W9-ADJ-296

Modern Roses: 12th Edition

The Comprehensive List of Roses in Cultivation or of Historical or Botanical Importance

Editors:

Marily A. Young
Columbus, NC

Phillip Schorr
St. Louis, MO

The American Rose Society
Shreveport, Louisiana
2007

Front Cover:

Gemini HT, pb, 1999, Zary, Dr. Keith W.; bud pointed, ovoid; flowers cream, blushing coral pink, 4½-5 in., 25-30 petals, high-centered, borne usually singly, moderate sweet fragrance; foliage large, deep green, glossy; prickles moderate; long stems; upright, spreading, tall (5½ ft.) growth; PP11691; [Anne Morrow Lindbergh × New Year]; int. by Bear Creek Gardens, 2000; Silver Medal, Monza, 1999. ARS Members' Choice, 2005. *Photo courtesy of Jackson & Perkins.*

 • ISBN: 978-1-59725-098-8

The American Rose Society
P.O. Box 30,000, Shreveport, Louisiana 71130-0030
Published by Pediment Publishing, a division of The Pediment Group, Inc. www.pediment.com

PREFACE

This book, *Modern Roses 12*, is the current edition in a series that dates back to 1930. Various editions have taken different approaches to the content of the publication, with recent editions serving as both a rose encyclopedia and as the official publication of rose registrations. The American Rose Society initiated a system for registering rose cultivars very early in its history, and was formally designated as the International Cultivar Registration Authority – Roses (ICRA-R) in 1955. However, satisfying the needs of rose society members, historians, researchers, and aficionados, in addition to meeting obligations as the ICRA-R, has become an impossible task for one volume.

Therefore, the American Rose Society has made the decision to publish two separate volumes: *Modern Roses 12*, which is a comprehensive listing of all rose cultivars and species documented during the research and preparation of the volume by its editors, and the *Official Registry of Rose Cultivars*, which focuses on registered cultivars and their identifying details.

Modern Roses 12 does not use any special typographical treatment to distinguish registered from non-registered cultivars, nor does it attempt to identify trademarks or other proprietary names. It does, however, use the American Rose Society's current standard of bold face type to indicate ARS approved exhibition names (AEN's).

Although we, the editors, cannot claim that *Modern Roses 12* is error-free, we have had a special advantage in preparing this book. The increasingly wide-spread use of the Internet and electronic mail have made it possible for us to establish contacts world-wide, with breeders, nurseries, botanists, and other rose lovers. We have tried to take advantage of this situation to improve the accuracy of our data, while still maintaining faithfulness to historical records. We realize that some rose cultivar names may strike modern readers as misspelled, odd, or even offensive. However, it is important to accept fact as fact and to realize that our perspective changes over time.

Phil Schorr Marily Young

ACKNOWLEDGMENTS

The publication of this book would not have been possible without the contributions of information and photographic material from several rose industry firms. In particular, we would like to thank Dickson Nurseries Limited, Roseraie Guillot, Heirloom Roses, Jackson & Perkins, W. Kordes Söhne, Nor'East/Greenheart Farms, Ross Roses, Weeks Wholesale Roses, and J. B. Williams and Associates for their financial support.

The efforts involved in producing this edition have been shared by many of our rose friends world-wide. For their willing help with research, we would like to thank Cassandra Bernstein (USA), Helga Brichet (Italy), Robert Edberg (USA), Dr. Lars-Åke Gustafson (Sweden), François Joyaux (France), Gregg Lowery (USA), Dr. Malcolm Manners (USA), Odile Masquelier (France), Dr. Yuki Mikanagi (Japan), Laurie Newman (AU), Roger Phillips (UK), Brigid & Charles Quest-Ritson (UK), Martin Rix (UK), Gerta Roberts (UK), Phillip Robinson (USA), Stephen Scaniello (USA), and Peter Schneider (USA).

We would also like to thank all the rose industry firms who so patiently answered our questions about their roses, and in particular to mention Thomas Proll of Kordes and Cheryl Malone of Heirloom. The photographic section of this book owes much to our American Rose Society photography contest winners, but especially to Rich Baer (USA) for his stunning work and his willingness to share additional material. We must also give tremendous thanks to our proof-reading team: Jane & Jim Delahanty, Crenagh & David Elliott, Steve Jones, Dr. Tony Liberta, George Meiling, and Jack Williams.

Finally, although it is an impossible to show enough appreciation, we must thank two people who have made very special contributions to this book: Professor Gianfranco Fineschi, and Jeannette Schorr. Without their support and encouragement, we would have given up long ago!

KEY TO ENTRIES

The format for a typical entry relies on the positional placement of specific descriptive data, as shown below. Not all entries will contain all elements of data.

Approved Exhibition Name Class, color, registration year, hybridizer; bud description; sepal description; flower description, including color, size, petal count, form, bloom habit, and fragrance; bloom frequency; foliage description; prickle description; stem description; growth habit; hip description; hardiness; patent number; subgenus[1], section[1], chromosome count[1]; parentage; comments; awards [1] subgenus, section, and chromosome count are present only on entries for species

International Cultivar Registration Authority Approved Horticultural Classifications

** Indicates Old Garden Rose

A	Alba**
Ayr	Ayrshire**
B & Cl B	Bourbon & Climbing Bourbon**
Bslt	Boursalt**
C	Centifolia**
Ch	China & Climbing China
D	Damask**
F & Cl F	Floribunda & Climbing Floribunda
Gr & Cl Gr	Grandiflora & Climbing Grandiflora
HBc	Hybrid Bracteata**
HCh	Hybrid China & Climbing Hybrid China**
HEg	Hybrid Eglanteria**
HFt	Hybrid Foetida**
HG	Hybrid Gigantea
HGal	Hybrid Gallica**
HKor	Hybrid Kordesii
HMoy	Hybrid Moyesii
HMsk	Hybrid Musk
HMult	Hybrid Multiflora**
HP & Cl HP	Hybrid Perpetual & Climbing Hybrid Perpetual**
HRg	Hybrid Rugosa
HSem	Hybrid Sempervirens**
HSet	Hybrid Setigera**
HSpn	Hybrid Spinosissima**
HT & Cl HT	Hybrid Tea and Climbing Hybrid Tea
HWich	Hybrid Wichurana
LCl	Large-Flowered Climber
Min & Cl Min	Miniature and Climbing Miniature
MinFl & Cl MinFl	Mini-Flora & Climbing Mini-Flora
Misc OGR	Miscellaneous OGR**
M & Cl M	Moss & Climbing Moss**
N	Noisette**
P	Portland**
Pol & Cl Pol	Polyantha and Climbing Polyantha
S	Shrub
T & Cl T	Tea & Climbing Tea**

American Rose Society Color Classifications

ab	apricot & apricot blend
dp	deep pink
dr	dark red
dy	deep yellow
lp	light pink
ly	light yellow
m	mauve & mauve blend
mp	medium pink
mr	medium red
my	medium yellow
ob	orange & orange blend
op	orange pink & orange pink blend
or	orange red & orange red blend
pb	pink blend
r	russet
rb	red blend
w	white, near white & white blend
yb	yellow blend

EXAMPLE:

Angelita Min, w, 1982, McGredy, Sam IV; bud small, ovoid, yellow; flowers pure white, 3 cm., 35-40 petals, decorative, borne in sprays, slight fragrance; recurrent; foliage small, dark, glossy; prickles numerous, needle, declining, light brown; growth low (10 in.), spreading; hips few, globular, orange; PP5849; [Moana × Snow Carpet]; int. in 1982; Gold Star of the South Pacific, Palmerston North, NZ, 1983

THE BERMUDA MYSTERY ROSES

The term "Bermuda mystery roses" was first used by Peter Harkness when he visited Bermuda in the late 1970's. The term refers to a number of cultivars which have been grown in Bermuda for many years – some since the mid-1700's. Efforts have been undertaken to document and preserve these roses, and to identify them when it is suspected that they are varieties imported year ago under long-forgotten names. Many of these cultivars are currently treated as "found" roses and, therefore, are not included in the body of the Modern Roses 12 text. However, the members of the Bermuda Rose Society are concerned that in time, no one will remember that these roses are of Bermudian origin. The following list is provided to assist their efforts in documenting the history of these cultivars.

Bermuda's Catherine Mermet T, w

Bermuda's Emmie Gray Ch, rb

Bermuda's Kathleen S, mr

Brightside Cream N, w

Carnation HCh, mp

Maitland White T, w

Miss Atwood T, ab

St. David's Ch, rb

Smith's Parish T, w (perhaps synonymous with Fortune's Five-Colored Rose)

Soncy T, ly

Spice Ch, w (perhaps synonymous with Hume's Blush)

Trinity T, w

Vincent Godsiff Ch, mr

À Balais – See **Comtesse de Chamoïs**, C

À Bois Brun HMult, mp, 1849, Vibert; flowers carminy pink, petals notched, often with a line in the middle, full, borne in clusters

À Bordures – See **Comtesse de Chamoïs**, C

À Bouquets – See **Argentée**, D

À Boutons Renversés – See **Boursault Rose**, Bslt

À Bractées – See ***R. bracteata*** (Wendland)

A Caen la Paix HT, m, Orard, Joseph; int. in 1994

A Capella HT, mr, 1984, Stoddard, Louis; flowers large, 35 petals, borne singly, slight fragrance; foliage large, medium green, matte; upright growth; [Command Performance × Tiffany]; Bronze Medal, ARC TG, 1984

À Coeur Jaune A, w, about 1810, Descemet; flowers white with yellow center

A Country Woman HT, dr, Zary; int. in 1997

À Douze Pétales – See **À Fleurs Presque Simples**, C

À Feuille de Chêne C, mp, before 1811, Trianon; bud round; flowers rose pink, medium, very full, borne in clusters of 5-7; foliage oval, close-set, deeply toothed; prickles few, weak

À Feuilles Bipinnées – See ***R. centifolia bipinnata*** (Thory), C

À Feuilles Cloquées – See **Bullata**, C

À Feuilles Crénelées C, lp, before 1804, Dupont; flowers delicate pink, small, full, borne in small clusters, moderate fragrance; foliage rounded, very deeply dentate; prickles small, almost straight

À Feuilles Crépues – See **Bullata**, C

À Feuilles Crispées – See ***R. centifolia bipinnata*** (Thory), C

À Feuilles de Bengale Misc OGR, before 1815, Descemet; hybrid canina

À Feuilles de Céleri – See ***R. centifolia bipinnata*** (Thory), C

À Feuilles de Chanvre – See **Cymbaefolia**, A

À Feuilles de Chanvre C, lp, before 1811; flowers pinkish white, dbl.; foliage long, slender, pointed, serrate

À Feuilles de Chou – See **Bullata**, C

À Feuilles de Fraxinelle Misc OGR, before 1815, Descemet; hybrid canina

À Feuilles de Frêne – See **Turneps**, S

À Feuilles de Groseillier – See ***R. centifolia bipinnata*** (Thory), C

À Feuilles de Pêcher A, w, before 1817, Pelletier; flowers medium, full; foliage pointed, regularly dentate; possibly synonymous with Cymbaefolia

À Feuilles de Persil – See ***R. centifolia bipinnata*** (Thory), C

À Feuilles d'Épine – See ***Hulthemia persica***

À Feuilles d'Ormé HGal, lp, before 1820, Descemet

À Feuilles Gaufrées – See **Bullata**, C

À Feuilles Penchées – See ***R. clinophylla*** (Thory)

À Fleur d'Anémone – See **De La Flèche**, M

À Fleur Double – See **La Moderne**, P

À Fleur d'un Rouge Pâle – See **Agathe Incarnata**, HGal

À Fleurs d'Anémone – See **Anémone**, M

À Fleurs de Rose Tremier de la Chine C, dp, before 1828, Pelletier; flowers rosy crimson, edged and mottled with blush, large, dbl., cupped; prickles few, gray; growth upright

À Fleurs Doubles – See **Double White**, HMsk

À Fleurs Doubles – See **Plena**, A

À Fleurs Doubles – See **Petite Hessoise**, HEg

À Fleurs Doubles Violettes Ch, m, before 1818

À Fleurs Doubles Violettes C, m, from France; flowers violet purple, medium, full, moderate fragrance

A Fleurs Gigantesques HGal, mp, 1813; flowers rich deep pink, large, very dbl.; bushy growth

À Fleurs Marbrée – See **Marmorea**, HGal

À Fleurs Panachées – See **Variegata**, C

À Fleurs Presque Simples C, mp, 1807, Charpentier; flowers small, 5-7 petals; foliage small, light green; prickles slightly hooked; growth upright, small (15-20 in.); hips small, elongate, red

À Fleurs Roses – See **Elisa**, A

A Fleurs Roses de Laffay HSem, Laffay, M.

À Fleurs Rouges Doubles – See **Red Damask**, D

À Fleurs Simples C, mp, before 1804, Dupont; flowers rose pink, medium, single to semi-dbl.

À Fleurs Simples Couleur de Cire – See ***R. foetida*** (Herrmann)

A. Geoffrey de St Hilaire HP, mr, 1878, Verdier; flowers medium, dbl.; tall growth

À Grand Cramoisi HGal, m, before 1818, Trianon; flowers very dark purple, semi-dbl.

À Gros Cul – See ***R. × francofurtana*** (Muenchhausen), Misc OGR

A. J. Herwig – See **Arend Herwig**, F

À Longs Pédoncule M, lp, 1854, Robert; bud pale green, mossy, long peduncles; flowers pink, flushed lilac, many petaled, 6 cm., dbl., globular, borne in clusters of 20-25; foliage small, round, soft green; vigorous growth

A Midsummer Nights Dream Gr, dr, 2003, Rawlins, R.; flowers red, reverse lighter, small, single, borne in large clusters; foliage medium green, semi-glossy; prickles medium, sharp, moderate; growth upright, 30 in., garden, decorative; [seedling × seedling]

A Night in June HT, or, 1935, Elmer's Nursery; flowers coral-red, very large, dbl.; foliage leathery; vigorous, bushy growth; [sport of Evening Star]

À Odeur de Noisette – See **Thisbé**, HCh

À Odeur de Punaise – See **Le Rire Niais**, C

À Odeur Ingrate – See **Le Rire Niais**, C

À Pedoncules Courbées HGal, lp, before 1829, Coquerel; flowers flesh pink

À Pétale Teinté de Rose – See ***R. × damascena subalba*** (Redouté), D

À Pétales Variés – See **York and Lancaster**, D

À Petites Fleurs – See **Enfant de France**, HGal

A Royal Bride HT, w, 2001, Rosen Tantau; flowers full, borne mostly solitary, slight fragrance; foliage medium size, medium green, glossy; prickles medium, straight, moderate; upright, tall (100 cm.) growth; garden, cut flower; [seedling × seedling]; int. by Eurosa, 2001

À Sept Pétales – See **À Fleurs Presque Simples**, C

A Shropshire Lad S, yb, 1997, Austin, David; flowers very dbl., 100 petals, rosette, borne in small clusters; foliage medium size, medium green, semi-glossy; prickles moderate; bushy, medium (5 × 4 ft.) growth; PP10607; int. by David Austin Roses, Ltd., 1996

A Thousand Cranes – See **Senbatsuru**, HT

À Tiges sans Épines – See **Inermis**, HSpn

A Whiter Shade of Pale HT, w, Pearce; flowers white with a touch of pink shading, large, dbl., high-centered, borne mostly singly, intense fragrance; recurrent; foliage semi-glossy; medium (3-4 ft.) growth; int. by Pocock's Roses, 2006

A. Boquet – See **A. Bouquet**, T

A. Bouquet T, w, 1873, Liabaud; flowers white, striped, large, full, borne in small clusters; probably extinct

A. Denis HT, my, 1935, Böhm, J.; flowers lemon-yellow, streaked carmine, large, dbl.; [Gorgeous × Marion Cran]

A. Drawiel HP, dr, 1887, Lévêque; flowers large, dbl.

A. Dvorak HT, op, 1933, Böhm, J.; flowers light pinkish orange, open, large, dbl.; foliage glossy, dark; bushy growth; [Mme Butterfly × Gorgeous]

A. G. A. Rappard HT, op, 1934, Buisman, G. A. H.; flowers salmon, verging on Neyron pink, well-shaped, dbl., slight fragrance; foliage glossy, bright green; vigorous, bushy growth

A. G. A. Ridder van Rappard – See **A. G. A. Rappard**, HT

A. G. Furness HT, mr, 1941, Clark, A.; flowers rich red; semi-climbing growth; [Sensation × unknown]

A. H. Kirk HT, op; flowers salmon pink with carmine, large, dbl.

A. K. Mishra HT, w, Pushpanjali; flowers large, milky white with broad petals, well formed; vigorous, hardy growth; int. in 1997

A. K. Williams – See **Alfred K. Williams**, HP

A. M. Ampère HP, dr, 1881, Liabaud; [Lion des Combats × unknown]

A. MacKenzie S, rb, 1985, Svedja, Felicitas; bud ovoid; flowers medium red, reverse lighter, 3 in., 45 petals, cupped, borne in clusters of 6-12; repeat bloom; foliage yellow-green, glossy, leathery; prickles purple; upright growth; [Queen Elizabeth × (Red Dawn × Suzanne)]; int. by Agriculture Canada, 1985

A. N. W. B. Rose HT, w, 1933, Buisman, G. A. H.; flowers white, tinted yellow, open, large, dbl.; very vigorous growth; [Frau Karl Druschki × Souv. de Claudius Pernet]

A. R. S. Centennial – See **American Rose Centennial**, Min

A. W. Jessep HT, dp, 1952, Clark, A.; flowers rich cerise-pink, large, 38 petals; vigorous growth

Aachener Dom – See **Pink Panther**, HT

Aafje Heynis HT, mr, 1964, Buisman, G. A. H.; flowers bright red, well-shaped, large; foliage glossy, light green; vigorous, upright growth; [Prima Ballerina × Salvo]

Aaland S, dp

Aalsmeer Gold HT, dy, 1978, Kordes; bud long, pointed; flowers deep yellow, 23 petals, high-centered, borne singly, slight fragrance; foliage glossy; vigorous, upright, bushy growth; PP4421; [Berolina × seedling]

Aasha HT, mr, Datta; flowers rose red, non-fading, classic; long stems; int. in 2003

Aasmeer HT, ob; flowers peachish-orange with yellow tones

Aba Saheb HT, ob, Chiplunkar; flowers show splashes and streaks of paler orange on both sides of the broad petals, full, high-centered; [sport of Modern Art]; int. by Decospin, 1993

Abailard HGal, lp, before 1826, Sommesson; flowers delicate pink, medium, very dbl.

Abaillard HGal, lp, 1845, Robert; flowers light pink and dark pink, marbled, medium, very dbl.

Abasanta HT, dp, 1956, Motose; bud pointed, cerise; flowers carmine, occasionally streaked white, large, dbl., moderate fragrance; foliage dark; compact growth; PP1527; [Red Columbia × (Red Columbia × Tausendschön sport)]

Abba Dabba Min, mr, 1980, Lyon; bud long, pointed; flowers 38 petals, borne 1-5 per cluster, slight fragrance; foliage small, medium green; prickles tiny, curved; compact, bushy growth; [Red Can Can × seedling]; int. in 1980

Abbaye de Cluny HT, ab, 1996, Meilland International SA; flowers orange apricot, 4 1/4 in., full, borne mostly singly; foliage medium size, dark green, semi-glossy; prickles moderate; bushy, medium (90 cm.) growth;

PP9609; [Just Joey × (MEIrestif × MEInarual)]; int. by The Conard-Pyle Co., 1993; Gold Medal, Belfast, 1995

Abbé André Reitter HT, lp, 1901, Welter; flowers light flesh pink, large, full, slight fragrance

Abbé Berlèze HGal, w, before 1845, Baumann; flowers white, shaded flesh, dbl.

Abbé Berlèze HP, dp, 1864, Guillot et Fils; [sport of Géant des Batailles]

Abbé Bramerel HP, dr, 1871, Guillot et Fils; flowers large, dbl.; [Géant des Batailles × unknown]

Abbé de la Haye B, mp, 1854, Robert; flowers glowing pink, large, full

Abbé de la Haye HT, mp, 1855, Bourbin; flowers bright pink, large, full

Abbé Garroute T, pb, 1902, Bonnaire; flowers coppery yellow and carmine pink, petals edged pink, large, full, intense fragrance; probably extinct

Abbé Girardin B, mp, 1881, Bernaix, A.; flowers carmine-pink, center darker, large, dbl.; [Louise Odier × Hermosa]

Abbé Giraudier HP, mr, 1869, Levet; flowers cherry red, very large, dbl.; [Géant des Batailles × Victor Verdier]

Abbé Lemire HT, dr, Orard; int. in 1997

Abbé Millot HT, lp, 1900, Corboeuf; flowers silvery pink, large, dbl.

Abbé Miolan Ch, m, 1839; flowers purple, striped white, dbl.

Abbé Reynaud HP, m, 1863, Guillot

Abbé Vénière HP, mp, 1867, Guillot; flowers shining pink, medium, semi-dbl. to dbl.; recurrent

Abbeyfield Gold – See **Golden Fairy Tale**, HT

Abbeyfield Rose HT, dp, 1984, Cocker, A.; flowers rose red, large, 35 petals, slight fragrance; foliage medium size, medium green, semi-glossy; bushy growth; [National Trust × Silver Jubilee]; int. by Cocker & Sons, 1985; Golden Prize, Glasgow, 1990

Abbotswood S, mp, 1954, Hilling; flowers lighter at edges, medium, semi-dbl.; growth habit similar to *R. canina*; [chance hybrid of *R. canina* × unknown garden variety]

Abby's Angel MinFl, dy, 2007, Wells, Verlie W.; flowers deep yellow, red on edge on first few petals, reverse deep yellow, 3 in., full, borne mostly solitary; foliage medium size, dark green, semi-glossy; prickles hooked, few; growth upright, tall (3½-4 ft.); exhibition; [seedling × Bees Knees]; int. by Wells MidSouth Roses, 2007

Abd-el-Kader HP, pb, 1861, Verdier, E.; flowers carmine, tinted dark purple, semi-dbl.

Abdul-Hamid – See **S. M. I. Abdul-Hamid**, HRg

Abeilard – See **Abailard**, HGal

Abel Carrière HP, dr, 1875, Verdier, E.; flowers velvety crimson, brighter center, large, 45 petals; [Baron de Bonstetten × seedling]

Abel Grand – See **Abel Grant**, HP

Abel Grant HP, lp, 1866, Damaizin; flowers silky whitish-pink, streaked lighter silver, large, dbl., intense fragrance; medium growth; [Jules Margottin × unknown]

Abelzieds HRg, mp, Rieksta, Dr. Dz.; flowers large, semi-dbl., slight fragrance; growth medium; [*R. rugosa alba* × Poulsen's Pink]; int. in 1957

Abendglut – See **Valiant Heart**, F

Abendröte HP, op, 1919, Ebeling; flowers light coral-red; compact growth; [Frau Karl Druschki × Juliet]; int. by Teschendorff

Aberdeen S, lp, Poulsen; flowers light pink, small, no fragrance; foliage dark; growth broad, bushy, 40-60 cm.; PP9457; int. as Rutland Cover, Poulsen Roser, 1988

Aberdeen Celebration F, ob, Cocker; int. in 1994

Aberdonian F, rb, 1976, Cocker; flowers golden bronze and scarlet, large, 20 petals, slight fragrance; foliage glossy; [(Evelyn Fison × Manx Queen) × (Sabine × Circus)]

Abhaya – See **Magic Medley**, HT

Abhisarika HT, rb, 1976; bud long, pointed; flowers red stripes on yellow background, 2½-3 in., 48 petals, high-centered; free blooming; foliage glossy, yellowish; vigorous growth; [induced sport of Kiss of Fire]; int. by IARI, 1975

Abhishek Gr, rb, IARI; flowers streaks and splashes of yellow and white on broad, crimson red petals; very floriferous; [sport of Jantar Mantar]; int. in 2003

Abiding Faith HT, dp, 1954, Montose; bud semi-ovoid; flowers deep rose-pink, 4-5 in., 20-35 petals, intense fragrance; vigorous, upright growth; PP1323; [La France × (Senator × Florex)]

Abiding Faith, Climbing Cl HT, dp, 1957, Motose

Abigail Adams Rose HMult, mp, Lowe, Mike; flowers fade to white, medium, semi-dbl., borne in small to large clusters, moderate fragrance; reliable repeat; growth low, spreading; groundcover; [*R. multiflora nana* × Sweet Chariot]; int. by Ashdown Roses, 2005

Abigaile F, pb, 1988, Tantau

Abington Park Northampton HT, op, 1997, Jones, L.J.; flowers very dbl., 41 petals, borne in small clusters; foliage medium size, medium green; some prickles; bushy, medium (3 ft.) growth; [Cynthia Brooke × Little Darling]

Able Min, yb, 2006, Tucker, Robbie; flowers yellow with orange edge, ¾ in., dbl., borne mostly solitary; foliage dark green, glossy; prickles small, slightly curved downward, red to brown, moderate; growth compact, medium (to 30 in.); exhibition, cut flower, landscape; [Cal Poly × Soroptimist International]; int. by Rosemania, 2007

Abol HT, w, 1927, Evans; flowers ivory-white tinted blush, large, dbl.; int. by Beckwith

Abondant Pol, mp, 1914, Turbat; flowers medium-large, dbl.

Abondante – See **Celsiana**, D

About Face Gr, ob, 2003, Carruth, Tom; flowers deep orange gold, reverse burnished red, 9-12 cm., full, borne mostly solitary, no fragrance; foliage large, dark green, semi-glossy; prickles moderate, average, almost straight, brown; growth upright, very vigorous, tall (180-200 cm.); garden decoration; [((O Sole Mio × seedling) × Midas Touch) × Hot Cocoa]; int. by Weeks Roses, 2005

Abracadabra HT, pb, 1991, Warriner, William A.; bud pointed, ovoid, deep pink/yellow; flowers purple pink, tan and yellow, 4½-5 in., full, high-centered, borne mostly singly, intense fragrance; foliage large, dark green, semi-glossy; some prickles; medium (90-120 cm.), upright, bushy growth; PP8590; [White Masterpiece × Tribute]; int. by Bear Creek Gardens, 1993

Abracadabra HT, rb; flowers deep red/brown petals with lemon yellow stripes; int. by Kordes, 2002

Abraham Darby S, ab, 1991, Austin, David; bud rounded, dark pink base with yellow; flowers pink peach-apricot, 3-4 in., very dbl., cupped, quartered, intense fragrance; foliage dark green, shiny; vigorous, bushy, angular growth; PP7215; [Yellow Cushion × Aloha]; int. by David Austin Roses, Ltd., 1985

Abraham Zimmerman HP, mr, 1879, Lévêque; flowers large, dbl.

Abraxas S, dr, VEG; flowers medium-large, dbl.; int. in 1973

Abricot HT, ab, 1929, Barbier; flowers apricot and coral-salmon, reverse coral-red; [Mrs Aaron Ward × Jean C.N. Forestier]

Abricotée T, ab, 1843, Dupuis; flowers apricot, margins flesh, dbl., cupped

Absent Friends F, ab, Dickson; flowers peach, reverse yellow, fading to pink, full, rosette, borne in large clusters, moderate fragrance; recurrent; foliage small, dark green, glossy; vigorous, bushy (100 cm.) growth; int. by Dickson Roses, 2006

Absolute – See **Absolute Hit**, MinFl

Absolute Hit MinFl, or, Poulsen; flowers orange-red, 5-8 cm., dbl., no fragrance; growth bushy, 40-60 cm.; int. by Poulsen Roser, 1996

Absolutely Min, yb, 1998, Saville, F. Harmon; bud medium, ovate; flowers pale to medium yellow, dusted apricot-pink, lighter reverse, 22 -40 petals, high-centered, borne singly and in small clusters, floriferous, slight fragrance; free flowering; foliage medium size, medium green, semi-glossy; few prickles; upright, compact, spreading, bushy, vigorous growth; PP11132; [Unnamed seedling × Rise 'n' Shine]; int. by Nor'East Miniature Roses, 1998

Abu HT, dp, VEG; flowers large, dbl.

Abundance F, mp, 1976, Gandy, Douglas L.; flowers 4½ in., 30 petals, slight fragrance; foliage dark; low, bushy growth; [seedling × Firecracker]; int. in 1974

Abundancia – See **Mary Hayley Bell**, S semi-dbl.

Aburae HT, yb, Ota

Abyssinian Rose – See **St John's Rose**, S

AC De Montarville – See **De Montarville**, HKor

AC Marie Victorin – See **Marie-Victorin**, HKor

AC William-Booth – See **William-Booth**, HKor

Academy Min, pb, 1983, McGredy, Sam IV; flowers small, 20 petals, slight fragrance; foliage small, medium green, semi-glossy; bushy growth; [Anytime × Matangi]; int. in 1982

Acadia – See **Trelleborg**, F

Acadia Sunrise F, or, 2001, Twomey, Jerry, and Lim, Ping; flowers rich orange, 4½ in., dbl., high-centered, borne mostly solitary, slight fragrance; foliage medium size, dark green, glossy; prickles moderate; growth upright, compact (4 ft.); garden decoration; [seedling × seedling]; int. by Bailey Nurseries, Inc., 2002

Acadian Ch, dp, 1987, James, John; flowers deep, bright pink, medium, 5 petals, intense fragrance; foliage small, medium green, matte; prickles fine; upright, bushy, hardy growth; [*R. nitida* × *R. chinensis semperflorens*]; int. in 1986

Acapella – See **Charlies Rose**, HT

Acapulco F, yb, 1962, Von Abrams; bud pointed; flowers yellow and light orange, often flushed pink, medium, 30-40 petals, cupped, borne in clusters; foliage dark, glossy; bushy, compact growth; [seedling × Masquerade]; int. by Peterson & Dering, 1962

Acapulco HT, rb, Dickson, Patrick; flowers mixture of scarlet, ivory and yellow, dbl., high-centered; int. in 1997

Acaritha HRg, Wartz

Accent F, mr, 1976, Warriner, William A.; bud ovoid; flowers cardinal-red, 2-2½ in., 25 petals, flat, slight fragrance; foliage small, dark, leathery; bushy, compact growth; PP3994; [Marlena × seedling]; int. by J&P, 1977

Acclaim HT, ob, 1982, Warriner, William A.; flowers orange, large, 34 petals; foliage medium green, semi-glossy; upright, bushy growth; PP5638; [Sunfire × Spellbinder]; int. by J&P, 1986

Accolade HT, rb, 1981, Dawson, George; bud ovoid; flowers bright red, shaded darker, 48 petals, high-centered, borne mostly singly, slight fragrance; foliage dark, matte; prickles hooked, brown; vigorous growth; [(Daily Sketch × Charles Mallerin) × Peter Frankenfeld]; int. by Rainbow Roses, 1979

Accord F, ab, 1969, Mason, P.; flowers apricot-peach, reverse carmine, well-formed, high-centered, borne in clusters, moderate fragrance; foliage dark; bushy growth; [Circus × seedling]; int. by P.G. Mason, 1965

Ace of Diamonds Min, mr, 1998, Bridges, Dennis A.; flowers bright medium red, good substance, 1-1½ in., full, high-centered, borne mostly singly and small clusters, intense fragrance; foliage small, dark green, semi-glossy; few prickles; stems strong; bushy, spreading, medium growth; Disease resistant; int. by Bridges Roses, 1998

Ace of Hearts – See **Herz As**, HT

Ace of Hearts – See **Asso di Cuori**, HT

Acervate Pol, mp, 1934, Miers

Acey Deucy Min, mr, 1983, Saville, F. Harmon; flowers small, 20 petals, high-centered, moderate fragrance; foliage small, medium green, semi-glossy; bushy growth; [(Yellow Jewel × Tamango) × Sheri Anne]; int. by Nor'East Min. Roses, 1982

Achantha Gr, dr, Viraraghavan, M.S. Viru; int. in 1987

Achievement HWich, dp, 1925, English; flowers deep rose pink shaded coral, small, full; foliage variegated; [sport of Dorcas]

Achille HGal, dr, before 1810, possibly Miellez; flowers deep velvety purple-red, 4 in., dbl.; prickles numerous, fairly hooked

Achille Pol, mp, 1936, Guinoisseau; flowers medium-large, semi-dbl.

Achille Cesbron HP, mr, 1894, Rousset; flowers very large, dbl.; [Mme Eugène Frémy × unknown]

Achille Gonod HP, mr, 1864, Gonod; flowers large, dbl.; [Jules Margottin × unknown]

Acidalie B, w, 1833, Rousseau; flowers white with blush center, large, dbl., globular; recurrent bloom; vigorous growth

Acqua Cheta HT, rb, 1962, Giacomasso; flowers magenta-red, reverse silvery, 50 petals; foliage dark; compact growth; [Crimson Glory × Peace]

Acropolis S, r, Meilland; flowers pink bronze, reverse lighter, dbl., cupped, borne in clusters; free-flowering; growth to 50-70 cm.; int. in 2002

Actrice HT, rb, 1966, Verschuren, A.; bud ovoid; flowers red and light pink, large, dbl.; foliage dark; [Tzigane × Kordes' Perfecta]; int. by Van Engelen

Ada Perry Min, op, 1978, Bennett, Dee; bud ovoid; flowers soft coral-orange, medium, 40 petals, high-centered, slight fragrance; foliage dark; vigorous, upright growth; [Little Darling × Coral Treasure seedling]; int. by Tiny Petals Nursery

Adagio HT, dr, 1979, Lens, Louis; bud very long, pointed; flowers blood-red, 3½-4 in., 28-35 petals, globular; foliage dark; vigorous, bushy growth; [seedling × Uncle Walter]; int. in 1971

Adagio – See **Home of Time**, HT

Adair Roche HT, pb, 1968, McGredy, Sam IV; flowers deep pink, reverse silver, well-formed, large, 30 petals; foliage glossy; [Paddy McGredy × Femina seedling]; int. by McGredy; Gold Medal, Belfast, 1971

Adam T, mp, 1833, Adam; flowers rich rosy-salmon, more yellow inside, 7-9 cm., semi-dbl. to dbl., globular, strong tea fragrance; [possibly Hume's Blush × Rose Edouard]

Adam Messerich B, mr, 1920, Lambert, P.; flowers rose-red, semi-dbl., cupped, intense raspberry fragrance; recurrent bloom; foliage glossy, light; vigorous, bushy growth; [Frau Oberhofgärtner Singer × (Louise Odier × Louis Philippe (Ch))]

Adam Paul HP, lp, 1852, Laffay; flowers very large, full, globular, moderate fragrance

Adam Rackles T, pb, 1905, Rommel; flowers marbled and spackled pink, very large, full, slight fragrance; [sport of Mme Caroline Testout]

Adam's Smile Min, dp, 1988, Saville, F. Harmon; flowers deep pink, medium, 23-27 petals, high-centered, borne usually singly and in sprays of 3-5, no fragrance; foliage medium size, medium green, semi-glossy; prickles long, thin, pointed slightly downward, gray-red; upright, bushy, medium growth; no fruit; PP6570; [(Rise 'n' Shine × Sheri Anne) × Rainbow's End]; int. by Nor'East Min. Roses

Added Touch Min, or, 1984, Lyon; bud small; flowers orange-red, touch of yellow in the center and back of petals, 20 petals; foliage small, medium green, semi-glossy; upright, bushy growth; [Dandy Lyon × seedling]

Addo Heritage HT, pb, Poulsen

Adela HT, pb, Viveros Fco. Ferrer, S L; flowers 32 petals; [Shocking Blue × Kardinal]; int. in 1991

Adela HT, lp, Kordes; flowers porcelain pink, dbl., high-centered, no fragrance; stems long; growth vigorous, tall; int. in 2001

Adelaide – See **Adelaide Hoodless**, S

Adélaïde Bougère B, m, 1852, Bougère; flowers velvety purple, shaded darker, large, full; possibly synonymous with Adèle Bougère

Adélaïde de Meynot HP, mp, 1882, Gonod; flowers bright cerise pink, rounded petals, large, moderate centifolia fragrance; quite remontant; numerous prickles; stems very dark green; growth upright

Adélaïde d'Orléans HSem, w, 1826, Jacques; bud small, dark pink; flowers pale rose, fading to cream/white, yellow stamens, 6-7 cm., semi-dbl., loosely cupped, borne in clusters; non-recurrent; lax, sprawling, vigorous (15 ft.) growth; [*R. sempervirens* × Parson's Pink]

Adelaide d'Orléans HP, mp, 1861, Robert; flowers medium pink, shaded lilac

Adelaïde Fontaine B, mp, 1856, Fontaine

Adelaide Hoodless S, dp, 1973, Marshall, H.H.; bud ovoid; flowers light red, medium, semi-dbl., slight fragrance; repeat bloom; foliage glossy; vigorous, bushy growth; [Fire King × (J.W. Fargo × Assiniboine)]; int. by Canadian Ornamental Plant Foundation, 1975

Adelaide Lee Min, pb, 1986, Stoddard, Louis; flowers white with red petal edges, 1 in., 25 petals, urn-shaped, borne singly; foliage medium green, matte; prickles few, green, straight; upright growth; [Gene Boerner × Magic Carrousel]

Adélaïde Moullé HWich, pb, 1902, Barbier; flowers lilac-pink, center carmine, 4 cm., dbl., borne in clusters; midseason bloom; foliage oval, slightly pointed, reflexed, smooth; prickles numerous, straight, slender, very sharp, dark brown; [*R. wichurana* × Souv. de Catherine Guillot]

Adelaide Pavié – See **Adèle Pavié**, N

Adelaide Tonight Min, mp, 1999, Thomson, George L.; flowers pink, reverse lighter, ½-¾ in., dbl., borne in large clusters; foliage medium size, medium green, semi-glossy; prickles moderate; spreading, medium (18-24 in.) growth; [Avandel × Little Mike]

Adèle HGal, mp, before 1814, Descemet; flowers medium, full

Adèle HT, dy, 1935, Lens; flowers clear gold, base deeper; [Roselandia × Clarice Goodacre]

Adèle Bernard N, w; flowers white with salmon pink, full

Adèle Bougère HT, dr, 1852, Robert; flowers velvety dark purple, full

Adèle Courtoisé HGal, dp, before 1842; flowers rosy red, small, very dbl.

Adèle Crofton HT, yb, 1928, Dickson, A.; flowers yellow overlaid scarlet-orange, dbl.

Adèle de Bellabre T, pb, 1888, Ducher fils; flowers coppery pink to reddish-peach, large, full; probably extinct

Adèle Descemet HGal, Descemet, M.

Adele Duttweiler – See **Royal Dane**, HT

Adele Frey Cl HT, dp, 1911, Walter; flowers large, very dbl.

Adèle Gérard HGal, lp; flowers light pink, aging to white, large, full

Adèle Heu HGal, m, 1816, Vibert; flowers purple-pink with white shadings, medium large, dbl., moderate fragrance

Adèle Mauzé P, lp, 1847, Vibert; flowers rose pink, medium to large, full

Adèle Pavie M, lp, 1850, Vibert; flowers flesh white to pink, 8 cm., dbl., rosette, moderate fragrance

Adèle Pavié N, lp, 1857, Moreau & Robert; flowers light pink, center crimson, shaded white, often yellow at base; [Lamarque × unknown]

Adèle Pradel – See **Mme Bravy**, T

Adèle Prévost HGal, lp, before 1836; flowers blush, center pink, large, dbl.; vigorous, upright growth

Adele Searll S, ab, Kordes; flowers apricot-pink, heavy, 100 petals, borne in large clusters, moderate sweet fragrance; growth semi-prostrate, compact, spreading; int. in 1999

Adéline C, pb, 1830, Vibert; flowers vivid rose, paler toward edge, dbl.; foliage dark; compact, branching growth

Adeline M, dp; bud well mossed; flowers lilac-rose, 2 in., dbl.; foliage light green; compact, well-branched growth

Adeline Genée F, my, 1967, Harkness; bud plump; flowers 4 in., 50 petals, borne in clusters; foliage glossy; low, bushy growth; [Paddy McGredy × seedling]

Adesmano HT, pb, Adam

Adiantifolia HRg, mp, 1907, Cochet-Cochet; foliage ferny

Adieu de Bordier HGal, mr; flowers vivid red, very dbl.

Aditya HT, dy, K&S; flowers long lasting, deep yellow, dbl., broad; int. by KSG Son, 1990

Admirable HGal, mr, before 1787; flowers scarlet red, full; prickles numerous, short; from Holland

Admirable Min, w, 1991, McCann, Sean; bud ovoid, sharply pointed sepals; flowers soft pink with darker accent, reverse ivory with pink accent, 2½ in., 38 petals, high-centered, borne usually singly, intense fruity fragrance; foliage large, medium green, semi-glossy; long, straight stems; upright, tall growth; [seedling × Admiral Rodney]; int. by Justice Miniature Roses, 1992

Admirable de Lille – See **Orphise**, HGal

Admirable Panachée – See **Comte Foy**, HGal

Admiral – See **Waves**, HT

Admiral – See **Sea Rodney**, Min

Admiral HT, mr, Tantau; int. by Rosen Tantau, 2002

Admiral de Rigny N, mp, before 1844; growth dwarf

Admiral Dewey HT, mr, 1899, Taylor; flowers rich creamy rose, shaded with gold-yellow and peach, large, dbl.; [sport of Mme Caroline Testout]

Admiral la Peyrouse – See **La Peyrouse**, HP

Admiral Rigney – See **Admiral de Rigny**, N

Admiral Rodney HT, pb, 1974, Trew, C.; flowers pale rose-pink, reverse deeper, 4-4½ in., 45 petals, intense fragrance; foliage large, glossy, dark; vigorous growth; int. by Warley Rose Gardens, 1973

Admiral Schley HT, r, 1901, Cook, J.W.; flowers red; [Col. Joffé × Général Jacqueminot]

Admiral Ward HT, rb, 1915, Pernet-Ducher; flowers crimson-red, shaded fiery red and velvety purple, large, dbl., globular; [seedling × Château de Clos Vougeot]

Admiration HT, rb, 1922, McGredy; flowers cream,

shaded vermilion, pointed, large, dbl.; foliage light green; moderately bushy growth

Admiration – See **Rosa Zwerg**, HRg

Admired Miranda S, lp, 1983, Austin, David; flowers opening flat, then reflexing, large, dbl., flat; foliage medium size, medium green, semi-glossy; upright growth; [The Friar × The Friar]; int. by David Austin, 1983

Adolf Deegen HT, pb, 1935, Böhm, J.; flowers rosy pink with fiery streaks, large; [Ophelia × Wilhelm Kordes]

Adolf Grille F, dp, 1940, Kordes; bud pointed, ovoid; flowers scarlet-carmine, 4-5 in., 25 petals, cupped, borne in clusters; foliage leathery, dark, wrinkled; vigorous, bushy, compact growth; [Dance of Joy × (Cathrine Kordes × E.G. Hill)]; int. by J&P

Adolf Horstmann HT, yb, 1973, Kordes, R.; flowers deep yellow-orange with pink overtones, 5 in., dbl., high-centered; foliage glossy; vigorous, upright growth; [Colour Wonder × Dr. A.J. Verhage]; int. by McGredy & Son, 1972

Adolf Kärger HT, my, 1918, Kordes, H.; bud long; flowers golden yellow, fading lighter in full sun, very large, full; foliage large, dark green; [Cissie Easlea × Sunburst]

Adolf Koschel HT, ab, 1918, Kordes, H.; bud long, pointed; flowers light orange yellow, nuanced red, large, very full, borne mostly solitary, moderate fragrance; foliage medium size, leathery, bronzy green; [Harry Kirk × Louise Catherine Breslau]

Adolf Papeleu F, w, RvS-Melle; [Maizières × Maria Mathilde]; int. in 1996

Adolph Gude HT, pb, 1941, Gude; flowers rose-pink, reverse darker, 5½-6 in., 30 petals, high-centered; very vigorous growth; [sport of Red Radiance]

Adolph Horstmann – See **Adolf Horstmann**, HT

Adolphe Brogniard HP, mp, 1868, Margottin; flowers carmine pink, large, full

Adolphe Noblet HP, dp, Ledechaux

Adonis HGal, dp, before 1814, Descemet; flowers bright pinky red, flat

Adonis HGal, lp, before 1829; flowers flesh pink, medium, full

Adonis HT, ly, 1921, Bees; flowers ivory-yellow, shaded lemon, dbl.; [Sunburst × American Beauty]; Gold Medal, NRS, 1920

Adora Pol, mp, 1936, Beckwith; bud deep flame-pink; flowers rose-pink, dbl.; vigorous, dwarf growth

Adora HT, op, Kasturi; flowers luminous coral to deep vermilion, well formed; long stems; int. by KSG Son, 1986

Adorable HT, lp, 1930, Eichholz; flowers flesh-pink; [sport of Columbia]

Adoration HT, op, 1940, Gaujard; bud long, pointed; flowers bright salmon, 5 in., 22 petals; foliage leathery; vigorous, bushy growth; [(Mme Joseph Perraud × seedling) × seedling]; int. by J&P

Adorn Min, pb, 1986, McDaniel, Earl; flowers medium pink blending lighter, reverse medium pink, 30 petals, high-centered, urn-shaped, borne singly; foliage medium size, dark, semi-glossy; prickles slender, light; medium, upright, bushy growth; [seedling × seedling]; int. by McDaniel's Min. Roses

Adriadne – See **Ariane**, HGal

Adrian F, Camprubi, C.

Adrian Bailey F, op, 1978, Bailey; bud globular; flowers orange-scarlet, large, 28 petals; foliage glossy; bushy, upright growth; [Fragrant Cloud × Evelyn Fison]

Adrian Reverchon HMult, mp, 1909, Lambert; flowers bright pink with white blaze, fading almost to white, 5-6 cm., single, borne in large clusters; autumn repeat

Adriana HT, ab; flowers pale cream deepening to creamy caramel, large, dbl., classic, moderate spicy fragrance; recurrent; foliage dark green, disease-resistant; well-branched, medium (30 in.) growth; int. by Fryer, 2000

Adriana Top Model F, ab, Laperrière; flowers apricot, slight fragrance; growth compact; int. by Roseraie Laperrière, 2005

Adrie Stokman HT, mp, 1948, Stokman; flowers darker pink than Briarcliff; [Parel van Aalsmeer × unknown]

Adrien de Montebello HP, dp, 1868, Margottin; flowers silky dark pink, medium, full

Adrien Marx HP, mr, 1866, Granger; flowers cherry red, large, full

Adrien Mercier F, rb

Adrien Schmitt HP, mr, 1889, Schmitt

Adrienne Berman HT, mr, 1996, Poole, Lionel; flowers very large, spiraled, with thick-textured petals, full, borne mostly singly, moderate fragrance; foliage large, dark green, semi-glossy; some prickles; upright, medium growth; [(Precious Platinum × Silver Jubilee) × Cardiff Bay]; int. by F. Haynes & Partners, 1997

Adrienne Christophe N, ab, 1869, Guillot; flowers coppery apricot yellow, shaded peach pink, sometimes deep yellow, very dbl.; foliage smooth, pale green; prickles long, sharp, brown

Adrienne de Cardoville C, lp, 1845, probably Verdier; flowers light rosy crimson, large, full, cupped; growth branching

Adrienne Leal F, dp, 1965, Leal; bud ovoid; flowers deep pink to soft mauve, medium, dbl.; foliage dark, leathery; vigorous, upright growth; [sport of Roundelay]

Adrienne Martin HT, dp, 1930, Buatois; flowers carmine, base yellow, very dbl., cupped; foliage glossy, dark; vigorous, bushy, low growth; [Recuerdo de Angel Peluffo × The Queen Alexandra Rose]

Advance HT, rb, 1940, LeGrice; flowers orange-flame, shaded cerise, reverse cerise, large, dbl.; foliage leathery, dark; long, strong stems; vigorous, bushy growth; [Comtesse Vandal × Mrs Sam McGredy]; int. by C-P

Advance Guard – See **Wilhelm Teetzmann**, F

Adventure – See **Aventure**, HT

Adventure HT, pb, Spek; flowers blush with pink edges and greenish guard petals, very large, full, high-centered, borne mostly singly; good repeat; stems long; florist rose; int. by Jan Spek Rozen, 2003

Adventure – See **Adventure Palace**, Min

Adventure Palace Min, dr, Poulsen; flowers dark red, 2 in., dbl. to full, cupped, no fragrance; foliage dark green, glossy; bushy, low (40-60 cm.) growth; int. by Poulsen Roser, 2005

Adversity MinFl, w, 2005, Goldstein, Jack J.; flowers white, reverse light yellow, 1¼ in., full, borne mostly solitary, moderate fragrance; foliage medium size, medium green, matte; prickles few, ¼ in., triangular, green; bushy, medium growth; [sport of Soroptimist International]; int. by Jack J. Goldstein, 2005

Advocate HT, mr, 1928, Dickson, A.; flowers crimson-scarlet, dbl.

Æbleblomst HMsk, lp, Petersen; int. in 1955

Aëlita S, w, 1952, Shtanko, E.E.; flowers white tinted green, large, 50 petals; foliage glossy; vigorous growth; [New Dawn × unknown]

Aennchen Müller – See **Ännchen Müller**, Pol

Aenne Burda HT, mr, 1973, Kordes; flowers blood-red, large, dbl., high-centered; foliage large, glossy; vigorous, upright, bushy growth

Aenne Kreis HT, ab, 1930, Kreis; flowers orange-yellow, reverse lighter, well-formed, dbl.; vigorous, branching growth; [sport of Wilhelm Kordes]

Aetna – See **Etna**, M

Affection MinFl, mr, Poulsen; flowers medium red, 5-8 cm., semi-dbl., no fragrance; foliage dark; growth bushy, 20-40 cm.; int. by Poulsen Roser, 2005

Affirm HT, mp, 1998, McMillan, Thomas G.; flowers high center, medium pink, 4 in., very dbl., high-centered, borne mostly singly or small clusters; foliage medium size, medium green, dull; numerous prickles; low, spreading growth; [seedling × seedling]; int. by Hortico, Inc., 1998

Afghan Rose – See ***R. ecae*** (Aitchison)

Aflame F, op, 1954, LeGrice; flowers orange-strawberry, 4 in., semi-dbl., borne in clusters; foliage dark, glossy; vigorous, low, spreading growth; [(Poulsen's Pink × Ellinor LeGrice) × Mrs Pierre S. duPont]

Africa Star HT, m, 1965, West; flowers 3½-4 in., 65 petals; foliage coppery; bushy growth; int. by Harkness

African Dawn HT, pb, Schreurs; int. by Australian Roses, 2004

African Queen HT, dp, Tantau; int. in 1996

African Sunset HT, ab, 1966, Herholdt, J.A.; flowers apricot-orange, pointed, 4½ in., dbl.; free growth; [Sutter's Gold × Chantré]

African Sunset HT, or, J&P; int. in 1994

After Dark S, dr, 2004, Ponton, Ray; flowers dark red, 3-4 in., semi-dbl., borne mostly solitary, slight fragrance; foliage medium size, medium green, semi-glossy; prickles medium, curved; stems wine-colored; upright, medium (4 ft.) growth; [Lillian Austin × San Gabriel]

After Glow Gr, op

After Midnight Min, dr, 1991, King, Gene; bud ovoid; flowers dark red, tips show darker edge, outer petals darker, medium, 28 petals, high-centered, borne singly, no fragrance; foliage medium size, medium green, semi-glossy; medium, upright growth; [(B.C. × Scamp) × Black Jade]; int. by AGM Miniature Roses, 1990

Afterglow HT, ab, 1930, Joseph H. Hill, Co.; flowers apricot-yellow, dbl.; [seedling × Souv. de Claudius Pernet]

Afterglow HT, ob, 1938, LeGrice; bud long, pointed, orange; flowers golden yellow, reverse golden orange, large, dbl.; foliage bluish green, glossy; long stems; vigorous, bushy growth; [sport of Mrs Sam McGredy]

Afterglow S, pb, Williams, J.B.; int. by Hortico, 2004

Afternoon Delight Min, mp, 1991, Jolly, Marie; flowers large, 21 petals, borne mostly singly and in small clusters, slight fragrance; foliage medium size, medium green, matte; few prickles; tall (45 cm.), upright, spreading, vigorous growth; [Party Girl × Fashion Flame]; int. by Rosehill Farm, 1992

Afternoon Delight – See **Floral Fairy Tale**, F

Agar HGal, pb, 1843, Vibert; flowers dark rose, spotted, medium, dbl., quartered, borne in clusters of 3-4, slight to moderate fragrance; foliage thick, clear green, large; numerous prickles

Agar HT, w, 1910, Brassac

Agate Pourpre HT, mr, 1967, Delbard-Chabert; flowers currant-red, 5-6 in., dbl., cupped; intermittent bloom; foliage dark, serrated; [Impeccable × Rome Glory]; int. by Cuthbert, 1965

Agatha – See **Francfort Agathé**, HGal

Agatha Christie F, dp, 1966, Buisman, G. A. H.; bud ovoid; flowers pink-red, dbl., borne in clusters; foliage dark; compact growth

Agatha Christie – See **Ramira**, LCl

Agatha Francofurtana – See **Francfort Agathé**, HGal

Agathe à Dix Coeurs HGal, m, before 1836, Lahaye; flowers lilac pink, edges lighter and spotted, medium

Agathe à Feuilles Glauques HGal, dp, before 1836, Noisette, E.; flowers medium, full

Agathe Admirable HGal, mp, about 1860, Miellez

Agathe Agréable D, mp, before 1814, Descemet

Agathe Agréable HGal, mp, about 1860, Miellez

Agathe Amédée – See **Amédée**, HGal

Agathe Amusante HGal, mp, about 1860, Miellez

Agathe Anaïs HGal, m, 1819, Vibert; flowers dark lilac pink, often marbled, full, semi-globular; Agathe group

Agathe Anna HGal, mp, before 1840, Vétillard; flowers bright pink

Agathe Athala HGal, op, before 1840, Garilland; flowers aurora-pink

Agathe Bécourt HGal, about 1860, Baumann

Agathe Carnée – See **Agathe Incarnata**, HGal

Agathe Couronnée – See **Marie-Louise**, D

Agathe Fatime – See **Fatime**, HGal

Agathe Incarnata HGal, lp, before 1811; sepals long; flowers silvery blush pink, small eye at center, medium, very dbl., quartered, flat, borne in small clusters, intense fragrance; foliage dark green, lightly serrated; numerous prickles; growth habit intermediate between the Gallicas and the Damasks; Agathe group; probably a hybrid of Gallica and Damask, from Holland

Agathe Majesteuse – See **Aimable Rouge**, HGal, 1819-1820

Agathe Marie-Louise – See **Agathe Incarnata**, HGal

Agathe Nabonnand – See **Mme Agathe Nabonnand**, T

Agathe Nouvelle – See **Héloïse**, HGal

Agathe Rose – See **Marie-Louise**, D

Agathe Royale – See **Royale**, HGal

Agathoïde HP, pb, 1860, Lebreton; flowers light pink with red tints, large, full

Age Tendre HT, dp, 1966, Croix, P.; bud long, pointed; flowers rose, large, dbl., high-centered; strong stems; vigorous growth; [Queen Elizabeth × Spartan]

Agemy HT, ob

Agemy Sport HT, dy

Agéna HT, op, 1970, Delbard-Chabert; bud long, pointed; flowers salmon-pink, large, dbl., moderate fragrance; foliage glossy, leathery; vigorous, bushy growth; [Chic Parisien × (Michèle Meilland × Mme Joseph Perraud)]; int. by Pepinieres G. Delbard, 1966

Agénor HGal, m, 1832, Vibert; flowers reddish-purple, medium, dbl.

Agkon HT, dp, Agel

Aglaé Adanson HGal, m, 1823, Vibert; flowers lilac pink, spotted with white, very large, dbl., cupped

Aglaia C, lp, before 1811, possibly Descemet; bud pink, pointed; flowers pink shading to lilac mixed with white, petals fluted, 2½ in., full, moderate fragrance; foliage slender, delicate

Aglaia HMult, ly, 1896, Schmitt; flowers straw-yellow to white, small, semi-dbl. to dbl., cupped, borne in very large clusters, moderate fragrance; seldom repeats; foliage glossy; vigorous growth; [*R. multiflora* × Rêve d'Or]; int. by Lambert, P., 1896

Agnes HRg, my, 1900, Saunders; flowers pale amber, center deeper, open, dbl., moderate fragrance; profuse, non-recurrent bloom; foliage light green, glossy, rugose; short stems; vigorous (6 ft.), bushy growth; very hardy; [*R. rugosa* × *R. foetida persiana*]; int. by Central Exp. Farm, 1922

Agnès Ageron HT, mr, 1958, Arles; flowers cerise-red, reverse tinted currant-red, well-formed; very vigorous growth; [Mme Méha Sabatier × Léonce Colombier]; int. by Roses-France

Agnes Barclay HT, yb, 1927, Clark, A.; flowers yellow and reddish-salmon; int. by NRS Victoria

Agnes Bernauer HT, lp, Kordes; bud globular; flowers clear pink with slight yellow base, dbl., moderate fragrance; int. in 1989

Agnes De Puy HT, dp, 1930, De Puy; flowers geranium-red veined gold, large, 22 petals, high-centered; long stems; very vigorous growth; hardy; [Lady Battersea × (Honeymoon × Mme Butterfly)]

Agnes Emily Carman HRg, mr, 1898, Carman; flowers bright crimson, large, dbl.; some repeat bloom; foliage large, rugose; vigorous (5 ft.) growth; possibly *R. rugosa* × Harison's Yellow

Agnes Glover HT, dr, 1924, Chaplin Bros.; flowers deep velvety crimson; [Admiral Ward × George Dickson]

Agnes Kruse F, 1936, Tantau; flowers velvety red, fiery, large; vigorous growth; [Mme Edouard Herriot × Eblouissant]

Agnes Laura Blackburn F, yb, 1990, Cants of Colchester, Ltd.; bud pointed; flowers bicolor yellow, medium, 5 petals, borne in sprays; [City of Portsmouth × seedling]; int. in 1989

Agnes Lucké HT, pb, 1960, Armbrust; bud long, pointed; flowers cerise-pink, reverse whitish pink, large to medium size, 50 petals, high-centered, moderate fragrance; foliage leathery; vigorous, upright growth; [Happiness × Peace, Climbing]; int. by Langbecker, 1959

Agnes Marguerite HT, or, 1953; flowers reddish-orange, shaded apricot; foliage glossy; int. by Bide

Agnes My Oh! F, ab, 2005, Michelle L. LeVan-Steklenski; flowers apricot blend, reverse light creamy apricot, 3½ in., dbl., borne mostly solitary; foliage medium size, medium green, semi-glossy; prickles small, straight and narrow, light green, moderate; growth compact, medium (3-4 ft.); hedge, garden decoration; [Fame × Anthony Meilland]; int. in 2007

Agnes Roggen HT, pb, 1926, Leenders, M.; flowers pale pink, reverse carmine, dbl.

Agnes Schilliger S, pb, Guillot-Massad; flowers full; int. by Roseraies Guillot, 2003

Agnes und Bertha HMult, lp, 1926, Bruder Alfons; bud dark pink; flowers small, single to semi-dbl., borne in large clusters; [Tausendschön × Dorothy Perkins]

Agnes Winchel HT, pb, 1989, Winchel, Joseph F.; bud pointed; flowers light pink with deep pink border, medium, 28 petals, high-centered, borne singly, slight fruity fragrance; foliage medium size, dark green, semi-glossy; prickles slightly hooked, medium, green; upright, medium growth; hips globular, medium, orange; PP7826; [Dorothy Anne × seedling]; int. by Coiner Nursery, 1990

Agni HT, or, G&L; flowers deep orange-red with blackish sheen, high-centered; long stems; int. in 1985

Agnihotri HT, dp, Kasturi; flowers large, rose red with lighter overtones at petal edges; int. by KSG Son, 1981

Agra HRg, lp, Rieksta; flowers large, loosely petaled, slight fragrance; growth to 1¼ m. tall and wide; int. in 1949

Agreement F, pb, 1971, LeGrice; flowers deep glowing pink, base golden, 3 in., 30 petals, high-centered; foliage glossy, bright green; tall, very free growth

Agrippina – See **Cramoisi Supérieur**, Ch

Agrippina, Climbing – See **Cramoisi Supérieur, Climbing**, Cl Ch

Ah Mow T, lp, Hay

Ahalya F, lp, Kasturi; flowers pale pink; continuous bloom; compact growth; [sport of Summer Snow]; int. by KSG Son, 1969

Ahimsa HT, my, 1996, Viraraghavan, M.S. Viru; bud golden; flowers large, clear yellow with darker centers, 5 in., full, borne mostly singly, moderate fragrance; foliage large, medium green, semi-glossy; no prickles; upright, medium (3 ft.) growth; [Mme Charles Sauvage × seedling]; int. by Hortico Roses, 1996

Ahlin F, ob, 1980, Fong; bud ovoid; flowers orange, 15 petals, high-centered, borne 4-6 per cluster, slight fragrance; foliage large, leathery; prickles hooked; upright growth; [seedling × Little Darling]

Ahoi F, or, 1964, Tantau, Math.; bud urn shaped; flowers bright orange-red, dbl., borne in clusters; low, bushy growth

Aïcha HSpn, dy, 1966, Petersen; bud long, pointed; flowers deep yellow, large, semi-dbl.; foliage light green; vigorous, bushy growth; [Souv. de Jacques Verschuren × Guldtop]

Aïda HT, mr, 1957, Mansuino, Dr. Ada; bud urn shaped; flowers clear rose-red, 5 in., 25 petals, cupped, intense fragrance; foliage leathery; vigorous, upright, symmetrical growth; PP1639; [Crimson Glory × Signora]; int. by J&P, 1956

Aigle Brun HGal, dr, before 1811; bud pointed; flowers blackish velvety bright crimson, 2½ in., semi-dbl.; few prickles

Aigle Noir HGal, dr, 1818, Godefroy (possibly Descemet); flowers velvety purple, medium, dbl.

Aigle Rouge – See **La Belle Sultane**, HGal

Aiglon HT, rb, 1961, Gaujard; bud long, pointed; flowers coppery red, reverse yellow, large, 38 petals; foliage glossy, light green; vigorous, upright growth; [Viola × Opera seedling]

Aileen F, ab, 1976, Wood; flowers light apricot, peach blended, large, dbl., moderate fragrance; upright, free growth; [sport of Elizabeth of Glamis]

Aimable Amie HGal, dp, before 1818, Trianon; flowers medium, dbl.

Aimable Beauté – See **L'Aimable Beauté**, HGal

Aimable Eléonore C, dp, before 1828, Coquerel; flowers medium, full

Aimable Emma – See **Belle Hélène**, HGal

Aimable Henriette HGal, mp; flowers carmine, medium

Aimable Pourpre HGal, dr, before 1811; bud round, flattened; flowers purple black, 3 in., semi-dbl., moderate fragrance; foliage elongated, finely dentate; from Holland

Aimable Rouge HGal, dp, 1819-1820, Vibert; flowers pink with hints of mauve, medium, very dbl., quartered, flat, borne mostly solitary, moderate fragrance; foliage small, clear green, round to eliptical; growth bushy, medium (1¼ m.)

Aimable Rouge HGal, mp, before 1845, Godefroy; flowers pink, edges whitish, medium, full, dahlia-like

Aimable Sophie – See **Belle Hélène**, HGal

Aimé Jacquet F, ab, Dorieux; flowers apricot-orange, fading pink, dbl., high-centered; low to medium growth; int. by Roseraies Dorieux, 2006

Aimé Plantier – See **Safrano**, T

Aimée Cochet HT, lp

Aimée Desprez N, m, about 1830, Desprez; flowers violet, center whitish pink, small, full

Aimée Vibert N, w, 1828, Vibert; bud pinking; flowers pure white, 5 cm., dbl., rosette, borne in small to medium clusters, strong musky fragrance; recurrent bloom; foliage semi-evergreen; nearly thornless; vigorous growth; [Champneys' Pink Cluster × a double form of *R. sempervirens*]

Aimée Vibert Scandens – See **Aimée Vibert, Climbing**, N

Aimée Vibert, Climbing N, w, 1841, Curtis

Aimée Vibert Jaune – See **Mme Brunner**, N

Ain't Misbehavin' Min, dr, 1990, McCann, Sean; flowers 5 petals; foliage small, green, semi-glossy; bushy growth; [Oonagh × (Pot Black × Black Jade)]; int. in 1991

Ain't She Sweet HT, or, 1993, Winchel, Joseph F.; flowers large, terra-cotta orange to deep orange-red, 3-3½ in., 30-35 petals, high-centered, borne mostly singly, intense spice and rose fragrance; foliage large, medium green, matte; some prickles; new stems dark red; medium, rounded, bushy growth; PP9071; [seedling × Dolly Parton]; int. by Weeks Roses, 1994

Air France HT, dr, 1964, Asseretto, A.; flowers red to cherry-red, medium, dbl., cupped, moderate fragrance; vigorous, bushy growth; PP2120; RULED EXTINCT 9/82 ARM; [seedling × Poinsettia]; int. by Pin-Blanchon, 1958

Air France Min, yb, 1983, Meilland, Mrs. Marie-Louise; bud oval, small; flowers light yellow, pink petal edges, 1½ in., 50 petals, cupped, borne in small clusters, no fragrance; free-flowering; foliage small, dark green, matte; prickles small, numerous; bushy (18 in.) growth; PP5180; [Minijet × (Darling Flame × Perle de Montserrat)]; int. in 1982

Air France Meillandina – See **Air France**, Min

Airain – See **Châtelet**, HT

Airborne F, dp, 1949, Leenders, M.; flowers deep pink, large, dbl.; vigorous growth; [Donald Prior × Rosamunde]

Aishwarya HT, dr, Kasturi & Sriram; flowers dark, velvety crimson with a blackish sheen, high-centered, moderate fragrance; recurrent; int. by KSG Son, 2001

Aisling F, w, 1966, Slattery; flowers ivory-cream, 4 in., dbl.; foliage small, glossy; very vigorous growth; [Queen Elizabeth × Allgold]

Ajaccio HT, mr, Croix, P.; int. in 1968

Ajanta HT, m, 1979, Takur; bud tapered; flowers 5-5½ in., 35-40 petals, high-centered, moderate spicy fragrance; foliage large, glossy; bushy growth; [(Lady X × unknown) × Memoriam]; int. by Doon Valley Roses, 1978

Aka Tombo Min, rb

Akane Fuji HRg, dp, Komatsu

Akash HT, m, Ghosh; flowers lilac pink, satiny petals, high-centered; int. in 1998

Akash Sundari HT, m, Pal, Dr. B.P.; flowers lilac pink with deep red flushes on outer petals, high-centered; int. in 1982

Akashdeep F, or, Chiplunkar; flowers bright pomegranate red, semi-dbl., borne in clusters; int. by Decospin, 1992

Akashi S, lp

Akatsuki HT, mr, Hiroshima; int. by Hiroshima Bara-en, 2005

Akebono HT, yb, 1964, Kawai; flowers light yellow flushed carmine, high pointed, large, 56 petals; foliage dark, glossy; vigorous, upright growth; [Ethel Sanday × Narzisse]

Akemi F, or, 1977, Keisei Rose Nurseries, Inc.; bud ovoid; flowers, 2-2½ in., 33 petals, cupped, slight fragrance; foliage dark; vigorous, upright growth; [(Sarabande × Hawaii) × (Sarabande × Ruby Lips)]

Akito F, w, 1973, Tantau, Math.; bud ovoid; flowers, dbl., borne in clusters; foliage medium size, medium green; upright, bushy growth; [Zorina × Nordia]

Akito HT, w, Tantau; flowers clear white, medium to large, dbl., high-centered, borne mostly singly; recurrent; stems medium to long; florist rose; int. by Rosen Tantau, 1998

Akogare HT, pb, Hiroshima; int. by Hiroshima Bara-en, 1998

Aksel Olsen Misc. OGR, mp, Gustavsson; [*R. helenae* × unknown]; very close in appearance and growth to *R. helenae*, its parent.; int. in 1998

Alabama HT, pb, 1976, Weeks; bud long, pointed; flowers deep pink, reverse near white, 3½-4 in., 25 petals, high-centered, moderate tea fragrance; foliage dark, leathery; upright growth; PP4008; [Mexicana × Tiffany]

Alabaster HT, w, 1963, Wyant; flowers, 5 in., 70-80 petals, high-centered, moderate fragrance; moderate, upright growth; [Blanche Mallerin × McGredy's Ivory]; int. by Wyant Nurs., 1961

Alabaster HT, w, Tantau; int. by Rosen Tantau, 2002

Aladdin F, mr, 1965, Verbeek; bud ovoid; flowers red, very dbl., borne in clusters; foliage dark; numerous prickles; [Miracle × Edith Piaf]

Aladdin Min, op, 1999, Schuurman, Frank B.; flowers, 1¾-2 in., full, borne in large clusters, moderate fragrance; foliage large, dark green, glossy; prickles moderate; spreading, tall growth; [Tinkerbell × Texas]; int. by Franko Roses New Zealand, 1995

Aladdin – See **Aladdin Palace**, MinFl

Aladdin Palace MinFl, ab, Poulsen; flowers apricot blend, 5-8 cm., 25 petals, slight wild rose fragrance; foliage dark; growth bushy, 40-60 cm.; PP15794; int. by Poulsen Roser, 2002

Aladdins Dream HT, dp, Twomey, Jerry; PP10149; [Silver Jubilee × Evening Star]; int. in 1995

Aladin Min, ob

Alain F, mr, 1948, Meilland, F.; bud ovoid; flowers bright carmine-red, semi-dbl., borne in clusters; foliage glossy, dark; upright, bushy growth; [(Guineé × Skyrocket) × Orange Triumph]; int. by C-P; Gold Medal, Geneva, 1948

Alain, Climbing Cl F, mr, 1957, Roth; flowers semi-dbl., borne in small clusters

Alain Blanchard HGal, m, 1839, Vibert; flowers purplish-crimson, becoming mottled giving a spotted look, semi-dbl., cupped, moderate fragrance; foliage medium green; vigorous, medium growth; [probably *R. centifolia* × *R. gallica*]; could be classified as a Centifolia, as it is probably a hybrid; possibly bred by Coquerel, and distributed by Vibert

Alain Blanchard Panachée HGal, pb; flowers identical to its parent, but with fewer petals and stripes instead of spots; [sport of Alain Blanchard]

Alain Souchon – See **Rouge Royale**, HT

Alamein F, mr, 1963, McGredy, Sam IV; flowers scarlet, 3 in., 10 petals, flat, borne in clusters; foliage dark; vigorous, bushy growth; [Spartan × Queen Elizabeth]; int. by McGredy

Alamode Min, w, 1997, Brown, Ted; flowers medium, single, borne in small clusters; foliage medium size, dark green, glossy; bushy, medium (2½ ft.) growth; [Esprit × Party Girl]

Alan Butterworth HT, ob, 2000, Rawlins, R.; flowers, 3¾ in., full, borne mostly solitary, slight fragrance; foliage dark green, glossy; prickles ½ in., triangular, moderate; growth upright, tall (5 ft.); garden decorative; [seedling × seedling]

Alan Sandys MinFl, mr, 2006, Thomson, George L.; flowers medium red, reverse lighter, 2 in., very full, borne in small clusters; foliage medium size, dark green, glossy; prickles medium, hooked, brown, moderate; growth compact, short (24 in.); garden decorative; [seedling × Europeana]; int. by Ross Roses, 2006

Alan Tew HT, op, McGredy; flowers deep salmon, large, dbl., high-centered, moderate fragrance; free-flowering; foliage glossy, leathery; growth medium; int. by Ludwig's Roses, 2003

Alan Titchmarsh S, dp, Austin, David; bud rounded; flowers very full, globular, moderate warm Old Rose fragrance; recurrent; slightly arching (4 ft.) growth; int. by David Austin Roses, 2006

Alanna Holloway HT, dr, 1974, Holloway; flowers ovoid; foliage glossy, leathery; very vigorous growth; [sport of Uncle Walter]

Alaska HT, w, 1949, Meilland, F.; flowers ivory-white, well-formed, large, 50 petals; vigorous, upright growth; [Peace × Blanche Mallerin]

Alaska Centennial Gr, dr, 1967, Morey, Dr. Dennison; bud long, pointed; flowers dark blood-red-scarlet, 3½-5 in., dbl., high-centered; foliage dark, leathery, glossy; vigorous, upright growth; [Siren × Avon]; int. by General Bionomics, 1967

Alastair McEwan F, ly, 2005, Rawlins, R.; flowers full, borne in small clusters, slight fragrance; foliage dark green, semi-glossy; upright, medium (1 m.) growth; garden; [Solitaire × (Baby Love × Amber Queen)]

Alba C, w, before 1775; flowers pure white, large, full

Alba – See ***R. rugosa alba*** (Rehder)

Alba – See **Fausse Unique**, D

Alba Bifera A, w, 1843, Augeul; flowers lilac white, 5-6 cm., very full; some repeat

Alba Carnea HP, lp, 1867, Touvais

Alba Flore Multiplici – See **Pompon Blanc**, HSpn

Alba Foliacea A, w, 1824

Alba Garcia HT, w, Viveros Fco. Ferrer, S L; flowers 26 petals, high-centered; [Shocking Blue × Carta Blanca]

Alba Maxima A, w, before 1867; flowers similar to Maiden's Blush, but center creamy, with a faint buff tinge on opening, aging to pure white, 4 in., dbl, flat, borne in clusters of 2-6, moderate fragrance; non-recurrent; foliage clear gray-green; growth to 6-8 ft.; a natural sport of *R.* × *alba semi-plena*, but with more petals

Alba Meidiland S, w, 1987, Meilland, Mrs. Marie-Louise; bud globular, small; flowers medium, very white, 3½-4 cm., 50-55 petals, cupped, borne in clusters of 8-15, no fragrance; free-flowering; foliage medium size, medium green, glossy; spreading growth, vigorous (4-5 ft.); PP6891; [*R. sempervirens* × Marthe Carron]; int. in 1985

Alba Meillandécor – See **Alba Meidiland**, S

Alba Meillandina Min, w, 1988, Meilland, Mrs. Marie-Louise; bud conical; flowers very dbl., 85-90 petals, flattened cup, borne singly and in small clusters, no fragrance; free-flowering; foliage small, medium green, semi-glossy; bushy (12 in.) growth; PP7347; [MEIdonq × (Darling × Jack Frost)]; int. by SNC Meilland & Cie, 1986

Alba Minima A, mp, Scarman; int. in 1997

Alba Mutabilis HP, 1865, Verdier; flowers delicate pink, clouded with deeper pink; sometimes classed as M

Alba Odorata HBc, w, 1834, Mariani; flowers yellowish-white, anthers yellow, large, full, flat, moderate fragrance; foliage 5-7 oval leaflets, glossy; prickles straight, large; stems wood greenish-purple; [*R. bracteata* × *R. roxburghii*]; often confused with Maria Leonida

Alba Plena – See ***R. banksiae banksiae*** (Aiton)

Alba Regalis – See **Great Maiden's Blush**, A

Alba Rosea – See **Celestial**, A

Alba Rosea – See **Beauté Tendre**, A

Alba Rosea – See **Mme Bravy**, T

Alba Rubifolia HWich, w, 1901, Van Fleet; flowers large, dbl., moderate fragrance; foliage glossy, evergreen; growth creeping

Alba Semi-plena A, w, before 1754; flowers medium, showing yellow stamens, 8-12 petals, strong fragrance; non-recurrent; foliage glaucous, gray-green; prickles strong, few; growth upright, large (12-15 ft.); large crop of red hips in fall

Alba Simplex HBc, w; flowers single; [*R. bracteata* × unknown]

Albania Min, Dot, Simon; int. in 1991

Albast HT, op, 1928, Van Rossem; bud ovoid; flowers salmon-pink, open, large, dbl.; foliage bronze, glossy; vigorous growth; [Morgenglans × Mrs Wemyss Quin]

Albatross HT, w, 1908, Paul, W.; flowers white, shaded pink, large, full

Albatross HWich, w; int. in 1988

Albéric Barbier HWich, w, 1900, Barbier; bud small, yellow; flowers creamy white, center yellow, 8 cm., dbl., borne singly or in small clusters, moderate fruity, sweet fragrance; non-recurrent; foliage glossy, dark; vigorous growth; [*R. wichurana* × Shirley Hibberd]

Alberich – See **Happy**, Pol

Albert F, op, 1962, Jones; flowers orange salmon, 50 petals, high-centered, borne in clusters; foliage glossy, bronze; vigorous, bushy, compact growth; int. by Hennessey

Albert Durand T, lp, 1906, Schwartz; flowers light carmine pink, shaded flesh white, center darker carmine, large, full; [Luciole × André Schwartz]

Albert Dureau HP, dr, 1869, Vigneron; flowers shining dark red, shaded scarlet, large

Albert Edward S, ly, 1970, Hillier; flowers creamy yellow, 1½-2 in., 5 petals, moderate fragrance; vigorous growth; [*R. spinosissima altaica* × *R. hugonis*]; int. in 1961

Albert Fourès T, rb, 1899, Bonnaire; flowers brick red with golden yellow, large, full

Albert-Georg Pluta Rose F, mr, Tantau, Math.; flowers luminous red, large, dbl.; int. in 1986

Albert Gilles HT, op, 1943, Mallerin, C.; flowers pink tinted coral; [Julien Potin × Mme Joseph Perraud]; int. by A. Meilland

Albert Hoffmann T, ly, 1904, Welter; flowers very large, dbl., intense fragrance; [Souv de Catherine Guillot × Maman Cochet]

Albert la Blotais HP, dr, 1881, Moreau et Robert

Albert la Blotais, Climbing Cl HP, mr, 1888, Pernet Père; flowers deep pink to light red, 11 cm., very dbl., flat, strong fragrance; [Gloire de Dijon × Général Jacqueminot]

Albert Maumené S, or, 1934, Sauvageot, H.; bud large, pointed, ovoid, copper-red; flowers carrot-red shaded copper, semi-dbl., cupped; recurrent; foliage glossy, dark; growth very vigorous, bushy, open; [Mme Edouard Herriot × *R. hugonis*]

Albert Pagé – See **Albert Payé**, HP

Albert Payé HP, lp, 1873, Touvais; flowers flesh-pink, large; vigorous growth

Albert Pike HT, dp, 1926, Vestal; flowers glowing cerise, flushed peach at times; [sport of Columbia]

Albert Poyet LCl, pb, Eve, A.; flowers cherry pink, cream at center, aging to crimson with light pink, 4 in., dbl., borne in small clusters, slight fragrance; int. in 1979

Albert Stopford T, lp, 1898, Nabonnand; bud long; sepals large; flowers dark crimson rose, large, full, borne mostly solitary, moderate fragrance; foliage large; prickles strong, numerous; growth vigorous; [Général Schablikine × Papa Gontier]

Albert Weedall HT, ly, 1997, Scrivens, Len; flowers large, dbl., borne in large clusters; foliage medium size, medium green, semi-glossy; some prickles; upright, tall (5ft.) growth; [seedling × seedling]; int. by F. Haynes & Partners

Alberta F, dp, 1995, Fleming, Joyce L.; flowers large, 10 petals, flat, borne in small clusters, slight fragrance; foliage medium size, dark green, semi-glossy; some prickles; growth compact, spreading, medium; [Carefree Beauty × Red Hot]; int. by Hortico

Alberta Hunter F, ly, 1985, French, Richard; flowers red stamens, large, 25 petals, cupped, borne singly; foliage medium size, dark, semi-glossy; prickles small, straight, red; medium, upright, bushy growth; hips small, globular, dull orange; [Eleanor Perenyi × Lillian Gish]

Albertan S, mp, 1962, Erskine; flowers bright pink, 15-18 petals; [Athabasca × unknown]

Albertina Sisulu S, w, Dickson; int. by Ludwig's Roses, 2004

Albertine HWich, op, 1921, Barbier; bud ovoid; flowers light salmon pink, tinted yellow, darker reverse, aging to light pink, 7-9 cm., semi-dbl. to dbl., cupped, borne in small clusters, moderate fragrance; non-recurrent; foliage dark green, glossy; prickles numerous, large; vigorous growth; [*R. wichurana* × Mrs Arthur Robert Waddell]

Alberto N. Calamet HT, mp, 1909, Soupert & Notting; flowers flesh pink, large, full

Alberton Amor HT, dp, Taschner; int. in 1995

Albinia S, op, Poulsen; int. in 1996

Albion HP, pb, 1870, Liabaud; flowers scarlet red, shaded orange, large, full, spherical

Albion HT, mp, 1985, Poulsen, Niels D.; flowers large, dbl., urn-shaped, borne singly, slight fragrance; foliage semi-glossy; bushy growth; [Frileuse × seedling]; int. by Vilmorin-Andrieux, 1969

Albion S, w, Skinner; bud cream; flowers dbl.; recurrent bloom; foliage leaflets small, firm, dark; growth to 4 ft.; hardy; [*R. laxa* hybrid]

Albo Pleno – See **Pompon Blanc**, HSpn

Albrecht Dürer S, ob, Tantau; flowers orange to apricot, large, very dbl.; int. by Rosen Tantau, 2003

Albuquerque Enchantment Min, rb, 1997, Moore, Ralph S.; flowers medium, dbl., borne in small clusters; foliage medium size, medium green, semi-glossy; medium (30-45 cm.) bushy, spreading growth; [Poker Chip × Cherry Magic]; int. by Sequoia Nurs.

Alcantara – See **Red Flower Carpet**, S

Alcazar F, or, 1961, Gaujard; bud pointed; flowers coppery red, 3 in., 18 petals; foliage glossy, bronze; bushy growth; [Jolie Princesse × (Opera × Miss France)]

Alcha S, mp

Alchemist – See **Alchymist**, S

Alchymist S, ab, 1956, Kordes; bud ovoid; flowers yellow shaded orange, pink and red, large, very dbl.; heavy, non-recurrent bloom; foliage glossy, bronze; vigorous, upright (6 ft.) growth; [Golden Glow × *R. rubiginosa* hybrid]

Alcide Vigneron HP, mp, 1862, Vigneron; flowers large, full

Alcime HGal, m, 1845, Vibert; flowers very dark violet, medium, dbl.

Alcime M, mr, 1861, Robert & Moreau; flowers purple-red, 8-10 cm., borne in large clusters

Alcine HGal, dp, 1834, Vibert; flowers deep rosy pink, spotted white, edged lilac-blush, large, dbl., cupped; vigorous, upright growth

Alcmaria F, mr, Verbeek; flowers blood red, large, dbl.; int. in 1971

Alconbury F, dp, 1996, Taylor, Franklin; flowers deep pink with touch of violet, medium, very dbl., high-centered, borne singly and in sprays; foliage medium size, dark green, semi-glossy; few prickles; tall (48 in.), upright, bushy growth; int. by Taylor's Roses, 1997

Aldégonde – See **Rouge Formidable**, HGal

Alden Biesen HMsk, lp, 2000, Lens, Louis; flowers medium pink, reverse lighter, 3-4 cm., single, borne in large clusters; recurrent; foliage medium size, dark green, semi-glossy; prickles moderate; upright, medium (4-5 ft.) growth; [Pleine de Grace × Pretty Pink]; int. by Louis Lens NV, 1996

Alec Rose F, or, 1969, McGredy, Sam IV; flowers scarlet, well-formed, borne in trusses; free growth; [Hassan × John Church]; int. by McGredy

Alecia Carol HT, mp, 2006, Mander, George; flowers luminous pink, reverse light pink, 5 in., full, borne in small clusters; foliage large, dark green, semi-glossy; prickles in., needle point, medium brown, moderate; growth bushy, tall (4-5 ft.); garden, exhibition; [Tiffany × Pascali]; int. by Hortico, Inc., 2006

Alec's Red HT, mr, 1971, Cocker, A. M.; flowers deep, bright crimson, 6 in., 45 petals, moderate fragrance; foliage matte, green; vigorous, upright growth; PP3056; [Fragrant Cloud × Dame de Coeur]; int. by J. Cocker & Sons, 1970; President's International Trophy, RNRS, 1970, Gold Medal, RNRS, 1970, Edland Fragrance Medal, ARS, 1969, ADR, 1973

Alec's Red, Climbing Cl HT, mr, 1976, Harkness; flowers dbl., borne singly or in small clusters; [sport of Alec's Red]

Alector Cramoisi HGal, dr, before 1811, Dupont; flowers velvety crimson red, large, dbl., moderate fragrance

Aleene Min, mp, 2001, Giles, Diann; flowers medium, full, borne mostly solitary, no fragrance; foliage medium size, medium green, matte; prickles small, straight, few; growth upright, medium; garden decorative, exhibition; [seedling × seedling]; int. by Giles Rose Nursery, 2001

Alegria F, ob; int. by deRuiter, 2001

Alegrias F, rb, 1981, Rose Barni; bud globular; flowers medium yellow, reverse orange-red, 23 petals, cupped, borne 3-6 per cluster, no fragrance; foliage medium size, glossy; prickles straight, reddish-green; upright, bushy growth; [seedling × Charleston seedling]; int. in 1978

Alejandra Conde Min, dr, Viveros Fco. Ferrer, S L; flowers 22 petals, rosette; [M Litigan × Scarlet Meillandina]

Alena Gr, ob, 1970, Raffel; flowers orange, large, dbl., cupped; foliage large, glossy, dark; vigorous, upright, bushy growth; [seedling × Tropicana]; int. by Port Stockton Nursery

Alessa LCl, mr, Jensen; int. in 1988

Aletha Min, yb, 2000, Schramm, Dwayne; flowers yellow, tinged pink, reverse yellow, small, full, borne mostly singly, slight fragrance; foliage small, light green, matte; few prickles; growth spreading, low (8-12 in.); [Orange Honey × Orange Honey]

Aletha June Min, lp, 2000, Moe, Mitchie; flowers full, high-centered, borne mostly singly, slight fragrance; foliage medium size, medium green, semi-glossy; few prickles; growth upright, medium (15-18 in.); [Grace Seward × Blue Peter]; int. by Mitchie's Roses and More

Alex Brackstone F, dy, 2006, Rawlins, Ronnie; flowers yellow, reverse yellow, 2½ in., full, borne in large clusters; foliage medium size, dark green, glossy; prickles ½ in., triangular, few; growth upright, medium (33 in.); garden decoration; [Baby Love × Amber Queen × Laura Ford × Goldbusch]

Alex C. Collie F, mr, Cocker; int. in 1996

Alex Dickson – See **Mme Pulliat**, HP

Alexa MinFl, dp, 2001, Moe, Mitchie; flowers deep pink, reverse light pink, 1½-2 in., dbl., high-centered, borne mostly singly, slight fragrance; foliage medium size, dark green, semi-glossy; prickles medium, straight, light green, few; growth spreading, tall (24-30 in.); garden decoration, exhibition; [Grace Seward × Blue Peter]; int. by Mitchie's Roses and More, 2001

Alexander HT, or, 1972, Harkness, R.; bud pointed; flowers bright vermilion-red, 5 in., 25 petals, high-centered, slight fragrance; foliage glossy; tall, vigorous growth; [Tropicana × (Ann Elizabeth × Allgold)]; int. by J. L. Harkness; ADR, 1974, James Mason Medal, RNRS, 1987, Gold Medal, Hambourg, 1973, Gold Medal, Belfast, 1974

Alexander Emslie HT, dr, 1918, Dickson, A.; flowers deep crimson, base slightly white, large, full, moderate fragrance

Alexander Hill Gray T, dy, 1911, Dickson, A.; flowers deep lemon-yellow, aging deeper, large; vigorous growth

Alexander Laquemont – See **Alexandre Laquement**, HGal

Alexander MacKenzie – See **A. MacKenzie**, S

Alexander Marghiloman HT, w, 1928, Mühle; flowers cream-white, center salmon; [Harry Kirk × unknown]

Alexander Milne Min, lp, 1987, Laver, Keith G.; flowers light pink, reverse cream, small, 35 petals, high-centered, borne singly; foliage small, medium green, semi-glossy; prickles straight, light brown; bushy, low growth; hips rounded, orange; [Corn Silk × Ice Princess]; int. by Springwood Roses

Alexander von Humboldt HKor, mr, 1960, Kordes, R.; flowers fiery blood red, occasionally flecked white, medium, dbl., rosette, borne in large clusters, slight fragrance; foliage glossy; vigorous (9-12 ft.) growth; [*R. × kordesii* × Cleopatra]; int. by Kordes

Alexandra – See **Alexander**, HT

Alexandra HT, yb, Kordes; int. in 1973

Alexandra – See **Princess Alexandra**, S

Alexandra HT, ly, Kordes; flowers pale yellow, dbl., high-centered, slight fragrance; stems 80 cm.; int. by W. Kordes Söhne, 2003

Alexandra Kordana Min, ab, Kordes; flowers bronzy with pink tones on reverse, dbl.; container rose; int. by W. Kordes Söhne

Alexandra Leek F, ob, 1995, Fleming, Joyce; flowers soft orange, medium, single, borne in small clusters, moderate fragrance; foliage medium size, medium green, semi-glossy; some prickles; growth upright, bushy, tall; [Masquerade × Mrs John Laing]; int. by Hortico

Alexandra Rose – See **The Alexandra Rose**, S

Alexandre Chomer HP, m, 1875, Liabaud; flowers velvety pruple, nuanced violet, large, full; prickles irregular, reddish

Alexandre Damaizin HP, mp, 1861, Damaizin

Alexandre Dumas HP, dr, 1861, Margottin; flowers velvety maroon, striped poppy, large, full

Alexandre Dumas D, lp, 1969, Fankhauser; flowers very dbl., cupped, borne in clusters, intense damask fragrance; abundant, non-recurrent bloom; foliage small, light green, glossy, leathery; vigorous, upright (6-8 ft.) growth; [Ma Perkins × *R. damascena versicolor*]

Alexandre Dupont HP, dr, 1892, Liabaud; flowers dark, velvety red, very large, dbl.; [Triomphe de l'Exposition × unknown]

Alexandre Dutitre HP, lp, 1878, Lévêque; flowers light bright pink, large, full; very remontant

Alexandre Fontaine HP, dp, 1860, Fontaine

Alexandre Girault HWich, pb, 1909, Barbier; bud rose-pink; flowers carmine-red, base salmon, reverse lighter, 6-7 cm., dbl., borne in small clusters, moderate fragrance; non-recurrent; foliage dark green, glossy; vigorous growth; [*R. wichurana* × Papa Gontier]

Alexandre Laquement HGal, m, before 1885; flowers violet spotted with red

Alexandre Trémouillet HWich, dp, 1903, Barbier; flowers blush white, tinted with rose and salmon center, 8-9 cm., dbl., borne in large clusters; foliage dark green, oval, glossy, heavily dentate; prickles numerous, upright; [*R. wichurana* × Souv de Catherine Guillot]

Alexandre von Humboldt HP, lp, 1869, Verdier, E.; flowers silvery pink, shaded carmine, large, full

Alexandria Rose S, rb, 1988, Williams, J. Benjamin; flowers ivory to white with light red washing on petal edge, deeper yellow at base, large, dbl., pointed; free-flowering; foliage large, dark green, glossy, disease-resistant; upright, bushy, vigorous, strong, hardy growth; [(Queen Elizabeth × Kordes' Perfecta) × Mount Shasta]

Alexandria's Rose Min, mp, 2004, Williams, Michael C. /Houston, John P; flowers medium pink, reverse outer part of petals have a whitening effect, 1½ in., dbl., borne singly and in small clusters, moderate fragrance; foliage medium size, dark green, semi-glossy; prickles slant down, moderate; growth upright, angular, medium to tall (18-24 in.); garden, exhibition; [seedling × seedling]; int. by The Mini Rose Garden

Alexandrine Bachmeteff HP, mr, 1852, Margottin

Alexandrine Chapuis HT, my, 1935, Vially; bud long, pointed, yellow, shaded carmine; flowers well-formed, large, dbl.; foliage bright green; [Feu Joseph Looymans × seedling]

Alexandrine de Belfroy HP, op, 1859, Fontaine

Alexia F, pb, 1983, Cants of Colchester, Ltd.; flowers cream blended pink, medium, 20 petals, moderate fragrance; foliage medium size, medium green, semi-glossy; upright growth; [Jubilant × seedling]; int. in 1984

Alexia Wilson F, ob, 1972, Horner, C. P.; flowers cream veined orange; [sport of Elizabeth of Glamis]

Alexis – See **L'Oréal Trophy**, HT

Alexis Lepère HP, mr, 1875, Vigneron; flowers very large, dbl.

Alezane HT, ab, 1935, Pahissa; bud urn shaped, reddish brown; flowers deep apricot, large, dbl., cupped, moderate fruity fragrance; foliage glossy, bronze, dark; very vigorous growth; [Angèle Pernet × Comtesse de Castilleja]; int. by J&P

Alfabia S, op, Noack; flowers coral, lighter reverse, 3 cm., 5-10 petals, cupped, flattening when open, borne in large sprays; recurrent; foliage dark green, glossy; prickles moderate, 5 mm., curved slightly downward; compact (3-4 ft.) growth; PP14441; [Korsami × seedling]; int. by Noack's Rosen, 2002

Alfi Min, dp, 1986, Olesen, Pernille & Mogens N.; flowers soft lavendar to pink, small, 40-45 petals, borne in large clusters and candelabras, no fragrance; foliage small, light green, glossy; compact growth, free flowering; PP5058; [Mini-Poul × Harriet Poulsen]; int. by Poulsen's Roses, 1981

Alfie Luv Min, op, 1991, Taylor, Pete & Kay; flowers orange-pink with lavender hue, yellow base, large, dbl., borne mostly singly, slight fragrance; foliage medium size, medium green, semi-glossy; some prickles; upright, medium (60 cm.) growth; [Azure Sea × seedling]; int. by Taylor's Roses, 1992

Alfieri HGal, m, 1833, Vibert; flowers lilac-pink, medium, dbl.

Alfred A. Buckwell HT, mr, 1952, Buckwell; flowers red, 3 in., 30 petals, high-centered; foliage dark, leathery; vigorous growth; [Hector Deane × Betty Uprichard]

Alfred Colomb HP, dp, 1865, Lacharme, F.; flowers strawberry-red, reflexes crimson-carmine, large, 45 petals, high-centered, intense fragrance; recurrent bloom; growth dense; [Général Jacqueminot × unknown]

Alfred de Dalmas M, lp, 1855, Laffay, M.; bud rose-colored; flowers light pink with blush edges, of poor quality, small, dbl., borne in corymbs; some recurrent bloom; very prickly; vigorous, straggling growth

Alfred de Rougemont HP, dr, 1863, Lacharme, F.; flowers crimson-magenta, well-formed, very large, dbl.; vigorous, upright growth; [Général Jacqueminot × unknown]

Alfred Dietrich HMult, rb, Mertens; flowers carmine with white stripes, dbl., slight fragrance; int. in 1980

Alfred K. Williams HP, mr, 1877, Schwartz, J.; flowers carmine-red, changing to magenta; [sport of Général Jacqueminot]

Alfred Leveau HP, mp, 1880, Vigneron; flowers carmine-rose, aging lighter, large, full, borne mostly solitary; foliage dark green; prickles few, chestnut brown; growth upright

Alfred Newton HT, yb, 1959, Kemp, M.L.; flowers pale yellow edged crimson, 5 in., 35-40 petals, high-centered; foliage dark; vigorous growth; [Moonbeam × Karl Herbst]

Alfred Pétot HT, dr, 1935, Buatois; bud elongated; flowers crimson, well-formed, large, dbl.; foliage dark; strong stems; very vigorous growth; [Jeanne Excoffier × Yves Druhen]

Alfred Sisley S, ob, Delbard; flowers orange and pink stripes with yellow reverse, full, slight fragrance; free-flowering; growth to 80 cm.; int. by Georges Delbard SA, 2005

Alfred W. Mellersh HT, op, 1918, Paul, W.; flowers salmon-yellow, shaded rose, center amber

Alfredo Moreira da Silva HT, yb, 1946, Mallerin, C.; bud long, pointed; flowers golden yellow tinted coral, large, semi-dbl.; foliage dark; very vigorous, upright growth; [Dr. Kirk × Peace]; int. by A. Meilland

Alfresco LCl, pb, 2000, Warner, Chris; flowers salmon blended with yellow, reverse pink, 4 in., 24 petals, borne in small clusters, moderate sweet fragrance; foliage medium size, dark green, semi-glossy; few prickles; growth climbing, upright, spreading, tall (9-10 ft.); walls, fences, pergolas; [Mary Sumner × Summer Wine]; int. by Warner's Roses, 2001

Alger HT, op, 1943, Gaujard; bud pointed; flowers clear pink, reverse salmon-pink, very large, dbl.; foliage leathery; vigorous growth

Algonquin S, pb, 1928, Central Exp. Farm; flowers purplish rose, center white, large, single, flat; non-recurrent; foliage dull, yellow-green; very vigorous (10 ft.) growth; hips large, bottle-shaped, red; hardy; [*R. rubrifolia* × *R. rugosa* hybrid seedling]

Ali-Baba F, or, 1963, Croix, P.; flowers large, 15-20 petals, borne in clusters; [(Corail × Baccará) × seedling]

Ali Pacha Chériff HP, mr, 1886, Lévêque, P.; flowers vermilion red, tinted blackish purple, large, full

Alibi F, w, 1961, deRuiter; flowers well-formed, 3-4 in., 30 petals; vigorous growth; [Kaiserin Auguste Viktoria × Pink Fragrance]

Alicante MinFl, dp, Poulsen; flowers deep pink to light red, 5-8 cm., dbl., no fragrance; foliage dark; growth bushy, 20-40 cm.; int. by Poulsen Roser, 2004

Alice A, w, about 1830, Parmentier; flowers white shaded flesh, medium, full

Alice Pol, mp, 1925, Spek; flowers pink, fringed, borne in large clusters; [Echo × Orléans Rose]

Alice S, pb, 1935, Wright, Percy H.; flowers dbl.; RULED EXTINCT 11/80 ARM; hybrid macounii

Alice HT, lp, 1981, Allender, Robert William; bud long; flowers light pink, darker center, 45 petals, high-centered, borne singly, no fragrance; shy bloom; foliage large; prickles long, red; spreading (to about 4 ft.) growth; [Royal Highness × Christian Dior]; int. in 1978

Alice Aldrich HRg, lp, 1901, Lovett, J.T.; flowers clear, bright pink, large, dbl.; repeat bloom; [*R. rugosa* × Colonel de Sansal, or Caroline de Sansal]; int. by Conard & Jones

Alice Amos F, pb, 1922, Spek; bud long, pointed; flowers cerise, white eye, single, borne in clusters on strong stem; very vigorous growth; [Tip-Top × seedling]; int. by Prior

Alice Bracegirdle HT, w, 2001, Bracegirdle, A.J.; flowers 5 in., full, high-centered, borne mostly solitary; foliage large, medium green, matte; prickles medium, straight, few; growth upright, medium (3½ ft.); exhibition; [sport of Sunderland Supreme]

Alice Chamrion Pol, lp, 1908, Dubreuil; flowers flesh pink

Alice Cory Wright HT, dp, 1910, Paul, W.; flowers large, full

Alice de Rothschild HT, w, 1920, Gemen & Bourg; flowers creamy white with pink reflections, center darker

Alice Dureau – See **Mme Alice Dureau**, HP

Alice Faye Min, rb, 1992, McCann, Sean; flowers full circle of red with distinct yellow eye from the bottom view, 2½ in., 22-24 petals; foliage large, medium green, semi-glossy; upright, tall growth; [seedling × seedling]; int. by Justice Miniature Roses, 1992

Alice Fontaine B, op, 1879, Fontaine; flowers light salmon pink, medium, full

Alice Furon HT, w

Alice Garnier – See **Mme Alice Garnier**, HWich

Alice Grahame HT, w, 1903, Dickson, A.; flowers ivory white, tinted salmon, very large, very dbl., moderate fragrance

Alice Gray – See **Scandens**, Ayr

Alice Hamilton Ch, dr, 1903, Nabonnand; bud long; flowers velvety crimson red, dbl., slight sweet fragrance; foliage dark green; [Bengale Nabonnand × Parsons' Pink China]

Alice Harding HT, my, 1937, Mallerin, C.; bud ovoid; flowers golden yellow, large, dbl.; foliage glossy, dark; vigorous growth; [Souv. de Claudius Pernet × Mrs Pierre S. duPont]; int. by J&P

Alice Hoffmann Ch, rb, 1897, Hoffmann; flowers pink, touched cherry

Alice Jarrett F, ob, 1999, Everitt, Derrick; flowers orange, reverse cream yellow, 3-3½ in., full, borne in small clusters, slight fragrance; foliage medium size, medium green, semi-glossy; prickles moderate; upright, tall (3-3½ ft.) growth; [(Mary Sumner × (L'Oreal Trophy × Edith Holden)) × Friendship]

Alice Kaempff HT, pb, 1921, Felberg-Leclerc; bud medium, long-pointed, pink with a light violet tint; flowers silvery rose-pink, center coppery yellow, large, dbl., globular, moderate fragrance; foliage medium size, glossy; [General MacArthur × Radiance]

Alice King Cl F, mr, 1988, Harrison, G.; flowers medium, luminous red, aging lighter, small, 40-50 petals, borne in sprays; foliage light green, glossy; prickles small, medium red; vigorous, slight perpetual growth; [Dublin Bay × seedling]

Alice Lee Min, pb, 1991, Taylor, Pete & Kay; bud pointed; flowers pink with color lighter towards edge of petals, giving a lavender cast. medium, 15-18 petals, high-centered, borne singly, slight fragrance; foliage medium size, medium green, semi-glossy; upright, bushy, medium growth; [Azure Sea × seedling]; int. by Taylor's Roses, 1990

Alice Lemon HT, w, 1912, Hill, E. G.

Alice Leroi M, pb, 1842, Vibert; bud well-mossed; flowers lilac-blush shaded rose, center deep rose, very large, dbl.; vigorous growth

Alice Lindsell HT, lp, 1902, Dickson, A.; flowers creamy white with a pink center, large, dbl., high-centered

Alice Manley HT, my, 1959, Joseph H. Hill, Co.; bud long, pointed; flowers mimosa-yellow, 3½-4 in., 45-50 petals, high-centered, slight fragrance; foliage leathery; vigorous, upright, bushy growth; PP1546; [seedling × Golden Rapture]; int. in 1958

Alice Marion Whyte HT, lp, 1932, Evans; flowers soft pink, fading pure white

Alice Mavis S, lp, Peden, G.H.; int. in 1994

Alice of Ingleside HT, 1910, Briggs

Alice Pat F, rb, 1982, Jerabek, Paul E.; bud ovoid; flowers red shading to white, reverse white shaded pink, 38 petals, flat, borne 1-6 per cluster, slight fragrance; foliage dark, glossy; prickles slightly hooked, reddish-tan; upright, short growth; [seedling × seedling]; Bronze Medal, ARC TG, 1983

Alice Springs LCl, lp, Peden; flowers cupped, cupped, moderate fragrance

Alice Stern HT, w, 1926, Gillot, F.; bud long, pointed; flowers white, center cream, sometimes salmon, large, 30-40 petals; foliage dark, bronze; vigorous, bushy growth; [Grange Colombe × Sunburst]

Alice Vena HGal, m, before 1867; flowers plum-purple, large, borne in clusters

Alice Vibert C, mr, 1855, Robert; flowers bright rose red, medium, full, globular

Alice Vigneron – See **Alcide Vigneron**, HP

Alice Wieman Pol, dp, 1970, Bodley; flowers pink, open, small, dbl., moderate fragrance; continuous bloom; growth moderate, bushy; PP2893; [seedling × Rita Sammons]

Alicia HT, pb, 1972, Lees; flowers rose-pink, edged cream, large, 36 petals; foliage dark; vigorous growth; [Golden Scepter × Ena Harkness]

Alicia HT, pb, 2000, Giles, Diann; flowers full, borne mostly singly, no fragrance; foliage medium size, light green, matte; prickles moderate; growth bushy, medium (4 ft.); [Vera Dalton × Tiffany]; int. by Giles Rose Nursery

Alicia Courage HT, pb, Courage; flowers pink with shades changing with weather, dbl., high-centered, moderate fragrance; growth medium; int. in 2002

Alicja LCl, lp

Alida HT, mr, 1938, Lens; bud long, pointed; flowers well-formed, very dbl.; foliage bright; vigorous, bushy growth; [Charles P. Kilham × E.G. Hill]

Alida Lovett HWich, lp, 1905, Van Fleet; bud long, pointed; flowers shell-pink, base shaded sulfur, 7-8 cm., dbl., borne in clusters of 3-10; non-recurrent; foliage glossy; vigorous, climbing growth; [*R. wichurana* × Souv de President Carnot]; int. by J.T. Lovett

Alie Dool HT, m, 2003, Rawlins, R.; flowers lavender pink, medium, dbl., borne in small clusters; foliage medium size, medium green, semi-glossy; prickles 1 cm., triangular, few; growth compact, short (28 in.); garden decoration; [Samara × (Seaspray × (Queen Elizabeth × *R. laxa*))]

Aliena MinFl, yb, 2002, Tucker, Robbie; flowers deep yellow with red edging, reverse light yellow, 1½-2 in., dbl., borne mostly solitary, no fragrance; foliage dark green, matte; prickles small, straight, green to brown, few; growth bushy, tall (4 ft.); [seedling × seedling]; int. by Rosemania, 2002

Aliénor d'Aquitaine HGal, mr, Rautio; int. in 1999

Aliette HT, 1958, Arles; flowers salmon-pink tinted orange, well-formed; vigorous, bushy growth; [Pres. Herbert Hoover × Signora]; int. by Roses-France

Alika HGal, mr, 1906; flowers brilliant red with no purple, many stamens, petalage variable, large, semi-dbl., moderate fragrance; vigorous growth; brought to the U.S. from St. Petersburg, Russia, by Prof. N. E. Hansen; int. by In commerce, 1930

Alina HT, w, Tantau; int. by Rosen Tantau, 2003

Aline HGal, lp, 1816, Vibert; flowers flesh pink, medium, full

Aline HT, or, 1950, Astolat Nursery; flowers peach, compact, 4 in., 22 petals; foliage dark; vigorous growth; [sport of Picture]

Aline Min, or, Laperrière; int. in 1994

Aline Rozey N, lp, 1884, Schwartz; sometimes classed as HP

Aline Sisley T, dr, 1874, Guillot fils; flowers red to purplish rose or violet/crimson, large, dbl.; foliage yellowish green; growth vigorous, semi-climbing

Alinka HT, ob, Kordes; int. in 1985

Alisha Min, pb, 1995, Spooner, Raymond A.; flowers soft pink with white margin on outer edge, medium, very dbl., borne mostly singly, no fragrance; foliage medium size, medium green, matte; few prickles; medium (20 in.), bushy growth; [Marriotta × seedling]; int. by Oregon Miniature Roses, 1995

Alison F, op, 1996, Cocker, James & Sons; flowers peach salmon, 3-3½ in., borne in large clusters; foliage medium size, medium green, glossy; some prickles; medium, upright, bushy growth; [Silver Jubilee × (Sabine × Circus)]; int. by James Cocker & Sons, 1995

Alison LCl, dp, McAllister; flowers vibrant pink, dbl.; dark green foliage; [sport of Dublin Bay]; int. by De Boer Roses, 2001

Alison Brown HT, dp, 1993, Brown, Mrs. Ann; flowers deep pink, 3-3½ in., full, borne mostly singly, some small clusters, intense fragrance; foliage medium size, dark green, semi-glossy; some prickles; medium (125 cm.), bushy growth; [sport of Ena Harkness]; int. by Brown, 1993

Alison Wheatcroft F, ab, 1959, Wheatcroft Bros.; flowers apricot flushed crimson; [sport of Circus]

Alistair Sheridan HT, ob, 1992, Pearce, C.A.; flowers orange, reverse orange, aging pinky orange, 4¾ in., dbl., urn-shaped, borne usually singly; foliage large, medium green, glossy; upright growth; [F seedling (HO79) × HT seedling (315)]; int. by The Limes New Roses, 1991

Alister Clark F, lp, 1999, Newman, Laurie; flowers 3-3½ in., full, borne in small clusters, intense fragrance; foliage small, dark green, glossy; prickles moderate; spreading, medium (3 ft.) growth; [sport of Marjory Palmer]; Marjory Palmer sport; int. by Reliable Roses, 1990

Alister Clark's Pink HT, lp, Clark, A.

Alister Stella Gray N, ly, 1894, Gray, A.H.; bud long, pointed; flowers pale yellow, center orange, fading to white, 6-7 cm., dbl., borne in small clusters, moderate fragrance; recurrent bloom; foliage small, glossy; vigorous, climbing growth; [William Allen Richardson × Mme Pierre Guillot]

Alister's Gift HG, lp, 2006, Viraraghavan, M.S. Viru; bud long, elegant; flowers light pink, reverse medium pink, 5 in., dbl., high-centered, borne in small clusters; foliage large, medium green, semi-glossy; prickles medium, pointing down, brown, moderate; growth bushy, tall (4 ft.); garden decorative, exhibition; [Naga Belle × Lady Mann]; int. by Roses Unlimited, 2007

Alix – See **Diadême de Flore**, HGal

Alix Roussel T, yb, 1908, Gamon; flowers yellow with salmon center, large, full

All Ablaze LCl, mr, 1999, Carruth, Tom; bud short, ovoid; flowers medium cherry red, ruffled, 4 in., 35 petals, borne in small clusters, slight spice fragrance; foliage medium size, dark green, semi-glossy; vigorous (12 ft.) growth; PP13107; [Don Juan × (Rosa soulieana seedling × Trumpeter)]; int. by Weeks Roses, 2000

All-American Bride HT, w, 2000, Williams, J. Benjamin; flowers white, delicate washed blush, reverse white, 4½-5 in., full, high-centered, borne mostly singly, moderate fragrance; foliage large, dark green, glossy, disease-resistant; few prickles; growth upright, bushy; very hardy; [White Masterpiece × Miss All-American Beauty]; int. by W. Atlee Burpee Co.

All Gold – See **Allgold**, F

All In One – See **Exploit**, LCl

All That Jazz S, op, 1991, Twomey, Jerry; bud pointed; flowers coral salmon blend, loose, 4½ in., 10-15 petals, cupped, loose, borne in sprays of 3-5, moderate damask fragrance; foliage medium size, dark green, glossy; prickles moderate; upright, bushy, medium growth; PP7978; [Gitte × seedling]; int. by DeVor Nurseries, Inc., 1991

Allalujah – See **Alleluia**, HT

Allamand-Ho S, pb, 1985, Buck, Dr. Griffith J.; bud ovoid; flowers pink and yellow blend, petals edged ruby red, color intensifying with age, 38 petals, cupped, borne in clusters of 1-6, moderate sweet fragrance; repeat bloom; foliage dark, leathery, semi-glossy; prickles awl-like, red-brown; erect, bushy growth; hardy; [(Hawkeye Belle × Prairie Star) × lobelle]; int. by Iowa State University

Allambie HT, Donovan, R.

Allanson Rose HT, or, Kordes; flowers bright vermilion intensifying to burnt orange in the sun, medium, dbl., high-centered, borne one to a stem and candelabras; free-flowering; foliage glossy green; growth medium, neat, upright; int. by Ludwig's Roses, 2001

Allard (form or hybrid of *R. xanthina*), dy; flowers chrome-yellow, dbl.; from the Botanic Gardens, Lyon, France

Allegeo '80 HT, or, 1985, Meilland, Mrs. Marie-Louise; flowers large, 35 petals, no fragrance; foliage medium size, medium green, semi-glossy; [(Diorette × Tropicana) × (seedling × (Diorette × Tropicana))]; int. by Meilland Et Cie, 1980

Allegra HGal, mp, 2003, Barden, Paul; flowers medium pink, reverse light pink, 3½-4 in., very full, borne in small clusters, intense fragrance; once blooming, for four to six weeks in Spring; foliage large, dark green, matte; prickles ¼ to ½ in., curved, reddish, few; bushy, arching growth, medium (5-6 ft.); [Duchesse de Montebello × St. Swithun]; int. in 2004

Allégresse HT, mr, 1952, Robichon; flowers red, becoming lighter, well-formed, very dbl.; strong stems; vigorous, upright growth; [Fantaisie × Sensation]; int. by Vilmorin-Andrieux

Allegretto HT, or, 1979, Huber; bud long, pointed; flowers 4 in., 14-17 petals, slight fragrance; foliage leathery; upright growth; [Fragrant Cloud × Sutter's Gold]; int. in 1975

Allegro HT, or, 1962, Meilland, Alain A.; flowers 3½-4½ in., 30 petals, high-centered, slight fragrance; foliage leathery, glossy; vigorous, bushy growth; PP2358; [(Happiness × Independence) × Soraya]; int. by URS, 1962; Gold Medal, The Hague, 1962, Gold Medal, Rome, 1962

Allegro HT, mr, Richardier; int. in 1999

Allegro Symphonie Min, ob, Meilland; flowers orange and yellow bicolor, color deepening, dbl.; int. by Meilland Richardier, 2004

Alleluia Cl Pol, Cazzaniga, F. G.; int. in 1960

Alleluia HT, rb, 1982, Delbard, Georges; flowers velvety deep red, silver reverse, large, of heavy substance, 30 petals; foliage deep green, glossy; [((Impeccable × Papa Meilland) × (Gloire de Rome × Impeccable)) × Corrida]

Alleluia HT, ab, Delbard; greenhouse cut flower; sold only in Australia; int. in 2003

Allen Box Pol, lp, 1928, Box, S.

Allen Brundrett HT, dr, Brundrett; int. in 1994

Allen Chandler Cl HT, mr, 1923, Chandler; bud long, pointed; flowers brilliant crimson, large, semi-dbl., borne 3-4 per cluster; recurrent bloom; foliage dark, leathery, glossy; vigorous, pillar growth; [Hugh Dickson × unknown]; int. by Prince; Gold Medal, NRS, 1923

Allen's Fragrant Pillar Cl HT, rb, 1931, Allen; bud long, pointed; flowers cerise, base flushed yellow, 4 in., dbl., open, borne mostly solitary, moderate fragrance; recurrent bloom; foliage glossy, bronze; long, strong stems; moderate climbing growth; [Paul's Lemon Pillar × Souv. de Claudius Denoyel]

Allen's Golden Climber LCl, ob, 1933, Allen; flowers dark yellow, reverse orange, 3½-4 in., dbl.; non-recurrent; foliage glossy

Allen's Jubilee – See **Jubilee**, HT

Allgold F, my, 1957, LeGrice; flowers bright buttercup-yellow, 3 in., 15-22 petals, borne singly and in large trusses, slight fragrance; foliage small, glossy, dark; vigorous growth; PP1665; [Goldilocks × Ellinor LeGrice]; Gold Medal, NRS, 1956

Allgold, Climbing Cl F, my, 1965, Gandy, Douglas L.; [sport of Allgold]; int. by Gandy's Roses, Ltd., 1961

Alliance F, dp, 1966, Delforge; bud ovoid; flowers light red and deep pink, large, dbl.; foliage soft; strong stems; very vigorous, bushy growth; [Rosita × Queen Elizabeth]

Alliance HT, w, 1985, Meilland, Mrs. Marie-Louise; flowers glowing white, large, no fragrance; foliage medium size, dark, matte; upright growth; [Rustica × Youki San]; int. by Meilland Et Cie, 1983

Alliance HT, rb, Keisei; flowers medium red, white reverse; int. by Meilland International, 2002

Alliance Franco-Russe T, my, 1899, Goinard; bud long; flowers tea-yellow, shading to salmon towards the center, large, dbl.; foliage large, bright green

Allie S, mp, 2000, Giles, Diann; flowers medium, full, borne mostly singly, no fragrance; foliage medium size, medium green, matte; prickles moderate; growth upright, tall; [sport of Auscrim]; int. by Giles Rose Nursery

Allison Sweetie Gr, mr, 1978, Miller, F.; bud long, pointed, oval; flowers 3-3½ in., 21-25 petals, high-centered, moderate fragrance; foliage large, glossy, dark; tall, vigorous growth; [Tropicana × Mister Lincoln]

Alliswell HT, w, 1956, Motose; bud ovoid; flowers white overcast pink, center cameo-pink, 5-6 in., 50-60 petals, peony-like, moderate fragrance; vigorous, bushy growth; PP1480; [Neige Parfum × (Charlotte Armstrong × Blanche Mallerin)]

Allotria F, or, 1959, Tantau, Math.; flowers orange-scarlet, 3 in., dbl., flat, borne in large clusters; foliage dark, glossy; vigorous growth; [Fanal × Cinnabar seedling]; int. in 1958

Allspice HT, my, 1976, Armstrong, D.L.; bud ovoid, pointed, deep yellow; flowers 4½ in., 35 petals, moderate honey and tea rose fragrance; foliage large, olive-green; vigorous, upright, bushy growth; PP4301; [Buccaneer × Peace]; int. by Armstrong Nursery, 1977

Allumbie – See **Allambie**, HT

Allure HT, pb, 1950, Swim, H.C.; bud long, pointed, carmine-rose; flowers Neyron rose, base yellow, 5-6 in., 28-30 petals, high-centered, slight fragrance; foliage leathery, glossy, light green; very vigorous, upright growth; [Mrs Pierre S. duPont × Charlotte Armstrong]; int. by Inter-State Nursery

Alluring HT, pb, 2003, McCann, Sean; flowers veined pink and cream, medium, full, borne in small clusters, moderate fragrance; foliage large, medium green, semi-glossy; growth upright, medium; garden, decorative; [seedling × seedling]

Allux Symphony – See **Symphony**, S

Alma HT, m; int. in 1980

Alma F, dr, Riethmuller; flowers dark crimson, dbl., borne in large clusters; dwarf growth; [Orange Triumph × Eutin]

Alma-atinskaj Aromatnaja HT, m, Besschetnowa; flowers large, very dbl.; int. in 1959

Alma Bierbauer S, op, Williams, J. Benjamin; flowers salmon pink with yellow eye and pink stamens, single; int. in 1997

Alma Blue – See **Alma**, HT

Alma June Seville HT, mp, 2006, Rawlins, Ronnie; flowers pink, reverse pink, 3 in., full, borne mostly solitary; foliage medium size, dark green, glossy; prickles triangular, moderate; growth upright, medium (36 in.); garden decorative; [Ingrid Bergman × Silver Anniversary]

Alma Mater HT, lp, 1929, Good & Reese; flowers lighter in color; [sport of Columbia]

Almandet HT, mp, Croix; int. in 1966

Almirante Américo Tomás HT, rb, 1955, Moreira da Silva; flowers geranium-red, reverse old-gold, large, dbl.; very vigorous growth; [Sultane × Peace]

Almond Glory Min, ab, 1991, Zipper, Herbert; flowers deep apricot, small, full, high, borne in small clusters, moderate fragrance; foliage small, dark green, glossy; few prickles; medium (30 cm.), compact growth; [Rise 'n' Shine × High Spirits]; int. by Magic Moment Miniature Roses, 1992

Almondeen HT, pb, 1983, Christensen, Jack E.; buds pointed; flowers almond and pink blend, large, dbl.; foliage large, medium green, semi-glossy; upright, bushy growth; PP5704; [Angel Face × First Prize]; int. by Armstrong Nursery, 1984

Almost Perfect Min, dr, 2003, Wells, Verlie W.; flowers dark velvet red, reverse red with white base, 1 in., full, borne mostly solitary, slight fragrance; foliage small, dark green, semi-glossy; prickles 1/16 in., straight; growth upright, medium (18 in.); garden, exhibition; [seedling × seedling]; int. by Wells MidSouth Roses, 2002

Almost Sunset HT, yb, Zary

Almost Wild Cerise S, lp; int. by Sanwell Nurseries, 2005

Almost Wild Embers S, or; int. by Sanwell Nurseries, 2005

Almost Wild Yellow S, my; int. by Sanwell Nurseries, 2005

Alnwick Castle S, pb, 2002, Austin, David; flowers dusty apricot-pink, 7 cm., very dbl., cupped, borne in small clusters, no fragrance; foliage medium size, medium green, semi-glossy, leathery, smooth; prickles medium, concave, brown, moderate; growth bushy, medium (120 cm.); garden decorative; [seedling × Ausgold]; int. by David Austin Roses, Ltd., 2001

Aloha Cl HT, mp, 1949, Boerner; bud ovoid; flowers rose-pink, reverse deeper, large, 58 petals, cupped, moderate fragrance; recurrent bloom; foliage leathery, dark; vigorous, pillar (8-10 ft.) growth; [Mercedes Gallart × New Dawn]; int. by J&P

Aloha HT, yb, Kordes; flowers yellow with reddish margin, medium size; stems 60 cm; greenhouse rose; int. by W. Kordes Söhne, 1999

Aloha HT, dy, McGredy; flowers golden yellow, dbl., classical; growth medium to tall; int. in 2000

Aloha LCl, ob, Kordes; flowers red-orange, apricot colored with some pink and red shades, medium size, very dbl., borne in clusters of up to ten blooms, slight fruity fragrance; recurrent; growth climbing, 8+ ft. tall; int. by W. Kordes Söhne, 2004; Certificate of Merit, Orléans, 2006

Alois Jirásek HT, ob, 1931, Böhm, J.; bud long, pointed; flowers dark orange, tinted brownish yellow, large, dbl.; foliage glossy; vigorous growth; [Mme Butterfly × Mrs George Shawyer]

Alouette Pol, op, 1971, Delforge; bud long, pointed; flowers salmon-orange, medium, semi-dbl., cupped; profuse, continuous bloom; foliage leathery; vigorous, bushy growth; [Ambassadeur Baert × seedling]

Aloysia Kaiser S, my, 1937, Lambert, P.; bud ochre-yellow; flowers reddish bright yellow, round, large, dbl., borne in clusters; seasonal bloom; vigorous growth; [Miss G. Mesman × Belle Doria]

Alpaïde de Rotalier HP, lp, 1863, Campy; flowers transparent light pink, large, full

Alpenfee HSet, lp, before 1890, Geschwind, R.; flowers dbl., borne in clusters, no fragrance; probably *R. setigera* × a Hybrid Perpetual

Alpenglühen – See **Alpine Glow**, F

Alpenglühen S, mr, Tantau; flowers bright signal-red with yellow stamens, borne in clusters; foliage fresh green, glossy; growth low and spreading, maximum 2 ft.; int. by Rosen Tantau, 2004

Alpengrüss F, Noack, Werner; int. in 1974

Alpenkonigin F, mr

Alpha HT, or, 1976, Paolino; flowers bright vermilion, 4 in., 20 petals; foliage leathery; [((Show Girl × Baccará) × Romantica) × (Romantica × Tropicana)]; int. by URS

Alpha Meidiland – See **Carefree Marvel**, S

Alpha Moe Min, ob, 1998, Moe, Mitchie; flowers cream white with orange edges, 1½ in., 6-11 petals, borne mostly singly, slight fragrance; foliage medium size, medium green, semi-glossy; few prickles; upright, medium (18 in.) growth; [Pink Petticoat × seedling]; int. by Mitchie's Roses & More, 1999

Alphaïde de Rotallier – See **Alpaïde de Rotalier**, HP

Alphee HT, Croix, P.; int. in 1972

Alphonse Belin HP, mr, 1863, Gautreau; flowers cherry red, large, full

Alphonse Damaizin HP, mr, 1861, Damaizin

Alphonse Daudet HT, ab, Meilland; flowers mimosa-yellow, veined in center with shrimp pink, 75-80 petals, quartered, moderate peach fragrance; foliage semi-glossy, disease-resistant; growth to 100-110 cm.; int. in 1997

Alphonse de Lamartine HP, lp, 1853, Ducher; flowers rosy blush, medium, dbl.; moderate growth

Alphonse Fontaine HP, mp, 1868, Fontaine; flowers carmine, shaded cherry red, large, full

Alphonse Karr HP, dr, 1845, Portemer

Alphonse Karr HP, lp, 1847, Feuillet; flowers bright pink, edges lighter, large, very full

Alphonse Karr T, m, 1878, Nabonnand, G.; flowers crimson-purple, center lighter, large, dbl.; [Duchess of Edinburgh × unknown]

Alphonse Maille HCh, dr, 1825, Boutigny; flowers dark purple-red, full

Alphonse Maille HT, mp, 1830, Laffay; flowers bright carmine, shaded purple

Alphonse Soupert HP, mp, 1883, Lacharme, F.; flowers rose pink, large, dbl., moderate fragrance; numerous prickles; [Jules Margottin × unknown]

Alphonse Troussard HT, 1951, Buatois

Alpin LCl, or, 1964, Combe; flowers bright orange-red, 3 in., dbl., borne singly or in small clusters; recurrent bloom; foliage dark, glossy; vigorous growth; [Spectacular × Toujours]; int. by Minier-Anges, 1960

Alpine HT, my, 1954, Grillo; bud long, pointed; flowers clear yellow, open, 5½ in., 30 petals; foliage leathery; vigorous, upright growth; [sport of Sunnymount]

Alpine Brier – See ***R. pendulina*** (Linnaeus)

Alpine Glow F, or, 1954, Tantau, Math.; bud deep orange-red; flowers vermilion-red, 3-4 in., 28 petals, cupped, borne in clusters of 4-10, moderate fragrance; foliage glossy; vigorous, bushy growth; PP1395; [Cinnabar × (Cinnabar × Käthe Duvigneau)]; int. by J&P, 1954

Alpine Gold Min, dy; growth short

Alpine Rock HT, w

Alpine Rose – See ***R. pendulina*** (Linnaeus)

Alpine Sunset HT, ab, 1975, Cants of Colchester, Ltd.; flowers peach-pink, apricot reverse, 7-8 in., 30 petals, moderate fragrance; foliage glossy, medium green; vigorous, upright growth; [Dr. A.J. Verhage × Irish Gold]; int. by G. Roberts, 1973

Alsace HT, op, 1946, Meilland, F.; flowers salmon-pink, base gold, 6 in., dbl.; foliage dark; free growth; [Peace × Mme Joseph Perraud]

Alsace S, dr, Pekmez, Paul; int. in 1992

Alsace-Lorraine HP, dr, 1879, Duval; flowers dark velvety red, large

Alsterufer HT, dr, 1909, Lambert, P.; flowers medium large, dbl., intense fragrance

Alt-marburg S, lp, Weihrauch; flowers large, dbl.; int. in 1979

Alt-Rothenburg HT, dp, 1939, Burkhardt; flowers large, dbl.

Alt Wien HT, pb, 1968, Prinz; flowers carmine-rose, 4 in., dbl.; foliage dark, glossy; compact growth; [sport of Queen of Bermuda]; int. by Wohlt, 1965

Altai Rose – See ***R. spinosissima altaica*** (Bean)

Altair S, pb, Barni; flowers light pink with salmon tones, dbl., rosette, borne in clusters of 8 to 10, slight fragrance; continuous; foliage small to medium size, medium green; growth vigorous, fast grower, 50-70 cm.; groundcover; [Frine × seedling]

Altalaris S, w, 1941, Skinner; bud large, pointed; flowers white, sometimes flushed pink, single, open; abundant, non-recurrent bloom; foliage leathery; numerous prickles; vigorous, bushy, growth; hips apple-shaped, bright red; [*R. spinosissima altaica* × *R. acicularis*]

Alte Liebe HT, or, Berger, A.; flowers large, dbl.; int. in 1974

Alte Liebe F, op, W. Kordes Söhne; flowers salmon-orange and pink, medium large, dbl.; int. in 1983

Altenburg F, or, Berger, A.; flowers medium large, dbl.; int. in 1977

Alter Ego HT, pb, Nirp; flowers hot pink with golden reverse; int. in 2003

Altesse HT, dp, 1950, Meilland, F.; bud ovoid; flowers strawberry-red, large, 35-40 petals, globular; vigorous, upright growth; [Vercors × Léonce Colombier]; int. by URS

Altesse – See **Anticipation**, HT

Altesse HT, ab, Richardier; flowers yellow and copper, dbl.; growth compact, uniform, medium (3 ft.); int. by Meilland Richardier, 1999

Altesse F, lp, Meilland; flowers light buff-colored pink, dbl., high-centered; greenhouse rose; int. by Meilland International, 2004

Altesse 75 HT, Meilland, L.; int. in 1975

Althea HT, mr, 1930, Pemberton; flowers glowing crimson, moderate damask fragrance; int. by Bentall

Altissima – See **Aigle Brun**, HGal

Altissimo LCl, mr, 1966, Delbard-Chabert; flowers blood-red, 4-5 in., 7 petals, cupped, borne singly or in small clusters; repeat bloom; foliage dark, serrated; tall growth; [Ténor × seedling]; int. by Cuthbert

Altmärker HT, yb, 1908, Türke; flowers ochre-yellow tinted garnet, large, dbl.; vigorous growth; [Kaiserin Auguste Viktoria × Luciole]

Alto – See **Alto Parade**, MinFl

Alto Parade MinFl, ab, Poulsen; flowers apricot blend, 5-8 cm., dbl., slight wild rose fragrance; bushy (20-40 cm.) growth; int. by Aldershot Greenhouses Ltd., 2004

Altonia (natural variation of *R. setigera*), mp; flowers brilliant pink, single to semi-dbl.

Altrusa Min, ob, Eagle; int. by Southern Cross Nurseries, 1998

Altus – See **Altissimo**, LCl

Alupka N, w, before 1900; flowers medium large, dbl., moderate fragrance; [sport of Maréchal Niel]; possibly synonymous with White Marechal Niel or Mme Hoste

Alvares Cabral F, mr, Moreira da Silva; flowers bright red; [Pinocchio × Alain]

Always HT, dr, 1958, Leon, Charles F., Sr.; bud long, pointed; flowers dark cardinal-red, 6 in., 28 petals, moderate fragrance; foliage leathery; vigorous growth; PP1692; [(Charlotte Armstrong × Applause) × Ena Harkness]

Always A Lady Min, m, 1988, Bennett, Dee; flowers pale mauve to lavender, medium, 25-30 petals, high-centered, borne usually singly or in sprays of 3-5, moderate damask fragrance; foliage medium size, medium green, semi-glossy; prickles hooked slightly downward, pale yellow; bushy, medium growth; hips globular, green-brown; PP7187; [Deep Purple × Dilly Dilly]; int. by Tiny Petals Nursery, 1987

Always a Smile S, ob, 2003, Horner, Colin P.; flowers tangerine, reverse pale orange, 9 cm., dbl., borne in large clusters; foliage large, dark green, glossy; prickles medium, slightly curved, moderate; growth upright, tall (5 ft.); garden decorative; [Wandering Minstrel × Golden Future]; int. by Warley Garden Roses, 2005

Always Love You F, dy, 2000, Umsawasdi, Dr. Theera; flowers medium, dbl., borne in small clusters, slight fragrance; foliage medium size, medium green, semi-glossy; prickles moderate; growth upright, bushy, medium; [Loving Touch × Lanvin]; int. by Certified Roses, Inc., 1999

Always Mine HT, dr, 1989, Marciel, Stanley G.; bud pointed, tapering; flowers deep red, large, 39 petals, cupped, borne singly, intense spicy fragrance; foliage large, dark green, glossy; prickles declining, pea green with cinnamon tinges; upright, tall growth; [Visa × Sassy]; int. by DeVor Nurseries, Inc.

Always Special Min, dr, Benardella; growth medium; int. in 2001

Alwyn's Favourite HT, my, 2007, Robert Webster; flowers full, borne in small clusters, moderate fragrance; foliage medium size, medium green, semi-glossy; prickles 6 mm., triangular, few; growth compact, short (24 in.); bedding, garden decorative; [((Royal Volunteer × Modern Art) × The Marquess of Bristol) × Jorja Julianna]

Aly Pacha Chérif – See **Ali Pacha Chériff**, HP

Ama F, or, 1955, Kordes; bud ovoid; flowers deep orange-scarlet, large, dbl., high-centered, borne in clusters (up to 20); foliage dark, glossy, leathery; vigorous, bushy growth; [Obergärtner Wiebicke × Independence]

Amabilis HGal, m, before 1845; flowers purple, streaked lilac, full, slight fragrance

Amabilis T, mp, about 1850, Robert

Amabilis T, mp, 1856, Touvais; flowers shining pink, large, full

Amabilis T, mp, 1857, Lartay; flowers large, full

Amadeus S, rb, 1991, Barni, V.

Amadeus LCl, dr, 2006; bud dark red; flowers dark red with little bluing, 8 cm., dbl., borne in clusters of 5-7; foliage large, dark green, very glossy; growth climbing, 8+ ft. tall; int. by W. Kordes' Söhne, 2003

Amadine P, mp

Amadis Bslt, dr, 1829, Laffay, M.; flowers deep crimson-purple, usually striped with white, 6-7 cm., semi-dbl., cupped, borne in small clusters; very early; non-remontant; foliage thin, pale; thornless; stems young wood whitish green, old wood red-brown; vigorous, upright growth; excellent pillar; [*R. chinensis* × *R. pendulina*]

Amaglia LCl, w; int. in 1980

Amalfi Pol, dy, 1971, Delforge; bud long, pointed; flowers deep yellow to salmon-pink, small, dbl., cupped; abundant,continuous bloom; foliage small, dark; moderate, bushy growth

Amalia HT, dr, 1994, Meilland, Alain A.; flowers 3-3½ in., full, borne mostly singly, no fragrance; foliage medium size, dark green, semi-glossy; numerous prickles; medium (100-120 cm.), upright growth; PP7718; [(Queen Elizabeth × Karl Herbst) × Papa Meilland]; int. by Sauvageot, 1986

Amalia Jung HT, mr, 1934, Leenders, M.; flowers crimson-red, large, dbl.; foliage glossy, cedar-green;

vigorous growth; [Mrs Henry Winnett × Lady Helen Maglona]

Amalie de Greiff HT, pb, 1912, Lambert, P.; flowers brick-rose, center salmon and orange-yellow, large, dbl., moderate fragrance; [Herrin von Lieser × Mme Mélanie Soupert]

Amalinda HT, mr

Amami HT, op, 1927, Easlea; flowers peach-pink, overlarge, 12-15 petals; foliage light; very vigorous growth

Amanda Min, dr, 1982, deRuiter; flowers medium, 20 petals, slight fragrance; foliage small, medium green, semi-glossy; bushy growth; [Scarletta × seedling]; int. by Fryer's Nursery, Ltd., 1977

Amanda F, ob, Noack, Werner; int. in 1979

Amanda F, my, 1979, Bees; bud globular; flowers large, 25 petals, high-centered, slight fragrance; foliage small, light green; upright growth; [Arthur Bell × Zambra]

Amanda Justine HT, rb, 2001, Hiltner, Martin J.; flowers medium red, white reverse, 4 in., full, high-centered, borne mostly solitary, or small clusters, no fragrance; foliage medium size, medium green, semi-glossy; prickles medium, hooked down, moderate; growth upright, medium (3-3½ ft.); garden decoration, exhibition; [Lynn Anderson × Amber Queen]

Amanda Kay Min, w, 1991, Justice, Jerry G.; bud ovoid; flowers white to near white, some pink shading, small, dbl., high-centered, borne singly, intense spicy fragrance; foliage small, medium green, glossy; bushy, low growth; [seedling × seedling]; int. by Justice Miniature Roses, 1991

Amanda Marciel HT, lp, 1989, Marciel, Stanley G.; bud slender and tapering; flowers very delicate pink, large, 26 petals, cupped, borne singly, slight spicy fragrance; foliage medium size, dark green, glossy; no prickles; upright, tall growth; [seedling × Pink Puff]; int. by DeVor Nurseries, Inc.

Amanda Patenaude – See **Amanda Patenotte**, P

Amanda Patenotte P, mp, 1845, Vibert; flowers pale rose, large, full, globular; foliage medium size, light green; few prickles; roses sold as Amanda Patenaude in the U.S. in recent years are almost certainly Joasine Hanet

Amandine HP, dp, 1846, Vibert; flowers large, full

Amandine Chanel S, pb, Guillot-Massad; flowers raspberry pink, reverse white, borne in clusters of 5-7; growth to 1 m.; int. by Roseraies Guillot, 2005

Amanecer HT, Dot, Pedro

Amanogawa F, ly, Suzuki; int. in 1956

Amara HT, pb, Gaujard; flowers two toned rosy pink, dbl., high-centered; int. in 1980

Amarancha F, ab

Amarante B, dr, 1859, Page; flowers carmine purple with cherry red, medium, full, cupped

Amarante Pol, mr, 1916, Barbier; flowers dark crimson, sometimes striped white, borne in clusters of 25-70

Amaretto LCl, w, Kordes; flowers cream with light pink tones in center, 8 cm., dbl., high-centered, borne singly and in small clusters, moderate fruity fragrance; recurrent; strong (8 ft.) growth; int. by W. Kordes Söhne, 2006

Amarillo HT, dy, 1961, Von Abrams; bud pointed; flowers deep yellow, 5 in., 30 petals; foliage leathery, light green; vigorous, upright growth; [Buccaneer × Lowell Thomas]; int. by Peterson & Dering, 1961

Amarillo F, dy, Select Roses, B.V.; int. in 1994

Amateur André Fourcaud HT, lp, 1903, Puyravaud; bud very long; flowers light pink, reverse darker, very large, dbl., high-centered, moderate fragrance; [Mme Caroline Testout × unknown]

Amateur E. Biron HT, op, 1928, Biron; flowers shrimp-pink, center tinted copper, reverse old-rose, camellia-like

Amateur Lopes HG, 1905, Cayeux; [Mme Berard × *R. gigantea*]

Amateur Teyssier HT, w

Amatsu-Otome HT, yb, 1960, Teranishi, K.; flowers golden yellow edged deep orange, 4½-5 in., 48 petals, high-centered, slight fragrance; foliage semi-glossy; vigorous, compact growth; [Chrysler Imperial × Doreen]; int. by Itami Rose Nursery

Amatsu-Otome, Cl Cl HT, yb; int. in 1967

Amaury Fonseca Pol, w, 1914, Soupert & Notting; flowers white, suffused light pink in fall, well-formed

Amazing – See **Amazing Palace**, MinFl

Amazing Grace HT, mp, 1973, Anderson's Rose Nurseries; flowers rich pink, high pointed, 5 in., 43 petals; [Carina × Mischief]

Amazing Grace – See **Myriam**, HT

Amazing Grace '07 HT, w, 2007, Chapman, Bruce; flowers 9 cm., full, borne mostly solitary; foliage large, dark green, glossy; prickles medium, hooked, brown, few; growth upright, tall (1½ m.); garden decoration; [White Spray × Aotearoa]; int. by Ross Roses, 2007

Amazing Palace MinFl, ab, Poulsen; bud pointed ovoid; flowers blend of apricot with orange and orange-red tones, 5-8 cm., 30-35 petals, deep cup, borne singly and in small clusters, slight fragrance; recurrent; foliage dark, glossy; prickles numerous, 10 mm, deeply concave; bushy, 40-60 cm. growth; PP15895; int. by Poulsen Roser, 2004

Amazon F, ob, 1992, Christensen, Jack E.; flowers orange bronze, large, well-formed, borne in neat clusters

Amazon Lady – See **Enchanted**, HT

Amazone T, my, 1872, Ducher; flowers yellow, reverse veined rose, well-formed; [Safrano × unknown]

Amazone LCl, mr, 1961, Delforge; flowers bright red; [sport of Spectacular]

Amazone F, mr, de Ruiter, G.

Ambasciatore Marco Fracisci T, lp

Ambassadeur Baert F, op, 1964, Delforge; flowers salmon; foliage bronze; low, compact growth; [Sumatra × seedling]

Ambassadeur Nemry F, dp, 1949, Leenders, M.; flowers deep rose-pink, reverse salmon-carmine, large, dbl.; vigorous growth

Ambassador HT, ob, 1930, Premier Rose Gardens; bud long, pointed; flowers bronze-salmon, large, dbl.; foliage leathery, dark; vigorous, bushy growth; [Mme Butterfly × Souv. de Claudius Pernet]

Ambassador HT, ob, 1977, Meilland; bud conical, large; flowers orange-red, reverse blended with golden yellow (orange-apricot), 4 in., 30-35 petals, cupped, borne mostly singly, slight fragrance; recurrent; foliage dark green, semi-glossy; prickles large, average number; bushy (4½ ft.) growth; PP4224; [((Meialfi × Meifan 00186F) × King's Ransom) × Whisky Mac]; int. by C-P, 1979

Ambassador HT, mr, Meilland; flowers velvety red, frilly; int. in 1995

Amber Cl Pol, 1908, Paul, W.; flowers pale amber, single; early; low growth; RULED EXTINCT; [Jersey Beauty × unknown]

Amber HT, 1930, Jordan, B.L.; flowers amber; RULED EXTINCT; [sport of Ophelia]; int. by Beckwith

Amber – See **Amber Hit**, MinFl

Amber Abundance – See **Hyde Park**, F

Amber Beauty F, pb, 1962, Leenders, J.; flowers pink tinted brown, dbl.; [Goldilocks × Lavender Pinocchio]

Amber Cloud HG, dy, 2006, Viraraghavan, M.S. Viru; flowers deep yellow-apricot, reverse deep yellow, 5 in., single, borne mostly solitary; foliage large, medium green, glossy; prickles large, triangular, pointing downward, grey brown, numerous; growth spreading, climbing, tall (up to 20 ft.); [Reve d'Or × Rosa gigantea]; int. by Roses Unlimited, 2006

Amber Cover S, ab, Olesen; bud ovate; flowers yellow-orange to apricot, 6 cm., 18-22 petals, open cup, borne in clusters of 5-15, slight honey fragrance; recurrent; foliage dark green, semi-glossy; prickles several, 4-7 mm., deeply concave, ocher; compact, bushy (2 ft.) growth; PP13292; [Amber Hit × Aspen]; int. by Poulsen, 2001; Bronze Medal, Gifu, 2006, Gold Medal, Monza, 2000

Amber Flash MinFl, ob, 1982, Williams, J. Benjamin; flowers medium, dbl., moderate fragrance; foliage medium size, dark, semi-glossy; PP5271; [Zorina × Starina]; int. by C-P

Amber Flush – See **Devotion**, HT

Amber Gem HBc, ob, 2003, Moore, Ralph S.; flowers orange/pink, reverse lt pink-white, 1½ in., full, borne in small clusters, slight fragrance; foliage small, medium green; prickles small, hooked, light green, few; growth compact, short (15 in.); pots, garden, borders; [Joycie × Out of Yesteryear]; int. by Sequoia Nurs., 2003

Amber Glo – See **Amber Glow**, LCl

Amber Glow LCl, ab, Nieuwesteeg; flowers apricot-yellow, dbl., slight rose fragrance; constant; growth to 2 × 2 m., low, vigorous; int. in 2004

Amber Gold HT, dy, 1962, Moro; bud ovoid; flowers deep golden yellow, 5-5½ in., 40-45 petals, cupped, moderate fragrance; foliage leathery; vigorous, upright growth; PP2301; [Golden Rapture × Golden Scepter]; int. by J&P, 1962

Amber Hit MinFl, ab, Poulsen; flowers orange and orange blend with tones of other hues, 5-8 cm., 25 petals, slight wild rose fragrance; growth bushy, 40-60 cm.; int. by Poulsen Roser, 2000

Amber Honey HT, ab

Amber Kordana Min, ab, Kordes; flowers amber yellow with pink tones as it ages, semi-dbl., opens quickly to flat, borne mostly singly; recurrent; foliage dark green; compact growth; container rose; int. by W. Kordes Söhne

Amber Light – See **Amberlight**, F

Amber Nectar F, ab, 1996, Mehring, Bernhard F.; flowers amber/apricot with amber yellow reverse, 2 in., full, borne in large clusters; foliage medium size, medium green, glossy; prickles moderate; upright, medium (60 cm.) growth; [Alexander × Sweet Magic]; int. by Henry Street Nurseries, 1997

Amber Panarosa S, ab; int. by Ludwig's Roses, 2004

Amber Queen F, ab, 1984, Harkness; bud plump; flowers apricot gold, large, 25-30 petals, cupped, borne in clusters of 3-7, moderate sweet and spicy fragrance; foliage large, copper red to medium green, semi-glossy; prickles reddish; low, compact, bushy growth; disease resistant; PP5582; [Southampton × Typhoon]; Rose of the Year, St. Albans, UK, 1984, Gold Star of the South Pacific, Palmerston North, NZ, 1988, Gold Medal, Orléans, 1987, Gold Medal, Genoa, 1986

Amber Ribbon Min, ab, 1987, Zipper, Herbert; bud pointed; flowers deep apricot to deep yellow at base, aging butterscotch, 1½-2 in., 22 petals, high-centered, borne singly or in sprays of 2-5, slight fragrance; foliage medium size, dark green, semi-glossy; upright, tall growth; [Rise 'n' Shine × Pot 'o Gold]; int. by Magic Moment Miniature Roses, 1987

Amber Rose – See **Parks' Yellow Tea-Scented China**, T

Amber Sands Min, ab, 1985, Hardgrove, Donald & Mary; flowers large, 35 petals, high-centered, slight fragrance; foliage medium size, medium green, semi-glossy; upright, bushy growth; [Fragrant Cloud × Poker Chip]; int. by Rose World Originals, 1984

Amber Spire S, ab, Kordes; int. in 1995

Amber Star – See **Jacob van Ruysdael**, F

Amber Star Min, ob, 1999, Mander, George & Pazdzierski, Jim; flowers amber/orange, reverse golden yellow, 1¾-2¼ in., full, borne in small clusters, slight fragrance; foliage medium size, dark green, glossy; prickles moderate; upright, tall (15-20 in.) growth; [sport of Glowing Amber]; int. by The Mini Rose Garden, 1999

Amber Sun Min, ob, 2001, Shuttleworth, Sam; flowers dark amber orange, reverse golden yellow, 4-6 cm., full, borne in small clusters, slight fragrance; foliage medium size, dark green, semi-glossy; prickles small (¼ in.), needlepoint, moderate; growth upright, tall (40-50 cm.); containers, garden, exhibition; [sport of Glowing Amber]; blooms open extremely slowly; int. by Select Roses, 2002

Amber Sun S, ab, Kordes; bud small, elongated, orange-yellow; flowers copper yellow, fading to cream yellow, 2 in., semi-dbl., cupped, borne in clusters of 5-8, moderate fragrance; free-flowering; foliage medium size, dark green, very glossy; bushy (50 × 60 cm.) growth; int. by W. Kordes Söhne, 2006

Amber Sunset Min, ob, 1996, Mander, George; flowers orange with orange and dark yellow reverse, 1¾-2 in., full, high-centered, star-shaped, no fragrance; foliage medium size, dark green, glossy, disease-resistant; some prickles; very vigorous, medium (40-50 cm.), bushy growth; [June Laver × Rubies 'n' Pearls]; int. by Select Roses, 1996

Amber Waves F, ab, 1999, Zary, Dr. Keith W.; bud copper/gold, pointed, ovoid; flowers amber yellow, reverse yellow/apricot, opens flat, 3½-4 in., full, cupped, borne singly and in small clusters, moderate fruity fragrance; foliage medium size, dark green, glossy; prickles moderate; upright, bushy, medium (3½ ft.) growth; PP11839; [seedling × Amber Queen]; int. by Bear Creek Gardens, Inc., 2001; Bronze Medal, Australian Nationall Rose Trials, 1999

Amberglo Min, r, 1989, Williams, Ernest D.; flowers small, 34 petals, intense fragrance; foliage small, dark green, semi-glossy; bushy, sturdy growth; [Tom Brown × Twilight Trail]; int. in 1988

Amberlight F, yb, 1961, LeGrice; flowers clear amber, 3½-4 in., dbl., borne in open clusters, intense fruity fragrance; vigorous, upright, bushy growth; PP2197; [(seedling × Lavender Pinocchio) × Marcel Bourgouin]; int. by Wayside Gardens, 1961

Amberlight – See **Fyvie Castle**, HT

Ambiance HT, lp, 1955, Delforge; bud long, pink, passing to cream; [Comtesse Vandal × Pres. Macia]

Ambiance HMsk, pb, 2000, Lens, Louis; flowers deep pink, reverse lighter, 1 in., single, borne in large clusters; recurrent; foliage small, dark green, semi-glossy; few prickles; compact low (50-60 cm.) growth; [*R. multiflora adenocheata* × Vanity]; int. by Louis Lens NV, 1994

Ambiance HT, yb; int. by NIRP, 1995

Ambiente HT, ly, Noack; bud rounded, greenish white; flowers cream white with yellowish center, dbl., high-centered, slight fragrance; recurrent; foliage dark green, medium size, glossy; growth robust, low (70 × 40 cm.), bushy; int. by W. Kordes Söhne, 2002

Ambossfunken HT, rb, 1961, Meyer; flowers coral-red streaked golden yellow, well-formed, large, 33 petals; bushy growth; int. by Kordes

Ambra F, ob, 1983, Rose Barni-Pistoia; flowers deep, large, 20 petals, cupped, borne in clusters of 3-5, slight fragrance; foliage medium size, brownish-green, glossy; prickles reddish; upright, bushy growth; [seedling × seedling]; int. in 1982

Ambre HT, ob, 1956, Gaujard; bud ovoid; flowers brilliant orange and yellow, very large, dbl., moderate fragrance; foliage glossy, dark; very vigorous, bushy growth; [Peace × seedling]

Ambre Solaire Pol, pb, 1966, Ebben; bud ovoid; flowers red, pink and yellow, dbl., borne in clusters; foliage dark; [Masquerade × seedling]

Ambridge Rose S, ab, 1994, Austin, David; flowers apricot-pink, 2½-3 in., very dbl., cupped, borne in small clusters; foliage medium size, dark green, semi-glossy; some prickles; small (2½ ft.), bushy growth; PP8679; [Charles Austin × seedling]; int. by David Austin Roses, Ltd., 1990

Ambrogio Maggi HP, mr, 1879, Pernet fils; flowers bright rose pink, very large, dbl., globular; very remontant; foliage light green; growth upright, vigorous; [John Hopper × unknown]

Ambroise Paré HGal, m, 1846, Vibert; flowers rose-purple, tinted carmine with mottling of pale lilac grey tones in cool, moist weather, dbl., rosette

Ambroise Verschaffelt HP, dr, 1858, Vindrin; flowers violet-red, large, full

Ambrosia F, ob, 1962, Dickson, Patrick; flowers amber, 2½-3 in., 7-10 petals, flat, borne in large clusters; foliage dark; vigorous, bushy growth; [seedling × Shepherd's Delight]; int. by A. Dickson

Ambrosia Gr, mp, 1999, Schuurman, Frank B.; flowers 2¾-3 in., full, borne in small clusters, moderate fragrance; foliage large, medium green, semi-glossy; prickles moderate; bushy, medium growth; [Sexy Rexy × New Year]; int. by Franko Roses New Zealand, 1996

Amdo HRg, mp, 1927, Hansen, N.E.; flowers medium, 16 petals, borne in clusters of 7-10; non-recurrent; [Tetonkaha × La Mélusine]

Amédée HGal, mp, 1827, Desportes; Agathe group

Amédée de Langlois B, m, 1872, Vigneron; flowers dark, velvety purple, medium, full, borne in small clusters

Amédée Philibert HP, m, 1879, Lévêque; flowers purple and red

Amefica HT, yb, Tantau; int. by Rosen-Tantau, 2002

Amélia – See **Belle Rosine**, S

Amélia A, mp, 1823, Vibert, J. P.; sepals foliaceous, persistent; flowers bright pink, anthers deep yellow, large, semi-dbl. to dbl., borne in clusters of 4-6, moderate fragrance; non-recurrent; foliage arching, simply serrate, gray-green, pointed-elliptical; prickles sparse, uneven, needle-like; hips large, oval

Amelia – See **Amelia Renaissance**, S

Amelia Anderson T, pb

Amelia Barter HT, mr, 1965, Barter; flowers bright scarlet tinted silvery, 5½ in., dbl.; foliage dark, glossy; [Queen Elizabeth × Claude]

Amelia Earhart HT, yb, 1932, Reymond; flowers golden yellow, center flushed pink, large, dbl.; vigorous growth; [Souv. de Claudius Pernet × (Louise Catherine Breslaux × Paul Neyron)]; int. by J&P

Amelia Fleming F, mp, 1995, Fleming, Joyce L.; flowers medium pink with pink tones, prominent stamens, medium, 5 petals, borne in clusters, moderate fragrance; foliage medium size, medium green, matte; upright (120-140 cm.) growth; [Marchenland × Bambula]; int. by Hortico Roses, 1994

Amelia Louise Min, mp, 1994, Haynes, F.; flowers small, full, borne mostly singly, slight fragrance; foliage small, medium green, semi-glossy; few prickles; low, bushy growth; [seedling × seedling]; int. by F. Haynes & Partners, 1993

Amelia Renaissance S, ab, Poulsen; flowers apricot blend, 10-15 cm., dbl., moderate fragrance; growth bushy, 100-150 cm.; PP15167; int. by Poulsen Roser, 2002

Amelia Rey Colaco F, Moreira da Silva, A.; int. in 1960

Amélie de Bethune HT, rb, 1923, Pernet-Ducher; flowers coral-red shaded carmine, medium, dbl.

Amélie de Mansfield HGal, mp, before 1842; flowers vivid pink, medium, dbl.

Amélie de Marsilly A, lp, 1818, Vibert; flowers light flesh pink, globular

Amélie d'Orléans HGal, dp, 1825, Cartier; flowers large, semi-dbl.

Amelie Fristel HT, yb, Adam; flowers yellow, outer petals turning orange and pink, dbl., high-centered; recurrent; foliage dark green; robust (3-4 ft.) growth; int. by Pep. de la Guerinais, 2006

Amélie Gravereaux HRg, mr, 1903, Gravereaux; bud ovoid; flowers medium red, fading to purplish, 10 cm., semi-dbl. to dbl., strong sweet fragrance; recurrent bloom; foliage dark, rugose; numerous prickles; vigorous, spiny growth; [(Général Jacqueminot × Maréchal Niel) × Conrad Ferdinand Meyer]

Amélie Hoste HP, lp, 1874, Gonod; flowers flesh pink, reverse darker, large, full

America N, ly, 1859, Page, G.; flowers light yellow-white with cream, tints of flesh pink, full; [Solfaterre × Safrano]

America HRg, mr, 1895, Harvard University Gardens/Paul; flowers bright crimson, large, semi-dbl.; hips long, red, ovate

America HMult, mp, 1915, Walsh; flowers pink, center white, 3-3½ cm., single, borne in large clusters (often to 75); [*R. wichurana* × *R. multiflora*]; sometimes classed as HWich

America LCl, op, 1975, Warriner, William A.; bud ovoid, pointed; flowers salmon, reverse lighter, imbricated, 3½-4½ in., 43 petals, borne singly and in small clusters, intense fragrance; foliage large, medium green; climbing (10-12 ft.) growth; PP3682; [Fragrant Cloud × Tradition]; int. by J&P, 1976

American Banner N, pb, 1879, Cartwright; flowers carmine striped white, small, semi-dbl., intense fragrance; probably extinct; [sport of Bon Silène]; int. by P. Henderson

American Beauty HP, dp, 1875, Lédéchaux; bud globular; flowers large, 50 petals, cupped, intense fragrance; sometimes recurrent bloom; vigorous growth; int. by Bancroft and Field Bros., 1886

American Beauty, Climbing HWich, dp, 1909, Farrell; flowers deep rose-pink, 7-8 cm., dbl., cupped, borne in small clusters, moderate damask fragrance; non-recurrent; foliage glossy; growth to 12-15 ft.; [(*R. wichurana* × Marion Dingee) × American Beauty]

American Belle HP, mp, 1893, Burton; [sport of American Beauty]

American Classic HT, dr, 1994, Winchel, Joseph F.; flowers dbl., borne mostly singly; foliage large, medium green, matte; some prickles; tall, upright growth; [seedling × seedling]; int. by Certified Roses, Inc., 1997

American Dawn HT, rb, 1976, Warriner, William A.; bud ovoid; flowers rose-red, base white, 4-5 in., 30 petals, high-centered; foliage glossy, dark; upright growth; [Personality × seedling]; int. by J&P

American Dream HT, dr, 1987, Winchel, Joseph F.; flowers deep red, large, 25 petals, high-centered, borne singly, slight damask fragrance; foliage medium size, medium green, semi-glossy; prickles average, dark brown, slightly recurved; upright, tall growth; hips round, average, medium size, medium orange; [(My Dream × Charles Mallerin) × seedling]; int. by Co-Operative Rose Growers, 1990; Gold Medal, ARC TG, 1986

American Fantasy HT, op, 1990, Twomey, Jerry; bud ovoid; flowers salmon pink, reverse lighter, large, 32 petals, cupped, borne singly, moderate fruity fragrance; foliage medium size, dark green, glossy; prickles declining, yellow with red tinge; upright, medium growth; [Sonia × seedling]; int. by DeVor Nurseries, Inc., 1990

American Flagship HT, mr, 1946, Lammerts, Dr. Walter; bud urn-shaped; flowers bright scarlet, 3½-4½ in., 15 petals, slight spicy fragrance; foliage leathery; vigorous, upright, bushy growth; [Crimson Glory × Crimson Glory]; int. by C.R. Burr

American Girl HT, mr, 1929, Maton; flowers large, dbl., high-centered; foliage leathery, dark; long stems; vigorous growth; [sport of Hollywood]

American Glory HT, dr, 1991, Twomey, Jerry; bud ovoid, pointed; flowers cardinal red, large, 28 petals, cupped, borne usually singly, slight damask fragrance; foliage medium size, dark green, semi-glossy; upright, bushy, medium growth; PP7973; [Portland Trailblazer × Silver Jubilee]; int. by DeVor Nurseries, Inc., 1991

American Heritage HT, yb, 1965, Lammerts, Dr. Walter; bud long, pointed; flowers ivory and salmon blend, becoming salmon, large, dbl., high-centered; foliage dark, leathery; tall growth; PP2687; [Queen Elizabeth × Yellow Perfection]; int. by Germain's

American Heritage, Climbing Cl HT, yb, 1973, Arora, Bal Raj; buds long pointed; flowers cream with pink edges, large, high-centered, borne mostly singly; foliage leathery, light green; [sport of American Heritage]; int. by The Rosery, India, 1971

American Hero HT, mr, Zary; flowers scarlet red, 4-6 cm., 35-40 petals, slight sweet fragrance; foliage glossy; stems long, nearly thornless; growth 5 × 4 ft.; PPRR; int. in 2002

American Home HT, dr, 1960, Morey, Dr. Dennison; bud ovoid; flowers 4½ in., 30 petals, cupped, intense fragrance; foliage leathery; vigorous, upright growth; PP2096; [Chrysler Imperial × New Yorker]; int. by J&P, 1960

American Honor HT, mp, 1993, Twomey, Jerry; flowers very dbl., high-centered, borne mostly singly; foliage medium size, dark green, semi-glossy; few prickles; medium (110 cm.), upright growth; PP9443; [Sheer Elegance × Silver Jubilee]; int. by DeVor Nurseries, Inc., 1993

American Independence – See **Air France**, Min

American Legion – See **Legion**, HT

American Pillar HWich, pb, 1902, Van Fleet; flowers carmine-pink, white eye, golden stamens, 5-6 cm., single, borne in clusters of 10-20; non-recurrent; foliage large, dark green, glossy; vigorous (15-20 ft.) growth; hips red; [(*R. wichurana* × *R. setigera*) × red Hybrid Perpetual]; int. by Conard & Jones, 1908

American Pride HT, 1928, Grillo; bud long, pointed; flowers pure white, outside petals occasionally tinted pink, 4½ in., 35 petals; foliage leathery; very vigorous growth; RULED EXTINCT 2/79 ARM; [sport of Grillodale]

American Pride HT, dr, 1978, Warriner, William A.; bud pointed, ovoid; flowers dark velvety red, 4-5 in., 33 petals, high-centered; foliage large, dark; tall, upright growth; PP4139; int. by J&P, 1974

American Rose Centennial Min, pb, 1991, Saville, F. Harmon; bud ovoid; flowers creamy white, edged soft pink, 1½ in., 50-55 petals, high-centered, borne singly or in sprays of 3-5, slight fragrance; foliage medium size, dark green, semi-glossy; bushy, medium growth; PP8181; [High Spirits × Rainbow's End]; int. by Nor'East Min. Roses, 1992

American Roseate HEg, dp, about 1840, Prince Nursery; flowers bright rose, semi-dbl.; vigorous growth

American Seedling HT, dp, 1904, Bissot; flowers dark rose pink, reverse darker; [Chatenay × Liberty]

American Shakira – See **Playrose**, HT

American Spirit HT, mr, 1986, Warriner, William A.; flowers large, 35 petals, high-centered, borne usually singly, no fragrance; foliage medium size, medium green, semi-glossy; upright, tall growth; PP6083; [seedling × American Pride]; int. by J&P, 1988

American White HEg, w, about 1840, Prince Nursery; flowers creamy white, semi-dbl.; vigorous growth

Americana HT, mr, 1961, Boerner; bud ovoid; flowers bright red, 5½ in., 28 petals, high-centered, moderate fragrance; foliage leathery; vigorous, upright growth; PP2058; [(Poinsettia × unknown) × New Yorker]; int. by J&P, 1961

America's Choice – See **H. C. Andersen**, F

America's Classic – See **American Classic**, HT

America's Junior Miss F, lp, 1964, Boerner; bud ovoid; flowers soft coral-pink, medium, dbl., moderate fragrance; foliage glossy; vigorous, bushy growth; PP2541; [Seventeen × Demure seedling]; int. by J&P, 1964

Amerlock S, op; flowers coral and rose, dbl., borne in small clusters; remontant; int. by Sauvageot, 1979

Ames 5 HMult, mp, 1932, Maney; flowers good size, borne in clusters; non-recurrent; thornless; stems red in winter; very vigorous growth; very hardy; [*R. blanda* × *R. multiflora*]; int. by Iowa State College

Ames 6 HMult, mp; [*R. blanda* × *R. multiflora*]

Ames Climber – See **Ames 5**, HMult

Amethyst HT, m, Urban, J.; flowers violet-pink, large, dbl.; int. in 1978

Améthyste HMult, m, 1911, Nonin; flowers violet-crimson, streaked with white, small, very dbl., borne in large trusses; non-recurrent; foliage glossy; stems long, arching; either a sport of Non Plus Ultra, or Non Plus Ultra × *R. multiflora*

Amethyste HT, m, Christensen

Ametista HT, m, Barni, V.; buds long, tapering; flowers strong, non-fading color, large, dbl., moderate fragrance; growth vigorous, 80-100 cm.; int. by Rose Barni, 1985

Amherst S, w, Poulsen; flowers white, small, no fragrance; foliage dark; growth broad, bushy, 60-100 cm.; PP16128; int. as Bright Cover, Poulsen Roser, 2003; First Prize, Hradec Králové, 2006, Silver Certificate, The Hague, 2006, Clarke Cunningham Shrub Award, Belfast, 2006

Ami Aminta HGal, before 1814, Descemet

Ami Charmet HP, dp, 1900, Dubreuil; flowers satiny China-rose pink, thick-petaled, very large, very dbl., camellia-like, borne in small clusters, moderate Gallica fragrance

Ami Chenault HT, Moreira da Silva, A.

Ami Clement F, dp

Ami des Jardins – See **Finale**, F

Ami Desvignes HT, mr, 1954, Privat; flowers base of petals veined coral, petals waved, large, semi-dbl.; foliage glossy; vigorous growth

Ami Dietrich HT, Moreira da Silva, A.

Ami F. Mayery HT, mr, 1938, Denoyel, Mme.; bud long, pointed, vermilion-red; flowers poppy-red, very large, dbl., cupped; foliage dark; stiff stems; vigorous growth; [Huguette Vincent × seedling]; int. by C. Chambard

Ami L. Cretté HT, rb, 1931, Chambard, C.; bud long, pointed, coppery oriental red; flowers crimson-red, reverse light coral-rose and yellow, medium to large, semi-dbl., cupped, moderate fragrance; foliage dark; very vigorous, bushy growth; int. by C-P

Ami Léon Chenault F, mr, 1929, Nonin; flowers dark garnet, slightly striated white, borne in clusters; [sport of Lafayette]

Ami Léon Pin HT, ly, 1947, Gaujard; bud long, pointed; flowers pale yellow, reverse pink, very large, dbl.; foliage dark; very vigorous growth

Ami Martin HP, or, 1906, Chédane-Guinoisseau; flowers vermilion orange-red, very large, very dbl.

Ami Poncet T, pb, 1903, Toussaint; flowers bright pink, edged light violet with salmon pink, very large, full; [Papa Gontier × unknown]

Ami Quinard HT, dr, 1927, Gaujard; bud long, pointed; flowers blackish garnet and coppery scarlet, medium, 17 petals, cupped, moderate fragrance; foliage leathery; vigorous growth; [Mme Méha Sabatier × (Mrs Edward Powell × *R. foetida bicolor*)]; possibly Mallerin instead of Gaujard; int. by C-P, 1930

Ami René Badel F, mr, 1961, Arles; bud pointed; flowers carthamus-red, 36 petals, high-centered; foliage bronze; [Belle Créole × (Gloire du Midi × Paul Crampel)]; int. by Roses-France

Amica HT, 1969, Cazzaniga, F. G.; flowers cinnabar-red, large, moderate fragrance; foliage light green; PP2827; [Coup de Foudre × Lampo]; int. by F. Giuseppe, 1966

Amie – See **Amie Renaissance**, S

Amie Renaissance S, lp, Poulsen; bud ovoid; flowers light pink with slight orange and yellow tints, 8-10 cm., 65 petals, deep cup, borne mostly singly, moderate floral fragrance; upright, bushy (100-150 cm.) growth; PP15158; [seedling × Clair Renaissance]; int. by Poulsen Roser, 2002

Amiga Mia S, mp, 1978, Buck, Dr. Griffith J.; bud ovoid, pointed; flowers empire-rose, 4-5 in., 30 petals, high-centered, moderate fragrance; foliage large, dark, leathery; vigorous, upright, bushy growth; [Queen Elizabeth × Prairie Princess]; int. by Iowa State University

Amigo F, mr, 1951, Whisler; bud short, pointed; flowers currant-red, 3-3½ in., 17-20 petals, cupped, moderate spicy fragrance; foliage leathery; upright, bushy growth; [World's Fair × Adolf Grille]; int. by Germain's

Amigo Roger Sucret F, Dot, Simon; int. in 1970

Aminta – See **Ami Aminta**, HGal

Amiral Cécile HP, m, 1850, Debeaumont; flowers purple-violet, medium to large, full, moderate fragrance

Amiral Courbet HP, mr, 1884, Dubreuil; bud oval; flowers bright carmine red with magenta tints, full, cupped; foliage pale green, matte; prickles scattered

Amiral Gravina HP, m, 1860, Moreau et Robert; flowers blackish purple, shaded with scarlet

Amiral Nelson HP, lp, 1859, Ducher; flowers light carmine pink, large, dbl.

Amirose F, yb, Delbard; flowers yellow with vermilion, dbl., borne in small clusters; int. by Sauvageot, 1980

Amistad Sincera HT, w, 1963, Camprubi, C.; bud ovoid; flowers pure white, 4-4½ in., 55 petals, high-centered to cupped, borne mostly singly, slight to moderate tea fragrance; recurrent; foliage large, dark green, leathery; prickles several, reddish-brown; vigorous, well-branched growth; PP2055; [Alaska × Virgo]; int. by C-P, 1963

Amitié HT, ob, 1951, Mallerin, C.; flowers coppery orange-yellow, well-shaped, large, dbl.; vigorous, branching growth; [Mandalay × Schéhérazade]; int. by EFR

Amitié HGal, pb; sometimes classed as D

Amleger HT, mr, 1973, Molina; flowers blood-red to cardinal-red, imbricated, 4½ in., 40 petals, cupped, slight tea fragrance; foliage dark, leathery; vigorous growth; [sport of Baccará]; int. by URS-Meilland, 1972

Amma HT, w, Ghosh; flowers light lemon yellow to pure white, high-centered, moderate fragrance; int. by KSG Son, 2006

Ammerland S, my, Noack, Werner; int. in 1986

Ammonit F, mp, Scholle; bud scrolled; flowers large, coral-rose, white eye, pink stamens, cupped, borne in cluster-flowering, intense damask fragrance; int. in 1974

Amor F, mp, 1958, deRuiter; bud pointed; flowers clear pink, medium, 22 petals; vigorous, bushy growth; [(Golden Rapture × Floribunda seedling) × (Golden

Rapture × Floribunda seedling)]; int. by Blaby Rose Gardens, 1957

Amor – See **Amor Hit**, Min

Amor Hit Min, dr, Olesen; bud globular; flowers dark red, reverse darker, 1-1½ in., very full, cupped, borne in clusters, very slight fragrance; recurrent; foliage dark green, glossy; prickles numerous, variable lenght, concave; vigorous, bushy (2 ft.) growth; PP15812; [seedling × seedling]; int. by Poulsen Roser, 2003

Amore F, mp, 1957, Riethmuller; flowers rosy pink, reverse lighter, medium, dbl.; foliage semi-glossy; moderate growth; [Orange Triumph × Spring Song]

Amore HT, rb, Kordes; flowers small, dark red with yellow reverse; [sport of Frisco]; greenhouse rose

Amore Kordana Min, dr, Kordes; flowers dbl.; container rose; int. by W. Kordes Söhne

Amoretta – See **Amorette**, Min

Amorette Min, w, 1980, deRuiter; bud long, pointed ovoid; flowers white, ivory center, 2 in., 50 petals, flat, borne 10-15 per cluster, slight fragrance; recurrent; foliage light, mid-green, leathery; prickles long, narrow, hooked slightly downward, red to brown; stems medium, slender; short, dense, bushy growth; patio; PP4493; [Rosy Jewel × Zorina]; int. by Fryer's Nursery, Ltd., 1979

Amoretto – See **Sebastian Kneipp**, HT

Amorosa HT, w, Kordes; flowers white, tinted pink, 4½ in., 30 petals, high-centered; int. by W. Kordes Söhne, 1995

Amorosa F, my, Fryer; flowers pale gold; int. by De Boer Roses, 2005

Amorosa F, Moreira da Silva, A.

Amorous HT, lp, 1986, Warriner, William A.; flowers shell pink, 30 petals, high-centered, borne singly, slight fruity fragrance; foliage large, medium green, glossy; upright, tall growth; [White Masterpiece × Marina]; int. by J&P

Amour Ardent – See **Burning Love**, F

Amourette Ch, mp; flowers rose-pink, edged lighter, large, pointed, petals recurving; foliage dark; stems red

Amoureuse HT, ab, 1960, Gaujard; flowers coppery yellow, large, 34 petals, borne singly; foliage large, medium green; [Peace × Rose Gaujard seedling]

Amours de Saverne F, rb, Sauvageot; flowers velvety red, silver reverse, dbl.; int. in 1999

Ampère HT, or, 1937, Meilland, F.; flowers nasturtium-red, edges lighter, reverse orange-yellow, very large, dbl.; foliage bright green; [Charles P. Kilham × Condesa de Sástago]

Amstelveen – See **Coral Meidiland**, S

Amsterdam F, or, 1976, Verschuren, Ted; bud ovoid; flowers clear orange-red, 2½ in., 12-15 petals; foliage glossy, brown-red; vigorous growth; [Europeana × Parkdirektor Riggers]; int. by Verschuren & Sons, 1972; Gold Medal, The Hague, 1972

Amulett HT, mr, 1932, Tantau; bud ovoid; flowers fiery red, very dbl., high-centered; foliage dark, glossy; vigorous, bushy growth; [Mrs Henry Winnett × Johanniszauber]; int. by C-P

Amulett Min, pb, Tantau; flowers rich pink, very dbl.; foliage medium green; wide, bushy (20 in.). growth; int. in 1991

Amurensis (form of *R. blanda carpohispida*), mp; flowers large, semi-dbl.; prickles sparsely armed; stems wood red; tall growth

Amy F, mp, 1954, Von Abrams; bud ovoid; flowers carmine-rose, 2½-3 in., 38 petals, high-centered, borne in loose clusters, moderate fragrance; foliage leathery; compact, dwarf growth; PP1455; [Show Girl × Fashion]; int. by Peterson & Dering, 1954

Amy Brown F, ob, 1978, Harkness; bud ovoid; flowers burnt-orange to fire-red, rounded, 2½-3 in., 28 petals, moderate fruity fragrance; foliage large, dark; low, bushy growth; [Orange Sensation × ((Highlight × Colour Wonder) × (Parkdirektor Riggers × Piccadilly))]

Amy Donelan F, m, 2006, Rawlins, R.; flowers lavender, 5 in., full, borne in small clusters; foliage medium size, medium green, glossy; prickles ½ in., triangular, few; growth medium (3½ ft.); garden decoration; [(Summerwine × (Montezuma × (Violacea × Montezuma))) × Golden Future]; int. in 2006

Amy Grant MinFl, lp, 1998, Tucker, Robbie; flowers light pink, varies by temperature, 1½-1¾ in., dbl., high-centered, borne mostly singly; foliage medium size, dark green, glossy; prickles few, small, slightly hooked downward; growth low (18-24 in.), upright; PP12270; [Loving Touch × White Masterpiece]; int. by Nor'East Miniature Roses, 1999

Amy Johnson LCl, mp, 1931, Clark, A.; bud ovoid; flowers lighter pink at edges, large, dbl., cupped, moderate fragrance; recurrent; foliage wrinkled; vigorous (12-15 ft.) growth; [Souv. de Gustave Prat × unknown]; int. by NRS Victoria

Amy Rebecca Min, dy, 1986, Jolly, Marie; flowers deep yellow, small, 38 petals, high-centered, borne usually singly; foliage small, medium green, semi-glossy; prickles small, brown; medium, upright growth; [Rise 'n' Shine × Summer Butter]; int. by Rosehill Farm, 1987

Amy Robsart HEg, dp, 1894, Penzance; flowers deep rose, center white, large, semi-dbl., moderate fragrance; summer bloom; foliage fragrant; vigorous growth; [*R. rubiginosa* × HP or B]; int. by Keynes, Williams & Co.

Amy Sis Min; int. in 1999

Amy Vanderbilt F, m, 1956, Boerner; bud globular; flowers lavender-lilac, 3 in., 70 petals, cupped, borne in pyramidal clusters, moderate fragrance; foliage dark, glossy; upright, bushy growth; PP1585; [(Lavender Pinocchio × unknown) × Lavender Pinocchio]; int. by J&P, 1956

Amy's Delight Min, mp, 1981, Williams, Ernest D.; bud ovoid; flowers clear medium pink, opening imbricated, 60 petals, borne usually singly, no fragrance; foliage small, medium green, very glossy; prickles straight, tan; compact, bushy growth; [Little Darling × Little Chief]; int. in 1980

Amy's Delight F, pb, Williams, J. B.; flowers shades of light pink to orange-red, semi-dbl., borne in clusters, moderate fragrance; abundant; int. by Hortico, Inc., 2001

Ana de Cuevas HT, yb, Viveros Fco. Ferrer, S L; flowers 24 petals, high-centered; [Bucaneer × Cocktail]

Ana Olga Steppuhn HT, ob, Vidal

Anabell F, ob, 1973, Kordes; flowers orange and silvery blend, well-formed, 4 in., 30 petals, moderate fragrance; foliage small; [Zorina × Colour Wonder]; int. by Dicksons of Hawlmark, 1972

Anabelle Min, mr, Benardella

Anacréon HGal, mp, 1828, Vibert; flowers carmine-pink, medium large, very dbl.

Anadia – See **Carefree Marvel**, S

Anaïs HSpn, dp, 1823, Bizard

Anaïs Charles – See **Charles-Anaïs**, C

Anaïs Ségalas HGal, pb, 1837, Vibert; flowers rosy crimson, edged rosy lilac, expanded, large, dbl., borne singly or in clusters of 2-5, moderate fragrance; foliage clear green, elliptical to round, with 3 leaflets; numerous prickles; branching growth; maybe be from Parmentier, introduced by Vibert; sometimes classified as C

Anaïse B, mp; flowers medium large, dbl.

Anant HT, pb, Chiplunkar; int. in 1991

Ananya HT, pb, Ghosh; flowers light pink and cream, changing to deep pink with petal tips cerise, well formed; int. in 1998

Anastasia HT, w, 1981, Greff, N.P.; bud ovoid, pointed; flowers 30 petals, high-centered, borne usually singly, no fragrance; recurrent; foliage large, dark; prickles bronze, turning brown with age; vigorous, dense growth; [John F. Kennedy × Pascali]; int. in 1980

Anathalie Chantrier HP, w, 1854, Cherpin; flowers white, edges shaded carmine, medium, full, semi-globular

Anatole HGal, mr, 1827, Noisette

Anatole de Montesquieu N, m, before 1835, Jacques; flowers violet-purple, medium, full

Anatole de Montesquieu HSem, w, before 1852, Van Houtte; bud pink; flowers small, dbl., borne in large, open clusters of 10-30, moderate musk fragrance

Ancelin HGal, dp, 1829, Noisette, E.; flowers deep rose, very large, dbl., borne in clusters of 5-7; foliage rounded, slightly dentate; prickles numerous, hooked; [*R. turbinata* × unknown]; a variety of *R. francofurtana*

Ancestry Min, mp, 1997, Jellyman, J.S.; flowers medium, 8-14 petals, borne in small clusters; foliage medium size, medium green, glossy; spreading, bushy, medium (30cm.) growth; [seedling × Party Girl]; int. by Federation of Family History Societies

Anchieta HT, (Brazil)

Anci Böhm – See **Anci Böhmova**, HMult

Anci Böhmova HMult, mp, 1929, Böhm, J.; bud medium, globular; flowers deep violet pink, large, full, globular, borne in large clusters; foliage small, sparse, gray-green, soft; [sport of Marietta Silva Tarouca]

Ancienne – See **Shailer's White Moss**, M

Ancienne Pivoine – See **Bourbon**, HGal

Ancient Art Min, op, 1985, Hardgrove, Donald L.; flowers orange-pink blend, yellow reverse, medium, dbl., slight fragrance; foliage medium size, medium green, matte; upright, bushy growth; [Rise 'n' Shine × Picnic]; int. by Rose World Originals

Anda Pol, rb, 1986, Lens, Louis; flowers dark red, white eye, 2 in., 5 petals, borne in clusters of 18-24, moderate fruity fragrance; prickles purple; bushy growth; [(Britannia × *R. moschata*) × (Little Angel × Europeana)]; int. in 1980

Andalusien F, mr, 1977; bud long, pointed; flowers red, 3 in., 34 petals, cupped; vigorous, bushy growth; [seedling × Zorina]; int. by Kordes, 1977; ADR, 1976

Andante HT, mr, 1962, Laperrière; flowers large, 40 petals; foliage bronze; vigorous, bushy growth; int. by EFR

Andante S, op, 1964, Buck, Dr. Griffith J.; bud ovoid, pointed; flowers light salmon-pink, medium, dbl., cupped, slight fragrance; repeat bloom; foliage dark, bronze, leathery; vigorous (5-6 ft.), upright, arching growth; [Sea of Fire × (Josef Rothmund × *R. laxa*)]; int. by Iowa State University, 1962

Andenken an Alma de l'Aigle HMsk, lp, 1948, Kordes; flowers light pink, blush at the base, 9 cm., full, moderate fragrance

Andenken an Alma de l'Aigle Ilsabella – See **Andenken an Alma de l'Aigle**, HMsk

Andenken an Breslau HWich, mr, 1913, Kiese; flowers carmine-red, 5-6 cm., dbl., borne in large clusters; foliage small, glossy

Andenken an Franz Heinsohn F, dr, 1985, Poulsen, S.; flowers medium, dbl., urn-shaped, borne in clusters, slight fragrance; upright, bushy growth; [D.T. Poulsen × seedling]; int. in 1938

Andenken an Gartendirektor Siebert HMult, pb, 1923, Kiese; flowers carmine-rose, with yellow, borne in clusters; [Eisenach × Polyantha seedling]

Andenken an Gustav Frahm – See **Gustav Frahm**, F

Andenken an Hermann Thiess F, or, Krause; flowers

medium large, semi-dbl.; int. in 1959

Andenken an J. Diering Cl HT, 1902, Hinner, W.

Andenken an Johannes Gehlhaar HT, w, 1925, Gehlhaar; flowers large, dbl.

Andenken an Kricker Hahn S, Weihrauch; int. in 1995

Andenken an Moritz von Fröhlich HT, mr, 1905, Hinner, W.; flowers carmine red, large, dbl.; [Mme Caroline Testout × possibly Princesse de Béarn]

Andersen's Yellow HT, my, 1985, Walter, J.C.; flowers large, dbl., slight fragrance; foliage medium size, dark, semi-glossy; [Queen Elizabeth × seedling]; int. by Kimbrew-Walter Roses, 1984

Andersonii S, mp, 1935; flowers bright pink, 2-2½ in., single, borne in clusters of 4-6; early summer; growth vigorous, branching (4-5 ft.); [chance hybrid of *R. canina* × possibly *R. arvensis*]; int. as *R. andersonii*, Hillier & Sons

Anderson's Double Lady's Blush HSpn, ly, about 1810, Anderson, George

Andie MacDowell MinFl, or, 2003, Williams, Michael C.; flowers medium orange, reverse lighter, 2½ in., dbl., borne in large clusters, no fragrance; foliage large, dark green, matte; prickles ¼ in., pointed down; growth upright, tall (2½ ft.); garden, exhibition, cutting; [unknown × unknown]; int. by Bridges Roses, 2004; Award of Excellence, ARS, 2004

Andorra HT, ab, 1976, Kordes; bud long, pointed; flowers large, 24 petals, high-centered, intense fragrance; foliage glossy, dark; vigorous, upright, bushy growth; [Dr. A.J. Verhage × seedling]; int. by Fey, 1973

André Brichet F, w, DVP Melle; flowers large, dbl, borne in clusters, moderate fragrance; foliage dense, disease-resistant; [Melrose × Mary Rose]; int. in 2001; Gold Medal, Le Roeulx, 2000, Gold Medal, Baden-Baden, 2000, Bronze Medal, The Hague, 2006

André Brunel S, mp, Panozzo, Bernard; flowers stable pink, 3½ in., full, pompon, intense fragrance; vigorous (3-4 ft.) growth; int. by Les Roses Anciennes de André Eve, 2006

André Chénier HP, m, 1851, Robert; flowers dark violet, medium, full, globular

André de Garnier des Garets HT, pb, 1899, Buatois; flowers bright pink, shaded coppery yellow, medium; [Luciole × Ophirie]

André Du Pont – See **Rouge Formidable**, HGal

André Durand HP, lp, 1871, Schwartz

Andre Eve HT, pb, Adams; flowers various shades of pink to rosy apricot; growth strong, 90-120 cm.; int. in 2002

André Fresnoy HP, rb, 1869, Pernet; flowers shining red, shaded deep purple, very large, full, globular; [Victor Verdier × unknown]

André Gamon HT, mp, 1908, Pernet-Ducher; flowers carmine

André le Nôtre – See **Betty White**, HT

André le Nôtre, Climbing Cl HT, mp, Meilland; flowers deeper in center, outer petals fading, full, cupped, moderate old rose fragrance; foliage disease-resistant; 7+ ft. growth; int. by Meilland Richardier, 2006

André le Troquer HT, ob, 1946, Mallerin, C.; flowers orange shading to apricot, 5 in., 30 petals, cupped; foliage very dark; very vigorous, upright growth; int. by A. Meilland; Gold Medal, Bagatelle, 1946, Gold Medal, NRS, 1951

André Leroy HP, lp, 1860, Pradel; int. in 1860

André Leroy d'Angers HP, mr, 1866, Trouillard; bud dark violet; flowers crimson, shaded with violet, often ill-formed, large, dbl.; vigorous growth; int. by Standish

André Louis HMult, w, 1920, Tanne; flowers white, center flesh-pink, full, borne in clusters of 4-5; sometimes classed as HWich; int. by Turbat

André Pernet HT, mr, 1956, Gaujard; bud long; flowers red, becoming lighter at center and purplish on outer petals, dbl.; foliage dark; very vigorous growth; [Peace × (Mme Elie Dupraz × unknown)]

André Schwartz T, mr, 1882, Schwartz, J.; flowers crimson, sometimes striped white

André Schwartz HT, mr, Tantau; flowers clear red, dbl., high-centered; recurrent; medium growth; int. by Ludwig's Roses, 2003

Andrea HT, ob; int. in 1968

Andrea Min, pb, 1978, Moore, Ralph S.; bud pointed; flowers deep pink, silver reverse, 1½ in., 20 petals, high-centered; foliage dark; vigorous, bushy, spreading growth; [Little Darling × unknown]; int. by Sequoia Nursery, 1978

Andrea – See **Andrea Parade**, MinFl

Andrea Jane HT, pb, McGredy; flowers large, edged red, suffusing to pink; int. by De Boer Roses, 2003

Andrea Jones F, pb, 2003, Rawlins, R.; flowers medium, dbl., borne in small clusters; foliage medium size, dark green, glossy; prickles hooked; growth upright, tall (5½ ft.); garden; [Golden Future × (Florange × Sealax)]; int. in 2003

Andrea Muraglia – See **Frau Betty Hartmann**, HT

Andrea Parade MinFl, m, Poulsen; flowers lavender and purple, 5-8 cm., dbl., no fragrance; foliage dark; growth bushy, 20-40 cm.; int. by Poulsen Roser, 2004

Andrea Stelzer HT, lp, Kordes; flowers clear soft pink, spiral centers, 25-30 petals, exhibition, borne one to a stem, slight fragrance; foliage very shiny, dark green; stems long and straight; growth tall and upright; int. by W. Kordes Söhne, 1992

Andreas Höfer HMult, mr, 1911, Kiese; flowers brilliant blood-red, small, full, borne in clusters of up to 30; foliage somber green; thornless; growth vigorous (3 m.); [Tausendschön × unknown]

Andrée Joubert HT, op, 1952, Mallerin, C.; bud very long, dark orange-coral; flowers pastel salmon, large; [Soeur Thérèse × Duquesa de Peñaranda]; int. by EFR

Andrée Lenoble Pol, dp, 1915, Turbat; flowers unfading rose or red

Andrée Palthey HT, mr, 1946, Gaujard; bud long, pointed; flowers bright red, large, very dbl.; foliage bronze; vigorous growth; [Mme Joseph Perraud × seedling]

Andrée Perrier HT, ob, 1932, Chambard, C.; bud long; flowers orange-yellow, shaded carmine, very large, dbl., cupped; [Souv. de F. Bohé × seedling]

Andrée Roux HT, rb, 1927, Pernet-Ducher; flowers coral-red, tipped carmine, reverse yellow; int. by Gaujard

Andrèe Sauvager HT, yb, 1935, Mallerin, C.; flowers light orange-yellow, large, dbl.

Andrée-Sophie Girard F, mr, 1958, Arles; flowers currant-red, edged silvery, dbl.; [Alain × Independence]; int. by Roses-France

Andrée Vanderschrick HWich, w, 1935, Buatois; bud greenish; flowers opening well, small, very dbl., borne in clusters; profuse seasonal bloom; foliage dark; very vigorous, climbing growth

Andres Battle HT, dr, 1951, Camprubi, C.; bud long, pointed; flowers crimson, large, dbl., high-centered; strong stems; vigorous growth; [Comtesse Vandal × Sensation]

Andrew Barton Patterson HT, ob, Allender, Robert William; int. in 1999

Andrew's Comfort S, ly; flowers light yellow, dbl., borne on every branch and stem; continuous bloom; growth neat, densely branched shrublet, 70 cm.; int. in 1996

Andrews Rose – See ***R. spinosissima andrewsii*** (Rehder)

Andrewsii M, mp, 1807; flowers soft blush tinted lavender pink with chartreuse stamens

Andromeda HT, pb, Ghosh; buds long; flowers medium pink with lighter reverse, large, full; free-flowering; strong growth; int. in 1998

Andromeda S, dp, Barni; flowers rose carmine, large, semi-dbl., moderate fruity fragrance; continuous; foliage medium size, shiny; growth to 50-70 cm.; groundcover; int. by Rose Barni, 2003

Andromeda – See **Andromeda Hit**, MinFl

Andromeda Hit MinFl, w, Poulsen; flowers white, 5-8 cm., dbl., slight fragrance; foliage dark; growth bushy, 20-40 cm.; int. by Poulsen Roser, 2004

Andulka HT, op, 1935, Brada, Dr.; bud long, pointed; flowers pink to salmon-pink, large, dbl.; vigorous, bushy growth; int. by Böhm

Andy Gray HT, pb, 2000, Rawlins, R.; flowers pink-apricot, reverse pink, medium, very full, borne in small clusters; foliage medium size, dark green, semi-glossy; prickles moderate; growth upright, tall (48 in.); [Solitaire × Abraham Darby]

Anémone – See **Provins Renoncule**, HGal

Anémone – See **De La Flèche**, M

Anémone M, mp, 1844, Mauget; flowers even crimson, center petals curling, 6 cm., dbl., cupped

Anemone S, lp, 1896, Geschwind/Schmidt; flowers silver pink, petals shell-shaped, 4 in., 5 petals, moderate fragrance; spring bloom, then scattered bloom; foliage glossy; vigorous, bushy growth; [*R. laevigata* × *R. odorata*]; int. by J.C. Schmidt

Anémone Ancienne – See **Ornement de la Nature**, HGal

Anémone Argentée HGal, m, before 1826, Barrier; flowers violet-purple; Agathe group

Anemone Rose – See **Anemone**, S

Anemonenrose – See **Anemone**, S

Anemonoides C, mr, 1814, Poilpre

Anemonoides – See **Anemone**, S

Anette F, Noack, Werner; int. in 1978

Angara HT, rb, 1983, Gupta, Dr. M.N. & Shukla, R.; flowers dark red with hues of orange; [sport of Montezuma]; int. by National Botanical Research Institute

Ange Divin Min, op, Lens; flowers salmon pink, very dbl., rosette; very floriferous; red tips on foliage; growth to 20-30 cm.; int. by Lens Roses, 1994

Angel S, w, 1983, deVor, Paul F.; flowers flora-tea, small, 35 petals, slight fragrance; foliage medium size, light green, semi-glossy; upright growth; [(Queen Elizabeth × seedling) × Jack Frost]; int. in 1982

Angel Bells HT, rb, 1964, Herholdt, J.A.; flowers ivory, flushed orange and red, well-formed, large, dbl., borne singly; foliage dark, glossy; bushy growth; [Peace × Rina Herholdt]; int. by Herholdt's Nursery

Angel Cream F, w, 1989, Ravi, Professor N.; bud broadly ovate; flowers creamy white, turning pure white; [sport of Angel Face]

Angel Darling Min, m, 1976, Moore, Ralph S.; flowers lavender, 1½ in., 10 petals, slight fragrance; foliage leathery; vigorous growth; PP4070; [Little Chief × Angel Face]; int. by Sequoia Nursery

Angel Delight HT, ab, 1977, Fryers Nursery, Ltd.; flowers peach shaded salmon and apricot buff, full, high-centered; [sport of Femina]; int. in 1976

Angel Dust Min, w, 1978, Bennett, Dee; bud ovoid; flowers small, 18-20 petals, high-centered; foliage dark; vigorous, upright, spreading growth; [Magic Carrousel × Magic Carrousel]; int. by Tiny Petals Nursery

Angel Eve – See **Baby Grand**, Min

Angel Eyes Min, dp, 1979, Lyon; bud ovoid; flowers

spinel-red, 1 in., 10 petals, slight fragrance; foliage small; very compact, bushy growth; int. in 1978

Angel Face F, m, 1968, Swim & Weeks; bud pointed; flowers deep mauve-lavender, petal edges blushed ruby, 3½-4 in., 25-30 petals, high-centered, borne in large clusters, intense strongly citrus fragrance; foliage dark, leathery, glossy; vigorous, upright, bushy growth; PP2792; [(Circus × Lavender Pinocchio) × Sterling Silver]; int. by C-P; John Cook Medal, ARS, 1971

Angel Face, Climbing Cl F, m, Haight (also Ruston, 1996); flowers ruffled, lavender-mauve, borne in best on old wood, intense fragrance; growth to 10-12 ft.; int. in 1981

Angel Gates HSem, pb

Angel Girl HT, pb, 1973, Wyant; flowers peach-pink; [sport of Bel Ange]

Angel Guiméra HT, my, 1926, Dot, Pedro; bud long, pointed; flowers amber-yellow, medium, dbl.; foliage large, thick; [Frau Karl Druschki × Souv. de Claudius Pernet]; int. by S. Dot

Angel Pink Cl Min, op, 1987, Moore, Ralph S.; flowers pink to soft coral pink, holds color, dbl., high-centered, borne in sprays of 3-7, slight fragrance; foliage medium size, light green, semi-glossy; prickles medium, brown, slightly hooked downwards; upright, tall, climbing (5-7 ft.) growth; no fruit; [Little Darling × Eleanor]

Angel Rose – See ***R. chinensis minima*** (Voss)

Angel Wings HT, yb, 1959, Lindquist; bud ovoid; flowers yellow, shading to white, edged pink, 3½-4 in., 23 petals, cupped, moderate fragrance; foliage leathery; upright growth; PP1865; [Golden Rapture × Girona]; int. by Howard Rose Co., 1958; Gold Medal, Portland, 1959

Angela F, yb, 1958, Kordes; flowers golden yellow shaded crimson, 2½ in., 28 petals, borne in trusses of 15-20, slight fragrance; very free bloom; foliage glossy, dark; vigorous, upright growth; [Masquerade × Golden Scepter]; int. by Henry Morse & Sons, 1957

Angela F, dp, 1984, Kordes; flowers deep pink, 35 petals, cupped, borne singly and in clusters; foliage medium size, medium green, glossy; bushy growth; [Yesterday × Peter Frankenfeld]; ADR, 1982

Angela HT, yb, J&P

Angela Daffey Min, lp, Hannemann, F.; int. in 1989

Angela Davis HT, pb, 2005, Poole, Lionel; flowers pink/apricot, reverse pink, 4-4½ in., dbl., borne singly and in small clusters, intense fragrance; foliage medium size, medium green, glossy; prickles moderate, medium, hooked down, light brown; bushy, medium (2½-3 ft.) growth; garden bedding, borders; [Silver Jubilee × Bernice Cooper]; int. in 2006

Angela Lansbury HT, pb, Twomey, Jerry; flowers soft color deepens on petal edges, dbl., high-centered, slight fragrance; foliage glossy, deep green; growth medium; PP10172; [Gitte × Silver Jubilee]; int. in 1995

Angela Marie HT, lp, 2000, Ohlson, John; flowers light pink, reverse lighter, 4 in., full, high-centered, borne mostly solitary, slight fragrance; foliage medium size, medium green, semi-glossy; numerous prickles; growth compact, medium (5 ft.); [First Prize × seedling]; int. in 2001

Angela Merici HT, w, Lens, Louis; int. in 1987

Angela Rippon Min, mp, 1976, deRuiter; flowers salmon-pink, patio, small, moderate fragrance; dwarf, compact growth; [Rosy Jewel × Zorina]; int. by Fryer's Nursery, Ltd., 1977

Angela Rose Taylor F, pb, 2004, Smith, Keith; flowers semi-dbl., borne in large clusters, intense fragrance; foliage medium size, medium green, semi-glossy; prickles 1½ cm., normal; growth upright, tall (2 m.); garden decorative; hedging; [Seedling (Hannah Gordon × Raspberry Ice) × unknown]; int. by Nieuwesteegs Rose Nursery, 2001

Angela's Choice F, pb, 1972, Gobbee, W.D.; flowers light pink, reverse deep pink, 3 in., 15 petals; foliage matte; vigorous, upright growth; [Dainty Maid × Anna Wheatcroft]

Angela's Rose – See **Angela Rose Taylor**, F

Angèle D, lp, before 1846; flowers light carmine pink, very large, very dbl.

Angèle HT, w, 1933, Vestal; bud ovoid; flowers creamy white, large, dbl., borne in clusters; foliage leathery; long stems; vigorous, bushy growth; [seedling × Kaiserin Auguste Viktoria]

Angèle d'Arnex HT, mp, 1912, Bernaix fils; flowers China pink with silvery lavender reflections, large, full

Angèle Fontaine HP, lp, 1877, Fontaine; flowers medium to large, full

Angèle Pernet HT, ob, 1924, Pernet-Ducher; bud ovoid; flowers reddish-orange shaded yellow, large, dbl., globular, moderate fruity fragrance; foliage dark, bronze, leathery; vigorous, bushy growth; [Bénédicte Seguin × HT]; Gold Medal, NRS, 1925, Gold Medal, Bagatelle, 1924

Angelglo Min, m, 1983, Williams, Ernest D.; flowers lavender, micro-mini, small, dbl., slight fragrance; foliage small, dark, semi-glossy; bushy growth; PP5356; [Angel Face × (Angel Face × Over the Rainbow)]; int. by Mini-Roses, 1982

Angelica – See **Angela**, F

Angelica Renae Min, pb, 1996, Wells, Verlie W.; flowers bright medium pink blend, full, high-centered, borne mostly singly, slight fragrance; foliage medium size, dark green, matte; some prickles; upright, bushy (24-30 in.) growth; [Anita Charles × seedling]; int. by Nor'East Min. Roses, 1996; AOE, ARS, 1996

Angelika F, dp; flowers small, deep pink, dbl., high-centered; greenhouse rose; int. by W. Kordes Söhne, 1993

Angelina S, pb, 1976, Cocker; flowers rose-pink, white eye and reverse, 3 in., 11 petals, borne in clusters; foliage matte, light green; bushy, spreading growth; [(Tropicana × Carine) × (Cläre Grammerstorf × Frühlingsmorgen)]; int. in 1976

Angelina Lauro HT, or, 1970, Lens; flowers medium, dbl.; foliage dark; int. by Spek, 1968

Angeline Lauro – See **Angelina Lauro**, HT

Angélique HGal, mr, about 1820, Descemet; flowers medium red, center brighter, large, very full

Angelique F, op, Swim, H.C.; bud ovoid; flowers coral-pink to salmon-pink, open, 2½-3 in., 20-25 petals, borne in clusters, slight fragrance; vigorous, spreading growth; [World's Fair × Pinocchio]; int. by C.R. Burr, 1961

Angelique – See **Ankori**, HT

Angélique Quétier M, m, 1839, Quétier; bud well mossed; flowers violet-rose, large, very dbl., cupped

Angelis HT, w, 1960, Dot, Pedro; bud long; flowers , 8-10 petals; upright, bushy growth; [Virgo × Ibiza]

Angelita Min, w, 1982, McGredy, Sam IV; bud small, ovoid, yellow; flowers pure white, 3 cm., 35-40 petals, decorative, borne in sprays, slight fragrance; recurrent; foliage small, dark, glossy; prickles numerous, needle, declining, light brown; growth low (10 in.), spreading; hips few, globular, orange; PP5849; [Moana × Snow Carpet]; int. in 1982; Gold Star of the South Pacific, Palmerston North, NZ, 1983

Angelita Ruaix HT, ob, 1940, Dot, Pedro; flowers orange-yellow, large, dbl., high-centered; foliage glossy, dark; very vigorous growth; [Duquesa de Peñaranda × Pres. Herbert Hoover]

Angelo Sgaravatti HT; int. in 1981

Angel's Angel F, or, 2006, Castillo, Angel; flowers orange-red, reverse pink and red, 4 in., single, borne in small clusters; foliage large, medium green, semi-glossy, disease-resistant; prickles medium, slightly hooked, moderate; growth spreading, medium (24 in.); garden decorative, exhibition; [Little Darling × Sarabande]; int. by Angel Roses, 2007

Angel's Blush Min, ab, 1996, William, Michael C.; flowers apricot, darkest color on the very edge of the petals, large, dbl.; foliage small, medium green, semi-glossy; few prickles; medium (50 cm.), upright growth; [seedling × unknown]; int. by The Mini Rose Garden, 1997

Angel's Blush – See **Gene Jones**, F

Angels Mateu HT, ab, 1934, Dot, Pedro; bud ovoid; flowers salmon, overlaid gold, large, 40 petals, globular, moderate blackberry fragrance; foliage dark; vigorous, bushy growth; [Magdalena de Nubiola × Duquesa de Peñaranda]; int. by C-P; Gold Medal, Rome, 1934, Gold Medal, Bagatelle, 1934

Angelus HT, w, 1921, Lemon; flowers white, center cream, large, 40-45 petals; foliage leathery, dark; vigorous growth; [Columbia × Ophelia seedling]

Angelus, Climbing Cl HT, w, 1933, Dixie Rose Nursery; flowers large, full, moderate fragrance; [sport of Angelus]

Angelus HT, ob, Gaujard; flowers orange, well-formed; int. in 1980

Angers-Rose Pol, mp, 1912, Delaunay

Angie F, lp, 2005, Paul Chessum Roses; flowers dbl., borne in small clusters, slight fragrance; foliage small, medium green, glossy; prickles medium; bushy, short growth; bedding, borders, containers; [seedling × seedling]; int. by Love4Plants Ltd, 2005

Angie Heatwole F, mp, 1996, Heatwole, Robert E.; flowers medium, dbl., borne in small clusters; foliage medium size, medium green, semi-glossy; few prickles; medium, upright growth; [seedling × Dreamer]

Angkor HT, mr, 1967, Delbard-Chabert; flowers carmine-red, large, dbl., globular; foliage bronze, glossy, leathery; vigorous, bushy growth; [Belle Rouge × (Rome Glory × Gratitude)]

Anglica Minor A, w; flowers center muddled, dbl.; foliage dark gray-green; dwarf growth

Angola F, dr, Moreira da Silva; [seedling × Alain]

Angora HT

Angus MacNeil F, op, 1967, Vincent; flowers salmon-pink and cream, well-formed, borne in clusters; foliage dark; free growth; [The Optimist × Ma Perkins]

Anibal David HT, my, 1961, Moreira da Silva

Anicet Bourgeois HP, mr, 1881, Moreau & Robert; flowers bright cherry red, large, full, cupped; [Senateur Vaisse × Mme Victor Verdier]

Anicka Pol, dr, 1940, Valàsek; flowers small, dbl.

Anika HT, dy, Haschke; flowers golden-yellow, dbl., high-centered, borne mostly singly, slight fragrance; recurrent; foliage dark green, glossy; stems long, strong; strong, upright, branching growth; int. in 1987

Anikall HT, dy, Haschke; int. in 1987

Animating – See **Bengale Animée**, Ch

Animo F, yb, 1962, deRuiter; flowers yellow, becoming copper-red, open, 2½ in., semi-dbl., borne in clusters; bushy growth; [Masquerade × Beauté]

Anirvan HT, rb, Ghosh; flowers bright scarlet with silvery reverse, large, well formed, moderate fragrance; free-flowering; int. in 2001

Anisley Dickson – See **Dicky**, F

Anita mp, 1965, de Ruiter; bud ovoid; flowers medium, very dbl., borne in clusters; foliage dark green

Anita F, pb, 1982, Swim, H.C. & Christensen, J.E.; bud ovoid, pointed; flowers large, 43 petals, borne in clusters of 3-7, slight tea fragrance; foliage large, glossy; prickles large; medium growth; [Rumba × Marmalade]; int. by Armstrong Nursery

Anita Charles Min, op, 1981, Moore, Ralph S.; bud pointed; flowers bright pink, reverse lighter pink-yellow blend, 43 petals, high-centered, borne singly, sometimes 2-3 per cluster, moderate tea fragrance; foliage small, leathery, matte; prickles straight; vigorous, upright, spreading growth; [Golden Glow × Over the Rainbow]

Anita Charles, Climbing Cl Min, op, Vidal

Anita M. S, op, 2004, Warner, Chris; flowers peach pink, reverse light pink, 7-8 cm., dbl., borne in small clusters, moderate fragrance; repeat flowering; foliage small, medium green, semi-glossy; prickles small, straight; growth bushy, medium (4 ft.); garden decorative; [Laura Ford × Chewbold [Lichtkonigin Lucia × (Angelina × (Flamenca × R bella))]]; pimpinellifolia-type; int. by Kristen Cedergren, 2004

Anita Pereire S, w, Orard; flowers single; [Anisley Dickson × *R. wichurana*]; int. by Orard, 1996

Anita Russell Min, mp, 2004, Jalbert, Brad; flowers pink, petals having pointed tips, 1¼ in., dbl., borne in small clusters, slight fragrance; foliage medium green, semi-glossy; prickles medium, green, moderate; growth upright, medium (14-16 in.); [Cherry Wine × Glowing Amber]; int. in 2001

Anita Stahmer F, dp, 1976, Kordes; bud long, pointed; flowers deep pink, 2½ in., 27 petals, high-centered, slight fragrance; foliage soft; vigorous, upright, bushy growth; [sport of Zorina]

Anita's Quartered Tropicana HT, mr; int. in 1998

Anitra Louisa F, rb, 2006, Rawlins, Ronnie; flowers red/pink striped, reverse red, medium, full, borne in small clusters, moderate fragrance; foliage medium size, medium green, semi-glossy; prickles ½ in., triangular, moderate; growth compact, medium (30 in.); garden decoration; [Kanagem × Candle in the Wind]

Anja F, op, Kordes; bud sharply pointed; flowers deep salmon intensifying to orange in sun, thick petals, dbl., high-centered, slight fragrance; prolific; growth medium; flora-tea; int. in 1993

Anjani Pol, rb, Kasturi; flowers red with prominent white eye, borne in large sprays; int. by KSG Son, 1970

Anjou – See **Anjou Palace**, S

Anjou S, op, Kordes

Anjou Festival F, mr, Pineau; int. in 1982

Anjou Palace S, mr, Poulsen; flowers medium red, 8-10 cm., 25 petals, no fragrance; foliage dark; growth bushy, 40-60 cm.; PP15507; int. by Poulsen Roser, 2002

Ankara HT, op, 1940, Meilland, F.; flowers salmon-orange, center coppery, very large, dbl., cupped; foliage leathery; vigorous, upright growth; [Joanna Hill × Mme Joseph Perraud]; int. by A. Meilland

Anke Schwarz HT, mr, Hetzel; int. in 1993

Ankori HT, ob, 1985, Kordes; flowers bright vermilion orange, well-formed, large, 40 petals; foliage medium size, medium green, matte; bushy growth; PP5012; [Mercedes × seedling]; int. in 1980

Ann S, mp, 1998, Austin, David; flowers 2½ in., single, borne in clusters; foliage medium size, medium green, semi-glossy; prickles moderate; bushy, medium (3 ft.) growth; int. by David Austin Roses, Ltd., 1997

Ann Aberconway F, ab, 1976, Mattock; flowers apricot-orange, 3 in., 20 petals; foliage dark, leathery; [Arthur Bell × seedling]; int. by The Rose Nurseries

Ann Barter HT, mr, 1962, Barter; flowers cerise, 5 in., 18 petals; foliage dark; vigorous growth; [Peace × Ena Harkness]

Ann Cox Chambers F, w, 2003, Carruth, Tom; flowers very pastel apricot to near white, 9-11 cm., dbl., borne in small clusters, slight fragrance; foliage medium size, dark green, semi-glossy; prickles moderate, average, straight, greenish brown; growth bushy, rounded, medium (90-110 cm.); garden decoration; [Moonstone × Marilyn Monroe]; int. by Weeks Roses, 2003

Ann Delforge HT, ob

Ann Elizabeth F, mp, 1962, Norman; flowers clear rose-pink, large, 15 petals, borne in open clusters; foliage glossy; vigorous, quite tall growth; int. by Harkness, 1962

Ann Elizabeth Vear HT, ab, 2003, Rawlins, R.; flowers apricot, reverse apricot yellow, medium, dbl., borne in small clusters; foliage medium size, medium green, matte; prickles 1 cm., triangular, few; growth compact, medium (30 in.); garden decoration; [(Baby Love × Amber Queen) × Amber Queen]

Ann Endt HRg, dr, 1979, Nobbs; bud long-sepaled; flowers medium, 5 petals, moderate cinnamon fragrance; foliage small, soft; [*R. rugosa* × *R. foliolosa*]; int. in 1978

Ann Factor HT, ab, 1974, Ellis & Swim; bud ovoid; flowers pastel apricot, large, very dbl., high-centered, intense fragrance; foliage large, glossy, bronze, leathery; vigorous, bushy growth; [Duet × Jack O'Lantern]; int. by Armstrong Nursery, 1975

Ann Henderson F, r; flowers coppery red-orange, coffee, bronze, medium, dbl., borne in clusters, moderate fragrance; repeats freely; foliage glossy, bronze green; growth rounded, medium (3 × 2 ft.); int. by Fryer, 2004

Ann Holbrook Min, yb, 1982, Dobbs, Annette E.; bud globular; flowers yellow-pink blend, small, dbl., slight fragrance; foliage small, medium green, glossy; spreading growth; [Patricia Scranton × Little Darling]

Ann Kercher HT, dp; flowers variable form, small

Ann Moore Min, or, 1981, Moore, Ralph S.; bud long, pointed; flowers 30 petals, high-centered, borne usually singly, moderate fragrance; foliage leathery, semi-glossy; prickles long; vigorous, bushy, upright growth; [Little Darling × Fire Princess]

Ann Reilly F, mp, 2004, Ballin, Don; flowers satiny, reverse slightly duller, 2½-3 in., very full, borne mostly solitary, no fragrance; foliage medium size, semi-glossy; prickles small to medium, slightly curved down; growth compact, medium; garden decoration; [sport of Olympiad]; int. by Pending, 2005

Anna – See **My Lady Kensington**, C

Anna HT, lp, Pekmez, Paul; bud cream white; flowers cream brushed with pink, dbl., exhibition, borne in small clusters, moderate fragrance; foliage bright green; growth vigorous, 4-5 ft.; int. by Carlton, 1998

Anna S, op, Carlsson-Nilsson; flowers color lighter toward petal edges, dbl.

Anna Aguilera F, Dot, Simon; int. in 1972

Anna Alexieff HP, mr, 1858, Margottin; flowers rose pink, large, dbl., cupped, borne in clusters of 3; medium, upright growth

Anna Caroline Maxwell HT, dr, 2000, Perry, Astor; flowers rich dark red, 4½ in., full, borne mostly singly, slight fragrance; foliage medium size, dark green, matte; few prickles; growth upright, tall; [Karl Herbst × Burgundy]; int. by Certified Roses, Inc.

Anna Chartron T, w, Schwartz, Vve.; flowers white tinted pink; [Kaiserin Auguste Viktoria × Luciole]

Anna de Diesbach HP, dp, 1858, Lacharme, F.; bud long, pointed; flowers deep pink, center darker, 5-6 in., 40 petals, cupped, intense fragrance; vigorous, tall growth; [La Reine × unknown]

Anna de Melun HP, dp, 1849, Vibert; flowers medium, full

Anna de Noailles HT, dr, 1941, Gaujard; flowers crimson-red, medium, semi-dbl., high-centered; very vigorous, bushy growth; [Étoile de Hollande × seedling]

Anna Fendi HT, ab, Barni; flowers intense apricot in the heart, fading to cream at the petal edges, large, dbl., moderate fragrance; growth to 90-100 cm.; int. by Rose Barni, 2004

Anna Ford Min, ob, 1980, Harkness; flowers deep salmon-orange, yellow eye, patio, small, 18 petals, borne in large clusters; foliage small, glossy; prickles small; low, bushy growth; [Southampton × Darling Flame]; Gold Medal, RNRS, 1981, President's International Trophy, RNRS, 1981, Gold Medal, Glasgow, 1989, Gold Medal, Genoa, 1987

Anna Fugier HT, w, 1903, Bonnaire; flowers white, center salmon pink, very large, very full

Anna Hartmannová HT, w, 1933, Brada, Dr.; flowers cream-white, very dbl.; [sport of Frau Luise Kiese]; int. by Böhm

Anna Jane F, or, 2006, Horner; flowers dbl., borne in small clusters; foliage medium size, medium green, glossy; prickles small, hooked, brown, numerous; growth upright, medium (3½ ft.); garden decorative; [(Baby Love × Golden Future) × Cocoa × Hot Chocolate]; int. by Warley Roses, 2007

Anna Jung T, mp, 1903, Nabonnand; flowers bright pink with salmon tints, center coppery, very large, semi-dbl., moderate fresh fragrance; foliage very large, dark green

Anna Katherine HT, w, 1994, Ortega, Carlos; flowers white blend, medium, dbl., borne mostly singly; foliage large, medium green, matte; some prickles; tall, upright growth; [Osiana × seedling]; int. by Aebi Nursery, 1994

Anna Leese – See **Chihuly**, F

Anna Livia F, op, 1985, Kordes, W.; flowers orange pink, large, 20 petals; foliage medium size, medium green, semi-glossy; bushy growth; [(seedling × Tornado) × seedling]; Golden Rose, The Hague, 1989, Golden Prize, Glasgow, 1991, Gold Medal, Orleans, 1987

Anna Louisa F, lp, 1967, deRuiter; flowers soft pink, 2½ in., dbl., borne in large clusters; vigorous, low, bushy growth; [Highlight × Valeta]

Anna Maria HT, dp, 1948, Ohlhus; bud ovoid; flowers rosy pink, 5 in., 40-70 petals, high-centered; foliage leathery, dark; vigorous, upright growth; [Soeur Thérèse × (Duquesa de Peñaranda × Mrs Pierre S. duPont)]; int. by C-P

Anna Maria de Montravel – See **Anne-Marie de Montravel**, Pol

Anna Marie – See **Anne Marie**, HSet

Anna Marie HP, 1928, Alfons

Anna Marie – See **Anna Maria**, HT

Anna Marie Min, ly, 2004, Rickard, Vernon; flowers light yellow, blushed medium pink in cool weather, 1¾ in., dbl., borne mostly solitary, no fragrance; foliage medium size, dark green, semi-glossy; prickles straight, red, numerous; growth spreading, tall (36 in.); exhibition, garden decoration; [Fairhope × Sweet Caroline]; int. by Almost Heaven Roses, 2004

Anna-Marie Côte – See **Anne-Marie Côte**, N

Anna Milam F, mp, 2000, Moe, Mitchie; flowers medium, petals ruffled, 3-4 in., full, high-centered, borne in large clusters; foliage medium size, medium green, semi-glossy; prickles moderate; growth vigorous, upright, tall (3-4 ft.); [Pristine × City of London]; int. by Mitchie's Roses and More

Anna Müller-Idserda F, mp, 1966, Buisman, G. A. H.; bud ovoid; flowers pink, medium, dbl.; foliage dark; [Duet × Juliette E. van Beuningen]

Anna Neagle HT, rb, 1937, McGredy; flowers bright currant-red, base sunflower-yellow, dbl.; foliage dark; free, branching growth

Anna Olivier T, pb, 1872, Ducher; flowers yellowish-flesh, shaded salmon, reverse rose, well-formed, large, dbl.; vigorous growth

Anna Olivier, Climbing Cl T, yb; flowers golden pink, large, full
Anna Pavlova HT, lp, Beales, Peter; flowers delicate pink, darker at base, large, dbl., globular, intense sweet fragrance; int. in 1981
Anna Poulsen – See **Anne-Mette Poulsen**, F
Anna Rübsamen HWich, mp, 1904, Weigand, C.; flowers clear pink, aging lighter, 4 cm., dbl., borne in compact clusters; vigorous growth
Anna Saheb HT, pb, Chiplunkar; int. in 1993
Anna Scharsach HP, mp, 1890, Geschwind, R.; flowers large, dbl.; [Baronne Adolphe de Rothschild × Mme Lauriol de Barney]
Anna Ségales – See **Anaïs Ségalas**, HGal
Anna Soupert HT, yb, 1934, Soupert, G.; flowers yellow, center orange, very large, cactus-dahlia form, dbl.; foliage bronze, dark; dwarf growth; [Sunburst × Prince de Bulgarie]; int. by C. Soupert
Anna Stave HT, w, 1973, Curtis, E.C.; bud ovoid; flowers white, tipped pink, medium, dbl., high-centered; foliage dark, soft; moderate, upright growth; [Pink Parfait × Kordes' Perfecta]; int. by Kimbrew, 1973
Anna-Toki Min, pb, 2000, Hamilton, Noel; flowers salmon pink, reverse silver white, medium, very full, borne in large clusters, slight fragrance; foliage medium size, dark green, glossy, disease-resistant; few prickles; growth spreading, low (24 in.); containers, borders; [seedling × seedling]; int. by Coming Up Roses, 2000
Anna Vena Pol, dr, Zyla; flowers medium, dbl.; int. in 1972
Anna Von Diesbach – See **Anna de Diesbach**, HP
Anna Watkins HT, ab, 1963; flowers deep cream shaded yellow, reverse apricot, well-shaped, 5 in., 30 petals; foliage dark, glossy; vigorous, upright growth; [Ena Harkness × Grand'mère Jenny]; int. by Watkins Roses, 1963
Anna Wheatcroft F, or, 1960, Tantau, Math.; flowers light vermilion, gold stamens, 4 in., single, borne in clusters, slight fragrance; foliage dark, glossy; vigorous growth; [(Cinnabar × unknown) × seedling]; int. by Wheatcroft Bros., 1960
Anna Yung T, dp, Nabonnand; int. in 1904
Anna Zinkeisen S, ly, 1983, Harkness; bud plump; flowers 30 petals, borne in clusters of 3-7, moderate musk fragrance; foliage small, light green, semi-glossy; prickles small; medium, spreading, dense growth; [seedling × Frank Naylor]; int. in 1983
Annabella HT, dy, 1940, Grillo; flowers light buff-gold, 5 in., 55 petals, moderate fragrance; RULED EXTINCT 5/83 ARM; [sport of Joanna Hill]
Annabella HT, my, 1983, Rose Barni-Pistoia; bud ovoid; flowers deeply cupped, medium, 35 petals, cupped, borne singly, no fragrance; foliage medium size, dark, matte; prickles straight, light yellow; upright growth; [Ambassador × seedling]
Annabelle – See **Anabell**, F
Annabelle Kolle F, dp, Hetzel; int. in 1993
Annan's Orchard M, dp
Annapolis S, dp, Poulsen; flowers deep pink to light red, small, dbl., cupped, borne in clusters, very slight fragrance; recurrent; foliage dark green, glossy; bushy, low (40-60 cm.) growth; int. as Soft Cover, Poulsen Roser, 2005; Gold Medal, Rome, 2006, Gold Medal, Le Roeulx, 2006
Annapurna – See **Faith Whittlesey**, HG
Annapurna HT, w, Dorieux; int. in 2001
Annaroy HT, pb, 1951, Shepherd; bud ovoid; flowers pink with slight salmon undertone, imbricated, 110 petals; foliage glossy; [Pink Princess × Los Angeles]; int. by Bosley Nursery
Ännchen Müller Pol, dp, 1907, Schmidt, J.C.; flowers warm rose, fading, large, dbl., cupped, borne in clusters; foliage glossy; vigorous, bushy growth; [Crimson Rambler × Georges Pernet]
Annchen Muller – See **Ännchen Müller**, Pol
Annchen von Tharau – See **Ännchen von Tharau**, HMult
Ännchen von Tharau HMult, w, 1886, Geschwind, R.; flowers creamy mother-of-pearl, darker at center, 7 cm., very dbl., borne in small clusters, moderate sweet fragrance; foliage glaucous; prickles moderate; [an Alba × an arvensis hybrid]
Anne HT, mr, 1925, Pemberton; flowers cherry-red, large, dbl., globular, moderate damask fragrance; foliage leathery; vigorous, bushy, compact growth
Anne Aymone – See **Anne-Aymone Giscard d'Estaing**, F single
Anne-Aymone Giscard d'Estaing F, w, Dorieux; flowers single; int. in 1993
Anne Béluze – See **Mme Anne Béluze**, B
Anne Boleyn S, lp, 2000, Austin, David; flowers soft warm pink, 3 in., 110 petals, rosette; foliage shiny, disease-resistant; almost thornless; arching growth; int. by David Austin Roses, Ltd., 1999
Anne Cocker F, op, 1971, Cocker, A.; flowers vermilion, 2½ in., 36 petals; foliage glossy, light to medium green; vigorous, upright growth; [Highlight × Colour Wonder]; int. by J. Cocker & Sons, 1970
Anne Colle HT, pb, Ludwig; int. by Ludwig's Roses, 2003
Anne Dakin LCl, pb, Holmes; flowers coral pink, medium, dbl., borne in small clsuters, slight fragrance; foliage glossy; int. in 1974
Anne de Boleyn S, lp, 1829, Girardon; bud pointed, long; flowers large, with delicate green pip, 3 in., semi-dbl., borne mostly solitary; foliage finely dentate, widely set; prickles numerous, straight, unequal; [Grosse Mohnkopfs Rose × unknown]
Anne de Bretagne Ch, mp, before 1836, Laffay; flowers bright pink, medium, dbl.
Anne de Bretagne HP, lp, 1849, Vibert; flowers flesh pink, large, full
Anne de Bretagne S, dp, 1979, Meilland, Mrs. Marie-Louise; bud conical; flowers 20 petals, shallow cupped; foliage semi-glossy; vigorous, upright growth; [((Malcair × Danse des Sylphes) × (Zambra × Zambra)) × Centenair]; int. in 1976
Anne Diamond HT, ab, 1989, Sealand Nurseries, Ltd.; bud pointed; flowers apricot, reverse pink, aging apricot, medium, 38 petals, urn-shaped, borne in sprays of 3 or 4; foliage medium size, dark green, semi-glossy; prickles slightly hooked, brown; upright, bushy growth; [Mildred Reynolds × Arthur Bell]; int. in 1988
Anne d'Ornano HT, m, 1967, Gaujard; bud long, pointed; flowers bright purple-crimson, very large, dbl.; foliage dark, leathery; vigorous, bushy growth; [John S. Armstrong × Rose Gaujard]
Anne Elizabeth HT, lp, Thomas, Dr. A.S.; int. in 1979
Anne Farnworth HT, rb, 1964, Court; flowers like parent, in sunset shades; [sport of Tzigane]
Anne Gregg HT, ab, 1994; flowers moderately large, 3-3½ in., dbl.; foliage large, dark green, matte; some prickles; medium (80 cm.), upright growth; [sport of Diorama]; int. by Rearsby Roses, Ltd., 1994
Anne Hall HRg, mp, Johnson; int. in 2002
Anne Harkness F, ab, 1978, Harkness; bud globular; flowers deep apricot, dbl., cupped, borne in trusses, slight fragrance; foliage medium green, semi-glossy; vigorous, upright, tall growth; [Bobby Dazzler × ((((Manx Queen × Prima Ballerina) × (Chanelle xPiccadilly)) × ((Manx Queen × Prima Ballerina) × (Chanelle xPiccadilly))) × (Chanelle × Piccadilly))]; int. in 1980
Anne Hathaway – See **Mrs Iris Clow**, F
Anne Hering Min, r, 1999, Moe, Mitchie; flowers pale russet, reverse lighter, yellow base, 1-2 in., dbl., high-centered; foliage medium size, medium green, semi-glossy; few prickles; upright, medium (15 in.) growth; [Fairhope × Wistful]; int. by Mitchie's Roses & More, 1999
Anne Jackson LCl, dp, 1973, Jackson, J.R.; flowers cerise, medium, 30-35 petals, cupped; foliage glossy, bronze; vigorous growth; [sport of Spectacular]
Anne Kercher HT, dp, 1980, Simpson, J.W.; bud long, pointed; flowers deep pink, 30 petals, high-centered, borne singly or 3 per cluster; foliage large, dense, medium green; prickles straight; vigorous, very bushy, compact growth; [First Prize × seedling]
Anne Laferrère HP, dr, 1916, Nabonnand, C.; flowers deep velvety blood-red; vigorous growth
Anne Laure S, dr, 1996, Guillot-Massad; flowers bright, blood red with golden stamens, single; growth to 4 ft.; int. by Roseraies Guillot, 1996
Anne Letts HT, pb, 1954, Letts; flowers rose-pink, reverse silvery, pointed, 4½ in., 28 petals, moderate fragrance; foliage glossy; bushy growth; [Peace × Charles Gregory]
Anne Leygues T, lp, 1905, Nabonnand, P.&C.; flowers flesh-pink; [Gén. Schablikine × Comtesse Bardi]
Anne Lorentz HT, lp, Spek; int. by Ludwig's Roses, 2005
Anne Marie HSet, dp, 1843, Feast; flowers pale rose, large, dbl., borne in clusters
Anne Marie HT, dp, 1970, Meilland; bud long, pointed; flowers deep pink, large, dbl., high-centered, intense fragrance; foliage dark, leathery; vigorous, branching growth; [Sutter's Gold × (Demain × Peace)]; int. as Anne Marie Trechslin, URS, 1969
Anne-Marie Côte N, w, 1875, Guillot; flowers pure white, sometimes tinted pink, medium, full, globular, borne in small clusters; foliage dark green; prickles long, straight
Anne-Marie de Montravel Pol, w, 1879, Rambaux; flowers pure white, of irregular form when fully open, sometimes showing stamens, 1½ in., dbl., moderate lily-of-the-valley fragrance; foliage dark green above, grayish beneath, glossy, 3-5 leaflets; prickles very few; dwarf, compact growth; [Dbl. flowered Multiflora × Mme de Tartas]
Anne Marie Laing F, lp, 1998, Shipway, John; flowers light pink, darker reverse, 4 in., very dbl., camellia-like, borne in large clusters; foliage medium size, dark green, dull; few prickles; upright, tall (110 cm.) growth; [(Iceberg × Anytime) × Sexy Rexy]; int. by F. Haynes Partners, 1998
Anne-Marie Milliat HT, w, 1939, Gaujard; bud very long; flowers large, very dbl.; very vigorous growth
Anne Marie Soupert HT, op, 1904, Soupert & Notting; flowers glossy carmine-salmon, very large, full; [Mme Edmé Metz × Mme Jules Grolez]
Anne Marie Trechslin – See **Anne Marie**, HT
Anne Marie Treschlin, Climbing Cl HT, pb
Anne McDonald F, pb, 1992, Spriggs, Ian Raymond; flowers rose pink and creamy yellow, classical, 3¼ in., 30 petals, high-centered, borne in clusters of 10-30; foliage medium green, glossy; medium to tall (1-3 m.), upright growth; [Granada × Kordes Perfecta]; int. by Treloar Roses Pty. Ltd., 1991
Anne-Mette Poulsen F, mr, 1935, Poulsen, S.; bud long, pointed; flowers bright crimson-red, darkening, large, dbl., borne in clusters; vigorous growth; [Ingar Olsson × seedling]; int. by McGredy, 1935
Anne Morrow Lindbergh HT, pb, 1993, Warriner, William A.; flowers pink, white, yellow blend, 3-3½ in.,

full, borne mostly singly, moderate fragrance; foliage medium to large, medium green, semi-glossy; some prickles; tall (150-160 cm.), upright growth; [seedling × seedling]; int. by Bear Creek Gardens, 1994

Anne no Omoide – See **Souv d'Anne Frank**, F

Anne of Geierstein HEg, dr, 1894, Penzance; flowers deep crimson, medium, single, moderate fragrance; summer bloom; foliage fragrant; vigorous growth; hips bright scarlet; [*R. rubiginosa* × HP or B]; int. by Keynes, Williams & Co.

Anne Poulsen – See **Anne-Mette Poulsen**, F

Anne Scranton F, lp, 1971, Dobbs, Annette E.; bud ovoid; flowers light pink, center flesh-white, medium, dbl.; foliage leathery; vigorous, upright growth; [Queen Elizabeth × Katherine T. Marshall]

Anne Vanderbilt HT, or, 1941, Brownell; bud pointed; flowers reddish-orange, open, 4-5 in., 28 petals, intense fragrance; foliage leathery, glossy; very vigorous, bushy growth; [seedling × Stargold]

Anne Wheatcroft – See **Anna Wheatcroft**, F

Anneka HT, yb, 1990, Harkness, R., & Co., Ltd.; bud ovoid; flowers high-centered to cupped to reflexed, medium, 45 petals, high-centered, borne usually singly or in sprays of 3-5, moderate fruity fragrance; foliage medium size, medium green, glossy; prickles slightly curved, medium, dark reddish; upright, medium growth; hips ovoid, medium to large, medium green; [Goldbonnet × Silver Jubilee]; int. by R. Harkness & Co., Ltd.

Anneke Doorenbos F, pb, 1956, Doorenbos; flowers silver-pink, reverse darker; [sport of Buisman's Triumph]; int. by Boerma

Anneke Koster Pol, dr, 1927, Koster, D.A.; flowers deep red; [sport of Greta Kluis]

Anneli MinFl, ob, 2004, McCann, Sean; flowers bright orange, reverse yellow, 1½ in., semi-dbl., borne in small clusters, moderate fragrance; foliage medium size, medium green, semi-glossy; prickles small, straight, green, moderate; growth compact, garden variety; [Kiss 'n' Tell × Bloomsday]; int. by Ashdowne, 2006

Annelies HMsk, lp, Lens; flowers small, light pink, rosette, borne in pyramidal clusters, slight fragrance; growth to 125-150 cm.; int. by Lens Roses, 2001

Anneliese HT, dr, Miessler, Herbert; int. in 1971

Anneliese HT, lp, Wänninger, Franz; flowers light pink to white, large, semi-dbl.; int. in 1990

Anneliesse Rothenberger – See **Oregold**, HT

Annelise Border S, mr, Poulsen; flowers medium red, small, no fragrance; foliage dark; growth tall (100-150 cm.), bushy; int. by Poulsen Roser, 1998

Annemarie Jacobs HT, dy, 1910, Jacobs; flowers dark golden yellow, shaded red, medium to large, full, moderate fragrance

Annemarie van Onsem F, mr, 1971, Institute of Ornamental Plant Growing; bud ovoid; flowers vivid red, open, medium, semi-dbl.; foliage large, glossy, dark; very vigorous, upright, bushy growth; [Circus × Korona]

Annerose F, or, Croix; flowers medium size, slow opening, long lasting, dbl., slight fragrance; young foliage reddish, turning dark green, glossy; growth to 50-70 cm.; int. in 1976

Anne's Delight Min, dp, 1982, Williams, Ernest D.; bud pointed; flowers 40 petals, high-centered, borne usually singly, slight fragrance; foliage small, dark, glossy; prickles long, thin; upright, bushy growth; [Little Darling × Over the Rainbow]; int. by Mini-Roses, 1981

Annette HT, op, 1952, Swim, H.C.; bud long, pointed; flowers salmon-pink, 4-4½ in., 20-25 petals, high-centered; foliage glossy, leathery, dark; vigorous, compact growth; [Charlotte Armstrong × Contrast]; int. by Earl May Seed Co.

Annette MinFl, mp, Olesen; flowers dbl., borne mostly solitary, slight fragrance; foliage dark green, glossy; growth bushy, low (40-60 cm.); PP12762; int. by Poulsen Roser, 1998

Annette Dobbs Min, op, 1991, Moore, Ralph S.; bud pointed; flowers coral-red, lighter reverse, ages slightly lighter, medium, 15 petals, flat, edges turned up, borne in sprays of 3-5, no fragrance; foliage medium size, medium green, semi-glossy; bushy, medium growth; [Anytime × Playgirl]; int. by Sequoia Nursery, 1990

Annette Elizabeth LCl, lp, Stewart, L.; [Clair Matin × Wedding Day]; int. in 1992

Annette Gatward HT, ab, 1954, Gatward; flowers peach, large, dbl.; foliage light green; upright growth; [Mrs Charles Lamplough × Barbara Richards]

Annette Gravereaux HT, my, 1929, Leenders, M.; bud large, ovoid; flowers lemon-yellow, shaded orange, very large, dbl.; foliage medium size, dark green; growth upright; [Mev. C. van Marwijk Kooy × Golden Emblem]

Annette Hit – See **Annette**, MinFl

Anni Jebens HT, dy, 1932, Kordes; bud large, long, pointed, golden yellow; flowers blood-red, reverse golden yellow, dbl., high-centered; foliage leathery, glossy, bronze; bushy, dwarf growth; [Charles P. Kilham × Mev. G.A. van Rossem]

Anni Welter M, mp, 1906, Welter; flowers large, full, moderate fragrance; [Crested Moss × La France]

Annick F, or, Fryer; flowers large, orange scarlet, dbl., borne singly and in trusses, moderate fragrance; foliage dense, lush; growth vigorous (90 cm.); int. by Fryer's Roses, 2002; Silver Medal, Glasgow, 2006

Annie S, ly, 1998, Bossom, W.E.; flowers cream yellow, 3 in., 8-14 petals, borne in large clusters; foliage large, dark green, semi-glossy; prickles moderate; spreading, medium growth; [Sexy Rexy × Forever Amber]

Annie HT, ob, 2006, Wilce, David Edward; flowers dbl., borne mostly solitary; foliage medium size, medium green, glossy; prickles moderate; growth upright, 90 cm.; [Silver Jubilee × Grandpa Dickson]; int. in 2006

Annie Beaufais F, or, deRuiter; int. in 1962

Annie Besant HT, w, 1910, Nabonnand; flowers flesh to cream with peach tints; growth upright

Annie Brandt HT, op, 1932, Mallerin, C.; bud long, pointed; flowers pink tinted coral, open, large, semi-dbl.; foliage leathery, glossy; very vigorous, bushy growth; [Mrs Pierre S. duPont × Colette Clément]; int. by C-P

Annie Burgess HP, lp, 1926, Burgess, S.W.; flowers pale pink, borne in clusters; early bloom; [Lyon Rose × Frau Karl Druschki]

Annie Cook T, rb, 1888, Cook, J.W.; flowers blush-tinted; probably extinct; [sport of Bon Silène]

Annie Crawford HP, mp, 1915, Hall; flowers bright pink, very large, 30-35 petals, high-centered; recurrent bloom; vigorous growth; Gold Medal, NRS, 1914

Annie de Metz HT, or, 1932, Mallerin, C.; bud large; flowers dbl., high-centered; [Golden Emblem × *R. foetida bicolor* seedling]; int. by C-P

Annie Drevet HT, rb, 1939, Caron, B.; bud long, yellow; flowers fiery red, reverse yellow, large, semi-dbl., cupped; foliage leathery, glossy, dark; vigorous growth; [Charles P. Kilham × (Kitchener of Khartoum × Mari Dot)]; int. by A. Meilland, 1939

Annie Dupeyrat HT, op, 1935, Mallerin, C.; bud ovoid; flowers very large, dbl.; foliage leathery; bushy growth; [Mrs T. Hillas × Elvira Aramayo]; int. by C-P

Annie East – See **Annie**, S

Annie Girardot HT, Kriloff, Michel; int. in 1979

Annie Laurie HT, pb, 1918, Stuppy Floral Co.; bud long, pointed; flowers flesh-pink, base yellow, large, dbl., cupped; foliage glossy; very vigorous growth; [sport of Ophelia]

Annie Laurie – See **Annie Laurie McDowell**, LCl

Annie Laurie HT, pb, 2003, Renfroe, Samuel; flowers full, borne mostly solitary; foliage medium size, medium green, semi-glossy; growth upright, tall (4-6 ft.); garden, exhibition; [sport of Virginia]

Annie Laurie McDowell LCl, mp, Rupert; int. by Ashdowne, 2001

Annie Laxton HP, mp, 1869, Laxton

Annie M. G. Schmidt S, lp; flowers borne in clusters; int. by Belle Epoque, 2001

Annie Nell S, mp, 2003, Ponton, Ray; flowers medium, full, borne in small clusters; foliage medium size, dark green, semi-glossy, disease-resistant; prickles medium, curved, moderate; growth upright, medium (4 ft.); specimen, hedge; [Lillian Austin × (Katy Road Pink × Reveil Dijonnaise)]

Annie R. Mitchell Min, ly, 1996, Moore, Ralph S.; flowers light yellow to white, 1½-2 in., full, borne in small clusters, moderate fragrance; foliage medium size, medium green, semi-glossy; few prickles; spreading, bushy, medium (15-18 in.) growth; [sport of Mary Hill]; int. by Sequoia Nursery, 1996

Annie Vibert N, w, before 1871, Vibert; flowers pink on opening, then white, medium, moderate fragrance; foliage glossy; stems long, arching; growth to (12 ft.)

Annie Wood – See **Mlle Annie Wood**, HP

Annie's Song F, lp, Spriggs, Ian Raymond; int. in 1990

Annirose – See **Annerose**, F

Anniversarie de Willemse HT, pb; flowers striped; int. by Willemse France, 2003

Anniversary HT, my, 1961, Byrum, Roy L.; bud ovoid; flowers yellow, 4-5 in., 55-60 petals, high-centered, moderate fragrance; foliage leathery, dark; strong stems; vigorous, upright growth; PP2084; RULED EXTINCT 5/81 ARM; [Mary Jo × Lamplighter]; int. by Hill, Joseph H., Co.

Anniversary HT, dr, 1981, Hoy, Lowel L.; bud long, pointed; flowers 23 petals, high-centered, borne 1-3 per cluster, moderate fragrance; foliage medium to large; prickles hooked down; upright growth; PP4986; [Love Affair × seedling]; int. by Joseph H. Hill, Co.

Anniversary F, lp, Matthews; flowers medium size, porcelain pink; int. in 1998; Gold Star of the South Pacific, Palmerston North, NZ, 1997

Ann's Rose Cl Min, op, 1996, Bell, Judy G.; flowers light orange pink, 1½ in., dbl., borne in small clusters; foliage medium size, light green, glossy; few prickles; tall (5 ft.), upright, pillar growth; int. by Michigan Mini Roses, 1996

Ann's Wedding HT, my, 1976, Rosemount Nursery; flowers very full, 4 in., 40 petals, moderate fragrance; foliage glossy, dark; free growth; [sport of Whisky Mac]

Annulet Pol, lp, 1935, Miers, A.

Anny Min, w, 1949, Dot, Pedro; long, leafy sepals; flowers pale pink fading white, micro-mini, ½ in., 30 petals; growth to 6 in; [Rouletii × Perla de Montserrat]

Anny Brandt HT, yb, 1951, Mallerin, C.; bud pointed; flowers creamy yellow, edges and reverse tinted lilac, petals waved, dbl.; vigorous growth; int. by EFR

Anny Muller – See **Ännchen Müller**, Pol

Anomalia B, mp, 1838, Bizard; flowers medium, full

Another Chance HT, w, 1994, Heyes, Alex; flowers medium, full, borne mostly singly, slight fragrance; foliage medium to large, medium green, matte; some prickles; medium-tall, bushy growth; [Mount Shasta × Saffron]; int. by Rainbow Roses, 1996

Anri HT, yb, 1997, Ohtsuki, Hironaka; flowers very dbl.; foliage large, dark green, glossy; few prickles; bushy, upright, medium (180cm.) growth; [Mme. Sachi × Yarna]

Ans Min, dr, 1990, Benardella, Frank A.; bud pointed; flowers shapely, burgundy wine-colored, borne on long stems, slight fragrance; foliage glossy; growth vigorous, tall

Anson Jones S, yb, 2005, Shoup, George Michael; flowers semi-dbl., borne mostly solitary, moderate fragrance; remontant; foliage large, dark green, semi-glossy; prickles moderate; growth upright, tall (5-6 ft.); hedge; [Carefree Beauty × Carefree Beauty × Mrs Oakely Fisher]; int. by Antique Rose Emporium, 2000

Antares S, pb, Barni, V.; int. in 1996

Anthea HT, yb, 1949, Bees; flowers pale yellow flushed rose, compact, 4-5 in., 20-25 petals; foliage dark; vigorous growth; [McGredy's Yellow × Phyllis Gold]

Anthea Fortescue F, pb, 1992, Pearce, C.A.; flowers pink, yellow center, buff reverse, 2½ in., dbl., urn-shaped, borne in sprays of 3-9, slight fragrance; foliage small, medium green, glossy, immune to powdery milde; low, spreading growth; [(F seedling × (P135)) × F seedling]; int. by The Limes New Roses, 1991

Anthea Turner HT, yb, 1997, Thomas, D.; flowers very dbl., 41 petals; foliage medium size, dark green, semi-glossy; few prickles; compact, medium growth; [Alec's Red × Harry Wheatcroft]; int. by C & K Jones

Anthéor HT, ab, 1948, Meilland, F.; bud long, furled; flowers reddish-apricot, dbl.; [(Joanna Hill × Duquesa de Peñaranda) × (Charles P. Kilham × Mme Joseph Perraud)]

Anthéros HP, mp, 1839, Lepage; flowers large, flat

Anthony S, lp, 2006, Beales, Amanda; flowers small, full, borne in large clusters; foliage medium size, dark green, glossy; prickles average, straight, numerous; growth bushy, short (1 m.); [Armada × Centenaire de Lourdes]; int. by Peter Beales Roses, 2002

Anthony Meilland F, my, 1994, Meilland, Alain A.; bud egg-shaped; flowers 3-3½ in., 27-30 petals, cupped, borne in small clusters, no fragrance; good repeat; foliage large, medium green, semi-glossy; prickles large; medium (3 ft.), bushy growth; PP8449; [(Sunblest × Mitzi 81) × Spek's Yellow]; int. by SNC Meilland & Cie, 1990

Anticipation HT, rb, 1990, Meilland; flowers red with silver/white reverse, medium, 35 petals, high-centered, borne singly, slight fragrance; foliage medium size, medium green, semi-glossy; bushy growth; [seedling × seedling]; int. by Co-Operative Rose Growers, 1991

Antico Amore HT, mp, 1988, Barni, V.; flowers pink with apricot tinge, color holds, dbl., cupped, intense fragrance; growth to 90-100 cm.

Antigone HT, yb, 1969, Gaujard; bud pointed; flowers yellow shaded red, large, dbl.; foliage light green, soft; vigorous, upright growth; [Rose Gaujard × Guitare]; Gold Medal, Bagatelle, 1967

Antigua HT, ab, 1974, Warriner, William A.; bud ovoid; flowers large, dbl., high-centered, slight fragrance; foliage leathery; vigorous, upright, bushy growth; PP3431; [South Seas × Golden Masterpiece]; int. by J&P; Gold Medal, Geneva, 1972

Antigua – See **Antigua Kordana**, Min

Antigua Kordana Min, pb, Kordes; bud ovoid; flowers light pink with deeper pink tones in center, 6 cm., 40-45 petals, cupped to flat, borne mostly singly, no fragrance; recurrent; foliage dark green, glossy; prickles numerous, 4-6 mm., triangular, elongated; upright (10 in.), bushy growth; containers; PP14902; [seedling × seedling]; int. by W. Kordes Söhne, 2002

Antike F, yb, W. Kordes Söhne; flowers reddish-yellow, medium, dbl.; int. in 1966

Antike 89 LCl, w, 2006; flowers cream with carmine edging, 10 cm., full, borne in large clusters; foliage dark green, very glossy, leathery; growth vigorous, heavy canes, slow climber to 2½ m.; int. by W. Kordes' Söhne, 1988

Antike Kordana Min, lp, Kordes; flowers pale pink with deeper center, dbl.; container rose; int. by W. Kordes Söhne

Antinea HT, op, 1934, Gaujard; flowers salmon-orange, base yellow, very large, dbl.; foliage glossy; very vigorous, bushy growth; [Julien Potin × seedling]; int. by H&S

Antiope HGal, pb, before 1815, Descemet; flowers pink with purple, medium, full

Antique F, rb, 1967, Kordes; flowers crimson and gold, borne in clusters; bushy growth; [Honeymoon × Circus]; int. by A. Dickson

Antique 89 – See **Antike 89**, LCl

Antique Abundance – See **English Sonnet**, F

Antique Artistry S, ab, Clements, John; flowers apricot-peach, 4 in., 95 petals, old-fashioned; foliage serrated, matte green; growth vigorous, compact (4 × 3 ft.); int. by Heirloom, 2000

Antique Brass HT, ab, Zary, K.; PP11617; int. by J&P, 1999

Antique Gold Min, yb, 1995, Laver, Keith G.; flowers deep chrome yellow tipped with red, small, full, borne mostly singly; foliage medium size, light green, semi-glossy; some prickles; spreading, medium growth; [seedling × seedling]; int. by Springwood Roses, 1996

Antique Lace F, mp, 1991, Strahle, B. Glen; bud ovoid; flowers medium pink, light pink center, medium, 25-35 petals, urn-shaped; foliage medium size, dark green, semi-glossy; bushy, medium growth; [seedling × Little Cameo]; int. by Coyier's Roses, 1990

Antique Nostalgia – See **Nostalgie**, HT

Antique Rose Min, mp, 1981, Moore, Ralph S.; bud pointed; flowers rose pink, mini-flora, medium, 38 petals, high-centered, borne usually singly, slight fragrance; foliage dark, semi-glossy; prickles straight, brown; vigorous, upright growth; [Baccará × Little Chief]

Antique Silk F, w, 1985, Kordes; flowers near white, flora-tea, large, 20 petals; foliage medium size, medium green, semi-glossy; upright, bushy growth; PP5411; [(Anabell × unknown) × seedling]; int. by W. Kordes Söhne, 1982

Antique Tapestry Min, rb, 1991, Clements, John K.; flowers burgundy and gold, large, dbl., high-centered, borne mostly singly, slight fragrance; foliage medium size, dark green, semi-glossy; few prickles; medium (40 cm.), upright growth; [Redgold × seedling]; int. by Heirloom Old Garden Roses, 1990

Antique Velvet Min, dr, 1993, Jobson, Daniel J.; flowers velvety dark red, large, dbl., borne in large clusters; foliage large, medium green, semi-glossy; few prickles; patio, tall, upright, bushy growth; [Valerie Joanne × (Party Girl × Pillow Talk)]; int. by Jobson, 1993

Antoine Alléon HP, 1872, Damaizin; flowers bright cherry red, center crimson, large, full

Antoine Devert T, w, 1880, Gonod; flowers white, tinted flesh and sulfur yellow, reverse salmon pink, large, full, cupped, moderate fragrance

Antoine Ducher HP, rb, 1866, Ducher; flowers violet-red, large; [Mme Domage × unknown]

Antoine Mermet T, dp

Antoine Mouton HP, mp, 1874, Levet; flowers deep rose, tinged with lilac, reverse silvery, large, full; foliage very serrated; few prickles; [La Reine × unknown]

Antoine Noailly HT, mr, 1958, Croix, P.; bud long; flowers clear red, scalloped petals; [seedling × Mme G. Forest-Colcombet]

Antoine Quihou HP, m, 1880, Verdier, E.; flowers velvety purple, large, full, moderate fragrance

Antoine Rivoire HT, lp, 1895, Pernet-Ducher; bud ovoid; flowers light pink shaded darker, imbricated, dbl.; foliage dark; vigorous growth; [Dr. Grill × Lady Mary Fitzwilliam]

Antoine Schurz HP, lp, 1890, Geschwind, R.; flowers flesh-white, very large, very dbl., cupped, quartered, moderate centifolia fragrance

Antoine Verdier HP, pb, 1871, Jamain, H.; flowers pink, shaded muddy lilac, dbl.

Antoine Weber T, mp, 1899, Weber; flowers soft, rosy flesh-pink, center lighter, large, dbl.

Antoinette A, w, before 1826, Descemet; flowers pure white, full, globular, moderate fragrance

Antoinette HT, ab, 1968, Patterson; bud long, pointed; flowers open, medium size, dbl.; foliage large, glossy, leathery; vigorous, upright growth; [Queen Elizabeth × Peace]; int. by Patterson Roses

Antoinette HT, ab, Kordes; int. in 1993

Antoinette Bouvagne T, w, 1842, Béluze; flowers flesh white, large, full

Antoinette Cuillerat Ch, w, 1897, Buatois; flowers bright white with coppery sulphur yellow base, lightly edged with carmine/violet; probably extinct

Antoinette Durieu T, dy, 1890, Godard; [Mme Caro × unknown]

Antoinette Massard N, mr, 1913, Nabonnand; flowers bright carmine-red, shaded vermilion, dbl.

Antonella HT, mp, 1964, Mondial Roses; bud globular; flowers camellia-pink, 5 in., dbl., high-centered; strong stems; vigorous growth

Antonella Fineschi F, Fineschi, G.; int. in 1985

Antonelliana HT, ob, 1952, Giacomasso; flowers orange and deep yellow tipped, well-formed, dbl.; foliage glossy; vigorous growth; [Gaiezza × Margaret McGredy]

Antonia F, w, 1980, Bazeley, B.L.; bud long, pointed; flowers blushed white, palest pink flush, well-formed, dbl., borne in large clusters, slight fragrance; vigorous, bushy, low growth; [sport of Tantau's Tip Top]; int. by Highfield Nursery, 1979

Antonia d'Ormois – See **Antonine d'Ormois**, HGal

Antonia Pahissa HT, ob, 1935, Pahissa; bud long, pointed; flowers rich orange, large, dbl., cupped; foliage glossy, dark; long stems; very vigorous, bushy growth

Antonia Ridge HT, mr, 1976, Paolino; flowers cardinal-red, 4-4½ in., 30 petals, high-centered; vigorous growth; [(Chrysler Imperial × Karl Herbst) × seedling]; int. by URS

Antonietta Ingegnoli Pol, pb, 1923, Ingegnoli; flowers golden pink, opening in two distinct tones on same plant, dbl.; [*R. wichurana* × *R. chinensis*]

Antonín Dvorák – See **A. Dvorak**, HT

Antonine d'Ormois HGal, lp, 1835, Vibert; flowers blush, fading at edge, small eye at center, petals recurved at the edge, small to medium, dbl., cupped, quartered, borne in clusters of 2-3; foliage dark green, small, pointed; prickles moderate

Antonine Verdier HT, lp, 1872, Jamain; flowers light carmine, large, full

Antonio Rolleri de Peluffo HT, dr, 1926, Soupert & Notting; bud large, ovoid; flowers brilliant red, center darker, very large, dbl., borne mostly solitary, moderate fragrance; [Gen. MacArthur × Mme Edouard Herriot]

Antoon van Dijk S, dp, DVP Melle; [Maizières × seedling]; int. in 2000

Anurag HT, pb, 1981, Division of Vegetable Crops and Floriculture; bud long, pointed; flowers Tyrian rose, 54 petals, high-centered, borne singly, intense fragrance; free-flowering; foliage large, smooth, light green; prickles hooked, brown; upright, bushy growth; [Sweet Afton × Gulzar]; int. in 1980

Anurupa HT, mp, Friends Rosery; int. in 1997

Anuschka F, or, 1978, Tantau, Math.; bud ovoid; flowers

large, 23 petals; foliage large; bushy, upright growth

Anuschka HT, dp, Tantau; int. in 2004

Anusheh F, rb, 1992, Payne, A.J.; flowers red with yellow reverse, medium, full, borne in large clusters, slight fragrance; foliage medium size, dark green, glossy; numerous prickles; medium, upright growth; [Len Turner × seedling]

Anusuya HT, m, Chakraborty, Dr. K.; flowers purple pink, large, dbl., high-centered, moderate sweet fragrance; int. in 1995

Anvil Sparks – See **Ambossfunken**, HT

Anvil Sparks, Climbing Cl HT, ob

Anydale HT, yb, 2005, Poole, Lionel; flowers yellow with pink edge, 4½ in., dbl., high, spiral center, borne mostly solitary, slight fragrance; foliage medium size, medium green, glossy; prickles medium, slightly hooked, brown, moderate; growth bushy, medium (1 m.); garden decoration; [Joanna Lumley × Healing Hands]; int. by Lionel Poole, 2006

Anytime Min, op, 1974, McGredy, Sam IV; flowers salmon-orange, purplish eye, ½-1 in., 12 petals, moderate fragrance; foliage dark; [New Penny × Elizabeth of Glamis]; also registered as Tick Tock, 1974; int. by McGredy Ltd., 1973

Anzac HT, op, 1943, Howard, F.H.; flowers azalea-pink with coppery scarlet sheen, 5 in., 42-50 petals, camellia-like, moderate fruity fragrance; foliage leathery; long stems; very vigorous, upright, compact growth; [Miss Rowena Thom × seedling]; int. by H&S

Aoraki Cl Min, w, 2003, Eagle, B & D; flowers white/pale pink, reverse white, sometimes darker pink on edges, 4 cm., semi-dbl., borne in small clusters, no fragrance; foliage medium size, medium green, matte; prickles slightly hooked; growth spreading, tall (300 cm.); garden, fences, pillars; [Jeanne Lajoie × seedling]; int. by Southern Cross Nurseries, 1994

Aorangi F, w, 1980, Murray, Nola; bud pointed; flowers cream, 3 in., 41 petals, high-centered, slight fragrance; foliage large; upright growth; [Arthur Bell × Red Devil]

Aorangi HT, w, Sandbrook; flowers white, of elegant form; growth medium to tall; int. in 1995

Aotearoa-New Zealand – See **New Zealand**, HT

Aozora HT, m, 1973, Suzuki, Seizo; flowers deep lilac-blue, large, dbl., high-centered; foliage large, leathery; vigorous, upright growth; [(Sterling Silver × unknown) × seedling]; int. by Keisei Rose Nursery, 1973

Apache S, yb, 1961, Von Abrams; bud ovoid, flushed red; flowers medium to buff-yellow, 5-6 in., 60 petals; foliage leathery; vigorous (5-6 ft.), spreading, open growth; [Fred Howard × Buccaneer]; int. by Peterson & Dering, 1961

Apache HT, op, Kordes; flowers bright pink-orange, medium, dbl., high-centered, borne mostly singly; recurrent; stems average 24 in.; florist rose; int. by W. Kordes Söhne, 2005

Apache Belle HT, rb, 1968, Sitton; bud ovoid; flowers orange-red, 5 in., very dbl., slight fragrance; foliage glossy; vigorous, upright, compact growth; PP2847; [sport of The Alamo]; int. by Co-Operative Rose Growers

Apache Princess Min, or, 1990, Twomey, Jerry; bud ovoid; flowers bright orange-red, medium, 38 petals, cupped, borne singly, slight fruity fragrance; foliage medium size, medium green, semi-glossy; prickles declining, purple; upright, medium growth; PP8064; [Cricket × Fireburst]; int. by DeVor Nurseries, Inc., 1990

Apache Tears F, rb, 1972, Pikiewicz; flowers cream to creamy pink, petals edged red, medium, dbl., high-centered, slight fragrance; foliage large, light; vigorous, bushy growth; [Karl Herbst × China Doll]; int. by Edmunds Roses, 1971

Apache Wells F, yb, 1971, Williams, J. Benjamin; bud ovoid; flowers canary-yellow, washed pink, medium-small, dbl., high-centered; foliage leathery; vigorous, bushy growth; [Circus × The Optimist]

Apachi – See **Tai-Gong**, F

Apart HRg, m, Uhl, J.; flowers mauve blend, dbl.; prolific fruit; int. in 1981

Apart Pavement – See **Apart**, HRg

Aparte – See **Spartan**, F

Apeles Mestres Cl HP, dy, 1931, Dot, Pedro; flowers sunflower-yellow, large, dbl., globular, moderate fragrance; occasional repeat; foliage dark, glossy; vigorous, climbing growth; [Frau Karl Druschki × Souv. de Claudius Pernet]; int. by C-P

Apéritif F, pb, 1973, Boerner; bud ovoid; flowers ivory, petals edged rose-pink, medium, dbl., high-centered, slight fragrance; foliage leathery; vigorous, upright, bushy growth; [seedling × Starbright]; int. by J&P, 1972

Apéritif HT, my, 1998, McGredy, Sam IV; flowers medium yellow, 4 in., dbl., borne mostly singly, slight fragrance; foliage large, light green, matte; prickles moderate; growth bushy, medium (110 cm.); [Solitaire × Sunbright]; int. by McGredy International

Apfelblüte Pol, w, 1907, Wirtz & Eicke; flowers light pink-white, small, dbl.; [Mme Norbert Levavasseur × unknown]

Apfelblüte S, w, Noack, Werner; flowers light pink-white, medium, semi-dbl.; int. in 1991

Aphrodite HT, or, 1928, Easlea; bud long, pointed; flowers coral-red, shaded gold, large, semi-dbl.; foliage dark, glossy; vigorous, bushy growth; [Hortulanus Budde × Toison d'Or]

Aphrodite, Climbing Cl HT, or, 1933, Hillock

Aphrodite HT, ab, Tantau; int. by Rosen Tantau, 2003

Apogée HT, ob, 1970, Delbard-Chabert; bud ovoid; flowers coppery, large, dbl., cupped, slight fragrance; foliage bronze, glossy; vigorous, upright growth; [(Queen Elizabeth × Provence) × ((Sultane × unknown) × Mme Joseph Perraud)]; int. by Pepinieres G. Delbard, 1966

Apolline B, mp, 1848, Verdier, V.; flowers bright rose-pink, large, full, cupped; [Pierre de St. Cyr × unknown]

Apollo HT, dy, 1941, Armstrong, J.A.; flowers golden yellow; [sport of Mme Joseph Perraud]; int. by Armstrong Nursery

Apollo, Climbing Cl HT, my, Leenders; bud reddish; int. in 1970

Apollo HT, my, 1971, Armstrong, D.L.; bud long, pointed; flowers soft sunshine yellow, large, dbl., moderate fragrance; foliage large, glossy, dark, leathery; vigorous, upright, bushy growth; PP3322; [High Time × Imperial Gold]; int. by Armstrong Nursery

Apollo – See **Apollo Parade**, Min

Apollo Parade Min, ab, Poulsen; flowers apricot blend, medium, semi-dbl., no fragrance; growth narrow, bushy, 20-40 cm.; PP11539; int. by Poulsen Roser, 1998

Apollo Tribute – See **Amazon**, F

Apollo XI – See **Apollo, Climbing**, Cl HT

Apollon – See **Superbe Cramoisie**, C

Apoman HT, yb, Adam

Apothecary's Rose – See ***R. gallica officinalis*** (Thory)

Apotheker Franz Hahne S, op, 1919, Müller, Dr. F.; flowers salmon-rose on orange-yellow ground, large, full, moderate fragrance

Apotheker Georg Höfer HT, or, 1900, Welter; flowers coppery-red, very large, very dbl.

Apotheker George Höfer, Climbing Cl HT, or, 1941, Vogel, M.; flowers very large, dbl.; [sport of Apotheker George Höfer]

Apotheose F, yb, 1963, Delforge; flowers Indian yellow edged red, becoming garnet-red; vigorous growth; [Arc-en-Ciel × seedling]

Appeal HT, mp, 1959, Fletcher; flowers clean pink, dbl., intense fragrance; long stems; vigorous, bushy growth; [Ena Harkness × Treasure]; int. by Tucker & Sons, 1957

Applause HT, dp, 1949, Swim, H.C.; bud long, pointed; flowers light red, 4-4½ in., 50 petals, high-centered; foliage leathery, dark; vigorous, upright, bushy growth; [Contrast × Charlotte Armstrong]; int. by Armstrong Nursery; Gold Medal, Bagatelle, 1947

Applause – See **Joy of Health**, F

Applause Min, ab, 1999, Saville, F. Harmon; flowers medium coral, reverse lighter, 1¼ in., dbl., slight fragrance; foliage small, medium green, semi-glossy; prickles moderate; upright, compact, low growth; PP13055; [Sequoia Gold × Sparks]; int. by Nor'East Miniature Roses, 2000; AOE, ARS, 2000

Apple Blossom HMult, lp, 1890, Dawson; [Dawson × *R. multiflora*]; possibly the same as the 1932 version from Burbank

Apple Blossom HT, mp, 1906, Cooling

Apple Blossom Pol, lp, 1908, Schultheis

Apple Blossom HMult, lp, 1932, Burbank; flowers light pink, center lighter, petals crinkled, semi-dbl., borne in huge clusters; vigorous growth; q-r; [Dawson × *R. multiflora*]; possibly bred by Dawson about 1890, and introduced by Stark Bros., in 1932

Apple Blossom Flower Carpet – See **Appleblossom**, S

Apple Rose – See ***R. villosa*** (Linnaeus)

Apple Seed S, mp, Keihan; int. by Keihan Gardening, 2000

Appleblossom S, lp, 1963, Skinner; flowers apple blossom-pink, dbl., cupped; recurrent bloom; bushy (2 ft.) growth

Appleblossom S, mp, Noack, Werner; flowers soft pink, 4 cm., semi-dbl., cupped, borne in clusters, slight fragrance; recurrent; growth low (2 × 3 ft.), bushy; groundcover; PP10239; int. in 1997

Appleblossom Festival S, pb, Williams, J. Benjamin; int. in 1999

Appledore F, lp, 1965, Allen, E.M.; flowers medium, 24 petals, moderate fragrance; foliage glossy; vigorous growth; [Karl Herbst × Pink Charming]

Applejack S, pb, 1973, Buck, Dr. Griffith J.; bud small, long, pointed, ovoid; flowers Neyron rose, stippled crimson, large, semi-dbl., intense fragrance; repeat bloom; foliage leathery; vigorous, upright, bushy growth; [Goldbusch × (Josef Rothmund × *R. laxa*)]; int. by Iowa State University

Appleton's Limelight HT, dy, 1934, Appleton; bud long, pointed; flowers deep golden yellow, open, large, semi-dbl.; foliage leathery, glossy; vigorous, bushy growth; [sport of Lady Forteviot]

Appreciation HT, mr, 1971, Gregory; flowers light red shading crimson, pointed, 4 in., 27 petals; foliage glossy; vigorous growth; [Queen Elizabeth × seedling]

Apps Rose F, ab, Kordes; int. in 1996

Apricot Abundance – See **Calliope**, F

Apricot Angel HT, ab; int. in 1999

Apricot Beauty S, ab, Rendu; int. in 1980

Apricot Bells HMsk, ab, 2000, Lens, Louis; buds apricot; flowers creamy apricot to pink and darker pink, 4 cm., semi-dbl., cupped, borne in large clusters, intense fragrance; recurrent; foliage large, brown to dark green, semi-glossy; prickles moderate; upright, tall (5 ft.) growth; [Trier × Mutabilis]; int. by Louis Lens NV, 1999

Apricot Brandy F, ab, 1970; flowers apricot, base yellow, 4 in., 22 petals, slight fragrance; foliage bronze-green; int. by Fryers Nursery, Ltd., 1972

Apricot Brandy Min, ab, Benardella; growth tall; int. in 1996

Apricot Castle – See **Lazy Days**, F

Apricot Charm Min, ab, 1987, Williams, Ernest D.;

flowers apricot, reverse slightly deeper, blending to yellow at base, 42 petals, high-centered, borne usually singly, slight fragrance; foliage small, dark green, glossy; prickles few, thin, light tan; bushy, spreading, medium growth; no fruit; [Gingersnap × Anita Charles]; int. by Mini-Roses, 1986

Apricot China F, mr; int. in 1996

Apricot Clementine Min, ab, Tantau; flowers long lasting, bright apricot; growth compact, vigorous; int. by Rosen Tantau, 2002

Apricot Cottage Rose – See **Sussex**, S

Apricot Crème Min, ab, 1989, Bell, Douglas & Judy; bud pointed; flowers light apricot, edges cream, reverse apricot to cream; [sport of Yellow Doll, Climbing]; int. by Michigan Mini Roses, 1989

Apricot Dawn HT, ab, 1938, Wyant; flowers apricot, base yellow; [sport of Golden Dawn]

Apricot Delicious Min, ab, Welsh; int. in 1996

Apricot Delight HT, ab, Delbard; bud long bud; flowers rich, deep apricot with broad petals, dbl., slight fragrance; growth medium; int. in 1978

Apricot Delight HT, ab, Attfield; flowers dbl., high-centered; tall growth; int. in 1999

Apricot Doll Min, ab, 1991, Laver, Keith G.; bud ovoid; flowers apricot, yellow center, reverse lighter, aging light apricot, medium, 30-35 petals, urn-shaped, borne usually singly and in sprays of 1-4, moderate fragrance; foliage small, medium green, matte; spreading, low growth; [Painted Doll × Painted Doll]; int. by Springwood Roses, 1990

Apricot Garland – See **Nice 'n' Easy**, S

Apricot Gem F, ab, Delbard-Chabert; flowers dbl.; int. in 1978

Apricot Glow LCl, ab, 1936, Brownell; flowers apricot, turning apricot-pink, 7 cm., dbl., borne in large trusses, intense fragrance; non-recurrent; foliage very glossy; numerous prickles; long stems; very vigorous (20 ft.) growth; [(Emily Gray × Dr. W. Van Fleet) × Jacotte]; int. by B&A, 1936

Apricot Hit Min, ab

Apricot Ice F, ab, Dickson; flowers light pastel apricot, darker in center, dbl., borne in clusters of 5-30, slight fragrance; growth slightly arching, bushy, vigorous, 3 ft.; int. by Dickson Nurseries, 2003

Apricot Impressionist LCl, ab, Clements, John; bud apricot bronze; flowers 4-5 in., 50 petals, moderate fragrance; recurrent; free standing (6-7 ft.) or supported (9-12 ft.) growth; PPAF; int. by Heirloom Roses, 2006

Apricot Kisses S, ab, 1999, Gear, Ian Robert; flowers dark apricot, aging to pale apricot, 2½ in., full, borne in small clusters, slight fruity fragrance; foliage medium size, medium green, new growth purple-red, semi-glossy; prickles moderate; spreading, bushy, medium (4-5 ft.) growth; patio climber; [Laura Ford × seedling]

Apricot Medinette Min, ab, 1985, Olesen, Pernille & Mogens N.; flowers apricot-orange, well-formed, small, 20 petals, borne in clusters; foliage leathery, glossy; prickles brown; spreading growth; [Mini-Poul × Mary Sumner]; int. by Ludwigs Roses Pty. Ltd., 1984

Apricot Midinette – See **Apricot Medinette**, Min

Apricot Mist Min, ab, 1987, Saville, F. Harmon; flowers apricot with tones of pink and yellow, medium, 40-45 petals, high-centered, borne singly; foliage small, dark green, glossy; prickles long, thin, straight, brown; bushy, low, profuse, compact, symmetrical growth; no fruit; PP6507; [Fantasia × Baby Katie]; int. by Nor'East Min. Roses

Apricot Mist Min, ab, Eagle, Barry & Dawn

Apricot Moon F, ab, Lowery/Eisen; flowers deep apricot-yellow, very dbl., intense anise, myrrh fragrance; [sport of Moonsprite]; int. by Vintage Gardens, 1995

Apricot Nectar F, ab, 1965, Boerner; bud ovoid; flowers pink-apricot, base golden, 4-4½ in., dbl., cupped, intense fruity fragrance; foliage glossy, dark; vigorous, bushy growth; PP2594; [seedling × Spartan]; int. by J&P, 1965

Apricot Nectar, Climbing Cl F, ab

Apricot Nectar - Dawson's Selection HT, ab, Dawson; larger form of Apricot Nectar; int. by Dawson Garden Centers, 2002

Apricot Panarosa S, ab, Kordes; int. by Ludwig's Roses, 2004

Apricot Parfait HT, ab, 1976, Warriner, William A.; bud ovoid; flowers apricot-pink blend, 4 in., 53 petals, high-centered, slight fragrance; foliage large, dark; upright growth; [seedling × South Seas]; int. by J&P

Apricot Parfait – See **Evelyn**, S

Apricot Passion HT, ab, 2000, Zary, Keith; flowers apricot-pink, reverse apricot yellow, medium, full, borne singly and in clusters, slight fragrance; foliage semi-glossy; growth medium, vigorous, upright; PP12202; [yellow HT seedling × Mirabella]; int. by Bear Creek Gardens

Apricot Perfection Min, ab, 1992, Clements, John K.; flowers soft apricot, small, dbl., high-centered, borne mostly singly, slight fragrance; foliage small, medium green, matte; some prickles; tall (50 cm.), upright, bushy growth; [My Louisa × seedling]; int. by Heirloom Old Garden Roses, 1990

Apricot Prince – See **Gingersnap**, F

Apricot Profusion F, ab, Kordes; bud slender, pointed, apricot colored; flowers deep cream-apricot, semi-dbl., open, borne in clusters; continuous bloom; foliage glossy; growth short, spreading, densely branched

Apricot Queen HT, ab, 1940, Howard, F.H.; bud pointed; flowers salmon-pink, base apricot-orange, large, 45 petals; foliage leathery; very vigorous, bushy growth; [Mrs J.D. Eisele × Glowing Sunset]; int. by H&S

Apricot Queen, Climbing Cl HT, ab, 1950, Maranda

Apricot Queen S, ab, Interplant; int. in 1999

Apricot Queen Elizabeth Gr, ab, Verschuren; flowers apricot yellow aging to buff and pale orange; int. in 1980

Apricot Silk HT, ob, 1965, Gregory, C.; flowers coppery orange, double, high-centered, borne several together; foliage deep green, glossy; [Souv de Jacques Verschuren × unknown]

Apricot Sky LCl, ab, Barni; flowers yellow cream and apricot, very dbl., cupped; growth to 8-20 ft.; int. by Rose Barni, 2004

Apricot Spice HT, ab, 1985, Sanday, John; flowers orange-apricot, medium, 35 petals; foliage medium size, medium green, matte; bushy growth; [City of Gloucester × seedling]

Apricot Summer F, ab, Kordes; int. in 1995

Apricot Sunblaze – See **Mark One**, Min

Apricot Sunblaze Min, yb, 1994, Meilland, Alain A.; flowers yellow edged in bright orange, 1½ in., dbl, high-centered, borne mostly singly, no fragrance; foliage small, dark green, glossy; few prickles; medium, bushy growth, compact; PP9033; [(Mark One × Yellow Meillandina) × Gold Badge]; int. by The Conard-Pyle Co., 1994

Apricot Surprise S, ab

Apricot Twist Min, ab, 1993, Moore, Ralph S.; flowers medium, dbl., borne in small clusters; foliage small, medium green, semi-glossy; few prickles; low (30-32 cm.), bushy, compact growth; PP9656; [Golden Angel × Sequoia Gold]; int. by Sequoia Nursery, 1994

Apricot Wine F, ab, 1980, Slack; flowers burnt apricot, 12 petals; foliage dark, glossy; low, compact growth; [Allgold × seedling]; int. in 1978

Apriheart Min, ab, 1984, Hardgrove, Donald L.; bud small; flowers light apricot, center deeper, small, dbl., borne singly, intense fragrance; foliage small, medium green, semi-glossy; prickles very few; bushy growth; [Picnic × Rise 'n' Shine]; int. in 1983

Aprikola F, ab, 2006; bud rounded, orange-yellow; flowers deep apricot yellow, change to apricot-pink, 6 cm., full, borne in small clusters, slight fruity, sourish fragrance; foliage medium size, dark green, very glossy, very disease-resistant; growth wide, medium, 70 cm.; int. by W. Kordes' Söhne, 2000

April HT, op, 2000, Horner, Colin P.; flowers orange-pink, aging more pink, reverse lighter, 8 cm., dbl., borne mostly singly; foliage medium size, medium green, semi-glossy; prickles moderate; growth bushy, medium (80 cm.); [Indian Summer × Beautiful Britain]; int. in 2002

April HT, dy, Schreurs; greenhouse rose; int. in 2002

April Fool's Day HT, lp, 1997, Gregory, C.; flowers medium, very dbl., borne in small clusters, moderate fragrance; foliage medium size, medium green, semi-glossy; some prickles; growth bushy, medium (2½-3 ft.); [sport of Silver Jubilee]; int. by Gregory Roses

April Hamer HT, pb, 1983, Bell, Ronald J.; flowers shell pink with bright pink edges, large, 40 petals, high-centered; foliage dark; vigorous, upright growth; [Mount Shasta × Prima Ballerina]; int. by Treloar Roses Pty. Ltd., 1998

April in Paris HT, pb, 2007, Zary, Keith W.; flowers pink cream blend, 4½ in., full, blooms borne mostly solitary; foliage medium size, dark green, glossy; prickles 8-10 mm., hooked downward, greyed-orange, few; growth upright, medium (5 ft.); [Pristine × New Zealand]; int. by Jackson & Perkins Wholesale, Inc., 2008

April Love S, mp, Clements, John; flowers soft, sweet pink, 4-5 cm., very full, cupped, heavy fruity, myrrh fragrance; profuse bloom; foliage rich, dark green; growth spreading (4-5 × 4-5 ft.); int. by Heirloom Roses, 2004

April Moon S, my, 1985, Buck, Dr. Griffith J.; bud small; flowers lemon yellow, 28 petals, cupped, borne 5-10 per cluster, moderate sweet fragrance; repeat bloom; foliage dark, leathery; prickles awl-like, tan; erect, short, bushy growth; hardy; [Serendipity × (Tickled Pink × Maytime)]; int. by Iowa State University, 1984

April Moore HT, w, 2007, Poole, Lionel; flowers white with pale pink, large, 5 in., full, borne mostly solitary; foliage medium size, dark green, glossy; prickles medium, slightly hooked down, brown, moderate; growth bushy, medium (3 ft.); garden decoration, borders; [Silver Anniversary × New Zealand]; int. by David Lister Roses, 2008

Aprilia HT, dp, 1937, Cazzaniga, F. G.; bud ovoid; flowers old-rose, open, very large, dbl.; foliage leathery; vigorous, upright growth; Gold Medal, Rome, 1937

Aprutina F, Borgatti, G.; int. in 1969

Apsara F, 1970, Pal, Dr. B.P.; bud ovoid; flowers salmon-pink, open, medium, semi-dbl.; foliage glossy; vigorous, upright, open growth; RULED EXTINCT 3/84 ARM; int. by Indian Agric. Research Inst., 1966

Apsara HT, pb, 1984, Pal, Dr. B. P.; flowers flesh pink with salmon shadings, strong fragrance; foliage medium size, leathery, round; stems long, uniform; growth upright; [Sonia × Sabine]; int. by K. S. G. Son, 1983

Aqua HT, mp, Schreurs; int. by Australian Roses, 2004

Aquarelle F, dy, 1979, Lens; bud ovoid; flowers open, 2 in., 18-25 petals, flat, moderate fruity fragrance; foliage dark; very vigorous growth; [Gold Strike × Golden Garnette]; int. in 1969

Aquarelle HT, yb, Tantau; int. by Rosen Tantau, 2002

Aquarelle HT, r, Croix

Aquarius Gr, pb, 1970, Armstrong, D.L.; bud ovoid; flowers medium pink blend, medium, dbl., high-centered, slight fragrance; foliage large, leathery; vigorous, upright, bushy growth; [(Charlotte Armstrong × Contrast) × (Fandango × (World's Fair × Floradora))]; int. by Armstrong Nursery, 1971; Gold Medal, Geneva, 1970

Aquarius HT, dp, Tantau; int. by Rosen Tantau, 2002

Aquarius Min, rb, Burston; int. by Burston Nurseries, 2004

Aquilla Bright HT, ob, 1988, Lea, R.F.G.; flowers medium, full, slight fragrance; foliage medium size, medium green, semi-glossy; upright growth; [Sunblest × Matador]

Aquitaine – See **Essex**, S

Ara Pacis HT, w, 1955, Giacomasso; bud tubular, well formed; flowers ivory-white edged reddish-purple, very large, 50 petals; foliage glossy, bright green; long stems; vigorous growth; [Peace × Marguerite Chambard]

Arabella HT, dp, 1918, Schilling/Tantau; flowers crimson-pink, pointed, large, full, moderate fragrance; vigorous growth; [sport of Mme Caroline Testout]

Arabella F, rb, Benny, David; flowers bright red with white reverse, dbl, borne in trusses; int. by Camp Hill Roses

Arabella's Rambler lp, Scarman; int. in 2001

Arabesque F, lp, 1978, Sanday, John; bud pointed; flowers soft pink, 3 in., 10 petals; vigorous growth; [(Gavotte × Tropicana) × Tropicana]

Arabesque F, Christensen; int. in 1988

Arabesque S, pb, Interplant; flowers striped; groundcover; spreading growth; int. in 1997

Arabia F, ob, 1986, Tantau

Arabia HT, r, Tantau; possibly synonymous with Tanibara/Arabia; int. by Rosen Tantau, 1999

Arabian Nights F, op, 1963, McGredy, Sam IV; flowers light salmon-orange, well-formed, 4½ in., 25 petals; vigorous growth; [Spartan × Beauté]; int. by McGredy & Son, 1963

Araby Gr, lp, 1973, Thomson; bud long, pointed; flowers light orchid-pink, center white, open, large, dbl.; foliage large, glossy, dark, leathery; vigorous, upright growth; [Honey Chile × Rose Merk]

Araceli Leyva HT, op, 1940, Dot, Pedro; bud long, pointed; flowers rose-salmon, large, dbl., cupped; foliage leathery; strong stems; vigorous, upright growth; [Mme Butterfly × Comtesse Vandal]

Arahina Min, dy; int. by Matthews Nursery, 2001

Arakan F, lp, 1968, Harkness; flowers dbl., borne in trusses; [Pink Parfait × Ivory Fashion]

Aramis HGal, pb, 1845, Vibert; flowers white striped with deep rose pink, medium, full, cupped

Aramis B, dp, 1849, Boyau; flowers dark pink, shaded light pink, medium, dbl.

Aramis F, dr, 1964, Laperrière; flowers bright scarlet, 3 in., semi-dbl., borne in clusters of 7-8; foliage dark; very bushy, compact growth; [Bel Ami × (Java × Alain)]; int. by EFR

Arashiyama HT, w, 1997, Kameyama, Yasushi; flowers large, 41 petals; foliage medium size, medium green, glossy; some prickles; medium (1-2m.) growth; [Garden Party × Pristine]

Aratama HT, yb, 1976, Takahashi, Takeshi; bud pointed; flowers yellow and red, 6 in., 25 petals, high-centered; foliage glossy, light green; vigorous growth; [Kordes' Perfecta × (Garden Party × Christian Dior)]

Aravali Princess HT, op, Pal, Dr. B.P.; int. in 1987

Arbelle F, or, Gaujard

ARC Angel HT, ob, Fryer, Gareth; flowers large, coppery salmon, dbl., high-centered, intense fragrance; recurrent; foliage dark green; growth vigorous and bushy, 3 ft.; int. in 1996

Arc de Triomphe HT, yb, 1955, Buyl Frères; bud globular; flowers yellow-copper, large, dbl., moderate fragrance; foliage glossy, olive-green; upright growth; RULED EXTINCT 1/86

Arc de Triomphe – See **Summer Fashion**, F

Arc-en-Ciel F, pb, 1961, Delforge; flowers rich yellow to salmon-pink, carmine and crimson, 65-70 petals, borne in tight clusters; foliage dark; growth moderate; [Masquerade × Maria Delforge]

Arcade Min, mr, Spooner, Raymond A.; int. in 1996

Arcadia HWich, dr, 1913, Walsh; flowers crimson-scarlet, 3 cm., dbl., rosette, borne in small clusters; very vigorous growth

Arcadia HT, rb, 1938, Gaujard; bud ovoid; flowers reddish-copper, very large, dbl.; foliage glossy; long stems; vigorous growth

Arcadia F, mp, Noack; int. by Noack's Roses, 2004

Arcadian – See **New Year**, Gr

Arcanto S, mp, Barni, V.; int. in 1995

Arcanum Min, ab, 2000, Tucker, Robbie; flowers creamy apricot, 4-7 cm., dbl., high-centered, borne mostly singly, no fragrance; foliage medium size, medium size, very glossy; some prickles; growth bushy, medium (20 in.); [seedling × Kristin]; int. by Rosemania, 2001

Arcata Light Yellow Wichurana – See **Weisse New Dawn**, LCl

Arch. Reventós HT, ab, 1935, Leenders, M.; bud ovoid, apricot; flowers cream-yellow, large, dbl.; foliage glossy, dark; vigorous, bushy growth

Arch. Reventós, Climbing Cl HT, Leenders, M.

Archange LCl, mr; int. in 2004

Archangel S, lp, 1980, Hawker, U.; flowers delicate pink, frilled, large, 9-10 petals, slight fragrance; foliage light green; tall growth; [Little Darling × Gypsy Moth]

Archduchess Charlotte Ch, dp, 1976, Earing, F.E.; bud pointed; flowers intense deep solid pink, 2½-3 in., 76 petals, cupped, moderate fragrance; profuse bloom early summer; foliage glossy, smooth; climbing growth; [sport of Archduke Charles]; int. by Kern Rose Nursery, 1975

Archduke Charles Ch, rb, before 1837, Laffay, M.; flowers rose with paler edges, aging to rich crimson, dbl.; moderate growth

Archévêque – See **La Provence**, HGal

Archiduc Charles – See **Belle Hélène**, HGal

Archiduc Charles – See **Archduke Charles**, Ch

Archiduc Joseph T, pb, 1892, Nabonnand, G.; flowers purplish pink, center flesh-pink; vigorous growth; [Mme Lombard × unknown]

Archiduchesse Elisabeth d'Autriche HP, mp, 1881, Moreau et Robert; flowers rose-pink, dbl.

Archiduchesse Elisabeth-Marie Pol, ly, 1898, Soupert & Notting; flowers canary-yellow fading white, imbricated, medium, dbl.; vigorous growth; [Mignonette × Luciole]

Archiduchesse Maria Immaculata T, mr, 1887, Soupert & Notting

Archiduchesse Marie-Dorothée Amélie – See **Erzherzogin Marie Dorothea**, HT

Archiduchesse Marie Marguerite HT, dp, 1889, Balogh; flowers large, full; [Général Jacqueminot × Mme Falcot]

Archiduchesse Thérèse-Isabelle T, w, 1834, Barbot; flowers white, tinted yellow at center, large, full

Archie Gray HT, dr, 1920, Dickson, H.; flowers deep crimson, shaded scarlet, dbl.

Archimède HP, w, 1852, Laffay; flowers light lilac-white, very large, full, cupped

Archimède T, mp, 1855, Robert; flowers pink, shaded chamois, center darker, very large, full, globular

Arctic Emerald S, w, 1982, James, John; bud globular, pointed; flowers white, with yellow-green center, small to medium, 12 petals, borne 1-5 per cluster; repeat bloom; foliage small, light green; low, compact growth; [Thérèse Bugnet × Europeana]; int. in 1978

Arctic Flame HT, mr, 1957, Brownell; bud medium, pointed; flowers bright crimson red, 5 in., 50-60 petals, high-centered, borne singly and in small clusters, moderate tea fragrance; free-flowering; foliage medium size, dark green; prickles several; stems long, stiff; vigorous (4 ft.), bushy growth; winter hardy ; PP1432; [(Queen o' the Lakes × Pink Princess) × Mirandy]; int. by Stern's Nursery, 1956

Arctic Glow S, rb, 1982, James, John; bud globular, pointed; flowers scarlet shading to white center, large, 28 petals, borne singly; repeat bloom; foliage dark, rough; compact growth; [Pike's Peak × Show Girl]; int. in 1978

Arctic Pink F, lp, 1966, Smith, E.; flowers pink fading lighter, 3 in., cupped, borne in trusses; vigorous growth; [sport of Dearest]

Arctic Rose – See ***R. acicularis*** (Lindley)

Arctic Snow Min, w, 1983, Williams, Ernest D.; flowers small, dbl., high-centered; foliage small, dark, glossy; upright, bushy growth; [Miniature seedling × Over the Rainbow]; int. by Mini-Roses

Arctic Sunrise Min, w, 1990, Barrett, F.H.; bud pointed; flowers small, 30 petals, flat, borne in sprays of 40-60, no fragrance; foliage small, medium green, glossy; prickles long, thin, small, pale tan; spreading, low growth; no fruit; [Snow Carpet × Tranquillity]; int. in 1989

Ardelle HT, w, 1955, Eddie, H.M.; bud long, pointed; flowers creamy white, 5 in., 72 petals, high-centered, moderate fragrance; foliage glossy; very vigorous, compact growth; PP2042; [Mrs Charles Lamplough × Peace]; int. by Harkness

Ardennes – See **Eye Appeal**, S

Ardente Cl F, op, Moreira da Silva; flowers salmon and orange; [seedling × Alain]

Ardoisée – See **Charles de Mills**, HGal

Ardoisée de Lyon HP, m, 1858, Damaizin; flowers violet-rose, very large, full, quartered; foliage dark green; vigorous growth

Ardon HWich, mp, 1925, Turbat; flowers bright Neyron rose, stained white, 5-6 cm., very full, borne in pyramidal clusters of 30-40; foliage small, glossy; nearly thornless

Ardore HT, mr, 1974, Calvino; bud ovoid, globular; flowers orient red, large, dbl., cupped, moderate fragrance; foliage large, dark, leathery; very vigorous, upright, bushy growth; PP2814; [seedling × Ninfa]

Ards Beauty F, my, 1984, Dickson, Patrick; bud large; flowers large, 20 petals, high-centered; foliage medium size, medium green, glossy; bushy growth; [(Eurorose × Whisky Mac) × Bright Smile]; int. in 1986; Gold Medal, RNRS, 1983

Ards Pillar HT, mr, 1903, Dickson, A.; flowers velvety crimson, large, semi-dbl., cupped

Ards Rambler Cl HT, or, 1908, Dickson, A.; flowers orange-red, dbl., intense fragrance

Ards Rover Cl HP, dr, 1898, Dickson, A.; flowers crimson, shaded maroon, large, dbl.; sometimes recurrent bloom; pillar growth

Arejay Min, ab, 1993, Kirkham, Gordon Wilson; flowers moderately small, dbl., borne in large clusters, slight fragrance; foliage small, medium green, glossy; few prickles; low, bushy growth; [seedling × seedling]; int. by Kirkham, 1995

Arena 91 HT, dp, Dey, S. C.; flowers large, full, well formed; int. by Horticulture Arena, 1991

Arena 92 HT, dp, Dey, S. C.; flowers very large, well formed

Arena 93 F, yb, Dey, S.C.; flowers deep yellow changing

to pink and deepening to red, borne in well-placed clusters; int. in 1993

Arena 94 F, mr, Dey, S. C.; flowers velvety red, borne in large clusters; growth vigorous; int. in 1994

Arena 95 HT, w, Dey, S. C.; flowers white with petal edges purple, large, well formed; int. in 1995

Arena's Dream Kordes, Kordes; PP11355; int. in 1998

Arend Herwig F, ob, 1966, Buisman, G. A. H.; bud ovoid; flowers orange-red, medium, dbl.; foliage dark; [Korona × Heureux Anniversaire]

Arethusa Ch, yb, 1903, Paul, W.; flowers yellow, tinted apricot, borne in small clusters, moderate fresh fragrance; foliage glossy, somewhat sparse; growth medium (3 × 3 ft.)

Argental HT, w, Croix

Argentée D, lp, before 1811; flowers satiny flesh pink, medium, borne in clusters of 5-20; foliage oval, pointed; numerous prickles

Argentina F, ab, 1941, Leenders, M.; flowers reddish-apricot, semi-dbl.; [Mev. Nathalie Nypels × Orange Glory]

Argentine Cramon – See **Mlle Argentine Cramon**, HT

Argosy HT, op, 1938, Clark, A.; flowers salmon, flushed pink, dbl.; long stems; [Souv. de Gustave Prat × seedling]; int. by NRS New South Wales

Argovia HT, pb, Huber; flowers strong pink with yellow in center; int. by Rosen Huber, 1998

Argyle HT, w, 1921, Dobbie; flowers creamy yellow to pure white, large, full; vigorous growth; [Mme Caroline Testout × Marquise de Sinéty]

Argyll HT, ly, 1918, Dobbie; flowers light yellow, fading to white, large, full; [Mme Caroline Testout × Marquise de Sinéty]

Aria F, op, 1957, deRuiter; flowers salmon shaded pink, large, dbl.; bushy growth; [Duchess of Rutland × Fashion]

Ariadne – See **Ariane**, HGal

Ariadne Ch, rb, 1918, Paul, W.; flowers bright crimson, center shaded yellow

Ariake HT, w, 1978, Teranishi, K.; bud globular; flowers ivory, 5 in., 47-50 petals, cupped, moderate fragrance; foliage light green; vigorous, upright growth; [(Lady × Garden Party) × seedling]; int. by Itami Rose Nursery, 1976

Ariana d'Algier – See **Complicata**, HGal

Ariane HGal, m, 1818, Vibert; flowers light purple-pink, medium, full; not the same as Vibert's Alba Ariane

Ariane A, 1818, Vibert; not the same as Vibert's HGal Ariane

Ariane de Vibert HGal, dp, about 1835, Vibert; flowers very large, very full; perhaps synonymous with Ariadne

Arianna HT, pb, 1968, Meilland, Louisette; flowers carmine-rose suffused coral, large, 35 petals, high-centered, slight fragrance; foliage dark, leathery; vigorous, upright, open growth; [Charlotte Armstrong × (Peace × Michèle Meilland)]; int. by URS; Gold Medal, Rome, 1965, Gold Medal, The Hague, 1965, Gold Medal, Bagatelle, 1965

Arianna HT, w, Meilland; possibly Arianna 85/Meikrusa

Aribau HT, mr, 1936, Dot, Pedro; bud long, pointed; flowers brilliant red, large, dbl.; foliage glossy; long stems; very vigorous growth; [Kitchener of Khartoum × Director Rubió]; int. by H. Guillot

Aridhra HT, pb, K & S; flowers cream to pale pink, full, well shaped; [sport of Raja Surendra Singh of Nalagarh]; int. in 2003

Ariel Cl T, pb, 1910, Paul; flowers coppery golden yellow over pink

Ariel HT, my, 1921, Bees; flowers golden yellow, streaked crimson, large, dbl., globular, moderate fragrance; foliage dark; long stems; vigorous, bushy growth; [Mme Edouard Herriot × Natalie Boettner]; Gold Medal, NRS, 1920

Arielle P, 1845, Vibert

Arielle HT, mp, Tantau; int. by Rosen Tantau, 2001

Arielle Dombasle LCl, yb, 1991, Meilland; flowers salmon yellow, reverse yellow, 3 in., semi-dbl.; int. in 1991

Aries F, mr, Burston; int. by Burston Nurseries, 2004

Arifa F, rb, Tantau; florist rose; int. by Rosen Tantau

Arioso HT, or, 1976, Paolino; flowers light vermilion, 5 in., 25 petals, slight fruity fragrance; foliage glossy, dark; very vigorous, upright growth; [(Paris-Match × Baccará) × Marella]; int. by URS

Arioso HT, pb, Meilland; flowers light pink with deeper pink edges, dbl., high-centered, moderate citrus fragrance; recurrent; moderate (100 cm.) growth; int. in 1995

Ariste HT, my, 1960, Jones; bud very pointed, deep yellow; flowers light yellow, medium, 5 petals; foliage dark, leathery; vigorous, bushy growth; [Joanna Hill × Souv. de Mme Boullet]; int. by Hennessey

Aristide – See **Mlle Aristide**, M

Aristide HSpn, mp, from Scotland

Aristide Briand HWich, m, 1928, Penny; flowers mauve-pink, reverse lighter, medium, semi-dbl., borne in clusters of 10-15, moderate fragrance; some repeat; [Yseult Guillot × unknown]

Aristide Dupuy HP, dp, 1866, Trouillard or Touvais; flowers slatey violet bordered bright pink, large, dbl.

Aristobule M, dp, 1849, Foulard; flowers dark rose with touches of clear rose, dbl.

Aristocrat HT, pb, 1949, Holmes, M.A.; bud long, pointed; flowers clear light pink, reverse darker, 4½-5 in., 28-35 petals, high-centered; foliage leathery, dark; very vigorous, upright growth; [sport of Pink Delight]; int. by Mortensen

Aristocrat Min, dp, 2002, White, Wendy R.; flowers deep pink/near red, reverse medium to dark pink, 2 in., full, borne mostly solitary; foliage medium size, dark green, semi-glossy; prickles 5/16 in., tapered and angled down, moderate; growth upright, compact, medium (14-18 in.); cutting, exhibition, garden; [June Laver × New Zealand]; int. by Nor' East Miniature Roses, 2002; Gold Medal, Rose Hills, 2006

Aristocrat HT, w, Chakraborty, Dr. K.; flowers creamy white with deep pink at petal edges, well-formed; very vigorous growth; int. in 2003

Aristote HGal, pb; a variety of *R. francofurtana*

Arizona Gr, ob, 1974, Weeks; bud urn-shaped; flowers golden bronze to orangy yellow, medium, 25-30 petals, high-centered, borne singly, intense sweet fragrance; foliage glossy, dark, leathery; long, cutting length stems; vigorous, upright, bushy growth; PP3568; [((Fred Howard × Golden Scepter) × Golden Rapture) × ((Fred Howard × Golden Scepter) × Golden Rapture)]; int. by C-P, 1975

Arizona Sunset Min, yb, 1985, Jolly, Nelson F.; flowers light yellow, flushed orange-red, medium, 20 petals, cupped; foliage small, medium green, semi-glossy; prickles slanted downward; bushy, spreading growth; PP6559; [Rise 'n' Shine × Zinger]; int. by Rosehill Farm

Arjun HT, or, 1981, Division of Vegetable Crops and Floriculture; bud long, pointed; flowers 35 petals, cupped, borne singly or 8 per cluster, slight fragrance; foliage large, smooth; prickles hooked; tall, upright growth; [Blithe Spirit × Montezuma]; int. in 1980

Arkansas HT, or, 1980, Weeks; bud ovoid, pointed; flowers paprika red-orange, 48 petals, urn-shaped, borne singly or 2-4 per cluster, slight spicy fragrance; foliage leathery; prickles long, oval-based, hooked downward; upright, vigorous growth; PP4700; [seedling × seedling]

Arkansas Rose – See ***R. arkansana*** (Porter)

Arkansas Sunshine F, my, 1965, Jones; flowers golden yellow, 30 petals, cupped, borne in clusters; foliage dark, leathery; vigorous, bushy growth; [Goldilocks × seedling]; int. by Hennessey, 1962

Arkavathi F, dp, Kasturi; int. in 1971

Arkle HT, or, 1978, Hughes Roses; bud cupped; flowers dark tangerine, 4 in., 45-50 petals, cupped, intense fragrance; foliage glossy; vigorous growth; [sport of Whisky Mac]

Arlene Francis HT, my, 1958, Boerner; bud long, pointed; flowers golden buttery yellow, 5 in., 25-30 petals, high-centered, borne mostly singly, intense sweet licorice fragrance; foliage dark, glossy; vigorous growth, upright, medium sized; PP1684; [(Eclipse × unknown) × Golden Scepter]; int. by J&P, 1957

Arlequin HGal, rb, before 1821, Vibert; flowers crimson marbled with pink, medium, full

Arlequin – See **Pourpre Marbrée**, HGal

Arlequin HP, rb, 1872, Taillandier; int. in 1872

Arlequin HT, ob, 1945, Gaujard; flowers orange-yellow and coppery red, very large, dbl., globular; foliage dark, glossy; bushy growth

Arles – See **Fernand Arles**, HT

Arles Dufour HP, m, 1863, Liabaud

Arlette F, rb, Poulsen; int. in 1996

Arm-Roy Beauty HT, mr, 1945, Armacost & Royston; very vigorous, tall growth; [sport of Better Times]

Armada S, mp, 1988, Harkness, R., & Co., Ltd.; flowers medium pink, aging slightly paler, medium, 17 petals, cupped, borne in sprays of up to 12; repeat bloom; foliage medium size, medium green, glossy; prickles slightly recurved, medium green; spreading growth; hips rounded, medium green; [New Dawn × Silver Jubilee]; int. by R. Harkness & Co., Ltd.

Armagh HT, ab, 1950, McGredy, Sam IV; flowers creamy pink, apricot and buff, pointed, large, 49 petals; foliage dark; free growth; [Sam McGredy × Admiration]

Armani S, mp, Poulsen; flowers medium pink, 8-10 cm., semi-dbl., no fragrance; foliage dark; growth bushy, 20-40 cm.; int. by Poulsen Roser, 2005

Armani Hit – See **Armani**, S

Arménie HT, ab, 1936, Buatois; bud purple-garnet; flowers blood-red, shaded, large, very dbl.; very vigorous, bushy growth; [Rhea Reid × Yves Druhen]

Armide A, lp, 1818, Vibert; flowers flesh with pale edges, medium, very dbl., borne in clusters, moderate fragrance; non-recurrent; foliage acutely serrated, veined, medium green; growth bushy, shrubby, 3 ft.; winter hardy, tolerates part shade

Armide N, mp, before 1836, Laffay; flowers pink, aging to lilac, medium, lightly dbl.

Armide P, mp, 1847, Vibert; flowers pink with salmon reflections, large, full, cupped

Armide HP, mp, 1858, Margottin

Armilla – See **Cherry-Vanilla**, Gr

Arminda HT, op, 1956, Camprubi, C.; bud ovoid; flowers bright pink tinted coral, large, very dbl., globular; foliage glossy; strong stems; vigorous growth; [Peace × Symphonie]

Armonia HT, mr, 1951, Cazzaniga, F. G.; bud long, pointed; flowers bright red, dbl., high-centered; foliage dark, leathery; long stems; very vigorous, upright growth

Armorique – See **White Nights**, S

Armosa – See **Hermosa**, Ch

Armoton – See **San Antonio**, Gr

Arnaud Delbard – See **First Edition**, F

Arndt LCl, lp, 1913, Lambert, P.; bud yellowish red; flowers pale salmony pink to medium, 4-5 cm., semi-dbl. to dbl., borne in clusters of 10-20; recurrent bloom; foliage dark; half-climbing growth; [Hélène × Gustav Grünerwald]

Arnelda Mae Min, lp, 1983, Pencil, Paul S.; bud small; flowers small, 30 petals, high-centered, borne singly and in clusters up to 7; foliage small, light green, matte; bushy growth; [Sheri Anne × seedling]

Arnhem Glory HT, dr, 1959, Verschuren; flowers deep velvety red, large; vigorous growth

Arnold Greensitt HT, yb, 1987, Greensitt, J.A.; flowers medium, full, intense fragrance; foliage large, light green, matte; bushy growth; [E.H. Morse × Summer Sunshine]; int. by Nostell Priory Rose Gardens, 1982

Arnold Rose HRg, mr, 1914, Dawson; flowers reddish-purple, semi-dbl.; some recurrent bloom; vigorous growth; [*R. rugosa* × Génèral Jacqueminot]; int. by Eastern Nursery

Arnoldiana – See **Arnold Rose**, HRg

Aroha HT, mp, 1987, Murray, Nola; flowers medium, soft pink, elongated, 43 petals, borne in sprays of 3-5, slight fragrance; foliage medium size, light green; prickles pointed, brown; tall growth; [Rifleman × Pascali]; int. in 1986

Aroma HT, mr, 1931, Cant, B. R.; bud ovoid; flowers crimson, large, dbl.; vigorous, bushy growth; int. by J&P

Aromatherapy HT, mp, 2005, Zary, Keith W.; flowers full, borne mostly solitary, intense fragrance; foliage large, dark green, glossy; prickles 7-9 mm., straight, greyed-yellow, moderate; growth upright, branching and vigorous, medium (150 cm.); [seedling × New Zealand]; int. by Jackson & Perkins Wholesale, Inc., 2005

Aromatic HT, pb; flowers blend of light and medium pinks, cupped, borne in clusters, intense fragrance; int. in 1970

Arosia HT, mp, Noack, Werner; int. in 1998

Arpége HT, Dorieux, Francois; int. in 1978

Arpege HT, Boerner, E. S.; PP2237

Arpeggio F, dp, 1961, Von Abrams; bud pointed; flowers light red, 3 in., 12-18 petals, borne in clusters; foliage dark, glossy; vigorous, compact growth; int. by Peterson & Dering, 1961

Arras Pol, mr, 1924, Turbat; flowers crimson-red; [sport of Triomphe Orléanais]

Arrillaga HP, lp, 1929, Schoener; flowers light pink, base golden, large, 50 petals, moderate fragrance; vigorous growth; [(a centifolia × Mrs John Laing) × Frau Karl Druschki]; int. by B&A

Arrogance HT, pb, 1978, Poulsen, Niels D.; flowers coral-pink, 4 in., 25 petals, slight fragrance; foliage dark, leathery; compact growth; [Mischief × John S. Armstrong]; int. by Poulsen, 1970

Arromanches F, op, Eve, A.; repeats well in fall; growth vigorous, 80-100 cm.; int. in 1975

Arrow – See **Calypso Hit**, MinFl

Arrow Folies F, m, J&P; flowers light ruby purple striped with white, dbl., borne in sprays; PP15082; greenhouse rose; int. by Meilland International, 2004

Arrow Hit – See **Calypso Hit**, MinFl

Arrow Patiohit – See **Calypso Hit**, MinFl

Arrowtown LCl, dy, Martin; buds apricot; flowers large, deep golden yellow; growth to 12-14 ft.; int. in 1982

Art Deco HMsk, mr, 2000, Lens, Louis; flowers medium red, 2 cm., single, borne in large clusters; recurrent; foliage medium size, medium green, semi-glossy; numerous prickles; upright, tall (7 ft.) growth, can be used as climber; [Pleine de Grace × Pretty Pink]; int. by Lens Roses, 1993

Artama HT, yb, 1978, Takahashi, Takeshi; bud pointed; flowers 25 petals, high-centered; foliage light green, pointed, glossy; few prickles; sturdy growth; [Kordes' Perfecta × (Garden Party × Christian Dior)]

Artek HT, dr, 1939, Kosteckij; flowers dark, velvety red, medium, dbl.

Artemis HT, w, Tantau; int. in 2003

Artémise HP, dp, 1851, Robert

Artful Dodger Min, rb, 1996, Burrows, Steven; flowers cherry red, cream reverse, 1 in., dbl., borne in large clusters; foliage medium size, dark green, glossy; some prickles; tall (45 cm.), upright, spreading, bushy growth; [Sheri Anne × Richard Buckley]; int. by Burrows Roses, 1997

Arthur Bell F, my, 1965, McGredy, Sam IV; flowers golden yellow fading to creamy yellow, large, 15 petals, intense sweet fragrance; foliage heavily veined; vigorous growth, medium to tall; [Cläre Grammerstorf × Piccadilly]; int. by McGredy

Arthur Bell, Climbing Cl F, my, 1976, Pearce, C.A.; int. by Limes Rose Nursery, 1979

Arthur Cook HT, dr, 1924, McGredy; bud long, pointed; flowers deep crimson, large, dbl.; foliage light, glossy; long, strong stems; vigorous, bushy, compact growth; Gold Medal, NRS, 1925

Arthur Cox Min, pb, 1997, Jellyman, J.S.; flowers medium, dbl., borne in small clusters; foliage medium size, medium green, semi-glossy; compact, medium growth; [Cotswold Gold × Peaches 'n' Cream]; int. by F. Haynes & Partners

Arthur de Sansal P, m, 1855, Cochet; flowers rich crimson-purple, fully damask-like, medium, dbl., cupped, intense fragrance; growth small, twiggy; [Géant des Batailles × unknown]; sometimes classed as HP

Arthur Hillier HMoy, dp, 1970, Hillier; flowers rose-crimson, 2½-3 in., 5 petals, slight fragrance; repeat bloom; vigorous growth; [*R. macrophylla* × *R. moyesii*]; int. by Hillier & Sons, 1961

Arthur J. Taylor HT, dr, 1947, Wheatcroft Bros.; flowers large, dbl.

Arthur Merrill F, mr, 2001, Horner, Heather M.; flowers medium red with paler reverse, 6 cm., dbl., borne in large clusters, slight fragrance; foliage medium size, medium green, glossy; prickles medium, slightly curved, moderate; growth bushy, medium (80 cm.); [Anna Ford × Black Jade]; int. by Battersby Roses, 2001

Arthur Oger HP, m, 1875, Oger; flowers purple/pink, very large, dbl.; [Gloire de Ducher × unknown]

Arthur R. Goodwin HT, or, 1909, Pernet-Ducher; flowers coppery orange-red, passing to salmon-pink, medium to large, full; [seedling × Soleil d'Or]

Arthur R. Goodwin, Climbing Cl HT, or

Arthur Scargill Min, mr, 1985, Thompson, M.L.; [sport of Amruda]

Arthur Schulte HT, rb, 1987, Williams, J. Benjamin; flowers cherry to blood red with ivory white at base of petals, large, 43 petals, high-centered, borne singly and in sprays of 1-3, moderate damask fragrance; foliage large, dark green, semi-glossy, disease-resistant; prickles medium-large, light green-bronze; upright, bushy, medium, very vigorous, some interbranching growth; hips rounded, medium size, pumpkin-orange; [(Colorama × unknown) × Chrysler Imperial]; int. by Krider Nursery, 1986

Arthur Vesey HT, mr; int. by Veseys Roses, 2005

Arthur Weidling HP, dp, 1932, Vogel; flowers large, full, moderate fragrance; [sport of Pride of Reigate]

Arthur Wood Min, dr, 2000, Giles, Diann; flowers medium, full, high-centered, borne mostly singly, no fragrance; foliage small, dark green, semi-glossy; prickles moderate; growth compact, medium; int. by Giles Rose Nursery

Arthur Young M, m, 1863, Portemer fils; flowers dark velvety purple, large, full, cupped; recurrent bloom; vigorous growth

Artista HT, pb, Delbard; flowers medium size, pink striped and painted yellow and white, dbl., no fragrance; growth compact, vigorous; int. by Ludwig's Roses, 2001

Artista Panarosa – See **Maurice Utrillo**, F

Artiste HT, my, 1965, Jones, J. A.; bud long, pointed, deep yellow; flowers single, borne singly and several together; foliage dark green, leathery; few prickles; growth vigorous, bushy; [Joanna Hill × Souv de Mme Boullet]; int. by Hennessey, 1960

Artiste F, w, 1986, Dorieux

Artistic F, ob, 1971, LeGrice; flowers orange, fading red, pointed, 2 in., 10-15 petals, moderate fragrance; foliage small

Artistic Licence HT, rb, 2007, Guest, M.; flowers red with variable yellow stripes, 4½ in., full, borne mostly solitary; foliage medium size, dark green, glossy; prickles ½ in., hooked, moderate; growth upright, tall (40 in.); garden decoration, exhibition; [seedling × Red Planet]; int. by Pocock's Roses, 2007

Artistry HT, op, 1998, Zary, Dr. Keith W.; flowers coral-orange and creamy coral reverse, 4½ in., 30-35 petals, high-centered, borne singly, full, best form and color in heat, slight fragrance; foliage large, dark green, semi glossy; prickles moderate; upright, bushy, tall growth; PP10230; [seedling × seedling]; int. by Bear Creek Gardens, Inc., 1997

Arturo Toscanini – See **Elegy**, HT

Aruba HT, mr, Spek; flowers medium size, bright red

Aruba-Caribe HT, pb, 1967, Boerner; bud ovoid; flowers rose-pink and ivory, 5 in., 38 petals, high-centered, intense fruity fragrance; foliage leathery; vigorous, upright growth; PP2779; [(Diamond Jubilee × unknown) × Fashion seedling]; int. by J&P

Aruna HT, or, 1970, Pal, Dr. B.P.; flowers bright orange-scarlet, medium, dbl., cupped; foliage glossy; bushy, compact growth; [Independence × seedling]; int. by Indian Agric. Research Inst., 1968

Arunima F, dp, 1976, IARI; bud ovoid; flowers deep pink, 2 in., 50 petals; foliage glossy; vigorous, bushy, compact growth; [Frolic × seedling]; int. in 1975

Arusha HT, mp; flowers 3 in., 30-35 petals; stems 50-70 cm length; greenhouse rose; int. by Terra Nigra B.V., 2004

Arva Leany A, w, 1911, Geschwind; flowers cream yellow with a delicate carmine tint, large, full, moderate fragrance; growth upright, semi-climbing

As de Coeur – See **Herz As**, HT

Asaborake HT, dy, 1984, Ota, Kaichiro; flowers deep yellow, sometimes tipped pink, large, 30 petals, high-centered, slight fragrance; foliage medium green, semi-glossy; bushy, upright growth; [(Golden Scepter × Narzisse) × Kordes' Perfecta]; int. in 1979

Asagumo HT, yb, 1973, Suzuki, Seizo; bud ovoid; flowers large, dbl., cupped; foliage glossy, dark; vigorous, upright growth; [(Peace × unknown) × Charleston seedling]; int. by Keisei Rose Nursery

Asam Rose HT, dp, Asami; int. in 1994

Asbach F, or, 1960, Leenders, M.; [Ambassadeur Nemry × Cinnabar]

Aschenbrödel Pol, 1903, Lambert, P.; flowers rose with salmon, small, dbl.; bushy, dwarf growth; [Petite Léonie × *R. foetida bicolor*]

Aschermittwoch LCl, w, 1955, Kordes; bud silvery gray; flowers silver-gray white, large, dbl., borne in large trusses; vigorous growth

Aschersoniana S, m, 1880, Münden; flowers bright, light purple, very numerous, small; numerous prickles; growth to 6 ft.; [*R. blanda* × *R. chinensis*]

Ascot F, ab, 1962, Dickson, Patrick; flowers salmon-coral, 4 in., 18 petals, borne in clusters; low growth; [Brownie × seedling]; int. by Dickson, A.

Ascot Bonnet F, m, 2000, Hetzel, Karl; flowers lilac mauve, reverse lilac, 6 cm., dbl., borne in large clusters; foliage medium size, medium green, glossy; few prickles; growth bushy, medium (80-90 cm.); [seedling × seedling]; int. by Eurosa

Ascot Jubilee HT, lp, Welsh, Eric

Asepala M, w, 1840, Foulard/Verdier; flowers white, shaded flesh, sometimes edged rose, petal edges curled, small, dbl.; compact, erect growth

Ash Wednesday – See **Aschermittwoch**, LCl

Asha HT, pb, Agarwal; flowers salmon pink with yellow reverse, large, exhibition, moderate fragrance; int. by Friends Rosery, 1968

Ashgrove Jubilee HT, pb, 1991, Welsh, Eric; flowers cream, shading to deep rose at edges, 30 petals, classic hybrid tea, borne singly, slight fragrance; foliage thick, shiny, dark green, obtuse at base; tall, upright growth; [Mascot × ((seedling × Red Lion) × Silver Lining)]; int. by Rose Hill Roses, 1990

Ashlesha Gr, op, K & S; flowers soft coral apricot, well formed; growth similar to Prima Donna; [sport of Prima Donna]; int. in 2003

Ashley S, ly, John Clements; flowers soft yellow, 4 in., 20 petals, cupped, borne in clusters, intense sweet fragrance; foliage light green; growth sturdy, upright, 4 × 3 ft.; PPAF; int. by Heirloom Roses, 2002

Ashley Marie Min, m, 1995, Bell, Judy G.; flowers light lavender, 1-1½ in., dbl., borne mostly singly; foliage small, dark green, semi-glossy; few prickles; low (14 in.), bushy growth; [Dale's Sunrise × Angel Face]; int. by Michigan Miniature Roses, 1996

Ashley's Surprise Min, m, King; flowers 2-3 in., moderate fragrance; growth tall (2-3 ft.); int. in 1997

Ashram HT, r, Tantau; flowers copper brown orange, dbl., moderate fruity fragrance; growth strong growing; int. by Rosen Tantau, 1998

Ashton MinFl, pb, 2005, Wells, Verlie W.; flowers light pink, reverse light pink edge, 1½-1¾ in., dbl., borne mostly solitary, no fragrance; foliage medium size, medium green, semi-glossy; prickles ¼ in., straight; growth compact, medium (2½ ft.); garden decorative, exhibition; [seedling × Louisville Lady]; int. by Wells Mid-South Roses, 2004

Ashwini '89 HT, dr, K&S; flowers crimson with deep velvety black overtones, large, full; int. in 1989

Asja HT, or, McGredy, Sam IV; int. in 1998

Askari HT, yb, J&P

Asmodée HGal, mr, 1849, Vibert; flowers rosy crimson, large, dbl.

Aspasia – See **Aspasie**, HGal

Aspasie HGal, lp, 1819, Vibert

Aspen S, my, 1996, Olesen, Pernille & Mogens N.; flowers dbl., borne in small clusters, slight fragrance; foliage medium size, dark green, semi-glossy; few prickles; low (14-16 in.), spreading growth; PP9637; int. by DeVor Nurseries, Inc., 1995; Certificate of Merit, Belgium, 1992, 2nd prize, Copenhagen, 1992

Aspen Snow HT, w; int. by Carlton Rose Nurseries, 2002

Aspirant Marcel Rouyer HT, ab, 1919, Pernet-Ducher; bud long, pointed; flowers apricot, tinted salmon-flesh, veined yellow, large, dbl.; foliage glossy, bronze; long, strong stems; very vigorous growth; [Sunburst × seedling]

Aspirant Marcel Rouyer, Climbing Cl HT, ab, 1934, Brenier, E.C.

Aspirin – See **Special Child**, F

Aspirin-Rose – See **Special Child**, F

Assemblage de Beauté(s) HGal, dr, 1823, Delaâge; flowers brilliant crimson, with a small button at center, medium, dbl., slight fragrance; foliage thick, somber green; few prickles; erect growth

Assiniboine S, dp, 1968, Marshall, H.H.; flowers purplish red, large to medium, semi-dbl., slight fragrance; intermittent bloom; foliage glossy; weak stems; vigorous growth; [Donald Prior × *R. arkansana*]; originally registered as HSuff; int. by Canada Dept. of Agric., 1962

Asso di Cuori HT, dr, 1983, Kordes, W.; bud large, ovoid; flowers 30 petals, cupped, moderate fragrance; foliage large, dark; prickles dark green; bushy growth; int. by John Mattock, Ltd, 1981

Asso di Cuori, Climbing Cl HT, dr, Barni; int. by Rosa Barni, 1979

Asso Francesco Baracca HT, pb, 1936, Giacomasso; bud long; flowers golden salmon, center deeper, well-formed, dbl.; long stems; vigorous growth; [Julien Potin × seedling]

Asta von Parpart HMult, m, 1909, Geschwind, R.; bud fat; flowers carmine pink to light purple, lighter edges and reverse, 4-5 cm., dbl., flat, quartered, borne in small clusters, slight sweet fragrance; repeats well; foliage glaucous, tinted blue, sometimes edged red; prickles large; [De La Grifferaie × a HP or B]

Asta von Parpat – See **Asta von Parpart**, HMult

Asterix Min, or, 1986, Lens, Louis; flowers small, 65 petals, flat, borne in clusters of 12-22, no fragrance; prickles hooked, brown; bushy growth; [(Little Red × (Little Angel × Robin Hood)) × Idée Fixe]; int. in 1980

Astolat Charm HT, pb, 1951, Astolat Nursery; flowers flesh-pink, base apricot, 4 in., 30 petals; foliage dark; vigorous growth; [sport of McGredy's Salmon]

Astor Perry HT, dy, 2004, Astor Perry; flowers full, borne mostly solitary, moderate fragrance; foliage medium size, dark green, semi-glossy; prickles average, recurved; growth upright, medium; garden decorative; [Irish Gold × Voo Doo]; int. by Burks, Larry, 2005

Astoria HT, ob, 1963, Delforge; bud pointed; flowers bright orange shaded coral; foliage bronze, glossy; [Opera × Demoiselle]

Astra HT, lp, 1890, Geschwind; flowers flesh pink, sometimes edged lighter, large, full, cupped, borne mostly solitary

Astra Min, mp, 1982, Williams, J. Benjamin; flowers pink, bright yellow stamens, small, 5 petals, borne singly and in small clusters; foliage small, medium green, semi-glossy; short, upright growth; [Pinafore × (Lilibet × Fairy Queen)]; int. by C-P

Astra HT, pb, deRuiter; int. in 1989

Astra – See **Soroptimist International**, Min

Astra Desmond LCl, yb

Astral HT, dp, 1976, Bees; flowers deep rose-pink, low-centered, 4 in., 24 petals, intense fragrance; recurrent; foliage glossy, dark; vigorous growth; [Tropicana × Pink Favorite]

Astral LCl, dr, Croix; flowers deep crimson, large; int. in 1983

Astre Brillant HGal, mp

Astrea Min, m, 1985, Barni, V.

Astrée A, mp, before 1842; flowers pink, changing to delicate lilac blush, very large, very dbl., globular; growth branching

Astrée HT, pb, 1956, Croix, P.; flowers medium pink, reverse shaded orange, large, dbl.; [Peace × Blanche Mallerin]

Astrée, Climbing Cl HT, op, Croix, P.; flowers apricot, edged pink, large, flat; int. in 1960

Astrid Gräfin von Hardenberg S, m, Tantau; flowers warm, intense Bordeaux-red, dbl., intense fragrance; growth to 4-5 ft.; int. by Rosen Tantau, 2002

Astrid Lindgren S, lp, Poulsen; flowers light apricot-pink, 10-15 cm., dbl., borne in clusters, slight raspberry fragrance; foliage dark, glossy; growth bushy, 6-8 ft.; int. in 1991

Astrid Späth – See **Frau Astrid Späth**, F

Astrid Späth Striped F, rb, 1933; flowers soft pink and white with bright carmine striping, slight fragrance; free-flowering; growth to 3 ft.; [sport of Frau Astrid Späth]

Astroïde F, rb; int. in 2004

Astrolabe HMult, mr, 1825, Garilland

Astrorose HT, mr, 1970, Porter; bud long, pointed; flowers cardinal-red to crimson, medium, dbl., moderate fragrance; foliage large, dark, bronze, leathery; vigorous growth; [Helene Schoen × Chrysler Imperial]; int. by Country Gardens Nurs., 1971

Asturias F, rb, 1956, Dot, M.; flowers red, reverse carmine, large, 40 petals, borne in corymbs; foliage glossy; strong stems; very vigorous growth; [Méphisto × Coralín]

Asuka Otome S, pb, 2001, Simizu, Jungi; flowers light pink with deep pink edge, small, single, slight fragrance; foliage small, medium green, matte; growth bushy; [Azumino × Azumino]

Asun Galindez de Chapa HT, pb, 1923, Ketten Bros.; flowers salmon-pink, reverse darker, base yellow; [Mons. Paul Lédé × Jacques Vincent]

Atago HT, or, Keisei Rose Nurseries, Inc.; flowers bright, well-formed

Atalanta LCl, 1927, Williams, A.; bud coppery pink; flowers flesh-pink, dbl.; [Paul Ploton × William Allen Richardson]

Atalante F, mr, 1958, Buyl Frères; flowers geranium-red, large; very vigorous growth

Atalante HT, rb, Adam; int. in 2002

Atar Gull HP, mp, 1858, Avoux / Crozy; flowers bright pink, medium

Atara HT, rb, 1985, Nevo, Motke; flowers medium red, flecked and striped near white, reverse near white with red; [sport of Suspense]; int. by Maoz Haim Rose Nursery, 1974

Atco Royale F, my, Fryer, Gareth; flowers large, pale amber, dbl., borne singly and in clusters, moderate fragrance; foliage bright green, dense; int. by Fryer's Roses, 1994

Atena HT, dy

Athabasca Sp, dp, 1930; flowers deep pink, 15-20 petals; non-recurrent; very vigorous growth; hardy; a *R. macounii* variant, found growing at Vilna, Alberta, Canada, about 1930

Athalie – See **Fanny Bias**, HGal

Athalie P, lp, 1851, Robert; flowers flesh pink, medium, full, cupped

Athalin B, mr, 1830, Jacques; flowers cherry-red, large, cupped

Athanase Coquerel B, m, 1853, Pradel; flowers reddish-violet, medium, full

Athelin HGal

Athena HT, w, 1985, Kordes, W.; flowers clear white, large, 35 petals, moderate fragrance; foliage large, medium green, matte; upright, bushy growth; [seedling × Helmut Schmidt]; greenhouse rose

Athene HT, lp, 1976, Murray & Hawken; bud green; flowers porcelain-pink, base yolk-yellow, 5½ in., 37 petals, intense apple fragrance; foliage large; moderate, bushy growth; [Peace × Diamond Jubilee]; int. by Rasmussen's, 1975

Athene HT, w, Benardella, Frank A.; bud long, pointed; flowers medium size, cream white, dbl., slight fragrance; long stems; growth tall; int. in 1996

Atherton HT, my, 1980, Perry, Astor; bud long, pointed; flowers 35 petals, urn-shaped, borne 1-3 per cluster, moderate fruity fragrance; foliage medium size, matte; prickles small, recurved; medium growth; [seedling × Sunblest]; int. in 1981

Athlete HT, rb, 1965, Barter; flowers nasturtium-red shaded gold, medium, 16 petals, slight fragrance;

foliage light green; bushy growth; [Tzigane × Claude]

Athlone F, yb, 1965, McGredy, Sam IV; flowers cream edged orange-scarlet, open, borne in clusters; foliage small, dark; free growth; [Circus × Cinnabar]

Atholl Grant HT, yb, 2000, Rawlins, R.; flowers yellow suffused red, reverse yellow, medium, very full, borne in small clusters, slight fragrance; foliage medium green, semi-glossy; prickles moderate; growth upright, medium (30 in.); [Chinatown × Remember Me]; int. in 2000

Athos F, ob, 1965, Laperrière; flowers bright orange, large, 28 petals; foliage dark; bushy growth; [Coup de Foudre × Soleil]; int. by EFR

Atida HT, dr, 1941, Sauvageot, H.; flowers velvety dark scarlet, well-formed, quite large, semi-dbl.; very vigorous growth; [Mme Van de Voorde × Dance of Joy]; int. by Sauvageot

Atida HT, mr, Sauvageot; flowers velvety red-purple, dbl.; int. in 1991

Atida 93 HT, Sauvageot, H.; int. in 1993

Atkins Beauty – See **Center Gold**, Min

Atlanta Min, mp, deRuiter; int. in 1992

Atlanta HT, dy, 1992, Lemrow, Dr. Maynard W.; flowers deep clear yellow, long-lasting color, 3-3½ in., dbl., borne mostly singly; foliage medium size, medium green, matte; some prickles; medium (90-120 cm.), upright, bushy, full growth; [Honor × Gingersnap]; int. by Weeks Roses, 1996

Atlantic Gr, or, 1956, Gaujard; flowers medium, semi-dbl., slight fragrance; foliage glossy, dark; [Peace × seedling]

Atlantic City F, rb, 1995, Jolly, Marie; flowers ivory white with dark red blend, large, full, borne mostly singly; foliage medium size, dark green, semi-glossy; few prickles; medium (105 cm.), compact growth; [Crimson Glory × Orange Honey]; int. by Paramount Nursery, 1996

Atlantic Star F, op, Fryer, Gareth; flowers large, soft salmon, dbl., borne in large clusters, moderate fragrance; almost constant; foliage dense, dark green; growth vigorous, 3 ft.; int. by Fryer's Roses, 1993

Atlantida HT, op, 1939, Pahissa; flowers coppery salmon, shaded peach; vigorous growth

Atlantis F, m, 1970, Harkness, R.; flowers deep mauve, 3 in., 5 petals, moderate fragrance; foliage glossy, purple tinted; [Orangeade × Lilac Charm]; int. by J. L. Harkness, 1969; Gold Medal, Rome, 1969

Atlantis – See **Atlantis Palace**, F

Atlantis Palace F, dy, Poulsen; flowers deep yellow, 5-8 cm., dbl., slight wild rose fragrance; foliage dark; growth bushy, 40-60 cm.; PP11638; int. by Poulsen Roser, 1998

Atlas HT, dr, 1970, Delbard-Chabert; bud long, pointed; flowers magenta-red edged darker, large, dbl., cupped; foliage dark, glossy; vigorous, upright, bushy growth; [Chic Parisien × Provence]; int. by Pepinieres G. Delbard, 1966

Atocha Gold S, my, 2006, Ray Ponton; flowers semi-dbl., borne mostly solitary; recurrent; foliage medium green, semi-glossy, disease-resistant; prickles medium, hooked, moderate; growth upright, spreading, medium; hips fragrant; [Lillian Austin × (Carefree Beauty × Reveil Dijonnais)]; int. in 2006

Atoll – See **Clarita**, HT

Atoll F, my, Richardier; int. in 2002

Atoll 99 LCl, Meilland; int. in 1999

Atom Bomb – See **Atombombe**, HEg

Atombombe HEg, mr, 1953, Kordes; bud pointed; flowers deep scarlet-orange, 2½ in., 28 petals, borne in clusters; very vigorous growth; [Obergärtner Wiebicke × Independence]

Atomflash – See **Atombombe**, HEg

Atomic White HT, ly, 1948, Brownell; bud long, pointed; flowers white, center tinted yellow, large, dbl., high-centered, moderate fragrance; vigorous, bushy growth; [Pink Princess × Shades of Autumn]

Atropurpurea – See **Subnigra**, HGal

Atropurpurea HRg, mr, 1899, Paul; flowers carmine-crimson, single, borne in clusters; early summer; vigorous (3-5 ft.) growth; [*R. rugosa* × *R.* × *damascena*]

Atropurpurea Pol, m, 1910, Levavasseur; flowers purple-red; [Mme Norbert Levavasseur × Perle des Rouges]

Attache HT, m; int. by Tantau, 2001

Attar of Roses HT, w, 1936, Cant, B. R.; bud globular; flowers creamy white, edged pink, dbl., cupped; foliage glossy, bronze; long, strong stems; vigorous, bushy, compact growth

Attila A, dp; flowers deep pink, large, semi-dbl., cupped

Attire HT, ob, Ghosh; buds long; flowers orange blended pink, large, dbl.; int. in 1999

Attleborough LCl, mr, 2006, Beales, Amanda; flowers medium red, reverse medium red, 10 cm., full, borne in large clusters; foliage medium size, medium green, glossy; prickles average, curved down, moderate; growth bushy, tall (3-4 m.), climbing; [Paul's Scarlet Climber × Parkdirektor Riggers]; int. by Peter Beales Roses, 2001

Attraction HT, lp, 1886, Dubreuil; bud ovoid; flowers light carmine, nuanced China pink, paler edging, full; foliage matte

Attraction HT, yb, 1931, Dickson, A.; flowers yellow and orange, dbl., globular; foliage glossy, bronze; dwarf, bushy growth

Attractive Cover S, dr, Poulsen; flowers dark red, 5-8 cm., slight wild rose fragrance; foliage dark; growth flat, bushy, 40-60 cm.; PP13270; int. by Poulsen Roser, 2000

Attraktion F, op, 1963, Tantau, Math.; bud long, pointed; flowers salmon-copper, reverse golden yellow, dbl., borne in large clusters; foliage glossy, dark; vigorous, bushy growth

Aubade HT, ob, 1963, Verbeek; flowers yellow-orange, medium, dbl.; foliage dark; [Docteur Valois × seedling]

Auberge de l'Ill S, pb, 2002, Eve; flowers pale pink, 3-4 cm., dbl., pompons, borne in large sprays, slight fragrance; repeats well; foliage medium size, medium green, glossy; prickles moderate; growth low, spreading, bushy (40-50 cm.); [Beauce × seedling]; int. by Les Roses Anciennes de André Eve, 2003

Aubrey Cobden HT, my, 1948, Mee; flowers clear yellow, medium, 30 petals; foliage glossy, stems red; free growth; [Oswald Sieper × seedling]; int. by Fryer's Nursery, Ltd.

Auckland Metro HT, w, 1988, McGredy, Sam IV; flowers large, creamy white, full, intense fragrance; foliage large, dark green, semi-glossy; bushy growth; [Sexy Rexy × (seedling × Ferry Porsche)]; int. by McGredy Roses International, 1988

Audace – See **Carefree Beauty**, S

Audie Murphy HT, mr, 1957, Lammerts, Dr. Walter; bud long, pointed, crimson; flowers 4½-5½ in., 20 petals, high-centered, moderate spicy fragrance; foliage semi-glossy, dark, bronze; vigorous, upright, bushy growth; PP1558; [Charlotte Armstrong × Grande Duchesse Charlotte]; int. by Roseway Nursery, 1956; Gold Medal, Portland, 1957

Audine HT, lp, 1950, Gatward; flowers shell-pink, reflexed, 22 petals, high-centered; foliage dark; vigorous, upright growth; [Percy Izzard × William Moore]

Audobon – See **Audubon**, S

Audrey HT, dr, 1922, Paul, W.; flowers deep crimson, well-formed, high-centered

Audrey Gardner Min, lp, 1990, Pearce, C.A.; bud rounded; flowers shell pink, reverse slightly darker, aging same, large, 45 petals, cupped, borne in sprays of 25-30, no fragrance; foliage small, medium green, semi-glossy; prickles pointed, red; bushy, medium growth; no fruit; [seedling × seedling]; int. by Rearsby Roses, Ltd., 1990

Audrey Harrison Cl HT, ab, 1971, Harrison; flowers pale apricot, 4 in., semi-dbl., intense fragrance; free bloom, early; foliage glossy, dark; [sport of Shot Silk]; int. by Harkness, 1969

Audrey Hepburn HT, lp, 1991, Twomey, Jerry; bud pointed; flowers blush pink, fading to lighter pink, large, 30-32 petals, moderate fruity fragrance; foliage medium size, dark green, glossy; upright, bushy, medium growth; PP7980; [Evening Star × Silver Jubilee]; int. by DeVor Nurseries, Inc., 1991

Audrey Marie F, mr, 1994, Dobbs, Annette E.; flowers medium red, medium, full, borne mostly singly, slight fragrance; foliage medium size, medium green, semi-glossy; some prickles; low (2½ ft.), bushy growth; [Tamanga × Anne Scranton]; int. by Michael's Roses, 1994

Audrey McCormack F, ab, 1999, Kenny, David; flowers soft apricot yellow, 3 in., full, borne in large clusters, moderate fragrance; foliage large, medium green, glossy; numerous prickles; spreading, bushy, medium (3 ft.) growth; [Golden Wedding × Bright Smile]

Audrey Mieklejohn HT, my, Delbard

Audrey Stell HT, pb, 1937, Stell; flowers soft strawberry-pink, reverse sulfur-yellow, semi-dbl.; foliage light; long, strong stems; vigorous, bushy growth; [sport of Soeur Thérèse]; int. by Stell Rose Nursery

Audrey Wilcox HT, rb, 1987, Fryers Nursery, Ltd.; flowers cerise red and silver cream, full, intense fragrance; foliage large, dark green, glossy; [Alpine Sunset × Whisky Mac]; int. in 1985

Audrey's Rose F, m, 2003, Rippetoe, Robert Neil; flowers deep mauve, reverse white, 2¼ in., dbl., borne mostly solitary, intense fragrance; foliage medium size, medium green, semi-glossy, disease-resistant; prickles small, slightly hooked, brown, few; growth bushy, short (2 ft.); bedding, hedges; [Lilac Charm × unknown]; int. by Robert Neil Rippetoe, 2002

Audubon S, mr; flowers 5 petals, no fragrance; growth to 3-4 ft.; int. by Antique Rose Emporium, 2005

Augie Boy Min, rb, 1995, Rennie, Bruce F.; flowers 1-1½ in., dbl., borne mostly singly; foliage medium size, medium green, glossy; few prickles; low (12-15 in.), compact growth; [Party Girl × California Dreaming]; int. by Rennie Roses International, 1994

August Kordes – See **Lafayette**, F

August Noack HT, dr, 1928, Kordes; bud long, pointed; flowers deep scarlet, open, large, dbl., high-centered; foliage bronze, dark; vigorous, bushy growth; [sport of Columbia]

August Noack, Climbing Cl HT, dr, 1935, Lens

August Seebauer F, dp, 1944, Kordes; bud long, pointed; flowers deep rose-pink, large, dbl., high-centered, borne in clusters; foliage glossy; vigorous growth; [Break o' Day × Else Poulsen]

Augusta – See **Solfaterre**, N

Augusta HRg, lp, 1953, Wright, Percy H.; flowers flat, intense fragrance

Augusta S, ab, 1995, Olesen, Pernille & Mogens N.; flowers peach, 2-3 in., dbl.; foliage small, medium green, dull; some prickles; low (24 in.), spreading growth; int. by Young's American Rose Nursery, 1995

Augusta Luise S, pb, Tantau; flowers large, pink to

peach, dbl., intense fruity fragrance; foliage dark green; medium growth; int. by Rosen Tantau, 2000

Auguste Barbier HWich, mp, 1900, Barbier; flowers medium pink to mauve; [L'Idéal × *R. wichurana*]

Auguste Buchner HP, m, 1880, Lévêque; flowers velvety dark purple, shaded scarlet, large, full, slight fragrance

Auguste Chaplain HP, mr, 1921, Tanne; flowers large, dbl.

Auguste Comte T, mp, 1896, Soupert & Notting; flowers outer petals carmine red, center flesh pink, large, dbl.; foliage dark green; [Marie Van Houtte × Mme Lombard]

Auguste Delobel LCl, mr, 1924, Turbat; flowers carmine, large white eye, yellow stamens, borne in clusters

Auguste Finon HMult, yb, 1923, Turbat; flowers golden yellow passing to coppery and salmon, borne in clusters; [Goldfinch × seedling]

Auguste Gervais HWich, ab, 1918, Barbier; flowers coppery yellow and salmon, fading white, 4-5 in., semi-dbl., borne in clusters, moderate fragrance; seasonal bloom; very vigorous, climbing growth; [*R. wichurana* × Le Progrès]

Auguste Guinoisseau HP, dr, 1853, Guinoisseau

Auguste Kordes Cl F, mr, 1928, Kordes; flowers light scarlet, borne in clusters; fine seasonal bloom, later intermittent; vigorous, climbing growth; [sport of Lafayette]

Auguste Mie HP, mp, 1851, Laffay; flowers glossy pink, silvery reverse, large, very full, globular; prickles numerous, straight; [sport of La Reine]

Auguste Neumann HP, mr, 1869, Verdier, V.; flowers poppy red, shaded fiery red, sometimes marbled white, large, full

Auguste Oger T, pb, 1855, Oger; flowers rose pink with copper tints, large, very full, globular

Auguste Renoir HT, mp, 1994, Meilland, Alain A.; bud ovoid; flowers Bengal pink, 3-4 in., 50-65 petals, cupped with flat center, borne mostly singly, moderate fragrance; repeats in flushes; foliage medium size, medium green, semi-glossy; numerous prickles; medium, bushy growth; PP9564; [(Versailles × Pierre de Ronsard) × Kimono]; int. by SNC Meilland & Cie, 1992

Auguste Rigotard HP, mr, 1871, Schwartz

Auguste Rivière T, yb, 1853, Lacharme

Auguste Rivière – See **Souv d'Auguste Rivière**, HP

Auguste Roussel LCl, pb, 1913, Barbier; flowers salmon-pink to flesh-pink, well-formed, petals undulated, large, semi-dbl., borne in clusters of 5-12; seasonal bloom; very vigorous, climbing growth; [*R. macrophylla* × Papa Gontier]

Auguste Vacher T, yb, 1853, Lacharme; flowers yellow, shaded copper, medium, full

Auguste Vermare HT, or, 1958, Arles; bud pointed; flowers coral-red; vigorous, upright growth; [Comtesse Vandal × seedling]; int. by Roses-France

Auguste Victoria S, dy; int. in 1999

Augustine Bertin HGal, dp, 1818, Vibert

Augustine Guinoiseau HT, lp, 1889, Guinoiseau fils; flowers white, tinted light flesh, large, full; [sport of La France]

Augustine Halem HT, dp, 1891, Guillot, J. B.; flowers carmine rose, shaded with purple, medium, full, globular

Augustine Margat B, mp; flowers bright pink, reverse lighter, medium, very full, cupped

Augustine Pourprée – See **Marie-Louise**, D

Augustus Hartmann HT, dp, 1914, Cant, B. R.; flowers Tyrian rose, large, dbl., slight fragrance; foliage rich green, leathery; vigorous growth; Gold Medal, NRS, 1914

Augustus Hartmann, Climbing Cl HT, Fineschi, G.; int. in 1980

Augustus Stone HT, ab, 1999, Poole, Lionel; flowers light apricot/amber, resist bad weather, 4-4½ in., full, borne in small clusters, moderate fragrance; foliage medium size, dark green, dull; some prickles; bushy, medium (3 ft.) growth; [Gavotte × Pot of Gold]; int. by David Lister, Ltd., 2000

Auld Lang Syne HT, ob, 1957, Motose; bud ovoid; flowers orange edged pale orange-yellow, 4 in., 35-45 petals, moderate fruity fragrance; bushy growth; PP1500; [Tawny Gold × (Talisman × Tawny Gold)]

Aunt Belle's Tea T, pb

Aunt Gerry HT, ly, 1992, Sheldon, John & Jennifer; flowers golden yellow, 3-3½ in., 35 petals, slight spicy fragrance; foliage medium size, medium green, semi-glossy; prickly peduncle; medium (90-120 cm.), upright, very vigorous growth; [sport of Lanvin]; int. by Trophy Roses, Ltd., 1992

Aunt Harriet HWich, rb, 1918, Van Fleet; flowers scarlet-crimson, white eye, yellow stamens, semi-dbl.; vigorous growth; [Apolline × *R. wichurana*]; int. by Phila. Farm Journal

Aunt Honey S, mp, 1985, Buck, Dr. Griffith J.; bud large, ovoid; flowers large, rose-pink shading lighter toward outer petals, 4-5 in., 36-42 petals, high-centered, borne 5-10 per cluster, moderate damask fragrance; repeat bloom; foliage medium size, dark olive-green; prickles awl-like, tan; erect, short, bushy growth; hardy; [Music Maker × Habanera]; int. by Iowa State University, 1984

Aunt Lucy S, w, Williams, J.B.; buds amber yellow; flowers ivory with yellow stamens, single; foliage dark green; growth upright, vigorous; int. by Hortico, 2003

Aunt Rosie HT, pb, 2001, Hiltner, Martin J.; flowers 3-3½ in., dbl., borne mostly solitary; foliage medium size, medium green, semi-glossy; prickles ¼ in., curving down, moderate; growth upright, medium (2½-3 ft.); garden decorative, exhibition; [Lynn Anderson × Dublin]

Aunt Ruth LCl, pb, 1995, Jerabek; flowers streaked medium pink, white eye, reverse white streaked pink, 3 in., semi-dbl., borne in small and large clusters, slight fragrance; foliage medium size, medium green, semi-glossy; few prickles; growth bushy, spreading

Auntie Louise Min, ob, 2004, Jalbert, Brad; flowers orange tinged pink, reverse lighter orange, 1¼ in., full, borne in small clusters, slight fragrance; foliage medium size, medium green, semi-glossy; prickles medium, reddish brown, numerous; growth spreading, medium (14-16 in.); containers, garden decorative; [Orange Honey × Sexy Rexy]; int. in 1999

Aunty Dora F, m, 1970, Deamer; flowers magenta, semi-dbl., borne in trusses; low growth; [Dearest × Lilac Charm]; int. by Warley Rose Gardens

Aunty Lil F, yb, 1995, Kenny, David; flowers yellow edged pink, fades to pink, medium, full, borne in large clusters, slight fragrance; foliage medium size, medium green, glossy; some prickles; medium, upright growth; [(Friesia × Kiskadee) × (Mary Sumner × Regensberg)]; int. in 1994

Aurea – See **Aureus**, T

Aurea HT, yb, 1948, Dot; flowers yellow, reverse red, well-formed, moderate fruity fragrance; foliage glossy; vigorous growth

Aurea HT, dy, Meilland; int. in 1987

Aureate HT, ob, 1932, Dickson, A.; flowers orange and scarlet to yellow, large, dbl.; foliage bronze; vigorous, bushy growth; Gold Medal, NRS, 1929

Aurelia Capdevila HT, pb, 1933, Dot, Pedro; flowers pink, base salmon; foliage dark; vigorous growth

Aurelia Liffa HSet, mr, 1886, Geschwind, R.; flowers carmine with magenta tints, 4-6 cm., dbl., borne in small clusters, slight fragrance; numerous prickles; growth tall (3-4 m.), upright; very winter hardy; [*R. setigera* × Marie Baumann]

Aurelia Weddle HT, or, Weddle, Von C.; flowers 65 petals, exhibition; heat tolerant; int. in 1995

Aurélien Igoult HMult, m, 1924, Igoult; flowers bluish-violet, shaded reddish, medium, semi-dbl.; vigorous, climbing growth; [Veilchenblau × seedling]; int. by Bruant

Aureola HT, my, 1934, Böhm, J.; flowers golden yellow; [sport of Mev. G.A. van Rossem]

Auréole HT, ob, 1951, Gaujard; bud large; flowers orange-yellow, semi-dbl.; foliage glossy, dark; very vigorous growth

Aureus T, yb, 1873, Ducher; flowers coppery yellow, medium, full

Auria HT, mr, Richardier; flowers clear red, very dbl., moderate citrus fragrance; growth to 70-100 cm.; int. in 1999

Auriol Pol, rb, 1930, Alderton

Auriu de Cluj F, yb, Wagner, S.; flowers flat, 15 petals, slight fragrance; foliage medium size, light green, glossy; int. in 1984

Aurora – See **Celestial**, A

Aurora HT, op, 1898, Paul, W.; bud very long; flowers salmon towards center, paler edges, large, full; foliage dark green

Aurora HMsk, ly, 1928, Pemberton; flowers yellow, passing to creamy white, medium, single, borne in small clusters, moderate fragrance; [Danaë × Miriam]

Aurora F, op, 1941, Leenders, M.; flowers salmon-pink tinted golden yellow and orange, dbl.; [Mev. Nathalie Nypels × seedling]; Gold Medal, Bagatelle, 1940

Aurora HKor, ob, 1956, Kordes; flowers orange-yellow outside, pinker within, large, dbl., borne in small clusters; non-recurrent; foliage dark green, glossy; vigorous growth; very hardy

Aurora F, my

Aurora HT, mr, Strnad

Aurora (variety of *R. acicularis*), mr; flowers have wide, thick petals, 5 petals, borne singly; non-remontant; foliage red and purple in fall; prickles to the end of the branch

Aurora Boreal HT, rb, 1935, Munné, B.; flowers geranium, shaded fiery red, semi-dbl.; foliage dark; very vigorous growth; [Étoile de Hollande × (Ville de Paris × Sensation)]

Aurore – See **Celestial**, A

Aurore HP, mp, 1861, Laffay, M.

Aurore Ch, yb, 1897, Widow Schwartz; flowers yellow passing to salmon-pink, loose; recurrent bloom; [Mme Laurette Messimy × unknown]

Aurore HT, pb, 1936, Capiago; flowers pink, base yellow, dbl.; vigorous growth

Aurore F, or

Aurore Boréale HP, mr, 1865, Oger; flowers large, full; remontant

Aurore de Guide B, dr, 1849, Thomas; flowers red, shaded violet, full, globular

Aurore de Jacques-Marie S, yb, Guillot-Massad; flowers white and pale yellow, fading pink, borne in small clusters; growth compact; int. by Roseraies Guillot, 2001

Aurore d'Enghien HGal, m, about 1830, Parmentier; flowers bright dawn pink, medium, full

Aurore d'Espagne HT, pb, 1966, Dot; bud long, pointed; flowers salmon-pink to nankeen yellow, medium, semi-dbl., cupped; vigorous growth; [Zambra × Queen Elizabeth]; int. by Minier

Aurore du Matin HP, mr, 1867, Rolland; flowers light red, reverse silvery, large, dbl., intense fragrance

Aurore Lassalle S, mp, Gilet; int. by Les Rosiers du Berry, 2005

Aurore Sand LCl, pb, 1964, Robichon; flowers two-tone soft pink and copper, 5 in., dbl., moderate fragrance; recurrent bloom; vigorous growth; [Mme Moisans × Odette Joyeux]; Gold Medal, Bagatelle, 1963

Ausonius HMsk, pb, 1932, Lambert, P.; buds oval, yellow-red; flowers yellowish-pink, center white, medium, semi-dbl., borne in pyramidal trusses of 20-50, moderate fragrance; free, recurrent bloom; foliage leathery; semi-climbing, bushy growth; [(Chamisso × Léonie Lamesch) × (Geheimrat Dr. Mittweg × Tip-Top)]

Austin Jace Min, m, 2005, Ellerman, Gigi; flowers mauve, reverse mauve, small, full, borne mostly solitary; foliage medium size, medium green, matte; prickles average, slight curve, few; growth bushy, medium; [sport of Black Jade]; int. in 2005

Austragold HT, my, 1980, McGredy, Sam IV; flowers non-fading yellow; stems strong; growth medium

Austral HT, Bees; int. in 1976

Australia Fair F, pb, 2001, Thomson, George L.; flowers soft pink, slightly darker reverse, 1 in., dbl., borne in large clusters, moderate fragrance; foliage medium size, medium green, semi-glossy; prickles medium, hooked, moderate, brown; growth compact, low (1 m.); garden decorative; [Tombot × (Madam President × unknown)]; int. by Ross Roses, 2001

Australia Felix HT, pb, 1919, Clark, A.; bud small, globular; flowers pink and silver shaded lavender, semi-dbl., cupped; foliage dark, glossy; vigorous, bushy growth; [Jersey Beauty × La France]

Australian Beauty Cl HP, mr, 1907, Kerslake; flowers crimson, moderate fragrance; [President × Lord Macaulay]

Australian Bicentennial HT, lp, Bell, Ronald J.; [Daily Sketch × Red Planet]; int. in 1987

Australian Centenary of Federation – See **Rebell**, HT, 2006

Australian Centre Gold – See **Center Gold**, Min

Australian Gold F, ab, 1981, Kordes; bud ovoid; flowers apricot-peach, 20 petals, borne 5 per cluster, moderate fragrance; foliage dark, leathery; prickles red; bushy growth; int. by John Mattock, Ltd, 1980

Australian Sunrise S, rb, 2001, Spriggs, Ian Raymond; flowers cherry red, darker reverse, 10 cm., single, borne in small clusters, intense fragrance; foliage medium size, dark green, semi-glossy; prickles moderate; growth upright, tall (1¾ m.); garden decorative, cutting; [Altissimo × (Munchen × Erfurt)]; int. by Thomas for Roses, 2000

Australia's Olympic Gold Rose Rose – See **Golden Eagle**, Gr

Australie HT, dp, 1907, Kerslake; flowers large, dbl.

Austriaca – See **Rosier d'Amour**, HGal

Austrian Brier – See ***R. foetida*** (Herrmann)

Austrian Copper – See ***R. foetida bicolor*** ((Jacquin) Willmott)

Austrian Yellow – See ***R. foetida*** (Herrmann)

Austriana F, mr, 2000, Tantau, Math.; flowers small, single, borne in large clusters, no fragrance; foliage medium size, dark green, glossy, disease-resistant; prickles moderate; growth compact, low; [seedling × seedling]; int. by Rosen Tantau, 1996

Autocrat HT, pb, 1925, Beckwith; flowers ochre to flesh-pink, reverse prawn-red, large

Autograph HT, pb, 2000, Mattia, John; flowers deep pink, reverse light pink, striped white, 4½ in., very full, high-centered, borne mostly singly, slight fragrance; foliage medium size, medium green, semi-glossy; prickles moderate; growth upright, medium (4-5 ft.); [sport of Signature]; int. in 2003

Autumn HT, ob, 1928, Coddington; bud deep burnt orange; flowers burnt-orange, streaked red, medium, 20-25 petals, cupped, moderate fragrance; foliage dark, glossy; [Sensation × Souv. de Claudius Pernet]

Autumn, Climbing Cl HT, ob, 1951, deVor, W.L.; int. by Amling-DeVor Nursery

Autumn Bliss MinFl, yb, 2005, Wells, Verlie, W.; flowers odd shade of yellow, 1 in., full, borne mostly solitary; foliage medium size, medium green, semi-glossy; prickles ¼ in., straight, few; growth upright, medium (2-3 ft.); exhibition, garden decorative; [seedling × seedling]; int. Wells' MidSouth Roses, by 2005

Autumn Bouquet S, mp, 1948, Jacobus; bud long, pointed; flowers carmine-rose-pink, large, dbl.; recurrent bloom; foliage leathery; vigorous, upright, compact growth; [New Dawn × Crimson Glory]; int. by B&A

Autumn Damask D, mp, before 1849; flowers pink, lighter at edges, less full than *R. × damascena*, dbl., borne singly or in small clusters, moderate fragrance; foliage light gray-green, oval, with 5-7 leaflets

Autumn Dawn Min, op, 1999, Bridges, Dennis A.; flowers orange-pink, reverse slightly lighter, 1¼ in., dbl.; foliage medium size, dark green, semi-glossy; prickles moderate; spreading, medium (2 ft.) growth; [Carrot Top × unknown]; int. by Bridges Roses, 2000

Autumn Days F, ob

Autumn Delight HMsk, w, 1933, Bentall; flowers white with red stamens, large, single, borne in large clusters, moderate fragrance

Autumn Dusk Gr, pb, 1976, Buck, Dr. Griffith J.; bud ovoid, pointed; flowers pale Tyrian rose and white, 3½-4½ in., 33 petals, high-centered; foliage leathery; upright, bushy growth; [Music Maker × (Dornröschen × Peace)]; int. by Iowa State University, 1975

Autumn Fire – See **Herbstfeuer**, HEg

Autumn Fire Min, or, 1983, Moore, Ralph S.; flowers small, semi-dbl.; foliage small, medium green, semi-glossy; bushy, very spreading growth; [Little Chief × Anytime]; int. by Moore Miniature Roses, 1982

Autumn Flame HT, ob, 1953, Thomson; bud long, pointed; flowers orange-yellow tinted red, 4 in., 35-40 petals, cupped; foliage dark, leathery; upright, bushy, compact growth; [Ednah Thomas × Autumn]

Autumn Frost Min, w, 1983, Rose, Euie; flowers medium, 35 petals, high-centered; foliage medium size, medium green, semi-glossy; bushy growth; [seedling × seedling]; int. by Little Gems Mini Rose Nursery

Autumn Glow HT, ob, 1979, Anderson's Rose Nurseries; bud pear shaped; flowers yellow-orange, 5 in., 55 petals, high-centered, slight fragrance; foliage small; bushy growth; [Pascali × Bayadère]; int. in 1978

Autumn Gold HT, yb, 1975, Weeks; bud pointed; flowers brown-butterscotch-yellow, 3½-4 in., 42 petals, globular, moderate fragrance; foliage glossy, dark, leathery; tall, upright growth; PP3710; [seedling × seedling]; int. by O. L. Weeks, 1974

Autumn Hues F, ob, 1962, Von Abrams; bud pointed; flowers orange, yellow and scarlet, 3-3½ in., 35 petals, high-centered, borne in clusters; foliage glossy; upright growth; [Pinocchio × Fred Edmunds]; int. by Peterson & Dering

Autumn Kiss Min, mp, 1994, Walsh, Richard Bruce; flowers medium salmon pink, medium, dbl., borne in small clusters, slight fragrance; foliage small, dark green, glossy; few prickles; medium, upright growth; [Ginger Meggs × Avandel]; int. by Fradee Nursery

Autumn Leaves – See **English Elegance**, S

Autumn Magic Min, ob, 1987, Jacobs, Betty A.; very long and feathery sepals; flowers bright golden-orange, with red at petal tips, reverse yellow, fading to red, 35 petals, high-centered; foliage medium size, dark green, semi-glossy; prickles very few; bushy, medium growth; no fruit; [Confetti × Anita Charles]; int. by Four Seasons Rose Nursery

Autumn Moon – See **Shu-getsu**, HT

Autumn Queen HT, ob, 1933, Vestal; bud long, pointed; flowers burnt-orange, pink, gold, open, semi-dbl.; foliage leathery, bronze; vigorous, bushy growth

Autumn Shades Min, lp, Hannemann, F.; [Silver Jubilee × Oz Gold]; int. by The Rose Paradise, 1997

Autumn Song – See **Pure Poetry**, F

Autumn Spice HT, ob, 2005, Smith, John T.; flowers brilliant orange, reverse yellow, 4½-5 in., full, high-centered, borne mostly solitary; foliage medium size, dark green, semi-glossy; prickles medium, straight slightly downward, red, moderate; growth compact, medium (3½-4 ft.); hedging; [Gemini × Donna Darling]; int. by same, 2007

Autumn Splendor MinFl, yb, 1999, Williams, Michael C.; flowers yellow tinted orange and red, 2 in., full, high-centered, borne mostly singly, slight fragrance; foliage large, medium green, semi-glossy; upright, tall (30-40 in.) growth; int. by The Mini Rose Garden, 1999; Award of Excellence, ARS, 1999

Autumn Spray F, yb, 1964, Norman; flowers gold edged red, 3 in., 40 petals, flat; foliage glossy; [Masquerade × Isobel Harkness]; int. by Harkness

Autumn Sunblaze Min, or, 1996, Selection Meilland; bud conical; flowers bright vermilion, reverse red, 4 cm., 40-45 petals, cupped, borne in clusters of 6-15, no fragrance; recurrent; foliage medium size, medium green, semi-glossy; prickles numerous, small, pinkish; medium (24 in.), bushy growth; heat tolerant; PP9652; [(Bonfire Night × Orange Symphonie) × Orange Jewel]; int. by Conard-Pyle Co., 1995

Autumn Sunlight LCl, or, 1965, Gregory; flowers orange-vermilion, medium, 30 petals, semi-globular, borne in small clusters, moderate fragrance; foliage glossy, bright green; [Spectacular × Goldilocks, Climbing]

Autumn Sunset S, ab, 1987, Lowe, Malcolm; flowers medium apricot, with touches of orange and golden yellow, fading lighter, 20 petals, cupped, intense fruity fragrance; repeat bloom; foliage medium size, medium green, glossy, disease-resistant; prickles curved, medium, red; bushy, tall, climbing growth; hips round, medium, orange; [sport of Westerland]; int. by Lowe's Own Root Roses, 1988

Autumn Tints HT, yb, 1914, Cant, B. R.; flowers coppery-pink with yellow, medium, dbl.

Autumnalis – See ***R. moschata*** (Herrmann)

Aux Cent Écus – See **Belle Laure**, HSpn

Auzou – See **Couture**, HCh

Ava Rose F, yb, McCann, Sean; flowers light yellow, flushed pink, semi-dbl., moderate fragrance; recurrent; medium (3-5 ft.) growth; [Playboy × unknown]; int. by Ashdown Roses

Avalanch II S, w, Williams, J. Benjamin; groundcover; spreading growth; int. in 1998

Avalanche HT, w, 1922, Lippiatt; flowers creamy white, center deeper, dbl.

Avalanche HT, w, 1936, Chambard, C.; bud long; flowers large; foliage slightly bronze; vigorous, bushy, compact growth

Avalanche F, w, Warriner, William A.; bud cream color; flowers cream changing to white, borne in clusters; growth vigorous, medium; int. in 1991

Avalanche HT, w; int. by K & M Nursery, 2004

Avalanche II – See **Avalanch II**, S

Avalanche Rose F, mr, 1986, Delbard; flowers large, dbl.; vigorous, bushy growth; [(François et Joseph Guy × (Sultane × Unknown)) × (Alain × Étoilede Hollande)]; int. in 1977

Avalanche Rose S, mp, Delbard; flowers single; int. by

Georges Delbard SA, 2002

Avalon HT, ab, 1935, Western Rose Co.; bud ovoid; flowers apricot-yellow, center deeper, very large, dbl., globular; foliage glossy, bronze; vigorous, bushy growth; [sport of Duchess of Atholl]; int. by Germain's

Avance S, mp, 1999, Barni, V.; flowers medium size, strong color, dbl., borne in large clusters; blooms all season; growth compact (40-60 cm.); int. by Rose Barni, 1999

Avandel Min, yb, 1977, Moore, Ralph S.; bud long, pointed; flowers pink-yellow blend, 1-1½ in., 23 petals, cupped to flat, moderate fruity fragrance; foliage medium to dark green, leathery; upright, bushy growth; PP4366; [Little Darling × New Penny]; int. by Sequoia Nursery; AOE, ARS, 1978

Avant-Garde HT, rb, Delbard; flowers striped; int. in 2003

Avant Garde HT, m, Schreurs, P.N.J.; flowers pale lilac with deeper edges, pointed petals, large, dbl., high-centered, borne mostly singly, slight fragrance; repeats in flushes; foliage dark green; few prickles; int. by Carlton Rose Nurseries, 2005

Avanti HT, rb, Teranishi; flowers single; int. in 1966

Avanti HT, dr, 1990, Warriner, William A. & Zary, Keith W.; bud ovoid, pointed; flowers dark red, hint of blue reverse, aging dark, dark red, large, 25-30 petals, high-centered, urn-shaped, slight fruity fragrance; foliage medium to large, dark green, matte to semi-glossy; upright, bushy, tall growth; [Royalty × Samantha]; int. by Bear Creek Gardens, 1990

Ave Maria Pol, w, 1933, Bohm; growth compact, low (24-32 in.); [sport of Ulster]

Ave Maria HT, w, 1960, Brownell; flowers pure white, well-formed, 4-6 in., dbl.; vigorous, bushy growth; RULED EXTINCT 12/85; [seedling × Break o' Day, Climbing]; int. by Stern's Nursery, 1957

Ave Maria HT, op; int. by Kordes, 1972

Ave Maria HT, op, 1986, Kordes, W.; flowers orange-salmon, large, 35 petals, high-centered, borne singly, moderate fragrance; foliage large, medium green, semi-glossy; prickles small; upright growth; [Uwe Seeler × Sonia]; int. by Kordes, 1981

Avebury LCl, lp, McLeod, J.; int. by Honeysuckle Cottage, 1995

Avenant – See **Belle Biblis**, HGal

Avenir B, mp, 1858, Lartay; flowers bright pink, center darker, large, full

Avenir HWich, lp, 1910, Corboeuf; flowers whitish pink, 3-4 cm., semi-dbl., borne in large clusters

Avenir HT, Godin; int. in 1980

Aventure HT, or, 1964, Croix, P.; flowers large, 55 petals, high-centered, slight fragrance; foliage leathery, glossy; vigorous, upright, bushy growth; PP2500; [(Corail × Baccará) × seedling]; int. by C-P, 1965

Aventure No. 2 HT, ob, Croix

Avenue's Red – See **Konrad Henkel**, HT

Aveu HT, dp, Croix; flowers large, dbl.

Aviateur Blériot HWich, yb, 1910, Fauque; flowers pale orange-yellow, fading white, 6-7 cm., 34 petals, borne in clusters, moderate magnolia fragrance; non-recurrent; foliage small, glossy, dark green; vigorous, climbing growth; [*R. wichurana* × William Allen Richardson]

Aviateur Michel Mahieu HT, mp, 1912, Soupert & Notting; flowers coral-red, center brighter, large, dbl., intense fragrance; [Mme Mélanie Soupert × Lady Ashtown]

Aviator Parmentier HT, op, 1941, Verschuren-Pechtold; bud long, pointed; flowers peach-pink to orange, 4-4½ in., 30-35 petals, high-centered; foliage glossy; very vigorous growth; [seedling × Briarcliff]; int. by J. Parmentier

Avignon F, my, 1974, Cants of Colchester, Ltd.; flowers dbl., 23 petals; foliage light, glossy; vigorous growth; [Zambra × Allgold]

Aviora HT, mr, 1960, Verbeek; flowers clear red, 40 petals; foliage glossy, dark; very large growth; [Happiness × seedling]

Avô Albina HT, rb, 1956, Moreira da Silva; flowers crimson, reverse silvery, large, high-centered; very vigorous growth; [Peace × Crimson Glory]

Avô Alfredo HT, rb, 1956, Moreira da Silva; flowers spectrum-red, reverse carmine; [seedling × Independence]

Avoca HT, mr, 1907, Dickson, A.; flowers crimson-scarlet, large, dbl., high-centered; very vigorous growth

Avocat Duvivier HP, m, 1875, Lévêque; flowers dbl.; [Général Jacqueminot × unknown]

Avocat L. Lambert HP, mp, 1884, Besson; flowers silky pink, center white, large, full

Avocet F, ob, 1983, Harkness, R., & Co., Ltd.; bud pointed; flowers orange edged vermilion, large, semi-dbl., borne in large clusters; foliage dark, glossy; prickles numerous, dark; medium, bushy growth; [Dame of Sark × seedling]; int. in 1984

Avon HT, dr, 1961, Morey, Dr. Dennison; bud ovoid; flowers 4½-5½ in., 23 petals, high-centered, intense fragrance; foliage leathery; vigorous, upright growth; PP2154; [Nocturne × Chrysler Imperial]; int. by J&P, 1961

Avon, Climbing Cl HT, dr, 1975, Kumar, S.

Avon – See **Niagara**, S

Avril Elizabeth Home – See **Heaven on Earth**, F

Avril Sherwood F, my, 1976, Sherwood; bud ovoid; flowers golden yellow fading to buttercup-yellow, 3-3½ in., 18 petals, slight fragrance; foliage glossy, dark, leathery; upright growth; [Pink Parfait × Allgold]; int. by F. Mason, 1975

Awakening LCl, lp, 1992, Böhm, J.; flowers medium, full, quartered, moderate fragrance; [sport of New Dawn]; brought from Czechoslovia to England by R. Balfour and re-introduced; int. as Probuzeni, Blatna, 1935

Award HT, mr, 1953, Taylor, C.A.; flowers velvety red; foliage very glossy, dark; short stems; vigorous growth; [Will Rogers × Mme Henri Guillot]

Awareness HT, dp, Fryer, Gareth; flowers bright pink, full, high-centered, borne singly and in clusters; recurrent; vigorous, medium growth; int. by Fryer's Roses, 1997

Awayuki S, w

Axeline LCl, mp

Axelle HT, Gaujard; int. in 1964

Ayaka F, w, Yasuda

Ayako Gr, ly, 1991, Maltagliati, Mark G.; flowers pale yellow cream, large, full, slight fragrance; foliage medium size, medium green, semi-glossy; medium, upright growth; [sport of Sonia]; int. by Nino-miya Nursery Co., 1990

Ayaori F, rb

Ayez – See **Spectabilis**, HSem

Aylsham S, dp, 1948, Wright, Percy H.; bud ovoid; flowers deep pink, large, dbl.; non-recurrent; foliage light green, glossy; vigorous (to 5 ft.) growth; [Hansa × *R. nitida*]

Ayrshire Queen Ayr, dr, 1835, Rivers; flowers purplish crimson, large, semi-dbl.; [Blush Ayrshire × Tuscany]

Ayrshire Rose Misc OGR, pb, 1790; buds rosy pink; flowers medium size, white, dbl., borne in heavy bloom; once bloomer; strong growth to 5-7 m.; very frost hardy

Ayrshire Splendens – See **Splendens**, Ayr

Ayrshirea – See **Ayrshire Rose**, Misc OGR

Azafran HT, my, Meilland; flowers saffron yellow, dbl., exhibition; greenhouse rose; int. by Meilland International, 2004

Azalea Rose Pol, mp, 1940, Griffing Nursery; flowers bright rose-pink, resemble azaleas; [sport of Ellen Poulsen]

Azeez F, op, 1969, Pal, Dr. B.P.; bud pointed; flowers coral-pink, reverse lighter, medium, dbl., high-centered; foliage leathery; upright, compact growth; int. by Indian Agric. Research Inst., 1965

Azelda HT, op, 1963, Matthews; bud long, pointed; flowers coral-rose, dbl., cupped; foliage glossy, light green; long stems; vigorous, upright growth; [Queen Elizabeth × Rosenelfe]

Aztec HT, or, 1957, Swim, H.C.; bud long, pointed; flowers scarlet-orange, 4-5 in., 25 petals, high-centered, moderate fragrance; foliage glossy, leathery; vigorous, spreading growth; PP1648; [Charlotte Armstrong × seedling]; int. by Armstrong Nursery, 1957

Aztec Gold Gr, dy, Winchel, J.; flowers golden yellow, dbl., very slight fragrance; foliage glossy; stems sturdy; tall growth; int. in 2006

Azubis – See **Indigoletta**, LCl dbl.

Azubis LCl, m, van den Laak; flowers large, lilac, intense fragrance; growth to 10 ft.; int. in 1981

Azulabria – See **Blue Peter**, Min

Azumino Cl Min, rb, Onodera; flowers single; int. in 1983

Azur F, m, 1979, Lens; bud ovoid; flowers deep lavender-mauve, pointed, 2½-3 in., 15 petals, intense fragrance; foliage dark reddish-green; vigorous, compact, bushy growth; [Sterling Silver × (Gold Strike × Golden Garnette)]; int. in 1967

Azure Sea HT, m, 1983, Christensen, Jack E.; flowers silvery lavender, petals edged ruby, deeper reverse, well-formed, large, 30 petals; foliage large, dark, matte; upright, bushy growth; PP5693; [(Angel Face × First Prize) × Lady X]; int. by Armstrong Nursery

Azusa Min, mr, Takatori

B. C. Min, dr, 1986, King, Gene; flowers dark red, reverse darker, 24 petals, high-centered; foliage small, medium green, matte; prickles long, hooked, brown; medium, upright, bushy growth; globular fruit; [Evelyn Fison × Magic Mist]; int. by AGM Miniature Roses

B. S. Bhatcharji HT, my, 1933, Dickson, A.; flowers buttercup-yellow, well-formed, large; foliage glossy, dark; vigorous growth

B. W. Price HT, mp, 1943, McGredy; bud long, pointed; flowers cerise-pink, open, large, 6-8 petals; foliage soft; vigorous, upright, bushy growth; [Night × Mme Butterfly]; int. by J&P

Babe Pol, pb, Hazelwood; int. in 1958

Babe Min, mp, Lougheed; int. by Lamrock's Little Roses, 2004

Babe Ruth HT, op, 1950, Howard, F.H.; bud ovoid; flowers coral, reverse rose-coral, 4-4½ in., 35-40 petals, cupped, moderate fragrance; foliage leathery, glossy, bronze; vigorous, upright growth; [Los Angeles × seedling]; int. by H&S

Babet D, lp, before 1838; flowers flesh pink, medium, full

Babette – See **Babet**, D

Babette HWich, mr, 1906, Walsh; flowers carmine-red, 4 cm., semi-dbl. to dbl., borne in large clusters; non-recurrent; foliage glossy; Ruled extinct 1970 ARA

Babette F, m, 1970, Gaujard; flowers lavender-pink, small, single, cupped, slight fragrance; foliage leathery, small; vigorous, bushy growth; [seedling × Eminence]

Babette HT, op, Kordes; flowers medium size, salmon pink, dbl., exhibition, no fragrance; stems medium; growth tall (2 m.); int. in 1999

Babette Stutzer – See **Babette**, HT

Babs – See **Coton Gold**, HT

Babt Deitz Pol, or, 1924, Opdebeeck; flowers oriental red, edged salmon, dbl.

Baby Abel Chatenay Pol, op, 1914, Altmüller; flowers salmon pink, medium, full

Baby Alan Pol, mp, 1930, Kessler; flowers shining pink, very dbl., daisy-like, borne in clusters; int. by J.T. Lovett

Baby Alberic Pol, ly, 1932, Chaplin Bros.; bud yellow; flowers creamy white, small, dbl.; recurrent bloom; vigorous growth

Baby Allan Pol, mp, 1930, Kessler; flowers glossy pink, small, very full

Baby Ashley Min, yb, 1985, King, Gene; flowers light yellow, petals edged light pink, 24 petals, borne singly and in cluster of 3-5; foliage small, dark, matte; prickles straight, small, light brown; bushy growth; int. by AGM Miniature Roses

Baby Austin Min, ab, 2002, Moore, Ralph S.; flowers peach/pink, peach/apricot reverse, micro-mini, 1 in., full, cupped/quartered, borne in small clusters, slight fragrance; foliage small, medium green, semi-glossy; prickles small, straight, few, green; growth bushy, short (10-12 in.); [Joycie × seedling]; int. by Sequoia Nursery, 2001

Baby Baccará Min, or, 1965, Meilland, Alain A.; flowers orange-scarlet, 1½ in., dbl.; foliage dark; [Callisto × Perla de Alcañada]; int. by URS

Baby Baccara Min, mr, Meilland; flowers dbl., borne in clusters; growth compact (40-45 cm.); int. by Meilland Richardier, 2002

Baby Ballerina Min, pb, Villegas; flowers deep pink lightening to white near the center, 5 petals, borne in clusters; spreading growth, 2 ft. high by 4-5 ft. wide; int. in 1997

Baby Bath Pol, mp, Robinson; flowers tiny, rosette, borne in tight clusters, moderate sweet fragrance; good repeat; very dwarf, compact growth; int. in 1989

Baby Betsy McCall Min, lp, 1960, Morey, Dr. Dennison; flowers micro-mini, 1 in., 20 petals, cupped, moderate fragrance; foliage leathery, light green; vigorous, dwarf, compact (8 in.) growth; PP1984; [Cécile Brünner × Rosy Jewel]; int. by J&P, 1960

Baby Bettina Min, or, 1981, Meilland, Mrs. Marie-Louise; bud ovoid; flowers vermilion, reverse carmine, deep, mini-flora, 15-20 petals, cupped, borne 3-11 per cluster, slight fragrance; foliage matte, dense; vigorous growth; [(Callisto × Perla de Alcañada) × Starina]; int. by Meilland Cie, 1977

Baby Betty Pol, mp, 1929, Burbage Nursery; bud ovoid, yellow, tinged red; flowers pink, base lighter, small, dbl., cupped; abundant, recurrent bloom; foliage leathery, dark, bronze; vigorous, compact, bushy growth; [Eblouissant × Comtesse du Cayla]

Baby Bio F, dy, 1977, Smith, E.; flowers deep golden yellow, patio, 3 in., 28 petals; foliage glossy; [Golden Treasure × seedling]; int. by Rosemont Nursery Co.; Gold Medal, Rome, 1976

Baby Blanket S, lp, 1993, W. Kordes Söhne; flowers medium, dbl., borne in large clusters, slight fragrance; foliage small, dark green, glossy; few prickles; medium (60-75 cm.), bushy, spreading (120-150 cm.) growth; [Weisse Immensee × Goldmarie]; int. by Bear Creek Gardens, Inc., 1993

Baby Blaze F, mr, 1954, Kordes, W.; bud ovoid; flowers cherry-red, white eye, 3 in., 33 petals, cupped, borne in clusters of 10-25, moderate fragrance; foliage light, glossy; vigorous, bushy, compact growth; PP1362; [World's Fair × Hamburg]; int. by J&P, 1954

Baby Bloomer Min, mp, 2007, Zary, Keith W.; flowers pure medium pink, 1-1½ in., semi-dbl., blooms borne in large clusters; foliage small, dark green, glossy; prickles 4-6 mm., straight, greyed-orange, few; growth spreading, medium (18 in.); [seedling × Boy Crazy]; int. by Jackson & Perkins Wholesale, Inc., 2007; Award of Excellence, ARS, 2006

Baby Boomer Min, mp, 2003, Benardella, Frank; flowers medium pink, reverse lighter pink, 1½ in., dbl., borne mostly solitary; foliage medium size, medium green, semi-glossy; prickles 3/16 in., angled slightly down, few; growth upright, spreading, bushy, tall (28-36 in.); garden decorative, cutting; PP14894; [Ivory Beauty × Kristin]; int. in 2002; Award of Excellence, ARS, 2003

Baby Bunting Min, dp, 1953, deVink, J.; flowers deep pink, 1½ in., 20 petals; [Ellen Poulsen × Tom Thumb]; int. by T. Robinson, Porchester Nursery

Baby Cakes Min, rb, 1995, Taylor, Pete & Kay; flowers white, edged red, opening to red and white appearance, small, dbl., borne mostly singly; foliage medium size, medium green, semi-glossy; few prickles; upright, bushy, medium (28 in.) growth; [Party Girl × Admiral Rodney]; int. by Taylor's Roses, 1996

Baby Carnaval – See **Baby Maskerade**, Min

Baby Carnival – See **Baby Maskerade**, Min

Baby Caroline Louise Min, w, 1998, Barker, S.J.L.; bud tall; flowers white, slight lemon center, white reverse, opening flat, 2 in., very dbl., high-centered, borne in small, well-formed clusters; foliage medium size, medium green, semi-glossy; prickles moderate; tall, bushy growth; [Sexy Rexy × Laura Ford]

Baby Cécile Brunner Min, lp, 1982, Moore, Ralph S.; flowers soft pink, 1 in., dbl., slight fragrance; recurrent; foliage small, medium green, matte; upright, bushy (12 in.) growth; [Cécile Brunner, Climbing × Fairy Princess]; int. by Moore Min. Roses, 1982

Baby Château F, mr, 1936, Kordes; bud ovoid, crimson; flowers red shaded garnet, large, dbl.; foliage glossy, bronze; very vigorous, bushy growth; [Aroma × (Eva × Ami Quinard)]

Baby Cheryl Min, lp, 1965, Williams, Ernest D.; bud pointed; flowers light pink, reverse lighter, micro-mini, small, dbl., moderate spicy fragrance; foliage leathery; vigorous, dwarf growth; [Spring Song × seedling]; int. by Mini-Roses

Baby Chicks Min, my

Baby Claire Min, pb, 2001, Sproul, James A.; bud pointed; flowers white to light pink, edged in darker pink, medium, 25-35 petals, high-centered, borne in small clusters, slight fragrance; foliage medium size, medium green, semi-glossy; prickles medium, few; growth compact, bushy, medium (24-30 in.); exhibition, garden decorative; [Fairhope × Hot Tamale]; int. by Sproul Roses by Design, 2001

Baby Crimson – See **Perla de Alcañada**, Min

Baby Darling Min, ab, 1964, Moore, Ralph S.; bud pointed; flowers apricot-orange, small, 20 petals; dwarf, bushy (12 in.) growth; PP2682; [Little Darling × Magic Wand]; int. by Sequoia Nursery, 1964

Baby Darling, Climbing Cl Min, ab, 1973, Trauger, F.; buds small, long pointed; flowers orange-apricot softening to peach pink, small, dbl, open, borne singly and several together; [sport of Baby Darling]; int. by Sequoia Nursery, 1972

Baby Diana Min, or, 1986, Saville, F. Harmon; flowers orange-red, yellow reverse, small, 20 petals, high-centered, borne usually singly; foliage small, medium green, semi-glossy; prickles long, thin, hooked, brown; bushy growth; PP5957; [Zorina × (Sheri Anne × Glenfiddich)]; int. by Nor'East Min. Roses

Baby Dioressence Min, m; growth short

Baby Doll – See **Tip-Top**, Pol

Baby Dominic Min, op, 1992, Bell, Judy G.; fringed sepals; flowers light orange-coral pink, micro-mini, ½ in., dbl., high-centered, borne in small clusters; foliage small, light green, matte; few prickles; low, compact, bushy growth; [Centergold × Cuddles]; int. by Michigan Mini Roses

Baby Donnie Min, mr; flowers scarlet-crimson, very long lasting, single, borne in clusters; growth dwarf; int. in 1972

Baby Dorothy – See **Maman Levavasseur**, Pol

Baby Eclipse Min, ly, 1984, Moore, Ralph S.; bud small; flowers small, semi-dbl.; foliage small, medium green, matte; bushy, spreading growth; [(*R. wichurana* × Floradora) × Yellow Jewel]; int. by Moore Min. Roses; AOE, ARS, 1984

Baby Elegance Pol, ab, 1912, Hobbies; flowers pale yellow-orange, single

Baby Face Min, lp, Laver, Keith G.; bud tapered; flowers light pink, very small, 35 petals, borne in large sprays, slight fragrance; foliage small, light green, matte; compact growth; [Popcorn × Popcorn]; int. in 1982

Baby Farbenkönigin Pol, dp, 1914, Altmüller; flowers medium

Baby Faurax Pol, m, 1924, Lille, L.; flowers violet, small, dbl., borne in large clusters; dwarf growth

Baby Garnette Min, mr, 1962, Morey, Dr. Dennison; flowers blood-red, small, dbl.; foliage dark; vigorous (10-12 in.), compact growth; [Red Imp × Sparkler]; int. by J&P

Baby Girl Min, yb, Clements, John; flowers butter yellow shading to bronzy copper., 1½ in., 5 petals; Profusion; foliage shiny, leathery, dark green; growth to 2½ × 2 ft.; int. by Heirloom, 2001

Baby Gloria Pol, or, 1936, Böhm, J.; flowers salmon-red, larger than parent; very dwarf (6-8 in.) growth; [sport of Gloria Mundi]

Baby Gold – See **Baby Gold Star**, Min

Baby Gold Star Min, dy, 1940, Dot, Pedro; bud pointed; flowers golden yellow, 14 petals; foliage small, soft; [Eduardo Toda × Rouletii]; int. by C-P

Baby Gold Star, Climbing Cl Min, dy, 1965, Williams, Ernest D.; int. by Mini-Roses, 1964

Baby Grand Min, mp, 1994, Poulsen Roser APS; flowers clear pink, medium, full, quartered, borne in small clusters, slight fragrance; foliage small, medium green, matte, very disease-resistant; some prickles; low (25-30 cm.), bushy, compact, rounded growth; [Egeskov × seedling]; int. by Weeks Roses, 1995

Baby Herriot – See **Étoile Luisante**, Pol

Baby Jack Min, w, Benardella; flowers white, adding pink tones in heat, dbl.; [sport of Figurine]; int. in 1999

Baby Jayne Cl Min, mp, 1959, Moore, Ralph S.; flowers soft pink, very small, 45 petals, borne in clusters; foliage small, glossy; growth to 3-4 ft.; [Violette × Zee]; int. by Germain's, 1957

Baby Katie Min, pb, 1979, Saville, F. Harmon; bud ovoid, pointed; flowers cream and pink blend, small, 28 petals, high-centered, slight fragrance; foliage matte, green; vigorous, compact, bushy growth; PP4471; [Sheri Anne × Watercolor]; int. by Nor'East Min. Roses, 1978

Baby Lilian Min; flowers begonia-rose, base tinted orange-yellow, rather large for the class, dbl.; foliage small, light, glossy; vigorous (12-15 in.) growth

Baby Love Min, dy, 1992, Scrivens, Len; bud small, pointed; flowers buttercup yellow, medium, 5 petals, borne mostly singly, slight licorice fragrance; foliage small, medium green, semi-glossy; some prickles; compact (3 ft.) growth; [(Sweet Magic × seedling) × (Sunblest × *R. davida elongata* seedling)]; int. in 1992

Baby Love Min, lp, Barni; flowers clear pink, dbl.; compact (30-35 cm.) growth; int. by Rose Barni, 1992

Baby Luke S, pb, 2005, Cockerham, John E.; flowers pink and yellow blend, reverse pink blend, aging to all-pink, 3-3½ in., single, borne mostly solitary; foliage medium size, medium green, semi-glossy; prickles varied, blade, numerous; growth upright, medium (3 ft); informal hedges, garden decoration; [Sheer Bliss × Gizmo]; int. in 2005

Baby Lyon Rose Pol, rb, 1916, Turbat; flowers coral-rose, shaded chrome-yellow or shrimp-red, dbl.

Baby Maria Min, dp

Baby Mascarade – See **Baby Maskerade**, Min

Baby Maskarade – See **Baby Maskerade**, Min

Baby Maskerade Min, rb, 1956, Tantau, Math.; bud ovoid; flowers yellow aging red, 1 in., 23 petals, slight fruity fragrance; foliage leathery; vigorous, compact (8 in. tall) growth; PP1580; [Tom Thumb × Masquerade]; int. by J&P, 1956

Baby Masquerade – See **Baby Maskerade**, Min

Baby Masquerade, Climbing Cl Min, rb, 1976, Sykes, R.O.; int. by Mini-Roses, 1974

Baby Mermaid – See **Happenstance**, HBc

Baby Michael Min, dp, 1991, Justice, Jerry G.; bud pointed; flowers deep rose pink, reverse medium pink with a touch of silver at base, medium, 38-40 petals, high-centered, borne singly, slight spicy fragrance; foliage medium size, dark green, semi-glossy; upright, medium growth; [seedling × seedling]; int. by Justice Miniature Roses, 1991

Baby Mine Pol, my, 1929, Moore, Ralph S.; flowers sulfur to butter-yellow; [Cécile Brunner, Climbing × unknown]

Baby Ophelia Min, lp, 1961, Moore, Ralph S.; bud pointed; flowers soft pink, 1 in., 33 petals; foliage glossy; vigorous, bushy (8-12 in.) growth; [(*R. wichurana* × Floradora) × Little Buckaroo]; int. by Sequoia Nursery, 1961

Baby Orange Triumph Min, or; flowers small, dbl.

Baby Paradise Min, m, 2003, Meilland International; flowers mauve, reverse mauve, 3-5 cm., very full, borne in small clusters, no fragrance; foliage medium size, medium green, semi-glossy; prickles moderate; growth bushy, medium (18-24 in.); garden decoration, containers; PPAF; [Savarain × (Playboy × Morrousel) × Meidanu]; int. by The Conard-Pyle Company, 2004

Baby Peace Min, yb, 1962, De Mott & Johnson, G.E.; bud urn shaped; flowers ivory-yellow tipped pink, ½-1 in., 50-55 petals, slight fragrance; very vigorous growth; PP2201; [sport of Peace]

Baby Pinocchio Min, pb, 1967, Moore, Ralph S.; bud ovoid; flowers salmon-pink blend, small, dbl., moderate fragrance; foliage glossy, leathery; vigorous, bushy growth; PP2967; [Golden Glow × Little Buckaroo]; int. by Sequoia Nursery

Baby Rambler, Climbing – See **Miss G. Mesman**, Cl Pol

Baby Rambler – See **Little Rambler**, Cl Min

Baby Romantica HT, yb, Meilland; flowers ocher yellow with pink edges, dbl.; greenhouse rose; int. by Meilland International, 2004

Baby Rosamunde Pol, mp, 1930, Kessler; flowers rose-pink, semi-dbl.; int. by J.T. Lovett

Baby Secret Min, w, Bridges, Dennis A.; flowers long, slender, white with salmon pink edges, dbl., exhibition; foliage glossy, dark green; stems long; growth slightly spreading; PPRR; int. in 1997

Baby Shannon Min, my, 2005, Denton, James A; flowers full, borne mostly solitary, no fragrance; foliage medium size, medium green, semi-glossy; prickles medium, straight, light brown, moderate; growth bushy, medium (24 in.); exhibition, garden decoration; [June Laver × Incognito]

Baby Sunbeam LCl, ab, 1934, Burbank; flowers light apricot, passing to cream-yellow, large yellow center, borne in large clusters; foliage bronze; very vigorous growth; int. by Stark Bros.

Baby Sunrise Min, ab, 1984, McGredy, Sam IV; bud small; flowers copper apricot, small, semi-dbl.; foliage small, medium green, semi-glossy; bushy growth; PP7031; [Dorola × Moana]

Baby Sylvia F, op, 1960, Fryers Nursery, Ltd.; flowers flesh-salmon-pink, 3 in., 25-30 petals; very vigorous growth; [Lady Sylvia × seedling]; int. in 1959

Baby Talisman – See **Presumida**, Min

Baby Talk F, m, 1980, Weeks; bud small, ovoid, pointed; flowers dusty mauve-pink, patio, 26 petals, borne mostly singly, moderate tea fragrance; foliage small to medium size, moderately thin; low to medium, compact, dense growth; PP4713; [Plain Talk × Angel Face]

Baby Tausendschön – See **Echo**, HMult

Baby Tom S, mr, 1997, Bossom, W.E.; flowers single, single, borne in small clusters; foliage small, light green, glossy; few prickles; spreading, medium (60 cm.) growth; [Eyepaint × Ballerina]

Baby Typhoon Min, ab, 1988, Halevi, A.M.; flowers bright, clear apricot, center golden-yellow, medium, 35-40 petals, high-centered, borne singly or in sprays of 3-5, moderate damask fragrance; foliage medium size, dark green, semi-glossy; prickles pointed, large, straw; bushy, spreading, tall growth; [sport of Gold Coin]

Baby Vougeot – See **Baby Château**, F

Babyface MinFl, w, 2001, Rawlins, R.; flowers 2 in., borne in large clusters, intense fragrance; foliage medium size, dark green, glossy; prickles moderate; growth bushy, medium (2 ft.); garden decorative; [Laura Ford × Margaret Merrill]; int. by Rearsby Roses, 2001

Babyflor Min, m, Tantau; flowers dbl., hybrid tea, borne in clusters; a good rose for containers; int. in 1992

Babylon HT, op, 1976, Bees; flowers deep coral-pink, low-centered, 5 in., 36 petals; foliage glossy, dark; moderately vigorous growth; [Tropicana × Pink Favorite]; int. by Sealand Nursery

Baby's Blush Ch, mp, Scarman; int. in 1995

Baby's Secret – See **Baby Secret**, Min

Bacardi HT, ob, 1987, Weeks, O.L.; flowers uniform iridescent coral-orange, fading lighter, small, 30 petals, high-centered, borne singly, slight fruity fragrance; foliage medium size, medium green, semi-glossy; prickles straight, small, reddish; upright, medium growth; PP6862; [seedling × seedling]; int. by Weeks Wholesale Rose Growers

Baccará HT, or, 1962, Meilland, F.; bud globular, medium; flowers geranium red, 3 in., 75 petals, cupped, opening flat, borne mostly singly; foliage dark green, leathery; bushy, upright growth; PP1367; [Happiness × Independence]; int. by URS, 1954

Baccará, Climbing Cl HT, or, 1965, Meilland; int. by URS

Baccara Blanca Min, w

Baccarat – See **Baccará**, HT

Bacchante HGal, dr, before 1811; flowers wine red, very dbl., moderate fragrance; foliage yellow-green, very dentate

Bacchus HP, mp, 1855, Paul, W.; flowers bright carmine, medium, full

Bacchus HP, mr, 1896, Paul, G.; flowers shining scarlet, shaded with glowing chestnut-brown, medium to large, full

Bacchus HT, dp, 1959, Dickson, A.; flowers cherry-pink, medium, 25 petals, moderate fragrance; vigorous growth; int. in 1951; Gold Medal, NRS, 1952

Back Home HT, ly, 1995, Giles, Diann; flowers 2½-4 in., full, borne mostly singly, intense fragrance; foliage medium size, light green, semi-glossy; few prickles; medium, spreading growth; [Dr A.J. Verhage × Midas Touch]; int. by Giles Rose Nursery, 1995

Bad Bergzabern HT, mr, Hetzel; int. in 1993

Bad Birnbach – See **Electric Blanket**, F

Bad Ems S, mp, Schultheis; int. in 1990

Bad Füssing F, mr, 1980, Kordes, W.; bud large; flowers brilliant red, 23 petals, cupped, borne in clusters, moderate fragrance; foliage glossy, dark; few prickles; vigorous, upright, bushy growth; [Gruss an Bayern × seedling]

Bad Homburg HT, ab, Eichelmann; int. in 1995

Bad Langensalza F, pb, 1954, Berger, W.; flowers carmine-pink, large, dbl.

Bad Nauheim – See **National Trust**, HT

Bad Naukeim – See **National Trust**, HT

Bad Neuenahr HKor, mr, 1958, Kordes, W.; bud ovoid; flowers deep crimson, 4 in., 50 petals, cupped, borne in clusters (to 15), moderate fragrance; foliage dark green, glossy, leathery; vigorous (6 ft.) growth

Bad Pyrmont F, or, 1976, Kordes; bud pointed; flowers 4 in., 40 petals, high-centered; abundant bloom; foliage dark, soft; vigorous, upright, bushy growth; [Duftwolke × seedling]; int. by Horstmann

Bad Salzuflen F, mp

Bad Wörishofen F, mr, 1976, Kordes, W.; bud ovoid; flowers 2½ in., 18 petals, cupped, slight fragrance; foliage dark, soft; vigorous, bushy growth; [Sarabande × Marlena]; int. in 1972

Bad Wörishofen 2005 – See **Emely Vigorosa**, F

Baden-Baden HT, dr, 1952, Kordes; flowers deep crimson, large, dbl.; foliage dark, leathery; vigorous, upright growth; [Poinsettia × Crimson Glory]

Badener Gold F, ob, McGredy, Sam IV; int. in 1974

Badia HT, Mansuino, Dr. Andrea

Badinage HT, op, 1951, Gaujard; flowers salmon-pink flushed coppery, 4-4½ in., 30 petals; foliage leathery, dark; vigorous growth; [Peace × seedling]

Badner Traberchampion HT, lp

Baedonthorp HT, w, 2000, Baer, Rich; flowers white, shading to light pink at edge, 5 in., full, high-centered, borne mostly singly, slight fragrance; foliage large, dark green, semi-glossy; prickles moderate; growth upright, medium (4-5 ft.); [sport of Signature]; int. by Edmunds Roses, 2002

Bagatelle HMult, w, 1908, Soupert & Notting; flowers white, washed very delicate pink, 4 cm., full, borne in large clusters; [Turner's Crimson Rambler × Mignonette]

Bagatelle HT, mr, 1943, Gaujard; bud large, oval; flowers bright red, very dbl.; foliage leathery; very vigorous, bushy growth

Bagdad HT, or, 1953, Swim, H.C.; bud ovoid to urn shape; flowers nasturtium-red to orange, becoming cupped, 4½ in., 48-55 petals, high-centered, intense fragrance; foliage glossy; very vigorous, bushy growth; PP1291; [Charlotte Armstrong × Signora]

Bagheera F, or, 1976, Kordes, W.; bud ovoid; flowers 4 in., 35 petals, high-centered; foliage glossy, dark; vigorous, upright growth; [Nordia × seedling]

Bagliore HT, mr, 1955, Aicardi, D.; flowers crimson-red; stiff stems; very vigorous growth

Bahama F, dr, 1968, Soenderhousen; flowers semi-dbl.; vigorous, low growth; [Fidélio × Hanne]

Bahia F, ob, 1973, Lammerts, Dr. Walter; bud ovoid; flowers orange, medium, dbl., cupped, moderate spicy fragrance; foliage glossy, dark, leathery; vigorous, upright, bushy growth; PP3525; [Rumba × Tropicana]; int. by Armstrong Nursery, 1974

Bahrs Lieveling F, mr, 1950, Leenders, M.; flowers velvety crimson-red; [Donald Prior × Orange Triumph]

Bailando HT, lp, Tantau; int. by Rosen Tantau, 2001

Bailey's Red – See **Karen Poulsen**, F

Bajazzo HT, rb, 1961, Kordes, R.; flowers velvety blood-red, reverse white, well-formed, large; vigorous, upright growth; int. by Kordes

Bakels F, Gaujard; int. in 1980

Bakewell Scots Briar HSpn, ly

Bakker's Newcomer HT, m

Bakker's Orange HT, ob, Bakker; flowers bright orange, dbl., high-centered, moderate soft fragrance; int. by Bakker France

Baladin F, Combe, M.

Balaji HT, ob, Patil, B.K.; int. in 1998

Balalaika F, dr, 1978, Hubner; bud ovoid; flowers blood-red, dbl.; foliage glossy; low, bushy growth; int. by O. Baum

Balcon LCl, or, 1962, Combe; bud ovoid; flowers geranium-red, open, 3 in., dbl.; foliage dark, glossy; very vigorous growth; [Spectacular × unknown]; int. by Minier, 1960

Balder S, mr, Carlsson-Nilsson; int. in 2001

Baldo Min, yb, 2003, Moe, Mitchie; flowers full, high-centered, borne mostly solitary, moderate fragrance; foliage medium size, medium green, semi-glossy; prickles small, straight, light tan, few; growth upright, medium; exhibition, garden decoration; [Hot Tamale × Elegant Beauty]; int. by Mitchie's Roses and More, 2003

Balduin HT, pb, 1896, Lambert, P.; flowers pink, edged darker, large, dbl.; vigorous growth; [Charles Darwin × Marie van Houtte]; int. by Dingee & Conard, 1901

Balduin – See **Sleepy**, Pol

Balduinus HT, r, DVP Melle; [Floirzel × Ingrid Bergman]; int. in 2000

Baléares HT, w, 1957, Dot, Simon; bud pointed; flowers base and reverse of petals white suffused carmine, deeper at edges, 35 petals; foliage dark, glossy; stiff stems; upright growth; [Peace × Flambee]

Bali Pol, 1960, Leenders, J.; flowers orange-yellow, open, large, 6 petals; foliage glossy, light green; bushy growth; [Masquerade × Golden Rain]

Bali-Hi HT, mp, 1960, Lowe; flowers peach-pink to shell-pink, medium, high-centered, moderate fragrance; foliage glossy; vigorous, upright growth; int. by Wm. Lowe & Son, 1959

Balinese HT, m, 1963, Boerner; bud ovoid; flowers brown and lavender tones, 4½-5 in., 35-40 petals, cupped, intense fruity fragrance; foliage glossy; vigorous, upright growth; [Grey Pearl × Brownie]; int. by J&P, 1963

Baljit HT, dp, 1980, Lucknow; bud pointed; flowers spirea-red, open but full, 5 in., 30-40 petals; long-lasting, profuse bloom; foliage dark, leathery; free growth; [sport of Velsheda]; int. in 1979

Balkan Star HT, m, Tapanchev; flowers large, dark pink to mauve, dbl., slight fragrance; int. in 1997

Ball of Snow N, w, 1887, Henderson

Ballade F, op, 1960, deRuiter; flowers deep orange-salmon, well-formed, 25 petals, borne in clusters; bushy growth; [Signal Red × Polyantha seedling]

Ballade F, lp, Tantau; int. in 1991

Ballady C, lp, 1934, Perrot; flowers large, dbl.

Ballerina HMsk, mp, 1937, Bentall; flowers bright soft pink, white eye, small, single, borne in very large clusters; vigorous (3 ft.) growth

Ballerina F, my, 1941, Leenders, M.; flowers naples yellow, large, dbl.

Ballerina Min, lp; flowers small, full, cupped, very slight fragrance; foliage dark green, glossy; bushy, low (20-40 cm.) growth; int. by Poulsen Roser, 1996

Ballerina, Climbing LCl, pb, 1997, Rearsby; flowers white in center, deepening to pink outer edge, reverse white, medium, semi-dbl., borne in large clusters, moderate fragrance; foliage medium size, light green, semi-glossy; some prickles; upright (15 ft.) growth; [sport of Ballerina]

Ballerina HT, lp, Kordes; flowers medium size, soft pink, dbl., high-centered; stems 60 cm length; greenhouse rose; int. by W. Kordes Söhne, 2001

Ballerina × *R. filipes* S, pb, Lens; bud pointed; flowers bright pink with white eye, fading white, single, borne in large clusters; once blooming; arching, tall (to 10 ft.) growth; int. after 1980

Ballerine HT, w, 1955, Buyl Frères; bud long; flowers satiny snow-white, open, medium, dbl.; foliage glossy; vigorous, bushy growth; int. by Delforge

Ballet HT, dp, 1959, Kordes, R.; flowers deep pink, 5 in., 52 petals, slight fragrance; foliage gray-green; vigorous, bushy growth; [Florex × Karl Herbst]; int. by A. Dickson

Ballet, Climbing Cl HT, op, 1962, Kordes

Ballet HT, dp, Kordes; bud round; flowers strong, stable pink, medium to large, dbl., high-centered; stems length 60 cm; florist rose; int. by W. Kordes Söhne, 1999

Ballila HT, mr, 1935, Bräuer; flowers medium, dbl.

Ballindalloch Castle F, dp, 1997, Cocker, Ann G.; flowers medium, very dbl., borne in large clusters; foliage medium size, medium green, glossy; some prickles; bushy, medium (2½ ft.) growth; [(Anne Cocker × Maxi) × Silver Jubilee]; int. in 1996

Balmain Climber LCl, lp; flowers single

Baltik F, m, VEG; flowers violet, large, dbl.

Baltimore HT, lp, 1898, Cook, J.W.; flowers blush tinted; [Mme Antoine Rivoire × Lady Mary Fitzwilliam]

Baltimore Beauty LCl, ly, 1927, Schluter; flowers buff-yellow, fading white, semi-dbl., borne in clusters; long, strong stems

Baltimore Belle HSet, lp, 1843, Feast; flowers pale blush to rose-white, small to medium, very dbl., borne in clusters of 6-12, moderate fragrance; non-recurrent; vigorous growth; [*R. setigera* × probably a Noisette]; Silver Medal, Hort Society of Maryland

Balusiana HGal, m, about 1845, from Austria; flowers lilac purple with silvery gray reflections

Balwant HT, ab, Phadtare; flowers non-fading apricot; [sport of Christian Dior]

Bambey HT, mr, 1980, Perry, Astor; bud long, pointed; flowers 60 petals, high-centered, intense fruity fragrance; foliage matte; prickles small, recurved; medium growth; [(Fragrant Cloud × Peace) × Alec's Red]; int. in 1981

Bambi F, mp, 1962, Watkins Roses; flowers bright pink, 2 in., 24 petals, borne in clusters; foliage dark; vigorous, bushy, low growth; [The Optimist × Korona]

Bambi F, mp, 1962, Von Abrams; bud pointed; flowers light apricot-pink, 3 in., 20 petals, cupped, borne in clusters; foliage glossy; vigorous, bushy, compact growth; int. by Peterson & Dering, 1962

Bambi Min, rb, Delbard; int. in 1998

Bambina F, w, 1962, Moreira da Silva; bud yellow; flowers large, semi-dbl., borne in clusters; [seedling × Virgo]

Bambino Min, mp, 1953, Dot, Pedro; [sport of Perla de Alcañada pink]

Bambino Min, or, 1997, Saville, F. Harmon; flowers small, micro mini, vibrant orange, full, borne in small clusters, no fragrance; foliage small, medium green, semi-glossy changing to matte; compact, bushy, low (to 14in.) growth; PP10980; [Sequoia Gold × Sparks]; int. by Nor'East Miniatures, 1998

Bambino Min, mp, Noack; flowers single; int. by Noack's Rosen, 2005

Bambolina Min, pb

Bamboo Rose – See ***R. watsoniana*** (Crépin)

Bambula F, op, 1971, Tantau, Math.; flowers 5 in., 28 petals, slight fragrance; foliage glossy, dark; int. by Wheatcroft & Sons, 1970

Banana Split Min, yb, 1987, Zipper, Herbert; flowers creamy yellow blushed with pink, medium, dbl.; foliage medium size, medium green, semi-glossy; upright, bushy growth; [Little Darling × Poker Chip]; int. by Magic Moment Miniature Roses

Banana Split S, yb, 2001, Giles, Diann; flowers striped, 4 in., full, borne mostly solitary, intense fragrance; foliage medium size, medium green, semi-glossy; prickles medium, straight, few; growth upright, compact, medium (3½ ft.); garden decorative; [Queen Margrethe × Scentimental]; int. by Giles Rose Nursery, 2001

Banana Splits HT, my, 2000, Rawlins, R.; flowers straw yellow, 4 in., full, borne in small clusters, slight fragrance; foliage medium size, light green, matte; prickles 1 cm., triangular, moderate; growth bushy, medium (39 in.); garden decorative; [Solitaire × (Baby Love × Amber Queen)]

Banaras Dawn HT, ab, 1979, Saxena; bud tapered; flowers apricot-buff, 4½ in., 30 petals, high-centered, intense fruity fragrance; foliage glossy, light green; vigorous growth; int. by Doon Valley Roses, 1977

Banater Rose HT, w, 1927, Mühle; flowers cream-white, center orange-yellow, dbl.; [Harry Kirk × unknown]

Banbridge F, pb, 1967, McGredy, Sam IV; flowers rose-red and yellow, well-shaped, 3 in., borne in clusters; [Mme Léon Cuny × Cläre Grammerstorf]

Banbridge, Climbing ClF, pb; int. in 1978

Banco HT, op, 1956, Laperrière; flowers salmon-pink

becoming gold tinted, well-formed, large, 50 petals; foliage bright green; vigorous, upright growth; [Peace × seedling]; int. by EFR

Banco 86 HT, dy, 1986, Laperrière; flowers intense yellow, 35 petals

Bandeau de Soliman – See **Charles X**, HGal

Banestu HGal, m, about 1845, Calvert

Bangalore S, mp, Poulsen; flowers soft medium pink, outer petals lighten, 8-10 cm., dbl., slight fragrance; foliage dark green, glossy; broad, bushy (40-60 cm.) growth; int. in 2004; Honorable Mention, Hradec Králové, 2006

Bangalore Palace – See **Bangalore**, S

Bangor F, or, 1972, Dickson, A.; flowers geranium-lake, ovate, large, 24 petals; foliage leathery; free growth; [Jubilant × Marlena]

Bangor Cathedral HT, dy, Kirkham, Gordon Wilson; int. in 1996

Bangsbo F, mp, Poulsen; flowers medium pink, 8-10 cm., 25 petals, no fragrance; foliage dark, glossy; growth bushy; int. by Poulsen Roser, 1996

Banjaran F, yb, 1970, Pal, Dr. B.P.; flowers gold and orange-red, small, dbl., cupped, borne in clusters, slight fragrance; foliage leathery; vigorous, upright, compact growth; int. by K.S.G. Son's Roses, 1969

Banjo HT, lp, Tantau; int. in 2002

Banks' Rose – See ***R. banksiae*** (Aiton)

Banksiae Alba – See ***R. banksiae banksiae*** (Aiton)

Banksiaeflora HSem, w; flowers white with cream center, small, very dbl.

Banksian Rose – See ***R. banksiae*** (Aiton)

Banner HT, pb, 1951, Raffel; flowers deep pink, striped white, moderate fragrance; [sport of Charlotte Armstrong]; int. by Port Stockton Nursery

Banquet F, w, Noack; int. by Noack's Rosen, 2002

Banquise HT, w, Laperrière; flowers pure white, well-formed; int. in 1974

Banshee S, mp, 1928, Origin unknown; flowers pink, troubled by balling, of poor texture, very dbl., moderate fragrance; non-recurrent

Bantry Bay LCl, mp, 1967, McGredy, Sam IV; flowers soft pink, reverse bright pink, 4 in., semi-dbl. to dbl., borne in small clusters; foliage large, semi-glossy; [New Dawn × Korona]; int. by McGredy

Banzai HT, rb, 1961, Meilland, Mrs. Marie-Louise; bud ovoid; flowers red, pink and cream blend, large, 30 petals, high-centered, slight fragrance; foliage leathery, dark; vigorous, bushy growth; PP2142; [Radar × Caprice]; int. by C-P, 1961

Banzai HT, my, 1976, Paolino; flowers canary-yellow, 4 in., 35 petals, cupped; vigorous growth; PP4013; [Coed × ((seedling × seedling) × Verla)]; int. by Meilland

Banzai '76 – See **Banzai**, HT, 1976

Banzai 83 HT, yb, Meilland; int. in 1983

Baptiste Desportes HP, mr, Trouillard; flowers large, full; good repeat

Baptiste Lafaye Pol, dp, 1910, Puyravaud; flowers carmine-pink, medium, dbl.

Bar-le-Duc HMult, mr, 1907, Soupert & Notting; flowers brick red to carmine, reverse carmine & copper, large, full; [Souv. de Pierre Notting × Crimson Rambler]

Baraguay HGal, lp, 1819, Hardy; flowers ashy-pink; foliage nearly thornless

Barakura S, lp, 2006, Beales, Amanda; flowers small, dbl., borne in large clusters; foliage small, light green, semi-glossy; prickles small, straight, few; growth spreading, short (60 cm.); groundcover, containers; [Bonica × Rambling Rector]; int. by Peter Beales Roses, 1998

Baralt – See **Altair**, S

Barba Blue – See **Barbe Blue**, HT

Barbara HT, rb, 1923, Paul, W.; flowers bright red, base yellow, reverse pale yellow, very large, semi-dbl.

Barbara HT, yb, 1962, Gaujard; flowers amber-yellow lightly flushed pink, 5 in., 20 petals, high-centered; foliage dark; very vigorous growth; int. by Gandy's Roses, Ltd., 1962

Barbara Allen S, w, Williams, J. Benjamin; flowers ivory with pink washing on petal edges, semi-dbl.; spreading growth; int. in 1999

Barbara Austin S, lp, 1999, Austin, David; flowers 3-4 in., 73 petals, borne mostly singly, moderate fragrance; foliage medium size, medium green, semi-glossy, good disease-resistant; prickles moderate; upright, medium (4 ft.) growth; PP11423; [Fair Bianca × seedling]; int. by David Austin Roses Ltd., 1997

Barbara Bush HT, pb, 1991, Warriner, William A.; flowers salmon pink where exposed to sun, lighter pink to ivory white where unexposed, 5 in., 25-30 petals, high-centered, borne mostly singly, moderate damask fragrance; foliage medium size, medium green, glossy; tall, upright, spreading growth; PP7542; [Pristine × Antigua]; int. by Bear Creek Gardens, 1991; Best Established Rose, Rose Hills, 2006

Barbara Carrera F, op, Beales, Peter; flowers bright orange salmon, softening with age, dbl., slight fragrance; foliage matte, dark green; growth short; int. in 1994

Barbara Dawson HT, lp, Dawson; [Mount Shasta × Saffron]; int. in 1987

Barbara Frietchie HT, dp, 1960, Silva; bud long, pointed; flowers rose-red, open, large, dbl.; vigorous, upright growth; [Heart's Desire × The Chief]; int. by Plant Hybridizers of Calif., 1959

Barbara Hauenstein HT, mp, Poulsen; flowers large, dbl.; int. in 1957

Barbara Hendrick HT, ab, Dorieux; int. by Roseraies Dorieux, 1998

Barbara Joyce Min, mr, 1999, Jolly, Betty J.; flowers 1½ in., 41 petals, borne in small clusters; foliage medium size, dark green, resistant, semi-glossy; few prickles; upright, medium (16 in.) growth; [Miss Dovey × Kristin]; int. by Langenbach

Barbara Mandrell Min, ab, 1991, King, Gene; bud pointed; flowers dark apricot changing to apricot-pink at 3/4 open, yellow base, aging to white, medium, 28 petals, high-centered, borne singly or in sprays of 3-10, slight fragrance; foliage medium size, medium green, matte; upright, medium growth; [(seedling × Party Girl) × Party Girl]; int. by AGM Miniature Roses, 1990

Barbara Mason HT, my, 1947, Moss; bud long, pointed; flowers medium, semi-dbl., high-centered; foliage glossy; vigorous, upright growth; [Eclipse × Luis Brinas]; int. by F. Mason

Barbara Meyer Gr, or, 1971, Meyer, H.M.; bud ovoid; flowers medium, very dbl., high-centered; foliage glossy, dark; vigorous, upright growth; [Queen Elizabeth × Tropicana]; int. by Aloe Vera Nursery

Barbara Oliva M, m, 2004, Barden, Paul; flowers violet-purple blend, reverse paler violet, 4 in., very full, borne in small clusters, intense fragrance; spring-blooming only; foliage medium size, dark green, matte; prickles ¼ in., mostly straight; growth bushy, arching canes when mature, medium (4-7 ft.); borders; [unidentified Centifolia Moss × self]; int. by The Uncommon Rose, 2005

Barbara Richards HT, yb, 1930, Dickson, A.; flowers yellow, reverse flushed pink, very large, dbl.; stems weak necks; vigorous, bushy growth

Barbara Robinson HT, w, 1925, Dickson, A.; bud long, pointed; flowers creamy white, large, dbl., high-centered

Barbara Straus HT, dr, 1978, Schwartz, Ernest W.; bud long, pointed; flowers 22 petals, borne singly; foliage glossy; spreading, upright growth; [Mister Lincoln × unknown]; int. by Flora World, Inc.

Barbara Ward HT, mr, 1931, Ward, F.B.; flowers crimson-scarlet, large, 42 petals; vigorous growth; [Royal Red × Columbia]

Barbararosa LCl, lp, Worl; flowers soft lilac pink fading to blush pink, single to semi-dbl., moderate fragrance; abundant bloomer; growth vigorous; int. by Vintage Gardens, 1980

Barbara's Rose HBc, yb; flowers single; int. in 1992

Barbarella Min, pb, 1983, Rose Barni-Pistoia; flowers deep pink, reverse creamy yellow, small, 20 petals, slight fragrance; foliage small, dark, matte; bushy growth; [seedling × seedling]; int. in 1981

Barbarina F, yb, Berger, A.; flowers large, dbl.; int. in 1965

Barbarossa HP, m, 1906, Welter; flowers carmine-purple, large, 55 petals; vigorous growth; [(Frau Karl Druschki × Captain Hayward) × Princesse de Béarn]

Barbe Blue HT, m

Barbeque F, mr, 1961, Dickson, Patrick; flowers rich red, 4 in., 30 petals, flat, borne in large clusters; foliage dark; vigorous, upright, bushy growth; [seedling × Lilli Marleen]; int. by A. Dickson, 1961

Barbetod – See **Bella di Todi**, HT

Barbie F, mp, 1976, Swim, H.C. & Ellis, A.E.; bud pointed, ovoid; flowers sweetheart, 2½ in., 35-40 petals, slight fragrance; foliage small, glossy; upright growth; PP4723; [Escort × Jazz Fest]; int. by Armstrong Nursery, 1977

Barbie Min, mp, 1998, Walden, John K.; flowers medium pink, long lasting, 2 in., 41 petals, borne in small clusters, slight fragrance; foliage medium size, dark green, semi glossy; prickles moderate; upright, low, suitable for pots growth; PP11416; [(seedling × Watercolor) × Red Minimo]; int. by Bear Creek Gardens, Inc., 1999

Barbie Dazzler HT, pb, 2004, Williams, J. Benjamin; flowers light pink blend, reverse deep pink, large, ruffled, 4½-5 in., dbl., borne mostly solitary, moderate fragrance; foliage large, dark green, glossy; prickles small-medium, curved down; vigorous, upright, tall, 3½-4 ft. growth; [Sonia × Boulie's Dream]; int. by J. B. Williams & Associates, 2004

Barbra Streisand HT, m, 1999, Carruth, Tom; flowers lavender, blushing darker, slow opening, 3½-4 in., 25-30 petals, borne in small clusters, intense fragrance; foliage large, dark green, glossy; prickles moderate; upright, bushy, medium (3-4 ft.) growth; PP13120; [(Blue Nile × (Ivory Tower × Angel Face)) × New Zealand]; int. by Weeks Roses, 2000

Barby HT, mp, Kordes; int. in 1995

Barby Kordana Min, mp, Kordes; flowers full; container rose; int. by W. Kordes Söhne

Barcarolle HT, mr, 1959, Laperrière; flowers crimson tinted geranium-red, large, 50 petals; vigorous, bushy growth; [Paulette × Tonnerre]; int. by EFR

Barcelona HT, dr, 1932, Kordes; bud long, pointed; flowers crimson, large, 75 petals, moderate spicy fragrance; foliage dark; vigorous growth; [(Sensation × Templar) × Lord Charlemont]

Barcelona 95 HT, w, Roses Noves Ferrer, S L; flowers 26 petals, high-centered; [FE-903021 × FE-89081]

Bardou Job B, dr, 1887, Nabonnand, G.; flowers crimson, shaded blackish, semi-dbl.; vigorous, semi-climbing growth; [Gloire des Rosomanes × Général Jacqueminot]

Barillet M, mr, 1850, Verdier, V.; flowers dark carmine, large, dbl., cupped

Barillet HP, 1867

Baringo HT, dp; flowers 9 cm., 30-35 petals; greenhouse rose; int. in 2004

Barkarole – See **Taboo**, HT

Barkhatnaia Krasavitsa HT, dr, 1938, Gubonen;

flowers velvety red, medium, semi-dbl., cupped; foliage dark; low growth

Barley Gold – See **Bowled Over**, F

Barley Sugar Cl Min, my, Peden, R.; int. in 1997

Barlow HP, dp, 1860, Ducher

Barn Dance S, op, 1975, Buck, Dr. Griffith J.; bud ovoid, long, pointed; flowers light salmon-pink, 2½-3½ in., 23 petals, cupped; foliage light to dark, leathery; [Tickled Pink × Prairie Princess]; int. by Iowa State University

Barna HT, dp, Ghosh; flowers florescent deep pink with violet tinge, well formed; free-flowering; int. in 2001

Barnard's Magic Day F, w, 2003, Horner, Colin P.; flowers cream-apricot, reverse white, 8 cm., full, borne in small clusters; foliage medium size, medium green, semi-glossy; prickles medium, curved, moderate; growth bushy, medium (80 cm.); garden decorative; [Bonica × Golden Celebration]; int. by Warley Garden Roses, 2003

Barni HT, ob; int. in 2004

Báró Natália Majthényi HSet, m, 1889, Geschwind; flowers violet-purple, tinted ash gray; [Souv. de President Lincoln × Mme Lauriol de Barny]

Barock HT, my, Tantau; int. in 1990

Barock S, yb, Tantau; flowers yellow to light yellow cream, very dbl., slight fragrance; heavy bloomer; foliage dark, very glossy; growth to 200-250 cm.; int. by Rosen Tantau, 2000

Barockes Bischofszell S, rb; flowers bright red with white reverse, dbl., high-centered; int. by Richard Huber AG, 2006

Baron Adolphe de Rothschild HP, m, 1862, Lacharme

Baron Alexandre de Vrints HP, pb, 1880, Gonod; flowers dark pink, striped with red over white, full, moderate fragrance; [Mme de Tartas × unknown]

Baron Chaurand HP, mr, 1869, Liabaud; flowers velvety scarlet, deep grenadine in center, large, full, cupped; prickles straight, very strong at base; growth upright; possibly a seedling of Mons Bonçenne

Baron Cuvier HGal, pb; flowers pink over violet-red, large, full

Baron de Bastrop S, dr, 2004, Ponton, Ray; flowers single, borne in small clusters, slight fragrance; foliage medium size, light green, semi-glossy; prickles medium; spreading, medium (4 ft.) growth; [San Felipe Noisette × Cameron Bohls]

Baron de Bonstetten HP, dr, 1871, Liabaud; flowers dark velvety crimson, large, 80 petals; sometimes recurrent bloom; vigorous, compact growth; [Général Jacqueminot × Géant des Batailles]

Baron de Gossard – See **Le Pérou**, HGal

Baron de Gossard HP, m, Gravereaux

Baron de Maynard – See **Baronne de Maynard**, N

Baron de Rothschild HP, m, 1862, Guillot; flowers dark carmine, shaded violet, aging to amaranth, large, full, moderate fragrance

Baron de Rothschild – See **Baron Adolphe de Rothschild**, HP

Baron de St. Triviers T, pb, 1882, Nabonnand; flowers flesh-pink, shaded to copper, large, semi-dbl., moderate fragrance; few prickles; growth vigorous; [Isabelle Nabonnand × unknown]

Baron de Wassenaër M, dp, 1854, Verdier, V.; flowers light crimson, dbl., cupped, borne in clusters; some repeat; vigorous growth

Baron de Wolseley HP, 1882, Verdier, E.; flowers velvety bright crimson with flame tints, large, full; foliage oval-rounded, serrated, delicate green; prickles numerous, short, pink; stems reddish-green; growth upright

Baron Elisi de St Albert – See **Gabriel Fournier**, HP

Baron Elisi de St Albert HP, dr, 1893, Widow Schwartz; flowers violet-red, aging to lilac-red, very large, full

Baron Ernest Leroy HP, dp, 1875, Garçon

Baron G. B. Gonella B, pb, 1859, Guillot Père; flowers medium-dark pink, large, full, some quartering, moderate fragrance; [Louise Odier × unknown]

Baron Giraud de l'Ain – See **Baron Girod de l'Ain**, HP

Baron Girod de l'Ain HP, rb, 1897, Reverchon; flowers bright red, petals edged white, dbl., slight fragrance; [sport of Eugène Furst]

Baron Girod de l'Ain Striped Sport

Baron Haussmann HP, mr, 1867, Lévêque; flowers light red, large, very dbl.

Baron Heckeren de Wassenaer HP, mp, 1852, Margottin; flowers bright pink, large, full

Baron J. B. Gonella – See **Baron G. B. Gonella**, B

Baron J. G. Gonella – See **Baron G. B. Gonella**, B

Baron Jacques Riston HT, op, 1936, Ketten Bros.; bud long, pointed; flowers salmon-pink, well-shaped, large, 45-50 petals; very vigorous growth; [Mme Butterfly × (Rev. David R. Williamson × Gorgeous)]

Baron Lassus de St Geniez HP, mp, Granger; flowers large, dbl.

Baron Meillandina Min, rb, 1987, Meilland, Mrs. Marie-Louise; flowers white with red edges, medium, dbl., umbrella-shaped; foliage small, medium green, glossy; bushy growth; PP6818; [Magic Carrousel × ((Alain × Mutabilis) × (Medar × Caprice))]; int. by Meilland Et Cie, 1986

Baron N. de Rothschild HP, mp, 1882, Lévêque; flowers bright carmine, large, full

Baron Nathaniel de Rothschild HP, mr, 1882, Lévêque; flowers bright crimson red, large, full; foliage dark green

Baron Palm HT, mr, 1913, Lambert, P.; flowers velvety red with deep yellowish-red and vermilion reflections, large, dbl., cupped, moderate fragrance; [Étoile de France × Mme Ravary]

Baron Peletan de Kinkelin HP, dr, 1864, Granger; flowers large, dbl.

Baron Sunblaze – See **Baron Meillandina**, Min

Baron Taylor HP, mr, 1880, Dugat; flowers light red, large, dbl.; [sport of John Hopper]

Baron T'Kind de Roodenbecke HP, m, 1897, Lévêque; flowers shaded purple

Baronesa de Ovilar HT, 1935, Munné, B.; flowers carmine tinted yellow, very large, dbl.; foliage dark; strong stems; very vigorous growth; [Sensation × Souv. de Claudius Pernet]

Baroness Henrietta Snoy – See **Baronne Henriette de Snoy**, T

Baroness Krayenhoff HT, pb, 1931, Buisman, G. A. H.; flowers peach-pink, center orange, very large, dbl.; foliage light green; long stems; vigorous, compact growth; [Mrs Henry Bowles × Lady Roundway]

Baroness Rothschild HP, lp, 1867, Pernet Père; flowers very soft rose, tinted white, large, 40 petals, cupped; some recurrent bloom; vigorous, erect growth; [sport of Souv. de la Reine d'Angleterre]

Baronesse HT, or, 1989, Tantau

Baronesse A. van Hövell tôt Westerflier HT, m, 1933, Leenders, M.; flowers carmine-purple, base yellow, large, dbl.; foliage bronze; very vigorous, bushy growth

Baronesse H. von Geyr HT, pb, 1928, Leenders, M.; flowers pale flesh and vermilion-red, dbl.; [(Farbenkonigin × Juliet) × Sunburst]

Baronesse M. van Tuyll van Serooskerken HT, pb, 1922, Leenders, M.; flowers rose and lilac-white, base apricot, semi-dbl.; [Jonkheer J.L. Mock × Mme Mélanie Soupert]

Baronesse Manon F, mp, 1938, Poulsen, S.; flowers clear pink, firm petals, 3 in.; foliage glossy, holly-like; vigorous, bushy growth; [Else Poulsen × Dame Edith Helen]; int. by C-P, 1952

Baronesse S. H. W. van Dedem HT, yb, 1923, Leenders, M.; flowers yellow and coppery, open, large, semi-dbl.; foliage dark, glossy; vigorous, bushy growth

Baronesse von Ittersum HMult, rb, 1910, Leenders, M.; flowers light crimson, shaded deeper, medium, semi-dbl., borne in clusters; free, non-recurrent bloom; foliage dark, glossy; vigorous, climbing (15 ft.) growth; [Crimson Rambler × Mme Laurette Messimy]

Baronin Anna von Lüttwitz HMult, lp, 1909, Walter; flowers cream-pink, 3½ cm., dbl., borne in large clusters, moderate musky fragrance; non-recurrent; [Euphrosine × Rösel Dach]

Baronin von Adelebsen S, mr, 1938, Vogel, M.; flowers medium, single

Baronne F, dp, Select; flowers 9 cm., 30-40 petals, high-centered; stems 50-70 cm; greenhouse rose; int. by Terra Nigra B. V., 2003

Baronne Ada T, w, 1897, Soupert & Notting; flowers cream with chrome yellow center, large, full, globular, intense fragrance; [Mme Lonbard × Rêve d'Or]

Baronne Adolphe de Rothschild – See **Baroness Rothschild**, HP

Baronne Berge – See **Mme la Baronne Berge**, T

Baronne C. Rochetaillée T, op, 1900, Dubreuil; flowers sulfur yellow, tinted salmon, large to very large, full, moderate fragrance

Baronne Charles de Gargan Cl T, ly, 1893, Soupert & Notting; flowers light daffodil yellow, center darker, large, full, moderate fragrance; [Mme Barthélemy Levet × Socrate]

Baronne Charles d'Huart HT, pb, 1910, Ketten Bros.; flowers lilac-rose suffused white, reflexed, dbl.; [Pharisaer × seedling]

Baronne Daumesnil B, mp, 1863, Thomas; flowers shining pink

Baronne de Beauverger HP, mr, 1867, Gautreau or Cochet; flowers cherry red

Baronne de Hoffmann T, rb, 1887, Nabonnand; flowers coppery, shaded red, large, dbl.

Baronne de Maynard N, w, 1865, Lacharme, F.; flowers white, edges tinged pink, medium, full, cupped, borne in small clusters; moderately vigorous growth; [Mlle Blanche Lafitte × Sapho]; sometimes classed as B

Baronne de Medem HP, mr, 1876, Verdier, E.; flowers bright carmine cerise-red, large, full, globular

Baronne de Nervo S, Delbard-Chabert; int. in 1969

Baronne de Noirmont B, mp, 1861, Granger; flowers purplish-pink, medium, full, cupped, borne in small clusters, moderate violet fragrance; sometimes classed as HP

Baronne de Prailly HP, mr, 1871, Liabaud, J.; flowers bright red, large, very full, globular; [Victor Verdier × unknown]

Baronne de Rothschild, Climbing – See **Baronne Edmond de Rothschild, Climbing**, Cl HT

Baronne de St Didier HP, mr, 1886, Leveque, P.; flowers crimson red, sometimes shaded lilac and purple, often edged white, very large, full

Baronne de Savigny T, mp, 1854, Desprez; flowers pink, center darker, large, full

Baronne de Schorlemmer HT, mp, Lens, Louis; flowers large, dbl.; int. in 1985

Baronne de Stael HGal, ob, 1820, Vibert; flowers salmon-pink, open, large, dbl.; vigorous, branching growth

Baronne de Vivario Pol, w, 1925, Soupert & Notting; flowers dbl., borne in clusters; [Orléans Rose × Jeanny Soupert]

Baronne d'Ivry HGal, w; flowers yellowish-white, aging to red, medium, very full, globular

Baronne Edmond de Rothschild HT, rb, 1970, Meilland; flowers ruby-red, whitish reverse, large, 40 petals, high-centered, intense fragrance; foliage glossy, leathery; vigorous growth (90-100 cm.); [(Baccará × Crimson King) × Peace]; int. by Meilland International, 1968; Gold Medal, Rome, 1968, Gold Medal, Lyon, 1968

Baronne Edmond de Rothschild, Climbing Cl HT, rb, 1979, Meilland, Mrs. Marie-Louise; flowers red with silver reverse, 14-16 cm., borne in small clusters, moderate fragrance; recurrent; foliage glossy; int. by Meilland & Co SNC, 1974

Baronne Finaz HT, mp, 1962, Gaujard; flowers bright pink, large, 35 petals, moderate fragrance; foliage glossy, dark; long stems; very vigorous, upright growth; [(Peace × unknown) × Opera]

Baronne G. Chandon – See **Socrate**, T

Baronne G. de Noirmont HT, pb, 1891, Cochet; bud rounded; flowers flesh pink with salmon, fading to blush white, large, full; foliage light green; prickles few, strong, reddish; growth upright

Baronne Gonella – See **Baron G. B. Gonella**, B

Baronne Gustave de St Paul HP, lp, 1894, Glantenet; flowers pale pink with silvery tints, 4½ in., dbl.

Baronne Hallez de Claparède HP, dr, 1849, Lebougre

Baronne Haussmann HP, mr, 1867, Verdier, E.

Baronne Henriette de Loew T, w, 1888, Nabonnand, G.; flowers pinkish white, center yellow, dbl.

Baronne Henriette de Snoy T, pb, 1897, Bernaix, A.; flowers flesh, reverse carmine-pink, well-formed, 9-10 cm., dbl., flat, borne in small clusters, slight fragrance; reliable repeat; vigorous growth; [Gloire de Dijon × Mme Lombard]

Baronne Jard-Panvillers HP, mp, 1880, Duval; flowers bright pink, large, full

Baronne Louise Uxkull HP, pb, 1871, Guillot; flowers bright flesh pink with carmine, very large, full

Baronne Maurice de Graviers HP, rb, 1866, Verdier, E.; flowers intense cerise red, tinted and shaded pink and carmine, reverse whitish, medium, full

Baronne Nathalie de Rothschild HP, lp, 1885, Pernet Père; flowers bright pink with silvery shadings, very large, very dbl., globular, moderate fragrance; growth upright; [Baronne Adolphe de Rothschild × unknown]

Baronne Nathaniel de Rothschild – See **Baronne Nathalie de Rothschild**, HP

Baronne Noirmont – See **Baronne de Noirmont**, B

Baronne Peletan – See **Baron Peletan de Kinkelin**, HP

Baronne Presval HP, dp

Baronne Prévost HP, mp, before 1841, Desprez; flowers rose-pink, shading lighter, large, dbl., flat, moderate fragrance; recurrent bloom; vigorous, erect growth

Baronne Prévost, Climbing Cl HP, mp

Baronne Surcouf S, mp, 1989, Briant

Baronne Vitat HP, mp, 1873, Liabaud; flowers very large, full, globular

Baroque S, m, Harkness; flowers magenta with small white eye and yellow stamens, semi-dbl.; growth low and spreading (2 × 3½ ft.); int. in 1995

Baroque Floorshow – See **Baroque**, S

Barossa Dream HT, ab, 1999, Schuurman, Frank B.; flowers apricot, reverse light apricot, 4½-5 in., dbl., borne mostly singly; foliage large, medium green, semi-glossy; prickles moderate; bushy, tall (3-4 ft.) growth; [City of Auckland × New Year]; int. by Franko Roses New Zealand, Ltd., 1995

Barricade LCl, mr, Combe, C.; flowers vermilion/orange, medium to large, dbl., borne in small clusters, no fragrance; int. in 1968

Barrie F, pb, 1973, Schloen, J.; bud ovoid; flowers salmon-pink, medium, dbl., cupped; free bloom; foliage glossy, light; [Sumatra × Fashion]

Barry Fearn – See **Schwarze Madonna**, HT

Barry Stephens HT, ab, 2000, Horner, Calvin L.; flowers apricot edged red, reverse lighter, 6 in., full, borne mostly singly, moderate fragrance; foliage large, dark green, semi-glossy; prickles moderate; upright, medium (3½ ft.) growth; [Typhoon × Benson & Hedges Gold]; int. by Battersby Roses, 2000

Barter's Pink HT, ob, 1965, Barter; flowers bright coral-pink, deeply veined, 4 in., dbl., slight fragrance; foliage light green; vigorous, bushy growth; [Queen Elizabeth × Claude]

Barthélemy Joubert HP, mr, 1877, Moreau et Robert; flowers bright cerise red, large, full

Barunka F, op, Urban, J.; flowers salmon-pink, large, very dbl.; int. in 1983

Bashful Pol, pb, 1958, deRuiter; flowers reddish-pink, white eye, small, single, borne in trusses; bushy, compact growth; int. by Gregory & Sons, 1955

Basier HT, w, 1955, Mallerin, C.; flowers pearly white, edges tinted pink, 3 in., 40 petals, high-centered, moderate fragrance; vigorous growth; [Mme Joseph Perraud × Independence]; int. by Wheatcroft Bros., 1954

Basildon Belle F, or, 1965, Maarse, G.; flowers vermilion; [sport of Anna Wheatcroft]; int. by Basildon Rose Gardens, 1964

Basildon Bond HT, ab, 1980, Harkness, R., & Co., Ltd.; flowers loose form, 27 petals, borne 1-3 per cluster; foliage large, medium green, very glossy; prickles large, straight; medium, upright growth; [(Sabine × Circus) × (Yellow Cushion × Glory of Ceylon)]; Gold Medal, Belfast, 1982

Basilika HT, op, VEG; flowers salmon-pink, large, dbl.

Bassino S, mr, 2006, W. Kordes' Söhne; flowers with ruffled petals and yellow stamens, 3 cm., single, cupped, borne in small, dense clusters; foliage small, glossy, dense; growth wide and bushy (25 cm.), canes at first upright, but later low

Bastei S, or, Schmadlak, Dr.; flowers deep orange shaded burnt umber, very dbl., flat, then recurved, no fragrance; int. in 1973

Bastogne HT, or, Grandes Roseraies; flowers vermilion, shaded darker, well-formed; foliage dark; very vigorous growth

Basye's Amphidiploid S, mp, 1955, Basye, Dr. Robert; flowers medium, single; prickles very numerous; growth very large; [*R. moschata abysinnica* × *R. rugosa rubra*]

Basye's Blueberry S, mp, Basye, Robert; int. in 1982

Basye's Legacy S, mp, Basye; flowers small, medium to dark pink, 5 petals, borne in small clusters, moderate fragrance; may repeat if kept deadheaded; growth spreading; can be used as a climber; int. by Ashdown, 2002

Basye's Myrrh-Scented Rose S, lp, Basye, Robert; int. in 1980

Basye's Purple Rose S, m, Basye, Robert; flowers large, velvety purple with gold stamens, single, moderate fruity fragrance; rough, sparse foliage; growth thick, erect, with prickly canes; [*R. rugosa* × *R. foliolosa*]; int. in 1968

Basye's Thornless – See **Commander Gillette**, S single

Bataclan S, dy, Tantau; int. in 2005

Baton Rouge – See **Attractive Cover**, S

Battersby Beauty HT, ly, 1997, Horner, Calvin; flowers medium, very dbl., borne mostly singly; foliage medium size, light green, semi-glossy; bushy, medium (90 cm.) growth; [Polar Star × (Elina × Remember Me)]; int. by Battersby Roses

Battle of Britain HT, yb, 1970, Gandy, Douglas L.; flowers yellow-orange, medium, 30 petals; [Miss Ireland × Summer Sunshine]; int. by Wheatcroft & Sons

Bavaria – See **Gruss an Bayern**, F

Bavaria München – See **Lazy Days**, F

Bavarian Girl – See **Schöne Münchnerin**, F

Bavarian Gold – See **Bayerngold**, F

Baviera d'Oro – See **Bayerngold**, F

Baxter Beauty T, ab, 1938, Clark, A.; flowers light yellow to sulphur overlaid outside with light salmon pink; [sport of Lorraine Lee]

Bay – See **Grove Cottage**, S

Bay – See **Bay Cottage**, S

Bay Cottage S, dp, Poulsen; flowers deep pink, small, single, borne in clusters, no fragrance; foliage dark; growth broad, bushy, 40-60 cm.; int. by Poulsen Roser, 2004

Bay Glow Min, yb

Bay of Bengal HT, m, Ghosh; flowers silver lilac with deeper petal edges and veins, dbl.; int. in 2001

Bayadère HT, ab, 1954, Mallerin, C.; flowers salmon-pink to canary yellow, tinted pink, large, 52 petals, high-centered; foliage dark, bronze; vigorous, bushy growth; [R.M.S. Queen Mary × seedling]; int. by Wheatcroft Bros., 1954; Gold Medal, NRS, 1954

Bayerngold F, my, 1990, Tantau; flowers clear yellow, medium, dbl., high-centered; foliage glossy; compact, low (40-50 cm.) growth; very winter hardy; among the healthiest of the yellows

Bayernland – See **Madison**, S

Bayernland Cover – See **Madison**, S

Bayerntraum HT, mp, Cocker; int. in 1999

Bayreuth S, rb, W. Kordes Söhne; flowers medium, dbl., moderate fragrance; int. in 1965

Be-Bop S, rb, 2003, Carruth, Tom; flowers light red with a large yellow eyezone, reverse yellow, 5½-7 cm., single, borne in large rounded clusters, slight fragrance; foliage medium size, medium green, semi-glossy; prickles moderate, average, almost straight, light tan; growth spreading, medium (80-100 cm.); garden decoration; [Santa Claus × *R. soulieana* derivative]; int. by Weeks Roses, 2003; Certificate of Merit, Adelaide, 2006

Be Glad HT, rb, 1988, McMillan, Thomas G.; flowers white changing to red, reverse white, aging deep pink, medium, 25-30 petals, high-centered, moderate fruity fragrance; foliage medium size, dark green, glossy; prickles normal; upright, medium growth; no fruit; [Paradise × Color Magic]; Silver Medal, ARC TG, 1988

Be My Valentine HT, mr, Williams, J.B.; flowers velvet red; int. by Hortico, 2003

Bea Wallace HT, dr, 2007, Burks, Larry; flowers deep red, reverse medium red, 5 in., full, borne mostly solitary; foliage medium size, dark green, semi-glossy; prickles average, recurved, green/brown, moderate; growth upright, tall (60 in.); garden decorative, exhibition; [seedling × seedling]; int. in 2007

Beach HT, r, Tantau; flowers medium size, tan/yellow, dbl.; heavy bloomer; greenhouse rose; int. by Rosen Tantau, 2001

Beach Baby F, ob, Benny, David; flowers warm orange to salmon, borne in large trusses; growth medium; int. by De Boer Roses, 2005

Beach Boy Min, my, 1982, Williams, Ernest D.; bud pointed; flowers golden buff, 48 petals, high-centered, borne usually singly, slight fragrance; foliage small, dark, slightly glossy; prickles short, tan; upright, bushy growth; [Tom Brown × seedling]; int. by Mini-Roses, 1981

Beach Girl HT, ab, Dorieux; flowers peach-apricot and yellow, dbl., high-centered, slight fragrance; growth to 4-5 ft.; int. in 1998

Beachcomber F, r, 1987, McGredy, Sam IV; flowers

medium, 6-14 petals, slight fragrance; foliage medium size, medium green, semi-glossy; bushy growth; [seedling × Colorbreak]; Gold Star of the South Pacific, Palmerston North, NZ, 1985

Beacon HT, 1952, Swim, H.C.

Beacon Belle Ayr, lp, 1919, Farquhar; flowers flesh passing to white, small, dbl., borne in clusters, moderate fragrance; [Orléans Rose × (Katharina Zeimet × *R. arvensis*)]

Beacon Lodge HT, dr, 1976, Ellick; flowers deep red, 4-5 in., 40-45 petals; foliage glossy, dark; very vigorous growth; [Chopin × Ena Harkness]

Beacon View HT, mr, 1977, Ellick, C. W.; flowers dbl, borne several together and in trusses; foliage large, long, pointed, medium green, semi-glossy; growth very vigorous; [Karl Herbst × Lathom Park]

Bean Rock HT, op, McGredy; flowers large, rich salmon pink, dbl., exhibition; growth medium; int. in 2001

Beatrice HT, mp, 1908, Paul, W.; flowers dark carnation pink tinted scarlet-vermilion, very large, very full

Beatrice F, dp, 1968, McGredy, Sam IV; flowers deep rose pink, dbl., borne in large sprays; [Paddy McGredy × (Kordes' Perfecta × Montezuma)]

Beatrice HT, lp, Barni, V.; flowers cream suffused with soft pink, darker at center, large, very dbl., high-centered, borne one bloom to a stem, moderate fragrance; foliage medium large; stems long; growth erect and vigorous, tall (90-110 cm.); int. by Rose Barni, 1995

Beatrice Berkeley HT, rb, Fitzhardinge

Beatrice Boeke HT, dp, 1966, Buisman, G. A. H.; bud ovoid; flowers pink-red, large, dbl.; [Montezuma × Detroiter]

Beatrice Jennings F, op, 2006, Rawlins, Ronnie; flowers vermilion/pink stripe, reverse vermilion, 2 in., semi-dbl., borne in small clusters, no fragrance; foliage medium size, dark green, glossy; prickles ½ in., triangle, moderate; growth upright, tall (42 in.); garden decoration; [Florange × Candle in the Wind]

Beatrice McGregor HT, dr, 1938, Clark, A.; flowers large, dbl.; [Sensation × seedling]; int. by NRS Victoria

Beatrice Samzin F, mp, Scholle, E.; flowers large, very dbl.; int. in 1970

Béatrix B, mr, 1865, Cherpin; flowers bright carmine red, medium to large, full, cupped, borne in small clusters; nearly thornless; growth upright; [Louise Odier × unknown]

Beatrix, Comtesse de Buisseret HT, mp, 1900, Soupert & Notting; flowers silver rose, aging to rosy carmine red, very large, dbl., moderate fragrance

Beau Carmin Ch, pb, before 1810, Descemet; flowers velvety carmine, shaded purple, medium, full

Beau Cramoisi Royal – See **Cramoisi Royal**, HGal

Beau Narcisse HGal, m, before 1828, Miellez; flowers purple, striped, medium, full, cupped

Beau Rose Misc OGR, mp

Beau Rose Primaplant Pol, dp, Vlaeminck; flowers large, dbl.; int. in 1963

Beaucaire Pol, rb, 1937, Grandes Roseraies; flowers edges chamois-pink, center coppery yellow, reverse coppery-red, dbl.; vigorous, dwarf growth

Beaujolais HT, mr, 1932, Croibier; flowers crimson-carmine, very large, dbl., globular; very vigorous growth; [Hadley × Laurent Carle]

Beaujolais HT, dr, Select; flowers 10 cm., 40 petals, high-centered; stems 60-80 cm long; greenhouse rose; int. by Terra Nigra, 2003

Beaulieu HP, 1883, Moreau et Robert

Beaulieu – See **Tequila Sunrise**, HT

Beaulieu S, mr, 1998, Rosen Tantau; flowers medium red, 2½ in., single, borne in large clusters, no fragrance; foliage medium size, dark green, glossy; prickles moderate; low, spreading (30 cm.) growth; [seedling × seedling]; int. by Eurosa, 1998

Beaulieu Abbey F, ab, 1964, Cobley; flowers creamy yellow suffused pink, well-formed, 4 in., dbl.; foliage dark, glossy, leathery; vigorous growth; [Masquerade × Docteur Valois]; int. by Blaby Rose Gardens

Beauregard LCl, Croix, P.; int. in 1972

Beauté HT, ab, 1953, Mallerin, C.; bud long; flowers light apricot, well-formed, large, dbl.; vigorous growth; [Mme Joseph Perraud × seedling]; int. by Wheatcroft Bros., 1954

Beauté d'Automne Pol, dp, 1918, Turbat; flowers bright rose-pink, dbl., borne in clusters of 50-70; [Phyllis × seedling]

Beauté de Billard HMult, mr, before 1855, Billard; flowers glowing scarlet, full

Beauté de France HT, w, 1920, Toussaint Mille Fils; flowers creamy white to pure white, inside yellow, dbl.; [Mme Mélanie Soupert × Kaiserin Auguste Viktoria]

Beauté de France HT, 1952, Gaujard; bud long, pointed; flowers brick flushed coppery, medium, dbl.; foliage leathery, dark; upright growth; [(Comtesse Vandal × seedling) × seedling]

Beauté de la Malmaison HGal, dr, before 1885; flowers deep red, marbled with violet, medium, full

Beauté de l'Europe T, op, 1881, Gonod; flowers light orange-pink, yellow base, large, dbl., intense fragrance; few prickles; [Gloire de Dijon × unknown]

Beauté de Lyon – See **Beauté Inconstante**, T

Beauté de Lyon HP, or, 1910, Pernet-Ducher; flowers coral-red, tinted yellow, large, dbl., globular, moderate fragrance; foliage brilliant green; prickles very large, red; [Soleil d'Or × seedling]; Gold Medal, Bagatelle, 1911

Beauté de Roulers HP, mp, 1860, de Cock

Beauté de Versailles – See **Georges Cuvier**, B

Beaute Francaise HP, mr, 1862, Lartay

Beauté Incomparable D, mr, 1860, Miellez

Beauté Inconstante T, ob, 1892, Pernet-Ducher; flowers orange to coppery red, shaded carmine and yellow, highly variable, 9-10 cm., semi-dbl. to dbl., moderate fragrance; vigorous growth; [Safrano × Earl of Eldon]; sometimes classed as a Noisette

Beauté Insurmontable HGal, dp, before 1811; flowers plumed deep pink and delicate pink and purple ground, small, dbl.; from Holland

Beauté Lyonnaise HT, w, 1895, Pernet-Ducher; flowers white tinted pale yellow, large; [Baronne Adolphe de Rothschild × unknown]

Beauté Orléanaise HWich, w, 1919, Turbat; bud salmon red; flowers white to flesh-pink, 4 cm., dbl., borne in small to medium clusters; foliage small, dark green, glossy

Beauté Rare – See **Sapho**, HGal

Beauté Renommée HGal, mr, before 1811; flowers red with purple tones to medium, 2 in., full; from Holland

Beauté Riante HGal, dp, before 1836, Calvert; flowers dark pink, aging to red, edges lighter, small to medium

Beauté Spatiale HT, mr, 1970, Delbard-Chabert; flowers velvety red, medium, semi-dbl., high-centered, slight fragrance; foliage bronze, soft; moderate, bushy growth; [Walko × Impeccable]; int. by Pepinieres G. Delbard, 1966

Beauté Superbe Agathée HGal, lp, before 1811; bud pointed; flowers small, very dbl., borne in small clusters, moderate fragrance; Agathe group

Beauté Suprême C, m, before 1846; flowers dark purple with bluish carmine, full

Beauté Surprenante HGal, w, before 1820, Descemet/ Vibert; flowers white, with a pink heart, medium; possibly synonymous with Beauté Supréme

Beauté Tendre HGal, dp, before 1810, Dupont; flowers deep pink, vinous white beneath, veined darker red above, large, very dbl.

Beauté Tendre A, lp, before 1813; flowers pale rose, nearly white edges, very large, full

Beauté Touchante HGal, mr, before 1813, Miellez

Beauté Virginale D, w, before 1811, Descemet; bud pointed, delicate pink; flowers blush white, medium, full, borne in clusters of 3-4; foliage oval, deeply toothed, ashy green

Beautiful Black HP, dr

Beautiful Bride – See **Maria Teresa**, S

Beautiful Britain F, or, 1983, Dickson, Patrick; flowers orange-red, reverse deeper, medium, 20 petals, borne in clusters; foliage medium size, medium green, semi-glossy; upright, bushy growth; [Red Planet × Eurorose]; int. by Dickson Nurseries, Ltd.; Rose of the Year, 1983

Beautiful Carpet – See **Wiltshire**, S

Beautiful Doll Min, mp, 1982, Jolly, Betty J.; flowers 25 petals, high-centered, borne singly and in small clusters; foliage small, dark, semi-glossy; bushy, spreading growth; [seedling × Zinger]; int. by Rosehill Farm

Beautiful Dreamer F, ob, 1976, Herholdt, J.A.; flowers orange to sunset-gold, pointed, 2-2½ in., 35 petals, slight fragrance; foliage glossy; [seedling × seedling]; int. by Roselandia, 1977

Beautiful Dreamer – See **Summer Dream**, F

Beautiful Fukuyama HT, or, Hiroshima; int. in 1986

Beautiful Nature S, pb; int. in 1999

Beautiful Sunday Min, mr, 1977, Takatori, Yoshiho; bud ovoid; flowers bright geranium-red, small, 60 petals, cupped; foliage glossy, dark, leathery; compact, bushy growth; [Camelot × Camelot seedling]; int. by Japan Rose Nursery

Beautiful Sunrise LCl, pb, 2000, Bossom, W.E.; flowers salmon with yellow center, light pink reverse, 5 cm., semi-dbl., borne in large clusters, slight fragrance; foliage small, medium green, semi-glossy, disease-resistant; prickles small, straight, few; growth spreading, tall (3 m.); walls, fences, pergolas; [Phyllis Bide × (Anytime × (Liverpool Echo × (Flamenca × *R. bella*)))]; int. as Cheers, Warner's Roses, 2001

Beauty HT, mr, 1931, Ward, F.B.; flowers american beauty red, but darker, very large, dbl.; long stems; vigorous growth; [(Crusader × Premier) × American Beauty]

Beauty Min, mr, Olesen; flowers dbl., 25-30 petals, no fragrance; foliage dark green, glossy; growth narrow, bushy, very low (20-40 cm.); int. in 1996

Beauty by Oger HT, pb, Select; flowers medium pink with outer petals turning darker as they open, 11 cm., 40 petals, high-centered; stems 60-80 cm long; int. by Terra Nigra, 2003

Beauty Cream F, w, 1956, Verschuren; flowers cream, large; foliage dark; vigorous, upright growth; int. by Gandy Roses, Ltd.

Beauty Fairy LCl, dp

Beauty from Within HT, ob, Orard; flowers deep golden center with pink edges on the outer petals, takes on an orange hue as, dbl., high-centered, then cupped; foliage dark green; straight stems; growth vigorous, upright, medium; int. in 2002; Trial Ground Certificate, Durbanville, 2006

Beauty of Badgen HT, lp, 1924, French, A.

Beauty of Beeston HP, dr, 1882, Frettingham; flowers velvety crimson, small, full

Beauty of Brisbane Pol, pb, 1932, Perrot; [sport of Goldlachs]

Beauty of Dropmore S, w, 1956, Skinner; flowers dbl.; non-recurrent; bushy, erect growth; [*R. spinosissima altaica* × *R. spinosissima* cultivar]

Beauty of England HP, dp

Beauty of Festival HT, Klimenko, V. N.; int. in 1955

Beauty of Glazenwood – See **Fortune's Double Yellow**, Misc OGR

Beauty of Glenhurst Ch, dp, 1985, Morley; growth semi-climbing (10 ft.); [Parsons' Pink China × unknown]; int. by Beauty of Glenhurst, 1983

Beauty of Greenmount N, dp, 1854, Pentland; flowers cherry pink with rose red shades, full

Beauty of Greenwood – See **Beauty of Greenmount**, N

Beauty of Hurst LCl, w, 1926, Hicks; flowers creamy buff, dbl.; foliage dark; very vigorous growth

Beauty of Leafland HSpn, pb, Erskine; flowers blend of pale pink and pale yellow, almost creamy white, 25-30 petals, intense fragrance; non-remontant; [Butterball × Haidee]

Beauty of New South Wales Pol, rb, 1931, Knight, G.; flowers bright crimson, center white, small, single, borne in clusters of 20; bushy, dwarf growth; [Orléans Rose × Alice Amos]

Beauty of Rosemawr T, pb, 1903, Van Fleet/Conard & Jones; flowers carmine rose veined vermilion and white, medium, dbl., slight fragrance; growth medium (3 × 2 ft.)

Beauty of Stapleford HT, rb, 1879, Bennett; flowers red and violet, well-formed, large, no fragrance; moderate growth; [Mme Bravy × Comtesse d'Oxford]; very prone to mildew

Beauty of the Prairies – See **Queen of the Prairies**, HSet

Beauty of the Thames HP, mp, 1876, Walker; flowers bright carmine, large, full

Beauty of Waltham HP, mr, 1862, Paul, W.; flowers rosy crimson, large, dbl.; recurrent bloom; vigorous growth; [Général Jacqueminot × unknown]

Beauty of Westerham HP, mr, 1864, Cattell

Beauty Queen F, mp, 1983, Cants of Colchester, Ltd.; flowers medium, dbl., intense fragrance; foliage large, dark, glossy; [English Miss × seedling]

Beauty Secret Min, mr, 1965, Moore, Ralph S.; bud pointed; flowers cardinal-red, 1½ in., dbl., high-centered; foliage small, glossy, leathery; vigorous, bushy growth; [Little Darling × Magic Wand]; int. by Sequoia Nursery; AOE, ARS, 1975, Miniature Rose Hall of Fame, ARS, 1999

Beauty Show – See **Shobha**, HT

Beauty Star – See **Liverpool Remembers**, HT

Beauty Temple HT, w, Chakraborty, Dr K.; flowers pure white, large; int. by KSG Son, 2005

Beautyglo Min, lp, 1985, Williams, Ernest D.; flowers small, 35 petals, high-centered; foliage small, dark, semi-glossy; bushy growth; PP6199; [Tom Brown × Black Jack]; int. by Mini-Roses

Beauty's Blush HRg, dp, 1955, Univ. of Saskatchewan; flowers deep pink, becoming lighter, dbl.; non-recurrent; vigorous (6 ft.) growth; hardy onthe Canadian prairies; [Tetonkaha × Pink Pearl]

Bébé Blanc Pol, w, 1922, Turbat; flowers dbl., borne in large clusters; dwarf growth

Bébé Fleuri Ch, mp, 1906, Dubreuil; flowers small, occasionally striped, semi-dbl.

Bébé Leroux Pol, w, 1901, Soupert; flowers medium, in trusses of 20-40; compact growth; [Mignonette × Archiduchesse Elisabeth-Marie]

Bebe Lune F, my, 1965, Delbard

Becca Godman F, pb, Wells; int. in 1998

Becker's Ideal – See **Ideal**, HT

Beckett's Single HGal, mp, Quest-Ritson

Becky HT, dp, 1925, Beckwith; flowers glowing rose-pink, single; vigorous growth

Becky Adams Min, m, 2001, Moe, Mitchie; flowers mauve, developing red petal tips in intense sun, 1½-2 in., full, high-centered, borne mostly singly, moderate fragrance; foliage medium size, dark green, Semi-glossy; prickles medium, hooked, red, moderate; growth spreading, medium (18-24 in.); exhibition, garden decorative; [Fairhope × Wistful]; int. by Mitchie's Roses and More, 2001

Bedazzled Min, dp, 1999, Walden, John K.; flowers 2-2½ in., full, borne in small clusters, slight fragrance; foliage dark green, semi-glossy; prickles moderate; compact, medium (20-24 in.) growth; PP12352; [sport of Hot Tamale]; int. by Bear Creek Gardens, Inc., 2000

Bedazzler S, mr; int. by Heirloom, 2003

Bedford Belle HT, mr, 1884, Laxton; flowers reddish-white, large, very full, cupped; foliage bluish green; [Gloire de Dijon × Souv du Comte de Cavour]

Bedford Crimson HT, dr, 1926, Laxton Bros.; flowers velvety crimson, well-formed, 40 petals; [Richmond × Château de Clos Vougeot]

Bedfordia HT, pb, 1931, Laxton Bros.; flowers pink, outer petals lighter, center salmon, 52 petals; vigorous growth

Bedont F, ab, Harkness; flowers light apricot, 4 in., 20-25 petals, spiral, moderate fragrance; recurrent; foliage dark green, glossy; vigorous, compact, upright (3-4 ft.) growth; int. by Edmund's Roses, 2006

Bedrich Smetana HT, w, 1933, Böhm, J.; flowers pearly white, open, very large, semi-dbl.; vigorous, bushy growth; [Modesty × Ophelia]

Beehive Gold – See **Goldfinch**, S

Beehive Gold Min, dy; flowers smallish, pure golden, non-fading; growth medium

Bee's Balm S, mp, J. B. Williams; flowers ruffled, single, slight fragrance; growth to 4 × 4 ft.; int. by Hortico, Inc., 2005

Bee's Frolic S, lp, 1980, Dawnay, Mrs. E.; bud small, pointed; flowers 14 petals, borne 2-3 per cluster, intense fragrance; repeat bloom; foliage medium size, matte; prickles small; upright, strong growth; [Schneezwerg × Clair Matin]; int. in 1976

Bees Knees Min, yb, 1998, Zary, Dr. Keith W.; flowers yellow/pink blend, 2½ in., full, borne in large clusters, slight fragrance; foliage medium size, dark green, dull; prickles moderate; growth bushy, tall (3 ft.); [seedling × Haute Pink]; int. by Bear Creek Gardens, Inc., 1998

Bee's Landing S, op, J. B. Williams; int. by Hortico, Inc., 2005

Beginnings S, pb, Williams, J.B.; flowers silvery pink, center lighter, showy stamens, single, flat, borne in clusters, slight fragrance; recurrent; growth to 4 ft.; int. by Hortico Inc., 2006

Begonia HT, op; flowers frilled and crimped petals, moderate fragrance; long stems; medium growth

Behold Min, my, 1996, Saville, F. Harmon; bud medium; flowers clear, bright medium yellow, reverse lighter, holds color, dbl., borne mostly singly, no fragrance; foliage medium size, medium green, semi-glossy; few prickles; upright, compact, medium (22-26 in.) growth; PP10249; [(Rise 'n' Shine × Sheri Ann) × (Heideroslein × Nozomi)]; int. by Nor'East Min. Roses, 1997

Bekola – See **Aalsmeer Gold**, HT

Bel-Air HT, dr, Swane; int. in 1986

Bel Ami F, mr, 1958, Laperrière; flowers large, dbl., borne in clusters of 7-8; bushy growth; [Michèle Meilland × Tonnerre]; int. by EFR

Bel Ami – See **Philippe**, F

Bel Ange HT, mp, 1962, Lens; flowers soft pink, reverse darker, 4½ in., 35 petals, moderate fragrance; foliage dark; vigorous growth; PP2579; [(Independence × Papillon Rose) × (Charlotte Armstrong × Floradora)]; int. as Belle Epoque, J&P, 1965; Gold Medal, Kortrijk, 1965

Bel Ange, Climbing Cl HT, mp, Ruston, D.; [sport of Bel Ange]; int. in 1970

Bel Canto HT, or, 1964, Mondial Roses; flowers bright geranium-red, well-formed; foliage coppery; upright growth

Bel Esprit HMsk, pb, 2000, Lens, Louis; flowers pale pink, center white, reverse lighter, 3-4 cm., single, borne in large, pyramidal clusters; recurrent; foliage medium green, dull, disease-resistant; prickles moderate; upright, medium (70-100 cm.) growth; [(*R. multiflora adenocheata* × Ballerina) × Puccini]; int. by Louis Lens NV, 1992

Bela Portuguesa – See **Belle Portugaise**, Cl T

Belami HT, op, 1986, Kordes, W.; flowers orange pink, large, 35 petals, high-centered, moderate fragrance; foliage medium size, dark, glossy; upright, bushy growth; [(Prominent × Carina) × Emily Post]; int. in 1985

Belami – See **Bremer Stadtmusikanten**, S

Belfast Belle HT, dy, 1990, Dickson, Patrick; flowers large, full, slight fragrance; foliage medium size, medium green, semi-glossy; upright, bushy growth; [seedling × Pot O' Gold]; int. by Dickson Nurseries, Ltd., 1991

Belfield (from Bermuda) – See **Slater's Crimson China**, Ch

Belgian Lace S, lp, 2000, Lens, Louis; flowers light pink, reverse lighter, 3-4 cm., dbl., flat, borne in small clusters; once blooming; foliage small, medium green, semi-glossy; prickles moderate; spreading, medium (80-120 cm.) growth; [Lovania × (Robin Hood × seedling)]; int. by Louis Lens NV, 1994

Belgic Blush – See **Blush Belgiques**, A

Belgic Provence – See **Blush Belgiques**, A

Belgic Rose – See **Blush Belgiques**, A

Belgica HT, dr, 1929, Buyl Frères; flowers crimson-red, shaded garnet, large, very dbl.; vigorous growth

Belgica Flore Rubricante – See **Blush Belgiques**, A

Belgica Rubra – See **Rouge de Belgique**, HGal

Belinda HMsk, mp, 1936, Bentall; flowers soft pink, medium, semi-dbl., borne in very large, erect trusses, moderate fragrance; vigorous (4-6 ft.) growth; a good hedge or pillar rose

Belinda F, ob, 1973, Tantau, Math.; bud ovoid; flowers copper to orange, medium, dbl., moderate fragrance; vigorous, upright, bushy growth; PP3382; [seedling × Zorina]; int. in 1971

Belinda's Dream S, mp, 1992, Basye, Robert; flowers 3¼-4¼ in., very full, borne in small clusters, moderate fruity, raspberry fragrance; repeat bloom; foliage medium size, medium green, matte; medium (5 × 4 ft.), bushy growth; [Jersey Beauty × Tiffany]; int. in 1989

Belinda's Rose – See **Belinda's Dream**, S

Bélisaire D, lp, before 1829; flowers pale or flesh pink, medium, very dbl., borne in small clusters; foliage pale green, regularly toothed; prickles numerous, uneven, enlarged at base

Belkanto LCl, mr, Noack; int. by Noack's Rosen, 2005

Bell Charmer Min, ob, 1992, Bell, Charles E., Jr.; flowers distinctive soft orange with light yellow petal base and reverse, large, full, slight fragrance; foliage medium size, medium green, semi-glossy; some prickles; medium (45-55 cm.), upright, bushy growth; [(Cherish × Avandel) × seedling]; int. by Kimbrew Walter Roses, 1993

Bell Ringer Min, dp, 1989, Bell, Charles E., Jr.; flowers deep pink, silver at base, small, 34 petals, slight fruity fragrance; foliage medium size, medium green, semi-glossy; upright, bushy growth; [(Fragrant Cloud × Avandel) × Bonny]; int. by Kimbrew Walter Roses, 1989

Bella T, w, 1890, California Nursery Co.; bud pointed; flowers large; probably extinct

Bella F, mr, deVor; PP11263; int. in 1995

Bella – See **Bella Renaissance**, S

Bella Christina F, rb, 2006, Mander, George; flowers dark red, reverse cream, 4½ in., full, borne in large clusters; foliage large, dark green, very glossy, disease-resistant; prickles in., needle-point, medium brown, moderate; growth upright, tall (4-5 ft.); garden decorative, exhibition; [Shades of Pink × Super Sun]; int. by Hortico, Inc., 2007

Bella di Monza – See **Belle de Monza**, Ch

Bella di Todi HT, dy, Barni; flowers yellow with apricot tones, outer petals lighter, 10-12 cm., very dbl., quartered, Intense fragrance; foliage medium size, dark green; growth to 80-100 cm.; [seedling × Antico Amore]; int. by Rose Barni, 2000

Bella Donna D, lp, Before 1844; flowers soft lilac-pink, large, with a small center eye, very dbl., flat, strong fragrance; foliage pale green

Bella Donna F, mr, 1964, Verbeek; bud ovoid; flowers bright red medium, dbl., borne in clusters; foliage dark; [(Baccará × unknown) × Miracle]

Bella Epoca – See **Bel Ange**, HT

Bella Minijet Min, ab, Meilland

Bella Multiflora HMult, mp, Uhl, J.; flowers large, borne in sprays; few prickles; arching growth; int. in 1994

Bella Nitida S, mp, Uhl, J.; flowers large; medium growth; very hardy; int. in 1994

Bella Notte S, dr, Hiroshima; groundcover; spreading growth; int. by Hiroshima Bara-en, 2002

Bella Renaissance S, my; flowers medium yellow, 8-10 cm., very dbl., borne in clusters, moderate fragrance; free-flowering; foliage dark, leathery; growth bushy, 3 × 4 ft.; PP12522; int. by Poulsen, 1995

Bella Roma – See **Bella'roma**, HT

Bella'roma HT, pb, 2004, Zary, Keith W.; flowers yellow pink blend, reverse yellow pink blend, 4-4½ in., 30 -35 petals, borne mostly solitary, intense fragrance; foliage dark green, glossy; prickles 5 mm., hooked slightly downward; growth upright, 4½ ft.; PP15075; [Sunbright × Kelbian]; int. by Jackson & Perkins Wholesale, Inc., 2003

Bella Rosa F, mp, 1982, Kordes, W.; flowers miniflora, large, 34 petals, slight fragrance; foliage small, medium green, glossy; bushy growth; [seedling × Traümerei]; Gold Medal, Durbanville, 1981, Gold Medal, Copenhagen, 1981, Gold Medal, Baden-Baden, 1983

Bella Via MinFl, w, 1991, Zipper, Herbert; flowers medium, full, high-centered, borne mostly singly, moderate fragrance; foliage medium size, dark green, matte; few prickles; medium (40 cm.), upright growth; [Rise 'n' Shine × Olympic Gold]; int. by Magic Moment Miniature Roses, 1992

Bella Vita HT, w; int. by K & M Nursery, 2005

Bella Weiss F, w, 1989, Kordes; flowers white version of Bella Rosa, no fragrance; growth to 60 cm.high × 40 cm.wide; [sport of Bella Rosa]

Bellard HGal, lp, Before 1842; flowers beautifully shaped, translucent shade of pink, light and bright, very dbl., moderate fragrance

Belle HT, lp, 1999, Hiltner, Martin; flowers light pink, reverse medium pink, 4½ in., dbl., borne mostly singly; foliage small, dark green, semi-glossy; prickles moderate; upright, medium (2½ ft.) growth; [First Prize × Handel]

Belle – See **Belle Hit**, MinFl

Belle Adélaide HGal, dp, Miellez; flowers cerise-red, very dbl., flat

Belle Aimable HGal, rb, before 1811; flowers pale red plumed white, small, dbl.; from Holland

Belle Allemand T, lp, 1841, Beluze, J.; flowers flesh pink, shaded rose pink, large, semi-dbl. to dbl.

Belle Alliance – See **Tricolore**, HGal

Belle Americaine HP, dp, 1837, Boll, Daniel

Belle Amour A, lp, before 1867; flowers soft pink with salmon tones, prominent yellow stamens, semi-dbl., moderate myrrh fragrance; growth to 5-6 ft.; found in Normandy, about 1950, but undoubtedly a much older variety; sometimes classed as D; int. by Found at a convent at Elboeuf in the 1940's

Belle Ange – See **Bel Ange**, HT

Belle Anglaise HP, mp, 1856, Ducher

Belle Anglaise HT, dy; int. in 1995

Belle Aspasie T, m, before 1836, Coquerel; flowers bright velvety purple, very large, semi-dbl.

Belle Aspasie N, dp, before 1836, Laffay; flowers medium, full

Belle au Bois Dormant S, pb, Kordes; flowers pink with salmon, full, some fragrance; growth vigorous, 100-120 cm.; int. in 1960

Belle Auguste D, lp, before 1824, Descemet/Vibert; flowers blush pink changing to nearly white, large, full

Belle Aurore – See **Celestial**, A

Belle Aurore A, lp, about 1815, Descemet; flowers light pink, tinted lilac

Belle Aurore HGal, lp, before 1836, Vibert; flowers flesh pink with lilac tints, large, full; sometimes classed as A

Belle Biblis HGal, m, 1815, Descemet, M.; flowers deep flesh pink, changing paler, large, dbl., moderate fragrance; growth erect

Belle Blanca LCl, w; flowers large, semi-dbl.; [probably a Belle Portugaise sport]

Belle Blonde HT, my, 1955, Meilland, F.; flowers yellow, center darker, well-formed; foliage glossy; bushy growth; [Peace × Lorraine]; int. by URS

Belle Bourbon – See **Rouge Formidable**, HGal

Belle Brun HGal, dr, before 1811; flowers velvety violet purple, large, semi-dbl.; [Aigle Brun × unknown]

Belle Camille HGal, pb, before 1820, Descemet; flowers lilac pink, aging to red, medium

Belle Cerise HGal, mr, about 1810, Descemet

Belle Champenoise HT, my, Orard; int. in 1997

Belle Chartronnaise T, pb, 1861, Lartay; flowers bright pink with canary yellow

Belle Chartronnaise HGal, m; flowers violet purple, full

Belle Clementine A, lp, before 1845; flowers mottled flesh-color; mottling in the blooms suggests *R. alba* × *R. gallica*

Belle Coquette S, mp; groundcover; spreading growth; int. in 1999

Belle Couronnée – See **Celsiana**, D

Belle Créole F, rb, 1958, Arles; flowers variegated red and brick-red, borne in clusters; foliage dark; vigorous, upright growth; [(Gruss an Teplitz × Independence) × (Floradora × Independence)]; int. by Roses-France

Belle Cuivrée HT, or, 1924, Pernet-Ducher; flowers coral-red, shaded coppery yellow, medium, semi-dbl.

Belle Danielle – See **Jack Wood**, F

Belle d'Aulnay HGal, mp, before 1824, Barrier; flowers full, moderate fragrance; sometimes attributed to Prévost

Belle d'Auteuil D, dp, before 1826, Prévost (?); flowers rosy lilac, large, full, globular; foliage short, round; prickles short; growth branching, robust

Belle d'Automne HT, Ducher, Ch.; int. in 1969

Belle de Baltimore – See **Baltimore Belle**, HSet

Belle de Bordeaux T, pb, 1861, Lartay (possibly Bernède); flowers pink with crimson center, large, dbl.; vigorous growth; [Gloire de Dijon × unknown]

Belle de Bourg-la-Reine HP, mp, 1859, Margottin; flowers large, full

Belle de Crécy HGal, m, 1829, Roeser (introduced by Hardy); sepals leafy; flowers cerise and purple, becoming lavender-gray, center green, medium, very dbl., flat, quartered, borne in small clusters; foliage dark green elongated, irregularly dentate; prickles numerous, dark brown, slightly hooked; stems slender; growth upright; sometimes classed as HCh

Belle de Dom S, pb, Guillot-Massad; int. in 1996

Belle de Florence – See **Belle de Monza**, Ch

Belle de Fontenay HGal, mr, before 1828, Boutigny; flowers glowing cherry red, edges lighter pink, medium, very full

Belle de Hesse – See **Illustre**, HGal

Belle de Juin F, Croix, P.; int. in 1974

Belle de Lille – See **Blush Boursault**, Bslt

Belle de Londres – See **Compassion**, LCl

Belle de Marly HGal, dp; flowers bright rose, shaded violet, large, dbl.

Belle de Monza Ch, mr, about 1825, Villaresi/Noisette; flowers light cherry red to light purple, medium, semi-dbl., cupped, borne in large clusters; re-introduced by Vibert about 1840

Belle de Normandy HP, mp, about 1890, California Nursery Co; flowers clear rose, shaded with rosy carmine and lilac, very large

Belle de Parme F, mp, 1962, Arles; flowers lilac-mauve; low, spreading growth; [(Lafayette × (Gruss an Teplitz × Independence)) × *R. rugosa rubra*]; int. by Roses-France

Belle de Provins HT, dr, 1954, Robichon; flowers velvety dark red, well-formed, large, dbl.; vigorous growth; [Crimson Glory × E.G. Hill]

Belle de Regnie S, mr, Dorieux; int. by Roseraies Dorieux, 2005

Belle de Remalard HMult, pb, d'Andlau; flowers small, bright pink with a whiter heart, borne in large sprays; one blooming in the spring only; growth vigorous and spreading, 5-6 m.; hips small, red; found growing from seed in garden by Mme d'Andlau at Rémelard; int. in 1998

Belle de Ségur A, lp, before 1828, Lelieur; flowers soft rosy flesh, edges blush, dbl., cupped; foliage dark; vigorous, upright growth

Belle de Stors HGal, m, about 1836, Lahaye; flowers purple pink, medium, full

Belle de Trianon P, lp, before 1826, Prévost

Belle de Vaucresson HGal, lp, before 1840, Dubourg or Prévost; flowers flesh pink, medium, very full

Belle de Vernier HCh, pb, before 1827, from Douai; flowers rosy crimson, marbled with dark purplish slate, medium, full, cupped; possibly synonymous with Belle Violette and/or De Vergnies

Belle de Vilmorin – See **Unique Carnée**, C

Belle de Yèbles HGal, mr, before 1835, Desprez; flowers bright red

Belle de Zelbes – See **Belle de Yèbles**, HGal

Belle des Jardins HGal, m, 1872, Guillot et Fils; flowers purplish violet-red, striped lilac and white, with a button center, dbl., cupped, borne singly or in small clusters, strong fragrance; foliage medium green, elliptical; prickles moderate; vigorous growth; [La Rubanée × unknown]

Belle des Massifs HP, mp, 1862; flowers bright carmine, dbl.

Belle des Neiges HT, w; int. by Fabre Graines, 2005

Belle d'Espinouse S, rb, Guillot-Massad; int. by Roseraies Guillot, 2006

Belle Dijonnaise – See **Zéphirine Drouhin**, B

Belle Doria HGal, pb, before 1847, Parmentier; flowers lilac, spotted and striped with white, carmine center, small to medium, full, cupped

Belle d'Orléans HP, m, 1851, Vigneron; flowers lilac pink

Belle d'Orléans N, w, 1902, Conard & Jones; flowers

white, sometimes tinted rose, small, borne in large clusters; remontant; growth semi-climbing

Belle d'Orléans LCl, or, 1958, Robichon; flowers reddish-crimson, 4½-5 in., dbl., borne in large clusters; recurrent bloom; foliage glossy; vigorous growth; [seedling × Independence]

Belle du Printemps HP, pb, 1863, Damaizin; flowers carmine, striped with darker carmine, large, dbl.

Belle du Seigneur HT, ab, Delbard; flowers large, coppered ocher two tone, holds well when open, dbl., high-centered; growth vigorous; int. by Georges Delbard SA, 2002

Belle Egarée – See **Mme Charles Damé**, HP

Belle Elisa – See **Elisa**, A

Belle Emilie d'Arlon HGal, lp, 1839, David; flowers flesh pink, shaded white, large, full

Belle Epoque – See **Bel Ange**, HT

Belle Époque HT, pb, 1965, Kriloff, Michel; flowers fuchsia-pink, reverse creamy, 6 in., 40 petals, moderate fragrance; foliage glossy; vigorous, upright growth; [Peace × Independence]; int. by Cramphorn's Nursery, 1963

Belle Epoque HT, ab, Fryer, Gareth; flowers golden bronze on upper surface, darker nectarine-bronze reverse, dbl., high-centered; quick to repeat; foliage medium green, glossy; growth vigorous, bushy; [Remember Me × Simba]; int. in 1994

Belle Epoque HT, mp; int. by Roseraies Barth, 2003

Belle Estelle – See **Estelle**, HSpn

Belle Étoile Gr, my, 1961, Lens; bud long, pointed; flowers golden yellow, well-formed, 25 petals, borne in clusters of 5-7; long stems; vigorous, upright growth; [Joanna Hill × Tawny Gold]

Belle Évêque – See **L'Évêque**, HGal

Belle Fabert P, dp, before 1825, Fabert; flowers rosy crimson, sometimes tinted with purple, very large, full, globular

Belle Flamande – See **Marie-Louise**, D

Belle Fleur – See **Damas Violacé**, D

Belle Fleur d'Anjou T, lp, 1873, Touvais; flowers shining flesh pink, very large, full

Belle Flore HGal, dr, before 1813, Descemet; flowers velvety violet crimson, darker at center, large, very dbl., moderate fragrance

Belle Florentine HGal, mp, before 1829, Boutigny; flowers large, full

Belle Galathée HGal, w, before 1813, Descemet; flowers flesh white

Belle Hébé Ch, lp, before 1815, Descemet; flowers bright flesh pink, center darker, medium, full

Belle Hébé HGal, mp, before 1836, Laffay; flowers bright pink, flesh center, large; Agathe group

Belle Hélène HGal, m, before 1818, Descemet; flowers delicate blush pink, large, very dbl., cupped

Belle Hélène HGal, dr, before 1829, Vibert; flowers intense purple, nuanced violet, medium, very full

Belle Hélène C, mp, before 1829, Boutigny; flowers large, full

Belle Hélène Ch, w, about 1835, Laffay

Belle Henriette M, lp, about 1830, Vibert

Belle Henriette HP, dr; flowers dark red, medium, full

Belle Herminie HGal, m, 1819, Coquerel; flowers bright purple-pink, spotted white, medium, semi-dbl.

Belle Hit MinFl, lp, Poulsen; flowers light pink, 5-8 cm., dbl., slight wild rose fragrance; foliage dark; growth bushy, 20-40 cm.; int. by Poulsen Roser, 2005

Belle Isidore Ch, mp; flowers bright carmine, shaded flesh pink, medium, full

Belle Isis HGal, lp, 1845, Parmentier; flowers flesh-pink, lighter at edges, with a central button, dbl., quartered, borne singly or in clusters of 2-3; foliage small, light green, rounded, coarsely toothed; numerous prickles; Agathe group

Belle Italienne – See **Achille**, HGal

Belle Ivryenne HP, dp, 1891, Lévêque; flowers large, dbl.

Belle Jardinière HP, lp, 1853, Avoux & Crozy

Belle Junon – See **Junon**, HGal

Belle Laure HSpn, w, 1817, Dupont/Vibert; flowers white, spotted purple at center, 2-2½ in., single; prickles straight, unequal, mixed with bristles

Belle Laure No. 1 – See **Belle Laure**, HSpn

Belle Laure No. 2 HSpn, w, 1818, Descemet/Vibert; flowers marbled white and purplish pink, 2-3 in., single; foliage ovate, simply dentate; prickles very numerous, dense, fine, unequal, almost straight; hips oval-globular, brown-black

Belle Léonide C, 1823, Bizard

Belle Léopoldine HGal, mp, before 1829, Boutigny

Belle Lilette HT, mr, 1926, Gemen & Bourg; flowers carmine-red, very large, dbl.

Belle Loire S, Croix, P.

Belle Lucile HGal, before 1810, Descemet

Belle Lyonnaise HP, mp, 1854, Lacharme

Belle Lyonnaise Cl T, ly, 1869, Levet, F.; flowers canary yellow, fading white, 10-11 cm., dbl., loosely quartered, borne mostly solitary, moderate fragrance; prickles large; vigorous, climbing growth; [Gloire de Dijon × unknown]

Belle Lyonnaise – See **Fürst Bismarck**, T

Belle Mâconnaise T, mp, 1870, Ducher; flowers large, full

Belle Marie – See **La Belle Marie**, T

Belle Marseillaise – See **Fellemberg**, Ch

Belle Mathilde – See **La Belle Mathilde**, HSpn

Belle Meillandina Min, dr, 1984, Meilland, Mrs. Marie-Louise; PP5038; [sport of Meillandina]; int. by Meilland Et Cie, 1980

Belle Mignonne HGal, lp, before 1819, Prévost; flowers light pink, inner petals often rayed white, small, dbl.

Belle Nanon B, dp, 1872, Lartay; flowers carmine

Belle Nantaise HT, w, 1901, Bahaud; flowers white tinted salmon pink, very large, full, moderate fragrance; [Mme Caroline Testout × Viscountesse Folkestone]

Belle Ninon HGal, m, before 1821, Boutigny; flowers dark lilac, edges lighter, medium, full, semi-globular

Belle Noisette – See ***R. × noisettiana*** (Thory), N

Belle Normande HP, w, Oger; flowers silvery rose; [sport of La Reine]

Belle of Berlin HT, mp, Tantau; bud long, slim; flowers 20 petals, slight fragrance; foliage medium size, dark, semi-glossy; stems long, slim; growth tall, upright; int. by Rosen Tantau, 1994

Belle of Portugal – See **Belle Portugaise**, Cl T

Belle of Punjab F, mp, 1969, Pal, Dr. B.P.; bud ovoid; flowers warm salmon pink, 52 petals, high-centered, borne singly and in clusters; foliage dark, glossy; very vigorous, compact growth; [Montezuma × Flamenco]; originally registered as HT; re-registered 1980 as F; int. by Indian Agric. Research Inst., 1965

Belle of Tasmania F, or, 1968, Holloway; bud pointed; flowers velvety scarlet, center darker, medium, dbl., high-centered; foliage glossy; vigorous, tall, compact growth; [Korona × Étoile de Hollande]

Belle Olympe HGal, mr, before 1820, Descemet

Belle Orléanaise HT, mp, 1902, Corboeuf; [Mme Caroline Testout × Mme Abel Chatenay]

Belle Parade HGal, m, before 1811; flowers carnation-cerise, with lilac tints, large, very dbl., borne in clusters of 6-8; foliage oval, dentate; few prickles; from Holland

Belle Poitevine HRg, mp, 1894, Bruant; bud long, pointed; flowers rose-pink to magenta-pink, large, semi-dbl., slight sweet fragrance; recurrent bloom; foliage dark, rugose; vigorous (3½-4 ft.), bushy growth; [Regeliana × unknown]

Belle Portugaise Cl T, lp, 1903, Cayeux, H.; bud very long, pointed (to 4 in.); flowers light flesh-pink, slightly darker reverse, 4-6 in., semi-dbl., slight damask/tea fragrance; long spring bloom; foliage long, narrow, light green; very vigorous (20 ft.) growth; not hardy north; [Souv de Mme Léonie Viennot × *R. gigantea*]

Belle Pourpre HGal, m, before 1813, from Holland; flowers dark violet purple

Belle Pourpre Violette – See **Belle Violette Foncé**, HGal

Belle Renaissance – See **Bella Renaissance**, S

Belle Rose HP, mp, 1864, Touvais; flowers bright pink, very large, full

Belle Rosine S, dp, before 1820, Descemet; flowers bright cerise pink, large, dbl., borne in clusters; foliage very villose beneath; prickles very hooked; stems crooked; hybrid turbinata

Belle Rosine HGal, dp, 1829 or 1830, Vibert; flowers deep pink, edged lighter, open, large, dbl.; erect growth

Belle Rouge HT, dr, 1956, Delbard-Chabert; flowers dark velvety red becoming carmine-purple, large; [(Happiness × unknown) × Impeccable]

Belle Rouge HT, dr, Delbard; flowers firm petaled, velvet red, dbl., high-centered, no fragrance; growth tall, grows easily; PP9915; int. in 1999

Belle Rubine – See **La Rubanée**, HGal

Belle sans Flatterie HGal, m, before 1806; flowers lilac-pink, lighter on the edges, heavily veined, with a center button, medium, very dbl., quartered, flat, borne usually solitary; foliage oblong, dark green; prickles very few; from Holland

Belle sans Pareille HGal, mp, before 1845, in Brussels; flowers shining carmine, aging to lilac, striped violet, globular, slight fragrance

Belle Siebrecht – See **Mrs W. J. Grant**, HT

Belle Siebrecht, Climbing – See **Mrs W. J. Grant, Climbing**, Cl HT

Belle Splendens HGal, before 1820, Descemet

Belle Stéphanie D, m, about 1825, Boutigny; flowers lilac pink, medium, full

Belle Story S, lp, 1985, Austin, David; flowers light pink, yellow stamens, large, 35 petals, cupped, intense fragrance; foliage medium size, medium green, semi-glossy; bushy growth; PP7213; [(Chaucer × Parade) × (The Prioress × Iceberg)]; int. by David Austin Roses, Ltd., 1984

Belle Suisse HT, mr, 1936, Heizmann, E.; flowers large, dbl.

Belle Sultane – See **La Belle Sultane**, HGal

Belle Sunblaze – See **Belle Meillandina**, Min

Belle Symphonie Min, mp, Meilland; int. in 1997

Belle Ternaux HGal, m, about 1825, Boutigny; flowers purple, shaded violet, small to medium, full

Belle Thérèse – See **Maiden's Blush**, A

Belle Vichysoise N, lp, 1895, Lévêque; flowers pink or pinkish white, small, very dbl., borne in clusters of 20-50; very vigorous growth; may have originally been introduced as Cornélie (Moreau-Robert, 1858); int. by Lévêque

Belle Victorine C, lp, before 1815, Descemet; flowers flesh pink, center darker, edges lighter, medium, full

Belle Villageoise – See **Panachée Pleine**, HGal

Belle Violette HCh, m, before 1830, De Vergnies; flowers bright violet, medium, full; possibly synonymous with Belle de Vernier and/or De Vergnies

Belle Violette Foncé HGal, m, before 1815, Descemet

Belle Virginie HGal, m, about 1814; flowers violet pink, medium, full; from Sèvres

Belle Yvrienne HP, rb, 1890, Lévêque; flowers brilliant

red, shaded white and carmine, very large, very full

Belles and Beaus S, rb, 1987, Adams, Dr. Neil D.; flowers red-white bicolor, floribunda type, medium, dbl., high-centered; foliage medium size, dark green, glossy, disease-resistant; upright, moderately hardy growth; [Little Darling × seedling]

Bellevue HT, yb, 1978, Poulsen, Niels D.; flowers dark yellow and apricot, edged red, 6 in., 23 petals; foliage glossy, leathery; vigorous, upright growth; [(Tropicana × Piccadilly) × Fru Jarl]; int. by Poulsen, 1976

Bellina F, op, 1959, Von Abrams; flowers shrimp-pink, 2-2½ in., 40 petals, high-centered, borne in large clusters, moderate fragrance; foliage glossy; low, compact growth; PP1915; [Pinocchio × (Fashion × Orange Triumph)]; int. by Peterson & Dering, 1958

Bellisima F, ob, 1999, Schuurman, Frank B.; flowers 2½ in., full, borne mostly singly, slight fragrance; foliage medium size, dark green, glossy; few prickles; upright, medium growth; [Lambada × Pot O' Gold]; int. by Franko Roses New Zealand, Ltd., 1998

Bellissima MinFl, or, 1989, Zipper, Herbert; flowers orange-red, darker along edges, medium, dbl., high-centered, borne singly, no fragrance; foliage medium size, medium green, semi-glossy; upright growth; [Pink Petticoat × Lady Rose]; int. by Magic Moment Miniature Roses, 1989

Bellissima HT, my, 1991, Laperrière; flowers pale yellow at the center, darker edges, dbl.

Bellona F, my, 1975, Kordes, R.; bud ovoid; flowers golden yellow, pointed, 3 in., 27 petals, slight fragrance; foliage light; very vigorous, upright growth; PP3790; [New Day × Minigold]; int. by J&P, 1976

Bellotte HGal, mp, before 1826, Vibert; flowers crimson pink, medium

Belmont HCh, lp, 1846, Vibert; flowers flesh, tinted pink, moderate Tea fragrance

Beloved HT, w, 1978, Hill, E.H.; bud tinted pink; flowers reflexing, 6-7 in., 33-35 petals; foliage glossy; [sport of Memoriam]; int. by Shropshire Roses

Beloved – See **Cesar E. Chavez**, HT

Béluze B, mr, about 1840, Béluze; flowers cherry red, medium, full

Belvedere – See **Princesse Marie**, HSem

Belvédère F, dr, 1928, Kiese; flowers velvety dark red, large, dbl.; vigorous, dwarf growth; [Eblouissant × Château de Clos Vougeot]

Belvédère HT, dr, 1955, Delforge; flowers large, deep red. large petals, moderate fragrance; [Reine Elisabeth × Christopher Stone]

Belvedere S, ob, Tantau; flowers orange-peach, large, long-lasting, very dbl., slight fragrance; foliage dark green, glossy; growth strong grower; int. by Rosen Tantau, 2002

Belvedere Park HT, dr, 1995, LeCroy, Jack; flowers dark red, edging to black, large, full, borne mostly singly; foliage medium size, dark green, glossy; few prickles; medium (4 ft.), spreading, bushy growth; [Swarthmore × First Prize]; int. by K&M Nursery, 1995

Ben Arthur Davis HT, yb, 1935, Bostick; flowers yellow, reverse pinkish gold, dbl., cupped; foliage leathery, glossy, dark; bushy growth; [sport of Edith Nellie Perkins]

Ben Britten – See **Benjamin Britten**, S

Ben Cant HP, dr, 1901, Cant, B. R.; flowers crimson, center darker, very large, 25 petals, high-centered, intense fragrance; vigorous growth; [Suzanne-Marie Rodocanachi × Victor Hugo]

Ben Chaplin HT, w, 2003, Chaplin, Mrs. Mavis; flowers medium red, changing to purple, large, single, borne mostly solitary, no fragrance; foliage medium size, medium green, matte; prickles 10mm., straight; growth upright, medium (60 cm.); [sport of Linclonshire Poacher]; int. by Mrs Mavis Chaplin, 2003

Ben-Hur Gr, mr, 1960, Lammerts, Dr. Walter; bud long, pointed; flowers crimson, 4-5 in., 23 petals, high-centered, moderate fragrance; foliage leathery, glossy; vigorous growth; PP2066; [Charlotte Armstrong × (Charlotte Armstrong × Floradora)]; int. by Germain's

Ben Stad LCl, pb, 1925, Undritz; flowers pink, center yellow, edged white, reverse flesh-pink; [Silver Moon × Mme Jules Grolez]; int. by B&A

Benardella's Pearl – See **Jilly Jewel**, Min

Bendigold F, or, 1978, Murley, J.J.; bud globular; flowers 3 in., dbl., moderate fragrance; foliage glossy, bronze; vigorous, upright growth; [Rumba × Redgold]; int. by Brundrett, 1979

Bénédicte Seguin HT, ob, 1918, Pernet-Ducher; flowers ochre, shaded coppery orange, large, dbl., moderate fragrance

Benedictus XV HT, w, 1917, Leenders, M.; bud large, long-pointed; flowers white, center toned rose-salmon, large, dbl., borne mostly solitary, moderate fragrance; [Jonkheer J.L. Mock × Marquise de Sinéty]

Benedikt Roezl HRg, lp, 1925, Berger, V.; flowers light carmine-rose, large, very dbl.; foliage rugosa-like; vigorous, very bushy growth; [(*R. rugosa* × unknown) × La France]; int. by Faist

Benelux F, dr, 1949, Leenders, M.; flowers crimson-red, semi-dbl.; [Donald Prior × Rosamunde]

Benelux Star HT, yb, 1997, RvS-Melle; flowers 4 in., 37 petals, cupped, moderate fragrance; foliage matte; strong grower growth; int. in 1997

Benevolence HT, or, 1986, Sanday, John; flowers rich vermilion, large, 35 petals, high-centered, moderate fragrance; foliage large, dark, semi-glossy; prickles long, narrow; bushy growth; [Vera Dalton × seedling]; int. in 1986

Bengal Centifolia Ch, pb, 1804, Noisette

Bengal Cramoisi Double – See **Sanguinea**, Ch

Bengal Crimson – See **Sanguinea**, Ch

Bengal Ordinaire – See **Pallida**, Ch

Bengal Rose – See **Slater's Crimson China**, Ch

Bengal Tiger F, or, 2000, Kralovetz, Timm R.; flowers orange-red blend, 3-4½ in., semi-dbl., borne singly, slight fragrance; foliage small, dark green edged in dark red, glossy; prickles moderate; growth speading, medium (3-3½ ft.); PP14048; int. by Chamblee's Rose Nursery, 2002

Bengale à Grandes Feuilles – See **Bengale Centfeuilles**, Ch

Bengale Angevin – See **Blush Boursault**, Bslt

Bengale Animée Ch, mp, before 1817, from England; flowers lilac pink, small

Bengale Animée des Anglais – See **Bengale Animée**, Ch

Bengale Centfeuilles Ch, pb, 1804, Noisette; flowers pink bordered with deep wine pink, medium, full, borne in small clusters; foliage large, dark green, elongated, flat, slightly toothed; numerous prickles; stems upright

Bengale Centifolia – See **Bengale Centfeuilles**, Ch

Bengale Cerise Ch, mr

Bengale Cypress – See **Blush Boursault**, Bslt

Bengale d'Automne Ch, dp, 1825, Laffay, M. (possibly Cartier); flowers deep rose, paler at the petal bases, large, moderate sweet, with a hint of pepper fragrance

Bengale Gontier Cl HCh, dp; flowers pink, with carmine tones and violet veins through the petals, 7 cm., dbl., borne in clusters; vigorous, tall (10-15 ft.) growth

Bengale Hollandaise – See **Maheca**, Bslt

Bengale Nabonnand Ch, dr, 1886, Nabonnand; flowers very dark velvety purplish red, with tints of copper and yellow

Bengale Noire – See **Pourpre Foncé**, HGal

Bengale Noisette – See ***R. × noisettiana*** (Thory), N

Bengale Œillet – See **Bengale Centfeuilles**, Ch

Bengale Pourpre – See **Pourpre**, Ch

Bengale Rouge HCh, dr, 1781; flowers small, dark red to purple, semi-dbl.; blooms from spring through autumn; possibly synonymous with Rose du Bengale/Sanguinea

Bengale Rouge Ch, mr, 1955, Gaujard; bud ovoid; flowers bright carmine-red, open, very large; recurrent bloom; foliage abundant; very vigorous growth; [Gruss an Teplitz × seedling]

Bengale Sanguinaire Ch, mr, 1838, Desprez; flowers crimson, petals concave, small, very dbl.

Bengale Violet – See **Reversa**, Bslt

Bengali Ch, dp, 1913, Nonin; flowers medium, full, slight fragrance

Bengali F, or, 1969, Kordes; bud ovoid; flowers red-orange, medium, dbl.; foliage dark; [Dacapo × seedling]; int. by Buisman, 1969

Bengt M. Schalin HEg, dp, 1956, Kordes; flowers rose-red, semi-dbl., borne in clusters (up to 10), slight fragrance; non-recurrent; foliage light green, leathery, glossy; very vigorous growth; [*R. kordesii* × Eos]

Benihime Min, mr; int. by Keisei, 1992

Benikanoko HT, rb; flowers striped; int. by Hiroshima, 1998

Beniowski HGal, m, before 1836, Coquerel; flowers purple, medium, full

Benita – See **Benita Stripe**, Min

Benita Gr, my, 1994, Dickson, Colin; flowers saffron yellow, 3 in., full, moderate fragrance; foliage medium size, medium green, semi-glossy; upright (90 cm.) to bushy growth; int. by Dickson Nurseries, Ltd., 1994

Benita Stripe Min, rb, Benardella, Frank; flowers striped; int. in 1992

Benjamin Britten S, or, 2002, Austin, David; flowers very dbl., cupped, borne in small clusters, intense fragrance; foliage medium size, dark green, semi-glossy; prickles medium, deep concave, red/brown, moderate; growth bushy, medium (120 cm.); garden decorative; [Ausfather × pink English-type shrub]; int. by David Austin Roses, Ltd., 2001

Benjamin Drouet HP, dr, 1878, Verdier, E.; flowers intense purplish red, brightened with fiery red, very large, full, borne in small clusters; foliage large, ovate, deeply toothed; prickles numerous, large, brownish green; growth vigorous

Benjamin Franklin HT, lp, 1969, Von Abrams; bud ovoid; flowers dawn-pink, large, 55 petals, high-centered; foliage dark, leathery; upright growth; int. by Roses by Edmunds, 1970

Benkey HT, Itami, B.; int. in 1969

Benmable Min, rb, Benardella, Frank; int. in 1996

Benmay Min, ob, Benardella, Frank; int. in 2001

Benmoon Min, m, Benardella, Frank; int. in 1992

Bennett's Seedling Ayr, w, 1840, Bennett ; bud pink; flowers pale pink, fading to white, 5 cm., semi-dbl. to dbl., borne in large clusters, strong musky fragrance; raised by Bennett, the gardener for Lord Manners at Thoresby; int. by Lord Manners at Thoresby, England

Bennewhampshire Min, yb, Benardella, Frank; int. in 2001

Benoist Pernin HP, mp, 1889, Myard; flowers bright velvety pink; [sport of Duchess of Edinburgh]

Benoit Cornet HP, mr, 1868, Cornet/Ducher; flowers poppy red

Benoit Friart HT, m, 1985, Rijksstation Voor Sierplantenteelt; flowers rosy lilac, medium, 47 petals, flat, borne singly and in clusters of up to 7, intense fragrance; foliage matte; upright growth; [Fragrant Cloud × Astrée]; int. in 1978

Benoît Pernin – See **Benoist Pernin**, HP
Benoni '75 – See **Vision**, HT, 1977
Ben's Gold HT, dy, Williams, J. Benjamin; flowers semi-dbl., star-shaped; int. in 1996
Ben's Pink Cluster S, pb, J. B. Williams; flowers red buds opening to pink clusters; int. by Hortico, 2004
Benson and Hedges – See **Benson and Hedges Gold**, HT
Benson and Hedges Gold HT, yb, 1979, McGredy, Sam IV; bud ovoid; flowers deep golden yellow flushed coppery red, medium, 33 petals; bushy growth; [Yellow Pages × (Arthur Bell × Cynthia Brooke)]; int. by Mattock; Gold Star of the South Pacific, Palmerston North, NZ, 1978
Benson & Hedges Special – See **Dorola**, Min
Bentall's Scarlet HT, or, 1935, Bentall; flowers bright scarlet; very vigorous growth
Bente HT, op; greenhouse rose; int. by Terra Nigra B. V., 2004
Bentveld HT, op, 1932, Posthuma; flowers carmine-orange, edges lighter than parent; vigorous growth; [sport of Charles P. Kilham]; int. by Low
Benvenuto LCl, mr, 1967, Meilland; flowers rose-red, medium, semi-dbl., borne in small clusters; recurrent bloom; prickles numerous, short; vigorous, climbing growth; [(Alain × Guinée) × Cocktail]; int. by URS
Bérangère M, lp, 1849, Vibert; flowers delicate pink, large, dbl.
Berberifolia Hardii – See **Hulthemia hardii**
Berceau Impérial HP, mp, 1856, Vigneron; flowers bright pink, moderate fragrance
Berceuse HT, my, 1950, Robichon; bud globular, yellow; flowers chamois, very large, very dbl.; foliage leathery; very vigorous, upright growth; [Signora × Mrs Pierre S. duPont]
Berendina – See **Pimprenelle**, S
Bérénice HGal, rb, 1818, Vibert; flowers rose and crimson, shaded with slate, large, dbl., globular; pendulous growth
Bérénice F, dr, Croix, P.; int. in 1979
Berenice S, pb, Barni, V.; flowers salmon, with pastel rose shading on outer petals, dbl.; no prickles; growth vigorous, spreading, groundcover (50-70 cm.); int. in 1993
Bérénice HGal, lp, before 1829, Racine; flowers light bright pink, medium, full, borne in small clusters
Berenice Neville HT, dy, 1995, Kirkham, Gordon Wilson; flowers medium to large, dbl., borne in small clusters; foliage medium size, dark green, semi-glossy; numerous prickles; medium, upright growth; [Tynwald × Bright Smile]; int. by Kirkham, 1996
Bergers Erfolg HRg, mr, 1925, Berger, V.; flowers fire-red with yellow stamens, 3-4 in., single, borne in clusters; occasionally recurrent bloom; foliage dark; very vigorous, bushy growth; [(*R. rugosa* × unknown) × Richmond]; int. by Pfitzer
Bergers Koralle F, op, Berger, W.; flowers dark salmon-pink, large, dbl.; int. in 1956
Bergers Morgenröte S, lp, Berger, W.; flowers creamy pink, medium, dbl.; int. in 1959
Bergers Roma HT, rb, Berger, W.; flowers large, dbl.; int. in 1965
Bergesloh Pol, mr, 1929, Vogel, M.; flowers carmine-red, small, dbl.
Bergfeuer F, Leenders, J.; int. in 1959
Bergfeuer Superior F, Leenders, J.; int. in 1968
Bergrat Otto Berger HT, w, 1924, Berger, V.; flowers creamy white to sulfur, center deeper, dbl.; [Pharisaer × Prince de Bulgarie]; int. by Faist
Bering – See **Bering Renaissance**, S
Bering Renaissance S, m, Poulsen; flowers mauve, 10-15 cm., dbl., intense fragrance; foliage dark; growth bushy, 100-150 cm.; int. by Poulsen Roser, 1997
Berkeley – See **Tournament of Roses**, Gr
Berkeley Beauty Min, m, 1988, Moore, Ralph S.; flowers picotee white, edged lavender to pink (striped), small, dbl., high-centered; foliage medium size, medium green, semi-glossy, abundant; prickles varying green to brown; bushy, medium, neat growth; [Pink Petticoat × Make Believe]; int. by Sequoia Nursery, 1987
Berkshire – See **Sommermärchen**, F, 2006
Berleburg F, dp, Poulsen; flowers 8-10 cm., 25 petals, no fragrance; foliage dark; growth bushy, 60-100 cm.; PP12904; int. by Poulsen Roser, 1996
Berleburg Castle – See **Berleburg**, F
Berlengas HT, Moreira da Silva, A.
Berlin S, ob, 1949, Kordes; bud long, pointed; flowers orange-scarlet, center golden, large, single, borne in large clusters; repeat bloom; foliage leathery, dark; prickles large; very vigorous, upright growth; [Eva × Peace]
Berlin Beauty HT, lp
Berliner Luft F, ob, Hauser; flowers orange-yellow, large, dbl., high-centered, borne in small clusters, slight fragrance; bushy, vigorous (80-100 cm.) growth; int. in 1985
Berlitz S, mr; int. by Michael's Premier Roses, 2001
Bermer Stadtmusikanten S, lp; int. by Kordes, 2000
Bermina, Cl. Cl F, ly, Ruston; flowers plae yellow, fading almost to white, full, moderate fragrance
Bermuda Pink HT, lp, 1975, Golik; bud ovoid; flowers flesh-pink, 4-5 in., 35-40 petals, globular, slight rose fragrance; foliage glossy, light; compact, moderate growth; [Queen of Bermuda × Montezuma]; int. by Dynarose, 1974
Bermuda Yellow Mutabilis HCh, ly, 2004, Watlington, Ronica; flowers light yellow, shaded pink towards petal edges, large, single
Bermuda's Emmie Gray Ch, rb; discovered in Bermuda.
Bermudiana HT, mp, 1966, Boerner; bud ovoid; flowers 5-6 in., 35-60 petals, high-centered, moderate fragrance; foliage leathery; vigorous, upright growth; PP2578; [Golden Masterpiece × unknown]; int. by J&P
Bern HT, dp, 1979, Huber; bud long, pointed; flowers deep pink, shallow, 4 in., 24 petals, intense spicy fragrance; foliage dark, leathery; spreading growth; [Crimson Glory × Lilac Charm]; int. in 1975
Bernadette HT, lp, 1964, Kelly; flowers large, dbl., high-centered; foliage dark, leathery; vigorous, bushy growth; [sport of Peace]
Bernadette HT, w, Dorieux; int. in 1976
Bernadette Chirac HRg, ab, 1986, Delbard-Chabert; flowers apricot, yellow and orange blend, large, 23 petals, cupped, slight fragrance; foliage rugose; vigorous, bushy growth; [*R. rugosa* × (First Edition × Floradora)]; int. in 1979
Bernadette Lafont S, dp, Sauvageto; flowers rose-fuchsia, very dbl., quartered, cupped; int. in 2004
Bernaix, Climbing Cl HT, dr, 1935, Shamburger, C.S.; [sport of Souv. d'Alexandre Bernaix]
Bernalene HT, ab, Kordes; int. in 1994
Bernalia S, mp, 1965, Bernal; flowers pink, center white, small, semi-dbl., borne in clusters, moderate fragrance; recurrent bloom; foliage bright green; vigorous growth; [Mosqueta × Cecilia]
Bernard P, op, 1836, unknown; flowers salmon-pink, medium, full, cupped; growth small; [sport of Rose du Roi]
Bernard Buffet HT, dp, Gaujard; flowers pink cyclamen rose, exhibition, slight fragrance; growth very bushy; int. by Rene Dessevre, 2003
Bernard Palissy B, mp, 1847, Vibert; flowers bright pink, striped garnet red, large, full, globular
Bernard Palissy HP, mp, 1863, Margottin; flowers bright carmine, very large, very full
Bernard Pivot F, dy, Orard; flowers bright yellow, dbl.; compact, strong growth; int. in 2002
Bernard Verlot HP, rb, 1874, Verdier, E.; flowers red-scarlet, center violet, full
Bernd Clüver F, mp, 1974, Reinold; bud pointed; flowers 2½-3 in., moderate fruity fragrance; moderate, upright growth; [Nordia × Sans Souci]
Bernd Weigel Rose F, mp, Tantau; flowers strong pink in center, fading to pale pink on the outer petals, dbl., borne in clusters; int. by Rosen Tantau, 2004
Bernensis S, mr, Meilland; flowers bright red, dbl.; good repeat; dark green, small foliage; growth to 40-60 cm.; groundcover; int. in 1994
Bernhard Daneke Rose – See **Showbiz**, F
Bernice HT, mp, 1927, Pemberton; flowers carmine-pink on yellow base, semi-dbl.
Bernice Pol, mp, 1937, Nicolas; bud ovoid; flowers brilliant cerise-pink, small, dbl., globular, borne in clusters; recurrent bloom; foliage glossy, light; dwarf growth; [Baby Tausendschon × Gloria Mundi]; int. by J&P
Bernice Cooper HT, pb, 2005, Poole, Lionel; flowers ivory with pink edge, 5 in., very full, high-centered, borne mostly solitary, moderate fragrance; foliage medium size, dark green, semi-glossy; prickles medium, triangular, brown, moderate; growth bushy, medium (30 in.); garden decoration, exhibition; [Pedrus Aquarius × New Zealand]; int. in 2006
Bernina F, w, deRuiter; flowers white, medium, full, slight fragrance; int. in 1979
Bernina, Climbing Cl F, w
Bernstein Pol, yb, VEG (S) Baumschulen Dresden; flowers dark yellow and copper, medium, dbl.; int. in 1972
Bernstein – See **Bernstein-Rose**, F
Bernstein-Rose F, dy, Tantau; flowers large, warm amber-yellow, very dbl., moderate fresh herb fragrance; growth to 50-60 cm.; int. in 1987
Bernstorff F, mp, Olesen; bud broad based ovoid; flowers medium pink, 8 cm., 75-80 petals, rosette, borne in clusters of up to 7, slight floral fragrance; recurrent; foliage dark; prickles numerous, 6 mm., linear to hooked; bushy (60-100 cm.) growth; PP15161; [seedling × Queen Margrethe]; int. by Poulsen Roser, 2003; Honorable Mention, Hradec Králové, 2006
Berolina F, my, 1976, Kordes; bud long, pointed; flowers high-centered, slight fragrance; foliage dark, soft; vigorous, upright growth; [Mabella × seedling]
Berries 'n' Cream LCl, pb, 1999, Olesen; flowers pink striped white, reverse same, 4-5 in., full, borne in large clusters, moderate apple fragrance; foliage large, medium green, glossy; few prickles; climbing, tall (10-12 ft.) growth; PP10639; [Evita × seedling]; int. as Calypso, Poulsen Roser ApS
Berry Berry Grape Min, m, King; int. in 1997
Berry Berry Red Min, mr, 1993, Taylor, Franklin; flowers medium red, large, dbl., borne mostly singly, slight fragrance; foliage medium size, medium green, semi-glossy; few prickles; medium (24 in.), upright, bushy growth; [Party Girl × Papa Meilland]; int. by Taylor's Roses, 1993
Berry Patch – See **Ruby**, Min
Bersagliera HT, dp, 1960, Luigi; bud globular; flowers crimson, phlox-pink and fuchsia-pink, medium, dbl.; strong stems; vigorous growth
Bert Hinkler Pol, dp, 1928, Harrison, A.
Bert Mulley – See **Edna Walling**, HMult
Bertha S, lp, 1946, Wright, Percy H.; flowers delicate

pink, very large, single, borne like hollyhock flowers; non-recurrent; erect stems; growth to 8 ft.; [(*R. rugosa* × Hybrid Perpetual) × (*R. multiflora* × *R. blanda*)]

Bertha Aikman HT, op, 1977, Simpson, J.W.; bud high pointed; flowers two-toned salmon-pink, 4 in., 45 petals, moderate fragrance; foliage matte; moderate, slightly spreading growth; [Gypsy Moth × Percy Thrower]; int. by Manawatu Rose Soc.

Bertha Gorst HT, mr, 1933, Beckwith; flowers crimson-cerise, base gold, veined bronze, very large, dbl.; foliage bronze; [sport of Autumn]

Bertha Kiese HT, my, 1913, Jacobs; flowers medium, semi-dbl.; [Kaiserin Auguste VIktoria × Undine]

Bertha Turner HT, op, 1925, Pemberton; flowers salmon-peach

Bertha von Suttner HT, ly, 1918, Verschuren; flowers light yellow with copper tints, medium, dbl.

Berthe Baron HP, lp, 1869, Baron-Veillard; flowers delicate rose shaded with white, large, dbl.; [Jules Margottin × unknown]

Berthe de Sansal HP, mp, about 1850, de Sansal, Desprez, or Jamain; flowers medium, full

Berthe du Mesnil de Mont Chauvau HP, lp, 1876, Jamain, H.; flowers light silvery rose pink, center lighter, medium, dbl.

Berthe Gaulis HT, rb, 1909, Bernaix fils; flowers light red over China pink, center darker, very large, full, moderate fragrance

Berthe Lévêque – See **Mlle Berthe Lévêque**, HP

Berthe Mallerin HT, or, 1960, Mallerin, C.; flowers red tinted orange, dbl.; strong stems; vigorous growth

Berthet HGal, m, before 1827, Cartier; flowers violet

Berti Gimpel HP, mp, 1913, Altmüller; flowers large, semi-dbl.; [Frau Karl Druschki × Fisher Holmes]

Bertin N, mp, about 1836, Bertin; flowers fresh pink, aging to purple pink, large, full

Bertram – See **Sneezy**, Pol

Bertram Park HT, mr, 1928, Burbage Nursery; flowers rosy crimson, base yellow, single, slight fragrance; [Eblouissant × Mme Edouard Herriot]

Berwick HSpn, pb; flowers rose shading to white at edges, large, semi-dbl.; growth low

Beryl Ainger HT, w, 1955; flowers cream, base golden yellow; [sport of The Doctor]; int. by F. Cant

Beryl Bach HT, yb, 1985, Harkness, R., & Co., Ltd.; flowers yellow, blended pink, large, 40 petals, moderate fragrance; foliage large, light green, matte; tall, upright growth; [Sunsprite × Silver Jubilee]; int. by R. Harkness & Co., Ltd.

Beryl Formby HT, yb, 1948, Fryers Nursery, Ltd.; flowers golden yellow shaded crimson, 36-40 petals; foliage glossy; bushy growth; [sport of McGredy's Sunset]

Beryl Formby, Climbing Cl HT, yb, 1956, Letts

Beryl Joyce HT, ob, Tantau; int. by Pocock's Roses, 2006

Beryl Wearmouth F, mp, 1974, Harkness; flowers 4½ in., 19 petals; foliage light green, matte; [(Ann Elizabeth × Orange Sensation) × Sea Pearl]

Besançon HT, op, Sauvageot; flowers rose-salmon, reverse carmine, 50-60 petals; growth to 80-90 cm.; int. in 1973

Beslan HT, mp, 2004, Ryan, Max; flowers medium pink, reverse white, 7½ cm., very full, borne mostly solitary, slight fragrance; recurrent; foliage medium size, dark green; prickles moderate, moderate; stems long; growth compact, bushy; exhibition; [Virgo × Signature]; int. by Same, 2002

Bess Lovett HWich, dp, 1915, Van Fleet; flowers light red, 7-8 cm., dbl., cupped, borne in clusters of 10-20, moderate fragrance; foliage dark green, glossy; vigorous, climbing growth; [*R. wichurana* × Souv du Président Carnot]; int. by J.T. Lovett

Bessie Brown HT, ly, 1899, Dickson, A.; flowers yellowish-white, large, very dbl.; foliage light, leathery, glossy

Bessie Chaplin HT, mp, 1921, Chaplin Bros.; flowers bright pink, center deeper, very dbl.; [Lady Pirrie × Gorgeous]; Gold Medal, NRS, 1923

Bessie Johnson HP, lp, 1873, Curtis; flowers light flesh pink, large, very dbl., globular; [sport of Abel Grand]

Bessie Johnson, Climbing Cl HP, dp, 1878, Paul, G.

Bessie Lee Pol

Bessy S, ob, Interplant; bud small, roundish; flowers gold-orange to apricot, medium size; foliage dark green, glossy; growth to 40-60 cm.; int. in 1998

Best Friend – See **Caprice de Meilland**, HT

Best Friend – See **My Best Friend**, Min

Best Friends Min, ob, 2001, Bridges, Dennis; flowers reverse yellow, 1½ in., dbl., borne mostly solitary, slight fragrance; foliage medium size, dark green, semi-glossy; prickles ¼ in., downward curved, moderate; growth compact, bushy, low (16-18 in.); garden, container, border, cutting; [Hot Tamale × select pollen]; int. by Bridges Roses, 2002; AOE, ARS, 2002

Best of 04 Min, yb, 2005, Wells, Verlie W.; flowers yellow orange blend, reverse orange edge to yellow, 1½-1¾ in., dbl., borne mostly solitary; foliage medium size, medium green, semi-glossy; prickles ¼ in., hooked; growth upright, slightly spreading, medium (2½ ft.); garden, exhibition; [seedling × seedling]; int. Wells' MidSouth Roses, by 2004

Best of Friends HT, my, Poulsen; flowers medium yellow, 8-10 cm., 25 petals, borne one to a stem, slight fragrance; foliage dark, glossy; growth bushy, 60-100 cm.

Best Regards, Climbing Cl HT, pb, 1940, Elmer, C.A.; int. by Germain's

Best Regards HT, pb, 1944, Morris; flowers pink bicolor, 6-7 in., 50-60 petals, dahlia-like; foliage leathery, dark; very vigorous, compact growth; [Soeur Thérèse × Signora]; int. by Germain's

Best Wishes HT, dp, 1960, Fisher, G.; bud long, pointed; flowers currant-red, 5½-6 in., 25-35 petals, high-centered, moderate fragrance; foliage leathery; strong stems; very vigorous growth; int. by Arnold-Fisher Co., 1959

Best Wishes, Climbing Cl HT, rb, Chessum, Paul; flowers red with gold reverse; variegated foliage; int. in 1996

Best Wishes Min, dp, Delbard; int. in 2001

Beta HT, pb, 2007, Chapman, Bruce; flowers full, borne mostly solitary; foliage medium size, dark green, glossy; prickles medium, hooked, brown, few; growth upright, medium (1½ m.); garden decoration; [Kardinal × St. Patrick]; int. by Ross Roses, 2007

Betano Beach F, rb, 1966, Fankhauser; bud long, pointed; flowers light salmon-pink, reverse scarlet and burnt crimson, medium, dbl., high-centered; foliage glossy, dark, leathery; vigorous, upright growth; [Ma Perkins × Detroiter]; int. by A. Ross & Son

Beth F, ly, 1968, O'Connell; flowers buff-yellow; [sport of Elizabeth of Glamis]; int. by Rumsey, 1966

Beth HSpn, lp, Mertens; flowers single; int. in 1973

Bethany Grace Min, mp, 2003, Chaffin, Lauren M.; flowers finish pink as they age, 2 in., very full, borne mostly solitary, slight fragrance; foliage medium size, dark green, semi-glossy; prickles slightly curved; growth upright, bushy, tall (18-24 in.); garden, containers; [unknown × unknown]; int. by Pixie Treasures Miniature Roses, 2003

Bethany Helena HT, pb, 1997, Poole, Lionel; flowers large, very dbl., borne mostly singly; foliage large, dark green, semi-glossy; upright, medium growth; [Tom Foster × Gavotte]

Betinho HT, rb, 1958, Moreira da Silva; flowers velvety red and brown; [Charles Mallerin × Monte Carlo]

Betsie Jane HT, ab, 1977, Tresise; bud long, pointed; flowers soft apricot-pink, large, dbl., moderate fragrance; foliage light green; tall, vigorous growth; [sport of Bewitched]; int. in 1976

Betsy Min, ob, 2003, Hough, Robin; flowers full, borne mostly solitary; foliage medium size, medium green, semi-glossy; prickles medium, slightly curved down, moderate; growth upright, medium (18-24 in.); exhibition; [sport of Pierrine]; int. in 2002

Betsy Jane S, pb, 2004, Mary C. Carle; flowers medium pink with white base, yellow stamens, 1 in., 5 petals, borne in clusters of 24-36, slight fragrance; quick repeat; foliage medium size, dark green, semi-glossy; small, hooked, brown, no prickle; growth spreading, medium (3-3½ ft.); garden; hips ruby; [Climbing Rainbow's End × unknown]; int. in 2004

Betsy McCall F, op, 1956, Boerner; bud ovoid; flowers shrimp-pink, open, 3-3½ in., 25-30 petals, borne in large clusters, moderate fragrance; foliage glossy; vigorous, bushy growth; PP1603; [seedling × Fashion]; int. by J&P

Betsy Murchison HT, dp, Desamero, Luis; flowers 34 petals, high-centered; [Southern Lady × seedling]

Betsy Ross HT, ob, 1931, Samtmann Bros.; flowers like parent but marked russet-orange; [sport of Talisman]

Betsy Ross HT, dr, 1970, Delbard; flowers deep red, large, dbl., high-centered, slight fragrance; vigorous, upright growth; [(Gloire de Rome × La Vaudoise) × Divine]; int. as La Passionata, Trioreau, & Pepinieres G. Delbard, 1969

Betsy Taaffe S, ab, Taaffe; [sport of Abraham Darby]

Betsy van Nes Pol, mr, 1914, van Ryn; flowers pure bright red, unusually large, semi-dbl.; [sport of Mrs W. H. Cutbush]

Bette Irene S, ab, 1987, Schneider, Peter; flowers apricot, reverse deeper, fading light pink, imbricated, medium, 9 petals, moderate fragrance; repeat bloom; foliage medium size, dark green, matte; prickles awl-like, medium, brown; upright, medium-tall growth; hips rounded, medium size, ornamental, bright red; [Dairy Maid × seedling]

Bettelstudent Pol, dp, 1909, Lambert; flowers dark carmine; [Euphrosyne × Sunset]

Better Homes & Gardens HT, pb, 1976, Warriner, William A.; bud ovoid; flowers rose, ivory reverse, 3-3½ in., 38 petals, high-centered, slight fragrance; foliage glossy, dark; medium-tall, upright growth; PP3956; [Tropicana × Peace]; int. by J&P, 1975

Better Homes & Gardens Diamond Jubilee HT, rb, 1997, Winchel, Joseph F.; flowers ivory cream, silvery with raspberry edges, 3 in., full, slight fragrance; foliage medium size, medium green, semi-glossy; upright, medium (5ft.) growth; [Lynn Anderson × seedling]; int. by Certified Roses, Inc.

Better Times HT, mr, 1934, Joseph H. Hill, Co.; flowers cerise, large, dbl., high-centered; foliage dark, leathery; very vigorous, compact growth; [sport of Briarcliff]

Better Times, Climbing Cl HT, mr, 1937, Parmentier, J.

Bettie Herholdt HT, w, 1978, Herholdt, J.A.; bud pointed; flowers ivory-white, 5½ in., 50 petals, moderate fragrance; vigorous growth; PP3923; [(White Swan × seedling) × Pascali]

Bettina HT, op, 1953, Meilland, F.; flowers salmon-orange, veined, well-formed, 4 in., 37 petals, moderate fragrance; foliage dark, glossy, bronze; vigorous growth; [Peace × (Mme Joseph Perraud × Demain)]; int. by URS

Bettina, Climbing Cl HT, op, 1959, Meilland, F.; flowers salmon pink at center, buff yellow at edges, large, moderate fragrance; int. by URS, 1958; Gold Medal, Geneva, 1959

Bettina '78 HT, op, 1976, Paolino; flowers coral, 4 in., 30 petals; foliage dark, leathery; vigorous growth; PP3857; [(Jolie Madame × Sunlight) × (Lady Elgin × Dr. A.J. Verhage)]; int. by URS, 1976

Bett's Cardinal Spirit F, dr, 1999, Walters, Betty & Richard; flowers cardinal red, 4½ in., dbl., borne in small clusters; foliage medium size, medium green, semi-glossy; few prickles; upright, medium (3 ft.) growth; [High Spirit × (Moody Blues × Melina)]

Bett's Lemon Cream F, ly, 2003, Walters, Betty and Richard; flowers full, borne in small clusters; foliage medium size, dark green, matte; prickles medium, hooked; growth upright, tall (1 m.); garden, exhibition; [Mt. Hood × Casino]; int. in 1995

Bett's Little Gem Min, mp, 1996, Walters, Betty & Richard; flowers medium pink with white ring around stamens, full, open, cupped, slight fragrance; foliage medium size, light green, semi-glossy; few prickles; upright, medium growth; [Pink Petticoat × unknown]

Bett's Little Rhapsody Min, op, 1996, Walters, Betty & Richard; flowers orange-pink, medium, 76 petals, borne mostly singly; foliage medium size, dark green with pink edge, glossy; upright, very compact, medium (3-4 ft.) growth; [Bett's White Delight × seedling]

Bett's Pink Lace Min, pb, 1996, Walters, Betty & Richard; flowers white with pink edge, changing to salmon pink, full, borne singly and in small clusters, intense fragrance; foliage medium size, dark green, glossy; few prickles; compact, low growth; [Pink Petticoat × seedling]

Bett's Snow Dancer F, w, 1999, Walters, Betty & Richard; bud hint of green, opening to white; flowers outer edge white with cream center, numerous golden stamens, 4½ in., full, borne in large clusters; foliage medium size, medium green, semi-glossy; some prickles; compact, medium (4 ft.) growth; [Mt Hood × Aorangi]

Bett's White Delight Min, w, 1992, Walters, Betty & Richard; flowers creamy white opening to pure white, rosette, 2½ in., 58-86 petals, borne in clusters of 5; foliage medium to dark green, matte; tall, compact growth; [Pink Petticoat × seedling]

Bett's White Sensation F, w, 2003, Walters, Betty and Richard; flowers white to cream, 8 cm., very full, borne in large clusters; foliage medium size, dark green, matte; prickles medium, hooked; growth upright, tall (1-2 m.); garden, exhibition; [Mt. Hood × Aorangi]; int. in 1995

Bett's Winter Holly Min, or, 2003, Walters, Betty and Richard; flowers very full, borne in small clusters; foliage small, dark green, glossy; prickles ½ cm., narrow; growth upright, tall (18 in.); garden; [Winter Magic × Irresistable]; int. in 1999

Betty HT, pb, 1905, Dickson, A.; flowers coppery rose, shaded yellow, large, dbl.; very vigorous growth

Betty, Climbing Cl HT, pb, 1926, Hohman

Betty HT, dr, 2000, Priestly, J.L.; flowers dark red, 9 cm., dbl., slight fragrance; medium size, light green, dull foliage; prickles moderate; compact, medium growth (3 ft.); [Satellite × Ena Harkness]

Betty Alden Cl Pol, lp, 1919, Farquhar; flowers appleblossom-pink passing to white, single; [Orléans Rose × (Katharina Zeimet × *R. arvensis* hybrid)]

Betty Baum HT, lp, 1927, Baum; flowers delicate pink, base yellow, dbl.; [sport of Premier]

Betty Bee Min, pb, 1984, Blazey, Daniel; flowers pink, white reverse, small, dbl., high-centered, no fragrance; foliage small, medium green, semi-glossy; compact, bushy growth; PP5448; [Little Darling × Toy Clown]; int. by Nor'East Min. Roses, 1983

Betty Berkeley T, mr, 1904, Bernaix, A.; bud long, ovoid; flowers bright red, medium, dbl.

Betty Bland S, dp, 1925, Skinner; flowers deep rose, fading pink, center deeper, dbl.; non-recurrent bloom; foliage rich green, soft; stems twigs ruby-red; vigorous (6 ft.), bushy growth; very hardy; [*R. blanda* × HP]

Betty Blossom HWich, mp, 1900, Dawson; flowers clear rose-pink, semi-dbl., borne in loose clusters; growth vigorous; pillar or bush; [*R. wichurana* × Mrs W.J. Grant]; int. by Eastern Nursery

Betty Boop F, rb, 1999, Carruth, Tom; bud pointed; flowers rosy edged, yellow at base when fresh, fading to white; bright stamens, 4 in., 6-12 petals, borne in small cluster of 3 to 5, moderate fruity fragrance; floriferous; foliage medium size, dark green, glossy, dark red new growth; prickles moderate; rounded, bushy, medium (4 ft.) growth; PP11517; [Playboy × Picasso]; int. by Weeks Roses, 1999

Betty Cuthbert HT, or, 1964, Palmer; bud long, pointed; flowers medium, very dbl.; foliage soft, glossy; very vigorous, upright growth; [sport of Roundelay]; int. by Palmer & Engall

Betty Driver F, pb, 1982, Gandy, Douglas L.; flowers pale peach and gold blend, yellow stamens, patio, large, semi-dbl.; foliage medium size, light green, semi-glossy; low, bushy growth; [seedling × Topsi]; int. by Gandy Roses, Ltd.

Betty Free F, mp, 1950, LeGrice; bud pointed; flowers Neyron rose, 25 petals, borne in clusters; vigorous growth; [sport of Fortschritt]

Betty Grace Clark HT, ob, 1933, Clarke Bros.; flowers orange-yellow, reverse streaked red, high-centered; vigorous, bushy growth; [sport of Marie Adélaide]

Betty Harkness F, ob, Harkness; flowers deep tangerine, 4 in., 24 petals, high-centered, moderate orange/clove fragrance; recurrent; foliage dark green, glossy; moderate (3 ft.) growth; int. in 1998

Betty Herholdt – See **Bettie Herholdt**, HT

Betty Hulton HT, dy, 1923, Dickson, A.; flowers deep saffron-yellow, dbl.; Gold Medal, NRS, 1923

Betty Lou Min, dp, 2004, Rickard, Vernon; flowers dark pink, blending to yellow at center when fully open, 1¾ in., dbl., borne mostly solitary, no fragrance; foliage medium size, dark green, glossy; prickles curved down, tan, numerous; growth spreading, tall (36 in.); [Fairhope × Ruby Baby]; int. by Almost Heaven Roses, 2004

Betty May Wood HT, ab, 1970, Wood; flowers apricot to buff, reverse coral-salmon, well-formed, 30 petals; foliage light green; free growth; [sport of Mischief]

Betty Morse HT, mr, 1950, Kordes; bud long, pointed; flowers 4 in., 25 petals; foliage olive-green; vigorous growth; [Crimson Glory × (Crimson Glory × Cathrine Kordes)]; int. by Morse

Betty Neuss HT, mp, 1974, Dawson, George; bud small, long, pointed; flowers pure pink, medium, dbl., slight fragrance; foliage small; very vigorous, upright growth; int. by C. Brundrett, 1973

Betty O HT, pb, 2006, Wells, Verlie W.; flowers light to medium pink, reverse light pink, 3½ in., full, borne in small clusters; foliage medium size, dark green, semi-glossy; prickles ⅜ in., straight, moderate; growth upright, medium (4 ft.); garden, exhibition; [Virginia × unknown]; int. by Wells' MidSouth Roses, 2006

Betty Paul HT, mp, 1988, Warner, A.J.; flowers medium pink blend, medium, 20-25 petals, high-centered, borne usually singly or in sprays; foliage medium size, medium green, semi-glossy, disease-resistant; prickles straight, medium, light brown; upright, medium, tall growth; hips ovoid, small, yellow-orange; [Queen Elizabeth × (Tiffany × Tropicana)]; Bronze Medal, ARC TG, 1987

Betty Pearson HT, w, 1929, Burbage Nursery; flowers cream, center apricot, petals shell-shaped, large

Betty Prior F, mp, 1935, Prior; bud ovoid, dark carmine; flowers carmine-pink, 5 petals, cupped, borne in clusters; vigorous, bushy growth; [Kirsten Poulsen × seedling]; int. by J&P, 1938; Gold Medal, NRS, 1933

Betty Prior, Climbing Cl F, mp, 1995, Cooper, Donell; flowers medium carmine pink, medium, 5 petals, borne in small clusters; foliage large, medium green, dull; some prickles; upright, spreading, medium growth; [sport of Betty Prior]; int. by Certified Roses, Inc., 1997

Betty Sheriff LCl, w, Sheriff

Betty Stielow HT, dp, 1928, Stielow Bros.; flowers dark pink, almost red at times, dbl.; [sport of Premier]

Betty Sutor HT, pb, 1929, McGredy; flowers pale pink, veined rose, reverse rosy, large, dbl.; foliage light, glossy; vigorous, bushy growth

Betty Uprichard HT, ab, 1922, Dickson, A.; bud long, pointed; flowers delicate salmon-pink, reverse carmine with coppery sheen, large, 20 petals, high-centered, intense fragrance; foliage large, light bronze green, leathery, glossy; very vigorous, tall growth; Gold Medal, NRS, 1921

Betty Uprichard, Climbing Cl HT, ab, 1936, Krause

Betty White HT, pb, Meilland Intl.; flowers light pink, darker toward center, large, 60-65 petals, cupped; foliage semi-glossy; growth to 90-110 cm.; PP13897; int. as André le Nôtre, Meilland, 2001

Betty Will S, pb, 1963, Erskine; flowers bright pink, lighter reverse, 35 petals; recurrent; foliage dark, leathery; some large prickles; red canes; tall growth; very hardy; [George Will × Betty Bland]

Betty Wilson Min, rb, 1998, Sheridan, John; flowers red, reverse yellow, 2 in., dbl., borne in small clusters; foliage medium size, light green, glossy; prickles few, small, hooked; upright, medium (2 ft.) growth; patio; [Sheila's Perfume × (Little Darling × seedling)]

Betty Wright Gr, m, 1988, Burks, Larry; flowers lilac-mauve, darker at tips, aging lighter lilac, semi-dbl., cupped, urn-shaped, slight fruity fragrance; foliage medium size, medium green, matte; prickles slight recurved, average, brown; bushy, medium growth; hips globular, average, orange-yellow; [Angel Face × seedling]; int. by Co-Operative Rose Growers

Betty's Baby MinFl, dp, 1994, Bell, Judy G.; flowers deep pink with white center, small, semi-dbl., borne in small clusters, no fragrance; foliage small, medium green, semi-glossy; few prickles; medium (12-14 in.), upright, bushy growth; [Twilight Trail × Charmglo]; int. by Michigan Mini Roses, 1995

Betty's Pride Min, rb

Betzel's Pink HT, op, 1955, Betzel; bud long; flowers coral-pink, 5 in., 55-60 petals, high-centered; foliage leathery, glossy; strong stems; vigorous, bushy growth; [sport of Pres. Herbert Hoover]; int. by Edmunds Roses, 1955

Beulah Belle S, mp, Rupert; flowers dbl., sometimes quartered, borne in along arching canes, strong fragrance; occasional repeat; foliage greyish-green; growth 7-8 ft.; good for pegging; int. by Ashdown Roses, 2001

Bev Dobson LCl, pb, 2000, Jerabek, Paul; flowers white with pink edge, 3 in., dbl., borne in small clusters, moderate fragrance; foliage medium size, medium green, semi-glossy, reddish when young; prickles moderate; growth climbing, spreading; int. by Freedom Gardens, 2001

Beverley Anne Ch, mr, 1987, Nobbs, Kenneth J.; flowers red-purple, open, 21 petals, flat, borne in sprays of 3-7, slight fragrance; foliage pivoted, serrated; no prickles; semi-dwarf growth; [seedling × seedling]

Beverley Stoop – See **Jaydon**, F

Beverly-Ann F, rb, 2000, Horner, Colin; flowers cerise purple, reverse lighter, 7 cm., dbl., borne in small clusters, moderate fragrance; foliage medium size, medium green, semi-glossy; numerous prickles; growth medium (90 cm.); [Anna Ford × (seedling × (Blessings × *R. moyesii fargesii*))]; int. by Warley Roses, 2003

Beverly Hills HT, ob, 1982, Delbard, Georges; flowers dark orange, greenhouse variety, borne in clusters; PP5673; [(Zambra × Orange Sensation) × (Zambra × (Orange Triumph × Floradora))]; int. as Malicorne, Pepinieres et Roseraies

Beverly Jayne S, lp, 1999, Jones, L.J.; flowers center deep pink, outer light pink, 1¼ in., 41 petals, borne in large clusters; foliage small, light green, dull; few prickles; upright, bushy, medium (3 ft.) growth; [Angela Rippon × New Dawn]

Beverly Kordana Min, op, Kordes; flowers coral pink, dbl.; container rose; int. by W. Kordes Söhne

Beverly Nicols HT, op, 1939, Burbage Nursery; flowers cream, reverse salmon, well-formed, large, high-centered; vigorous growth

Beverly Watson HT, w, Kordes; bud creamy white; flowers white with a delicate tan tint, full, cupped, slight fragrance; free-flowering; long, firm stems; tall growth; int. in 1997

Bewitched HT, mp, 1967, Lammerts, Dr. Walter; bud urn shaped; flowers cotton candy pink, 5 in., 27-30 petals, high-centered, borne singly, moderate damask fragrance; foliage large, apple green, glossy; new stems and foliage is red; vigorous, medium, rounded growth; PP2755; [Queen Elizabeth × Tawny Gold]; int. by Germain's; Gold Medal, Portland, 1967

Bewitched, Climbing Cl HT, mp; int. in 1989

Bewitched – See **Berleburg**, F

Bezruc HT, mr, 1938, Böhm, J.; flowers large, dbl.

Bhagmati F, mr, 1979, Viraraghavan, M.S. Viru; bud ovoid; flowers 2½-3 in., 15-20 petals, cupped, slight fragrance; foliage glossy, light green; dwarf, vigorous, bushy growth; [Charleston × ((Roman Holiday × Flamenco) × Goldgleam)]; int. by KSG Roses, 1977

Bhanu HT, yb, K&S; flowers cream to yellow with pink, full, well formed, moderate fragrance; int. by KSG Son, 1990

Bharami – See **Bharani**, Min

Bharani Min, m, 1984, Kasturi; flowers small, mauve with white eye, semi-dbl.; foliage small, light green, matte; upright growth; [seedling × seedling]; int. by KSG Son, 1973

Bhargav HT, op, K&S; flowers coral pink, dbl., classic, slight tea fragrance; int. by KSG Son, 1993

Bhavani HT, op, Kasturi; flowers salmon orange to vermilion, spiral; int. by KSG Son, 1986

Bhim HT, dr, 1970, IARI; bud long, pointed; flowers scarlet-red, open, large, very dbl.; abundant, intermittent bloom; vigorous, upright growth; [Charles Mallerin × Delhi Princess]; int. by Div. of Vegetable Crops & Flori.

Bi-Centennial Rose – See **The Australian Bicentennial**, HT

Bianca HT, w, 1913, Paul, W.; bud long, pointed; flowers pale peach tinted pinkand violet, center shaded rose, medium, dbl.; RULED EXTINCT 3/83 ARM

Bianca HT, w, 1927, Pemberton; flowers white, sometimes lightly flushed cream or pink, well-formed, dbl., moderate fragrance; RULED EXTINCT 3/83 ARM

Bianca HT, w, Kuhn; bud slim bud; flowers clean white, large, slight fragrance; dark green leaves; growth upright, strong; int. in 1987

Bianca Min, w, Olesen; flowers dbl., 25-30 petals, borne mostly solitary, moderate fragrance; foliage medium green, semi-glossy; growth bushy, very low (20-40 cm.); int. in 1996

Bianca Camelia HT, w, 1933, San Remo Exp. Sta.; bud ovoid, pointed; flowers snow-white, center light blush-yellow, very large, 23-25 petals; foliage light green; very vigorous, upright growth; [Nuntius Pacelli × Sachsengruss]

Bianca Parade Min, w, Poulsen; flowers white, medium, dbl., moderate fragrance; growth bushy, 20-40 cm.; int. by Poulsen Roser, 1996

Bianco Min, w, 1983, Cocker, James; flowers patio, small, 35 petals; foliage medium size, medium green, semi-glossy; bushy growth; [Darling Flame × Jack Frost]; int. by Cocker & Sons

Bibi Maizoon S, dp, 1995, Austin, David; flowers have cabbage rose form early, opening to cupped, rich pink, 7 cm., 41 petals, cupped, borne in small clusters, moderate fragrance; medium size, dark green, semi-glossy foliage; some prickles; strong, arching growth; 4 × 4 ft.; int. by David Austin Roses, 1989

Bibi Mezoon – See **Bibi Maizoon**, S

Bibiché F, ob, Dorieux, Francois; int. in 1974

Bibiché, Climbing Cl F, ob, Dorieux, Francois; int. in 1980

Bicentenaire de George Sand S, mp, Gilet; int. by Les Rosiers du Berry, 2005

Bicentenaire de Guillot S, dp, Guillot; free-flowering; foliage dense, healthy; growth vigorous; int. by Roseraies Guillot, 2004

Bicentennial F, rb, 1973, Meyer, C.; flowers deep pink and red blend, medium, dbl., high-centered, slight fragrance; foliage leathery; vigorous, upright, bushy growth; PP3802; int. by C-P, 1975

Bichette HT, mp, 1970, Verschuren, A.; flowers Persian rose, large, 20-25 petals; foliage dark, leathery; vigorous, upright growth; [Diamond Jubilee × seedling]; int. by Stassen, 1968

Bico Min, yb, Poulsen Roser; int. in 2000

Bicolette HT, rb, Tschanz, E.; flowers rusty red with cream reverse, dbl., high-centered; recurrent; int. in 1980

Bicolor – See ***R. spinosissima bicolor*** (Andrews)

Bicolor M, pb, 1855, Lacharme; flowers pink, spotted with violet, medium, dbl.; some repeat

Bicolore HP, w, 1877, Oger; flowers white with pink edge, aging to frosty pink, full, flat

Bicolore Incomparable HP, pb, 1861, Touvais; flowers deep pink, darker at center, striped with lighter pink, medium, full; sometimes classed as HGal or M

Bicolore Nana HSpn, w, Smith; flowers cream, flecked with carmine, medium, single; growth dwarf

Bicolour HT, rb; int. in 2004

Biddulph Grange S, rb, Fryer, Gareth; flowers velvety bright red with white base and reverse, semi-dbl., borne in large trusses, slight fragrance; bushy (3-4 ft.) growth; int. by Fryer's Roses, 1988; Gold Medal, Glasgow, 1991

Biddy Min, pb, Benardella, Frank; flowers soft pink with creamy yellow in the heart, 54 petals; good repeat; foliage medium green; growth bushy, 35 cm.

Bidentate Mountain Rose – See ***R. arvensis*** (Hudson)

Biedermeier HT, pb, Tantau; flowers white with pink edges, large, very dbl., borne in sprays; greenhouse rose; int. by Rosen Tantau, 2002

Biedermeier Min, rb; flowers cherry red and creamy white; int. by Richard Huber AG, 2006

Bien-Aimée HGal, mr, before 1845; flowers shining fiery red, full, moderate fragrance

Bienkie F, op; flowers between coral and apricot, small, dbl., exhibition, borne in large sprays and singly; repeats well; neat growth; int. by Kordes, 1995

Bienvenu Gr, ob, 1969, Swim & Weeks; bud long, pointed; flowers reddish-orange, large, 70 petals, high-centered, intense fragrance; foliage leathery, matte; vigorous, upright growth; PP3007; [Camelot × (Montezuma × War Dance)]; int. by Weeks Wholesale Rose Growers

Bienvêtu – See **Mons Gustave Bienvêtu**, HRg

Bifera Coronata – See **Celsiana**, D

Bifera Italica HGal, lp, before 1811, from Italy; bud pointed; flowers medium, dbl., borne in clusters; foliage light green; few prickles

Big and Beautiful Min, ab, 1999, Bennett, Dee; flowers deep apricot, 1-1½ in., full, borne mostly singly, slight fragrance; foliage medium size, medium green, semi-glossy; prickles moderate; upright, bushy, tall (5-6 ft.) growth; [Futura × Jean Kenneally]; int. by Tiny Petals, 2000

Big Apple HT, mr, 1984, Weeks, O.L.; flowers large, dbl., moderate fragrance; foliage large, medium green, matte to semi-glossy; upright, spreading growth; [Mister Lincoln × (Suspense × King's Ransom)]; int. by Weeks Wholesale Rose Growers, 1984

Big Apple HT, pb, Jackson & Perkins; bud ivory; flowers rose pink with carmine petal edges, large, dbl., exhibition, intense fragrance; strong growth, 100-120 cm.; int. by Rose Barni, 2003

Big Apricot Min, ab, Wells

Big Bang F, or, 1981, Barni-Pistoia, Rose; bud pointed; flowers deep orange-red, shallow-cupped, 13 petals, cupped, borne 5-10 per cluster, no fragrance; foliage matte, light green; prickles reddish-green; bushy growth; [Sarabande × Sarabande seedling]; int. in 1980

Big Ben HT, dr, 1964, Gandy, Douglas L.; flowers well-formed, 5-6 in.; foliage dark; tall growth; [Ena Harkness × Charles Mallerin]

Big Bowie S, ob, J. B. Williams; flowers apricot and orange blend, dbl., moderate fragrance; repeats well; growth strong grower to 5 ft.; int. by Hortico, 2005

Big Chief – See **Portland Trailblazer**, HT

Big Daddy HT, or, 1994, McGredy, Sam IV; flowers scarlet-orange, 3 in., full; foliage large, medium green, semi-glossy; bushy (100 cm.) growth; [Howard Morrison × Mme Delbard]; int. by McGredy Roses International, 1994

Big Duke HT, dp, 1991, Weddle, Von C.; bud pointed; flowers deep pink, silvery pink reverse, large, dbl., high-centered, borne usually singly, moderate fruity fragrance; foliage large, medium green, semi-glossy; upright, tall growth; [The Duke × seedling]

Big Jack Charlton HT, w, 1994, Poole, Lionel; flowers ivory, pale pink edge, 3-3½ in., full, borne mostly singly, slight fragrance; foliage large, dark green, glossy; some prickles; medium (85 cm.), upright growth; [Gavotte × Queen Esther]; int. by Battersby Roses, 1995

Big Jim Larkin HT, rb, 1998, McCann, Sean; flowers red with silver reverse, silvers flecks on top surface, 4½-5 in., very dbl., borne in large clusters; foliage large, dark green, semi-glossy; free blooming, spreading, medium (4 ft.) growth; [Lady in Red × Old Master]; int. by Hughes Roses, 1999

Big John Min, mr, 1980, Williams, Ernest D.; bud pointed; flowers deep medium red, base yellow, 1-1½ in., 42

petals, high-centered; foliage small, glossy, bronze; upright, bushy growth; PP4754; [Starburst × Over the Rainbow]; int. by Mini-Roses, 1979

Big John – See **Te Awamutu Centennial**, HT

Big John – See **Galleria**, HRg

Big Pink HT, dp, 2000, Lindquist, Jr., Robert; flowers full, 25-31 petals, high-centered, borne mostly singly; large, medium green, semi-glossy foliage; spreading, pillar, tall (4-8 ft.) growth; introduced originally prior to 1940

Big Purple – See **Stephens' Big Purple**, HT

Big Red HT, dr, 1967, Meilland, Mrs. Marie-Louise; bud pointed; flowers 4½-6 in., 52 petals, high-centered, slight fragrance; foliage leathery; vigorous, upright, bushy growth; PP2693; [Chrysler Imperial × seedling]; int. by C-P

Big Splash Cl HT, rb, 1969, Armstrong, D.L.; bud pointed; flowers flame-red, reverse lighter, base yellow, large, dbl., high-centered; foliage glossy, leathery; vigorous, climbing (8-10 ft.) growth; [Buccaneer × Bravo]; int. by Armstrong Nursery

Big Time HT, dp; flowers dbl., exhibition, borne mostly one to a stem; int. by Interplant, 2001

Biggi HT, yb, 1976, Kordes; bud ovoid; flowers 4½ in., 27 petals, high-centered, moderate fragrance; intermittent bloom; foliage glossy, dark; vigorous, upright growth; [Dr. A.J. Verhage × seedling]; int. by Fey, 1975

Bignonia N, yb, 1874, Levet; flowers golden orange, full

Bigoudi Min, rb, Meilland; flowers red and yellow striped, medium, dbl.; growth to 40-45 cm.; int. in 2001

Bihanga HT, ob, Ghosh; flowers flower orange with pink blend, reverse golden yellow, large, dbl., high-centered; int. in 2001

Bijarre – See **Francfort Agathé**, HGal

Bijou Pol, lp, 1932, deRuiter; flowers old rose; int. by Sliedrecht & Co.

Bijou MinFl, pb, Lens, Louis; int. in 1991

Bijou S, dy, Barni, V.; flowers creamy yellow, small, borne in large sprays, covering the plant; growth low, spreading, 40-60 cm.; int. by Rose Barni, 1999

Bijou de Couasnon HP, dr, 1886, Vigneron; flowers intense velvety red, large, full; growth upright; [Charles Lefebvre × unknown]

Bijou de Lyon HMult, w, 1882, Schwartz; flowers small, full, borne in clusters

Bijou de Royat-les-Bains Ch, mp, 1891, Veysset; flowers medium pink, marbled with carmine medium, dbl.; [Hermosa × unknown]

Bijou des Amateurs HGal, dr, before 1830, Jacquemet-Bonnefont; flowers dark cerise, medium to large, full

Bijou des Prairies – See **Gem of the Prairies**, HSet

Bijou d'Or – See **Golden Jewel**, Min

Bijou Superior Pol, lp, deRuiter; flowers have more lasting color; [sport of Bijou]

Bikini Red HT, mr, 1976, Golik; bud ovoid; flowers rose-red, tinged white, ruffled, 5 in., 40 petals, moderate fruity fragrance; foliage glossy, dark; [Queen of Bermuda × Peace]; int. by Dynarose, 1974

Bila Junior Miss HT, w, Strnad

Bilitis F, or, 1978, Gaujard; flowers vermilion-red, center yellow; [Tabarin × Golden Slippers]; int. in 1969

Bill Beaumont F, mr, 1983, Fryer, Gareth; flowers crimson, 20 petals, slight fragrance; foliage medium size, medium green, matte; bushy growth; [Evelyn Fison × Redgold]; int. by Fryer's Nursery, Ltd., 1982

Bill Cone Min, mr, 1989, Williams, Michael C.; bud ovoid; flowers medium, 35 petals, cupped, borne usually singly; foliage medium size, medium green, semi-glossy; prickles light green, globular; upright, tall growth; hips round, green to orange-yellow; [Heartland × Anita Charles]; int. by The Rose Garden & Mini Rose Nursery

Bill Daisey HT, mr, J. B. Williams; int. by Hortico, Inc., 2005

Bill Grant S, w, Clements, John; flowers white with gold stamens., 1 in., 5 petals, borne in clusters; free-flowering; foliage medium green, glossy; bushy (3-4 ft.), arching growth; int. by Heirloom, 2001

Bill Heath HT, w, 2007, Poole, Lionel; flowers upper ivory, tinged pink, reverse same, very large, 6 in., single, high-centered, borne mostly solitary; foliage dark green, glossy; prickles large, hooked down, dark brown, moderate; growth upright, medium (3 ft.); exhibition; [Brad × New Zealand]; int. in 2007

Bill Hunt HT, op, 1976, Blakemore; flowers deep coral, medium, 30 petals; foliage glossy; fairly vigorous growth; [Mischief × Serenade]

Bill Slim F, op, 1986, Harkness; bud globular; flowers salmon, deep pink reverse, large, 30 petals, borne singly or in clusters, slight fragrance; foliage glossy; bushy, spreading growth; [seedling × Silver Jubilee]; int. in 1987

Bill Temple HT, w, 1976, Harkness; flowers cream, 5-6 in., 30 petals, slight fragrance; foliage glossy, dark; [Crimson Halo × Piccadilly]

Bill Warriner F, op, 1998, Warriner, William A. & Zary, Keith W.; bud pointed, ovoid; flowers coral pink, ruffled edges, 3½-4 in., full, borne in large clusters, slight sweet fragrance; foliage medium size, dark green, semi-glossy; prickles moderate, straight; compact (3 ft.) growth; PP9494; [Sun Flare × Impatient]; int. by Bear Creek Gardens, Inc., 1997

Billard HP, op, before 1845, Billard; flowers bright peach-pink, large, very full, moderate fragrance

Billard et Barré Cl T, my, 1898, Pernet-Ducher; flowers deep buff, edges lighter, 9 cm., dbl., strong tea fragrance; [Mlle Alice Furon × Duchesse d'Auerstadt]

Billie and Lew HWich, m, Nobbs; int. in 1995

Billie Teas Min, dr, 1992, Hooper, John C.; flowers 1½ in., full, borne mostly singly, no fragrance; foliage medium size, medium green, matte; some prickles; medium (38-45 cm.), upright growth; [seedling × Merrimac]; int. by Kimbrew Walter Roses, 1992; AOE, ARS, 1993

Billionaire HT, mr, 1973, Warriner, William A.; bud ovoid, long, pointed; flowers large, dbl., high-centered, slight fragrance; foliage leathery; vigorous, upright growth; PP3381; [Fragrant Cloud × Proud Land]; int. by J&P

Billy S, rb, Hauser; int. in 1993

Billy Boiler Cl HT, mr, 1927, Clark, A.; flowers glowing red, semi-dbl.; vigorous, tall growth; [Black Boy × unknown]; int. by NRS Victoria

Billy Boy HT, my, 1926, McGredy; flowers sunflower-yellow, semi-dbl.; [Golden Emblem × Christine]; int. by Beckwith

Billy Boy Min, mr, 1990, Moore, Ralph S.; bud pointed, short; flowers small, 15-18 petals, cupped, borne usually singly; foliage small, medium green, matte, dense; prickles slender, straight, small, brownish; bushy, low to medium, compact growth; [Anytime × Happy Hour]; int. by Sequoia Nursery

Billy Fury Min, lp, 2005, Paul Chessum Roses; flowers single, borne in small clusters; foliage medium size, dark green, glossy; prickles large, long, pink, numerous; growth compact, medium (24 in.); bedding, containers; [seedling × seedling]; int. by World of Roses, 2005

Billy Graham HT, lp, 1998, Zary, Dr. Keith W.; bud long, pointed; flowers light pink, 5 in., 25-30 petals, high-centered, borne singly, slight sweet fragrance; foliage large, dark green, glossy; prickles moderate; growth upright, tall (5 ft.); PP11049; [Honor × Color Magic]; int. by Bear Creek Gardens, Inc., 1998

Bimboro HT, dr, 1979, W. Kordes Söhne; bud globular; flowers 3-3½ in., 46 petals, high-centered, moderate fragrance; foliage glossy; vigorous, bushy, upright growth; [seedling × Kardinal]; int. by Willemse

Binapani HT, w, Dey, S. C.; flowers large, pastel cream with shades at petal edges, dbl.; floriferous

Bing Crosby HT, ob, 1980, Weeks; bud ovoid; flowers strong clear orange, 5 in., 40-45 petals, cupped, borne mostly singly, slight light spice fragrance; foliage medium size, heavy, leathery, wrinkled, dark; prickles long hooked downward; long stems; vigorous, upright, bushy growth; PP4695; [seedling × First Prize]

Bingo HT, dr, 1956, Robichon; bud pointed; flowers cardinal-red, 4-5 in., 55 petals, high-centered, intense fragrance; foliage glossy; upright growth; PP1392; [((Hadley × unknown) × Ami Quinard) × Crimson Glory]; int. by Ilgenfritz Nursery, 1955

Bingo Meidiland – See **Carefree Delight**, S

Bingo Meillandecor – See **Carefree Delight**, S

Bingo Queen Min, pb, 1996, Bennett, Dee; flowers light pink with medium pink inner petals, 1½ in., full, high-centered; foliage medium size, medium green, semi-glossy; prickles moderate; bushy, medium (50-60 cm.) growth; [Brandy × Jean Kenneally]; int. by Tiny Petals Nursery, 1997

Bipinnata – See ***R. centifolia bipinnata*** (Thory), C

Bipontina S, mr, Huber; int. by Richard Huber AG, 1988

Bipontina 650 S, pb, Huber; flowers bright pink with white eye, semi-dbl., flat, borne in large sprays; very willing bloomer; light green foliage; tall (150 cm.) and spreading growth; int. by Richard Huber AG, 2002

Bir-Hackeim HT, mr, 1946, Mallerin, C.; bud long, pointed; flowers fiery red, open, semi-dbl., cupped; very vigorous, upright, bushy growth; int. by A. Meilland

Bird of Fire HT, yb, 1992, Taylor, Thomas E.; flowers yellow blending to reddish edges, reverse yellow, aging lighter, 4-4¾ in., 25-30 petals, high-centered; foliage medium size, dark green, semi-glossy, leathery, reddish w; upright, bushy, medium growth; [Fragrant Delight × Sunsilk]; int. by National Kirtland's Warbler Recovery Team

Birdie Blye HMult, mp, 1904, Van Fleet; bud long, pointed, carmine; flowers rose-pink, 7-8 cm., dbl., cupped, borne in small clusters; recurrent bloom; foliage light green; vigorous (4-5 ft.) growth; [Helene × Bon Silene]; int. by Conard & Jones

Birdsong LCl, mp, 1991, Seward, Grace; flowers small, semi-dbl., borne in very large clusters, moderate fragrance; foliage small to medium size, medium green, semi-glossy; few prickles; tall (300+ cm.), spreading, large, rambling growth; [seedling × seedling]

Birdy HT, rb, Tantau; flowers red with yellow center and reverse, medium, dbl., cupped, borne mostly singly; recurrent; stems moderate; greenhouse rose; int. by Rosen Tantau, 1997

Birendranath HT, pb, Chakraborthy, Dr K.; flowers cream white with pronounced raspberry color blend, dbl., high-centered, moderate fragrance

Birgitta HT, dr, 1961, de Boer; bud ovoid; flowers large, dbl.

Birgitte de Villenfagne HMsk, pb

Birichina F, (Italy)

Birmingham Boerner F, w, 1976, Schoepfle; flowers light flesh-pink turning white; [sport of Gene Boerner]

Birmingham Post F, dp, 1968, Watkins Roses; flowers deep pink, large, dbl.; foliage leathery; vigorous growth; [Queen Elizabeth × Wendy Cussons]

Birthday Boy F, m, Tantau; int. by Layham Garden Center & Nursery, 2005

Birthday Candle HT, rb, Teranishi; int. in 2003

Birthday Girl – See **Cocorico**, F

Birthday Party Min, mp, 1979, Strawn; bud ovoid; flowers pink, 1½-2 in., 28 petals, high-centered, moderate fragrance; foliage dark; upright, spreading growth; PP4637; [Attraktion × Sheri Anne]; int. by Pixie Treasures Min. Roses

Birthday Present Cl HT, dr, 1950, Toogood; bud ovoid; flowers dark velvet red, 20 petals, high-centered, intense fragrance; non-recurrent; foliage dark, leathery; vigorous, climbing growth; [Guineé × Rouge Mallerin]

Birthday Wishes HT, rb, 1997, Guest, M.M.; flowers large, very dbl., borne mostly singly; foliage large, dark green, glossy; some prickles; upright, medium (30in.) growth; [Fragrant Cloud × Honey Favourite]

Birthday Wishes – See **Shrimp Hit**, MinFl

Biscay Min, mp, 1989, Bridges, Dennis A.; bud ovoid; flowers medium pink, reverse slightly darker, medium, 26 petals, high-centered, borne usually singly, slight fragrance; foliage medium size, medium green, semi-glossy; prickles slightly downward pointed, medium, deep pink; upright, medium growth; [Summer Spice × seedling]; int. by Bridges Roses, 1989

Bischof Dr Korum HT, pb, 1921, Lambert, P.; flowers yellowish-rose, dbl., moderate fragrance; [Frau Karl Druschki × Laurent Carle]

Bischofsstadt Paderborn S, or, 1964, Kordes, R.; flowers cinnabar-scarlet, semi-dbl., saucer-shaped; vigorous (3-4 ft.), bushy growth; ADR, 1968

Bischofzell HT, rb, Huber; int. by Richard Huber AG, 2005

Bishop Darlington HMsk, ab, 1926, Thomas; bud ovoid; flowers cream to flesh-pink, with yellow glow, 10-11 cm., 17 petals, cupped, borne in small clusters, moderate fruity fragrance; recurrent bloom; foliage bronze, soft; semi-climbing growth; [Aviateur Bleriot × Moonlight]; int. by H&S, 1928

Bishop Elphinstone F, dr, 1993, Cocker, James; flowers crimson, medium, full, borne in large clusters, slight fragrance; foliage large, dark green, semi-glossy; some prickles; tall (3 ft.), upright growth; [seedling × (Tropicana × Baccara)]; int. by James Cocker & Sons, 1994

Bishop of Sherwood HT, op, 1977, Bracegirdle; flowers pale salmon flushed pink, 5 in., 34 petals, intense fragrance; vigorous, upright growth; [Mischief × (Wendy Cussons × Peace)]

Bishop Rose – See **L'Évêque**, HGal

Bishop's Castle S, mp, 2006; flowers very full, borne in small clusters; foliage medium size, dark green, matte; prickles medium, hooked downward, medium red, moderate; growth bushy, vigorous, medium (120 cm.); garden decorative; [seedling × seedling]; int. by David Austin Roses, Ltd., 2006

Bishop's Paul Neyron HP, mp, Ruston?; flowers similar to Paul Neyron; seedling from Paul Neyron

Bishop's Rambler HWich, dr, Scarman; int. in 1996

Bishop's Rose C, pb; vigorous (to 5 ft.) growth; [apparently *R. gallica* × *R. centifolia*]

Bit o' Gold Min, dy, 1982, Williams, Ernest D.; bud ovoid; flowers deep yellow, imbricated petals, very small, 40 petals, moderate fragrance; foliage small, dark, semi-glossy; compact, bushy growth; PP5306; [seedling × Golden Angel]; int. by Mini-Roses, 1981

Bit o' Magic Min, pb, 1980, Williams, Ernest D.; bud pointed; flowers deep pink, reverse nearly white, micro-mini, 1 in., 50 petals, high-centered; foliage small, dark, glossy; compact, spreading growth; PP4729; [Over the Rainbow × Over the Rainbow]; int. by Mini-Roses, 1979

Bit o' Spring Min, pb, 1981, Williams, Ernest D.; bud long, pointed; flowers medium buffy pink, reverse lighter yellow-pink, 45 petals, high-centered, borne usually singly, moderate fragrance; foliage deep green, matte; prickles thin, tan curved down; upright, bushy growth; [Tom Brown × Golden Angel]; int. in 1980

Bit o' Sunshine Min, dy, 1956, Moore, Ralph S.; flowers bright buttercup-yellow, 1½ in., 18-20 petals, moderate fragrance; bushy (12-14 in.), compact growth; PP1631; [Copper Glow × Zee]; int. by Sequoia Nursery

Bit of Honey Min, dy, 1980, Vastine, Gilbert; flowers 48 petals; [sport of Sunnydew]; int. by Gulf Stream Nursery

Bit of Paradise Min, m; int. by Giles Nursery, 1999

Bitten Clausen – See **Scented Memory**, HT

Biva HT, pb, Ghosh; flowers large, pale pink turning deeper, dbl., high-centered, intense tea fragrance; int. by KSG, 2001

Bizarre HGal, m, before 1836, Calvert; flowers dark purple/pink, aging to dark purple, small to medium, full

Bizarre Changeant – See **Pourpre Marbrée**, HGal

Bizarre Marbrée HGal, rb, before 1848; flowers red, marbled with white

Bizarre Triomphant(e) – See **Charles de Mills**, HGal

Blå Måndag – See **Blue Moon**, HT

Blaby Courier HT, mr, 1956, Verschuren; bud deep crimson; flowers vivid scarlet; strong stems; int. by Blaby Rose Gardens

Blaby Jubilee – See **Dries Verschuren**, HT

Blaby's Monarch HT, lp, 1960, Verschuren; flowers rose-pink, 5-6 in., 40 petals, high-centered; foliage light green; vigorous growth; [Briarcliff × seedling]; int. by Blaby Rose Gardens, 1960

Black Baccara HT, dr, 2004, Meilland International; flowers dark red, reverse dark red, 8 cm., full, borne mostly solitary, no fragrance; foliage dark green, glossy; growth upright, tall (up to 6 ft.); cutting; PP13152; [Meifota × Meilouzou]; int. by The Conard-Pyle Company, 2002

Black Beauty HT, dr, 1976, Delbard; flowers garnet-red, large, dbl., slight fragrance; bushy growth; [(Gloire de Rome × Impeccable) × Papa Meilland]; int. by Bees, 1973

Black Beauty HT, dr, Hiroshima; int. by Hiroshima Bara-en, 1994

Black Beauty – See **Black Beauty 99**, F

Black Beauty 99 F, rb, Kordes; flowers small, blackish red with yellow reverse, dbl., high-centered; PP11185; [sport of Frisco]; greenhouse rose; int. by W. Kordes Söhne, 1999

Black Bess F, dr, 1939, Kordes; bud long, pointed; flowers blackish crimson, semi-dbl., high-centered, borne in clusters; foliage dark, bronze; vigorous, bushy growth; [Dance of Joy × Crimson Glory]; int. by Morse

Black Bourbon B, dr

Black Boy LCl, dr, 1919, Clark, A.; flowers very dark red, petals satiny, 3 in., semi-dbl., moderate fragrance; foliage sparse, wrinkled, light; vigorous growth; [Étoile de France × Bardou Job]; int. by NRS South Australia

Black Boy M, dr, 1959, Kordes; bud ovoid, lightly mossed; flowers deep crimson, large, very dbl., intense fragrance; non-recurrent; foliage light green, leathery; vigorous, upright, bushy growth; [World's Fair × Nuits de Young]; int. in 1958

Black Butterfly – See **Kurocho**, F

Black Cherry F, dr, 2007, Zary, Keith W.; flowers 3-3½ in., 20 -25 petals, blooms borne in large clusters; foliage medium size, medium green, glossy; prickles 8-10 mm., hooked downward, greyed-orange, moderate; growth bushy, medium (3½ ft.); [seedling × seedling]; int. by Jackson & Perkins Wholesale, Inc., 2006

Black Delight HT, dr, G&L; flowers deep, blackish red, dbl., well formed; free-flowering; int. in 1985

Black Fire Pol, dr, 1971, Delforge; bud ovoid; flowers open, medium, dbl., slight fragrance; foliage dark, soft; vigorous, bushy growth; [Red Favorite × seedling]

Black Garnet HT, dr, 1980, Weeks; bud ovoid, pointed; flowers dark, black-red, velvety, 5½ in., 50-55 petals, high-centered, borne singly or 2-3 per cluster, slight tea fragrance; foliage medium to large, moderately leathery, dark grayish-green; prickles short to medium, hooked downward; bushy, upright, branching growth; PP4738; [Mister Lincoln × Mexicana]

Black Gold Min, dr, Clements, John K.; int. in 1996

Black Heart Min, dr, 2006, Hopper, Nancy; flowers velvety dark red, 2 in., single, borne mostly solitary; foliage medium size, medium green, semi-glossy; growth bushy, medium (15 in.); [Scarlet Moss × Black Jade]; int. in 2006

Black Ice F, dr, 1972, Gandy, Douglas L.; flowers 4 in., 24 petals, slight fragrance; foliage glossy, dark; [(Iceberg × Europeana) × Megiddo]

Black Jack Min, dr, 1983, Williams, Ernest D.; flowers deep red, golden stamens, small, 40 petals, high-centered; foliage small, dark, semi-glossy; bushy growth; PP5671; [Tom Brown × Over the Rainbow]; int. by Mini-Roses

Black Jade Min, dr, 1985, Benardella, Frank A.; bud near black; flowers deep red, 1-1½ in., 35 petals, high-centered, borne singly, no fragrance; foliage medium size, dark, semi-glossy; upright growth; PP5925; [Sheri Anne × Laguna]; int. by Nor'East Min. Roses; AOE, ARS, 1985

Black Knight HT, dr, 1934, Hillock; flowers crimson shaded blackish, 30-35 petals; foliage glossy, dark; vigorous growth; [Ami Quinard × Château de Clos Vougeot]

Black Lady HT, dr, 1977, Tantau, Math.; bud globose; flowers blackish-red, medium, dbl., intense fragrance; foliage matte; bushy growth; int. in 1976

Black Magic Cl HT, dr, 1953, Hamilton; flowers blackish crimson, medium, dbl., intense fragrance; occasional repeat bloom; [Guineé × unknown]

Black Magic HT, dr, Tantau; bud almost black, pointed, ovoid buds; flowers dark garnet with darker edges, 4-5 in., 30 petals, exhibition, slight sweet fragrance; dark green, glossy foliage; upright growth; PP10650; int. in 1997

Black Magic Min, dr, 2003, Eagle, B & D; flowers dbl., borne in small clusters, slight fragrance; foliage medium size, dark green, glossy, disease-resistant; prickles small, straight; growth upright, medium (40-50 cm.); garden, exhibition; [Patio Prince × Black Jade]; int. by Southern Cross Nurseries, 1997

Black Moss – See **Nuits de Young**, M

Black Night HT, dr, 1979, Huber; bud long; flowers 4 in., 26 petals; foliage dark, leathery; vigorous, upright growth; [Fragrant Cloud × Pharaoh]; int. in 1975

Black Opal HT, dr, 1957, Ulrick, L.W.; flowers dark velvety red; [Mirandy × Tassin]

Black Pearl – See **Perle Noire**, HT

Black Pearl – See **Kuroshinju**, HT

Black Prince HP, dr, 1866, Paul, W.; flowers dark crimson shaded black, large, dbl., cupped; recurrent bloom; vigorous growth; [Pierre Notting × unknown]

Black Ruby HT, dr, 1970, Delbard-Chabert; flowers center crimson, large, 40 petals, cupped; tall growth; [Rome Glory × Impeccable]; int. by Cuthbert, 1965

Black Ruby LCl, mr

Black Sapphire Min, dr, 1995, Laver, Keith G.; flowers full, borne mostly singly; foliage medium size, medium green, glossy; few prickles; patio, upright, medium growth; [Royal Victoria × seedling]; int. by Springwood Roses, 1995

Black Satin HT, dr, 1988, Betts, John; flowers 30 petals, high-centered, borne singly, slight fragrance; foliage medium size, dark green, semi-glossy; prickles few, pointed slightly down, small, light brown; upright, medium growth; hips rounded, medium size, red; [Folklore × Loving Memory]; int. by Wisbech Plant Co., 1987

Black Shadow HT, dr; int. by Carmel Rose Farm, 2005

Black Swan HT, dr, Asami; int. in 1988

Black Tarquin Cl HT, dr, 1955, Eacott; flowers dark crimson-maroon; vigorous growth; [Honour Bright × Guinee]

Black Tea HT, r, 1986, Okamoto, K.; flowers brown, 32 petals, urn-shaped, borne usually singly, slight fragrance; foliage medium size, dark, semi-glossy; prickles deep brown, hooked; medium, bushy growth; [Hawaii × (Aztec × (Goldilocks × Fashion))]; int. by K. Hirakata Nursery, 1973

Black Velvet HT, dr, 1960, Morey, Dr. Dennison; bud ovoid; flowers 5-5½ in., 28 petals, high-centered, intense fragrance; foliage leathery, dark; vigorous, upright growth; PP2182; [New Yorker × Happiness]; int. by J&P, 1960

Black Velvet – See **Schwarzer Samt**, HKor

Blackberry Blossom Pol, w, Semple; int. in 1980

Blackberry Nip HT, m, 1996, Somerfield, Rob; flowers deep purple, very dbl., borne mostly singly, intense fragrance; foliage medium size, medium green, semi-glossy; some prickles; upright, medium growth; [Deep Secret × Old Port]

Blackberry Rose – See ***R. rubus*** (Léveillé & Vaniot)

Blackboy – See **Black Boy**, LCl

Bladud HP, pb, 1896, Cooling; flowers dark carnation, becoming coppery pink, edged silvery white, large, full, globular

Blairii No. 1 HCh, mp, 1845, Blair; flowers bright rose, sometimes tinged red, large, semi-dbl., cupped, intense fragrance; branching growth; liable to injury from severe cold; [A China (probably Parks' Yellow Tea-scented China) × a hardy rose (possibly Tuscany)]

Blairii No. 2 HCh, lp, 1845, Blair; flowers rosy blush, large, dbl., moderate fragrance; blooms over a long period; vigorous (up to 15 ft hardy; [a China (probably Parks' Yellow Tea-scented China) × a hardy rose (probably Tuscany)]

Blairii No. 3 HCh, mp, 1845, Blair

Blake Hedrick HT, mr, 2004, Edwards, Eddie & Phelps, Ethan; flowers full, borne mostly solitary, slight fragrance; foliage medium size, dark green, glossy; prickles small; upright, medium (5 ft.) growth; exhibition; [Veteran's Honor × Hot Princess]; int. in 2005

Blakeney's Red HT, mr, 1962, Blakeney; bud long, pointed; flowers currant-red, base yellow, 5 in., 45 petals, high-centered; foliage leathery; moderate, bushy growth; [Karl Herbst × Peace]; int. by Eddie, 1962

Blanc à Fleurs Doubles – See **Pompon Blanc**, HSpn

Blanc à Fleurs Pleines – See **Plena**, HSem

Blanc Ancien – See ***R. banksiae banksiae*** (Aiton)

Blanc Carné – See **Shailer's White Moss**, M

Blanc de Neige – See ***R. laevigata*** (Michaux)

Blanc de Vibert P, w, 1847, Vibert; flowers small white, full of petals, dbl., moderate damask perfume fragrance; sometimes recurrent bloom; foliage light green; slender and upright growth

Blanc Dot – See **Blanche Dot**, HT

Blanc Double de Coubert HRg, w, 1892, Cochet-Cochet; bud pleasing; flowers half-open white, fairly large, semi-dbl. to dbl., intense even at night fragrance; repeat bloom; foliage very rugose; vigorous (5-7 ft.) growth; [*R. rugosa* × Sombreuil]

Blanc Lafayette – See **Dagmar Späth**, F

Blanc Meillandécor – See **White Meidiland**, S

Blanc Ordinaire – See **Plena**, A

Blanc Parfait – See **Pompon Blanc Parfait**, A

Blanc Pur Misc OGR, w, 1827, Mauget; flowers pure white, large, dbl., borne in large clusters, moderate fragrance; prickles large

Blanc Queen Elizabeth – See **White Queen Elizabeth**, F

Blanca F, w, 1966, Lens; flowers pure white, large, dbl., borne in clusters, slight fragrance; vigorous growth; [Purpurine × (Papillon Rose × Sterling Silver)]

Blanca – See **Blanca Parade**, MInFl

Blanca Parade MInFl, w, Poulsen; flowers white, 5-8 cm., dbl., no fragrance; foliage dark; growth bushy, 20-40 cm.; PP15084; int. by Poulsen Roser, 2001

Blanche – See **Shailer's White Moss**, M

Blanche – See **À Coeur Jaune**, A

Blanche à Coeur Jaune – See **À Coeur Jaune**, A

Blanche Amiet HT, op, 1921, Turbat; flowers coppery salmon, passing to clear rose

Blanche Anglaise – See **White Bath**, M

Blanche Cascade S, w, Delbard; bud white with pink edge; flowers very white, semi-dbl., flat, borne in clusters, slight citronnelle fragrance; almost constant bloom; growth to 50-100 cm.; int. by Georges Delbard SA, 2000

Blanche Colombe LCl, w, Delbard; bud tinted lemon; flowers pure white, 3½-4 in., dbl., borne mostly solitary; vigorous growth; int. by Georges Delbard SA, 1995

Blanche Comète HT, w, 1982, Delbard, Georges; flowers dbl., borne in clusters; [(Virgo × Peace) × (Goldilocks × Virgo)]; int. by Delbard Roses

Blanche de Bath – See **White Bath**, M

Blanche de Beaulieu HP, w, 1850, Margottin; flowers white, shaded pink, full, cupped

Blanche de Belgique A, w, before 1848; sepals long; flowers pure white, center tinted sulphur, stamens visible, very large, semi-dbl. to dbl., borne in clusters of 3-4, moderate fragrance; foliage somber grey-green, deeply dentate; tall, arching growth

Blanche de Bernède HP, w, 1852, Bernède; flowers pure white, large, full

Blanche de Méru HP, w, 1869, Verdier, C.; flowers lightly blushing white, aging to pure white, large, full, borne in small clusters; [Jules Margottin × unknown]

Blanche de Portemer HP, lp, 1851, Portemer; flowers flesh white, large, full

Blanche de Soleville T, w, 1854, Pradel; flowers white, shaded cherry red, large, full

Blanche d'Italie M, w, about 1835, Prévost; flowers medium, dbl., moderate fragrance

Blanche d'Orléans N, w; flowers pure white, large, full

Blanche Dot HT, w, 1962, Dot, Pedro; flowers snow-white, well-formed, large, 33 petals; [White Knight × Virgo]

Blanche Double – See **Alba**, C

Blanche du Roi – See **Célina Dubos**, D

Blanche Duranthon – See **Mme Lucien Duranthon**, T

Blanche Frowein HMult, yb, 1916, Leenders, M.; flowers coppery yellow, 5-6 cm., full; remontant

Blanche Lafitte – See **Mlle Blanche Laffitte**, B

Blanche Mallerin HT, w, 1941, Mallerin, C.; bud long, pointed; flowers pure white, 4 in., 33 petals, high-centered; foliage leathery, glossy; vigorous growth; PP594; [Edith Krause × White Briarcliff]; int. by A. Meilland

Blanche Messigny HT, ly, 1923, Gillot, F.; flowers creamy yellow, large, 45 petals; vigorous, bushy growth

Blanche Moreau M, w, 1880, Moreau et Robert; bud well mossed; flowers pure white, large, dbl., borne in clusters, moderate fragrance; some repeat bloom; lax growth; [Comtesse de Murinais × Perpetual White Moss]

Blanche Mousseuse – See **White Bath**, M

Blanche Nabonnand T, w, 1883, Nabonnand, G.; flowers creamy white tinged lemon or flesh, dbl., globular

Blanche Neige Pol, w, 1929, Koster

Blanche Neige – See **Snow Carpet**, Min

Blanche Nouvelle – See **White Bath**, M

Blanche Odorante HT, w, 1952, Caron, B.; bud very long, pointed; flowers purest white, large, very dbl.; vigorous growth; [Pole Nord × Neige Parfum]; int. by EFR

Blanche Pasca – See **Pascali**, HT

Blanche Rebatel Pol, pb, 1889, Bernaix, A.; flowers carmine and white

Blanche Roberts – See **Blanche Moreau**, M

Blanche Semi-Double HSpn, w, before 1819; flowers semi-dbl.

Blanche Simon w, 1862, Moreau et Robert; flowers white, green pip at center, large, dbl.

Blanche Simple HGal, w

Blanche Superbe – See **Blanche de Belgique**, A

Blanche Unique – See **White Provence**, C

Blanche-Vibert – See **Blanc de Vibert**, P

Blanche Wimer Min, pb, 1986, Shaw, Dr. John; flowers light yellow and pink blend, 66 petals, cupped, borne usually singly, slight fruity fragrance; foliage medium size, medium green, semi-glossy; prickles slightly hooked, reddish-green; tall, upright growth; no fruit; [Pink Petticoat × seedling]

Blanchefleur C, w, 1835, Vibert; sepals long; flowers white tinted blush, medium, dbl., cupped and quartered, borne in clusters of 4-8, intense fragrance; foliage gray-green, oblong-pointed; prickles moderate; broad, vigorous growth

Blanda – See **Agathe Incarnata**, HGal

Blanda Egreta HMult, mp, 1926, Bruder Alfons; flowers single; nearly thornless; [sport of Tausendschön]

Blandford Rose HGal, mp, about 1791

Blandine Choupette HT, rb; int. in 2000

Blanik F, dr, Vecera, L.; flowers medium, dbl.; int. in 1964

Blarney Cl HT, mp, 1934, Howard Rose Co.; flowers pink, base apricot, dbl.; recurrent bloom; foliage leathery, dark; vigorous, climbing growth; [sport of Irish Charm]

Blässe Niederlandische Rose – See **Agathe Incarnata**, HGal

Blastoff F, ob, 1993, Moore, Ralph S.; flowers scarlet orange, white reverse, petals ruffled, 1½-2 in., 35-40 petals, quartered, borne in large clusters, slight slight spice fragrance; foliage medium size, dark green, semi-glossy; numerous prickles; medium (100-120 cm.), upright growth; PP9405; [Orangeade × Little Artist]; int. by Weeks Roses, 1995

Blatenskà Kràlovna HWich, mp, 1937, Böhm, J.; flowers dbl.

Blatná HT, dr, 1927, Böhm, J.; flowers velvety dark red, dbl.; dwarf growth; [Lieutenant Chaure × Oskar Cordel]

Blaue Adria HT, mr; int. in 2002

Blauwe Donau F, m, 1975, Verschuren, Ted; bud ovoid; flowers open, 3 in., 10-12 petals, intense fragrance; foliage glossy; bushy growth; [Orangeade × Sterling Silver]; int. by Verschuren & Sons, 1973

Blaydon Races F, yb, 1976, Wood; flowers scarlet shading to yellow, 2½ in.; foliage glossy, dark, leathery; vigorous, tall, upright growth; [Bobby Shafto × (Arthur Bell × Piccadilly)]

Blaze LCl, mr, 1932, Kallay; flowers bright scarlet, 2-3 in., 20-25 petals, cupped, borne in large clusters; recurrent bloom; foliage leathery, dark; very vigorous, climbing growth; distributed as Paul's Scarlet Climber × Gruss an Teplitz, but may be a sport of the former; int. by J&P

Blaze Away F, or, 1979, Sanday, John; bud pointed;

flowers scarlet-vermilion, large, 7 petals; vigorous, bushy growth; [(Karl Herbst × Crimson Glory) × Sarabande]

Blaze Improved – See **Demokracie**, LCl

Blaze of Glory LCl, ob, Zary, Keith; bud pointed ovoid; flowers bright coral/orange/red, 4 in., 25 petals, cupped, slight musk fragrance; recurrent; foliage dark green, glossy; vigorous (12-14 ft.) growth; int. in 2004

Blaze Superier – See **Demokracie**, LCl

Blazing Lights HT, ob, K&S; int. in 1995

Bleak House HRg, mp; int. by Bleak House, 1995

Blenheim – See **Schneesturm**, S

Bles Bridges HT, dr, Kordes; flowers dark red, slow to open, good petal substance, 3-4 in., 28-33 petals, exhibition, no fragrance; dark green, glossy foliage; short stems; growth to 3-4 ft.; int. in 1996

Blésine – See **Blessings**, HT

Blesma Soul HT, lp, 1981, Anderson's Rose Nurseries; bud long, pointed; flowers 36 petals, borne singly or in small clusters, intense fragrance; foliage light green; prickles large based, reddish-brown; upright growth; [Pascali × Fragrant Cloud]; int. in 1982

Bless My Time Gr, lp, 1983, Orr, Rudolph F.; flowers clear light pink, veins sometimes darker; [sport of Queen Elizabeth]

Blessed Event Min, pb, 1993, Laver, Keith G.; flowers white suffused pink, large, full, borne singly and in small clusters, slight fragrance; foliage medium size, dark green, matte; some prickles; low (25-30 cm.), upright growth; [Enjoy × (June Laver × Party Girl)]; int. by Springwood Roses, 1993

Blessings HT, op, 1967, Gregory; flowers medium coral-salmon, large, 30 petals, high-centered, moderate fragrance; [Queen Elizabeth × seedling]; int. in 1968

Blessings, Climbing Cl HT, op, Gregory; flowers salmon, fading to soft pink, dbl., high-centered; foliage dark green; strong growth, 8 ft. and greater; int. in 1972

Bleu – See **Charles de Mills**, HGal

Bleu Céleste – See **Celestial**, A

Bleu Magenta HMult, m, 1900, Van Houtte; flowers dark crimson-purple, sometimes flecked white, 6-7 cm., dbl., flat, borne in medium clusters, moderate fragrance; foliage dark; nearly thornless; [Turner's Crimson Rambler × unknown]; French origin; 'Bleu Violette' probably has precedence as correct name

Bleu Violette – See **Bleu Magenta**, HMult

Blickfang F, dr, VEG; flowers reddish-violet, large, very dbl.

Bliss S, dp, 2006, Beales, Amanda; flowers deep pink, reverse deep pink, 10 cm., very full, borne in small clusters; foliage medium size, medium green, matte; prickles average, straight, moderate; growth bushy, short (60 cm.); containers, landscape; [Comte de Chambord × Centenaire de Lourdes]; int. by Peter Beales Roses, 2000

Blithe Spirit HT, lp, 1964, Armstrong, D. L. & Swim, H. C.; flowers medium, dbl., slight fragrance; foliage leathery; vigorous, spreading, upright growth; PP2653; [Fandango × seedling]; int. by Armstrong Nursery, 1964

Blizzard Min, w, 1991, Warriner, William A.; bud pointed; flowers medium, full, no fragrance; foliage small, dark green, glossy; low, spreading, compact growth; [Petticoat × Orange Honey]; int. by Bear Creek Gardens

Bloemfontein F, ob, Kordes; flowers warm orange with a yellow base, medium, semi-dbl., moderate fragrance; growth medium; int. in 1988

Blöhm & Voss F, or; flowers bright orange-scarlet good trusses

Blois S, w, Olesen; bud pointed ovoid; flowers pure white, 4 cm., 25 petals, high-centered, then flat, borne in clusters of 3-7, slight floral fragrance; free-flowering; foliage semi-glossy; prickles few, 8 mm., hooked downward; upright (3 ft.), bushy growth; PP15810; [Bernina × seedling]; int. by Poulsen Roser, 2003

Blonde Bombshell F, my, 1995, Bees of Chester; flowers medium yellow, fading to pale yellow with pink edging, full, borne in small clusters, slight fragrance; medium size, dark green, glossy foliage; numerous prickles; growth strong, bushy, upright grower to 3 ft.; int. by L.W. van Geest Farms, 1995

Blondie F, my, 1987, Warriner, William A.; flowers medium yellow, fading slightly, medium, 25 petals, high-centered, borne usually singly, slight fruity fragrance; foliage medium size, light green, semi-glossy; prickles straight, medium; upright, bushy, medium growth; no fruit; [(Bridal Pink × Golden Wave) × Gold Rush]; int. by J&P

Blondie HT, op, Laperrière; flowers salmon, high-centered; int. by Laperriere, 1988

Blondine HT, lp, 1954, Grillo; bud pointed, globular; flowers blush-pink, 4 in., 60 petals; foliage leathery; upright growth; [sport of Catalina]

Blondine Cl HT, w, Arles; flowers pearl-white, well-formed, large; foliage clear green; vigorous growth; [Comtesse Vandal, Climbing × Michèle Meilland, Climbing]; int. by Roses-France

Blood – See **Hector**, HGal

Blood d'Angleterre – See **Hector**, HGal

Blood-red China Rose – See **Sanguinea**, Ch

Bloodstone HT, or, 1951, McGredy, Sam IV; flowers large, 24 petals, high-centered; foliage dark, coppery green; vigorous growth; [The Queen Alexandra Rose × Lord Charlemont]

Bloomer Girl Min, op, 1984, Bennett, Dee; flowers soft vermilion to medium pink, small, 35 petals, slight fragrance; foliage medium size, medium green, semi-glossy; upright, bushy growth; PP5523; [Futura × Pink Petticoat]; int. by Tiny Petals Nursery, 1983

Bloomerick HGal, m, before 1845, Calvert; flowers light lilac pink, aging lighter, medium, full

Bloomfest Min, ab, 1999, Bell, Judy G.; flowers 1 in., dbl., borne in small clusters; foliage medium size, medium green, dull; few prickles; compact, low (14 in.) growth; [Rise 'n' Shine × unknown]; int. by Michigan Mini Roses, 1999

Bloomfield Abundance F, lp, 1920, Thomas; flowers light salmon-pink, dbl.; foliage glossy, dark; bushy growth; [Sylvia (rambler, Paul, 1912) × Dorothy Page-Roberts]; int. by B&A; Gold Medal, Portland, 1919

Bloomfield Acrobat HT, dp, 1929, Thomas; flowers full, moderate fragrance; [Mme Abel Chatenay × Mme Butterfly]

Bloomfield Beauty HT, op, 1929, Thomas; flowers carmine-orange, large, full, moderate fragrance; [Bloomfield Exquisite × Hoosier Beauty]

Bloomfield Beverly HT, or, 1924, Thomas; flowers orange-crimson, dbl.; vigorous growth; [Mary, Countess of Ilchester × Mme Edouard Herriot]

Bloomfield Brilliant LCl, op, 1931, Thomas; flowers light salmon with orange glow, large, 18 petals; vigorous growth; [Mme Abel Chatenay × Kitty Kininmonth]; int. by H&S

Bloomfield Comet HMsk, op, 1924, Thomas; bud long, pointed, reddish orange; flowers orange, base yellow, large, 5 petals; foliage sparse, light bronze, soft; [Duchess of Wellington × Danaë]; int. by B&A

Bloomfield Completeness HMsk, ab, 1931, Thomas; flowers deep orange-yellow, dbl., moderate fragrance; continuous; [Bloomfield Perfection × Mme Butterfly]

Bloomfield Courage HWich, rb, 1925, Thomas; flowers dark velvety red, center white, prominent yellow stamens, 3 cm., single, borne in medium to large clusters, no fragrance; non-recurrent; foliage dark; few prickles; vigorous, climbing or pillar (20 ft.) growth; hips small, red; int. by H&S

Bloomfield Culmination HMsk, pb, 1924, Thomas; bud long, pointed; flowers rose-pink, center white, 3 in., single; recurrent bloom; foliage leathery; moderately vigorous growth; [Sheila Wilson × Danaë]; int. by B&A

Bloomfield Dainty HMsk, my, 1924, Thomas; bud long, pointed, deep orange; flowers clear canary-yellow, 2 in., single, moderate fragrance; foliage glossy; moderately vigorous growth; [Danaë × Mme Edouard Herriot]; int. by B&A

Bloomfield Dawn HMsk, pb, 1931, Thomas; bud long, slender, rose-pink; flowers light pink, base yellow, reverse deep pink, large, semi-dbl.; long, strong stems; [a climbing rose × Bloomfield Progress]; int. by Armstrong Nursery

Bloomfield Decoration HMsk, pb, 1925, Thomas; flowers cerise-pink, center white, prominent golden stamens, open, single; foliage glossy; [Sylvia × Arndt]; int. by H&S, 1927

Bloomfield Discovery HMsk, pb, 1925, Thomas; flowers pink, reverse darker, large, single; foliage dark; moderately vigorous growth; [Danaë × (Frau Karl Druschki × Mme Caroline Testout)]; int. by B&A

Bloomfield Dream T, pb, 1924, Thomas; flowers medium pink with saffron yellow, reverse pink with wine-red, dbl., moderate fragrance; [Rêve d'Or × unknown]

Bloomfield Endurance – See **W. Freeland Kendrick**, LCl

Bloomfield Experiment Cl HP, my, 1929, Thomas; flowers citron yellow, full, slight fragrance; [Frau Karl Druschki × Frau Ida Münch]

Bloomfield Exquisite Cl HT, mp, 1924, Thomas; flowers clear pink, dbl.; recurrent bloom; vigorous growth; [Gloire de Dijon × Gruss an Teplitz]; int. by H&S

Bloomfield Fascination HMsk, ly, 1924, Thomas; flowers light canary yellow, small, dbl.; foliage rich bronze green, soft; [Danaë × Mme Laurette Messimy]; int. by B&A

Bloomfield Favorite HMsk, w, 1924, Thomas; bud deep salmon; flowers pinkish cream, 1½ in., dbl.; [Debutante × Moonlight]; sometimes classed as HWich

Bloomfield Flame HT, rb, 1930, Thomas; bud long, pointed, flame-red; flowers crimson-flame, center orange-yellow, large, 22 petals, moderate spicy fragrance; foliage leathery, glossy, dark bronze; vigorous, bushy growth; [Louise Crette × Mme Charles Lutaud]; int. by H&S

Bloomfield Giant HT, op, 1929, Thomas; flowers silvery salmon pink, large, very full, moderate fragrance; [Mme Abel Chatenay × Mme Butterfly]

Bloomfield Gipsy T, ob, 1929, Thomas; flowers shining orange, full; [Rêve d'Or × Rosomane Narcisse Thomas]

Bloomfield Gold T, ob, 1929, Thomas; flowers coppery orange; [Gloire de Dijon × Rosomane Narcisse Thomas]

Bloomfield Improvement – See **Ednah Thomas**, Cl HT

Bloomfield Loveliness – See **Sophie Thomas**, Cl HT

Bloomfield Lustre LCl, op, 1931, Thomas; flowers salmon-pink, base yellow, dbl.; [Hortulanus Budde × Souv. de Mme Léonie Viennot]; int. by H&S

Bloomfield Magic LCl, op, 1924, Thomas; flowers light salmon to cream, flat; moderately vigorous growth; [Gloire de Dijon × Frau Berta Gurtler]

Bloomfield Mystery LCl, lp, 1924, Thomas; flowers silver-pink, tinged yellow, 2 in., flat; moderately vigorous growth; [Blanche Frowein × Bloomfield Abundance]; int. by B&A

Bloomfield Perfection HMsk, w, 1925, Thomas; bud

ovoid, orange and pink; flowers cream-yellow suffused lilac, large, dbl.; recurrent bloom; [Danaë × Bloomfield Abundance]; int. by B&A, 1927

Bloomfield Perpetual HP, w, 1920, Thomas; flowers resembling *R. laevigata*, single; [Iceberg × Frau Karl Druschki]; int. by B&A

Bloomfield Progress HT, mr, 1920, Thomas; flowers glowing red, dbl.; vigorous growth; [Mary, Countess of Ilchester × General MacArthur]; int. by B&A

Bloomfield Quakeress Cl T, ly, 1931, Thomas; flowers small, semi-dbl.; free recurrent bloom; foliage glossy, light; long stems; vigorous growth; [Safrano × unknown]; int. by Armstrong Nursery

Bloomfield Rocket LCl, dp, 1925, Thomas; flowers dark pink, center lighter, very large, single; very vigorous (6-8 ft.) growth; [Mme Caroline Testout × Ulrich Brunner Fils]; int. by B&A

Bloomfield Ruby Cl HT, mr, 1929, Thomas; flowers ruby red, large; [Hortulanus Budde × Souv de Mme Leonie Viennot]

Bloomfield Star Cl Pol, ob, 1929, Thomas; flowers orange with canary yellow

Bloomfield Success HT, ob, 1929, Thomas; flowers orange with canary yellow to creamy yellow, shaded lilac, dbl., moderate fragrance; [Laurette Messimy × Danae]

Bloomfield Vanity HFt, or, 1929, Thomas; flowers coral-red, large; [Rêve d'Or × Lutea hybrid]

Bloomfield Velvet Cl HT, mr, 1929, Thomas; flowers large, full, moderate fragrance; [Crimson Queen × Kitty Kininmonth]

Bloomfield Victory HWich, lp, 1929, Thomas; flowers light flesh pink, tinted darker pink, slight fragrance; [Aviateur Blériot × Yvonne Rabier]

Bloomfield Volcano HFt, mr, 1929, Thomas; flowers dark fiery red, large, semi-dbl.; [Louise Crette × The Queen Alexandra Rose]

Bloomin' Easy S, mr, 1988, Christensen, Jack E.; flowers clear, bright red, medium, 22-25 petals, urn-shaped, borne singly, moderate tea fragrance; repeat bloom; foliage large, medium green, glossy; prickles hooked slightly downward, medium, red; upright, bushy, medium growth; hips round, medium size, bright red-orange; PP7157; [Trumpeter × Simplicity]; int. by Armstrong Nursery, 1987

Bloomin' Pretty LCl, w, Williams, J. Benjamin; flowers white with pale pink paint, semi-dbl.; int. in 1999

Blooming Carpet – See **Flower Carpet**, S

Blooming Marvelous Min, dp

Bloomsday F, ob, 1981, McCann, Sean; flowers orange, marked brown, reverse deep gold, loose, 28 petals, borne in clusters of 4-5; foliage matte, green; prickles straight, red-brown; vigorous, upright growth; [Belinda × (Maxi × Joyfulness)]; int. by Hughes Roses

Bloomtown Min, pb, 1993, Taylor, Franklin "Pete" & Kay; flowers pink petals with slightly darker edges, reverse cream, large, dbl., borne in small clusters; foliage medium size, medium green, semi-glossy; some prickles; medium (24 in.), upright, spreading growth; [Party Girl × Andrea]; int. by Taylor's Roses, 1993

Blossom HT, pb, 1925, Beckwith; flowers red over peach-pink, reverse pinkish yellow

Blossom Blanket S, w, 2001, Dickson, Colin; bud palest pink; flowers with prominent yellow stamens, 5 cm., dbl., borne in small clusters, moderate apple fragrance; foliage small, medium green, glossy, red when young; prickles small, few; growth spreading, low (60 × 110 cm.); garden decorative; [seedling × The Fairy]; int. as To Mummy, Dickson Nurseries, Ltd., 2001

Blossom Hill F, ob, 1957, Kordes; flowers orange, 2½ in., 10 petals, cupped, borne in clusters; foliage dark, glossy; vigorous, upright, bushy growth; int. by Morse

Blossom Magic LCl, mp, Meilland; flowers medium size, clear pink; growth vigorous, relaxed, easy growing climber; int. in 1994

Blossomtime LCl, mp, 1951, O'Neal; bud pointed; flowers pink, reverse deeper, 4 in., 38 petals, high-centered, borne in small clusters, intense fragrance; repeat bloom; tall shrub or moderate climbing (6-7 ft.) growth; PP1240; [New Dawn × a Hybrid Tea]; int. by Bosley Nursery

Blue Angel F, m, 1992, Rennie, Bruce F.; flowers medium, dbl., borne mostly singly; foliage medium size, dark green, semi-glossy; few prickles; medium, bushy growth; [Lavonde × Shocking Blue]; int. by Rennie Roses International

Blue Bajou F, m, Kordes; flowers silvery lilac to lavender blue with large, rounded petals, dbl., rounded, slight fragrance; dark green, glossy foliage; opens like a water lily; int. in 1993

Blue Bajou, Climbing ClF, m, Ichibashi; int. in 1998

Blue Bayou – See **Blue Bajou**, F

Blue Bell HT, rb, Meilland; bud conical, large; flowers currant red with magenta reverse, 4-5 in., 20-25 petals, cupped, borne mostly singly, no fragrance; good repeat; foliage medium size, medium green, semi-glossy; numerous prickles; erect (4-5 ft.) growth; PP10948; [Livia × (White Success × Candia)]; greenhouse rose; int. in 1997

Blue Bells – See **Blue Bell**, HT

Blue-Bijou – See **Blue Bajou**, F

Blue Bird F, m, Dey, S. C.; flowers blue-violet, borne in large clusters; [sport of Fraternity]; int. in 1989

Blue Bird HT, Poulsen

Blue Boy M, m, 1959, Kordes; bud ovoid; flowers deep reddish-violet, large, dbl., high-centered, intense fragrance; non-recurrent; foliage light green, glossy; vigorous (3 ft.), upright, bushy growth; [Louis Grimmard × Independence]; int. in 1958

Blue Boy S, m, Interplant; groundcover; spreading growth; int. in 2001

Blue Boy HT, m

Blue Carpet – See **Cosette**, F dbl.

Blue Chateau HT, m, 1999, Teranishi, K.; flowers pale violet, 50 petals, high-centered; growth to 4 ft.; [Madame Violet × seedling]; int. by Itami Rose Nursery, 1994

Blue Chip F, m, 1983, Warriner, William A.; flowers medium, 20 petals; foliage medium size, medium green, semi-glossy; bushy, upright growth; PP5684; [Heirloom × Angel Face]; int. by J&P

Blue Cupido Min, m, deRuiter; PP9735; int. in 2003

Blue Curiosa HT, m, Pouw; PP10918; originally a greenhouse rose.; int. by De Ruiter, 1997

Blue Danube – See **Blauwe Donau**, F

Blue Delight HT, m, Kasturi; flowers orchid mauve, dbl., intense fragrance; int. in 1980

Blue Diamond HT, m, 1963, Lens; flowers lavender, 4 in., 35 petals; foliage dark, coppery; vigorous, compact, bushy growth; [Purpurine × (Purpurine × Royal Tan)]

Blue Fairy S, m, Kordes; flowers lavender, semi-dbl., borne in clusters; int. by Roses N.W., 2004

Blue For You F, m, 2006, James, Peter J.; flowers lilac, reverse lighter, 3-4 in., semi-dbl., borne in large clusters; foliage medium size, medium green, semi-glossy; prickles straight, few; growth bushy, medium (3 ft.); garden decorative; [Rogscriv (Natural Beauty) × Seedling (Floribunda dark purple)]; int. by Christopher Warner, 2007

Blue Friendship S, m, Verschuren; flowers small, semi-dbl.; repeats well; groundcover; spreading growth; int. in 1984

Blue Girl – See **Cologne Carnival**, HT

Blue Girl, Climbing – See **Kölner Karneval, Climbing**, Cl HT

Blue Glow HT, m, 1983, Cattermole, R.F.; bud pointed; flowers pinkish-mauve, 45 petals, high-centered, borne singly and 3-5 per cluster, slight fragrance; foliage light green; prickles light brown, triangular; upright, branching growth; [Silent Night × Blue Moon]

Blue Heaven HT, m, 1971, Whisler, D.; bud ovoid; flowers large, dbl., high-centered, intense fragrance; foliage large, glossy; vigorous, upright growth; PP3818; [(Sterling Silver × Simone) × Song of Paris]; patent application says parentage is Simone × Sterling Silver; int. by Gro-Plant Industries

Blue Ice Min, m, 1993, Laver, Keith G.; flowers lavender, petals reflex upon opening, large, full, borne mostly singly, moderate fragrance; foliage small, medium green, semi-glossy; some prickles; low (25-30 cm.), upright, bushy growth; [June Laver × Apricot Doll]; int. by Springwood Roses, 1993

Blue Jay F, m

Blue Light HT, m, Ito; int. in 1995

Blue Magenta HT, m; int. in 2002

Blue Magic Min, m; int. in 1986

Blue Magic HT, Dot, Pedro

Blue Margrethe HWich, m; from Germany

Blue Mist Min, m, 1975, Moore, Ralph S.; bud short, rounded; flowers soft pink to lavender, micro-mini, small, 23 petals, intense fragrance; foliage soft; vigorous, bushy, rounded growth; [seedling × seedling]; int. by Sequoia Nursery, 1970

Blue Monday – See **Blue Moon**, HT

Blue Monday, Climbing – See **Blue Moon, Climbing**, Cl HT

Blue Moon HT, m, 1965, Tantau, Math.; bud long, pointed; flowers lilac, 4 in., 40 petals, intense fragrance; vigorous growth; [(Sterling Silver × unknown) × seedling]; int. by Wheatcroft Bros., 1964; Gold Medal, Rome, 1964, ADR, 1964

Blue Moon, Climbing Cl HT, m, 1981, Mungia (also Jackson, 1978); flowers lilac mauve, 12 cm., dbl., strong fragrance; PP5049; [sport of Blue Moon]; int. by Montebello Rose Co., Inc.

Blue Nile HT, m, 1980, Delbard, Georges; bud ovoid, pointed; flowers deep lavender, 5 in., 28-30 petals, high-centered, borne singly or 2-3 per cluster, intense fruity fragrance; foliage large, olive green; prickles short, hooked downward; tall, upright, spreading growth; PP4671; [(Holstein × Bayadere) × (Prelude × Saint-Exupery)]; int. as Nil Bleu, Sauvageot, 1977

Blue Ocean HT, m, Hande, Dr Y. K.; flowers light mauve with deeper edges, dbl., high-centered; int. in 1983

Blue Ovation Min, m, deRuiter; int. in 2000

Blue Parfum HT, m, 1978, Tantau, Math.; bud ovoid; flowers mauve-blush, large, dbl.; foliage glossy; bushy, upright growth; int. in 1977

Blue Perfume – See **Blue Parfum**, HT

Blue Peter Min, m, 1983, deRuiter, George; flowers lilac-purple, patio, small, semi-dbl.; foliage small, light green, semi-glossy; bushy growth; [Little Flirt × seedling]; int. by Fryer's Nursery, Ltd.

Blue Rambler – See **Veilchenblau**, HMult

Blue Ribbon HT, m, Christensen, Jack E.; bud ovoid; flowers medium lavender, 5-6 in., 35-40 petals, borne mostly singly, intense sweet citrus-blossom fragrance; foliage large, medium green, semi-glossy; upright growth; PP6000; [(Angel Face × First Prize) × Blue Nile]; int. by Armstrong Nursery, 1986

Blue River HT, m, 1974, Kordes; bud long, pointed; flowers mauve-magenta, large, dbl., cupped, intense fragrance; foliage glossy; vigorous, upright growth; RULED EXTINCT 6/84 ARM; [Mainzer Fastnacht × Silver Star]; int. by Horstmann, 1973

Blue River HT, m, 1984, Kordes, W.; bud large; flowers lilac, shaded deeper at petal edges, large, 35 petals, high-centered, intense fragrance; foliage medium size, medium green, semi-glossy; upright growth; [Blue Moon × Zorina]; int. in 1984

Blue Rosalie – See **Veilchenblau**, HMult

Blue Skies HT, m, 1983, Buck, Dr. Griffith J.; flowers large, 35 petals, moderate fragrance; foliage large, semi-glossy; upright, bushy growth; PP5756; [((Sterling Silver × Intermezzo) × (Sterling Silver × Simone)) × (Music Maker × (Blue Moon × Tom Brown))]; int. by J.B. Roses, Inc., 1984

Blue Sky – See **Aozora**, HT

Blue Sky HT, m, Dot; flowers lavender, high-centered, moderate fragrance; int. in 1982

Blue Star, Climbing Cl HT, m, 1963, Thompson, M.L.; flowers lavender-blue, small, dbl., flat, borne in clusters, slight fragrance; profuse, non-recurrent bloom; foliage glossy; vigorous (8 ft.) growth; PP2448

Blue Star LCl, m, Clements, John; flowers old fashioned style, lavender and purple, 3 in., 50 petals, cupped, intense expensive perfume fragrance; blue-green foliage; growth to 8-10 ft.; int. by Heirloom Roses, 2003

Blue Time HT, m, Teranishi; int. by Itami Rose Garden, 2005

Blue Violet HT, m, Perry; int. in 1981

Blue Work HT, m

Bluebell – See **Blue Bell**, HT

Blueberry Hill F, m, 1999, Carruth, Tom; bud plump, pointed, dark lilac; flowers clear lilac, curved petals, golden stamens, 4 in., single, high-centered, borne in small clusters, moderate apple fragrance; foliage very serrated, large, dark green, glossy; prickles moderate; upright, medium, rounded, bushy (3-4 ft.) growth; PP10072; [Crystalline × Playgirl]; int. by Weeks Roses, 1997

Blueblood Min, mr, 1982, Laver, Keith G.; flowers velvety texture, small, 55 petals; foliage small, deep green, semi-glossy; spreading growth; PP5851; [Dwarfking '78 × Hokey Pokey]

Bluenette – See **Blue Peter**, Min

Blues LCl, mp, Poulsen; flowers medium pink, 5-8 cm., 25 petals, no fragrance; foliage dark; growth bushy, 100-150 cm.; int. by Poulsen Roser, 2004; Gold Medal, Rome, 2006

Bluesette F, m, 1986, Lens, Louis; flowers lilac, 2 in., 50 petals, flat, borne in clusters of 3-18, slight fragrance; prickles dark green; bushy growth; [Little Angel × (Westmauve × Blue Diamond)]; int. in 1984

Bluewunder – See **Flower Power**, F

Bluhendes Barock F, mp, Noack, Werner; int. in 1997

Blühwunder – See **Flower Power**, F

Blumen Dankert HMult, mp, 1904, Kiese; flowers carmine-pink, 3½ cm., dbl., borne in large clusters, no fragrance; few prickles; growth vigorous, upright (3 m.)

Blumenschmidt T, yb, 1906, Schmidt, J.C.; flowers primrose-yellow, outer petals rose-pink, full; [sport of Mlle Franziska Kruger]

Blumenschmidt's Elfenkönigin HT, w, 1939, Weigand, C.; flowers ivory-white, center orange, very large, dbl., high-centered, moderate lily-of-the-valley fragrance; long, strong stems; bushy, dwarf growth; [Ophelia × Julien Potin]; int. by Schmidt, J.C.

Blumenschmidts Sonntagskind F, mp, 1945, Vonholdt; flowers medium, dbl.

Blush M, m, before 1838, Hooker; flowers lilac blush, medium, dbl.; foliage very dense; growth erect

Blush Min, mp, Olesen; flowers dbl., 25-30 petals, no fragrance; foliage medium green, semi-glossy; growth bushy, very low (20-40 cm.); int. by Poulsen Roser, 2000

Blush Baby Min, Pearce, C.A.; int. in 1986

Blush Belgic – See **Blush Belgiques**, A

Blush Belgiques A, lp; flowers blush pink, large, dbl.

Blush Boursault Bslt, pb, before 1824; flowers blush, center deep flesh, very large, tending to ball, pendulous, very dbl., globular, borne in small clusters; foliage remains longer than other boursaults; thornless; pendulous growth; apparently a hybrid of Red Boursault and *R. odorata*; credited to various breeders, including Noisette and Vilmorin

Blush China HCh, lp, 1903, Cant, B. R.; flowers medium, semi-dbl.

Blush Damask D, lp, before 1806; flowers center rose, shading to pale blush on outside petals, small, dbl., quartered, moderate fragrance; non-recurrent; foliage dark green, elliptical, with 5-7 leaflets

Blush Gallica – See **Blush Damask**, D

Blush Hip A, lp, before 1846; flowers delicate soft pink, green eye, medium, dbl., flat, borne singly and in clusters of 3-6; foliage gray-green, deeply dentate; growth vigorous, branching; a form of Cuisse de Nymphe, according to G.S. Thomas

Blush Knock Out – See **Blushing Knock Out**, S

Blush Maman Cochet – See **William R. Smith**, T

Blush Monthly – See **Old Blush**, Ch

Blush Moss M, lp, before 1854; flowers blush, center pinkish when first open, well-mossed, large, dbl., cupped; moderate branching growth

Blush Musk – See **Fraser's Pink Musk**, N

Blush Noisette N, w, before 1817, Noisette; bud crimson; flowers pinkish white, tinted lilac, edges lighter, 4 cm., cupped, borne in large, upright clusters, moderate fragrance; recurrent; foliage dark; nearly thornless; stems reddish; growth vigorous (8-10 ft.); [Champneys' Pink Cluster × unknown]

Blush o' Dawn – See **Flush o' Dawn**, HT

Blush of Success F, pb, Poulsen; flowers pink blend, 5-8 cm., dbl., no fragrance; growth bushy, 60-100 cm.; PP15053; int. by Poulsen Roser, 2003

Blush Queen HT, lp, 1924, Cant, F.; flowers blush-pink, dbl.

Blush Rambler HMult, lp, 1903, Cant, B. R.; flowers blush-pink, pale at the center, 4 cm., semi-dbl., cupped, borne in large clusters; non-recurrent; vigorous, climbing (10-12 ft.) growth; [Crimson Rambler × The Garland]

Blushing Beauty LCl, lp, 1934, Burbank; flowers three-toned shell-pink, very large; very vigorous growth; int. by Stark Bros.

Blushing Beauty HT, w, 2000, Dykstra, Dr. Michael; flowers white and pink blend, reverse light pink, 4-5 cm., full, exhibition, borne mostly singly, slight fragrance; foliage medium size, medium green, glossy; prickles moderate; growth upright, medium; [Pristine × Touch of Class]; int. by Cecil Godman's Show Roses, 2001

Blushing Blue Min, m, 1988, Rennie, Bruce F.; flowers lavender with magenta edge, yellow-tan at base, medium, 30-35 petals, high-centered, borne usually singly; repeat bloom; foliage medium size, medium green, semi-glossy; prickles straight, medium, transparent yellow-green; upright, bushy growth; hips rounded, medium size, orange; [Shocking Blue × Twilight Trail]; int. by Rennie Roses International, 1989

Blushing Bride HT, w, 1918, Dickson, H.; flowers white, center blush, dbl.; RULED EXTINCT 5/90

Blushing Bride HT, W, 1930, Joseph H. Hill, Co.; flowers white tinged pink, large, dbl.; vigorous growth; RULED EXTINCT 5/90; [Mme Butterfly × Premier]

Blushing Bride HT, w, 1990, Greenwood, Chris; flowers moderately large, dbl., intense fragrance; foliage large, dark green, semi-glossy; upright, bushy growth; [sport of Silverado]

Blushing Bride F, lp, Harkness; int. in 1998

Blushing Cheeks HT, mp, Dickson; int. in 1970

Blushing Dawn Min, pb, 1985, Weeks, Michael W.J.; flowers creamy white, peach pink eye, yellow stamens, petals painted peach pink, 7-8 petals, moderate fragrance; foliage medium size, dark, matte; low, bushy growth; [Jeanne Lajoie × Eyepaint]; int. in 1983

Blushing Groom Min, w, 1982, McCann, Sean; flowers near white, small, 35 petals, slight fragrance; foliage small, dark, semi-glossy; upright growth; [Rise 'n' Shine × Karl Herbst]; int. in 1983

Blushing Jewel Min, lp, 1959, Morey, Dr. Dennison; bud ovoid; flowers blush-pink, overcast rose-pink, open, ½-¾ in., 45-50 petals, moderate fragrance; low, compact growth; PP1906; [Dick Koster × Tom Thumb]; int. by J&P, 1958

Blushing June F, or, 1996, LeCroy, Jack; flowers orange, vivid stamens, large, 6-14 petals, borne mostly singly, slight fragrance; foliage medium size, medium green, semi-glossy; some prickles; upright, medium growth; [Altissimo × Frances Ashton]

Blushing Knock Out S, lp, Yoder Bros.; flowers light pink aging to shell pink, medium, single, cupped to flat, borne singly and in small clusters, no fragrance; free-flowering; foliage mossy green with blue hues; prickles mostly on lower portions of canes; compact (2-3 ft.), spreading growth; PP14700; [sport of Knock Out]; int. by Conard Pyle, 2004

Blushing Knockout – See **Blushing Knock Out**, S

Blushing Lucy HWich, lp, 1938, Williams, A.; flowers pale pink with a white eye, semi-dbl., borne in large clusters; profuse, late bloom; foliage glossy; growth vigorous

Blushing Maid – See **Rocky**, LCl

Blushing Panarosa S, lp, Delbard; int. by Ludwig's Roses, 2004

Blushing Pink Iceberg – See **Pink Iceberg**, F

Blushing Queen Gr, w, 1976, Baker, Larry; bud pointed; flowers near white, center blush-pink, 38-40 petals, high-centered; vigorous, upright growth; [sport of Queen Elizabeth]

Blushing Rose – See **Coy Colleen**, HT

Blushing Yuki HT, rb, 2006, Viraraghavan, M.S. Viru; flowers red and dark pink with white in center, reverse white, hand-painted, 4 in., dbl., borne mostly solitary; foliage large, medium green, semi-glossy; prickles medium, slender, pointing down, light brown, moderate; growth bushy, medium (3 ft.); garden decorative; [Silver Jubilee × Priyatama]; int. by Roses Unlimited, 2006

Blutpurpurne Rose – See **Sanguineo-Purpurea Simplex**, HGal

Blythe Spirit S, my, 2000, Austin, David; flowers soft yellow, 2¼ in., 51 petals, loose, borne in large sprays, moderate musk fragrance; foliage bright green, matte; bushy growth; int. by David Austin Roses, 1999

Bo HT, op, Pekmez, Paul; int. in 1997

Bo-Peep Min, mp, 1950, deVink; bud ovoid, pointed; flowers rose-pink, micro-mini, very small, 28 petals, cupped; foliage small, glossy; bushy, dwarf (5-8 in.) growth; [Cécile Brunner × Tom Thumb]; int. by C-P

Boadicea T, mp, 1901, Paul, W.; flowers creamy pink edged with rose, large, dbl., moderate fragrance; growth vigorous

Boardwalk HT, pb, 2004, Edwards, Eddie & Phelps, Ethan; flowers pink blend, reverse pink blend, 4-5 in, full, borne mostly solitary; foliage dark green, semi-glossy; prickles small, hooked; growth upright, medium; exhibition; [White Success × Hot Princess]; int. in 2005

Bob & Linda HT, pb, 2005, Smith, John T.; flowers dark pink with darker edges, reverse white, 4-4½ in., full, high-centered, borne mostly solitary, no fragrance; foliage medium size, dark green, semi-glossy; prickles medium, straight, red, moderate; growth compact, medium (3½-4 ft.) hedging, exhibition; [Gemini × Donna Darling]; int. in 2007

Bob Collard F, mr, 1987, Turley, V.G.; flowers very luminous, brilliant red, reverse deeper red, medium, 11 petals, cupped, borne singly or in sprays of 5-10, slight fruity fragrance; foliage medium size, medium green, glossy; upright, bushy, medium growth; hips round, cupped, average, red; [Happiness × Copenhagen]

Bob Davison HP, mr, before 1910, Dickson, A.; bud large; flowers glossy scarlet, shaded crimson, large, very full

Bob Fleming F, w, Fleming; int. by Hortico Roses, 2004

Bob Greaves F, ob, Fryer, Gareth; flowers bright orange-salmon, dbl., exhibition, slight fragrance; leathery foliage; int. in 1998

Bob Hope HT, mr, 1966, Kordes, R.; bud urn-shaped; flowers scarlet red, 6 in., 35-40 petals, high-centered, borne mostly singly, intense damask fragrance; foliage dark, leathery; vigorous, tall, upright growth; PP2734; [Friedrich Schwartz × Kordes' Perfecta]; int. by J&P

Bob Kennedy HT, Ingegnoli

Bob Thomas HT, pb, 2000, Webster, Robert; flowers pale salmon pink shades, medium size, full, borne mostly singly, slight fragrance; foliage medium size, medium green, semi-glossy; prickles moderate; upright, medium (30 in.) growth; [The Marquess of Bristol × Warm Wishes]

Bob Woolley HT, ab, 1970, Sanday, John; flowers peach-pink, reverse lemon, 5 in., 60 petals, slight fragrance; foliage matte, green; [Gavotte × Golden Scepter]

Bobbie Darlene HT, lp, 2001, Caruthers, Carlton & Bobbie; flowers medium to large, full, high-centered, borne mostly solitary, slight fragrance; foliage medium size, medium green, semi-glossy; growth upright, medium; garden decorative, exhibition; [sport of Touch of Class]; int. by K&M Nursery, 2004

Bobbie James HWich, w, 1970, Thomas, G. S.; flowers creamy white, 2 in., 7-9 petals, cupped, borne in large clusters, intense fragrance; foliage large, glossy; vigorous growth; int. by Sunningdale Nurseries, 1961

Bobbie Lucas F, op, 1967, McGredy, Sam IV; flowers deep salmon-orange, well-formed, large, borne in clusters; foliage dark; [Margot Fonteyn × Elizabeth of Glamis]

Bobbie Robbie – See **Souv de J. Chabert**, F

Bobbie Vesely HT, pb, 1996, Sheldon, John, Jennifer & Robyn; flowers medium pink blend, reverse medium pink with yellowish tinge, full; foliage medium size, medium green, dull; prickles moderate; upright, medium growth; [Pristine × Gold Medal]; int. by Sheldon, 1995

Bobbink White Climber LCl, w, 1951, Jacobus; flowers creamy yellow to pure white, 3 in., 45-50 petals, moderate fragrance; recurrent bloom; foliage dark, glossy; vigorous, climbing growth; [Dream Girl × seedling]; int. by B&A

Bobby Charlton HT, pb, 1975, Fryer, Gareth; flowers deep pink, reverse silver, well-formed, 6 in., 38 petals, moderate spicy fragrance; foliage dark, leathery; [Royal Highness × Prima Ballerina]; int. by Fryer's Nursery, Ltd., 1974; Gold Medal, Portland, 1980, Gold Medal, Baden-Baden, 1976

Bobby Dazzler F, ab, 1972, Harkness; flowers blush, shaded rich apricot, 3 in., 50 petals, slight fragrance; foliage small, matte; [(Vera Dalton × Highlight) × (Ann Elizabeth × Circus)]

Bobby Shafto HT, my, 1967, Wood; [sport of Piccadilly]

Bobino F, mr

Bobo HT, mr, 1980, Perry, Astor; bud long; flowers 30 petals, urn-shaped, borne singly, intense fruity fragrance; int. in 1981

Bobolink Min, dp, 1960, Moore, Ralph S.; flowers rose-pink, base near white, 1-1½ in., 50 petals, slight fruity fragrance; foliage leathery, glossy; vigorous, bushy (18 in.) growth; PP2009; [(*R. wichurana* × Floradora) × (Oakington Ruby × Floradora)]; int. by Sequoia Nursery, 1959

Bobo's Rose F, dr, 2005, Rawlins, R.; flowers dr, reverse dr, 10 cm., full, borne in small clusters; foliage medium size, medium green, semi-glossy; growth upright, medium; garden decorative; [Florange × Ingrid Bergman]

Bobravka S, op, Urban, J.; flowers dark orange-pink with red tones, medium, dbl.; int. in 1975

Bobrinski – See **Comte de Bobrinsky**, HCh

Bob's Peach Min, op, 1997, Webster, Robert; flowers medium, dbl., borne in large clusters; foliage large, medium green, glossy; numerous prickles; growth bushy, tall (28 in.); [Robin Redbreast × Pot O'Gold]; int. by Handley Rose Nursery, 1998

Bocca Negra HMult, dr, 1910, Dubreuil; flowers purple-crimson, center white, 3-5 cm., cupped, borne in medium to large clusters, moderate musky fragrance; vigorous growth

Boccaccio F, or, 1965, Verschuren, A.; flowers bright scarlet-red, large, 30-40 petals, borne in clusters; foliage glossy; vigorous, upright growth; [Atombombe × seedling]; int. by Stassen Junior, 1963

Boccace HP, dp, 1859, Moreau et Robert; flowers bright carmine, large, full; foliage dark, rough

Bocher HT, pb, 1990, Rodgers, Shafner R.; flowers very dbl.; foliage medium size, medium green, matte; upright growth; [Prima Ballerina × Alec's Red]

Bodhisatva – See **Magic East**, S

Boeing HT, w; flowers 10 cm., 30-35 petals, high-centered; greenhouse rose; int. by Terra Nigra B.V., 2004

Bohemia HT, mp, 1928, Böhm, J.; flowers pure rose-pink, semi-dbl.; [Mrs Franklin Dennison × Mrs Henry Morse seedling]

Bohémienne HT, or, 1954, Mallerin, C.; flowers 45 petals; bushy growth; int. by EFR

Böhm Junior HT, dp, 1935, Böhm, J.; flowers carmine-red, dbl.; foliage glossy; bushy growth; [Laurent Carle × (Paul's Scarlet Climber × Ethel Somerset)]

Böhm Senior HT, mr, 1938, Böhm, J.; flowers large, dbl.

Böhmorose HT, mp, 1935, Böhm, J.; flowers rosy carmine to light rose-pink, very large, dbl.; foliage glossy, dark; very vigorous growth; [Gen. MacArthur × Laurent Carle]

Böhmova Azurovà HP, m, 1934, Böhm, J.; flowers dark violet-pink, large, dbl.

Böhmova Popelka Pol, dr, 1934, Böhm, J.; flowers dark blood-red; foliage curiously variegated

Böhm's Climber Cl HT, mr, before 1935, Böhm, J.; flowers light to medium crimson, medium, dbl., moderate fragrance

Böhm's Triumph HT, dr, 1934, Böhm, J.; flowers very large, semi-dbl., high-centered; foliage dark; vigorous, bushy growth; [Vaterland × Lord Charlemont]

Boieldieu HP, mr, 1877; flowers cherry red, very large; [Jules Margottin × Baronne Prévost]; int. by Margottin, 1877

Boileau HP, mp, 1883, Moreau-Robert; flowers satiny pink, large, full, cupped; [Victor Verdier × unknown]

Bojangles Min, dy, 1982, Warriner, William A.; flowers deep yellow, small, 20 petals, no fragrance; foliage small, light green, semi-glossy; upright, bushy growth; PP4990; [Spanish Sun × Calgold]; int. by J&P, 1983

Bojangles F, ob, Bell; short growth; int. by Bell Roses Ltd., 2001

Boksburg Fantasia HT, mr, 1988, W. Kordes Söhne; flowers large, 23 petals, borne in sprays of 1-3, moderate fragrance; foliage medium green; prickles needle point, brown; tall, well-branched growth; [seedling × seedling]; int. by Ludwigs Roses Pty. Ltd., 1988

Bolchoi – See **Bolshoï**, HT

Bolchoï HT, rb; flowers yellow gold, bordered with strong red, 45 petals, intense fragrance; good repeat bloom; dark green, leathery foliage; growth to 3-5 ft.; int. by Meilland, 1996

Boléro HT, rb, 1937, Gaujard; flowers nasturtium-red and gold, dbl.; foliage leathery; long stems; very vigorous, bushy growth

Boléro F, ob, 1958, Buyl Frères; bud pointed; flowers orange, large, dbl.; very vigorous growth

Bolero HT, Pironti, N.; int. in 1963

Bolero HT, w, Meilland; flowers dbl., high-centered, borne mostly singly; recurrent; florist rose; int. by Meilland Intl., 1998

Bolero LCl, w, Olesen; flowers white, 8-10 cm., 14 petals, slight wild rose fragrance; foliage dark; growth bushy, 200-300 cm.; PP12683; int. by Poulsen Roser, 1999

Bolero – See **Bolero 2004**, F

Bolero 2004 F, w, 2004, Meilland International; flowers large, very full, borne in small clusters, intense fragrance; foliage large, dark green, glossy; growth spreading, medium (3-4 ft.); garden; [(Kimono × Ausreef) × Delge]; int. by The Conard-Pyle Company, 2004

Bolivar F, pb, 2006, Martin, Robert B., Jr.; flowers hot fuchsia pink, reverse cream with yellow heart, 3 in., full, borne mostly solitary; foliage medium size, dark green, glossy, disease-resistant; prickles medium, slightly hooked, brown, few; growth upright, medium (36 in.); exhibition, garden decorative; [Silver Jubilee × Steppin' Out]; int. by Edmunds Roses, 2006

Bolshoï HT, or, Meilland; flowers orange-red with yellow reverse, dbl.; recurrent; vigorous growth; int. in 1996

Bombon Min, Dot, Simon; int. in 1967

Bon Accord HT, pb, 1967, Anderson's Rose Nurseries; flowers pink shaded silver, high-pointed, 4½ in.; foliage glossy; [Prima Ballerina × Percy Thrower]; int. in 1967

Bon-Bon F, pb, 1973, Warriner, William A.; bud ovoid; flowers deep rose-pink, reverse white, large, semi-dbl., slight fragrance; foliage dark; vigorous, bushy growth; PP3555; [Bridal Pink × seedling]; int. by J&P, 1974

Bon Chance – See **Mike's Old-Fashioned Pink**, S

Bon Silène T, dp, before 1837, Hardy; bud well-formed; flowers deep rose, large, dbl., moderate fragrance; recurrent bloom; vigorous growth

Bon Silène Blanc T, ly, 1885, Morat; flowers pale yellow to creamy white, large; [sport of Bon Silène]

Bon Voyage – See **Voeux de Bonheur**, HT

Bona Weillschott HT, rb, 1889, Soupert & Notting; flowers vermilion pink, center orange-red, large, full, moderate fragrance; [Bon Silène × Marie Baumann]

Bonanza HT, yb, 1957, Verbeek; flowers yellow shaded red, slight fragrance; foliage dark; vigorous growth; RULED EXTINCT 5/82 ARM

Bonanza S, yb, 1982, Kordes, W.; flowers yellow tipped red, large, 20 petals, slight fragrance; foliage medium size, dark, glossy; upright growth; [seedling × Arthur Bell]; int. by Kordes, 1983; ADR, 1984

Bonanza HT, ab, Kordes; flowers apricot with pink on outer petals, medium; [sport of Sioux]; int. by W. Kordes Söhne, 2002

Bonanza Kordana Min, ab, Kordes; flowers apricot-pink, full; container rose

Bonapart – See **Electric Blanket**, F

Bonavista HRg, lp, 1978, Svedja, Felicitas; bud ovoid; flowers open, 2 in., 20 petals, intense fragrance; abundant, repeat bloom; foliage yellow-green; upright, bushy growth; [Schneezwerg × Nemesis]; int. by Canada Dept. of Agric.

Bonbon – See **Bonbon Hit**, MinFl

Bonbon Hit MinFl, yb, Poulsen; flowers yellow blend, 5-8 cm., semi-dbl., slight wild rose fragrance; foliage dark; growth bushy, 40-60 cm.; int. by Poulsen Roser, 1992

Bonbori LCl, ob, 1977, Suzuki; flowers orange, with apricot yellow reverse; [Golden Slippers × (Joseph's Coat × Circus)]; int. by Keisei, 1973

Bond Street HT, op, 1965, McGredy, Sam IV; flowers deep salmon-pink, 4½ in., 75 petals; [Radar × Queen Elizabeth]; int. by McGredy

Boneyard Yellow F, my; int. in 1996

Bonfire HWich, mr, 1928, Turbat; flowers brilliant scarlet red, lighter reverse to medium, 4-5 cm., dbl., rosette, borne in clusters of 20-25; foliage light green, small, glossy; very vigorous growth; [Turner's Crimson Rambler × *R. wichurana*]

Bonfire – See **Bonfire Night**, F

Bonfire Min, rb, 2006, Benardella, Frank; flowers bright red with lighter reverse, medium, full, hybrid tea, borne singly and in sprays; foliage medium size, dark green, matte; prickles -¼ in., top angled down; bottom curved, very light green; growth upright, well branched; vigorous, medium (24-30 in.); garden decoration; [Ruby × Timeless]; int. by Nor'East Miniature Roses/ Greenheart Farms, Inc., 2007; Award of Excellence, ARS, 2007

Bonfire Night F, rb, 1972, McGredy, Sam IV; flowers red, shaded yellow-orange, large, 19 petals, globular, slight fragrance; foliage matte; [Tiki × Variety Club]; int. by McGredy & Son, 1971

Bonfire of Artec HT

Bonhomme Min, w, 1986, Laver, Keith G.; [sport of Blueblood]

Bonica F, or, 1959, Meilland, F.; flowers scarlet, 70 petals, high-centered, borne in clusters, slight fragrance; foliage dark, leathery; vigorous, bushy growth; PP1673; [(Alain × Independence) × Moulin Rouge]; int. by URS

Bonica S, mp, 1985, Meilland, Mrs. Marie-Louise; bud ovoid, small; flowers medium pink center, lighter at edges, 6 cm., 53 petals, cupped, borne in clusters of up to 20, no fragrance; free-flowering; foliage small, dark green, semi-dull; prickles small, hooked down; bushy, low (80 cm.) growth; PP5105; [(*R. sempervirens* × Mlle Marthe Carron) × Picasso]; int. by Meilland Et Cie, 1981; Rose Hall of Fame, WFRS, 2003, ADR, 1983

Bonica, Climbing LCl, mp; int. in 1994

Bonica '82 – See **Bonica**, S

Bonica 82, Climbing – See **Bonica, Climbing**, LCl

Bonica Meidiland – See **Bonica**, S

Bonita LCl, dr, 1958, Knight, A.T.; flowers crimson, medium, 15 petals, borne in clusters of 3-8; foliage dark, glossy; vigorous (10-15 ft.) growth

Bonita – See **Bonita Renaissance**, S

Bonita Renaissance S, pb, Olesen; bud pointed ovoid; flowers mainly soft pink with some yellow-orange tones when first opening, 4 in., 45 petals, rosette, borne in clusters of 5 or 6, intense sweet fragrance; recurrent; foliage medium to dark green, glossy; prickles moderate, 6 mm., concave, tan to brown; bushy (100-150 cm.) growth; PP15887; [seedling × Clair Renaissance]; int. by Poulsen Roser, 2001; Bronze Certificate, The Hague, 2006

Bonjour Gr, mr, 1965, Gaujard; flowers bright red, medium, dbl.; foliage leathery; very vigorous, bushy growth; [Mignonne × Miss Universe]

Bonmoon – See **Silver Dawn**, S

Bonn HMsk, or, 1950, Kordes; flowers orange-scarlet, 4 in., 25 petals, borne in trusses of 10, moderate musk fragrance; foliage glossy; upright, bushy (4-5 ft.) growth; [Hamburg × Independence]

Bonne Chere S, rb, 1986, James, John; flowers bright velvet red, creamy eye, large, 5 petals, borne in large clusters, slight fragrance; repeat blooming; foliage medium size, dark, leathery; vigorous, arching (to 4 ft.) growth; [(*R. nutkana* × Baronne Prevost) × Alika]; int. in 1985

Bonne Fête HT, or, 1960, Delbard-Chabert; bud long, pointed; flowers orange-coral, large, 25-30 petals; foliage leathery, glossy; strong stems; vigorous, bushy growth; [Independence × Barcelona]

Bonne Geneviève HCh, m, 1826, Chevrier/Laffay; flowers bright purple, center garnet, large, full

Bonne Nouvelle – See **Good News**, HT

Bonne Nuit, Climbing Cl HT, dr, 1964, Kashimoto; int. by Itami Rose Nursery

Bonne Nuit HT, dr, 1968, Combe; bud pointed; flowers blackish red, medium, dbl., high-centered, moderate fragrance; foliage sparse, glossy; bushy growth; int. by Wyant, 1966

Bonnie S, dp, 1956, Wright, Percy H.; growth similar to Aylsham but taller and more rapid and vigorous; [Hansa × *R. nitida*]

Bonnie Anne HT, pb, 1976, MacLeod; flowers pink, reverse yellow and pink, 3-3½ in., 30 petals, moderate fragrance; foliage large, dark, glossy; [Prima Ballerina × Wendy Cussons]

Bonnie Belle HWich, mp, 1911, Walsh; flowers rose pink, lighter towards edges, 5 cm., single, borne in medium to large clusters; foliage glossy; growth to 8-10 ft.

Bonnie Bess HT, op, 1929, Dale; flowers deep coral-pink, suffused copper, dbl.; [Wilhelm Kordes × (Crusader × Sunburst)]

Bonnie Doone Cl HT, yb, 1941, Clark, A.; [City of Little Rock seedling × seedling]

Bonnie Hamilton F, or, 1976, Cocker; flowers vermilion-red, well-formed, 2½ in., 26 petals, slight fragrance; foliage dark; [Anne Cocker × Allgold]

Bonnie Jack F, ly, 2000, Bennett, Dee; flowers full, high-centered, borne in small clusters, slight fragrance; foliage medium size, medium green, matte; prickles moderate; growth upright, tall (4-5 ft.); [Irish Gold × Party Girl]; int. by Tiny Petals Nursery, 2001

Bonnie Jane Pol, dp; int. in 2000

Bonnie Jean HT, rb, 1933, Archer; flowers carmine-cerise, base white, large, single; vigorous growth

Bonnie Maid F, pb, 1951, LeGrice; flowers silvery pink reverse deep pink, 3 in., 17 petals, borne in clusters of 5-8; foliage leathery, dark; vigorous, bushy growth; Gold Medal, NRS, 1955

Bonnie Pink F, lp, 1964, Boerner; bud ovoid; flowers geranium-pink overcast begonia-rose, with upright center petals, 4½ in., 35-40 petals, high-centered, moderate fragrance; foliage glossy; vigorous, upright growth; PP2411; [(White Garnette × unknown) × Hawaii]; int. by J&P

Bonnie Prince HMult, w, 1916, Cook, T.N.; bud small, pointed; flowers white, center tinged yellow, medium, dbl., cupped, borne in medium clusters, moderate fragrance; foliage medium size, glossy, thick; excellent pillar growth; hips round, 1/2 in., red; [White Tausendschön × Wichurana seedling]; int. by Portland Rose Soc., 1924

Bonnie Prince Charlie HT, mr, 1960, Cuthbert; bud pointed; flowers bright red, well-formed, dbl.

Bonnie Prince Charlie's Rose – See **Alba Maxima**, A

Bonnie Rosalie F, w, 2006, Rippetoe, Robert Neil; flowers white-pink edge, reverse white, red stamens, 2-2½ in., single, borne mostly solitary, moderate clove fragrance; foliage medium size, medium green, matte; prickles medium, slightly hooked, red brown, moderate; growth bushy, medium (3 × 3 ft.); landscape, bedding; [Sweet Vivien × unknown]; int. by Robert Neil Rippetoe, 2006

Bonnie Scotland HT, dp, 1976, Anderson's Rose Nurseries; flowers light red, 5 in., 43 petals, high-centered, intense damask fragrance; foliage glossy; [Wendy Cussons × Percy Thrower]

Bonny Min, mp, 1975, Kordes; flowers deep pink, lighter reverse, dbl., globular, slight fragrance; foliage small, light, wrinkled; dwarf growth; [Zorina × seedling]; int. in 1974

Bonny LCl, lp, Kordes; bud small, deep pink; flowers pure pink, 5 cm., borne in large clusters; profuse spring bloom, non-recurrent; medium green, glossy foliage; vigorous growth to 10 ft.; int. by W. Kordes Söhne, 1998

Bonny Kordana Min, dp, Kordes; flowers soft, deep pink, full; container rose; int. by W. Kordes Söhne

Bonsoir HT, mp, 1967, Dickson, A.; bud ovoid; flowers peach-pink, 6 in., dbl., intense fragrance; foliage glossy; int. by A. Dickson & Sons, 1968

Bonza F, op, Bell; int. by Bell Roses Ltd., 2001

Booful HT, dr, 2000, Priestly, J.L.; flowers full; foliage medium size, light green, dull; prickles moderate; growth compact, medium (3 ft.); [sport of Delsatel]

Boogie-Woogie LCl, mp, Poulsen; flowers medium pink, 8-10 cm., dbl., slight wild rose fragrance; foliage reddish green; growth bushy, 100-150 cm.; PP15102; int. by Poulsen Roser, 2002

Booker T. Washington HMult, dr, 1930, Turbat; flowers deep maroon, borne in clusters; int. by C-P

Boomerang Min, rb, 1992, Spooner, Raymond A.; flowers red and white, large, full, borne in small clusters, no fragrance; foliage medium size, medium green, semi-glossy; some prickles; medium, bushy growth; [seedling × seedling]; int. by Oregon Miniature Roses, 1993; AOE, ARS, 1993

Bopeep – See **Bo-Peep**, Min

Bora Bora – See **Ashram**, HT

Bordeaux HMult, mr, 1908, Soupert & Notting; flowers wine-red, 3½ cm., dbl., borne in large clusters, slight fragrance; non-recurrent; very vigorous growth; [Crimson Rambler × Mlle Blanche Rebatel]

Bordeaux – See **Bordeaux Palace**, MinFl

Bordeaux des Dames – See **Petite de Hollande**, C

Bordeaux Kordana Min, or, Kordes; flowers orangey-red, small, dbl., cupped, borne singly and in small clusters; compact, small growth; container rose; int. by W. Kordes Söhne, 1998

Bordeaux Kordana Min, dr, Kordes; flowers small, dbl., cupped to flat, borne mostly singly; recurrent; foliage dark green; compact growth; container rose; int. in 2005

Bordeaux Palace MinFl, mr, Poulsen; flowers medium red, 5-8 cm., 25 petals, no fragrance; foliage dark; growth narrow, bushy, 40-60 cm.; PP15874; int. by Poulsen Roser, 2004

Border Beauty F, mr, 1958, deRuiter; flowers bright scarlet, 2-2½ in., semi-dbl., borne in very large trusses (10-12 in); foliage dark, glossy; vigorous, upright growth; [Floribunda seedling × Signal Red]; int. by Gregory & Son, 1957

Border Coral F, op, 1958, deRuiter; flowers coral-salmon, 2-2½ in., semi-dbl., borne in trusses; foliage dark, glossy; vigorous, spreading growth; [Signal Red × Fashion]; int. by Gregory & Son, 1957

Border Coral, Climbing Cl F, op, 1965, Sanday, J.; int. by Sanday; Gregory

Border Gem F, pb, 1961, Morey, Dr. Dennison; bud ovoid; flowers geranium-pink, center light salmon-orange, 2½-3 in., 20 petals, borne in clusters, moderate fragrance; foliage leathery; compact, low growth;

PP2059; [(Navajo × Golden Dawn) × Pinocchio]; int. by J&P, 1961

Border Gold F, dy, 1966, Morey, Dr. Dennison; bud ovoid; flowers medium to deep yellow, very dbl.; foliage dark, leathery; vigorous, low, bushy growth; [Allgold × Pigmy Gold]; int. by General Bionomics

Border King Pol, mr, 1952, deRuiter; flowers bright strawberry-red, small large truss, 16 petals; foliage dark, glossy; very vigorous growth; int. by Gregory

Border King, Climbing Cl Pol, mr, 1960, Gregory

Border Princess F, op, 1951, Verschuren-Pechtold; flowers coral-pink shaded orange, reflexed, 3 in., 22 petals, high-centered; foliage light, glossy; vigorous growth; int. by Bentley

Border Queen F, op, 1951, deRuiter; flowers salmon-pink, center paler, reverse darker truss, 2½ in., 9 petals; foliage leathery, olive-green; vigorous, compact growth; int. by Gregory; Gold Medal, NRS, 1950

Borderer Pol, pb, 1918, Clark, A.; flowers salmon, fawn and pink, semi-dbl.; dwarf, spreading growth; [Jersey Beauty × unknown]; int. by NRS Victoria

Bordura de Nea F, w, Wagner, S.; bud short; flowers small to medium sized, white-pink, 8 petals, flat, borne in clusters, slight fragrance; foliage small, semi-glossy, medium green; [Bonica '82 × Incandescent]; int. by Res. Stn. f. Fruit Growing, Cluj, 1995

Bordure Pol, mp, 1911, Barbier; flowers carmine-pink, small, dbl.; [Universal Favorite × unknown]

Bordure Blanche F, w, Delbard; flowers white, small, blooms open flat, borne in large clusters; low (50-100 cm.), bushy growth; int. in 1997

Bordure Camaïeu F, ob, Delbard; buds orange-yellow; flowers have tones of orange and yellow, turning pink as they age, semi-dbl., flat, borne in clusters; growth to 50-100 cm.; int. by Georges Delbard SA, 2002

Bordure d'Or F, my, Delbard

Bordure Magenta F, dp, Delbard; flowers magenta, borne in large clusters; growth to 50-60 cm.; int. by Georges Delbard SA, 2004; Certificate of Merit, Belfast, 2006

Bordure Nacrée Min, ly, 1986, Delbard; flowers creamy light yellow, small, 38 petals, no fragrance; low, bushy growth; [(Orléans Rose × Francois et Joseph Guy) × (Goldilocks × DELtorche)]; int. in 1973; Gold Medal, Baden-Baden, 1972

Bordure Rose – See **Strawberry Ice**, F

Bordure Rose Number 2 F, mp, Delbard; growth low, dense, vigorous; int. by Georges Delbard SA, 1993

Bordure Vermillon F, rb, Delbard; flowers red-copper, cream-red reverse, borne in clusters; constant bloom; growth to 50-100 cm.; int. in 1990

Bordure Vive Pol, mp, Delbard; flowers rose-cyclamen, rose-silver reverse, dbl., borne in small clusters; growth small (39 cm.); borders, containers; int. in 1985

Bordurella F, pb

Borealis HKor, w, 1980, James, John; bud globular, pointed; flowers 27 petals, high-centered, borne singly, moderate sweet fragrance; repeat bloom; foliage shiny; prickles gray; bushy growth; [Blanche Mallerin × Leverkusen]

Born Again – See **Renaissance**, HT

Born Free Min, or, 1978, Moore, Ralph S.; bud long, pointed; flowers brilliant orange-red, 1½ in., 20 petals; foliage dark; bushy, upright growth; PP4454; [Red Pinocchio × Little Chief]; int. by Sequoia Nursery

Borsalino S, mr, Interplant; int. in 1987

Borussia – See **Cottage Maid**, S

Boryana HT, dr, 1985, Staikov, Prof. Dr. V.; flowers large, 55 petals; foliage dark, glossy; vigorous, upright growth; [Tallyho × Spartan]; int. by Kalaydjiev and Chorbadjiiski, 1977

Boscobel Min, ob, 1991, King, Gene; flowers orange to burnt orange, small, dbl., borne mostly singly, no fragrance; foliage medium size, light green, matte; upright, medium growth; [(Cheers × Rainbow's End) × Breezy]; int. by AGM Miniature Roses

Boseyeball S, mr, 1997, Bossom, W.E.; flowers single, single, borne in small clusters; foliage small, light green, glossy; few prickles; spreading, medium (60 cm.) growth; [Eyepaint × Ballerina]

Bosom Buddy HT, or, Wells; int. in 1992

Bossa Nova HT, dy, 1964, McGredy, Sam IV; flowers deep golden yellow, 4 in., 28 petals, high-centered; foliage dark; [Leverkusen × Buccaneer]; int. by McGredy

Bossa Nova F, mp, Olesen; flowers flower light on edges, deeper in heart, 5-8 cm., full, borne in clusters; recurrent; foliage dark, glossy; growth bushy, 100-150 cm.; PP12523; [seedling × The Fairy]; int. by Poulsen Roser, 1996

Bossuet HP, about 1836, Vibert

Bossuet HGal, mr, before 1846; flowers scarlet, edges darker

Bossuet, Aigle de Meaux HT, m, J&P; int. by Roseraies Guillot, 2005

Boston HT, mp, 1917, Montgomery Co.; flowers dbl.; [Mrs George Shawyer × seedling]

Boston Beauty Pol, mp, 1919, Farquhar; flowers clear pink, dbl.; [Orléans Rose × (Katharina Zeimet × Old Ayrshire rose)]

Boston Rambler – See **Farquhar**, HWich

Bosum Buddy HT, op, 2003, Wells, Verlie W.; flowers full, borne mostly solitary; foliage medium size, dark green, semi-glossy; prickles ¼ in., hooked; growth upright, medium; garden, exhibition; [Friendship × Dolly Parton]; int. by Wells MidSouth Roses, 2003

Botanica F, pb, 1998, Thomson, George L.; flowers pink with touch of lilac, 2 in., 26-41 petals, borne in large clusters; foliage medium size, medium green, dull; prickles moderate; bushy, medium (3-3½ ft.) growth; [Avandel × Madam President]

Botaniste Abrial – See **Lowell Thomas**, HT

Botaniste Henri Grimm F, my, 1958, Gaujard, R.; flowers golden to straw-yellow, becoming pink tinted, large, borne in clusters; vigorous growth; [Goldilocks × Fashion]; int. by G. Truffaut

Botany Bay HT, rb, J&P?; flowers deep coral-red with a cream center, dbl., slight fragrance; medium growth; possibly from 1988; int. in 1988

Botero HT, mr; flowers very dbl., high-centered; growth to 100-120 cm.; int. by Meilland, 2002

Bottanix F, or, McGredy; flowers bright orange-red, borne in clusters; mid-green foliage; int. by Gandy's Roses Ltd, 2003

Botticelli F, mp, Meilland; flowers 50-55 petals, well-formed, borne in clusters; good repeat; growth compact (70-80 cm.); Certificate of Merit, Belfast, 2006

Botzaris D, w, before 1856; flowers creamy white, medium size, very dbl., flat, quartered; non-recurrent; foliage light green; growth to 4 × 3 ft., vase-shaped

Boudoir HT, pb, 1942, Meilland, F.; flowers Tyrian rose, reverse white, large, 50 petals, high-centered; foliage leathery; vigorous, upright, bushy growth; [Ampere × (Charles P. Kilham × Margaret McGredy)]; int. by C-P

Boudoir S, pb, Clements, John K.; flowers soft medium pink with ivory reverse, 4 in., dbl., loosely cupped; compact (4 × 3 ft.) growth; int. in 1995

Bougainville N, pb, 1822, Cochet/Vibert; bud crimson-purple, round; flowers pink in center, becoming paler and tinged with lilac at the base, 4 cm., very dbl., cupped, borne in large clusters, slight fragrance; foliage narrow, glossy; numerous prickles

Bougère T, op, 1832, Bougère; flowers deep salmon, shaded bronze, large, full, cupped; growth vigorous; probably extinct

Bougère – See **Clotilde**, T

Boula de Nanteuil – See **Comte de Nanteuil**, HGal, 1834

Boule de Nanteuil – See **Comte de Nanteuil**, HGal, 1834

Boule de Neige – See **Globe White Hip**, C

Boule de Neige B, w, 1867, Lacharme, F.; flowers pure white, compact, dbl., moderate fragrance; occasional recurrent bloom; foliage dark; [Mme Blanche Lafitte × Sappho]; sometimes classified as N

Boule d'Hortensia – See **Aimable Rouge**, HGal, 1819-1820

Boule Hortensia – See **Majestueuse**, HGal

Boulie's Dream S, ob, 1998, Williams, J. Benjamin; flowers orange-red inside, yellow reverse, 4½-5 in., full, borne singly and in large clusters, intense fragrance; foliage large, dark green, semi-glossy; few prickles; strong, vigorous, upright, climbing, arched growth; [Folklore × self]; int. by J. Benjamin Williams & Associates, 1999

Boulie's Favorite S, mp, Williams, J.B.; int. by Hortico, 2004

Bountiful F, pb, 1972, LeGrice; flowers strawberry-salmon, reverse deeper, 3 in., 33 petals, high-centered; foliage small; tall, erect growth; [Vesper × seedling]

Bountiful Abundance S, op; flowers dainty coral pink, dbl., borne in clusters; blooms all season; prostrate groundcover growth; int. in 2000

Bounty HT, w, Select; flowers pure white, 9 cm., very full, high-centered, borne mostly singly; recurrent; stems long; florist rose; int. by Terra Nigra BV, 2005

Bouquet F, dp, 1940, Tantau; flowers deep pink, 33 petals, cupped; foliage dark, leathery; vigorous, bushy, compact growth; [Ingar Olsson × Heidekind]; int. by C-P

Bouquet Blanc HP, w, 1856, Robert; flowers white to light pink, medium, dbl.

Bouquet Blanc Pol, w, 1914, Corrard; flowers pure white with some yellow towards center, medium, dbl.

Bouquet Charmant HSet, lp, about 1810, Descemet

Bouquet Charmant HGal, mp, before 1811; flowers rosy purple, large, dbl.; from Holland

Bouquet de Flore B, mr, 1839, Bizard; flowers light carmine red, very large, dbl., cupped; foliage dark green

Bouquet de la Mariée – See **Bouquet de Marie**, N

Bouquet de Marie N, w, 1858, Damaizin; flowers light greenish-white, fading to pure white, 6 cm., dbl., borne in small clusters; foliage light green; prickles numerous, short

Bouquet de Mühlenbeck HGal, about 1860, Baumann

Bouquet de Neige Pol, w, 1900, Vilin; flowers bright white, medium, dbl., borne in clusters of 20-30

Bouquet de Venus HGal, lp, before 1819; bud elongate; flowers silky flesh pink, mixed with touches of white, large buttoned center, small, very dbl., pompon; foliage light green, round; prickles moderate; stems slender, yellowish; growth small, compact; Agathe group; Lerouge claims to have received it from Malmaison

Bouquet des Fleurs – See **Bouquet de Flore**, B

Bouquet d'Or N, yb, 1872, Ducher; flowers buff yellow, center coppery salmon, 9 cm., dbl., flat; [Gloire de Dijon × unknown]

Bouquet d'Or HT, ly, 1922, Lippiatt; flowers light golden yellow, well-formed; vigorous growth

Bouquet d'Otto HGal, before 1860, Baumann

Bouquet Fait S, pb, 1986, Lens, Louis; flowers medium pink with a white eye, 2 in., semi-dbl., borne singly and in small clusters, intense fragrance; non-recurrent; foliage grayish green, hairy; bushy (to 5 ft.) growth; [*R. mollis* × Complicata]; int. in 1985

Bouquet Parfait – See **Royale**, HGal

Bouquet Parfait HMsk, pb, 2000, Lens, Louis; flowers pale pink to cream, reverse lighter, 2 in., full, globular, borne in large clusters; recurrent; foliage medium size, dark green, glossy, disease-resistant; few prickles; upright, medium (4-5 ft.) growth; [(*R. multiflora adenocheata* × Ballerina) × White Dream]; int. by Louis Lens BV, 1989

Bouquet Rose HWich, mp, 1912, Theunis/Eindhoven; flowers rose pink to lilac-white, 1½-2 in., full, borne in medium clusters; [Turner's Crimson Rambler × Ernst Grandpierre]

Bouquet Rose Pol, lp, 1928, Granger-Gaucher; flowers flesh-pink and peach-blossom, borne in clusters of 30-40; int. by Turbat

Bouquet Rose de Vénus – See **Bouquet de Venus**, HGal

Bouquet Rouge F, mr, 1963, Arles; flowers large, 45 petals, borne in clusters of 14-16; vigorous growth; [(Gruss an Teplitz × Independence) × (Independence × Floradora)]; int. by Roses-France

Bouquet Superbe – See **Bouquet Charmant**, HGal

Bouquet Tout Fait – See **Red Damask**, D

Bouquet Tout Fait N, w, before 1836, Laffay, M.; sepals long, foliolate; flowers creamy white, 3-4 cm., semi-dbl., borne in large clusters; repeats well

Bouquet Vanille S, w, Delbard; int. in 1993

Bouquetterie Min, mr; flowers bright red, borne in clusters; free-flowering

Bourbon HGal, pb, before 1811; bud delicate pink, pointed; flowers striped and mottled with pink and a pale ground, medium, semi-dbl., moderate fragrance

Bourbon Jacques – See **Rosier de Bourgon**, B

Bourbon Queen – See **Queen of Bourbons**, B, 1834

Bourbon Rose B, dp, 1817; flowers pink, red or purple, 3 in., semi-dbl., borne solitary or in few-flowered clusters, moderate applesauce fragrance; some repeat; foliage large, thick, edged purplish-red when young, with 5-7 leaflets; stems bright green with purple shading; growth compact, vigorous; brought to France from Réunion (Ile de Bourbon); probably *R. chinensis* × Quâtre Saisons

Bourgogne S, mr, Interplant; flowers single; int. in 1983

Bourgogne No. 2 S, mr, Adam, M.; int. in 1996

Bournonville – See **Pink Fizz**, LCl

Boursault Rose Bslt, mp, about 1810; flowers pink to purple, often showing a white stripe, semi-dbl., nodding, in corymbs; non-recurrent; foliage medium size, bright green, deeply serrated; stems long, flexible, reddish-purple; climbing to 12 ft. growth; subglobose, smooth fruit; very hardy; [probably *R. pendulina* × a China (possibly *R. chinensis*)]; possibly bred in 1810 by Cugnot and sent to the garden of Henri Boursault

Bouton d'Or T, dy, 1867, Guillot; flowers dark golden yellow, reverse whitish yellow, very full; [Canari × unknown]

Boutonniere HT, op, 1940, Lammerts, Dr. Walter; flowers salmon-pink, 3 in., 40-50 petals; foliage dark, glossy, bronze; vigorous, bushy, compact growth; [Lulu × Mrs Sam McGredy]; int. by Armstrong Nursery

Boutons d'Unique HSpn, mp, 1821, Cartier

Bouzloudja HT, mr, 1985, Staikov, Prof. Dr. V.; flowers large, 40 petals, slight fragrance; foliage dark, glossy; vigorous, bushy growth; [Sarah Arnot × Rina Herholdt]; int. by Kalaydjiev and Chorbadjiiski, 1974

Bow Bells S, dp, 1994, Austin, David; flowers deep pink, medium, dbl., borne in large clusters, moderate fragrance; foliage medium size, medium green, semi-glossy; some prickles; upright, bushy (47 in.) growth; [seedling × Graham Thomas]; int. by David Austin Roses, Ltd., 1991

Bowie Pink S, mp

Bowie Pink Lady HT, lp, Williams, J. Benjamin; bud dark pink; flowers soft pink with hint of lemon at heart, high-centered; int. by Hortico, 1995

Bowie White Patio Min, w, Williams, J. Benjamin

Bowie Yellow Blush Gr, ly, Williams, J.B.; int. by Hortico, 2004

Bowie Yellow Patio MinFl, my, Williams, J. Benjamin; flowers high-centered, high-centered; int. in 1995

Bowled Over F, ab, 2001, Rosen Tantau; flowers amber yellow, reverse amber yellow, 5 cm., dbl., borne in small clusters; foliage small, medium green, glossy; prickles moderate; growth compact, medium; garden decoration, containers; [seedling × seedling]

Boy Crazy S, dp, 1992, Dickson, Patrick; flowers deep pink, petal base has cream colored "half moon", heavy petal substance, medium, dbl.; foliage medium size, dark green, glossy; some prickles; patio; medium (90 cm.), upright, bushy growth; [Sweet Magic × DICmerlin]; int. by Bear Creek Gardens, 1992

Boy O Boy S, mr, 1999, Dickson, Colin; flowers 2¾-3 in., semi-dbl.; foliage small, medium green, glossy; prickles moderate; flori-shrub; bushy, spreading (30 in.) growth; [Little Prince × Eye Opener]; int. by Dickson Nurseries, Ltd., 1996

Boy Scout HT, or, 1946, Duehrsen; bud long, pointed; flowers flame, large, dbl., high-centered; foliage dark, glossy; very vigorous, upright, bushy growth; [Joanna Hill × Olympiad]; int. by California Roses

Boys' Brigade Min, mr, 1984, Cocker, Ann G.; flowers medium, patio, 5 petals, borne in clusters, no fragrance; foliage small, medium green, semi-glossy; bushy growth; [(Darling Flame × Saint Alban) × (Little Flirt × Marlena)]; int. by Cocker & Sons, 1984

Bozena Nemcová HT, dp, 1931, Böhm, J.; flowers pure dark pink, very large, dbl., cupped; foliage bronze, thick; strong stems; vigorous growth; [Sylvia × Priscilla]

Brad HT, ab, 1999, Poole, Lionel; flowers 5½ in., full, borne mostly singly, moderate fragrance; foliage medium size, medium green, dull; few prickles; bushy, medium (3 ft.) growth; [Gavotte × Ravenswood]

Bradgate HT, yb, 1971, Worth; flowers yellow and deep red bicolor, pointed, 4-5 in., 27 petals, slight fragrance; foliage dark; free growth; [sport of Piccadilly]; int. by Wm. Lowe & Sons, 1970

Bradley Craig F, or, 1987, McGredy, Sam IV; flowers scarlet, medium, dbl., slight fragrance; foliage medium size, medium green, glossy; bushy growth; [Tojo × Montana]; int. in 1986

Bradova Germania HFt, op, 1932, Brada, Dr.; flowers coppery-pink, large, semi-dbl.

Bradova Lososova Druschki HP, op, 1937, Brada, Dr.; flowers salmon-pink, large

Bradwardine – See **Rose Bradwardine**, HEg

Braham Datt HT, lp, 2005, Shastri, N.V.; flowers light pink, reverse light pink, 4½ in., full, borne mostly solitary, moderate fragrance; foliage medium size, medium green, semi-glossy; prickles medium, crooked; growth compact, medium (3½ ft.); [Sahasradhara × Pristine]; int. by Shastri. N.V., 1996

Braine l'Alleud HT, Delforge, H.; int. in 1984

Braiswick Beatuy HMult, pb, 1912, Cant, F.; flowers silky pink, base bronze-pink, center tinted scarlet, moderate fragrance

Braiswick Charm HWich, ob, 1914, Cant, F.; flowers orange-yellow, edges almost white, borne in clusters; foliage dark, glossy, leathery; long, strong stems; very vigorous growth

Braiswick Fairy HMult, dp, 1912, Cant, F.; flowers darp pink, aging lighter, semi-dbl.

Braiswick Gem HMult, my, 1912, Cant, F.; flowers nankeen yellow, moderate fragrance

Bramble Bear Min, ab, Benardella, Frank; int. in 1997

Bramble-Leaved Rose – See ***R. setigera tomentosa*** (Torrey & Gray)

Brandenburg HT, or, 1965, Kordes, R.; flowers deep salmon, reverse darker, 5 in., 40 petals, high-centered; vigorous, upright growth; PP2810; [(Spartan × Prima Ballerina) × Karl Herbst]; int. by McGredy

Brandenburg Gate HT, mr, 1991, Warriner, William A.; flowers red with light reverse, large, full, exhibition, moderate fragrance; foliage large, medium green, matte; tall, upright growth; [seedling × Madras]; int. by Bear Creek Gardens, 1990

Brandon LCl, mr, 1964, Combe; bud long, pointed; flowers dark carmine-red, large, dbl., borne mostly solitary; very free, recurrent bloom; vigorous growth

Brandon's Dream HT, pb, 2003, Wells, Verlie W.; flowers large, full, borne mostly solitary, intense fragrance; foliage large, medium green, semi-glossy; prickles in., straight; growth upright, tall; garden decoration; [seedling × seedling]; int. by Wells MidSouth Roses, 2003

Brandy HT, ab, 1981, Swim, H.C. & Christensen, J.E.; bud long, pointed; flowers deep apricot, 5 in., 25-30 petals, high-centered, borne mostly singly, slight tea fragrance; foliage large, dark green; prickles straight; vigorous, medium growth; PP5168; [First Prize × Dr. A.J. Verhage]; int. by Armstrong Nursery

Brandy, Climbing Cl HT, ab, Swane; [sport of Brandy]; int. in 1994

Brandy Butter HT, ob, 1980, Northfield, G.; bud long, pointed; flowers pale gold, 28 petals, high-centered, borne 4-5 per cluster, moderate fragrance; foliage mid-green; prickles thick, triangular-shaped; tall, upright growth; [Fred Gibson × Royal Gold]

Brandy Snap HT, ob, 1999, Dickson, Colin; flowers orange/bold, large, full, borne mostly singly, intense fragrance; foliage medium size, medium green, glossy; prickles moderate; upright, medium (30 in.) growth; [seedling × seedling]; int. by Dickson Nurseries Ltd., 1999

Brandyglow – See **Vanessa Belinda**, F

Brandypink – See **Ronald George Kent**, F

Brandysnap – See **Brandy Snap**, HT

Brandywine HT, ly, 1941, Thompson's, J.H., Sons; bud long, pointed; flowers buff-yellow, 4-5 in., 25-30 petals; foliage olive-green, leathery; very vigorous, upright growth; [seedling × Souvenir]; int. by C-P; John Cook Medal, ARS, 1945

Brasero F, mr, Kordes; flowers large; int. by Sauvageot, 1978

Brasier HT, mr, 1937, Mallerin, C.; flowers flame-scarlet, large, dbl.; foliage glossy; very vigorous, bushy growth; [Charles P. Kilham × seedling]; int. by C-P

Brasilia HT, rb, 1967, McGredy, Sam IV; flowers scarlet, reverse gold, 4 in., dbl., slight fragrance; PP3071; [Kordes' Perfecta × Piccadilly]; int. by McGredy & Son, 1968

Brass Band F, ab, 1993, Christensen, Jack E.; flowers melon orange and yellow bicolor, 3-3½ in., 30-35 petals, borne in small clusters, slight fruity fragrance; foliage large, dark green, semi-glossy; some prickles; medium (100 cm.), upright, bushy growth; PP9171; [Gold Badge × seedling]; int. by Bear Creek Gardens, Inc., 1994

Brass Monkey LCl, ab, Harkness; flowers peach-apricot, changing to amber, dbl., cupped, dahlia-like; moderate growth; int. in 1998

Brass Ring Min, ob, 1981, Dickson, Patrick; bud pointed; flowers coppery orange, fading to rose pink, patio, dbl., flat, borne in large clusters; foliage small, pointed, glossy; upright, arching growth; PP4991; [Memento × Nozomi]; int. by J&P

Braunwald S, w

Brautzauber F, w, Noack; int. in 2001

Bravado F, dr, 1986, Warriner, William A.; flowers 26 petals, high-centered, borne usually singly, slight fragrance; foliage medium size, dark, semi-glossy; prickles medium, red to brown, hooked downward; medium, upright growth; PP5978; [seedling × Gabriella]; int. by J&P, 1987

Brave Heart F, mp, 1996, Horner, Heather M.; flowers high-pointed, 4 in., dbl., borne in small clusters; foliage large, medium green, semi-glossy; some prickles; medium (100 cm.), upright growth; [(Prominent × Southampton) × Bright Smile]; int. by Battersby Roses, 1998

Brave Patriot S, mr, 2003, Buck; flowers single, borne in small clusters, moderate fragrance; foliage medium size, dark green, semi-glossy; prickles 1/4 in., straight, moderate; growth upright, tall (6 ft.); hedge or specimen shrub; [sport of Maytime]; int. by Roses Unlimited, 2002

Braveheart – See **Gordon's College**, F

Braveheart S, dr, Clements, John K.; flowers deep royal red with velvety texture, 4 in., 37 petals; dark green foliage; growth to 3½ × 4 ft; [Tamango × The Dark Lady]; int. by Heirloom Roses, 1998

Bravo HT, mr, 1951, Swim, H.C.; bud ovoid; flowers cardinal-red, 4-5 in., 35 petals, high-centered, borne in clusters; foliage leathery; vigorous, upright, moderately bushy growth; [World's Fair × Mirandy]; int. by Armstrong Nursery

Bravo Min, mr, Poulsen; flowers medium red, medium, dbl., no fragrance; foliage dark; growth bushy, 20-40 cm.; PP10629; int. by Poulsen Roser, 1998

Bravo Parade – See **Bravo**, Min

Braz Ornelas HT, Moreira da Silva, A.

Brazerade LCl, mr

Brazier – See **Brasier**, HT

Brazil HT, rb, 1947, Caron, B.; bud long, pointed; flowers saturn-red, reverse saffron-yellow, well-shaped, dbl.; foliage light green; int. by URS

Bread 'n' Butter Min, ob, 1985, Bennett, Dee; flowers golden orange blended yellow, 5 cm., 28 petals, cupped, borne usually singly, some small clusters, moderate fragrance; recurrent; foliage medium size, medium green, semi-glossy; prickles moderate, slender, hooked slightly downward; stems long; upright, bushy growth; hips globular, orange; PP6135; [Arizona × Orange Honey]; int. by Tiny Petals Nursery, 1985

Break o' Dawn Cl Min, pb, 1983, Williams, Ernest D.; flowers white with deep pink edges, white reverse, small, 35 petals, slight fragrance; foliage small, dark, glossy; upright, bushy, climbing growth; [Little Darling × Over the Rainbow]; int. by Mini-Roses, 1982

Break o' Day Pol, pb, 1937, Archer; flowers copper-pink, center yellow, fading to shell-pink, semi-dbl., cupped, borne in clusters; recurrent bloom; vigorous growth

Break o' Day HT, ob, 1939, Brownell; flowers orange shades, large, 50 petals, intense fragrance; vigorous growth; [seedling × Glenn Dale]

Break o' Day, Climbing Cl HT, ob, 1944, Brownell; flowers pale pink, apricot at center, large, full

Breakaway Min, mr, 1981, Lyon, Lyndon; bud ovoid, pointed; flowers 23 petals, borne singly, slight fragrance; foliage small, medium green; prickles straight, tiny, brownish-green; compact, upright, bushy growth; [Dandy Lyon × seedling]; int. in 1980

Breath of Heaven S, mr, 2000, Hamilton, Noel; flowers cerise red, reverse lighter, medium size, 70 petals, exhibition, borne mostly singly; foliage medium size, medium green, semi-glossy; prickles moderate; upright growth, 4½ ft.; [(Heavenly Scent × seedling) × seedling]; int. by Coming Up Roses, 2002

Breath of Life LCl, ab, 1980, Harkness & Co., Ltd.; bud plump; flowers apricot to apricot-pink, large, 33 petals, borne singly or in small clusters, moderate fragrance; foliage semi-glossy; prickles large, straight, reddish; upright (to 8 ft.) growth; [Red Dandy × Alexander]; int. in 1981

Breath of Spring Min, my, 2001, Bridges, Dennis; flowers 1 in., dbl., borne mostly solitary; foliage large, dark green, semi-glossy; prickles in., straight, moderate; growth upright, tall (2½ ft.); garden decorative, containers, cutting; PPAF; [(Summer Sunset × select pollen) × select pollen]; int. by Bridges Roses, 2002

Breathless HT, dp, 1993, Warriner, William A.; three sepals moderately bearded; flowers deep pink, 3-3½ in., dbl., borne mostly singly, moderate fragrance; foliage large, medium green, purple-red when young, semi-glossy; some prickles; tall (150 cm.), upright growth; PP8595; [seedling × Chrysler Imperial]; int. by Bear Creek Gardens, Inc., 1993

Breathtaking HT, dp, 1982, Leon, Charles F., Sr.; bud ovoid, long, pointed; flowers deep pink, 40 petals, high-centered, intense damask fragrance; foliage medium to large, medium green, semi-glossy; upright, bushy growth; [(Pink Silk × unknown) × (Pink Parfait × Wendy Cussons)]; int. in 1981

Breathtaking HT, my; flowers crisp, rich yellow, 4 in., 30 petals, old-fashioned form, moderate fruity/tea fragrance; bright, lime green foliage; growth to 4 × 3 ft.; int. by Harkness, 2003

Bredon S, ab, 1985, Austin, David; flowers medium, dbl.; repeat bloom; foliage small, light green, matte; upright growth; [Wife of Bath × Lilian Austin]; int. by David Austin Roses, Ltd., 1984

Breeze – See **Breeze Parade**, Min

Breeze Hill HWich, ab, 1926, Van Fleet; flowers flesh tinted apricot, center rose, paling, 3 in., 55 petals, cupped, borne in clusters, moderate fragrance; non-recurrent; foliage small, round matte; growth bushy, heavy canes; [*R. wichurana* × Beauté de Lyon]; int. by American Rose Society

Breeze Parade Min, ab, Poulsen; flowers apricot blend, medium, dbl., no fragrance; growth bushy, 20-40 cm.; PP13426

Breezy Min, ob, 1984, Saville, F. Harmon; bud small; flowers bright orange-red, yellow reverse, small, 20 petals, high-centered, borne in sprays; foliage small, medium green, semi-glossy; upright growth; [Sheri Anne × seedling]; int. by Nor'East Min. Roses

Bregina F, or, 1965, deRuiter; flowers vermilion-red; [sport of Mandrina]

Bremer Stadtmusikanten S, pb, 2006, W. Kordes' Söhne; bud rounded, cream yellow, suffused reddish; flowers cream pink with darker center, 8 cm., full, camellia-like, borne mostly in large clusters, slight sweetish fragrance; foliage medium size, dark green, glossy; bushy, tall (120 cm.) growth; int. by W. Kordes' Söhne, 2000

Brenda HEg, lp, 1894, Penzance; flowers peach-blossom-pink, single; foliage fragrant; very vigorous growth; int. by Keynes, Williams & Co.

Brenda Ann HT, dy, 1975, Watts; flowers amber-yellow, 5 in., 37 petals, slight fragrance; foliage glossy, tinted bronze; vigorous, tall, upright growth; [sport of Piccadilly]; int. in 1973

Brenda Burg S, ob, Clements, John K.; int. in 1999

Brenda Colvin LCl, lp, 1970, Colvin; flowers apple-blossom pink, 1 in., 5 petals, borne in trusses, strong sweet-musk fragrance; foliage dark, glossy; very vigorous growth; int. by Sunningdale Nursery

Brenda Lee Min, yb, 1991, Williams, Michael C.; bud pointed; flowers red edge to yellow base, small, 20 petals, urn-shaped; foliage small, medium green, semi-glossy; bushy, low, compact growth; [Rise 'n' Shine × Rainbow's End]; int. by The Rose Garden & Mini Rose Nursery, 1991

Brenda Mowery A, lp, 2003, Starnes, John A. Jr.; flowers light pink, reverse light pink, 3½ in., very full, borne in small clusters, intense complex, spicy fragrance; foliage large, dark green, matte, disease-free; prickles moderate, 1/4 in., curved, brown, moderate; growth upright, rampant vigor, tall (8-10 ft.); pillar; very hardy; [Alba maxima × Alfred Colomb]; int. by John A. Starnes Jr., 2002

Brenda of Tasmania F, w, 1971, Holloway; bud ovoid; flowers white, center pink, large, dbl., cupped; foliage large, glossy; upright, bushy growth; [sport of Queen Elizabeth]

Brendan Maguire F, or, 2004, Kenny, David; flowers orange-red, reverse yellow, 7½ cm., dbl., borne in small clusters, slight fragrance; foliage large, dark green, glossy, disease-resistant; prickles medium, hooked; growth upright, tall (120 cm); garden decoration; [Laura Ford × Fellowship]; int. in 2006

Brenda's Fragrance HT, pb, 1967, Smith, W.H.; flowers cerise edged white, high-centered; foliage leathery; vigorous growth; [Lieutenant Chaure × Hector Deane]

Brennende Liebe – See **Burning Love**, F

Brennpunkt F, mr, Haenchen, E.; int. in 1972

Brennus HCh, dr, 1830, Laffay, M.; flowers deep red, shaded with violet, large, full, flat; sometimes classed as B

Brentwood Hedger HRg, dp, Brentwood; name for a group of rugosa seedlings, not an individual cultivar; int. by Brentwood Bay Nurseries, 2005

Brentwood Style F, ab, 2002, Horner, Colin P.; flowers apricot, light yellow reverse, 6 cm., dbl., borne in small clusters, slight fragrance; foliage medium size, medium green, semi-glossy; prickles small, curved, moderate; growth bushy, medium (1 m.); garden decorative; [Warm Welcome × Pretty Lady]; int. by Warley Rose Garden, 2003

Bresilienne Pol, dr, 1971, Delforge; bud long, pointed; flowers deep red, medium, dbl., cupped; foliage bronze, leathery; vigorous, dwarf, bushy growth; [Red Favorite × Ena Harkness]

Brett's Rose Min, yb, Benardella, Frank; int. in 2001

Brewood Belle LCl, mr, Scarman; int. in 1996

Brian MinFl, mr, Barni, V.; flowers bright red, dbl.; growth to 35-40 cm.; int. by Rose Barni, 1995

Brian Donn Min, dr, 1991, Bennett, Dee; bud ovoid; flowers darkest ruby red to maroon, dark ruby red reverse, ages only slightly lighter, medium, 35-45 petals, high-centered, moderate damask fragrance; foliage medium size, medium green, semi-glossy; bushy, medium growth; [Intrique × Big John]; int. by Tiny Petals Nursery, 1990

Brian Lee Min, m, 1986, Bennett, Dee; flowers dark red, aging mauve, 28 petals, high-centered, urn-shaped, borne in small clusters; foliage medium size, dark, semi-glossy; prickles small reddish; medium, upright, bushy growth; hips in.; globular, brown-green; PP6789; [Carrousel × Plum Duffy]; int. by Tiny Petals Nursery

Brian Rix S, mp, Harkness; flowers lilac pin, intense fragrance; growth to 100 cm.; int. by R. Harkness & Co, 1999

Briana's Rose F, lp; int. in 2001

Briand-Paneuropa HT, mp, 1931, Böhm, J.; flowers carmine-rose, base yellow, very large, dbl.; vigorous growth; [Franklin × Willowmere]

Brianna HT, ly, 1992, Marciel, Stanley G.; flowers canary yellow, 3-3½ in., full, borne mostly singly, moderate fragrance; foliage large, medium green, semi-glossy; few prickles; upright (152 cm.) growth; [(Seedling 82249-1 75062-1 × Excitement) × (75062-1 × Cocktail)]; int. by DeVor Nurseries, Inc.

Brian's Song S, op, 1978, Smith, R.L.; flowers 4 in., 35 petals, high-centered, moderate fragrance; intermittent bloom; foliage large, glossy, dark; [Independence × Pike's Peak]; int. by Smith's Greenhouse & Nursery

Briant Hill Min, ob, Poulsen; int. in 1994

Briarcliff HT, pb, 1926, Pierson, P.M.; flowers center deep rose-pink, outer petals lighter; [sport of Columbia]

Briarcliff, Climbing Cl HT, pb, 1929, Parmentier, J.

Briarcliff Brilliance HT, dp, 1932, Pierson, P.M.; flowers rose to rose-red, large, dbl.; vigorous growth; [sport of Briarcliff]

Briarcliff Supreme HT, pb, 1947, Hinner, P.; bud long, pointed; flowers briarcliff pink, very large, dbl.; foliage dark; very vigorous, upright growth; [sport of Briarcliff]; int. by Bauské Bros. & Hinner

Bricky HT, r, Delbard; flowers brick orange, adding brown tones as it ages, dbl., high-centered, borne mostly singly, moderate fragrance; recurrent; medium growth; int. in 2005

Bridal Blush HT, w, 1990, Twomey; bud ovoid; flowers white with pink margins, petals imbricated, large, 75 petals, cupped, borne singly; foliage medium size, dark green, semi-glossy; prickles variable, green with brownish-orange; growth upright, medium; [Queen Elizabeth × Helmut Schmidt]; int. by DeVor Nurseries, Inc, 1990

Bridal Bouquet HT, w, 1976, Ormerod; flowers 3-4 in., 23 petals; foliage matte, green; vigorous, compact growth; [sport of Lady Sylvia]

Bridal Delight HT, lp, Day; [sport of Bridal White]

Bridal Meillandina – See **Bridal Sunblaze**, Min

Bridal Pink F, mp, 1967, Boerner; bud ovoid, pointed, long; flowers large, pink blended with cream, 30-35 petals, high-centered, borne in small clusters or singly, moderate spicy fragrance; foliage leathery; vigorous, upright, bushy growth; PP2851; [(Summertime × unknown) × (Spartan × unknown)]; int. by J&P

Bridal Robe HT, w, 1955, McGredy, Sam IV; flowers ivory-white, high-pointed, 4 in., 54 petals, moderate fragrance; foliage glossy, olive-green; vigorous growth; [McGredy's Pink × Mrs Charles Lamplough]; Gold Medal, NRS, 1953

Bridal Shower HT, w, deVor; int. in 1996

Bridal Shower F, lp, 1998, Zary, Dr. Keith W.; flowers light pink, 4 in., very dbl., borne in small clusters, slight fragrance; foliage medium size, dark green, glossy; prickles moderate; upright, bushy, tall (4 ft.) growth; PP11220; [seedling × Sunflare]; int. by Bear Creek Gardens, Inc., 1999

Bridal Sonia Gr, mp

Bridal Sunblaze Min, w, 1996, Meilland International SA; flowers 2 in., 30-40 petals, borne in small clusters; foliage large, dark green, dull; few prickles; compact, medium (18 in.) growth; PP10002; [(MEIringa × Schneewitchen) × (MEIzogrel × MEIlarco)]; int. by The Conard-Pyle Co., 1996

Bridal Veil F, ly, 1954, Boerner; bud ovoid, cream; flowers white overcast seafoam-yellow, open, 2½ in., 75-80 petals, borne in clusters, intense fragrance; vigorous, bushy growth; PP1347; [(Pinocchio × unknown) × Pigmy Gold]; int. by Stark Bros., 1954

Bridal White – See **Tricia**, F

Bridal Wreath HWich, 1909, Manda

Bride, Climbing – See **Ruth Vestal**, Cl T

Bride – See **Hanayome**, HT

Bride HT, lp, Fryer, Gareth; flowers soft pink, 4¼ in., 21 petals, high-centered, moderate tea fragrance; vigorous growth, 4 × 3 ft.; int. in 1995

Bride of Abydos – See **La Fiancée d'Abydos**, T

Bride of Colmar Gr, mr, Williams, J.B.; flowers bright red, fading to light pink with age, single, flat; recurrent; foliage dark green; growth to 4 ft.; int. by Hortico, Inc., 2004

Bride of Lille – See **Triomphe de Lille**, D

Bride's Blush HT, w, 1923, Amling Co.; flowers creamy white, at times blush-pink, 6 petals; [sport of Columbia]

Bride's Dream HT, lp, 1985, Kordes, R.; bud long, pointed, ovoid; flowers very pale pink, 5 in., 25-30 petals, high-centered, borne singly, slight fragrance; foliage large, medium green, matte; prickles dark brown; tall, upright growth; [Royal Highness × seedling]; int. by Ludwigs Roses Pty. Ltd., 1984

Bride's Maid F, dp, Ghosh; int. in 2001

Bride's Maid w

Bride's White F, w, 1970, Mansuino, Q.; flowers pure white, small, dbl., cupped; vigorous, upright, bushy growth; PP2833; int. by Carlton Rose Nurseries, 1968

Bridesmaid T, lp, 1893, Moore; flowers clear silvery pink; [sport of Catherine Mermet]; like its parent except in color

Bridesmaid, Climbing Cl T, lp, 1897, Dingee & Conard; flowers clear rose-pink with crimson shading, 10-12 cm.; [sport of Bridesmaid]

Bridge of Sighs LCl, ab, Harkness; flowers amber to rich, deep apricot, petals drop cleanly, 3-4 in., 18 petals, slight fragrance; rapid repeat; growth to 10 ft., with pliable canes; int. by Harglow, 2001

Bridget HT, op, 1947, Fletcher; bud long, pointed; flowers brilliant orange-scarlet, base bright golden yellow, 4-5 in., 35-40 petals, flat; foliage glossy, bright green; [Mrs Henry Bowles × Phyllis Gold]; int. by Tucker

Bridget F, dp, Kordes; flowers full, high-centered, borne in clusters, no fragrance; consistent bloomer; neat, compact growth to 80 cm.; int. in 1993

Bridget HMsk, ab, Clements, John K.; int. in 1996

Bridget Mary S, dp, 2006, Treloar, R.V.; flowers full, borne in small clusters; foliage medium size, medium green, matte; prickles 5 mm., hooked, brown, moderate; growth bushy, medium (1 m.); [sport of Mary Rose]; int. in 2007

Bridget's Joy HT, lp, 1997, Johnstone, Leonard E.; flowers very dbl., borne mostly singly; foliage medium size, medium green, semi-glossy; compact, medium (140cm.) growth; [sport of Coral Fiesta]

Bridgwater Pride F, op, 1982, Sanday, John; flowers rich salmon, medium, 20 petals; foliage medium size, dark, semi-glossy; bushy, compact growth; [Vera Dalton × Allgold]; int. by Sanday Roses, Ltd.

Brie-Rose T, 1913, Boulanger; [sport of Mme Bérard]

Brier Bush – See ***R. canina*** (Linnaeus)

Brigadeiro França Borges F, or, 1960, Moreira da Silva; flowers bright orange-red; [Independence × seedling]

Brigadoon HT, pb, 1991, Warriner, William A.; bud ovoid, pointed; flowers pink near center, coral pink at petal margin, rose pink and cream reverse, 5 in., 35-40 petals, high-centered, borne mostly singly, moderate spicy fragrance; foliage medium size, dark green, semi-glossy; upright, spreading, tall growth; PP8591; [seedling × Pristine]; int. by Bear Creek Gardens, 1992

Bright Angel S, yb, 1978, Smith, R.L.; bud ovoid; flowers light yellow, edged pink, 4 in., 48 petals, high-centered, intense fragrance; intermittent bloom; foliage large, glossy, dark; vigorous, bushy growth; [Dornroschen × Golden Wings]; int. by Smith's Greenhouse & Nursery

Bright Beam Gr, pb, 1974, Fuller; bud ovoid; flowers cream, edged pink, large, dbl., cupped, moderate fragrance; profuse, intermittent bloom; foliage glossy, dark; very vigorous, upright growth; [Peace × Little Darling]; int. by Wyant, 1972

Bright Beauty HT, or, Delbard

Bright Boy HT, mr, 1948, Clark, A.; flowers brilliant red

Bright Carpet S, mp; groundcover; spreading growth; int. by Heirloom Roses, 2004

Bright Cover – See **Amherst**, S

Bright Day Cl Min, rb, 2002, Warner, Chris; flowers dbl., borne in small clusters, slight fragrance; foliage medium green, glossy; prickles small, straight, few; growth upright, tall (6 ft.); fences, walls, pillars; int. by Warner's Roses, 2003

Bright Delight F, yb, 2005, McMillan, Thomas; flowers dark yellow with pink highlights, reverse dark yellow, 2½ in., full, borne in small clusters, no fragrance; foliage small, dark green, glossy; prickles medium, triangular, few; growth compact, short (2½ ft.); garden decorative; [Yellow Flurette × Rainbow's End]; int. in 2006; Bronze Certificate, ARC Trial Gardens, 2005

Bright Eyes F, yb, 1948, Duehrsen; bud ovoid; flowers light yellow to primrose, medium, large truss, 25 petals, slight fragrance; foliage leathery, glossy, dark; dwarf growth; RULED EXTINCT 6/83 ARM; [Joanna Hill × (Heidekind × Betty Uprichard)]; int. by H&S

Bright Eyes F, or, 1983, Sanday, John; flowers yellow stamens, medium, dbl.; foliage medium size, dark, matte; bushy growth; [seedling × Circus]; int. by John Sanday Roses, Ltd.

Bright Eyes – See **Our Molly**, S

Bright Fire Cl HT, dr, 1977, Pearce; flowers crimson, shaded darker, 4½ in., 15 petals, slight fragrance; foliage glossy, dark; free growth; [Parkdirektor Riggers × Guinee]; originally registered as LCl

Bright Fire LCl, or, Pearce; buds urn shaped, pointed; flowers bright orange-vermillion, 5-6 in., 40 petals; foliage dark green and leathery; growth to 10-12 ft.; int. in 1997

Bright Garbs F, or, 1978, Hardikar, Dr. M.N.; bud pointed; flowers 2½ in., 12 petals, moderate fragrance; foliage large; dwarf growth; [Orangeade × seedling]

Bright Ideas LCl, pb, 2003, Horner, Colin P.; flowers pink with white stripes, reverse paler, 8 cm., dbl., borne in large clusters, moderate fragrance; foliage medium size, medium green, glossy; prickles medium, almost straight, moderate; growth upright, medium (2 m.); garden decorative; [Lichterloh × Tall Story × [Southhampton × ((New Penny × White Pet) × Stars 'n' Stripes))]; int. by Peter Beales Roses, 2003

Bright Jewel Min, pb; bud pointed; flowers rose-pink, white center, very small, semi-dbl., borne in clusters; low, compact growth

Bright Lights Min, pb, 1996, Apple, Ken; flowers dark pink with bright yellow stripe on some petals, reverse, dbl.; foliage medium size, medium green, semi-glossy; numerous prickles; upright, medium (24 in.) growth; [Red Delight × Hurdy Gurdy]; int. by K&C Roses, 1997

Bright Meadow – See **Yasnaya Poliana**, HT

Bright Melody S, mr, 1985, Buck, Dr. Griffith J.; bud ovoid, pointed; flowers large, 30 petals, cupped, borne 1-10 per cluster, slight fragrance; repeat bloom; foliage medium-large,dark olive green, leathery; prickles awl-like, tan; erect, bushy growth; [Carefree Beauty × (Herz As × Cuthbert Grant)]; int. by Iowa State University, 1984

Bright Minijet Min, dp, Meilland

Bright Morning HT, my, 1958, Ratcliffe; flowers golden yellow

Bright Pink Iceberg – See **Brilliant Pink Iceberg**, F

Bright Red Pol, dr, 1938, deRuiter; flowers velvety dark red, dbl., borne in large clusters; bushy growth

Bright Sight Min, ob, 1993, Bell, Judy G.; flowers light orange, medium, full, borne in large clusters, no fragrance; foliage small, medium green, matte; few prickles; upright (18 in.), bushy growth; [Charmglo × Poker Chip]; int. by Michigan Miniature Roses, 1994

Bright Smile F, my, 1980, Dickson, Patrick; bud pointed; flowers empire yellow, convex, small, 15 petals, flat, borne 15 per cluster; foliage dense, mid-green; prickles concave, purple; bushy, medium growth; [Eurorose × seedling]; int. in 1981; Gold Medal, Belfast, 1982

Bright Smile, Climbing Cl F, my, Vidal; int. after 1981

Bright Spark – See **Centenaire de Lourdes Rouge**, F

Bright Star S, or, Williams, J. Benjamin; flowers single; int. by Hortico, 1999

Bright Wings HT, op, 1942, Mallerin, C.; bud long, pointed, rosy orange; flowers centers orange shading to pink, large, 22 petals, cupped, moderate fruity fragrance; foliage bronze; strong stems; vigorous, bushy growth; [Mme Arthaud × Annie Drevet]; int. by A. Meilland

Brightfire – See **Bright Fire**, LCl

Brightness HT, rb, 1959, Fryers Nursery, Ltd.; bud long, pointed; flowers scarlet, reverse golden yellow, merging to orange, 4½-5½ in., 28-35 petals, high-centered, intense fragrance; foliage leathery, glossy; bushy, moderately vigorous growth; PP1917; [sport of Doreen]; int. in 1958

Brightness of Cheshunt HP, mr, 1881, Paul, G.; flowers shining brick red, full; [Duke of Edinburgh × unknown]

Brighton Beauty T, mr, 1891, Bragg

Brighton Cardinals Min, rb, 2005, Wells, Verlie W.; flowers white with red edges, reverse white, ¾ in., full, high-centered, borne mostly solitary; foliage medium size, medium green, semi-glossy; prickles ¼ in., straight, moderate; growth upright, medium (2-3 ft.); exhibition, garden decorative; [seedling × seedling]; int. by Wells Mid-South Roses, 2005

Brightside Min, or, 1975, Moore, Ralph S.; flowers 1 in., 25 petals, high-centered, moderate fragrance; foliage small, matte; upright, bushy growth; [Persian Princess × Persian Princess]; int. by Sequoia Nurs., 1974

Brigitte Bardot HT, rb, Orard; flowers red striped with white, dbl.; growth to 100 cm.; int. in 2002

Brigitte de Landsvreugd HMult, w, Mertens; flowers semi-dbl., borne in large clusters; int. in 1988

Brigitte de Villenfagne HMsk, lp, 2000, Lens, Louis; flowers pale pink, white center, reverse lighter, 1 in., single, borne in large clusters, moderate fragrance; recurrent; foliage medium size, medium green, semi-glossy, disease-resistant; prickles moderate; growth upright, tall (125-150 cm.); hedge, border; [*R. multiflora adenocheata* × (*R. multiflora nana* × Ballerina)]; int. by Louis Lens NV, 1993

Brigitte Fossey HT, ab, Dorieux; int. by Roseraies Dorieux, 2000

Brigitte Jourdan F, or, 1962, Arles; bud ovoid; flowers pomegranate-red, large, dbl., globular, slight fragrance; foliage dark, glossy; vigorous, bushy growth; [Belle Créole × Independence]; int. by Roses-France, 1960

Brillant HT, mr, 1952, W. Kordes Söhne; flowers somewhat large, semi-dbl., moderate fragrance

Brillant S, or, W. Kordes Söhne; flowers medium, dbl.; int. in 1983

Brillante HGal, mp, about 1810, Descemet; flowers bright pink, large, full

Brilliance F, or, 1959, Boerner; bud ovoid; flowers coral, 2 in., 50 petals, cupped, moderate fragrance; foliage glossy; compact growth; PP1799; [seedling × Independence]; int. by J&P, 1959

Brilliancy HT, or, 1936, LeGrice; flowers brilliant scarlet, dbl.; foliage leathery; short stems; bushy growth; [Étoile de Hollande × Daily Mail Scented Rose]

Brilliant – See **Detroiter**, HT

Brilliant Betty HT, pb, 2000, Singer, Steven J.; flowers bright pink, reverse light pink, 4-5 in., full, borne mostly singly; foliage medium size, medium green, semi-glossy; prickles moderate; upright growth to 4-6 ft.; [Great Scott × King of Hearts]; int. by Wisconsin Roses, 2001

Brilliant Cover – See **Old Charleston**, S

Brilliant Echo Pol, mp, 1927, Western Rose Co.; flowers rosy pink; [sport of Echo]

Brilliant Flower Circus F, ob, Kordes; flowers brilliant orange, 2.5 in., full, cupped, borne in clusters, slight sweet fragrance; recurrent; moderate (30-40 in), compact growth; int. by Wayside Gardens, 2007

Brilliant Hit – See **Carrot Top**, Min

Brilliant King F, mr, 1961, Leenders, J.; flowers bright red, shallow, 4 in., 32 petals, cupped; [Cocorico × Orange Delight]

Brilliant Light – See **Kagayaki**, F

Brilliant Meillandina Min, or, 1985, Meilland, Mrs. Marie-Louise; flowers 15 petals, cupped, borne in clusters of 3-20, no fragrance; foliage dark, semi-glossy; [Parador × (Baby Bettina × Duchess of Windsor)]; int. by Meilland Et Cie, 1975

Brilliant Pink Iceberg F, pb, 1999, Weatherly, Lilia; flowers deep pink, reverse white, 3½-4 in., dbl., borne in large clusters, moderate fragrance; foliage large, light green, glossy; few prickles; upright, rounded, medium (30-36 in.) growth; PP12645; [sport of Pink Iceberg]; int. by Swane Bros. Pty. Ltd., 1999

Brilliant Red HT, mr, 1938, Lens; bud very long, pointed; flowers brilliant red, well-formed, very large, dbl.; foliage bright green; vigorous, bushy growth; [Charles P. Kilham × Étoile de Hollande]

Brilliant Rosamini Min; int. in 2000

Brilliant Star F, mr, 1965, Watkins Roses; flowers bright red, center shaded yellow, 2½-3 in., 12-20 petals, borne in clusters; foliage glossy; vigorous growth; [Masquerade × Dicksons Flame]

Brilliant Vigorosa – See **Diamant**, F

Brimoon – See **Moonlight and Roses**, Min

Brindis LCl, rb, 1962, Dot, Simon; flowers geranium-red, center light yellow to medium, 2-2½ in., single, borne in small clusters, no fragrance; foliage dark; vigorous growth; [Orange Triumph, Climbing × (Phyllis Bide × Baccará)]

Brinessa HT, pb, Delforge; flowers different shades of pink, 10 cm., very dbl., high-centered, intense fragrance; dark green, glossy, leathery foliage; strong stems; erect, upright growth to 80 cm.; int. in 1985

Briosa F, yb, Barni, V.

Brisbane Blush F, pb, Long, P.; [(Golden Slippers × Lavendula) × Prima Ballerina]; int. in 1993

Brise Parfumée F, mr, 1950, Truffaut, G.; bud pointed; flowers dbl., borne in clusters; foliage glossy, bronze; numerous prickles; stems bark and twigs reddish brown; very vigorous growth; [Böhm's Triumph × Baby Chateau]

Bristol HT, rb, 1968, Sanday, John; flowers bright crimson, reverse lighter, large, dbl.; foliage dark; compact growth; [Gavotte × Tropicana]

Bristol Post HT, op, 1972, Sanday, John; flowers pale salmon-pink, base orange, pointed, 4½ in., 29 petals; foliage slightly glossy, dark; upright growth; [Vera Dalton × Parasol]

Britannia HT, 1916, Dobbie

Britannia Pol, rb, 1929, Burbage Nursery; flowers crimson, center white, small, single, borne in clusters of 30-40; recurrent bloom; foliage small, leathery, light; compact, bushy growth; [Coral Cluster × Eblouissant]

Britannia HT, ob, Fryer, Gareth; flowers apricot and gold, changing to nectarine and orange as it opens, dbl., high-centered, borne profusely, moderate fragrance; growth free branching, medium (75 cm.); int. in 1998

Britannica Pol, rb

Brite Blue HT, m; flowers of blue mauve with deep lavender shades and a red purple finish, intense fragrance; florist rose; int. in 1984

Brite Eyes LCl, pb, Radler; flowers medium pink with white eye and yellow stamens, 7-10 petals, shallow cup, borne in clusters, moderate fragrance; recurrent; foliage disease-resistant; compact (6-8 ft.) growth; int. in 2006

Brite Lites – See **Princess Alice**, F

Britestripe Min, rb, 1991, Clements, John K.; flowers soft pink, striped bright red, medium, full, borne in small clusters, no fragrance; foliage small, medium green, semi-glossy; some prickles; medium (30 cm.), bushy, compact growth; [Pinstripe × seedling]; int. by Heirloom Old Garden Roses, 1990

Britestripes – See **Britestripe**, Min

British Columbia Centennial HT, pb, 1972, Boerner; bud ovoid; flowers light rose-pink, reverse white, large, dbl., high-centered, slight fragrance; foliage leathery; vigorous growth; [Pink Masterpiece × seedling]; int. by Pan American Bulb Co.

British Queen HT, w, 1912, McGredy; flowers creamy white, center flushed, large, dbl., high-centered; foliage light green, soft; long, weak stems; bushy growth; Gold Medal, NRS, 1912

Brittany Noel S, w, J. B. Williams; flowers dbl., pompon, borne in clusters of pure white blooms; groundcover; spreading growth to 2 ft.; int. by Hortico, 2005

Brittany's Glowing Star – See **Amber Star**, Min

Brno HT, ob, 1933, Böhm, J.; flowers maroon, orange, gold, open, large, semi-dbl.; foliage glossy; vigorous, bushy growth; [Souv. de George Beckwith × Rosemary]

Broadcaster Gr, or, 1971, Perry, Anthony; bud ovoid; flowers medium, dbl., slight fragrance; foliage dark; vigorous growth; [Queen Elizabeth × Circus]; int. by Conklin, 1969

Broadlands – See **Sonnenschirm**, S

Broadway HT, yb, 1985, Perry, Anthony; bud pointed; flowers golden yellow, blended orange-pink, well-formed, 4-4½ in., 30-35 petals, high-centered, borne singly, moderate spice and damask fragrance; foliage medium to large, dark, semi-glossy; upright growth, moderately tall; PP5827; [(First Prize × Gold Glow) × Sutter's Gold]; int. by Cooperative Rose Growers, 1986

Broadway LCl, ab, Clark, A.; flowers apricot, large, single, flat; spring-blooming; healthy evergreen foliage

Brocade HT, pb, 1960, Combe; bud ovoid; flowers soft rose, base cream-white, 4-5 in., 54 petals, cupped, moderate fragrance; foliage leathery; vigorous, upright growth; PP1856; [Charlotte Armstrong × Baiser]; int. by Hémeray-Aubert

Brocade S, w, Williams, J. Benjamin; flowers ivory with mauve tint, dbl.; int. in 1998

Brocéliande HT, rb, Adam; flowers fuchsia with lilac, ivory, and yellow stripes, dbl.; int. in 2002

Brög's Canina (strain of *R. canina*), lp; almost thornless; vigorous growth; in use as an understock; int. by Brög

Brokat HT, r, Tantau; flowers golden yellow with brownish red; int. by Rosen Tantau, 2003

Bronze Min, ob, Olesen; flowers dbl., 25-30 petals, no fragrance; foliage dark green, glossy; growth bushy, very low (20-40 cm.); PP11500

Bronze Baby MinFl, yb, Pearce

Bronze Beauty F, ob, 1975, Warriner, William A.; bud ovoid-pointed; flowers golden yellow to orange-yellow, open, 4 in., 27 petals, slight fragrance; foliage large, leathery; vigorous growth; [Electra × Woburn Abbey]; int. by J&P, 1974

Bronze Bedder HT, yb, 1920, Paul, W.; flowers bronzy yellow, large, single

Bronze Masterpiece HT, ab, 1960, Boerner; bud long;

flowers bronze-apricot, becoming orange-yellow, 5½-6 in., 48 petals, high-centered, moderate fragrance; foliage leathery, glossy; vigorous, upright growth; PP2000; [Golden Masterpiece × Kate Smith]; int. by J&P, 1960; Gold Medal, Geneva, 1958

Bronze Star HT, ab, 2000, Weeks, O.L.; bud globular; flowers amber-apricot, reverse gold-apricot, petals scalloped, 4-5 in., 19-26 petals, cupped, borne mostly singly, intense spicy fragrance; recurrent; foliage large, medium green, semi-glossy; prickles numerous, 1 cm., hooked, brown; bushy, tall (4-5 ft.) growth; PP15020; [Just Joey × seedling]; int. by Conard-Pyle Co., 2000

Bronze Sunset HT, ab, 2001, Coiner, Jim; flowers medium, semi-dbl., borne in small clusters, no fragrance; foliage medium size, light green, matte; prickles 1/16 in., few; growth compact, medium; garden decorative; [seedling × seedling]

Brook – See **Seseragi**, HT

Brook Song S, my, 1985, Buck, Dr. Griffith J.; flowers imbricated form, large, 40 petals, borne singly and in clusters of up to 8; repeat bloom; foliage leathery, dark; prickles awl-like, tan; erect growth; hardy; [Prairie Star × Tom Brown]; int. by Iowa State University, 1984

Brookdale Giant White – See **Jackman's White**, HT

Brooks' Red HT, mr, 2000, Brooks, Warren; flowers medium red, reverse blushing red to yellow, 5 in., full, high-centered, exhibition, borne mostly singly, slight fragrance; good repeat; foliage large, dark green, semi-glossy; prickles moderate; long, strong stems; growth upright, tall (5 ft.); int. by Johnny Becnel Show Roses, 2000

Brookville HT, ly, 1942, Brookville Nursery; flowers cream-yellow; [sport of Leonard Barron]

Broomfield Novelty – See **Margaret Anderson**, LCl

Brother Cadfael S, mp, 1995, Austin, David; flowers rich pink, 45 petals, cupped, intense old rose fragrance; foliage dark green; prickles few thorns; straight stems; strong, bushy growth; PP8681; int. by David Austin Roses, 1990

Brother John F, ab; flowers apricot in center, fading to blush pink on outer petals, full, rosette; int. by Roses Unlimited, 2004

Brother Sun Gr, my, 1998, Fleming, Joyce L.; flowers medium yellow, deeper color at base, flattened top, long lasting, 2½-3 in., 41-50 petals, borne mostly singly, moderate fragrance; foliage medium size, medium green, dull; prickles moderate; compact, upright growth; [Goldener Olymp × Australian Gold]; int. by Hortico, Inc., 1997

Brother Wilfred HT, mp, 1976, Wood; [sport of Alec's Red]

Brothers Grimm Fairy Tales – See **Gebrüder Grimm**, F

Brown County Splendor S, yb, 1985, Williams, J. Benjamin; flowers ivory to yellow blended with peach to orange-red, large, 35 petals; foliage large, dark, semi-glossy; upright, spreading growth; [Paul's Lemon Pillar × (Garden Party × Command Performance)]; int. by Krider Nursery, 1984

Brown Study F, r, 1999, Jerabek, Paul E.; flowers russet, turning brown, darker at edges, 2¾ in., dbl., borne singly and in small clusters; foliage medium size, dark green, semi-glossy; prickles moderate; spreading, medium (3 ft.) growth; int. by Freedom Gardens, 1998

Brown Sugar Min, ab, 1995, Taylor, Pete & Kay; flowers medium, dbl., borne mostly singly; foliage medium size, dark green, glossy; some prickles; upright, bushy, medium (30 in.) growth; [Party Girl × Julia's Rose]; int. by Taylor's Roses, 1996

Brown Velvet F, r, 1983, McGredy, Sam IV; flowers orange, tinged brownish, medium, 35 petals; foliage medium size, dark, glossy; upright, medium to tall growth; [Mary Sumner × Kapai]; int. in 1982; Gold Star of the South Pacific, Palmerston North, NZ, 1979

Brownell Yellow Rambler HMult, my, 1942, Brownell; flowers petals recurved, dbl., borne in more open clusters than Dorothy Perkins, slight fragrance; [(Emily Gray × Ghislaine de Feligonde) × Golden Glow]

Brownell's Everblooming Pillar No. 73 – See **Scarlet Sensation**, LCl

Brownie F, r, 1960, Boerner; bud ovoid, tan shades, edged pinkish; flowers brownish tan, reverse yellow, 3½-4 in., 38 petals, cupped, borne in small clusters, moderate fragrance; foliage leathery; vigorous, upright, bushy growth; [(Lavender Pinocchio × unknown) × Grey Pearl]; int. by J&P, 1959

Brownlow Hill Rambler – See **Mme Alice Garnier**, HWich

Browsholme Rose Ayr, w, 1900

Brucella – See **Bruoscella**, HT

Brundrette Centenary S, dp

Brunella Min, mr

Brunette HGal, about 1810, Descemet

Brunette F, yb, 1979, Lens; bud ovoid; flowers amber-yellow to orange, 1½-2½ in., 25 petals, cupped; foliage glossy; [(Purpurine × Lavender Pinocchio × Fillette) × (Gold Strike × Golden Garnette)]; int. by Spek, 1970

Bruno Perpoint S, mp, Guillot-Massad; int. by Roseraies Guillot, 1998

Bruno, Golden Boy F, yb, 2004, Horner, Colin P.; flowers amber yellow, reverse deeper, 7 cm., dbl., borne in small clusters, moderate fragrance; foliage medium size, medium green, semi-glossy; prickles medium, curved; upright, tall (5 ft.)growth; garden decorative; [(Golden Future × Baby Love) × Beautiful Britain]; int. by Unknown at this time

Brunonii Himalayica – See **Paul's Himalayan Musk Rambler**, HMsk

Bruoscella HT, dy, 1986, Lens, Louis; flowers golden yellow, large, 35 petals, high-centered, urn-shaped, borne singly or in small clusters, intense fragrance; prickles dark green; upright, bushy growth; [Peace × Golden Garnette]; int. in 1980

Brushstrokes F, yb, 1999, Guest, M.M.; flowers yellow and red striped, reverse paler, large, full, borne in small clusters; foliage medium size, dark green, glossy; few prickles; upright, medium (28 in.) growth; [seedling × Solitaire]; int. by A. J. Palmer & Son, 1999

Brutus – See **Brennus**, HCh

Bruun F, Delforge, H.; int. in 1995

Bruxelles – See **Bruoscella**, HT

Bryan LCl, my, Mekdeci; int. in 1993

Bryan F, ob, 2001, Giles, Diann; flowers orange and white, 3 in., dbl., borne in large clusters, slight fragrance; foliage medium size, medium green, glossy; prickles small, straight, numerous; growth spreading, medium; garden decorative, exhibition; [Queen Margrethe × Betty Boop]; int. by Giles Rose Nursery, 2001

Bryan Freidel Pink Tea T, w

Bryce Canyon – See **Frederiksborg**, F

Brymore Jubilee HT, my, 2002, Poole, Lionel; flowers full, high-centered, borne mostly solitary, slight fragrance; foliage medium size, dark green, glossy; prickles medium, triangular, moderate; growth upright, bushy, vigorous, medium; exhibition, bedding; [Tom Foster × Ravenswood Village]; int. by David Lister Roses, 2002

Bryte White HT, w

Bubble Bath HMsk, lp, Matson; flowers soft pink, dbl., borne in clusters; growth large, cascading shrub, can be trained as a climber; [Kathleen × Climbing Cecile Brunner]; int. in 1980

Bubble Gum Min, pb, 1999, Buster, Larry S.; flowers pink, reverse ivory, 1¼ in., dbl., borne mostly singly; foliage medium size, medium green, semi-glossy; prickles moderate; upright, tall (2 ft.) growth; [Garden State × seedling]; int. by Kimbrew-Walter Roses, 1998

Bubble Gum Mega Brite Min, mp, J&P; PP11299; int. by Bear Creek Gardens, 2000

Bubbles Min, yb, 1986, Zipper, H.; flowers medium yellow, shaded pink and coral, 35 petals, borne singly and in small clusters; foliage medium size, medium green, semi-glossy; upright, spreading growth; [(Little Darling × (Roundabout × Redgold)) × (Maytime × Poker Chip)]; int. by Magic Moment Miniature Roses

Bubbles Min, mp, Fryer, Gareth; flowers brilliant, satin pink, borne in heavily in clusters; good repeat; growth low (to 40 cm.); int. by Fryer's Roses, 1998

Bubikopf MinFl, pb, Tantau, Math.; int. in 1986

Bucaroo – See **Simon Estes**, S

Buccaneer Gr, my, 1952, Swim, H.C.; bud urn-shaped; flowers buttercup-yellow, 3-3½ in., 30 petals, cupped, moderate fragrance; foliage dark, leathery; vigorous, upright, tall growth; [Golden Rapture × (Max Krause × Capt. Thomas)]; int. by Armstrong Nursery; Gold Medal, Geneva, 1952

Buckaroo S, pb, Buck; int. by Roses Unlimited, 2003

Buckeye Belle S, pb, 1956, Garwood; bud globular; flowers pale to deep pink, open, 1½ in., 15 petals, borne in compact clusters; abundant, recurrent bloom; foliage dark; vigorous, upright, bushy growth; [*R. hugonis* × seedling]

Buck's Fizz – See **Gavnø**, F

Bucred S, rb, Buck; int. by Roses Unlimited, 2005

Bucroo – See **Simon Estes**, S

Bud Meyers MinFl, ob, 2006, McCann, Sean; flowers orange, reverse lighter, 1½-2 in., single, borne mostly solitary; foliage small, dark green, semi-glossy; prickles small, hooked, tan, moderate; growth compact, short (3 ft.); [Bloomsday × seedling]; int. by Ashdown Roses Ltd, 2006

Budapest HT, ab

Budatetini T, ob, Mark; int. in 1960

Buenos Aires F, r, 1957, Silva; flowers burnt brick to dark red-ochre, dbl.; low growth; [Mme Henri Guillot × Pinocchio]

Buff Beauty HMsk, ab, 1939, Bentall, Ann; flowers apricot-yellow, 4 in., 50 petals, borne in clusters of 8-12, moderate fragrance; foliage large, medium green, semi-glossy; vigorous (to 6 ft.) growth; [William Allen Richardson × unknown]

Buff King LCl, ab, 1939, Horvath; bud ovoid, deep amber; flowers amber and buff, large, cupped; foliage glaucous green; long, strong stems; very vigorous (10-12 ft.) growth; int. by Wayside Gardens Co.

Buffalo HRg, dp, Uhl, J.; int. in 1989

Buffalo-Bill HP, lp, 1889, Verdier, E.; flowers very light pink, large, full, flat

Buffalo Bill – See **Regensberg**, F

Buffalo Gal HRg, dp, Uhl, J.; flowers lavender-pink, dbl., loose, borne in clusters, intense fragrance; foliage large, light green, wrinkled, shiny; growth upright, 3-4 ft.; int. in 1989

Buffon P, lp, before 1821; flowers pale rose, large, very dbl.

Buffon HP, mp, 1859, Guillot

Buffy Min, ab, 1987, King, Gene; flowers light apricot, reverse deeper, darker towards center, medium, 20 petals, high-centered, slight fragrance; foliage medium green, matte; prickles slightly hooked, light brown; mini-flora; bushy spreading growth; hips oval, green; [Vera Dalton × Party Girl]; int. by AGM Miniature Roses, 1987

Buffy Sainte-Marie HT, op, 1996, Mander, George; flowers blend of salmon, orange and pink with yellow center 3¼-4¼ in., dbl.; foliage medium size, dark green, glossy, disease-resistant; very vigorous, medium (70-90 cm.), bushy growth; [June Laver × Rubies 'n' Pearls]; int. by Select Roses, 1996

Bugatti HT, m, W. Kordes Söhne; bud urceolate; flowers magenta-purple, 10 cm., 50-55 petals, cupped, borne mostly singly, slight fragrance; recurrent; foliage large, dark green, glossy; prickles numerous, 8-10 mm., hooked downward; stems 70 cm; vigorous, upright growth; PP14176; [seedling × seedling]; florist rose; int. in 2002

Bugle Boy F, dy, 1989, Christensen, Jack E.; bud ovoid, pointed; flowers deep yellow, good substance, medium, 35 petals, cupped, borne in sprays of 5-6, slight tea fragrance; foliage medium size, medium green, very glossy; prickles hooked slightly downward, medium, red to tan; bushy, medium growth; fruit unknown; [Sunsprite × (Katherine Loker seedling × Gingersnap)]; int. by Bear Creek Gardens, 1988

Buisman's Glory F, mr, 1952, Buisman, G. A. H.; flowers currant-red, open, medium, single; foliage light green; [Karen Poulsen × Sangerhausen]

Buisman's Gold F, dy

Buisman's Triumph F, mp, 1952, Buisman, G. A. H.; flowers bright pink, becoming lighter, large, 13 petals; foliage dark; vigorous growth; [Käthe Duvigneau × Cinnabar]

Buisson Ardent Gr, mr, 1956, Gaujard; flowers bright red, medium; foliage dark; [Peace × seedling]

Buisson d'Or HFt, my, 1928, Barbier; flowers canary-yellow, dbl.; good seasonal bloom; growth to 3-5 ft.; [Mme Edouard Herriot × Harison's Yellow]

Bukala LCl, ob

Bukavu HMsk, dp, 2000, Lens, Louis; flowers deep pink, reverse lighter, 4-5 cm., single, borne in large clusters; recurrent bloom; foliage medium size, dark green, glossy; prickles moderate; upright, medium (80-120 cm.) growth; [Britannia × Rush]; int. by Louis Lens NV, 1998; Gold Medal, Geneva, 1999

Bullata C, mp, 1809; flowers deep rose, vary large, 3 in., very dbl., globular, borne mostly singly or in clusters on long, slender peduncles, intense fragrance; summer bloom; foliage very large, thick, and crinkled like lettuce; becoming bronze-tinted in late summer

Bull's Eye HT, dr; flowers 11 cm., 30-40 petals, high-centered; greenhouse rose; int. by Terra Nigra, 2002

Bull's Red HT, mr, 1976, McGredy, Sam IV; bud ovoid; flowers brilliant crimson, 4 in., 28 petals, high-centered; foliage dark; tall, upright growth; [Sympathie × Irish Rover]; int. by McGredy Roses International, 1977

Bundesrat Häberlin HFt, yb, 1940, Soupert & Notting; flowers medium, dbl.

Bundle of Joy Min, lp, 2003, Eagle, B & D; flowers light pink with slightly deeper pink in center, 5 cm., full, borne mostly solitary, no fragrance; foliage medium size, medium green, matte, disease-resistant; prickles small, slightly hooked; growth upright, tall (60 cm.); [Magic Carrousel × unknown (open pollinated]; int. by Southern Cross Nurseries, 2000

Bunker Hill HT, dp, 1949, Fisher, G.; bud pointed; flowers rose-red, large, 25-40 petals, high-centered; foliage leathery, dark; very vigorous, bushy growth; [Rome Glory × Better Times]; int. by Arnold-Fisher Co.

Bunny Hop Cl Min, mp, 1993, Zary, Dr. Keith W.; flowers medium, dbl., borne in large clusters, slight fragrance; foliage small, dark green, semi-glossy; some prickles; upright (180 cm.), spreading, climbing growth; [Pink Pollyanna × seedling]; int. by Bear Creek Gardens, Inc., 1995

Bunte Frau Astrid Späth Pol, lp, 1940, Vogel, M.; flowers light pink with red, medium, semi-dbl.

Bunte Provinrose – See **Variegata**, C

Bunter Kobold MinFl, yb, Dickson, Patrick; int. in 1995

Burbank T, pb, 1900, Burbank; flowers light pink and crimson, 3-3½ in., dbl.; foliage glossy; Hermosa × Bon Silene seedling, or seedling of Hermosa × Bon Silene; Gold Medal, St. Louis World's Fair, 1904

Buret T, m, about 1860, Buret; flowers bluish-red with violet, sometimes edged white, full, globular

Burg Baden LCl, mp, Kordes; flowers pale crimson, medium, single, borne in large clusters; int. in 1955

Burgemeester Berger HT, lp, 1934, Leenders Bros.; flowers soft pink, marked white; vigorous growth; [sport of Dame Edith Helen]

Burgemeester Sandberg HT, op, 1920, Van Rossem; flowers silvery pink, shaded coral-rose-pink, dbl.; [Pharisaer × Lady Alice Stanley]

Burgemeester van Oppen HT, my, 1939, Leenders, M.; flowers golden yellow; [Golden Ophelia × Pardinas Bonet]

Bürgermeister Christen HT, dp, 1911, Bernaix, A.; flowers large, dbl.; [Mme Caroline Testout × Fisher-Holmes]

Burgess Pink Min, mp; int. by Burgess Seed and Plant

Burgess Red Min, mr; int. by Burgess Seed and Plant

Burgess Yellow Min, my; int. by Burgess Seed and Plant

Burghausen S, mr, 2006; flowers light red with ruffled petals, 8 cm., dbl., cupped, borne in small clusters and trusses with many flowers; foliage semi-glossy; bushy, upright, arching growth with heavy, well-branched canes; int. by W. Kordes' Söhne, 1991

Burgund HT, dr, 1977, Kordes, W.; bud long, pointed; flowers 4 in., 30 petals, high-centered; vigorous, bushy growth; [Henkell Royal × seedling]

Burgund '81 – See **Loving Memory**, HT

Burgundiaca – See **Petite de Hollande**, C

Burgundian Rose HGal, pb, before 1650; flowers deep pink suffused purple, center paler, 1 in., dbl., rosette; foliage dark gray-green; few prickles; compact (18 in.) growth

Burgundy HT, mr, 1939, H&S; flowers wine-red broad, evenly arranged petals, dbl.; very vigorous growth; [Vaterland × seedling]

Burgundy Ice – See **Burgundy Iceberg**, F

Burgundy Iceberg F, m, Weatherly, Lilia; bud pointed to somewhat ovoid; flowers deep purple-red, lighter reverse, with velvety texture, 3-4 in., 25-30 petals, somewhat cupped, borne in clusters, slight honey fragrance; recurrent; foliage semi-glossy; prickles very few, medium, straight, angled slightly downward; bushy, medium (3 ft.) growth; hips obovate to ovoid ; PP16198; [sport of Brilliant Pink Iceberg]; int. by Prophyl Pty Ltd/Swanes Nurseries Australia Pty Ltd, 2003; Marion de Boehme Memorial Award, National Trial Garden of Australia, 2005, Gold Medal, National Trial Garden of Australia, 2005, Best Floribunda, Rose Hills, 2005

Burgundy Popwell HT, w, 2006, Popwell, Larry G., Sr; flowers white/pink edges, reverse white/pink edges, 2¾ in., full, borne mostly solitary; foliage medium size, medium green, semi-glossy; prickles moderate; growth bushy, up to 5 ft.; [Crystailine × Love]; int. by Popwell, Larry G., Sr, 2006

Burgundy Queen – See **James Biddle**, HT

Burgundy Rose – See **Burgundian Rose**, HGal

Burgundy Trail Cl Min, dr

Burke P, m, 1860, Moreau & Robert; flowers slatey lilac

Burkhard – See **Grumpy**, Pol

Burkhardt – See **Grumpy**, Pol

Burlington S, dr, Olesen; bud short, globular; flowers dark red, 1½-2 in., 40-50 petals, cupped, borne in large clusters, slight floral fragrance; recurrent; foliage dark green, matte; prickles numerous, 4-5 mm, slightly concave, tan; broad, bushy (2 ft.) growth; PP12563; [Unnamed seedling × seedling]; int. as Velvet Cover, Poulsen, 1995

Burma Star F, ab, 1975, Cocker; flowers light apricot yellow, large, 22 petals, moderate fragrance; foliage large, glossy; [Arthur Bell × Manx Queen]; int. in 1974

Burnaby HT, w, 1954, Eddie; flowers creamy white, 4-6 in., 56 petals, high-centered, slight fragrance; foliage dark, glossy; vigorous, bushy growth; PP1314; [Phyllis Gold × Pres. Herbert Hoover]; int. by Peterson & Dering; Gold Medal, Portland, 1957, Gold Medal, NRS, 1954

Burnet Irish Marbled – See **Irish Rich Marbled**, HSpn

Burnet Rose – See ***R. spinosissima*** (Linnaeus)

Burning Desire HT, mr, 2000, Zary, Keith; flowers velvety crimson red, 5 in., full, exhibition, borne mostly singly, no fragrance; foliage large, dark green, glossy; prickles moderate; upright growth to 5 ft.; PP12200; [Macauck × Poulman]; int. by Bear Creek Gardens, Inc, 2001

Burning Desire HT, ab, Delbard; int. in 2001

Burning Ember LCl, rb, 2000, Brown, Ted; flowers cream, center fading to medium red petal edges, reverse cream, frilled edges, 3½ in., 8-14 petals, borne in small clusters; foliage medium size, medium green, semi-glossy; prickles moderate; climbing, upright, medium (8-10 ft.) growth; [Esprit × Night Light]; int. in 2000

Burning Glow – See **Burning Gold**, F

Burning Gold F, ob, Poulsen; bud deep orange-red buds; flowers bright orange; vigorous growth; int. in 1990

Burning Love F, mr, 1956, Tantau, Math.; flowers scarlet, 4 in., 22 petals, borne in trusses of 3-5, moderate fragrance; foliage dark, glossy; vigorous, bushy growth; [Fanal × Crimson Glory]; int. by Wheatcroft Bros., 1956; Gold Medal, Baden-Baden, 1954

Burning Sky – See **Paradise**, HT

Burnleigh F, lp; int. in 1999

Burnt Orange F, ob, 1976, Hamilton; flowers deep orange; [sport of Woburn Abbey]; int. in 1973

Burr Rose – See ***R. roxburghii*** (Trattinnick)

Burr's Multiflora (clone of *R. multiflora*); growth vigorous; used as understock; used for understock

Burwah Cl HT, dp, 1953, Ulrick, L.W.; flowers deep rose-pink, large, dbl., cupped; very vigorous climbing growth; [Editor McFarland × Black Boy]

Busard Triomphant – See **Charles de Mills**, HGal

Bush Baby Min, pb, 1984, Pearce, C.A.; flowers small, 35 petals, slight fragrance; foliage small, medium green, matte; bushy growth; int. by Limes Rose Nursery, 1985

Bush Garden Climber LCl, op, Thomas

Bush Walk HRg, dr; int. by Bell Roses Ltd, 2001

Bushfire HWich, mr, 1917, Clark, A.; flowers bright crimson, yellow zone around center, small, very large, dbl.

Bushfire S, ob, Poulsen; flowers fiery orange, medium, dbl., high-centered, borne mostly singly; good repeat; young foliage purple-red; vigorous growth to 2 m.

Bushu HT, ob, 1985, Yasuda, Yuji; bud ovoid; flowers orange-red, reverse lighter, large, 35 petals, high-centered, no fragrance; foliage medium size, dark, semi-glossy; prickles slanted downward; tall, vigorous, upright growth; [Dolce Vita × Roklea]

Bushveld Dawn – See **Cary Grant**, HT

Busy Min, dp

Busy Bee – See **Electric Blanket**, F

Busy Bee Min, ab, 2001, Saville, F. Harmon; flowers coral-orange, soft yellow reverse, 1¼ in., full, borne in small clusters, slight fragrance; continuous; foliage medium size, dark green, matte; prickles ¼ in., thin, straight, numerous; growth compact, bushy, medium

(14-20 in.); garden decorative, containers; [Sequoia Gold × Sparks]; int. by Nor'East Miniature Roses, 2001

Busy Lizzie F, mp, 1971, Harkness; flowers pink, 2 in., 12 petals; foliage glossy, dark; [(Pink Parfait × Masquerade) × Dearest]; int. by R. Harkness & Co., 1970

Busybody HT, dy, 1929, Clark, A.; flowers rich chrome-yellow, small; [Georges Schwartz × Lena]; int. by Hazlewood Bros.

Buta HT, w, Cant, B. R.; flowers pure white, well-formed

Butter Cream MinFl, my, 2003, Martin, Robert B., Jr.; flowers my, reverse my, 2 in., full, borne mostly solitary, no fragrance; foliage medium size, medium green, s`emi-glossy; prickles small, straight, black, few; growth upright, tall (30 in.); exhibition, cutting, borders; [Anne Morrow Linbergh × Fairhope]; int. by RoseMania.com, 2003

Butter 'n' Sugar Min, w, 1994, Berg, David H.; flowers vary from white to yellow shading to white, large, very dbl., borne mostly singly; foliage medium size, medium green, semi-glossy; few prickles; low (15-18 in.), spreading growth; [Klima × (Intrigue × Poker Chip)]

Butterball S, ly, 1950, Skinner; flowers creamy yellow, single; non-recurrent; foliage small; prickly, arching branches; growth spinosissima type; 6 ft.; hips large, rounded, reddish

Buttercream Ch, ab, 2003, Rippetoe, Robert Neil; flowers light yellow, often deep yellow in cool weather, fading to creamy white, 2¼ in., dbl., borne mostly solitary, no fragrance; foliage medium size, medium green, semi-glossy; prickles medium, slightly curved, brown, few; growth compact, medium (3 ft.); hedge, specimen, standards; ['Mutabilis' × Unknown, probably selfed seedling]; int. by Robert Neil Rippetoe

Buttercream HT, ly, 2004, Zary, Keith W.; flowers light yellow, reverse light yellow, 5 in., full, borne mostly solitary, moderate fragrance; foliage large, dark green, glossy; prickles 4-6 mm., hooked slightly downward; growth upright, tall (5 ft.); specimen, garden; PP13925; int. by Jackson & Perkins Wholesale, Inc., 2003

Buttercup HWich, my, 1909, Paul, W.; bud light orange; flowers bright yellow, fading to lemon and cream, small, single to semi-dbl.; foliage small, dark green, glossy; few prickles

Buttercup HT, ab, 1929, Towill; flowers apricot-yellow, dbl., cupped

Buttercup HT, my, 1930, Dobbie; flowers buttercup-yellow, well-formed, semi-dbl.; vigorous growth

Buttercup – See **Buttercup 98**, S

Buttercup 98 S, dy, 2000, Austin, David; flowers golden yellow, upper petals fade to deep pink, reverse apricot, 9 cm., dbl., borne in small clusters; foliage medium size, medium green, dull; few prickles; branching, medium (4 ft.) growth; [Graham Thomas × seedling]; int. by David Austin Roses, 1998

Buttercurls S, dy, possibly from Delbard; int. in 2003

Butterflies S, ob, 1997, Mekdeci, Dr. Anthony Casimir; flowers medium, single, borne in large clusters; foliage medium size, medium green, semi-glossy; bushy (5ft.) growth; [Dornroschen × Golden Wings]; int. by Hortico, 1989

Butterflies S, my, Ilsink; flowers large, bright yellow with golden stamens, single; continuous bloom; low, spreading growth; int. in 1996

Butterflies LCl, rb

Butterflies Cover – See **Telluride**, S

Butterflies of Gold HT, my, 1939, Brownell; [Mrs Arthur Curtiss James × unknown]

Butterfly HT, rb, Herholdt; bud pointed buds; flowers cream changing to red with sun exposure, flat

Butterfly Glow HT, or, 1969, Barter; flowers vermilion, large, 20 petals; foliage dark; free growth; [Centre Court × Carla]

Butterfly Kisses F, my, 1999, Giles, Diann; flowers medium, single, borne in small clusters; foliage medium size, medium green, semi-glossy; few prickles; upright, spreading, medium growth; [Sun Flare × Summer Snow]; int. by Giles Rose Nursery, 1999

Butterfly Papilio – See **Motylek**, HT

Butterfly Wings F, pb, 1977, Gobbee, W.D.; flowers ivory, petals edged pink, 4-4½ in., 12 petals, flat, borne in clusters, moderate fragrance; foliage large; [Dainty Maid × Peace]; int. by Harkness, 1976

Buttermere HWich, yb, 1932, Chaplin Bros.; flowers creamy yellow flushed pink, 6 cm., semi-dbl., borne in large trusses, moderate fragrance; foliage glossy; numerous prickles; vigorous, erect growth

Buttermilk Sky F, ab, 2002, McCann, Sean; flowers apricot cream with yellow hints, medium, full, borne in large clusters, intense fragrance; foliage medium size, dark green; prickles moderate; growth upright, medium; garden decorative; [Laura's Laughter × Ulster Monarch]; int. in 2003

Buttermint Min, my, 1993, Moore, Ralph S.; flowers large, dbl., borne mostly singly, slight fragrance; foliage medium size, medium green, semi-glossy; few prickles; medium to tall (36-40 cm.), upright, bushy growth; [Pink Petticoat × Gold Badge]; int. by Sequoia Nursery, 1994

Butterscotch HT, yb, 1942, Joseph H. Hill, Co.; bud long, pointed; flowers lemon-chrome, reverse pale orange-yellow, 4½-5½ in., 28 petals, slight fragrance; foliage leathery, glossy, dark; upright, compact growth; [Souv. de Claudius Pernet × R.M.S. Queen Mary]; int. by Wayside Gardens Co., 1946

Butterscotch LCl, r, 1986, Warriner, William A.; flowers tannish-orange, loose, 25 petals, cupped, borne in clusters of 3-5; foliage medium size, medium green, semi-glossy; no fruit; PP5895; [(Buccaneer × Zorina) × Royal Sunset]; int. by J&P

Butterscotch Dream Min, op; int. in 2005

Buttons Min, w, 1981, Lemrow, Dr. Maynard W.; bud globular; flowers 35 petals, borne singly, no fragrance; foliage very tiny, smooth; no prickles; compact growth; [seedling × seedling]

Buttons Min, or, 1987, Dickson, Patrick; flowers medium, dbl., slight fragrance; foliage small, medium green, glossy; patio; bushy growth; [(Liverpool Echo × Woman's Own) × Memento]

Buttons 'n' Bows Min, dp, 1981, Poulsen Roser APS; bud small; flowers deep pink, reflexing at maturity, 28 petals, high-centered and cupped, borne singly and in sprays, moderate fruity fragrance; recurrent; prickles straight; compact, upright growth; [Mini-Poul × Harriet Poulsen]; int. by Windy Hill Nursery, 1980

Buxom Beauty – See **Parole**, HT

Buzby F, or, 1978, Plumpton, E.; flowers light vermilion, conical, 1½ in., 11 petals, slight fragrance; dwarf, compact, upright growth; [Irish Mist × Topsi]

Buzzy's White Seedling N, w

By Appointment F, ab, 1990, Harkness, R., & Co., Ltd.; bud ovoid; flowers pale buff apricot, aging paler, medium, 22 petals, urn-shaped, becoming cupped, slight fragrance; foliage medium size, dark green, semi-glossy; prickles rather narrow, medium, dark reddish-green; upright, medium growth; [Anne Harkness × Letchworth Garden City]

By Design Min, ob, 1992, Laver, Keith G.; flowers orange, large, full, high-centered, borne in small clusters, slight fragrance; foliage medium size, medium green, semi-glossy; some prickles; medium (40-50 cm.), bushy-growth; [(Breezy × Julie Ann) × (June Laver × Painted Doll)]; int. by Springwood Roses

By Joe Min, w, 1990, Gatty, Joseph; bud pointed; flowers ivory white, 25 petals, high-centered, borne singly; foliage medium size, dark green, matte; upright, bushy, tall growth; [Pink Petticoat × Pink Petticoat]; int. by Keith Keppel, 1990

Byala Valentina Gr, w, 1986, Staikov, Prof. Dr. V.; flowers creamy white, large, 25 petals, slight delicate fragrance; foliage dark, glossy; vigorous, upright growth; [Queen Elizabeth × seedling]; int. by Kalaydjiev and Chorbadjiiski, 1974

C. A. Fletcher HT, dp, 1947, Fletcher; flowers clear rose-crimson, well-formed, 5-6 in., 35-40 petals; vigorous growth; [May Wettern × Mrs Henry Bowles]; int. by Tucker

C. Chambard HT, 1934, Bel; flowers deep yellow, reverse tinted red, dbl., cupped; foliage dark; vigorous growth

C. F. Worth – See **Mme Charles Frédéric Worth**, HRg

C. Gaudefroy N, dp, 1901, Bonnaire; flowers carmine pink, center brick red, medium

C. H. Middleton HT, dr, 1939, Cant, B. R.; flowers dark crimson, large, very dbl., high-centered; foliage glossy; long stems; vigorous, bushy growth

C. S. R. HP, 1934, Böhm, J.; flowers white with pink striping, large, dbl.

C. V. Haworth HT, dr, 1917, Dickson, A.; flowers intense black-scarlet with rich crimson, with massive shell-shaped petals; vigorous growth; Gold Medal, NRS, 1919

C. V. Haworth, Climbing Cl HT, dr, 1932, Cant, F.

C. W. Cowan HT, mr, 1912, Dickson, A.; bud short, pointed; flowers warm carmine-cerise, large, dbl., rather flat, moderate fragrance

C. W. S. – See **Canadian White Star**, HT

Cabana HT, pb, 2001, Zary, Keith; buds long, pointed, ovoid; flowers rose pink with light yellow stripes., 4½ in., 25-30 petals, borne mostly solitary, slight spicy fragrance; foliage medium size, dark green, glossy; prickles moderate; growth upright, tall (5 ft.); garden decorative; PP13089; [pink HT seedling × striped HT seedling]; int. by J&P, 2002

Cabaret F, or, 1964, deRuiter; flowers vermilion-salmon, 2½ in., 35-40 petals, camellia-like, borne in clusters; vigorous, upright growth; RULED EXTINCT 6/83 ARM; [Dacapo × Floribunda seedling]; int. by Blaby Rose Gardens, 1963

Cabaret Min, dr, 1983, Warriner, William A.; bud small; flowers small, 35 petals; foliage small, medium green, semi-glossy; upright, bushy growth; PP5576; [(Fire Princess × Mary DeVor) × (seedling × Caliente)]; int. by J&P

Cabaret HT, rb, Laperrière; flowers creamy white blended with carmine red, dbl., high-centered, moderate fragrance; int. in 1992

Cabbage Rose (Gerard) C, mp, before 1596; flowers rose pink, outer petals larger and lighter, 3 in., very dbl., globular, borne singly or in clusters, moderate fragrance; summer blooming; foliage egg-shaped, pointed, usually with 5 leaflets; prickles moderate, uneven, scythe-shaped; growth branching, tall (5 ft.); hips almost round, rare; mentioned as early as about 410 B.C. by Herodotus

Cacaphony HT, op, 1975, Golik; flowers pink tinged orange, 4 in., 28 petals, moderate fruity fragrance; foliage glossy, dark; [Baccará × Golden Showers]; int. by Dynarose, 1974

Cachet MinFl, w, 1997, Tucker, Robbie; flowers full, high-centered, borne mostly singly, no fragrance; foliage medium size, medium green, semi-glossy; upright, tall (3 ft.) growth; PP10828; [seedling × seedling]; int. by Rose Hill Nursery, 1998

Cacilda Backer HT, ab; from Brazil

Cacophony Min, rb; flowers white with irregular stripes, dots and patches of red, no fragrance; growth compact, shrubby, spreading plant; int. in 2000

Cactus Blanc Pol, w, 1970, Delbard-Chabert; bud globular; flowers creamy white, small, dbl., cupped, borne in clusters; foliage light green, glossy; moderate, bushy growth; [(Orléans Rose × Orléans Rose) × ((Francais × Lafayette) × (Orléans Rose × Goldilocks))]; int. by Pepinieres G. Delbard, 1967

Caddy HT, my, 1943, Meilland, F.; bud large, well formed, yellow; vigorous growth; [Soeur Thérèse × Prof. Deaux]

Cadenza LCl, dr, 1967, Armstrong, D.L.; bud ovoid; flowers dark scarlet, 2½-3 in., dbl., slightly cupped, borne in clusters; recurrent bloom; foliage glossy, dark, leathery; compact, moderate growth; PP2915; [New Dawn × Embers, Climbing]; int. by Armstrong Nursery

Cadette F, ab, 1979, Lens, Louis; bud pointed; flowers pastel pink-apricot, 2 in., 35 petals, cupped, moderate fruity fragrance; foliage glossy, dark; vigorous, upright growth; [Poupee × Fillette]; int. in 1971

Cadillac HT, op, Kordes; int. in 1990

Cadillac F, or, Poulsen; flowers orange-red, 5-8 cm., 25 petals, slight wild rose fragrance; foliage dark; growth bushy, 60-100 cm.; PP15819; int. by Poulsen Roser, 2003

Cadillac DeVille – See **Moonstone**, HT

Cadiz F, my, Poulsen; flowers medium yellow, 5-8 cm., 25 petals, no fragrance; foliage dark; growth bushy, 60-100 cm.; int. by Poulsen Roser, 2005

Cæcilie Scharsach HP, lp, 1887, Geschwind, R.; flowers flesh white fading to white, large, very dbl., intense fragrance; [Jules Margottin × unknown]

Caesar HT, mr, 1982, van Veen, Jan; bud ovoid; flowers cardinal red, 33 petals, high-centered, borne 2-3 per cluster, slight tea fragrance; foliage leathery, medium green, semi-glossy; prickles red; upright, branched growth; PP4992; [Ilona × seedling]; int. by Carlton Rose Nurseries

Caesar's Rose Min, dr, 1996, Bell, Judy G.; flowers dark red with yellow stamens, 1-1½ in., single, borne mostly singly, no fragrance; foliage small, dark green, matte; prickles numerous dark red, short; upright, medium (15-18 in.) growth; winter hardy; [Jean Kenneally × Angel Face]; int. by Michigan Mini Roses, 1997

Café F, r, 1956, Kordes; flowers coffee-with-cream color, very dbl., flat, borne in clusters; foliage olive-green; vigorous growth; [(Golden Glow × *R. kordesii*) × Lavender Pinocchio]; int. by McGredy

Café Olé Min, r, 1990, Moore, Ralph S.; bud pointed; flowers medium to large, 40-50+ petals, cupped, borne singly or in sprays of 3-5, moderate spicy fragrance; foliage medium to large, medium green, dull to semi-glossy; prickles slender, hooked downward, brown; upright, bushy, tall, vigorous growth; hips round, orangish; [sport of Winter Magic]; int. by Sequoia Nursery

Cafougnette HT, op, 1956, Dorieux; flowers soft orange-salmon, reverse carmine-red, open, well-shaped; foliage dark; strong stems; [Happiness × Peace]; int. by Pin

Cagul HT, op, Moreira da Silva, A.; flowers salmon-orange and pink, large, very dbl.; int. in 1971

Cahto Maid S, lp

Caid Pol, ob, 1971, Delforge; bud ovoid; flowers orange, medium, dbl.; repeat bloom; foliage leathery; vigorous, bushy growth; [Orangeade × seedling]

Cairngorm F, ob, 1974, Cocker; flowers tangerine and gold, 2½ in., 25 petals, slight fragrance; foliage glossy, dark; upright growth; [Anne Cocker × Arthur Bell]; int. by J. Cocker & Sons, 1971

Caitlin Min, w, 1987, Travis, Louis R.; flowers flesh pink fading white, small, 12-15 petals, urn-shaped, borne in sprays, slight spicy fragrance; foliage small, medium green, semi-glossy; prickles straight, tan-brown; bushy, low growth; no fruit; [Fairy Moss × Fairy Moss]

Caitlin May Min, ab, 2003, Jellyman, J.S.; flowers apricot-white, reverse white, 2 in., dbl., borne in small clusters, moderate fragrance; foliage medium size, medium green, semi-glossy; prickles 3 mm., curved, few; growth compact, medium (2½ ft.); garden decoration; [Marylin Ross × (Jean Kenneally × (Sue Lawley × Sue Lawley))]

Cajun Dancer Min, rb, 1993, Taylor, Franklin "Pete" & Kay; flowers red with white eye, light reverse, large, 6-14 petals, borne singly and in large clusters; foliage medium size, dark green, semi-glossy; some prickles; tall (36 in.), upright, bushy growth; [Party Girl × unknown]; int. by Taylor's Roses, 1993

Cajun Firelight HT, or, 2001, Edwards, Eddie; flowers 4½-5 in., full, borne mostly solitary, moderate fragrance; foliage medium size, dark green, glossy; prickles rounded, few; growth upright, tall (5-6 ft.); garden decorative, exhibition; [seedling × seedling]; int. by Johnny Becnel Show Roses, 2001

Cajun Moon HT, w, 2001, Carruth, Tom; flowers white edged pink, 11-13 cm., full, high-centered, borne mostly solitary, slight fragrance; foliage large, dark green, semi-glossy; prickles very few, average, straight; growth upright, tall (140 to 170 cm.); garden decoration, exhibition; [Crystalline × Lynn Anderson]; int. by Johnny Becnel Show Roses, 2001

Cajun Pearl HT, lp, 2003, Edwards, Eddie; flowers reverse light pearl pink, 5½ in., full, borne mostly solitary; foliage medium size, dark green, glossy; growth upright, medium (5 ft.); exhibition; [Cajun Moon × Fantasy]; int. by Johnny Becnel Show Roses, 2003

Cajun Queen – See **Deidre Hall**, HT

Cajun Signature HT, w, 2004, Meyer, Larry & Doris; flowers white with raspberry edges, reverse white with lighter edge, 4½-5 in., full, borne mostly solitary; foliage large, dark green, semi-glossy; prickles 3/8 in., slightly hooked; growth bushy, tall (3½-5 ft.); garden decoration, exhibition; [sport of Jacnor]; int. by Johnny Becnel Show Roses, Inc., 2004

Cajun Spice Min, ob, 1993, Taylor, Franklin; flowers bright orange, white eye, light reverse, large, semi-dbl., borne mostly singly, no fragrance; foliage medium size, medium green, semi-glossy; some prickles; medium (24 in.), upright, bushy growth; [Party Girl × Baby Diana]; int. by Taylor's Roses, 1993

Cajun Spice HT, or, McMillan, Thomas G.; flowers lustrous orange-red, dbl., high-centered; int. in 1996

Cajun Spice, Climbing Cl HT; flowers large, vermilion, full; growth sturdy, vigorous plant; [sport of Cajun Spice]; int. by KSG Son, 2003

Cajun Sunrise HT, pb, 2000, Edwards, Eddie; flowers pink yellow, 4-4½ in., full, high-centered, borne mostly singly, slight fragrance; foliage medium size, medium green, semi-glossy; few prickles; growth upright, medium (4-5 ft.); [Crystalline × Elegant Beauty]; int. by Johnny Becnel Show Roses, 2001

Cal Poly Min, my, 1991, Moore, Ralph S.; flowers

non-fading, large, dbl., borne in small clusters; foliage medium size, medium green, semi-glossy; few prickles; medium (24 cm.), upright, bushy growth; PP8453; [(Little Darling × Yellow Magic) × Gold Badge]; int. by Sequoia Nursery, 1992; AOE, ARS, 1992

Cal Poly, Cl Cl Min, my, Moore, Ralph; int. by Sequoia Nursery, 2000

Calapuno S, dy, Noack; flowers creamy gold, 8 cm., dbl., cupped, slight fragrance; recurrent; growth to 4-5 ft.; int. by Noack Rosen, 2005; Bronze Medal, Baden-Baden, 2006

Calay Min, my, 1982, Robinson, Thomas, Ltd.; flowers lemon yellow, small, semi-dbl.; foliage small, dark, glossy; upright, bushy growth; [Rumba × New Penny]; int. by T. Robinson, Ltd.

Calcutta 300 HT, pb, V&B; flowers large, bright pink with stripes and patches of white, broad petals, dbl.; free-flowering; [sport of Taj Mahal]; int. in 1994

Caldwell Pink – See **Pink Pet**, Ch

Caldwell Pink Cl. – See **Pink Pet, Climbing**, Cl Ch

Caledonia HT, w, 1928, Dobbie; bud long, pointed; flowers large, 25 petals, high-centered; foliage leathery, dark; vigorous growth; RULED EXTINCT 7/83 ARM

Caledonia, Climbing Cl HT, w, 1936, Bel; flowers ivory-white, full; fairly good rebloom

Caledonian HT, ly, 1983, Mayle, W.J.; flowers creamy yellow, large, dbl.; foliage medium size, medium green, semi-glossy; bushy growth; [Kordes' Perfecta × Irish Gold]

Calgary HT, mr, Twomey, Jerry; int. in 1997

Calgold Min, dy, 1977, Moore, Ralph S.; bud pointed; flowers deep clear yellow, 1½ in., 23 petals, slight fragrance; foliage small to medium size, glossy; bushy growth; PP4230; [Golden Glow × Peachy White]; int. by Sequoia Nursery

Calibra HT, or; flowers orange-red, small, dbl., high-centered; PP9043; int. by Kordes, 1994

Calibra Kordana Min, ob, Kordes; flowers orange, full; container rose; int. by W. Kordes Söhne

Calico HT, pb, 1976, Weeks; flowers pink, yellow reverse, 3½-4 in., dbl., globular, slight tea fragrance; foliage dark; vigorous, upright to spreading growth; PP4006; [seedling × Granada]; int. by Weeks Wholesale Rose Growers

Calico Doll Min, ob, 1979, Saville, F. Harmon; bud ovoid, pointed; flowers orange, striped yellow, 1-1½ in., 18 petals, cupped; foliage dark; compact growth; [Rise 'n' Shine × Glenfiddich]; int. by Nor'East Min. Roses

Calico Star F, yb, 1978, Fong; bud ovoid; flowers golden yellow, edged red, 4 in., 25-30 petals, high-centered, slight fragrance; upright growth; [Circus × Lavender Girl]; int. by United Rose Growers, 1976

Caliente F, dr, 1974, Warriner, William A.; bud ovoid-pointed; flowers deep pure red, medium, dbl., high-centered; foliage large, leathery; very vigorous, bushy growth; [seedling × seedling]; int. by J&P

Caliente Min, dr, 2005, Benardella, Frank A; flowers dark red, reverse medium red, 2 in., full, borne mostly solitary, moderate fragrance; foliage medium size, dark green, semi-glossy, disease-resistant; prickles ¼ in., slight curved and angled down, moderate; growth upright, bushy, medium (2 × 2 ft.); exhibition, garden decorative; hardy; [Ruby × Timeless (HT-Zary)]; int. by Nor'East Miniature Roses, 2004; AOE, ARS, 2006

California HP, mp, 1905, California Nursery Co.; flowers rosy pink

California HT, ob, 1916, H&S; flowers deep orange, base golden yellow, large, full, moderate fragrance

California HT, ob, 1940, Howard, F.H.; bud long, pointed; flowers ruddy orange, reverse overlaid pink, 5-6 in., 30 petals, moderate fruity fragrance; foliage leathery, glossy; vigorous, bushy, spreading growth; [Miss Rowena Thom × Lady Forteviot]; int. by H&S, 1937

California, Climbing Cl HT, ob, 1953, Howard, A.P.; int. by H&S

California Beauty HT, my, 1926, Pacific Rose Co.

California Beauty HT, dp, 1935, Proietti; bud long, pointed to ovoid; flowers deep bright pink, very large, dbl.; foliage leathery, dark; vigorous growth; [Dame Edith Helen × Hollywood]

California Blonde Min, yb, 1993, Rennie, Bruce F.; flowers medium, dbl., slight fragrance; foliage medium size, medium green, semi-glossy; few prickles; medium, upright growth; [Party Girl × Tooth of Time]; int. by Rennie Roses International, 1995

California Centennial HT, dr, 1949, Howard, F.H.; bud long, pointed; flowers 3½-4 in., 28 petals, high-centered, intense fragrance; foliage leathery, bronze; vigorous, upright growth; [Tango × Mauna Loa]; int. by H&S

California Dreaming Min, mr, 1986, Rennie, Bruce F.; flowers medium red, reverse lighter, 28 petals, high-centered, borne usually singly, moderate fruity fragrance; foliage medium size, dark, semi-glossy; prickles tiny, maroon; medium, bushy growth; hips globular, yellow-orange; [Julie Ann × Black Jack]; int. by Rennie Roses International, 1987

California Girl Min, ab, 1986, Rennie, Bruce F.; flowers apricot, reverse yellow blend, 28 petals, high-centered, borne singly, moderate fruity fragrance; foliage medium to large, medium green, semi-glossy; prickles small; bushy, spreading growth; hips orange-red; [Julie Ann × Red Love]; int. by Rennie Roses International, 1987

California Glory HT, rb, 1995, Ortega, Carlos; flowers 3-3½ in., very dbl., borne mostly singly; foliage medium size, dark green, matte; numerous prickles; tall (150 cm.), upright growth; [Osiana × Kardinal]; int. by Aebi Nursery

California Gold Pol, ab, 1934, Smith, J.; flowers orange-yellow, dbl., globular, borne in clusters; foliage leathery, light; long stems; very vigorous, bushy growth; [sport of Gloria Mundi]

California Ground Rose – See ***R. spithamea*** (Watson)

California Heart MinFl, or, 2004, Bennett, Dee; flowers orange-red, reverse orange, medium, dbl., high-centered, borne mostly solitary, slight fragrance; foliage medium size, medium green, semi-glossy, disease-resistant; stems long; growth bushy, medium (18-30 in.); garden, containers, exhibition; [Futura × Jean Kenneally]; int. by Tiny Petals Nursery, 2003

California Sun Min, ab, 1988, Rennie, Bruce F.; flowers golden apricot, opening to golden center, reverse lighter, 30-35 petals, high-centered, no fragrance; foliage large, medium green, matte; prickles straight, medium, pinkish; upright, tall growth; patio, containers; hips rounded, medium, yellow-orange; [Shocking Blue × Rise 'n' Shine]; int. by Rennie Roses International, 1989

California Surf Min, w, 1988, Rennie, Bruce F.; flowers creamy white with peachy-pink edging, small, 20 petals, urn-shaped, borne usually singly, slight fragrance; foliage small, medium green, semi-glossy; prickles straight, small, reddish-brown; upright growth; hips round, small, yellow-orange; [seedling × seedling]; int. by Rennie Roses International, 1988

California Wild Rose – See ***R. californica*** (Chamisso & Schlechtendahl)

California's Favorite HT, op, 1949, Raffel; bud long, pointed; flowers light salmon-pink, base yellow, large; foliage soft; vigorous, bushy growth; [sport of Stockton Beauty]; int. by Port Stockton Nursery

Caline HT, op, 1958, Ducher, Ch.; flowers soft geranium-red, medium, 33 petals; foliage clear green; vigorous, upright growth; int. by EFR

Calizia S, op, Noack; int. by Pep. Allavoine, 2006

Calliope HP, pb, 1853; flowers cherry-carmine, center white, medium, very full

Calliope HP, mp, 1879, Moreau & Robert; flowers bright silky pink, center darker, large, full

Calliope S, mp, Barni, V.; int. in 1985

Calliope F, ab, Harkness; flowers apricot in center fading to light pink on outer petals, dbl., borne in large clusters, moderate fragrance; good rebloom; upright growth to 3 × 2 ft.; int. by R. Harkness & Co, 1998

Callista S, w, 2005, Rippetoe, Robert Neil; flowers white, becoming pink and apricot in cool weather, 3-5 in., full, borne mostly solitary, intense fragrance; foliage medium size, medium green, semi-glossy; prickles medium, straight, tan, moderate; growth bushy, tall (4-6 ft.); [Sweet Afton × Abraham Darby]; int. in 2005

Callisto HMsk, my, 1920, Pemberton; flowers golden yellow, small, rosette, borne in clusters; recurrent bloom; foliage dark green; growth branching, bushy, 3-4 ft.; [William Allen Richardson × William Allen Richardson]

Callum's Glow – See **Amber Sun**, Min

Calocarpa HRg, mp, 1894, Bruant; flowers rose-colored, 4-4½ in., single; hips abundant, scarlet, shiny; [*R. rugosa* × Parsons' Pink China]

Calumet Min, yb, 1985, Eagle, Barry & Dawn; flowers creamy yellow, petals edged with pink, 30 petals, high-centered, borne 1-3 per cluster; foliage medium green, semi-glossy; prickles very few, small, red; upright, bushy growth; [Golden Angel × Golden Angel]; int. by Southern Cross Nursery

Calvert – See **Globe White Hip**, C

Calypso – See **Blush Boursault**, Bslt

Calypso F, or, 1959, Boerner; bud globular; flowers orange-red, reverse red, loose, 3-3½ in., 18 petals, cupped, borne in large, pyramidal trusses, intense damask fragrance; foliage dark, leathery; vigorous, bushy growth; PP1624; [Geranium Red × Fashion]; int. by Stuart, 1957

Calypso HT, pb, Tantau; flowers light salmon-pink, shaded cerise pink, large, dbl., exhibition, moderate Damask and fruit fragrance; dark, glossy foliage; int. in 1988

Calypso – See **Berries 'n' Cream**, LCl

Calypso D, lp, Vibert; flowers rosy blush with paler edges, large, dbl., cupped

Calypso Hit MinFl, dr, Poulsen; flowers dark red, 5-8 cm., dbl., no fragrance; foliage dark; growth bushy, 40-60 cm.; PP11541; int. by Poulsen Roser, 1998

Calypso Petite C, mp, before 1820, Descemet; flowers bright crimson, very large, very dbl., borne in large clusters

Camaieu – See **Camaieux**, HGal

Camaieux HGal, m, 1830, Gendron; flowers white and pale rosy purple, striped, with a small button at center, small, dbl., flat, rosette, borne singly or in clusters of 2-3, moderate fragrance; foliage small, thick, dark green; prickles small; vigorous, rather dwarf growth; int. by Vibert, 1830

Camaieux F, rb

Camaieux Fimbriata HGal, m, Bell; int. in 1980

Camaieux Reversion HGal, m, Robinson; flowers rich rose purple subdued with an overlay of pink, moderate fragrance; sport of Camaieux (or reversion); int. in 1985

Camara HT, or, 1979, Delbard; flowers orange-vermilion, petals recurved, 4-5 in., 33 petals, slight fragrance;

PP4332; [((Chic Parisien × Tropicana) × (Gloire de Rome × Impeccable)) × (Tropicana × Samourai)]; int. in 1978

Camargue – See **Telford's Promise**, S

Camay HT, dp, 1959, Fletcher; flowers deep rose-pink to carmine, 5 in., 40 petals; foliage light green; vigorous growth; [Ena Harkness × C.A. Fletcher]; int. by Tucker

Cambrai HFt, yb, 1920, Smith; flowers light orange-yellow, medium, dbl.; [sport of Mme Edouard Herriot]

Cambria S, lp

Cambridge S, m, Poulsen; bud short, ovoid; flowers mauve, 5 cm., semi-dbl. to dbl., cupped, borne in clusters, slight wild rose fragrance; recurrent; foliage dark green, glossy; growth broad, bushy, 60-100 cm.; PP12520; [Unnamed seedling × Dorus Rijkers]; int. as Lavender Cover, Poulsen Roser, 1997

Cambridgeshire – See **Carpet of Color**, S

Camden MinFl, m, 2002, Hough, Robin; flowers red with mauve tinge, fading to pink with mauve, 1½-2 in., dbl., high-centered, borne mostly solitary, slight fragrance; foliage large, medium green, glossy; prickles long, straight, moderate; growth upright, tall (3 ft.); exhibition; [Black Jade × Mollycita]

Caméléon Ch, mr, about 1827, Desprez; flowers crimson

Caméléon T, pb, about 1830, Laffay; flowers pink, shaded carmine, medium, full, cupped, moderate fragrance

Caméléon Ch, pb, from Angers; flowers rose pink, shaded and striped with carmine

Cameleon F, yb, 1961, Verschuren, A.; flowers yellow, pink and orange, 22-27 petals, borne in large clusters; foliage dark, glossy; upright, compact, bushy, symmetrical growth; [Masquerade × seedling]; int. by van Engelen

Camélia HT, or, 1948, Heizmann & Co.; bud pointed; flowers fiery vermilion-red, medium, semi-dbl., cupped; foliage glossy, dark; vigorous, bushy growth; [Vainqueur × (Charles P. Kilham × Katharine Pechtold)]; Gold Medal, Geneva, 1948

Camelia F, dp, 1953, Klyn; flowers cerise-pink, medium, borne in clusters; strong stems; moderate growth; [Pinocchio × seedling]

Camélia Rose Ch, lp, about 1830, Prévost; flowers bright rosy pink, shaded lilac, medium, dbl., cupped; foliage dark green; sometimes classed as N

Cameliarose F, lp, 1960, Croix, P.; flowers soft pink, camellia-like; very free bloom, especially in autumn; upright growth; [Mme Joseph Perraud × Incendie]; int. by Minier

Camella – See **Camilla**, HT

Camelot Gr, op, 1965, Swim & Weeks; bud ovoid; flowers shrimp-pink, 3½-4 in., 48 petals, cupped, borne in clusters, moderate spicy fragrance; foliage leathery, glossy, dark; vigorous, tall growth; PP2371; [Circus × Queen Elizabeth]; int. by C-P

Camelot, Climbing Cl Gr, op; int. after 1965

Cameo Pol, op, 1932, deRuiter; flowers salmon-pink, turning soft orange-pink; [sport of Orléans Rose]; int. by J&P

Cameo, Climbing – See **Pink Cameo**, Cl Min

Cameo Cream – See **Caroline de Monaco**, HT

Cameo Perfume – See **Renaissance**, HT

Cameo Queen Min, pb, 1986, Bridges, Dennis A.; flowers light pink, reverse blends of pink, mini-flora, 34 petals, high-centered, borne usually singly; foliage large, medium green, semi-glossy; prickles medium, long, light; medium, bushy growth; [Heartland × seedling]

Cameo Superior Pol, mp, deRuiter; flowers have more lasting color; [sport of Cameo]

Cameron Bohls S, dr, 2000, Ponton, Ray; flowers single, borne in small clusters; quick repeat; foliage medium size, dark green, glossy; prickles moderate; upright, medium growth; orange hips; [Carefree Beauty × Lichterloh]

Camilla HT, dp, 1954, Aicardi, D.; bud ovoid; flowers strawberry-red, loosely formed, large, 30-36 petals; very vigorous growth; [Fiamma × Talisman]; int. by Olivieri

Camilla HT, ab; int. in 2000

Camilla – See **Camilla Parade**, MinFl

Camilla Parade MinFl, w, Poulsen; flowers white with faint pink cast, 2 in., 70 petals, high-centered, borne mostly singly, slight floral fragrance; recurrent; foliage dark green, glossy; prickles moderate, 4 mm; stems 6 in.; bushy, compact (20-40 cm.) growth; PP15142; [Patricia Kordana × Peach Parade]; int. by Poulsen Roser, 2002

Camilla Sunsation S, dp, Kordes; flowers deep pink, small, dbl., borne in clusters, no fragrance; prostrate, groundcover growth; int. in 1997

Camille HT, lp, 1993, Warriner, William A.; flowers light pink, near white, 3-3½ in., very dbl., borne mostly singly; foliage large, dark green, semi-glossy; some prickles; medium (120 cm.), upright, bushy growth; [Honor × Fragrant Memory]; int. by Bear Creek Gardens, 1995

Camille Bernardin HP, rb, 1865, Gautreau; flowers red with white, very large, dbl., intense fragrance; [Général Jacqueminot × unknown]

Camille Bouland A, lp, before 1826, Prévost; flowers delicate rose, medium, very dbl., globular

Camille Pissarro F, yb, Delbard, Georges; flowers yellow, striped and shaded with red, pink, orange and white, dbl.; dark green foliage; int. in 1996

Camille Raoux – See **Camille Roux**, T

Camille Rose S, mp, 2006, Jerabek, Paul; flowers very full, borne in small clusters; foliage dark green, semi-glossy; prickles medium, straight, red, moderate; growth upright, bushy, wide and tall (5-6 ft.); hedging; [unknown × unknown]; int. by Calvin W. Schroeck, 2007

Camille Roux T, mr, 1885, Nabonnand; flowers bright red, pinkish at petal edges, large, full, globular; prickles large, few; growth vigorous, bushy

Camillo Schneider HT, mr, 1922, Kordes; flowers clear blood-red, dbl.; [Lieutenant Chaure × Comte G. de Rochemur]

Camisole F, ab, 2001, Zary, Keith; bud pointed, ovoid; flowers 4 in., full, borne in small clusters, moderate fragrance; foliage large, dark green, glossy; prickles moderate; growth upright, medium (3½ ft.); garden decorative; PP13210; [Impatient × Amber Queen]; int. by J&P, 2002

Camoëns HT, mp, 1881, Schwartz, J.; flowers bright rose, center shaded yellow, very large, full, moderate fragrance; foliage semi-glossy, bronzed; prickles strong, widely-spaced; moderately vigorous growth; [Antoine Verdier × unknown]

Camp David HT, dr, Tantau; flowers very dark red, dbl., high-centered, intense fragrance; growth small, sturdy, compact plant; int. in 1984

Campanela – See **Campanile**, LCl

Campanile LCl, dp, 1967, Delbard-Chabert; bud globular; flowers deep magenta-pink, 4 in., dbl., borne singly and in small clusters, moderate fragrance; repeat bloom; foliage glossy, leathery, bronze; vigorous, climbing growth; [(Queen Elizabeth × Provence) × ((Sultane × unknown) × Mme Joseph Perraud)]

Campfire Cl Pol, or, 1956, Fryers Nursery, Ltd.; flowers orange-scarlet, small, rosette, borne in clusters; vigorous (6-8 ft.) growth; [sport of Cameo]

Campfire Min, or, 1991, Williams, J. Benjamin; bud pointed; flowers fiery orange neon red, ages deeper, medium, 26 petals, high-centered, borne singly, moderate damask fragrance; foliage medium size, dark green, semi-glossy; upright, bushy growth; [Marina × Starina]; int. by White Rose Nurseries, Ltd., 1990

Campfire Arteka – See **Kostior Arteka**, F

Campfire Girl HT, op, 1946, Duehrsen; bud long, pointed; flowers deep salmon, large, dbl., high-centered; foliage dark, leathery; vigorous, upright, bushy growth; [Joanna Hill × Gruss an Aachen]; int. by California Roses

Camphill Glory HT, pb, 1980, Harkness, R., & Co., Ltd.; flowers creamy pink, large, 54 petals, high-centered, borne singly, slight fragrance; foliage medium green, matte; numerous prickles; vigorous, branching growth; [Elizabeth Harkness × Kordes' Perfecta]; int. in 1981

Campina HT, lp, 1937, Lens; bud long; flowers flesh-pink; very vigorous growth; [Comtesse Vandal × White Briarcliff]

Camping Pol, pb, 1967, Grabczewski; flowers deep lavender-pink with white eye, small, single, globular, borne in large clusters; foliage small, olive-green; low, bushy growth; [sport of Paul Crampel]

Camrose S, mp, Twomey, Jerry; int. in 1998

Camuzet HCh, m, before 1829, Camuzet; flowers dark purple

Camuzet Carné HCh, op, 1829, Camuzet; flowers peach-pink aging to flesh white, large, full

Canadian Belle T, ab, 1907, Conard & Jones; flowers creamy-buff with deep apricot center, shaded with rose and amber, moderate fragrance

Canadian Centennial F, or, 1965, Boerner; bud ovoid; flowers coral-red, medium, dbl., cupped, moderate fragrance; foliage glossy; vigorous, upright, compact growth; PP2628; [(Pinocchio × unknown) × Spartan]; int. by J&P

Canadian Dream F, m, 1997, Brown, Ted; flowers single, 3 in., single, borne in small clusters; foliage medium size, dark green, glossy; upright, tall (4½ × 6ft.)growth; [Nymphenburg × seedling]

Canadian Jubilee HT, op, 1927, Dunlop; flowers Indian red to pink, base orange, dbl.; [Priscilla × Commonwealth]

Canadian Northlight HT, dp, 1984, Mander, George; flowers large, 28 petals, high-centered, borne in clusters of 6-9, light fragrance; foliage medium green, leathery; prickles dark red; spreading growth; [(Fragrant Cloud × Diamond Jubilee) × Super Sun]

Canadian Sunset HT, rb, 1996, Williams, J. Benjamin; flowers red with yellow reverse, large, dbl., borne mostly singly, moderate fragrance; recurrent; foliage large, mahogany to dark green, glossy, disease-resistant; vigorous, upright (3½-4 ft.), bushy growth; [Oregold × Tropicana]; int. as Spirit of Ocean City, J. B. Williams & Assoc.

Canadian White Star HT, w, 1980, Mander, George; flowers opening to multi-pointed star, 43 petals, high-centered, borne singly; foliage dark, leathery, glossy; prickles slightly hooked; vigorous, upright growth; PP5852; [Blanche Mallerin × Pascali]; int. by Hortico Roses, 1985

Canadiana – See **Imperial Gold**, HT

Canari T, my, 1852, Guillot père; flowers canary yellow, medium, full, borne in small clusters

Canarias HT, mr, 1964, Dot, Pedro; flowers bright red, large; int. by Minier

Canarienvogel Pol, 1903, Welter; flowers saffron-yellow and amber-yellow stained pink and purple, semi-dbl.; strong stems; vigorous growth; [Étoile de Mai × Souv. de Catherine Guillot]

Canarina ; int. in 1965

Canary T, my, 1852, Guillot Père; bud small, well formed; flowers canary-yellow; growth rather weak

Canary HT, ly, 1929, Dickson, A.; bud golden yellow, edges flushed; flowers light yellow, deepening, spiral, high-centered; branching growth

Canary HT, yb, 1976, Tantau, Math.; flowers yellow, petals marked orange, well-formed, medium, dbl.; int. by Krussmann, 1972

Canary Min, my; flowers primuline-yellow, semi-dbl., star-shaped

Canary HSpn, ly

Canary Bird S, dy, 1907; flowers golden yellow, aging to cream, medium, 5 petals; hips blackish-purple; originally thought to be a form of *R. xanthina*, but more probably a hybrid of *R. xanthina* × *R. hugonis* or *R. pimpinellifolia*

Canary Charm HT, my, 1969, Knight, G.; flowers very large, dbl., high-centered; foliage dark, leathery; free growth; [sport of Wiener Charme]

Canary Diamond HT, dy, 2002, Weeks, O.L.; flowers bright canary yellow, 4 in., dbl., borne mostly solitary, moderate fragrance; foliage large, dark green, semi-glossy; prickles few, average, curved; growth upright, medium (5 ft.); garden decorative; [Summer Sunshine × Georgia]; int. by Certified Roses, Inc., 2002

Canasta HT, mr, 1966, Gaujard; bud long, pointed; flowers bright red, large, dbl., high-centered; very vigorous, upright growth; [Karl Herbst × Miss Universe]

Canasta, Climbing Cl HT, mr; int. after 1966

Canberra HT, op, 1927, Burbage Nursery; flowers carmine, reverse buff at base, shading to salmon-pink; [Donald MacDonald × The Queen Alexandra Rose]

Canberra HT, mp, 1928, Harrison; flowers very dbl.

Canberra Pol, op, 1935, Knight, G.; flowers salmon-coral-pink; [sport of Gloria Mundi]

Canberra Rose F, pb, 1999, Thomson, George L.; flowers medium pink, reverse darker, 3 in., 16-40 petals, borne in large clusters; foliage medium size, dark green, glossy; prickles moderate; upright, medium (3-4 ft.) growth; [Watercolour × Madam President]; int. by Ross Roses, 2000

Cancan F, ob, 1969, Jelly; bud short, pointed; flowers mandarin-red, small, dbl., moderate spicy fragrance; foliage leathery; PP2902; int. by E.G. Hill Co.

CanCan HT, ob, 1985, LeGrice, E.B.; flowers orange, large, 24 petals, intense fragrance; foliage large, dark, semi-glossy; bushy growth; [Just Joey × (Superior × Mischief)]; int. in 1982

Cancan Swirl F, m, 2003, McCann, Sean; flowers have lighter edges, large, full, flat, borne in large clusters, moderate fragrance; foliage medium size, medium green, semi-glossy; prickles moderate; growth upright, medium; garden decorative; [Gentle Annie × Charles de Gaulle]; int. in 2003

Cancer F, w, Burston; int. by Burston Nurseries, 2004

Cancun HT, or, 1999, Carruth, Tom; flowers dark orange-red, 5-6 in., full, borne mostly singly, slight fragrance; foliage large, dark green, glossy; prickles moderate; upright, medium (3½-4 ft.) growth; [Ingrid Bergman × All That Jazz]; int. by Spring Hill Nurseries, Co., 1999

Candelabra Gr, ob, 1998, Zary, Dr. Keith W.; bud long, pointed; flowers coral-orange, 4 in., 20-25 petals, borne in small clusters, slight tea fragrance; foliage medium size, dark green, glossy; prickles moderate; bushy, medium tall growth; PP11016; [Tournament of Roses × seedling]; int. by Bear Creek Gardens, 1999

Candella HT, rb, 1990, McGredy, Sam IV; flowers large, dbl.; foliage large, dark green, glossy; bushy growth; PP9239; [Howard Morrison × Esmeralda]; int. by McGredy Roses International

Candeur F, w, 1986, Delbard; flowers large, 30 petals, high-centered, no fragrance; low, upright growth; [((Robin Hood × Virgo) × (Frau Karl Druschki × (Queen Elizabeth × Provence))) × (Virgo × Peace)]; int. in 1978; Gold Medal, Baden-Baden, 1978

Candeur Lyonnaise HP, w, 1913, Croibier; bud long, pointed; flowers white, sometimes tinted pale yellow, large, dbl.; very vigorous growth; [Frau Karl Druschki × unknown]

Candia HT, rb, 1985, Meilland, Mrs. Marie-Louise; flowers red and yellow blend, large, 38 petals, high-centered; foliage large, light green; PP4705; [Matador × (Tropicana × Flirt)]; int. by Meilland Et Cie, 1978

Candice Min, pb, 1987, Zipper, Herbert; flowers medium, dbl.; foliage medium size, medium green, semi-glossy; upright growth; [Libby × Queen Elizabeth]; int. by Magic Moment Miniature Roses

Candid HT, w, Delbard

Candid Prophyta HT, ab, de Ruiter; PP10531; int. by De Ruiter's New Roses Int.

Candida HT, yb, 1964, Leenders, J.; flowers creamy yellow, center salmon, well-formed; [Tawny Gold × Golden Scepter]

Candide A, w, 1831, Vibert; flowers white, tinged with fawn, medium, full

Candide HT, Gaujard; int. in 1970

Candide – See **Gavnø**, F

Candle in the Wind S, ob, McGredy; flowers oriental orange-red with fine brush strokes of white, 4 in., 9 petals; foliage rich green; growth upright, 4 × 2½ ft.; int. in 2002

Candle Light Cl Min, yb, Warner, Chris; int. in 1995

Candleflame Min, yb, 1956, Moore, Ralph S.; bud slender; flowers red, yellow and orange, 5 petals; foliage leathery; vigorous (10 in.), bushy growth; [(Soeur Thérèse × Julien Potin) × (Eblouissant × Zee)]; int. by Sequoia Nursery

Candleglow HT, yb, 1951, Whisler; bud long, pointed; flowers yellow washed shrimp-pink, 5-6 in., 38 petals, cupped, slight fragrance; foliage glossy, dark; vigorous, upright growth; [Golden Rapture × (seedling × Joanna Hill)]; int. by Germain's

Candlelight HT, my, 1932, Horvath; flowers yellow, deeper in hot weather, large, dbl., high-centered, moderate fragrance; foliage glossy; bushy growth; RULED EXTINCT 9/81 ARM; [Souv. de Claudius Pernet × Mme Butterfly]; int. by Bosley Nursery

Candlelight HT, dy, 1982, Christensen, J.E. & Swim, H.C.; bud ovoid, pointed; flowers deep yellow, spiraled, 30 petals, borne mostly singly; foliage large, semi-glossy; prickles large-based; medium-tall, upright, branching growth; PP5398; [Shirley Laugharn × (Bewitched × King's Ransom)]; int. by Armstrong Nursery

Candlelight S, dy, Tantau; flowers unfading deep yellow, full, cupped, intense fragrance; long, strong stems; int. by Rosen Tantau, 2002

Candy HT, ob, 1950, Brownell; bud long, pointed; flowers apricot-orange, medium, dbl., high-centered, moderate fragrance; vigorous, upright, compact, bushy growth; [Pink Princess × Shades of Autumn]

Candy Apple Gr, mr, 1975, Weeks, O.L.; bud ovoid; flowers bright apple red, 5 in., 40-45 petals, cupped, borne in small clusters, slight tea fragrance; foliage matte, olive-green; upright, medium, bushy growth; PP3748; [Jack O'Lantern × (seedling × El Capitan)]; int. by O. L. Weeks, 1975

Candy Cane Cl Min, pb, 1959, Moore, Ralph S.; flowers deep pink, striped white, 1½ in., 13 petals, borne in loose clusters; vigorous, upright (to 4 ft.) growth; PP1951; [seedling × Zee]; int. by Sequoia Nursery, 1958

Candy Corn Min, ob, 1999, Taylor, Franklin "Pete" & Kay; flowers orange-yellow, 1¼ in., single, borne mostly singly; foliage medium size, medium green, semi-glossy; few prickles; upright, bushy, medium (18 in.) growth; int. as Sweet Amy, Taylor's Roses, 1998

Candy Cover – See **Nashville**, S

Candy Cream HT, pb, Ghosh; flowers large, cream white with tips of petals and edges cerise pink, full; int. in 1999

Candy Favourite HT, pb, 1970, Heath, W.L.; flowers carmine, striped pale rose, 4½-5 in., 25 petals, slight fragrance; foliage very glossy; vigorous growth; [sport of Pink Favorite]

Candy Flo HT, rb

Candy Floss F, lp, 1960, Fryers Nursery, Ltd.; flowers bright pink, 3 in., 40 petals, rosette, borne in large clusters, slight fragrance; very vigorous growth; [Lilibet × seedling]; int. in 1959

Candy Land LCl, pb, 2006, Carruth, Tom; flowers rose pink with yellow-white stripes, 9-11 cm., dbl., hybrid tea form, borne in large clusters; recurrent; foliage large, bright medium green, glossy; prickles average, almost straight, brown, moderate; growth spreading, climbing, canes up to 200 cm. long; garden decoration; [Rosy Outlook × Pretty Lady]; int. by Weeks Roses, 2007

Candy Mountain S, dp, 1998, Walden, John K.; flowers deep pink, 1½-2 in., single, borne in large clusters; foliage small, medium green, dull; prickles moderate; bushy, arching, low (2 ft.) growth; PP10616; [Sweet Chariot × seedling]; int. by Bear Creek Gardens, Inc., 1997

Candy Pink Min, lp, 1969, Moore, Ralph S.; bud ovoid; flowers small, dbl.; foliage small, leathery; vigorous, dwarf, bushy growth; [(*R. wichurana* × Floradora) × (Oakington Ruby × Floradora)]; int. by Sequoia Nursery

Candy Rain – See **Abraham Darby**, S

Candy Rose S, rb, 1982, Meilland, Mrs. Marie-Louise; bud conical; flowers deep pink, reverse medium red, 2 in., 15-20 petals, borne in clusters, no fragrance; foliage small, medium green, semi-glossy; arching, spreading growth; PP6385; [(*R. sempervirens* × Mlle Marthe Carron) × ((Lilli Marleen × Evelyn Fison) × (Orange Sweetheart × Fruhlingsmorgen))]; int. by Meilland Et Cie, 1980

Candy Stick – See **Candystick**, HT

Candy Stripe HT, pb, 1963, McCummings; flowers dusty pink streaked (striped) lighter; PP2278; [sport of Pink Peace]; int. by C-P, 1964

Candy Sunblaze Min, dp, 1991, Selection Meilland; bud ovoid, large; flowers deep pink, 6-7 cm., 85-95 petals, globular, then cupped, borne in clusters of 1-5, slight fragrance; recurrent; foliage medium size, dark green, glossy; prickles medium, light tan; tall, bushy, upright growth; PP7621; [sport of Lady Sunblaze]; int. by The Conard-Pyle Co., 1992

Candy Tower HT, op

Candyfloss Min, dp; int. by Burston Nurseries, 2005

Candystick HT, pb, 1976, Williams, J. Benjamin; flowers deep pink striped white; [sport of Better Times]; int. as Red-n-White Glory, Lakeland Nursery Sales, 1975

Candystripe – See **Candy Stripe**, HT

Caneghem – See **Kanegem**, F

Canibo – See **Bonica, Climbing**, LCl

Canicule – See **Sonnenschirm**, S

Canigó HT, w, 1927, Dot, Pedro; flowers dbl.; [Antoine Rivoire × Mme Ravary]

Cannabina – See **À Feuilles de Chanvre**, C

Cannes Festival HT, yb, 1951, Meilland, F.; flowers Indian yellow veined amber, pointed, 4 in., 35 petals; foliage dark; vigorous, upright, branching growth; [Peace × Prinses Beatrix]; int. by URS

Cannes Festival – See **Cannes Festival 83**, HT

Cannes Festival 83 HT, yb, Meilland, Alain A.; flowers

Indian-yellow, edged with orange, large, dbl.; int. in 1983

Cannes La Coquette HT, op, 1877, Nabonnand

Canonvale HSpn, m; flowers white to blush pink with lilac at petal base, medium, semi-dbl., borne in clusters, strong sweet fragrance; growth small, compact (1 m.); hips small, round, black

Canoodling MinFl, ob, 2004, McCann, Sean; flowers deep orange with yellow markings, 1½ in., semi-dbl., borne in small clusters, no fragrance; foliage small, dark green, semi-glossy; prickles small, straight, brown, moderate; growth upright, medium; garden; [San Francisco Sunset × seedling.]; int. in 2004

Cantab S, dp, 1927, Hurst; bud long, pointed; flowers deep pink, base white, prominent yellow stamens, large, single, saucer-shaped; non-recurrent; foliage dark, 7-9 leaflets; growth to 6-8 ft.; [*R. nutkana* × Red-Letter Day]

Cantabile S, lp, 1964, Buck, Dr. Griffith J.; bud ovoid; flowers light camellia-rose shaded darker, medium, 25 petals, moderate fragrance; repeat bloom; foliage leathery, bronze; vigorous, upright (5 ft.) growth; [Harmonie × (Josef Rothmund × *R. laxa*)]; int. by Iowa State University, 1962

Cantabrigiensis S, ly, 1935; flowers cream to pale yellow, 2¼ in., single; [*R. hugonis* × *R. sericea*]; introduced by Cambridge Botanic Garden

Cantate F, ob, 1959, van de Water; flowers orange; [sport of Red Favorite]; int. by Spek

Canterbury S, mp, 1969, Austin, David; flowers rose-pink, medium, 12 petals; repeat bloom; [(Monique × Constance Spry) × seedling]

Canterbury – See **Scoop Jackson**, Gr

Canterbury – See **Perpetually Yours**, LCl

Canterbury Pride Min, r, 1992, Reynolds, Ted; flowers 1½ in., very dbl.; foliage small, medium green, semi-glossy; low (28 cm.), upright growth; [Hot Chocolate × miniature seedling]; int. by Reynolds Roses

Cantilena Bohemica HT, dp, Havel; flowers carmine-pink, large, very dbl.; int. in 1977

Cantilena Moravica HT, yb, Havel; int. in 1981

Canyon Cupido Min, yb, de Ruiter; PP10818; int. in 2002

Canyonlands F, op, Poulsen; flowers orange pink, 8-10 cm., dbl., no fragrance; foliage dark; growth bushy, 60-100 cm.; int. as Fredensborg, Poulsen Roser, 1996

Canzonetta F, or, 1953, San Remo Exp. Sta.; bud ovoid, cardinal-red; flowers orange-red, reverse yellow suffused red, open, large, 10-12 petals, borne in clusters of 25-40; foliage dark, glossy, leathery; vigorous, bushy growth; [Lawrence Johnston × Fashion]; int. by Sgaravatti

Canzonetta F, or, Noack; int. by Noack's Rosen, 2005

Cap Horn Gr, op, Dorieux; int. by Roseraies Dorieux, 2001

Cap Horn, Climbing Cl Gr, op, Dorieux; int. by Roseraies Dorieux, 2005

Cape Cod S, lp, 1995, Olesen, Pernille & Mogens N.; flowers soft pink, 2-3 in., 5 petals, borne in large clusters; foliage small, medium green, semi-glossy; few prickles; medium (36-42 in.), spreading growth; PP9641; int. by Young's American Rose Nursery, 1995; Silver Medal, Bundesgartenshau GER, 1991

Cape Coral HT, ab, 1964, Boerner; bud ovoid; flowers orange-coral, 5 in., 50-55 wavy petals, cupped, moderate fragrance; foliage leathery, glossy, veined red; long, strong stems; vigorous, bushy growth; PP2400; [Spartan × Golden Masterpiece]; int. by J&P, 1964

Cape Hatteras Min, w, 1988, Bridges, Dennis A.; flowers medium, 40 petals, high-centered, borne singly, slight spicy fragrance; foliage medium size, dark green, glossy; prickles long, pointed, medium pink-tan; upright, medium, vigorous growth; [Rise 'n' Shine × seedling]; int. by Bridges Roses

Cape Horn S, pb; flowers ivory white with pink and red edges, semi-dbl.; growth to 4 ft.

Capel Manor College F, op, 1991, Bossom, W.E.; bud pointed; flowers golden peach, medium, 10 petals, flat, borne in sprays of 20-36; foliage medium size, medium green, glossy; tall, upright, very vigorous growth; [Anne Harkness × Greensleeves]

Capeline LCl, mp, 1967, Hémeray-Aubert; flowers Tyrian rose, semi-dbl., high-centered; recurrent bloom; foliage leathery; vigorous growth; [Etendard × Diane d'Urfe]

Capella HT, ab, 1985, Meilland, Mrs. Marie-Louise; flowers large, 35 petals; foliage medium size, dark, matte; PP4868; [seedling × Banzai]; int. by Meilland Et Cie, 1979

Caper F, dr, 1976, Warriner, William A.; bud long, pointed; flowers open, 2-2½ in., 25 petals, slight fragrance; foliage dark; upright growth; PP3937; [seedling × Mary DeVor]; int. by J&P

Capistrano HT, mp, 1949, Morris; bud ovoid; flowers bright pink, 6 in., 36 petals, globular, moderate fragrance; foliage leathery; vigorous, upright growth; int. by Germain's

Capistrano, Climbing Cl HT, mp, 1952, Germain's

Capitaine Basroger M, rb, 1890, Moreau et Robert; flowers bright carmine-red, shaded purple, large, dbl.; very vigorous, almost climbing growth

Capitaine Dyel de Graville B, pb, 1905, Boutigny; flowers pink with darker center, very large, very dbl.; very remontant; [sport of Souv de la Malmaison]

Capitaine Georges Dessirier HT, dr, 1919, Pernet-Ducher; bud large, globular; flowers dark velvety red, shaded crimson, large, dbl., borne mostly solitary, moderate fragrance; [Château de Clos Vougeot × unknown]

Capitaine John Ingram M, m, 1855, Laffay, M.; bud well mossed; flowers variously described as dark purple, velvety crimson and reddish-purple, dbl., moderate fragrance; vigorous growth

Capitaine Jouen HP, mr, 1900, Boutigny; flowers vivid crimson, very large, dbl.; [Eugene Furst × Triomphe de l'Exposition]

Capitaine Lamure HP, m, 1870, Levet

Capitaine Lefort T, dp, 1888, Bonnaire; bud long, large; flowers purplish rose, reverse paler, 5-5½ in.; [Socrate × Catherine Mermet]

Capitaine Millet T, mr, 1901, Ketten Bros.; flowers bright red, reverse purplish, base golden, large, dbl.; [Général Schablikine × Mme A. Etienne]

Capitaine Paul HP, 1867, Boyau

Capitaine Peillon HP, m, 1893, Liabaud; flowers purple-pink, large, dbl.

Capitaine Rénard P, pb, before 1843; flowers pale flesh pink,striped with crimson, large, very full

Capitaine Rognat HP, mr, 1864, Guillot; flowers glowing scarlet, large, full, cupped

Capitaine Sissolet HCh, mp, before 1841; flowers rosy lilac, large, very dbl., cupped; vigorous, branching growth; sometimes classed as B

Capitaine Soupa HT, dp, 1902, Laperrière; flowers carmine-pink, very large, dbl.; [Mme Caroline Testout × Victor Verdier]

Capitaine Soupa, Climbing Cl HT, dp, 1938, Vogel, M.; flowers carmine-pink, large, dbl.; [sport of Capitaine Soupa]

Capitaine Williams HGal, dr, before 1843; flowers deep carmine red, medium, very dbl., moderate fragrance

Capitalia HT, Ansaloni

Capitole F, mp, Laperrière; flowers rose-cyclamen, 20 petals; int. by Sauvageot, 1986

Capitoule – See **Capitoule Palace**, MinFl

Capitoule Palace MinFl, dr, Poulsen; flowers dark red, 5-8 cm., dbl., slight wild rose fragrance; foliage dark; growth bushy, 40-60 cm.; PP15645; int. by Poulsen Roser, 2002

Caporosso HRg, mr, Mansuino, Q.; int. in 1975

Cappa Magna F, mr, 1967, Delbard-Chabert; flowers have yellow stamens and wavy petals, 4 in., 8-10 petals, cupped, borne in clusters of 20-30; foliage dark, glossy, large; upright growth; [Tenor × unknown]; int. by Cuthbert, 1967

Cappuccino HT, ob, Teranishi; int. in 1998

Cappuccino HT, dy, Tantau; flowers cream-yellow with deeper ocher in center, medium, dbl., high-centered; foliage dark, slightly glossy; few prickles; greenhouse rose; int. in 1999

Cappuccino HT, dy, Tantau; flowers creamy white to tan-gold, 8 cm., full, cupped, moderate fruity fragrance; low to moderate growth; int. by Rosen Tantau, 2005

Capreolata – See **Ayrshire Rose**, Misc OGR

Capreolata Ruga Misc OGR, mp, 1820

Capri F, op, 1960, Fisher, E. G.; bud conical; flowers bright coral, reverse lighter, 3-3½ in., 38 petals, high-centered, borne in small clusters, slight fragrance; foliage bright green, glossy, leathery; vigorous growth; PP1453; [Fashion × Floradora]; int. by Wyant Nurs., 1960

Capri HT, ab

Capri Sun HT, ob, Tantau; int. in 1991

Caprice HT, or, 1934, Leenders, M.; bud long, pointed; flowers orient red and peach-red, large, dbl.; foliage glossy, light; vigorous growth; [seedling × Gwyneth Jones]

Caprice HT, pb, 1948, Meilland, F.; bud ovoid; flowers deep pink, reverse cream, large, 24 petals; foliage dark, leathery; vigorous, upright, bushy growth; [Peace × Fantastique]; int. by C-P

Caprice, Climbing Cl HT, or, 1951, Lens

Caprice – See **Denise Grey**, S

Caprice – See **Caprice de Meilland**, HT

Caprice HT, dp, Meilland; int. in 2004

Caprice de Meilland HT, mp, Meilland; flowers pink tinted mauve, large, full, high-centered, strong fruity fragrance; foliage semi-glossy; growth to 100 cm.; int. in 1998

Caprice des Dames HCh, pb, before 1831, Miellez; flowers dark purple/pink, small, flat; foliage oval lanceolate, sharply dentate; growth dwarf (6 in.); Lawrenciana

Caprice du Zéphyre – See **Marie-Louise**, D

Capricious Min, lp, 2002, McCann, Sean; flowers medium, full, borne mostly solitary; foliage medium size, medium green, semi-glossy; few prickles; growth upright, medium; exhibition; [Kiss 'n' Tell × Kristin]

Capricorn HGal, dp, 1819, Miellez; flowers bright pink, medium, full

Capricorn F, rb, 1961, Verschuren; flowers scarlet, reverse silver, 2 in., 16 petals, borne in large clusters; foliage dark, dull, leathery; very vigorous growth; int. by Blaby Rose Gardens, 1961

Capricorn F, w, Burston; int. by Burston Nurseries, 2004

Capricornus C, mr, before 1811; bud pointed; flowers intense velvety red, 2 in., very dbl.; foliage glaucous green

Capriole F, mp, 1959, Tantau, Math.; bud cherry-red; flowers vivid pink, stamens prominent, medium, semi-dbl., borne in large clusters; foliage dark, semi-glossy; vigorous, dwarf, bushy growth; [Red Favorite × Fanal]; int. in 1956

Captain Bligh HT, mp, 1939, Fitzhardinge; bud long, pointed; flowers silvery rose, large, very dbl.; foliage leathery, dark; very vigorous growth; [Gustav Grünerwald

× Betty Uprichard]; int. by Hazlewood Bros.

Captain Blood HT, dr, 1938, Melville Bros.; bud ovoid; flowers scarlet and crimson, dbl., cupped; foliage leathery; vigorous, bushy growth; [Gen. MacArthur × E.G. Hill]; int. by R. Murrell

Captain Christy HT, lp, 1873, Lacharme, F.; flowers soft flesh-pink, center darker, large, 40 petals, globular, slight fragrance; wide, compact growth; [Victor Verdier × Safrano]

Captain Christy, Climbing Cl HT, lp, 1881, Ducher; flowers delicate flesh, deeper in center, large, full, globular, strong fragrance; [sport of Captain Christy]

Captain Christy Panaché HT, pb, 1896, Letellier; flowers striped white and pink; [sport of Captain Christy]

Captain Cook F, op, 1976, McGredy, Sam IV; flowers orange-salmon, 4 in., 10 petals, moderate fragrance; foliage glossy; growth medium; [Irish Mist × seedling]; int. by Mattock, 1977

Captain F. Bald HT, dr, 1919, Dickson, A.; flowers scarlet-crimson, velvety black sheen, dbl.

Capt. F. S. Harvey-Cant HT, pb, 1923, Cant, F.; bud long, pointed; flowers peach-pink, reverse deep pink, very large, dbl.; foliage dark, leathery; vigorous, bushy growth; Gold Medal, NRS, 1922

Captain George C. Thomas – See **Captain Thomas**, Cl HT

Captain Glisson HT, dy, 1935, Joseph H. Hill, Co.; bud long, pointed; flowers dark yellow, edged lighter, large, 28-30 petals; very vigorous, compact growth; [Joanna Hill × Sweet Adeline]

Captain Harry Stebbings HT, dp, 1980, Stebbings; bud long, pointed; flowers deep pink, 5-6½ in., 43 petals, high-centered, intense fruity fragrance; foliage large, leathery; upright, bushy growth; [seedling]; int. by Country Garden Nursery

Captain Hayward HP, dp, 1893, Bennett; flowers light crimson, edged lighter, large, 25 petals, high-centered; sparsely recurrent; vigorous growth; hips large, orange; [Triomphe de l'Exposition × unknown]

Captain Hayward, Climbing Cl HP, dp, 1906, Paul; flowers pinkish-crimson, lighter at edges, 10-12 cm., semi-dbl., cupped, strong fragrance; [sport of Captain Hayward]

Captain Ingram – See **Capitaine John Ingram**, M

Captain Kidd HSet, mr, 1934, Horvath; flowers blood-red, 10 cm., dbl., open, cupped, moderate fragrance; non-recurrent; foliage leathery, dark; prickles long; long, strong stems; very vigorous, climbing or tall pillar growth; [(*R. setigera* × unknown) × Hoosier Beauty]

Captain Kilbee Stuart HT, dr, 1922, Dickson, A.; bud long, pointed; flowers scarlet-crimson, very large, dbl.; moderate growth; Gold Medal, NRS, 1922

Captain Kilby F, mr, 1955, deRuiter; flowers blood-red, medium, semi-dbl., borne in large trusses, moderate fragrance; foliage glossy, parsley-green; very vigorous growth; int. by Gandy Roses, Ltd., 1955

Captain Philip Green T, pb, 1899, Nabonnand; bud long; flowers cream with carmine, large, full; prickles strong; growth vigorous; [Marie Van Houtte × Devoniensis]

Capt. Robinson Sp, dp, Robinson, C.H.; flowers 13 petals; non-recurrent; foliage small, dark; few prickles; growth to 1 ft.

Capt. Ronald Clerk HT, or, 1923, McGredy; flowers vermilion-scarlet, semi-dbl.

Capt. Ronald Clerk, Climbing Cl HT, or, 1935, Austin & McAslan

Captain Samuel Holland S, mr, 1991, Ogilvie, Ian S.; flowers medium, dbl., slight fragrance; foliage medium size, medium green, glossy; spreading, medium growth; [(*R. kordesii* × (Red Dawn × Suzanne)) × ((*R. kordesii* × Red Dawn × Suzanne) × (Red Dawn × Suzanne))]; int. by Agriculture Canada, 1990

Captain Sassoon HT, dr, 1938, Gaujard; flowers dark crimson; vigorous growth

Captain Scarlet Cl MinFl, mr; flowers scarlet red, 2 in., semi-dbl., shallow cup, borne in clusters, flowers all the way up the plant; recurrent; foliage dark green, glossy; tall (6-8 ft.) growth

Captain Thomas Cl HT, ly, 1935, Thomas; bud long, pointed; flowers lemon to cream, red stamens, large, single, borne in small clusters, moderate fragrance; recurrent bloom; foliage glossy, light; climbing or pillar (10 ft.) growth; [Bloomfield Completeness × Attraction]; int. by Armstrong Nursery, 1938

Captain Watkins Pol, dp, Heyde, C.W.

Captain Williams – See **Capitaine Williams**, HGal

Captain Woodward HP, dp; flowers light red

Captivation Min, or, 1991, King, Gene; flowers medium, full, borne mostly singly, slight fragrance; foliage medium size, light green, matte; some prickles; upright (60-70 cm.), bushy growth; [(Arthur Bell × Little Jackie) × Little Jackie]; int. by AGM Miniature Roses, 1992

Captivator HT, mp, 1942, Joseph H. Hill, Co.; [sport of Better Times]

Capuchonnée D, mp, 1820, Bozérian

Capucine Chambard HFt

Cara Bella – See **Carabella**, F

Cara Mia HT, mr, 1969, McDaniel, G.K.; bud ovoid; flowers large, dbl., moderate fragrance; foliage dark; vigorous, upright growth; PP3059; int. by Carlton Rose Nurseries

Cara Mia, Climbing Cl HT, mr; int. in 1976

Carabella F, yb, 1960, Riethmuller; bud pointed, apricot; flowers cream edged pink, open, single, borne in clusters; foliage glossy, light green; moderate, bushy growth; [Gartendirektor Otto Linne × seedling]

Caraibes HT, Combe, M.; int. in 1970

Caramba HT, rb, 1970, Tantau, Math.; bud pointed; flowers bright red, reverse white, well-formed, large, 45 petals; foliage glossy; upright growth; int. by Wheatcroft & Sons, 1967

Caramba S, ob; bud rounded; flowers apricot orange, 7 cm., 20 petals, high-centered, borne in small clusters, slight sweet fragrance; recurrent; foliage leathery; prickles few, 9 mm., hooked downward; vigorous, bushy, flat (2 ft. × 3 ft.) growth; PP13396; [seedling × seedling]; int. by Rosen Tantau, 2002

Carambole – See **Caesar**, HT

Caramel Antike F, ab, Kordes; flowers honey-yellow to apricot, full, cupped, borne mostly in clusters, moderate fragrance; recurrent; moderate growth; int. in 2005

Caramel Creme HT, my, 1980, Weeks, O.L.; bud ovoid; flowers caramel yellow, 30 petals, cupped, borne singly, slight spicy fragrance; foliage finely serrated; prickles long, hooked downward; bushy, moderate growth; PP4706; [(Sunbonnet × Mister Lincoln) × Oldtimer]

Caramel Kisses Min, m, 2007, Zary, Keith W.; flowers tan lavender blend, 1½-2 in., dbl., borne in small clusters; foliage small, dark green, glossy; prickles 4-6 mm., straight, greyed-orange, few; growth compact, medium (32-40 in.); [Kaleidoscope × Chipmunk]; int. by Jackson & Perkins Wholesale, Inc., 2008

Caramella HT, ab, Meilland; int. in 1986

Caramella S, my, 2006; flowers large, amber yellow, 10 cm., full, nearly quartered, borne in small clusters; foliage large, green, semi-glossy; vigorous, erect, upright growth to 120 cm.; int. by W. Kordes' Söhne, 2001

Caramella Kordana Min, ab, Kordes; flowers copper center, outer petals yellow tinged with pink, full; container rose; int. by W. Kordes Söhne

Caravelle HT, mr, 1964, Mondial Roses; flowers bright cherry-red, large, dbl., high-centered; strong stems; vigorous, upright growth; [Better Times × seedling]

Carcassonne F, ab, Olesen; bud short, pointed, broad-based; flowers apricot-pink, 8 cm., 28-35 petals, deep cup, borne in clusters, slight fragrance; recurrent; foliage glossy, disease-resistant; prickles moderate, 7 mm., hooked downward; bushy (60-100 cm.) growth; PP15232; [seedling × Queen Margrethe]; int. in 2003; Golden Rose, Kortrijk, 2006

Cardeal de Rohan F, dr, 1957, Moreira da Silva; flowers deep red, semi-dbl.

Cardiff Bay HT, mr, 1993, Poole, Lionel; flowers 3-3½ in., full, borne mostly singly, intense fragrance; foliage medium size, red changing to dark green, matte; some prickles; medium (105 cm.), upright growth; [seedling × Loving Memory]; int. by F. Haynes & Partners, 1994

Cardinal HT, mr, 1904, Cook, J.W.; flowers deep rich crimson tinted golden at center, medium, full, flat; RULED EXTINCT 12/85 ARM; [Liberty × seedling]

Cardinal MinFl, dr, Olesen; flowers dbl., borne mostly solitary, slight fragrance; foliage dark green, glossy; growth bushy, low (40-60 cm.)

Cardinal de Richelieu HGal, m, before 1847, Parmentier; flowers dark purple, small, very dbl., moderate fragrance; foliage elliptical, dark green; few prickles; bushy, compact growth; sometimes classed as HCh; int. by Van Houtte

Cardinal Hume S, m, 1984, Harkness, R., & Co., Ltd.; bud pointed; flowers violet-purple, 31 petals, cupped, borne in clusters of 3 or more, moderate musk fragrance; repeat bloom; foliage variable shades of green, matte; prickles small; medium, spreading growth; [((seedling × (Orange Sensation × Allgold)) × *R. californica*) × Frank Naylor]

Cardinal Mercier HT, op, 1930, Lens; flowers salmon-pink tinted orange, very large, full, globular; foliage bronze; vigorous growth

Cardinal Patrizzi HP, dr, 1857, Trouillard; flowers velvety purplish red tending towards black, edges bright flame, medium, very full; [Géant des Batailles × unknown]

Cardinal Richelieu – See **Cardinal de Richelieu**, HGal

Cardinal Song Gr, mr, 1993, Selection Meilland; flowers 3-3½ in., very dbl., borne mostly singly; foliage large, dark green, glossy; some prickles; medium, semi-erect growth; PP8847; [Olympiad × (Michel Lis Le Jardinier × Red Lady)]; int. by The Conard-Pyle Co., 1992

Cardinale de la Puma HT, dp, 1938, Leenders, M.; flowers carmine-red, large, semi-dbl.; foliage glossy; vigorous, bushy growth; [Mgr. Lemmens × Lord Charlemont]; Gold Medal, Rome, 1937

Cardinals Hat HT, mr, 1960, Leenders, J.; [Souv. de Jacques Verschuren × Charles Mallerin]

Cardinal's Robe HT, ob, 1994, McGredy, Sam IV; flowers orange blend, 3 in., full, slight fragrance; foliage large, medium green, matte; bushy (100 cm.) growth; PP10696; [Waiheke × Las Vegas]; int. as Susan Devoy, McGredy Roses International, 1994

Carding Mill S, ab, 2004; flowers apricot, reverse yellow blend, 7½ cm., very full, borne in small clusters, moderate fragrance; foliage medium size, medium green, semi-glossy; prickles medium, hooked downward; growth bushy, vigorous, medium (120 cm.); garden decorative; [Ausland × seedling (yellow English type shrub)]; int. by David Austin Roses, Ltd., 2004

Cardon HCh, m, before 1830, Cardon; flowers bright purple, center lighter

Care 2000 S, pb, 2006, Beales, Amanda; flowers soft pink, reverse pink with salmon highlights, 10 cm., dbl., borne in small clusters; foliage medium size, medium green, semi-glossy; prickles average, straight, moderate; growth bushy, short (1 m.); containers; [Kathleen Ferrier

× La Sevillana]; int. by Peter Beales Roses, 1999

Care Deeply Min, ab, 1983, Lyon, Lyndon; flowers medium, 35 petals, moderate fragrance; foliage medium size, medium green, semi-glossy; upright, bushy growth; [Honey Hill × seedling]; int. by L. Lyon Greenhouses, 1982

Carefree F, dp, 1959, Fletcher; flowers rose bengal, camellia form, medium, 75 petals, borne in clusters; foliage dark; free growth; [Alain × Pinocchio]

Carefree Beauty S, mp, 1979, Buck, Dr. Griffith J.; bud ovoid, long, pointed; flowers light rose, 4½ in., 15-20 petals, moderate fragrance; repeat bloom; foliage olive-green, smooth; vigorous, upright, spreading growth; PP4225; [seedling × Prairie Princess]; int. by C-P, 1977

Carefree Beauty – See **Carefree Delight**, S

Carefree Days – See **Belle Symphonie**, Min

Carefree Delight S, pb, 1994, Meilland; bud short, ovoid; flowers dark pink fading to light pink at center, slight eye effect, reverse lighter, 2-2½ in., 5-10 petals, flat cup, borne mostly in clusters, slight fragrance; free-flowering; foliage small, dark green, glossy; numerous prickles; arching, medium (2½ ft.) growth; PP8841; [(Eyepaint × Nirvana) × Smarty]; int. by SNC Meilland Et Cie, 1991

Carefree Marvel S, dp, 2003, Meilland International; bud globular, small; flowers 2 in., 24-28 petals, flattened, borne in large clusters, no fragrance; free-flowering; foliage medium green, glossy; prickles moderate; growth spreading, medium (2-3 ft.); groundcover, landscape, containers; PP16030; [Flower Carpet × (Magic Meidiland × Immensee)]; int. by The Conard-Pyle Company, 2003

Carefree Sunshine S, ly, 2001, Radler, William J.; flowers 3 in., single, borne in small clusters, no fragrance; foliage medium size, light green, matte; prickles moderate; growth upright (3½-4 ft.); landscape; very resistant to blackspot; PP13063; [seedling × seedling]; int. by The Conard-Pyle Co., 2001

Carefree Tapestry S, ob; flowers orange and yellow, small, borne in clusters; foliage glossy, green; groundcover; spreading growth; int. by Northland Rosarium, 2003

Carefree Wonder S, pb, 1990; bud pointed, ovoid; flowers medium pink with light pink reverse, aging to medium pink, 4-4½ in., 26-30 petals, cupped, borne in sprays of 1-4, slight fragrance; free-flowering; foliage medium size, medium green, semi-glossy; prickles narrow, reddish; bushy, medium growth; suitable for hedges; hips oval, reddish-brown; hardy; PP7783; [(Prairie Princess × Nirvana) × (Eyepaint × Rustica)]; int. as Dynastie, Selection Meilland, 1978

Careless Love HT, pb, 1955, Conklin; flowers deep pink, streaked (striped) and splashed white; PP1582; [sport of Red Radiance]; int. by Golden State Nursery, 1955

Careless Moment Min, pb, 1978, Williams, Ernest D.; bud long, pointed; flowers white, lightly edged pink, 1-1½ in., 45 petals, high-centered, moderate fragrance; foliage small; bushy, spreading growth; PP4426; [Little Darling × Over the Rainbow]; int. by Mini-Roses, 1977

Caress HT, yb, 1935, Dickson, A.; flowers pale buttercup yellow, tinted rose, edged salmon-carmine, dbl.; foliage bright green, leathery; vigorous growth

Carezza HT, op, Barni, V.; buds elegant; flowers rose-salmon turning coral-red in sun, dbl., high-centered, borne one to a stem; erect growth to 90-110 cm.; int. in 1996

Caribbean Gr, ab, 1992, Kordes, W.; flowers apricot orange/yellow blend with yellow reverse, 3-3½ in., 30-40 petals, high-centered, borne in small clusters, moderate fragrance; foliage large, dark green, semi-glossy, with red mid-vein and margins; numerous prickles; medium (110-125 cm.), upright, bushy growth; PP8592; [Mercedes × (New Day × seedling)]; int. by Bear Creek Gardens, 1994

Caribbean Dawn – See **Maxi Vita**, F

Caribbean Queen Min, r, 1986, Rennie, Bruce F.; flowers apricot-copper, reverse yellow, 33 petals, high-centered, borne singly, slight fragrance; foliage small to medium size, medium green, semi-glossy; prickles medium, orange-red; vigorous, bushy growth; hips ovoid, yellow; [Sunday Brunch × Gold Mine]; int. by Rennie Roses International, 1987

Caribe Min, ab, 1982, Warriner, William A.; flowers apricot, semi-dbl.; foliage small, light green, semi-glossy; upright, bushy growth; PP5246; [Bridal Pink × Fire Princess]; int. by J&P, 1983

Caribia – See **Harry Wheatcroft**, HT

Caribia, Climbing – See **Harry Wheatcroft, Climbing**, Cl HT

Caribia Twist HT, rb; int. by Bell Roses, 2004

Caribou HRg, w, 1946, Preston; bud pointed; flowers large, 5 petals, flat, slight fragrance; non-recurrent bloom; foliage glossy, leathery, dark, rugose, scented like sweetbrier; bushy, vigorous growth; ornamental fruit; very hardy; [Ross Rambler × ((*R. rugosa* × *R. eglanteria*) × seedling)]; int. by Central Exp. Farm

Carike Keuzenkamp – See **Kanegem**, F

Carillon HT, or, 1935, Nicolas; bud long, pointed, scarlet-orange; flowers brilliant flame, paling, large, semi-dbl.; foliage glossy, light; bushy growth; [Charles P. Kilham × Mrs Pierre S. duPont]; int. by J&P

Carillon HT, dy, 1953, Moulin-Epinay; bud long, pointed, deep yellow spotted carmine; flowers medium, 30-35 petals; vigorous growth; [(Soeur Thérèse × Orange Nassau) × Orange Nassau]; int. by Vilmorin-Andrieux

Carina HT, mp, 1963, Meilland, Alain A.; flowers 5 in., 40 petals, high-centered, moderate fragrance; foliage leathery; upright, bushy growth; PP2378; [White Knight × (Happiness × Independence)]; int. by Moerheim, 1963; ADR, 1966

Carina, Climbing Cl HT, mp, 1970, Meilland; [sport of Carina]; int. by URS, 1968

Carina Spire HT, pb, Kordes; flowers silvery pink on inside, strong pink on reverse, dbl., high-centered; good repeat bloom; growth bushy, tall (to 2 m.); int. in 1999

Carina Superior HT, w, 1977, Takatori, Yoshiho; bud pointed; flowers white, reverse light pink, 5 in., 35-40 petals, high-centered, moderate fragrance; foliage leathery; upright, bushy growth; [sport of Carina]; int. by Japan Rose Nursery, 1978

Carine HT, op, 1911, Dickson, A.; bud long, pointed; flowers orange-carmine tinted buff, well-formed; strong stems; vigorous growth

Carinella HT, w, Meilland; int. in 1973

Caring Min, mp; int. in 2003

Caring For You Cl F, pb, 1997, Bossom, W.E.; flowers large, 41 petals, borne in small clusters; foliage medium size, medium green, semi-glossy; some prickles; climbing (15 ft.) growth; [English Miss × Summer Wine]

Caring For You HT, lp, 2000, Cocker, A.G.; flowers large, light pink, full, high-centered, borne mostly singly; foliage large, medium green, glossy; prickles moderate; upright, tall growth; [Pristine × National Trust]; int. in 2000

Carinita Min, pb, Meilland; int. in 1995

Carioca HT, ab, 1942, Chase; bud long; flowers 4½ in., 25-38 petals, high-centered; foliage dark, glossy, leathery; vigorous, upright growth; [sport of Talisman]; int. by J&P

Carioca HT, ob, 1951, Lens; bud semi-ovoid; flowers tangerine-orange, large, dbl., globular; foliage bright bronze green; long, strong stems; very vigorous growth; [Rubin × Mme Henri Guillot]

Carioca HT, pb, Teranishi; int. in 1989

Carissima HWich, lp, 1905, Walsh; flowers delicate flesh, carnation-like, small, petals quilled, dbl., rosette, borne in large clusters, moderate fragrance; foliage glossy

Caritas HT, mp, Urban, J.; flowers large, dbl.; int. in 1970

Caritas HT, ob, Poulsen; flowers orange and orange blend, 8-10 cm., 25 petals, borne one to a stem, slight fragrance; foliage reddish green; growth bushy, 60-100 cm.; PP13295; int. by Poulsen Roser, 2001

Carito MacMahon HT, my, 1934, Dot, Pedro; bud large, ovoid; flowers dbl., cupped; foliage glossy, dark; strong stems; vigorous growth; [Mrs Pierre S. duPont × Cayetana Stuart]

Carl Coërs HP, rb, 1865, Granger; flowers bright red with dark purple, very large, full

Carl Kempkes F, dr, 1937, Kordes; bud long, pointed; flowers crimson, open, large, semi-dbl., borne in clusters; foliage glossy, dark; strong stems; vigorous, bushy growth; [Dance of Joy × Mary Hart]; int. by Späth

Carl Philip – See **Mariandel**, F

Carl Philip Kristian IV – See **Mariandel**, F

Carl Red HT, mr; flowers dbl., high-centered; int. by Interplant, 1992

Carla S, mr, 1963, Erskine; [Will Alderman × Hansa]

Carla HT, op, 1963, deRuiter; flowers soft salmon-pink, 3½-5 in., 26 petals, moderate fragrance; foliage dark; vigorous growth; PP2401; [Queen Elizabeth × The Optimist]; int. by Ball Seed Co., 1968

Carla, Climbing Cl HT, op, 1970, Riethmuller, F.; buds large, long pointed; flowers soft salmon, large, dbl, high-centered, borne singly, moderate fragrance; foliage medium size, dark green, leathery; growth vigorous, climbing; [sport of Carla]

Carla Ann Gr, yb, 2006, Horner, Calvin; flowers yellow/pale peach, reverse pale peach, 3 in., dbl., borne in small clusters; foliage medium size, light green, matte; prickles medium, hooked, green, few; growth upright, tall (5 ft.); garden decorative; [(Rosemary Harkness × Remember Me) × Friendship]; int. by Horner, 2007

Carla Fineschi Cl T, rb, Eve, Guy; flowers carmine red, reverse silvery red, 4-5 cm., semi-dbl., borne in large clusters, slight fragrance; good repeat; foliage medium size, medium green, semi-glossy; prickles moderate to numerous; growth to 2½-3 m.; [(Étendard × unknown) × Don Quichotte]; int. by Andre Eve, 2002

Carlea S, mp, 1965, Wright, Percy H.; flowers similar to Victory Year but darker and more abundant; non-recurrent; [Betty Bland × unknown]

Carley – See **Carley Regan**, Min

Carley Regan Min, mr, Jalbert; flowers hybrid tea form; growth to 16-18 in.; int. by Lamrock's Little Roses, 2004

Carley's Rose – See **Carley Regan**, Min

Carlita – See **Kamchin**, HT

Carlos Beauty (variety of *R. acicularis*), mp, Erskine; flowers bright pink, 12-15 petals

Carlos Dawn S, dp, Erskine; int. in 1950?

Carlos Perpetual S, lp, Erskine

Carlos Red S, dr, Erskine

Carlos Reis Cl HT, mr, Moreira da Silva; flowers purplish red; [Étoile de Hollande, Climbing × Pres. Herbert Hoover]

Carl's Rose Min, m, 1985, Lemrow, Dr. Maynard W.; flowers small, 35 petals, high-centered, borne in sprays; foliage small, medium green, semi-glossy; low, upright growth

Carlsham S, mp, 1964, Erskine; flowers rose-pink, large, 25 petals; recurrent bloom; foliage glossy; [Hansa × *R. nitida*]

Carmagnole F, w, 1991, Delbard & Chabert; flowers white cream with soft pink, medium, 20-25 petals, cupped, slight fragrance; foliage dark green; bushy (80-100 cm.) growth; [(Milrose × Legion d'Honneur) × (Zambra × Orange Sensation)]; int. in 1990

Carmel Bice F, pb, 1959, Riethmuller; bud ovoid; flowers pink, reverse lighter, semi-dbl., borne in clusters; foliage leathery, glossy; vigorous, upright growth; [Gartendirektor Otto Linne × seedling]

Carmel Sunset HT, ab, 1998, McGredy, Sam IV; flowers apricot blend, 4½ in., dbl., borne mostly singly; foliage large, medium green, dull; prickles moderate; bushy, tall (120 cm.) growth; [Freude × Silver Jubilee]; int. by McGredy, Sam, 1997

Carmela Min, ob, 1986, Moore, Ralph S.; bud lightly mossed; flowers orange, yellow center, small, 15 petals, borne in sprays of 3-5, slight fragrance; foliage small, light green, matte; prickles small, brownish; medium, bushy, spreading growth; hips small, ovoid to globular, orange; [Fairy Moss × Yellow Jewel]; int. in 1980

Carmela – See **Georgeous**, Min

Carméline S, lp, Guillot-Massad; flowers soft, pale pink, full, cupped form; int. by Roseraies Guillot, 2000

Carmelita HT, mr, 1933, Spanbauer; bud ovoid; flowers vivid red, large, dbl., high-centered; foliage dark; very vigorous, bushy growth; [Matchless × Milady]

Carmelita F, my, Poulsen; flowers medium yellow, 8-10 cm., dbl., no fragrance; foliage dark; growth bushy, 100-150 cm.; int. by Poulsen Roser, 1998

Carmelita Castle – See **Carmelita**, F

Carmen Cl T, lp, 1888, Dubreuil; flowers buff pink at opening, very dbl.; [Souv de la Malmaison × unknown]

Carmen HRg, mr, 1907, Lambert, P.; flowers crimson, stamens yellow, large, single, borne in clusters; foliage dark; vigorous growth; [*R. rugosa rosea* × Princesse de Béarn]

Carmen HT, dr, 1956, Delforge; flowers deep red, well-formed, large, dbl.; foliage dark; moderate growth; [Crimson Glory × seedling]

Carmen HT, or, Tantau; flowers deep orange-red, dbl., well-formed, borne mostly singly, intense fragrance; recurrent; stems long; medium growth; int. in 1986

Carmen F, dr, 1987, Warriner, William A.; flowers deep red, very little fading, small, 30 petals, high-centered, borne usually singly, no fragrance; foliage medium size, dark green, semi-glossy; upright, bushy growth; PP6070; [seedling × Samantha]; int. by J&P, 1986

Carmen F, mr, Roman, G., and Wagner, S.; flowers light carmine red, small to medium, semi-dbl., borne in clusters; foliage medium to large, dark green, glossy; [Candy Rose × Yesterday]; int. by Res. Stn. for Hort., 1999

Carmen – See **Sensuous Parade**, Min

Carmen HT, dr, Tantau; flowers dark velvet red, dbl., high-centered; few prickles; long stems; greenhouse rose

Carmen de Bencomo HT, Camprubi, C.

Carmen Miranda HT; from Brazil

Carmen Papandrea Min, dp, 1989, Papandrea, John T.; flowers deep pink; [sport of Magic Carrousel]

Carmen Sistachs Pol, 1936, Dot, Pedro; flowers rose-pink, base old-gold, dbl., borne in clusters; foliage sparse, small, soft, light; small vigorous, bushy growth

Carmen Sylva HT, yb, 1891, Heydecker; flowers yellowish-white with pink, large, dbl.; [Baronne Adolphe de Rothschild × Mme Barthélemy Levet]

Carmen Talón HT, dr, 1953, Dot, Pedro; bud oval; flowers velvety dark red, large, 35 petals; strong stems; vigorous growth; [Charles Mallerin × Satan]

Carmen Tessier HT, dr, 1964, Mondial Roses; bud long, pointed; flowers crimson-red, open, dbl.; foliage leathery; vigorous, bushy growth; [seedling × Independence]

Carmencita Min, w, 1954, Camprubi, C.; bud ovoid; flowers pure white, 55 petals; foliage clear green; vigorous growth; [Lady Sylvia × Perla de Alcanada]

Carmenetta S, lp, 1923, Central Exp. Farm; flowers pale pink, medium, single, borne in clusters; foliage leathery, reddish; growth vigorous(7 ft), spreading (11 ft.); very hardy; [*R. rubrifolia* × *R. rugosa*]

Carmin Brillant HGal, mr, before 1813; flowers light purple, carmine in center, medium, very dbl.; from Holland

Carmin d'Yèbles Ch, mr, 1839, Desprez; flowers carmine red, full, cupped, moderate fragrance

Carmin Velouté Ayr, mp; flowers bright carmine pink, very full

Carmine Button Min, dp

Carmine Panarosa S, mr, Delbard; int. in 2004

Carmine Pillar – See **Paul's Carmine Pillar**, HMult

Carmosina – See **Admirable**, HGal

Carmosina – See **Cramoisie**, HGal

Carmosine HT, mr, Laperriere, L.; flowers bright crimson, dbl., high-centered; int. in 1982

Carnation Rose – See **Great Maiden's Blush**, A

Carnaval F, rb, 1987, Kordes, W.; flowers white with red edges, large, full, no fragrance; foliage medium size, dark green, matte; bushy growth; [seedling × (Die Krone × Simona)]; int. in 1986

Carnaval de Rio F, ob, 1982, Delbard, Georges; flowers orange, dbl., borne in clusters; [(Zambra × Orange Sensation) × (Zambra × (Orange Triumph × Floradora))]; int. by Delbard Roses

Carné – See **Great Maiden's Blush**, A

Carné – See **Vilmorin**, M

Carné – See **Agathe Incarnata**, HGal

Carnea – See **Unique Carnée**, C

Carnea Double – See **Double Carnée**, HSpn

Carnea Virginalis – See **Beauté Virginale**, D

Carnée – See **Victoria**, HFt

Carnée Double – See **Double Carnée**, HSpn

Carnet de Bal HT, Dorieux, Francois; int. in 1972

Carnival HT, op, 1939, Archer; flowers glowing orange to soft cerise, dbl.; foliage glossy, light; vigorous growth; RULED EXTINCT, 1/88

Carnival Glass Min, ob, 1979, Williams, Ernest D.; bud pointed; flowers yellow-orange blend, 1-1½ in., 38 petals, slight fragrance; foliage small, glossy, bronze; bushy, spreading growth; [seedling × Over the Rainbow]; int. by Mini-Roses

Carnival Parade Min, yb, 1979, Williams, Ernest D.; bud long, pointed; flowers golden yellow, edged red, 1 in., 45 petals, high-centered, slight fragrance; foliage small, dark, glossy; upright, bushy growth; PP4580; [Starburst × Over the Rainbow]; int. by Mini-Roses

Carnival Queen HT, mr, 1965, Armbrust; bud long, pointed; flowers luminous red, large, semi-dbl.; vigorous growth; [(Tassin × Priscilla) × Charlotte Armstrong]; int. by Langbecker

Carol – See **Carol Amling**, F

Carol HT, pb, 1964, Herholdt, J.A.; flowers cyclamen-rose, becoming orchid at edge, center apricot, well-formed, 45 petals; no prickles; moderate growth; [Queen Elizabeth × Confidence]; int. by Herholdt's Nursery

Carol, Climbing – See **Carol Amling, Climbing**, Cl F

Carol Amling F, mp, 1953, Amling, C.M. & Beltran; flowers deep rose-pink, edged lighter; [sport of Garnette]; int. by Amling Bros.

Carol Amling, Climbing Cl F, mp; int. by C. Newberry & Son

Carol Ann Pol, op, 1940, Kluis; flowers orange-salmon, 1-1½ in., 35-45 petals, cupped, borne in tight clusters; recurrent bloom; dwarf (12 in. or less) growth; [sport of Marianne Kluis Superior]; int. by Klyn

Carol Ann F, mr, 1990, Pearce, C.A.; bud rounded; flowers scarlet, loose, medium, 42 petals, borne in sprays of 3-15; foliage large, medium green, semi-glossy; prickles straight, large, red; spreading, medium growth; [Geraldine × seedling]; int. by Rearsby Roses, Ltd., 1990

Carol Ann HT, dr, 2002, Ohlson; flowers dark red, lighter reverse, 4-5 in., full, high-centered, borne mostly solitary, slight fragrance; foliage large, medium green, semi-glossy; prickles hooked, moderate; growth upright, tall (5-6 ft.); [First Prize × Mister Lincoln]

Carol Ann Min, lp, Welsh

Carol Howard HT, mp, 1935, Pfitzer; bud long, pointed; flowers rose-pink, very large, peony-like; foliage dark; vigorous growth; int. by P.J. Howard

Carol-Jean Min, dp, 1977, Moore, Ralph S.; bud pointed; flowers deep pink, 1 in., 22 petals, slight fragrance; foliage small to medium size, dark; upright, very bushy growth; PP4277; [Pinocchio × Little Chief]; int. by Sequoia Nursery

Carol-Joy HT, mr, Allender, Robert William; int. in 1991

Carola S, dp, Noack, Werner; flowers cherry pink shaded salmon-rose with a white eye, large, semi-dbl.; compact growth; int. in 1988

Carole Anne HT, my, Thames; flowers chrome yellow, large; free-flowering; int. in 1986

Carole Bouquet HT, lp; int. in 2000

Carole Lovett F, r, 2000, Bossom, Bill; flowers russet, medium, dbl., borne in small clusters; foliage medium green, semi-glossy; prickles moderate; upright growth to 3 ft.; [Edith Holden × Sexy Rexy]; int. in 2000

Carolin – See **Coralin**, Min

Carolin Reiberl F, dp, Hetzel; int. in 1992

Carolina Bank – See **Caroline Bank**, HMult

Carolina Budde HMult, mr, 1913, Leenders; flowers crimson, 6 cm., full, no fragrance; foliage glossy; [Turner's Crimson Rambler × Léonie Lamesch]

Carolina Classic HT, pb, 1992, Bridges, Dennis A.; flowers medium pink edged deeper pink, 3-3½ in., very dbl., borne mostly singly; foliage medium size, medium green, matte; few prickles; medium (90-100 cm.), upright growth; [Just Lucky × Flaming Beauty]; int. by Bridges Roses

Carolina Daza HT, my, Viveros Fco. Ferrer, S L; flowers 28 petals, high-centered; [Zambra × Kolner Karneval]

Carolina Lady Min, mr, 2000, Williams, Michael C.; flowers medium to dark red, reverse medium red, white at base, 2 in., full, exhibition, borne mostly singly, no fragrance; foliage medium size, dark green, semi-glossy; few prickles; upright, medium (18-24 in.) growth; [seedling × select pollen]; int. by Mini Rose Garden, 2000

Carolina Moon HT, my, 1990, Bridges, Dennis A.; bud pointed; flowers medium yellow, fading slightly, 28 petals, high-centered, borne singly, intense fruity fragrance; foliage medium size, medium green, semi-glossy; prickles pointed slightly downward, medium, deep pink; upright, tall, vigorous growth; [Just Lucky × Thriller]; int. by Bridges Roses, 1990

Carolina Morning Min, rb, 1990, Williams, Michael C.; bud pointed; flowers red with yellow center, aging red, small, 20 petals, high-centered, borne singly and in small clusters, no fragrance; foliage small, medium green, semi-glossy; prickles straight, small, red; bushy, medium growth; hips round, orange; [Rise 'n' Shine × Rainbow's End]; int. by The Rose Garden & Mini Rose Nursery, 1990

Carolina Rose – See ***R. carolina*** (Linnaeus)

Carolina Sunset LCl, rb, 1990, Jeremias, Lephon L.; bud ovoid; flowers crimson, gold reverse, dbl., cupped, borne in sprays of 3-7; foliage average, dark green, matte; growth upright, tall (10-12 ft.); [seedling × seedling]

Caroline T, lp, 1829, Guérin; bud firm, red, ovoid; flowers light pink with yellowish center, medium, full, cupped, borne in small clusters, moderate centifolia fragrance; foliage oval to round; prickles few, small; probably extinct

Caroline HT, op, 1955, Gaujard; flowers cinnabar-salmon, very large, 70 petals; foliage dark, glossy, leathery; very vigorous, bushy growth; [Peace × seedling]

Caroline Anne HT, my, Thomas; int. in 1986

Caroline Bank HMult, lp, before 1890, Geschwind, R.; flowers crimson, flecked with white, fading to pink with lilac tints, medium, dbl., flat; [De La Grifferaie × a HP or B]; sometimes classed as HSet

Caroline Brian MinFl, ob; int. in 1997

Caroline Budde HMult, dr, 1913, Leenders, M.; flowers crimson-red, large, dbl.; foliage dark; vigorous growth; [Crimson Rambler × Léonie Lamesch]

Caroline Clarke HT, op, 1997, Horner, Heather M.; flowers large, full, borne in small clusters, moderate fragrance; foliage medium size, medium green, semi-glossy; some prickles; bushy, medium (90 cm.) growth; [(Prominent × Southampton) × New Year]; int. by Warley Rose Gardens, Ltd.

Caroline Cook T, ab, 1871, Cook; [Safrano × unknown]

Caroline d'Angleterre A, lp, 1822, Calvert; flowers pale pink, small, full, globular; prickles sparse, red, aciculate; stems slender

Caroline d'Arden HP, mp, 1888, Dickson, A.; flowers delicate pure pink, very large, dbl., intense fragrance; foliage large; [Alfred K. Williams × Marie Baumann]

Caroline Davison F, op, 1980, Harkness, R., & Co., Ltd.; flowers medium salmon-pink, mini-flora, small, 16 petals, borne in small clusters; foliage small, dark reddish-green; prickles straight, dark green; low, bushy growth; [Tip Top × Kim]; int. in 1979

Caroline de Berri – See **Foliacée**, C, before 1808

Caroline de Berry Ch, w; flowers flesh white, medium, full, cupped

Caroline de Monaco HT, w, 1993, Meilland, Alain A.; bud conical, large; flowers cream white, 3-4½ in., 40-45 petals, borne mostly singly, no fragrance; good repeat; foliage large, dark green, semi-glossy; prickles large; medium, bushy growth; PP7622; [Chicago Peace × Tchin-Tchin]; int. by Conard-Pyle, 1993

Caroline de Rosny – See **Caroline**, T

Caroline de Sansal HP, mp, 1849, Desprez; flowers pink, center darker, large, dbl., flat; recurrent bloom; vigorous growth; [Baronne Prévost × unknown]

Caroline d'Erard B, w, 1850, Cochet; flowers flesh white, edges lighter, medium, full

Caroline Emmons F, rb, 1962, Boerner; bud ovoid; flowers scarlet-red, large, 55-60 petals, cupped, intense geranium fragrance; foliage leathery; vigorous, upright, bushy growth; PP2130; [(Geranium Red × Fashion) × (Diamond Jubilee × Fashion)]; int. by Home Nursery Products Corp., 1962

Caroline Esberg LCl, mp, 1926, Diener; flowers dull rose, dbl., borne in clusters

Caroline Hairston S, ab; flowers large, buff to pink, held above the foliage, double, cupped to flat, some fragrance; remontant; growth large (5-6 ft.); hardy to -10ºF; [Buff Beauty × Heritage]; int. by Antique Rose Emporium, 2004

Caroline Kaart HT, op, 1964, Buisman, G. A. H.; flowers salmon-pink veined dark red, large; foliage glossy; upright growth; [Bayadère × Ballet]

Caroline Küster – See **Mme Caroline Küster**, N

Caroline Louise HT, mp, 2000, McCann, Sean; flowers large, full, borne mostly solitary, intense fragrance; foliage large, dark green, very matte; numerous prickles; growth spreading; [Prima Ballerina × Fragrant Cloud]

Caroline Maille C, mp, about 1825, Boutigny; flowers semi-dbl.

Caroline Marniesse N, w, 1848, Roeser; bud pink; flowers creamy white, 5 cm., dbl., globular, borne in clusters of 3-9, slight musky fragrance; blooms throughout summer; probably synonymous with Duchesse de Grammont

Caroline Nicholson Min, mp, 2006, Paul Chessum Roses; flowers dbl., borne in small clusters; foliage medium size, medium green, semi-glossy; prickles small, short, pink, few; growth bushy, tall (2 ft.); bedding, borders, containers; int. by World of Roses, 2005

Caroline Oldrey HT, lp, 1998, Jones, L.J.; flowers pale pink, high-centered, 2½-3 in., 41-45 petals, borne mostly singly; foliage medium size, medium green, semi-glossy; prickles moderate; medium, compact, upright growth; [Solitaire × Prima Ballerina]; int. by Haynes Roses, 1997

Caroline Plumpton F, dp, 1976, Plumpton, E.; flowers deep Neyron rose, edged lighter, 2½ in., 20-25 petals, slight fragrance; foliage matte, green; very free growth; [Red Lion × seedling]

Caroline Riguet B, lp, 1857, Lacharme; flowers whitish pink

Caroline Schmitt – See **Mme Caroline Schmitt**, N

Caroline Ternaux N, w, about 1840, Laffay; flowers pure white, large, full

Caroline Testout – See **Mme Caroline Testout**, HT

Caroline Testout, Climbing – See **Mme Caroline Testout, Climbing**, Cl HT

Caroline Victoria HT, w, Harkness; flowers ivory, dbl., high-centered, intense fragrance; moderate growth; int. by R. Harkness & Co., 2006

Carolyn – See **Coralin**, Min

Carolyn HT, mp, 1998, McGredy, Sam IV; flowers medium pink, 4 in., very dbl., borne mostly singly; foliage large, light green, dull; prickles moderate; bushy, medium (110 cm.) growth; [(((Courvoisier × Arthur Bell) × Traumerei) × (Tojo × Vienna Woods)]; int. by McGredy, Sam, 1995

Carolyn Ann Min, mp, 1985, Hooper, Clint; flowers small, 20 petals; foliage medium size, medium green, semi-glossy; bushy growth; [Gene Boerner × Baby Katie]; int. by Kimbrew Walter Roses

Carolyn Dean LCl, mp, 1941, Moore, Ralph S.; bud long, pointed; flowers bright pink, 1¾ in., single, borne in clusters; recurrent bloom; foliage glossy; growth to 5 ft.; [Étoile Luisante × Sierra Snowstorm]; int. by Sequoia Nursery

Carolyn Dianne F, lp, 1964, Patterson; flowers medium, dbl., moderate fragrance; foliage glossy; vigorous, compact growth; PP2749; [Ma Perkins × Pinocchio]; int. by Patterson Roses

Carolyn Elizabeth Min, m, 2003, Sproul, James A.; flowers 1½ in., dbl., borne in small clusters, intense fragrance; foliage large, medium green, matte; few prickles; growth bushy, 30-36 in; garden decoration; [Chipmunk × Stainless Steel]; int. by Sproul Roses By Design, 2002

Carolyn's Passion MinFl, my, 2006, Williams, J. Benjamin; flowers yellow, petals quilling with age, 1-1½ in., dbl., high-centered, borne in small clusters, moderate fragrance; recurrent; foliage small, medium green, matte; prickles small, straight, light tan, moderate; growth compact, short (12 in.); containers, hedging; [Hershey's Yellow × Yellow Butterfly]; int. in 2005

Caron F, pb, 1972, Langdale, G.W.T.; flowers white and pink, 3 in., 38 petals; foliage semi-glossy; upright growth; [Kordes' Perfecta × Saratoga]

Carosi HT, Wituszynski, B.; int. in 1969

Carouge HT, dr, 1978, Gaujard; flowers crimson-red, dbl.; [Marylene × Credo]

Carousel HT, pb, Kordes; flowers cream with pink to red edges, medium; greenhouse rose; int. by W. Kordes Söhne, 2002

Carousel F, w; int. by Burston Nurseries, 2006

Caroyal HRg, mr, Erskine; int. by Sheila Holmes

Carpet of Color S, rb, Kordes; int. by Heirloom Roses

Carpet of Gold HWich, my, 1939, Brownell; bud golden yellow; flowers golden yellow, aging to lemon yellow, 2-3 in., single to semi-dbl.; some repeat; foliage glossy; trailing growth, 12-15 ft.; [(Emily Gray × Aglaia) × Golden Glow]

Carriage Dorizy B, m, 1849, Dorizy; flowers bright garnet purple, medium, full

Carrie Corl Gr, mr, 1969, Germain's; bud ovoid; flowers large, dbl.; foliage dark, leathery; vigorous growth; [Queen Elizabeth × ((Queen Elizabeth × unknown) × Happiness)]; int. by Flower of the Month

Carrie Jacobs Bond HT, mp, 1935, Howard, F.H.; bud ovoid; flowers rose-pink, center flushed crimson, large, very dbl.; foliage leathery, dark; long stems; vigorous growth; [Premier Supreme × Lady Leslie]; int. by Dreer

Carrie Jacobs Bond, Climbing Cl HT, mp, 1940, H&S

Carrot Top Min, ob, 1991, Olesen, Pernille & Mogens N.; bud ovoid, slightly pointed; flowers orange to orange-red, clear lasting color, medium, 18-22 petals, high-centered to cupped, borne singly or in small clusters, slight fragrance; prolific bloom; foliage medium size, medium green, matte; prickles few, long, straight, angled downward, brown; low (40-50 cm.), bushy, compact growth; hips short, globular, orange; PP9048; [seedling (F) × seedling (Min)]; int. by Weeks Roses, 1994

Carrousel Gr, mr, 1950, Duehrsen; flowers medium, 20 petals; foliage leathery, dark, glossy; vigorous, upright, bushy growth; [seedling × Margy]; int. by Elmer Roses Co.; Gold Medal, ARS, 1956, Gold Medal, Portland, 1955

Carrousel, Climbing Cl Gr, mr, 1960, Weeks; PP1990; int. by Elmer Roses Co., 1959

Carrousel Maid Min, rb

Carry Nation F, w, 1960, Silva; bud ovoid; flowers white, center cream, small, semi-dbl., globular, borne in clusters, slight fragrance; foliage soft, glossy; vigorous, low growth; [Pinocchio × Katharina Zeimet]; int. by Plant Hybridizers of Calif., 1959

Carte Blanche HT, w, 1976, Paolino; flowers flora-tea, 4 in., 38 petals; foliage matte; vigorous growth; PP3804; [(Carina × White Knight) × Jack Frost]; int. by URS

Carte Blanche F, w; flowers pure white, full; growth to 90-100 cm.; int. by Meilland, 2000

Carte d'Or – See **Supra**, HT

Carte d'Or F, my; flowers non-fading bright yellow, dbl., moderate fragrance; growth compact (65-75 cm.); int. by Meilland, 2002

Carte Noir F, dr, Meilland; flowers black-red; greenhouse rose; int. by Meilland International, 1998

Carte Rose F, lp

Carter HT, dp, 2002, Ohlson, John; flowers full, borne mostly solitary, intense fragrance; foliage medium size, medium green, semi-glossy; prickles hooked, moderate; growth upright, medium (4-5 ft.); [First Prize × Intrigue]

Carthage Rose – See **Summer Damask**, D

Cartier S, pb, Poulsen; flowers pink blend, 8-10 cm., dbl., slight fragrance; foliage dark; growth bushy, 20-40 cm.; int. by Poulsen Roser, 2004

Cartier Hit – See **Cartier**, S

Cartoon F, pb, Spek; flowers pink with green on guard petals, 3 in., 40-45 petals, cupped, borne singly and in sprays; recurrent; prickles moderate; stems long; florist rose; int. by Jan Spek Rozen, 2005

Cartwheel Min, rb, 1989, Warriner, William A.; bud

ovoid; flowers red and white picotee, small, 20 petals, cupped, borne singly; foliage small, medium green, matte; prickles hooked, small, tan; low, bushy growth; PP7508; [Libby × seedling]; int. by Bear Creek Gardens, 1990

Caruso – See **Rouge Royale**, HT

Cary Grant HT, ob, 1987, Meilland, Mrs. Marie-Louise; flowers vivid orange blend, lighter at petal base, 5 in., 35-40 petals, high-centered, borne singly, opening slowly, intense spicy fragrance; foliage medium size, dark green, glossy; prickles slightly recurved, light green-straw; upright, medium growth; hips ovoid, green-red-orange; PP6792; [(Pharaoh × Königin der Rosen) × ((Zambra × Suspense) × King's Ransom)]; int. by Wayside Gardens Co., 1987

Caryatide HT, dr, 1955, Buyl Frères; bud long, pointed; flowers semi-dbl.; strong stems; upright growth; [Hens Verschuren × Poinsettia]

Caryophyllata – See **Œillet**, C

Casa Blanca LCl, w, 1968, Sima; bud tinged carmine-pink; flowers semi-dbl., flat, borne in clusters; intermittent bloom; foliage medium size, dark green, glossy; vigorous, climbing growth; [New Dawn × Fashion]

Casa Blanca – See **Casablanca**, F

Casa Loma S, dp, Hortico; flowers deep pink, large, full, quartered, cupped, moderate fragrance; growth to 5 ft.; int. by Hortico Inc., 1996

Casablanca F, w, Select; flowers intermediate, sweetheart-size; int. in 2003

Casanova HT, ly, 1964, McGredy, Sam IV; flowers straw-yellow, 6 in., 38 petals, high-centered; [Queen Elizabeth × Kordes' Perfecta]; int. by Fisons Horticulture

Cascabel F, rb, 1957, Dot, Pedro; flowers red, reverse pearly, passing to carmine, 45-50 petals, globular, borne in clusters; foliage glossy; very vigorous, upright, compact growth; [Méphisto × Perla de Alcañada]

Cascade LCl, mr, 1951, Mallerin, C.; flowers bright crimson, with white flecks at center, 2½ in., single to semi-dbl., borne in large clusters; very vigorous growth; [Holstein × American Pillar]; int. by EFR

Cascade HT, w, Strahle, B. Glen; PP7382; int. in 1990

Cascade LCl, pb, Poulsen; flowers pink blend, 8-10 cm., slight wild rose fragrance; foliage reddish green; growth bushy, 100-150 cm.; int. as Nordina, Poulsen Roser, 2000

Cascade Blanche – See **Blanche Cascade**, S

Cascadia HMsk, lp, 1925, Thomas; flowers blush-pink paling to white, 1 in., 15 petals, borne in clusters, slight fragrance; recurrent bloom; foliage glossy, dark; tall growth; [Mme d'Arblay × Bloomfield Abundance]; int. by B&A; Gold Medal, Portland, 1922

Cascading White – See **Blossom Blanket**, S

Casey's Blush Min, ab, 2001, Bell, Judy G.; flowers flesh-pink, medium, full, borne mostly solitary, no fragrance; foliage medium size, medium green, semi-glossy; prickles small, straight, few; growth upright, bushy; garden decorative, containers, exhibition; [Jean Kenneally × Rainbow's End]; int. by Michigan Mini Roses, 2001

Cashmere HT, ab, 1980, Weeks, O.L.; bud pointed; flowers soft apricot, 30 petals, globular, borne singly and 3-5 per cluster, slight spicy fragrance; foliage leathery, dark; prickles long, hooked; vigorous, bushy growth; PP4736; [Tanya × Jack O'Lantern]

Casilda Becker – See **Cacilda Backer**, HT

Casimir Delavigne P, mr, 1848, Vibert; flowers violet-red and crimson, nuanced lilac, 8-9 cm., full, globular

Casimir Moullé HWich, pb, 1910, Barbier; flowers purplish pink, reverse silvery pink, 4-5 cm., very dbl., flat, borne in clusters of 20-50; foliage medium green, glossy; [*R. wichurana* × Mme Norbert Levavasseur]

Casino LCl, ly, 1963, McGredy, Sam IV; flowers soft yellow, well-formed, 4½ in., dbl., borne mostly solitary, moderate fragrance; recurrent bloom; foliage dark, glossy; vigorous (10 ft.) growth; [Coral Dawn × Buccaneer]; int. by McGredy & Son, 1963; Gold Medal, NRS, 1963

Casper – See **Magna Charta**, HP

Casque d'Or F, my, 1986, Delbard; flowers well-shaped, 4 in., 30 petals, no fragrance; vigorous, upright, bushy growth; [(Zambra × Jean de la Lune) × (Michèle Meilland × Tahiti)]; int. in 1979

Cassandra HT, mr, 1966, Dorieux; flowers cherry, 4½ in., high-centered; foliage dull, serrated; free growth; [(Karl Herbst × Ena Harkness) × (Christian Dior × Peace)]; int. by Bees

Cassandra F, or, Noack, Werner; int. in 1998

Cassandre LCl, mr, Meilland; flowers light red aging to rich carmine pink, medium, borne in small clusters, moderate fragrance; growth pillar climber; int. in 1989

Cassie – See **Snowbelt**, Pol

Casta Diva HT, w, 1983, Rose Barni-Pistoia; flowers large, clear white with cream center, 35 petals, cupped, no fragrance; foliage large, dark, glossy; prickles flat, yellow; upright growth; [Pascali × seedling]; int. in 1982

Castanet F, op, 1960, Boerner; bud ovoid; flowers orange-pink, reverse lighter, large, 45 petals, moderate fragrance; upright, bushy growth; PP1840; [Chic × Garnette seedling]; int. by J&P, 1959

Castel – See **Versailles**, HT

Castella S, mr, 1985, Tantau, Math.; flowers medium, semi-dbl.; foliage large, dark, semi-glossy; upright growth; int. in 1984

Castellana F; from Italy

Castilian HT, ob, Williams, J. Benjamin; flowers ivory in heart, orange on outer part of petals, spreading toward heart as it ages, dbl., high-centered, intense fragrance; recurrent; stems long; medium (4 ft.) growth; int. in 1996

Castilian Rose – See **Summer Damask**, D

Castle Hill Min, dp, 1990, Zipper, Herbert; bud pointed; flowers deep pink with mauve undertones, shading lighter towards base, dbl., high-centered, no fragrance; foliage medium size, medium green, semi-glossy, highly mildew-resistant; prickles curved, small, tan; bushy, low growth; hips round, small, light orange; [Sheri Anne × Red Devil]; int. by Magic Moment Miniature Roses, 1990

Castle Howard Tercentenary – See **Goldschatz**, F

Castle Hyde S, dr, 2001, Kenny, David; flowers dark velvety red, old fashioned, 4 in., full, borne in small clusters; foliage large, medium green (light green when young), semi-glossy; prickles large, hooked, numerous; growth spreading, bushy, tall (4 ft.); garden decorative; [((Mary Sumner × Kiskadee) × Bassino) × Purple TIger]

Castle of Dreams S, my

Castle of Mey F, ob, 1992, Cocker, James; flowers orange gold, medium, dbl., borne in small clusters; foliage medium size, dark green, semi-glossy; some prickles; medium, bushy growth; [Anne Cocker × (Yellow Pages × Silver Jubilee)]; int. by James Cocker & Sons

Castor – See **Castore**, S

Castore S, lp, Barni, V.; flowers pink with base of petals lighter, semi-dbl., borne in large corymbs, moderate fragrance; spreading, bushy growth to 70-90 cm.; int. in 1987

Catalina HT, pb, 1939, San Remo Exp. Sta.; bud long, pointed, carmine, reverse salmon; flowers carmine suffused yellow and rose, very large, 23 petals; foliage dark, glossy; very vigorous growth; [Pres. Herbert Hoover × Katharine Pechtold]

Catalina HT, op, 1940, Grillo; bud very long, coral-pink edged old-rose; flowers salmon to shrimp-pink, 4½ in., 25-30 petals, high-centered; very vigorous, upright growth; [sport of Joanna Hill]

Catalina S, lp, Poulsen; flowers light pink, 8-10 cm., dbl., no fragrance; foliage dark; growth bushy, 20-40 cm.; int. by Poulsen Roser, 2005

Catalina Gr, ab, 2007, Zary, Keith W.; flowers apricot-pink, 4½ in., full, blooms borne in small clusters; foliage medium size, dark green, glossy; prickles 8-10 mm., straight, greyed-orange, moderate; growth upright, tall (5 ft.); [Color Magic × seedling]; int. by Jackson & Perkins Wholesale, Inc., 2008

Catalina Frau HT, lp, Viveros Fco. Ferrer, S L; flowers 28 petals, high-centered; [FE-85146 × Osiana]

Catalina Palace – See **Catalina**, S

Catalonia HT, or, 1933, Dot, Pedro; flowers bright orange-crimson, shaded gold, large, very dbl., globular; foliage dark; bushy growth; [(Shot Silk × Mari Dot) × Jean C.N. Forestier]; int. by C-P

Catalunya – See **Gruss an Teplitz, Climbing**, Cl HCh

Caterpillar S, lp, 1985, Olesen, Pernille & Mogens N.; flowers small, dbl., borne in large trusses, no fragrance; foliage small, dark, glossy; growth broad, bushy, tall (100-150 cm.); [Temple Bells × seedling]; int. by D.T. Poulsen, 1984

Catharina Klein HT, pb, 1930, Berger, V.; bud ovoid; flowers bright pink, yellow background, large, very dbl.; foliage rich green; very vigorous growth; [Mrs Franklin Dennison × Hadley]; int. by Münch & Haufe

Cathay F, ly, 1957, Swim, H.C.; flowers 3½-4½ in., 35-40 petals, high-centered; foliage glossy, leathery; vigorous, compact growth; [Fandango × Pinocchio]

Cathcart Bedder HT, op, 1939, Austin & McAslan; flowers salmon-shrimp-pink; foliage bronze; vigorous, bushy growth

Cathedral F, ab, 1973, McGredy, Sam IV; flowers apricot shading salmon, 4-5 in., 22-25 petals, borne in small clusters, slight anise fragrance; foliage glossy, olive-green; growth bushy, medium, compact; [Little Darling × (Goldilocks × Irish Mist)]; int. as Coventry Cathedral, McGredy & Son, 1972; Gold Star of the South Pacific, Palmerston North, NZ, 1974, Gold Medal, Portland, 1974

Cathedral City – See **Domstadt Fulda**, F

Cathedral Peak HT, w, J&P; int. in 1995

Cathedral Splendour F, op, Harkness, R.; flowers rich, satiny pink, 4-5 cm., 24 petals, high-centered, borne on long stems, intense fragrance; dark green foliage; growth quick, to 4-5 ft.; int. in 1995

Catherine Anne Min, w, 1999, Goodall, G. T.; flowers medium, dbl., borne in small clusters; foliage medium size, medium green, semi-glossy; numerous prickles; bushy, tall (3 ft.) growth; [Rise 'n' Shine × City of London]

Catherine Bell Cl HP, pb, 1877, Bell & Son

Catherine Blackburn Pol, pb, Matthews, W.J.

Catherine Bonnard B, dp, 1871, Guillot fils; flowers cerise pink, medium, full; non-remontant; foliage dull green; numerous prickles; sometimes classed as HCh

Catherine Cookson HT, lp, 1987, Greensitt, J.A.; flowers large, full, moderate fragrance; foliage large, dark green, glossy; bushy growth; [Gavotte × King's Ransom]; int. by Nostell Priory Rose Gardens, 1985

Catherine de Würtemberg M, lp, 1843, Robert; bud well mossed; flowers soft pink, large, very dbl., globular; vigorous growth; sometimes attributed to Vibert

Catherine Deneuve HT, op, Meilland; flowers rose with light salmon, 20-25 petals, high-centered, borne mostly singly; good repeat; foliage glossy; vigorous, compact (3 ft.) growth; int. in 1981

Catherine Frances HT, lp, 2001, Jacobs, Mrs. Margaret; flowers pale pink, 14 cm., dbl., borne mostly solitary, intense fragrance; foliage medium size, medium green, glossy; prickles 7 mm., moderate; growth bushy, medium (120 cm.); garden decorative, exhibition; [Mt. Shasta × (Apogee × Ena Harkness)]

Catherine Ghislaine D, m, 1885; flowers violet-pink, fading to white, small, semi-dbl., moderate fragrance

Catherine Graham HT, pb, 2007, Ballin, Don; flowers light pink, darker at center, greenish-yellow petal hinge, 4-5 in., full, borne mostly solitary; foliage large, medium green, semi-glossy; prickles small to medium, slightly hooked angled down, light green; growth upright, tall (5-6 ft.); garden decoration, exhibition; [sport of Izy]

Catherine Guelda S, m, 2006, Zlesak, David C.; flowers 2½ in., full, borne in small clusters; foliage medium size, medium green, matte; prickles moderate; growth upright, medium; [Polyantha seedling × Therese Bugnet]; int. in 2006; Silver Certificate, ARS/ARC

Catherine Guillot B, dp, 1860, Guillot fils; flowers carmine-rose, large, dbl.; vigorous growth; [Louise Odier × unknown]

Catherine Langeais HT, mr, 1965, Hémeray-Aubert; flowers carmine-red, well-formed, 46 petals, high-centered; vigorous, upright growth; [Michèle Meilland × Berthe Mallerin]

Catherine Marie HT, mp, 1991, Wambach, Alex A.; bud pointed; flowers medium to shell pink, 26 petals, high-centered, intense fragrance; foliage medium size, medium green, semi-glossy; [Pristine × Captain Harry Stebbings]; int. in 1995

Catherine McAuley F, dy, Bear Creek Gardens; int. in 1993

Catherine Mermet T, lp, 1869, Guillot et Fils; bud well-shaped; flowers flesh-pink, edges tinted lilac-pink, large, dbl.; vigorous growth

Catherine Mermet, Climbing Cl T, lp, 1913, Cant, F.

Catherine Nelson LCl, mp; int. by Nelson's Florida Roses, 2005

Catherine Pericard F, Pineau; int. in 1981

Catherine Seyton HEg, lp, 1894, Penzance; flowers soft pink, with prominent yellow stamens, single, moderate fragrance; non-recurrent; foliage fragrant (apple); vigorous growth; int. by Keynes, Williams & Co.

Catherine Soupert HP, w, 1879, Lacharme, F.; flowers white, washed peach-pink, large, full; [Jules Margottin × unknown]

Catherine II Ch, lp, 1832, Laffay, M.; flowers flesh pink, medium, full

Catherine von Wurtemburg M, m, 1843, Robert

Cathie HT, m, 1999, Priestly, James L.; flowers mauve, outer petals edges shaded light red, large, full; foliage medium size, dark green, dull; upright, tall (4 ft.) growth; [Paradise × unknown]

Cathie Irwin Gr, ob, Kordes

Cathrine Kordes HT, dr, 1930, Kordes; bud long, pointed, blood-red, shaded black; flowers dark scarlet, large, dbl.; foliage dark (blood-red when young), leathery; very vigorous growth; [(Mme Caroline Testout × Willowmere) × Sensation]; int. by H&S

Cathrine Kordes, Climbing Cl HT, dr, 1938, Krohn; flowers crimson, reverse lighter, 5 in., dbl., globular; int. by Kordes

Cathy Anne HT, r, 1990, Wilson, George D.; bud pointed; flowers 25 petals, high-centered, borne singly; foliage small, dark green; prickles long, slender, red; long, straight stems; medium growth; [Judith Morton × Sylvia]

Catinat HGal, m, 1838, Vibert; flowers violet, spotted with purple, medium, full

Catinat HP, mr, 1874, Oger

Cato HMult, lp, 1904, Gratama; bud crimson red; flowers pink-yellow, 2 in., dbl., borne in clusters of 20-25; foliage shallowly dentate, dark green, glossy; prickles small, recurved

Catorce de Abril HT, yb, 1932, Padrosa; flowers yellow streaked red

Catriona Annette LCl, pb; int. in 2000

Cat's Meow F, ob, 1996, Desmet, Paul; flowers medium orange, petal base medium yellow, bright orange, buff, large, 29-31 petals, slight fragrance; foliage medium size, dark green, semi-glossy; numerous prickles; growth upright, tall (40 in.); [Colour Wonder × unknown]; int. by Desling Farms

Cauldron HT, pb, 1970, Waterhouse Nursery; flowers rose-pink to yellow, 4½ in., 23 petals, moderate fragrance; foliage glossy, dark; RULED EXTINCT 6/83 ARM

Cauldron S, mp, 1983, Holliger, Franc; flowers small, 5 petals, slight fragrance; foliage medium size, mid-green, matte; upright growth; [*R. rubrifolia* × *R. nutkana*]

Cauvery HT, dr, Kasturi; flowers medium, non-fading blackish crimson, ruffled petals, dbl.; int. in 1973

Cavalcade F, rb, 1950, Verschuren-Pechtold; bud ovoid; flowers oxblood-red and yellow, changing daily to crimson, carmine and silvery pink, 32 petals, intense fruity fragrance; foliage glossy, dark; vigorous, bushy growth; int. by Stuart

Cavalcade, Climbing Cl F, rb, 1957, Gandy, Douglas L.

Cavalier HT, ob, 1939, Samtmann Bros.; flowers burnt-orange to cream-buff, dbl.; [sport of Mrs Franklin D. Roosevelt]

Cavallii – See **Ravellae**, HSpn

Cavriglia HT, Fineschi, G.; int. in 1989

Cayenne HT, ob, 1975, Warriner, William A.; bud short, pointed; flowers deep orange, 3-4 in., 38 petals, slight fragrance; upright growth; PP3779; [South Seas × seedling]; int. by J&P, 1976

Cayetana Stuart HT, my, 1931, Dot, Pedro; bud long, pointed; flowers very large, dbl., cupped; foliage dark, glossy; very vigorous, bushy growth; [Isabel Llorach × (Constance × Sunburst)]; int. by C-P; Gold Medal, Bagatelle, 1930

Cechoslavia HT, w, 1921, Berger, V.; flowers milky white suffused salmon-carmine, center golden yellow, dbl.; [Pharisaer × Mme Antoine Mari]; int. by A. Berger

Cecil HT, my, 1926, Cant, B. R.; flowers golden yellow, 4 in., 5 petals, borne in large clusters; bushy growth

Cecil, Climbing Cl HT, my, 1940, Chaffin; int. by Armstrong Nursery

Cecil Earl S, w, J. B. Williams; flowers 5 petals, slight fragrance; foliage dark green; growth to 4 × 3 ft.; int. by Hortico, Inc., 2005

Cécile Brünner – See **Mlle Cécile Brünner**, Pol

Cécile Brünner, Climbing – See **Mlle Cécile Brünner, Climbing**, Cl Pol

Cecile Brunner, Everblooming Climbing Cl Pol, lp, Siskiyou; flowers delicate, soft pink, sweetheart size, 2 in., 18 petals, moderate pepper/spice fragrance; vigorous growth, 14-20 ft.; int. in 1996

Cecile Custers HT, pb, 1914, Leenders, M.; flowers lilac-rose, reverse deep rose-pink, dbl.; [Mme Abel Chatenay × Violet Liddell]

Cecile Lens Min, mp

Cecile Mann HT, mr, 1939, Clark, A.; vigorous growth; [Mrs Albert Nash × seedling]; int. by Brundrett

Cécile Ratinckx HT, my, 1924, Vandevelde; flowers coppery yellow, large, full; foliage glossy; [Louise Catherine Breslau × Mme Edouard Herriot]

Cécile Verlet HT, yb, 1926, Walter, L.; flowers yellow, passing to rose-pink; [Marianna Rolfs × Nordlicht]

Cécile Walter HT, op, 1926, Mallerin, C.; bud long, pointed; flowers coral-pink to coppery pink, base gold, very large, 28 petals, cupped; foliage rich green, leathery; vigorous growth; [(Mme Mélanie Soupert × Mme Edouard Herriot) × seedling]; int. by C-P

Cecilia S, pb, 1980, James, John; bud globular, pointed; flowers light pink blended darker pink, 25 petals, carnation-like, borne singly, moderate spicy fragrance; foliage small, pointed, glossy; prickles hooked; vigorous, compact, bushy growth; [(*R. wichurana* × Baronne Prevost) × (*R.* × *odorata*)]

Cecilia 89 F, ab, Hannemann, F.; [Oz Gold × Eye Paint]; int. by The Rose Paradise, 1992

Cecilio Rodriguez HT, dr, 1950, Camprubi, C.; bud long, pointed; flowers dark velvety red, large, dbl., high-centered; foliage dark; strong stems; very vigorous growth; [Tassin × Eugenio d'Ors]

Cecilitas Min, lp

Cecil's Bright Apricot HT, ab, Godman; int. in 1996

Cecily Gibson F, rb, 1991, Everitt, Derrick; bud ovoid; flowers currant red, yellow base, medium, 35 petals, cupped, borne in sprays of 3-6, slight to moderate fragrance; foliage medium to large, dark green, glossy; bushy, medium to tall growth; [Southampton × (Arthur Bell × Maigold × Glenfiddich)]; int. in 1990

Cecily Phippen Marks S, lp, 2007, Williams, J. B.; flowers medium, dbl., borne in small clusters, moderate fragrance; foliage medium size, dark green, semi-glossy; prickles ¼ in., moderate; growth compact, medium; [Rose Parade × seedling]

Cedar Crest College F, dy, 1992, Williams, J. Benjamin; flowers deep golden yellow, medium, 6-14 petals, borne in small clusters; foliage medium size, dark green, glossy; few prickles; medium (3-4 ft.), upright, bushy growth; [Ivory Fashion × Sunsprite]; int. in 1993

Cedric Adams HT, dr, 1949, Brownell; bud ovoid; flowers scarlet to carmine, large, dbl., high-centered, moderate fragrance; foliage dark, bronze; vigorous growth; [Pink Princess × Crimson Glory]

Cee Dee Moss S, pb, 1991, Moore, Ralph S.; bud pointed; flowers pink with occasional white stripe, lighter reverse, ages lighter, 2½-3¼ in., dbl., cupped, loose, borne in sprays of 3-5; foliage medium size, light green, glossy; bushy, spreading, medium growth; [Carolyn Dean × seedling]; int. by Sequoia Nursery, 1990

Cearcee HT, ob, Gokhale; int. in 1995

Cel Blau – See **Blue Sky**, HT

Celamire – See **Sophie de Bavière**, A

Celeb S, op, McCann, Sean; flowers soft orange pink, 3 in., dbl., slight fragrance; repeatbloom; growth upright, bushy, medium (4-5 ft.); int. by Ashdown Roses, 2004

Celebrate America HT, mr, 1991, Rosen Tantau; flowers crimson red, 4-4¾ in., 45-55 petals, high-centered, borne usually singly; foliage large, medium green, semi-glossy; upright, spreading, medium growth; PP7333; [seedling × seedling]; int. by Bear Creek Gardens, 1990

Celebrate Life Min, ob, 2005, Moore, Ralph S.; flowers orange, reverse orange/pink, 1½ in., semi-dbl., borne in small clusters, slight fragrance; foliage medium size, medium green, semi-glossy; no prickles; bushy, medium (15 in.) growth; containers, borders; [Golden Gardens × Sequoia Ruby]; int. by Sequoia Nurs., 2005

Celebration F, op, 1962, Dickson, Patrick; flowers light salmon red with ivory disc, reverse peach, 3 in., 30 petals, cupped, borne in clusters, slight fragrance; foliage light green; vigorous, bushy growth; [Dickson's Flame × Circus]; int. by A. Dickson

Celebration – See **Myriam**, HT

Celebration Days HT, mp, Thames Valley Rose Growers; flowers shell pink, color deepening at the edges; int. in 1987

Celebration 2000 – See **Rabble Rouser**, S

Celebrity HT, pb, 1945, E.G. Hill, Co.; bud pointed; flowers pink, base shaded yellow, 6-7 in., 30-35 petals, high-centered, moderate spicy fragrance; foliage leathery, dark; vigorous, bushy growth; RULED EXTINCT 1/88; [Golden Rapture × Carmelita]

Celebrity HT, dy, 1988, Weeks, O.L.; bud pointed, large; flowers deep yellow, aging clear yellow, 4½-5 in., 30-35 petals, high-centered, borne usually singly, moderate fruity fragrance; foliage large, dark green, glossy; prickles pointed slightly downward, small, yellow-brown; upright, bushy, medium growth; PP7264; [(Sunbonnet × Mister Lincoln) × Yello Yo Yo]; int. by Weeks Roses

Celebrity HT, dr, Select; flowers 11 cm., 30-35 petals, high-centered, borne mostly singly; greenhouse rose; int. by Terra Nigra BV, 2003

Celery-Leaved Rose – See ***R. centifolia bipinnata*** (Thory), C

Céleste – See **Celestial**, A

Céleste – See **Grand Sultan**, HGal

Céleste Blanche – See **Celestial**, A

Celeste Mahley F, pb, 1974, Byrum; bud long, pointed; flowers medium, dbl., slight fragrance; foliage leathery; vigorous, upright, bushy growth; [Seventeen × Gemini]; int. by J.H. Hill Co., 1972

Celestial A, lp, before 1810; flowers light blush, golden stamens, large, semi-dbl. to dbl., cupped, intense sweet fragrance; non-recurrent; foliage bluish, large, with 5-7 leaflets; vigorous (to 6 ft.) growth; from Holland; possibly introduced to France by Charpentier

Celestial HSpn, lp, about 1854; flowers pale flesh, small, dbl., intense fragrance; low growth; [*R. rubiginosa* × *R. spinosissima*]; sometimes listed as HEg

Celestial HT, lp, 1924, Myers & Samtmann; flowers light pink, edged paler, dbl.; [sport of Premier]

Celestial Star F, or, 1969, Pal, Dr. B.P.; bud ovoid; flowers dbl., borne in clusters; foliage glossy; vigorous, compact growth; int. by Indian Agric. Research Inst., 1965

Célestine Ch, w, about 1825, Laffay; flowers pure white, full

Célestine HGal, cp, before 1836, Vibert

Célestine HP, mp, before 1848; flowers bright pink, full, cupped

Célestine D, lp, before 1826, Coquerel

Celestis – See **Celestial**, A

Celia HT, mp, 1906, Paul, W.; flowers silky pink, large, full

Celia HT, mr; int. in 2003

Celia Walker F, rb, 1962, Fletcher; flowers cherry-red, reverse silver, 3 in., 15-20 petals, borne in clusters; foliage dark, glossy; vigorous, upright growth; [Alain × Golden Scepter]; int. by Tucker & Sons, 1962

Celica HT, mp, 1985, Meilland, Mrs. Marie-Louise; flowers large, 20 petals; foliage medium size, dark, semi-glossy; upright growth; PP5683; [seedling × ((Zambra × (Baccará × White Knight) × Golden Garnette) × seedling)]; int. by Meilland Et Cie, 1981

Celientje HT, ly; int. in 1997

Célina M, m, before 1843, Hardy; bud heavily mossed; flowers reddish-purple, center occasionally streaked white, large, dbl.

Celina S, dy, Noack, Werner; bud pointed; flowers lemon yellow, fading as they age, 2 in., 10-15 petals, cupped, borne in large sprays, slight fragrance; free-flowering; foliage medium size, light green, glossy; prickles average, 5 mm., slightly curved down, brown; vigorous (60-80 cm.), spreading, groundcover growth; hips small, round, green with reddish tint; PP10527; [Immensee × Westfalengold]; int. in 1997

Célina Dubos D, w, 1849, Dubos; flowers pale pink, nearly white, intense fragrance; sometimes recurrent bloom; [probably a sport of Rose du Roi]; Damask Perpetual

Céline B, mp, about 1835, Laffay, M.; flowers pale rose, large, dbl., cupped, borne in large clusters; does not repeat; very vigorous growth

Céline – See **Célina**, M

Céline HCh, m, 1855, Robert; flowers carmine-purple

Céline Bourdier P, mr, 1852, Robert; flowers red shaded with lilac, 2½ in., full

Céline Briant M, lp, 1853, Robert; flowers 5-6 cm., full, rosette, borne in clusters of 8-12; freely remontant

Céline Delbard F, ob, 1986, Delbard, G.; flowers salmon, silver reverse, large, 23 petals, cupped, borne in clusters, no fragrance; recurrent; foliage dark green; bushy, rounded growth; [seedling × (Milrose × Legion d'Honneur)]; int. in 1983

Celine Dion S, ob, 2000, Williams, J. Benjamin; flowers bright orange with lighter reverse, 3-3½ in., single, borne in large clusters, moderate fragrance; foliage medium size, dark green, semi-glossy, disease-free; prickles few, very small, curved down; growth compact, bushy (2½-3 ft.); bedding, containers, cutting; hardy; [Fifth Ave. × Tropicana]; int. by J.C. Bakker & Sons, 2000

Céline Dubois – See **Célina Dubos**, D

Céline Forestier N, ly, 1842, Trouillard; flowers pale yellow, buff, with slight touches of pink, darker at center, 6-8 cm., dbl., frequently quartered, borne singly or in small clusters, moderate fragrance; repeat blooming; foliage dark, glossy; vigorous (to 6 ft.) growth; [Champneys' Pink Cluster × a Tea rose]; probably re-introduced as Lusiadas by da Costa (Portugal)

Céline Gonod B, mr, 1861, Gonod; flowers silvery red, edged bright pink, full, globular

Célinette Chataigne B, mp, 1880, Brassac; flowers medium

Cels – See **Celsiana**, D

Cels Multiflora – See **Cels Multiflore**, T

Cels Multiflore T, lp, 1836, Hardy/Cels; flowers flesh pink with darker center, medium, full, cupped; very recurrent

Celsiana D, lp, before 1817; flowers silky pale pink, petals crinkled, with golden stamens, 4 in., semi-dbl., borne in cluster of 3-4, moderate fragrance; non-recurrent; foliage oval, smooth, grayish-green, reverse lighter, fragrant; vigorous, upright (4-5 ft.) growth; from Holland; introduced to France by Cels

Celtic Cream HT, my, Dickson; buds pointed, lime lemon; flowers large, rich golden cream, moderate fragrance; growth medium to tall; int. in 1999

Celtic Honey S, ab, Dickson; buds apricot salmon; flowers non-fading honey toned apricot, dbl., exhibition; growth medium to tall; int. in 2000

Celtic Pride – See **Marjorie Marshall**, S

Cendres de Napoléon B, m, 1841, Béluze; flowers lilac pink with violet, medium, full

Cendrillon HT, mp, 1951, Gaujard; bud very large; flowers salmon, dbl.; foliage leathery; very vigorous, upright growth

Cent Feuilles – See **Cabbage Rose**, C

Centenaire de Lourdes F, mp, 1958, Delbard, G.; flowers soft rose, 3½-4 in., semi-dbl., borne in clusters of 5-10; vigorous, bushy growth; [(Frau Karl Druschki × seedling) × seedling]

Centenaire de Lourdes, Climbing Cl F, mp, Delbard; flowers large, dbl.; glossy, dark green foliage; few prickles; growth to 3 m.; int. by Georges Delbard SA, 2005

Centenaire de Lourdes Rose – See **Centenaire de Lourdes**, F

Centenaire de Lourdes Rouge F, mr, Delbard; flowers borne in clusters, intense jasmine fragrance; good rebloom; bushy growth, 50-100 cm.; int. by Georges Delbard SA, 1992

Centenaire du Tour de France HT, my, Delbard; int. by Georges Delbard SA, 2004

Centenaire du Vesinet Gr, op, 1979, Pineau; bud pointed; flowers salmon-orange, 3 in., 32 petals, slight fragrance; vigorous, upright growth; [Sonia × Prominent]; int. by Searn, 1977

Centenary F, dp, 2006; flowers semi-dbl., borne in small clusters; bushy, medium (100 cm.) growth; int. as NDR 1 - Radio Niedersachsen, W. Kordes' Söhne, 1996

Centenary College HT, dr, 1983, Christensen, Jack E.; flowers deep red, large, 35 petals, intense fragrance; foliage large, medium green, matte; vigorous, upright, tall growth; [Angel Face × Typhoo Tea]; int. by Armstrong Nursery, 1982

Centenary of Federation – See **Betty Boop**, F

Centennaire de Lourdes – See **Centenaire de Lourdes**, F

Centennial HT, ob, 1953, Mallerin, C.; bud ovoid; flowers peach-red, reverse orange-buff, 4-4½ in., 40-45 petals, high-centered, moderate fragrance; foliage rich green; vigorous, bushy growth; PP1384; [seedling × Orange Nassau]; int. by J&P

Centennial Gr, ab, Ping Lim; flowers apricot to light yellow, fading to creamy white, 2½ in., 22 petals, high-centered, borne in clusters; recurrent; foliage bronze tinged; stems long; low (2-3 ft.) growth; int. by Easy Elegance Roses, 2006

Centennial Gold HT, my

Centennial Miss Min, dr, 1952, Moore, Ralph S.; flowers deep wine-red, base tinged white, 1 in., 60 petals, moderate fragrance; foliage small, dark, leathery, glossy; no prickles; dwarf (10-12 in.), bushy growth; PP1301; [Oakington Ruby × Oakington Ruby]; int. by Sequoia Nursery

Centennial Rose S, dy, Ludwig; int. by Ludwig's Roses, 2003

Centennial Star HT, yb, 1996, Meilland International SA; bud conical; flowers yellow with pink edge, 4¾ in., 50 petals, borne usually singly, slight fragrance; free-flowering; foliage large, dark green, semi-glossy; numerous prickles; bushy, medium (3 ft.) growth; PP10668; [(Peace × Landora) × Kings Ransom]; int. by Conard-Pyle Co., 1996

Centennial Sweetheart Cl F, mr, 1960, Greene; bud globular; flowers bright red, large, 25 petals, borne in large clusters, intense fragrance; foliage glossy, light green; very vigorous growth; PP1871; [sport of Alain]; int. in 1959

Center Gold Min, dy, 1981, Saville, F. Harmon; bud pointed; flowers deep yellow, sometimes near white, 60 petals, high-centered, borne singly or up to 12 per cluster, moderate spicy fragrance; foliage glossy, textured; prickles long, thin, slanted downward; upright, compact growth; [Rise 'n' Shine × Kiskadee]; int. by American Rose Foundation; AOE, ARS, 1982

Centerpiece Min, mr, 1985, Saville, F. Harmon; flowers deep medium red, small, 35 petals, high-centered; foliage small, dark, semi-glossy; bushy growth; PP5692; [(Sheri Anne × Tamango) × (Sheri Anne × (Yellow Jewel × Tamango))]; int. by Nor'East Min. Roses, 1985; AOE, ARS, 1985

Centfeuilles Anglais – See **Rubra**, C

Centfeuilles de Bordeaux – See **Petite de Hollande**, C

Centfeuilles Foliacée – See **Foliacée**, C, before 1808

Centfeuilles Nain – See **Pompon Varin**, C

Centfeuilles Roses – See **Centifolia Rosea**, HP

Centifolia a Fleurs Doubles Violettes C, m

Centifolia d'Avranches – See **Duchesse de Grammont**, D

Centifolia Foliacea C, mp, 1810

Centifolia Minima – See **Rouletii**, Ch

Centifolia Muscosa – See **Communis**, M

Centifolia Rosea HP, mp, 1863, Touvais; flowers bright rose, large, cupped; foliage crinkled, light green wood with many red prickles; vigorous growth; [La Reine × unknown]

Centifolia Unica – See **Rubra**, C

Centifolia Variegata – See **Variegata**, C

Central Park S, ab, 1995, Olesen, Pernille & Mogens N.; flowers peach, bright yellow stamens, fading white, 2 in., dbl., borne in small clusters; foliage small, medium green, glossy; few prickles; low (2 ft.), spreading growth; PP9665; int. by Young's American Rose Nursery, 1995

Centre Court HT, w, 1964, Barter; flowers white, center tan, well-shaped, 4 in., 38 petals; foliage dark; vigorous growth; [Eden Rose × Ena Harkness]

Centre Stage S, lp, 2000, Warner, Chris; flowers light pink with paler reverse, small, single, borne in large clusters, slight fragrance; foliage small, medium green, glossy; prickles small, curved, moderate in number; growth spreading, very low; groundcover; [Eyeopener × (*R. luciae* × Laura Ashley)]; int. by Warner's Roses, 2001

Centrex Gold F, my, 1977, Smith, E.; flowers 3 in., 25 petals, slight fragrance; foliage matte, green; [Alison Wheatcroft × Chinatown]; int. by Wheatcroft, 1975

Centro de Lectura HT, mr, 1959, Dot, M.; flowers crimson, 40 petals; foliage glossy, bright green; long strong stems; vigorous growth; [Texas Centennial × Peace]

CentrO-Rose S, mr, Tantau; bud pointed ovoid; flowers strong red, 6 cm., 20-22 petals, high-centered, borne in clusters of 6-15, no fragrance; recurrent; fresh green, glossy foliage; prickles 5 mm., hooked downward, brown; compact (2 ft.), bushy, groundcover growth; no hips; PP12190; [Footloose × seedling]; int. by Rosen Tantau, 2002

Centurio HT, dr, 1978, Verschuren, Ted; flowers lasting well; moderate, bushy growth; [Orangeade × Baccará]; int. by Verschuren, 1974

Centurion F, dr, 1976, Mattock; flowers blood-red, shaded crimson, 3 in., 30 petals, slight fragrance; foliage glossy, dark; [Evelyn Fison × seedling]; int. in 1975

Century Sunset HT, dr, 1999, Tantau; flowers 4½-5 in., full, borne mostly singly, slight fragrance; foliage large, dark green, semi-glossy; prickles moderate; upright, medium (2-2½ ft.) growth; int. as Herz As, Rosen Tantau, 1998

Century 21 HT, lp, Morey, Dr. Dennison; bud ovoid; flowers shell-pink, reverse slightly darker, large, dbl., high-centered, moderate fragrance; foliage glossy; vigorous growth; [Condessa de Sástago × Soeur Thérèse]; int. by J&P, 1962

Century Two HT, mp, 1971, Armstrong, D.L.; bud long, pointed; flowers large, hot pink, 5 in., 30-35 petals, high-centered, borne singly, moderate damask fragrance; foliage leathery; vigorous, upright, bushy growth; PP3340; [Charlotte Armstrong × Duet]; int. by Armstrong Nursery

Cera F, r, DVP Melle; flowers deep pink to light red, dbl., borne in large clusters; recurrent; foliage dark green, disease-resistant; growth to 3 ft.; [Melglory × Guirlande d'Amour]; int. in 1998; Golden Rose, The Hague, 2006, Gold Medal, Lyon, 2000, Gold Medal, Hradec Kralove, 2000

Ceremony F, w, 1979, Lens, Louis; bud cupped; flowers pure white, 2½ in., 40-45 petals; foliage leathery; very bushy growth; [Tiara × Pascali]; int. in 1970

Ceres HMsk, lp, 1914, Pemberton; flowers pale blush, tinted light yellow, stamens bright yellow, semi-dbl.; profuse seasonal bloom; shrub growth

Ceres HT, ob, 1922, Spek; flowers deep orange, center salmon, large, full; [Sunburst × Mme Edmond Rostand]

Ceres Min, or, Tantau; int. in 1994

Cerise – See **Belle Rosine**, S

Cerise N, pb; flowers bright pink, mixed with cherry and coral-red, large, full, globular

Cerise HT, dp, 1945, Tantau; flowers deep pink, large, 25 petals; foliage dark, leathery; vigorous, upright growth; [Crimson Glory × Sterling]

Cerise S, dp, Delbard

Cerise Bouquet S, dp, 1958, Kordes; flowers cerise-crimson, semi-dbl., loose, then flat, moderate fragrance; foliage small, grayish; open, arching growth; [*R. multibracteata* × Crimson Glory]; a different rose may have been introduced under this name by Tantau, about 1937, but Kordes confirms this one is theirs

Cerise d'Angers Ch, about 1834, from Angers

Cerise Dawn HT, dr, 1989, Marciel, Stanley G.; bud urn-shaped; flowers magenta, reverse Tyrian purple, aging without discoloration, large, 30 petals, globular, slight damask fragrance; foliage large, dark green, semi-glossy; prickles declining and well spaced apart, pea green; upright, tall growth; [Carina × Angel Face]; int. by DeVor Nurseries, Inc.

Cerise d'Enghien HGal, mp, about 1830, Parmentier; flowers bright carmine, medium, full

Cerise d'Orlin HGal, dp; flowers deep pink, reverse silver, loose, semi-dbl.

Cerise Rouge S, mr

Cerise Talisman HT, dp, 1933, Clarke Bros.; flowers cerise; [sport of Talisman]

Cérisette la Jolie – See **Surpasse Tout**, HGal

Cernousek HT, Strnad

Certinia S, w, Noack; flowers creamy white, occasional rose pink petal edge, 8 cm., dbl., borne in clusters; recurrent; vigorous (5 ft.) growth; int. by Noack Rosen, 2006

Cervanek HT, or, Strnad

Cervanky Cl HT, dy, 1935, Böhm, J.; flowers large, dbl.

Cervantes S, mr

Cervena Gloria Dei HT, mr, Strnad

Cervena Super Star HT, dr, Strnad; int. in 1976

Cervia – See **Floral Fairy Tale**, F

Cerys Ann HT, yb, 1997, Guest, M.M.; flowers medium, very dbl., borne mostly singly; foliage large, dark green, glossy; some prickles; bushy, medium (30 in.)growth; [Fulton Mackay × Freedom]

César S, yb, Meilland; flowers creamy yellow with pink, very large, dbl.; int. in 1993

César Beccaria HGal, w, 1855, Robert; flowers white, striped and spotted lilac and pink, large, dbl., flat

Cesar E. Chavez HT, dr, 2004, Zary, Keith W.; flowers 5 in., 30-35 petals, borne mostly solitary, slight fragrance; foliage large, dark green, glossy; prickles 5-7 mm., hooked slightly downward; growth upright, tall (6 ft.), specimen, garden decoration; PP14104; [Olympiad × Ingrid Bergman]; int. by Jackson & Perkins Wholesale, Inc., 2002

César Jules B, dp, 1865, Verdier, E.; flowers dark cherry pink, large, full

Ceská Pohadka Pol, rb, 1933, Böhm, J.; flowers red, salmon, rose and white, borne in clusters; very vigorous, dwarf growth; [sport of Golden Salmon]

Ceské 'Praci cest' LCl, Vecera, L.; flowers small, dbl.; prickles large; int. in about 1970

Césonie M, dp, 1859, Moreau et Robert; flowers carmine-crimson, large, dbl., borne in large clusters; some repeat; compact growth

Césonie P, dp, before 1836, Vibert; flowers dark rose, large, full

Cestiflora HSpn, ly; flowers sulfur-yellow; early bloom; foliage finely divided; growth to 3-4 ft.; hips glossy, black

Cetina – See **Setina**, Cl HCh

Cevennes – See **Heidesommer**, F

Cha Cha Min, ob, 1983, Cocker, James; flowers orange-red with yellow eye, dbl., slight fragrance; foliage small, medium green, semi-glossy; bushy growth; [(Wee Man × Manx Queen) × Darling Flame]; int. by Cocker & Sons, 1983

Chablis HT, w, 1984, Weeks, O.L.; flowers creamy white, medium-large, dbl., high-centered, slight fragrance; foliage large, medium green, matte; upright growth; [seedling × Louisiana]; int. by Weeks Wholesale Rose Growers, 1984

Chacita F, dr, 1947, Boerner; bud ovoid, globular; flowers deep red, medium, dbl., cupped, borne in clusters; foliage dark, leathery; vigorous, bushy growth; [Pinocchio × Crimson Glory]

Chacok – See **Pigalle**, F

Chaim Soutine HT, pb, Delbard; bud longs, pointed; flowers with variations of deep pink and white on every petal, large, dbl., high-centered, borne mostly singly, no fragrance; growth vigorous, 4-5 ft.; PP11502; int. in 2001

Chaldean HT, yb, 2002, Cowlishaw, Frank; flowers yellow with orange reverse, 5 in., full, borne mostly solitary, slight fragrance; foliage medium green, semi-glossy; prickles moderate, up to 10 mm., curved and hooked; growth upright, medium (3 ft.); bedding; [Fellowship × Summer Love]

Chalice HT, ab, 1960, Verschuren, H. A.; bud ovoid, pointed; flowers apricot-yellow, 5½-6 in., 55-60 petals, high-centered, intense fragrance; foliage leathery, glossy; vigorous, upright growth; PP1961; [Orange Delight × Golden Rapture]; int. by J&P, 1959

Chalice Well HMult, pb, McLeod, J.; [*R. multiflora* × unknown]; int. by Honeysuckle Cottage, 1995

Challenge F, dr, 1962, Fletcher; flowers deep blood-red, 2 in., 20 petals, camellia-like, borne in clusters; foliage dark; bushy, low growth; [Alain × Pinocchio]; int. by Tucker & Sons, 1962

Challenger HT, dr, 1938, Cant, B. R.; flowers dark crimson, very large, dbl., high-centered; foliage leathery, dark; long stems; vigorous, bushy growth; RULED EXTINCT, 6/89

Challenger HT, dr, 1989, Tracy, Daniel; bud ovoid; flowers dark red, reverse medium red, medium, 25 petals, high-centered, urn-shaped, borne in sprays of 2-3, moderate fragrance; foliage medium size, semi-glossy; prickles angled downward, small, orange blend; upright, medium growth; hips pear-shaped, small, orange blend; [Jacqueline × seedling]; int. by DeVor Nurseries, Inc., 1987

Challis Gold HT, dy, 1987, Greensitt, J.A.; flowers medium, 15-20 petals, high-centered; foliage medium size, medium green, glossy; spreading growth; [sport of Gold Dot]; int. by Nostell Priory Rose Gardens, 1983

Chalom HT, Moreira da Silva, A.

Chamba Princess F, op, 1971, Pal, Dr. B. P.; flowers salmon-pink, open, medium, semi-dbl., slight fragrance; intermittent bloom; foliage leathery; moderate, bushy growth; int. by Indian Council of Ag. Research, 1969

Chambe di Kali HT, mp, 1984, Pal, Dr. B.P.; flowers large, 22 petals, high-centered, borne singly, slight fragrance; foliage large, dark, glossy; prickles green to brown; medium, compact growth; [Bewitched × seedling]; int. by K.S.G. Son's Roses, 1983

Chambord F, mp, 1960, Delforge; bud pointed; flowers pink, becoming darker, open, large, dbl., borne in clusters; foliage bronze; bushy growth; [Roquebrune × Queen Elizabeth]

Chambord F, my, Poulsen; flowers medium yellow, 8-10 cm., 25 petals, no fragrance; growth bushy, 60-100 cm.; PP16143

Chameleon – See **Émilie Gonin**, T

Chameleon HT, or, 1918, Dickson, A.; flowers flame, edged cerise; [Lyon Rose × unknown]

Chameleon Min, yb, Welsh, Eric; [Wee Beth × (Starina × unknown)]; int. by Biotech Plants Pty, Ltd., 1995

Chameleon – See **Pur Caprice**, S

Chami HMsk, mp, 1929, Pemberton; flowers bright rose-pink, stamens yellow, medium, single, intense fragrance; recurrent bloom; bushy growth

Chamisso HMult, pb, 1922, Lambert, P.; flowers flesh-pink, center yellowish-white to medium yellow, 5-6 cm., semi-dbl., borne in large clusters, moderate fragrance; profuse, recurrent bloom.; foliage bronze; long stems; vigorous, trailing growth; [Geheimrat Dr. Mittweg × Tip-Top]

Chamoïs – See **Comtesse de Chamoïs**, C

Chamois C, mp, before 1824, Mme Chamois

Chamoïs T, ly, 1869, Ducher; bud deep apricot; flowers fawn yellow, somtimes changing to coppery yellow, medium, semi-dbl.

Chamois Doré F, ab, 2000, Lens, Louis; flowers pale apricot, reverse lighter, 6 cm., dbl., borne in small clusters; recurrent; foliage medium size, medium green, semi-glossy; few prickles; bushy, low (60-70 cm.) growth; [LLX7952 × Goldtopaz]; int. by Louis Lens, 1990

Champ Weiland HT, mp, 1915, Weiland & Risch; flowers clear pink; foliage glowing, reddish; [sport of Killarney]

Champagne HT, yb, 1961, Lindquist; bud pointed, ovoid; flowers buff shaded apricot, 4-5 in., 28 petals, high-centered, moderate fragrance; foliage leathery, dark; vigorous, upright, bushy growth; PP2151; [Charlotte Armstrong × Duquesa de Peñaranda]; int. by Howard Rose Co., 1961

Champagne – See **Antique Silk**, F

Champagne Cocktail F, yb, 1983, Horner, Colin P.; flowers pale yellow, flecked and splashed pink, yellow reverse, medium, 20 petals, borne in clusters of 3-5, moderate fragrance; foliage medium size, medium green, glossy; bushy growth; [Old Master × Southampton]; int. in 1985; Gold Medal, Glasgow, 1990

Champagne Dream Min, ab; int. in 2004

Champagne Moment – See **Lions-Rose**, F

Champagne on Ice Min, r, Rasmussen; int. by Rasmussen's Nursery, 2002

Champagne Patio Min, ab; int. in 2003

Champagne Pearl F, ab, W. Kordes Söhne; flowers large, apricot cream with a green shade as they age, dbl., borne in large clusters; int. in 1983

Champagne Time Min, ab, Benardella, Frank; int. in 1996

Champagner – See **Antique Silk**, F

Champagnerperle – See **Champagne Pearl**, F

Champion HT, yb, 1976, Fryer, Gareth; flowers yellow-cream, flushed red and pink, 7-8 in., 50-55 petals, moderate fragrance; foliage large, light; [Irish Gold × Whisky Mac]; int. by Fryer's Nursery, Ltd., 1976

Champion F, or, Noack, Werner; int. in 1988

Champion, Climbing Cl HT, yb, 1999, Kameyama, Yasushi; flowers yellow-cream, flushed red and pink, 3-3½ in., 50-55 petals, high-centered; foliage large, medium green; climbing (12 ft.) growth; [sport of Champion]; int. by La Vie en Rose Co., Ltd., 1998; Gold Medal, Japan (JRC), 1997

Champion of the World HP, mp, 1894, Woodhouse; flowers rose-pink, large, dbl.; seasonal bloom; vigorous growth; [Hermosa × Magna Charta]

Champlain HKor, dr, 1983, Svedja, Felicitas; flowers large, bright medium red with darker petal tips, 2½ in., 30 petals, borne in small clusters, slight fragrance; repeat bloom; foliage small, dark yellow-green; prickles straight, yellow-green; bushy growth, 3 ft.; hardy; [(*R. kordesii* × seedling) × (Red Dawn × Suzanne)]; int. by Agriculture Canada, 1983

Champneyana – See **Champneys' Pink Cluster**, N dbl.

Champneys' Bengal Rose Ch, mp, about 1800, Champneys

Champneys' Pink Cluster N, lp, before 1810, Champneys; flowers dbl., borne in large clusters, moderate musky-sweet fragrance; recurrent bloom; moderately vigorous growth; moderately hardy; [*R. moschata* × Parsons' Pink China]

Champneys' Rose – See **Champneys' Pink Cluster**, N dbl.

Champs de Mars HP, pb, 1867, Verdier, E.; flowers carmine, shaded violet, large, full

Champs-Elysées HT, dr, 1958, Meilland, F.; flowers rich crimson-red, large, 35 petals, cupped, slight fragrance; vigorous, bushy growth; [Monique × Happiness]; int. by URS, 1957; Gold Medal, Madrid, 1957

Champs-Elysées, Climbing Cl HT, dr, 1969, Meilland; [sport of Champs-Elysees]; int. by URS

Chancelier d'Angleterre HGal, mr, before 1836, Calvert; flowers bright red, medium, full

Chandelle F, lp, 1958, Lens; flowers light pink, reverse darker, well-formed, medium, dbl., borne in clusters; foliage bronze; vigorous, compact growth; [Gretel Greul × (Lady Sylvia × Fashion)]

Chanderi HT, lp, 1968, Singh, R. S.; bud long, pointed; flowers light pink, edged deeper, medium, dbl., high-centered, slight fragrance; foliage soft; moderate, upright, compact growth; [Peace × seedling]

Chandon Rose HT, pb, Delbard; int. in 2003

Chandos Beauty HT, pb; flowers medium pink in center, petals fading to light pink as they open, 40 petals, intense fruity & spicy fragrance; recurrent; growth to 3 ft.; int. by Harkness, 2005

Chandrama F, w, 1981, Division of Vegetable Crops and Floriculture; bud pointed; flowers 25 petals, borne in clusters of 3-6, slight fragrance; foliage dark; prickles straight, brown; spreading growth; [White Bouquet × Virgo]; int. in 1980

Chandrika Min, w, Kasturi; flowers greenish white to pure white, pompon, borne in clusters; int. by KSG Sons, 1978

Chanel HT, dp, Juneida; int. in 1995

Chanelle F, op, 1960, McGredy, Sam IV; flowers peach-pink shaded rose-pink, well-formed, 3 in., 20 petals, borne in clusters, moderate fragrance; foliage dark, glossy, pointed; vigorous, bushy growth; [Ma Perkins × (Fashion × Mrs William Sprott)]; int. by McGredy & Son, 1959; Gold Medal, Madrid, 1959

Change of Heart HT, pb, 2007, Zary, Keith W.; flowers medium pink, reverse white, 4½ in., full, borne mostly solitary; foliage medium size, dark green, glossy; prickles 8-10 mm., hooked, greyed-orange, moderate; growth upright, tall (5 ft.); [seedling × seedling]; int. by Jackson & Perkins Wholesale, Inc., 2007

Changeante – See **White Provence**, C

Changing My Habits Min, r, 2006, Hopper, Nancy; flowers light tan, aging to mauve, 1¾ in., very full, borne mostly solitary; foliage medium size, medium green, matte; prickles ½ in., tan, few; growth bushy, short (12 in.); [Winter Magic × Cafe Ole]; int. in 2006

Chanoine Tuaillon HT, dp, 1931, Gillot, F.; bud persian red; flowers carmine, very large, dbl., globular; very vigorous growth; [Betty Uprichard × Lucie Nicolas Meyer]

Chanson d'Été – See **Summer Song**, F

Chantal HT, w, 1958, Moulin-Epinay; bud long, ovoid; flowers ivory, center yellow, edged carmine, very large, 60 petals; vigorous, bushy, upright growth; [Mme Charles Sauvage × Carillon]

Chantal S, ab, Williams, J.B.; flowers soft apricot-pink with lighter center, golden stamens, semi-dbl., flat, moderate fragrance; recurrent; low (2 ft.) growth; int. by Hortico, Inc., 2006

Chantal Mérieux S, mp, Guillot-Massad; flowers very dbl., quartered; growth to ¾ m.; int. by Guillot-Massad, 2000

Chantana HT, pb, Umsawasdi, Dr. Theera; flowers 3-3½ in., full, borne mostly singly, intense fragrance; foliage medium size, medium green, matte; some prickles; tall, upright, bushy growth; [Azure Sea × Mister Lincoln]; int. in 1995

Chantebrise LCl, mr, Croix, P.; int. in 1969

Chanteclerc F, mr, 1956, Gaujard; flowers bright red, large; foliage bright green; bushy growth; [Peace × seedling]

Chantefleur F, op, Laperriere, L.; flowers rose-salmon; growth to 60-70 cm.; int. in 1958

Chantelle HT, ab, Kordes; flowers light apricot, pink tones on reverse, large, dbl., high-centered, borne mostly singly; recurrent; stems long; int. by W. Kordes Söhne, 2005

Chanterelle – See **Cynthia**, HT, 1976

Chantilly HT, or, 1964, Verschuren, A.; flowers orange to red-lead, 40 petals; foliage glossy, dark; strong stems; vigorous growth; [Baccará × seedling]; int. by van Engelen

Chantilly HT, w, Grandiflora Nurseries; int. in 2002

Chantilly Lace HT, m, 1979, deVor, Paul F.; bud long; flowers red-purple, 4-5 in., 35 petals, high-centered, intense fragrance; foliage glossy; vigorous growth; PP4665; [Blue Moon × Angel Face]; int. by DeVor Nurseries, Inc., 1978

Chantoli – See **Sunset Celebration**, HT

Chantré HT, ob, 1959, Kordes, R.; bud long, pointed; flowers orange and golden yellow, 5 in., 20-25 petals, high-centered, moderate fragrance; foliage dark, leathery; very vigorous, upright, bushy growth; [Fred Streeter × Antheor]; int. in 1958

Chantre, Climbing Cl HT, ob, 1974, Arora, B. R.; buds large, long pointed; flowers orange and golden yellow, large, very dbl., high-centered, borne singly; foliage medium size, dark green, leathery; growth vigorous, upright (300 cm.); [sport of Chantre]; int. by The Rosery, 1973

Châpeau de Napoléon – See **Crested Moss**, C

Chapel Bells S, lp, Williams, J.B.; flowers delicate pink, semi-dbl., slight fragrance; foliage glossy, dark green.; hardy to -20ºF; int. by Hortico, 2003

Chapelain d'Arenberg HGal, mp, before 1847, possibly Parmentier; flowers bright pink, medium

Chaperon Rouge F, mr, 1951, Vilmorin-Andrieux; bud globular; flowers velvety crimson, center darker, open, medium, very dbl.; foliage glossy, bronze, dark; vigorous, upright growth; [Crimson Glory × (Baby Chateau × seedling)]

Chaplin's Crimson Glow HWich, rb, 1930, Chaplin Bros.; flowers deep crimson, base white, large, dbl.

Chaplin's Pink Climber HWich, mp, 1928, Chaplin Bros.; flowers bright pink, reverse lighter, stamens golden yellow, 6-7 cm., semi-dbl., flat, borne in large clusters; non-recurrent; foliage large, dark green, glossy; very vigorous growth; [Paul's Scarlet Climber × American Pillar]; Gold Medal, NRS, 1928

Chaplin's Pink Companion LCl, lp, 1961, Chaplin, H.J.; flowers silvery pink, 2 in., 22 petals, borne in clusters of up to 30, moderate fragrance; non-recurrent; foliage glossy; vigorous growth; [Chaplin's Pink Climber × Opéra]; int. by Chaplin & Sons

Chaplin's Triumph HT, dr, 1936, Chaplin Bros.; bud long, pointed; flowers deep velvety crimson; foliage dark; vigorous growth

Charade F, op, 1965, Herholdt, J.A.; flowers coral-cerise tinted salmon, pointed, 3 in., dbl., borne in clusters; foliage glossy; free growth; [Queen Elizabeth × seedling]

Charade F, dr, 1988, Joseph H. Hill, Co.; flowers cardinal-red, small, 20-25 petals, high-centered, borne in sprays of 2-5; foliage medium size, dark green, semi-glossy; prickles straight, medium, lilac; mini flora bushy, profuse growth; PP6669; [Cindy × Sassy]; int. by DeVor Nurseries, Inc., 1988

Chardonnay – See **Nobilo's Chardonnay**, HT

Charentes – See **Astrid Lindgren**, S

Chariot of Roses Min, dr, 1986, Fischer, C.&H.; flowers 25 petals, borne singly; foliage small, dark, matte; prickles small, nearly straight, reddish; long, pendulous growth; small, globular fruit; [seedling × Fairy Moss]; int. by Alpenflora Gardens

Chariots of Fire LCl, dr, Williams, J. Benjamin; free-standing, climbing growth; int. by Hortico, 1996

Chariotteer HT, rb, J. B. Williams; flowers red and white; int. by Hortico, Inc., 2004

Charisma HT, or, 1974, Meilland; RULED EXTINCT 3/77 ARM; int. by C-P, 1977

Charisma F, rb, 1977, Jelly, R. G.; bud ovoid; flowers scarlet and yellow, 2-2½ in., 40-50 petals, high-centered, borne in small clusters, slight fruity fragrance; foliage medium size, dark green, glossy, leathery; vigorous, bushy, upright growth; PP4173; [Gemini × Zorina]; int. by C-P; Gold Medal, Portland, 1976

Charisma F, mr, Zary; int. in 2002

Charisma, Climbing Cl F, rb, Katsuri & Sriram; very free flowering; [sport of Charisma]; int. by KSG, 2004

Charisma F, ly, Pearce

Charismatic MinFl, rb, 2003, Clemons, David; flowers edged red, white to light yellow base, reverse white, red edge intensifies in bright sun, 1½-2 in., dbl., borne mostly solitary, no fragrance; foliage medium size, medium green, semi-glossy; few prickles; growth upright, tall (24-36 in.); exhibition, garden decoration; [Ruffian × Kristin]; int. by David E. Clemons, 2004

Charity HT, mr, 1953, Taylor, C.A.; flowers bright velvety red, 5 in., 40-50 petals, high-centered; foliage glossy; vigorous, upright, bushy growth; [Will Rogers × Mme Henri Guillot]

Charity – See **Charity 97**, S

Charity 97 S, yb, 2000, Austin, David; flowers apricot-yellow, 3 in., very full, borne in small clusters, intense fragrance; foliage medium size, dark green, glossy; prickles moderate; upright, bushy, medium (3 ft.) growth; PP11483; [Graham Thomas × seedling]; int. by David Austin, 1997

Charivari S, yb, 1971, Kordes, R.; bud ovoid; flowers golden yellow to salmon, large, dbl., cupped; foliage glossy; vigorous, upright, bushy growth; [Königin der Rosen × Goldrausch]

Charlemagne HP, dp, 1836, Dorisy; flowers bright pink, large, very full; growth to 4 ft.

Charlemagne HP, mr, 1863, Oger; flowers shining cherry red, large, full, globular

Charlemagne – See **Président Dutailly**, HGal

Charles Albanel HRg, mr, 1983, Svedja, Felicitas; flowers medium, 20 petals, moderate fragrance; repeat bloom; foliage yellow-green, rugose; prickles straight, gray-green; groundcover; low, spreading growth; [Souv. de Philemon Cochet × seedling]; int. by Agriculture Canada, 1983

Charles-Anaïs C, 1824, Bizard

Charles Austin S, ab, 1981, Austin, David; bud globular; flowers apricot tinged pink, fading to light pink, rosette, 70 petals, borne singly and in small clusters, moderate fragrance; foliage medium green, dense; prickles hooked, red; vigorous, upright, bushy growth; [Chaucer × Aloha]; int. by David Austin Roses, Ltd., 1973

Charles Aznavour – See **Matilda**, F

Charles Baltet HP, mp, 1877, Verdier, E.; flowers bright carmine pink, large, full

Charles Bonnet HP, dp, 1884, Bonnet; flowers dark rose, medium, dbl.; repeat bloom

Charles Cretté HT, mp, 1917, Chambard, C.; flowers velvety rose, large

Charles Darwin HP, mp, 1879, Laxton Bros.; flowers brownish crimson, large; [Pierre Notting × Mme Julia Daran]; int. by W. Paul

Charles Darwin S, my, 2002, Austin, David; flowers very dbl., borne in small clusters, moderate fragrance; foliage medium size, medium green, semi-glossy; prickles medium, hooked downwards, brown, few; growth bushy, branching, medium (1 m.); garden decorative; PP13992; [peachy pink english-type shrub × yellow english-type shrub]; int. by David Austin Roses, Ltd., 2001; Bronze Medal, Gifu, 2006

Charles de Franciosi T, yb, 1890, Soupert & Notting; bud long, well-formed, red-orange; flowers chrome yellow with salmon, outer petals tinted pink; large, full, rosette, borne mostly solitary; [Sylphide × Mme Crombez]

Charles de Gaulle HT, m, 1976, Meilland, Mrs. Marie-Louise; flowers lilac, 3½-4 in., 38 petals, cupped, intense fragrance; vigorous growth; [(Sissi × Prelude) × (Kordes' Sondermeldung × Caprice)]; int. by URS, 1974

Charles de Lapisse HT, lp, 1910, Laroulandie; flowers pale blush-pink, very large, full; [sport of Mme Caroline Testout]

Charles de Legrady T, dr, 1884, Pernet-Ducher; flowers red, richly shaded with violet crimson, large, full, intense fragrance

Charles de Mills HGal, dr, before 1790; flowers dark, velvety violet-crimson, medium, very dbl., flat, reqularly quartered, slight fragrance; foliage elliptical, dark green; few prickles; from Holland

Charles Desprez B, dp, 1831, Desprez; flowers medium, full

Charles Dickens HP, mp, 1886, Paul, W.; flowers full

Charles Dickens F, op, 1971, McGredy, Sam IV; flowers rosy salmon, 3 in., 16 petals, slight fragrance; [Paddy McGredy × Elizabeth of Glamis]; int. by McGredy & Son, 1970

Charles Dillon F, mp, 1971, Wood; flowers soft pink, large, 24 petals, slight fragrance; foliage dark; low, bushy growth; [Orangeade × Piccadilly]; int. by Homedale Nursery, 1970

Charles Dingee – See **William R. Smith**, T

Charles Duval B, mp, 1841, Duval, C.; flowers variable pink, large, full, cupped; growth erect

Charles Duval HP, mr, 1847, Laffay, M.; flowers scarlet, dbl., cupped; vigorous growth

Charles E. Shea HT, mp, 1917, Hicks; flowers rich pink; [sport of Mrs George Shawyer]

Charles Eyck F, yb

Charles F. Warren HT, mp, 1960, Mee, O.; flowers rose-pink, well-formed, large, 40 petals, moderate fragrance; vigorous growth; [Wilfred Pickles × Karl Herbst]

Charles Fargas HT, pb, 1935, Dot, Pedro; flowers large, dbl.

Charles Fontaine HP, dr, 1868, Fontaine; flowers dark red, shaded purple, large, full

Charles Gater HP, mr, 1893, Paul; flowers red, 40 petals, globular; vigorous growth

Charles Getz HBank, lp, 1871, Cook

Charles Gregory HT, ob, 1947, Verschuren; flowers vermilion, shaded gold, well-formed, 22 petals; foliage dark, glossy; vigorous growth; int. by Gregory

Charles Gregory, Climbing Cl HT, ob, 1960, Gregory

Charles H. Rigg HT, mr, 1931, Chaplin Bros.; flowers bright red fading to pink, dbl.; large stout, erect stems; vigorous growth

Charles Hamlet Butler S, lp, 2002, Andresen, Terry; flowers single, borne mostly solitary, no fragrance; foliage medium size, light green, matte; prickles small, straight, thin, dark green, moderate; growth bushy, medium; [sport of Mary Rose]; int. by Muncy Roses, 2003

Charles Henry HT, mr, 1967, Hooney; flowers crimson; foliage dark; vigorous, upright growth; [Ena Harkness × Lady Sylvia]

Charles J. Grahame HT, mr, 1905, Dickson, A.; flowers dazzling scarlet, well-formed, large, dbl., intense fragrance; vigorous growth

Charles K. Douglas HT, mr, 1919, Dickson, H.; bud long, pointed; flowers large, 28 petals; foliage dark; vigorous growth

Charles K. Douglas, Climbing Cl HT, mr, 1934, Leenders Bros.

Charles Kuralt S, mp, Clements, John K.; flowers open coral, fading to pink, 3½ in., 20 petals, borne in clusters of 5-12; upright, study growth, 4½ × 5 ft.; PPAF; int. by Heirloom Roses, 1999

Charles Lamb HP, mr, 1884, Paul, W.; flowers light, glossy cerise-red, large, full

Charles Lawson B, dp, 1853; flowers vivid rose, very large, full; prickles unequal, numerous; vigorous, compact growth; introduced by Lawson

Charles Lee HP, dp, 1868, Gautreau; flowers dark vermilion, shaded bright scarlet, large, full

Charles Lefèbvre HP, dr, 1861, Lacharme, F.; flowers reddish-crimson, shaded purple, large, 70 petals, cupped, moderate fragrance; bloom often recurrent; vigorous, tall growth; [Général Jacqueminot × Victor Verdier]

Charles Lefèbvre, Climbing Cl HP, dr, 1875, Cranston

Charles Lemayeux HGal, dp, before 1885; flowers deep carmine, large, full

Charles Lemoine HGal, m, before 1885; flowers velvety purple lilac, medium, full

Charles Louis No. 1 HCh, mr, 1840, Foulard/Verdier; bud round; sepals long; flowers deep cherry red, large, full, moderate fragrance; foliage fresh green, purplish when young

Charles Mallerin HT, dr, 1951, Meilland, F.; flowers blackish crimson, 6 in., 38 petals, flat; foliage leathery, dark; vigorous, irregular growth; [(Rome Glory × Congo) × Tassin]; int. by C-P

Charles Mallerin, Climbing Cl HT, dr, 1960, Balducci & Figli; buds large, shapely; flowers deep, velvet red, intense fragrance; vigorous, loose growth

Charles Margottin HP, mr, 1863, Margottin; flowers carmine red, with flame-red at center, very large, full, slightly cupped, moderate fragrance; foliage slightly crimped, dark green; prickles few, small, upright; stems reddish, smooth; [Jules Margottin × unknown]

Charles Martel HGal, pb, 1840, Parmentier; flowers slate pink, shaded purple, center carmine, large, full

Charles Martel B, mr, 1847, Guillot; flowers dark garnet, shaded crimson, medium, full

Charles Martel HP, dr, 1876, Oger; flowers purple-red, sometimes with a violet tinge, very large, dbl.

Charles Métroz Pol, dp, 1900, Schwartz; flowers China pink tinted salmon pink and carmine, small; foliage bright green, glossy

Charles P. Kilham HT, or, 1926, McGredy; flowers

red-orange, fading to lincoln red, well-formed, large, 32 petals; vigorous, bushy growth; int. by Beckwith; Gold Medal, NRS, 1927

Charles P. Kilham, Climbing Cl HT, or, 1931, Howard Rose Co. (also Morse, 1934)

Charles Quint HGal, m, 1856, Robert; flowers lilac-rose and white, medium, full, globular

Charles Ravolli T, dp, Pernet Père; flowers carmine-rose; moderate growth

Charles Rennie Mackintosh S, pb, 1994, Austin, David; flowers lilac pink, medium, very dbl., borne in small clusters; reliable repeat; foliage medium size, dark green, matte; growth medium (110 cm.), bushy; PP8155; int. by David Austin Roses, Ltd., 1988

Charles Robin B, m, 1853, Vigneron; flowers light purple

Charles Rouillard HP, lp, 1852, Laffay

Charles Rovelli T, rb, 1876, Pernet père; flowers brilliant carmine, changing to silver rose, center and base of petals golden yellow, very full, globular

Charles XII B, dp; flowers strong pink with touches of lilac, 5 in., moderate fragrance; growth tall, bushy; int. by Dickerson, Brent, 2004

Charles Turner HP, mr, 1868, Verdier, E.; flowers glowing red, very large, full; growth tall

Charles Turner HP, mr, 1869, Margottin; flowers crimson-vermilion, large, dbl., flat; prickles numerous, dark red

Charles Verdier HP, mp, 1867, Guillot; flowers bright pink, edged lighter, very large, full; [Victor Verdier × unknown]

Charles Wagner HP, mr, 1907, Van Fleet/Conard & Jones; flowers clear bright red, approaching scarlet, large, dbl., borne in clusters of 3-5; foliage dark green; [Jean Liabaud × Victor Hugo]

Charles William HT, pb, 1989, Cattermole, R.F.; bud urn-shaped; flowers carmine rose, reverse lighter, yellow at base, petals pointed, reflexed, 56 petals, no fragrance; foliage matte, medium green, large; prickles light brown; upright, tall growth; [Bradenburg × Command Performance]

Charles Wood HP, rb, 1864, Portemer; flowers red shaded with crimson, reverse white, very large, full

Charles × HGal, mr, before 1826, Descemet; flowers glossy crimson

Charleston F, yb, 1965, Meilland, Alain A.; bud pointed; flowers yellow flushed crimson, becoming crimson, 3 in., 20 petals, borne in clusters, slight fragrance; foliage dark, leathery, glossy; upright, compact growth; [Masquerade × (Radar × Caprice)]; int. by URS

Charleston, Climbing Cl F, yb, 1966, Rumsey, R.H. (also Keisei, 1978); flowers yellow with red edges; int. by Rumsey, 1966

Charleston HP, mp

Charleston 88 – See **Louis de Funes**, HT

Charlie Min, mr, 1984, King, Gene; flowers small, 35 petals, high-centered; foliage small, dark, matte; upright, bushy growth; [seedling × Big John]

Charlie Brown Min, rb, 1996, Moore, Ralph S.; flowers red and white stripe, 1-1¼ in., 8-14 petals, borne singly or in small clusters; foliage small, medium green, semi-glossy; few prickles; compact, bushy, low (12-15 in.) growth; [seedling × Pinstripe]; int. by Sequoia Nursery, 1997

Charlie Chaplin HT, ab, Tschanz, E.

Charlie Dimmock – See **Charlies Rose**, HT

Charlie McCarthy Pol, w, 1955, Wiseman; bud creamy white; flowers pure white, 1½-2 in., 28 petals, borne in clusters, moderate fragrance; foliage glossy, leathery, dark; dwarf, compact growth; [Mrs Dudley Fulton × Mermaid]; int. by H&S, 1955

Charlie Perkins HT, dr, 1970, Zombory; bud long, pointed; flowers overlaid black, large, semi-dbl.; foliage large, glossy, dark, bronze, leathery; very vigorous, upright, bushy growth; [Carrousel × Circus]; int. by General Bionomics

Charlie's Aunt HT, pb, 1965, McGredy, Sam IV; flowers cream, heavily suffused rose, high-pointed, 5 in., 65 petals; foliage dark; [Golden Masterpiece × Karl Herbst]; int. by Geest Industries

Charlies Rose HT, pb, 2000, Tantau, Math.; bud long, pointed; flowers pink, reverse silver pink, 14-15 cm., full, borne mostly singly, intense fragrance; foliage large, dark green, semi-glossy; numerous prickles; upright, vigorous growth, 100-120 cm; [seedling × seedling]; int. by Rosen Tantau, 1998

Charlie's Uncle HT, rb, 1976, Haynes; flowers cream, suffused carmine, 5-6 in., 40 petals, high-centered, slight fragrance; foliage large, leathery; [sport of Charlie's Aunt]; int. in 1975

Charlotte HT, op, 1941, Duehrsen; bud long, pointed; flowers salmon-pink and coral, base gold, dbl., high-centered; foliage glossy; vigorous, bushy growth; [Joanna Hill × Golden Dawn]; int. by California Roses

Charlotte LCl, Zampini, P.; PP2284

Charlotte S, ly, 1994, Austin, David; flowers soft yellow, 3-3½ in., very dbl., borne in small clusters; foliage medium size, medium green, semi-glossy; few prickles; medium (100 cm.), upright, bushy growth; [seedling × Graham Thomas]; int. by David Austin Roses, Ltd., 1993

Charlotte HT, mr, Tantau; PP11020; int. in 1997

Charlotte Anne F, m, 1993, Blankenship, Paul; flowers lavender, medium, 5 petals, borne in small clusters; foliage medium size, dark green, glossy; some prickles; medium, spreading growth; [sport of Playgirl]; int. by Roses Unlimited, 1994

Charlotte Armstrong HT, dp, 1940, Lammerts, Dr. Walter; bud long, pointed, blood-red; flowers deep pink to cerise, 3-4 in., 35 petals, moderate fragrance; foliage dark, leathery; vigorous, compact growth; [Soeur Thérèse × Crimson Glory]; int. by Armstrong Nursery; John Cook Medal, ARS, 1941, NRS, 1950, Gertrude M. Hubbard, ARS, 1945, Gold Medal, Portland, 1941

Charlotte Armstrong, Climbing Cl HT, dp, 1942, Morris; bud long, pointed; flowers deep pink, moderate fragrance; int. by Armstrong Nursery, 1942

Charlotte Brownell HT, yb, Brownell, H.C.; flowers buff with chrome yellow center and pink tint on edges, 4-5 in., dbl., high-centered; growth to 3-4 ft.; very winter hardy; PP3374

Charlotte Chevalier HT, dy, 1916, Chambard, C.; flowers dark canary-yellow; [sport of Arthur R. Goodwin]

Charlotte Corday HP, dr, 1864, Joubert

Charlotte de Lacharme HGal, pb, before 1824, Vibert; flowers purple-pink plumed and spotted with white and pale pink, medium, dbl.

Charlotte E. van Dedem HT, my, 1937, Buisman, G. A. H.; bud long, pointed; flowers large, semi-dbl.; foliage glossy; vigorous growth; [Roselandia × Ville de Paris]; Gold Medal, Portland, 1938

Charlotte Elizabeth Gr, dp, 1965, Norman; flowers deep rose-pink, 3-4 in., 26 petals, high-centered, borne in clusters; foliage glossy; int. by Harkness

Charlotte Gillemot HT, pb, 1894, Guillot; flowers milk white with salmon and rose pink, large, full, moderate fragrance

Charlotte Ives F, pb, 1965, Warren; bud globular; flowers rose-pink, center light yellow, open, medium, single, borne in clusters; compact, upright, bushy growth; [Ma Perkins × Rose Gaujard]

Charlotte Jan S, mp, 2005, Williams, J. Benjamin; flowers 3 in., dbl., old-fashioned, borne in small clusters, moderate fragrance; remontant; foliage medium size, medium green, semi-glossy; prickles medium, curved down, light green, few; growth compact, medium (3-3½ ft.); beds, hedging, landscaping; [Rose Parade × Jin Bowie]; int. in 1999

Charlotte Kemp HWich, m, Nobbs; int. in 1997

Charlotte Klemm Ch, or, 1905, Türke; flowers red shaded orange, medium, semi-dbl.; probably extinct; [Alfred Colomb × Cramoisi Supérieur]

Charlotte Mackensen HMult, mr, 1938, Vogel, M.; flowers carmine red with silvery reverse, 7-8 cm., dbl., borne in tight clusters

Charlotte Maertz Pol, mr, 1913, Altmüller; flowers red with silvery reflections

Charlotte Marie S, pb, 1998, Fleming, Joyce L.; flowers pale pink, light at the base, pale reverse, 3 in., single, borne in small clusters; foliage medium size, narrow, dark green, semi-glossy; prickles moderate; low, compact, upright growth; [Marchenland × *R. virginiana*]; int. by Hortico, Inc., 1997

Charlotte Pate HT, yb, 1971, MacLeod; bud globular; flowers pink, yellow reverse, large, 25 petals; foliage medium size, medium green, glossy; [Wendy Cussons × Golden Sun]

Charlotte Rampling HT, mr, Meilland; flowers velvety red, large, 80 petals, moderate fragrance; growth to 70-80 cm.; int. in 1988

Charlotte Searle HT, mr, Kordes

Charlotte Séguier HP, lp, 1849, Béluze; flowers flesh pink, tinted lilac at edges, large, full; very remontant

Charlotte von Rathlef HWich, dp, 1936, Vogel, M.; flowers deep pink, lighter at edges, small, very dbl., borne in small clusters; non-recurrent; foliage leathery, dark; vigorous, climbing growth; [Fragezeichen × American Pillar]; int. by Heinemann

Charlotte Wheatcroft F, mr, 1959, Wheatcroft Bros.; flowers bright scarlet, large, single, borne in large trusses; foliage dark, glossy; vigorous, tall growth; int. in 1958

Charlotte Wierel Pol, w, 1926, Walter, L.; flowers cream-white, center bright rose-pink; vigorous growth; [Bebe Leroux × Helene Videnz]

Charlottenhof S, mr, 1938, Vogel, M.; flowers medium, dbl.

Charlotte's Rose F, ab, 2006, Burks, Larry; flowers pastel apricot, reverse pink to apricot, 3 in., semi-dbl., borne in small clusters; foliage medium size, medium green, semi-glossy; prickles average, slightly recurved, brown to dark tan, moderate; growth compact, medium (24-36 in.); garden decorative; [seedling × seedling]; int. in 2006

Charlye Rivel HT, dr, Roses Noves Ferrer, S L; flowers 32 petals, high-centered; [Jack-8301365 × Inedita]

Charm HT, op, 1920, Paul, W.; bud reddish orange, shaded pink and copper; flowers coppery yellow

Charm – See **Charme**, HT

Charm Bracelet Min, dy, 1992, Christensen, Jack E.; flowers dark yellow, aging to pink, red blush on tips of outer petals, medium, very dbl., slight fragrance; foliage small, dark green, semi-glossy; some prickles; low (45 cm.), bushy, compact growth; [Fool's Gold × seedling]; int. by Bear Creek Gardens, 1992

Charm of Paris HT, mp, 1965, Tantau, Math.; flowers pink, large, 48 petals; vigorous growth; [Prima Ballerina × Montezuma]; int. by Wheatcroft Bros.; Edland Fragrance Medal, ARS, 1966

Charmaine Pol, mp, 1929, Burbage Nursery; flowers pink tinged salmon, open, dbl., borne in sprays; recurrent bloom; foliage bright, glossy; long stems; very vigorous, bushy growth; [Evelyn Thornton × unknown]

Charmant Min, mr, 1987, Kordes, W.; flowers small, 40 petals; foliage small, medium green, semi-glossy; bushy growth; [((seedling × Tornado) × KORkonig) × Trumpeter]

Charmant Min, pb, 2006; bud small, pointed; flowers pure pink with a yellow-white center, cream reverse, 4 cm., full, pompon, borne singly and in clusters, slight, sweetish fragrance; foliage small, dark green, very glossy; growth bushy, short (50 cm.); int. by W. Kordes' Söhne, 1999; Silver Certificate, The Hague, 2006

Charmant HT, ab, Kordes; flowers creamy apricot with green tints on some petal edges, large, dbl., high-centered, borne mostly singly; recurrent; stems long; upright growth; int. by W. Kordes Söhne, 2005

Charmant Isidore HGal, m, before 1829, Boutigny; flowers lilac

Charme HT, dp, 1930; bud long, pointed; flowers cherry-red, large, dbl.; foliage glossy; vigorous growth; int. by Rice Bros. Co.

Charme d'Amour – See **Liebeszauber**, HT, 1959

Charme de Paris F, ob, Delbard, Georges; flowers salmon-orange with rose-salmon reverse, dbl.; int. in 1979

Charme de Vienne – See **Vienna Charm**, HT

Charmed MinFl, ab, 2001, Bridges, Dennis; flowers 2¼ in., dbl., borne mostly solitary, slight fragrance; prickles in., straight, pointing slightly down, few; growth upright, tall (2½-3 ft.); garden decorative, exhibition, cutting; PPAF; [Purple Dawn × select pollen]; int. by Bridges Roses, 2002

Charmente HT, lp, 1979, Huber; bud globular; flowers 4 in., 42 petals; foliage bright green, leathery; upright, spreading growth; [Fragrant Cloud × Ena Harkness]; int. in 1975

Charmer HT, lp, 1923, Schoener; flowers silvery pink; [(Pharisaer × unknown) × Joseph Hill]; int. by Doyle

Charmer HT, lp, 1934, Dickson, A.; flowers light pink, center shaded salmon, large, dbl., high-centered; foliage leathery; vigorous, free branching growth; Gold Medal, NRS, 1932

Charmer Min, w, 2004, Benardella, Frank; flowers ivory with pink at base, reverse ivory and pink, 1½-1¾ in., dbl., borne mostly solitary, slight fragrance; foliage medium size, medium green, semi-glossy; prickles ¼ to in., pointed slightly down; growth upright, well-branched, medium (18 in.); garden decoration, cutting; int. by Nor East Miniature Roses, 2004

Charmglo Min, pb, 1981, Williams, Ernest D.; bud long, pointed; flowers creamy white painted deep pink, reverse lighter, 35 petals, high-centered, borne usually singly, slight fragrance; foliage small, medium to dark green, slightly matte; prickles long, thin, brown, curved down; bushy, compact growth; [seedling × Over the Rainbow]; int. by Mini-Roses, 1980

Charmi HMsk, mp, 1929, Pemberton; flowers light to dark pink, medium, semi-dbl.

Charmian S, mp, 1983, Austin, David; flowers large, dbl.; foliage medium size, medium green, semi-glossy; spreading growth; [seedling × Lilian Austin]; int. by David Austin Roses, Ltd., 1982

Charming HT, mp, 1922, Van Rossem; flowers salmon-pink, reverse coral-pink, semi-dbl.; [Alexander Hill Gray × Mme Edouard Herriot]

Charming – See **Charming Parade**, Min

Charming Bells – See **Caterpillar**, S

Charming Cover S, mr, Olesen; bud pointed-ovoid; flowers medium red with orange overtones, 5 cm., 14-16 petals, shallow cup, borne in large panicles, very slight fragrance; recurrent; foliage dark green, glossy; prickles moderate, linear to deeply concave, tan; bushy, compact (80 cm.) growth; PP12681; [seedling × seedling]; int. in 2000

Charming Diana HT, mp, 1998, Twomey, Jerry; flowers pink, reverse medium, 6 in., dbl., borne singly, very large; foliage large, dark green, glossy; numerous prickles; bushy, medium growth

Charming Maid F, ob, 1953, LeGrice; bud orange-salmon; flowers salmon, base golden, 4-4½ in., 5-6 petals, borne in trusses, moderate fragrance; foliage dark, glossy; PP2209; [Dainty Maid × Mrs Sam McGredy]; Gold Medal, NRS, 1953

Charming Parade Min, or, Poulsen; flowers orange-red, medium, semi-dbl., no fragrance; foliage dark; growth bushy, 20-40 cm.

Charming Princess HT, yb, 1926, Hancock; flowers deep yellow, edged vermilion large, dbl.; foliage dark; vigorous growth; [sport of The Queen Alexandra Rose]

Charming Rosamini Min, ob, deRuiter

Charming Rose HT, lp

Charming Unique HT, mp, deRuiter; PP11175; int. by De Ruiter's New Roses Intl.

Charming Vienne – See **Vienna Charm**, HT

Charpentier – See **Estelle**, HSpn

Charter 700 F, my, Fryer, Gareth; flowers bright yellow, large, dbl., exhibition, borne in well-spaced clusters; good rebloom; growth upright to 2 ft.; int. in 1993

Chartreuse HT, my, 1940, Mallerin, C.; bud long; flowers canary-yellow, dbl.; foliage glossy; bushy growth; [Soeur Thérèse × Angels Mateu]; int. by A. Meilland

Chartreuse – See **Solitaire**, HT

Chartreuse de Parme S, m, Delbard, Georges; flowers rosy mauve, full, intense floral & citrus fragrance; growth to 3 ft.; int. by Georges Delbard SA, 1996

Charugandha HT, mr, 1974, IARI; buds large, long, pointed; flowers velvety crimson-red, very large, dbl, high-centered, borne singly and several together; foliage medium size, green, soft; growth vigorous, upright (90 cm.); [Delhi Princess × Eiffel Tower]

Chase Beauty HT, dr, 1947, Chase; bud long; flowers rich dark red, 5½ in., 35-45 petals, high-centered; foliage dark; very vigorous, tall growth; [sport of Better Times]; int. by Chase Gardens

Chasin' Rainbows Min, rb, 1989, Saville, F. Harmon; bud ovoid; flowers very brilliant yellow, edged red with scarlet becoming more red with age, 21 petals, high-centered, slight spicy fragrance; foliage small, dark green, semi-glossy; prickles long, thin, angled, light brown; bushy, low growth; no hips; PP7058; [Zorina × Rainbow's End]; int. by Nor'East Min. Roses, 1988

Chastity Cl HT, w, 1924, Cant, F.; flowers pure white, base lemon, 3½-4 in., dbl., high-centered, borne in small to medium clusters; non-recurrent bloom; foliage light, glossy; vigorous growth

Chastleton HP, lp, 1800; flowers large, very dbl.

Château – See **Baby Château**, F

Château Angelus – See **White Nights**, S

Chateau Canon S, dr, McGredy, Sam IV

Château d'Amboise HT, dr, 1989, Delbard & Chabert; flowers dark red, opening bright, long, 23-30 petals; foliage bright; vigorous growth; [(Tropicana × unknown) × ((Rome Glory × Impeccable) × (Rouge Meilland × Soraya))]

Château de Bagnols F, lp, Orard

Château de Beauregard F, yb, Sauvageot; flowers creamy white with pale yellow centers and cerise edges, dbl.; int. in 2000

Château de Chenonceaux HT, mp, 1978, Gaujard; flowers brilliant pink, large, 45 petals; tall growth; [Americana × Queen Elizabeth]; int. in 1973

Château de Clos Vougeot HT, dr, 1908, Pernet-Ducher; flowers deep velvety red, 75 petals, intense damask fragrance; foliage dark, leathery; sprawling growth

Château de Clos Vougeot, Climbing Cl HT, dr, 1920, Morse; bud very large; flowers deep velvety red, turning darker with age, 10-12 cm., full, peony-shaped; foliage leathery, glossy; [sport of Château de Clos Vougeot]

Château de Filain F, op, Sauvageot; flowers rose-salmon, dbl.

Château de Gros-Bois N, dy, 1909, Laperrière; flowers golden yellow, semi-dbl.; recurrent; [Mme Pierre Cochet × unknown]

Château de la Juvénie S, lp, 1901, Gravereaux; flowers soft, pale pink, small; non-recurrent; pillar growth to 2½ m.

Château de Namur HGal, pb, before 1842; flowers very dark violet, striped white, crimson center, medium, full; possibly from Quétier, but more probably from Parmentier

Château de Vaire S, dr, 1934, Sauvageot, H.; flowers deep velvety red, large, dbl., cupped; non-recurrent; foliage bronze, dark; bushy (3½-6½ ft.) growth; moderately hardy; [Charles K. Douglas × *R. macrophylla*]

Château de Vaumarcus S, op; flowers orange-nasturtium pink, medium, dbl., classic hybrid tea form, slight fragrance; floriferous; growth to 5 ft.; int. by Alain Tschanz SA, 2000

Château de Versailles – See **Guy Laroche**, HT

Château des Bergeries T, ly, 1886, Widow Lédéchaux; bud large; flowers pale canary yellow, darker at center, large, very full, globular

Château du Rivau HMult, w, Eve; flowers with yellow stamens, 3-4 cm., single, borne in broad sprays, slight fragrance; non-recurrent; foliage large, dark green, semi-glossy; prickles moderate; vigorous growth to 5-8 m.; int. by Andre Eve, 2004

Château Frontenac S, dp

Château la Croix HT, ab, Dorieux; int. as Chateau la Croix, Roseraies Dorieux, 1995

Château La Salle HT, yb, 1966, Morey, Dr. Dennison; bud long, pointed; flowers buff-yellow, large, dbl., high-centered; foliage dark, leathery; vigorous, bushy, compact growth; [Joanna Hill × Ellinor LeGrice]; int. by General Bionomics

Château Luegg – See **Schloss Luegg**, HMult

Chateau Merlot – See **CentrO-Rose**, S

Chateau Montrose – See **Jutland**, F

Chateau Pavie – See **Tivoli Gardens**, HT

Château Pelles HT, lp, 1927, Mühle; bud cream-white; flowers soft pink, shaded salmon, dbl.; [Harry Kirk × unknown]

Châteauroux F, or, Croix, P.

Châtelaine F, op, 1960, Lens; bud pointed; flowers coral overcast salmon, well-formed, 3 in., 32 petals, borne in small clusters, moderate fragrance; foliage glossy, coppery; vigorous growth; [(Peace × seedling) × Fashion]; int. in 1957

Châtelaine de Lullier HT, mr, Meilland; flowers carmine-red, large, dbl.; int. in 1987

Châtelaine de Lullier – See **Rendez-vous**, HT

Châtelet HT, mp, 1952, Moulin-Epinay; bud globular, coral; flowers pink heavily tinted salmon, medium, very dbl.; [Yvonne Plassat × seedling]; int. by Vilmorin-Andrieux

Châtillon Rambler HWich, mp, 1913, Nonin; flowers salmon-pink, 3 cm., semi-dbl., cupped, borne in large clusters; growth to 15-20 ft.; [Dorothy Perkins × Turner's Crimson Rambler]

Châtillon Rose Pol, mp, 1923, Nonin; flowers bright pink, semi-dbl., cupped, borne in large clusters; foliage glossy; bushy (1-2 ft. growth; [Orléans Rose × seedling]

Chatillon White – See **White Chatillon**, Pol

Chatsworth – See **Footloose**, S

Chattem Centennial Min, or, 1979, Jolly, Betty J.; bud ovoid; flowers medium, 38 petals, cupped, slight fruity fragrance; upright, bushy growth; PP4564; [Orange Sensation × Zinger]; int. by Rosehill Farm

Chattem Centennial, Climbing Cl Min, or, 1991, Jolly, Marie; bud ovoid; flowers orange-red, aging light orange, medium, 38 petals, cupped, loose, borne usually singly or in sprays of 3-5, slight fruity fragrance; foliage medium size, light green, matte; tall (4-6 ft.) growth; [sport of Chattem Centennial]; int. by Rosehill Farm, 1991

Chatter F, mr, 1947, Boerner; flowers velvety bright crimson, 14 petals, cupped, borne in large clusters; bushy, compact growth; [World's Fair × Betty Prior]; int. by J&P

Chatter, Climbing Cl F, mr, 1960, Schmidt, K.; flowers light red, medium, semi-dbl., moderate fragrance

Chatterbox F, ob, 1973, Sanday, John; flowers bright orange-vermilion, rosette, 2 in., 16 petals; foliage glossy; dwarf growth; [Sarabande × Circus]

Chattooga Min, dp, 2004, Michael C Williams; flowers 2 in., dbl., borne mostly solitary, no fragrance; foliage large, dark green, matte; prickles in., curved down; growth upright, tall (24-36 in.); garden decoration, cutting, exhibition; [Pierrine × unknown]; int. by Bridges Roses, 2005; Award of Excellence, ARS, 2005

Chaucer S, mp, 1981, Austin, David; bud globular; flowers rose pink in center, paling toward edges, full, cupped, borne singly and in small clusters, intense fragrance; foliage medium green; prickles slightly hooked, red; vigorous, upright, bushy growth; PP10618; [seedling × Constance Spry]; int. by David Austin Roses, Ltd., 1970

Chaumant – See **Maiden Voyage**, F

Cheaky Monkey Min, dp, Jalbert; int. by Harvest Moon Farms, 2005

Checkers Min, mr, 1990, Chaffin, Lauren M.; bud pointed; flowers medium red, aging darker, 20 petals, high-centered, borne singly, slight spicy fragrance; foliage small, medium green, semi-glossy; prickles needle-shaped, tan; bushy, low growth; rarely forms fruit; [Deep Purple × Happy Hour]; int. by Pixie Treasures Min. Roses

Checkmate MinFl, rb, 2002, Tucker, Robbie; flowers orange-pink with white at base, reverse light orange-pink, 2½-3 in., full, borne mostly solitary, slight fragrance; foliage large, medium green, matte; prickles medium, straight, green to brown, moderate; growth bushy, tall (3½ ft.); garden decorative, exhibition; [seedling × seedling]; int. by Rosemania, 2002

Chédane-Guinoisseau – See **Mons Chédane-Guinoisseau**, HRg

Cheek to Cheek LCl, w, Poulsen; flowers white with pink tinge, 5-8 cm., full, cupped, borne mostly in clusters, very slight fragrance; recurrent; foliage dark green, glossy; bushy, tall (150-200 cm.) growth; int. as Salsa, Poulsen Roser, 2002

Cheer F, mp, 1941, Kordes; flowers deep rose-pink, open, 4 in., semi-dbl., borne in clusters; foliage leathery; vigorous, upright growth; RULED EXTINCT 1/84 ARM; [Dance of Joy × Golden Rapture]; int. by J&P

Cheer Up Min, ob, 1986, Bennett, Dee; flowers deep orange, 28 petals, high-centered, urn-shaped, borne usually singly and in small clusters, slight fragrance; foliage medium size, dark, semi-glossy; prickles small, red; medium, upright, bushy growth; hips globular, 1/2 in., green and brown; PP6456; [Futura × Bread 'n' Butter]; int. by Tiny Petals Nursery

Cheerful HT, ob, 1915, McGredy; flowers orange-flame, base yellow, very large, dbl.; foliage rich green, glossy

Cheerful Charlie F, mr, 2004, Cocker, A.G.; flowers semi-dbl., borne in small clusters; foliage medium size, medium green, glossy; prickles 6 mm., straight; growth compact, medium (2-2½ ft.); garden decorative; [Drummer Boy × Abbeyfield Rose]; slight swirling of petals; int. by James Cocker & Sons, 2004

Cheerful Days HT, dy, Bell; int. by Bell Roses, 2001

Cheerfully Pink F, op, 2001, Coiner, Jim; flowers medium pink, pink blend reverse, 2½ in., semi-dbl., borne in large clusters, no fragrance; foliage medium size, medium green, semi-glossy; prickles small, regular, moderate; growth bushy, tall (4 ft.); [seedling × seedling]

Cheerfulness F, op, 1981, Everitt, Derrick; flowers orange, pink and yellow blend, 8 petals, borne 10 per cluster; foliage small; prickles small, brown; compact growth; [seedling × seedling]; int. by Gandy Roses, Ltd.

Cheerie – See **Chérie**, F, 1931

Cheerio – See **Chérie**, F, 1931

Cheerio Pol, dp, 1937, Archer; flowers carmine-cerise, large, semi-dbl., cupped, borne in clusters, slight fragrance

Cheerio – See **Playboy**, F

Cheerleader Min, dr, 1986, Moore, Ralph S.; flowers small, very dbl., borne in sprays of 5-10; foliage small, medium green, semi-glossy; bushy, spreading growth; no fruit; PP5977; [Fairy Moss × Orange Honey]; int. by Moore Min. Roses, 1985

Cheers Min, ob, 1984, Saville, F. Harmon; flowers orange-red, cream reverse, 20 petals; foliage small, medium green, semi-glossy; compact, bushy growth; [Poker Chip × Zinger]; int. by Nor'East Min. Roses

Cheers – See **Kampai**, HT

Cheers To You S, yb; growth to 3-4 ft.; int. by B&B Nursery, 2001

Cheery Chatter Min, mr, 1984, Lyon, Lyndon; flowers medium, 20 petals; foliage small, medium green, semi-glossy; upright, bushy growth; [Dandy Lyon × seedling]; int. by L. Lyon Greenhouses

Cheese Cake Min, w, 1997, Brown, Ted; flowers medium, dbl., borne mostly singly; foliage medium size, dark green, glossy; bushy, medium (5 ft.) growth; [Esprit × seedling]

Chelsea HT, mr, 1950, LeGrice; flowers carmine shaded orient red, 4 in., dbl.; vigorous, compact growth; RULED EXTINCT 6/86

Chelsea Min, mp, 1986, Moore, Ralph S.; lacy sepals; flowers small, 25 petals, cupped, borne in clusters of 5 or more, slight fragrance; foliage small to medium size, medium green, semi-glossy; upright, bushy growth; hips few, globular, medium size, orange; [(Little Darling × Yellow Magic) × Crested Jewel]; int. by Sequoia Nursery

Chelsea HT, pb, 1997, Ortega, Carlos; flowers medium, dbl., borne mostly singly; foliage small, dark green, semi-glossy; upright, medium (4-5 ft.)growth; [Lauren Elizabeth × Paul's Pink]; int. by Aebi Nursery

Chelsea Belle Min, mr, 1991, Taylor, Pete & Kay; bud pointed; flowers medium red with white base, whitish reverse, aging lighter, medium, 28-30 petals, high-centered, borne mostly singly, moderate fragrance; foliage medium size, medium green, semi-glossy; upright, bushy, medium growth; [Azure Sea × Party Girl]; int. by Taylor's Roses, 1990

Chelsea Brittlyn Min, mp, 2006, Smith, Joseph and Brenda; flowers full, borne mostly solitary; foliage medium size, dark green, semi-glossy; prickles small, tan/red, moderate; growth compact, medium (30 in.); [sport of Aristocrat]; int. in 2007

Chelsea Gold F, ab, 1985, Sealand Nurseries, Ltd.; flowers medium, 20 petals; foliage medium size, medium green, semi-glossy; numerous prickles; bushy growth; [Arthur Bell × Elizabeth of Glamis]

Chelsea Morning S, ab, 2001, Zary; buds pointed, ovoid; flowers pink and apricot blend, aging to more intense pink, 4-5 cm., 40 petals, saucer-shaped, borne mostly solitary, moderate fruity fragrance; foliage medium size, dark green, glossy; prickles moderate; growth upright, medium (5 ft.); garden decorative; PP14755; [New Year × French Perfume]; int. by J&P, 2002

Chelsea Pensioner Min, mr, 1983, Mattock, John, Ltd.; flowers scarlet, small, 20 petals, slight fragrance; foliage small, dark, semi-glossy; bushy growth; patio, containers; [(Gold Pin × unknown) × seedling]; int. by John Mattock, Ltd., 1982

Chénédolé HCh, or, about 1840, Thierry; flowers crimson, small, dbl., cupped, moderate fragrance; very prickly; vigorous, upright growth

Chénier HCh, mp, about 1825, Laffay; flowers bright pink

Chenonceaux – See **Château de Chenonceaux**, HT

Cheré Michelle Min, op, 1986, Jolly, Marie; flowers white with coral pink petal edges, small, 30 petals, high-centered; foliage medium size, medium green, semi-glossy; prickles small, cream to light brown, hooked downward; medium, upright growth; hips medium, globular, orange-green; [Sheri Anne × Anita Charles]; int. by Rosehill Farm, 1987

Chérie F, mp, 1931, Morse; flowers bright rose-pink, small, dbl., cupped, borne in clusters; foliage leathery; vigorous, bushy growth; [sport of Else Poulsen]

Cherie – See **Cerise**, N

Chérie F, ob, 1964, Gaujard; bud long; flowers bright orange, reverse coppery, well-formed, dbl.

Cherie S, dp; flowers single; int. by Jan Spek Rozen, 2002

Cherish F, op, 1979, Warriner, William A.; bud short, flat; flowers coral-pink, 3 in., 28 petals, high-centered, slight fragrance; foliage large, dark; compact, spreading growth; PP4331; [Bridal Pink × Matador]; int. by J&P, 1980

Cherokee HT, mr; flowers bright red, round, dbl.; int. by Carlton Roses, 2004

Cherokee Fire Min, dr, 1982, Lyon, Lyndon; flowers deep red, medium, semi-dbl.; foliage medium green, semi-glossy; upright, bushy growth; [Merry Christmas × seedling]; int. by L. Lyon Greenhouses

Cherokee Rose – See ***R. laevigata*** (Michaux)

Cherries 'n' Cream Min, rb, King; int. in 1997

Cherries 'n' Cream S, m, 2005, Zary, Keith W.; flowers cherry-maroon and white, handpainted, reverse white, 10-12 cm., 20 petals, borne in large clusters, intense fragrance; foliage large, dark green, glossy; prickles 10-12 mm., straight, greyed-orange, moderate; growth upright, very vigorous, tall (180 cm.); PP16705; [Pure Poetry × Fabulous!]; int. by Jackson & Perkins Wholesale, Inc., 2005

Cherries Jubilee HWich, mr, Clements, John K.; flowers cherry scarlet-red with golden centers, 1½ in., 5-8 petals, borne in large clusters; profuse, non-recurrent; rich green foliage; vigorous climbing growth to 14 ft.; PPAF; int. in 1999

Cherrio F, dp, 1937, Archer; flowers carmine-cerise, large, semi-dbl., cupped, borne in clusters; vigorous, compact growth

Cherrio F, mp, 1948, Kordes; flowers light pink, reverse darker, semi-dbl.; vigorous, bushy growth; [Holstein × Sapho]

Cherry HT, pb, 1928, McGredy; flowers brilliant carmine-pink flushed yellow, lower half yellow, large, dbl., high-centered; vigorous, bushy growth

Cherry, Climbing Cl HT, pb, 1934, Savage Nursery

Cherry – See **Cherry Parade**, Min

Cherry Blossom F, mp, 1964, Verschuren, A.; bud orient red; flowers rose-pink to camellia-pink, 26 petals, borne in clusters; foliage glossy, dark; compact growth; [Fashion × seedling]; int. by van Engelen

Cherry Blossom Clam – See **Sakuragai**, F
Cherry Blossom Haze – See **Sakura-Gasumi**, F
Cherry Blossom Viewing on the River – See **Hanami-Gawa**, Cl Min
Cherry Bomb Min, ob, 1991, Jolly, Marie; flowers orange, medium, very dbl., borne mostly singly, no fragrance; foliage small, medium green, semi-glossy; few prickles; medium, upright growth; [Fashion Flame × Sheri Anne]; int. by Rosehill Farm, 1991
Cherry Brandy HT, ob, 1965, Tantau, Math.; flowers orange, 5 in., 30 petals; foliage dark, glossy, leathery; very vigorous, upright growth
Cherry Brandy '85 HT, ob, 1985, Tantau, Math.; flowers orange, large, 35 petals, no fragrance; foliage large, medium green, glossy; upright growth; Gold Medal, Belfast, 1989
Cherry Charm LCl, pb, 1976, MacLeod; flowers deep pink, reverse silver pink, 5 in., 25 petals; non-recurrent; foliage dark; [Norwich Salmon × (Seedling sport × Peeping Tom)]
Cherry Cheerful Pol, rb, 1995, Jobson, Daniel J.; flowers cherry red with white shadings, small, 6-14 petals, borne in large clusters; foliage medium size, medium green, glossy; compact, spreading, bushy, medium (3 × 5 ft.) growth
Cherry Chinks – See **Wettra**, F
Cherry Cola HT, dr
Cherry Cordial Min, rb, 1997, Wells, Verlie W.; flowers medium, bright red with white reverse, very dbl., borne mostly singly; foliage medium size, dark green, semi-glossy; upright, medium growth; [Magic Carrousel × seedling]; int. by Kimbrew-Walter Roses, 1997
Cherry Cover – See **Key West**, S
Cherry Cream Gr, op; flowers creamy white and salmon blend, dbl.; int. in 1995
Cherry Drop Ch, rb, 2003, Rippetoe, Robert Neil; flowers light red, 2 in., very full, borne in small clusters, moderate cherry-candy fragrance; foliage medium size, dark green, semi-glossy; prickles medium, hooked, brown, moderate; growth spreading, angular, medium (3-4 ft.); hedge, specimen, bedding; [sport of Serratipetala]; int. in 2002
Cherry Folies F, rb, Meilland; flowers cherry red with white reverse; greenhouse rose; int. by Meilland Intl, 2004
Cherry Garland LCl, mr, Taschner, Ludwig; flowers cherry red, medium, full, pompon, borne in clusters; foliage glossy; stems long, supple; rapid, tall growth; int. by Ludwig's Roses, 2005
Cherry Gem Min, mr, Bell; flowers dbl., no fragrance; growth compact (16 in.)
Cherry Girl HT, mp, Kordes; flowers strong pink, large, dbl.; stems 55 cm.; [sport of Cherry Lady]; int. by W. Kordes Sohne, 2002
Cherry Glow Gr, mr, 1959, Swim, H.C.; flowers cherry-red, 3-4 in., 23 petals, cupped, moderate spicy fragrance; foliage leathery, glossy; vigorous, upright growth; [Floradora × First Love]; int. by C.R. Burr, 1959
Cherry Glow – See **Sweet Cherry**, HT
Cherry Gold – See **Polo Club**, HT
Cherry Hi Min, dr, 1996, Moore, Ralph S.; flowers dark red, reverse slightly lighter, 1½ in., very dbl., borne in small clusters, no fragrance; few prickles; PP11099; [Show 'n' Tell × Sincerely Yours]; int. by Sequoia Nursery, 1997
Cherry Jubilee S, mr, 1991, Warriner, William A.; flowers light to medium red, medium, dbl., no fragrance; foliage medium size, medium green, semi-glossy; upright, bushy growth; [seedling × Simplicity]; int. by Bear Creek Gardens, 1991
Cherry Kordana Min, mr, Kordes; flowers cherry red; int. by W. Kordes Söhne
Cherry Lady HT, mr, Kordes; int. by W. Kordes Söhne, 1999
Cherry Lips F, dp, Williams, J. Benjamin; flowers fluorescent hot pink, dbl.; profuse; compact growth; int. by Hortico, 1997
Cherry Magic Min, dr, 1988, Moore, Ralph S.; flowers deep red, reverse lighter red with silver sheen, aging lighter, 25 petals, high-centered; foliage small, medium green, matte; prickles short, small, brown; bushy, spreading, low growth; hips round, small, orange-red; PP7061; [Anytime × Lavender Jewel]; int. by Sequoia Nursery
Cherry Meidiland S, rb, 1995, Meilland; bud oval, medium; flowers red with a white eye, reverse lighter, 2 in., 5 petals, flat cup, borne in small clusters, no fragrance; good repeat; foliage medium size, dark green, semi-glossy; prickles numerous, medium; upright, bushy growth (5½-6 ft.); PP9251; [Pink Meidiland × (Regensberg × Fair Play)]; int. by Conard-Pyle Co.; Gold Medal, Geneva, 1994
Cherry Meillandecor – See **Cherry Meidiland**, S
Cherry Page HT, pb, 1914, Easlea; flowers carmine-pink, base yellow; [Duchess of Bedford × Le Progres]
Cherry Parade Min, dp, Poulsen; flowers deep pink, medium, dbl., no fragrance; foliage dark; growth bushy, 20-40 cm.; PP12738; int. by Poulsen Roser, 1999
Cherry Parfait Gr, rb, 2001, Meilland International; bud conical; flowers white with red edges, 5 in., 30-35 petals, high-centered, borne in small clusters, no fragrance; foliage medium size, dark green, semi-glossy; prickles medium, moderate; growth bushy, medium (4-5 ft.); specimen, landscape; PP12802; [Meichoiju × (Meidanu × Macman)]; int. by The Conard-Pyle Company, 2000; Trial Ground Certificate, Durbanville, 2006, Golden Rose, Rose Hills, 2006, AARS, 2003
Cherry Pastel Min, mr, 1997, Williams, J. Benjamin; flowers bright cherry red, medium, dbl., borne mostly singly, moderate fragrance; [Red Sunblaze × Pink Sweetheart]; int. by Paramount Roses, 1997
Cherry Pie HT, dp, 1967, Gaujard; flowers deep rose-pink, 4½ in., dbl., high-centered, slight fragrance; int. by Gandy Roses, Ltd., 1965
Cherry Red HMoy, mr; flowers rich cherry red; [*R. moyesii fargesii* × unknown]
Cherry Ripe HT, mr, before 1922, Paul, W.
Cherry Ripe F, mr, 1949, Heers; flowers scarlet, small, 70 petals; intermittent bloom; vigorous growth; [sport of Orange Triumph]; int. by Pacific Nursery
Cherry-Rose HT, mp, 1946, Brownell; bud long, pointed; flowers cherry-rose, very large, dbl., high-centered, moderate fragrance; foliage glossy; very vigorous, upright, compact growth; [Pink Princess × Crimson Glory]
Cherry Rose Min, dp
Cherry Sunblaze Min, mr, 1993, Hutton, R.J.; flowers bright red, non-fading, 1-1½ in., 40-25 petals, borne in small clusters; foliage medium size, dark green, semi-glossy; some prickles; medium (35 cm.), bushy growth; PP8448; [Coppelia × Magic Carrousel]; int. by Conard-Pyle, 1993
Cherry-Vanilla Gr, pb, 1973, Armstrong, D.L.; bud pointed; flowers pink, center creamy yellow, medium, dbl., cupped; foliage dark, leathery; vigorous, upright, bushy growth; [Buccaneer × El Capitan]; int. by Armstrong Nursery
Cherry-Vanilla, Climbing Cl Gr, pb, Fineschi; flowers lemon yellow, changing to white with deep pink edges, very large, dbl.; int. in about 1990
Cherry Velvet HT, dp, 1989, Olesen, Pernille & Mogens N.; flowers deep pink, large, 20 petals, moderate fragrance; foliage large, medium green, glossy; upright, vigorous growth; [Vision × seedling]; int. by Poulsen Roser ApS, 1987
Cherry Wine Min, mr, 1993, Jalbert, Brad; flowers medium, full, borne mostly singly, slight fragrance; foliage medium size, medium green, matte; some prickles; medium (30-35 cm.), spreading growth; [Dee Bennett × Winsome]; int. by Select Roses, 1994
Cherryade S, dp, 1961, deRuiter; flowers deep pink, well-formed, 4 in., 40 petals; foliage dark; vigorous, tall growth; [New Dawn × Red Wonder]
Cherub HMult, pb, 1923, Clark, A.; flowers pink and salmon, small, semi-dbl., cupped; remontant; foliage rich green, glossy, wrinkled; very vigorous, climbing growth; [Claire Jacquier × unknown]; cultivar currently in commerce is probably not correct; int. by Brundrett
Cherubim – See **Cherub**, HMult
Chervena Ghita HT, mr, 1986, Staikov, Prof. Dr. V.; flowers bright cerise, large, 75 petals, borne in clusters; foliage dark, glossy; vigorous, upright growth; [General Stefanik × Peace]; int. by Kalaydjiev and Chorbadjiiski, 1974
Cheryl's Delight Min, pb, 1985, Williams, Ernest D.; flowers medium pink, reverse white, small, 35 petals, slight fragrance; foliage small, dark, semi-glossy; bushy growth; PP5910; [Little Darling × Over the Rainbow]; int. by Mini-Roses, 1984
Chesapeake Min, lp, 1984, Jolly, Nelson F.; flowers small, 50 petals; foliage medium size, medium green, semi-glossy; bushy growth; [Rise 'n' Shine × (Helen Traubel × First Prize)]; int. by Rosehill Farm
Chesapeake Sunset F, ob, Williams, J. Benjamin; flowers orange-yellow blend, dbl.; int. by Hortico, 1999
Cheshire HT, my, 1999, Fryer, Gareth; flowers golden honey yellow, large, dbl., borne in small clusters, moderate fragrance; foliage large, dark green, semi-glossy; prickles moderate; upright, medium (3 ft.) growth; int. by Fryer's Nurseries, Ltd., 1999
Cheshire S, mp, Kordes; flowers medium pink in center, outer petals pale pink to white, full, rosette, no fragrance; growth short (2 × 3 ft.), broad; int. in 2001
Cheshire Cream F, w, 1976, Holmes, R.; flowers soft buff, becoming cream, 2½ in., 50 petals, moderate spicy fragrance; foliage small, glossy; low growth; [(Anna Wheatcroft × Ivory Fashion) × (Buff Beauty × Masquerade)]; int. by Fryer's Nursery, Ltd.
Cheshire Lady HT, pb, 1970, Dale, F.; flowers bright pink to scarlet, large, 30-40 petals; free growth; [Fragrant Cloud × Gavotte]
Cheshire Life HT, or, 1973, Fryer, Gareth; flowers vermilion, 5 in., 36 petals, spiral-shaped, slight fragrance; foliage dark, leathery; [Prima Ballerina × Princess Michiko]; int. by Fryer's Nursery, Ltd., 1972
Cheshire Regiment HT, ab, Fryer, Gareth
Cheshunt Hybrid Cl HT, mr, 1872, Paul; flowers red shaded violet, large, dbl.; vigorous growth; [Mme de Tartas × Prince Camille de Rohan]; sometimes referred to as the first Hybrid Tea
Cheshunt Scarlet HP, mr, before 1902, Paul; flowers scarlet crimson, semi-dbl.
Chess F, m, 1993, Ilsink, G.P.; flowers deep purple, medium, full, borne in sprays, no fragrance; foliage medium size, dark green, glossy; few prickles; medium (55 cm.), upright growth; int. by Interplant B.V., 1991
Chess Man Min, mr, 1997, Giles, Kevin; flowers medium, very dbl., borne mostly singly; foliage medium size, dark green, dull; upright, medium (3 ft.) growth; [Chrysler Imperail × select pollen]; int. by Giles Rose Nursery
Chessum's Choice Sp, w, 1986, Chessum, Paul; [sport of Pfander's Canina]; strain of *R. canina*; used as a stem

of standard (tree) roses; int. by Alan Thompson, 1988

Chester F, my, 1977, Bees; flowers golden yellow, 3 in., 15 petals, slight fragrance; foliage glossy, dark; vigorous growth; [Arthur Bell × Zambra]; int. in 1976

Chester Cathedral HT, ab, 1991, Cowlishaw, Frank; bud pointed; flowers light apricot, reverse cream to very light gold, medium, dbl., high-centered, borne usually singly, slight fragrance; foliage medium size, dark green, glossy; low, bushy growth; [Honey Favorite × Piccadilly]

Chestnut rose – See ***R. roxburghii*** (Trattinnick)

Chevalier Angelo Ferrario T, dr, 1895, Bernaix; flowers carmine-purple, large, full

Chevalier Nigra HP, dr, 1865, Damaizin/Verdier

Chevreul M, mp, 1887, Moreau et Robert; flowers salmon-pink, well mossed; large fruit, colorful in fall

Chevreuse – See **Westfalenpark**, S

Chévrier – See **Miralda**, HCh

Chevy Chase HMult, dr, 1939, Hansen, N.J.; flowers dark crimson, small, 65 petals, borne in clusters of 10-20, moderate fragrance; non-recurrent; foliage soft, light green, wrinkled; vigorous, climbing (to 15 ft.) growth; [*R. soulieana* × Eblouissant]; int. by B&A; Dr. W. Van Fleet Medal, ARS, 1941

Cheyenne Cl HT, lp, 1962, Von Abrams; bud long, pointed; flowers light pink, coral-pink at base, 4-5 in., 30-40 petals, high-centered, slight fragrance; foliage leathery; vigorous (6-7 ft.) growth; RULED EXTINCT 1/85 ARM; [Queen Elizabeth × seedling]; int. by Peterson & Dering, 1962

Cheyenne Min, ab, 1985, Spooner, Raymond A.; flowers golden apricot, 20 petals, borne singly; foliage medium size, medium green, semi-glossy; upright growth; [Rise 'n' Shine × Center Gold]; int. by Oregon Miniature Roses, 1984

Cheyenne Frontier HT, w, 1972, Adams, M.R.; bud large; flowers white, slowly changing to red, medium, dbl., high-centered, slight fragrance; foliage large, glossy, dark; moderate, upright growth; [(Charlotte Armstrong × Vogue) × Peace]

Chez Vito HT, mr, 1973, Meilland; bud ovoid; flowers medium red, reverse lighter, medium, dbl., high-centered, moderate fragrance; foliage large, leathery; vigorous, upright, bushy growth; [Paris-Match × (Baccará × Happiness)]; int. by C-P

Chi Dan Hóng Xîn HCh, mr, from China

Chi lo Sà? HT, yb, 1965, Fratelli Giacomasso; flowers yellow suffused red; [(Peace × Fiaba) × seedling]

Chi Long Han Zhu – See **White Pearl in Red Dragon's Mouth**, Ch

Chianti S, m, 1967, Austin, David; flowers purplish maroon, semi-dbl., borne in small clusters, moderate fragrance; repeat bloom; foliage dark, glossy; vigorous growth; [Dusky Maiden × Tuscany]; int. by Sunningdale Nursery, 1967

Chianti F, dy, Select; int. by Terra Nigra BV, 2003

Chiarastella HT, rb, 1948, Fratelli Giacomasso; flowers rose-red and yellow bicolor, well-formed, large, dbl.; foliage glossy; strong stems; vigorous growth; [Julien Potin × Mme G. Forest-Colcombet]

Chibi F, Shinoda, D. S. & Umeda, G. Y.; PP3840

Chic F, pb, 1953, Boerner; bud ovoid; flowers geranium-pink, 2½ in., 68 petals, cupped, borne in clusters, moderate fragrance; vigorous, branching growth; PP1286; [(Pinocchio × unknown) × Fashion]; int. by J&P

Chic – See **Chic Parade**, MinFl

Chic Folies F, dp, Meilland; flowers magenta pink, dbl.; florist rose; int. by Meilland Intl, 2004

Chic Parade MinFl, lp, Poulsen; flowers light pink, 5-8 cm., dbl., no fragrance; foliage dark; growth bushy, 20-40 cm.; PP15405; int. by Poulsen Roser, 2001

Chic Parisien F, op, 1956, Delbard-Chabert; flowers coral-pink, center darker, well-formed, dbl., borne in clusters of 4-8; foliage dark; vigorous growth

Chica HT, lp, Kordes; int. in 1998

Chica Kordana – See **Chica Kordana Mini Brite**, Min

Chica Kordana Mini Brite Min, dp, Kordes; bud long, pointed ovoid; flowers 1¾ in., 40-45 petals, high-centered, flattens, borne singly and in small clusters, no fragrance; free-flowering; foliage leathery, glossy; prickles few, short, hooked downward; stems strong; vigorous, upright (20-22 in.), compact growth; PP11154; [Korialie × seedling]; int. by W. Kordes Söhne, 1998

Chicago HT, m, 1928, Aldous; flowers soft mauve-pink, dbl.; [sport of Premier]

Chicago Peace HT, pb, 1962, Johnston; flowers phlox-pink, base canary-yellow, 5-5½ in., 50-60 petals, cupped, borne mostly singly, slight fragrance; recurrent; foliage large, dark green, leathery, glossy; tall growth; PP2037; [sport of Peace]; int. by URS; Gold Medal, Portland, 1961

Chicago Peace, Climbing Cl HT, pb, Brundrett; [sport of Chicago Peace]; int. in 1978

Chichi Rose F, op

Chick-a-dee Min, mp, 1990, Moore, Ralph S.; bud pointed; flowers medium pink with occasional white stripes, reverse similar, 40-50 petals, high-centered, slight fragrance; foliage small, medium green, matte to semi-glossy; prickles small, hooked downward, brownish; bushy, low, compact, rounded growth; [Cécile Brunner × (Dortmund × (Fairy Moss × Little Darling × Ferdinand Pichard))]; int. by Sequoia Nursery

Chick-A-Dee, Climbing Cl Min, mp, 2000, Moore, Ralph S.; flowers medium pink, 4-7 cm., full, borne in large clusters; foliage medium size, dark green, glossy; few prickles; growth upright, spreading to 6 ft tall; [sport of Chick-A-Dee]; int. by Sequoia Nurs.

Chickasaw Rose – See ***R. bracteata*** (Wendland)

Chidori – See **Ryokkoh**, F

Chief – See **The Chief**, HT

Chief Justice Holmes Cl HT, dr, 1935, Schoener; flowers very dark red; [Jules Margottin × Château de Clos Vougeot]; Gold Medal, Portland, 1936

Chief Seattle HT, yb, 1951, Swim, H.C.; bud conical; flowers buff and old-gold, center shrimp-red, 4-5 in., 55 petals, high-centered, moderate fragrance; foliage glossy; tall growth; [Charlotte Armstrong × Signora]; int. by Armstrong Nursery

Chieftain HT, rb, 1936, Montgomery Co.; bud ovoid; flowers brilliant red, base yellow, large, dbl., high-centered; foliage leathery, dark; vigorous growth; [Hadley × Talisman]

Chiffon HT, lp, 1940, Grillo; flowers blush-pink, tinted light lavender, 5½ in., 30 petals; [sport of Regina Elena]

Chihuly F, rb, 2003, Carruth, Tom; flowers yellow blushing to orange, sometimes with subtle striping, finishing red, reverse more yellow with less blue, 9-11 cm., dbl., borne in small clusters, slight fragrance; foliage medium size, dark green, glossy; prickles moderate, average, straight, brown; stems dark red when new; growth bushy, medium (100-120 cm.); garden decoration; PP15076; [Scentimental × Amalia]; int. by Weeks Roses, 2004; Certificate of Merit, Rose Hills, 2006, Certificate of Merit, Palmerston, NZ, 2006

Chilcote Rose – See ***R. roxburghii*** (Trattinnick)

Child of Achievement – See **Bella Renaissance**, S

Child of France – See **Enfant de France**, HGal

Childhood Memories LCl, mp, Fergusson; int. in 1997

Childling C, mp, before 1759; sepals long; flowers large; foliage similar to *R.* × *centifolia*; frequently showing proliferation

Childs' Jewel HT, yb, 1902, Childs; flowers varying from dark copper-yellow to lighter, or vermilion with apricot yellow, medium, dbl.; [sport of Killarney]

Child's Play Min, pb, 1991, Saville, F. Harmon; flowers porcelain white with pink edges, 1½ in., 20 petals, high-centered, borne singly or in small clusters, moderate sweet fragrance; foliage medium size, dark green, matte; upright, medium growth; PP8175; [(Yellow Jewel × Tamango) × Party Girl]; int. by Nor'East Min. Roses; AOE, ARS, 1993

Chili Pepper Min, or, 1997, Giles, Diann; flowers medium, very dbl., borne in small clusters; foliage large, dark green, glossy; bushy, medium (1½-2 ft.) growth; [Vera Dalton × select pollen]; int. by Giles Rose Nursery

Chili Pepper F, mr, Select; int. by Terra Nigra BV, 2003

Chill Out Min, m, 1999, Giles, Diann; flowers large, dbl., borne mostly singly; foliage large, medium green, semi-glossy; few prickles; upright, tall growth; [Lavender Sweetheart × Herbie]; int. by Giles Rose Nursery, 1999

Chilterns – See **Red Ribbons**, S

Chimène – See **Sue Hipkin**, HT

Chimo S, mr, 1992, Ilsink, Peter; flowers red aging dark red, 1¼ in., 5 petals, cupped, borne singly; repeat bloom; foliage medium size, medium green, glossy; low (90 cm.), spreading growth; [seedling × Immensee]; int. by W. Kordes Sohne, 1988

Chin Chin – See **Promise**, HMult

Chin Chin China Ch, ly, 1909, Hobbies; [sport of Mme Eugene Résal]

China Belle HCh, pb, 1980, James, John; bud ovoid; flowers light and medium pink blend with yellow, dbl., cupped, borne 5-7 per cluster, slight fruity fragrance; foliage glossy; prickles curved, red; short stems; compact, bushy, upright growth; [(Doubloons × Holiday) × Slater's Crimson China]

China Doll Pol, mp, 1946, Lammerts, Dr. Walter; bud pointed; flowers China-rose, base mimosa-yellow, 1-2 in., 24 petals, cupped, borne in large trusses, slight tea fragrance; foliage leathery, with mostly 5 leaflets (similar to Pinkie); dwarf (18 in.), bushy growth; [Mrs Dudley Fulton × Tom Thumb]; int. by Armstrong Nursery

China Doll, Climbing Cl Pol, mp, 1978, Weeks; flowers bright pink, 5 cm., dbl., borne several to a stem on laterals from climbing canes, slight tea to spicy fragrance; recurrent; foliage glossy; prickles very few, short, hooked downward; vigorous, tall (4-6 ft.) growth; PP4323; [sport of China Doll]; int. by Weeks Wholesale Rose Growers, 1977

China Girl F, my, Tantau; flowers strong lemon yellow, 4 in., very full, cupped, borne in clusters, slight fragrance; good repeat; strong, compact (2-3 ft.) growth; int. by Rosen Tantau, 2006

China Rose – See ***R. chinensis*** (Jacquin)

China Sunrise HT, ab, 2001, Newman, Laurie; flowers light apricot, darker reverse, 8 cm., 25-30 petals, borne mostly solitary, intense fragrance; foliage medium size, dark green, glossy; prickles moderate, medium, slightly curved; upright, medium (1½ m.) growth; [Parador × Jocelyn]; int. by Reliable Roses, 2001

Chinaberry Min, yb, Benardella, Frank; int. by Bell Roses

Chinatown F, dy, 1965, Poulsen, Niels D.; flowers yellow, sometimes edged pink, 4 in., dbl., borne in clusters, intense fragrance; foliage dark; vigorous, tall, bushy growth; [Columbine × Clare Grammerstorf]; int. by A. Dickson; Gold Medal, NRS, 1962

Chinatown Moss M, rb

Chinese Lantern Min, rb, 1987, Jacobs, Betty A.; flowers hand-painted red, yellow and white, reverse light pink, fading red and white, 15 petals, slight spicy fragrance; foliage medium size, medium green, red when young, glossy; bushy, spreading, medium growth; hips round, medium, red-orange; [Avandel × Old Master]; int. by Four Seasons Rose Nursery, 1986

Chinese Monthly Rose – See **Slater's Crimson China**, Ch

Chinese Puzzle MinFl, rb, 1999, Giles, Diann; flowers small, dbl., borne in large clusters; foliage small, dark green, glossy; numerous prickles; climbing, tall growth; [Vera Dalton × Roller Coaster]; int. by Giles Rose Nursery, 1999

Chingari F, yb, 1976, Pal, Dr. B.P.; bud pointed; flowers aureolin to currant-red, open, 3 in., 17 petals; foliage glossy; vigorous, bushy, compact growth; [Charleston × seedling]; int. by Laveena Roses, 1975

Chinquapin Rose – See ***R. roxburghii*** (Trattinnick)

Chipie F, ab, 1978, Poulsen, Niels D.; flowers rose-begonia to apricot, open, 4 in., 24 petals; foliage light green; bushy growth; [(Elizabeth of Glamis × (Heidelberg × 8366-2)) × (Pernille Poulsen × (Danish Gold × Mischief))]; int. by Vilmorin-Andrieux, 1974

Chipmonk – See **Chipmunk**, Min

Chipmunk Min, r, 1991, Chaffin, Lauren M.; flowers tannish brown blending with mauve when full blown, large, full, borne mostly singly, moderate fragrance; foliage medium size, medium green, semi-glossy; few prickles; medium (30 cm.), bushy, neat, compact growth; [Deep Purple × Rainbow's End]; int. by Pixie Treasures Min. Roses, 1992

Chippendale S, ob, Tantau; flowers deep orange, outer petals lighter, 4 in., full, cupped, intense fragrance; good repeat; foliage dark green, glossy; strong (80-100 cm.) growth; int. by Rosen Tantau, 2006

Chipper Min, ab, 1966, Meilland, Alain A.; bud ovoid; flowers salmon-pink, small, dbl., slight fragrance; foliage glossy, leathery; vigorous, dwarf growth; PP2764; [((Dany Robin × unknown) × Fire King) × Perla de Montserrat]; int. by C-P

Chippewa S, mp, Central Exp. Farm; flowers rose-pink, semi-dbl., borne in clusters; foliage leathery, bronze

Chiquita LCl, op, 1938, Moore, Ralph S.; flowers orange-yellow to coppery orange and salmon-pink, base yellow; RULED EXTINCT 1/88; [Sierra Snowstorm × Étoile Luisante]; int. by Brooks & Son

Chiquita Min, dr, 1988, Moore, Ralph S.; flowers rich, dark red with fluorescent glow, 20 petals, flat, borne singly, slight fragrance; foliage small, medium green, matte; prickles hooked, short, brown; upright, bushy, medium growth; few to no hips; [Anytime × Happy Hour]; int. by Sequoia Nursery

Chiquito F, or, de Ruiter; int. by Sauvageot, 1977

Chiraz HT, pb, 1986, Kriloff, Michel; flowers creamy white, flushed pink, petals edged carmine red, large; foliage dark; dense growth; [Kordes' Perfecta × Peace]

Chireno S, dp, 2002, Ponton, Ray; flowers 3-4 in., single, borne mostly solitary; foliage medium size, medium green, semi-glossy; prickles medium, straight, few; growth upright, spreading, medium (4 ft.); landscape; [Carefree Beauty × Mutabilis]; int. by Chamblee's Rose Nursery, 2002

Chiripa F, mr, 1957, de Dot, G.F.; bud pointed; flowers red, reverse carmine, 26 petals, borne in clusters of 3-5; foliage bright green; upright, compact growth; [Radar × (Rosalia Riviera × Independence)]

Chit Chat Min, my, 1999, Bridges, Dennis A.; flowers ¾ in., full, borne mostly singly, no fragrance; foliage medium size, dark green, semi-glossy; few prickles; compact, bushy, medium (18-20 in.) growth; [Cal Poly × unknown]; int. by Bridges Roses

Chitchor F, pb, 1974, Pal, Dr. B.P.; buds medium, pointed; flowers white suffused with pink, medium, dbl, open, borne several together; foliage light green, soft; growth very vigorous, bushy (95 cm.); [Pink Parfait × unknown]; int. by IARI, 1972

Chitina – See **Aspen**, S

Chitra HT, ob, IARI; flowers tangerine orange with white stripes; free-flowering; [sport of Janina]; int. in 1995

Chitralekha HT, or, 1974, IARI; buds large, long pointed; flowers ruby-red to signal-red, large, dbl, high-centered, borne singly, slight tea fragrance; foliage medium size, soft; growth vigorous, bushy (65 cm.); [Montezuma × Baccara]; int. in 1972

Chitrarajini HT, pb, Kasturi; flowers ivory with a tinge of pink, becoming deeper rose red, dbl., high-centered; int. by KSG Son, 1985

Chitwan HT, my, 1973, Indian Agri. Research Institute; buds large, long pointed; flowers primrose-yellow, large, very dbl., high-centered, borne mostly singly; foliage medium size, light green, soft; growth vigorous, compact, bushy; [Western Sun × Golden Splendor]

Chivalry HT, rb, 1978, McGredy, Sam IV; flowers red, yellowish reverse, large, 35 petals; foliage glossy, dark; PP4281; [Peer Gynt × Brasilia]; int. by Mattock, 1977

Chiyo HT, dp, 1976, Ota, Saku; bud long, pointed; flowers deep pink, 4-4½ in., 25 petals, high-centered, slight fruity fragrance; foliage glossy, medium to dark green; vigorous, upright growth; [Karl Herbst × Chrysler Imperial]; int. by Eastern Roses, 1975

Chloe – See **Chloe Renaissance**, S

Chloe – See **Chloe's Star**, Min

Chloe of Childerly F, or, 2002, Bossom, Bill; flowers large, semi-dbl., borne in small clusters, slight fragrance; foliage dark green, semi-glossy; prickles in., triangular, moderate; growth upright, medium (3 ft.); garden decorative; [Sexy Rexy × Forever Amber]

Chloe Renaissance S, lp, Poulsen; flowers light pink, 10-15 cm., dbl., intense fragrance; foliage dark; growth bushy, 100-150 cm.; PP15467; int. by Poulsen Roser, 2001

Chloe's Star Min, my, 2002, Pazdzierski, Jim; flowers dbl., high-centered, borne in small clusters, slight fragrance; foliage medium size, dark green, glossy; prickles ¼ in., needle-point, moderate; growth upright (20-24 in.); garden decorative, exhibition, containers; [sport of Brittany's Glowing Star]; int. as Chloe, Select Roses, 2002

Chloris A, lp, before 1820, Descemet; flowers soft pink, many-petaled, reflexing with a button eye, medium, dbl., borne in clusters of 4-6, slight fragrance; foliage dark, leathery, bluish-green; very few prickles; vigorous (to 4-5 ft.) growth

Chloris HT, mr, 1890, Geschwind; flowers light purple-crimson, very large, full

Chobee F, mr, 1993, Giles, Diann; flowers medium, full, borne mostly singly, slight fragrance; foliage medium size, medium green, matte; few prickles; medium, bushy growth; [seedling × Congratulations]; int. by Giles Rose Nursery, 1993

Chocolate Prince – See **Terracotta**, HT

Chocolate Ruffles F, r; int. by Hole's Greenhouses & Gardens, 2005

Choo-Choo Centennial Min, lp, 1980, Jolly, Betty J.; bud ovoid; flowers light pink, edged darker, reverse white, small, 68 petals, high-centered, borne in clusters, slight fragrance; foliage matte, light green; prickles straight; compact, bushy growth; PP4849; [Rise 'n' Shine × Grand Opera]; int. by Rosehill Farm

Choo-Choo's Baby Min, rb, 1981, Jolly, Betty J.; bud urn-shaped; flowers red, shaded to yellow at base, 26 petals, flat, borne singly and in pairs, slight fragrance; foliage tiny, light green; no prickles; low, branching, dense growth; [Watercolor × Watercolor seedling]; int. by Rosehill Farm, 1980

Chopin HT, mr, 1968, Ellick; flowers 4-6 in., 38 petals; foliage medium to light green; vigorous growth; [Montezuma × Christian Dior]

Chopin – See **Fréderic Chopin**, HT

Chorale S, lp, 1978, Buck, Dr. Griffith J.; bud ovoid, pointed; flowers pale pink, large, 48 petals, high-centered; foliage dark, leathery; vigorous, upright, bushy growth; [(Ruth Hewitt × Queen Elizabeth) × (Morning Stars × Suzanne)]; int. by Iowa State University

Chorus F, or, 1976, Paolino; flowers vermilion-red, 4 in., 35 petals, borne several together, slight fruity fragrance; foliage glossy; vigorous growth; [Tamango × (Sarabande × Zambra)]; int. by URS, 1975; ADR, 1977

Chorus, Climbing Cl F, or, Meilland; int. in 1986

Chorus Girl F, or, 1970, Robinson, H.; flowers vermilion, 3 in., 16 petals, high-centered; foliage dark, coppery; [Highlight × seedling]; int. by Victoria Nursery

Chorus Line S, dr, 1992, Zary, Keith & Warriner, William; flowers red, cream base, 3-3½ in., 16-20 petals, borne in small clusters; foliage large, dark green, semi-glossy; some prickles; medium (120-135 cm.), upright, bushy, very vigorous growth; [Razzle Dazzle × seedling]; int. by Bear Creek Gardens

Chot Pestitele HP, mp, 1932, Böhm, J.; bud oblong; flowers rose-pink, 6 in., 22 petals, flat; foliage glossy; [sport of Frau Karl Druschki]

Chota F, or, 1976, Sheen; flowers light vermilion, large, 50 petals, slight fragrance; foliage small, semi-glossy; moderately low growth; [Violet Carson × Korona]

Chou – See **Cabbage Rose**, C

Chouette Pol, dr, 1969, Delforge; bud ovoid; flowers dark fire-red, large, dbl.; foliage dark, soft; vigorous, bushy growth; [Atlantic × seedling]

Chowan HT, ob, 1995, Perry, Astor; flowers 4¾ in., full, high-centered, borne mostly singly, moderate fragrance; recurrent; foliage large, medium green, dull; some prickles; tall (160 cm.), upright growth; [Folklore × Hot Pewter]; int. by Hortico Roses, 1995

Chremesina Scintilland – See **Admirable**, HGal

Chris LCl, my, Kirkham, Gordon Wilson; flowers rich yellow with orange shadings on outer petals, large, dbl., high-centered, moderate fragrance; vigorous growth to 8-10 ft.; int. in 1999

Chris Evert HT, ob, 1996, Carruth, Tom; flowers clear orange-yellow blushing red, reverse with less blush, full, high-centered, borne singly, moderate fruity fragrance; foliage clean, medium size, dark green, semi-glossy; prickles moderate; upright, compact, medium (3-4 ft.) growth; PP10071; [Voodoo × (Katherine Loker × Gingersnap)]; int. by Spring Hill Nurseries Co., 1996

Chris Jolly MinFl, or, 1985, Jolly, Nelson F.; flowers medium, 40 petals, high-centered, slight fragrance; foliage medium size, medium green, semi-glossy; upright, bushy growth; [(Orange Sweetheart × Zinger) × Rise 'n' Shine]; int. by Rosehill Farm

Chris Rabe F, w, 2002, Chaney, William E.; flowers borne in small clusters, slight fragrance; foliage small, medium green, semi-glossy; prickles small, thin, curved downward, green, moderate; growth compact, short; [floribunda seedling × miniature seedling]

Chriss and Dianni Sp, w; used as understock; clone of *R. multiflora*

Chrissie MacKellar HT, op, 1913, Dickson, A.; bud crimson-carmine on deep madder; flowers orange-pink, reverse deeply zoned orange, semi-dbl.

Christa Min, w, 1993, Chaffin, Lauren M.; flowers large, full, high-centered, borne mostly singly, slight fragrance; foliage medium size, medium green, semi-glossy, disease-resistant; some prickles; long stems; tall (45 cm.), upright, vigorous growth; [Honor × Rise 'n' Shine]; int. by Pixie Treasures Min. Roses, 1993

Christel von der Post HT, dy, 2006; bud large, elongated; flowers medium size, lasting color, 10 cm., full, high-centered, borne mostly solitary, moderate fragrance; foliage fresh green, glossy; bushy, upright, vigorous growth to 3 ft.; int. by W. Kordes' Söhne, 1990

Christian F, m; PPAF; int. by Bear Creek Gardens, 2000

Christian Curle HWich, lp, 1910, Cocker; flowers flesh-pink, small, full; [sport of Dorothy Perkins]

Christian Dior HT, mr, 1959, Meilland, F.; bud ovoid, pointed; flowers clear true red, 4-4½ in., 45-50 petals, high-centered, borne mostly singly, slight soft spice fragrance; foliage leathery, glossy; long stems; vigorous, upright, bushy growth; PP1943; [(Independence × Happiness) × (Peace × Happiness)]; int. by URS, 1958; Gold Medal, Geneva, 1958

Christian Dior, Climbing Cl HT, mr, 1966, Chang, Chi-Shiang

Christian Püttner HP, m, 1862, Oger; flowers bright purple, shaded pomegranate, large, full

Christian Schultheis S, pb, Schultheis; flowers deep pink, paler reverse, large, very dbl., cupped; dark green, glossy foliage; strong growth to 5 ft. tall and wide; int. by Rosen von Schultheis, 2000

Christiana Wood HT, mr, 1979, Wood, J.; bud ovoid; upright, bushy growth; [sport of Tropicana]; int. in 1975

Christiane Horbiger F, w

Christina HT, pb, 1959, Crouch; flowers pink, reverse currant red, dbl.; very vigorous growth; RULED EXTINCT 12/85 ARM; [Granat × Radiance]; int. by Roseglen Nursery

Christina HT, pb, 1986, Staikov, Prof. Dr. V., Kalaydjieve & Chorbadjiiski; flowers deep pink, reverse light pink, large, 45 petals; foliage leathery, glossy; vigorous, upright growth; [Rina Herholdt × seedling]; int. in 1977

Christina HT, my, 1990, Select Roses, B.V.; bud pointed; flowers bright lemon-yellow, non-fading, medium to large, 43 petals, cupped, borne singly, no fragrance; foliage large, dark green, glossy; prickles declining, light red; upright, tall growth; [Eliora × seedling]; int. by DeVor Nurseries, Inc., 1990

Christina Atherton HT, op, 1979, McGredy, Sam IV; flowers salmon-pink, 4 in., 33 petals, high-centered, slight fragrance; free growth; [Tiki × seedling]; int. in 1978

Christina Nilsson HP, mr, 1861, Jamain; flowers cerise red, very large, full, cupped; [Général Jacqueminot × unknown]

Christine HT, dy, 1918, McGredy; flowers deep golden yellow, small, moderate fragrance; foliage dark, glossy; Gold Medal, NRS, 1916

Christine, Climbing Cl HT, dy, 1936, Willink; flowers golden-yellow, small, dbl.; growth to 15 ft.

Christine S, ob, Clements, John K.; flowers flame-orange, 4 in., 5-7 petals; leathery, dark green foliage; upright growth, 4-6 ft; PPAF; int. by Heirloom Roses, 1998

Christine S, ab; int. in 2001

Christine HT, ab, Kordes; int. by W. Kordes Söhne

Christine de Noué – See **Mlle Christine de Noué**, T, 1890

Christine Gandy F, dp, 1959, deRuiter; flowers deep pink, 3 in., semi-dbl., borne in small clusters, moderate fragrance; foliage dark; vigorous growth; [Polyantha seedling × Fashion]; int. by Gandy Roses, Ltd., 1958

Christine Horbiger – See **Mount Hood**, HT

Christine Lanson HT, ob

Christine Marina F, m, 2003, McCann, Sean; flowers edged lighter, large, full, flat, borne in large clusters, moderate fragrance; foliage medium size, medium green, semi-glossy; prickles moderate; growth upright, medium; garden decorative; [Gentle Annie × Charles de Gaulle]; int. in 2003

Christine Prior HT, rb, 1924, McGredy; flowers deep rosy red, flushed yellow and peach, base yellow, semi-dbl.

Christine Weinert Min, or, 1976, Moore, Ralph S.; flowers brilliant scarlet, shaded deeper, flat to rounded, 1 in., 25 petals, moderate fragrance; foliage small, leathery; upright, bushy growth; PP4030; [(Little Darling × Eleanor) × (Little Darling × Eleanor)]; int. by Sequoia Nursery

Christine Wright HWich, mp, 1909, Farrell; flowers wild-rose-pink, fading to pale, silvery pink, 7-9 cm., semi-dbl., cupped, borne singly and in small clusters, moderate fragrance; foliage glossy; long stems; growth to 12-15 ft.; [(*R. wichurana* × Marion Dingee) × Mme Caroline Testout]

Christine Wunderlich HT, op, 1934, Wunderlich; flowers yellowish-orange-pink, large; very vigorous growth; [sport of Golden Ophelia]

Christine's Dream HT, rb, 2002, Bridges, Dennis; flowers medium red, reverse pink-white, medium, full, borne mostly solitary, moderate fragrance; foliage medium size, dark green, semi-glossy; prickles moderate; growth vigorous, upright, medium (4½-5½ ft.); garden, exhibition, cutting; [King of Hearts × Thriller]; int. by Bridges' Roses, 2002

Christingle F, or, 1985, Harkness, R., & Co., Ltd.; flowers large, 35 petals; foliage medium size, dark, semi-glossy; bushy growth; [Bobby Dazzler × Alexander]; int. in 1987

Christmas Beauty HT, dr, 1942, Krowka; flowers darker red than parent, 4½-5 in., 25-30 petals; foliage blue-green, leathery; vigorous growth; [sport of Better Times]

Christmas Card HT, ly, 1995, Sheldon, John & Robin; flowers light yellow, fading to white on outer petals, large, full, borne mostly singly, moderate fragrance; foliage medium size, medium green, matte; upright, medium growth; [Spirit of Glasnost × Lanvin]

Christmas Cheer HT, mr, 1957, Joseph H. Hill, Co.; bud long, pointed; flowers cherry-red, 4½-5½ in., 45-50 petals, high-centered, slight fragrance; foliage dark, leathery; vigorous, upright growth; PP1468; [Sister Kenny × Happiness]

Christmas Red HT, mr, 1948, Brownell; bud large, long, pointed; flowers spectrum-red, open, dbl., moderate fragrance; foliage glossy; bushy, dwarf growth; [Pink Princess × Crimson Glory]

Christmas Snow HMult, w, Clements, John; flowers pure white, 2½ in., 60 petals, cupped, borne in large clusters; non-recurrent; rich green foliage; vigorous, climbing growth, 14 ft.; PPAF; int. by Heirloom Roses, 2000

Christobel HT, ab, 1937, Croibier; flowers apricot-yellow shaded salmon, very large, dbl.; foliage glossy; very vigorous, bushy growth; [Frau Karl Druschki × Mme Butterfly]

Christoph Colombus – See **Christopher Columbus**, HT

Christoph Weigand HT, lp, 1928, Weigand, C.; flowers very large, dbl., high-centered; foliage rich green, wrinkled; vigorous growth; [Frau Karl Druschki × Souv. de Claudius Pernet]

Christophe Colomb – See **Cristoforo Colombo**, HT

Christophe Colomb – See **Christopher Columbus**, HT

Christophe Colomb, Cl. Cl HT, or, Meilland; flowers much like the bush form, large, dbl.; dark green foliage; growth to 2 m. and more

Christophe Colombe P, m, 1854, Robert; flowers amaranth purple, darker at center, 11-13 cm., full, flat

Christophe Colomb, Gpt. – See **Christophe Colomb, Cl.**, Cl HT

Christophe Combejean Gr, rb, Guillot-Massad; bud pointed; flowers red, striped yellow which fades to white, borne in clusters of 5-7; int. by Roseraies Guillot, 2005

Christopher Min, mr, 1988, Bennett, Dee; flowers medium red, medium, 30-35 petals, high-centered, borne usually singly or in sprays of 3-5; foliage medium size, medium green, semi-glossy; prickles hooked slightly downward, yellow-red; upright, medium growth; hips globular, green-brown; PP7191; [Futura × Big John]; int. by Tiny Petals Nursery

Christopher HT, mr, Cocker; flowers bright red, dbl., high-centered; dark green glossy foliage; upright, compact growth, 2½ ft.; [Anne Cocker × National Trust]; int. in 1993

Christopher Columbus HT, ob, 1992, Selection Meilland; bud oval, large; flowers orange blend/copper, 4-5 in., 25-27 petals, cupped, borne mostly singly, slight fragrance; good repeat; foliage large, dark green, semi-glossy; prickles numerous, large; medium (120-140 cm.), upright growth; PP8496; [Coppélia 76 × (Ambassador × MEInaregi)]; Gold Medal, Durbanville, 1990

Christopher Columbus – See **Nashville**, S

Christopher Marlowe S, or, 2004; flowers orange-red, reverse yellow blend & orange-red, 7½ cm., very full, borne in small clusters, moderate fragrance; foliage medium size, dark green, semi-glossy; prickles medium, deeply concave; growth bushy, branching, short (90 cm.); garden decorative; PP14943; [seedling (medium pink shrub) × Golden Celebration]; int. by David Austin Roses, Ltd., 2002; Bronze Medal, Adelaide, 2006

Christopher Milton HT, dp, 1967, Martin, W.A.; bud long, pointed, light red; flowers medium pink, edged lighter, large, dbl., high-centered; foliage dark, glossy; very vigorous, upright growth; [sport of Christian Dior]

Christopher Popwell HT, dr, 2006, Popwell, Larry G., Sr; flowers large, semi-dbl., borne mostly solitary; foliage medium size, medium green, semi-glossy; prickles moderate; growth bushy, 30 in.; [Altissimo × Love]; int. in 2006

Christopher Stone HT, mr, 1935, Robinson, H.; bud long, pointed; flowers large, 30 petals, moderate damask fragrance; foliage bright green; vigorous growth; int. by Wheatcroft Bros., 1935; Gold Medal, Portland, 1937, Gold Medal, NRS, 1934

Christopher Stone, Climbing Cl HT, mr, 1942, Marsh's Nursery; flowers intense red-scarlet flowers with maroon-scarlet flush to outer petals, 5 in., semi-dbl.

Chromatella N, ly, 1843, Coquereau; flowers creamy white, center yellow, large, very dbl., globular, quartered, moderate fragrance; vigorous, climbing growth; [Lamarque × unknown]

Chrysandra S, dp, Weihrauch; flowers carmine-pink, large, semi-dbl.; int. in 1983

Chryscinn – See **Belle Epoque**, HT

Chrysler Min, pb, Benardella, Frank; int. by Treloar Roses, 2003

Chrysler Imperial HT, dr, 1952, Lammerts, Dr. Walter; bud long, pointed; flowers deep red, velvety, 4½-5 in., 45-50 petals, high-centered, borne singly; foliage dark, semi-glossy; vigorous, compact growth; [Charlotte Armstrong × Mirandy]; int. by Germain's; John Cook Medal, ARS, 1964, James Alexander Gamble Fragrance Medal, ARS, 1965, Gold Medal, Portland, 1951, Gold Medal, ARS, 1956

Chrysler Imperial, Climbing Cl HT, dr, 1958, Begonia, P.B.; flowers dark red, velvety, very dbl., intense fragrance; PP1528; [sport of Chrysler Imperial]; int. by Germain's, 1956

Chrystelle HT, or, 1979, Godin, M.; bud oval; flowers deep, large, 30-35 petals, cupped; foliage dark; [(Lady

Zia × Wizo) × Silver Lining]; int. in 1975

Chryzia HT, dp, 1970, Wyant; bud long, pointed; flowers light red, large, dbl.; vigorous, upright, bushy growth; [Chrysler Imperial × Lady Zia]

Chuckles F, dp, 1955, Shepherd; bud long, pointed; flowers deep pink, white eye, large, 11 petals, borne in large clusters, moderate fragrance; foliage dark, leathery; vigorous, bushy growth; PP1608; [(Jean Lafitte × New Dawn) × Orange Triumph]; int. by Bosley Nursery, 1955

Chula Vista Min, dr, 1992, Bennett, Dee; flowers medium, full, high-centered, borne mostly singly, slight fragrance; foliage small, medium green, semi-glossy, disease-resistant; some prickles; long stems; medium (60-80 cm.), bushy growth; [Christian Dior × Brian Lee]; int. by Tiny Petals Nursery, 1993

Chumki HT, pb, Ghosh; flowers creamy pink with outer edges and reverse of deeper pink, well formed; int. by KSG, 2001

Chunga – See **Ralph's Creeper**, S

Church Mouse Min, r, 1989, Jacobs, Betty A.; bud pointed; flowers tan-brown, with yellow at base, aging light lavender-brown, 20 petals, moderate sweet fragrance; foliage large, medium green, matte; prickles slightly declining, small, red to tan; low, bushy, compact growth; no fruit; [Angel Face × Plum Duffy]; int. by Sequoia Nursery, 1989

Ciak LCl, rb, Barni, V.; flowers red with golden yellow halo in center, single, borne in clusters, no fragrance; growth to 8-20 ft.; int. by Rose Barni, 1994

Ciana Rose Min, lp, 2002, McCann, Sean; flowers medium, dbl., borne in large clusters; foliage medium size, medium green, semi-glossy; few prickles; growth compact, medium; garden decorative; [Kiss 'n' Tell × Sexy Rexy]

Ciao S, or, Hiroshima; groundcover; spreading growth; int. by Hiroshima Bara-en, 2002

Cibles HRg, mr, 1893, Kaufmann; flowers bright red, base yellow, medium, single; vigorous, upright growth; [*R. rugosa rubra* × Perle de Lyon]

Cicely Lascelles Cl HT, op, 1932, Clark, A.; flowers pink shaded salmon, reverse darker, 12 cm., semi-dbl.; recurrent; growth very vigorous; pillar; [Frau Oberhofgartner Singer × Scorcher]

Cicely O'Rorke Cl HT, mp, 1937, Clark, A.; flowers pink, shaded salmon, large, semi-dbl., cupped; recurrent bloom; long stems; very vigorous, climbing or pillar growth; [Souv. de Gustave Prat × seedling]; int. by NRS Victoria

Cidade de Lisboa LCl, pb, 1939, Moreira da Silva; bud long, pointed; flowers salmon-pink, edged yellow, large, semi-dbl., high-centered; long stems; vigorous growth; [Belle Portugaise × Mme Edouard Herriot]

Cider Cup Min, ob, 1987, Dickson, Patrick; flowers medium, dbl.; foliage medium size, medium green, glossy; patio growth; [Memento × (Liverpool Echo × Woman's Own)]; int. in 1988

Ciel Bleu HT, m, Dot, Simon; int. in 1982

Cilly Michel HT, or, 1928, Felberg-Leclerc; flowers nasturtium-red, large, dbl.; [Mme Mélanie Soupert × Felbergs Rosa Druschki]

Cimarosa F, op, 2000, Lens, Louis; flowers orange-pink, 7-8 cm., very full, borne in small clusters, intense fragrance; recurrent bloom; foliage medium size, brown-green, glossy; prickles moderate; growth bushy, medium (2 ft.); [Little Angel × Fragrant Delight]; int. by Louis Lens NV, 1989

Cimarron HT, pb, 1938, Hillock; bud spiraled, almost red; flowers ruffled, salmon, reverse deep pink; vigorous, compact growth; [Nellie E. Hillock × Golden Dawn]

Cina HT, ob, 1978, Gaujard; bud full; flowers brilliant coral, flushed salmon; foliage large; [Premiere Ballerine × Femina]; int. in 1973

Cinderella N, pb, 1859, Page; flowers salmon-pink to carmine-pink

Cinderella HWich, dp, 1909, Walsh; flowers deep pink, petal tips quilled, small, dbl., borne in large clusters; free, non-recurrent bloom; vigorous growth

Cinderella Min, w, 1953, deVink; flowers satiny white tinged pale flesh, very small, 1 in., 55 petals, moderate spicy fragrance; no prickles; upright growth; [Cécile Brunner × Tom Thumb]; int. by C-P

Cinderella, Climbing Cl Min, w, 1975, Sequoia Nursery; int. by Moore Miniature Roses, 1975

Cinderella Min, m, Schuurman; flowers deep vibrant mauve, dbl.; growth medium to tall; int. by De Boer Roses, 1999

Cinderella S, lp, 2006; flowers soft pink, 10 cm., very dbl., cupped, borne in clusters of 4-6, moderate fruity/apple fragrance; foliage medium size, dark green, very glossy, dense; growth very bushy, well branched, upright, 4-5 ft.; int. by W. Kordes' Söhne, 2003

Cinderella HT, mp, Kordes; flowers medium pink, turning lighter as it opens, large, full, high-centered, borne mostly singly; recurrent; prickles nearly absent; stems long; int. by W. Kordes Söhne, 2006

Cinderella Gold Min, my, 1995, Moore, Ralph S.; flowers small, dbl., borne mostly singly and in small clusters; foliage small, light green, semi-glossy; no prickles; low (15 cm.) bushy growth; [Cal Poly × Cal Poly]; int. by Sequoia Nursery, 1996

Cinderella Kordana Min, mp, Kordes; flowers soft pink, full; container rose; int. by W. Kordes Söhne, 2005

Cinderella's Midnight Rose HT, mp, 1978, Bernard; flowers rich pink, 4-5 in., slight fragrance; foliage glossy; vigorous growth

Cindy Min, dp, 1985, Williams, Ernest D.; flowers deep pink, well-formed, small, dbl.; foliage small, dark, glossy; [Tom Brown × Over the Rainbow]; int. by Mini-Roses

Cindy – See **LeAnn Rimes**, HT

Cindy – See **Cindy de Meilland**, F

Cindy de Meilland F, pb, Meilland; flowers pale pink edged with dark pink; greenhouse rose; int. by Meilland Intl., 1997

Cineraire Ch, rb, 1970, Lambert; flowers rich red, center white, very small, 5 petals, cupped, borne in trusses; int. by E. Murrell, before 1964

Cinerama HT, pb, 1966, Herholdt, J.A.; flowers salmon, reverse buff-yellow, pointed, 4½-5 in.; vigorous growth; [seedling × Tzigane]

Cineraria Pol, rb, 1909, Lambert; flowers light red, white in center, small, single

Cineraria Pol, m, 1934, Leenders, M.; flowers carmine-purple, center white, open, large, semi-dbl.; foliage soft; vigorous, bushy growth; [Miss Edith Cavell × Tip-Top]

Cingallegra HT, yb, 1958, Cazzaniga, F. G.; bud well shaped; flowers lemon-yellow, edged pinkish, dbl.; long, strong stems; [Golden Scepter × Crimson Glory]

Cinnabar F, or, 1945, Tantau; bud small, globular; flowers vermilion to scarlet, semi-dbl., cupped, borne in clusters, slight fragrance; recurrent; foliage leathery; bushy, upright growth; [Baby Chateau × *R. roxburghii*]

Cinnabar Improved F, or, 1951, Tantau; flowers orange-scarlet, semi-dbl., borne in trusses; [(Cinnabar × Kathe Duvigneau) × Cinnabar]

Cinnamon Delight Min, r, 1993, Williams, Ernest D.; flowers russet with deep yellow base, medium, full, borne mostly singly, intense fragrance; foliage small, dark green, semi-glossy; few prickles; medium (40 cm.), upright growth; [seedling × Twilight Trail]; int. by Mini Roses of Texas, 1993

Cinnamon Rose – See ***R. cinnamomea*** (Linnaeus)

Cinnamon Toast Min, r, 1986, Saville, F. Harmon; flowers russet brown, small, 28 petals, high-centered; foliage small, medium green, semi-glossy; prickles small, red; low, upright, bushy growth; [Zorina × (Sheri Anne × Glenfiddich)]; int. by Nor'East Min. Roses

Cinnamon Twist F, ob, 2007, Zary, Keith W.; flowers orange turning coral-orange, 5 in., 25-30 petals, blooms borne mostly solitary; foliage medium size, dark green, glossy; prickles 6-8 mm., straight, greyed-orange, moderate; growth compact (3½ ft.); [seedling × Outrageous]; int. by Jackson & Perkins Wholesale, Inc., 2007

Cinzia ; int. in 1996

Circé M, pb, 1855, Robert; flowers delicate pink spotted with white, 4-6 cm., full, flat; some repeat

Circe HT, lp, 1916, Paul, W.; flowers whitish-pink shaded with carmine, base deep yellow, large, dbl.

Circé F, or, 1979, Gaujard; bud long; flowers brilliant orange-red, 1½-2 in., 16 petals; foliage large, dark; vigorous, compact growth; [Guitare × Prominent]

Circumpolar Rose – See ***R. acicularis*** (Lindley)

Circus F, yb, 1956, Swim, H.C.; bud urn-shaped; flowers yellow marked pink, salmon and scarlet, 2½-3 in., 45-58 petals, high-centered, borne in large, ruffled clusters, moderate tea to spicy fragrance; foliage semi-glossy, leathery; bushy growth; PP1382; [Fandango × Pinocchio]; int. by Armstrong Nursery, 1956; Gold Medal, NRS, 1955, Gold Medal, Geneva, 1955

Circus, Climbing Cl F, yb, 1961, House; PP2074; int. by Armstrong Nursery

Circus HT, yb, Kordes; flowers medium, intense yellow with red on petal tips, full, high-centered, borne mostly singly; greenhouse rose

Circus Clown Min, rb, 1991, Moore, Ralph S.; flowers medium, semi-dbl., borne mostly singly or in small clusters, slight fragrance; foliage small, medium green, semi-glossy; few prickles; low (18-22 cm.), bushy, compact growth; [Pink Petticoat × Make Believe]; int. by Sequoia Nursery, 1992

Circus Days Gr, rb, William, J.B.; flowers ivory white edged red, ruffled, dbl.; int. by Hortico, 2003

Circus Knie HT, yb, 1979, Huber; bud long, pointed; flowers 3½-4 in., 32-38 petals, cupped, slight fragrance; foliage dark, leathery; [Moulin Rouge × Peace]; int. in 1975

Circus Minijet Min, yb, Meilland; int. by Australian Roses, 2003

Circus 99 – See **Circus**, HT

Circus Parade F, yb, 1964, Begonia, F.B. & DeVor, P.; flowers yellow-orange overlaid with crimson which spreads down petals, redder than Circus; growth more vigorous than Circus; PP2150; [sport of Circus]; int. by Armstrong Nursery, 1963

Cisco F, dy, 1993, Strahle, Robert; flowers medium, full, borne in small clusters, slight fragrance; foliage medium size, medium green, glossy; medium (60 cm.), upright growth; [Escort × Golden Nugget]; int. by Carlton Rose Nurseries, 1989

Cissie Min, mp, 1979, Bennett, Dee; bud long, pointed; flowers 1 in., 18-20 petals, high-centered, borne singly, slight fragrance; foliage dark green with touches of red and bronze on edges; prickles small, thin; bushy, upright growth; PP4730; [Gene Boerner × Elfinesque]; int. by Tiny Petals Nursery

Cissie Easlea HT, my, 1913, Pernet-Ducher; bud oval, pale buff; flowers clear saffron yellow, with carmine center, large, full, globular; foliage green-bronze; few prickles; [Melanie Soupert × Rayon d'Or]

Citation Gr, dr, 1986, Hoy, Lowel L.; flowers dark red, reverse lighter, 35 petals, high-centered, borne in sprays of 2-3; foliage large, dark, semi-glossy; prickles short, lilac, hooked downward; medium, bushy growth; hips globular, light orange; [seedling × seedling]; int. by Joseph H. Hill, Co., 1982

Citrina HT, dy

Citron HT, ly, 1942, Gaujard; flowers buff, shaded copper, 28 petals, cupped; foliage reddish; vigorous growth; [Julien Potin × seedling]; int. by J&P

Citron-Fraise – See **Little Gigi**, S

Citronella F, ly, 1946, Leenders, M.; flowers lemon-yellow, 15 petals, globular, borne in clusters; foliage glossy; branching growth; [Mev. Nathalie Nypels × Donald Prior]; int. by Longley

Citronella HT, ly, 1999, Schuurman, Frank B.; flowers 4½-5 in., full, borne mostly singly, slight fragrance; foliage large, medium green, glossy; prickles moderate; upright, tall growth; [sport of La Parisienne]; int. by Franko Roses New Zealand, Ltd., 1998

Citrus Candy Min, ob, 2000, Giles, Diann; flowers orange, medium size, full, exhibition, borne mostly singly, no fragrance; foliage medium size, medium green, dull; prickles moderate; upright, medium growth; [Little Darling × Rainbow's End]; int. by Giles Rose Nursery, 2000

Citrus Splash S, ob, 2007, Zary, Keith W.; flowers orange yellow striped, 3½ in., dbl., blooms borne in small clusters; foliage medium size, dark green, glossy; prickles 6-8 mm., hooked downward, greyed-orange, moderate; growth upright, medium (4½ ft.); [seedling × seedling]; int. by Jackson & Perkins Wholesale, Inc., 2008

Citrus Tease F, mp, 2000, Zary, Keith; flowers large, dbl., high-centered, borne in small clusters; foliage medium size, dark green, glossy; prickles moderate; upright, bushy growth (3½ ft.); PP12116; [Pink Pollyanna × Gnome World]; int. by Bear Creek Gardens, 2001

City Girl LCl, pb, 1993; flowers large, light rose pink with primrose base and salmon pink reverse stained yellow, 4¾ in., 12 petals, borne in sprays of 3-5, moderate fruity fragrance; foliage large, dark green, glossy; upright, tall, climbing growth; [Armada × Compassion]; int. by Harkness, 1985

City Lights MinFl, dy, Poulsen; int. in 1992

City Livery F, my, Harkness; flowers full, borne in clusters; growth to 3 ft.; PPAF; int. by Harkness & Co, 2001

City of Adelaide – See **Jacqueline Nebout**, F

City of Alexandria – See **Alexandria Rose**, S

City of Auckland HT, ob, 1982, McGredy, Sam IV; flowers large, deep gold and orange with a bit of pink, dbl., intense fragrance; foliage medium green, semi-glossy; growth bushy, medium; [Benson & Hedges Gold × Whisky Mac]; int. by McGredy Roses International, 1981

City of Bath HT, pb, 1976, Sanday, John; flowers deep candy-pink, reverse lighter, 4 in., 55 petals, moderate fragrance; foliage matte, green; [Gavotte × Buccaneer]; int. in 1969

City of Belfast F, or, 1968, McGredy, Sam IV; flowers bright red, dbl., cupped, borne in trusses; foliage glossy; PP3070; [Evelyn Fison × (Circus × Korona)]; int. by McGredy; Gold Medal, RNRS, 1967, President's International Trophy, RNRS, 1967, Gold Star of the South Pacific, Palmerston North, NZ, 1969, Gold Medal, The Hague, 1976

City of Benalla HT, op, 1983, Dawson, George; bud globular, pointed; flowers carmine, opening with outer petals paling, inner petals coral, dbl., high-centered; foliage dark, dense, glossy; prickles brown, hooked down; vigorous, tall growth; [My Choice × Extravaganza]; int. by Rainbow Roses

City of Birmingham – See **Esprit**, S

City of Bradford F, or, 1986, Harkness; flowers small to medium, semi-dbl., cupped, borne in large clusters; foliage dark, semi-glossy; medium, upright growth; [(Manx Queen × Whisky Mac) × ((Highlight × Colour Wonder) × (Parkdirektor Riggers × Piccadilly))]

City of Cardiff HT, rb, 1992, Poole, Lionel; flowers 3-3½ in., very dbl., borne mostly singly; foliage medium size, medium green, matte; some prickles; medium, upright growth; [Lady Sylvia × Chicago Peace]; int. in 1993

City of Carlsbad F, ob, 2000, Carruth, Tom; flowers orange striped white, 9-11 cm., dbl., borne in small clusters, slight fragrance; foliage large, dark green, glossy; prickles moderate; upright, bushy (80-120 cm.) growth; PP13512; [Rosy Outlook × Scentimental]; int. by Armstrong Garden Centers, 2001

City of Christchurch HT, op, McGredy, Sam IV; flowers deep salmon pink to vermilion, pointed petals; growth medium; int. in 1988

City of Dunedin Min, yb, 1995, Reynolds, Ted; flowers old gold changing to yellow then white with red edge, small, full, borne in small clusters; foliage medium size, medium green, glossy; few prickles; upright, medium growth; [(Rise 'n' Shine × seedling) × Rainbow's End]; int. by Wallises Nursery, 1995

City of Gisborne HT, op, 1968, Appleyard; bud long, pointed; flowers pink shaded orange-yellow, large, semi-dbl., high-centered; foliage glossy; vigorous, upright growth; [Prima Ballerina × Prima Ballerina]

City of Glasgow HT, ab, 1970, Haynes; flowers apricot, suffused pink; [sport of Femina]

City of Gloucester HT, dy, 1970, Sanday, John; flowers saffron-yellow shaded gold, large, dbl., high-centered; vigorous growth; [Gavotte × Buccaneer]; int. in 1970

City of Goulburn F, yb, Swane; flowers blend of yellow, copper and gold, dbl., cupped; growth to 3-4 ft.; int. by Swane's Nurseries, 1995

City of Hamilton F, ob, 1972, Dickson, A.; flowers orange and gold, large, dbl.; foliage dull; free growth; [Innisfree × Elizabeth of Glamis]

City of Harvey HWich, op, 1944, Wiseman; flowers pink tinted orange, small, semi-dbl., cupped, borne in clusters; profuse bloom, not repeated; foliage dark, glossy; growth to 12 ft.; [*R. wichurana* × Orléans Rose]

City of Hereford HT, mp, 1967, LeGrice; flowers carmine-pink, pointed, 6 in.; foliage dark; [Wellworth × Spartan]

City of Ichalkaranji HT, pb, Chiplunkar; int. in 1989

City of Invercargill HT, dp, 1996, Reynolds, Ted; bud very dark red; flowers deep pink, large, very dbl., borne mostly singly; foliage medium size, medium green, glossy, disease-free; few prickles; upright, medium growth; [Westerland × Perfume Delight]; int. by Ted Reynolds Roses International, 1996

City of Joy HT, dr, Chakroborty; flowers velvety crimson red, full; int. by KSG, 2003

City of Kingston F, or, 1973, Schloen, J.; bud ovoid; flowers medium, very dbl., globular; foliage dark, leathery; moderate, bushy growth; [Malibu × Independence]

City of Leeds F, op, 1966, McGredy, Sam IV; flowers salmon, 4½ in., 19 petals, borne in clusters, slight fragrance; foliage dark; [Evelyn Fison × (Spartan × Red Favorite)]; int. by McGredy; Gold Medal, RNRS, 1965

City of Little Rock HT, mp, 1924, E.G. Hill, Co.; flowers hydrangea-pink, open, semi-dbl.; vigorous growth; int. by Vestal

City of London F, lp, 1987, Harkness, R., & Co., Ltd.; flowers light pink, fading to blush, large, dbl., intense fragrance; foliage medium size, medium green, glossy, ovate to pointed; prickles small, reddish, sparse; bushy growth; [Radox Bouquet × Margaret Merril]; int. by The Rose Gardens, 1988; Gold Medal, LeRoeulx, 1985

City of Manchester HT, pb, 1987, Greensitt, J.A.; flowers large, dbl., moderate fragrance; foliage large, dark green, semi-glossy; bushy growth; [Gavotte × Red Lion]; int. by Nostell Priory Rose Gardens, 1982

City of Newcastle HT, yb, 1976, Wood; flowers yellow, tinged salmon-orange, 5 in., 35 petals; foliage semi-glossy; vigorous, tall, upright growth; [Arthur Bell × Mischief]

City of Newcastle Bicentennary – See **Veterans' Honor**, HT

City of Norwich HT, mr, 1949, Kordes; bud ovoid; flowers scarlet-crimson, well-formed, 6 in., 35 petals; foliage leathery; [Crimson Glory × (Crimson Glory × Cathrine Kordes)]; int. by Morse

City of Nottingham F, or, 1962, deRuiter; flowers orange-scarlet, 2½ in., 30-40 petals, rosette, borne in clusters; foliage dark; vigorous, bushy, compact growth; [seedling × Moulin Rouge]

City of Oelde S, mp, 2006, Beales, Amanda; flowers semi-dbl., borne in small clusters; foliage medium size, dark green, semi-glossy; prickles average, straight, few; growth bushy, 1¼ m.; [Bonica × Maigold]; int. by Peter Beales Roses, 2002

City of Panjim HT, pb, Kasturi; flowers pink and off-white; int. by KSG Son, 1972

City of Pilsen – See **Plzen**, HT

City of Portland – See **Mme Caroline Testout**, HT

City of Portland F, mr, 1977, Takatori, Yoshiho; bud pointed; flowers geranium-red, base primrose-yellow, 2½-3½ in., 5 petals; foliage glossy; very free growth; [seedling × Cocktail seedling]; int. by Japan Rose Nursery

City of Portsmouth F, ob, 1976, Cants of Colchester, Ltd.; flowers copper, 3-4 in., 25 petals, moderate fragrance; foliage bronze; tall growth

City of Pretoria F, ab, Kordes; flowers deep orange-apricot with cream reverse, dbl., cupped, borne in large clusters, no fragrance; growth well rounded plant, 5 ft

City of Sails LCl, mp, Matthews; int. by Matthews Nurseries, 2000

City of San Diego S, rb, 2000, Carruth, Tom; flowers cherry red, reverse lighter red, finishing purple-red, 2-3 in., dbl., borne in large clusters, slight fragrance; foliage medium size, medium green, glossy; spreading, bushy (5-6 ft.) growth; PP13511; [Red Fairy × Raven]; int. by Armstrong Garden Center, 2001

City of San Francisco F, mr, 2000, Carruth, Tom; flowers clear, lasting, pure red, ruffled petals, 3-4 in., dbl., borne in small clusters; foliage medium size, dark green, semi-glossy; prickles moderate; compact (80-100 cm.), bushy growth; PP13513; [Santa Claus × (Playboy × Olympiad)]; int. by Armstrong Garden Center, 2001

City of Sheffield HT, yb, 1987, Greensitt, J.A.; flowers medium, dbl., intense fragrance; foliage medium size, medium green, matte; spreading growth; [sport of Diorama]; int. by Nostell Priory Rose Gardens, 1978

City of Springfield F, rb, 1989, Pencil, Paul S.; flowers non-fading, medium, 34 petals, borne in sprays of 6-10; bushy, hardy growth; [Pink Parfait × Roman Holiday]

City of Timaru – See **Crocus Rose**, S

City of Wangaratta HT, mr, Dawson; int. in 1985

City of Warwick – See **Grand Marshall**, HT

City of Welland HT, yb, Kordes; flowers dbl.; foliage deep green, glossy; upright growth; int. in 1996

City of Windsor – See **Liebeszauber**, HT, 2006

City of Windsor HT, ob; int. by Enderlein Nurseries, 1999

City of Worcester HT, mr, 1983, Scrivens, L.; flowers large, 35 petals, high-centered, moderate fragrance; foliage medium size, medium green, matte; [Red Planet × (Ena Harkness × Fragrant Cloud)]

City of York LCl, w, 1945, Tantau; bud buff yellow;

flowers creamy white, small to medium, 15 petals, cupped, borne in clusters of 7-15, moderate fragrance; may repeat; foliage glossy, leathery; vigorous, climbing growth; [Dorothy Perkins × Professor Gnau]; int. by C-P; Gold Medal, ARS, 1950

Ciudad de Oviedo C, mp, before 1932; from Spain

Ciudad de Oviedo C, mp; flowers single; from Spain

Clair – See **Clair Renaissance**, S

Clair de Lune HT, m, 1967, Gaujard; bud pointed; flowers large, dbl.; foliage leathery; vigorous, upright growth; [Eminence × Viola]

Clair Matin LCl, mp, 1962, Meilland, Mrs. Marie-Louise; bud pointed; flowers have 15 petals, cupped, borne in rounded clusters, moderate sweetbriar fragrance; foliage dark, leathery; vigorous (10-12 ft.), well-branched growth; PP2186; [Fashion × ((Independence × Orange Triumph) × Phyllis Bide)]; int. by URS, 1960; Gold Medal, Bagatelle, 1960

Clair Renaissance S, lp, Olesen; flowers light pink, 8-10 cm., full, intense fragrance; foliage dark; growth bushy, 100-150 cm.; int. by Poulsen Roser, 1995

Claire HMult, mp, before 1866; flowers carmine pink, cupped

Claire HT, pb, Dawson; int. in 1987

Claire – See **Claire Rose**, S

Claire Carnot N, yb, 1873, Guillot; flowers yellow, bordered with white and carmine rose, medium, full, cupped, borne in small clusters

Claire Chazal HT, w, Adam; flowers white with bright pink edges, dbl., globular, slight fragrance; moderate (80-100 cm.) growth; int. by Pepinieres de la Guerinais, 2006

Claire Desmet HT, my, 1932, Buatois; flowers golden yellow, very dbl., cupped; foliage leathery, bronze; long, strong stems; vigorous, bushy growth; [Margaret Dickson Hamill × Souv. de Claudius Pernet]

Claire d'Olban HGal, dp, 1825, Vibert; flowers deep pink with pale edges, medium, full; numerous prickles

Claire-France HT, mp, 1964, Mondial Roses; bud pointed; flowers clear pink, large, 40 petals, high-centered; foliage glossy; vigorous, upright growth

Claire Godard T, w, 1894, Godard; flowers pure white, large, full

Claire Jacquier N, ly, 1888, Bernaix, A.; flowers yellow, fading to creamy yellow, 3 cm., semi-dbl., borne in clusters of 5-10, moderate musky fragrance; occasional autumn repeat; very vigorous growth; [possibly *R. multiflora* × Tea rose]

Claire Jolly HMsk, mp, 2000, Lens, Louis; flowers medium pink, paler center, small, semi-dbl., borne in large clusters; recurrent; foliage small, medium green, glossy, disease-resistant; prickles moderate; upright, low (60 cm.) growth; hedge; [(*R. multiflora adenocheata* × Ballerina) × The Fairy]; int. by Louis Lens BV, 1991

Claire Laberge HRg, mp, 2001, Fleming, Joyce; flowers medium pink with lighter pink reverse, 5-6 cm., borne in small clusters, intense fragrance; continuous; foliage medium size, medium green, semi-glossy; prickles 1½ cm., numerous; growth bushy, medium (5 ft.); hedging, specimen; hardy, disease-resistant; [Jens Munk × Scabrosa]; int. by Hortico, Inc., 2001

Claire Rayner – See **Pandemonium**, F

Claire Rose S, mp, 1991, Austin, David; flowers very large, full, cupped, intense fragrance; foliage clear green; bushy, vigorous growth; [Charles Austin × (seedling × Iceberg)]; int. by David Austin Roses, Ltd., 1988

Claire Scotland Min, ab, 1992, Cocker, James; flowers light apricot-pink, large, dbl., borne in small clusters; foliage medium size, medium green, semi-glossy; some prickles; patio; low (50-80 cm.), bushy growth; [(National Trust × Wee Man) × Darling Flame]; int. by James Cocker & Sons, 1990

Claire's Dream HT, mr, 2001, Guest, M.; flowers 4-5 in., full, borne mostly solitary, moderate fragrance; foliage large, dark green (red when young), glossy; prickles up to ½ in., hooked, moderate; growth upright, tall (40 in.); garden decorative, exhibition; [Gordon's College × Red Planet]; int. by Denham Court Nursery, 2002

Clairette HT, mp, Croix, P.; int. in 1974

Clanwilliam HT, op

Clara Min, op, Viveros Fco. Ferrer, S L; flowers 20 petals, rosette; [M Litigan × Inedita]; int. in 1986

Clara HT, ab, 1995, Sheldon, John & Robin; flowers unusual apricot, medium, full, borne mostly singly; foliage medium size, medium green, matte; upright, medium growth; [Nantucket × Lovely Lady]

Clara F, lp, Barni; flowers pastel pink, dbl., borne in small clusters, intense fragrance; recurrent bloom; bronzy foliage; growth to 2½-3 ft.; int. by Rose Barni, 2004

Clara – See **Clara Parade**, MinFl

Clara Barton HT, ab, 1898, Van Fleet; flowers delicate amber pink, 3-3½ in., dbl., moderate fragrance; [American Beauty × Clotilde Soupert]

Clara Bow Cl HT, yb, 1927, Padella Rose Co.; flowers yellow stained crimson, dbl.; growth to 12-15 ft.; [sport of Golden Emblem]; int. by Germain's

Clara Cochet HP, lp, 1886, Lacharme, F.; flowers light pink, center brighter pink, very large, dbl., globular; [Jules Margottin × unknown]

Clara Curtis HT, my, 1922, Dickson, A.; flowers rich golden yellow, very dbl.; Gold Medal, NRS, 1919

Clara d'Arcis – See **Mme Clara d'Arcis**, HT

Clara Eileen F, ob, 2006, Rawlins, Ronnie; flowers orange/yellow, reverse yellow, 2½ in., full, borne in small clusters; foliage medium size, medium green, glossy; prickles ½ in., triangular, moderate; growth upright, medium (36 in.); garden decoration; [Chinatown × Remember Me]

Clara Granato F, mr

Clara Munger LCl, m, Munger; flowers lavender

Clara Parade MinFl, w, Poulsen; flowers white, 5-8 cm., dbl., no fragrance; growth bushy, 20-40 cm.; int. by Poulsen Roser, 2004

Clara Sylvain T, w, 1838; flowers pure white with cream, large, full

Clara Watson HT, w, 1894, Prince; flowers mother-of-pearl white, center peach, dbl.

Clara's Surprise HT, mp, 1998, Kirkham, Gordon Wilson; flowers lilac pink, high centered, medium size, full, high-centered, borne in small clusters, moderate fragrance; foliage medium size, dark green, semi-glossy; few prickles; compact, low growth; [Seaspray × Admiral Rodney]

Clare HT, pb, 1972, MacLeod; flowers cream, edged rose-pink, 5½ in., 35 petals, high-centered; foliage large, medium green, semi-glossy; vigorous, tall growth; [Ethel Sanday × Rose Gaujard]

Clare de Escofet HT, w, 1920, Easlea; flowers delicate flesh-white, very large, dbl.

Cläre Grammerstorf F, dy, 1957, Kordes; bud ovoid; flowers large, dbl., high-centered; foliage leathery, glossy; vigorous, bushy growth; [Harmonie × (*R. rubiginosa* × unknown)]

Clare Helen HT, lp, 1985, Owen, Fred; [sport of Gail Borden]

Clarence House LCl, w, 2006, Beales, Amanda; flowers light yellow, reverse white, 10 cm., very full, borne in small clusters; foliage medium size, dark green, glossy; prickles average, straight, moderate; growth upright, spreading, medium (3-4 m.), climbing; [City of York × Aloha]; int. by Peter Beales Roses, 2000

Claret Min, m, 1978, Saville, F. Harmon; bud short, pointed; flowers 1 in., 48 petals, cupped; very compact, spreading. growth; [Little Chief × Little Chief]; int. by Nor'East Min. Roses, 1977

Claret HT, dr, Fryer; bud large, almost black; flowers velvety, dark crimson, dbl., high-centered, borne in trusses, moderate fragrance; recurrent; bushy, medium (3 ft.) growth; int. by Fryers Roses, 2005

Claret Cup Min, rb, 1962, Riethmuller; bud globular; flowers dark red, white eye, small, dbl., borne in clusters, moderate fragrance; foliage leathery, dark; vigorous, bushy, compact growth; [Spring Song × Eutin]; int. by Hazelwood Bros., 1962

Clarice Goodacre HT, w, 1916, Dickson, A.; bud pointed; flowers ivory-white, shaded chrome, dbl., high-centered; foliage dark, soft; vigorous, bushy growth

Clarice Weston Flower Maker HT, lp, 2006, Cowlishaw, Frank; flowers light pink, shaded fawn, reverse light pink and fawn blend, petal edges serrated, 3 in., dbl., borne mostly solitary; foliage medium size, medium green, semi-glossy; prickles up to 8mm., straight, green/brown, moderate; growth upright (2 ft.); garden decorative; [Alexander × Forever Royal]; int. in 2008

Clarice Wood Min, mr, 2001, Jellyman, J.S.; flowers 2 in., dbl., borne in small clusters, no fragrance; foliage small, dark green, glossy; prickles small, curved, few; growth upright, bushy, medium (18 in.); bedding, containers; [Jean Kenneally × Merrie]

Claridge F, mp, 1985, Pekmez, Paul; flowers large, 35 petals, moderate fragrance; foliage medium size, light green, semi-glossy; upright growth; [seedling × seedling]; int. in 1984

Clarinda F, mr, 2001, Cocker, A.G.; flowers medium, semi-dbl., borne in large clusters, slight fragrance; foliage medium size, dark green, glossy; prickles 6 mm., straight, moderate; growth bushy, medium (2-2½ ft.); garden decorative; [Drummer Boy × Playboy]; int. by James Cocker & Sons, 2002

Clarion Call F, op, 1995, Fleming, Joyce L.; flowers orange-pink with red-salmon hues, medium, 6-14 petals, borne singly and in clusters of up to 5, slight fragrance; foliage medium size, medium green, matte; bushy (to 75 cm.) growth; [Canadian Centennial × Traumerei]; int. by Hortico Roses, 1994; Best Seedling, ARS, 1991

Clarissa Min, ab, 1982, Harkness, R., & Co., Ltd.; flowers small, 43 petals, high-centered, borne in large clusters; foliage small, dark, glossy; prickles small; tall, upright growth; [Southampton × Darling Flame]; int. by Harkness New Roses, Ltd., 1983; Gold Star of the South Pacific, Palmerston North, NZ, 1982

Clarissa Dana HT, pb, 1933, Nicolas; flowers brilliant pink with amber glow, large, dbl., high-centered; vigorous growth; [(HT × La France) × Marechal Niel]; int. by J&P

Clarita HT, or, 1972, Meilland; flowers vermilion, 5 in., 30-35 petals, high-centered, slight fragrance; foliage dark; very vigorous, upright growth; [Tropicana × (Zambra × Romantica)]; int. by L. Dol, 1971; Gold Medal, Lyon, 1971, Gold Medal, Geneva, 1971

Clarity F, w, 1993, Jobson, Daniel J.; flowers white with cream center, medium, dbl., borne in small clusters; foliage large, dark green, glossy; some large prickles; medium, upright, bushy growth; [Pristine × (Party Girl × Laureate)]; int. by Jobson, 1993

Clark Ochre Seedling Cl HT, dy, Clark

Clark Pink Cl HT, mp, Clark

Clarke's Multiflora Sp, w; thornless; clone of *R. multiflora*; used for understock

Clark's Tea HT, mp

Class Act F, w, 1988, Warriner, William A.; bud long, pointed ovoid; flowers clear white, 3-4 in., 15-20 petals, high-centered, opening flat, borne in sprays of 3-6, slight fruity fragrance; recurrent; foliage medium size, dark green, semi-glossy; prickles moderate, long, narrow; stems strong, short; upright, bushy, medium growth; hips bright orange; PP6515; [Sun Flare × seedling]; int. by J&P; Gold Star of the South Pacific, Palmerston North, NZ, 1990, Gold Medal, Portland, 1989

Class of '73 MinFl, pb, 2003, Tucker, Robbie; flowers light pink with dark edging, 1½ in., dbl., borne mostly solitary, no fragrance; foliage medium green, semi-glossy; thornless; growth upright, medium (to 24 in.); exhibition, cut flower, garden; [Sam Trivitt × Dancing Flame]; int. by Tucker, Robbie (Rosemania), 2004

Classic HT, dp, Kasturi & Sriram; flowers large, deep rose pink, intense fragrance; vigorous growth; int. by KSG Son, 1997

Classic Beauty HT, pb, 1994, Winchel, Joseph F.; flowers cream and dark pink blend with yellow base, 3-3½ in., dbl., borne mostly singly; foliage medium size, medium green, matte; some prickles; medium, bushy growth; int. by Certified Roses, Inc., 1997

Classic Chic Min, ob, 1986, McDaniel, Earl; flowers orange, 35 petals, high-centered, borne usually singly; foliage medium size, dark, semi-glossy; prickles few, slender; medium, upright growth; [seedling × seedling]; int. by McDaniel's Min. Roses

Classic Duet HT, mp, Kordes; flowers medium, full, high-centered, borne mostly singly; recurrent; stems moderately long; [sport of Duett]; int. by W. Kordes Söhne, 2005

Classic Love Min, mp, 1983, Lyon, Lyndon; flowers small, 20 petals, borne in clusters; foliage small, medium green, semi-glossy; upright, bushy growth; [Baby Betsy McCall × seedling]; int. by L. Lyon Greenhouses

Classic Orange Min, ob; int. in 1997

Classic Sunblaze Min, mp, 1985, Meilland, Mrs. Marie-Louise; bud conical, small; flowers rich pink, 1½-2 in., 40 petals, borne mostly singly; foliage medium size, dark green, matte; prickles medium, fairly numerous; growth short (15 in.), bushy; PP5958; [sport of Pink Sunblaze]; int. by SNC Meilland & Cie

Classic Touch HT, lp, 1991, Hefner, John; flowers large, full, borne mostly singly; foliage large, medium green, semi-glossy; tall, upright growth; [sport of Touch of Class]; int. by Co-Operative Rose Growers, 1993

Classical Velvet HT, mr, 1992, Hoy, Lowel L.; flowers 5¼ in., 25 petals, borne in sprays of 4-5; foliage medium size, dark green, semi-glossy; upright, bushy, tall growth; [Anniversary × seedling]; int. by DeVor Nurseries, Inc.

Classie Lassie Gr, pb, 1990, Winchel, Joseph F.; bud pointed; flowers ivory-pink, with salmon pink edges, aging to salmon, 25-30 petals, high-centered, oval-shaped, moderate fruity fragrance; foliage medium size, medium green, glossy, disease-resistant; prickles average, brown-green, slightly recurved; bushy, medium growth; [Touch of Class × seedling]; int. by Co-Operative Rose Growers, 1991

Classy Min, yb, 1987, Travis, Louis R.; flowers yellow with pink overlay, small, 13-18 petals, high-centered, borne singly, intense spicy fragrance; foliage small, medium green, semi-glossy; prickles straight, very few, tan-brown; bushy, low growth; hips round, green-orange; [Yellow Jewel × Yellow Jewel]

Classy HT, mr, E.G. Hill, Co.; int. in 1992

Classy Carol HT, pb, Delaney, Larry; flowers white blushed salmon, 4-6 in., 30 petals, decorative, borne one to a stem, slight fragrance; dark green, glossy foliage; stems long and straight; well behaved, 4-5 ft. growth; int. by Edmunds' Roses, 2005

Classy Lady HT, ab; int. by Chichester Roses, 2005

Claude HT, mr, 1950, Mallerin, C.; flowers bright orient red, 6-7 in., 35 petals; foliage glossy, dark; vigorous, upright growth; [(Comtesse Vandal × Brazier) × seedling]; int. by Wheatcroft Bros.

Claude Bernard HP, dp, 1878, Liabaud; flowers large, full, globular; [Jules Margottin × unknown]

Claude Henry McLean S, dr, Gawron; int. in 1995

Claude Jacquet HP, dr, 1892, Liabaud; flowers dark red/purple, very large, dbl.

Claude Levet HP, mr, 1872, Levet

Claude Million HP, dr, 1863, Verdier, E.; flowers scarlet-crimson, touched with rose and violet, velvety, large, full, cupped

Claude Monet HT, rb, J&P; flowers striped, with patches of red, yellow and orange-pink, medium, dbl.; growth vigorous, medium; int. in 1992

Claude Petit HT, mp, 1936, Buatois; flowers soft salmon-pink, stamens yellow, very dbl., high-centered; vigorous growth; [Mlle Marie Mascuraud × Beauté de Lyon]

Claude Rabbé HWich, dp, 1941, Buatois; flowers carmine-pink, 7 cm., borne in clusters of 6-10

Claude's Cracker HT, dr, 2006, Rawlins, Ronnie; flowers crimson, 3 in., full, borne mostly solitary; foliage large, dark green, glossy; prickles ½ in., triangular, few; growth upright, medium (36 in.): garden decoration; [seedling × Ingrid Bergman]

Claudia F, pb, 1959, Broadley; flowers deep cherry-coral, dbl.; vigorous growth; [Ma Perkins × Geranium Red]; int. by Roseglen Nursery

Claudia HT, mp, Meilland; bud ovoid, large; flowers orient pink, reverse lighter, 4 in., 30-35 petals, cupped, borne mostly singly, slight fragrance; good repeat; foliage large, medium green, semi-glossy; prickles few, and often none on young stems; stems 60-80 cm under greenhouse conditions; erect (2-3 ft.) growth; PP10173; [Meitalmin × (Meidiaplou × Delpoid)]; greenhouse rose; int. in 1997

Claudia – See **Claudia Parade**, MinFl

Claudia Augusta N, w, 1856, Damaizin; flowers white with cream center, large, full; foliage dark green

Claudia Cardinale S, my, Guillot-Massad; flowers warm yellow-amber, incurving, full, globular, domed form, moderate fragrance; glossy foliage; growth to 5 ft.; int. by Roseraies Guillot, 1997

Claudia Parade MinFl, lp, Poulsen; flowers light pink, 5-8 cm., dbl., no fragrance; foliage dark; growth bushy, 20-40 cm.; PP13454; int. by Poulsen Roser, 2000

Claudie Augustin – See **Claudia Augusta**, N

Claudine A, w, 1823, Vibert; sepals foliaceous; flowers medium, semi-dbl.

Claudius HT, rb, 1910, Cant, B.; flowers glowing fire red with salmon pink, large, full

Claudius Levet T, pb, 1886, Levet; flowers carmine rose, salmon center, large, full

Claudy Chapel HT, yb, 1930, Beaumez; flowers deep yellow and coppery, to salmon-pink, large, dbl.; vigorous growth; int. by Delhaye

Claus Groth HSpn, ob, 1951, Tantau; flowers salmon-orange shaded apricot-yellow, large, dbl., intense spinosissima fragrance; foliage dark; vigorous, bushy (5 ft.) growth; large fruit; [R.M.S. Queen Mary × *R. spinosissima*]

Clear Moon HT, my, 2007, Iwata, Masaaki; flowers dbl., borne mostly solitary; foliage medium size, medium green, semi-glossy; growth upright, medium; cutting; [Kamakura × (Golden Heart × Hoshizukuyo)]; int. by Ibaraki Barakai, 2007

Clear Oceans HT, w; flowers medium, full, high-centered; int. in 2001

Clematis HWich, rb, 1924, Turbat; flowers dark red, prominent white eye, 2 cm., single, borne in clusters of 40-50, no fragrance; foliage small, glossy; vigorous, climbing growth

Clémence Beaugrand – See **Mme Clémence Beauregard**, M

Clémence Isaure HGal, dp, about 1835, Vibert; flowers deep pink, center crimson, large, full

Clémence Isaure HP, op, 1851, Robert; flowers salmon pink, medium, full, globular

Clémence Isaure HEg, pb, Trattinnick; flowers pink over white, medium, single

Clémence Joigneaux HP, mr, 1861, Liabaud; flowers bright red, tinted with lilac, very large, full

Clémence Lartay HP, mr, 1860, Lartay

Clémence Raoux HP, mp, 1869, Granger; flowers bright pink, shaded silvery pink, large, full, quartered, moderate fragrance; foliage dark green, glossy; prickles straight, flat

Clémence Robert M, mp, 1863, Robert et Moreau; bud heavily mossed; flowers bright pink, 9-11 cm., full, borne in clusters; sometimes recurrent bloom

Clément Marot HP, m, 1860, Oger

Clément Nabonnand T, yb, 1877, Nabonnand

Clément Pacaud HT, dp, 1916, Chambard, C.; flowers brilliant carmine, large, full

Clementina HT, pb, 1961, Dot, Pedro; flowers carmine and rosy white bicolor; [Grand Gala × Vicky Marfá]

Clementina Carbonieri T, yb, 1913, Bonfiglio, A.; bud long, reddish-yellow; flowers light violet pink, medium, full; growth medium (3 × 2 ft.); [Kaiserin Auguste Viktoria × Souv de Catherine Guillot]

Clémentine HGal, mp, 1818, Vibert

Clémentine HEg, pb, before 1824, Descemet; flowers white with carmine red edges, with striped, medium, semi-dbl.; foliage darker green, glossy; hips dark red, very large, flattened cone-shaped; synonymous with Janet's Pride, as reintroduced by W. Paul

Clementine Min, ob, Tantau; flowers apricot-orange, dbl., borne in clusters; dark green foliage; int. by Rosen Tantau, 1997

Clémentine Duval B, mp, 1847, Laffay, M.; flowers bright rose, cupped; sometimes classed as HP

Clémentine Séringe HP, mp, 1840, Wood; flowers rose-pink, dbl.

Cleo HT, lp, 1981, Bees; flowers soft light pink, 37 petals, high-centered, borne singly and in pairs, slight fragrance; foliage light green, semi-matte; prickles red; strong, bushy growth; [Kordes' Perfecta × Prima Ballerina]

Cleonagh Ann F, mp, 2001, Horner, Colin P.; flowers medium pink, paler reverse, 7 cm., dbl., borne in small clusters, slight fragrance; foliage medium size, medium green, glossy; prickles medium, slightly curved, moderate; growth spreading, medium (1 m.); garden decorative; [Armada × ((seedling × (Robin Redbreast × *R. bella*)) × Remember Me)]; int. by Warley Rose Gardens, 2002

Cleopatra T, pb, 1889, Bennett; flowers flesh colour shaded with rose, large, full

Cleopatra HT, rb, 1956, Kordes; flowers scarlet, reverse old-gold, well-formed, medium, 45 petals, moderate fragrance; foliage dark, glossy; vigorous growth; [(Walter Bentley × Condesa de Sástago) × Golden Scepter]; int. by Wheatcroft Bros., 1955; Gold Medal, NRS, 1955

Cleopatra – See **Kleopatra**, HT

Cleora Min, mp, 1976, Dobbs; bud globular; flowers medium pink, reverse darker, 1½ in., 50 petals, flat; foliage small, light, leathery; vigorous growth; [Fairy Moss × Fairy Moss]; int. by Port Stockton Nursery, 1977

Cléosthène HP, m, before 1866; flowers lilac pink, very large, full

Cleveland Bouquet HT, op, 1940, Horvath; flowers shrimp-pink with salmon-pink undertone, open, semi-dbl.

Cleveland I HT, yb, 1916, Dickson, A.; flowers coppery yellow

Cleveland II HT, pb, 1916, Dickson, H.; bud long; flowers antique pink, shaded reddish-copper, base copper-yellow, large, full, high-centered, moderate fragrance

Clever Gretel S, pb, Kordes; int. by Ludwig's Roses, 2003

Cliché HT, pb, 2001, Gareth Fryer; flowers medium pink, light yellow reverse, 5 in., full, borne mostly solitary; foliage medium size, dark green, glossy; prickles ½ in., straight, few; growth upright, tall (5-6 ft.); garden decorative, exhibition, cutting; [Grandpa Dickson × Sweetheart]; vigorous; prefers warmer climates; int. by Edmunds' Roses, 2002

Cliff Richard F, pb, Van Geest; flowers medium pink, silver reverse; foliage glossy, mid-green; upright growth, 4-5 ft.; int. in 1993

Cliffs of Dover S, w, 1995, Olesen, Pernille & Mogens N.; flowers white, bright yellow stamens, 1-1½ in., 5 petals, borne in small clusters, no fragrance; foliage small, dark green, glossy; few prickles; low (36 in.), arching, spreading growth; PP9650; [seedling × seedling]; int. by Young's American Rose Nursery, 1995

Cliffs of Dover Cover – See **Cliffs of Dover**, S

Clifton Moss – See **White Bath**, M

Climentina HT, mp, 1955, Klimenko, V. N.; flowers rosy pink, large; [Independence × Peace]

Clinora Cl HT, dy, 1979, Orard, Joseph (also Tantau, 1978, NR); bud pointed; flowers pure, dark yellow, large, intense fragrance; [sport of Sunblest]; int. by Pekmez, 1978

Clio HGal, mr, before 1820, Descemet; flowers carmation red

Clio HP, lp, 1894, Paul, W.; flowers flesh, large, very dbl., globular, borne in clusters; seasonal bloom; foliage rich green; vigorous growth

Clio HT, or, Gaujard; flowers luminous Indian red, large

Clitus Ch, m, 1853, Bernède; flowers purple-pink aging to carmine, large, full

Clive Beck HT, yb, Kordes; flowers sand yellow with coral pink edges, large, dbl., high-centered, no fragrance; long stems; upright growth, 7 ft.; int. by Ludwig's Roses, 2001

Clive Lloyd HT, dp

Clivia HT, ob, 1985, Kordes, W.; bud ovoid; flowers salmon orange-red blend, 30 petals, high-centered, borne singly; foliage medium size, medium green, matte; prickles brown; upright, bushy growth; [Mercedes × (Sonia × Uwe Seeler)]; int. in 1979

Clo-Clo HT, pb, 1985, Pekmez, Paul; flowers 20 petals; foliage dark; upright growth; [Emily Post × Bellona]; int. in 1984

Clochemerle HT, mr, 1989, Delbard & Chabert; flowers large, 38 petals, cupped, slight fragrance; foliage matte; vigorous, bushy growth; [seedling × ((Michele Meilland × Karla) × seedling)]; int. in 1988

Clodagh McGredy HT, ab, McGredy; flowers soft golden amber, ruffled petals, dbl., moderate fragrance; matte foliage; compact (2½ ft.), bushy growth; int. in 2001

Cloris Adriana HT, dp, 1997, Poole, Lionel; flowers high-centered, large, 41 petals, borne mostly singly; foliage large, dark green, dull; some prickles; spreading, bushy, medium growth; [Blue Moon × Gavotte]

Clos de la Pellerie HT, or, 1988, Delbard-Chabert; flowers medium vermilion red, long, large, 25-35 petals, slight fragrance; foliage large; good, vigorous, bushy growth; [(Spartan × Baccará) × seedling]

Clos Fleuri S, Delbard-Chabert; int. in 1970

Clos Fleuri Bicolore – See **Ville du Perreux**, F

Clos Fleuri Blanc F, w, 1989, Delbard & Chabert; flowers large, 40 petals, slight fragrance; foliage bright; semi-climbing, vigorous growth; [(Milrose × Legion d'Honneur) × Candeur]; int. by Georges Delbard SA, 1988

Clos Fleuri Champagne F, ab, Delbard; flowers medium, honey-champagne with some pink petal edges, dbl., high-centered, slight fragance fragrance; recurrent bloom; growth to 2 ft.; int. in 1990

Clos Fleuri d'Or F, ob, Delbard; flowers orange and gold shades, dbl., borne in clusters; growth to 2 ft.; int. in 1990

Clos Fleuri Jaune F, my, 1989, Delbard & Chabert; flowers yellow, shaded ochre, opening to yellow-amber, large, 18 petals, slight fragrance; foliage bright; semi-climbing, vigorous growth; [(Orléans Rose × Goldilocks) × Parure d'Or]; int. in 1988

Clos Fleuri Rose F, mp, 1989, Delbard & Chabert; flowers medium, 30 petals, borne in clusters; foliage bright; bushy, vigorous growth; [(Zambra × Orange Sensation) × (Robin Hood × Virgo)]; int. in 1988

Clos Fleuri Rose No. 2 F, mp, Delbard; flowers pure rose pink, full; low growth; int. in 1994

Clos Fleuri Rouge F, mr, 1989, Delbard & Chabert; flowers medium, 20 petals, flat, slight fragrance; foliage bright; bushy, vigorous growth; [Orléans Rose × Queen Elizabeth]; int. in 1988

Clos Fleuri Vermilion F, or, Delbard; flowers bright vermilion, semi-dbl. to dbl., cupped to open, borne in clusters of 5 to 10; recurrent; foliage dark bronzy green, glossy; growth to 2-3 ft.; int. as Clos Fleuri Vermillon, Georges Delbard SA, 2005

Clos Vougeot F, mr, 1986, Delbard-Chabert; flowers medium, 28 petals, no fragrance; bushy growth; [(Alain × Charles Mallerin) × (Lafayette × Walko)]; int. in 1983

Close to You HT, ly; int. in 2006

Close Up – See **Carmel Sunset**, HT

Closer to Heaven LCl, dr, 2004, Moore, Ralph S.; sepals frilly; flowers deep ruby red, reverse medium red, 3½ in., semi-dbl., borne in large clusters, slight fragrance; early summer bloom; foliage medium size, dark green, semi-glossy; prickles, hooked; growth upright, climbing, cascading, medium (7-10 ft.); pillar; [(*R. wichuraiana* × Floradora) × (Queen Elizabeth × Crested Moss)]; int. by Sequoia Nurs., 2005

Clotaria HT, mr, 1936, San Remo Exp. Sta.; flowers bright fuchsia-red, well-formed, medium, 26-28 petals; foliage dark, glossy; vigorous, upright, bushy growth; [Gruss an Coburg × J.C. Thornton]

Cloth of Gold – See **Chromatella**, N

Clothilde HGal, lp, 1867, Coquerel

Clothilde Roland HP, mr, 1867, Roland; flowers cherry red, large, full

Clothilde Sigrist T, mp, 1907, Bidaud; flowers pink, striped darker pink, large, full

Clothilde Soupert T, mp, 1883, Levet; flowers carmine-pink, large, very full; [Gloire de Dijon × unknown]

Clotilde – See **Bougère**, T

Clotilde T, mp, 1867, Roland; flowers medium pink with violet pink, very large, full

Clotilde Soupert Pol, w, 1890, Soupert & Notting; flowers pearly white, center soft rose-pink, large, very dbl., borne in clusters, moderate fragrance; foliage rich green, soft; bushy (10-20 in.) growth; [Mignonette × Mme Damaizin]

Clotilde Soupert, Climbing Cl Pol, w, 1896, Berckmans, P.J., Co. (also Dingee & Conard, 1901); flowers borne in small clusters, moderate tea fragrance; good repeat

Cloud Dancer Gr, w, 1995, Burks, Larry; flowers white blend, dbl., borne in small clusters; foliage medium size, medium green, semi-glossy; few prickles; upright, medium growth; [White Queen Elizabeth × unknown]; int. by Certified Roses, Inc., 1995

Cloud Nine Min, w, 1982, Warriner, William A.; flowers medium, semi-dbl.; foliage light green, matte; spreading growth; PP5557; [Bon Bon × Calgold]; int. by J&P, 1984

Cloud Nine S, w, Williams, J. Benjamin; flowers white touched with apricot, moderate fragrance; int. by Hortico Inc., 1999

Cloud Nine HT, mp, Fryer; flowers bright, glowing pink, large, dbl., classically structured, moderate fragrance; growth to 110 cm.; int. by Fryer's Roses, 2004

Cloudland HT, m, 1994, Perry, Astor; flowers 3-3½ in., full, moderate fragrance; foliage large, medium green, matte; upright (150 cm.) growth; [Blue Moon × Paradise]; int. by Perry Roses, 1995

Clouseau Min, mr, 1995, Taylor, Pete & Kay; flowers medium red, cream reverse, large, full, borne mostly singly; foliage medium size, dark green, semi-glossy; some prickles; upright, bushy, medium (48 in.) growth; [Azure Sea × Marijke Koopman]

Clove Scented Musk Misc OGR, w

Clovelly HT, dp, 1924, Hicks; flowers carmine-pink, well-formed; vigorous growth; Gold Medal, NRS, 1924

Cloverdene HT, pb

Clovis HP, m, 1868, Ledéchaux; flowers purple-pink

Club F, mr, 1957, Gaujard; flowers bright red, open, medium, single; foliage glossy, bronze; very vigorous, bushy growth; [Peace × Opera seedling]

Clubrose Lydia – See Lydia

Clubrose Scala F, rb, 1973, Kordes; flowers blood-red and orange, medium, dbl., globular; foliage glossy, dark, leathery, bronze; vigorous, upright, bushy growth; [Marlena × seedling]

Clydebank Centenary F, or, 1988, Cocker, James & Sons; flowers orange-vermilion red, medium, 15-25 fimbriated petals; foliage medium size, medium green, matte; upright growth; [((Highlight × Colour Wonder) × (Parkdirektor Riggers × Piccadilly)) × Darling Flame]

Clytemnestra HMsk, op, 1915, Pemberton; bud copper; flowers salmon-chamois, ruffled, small, 18-20 petals, borne in clusters, moderate fragrance; recurrent bloom; foliage leathery, dark; bushy (3-4 ft.), spreading growth; [Trier × Liberty]; Gold Medal, NRS, 1914

Cnos × HT, my, 1957, Bronisze (Poland) State Nursery; flowers golden yellow tinged copper; vigorous growth; [Bettina × unknown]

Coachman F, mr, Williams, J.B.; flowers cherry-red, outer petals lighter, dbl., pompon, borne in clusters; recurrent; foliage glossy; int. by Hortico, Inc., 1996

Coalite Flame HT, or, 1976, Dickson, A.; flowers 5 in., 60 petals, moderate fragrance; foliage large, matte; [Fragrant Cloud × Red Planet]; int. by Dickson's of Hawlmark, 1974

Coby Fankhauser HT, my, 1971, Fankhauser; flowers buttercup-yellow, large, dbl., high-centered; foliage leathery; vigorous, upright, bushy growth; [John S. Bloomfield × Elizabeth Fankhauser]

Cocarde – See **Majestueuse**, HGal

Cocarde A, mp, about 1810, Descemet; flowers bright pink, edges lighter

Cocarde Jacobée HGal, mr, 1824, in Brussels

Cocarde Jaune HT, pb, 1933, Ketten Bros.; bud large, long, pointed, reddish salmon; flowers yellowish-salmon, base yellow, reverse coral-red, dbl., cupped; foliage dark; vigorous, bushy growth; [Diana × Marie Adélaide]

Cocarde Pâle HGal, lp, before 1813, Pradel, H.; flowers bright, light pink, edges lighter

Cocarde Rouge HGal, mp, about 1825, Vibert; flowers bright glowing pink

Cocarde Royale – See **Grand Monarche**, HGal

Coccinea HBc, dr, before 1835

Coccinea T, m, about 1840, Cels; flowers dark purple, medium, full

Coccinea HMult, pb, 1843, Legris; bud round, fat; flowers varied, white, pink, and scarlet, 2½-3 in., full, borne in clusters of up to 30; not recurrent; sometimes attributed to Van Houtte

Coccinée Superbe – See **Le Vingt-Neuf Juillet**, HCh

Coccinelle LCl, or, 1956, Buyl Frères; flowers bright geranium-red

Cochineal Glory HT, mr, 1937, Leenders, M.; bud pointed; flowers open, large, semi-dbl.; vigorous, bushy growth

Cochineal Glory, Climbing Cl HT, mr, 1945, Vogel, M.; flowers large, semi-dbl.

Cock A Doo – See **Cockadoo**, F

Cockadoo F, dr, Cocker; int. in 1984

Cockle Shells Min, pb, 1985, Leon, Charles F., Sr.; flowers pale yellow tinged deep pink, medium, 35 petals; foliage medium; bushy, spreading growth; [(Kathy Robinson × seedling) × (Janna × seedling)]

Cocktail S, rb, 1958, Meilland, F.; bud pointed; flowers geranium red, base primrose yellow, 2½ in., 5 petals, borne in clusters, slight spicy fragrance; foliage leathery, glossy; vigorous, semi-climbing growth; shrub or hedge; PP1821; [(Independence × Orange Triumph) × Phyllis Bide]; int. by URS, 1957

Cocktail '80 HT, my, 1977, Meilland, Mrs. Marie-Louise; bud elongated; flowers 5 in., 20 petals, high-centered; foliage dark; very vigorous growth; int. by Meilland

Coco F, yb, 1976, Fryer; flowers deep golden yellow with orange-pink, 3 in., 20-25 petals, borne in small clusters; foliage glossy; [Pernille Poulsen × Redgold]; int. by Fryers Nursery, Ltd., 1975

Coco LCl, or, Kordes; int. in 1989

Coco Min, ob, Poulsen; flowers orange and orange blend, medium, dbl., no fragrance; growth bushy, 20-40 cm.; PP15083; int. by Poulsen Roser, 2002

Coconut Ice HT, pb, 1991, Walker, D.R.; bud large, pointed; flowers pink blend with mauve shadings, medium, full, high-centered, borne 1-3 per stem, slight fragrance; foliage medium green, semi-glossy; tall, vigorous growth; [Alexander × Vol de Nuit]

Coconut Ice LCl, w, 2003, Horner, Colin P.; flowers white suffused with pink, reverse white, 7 cm., full, borne in large clusters, moderate fragrance; foliage medium size, medium green, matte; prickles small, curved, moderate; growth upright, medium (2 m.); garden decorative; [Leverkusen × (seedling × Immensee)]; int. by D&S Nurseries, 2003

Cocorico F, or, 1951, Meilland, F.; bud pointed; flowers geranium-red, 3 in., 8 petals, borne in clusters, moderate spicy fragrance; foliage glossy, bright; vigorous, upright, bushy growth; [Alain × Orange Triumph]; int. by URS, 1951; Gold Medal, NRS, 1951, Gold Medal, Geneva, 1951

Cocorico, Climbing Cl F, or, 1964, Ruston, D.

Cocorico F, pb, Meilland; flowers ivory with rose-carmine edges, semi-dbl., cupped, borne in clusters; recurrent; foliage dark green, glossy, thick; medium growth

Cocotte HT, mp, 1957, Gaujard; flowers bright salmon, large, dbl., moderate fragrance; foliage bronze; upright growth; [Peace × (Fashion × Vogue)]

Coed F, my, 1971, Jelly; bud short, pointed; flowers medium, dbl., high-centered, slight fragrance; foliage dark, leathery; vigorous, upright growth; PP3166; [Golden Garnette × seedling]; int. by E.G. Hill Co.

Coelina – See **Célina**, M

Coelina Dubos – See **Célina Dubos**, D

Coeur Aimable HGal, m, about 1860, Miellez; flowers crimson-purple, medium, full

Coeur d'Alene HRg, mp; int. in 1996

Coeur d'Amour – See **Red Devil**, HT

Coeur de Lion HP, mp, 1867, Paul, W.; flowers shining pink with light pink, large, dbl.

Coeur d'Or – See **Heart of Gold**, HWich

Coeur Farouche S, m, Delbard; int. in 1993

Coeur Noir HGal, dr, about 1860, Miellez

Coeur Tendre D, dp, about 1860, Miellez

Coffee Bean Min, r, 2006, Bedard, Christian; flowers smoky chocolate-orange, reverse cinnamon-orange, 3-4 cm., dbl., borne mostly solitary; foliage medium size, dark green, very glossy; prickles small, sligtly hooked, beige-brown, few; growth compact, bushy, short (30-50 cm.); garden decoration, exhibition; [Santa Claus × Hot Cocoa]; int. by Weeks Roses, 2008

Coffee Country F, m, 1997, Viraraghavan, M.S. Viru; flowers russet and coffee brown, mauve suffusion, light yellow reverse, 4 in., dbl., borne in small clusters; foliage medium size, medium green, semi glossy; spreading, medium (3 ft.) growth; [(Zorina × Cecile Brunner) × (The Fairy × Nordia)]; int. by Hortico

Coffee Ovation Min, r, de Ruiter; int. in 2000

Cognac F, ab, 1959, Tantau, Math.; flowers apricot, reverse darker, stamens dark amber, large, dbl., borne in small clusters; foliage glossy, dark olive-green; moderate growth; [Alpine Glow × Mrs Pierre S. duPont]; int. in 1956

Cognac, Climbing Cl F, ab, 1962, Kordes

Coimbra HT, dp, 1953, Moreira da Silva; flowers cerise-pink, large, dbl., high-centered; [Heinrich Wendland × Crimson Glory]

Colbert HT, pb, 1991, Delbard-Chabert; flowers creamy white, delicately shaded porcelain pink, large, 27-35 petals, cupped, slight fragrance; foliage dark green, flat; bushy (80-100 cm.) growth; [((Peace × Bettina) × (President Herbert Hoover × Tropicana)) × Chateau de Versailles]; int. in 1990

Colby School F, lp, 2006, Beales, Amanda; flowers creamy white to blush pink, deeper in center, medium, dbl, cushion-like, borne mostly solitary, slight fragrance; foliage medium green, glossy; prickles straight, few; bushy, compact, low growth; [Bonica × Great Ormond Street]; int. by Peter Beales Roses, 2005

Colcestria Cl HT, pb, 1916, Cant, B. R.; flowers rose to silver-pink, reverse darker, petals reflexed, 4-5 in., dbl., borne singly or in small clusters, intense damask fragrance; foliage light

Colchester – See **Randers**, F

Colchester Beauty F, dp, 1992, Pawsey, P.R.; flowers candy pink, medium, 6-14 petals, borne mostly singly; foliage medium size, dark green, semi-glossy; some prickles; medium (60-80 cm.), bushy growth; [English Miss × seedling]; int. by Cants of Colchester Ltd., 1989

Colchester Castle F, ab, Poulsen; int. by Cants of Colchester, 2005

Colchester Evening Gazette F, mr, 1972, Cants of Colchester, Ltd.; flowers bright red, 2 in., 40-50 petals, rosette, slight fragrance; foliage light; very free growth; [Evelyn Fison × Etendard]

Colchester Gazette – See **Colchester Evening Gazette**, F

Coleraine HT, lp, 1971, McGredy, Sam IV; flowers pale pink, large, 49 petals, high-centered, slight fragrance; foliage light; free growth; [Paddy McGredy × (Mme Léon Cuny × Columbine)]; int. by McGredy & Son, 1970

Cole's Pink Lafayette F, mp, 1930, Cole Nursery Co.; flowers rose-pink, semi-dbl.; [sport of Lafayette]

Cole's Settlement S, w, 2006, Shoup, George Michael; flowers single, borne in small clusters, moderate fragrance; remontant; foliage large, medium green, semi-glossy; few prickles; growth bushy, tall, (6 ft.); hedging; [((Carefree Beauty × Heritage) × Bayse's Blueberry) × Heritage]; int. by Antique Rose Emporium, 1998

Coletta Montanelli HT, dy, 1976, Kordes; bud globular; flowers deep yellow, 4 in., 32 petals, high-centered, slight fragrance; foliage dark, soft; vigorous, upright, bushy growth; [seedling × Peer Gynt]; int. by Barni, 1975

Colette N, pb, 1932, Schwartz, A.; flowers nankeen yellow at center, shaded salmon-pink, large; foliage glossy, light; very vigorous growth; RULED EXTINCT 7/90; [William Allen Richardson × Mme Laurette Messimy]

Colette HT, mp, 1991, Warriner, William A. & Zary, Keith W.; bud ovoid, pointed; flowers medium soft pink, aging slightly paler, large, 25-30 petals, urn-shaped, borne usually singly, slight damask fragrance; foliage large, dark green, semi-glossy; upright, bushy, tall growth; [Lorena × seedling]; int. by Bear Creek Gardens, 1990

Colette LCl, mp, 1996, Meilland International SA; bud conical, small; flowers ruffled, 3-3½ in., 135 petals, borne in small clusters, intense fragrance; good repeat; foliage small, dark green, glossy; prickles numerous, small to medium; spreading, medium (2 m.) growth; PP9994; [(Fiona × Friesia) × Prairie Princess]; int. as Colette John Keats, The Conard-Pyle Co., 1995

Colette Berges HT, mr, 1940, Dot, Pedro; flowers crimson, medium, 45 petals, high-centered, moderate damask fragrance; vigorous growth; [Red Columbia × Ami Quinard]

Colette Clément HT, ob, 1932, Mallerin, C.; flowers reddish-orange, medium, semi-dbl.; foliage glossy, dark; vigorous growth; [(Mme Mélanie Soupert × Mme Edouard Herriot) × (Mrs Edward Powell × *R. foetida bicolor*)]; int. by C-P

Colette Jelot F, yb, 1942, Meilland, F.; flowers amber-yellow shaded currant-red, open, medium, semi-dbl., borne in clusters; foliage soft; dwarf growth; [Ampere × (Charles P. Kilham × (Charles P. Kilham × Capucine Chambard))]; int. by A. Meilland

Colette Pappin Glynn Min, w, 2001, McCann, Sean; flowers white with yellow center, small, dbl., borne in small clusters; foliage small, medium green, semi-glossy; few prickles; growth compact, low; [Someday Soon × Kent]

Colibre – See **Colibri**, Min

Colibre 79 Min, ob, 1979, Meilland; flowers golden yellow, edged and veined orange; int. in 1979

Colibre 80 – See **Colibre 79**, Min

Colibri Pol, ly, 1898, Lille; flowers soft yellow, fading

Colibri Min, ob, 1959, Meilland, F.; bud ovoid; flowers bright orange-yellow, small, dbl., borne in clusters, slight fragrance; foliage glossy; bushy growth; [Goldilocks × Perla de Montserrat]; int. by URS, 1958; Golden Rose of The Hague, The Hague, 1962

Colibri 80 Min, Meilland, Alain A.; int. in 1980

Colin Kelly HT, dp, 1945, Krebs; bud pointed; flowers cerise-red, very large, dbl.; foliage leathery; upright, bushy growth; [E.G. Hill × The Queen Alexandra Rose]; int. by Marsh's Nursery

Colin Kelly, Climbing Cl HT, dp, Marsh's Nursery

Colinda HT, mr; PP11052; int. in 1997

Colin's Fubar HT, lp, 2000, McCann, Sean; flowers soft pink, veined, medium, dbl., globular, borne mostly singly, moderate fragrance; foliage medium size, medium green, semi-glossy; few prickles; growth upright; [Pink Favorite × Fragrant Cloud]

Colin's Salmon HT, op, Bell, Ronald J.; [sport of Bel Ange]; int. in 1970

Colisée F, mr, 1965, Gaujard; bud pointed; flowers coppery pink, open, medium, semi-dbl.; foliage dark, glossy; very vigorous, bushy growth; [Atlantic × Circus]; int. by Ilgenfritz Nursery

Colleen HT, mp, 1914, McGredy; bud high pointed;

flowers bright rose shaded rose-pink, large, dbl.; vigorous growth; Gold Medal, NRS, 1913

Colleen HT, pb, Kordes; flowers large, creamy white and pink blend, dbl.; medium to tall growth; int. in 1994

Colleen Little Min, my, 1992, Little, Lee W.; flowers medium, full, high-centered, borne usually singly or in sprays of 5-7, slight fragrance; foliage small, dark green, semi-glossy, disease-resistant; some prickles; medium (26-30 cm.), upright, bushygrowth; [Luis Desamero × Cheyenne]; int. by Oregon Miniature Roses, 1992

Colleen Mary HT, dr, 2003, Meilland International; flowers 8-10 cm., full, borne in small clusters; foliage medium green, Matte; prickles moderate; growth upright (5-6 ft.); garden, cutting; [(Duc de Windsor × Chrysler Imperial) × Rouge Meilland]; int. by The Conard-Pyle Company, 2003

Colleen Moore HT, dr, 1944, Joseph H. Hill, Co.; flowers velvety carmine, open, 4-4½ in., dbl.; foliage leathery, dark; strong stems; vigorous, upright growth; [((De Luxe × Senior) × Premier) × Chieftain]; int. by Bosley Nursery

College Avenue Columbia HT, dp

College Avenue #10 – See **Heinrich Wendland**, HT

Collegiate 110 F, my, Dickson, Patrick; flowers open, clear yellow, no fragrance; growth to 3 ft.; int. by Ludwig's Roses

Collegiate Pride HT, mr, Bell; int. in 1989

Cologne – See **Köln am Rhein**, HKor

Cologne Gr, m, 1998, McGredy, Sam IV; flowers mauve, 4½ in., dbl., borne in small clusters, intense fragrance; foliage large, medium green, matte; prickles moderate; bushy, medium (110 cm.) growth; [Harmonie × Lagerfeld]; int. by McGredy, 1996

Cologne Carnival – See Kölner Karnival

Coloma's Gold Min, yb, Fischer; [sport of Work of Art]; int. in 1998

Colombe HT, Croix, P.; int. in 1976

Colombina HT, pb, Barni, V.; flowers white with deep pink edges which spread with age, dbl., high-centered, borne mostly singly, no fragrance; few prickles; growth to 3 ft.; int. by Rose Barni, 1985

Colombine – See **Columbine**, F

Colonel Campbell Watson HT, mp, 1936, Bees; bud pointed; flowers salmon-pink, dbl., high-centered; foliage soft; long stems; vigorous growth; [Joan Howarth × Portadown]; Gold Medal, NRS, 1935

Colonel Combe B, m, 1856, Pradel; flowers lilac pink, globular, moderate fragrance

Colonel Dazier HT, w, 1927, Ketten Bros.; flowers rosy white, reverse bright rose, base golden yellow, dbl.; [Le Progrés × Jonkheer J.L. Mock]

Colonel de Rougemont HP, pb, 1853, Lacharme

Colonel de Sansal HP, mr, 1875, Jamain, H.; flowers velvety carmine shaded deep carmine, large, full

Colonel Félix Breton HP, rb, 1883, Schwartz; flowers velvety grenadine red at center, outer petals violet, amaranth reverse, large, full, borne singly or in small clusters; foliage light green; prickles moderate, red, slightly hooked

Colonel Foissy HP, mp, 1849, Margottin; sepals often foliaceous; flowers bright cherry-cerise, medium, dbl., borne in clusters of 5-10; foliage dark green, irregularly dentate; prickles very numerous, reddish

Colonel Gravereaux HT, op, 1940, Mallerin, C.; flowers salmon-coral, reverse yellow; strong stems; vigorous, upright growth; int. by A. Meilland

Colonel Joffé T, mr, 1893, Liabaud; flowers purplish red, petals wrinkled, flat

Colonel Leclerc HT, mp, 1909, Pernet-Ducher; flowers Tyrian pink, dbl.; [Mme Caroline Testout × Horace Vernet]

Colonel Lindbergh Pol, op, 1928, Kromhout; flowers salmon-orange; [sport of Juliana Rose]; int. by Vuyk van Nees

Colonel Nicolas Meyer HT, mr, 1934, Sauvageot, H.; bud pointed; flowers brilliant velvety red, open, dbl.; foliage leathery; strong stems; vigorous, bushy growth; [La Maréchale Petain × Edouard Mignot]

Colonel Oswald Fitzgerald HT, dr, 1917, Dickson, A.; flowers dark velvety crimson, well-formed, dbl.; vigorous, branching growth

Colonel R. S. Williamson HT, lp, 1907, Dickson, A.; flowers white, center deep blush, large, dbl., high-centered; foliage glossy, dark; vigorous, open growth

Colonel R. S. Williamson, Climbing Cl HT, w, 1920, Dingee & Conard; [sport of Colonel R. S. Williamson]

Colonel Robert Lefort M, dr, 1864, Verdier, E.; flowers purple-red

Colonel Sharman-Crawford HT, mr, 1933, Dickson, A.; flowers rich velvety crimson, large, dbl., high-centered; foliage leathery; long, strong stems; vigorous, bushy growth; Gold Medal, NRS, 1931

Colonel Souflot HP, mr, 1862, Vigneron

Colonel Svec – See **Plukovnik Svec**, HT

Colonel Tillier B, m; flowers lilac pink, medium, full

Colonia – See **Exploit**, LCl

Colonial Days S, dr, 2002, Giles, Diann; flowers large, very dbl., borne mostly solitary; foliage medium size, medium green, matte; prickles small, straight; growth upright, medium; garden decorative; [Fishermen's Friend × Squire]; int. by Muncys Rose Emporium, 2000

Colonial White – See **Sombreuil**, LCl

Color Burst – See **Colorburst**, Gr

Color Carnival – See **Colour Carnival**, F

Color Girl F, pb, 1966, Fuller; bud ovoid; flowers whitish, edged red, medium, dbl., high-centered; foliage dark, leathery; bushy, low growth; [Little Darling × Cocorico]; int. by Wyant

Color Guard Min, mp, 1991, Jolly, Marie; flowers 2 in., 25 petals, borne mostly singly, no fragrance; foliage medium size, medium green, matte; few prickles; upright (20 cm.), bushy, very hardy growth; [Anita Charles × Poker Chip]; int. by Rosehill Farm, 1993

Color-Guard LCl, dp, 2002, Jones, Ken; flowers full, borne mostly solitary, moderate fragrance; foliage medium size, dark green, semi-glossy; prickles large, curved, numerous; growth spreading, very vigorous, tall (20-30 ft.); fences; [seedling × First Prize]

Color Magic HT, pb, 1977, Warriner, William A.; bud long; flowers pale salmon blushing pink, 5 in., 25-30 petals, flat, borne singly, intense fruity fragrance; foliage large, dark green; upright growth; PP3998; [seedling × Spellbinder]; int. by J&P, 1978

Color Purple Min, m, 1991, Clements, John K.; flowers rich deep purple, medium, very dbl., borne mostly singly, moderate fragrance; foliage medium size, dark green, holly-like, glossy; few prickles; low (25 cm.), spreading, compact growth; [Angel Face × seedling]; int. by Heirloom Old Garden Roses, 1990

Color Purple – See **The Colour Purple**, Min

Color Wonder Min, yb, Clements, John; flowers bright yellow, changing to wine purple, 1¼ in., 5 petals; continuous bloom; bushy growth, 2½-3 ft high, 2 ft wide; int. by Heirloom Roses, 2001

Colorado HT, Combe, M.; int. in 1970

Colorado F, mp, Select Roses, B.V.

Colorama HT, rb, 1968, Meilland, Mrs. Marie-Louise; bud ovoid; flowers red with yellow reverse, large, dbl., cupped, moderate fragrance; foliage very glossy; vigorous, upright, bushy growth; PP2862; [Suspense × Confidence]; int. by C-P

Coloranja – See **Mustang**, HT

Colorbreak – See **Brown Velvet**, F

Colorburst Gr, dp, Twomey, Jerry; flowers borne in small clusters; good repeat; PP10113; int. in 1995

Coloso HT, mp, 1962, Dot, Simon; flowers 50 petals; very vigorous growth; [Chrysler Imperial × (Peace × Queen Elizabeth)]

Colossal – See **Colossal Meidiland**, S

Colossal Meidiland S, mr, Meilland; flowers bright red, medium size, dbl., borne in clusters; recurrent bloom; int. in 2000

Colossus HT, dy, 1998, Perry, Astor; flowers golden yellow, medium sized, full, borne in small clusters, moderate fragrance; foliage medium size, medium green, glossy; growth upright, medium (5 ft.); [Folklore × Golden Gate]; int. by Certified Roses, Inc., 1999

Colour – See **Colour Parade**, MinFl

Colour Carnival F, yb, 1962, LeGrice; flowers primrose-yellow edged pink, well-formed, 3 in., 50 petals, borne in clusters; vigorous, low, bushy growth; int. by Wayside Gardens Co., 1962

Colour Glow F, ob, 1971, Butter; flowers orange, reddening to flame, large, 36 petals, globular, slight fragrance; vigorous growth; [Tropicana × Masquerade]; int. by Wood End Gardens, 1969

Colour Harmony HT, pb, Ghosh; int. by KSG, 1998

Colour Hit – See **Colour Parade**, MinFl

Colour Magic MinFl, pb; int. in 1999

Colour Parade F, yb, 1991, Laver, Keith G.; flowers yellow turning to red, small, full, borne in small clusters, slight fragrance; foliage medium size, medium green, glossy; some prickles; low (45 cm.), bushy growth; [Breezy × Julie Ann]; int. by Springwood Roses, 1992

Colour Parade MinFl, or, Poulsen; bud long, pointed, ovoid; flowers orange-red, 5 cm., 25-35 petals, borne usually in small clusters, very slight fragrance; recurrent; foliage dark green, glossy; prickles average, 3-4 mm., straight; bushy, compact (20-40 cm.) growth; PP13138; [seedling × Charming Parade]; int. by Poulsen Roser, 1998

Colour Patiohit – See **Colour Parade**, MinFl

Colour Sergeant F, or, 1972, Harkness; flowers 4 in., 20 petals; foliage glossy; [Queen Elizabeth × (Ann Elizabeth × Circus)]; int. by R. Harkness & Co., 1970

Colour Wonder HT, ob, 1964, Kordes, R.; bud ovoid; flowers orange-coral, reverse cream, large, 50 petals, slight fragrance; recurrent; foliage glossy, bronze; prickles numerous, large; vigorous, bushy growth; [Kordes' Perfecta × Tropicana]; int. by McGredy, 1964; Gold Medal, Belfast, 1966, ADR, 1964

Colour Wonder HT, pb, Dey, S. C.; flowers large, creamy ivory to apricot-pink to light red; int. in 2000

Colourama – See **Colorama**, HT

Colourbox F, yb, Benardella, Frank; int. in 2001

Coluche F, mr; flowers luminous red, dbl., borne in large clusters; recurrent; foliage semi-glossy; growth to 60-80 cm.; int. by Meilland, 2002

Columbia HWich, mp, 1903, Hooper Bro. & Thomas; non-recurrent; moderately vigorous growth; [seedling × Mme Caroline Testout]

Columbia HT, mp, 1916, E.G. Hill, Co.; bud long, pointed; flowers glistening rose-pink, large, 65 petals, intense fragrance; foliage dark; vigorous growth; [Ophelia × Mrs George Shawyer]; Gold Medal, Portland, 1919, Gertrude M. Hubbard, ARS, 1919

Columbia, Climbing Cl HT, mp, 1920, Totty (also Hill (1920), Vestal (1923), and Lens (1929)); bud very large, long-pointed; flowers pink changing to brighter pink, large, very full; [sport of Columbia]

Columbian Climber – See **Columbia, Climbing**, Cl HT

Columbine F, yb, 1956, Poulsen, S.; flowers creamy yellow tinged pink, well-formed, borne in open clusters; foliage glossy; vigorous growth; [Danish Gold × Frensham]; int. by McGredy

Columbine – See **Columbine Parade**, MinFl

Columbine Parade MinFl, lp, Poulsen; flowers light pink, 5-8 cm., dbl., no fragrance; foliage dark; growth bushy, 20-40 cm.; PP13487; int. by Poulsen Roser, 2000

Columbus F, dp, 1990, Carruth, Tom; bud ovoid, pointed; flowers deep rose pink, fading very little, large, 28-35 petals, high-centered, borne usually singly, slight fragrance; foliage large, medium green, dull; prickles almost straight, slightly hooked, medium, pinkish-brown; bushy, medium growth; PP8183; [seedling × Bridal Pink]; int. by Weeks Roses, 1991

Columbus Queen HT, pb, 1962, Armstrong, D.L., & Swim, H. C.; bud ovoid, pointed; flowers light pink, reverse darker, 4 in., 24-30 petals, high-centered, slight fragrance; foliage leathery, dark; vigorous, upright growth; PP2170; [La Jolla × seedling]; int. by Armstrong Nursery, 1962; Gold Medal, Geneva, 1961

Columella HGal, dr, 1841, Vibert; flowers rich rosy crimson, often shaded violet, medium, full, cupped

Columelle – See **Columella**, HGal

Columelle HGal, m, 1860, Moreau et Robert; flowers lilac-pink center, lighter at edges, very full; sometimes classed as D

Colysée – See **Colisée**, F

Come Lei HT, Giacomasso; int. in 1968

Comedie F, Combe, M.; int. in 1977

Comedy MinFl, yb, 2000, Giles, Diann; flowers medium size, yellow blend, full, borne in small clusters, no fragrance; foliage medium size, medium green, dull; few prickles; upright, medium growth; [Little Darling × Rainbow's End]; int. by Giles Rose Nursery, 2000

Comendador Nogueira da Silva HT, rb, 1961, Moreira da Silva; flowers dark red, reverse silvery; [Confidence × Independence]

Comet Cl F, pb, 1934, Mesman; flowers flesh pink, shaded salmon-yellow, large, very dbl., slight fragrance; foliage leathery; short, strong stems; [sport of Gruss an Aachen]; int. by Bosley Nursery

Comet Tail F, m, Zary; flowers striped; int. by Bear Creek Gardens

Comice de Seine-et-Marne Ch, mr, 1842, Desprez; flowers scarlet, shaded carmine, full, cupped

Comice de Tarn-et-Garonne B, mr, 1852, Pradel; flowers carmine red, medium, full, intense fragrance

Commanche Gr, or, 1968, Swim & Weeks; bud pointed; flowers bright, medium, dbl., high-centered; foliage leathery; vigorous, upright, bushy growth; PP2855; [Spartan × (Carrousel × Happiness)]; int. by C-P

Command Performance HT, or, 1970, Lindquist; bud ovoid; flowers medium, dbl., high-centered, intense fragrance; foliage leathery; vigorous, tall, bushy growth; PP3063; [Tropicana × Hawaii]; int. by Howard Rose Co.

Commandant Beaurepaire HP, pb, 1875, Moreau-Robert; flowers intense rose pink, striped purple and violet, spotted white, large, dbl., cupped; occasional repeat; foliage light green; prickles spiny; vigorous growth; originally put in commerce under this name and classified as HGal; later renamed Panachée d'Angers and reclassed after some remontancy was noted

Commandant Cousteau – See **Lasting Love**, HT

Commandant Cousteau, Climbing Cl HT, dr, Adam; flowers velvety dark red, dbl., moderate fragrance; recurrent; foliage dark green to reddish green; vigorous (10 ft.) growth; [sport of Commandant Cousteau]; int. in 2004

Commandant Félix Faure HP, mr, 1901, Boutigny; flowers light crimson-red, tinted vermilion, 25 petals, cupped; vigorous, upright growth

Commandant L. Bartre HT, rb, 1920, Schwartz, A.; flowers dark carmine-red, tinted brilliant pink, dbl.; vigorous growth; [Lady Ashtown × Louis van Houtte]

Commandant Letourneux HT, dp, 1903, Bahaud; flowers carmine-pink, very large, very dbl.; [sport of Joséphine Marot]

Commandant Mansuy HP, mr, 1869, Vigneron; flowers fire-red, large, full

Commandant Marchand T, my, 1900, Puyravaud; flowers yellow, center darker, petals edged cream, large, full, moderate fragrance; [Gloire de Dijon × unknown]

Commandatore Francesco Ingegnoli Cl HT, or, 1923, Ingegnoli; flowers geranium-red

Commander Gillette S, mp; flowers single; some repeat; thornless; [*R. carolina alba* × Hugh Dickson]

Com. Sukumar Da HT, lp, Pushpanjali; flowers ivory pink, moderate fragrance; int. in 1997

Commandeur Jules Gravereaux HP, mr, 1908, Croibier; bud pointed; flowers dazzling red, center shaded maroon, large, peony-like, dbl.; vigorous growth; [Frau Karl Druschki × Liberty]

Commandeur Jules Gravereaux, Climbing Cl HP, mr, 1925, Belouet; int. by Grandes Roseraies

Commando HT, op, 1945, Howard, F.H.; bud long, pointed; flowers orange-buff, suffused pink, 5 in., 30-35 petals, camellia-like; foliage leathery, glossy; upright, bushy growth; [Mrs J.D. Eisele × Glowing Sunset]; int. by H&S

Commitment LCl, dr, Clements, John K.; int. by Heirloom Roses, 1995

Common Blush China – See **Old Blush**, Ch

Common Centifolia – See **Cabbage Rose**, C

Common China – See **Old Blush**, Ch

Common Monthly – See **Old Blush**, Ch

Common Moss – See **Communis**, M

Common Pink China – See **Old Blush**, Ch

Common Pompon – See ***R. × centifolia pomponia*** (Lindley), C

Common Purple Boursault – See **Reversa**, Bslt

Common Red China – See **Slater's Crimson China**, Ch

Commonwealth HT, dp, 1923, Montgomery Co.; bud pointed; flowers deep pink, large, dbl.; foliage leathery, rich green; [Ophelia × seedling]; int. by A.N. Pierson

Commonwealth F, pb, 1948, Kordes; flowers crimson with white eye, 10 petals, borne in clusters; foliage leathery; [Col. Nicolas Meyer × Holstein]; int. by Morse

Commonwealth Glory HT, ab; flowers large, peach-apricot in center, outer petals pearly pink to ivory, 7 in., 30-35 petals, high-centered, borne mostly singly, moderate fruity fragrance; recurrent; foliage glossy; stems long; upright (3-5 ft.) growth; int. by Harkness, 1998

Communique S, pb, Williams, J.B.; flowers soft pink with ivory center, semi-dbl., flat, moderate fragrance; recurrent; growth to 3 ft.; int. by Hortico Inc., 2006

Communis M, mp, before 1720; sepals, peduncles and calyx glandular, mossy; flowers large, dbl.; [sport of *R. centifolia*]; the presence of 'moss' on the peduncles and calice is highly variable and unstable, and likely to revert; because of the variability, this rose entered commerce under many different names

Community Banquet HT, lp, 2007, Bell, Ron; flowers large, 10 cm., full, borne mostly solitary; foliage medium size, dark green, semi-glossy; prickles medium, hooked, brown, few; growth upright, medium (1½ m.); garden decorative; [(Daily Sketch × unknown) × Red Planet]; int. by Ross Roses, 2007

Compactilla HSpn, ly; flowers small, creamy ivory with yellow stamens, single

Compassion LCl, op, 1973, Harkness; flowers salmon pink shaded apricot, large, 36 petals, borne singly or in small clusters, moderate sweet fragrance; foliage large, dark; prickles large, reddish; medium, bushy growth; [White Cockade × Prima Ballerina]; Gold Medal, Baden-Baden, 1973, Edland Fragrance Medal, ARS, 1973, ADR, 1976

Compassionate Friend F, lp, 1993, Harkness; flowers medium pink, lighter at center, reverse light pink, 4 in., 24 petals, borne in sprays of 5-7, moderate fruity fragrance; foliage medium size, medium green, semi-glossy; spreading, low growth; [seedling × Memento]; int. by Harkness New Roses, Ltd., 1985

Compassionate Friends Gr, ly, 2000, Walsh, Richard; flowers semi-dbl., 6-14 petals, borne in small clusters; foliage medium size, light green, semi-glossy; few prickles; upright, tall growth; [(Ginger Heggs × City of Leeds) × Gold Medal]

Complicata HGal, pb; flowers deep pink, white eye, yellow stamens, large, single; rampant (to 6 ft.) growth; probably *R. gallica* × *R. canina*

Comptoire des Bourbons B, mp

Comrade HT, mr, 1948, Dickson, A.; flowers scarlet-crimson, well-formed, medium

Comte Adrien de Germiny HP, mp, 1881, Lévêque; flowers bright rose pink, large, full; very remontant; foliage dark green; [Jules Margottin × unknown]

Comte Alphonse de Serenyi HP, pb, 1865, Touvais; flowers bright carmine, shaded purple and garnet, large, full

Comte Amédé de Foras T, pb, 1900, Gamon; flowers China pink shaded with saffron, full, moderate sweet fragrance; [Luciole × G. Nabonnand]

Comte Bobrinsky – See **Comte de Bobrinsky**, HCh

Comte Cavour HP, mp, 1856, Vigneron; flowers bright pink, large, full, moderate fragrance

Comte Cavour HP, pb, 1859, Liabaud

Comte Chandon T, my, 1894, Soupert & Notting; flowers outer petals light yellow, center bright chrome yellow, large, full; [Lutea Flora × Coquette de Lyon]

Comte Charles d'Harcourt HP, mr, 1897, Lévêque; flowers bright carmine red, large, full; foliage dark green

Comte de Beaufort HP, m, 1858, Boyau; flowers purple, shaded darker, medium, full

Comte de Bobrinsky HCh, dp, 1849, Marest; flowers carmine-pink, medium, dbl.; sometimes classed as HP

Comte de Boubert Ch, lp, before 1855; flowers bright pink, shaded flesh pink, large, full

Comte de Cavour – See **Comte Cavour**, HP, 1859

Comte de Chambord P, pb, about 1860, Moreau-Robert; flowers pink tinted lilac, very dbl., flat, intense fragrance; vigorous, erect growth; confused in commerce with Mme Boll

Comte de Colbert – See **Comtesse de Colbert**, B

Comte de Falloux HP, dp, 1863, Trouillard or Standish; flowers crimson-pink; int. by Standish & Noble, 1863

Comte de Flandres HP, dr, 1881, Lévêque, P.; flowers velvety blackish purple red, shaded carmine, very large, full; foliage brownish-green; [Mme Victor Verdier × unknown]

Comte de Grassin HP, dp, 1890, Corboeuf; flowers dark pink, shaded carmine, large, full; [General Jacqueminot × La France]

Comte de Grivel T, ly, 1871, Levet; flowers straw yellow, dbl.

Comte de Montalivet HP, 1846, Mondeville

Comte de Montessier HP, mp, 1852, Berger

Comte de Montijo B, m, 1855, Fontaine; flowers velvety dark purple, shaded violet, full

Comte de Mortemart HP, mp, 1880, Margottin fils; flowers clear pink, very large, full, intense fragrance

Comte de Murinais HGal, dr; flowers slate-red, marbled, large

Comte de Nanteuil HGal, m, 1834, Roeser; flowers crimson purple, center sometimes fiery crimson, reverse silvery, large, dbl., irregularly quartered, borne in clusters of 2-4, moderate fragrance; foliage medium green, elliptical, deeply toothed; prickles very thin; branching growth

Comte de Nanteuil HGal, pb, 1852, Quétier; flowers bright rose with crimson edges, sometimes with a green center, large, dbl., cupped; vigorous growth; [Boule de Nanteuil × unknown]

Comte de Paris HP, m, 1839, Laffay, M.; flowers purplish pink, very large, full, cupped; very remontant; growth erect

Comte de Paris T, lp, 1839, Hardy; flowers very large, full, moderate fragrance

Comte de Paris HP, dp, 1864, Verdier, E.; flowers pink over cherry, large, full

Comte de Paris HP, rb, 1886, Lévêque; flowers poppy red, shaded with bright purple and crimson, large, full

Comte de Raimbaud – See **Comte Raimbaud**, HP

Comte de Sembui – See **Jean Ducher**, T

Comte de Taverna T, ly, 1872, Ducher; flowers whitish yellow, darker at center, large, very full

Comte de Thun-Hohenstein – See **Comte Frédéric de Thun-Hohenstein**, HP

Comte de Torres Cl HT, op, 1906, Schwartz, A.; flowers coppery salmon-pink, large, dbl., borne in small to medium clusters; prickles large; [Kaiserin Auguste Viktoria × Mme Bérard]

Comte d'Epremesnil HRg, m, 1882, Nabonnand; flowers violet-pink, large, semi-dbl.

Comte d'Eu B, mr, 1844, Lacharme

Comte F. de Chavagnac HT, mp, before 1929; flowers peach-blossom-pink, center rosy carmine; [Antoine Rivoire × Zéphirine Drouhin]

Comte F. de Chavagnac, Climbing Cl HT, mp, 1929, Siret-Pernet; flowers orange pink, rosy carmine at center, medium, full; foliage light green; nearly thornless; [Antoine Rivoire × Zéphirine Drouhin]

Comte Florimond de Bergeyck HP, rb, 1879, Soupert & Notting; flowers pink-brick, tinted orange-red, large, very full

Comte Foy HGal, lp, 1827, Lecomte; flowers pale rose, aging lilac, whitish-violet at edges, very large, dbl., cupped, borne singly or in clusters of 2-3, slight fragrance; foliage small, round, light green; no prickles

Comte Foy HGal, rb; flowers white, striped red

Comte Foy de Rouen – See **Comte Foy**, HGal, 1827

Comte Frédéric de Thun-Hohenstein HP, dr, 1880, Lévêque; flowers deep reddish-crimson, tinted carmine, large, full, moderate fragrance; foliage large, dark green; prickles numerous, small, white

Comte G. de Rochemur HT, 1911, Schwartz, A.; flowers bright scarlet, large, dbl.; [Xavier Olibo × Gruss an Teplitz]

Comte G. de Roquette-Buisson T, mp, 1887, Nabonnand; flowers bright pink, large, very full, moderate fragrance; [Reine Maria Pia × unknown]

Comte Galatine HT, pb, 1901, Brauer; flowers dark flesh pink, shaded yellow-red, reverse carmine

Comte H. de Choiseul HFt, op, 1894, Pernet-Ducher; flowers salmon-orange, salmon-pink at center, shaded yellow at base, large, full; [Lady Mary Fitzwilliam × Souv de Mme Levet]

Comte Henri Rignon HT, yb, 1885, Pernet-Ducher; flowers coppery yellow with salmon pink center, large to very large, full, cupped; [Baronne Adolphe de Rothschild × Ma Capucine]

Comte Horace de Choiseul HP, mr, 1879, Lévêque; flowers fiery vermilion with scarlet, velvety, large, full, moderate fragrance

Comte Lelieur – See **Rose du Roi**, P

Comte Litta HP, rb, 1866, Verdier, E.; flowers velvety scarlet, shaded grenadine-violet, large, full

Comte Odart HP, mr, 1850, Dupuy-Jamain; flowers bright red, aging to violet, 8-9 cm., full, quartered; foliage rounded, dark green; prickles nearly straight, deep maroon, numerous; stems short, brown-green

Comte Raimbaud HP, mr, 1867, Rolland; flowers crimson, large, dbl.

Comte Raoul Chandon HP, rb, 1896, Lévêque; flowers vermilion tinted with brown, large, full

Comte-Robert – See **Maurice Bernardin**, HP

Comtes des Champagne S, yb, 2002, Austin, David; flowers medium yellow fading to white, 7 cm., semi-dbl., borne in small clusters, moderate fragrance; foliage medium size, medium green, semi-glossy, leathery, smooth, disease-resistant; prickles medium, deep concave, red, few; growth bushy, medium (120 cm.); garden decorative; [pink English-type shrub × Tamora]; int. by David Austin Roses, Ltd., 2001; Certificate of Merit, Adelaide, 2006

Comtesse Alban de Villeneuve T, pb, 1881, Nabonnand; flowers coppery pink, shaded scarlet, full; growth vigorous

Comtesse Anna Thun T, yb, 1887, Soupert & Notting; flowers golden orange-yellow, large, full, cupped, intense fragrance; [Sylphide × Mme Camille]

Comtesse Anne de Bruce HT, pb, 1937, Mallerin, C.; bud pointed; flowers coppery pink to nasturtium-red, very large, semi-dbl., cupped; foliage glossy; very vigorous growth; [Charles P. Kilham × (Mrs Pierre S. duPont × (*R. foetida bicolor* × unknown))]; int. by H. Guillot

Comtesse Antonia Migazzi HP, mp, 1889, Benkö, Dr.; flowers silvery rose, large, full; [sport of Mabel Morrison]

Comtesse Barbantane – See **Comtesse de Barbantane**, B

Comtesse Bardi T, yb, 1896, Soupert & Notting; flowers dull reddish-yellow, center coral-red with gold tints, large, dbl., moderate fragrance; [Rêve d'Or × Mme Lombard]

Comtesse Bardi T, yb, 1900, Nabonnand; flowers canary-yellow, center fawn, edges shaded carmine, large, dbl.; [Safrano × Château des Bergeries]

Comtesse Beatrix de Buisseret – See **Beatrix, Comtesse de Buisseret**, HT

Comtesse Bertrand de Blacas HP, mp, 1888, Verdier, E.; flowers soft bright rose, large, full, globular, cupped; foliage very large, light green, elliptical, irregularly serrated; prickles few, straight, pink; growth erect

Comtesse Branicka HP, lp, 1888, Lévêque; flowers delicate silvery pink, large, dbl.

Comtesse Brigitte Chandon-Moet HT, ab, Dorieux; int. in 1997

Comtesse Brigitte de la Rochefoucauld S, pb, Dorieux; flowers striped; int. by Roseraies Dorieux, 2002

Comtesse Cahen d'Anvers HP, mp, 1885, Lédéchaux; flowers deep pink, large, dbl., globular, moderate fragrance; foliage dark green; growth upright; [La Reine × unknown]

Comtesse Cécile de Chabrillant HP, pb, 1858, Marest; flowers satiny pink, silvery reverse, medium, dbl., globular; foliage dark, leathery; prickles numerous small, dark; [Jules Margottin × unknown]

Comtesse Cécile de Forton Cl T, pb, 1916, Nabonnand, G.; flowers rose-peach, very large, dbl.

Comtesse d'Alcantara – See **Home & Country**, HT

Comtesse d'Ansembourg HT, ly, 1918, Leenders, M.; flowers yellowish-white, dbl.; [Étoile de France × Marquise de Sinéty]

Comtesse de Baillet HGal, w, 1827, from Courtray

Comtesse de Barbantane B, lp, 1858, Guillot Père; flowers blush, shaded with rose, large, full, cupped, borne in small clusters; [Reine des Ile-Bourbons × unknown]; sometimes classed as HP

Comtesse de Bardi – See **Comtesse Bardi**, T, 1896

Comtesse de Bouchard – See **Comtesse de Bouchaud**, N

Comtesse de Bouchaud N, my, 1890, Guillot et Fils; flowers saffron yellow, very large

Comtesse de Bresson HP, lp, 1873, Guinoiseau, B.; flowers bright pink, petal edges white, large, dbl.; [Jules Margottin × unknown]

Comtesse de Brossard T, my, 1862, Oger; flowers canary yellow, medium, full

Comtesse de Camondo – See **Mme la Comtesse de Camondo**, HP

Comtesse de Caserta T, mr, 1877, Nabonnand, G.; flowers coppery-red, large

Comtesse de Cassagne HT, mp, 1919, Guillot, M.; flowers coppery rose, shaded bright rose, sometimes entirely yellow, large, dbl., moderate fragrance

Comtesse de Castilleja HT, op, 1926, Chambard, M.; bud orange; flowers coral, cupped; foliage dark; strong stems; very vigorous growth; [(Mme Edouard Herriot × Juliet) × seedling]

Comtesse de Chabrillant Blanche – See **Mme Lefrançois**, HP

Comtesse de Chamoïs C, mp, about 1810, Descemet; flowers small, full, semi-globular; foliage large, oval-rounded; growth vertical

Comtesse de Chaponnay HG, lp, 1924, Nabonnand, P.; flowers creamy pink, center bright salmon-pink, very large, full, cupped, strong fragrance; [*R. gigantea* × Mme Hoste]

Comtesse de Choiseul – See **Mlle Marie Rady**, HP

Comtesse de Colbert B, m, about 1846, from Angers; flowers purple, medium, full

Comtesse de Coursy HP, dp, 1862, Lévêque; flowers pink over red

Comtesse de Coutard HCh, mp, 1829, Noisette, E.; flowers large, very dbl., borne in clusters of 5-7; foliage elongate, glabrous, lightly dentate; prickles numerous, unequal

Comtesse de Falloux HP, mp, 1867, Trouillard; flowers pink, nuanced mauve, very large, very full

Comtesse de Flandres HP, lp, 1878, Verdier, E.; flowers light silvery pink, center bright pink, large, dbl., cupped; foliage delicate green, deeply toothed; few prickles; growth upright

Comtesse de Fresnel N, m, before 1835, Prévost; flowers lilac pink, with dark pink-purple, medium, full

Comtesse de Fressinet de Bellanger HP, lp, 1885, Lévêque; flowers flesh pink, very large, full; foliage light green

Comtesse de Frigneuse T, my, 1885, Guillot et Fils; flowers large, dbl.; [Mme Damaizin × unknown]

Comtesse de Galard-Béarn N, ly, 1893, Bernaix, A.; flowers light yellow with pink tones, 7-9 cm., dbl., strong tea fragrance

Comtesse de Greffulhe HP, pb, 1896, Lévêque; flowers carmine, shaded fiery red with dark purple, large, full

Comtesse de Jaucourt – See **Mme la Comtesse de Jaucourt**, HP

Comtesse de la Morandière HT, op, 1929, Chambard, C.; flowers shrimp-pink, reverse coral-red, dbl.

Comtesse de Labarthe – See **Duchesse de Brabant**, T

Comtesse de Lacépède HGal, lp, 1840, Duval/Verdier; flowers silvery blush, center sometimes rosy, large, dbl.; moderate growth; sometimes classed as HCh

Comtesse de Leusse T, mp, 1878, Nabonnand; flowers large, soft medium pink, dbl.

Comtesse de Ludre HP, mr, 1879, Verdier; flowers

carmine, edged white, very large, full, cupped, strong fragrance

Comtesse de Marnes HP, pb, 1854, Desprez; flowers lilac pink, shaded dark crimson, large, full

Comtesse de Martel HT, mp, 1939, Meilland, F.; flowers carnation-pink, center coppery, very large; very vigorous growth; [Charles P. Kilham × Margaret McGredy]

Comtesse de Medina Coeli HP, mr, 1864, Marest; flowers glowing red, large, full

Comtesse de Murinais M, w, 1843, Vibert; flowers flesh, opening white, large, dbl.; non-recurrent; growth to 4-5 ft.

Comtesse de Murinais HGal, lp, 1843, Robert; flowers large, full

Comtesse de Nadaillac T, ab, before 1910, Guillot; flowers coppery yellow, centers salmon

Comtesse de Noë M, m, 1846, Portemer; flowers shining purple-carmine, shaded dark lilac, medium, very full; remontant

Comtesse de Noghera T, op, 1902, Nabonnand; flowers light salmon-pink, very large, very dbl.; [Reine Emma des Pays-Bas × Paul Nabonnand]

Comtesse de Palikao HP, lp, 1865, Pernet; flowers flesh pink, shaded white, large, full

Comtesse de Panisse T, pb, before 1910; flowers rosy buff, shaded with carmine and violet; large, full

Comtesse de Paris HP, pb, 1864, Verdier, E.; flowers bright pink, petal edges tinted white, reflexed, 10-12 cm., full, globular; foliage dark green; [Victor Verdier × unknown]; re-released by Lévêque in 1882

Comtesse de Paris HT, dy, Briant; int. in 1993

Comtesse de Polignac HP, dr, 1862, Granger; flowers poppy red, velvety, tinted flame, and purple, medium, dbl.

Comtesse de Provence HT, mp, 2001, Meilland, A.; bud conical; flowers medium coral-pink, 5 in., 80 petals, cupped, borne mostly solitary, intense fragrance; recurrent; foliage large, medium green, semi-glossy; prickles moderate, hooked downward; growth upright, medium (5½ ft.); hips smooth, rounded, yellow-green; PP13860; [(Centenaire de Lourdes × Duc de Windsor) × Regatta]; int. by The Conard-Pyle Company, 2001

Comtesse de Rességuier B, mp, 1842, Béluze; flowers silver pink, medium, full, cupped

Comtesse de Rocquigny B, lp, 1874, Vaurin; flowers white, tinted with rosy salmon, medium, full, globular

Comtesse de Roquette-Buisson HP, lp, 1888, Lévêque; flowers light pink, tinted both darker and lighter, very large; foliage very large, light green

Comtesse de Rosemond-Chabeau de Lussay T, op, 1887, Chauvry; flowers salmon pink, center bright pink over coppery yellow base, reverse China pink, large, full

Comtesse de Saxe T, w, 1904, Soupert & Notting; flowers porcelain white, tinted yellow, large, very full, moderate fragrance; [Leonie Osterrieth × Souv de Mme Eugene Verdier]

Comtesse de Séguier HP, mr, 1861, Samson; flowers bright red

Comtesse de Seguier HP, mr, 1848, Verdier, V.

Comtesse de Ségur S, mp, Delbard; flowers light rose pink, petals dahlia-like, very dbl., moderate rose & raspberry fragrance; int. by Georges Delbard SA, 1994

Comtesse de Ségur C, lp, 1848, Verdier, V.; flowers pale flesh, medium, full

Comtesse de Serenye HP, lp, 1874, Lacharme, F.; flowers soft pink, very large, full; foliage dark green, regularly dentate; prickles flattened, hooked; [La Reine × unknown]

Comtesse de Turenne HP, lp, 1853, Oger; flowers flesh pink, lilac centered

Comtesse de Turenne HP, lp, 1867, Verdier, E.; flowers flesh pink, large, full; foliage dark green

Comtesse de Vallier HP, 1866, Damaizin

Comtesse de Vezins – See **Vicomtesse de Vezins**, HP

Comtesse de Vitzthum T, my, 1890, Soupert & Notting; flowers light yellow outer petals, bright yellow center, large, full

Comtesse de Woronzoff – See **Regulus**, T

Comtesse Diana HT, or, Hetzel; int. in 1989

Comtesse Doria M, m, 1854, Portemer fils; flowers purple-pink, shaded salmon, heavily mossed

Comtesse d'Orléans HP, w, 1854, Descemet; flowers lilac-flesh-white, medium, full

Comtesse d'Oxford HP, mr, 1869, Guillot Père; flowers bright velvety carmine red, sometimes with violet tones, large, dbl., globular, moderate fragrance; recurrent bloom; [Victor Verdier × unknown]

Comtesse du Barry F, ly, Verschuren; flowers light sulpher yellow, 5-6 cm., 50-60 petals, borne in large clusters; growth to 60 cm.

Comtesse du Cayla Ch, ob, 1902, Guillot, P.; flowers nasturtium-red, tinted orange, semi-dbl., flat, moderate fragrance; recurrent bloom; foliage dark, glossy; vigorous growth; [(Rival de Pæstum × Mme Falcot) × Mme Falcot]

Comtesse Duchatel HP, m, 1842, Laffay; flowers purple pink, medium to large, very full, cupped

Comtesse Dusy T, w, 1893, Soupert & Notting; bud long; flowers large, full, moderate fragrance

Comtesse Emmeline de Guigné T, pb, 1903, Nabonnand; bud long, ovoid, coppery carmine; flowers delicate flesh-pink, coppery center, very large, full; foliage dark green; growth bushy, vigorous; [Papa Gontier × Comtesse Festetics Hamilton]

Comtesse Eva Starhemberg T, yb, 1890, Soupert & Notting; bud long; flowers cream yellow, center chrome-ochre, edge of outer petals tinted pink, large, full; [Étendard de Jeanne d'Arc × Sylphide]

Comtesse Eva Starhemberg, Climbing Cl T, yb, 1917, Glen St. Mary Nurs.; [sport of Comtesse Eva Starhemberg]

Comtesse Festétics Hamilton T, pb, 1892, Nabonnand; bud long, elegant; flowers carmine red with coppery tints in center, large, full, borne mostly solitary; foliage very large, wavy, dark green; prickles numerous, strong; growth vigorous

Comtesse Fressinet de Belanger HP, mp, 1886, Lévêque; flowers rose

Comtesse Georges de Roquette-Buisson N, my, 1885, Nabonnand; flowers bright yellow, fading to cream, medium, dbl., globular

Comtesse Georges de Roquette-Buisson HP, mp, 1899, Lévêque

Comtesse Hélène Mier HP, lp, 1876, Soupert & Notting; flowers light satiny pink, tinted darker, large, full

Comtesse Henrietta Combes HP, pb, 1881, Schwartz, J.; flowers satin-rose with silvery reflections, full, centifolia-like; very remontant

Comtesse Horace de Choiseul T, pb, 1886, Lévêque; flowers dark pink, shaded coppery yellow, large, full

Comtesse Icy Hardegg HT, dp, 1911, Soupert & Notting; flowers carmine, large, dbl.; [Mrs W.J. Grant × Liberty]

Comtesse Jeanne de Flandre – See **Flamingo Meidiland**, S

Comtesse Julie de Schulenburg HP, dr, 1889, Soupert & Notting; flowers red with purple, dark velvety brown at center, large, full, rosette, moderate fragrance

Comtesse Julie Hunyady T, yb, 1888, Soupert & Notting; flowers yellow shaded greenish, edged with pink, large, full

Comtesse Lacépède – See **Comtesse de Lacépède**, HGal

Comtesse Lily Kinsky T, w, 1895, Soupert & Notting; flowers pearly white with yellowish tint in center, full; [Marie Van Houtte × Victor Pulliat]

Comtesse Louise de Kergorlay HP, m, 1860, Touvais; flowers bright purple, large, full

Comtesse Maggi Starzunska T, pb, 1911, Nabonnand

Comtesse Maria Cristina Pes HT, mp, 1911, Bernaix fils; flowers glowing China pink, large, full

Comtesse Marie de Bourges HP, mp, 1853, Cherpin; flowers glowing carmine pink, center garnet, large, full

Comtesse Mélanie de Pourtales HT, w, 1914, Walter; flowers creamy white, outer petals shaded red; [Frau Karl Druschki × Mme Ravary]

Comtesse Moens de Fernig HT, dr, 1961, Verbeek; flowers wine-red, 25 petals; vigorous growth; [Poinsettia × seedling]

Comtesse Molé Ch, mp, before 1866; flowers bright pink, shaded grenadine, very large, full, cupped

Comtesse Nathalie de Kleist HP, op, 1881, Soupert & Notting

Comtesse O'Gorman HP, rb, 1888, Lévêque; flowers red and violet, large, full; foliage glaucous green

Comtesse O'Gorman T, pb, 1892, Nabonnand; flowers China pink, golden yellow at base, medium, dbl., moderate fragrance; [Baron de St. Triviers × unknown]

Comtesse Olivier de Lorgeril T, op, 1901, Bernaix; flowers peach pink shaded capucine-yellow, reverse light coppery red, large, full

Comtesse Ouwaroff – See **Duchesse de Brabant**, T

Comtesse Panarosa – See **Comtesse de Ségur**, S

Comtesse Prozor HG, pb, 1922, Nabonnand, P.; flowers salmon-rose, reverse coral-red; [*R. gigantea* × Comtesse de Bouchaud]

Comtesse Renée de Béarn HP, dr, 1896, Lévêque, P.; flowers carmine, brightened with blackish purple, tinted flame, large, full; foliage glaucous green

Comtesse Renée de Mortemart T, w, 1893, Godard; flowers creamy white, golden at base, large, full, moderate fragrance

Comtesse Riza du Parc T, mp, 1876, Schwartz, J.; flowers rose to carmine, large, dbl., globular; [Comtesse de Labarthe × unknown]

Comtesse Sophie Torby T, ob, 1902, Nabonnand; flowers peachy-red with orange shading, intense fragrance; [Reine Emma des Pays-Bas × Archiduc Joseph]

Comtesse Vaillant HP, m, 1854, Margottin; flowers light violet, sometimes shaded dark violet, large, full

Comtesse Vally de Serenye HP, 1875, Fontaine

Comtesse Vandal HT, pb, 1932, Leenders, M.; flowers salmon-pink, reverse coppery pink, large, 30 petals, high-centered, moderate fragrance; foliage leathery; bushy growth; [(Ophelia × Mrs Aaron Ward) × Souv. de Claudius Pernet]; int. by J&P; Gold Medal, Bagatelle, 1931

Comtesse Vandal, Climbing Cl HT, op, 1936, J&P; flowers bright crimson, interior chamois, very large, full, moderate fragrance; [sport of Comtesse Vandal]

Comtesse Vandale – See **Comtesse Vandal**, HT

Comtesse Vandale, Climbing – See **Comtesse Vandal, Climbing**, Cl HT

Concert – See **Berries 'n' Cream**, LCl

Concertino F, or, 1979, Meilland, Mrs. Marie-Louise; flowers cherry-red, medium, 20 petals, cupped, slight fragrance; foliage matte, dark; vigorous, bushy growth; [((Fidélio × Fidélio) × (Zambra × Zambra)) × Marlena]; int. by Meilland et Cie, 1976

Concertino Min, dp, 1988, Meilland, Alain A.; flowers cardinal-pink, medium, full, no fragrance; foliage small, medium green, semi-glossy; bushy, compact growth; [(Anytime × Julita) × Lavender Jewel]; int. by SNC Meilland & Cie

Concerto F, mr, 1953, Meilland, F.; PP1244; [Alain × Floradora]; int. by URS; President's International Trophy, RNRS, 1953, Gold Medal, NRS, 1953

Concerto, Climbing Cl F, mr, 1970, Truffant, G.; [sport of Concerto]; int. by URS, 1968

Concerto S, ab, Meilland; flowers light ochre pink; growth to 100 cm.; int. by Meilland Intl, 1994

Concerto 94 – See **Concerto**, S

Conch Shell Climber LCl, pb, 2006, Starnes, John A., Jr.; flowers shell pink, 2½-3 in., very full, borne mostly solitary, slight apple/tea fragrance; very remontant; foliage medium size, medium green, semi-glossy, disease-resistant; prickles ¼ in., sharply curved, light brown, moderate; growth upright, climbing, medium (8-12 ft.); pillar/climber; [wichurana rambler × Sunflare]; int. in 2006

Conchita Pol, op, 1935, Jordan, H.; flowers clear salmon, dbl., cupped, borne in clusters; foliage glossy; vigorous growth; int. by Low, 1935

Concorde – See **Forever Yours**, HT

Concorde F, pb, Meilland; flowers carmine pink with yellow heart, 3½-4 in.; growth to 30 in.; int. in 1995

Concorde 92 HT, dy, Meilland, Alain A.; flowers large, dark lemon yellow, loose; int. by Meilland, 1992

Concordia HT, mp, 1924, Brix; flowers glowing pink, edged silver-pink, semi-dbl.; int. by Teschendorff

Concordia HT, rb, 1946, Giacomasso; flowers red, reverse deep yellow, well-formed, dbl.; vigorous growth; [Charles P. Kilham × Crimson Glory]

Condesa da Foz – See **Rêve d'Or**, N

Condesa de Barcelona HT, yb, Viveros Fco. Ferrer, S L; flowers 26 petals, high-centered; [Mount Shasta × Helmut Schmidt]

Condesa de Benahavis HT, mp, 1949, La Florida; flowers salmon-pink, well-formed; [Étoile de Hollande × Sensation]

Condesa de Glimes F, pb, Bofill; flowers begonia-pink, center ochre-yellow, single; int. by Torre Blanca

Condesa de Mayalde HT, rb, 1956, Dot, Pedro; bud pointed; flowers white edged carmine, 30 petals, high-centered; foliage glossy; compact, upright growth; [Peace × Flambee]

Condesa de Mayalde, Climbing Cl HT, w, 1964, Samuels

Condesa de Munter HT, or, 1932, Munné, B.; flowers geranium-red, tinted orange-yellow, large, semi-dbl., cupped; long, strong stems; vigorous growth; [Souv. de Josefina Plà × Souv. de Claudius Pernet]

Condesa de Saldanha HT, ob, 1961, Munné, M.; flowers reddish-orange, mottled yellow, large, 45 petals; vigorous growth

Condesa de Sástago HT, pb, 1932, Dot, Pedro; bud ovoid; flowers deep pink, reverse yellow, large, 55 petals, cupped, moderate fragrance; foliage glossy, dark; vigorous, tall growth; [(Souv. de Claudius Pernet × Maréchal Foch) × Margaret McGredy]; int. by C-P; Gold Medal, Rome, 1933

Condesa de Sástago, Climbing Cl HT, pb, 1936, Vestal; flowers oriental red and yellow, large, full, moderate fragrance; [sport of Condesa de Sástago]

Condesa de Villarrea HT, mr, 1960, Dot, M.; flowers crimson, reverse cardinal-red, large, 35 petals; long, stiff stems; vigorous growth; [Chrysler Imperial × Texas Centennial]

Conditorum HGal, dr; flowers pale pink, large, semi-dbl.; recorded in 1900, but undoubtedly a very old form; perhaps identical with Parkinson's Hungarian Rose

Condoleezza F, pb, 2006, Moore, Ralph S.; bud lightly mossed; flowers pink, reverse yellow, with wavy petals, 2 in., semi-dbl., borne in small clusters; foliage medium size, medium green, semi-glossy; prickles small, straight, green, moderate; growth compact, medium (2-4 ft.); specimen, border, cut flower; [Lemon Delight × Angel Face]; int. by Sequoia Nurs., 2006

Conestoga S, w, 1946, Preston; bud ovoid; flowers open, 2 in., 30 petals, borne in clusters; non-recurrent; foliage soft, sparse, small; upright, vigorous growth; hardy; [Betty Bland × seedling]; int. by Central Exp. Farm

Confection Min, mp, 1989, Warriner, William A.; bud ovoid, pointed; flowers pink with yellow to cream base, medium, very dbl., high-centered, borne usually singly, slight fragrance; foliage medium size, dark green, matte; prickles straight to slightly hooked, light green; low, bushy growth; PP6518; [seedling × seedling]; int. by Bear Creek Gardens, 1988

Confederation HT, mp, 1964, Golik; flowers compact, large, 70 petals; foliage dark, glossy; moderate, vigorous growth; [Queen o' the Lakes × Serenade]; int. by Ellesmere Nursery

Conference 63 HT, dr, 1965, Quentin; flowers deep crimson, 4½ in., dbl.; foliage light green; tall growth

Confetti – See **Konfetti**, HT

Confetti F, rb, 1980, Swim, H.C. & Christensen, J.E.; bud ovoid; flowers deep yellow, aging orange-red, 18-25 petals, high-centered, borne 3-7 per cluster, slight tea fragrance; foliage medium green; prickles hooked downward; upright growth; PP5399; [Jack O'Lantern × Zorina]; int. by Armstrong Nursery, 1983

Confidence HT, pb, 1951, Meilland, F.; bud ovoid; flowers pearly light pink to yellow blend, large, 28-38 petals, high-centered, moderate fragrance; foliage dark, leathery; vigorous, upright, bushy growth; [Peace × Michèle Meilland]; int. by URS, 1951; Gold Medal, Bagatelle, 1951

Confidence, Climbing Cl HT, pb, 1961, Hendrickx; int. by URS

Confidence HT, w, 1995, Meilland; bud elongated, medium; flowers creamy white with pink petal tips, 5 in., 35 petals, borne mostly singly, slight fragrance; recurrent; foliage dark green, glossy; prickles few, small; growth upright (2-3 ft.); PP9223

Conga HT, my, Tantau; flowers golden-yellow, medium, dbl., high-centered, borne mostly singly; recurrent; stems long; florist rose; int. by Rosen Tantau, 2000

Congo HT, dr, 1943, Meilland, F.; bud long, pointed; flowers velvety maroon, open, medium, dbl.; foliage leathery, bronze; bushy, dwarf growth; [Admiral Ward × Lemania]; int. by A. Meilland

Congolaise HT, dr, Tantau; flowers velvety dark red, well-formed, large, dbl.; vigorous growth

Congratulations HT, op, 1979, W. Kordes Söhne; bud long, pointed; flowers medium pink, 4½ in., 42 petals, high-centered, moderate fragrance; foliage semi-glossy; vigorous, upright, bushy growth; [Carina × seedling]; ADR, 1977

Congratulations – See **Kotobuki**, HT

Coniston – See **Comtes des Champagne**, S

Connie Min, dy, 1991, Jerabek, Paul E.; bud pointed; flowers dark yellow fading to light yellow, 11 petals, flat, borne singly or in small clusters, slight fragrance; foliage medium size, dark green, glossy; bushy, medium (36 cm.), very dense growth; [unknown × unknown]

Connie Crook F, mr, 1997, Bossom, W.E.; flowers large, very dbl., borne in large clusters; foliage large, dark green, glossy; few prickles; upright, tall (120 cm.) growth; [seedling × Selfridges]

Connie Lohn Min, lp, 2003, Barden, Paul; buds mossed; flowers very small, 1 in., dbl., borne in large clusters; foliage small, medium green, semi-glossy; prickles to ¼ in., straight, mossy; growth compact, short (12 in.); specimen, containers, borders; [Dresden Doll × Dresden Doll]; int. in 2003

Connie Mack F, dr, 1952, Duehrsen; flowers dark velvety crimson, medium, 25 petals, borne in clusters; foliage glossy, dark; vigorous growth; [seedling × Margy]; int. by H&S

Connie's Choice – See **Paul Potter**, S

Connoisseur S, m, William, J.B.; buds tall, elegant; flowers purple-burgundy with pink stripes, borne in large clusters; foliage glossy; int. by Hortico Inc., 2003

Conqueror HT, ly, 1929, Chaplin Bros.; flowers saffron-yellow, fading pale yellow, 15 petals; vigorous, bushy growth

Conqueror's Gold F, yb, 1985, Harkness, R., & Co., Ltd.; flowers yellow, edged orange-red, 18 petals, cupped, borne in clusters of up to 7, slight fragrance; foliage medium size, dark semi-glossy; medium, bushy growth; [Amy Brown × Judy Garland]

Conquest F, my, 1994, Harkness; flowers large, 30 petals, borne in sprays of 7-10, slight spicy fragrance; foliage medium size, light green, glossy; bushy, medium growth; [Dame of Sark × Bright Smile]; int. by Harkness New Roses, Ltd., 1994

Conquete HT, Combe, M.; int. in 1967

Conquistador LCl, mr, Pineau; flowers vermilion, 3 in., semi-dbl., moderate fragrance; foliage glossy; int. in 1983

Conquistador LCl, mr, Fryer; flowers velvety red, dbl.; growth to 10-12 ft.; int. in 2005

Conrad Ferdinand Meyer HRg, lp, 1899, Müller, Dr. F.; flowers silver pink, large, dbl., cupped, borne in clusters, intense fragrance; repeat bloom; foliage leathery; vigorous (8-10 ft.), good pillar rose, bushy growth; [*R. rugosa* × Gloire de Dijon]

Conrad Hilton F, my, 1962, Shepherd; bud ovoid; flowers golden yellow, outer petals sometimes white, 2½ in., 30-45 petals, flat; foliage leathery, dark, glossy, crinkled; very vigorous, upright, bushy growth; [(Dupontii × Pinocchio) × (Goldilocks × Feu Pernet-Ducher)]; int. by Bosley Nursery, 1962

Conrad O'Neal S, dp, 1968, O'Neal; bud ovoid; flowers deep pink, medium, very dbl., intense fragrance; foliage dark, glossy; vigorous, upright growth; [(Blossomtime × unknown) × Don Juan]; int. by Wyant, 1966

Conrad's Crimson S, rb, 1972, Eacott; flowers crimson, shaded purple, 3 in., 30 petals, flat; early bloom; foliage light green to bronze; [Sweet Sultan × Conrad F. Meyer]

Conservation Min, pb, 1986, Cocker, James & Sons; flowers medium, semi-dbl., slight fragrance; foliage small, light green, semi-glossy; bushy growth; [((Sabine × Circus) × Maxi) × Darling Flame]; Gold Medal, Dublin, 1986

Conservency Rose F, mp, 1996, Pallek, Ruth; flowers vibrant pink, some varigation, not solid pink, long lasting, 1½ in., 30 petals; foliage medium size, medium green, glossy, disease-resistant; some prickles; medium (20 in.), bushy growth; int. by Carl Pallek & Son Nurseries, 1995

Consolata HT, yb, 1936, Capiago; bud pointed; flowers yellow and coppery nasturtium-red; foliage bronze; long, strong stems

Conspicuous HT, mr, 1930, Dickson, A.; flowers glowing scarlet, very large, dbl.; vigorous growth; int. by B&A, 1932

Constance HT, my, 1915, Pernet-Ducher; flowers yellow to golden yellow, medium, dbl., high-centered; foliage rich green, glossy; bushy growth; [Rayon d'Or × unknown]; Gold Medal, Bagatelle, 1916

Constance, Climbing Cl HT, my, 1927, Pacific Rose Co.

Constance des Hollandaises – See **My Lady Kensington**, C

Constance Casson HT, pb, 1920, Cant, B. R.; flowers carmine, flushed apricot, dbl.; [Queen Mary × Gorgeous]

Constance Fettes F, ab, 1993, Cocker; flowers medium, full, borne in small clusters, moderate fragrance; foliage medium size, medium green, glossy; some prickles; medium (2½ ft.), upright, bushy growth; [(Fragrant Cloud × Alexander) × Sunblest]; int. by James Cocker & Sons, 1993

Constance Finn F, lp, Harkness; flowers very dbl., moderate fragrance; recurrent; upright, vase shaped growth to 3 ft; int. by R. Harkness & Co, 1997

Constance Morley HT, ob, 1982, Gregory, C. & Sons, Ltd.; flowers orange-gold tinged red, diffused center, 39 petals, borne singly, slight fragrance; foliage dark, glossy; prickles elongated, orange; spreading, bushy growth; [Piccadilly × seedling]; int. in 1981

Constance Spry S, lp, 1961, Austin, David; flowers rose pink, 5 in., 55-70 petals, cupped, borne in clusters, moderate myrrh fragrance; foliage dark; vigorous (5-6 ft.) growth; [Belle Isis × Dainty Maid]; int. by Sunningdale Nurseries, 1961

Constant Lusseau HP, mp, 1864, Trouillard; flowers bright carmine, shaded violet, medium, full

Constantia HT, mp, 1960, Herholdt, J.A.; bud pointed; flowers Neyron rose, well-formed, 4-4½ in., 40 petals; moderate growth; [Baccará × Grace de Monaco]; int. by Herholdt's Nursery

Constanza HT, ob, 1967, Tantau, Math.; bud pointed; flowers orange, well-formed, large, 25-30 petals; foliage dark, glossy; upright, bushy growth; int. by Wheatcroft Bros.

Constanze HT, ob, Tantau; int. in 1992

Constanze Spry – See **Constance Spry**, S

Constellation HT, ob, 1949, Gaujard; bud long, pointed; flowers coppery orange, well-formed, very large; very vigorous, erect growth; [Peace × seedling]

Constellation LCl, ab; flowers cream and apricot, moderate fragrance; growth to 8-10 ft.; int. by Hortico, 1999

Constellation Min, w, 2000, Saville, F. Harmon; flowers near white, medium, 35-40 petals, high-centered, borne mostly singly; foliage medium size, dark green, semi-glossy to glossy; no prickles until plant matures, then few; upright, spreading, well-branched, medium (24-28 in.) growth; PP12652; [Sachet × New Zealand]; int. by Nor'East Mini Roses, 1999

Consul M. Mezin HT, Verbeek

Contempo F, ob, 1970, Armstrong, D.L.; bud ovoid; flowers orange blending to gold, medium, dbl., high-centered, moderate fragrance; foliage light, leathery; vigorous, bushy growth; PP3102; [Spartan × (Goldilocks × (Fandango × Pinocchio))]; int. by Armstrong Nursery, 1971

Contentment HT, pb, 1956, Boerner; bud globular; flowers soft pink suffused yellow, 5½ in., 65-70 petals, high-centered, intense fragrance; foliage glossy, leathery; vigorous, upright growth; PP1644; [(seedling × Lilette Mallerin) × Orange Delight]; int. by J&P

Contessa S, dp, 1987, Warriner, William A.; flowers deep pink with yellow center, reverse deep pink, fading slightly, 6-10 petals, flat, slight spicy fragrance; fast cycle; foliage medium size, medium green, semi-glossy; prickles straight, long, green-brown; upright, tall growth; PP6577; [Sunsprite × seedling]; int. by J&P

Contessa Cecilia Lurani HT, dp, 1902, Brauer; flowers deep pink with salmon red, large to very large, full, moderate fragrance; [Kaiserin Auguste Viktoria × Principessa di Napoli]

Contessa Mona Bismark Gr

Contiki HT, ab, 2004, Wilke, William; flowers apricot, pink, and cream, reverse light pink, 4½-5½ in., dbl., borne mostly solitary, slight fragrance; foliage medium size, medium green, semi-glossy; prickles ¼ in., curved downwards; growth bushy, medium (4-5 ft.); garden, exhibition; [unknown × unknown]

Continental HT, mr, 1966, Lammerts, Dr. Walter; bud ovoid; flowers cardinal-red, large, dbl., moderate fruity fragrance; foliage leathery; vigorous, upright growth; PP2751; [Baccará × Yuletide]; int. by Amling-DeVor Nursery

Contrast HT, pb, 1937, H&S; flowers China-pink and bronze, reverse white and bronze, large, dbl., high-centered, moderate fragrance; foliage leathery, glossy; very vigorous, bushy, compact growth; [seedling × Talisman]

Contribute HT, my, Dawson; int. in 1977

Conundrum MinFl, yb, 2002, Tucker, Robbie; flowers yellow with red edging, deepening with age, 2-3 in., dbl., high-centered, borne mostly solitary, slight fragrance; foliage medium size, dark green, semi-glossy; prickles regular, few; growth upright, medium (2-2½ ft.); exhibition, cutting, garden decorative; [Cal Poly × Kristin]; int. by Rosemania, 2002

Convivial Cl Min, ab, 2003, McCann, Sean; flowers light apricot, finishing white, small to medium, dbl., quartered, borne in small clusters, no fragrance; foliage medium size, dark green, semi-glossy; stems long; growth spreading, medium; [(S.W.A.L.K. × Kiss 'n' Tell) × New Dawn]

Conway Jones HT, 1913, Dickson

Cookie LCl, or, Meilland; flowers scarlet red-orange, dbl.; growth climbing (2½ m.); int. by Meilland-Richardier, 2001

Cool Breeze HT, lp, Spek; bud large; flowers soft, delicate pink, full, high-centered; int. by Carlton, 2002

Cool Dude Min, m, 1995, Rennie, Bruce F.; flowers 1 in., dbl., borne mostly singly; foliage small, medium green, semi-glossy; no prickles; low (10-12 in.), compact growth; [seedling × Blushing Blue]; int. by Rennie Roses International, 1995

Cool Water HT, w, Schreurs; int. by Australian Roses, 2004

Cool Wave Min, w, 1987, Zipper, Herbert; flowers white with hints of yellow at petal base, medium, dbl., high-centered; foliage medium size, medium green, matte; [Poker Chip × Pink Parfait]; int. by Magic Moment Miniature Roses

Coolidge – See **I. X. L.**, HMult

Coolness F, w, 1959, Boerner; bud ovoid, cream; flowers 2½-3 in., 55-60 petals, moderate fragrance; foliage leathery, glossy; vigorous, bushy, compact growth; [(Glacier × unknown) × (Starlite × unknown)]; int. by J&P, 1959

Coon Carnival F, yb, 1985, Kordes, R.; bud ovoid; flowers yellow, changing to pink and red, large, 56 petals, borne singly or in clusters of up to 7, slight fragrance; foliage matte, green; prickles straight, brown; medium, bushy growth; [seedling × seedling]; int. by Ludwigs Roses Pty. Ltd., 1981

Cooperi – See **Cooper's Burmese**, HG

Cooperoo Emblem Pol, m, Harrison, A.

Cooper's Burmese HG, w, 1927; flowers near white, large, single; foliage glossy; vigorous (to 20 ft.) growth; [possibly a natural hybrid of *R. gigantea* × *R. laevigata*]; collected as seed from Burma by Roland Cooper

Cooran F, dp, 1953, Ulrick, L.W.; bud long, pointed; flowers deep rose-pink, very large, dbl., borne in clusters; very vigorous growth; [Mrs Tom Henderson × Ming Toy]

Coorg – See **Coffee Country**, F

Cooroy F, mp, 1953, Ulrick, L.W.; flowers rose-pink, very dbl., high-centered, borne in clusters; [Mrs Tom Henderson × Mrs Tom Henderson]

Copacabana LCl, or, 1966, Dorieux; flowers vermilion, tinted brown, large, 40 petals, globular, borne in small clusters; foliage dark green; [Coup de Foudre × unknown]; int. by Bees

Copacabana F, ob, Dorieux; int. in 1995

Copacabana – See **Macha Méril**, HT

Copenhagen Cl HT, mr, 1964, Poulsen, Niels D.; flowers scarlet, 5 in., dbl., borne in small clusters, moderate fragrance; foliage large, coppery dark green; vigorous growth; [Hakuun × Ena Harkness]; int. by McGredy

Copia F, mr, 1964, Mondial Roses; flowers bright cardinal-red, large, semi-dbl.; vigorous, bushy growth; [(Independence × seedling) × Tour de France]

Coppa Nob F, op, Cocker; int. in 1982

Coppélia HT, ob, 1952, Meilland, F.; flowers rosy shades, deepening to orange, medium, 28 petals, cupped; foliage leathery; vigorous, upright growth; [Peace × Europa]

Coppelia S, dp, Kordes

Coppélia 76 F, op, Meilland; flowers medium, dbl.; int. in 1976

Copper Arch LCl, ob, Kordes; buds golden, shapely; flowers copper-bronze, medium size, dbl., star shaped, borne singly and in large clusters; recurrent bloom; free-standing growth, or draped over a support; int. in 1991

Copper Climber LCl, op, 1938, Burbank; bud pointed, coppery; flowers glowing coppery salmon, edged pink, large; int. by Stark Bros.

Copper Coronet HT, ab, 1987, Strange, J.F.; flowers coppery amber, reverse blush pink, fading amber and cream, large, 60 petals, high-centered, slight fragrance; foliage medium size, medium green, semi-glossy; upright, medium growth; [Ginger Rogers × Royal Highness]

Copper Crown S, op, 1992, Williams, J. Benjamin; flowers rusty copper with orange center, large, 5 petals, slight fragrance; foliage medium size, dark green, semi-glossy; upright (4 × 4 ft.), bushy growth; [Westerland × Orange Velvet]; int. by Hortico Roses, 1992

Copper Delight F, ob, 1956, LeGrice; flowers clear orange, large, 14 petals, borne in large clusters; foliage olive-green; vigorous, upright, bushy growth; [Goldilocks × Ellinor LeGrice]

Copper Gem HT, ab, Cocker; flowers rich copper; strong stems; medium growth; int. in 1984

Copper Glow LCl, ob, 1940, Brownell; flowers coppery yellow, 4 in., 27 petals, intense fragrance; seasonal bloom; foliage dark green, glossy; vigorous, climbing (20 ft.), open habit growth; [Golden Glow × Break o' Day]

Copper Kettle F, ob, 1978, Williams, J. Benjamin; bud elongated, tangerine; flowers brilliant copper-orange and yellow, 2½-3½ in., 28 petals, high-centered, moderate fragrance; foliage glossy, dark bronze green; upright growth; hardy to -20ºF; [Queen Elizabeth × Golden Slippers]; int. by J.B. Williams & Associates

Copper King HT, dy, 1982, Herholdt, J.A.; flowers copper-gold, large, 35 petals; foliage dark, glossy; upright growth; [Vienna Charm × seedling]

Copper Luster HT, op, 1945, Roberts; flowers coppery pink, loosely, large, 23 petals, cupped; foliage glossy, bronze; vigorous, upright growth; [Better Times × Orange Nassau]; int. by Totty

Copper Nugget HT, op, 1942, Lammerts, Dr. Walter; bud ovoid to urn shaped; flowers orange-salmon, small, 50-60 petals, high-centered; foliage leathery, glossy, dark; strong stems; dwarf, bushy growth; [Charles P. Kilham × Capt. Thomas]; int. by Armstrong Nursery

Copper Pot F, ob, 1968, Dickson, A.; flowers orange-yellow, deeper reverse, large, 15 petals, borne in trusses; foliage glossy, bronze; tall growth; [seedling × Golden Scepter]

Copper Ruffles Min, or, 1983, Dobbs, Annette E.; flowers small, dbl., high-centered, slight fragrance; foliage small, medium-green, semi-glossy; upright growth; [Anytime × Sheri Anne]; int. in 1982

Copper Star MinFl, ob, Clements, John; flowers bronzy copper, 2½ in., single, flat, star-shaped, moderate fresh fragrance; recurrent; foliage small, dark green; bushy, compact (30 in.) growth; int. by Heirloom Roses, 2007

Copper Sunset Min, ob, 1988, Saville, F. Harmon; bud pointed; flowers coppery-orange, flushed orange-red, reverse medium red, 21 petals, high-centered; foliage medium size, dark green, semi-glossy; prickles long, thin, slanted, gray-red; upright, medium, angular growth; hips ovoid, orange; PP7032; [Acey Deucy × Rainbow's End]

Copperkins HT, ob, 1957, Ratcliffe; bud long, pointed, dark orange-flame; flowers orange, well-formed, 25 petals, intense fruity fragrance; foliage glossy; vigorous growth; [Mme Henri Guillot × Golden Scepter]

Coppers Grand S, mr; int. in 1997

Coppertone – See **Oldtimer**, HT

Coppery Heart S, yb, 1958, Gaujard; flowers coppery yellow shaded red, large, dbl.; repeat bloom; foliage dark, glossy; long stems; very vigorous growth; [Peace × Conrad Ferdinand Meyer]

Copy Cat Min, mp, 1986, Moore, Ralph S.; [sport of Beauty Secret]; int. by Moore Min. Roses, 1985

Coq de Roche HT, dr, 1945, Meilland, F.; flowers blood-red, large, very dbl.; very vigorous growth; [Duquesa de Peñaranda × J. B. Meilland]

Coquellicot HT, or, 1942, Meilland; flowers orange-red with gold, medium, semi-dbl.

Coquette – See **Bertram Park**, HT

Coquette HT, lp, 1929, Dobbie; flowers pale flesh-pink, well-formed; vigorous growth

Coquette Pol, mr, 1929, Geary; flowers bright vermilion, base yellowish, large; [Éblouissant × Mme Edouard Herriot]

Coquette HT, w, 1976, Warriner, William A.; bud long; flowers 4 in., 30-35 petals, high-centered; foliage light green, reddish underneath; upright growth; [seedling × seedling]; int. by J&P

Coquette Bordelaise HP, pb, 1896, Duprat; flowers dark pink with white stripes, very large, dbl.; [sport of Mme Georges Desse]

Coquette de Lyon HP, lp, 1859, Lacharme, F.; flowers flesh-pink

Coquette de Lyon T, ly, 1872, Ducher; flowers canary-yellow, medium size

Coquette de Melun B, lp, Varengot; flowers flesh pink, medium, full

Coquette des Alpes B, w, 1867, Lacharme, F.; flowers white tinged blush, medium to large, dbl., semi-cupped; very remontant; vigorous growth; [Mlle Blanche Lafitte × Sappho (Damask Perpetual)]

Coquette des Blanches B, w, 1871, Lacharme, F.; bud fat; flowers white, lightly washed pink, 10 cm., dbl., cupped, moderate fragrance; vigorous growth; [Mlle Blanche Lafitte × Sappho (Damask Perpetual)]; sometimes classified as N

Coquina HWich, pb, 1909, Walsh; flowers rose-pink fading lighter, base creamy white, single, cupped, borne in large clusters, moderate fragrance; foliage dark, almost evergreen; stems long, strong; very vigorous (20-24 ft.) growth

Cora HGal, m, 1827, Lecomte or Savoureux; flowers velvety purple-violet, shaded red, small, dbl., borne in clusters of 3-4; prickles scattered, fine; growth erect, small

Cora HP, mp, 1859, Touvais or Guillot; flowers bright pink, medium; [Général Jacqueminot × unknown]

Cora Ch, yb, 1899, Schwartz; flowers yellow and orange, shaded carmine, medium, full

Cora à Pétales Variés yb, before 1819; flowers yellowish-pink, large

Cora L. Barton N, 1840, Buist; [Lamarque × unknown]

Cora Marie HT, mr, 1987, Kordes, W.; flowers large, dbl., no fragrance; foliage large, dark green, semi-glossy; upright growth; [Ankori × seedling]; int. in 1986

Corail LCl, pb, 1931, Schwartz, A.; flowers light peach-blossom-pink, reverse coral-pink and carmine, opening well, dbl.; recurrent bloom; foliage bright, glossy; very vigorous growth; [William Allen Richardson × Orléans Rose]

Coral HT, pb, 1931, Dickson, A.; flowers bright coral, base buttercup-yellow, dbl., globular; wiry erect stems; vigorous growth

Coral Min, rb, Olesen; flowers dbl., 25-30 petals, borne mostly solitary, no fragrance; foliage dark green, glossy; int. in 1996

Coral HT, dy, Roses Noves Ferrer, S L; flowers 22 petals, high-centered; [FE-87518 × K-861242-1]

Coral LCl, mp; foliage massive; vigorous, climbing growth; half-hardy; [*R. sinowilsonii* × seedling]; int. by F.C. Stern

Coral 'n' Gold Min, op, 1995, Mander, George; flowers coral/salmon/pink blend inside, yellow/cream reverse, some yellow stripes, full, borne in small clusters, no fragrance; foliage medium size, medium green, semi-glossy; few prickles; bushy, medium (40-45 cm.) growth; [June Laver × Rubies 'n' Pearls]; int. by Select Roses, 1995

Coral Anne Griffiths HT, mp, 1979, Henson; bud very tight; flowers 72 petals, moderate fragrance; foliage glossy, dark; very large (6 in.) very vigorous growth; [sport of Red Devil]; int. in 1978

Coral Bay HT, op, 1972, Swim & Weeks; bud ovoid; flowers silvery coral-orange, medium, dbl., cupped, moderate fragrance; foliage glossy, leathery; vigorous growth; PP3243; [seedling × seedling]; int. by Weeks Wholesale Rose Growers, 1971

Coral Beauty Pol, mp, 1941, deRuiter; flowers spinel-pink, 1½ in., dbl., flat, borne in clusters; vigorous, branching growth; [sport of Orléans Rose]; int. by J&P

Coral Belle F, ob, 1962, Jelly; bud pointed, ovoid; flowers vermilion, 1½-2½ in., 45 petals, high-centered; foliage leathery; strong stems; vigorous, upright growth; [Stoplite × Orange Sweetheart]; int. by E.G. Hill Co., 1962

Coral Bells Pol, op, J&P; flowers coral pink, medium, dbl.; int. in 1962

Coral Border – See **Coral Gables**, S

Coral Button Min, op

Coral Cameo Min, dp, 1986, Moore, Ralph S.; flowers deep pink, dbl., high-centered, borne singly and in small sprays; foliage small, medium green, semi-glossy; prickles very few; medium, upright, bushy growth; hips small, globular, orange; [Little Darling × Anytime]; int. by Moore Min. Roses, 1982

Coral Carpet MinFl, mp, Williams, J. Benjamin; flowers coral pink to light pink; groundcover; spreading growth; int. in 1997

Coral Cascade F, or, 1980, James, John; flowers coral-red, 50-75 petals, globular, borne singly or 3-5 per cluster, slight carnation fragrance; foliage opens russet, turning dark green, glossy; prickles reddish-gray; vigorous, compact, bushy growth; [Van Bergen × Pink Hat sport]

Coral Chateau HT, op, Teranishi; int. in 1998

Coral Cluster Pol, op, 1920, Murrell, R.; flowers coral-pink; [sport of Orléans Rose]; Gold Medal, NRS, 1921

Coral Cover S, op; groundcover; spreading growth; int. by Enderlein Nurseries, 2002

Coral Creeper LCl, dp, 1938, Brownell; bud deep red; flowers coral to light pink, 3 in., semi-dbl., borne singly or in small clusters, strong musky fragrance; foliage dark green, glossy, leathery; numerous prickles; upright stems; very vigorous growth; [(Dr. W. Van Fleet × Emily Gray) × Jacotte]

Coral Crown F, or, 1960, Von Abrams; flowers coral-red, 3 in., 35 petals, high-centered, borne in clusters, moderate fragrance; foliage glossy; low, compact growth; PP1991; [Else Poulsen × (Fashion × Orange Triumph)]; int. by Peterson & Dering, 1959

Coral Cup Pol, op, 1936, B&A; flowers soft coral, very dbl., cupped, borne in clusters; profuse, repeated bloom; very vigorous, bushy growth; [sport of Gloria Mundi]

Coral Cushion S, op; int. by Hortico, 2004

Coral Dawn LCl, mp, 1952, Boerner; bud ovoid; flowers coral pink, aging to rose pink, lighter edges, 6-8 cm., 30-35 petals, cupped, borne singly or in small clusters, moderate fragrance; remontant; foliage wide, dark green, glossy; vigorous (8-12 ft.) growth; [(New Dawn × unknown) × seedling]; int. by J&P

Coral Delight Gr, op, Hiroshima; [sport of Cream Delight]; int. by Hiroshima Bara-en, 2001

Coral Destiny HT, op, 1983, Perry, Anthony; flowers medium coral pink, large, 35 petals, slight fragrance; foliage medium green, semi-glossy; upright growth; [Joanna Hill × Queen Elizabeth]; int. by Ball Seed Co., 1984

Coral Drops HMoy, op, before 1927; flowers pale coral-pink, single; non-recurrent

Coral Fairy HWich, pb, 1995, Moore, Ralph S.; flowers 1½ in., single, borne in large clusters; foliage small, dark green, semi-glossy; few prickles; tall (3-4 m.), upright, bushy, spreading growth; [(*R. wichurana* × Floradora) × Hallelujah]; int. by Sequoia Nursery, 1995

Coral Fantasy Min, ab, 1982, Lyon, Lyndon; flowers medium, 34 petals; foliage medium green, semi-glossy; vigorous, upright, bushy growth; [Dandy Lyon × seedling]; int. by L. Lyon Greenhouses

Coral Fiesta HT, or, 1983, Dot, Simon; flowers large, 45 petals, cupped, no fragrance; foliage large, dark, matte; prickles light yellow; bushy growth; [seedling × seedling]; int. by Rose Barni-Pistoia

Coral Fiesta, Climbing Cl HT, or, Barni; flowers coral and vermilion; growth to 10-25 ft.; int. by Rose Barni, after 1983

Coral Floc F, or, Dot

Coral Flower Carpet – See **Alfabia**, S

Coral Gables S, op, Poulsen; bud pointed, ovoid to globular; flowers coral pink, 3 in., 60-70 petals, borne in large clusters, very slight fragrance; recurrent; foliage small, dark green, glossy; prickles several, 5-6 mm., hooked downward; vigorous, bushy (100 cm.), slightly arching growth; PP12471; [seedling × Bonica]; int. as Coral Border, Poulsen Roser, 1998

Coral Galaxy F, op, Zary; int. by Bear Creek Gardens

Coral Gem F, pb, 1959, Boerner; bud ovoid; flowers light coral-pink, open, 2½ in., 40-45 petals, cupped, borne in clusters, moderate fruity fragrance; foliage leathery, dark; vigorous, bushy growth; PP1797; [((Pinocchio × Mrs Sam McGredy, Climbing) × (Pinocchio × Mrs Sam McGredy, Climbing)) × Fashion]; int. by J&P, 1959

Coral Glow LCl, op, 1964, Croix, P.; flowers salmon-pink, borne in clusters; [Spectacular × seedling]; int. by Minier

Coral Hush – See **Mother's Rose**, HT

Coral Ice HT, op, Interplant; int. in 1996

Coral Island Min, op

Coral Meidiland S, mp, 1994, Meilland, Alain A.; bud conical, small; flowers scarlet pink, medium, 5 petals, cupped, borne in small clusters, no fragrance; free-flowering; foliage small, medium green, semi-glossy; prickles numerous, small to medium; medium (70-90 cm.), bushy growth; PP9777; [(Immensee × Green Snake) × (Temple Bells × Red Cascade)]; int. as Sandton City, SNC Meilland & Cie

Coral Midinette – See **Salmo**, S

Coral Mist HT, op, 1966, Patterson; bud ovoid; flowers coral-pink, dbl., high-centered; foliage glossy, light green; vigorous, bushy, open growth; [Spartan × Good News]; int. by Patterson Roses

Coral Pagode MinFl, pb, Poulsen; flowers pink blend, 5-8 cm., dbl., borne in clusters, no fragrance; foliage dark; cascading growth, hanging basket type; PP13593; int. by Poulsen Roser, 2000

Coral Palace – See **Countess Celeste**, S

Coral Panarosa S, op, Kordes; flowers large, coral, full, no fragrance; growth tall (2 m.), thick; int. in 2001

Coral Pastel MinFl, op, Williams, J.B.; int. by Hortico, 2003

Coral Pillar Cl HT, mr, 1945, Lammerts, Dr. Walter; flowers geranium-pink, large, dbl., high-centered; foliage glossy, dark; very vigorous, upright growth; [Crimson Glory × Capt. Thomas]; int. by Univ. of Calif.

Coral Princess F, ob, 1966, Boerner; bud ovoid; flowers coral-orange, large, 25 petals, cupped, moderate fragrance; foliage leathery; vigorous, bushy growth; PP2635; [((Fashion × unknown) × (Garnette × Unknown)) × Spartan]; int. by J&P

Coral Prophyta HT, op, de Ruiter; int. by De Ruiter's New Roses Intl.

Coral Queen HT, or, 1928, Reeves; flowers coral-red, large, dbl., cupped; foliage dark, glossy; long, strong stems; vigorous, bushy growth; [sport of The Queen Alexandra Rose]

Coral Queen Elizabeth F, op, 1966, Gregory; flowers coral-salmon, 3 in., dbl., borne in clusters; foliage glossy; very vigorous growth; [Queen Elizabeth × seedling]

Coral Reef HT, mp, 1948, Joseph H. Hill, Co.; bud long, pointed; flowers pink, medium, 25-30 petals, moderate fragrance; foliage leathery, wrinkled, dark; vigorous, upright, bushy growth; [Joanna Hill × R.M.S. Queen Mary]

Coral Reef Min, op, 1985, Cocker, Ann G.; flowers orange, patio, medium, semi-dbl., slight fragrance; foliage small, medium green, glossy; bushy growth; [(Darling Flame × St. Albans) × Silver Jubilee]; int. by Cocker & Sons

Coral Reef Min, mp, 2004, Jalbert, Brad; buds heavily mossed, sticky, scented; flowers 1 in., full, borne mostly solitary, slight fragrance; foliage dark green, glossy; prickles small, green, numerous; growth compact, short, pot or garden; [Dresdon Doll × Silver Jubilee]; int. in 2000

Coral Rosamini Min, op

Coral Rose – See ***R. saturata*** (Baker)

Coral Sand F, op, 1991, Rennie, Bruce F.; flowers coral, large, full, borne mostly singly, intense fragrance; foliage medium size, medium green, semi-glossy; bushy growth; [Paul Shirville × Shocking Blue]; int. by Rennie Roses International, 1991

Coral Satin LCl, op, 1960, Zombory; bud ovoid; flowers coral pink, reverse lighter, 3½-4 in., 25 petals, high-centered, borne in small clusters, moderate fragrance; foliage dark green, glossy; numerous prickles; vigorous (6-8 ft.) growth; PP2098; [New Dawn × Fashion]; int. by J&P, 1960

Coral Sea HT, dp, 1942, Joseph H. Hill, Co.; bud globular, old-rose; flowers light red, large, 40-45 petals, high-centered; foliage leathery, dark; long, strong stems; vigorous, upright, much branched growth; [Katharine Pechtold × R.M.S. Queen Mary]

Coral Sea – See **Orange Passion**, HT

Coral Silk F, op, 1972, Gregory; flowers coral and peach, 3 in., 18 petals, flat; foliage glossy, dark; very free growth

Coral Spire HT, mp, Kordes; flowers large, clear coral-pink, dbl., high-centered, no fragrance; foliage large, leathery, deep green; tall, upright, vigorous growth; int. in 1994

Coral Sprite Min, mp, 1989, Warriner, William A.; bud ovoid, pointed; flowers medium, very dbl., urn-shaped, borne in sprays of 3-18, no fragrance; foliage medium size, dark green, matte; prickles straight to slightly angled downward, yellow-green; bushy, spreading, low growth; PP7717; [Merci × Party Girl]; int. by Bear Creek Gardens, 1989

Coral Star HT, op, 1967, Robinson, H.; flowers coral-pink, well-formed, medium; vigorous, upright growth; [Tropicana × Stella]

Coral Sunblaze Min, op, Meilland; bud ovoid; flowers soft coral pink, 2 in., 65-110 petals, flat cupped, borne singly and in small clusters, no fragrance; free-flowering; foliage dark green, semi-glossy; prickles sharply pointed, 6 mm., yellow-green; bushy (2 ft.), spreading growth; PP15500; [(Parador × Swany Mimi) × Air France]; int. by Greenheart Farms, 2004

Coral Sunset HT, or, 1965, Boerner; bud ovoid; flowers coral-red, large, dbl., moderate fragrance; foliage dark, leathery; vigorous growth; [(Garnette × unknown) × Hawaii]; int. by J&P, 1964

Coral Treasure Min, ob, 1972, Moore, Ralph S.; bud ovoid; flowers coral-orange, medium, dbl.; foliage glossy, leathery; dwarf, bushy growth; [seedling × Little Buckaroo]; int. by Sequoia Nursery, 1971

CoralGlo F, op, 1960, Boerner; bud ovoid; flowers orange-rose, large, 42 petals, cupped; foliage bronze; bushy growth; [Independence × Fashion]; int. by Stark Bros., 1960

Corali LCl, rb, 1931, Dot, Pedro; flowers coral-red to rosy salmon; profuse seasonal bloom; foliage bright green; vigorous growth

Coralie D, lp, before 1848; flowers soft pink, lighter at edges, medium, very dbl., cupped; foliage grayish-green, small; vigorous growth

Coralie M, lp, about 1860, Miellez; flowers flesh, well-formed, medium, dbl.

Coralie HMult, pb, 1919, Paul, W.; bud coral; flowers coral-red to deep pink, 6-7 cm., dbl.; non-recurrent; foliage glossy; vigorous growth; [Hiawatha × Lyon Rose]

Coralin Min, or, 1955, Dot, M.; flowers coral-red, 40 petals; low, compact growth; [Méphisto × Perla de Alcañada]

Coralín Superb Min, dr, 1958, Will; [sport of Coralín]; int. by Kordes

Coraline LCl, ab, Eve, Andre; flowers salmon-apricot, 15-20 petals; heavy spring bloom, then recurrent; growth to 2-4 m.; int. by Andre Eve, 1976

Coraline S, mp, Tschanz, Gisèle; flowers pure pink, large, full; floriferous; growth to 3 ft.; int. by Alain Tschanz SA, 2003

Coralita LCl, or, 1964, Zombory; bud ovoid, deep red; flowers orange-coral, 4 in., 40-45 petals, moderate fragrance; foliage dark, leathery; vigorous (6-8 ft.) growth; PP2531; [(New Dawn × Geranium Red) × Fashion]; int. by J&P; David Fuerstenberg Prize, ARS, 1968

Coralitos Min, op, 1999, Schuurman, Frank B.; flowers 1 in., dbl., borne in small clusters; foliage small, medium green, semi-glossy; prickles moderate; spreading, low (12-16 in.) growth; int. by Franko Roses New Zealand, Ltd., 1996

Corallina T, rb, 1900, Paul, W.; flowers coppery red, large, dbl.

Corallina, Climbing Cl T, mp, 1930, Neisser; flowers carmine with vermilion

Corallina MinFl, ob, Barni, V.; int. in 1993

Coralline Pol, or, 1938, Smith, J.; flowers borne in very large clusters; profuse, repeated bloom; very rampant growth; [Gloria Mundi × Golden Salmon Superieur]; int. by Eddie

Corallovy Surprise HT, Klimenko, V. N.; int. in 1982

Corbeille Royale HT, mp, 1956, Buyl Frères; bud globular; flowers salmon-pink, dbl.; vigorous, upright growth

Cordelia HT, ab, 1976, LeGrice; flowers peach shaded deeper, pointed, 4-4½ in., 20 petals, moderate fragrance; foliage dark; tall growth; int. by Roseland Nurs., 1975

Cordelia S, mp, 2001, Austin, David; flowers semi-dbl., borne in small clusters, moderate fragrance; foliage medium size, dark green, matte, disease-resistant; prickles medium, hooked downward, few; growth upright, medium (105 cm.); garden, decorative; [seedling × seedling]; int. by David Austin Roses, Ltd., 2000

Cordelia de Grey S, dp, 1995, de Grey, Cordelia; flowers deep, bright pink with white eye, golden stamens, 2 in., 5 petals, borne in small clusters, slight fragrance; foliage small, dark green, dull; numerous prickles; medium, upright growth, arching canes

Cordial HT, mp, 1961, Verbeek; bud ovoid; flowers pink, medium, dbl., borne in clusters; foliage dark; [Satisfaction × seedling]

Cordoba S, or, Poulsen; flowers orange-red, 5-8 cm., full, classic hybrid tea form, very slight fragrance; foliage dark green, glossy; bushy (60-100 cm.) growth; int. by Poulsen Roser, 2005

Cordon Bleu HT, ab, 1990, Harkness, R., & Co., Ltd.; bud pointed; flowers apricot with begonia pink reverse, deepening to apricot with aging, 20 petals, cupped, moderate fruity fragrance; foliage medium to large, dark green, glossy; prickles recurving, average, reddish; upright, medium growth; [Basildon Bond × Silver Jubilee]; int. by R. Harkness & Co., Ltd., 1991

Cordon Rouge LCl, or, Combe; flowers vermilion, 3 in., dbl.; int. in 1970

Cordula F, or, 1973, Kordes, R.; bud globular; flowers red-orange, medium, dbl., slight fragrance; foliage dark, bronze, leathery; vigorous, dwarf, bushy growth; [Europeana × Marlena]; int. by Kordes, 1972

Corehead HT, mr, 1960, Dicksons of Hawlmark; flowers bright crimson; [Ena Harkness × Hazel Alexander]

Corimbosa – See **Red Damask**, D

Corina HT, pb, 1992, Warriner, William A. & Zary, Keith W.; flowers salmon pink with darker edges and lighter, almost cream, reverse, medium, full, high-centered, moderate fragrance; foliage large, dark green, matte; few prickles; medium (150 cm.), upright growth; [Bridal Pink × Kardinal]; int. by Bear Creek Gardens, 1993

Corinium F, m, 1970, Cooper; flowers mauvish pink, 3 in., 48-50 petals, full rosette; foliage semi-glossy; [sport of Alamein]

Corinna T, pb, 1893, Paul, W.; bud long; flowers flesh pink, shaded with rose and tinted with coppery-gold, medium, dbl.

Corinne F, ab, 1997, Brown, Ted; flowers medium, dbl., borne in small clusters; foliage medium size, dark green, glossy; bushy, medium (30 in.)growth; [Esprit × Indian Summer]

Corinne's Choice Min, w, 2004, Meagher, William E.; flowers 1¼ in., full, high-centered, star-shaped, borne mostly solitary; foliage medium size, dark green, matte; prickles in., needle-like; growth bushy, medium (18 in.); garden decoration, exhibition; [Hot Tamale × Reiko]

Corky F, rb, 1991, Zipper, Herbert; flowers white with red edges, white reverse, 3-3½ in., full, borne in small clusters, slight fragrance; foliage large, dark green, semi-glossy; few prickles; medium (100 cm.), bushy growth; [Tamango × seedling]; int. by Magic Moment Miniature Roses, 1992

Corlia HT, or, 1921, Bees; flowers terra-cotta; moderate growth

Corne Herholdt F, pb

Cornelia HT, pb, 1919, Scott, R.; flowers light pink, base orange, dbl.; [Ophelia × Mrs Aaron Ward]

Cornelia HMsk, pb, 1925, Pemberton; flowers strawberry flushed yellow, small, dbl., rosette, borne in flattish sprays; recurrent bloom; foliage dark bronze, leathery, glossy; very vigorous growth

Cornelia – See **Cornelia Hit**, MinFl

Cornelia Cook T, w, 1855, Cook; flowers creamy white, tinged lemon-yellow and flesh, well-formed, dbl., moderate fragrance; vigorous growth; [Devoniensis × unknown]

Cornelia Hit MinFl, my, Poulsen; flowers medium yellow, 5-8 cm., full, cupped, borne mostly singly, no fragrance; recurrent; foliage dark green, glossy; growth bushy, 20-40 cm.; int. by Poulsen Roser, 2003

Cornelia Patiohit – See **Cornelia Hit**, MinFl

Cornélie – See **Belle Vichysoise**, N

Cornélie Koch – See **Cornelia Cook**, T

Cornelis Timmermans HT, pb, 1919, Timmermans; flowers clear pink, edged deep yellow, very large, dbl., moderate fragrance; [Pharisaer × Le Progres]

Corner HT, pb, 1945, Wyant; bud pointed; flowers cerise, base yellow, reverse yellow washed pink, 4½ in., 20 petals; foliage leathery, glossy, dark; vigorous, bushy growth; [Soeur Thérèse × seedling]

Cornet HP, m, 1845, Lacharme, F.; flowers rose tinted with purple, very large, very dbl., cupped, moderate centifolia fragrance; vigorous, branching growth

Cornsilk Min, ly, 1983, Saville, F. Harmon; flowers light pastel yellow, small, 40 petals, high-centered, borne mostly singly, moderate fragrance; foliage medium size, medium green, semi-glossy; vigorous, bushy growth; PP5164; [Rise 'n' Shine × Sheri Anne]; int. by Nor'East Min. Roses; AOE, ARS, 1983

Corolle LCl, mr, 1962, Dot, Simon; flowers semi-dbl., 12 petals, slight fragrance; foliage glossy; vigorous growth; [Spectacular × Cocktail]

Corona de Oro – See **Gold Crown**, HT

Coronado HT, rb, 1961, Von Abrams; bud long, pointed; flowers red, reverse yellow, 5-6 in., 40 petals, high-centered, moderate fragrance; foliage glossy, dark; vigorous, upright growth; PP2162; [(Multnomah × Peace) × (Multnomah × Peace)]; int. by Peterson & Dering, 1960

Coronado, Climbing Cl HT, Ansaloni

Coronation HWich, rb, 1911, Turner; flowers red, lightly striped white, small, semi-dbl., rosette, borne in clusters

Coronation HP, mp, 1913, Dickson, H.; flowers flesh, shaded bright shrimp-pink, well-formed, large, 50 petals; recurrent bloom; stems smooth wood; vigorous growth; Gold Medal, NRS, 1912

Coronation – See **Peacekeeper**, F

Coronation Gold HT, yb, 1954, Cox; flowers golden yellow flushed crimson, large, intense damask fragrance; foliage glossy; vigorous growth; RULED EXTINCT 1980; [Signora × Peace]

Coronation Gold F, ab, 1978, Cocker, A.; bud globular; flowers golden yellow to apricot, 4 in., 27 petals; foliage glossy; vigorous, upright growth; [(Sabine × Circus) × (Anne Cocker × Arthur Bell)]; int. by Cocker

Coroneola – See **Double White**, HMsk

Coronet HT, lp, 1897, Dingee-Conard; bud deep carmine; flowers silvery carnation pink, very large, full, round; [Paul Neyron × Bon Silène]

Coronet Pol, yb, 1912, Paul, W.; flowers yellow tinted pink

Coronet F, dr, 1957, deRuiter; flowers deep crimson, 3 in., 17 petals, borne in clusters; foliage dark, glossy; vigorous, upright growth; [Independence × Red Wonder]; int. by Blaby Rose Gardens

Coronet Supreme HT, mp, 1955, Jelly; bud short, pointed; flowers rose-pink, 4-5 in., 45-65 petals, moderate fragrance; foliage dark, glossy; very vigorous, upright growth; PP1374; [seedling × Golden Rapture]; int. by E.G. Hill Co.

Corp de Ballet F, dp, Hiroshima; int. by Hiroshima Bara-en, 2004

Corporal Johann Nagy HSet, dp, 1890, Geschwind, R.; bud fat; flowers crimson and violet, 6-7 cm., dbl., no fragrance; foliage rounded, tinged purple when young; [De La Grifferaie × a HP or B]

Corpus Christi HT, dr, 1985, Weeks, O.L.; flowers large, 35 petals; foliage large, medium green, semi-glossy; upright, bushy, spreading growth; PP5854; [seedling × Night Time]; int. by Weeks Wholesale Rose Growers

Corrida Gr, Delbard-Chabert; int. in 1969

Corrie Koster Pol, dp, 1923, Koster, M.; flowers light coral-red, opening to deep pink, semi-dbl., borne in clusters; [sport of Juliana-Roos]; int. by Royer

Corroboree HT, m, 1969, Fankhauser; bud long, pointed; flowers lilac-mauve, open, very large, dbl., intense damask fragrance; foliage glossy; vigorous, upright growth; [Baccará × My Choice]

Corry HT, or, Kordes; int. in 1978

Corsage F, w, 1965, Belden; flowers small, semi-dbl., globular, borne in clusters; foliage soft; vigorous, bushy growth; [Blanche Mallerin × White Swan]; int. by Wyant

Corsage MinFl, w, Williams, J.B.; flowers white with faint pink tint in center, dbl., globular, slight fragrance; int. by Hortico, 2004

Corsair F, or, 1985, Sanday, John; flowers medium, 20 petals; foliage medium size, dark, glossy; bushy growth; [(Vera Dalton × Stephen Langdon) × Fiesta Flame]; int. by Sanday Roses, Ltd.

Corsaire HT, Combe, M.; int. in 1974

Corsica F, pb, 1964, Verschuren, A.; flowers salmon-pink edged dark pink to red, 20 petals; foliage dark, glossy; vigorous, bushy growth; int. by van Engelen

Corso HT, ob, 1976, Cocker; flowers coppery orange, 4½ in., 33 petals; foliage glossy, dark; [Anne Cocker × Dr. A.J. Verhage]

Corso Fleuri F, dr, 1956, Mondial Roses; flowers scarlet-red, petals waved, semi-dbl.; dwarf, compact growth; [sport of Red Favorite]

Cortège LCl, ab, Combe, M.; flowers pale orange, fading to soft apricot, 3 in., borne singly or in small clusters; int. in 1976

Corvedale S, pb, 2002, Austin, David; flowers dusty rose pink, 7 cm., dbl., cupped, borne in small clusters, moderate fragrance; foliage large, medium green, semi-glossy; prickles medium, deep concave, brown, few; growth bushy, medium (150 cm.); garden decorative; [Charles Rennie Mackintosh × deep red English-type shrub]; int. by David Austin Roses, Ltd., 2001

Corvette HT, or, Kordes; flowers large, bright orange-red, dbl., high-centered; PP11189; greenhouse rose; int. in 1997

Coryana S, mp, 1926, Hurst, C.C.; flowers rich pink, 2½ in., single; few prickles; tall (8 ft.), shrub growth; [*R. macrophylla* × *R. roxburghii*]

Corylus S, mp, 1988, LeRougetel, Hazel; flowers open, medium, single, borne usually singly or in sprays of 2-4, slight fragrance; foliage medium size, dark green, deep veined; prickles small, light brown; bushy growth; hips round, medium, scarlet; [*R. nitida* × *R. rugosa rubra*]; int. by Peter Beales, 1988

Cosetta F, ob, 1985, Bartolomeo, Embriaco; flowers light orange, reverse deeper with reddish shadings, medium, 30 petals, no fragrance; foliage medium size, dark, matte; [Zorina × Sole di San Remo]; int. in 1984

Cosette F, mp, 1987, Harkness, R., & Co., Ltd.; flowers dbl., slight fragrance; foliage small, medium green, matte; prickles small, dark; low, spreading growth; patio; [seedling × Esther's Baby]

Cosima F, or, 1983, Tantau, Math.; flowers medium, 20 petals, no fragrance; foliage large, dark, glossy; int. in 1981

Cosima – See **Arielle**, HT

Cosimo Ridolfi HGal, m, 1842, Vibert; flowers old-rose to lilac, spotted crimson, medium, full, cupped; foliage soft green; compact growth

Cosmic Min, ob, 1997, Bridges, Dennis A.; flowers light to medium orange with light yellow reverse, medium, full, borne in small clusters, slight fragrance; foliage large, medium green, semi-glossy; upright (24-26 in.), bushy growth; int. by Bridges Roses

Cosmo HMsk, lp, Robinson; flowers creamy blush, frilly, 2 in.; int. by Vintage Gardens, 2000

Cosmopoliet – See **Cosmopolitan**, F

Cosmopolit – See **Cosmopolitan**, F

Cosmopolitan F, mp, 1955, Buisman, G. A. H.; flowers borne in large clusters; bushy growth; [Silberlachs × seedling]

Cosmos HT, w, Combe; flowers pure white, 30 petals, high-centered, moderate fragrance; foliage matte; growth to 80 cm.; int. in 1993

Cosmos LCl, lp, Olesen; bud broad based; flowers light pink, 5 cm., 50-55 petals, rosette, borne in large clusters, flowers evenly top to bottom, slight fragrance; recurrent; foliage dark green, glossy; prickles numerous, 5 mm., hooked downward; growth broad, bushy, 200-300 cm.; PP15482; [Red Paillette × seedling]; int. by Poulsen Roser, 2002

Costa Dorada HT, Dot; int. in 1967

Cote d'Azur HT, m; int. in 1998

Côte Jardins F, mp, Orard; int. in 2001

Cote Rotie – See **Grand Amour**, HT

Cotillion F, yb, 1969, Byrum, Roy L.; bud ovoid; flowers yellow, edged pink, medium, high-centered, slight fragrance; foliage leathery; vigorous, upright growth; PP2978; [Rumba × Golden Garnette]; int. by J. H. Hill Co., 1967

Cotillion F, m, 1999, Zary, Dr. Keith W.; bud pointed, ovoid; flowers lavender, reverse pale lavender, 4 in., 41 petals, rosette, borne in large clusters, intense sweet fragrance; foliage medium size, dark green, glossy; prickles moderate; upright, spreading (3½ ft.) growth; PP11562; [seedling × Shocking Blue]; int. by Bear Creek Gardens, Inc., 1999; Gold Medal, Rome, 1998

Cotlands Rose – See **Autumn Splendor**, MinFl

Coton Gold HT, dy, 1984, Babb, J.T.; flowers glowing yellow; [sport of Whisky Mac]

Cotorrita Real Pol, pb, 1931, Padrosa; flowers white, rose and yellow, small, very dbl., globular, borne in clusters; profuse, repeated bloom; vigorous growth

Cotswold Charm HT, dp, 1967, Bennett, V.G.T.; flowers magenta, high-centered; foliage dark, leathery; moderate growth; [(Ophelia × unknown) × William Moore]

Cotswold Gold Min, ob, 1992, Jellyman, J.S.; flowers orange, medium, 6-14 petals, borne in small clusters, slight fragrance; foliage small, medium green, semi-glossy; few prickles; low (20 cm.), bushy growth; [Tony Jacklin × Judy Fischer]; int. in 1993

Cotswold Sunset F, pb, 1992, Jellyman, J.S.; flowers gold, pink edge, pale pink, moderately full, 3-3½ in., dbl., high-centered, borne in small clusters; foliage medium size, dark green, glossy; some prickles; medium (80-90 cm.), upright, compact growth; [(Cairngorm × unknown) × (Alexander × Wembley)]; int. in 1993

Cottage Dream – See **Pink Fire**, F

Cottage Garden Min, ob, 1992, Harkness, R., & Co., Ltd.; flowers deep, rich orange, large, full, borne in large clusters; foliage small, dark green, glossy; some prickles; low (60 cm.), upright growth; [Clarissa × Amber Queen]; int. by Harkness New Roses, Ltd.

Cottage Garden – See **Mix 'n' Match**, S

Cottage Maid – See **Perle des Panachées**, HGal

Cottage Maid S, my, Poulsen; flowers medium yellow, 8-10 cm., semi-dbl., borne in large clusters, slight wild rose fragrance; recurrent bloom; foliage dark; growth broad, bushy, 100-150 cm.; int. as Odense By-Rose, Poulsen Roser, 1990; Rose of the Year, Auckland, NZ, 1997

Cottage Pink HMult, mp; flowers single

Cottage Rose S, mp, 1994, Austin, David; flowers warm pink, medium, very full, borne in large clusters, moderate fragrance; foliage medium size, medium green, semi-glossy; numerous prickles; medium (40 in.), upright, bushy growth; [Mary Rose × Wife of Bath]; int. by David Austin Roses, Ltd., 1991

Cottage Rose S, mp; groundcover; spreading growth; int. by Richlyn Nurseries, 2002

Cottage White HMult, w; flowers single

Cotton Candy HWich, mp, 1952, Moore, Ralph S.; bud well-formed; flowers 2½ in., very dbl., borne in clusters; foliage very glossy, turning to autumn colors; vigorous (10-15 ft.) growth; [*R. wichurana* × seedling (F with *R. multibracteata* ancestry)]; int. by Sequoia Nursery

Cotton Top F, w, 1960, Joseph H. Hill, Co.; bud short, pointed; flowers 2-3 in., 45-50 petals, flat, slight fragrance; foliage leathery; vigorous, upright, well-branched growth; PP1886; [seedling × White Butterfly]; int. by J. H. Hill co., 1962

Cottontail Min, w, 1983, Strawn, Leslie E.; flowers small, 33 petals, borne in large clusters; foliage medium size, medium green, semi-glossy; upright, bushy growth; PP5436; [Pink Petticoat × Pink Petticoat]; int. by Pixie Treasures Min. Roses

Coucher de Soleil – See **Coral Sunset**, HT

Coucou F, dy, Dorieux; int. in 1982

Cougar MinFl, rb, 2000, Moe, Mitchie; flowers medium red, reverse light pink, 1-1½ in., full, high-centered, borne mostly singly; foliage large, medium green, semi-glossy; few prickles; growth vigorous, upright, tall (24-30 in.); [Klima × select pollen]; int. by Mitchie's Roses & More, 2000

Couleur de Brennus HGal, mr, before 1857; flowers medium, dbl.; slender, shrubby growth

Couleur de Chair – See **Vilmorin**, M

Couleur de Feu C, or, before 1908; flowers fiery orange, medium, full

Couleur de Sang – See **Admirable**, HGal

Count Bawbrinzki – See **Comte de Bobrinsky**, HCh

Countenance HT, mr, Williams, J.B.; flowers scarlet red, full, cupped, quartered, moderate fragrance; growth to 4 ft.; int. by Hortico Inc., 2005

Countess Bertha – See **Duchesse de Brabant**, T

Countess Cadogan HT, lp, 1978, Buss; bud long, pointed; flowers 4½ in., 40-45 petals, high-centered; foliage light green, leathery; very vigorous, upright growth; [sport of Carlita]; int. by H. Buss Nursery

Countess Celeste S, op, 1999, Poulsen Roser APS; flowers coral pink, old-fashioned form, 2½-3 in., very dbl., borne in small clusters, moderate fragrance; foliage medium size, dark green, glossy; prickles moderate; compact, rounded low (20-24 in.) growth; PP10923; [Queen Margrethe × seedling]

Countess Clanwilliam HT, mr, 1915, Dickson, H.; flowers pinkish cherry-red, dbl., high-centered; foliage rich green; bushy growth; Gold Medal, NRS, 1913

Countess M. H. Chotek – See **Gräfin Marie Henriette Chotek**, HMult

Countess Mary Cl HT, mp, 1933, Dixie Rose Nursery; [sport of Mary, Countess of Ilchester]

Countess Mary of Ilchester – See **Mary, Countess of Ilchester**, HT

Countess of Annesley HT, pb, 1905, Dickson, A.; flowers flesh pink with salmon, medium, moderate fragrance

Countess of Caledon HT, lp, 1897, Dickson, A.; flowers blush pink, center darker, large

Countess of Dalkeith F, rb, 1958, Dobbie; flowers vermilion flushed orange, very dbl., intense fragrance; vigorous growth; [sport of Fashion]; int. by Dobbie & Co., 1957

Countess of Derby HT, w, 1906, Dickson, A.; flowers creamy white with pink tints, large, dbl.

Countess of Elgin HT, op, 1925, Ferguson; flowers salmon-pink, reverse deep rose-pink; vigorous growth; [sport of Mme Edouard Herriot]

Countess of Glasgow HSpn, dr, before 1817, from England

Countess of Gosford HT, op, 1906, McGredy; flowers salmon-pink, long pointed, large, dbl.; Gold Medal, NRS, 1905

Countess of Ilchester – See **Mary, Countess of Ilchester**, HT

Countess of Lieven Ayr, w; flowers creamy white, medium, semi-dbl., cupped

Countess of Lonsdale HT, dy, 1919, Dickson, H.; flowers dbl.

Countess of Oxford – See **Comtesse d'Oxford**, HP

Countess of Pembroke HT, pb; flowers pink shaded darker, large, very dbl.; vigorous growth

Countess of Roseberry HP, mr, 1879, Postans; flowers carmine red, large, full, cupped; foliage dark green; few prickles; [Victor Verdier × unknown]

Countess of Shaftesbury HT, pb, 1912, Dickson, H.; flowers silvery carmine, edged pearl pink, large, full

Countess of Stradbroke Cl HT, dr, 1928, Clark, A.; bud ovoid; flowers dark glowing crimson, well-shaped, very large, dbl., globular, borne singly or in small clusters, intense fragrance; free, recurrent bloom; foliage rich green, wrinkled; vigorous growth; [Walter C. Clark × unknown]; int. by Hazlewood Bros.

Countess of Warwick HT, my, 1919, Easlea; flowers lemon-yellow, edged pink, large, dbl.; foliage dark olive green

Countess of Wessex S, w, 2006, Beales, Amanda; flowers full, borne in large clusters; foliage medium size, dark green; prickles average, hooked, moderate; growth upright, medium (1½ m.); garden decoration, containers, hedging; [Bonica × Maigold]; int. by Peter Beales Roses, 2006

Countess Sonja – See **Gräfin Sonja**, HT

Countess Vandal – See **Comtesse Vandal**, HT

Countess Vandal, Climbing – See **Comtesse Vandal, Climbing**, Cl HT

Country Dancer S, dp, 1972, Buck, Dr. Griffith J.; bud ovoid; flowers rose-red, large, dbl., moderate fragrance; repeat bloom; foliage large, glossy, dark, leathery; vigorous, dwarf, upright, bushy growth; [Prairie Princess × Johannes Boettner]; int. by Iowa State University, 1973

Country Doctor HT, lp, 1952, Brownell; bud long, pointed to ovoid; flowers silvery pink, large, dbl., high-centered, moderate fragrance; foliage glossy; vigorous, bushy growth; [Pink Princess × Crimson Glory]

Country Fair S, lp, Harkness; flowers 2 in., semi-dbl., borne in clusters; free-flowering; rounded (4 ft.) growth; int. in 1998

Country Garden Cl F, dp, 1996, Bossom, W.E.; flowers bright pink, white center, 4 in., 8-14 petals, borne in large clusters; foliage medium size, light green, glossy; few prickles; spreading, climbing, tall (15 ft.) growth; [Anne Harkness × seedling]

Country Girl F, mr, 1960, Temmerman; bud ovoid; flowers geranium-red, medium, dbl.; vigorous growth; [Independence × Salmon Perfection]; int. by Schraven, 1958

Country Girl, Climbing Cl F, mr, 1962, Buyl Frères

Country Girl – See **Emsie Girl**, HT

Country Gold – See **Sommermond**, F

Country Heritage – See **Our Jubilee**, HT

Country Joy Min, pb, 1984, Moore, Ralph S.; flowers light pink, yellow reverse, small, dbl.; foliage small, medium green, matte; compact growth; [Pinocchio × Yellow Jewel]; int. by Moore Min. Roses

Country Lady HT, ob, 1987, Harkness, R., & Co., Ltd.; flowers burnt orange, reverse suffused pale scarlet, fading orange-salmon, 25 petals, slight spicy fragrance; foliage medium size, medium green, semi-glossy; prickles decurved, medium, reddish; bushy, medium, high-shouldered growth; hips ovoid, medium, green; [Alexander × Bright Smile]; int. in 1988

Country Lass – See **Baby Blanket**, S

Country Life F, op, Harkness; flowers orange-salmon, 3½ in., semi-dbl., cupped, borne singly and in small clusters; recurrent; compact (3½ ft.), bushy growth; int. in 1998

Country Living S, lp, 1994, Austin, David; flowers pale pink, 3-3½ in., very dbl., borne in small clusters; foliage medium size, medium green, semi-glossy; some prickles; upright, bushy (41 in.) growth; [Wife of Bath × Graham Thomas]; int. by David Austin Roses, Ltd., 1991

Country Maid F, lp, 1972, Whartons Roses; low, compact growth; [sport of Tip Top]; int. by Deamer, 1971

Country Marilou – See **Mary Rose**, S

Country Morning Min, yb, 1986, Florac, Marilyn; flowers light yellow, blended pink, dbl., high-centered, borne singly, moderate spicy fragrance; foliage medium size, medium green, semi-glossy; prickles small, reddish; medium, upright growth; [Avandel × Young Love]; int. by MB Farm

Country Music S, dp, 1972, Buck, Dr. Griffith J.; bud ovoid; flowers Neyron rose, large, dbl., moderate fragrance; intermittent bloom; foliage large, leathery; vigorous, dwarf, upright, bushy growth; [Paddy McGredy × ((World's Fair × Floradora) × Applejack)]; int. by Iowa State University, 1973

Country Music S, pb, Harkness; int. in 1998

Country Pride LCl, ab

Country Prince – See **Royal Bassino**, S

Country Song S, lp, 1985, Buck, Dr. Griffith J.; bud ovoid; flowers large, 28 petals, cupped, borne 1-5 per cluster, moderate myrrh fragrance; repeat bloom; foliage leathery, dark; prickles awl-like, brown; erect, bushy growth; hardy; [Carefree Beauty × The Yeoman]; int. by Iowa State University, 1984

Country Song – See **Moon River**, S

Countryman S, pb, 1978, Buck, Dr. Griffith J.; bud

ovoid, pointed; flowers light rose-bengal, 4-5 in., 25-30 petals, cupped, moderate fragrance; foliage large, dark, leathery; vigorous, upright, spreading, bushy growth; [(Improved Lafayette × Independence) × Maytime]; int. by Iowa State University

Countryside Rose S, ab; int. by Love4Plants Ltd, 2004

Countrywoman HT, my, 1978, Dawson, George; bud globular; flowers lemon-yellow, medium, dbl.; foliage leathery; bushy growth; [seedling × Peace]; int. by Australian Roses

County Fair F, mp, 1960, Swim, H.C.; bud ovoid, pointed; flowers medium to dark pink, fading much lighter, 2½-3 in., 8-10 petals, flat, borne in clusters, slight fragrance; foliage leathery, dark, semi-glossy; vigorous, bushy growth; PP1897; [Frolic × Pink Bountiful]; int. by Armstrong Nursery, 1960

County Fair, Climbing Cl F, mp; int. in 1989

County Girl F, op, 1999, Horner, Colin P.; flowers orange, pink cream striped, reverse paler striped, ages more salmon, 4 in., dbl., borne in small clusters; foliage medium size, medium green semi-glossy; prickles moderate; bushy, medium (3 ft.) growth; [Alexander × (Southampton × ((New Penny × White Pet) × Stars 'n' Stripes))]; int. by Grange Farm Nursery, 2001

County of Cheshire – See **Cheshire**, S

Coup de Coeur LCl, mr, Maillard

Coup de Foudre F, or, 1956, Hémeray-Aubert; bud well-formed; flowers fiery red, cupped; foliage glossy, bronze; vigorous growth; [(Peace × Independence) × Oiseau de Feu]

Coup de Foudre, Climbing Cl F, Fineschi, G.; int. in 1976

Coupe d'Hébé B, dp, 1840, Laffay, M.; flowers deep pink, waxy texture, large, very dbl., cupped; foliage glossy; vigorous, erect growth; [Bourbon × *R. chinensis* hybrid]

Coupe d'Or HWich, my, 1930, Barbier; flowers canary-yellow, aging lighter, 2 in., dbl., cupped, moderate fragrance; foliage rich green, leathery, glossy; vigorous, climbing or trailing growth; [Jacotte × unknown]

Coupe d'Or – See **Gold Cup**, F

Courage HT, dr, 1923, McGredy; flowers deep brilliant maroon-crimson, very large, dbl., high-centered, intense fragrance; foliage rich green, leathery; bushy, dwarf growth

Courage HT, rb, 1941, Mallerin, C.; flowers red tinted yellow, open, very large, dbl.; vigorous, bushy growth; [seedling × Brazier]; int. by A. Meilland

Courage – See **Niccolo Paganini**, F

Courage HT, dr, Poulsen; flowers dark red, lighter reverse, 10-15 cm., full, high-centered, borne one to a stem, slight fragrance; recurrent; foliage matte; bushy (3-4 ft.) growth; int. by Poulsen Roser, 1998

Courageous – See **Madrigal**, S

Courageous Indira HT, ob, Chandrakant More; flowers orange vermilion with white stripes and streaks; int. in 1991

Courier HG, pb, 1930, Clark, A.; bud pale pink; flowers pink on white ground, 8-9 cm., dbl., borne in small clusters; foliage large; vigorous, climbing growth; [*R. gigantea* × Archiduc Joseph]; int. by Brundrett

Couronne de Salomon HGal, dp, before 1819; flowers very intense pink, large, very dbl., flat; growth upright

Couronne de Vibert HCh, mp, 1825, Bizard

Couronne d'Or – See **Gold Crown**, HT

Couronne Impériale HGal, m, about 1810, Descemet; flowers light violet, becoming purple, shaded lighter, large, full

Couronnée HGal, m, about 1811; flowers light violet, large

Court Jester F, ob, 1980, Cants of Colchester, Ltd.; flowers orange, reverse yellow, high-centered, borne 5-7 per cluster, slight fragrance; foliage mid-green, glossy; prickles large, hooked, red-brown; tall, upright growth

Courtin HGal, lp, 1824, Cartier; flowers flesh pink

Courtisane HT, or, Gaujard; flowers large, dbl.; int. in 1965

Courtney Min, rb, 1999, Giles, Diann; flowers red, reverse gold, 1½ in., dbl., borne in small clusters; foliage medium size, dark green, glossy; numerous prickles; spreading, low (1½ ft.) growth; [Princess Celest × Rainbow's End]; int. by Giles Rose Nursery, 1999

Courtney Carol F, ab, 2004, Horner, Colin P.; flowers orange/apricot, reverse pale apricot, 2½ in., dbl., borne in large clusters; foliage medium size, medium green, semi-glossy; prickles small, straight; growth compact, medium (2½-3 ft.); garden decorative; [(Laura Ford × Goldbusch) × Margaret Ann Silverstein]; int. by Warley Rose Gardens Ltd., 2007

Courtney Page HT, dr, 1922, McGredy; flowers velvety dark scarlet-crimson, dbl.; Gold Medal, NRS, 1920

Courtoisie F, ob, 1985, Delbard, Georges; flowers orange, reverse orange blended with yellow, large, 20 petals, moderate fragrance; foliage medium size, medium green; bushy growth; [Avalanche Rose × Fashion seedling]; int. by Pepinieres et Roseraies G. Delbard, 1984

Courtosie des Relais et Châteaux – See **Courtoisie**, F

Courtship HT, mp, 1955, Shepherd; bud conical; flowers cerise-pink, reverse lighter, 4-5 in., 28 petals, high-centered; foliage dark; vigorous, bushy growth; PP1511; [Mme Henri Guillot × Peace]; int. by Bosley Nursery, 1955

Courvoisier F, dy, 1971, McGredy, Sam IV; flowers large, 49 petals, high-centered, intense fragrance; foliage glossy, dark; [Elizabeth of Glamis × Casanova]; int. by McGredy

Cousin Essie S, w, 1996, Robertson, Myrtle; flowers 1½ in., 8-14 petals, moderate fragrance; foliage medium size, medium green, semi-glossy; few prickles; spreading, bushy, tall, (6 ft.) growth; [Honeyflow × unknown]; int. by Honeysuckle Cottage Nursery, 1988

Couture HCh, m, about 1825, Cartier; flowers bright violet

Cova da Iria HT, rb, 1963, Moreira da Silva; flowers light red, reverse gold; [seedling × Crimson Glory]

Covent Garden HT, rb, 1919, Cant, B. R.; flowers rich deep crimson flushed plum-black on reverse; foliage leathery, glossy; vigorous growth; Gold Medal, NRS, 1918

Covent Garden – See **Cream Abundance**, F

Coventrian F, dp, 1962, Robinson, H.; flowers ruby-cerise, well-formed, 3-3½ in., 30 petals, borne in large clusters; foliage dark, glossy; vigorous, bushy growth; [Highlight × seedling]

Coventry Cathedral – See **Cathedral**, F

Cover Girl HT, ob, 1960, Von Abrams; bud long, pointed; flowers orange, copper and gold, 5 in., 28-35 petals, high-centered, slight fragrance; foliage glossy, dark; upright, bushy growth; PP2020; [Sutter's Gold × (Mme Henri Guillot × seedling)]; int. by Peterson & Dering, 1959

Cowichan Super Cl HT, op, 1976, Meier, V. C.; flowers orange-salmon, 5 in., 30-35 petals, intense fragrance; bloom repeats; foliage glossy; tall, very vigorous growth; int. by Tamarack Roses, 1975

Cowra Rose Gr, mp, J&P; int. in 2000

Cox's Pink Polyantha Pol, mp

Cox's Red Polyantha Pol, mr

Coy Colleen HT, w, 1953, McGredy, Sam IV; bud pointed, rosy white; flowers milky white, well-formed, borne in clusters; foliage glossy; vigorous growth; [(Modesty × Portadown Glory) × Phyllis Gold]

Cracker HWich, mr, 1920, Clark, A.; flowers bright red with prominent stamens, 7-8 cm., single; sometimes classed as HG

Cracker, Climbing – See **Cracker**, HWich

Crackerjack F, rb, 1960, Fryers Nursery, Ltd.; flowers scarlet flushed yellow, 20 petals, borne in clusters, moderate fragrance; free growth; [Fashion × Masquerade]; int. in 1959

Crackerjack F, ob, Olesen; int. in 1989

Crackling Fire Min, ob, 1999, Walden, John K.; flowers copper orange, reverse deep red-orange, 2-2¼ in., 20-40 petals, borne in small clusters, no fragrance; foliage medium size, dark green, semi-glossy; prickles moderate; upright, compact, low (14-18 in.) growth; PP12322; [seedling × Rainbow's End]; int. by Bear Creek Gardens, Inc., 1999

Craig Christie F, dr, 2006, Paul Chessum Roses; flowers dbl., borne in small clusters, slight fragrance; foliage medium size, medium green, glossy; prickles large, long, red, few; growth compact, medium (24 in.); bedding, containers; [seedling × seedling]; int. by World of Roses, 2005

Craighall Climbing Rose Ayr, w, 1828; flowers dbl.; possibly a natural hybrid between *R. arvensis* and a form of *R. alba*

Craigweil HT, pb, 1929, Hicks; flowers silvery cerise-pink, reverse deeper, dbl.; strong stems; vigorous growth; [Mme Abel Chatenay × unknown]

Cramoisi – See **Rubra**, C

Cramoisi – See **Burgundian Rose**, HGal

Cramoisi – See **Tinwell Moss**, M

Cramoisi Brillant – See **Temple d'Apollon**, HGal

Cramoisi des Alpes HGal, mr, before 1829, Trébucien; flowers bright purplish red, dbl.; heavy, non-recurrent bloom

Cramoisi Éblouissant Ch, dr, 1839, possibly Laffay; flowers medium, dbl.

Cramoisi Foncé Velouté M, dr; flowers deep velvety crimson

Cramoisi Incomparable – See **Velours Pourpre**, HGal

Cramoisi Majeur – See **Hector**, HGal

Cramoisi Picoté HGal, rb, 1834, Vibert; flowers crimson, streaked and mottled (striped & spotted) darker, 2 in., very dbl., moderate fragrance

Cramoisi Royal HGal, about 1810, Descemet

Cramoisi Simple HWich, rb, 1901, Barbier; flowers deep crimson red with white center, 4 cm., single to semi-dbl., borne in large, upright panicles; foliage light green, glossy; prickles moderate, pink, large; [*R. wichurana rubra* × Turner's Crimson Rambler]

Cramoisi Supérieur Ch, mr, 1832, Coquereau; flowers crimson-red, small, dbl., cupped, borne in large clusters; recurrent bloom; vigorous growth

Cramoisi Supérieur, Climbing Cl Ch, mr, 1885, Couturier; flowers crimson, medium, semi-dbl., cupped; [Cramoisi Supéieur × unknown]; possibly the same as Mme Couturier-Mention or Rev. James Sprunt

Cramoisie HGal, dr, before 1791; flowers crimson-red, turning to purple, medium, dbl.

Cramoisie Éblouissante HGal, dr, before 1811, from Holland; flowers crimson purple, very dbl.; foliage long, very dentate; prickles numerous, small, flexible

Cramoisie Triomphante HGal, dp, before 1811, from Holland; flowers crimson, plumed with lighter pink, small, moderate fragrance

Cranbrook Pol, m, 1921, Matthews, W.J.

Crane – See **Tan Cho**, HT

Crane Viewing – See **Tsurumi 90**, HT

Crarae HT, yb, 1986, McKirdy, J.M.; flowers deep yellow

marked with scarlet, large, 35 petals, slight fragrance; foliage medium size, dark, glossy; bushy growth; [Piccadilly × Fred Gibson]; int. by John Sanday Roses, 1981

Crathes Castle F, mp, 1980, Cocker, James; flowers 18 petals, borne 12-15 per cluster; foliage large, dark, glossy; prickles triangular; rounded, bushy growth; [Dreamland × Topsi]

Crazy Dottie Min, ob, 1988, McCann, Sean; flowers orange-red with star-shaped copper center, small, 5 petals; foliage small, medium green, semi-glossy; bushy growth; [Rise 'n' Shine × (Sheri Anne × Picasso)]

Crazy For You – See **Fourth of July**, LCl

Crazy Horse HT, rb, Delbard; flowers basic white, striped, dotted and flecked with red, medium, dbl., no fragrance; numerous prickles; growth relatively compact and dense; PP10621; int. in 2001

Crazy Quilt Min, rb, 1980, Moore, Ralph S.; bud pointed; flowers red and white striped, dbl., flat, borne singly or in clusters of 3 or more; foliage medium green; prickles small, straight; compact, bushy growth; [Little Darling × seedling]; int. by Sequoia Nursery

Crazy Spire HT, or; flowers striped and spotted orange-red and yellow, dbl., high-centered, no fragrance; growth upright and slightly arching, 6 ft.; int. in 1995

Cream Abundance F, w; flowers creamy color, 3½-4 in., 50 petals, borne in clusters that cover the bush; repeats well; foliage dark green; growth rounded (3 × 3 ft.); int. by Harkness, 1999

Cream Chica Kordana Min, lp, Kordes

Cream Cracker HT, lp, 1933, Dickson, A.; flowers creamy buff, reverse shaded salmon, large, dbl.; vigorous growth; RULED EXTINCT 10/78 ARM

Cream Cracker HT, w, 1979, Murray, Nola; bud pointed; flowers cream, high-centered, 4½ in., 38 petals, borne singly, intense apple fragrance; foliage large, matte; often thornless; bushy growth; [Columbine × Iceberg]; int. by Rasmussen's

Cream Delight Gr, lp, 1983, Schuurman, Frank B.; flowers full; foliage medium size, medium green, glossy; upright growth; [sport of Sonia]

Cream Delight HT, ab, Douglas; flowers cream, centered apricot; [sport of Nitouche]; int. in 1987

Cream Dream HT, w, Kordes; flowers medium, clear cream color, dbl., high-centered; recurrent bloom; PP11387; [sport of Dream]; int. in 1997

Cream Gold Min, my, 1978, Moore, Ralph S.; bud long, pointed; flowers dbl., 38 petals, high-centered; compact, spreading growth; [Golden Glow × seedling]; int. by Sequoia Nursery

Cream Midinette Min, w, Pearce; int. by Ludwig's Roses, 2003

Cream Peach F, w, 1976, Sheridan; flowers cream, edged pink, 3-4 in., 15-20 petals, slight fragrance; foliage large, glossy; very free growth; [Paddy McGredy × seedling]

Cream Prophyta HT, w, de Ruiter; int. by DeRuiter's New Roses Intl.

Cream Puff MinFl, pb, 1981, Bennett, Dee; bud ovoid; flowers cream blushed pink, 18 petals, borne singly or in clusters of 3; foliage dark, semi-glossy; prickles long; spreading, bushy growth; [Little Darling × Elfinesque]; int. by Tiny Petals Nursery

Cream Puff, Climbing Cl Min, pb, Trimper, K.; [sport of Cream Puff]; int. in 1996

Cream Silk Min, w; int. by Love4Plants Ltd, 2005

Cream Sunsation S, w, Kordes; buds deep cream, pointed, smallish; flowers white, borne in clusters, no fragrance; foliage glossy, deep green, dense; prostrate, groundcover growth; int. in 1996

Cream Trip HRg, w, Bell; prickles very few; int. by Bell Roses Ltd, 2001

Credo HT, mr, 1965, Gaujard; flowers purplish red, medium, dbl., high-centered; foliage leathery; vigorous, upright growth; [Eminence × John S. Armstrong]

Cree S, lp, 1932, Central Exp. Farm; flowers pale pink fading to white, large, single; early bloom, non-recurrent; foliage glossy, bright green; vigorous growth; [*R. rugosa albo-plena* × *R. spinosissima hispida*]

Creeping Everbloom LCl, mr, 1939, Brownell; flowers 4 in., 30 petals, borne in clusters, moderate fragrance; recurrent bloom; growth to 3 ft.; [Frederick S. Peck × (Général Jacqueminot × Dr. W. Van Fleet)]

Creepy – See **Ralph's Creeper**, S

Creina Murland HT, dy, 1934, Dickson, A.; flowers sunflower-yellow, deepening, dbl.; foliage glossy; very vigorous growth

Crême S, lp, 1895, Geschwind, R.; flowers pale yellowish-pink, 4-5 cm., semi-dbl., borne in clusters of 10-15, strong musk fragrance; good autumn repeat; numerous prickles; very hardy; [(*R. canina* × Tea) × (*R. canina* × Bourbon)]

Creme Abundance – See **Cream Abundance**, F

Crème Anglais LCl, ly, Gandy; flowers soft yellow, dbl., borne in trusses; recurrent bloom; foliage pale green, plentiful; growth to 12-14 ft.; int. by Gandy's Ltd, 2004

Crème Brulee S, ly; flowers large, soft yellow, self-cleaning, dbl.; recurrent bloom; groundcover; spreading (24 × 36 in.) growth; int. by Northwest Horticulture, 2005

Crème Brulée S, pb, Gandy; flowers peach tinted copper, large, semi-dbl.; recurrent bloom; foliage glossy; growth to 12-15 ft.; int. by Gandy's Ltd, 2004

Créme Caramel – See **Pure Gold**, S

Crème de la Crème LCl, w, Gandy; flowers creamy white, 60 petals; recurrent bloom; foliage olive-green; growth to 12 ft.; int. by Gandy's Ltd, 1998

Crème Glacée Min, ly, 1989, Laver, Keith G.; bud pointed; flowers small, 23 petals, urn-shaped, borne singly, slight fragrance; foliage small, medium green, matte; prickles pointed and straight out, white-beige; bushy growth; hips globular, orange; [June Laver × Summer Butter]; int. by Springwood Roses, 1990

Creme Tausendschön HMult, w

Crenata – See **À Feuilles Crénelées**, C

Créole HT, dr, 1962, Gaujard; bud long, pointed; flowers purplish, red base coppery, large, dbl.; foliage dark, glossy; very vigorous, bushy growth; [Peace × Josephine Bruce]

Crêpe de Chine HT, mr, 1983, Delbard, Georges; flowers large, 20 petals; foliage glossy, clear green, dense; prickles bronze-red; vigorous, upright, bushy growth; [Joyeux Noel × (Gloire de Rome × Impeccable)]; int. by Delbard, 1970; Gold Medal, Madrid, 1970

Crepe Myrtle F, mr, 1937, Dixie Rose Nursery; growth to 5 ft.; [sport of Permanent Wave]

Crepe Rose – See **Paul Perras**, HP

Crepe Suzette Min, ob, 1987, Travis, Louis R.; flowers deep yellow with orange overlay, fading white with orange-red, 25-30 petals, high-centered, moderate fruity fragrance; foliage small, medium green, semi-glossy; prickles bowed, tan-brown; bushy, low growth; no fruit; [Orange Honey × Orange Honey]

Crépuscolo HT, ob, 1955, Aicardi, D.; flowers copper, pointed, dbl.; strong stems; upright growth; [Julien Potin × Sensation]; int. by Giacomasso

Crépuscule N, ab, 1904, Dubreuil; flowers copper orange, fading to apricot-yellow, 8-9 cm., semi-dbl., borne in small clusters, intense sweet, musky fragrance; tall growth

Crescendo F, mp, Noack; int. by Noack's Rosen, 2004

Crescendo HT, rb; flowers bright red, base touched with white, well-formed, large, dbl.; tall growth

Crescent Moon Cl Min, my, 2001, Moe, Mitchie; flowers 1-1½ in., dbl., borne in small clusters, slight fragrance; foliage small, medium green, semi-glossy; growth vigorous, upright, spreading, tall (30-36 in.); garden decoration; [Klima × Blue Peter]; int. by Mitchie's Roses and More, 2002

Cresset Gr, mr, 1961, Francis Hastings; bud long, pointed; flowers scarlet, semi-dbl., high-centered, borne in clusters, moderate fragrance; foliage leathery, glossy, dark; vigorous, bushy growth; [Queen Elizabeth × Cocorico]; int. by F. Mason & Son, 1961

Cressida S, ab, 1992, Austin, David; flowers apricot peach, 3-3½ in., very dbl., borne in small clusters; foliage small, light green, semi-glossy; some prickles; tall (70 in.), upright growth; int. by David Austin Roses, Ltd., 1983

Crested Damask D, mp, 2004, Barden, Paul; flowers medium warm pink, reverse darker pink, 3½ in., very full, borne in small clusters, intense fragrance; late spring bloom; foliage medium size, medium green, semi-glossy, blackspot-resistant; prickles ½ in., curved, brown-red; upright, arching growth, tall (5-7 ft.); specimen; [Marbrée × Crested Jewel]; int. in 2005

Crested Jewel M, mp, 1971, Moore, Ralph S.; bud long, pointed, mossed like Crested Moss; flowers bright rose-pink, medium, semi-dbl., high-centered; foliage leathery; vigorous growth; [Little Darling × Crested Moss]; int. by Sequoia Nursery

Crested Marvel F, dp, Moore; sepals long, fern-like, fluffy, much like those of Chapeau de Napoleon; flowers semi-dbl., borne in dense clusters, moderate fragrance; compact, medium growth; int. by Ludwig's Roses, 2005

Crested Moss C, mp, 1827, Kirche/Roblin/Vibert; very heavily mossed, with 2 pairs of sepals joined and the 3rd separate; flowers rosy pink, medium to large, very full; probably a seedling of *R. centifolia*, rather than a sport; discovered by Kirche in the ruins of an old villa near Fribourg, Switzerland, then sent to Robbin and put in commerce by Vibert

Crested Provence – See **Crested Moss**, C

Crested Provins – See **Crested Moss**, C

Crested Sweetheart LCl, mp, 1988, Moore, Ralph S.; flowers medium rose pink, large, very dbl., cupped, borne in sprays of 3-5, intense damask fragrance; foliage large, medium green, matte, rugose; prickles small, gray to brown; upright, tall growth; [Little Darling × Crested Moss]; int. by Wayside Gardens Co., 1988

Cri-Cri Min, ob, 1959, Meilland, F.; flowers salmon shaded coral, small, dbl.; foliage leathery; dwarf, very bushy growth; [(Alain × Independence) × Perla de Alcañada]; int. by URS, 1958

Cricket Min, ob, 1978, Christensen, Jack E.; bud ovoid; flowers light orange to yellow, 1-1½ in., 25 petals, globular, slight fragrance; foliage dark; upright, bushy growth; PP4663; [Anytime × Katherine Loker]; int. by Armstrong Nursery

Cricket Cl. Cl Min, ob

Cricks – See **Yorkshire Provence**, C

Cricri – See **Cri-Cri**, Min

Crignon de Montigny HGal, dr, before 1842; flowers violet red, medium, full

Crimean Night HT, dr, USSR

Crimean Sweetbrier – See ***R. horrida*** (Fischer)

Crimewatch Rose F, my; int. by World of Roses, 2006

Crimson – See **Tinwell Moss**, M

Crimson Min, dr, Poulsen; int. in 2000

Crimson Beauty HT, dr, 1930, Dingee & Conard; flowers crimson, dbl.; very vigorous growth; [Hoosier Beauty × Crimson Champion]

Crimson Beauty HT, dr, 1935, LeGrice; flowers red,

shaded scarlet and maroon, large, dbl.; foliage leathery; vigorous growth; [Daily Mail Scented Rose × Étoile de Hollande]

Crimson Bedder HP, mr, 1874, Cranston; flowers bright grenadine, large, dbl.

Crimson Bedder HMult, mp, 1896, Cooling; flowers single

Crimson Blush A, dr, Sievers; flowers large, very dbl., moderate fragrance; growth medium

Crimson Bouquet Gr, dr, 1999, Kordes; flowers dark garnet red, reverse shiny dark red, good substance, 4-4½ in., 20-25 petals, high-centered, borne in large clusters, slight sweet fragrance; foliage large, dark green, glossy; prickles large; upright, medium (4½ ft.) growth; PP12001; [Bad Füssing × Ingrid Bergman]; int. by Bear Creek Gardens, Inc., 2000

Crimson Boursault – See **Amadis**, Bslt

Crimson Brocade HT, dr, 1962, Robinson, H.; flowers bright scarlet-crimson, large, high-centered; strong stems; vigorous growth

Crimson Cascade LCl, dr, Fryer, Gareth; flowers medium size, dark red, dbl., high-centered, borne in clusters; recurrent bloom; dense, glossy foliage; vigorous growth, 8 ft; int. in 1991

Crimson Champion HT, dr, 1916, Cook, J.W.; flowers velvety crimson-red, dbl.; dwarf growth; [Étoile de France × seedling]

Crimson Chatenay HT, dr, 1915, Merryweather; [Mme Abel Chatenay × Leuchtfeuer]

Crimson China Rose – See **Slater's Crimson China**, Ch

Crimson-Coloured Provins Rose – See **Cramoisie**, HGal

Crimson Conquest HWich, dr, 1931, Chaplin Bros.; flowers scarlet crimson, 2½ in., semi-dbl., borne in small clusters, moderate fruity fragrance; foliage large, glossy; vigorous growth; [sport of Red-Letter Day]

Crimson Crown HT, mr, 1905, Dickson, A.; flowers red, middle yellowish-white, medium, semi-dbl.

Crimson Damask D, dr, 1901, Turner; flowers crimson, semi-dbl.

Crimson Dawn F, rb, 1970, Ellick; flowers crimson to carmine, 3½-4½ in., 20 petals; foliage dark; vigorous growth; [(Anne Poulsen × Dainty Maid) × (Bonn × Opera)]

Crimson Delight S, mr, 1992, Hoy, Lowel L.; flowers 2½ in., dbl., borne in sprays of 3-4; foliage medium size, medium green, semi-glossy; upright, bushy, low growth; [Volare × seedling]; int. by DeVor Nurseries, Inc.

Crimson Descant LCl, mr, 1972, Cants of Colchester, Ltd.; flowers crimson, 5 in., 30 petals, borne singly and in small clusters; foliage dark green, glossy; [Dortmund × Etendard]

Crimson Diamond HT, dr, 1947, Lammerts, Dr. Walter; bud long, pointed; flowers crimson-red, open, large, 35-40 petals; bushy growth; [Crimson Glory × Charlotte Armstrong]; int. by L.C. Lovett

Crimson Duke HT, mr, 1963, Meilland, Alain A.; bud ovoid; flowers crimson, 4-5 in., 45-55 petals, high-centered, moderate fragrance; foliage leathery, dark; vigorous, upright, bushy growth; PP2348; [(Happiness × Independence) × Peace]; int. by C-P, 1963

Crimson Elegance HT, dr, 1990, Leon, Charles F., Sr.; bud rounded; flowers crimson/scarlet, crimson reverse, aging darker red, 40 petals, high-centered, borne usually singly; foliage medium size, medium green, semi-glossy; upright, bushy, tall growth; [Big Red × Swarthmore]; int. by Oregon Grown Roses, 1990

Crimson Emblem HT, dr, 1916, McGredy; flowers brilliant crimson-scarlet, large, dbl., cupped; vigorous growth

Crimson Erecta HT, 1954, Cazzaniga, F. G.

Crimson Fire S, mr; flowers bright red with bright yellow center, single, flat; free-flowering; foliage glossy, medium green; mounding growth to 3 ft.; hips bright orange-red; int. by Stark Bros, 2005

Crimson Floorshow S, dr, Harkness; flowers bright crimson, opening to show golden stamens, 2¾ in., dbl.; foliage leathery, dark green; mounding, spreading growth (2½ × 4 ft.); int. in 1999

Crimson Fragrance HT, dr, 1980, Wright, R. & Sons; bud long, slender; flowers 38 petals, borne singly, intense fragrance; foliage slender, mid-green; prickles reddish-bronze; branching, upright growth; [Fragrant Cloud × seedling]

Crimson Gem Min, dr, 1974, deRuiter; bud ovoid; flowers deep red, medium, very dbl., cupped; foliage bronze, soft; vigorous, bushy growth; [Lillan × Polyantha seedling]; int. by C-P

Crimson Globe – See **Dr Rocques**, B

Crimson Globe M, dr, 1890, Paul, W.; flowers deep crimson, large, dbl., globular; vigorous growth

Crimson Glory HT, dr, 1935, Kordes; bud long, pointed; flowers deep velvety crimson, 5 in., 30-35 petals, cupped, borne mostly singly, intense damask fragrance; foliage leathery; vigorous, bushy, spreading growth; [Cathrine Kordes × W.E. Chaplin]; int. by Dreer; James Alexander Gamble Fragrance Medal, ARS, 1961, Gold Medal, NRS, 1936

Crimson Glory, Climbing Cl HT, dr, 1942, Millar (also Richardson, 1944, J&P, 1946); flowers richer crimson than bush form, 10-12 cm., intense fragrance; int. by Millar Bros, 1941

Crimson Glow HWich, mr, 1930, Chaplin; flowers glowing carmine, semi-dbl.; [Paul's Scarlet Climber × American Pillar]

Crimson Glow Pol, dr, 1945, Lammetts; flowers oxblood-red, semi-dbl., cupped; foliage glossy, dark; vigorous, upright growth; [Night × Mrs Dudley Fulton]; int. by Univ. of Calif.

Crimson Glow – See **Our Princess**, F

Crimson Grandiflora HMult, mr, 1912, Ghys; flowers purple red, 6 cm., full, borne in large clusters; very late spring bloom

Crimson Halo HT, dr, 1964, Park; flowers deep rose-red, 5 in., 30 petals, globular; vigorous growth; [Karl Herbst × Crimson Glory]; int. by Harkness

Crimson King HT, dr, 1943, Kordes; bud ovoid, long, pointed; flowers deep velvety crimson, large, dbl., high-centered, intense damask fragrance; foliage leathery; vigorous, bushy growth; [Crimson Glory × Kardinal]; int. by C-P

Crimson Knight S, mr, Williams, J.B.; flowers crimson, borne in masses, moderate fragrance; int. by Hortico, 1997

Crimson Knight Mega Brite Min, dr, Walden; PP11158; int. by Bear Creek Gardens, 1999

Crimson Lace F, dr, 1998, Zary, Dr. Keith W.; flowers dark red, old-fashioned, 3-3½ in., dbl., borne in small clusters, slight fragrance; foliage medium size, dark green, glossy; prickles moderate; compact, medium growth; PP10284; [Esprit × Razzle Dazzle]; int. by Bear Creek Gardens, Inc., 1997

Crimson Mme Desprez B, dr; flowers crimson, large, cupped

Crimson Masse – See **Liberté**, F

Crimson Medinette Min, dr, 1985, Olesen, Pernille & Mogens; flowers small, 33 petals, borne in clusters of 3-5, no fragrance; foliage small, leathery; prickles straight brown; dense growth; [seedling × Pygmae]; int. by Ludwigs Roses Pty. Ltd., 1984

Crimson Meidiland – See **Crimson Meillandecor**, S

Crimson Meillandecor S, dr; flowers luminous red, dbl., borne in small clusters; growth to 90-120 cm.; int. by Meilland, 1996

Crimson Minijet Min, dr, Meilland; int. by Australian Roses

Crimson Minuetto Min, dr, 2000, Meilland International; flowers very full, borne in small clusters, no fragrance; foliage medium size, dark green, matte; prickles moderate; growth compact, medium (8-12 in.); int. by Conard-Pyle Co., 1999

Crimson Moos – See **Tinwell Moss**, M

Crimson Moss – See **Tinwell Moss**, M

Crimson Orléans Pol, dr, 1922, Koster, M. (also Laxton, 1923); [sport of Orléans Rose]

Crimson Pillar LCl, rb, 2003, Meilland International; flowers medium red, reverse white, 4 in., dbl., borne in small clusters, no fragrance; foliage dark green, semi-glossy; numerous prickles; growth climbing, tall (to 10 ft.); hardy to 0°F; PPAF; int. by The Conard-Pyle Company, 2003

Crimson Promise Min, dr, 1994, Sproul, James A.; flowers antique, smoky dark red, 1¼-1¾ in., full, borne mostly singly, no fragrance; foliage medium size, dark green, semi-glossy, disease-resistant; few prickles; medium (20 in.), bushy growth; [Avandel × Chrysler Imperial]

Crimson Queen HP, dr, 1890, Paul; flowers velvety crimson, shaded with fiery red and maroon, very large, globular

Crimson Queen HT, dr, 1912, Montgomery, A.; flowers rich crimson, turning blue with age, very large, dbl., globular; vigorous growth; [(Liberty × Richmond) × Gen. MacArthur]

Crimson Rambler HMult, mr, 1893, Turner; flowers bright crimson, fading toward blue, 3½-4 cm., semi-dbl. to dbl., borne in pyramidal corymbs, no fragrance; heavy, non-recurrent bloom; foliage light, leathery, glossy, disposed to mildew; very vigorous, climbing (15-24 ft.) growth; int. by Turner, 1893

Crimson Rambler Remontant – See **Flower of Fairfield**, HMult

Crimson Rosamini Min, mr

Crimson Rosette F, dr, 1948, Krebs; bud small, ovoid; flowers dark crimson, rosette, 1-1½ in., 30 petals, borne in clusters; foliage leathery, dark; vigorous, bushy, dwarf growth; int. by H&S

Crimson Shower HWich, mr, 1951, Norman; flowers clear crimson, lighter reverse, 1¼ in., 20 petals, pompon, borne in loose clusters; foliage small, dark green, glossy; vigorous (10 ft.) growth; [Excelsa × unknown]; int. by Harkness

Crimson Spire – See **Liebeszauber**, HT, 2006

Crimson Star Min, rb, 2000, Denton, J.A.; flowers crimson red, reverse golden yellow, 4-6 cm., full, high-centered, borne in small clusters; foliage medium size, medium green, semi-glossy; few prickles; growth upright, medium (16-20 in.); exhibition; [(June Laver × (Rubies 'n' Pearls × unknown)) × Glowing Amber]

Crimson Superb – See **Mogador**, P

Crimson Tide HT, mr, 1983, McGredy, Sam IV; flowers crimson, large, 35 petals, high-centered, borne singly; foliage large, dark, leathery; upright growth; [seedling × seedling]; int. by Roses by Fred Edmunds

Crimson Velvet F, dr; flowers medium, single

Crimson Volunteer S, dr, Williams, J.B.; flowers velvet red, borne mostly one to a stem; int. by Hortico, 2002

Crimson Wave F, mr, 1972, Meilland; flowers cardinal-red, shaded cherry, 4-5 in., 25-30 petals, slight apple fragrance; foliage large, semi-matte, dark; vigorous, upright growth; [Zambra × (Sarabande × (Goldilocks × Fashion))]; int. by L. Dol

Crinkles Min, w, 1990, Frock, Marshall J.; bud ovoid;

flowers white, aging with flecks of red, slow to fade, crinkled center, 60 petals, high-centered, slight fragrance; foliage medium size, dark green, semi-glossy; prickles straight, short, red; upright, bushy, medium growth; fruit not observed; [Rise 'n' Shine × seedling]

Crinoline LCl, or, 1967, Hémeray-Aubert; flowers semi-dbl., cupped; recurrent bloom; foliage bronze; vigorous, climbing growth; [Diane d'Urfe × Étendard]

Criollo F, dp, Noack; int. by Noack's Rosen, 2005

Crispata HRg, lp, 1902, Kiese; flowers light carmine, single

Crispé Mousseux – See **Crested Moss**, C

Crispin-Morwenna Min, or, 1980, Harkness, R., & Co., Ltd.; flowers salmon-red, small, 25 petals, cupped, borne 3-7 per cluster, slight spicy fragrance; foliage small, dark, glossy; prickles reddish; low, spreading growth; [(Vera Dalton × (Chanelle × Piccadilly)) × Little Buckaroo]

Crissy Min, ob, 1979, Strawn; bud pointed; flowers deep bright coral, 1½-2 in., 20-25 petals, slight fragrance; foliage dark; PP4638; [Liverpool Echo × Sheri Anne]; int. by Pixie Treasures Min. Roses

Cristal HT, ob, 1937, Gaujard; bud long, pointed; flowers orange-yellow, large, dbl.; foliage leathery, light; vigorous, bushy growth; [Julien Potin × seedling]

Cristata – See **Crested Moss**, C

Cristel Palace – See **Crystal**, F

Cristian F, m, (METset)

Cristin Cira Gr, op, 1996, Vanderkruk, William; flowers orange, yellow, salmon blend, dbl., borne in small clusters, slight fragrance; foliage large, medium green, semi-glossy; some prickles; upright, medium growth; int. by Hortico Roses, 1995

Cristina HT, Zandri, R.; int. in 1972

Cristina Vidal F, my, Vidal

Cristobal Colon – See **Christopher Columbus**, HT

Cristoforo Colombo HT, yb, 1953, Aicardi, D.; bud long; flowers reddish-yellow, reverse tinged pink, large, 25-35 petals; foliage glossy; long stems; very vigorous growth; RULED EXTINCT 4/92; [Julien Potin × Frau Karl Druschki]; int. by V. Asseretto

Cristoforo Colombo – See **Christopher Columbus**, HT

Criterion HT, dp, 1966, deRuiter; flowers rose-red, 5 in., dbl., high-centered, moderate fragrance; recurrent; foliage dark; vigorous, tall growth; [(Independence × Signal Red) × Peace]

Criterion, Cl. Cl HT, mr, Gressard; int. in 1978

Crock O' Gold HT, my, 1970, Anderson's Rose Nurseries; flowers clear golden yellow, 4½ in., 30-35 petals, high-centered; [sport of Beauté]

Crocus Rose S, w, 2001, Austin, David; flowers very full, borne in small clusters, moderate fragrance; foliage medium size, medium green, semi-glossy, disease-resistant; prickles medium, slightly hooked downward, moderate; growth bushy, medium (1¼ m.); garden decorative; PP14092; [seedling × Golden Celebration]; int. by David Austin Roses, Ltd., 2000

Croft Original HT, RB, 1972, Cocker; flowers old-gold and red, 5 in., 30 petals, moderate fragrance; foliage light; int. by Wheatcroft Bros.

Croix Blanche HT, w, Croix, P.; flowers dbl., borne singly and in small clusters; int. in 1984

Croix d'Honneur HGal, mr, about 1830, Prévost; flowers bright red, small, full

Croix d'Honneur HCh, w, 1852, Dorisy; flowers flesh white, reverse pink, large, dbl.

Croix d'Or HT, my, Croix; flowers golden yellow, 4 in.; int. in 1985

Croix d'Or, Climbing Cl HT, my, Croix, P.

Croix Mauve S, m, Croix, P.; int. by Croix, 2004

Croix Verte – See **Rose Verte**, HT

Cromwell School Misc OGR, rb

Crowd Pleaser HT, dp, 2000, Greenwood, Chris; flowers cerise pink, brushed with cream on reverse, 9-11 cm., 25-30 petals, high-centered, borne mostly singly; upright, tall growth; PP14138; [sport of Lynn Anderson]; int. by Weeks Roses, 2001

Crown – See **Louis-Philippe**, Ch

Crown Jewel F, or, 1965, Boerner; flowers bright orange-red, medium, dbl., borne in clusters, moderate fragrance; foliage dark, leathery; moderate growth; PP2590; [Pink Bountiful × Spartan]; int. by J&P

Crown of Gold HT, yb, 1937, Duehrsen; bud pointed; flowers deep gold, edged lemon-yellow, large, dbl., high-centered; foliage light green, leathery, vigorous growth; [seedling × Joanna Hill]; int. by H&S

Crown of Jewels – See **Little Beauty**, F

Crown Prince HP, rb, 1880, Paul & Son; flowers reddish-crimson tinged with purple; [Duke of Edinburgh × unknown]

Crown Princess Margareta S, ab, 2000, Austin, David; flowers bright apricot orange, 3 in., very dbl., cupped, borne in small clusters, intense fruity fragrance; foliage medium size, bronze when young, semi-glossy; almost thornless; strong, arching growth to 1½ m.; PP13484; [seedling (apricot English shrub) × Abraham Darby]; int. by David Austin Roses, Ltd., 1999

Crown Princess Mary HT, w, 2006, Thomson, George L.; flowers varying from ivory and cream to light pink, reverse cream, 7-10 cm., very full, borne in small clusters; foliage medium size, glossy; prickles small, hooked, brown, few; growth bushy, (1¼-1½ m.); garden decorative; [(The Wild One × Frances Phoebe) × Ophelia]; int. by Ross Roses

Crowning Glory S, rb, 2001, Dickson, Colin; flowers red with yellow center, 4-5 cm., dbl., borne in large clusters, slight fragrance; foliage medium size, medium green, semy-glossy; prickles medium, few; growth spreading, tall (115 × 140 cm.), vigorous; garden decorative; [Duchess of York × New Penny]; int. by Dickson Nurseries Ltd., 2001

Crucenia – See **Hot Pewter**, HT

Crumble Bar F, ab, LeGrice; flowers in shades of copper, apricot and old gold, medium size, 50-60 petals, borne in clusters; moderate rebloom; relatively low growth; int. in 1982

Crusader HT, dr, 1920, Montgomery Co.; flowers crimson-red, center brighter, large, 65 petals; foliage leathery, rich green; vigorous growth; int. by A.N. Pierson

Crystal Min, pb, 1985, Bridges, Dennis A.; flowers light pink, deep pink reverse, small, 35 petals, high-centered; foliage large, dark, glossy; bushy growth; [Zinger × seedling]; int. by Bridges Roses

Crystal F, lp, Poulsen Roser APS; flowers creamy pink, 8-10 cm., dbl., slight wild rose fragrance; foliage dark; growth bushy, 40-60 cm.; int. by Poulsen Roser, 1996

Crystal Brook HWich, pb, Sutherland; flowers single; int. in 1994

Crystal Fairy Pol, w, Spek; flowers snowy with touches of soft pink blush; low, spreading growth; PPAF; int. by J&P, 2001

Crystal Lavender – See **Lavender Crystal**, Min

Crystal Palace – See **Crystal**, F

Crystal River Gr, ly, 2006, Castillo, Angel; flowers dbl., borne in small clusters; foliage large, dark green, glossy, disease-resistant; prickles medium, straight, moderate; growth upright, tall (48 in.); garden decorative; exhibition; [red blend HT seedling × Golden Unicorn]; int. by Angel Roses, 2007

Crystal Star Min, w, 1994, Muha, Julius; flowers medium, full, borne mostly singly and in small clusters, slight fragrance; foliage small, medium green, semi-glossy; some prickles; medium growth; [Pink Petticoat × Tooth of Time]; int. by Mori Miniature Roses, 1994

Crystal White HT, w, 1965, Boerner; flowers clear white, large, dbl., high-centered, moderate fragrance; foliage leathery; moderate, bushy growth; PP2553; [Princess White × White Queen]; int. by J&P

Crystalline HT, w, 1987, Christensen, Jack & Carruth, Tom; bud medium, pointed ovoid; flowers pure white, 5-5½ in., 30-35 petals, high-centered, cupped, borne usually singly, some small clusters, moderate spicy or sweet tea fragrance; recurrent; foliage medium size, medium green, semi-glossy; prickles normal, long, hooked downward, light green-tan; upright, bushy, tall growth; hips globose, large, orange; PP6714; [Bridal Pink × (Blue Nile × (Ivory Tower × Angel Face))]; int. by Armstrong Nursery, 1986

Crystal's Double Dark Red HT, dr

Csárdás F, op, Berger, W.; flowers luminous orange-pink, large, dbl.; int. in 1965

Csl Cerveny Kriz Pol, mr, 1928, Böhm, J.; flowers small, dbl.

Csl Legie Cl HT, dr, 1933, Böhm, J.; flowers dark scarlet, dbl.

Cuba HT, rb, 1926, Pernet-Ducher; flowers cardinal-red, tinted yellow, fading quickly, large, semi-dbl., globular, intense fragrance; foliage dark, bronze; very vigorous growth

Cubana S, ab, 2006; flowers apricot fading to pink, 5 cm., dbl., borne in small clusters; foliage small, glossy; growth spreading, short (50 cm.); int. by W. Kordes' Söhne, 2001

Cuddle Up Min, yb, 1991, Bennett, Dee; bud ovoid; flowers creamy yellow with coral pink blush, medium, 25-30 petals, high-centered, moderate fruity fragrance; foliage medium size, medium green, semi-glossy; bushy, medium growth; [Lagerfeld × My Delight]; int. by Tiny Petals Nursery, 1990

Cuddles Min, op, 1978, Schwartz, Ernest W.; bud ovoid; flowers deep coral-pink, 1-1½ in., 55-60 petals, high-centered, slight fragrance; compact growth; PP4291; [Zorina × seedling]; int. by Nor'East Min. Roses; AOE, ARS, 1979

Cuisse de Nymphe – See **Great Maiden's Blush**, A

Cuisse de Nymphe à Ovaire Lisse – See **Maiden's Blush**, A

Cuisse de Nymphe Émue – See **Maiden's Blush**, A

Cuisse de Nymphe Grande – See **Great Maiden's Blush**, A

Cuivré – See ***R. foetida bicolor*** ((Jacquin) Willmott)

Culverbrae S, dr, 1972, Gobbee, W.D.; flowers crimson-purple, 3½-4 in., 58 petals, intense fragrance; some repeat bloom; foliage light; vigorous growth; [Scabrosa × Francine]

Cumba Meillandina Min, ob, 1994, Meilland, Alain A.; flowers large, very dbl., borne in small clusters; foliage large, medium green, semi-glossy; some prickles; medium, bushy growth; [Orange Honey × (Darling Flame × Tapis Jaune)]; int. by SNC Meilland & Cie, 1992

Cumba Meillandina, Climbing Cl Min, ob, Meilland; int. in 2003

Cumbaya S, pb, Meilland; flowers pink with white eye, yellow stamens, medium, single, borne in large clusters; growth low, spreading (50 cm.); int. by Meilland Richardier, 2000

Cumbaya HT, r, Meilland; flowers dusty orange-red with tan at base of petals, dbl., high-centered, borne mostly singly; recurrent; int. by Meilland Intl., 2005

Cumberland – See **Rubra**, C

Cumberland Belle Cl M, lp, 1900, Dreer; flowers silvery pink, well mossed, small, very dbl.; [sport of Princesse Adélaide]

Cunningham Lady Banks S, ly, 1900
Cunningham West Climber N, ly, 1900
Cup Final HT, or, 1988, McGredy, Sam IV; flowers large, dbl., slight fragrance; foliage medium size, medium green, semi-glossy; upright growth; [Benson & Hedges Gold × (Kalahari × Papa Meilland)]; int. by McGredy Roses International, 1988
Cup of Joy HT, mp, 2006, Newman, Laurie; flowers soft pink, 4 in., full, borne mostly solitary; foliage medium green, semi-glossy; prickles small, moderate; growth upright, medium; [China Sunrise × Vol de Nuit]; int. by Reliable Roses, 2007
Cupcake Min, mp, 1981, Spies, Mark C.; bud ovoid; flowers clear medium pink, long lasting, 60 petals, high-centered, borne 1-5 per cluster, no fragrance; foliage glossy; no prickles; compact, bushy growth; PP4835; [Gene Boerner × (Gay Princess × Yellow Jewel)]; int. by Nor'East Min. Roses; AOE, ARS, 1983
Cupid Cl HT, lp, 1915, Cant, B. R.; flowers glowing flesh, tinted peach, 4-5 in., single, borne in small clusters, moderate fragrance; non-recurrent; foliage large, light green; vigorous, pillar growth; hips large, orange, pear-shaped
Cupido Min, lp, Maarse, G.; flowers shell-pink; growth to 6 in.
Cupidon F, dr, 1966, Gaujard; flowers brilliant crimson, small, semi-dbl., cupped; foliage leathery; vigorous, bushy growth; [Chanteclerc × Red Favorite]
Cupid's Beauty Min, ob, 1979, Williams, Ernest D.; bud long, pointed; flowers light orange and cream, 1½ in., 40-45 petals, high-centered, moderate fragrance; foliage small, dark; compact, spreading growth; PP4581; [seedling × Over the Rainbow]; int. by Mini-Roses, 1978
Cupid's Charm F, pb, 1964, Fuller; bud pointed; flowers salmon-pink, medium, 22 petals; vigorous, bushy growth; [Little Darling × First Love.]; int. by Wyant
Cupid's Heart HT, rb; int. in 1997
Cupid's Mark Min, pb; int. by Ashdown Roses, 2005
Cupie Doll Min, lp, 1983, Bennett, Dee; flowers light pink with fine coral edging on petals, heavy substance, 25 petals, high-centered, slight fragrance; foliage small, medium green, semi-glossy; upright, bushy growth; [seedling × Coral Treasure]; int. by Tiny Petals Nursery
Curé de Charentay HP, dr, 1867, Ducher; flowers dark garnet purple, very large, full
Curiace T, yb, 1860, Bernède; flowers yellowish-white, edged pink, medium, full
Curiosa – See **My Girl**, F
Curiosa, Climbing F, op
Curiosity HT, rb, 1972, Cocker; flowers scarlet, reverse gold, 4 in., 35 petals, cupped; foliage variegated, green and white; [sport of Cleopatra]
Curiosity, Climbing – See **Best Wishes, Climbing**, Cl HT
Curly Locks Min, lp, 1954, Robinson, T.; flowers soft pink; dwarf, compact growth
Curly Pink HT, mp, 1948, Brownell; bud long, pointed, rose-red; flowers 3½-5 in., dbl., moderate fragrance; foliage glossy, dark; vigorous, compact growth; [Pink Princess × Crimson Glory]
Current Affair Min, dr, 1991, Gruenbauer, Richard; flowers red, reverse red with yellow, ages dark pink, medium, 80 petals, cupped, no fragrance; foliage medium size, dark green, semi-glossy; upright, medium growth; [Red Ace × seedling]; int. by Flowers 'n' Friends Miniature Roses, 1993
Curtain Call HT, dp, 1978, Weeks; bud pointed; flowers cherry-red, 4-5 in., 32-35 petals, high-centered, slight fragrance; foliage dark, leathery; vigorous, growth; PP4282; [First Prize × seedling]; int. by Weeks Roses
Curtis Yellow HT, my, 1974, Curtis, E.C.; flowers clear yellow, large, dbl., high-centered, moderate fragrance; foliage light, leathery; vigorous, upright growth; [Golden Scepter × Miss Hillcrest]; int. by Kimbrew, 1973
Cuthbert Grant S, dr, 1967, Marshall, H.H.; bud ovoid; flowers deep purplish red, large, semi-dbl., cupped, slight fragrance; intermittent bloom; foliage glossy; vigorous, bushy growth; [(Crimson Glory × Assiniboine) × Assiniboine]; originally registered as hybrid suffulta; int. by Canada Dept. of Agriculture
Cutie Min, mp, 1952, Moore, Ralph S.; bud pointed; flowers clear pink, base white, 1 in., 16 petals, flat, slight fragrance; foliage small, glossy, bright green; prickles very few; dwarf (10 in.), bushy growth; PP1302; [Dancing Doll × Oakington Ruby]; int. by Sequoia Nursery
Cutie Min, w, Tantau; int. by Pocock's Roses, 2006
Cutie Pie Min, ly, 1989, Rennie, Bruce F.; bud ovoid; flowers light to medium yellow, small, 23 petals, high-centered, borne usually singly and in small clusters, moderate fruity fragrance; foliage small, dark green, glossy; prickles straight, small, yellow-red; bushy, low growth; hips globular, very small, yellow-orange; [Tangerine Mist × California Girl]; int. by Rennie Roses International, 1989
Cuwaert HT, Delforge, H.; int. in 1992
Cuyahoga – See **Berleburg**, F
Cybele HT, Hauser, V.; int. in 1962
Cybelle S, m, Guillot-Massad; flowers bright reddish-purple, full, cupped, borne in clusters of 3-5; dark, glossy foliage; growth to 4 ft.; int. by Roseraies Guillot, 2000
Cyclamen F, mp, 1959, Delbard-Chabert; bud long; flowers 3 in., semi-dbl., borne in sprays of 4-6; vigorous, bushy growth; [((Frau Karl Druschki × unknown) × (Orange Triumph × Unknown)) × ((Orange Triumph × unknown) × Tonnerre)]
Cyclamen – See **Cyclamen La Sevillana**, F
Cyclamen La Sevillana F, pb, Orard; int. in 1992
Cyclamen Meillandecor – See **Fuchsia Meidiland**, S
Cyclope Pol, m, 1909, Dubreuil; flowers velvety carmine purple, lined white, with pale yellow stamens, borne in clusters of 10-20; [Mme Norbert Levavasseur × unknown]
Cygne Blanc – See **White Swan**, HT
Cygne Noir HT, dr
Cymbaefolia A, w, 1807, Flobert/Pelletier; flowers matte white, small, semi-dbl. to dbl., borne in clusters; foliage whitish and cottony beneath, simple, elongate; nearly thornless; possibly synonymous with À Feuilles de Pêcher
Cymbaline S, lp, 1983, Austin, David; flowers medium, dbl.; foliage medium size, medium green, semi-glossy; spreading growth; [seedling × Lilian Austin]; int. by David Austin Roses, Ltd., 1982
Cymbeline – See **Cymbaline**, S
Cynosbatos – See ***R. canina*** (Linnaeus)
Cynosure HT, rb, 1978, Hardikar, Dr. M.N.; bud ovoid; flowers red, striped pink, 4½ in., 50 petals, intense fragrance; foliage glossy, soft; vigorous, upright growth; [Scarlet Knight × Festival Beauty]; int. in 1973
Cynthia HT, mr, 1934, Verschuren-Pechtold; flowers rich oriental red, dbl.; int. by H&S
Cynthia HT, dp, 1976, Warriner, William A.; bud long; flowers deep pink, 5 in., 35 petals, high-centered, moderate fragrance; foliage large, matte, light; tall, upright growth; PP3838; [seedling × Bob Hope]; int. by J&P
Cynthia Ann Parker HT, w, 1929, Vestal; flowers white tinged yellow or cream, dbl.
Cynthia Brooke HT, yb, 1943, McGredy; flowers empire yellow, reverse light salmon, 4 in., 45 petals, globular, moderate fruity fragrance; foliage leathery, dark; moderate, compact, bushy growth; [Le Progres × (Mme Mélanie Soupert × Le Progres)]; int. by J&P
Cynthia E. Hollis HMult, lp, Dawson; flowers pale pink, dbl.; foliage small, glossy; int. by Eastern Nursery
Cynthia Forde – See **Miss Cynthia Forde**, HT
Cynthia Westcott F, mp, Williams, J. Benjamin; flowers medium pink fading to ivory pink, 4 in., moderate fragrance; growth to 3 ft.; int. in 1997
Cynthie I HGal, lp, before 1820, Descemet, M.; flowers pale rose, circumference almost blush, large, dbl., cupped; erect, moderate growth
Cynthie II HGal, m, before 1820, Descemet/Vibert; flowers lilac-garnet, aging to purple-violet, reverse creamy white, large, full, cupped
Cyprienne Pol, mr, 1969, Delforge; bud ovoid; flowers light brilliant red, large, dbl.; abundant, continuous bloom; foliage glossy, light; moderate, bushy growth; [Sumatra × Fashion]
Cypris – See **Blush Boursault**, Bslt
Cyrano HT, rb, 1954, Gaujard; flowers bright red shaded purple, large, dbl.; long stems; very vigorous, upright growth; [(Opera × seedling) × seedling]
Cyril Fletcher HT, w, 1983, Bees; flowers creamy white, large, 35 petals, cabbage-like; foliage medium size, dark, semi-glossy; upright, bushy growth; [Fragrant Cloud × Whisky Mac]
Cyril Gully HT, lp, 2002, Poole, Lionel; flowers full, high-centered, borne mostly solitary, slight fragrance; foliage medium size, medium green, semi-glossy; prickles medium, slightly hooked, moderate; growth upright, bushy, vigorous, medium (1 m.); garden, exhibition; [(Hazel Rose × Cardiff Bay) × New Zealand]; int. by David Lister Roses, 2003
Cystic Fibrosis – See **65 Roses**, S
Czardas HT, rb, 1956, Delforge; flowers red, becoming pink; vigorous growth; [Tango × seedling]

D. Ana Guedes HT, ob, 1938, Moreira da Silva; bud ovoid; flowers orange and salmon-pink, veined yellow, large, dbl., cupped; foliage soft; vigorous, bushy growth; [Angèle Pernet × Mme Méha Sabatier]

D. Angelica Pereira da Rosa HT, pb, 1936, Moreira da Silva; flowers pink, shaded golden orange, reverse red, open, very large, dbl.; foliage light; [Angèle Pernet × Edith Nellie Perkins]

D. D. Ruaux HT, ob, Dorieux; int. in 1998

D. H. Lawrence HT, yb, 1985, McCarthy, Mrs. Rosemary; [sport of Gay Gordons]; int. by Rosemary Roses

D. Laura Pinto d'Azevedo HT, pb, 1936, Moreira da Silva; flowers shrimp-pink, center coral-red, base orange-yellow, very large, dbl., high-centered; foliage light, soft; [Pink Pearl × Constance]

D. Malvina Loureiro F, Moreira da Silva, A.

D. Maria Antonia Pacheco HT, mp, 1935, Moreira da Silva; flowers deep carmine-pink, well-formed, large, dbl.; foliage rich green, glossy; vigorous growth; [Mme Butterfly × Johanniszauber]

D. Maria do Carmo de Fragoso Carmona HT, pb, 1939, Moreira da Silva; bud long, pointed; flowers flesh-pink, edged yellow, large, dbl., high-centered; foliage glossy; long stems; vigorous growth; [Charles P. Kilham × Souv. de Claudius Pernet]

D. Maria José de Melo HT, op, Moreira da Silva; flowers salmon-pink

D. Maria Navarro HT, rb, 1962, Moreira da Silva; flowers carmine; [First Love × Paramount]

D. Silvia Ferreira HT, ob, Moreira da Silva; flowers salmon and red, reverse old-gold

D. T. Poulsen F, mr, 1930, Poulsen, S.; flowers bright blood-red, open, semi-dbl.; foliage dark, leathery; bushy growth; [Orléans Rose × Vesuvius]

D. T. Poulsen Improved F, mr, 1940, Van der Vis; bud small, globular, blood-red; flowers solid cherry-red, open, 30-35 petals; foliage leathery, wrinkled, dark; short, strong stems; vigorous, compact, bushy growth; int. by C-P

Dab HT, ab, 1985, Bridges, Dennis A.; flowers apricot center, pink reverse, petals tipped deep pink, large, 35 petals, high-centered, no fragrance; foliage large, dark, glossy; bushy growth; [Lady X × Flaming Beauty]; int. by Bridges Roses, 1985

Dacapo F, op, 1961, deRuiter; flowers deep salmon-pink, 3-4 in., 28 petals, borne in clusters, slight fragrance; vigorous, compact, bushy growth; [Fashion × Floribunda seedling]; int. by Horstmann

Dacapo LCl, mr, Olesen; bud pointed ovoid, broad base; flowers medium red, 2 in., 25-30 petals, rosette, borne in large clusters, very slight fragrance; recurrent; foliage dark green, glossy; prickles numerous, 10 mm., hooked downward; bushy (150-200 cm.) growth; PP16502; [Bassino × seedling]; int. by Poulsen Roser, 2004

Daddies Girl HT, yb, 1963, McTeer, Gilbert; flowers milky white flushed pink, base golden, 5-6 in., 40 petals; foliage dark; vigorous, spreading growth; [McGredy's Ivory × Peace]

Daddy Anstey HT, dy, 2005, Rawlins, R.; flowers deep yellow, reverse blend of yellow and orange pink, 11 cm., full, borne mostly solitary, slight fragrance; foliage medium size, dark green, glossy; upright, tall (110 cm.) growth; [Solitaire × (Baby Love × Tequila Sunrise)]

Daddy's Girls F, ab; flowers orangey-apricot, full; int. by Roses Unlimited, 2006

Daddy's Pink A, lp

Dady F, mp, 1978, Gaujard; [Mignonne × seedling]; int. in 1975

Dafne S, pb, Barni, V.; int. in 1995

Dagenham Show F, ob, 1976, Warley Rose Gardens; flowers salmon-orange, large, 25 petals; foliage matte; bushy growth; [Elizabeth of Glamis × seedling]

Dagmar F, mr, Urban, J.

Dagmar Hastrup HRg, lp, 1914, Hastrup; flowers silvery pink, 5 petals; foliage crinkled, rich green; low growth; [*R. rugosa* × unknown]; int. in about 1914

Dagmar Späth F, w, 1936, Wirtz & Eicke; flowers white, edge flushed pink, fading pure white; [sport of Lafayette]; int. by Spath

Dagmar Späth, Climbing Cl F, w, 1940, Buisman, G. A. H.; also Howard Rose Co., 1943, Huber, 1961

D'Aguesseau HGal, mr, 1836, Parmentier or Vibert; flowers crimson at center, shaded purple-mauve on the edges, aging to violet, with a small center button, small, dbl., flat, borne singly or in clusters of 2-3, moderate fragrance; foliage thick, medium green; few prickles; compact, erect growth

Dahlila F, yb, 1962, Leenders, J.; flowers yellow, becoming red; [Golden Perfume × Peace]

Daichi Mao HT, mp, Teranishi; int. by Itami Rose Garden, 2004

Daidala F, m, 1976, Kordes; bud ovoid; flowers 4 in., 35 petals, high-centered, slight fragrance; foliage dark, soft; vigorous, upright, bushy growth; [seedling × Silver Star]; int. by Willemse, 1975

Daily Express HT, ab, Fryer, Gareth; int. in 1986

Daily Herald HT, yb, 1942, Robinson, T.; bud pointed; flowers yellowish-orange, 4-5 in., dbl., cupped; foliage glossy, dark; vigorous, upright growth; int. by J&P

Daily Mail Rose – See **Mme Édouard Herriot**, HT

Daily Mail Rose, Climbing – See **Mme Édouard Herriot, Climbing**, Cl HT

Daily Mail Scented Rose HT, rb, 1927, Archer; flowers crimson, shaded maroon and vermilion, reverse dark crimson, petals imbricated, intense damask fragrance; [Château de Clos Vougeot × Kitchener of Khartoum]; Cup for Best New Scented Seedling, Daily Mail, 1927

Daily Mail Scented Rose, Climbing Cl HT, rb, 1930, Archer

Daily Post – See **Raven**, S

Daily Sketch F, pb, 1961, McGredy, Sam IV; flowers petals silver, edged deep pink, well-formed, large, 46 petals, borne in clusters, moderate fragrance; foliage dark; vigorous, bushy growth; [Ma Perkins × Grand Gala]; int. by McGredy & Son, 1961; Gold Medal, NRS, 1960

Daily Telegraph – See **Gilda**, F

Daimonji HT, or, 1986, Shibata, T.; flowers large, 48 petals, high-centered, borne usually singly, slight fragrance; foliage medium size, dark; medium, bushy growth; [seedling × (Miss Ireland × Polynesian Sunset)]; int. by K. Hirakata Nursery, 1981

Dainty T, yb, before 1910, Paul; flowers primrose yellow, edged & tipped with carmine, large, borne in clusters

Dainty HT, pb, 1921, Dickson, H.; flowers rosy apricot, tinted cherry-pink, edges and reverse deeper pink, dbl.

Dainty Pol, op, 1931, deRuiter; flowers salmon-pink, cupped

Dainty Bess HT, lp, 1925, Archer; flowers soft rose-pink, very distinct maroon stamens, broad, fimbriated petals, 5 in., single, borne in clusters of 5-9, moderate tea fragrance; foliage leathery, dark green; vigorous growth; [Ophelia × Kitchener of Khartoum]; Gold Medal, NRS, 1925

Dainty Bess, Climbing Cl HT, lp, 1935, van Barneveld; flowers pale lilac pink, darker reverse, prominent maroon stamens, large, single; [sport of Dainty Bell]; int. by California Roses

Dainty Bouquet Min, mp, 1994, Laver, Keith G.; flowers clear pink, medium, very dbl., borne mostly singly, slight fragrance; foliage medium size, medium green, semi-glossy; some prickles; medium (20 cm.), upright, spreading growth; [seedling × Pink Bouquet]; int. by Springwood Roses, 1994

Dainty Dawn Pol, mp, 1931, Knight, G.; flowers cerise-pink to mauve, semi-dbl., cupped, borne in clusters; foliage bronze; [Amaury Fonseca × Annchen Müller]

Dainty Delight Cl HT, mp, 1949, Duehrsen; bud ovoid; flowers darker pink than Dainty Bess, medium, semi-dbl., globular, borne in clusters; foliage glossy; vigorous (6-8 ft.) growth; [Ednah Thomas × Dainty Bess]; int. by California Roses

Dainty Dinah Min, op, 1982, Cocker, James; flowers medium salmon-pink, patio, small, semi-dbl., slight fragrance; foliage small, medium green, semi-glossy; bushy growth; [Anne Cocker × Wee Man]; int. by Cocker & Sons, 1981

Dainty Double Pink Cushion Rose – See **The Fairy**, Pol

Dainty Lady HT, mp, 1959, Peden, G.H.; bud long, pointed; flowers pink, medium, dbl., high-centered; foliage leathery; vigorous, upright, compact growth; [(Girona × Pres. Herbert Hoover) × Michèle Meilland]

Dainty Lady F, op, 1963, Fryers Nursery, Ltd.; flowers coppery salmon-pink, well-formed, borne in clusters; moderate growth; [Baby Sylvia × seedling]

Dainty Maid F, pb, 1940, LeGrice; bud pointed, cerise; flowers silvery pink, reverse carmine, single, borne in clusters; foliage leathery, dark; vigorous, compact, bushy growth; [D.T. Poulsen × seedling]; int. by C-P; Gold Medal, Portland, 1941

Dainty Star F, mr, 1973, Khanna, K. R., & Lata, P.; buds medium, pointed; flowers light crimson, medium, semi-dbl., open, borne mostly singly; foliage medium size, dark green, soft; few prickles; growth very vigorous, upright, open; [Dusky Maiden × Docteur Valois]

Dainty Superior Pol, op, deRuiter; flowers have more lasting color; [sport of Dainty]

Dairy Maid F, ly, 1957, LeGrice; bud yellow, splashed carmine; flowers cream, fading white, large, 5 petals, borne in large clusters; foliage glossy; vigorous growth; PP1792; [(Poulsen's Pink × Ellinor LeGrice) × Mrs Pierre S. duPont]

Daisy HT, mp, 1898, Dickson, A.; flowers silvery carnation pink, large, full, moderate fragrance

Daisy HT, ob, 1923, Hicks; flowers orange-flamed; [sport of Mme Edouard Herriot]

Daisy Brasileir HMult, rb, 1918, Turbat; flowers bright red and purple-red, anthers yellow, 3 cm., single, borne in clusters of 30; foliage dark green; hips orange-red

Daisy Bud HT, pb, 1933, Dickson, A.; bud well shaped; flowers rosy pink, shaded carmine and silver, large

Daisy Doll Min, pb, 1977, Lyon; bud long, pointed; flowers rose-pink, open, 1½ in., 20-25 petals; foliage tiny; compact, upright growth; [Little Amy × seedling]; int. by L. Lyon Greenhouses

Daisy Dumas HT, rb, 1965, White, T. Howland; flowers bright red, reverse gold edged red, medium, dbl., slight fragrance; foliage dark; bushy growth; [seedling × (Tzigane × seedling)]; int. by A. Ross & Son, 1962

Daisy Hill S, mp, about 1906, Smith; flowers pale silvery blush, suffused with peach, medium, single, moderate fragrance; growth to 8 ft.; abundant fruit; [*R. waitziana macrantha* × *R. chinensis*]

Daisy Hillary F, op, 1963, Mell; bud pointed; flowers salmon-pink, large, dbl., high-centered, borne in clusters; foliage leathery; vigorous, bushy growth; [sport of Spartan]

Daisy Kordana Min, lp, Kordes; flowers soft pink, dbl.; container rose; int. by W. Kordes Söhne

Daisy Lane S, dr, 2000, McCann, Sean; flowers black-red, medium, semi-dbl., borne in small clusters, slight fragrance; foliage medium size, medium green, semi-glossy; some prickles; growth upright; garden decorative; [Lady in Red × Fountain]

Daisy Mae HT, dy, 1987, Stoddard, Louis; flowers deep yellow, reverse medium yellow, large, 6 petals, flat, borne singly; foliage large, dark green, semi-glossy; prickles large, red down-curved, fading gray-tan; upright, tall growth; hips round to ovoid, russet-yellow; [Golden Showers × Golden Sun]

Daisy May Rogers HMsk, w, 1996, Muia, Charlotte R.; flowers 1 in., single, borne in large clusters, slight fragrance; foliage small, medium green, semi-glossy; prickles small, moderate; compact, spreading, medium (4 × 5 ft.) growth; [Mozart × unknown]; int. by My Green Thumb, 1992

Daisy Rose F, pb, 1982, Kordes, W.; flowers pink with white eye, small, 5 petals, borne in large clusters; foliage medium size, medium green, semi-glossy; bushy growth; [Robin Hood × Topsi]

Dakar HT, pb, 1932, Gaujard; flowers silvery pink, striped rose-pink, large; long, strong stems; [Julien Potin × seedling]

Dakar HT, dy, Interplant; greenhouse rose; int. by Grandiflora Nurseries, 2002

Dakota Min, mr, 1991, McGredy, Sam; flowers bright clear red, showing golden stamens, medium, semi-dbl., borne singly or with 2 side buds; foliage small, medium green, semi-glossy; growth bushy (32 cm.); [Volare × Eyeopener]; int. by Oregon Miniature Roses, 1992

Dakota HT, dr; flowers dbl., high-centered, borne one per stems; foliage medium size, dark green, matte

Dakota Sun S, my, 2005, Smith, Robert L.; flowers 4 in., single, borne in small clusters, no fragrance; foliage medium green, glossy; prickles ½ in., wide-based; growth upright, medium (4 × 3 ft.); garden decoration; hardy to -30ºF; [Prairie Harvest × Shrub seedling]; int. by Sam Kedem

Dakota's Song S, ab, 2005, Smith, Robert L.; flowers apricot-pink, reverse yellow blend, 3 in., single, borne in small clusters, moderate fragrance; foliage medium size, medium green, semi-glossy; prickles in., wide based; growth upright, medium (3½ × 2 ft.); garden; hardy to -30ºF; [Prairie Harvest × (Golden Unicorn × Applejack)]; int. by Sam Kedem

Dale Farm F, or, 1975, Smith, E.; flowers vermilion, 3 in., 25 petals, moderate fragrance; foliage dark; vigorous growth; int. by Wheatcroft & Sons, 1973

Dale's Sunrise Min, yb, 1991, King, Gene; flowers yellow tipped medium pink, fading pink, small, dbl., borne mostly singly, slight fragrance; foliage small, medium green, semi-glossy; upright, bushy, medium growth; [((B.C. × Scamp) × Rainbow's End) × Tobo]; int. by AGM Miniature Roses, 1990

Dalila HT, rb, 1943, Gaujard; bud long, pointed; flowers brilliant coppery red, large, semi-dbl.; foliage leathery; vigorous, erect growth; [Souv. de Claudius Pernet × seedling]

Dalila F, ob, 1958, Buyl Frères; flowers orange, dbl.

Dallas HT, rb, 1965, Hunter; flowers crimson-carmine, base primrose-yellow, very large, 40 petals; foliage dark, glossy; vigorous growth; [sport of Peace]; int. by Waterhouse Nursery, 1963

Dallas – See **Cora Marie**, HT

Dallas Gold HT, yb, 1987, Winchel, Joseph F.; flowers large, heavy, 25 petals; foliage medium size, dark green, glossy; bushy growth; [seedling × Flaming Beauty]; int. by Kimbrew Walter Roses, 1987; Silver Medal, ARC TG, 1984

Dalli Dalli F, dr, 1979, Tantau, Math.; bud ovoid; flowers medium, dbl., cupped, slight fragrance; foliage very glossy; upright, bushy growth; int. in 1977; ADR, 1975

Dalton's Gold Min, dy, Dickson; buds golden; flowers dbl.; growth medium; int. in 1999

Dalvey HT, dp, 1971, MacLeod; flowers deep pink, 5½ in., high-centered; foliage medium size, light green, matte; vigorous growth; [Peeping Tom × seedling]

Dama di Cuori – See **Dame de Coeur**, HT

Damara Min, mr, 2006, Hopper, Nancy; flowers bright, velvety red, 2¼ in., dbl., borne mostly solitary; foliage medium green, matte, new growth is reddish; prickles ¼ in., brown, moderate; growth bushy, medium (16 in.); [unnamed red × unnamned red]; int. in 2006

Damas de Yuste – See **Liberty Bell**, HT

Damas Franklin D, pb, 1853, Robert; flowers flesh-pink, shading to silver

Damas Monstrueux – See **Arielle**, P

Damas Mousseux – See **Tinwell Moss**, M

Damas Violacé D, m, 1820, Godefroy; flowers pale flesh pink with purple-violet, medium, very full; few prickles

Damascena Petala Variegata – See **York and Lancaster**, D

Damask Monthly – See **Autumn Damask**, D

Damask Rose – See **Summer Damask**, D

Dame Blanche D, w, before 1830, Miellez; bud red; flowers flesh white, large, dbl.

Dame Blanche HWich, w, 1923, Turbat; flowers greenish white, stamens yellow, single, borne in clusters; non-recurrent bloom; vigorous growth

Dame Blanche HT, w, 1927, Mühle; flowers white tinged green, dbl.; [Stadtrat Glaser × unknown]

Dame Cath F, lp, 1998, McGredy, Sam IV; flowers light pink, 2¾ in., semi-dbl., borne in small clusters; foliage medium size, dark green, dull; prickles moderate; bushy, low (50 cm.) growth; [Chaumant × (Seaspray × Freegold)]; int. by McGredy, 1997

Dame Catherine HT, dy, 1937, Cant, B. R.; bud ovoid; flowers golden yellow, large, dbl., high-centered; foliage glossy; long stems; vigorous, bushy growth

Dame de Coeur HT, mr, 1959, Lens; flowers cherry-red, large, dbl., moderate fragrance; foliage dark, glossy; vigorous growth; [Peace × Independence]; int. in 1958

Dame de Coeur, Climbing Cl HT, mr, 1985, Mungia, Fred A., Sr.; upright growth, 8-10 ft.; [sport of Dame de Coeur]; int. in 1984

Dame de København – See **Princess Marianna**, S

Dame de L'Etoile F, w, Adam, M.; int. in 1994

Dame Edith Helen HT, mp, 1926, Dickson, A.; flowers glowing pink, very large, full, cupped, moderate fragrance; not very free bloom; foliage leathery; long, strong stems; vigorous, bushy growth; [Mrs John Laing × a Pernetiana]; Gold Medal, NRS, 1926

Dame Edith Helen, Climbing Cl HT, mp, 1930, H&S; flowers dark pink, very large, very full; [sport of Dame Edith Helen]

Dame Elisabeth Murdock – See **Speelwark**, HT

Dame Joyce Frankland HT, my, 1989, Horner, Colin P.; bud globular, greenish-yellow; flowers large, 32 petals, urn-shaped, borne singly, slight fragrance; foliage large, medium green, glossy; prickles straight, medium, light brown; bushy growth; hips ovoid, large, yellow; [(Honey Favorite × Dr. A.J. Verhage) × Pot O'Gold]

Dame of Sark F, ob, 1976, Harkness; flowers orange flushed red, reverse yellow, 4½ in., 33 petals; foliage large, dark; [(Pink Parfait × Masquerade) × Tablers' Choice]

Dame Prudence S, lp, 1969, Austin, David; flowers soft pink, reverse lighter, medium, 65 petals, flat; [Ivory Fashion × (Constance Spry × Ma Perkins)]

Dame Roma HT, op, 2004, Thomson, George L.; flowers salmon pink, reverse lighter, 15 cm., very full, borne mostly solitary; foliage large, medium green, glossy; prickles medium, hooked; growth upright, tall (5½-7 ft.); garden decorative; [Sweetheart × Kardinal 89]; int. by Ross Roses, 2004

Dame Vera Lynn F, or, 1986, Pearce, C.A.; flowers brick red, large, 20 petals; foliage medium size, dark, semi-glossy; upright growth; [seedling × seedling]; int. by Limes Rose Nursery

Dame Wendy F, mp, Cants of Colchester, Ltd.; int. in 1991

Dames de Chenonceau S, lp, Delbard; flowers very dbl., intense rose, orange and apricot fragrance; int. in 2002

Dames Patronesses d'Orléans HP, dr, 1877, Vigneron; flowers crimson red, large

Damien's Amulet T, lp

Damon Runyon HT, mr, 1955, Duehrsen; bud ovoid; flowers crimson, 4-5½ in., 50 petals, high-centered, moderate fragrance; foliage glossy, coppery green; vigorous, upright, bushy growth; PP1441; [Major Shelley × Heart's Desire]; int. by H&S, 1954

Dan Poncet S, pb, Massad-Guillot; flowers small, chubby, crimson pink, pointed petals, some fragrance; foliage dark green; growth bushy, 70 cm.; int. by Roses Guillot, 2000

Dana HT, mp, 1982, Swim, H.C. & Ellis, A.E.; bud long, pointed; flowers 38 petals, spiraled, formal, borne singly, sometimes 3 per cluster, slight carnation fragrance; foliage large, semi-glossy; prickles long, straight; tall, upright, bushy growth; PP4707; [White Satin × Bewitched]; int. by Armstrong Nursery

Danaé HGal, lp, 1854, Robert; flowers flesh pink, shaded violet, medium, full

Danaé HP, pb, 1865, Touvais; flowers translucent pink, shaded cherry red, large, full

Danaë HMsk, ly, 1913, Pemberton; flowers pale buff-yellow, fading white, borne in clusters; recurrent bloom; growth to 6 ft.; [reputedly Trier × Gloire de Chedane-Guinoiseau]

Danara Min, rb, 2006, Hopper, Nancy; flowers blended dark red and mauve, reverse red, 3½ in., full, borne mostly solitary; foliage medium size, medium green, semi-glossy; prickles ¼ in., yellow, few; growth bushy, medium (16 in.); [single red mini × Sweet Chariot]; int. in 2007

Dance of Joy F, mr, 1931, Sauvageot, H.; flowers vivid scarlet-crimson, large, dbl.; foliage dark; vigorous growth; [Paul's Scarlet Climber × seedling]; Gold Medal, Bagatelle, 1931

Dance of Joy 95 F, mr, Sauvageot, H.; flowers vermilion, dbl.; int. in 1995

Dance of Spring – See **Harunomai**, F

Dancer Min, m; int. by Ashdown Roses, 2005

Dancing Butterflies LCl, ab

Dancing Dawn F, lp, 2005, Webster, Robert; flowers peach, pronounced red stamens, 2½ in., semi-dbl., borne in small clusters, moderate fragrance; foliage small, dark green, semi-glossy; prickles 5 mm., slightly hooked, moderate; compact, short (30 in.) growth; bedding; [Arizona Sunset × (Indian Summer × ((Matangi × Memorium) × Gold Bunny))]; int. by Handley Rose Nurseries, 2004

Dancing Doll Cl F, dp, 1952, Moore, Ralph S.; bud small, pointed; flowers deep rose-pink, 10-14 petals, cupped, borne in clusters; profuse, repeated bloom; foliage leathery, glossy; vigorous, climbing or spreading (10 ft.) growth; [Étoile Luisante × seedling]; int. by Marsh's Nursery

Dancing Fairies S, dp, DeVor; flowers deep, velvet pink with prominent golden stamens, 2 in., 15 petals, open, borne in dense clusters, no fragrance; glossy green foliage; wiry, curved stems; growth that of a broad floribunda; int. by Ludwig's Roses, 2002; Trial Ground Certificate, Durbanville, 2006

Dancing Fan – See **Maiogi**, HT

Dancing Fire HT, ob, 2000, Giles, Diann; flowers orange, 5 in., full, exhibition, borne mostly singly; foliage large, medium green, semi-glossy; numerous prickles; upright, medium growth; [sport of Soaring Wings]; int. by Giles Rose Nursery, 2000

Dancing Flame Min, yb, 2001, Tucker, Robbie; flowers yellow with red edges, 1½-2 in., dbl., borne mostly solitary, no fragrance; foliage medium size, medium green, glossy; prickles medium, hooked downward, light green to brown; growth upright, medium (24 in.); exhibition, garden decorative, cutting; [seedling × Kristin]; int. by Rosemania, 2001

Dancing Girl – See **Carte d'Or**, F

Dancing in the Wind HMsk, pb, Clements, John K.; int. in 1995

Dancing Pink F, dp, 1993, Henson, R.W.; flowers deep pink, 3-3½ in., 6-14 petals, borne in large clusters; foliage medium size, medium green, semi-glossy; some prickles; medium (75 cm.), bushy growth; [Southampton × Dortmund]; int. in 1993

Dancing Queen HT, pb, Tantau; flowers pink with green edge; int. by Australian Roses, 2004

Dancing Queen LCl, mp, Fryer; flowers bright pink, dbl., high-centered; recurrent bloom; foliage dark green; vigorous growth, 2-3 m.; int. by Fryer's Roses, 2005

Dancing Silk HT, op, 1966, Barter; flowers coral-pink, reflexed, 5 in.; foliage light green; vigorous growth; [Ena Harkness × McGredy's Yellow]

Dancing Team F, ab, Takatori; int. by Takatori Roses

Dandee Min, dr, 1983, Meredith, E.A. & Rovinski, M.E.; bud globular; flowers 35 petals, flat, borne singly; foliage medium size, dark, semi-glossy; upright growth; [seedling × Libby]; int. by Casa de Rosa Domingo

Dandenong MinFl, or; flowers rich orange-red, exhibition; growth strong; int. by Classic Miniature Roses

Dandy Pol, op, 1945, Wiseman; flowers light orange-pink, small, semi-dbl., cupped; profuse, non-recurrent bloom; foliage wrinkled, glossy, dark; very vigorous growth; [Gloria Mundi × unidentified species rose]

Dandy Dick F, mp, 1967, Harkness; flowers well-formed, large, 25 petals, borne in clusters, moderate spicy fragrance; foliage light; [Pink Parfait × Red Dandy]

Dandy Lyon Min, dy, 1979, Lyon; bud long, pointed; flowers buttercup-yellow, 2 in., 30 petals, moderate fragrance; foliage small, dark, glossy; compact, bushy growth; [seedling × Sunspot]; int. in 1978

Dani HT, or, Kordes; flowers medium size, luminous orange-red, dbl.; growth strong, medium; int. by W. Kordes Söhne

Dania – See **Toprose**, F

Danica S, w, Noack, Werner; flowers single; low, spreading growth; int. by Noack's Rosen, 1997

Daniel HT, rb, 1943, Mallerin, C.; bud long, pointed; flowers capucine-red on golden yellow base, dbl., cupped; foliage dark, glossy; vigorous, bushy growth; int. by A. Meilland

Daniel HT, dr, Williams, J. Benjamin; flowers large, high-centered, intense fragrance; int. by Hortico Inc., 1995

Daniel Boon S, dr, Williams, J.B.; flowers large flowered dark red.; int. by Hortico, 2004

Daniel Boone HT, dr, Morey, Dr. Dennison; flowers dusky red, large, dbl., globular; vigorous growth

Daniel Gélin – See **Wandering Minstrel**, F

Daniel Greenway HT, dy, 2004, Paul Chessum Roses; flowers 10 cm., dbl., borne mostly solitary, slight fragrance; foliage large, medium green, matte; prickles medium, green, moderate; growth upright, tall (110 cm.); bedding, borders, containers; [seedling × seedling]; int. by Love4Plants Ltd, 2004

Daniel Lacombe HMult, yb, 1885, Allard; flowers yellow washed pink, 5-6 cm., dbl., flat, borne in large clusters; some autumn repeat; almost thornless; growth vigorous, arching (6-7 m.); [*R. multiflora* × Margarita]

Daniel Lesueur HRg, ly, 1908, Gravereaux; bud salmon-pink to coppery pink; flowers large, dbl., cupped; foliage medium size, elliptical, not rugose; [(Pierre Notting × Safrano) × *R. rugosa*]

Daniel Philip F, mr, 1999, Fleming, Joyce L.; flowers 1¼-1½ in., semi-dbl., borne in small clusters; foliage small, medium green, semi-glossy, disease-resistant; prickles moderate; upright, medium (6 ft.) growth; [(Morden Fireglow × unknown) × seedling]; int. by Hortico, Inc., 1999

Daniela Min, lp, Kordes; flowers dbl., rosette, borne in clusters; foliage fresh green, semi-glossy; growth bushy, compact (10 in.); int. by W. Kordes Söhne, 1987

Danielle HT, w, Cocker; int. in 1992

Danielle Min, mp, 1997, Brown, Ted; flowers medium pink, fading to light pink, 1½ in., full, borne in small clusters, intense fragrance; foliage medium size, medium green, semi-glossy; bushy, medium (18 in.) growth; [Esprit × seedling]

Danielle Darrieux HT, pb, 1948, Gaujard; bud long, pointed; flowers salmon suffused yellow, reverse salmon-orange-pink, very large, dbl.; very vigorous, bushy growth

Danielle Robyn HT, rb, 1971, Hastie; bud globular; flowers pinky red and creamy white bicolor, large, dbl., high-centered; intermittent bloom; foliage glossy, dark; bushy growth; [Grand Gala × Western Sun]

Danina – See **Cara Mia**, HT

Daniphyl HT, mr, 1978, Ellick; flowers mandarin-red, 4-5 in., 45-50 petals; foliage semi-glossy, light; vigorous, upright growth; [Puccini × Chopin]; int. by Excelsior Roses

Danish Min, pb, Olesen; flowers dbl., borne mostly solitary, no fragrance; foliage dark green, glossy; growth bushy, very low (20-40 cm.); PP10809; int. in 1998

Danish Gold F, yb, 1949, Poulsen, S.; flowers yellow fading to creamy white, 2½-3 in., 5-9 petals, moderate spicy fragrance; foliage glossy; vigorous, compact growth; [(Golden Salmon × Souv. de Claudius Pernet) × Julien Potin]; int. by McGredy; Gold Medal, NRS, 1949

Danish Pink F, dp, 1965, Soenderhousen; flowers deep pink, almost full, medium, 2-2½ in., single, borne in large clusters, moderate fruity fragrance; vigorous, tall growth; int. by Hoersholm Nursery

Danmark HT, mp, 1891, Zeiner-Larsen; flowers silvery rose-red, large, dbl., cupped, intense fragrance; [sport or seedling of La France]

Dannenberg HT, op, 1916, Kiese; flowers coral pink, large, dbl.; [Gruss an Teplitz × Lyon Rose]

Dannie's Smile HT, lp, 1994, Maxheimer, Joanne; flowers medium, full, borne mostly singly; foliage medium size, dark green, matte; some prickles; medium, spreading growth; [sport of Elizabeth Taylor]; int. by Giles Rose Nursery, 1993

Danny Boy LCl, or, 1969, McGredy, Sam IV; flowers orange vermilion, fading to salmon pink, large, borne in small clusters, intense fragrance; recurrent bloom; foliage dark; [Uncle Walter × Milord]; int. by McGredy & Son

Danny Boy S, dr, Clements, John; flowers rich deep crimson-red showing a distinct mossing effect, 2½ in., 15 petals; foliage rich, dark green.; growth compact (3 × 3½ ft.), shrubby; int. by Heirloom, 2000

Danny Boy F, ob, Dickson; flowers rusty orange, dbl., borne singly and in clusters; int. by Dickson Nurseries Ltd., 2001

Danny Thomas Min, or, 1980, Wells, V.W., Jr.; flowers with yellow stamens, 35 petals, borne usually singly, moderate fragrance; foliage dark; prickles straight; compact growth; [Rose Hills Red × Rose Hills Red]; int. by Lou McGuire

Danse Azteque Min, yb, 1984, Gailloux, Gilles; flowers yellow-pink blend, medium, semi-dbl., flat, slight fragrance; foliage medium size, medium green, semi-glossy; vigorous, upright growth; [Baby Masquerade × unknown]; int. in 1985

Danse des Étoiles F, or, 1979, Godin, M.; bud ovoid; flowers red-orange, deep, 2½ in., 15-18 petals, cupped; foliage light green; [Orangeade × Orange Sensation]; int. in 1973

Danse des Sylphes LCl, or, 1959, Mallerin, C.; flowers rich red suffused geranium-red, 2½ in., dbl., globular, borne in small clusters; foliage glossy; very vigorous growth; [Spectacular × Toujours]; int. by URS

Danse de Feu – See **Spectacular**, LCl

Danse du Printemps LCl, lp, 1954, Combe; flowers light crimson pink, 7-8 cm., semi-dbl. to dbl.; infrequent repeat

Danubio Azul HT, m, 1957, Camprubi, C.; flowers lilac, medium, dbl., cupped; upright growth; [Tristesse × Independence]

Danyrose HT, mp, Croix, P.; int. in 1975

Danzig HT, dr, 1940, Tantau; flowers shining dark red, medium, dbl., borne in clusters; upright growth; [Hadley × Kardinal]

Danzille – See **Mme Bravy**, T

Daphne HSpn, dp, before 1817, from England; flowers full

Daphné HGal, dp, 1819, Vibert; flowers rose carmine touched with mauve, medium, dbl., globular

Daphne HMsk, lp, 1912, Pemberton; flowers blush-pink, small, semi-dbl., borne in clusters, moderate fragrance; vigorous growth

Daphne HT, lp, 1925, Dobbie; flowers soft pink, flushed rose, well-formed, dbl.

Daphne Claire Jones LCl, or, 1994, Kirkham, Gordon Wilson; flowers 3-3½ in., dbl.; foliage large, dark green, semi-glossy; numerous prickles; tall, upright growth; [Parkdirektor Riggers × seedling]; int. by Kirkham, 1996

Daphne Gandy F, mr, 1952, Leenders, M.; flowers blood-red, 3 in., borne in large trusses; foliage dark; vigorous growth; [Farida × Crimson Glory]; int. by Gandy Roses, Ltd.

Daphnis HT, mp, 1978, Gaujard; flowers brilliant pink, very large; upright growth; [Marylène × Mignonne]; int. in 1974

Dapple Dawn S, lp, Austin, David; flowers soft pink, large, single, slight musk fragrance; growth 5 × 4 ft.; [sport of Red Coat]; int. by David Austin Roses, 1983

Dara HT, ob, 1991, Wambach, Alex A.; flowers medium, 30 petals, high-centered, borne usually singly, intense fragrance; foliage medium size, medium green, semi-glossy; upright growth; [Olympiad × Just Joey]; int. in 1995

Darby HT, mp, 1993, Marciel, Stanley G. & Jeanne A.; flowers medium, dbl., borne mostly singly, no fragrance; foliage large, dark green, semi-glossy; some prickles; tall, upright growth; [Dolores × Cerise Dawn]; int. by DeVor Nurseries, Inc., 1993

Darby O'Gill Min, ob, 1996, McCann, Sean; flowers orange with creamy white striping, 1½ in., 18 petals, borne mostly singly, slight fragrance; foliage medium size, dark green, glossy; some prickles; upright, medium (24-26 in.) growth; PPAF; [Tattooed Lady × Lady in Red];

int. by Justice Miniature Roses, 1996

Darcelle Min, w, 1991, Spooner, Raymond A.; flowers medium, single, borne in sprays of 3-5, slight fragrance; foliage small, medium green, semi-glossy; bushy, low (13 cm.), very compact growth; [(Whistle Stop × Popcorn) × Nozomi]; int. by Oregon Miniature Roses, 1991

d'Arcet M, dr, 1851, Robert; flowers scarlet red, medium to large, dbl.

Darcey Bussell S, rb, 2006; flowers 10 cm., very full, borne in small clusters; foliage medium size, medium green, matte; prickles medium, concave, curved inward, red, moderate; growth bushy, vigorous, medium (120 cm.); garden decorative; [seedling × seedling]; int. by David Austin Roses, Ltd., 2006

Dardanelle HT, mr, 1926, Vestal; flowers cherry-rose, dbl.; foliage wrinkled, dark; bushy growth; [Premier × Ophelia]

Darien F, dr, 2006, Castillo, Angel; flowers long-lasting, 3 in., very full, old-fashioned, borne in small clusters; foliage medium size, dark green, glossy; prickles medium, slightly hooked, moderate; growth spreading, medium (34 in.); garden decorative, exhibition; [Fragrant Cloud × Eyepaint]; int. by Angel Roses, 2007

Darius Ch, m, 1827, Laffay; flowers lilac-purple, medium to large, very dbl., slight fragrance

Darius HGal, mr; flowers vivid red, large, dbl.

Dark Boy HT, dr, 1970, Pal, Dr. B.P.; bud ovoid; flowers velvety dark maroon-red, medium, dbl., slight fragrance; foliage soft; moderate, upright, open growth; [Nigrette × seedling]; int. by Indian Agric. Research Inst., 1965

Dark Eyes – See **Biddulph Grange**, S

Dark Lady – See **The Dark Lady**, S

Dark Lulu HT, dr, Kordes; flowers dark red with cream, medium, dbl., high-centered, borne mostly singly; recurrent; stems long; [sport of Lulu]; int. by W. Kordes Söhne, 2005

Dark Mirage Min, dr, 1996, McCann, Sean; flowers velvety dark red with very dark shading at tip, reverse dark shadows, 2 in., full, high-centered, borne mostly singly, intense fragrance; foliage medium size, dark green, glossy, highly serrated; stems long; medium (18-20 in.) growth; PPRR; [Lady in Red × Fountain]; int. by Justice Miniature Roses, 1997

Dark Secret HT, dr, 1937, Amling Co.; flowers large, dbl., globular; foliage leathery; short stems; dwarf growth; [Radiance × Hollywood]

Darling HT, lp, 1956, Taylor, C.A.; bud ovoid; flowers large, dbl., moderate fruity fragrance; foliage dark, glossy; vigorous, bushy growth; [Pink Princess × Charlotte Armstrong]; int. by California Nursery Co.

Darling – See **Cream Delight**, Gr full

Darling HT, op, Noack, Werner; int. in 1985

Darling HT, mp, Kordes; int. in 1994

Darling Annabelle HT, w, 1992, Perry, Astor; flowers white with faint pink center, 7-10 cm., full, high-centered, moderate fragrance; foliage large, medium green, matte; growth upright (170 cm.); [South Seas × Peace]; int. by Hortico Roses, 1993

Darling B LCl, op, 2001, Horner, Colin P.; flowers orange/pink, pale pink reverse, luminescent in bright sunlight, 8 cm., semi-dbl., borne in small clusters, moderate fragrance; foliage medium size, medium green, semi-glossy; prickles medium, curved, moderate; growth upright, tall (3 m.); garden decorative; [Warm Welcome × Summer Wine]; int. by Pocock's Roses, 2002

Darling Diane F, pb, 1995, Bossom, W.E.; flowers lavender pink blend, 3-3½ in., full, slight fragrance; foliage large, dark green, semi-glossy; tall, upright growth; [Champagne Cocktail × seedling]

Darling Flame Min, or, 1971, Meilland; flowers mandarin-red to vermilion-red, yellow anthers, 1½ in., 25 petals, globular, slight fruity fragrance; foliage glossy, dark; vigorous growth; [(Rimosa × Josephine Wheatcroft) × Zambra]

Darling Jenny HT, pb, 1996, Poole, Lionel; flowers deep pink shaded peach, large, full, borne mostly singly, slight fragrance; foliage medium size, dark green, semi-glossy; some prickles; bushy, medium growth; [Solitaire × Gavotte]; int. by Poole, 1997

Darlow's Enigma HMsk, w, Darlow; flowers pure white with golden stamens, 1½ in., 5-8 petals, borne in clusters of 50-100, intense sweet, honey fragrance; good rebloom; foliage dark green; growth large, 10 × 10 ft.; [seedling of unknown parentage]; int. by Heirloom Roses, 1995

D'Artagnan D, dr, 1969, Fankhauser; flowers wine-red, dbl., cupped, borne in clusters, intense damask fragrance; non-recurrent; foliage dark, leathery, wrinkled; vigorous, upright (6 ft.) growth; [Ma Perkins × York and Lancaster]

D'Artagnan F, ob, Laperrière

Darthuizer Orange Fire – See **Orange Fire**, F

Dart's Dash HRg, dr; flowers large, purple red, dbl., flat, intense sweet fragrance; foliage dark green; few prickles; growth bushy, spreading

Dart's Defender S, m, Darthuis; flowers mauve to violet-pink; growth 5 × 5 ft.; int. in 1971

Dart's Presence S, or; int. by Brochet-Lanvin, 2005

Dart's Red Dot S, mr, Interplant; low, spreading growth; int. in 1989

Darzens HP, op, 1860, Ducher

Das Goldene Prag – See **Zlatá Praha**, HT

Dasher Min, mr, 1993, Spooner, Raymond A.; flowers large, full, borne mostly singly, slight fragrance; foliage medium size, medium green, semi-glossy; some prickles; medium (40 cm.), upright, bushy growth; [Maurine Neuberger × seedling]; int. by Oregon Miniature Roses, 1994

D'Assas HP, pb, 1850, Vibert; flowers dark pink, tinged crimson, petals somewhat fringed, medium, dbl.; vigorous, straggling growth

Datin Melleney HT, pb, Delbard; buds pointed, pink cream; flowers large, cream with coral edges, coral spreads with exposure to sun, dbl., high-centered; recurrent bloom; growth tall, vigorous; int. by Ludwig's Roses, 2002

Daughter Margaret S, w, 1986, Nobbs, Kenneth J.; flowers peach, fading to white, 48 petals, borne in clusters of 2-6, slight fragrance; repeat bloom; foliage typical China; prickles broad, pink; compact growth; [Mutabilis × Cornelia]; int. in 1985

Dauntless HT, pb, 1949, Davis; bud long, pointed; flowers pink, reverse yellow, large, 60 petals, high-centered; foliage leathery, dark; upright growth; [Crimson Glory × Feu Pernet-Ducher]

Dauphine F, op, 1955, Gaujard; bud ovoid; flowers pink shaded salmon, open, large, dbl., borne in clusters; very vigorous growth; [seedling × Opera seedling]

Dauphine, Climbing Cl F, op, 1959, Gaujard

Dave Davis HT, dr, 1965, Davis, C. A.; bud long, pointed; flowers dark velvety red, large, 60 petals, high-centered, intense fragrance; foliage leathery; moderate growth; [seedling × Charles Mallerin]; int. by Wyant

Dave Hessayon HT, mp, 1990, Driscoll, W.E.; flowers full, moderate fragrance; foliage medium size, medium green, glossy; bushy growth; [Silver Jubilee × Pink Favorite]; int. by Rosemary Roses, 1989

Dave McQueen F, mr, 2005, Paul Chessum Roses; flowers light red, 6 cm., dbl., borne in small clusters, slight fragrance; foliage medium size, medium green, semi-glossy; prickles small; bushy, medium growth; bedding, borders, containers; [seedling × seedling]; int. by Love4Plants Ltd, 2005

David Arnot HT, rb; flowers bright scarlet, reverse old-gold; vigorous growth

David Barber S, w; bud white with rose tints; flowers white, dbl., pompon, borne in clusters of 10-12, slight fragrance; recurrent; foliage medium green; stems reddish; low (16 × 48 in.), spreading, groundcover growth; int. by Northwest Horticulture, 2005

David Charles Armstrong HT, mr, 1992, Driscoll, W.E.; flowers coral-red, 3-3½ in., full, borne mostly singly, slight fragrance; foliage medium size, medium green, semi-glossy; some prickles; tall (106 cm.), upright growth; [Silver Jubilee × Fragrant Cloud]; int. in 1993

David D. Bernstein Cl Min, mr, 2006, Paul Chessum Roses; flowers dbl., borne mostly solitary; foliage medium size, dark green, semi-glossy; prickles large, sharp, pink, moderate; growth upright, medium (36 in.); [seedling × seedling]; int. by World of Roses, 2005

David Dot Min, Dot, Simon; int. in 1978

David Gilmore HT, mr, 1923, Dickson, H.; flowers brilliant scarlet

David Gold HT, rb, 1957, Robinson, H.; flowers cherry-cerise tinted golden yellow, 6 in., high-centered, intense fragrance; foliage dark, glossy; very vigorous growth; [Shot Silk × Peace]

David Harum HT, op, 1904, Hill, E. G.; flowers peach pink, very large, very full

David Leek F, dp, Fleming, Joyce L.; flowers dark, smoky pink to red, dbl., moderate fragrance; good repeat; growth to 4 ft.; int. by Hortico Inc., 1996

David Mace HT, mr, 2003, Thomas, D.; flowers large, very full, borne mostly solitary; foliage large, dark green, semi-glossy; numerous prickles; growth upright, medium; [Gavotte × (Jan Guest × Red Devil)]; int. by Ivor Mace, 2003

David McKee HT, mr, 1933, Dickson, A.; flowers carmine-red, large, dbl., high-centered; foliage leathery; vigorous, bushy growth

David O. Dodd HT, mr, 1926, Vestal; flowers rich crimson flushed scarlet, large, dbl.; foliage glossy; bushy growth

David O. Dodd, Climbing Cl HT, mr, 1937, Howard Rose Co.

David Pradel T, m, 1851, Pradel; flowers pale rose and lavender, mottled, very large, full, globular, intense fragrance

David R. Williamson – See **Rev. David R. Williamson**, HT

David Ruston HT, pb

David Thompson HRg, mr, 1979, Svedja, Felicitas; bud ovoid; flowers with yellow stamens, 2½ in., 25 petals, intense fragrance; upright growth; [(Schneezwerg × Frau Dagmar Hartopp) × seedling]; int. by Canada Dept. of Agric.

David Whitfield F, mp, Gandy; flowers large, clear China rose, dbl., borne in open trusses; compact, upright growth; int. by Gandy's Roses, 1991

David Wilson HT, ab, 2002, Rawlins, R.; flowers apricot-yellow, orange-yellow reverse, medium, full, borne in small clusters, moderate fragrance; foliage large, medium green, glossy; prickles medium, pointed; growth upright, tall (3 ft.); garden decorative; [Southampton × Sweet Heart]; int. by Interose-Rearsby, Ltd., 2007

Davidoff HT, op, Guillot; buds slender, pointed; flowers dbl., borne singly and in clusters; foliage dark green, semi-glossy; int. by Roses Guillot, 1984

David's Star F, w, Horner; int. by Warley Rose Garden, 2005

Davina Jane HT, ob, 1997, Rawlins, R.; flowers very dbl., borne mostly singly, no fragrance; foliage medium size, medium green,semi-glossy; upright, medium (3 ft.) growth; [Sexy Rexy × Corso]

Davit Dot S, mr

Davy Crockett F, dr, 1956, deRuiter; flowers large, dbl.;

vigorous growth; [Étoile de Hollande × Floribunda seedling]; int. by Gandy Roses, Ltd.

Dawn Cl HT, mp, 1898, Paul, G.; flowers silvery rose pink, semi-dbl.; [Mme Caroline Testout × Mme Paul]

Dawn HT, op, 1953, Jelly; bud long, pointed; flowers salmon-pink, base yellow, 5-6 in., 28-36 petals, high-centered, moderate spicy fragrance; vigorous, upright growth; PP1316; int. by E.G. Hill Co

Dawn Chorus HT, ob, 1994, Dickson, Colin; buds vivid orange; flowers orpiment orange with buttercup yellow at base, medium, dbl., borne in large clusters; foliage medium size, medium to dark green, glossy; some prickles; medium (74 cm.), upright to bushy growth; [Wishing × Peer Gynt]; int. by Dickson Nurseries, Ltd., 1993; Gold Medal, Dublin, 1991, Rose of the Year, RosesUK, 1993

Dawn Cover S, mr, Poulsen; flowers medium red, 5-8 cm., single, no fragrance; foliage dark; growth bushy, 40-60 cm.; int. by Poulsen Roser, 2005

Dawn Creeper S, dp, 1995, Williams, J. Benjamin; flowers deep pink, small, semi-dbl., borne in small clusters; foliage small, dark green, glossy; some prickles; low (10-12 in.), spreading growth; [The Fairy × (Sea Foam × Sea Foam)]; int. by J. Benjamin Williams, 1996

Dawn Fragrance LCl, op, 1969, Mason, P.G.; flowers salmon-flesh, flushed rose-pink, well-formed, cupped; intermittent bloom; foliage dark, leathery; vigorous growth; [Blossomtime × (Blossomtime × unknown)]

Dawn Haggie HT, op, Kordes; flowers firm-petaled, soft salmon, slow opening, dbl., borne mostly singly, no fragrance; recurrent; sturdy stems; growth medium; int. in 1997

Dawn Mist F, pb, 1962, Boerner; bud ovoid; flowers reddish-pink, base yellow, 3 in., 30-35 petals, cupped, intense spicy fragrance; foliage leathery, glossy; vigorous, bushy, compact growth; PP2113; [(Goldilocks × Pinocchio) × Vogue]; int. by Home Nursery Products Corp., 1962

Dawn Pink F, mp, 1962; bud apricot; flowers pink, rosette form, large, 45-50 petals, borne in clusters, moderate fragrance; foliage light green; vigorous, upright growth; [Magenta × Ma Perkins]; int. by Anderson's Rose Nurseries, 1962

Dawn Sunsation – See **Maxi Vita**, F

Dawn Weller F, op, Poulsen; flowers large, copper colored, dbl., borne in clusters; glossy green foliage; vigorous, tall growth; int. in 1995

Dawnglow HT, pb, 1937, Burbank; flowers flesh-pink, large, dbl., high-centered

Dawning, Climbing LCl, op, 1956, Bennett, H.; flowers salmon-pink; foliage glossy; vigorous growth; [New Dawn × Margaret McGredy]; int. by Pedigree Nursery

Dawnlight F, pb, 1959, Motose; bud ovoid; flowers soft pink, 2-2½ in., 30-35 petals, flat, slight fragrance; foliage leathery, light green; thornless; vigorous, bushy growth; PP1740; [Summer Snow, Climbing × Summer Snow]; int. by G.B. Hart, Inc., 1958

Dawns Early Light HT, w, 1977, Linscott; bud long, palest pink; flowers white, faintly edged pale pink, pointed, long-lasting, 3½-4 in., 6 petals, intense fragrance; foliage light; tall growth; [Vesuvius × Vesuvius]; int. in 1972

Dawson HMult, mp, 1888, Dawson; flowers bright rose-pink with white centers, fading lighter, 3 cm., semi-dbl., borne in clusters of 10-20, moderate fragrance; non-recurrent; vigorous (10-25 ft.) growth; [*R. multiflora* × Général Jacqueminot]; int. by Strong

Dawsoniana – See **Dawson**, HMult

Dawson's Climber Cl HT, pb, Dawson; int. in 1960

Dawson's Delight HT, pb, Dawson; flowers cerise pink with straw yellow reverse, veined pink, dbl., moderate fragrance; tall growth; int. in 1978

Dawson's Yellow Climber LCl, my

Day Break – See **Daybreak**, HMsk

Day Breaker F, ab, 2003, Fryer, Gareth; flowers medium, pastel peach with yellow, 4 in., 30-35 petals, borne singly and in small clusters; foliage medium size, dark green, glossy; prickles large, almost straight, light brown to green, none; growth bushy, medium; exhibition, cutting garden decoration; PP15334; [Silver Jubilee × (Pensioners Voice × Cheshire Life)]; int. by Edmunds' Roses, 2004; AARS, 2004

Day Dream HT, dp, 1971, Armstrong, D.L.; bud long, pointed; flowers deep pink, large, dbl.; foliage glossy, leathery; vigorous, upright, bushy growth; PP3077; [Helen Traubel × Tiffany]; int. by Armstrong Nursery, 1969

Day Glow Min, dp, 1989, Warriner, William A.; bud ovoid, pointed; flowers deep pink, fading lighter, medium, 60 petals, high-centered, borne usually singly, slight fragrance; foliage medium size, dark green, matte; prickles straight, short; low growth; [Petticoat × Red Jewel]; int. by Bear Creek Gardens, 1988

Day Is Done HT, or, 1985, Schneider, Peter; flowers large, 35 petals, high-centered; foliage large, dark, semi-glossy; [Die Welt × Rosalynn Carter]

Day Light F, ab, 1992, Ilsink, G.P.; flowers apricot-yellow, apricot and light pink reverse, aging to champagne, 3¼ in., dbl.; foliage medium size, dark green, matte; upright, medium (36-48 cm.) growth; [seedling × New Year]; int. by Interplant B.V., 1991

Day of Triumph HT, mp, 1956, Meilland, F.; bud ovoid; flowers pink edged lighter, 5½ in., 50-65 petals, cupped, moderate fragrance; foliage leathery; vigorous, upright, bushy growth; PP1358; [Peace × Europa]; int. by URS, 1953

Daybreak HMult, op, 1909, Dawson; flowers deep salmon-pink, borne in clusters; late; [*R. wichurana* × *R. chinensis*]; int. by Eastern Nursery

Daybreak HMsk, my, 1918, Pemberton; flowers golden yellow, medium, single, moderate fragrance; recurrent bloom; foliage dark; vigorous, bushy growth; [Trier × Liberty]

Daybreak HT, pb, 1935, Laxton Bros.; bud large, long, pointed; flowers salmon-pink and yellow, very dbl., high-centered; foliage leathery; long stems; very vigorous growth; [Violet Simpson × Ivy May]

Daybreak – See **Rassvet**, HT

Daybreak S, dp, 1960, Erskine; flowers deep pink, 25-30 petals, moderate fragrance; non-remontant, but long blooming season; [Hansa × *R. woodsii*]

Daybreak – See **Akatsuki**, HT

Daybreak Min, ab; flowers rich apricot-pink; good repeat; growth to 18-24 in.

Daydream Cl HT, lp, Clark, A.; flowers blush pink, shading to a white center, ruffled, large, single to semi-dbl.; growth vigorousd bush or pillar; [Souvenir de Gustave Prat × Rosy Morn]; int. by Hazelwood Bros., 1925

Daydream – See **Len Turner**, F

DayDream S, m, 2004, Lim, Ping; flowers fuchsia pink, reverse deeper fuchsia pink, small, 10 petals, borne in large clusters; foliage small, dark green, glossy; prickles ¼ cm., awl; growth compact, medium (2 ft.); garden decoration, containers; PP15736; [Lavender Dream × Henry Kelsey]; int. by Bailey Nurseries, Inc., 2004; AARS, 2005

Daydream Min, ab; int. by Burston Nurseries, 2005

Daylight HT, pb, 1939, Hansen, N. J.; flowers creamy blush-pink, base yellow, 4 in., very dbl., high-centered; foliage soft; vigorous growth; RULED EXTINCT 4/92 ARM; [Grange Colombe × Los Angeles]; int. by B&A

Daylight Katy F, my, 1987, Schneider, Peter; flowers bright yellow, fading slightly paler, medium, 22 petals, urn-shaped, borne in sprays of 3-15; foliage medium size, bronze-green, semi-glossy; prickles pointed, medium, reddish; bushy, low growth; hips round, small, red; [Bright Smile × (Princess Michael of Kent × Party Girl)]

Daylight's Glow Min, my, 2006, Hopper, Nancy; flowers 1¾ in., dbl., borne mostly solitary; foliage medium green, matte; prickles ¼ in., tan, few; growth bushy, 10 in.; [sport of Tobo]; int. by Nancy hopper, 2006

Daytona HT, dp, Olij; PP10189; int. in 1997

Dazla HT, rb, 1930, Cant, B. R.; bud long, pointed; flowers orange-scarlet, base and reverse golden yellow, wavy petals, 6 in., semi-dbl.; foliage dark; vigorous growth

Dazla, Climbing Cl HT, rb, 1950, Cant, B. R.

Dazzla – See **Wapiti**, F

Dazzler – See **Leonie**, F dbl.

Dazzler – See **Wapiti**, F

Dazzler Min, pb, Kasturi; flowers dark pink with prominent white eye, borne in large clusters; low growth; int. in 1992

Dazzler MinFl, op, Genesis; int. in 1995

Dazzler Min, yb, 1997, Kelly, Martin; flowers medium, light yellow, reverse lighter yellow with light red tips and edges, 1¾ in., dbl., borne mostly singly; foliage medium size, dark green, semi-glossy; upright, medium growth; PP10333; [Rainbow's End × Kristin]; int. by Nor'east Miniature Roses, 1998

Dazzling Beauties Min, ob, Moore, Ralph; flowers blend of yellow, gold, orange and red, dbl., high-centered, borne in large clusters, no fragrance; constant bloom; stems short; vigorous growth, neat rounded shape; int. by Ludwig's Roses, 2001

Dazzling Delight F, op, 2004, Cocker, A.G.; flowers deep salmon, reverse lighter, 2½ in., dbl., borne in large clusters, slight fragrance; foliage medium size, medium green, glossy; prickles 6 mm., straight; growth bushy, medium, garden decorative; [Anisley Dickson × Pristine]; int. by James Cocker & Sons, 2004

Dazzling Red HWich, mr, 1914, Manda; flowers ruby red

De Bordeaux – See **Petite de Hollande**, C

De Bruxelles – See **Agathe Incarnata**, HGal

De Candolle HSpn, w, about 1830, Prévost; flowers white, edges marbled pink, sometimes striped, single

De Candolle HCh, m, about 1845, Calvert; flowers violet-purple

De Candolle M, lp, 1857, Portemer fils; flowers soft pink or rose-tinted, large, dbl.

De Candolle HWich, op, 1913, Robichon; bud yellow; flowers deep yellow to salmon yellow, medium, full, borne in clusters of 30-40; [*R. wichurana* × Eugenie Lamesch]

De Chartres HCh, lp, before 1829, Laffay; flowers very small, dbl.; growth dwarf (3-5 in.); Lawrenciana

De Esmée HT, lp, deRuiter; int. by De Ruiter's New Roses, 2001

De Flandre – See **Agathe Incarnata**, HGal

De Greeff's Jubilee F, dr, 1982, Verschuren, Ted; flowers large, semi-dbl., slight fragrance; foliage medium size, dark, semi-glossy; bushy growth; [Diablotin × Gisselfeld]; int. by Verschuren & Sons, 1980

De Hollande – See **Majestueuse**, HGal

De Kat HT, w; int. in 1995

De La Flèche M, dr, 1824, Lemeunier; flowers purple red, 1½ in., dbl., cupped; foliage reddish when young, dark green, rather small, elongate; prickles numerous, unequal, straight

De la Grifferaie HMult, dp, 1845, de Grille/Vibert; flowers carmine to pink, fading almost to white, 8 cm., dbl., round and flat, borne in clusters of 10-15, moderate fragrance; non-recurrent; foliage large, round, rugose, matte; nearly thornless; growth robust, arching, tall (3 m.); [*R. multiflora platyphylla* × a form of *R. gallica*]

De la Maître-Ecole – See **Rose de La Maître-Ecole**, HGal

De la Malmaison HGal, lp, before 1826, Pelletier; flowers medium to large, full; Agathe group

De la Mothe HP, mp, 1858, Avoux / Crozy; flowers very large, very full

De la Reine – See **Regina Dicta**, HGal

De la Reine – See **Reine des Fleurs**, HP

De l'Ile – See **Blush Boursault**, Bslt

De Luxe HT, rb, 1931, White Bros.; flowers bright velvety scarlet, reverse red, semi-dbl.; [sport of Premier]; int. by Liggit

De Marienbourg HSpn, w, before 1820, Redouté, H.; flowers whitish, streaked with red points at the tip, medium, single; foliage glaucous, oval; prickles unequal, almost straight

De Meaux White – See **Rose de Meaux White**, C

De Mon Fils A, mp, before 1815, Descemet

De Montarville HKor, mp, 1999, Agriculture et Agroalimentaire Canada; flowers medium pink, reverse light pink, 3 in., dbl.; foliage small, blue-green, dull; few prickles; compact, medium growth; PP11635; [((Queen Elizabeth × Arthur Bell) × (*R. kordesii* × seedling)) × (Red Pinocchio × (Joanna Hill × *R. spinosissima altaica*))]

De Naples P, about 1810, Descemet

De Reims – See **Petit St François**, C

De Rennes Ch, m, about 1840, Prévost; flowers bright, glowing purple

De Ruiter's Herald Pol, dr, 1949, deRuiter; flowers blood-red, prominent yellow stamens, small, 6 petals, borne in large trusses; foliage glossy, dark; vigorous, bushy growth; [Orange Triumph × seedling]; int. by Gregory; Gold Medal, NRS, 1948

De St Barthélémy P, m, 1820, Delaâge; flowers violet-purple, aging to deep pink, medium, dbl.

De Schelfhout HGal, lp, before 1847, Parmentier; flowers whitish pink, medium, dbl.

De Tous Mois HMsk, w, before 1828

De Van Eeden – See **L'Obscurité**, HGal

Dean Collins Gr, dp, 1953, Lammerts, Dr. Walter; bud ovoid, red; flowers deep pink, 4½-5 in., 53 petals, slight fragrance; foliage dark, glossy, leathery; vigorous growth; PP1279; [Charlotte Armstrong × Floradora]; int. by Roseway Nursery

Dean Hole HT, pb, 1904, Dickson, A.; flowers silvery carmine, shaded salmon, very large, dbl., moderate fragrance; [sport of Mme Caroline Testout]

Dean of Windsor HP, mr, 1878, Turner; flowers vermilion with scarlet, large, full, moderate fragrance

Deane Ross S, pb, 2004, Thomson, George L.; flowers lavender pink, reverse darker, 10 cm., very full, borne in small to large clusters, intense fragrance; foliage medium size, dark green, matte; prickles small, hooked; growth spreading, short (3-4 ft.); garden decorative; [Gertrude Jekyll × Anna Oliver × Tomone (Mrs Mary Thomson)]; int. by Ross Roses, 2002

Deanna S, pb, 2004, Ponton, Ray; flowers pink stripe, 3-4 in., single, borne mostly solitary, intense fragrance; foliage medium size, medium green, semi-glossy; prickles large, hooked, moderate; growth upright, medium (4 ft.); [Katy Road Pink × Fourth of July]

Dear Daughter F, dp; int. by Burston Nurseries, 2005

Dear Eleanor Min, lp, 1999, Giles, Diann; flowers dbl., borne mostly singly; foliage medium size, dark green, dull; few prickles; upright, medium growth; [Party Girl × Snow Bride]; int. by Giles Rose Nursery, 1999

Dear One – See **Kara**, Min

Dear One F, lp, Benny; flowers porcelain pink, high-centered; good repeat; growth medium; int. by Camp Hill Roses, 1998

Dear Prudence F, pb, 1995, Taylor, Pete & Kay; flowers light pink blushing with darker pink edges, medium, dbl., borne in large clusters; foliage medium size, medium green, semi-glossy; some prickles; upright, bushy, medium (38 in.) growth; [seedling × seedling]; int. by Taylor's Roses, 1996

Dearest F, pb, 1960, Dickson, A.; flowers rosy salmon-pink, gold stamens, well-formed, large, 30 petals, borne in clusters, moderate fragrance; foliage dark, glossy; vigorous, bushy growth; [seedling × Spartan]; Gold Medal, NRS, 1961

Dearest, Climbing Cl F, pb, Ruston, D.; int. in 1970

Dearest One – See **Cara Mia**, HT

Dearly Departed HT, mr; int. by Burston Nurseries, 2005

Debbie Min, yb, 1966, Moore, Ralph S.; flowers yellow, edges becoming pink, small, dbl., moderate fragrance; foliage small, leathery; bushy, low, sometimes semi-climbing growth; PP2911; [Little Darling × Zee]; int. by Sequoia Nursery

Debbie S, dp, Poulsen

Debbie Dawn F, lp, 1997, Rawlins, R.; flowers medium, dbl., borne in small clusters; foliage medium size, dark green, semi-glossy; upright (2½ ft.) growth; [Margaret Merril × Melrose]

Debbie-Karen HT, mp, 1984, Burdett, H.J.; flowers 4½-5½ in., dbl., high-centered, borne singly, slight fragrance; foliage large, light green, semi-glossy; vigorous, upright growth; [seedling × seedling]; int. in 1983

Debbie Lynn HT, dr, 1992, Jerabek, Paul E.; flowers dbl., 36 petals, high-centered, urn-shaped, borne usually singly; foliage medium size, dark green, semi-glossy; upright, bushy, medium growth; int. in 1986

Debbie Thomas HT, rb, 1996, Thomas, D.; flowers crimson, lighter reverse, large, very dbl., high-centered; foliage medium size, medium green, semi-glossy; numerous prickles; upright, tall growth; [City of Gloucester × My Joy]; int. by F. Haynes & Partners, 1992

Debidue Min, dp, 1991, Williams, Michael C.; flowers magenta, medium, full, borne mostly singly; foliage medium size, dark green, semi-glossy; some prickles; medium (12 cm.), upright growth; PP8690; [Jazz Fest × Party Girl]; int. by The Rose Garden & Mini Rose Nursery, 1992; AOE, ARS, 1992

Debonair HT, my, 1946, Lammerts, Dr. Walter; bud ovoid; flowers primrose-yellow, 3-4½ in., 28-35 petals, high-centered; foliage leathery, glossy, dark; very vigorous, upright, bushy growth; [Golden Rapture × seedling]; int. by Armstrong Nursery

Debonnaire S, dp; flowers glowing deep pink, large, very dbl., borne in clusters, strong sweet fragrance; free-flowering; foliage dark green, glossy; growth upright, medium tall; int. by Harkness, 2004

Deborah S, mp, Meilland; flowers dbl., cupped, borne in small clusters; foliage glossy green; growth to 100-110 cm.; int. in 1990

Deborah Beggs Moncrief – See **Tiger**, HT

Deborah Beggs Moncrief – See **Deborah Moncrief**, HT

Deborah Devonshire F, pb, 1997, Bossom, W.E.; flowers very dbl., 41 petals, old-fashioned, borne in small clusters; foliage medium size, dark green, glossy; few prickles; bushy, medium (90 cm.) growth; [Pearl Drift × CherryAde]

Deborah Moncrief HT, pb, 1991, Williams, J. Benjamin; flowers pink with ivory blend, large, full, borne mostly singly, intense fragrance; foliage large, dark green, matte; few prickles; medium (3 ft.), bushy, spreading growth; [Carla × Sonia]; int. by Hortico, Inc., 1991

Debra Gaye Min, op, 1985, Bennett, Dee; flowers orange-pink, soft yellow reverse, medium, 38 petals, high-centered; foliage medium size, medium green, semi-glossy; bushy, upright growth; PP6136; [Futura × Fairest of Fair]; int. by Tiny Petals Nursery

Deb's Delight F, pb, 1983, LeGrice, E.B.; flowers silvery salmon-pink blend, patio, medium, 35 petals, moderate fragrance; foliage medium size, medium green, semi-glossy; low, bushy growth; [Tip Top × seedling]

Debut Min, rb, 1988, Selection Meilland; flowers luminous scarlet blending to cream to yellow at base, aging, 1¾ in., 15-20 petals, cupped, borne singly and in clusters, no fragrance; recurrent; foliage medium size, dark green, semi-glossy; prickles slender, few, straw; bushy (16-20 in.) growth; hips ovoid, few, dull orange-red; PP6791; [Coppelia × Magic Carrousel]; int. by C-P, 1989

Debutante HWich, lp, 1902, Walsh; flowers rose-pink, fading to cameo-pink, small, dbl., rosette, borne in large clusters, moderate sweetbriar fragrance; non-recurrent; foliage dark, glossy; short stems; growth to 6-8 ft.; [*R. wichurana* × Baroness Rothschild]

Debutante F, mp, 1985, Warriner, William A.; flowers small, 20 petals; foliage medium size, medium green, matte; bushy growth; PP5729; [Bridal Pink × Zorina]; int. by J&P

Deccan Delight F, yb, Chiplunkar; flowers yellow to apricot orange, changing to orange and white; [sport of Anita]; int. in 1985

Deccan Deluxe HT, m, Chiplunkar; flowers pale pink, dbl.; [sport of Dr B. P. Pal]; int. in 1988

Decea Ann F, ab, 1976, Horsfield; flowers flushed peach-pink, 3½-4 in., 26 petals, intense fragrance; foliage dark, leathery; upright growth; [Queen Elizabeth × Elizabeth of Glamis]

Deception HT, dp, 1923, Beckwith; flowers deep rose, large; Gold Medal, NRS, 1923

Déclic S, m, Croix; flowers lilac pink, 3 in., dbl., borne in large clusters; foliage glossy; int. in 1988

Décor LCl, or, 1951, Mallerin, C.; flowers bright scarlet, semi-dbl., borne in clusters; foliage leathery; vigorous growth; [(Love × Paul's Scarlet Climber) × Demain]; int. by URS

Decor Arlequin S, rb, 1979, Meilland, Mrs. Marie-Louise; flowers strawberry-red and yellow, medium, 18 petals, cupped; foliage dark; very vigorous, upright growth; [((Zambra × Zambra) × (Suspense × Suspense)) × Arthur Bell]; int. as Meilland Decor Arlequin, Meilland & Co SNC, 1977; Gold Medal, Rome, 1975

Decor Rose – See **Anne de Bretagne**, S

Décor Terrasse ClMin, dy, Meilland; int. in 2002

Décora C, mp; flowers clear rose, small, very dbl., slight fragrance; intermediate between Rose de Meaux and Spong

Decorat – See **Freude**, HT

Décoration de Geschwind – See **Geschwind's Orden**, HMult

Decorator HT, rb, 1913, Hobbies; bud bright carmine, striped yellow; flowers reddish-yellow, large, semi-dbl.

Decorator HT, yb, 1914; flowers bright cream yellow, striped glowing red, semi-dbl.; from Brasil

Decorator HT, rb, 1936, Dickson, A.; flowers brilliant carmine, base orange-yellow; foliage glossy; very vigorous growth

Dedication F, ly, 1968, Harkness; flowers creamy ivory, dbl., borne in trusses; foliage glossy; [Pink Parfait × Circus]

Dee Bennett Min, ob, 1989, Saville, F. Harmon; flowers yellow and orange becoming orange-yellow, medium, 25 petals, high-centered, borne usually singly, slight fruity fragrance; foliage medium size, dark green, semi-glossy; prickles long, thin, curved, gray-orange; bushy, medium growth; no fruit; PP6951; [Zorina × (Sheri Anne × (Yellow Jewel × Tamango))]; int. by Nor'East Min. Roses, 1989; AOE, ARS, 1989

Dee Dee F, my, Meilland; flowers saffron yellow, dbl.,

high-centered; greenhouse rose; int. by Meilland Intl., 1998

Dee Dee Bridgewater LCl, mp, Meilland; flowers large, dbl., moderate fragrance; growth to 7 ft.; int. by Meilland Richardier, 2004

Deep Purple F, m, 1979, Kordes, R.; bud ovoid, pointed; flowers mauve-pink, imbricated, 3-4 in., 30-45 petals, moderate fragrance; foliage glossy, dark; vigorous, upright, bushy growth; PP4672; [Zorina × Silver Star]; int. by Armstrong Nursery, 1980

Deep Secret HT, 1946, Hildebrandt; flowers rich red becoming darker, compact; RULED EXTINCT 4/77 ARM; [Matchless × seedling]

Deep Secret HT, dr, 1977, Tantau, Math.; flowers deep crimson, 4 in., 40 petals, intense fragrance; foliage glossy, dark; vigorous, upright, medium growth; int. by Wheatcroft, 1977; ADR, 1978

Deep Velvet Min, dr, 1981, Jolly, Betty J.; flowers 33 petals, high-centered, urn-shaped, borne singly and 2-3 per cluster, slight fragrance; foliage tiny, medium green; prickles straight; bushy, compact growth; [(Grand Opera × Jimmy Greaves) × Baby Katie]; int. by Rosehill Farm

Deepika F, rb, 1976, IARI; bud pointed; flowers 2 in., 15 petals; free bloom, fairly lasting; foliage glossy, dark; vigorous, upright, open growth; [Shepherd's Delight × seedling]; int. in 1975

Deepshikha F, mr, 1976, IARI; bud pointed; flowers open, 2½ in., 35 petals, slight tea fragrance; foliage glossy, light; vigorous, compact, bushy growth; [Sea Pearl × Shola]; int. in 1975

Déesse HT, rb, 1957, Gaujard; bud long, pointed, white; flowers red spreading from outside to center petals, ending crimson, dbl.; vigorous, upright growth; [Peace × seedling]

Déesse Flore D, lp, 1827, Vibert; flowers blush white, center cerise pink, small to medium, full; growth branching

Defiance HT, mr, 1907, Hill, E. G.; flowers rich red, large, full; [Lady Battersea × Gruss an Teplitz]

Defiance HT, dr, 1914, Kress; flowers dark velvety red, 5-6 in., dbl.; foliage dark; vigorous growth; [Gruss an Teplitz × Étoile de France]

Degenhard – See **Doc**, Pol

DeGrazia's Pink Min, mp, 1983, Williams, Ernest D.; flowers small, of heavy substance, dbl., slight fragrance; foliage small, dark, glossy; bushy growth; [(seedling × Over the Rainbow) × (seedling × Over the Rainbow)]; int. by Mini-Roses

Deidre Hall HT, yb, 2005, Edwards, Eddie & Phelps, Ethan; flowers yellow blend, 5-6 in., full, high-centered, borne in small clusters, no fragrance; foliage large, dark green, glossy; prickles moderate; growth upright, tall, (5-6 ft.); garden, exhibition; [seedling × Santa Fe]

Déjà Vous Min, ab, 1986, Jolly, Nelson & Marie; bud pointed; flowers light apricot, aging lighter, large, 50 petals, high-centered, borne usually singly, slight fragrance; foliage medium size, medium green, semi-glossy; no prickles; medium, upright, spreading growth; no fruit; [Anita Charles × Sheri Anne]; int. by Rosehill Farm, 1987

Dekora HT, mp, Kordes; flowers bright pink to hot pink, medium, dbl., high-centered, borne mostly singly; recurrent; prickles very few; stems long; florist rose; int. by W. Kordes Söhne, 2005

Del Mar Fair F, dp, 1993, Bennett, Dee; flowers deep pink, 3-3½ in., full, borne in large clusters, moderate fragrance; foliage medium size, medium green, semi-glossy; some prickles; medium, upright, bushy growth; [Gene Boerner × Pucker Up]; int. by Tiny Petals Nursery, 1994

Delambre P, dp, 1863, Moreau et Robert; flowers carmine, darker at center, edges tinted lilac, dbl., quartered, borne in clusters, moderate sweet fragrance; remontant

Delany Sisters Gr, pb, 1997, Williams, J. Benjamin; flowers white with orange-pink highlights on outer petal edges, large, dbl., cupped, ruffled, borne mostly singly and in large clusters, intense fragrance; foliage large, dark green, semi-glossy; upright, bushy, tall (4½-5 ft.) growth; [Love × Handel]; int. by Hortico Inc., 1997

Delbara – See **Strawberry Ice**, F

Delbard F, or, Delbard-Chabert; flowers light orange-red, large, dbl.

Delbard's Orange Climber LCl, or, 1965, Delbard-Chabert; bud ovoid; flowers medium, dbl., high-centered, borne in small clusters; repeat bloom; foliage dark, glossy, leathery; vigorous, climbing, well branched growth; PP2573; [Spectacular × (Rome Glory × La Vaudoise)]; int. by Armstrong Nursery, 1963

D'Eleganta – See **Touch of Class**, HT

Delgramo F, m, Delbard; flowers dbl.

Delhi Apricot HT, ab, 1970, Pal, Dr. B.P.; bud pointed; flowers apricot-yellow, medium, dbl., slight fragrance; foliage light green, soft; moderate, bushy growth; int. by Indian Agric. Research Inst., 1964

Delhi Brightness F, op, 1970, Pal, Dr. B.P.; flowers open, medium, semi-dbl.; foliage glossy; vigorous, upright growth; int. by Indian Agric. Research Inst., 1963

Delhi Daintiness F, lp, 1970, Pal, Dr. B.P.; bud pointed; flowers light pink, reverse darker, medium, semi-dbl.; foliage glossy; vigorous, upright, compact growth; int. by Indian Agric. Research Inst., 1963

Delhi Maid F, ob, 1970, Pal, Dr. B.P.; bud pointed; flowers flame-orange, base gold, open, medium, single; foliage dark, glossy; vigorous, upright, compact growth; int. by Indian Agric. Research Inst., 1963

Delhi Pink Pearl HMult, lp, 1970, Pal, Dr. B.P.; bud ovoid; flowers pearly pink, open, medium, semi-dbl.; foliage glossy, light green; very vigorous, compact growth; [sport of Echo]; int. by Indian Agric. Research Inst., 1962

Delhi Prince F, dp, 1970, Pal, Dr. B.P.; bud pointed; flowers glowing deep pink, open, medium, semi-dbl., slight fragrance; foliage glossy; vigorous, bushy growth; int. by Indian Agric. Research Inst., 1963

Delhi Princess F, mp, 1969, Pal, Dr. B.P.; bud ovoid, cerise-red; flowers deep pink, open, large, semi-dbl., borne in clusters, slight fragrance; foliage glossy, bronze; very vigorous, compact growth; int. by Indian Agric. Research Inst., 1963

Delhi Rosette F, ob, 1970, Pal, Dr. B.P.; bud ovoid; flowers bright orange-scarlet, open, medium, 28 petals; foliage dark, glossy; vigorous, compact growth; int. by Indian Agric. Research Inst., 1965

Delhi Sherbet F, mp, 1970, Pal, Dr. B.P.; bud ovoid; flowers deep rose-pink, medium, dbl., intense fragrance; foliage glossy; vigorous, bushy, compact growth; [Gruss an Teplitz × seedling]; int. by Indian Agric. Research Inst., 1963

Delhi Starlet Min, ly, 1970, Pal, Dr. B.P.; bud pointed; flowers open, small, semi-dbl., slight musk fragrance; foliage small, glossy; dwarf, compact growth; [Goudvlinder × seedling]; int. by Indian Agric. Research Inst., 1963

Delhi Sunshine HT, yb, 1970, Pal, Dr. B.P.; bud pointed; flowers deep cream, reverse flushed pink, medium, dbl.; foliage light green; bushy, open growth; [Mme Charles Sauvage × seedling]; int. by Indian Agric. Research Inst., 1963

Delhi White Pearl LCl, w, 1969, Pal, Dr. B.P.; bud ovoid; flowers pearly white, dbl., borne in clusters, slight fragrance; repeat bloom; foliage glossy; vigorous growth; [Prosperity × seedling]; int. by Indian Agric. Research Inst., 1963

Délia HT, op, Guillot-Massad; flowers coppery pink, dbl., slight wild rose fragrance; foliage disease-resistant; stems flexible; growth shrubby; int. by Roseraies Guillot, 2004

Delicado HT, op, 1954, Lowe; flowers shell-pink shaded peach, well-shaped, 6 in.; moderate growth

Delicata HRg, lp, 1898, Cooling; flowers soft lilac-pink, large, semi-dbl., moderate fragrance; recurrent bloom; vigorous growth

Délicate HGal, mr, before 1827, Dubourg; flowers cherry red with bright lilac

Delicate Beauty HT, w, Kordes; buds pointed, light cream-yellow; flowers white to ivory, dbl., high-centered; recurrent; growth vigorous, spreading, medium

Delicate Lady HT, w, 2004, Sheldon, John; flowers white with pink at center, aging to pure white, reverse white, 4-6 in., full, borne mostly solitary, moderate fragrance; foliage dark green, semi-glossy; prickles medium, pointed, maroon, aging to green; growth upright, medium (4-6 ft.); exhibition, garden decoration; [Sheer Bliss × Headliner]; int. by Certified Roses, Inc, 2004

Delicate Sunsation S, w, Kordes ; buds long, pointed; flowers large, deep cream brushed with light pink, dbl.; constant bloom; growth neat, compact, prostrate; int. in 1998

Delicate Wine – See **Vino Delicado**, HT

Delicia – See **Elegant Beauty**, HT

Delicia HRg, dp, Kordes; bud very long, pointed; flowers deep pink, 4 in., dbl., intense sweet fragrance; recurrent; foliage large, dark green, glossy; numerous prickles; vigorous, erect, bushy growth to 7 ft.; int. by W. Kordes Söhne, 2003

Délicieuse HGal, mp, about 1830, Vibert; flowers bright pink, medium, full

Delicious HT, yb, 1933, Sauvage; flowers yellow, shaded peach, large, semi-dbl.; [sport of Los Angeles]

Delicious Min, mp, 1995, Welsh, Eric; flowers small, full, borne in small clusters, intense fragrance; foliage small, medium green, semi-glossy; few prickles; tall (65-70 cm.), upright, compact growth; [Avandel × ((seedling × Friesia) × seedling)]; int. by Rose Hill Roses, 1994

Délie Communaudat HT, yb, 1933, Buatois; flowers Naples yellow, shaded and edged carmine, dbl., cupped, moderate fragrance; foliage leathery; very vigorous, bushy growth; [Mme Charles Detreaux × Mme Edouard Herriot]

Delight HWich, rb, 1904, Walsh; flowers bright carmine, base white, stamens yellow, medium to large, semi-dbl., cupped; foliage glossy; long stems; very vigorous, climbing (15-20 ft.) growth

Delight F, dp; int. in 2005

Delight MinFl, ab, Olesen

Delight Hit – See **Delight**, MinFl

Delightful HT, pb, 1931, McGredy; flowers rose, base yellow, reverse amber-yellow, large, dbl., high-centered; foliage glossy; vigorous growth; [George Dickson × unknown]

Delightful HT, yb, 1956, Brownell; bud pointed; flowers straw-yellow, base shaded red, 4-5 in., 35-50 petals, high-centered, moderate fragrance; upright, compact growth; PP1372; [Curly Pink × Shades of Autumn]

Delightful Kiwi HT, lp, 1989, Cattermole, R.F.; bud tapering; flowers blush pink aging to creamy pink, medium, 45 petals, urn-shaped, borne singly; foliage light green, large, shiny; prickles light brown, very few; upright, branching growth; [Silent Night × (Prima Ballerina × Irish Mist)]; int. by South Pacific Rose Nursery, 1988

Delightful Lady HT, lp, 1983, Attfield, B.B.; flowers large, 30-35 petals, high-centered, borne singly in spring, 3-5 per cluster in autumn, slight fragrance; foliage semi-glossy; prickles brown; medium-tall growth; [Pascali × Merry Widow]

Delightful Pink F, mp, 1959, Boerner; bud ovoid; flowers pink, medium, 40-45 petals, cupped, borne in clusters, moderate fragrance; vigorous, upright growth; PP1803; [Chic × Demure]; int. by J&P, 1959

Delilah HT, m, 1999, Schuurman, Frank B.; flowers 4 in., dbl., borne mostly singly, no fragrance; foliage large, medium green, glossy; few prickles; upright, tall (3-4 ft.) growth; PP10918; [seedling × Osiana]; int. by Franko Roses New Zealand, Ltd., 1995

Delille M, w, 1852, Robert; flowers blush-white, nicely mossed, semi-dbl.; may repeat

Della Balfour S, ab, Harkness; flowers golden peach-orange, 4 in., dbl., borne in clusters, slight lemony fragrance; recurrent; foliage dark green, lush; growth to 8 ft.; [Rosemary Harkness × Elena]; int. in 1994

Della Reese HT, m, 2003, Carruth, Tom; flowers magenta, 11-14 cm., full, borne mostly solitary, intense fragrance; foliage large, dark green, glossy; prickles moderate, medium, almost straight, light brown; growth upright, tall (120-140 cm.); garden decoration; PPAF; [The Roseanne Rose × Blue Nile]; int. by Armstrong Garden Centers, Inc., 2005

Deloitte & Touche S, ab, Kordes; flowers a blend of peach and apricot with tones of bright orange; growth low and spreading; int. in 1996

Delore HT, ly, Kordes; flowers creamy buff shading to light apricot, high-centered, borne singly and in small clusters; growth medium to tall, strong and healthy; [sport of Folklore]; int. in 1982

Delphin HT, m, VEG; flowers violet-pink, large, dbl.

Delphine Gaudot T, w, 1840, Béluze; flowers cream white, medium, full

Delphine Gay HGal, m, about 1820, Vibert; flowers bright bluish-red, sometimes striped, medium, full

Delphine Gay D, w, 1823, Vibert; flowers white, shaded flesh pink, medium to large, full

Delphine Gay HP, w, 1847, Vibert

Delphiniana – See **Enfant de France**, HGal

Delphinie M, mp, before 1846; flowers rose pink, small, dbl., cupped

Delta – See **Break o' Day**, HT

Delta Dawn HT, my, 1999, Iverson, Halvor; flowers 5 in., full, borne mostly singly, intense fragrance; foliage medium size, medium green, semi-glossy; few prickles; upright, medium (5 ft.) growth; [sport of Out of Africa]

Delta Gamma HT, ly, 1977, Kimbrew-Walter Roses; bud pointed; flowers creamy white, base pale yellow, 4-4½ in., 38 petals, high-centered, moderate spicy fragrance; foliage dark; vigorous, upright, bushy growth; [Queen Elizabeth × Mount Shasta]

Delta Gold HT, yb, 1988, Perry, Anthony; flowers red and yellow blend, reverse red-yellow, medium, 35 petals, urn-shaped, slight fragrance; foliage medium size, dark green, glossy; prickles slight recurved, average, dark; strong stems; bushy, medium growth; hips round, average, orange; [Arizona × World Peace]; int. by Co-Operative Rose Growers, 1989

Delta Queen HT, mp; int. in 1998

Deltou F, Delbard, Georges; int. in 1986

Delveen P, mp, 1930, Alderton

Demain HT, mr, 1945, Mallerin, C.; bud pointed; flowers brilliant cardinal-red, reverse saffron-yellow, semi-dbl., cupped; very vigorous, upright growth; [Mrs Pierre S. duPont × Dr. Kirk]; int. by A. Meilland

Dembrosky – See **Dembrowski**, HP

Dembrowski HP, dr, 1849, Vibert; flowers deep crimson-violet; sometimes classed as B

Demetra F, yb, Barni; bud large buds; flowers cream clear apricot with deeper tones in center, full, high-centered; repeats quickly; vigorous growth, 2-3 ft.; int. by Rose Barni, 2003

Demitasse Min, m, 2001, Zary, Keith; flowers magenta, 2½ in., full, borne in large clusters, moderate fragrance; foliage small, medium green, glossy; prickles moderate; growth compact, low (2½ ft.); garden decorative; PP12996; [La Marne × lavender miniature seedling]; int. by J&P, 2002

Demoiselle HT, pb, 1960, Delforge; flowers soft pink becoming darker, open, medium, 25-30 petals; foliage bronze; vigorous, bushy growth; [Peace × Opera]

Demokracie LCl, dr, 1935, Böhm, J.; flowers medium to large, 8 cm., dbl., borne singly or in small clusters, no fragrance; said to be recurrent

Demon – See **Bonica**, S

Démone HT, dr, 1967, Tantau, Math.; bud ovoid; flowers medium, dbl., intense fragrance; foliage dark; int. by Buisman, 1965

Demure F, dp, 1952, Boerner; bud ovoid; flowers rose-pink, 2 in., 52 petals, flat, borne in clusters; foliage leathery; vigorous, compact growth; [Garnette × seedling]; int. by J&P

Denali HT, w, 2004, Edwards, Eddie & Phelps, Ethan; flowers large, petals very wide, 5-5½ in., full, high-centered, borne mostly solitary, moderate fragrance; recurrent; foliage medium size, dark green, semi-glossy; prickles small, hooked; growth upright, tall (5-6 ft.); exhibition; [Crystalline × White Success]; int. in 2005

Deneb LCl, dy

Denice HT, w, Spek; flowers pure white, 12 cm., 35-40 petals, high-centered, borne mostly singly; recurrent; numerous prickles; stems long; int. by Jan Spek Rozen, 2005

Denis Hélye HP, mr, 1864, Gautreau; flowers rosy crimson; vigorous growth

Denis Hélye M, m, 1864, Lévis; flowers violet-purple

Denise HT, my, 1955, Buyl Frères; bud oval; flowers citron-yellow, open, large, dbl.; foliage glossy, clear green; vigorous, bushy growth; [Peace × Brandywine]; int. by Delforge

Denise – See **Denise Parade**, MinFl

Denise-Anne F, op, 1973, Ellick; flowers blush-pink to orange-apricot, 4 in., 30-35 petals; foliage small, glossy, dark; vigorous growth; [(Memoriam × Orange Sensation) × (Peace × Memoriam)]; int. by Radway Roses

Denise Cassegrain Pol, w, 1922, Grandes Roseraies; flowers snow-white, very dbl., borne in clusters of 30-40

Denise Chambard HT, yb, 1940, Chambard, C.; bud long, carmine-yellow; flowers sulfur-yellow, shaded carmine, large, cupped; foliage bright green; strong stems; vigorous, upright growth; int. by Orard

Denise Dewar HT, dr, 1968, Trew, C.; flowers crimson, pointed; foliage bronze-green; free growth; [Isabelle de France × Karl Herbst]

Denise Grey S, lp, Meilland; flowers clear rose; int. in 1988

Denise Hale HT, pb, 1996, Wambach, Catherine; flowers light cream pink, darker edge, lighter reverse, 4½ in., full, borne singly; foliage medium size, dark green, semi-glossy; prickles moderate; upright, medium growth; [Elsie Melton × seedling]; int. by Certified Roses, Inc., 1996

Denise Hilling HMoy, dp

Denise Lefeuvre HT, rb, 1930, Chambard, C.; flowers nasturtium-red, center yellow, reverse bright red, large, dbl., cupped; strong stems; very vigorous growth

Denise McClelland HT, dr, 1965, Riethmuller; flowers claret-red, large, 30 petals, moderate fragrance; foliage dark, leathery, glossy; vigorous, upright, bushy growth; [Amy Johnson × New Yorker]; int. by Akhurst, 1964

Denise Parade MinFl, w, Olesen; bud pointed ovoid; flowers ivory white, 5-6 cm., 13-15 petals, high-centered, borne mostly singly, very slight fragrance; free-flowering; foliage dark green, matte; few prickles; bushy (20-40 cm.) growth; PP14309; [Patricia Kordana × seedling]; container rose; int. as Denise, Poulsen Roser, 2001

Denk an Mich F, mr; flowers geranium red; int. by Richard Huber AG, 2006

Denman HT, ly, 1989, Sealand Nurseries, Ltd.; flowers creamy yellow, large, 35 petals, urn-shaped, borne in sprays of 2-3, intense fragrance; foliage large, dark green, glossy; prickles medium, red; upright growth; [Mildred Reynolds × Arthur Bell]

Denny Arter LCl, yb, 2003, Starnes, John A. Jr.; flowers buff yellow, reverse ivory-cream, 3 in., dbl., borne in small clusters, moderate fragrance; very remontant; foliage small, light green, semi-glossy; prickles small, straight, beige, moderate; stems very pliable; spreading (7 ft.) growth; shrub or pillar; [Francis E. Lester × Graham Thomas]; int. by High Country Roses, 2005

Denny Boy F, yb, 1949, Marsh; bud small, ovoid; flowers orange-yellow, becoming redder, reverse sulfur-yellow, very dbl., cupped; very vigorous, bushy, dwarf growth; [Pinocchio × Mrs Erskine Pembroke Thom]; int. by Marsh's Nursery

Denoyel – See **Souv de Claudius Denoyel**, Cl HT

Dentelle S, mp, Huber; int. by Rosen Huber, 2005

Dentelle de Bruges S, w, 2000, Lens, Louis; flowers white, 2-3 cm., semi-dbl., borne in large clusters, moderate fragrance; non-recurrent; foliage medium size, medium green, semi-glossy; prickles moderate; bushy, tall (5-6 ft.) growth; [Seagull × Muhle Hamsdorf]; int. in 1990

Dentelle de Bruxelles S, mr, 2000, Lens, Louis; flowers dark carmine red, 1 in., semi-dbl., borne in large clusters; recurrent; foliage dark green-reddish, semi-glossy; prickles moderate; bushy, tall (5-6 ft.), arching growth; [Kiftsgate × Violet Hood]; int. in 1988

Dentelle de Malines S, lp, 2000, Lens, Louis; flowers pale pink to cream, reverse lighter, small, dbl., flat, borne in large clusters; foliage dark green, glossy; prickles moderate; bushy, tall (5-6 ft.) growth; [*R. filipes* × (Robin Hood × Baby Faurax)]; int. in 1986

Denver's Dream Min, ob, 1995, Saville, F. Harmon; flowers copper orange with red reverse, small, full, cupped, borne mostly singly, no fragrance; foliage medium size, dark green, semi-glossy; medium (16-20 in.), upright growth; PP9435; [Gingersnap × Klima]; int. by Nor'East Min. Roses, 1994

Denyse Ducas HWich, yb, 1953, Buatois; flowers golden yellow, carmine red exterior, 4½ in.

Député Debussy Cl HT, w, 1902, Buatois; flowers flesh white, yellow nub

Der Krad HT, dr, 1962, Wyant; bud long, pointed; flowers maroon-red, striped darker, 3½ in., dbl., high-centered; foliage glossy; vigorous, bushy growth; [Ami Quinard × Crimson Glory]

Derby F, or, 1963, Gaujard; bud ovoid; flowers medium, semi-dbl.; foliage light green, soft; very vigorous, bushy growth; [Miss France × seedling]

Derby-Hagen Gmelin Rose – See **Melody Parfumée**, Gr

Derdinger Sommer F, mp, Hetzel; int. in 1991

Dereham Pride Pol, dr, 1932, Norfolk Nursery; flowers darkest crimson; vigorous, dwarf growth; [Éblouissant × Orange King]

Derek Nimmo HT, ob, 1981, McGredy, Sam IV; bud ovoid; flowers orange-red, silvery reverse, 30 petals, borne singly and in small clusters; foliage medium green; prickles red; vigorous growth; [seedling × seedling]; int. by John Mattock, Ltd.

Dernburg HT, pb, 1916, Krüger; flowers bright rose, shaded coral-red and yellow, large, dbl.; [Mme Caroline Testout × Souv d'Aimée Terrel des Chênes]

Derrich Gardner – See **Flame of Fantasy**, HT

DeRuiter's Herald – See **De Ruiter's Herald**, Pol

Des Alpes sans Épines – See **Bourbon**, HGal

Des Peintres – See **Rubra**, M

Des Peintres – See **Rose des Peintres**, C

Des Poêtes D, mp, about 1825, Cartier

Descanso Dream Min, w, 1995, Carruth, Tom; flowers white blend, small, dbl., no fragrance; foliage small, dark green, semi-glossy; few prickles; low (25-30 cm.), bushy, compact growth; [Origami × Little Artist]; int. by Weeks Roses, 1994

Descanso Pillar LCl, pb, 1952, Lammerts, Dr. Walter; bud urn-shaped, carmine to scarlet-red; flowers begonia-rose to deep rose-pink, inside varying to scarlet, 4½-5 in., 33 petals, high-centered; recurrent bloom; foliage dark, glossy; growth to 6-7 ft.; [Crimson Glory × Capt. Thomas]; int. by Germain's

Descemet C, mp, before 1820, Descemet; flowers bright pink, changing to pale rose, very large, dbl., cupped; growth branching

Descemet B, w, 1847, Vibert; flowers flesh-white, tinted mauve, medium

Deschamps HGal, pb, about 1830, Charpentier or Parmentier; flowers light pink, shaded bright pink, medium, full

Deschamps N, mr, 1877, Deschamps; flowers cherry-red, 6-7 cm., cupped, borne in small clusters; good repeat; numerous prickles; vigorous growth; possibly synonymous with Longworth Rambler

Desdechardo HT, dp, 1980, Taylor, W.J.; flowers deep pink; [sport of Red Lion]

Desdemona HT, lp, 1912, Paul, W.; flowers opaque light pink, large, dbl., globular, intense fragrance

Desdémona P, mr, 1841, Vibert; flowers carmine red, medium, dbl.; some autumn repeat

Desert Charm Min, dr, 1973, Moore, Ralph S.; flowers deep red, medium, dbl., high-centered; foliage dark, leathery; vigorous, dwarf, bushy growth; [Baccará × Magic Wand]; int. by Sequoia Nursery

Desert Dance F, ob, 1977, Herholdt, J.A.; bud pointed; flowers orange, reverse gold, 3 in., 15-18 petals, cupped, slight fragrance; foliage glossy; moderaterly tall growth; [Impala × seedling]; int. in 1975

Desert Dawn Gr, yb; int. in 1998

Desert Dream HT, lp, 1955, McGredy, Sam IV; flowers buff-pink, high pointed, 5 in.; foliage light green; very vigorous growth; [R.M.S. Queen Mary × Mrs Sam McGredy]; int. by Kordes

Desert Glow – See **Della Balfour**, S

Desert Island F, ab, Dickson; flowers creamy caramel, outer petals lighter, medium, 32 petals, high-centered, moderate, pleasing fragrance; foliage medium size, medium green, glossy; growth bushy to spreading, 3 ft.; [White Diamond × Apricot Ice]; int. by Dickson Nurseries, 2005

Desert Magic S, pb, 2005, Singer, Judith A; flowers hot pink to deep smoky russet pink, reverse medium to deep pink, petal edges scalloped, 5½ in., semi-dbl., borne mostly solitary, no fragrance; foliage medium size, dark green, semi-glossy; prickles small, slightly curved, beige to light brown, few; growth medium; [Sonia × Blue Girl]; int. in 2006

Desert Orchid S, ly, 2001, Rawlins, R.; flowers 3 in., full, borne in large clusters, moderate fragrance; foliage medium size, medium green, semi-glossy; prickles pointed, moderate; growth upright, medium (3 ft.); garden decorative; [Solitaire × (Mountbatten × (Angelina × (Flamenco × *R. bella*)))]; int. by Rearsby Roses, 2001

Desert Peace HT, yb, 1992; bud conical, large; flowers yellow edged with red, 14 cm., 22 petals, borne mostly singly, some small clusters, slight fragrance; good repeat; foliage large, dark green, glossy; prickles numerous, large; tall (120-130 cm.), upright growth; PP8248; [(Sonia × Rumba) × (Piccadilly × Chicago Peace)]; int. by C-P, 1991

Desert Sands F, ab, 1977, Bees; flowers deep apricot, 4½ in., 30 petals, intense fragrance; vigorous growth; [Arthur Bell × Elizabeth of Glamis]; int. in 1976

Desert Song HT, rb, 1948, Fletcher; flowers glowing reddish-copper, 4-5 in., 40-45 petals, peony-like; foliage glossy, bronze; [Mrs Sam McGredy × Golden Dawn]; int. by Tucker

Desert Spice – See **France Libre**, HT

Desert Storm Min, op, 1991, Gruenbauer, Richard; bud ovoid; flowers orange in summer, pink in cold weather, medium, dbl., urn-shaped, borne singly; foliage medium size, dark green, semi-glossy; upright, medium growth; [Libby × Rise 'n' Shine]; int. by Flowers 'n' Friends Miniature Roses, 1991

Desert Storm S, or, Williams, J. Benjamin; int. in 1997

Desert Sun HT, dy, deVor; int. in 1996

Desert Sunset Gr, or, 1962, Booy, H.; bud ovoid; flowers 3-4 in., 10 petals, cupped; foliage glossy; upright growth; [Floradora × Chrysler Imperial]; int. by Booy Rose Nursery

Desfontaines HGal, mp, about 1825, Cartier; flowers bright carmine, medium, dbl.

Desgaches B, mp, 1840, Desgaches; flowers carmine pink, large, full, borne in small clusters; sometimes classed as Ch

Desgaches HP, mr, 1850, Lacharme; flowers bright red, exterior petals bordered crimson, medium, full; foliage delicate green; prickles numerous, irregular

Desi HT, yb, Rupprecht-Radke; flowers golden yellow with red stripes, large, dbl.; int. in 1964

Designer Sunset S, ob; flowers pink, orange, and yellow; growth to 2 ft.; int. in 2003

Designer's Choice Gr, yb, 1989, deVor Nursery; bud pointed; flowers yellow marked orange, medium, 30 petals, high-centered, borne usually singly and in small clusters; foliage medium size, dark green, glossy; prickles slight recurved, small, brown; upright, medium growth; hips ovoid, small, orange; [Prominent × Bengali]; int. by Co-Operative Rose Growers, 1989

Désir HT, rb, 1945, Gaujard; flowers purplish red, large, dbl.; foliage glossy; very vigorous, bushy growth

Desire HT, mr, 1953, Obertello; bud ovoid; flowers cardinal-red, 5 in., 35-45 petals, high-centered, moderate fragrance; foliage dark; upright, compact growth; PP1289; [sport of Pink Delight]; int. by Amling-DeVor Nursery

Désiré Bergera HWich, pb, 1910, Barbier; flowers coppery rose, center brighter, 5-6 cm., dbl., borne in clusters of 2-6, moderate tea fragrance; seasonal bloom; foliage small, dark green, glossy; vigorous growth; [*R. wichurana* × Aurore]

Desirée HT, lp, 1985, Tantau, Math.; flowers large, 35 petals; foliage large, dark, semi-glossy; upright growth; int. in 1985

Desireé S, pb, Clements, John; flowers rich peach with highlights at the center, shading to delicate peach-pink towards edges, 4 in., 20 petals, borne in clusters, intense fruity myrrh fragrance; blooms in abundance; mid-green foliage with reddish, serrated edges; upright growth to 3 ft.; int. by Heirloom, 2004

Désirée Clary Gr, lp, Guillot-Massad; int. by Roseraies Guillot, 2002

Desirée Fontaine HP, dr, 1884, Fontaine; flowers deep rich grenadine, tinted with bluish violet, large, full, cupped, borne 4-5 per cluster

Désirée Parmentier HGal, lp, before 1841, Parmentier; flowers vivid pink, large, dbl., flat; bushy growth

Desmond Gatward HT, mr, 1966, Kemp, M.L.; flowers cerise-crimson, well-formed, 4½ in.; foliage red-bronze; free growth; [Karl Herbst × Dicksons Red]

Desmond Johnston HT, mr, 1927, McGredy; flowers brilliant scarlet, base orange, reverse veined orange, large, dbl., high-centered; foliage rich green, leathery, glossy; short stems; bushy growth; Gold Medal, NRS, 1927

Desmond Wilcox F, mr; int. by Love4Plants Ltd, 2004

Desparado F, yb, 1968, Harkness; flowers yellow shaded pink, semi-dbl., borne in trusses; [Pink Parfait × Masquerade]

Desprez N, op, 1838, Desprez; flowers dawn pink to flesh pink, aging to pink with coppery yellow center, reverse lighter

Desprez à Fleur Jaunes – See **Jaune Desprez**, N

Dessert F, rb, VEG; flowers red with white, medium, semi-dbl.

Dessy F, Williamson

Destin HT, mr, Croix, P.; int. in 1961

Destin, Climbing Cl HT, mr

Destino HT, pb, Camprubi, C.; flowers salmon-pink, becoming lilac-pink, well-formed, 45 petals; foliage dark; upright growth

Destiny HT, dr, 1935, Beckwith; bud long, pointed, well shaped; flowers rich crimson-scarlet shaded blackish, dbl.; foliage dark, leathery; vigorous, bushy growth

Destiny F, w, Meilland; int. in 1989

Destiny's Dream LCl, my, 2006, Webster, Robert; flowers straw yelllow, 2 in., very full, borne in large clusters; foliage small, medium green, semi-glossy; prickles 3 mm., needle, moderate; growth upright, short (6-8 ft.); pillar climber; [Laura Ford × The Marques of Bristol]; int. by Handley Rose Nurseries, 2006

Detroiter HT, dr, 1952, Kordes; bud long, pointed; flowers 5½ in., 23 petals, high-centered; vigorous, upright, bushy growth; [Poinsettia × Crimson Glory]; int. by J&P; Gold Medal, NRS, 1952

Detroiter, Climbing Cl HT, dr, 1960; int. by J&P

Detty HT, or, Adam

Deuil de Colonel Denfert HP, dr, 1878, Margottin Père; flowers velvety purplish black, large, full

Deuil de Dr Reynaud B, dp, 1862, Pradel; flowers deep crimson pink, large, dbl., intense fragrance

Deuil de Duc d'Orleans B, m, 1845, Lacharme, F.; flowers deep purple, large, very dbl.; foliage dark green; nearly thornless

Deuil de Dunois HP, dr, 1873, Lévêque; flowers blackish-red, dbl.

Deuil de la Duchesse d'Orléans B, m, 1858, Pradel; flowers glowing purple

Deuil de l'Empereur du Mexique HP, m, 1867, Cordier; flowers dark purple

Deuil de Paul Fontaine M, m, 1873, Fontaine; bud somewhat mossy; flowers purple-red, reverse mahogany, cupped; repeat bloom; very prickly; vigorous growth

Deuil du Colonel d'Enfer – See **Deuil de Colonel Denfert**, HP

Deuil du Maréchal Mortier HCh, dr, before 1841; flowers velvety maroon purple, sometimes marbled with white, large, full, cupped

Deuil du Prince Albert HP, dp, 1862, Lapente; flowers dark carmine, medium, full, globular, moderate fragrance

Deutsche Hoffnung HT, yb, 1920, Kiese; flowers salmon-yellow to apricot-yellow; [Mme Caroline Testout × Grossherzogin Feodora von Sachsen]

Deutsche Welle F, m, Leenders; int. in 1983

Deutsches Danzig Pol, pb, 1935, Lambert, P.; flowers carmine-pink with white, small, single

Deutsches Rosarium Dortmund – See **Rosarium Dortmund**, LCl

Deutschland HT, yb, 1910, Kiese; flowers cream, opening to golden yellow, faint rose in the center, large; [Frau Karl Druschki × Soleil d'Or]

Devi Gayatri F, w, Sen; flowers creamy white, borne in clusters; vigorous, shrubby growth; int. in 1992

Devienne l'Ami – See **Devienne-Lamy**, HP

Devienne-Lamy HP, mr, 1868, Lévêque; flowers deep carmine, large, dbl., cupped, globular

Devil Dancer HT, mr, 1980, Hawken, Una; bud ovoid; flowers brilliant brick-red, 4 in., 5 petals, slight fragrance; foliage dark; bushy growth; [Sonora × Matangi]

Devil's Dance F, mr

Devon – See **Cottage Maid**, S

Devon – See **Madison**, S

Devon Maid LCl, pb, 1977, Warner, Chris; flowers light pink, reverse medium pink, large, 22 petals, borne in clusters of 3-4, moderate fruity fragrance; foliage large, medium green, glossy; prickles large, curved, orange; needs support; vigorous, spreading, tall growth; hips ovoid, orange; [Casino × Elizabeth of Glamis]; int. by Warner's Roses

Devoniensis T, w, 1838, Foster; flowers creamy white, center sometimes tinged blush, very large, dbl.; recurrent bloom; very vigorous growth; [probably Park's Yellow × Smith's Yellow]; int. by Lucombe, Prince & Co., 1841

Devoniensis, Climbing Cl T, w, 1858, Pavitt; bud pink; flowers creamy white, tinted pink or yellow at center, 4 in., full, intense tea fragrance; recurrent; growth large, 10-15 ft; [sport of Devoniensis]; int. by Curtis

Devonshire Maid LCl, mp; int. in 1993

Devotion F, pb, 1971, Harkness; flowers light pink, flushed deeper, 4½ in., 32 petals; foliage light; [Orange Sensation × Peace]

Devotion HT, ab, Ilsink; flowers apricot-orange, dbl.; growth upright, bushy; int. in 2003

Devotion F, ab, Dickson; int. by Battersby Roses, 2004

Dew Drop Min, rb, 1991, Zipper, Herbert; flowers red with white eye, medium, single, borne mostly singly, slight fragrance; foliage small, dark green, semi-glossy, very disease-resistant; few prickles; low (12 in.), compact growth; [Sheri Anne × Priscilla Burton]; int. by Magic Moment Miniature Roses, 1992

Dewdrop HT, lp, 1921, McGredy; flowers pale pink to pale rose; RULED EXTINCT 11/91 ARM

Dewey F, dr, 2001, Giles, Diann; flowers medium, dbl., borne in small clusters, no fragrance; foliage large, dark green, matte; prickles medium, straight, moderate; growth bushy, medium; garden decorative; [Vera Dalton × Red Simplicity]; int. by Giles Rose Nursery, 1999

Dezent HT, ly, VEG; flowers yellowish-white, large, dbl.

Diablotin F, mr, 1965, Delbard-Chabert; flowers 2-3 in., 17 petals, borne in small clusters, no fragrance; bushy, compact growth; [Orléans Rose × Fashion]; int. by Delbard, 1961

Diablotin, Climbing Cl F, mr, 1986, Delbard; [sport of Diablotin]; int. in 1970; Gold Medal, Rome, 1970, Gold Medal, Paris, 1970, Gold Medal, Geneva, 1970

Diabolo HWich, rb, 1908, Fauque & fils; flowers velvety crimson, white center, golden stamens, 7-8 cm., single to semi-dbl., borne in large clusters, no fragrance; foliage dark green; prickles small, crimson, numerous; [*R. wichurana* × Xavier Olibo]

Diabolo F, op, 1959, Gaujard; flowers bright salmon, medium, semi-dbl., cupped, slight fragrance; foliage bronze; short stems; very vigorous, bushy growth; [Jolie Princesse × (Alain × Miss France)]

Diadeem – See **Diadem**, F dbl.

Diadem HT, ob, 1922, McGredy; flowers orange-crimson suffused salmon and yellow, very large, dbl., high-centered; foliage rich green, leathery, glossy; vigorous, bushy growth

Diadem F, mp, Tantau; flowers dbl., borne in clusters, slight fragrance; foliage medium green; medium to tall growth; int. in 1986; Gold Medal, Durbanville, 1987

Diadême de Flore HGal, m, before 1835, Descemet/Vibert; flowers lilac pink, edges lighter, large

Diamant Pol, w, 1908, Robichon; bud conical; flowers sulphur-white, petals fringed and ruffled, large, borne in clusters of 6-12, moderate almond fragrance; [sport of Marie Pavie]

Diamant F, or, 1962, Kordes, R.; bud ovoid; flowers bright orange-scarlet, well-formed, large, 40 petals, borne in clusters, slight fragrance; foliage dark, glossy; vigorous, upright growth; PP2445; int. by A. Dickson

Diamant S, w, 2006; bud small, pointed, oval; flowers pure white with large golden stamens, 6 cm., semi-dbl., flat, borne in small clusters, no fragrance; recurrent; foliage small, dark green, glossy, dense; groundcover; bushy (2 ft.) growth; int. by W. Kordes' Söhne, 2001; Gold Certificate, The Hague, 2006

Diamant Rose HMsk, pb, 2000, Lens, Louis; flowers light pink, reverse lighter, 1 in., single, borne in large clusters; recurrent; foliage small, medium green, glossy, disease-resistant; few prickles; upright, bushy, low (2-3 ft.) growth; [(*R. multiflora adenocheata* × Ballerina) × seedling]; int. by Louis Lens NV, 1995

Diamantina HT, op, 1949, Giacomasso; flowers salmon and rose, large; strong stems; [Julien Potin × Ophelia]

Diamond – See **Diamant**, F

Diamond – See **Diamond Victory**, S

Diamond – See **Diamant**, S

Diamond Anniversary Min, m, 1996, Moore, Ralph S.; flowers mauve, reverse mauve or slightly lighter, 1½ in., 40 petals, borne in small clusters; few prickles; PP11063; [Joycie × Cherry Magic]; int. by Sequoia Nursery, 1997

Diamond Border – See **Diamond Head**, S

Diamond Days Forever F, w, Fryer; flowers white with creamy centers, dbl., high-centered, borne usually in clusters; recurrent; foliage dark green, glossy; medium, bushy growth; int. by Fryers Roses, 2006

Diamond Doll Min, ly, 1996, Bell, Judy G.; flowers light yellow, darker yellow center, petals quilled and reflexed, 1½ in., full, borne in small clusters, intense fragrance; foliage medium size, medium green, matte; few prickles; upright growth, 18 in.; medium (18 in winter hardy; [Rise 'n' Shine × Angel Face]; int. by Michigan Mini Roses, 1997

Diamond Gray HT, m, Teranishi; int. in 2004

Diamond Head S, w, Poulsen; flowers white, 8-10 cm., slight wild rose fragrance; dark foliage; growth bushy, 100-150 cm.; PP12568; int. as Diamond Border, Poulsen Roser, 1997

Diamond Jewel Min, w, 1959, Morey, Dr. Dennison; bud globular; flowers white, overcast blush-pink, ½-¾ in., 45-50 petals, cupped; compact, low, open growth; PP1908; [Dick Koster × Tom Thumb]; int. by J&P, 1959

Diamond Jubilee HT, ly, 1947, Boerner; bud ovoid; flowers buff-yellow, 5-6 in., 28 petals, cupped, moderate fragrance; foliage leathery; upright, compact growth; [Marèchal Niel × Feu Pernet-Ducher]; int. by J&P

Diamond Victory S, w, Poulsen; flowers white, 8-10 cm., 25 petals, moderate fragrance; foliage dark; growth bushy, 20-40 cm.; PP15889; int. by Poulsen Roser, 2000

Diamond Wishes – See **Misty**, Min

Dian Min, dp, 1958, Moore, Ralph S.; flowers soft red, 1 in., 45 petals, moderate apple fragrance; foliage small, dark, glossy; vigorous (15 in.), bushy growth; PP1808; [(*R. wichurana* × Floradora) × (Oakington Ruby × Floradora)]; int. by Sequoia Nursery, 1957

Diana HP, dp, 1873, Paul

Diana HT, mp, 1921, Bees; flowers Malmaison pink, very large, dbl., globular, moderate fragrance; vigorous growth; [Mrs Frank Workman × Sunburst]

Diana Pol, op, 1922, Spek; flowers bright orange shaded pink, large, semi-dbl.

Diana F, my, 1978, Tantau, Math.; bud globular; flowers medium, dbl., slight fragrance; foliage medium size, glossy; vigorous, upright growth

Diana – See **Diana, Princess of Wales**, HT

Diana Allen HT, op, 1939, Clark, A.; flowers salmon-pink, small, dbl.; short stems; bushy, compact growth; [Mrs Aaron Ward × seedling]; int. by NRS New South Wales

Diana Armstrong HT, dy, 1992, Thompson, Robert; flowers medium, full, borne mostly singly, intense fragrance; foliage medium size, medium green, semi-glossy; some prickles; upright (80 cm.) growth; [seedling × Prima Ballerina]; int. by Battersby Roses, 1993

Diana Cant HT, rb, 1928, Cant, B. R.; flowers carmine-red, base flushed orange, dbl.; [Isobel × seedling]

Diana Festival Min, lp, Laver, Keith G.; int. in 1996

Diana H. Gupta HT, op, 1999, Jellyman, J.S.; flowers orange-pink, reverse pale lemon yellow with faint white striping, 3 in., full, borne in small clusters, slight fragrance; foliage medium size, medium green, semi-glossy; few prickles; upright, bushy, medium (3 ft.) growth; [Gavotte × Bill Temple]

Diana Holman F, m, 2006, James, Peter J.; flowers purple, reverse lighter, 3-4 in., full, borne in large clusters; foliage medium size, dark green, semi-glossy; prickles straight, moderate; growth vigorous, bushy, tall (4 ft.); garden decoration; [Natural Beauty × Rhapsody in Blue]; int. by Peter J James, 2007

Diana Maxwell HT, ob, 1957, Kemp, M.L.; flowers orange-cerise, high pointed, 5 in., 45 petals; foliage bronze; vigorous growth; [Ena Harkness × Sam McGredy]

Diana Menhuin HT, dy, 1963, LeGrice; flowers deep buttercup-yellow, 5½ in., 30 petals, globular; foliage dark, glossy; vigorous, upright growth; [(Golden Masterpiece × Ellinor LeGrice) × Forward]

Diana Rowden LCl, op, 1977, Hawker; flowers deep copper-salmon to rose-pink, 5-6 in., 30 petals, intense fragrance; profuse, continuous bloom; foliage large, copper to green; [Mrs Sam McGredy, Climbing × Red Dandy]; int. by Harkness

Diana, Princess of Wales HT, pb, 1998, Zary, Keith W.; flowers pink cream blend, reverse pink cream blend, 5 in., full, borne mostly solitary, moderate fragrance; foliage large, medium green, glossy; prickles 6-8 mm., hooked upward; growth upright, well branched, tall (5-5½ ft.); specimen, garden; PP11482; [Anne Morrow Lindbergh × Sheer Elegance]; int. by Bear Creek Gardens, 1999

Diane HT, yb, 1958, Gaujard; flowers clear yellow, center orange-yellow, well-formed, large; vigorous growth; [Peace × (seedling × Opera)]

Diane HT, yb, Dawson, George; int. in 1976

Diane de Bollvillers T, w, before 1884, Baumann; flowers cream white, shaded pink, large, very full

Diane de Broglie HT, ob, 1929, Chambard, C.; flowers coral-orange, very large, dbl., cupped; foliage dark; strong stems; very vigorous growth

Diane de Poitiers HT, dp; flowers pure pink; growth to 3-4 ft.

Diane d'Urfé HT, w, 1958, Croix, A.; flowers white, becoming red-edged; vigorous growth; [Peace × Incendie]; int. by Minier

Dianna Kay Min, or, 1982, Dobbs, Annette E.; flowers small, 20 petals, no fragrance; foliage small, medium green, semi-glossy; upright growth; [Anytime × Sheri Anne]

Dianne Feinstein HT, yb, 1980, Fong, William P.; bud ovoid; flowers 23 petals, high-centered, borne singly, moderate fragrance; foliage dark; prickles triangular; vigorous, spreading growth; [McGredy's Yellow × Sutter's Gold]

Dianthaeflora – See **Œillet**, C

Dianthiflora – See **Fimbriata**, HRg

Diany Binny LCl, w, 1976, Binny; flowers pure white with prominent yellow stamens, 2 in., 5 petals, borne in clusters of 10-20, intense fragrance; foliage gray-green; [Kiftsgate × *R. rubrifolia*]

Diapason HT, mp, 1970, Delbard-Chabert; flowers porcelain pink, medium, 40 petals, globular, moderate fragrance; foliage bronze, glossy; very vigorous, bushy growth; [Chic Parisien × ((Sultane × unknown) × Mme Joseph Perraud)]; int. by Pepinieres G. Delbard, 1966

Diavoletta ; int. in 1966

Dic Della HT, dp, Chiplunkar; int. in 1996

Dicdella HT, dp, Chiplunkar; flowers large, deep pink, full, high-centered; [sport of Ace of Hearts]; int. in 1996

Dicdip HT, pb, 1985, Dickson, Patrick; flowers large, 32 petals, moderate fragrance; foliage medium size, purple when young; upright, bushy growth; [Eurorose × Typhoon]; int. in 1974

Dicfate F, mp, 1985, Dickson, Patrick; flowers medium, 18 petals, slight fragrance; foliage medium size, medium green; upright, bushy growth; [Futura × (Pye Colour × Prominent)]; int. in 1975

Dick Balfour S, w; flowers white blush; recurrent bloom; groundcover; spreading growth

Dick Koster Pol, dp, 1929, Koster, D.A.; flowers small, deep pink, dbl., cupped, borne in clusters; recurrent bloom; growth mounded, low, spreading; [sport of Anneke Koster]

Dick Koster Fulgens Pol, dp, 1940, Koster, M.; flowers light red, semi-dbl., borne in clusters; low, compact growth

Dick Koster Superior Pol, mr, 1955, Koster, D.A.; flowers rosy red; [sport of Dick Koster]

Dick Lindner HT, mp; flowers coral pink, dbl., high-centered; growth vigorous, medium; int. in 1996

Dick Tracy Min, rb, Dickson

Dick Wilcox HT, dr, 1949, Brownell; bud long, pointed to ovoid; flowers rose-red, 4-5½ in., 50-60 petals, high-centered, moderate fragrance; foliage dark; vigorous growth; [Pink Princess × Crimson Glory]

Dick's Delight Min, dp, 1999, Dickson, Colin; flowers 1¼ in., full, borne in large clusters; foliage small, dark green, glossy; prickles moderate; patio; compact to spreading, low (24 in.) growth; [seedling × The Fairy]; int. by Dickson Nurseries, 1999

Dickson's Bouquet HT, ab, 1938, Dickson, A.; flowers salmon, carmine and apricot, blended saffron, dbl.; long, wiry stems; vigorous growth

Dickson's Centennial HT, mr, 1936, Dickson, A.; bud pointed; flowers crimson to scarlet, loosely formed, very large; foliage bronze; long, strong stems; vigorous, bushy growth; int. by J&P, 1937

Dickson's Delight HT, ob, 1938, Dickson, A.; flowers vivid orange, heavily shaded scarlet-orange; foliage bronze-green; vigorous growth

Dickson's Flame F, or, 1959, Dickson, A.; flowers scarlet-flame, large, dbl., borne in trusses, slight fragrance; vigorous growth; [(Independence × unknown) × Nymph]; int. in 1958; President's International Trophy, NRS, 1958, Gold Medal, NRS, 1958

Dickson's Jubilee – See **Lovely Lady**, HT

Dickson's Perfection HT, pb, 1937, Dickson, A.; flowers shrimp-pink, base orange-yellow, large, dbl.; very vigorous growth; int. by Port Stockton Nursery

Dickson's Red HT, dr, 1938, Dickson, A.; flowers velvety crimson-scarlet, large, 18 petals, cupped, intense spicy fragrance; foliage leathery, dark; vigorous, bushy growth; Gold Medal, Portland, 1941, Gold Medal, NRS, 1939

Dickson's Wonder HT, ob, Dickson; int. in 1978

Dicky F, op, 1984, Dickson, Patrick; flowers reddish salmon-pink, reverse lighter, large, 35 petals, slight fragrance; foliage medium size, medium green, glossy; bushy growth; [Cathedral × Memento]; int. in 1983; Gold Medal, RNRS, 1984, President's International Trophy, RNRS, 1984

Didot HSpn, w, from Scotland; flowers blush white

Die Berühmte – See **Illustre**, HGal

Die Bloemhoffer HT, w, Kordes; bud pointed, urn shaped; flowers cream, outer petals cream tinted green, dbl., exhibition, no fragrance; growth to 4-5 ft.; int. by Ludwig's Roses, 2001

Die Krone HT, dy

Die Mutter von Rosa HT, lp, 1906, Verschuren; flowers medium, dbl.

Die Präsidentin HT, w, 1928, Mühle; flowers marble white, center soft yellow, semi-dbl.; [Harry Kirk × unknown]

Die Rheinpfalz F, ob, Hetzel; int. in 1993

Die Schöne Tölzerin S, mp, Schultheis; flowers lasting pink, medium, very dbl., almost quartered; growth broad, upright, 5 ft; int. by Rosen von Schultheis, 2001

Die Schonste HT, w; int. in 1998

Die Spree HT, lp, 1907, Nauke; flowers flesh pink, satiny whitish pink in center, large, dbl., moderate fragrance

Die Welt HT, ob, 1976, Kordes; bud long, pointed; flowers orange, red and yellow blend, 4½ in., 25 petals, high-centered, borne mostly singly, slight fragrance; foliage glossy; vigorous, upright, very tall, bushy growth; [seedling × Peer Gynt]

Diener's Blue HMult, m, 1926, Diener; flowers violet, 2 in., dbl., borne in heavy clusters; almost thornless; vigorous growth

Diener's Rose Understock HMult, rb, 1932, Diener; bud long; flowers rose-red shaded purple, stamens yellowish, 2 in., 10 petals, borne in clusters; foliage small, notched; climbing or trailing growth; producing much new wood in a season; [Veilchenblau × Veilchenblau sport]

Dieter Wolf Pol, or, 1978, Buisman, G. A. H.; flowers salmon-orange, semi-dbl.; foliage glossy, dark; vigorous, compact growth; [Tropicana × Jiminy Cricket]; int. in 1969

Dietlikon HT, mr, Huber; flowers cherry-red, dbl., high-centered; int. by Rosen Huber, 2005

Dietrich Woessner F, w, Huber; flowers creamy white, center tinted yellow in autumn, 6 cm., dbl., borne in clusters of 4-6; new foliage copper red, turning dark green; growth to 2-3½ ft., somewhat irregular; int. by Rosen Huber, 2001

Dieudonné HCh, dr, 1827, Mauget; flowers crimson purple, very small; Lawrenciana

Different Charm MinFl, or, 2004, McCann, Sean; flowers orange-red, reverse lighter red, 2½ in., very full, borne mostly solitary, slight fragrance; foliage medium size, medium green, semi-glossy; prickles small, straight; growth compact (2½ ft.); garden decoration; [unknown × unknown]; int. by Ashdown Roses, Ltd., 2004

Dignity HT, w, 1940, LeGrice; bud long, pointed; flowers creamy white, dbl.; foliage leathery; vigorous, bushy, compact growth

Dikgang Moseneke S, mr, Kordes; int. by Ludwig's Roses, 2002

Dil-Ki-Rani HT, lp, Pal, Dr. B.P.; int. in 1985

Diletta HT, mr, Barni, V.; flowers large, brilliant geranium red, dbl., high-centered, moderate fragrance; foliage bronzy green; growth vigorous, erect, 3-4 ft; int. in 1985

Dilly Dilly MinFl, m, 1985, Bennett, Dee; flowers lavender, medium, 35 petals, high-centered, moderate fragrance; foliage medium size, medium green, semi-glossy; upright growth; PP6141; [Chrysler Imperial × Plum Duffy]; int. by Tiny Petals Nursery, 1984

Dilly's Wiederkehr HFt, 1925, Schwartzbach; flowers large, dbl.

Dily's Allen HT, ob, 1952, Norman; bud long, pointed, ovoid; flowers orange-red, base saffron, 4 in.; foliage glossy, dark bluish green; vigorous, bushy growth; [Mrs Sam McGredy × seedling]; int. by Harkness

Dimity HT, pb, 1956, Taylor, C.A.; bud ovoid, pointed; flowers ivory to pure white, edged pink, large, dbl., cupped; foliage dark, leathery; upright, bushy growth; [Peace × seedling]

Dimples F, ly, 1968, LeGrice; flowers canary-yellow to ivory, semi-dbl., borne in trusses; foliage glossy

Dina Gee HT, rb, 2005, Smith, John T.; flowers red, reverse white, 4-5 in., full, high-centered, borne mostly solitary, no fragrance; foliage medium size, medium green, matte; prickles large, straight, light red, moderate; growth upright, tall (4½- 5 ft.) pillar; [Moonstone × Signature]; int. in 2007

Dinah HT, dr, 1920, Paul, W.; flowers deep crimson, shaded darker

Dinah Shore HT, dp, 1942, Grillo; flowers cerise-pink, 5 in., 65 petals, globular, intense fragrance; foliage glossy, dark; vigorous, upright growth; [sport of Jewel]

Dingee & Conard HP, mr, 1875, Verdier, E.; flowers shining poppy red, large, full, moderate fragrance

Dinky Min, or, 1986, Bridges, Dennis A.; flowers orange-red, reverse orange, 20 petals, urn-shaped, borne usually singly; foliage medium size, medium green, semi-glossy; prickles long, light red; upright growth; [Sheri Anne × seedling]

Dinky HMsk, dp, Velle-Boudolf; flowers pink fuchsia, full, borne in large, pyramidal sprays; recurrent; growth to 4 ft.; int. by Louis Lens, 2003; Golden Rose, Orléans, 2006

Dinsmore – See **Mme Charles Wood**, HP

Diny Hage HT, dr, 1956, Leenders, M.; flowers crimson-red, large, dbl.; vigorous growth; [Ambassadeur Nemry × Crimson Glory]

Dionisia F, yb, Barni; flowers white with yellow in the heart and deep pink edges, semi-dbl., borne in clusters, slight fruity fragrance; growth to 3-4 ft.; int. by Rose Barni, 2003

Diorama HT, yb, 1965, deRuiter; flowers apricot-yellow, 4½ in., dbl., high-centered; vigorous, upright growth; [Peace × Beauté]

Diorama, Climbing Cl HT, yb; int. after 1965

Dioressence Gr, m, 1985, Delbard, Georges; flowers lavender, well-formed, large, 35 petals, intense fragrance; foliage large, medium green, semi-glossy; bushy growth; [((Holstein × Bayadère) × Prelude) × seedling]; int. by Pepinieres et Roseraies G. Delbard, 1984

Diorette – See **Cancan**, F

Diplomat HT, dr, 1962, Boerner; bud ovoid; flowers current red edged blood-red, 3½-4 in., 50-55 petals, cupped, moderate fragrance; foliage leathery, dark; vigorous, upright growth; PP2114; [(Poinsettia × Tawny Gold) × Detroiter]; int. by Home Nursery Products Corp., 1962

Diplomatka F, mr, Klimenko, V. N.; flowers blood red, large, dbl.; int. in 1967

Diputacion de Tarragona HT, ob, 1970, Dot, Pedro; bud pointed; flowers orange-coral, large, 35 petals, high-centered, moderate fragrance; foliage glossy, bronze; upright, compact growth; [Baccará × (Chrysler Imperial × Soraya)]; int. by Rosas Dot, 1967

Directeur Alphand HP, m, 1883, Lévêque; flowers blackish purple, large, dbl.

Directeur Constantin Bernard HT, m, 1886, Soupert & Notting; flowers delicate magenta pink on a silvery ground, large, very full; [Abel Grand × Mlle Adèle Jougant]

Directeur Donatien Lelievre F, ob, 1959, Privat; flowers coppery orange, medium, dbl.

Directeur Guérin HT, ob, 1935, Gaujard; flowers orange-yellow, center coppery, overlarge, dbl.; foliage light; long stems; very vigorous growth

Directeur N. Jensen HP, m, 1883, Verdier, E.; flowers purple/pink, large, dbl.

Directeur René Gérard T, yb, 1892, Pelletier; flowers canary yellow, tinted China pink, edges shaded magenta, large, full; [Mme Falcot × Marquise de Vivens]

Director Plumecock – See **Président Plumecocq**, HT

Director Rubió HT, rb, 1929, Dot, Pedro; flowers magenta-red, very large, semi-dbl.; stiff stems; dwarf, bushy growth; [O. Junyent × Jean C.N. Forestier]; int. by C-P

Direkteur H. J. Bos S, pb; flowers large, borne in clusters; recurrent

Dir. Rijnveld F, or; flowers medium size, bright, semi-dbl.; recurrent; int. by Belle Epoque, 2001

Direkteur Rikala – See **Direktor Rikala**, F

Direktor Benschop – See **City of York**, LCl

Direktor Eric Hjelm Pol, rb, 1927, Koster, D.A.; flowers red; [sport of Prasident Hindenburg]

Direktor Hjelm – See **Direktor Eric Hjelm**, Pol

Direktor Rebhuhn HT, ob, 1929, Kordes; flowers orange, center reddish, dbl.; [Mme Butterfly × Angèle Pernet]

Direktor Rikala F, mp, 1934, Koster, D.A.; [sport of Lafayette]; possibly synonymous with Frau Astrid Späth

Direktor Struve Pol, w, 1924, van Nes; [sport of Echo]

Dirigent HMsk, mr, 1959, Tantau, Math.; bud pointed; flowers blood-red, semi-dbl., borne in clusters of up to 28, slight fragrance; recurrent bloom; foliage leathery; vigorous (4 ft.) growth; [Fanal × Karl Weinhausen]; int. in 1956; ADR, 1958

Disco HT, rb, 1980, Weeks, O.L.; bud medium to long, pointed; flowers medium red, reverse cream, 30 petals, high-centered, borne singly and 2-4 per cluster, slight spicy fragrance; foliage leathery, dark; prickles hooked downward; tall, upright growth; PP4737; [Sunrise-Sunset × seedling]

Disco F, pb, Harkness

Disco Dancer F, or, 1984, Dickson, Patrick; flowers orange scarlet, medium, semi-dbl.; foliage medium size, medium green, glossy; bushy growth; [Cathedral × Memento]; Gold Medal, The Hague, 1982

Discovery Gr, pb, 1959, deRuiter; flowers soft pink shaded apricot, 5-6 in., dbl., intense fragrance; vigorous growth; [(Peace × Christopher Stone) × Floribunda seedling]; int. by Blaby Rose Gardens, 1958

Discovery S, mp, Clements, John; flowers 4 in., 50 petals, deeply cupped, old-fashioned, slight myrrh fragrance; good repeat bloom; foliage lime green; growth upright, dense (3½ ft.); int. by Heirloom Roses, 2004

Discretion HT, pb, 1952, Gaujard; flowers salmon-pink shaded copper, large, 28 petals; foliage glossy; [Peace × seedling]

Disguise F, rb, William, J.B.; bud coral red; flowers creamy white in center, red on outer petals spreading toward center, semi-dbl. to dbl., slight fragrance; growth to 3 ft.; int. by Hortico, Inc., 2006

Disneyland – See **Disneyland Rose**, F

Disneyland Rose F, op, 2005, Walden, John K. & Zary, Keith W.; flowers orange pink blend, reverse orange pink blend, 7½ cm., 30-35 petals, borne in small clusters, slight fragrance; foliage medium size, dark green, glossy; prickles 5-7 mm., hooked downward, greyed-orange, moderate; growth upright, branching, compact, short (70-80 cm.); PP15114; [Sequoia gold × Hot Tamale]; int. by Jackson & Perkins Wholesale, Inc., 2004; Gold Medal, Rose Hills, 2006

Dispetto S, rb, Barni; flowers striped red and white, pattern variable, borne in clusters, slight fragrance; recurrent; foliage large, glossy; vigorous (50-70 cm.), spreading growth; int. by Rose Barni, 2006

Display F, pb, 1956, Arnot; flowers salmon-pink, becoming cherry-pink, well-formed, 2½ in., 13 petals, borne in large clusters; foliage glossy, bronze-green; very vigorous growth; [Orange Triumph × Golden Scepter]; int. by Croll

Disque d'Or – See **Goldstar**, HT

Disraeli S, mr, 1987, Adams, Dr. Neil D.; flowers medium, full, no fragrance; foliage large, dark green, glossy; upright, bushy, tall, broad growth; [Hamburger Phoenix × seedling]

Distant Drums S, m, 1985, Buck, Dr. Griffith J.; bud ovoid, pointed; flowers rose-purple, imbricated, large, 40 petals, borne singly and in clusters of up to 10, intense myrrh fragrance; repeat bloom; foliage medium-large, dark, leathery; prickles awl-like, brown; vigorous, erect, bushy growth; [September Song × The Yeoman]; int. by Iowa State University, 1984

Distant Sounds HT, pb, Webb; flowers clear pink with lighter reverse, dbl., high-centered, star shape, no fragrance; growth medium; int. in 1996

Distant Thunder S, m, Clements, John; flowers lavender-pink with hints of brown and gold (much like Distant Drums), 3½-4 in., 30 petals, strong fruity, myrrh fragrance; foliage reddish-bronze early, aging to deep olive-green, serrated red edges; growth compact (3 × 3 ft.), very bushy plant with foliage to the ground; int. by Heirloom Roses, 2002

Distinct F, rb, 1953, Boerner; flowers spectrum-red with white eye, imbricated, small, 25-30 petals, cupped, borne in rounded clusters; foliage glossy; vigorous, compact growth; [Triomphe Orléanais × Mrs Pierre S. duPont]; int. by J&P

Distinction HT, ab, 1882, Bennett; flowers shaded peach, dbl., cupped; either Mme de St. Joseph × Eugène Verdier, or Mabel Morrison × Devoniensis

Distinction F, dp, 1927, Turbat; flowers deep rose-pink, center brighter; [sport of Lafayette]

Distinction, Climbing Cl F, dp, 1935, Lens, Louis; flowers medium, semi-dbl.

Ditto Min, dr, 1986, Lyon, Lyndon; flowers very small, 14 petals, borne usually singly; foliage small, medium green, matte; no prickles; low, bushy growth; [Baby Betsy McCall × seedling]; int. by M.B. Farm Min. Roses, Inc.

Diva HT, dr, 1978, Poulsen; flowers dark velvety red, 6 in., 30 petals, slight fragrance; foliage dark; spreading growth; [Sonia × Gisselfeld]; int. in 1976

Diva HT, dy, Cocker; int. in 1995

Diversity HT, rb, K&S; flowers medium, pale salmon base, scarlet and yellow with yellow stripes; int. by KSG Son, 1995

Dividend HT, dy, 1931, Clark, A.; flowers rich yellow, dbl., globular; foliage dark; dwarf growth; [Franz Deegen × seedling]; int. by NRS Victoria

Divine HT, mr, 1964, Delbard-Chabert; bud dark purplish; flowers cardinal-red, well-formed, large, 45 petals; foliage bright green; strong stems; vigorous, upright growth; Gold Medal, Geneva, 1964

Divine Lady F, op, 1966, Lens, Louis; flowers salmon-pink suffused brownish, dbl.; very vigorous, dense growth; [Circus × Queen Elizabeth]

Dixie HT, op, 1925, Gray, W.R.; flowers salmon-pink, more large, dbl., cupped; [sport of Radiance]

Dixie Belle HT, lp, 1963, Boerner; bud ovoid, rose-pink; flowers 5-5½ in., 38 petals, cupped, moderate fragrance; foliage leathery; vigorous, upright growth; PP2302; [Golden Masterpiece × seedling]; int. by J&P, 1963

Dixie Climber Cl HT, ob, 1935, Watkins, A.F.; flowers salmon and gold; [sport of Gov. Alfred E. Smith]; int. by J&P

Dixie Dazzle Min, ob, 1991, King, Gene; bud ovoid; flowers orange-red to yellow, small, 16 petals, high-centered, no fragrance; foliage small, medium green, semi-glossy; upright, low growth; [(Rainbow's End × Miss Dovey) × Jennie Anne]; int. by AGM Miniature Roses, 1990

Dixie Dream – See **Festival**, HT

Dixie Holiday HT, mr, 1968, Garrison; bud long, pointed; flowers medium, dbl., high-centered; foliage bronze, leathery; very vigorous growth; [sport of Étoile de Hollande]; int. by Kimbrew

Dixieland Min, rb, 1992, Bridges, Dennis A.; flowers in shades of vibrant pink, red and white intensifying with sun, large, dbl., high-centered; foliage medium size, medium green, semi-glossy; no prickles; tall (50-60 cm.), upright growth; [Fancy Pants × seedling]; int. by Bridges Roses, 1992

Dixieland Linda Cl HT, ab, 1997, Beales, Peter; flowers very dbl., 41 petals, borne in small clusters; foliage medium size, dark green, glossy; upright, medium (8-10ft.)growth; [sport of Aloha]; int. by Peter Beales Roses, 1996

Dizzy F, Delforge, H.; int. in 1974

Dizzy Heights LCl, mr, 1999, Fryer, Gareth; flowers bright red, reverse same, 5-5½ in., dbl., borne in large clusters, slight fragrance; foliage medium size, dark green, semi-glossy; prickles moderate; upright, tall (7-10 ft.) growth; int. by Fryer's Nurseries, Ltd., 2000

Do-Si-Do S, mp, 1985, Buck, Dr. Griffith J.; flowers medium lavender-pink, large, cupped, borne 3-10 per cluster, moderate fragrance; repeat bloom; foliage dark olive green, leathery, glossy; prickles awl-like, tan; vigorous, erect, bushy growth; hardy; [(Autumn Dusk × Solitude) × Wanderin' Wind]; int. by Iowa State University, 1984

Doamna in Mov HT, m, Wagner, S.; flowers large, 28 petals, strong fragrance; foliage large, medium green, glossy, healthy; [Lavendula × Mainzer Fastnacht]; int. by Res. Stn. for Hort., 2003

Doc Pol, mp, 1958, deRuiter; flowers phlox-pink, small, 15 petals, borne in large trusses; compact growth; [Robin Hood × Polyantha seedling]; int. by Gregory & Son, 1954

Docile F, mp, Eve, A.; buds round; flowers pink with ruffled petals, dbl., borne in clusters of 3-5; growth to 3 ft.; int. by Les Roses de Anciennes de André Eve, 1995

Docteur Berthet B, mr, 1858, Damaizin; flowers shining cherry red with carmine, large, full

Docteur Brière B, pb, 1860, Vigneron; flowers cerise pink with yellow stamens, full, cupped, moderate fragrance

Docteur F. Debat – See **Doctor F. Debat**, HT

Docteur Hurta – See **Dr Hurta**, HP

Docteur Leprestre B, dr, 1852, Oger; flowers bright velvety purplish-red, large, full; foliage olive green

Docteur Leprêtre – See **Docteur Leprestre**, B

Docteur Louis Escarras HT, rb, 1922, Nabonnand, C.; flowers dark salmon-red shaded carmine-pink, 120 petals; [Constance × seedling]

Docteur Marjolin M, dp, 1860, Robert et Moreau; flowers bright red-pink, 7-9 cm., dbl., very globular

Docteur Morel HT, m, 1946, Laperrière; flowers carmine with chrome-yellow reflections, large, 40-45 petals; foliage dark; vigorous, upright growth; [Edith Nellie Perkins × Pres. Herbert Hoover]

Docteur Reymont HMult, w, 1907, Mermet; flowers pure white on pale green base, 3 cm., dbl., borne in medium, pyramidal clusters; numerous prickles; [Turner's Crimson Rambler × unknown]

Docteur Robert Salmont HT, yb, 1946, Gaujard; bud pointed; flowers capucine and yellow, reverse tinted chrome, base coppery; foliage dark; vigorous growth

Docteur Valois HT, rb, 1950, Mallerin, C.; flowers geranium shaded vermilion, reverse yellow, 4 in., semi-dbl.; foliage dark, glossy; vigorous, bushy growth; [(Annie Drevet × Condesa de Sástago) × Vive la France]; int. by URS

Dr A. Hermans HT, ly, 1906, Verschuren; flowers yellowish-pink, large, very full; [Rosa Verschuren × unknown]

Dr A. I. Petyt HT, rb, 1924, Burrell; flowers maroon-crimson shaded scarlet, large, dbl., high-centered; vigorous, bushy growth; [(George Dickson × unknown) × Edward Mawley]

Dr A. J. Verhage HT, dy, 1961, Verbeek; flowers large, petals wavy, 22-30 petals, intense fragrance; foliage dark, glossy; vigorous, bushy growth; PP2105; [Tawny Gold × (Baccará × seedling)]; patent issued as Golden Wave; re-registered as Golden Wave, 1968; int. by Carlton Rose Nurseries

Dr A. J. Verhage, Climbing Cl HT, dy, 1968, Blaby Rose Gardens

Dr A. S. Thomas HT, rb, 1951, Clark, A.; bud long, pointed; flowers dark crimson shaded darker, large, 60 petals, high-centered; foliage leathery, dark; vigorous, fairly compact growth; int. by NRS Victoria

Dr A. Svehla HT, rb, 1935, Böhm, J.; flowers dark carmine, very large, dbl.; bushy growth; [Col. Leclerc × Gen. MacArthur]

Dr A. von Erlach HT, pb, 1932, Soupert & Notting; bud nankeen yellow and salmon; flowers pink and straw-yellow, stamens yellow, semi-dbl., cupped; stiff stems; vigorous growth; [Prince de Bulgarie × Mrs S.K. Rindge]

Doctor Abrahams HT, ab, Hallows; int. in 1991

Dr Adam Christman Gr, dr, 1987, Williams, J. Benjamin; flowers dark crimson red to scarlet, large, full, borne in large sprays, slight fragrance; foliage large, dark green, semi-glossy; upright growth; [Queen Elizabeth × Chrysler Imperial]

Doctor Albert Schweitzer HT, pb, 1961, Delbard-Chabert; flowers opal-pink, reverse rose-red, well-formed, 5-6 in., 30-35 petals; foliage leathery, glossy; vigorous, upright bushy growth; [Chic Parisien × Michele Meilland]

Dr Andrew Carnegie HT, pb, 1927, Ferguson, R.C.; flowers light silvery pink, base yellowish; [sport of Mrs Henry Morse]; int. by Dreer, 1930

Dr Andry HP, mr, 1864, Verdier, E.; flowers rosy crimson, medium, 45 petals, cupped; foliage glossy; vigorous, upright growth; [Victor Verdier × unknown]

Dr Antonin Joly HP, op, 1886, Besson; flowers salmon-pink, large, very dbl.; [Baronne Adolphe de Rothschild × unknown]

Dr Arnal HP, mr, 1848, Roeser

Dr Auguste Krell HP, rb, 1877, Verdier, E.; flowers carmine cerise red, shaded purple, whitish reverse, large, full; foliage dark green, finely dentate; prickles numerous, unequal, straight, pink

Dr Augustin Wibbelt HT, yb, 1928, Leenders, M.; flowers golden yellow, shaded orange, large, semi-dbl., moderate fragrance; foliage medium size, light green; [sport of Los Angeles]

Dr Augusto de Castro HT, rb, 1954, Moreira da Silva; flowers bright red, reverse yellow; [Sultane × Peace]

Dr B. Benacerraf Min, pb, 1988, Miller, F.; flowers white to light pink, dark pink borders, opening to light pink, 15-20 petals; foliage ovoid, medium green, matte, disease-resistant; vigorous, compact growth; [(Double Delight × Simplex) × Magic Carrousel]

Dr B. G. Kane – See **Dr Kane**, HT

Dr B. P. Pal HT, m, 1981, Division of Vegetable Crops and Floriculture; bud long, pointed; flowers solferino purple, 70 petals, high-centered, borne singly; foliage dark, leathery; prickles straight, brown; upright growth; [seedling × seedling]; int. in 1980

Dr Baillet T, m, 1903, Corboeuf; flowers violet with white reflections, striped yellow

Dr Baillon HP, dr, 1878, Margottin père; flowers bright crimson, shaded purple, large, full

Dr Barnardo F, dr, 1968, Harkness; flowers crimson, large, 30 petals, borne in trusses; upright, bushy growth; [Vera Dalton × Red Dandy]

Doctor Behring HT, m, 1979, Dot, Simon; bud pointed; flowers red-purple, 4 in., 35 petals, cupped, moderate fragrance; foliage dark; tall, upright growth; [Amanecer × Tanya]

Dr Belville Cl HT, ob, 1931, Thomas; flowers orange-crimson, base yellow, open, large, semi-dbl., moderate fragrance; profuse spring bloom, then scattered; very vigorous (12 ft.) growth; [Barbara × Sunstar]; int. by H&S

Dr Benjamin Pal HT, mp, IARI; flowers dbl., well formed; int. in 1993

Dr Berthet T, mp, 1879, Pernet; flowers bright pink, large, full

Dr Bharat Ram HT, ab, IARI; flowers apricot with shades of pink, high-centered; profuse bloom; int. in 2000

Dr Bob Harvey HT, lp, 1993, Winchel, Joseph F.; flowers soft pink, medium, full, no fragrance; foliage medium size, medium green, matte; bushy growth; [seedling × seedling]; int. by Coiner Nursery

Dr Brada's Rosa Druschki HP, mp, 1934, Brada, Dr.; flowers very large, dbl.

Dr Branscom HT, ab, 1947, Danegger; bud pointed; flowers peach-blossom flushed apricot-pink, large, dbl., moderate spicy fragrance; upright growth; [sport of Pink Dawn]; int. by J.T. Lovett

Dr Bretonneau HP, m, 1858, Trouillard; flowers violet-red, medium, dbl.; [Géant des Batailles × unknown]

Dr Brownell HT, yb, 1964, Brownell, H.C.; bud long, pointed; flowers buff, center chrome-yellow, 5½ in., 34 petals, high-centered, intense fragrance; foliage glossy, dark; vigorous, upright growth; PP2499; [Helen Hayes × Peace]; int. by Brownell Sub-Zero Roses, 1964

Dr Burt LCl, rb, 1942, Brownell; bud long, pointed; flowers deep red to pink flushed orange, large, 45 petals; non-recurrent; foliage glossy, light; very vigorous, climbing (to 20 ft.), branching growth; [Coral Creeper × seedling]

Dr Carabare HT, m; flowers purple/pink, large, dbl.

Dr Carbonaro HT, pb, 1958, Moreira da Silva; flowers rose, reverse silver; [Happiness × Grand'mere Jenny]

Dr Carneiro Pacheco HT, rb, 1938, Moreira da Silva; flowers carmine, open, large, dbl.; foliage glossy, light; vigorous, bushy growth; [Mev. G.A. van Rossem × Sir David Davis]

Dr Cathrall HT, pb, 1966, Hills; flowers deep pink, reverse lighter, 4½-5 in.; foliage dark, leathery; vigorous growth; [sport of Hector Deane]

Dr Cazeneuve HT, dr, 1899, Dubreuil; bud deep purple-black; flowers dark velvety crimson, large, dbl.

Dr Charles T. Beaird Gr, op, 1999, Wambach, Catherine; flowers coral, medium, dbl., borne mostly singly and in small clusters; foliage medium size, medium green, semi-glossy; prickles moderate; upright, spreading, medium growth; int. by Certified Roses, Inc., 2000

Dr D. F. Malan HT, dr, 1960, Herholdt, J.A.; bud pointed; flowers very dark maroon, large, 45-50 petals; upright growth; [Happiness × Mirandy]; int. by Herholdt's Nursery

Dr Darley HT, mp, 1980, Harkness, R., & Co., Ltd.; flowers rose bengal, 45 petals, globular, borne usually singly; foliage mid-green, semi-glossy; prickles narrow, reddish; upright, bushy growth; [Red Planet × (Carina × Pascali)]; int. in 1981; Gold Medal, Munich, 1983

Dr de Chalus HP, mr, 1871, Touvais; flowers scarlet, center velvety, reverse pink, very large, full

Dr Debat – See **Doctor F. Debat**, HT

Doctor Dick HT, op, 1986, Cocker, James & Sons; flowers orange-coral, large, dbl., high-centered, slight fragrance; foliage large, medium green, matte; upright growth; [Fragrant Cloud × Corso]

Dr Dielthem HGal, mp, before 1866; flowers bright pink, large, very full

Doctor Domingo Pereira Cl T, pb, 1925, de Magalhaes; flowers lilac-rose, center yellow, large, dbl., moderate fragrance

Doctor Dorothy F, pb, 1997, Jones, L.J.; flowers medium, 41 petals, borne in small clusters; foliage medium size, medium green, semi-glossy; some prickles; upright, medium (5ft.)growth; [Jubilee × Little Darling]

Dr E. M. Mills S, yb, 1926, Van Fleet; flowers primrose suffused pink, becoming darker, 2-2½ in., semi-dbl., globular; early; foliage small, dark; growth bushy (to 4 ft.); [*R. hugonis* × Radiance]; int. by American Rose Society

Dr Eckener HRg, pb, 1930, Berger, V.; flowers coppery rose on yellow ground, aging soft pink, large, semi-dbl., cupped; repeat bloom; vigorous (5-6 ft.) growth; [Golden Emblem × Hybrid Rugosa]; int. by Teschendorff, 1930

Dr Edvard Benes HT, rb, 1935, Böhm, J.; flowers red with many white streaks, very large, dbl.; bushy growth; [sport of Étoile de France]

Dr Edward Deacon HT, ob, 1926, Morse; flowers deep salmon-orange to shrimp-pink, large, dbl., globular; vigorous, bushy growth; [Mme Edouard Herriot × Gladys Holland]

Dr Edwin J. Cohn HT, my, 2001, Perry, Astor; flowers 4 in., dbl., borne mostly solitary, slight fragrance; foliage medium size, dark green, semi-glossy; prickles average, recurved, moderate; growth upright, medium; garden decorative; [seedling × seedling]; int. by Certified Roses Inc., 2002

Dr Eileen O'Neil F, op, Harkness; growth to 1 m.; int. by R. Harkness & Co Ltd, 2001

Doctor Eldon Lyle Gr, dr, 1968, Mackay; bud pointed; flowers medium, dbl., high-centered, moderate fragrance; foliage soft, bronze; vigorous, compact growth; PP2942; [President Eisenhower × Suspense]; int. by Texas Rose Research Foundation

Dr Elizabeth Neumann HT, lp, 2001, Byrnes, Robert L.; flowers light pink, blush pink reverse, 4 in., full, high-centered, borne mostly solitary, intense fragrance; foliage medium green, semi-glossy, disease-resistant; few prickles; growth upright, medium; [Morden Centennial × unknown]; int. by Overbrooke Gardens, 2001

Dr Ernst Mühle HT, pb, 1928, Mühle; flowers rose-pink, with salmon-white reflex, very large, very dbl.; [Mme Edmée Metz × unknown]

Dr F. Debat – See **Doctor F. Debat**, HT

Doctor F. Debat HT, pb, 1952, Meilland, F.; bud ovoid, pointed; flowers bright pink tinted coral, 5-6 in., 25-30 petals, high-centered; foliage leathery, dark; vigorous, upright growth; [Peace × Mrs John Laing]; int. by C-P; Gold Medal, NRS, 1950

Dr F. Débat, Climbing Cl HT, pb, 1955, Barni, V.; flowers deep pink, lighter at edges, very large; int. by URS

Dr F. G. Chandler – See **Dickson's Red**, HT

Dr F. L. Skinner HSpn, yb, Simonet; flowers amber-yellow-pink, high-centered; growth very tall, almost climbing habit; very hardy; [Joanna Hill × *R. spinosissima altaica*]

Dr F. Weigand HT, mr, 1930, Weigand, C.; flowers cherry-red, dbl.; [Mme Caroline Testout × Hadley]

Dr Faust F, yb, 1957, Kordes, R.; flowers golden yellow shaded orange-pink, 2 in., 25 petals, borne in large clusters; foliage dark, glossy; vigorous, bushy growth; [Masquerade × Golden Scepter]; int. as Faust, A. Dickson; Gold Medal, NRS, 1956

Dr Félix Guyon T, dy, 1901, Mari; flowers dark yellow, center lighter, with shades of orange and apricot, very large, intense fragrance; foliage dark green

Dr Ferrandiz HT, ob, Camprubi, C.; flowers deep orange-red; vigorous growth

Dr Fleming HT, pb, 1960, Dot, M.; flowers soft pink, flushed crimson, well-formed, 40 petals; vigorous growth; [Queen Elizabeth × Baleares]

Dr Franco Nogueira HT, Moreira da Silva, A.

Dr G. Krüger HT, dr, 1913, Ulbrich; bud long; flowers carmine and crimson, large, very dbl.; foliage large, dark green; [(Mme Victor Verdier × (Mme Caroline Testout × unknown)) × Mme Falcot]; int. by Kiese

Dr Gallwey LCl, w, 1937, Reiter; flowers snow-white, 2 in., single, borne in large clusters; profuse bloom; very vigorous growth

Dr Gentil HT, Moreira da Silva, A.

Dr Georges Leger HT, mr, 1935, Gebrüder Ketten; flowers blood red, large, dbl., slight fragrance

Dr Georges Martin HP, mr, 1908, Vilin; flowers carmine-pink, very large, very dbl.; [Mme Prosper Laugier × L'Ami E. Daumont]

Doctor Goldberg HT, my, 1990, Gandy, Douglas L.; flowers large, golden yellow, full, intense fragrance; foliage large, dark green, matte; upright growth; [Royal Dane × Dutch Gold]; int. by Gandy Roses, Ltd., 1989

Dr Grandvilliers T, pb, 1893, Perny; bud very long; flowers yellowish-pink with darker pink, medium, dbl., borne in small clusters; prickles numerous, hooked; [Isabelle Nabonnand × Aureus]

Doctor Griffith Buck HT, 1977, Patterson; buds large, globular; flowers 40-45 petals, high-centered, borne singly and several together in irregular clusters; foliage soft green; growth very vigorous; [San Francisco × Peace]; int. by Patterson Roses

Dr Grill T, op, 1886, Bonnaire; flowers rose shaded coppery; [Ophirie × Souv. de Victor Hugo]

Dr Guarnero HT, dp, 1958, Moreira da Silva; flowers deep rose, well-formed, large, dbl.; vigorous, bushy growth; [Happiness × Grand'mere Jenny]

Dr Guépin HP, dr, 1872, Moreau & Robert; flowers glowing velvety red, shaded dark violet, large, full, moderate fragrance; [Duc de Cazes × unknown]

Dr Guilherme Pereira da Rosa HT, mr, 1955, Moreira da Silva; flowers cherry-red, well-formed; moderate growth; [Charles Mallerin × Lisboa]

Dr H. E. Rumble Min, mr, 1982, Hooper, John C.; flowers scarlet red, small, 30 petals, cupped, no fragrance; foliage large, light green; prickles small, brown; vigorous, upright growth; [Born Free × Westmont]; int. in 1981

Dr H. I. Gallagher HT, yb, 1990, Anderson, Mrs. Etta S.; bud ovoid; flowers yellow with bright pink on petal tips, reverse same, 35-50 petals, high-centered, intense spicy fragrance; foliage medium size, bronze-medium green, semi-glossy heavy, disease-resistant; prickles medium, bronze-green; bushy, medium to tall growth; [Spellbinder × Irish Gold]; int. in 1989; Bronze Medal, ARC TG, 1989

Dr Harry Upshall S, pb, 1993, Fleming, Joyce L.; flowers pinking yellow, center blush, prominent stamens, medium, full, moderate fragrance; non-recurrent; foliage small, medium green, matte; bushy, spreading (2 m.) growth; [Liverpool Echo × *R. foetida persiana*]; int. by Hortico Roses, 1993

Dr Heinrich Lumpe HT, pb, 1928, Berger, V.; flowers light rose-pink, base yellow, large, dbl., high-centered; strong stems; very vigorous, bushy growth; [Constance × Admiral Ward]; int. by A. Berger

Dr Helfferich HT, pb, 1919, Lambert, P.; bud very large, ovoid, rose-orange; flowers rose, center yellowish-orange, edged silvery, very large, dbl., cupped, borne singly or in small clusters, moderate fragrance; foliage medium size, glossy; growth upright; [Gustav Grunerwald × Mrs Aaron Ward]

Dr Hénon HP, w, 1855, Lille

Dr Henri Neuprez HWich, ly, 1913, Tanne; flowers canary-yellow to sulfur-white; [*R. wichurana* × Mme Barthelémy Levet]

Dr Herbert Gray S, lp, 1998, Austin, David; flowers clear light pink, reverse medium pink, large, 75-80 petals, cupped, borne in small clusters; foliage small, dark green, glossy; few prickles; spreading, medium (3 ft.) growth; [Heritage × seedling]; int. by David Austin Roses, Ltd., 1998

Dr Herbert Hawkesworth HT, dr, 1927, Bees; flowers deep crimson, center almost black

Dr Hermann Schulze-Delitzsch F, ab, Liebig; flowers creamy yellow to white with darker apricot-orange center, full, low-centered, borne in clusters, moderate fragrance; free-flowering; foliage dark green, glossy; bushy (3-4 ft.) growth; int. by Rosen-Union, 2000

Dr Hess von Wichdorf HT, rb, 1936, Vogel, M.; flowers red, shaded rose-lilac, large, dbl., high-centered; vigorous, bushy growth; [sport of Frank W. Dunlop]; int. by Heinemann

Dr Hoffmann HT, my, 1904, Welter

Dr Hogg HP, dr, 1880, Laxton; flowers deep violet-red, medium, dbl.

Dr Homi Bhabha HT, w, 1970, Pal, Dr. B.P.; bud long, pointed; flowers white, center somtimes tinted cream, large, very dbl., high-centered, slight fragrance; foliage leathery; vigorous, upright growth; [Virgo × seedling]; int. by Indian Agric. Research Inst., 1968

Dr Homi Bhabha, Climbing Cl HT, w, 1976, IARI

Dr Hooker HP, mr, 1876, Paul, G.; flowers scarlet-carmine, shaded violet, large, full; [Duke of Edinburgh × unknown]

Dr Huas HT, w, 1903, Corboeuf-Marsault; flowers flesh white, large, full, cupped, moderate fragrance; [Souv du Président Carnot × Mme Caroline Testout]

Dr Huey HWich, dr, 1914, Thomas; flowers crimson-maroon, anthers light yellow, 2 in., 15 petals, borne in clusters of 3-4; foliage rich green; nearly thornless; [Ethel × Gruss an Teplitz]; sometimes classed as LCl; int. by B&A, 1920; Gertrude M. Hubbard, ARS, 1924

Dr Hurta HP, m, 1867, Geschwind; flowers purplish pink, large, full, flat

Dr Ingomar H. Blohm HP, dr, 1919, Lambert, P.; flowers dark carmine-red, shaded chestnut-brown, large, dbl., intense fragrance

Dr Ingrid – See **Caritas**, HT

Dr J. Campbell Hall HT, op, 1905, Dickson, A.; flowers coral pink, white reflections, large, full

Dr J. G. Fraser HT, ab, 1926, Easlea; flowers salmon-apricot, suffused vermilion-pink; vigorous growth; [St. Helena × Muriel Dickson]

Dr J. H. Nicolas LCl, mp, 1940, Nicolas; flowers rose-pink, 5 in., 50 petals, globular, borne in clusters of 3-4, moderate fragrance; recurrent bloom; foliage dark, leathery; vigorous, pillar (8 ft.) growth; [Charles P. Kilham × Georg Arends]; int. by J&P

Dr Jack Bender HT, pb, 1993, Bridges, Dennis A.; flowers pink and white, 3-3½ in., full, borne in flowers borne mostly singly; foliage medium size, dark green, semi-glossy; numerous prickles; bushy, spreading (120 cm.) growth; [Lady X × Flaming Beauty]; int. by Bridges Roses, 1993

Doctor Jackson S, mr, 1992, Austin, David; flowers scarlet, golden stamens, medium, 5 petals, borne mostly singly, no fragrance; foliage medium size, medium green, semi-glossy; few prickles; medium (120 cm.), spreading growth; int. by David Austin Roses, Ltd., 1987

Dr Jaime Lopes Dias HT, mp, 1961, Moreira da Silva; flowers large; [Confidence × Juno]

Dr Jamain HP, mr, 1851, Jamain; flowers bright crimson, fading to pink, full; foliage brownish red when young, glabrous, finely dentate; prickles enlarged at base, very sharp, slightly hooked

Dr Jo F, ob; flowers peach apricot, mid-sized., dbl., borne in clusters., moderate fragrance; blooms throughout the season.; well foliaged, lush; growth upright, moderate (3 ft.) grower; int. by Fryer, 2000

Dr John Dickman MinFl, m, 2002, Bridges, Dennis; flowers mauve, edged red, reverse mauve, 2 in., dbl., borne mostly solitary; foliage medium size, medium green, semi-glossy; few prickles; growth upright, tall (36 in.); exhibition, cutting, garden; [Purple Dawn × select pollen]; int. by Bridges' Roses, 2003

Dr John Snow HT, w, 1979, Gandy, Douglas L.; flowers creamy white, 5 in., 35 petals, high-centered; foliage light green; tall growth; [Helen Traubel × seedling]

Dr Joseph Drew HT, yb, 1918, Page; flowers salmon-yellow, suffused pink, large, dbl., moderate fragrance; foliage dark green; [Mme Mélanie Soupert × Comtesse Icy Hardegg]; int. by Easlea

Dr Jules Bouché – See **Mme Jules Bouché**, HT

Dr Julliard HP, dr, 1851, Lacharme; flowers garnet purple, shaded carmine, large, full

Dr K. C. Chan Min, my, 1987, Bennett, Dee; flowers medium yellow, fading pale yellow, medium, 25-30 petals, urn-shaped, borne usually singly, slight fragrance; foliage medium size, medium green, semi-glossy; prickles slender, straight, reddish; mini-flora; upright, bushy, medium growth; hips globular, medium, brown; [Irish Gold × Rise 'n' Shine]; int. by Tiny Petals Nursery, 1986

Dr Kane N, my, 1856, Pentland; flowers sulphur yellow, large

Dr Kane HT, mp, Shastri; flowers large, luminous pink, full, high-centered; int. in 1999

Dr Karel Kramár HT, dr, 1937, Böhm, J.; flowers large, dbl.

Dr Kater Pol, dr, 1925, Struwe; flowers velvety dark red, shaded blackish, small, full; [sport of Orléans Rose]

Dr Kidwai HT, pb, 1999, Chiplunkar, C. R.; flowers light pink, edges blended magenta, reverse light pink, 3-4 in., full, borne mostly singly; foliage medium size, medium green, semi-glossy; prickles moderate; upright, tall (4-5 ft.) growth; [Paradise × (Paradise × Oklahoma)]; int. by KSG Roses, 1998

Dr Kirk HT, op, 1940, Mallerin, C.; bud long, pointed; flowers coral, shaded nasturtium-yellow, very large, 35 petals, high-centered; vigorous growth; [Charles P. Kilham × *R. foetida bicolor* hybrid]; int. by A. Meilland

Dr Lande T, op, 1902, Berger, V.; flowers deep salmon pink, darker in hot weather, large, semi-dbl., moderate fragrance

Dr Larrey HP, m, 1866, Moreau & Robert; flowers velvety purple, shaded carmine, medium, full

Dr Laude – See **Dr Lande**, T

Dr Lindley HP, dp, 1866, Paul, W.; flowers dark carmine, large, full

Dr Lopez Diaz HT, Moreira da Silva, A.

Dr M. Euwe HT, pb, 1936, Buisman, G. A. H.; bud pointed; flowers salmon, tinted yellow and pink, dbl., intense fragrance; foliage leathery, bronze; bushy growth

Dr M. S. Randhawa HT, pb, Pal, Dr. B.P.; flowers large, outside creamy white, inside splashed and edged deep pink, dbl., moderate fragrance; int. in 1989

Dr Manuel Alves de Castro HT, rb, Moreira da Silva; flowers red, reverse golden yellow

Dr Margaretha F, dr, 1960, Maarse, G.; flowers velvety dark red, medium, dbl., borne in large clusters; vigorous, bushy growth; [(Red Pinocchio × unknown) × Alain]

Dr Margrethe – See **Queen Margrethe**, S

Dr Mark Weston Min, mr, 2005, Spooner, Ray; flowers medium, full, borne mostly solitary, no fragrance; foliage medium size, medium green, semi-glossy; prickles few, in., pointed; bushy, medium (14-18 in.) growth; garden decoration, exhibition; [seedling × seedling]; int. by Oregon Miniature Roses, 2005

Dr Martin Luther S, w, Scholle; buds long, slim; flowers bright white, opening quickly, with golden stamens, dbl., moderate fragrance; recurrent; growth to 5 ft.; int. in 2000

Dr Marx HP, mr, 1842, Laffay, M.; flowers crimson red, very large, full, cupped; growth erect

Dr Maximo de Carvalho HT, dr, 1960, Moreira da Silva; flowers crimson-red; [Crimson Glory × Charles Mallerin]

Dr Mazaryk HP, lp, 1930, Böhm, J.; flowers large, dbl.

Dr McAlpine F, dp, 1981, Pearce, C.A.; flowers deep rose-pink, large, 30 petals, high-centered, borne singly and in clusters of up to 10, intense fragrance; foliage dark; prickles straight, red; low, bushy growth; patio, containers; int. by Limes Rose Nursery, 1983

Dr Mendes Correia HT, mr, 1938, Moreira da Silva; bud pointed; flowers bright red, very large, dbl.; foliage soft; vigorous, bushy growth; [Frau Margarete Oppenheim × Hortulanus Budde]

Dr Mengelberg F, dr, 1952, Leenders, M.; flowers deep blood-red, large, semi-dbl.; very vigorous growth

Dr Merkeley HSpn, dp, 1924; flowers deep pink, small, dbl., moderate fragrance; non-recurrent; low to medium growth; double pink wild form of *R. pimpinellifolia*; named in honor of Dr. Merkeley, who first grew it in Canada; discovered in eastern Siberia; int. by Skinner, 1924

Dr Miroslav Tyrs HP, rb, 1932, Böhm, J.; flowers crimson, shaded darker, very large; [sport of Anna de Diesbach]

Dr Morse HT, m

Dr Müller HFt, op, 1905, Müller, Dr. F.; flowers salmon-pink with touches of red, medium, semi-dbl.

Dr Müller's Rote HT, m, 1920, Müller, Dr. F.; flowers purple/pink, medium, dbl., intense fragrance; sometimes classed as HP

Dr Murphy's Magic Touch Min, m, 2000, Bennett, Dee; flowers mauve, 1½-2 in., full, exhibition, borne mostly singly; foliage medium size, medium green, dull; prickles moderate; growth bushy, tall (3 ft.); [Lagerfeld × Brian Lee]; int. by Tiny Petals Nursery, 2001

Dr Néran B, mr, 1856, Bernéde; flowers cherry red

Dr Nicolas Welter HT, op, 1912, Soupert & Notting; flowers delicate salmon pink, center darker, very large, dbl., moderate fragrance; [Mme Mélanie Soupert × Mme Segond Weber]

Dr Noshir Wadia HT, rb, 1999, Chiplunkar; flowers bright red, white stripes, reverse light red with stripes, 3-4 in., dbl., borne mostly singly; foliage large, dark green, glossy; numerous prickles; compact, medium (4-5 ft.) growth; [sport of Norma]; int. by KSG Roses, 1992

Dr O'Donel Browne HT, pb, 1908, Dickson, A.; flowers carmine-rose, large, well-formed, dbl.; vigorous growth

Dr Oliveira Salazar HT, ob, 1955, Moreira da Silva; flowers salmon and yellow shaded carmine, large, very dbl.; [Mme Marie Curie × Peace]

Dr P. G. Purohit F, pb, Chiplunkar; int. in 2001

Dr Pasteur HT, dp, 1887, Moreau-Robert; bud very long, globular; flowers soft rosy crimson, satiny, large, full; foliage dark green

Dr Paul Menzel HT, mp, Lucke, G.; flowers carmine-pink, large, dbl.; int. in 1980

Dr Petyt – See **Dr A. I. Petyt**, HT

Dr Pouleur T, rb, 1897, Ketten Bros.; flowers carmine and copper-red, outer petals striped reddish-pink, medium, full, globular, moderate fragrance; growth vigorous; [Lady Zoë Brougham × Alphonse Karr]

Dr R. Maag – See **Colorama**, HT

Dr Rafael Duque HT, rb, 1938, Moreira da Silva; flowers velvety purplish red, large; [Frau Margarete Oppenheim × Hortulanus Budde]

Dr Raimont Pol, mp, 1888, Alégatière; flowers carmine pink, aging to violet pink, darker center, medium, full, moderate fragrance; [Général Jacquiminot × unknown]

Dr Reiner Klimke F, lp, Noack, Werner; int. in 1988

Dr Renata Tyrsová LCl, op, 1937, Böhm, J.; flowers salmon-pink, 4 in., semi-dbl., globular, borne singly or in small clusters, moderate damask fragrance

Dr Ricaud Pol, lp, 1907, Corboeuf; flowers salmony flesh on copper ground, large, dbl., borne in large clusters, moderate fragrance; [White Pet × unknown]

Dr Richard Legler HT, pb; flowers shrimp-pink changing to old-rose and orange, moderate fruity fragrance; moderate growth

Dr Robert Huey – See **Dr Huey**, HWich

Doctor Robert Korns HMsk, ab, Lettunich; flowers small, borne in clusters, no fragrance; recurrent; growth arching, 6 ft; int. in 1996

Dr Rocques B, mp, 1839, Desprez; flowers bright carmine, medium, full, globular

Dr Rouges Cl T, rb, 1893, Schwartz; flowers deep coppery-red with orange shading, petals reflexed, 8 cm., dbl., moderate tea fragrance; very remontant

Dr Ruschpler HP, dp, 1856, Ruschpler; flowers silky pink, center brighter, large, full

Dr S. S. Bhatnagar F, dr, IARI; int. in 1994

Dr Scheiner HT, dr, 1929, Böhm, J.; flowers large, dbl.

Dr Schnitzler – See **Emin Pascha**, HT

Dr Scott (strain of *R. multiflora*), w; foliage mildew-resistant; growth used as understock

Dr Selma Lagerlof HRg, mp

Doctor Sewell HP, mr, before 1910; flowers crimson, shaded with purple, cupped

Dr Skinner – See **Dr F. L. Skinner**, HSpn

Dr Spitzer HP, pb, 1862, Geoffre; flowers bright carmine, shaded violet, reverse purple, large, full

Dr Sybil Johnson HT, dr, 1993, Stainthorpe, Eric; flowers medium, full, borne mostly singly, moderate fragrance; foliage medium size, medium green, semi-glossy; some prickles; medium (85 cm.), upright growth; [Tropicana × Prima Ballerina]; int. by Battersby Roses, 1994

Dr Tomin HT, Tagashira, Kazuso; int. in 1990

Dr Trigo de Negreiros HT, dr, 1954, Moreira da Silva; bud long, pointed; flowers deep red, large; very vigorous growth; [Charles Mallerin × Lisboa]

Dr Troendlin – See **Oberbürgermeister Dr Troendlin**, HT

Dr Troy Garret MinFl, mr, 2005, Wells, Verlie W.; flowers medium red, reverse light red, 2 in., full, high-centered, borne mostly solitary, moderate fragrance; foliage large, medium green, semi-glossy; prickles moderate, ¼ in., straight; growth upright, tall (3½-4 ft.); garden decorative, exhibition; [seedling × Memphis King]; int. by Wells MidSouth Roses, 2005

Dr Valois HT, 1950, Mallerin, C.

Dr van de Plassche Pol, mp, 1968, Buisman, G. A. H.; bud ovoid; flowers pink, medium, semi-dbl.; foliage dark; [Heureux Anniversaire × Allotria]

Dr van Rijn HT, my, 1952, Leenders, M.; bud ovoid; flowers lemon-yellow, large, dbl., high-centered; foliage light green, glossy; vigorous, bushy growth

Dr Vazquez HT, op, 1935, Camprubi, C.; flowers salmon, open, medium, semi-dbl.; foliage glossy; upright growth; [Duchess of Atholl × Margaret McGredy]

Dr Vingtrinier HP, dp, 1863, Fontaine; flowers bright carmine with cherry red, large, full

Dr W. E. Hadden HT, rb, 1934, McGredy; flowers raspberry-red, flushed yellow, deepening at base, well-formed; foliage dark; long, strong stems; vigorous growth

Dr W. Van Fleet LCl, lp, 1910, Van Fleet; bud pointed; flowers cameo-pink fading flesh-white, 8-10 cm., dbl., moderate fragrance; non-recurrent; foliage dark, glossy; vigorous, climbing (15-20 ft.) growth; [(*R. wichurana* × Safrano) × Souv. du Prés. Carnot]; int. by P. Henderson

Dr Wauer HT, dp, 1902, Brauer; flowers dark carmine, aging lighter, very large, very full, globular

Dr William Gordon HP, mp, 1905, Paul, W.; flowers satiny carnation pink, large

Dr Wolfgang Pöschl – See **Canadian White Star**, HT

Dr Zamenhof HWich, rb, 1935, Brada, Dr.; flowers crimson-red, base yellow, 12-14 cm., semi-dbl., loose, borne in small clusters, intense fragrance; very vigorous growth; [*R. wichurana* × seedling]; int. by Böhm

Dr Zumel HT, Kordes, R.

Doctor's Wife HT, op, 1967, Von Abrams; bud long, pointed; flowers salmon-pink, large, dbl., high-centered; foliage dark, glossy, leathery; vigorous, upright growth; int. by Edmunds Roses

Dog Rose – See ***R. canina*** (Linnaeus)

Doktor Sieber – See **Toniro**, HT

Dolce Luna HT, mp, Barni; flowers soft lilac pink, 10 cm., dbl., moderate fragrance; foliage large, medium green; growth erect, 100-120 cm.; [Mount Shasta × Rinascimento]; int. by Rose Barni, 2000

Dolce Vita HT, op, 1986, Delbard; flowers rosy salmon, large, 37 petals, high-centered; vigorous, upright, bushy growth; [Voeux de Bonheur × (Chic Parisien × (Michele Meilland × Mme Joseph Perraud))]; int. in 1971

Dolcezza S, mp

Dollar-Rose HT, mr, 1936, Tantau, Math.; flowers carmine-red, medium, dbl.

Dollie B Min, rb, 1982, Robinson, Thomas, Ltd.; flowers medium red, silver reverse, small, 35 petals; foliage small, dark green, red edges, glossy; bushy growth; [Parkdirektor Riggers × Darling Flame]

Dolly F, dp, 1978, Poulsen, Niels D.; flowers 2½-3 in., 20 petals; foliage glossy, dark; bushy growth; [(Nordia × Queen Elizabeth) × (seedling × Mischief)]; int. by Poulsen, 1975; Gold Medal, Baden-Baden, 1973, ADR, 1987

Dolly Brownell F, lp, 1926, Brownell; flowers color same as Dr W van Fleet; [Dr. W. Van Fleet × unknown]

Dolly Darling HT, mp, 1949, Brownell; bud long, pointed, red; flowers lustrous pink, open, 4-5 in., 20 petals, moderate fragrance; foliage glossy; vigorous, compact growth; [Pink Princess × Crimson Glory]

Dolly Dot MinFl, dy, J&P; int. in 1998

Dolly Madison HT, dy, 1935, Hillock; flowers golden yellow; vigorous growth; [sport of Mrs Pierre S. duPont climbing seedling]

Dolly Parton HT, or, 1985, Winchel, Joseph F.; flowers luminous orange-red, large, 35 petals, borne mostly singly, intense fragrance; foliage large, medium green, semi-glossy; upright growth; PP5608; [Fragrant Cloud × Oklahoma]; int. by C-P, 1984; Bronze Medal, ARC TG, 1982

Dolly Varden HRg, ab, 1914, Paul; bud deep yellow; flowers light apricot-pink, base yellow, large, semi-dbl.; recurrent bloom; vigorous growth

Dolly Varden Pol, mp, 1930, deRuiter; flowers clear pink, dbl.

Dolly's Forever Rose S, rb, 2006, Barden, Paul; bud slightly mossy; flowers vermilion-red, reverse medium yellow, 2½-3 in., dbl., borne in small clusters; foliage medium size, dark green, glossy; prickles ¼ in., slightly curved, brown, numerous; growth bushy, medium (3-4 ft.); specimen, borders, containers; [((Little Darling × Lemon Delight) × Angel Face) × Scarlet Moss]; int. in 2007

Dolly's Sister HT, op, 1989, Taylor, Thomas E.; flowers medium coral-pink; [sport of Dolly Parton]; int. by Michigan Mini Roses, 1989

Dolly's Sister Gr, or, Williams, J. Benjamin; flowers large, brilliant orange-red, dbl., high-centered, intense fragrance; int. by Hortico Inc, 1999

Dolomiti HT, ab, 1933, Ingegnoli; bud pointed; flowers flesh, with yellow reflex, very large, dbl.; foliage dark; strong stems; vigorous growth

Dolores HT, pb, deVor

Dolores Hope HT, dp, 2003, Carruth, Tom; flowers cerise pink, 12-14 cm., full, high-centered, borne mostly solitary, slight fragrance; foliage large, dark green, semi-glossy; prickles average, almost straight, brown, moderate; growth upright, to slightly spreading, tall (140-160 cm.); garden decoration; [Crystalline × Ingrid Bergman]; int. by Armstrong Garden Centers, Inc., 2004

Dolores Marie MinFl, m, 2001, Tucker, Robbie; bud on very long peduncle; flowers mauve with dark edge, 2½-3 in., very full, old-fashioned, borne mostly solitary, intense fragrance; foliage medium green, matte; prickles very small, straight downward, reddish-brown; growth upright, medium (18 in.); exhibition, garden decorative, cutting; [seedling × Scentsational]; int. by Rosemania, 2001

Domaine de Chapuis S, m, 1901, Roseraie de l'Hay; flowers violet-red; growth tall

Domaine de Charance HT, mp, Guillot-Massad; flowers clear pink, borne singly and in small clusters; foliage medium green, glossy; growth to 80 cm.; int. by Roseraies Guillot, 2005

Domaine de Courson, Climbing LCl, pb, Meilland; flowers pale pink with carmine pink tints, dbl., moderate fragrance; growth vigorous, 8 ft and up; int. in 1995

Domaine de Saint-Jean de Beauregard S, mp, Delbard; flowers full, pompon, borne in clusters; free-flowering; vigorous (2-3 ft.) growth; int. by Georges Delbard SA, 2006

Dombrowski – See **Dembrowski**, HP

Dométile Bécar – See **Dometil Beccard**, C

Dometil Beccard C, pb, before 1853; flowers light pink, striped with white, large, full, cupped, moderate fragrance; possibly synonymous with *R. centifolia variegata*

Dometille Baccard – See **Dometil Beccard**, C

Domila HT, op, Laperrière; int. in 1971

Domina HT, op, 1943, Heizmann, E.; flowers salmon-pink, large, dbl.

Dominant HT, op, 1966, Boerner; bud ovoid; flowers salmon-pink, medium, dbl., borne in clusters, slight fragrance; foliage dark; [Golden Masterpiece × Spartan]; int. by Spek, 1964

Dominator F, mp, 1961, deRuiter; flowers 3 in., semi-dbl., borne in clusters; vigorous, upright growth; [New Yorker × The Optimist]

Domingo F, dy, Select; int. by Terra Nigra, 2003

Dominic Boccardo – See **Dometil Beccard**, C

Dominie Sampson HSpn, lp, before 1848; flowers soft pink, marbled blush, semi-dbl.; very early, non-recurrent; foliage finely divided; dense, shrubby (3-4 ft.) growth; hips glossy, black

Dominique Min, lp, 1981, Bennett, Dee; bud ovoid; flowers light peachy pink, 30 petals, high-centered, intense apple fragrance; foliage medium green, arrow-shaped; prickles curved; upright growth; [Electron × Little Chief]; int. by Tiny Petals Nursery

Dominique Daran HP, m, 1860, Touvais; flowers velvety purple, large, full, cupped

Dominique Loiseau S, w, Delbard; flowers pure white with golden stamens, moderate fragrance; growth to 2 ft.; int. by George Delbard SA, 2005

Domino HT, dr, 1956, Gaujard; bud long, pointed; flowers dark crimson, medium; foliage dark; [Peace × seedling]

Domino Min, mr, Tantau; int. in 1994

Domkapitular Dr Lager HT, pb, 1903, Lambert, P.; flowers rose and carmine; [Mme Caroline Testout × Princesse de Bassaraba de Brancovan]

Domstadt Fulda F, or, 2006, W. Kordes' Söhne; flowers dazzling orange-red, 7 cm., dbl., borne mostly solitary; foliage dark green, glossy; growth vigorous, upright, 80 cm.; int. by W. Kordes'' Söhne, 1994; Gold Medal, Dublin

Domus Aurea HT, my, 1940, Aicardi, D.; flowers pure yellow; foliage dark, glossy; strong stems; very vigorous growth; [Julien Potin × Yellow seedling]; int. by Giacomasso

Don Alvarès B, mp, 1842, Boyau; flowers medium, full

Don Alvart – See **Don Alvarès**, B

Don Bosco HT, Dorieux, Francois; int. in 1976

Don Bosco HT, op, Laperriere, L.; int. in 1989

Don Bradman HT, rb, 1938, Wheatcroft Bros.; bud long, shapely; flowers coppery claret, fading to silvery pink, 40-50 petals

Don Cartwright F, mr, Jellyman, J. S.; flowers velvety red, medium, dbl, borne in small clusters, slight fragrance; foliage medium size, medium green, semi-glossy; growth upright, compact, medium (2½ ft.); [seedling × (Tony Jacklin × Andrea)]; int. in 1997

Don Charlton HT, pb, 1991, Thompson, Robert; flowers deep rose pink with silver reverse, large, very full, moderate fragrance; foliage large, dark green, glossy; upright growth; [Silver Jubilee × (Chicago Peace × Doris Tysterman seedling)]; int. by Battersby Roses, 1990

Don de Guérin HGal, dp, before 1846; flowers bright rose, sometimes shaded with light purple, large, full

Don Don Min, dr, 1977, Williams, Ernest D.; flowers red, reverse blending near white at base, 1-1½ in., 60 petals, moderate fragrance; foliage small, glossy, bronze; upright, bushy growth; [seedling × Over the Rainbow]; int. by Mini-Roses, 1976

Don José HT, op, 1922, Clark, A.; flowers salmon-pink, semi-dbl.; [Archiduc Joseph × seedling]; int. by NRS Victoria

Don Juan LCl, dr, 1958, Malandrone; bud ovoid; flowers velvety crimson red, 5 in., 30-35 petals, cupped, intense fragrance; recurrent bloom; foliage dark green, glossy, leathery; growth climbing, 12-14 ft; PP1864; [(New Dawn × unknown) × New Yorker]; int. by J&P

Don Marshall Min, dr, 1982, Moore, Ralph S.; flowers medium red, reverse blackish-red, small, 35 petals, high-centered, slight fragrance; foliage small, dark, matte; bushy, spreading growth; [Baccará × Little Chief]; int. by Moore Min. Roses

Don Pedro D, lp, before 1811; flowers delicate blush white-pink, 3 in., dbl., moderate fragrance; foliage elongate, pale green, glaucous; sometimes classed as M

Don Quichotte F, rb, 1970, Robichon; flowers cherry-red, base yellow, well-formed, large, dbl., borne in clusters, slight fragrance; foliage glossy, leathery; vigorous, upright growth; [Charles Gregory × Marcelle Auclair]; int. by Ilgenfritz Nursery, 1964

Don Quixote – See **Don Quichotte**, F

Don Rose HT, pb, 1943, Mallerin, C.; bud long, pointed, carmine-red; flowers coppery pink, open, large, 40 petals, cupped; foliage leathery, bluish green; vigorous, upright, bushy, rather compact growth; [Soeur Thérèse × seedling]; int. by C-P

Don Vogt F, w, 2004, Vogt, Don; flowers small, semi-dbl., borne mostly solitary, slight fragrance; foliage medium size, medium green, matte; prickles small, hooked, none; growth bushy, medium; exhibition, garden decoration; [Blueberry Hill × unknown]; int. by Maryanne Sievers, 2004

Doña Clara HT, m, 1965, Camprubi, C.; bud ovoid; flowers purplish pink, large, 50 petals, high-centered; vigorous growth

Dona Isaura Alexandrina HP, 1891, Alexandrino, Domingos

Doña Maria HSem, w, 1828, Vibert; flowers white, tinted pink to medium, 5-6 cm., semi-dbl., flat to cupped, borne in small clusters, moderate musk fragrance; foliage pale green; possibly synonymous with Princesse Marie

Doña Sol HGal, w, about 1830, Vibert; probably extinct; not the same as the HGal of the same name, Vibert, 1842

Doña Sol HGal, rb, 1842, Vibert; flowers currant red, spotted lighter pink or white, medium, very dbl.; supercedes an earlier (Vibert; 1830) white cultivar of the same name

Donald Davis F, or, 1992, Warner, Chris; flowers vermilion, medium, dbl., borne in small clusters; foliage medium size, medium green, semi-glossy; few prickles; medium (90 cm.), upright growth; [Anne Harkness × Beautiful Britain]

Donald Macdonald HT, ob, 1916, Dickson, A.; flowers orange-carmine, semi-dbl., borne in clusters; dwarf growth; Gold Medal, NRS, 1916

Donald Prior F, mr, 1938, Prior; bud ovoid; flowers bright scarlet flushed crimson, 3 in., 11 petals, cupped, borne in large clusters; foliage leathery, dark; vigorous, bushy growth; [seedling × D.T. Poulsen]; int. by J&P

Donald Prior, Climbing Cl F, mr, Farr

Donald Thomas Heald F, yb, 1994, Kirkham, Gordon Wilson; flowers small, semi-dbl., borne in small clusters, slight fragrance; foliage medium size, dark green, semi-glossy; numerous prickles; patio; low, compact growth; [seedling × Bright Smile]; int. in 1996

Donaldo HT, rb, 1980, Murray, Nola; bud ovoid; flowers red to pink, shapely, 4 in., 35 petals; foliage large, glossy, dark; tall growth; [Honey Favorite × Rose Gaujard]

Donatella – See **Granada**, HT, 1963

Donau HWich, m, 1913, Praskac; flowers purple-violet, fading to steely blue, 5 cm., semi-dbl., borne in clusters of 20-30, moderate lily-of-the-valley fragrance; foliage large; few prickles; [Erinnerung an Brod × *R. wichurana rubra*]

Donau! – See **Donau**, HWich

Donauprinzessin F, mp, Noack, Werner; int. in 1994

Donauwalzer – See **Conqueror's Gold**, F

Donauwelle S, m, Weihrauch; low, spreading growth; int. in 1991

Doncasterii HMoy, dp, 1930, Hurst, C.C.; flowers bright deep pink to light red, 2 in., single; foliage purplish-green; stems plum colored; arching growth (to 6 ft.); hips flagon-shaped, large, red; possibly *R. moyesii* × *R. macrophylla*; int. as *R. macrophylla doncasterii*, J. Burrell & Co., about 1930

Donella – See **Don Cartwright**, F

Donna Clara HT, pb, Leenders, M.; flowers buff, reverse strawberry-pink

Donna Darlin' HT, rb, 1993, Winchel, Joseph F.; flowers yellow blending pink to bright red, medium, dbl., slight fragrance; foliage large, dark green, semi-glossy; some prickles; medium (4 ft.), bushy growth; PP10112; [seedling × Double Delight]; int. by Coiner Nursery, 1994

Donna Fanny Cavalieri HT, 1953, San Remo Exp. Sta.

Donna Faye Min, lp, 1976, Schwartz, Ernest W.; bud pointed; flowers 1 in., 27 petals, high-centered, moderate fragrance; upright growth; [Ma Perkins × Baby Betsy McCall]; int. by Nor'East Min. Roses

Donna Jean F, m, 1991, Taylor, Pete & Kay; flowers mauve with white eye, medium, semi-dbl., borne singly and in small clusters, no fragrance; foliage medium size, dark green, semi-glossy; medium, upright, bushy growth; [Azure Sea × Party Girl]; int. by Taylor's Roses, 1991

Donna Kordana Min, dr, Kordes; flowers wine red, full, borne singly and in small clusters; recurrent; compact growth; containers; int. by W. Kordes Söhne

Donna Marella Agnelli HT, lp, Barni, V.; flowers dbl., high-centered; dark green foliage; growth strong, 3 ft.; int. by Rose Barni, 1988

Donna Margaret HT, w, 2000, Horner, Colin P.; flowers white with pink edge, reverse white, large, full, borne mostly singly; foliage medium size, dark green, semi-glossy; few prickles; growth upright, medium (3 ft.); [Pristine × Esmeralda]; int. in 2002

Donna Maria – See **Doña Maria**, HSem

Donna Maria – See **Donna Marie**, HSem

Donna Marie HSem, w, 1830, Vibert; flowers pure white, small, very dbl.

Donna Rose F, my, 2003, Webster, Robert; flowers large, dbl., borne in small clusters; foliage medium size, dark green, glossy; prickles 8 mm., slightly hooked; growth bushy, medium (30 in.); bedding; [((Robin Redbreast × Typhoon) × The Lady) × Indian Summer]; int. by Handley Rose Nurseries, 2004

Donna Silva Carmine F, Cazzaniga, F. G.; int. in 1974

Donna's Rambler w, Scarman; int. in 2001

Donnaway – See **Donnaway Hit**, MinFl

Donnaway Hit MinFl, ab, Poulsen; flowers apricot blend, 5-8 cm., dbl., slight fragrance; foliage dark; growth bushy, 20-40 cm.; int. by Poulsen Roser, 2004

Dony Robin F, op, 1959, Meilland, F.; bud pointed; flowers salmon-pink, open, medium, dbl., borne in clusters, slight fragrance; foliage leathery; vigorous, compact growth; [Goldilocks × Fashion]; int. as Dany Robin, URS, 1958

Doorenbos Selection HSpn, dr, Doorenbos; flowers rose-purple, yellow stamens, single; small, fine foliage; growth short, dense

Dooryard Delight HT, pb, 1940, Horvath; bud short, pointed, spiraled; flowers light pink, reverse rose-pink, petals sharply pointed, 2½ in., dbl.; recurrent bloom; foliage leathery; vigorous, bushy growth; [*R. setigera* × Lady Alice Stanley]; int. by Wyant

Dopey Pol, mr, 1958, deRuiter; flowers crimson-red, small, semi-dbl., borne in trusses; compact growth; [Robin Hood × Polyantha seedling]; int. by Gregory & Son, 1954

Dora HT, op, 1906, Paul, W.; flowers silvery peach pink, very large, full

Dora HT, or, 1978, Gaujard; bud long; flowers brilliant orange-red, dbl.; foliage bronze; [Tanagra × Rubens]; int. in 1975

Dora Delle Min, pb, 1991, Taylor, Pete & Kay; flowers light pink with lavender hue, lighter in center, reverse creamy white, medium, full, high-centered, borne usually singly, moderate fragrance; foliage medium size, medium green, semi-glossy; medium, upright growth; [Azure Sea × Jean Kenneally]; int. by Taylor's Roses, 1991

Dora Hansen HT, mp, 1908, Jacobs; bud long, pointed; flowers thulite-pink, open, large, dbl.; [Mme Caroline Testout × Mme Jules Grolez]

Dora Stober HT, w, 1925, Leenders, M.; flowers white shaded yellow, dbl.

Dorabella HT, Barni, V.; int. in 1986

Dorada HT, ab, Barni, V.; flowers intense ocher-apricot, dbl., intense fragrance; growth open, vigorous, 2½-3 ft.; int. in 1998

Doralta HT, Dorieux, Francois; int. in 1979

Dorandi – See **Harlequin**, HT

Dorcas HWich, pb, 1922, English; flowers deep rose-pink to coral-pink, base yellow, 3 cm., dbl., borne in large clusters; foliage small, semi-glossy; vigorous growth

Dorcas S, pb, 1985, Buck, Dr. Griffith J.; bud ovoid, pointed; flowers light pink, pale yellow blend, flecked deeper pink, 40 petals, cupped, slight fragrance; repeat bloom; foliage dark, leathery; prickles awl-like, tan; erect, bushy growth; hardy; [Minigold × Freckle Face]; int. by Iowa State University, 1984

Doreen HT, ob, 1951, Robinson, H.; flowers deep golden orange flushed scarlet, well-formed; foliage dark; vigorous growth; [Lydia × McGredy's Sunset]; int. by Baker's Nursery

Doreen Farrow Gr, ob, 2003, Everitt, Derrick; flowers orange-vermilion, reverse paler, large, full, borne in small clusters, moderate fragrance; medium size, medium green, semi-glossy foliage; prickles medium, hooked; growth upright, tall (3 ft.); garden decorative; [Solitaire × Mary Sumner × (L'Oreal Trophy × Edith Holden)]; int. in 2004

Doreen Johnson HT, lp, 1977, Dawson, George; bud long, pointed; flowers pale pink, dbl.; foliage large, light; vigorous, bushy growth; [(Great Venture × Fort Vancouver) × Memoriam]; int. by Australian Roses

Doreen Thorn HT, pb, 1934, Cant, F.; flowers deep pink, base yellow, well-shaped, large, dbl.; vigorous growth

Doreen Wells F, or, 1970, Watkins Roses; flowers orange-scarlet, 3 in., 25 petals, flat; foliage glossy, dark; low, bushy growth; [Soraya × Circus]

Doric F, yb, 1963, LeGrice; flowers golden salmon, large, 40 petals, borne in well-spaced clusters; foliage glossy; vigorous, compact growth; [Masquerade × Korona]

Dorienne HT, mr, 1958, Buyl Frères; bud short; flowers large, 34 petals, cupped; bushy, spreading growth; [Mrs Nieminen × seedling]

Dorina Neave HT, pb, 1926, Pemberton; flowers silvery pink, large, dbl., globular; stiff stems; compact growth

Dorinda S, pb, Peden, R.; int. in 1998

Doris HT, rb, 1939, Spandikow; flowers cerise striped white; [sport of Briarcliff]

Doris Ann Min, dr, 1987, Wambach, Alex A.; flowers small, full; foliage small, medium green, matte; [Black Jade × Tiki]

Doris Archer F, rb, 1962; flowers yellow, bronze and red, well-formed, 4 in., 30-35 petals, borne in clusters, moderate fragrance; foliage glossy; vigorous, compact growth; [Circus × seedling]; int. by Fryers Nursery, Ltd., 1962

Doris Bennett Min, pb, 2002, Moore, Ralph S.; flowers dark pink, reverse medium pink, 1-1½ in., very full, borne in small clusters; foliage medium size, medium green, Semi-glossy; prickles small, straight, green, few; growth spreading, short (12-15 in.); containers, garden, borders; int. by Sequoia Nurs., 2002

Doris Dickson HT, ob, 1924, Dickson, S.; flowers orange-cream, veined cherry-red; foliage very dark; stiff, wiry stems; vigorous growth

Doris Dowman HT, mp, 1997, Horner, Colin P.; flowers large, very dbl., borne mostly singly; foliage large, medium green, glossy; some prickles; compact, medium (3ft.) growth; [Silver Jubilee × (seedling × Karlsruhe)]; int. by Battersby Roses

Doris Downes LCl, pb, 1932, Clark, A.; flowers pink, aging to pale crimson very large, 11-15 cm., semi-dbl., cupped, intense fragrance; early; nearly thornless; climbing growth; hybrid gigantea; int. by NRS Victoria

Doris Findlater HT, ab, 1936, Dickson, A.; flowers light apricot, reverse flushed reddish-salmon and carmine, dbl.; vigorous growth

Doris Grace Robinson HT, w, 1943, Bees; bud pointed; flowers creamy white, well-shaped, large; foliage olive-green; vigorous, upright growth

Doris Howard F, mr, 1957, Wheatcroft Bros.; flowers blood-red, borne in large clusters; vigorous, bushy growth

Doris J. Robertson HT, lp; flowers whitish-pink, large, dbl.

Doris Morgan Min, dp, 2003, Bridges, Dennis; flowers 1 in., dbl., borne mostly solitary, moderate fragrance; foliage medium size, medium green, semi-glossy; prickles ¼ in., straight, moderate; growth upright, bushy, tall (28-32 in.); garden, exhibition, cutting; [Jennifer × select pollen]; int. by Bridges' Roses, 2003; Award of Excellence, ARS, 2003

Doris Norman F, or, 1959, Norman; flowers bright orange, to open, 2 in., 30 petals, high-centered, borne in small clusters; foliage purplish to dull green; vigorous, bushy growth; [Paul's Scarlet Climber × Mary]; int. by Harkness, 1958

Doris Osborne HT, mr, 1937, Clark, A.; bud pointed; flowers ruby-cerise, semi-dbl.; bushy growth; [Mme Abel Chatenay × seedling]; int. by NRS Victoria

Doris Page HSpn, ly, Page, Doris; flowers creamy yellow, small, single, flat; foliage serrated, fern-like; growth to 3 ft.; int. by Brentwood Bay Nursery, 2005

Doris Pleasance HT, w, 1979, Brewer; flowers blush-pink to white; [sport of Queen Elizabeth]

Doris Reese HT, my, 1996, Sheldon, John, Jennifer & Robyn; bud urn-shaped with tips of petals folding downward; flowers medium yellow, center of rose darker than outer petals, 4 in., full, high-centered, moderate fragrance; foliage medium size, dark green, semi-glossy; prickles moderate; upright, medium (3 ft.) growth; [seedling × Lanvin]

Doris Ryker – See **Dorus Rijkers**, Pol

Doris Trayler HT, yb, 1924, McGredy; bud pointed, orange; flowers yellow, reverse flushed crimson and orange, large, dbl., high-centered; foliage light green, leathery, glossy; bushy, dwarf, compact growth

Doris Tysterman HT, ob, 1976, Wisbech Plant Co.; flowers tangerine and gold, 4-5 in., 28 petals, slight fragrance; foliage glossy; upright growth; [Peer Gynt × seedling]; int. in 1975

Dornröschen S, pb, 1960, Kordes, R.; bud well-shaped; flowers salmon to deep pink, reverse yellow, large, dbl., borne in clusters; recurrent bloom; upright, well-branched growth; [Pike's Peak × Ballet]

Dornröschenschloss Sababurg S, mp, 2006; flowers pure pink, 10 cm., very full, high-centered, borne mostly solitary; foliage dark green, very glossy, leatherly, ruffled; growth upright, robust, 4 ft.; int. by W. Kordes' Söhne, 1993

Dorola Min, dy, 1982, McGredy, Sam IV; flowers medium, 26 petals, moderate fragrance; foliage small, medium green, semi-glossy; bushy growth; [Darling Flame × New Day]; int. by McGredy Roses International, 1983

Dorothe HT, my, 1980, LeGrice, E.B.; bud pointed; flowers 48 petals, borne singly, slight fragrance; foliage glossy, medium green; prickles large, curved, light brown; vigorous, upright growth; [Irish Gold × Dr. A.J. Verhage]

Dorothea Furrer HT, dr

Dorothea Howard HT, pb, 1985, Barclay, Hilary M.; flowers light pink, deeper pink reverse, well-formed, large, 30 petals, borne singly, moderate tea fragrance; foliage medium green, glossy; many hooked, brown prickles; [First Prize × Roundelay]; int. in 1978

Dorothee Heidorn Bslt, mp; flowers small, borne in large clusters; recurrent in late summer; growth to 8-12 ft.; reintroduced in 1995

Dorothy HT, lp, 1905, Dickson; flowers flesh pink, large, full; [Mme Caroline Testout × unknown]

Dorothy, Climbing Cl HT, pb, 1935, Bostick; [sport of Dorothy Page-Roberts]

Dorothy LCl, or; flowers smoky Mandarin orange, large, single; int. by Heirloom Roses, 1997

Dorothy F, ab, 2004, Cocker, A.G.; flowers apricot, reverse lighter, 2½ in., dbl., borne in large clusters, slight fragrance; foliage medium size, medium green, glossy; prickles 6 mm., straight; growth upright, medium (2½-3 ft.); garden decorative; [Gingernut × seedling]; int. by James Cocker & Sons, 2004

Dorothy A. Golik HT, ob, 1976, Golik; bud ovoid; flowers orange to flaming red, 4 in., 35 petals, high-pointed, moderate spicy fragrance; foliage glossy; moderate growth; [Tropicana × Peace]; int. by Dynarose, 1973

Dorothy Anderson HT, lp, 1949, McGredy; flowers large, 33 petals, high-centered; free growth; [Sam McGredy × George Dickson]

Dorothy Anne HT, pb, 1985, Winchel, Joseph F.; flowers white blending to deep pink at edges, large, 35 petals; foliage medium size, dark, semi-glossy; upright growth; PP6100; [First Prize × Lady X]; int. by Kimbrew-Walter Roses

Dorothy Broster HT, mp, 1978, Ellick; flowers azalea-pink, 5 in., 45 petals; foliage dark; very vigorous growth; [Blue Moon × Karl Herbst]; int. by Excelsior Roses

Dorothy Dennison HWich, lp, 1909, Dennison; flowers pale salmon pink, small, full, borne in large clusters; foliage light green, glossy; [sport of Dorothy Perkins]

Dorothy Dix Pol, mp, 1923, Hicks; flowers rose-pink, borne in clusters

Dorothy Donnelly HT, mr, 1997, Poole, Lionel; flowers large, very dbl., borne mostly singly; foliage medium size, dark green, semi-glossy; upright, bushy, medium growth; [Adrienne Berman × (Royal William × Gabi)]

Dorothy Douglas HT, rb, 1924, Dobbie; flowers vivid cerise-pink

Dorothy Drowne HWich, pb, 1924, Brownell; flowers white to pink, center crimson and scarlet; [Sodenia × unknown]

Dorothy Fowler HRg, mp, 1938, Skinner; flowers clear pink, well-formed, 3-3½ in., semi-dbl.; non-recurrent; growth to 3 ft.; [*R. rugosa* × (*R. acicularis* × *R. spinosissima*)]

Dorothy Goodwin HT, yb, 1954, Goodwin; flowers yellow tipped cerise-pink, well-formed, 4 in., 32 petals; foliage dark holly-green; vigorous growth; [sport of Peace]; int. by Gregory

Dorothy Grace Cl Min, pb, 1986, Dobbs, Annette E.; flowers yellow with pink petal edges, small, 25 petals, high-centered, borne in sprays of 3-5, no fragrance; foliage small, medium green, semi-glossy; prickles very few, brown, hooked downward; upright, climbing (to 6 ft.) growth; [Little Darling × Rise 'n' Shine sport]; int. by Port Stockton Nursery

Dorothy Hilda Wood HT, rb, 2006, Rawlins, Ronnie; flowers dark red, reverse gold, 2½ in., very full, borne mostly solitary; foliage medium size, dark green, glossy; prickles ½ in., triangular, few; growth upright, tall (43 in.); garden decoration; [Chinatown × Ingrid Bergman]; int. in 2006

Dorothy Hodgson HT, ob, 1930, Cant, F.; flowers orange-cerise, veined darker, well-formed, large; vigorous growth

Dorothy Howarth Pol, op, 1921, Bees; flowers coral-pink, tinted salmon, open, dbl., borne in clusters; foliage dark; bushy growth; [Léonie Lamesch × Annchen Müller]

Dorothy James HT, pb, 1939, C-P; flowers peach-pink reverse deep rose; [sport of Golden Dawn]

Dorothy Jeavons HMult, w, 1912, Bakers; flowers white, lightly shaded yellow; [sport of Blush Rambler]

Dorothy King HT, rb, 1924, King; flowers scarlet-crimson and maroon, semi-dbl.

Dorothy Lee HT, pb, 1929, Morse; flowers silvery shell-pink, base golden yellow, dbl.

Dorothy Lewis HT, dr, 2001, Everitt, Derrick; flowers dark red shaded russet, varying with weather conditions, 10 cm., full, borne in small clusters, slight fragrance; foliage medium size, dark green, semi-glossy; prickles small, slightly hooked, moderate; growth upright, low to medium (75-90 cm.); garden decorative; [((L'Oreal Trophy × Edith Holden) × (Mary Sumner × (Silver Jubilee × L'Oreal Trophy))) × (Mary Sumner × (L'Oreal Trophy × Edith Holden))]

Dorothy Lloyd HT, yb, 1998, Sheridan, John; flowers grey with brown center, reverse grey, 4 in., dbl., borne in small clusters; foliage medium size, medium green, semi-glossy; prickles few, medium, straight; bushy, medium (2½ ft.) growth; [Cream Peach × Paradise]

Dorothy Marie HT, dp, 1935, Scittine; [sport of Talisman]; int. by Lainson

Dorothy May Cooper Min, w, 1976, Ellick; flowers pure white, 1-2 in., 25-30 petals; foliage dark; very vigorous growth; [*R. roulettii* × Memoriam]

Dorothy McGredy HT, rb, 1936, McGredy; flowers deep vermilion, base and reverse yellow, well-shaped; foliage cedar-green; strong stems; vigorous growth

Dorothy Mollison HT, dr, 1930, Clark, A.; flowers dark crimson; [Mrs R.C. Bell × seedling]; int. by NRS Victoria

Dorothy Page-Roberts HT, pb, 1907, Dickson, A.; flowers coppery pink, suffused yellow, open, very large, dbl.; vigorous growth

Dorothy Peach HT, yb, 1957, Robinson, H.; flowers deep yellow flushed pink, 5 in., 37 petals, high-centered, moderate fragrance; foliage dark, glossy; vigorous growth; [Lydia × Peace]; Gold Medal, NRS, 1959

Dorothy Peach, Climbing Cl HT, yb, 1963, Watkins Roses

Dorothy Perkins HWich, lp, 1901, Miller; flowers bright carminy pink, lighter reverse, 4-5 cm., dbl., rosette, borne in large clusters, moderate fragrance; foliage small, dark, glossy; very vigorous (10-20 ft.) growth; [*R. wichurana* × Mme Gabriel Luizet]; int. by J&P

Dorothy Ratcliffe HT, rb, 1910, McGredy; flowers coral-red shaded fawn-yellow; vigorous growth

Dorothy Rose Min, or, 1998, Jones, Steve; flowers white with orange, red-orange, and/or red stripes, 2 in., single, borne in small clusters; foliage medium size, medium green, semi glossy; growth upright, tall (4 ft.); [Sarabande × Peggy T]; int. by Almost Heaven Roses, 2005

Dorothy Superior – See **Super Dorothy**, HWich

Dorothy Vietor Munger Gr, op, 2001, Burks, Larry; flowers coral, coral to salmon reverse, 4½ in., full, borne mostly solitary, moderate fragrance; foliage medium size, medium green, semi-glossy; prickles moderate; growth upright, medium; garden decorative; [(Camelot × unknown) × (Tropical Paradise × unknown)]; int. by Certified Roses, Inc., 2002

Dorothy Virginia Min, ly, 1999, Bell, Judy G.; flowers medium, dbl., borne mostly singly; foliage large, dark green, semi-glossy; few prickles; upright, medium growth; [Loving Touch × unknown]; int. by Michigan Mini Roses, 1999

Dorothy Wheatcroft F, mr, 1962, Tantau, Math.; flowers oriental red shaded darker, large, 18 petals, borne in clusters of 13, slight fragrance; foliage bright green; vigorous, bushy growth; int. by Wheatcroft Bros., 1961; Gold Medal, NRS, 1961

Dorothy Whitney Wood HT, op, Fryer, Gareth; int. in 1992

Dorothy Wilson F, ob, Beales, Peter; flowers vermilion orange, highlighted with yellow, dbl.; foliage mid-green, healthy; growth tidy and bushy, 2½ ft; int. in 1995

Dorothy's Gem S, ab, 2000, Harris, Dorothy; flowers peach, pink and yellow, reverse peach, pink, and white, medium, full, borne in small clusters, moderate fragrance; foliage medium size, medium green, semi-glossy; growth climbing, spreading, tall; [sport of Leverkusen]; int. in 1998

Dorothy's Regal Red HT, mr, 1984, Jerabek, Paul E.; flowers large, 58 petals, borne in small clusters, intense fragrance; foliage medium dark, glossy; bushy growth

Dorotka Darling Min, pb, 1991, Sudol, Julia; flowers pink and cream blend, medium, full, well-formed, borne mostly singly, sometimes in small clusters, slight fragrance; foliage medium size, dark green, semi-glossy, clean and abundant; some prickles; tall (60-80 cm.), upright growth; [Orange Darling × unknown]

Dorris Lee Min, ab, 1994, Wells, Verlie W.; flowers apricot blend, large, full, borne singly and in small clusters, moderate fragrance; foliage dark green, semi-glossy; some prickles; medium, upright growth; [seedling × Party Girl]; int. by Wells Midsouth Roses, 1994

Dorrit F, ob, 1970, Sonderhousen; flowers orange-yellow, full, flat, borne in trusses

D'Orsay Rose Misc OGR, dp; bud deep pink; long sepals; flowers deep pink, outer petals fading to pale pink receptacle wide, dbl.; summer bloom; foliage leaflets 5-7, leaden green; prickles paired below each leaf; erect growth to 5 ft.

Dorsland – See **Exploit**, LCl

Dortmund HKor, mr, 1955, Kordes' Sohne, W.; bud long, pointed; flowers red, white eye, 11-12 cm., single, open, borne in large clusters, moderate fragrance; recurrent bloom; foliage dark, very glossy; vigorous, climbing growth; hips numerous, orange; [seedling × *R. × kordesii*]; Gold Medal, Portland, 1971, ADR, 1954

Dortmunder Kaiserhain S, lp, Noack, Werner; flowers medium-large, dbl.; int. in 1995

Dorus Rijkers Pol, op, 1942, Leenders, M.; flowers salmon-pink, dbl., borne in clusters, moderate fragrance; recurrent bloom; foliage light green; vigorous, upright growth; int. as Doris Ryker, Klyn

Dot Com Min, dr, 2000, Moe, Mitchie; flowers very small, ½ in., semi-dbl., high-centered, borne mostly singly; foliage small, dark green, semi-glossy; few prickles; growth upright, medium (12 in.); [Vista × select pollen]; int. by Mitchie's Roses and More, 2000

Dothan HT, mp, 1984, Perry, Astor; flowers large, 35 petals, high-centered, slight fragrance; foliage large, medium green, matte; upright growth; [Koppies × King of Hearts]; int. by Perry Roses, 1984

Dotty HT, dy, 1931, Towill; flowers bronze-yellow, large, semi-dbl., globular; foliage glossy; long stems; very vigorous growth; [Souv. de Claudius Pernet × *R. foetida bicolor* seedling]

Dotty Bass HT, dr, 1970, Bass; bud long, pointed; flowers medium, dbl.; foliage dark, leathery; vigorous, upright growth; int. by DeVor Nurseries, Inc., 1968

Dotty Louise S, dr, Rupert; buds slender; flowers satiny dark reddish-purple, borne in clusters of 3, moderate fragrance; recurrent; new growth thornless, at base of older canes; growth to 5 ft.; int. by Ashdown, 2001

Double – See **Plena**, A

Double Blanche – See **Double White Burnet**, HSpn

Double Blush – See **Victoria**, HFt

Double Blush Burnet HSpn, pb, before 1821; flowers center blush, fading at edges, reverse white, medium, full; possibly the same as Double Carnée, or *R. pinpinellifolia rubra* (Redouté)

Double Brique HGal, pb, before 1842; flowers rosy pink, shading silver toward outside, dbl.

Double Bubble Min, mp, Zary; PP10929; int. in 1997

Double Carlos Red S, dr, Erskine; hybrid acicularis

Double Carnée HSpn, w, before 1826, Prévost; sepals glabrous; flowers flesh, small, dbl.; numerous prickles; possibly the same as Double Blush Burnet

Double Cherokee – See **Fortuniana**, Misc OGR

Double Cinnamon – See ***R. majalis*** (Herrmann) dbl.

Double Cream HG, w, 2006, Brichet, Helga; flowers large, full, borne mostly solitary; foliage large, medium green, glossy; prickles moderate; growth rampant, tall; [*R. gigantea* × unknown]; int. by Le Rose di Piedimonte, 2006

Double Dark Marbled HSpn, rb, Brown; flowers red mottled purple, small, semi-dbl.; early; possibly the same as Double Purple

Double Date Min, op, 1993, Laver, Keith G.; flowers orange pink, medium, very dbl., borne mostly singly, slight fragrance; foliage small, medium green, semi-glossy; some prickles; low, upright, bushy growth; [((Breezy × June Laver) × (Breezy × June Laver)) × seedling]; int. by Springwood Roses

Double Delight HT, rb, 1976, Swim, H.C. & Ellis, A.E.; bud long, pointed to urn-shaped; flowers creamy white becoming strawberry-red, 5½ in., 30-35 petals, high-centered, borne mostly singly, intense spicy fragrance; foliage large, deep green; upright, spreading, bushy growth; PP3847; [Granada × Garden Party]; int. by Armstrong Nursery; Hall of Fame, WFRS, 1985, James Alexander Gamble Fragrance Medal, ARS, 1986, Gold Medal, Rome, 1976, Gold Medal, Baden-Baden, 1976

Double Delight, Climbing Cl HT, rb, 1983, Christensen, Jack E.; flowers creamy white, broadly edged with crimson, 14-16 cm., borne mostly on second year wood, intense fragrance; intermittent flowering after spring flush; strong (8-10 ft.) growth; PP5155; [sport of Double Delight]; int. by Armstrong Nursery, 1985

Double Delight Supreme HT, rb, Chiplunkar; int. in 1993

Double Else Poulsen – See **Else's Rival**, F

Double Feature Gr, m, 1976, Williams, J. Benjamin; bud pointed; flowers reddish-purple, reverse yellow, 4 in., 28 petals, high-centered, slight damask fragrance; foliage large, dark; vigorous, upright growth; [Angel Face × Granada]; int. by Lakeland Nursery Sales, 1975

Double French Rose – See ***R. gallica officinalis*** (Thory)

Double Glee S, mp, Joyce Fleming; int. by Hortico, Inc., 2005

Double Gold MinFl, yb, 2002, White, Wendy R.; flowers light yellow, reverse golden yellow, 2½-3¼ in., full, borne mostly solitary, intense fragrance; foliage medium size, dark green, glossy; prickles straight or slightly angled down, moderate; growth upright, spreading, medium (18-30 in.), exhibition, cut flower; PP16056; [((Zorina × Baby Katie) × June Laver) × Old Glory]; int. by Nor' East Miniature Roses, 2003

Double Happy HT, rb, 1999, Schuurman, Frank B.; flowers bi-color red and yellow, large, dbl., borne mostly singly; foliage medium size, dark green, semi-glossy; prickles moderate; upright, medium (30-36 in.) growth; [Louise Gardner × Goldmarie]; int. by Franko Roses New Zealand, Ltd., 1999

Double Helix HT, pb, 2005, Shastri, N.V.; flowers pink and cream, 12 cm., very full, borne mostly solitary, intense fragrance; foliage medium size, dark green, matte; prickles medium, crooked; growth bushy, medium (36 in.); garden, exhibition; [Sheer Bliss × Cary Grant]; int. by N.V.Shastri, 1998

Double Hugonis S, ly, before 1932; flowers dbl.

Double Jaune – See **Multiplex**, Misc OGR

Double Joy Min, op, 1979, Moore, Ralph S.; bud long, pointed; flowers 1½ in., 35 petals, moderate fragrance; foliage small, matte, green; bushy growth; PP4619; [Little Darling × New Penny]; int. by Sequoia Nursery

Double Knock Out S, mr, 2004, Radler, William; flowers red, reverse red, 4 cm., full, borne in small clusters, no fragrance; foliage small, medium green, semi-glossy; growth bushy, medium (3-4 ft.); garden decoration; PP16202; [(Carefree Beauty × unknown) × (Razzle Dazzle × unknown)]; int. by The Conard-Pyle Company, 2004

Double Mme Butterfly – See **Annie Laurie**, HT, 1918

Double Marbrée – See **Maculata**, HSpn

Double Ophelia HT, lp, 1916, E.G. Hill, Co.; flowers similar to Ophelia, but with twice as many petals; [Ophelia × seedling]

Double Orléans Pol, mr, 1924, Hicks; flowers rosy crimson, center white; [sport of Orléans Rose]

Double Perfection HT, rb, 1988, Winchel, Joseph F.; flowers red, reverse white, aging darker red, reverse cream, 4½ in., dbl., high-centered, borne singly, slight fragrance; recurrent; foliage medium size, dark green, semi-glossy; prickles average, slightly recurved, medium size, brown; bushy, upright, medium growth; hips round, average, orange; PP6705; [(My Dream × First Prize) × seedling]; int. by Co-Operative Rose Growers

Double Pink HSpn, mp, from Scotland

Double Pink Edine – See **Double Pink**, HSpn

Double Pink Killarney HT, mp, 1910, Scott; flowers large, very dbl.

Double Pink Memorial Rose – See **Universal Favorite**, HWich

Double Purple HSpn, rb, before 1820; flowers dark lake, inclining to purple, lighter reverse, 2-2½ in., semi-dbl., cupped; hips black, globular, slightly flattened; possibly synonymous with Double Dark Marbled

Double Red – See **Rouge**, HSpn

Double Red – See **La Belle Distinguée**, HEg

Double Scarlet HEg, mr; flowers bright rosy red, dbl.; weak growth

Double Scarlet Sweet Briar – See **La Belle Distinguée**, HEg

Double Scotch White – See **Double White Burnet**, HSpn

Double Star Min, w, 1978, Dobbs, Annette E.; bud ovoid; flowers 10 petals, borne 2-5 per cluster; foliage small, firm, disease-resistant; no prickles; vigorous growth; [Fairy Moss × Fairy Moss]; int. by Small World Min. Roses

Double Talk F, rb, 1980, Weeks, O.L.; bud ovoid, pointed; flowers medium red, creamy white reverse, petals rolled loosely outward, 48 petals, cupped, slight spicy fragrance; foliage glossy, slightly wrinkled, dark; prickles long, hooked downard; compact growth; PP4710; [Plain Talk × Suspense]

Double Time HT, rb

Double Treat Min, yb, 1986, Moore, Ralph S.; bud mossy; flowers bright red and orange-yellow, striped, mini-moss, dbl., cupped, borne usually singly; foliage small to medium size, medium green, semi-glossy; prickles slender, brown; medium, upright, bushy growth; hips small, globular with numerous spines, orange; [Arizona × ((Fairy Moss × Fairy Moss) × (Little Darling × Ferdinand Pichard))]; int. by Sequoia Nursery, 1985

Double Trouble Min, ob, 2000, Bell, Judy; bud round; flowers light orange, 1 in., full, HT form, borne in large clusters, no fragrance; foliage medium size, medium green; few prickles; growth very full, bushy, upright (18 in.); [Party Girl × Gingersnap]; int. by Michigan Mini Roses, 2001

Double White HMsk, w, before 1629; flowers dirty white, medium, semi-dbl.; no repeat; prickles numerous, hooked

Double White – See **Double White Burnet**, HSpn

Double White HEg, w; flowers flesh-white, dbl.; vigorous growth

Double White – See **Elegans**, Ayr semi-dbl.

Double White Altaica – See **Double White Burnet**, HSpn

Double White Burnet HSpn, w, before 1818; flowers ivory-white, 2-3 in., semi-dbl., intense fragrance; vigorous growth

Double White Cherokee Sp, w; flowers semi-dbl.; a form of *R. laevigata*

Double White Killarney – See **Killarney Double White**, HT

Double White Lady Banks Rose – See ***R. banksiae banksiae*** (Aiton)

Double White Memorial Rose – See **Manda's Triumph**, HWich

Double White Moss – See **Shailer's White Moss**, M

Double White Noisette – See **Plena**, HSem

Double White Rugosa – See ***R. rugosa albo-plena*** (Rehder) dbl.

Double White Scots – See **Double White Burnet**, HSpn

Double White Striped Moss – See **Panachée Pleine**, M

Double Yellow – See **Williams' Double Yellow**, HFt

Double Yellow Scots Rose – See **Williams' Double Yellow**, HFt

Doubloons HSet, my, 1934, Horvath; bud ovoid, deep saffron-yellow; flowers rich gold, fading to lemon yellow, 5-7 cm., dbl., cupped, borne in large clusters, moderate fragrance; intermittent repeat; foliage glossy; vigorous growth; not dependably hardy; [(*R. setigera* × *R. wichurana*) × *R. foetida bicolor* hybrid]; int. by J&P; David Fuerstenberg Prize, ARS, 1936

Douce Symphonie – See **Debut**, Min

Douceur Normande – See **Coral Meidiland**, S

Douchka – See **Mary DeVor**, F

Doué Rambler HWich, mp, 1921, Begault-Pigné; flowers bright pink, borne in well-filled clusters

Douglas Ch, dr, 1848, Verdier, V.; flowers crimson, medium; vigorous growth; probably extinct

Douglas Gandy S, op, Gandy; flowers 4 in., 24 petals, borne in small clusters; recurrent; rich green foliage; growth vigorous, upright, 4-5 ft; [Graham Thomas × seedling]; int. by Heirloom Roses, 2000

Douglas MacArthur HT, pb, 1943, Howard, F.H.; bud long, pointed; flowers Delft rose, base slightly bronze, 4-4½ in., 24-30 petals, high-centered; foliage leathery; long stems; vigorous, upright, bushy, compact growth; [Mrs J.D. Eisele × Glowing Sunset]; int. by H&S

Douglas MacArthur, Climbing Cl HT, pb, 1949, Howard, F.H.; int. by H&S

Douglass – See **Douglas**, Ch

Doulce France F, pb, 1964, Mondial Roses; bud round; flowers clear pink flushed apricot, large, dbl.; vigorous, upright growth; [(Peace × seedling) × Lady Sylvia]

Dourada HT, dy, 1957, Moreira da Silva; flowers well-formed, dbl.; very vigorous growth; [Mme Marie Curie × Julien Potin]

Doutz S, lp, Beales, Amanda; int. in 1994

Doux Parfum – See **Typhoo Tea**, HT

Dove S, lp, 1986, Austin, David; flowers medium, dbl.; foliage medium size, dark, semi-glossy; spreading growth; [Wife of Bath × Iceberg seedling]; int. by David Austin Roses, 1984

Dove Dale S, mp, 1998, Mather, Wendy; flowers medium pink, 3 in., 41 petals, borne in small clusters; foliage medium size, dark green, glossy; prickles moderate, medium, straight; spreading, low (3 × 6 ft.) growth; [seedling × seedling]

Dovedale HT, rb, 1976, Moorhouse & Thornley; flowers cream, petals edged carmine, 5 in., 42 petals; foliage dark; low, bushy growth; [Fragrant Cloud × Stella]; int. in 1975

Dovedale – See **Dove**, S

Downland Cherry HT, mr, 1954, Ratcliffe; flowers light cerise shaded scarlet, intense spicy fragrance; foliage dark, leathery, dull green; vigorous growth; [Vanessa × Shot Silk]

Downland Lustre HT, yb, 1955, Ratcliffe; bud bronzy gold; flowers maize-yellow, reverse orange, medium, dbl., intense spicy fragrance; compact, bushy growth; [Vanessa × Shot Silk]

Downunder S, dr, Peden, R.

Doyen Théodore Cornet HP, mr, 1900, Bénard or Corboeuf; flowers currant red

Dr Michael Noble Min, ob, 2006, Mander, George;

flowers orange, reverse dark yellow, 2½ in., full, borne in small clusters; foliage medium size, dark green, glossy, disease-resistant; prickles ¼ in., hooked, light brown, moderate; growth bushy, medium (20-24 in.); garden, containers, exhibition; [Hot Tamale × Rubies 'n' Pearls]; int. by Select Roses, 2007

Dragon Wings – See ***R. sericea pteracantha*** (Franchet)

Dragon's Blood S, r, 2005, Barden, Paul; flowers deep orange/purple, reverse Chinese red, 3½ in., dbl., borne in small clusters; foliage medium size, dark green, semi-glossy, new growth deep plum; prickles moderate, in., hooked, deep red; growth bushy, arching canes with age, medium (5 × 5 ft.); specimen, borders; [((Little Darling × Yellow Magic) × Grandmother's Hat) × Brown Velvet]; int. in 2007

Dragon's Eye HCh, dr, 1992, Clements, John K.; flowers medium, very dbl., high-centered, borne mostly singly; foliage small, dark green, semi-glossy; some prickles; medium (70 cm.), bushy, compact growth; [seedling × seedling]; int. by Heirloom Old Garden Roses, 1991

Dragon's Fire Min, rb, 1993, Williams, Ernest D.; flowers bright red with deep yellow at base of petals, yellow reverse, medium, full, moderate fragrance; foliage small, medium green, semi-glossy; few prickles; medium (35 cm.), upright, compact growth; [Starburst × Twilight Trail]; int. by Mini Roses of Texas, 1993

Drambuie HT, rb, 1972, Anderson's Rose Nurseries; flowers orange-red, reverse red, high pointed, 5 in., 28-30 petals, intense fragrance; foliage glossy; vigorous, bushy growth; [sport of Whisky Mac]; int. in 1973

Dream HT, op, 1938, Dramm; flowers geranium-pink, 4½ in., 50-60 petals; strong stems; [sport of Better Times]

Dream HT, pb; flowers medium, pastel pink, lightly flushed apricot and salmon, dbl., high-centered, borne mostly singly; recurrent; PP11269; greenhouse rose; int. by Kordes, 1979

Dream S, my, Poulsen; flowers medium yellow, 8-10 cm., dbl., no fragrance; foliage dark; growth bushy, 40-60 cm.; PP13278; int. by Poulsen Roser, 2000

Dream F, pb; int. in 2005

Dream Baby Min, lp, 1993, Rennie, Bruce F.; flowers medium, dbl., borne mostly singly, slight fragrance; foliage small, medium green, semi-glossy; few prickles; medium, bushy growth; [Party Girl × Silver Phantom]; int. by Rennie Roses International, 1993

Dream Blush HT, lp, 1999, Twomey, Jerry; flowers 5 in., dbl., borne in small clusters, slight fragrance; foliage large, medium green, semi-glossy; few prickles; compact, medium (4 ft.) growth; PP11527; [Evening Star × Marijke Koopman]

Dream Boat – See **Dreamboat**, Min

Dream Cloud S, pb, 1985, Christensen, Jack E.; flowers light to dark salmon-pink, 20 petals, borne in large pyramidal clusters, slight fragrance; foliage medium size, long, narrow, medium green, matte; spreading, bushy, semi-pendulous growth; PP5998; [Zorina × Gartendirektor Otto Linne]; int. by Armstrong Nursery, 1985

Dream Come True HT, ly, 2005, Clark, Linda; flowers medium, full, borne mostly solitary, slight fragrance; foliage medium size, dark green, glossy; prickles moderate; growth upright, medium; [sport of Vanilla Perfume]; int. in 2005

Dream Come True Gr, yb, 2006, Pottschmidt, Dr. John; flowers yellow edged with cerise pink, reverse similar but with more yellow, 10-12 cm., 40 petals, borne mostly solitary, slight tea fragrance; recurrent; foliage large, dark green, matte; prickles average, almost straight, beige, moderate; stems long; growth upright, tall (170 to 200 cm.); garden decoration; [(Touch of Class × unknown) × unknown]; int. by Weeks Roses, 2008

Dream Dolly F, op, J&P; int. in 1993

Dream Dust F, mp, 1968, Gardner, B.C.; bud pointed; flowers small, dbl., borne in clusters, slight fragrance; foliage leathery; very vigorous, spreading growth; [(Lavender Girl × unknown) × (Little Darling × unknown)]

Dream Girl LCl, pb, 1944, Jacobus; flowers salmon-pink overlaid apricot, large, 55-65 petals, flat, borne in small clusters, intense fragrance; recurrent bloom; foliage dark green, glossy; climbing growth; pillars; [Dr. W. Van Fleet × Senora Gari]; int. by B&A

Dream Kid F, mp, Bell; int. by Bell Roses, 2003

Dream Kordana Min, mp, Kordes

Dream Lover Min, lp, 1995, Rennie, Bruce F.; flowers 1-1½ in., full, borne mostly singly, moderate raspberry fragrance; foliage medium size, medium green, glossy; some prickles; medium (18 in.), upright growth; [Pink Sheri × Innocent Blush]; int. by Rennie Roses International, 1995

Dream Lover MinFl, mp, Pearce; int. in 1998

Dream On F, mr, 2000, Delves, P.R.; flowers medium red, reverse lighter, medium size, dbl., borne in small clusters; foliage medium size, medium green, semi-glossy; prickles moderate; growth compact, low; [sport of Fryminicot]; int. by Woolhouse Nursery, 2000

Dream Orange HT, or, 1999, Twomey, Jerry; flowers large, full, borne in small clusters; foliage medium size, medium green, semi-glossy; prickles moderate; bushy, medium (5 ft.) growth; PP11525; [Cherish × (Evening Star × Trumpeter)]; int. in 2000

Dream Palace – See **Dream**, S

Dream Parade HT, op, 1938, Hillock; flowers amber in spring, seashell-pink in hot weather, burnt-orange, dbl.; vigorous growth; [sport of Condesa de Sástago]

Dream Pink HT, mp, 1999, Twomey, Jerry; flowers large, dbl., borne mostly singly, moderate fragrance; foliage large, medium green, glossy; prickles moderate; upright, medium (4 ft.) growth; PP11524; [White Masterpiece × Silver Jubilee]; int. in 2000

Dream Red HT, mr, 1999, Twomey, Jerry; flowers large, borne in small clusters; foliage medium size, dark green, glossy; prickles moderate; bushy, medium (5 ft.) growth; PP11503; [Esmeralda × Fireburst]

Dream Ruffles F, rb; int. in 2002

Dream Scarlet HT, mr, 2002, Twomey, Jerry; flowers very full, borne in very large clusters, moderate fragrance; foliage large, medium green, matte; prickles 6-12 mm., slanting downward, numerous; growth upright (1½ m.); garden decorative; PP15396; [Karma × unknown]; int. by Tesslaar International, 2002

Dream Sequence – See **Astrid Lindgren**, S

Dream Time HT, mp, 1977, Bees; flowers 5 in., 38 petals, high-centered; foliage light green; moderately vigorous growth; [Kordes' Perfecta × Prima Ballerina]

Dream Time Min, op, Benardella, Frank; flowers large, coral pink fading to pink, dbl.; growth tall; int. in 1999

Dream Waltz F, dr, 1970, Tantau, Math.; flowers large, dbl., borne in trusses; foliage glossy; int. by Wheatcroft & Sons, 1969

Dream Weaver Cl F, op, 1998, Zary, Dr. Keith W.; bud short, pointed; flowers coral pink, 3-3½ in., full, rosette, borne in large clusters, slight rose fragrance; foliage large, dark green, glossy; prickles moderate; growth tall, spreading, arching, climbing; PP9492; [seedling × Lady of the Dawn]; int. by Bear Creek Gardens, Inc., 1997

Dream White HT, w, Twomey, Jerry; int. by Edmunds, 2004

Dream Yellow HT, my, 1999, Twomey, Jerry; flowers 5 in., dbl., borne mostly singly, intense fragrance; foliage medium size, medium green, semi-glossy; prickles moderate; upright, medium (3 ft.) growth; PP11528; [(Sonia × Prominent) × Whisky Mac]

Dreamboat Min, my, 1982, Jolly, Betty J.; flowers medium, 60-70 petals, high-centered, slight fragrance; bushy, spreading growth; [Rise 'n' Shine × Grand Opera]; int. by Rosehill Farm, 1982

Dreamboat HT, lp, Dawson; int. in 1995

Dreamcatcher Cl Min, rb, 1995, McCann, Sean; flowers medium to dark red striped with white, 2-2½ in., 35-40 petals, borne singly, moderate damask fragrance; foliage medium size, medium green, glossy; tall, spreading growth; PPRR; [Lady in Red × ((Rose Gilardi × Wit's End) × (Remember Me × Stars 'n' Stripes))]; int. by Justice Miniature Roses, 1995

Dreamcoat Min, yb, 1996, McCann, Sean; flowers medium to dark yellow with scarlet accent, fades to reddish, 2½ in., dbl.; foliage large, dark green, semi-glossy; upright, tall (4-6 ft.) growth; PPRR; [Lady in Red × Joseph's Coat]; int. by Justice Miniature Roses, 1997

Dreamer Min, mp, 1991, Saville, F. Harmon; bud ovoid, pointed; flowers dusty pink, medium, 20 petals, cupped, borne singly or in sprays of 3-5, no fragrance; foliage medium size, dark green, semi-glossy; upright, bushy, medium growth; PP7757; [Baby Katie × Shocking Blue]; int. by Nor'East Min. Roses, 1991

Dreamgirl – See **Dream Girl**, LCl

Dreamglo Min, rb, 1979, Williams, Ernest D.; bud long, pointed; flowers white, tipped and blended red, 1 in., 50 petals, high-centered, slight fragrance; foliage small, dark; upright growth; PP4579; [Little Darling × Little Chief]; int. by Mini-Roses, 1978

Dreaming – See **Träumerei**, F

Dreaming – See **Dreaming Parade**, Min

Dreaming HWich, lp, Clements, John; flowers blush with large group of golden stamens, 1½ in., single, flat, borne in clusters, moderate sweet/honey fragrance; recurrent; rambling (10-15 ft.) growth; PPAF; int. by Heirloom Roses, 2006

Dreaming Free S, m, 2001, Lim, Ping; flowers deep mauve, reverse lighter mauve, 2½ in., single, borne in large clusters, slight fragrance; foliage medium size, medium green, semi-glossy, disease-resistant; few prickles; growth spreading, low (2-3 ft.); garden, groundcover; [seedling × Ballerina]; int. by Bailey Nurseries, Inc., 2002

Dreaming Parade Min, op, Poulsen; flowers coral-red, medium, dbl., no fragrance; foliage dark; growth bushy, 20-40 cm.; int. by Poulsen Roser, 1996

Dreaming Spires LCl, dy, 1973, Mattock; flowers bright golden yellow, 3 in., 25 petals, high-centered, intense fragrance; repeat bloom; foliage dark; [(Arthur Bell × unknown) × Allgold]; Gold Medal, Belfast, 1977

Dreamland – See **Traumland**, F

Dreamland HT, ob, 1995, Sheldon, John & Robin; flowers orange blend tipped with darker orange, dbl., borne mostly singly; foliage medium size, medium green, matte; upright, medium growth

Dreamrider Min, yb, 1998, Williams, Ernest D.; flowers med. yellow, pink edge, reverse yellow, 1¾ in., very dbl., borne mostly singly; foliage medium size, medium green, semi-glossy; few prickles; upright, bushy, medium (18 in.) growth; [Sue Jo × Twilight Trail]; int. by Texas Mini Roses, 1997

Dreams Come True – See **Senator Burda**, HT

Dreamsicle Min, ob, 1992, Taylor, Franklin "Pete" & Kay;

flowers creamy white edged with orangish pink edges, reverse same, large, dbl.; foliage small, medium green, semi-glossy; some prickles; medium (36 cm.), compact growth; [Poker Chip × Party Girl]; int. by Taylor's Roses, 1993

Dreamtime – See **Dream Time**, HT

Dreamtime – See **Dream Time**, Min

Dreamward HT, yb, 1996, Perry, Astor; flowers light yellow with pink blush, 4½ in., dbl., borne mostly singly; prickles moderate; [Peace × Granada]; int. by Certified Roses, Inc., 1997

Dreamy Min, yb, 1987, Bennett, Dee; flowers cream, edges blushed pink, reverse cream with more intense blush, 20-25 petals; foliage medium size, medium green, semi-glossy; prickles slender, small, reddish, slanted downward; upright, medium growth; hips globular, medium, brown; [Irish Gold × Party Girl]; int. by Tiny Petals Nursery

Drei Gleichen HFt, ly; flowers medium, semi-dbl.

Dreienbrunnen Pol, mr, Berger, W.; flowers small, dbl.; int. in 1957

Dresden HT, w, 1961, Robichon; bud ovoid; flowers white lightly suffused pink, 4-5 in., 60 petals, high-centered, intense fragrance; foliage leathery, dark; very vigorous, upright growth; PP1857; [Ophelia × Cathrine Kordes]; int. by Ilgenfritz Nursery, 1961

Dresden Doll Min, lp, 1976, Moore, Ralph S.; bud mossy; flowers soft pink, 1½ in., 18 petals, cupped, moderate fragrance; foliage glossy, leathery; low, bushy, compact growth; PP4026; [Fairy Moss × Moss seedling]; int. by Sequoia Nursery, 1975

Dresdner Gelbe No. 79311 F, dy, VEG; flowers medium-large, semi-dbl.

Dresselhuys – See **Petite Penny**, F

Dries Verschuren HT, my, 1963, Verschuren, A.; bud pointed; flowers buttercup-yellow, well-formed, large, 25 petals, moderate fragrance; foliage glossy, bronze; vigorous, upright, bushy growth; [Golden Rapture × seedling]; int. by Blaby Rose Gardens, 1961

Drifter's Escape F, or, 1971, Greenway; flowers vermilion, 3-3½ in., 10 petals; foliage glossy, reddish when young; [Orangeade × Orange Sensation]

Dronning Alexandrine HT, dp, 1985, Poulsen, S.; flowers deep pink, medium, dbl., urn-shaped, no fragrance; foliage medium green, semi-glossy; medium, bushy growth; int. by Poulsen, 1926

Dronning Ingrid – See **Caritas**, HT

Dronning Margrethe – See **Queen Margrethe**, S

Dronningen af Danmark – See **Königin von Dänemark**, A

Dropmore Yellow HFt, my, Skinner; [*R. foetida* × *R. spinosissima altaica*]

Drottning Margretha – See **Queen Margrethe**, S

Drottning Silvia – See **Jardins de Bagatelle**, HT

Drottningholm – See **Rosenborg**, F

Droujba F, yb, 1985, Staikov, Prof. Dr. V.; flowers yellow, shaded red, small, 42 petals, cupped, borne in clusters of 5-30, moderate tea fragrance; foliage dark, glossy; bushy growth; [Masquerade × Rumba]; int. by Kalaydjiev and Chorbadjiiski, 1975

Dru Min, dy, 1985, Hunt, W. Henry; flowers small, 35 petals, high-centered; foliage medium size, medium green, semi-glossy; upright, bushy growth; int. in 1986

Drummer Boy F, mp, 1965, Lammerts, Dr. Walter; bud ovoid; flowers soft carmine-rose, small, dbl., borne in large clusters, slight fragrance; foliage leathery; vigorous, tall growth; PP2722; [Pinocchio × Queen Elizabeth]; int. by Germain's, 1964

Drummer Boy F, dr, 1987, Harkness, R., & Co., Ltd.; flowers deep, vivid, bright scarlet, fading slightly paler, loose, 15 petals, cupped, slight spicy fragrance; foliage small, medium green, semi-glossy, oval-pointed; prickles fairly straight, small, purplish-red; patio; spreading, low growth; hips ovoid, small, greenish; [(Wee Man × (Southampton × Darling Flame)) × Red Sprite]

Drummer Girl – See **Drummergirl**, S

Drummergirl S, dp; flowers small, single; non-recurrent; int. in 2000

Drummond's Thornless Bslt, mp, before 1846, Drummond; flowers rosy carmine, aging lighter, large, semi-dbl., cupped

Druschka HP, dp, 1932, Kordes, W.; flowers carmine-pink, large, dbl.

Druschki – See **Frau Karl Druschki**, HP

Druschki Rubra HP, mr, 1929, Lambert, P.; flowers crimson lightening to scarlet around edges, dbl.; [Frau Karl Druschki × Luise Lilia]

Du Luxembourg N, m, 1829, Hardy; flowers rosy purple, large, full

Du Maître d'École – See **Rose de La Maître-Ecole**, HGal

Du Pont – See **Rouge Formidable**, HGal

Du Pré Tell S, pb, 2001, Brown, Ted; flowers blush pink to light pink with deeper petal edges, light pink reverse, mauve, 4½ in., semi-dbl., borne in small clusters, moderate fragrance; foliage medium size, dark green, glossy; prickles small, hooked, moderate in number; growth medium (4-6 ft.); garden decorative; [sport of Jacqueline du Pré]

Duarte de Olivera N, op, 1879, Brassac; flowers salmon rose, coppery at base, 7-8 cm., full, borne in small clusters, moderate tea fragrance; good repeat; [Ophirie × Rêve d'Or]

Dublin HT, mr, 1983, Perry, Astor; flowers large, smoky red, 5 in., 35-40 petals, high-centered, borne mostly singly, intense raspberry fragrance; foliage large, medium green, matte; long, straight stems; upright growth; [(seedling × Mister Lincoln) × Ann Letts]; int. by Perry Roses, 1983

Dublin Bay LCl, mr, 1976, McGredy, Sam IV; bud ovoid; flowers pure dark red, edges darker, 4½ in., 25 petals, moderate fragrance; foliage dark green, glossy; climbing growth; [Bantry Bay × Altissimo]; int. by McGredy Roses Internat'l, 1975; Rose of the Year, Auckland, NZ, 1993

Dubonnet Pol, dr, 1959, Jelly; bud small; flowers cardinal-red, dbl., slight fragrance; foliage leathery; vigorous growth; PP1675; [sport of Stoplite]; int. by E.G. Hill Co., 1958

Dubourg HCh, w, 1826, Dubourg; flowers white, shaded lilac-violet, very large

Duc d'Angoulême C, dp, 1821, from Holland; flowers vivid rose pink, medium, full

Duc d'Angoulême – See **Duchesse d'Angoulême**, HGal, 1835

Duc d'Angoulême – See **Duchesse d'Angoulême**, HGal, before 1860

Duc d'Anjou HP, dr, 1862, Boyau; flowers crimson, shaded with dark red, very large, full; foliage dark green

Duc d'Arenberg HGal, m, before 1836; flowers deep violet rose, edges tending to lilac, large, full, borne in small clusters; growth erect

Duc d'Audiffret-Pasquier HP, rb, 1887, Verdier, E.; flowers carmine red with bright purplish hue, center brighter, sometimes bordered white, large, full; foliage somber green, oblong, irregular, deep serration; prickles numerous, unequal, straight, think, yellowish; growth upright

Duc d'Aumale B, dp, 1858; flowers bright glowing pink, shaded purple, very large, full

Duc de Bassano HP, dp, 1862, Portemer; flowers velvety dark carmine, large, full

Duc de Bavière HGal, dp, 1824, in Brussels; flowers large, full

Duc de Bavière – See **Duchesse d'Angoulême**, HGal, before 1860

Duc de Beaufort HGal, pb, about 1825, from Belgium; flowers flesh with violet over carmine, medium, full

Duc de Berry HGal, m, before 1845, Prévost; flowers dark violet purple, medium, full

Duc de Bordeaux HGal, pb, 1820, Vibert; flowers rosy lilac, large, dbl.

Duc de Brabant C, mp, before 1842; flowers bright pink, medium to large, dbl.; foliage dark green, elongate; prickles numerous, hooked; growth vigorous, tall

Duc de Bragance – See **Duchesse de Bragance**, HP

Duc de Cambridge D, m, before 1841, Laffay; flowers deep purplish rose, edged crimson, large, dbl., flat, regular, moderate fragrance; foliage dark, edged reddish brown when young

Duc de Cazes B, m, before 1848; flowers lilac pink, very full, cupped

Duc de Cazes Ch, dr, about 1850; flowers velvety dark red-purple, large, full

Duc de Cazes HP, m, 1861, Touvais; flowers velvety purple, dbl., cupped; [Général Jacqueminot × unknown]

Duc de Chartres D, lp, 1820, Godefroy; flowers medium

Duc de Chartres HCh, mr, 1827, Hardy; flowers bright red

Duc de Chartres HP, dr, 1876, Verdier, E.; flowers violet purple red tinted crimson, plumed flame and carmine, large, full, borne mostly solitary; foliage rough, dark green; prickles numerous, recurved

Duc de Choiseul C, pb; flowers pale rose colour, with a deep carmine center

Duc de Constantine Ayr, mp, 1857, Soupert & Notting; flowers bright lilac-pink, fading to silvery pink, 7-8 cm., full, cupped; non-recurrent

Duc de Crillon B, mr, 1860, Robert et Moreau; flowers brilliant red, changing to bright rose, large, full, flat

Duc de Devonshire Ch, pb, 1852, Laffay; flowers lilac pink, striped white, large, full, cupped

Duc de Devonshire HP, mp, 1857, Vibert

Duc de Fitzjames HGal, dr, before 1835; flowers very dark crimson, shaded purple; from France

Duc de Grammont T, pb, 1825, Laffay

Duc de Grillon – See **Duc de Crillon**, B

Duc de Guiche HGal, m, 1821, possibly Sèvres; flowers light reddish-violet, lilac at edges, large, dbl., flat, quartered, borne singly or in clusters of 2-3, moderate fragrance; foliage medium green, elliptical; prickles moderate

Duc de Magenta T, ab, 1859, Margottin; flowers flesh shaded fawn, large, dbl.

Duc de Marlborough HP, dr, 1884, Lévêque; flowers bright crimson red, large, full; very remontant; foliage dark green

Duc de Montpensier HP, dr, 1875, Lévêque; flowers red, tinted crimson and brown, large, dbl., moderate fragrance; prickles hooked

Duc de Mortemart HT, dp, 1901, Godard; flowers carmine-pink, tinted bronze, large, full; [La France de 89 × Reine Emma de Pays-Bas]

Duc de Rohan – See **Duchesse de Rohan**, HP

Duc de Ruschpler – See **Dr Ruschpler**, HP

Duc de Sussex D, lp, before 1841, Laffay; flowers pale pink, center velvety ruby, large, dbl., globular; sometimes classed as HCh

Duc de Valmy HGal, m; flowers light purplish rose, marbled purple, large, dbl., cupped

Duc de Wellington – See **Duke of Wellington**, HP

Duc d'Enghien HGal, mr, about 1830, Parmentier; flowers cherry red, shaded dark violet, medium, full

Duc d'Estrée – See **Henri Lecoq**, B

Duc d'Harcourt HP, mr, 1863, Moreau et Robert; flowers carmine red, outer petals light carmine, large, dbl., borne in small clusters; foliage somber green; prickles long, straight

Duc d'Orléans HGal, pb, 1830, Vibert; flowers cherry rose, covered with small white spots, large, dbl., cupped

Duc d'Orléans HP, mr, 1888, Verdier, E.; flowers vermilion, shaded carmine, large, full

Duc d'Ossuna HP, dr, 1855, Avoux & Crozy

Duc d'York A, w, before 1818, Miellez; flowers flesh white, large, dbl.; thornless; stems reddish

Duc Engelbert d'Arenberg HT, w, 1899, Soupert & Notting; flowers alabaster white, center flesh pink, very large, full, moderate fragrance; [Mme Lombard × Belle Siebrecht]

Duc Meillandina – See **Classic Sunblaze**, Min

Ducher Ch, w, 1869, Ducher; bud tinted pink; flowers pure white to medium, 2½-3 in., dbl., flat, borne singly or in small clusters; foliage light green, glossy, narrow; vigorous growth

Duchess HT, mp, 1977, Van Veen; bud ovoid; flowers cameo-pink shaded deeper, 4-4½ in., dbl., high-centered, moderate fragrance; foliage glossy, leathery; bushy, upright growth; PP4241; [White Satin × seedling]; int. by Carlton Rose Nurseries, 1976

Duchess of Abercorn HT, pb, 1919, Dickson, H.; flowers creamy white edged bright rose, dbl.

Duchess of Albany HT, dp, 1888, Paul, W.; flowers deep pink, very large, full, globular; [sport of La France]

Duchess of Atholl HT, ob, 1928, Dobbie; flowers vivid orange, flushed old-rose, large, dbl., cupped; foliage bronze, leathery; vigorous growth

Duchess of Atholl, Climbing Cl HT, ob, 1933, Howard Rose Co.

Duchess of Bedford HP, mr, 1879, Postans, R.B.; flowers bright medium red, large, dbl., globular; [Charles Lefebvre × unknown]; int. by W. Paul & Sons

Duchess of Connaught HT, pb, 1879, Bennett; flowers deep silvery pink, large, globular, intense fragrance; growth dwarf; [Adam × Duchesse de Vallombrosa]

Duchess of Connaught HP, dr, 1882, Standish & Noble; flowers crimson red shaded velvety purple-black, large, full, globular, moderate fragrance; growth medium to tall

Duchess of Cornwall HT, op; flowers salmon-pink, full, cupped; free-flowering; foliage glossy

Duchess of Edinburgh T, dr, 1874, Nabonnand, G.; flowers crimson, becoming lighter, large, dbl.; moderate growth; [Souv de David d'Angers × unknown]; int. by Veitch

Duchess of Edinburgh HP, lp, 1874, Bennett; flowers delicate silvery pink, center brighter, large, full

Duchess of Fife HP, lp, 1893, Cocker; flowers delicate silvery pink, large, dbl., cupped, intense fragrance; [sport of Countess of Rosebery]

Duchess of Kent Ch, w, 1840, possibly Laffay; flowers creamy white, sometimes edged with rose pink, small, full, cupped

Duchess of Kent F, dp, 1968, Waterhouse, W.P.; flowers rose-Neyron-red, cupped, borne in trusses; low, bushy growth; [sport of Katharine Worsley]; int. by Waterhouse Nursery

Duchess of Marlborough HT, pb, 1922, Nabonnand, P.; flowers brilliant lilac-rose, reverse carmine-crimson, dbl.; [(Jonkheer J.L. Mock × unknown) × Beauté de Lyon]

Duchess of Montrose HT, rb, 1929, Dobbie; flowers vermilion-crimson, large

Duchess of Norfolk HP, mp, 1853, Margottin; flowers carmine pink, medium, full

Duchess of Normandy HT, pb, 1912, Le Cornu; flowers soft salmon-flesh, overlaid yellow, large, dbl., high-centered; vigorous, branching growth; [sport of Dean Hole]

Duchess of Paducah HT, w, 1971, Williams, J. Benjamin; bud ovoid; flowers white, edge flushed red, large, dbl., high-centered; foliage large, glossy, dark, leathery; vigorous, upright growth; [Kordes' Perfecta × Peace]

Duchess of Portland P, mr, about 1770; flowers bright scarlet, with prominent golden stamens, large, semi-dbl., moderate fragrance; occasional repeat in autumn; foliage clear green; bushy, moderate growth; possibly Red Quatre Saisons × *R. gallica officinalis*

Duchess of Rutland F, dp, 1956, deRuiter; flowers rich carmine-pink, small, semi-dbl., borne on large trusses; vigorous growth; int. by Gandy Roses, Ltd.

Duchess of Sutherland HP, lp, 1839, Laffay, M.; flowers rosy pink, large, dbl.; vigorous growth

Duchess of Sutherland HT, pb, 1912, Dickson, A.; flowers rose-pink shaded lemon on white base, large, dbl., high-centered, moderate sweetbriar fragrance; foliage glossy, olive-green; vigorous growth

Duchess of Wellington HT, ly, 1909, Dickson, A.; bud pointed; flowers buff-yellow, deeper toward center, open, large, 17 petals; foliage leathery; long, strong stems; bushy growth

Duchess of Wellington, Climbing Cl HT, ly, 1924, Howard Rose Co.

Duchess of Westminster HT, pb, 1879, Bennett; flowers satiny pink shaded carmine, large, dbl., slight Tea fragrance; moderate growth; [Adam × Marquise de Castellane]

Duchess of Westminster HT, mp, 1911, Dickson, A.; flowers clear rose-pink, dbl., moderate fragrance

Duchess of Windsor – See **Permanent Wave**, F

Duchess of York HP, op, 1897, Cocker; flowers salmon pink

Duchess of York HT, yb, 1925, Dickson, S.; flowers deep golden yellow, center tangerine, very well-formed, large, dbl.; vigorous growth

Duchess of York F, or, 1994, Dickson, Colin; flowers mandarin red suffused with sulfur yellow, small, full, borne in small clusters, slight fragrance; foliage medium size, medium green, semi-glossy; some prickles; low (56 cm.), bushy growth; patio; [Little Prince × Gentle Touch]; int. as Sunseeker, Dickson Nurseries, Ltd.

Duchesse d'Abrantes M, lp, 1851, Robert; flowers light pink with dark pink shading, large, dbl., rosette

Duchesse d'Albe T, yb, 1903, Lévêque; flowers yellowish-salmon, shaded coppery purple rose, base golden yellow, dbl., globular

Duchesse d'Angoulême – See **Agathe Incarnata**, HGal

Duchesse d'Angoulême HGal, mp, 1835, Vibert; flowers translucent pink, lighter on the border, dbl., irregularly quartered, borne in clusters of 3-4; foliage pointed, lanceolate, light green; few prickles

Duchesse d'Angoulême HGal, lp, before 1860, Miellez; flowers blush-lilac, mottled crimson, medium, dbl., cupped; moderate, upright growth; [probably Gallica × Centifolia hybrid]

Duchesse d'Anjou HT, mr, 1979, Godin, M.; bud pointed; flowers crimson-red, 3-3½ in., cupped, slight fragrance; foliage dark; vigorous growth; [Wizo × Soraya]; int. in 1976

Duchesse d'Aoste HP, mr, 1867, Margottin; flowers rich vivid rose, large, very dbl., flat, moderate fragrance; foliage light green; prickles carmine, laterally flattened, recurved, unequal

Duchesse d'Arenberg HGal, m; flowers violet pink, large, full

Duchesse d'Assuma – See **Duchesse d'Ossuna**, HP

Duchesse d'Auerstädt N, my, 1888, Bernaix, A.; flowers golden yellow, touched with apricot at center, 11 cm., very full, cupped, borne mostly solitary, moderate tea fragrance; [Reve d'Or × unknown]

Duchesse de Berry HGal, pb, 1820, Vibert; flowers light pink, shaded carmine, large, semi-dbl.

Duchesse de Berry Ch, dp, 1827, Mauget; flowers full

Duchesse de Brabant T, lp, 1857, Bernède; flowers soft rosy pink, large, 45 petals, cupped, intense fragrance; vigorous, spreading growth

Duchesse de Brabant, Climbing Cl T, pb, about 1900; flowers pale coral pink, fading to medium pink, darker reverse, strong tea fragrance

Duchesse de Bragance HP, mp, 1886, Verdier; flowers delicate satiny pink, tinted brighter pink, very large, dbl.; foliage dark green, oval, irregularly toothed; prickles unequal, short, straight, brown; growth upright

Duchesse de Buccleugh HGal, rb, 1837, Vibert; flowers medium pink, edges tinged lavender, small button at center, large, dbl., cupped, moderate fragrance; foliage elliptical, gray-green, large; nearly thornless; growth vigorous, tall (2 m.)

Duchesse de Cambacérès HP, m, 1854, Fontaine; flowers carmine pink with distinct purplish tones, large, dbl., globular, cupped, borne in large clusters; foliage thick, large, glaucous green, slightly rugose; prickles numerous, gray-brown, unequal, slightly hooked; vigorous growth

Duchesse de Caylus HP, dp, 1864, Verdier, C.; flowers brilliant carmine-pink, well-formed, large, full, globular, moderate fragrance; moderate growth; [Alfred Colomb × unknown]

Duchesse de Chartres HP, mp, 1875, Verdier, E.; flowers bright velvety pink, reverse lighter, very large, full

Duchesse de Coutard C, lp, before 1885; flowers medium, full; possibly synonymous with Comtesse de Coutard

Duchesse de Dino HMult, lp, before 1860, Baumann; flowers flesh white, medium, semi-dbl.

Duchesse de Dino HP, dr, 1889, Lévêque; flowers blackish crimson, tinted carmine and velvety purple, very large, dbl.; foliage dark green; growth tall

Duchesse de Galliera HP, pb, 1847, Portemer; flowers bright rose shaded flesh, large, dbl., cupped; foliage ovate, mostly serrated; prickles numerous, nearly straight, very sharp, brownish-red

Duchesse de Galliera HP, mp, 1887, Verdier, E.; flowers rose-pink

Duchesse de Germantes C, lp; int. in 1988

Duchesse de Grammont D, mp, 1825, Cels

Duchesse de Grammont N, w, before 1838; flowers flesh, small, dbl., borne in small clusters, moderate fragrance; probably synonymous with Caroline Marniesse

Duchesse de Guermantes M, mp, Morley, Dr B.; int. in 1988

Duchesse de Kent – See **Duchess of Kent**, Ch

Duchesse de la Mothe-Houdancourt HT, dp, 1907, Mille-Toussaint; flowers carmine pink shaded vermilion pink, nuanced straw yellow and coppery red, large, dbl., moderate fragrance; [Mme Abel Chatenay × Maman Cochet]

Duchesse de la Tremoille M, dp, Morley, Dr B.; int. in 1988

Duchesse de Magenta HP, lp, 1859, Guillot père

Duchesse de Mecklemburg T, ly; flowers straw yellow, shaded pink, large, semi-dbl., cupped

Duchesse de Medina Coeli – See **Comtesse de Medina Coeli**, HP

Duchesse de Montebello HGal, lp, 1824-1825, Laffay, M.; flowers pale pink, almost white at edges, with a small center button, small to medium, very dbl., rosette, borne singly or in clusters of 2-3, moderate fragrance; foliage small, rounded, light green; few prickles; erect, compact growth; sometimes classed as HCh

Duchesse de Montmorency P, mp, 1844, Lévêque, R.; flowers satiny rose pink, shaded lilac, large, dbl., globular; some autumn repeat

Duchesse de Montpensier HP, lp, 1846, Margottin

Duchesse de Norfolk B, m, Wood; flowers purple-carmine, large, full, moderate fragrance

Duchesse de Portland – See **Duchess of Portland**, P

Duchesse de Reggio – See **Fanny Bias**, HGal

Duchesse de Rohan HP, pb, before 1867, from France (possibly Lévêque); flowers rosy crimson, margined with lilac, compact, large, dbl.

Duchesse de Savoie HT, mr, Laperriere, L.; int. in 1988

Duchesse de Sutherland – See **Duchess of Sutherland**, HP

Duchesse de Talleyrand HT, yb, 1944, Meilland, F.; bud pointed; flowers egg-yolk-yellow to chrome-yellow, dbl.; well branched growth; [Mme Joseph Perraud × Fred Edmunds]

Duchesse de Thuringe B, w, 1847, Guillot Père; flowers white tinted lilac, large, full, borne in small clusters

Duchesse de Vallombrosa HP, ab, 1875, Schwartz, J.; flowers flesh shaded rose, large, dbl.; [Jules Margottin × unknown]

Duchesse de Vallombrosa T, rb, 1879, Nabonnand; flowers coppery red, very large, full, borne in small clusters

Duchesse de Vendome HT, rb, 1924, Nabonnand, P.; flowers crimson, coppery reflexes, reverse yellow, dbl.; [Souv. de Gilbert Nabonnand × Juliet]

Duchesse de Verneuil M, pb, 1856, Portemer fils; bud heavily mossed; flowers flesh-pink deepening to salmon-pink, camellia-like

Duchesse d'Istrie – See **William Lobb**, M

Duchesse d'Orléans – See **Lustre d'Église**, HGal

Duchesse d'Orleans HGal, mp, 1821, Laffay, M.

Duchesse d'Orléans C, lp, 1837, Vibert

Duchesse d'Orleans HP, m, 1851, Quétier; flowers carmine-lilac, reverse white, large, very full; [probably a La Reine seedling]

Duchesse d'Orléans T, w, about 1860, Robert; flowers white, shaded flesh pink, center darker, large, very full

Duchesse d'Orléans – See **Jean-Baptiste Casati**, HP

Duchesse d'Ossuna HP, dp, 1877, Jamain, H.; flowers vermilion rose, large, full

Duchesse Hedwige d'Arenberg HT, mp, 1899, Soupert & Notting; flowers silky pink with silvery reflections, center darker, very large, full, moderate fragrance; [Belle Siebrecht × Mme Caroline Testout]

Duchesse Marie Salviati T, ob, 1889, Soupert & Notting; bud long; flowers orange-yellow tinted pink, full, moderate violet fragrance; [Mme Lombard × Mme Maurice Kuppenheim]

Ducis M, lp, 1857, Robert et Moreau; flowers light pink shaded with lilac, 7-8 cm., full, flat, borne in small clusters

Dudley Cross – See **Mrs Dudley Cross**, T

Duet HT, mp, 1960, Swim, H.C.; bud ovoid; flowers light pink, reverse dark pink, ruffled, 4 in., 25-30 petals, high-centered, borne singly and in small clusters, slight tea fragrance; foliage leathery, dark green, glossy; vigorous, upright growth; PP1903; [Fandango × Roundelay]; int. by Armstrong Nursery, 1960; Gold Medal, Baden-Baden, 1959

Duet – See **Rendan**, F

Duet Supreme HT, pb, 1990, Patterson, William; bud rounded; flowers light to medium pink blend, medium pink reverse, 35 petals, urn-shaped, slight fragrance; foliage medium size, dark green, semi-glossy; [sport of Duet]; int. by Roses Unlimited, 1990

Duett F, or, Noack, Werner; int. in 1982

Duett HT, pb, Kordes; flowers medium, cream colored with touch of pink; int. by W. Kordes Söhne, 2001

Duett Kordana Min, pb, Kordes ; bud between urceolate and ovate; flowers cream with pink, 2 in., 40 petals, cupped, borne mostly singly, no fragrance; recurrent; foliage dark green, matte; prickles moderate, 3-4 mm., triangular, elongated; compact, upright growth; PP15059; [seedling × seedling]; container rose; int. by W. Kordes Söhne

Duffey's Delight HT, dr, 1977, Duffey; bud long, pointed; flowers velvety dark red, 5-6 in., 60 petals, high-centered, slight fragrance; foliage dark; very vigorous, upright growth; [sport of Norman Hartnell]; int. in 1976

Duftbella F, dr, 1975, Hetzel; bud ovoid; flowers dark velvet red, center lighter, large, dbl., intense fragrance; vigorous, bushy growth; [Fragrant Cloud × (Monique × Mardi Gras)]; int. by GAWA, 1973

Duftendes Weisskirchen F, mp, Hetzel; int. in 2002

Duftes Berlin HT, ob, Cocker; int. in 1988

Duftfestival – See **Botero**, HT very dbl.

Duftgold – See **Fragrant Gold**, HT

Duftparadies F, dr; int. in 1966

Duftrausch F, mp, 1972, Tantau, Math.; bud globular; flowers semi-dbl.; foliage soft; upright growth; RULED EXTINCT 4/85 ARM; [unknown × unknown]; int. by Horstmann

Duftrausch HT, mp, 1985, Tantau, Math.; flowers large, dbl.; foliage medium size, medium green, semi-glossy; upright growth; int. in 1986

Duftstar HT, dr, 1976, Kordes; bud long, pointed; flowers 4 in., 24 petals, high-centered, intense fragrance; foliage dark, soft; vigorous, upright growth; [seedling × Papa Meilland]; int. by Dehner & Co., 1974

Duftstern HT, op, Noack, Werner; buds long, cylindrical; flowers coral-orange to orange pink, large petals, dbl., well-formed, moderate fragrance; recurrent; foliage deep, burgundy-colored new growth; int. in 1973

Duftwolke – See **Fragrant Cloud**, HT

Duftwunder F, ob, 1972, Hetzel; flowers yellowish-orange, large, very dbl.; moderate, upright growth; [Fragrant Cloud × Goldmarie]

Duftzauber – See **Fragrant Charm**, HT

Duftzauber '84 – See **Royal William**, HT

Duhamel Dumonceau HP, mr, 1872, Vilin; flowers bright red, shaded violet at edges, large, dbl., moderate fragrance; sometimes classed as B

Duiliu Zamfirescu HT, mr, 1938, Palocsay, R.; flowers large, dbl.

Duisburg HT, dp, 1908, Hinner, W.; flowers carmine-pink, large, dbl.

Dukat LCl, my, 1959, Tantau, Math.; bud red-tipped; flowers golden yellow, lighter at edges, 4½ in., dbl., moderate fragrance; foliage glossy, leathery; vigorous (10-16 ft.), upright growth; [Mrs Pierre S. duPont × Golden Glow]; int. in 1955

Dukat HT, dy, Tantau; int. by Rosen Tantau, 1999

Dukat HT, my, Brabec

Dukata Min, ob, 2006, Hopper, Nancy; flowers orange with pink edge, reverse dark orange, 2½ in., semi-dbl., borne mostly solitary; foliage medium size, medium green, semi-glossy; prickles ¼ in., red/tan, moderate; growth bushy, medium (16 in.); [Tobo × Pierrine]

Duke Meillandina – See **Classic Sunblaze**, Min

Duke of Albany HP, dr, 1882, Paul; flowers vivid crimson when first opening, changing darker as the flowers expand, very large, very full

Duke of Argyll HSpn, pb

Duke of Cambridge – See **Duc de Cambridge**, D

Duke of Connaught HP, rb, 1875, Paul; flowers dark velvety crimson flushed brighter, large, dbl.; vigorous growth

Duke of Connaught HT, mr, 1879, Bennett; flowers rose-crimson, very large, with a tendency to ball, dbl.; moderate growth; [Adam × Louis van Houtte]

Duke of Edinburgh HP, dr, 1868, Paul; flowers deep red, large, dbl.; vigorous, erect growth; [Général Jacqueminot × unknown]

Duke of Edinburgh – See **The Gold Award Rose**, F

Duke of Fife HP, dr, 1892, Cocker & Sons; flowers deep crimson-scarlet, large, full; [sport of Étienne Levet]

Duke of Normandy HT, lp, 1921, Jersey Nursery; flowers silvery pink; [St. Helena × George Dickson]

Duke of Paducah HT, rb, 1971, Williams, J. Benjamin; bud ovoid; flowers dark velvety crimson, large, dbl., slight fragrance; foliage large, glossy, dark, leathery; vigorous, bushy growth; [Grand Gala × Josephine Bruce]

Duke of Teck HP, dp, 1880, Paul; flowers deep pink, large, 40 petals, globular, moderate fragrance; vigorous growth; [Duke of Edinburgh × unknown]

Duke of Wellington HP, dr, 1864, Granger; flowers velvety crimson-red, large, dbl., cupped; vigorous growth; [Lord Macaulay × unknown]

Duke of Wellington – See **Rosiériste Jacobs**, HP

Duke of Windsor HT, ob, 1968, Tantau, Math.; bud pointed; flowers orange, well-formed, large, 27 petals, intense fragrance; foliage dark, glossy; very vigorous, upright growth; int. by Wheatcroft & Sons, 1967; Edland Fragrance Medal, ARS, 1968, ADR, 1970

Duke of York Ch, pb, 1894, Paul & Son; flowers rosy-pink and white to crimson, variable

Duke Sunblaze – See **Classic Sunblaze**, Min

Duke Wayne – See **Big Duke**, HT

Dulce Bella T, op, 1890, Bennett; flowers coppery pink, large, full

Dulcinea HT, mr, 1965, Verschuren, A.; flowers oriental red, edged darker, reverse yellow, large, 50-55 petals; foliage dark, glossy; upright, bushy growth; [Condesa de Sástago × seedling]; int. by Stassen, 1963

Dumbo F, mr, 1956, Combe; flowers bright cherry-red, very large, semi-dbl.; foliage dark; very vigorous growth; [Mme G. Forest-Colcombet × Independence]

Dumnacus HP, mp, 1880, Moreau & Robert; flowers carmine pink, very large, full, cupped; [Countess of Oxford × unknown]

Dumortier HGal, pb, before 1843, Parmentier; flowers light red with silvery reflex, medium, very dbl., flat

Duncan Reade-Hill HT, ob, 2000, Poole, Lionel; flowers orange, medium, dbl., borne mostly singly, moderate fragrance; foliage medium size, dark green, semi-glossy; prickles moderate; growth upright, bushy, vigorous (3 ft.); [Golden Splendour × Doris Tysterman]

Duncan's Rose S, dp, Poulsen; flowers single, borne in clusters, no fragrance; recurrent; foliage glossy; [Johannesburg Garden Club × unknown]; int. in 1998

Dundee HSpn, w, before 1832, Austin, R.; flowers white blotched pink, reverse pure white, dbl., cupped; moderate growth

Dundee Rambler Ayr, lp, before 1838, Martin; flowers white edged with pale pink, fading to white, 5 cm., dbl., borne in medium clusters, slight sweet, musky fragrance; thought to be *R. arvensis* × a Noisette

Dune LCl, my, Delbard; flowers pure yellow, large, dbl., borne in clusters, intense fragrance; good repeat; growth to 8 ft.; int. by George Delbard SA, 1993

Dunkelrote Ellen Poulsen – See **Red Ellen Poulsen**, Pol

Dunkelrote Hermose B, dr, 1899, Geissler; flowers dark carmine red; foliage glossy; [Reine Marie Henriette × Hermosa]

Dunkelrote Tausendschön HMult, dr, 1942, Vogel, M.; flowers dbl., borne in small clusters; [Tausendschön × unknown]

Dunkerque HT, op, 1940, Laperrière; bud pointed, ovoid; flowers bright pink, slightly coppery, very large,

30 petals; foliage clear olive-green; long, strong stems; vigorus, upright, branching growth; [Charles P. Kilham × seedling]; Gold Medal, Bagatelle, 1940

Dunkirk HT, mr, 1947, Dickson, A.; flowers rose-red, 4-5 in., 36 petals; foliage glossy

Dunton Gold HT, ob, 1966, Dunton Nursery; flowers deep golden yellow-orange and pink tipped, 6 in., high-centered, moderate fragrance; foliage glossy; vigorous growth; [sport of Tzigane]

Dunwich Rose HSpn, ly; flowers soft lemon yellow to white, small, single, borne along arching canes, very early bloomer; fern-like foliage; prickles numerous, bristly; low, spreading, groundcover growth; int. in 1956 or before

Dunwichiensis – See **Dunwich Rose**, HSpn

Duo F, or, 1955, Gaujard; flowers coppery orange, open, petals fringed, medium, single; foliage dark; very vigorous growth; [Peace × seedling]

Duo Unique HT, pb, deRuiter; int. by De Ruiter's New Roses Intl, 2001

Dupetit Thouars B, mp, 1844, Portemer; flowers bright pink, large, full

Duplex – See **Alba Semi-plena**, A

Duplex – See **Rose d'Amour**, Misc OGR

Duplex Misc OGR, mp, before 1770; sepals foliaceous; flowers clear pink, medium, semi-dbl., slight fragrance; foliage downy, gray-green; prickles heavy; chance garden hybrid of *R. pomifera* × unknown

Dupont Rose – See **Dupontii**, Misc OGR

Dupontii Misc OGR, w, 1817; flowers blush, aging to creamy white, 3 in., single, perfectly circular shape, borne in small corymbs, slight musk fragrance; early summer; hips large, round, golden-orange; [perhaps descended from *R. gallica* × *R. moschata* hybrid]

Dupuy-Jamain HP, mr, 1868, Jamain, H.; flowers cerise-red, well-formed, 30 petals; vigorous growth

Dupuytren HGal, dr, 1823, Cartier; flowers very bright crimson, black velvet in center, cupped

Duquesa T, lp, 2005, Turner, James C.; flowers light pink with peach tones at center, medium, very full, borne in small clusters, intense fragrance; foliage medium size, medium green, semi-glossy; prickles moderate; [Mons. Tillier × Duchesse de Brabant]; int. in 2005

Duquesa de Peñaranda HT, ob, 1931, Dot, Pedro; bud pointed; flowers shades of orange, large, 35 petals, cupped, moderate fragrance; foliage rich green, glossy; vigorous growth; [Souv. de Claudius Pernet × Rosella]; int. by C-P; Gold Medal, Portland, 1933

Duquesa de Peñaranda, Climbing Cl HT, ob, 1940, Germain's

Dura S, w

Durban July F, rb, 1982, Kordes, W.; flowers yellow, orange to red, medium, semi-dbl.; foliage medium size, medium green, semi-glossy

Durbanville Flame HT, ab; flowers peach-apricot with orange edges, dbl., exhibition; firm, medium long stems; growth vigorous, tall, 5-6 ft; int. in 2001

Durgapur Delight HT, lp, Gupta; flowers flower light porcelain pink; free-flowering; growth vigorous; [sport of Montezuma]; int. in 1980

Durgapur Jubilee HT, pb, Ghosh; flowers light pink with deeper petal edges, high-centered; int. in 1998

Durham Pillar HMult, mr, 1960, Risley; bud globular; flowers rose-red, small, single, cupped, borne in clusters, slight fragrance; free, recurrent boom; foliage dark, leathery, glossy; moderate climbing or trailing growth; [Chevy Chase × seedling]; int. in 1958

Durham Prince Bishops HT, op, 1991, Thompson, Robert; flowers orange, flushed pink, medium, full, moderate fragrance; foliage large, dark green, glossy; bushy growth; [Silver Jubilee × Doris Tysterman]; int. by Battersby Roses, 1989

Dusky Dancer – See **Raven**, S

Dusky Maiden F, dr, 1947, LeGrice; flowers deep crimson scarlet, 3 in., single, borne in trusses, moderate fragrance; foliage dark; vigorous growth; PP2210; [(Daily Mail Scented Rose × Étoile de Hollande) × Else Poulsen]; Gold Medal, NRS, 1948

Dusky Red HT, dr, 1974, Wyant; flowers medium red, veined, large, dbl., high-centered, intense fragrance; intermittent bloom; foliage dark, leathery; vigorous, upright, bushy growth; [Karl Herbst × Big Red]; int. in 1972

Düsterlohe S, dp, about 1931, Kordes; flowers rose-red, 3 in., single to semi-dbl., borne singly and in small clusters; non-recurrent bloom; foliage dark green; vigorous, climbing growth; not dependably hardy; [Venusta Pendula × Miss C.E. van Rossem]

Düsterlohe I – See **Düsterlohe**, S

Düsterlohe II S, mr, 1941, Kordes; flowers light red, large, single; hybrid macrantha

Dusty Pink F, lp, 1961, Jelly; bud ovoid, long, pointed; flowers 3-3½ in., 50-60 petals, high-centered, moderate fragrance; vigorous, upright growth; PP2164; [Garnette × Garnette seedling]; int. by E.G. Hill Co., 1961

Dusty Red Min, dr, 2003, Wells, Verlie W.; flowers full, borne mostly solitary; foliage medium size, dark green, semi-glossy; prickles ¼ in., hooked, moderate; growth upright, medium (18-24 in.); garden, exhibition; [seedling × seedling]; int. by Wells Mid-South Roses, 2002

Dusty Rose Min, m, 1975, Morey, Dr. Dennison; flowers reddish-purple, 1½ in., 40-50 petals, high-centered, moderate spicy fragrance; foliage dark; upright growth; [Amy Vanderbilt × Cécile Brunner]; int. by Pixie Treasures Min. Roses, 1974

Dusty Springfield F, lp, 2001, Horner, Colin P.; flowers soft light pink, reverse paler, 7 cm., full, borne in small clusters, moderate fragrance; foliage medium size, medium green, semi-glossy; prickles medium, curved, moderate; growth compact, medium (70 cm.); garden decorative; [seedling × Matsukawa Rose]; int. by Warley Rose Gardens, 2003

Dutch Bengal – See **Maheca**, Bslt

Dutch Gold HT, my, 1977, Wisbech Plant Co.; flowers golden yellow, 6 in., 32-34 petals, moderate fragrance; foliage glossy, dark; vigorous growth; [Peer Gynt × Whisky Mac]; int. in 1978

Dutch Hedge HRg, lp, 1958, Nyveldt; flowers small, single; hips orange-red; [(*R. rugosa rubra* × *R. cinnamomea*) × *R. nitida*]

Dutch Miss Min, pb, 1987, Bridges, Dennis A.; flowers light pink veining to white base, fading slightly, medium, 22 petals, high-centered, borne singly, slight fragrance; foliage medium size, dark green, glossy; prickles straight, pointed, medium, tan; upright, medium growth; [Summer Spice × seedling]

Dutch Provence – See ***R. centifolia batavica*** (Clusius), C

Dwarf Austrian Rose – See **Rosier d'Amour**, HGal

Dwarf Crimson Rambler – See **Mme Norbert Levavasseur**, Pol

Dwarf Fairy – See **Zwergenfee**, Min

Dwarf King – See **Dwarfking**, Min

Dwarf King 78 – See **Zwergkönig 78**, MinFl

Dwarf Pavement – See **Rosa Zwerg**, HRg

Dwarf Queen – See **Queen of the Dwarfs**, Min

Dwarf Queen '82 Min, mp, 1985, Kordes, W.; bud deep pink; flowers lighten as they open, 4 cm., 35 petals, shallow cup, rosette, borne in clusters, slight fragrance; recurrent; foliage small, medium green, glossy; bushy (20 in.) growth; [Zwergkönig 78 × Sunday Times]

Dwarfking Min, mr, 1956, Kordes; flowers carmine, small, 25 petals, cupped, borne singly and in clusters, slight fragrance; foliage glossy; compact (8-10 in.) growth; PP1577; [World's Fair × Tom Thumb]; int. by J&P

d'Yèbles B, m, about 1830, Desprez; flowers violet-purple, medium, full

Dyllan's Mom MinFl, rb, 2001, Bryan Epstein; flowers red/orange/yellow, yellow/red reverse, 2 in., dbl., high-centered, borne mostly solitary, slight fragrance; foliage large, dark green, matte; growth upright, tall (3-4 ft.); garden decorative, exhibition; [Fireworks × Perfect Moment]

Dyna – See **Bingo**, HT

Dynamite LCl, dr, 1992, Warriner, William A.; flowers bright red, 4-4½ in., 30 petals, borne in small clusters, slight citrus fragrance; foliage large, dark green, glossy, resistant to powdery mildew; some prickles; tall (150-185 cm.), upright, spreading, arching growth; PP8741; [seedling × Simpathie]; int. by Bear Creek Gardens

Dynastie – See **Carefree Wonder**, S

Dynastie Piccard HT, pb, Meilland; flowers light pink with deeper pink edges, dbl., high-centered, borne mostly singly; florist rose; int. in 2002

Dynasty HT, ob, 1990, Warriner, William A.; bud pointed; flowers bright orange with yellow blending at petal base, aging to coral, 30 petals, cupped, no fragrance; foliage medium size, medium green, semi-glossy; prickles hooked down slightly, red to yellow-green; upright, spreading, tall growth; PP6443; [seedling × seedling]; int. by Bear Creek Gardens, 1991

Dynasty HT, pb, Keisei; flowers inner petals tan, outer petals dusty pink, dbl., informal; growth medium, open; int. in 1992

Dzambul HP, mr, 1938, Kosteckij; flowers medium, dbl.

E. B. LeGrice LCl, w, 2001, Kull, Amelita E.; flowers white, light pink reverse, 3 in., semi-dbl., borne in large clusters; foliage large, dark green, glossy; prickles small, slightly hooked, few; growth climbing (12-15 ft.); [sport of Pearl Drift]

E. E. Saskavá HT, dy, 1933, Böhm, J.; flowers large, dbl.

E. G. Hill HT, mr, 1929, E.G. Hill, Co.; bud ovoid; flowers dazzling scarlet, well-formed, very large, dbl., intense damask fragrance; vigorous growth

E. G. Hill, Climbing Cl HT, mr, 1942, Marlin

E. Godfrey Brown HT, dr, 1919, Dickson, H.; flowers deep reddish-crimson, dbl.

E. H. Morse – See **Ernest H. Morse**, HT

E. H. T. Broadwood HT, 1916, Dickson, H.

E. I. Farrington F, mr, 1953, Brownell; flowers cardinal-red to blood-red, turning almost crimson, 3½-4 in., 50-60 petals, high-centered, moderate fragrance; vigorous, spreading growth; PP1404; [Queen o' the Lakes × seedling]

E. J. Baldwin HT, my, 1952, Robinson, H.; flowers rich golden yellow, high pointed, well-formed, large, 30-40 petals; foliage dark; vigorous, upright, branching growth; [Phyllis Gold × seedling]; int. by Baker's Nursery

E. J. Ludding HT, pb, 1931, Van Rossem; flowers carmine-pink shaded coral-red and salmon, open, large, dbl.; bushy growth; [Ophelia × Hill's America]; int. by Prior

E. J. Moller HT, dr, 1924, Moller; flowers intense red, deepening toward black, dbl.; [George Dickson × unknown]

E. N. Ward Pol, pb, Kershaw

E. P. H. Kingma HT, ab, 1919, Verschuren; flowers apricot and orange-yellow, medium, dbl.; [Mme Edouard Herriot × Duchess of Wellington]

E. Pemberton Barnes HT, pb, 1928, Pemberton; flowers light pink, shaded cerise

E. V. Lucas HT, dr, 1934, McGredy; flowers dark velvety crimson, large, semi-dbl., borne in sprays; foliage dark; vigorous, upright, branching growth

E. Veyrat Hermanos Cl T, pb, 1895, Bernaix, A.; bud long, pointed; flowers apricot and carmine-pink, reflexes violet-rose, 9-10 cm., dbl., borne in small clusters, intense tea fragrance; vigorous growth

E. Veyrath Hermanos – See **E. Veyrat Hermanos**, Cl T

E. Y. Teas HP, mp, 1874, Verdier, E.; flowers bright red, large, full, globular, intense fragrance; [Alfred Colomb × unknown]

Eads F, pb, 1991, Burks, Larry; flowers pink and yellow, medium, semi-dbl., borne in small clusters, slight fragrance; foliage medium size, medium green, semi-glossy; low, compact growth; [(seedling × Pinocchio) × seedling]; int. by Specialty Roses, 1991

Eagle HT, dr, 1985, Verschuren, Ted; flowers large, 28 petals, cupped, borne in sprays of 3-5, moderate fragrance; foliage large, dark, semi-glossy; bushy, tall growth; [Centurio × Red Planet]; int. by H.A. Verschuren, 1984

Eagle Wings F, m, 1986, Lens, Louis; flowers white, shaded lilac, 2 in., 5 petals, borne in clusters of 3-24, moderate spicy fragrance; foliage very dark; prickles hooked, brown; bushy growth; [seedling × Picasso]; int. in 1982

Earl Beatty HT, dr, 1923, Chaplin Bros.; flowers deep crimson, large, dbl., cupped; bushy growth; [Hoosier Beauty × George Dickson]

Earl Godard Bentinck HT, mr, 1931, Buisman, G. A. H.; flowers red, base orange, large, dbl.; very vigorous growth; [Pharisaer × Covent Garden]

Earl Haig HT, mr, 1921, Dickson, A.; flowers brick-red, large, dbl.; prickles few thorns; vigorous, bushy growth; Gold Medal, NRS, 1920

Earl of Beaconsfield – See **Lord Beaconsfield**, HP

Earl of Dufferin HP, dr, 1887, Dickson, A.; flowers velvety crimson, shaded chestnut-red, very large, 53 petals, globular; vigorous growth

Earl of Eldon N, ob, 1872, Eldon/Coppin; flowers coppery orange, 7 cm., dbl., flat, borne in small clusters, moderate tea fragrance

Earl of Gosford HT, dr, 1912, McGredy; flowers dark crimson scarlet, large, dbl., intense fragrance

Earl of Mexborough T, mp, 1902, Brauer

Earl of Pembroke HP, mr, 1882, Bennett; flowers carmine-red, large, dbl.; [Marquise de Castellane × Maurice Bernardin]

Earl of Warwick HT, lp, 1904, Paul, W.; flowers pale pinkish buff, reverse livid pink, large, dbl.; [Souv. de S.A. Prince × Mrs W.J. Grant]

Earldomensis S, my, 1934, Page; flowers bright yellow; growth to 6 ft.; [*R. hugonis* × *R. omeiensis pteracantha*]

Early Bird F, mp, 1965, Dickson, Patrick; flowers rose-opal, well-formed, 4 in., dbl.; free growth; [Circus × Fritz Thiedemann]; int. by A. Dickson & Sons, 1965

Early Blush HRg, pb, Wheen, G.; [*R. rugosa* × unknown]; int. by Gretchen's

Early Mist Min, w, 1972, Van de Yssel; flowers cream, 2 in., 25 petals, globular, slight fragrance; foliage dull, light; vigorous growth; int. by Warmerdam, 1970

Early Morn HT, lp, 1944, Brownell; flowers shell-pink, large, dbl., high-centered, moderate fragrance; foliage glossy; long stems; vigorous growth; [(Dr. W. Van Fleet × Général Jacqueminot) × Break o'Day]

Early Peace – See **Molodost Mira**, HT

Early Ray HT, dy, 2001, Giles, Diann; flowers large, dbl., borne mostly solitary, moderate fragrance; foliage medium size, dark green, matte; prickles medium, straight, few; growth upright, low; garden decorative; [Dr. A.J. Verhage × Stroke o' Luck]; int. by Giles Rose Nursery, 1999

Early Red HSpn, rb; flowers carmine-red with gold, medium-large, semi-dbl.; [*R. pimpinellifolia* × Claudius Denoyel]

Early Spring – See **Soshun**, F

Earth Song Gr, dp, 1976, Buck, Dr. Griffith J.; bud long, pointed to urn-shaped; flowers Tyrian red to Tyrian rose, 4-4½ in., 25-30 petals, cupped, moderate fragrance; foliage glossy, dark, leathery; upright, bushy growth; [Music Maker × Prairie Star]; int. by Iowa State University, 1975

Earthquake Min, rb, 1984, Moore, Ralph S.; flowers striped red and yellow, reverse yellow, small, dbl., no fragrance; foliage small, medium green, semi-glossy; upright, bushy growth; PP5791; [Golden Angel × seedling]; int. by Moore Min. Roses, 1984

Earthquake, Climbing Cl Min, rb, 1991, Moore, Ralph S.; bud rounded; flowers red/yellow stripes, yellow reverse, aging similar, medium, 40 petals, urn-shaped, borne usually singly or in sprays of 3-5, no fragrance; foliage small, medium green, semi-glossy; upright, tall growth; [sport of Earthquake]; int. by Sequoia Nursery, 1991

Easlea's Golden Rambler HWich, yb, 1932, Easlea; flowers rich buff-yellow marked crimson, 4 in., 35 petals, flat, borne singly or in small clusters, moderate fragrance; non-recurrent; foliage leathery, rich olive-green; vigorous, climbing growth; int. by Totty; Gold Medal, NRS, 1932

East Anglia HT, mp, 1939, Morse; flowers aurora-pink; [sport of Golden Dawn]

East Europe F, mp, Urban, J.

Easter Min, my, Olesen; flowers dbl., borne mostly solitary, moderate fragrance; foliage dark green, glossy; growth bushy, very low (20-40 cm.)

Easter Bonnet HT, op, 1983, Burks, Joe J.; [sport of Queen Elizabeth]; int. as Super Derby, Co-Operative Rose Growers, 1982

Easter Bunny Min, m, 1995, Rennie, Bruce F.; flowers 2 in., 5 petals, borne mostly singly; foliage large, medium green, semi-glossy; few prickles; tall (2 ft.), upright growth; [Lavonde × seedling]; int. by Rennie Roses International, 1992

Easter Morn – See **Easter Morning**, Min

Easter Morning Min, w, 1960, Moore, Ralph S.; bud pointed; flowers ivory-white, 1½ in., 60-70 petals; foliage leathery, glossy; vigorous, dwarf (12-16 in.) growth; PP2177; [Golden Glow × Zee]; int. by Sequoia Nursery, 1960

Easter Parade F, yb, 1951, Whisler; bud ovoid, golden yellow; flowers salmon-pink and cerise, reverse yellow, becoming light carmine, 2½-3½ in., 50-55 petals; foliage dark, glossy, bronze; vigorous, bushy growth; [Sunshine × Herrenhausen]; int. by Germain's

Eastern Gem T, w, 1905, Conard & Jones; flowers creamy white, shaded light pink and yellow

Easy Min, rb, 1992, Zipper, Herbert; flowers red and white, medium, very dbl., borne in small clusters, no fragrance; foliage small, dark green, glossy; few prickles; medium (35 cm.), bushy growth; [Pink Petticoat × Banana Split]; int. by Magic Moment Miniature Roses

Easy Cover – See **Pebble Beach**, S

Easy Going F, yb, 1999, Harkness; flowers deep gold apricot, overlaid with peach when fresh, 3½-4 in., 26-30 petals, borne in small clusters, moderate fruity fragrance; foliage large, very bright, light green, glossy; numerous prickles; upright, bushy, medium (3-3½ ft.) growth; PP10478; [sport of Livin' Easy]; int. by Weeks Roses, 1999

Easy Orange F, ob, 1995, Jobson, Daniel J.; flowers bright orange, medium, full, borne in small clusters, moderate fragrance; foliage medium size, dark green, glossy; numerous prickles; upright, medium growth; [(Valerie Jeanne × Eyepaint) × Laureate]

Easy to Cut HMsk, lp, 2000, Lens, Louis; flowers light pink, reverse lighter, 2-2½ in., semi-dbl., borne in large clusters, moderate fragrance; recurrent; foliage medium size, medium green, semi-glossy; few prickles; upright, bushy, medium (3-4 ft.) growth; [(Trier × Pinocchio) × (Seagull × Ballerina)]; int. by Louis Lens BV, 1997

Easy Vibes F, op, 1999, Giles, Diann; flowers medium, dbl., borne in small clusters; foliage medium size, dark green, glossy; few prickles; compact, medium growth; [Sun Flare × Easy Living]; int. by Giles Rose Nursery, 1998

Ebb Tide HT, ab, 1961, Von Abrams; bud long, pointed; flowers light yellowish-pink, 5 in., 28 petals, high-centered; foliage glossy; vigorous, upright, compact growth; [(Sutter's Gold × seedling) × Peace]; int. by Peterson & Dering, 1961

Ebb Tide F, m, 2004, Carruth, Tom; flowers deep smoky purple, 8-10 cm., full, old-fashioned, borne in small clusters, intense clove fragrance; foliage medium size, dark green, semi-glossy; prickles average, almost straight; growth upright, medium (60 to 80 cm.); garden decoration; [((Sweet Chariot × Blue Nile) × Stephen's Big Purple) × ((International Herald Tribune × *R. soulieana* derivative) × (Sweet Chariot × Blue Nile))]; int. by Weeks Roses, 2006

Ebby S, dy, 2005, Williams, Benjamin R.; flowers semi-dbl., high-centered, borne in small clusters, moderate fragrance; foliage medium size, dark green, semi-glossy; prickles moderate, straight; growth compact, medium (36 in.); garden decorative; [Ben's Gold × Eclipse]; int. by Williams, J. Benjamin, 2005

Ebène HP, m, 1844, Boyau; flowers violet-purple, medium, full

Eberhard Jung Pol, mr, 1930, Schmitt, L.; flowers small, semi-dbl.

Eberwein – See **Dopey**, Pol

Éblouissant Pol, dr, 1918, Turbat; flowers dazzling deep red, very dbl., globular, borne in clusters; foliage bronze, glossy; bushy growth; [Bengale Rose × Cramoisi Superieur]

Ebony Gr, dr, 1960, Von Abrams; bud ovoid; flowers velvety dark red, 3-4 in., 20-30 petals, high-centered, slight fragrance; foliage glossy; vigorous, upright growth; PP2137; [Carrousel × Charles Mallerin]; int. by Peterson & Dering, 1960

Eboracum LCl, w, 1977, Powell, G.; flowers creamy white, yellow at base, 2½-3 in., 30-35 petals, borne singly and several together, moderate sweet fragrance; reliable repeat; foliage glossy; growth strong; hardy; [Casino × Ice White]

Écarlate HT, mr, 1907, Boytard; flowers brilliant scarlet, somewhat like Grüss an Teplitz, open, small, semi-dbl.; foliage rich green, glossy; vigorous, bushy growth; [Camoens × unknown]

Ecco Min, dy, Olesen; flowers dbl., no fragrance; foliage medium green, semi-glossy; growth bushy, very low (20-40 cm.); int. in 2000

Ecco Parade – See **Ecco**, Min

Echizo HT, Camprubi, C.

Echo Pol, pb, 1914, Lambert, P.; flowers varying (like Tausendschön) from dark pink to almost white, semi-dbl., cupped; reliable repeat; bushy growth; [sport of Tausendschön]

Echo S, op, Lens, Louis; flowers pink-salmon, dbl., borne in large clusters; vigorous growth, 80-120 cm; int. by Louis Lens, 1970

Éclair HP, dr, 1883, Lacharme, F.; flowers very dark red shaded blackish, well-shaped, small, dbl.; tall growth; [Général Jacqueminot × unknown]

Eclair de Jupiter HP, mr; flowers rose red, shaded glowing garnet purple, large, full

Eclair de Jupiter N, mr; flowers scarlet, shaded violet, large, dbl.

Éclaireur HP, dr, 1895, Vigneron; flowers dark bright red, exterior petals velvety, large, dbl., cupped, borne mostly solitary, moderate fragrance; very remontant; foliage dark green; [Duhamel Dumonceau × unknown]

Eclaireur F, Godin, M.; int. in 1971

Eclat de Haute Bretagne HT, ab, Adam; flowers rosy apricot, reverse lighter, dbl., globular, intense fragrance; to 70-90 cm. growth; int. by Pepinieres de la Guerinais, 2006

Éclatant Ch, mp, before 1836, Prévost; bud dark purple; flowers carmine

Éclatante HGal, mr, about 1860, Miellez

Éclatante HP, rb, 1862, Guillot; flowers poppy red with purple-violet, medium, full

Eclipse HT, ly, 1935, Nicolas; bud remarkably long, pointed, deep gold, with long, narrow; flowers golden yellow, loose, 28 petals, moderate fragrance; foliage leathery, dark; vigorous, bushy growth; [Joanna Hill × Federico Casas]; int. by J&P; Gold Medal, Rome, 1935, Gold Medal, Portland, 1935, Gold Medal, Bagatelle, 1936, David Fuerstenberg Prize, ARS, 1938

Eclipse F, pb, Sauvageot; int. in 1997; Golden Rose, Geneva, 1996

Eclipse, Climbing Cl HT, ly

Ecole de Barbizon LCl, m, Dorieux; int. by Roseraies Dorieux, 2005

Ecole d'Écully HT, op, Laperrière; flowers light salmon with saffron yellow at base, dbl.; int. in 1988

Ecstasy HT, yb, 1935, Dickson, A.; flowers pale yellow shaded bronze and cerise, dbl.; erect, branching growth

Ecstasy HT, dr, Kordes; buds large, pointed; flowers crimson, deepening to magenta, full, intense fragrance; nearly thornless flowering stems; growth medium; int. in 1994

Ed Steer HT, mr, 1999, Poole, Lionel; flowers 5 in., full, borne mostly singly, slight fragrance; foliage medium size, dark green, semi-glossy; prickles moderate; upright, medium (30 in.) growth; [(Royal William × Gabi) × Adrienne Berman]

Edda LCl, lp, 1929, Lodi; flowers pale pink, slightly darker center, 9-10 cm., very dbl.; [Reine Marie Henriette × Boncenne]

Edda S, mr, 1969, Lundstad; flowers clear rose-red, open, medium, 16 petals, borne in clusters; profuse, repeated bloom; foliage dark, glossy, leathery; vigorous growth; [Lichterloh × Scharlachglut]

Eddan S, rb, 2000, Makosch, Joachim; flowers dark red, reverse deep pink, medium size, full, borne mostly singly, intense fragrance; foliage medium size, light green, dull; few prickles; spreading, tall (4 ft.) growth; [sport of Auslo]; int. in 1987

Eddie HT, mr, 2004, Walsh, Richard; flowers medium red with yellow at petal base, 10 cm., full, borne mostly solitary, slight fragrance; foliage medium size, dark green, glossy, bronze when new; prickles medium, pointed; growth upright, tall (2 m.); garden; cutting; [Living × Uwe Seeler]; int. in 2003

Eddie's Advent HT, lp, 1938, Eddie; flowers pale buff, tipped pink, fading almost white, large, dbl., high-centered; foliage leathery; vigorous growth; [Mrs Sam McGredy × Edith Krause]

Eddie's Cream F, w, 1956, Eddie; flowers cream, large, dbl., borne in clusters, moderate apricot fragrance; vigorous growth; [Golden Rapture × Lavender Pinocchio]; int. by Harkness

Eddie's Crimson HMoy, mr, 1956, Eddie; flowers blood-red, 4-5 in., semi-dbl.; non-recurrent; vigorous (9-10 ft.) growth; large, globular fruit; [Donald Prior × *R. moyesii* hybrid]

Eddie's Jewel HMoy, mr, 1962, Eddie; flowers fiery red, semi-dbl.; recurrent bloom; few prickles; stems bark red; vigorous (8-9 ft.) growth; [Donald Prior × *R. moyesii* hybrid]

Eddie's Multiflora (clone of *R. multiflora*); used for understock

Edel HT, w, 1919, McGredy; flowers ivory-white, passing to pure white, well-formed, very large, dbl.; vigorous growth; [Frau Karl Druschki × Niphetos]

Edelweiss HP, w, 1925, Dienemann; flowers medium, full; [Frau Karl Druschki × unknown]

Edelweiss – See **Snowline**, F

Eden – See **Pierre de Ronsard**, F

Eden Min, mp, Olesen; flowers dbl., 25-30 petals, no fragrance; foliage medium green, semi-glossy; growth bushy, very low (20-40 cm.); int. in 1996

Eden Climber – See **Pierre de Ronsard**, F

Eden Ellen F, ab, 1985, Schneider, Peter; flowers medium, 35 petals, slight fragrance; foliage medium size, medium green, matte; bushy growth; [seedling × seedling]; int. in 1984

Eden Folies – See **Mimi Eden**, Min

Eden Romantica F, pb, Meilland; flowers light orient pink and light green, very full, globular, borne in sprays; PP15501; greenhouse rose; int. by Meilland Intl, 2004

Eden Rose HT, dp, 1950, Meilland, F.; bud ovoid; flowers Tyrian rose, 4½ in., 50-60 petals, cupped; foliage glossy, bright dark green; vigorous, upright growth; [Peace × Signora]; int. by URS, 1950; Gold Medal, NRS, 1950

Eden Rose, Climbing Cl HT, dp, 1962, Meilland, Alain A.; flowers deep pink, fading to medium pink, lighter reverse, 12-14 cm., strong fragrance; int. by URS

Eden Rose 85 – See **Pierre de Ronsard**, LCl

Eden Sungold F, my, 1977, Herholdt, J.A.; flowers pure yellow, 3 in., 30-35 petals, slight fragrance; semi-dwarf growth; [seedling × seedling]; int. in 1976

Edgar Andreu HWich, mr, 1912, Barbier; flowers bright blood-red, streaked white, reverse lighter, 7 cm., dbl., borne in clusters of 7-15; foliage small, dark green, glossy; [*R. wichurana* × Cramoisi Supérieur]

Edgar Blanchard HT, lp, 1912, Duron; flowers pink shading to white, large, dbl.; [Frau Karl Druschki × unknown]

Edgar Degas S, rb, Delbard; flowers red irregularly striped yellow and pink, semi-dbl.; foliage dark green, glossy; growth to 2-3 ft.

Edgar Jolibois HP, mr, 1883, Verdier, E.; flowers velvety scarlet, shaded with carmine, poppy and violet, large, full

Edgar M. Burnett HT, pb, 1914, McGredy; flowers flesh-pink, center dark pink, very large, dbl., moderate fragrance; Gold Medal, NRS, 1913

Edie Anne HT, mp; int. in 1997

Edina B, mp, 1849, Boyau; flowers bright pink, medium, full

Edina HT, w, 1934, Dobbie; flowers white, occasionally flushed pink, well-formed; foliage bronze red passing togreen; vigorous growth

Edisto MinFl, rb, 2007, Williams, Michael C.; flowers medium red, reverse medium red/yellow, medium, full, borne mostly solitary; foliage medium size, dark green, matte; prickles ¼ in., slightly curved down, reddish brown, moderate; growth upright, medium (30-36 in.); garden decoration, exhibition; [Chelsea Belle × unknown]; int. by Bridges Roses, 2007

Edith Bellenden HEg, mp, 1895, Penzance; flowers pale rose, small, single, borne in clusters; foliage fragrant; vigorous growth; very hardy

Edith Cavell – See **Miss Edith Cavell**, Pol

Edith Cavell HT, ly, 1918, Chaplin Bros.; flowers pale lemon-white, large, dbl.

Edith Clark HT, mr, 1928, Clark, A.; flowers fiery red, dbl., globular; foliage rich green; dwarf growth; [Mme Abel Chatenay × seedling]; int. by Hackett

Edith de Martinelli F, op, 1958, Arles; flowers salmon-pink, well-formed; vigorous growth; [(Gruss an Teplitz × Independence) × Floradora]; int. by Roses-France; Gold Medal, Geneva, 1958

Edith de Martinelli, Climbing Cl F, op, 1983, Orard, Joseph; growth climbing (to 3 m.); int. by Pekmez

Edith de Murat B, w, 1858, Ducher; flowers flesh, changing to white, petals somewhat fringed, medium, full

Edith Dennett F, op, 1974, Holmes, R.; flowers salmon-pink, 2-3 in., 24-30 petals, rosette, slight fragrance; foliage glossy; free growth; int. by Fryer's Nursery, Ltd., 1973

Edith d'Ombrain HT, w, 1902, Dickson; flowers white with touches of light pink, large, full

Edith Dombrain – See **Edith d'Ombrain**, HT

Edith Felberg HT, w, 1931, Felberg-Leclerc; flowers cream, center slightly darker, rather, dbl., cupped; foliage leathery; [seedling × Souv. de H.A. Verschuren]

Edith Hayward Cl HT, lp, 1967, Hayward; flowers pastel pink, large, dbl., high-centered; recurrent bloom; foliage glossy, dark; vigorous growth; [Fontanelle × Gen. MacArthur]

Edith Hazelrigg HT, ob, 1953, Cant, F.; flowers orange-cerise, pointed, 25 petals; foliage dark; vigorous growth

Edith Holden F, r, 1988, Warner, Chris; flowers russet-brown with yellow center, reverse slightly paler, aging slate grey, 15 petals, shallow cup, slight fragrance; free-flowering; foliage medium size, medium green, glossy; prickles very few; upright, tall, robust growth; hips rounded, small, orange; [Belinda × (Elizabeth of Glamis × (Galway Bay × Sutter's Gold))]; int. by E.B. LeGrice Roses, Ltd., 1988

Edith Krause HT, w, 1930, Krause; flowers greenish white, large, 30 petals, high-centered; very vigorous growth; [Mrs Charles Lamplough × Souv. de H.A. Verschuren]; int. by J&P

Edith Mary Mee HT, or, 1936, Mee; flowers vivid orient red, flushed orange, base yellow, dbl.; foliage dark, leathery; vigorous, bushy, compact growth; int. by Beckwith

Edith Nellie Perkins HT, op, 1928, Dickson, A.; flowers salmon-pink, flushed orange, reverse orange-red, shaded orange, 35-40 petals; few prickles; vigorous, bushy growth

Edith Nellie Perkins, Climbing Cl HT, op, 1936, H&S; Howard Rose Co.

Edith Oliver HT, lp, 1984, Singleton, C.H.; flowers soft light pink, large, 35 petals, borne in clusters of 4, moderate fragrance; foliage medium size, medium green, semi-glossy; prickles brownish-red; bushy growth; [Pink Parfait × seedling]; int. in 1980

Edith Part HT, pb, 1913, McGredy; flowers rich red, suffused deep salmon and coppery yellow

Edith Piaf HT, m, 1965, Verbeek; bud ovoid; flowers purple-red, large, dbl., slight fragrance; foliage dark; [Poinsettia × (Baccará × seedling)]; int. in 1962

Edith Piaf HT, dr, Meilland; bud conical and elongated; flowers velvet red, 4-5 in., 20 petals, high-centered, borne mostly singly, no fragrance; good repeat; foliage dark green, glossy; prickles few, small; growth erect (4-5 ft.); PP10633; [Hidalgo × Jelvanica]; greenhouse rose; int. by Meilland Intl, 1999

Edith Roberts HT, ab, 1969, Roberts, P.D.; flowers 5 in., high-centered; foliage glossy, dark; [sport of Dorothy Peach]

Edith Schurr S, yb, 1976, Stanard; bud globular, sulfur-yellow; flowers light yellow, center pink, 5 in., 60 petals, intense damask fragrance; recurrent bloom; foliage glossy; spreading growth; [(Wendy Cussons × Gavotte) × Leverkusen]; int. by Edmunds Roses

Edith Southgate Cl Min, pb, 1997, Barker, S.J.L.; flowers medium, dbl., borne mostly singly; foliage medium size, medium green, semi-glossy; some prickles; upright, medium (5ft.)growth; [Laura Ford × Admiral Rodney]

Edith Turner HP, lp, 1898, Turner; flowers light flesh pink, petals edged white

Edith Willkie HT, pb, 1943, Joseph H. Hill, Co.; bud long, pointed; flowers vivid pink, base lemon-chrome, 4½-5 in., 25-30 petals; foliage leathery, dark; vigorous, upright, compact growth; [Joanna Hill × R.M.S. Queen Mary]; int. by H&S, 1946

Edith Yorke HMult, lp, 1953, Miller, A.I.; flowers light almond-pink, semi-dbl., rosette, borne in trusses; foliage light green; very vigorous growth; [Havering Rambler × seedling]; int. by Jackman

Editor McFarland HT, mp, 1931, Mallerin, C.; flowers glowing pink, slightly suffused yellow, large, 30 petals; vigorous, bushy growth; [Pharisaer × Lallita]; int. by C-P

Editor McFarland, Climbing Cl HT, mp, 1948, Roseglen Nursery

Editor Stewart LCl, rb, 1939, Clark, A.; flowers crimson, sometimes flecked with white, fading to dark purple/pink, large, semi-dbl.; foliage bronze; long stems; growth vigorous; pillar or large bush; hybrid gigantea; int. by NRS Victoria

Editor Tommy Cairns HT, pb, 1991, Winchel, Joseph F.; flowers bright pink, light pink reverse, medium, 32-40 petals, borne mostly singly, slight fragrance; foliage medium size, medium green, semi-glossy; upright, medium growth; [seedling × seedling]

Edmée Cocteau – See **Mme Edmée Cocteau**, Cl HT

Edmée et Roger HT, op, 1903, Ketten Bros.; bud long; flowers flesh, center salmon flesh pink, darker ground, large; [Safrano × Mme Caroline Testout]

Edmond Charles-Roux HT, Dorieux, Francois; int. in 1990

Edmond de Biauzat T, op, 1885, Levet; flowers peach, tinted with salmon, large, full

Edmond Deschayes – See **Edmond Deshayes**, HT

Edmond Deshayes HT, ly, 1901, Bernaix, A.; flowers yellowish-white, large, dbl.

Edmond Duval HGal, mp, about 1835, Parmentier

Edmond Proust HWich, mr, 1903, Barbier; flowers pale rose and carmine, darker at center, 5-6 cm., very dbl., borne in clusters of 3-6, moderate fragrance; sparse seasonal bloom; foliage glossy; short stems; growth to 5-8 ft.; [*R. wichurana* × Souv. de Catherine Guillot]

Edmond Sablayrolles T, pb, 1888, Bonnaire; flowers hydrangea pink with peach/yellow, aging to bright carmine pink, large; [Souv de Victor Hugo × Mme Cusin]

Edmond Wood HP, mr, 1875, Verdier, E.; flowers cherry red, reverse carmine, large, full

Edmonton S, mp, Poulsen; flowers medium pink with mauve tones, 5-8 cm., semi-dbl. to dbl., cupped, borne in clusters, very slight fragrance; recurrent; foliage dark green, glossy; growth bushy (60-100 cm.); int. by Poulsen Roser, 2005

Edmund M. Mills HT, ob, 1927, Hieatt; flowers rosy flame, base deep gold, open, large, semi-dbl.; foliage dark, leathery; very vigorous, upright growth; [Red Radiance × Padre]

Edmund Rice HT, dp, 1992, Welsh, Eric; bud classic HT form; flowers light red, non-fading, petals pointed and reflexed, 5 in., 45-50 petals, high-centered, borne 5-7 per cluster and singly, moderate fragrance; repeats quickly; foliage very red when young, dark green, shiny, leathery; bushy, upright (4 ft.) growth; [Red Lion × Pink Silk]; int. by Christian Bros. College, 1992

Edna-Chris F, w, 1978, Ogden; bud pointed; flowers off-white, large, 30 petals, slight fragrance; foliage matte, green; tall, upright growth; [sport of Gene Boerner]

Edna Kaye HT, lp, 1959, Kemp, M.L.; flowers light pink tinted buff, 5 in., 56 petals; foliage bronze; free growth; [Directeur Guerin × Mirandy]

Edna Marie Min, lp, 1988, Moore, Ralph S.; flowers very soft pink, soft yellow base, aging becomes near white, 20 petals, high-centered, slight fruity fragrance; foliage small, light green, semi-glossy; prickles small, brown; upright, bushy, medium growth; [Pinocchio × Peachy White]; int. by Sequoia Nursery

Edna Mary F, dp, Horner; int. by Warley Rose Gardens, 2005

Edna Walling HMult, w, 1940, Clark or Mulley; flowers white to light rose pink, small, single, borne in clusters of 5-20; vigorous, climbing growth

Edna Wilson HT, my, 1983, Griffiths, Trevor; flowers large, dbl., moderate fragrance; foliage glossy; upright, vigorous growth; [sport of Beauté]; int. by T. Griffiths, Ltd., 1973

Ednah Thomas Cl HT, op, 1931, Thomas; flowers salmon-rose, large, dbl.; recurrent bloom; strong stems; vigorous, climbing growth; [seedling climber × Bloomfield Progress]; int. by H&S

Edo Bergsma HT, pb, 1932, Buisman, G. A. H.; bud pointed; flowers bright flesh and peach, large, intense fragrance; [Capt. F.S. Harvey-Cant × Étoile de Hollande]

Edon F, ab, Kordes

Edouard André HP, dr, 1880, Verdier, E.; flowers red, tinged with purple, large, full; foliage light green, oblong, finely dentate; prickles numerous, irregular, pointed, pink; growth upright

Edouard André le Botaniste – See **Edouard André**, HP

Edouard Desfossés B, m, 1840, Renard; flowers bright lilac pink, large, full

Edouard Dufour HP, dp, 1877, Lévêque; flowers dark carmine with brown tints, large, full, moderate fragrance; [Annie Wood × unknown]

Edouard Fontaine HP, mp, 1878, Fontaine; flowers frosty pink, large, full

Edouard Gautier T, yb, 1883, Pernet-Ducher; flowers have outer petals white, slightly pink on reverse, interior buff yellow with light pink, full, globular; [Devoniensis × unknown]

Edouard Guillot HT, op, Guillot-Massad; flowers salmon pink with slight yellow edges, borne in clusters of 3-5; foliage medium green, semi-glossy; int. by Roseraies Guillot, 2005

Edouard Hervé HP, dr, 1884, Verdier, E.; flowers dark currant red, large, full; foliage dark green, oblong, deeply toothed; prickles long, unequal, very sharp

Edouard Jesse – See **Edward Jesse**, B

Edouard Lefort HP, mr, 1886, Verdier, E.; flowers scarlet-carmine, shaded shining purple, large, very full

Edouard Mignot HT, m, 1927, Sauvageot, H.; flowers purplish garnet-red, reverse amaranth, dbl.; bushy growth; int. by F. Gillot

Edouard Morren – See **Edward Morren**, HP

Edouard Morren HP, dp, 1869, Granger; flowers silky carmine pink, tinted cherry red, very large, full; [Jules Margottin × unknown]

Édouard Pinaert HP, dr, 1877, Schwartz; flowers dark currant-red, edged in crimson, large, full, globular; foliage dark green; prickles numerous, slightly curved; growth upright; [Antoine Ducher × unknown]

Edouard Pynaert – See **Édouard Pinaert**, HP

Edouard Renard HT, mr, 1933, Dot, Pedro; flowers carmine, base yellow; long, stiff stems

Edu Meyer HT, rb, 1904, Lambert

Eduard Schill HT, or, 1931, Kordes; flowers brick-red shaded nasturtium-yellow, very large, semi-dbl., cupped; foliage glossy; vigorous growth; [Charles P. Kilham × Mev. G.A. van Rossem]

Eduardo Toda HT, my, 1947, Dot, Pedro; bud pointed; flowers sunflower-yellow; [Ophelia × Julien Potin]

Edward Behrens HT, dr, 1921, Kordes; flowers very dark velvety crimson, very large, dbl.; [Richmond × Admiral Ward]

Edward Bohane HT, or, 1915, Dickson, A.; flowers velvety crimson-orange to scarlet, large, very full, moderate fragrance

Edward Colston F, dr, 1990, Sanday, John; bud rounded; flowers dark red with medium red reverse, aging dark red, 40-45 petals, cupped, borne in sprays of 3-5, slight fruity fragrance; foliage medium size, medium green, matte; prickles barbed, red; upright, medium growth; no fruit; [Vera Dalton × Stephen Langdon]; int. by John Sanday Roses, Ltd., 1982

Edward Hyams S, yb; collected by Edward Hyams from Sharud in Iran in 1972; hybrid Persica; int. in 1972

Edward Jesse B, m, about 1840, Laffay; flowers dark purple, shaded crimson, medium, dbl., cupped

Edward Little Star F, m, 2001, Horner, Colin P.; flowers mauve with pink stripes, lavender reverse, small, single, borne in small clusters, moderate fragrance; foliage medium size, medium green, matte; prickles moderate, small, curved; growth upright, tall (170 cm.); garden decorative; [The Painter × Frantasia]; int. by Warley Rose Nurseries, 2006

Edward Mawley HT, dr, 1911, McGredy; bud almost black; flowers dark crimson, large, 18 petals, high-centered; bushy growth; Gold Medal, NRS, 1910

Edward Morren HP, mr, 1868, Granger; flowers deep cherry-rose, large, dbl., flat; vigorous growth; [Jules Margottin × unknown]

Edward VII Pol, mp, 1911, Low; flowers clear pink, small; [sport of Mme Norbert Levavasseur]

Edwardian Lady – See **Edith Holden**, F

Edwin F. Smith HT, 1918, Byrnes

Edwin Lonsdale HWich, dy, 1919, Dickson, H.; flowers bright light orange with citron yellow, fading to white, full; [*R. wichurana* × Safrano]

Edwin Markham HT, mp, 1923, Clarke Bros.; flowers bright rose-pink suffused silvery, dbl.; [Ophelia × Hoosier Beauty]

Edwin T. Meredith HT, ob, 1978, Warriner, William A.; bud ovoid, pointed; flowers coral-pink, 5 in., 30 petals, flat, slight fragrance; bushy, upright growth; PP4648; [Futura × First Prize]; int. by J&P, 1979

Efekto 21 – See **Les Amoureux de Peynet**, F

Effective LCl, mr, 1913, Hobbies; bud long; flowers crimson, 4 in., dbl., cupped, borne singly or in small clusters, moderate fragrance; intermittent repeat; very vigorous growth; [(Gen. MacArthur × unknown) × Paul's Carmine Pillar]

Effekt HT, rb, 1935, Krause; flowers scarlet-red, reverse flushed golden yellow, large, dbl., cupped; vigorous, bushy growth; [I Zingari × seedling]

Effekt F, dr, Berger; int. in 1975

Egalité F, m, 1946, Leenders, M.; bud pointed; flowers pale lilac-rose, 4 in., 25 petals, borne in trusses; foliage bronze; vigorous, branching growth; [Irene × seedling]; int. by Longley

Egas Monitz HT, Moreira da Silva, A.

Egeria HP, lp, 1874, Paul, W.; flowers delicate flesh pink, nuanced carmine and washed with white, large, full, semi-globular; [Jules Margottin × unknown]

Egeskov F, mp, 1985, Olesen, Pernille & Mogens N.; bud long, pointed ovoid; flowers bright medium pink, 20 petals, cupped, borne in large clusters, slight fragrance; foliage medium size, light green, glossy; prickles moderate, 4 mm., concave, greyed-orange; bushy growth; PP13835; [Tornado × Matangi]; int. by D.T. Poulsen, 1982

Eglanteria Lutea – See ***R. foetida*** (Herrmann)

Eglanteria Punicea – See ***R. foetida bicolor*** ((Jacquin) Willmott)

Eglantier – See ***R. arvensis*** (Hudson)

Eglantier Rouge – See ***R. rubiginosa*** (Linnaeus)

Eglantine – See ***R. rubiginosa*** (Linnaeus)

Eglantine Pol, dp, 1930, Soupert & Notting; flowers carmine, center white, many yellow stamens, single; small vigorous, dwarf, bushy growth; [Amaury Fonseca × Rodhatte]

Eglantine Guillot – See **Mlle Eglantine Guillot**, F

Eglantyne S, lp, 1994, Austin, David; flowers light, delicate pink, 3-3½ in., very dbl., cupped, borne in small clusters; foliage medium size, medium green, matte; some prickles; medium (115-130 cm.), bushy growth; PP9526; [seedling × Mary Rose]; int. as Eglantyne, David Austin Roses, Ltd., 1994

Egmont Behrens LCl, dr, Kordes; flowers deep velvet red, maturing to magenta burgundy, large, dbl., cupped, borne in clusters, moderate fragrance; recurrent; growth tall (10 ft.); int. by Ludwig's Roses, 2002

Egoli HT, dy, Kordes; int. in 1995

Egon Schiele – See **Astrid Lindgren**, S

Egyptian Treasure S, ob, 1974, Gandy, Douglas L.; flowers orange, 4 in., 16 petals, slight fragrance; foliage dark, glossy; [(Coup de Foudre × S'Agaro) × Vagabonde]; int. by Gandy's Roses, Ltd., 1973

Ehigasa F, yb, Keihan; int. in 1974

Eichsfeldia HMult, ly, 1925, Bruder Alfons; flowers yellowish-white, 3-4 cm., single, borne in small clusters, moderate musky fragrance; foliage glossy

Eiffel Tower HT, mp, 1963, Armstrong, D.L. & Swim, H. C.; bud long, urn-shaped; flowers 3½-5 in., 35 petals, high-centered, intense fragrance; foliage leathery, semi-glossy; vigorous, upright growth; PP2332; [First Love × seedling]; int. by Armstrong Nursery, 1963; Gold Medal, Rome, 1963, Gold Medal, Geneva, 1963

Eiffel Tower, Climbing Cl HT, mp, 1970, Laveena Roses; [sport of Eiffel Tower]; int. in 1967

Eiffelturm – See **Eiffel Tower**, HT

Eiko HT, yb, 1978, Suzuki, Seizo; bud pointed; flowers yellow and scarlet, pointed, 5-6 in., 30-35 petals; foliage large, glossy, light green; vigorous growth; [(Peace × Charleston) × Kagayaki]; int. by Keisei Rose Nursery

Eileen Bee HT, lp, 2007, Poole, Lionel; flowers large, 5½ in., full, borne mostly solitary; foliage large, dark green, glossy; prickles small, narrow, pointed, dark brown, few; growth bushy, medium (2½ ft.); garden decorative, exhibition; [Hazel Rose × Duncan Reed Hill]; int. by David Lister Roses, 2008

Eileen Boxall HT, dr, 1948, Boxall; flowers cerise, 5 in., 18 petals; foliage dark; vigorous growth; [sport of Betty Uprichard]

Eileen Dorothea HT, mr, 1931, Dickson, A.; bud pointed; flowers crimson-scarlet, edged darker, base yellow, dbl., high-centered; foliage deeply serrated; vigorous growth

Eileen Loow – See **Eileen Low**, Pol

Eileen Louise HT, mp, 1985, Brown, Harry G.L.S.; [sport of Admiral Rodney]

Eileen Low Pol, mp, 1911, Levavasseur; flowers China pink, grading to cream at base of petals, medium, dbl.; [Mme Norbert Levavasseur × Orléans Rose]

Eileen Whyte F, op, 2002, Horner, Colin P.; flowers salmon/orange, lighter reverse, 8 cm., dbl., borne in small clusters, moderate fragrance; foliage medium size, medium green, glossy; prickles medium, curved, moderate; growth upright, medium (1 m.); garden decorative; [Playmate × (Buttons × (Korp × Southampton))]; int. by Warley Rose Gardens, 2006

Eileen's Rose HT, op, 2006, Horner, Colin; flowers salmon pink, reverse salmon pink, 6 cm., dbl., borne in small clusters; foliage medium size, dark green, glossy; prickles up to ½ in., variable pointed, numerous; growth compact, medium (2½-4 ft.); garden decorative; [Pristine × Silver Jubilee]; int. by Warley Rose Gardens Ltd, 2007

Eisenach HWich, mr, 1910, Kiese; flowers bright red, small, single, borne in large clusters; very vigorous growth

Eisprinzessin HT, pb

Ekstasse – See **Ecstasy**, HT

Ekta HGal, mp, 1927, Hansen, N.E.; flowers medium, single to semi-dbl., moderate fragrance; non-recurrent; [Alika × American Beauty]

El Areana HSpn, w, 1911, Geschwind; flowers semi-dbl., borne singly on small stalks; early summer; foliage small, light green, matte; numerous prickles; growth low, compact

El Capitan Gr, mr, 1960, Swim, H.C.; flowers cherry to rose-red, 3½-4½ in., 30 petals, high-centered, borne in small clusters, slight fragrance; foliage dark, glossy; vigorous, upright, bushy growth; PP1796; [Charlotte Armstrong × Floradora]; int. by Armstrong Nursery, 1959; Gold Medal, Portland, 1959

El Capitan, Climbing Cl Gr, mr, 1963, Armstrong, D.L.; PP2697

El Catala Gr, rb, 1981, Buck, Dr. Griffith J.; bud ovoid, pointed; flowers medium red, reverse light pink, 35 petals, cupped, borne 1-8 per cluster, slight fragrance; foliage large, glossy; prickles awl-like; erect, slightly bushy growth; [Wanderin' Wind × ((Dornroschen × Peace) × Brasilia)]; int. by Iowa State University

El Chocón HT, dp

El Cid HT, or, 1969, Armstrong, D.L.; bud ovoid; flowers orange-red early, becoming more vivid red, 4-4½ in., 30-35 petals, high-centered to cupped, borne usually singly, some small clusters, very slight fragrance; recurrent; foliage medium size, olive green, semi-glossy, soft; prickles numerous, long, hooked slightly downward, yellowish-brown; stems medium, strong; vigorous, upright, bushy growth; PP3075; [Fandango × Roundelay]; int. by Armstrong Nursery; Gold Medal, Rome, 1969

El Dorado HT, yb, 1972, Armstrong, D.L.; flowers golden yellow, edged reddish, open, large, dbl., high-centered, intense fragrance; foliage large, glossy, leathery; vigorous, upright growth; PP3348; [Manitou × Summer Sunshine]; int. by Armstrong Nursery

El Paso HT, yb, 1988, Ohlson, John; flowers light yellow on outer petals, deep yellow on inner petals, reverse light yellow, dbl., high-centered, borne usually singly, slight spicy fragrance; foliage medium size, medium green, semi-glossy; prickles straight, medium, greenish-brown; bushy, medium, floriferous growth; [First Prize × Arlene Francis]; Bronze Medal, ARC TG, 1988

El Toro – See **Uncle Joe**, HT

Elaina Min, m, 1991, Zipper, Herbert; flowers medium, full, high-centered, borne in small clusters, moderate fragrance; foliage small, dark green, semi-glossy; few prickles; medium (35 cm.), bushy growth; [Blue Nile × Big John]; int. by Magic Moment Miniature Roses, 1992

Elaina Rothman HT, mp, 2002, Poole, Lionel; flowers full, borne mostly solitary, slight fragrance; foliage medium size, medium green, semi-glossy; prickles medium, long, pointed, moderate; growth upright, medium (2½ ft.); garden decorative, exhibition; [Gavotte × Spirit of the Heath]; int. by David Lister Roses, 2002

Elaine HT, yb, 1908, Paul, W.; flowers citron yellow with pink tints, large, full

Elaine HT, mp, 1950, Robinson, H.; flowers rose-pink, large, very dbl., high-centered; [Mrs A.R. Barraclough × Lady Sylvia]; int. by Baker's Nursery

Elaine HT, ab, 1951, Boerner; bud pointed; flowers 4½ in., 35-45 petals, high-centered; foliage leathery; very vigorous, upright growth; [Eclipse × R.M.S. Queen Mary]; int. by J&P

Elaine Frawley Pol, m, 2000, Weatherly, Lilia; flowers mauve-pink, tinted blue, reverse lighter, 1-2 in., very full, borne in small clusters, slight fragrance; foliage medium size, medium green, matte; few prickles; stems compact, low (less than 3 ft); [Cornelia × unknown]; int. by Sandy Bay Harrier Club, 1996

Elaine Greffulhe T, w, 1892, Cochet; flowers bright white, center sulfer yellow, large, very full

Elaine Holman HT, pb, 1976, Watson; bud long, pointed; flowers 3½-4 in., 50 petals, high-centered, moderate fragrance; foliage soft; vigorous growth; [Red Devil × Avon]; int. in 1975

Elaine Stuart HT, w, 1932, Edwards; flowers cream, center yellow; long stems; [Antoine Rivoire × Lillian Moore]

Elaine White F, w, 1959, Riethmuller; bud pointed; flowers cream, white and pink, open, small, semi-dbl., borne in clusters; foliage leathery; very vigorous, upright growth; [Gartendirektor Otto Linne × seedling]

Elaine's Choice F, pb, 1973, Ellick; flowers pale pink-apricot, yellow blend, 5 in., 40 petals, intense fragrance; foliage semi-glossy; vigorous growth; [Orange Sensation × Peace]; int. by Excelsior Roses, 1972

Élan F, my, Croix, P.; int. in 1960

Elation HT, dy, 1974, Warriner, William A.; bud long, pointed; flowers large, dbl.; foliage large, glossy, dark, leathery; vigorous, upright growth; [Buccaneer × seedling]; int. by Dickson's of Hawlmark

Elba HT, dr, 1963, Moreira da Silva; flowers deep red, reverse gold; [Confidence × Crimson Glory]

Elbefreude F, mr, Schmadlak, Dr.; flowers vermilion, large, dbl.; int. in 1983

Elbeglut Pol, dr, Schmadlak, Dr.; flowers large, semi-dbl.; int. in 1978

Elbegold Pol, dy, Schmadlak, Dr.; flowers golden yellow, medium, dbl.; int. in 1973

Eldora Harvey HT, pb, 1930, Harvey; flowers pink, center tinted lavender, reverse dark pink, dbl.; [Red Radiance × Maman Cochet]

Eldorado HT, ob, 1923, H&S; flowers copper, suffused orange and salmon, very large, dbl.; bushy growth; [seedling × Mme Edouard Herriot]

Eldorado F, dy, Christensen, Jack E.; flowers bright yellow to gold, well formed; free-flowering; growth medium to low; int. by J&P, 1992; Rose of the Year, Auckland, NZ, 1994

Eldorado HT, ob, Tantau; int. in 2004

Eleanor Min, op, 1960, Moore, Ralph S.; bud long, pointed; flowers coral-pink, aging darker, 1 in., 20-30 petals; foliage leathery, glossy; upright, bushy (12 in.), growth; PP2175; [(*R. wichurana* × Floradora) × (seedling × Zee)]; int. by Sequoia Nursery, 1960

Eleanor – See **Bering Renaissance**, S

Eleanor Annelise F, pb, 2002, Cocker, Anne G.; flowers peach pink, lighter reverse, 2 in., dbl., borne in large clusters, moderate fragrance; foliage medium size, very dark green, very glossy; prickles 9 mm., straight, moderate; growth upright, medium (2½ ft.); garden decorative; [Fragrant Delight × Clydebank Centenary]; int. by James Cocker & Sons, 2002

Eleanor Frances HT, dy, 1971, Green Acres Rose Nursery; flowers deep aureolin-yellow, 5 in., 28 petals; foliage glossy, leathery; vigorous, tall, upright growth; [Vienna Charm × seedling]; int. by V. E. Smith

Eleanor Henning HT, op, 1920, Easlea; bud pointed; flowers salmon-pink

Eleanor of Aquitaine – See **Aliénor d'Aquitaine**, HGal

Eleanor Perenyi Gr, yb, 1986, French, Richard; flowers yellow flushed apricot, reverse yellow flushed salmon, loose, 25 petals, moderate fruity fragrance; foliage medium size, dark, semi-glossy; prickles very few, hooked, small, red; medium, upright growth; hips small, globular, orange-red; [America × Sunsong]

Electra HMult, ly, 1900, Veitch; flowers yellow, fading white, medium, dbl., globular; foliage rich green, glossy; very vigorous, climbing growth; ruled extinct 1971 ARA; [*R. multiflora* × William Allen Richardson]

Electra HT, my, 1971, Boerner; flowers open, large, dbl., slight fragrance; foliage large, glossy, leathery; vigorous, upright growth; PP2979; [Eclipse × seedling]; int. by J&P, 1970

Electra S, dy, Winchell; flowers dbl., borne in clusters, slight fruity fragrance; free-flowering; growth moderate, much like a floribunda; PPAF; int. in 2006

Electric Blanket F, op, 2006; flowers salmon to coral pink, 4 cm., full, borne in trusses; foliage medium size, glossy; growth compact, low (1½ × 2 ft.); groundcover; int. as Bad Birnbach, W. Kordes' Söhne, 1999

Electron HT, dp, 1971, McGredy, Sam IV; flowers shocking pink, 5 in., 32-40 petals, high-centered, borne mostly singly, intense fragrance; foliage large, dark green, glossy; stems fully branched; upright, medium, bushy growth; PP3226; [Paddy McGredy × Prima Ballerina]; int. by McGredy & Son, 1970; Gold Medal, The Hague, 1970, Gold Medal, RNRS, 1969, Gold Medal, Portland, 1973, Gold Medal, Belfast, 1972

Élégance – See **Elegans**, Bslt

Elegance HWich, my, 1937, Brownell; flowers yellow, fading white at edges, reverse darker, 6 in., 48 petals, moderate fragrance; foliage large, dark green, glossy; prickles broad, red; vigorous growth; [Glenn Dale × (Mary Wallace × Miss Lolita Armour)]

Elégance HT, pb, 1955, Buyl Frères; bud globular; flowers rose-copper, large, dbl., moderate fragrance; foliage dark, leathery; moderate growth

Elegance HT, pb, Meilland; flowers light pink edged with dark pink, dbl., high-centered; PP10003; greenhouse rose; int. by Meilland Intl, 1996

Elegance Min, or, Olesen; bud short, pointed ovoid; flowers orange-red, medium, 25 petals, rosette, borne in clusters of 6-8; recurrent; foliage dark green, glossy; prickles few, 4 mm., hooked, greyed-orange; growth compact, bushy (40-60 cm.); PP15384; [seedling × seedling]; int. by Poulsen Roser, 2003; Honorable Mention, Hradec Králové, 2006

Elegance Min, m; recurrent; growth medium

Elegance Champagne HT, op, Teranishi; int. by Itami Rose Garden, 2005

Elegance Hit – See **Elegance**, Min

Elegans Bslt, rb, before 1844; flowers purple and crimson, often striped or spotted white, medium, semi-dbl., borne in very large clusters; probably synonymous with Amadis

Elegans Ayr, w; flowers semi-dbl., borne in large clusters; very vigorous growth

Elegant Beauty HT, ly, 1982, Kordes, W.; flowers light yellow flushed pink, large, 20 petals; foliage large, dark, matte; upright, bushy growth; [New Day × seedling]

Elegant Design F, pb, 1994, Moore, Ralph S.; sepals crested; flowers medium, dbl., borne in small clusters; foliage medium size, medium green, matte; few prickles; medium to tall (45-60cm.), upright, bushy growth; [Little Darling × Crested Jewel]; int. by Sequoia Nursery, 1995

Elegant Fairy Tale – See **Bremer Stadtmusikanten**, S

Elegant Pearl Min, w, 1983, Interplant; flowers creamy white, patio, dbl., borne in large clusters; foliage small, medium green, glossy; prickles few, medium; bushy growth; [seedling × Nozomi]

Elegant Pink Min, pb, 2005, Rickard, Vernon; flowers light pink, reverse medium pink, 1½ in., dbl., borne mostly solitary, no fragrance; foliage medium size, dark green, semi-glossy; prickles ¼ in., straight, brown, few; growth upright, medium (24 in.); exhibition-garden; [Fairhope × mixed pollen]; int. by Almost Heaven Roses, 2005

Elegant Touch HT, pb, 2001, Twomey, Jerry, and Lim, Ping; flowers deeper pink, reverse lighter pink, 5 in., dbl., high-centered, borne mostly solitary; foliage medium size, dark green, glossy; prickles moderate; growth upright, low (3-4 ft.); garden; [seedling × Sheer Elegance]; int. by Bailey Nurseries, Inc., 2002

Eleganta Min, mr

Élégante HGal, lp, before 1820, Hardy; flowers light pink, very large

Élégante HP, lp, 1847, Laffay; flowers large, full

Élégante HMult, mr, 1859, Laurentius; flowers cherry red

Élégante T, pb, 1882, Guillot; flowers China rose, aging to dawn pink, base coppery yellow, medium to large, dbl.

Élégante HT, ly, 1918, Pernet-Ducher; bud pointed; flowers creamy yellow, large, dbl., globular; branching growth

Élégante, Climbing LCl, w; bud long, slender; flowers white, center creamy yellow; foliage dull; possibly a HMult by Laffay, about 1835; int. by LeGrice Roses

Eleganza HT, lp; flowers creamy pink, 35 petals, classic hybrid tea, slight fragrance; tall growth; PPAF; int. in 2006

Eleghya Gr, dr, 1985, Staikov, Prof. Dr. V.; flowers deep blackish-red, 80 petals, cupped, borne in clusters of 2-5; foliage dark; bushy growth; [Spectacular × seedling]; int. by Kalaydjiev and Chorbadjiiski, 1975

Elegy HT, or, 1971, Meilland; flowers vermilion, 5½ in., 30 petals, globular; foliage semi-matte, dark; vigorous growth; [((Happiness × Independence) × Sutter's Gold) × ((Happiness × Independence) × Suspense)]

Elektra HT, ly, Rupprecht-Radke; flowers yellowish-white, large, dbl.; int. in 1964

Elektron – See **Electron**, HT

Elena Castello HT, pb, 1932, Munné, B.; flowers apricot-yellow to rose, semi-dbl.; vigorous growth; [Mme Butterfly × Angèle Pernet]

Eleonora LCl, dy, Barni, V.

Eleonore F, Noack, Werner; int. in 1973

Eléonore Berkeley HMult, m, 1900; flowers pale mauve-pink; [*R. multiflora* × Mme Luizet]

Eleta HT, mp, 1934, Dahlgren; bud pointed; flowers clear rose-pink, large, 65 petals, high-centered; vigorous growth; [Sensation × seedling]; int. by Kemble-Smith Co.

Elettra HT, op, 1940, Aicardi, D.; flowers copper-pink suffused reddish-yellow, large, dbl., high-centered; foliage leathery; very vigorous growth; [Julien Potin × Sensation]; int. by Giacomasso

Eleusine HT, m

Elf Min, dr

Elfe F, w, 1951, Tantau; bud pointed; flowers white tinted rose, petals shell-shaped, large, borne in clusters, intense fragrance; foliage glossy, dark; vigorous, upright, bushy growth; ruled extince, ARA 1985; [Swantje × Hamburg]

Elfe HT, lp, 1985, Tantau, Math.; flowers medium, 20 petals; foliage medium size, medium green, matte; upright growth; int. in 1982

Elfe LCl, w, Tantau; flowers large, ivory with green tint, full, slight fruity fragrance; recurrent; foliage large; growth vigorous, 8-10 ft.; int. by Rosen Tantau, 2001

Elfe Supreme F, mp; flowers rose-pink; [sport of Rosenelfe]

Elfenreigen S, dp, 1939, Krause; flowers deep rose-pink, center brighter, petals shell-shaped large, single; profuse, non-recurrent bloom; foliage reddish orange, later gray-green; very vigorous (5 ft.) growth; [Daisy Hill × seedling]; hybrid macrantha

Elfie's Joy HT, mp, 1995, Dry, Elfie; flowers medium pink, darker edges, lighter reverse, 5 in., full, borne mostly singly, moderate fragrance; foliage large, medium green, semi-glossy; numerous prickles; upright, medium growth; [sport of Sheer Elegance]; int. by Consolidated Nurseries, Inc., 1995

Elfin F, or, 1939, Archer; flowers cherry-rose shaded orange-salmon, 4½ in., dbl., borne in clusters; growth low growing; RULED EXTINCT 12/85

Elfin – See **Alfi**, Min

Elfin Charm Min, pb, 1975, Moore, Ralph S.; bud short, pointed; flowers phlox-pink, 1 in., 65 petals, moderate fragrance; foliage small, glossy, leathery; bushy, compact growth; [(*R. wichurana* × Floradora) × Fiesta Gold]; int. by Sequoia Nursery, 1974

Elfinesque Min, op, 1974, Morey, Dennison; bud pointed; flowers coral-orange to bright pink, small, semi-dbl., slight fragrance; foliage small, glossy, leathery; vigorous, dwarf, upright, bushy growth; [(Little Darling × unknown) × Yellow Bantam]; int. by Pixie Treasures Min. Roses, 1973

Elfinglo Min, m, 1978, Williams, Ernest D.; bud ovoid; flowers red-purple, micro-mini, ½ in., 33 petals, cupped, moderate fragrance; foliage small, glossy; compact growth; [Little Chief × Little Chief]; int. by Mini-Roses, 1977

Elfrid – See **Wiltshire**, S

Elgin Festival – See **Charlotte**, S

Eliane HT, ab, 1960, Gaujard; flowers bright salmon, well-formed, large, moderate fragrance; foliage dark; vigorous growth; [Mme Joseph Perraud × *R. foetida bicolor* hybrid]; int. by Gandy Roses, Ltd., 1959

Eliane Gillet S, w, Guillot-Massad; bud white splashed with red; flowers white, full, cupped; foliage glossy; growth bushy shrub, 3 ft.; int. by Roseraies Guillot, 1998

Elias S, pb, Buck; flowers deep pink with white eye, open; int. by Roses Unlimited, 2005

Elida HT, or, 1970, Tantau, Math.; flowers vermilion, large, 30 petals, high-centered, moderate fragrance; foliage dark, glossy; vigorous, branching growth; int. by Wheatcroft & Sons, 1966

Elie Beauvillain Cl T, mp, 1887, Beauvillain; flowers buff edges, coppery pink at center, 9-10 cm., dbl., borne in large clusters, moderate tea fragrance; prickles numerous, large; vigorous growth; [Gloire de Dijon × Ophirie]

Elie Lambert HP, mr, 1898, Lambert, E.; flowers bright carmine, large, full, globular

Elie Morel HP, m, 1867, Boucharlat

Elina HT, ly, 1984, Dickson, Patrick; flowers pale yellow to ivory, luminous, 5-5½ in., 30-35 petals, high-centered, borne singly; foliage large, dark, glossy; long stems; vigorous, tall growth; [Nana Mouskouri × Lolita]; int. in 1985; Rose Hall of Fame, WFRS, 2006, Gold Star of the South Pacific, Palmerston North, NZ, 1987, ADR, 1987

Elina-la-Jolie HGal, mr, before 1815, Descemet

Elisa A, lp, before 1810, Charpentier; flowers delicate pink, lighter at edges, 2-3 in., semi-dbl., borne in clusters of 6-8; foliage large, oval, light green, deeply toothed; prickles straight, very long

Elisa HT, mp, 1983, Rose Barni-Pistoia; flowers large, 40 petals, cupped, no fragrance; foliage large, light green, matte; upright growth; [seedling × Blessings]; int. in 1981

Elisa Blanche – See **Elisa**, A

Élisa Boëlle HP, w, 1869, Guillot Père; flowers white, tinted with rose, medium, full, circular, cupped; vigorous growth; [Mme Récamier × unknown]

Elisa Descemet HGal, lp, about 1810, Descemet; flowers glossy light pink, aging to flesh pink, large

Elisa Fugier T, w, 1890, Bonnaire; bud very long; flowers pure white lightly tinted soft yellow at center, very large, very full; [unnamed Tea × Niphetos]

Elisa Mercoeur HCh, mp, 1842, Vibert; flowers carmine pink, reverse lighter, large, full, cupped

Elisa Robichon HWich, mp, 1901, Barbier; flowers salmon-pink, fading pinkish buff, 4-5 cm., semi-dbl., open, borne in clusters of 5-10; some intermittent repeat; foliage dark, glossy; short, strong stems; vigorous, climbing (10 ft.), or trailing growth; [*R. luciae* × L'Ideal]

Elisabeth HMult, lp, 1926, Bruder Alfons; flowers light, creamy pink, 3 cm., dbl., borne in small clusters, moderate fragrance; nearly thornless; [Wartburg × unknown]

Elisabeth – See **Elizabeth of Glamis**, F

Elisabeth Barnes HT, op, 1907, Dickson, A.; flowers silky salmon pink, shaded yellow, reverse dark pink with coppery yellow, large, full, moderate fragrance

Elisabeth Didden HT, mr, 1918, Leenders, M.; flowers glowing carmine-red and scarlet, semi-dbl.; [Mme Caroline Testout × General MacArthur]

Elisabeth Faurax HT, w, 1937, Meilland, F.; bud pointed; flowers white, lightly shaded ivory, large, very dbl.; long stems; upright growth; [Caledonia × Mme Jules Bouche]

Elisabeth Faurax, Climbing Cl HT, w, 1937, Meilland, F.

Elisabeth Pollon HT, ob, 2000, Wambach, Catherine; flowers orange blend, 4 in., full, borne mostly singly; foliage medium size, dark green, semi-glossy; few prickles; upright, medium growth; [Elsie Melton × King of Hearts]; int. by Certified Roses, 2000

Elisabeth Tschudin F, mp, Hetzel; int. in 1981

Elisabeth Vigneron HP, lp, 1865, Vigneron; flowers light pink, darker within, very large, very full; foliage light green; prickles numerous, chestnut; growth upright, vigorous; [Duchesse de Sutherland × unknown]

Elise – See **Elsie**, HWich

Elise HT, w, 1969, Edmunds, F.; [sport of Prima Ballerina]; int. by Roses by Edmunds

Elise Fleury – See **Elyse Flory**, Ch

Elise Heymann T, yb, 1891, Strassheim; flowers coppery yellow, center peach-pink, reverse chrome yellow; very large, full; [Mme Lombard × Mont Rosa]

Elise Lemaire HP, lp, before 1886; flowers delicate pink, medium; foliage dark green, glossy; nearly thornless

Elise Noelle LCl, mr, 1991, Alde, Robert O.; flowers medium, dbl., borne in small clusters, slight fragrance; foliage medium size, medium green, semi-glossy; climbing (10 ft.) growth; [Dublin Bay × Burgund]

Elise Rovella HGal, mp, before 1842, Roseraie de l'Hay; flowers rosy pink, medium, dbl.; tall growth

Elise Sauvage T, yb, 1838, Miellez; flowers orange to yellow, sometimes yellow to white

Elise Tesch HT, yb, 1912, Altmüller, Johann; flowers Indian yellow with orange, large, very full; [sport of Mme Ravary]

Elise Vigneron – See **Elisabeth Vigneron**, HP

Elisio S, dp, Availishivilli; flowers bright pink, borne in clusters; recurrent; tall growth; int. in 1998

Eliska Krásnohorská HP, mp, 1932, Böhm, J.; flowers brilliant pink, large, semi-dbl., high-centered; foliage soft, bronze; bushy growth; [Capt. Hayward × Una Wallace]

Elite HT, yb, 1936, Tantau; bud pointed, red; flowers salmon-pink and yellow blend, very large, dbl., high-centered; foliage leathery, light; upright growth; [Charles P. Kilham × Pres. Herbert Hoover]; int. by J&P, 1941

Elite HT, ly, Fryer; flowers deep cream to yellow, small, dbl., high-centered, borne in abundant bloom; recurrent; growth vigorous, 4-5 ft.; int. by Ludwig's Roses, 2004

Eliza S, mp, 1961, Skinner; flowers clear pale rose, borne in clusters; non-recurrent; foliage dark, glossy; bushy, erect (3 ft.) growth

Eliza F, w, 2002, Giles, Diann; flowers medium, single, borne in small clusters; foliage medium size, light green, semi-glossy; prickles medium, straight, few; growth compact, medium; garden decoration, exhibition; [sport of Charlotte Anne]; int. by Giles Rose Nursery, 2001

Eliza HT, mp, 2006; flowers silvery pink, small, full, borne in small clusters; growth compact, medium (90 cm.); PP9752; int. by W. Kordes' Söhne, 2004; Gold Medal, Belfast, 2006

Eliza Balcombe HP, w, 1842, Laffay, M.; sepals very long; flowers white, pale flesh at center; foliage gray-green

Eliza Kordana Min, dp, Kordes; compact growth; int. by W. Kordes Söhne

Eliza Wren Pol, lp, Williamson; int. in 1997

Elizabeth HT, dp, 1911, Cant, B. R.; flowers deep carnation pink at the center, lighter towards edges, large, dbl., moderate fragrance; [Frau Karl Druschki × unknown]

Elizabeth Pol, mp, 1937, Letts; flowers rich salmon, semi-dbl., borne in large clusters

Elizabeth F, dp, 2004, Cocker, A.G.; flowers rose pink, 1½ in., full, borne in large clusters; foliage small, medium green, glossy; prickles 6 mm., straight; growth compact, bushy, short (2 ft.); garden decorative, containers; [Claire Scotland × Princess Alice]; int. by James Cocker & Sons, 2004

Elizabeth Abler Min, mr, 1991, Bennett, Dee; flowers medium red, opening to paler red at center, micro-mini, semi-dbl., high-centered, borne mostly singly, moderate fragrance; foliage small, medium green, semi-glossy; no prickles; low (20-30 cm.), bushy, compact growth; [(Christian Dior × Brian Lee) × unknown]; int. by Tiny Petals Nursery, 1992

Elizabeth Ann F, ob, 1993, Kirkham, Gordon Wilson; flowers bronze and gold, medium, dbl., borne in small clusters; foliage medium size, medium green, glossy; some prickles; medium, upright growth; [Kathleen's Rose × Eurorose]; int. by Kirkham, 1995

Elizabeth Arden HT, w, 1929, Prince; flowers pure white, dbl.; [Edith Part × Mrs Herbert Stevens]; Gold Medal, NRS, 1929

Elizabeth Brow – See **Elizabeth Rowe**, M

Elizabeth Casson F, lp, Harkness; flowers pale pink with lilac tones, borne in large clusters, moderate fruity fragrance; repeats well; growth bushy, robust; int. by R. Harkness & Co., 2005

Elizabeth Cone HT, lp, 1954, Cone; flowers flesh-pink, well-shaped; vigorous, low growth; [sport of Picture]; int. by Roger

Elizabeth Cullen HT, mr, 1921, Dickson, A.; flowers rich scarlet-crimson, semi-dbl.; Gold Medal, NRS, 1917

Elizabeth Dorothy HT, my, Allender, Robert William; int. in 1984

Elizabeth Fankhauser HT, op, Fankhauser, D.; bud large, long, pointed; flowers pure porcelain pink, edged deep crimson, very dbl., high-centered, borne singly and several together; foliage dark green, leathery, glossy; growth compact, medium; [Ma Perkins × Burnaby]; int. in 1965

Elizabeth Hamlin LCl, pb, 1987, Nobbs, Kenneth J.; flowers blush pink, fading to white, small, 5 petals, cupped, borne in mass clusters, slight fragrance; foliage medium size, pennate, with 5-7 leaflets; few prickles; rampant growth; [seedling × seedling]; int. in 1986

Elizabeth Harbour HT, pb, 1986, Harbour, E.R.; bud pointed; flowers light pink, dark pink reverse, 3 in., 30 petals, borne singly, slight fragrance; foliage medium size, medium green, semi-glossy; upright (3 ft.), bushy growth; [Elizabeth of Glamis × HT seedling (dark red)]; int. in 1985

Elizabeth Harkness HT, ly, 1969, Harkness; flowers off-white to creamy buff, often with pastel yellow and pink, 28 petals; foliage dark; upright, bushy growth; [Red Dandy × Piccadilly]

Elizabeth Harkness, Climbing Cl HT, w, 1973, Harkness; flowers pale yellow, fading to buff, 5-6 in.; [sport of Elizabeth Harkness]

Elizabeth Harwood LCl, lp

Elizabeth Hassefras Pol, mp, 1951; flowers buttercup form, glistening rose-pink with many stamens; int. by B&A

Elizabeth Heather Grierson LCl, lp, 1988, Mattock, John, Ltd.; bud coral pink; flowers soft pink, reverse darker, medium, dbl., borne in small clusters, moderate fragrance; foliage medium size, dark green, semi-glossy; upright growth; [Bonfire Night × Dreaming Spires]; int. by The Rose Nursery, 1986

Elizabeth Lee HT, dr, 1935, Chaplin Bros.; flowers dark velvety red, well-shaped

Elizabeth Marie HT, rb, 2007, Greenwood, Chris; flowers bright red, reverse white, 4-5 in., dbl., borne mostly solitary; foliage medium green, semi-glossy; prickles ¼ in., hooked downward, green, moderate; growth upright; [Stainless Steel × Rosie O'Donnell]

Elizabeth Munn Min, pb, 1993, McCann, Sean; flowers mainly pink with lighter reverse, dbl., flat, borne in small clusters; foliage medium size, medium green, semi-glossy; some prickles; medium, upright growth; int. by McCann, 1993

Elizabeth Navarro Pol, lp, 2001, Martin, Robert B., jr.; bud elongated, pointed, brushed pink on reverse; flowers 2 cm., dbl., borne in large clusters, no fragrance; foliage medium size, light green, matte; prickles medium, pointed, few; growth upright, medium (24-30 in.);

borders; [Nastarana × Nastarana]

Elizabeth of Glamis F, op, 1964, McGredy, Sam IV; flowers light orange-salmon, 4 in., 35 petals, flat, borne in clusters, intense fragrance; vigorous, compact bushy growth; PP2721; [Spartan × Highlight]; int. by McGredy, 1964; Gold Medal, NRS, 1963, President's International Trophy, NRS, 1963

Elizabeth of York HT, dp, 1928, Dobbie; bud large, pointed, cerise; flowers cerise-pink, 27 petals, high-centered; foliage dark, glossy; prickles few thorns

Elizabeth Park Centennial HT, pb, 2007, Mattia, John P.; flowers pink and white, 5-6 in., dbl., borne mostly solitary; foliage medium size, medium green, semi-glossy; prickles small, hooked, greenish-yellow, few; growth upright, medium (4-5 ft.); [Pretoria × Signature]; int. by Pride's Corners Farms, 2007

Elizabeth Philp F, ab, 1977, Philp, J.B. & Son; flowers creamy peach; [sport of Liverpool Echo]

Elizabeth Rowe M, mp, before 1888; flowers satiny pink, very large, dbl., moderate fragrance

Elizabeth Scholtz Gr, yb, 1988, Williams, J. Benjamin; flowers deep yellow with orange washing, reverse yellow with orange, full, high-centered, moderate damask fragrance; foliage large, plum-red to dark green, glossy; upright, bushy growth; [(Granada × Oregold) × (Arizona × Sunblest)]

Elizabeth Stuart S, ab, Massad-Guillot; flowers apricot with pink tones, moderate fragrance; foliage glossy; growth shrubby, 1 m.; int. by Roseraies Guillot, 2004

Elizabeth Taylor HT, dp, 1986, Weddle, Von C.; flowers deep pink with smoky edges, 4½-5 in., 30-35 petals, high-centered, borne usually singly, moderate spicy fragrance; foliage large, dark, semi-glossy; long stems; upright growth; PP6492; [First Prize × Swarthmore]

Elizabeth W. Adam HT, dp, 1926, Adam & Craigmile; flowers pink veined crimson, base yellow, 50 petals

Elizabeth Zeigler HWich, dp, 1917, Pierson, A.N.; flowers deep rose-pink; [sport of Dorothy Perkins]

Elka Gaarlandt Pol, dp, 1966, Buisman, G. A. H.; bud ovoid; flowers medium, dbl., borne in large clusters; foliage dark; [Hobby × Kathleen Ferrier]; Gold Star of the South Pacific, Palmerston North, NZ, 1970

Elke Fair LCl, ab, 2000, Bossom, Bill; flowers peach, straw reverse, red edge, frilly petals, 2¾ in., single, borne in large clusters; foliage large, medium green, semi-glossy; prickles moderate; climbing, spreading, tall (8 × 8 ft.) growth; [Southampton × Eyepaint]; int. by Bossom, 2000

Elke Gönewein HT, op, Gönewein; flowers bright salmon-pink, dbl., urn-shaped; recurrent; moderate (3-4 ft.) growth; int. by Rosen Gönewein, 1974

Ella Bodendorfer HMult, w, 1913, Paul; flowers cream white, speckled red with age, full

Ella Gordon HP, mr, 1883, Paul, W.; flowers glowing cherry red, large, full, globular; [Mme Victor Verdier × unknown]

Ella Guthrie HT, mp, 1937, Clark, A.; flowers large, dbl.; vigorous growth; [Premier × seedling]; int. by NRS Victoria

Ella McClatchy HMult, mp, 1926, Diener; flowers rose, single, borne in clusters; sometimes recurrent bloom; thornless

Ella Scott HWich, dp, 1925, Scott, G.J.; flowers deep rose-pink, approaching red, dbl., borne in clusters of 15-20; prickles few thorns; vigorous, climbing growth; [Orléans Rose × Chance seedling]; int. by Brundrett (NRS Victoria)

Ellamae Min, ab, 1986, Saville, F. Harmon; flowers 35 petals, high-centered, borne singly and in sprays of 3-5, moderate fragrance; foliage medium size, dark, glossy; prickles long, thin; medium, upright, bushy growth; PP6053; [Zorina × (Sheri Anne × Glenfiddich)]; int. by Nor'East Min. Roses

Elle – See **Nobility**, HT

Elle S, dp, 1981, Lundstad, Arne; bud pointed; flowers deep pink, 16 petals, borne 3-5 per cluster, intense fragrance; non-recurrent; foliage light green, 5-7 leaflets; prickles curved gray; vigorous, upright dense growth; [Schneezwerg × Splendens]; int. by Agricultural University of Norway, 1980

Elle HT, pb, 2003, Meilland International; flowers light pink, reverse orange pink, large, 50-55 petals, borne mostly solitary, intense fragrance; foliage large, dark green, glossy; growth bushy, short (5 ft.); garden, cutting; PPAF; [Purple Splendour × (Chicago Peace × Meikinosi)]; int. by Meilland Richardier, 2000; AARS, 2005

Ellen HT, dp, 1929, Hinner, P.; bud pointed; flowers unvarying dark pink, large, very dbl.; bushy growth; RULED EXTINCT 12/85; [sport of Premier]; int. by Gould

Ellen S, ab, 1986, Austin, David; flowers old rose form, large, dbl., intense fragrance; foliage large, medium green, semi-glossy; bushy growth; int. in 1984

Ellen Drew HP, lp, 1896, Drew; flowers light silvery pink with peach reflections, large, full; [sport of Duchesse de Morny]

Ellen Griffin Min, lp, 1988, Hefner, John; flowers medium, dbl.; foliage medium size, medium green, semi-glossy; upright, bushy growth; [Uwe Seeler × Party Girl]; int. by Kimbrew Walter Roses, 1988

Ellen Hamlyn S, dy, Dorieux

Ellen Mary HT, dr, 1963, LeGrice; flowers well-formed, 5 in., 34 petals, moderate fragrance; vigorous, upright growth; [Wellworth × Independence]

Ellen Poulsen Pol, mp, 1911, Poulsen, D.T.; flowers bright cherry-pink, large, dbl., borne in clusters; recurrent bloom; foliage glossy, dark; bushy growth; [Mme Norbert Levavasseur × Dorothy Perkins]; int. by Teschendorff

Ellen Poulsen Lysrosa Pol, op, 1938, Poulsen; flowers light salmon-pink, medium, dbl.

Ellen Poulsen Mork Pol, dr, 1985, Poulsen, S.; [sport of Ellen Poulsen]; int. in 1928

Ellen Terry HT, ly, 1925, Chaplin Bros.; flowers soft sulfur-cream, outer petals soft peach, well-shaped; upright, vigorous growth

Ellen Tofflemire HGal, m, 2001, Barden, Paul; flowers mauve/purple blend, 3-3½ in., very full, borne in small clusters, moderate fragrance; early summer; foliage medium size, medium green (bright green when young), matte, crinkled; prickles ¼ in., straight, brown, moderate; growth upright, short (3-4 ft.); hedging, specimen; [Tuscany Superb × Othello]

Ellen Willmott HT, lp, 1898, Bernaix, A.; flowers silvery flesh to shell-pink, dbl., cupped; very vigorous growth

Ellen Willmott HT, yb, 1936, Archer; flowers creamy lemon, flushed rosy pink, large, single; foliage leathery, dark; vigorous, upright growth; [Dainty Bess × Lady Hillingdon]

Ellen Zinnow HT, my, 1930, Krause; flowers yellow, shaded coppery orange and pink, dbl.; [Souv. de H.A. Verschuren × Sunstar]

Ellen's Joy S, lp, 1990, Buck, Dr. Griffith J.; bud ovoid; flowers light shell pink, aging lighter, medium, 23 petals, cupped, borne singly and in small clusters, moderate fruity fragrance; repeat bloom; foliage medium size, medium green, semi-glossy; prickles awl-like, rusty-green; upright, bushy, spreading, medium, winter hardy growth; hips globular, orange-red; [Vera Dalton × (Dornroschen × (Tickled Pink × Applejack))]; int. by Historical Roses, 1991

Ellesmere HT, w, 1927, Allen; flowers ivory-white to pure white; prickles few thorns; [Ophelia × unknown]

Elli Hartmann HT, my, 1913, Welter; flowers yellowish old-gold, dbl.; [(Souv. du Pres. Carnot × Mme Mélanie Soupert) × Marechal Niel]

Elli Knab HT, pb, 1934, Kordes; flowers flesh-cream flushed bright rose, veined vermilion, very large, dbl., high-centered; foliage leathery; upright, very vigorous growth; [Cathrine Kordes × W.E. Chaplin]

Elli Knab, Climbing Cl HT, pb, 1959, Tantau; int. in 1953

Ellinor LeGrice HT, my, 1949, LeGrice; bud ovoid; flowers 5-5½ in., 50 petals, cupped, moderate fruity fragrance; foliage leathery, glossy, dark; vigorous, upright growth; [Mrs Beatty × Yellowcrest]

Ellinor LeGrice, Climbing Cl HT, my, 1959, LeGrice

Elliot's Clementine HT, m, Elliot, Charles P.; flowers deep pink with mauve tones, 3½ in., very full, borne mostly solitary, slight fragrance; growth medium, upright, well-branched

Ellis Wood F, yb, 1983, Gateshead Metro. Borough Council; [sport of Arthur Bell]

Elmar Gunsch F, w, Scholle; flowers white with touch of yellow in center, small, dbl.; growth to 2-3 ft.; int. in 2001

Elmhurst HT, pb, 1985, Perry, Astor; flowers large, peachy pastel pink with yellow, 5 in., 30-35 petals, high-centered, borne mostly singly, moderate fruity fragrance; foliage medium size, medium green, matte; upright growth, moderately tall; [Granada × Helmut Schmidt]; int. by Perry Roses

Elmira HRg, mr, 1978, Svedja, Felicitas; bud ovoid; flowers bright red, open, 1½-2 in., 25 petals, intense fragrance; foliage yellow-green; upright, bushy growth; [Schneezwerg × Old Blush]; int. by Canada Dept. of Agric., 1977

Elmshorn S, dp, 1951, Kordes; flowers deep pink, pompom type, 1 in., 20 petals, cupped, borne in large trusses (to 40); recurrent bloom; foliage glossy, wrinkled,light green; [Hamburg × Verdun]; int. by Morse; ADR, 1950

Elna HMult, lp, Petersen; int. in 1964

Elna Noack Pol, or, Schmid, P.; flowers orange-red, medium, semi-dbl.; int. in 1960

Elnar Tonning HT, dp, 1926, Gyllin; flowers fuller and darker; [sport of Ophelia]

Elodea HT, ly, Roses Noves Ferrer, S L; flowers 22 petals, high-centered; [FE-87518 × K-861242-1]

Eloira HT, my, 1982, van Veen, Jan; flowers large, 35 petals, no fragrance; foliage medium size, medium green, semi-glossy; upright growth; [Elvira × seedling]; int. by G. Verbeek, 1981

Éloïse – See **Héloïse**, HGal

Eloise MinFl, mp, 2003, Fleming, Joyce L.; flowers medium, dbl., borne in small clusters; foliage medium size, medium green, semi-glossy, disease-resistant; growth spreading, open, medium (to 24 in.); hanging baskets, rock gardens; [Alberta × Lavender Dream]; int. in 2003

Elongata – See **Argentée**, D

Eloquence F, m, 1986, Warriner, William A.; flowers lavender, mini-flora, small, 20 petals, flat, borne singly and in clusters, slight spicy fragrance; foliage medium size, medium green, matte; upright, bushy growth; PP6010; [(Merci × Faberge) × Angel Face]; int. by J&P

Elouise – See **Héloïse**, HGal

Elsa Arnot HT, pb, 1960, Arnot; flowers golden yellow shaded pink and cerise, 4 in., 32 petals; foliage glossy; vigorous, upright growth; [Ena Harkness × Peace]; int. by Croll, 1959; Gold Medal, NRS, 1959

Elsa Knoll HT, op, 1968, Morey, Dr. Dennison; flowers shrimp-pink, large, 30 petals, high-centered, intense fragrance; foliage dark, glossy, leathery; vigorous, upright growth; [First Love × Castanet]; int. by General Bionomics, 1966

Elsbeth F, lp, 1963, deRuiter; flowers soft pink, dbl., borne in clusters; foliage dark; [sport of Valeta]

Elsbeth Meyer Pol, dr, 1940, Vogel, M.; flowers medium, semi-dbl.

Else HT, mr, 1929, Vogel, M.; flowers medium, dbl.

Else Chaplin Pol, dp, 1937, Chaplin Bros.; flowers deep rich pink, semi-dbl., borne in large trusses; vigorous growth

Else Kreis – See **Frau Elise Kreis**, Pol

Else Poulsen F, mp, 1924, Poulsen, S.; flowers bright rose-pink, 2 in., 10 petals, borne in clusters; foliage dark, bronze, glossy; vigorous, bushy growth; [Orléans Rose × Red Star]

Else Poulsen, Climbing Cl F, mp, 1932, Ley

Else Poulsen Meldugsfri F, mp, 1986, Poulsen, S.; [sport of Else Poulsen]; int. by Poulsen's Roses, 1937

Else Poulsen Morkrod F, dr, 1985, Poulsen, S.; [sport of Else Poulsen]; int. in 1934

Else's Rival F, mr, 1938, Boer Bros.; flowers carmine red, more, dbl.; healthier growth than parent; [sport of Else Poulsen]

Elsie HWich, lp, 1910, Paul, W.; flowers flesh pink with deeper centers, 4 cm., full, rosette, borne in clusters of 10-30; foliage glossy

Elsie LCl, lp, 1934, Chaplin Bros.; flowers soft pink, single; foliage dark, glossy; very vigorous growth

Elsie Allen HT, lp, 1972, Allen, L.C.; flowers pale pink, medium, dbl., high-centered, slight fragrance; vigorous, bushy growth; [sport of Montezuma]; int. by E.T. Welsh, 1971

Elsie Beckwith HT, mp, 1922, Beckwith; flowers rich rosy pink, center deeper, large, dbl., high-centered; foliage dark, shaded red, leathery; upright growth; [(Ophelia × unknown) × Mev. Dora van Tets]

Elsie Boldick Min, mr, 1978, Dobbs, Annette E.; bud ovoid, mossy; flowers single, borne 1-5 per cluster; foliage small, soft; growth to 15 in.; [Fairy Moss × Fairy Moss]; int. by Small World Min. Roses

Elsie de Radt – See **Golden Fairy Tale**, HT

Elsie Devy F, m, 1967, Fankhauser; bud ovoid; flowers soft lavender-pink, reverse mauve-pink, dbl., high-centered; foliage light green, leathery; very vigorous, upright, bushy growth; [Ma Perkins × Detroiter]

Elsie May LCl, mp, Hamilton; int. in 1992

Elsie Melton HT, pb, 1991, Wambach, Alex A.; bud pointed; flowers large, dbl., high-centered, borne usually singly, moderate fruity fragrance; foliage large, dark green, semi-glossy; upright, tall growth; [Pristine × King of Hearts]; int. by Alex A. Wambach, 1990

Elsie Warren F, ab, 1990, Milner, William; flowers apricot with lemon yellow eye, medium, dbl., moderate fragrance; foliage large, medium green, semi-glossy; upright growth; [Arthur Bell × Arthur Bell]; int. by Battersby Roses, 1990

Elsie Wright F, dr, 1983, Cattermole, R.F.; bud long, pointed; flowers large, 15 petals, borne usually singly, sometimes 3 per cluster, intense damask fragrance; foliage medium size, medium green, glossy; prickles light brown; upright growth; [Crimson Glory × Crimson Glory]

Elsiemae Min, op, 1986, Dobbs, Annette E.; flowers light coral pink, 25 petals, high-centered, borne in sprays of 2-4; foliage medium size, medium green, semi-glossy; prickles very few straight, light brown; tall, bushy growth; [Anne Scranton × Patricia Scranton]; int. by Port Stockton Nursery

Elsinore F, mr, 1958, Lindquist; flowers bright scarlet, semi-dbl., borne in large, open clusters; [Floradora × Pinocchio]; int. by McGredy & Son, 1957; Gold Medal, NRS, 1957

Elusive F, pb, 1993, Jobson, Daniel J.; flowers soft pink/cream blend, medium, dbl., borne in small clusters; foliage medium size, dark green, semi-glossy; some prickles; medium, upright, bushy growth; [(Party Girl × Laureate) × Ivory Fashion]; int. by Jobson, 1993

Elveshörn S, mp, 1985, Kordes, W.; flowers medium, 35 petals; foliage medium size, dark, semi-glossy; bushy, spreading growth; [The Fairy × seedling]

Elvira HT, ab, 1982, van Veen, Jan; flowers large, 35 petals, no fragrance; foliage medium size, medium green, semi-glossy; upright growth; [Zorina × Dr. A.J. Verhage]; int. by G. Verbeek, 1978

Elvira HEg, lp; flowers flesh, medium, semi-dbl.; vigorous growth

Elvira Aramayo HT, mr, 1922, Looymans; flowers Indian red, petals curling lengthwise, medium, semi-dbl.; bushy growth; [Feu Joseph Looymans × (Leslie Holland × Rayon d'Or)]; Gold Medal, Bagatelle, 1922

Elvira Aramayo, Climbing Cl HT, mr, 1933, Ingegnoli; flowers copper-orange-red, medium, semi-dbl., moderate fragrance; [sport of Elvira Aramayo]

Elvire – See **Poniatowsky**, HEg

Elvire Popesco HT, my, 1949, Gaujard; bud long, pointed; flowers golden yellow, large, 25 petals; foliage bronze; very vigorous, upright growth; [Comtesse Vandal × seedling]

Elvis Min, mr, 1979, Wells, V.W., Jr.; bud pointed, ovoid; flowers medium red, base white, 1 in., 60-70 petals, high-centered, borne singly and in clusters of 5, slight tea fragrance; recurrent; foliage dark green, glossy; prickles several, long, nearly straight; vigorous (14-16 in.) growth; PP4760; [Judy Fischer × seedling]; int. in 1978

Elvis – See **Miss Elvis**, HT

Elvis HT, w, Adam; flowers ivory washed with pink, large, very dbl.; int. in 2004

Elwina Min, or

Elyse Flory Ch, lp, 1852, Guillot père; flowers bright pink, paling at edges, medium to large, full

Elysée S, lp, Poulsen; flowers light pink, 5-8 cm., full, slight fragrance; foliage dark; growth bushy, 60-100 cm.; PP15859; int. by Poulsen Roser, 2003

Elysium F, mp, 1961, Kordes, R.; bud pointed; flowers salmon-pink, well-formed, large, 35 petals, cupped, moderate fragrance; foliage glossy; vigorous, tall, growth

Emaline Rouge HT, dr, 1938, Hofmann; flowers deep red; [sport of Better Times]

Emanuel S, ab, 1992, Austin, David; flowers apricot-pink, opening rosette, 3-3½ in., dbl., flat, borne in small clusters; foliage small, medium green, semi-glossy; some prickles; medium (43 in.), bushy growth; [(Chaucer × Parade) × (seedling × Iceberg)]; int. by David Austin Roses, Ltd., 1985

Emanuel – See **Crocus Rose**, S

Embajador Lequerica HT, pb, 1962, La Florida; bud pointed; flowers strawberry-pink, reverse Indian yellow at base passing to brick red at edge, 30 petals; vigorous growth

Embassy HT, yb, 1967, Sanday, John; flowers light gold veined and edged carmine, pointed, large, dbl.; foliage glossy; [Gavotte × (Magenta × Golden Scepter)]

Embassy Regal HT, pb, 1976, Sanday, John; flowers cream overlaid peach-pink, 5 in., 30 petals, moderate fragrance; [(Gavotte × Ethel Sanday) × (Crimson Glory × seedling)]

Ember Min, or, 1994, Saville, F. Harmon; flowers small, dbl., borne mostly singly, no fragrance; foliage small, medium green, semi-glossy; few prickles; medium (16-22 in.), upright, bushy, compact growth; [Copper Sunset × (Zorina × Baby Katie)]; int. by Nor'East Min. Roses, 1995

Emberglow HT, mp, 1935, Grillo; flowers rich salmon-pink, 5 in., 50 petals; foliage leathery; long stems; vigorous growth; [sport of Souvenir]

Embers F, mr, 1953, Swim, H.C.; bud ovoid; flowers scarlet, 2½-3 in., 23 petals, high-centered, borne in clusters, moderate spicy fragrance; foliage dark, semi-glossy; vigorous, bushy, compact growth; [World's Fair × Floradora]; int. by Armstrong Nursery

Embers S, yb, Delbard

Emblem HT, my, 1981, Warriner, William A.; flowers 25 petals, high-centered, borne singly, no fragrance; foliage glossy, dark; prickles straight, long, light green; upright growth; PP4847; [seedling × Sunshine]; int. by J&P

Embrace Pol, lp, 1974, Byrum; flowers medium, very dbl., high-centered, slight fragrance; foliage leathery; vigorous, upright, bushy growth; [Seventeen × Jack Frost]; int. by J.H. Hill Co., 1972

Embrasement F, mr, 1956, Delbard-Chabert; flowers fiery red, dbl., borne in clusters of 8-12; foliage bronze; vigorous growth

Embruixada – See **Violetera**, HT

Emden HP, dp, 1915, Schmidt; flowers large, full; [Frau Karl Druschki × Veluwezoom]

Emélie Fontaine HP, pb, 1881, Fontaine; flowers bright carmine with fiery purple, large, very full

Emely HT, w, Kordes; flowers large, off-white, dbl., moderate fragrance; healthy, robust growth; int. in 1998

Emely Min, mp, Kordes; int. by NewFlora, 2005

Emely 2000 HT, w, Kordes; int. by W. Kordes Söhne, 2002

Emely Kordana Min, w, Kordes; flowers cream, dbl., high-centered; container rose; int. by W. Kordes Söhne

Emely Vigorosa F, dp, Kordes; flowers carmine-pink, 7 cm., semi-dbl., shallow cup, borne in large clusters, slight fragrance; recurrent; foliage dark green, semi-glossy, dense; upright (2 ft.), bushy growth; int. as Bad Wörishofen 2005, W. Kordes Söhne, 2006

Emera – See **Flower Carpet**, S

Emera Pavement – See **Flower Carpet**, S

Emerald – See **Emerald Hit**, MinFl

Emerald Dream F, w, 1976, Williams, J. Benjamin; bud pointed, light to apple green; flowers white to ivory, center green, 1½-2 in., 12 petals, flat, loosely cupped, slight fruity fragrance; foliage dull, very dark, leathery; low, compact growth; [Pinafore × Ivory Fashion]; int. by Lakeland Nursery Sales, 1975

Emerald Hit MinFl, w, Poulsen; flowers white, 5-8 cm., dbl., no fragrance; growth bushy, 20-40 cm.; int. by Poulsen Roser, 2004

Emerald Mist – See **Mint Julep**, HT

Emerance HGal, w, before 1910; flowers cream, centers pale lemon, medium, full

Emeraude d'Or HT, yb, 1967, Delbard-Chabert; flowers yellow suffused carmine-pink, petals serrated, 5 in.; vigorous growth; [Sultane × Queen Elizabeth]; int. by Cuthbert, 1965

Emerickrose HMult, lp, 1922, Bruder Alfons; flowers light pink, white center to medium, 5 cm., dbl., borne in medium clusters, moderate fragrance; [Tausendschön × unknown]

Emi F, ob, Keisei; flowers orange blend with grey tones; int. by Keisei Rose Nurseries, 2005

Emil Kruisius F, my, 1943, Tantau; bud long, pointed; flowers large, 25-30 petals, borne in clusters; foliage glossy, light green; vigorous, bushy growth; [Golden Rapture × (Johanna Tantau × Eugenie Lamesch)]

Emil Nolde S, dy, Tantau; flowers intense yellow, large, dbl., cupped, borne in free blooming, moderate fragrance; recurrent; foliage medium green, glossy; growth to 3-4 ft.; int. in 2002

Émile Audusson T, 1842, Audusson

Emile Bardiaux HP, 1889, Lévêque, P.; flowers bright carmine red, tinted poppy and deep violet, large, full; foliage dark green, very large; [Mme Isaac Pereire × unknown]

Émile Charles HT, or, 1922, Bernaix, P.; flowers coral-red, medium, full; [sport of Mme Edouard Herriot]

Emile Courtier B, mp, 1837, Portemer; bud round; flowers lilac pink, medium, full, flat, borne in clusters of 4-5; foliage dark green, deeply dentate; prickles short, red, numerous

Emile Cramon HT, or, 1937, Chambard, C.; bud pointed; flowers coppery carmine, stamens chrome-yellow, very large; foliage dull green; very vigorous growth

Émile Fortépaule HWich, w, 1902, Barbier; flowers white, flushed salmon, 5-7 cm., dbl., globular, borne in large clusters, moderate tea rose fragrance; foliage dark green, oval-oblong, regularly dentate; prickles hooked, red; vigorous growth; [*R. wichurana* × Souv. de Catherine Guillot]

Emile J. Le Duc HT, mr, 1931, Le Duc; flowers scarlet-crimson, larger and stronger than the parent; [sport of Scott's Columbia]

Emile Nérini HWich, dp, 1911, Nonin; flowers carmine-pink with white, 5 cm., semi-dbl., borne in medium clusters; foliage large; few prickles; [Turner's Crimson Rambler × Dorothy Perkins]

Emilia Plantier N, ly, 1878, Schwartz; flowers light coppery yellow, medium large to large, dbl., moderate fragrance; foliage glossy

Emilie M, w, before 1885, Roseraie de l'Hay; flowers small, folded center, full

Emilie Courtier – See **Emile Courtier**, B

Émilie Dupuy Cl T, op, 1870, Levet; flowers light coppery-pink, fading to cream, large, dbl., moderate fragrance; [Mme Flacot × Gloire de Dijon]

Émilie Gonin T, w, 1896, Guillot; flowers ivory white, tinted with orange and fawn, edged with bright carmine, very large, full, moderate fragrance

Emilie Hausburg HP, m, 1868, Lévêque; flowers lilac-rose, large, dbl.

Emilie Plantier B, mp, about 1845, Plantier; flowers bright pink, large, full

Emilie Verachter HGal, mp, 1840, Parmentier; flowers medium, full, quartered; foliage small; few prickles; growth upright; hips rounded

Emilien Guillot S, or, Guillot-Massad; flowers bright orange-red, 5 in., full, cupped; continuous bloom; foliage dark green; int. by Roseraies Guillot, 2001

Emilo Feliu HT, op, Viveros Fco. Ferrer, S L; flowers 28 petals, high-centered; [Zambra × Osiana]

Emily HT, lp, 1949, Baines; flowers soft pink, 5-6 in., 40 petals, moderate fragrance; foliage dark; vigorous, upright growth; [Mme Butterfly × Mrs Henry Bowles]; int. by F. Cant

Emily S, lp, 1994, Austin, David; flowers pale pink, 3-3½ in., very dbl., borne in small clusters, moderate fragrance; foliage medium size, medium green, semi-glossy; numerous prickles; upright, bushy (30 in.) growth; PP8838; [The Prioress × Mary Rose]; int. by David Austin Roses, Ltd., 1992

Emily Carr S, mr, Ag Canada; flowers bright red, semi-dbl., shallow cup to flat, mild fragrance; foliage dark green; growth compact (2 ft.); winter hardy to -40ºF; int. by Aubin Nurseries, 2007

Emily Dodd HT, w, 1927, Dickson, A.; flowers milk-white, center cream, large, dbl.

Emily Gray HWich, dy, 1917, Williams, A.; flowers deep golden buff, stamens yellow, 6-7 cm., 25 petals, cupped, borne in small clusters, moderate tea fragrance; non-recurrent; foliage large, very glossy, dark, bronze-green; vigorous, climbing growth; [Jersey Beauty × Comtesse du Cayla]; int. by B.R. Cant; Gold Medal, NRS, 1916

Emily Hough HT, lp, 1991, Hough, Robin; flowers white, blushing pink toward center, more pink in cooler weather, large, dbl., high-centered, borne mostly singly, slight fragrance; foliage large, medium green, semi-glossy; some prickles; medium, upright growth; [sport of Touch of Class]; int. by Robin Hough, 1993

Emily Laxton HP, mr, 1878, Laxton; bud globular, pointed; flowers rich cherry-rose, large, full; [Jules Margottin × unknown]

Emily Louise MinFl, dy, Harkness; flowers yellow with faun and pink tints, single; medium growth; int. in 1990

Emily Post HT, mp, 1975, Byrum; flowers soft medium pink, 3½-4 in., 48 petals, high-centered, moderate fragrance; upright, bushy growth; PP3749; [Eternal Sun × Carina]; int. by J.H. Hill Co., 1974

Emily Rhodes LCl, mp, 1937, Clark, A.; flowers vermilion pink, large, semi-dbl. to dbl., cupped, moderate fragrance; reliable repeat; vigorous, climbing or pillar growth; [Golden Ophelia × Zephirine Drouhin]; int. by NRS Victoria

Emily Victoria F, op, 1994, Bossom, W.E.; flowers salmon pink, medium, very dbl., borne in small clusters; foliage medium size, medium green, semi-glossy; some prickles; low to medium (60 cm.), bushy, compact growth; [Conservation × (Pearl Drift × Highfield)]

Emily's Rose Cl Min, lp, Warner; flowers soft pink, dbl.; int. in 2001

Emin Pascha HT, dp, 1894, Drögemüller; flowers deep carmine, rose shaded crimson, 11 cm., dbl.; some autumn repeat; [Gloire de Dijon × Louis Van Houtte]

Emina HT, rb, 2006, Viraraghavan, M.S. Viru; flowers claret red, reverse yellow, up to 4 in, dbl., borne mostly solitary; foliage large, dark green, semi-glossy; prickles small, long,slender, triangular base, dark brown, few; growth bushy, medium (4 ft.); [bicolor hybrid tea × Sirohi Sunrise]; hybrid gigantea heritage; int. by Roses Unlimited, 2006

Éminence HT, m, 1962, Gaujard; flowers lavender, large, 40 petals, intense fragrance; foliage leathery, light green; vigorous, upright growth; PP2455; [Peace × (Viola × seedling)]; int. by Ilgenfritz Nursery, 1965

Eminence F, mr, Kordes, R.; bud large, ovoid, scarlet; flowers scarlet red, chromium yellow at base, 4-4½ in., 40-45 petals, high-centered, borne singly and several together in irregular clusters, slight fragrance; foliage medium size, medium green, leathery, glossy; prickles medium, hooked downward, moderate

Éminence, Climbing Cl HT, m, Gaujard; [sport of Éminence]; int. in 1972

Emir HT, rb, 1960, Verbeek; flowers yellow with orange-red, 6 in., 45 petals; foliage glossy; free growth; [seedling × Peace]

Emjay Skiba Min, mp, 1990, Skiba, Norman A.; bud pointed; flowers medium pink, outer petals lighter, large, 45 petals, high-centered, borne usually singly, moderate fruity fragrance; foliage large, dark green, edged red, semi-glossy; prickles sharp, pointed slightly downward, light green; bushy, tall growth; hips round, dark green-orange; [Sonia × Pink Petticoat]

Emma F, dp, 1980, Pearce, C.A.; flowers deep pink, 70 petals, borne 6-10 per clusters; foliage dark, glossy; prickles large; upright, branching growth; [Chanelle × Prima Ballerina]; int. by Limes Rose Nursery

Emma HT, lp, Meilland; flowers off-white with a pink tip, full, classic form; PP12499; int. by Meilland Intl, 1996

Emma Agnes HT, ob; int. in 2004

Emma Brady F, yb, 2003, Webster, Robert; flowers yellow, pink stripes, reverse pale yellow, 2½ in., dbl., borne in large clusters; foliage medium size, medium green, glossy; prickles 10-12 mm., straight; growth bushy, medium (30 in.); bedding; [Fairhope × Crazy for You]; int. in 2004

Emma Carter F, mp, 2004, Paul Chessum Roses; flowers semi-dbl., borne in small clusters, slight fragrance; foliage medium size, dark green, semi-glossy; growth upright, tall (100 cm.); beds, borders, hedges; [seedling × seedling]; int. by Love4Plants Ltd, 2004

Emma Clare HMult, pb; int. in 1994

Emma de Meilland – See **Emma**, HT

Emma Jane F, op, 1970, Sanday, John; flowers salmon-pink, base orange, 3 in., 16 petals; [Vera Dalton × (Masquerade × (Independence × Unknown))]

Emma Kate F, mr, 1992, Jellyman, J.S.; flowers light red with lighter reverse, 35 petals, borne in clusters of 4-10, moderate fruity fragrance; foliage medium size, dark green, glossy; upright, bushy, medium growth; [Tony Jacklin × Cairngorm]

Emma May HT, mp, 1999, Sheridan, John; flowers light pink, reverse deeper pink, 5-6 in., dbl., high-centered, borne mostly singly; foliage large, dark green, semi-glossy; prickles moderate; upright, medium (3½ ft.) growth; [Silver Jubilee × Dr A. J. Verhage]; TGC, RNRS, 1989

Emma Mitchell Min, ob, 1992, Horner, Colin P.; flowers orange/vermillion striped white, light orange reverse, aging light orange, 1¼ in., 12 petals, slight fruity fragrance; foliage small, medium green, semi-glossy; bushy, low growth; int. by Battersby Roses, 1993

Emma Vidal HT, dy, Vidal

Emma Vidal, Climbing Cl HT, dy, Vidal

Emma Wright HT, op, 1918, McGredy; flowers orange shaded salmon, large, semi-dbl., moderate fragrance; foliage rich green, glossy; dwarf growth

Emma Wright, Climbing Cl HT, op, 1932, Cant, F.

Emmanuella de Mouchy HG, mp, 1922, Nabonnand, P.; bud long, pale pink; flowers delicate transparent rose-pink, very large, semi-dbl., borne singly or in small clusters, intense fragrance; [*R. gigantea* × Lady Waterlow.]

Emmanuelle – See **Leaping Salmon**, LCl

Emmeline HCh, w, before 1829, Boutigny; flowers flesh white, edges tinted violet, cupped

Emmeline M, w, 1859, Robert & Moreau; flowers pure white, petals curly, 2½ in., full, rosette, borne in small clusters

Emmeline – See **Madeline**, HEg

Emmeline HT, my, 1921, Paul, W.; bud pure deep yellow; flowers lemon-yellow

Emmeloord Pol, or, 1973, Buisman, G. A. H.; bud cupped; flowers semi-dbl., round; foliage glossy, dark; [Olala × Finale]

Emmerdale F, mp, 1984, Greensitt, J.A.; flowers medium, 35 petals, moderate fragrance; foliage medium size, medium green, semi-glossy; bushy growth; [seedling × Pink Parfait]; int. by Nostell Priory Rose Gardens, 1983

Emmie Koster Pol, dr, 1956, Koster, D.A.; flowers deep red; [sport of Dick Koster]

Emmy Min, op, Barni, V.; flowers coral-salmon, dbl., high-centered; growth to 14-16 in.; int. by Rose Barni, 1993

Emotion B, w, 1862, Guillot père; flowers white, touched with pink, medium, full

Emotion B, pb, 1879, Fontaine; flowers pearl-pink, slightly domed, moderate fragrance; recurrent; stems smooth

Emotion – See **President Kekkonen**, F

Emotion – See **Emotion Parade**, Min

Emotion F, dp

Emotion Parade Min, dp, Poulsen; flowers deep pink, medium, dbl., no fragrance; foliage dark; growth bushy, 20-40 cm.; int. by Poulsen Roser, 1997

Emozione HT, ab, Barni, V.; flowers large, color stable, dbl.; foliage medium size, dark green; vigorous, upright (2½-3 ft.) growth; similar to Valencia, but color more intense and stable; int. by Rose Barni, 1999

Empereur HGal, dr, before 1810; flowers dark red with lilac

Empereur de Russie HGal, m, about 1840, Prévost; flowers lilac pink, medium to large, full

Empereur du Brésil HP, rb, 1880, Soupert & Notting; flowers violet-brown with magenta over varnished red, shaded carmine, very large, very full, globular

Empereur du Maroc HP, dr, 1858, Guinoiseau, B.; flowers crimson, tinged purple, very distinct, small, 40 petals, moderate fragrance; low, compact growth; [Geant des Batailles × unknown]; int. by E. Verdier

Empereur Napoléon III HP, dr, 1855, Granger

Empereur Nicolas II T, dr, 1903, Lévêque; bud large, long; flowers dark rich crimson, flamed with scarlet, very large, full; foliage dark green

Emperor HP, dr, 1883, Paul, W.; flowers very dark red, nearly blackish, small, full

Emperor HT, dr, 1958, Kuramoto, H.; bud urn shaped; flowers rose-red becoming darker, 3-3½ in., 35-45 petals, high-centered, intense fragrance; foliage glossy; vigorous, compact growth; PP1813; [sport of Pink Delight]

Emperor HT, mr, J&P; PP11047; int. in 1997

Emperor HT, ly, McGredy; flowers cream with deeper golden yellow in the center, dbl., high-centered; foliage large; growth bushy, 3 ft.; int. by McGredy Roses International, 1999

Empire Granger HT, mr, 1970, Morey, Dr. Dennison; bud long, pointed; flowers velvety blood-red, very large, dbl.; foliage large, glossy, dark, bronze, leathery; very vigorous, upright, bushy growth; [Rose Bowl × Hallmark]; int. by Country Garden Nurs.

Empire Queen HT, mr, 1925, Easlea; flowers brilliant cerise, large, dbl.; upright growth; [Cherry Page × Vanessa]

Empire State HT, mr, 1934, Nicolas; bud pointed; flowers velvety scarlet, base golden yellow, large, dbl., high-centered; foliage leathery; vigorous growth; int. by J&P

Empreinte HT, m, Dorieux; flowers violet-purple-red, dbl., cupped, intense fragrance; growth 100-120 cm.

Empress HT, dr, 1933, Chaplin Bros.; flowers dark cerise and red, well-formed; vigorous, upright growth; [(Ophelia × unknown) × seedling]

Empress Alexandra – See **Empress Alexandra of Russia**, T

Empress Alexandra of Russia T, rb, 1897, Paul, W.; flowers carmine red, tinted with orange and tipped with fiery red, large, full, globular, intense fragrance

Empress Eugénie – See **Impératrice Eugénie**, B

Empress Farah – See **Imperatrice Farah**, HT

Empress Josephine – HGal, pb, before 1815, Descemet; flowers cerise pink, lighter at edges, dbl., borne singly and in small clusters; foliage elliptical, veined

Empress Marie of Russia – See **Impératrice Maria Féodorowna de Russie**, T

Empress Michiko HT, lp, Dickson, Patrick; flowers blush pink, dbl., high-centered, moderate tea rose fragrance; good rebloom; foliage light green, healthy; numerous prickles; growth short (3 ft.); int. in 1992

Empress of China Cl Ch, mp, 1896, Jackson; flowers soft dark red, aging to light pink, 6 cm., semi-dbl. to dbl., slight fruity fragrance; foliage small; few prickles

Empress of India HP, dr, 1876, Laxton; flowers velvety crimson and purple, medium, globular, moderate fragrance; foliage dark green; [Triomphe des Beaux-Arts × unknown]

Empress of the North – See ***R. rugosa plena*** (Byhouwer)

Emsie Girl HT, ob, 1999, Williams, J. Benjamin; bud pointed; flowers creamy white with bright orange edge, dbl.; [Garden Party × American Heritage]; int. by J. B. Williams & Assoc.

Ena Baxter HT, or, 1990, Cocker, James & Sons; bud pointed; flowers salmon pink, reverse salmon red, medium, 26 petals, high-centered, borne in sprays of 5-9, slight fragrance; foliage large, medium green, glossy; prickles triangular, average, green; bushy, medium growth; hips urn-shaped, large, brown; [HARkrispin × Silver Jubilee]; int. in 1989; Gold Medal, Glasgow, 1994

Ena Gladstone HT, dp, 1936, Chaplin Bros.; flowers carmine-pink, base yellow, well-shaped, large

Ena Harkness HT, mr, 1946, Norman; flowers large, dbl., high-centered; foliage leathery; vigorous, upright growth; [Crimson Glory × Southport]; int. by Harkness, 1946; Gold Medal, Portland, 1955, Gold Medal, NRS, 1945

Ena Harkness, Climbing Cl HT, mr, 1954, Gurteen & Ritson (also Murrell, 1954); flowers bright crimson, 12-13 cm., intense fragrance; [sport of Ena Harkness]

Enchanted HT, mp, J&P; int. in 1995

Enchanted Autumn Gr, ob, 1976, Buck, Dr. Griffith J.; bud ovoid, pointed; flowers orange, 4-4½ in., 33 petals, cupped; foliage glossy, dark, coppery; upright, bushy growth; [(Queen Elizabeth × Ruth Hewitt) × Whisky]; int. by Iowa State University, 1975

Enchanter HT, dp, 1903, Cook, J.W.; flowers deep pink, large, full; [Mme Caroline Testout × Mlle Alice Furon]

Enchanting Days HRg, dr, Bell; flowers claret wine color with prominent yellow stamens, semi-dbl.; compact growth; int. by Bell Roses, 2001

Enchantment HT, pb, 1946, E.G. Hill, Co.; bud long, pointed; flowers shell-pink, base yellow, 6 in., 35 petals; foliage leathery; vigorous, upright growth; [R.M.S. Queen Mary × Eternal Youth]; int. by J&P

Enchantment – See **Sanka**, HT dbl.

Enchantment – See **Queen Margrethe**, S

Enchantress – See **L'Enchantresse**, HGal

Enchantress T, w, 1896, Paul & Son; flowers cream white

Enchantress T, mp, 1904, Cook, J.W.; flowers rose-pink

Enchantress HRg, dr; flowers velvety blood-red, very dbl.; extra strong and hardy

Encore F, mp, 1958, Von Abrams; bud pointed; flowers creamy pink, reverse rose-pink, 3 in., 10-14 petals, cupped, borne in large clusters, slight spicy fragrance; foliage glossy; vigorous, upright, bushy growth; PP1662; ruled extinct ARA 1984; [Else Poulsen × Capt. Thomas]; int. by Peterson & Dering, 1958

Encore HT, dr, 1984, Warriner, William A.; flowers large, 20 petals; foliage medium size, dark, semi-glossy; upright growth; PP5658; [seedling × Samantha]; int. by J&P

Endearment HT, op, 1989, Taylor, Thomas E.; bud pointed; flowers creamy pink, reverse coral pink, large, 10 petals, borne usually singly, slight sweet fragrance; foliage large, medium green, matte; prickles straight, medium, light brown; upright, tall growth; no fruit; [Gladiator × First Prize]; int. by Michigan Mini Roses, 1989

Endeavour Min, ab, 1993, Taylor, Franklin; flowers apricot with yellow base, reverse slightly darker, color fading with age, large, full, slight fragrance; foliage medium size, medium green, semi-glossy; few prickles; medium, upright growth; [Party Girl × Azure Sea]; int. by Taylor's Roses, 1993

Endless Dream HT, mp, 1990, Twomey, Jerry; bud pointed; flowers medium, soft pink, large, 32 petals, cupped, borne singly, moderate musk fragrance; foliage large, dark green, semi-glossy; prickles declining, grayish-white with black spots; upright, medium growth; PP7561; [Emily Post × (Sweepstakes × Silver Jubilee)]; int. by DeVor Nurseries, Inc., 1990

Endless Love Min, mr, 1982, Lyon, Lyndon; flowers medium, 35 petals; foliage medium size, dark, semi-glossy; upright, bushy growth; [Red Can Can × seedling]

Endless Summer Min, op, 1989, Rennie, Bruce F.; bud pointed; flowers shrimp-pink, reverse light pink, small, 33 petals, high-centered, borne singly, slight spicy fragrance; foliage small, dark green, semi-glossy; prickles straight, small, transparent to brown; low, bushy growth; no fruit; [Paul Shirville × California Dreaming]; int. by Rennie Roses International, 1990

Endless Summer – See **Tokonatsu**, HT

Endless Tale Cl HT, my, 1956, Motose; bud ovoid, deep yellow; flowers amber-yellow, outer petals creamy, 6-7 in., 30-35 petals; abundant, intermittent bloom; foliage leathery; vigorous (20+ ft.) growth; [Lestra Hibberd, Climbing × Lestra Hibbard sport]

Endora Min, pb, 1991, Zipper, Herbert; flowers cream, edged deep pink, large, full, high-centered, borne mostly singly, slight fragrance; foliage small, medium green, semi-glossy; few prickles; medium (35 cm.), upright growth; [Pristine × High Spirits]; int. by Magic Moment Miniature Roses, 1992

Enduring Love HT, yb, Pallek; int. in 1998

Enduring Spirit – See **Egeskov**, F

Enemy of War HT, pb, 1987, Hardikar, Dr. M.N.; flowers open, 50-60 petals, slight fragrance; foliage large, dark green, glossy, leathery; prickles beak-shaped, light green to deep brown; very vigorous, profuse growth; [Festival Beauty × Gynosure]; int. in 1986

Enfant d'Ajaccio – See **Souv d'Anselme**, B

Enfant de France HGal, m, about 1802, from Holland; bud round; flowers carminy crimson with light purple, medium, full, pompon; foliage dark green, small, oblong ovate; prickles numerous, small, unequal, almost straight; hips pyriform, red; Agathe group

Enfant de France – See **Beauté Tendre**, A

Enfant de France HGal, lp, before 1824, from Brussels; flowers flesh pink, small to medium, full; Agathe group

Enfant de France HP, lp, 1860, Lartay; flowers silvery pink, edged white, very large, very dbl., moderate fragrance

Enfant de France de Bruxelles – See **Enfant de France**, HGal

Enfant de la Libarde N, my, 1904, Chauvry

Enfant de Lyon – See **Narcisse**, T

Enfant d'Orléans Pol, m, 1929, Turbat; flowers Neyron rose, tinted purple, fading lighter, borne in clusters

Enfant Trouvé T, mp, 1861, Lartay

Enfield in Bloom F, my, 1996, Bossom, W.E.; flowers deep yellow, reddish tinge to petal edge, reverse lighter yellow, large, full, slight fragrance; foliage large, medium green, semi-glossy; prickles moderate; upright, tall (115 cm.) growth; [Anne Harkness × Greensleeves]

Engagement Gr, op, 1969, Patterson; bud globular; flowers coral-pink, large, dbl., high-centered; foliage dark, leathery; vigorous, bushy growth; [Ma Perkins × Montezuma]; int. by Patterson Roses, 1968

Engagement HT, lp, Tantau; flowers very large, dbl., high-centered; stems very long; greenhouse rose; int. by Rosen Tantau, 2003

Engelmann's Quest S, my, 2005, Shoup, George Michael; flowers single, borne in small clusters, slight fragrance; remontant; foliage medium size, dark green, semi-glossy; prickles moderate; growth compact, medium (3-4 ft.); containers, borders; hips small; hardy to -20ºF; [(The Fairy × *R. wichurana*) × Baby Love]; int. by Antique Rose Emporium, 2000

Enghien HT, ob, RvS-Melle; [Silver Jubilee × seedling]; int. in 1991

Eng. D. José de Mendia HT, mp, Moreira da Silva; flowers rosy salmon

Eng. Duarte Pacheco HT, dr, 1938, Moreira da Silva; flowers blackish crimson, large, very dbl., cupped; dwarf growth; [Hadley × Presidente Carmona]

Eng. Pereira Caldas HT, mp, 1954, Moreira da Silva; flowers salmon-pink, base yellow

Eng. Pulide Garcia HT, yb, 1961, Moreira da Silva; flowers yellow stained pink; [Grand'mere Jenny × Michele Meilland]

Eng. Vitória Pires HT, dr, 1954, Moreira da Silva; flowers velvety dark red

England's Glory HT, lp, 1904, Wood; flowers flesh-pink with a rosy center, large, dbl.; [(Gloire de Dijon × Mrs W. J. Grant) × unknown]

England's Rose S, w, 2000, Austin, David; flowers pale apricot in center, fading to cream, rounded, 3 in., 118 petals, rounded, borne in small clusters, moderate tea fragrance; foliage slighly glossy, dark green; bushy growth; PP13299; [seedling (pink English shrub) × seedling (yellow English shrub)]; int. as Ludlow Castle, David Austin Roses, 1999

England's Rose (Germany) – See **Jude the Obscure**, S

Englemann's Quest S, dy; flowers Yellow, single, Yes fragrance; Repeat bloom.; growth to 3-4 ft.; int. in 2004

English Apricot – See **Lucetta**, S

English Courtyard HT, m, 2003, Rawlins, R.; flowers medium, full, borne in small clusters, slight fragrance; foliage medium size, dark green, semi-glossy; prickles ½ in., triangular, moderate; growth bushy, tall (42 in.); garden decoration; [Solitaire × (Kanagem × Abraham Darby)]

English Dawn – See **Dapple Dawn**, S

English Elegance S, ob, 1986, Austin, David; flowers large, dbl., moderate fragrance; foliage medium size, medium green, semi-glossy; upright growth; PP7557

English Estates HT, yb, 1992, Thompson, Robert; flowers deep yellow edged red, medium, full, borne mostly singly, intense fragrance; foliage medium size, dark green, glossy; some prickles; upright (80 cm.) growth; [Whisky Mac × Catherine Cookson]; int. by Battersby Roses, 1991

English Garden S, ab, 1991, Austin, David; flowers soft apricot yellow, very large, very dbl., cupped, intense fragrance; foliage clear green; bushy, vigorous growth; PP7214; [Lilian Austin × (seedling × Iceberg)]; int. by David Austin Roses, Ltd., 1988

English Hedge HRg, mp, 1959, Nyveldt; flowers pink, small, single; hips red; [(*R. rugosa rubra* × *R. cinnamomea*) × *R. nitida*]

English Holiday F, yb, 1976, Harkness; flowers yellow, blended with salmon, 4 in., 33 petals, moderate fragrance; foliage large, glossy; [Bobby Dazzler × Goldbonnet]; int. in 1977

English Lavender Min, m, Bell; flowers deep lavender, moderate fragrance; short growth

English Miss F, lp, 1977, Cants of Colchester, Ltd.; flowers pale pink, 2½ in., 60 petals, borne in clusters, intense fragrance; foliage dark purple to dark green; [Dearest × The Optimist]

English Perfume Gr, m, 1999, Zary, Dr. Keith W.; flowers lavender blend, 5 in., 41 petals, intense fragrance; foliage medium size, dark green, semi-glossy; prickles moderate; upright growth; PP12220; [seedling × Carefree Wonder]; int. by Bear Creek Gardens, Inc., 1999

English Porcelain Min, lp, 1994, Moore, Ralph S.; flowers medium, dbl., borne mostly singly, slight fragrance; foliage medium size, medium green, matte; no prickles; low to medium (28-34 cm.), bushy, spreading, compact growth; [Anytime × Angel Face]; int. by Sequoia Nursery, 1995

English Sachet HT, lp, 1999, Zary, Dr. Keith W.; flowers cupped, ruffled, almost quartered, delicate petals, 4-4½ in., 40-50 petals, cupped, borne mostly singly, intense sweet fragrance; foliage medium size, medium green, matte; prickles moderate; upright, spreading, tall (5 ft.) growth; PP12118; [Summer Fashion × Silver Jubilee]; int. by Bear Creek Gardens, Inc., 1999

English Sonnet F, ab, 1989, Harkness; bud ovoid, reddish-apricot; flowers apricot with pink tints, 4 in., very dbl., cupped, borne singly or in small clusters, intense fruity fragrance; foliage medium size, dark green, glossy; prickles moderate; upright, spreading, medium (3 ft.) growth; [silver Jubilee × Dr A. J. Verhage]; int. by Harkness New Roses, 1988

English Violet S, dp, Austin, David

English Wedding Day – See **Wedding Day**, LCl

English Yellow – See **Graham Thomas**, S

Enhance S, ly, 1992, Sanday, John; flowers soft apricot yellow, 1½ in., dbl., borne in large clusters, moderate fragrance; foliage medium size, medium green, glossy; some prickles; low (25 cm.), spreading growth; [Malmesbury × The Fairy]; int. by John Sanday Roses Ltd.

Enid Pol, lp, 1936, Prior; flowers pale pink, borne in clusters; foliage light; upright growth

Enigma HT, rb, deRuiter

Enigma Variation S, mp; flowers pure pink, outer petals lighter, very full, cupped, quartered, moderate fragrance; recurrent; [sport of Sir Edward Elgar]; int. by Vintage Gardens, 2006

Enjoy Min, pb, 1989, Laver, Keith G.; bud pointed; flowers blush pink edged deeper pink, reverse white, small, 22 petals, high-centered, borne singly; foliage small, medium green, disease-resistant; prickles straight, very small, sparse, light brown; upright, low growth; hips ovoid, orange; [(Moulin Rouge × seedling) × Party Girl]; int. by Springwood Roses, 1989

Ennio Morlotti F, mp, 1976, Cazzaniga, F. G.; bud globular; flowers clear pink, 2½-3 in., 35 petals, high-centered, intense fragrance; foliage glossy; vigorous, upright growth; [Fashion × Queen Elizabeth]; int. in 1973

Enric Palau HT, m, Dot

Ensa de Rennes HT, dp, Adam, M.; int. in 1997

Entente Cordiale HT, yb, 1908, Guillot, P.; flowers nasturtium-red, base yellow. large, dbl., loose, borne in small clusters; [Mme Caroline Testout × Soleil d'Or]

Entente Cordiale HT, w, 1909, Pernet-Ducher; flowers creamy white, tinged carmine at edges; [Mme Abel Chatenay × Kaiserin Auguste Viktoria]

Enterprise F, pb, 1958, Kordes; flowers deep pink edged peach, 2 in., 20 petals, borne in large clusters, moderate fragrance; foliage dark, glossy, vigorous; upright, bushy growth; [Masquerade × seedling]; int. by Morse & Sons, 1956

Enver Pascha HT, lp, 1916, Kiese; flowers fleshy white, outside soft pink, dbl.

Envy HT, w, Zary; buds green; PP11633; int. by Bear Creek Gardens, 1999

Enzo Fumagalli F, mp, 1966, Cazzaniga, F. G.; bud globular; flowers salmon-pink, medium, very dbl.; abundant, intermittent bloom; foliage glossy; vigorous, bushy growth; [Mount Shasta × Papillon Rose]

Eos HMoy, rb, 1950, Ruys; bud ovoid; flowers sunset-red becoming brighter, center light pink, semi-dbl., cupped, borne in small clusters; non-recurrent; foliage leathery, glossy; shrub or pillar (to 6 ft.) growth; [*R. moyesii* × Magnifica]

Epic F, mp, 1989, Cattermole, R.F.; bud tapering; flowers medium, dbl., flat, borne in sprays of 3-6, moderate spicy fragrance; foliage bronze to dark green, glossy; prickles brown; upright, bushy growth; [Silent Night × Irish Mist]; int. by South Pacific Rose Nursery

Épidor HT, dy, 1982, Delbard, Georges; flowers large, 35 petals, slight fragrance; foliage large, medium green, matte; bushy growth; [(Peace × Marcelle Gret) × (Velizy × Jean de la Lune)]; int. in 1981

Epinal F, Croix, P.; int. in 1994

Épineux de la Chine – See **Fortuniana**, Misc OGR

Epoca Gr, dr, 1986, Lens, Louis; flowers very dark red, large, 45 petals, high-centered, borne in sprays of 3-18, no fragrance; foliage very dark; prickles brown-green; upright, bushy growth; [seedling × seedling]; int. in 1966

Epoca Mondadori – See **Epoca**, Gr

Éponine HGal, m, before 1829, Coquerel; flowers slatey lilac pink, shaded red, medium, very full

Eponine HMsk, w, before 1835; flowers medium, dbl., cupped, borne in large clusters, moderate fragrance

Epos Pol, mr, 1971, Delforge; bud ovoid; flowers medium, semi-dbl., cupped; foliage bronze, leathery; vigorous, upright growth; [Tommy Bright × seedling]

Equinox MinFl, ob, 2005, Tucker, Robbie; flowers orange and white, reverse white, medium, full, borne mostly solitary, no fragrance; foliage medium size, medium green, matte; prickles moderate, ¼ to ½ in., slightly curved downward, light green to brown; growth upright, medium (30 in.); exhibition, cut flower, garden; [Proprietary Seedling × Memphis King]; int. by Rosemania, 2005

Erato HMult, dp, 1937, Tantau; bud pointed; flowers small, semi-dbl., borne in medium clusters; foliage glossy; long stems; very vigorous climbing growth; [(Ophelia × *R. multiflora*) × Florex]

Erbprinzessin Leopold von Anhalt HT, ly, 1933, Behrens; flowers whitish-yellow, large, dbl.

Eremit de Granval – See **De Rennes**, Ch

Erfurt HMsk, pb, 1939, Kordes; bud long, pointed; flowers medium pink, yellow toward base, large, semi-dbl., borne in clusters, intense musk fragrance; recurrent bloom; foliage leathery, wrinkled, bronze; vigorous (5-6 ft.), trailing, bushy growth; [Eva × Reveil Dijonnais]

Eric F, mr, 1965, Hémeray-Aubert; bud ovoid; flowers medium, semi-dbl., cupped; foliage dark, glossy, leathery; vigorous growth; [Alain × Coup de Foudre]

Eric B. Mee HT, mr, 1937, Mee; flowers vivid cerise, well-shaped, small; int. by Beckwith

Eric Green HT, yb, 2003, Rawlins, R.; flowers yellow picotee, medium, dbl., borne in small clusters; foliage medium size, medium green, semi-glossy; prickles 1 cm., triangular, moderate; growth upright, short (30 in.); garden; [Solitaire × (Tango × Tequila Sunrise)]

Eric Hobbis HT, pb, 1966, Sanday, John; flowers pink, reverse peach, 4½ in., high-centered; low growth; [Gavotte × Peace]

Eric Holroyd HT, mr, 1925, Chaplin Bros.; flowers bright scarlet, base shaded gold

Eric Louw HT, mr, 1964, Herholdt, J.A.; bud pointed; flowers cyclamen-red, well-formed, 35-40 petals; foliage leathery, glossy; strong stems; vigorous, bushy growth; [Queen Elizabeth × Confidence]; int. by Herholdt's Nursery

Eric Tabarly LCl, dr, Meilland; bud medium, ovoid; flowers crimson, 4½ in., 95-100 petals, cupped, borne in small clusters, intense fragrance; recurrent; foliage medium to dark green, semi-glossy; prickles average, 5 mm. or more, hooked slightly downward; growth to 7 ft. and more; hips pitcher shaped, 3 cm. in diameter, olive green with orange shadings; PP15052; [Cappa Magna seedling × Ulmer Münster]; int. by Meilland, 2003

Eric The Red Min, mr, Welsh

Eric von Melnibonée S, op, Weihrauch; flowers yellowish salmon-pink, large, dbl.; int. in 1983

Erica F, or, 1964, Herholdt, J.A.; flowers orange-scarlet, frilled, semi-dbl., borne in large clusters; [seedling × Montezuma]; int. by Herholdt's Nursery

Erica – See **Eyeopener**, S

Erica Herholdt F, or, Herholdt, J.A.; flowers large, semi-dbl.; int. in 1964

Erich Frahm F, mr, 1939, Kordes; bud long, pointed, yellowish red; flowers carmine-scarlet, center yellow, petals shell-shaped, open, borne in umbels of up to 20; foliage dark, glossy, leathery; vigorous growth, very branching.; [Dance of Joy × Mary Hart]; int. by Timm

Eric's Choice Min, or, 2005, Webster, Robert; flowers

semi-dbl., borne in large clusters, slight fragrance; foliage medium size, dark green, glossy; prickles moderate, 5 mm., slightly hooked; growth compact, short (12 in.); bedding; [Pink Petticoat × Darling Flame]

Erie S, lp, 1946, Preston; flowers pale pink, 5 petals, borne in clusters; very free, non-recurrent bloom; foliage dark, fragrant (sweetbriar); vigorous, spreading growth; hips bottle-shaped, bright red; hardy; int. by Central Exp. Farm

Erie Treasure HRg, w, Wedrick; flowers blush to white, dbl.; recurrent bloom; foliage wrinkled; vigorous (6 ft.), bushy growth; [Souv. de Pierre Leperdrieux × Nova Zembla]

Erik Hjelm HT, op, 1929, Kordes; flowers pure salmon-pink, very dbl.; [Lieutenant Chaure × Sachsengruss]

Erika HT, mp, Asami; int. in 1990

Erika My Love Min, my, 1993, Armstrong, James L.; flowers yellow with white tips, 2-3 in., 25-30 petals, borne mostly singly; foliage medium green, semi-glossy; some prickles; tall (72 cm.), upright growth; [Rise 'n' Shine × seedling]

Erika Pluhar HT, dr

Erika Teschendorff HT, mr, 1949, Berger, V.; bud long, pointed; flowers fiery scarlet, open, very large, dbl., globular; foliage glossy, dark; very vigorous, upright growth; int. by Teschendorff

Erikonig HMult, m, 1886, Geschwind, R.

Erin Alonso Min, my, 2003, Alonso, Peter G. Jr.; flowers full, high-centered, borne mostly solitary, no fragrance; foliage medium size, dark green, semi-glossy; prickles in., sharp, green to brown, moderate; growth upright, tall (36-48 in.); garden decoration, exhibition; [sport of Bees Knees]; int. by Peter G. Alonso Jr., 2002

Erin Elise F, or, 2005, Jellyman, J.S.; flowers single, borne in small clusters, moderate fragrance; foliage medium size, medium green, semi-glossy; prickles moderate, mm., curved; growth upright, compact, medium (2-2½ ft.); bedding, containers; [Fragrant Cloud × Baby Love]; int. by Not Decided

Erin Fleming LCl, mp, 1997, Fleming, Joyce L.; flowers medium to deep pink, medium size, 41 petals, borne singly and in large clusters, up to 15 buds per cluster, moderate fragrance; foliage medium size, dark green, glossy; upright, tall growth; [Sunsation × Henry Kelsey]; int. by Hortico Inc, 1995

Erinnerung an Brod HSet, rb, 1886, Geschwind, R.; flowers cerise through crimson to purple, paler at center, 8 cm., dbl., quartered, flat, moderate fragrance; very remontant; [(*R. setigera* × unknown) × Génie de Châteaubriand]; sometimes classed as HP

Erinnerung an Brod × Belle Siebrecht LCl, m, 1930, Krüger

Erinnerung an Schloss Scharfenstein HT, m, 1892, Geschwind, R.; flowers purple/pink, large, dbl., intense fragrance

Erlkönig – See **Roi des Aunes**, S

Erna HWich, lp, 1929, Vogel, M.; flowers pale salmon pink, reverse darker, 4 cm., dbl., borne in small clusters; foliage dark green, glossy

Erna Baltzer HT, my, 1954, Leenders, M.; flowers golden yellow, medium; vigorous growth; [Tawny Gold × Gaudia]

Erna Doris F, op, 1986, Lens, Louis; flowers medium salmon pink, 24 petals, high-centered, borne in clusters of 3-12, slight fragrance; foliage small, medium green; prickles small, hooked, brown-green; upright, bushy growth; [Little Angel × Elizabeth of Glamis]; int. in 1985

Erna Grootendorst F, dr, 1938, Grootendorst, R.; flowers deep velvety crimson, large, semi-dbl.; foliage glossy, dark; bushy growth; [Bergers Erfolg × Gloria Mundi]

Erna Teschendorff Pol, mr, 1911, Teschendorff; flowers strawberry-red, open, small, semi-dbl.; foliage rich green, soft; bushy growth; [sport of Mme Norbert Levavasseur]

Ernest Bonçenne HP, mp, 1868, Cherpin/Liabaud; flowers bright pink, edges and reverse lighter pink, medium, full

Ernest H. Morse HT, mr, 1965, Kordes; flowers turkey-red, 4 in., 30 petals, intense fragrance; foliage leathery; vigorous growth; int. by Morse, 1964; Gold Medal, RNRS, 1965

Ernest H. Morse, Climbing Cl HT, mr; int. after 1964

Ernest Laurent HT, lp, 1914, Viaud-Bruant; flowers whitish pink, large, dbl., moderate fragrance

Ernest May HT, Seale; int. by Seale Nurseries, 2003

Ernest Metz T, mp, 1888, Guillot, J. B.; flowers rose-pink, center darker, large, dbl.

Ernest Morel HP, dr, 1898, Cochet, P.; flowers bright garnet-red, full; growth tall; [Général Jacqueminot × unknown]

Ernest Prince HP, mr, 1881, Ducher; flowers light red, darker at center, reverse silvery, very large, full, globular; foliage dark green; numerous prickles; growth upright; [Antoine Ducher × unknown]

Ernestine Cosme HWich, rb, 1926, Turbat; flowers brilliant red, with large white eye, single, borne in clusters of 75; numerous prickles; very vigorous, climbing growth

Ernestine de Barante HP, mp, 1843, Lacharme

Ernest's Blue HT, m, LeGrice; flowers full, high-centered, moderate fragrance; very long stems; compact, strong, medium growth; int. in 1990

Ernie Min, m, 1989, Bennett, Dee; bud ovoid; flowers light mauve, medium, 48 petals, urn-shaped, borne occasionally singly and in clusters of 6-12, moderate fruity fragrance; foliage medium size, medium green, semi-glossy; prickles hooked slightly downward, pale yellow-brown, few; upright, bushy, tall growth; hips globular, yellow-brown; [Blue Nile × Blue Mist]; int. by Tiny Petals Nursery

Ernie Pyle HT, mp, 1946, Boerner; bud long, pointed; flowers deep rose-pink, reverse deeper, 4½-5 in., 35-40 petals, cupped; foliage leathery; vigorous, upright, bushy growth; [((Royal Red × Talisman) × Seedling (red)) × (Talisman × Nutneyron)]; int. by J&P

Ernistine Audio D, m, before 1842, Audio; flowers bluish pink, full, moderate fragrance

Ernnst Hempel HT, lp, 1907, Mietzsch; flowers large, full

Ernst Dechant HWich, w, 1928, Vogel, M.; flowers white with yellow tints, small, semi-dbl., borne in small clusters

Ernst G. Dörell HMult, dp, 1887, Geschwind, R.; flowers carmine, 3-4 cm., dbl., cupped

Ernst Grandpierre HWich, w, 1902, Weigand, C.; flowers pale cream, base yellow, 5-6 cm., dbl., open, borne in large clusters; sparse bloom; foliage light, glossy; growth to 8-10 ft.; [*R. wichurana* × Perle des Jardins]

Eroica HT, dr, 1968, Tantau, Math.; bud ovoid; flowers velvety dark red, well-formed, large, 33 petals; foliage dark, glossy; vigorous, upright growth; int. by Wheatcroft & Sons, 1969; ADR, 1969

Eroika – See **Eroica**, HT

Eros F, dp, 1955, Maarse, G.; flowers deep rosy pink shaded brick-red, base yellow; dwarf, compact growth; [Pinocchio × unknown]

Eros HT, ob, Barni, V.; flowers orange vermilion, large, full, high-centered, no fragrance; recurrent; foliage clear, bright green; growth medium; int. by Rose Barni, 1990

Erotica – See **Eroica**, HT

Erotika – See **Eroica**, HT

Erskine (form of *R. blanda*), mp, Hansen, N.E.

Erubescens – See **Celestial**, A

Eruption HT, mr, 1934, Van Rossem; flowers fiery scarlet-red, large, semi-dbl.; foliage sea-green; bushy growth; [Red-Letter Day × Columbia]

Erwin Hüttmann HWich, dp, 1941, Krause; flowers rose-red, medium, dbl., intense fragrance

Erzherzog Franz Ferdinand T, pb, 1892, Soupert & Notting; flowers peach-red on yellow, peony-like, reverse often striped magenta red, large, full, cupped

Erzherzogin Marie Dorothea HT, yb, 1892, Balogh; flowers yellowish rose-red, large, very full; [Mme Falcot × Général Jacqueminot]

Esa HT, pb, Ghosh; flowers pastel pink with rich, deeper center, very full, well formed; int. in 2001

Esbank HT, mp, 1916, Dobbie

Escada F, mr, Tantau; int. by Rosen Tantau, 1994

Escalade Cl HT, mr, 1962, Combe; bud pointed; flowers carmine, large, high-centered; vigorous growth; [Spectacular × Charlotte Armstrong]; int. by Vilmorin-Andrieux

Escapade F, m, 1967, Harkness; flowers magenta-rose, center white, 3 in., 12 petals, borne in clusters; foliage glossy, light green; [Pink Parfait × Baby Faurax]; Gold Medal, Belfast, 1969, Gold Medal, Baden-Baden, 1969, ADR, 1973

Escimo – See **Eskimo**, F

Escimo – See **Silver Ghost**, S

Escimo Kordana Min, w, Kordes; flowers full; container rose; int. by W. Kordes Söhne

Esco Rose F, Gregory, C.

Escort F, dr, 1963, Swim & Weeks; bud pointed to urn-shaped; flowers small to medium, 30 petals, high-centered; foliage dark, leathery; vigorous, bushy growth; PP2436; [Spartan × Garnette]

Escultor Clará HT, m, 1956, Dot, Pedro; bud pointed; flowers purple-garnet, reverse magenta, large, 30 petals, high-centered, moderate fragrance; foliage dark, glossy; very vigorous, upright, compact growth; [Lilette Mallerin × Floradora]

Escurial HT, mr, 1970, Delbard-Chabert; flowers velvety cardinal-red, medium, semi-dbl., high-centered, slight fragrance; foliage dark, glossy; vigorous, bushy growth; [Gay Paris × Impeccable]; int. by Laxton & Bunyard, 1967

Eskil HT, yb, 1939, Ringdahl; flowers light yellow overlaid red and orange; [sport of Mrs Franklin D. Roosevelt]

Eskimo F, w, Kordes; flowers small, dbl., high-centered; PP8580; greenhouse rose; int. in 1991

Esmé HT, w, 1920, Cant, B. R.; flowers cream-white, edged rosy carmine, dbl.; [Mme Edouard Herriot × seedling]

Esme Euvrard HT, lp, Kordes; flowers tend to light pink, petals creped, 4-4½ in., dbl., borne mostly singly; upright, tall (4 ft.) growth; int. in 1992

Esmeralda A, lp, 1847, Verdier; flowers delicate flesh, margins white, medium, full

Esmeralda HP, mp, 1862, Fontaine; flowers bright pink

Esmeralda HT, w, 1888, Geschwind; flowers flesh white, aging to lilac pink, large, full

Esmeralda F, dp, 1957, Riethmuller; flowers deep rose-pink, reverse lighter, small, dbl., borne in very large clusters, moderate fragrance; vigorous growth; [Gartendirector Otto Linne × seedling]

Esmeralda – See **Keepsake**, HT, 1981

Esmeralda Kordana Min, dp, Kordes; flowers full, high-centered; container rose; int. by W. Kordes Söhne

Especially for You HT, my, Fryer, Gareth; flowers bright, unfading mimosa yellow, large, dbl., borne singly and in clusters, moderate fragrance; growth medium; int. by Fryer's Roses, 1996

Espérance T, 1905, Dubourdieu/Chauvry

Espérance HT, lp, deRuiter; PP14663; int. by De Ruiter's New Roses, 2001

Esperanto HT, my, 1932, Böhm, J.; flowers pure yellow,

very large, 60 petals, globular; [sport of Miss Lolita Armour]

Esperanto Jubileo HT, pb, 1987, Sanday, John; flowers cream, edged deep rose pink, yellow suffused at base, large, dbl., slight fragrance; foliage medium size, medium green, matte; bushy growth; [Gavotte × Piccadilly]

Espéranza F, mr, 1966, Delforge; bud ovoid; flowers bright red, large, dbl., borne in clusters; foliage dark, bronze, leathery, glossy; upright growth; [Donald Prior × Reverence]; originally registered as Pol; Gold Medal, The Hague, 1968, Gold Medal, Baden-Baden, 1968

Esplanade HT, dr, 1961, Verbeek; flowers 40 petals; foliage glossy; vigorous growth; [Soraya × seedling]

Espoir HT, pb, 1947, Lens; bud long, pointed; flowers pink, center light salmon-pink, large, 35 petals, slight fragrance; abundant bloom; foliage soft; bushy growth; RULED EXTINCT 6/83; [Charles P. Kilham × Neville Chamberlain]

Espoir F, op, 1958, Combe; flowers rich salmon, 4½ in., 50 petals, rosette, moderate fragrance; vigorous, low, bushy growth; RULED EXTINCT 6/83 ARM; [(Oiseau de Feu × Fashion) × (Independence × seedling)]; int. by Japan Rose Society

Espoir HT, mr, Meilland; flowers velvety red, large, 35 petals; foliage matte; int. by Sauvageot, 1981

Espoir HCh, w, 1983, Gailloux, Gilles; bud small; flowers small, single, slight fragrance; foliage very small, medium green, semi-glossy; upright, spreading growth; [HCh seedling × HCh seedling]

Espresso F, r, Spek; flowers light russet, deeper reverse, 9 cm., 25-30 petals, high-centered, borne mostly singly; recurrent; few prickles; stems long; int. by Jan Spek Rozen, 2005

Esprit F, or, GPG; int. in 1985

Esprit S, dr, 1987, Kordes, W.; flowers deep red, aging darker, medium, 12 petals, flat, borne in sprays of 5-7, no fragrance; repeat bloom; foliage small, medium green, semi-glossy; prickles medium, tan, slightly down pointed; upright, bushy, tall growth; no fruit; PP6117; [seedling × Chorus]; int. by J&P, 1989

Esprit HT, mp, Kordes; int. by W. Kordes Söhne, 2002

Esprit Kordana Min, mr, Kordes

Essence HT, dr, 1930, Cant, B. R.; bud pointed; flowers rich scarlet-crimson, becoming bluish, outer petals slightly fimbriated, cupped, moderate damask fragrance

Essence, Climbing Cl HT, dr, 1938, Western Rose Co.

Essence HT, op, deRuiter; int. by De Ruiter's New Roses, 2001

Essex S, mp, Poulsen; flowers medium to deep pink, small, single, no fragrance; foliage dark, glossy; low (60-100 cm.),spreading growth; int. as Pink Cover, Poulsen Roser, 1991

Essie Lee MinFl, ob, 1992, Bell, Judy G.; flowers white with orange picotee down ½ of petals, white to light orange reverse, small, full, globular, no fragrance; foliage small to medium size, dark green, semi-glossy; few prickles; upright (46 cm.), bushy growth; [Tennessee × Tennessee]; int. by Michigan Mini Roses, 1994

Estafette F, dr, 1964, Delforge; flowers open, 2½-3 in., semi-dbl., borne in clusters; foliage dark, glossy; vigorous growth; [Alain × Elmshorn]; int. by Delforge & Son, 1962

Estelle HGal, mp, before 1810; flowers flesh pink, medium, very dbl., intense fragrance

Estelle HSpn, lp, before 1820, Vibert; flowers flesh pink, medium, semi-dbl., borne in clusters; sometimes repeats in autumn; possibly synonymous with Jenny, Dupont, before 1810

Estelle HT, r, Olij, Huibert W; flowers ochre shaded with brown, creamy yellow on reverse, dbl., high-centered, borne mostly singly, slight fragrance; foliage dark bronze-green, glossy; growth upright (5 ft.); PP10844; int. in 1997

Estelle HT, op, Croix

Estelle de Meilland – See **Estelle**, HT

Estelle Pradel – See **Esther Pradel**, T

Estepona – See **Estepona Hit**, MinFl

Estepona Hit MinFl, ob, Poulsen; flowers orange blend, 5-8 cm., dbl., no fragrance; foliage dark; growth bushy, 20-40 cm.; int. by Poulsen Roser, 2004

Esterel – See **Heidekind**, S

Esther HGal, pb, 1845, Vibert; flowers blush pink petals overlaid magenta, pompon, moderate sweet, spicy fragrance; basal canes nearly smooth; possibly synonymous with Duchesse d'Oldenburg, Calvert, about 1845

Esther F, ob, 1954, San Remo Exp. Sta.; bud pointed, turkey-red; flowers golden orange, reverse lighter, open, large, 7-8 petals, borne in clusters; foliage glossy, bright green; long stems; very vigorous, bushy growth; [Cocorico × Canzonetta]

Esther HT, lp, Kordes; flowers light pink, medium, dbl., high-centered; int. by W. Kordes Söhne, 1999

Esther Ellen F, ob; int. by Hortico, Inc., 2005

Esther Geldenhuys HT, op, 1988, W. Kordes Söhne; flowers light coral pink, petals clam-shaped, large, 32 petals, borne singly, moderate fragrance; foliage glossy, purple to medium green; prickles concave, yellow-brown; vigorous, very tall, well-branched growth; [seedling × seedling]; int. by Ludwigs Roses Pty. Ltd., 1988

Esther Jasik MinFl, w, 1997, Zipper, Herbert; flowers large, 41 petals, borne mostly singly, slight fragrance; foliage medium size, dark green, dull; few prickles; upright, tall (3ft.) growth; [Shocking Blue × Pink Petticoat]; int. by Island Roses

Esther Jerabek F, mp, 1979, Jerabek, Paul E.; flowers 18 petals; spreading growth; [sport of The Fairy]

Esther O'Farim – See **Matador**, F

Esther Peiro F, or, Roses Noves Ferrer, S L; flowers 26 petals, high-centered; [Lamada × K-881543-02]

Esther Pradel T, ab, 1860, Pradel; bud pure white; flowers chamois, aging to salmon, medium, full; foliage large, dark green, glossy

Esther Rantzen F, ob, 1982, Dwight, Robert & Sons; flowers medium, semi-dbl., moderate fruity fragrance; foliage medium size, medium green, semi-glossy; upright, bushy growth; [Spartan × Orangeade]

Esther's Baby Min, mp, 1979, Harkness; bud pointed; flowers Persian rose, patio, medium, flat; foliage small, glossy; low, spreading growth; [(Vera Dalton × (Chanelle × Piccadilly)) × Little Buckaroo]

Estima S, lp, Noack; low, spreading, groundcover growth; int. by Noack's Rosen, 1998

Estima Min, op

Estralia – See **Pixie Pearl**, Min

Estralita – See **Pixie Pearl**, Min

Estrellita de Oro – See **Baby Gold Star**, Min

Estru F, lp, 1976, deRuiter; flowers patio, 1½ in., 50 petals; foliage small, glossy, dark; low, compact growth; [Rosy Jewel × Floribunda seedling]; int. in 1975

Étain HWich, op, 1953, Cant, F.; flowers salmon-pink, 5-6 cm., borne in large clusters; foliage small, glossy, dark green, almost evergreen; very vigorous growth

Été Parfumé – See **Typhoo Tea**, HT

Étendard HWich, mr, 1956, Robichon; flowers scarlet red, 8 cm., dbl., borne in small clusters, moderate fragrance; recurrent bloom; foliage very glossy, leathery; vigorous growth; [New Dawn × seedling]

Étendard de Jeanne d'Arc – See **Jeanne d'Arc**, N

Étendard de Lyon HP, mr, 1885, Gonod; flowers glossy peony red with metallic reflections, large, full

Étendard de Marengo HP, mr, 1848, Armand, Étienne; flowers dark scarlet with carmine, large, very full, cupped

Éterna HT, lp, 1979, Delbard-Chabert; bud long; flowers light carmine pink, 4-5 in., 28-32 petals; vigorous, upright growth; PP4440; [((Michèle Meilland × Carla) × (Dr. Schweitzer × Tropicana)) × (Queen Elizabeth × Provence)]; int. in 1978

Eterna Giovanezza – See **Eternal Youth**, HT

Eternal HT, ob, Delbard; int. by Australian Roses, 2003

Eternal Flame LCl, ob, 1955, Brownell; flowers light orange, 3-4 in., 12-19 petals, moderate fragrance; upright, climbing growth; PP1439; [seedling × Queen o' the Lakes]

Eternal Flame F, ob, Interplant; int. in 1992

Eternal Flame – See **Gebrüder Grimm**, F

Eternal Sun HT, or, 1966, Joseph H. Hill, Co.; bud ovoid; flowers vermilion, large, dbl., high-centered, slight fragrance; foliage dark, leathery; vigorous, upright, bushy growth; PP2689; [seedling × Jacqueline]

Eternal Youth HT, lp, 1937, Aicardi, D.; bud long, pointed; flowers suffused orange-salmon, 4-5 in., 50 petals, cupped, intense fragrance; foliage leathery; vigorous, upright, bushy growth; [Dame Edith Helen × Julien Potin]; int. by J&P

Eternally HT, rb, Hiroshima; int. by Hiroshima Bara-en, 1997

Eternally Yours – See **Candella**, HT

Eternité F, mr, 1947, Gaujard; flowers scarlet, 4-5 in., 25 petals; foliage dark; very free growth; [Mme Joseph Perraud × Holstein]

Eternity Gr, rb, 1991, Twomey, Jerry; flowers red/cream bicolor, medium, full, borne in large clusters, moderate fragrance; foliage medium size, dark green; some prickles; tall (6 ft.), upright growth; PP8413; [Gitte × Silver Jubilee]; int. by DeVor Nurseries, Inc., 1991

Ethel HWich, lp, 1912, Turner; flowers flesh-pink, small, semi-dbl., borne in large clusters; foliage glossy; vigorous growth; [Dorothy Perkins × unknown]

Ethel Austin F, dp, 1984, Fryers Nursery, Ltd.; flowers deep pink with lighter pink center, large, 20 petals, high-centered, moderate fragrance; recurrent; foliage large, medium green, semi-glossy; upright growth; [Pink Parfait × Redgold]

Ethel Brownlow T, op, 1887, Dickson, A.; flowers salmon pink, large; foliage glossy

Ethel Chaplin HT, my, 1926, Chaplin Bros.; flowers soft lemon-yellow, dbl.

Ethel Dawson HT, rb, Dawson, George; [Red Meillandina × seedling]; int. before 1987

Ethel Dickson HT, dp, 1917, Dickson, H.; flowers deep salmon-rose with silvery flesh reflexes, large, dbl.

Ethel James HT, dp, 1921, McGredy; flowers softer carmine-red than Isobel, flushed orange-scarlet, center yellow, 5 petals; bushy growth; Gold Medal, NRS, 1920

Ethel Malcolm HT, w, 1909, McGredy; flowers ivory-white, very large; vigorous growth; Gold Medal, NRS, 1909

Ethel Orr Min, mr, 1987, Williams, Ernest D.; flowers small, 35 petals, high-centered, borne usually singly or in sprays of 3-5, slight fragrance; foliage small, medium green, glossy; prickles few, small, tan; upright, bushy, medium, profuse growth; no fruit; [Miniature seedling × Big John]; int. by Mini-Roses

Ethel Sanday HT, yb, 1954, Mee; flowers yellow flushed apricot, well-formed, 4-5 in., 34 petals; foliage dark; vigorous, upright growth; [Rex Anderson × Audrey Cobden]; int. by Sanday; Gold Medal, NRS, 1953

Ethel Sloman HT, mr, 1966, Fankhauser; bud ovoid; flowers crimson, very dbl.; foliage leathery; compact, bushy growth; [Baccará × My Choice]

Ethel Somerset HT, mp, 1921, Dickson, A.; bud pointed; flowers shrimp-pink, large, dbl., high-centered, intense fragrance; vigorous, branching growth

Ethel Utter LCl, my, Wilber; bud cherry-red; flowers dbl.

Ethical F, rb, Dawson; int. in 1995
Étienette Desbrosses D, about 1828, from Angers
Etienne Dubois HP, dr, 1873, Damaizin; flowers deep velvety crimson, large, dbl.
Étienne Levet HP, mr, 1871, Levet Père; flowers carmine-red, large, 70 petals; sometimes recurrent bloom; vigorous, erect growth; [Victor Verdier × unknown]
Étienne Levet, Climbing Cl HP, mp; [sport of Étienne Levet]
Étienne Rebeillard HT, pb, 1924, Pernet-Ducher; flowers flesh-pink, suffused golden, semi-dbl.
Étincelante HT, dr, 1913, Chambard, C.; flowers brilliant red, tinted purple, large, dbl., moderate fragrance; [Gruss an Teplitz × Étoile de France]
Étincelle HT, or, 1958, Moulin; flowers bright red tinted orange, medium, 40-45 petals; low, bushy growth; [Crimson Glory × seedling]; int. by Vilmorin-Andrieux
Etna M, dr, 1845, Vibert; flowers crimson shaded purple, large, very mossy, very dbl., cupped, moderate fragrance
Etna HT, dr, 1924, Looymans; flowers deep crimson-maroon, semi-dbl.; [Red-Letter Day × H.V. Machin]; int. by Prior
Etna – See **Etna Parade**, Min
Etna F, ob; int. by Pépinières de la Saulaie, 2005
Etna Parade Min, or, Poulsen; flowers orange-red, medium, dbl., no fragrance; growth bushy, 20-40 cm.; int. by Poulsen Roser, 2004
Étoile d'Alaï HMsk, mr, 1946, Meilland, F.; flowers brilliant red, prominent golden stamens, medium, very dbl.; repeat bloom; bushy growth; [Skyrocket × unknown]
Étoile de Belgique HT, mr, 1946, Lens; flowers brilliant red, very large, dbl.; foliage bronze; vigorous, bushy growth; [Charles P. Kilham × Étoile de Hollande]
Étoile de Belgique HT, mr, 1956, Buyl Frères; bud ovoid; flowers geranium-red, large, dbl.; bushy, spreading growth; [Independence × Happiness]
Étoile de Bologne – See **Stella di Bologna**, HT
Étoile de Feu HT, op, 1921, Pernet-Ducher; flowers salmon-pink and coral-red, large, dbl., globular; foliage bronze; vigorous, bushy, branching growth
Étoile de Feu, Climbing Cl HT, ob, 1930, H&S
Étoile de France HT, dr, 1904, Pernet-Ducher; bud pointed; flowers dark rose-red, center cerise, medium to small, dbl., cupped; bushy growth; [Mme Abel Chatenay × Fisher Holmes]
Étoile de France, Climbing Cl HT, dr, 1915, Howard Rose Co.
Étoile de Hollande HT, mr, 1919, Verschuren; flowers bright red, very large, 35-40 petals, cupped, intense damask fragrance; foliage soft; growth moderate (to 3 ft.), branching; [Gen. MacArthur × Hadley]
Étoile de Hollande, Climbing Cl HT, mr, 1931, Leenders, M.; flowers rich velvet crimson, very large, dbl., cupped, intense old rose fragrance; [sport of Étoile de Hollande]
Étoile de la Malmaison A, lp, before 1844; flowers flesh, fading to French white, medium to large, full, cupped; foliage dark, dull green, thick; growth erect
Étoile de Lyon T, my, 1881, Guillot fils; bud large, full; flowers golden yellow, fading to ivory, 8-10 cm., dbl., moderate fragrance; sparse intermittent bloom; foliage soft; short, weak stems; bushy growth; [Mme Charles × unknown]
Étoile de Mai Pol, ly, 1893, Gamon; flowers sulfur-white, small, dbl.; vigorous growth
Étoile de Poitevine HT, rb, 1910, Bruant; flowers velvety red, striped pink and white; [Étoile de France × unknown]
Étoile de Portugal HG, dp, 1903, Cayeux, H.; flowers rose-red to salmon, large, dbl., loose; [*R. gigantea* × Reine Marie Henriette]
Étoile d'Or Pol, ly, before 1910; flowers small
Étoile d'Or HT, yb, 1931, Pernet-Ducher; flowers golden yellow, reverse shaded orange, large, semi-dbl.; upright, bushy growth; int. by Gaujard
Étoile du Berger B, w, 1841, Béluze; flowers flesh white, medium, full
Étoile du Matin B, dp, 1851, Bernède; flowers pink aging to violet, medium, full
Étoile du Nord HP, mr, 1854, Fontaine; flowers bright cherry red, shaded garnet purple, medium, full, globular
Étoile du Nord HP, dr, 1859, Bernède
Étoile Luisante Pol, mr, 1918, Turbat; bud pointed; flowers cerise-red, shaded coppery, semi-dbl., high-centered, borne in clusters; foliage bronze, glossy; prickles few thorns; long stems; bushy growth; int. by Michell
Etoile Rouge Min, rb
Etrusca HT, ob, Barni; bud globous; flowers soft orange, fading to bright apricot, full, cupped, then pompon, moderate fragrance; recurrent; foliage bronze red when young, then dark green; moderate (80-100 cm.) growth; int. by Rose Barni-Pistoia, 2006
Etty van Best HT, ly, 1934, Buisman, G. A. H.; flowers white, shaded yellow, dbl.; foliage leathery; vigorous growth; [Pharisaer × Souv. de H.A. Verschuren]
Etude LCl, dp, 1965, Gregory; bud coral; flowers deep peachy rose-pink, 8 cm., semi-dbl., borne in clusters, moderate fragrance; recurrent bloom; foliage glossy, light green; [Spectacular × New Dawn]
Eucharis HGal, dp, before 1820, Descemet, M. (?); flowers bright rose, edged lighter, large, dbl.
Eudoxie HGal, dp, before 1820, Descemet
Eudoxie D, mp, before 1848; flowers vivid rose with lilac tints twards the edge, large, dbl., cupped; numerous prickles; growth branching, vigorous; possibly synonymous with the HGal of the same name
Eugène Appert HP, dr, 1860, Trouillard; flowers velvety crimson-maroon, medium, full; [sport of Géant des Batailles]
Eugène Barbier HP, dy, 1920, Barbier; flowers brilliant canary-yellow, shaded coppery golden yellow, dbl., globular; prickles few thorns; upright growth; [Frau Karl Drushchki × Rayon d'Or]
Eugène Boullet HT, dr, 1909, Pernet-Ducher; flowers crimson-red, shaded carmine, large, dbl., globular, borne mostly solitary; foliage bronze green; vigorous growth; [Liberty × Étoile de France]
Eugène Bourgeois – See **René Denis**, N
Eugène Bréon B, op, 1847, Paillet; flowers salmon pink with flesh, large, full
Eugène de Beauharnais Ch, dr, 1838, Hardy; flowers purple, large, dbl., moderate fragrance
Eugène de Luxembourg – See **Prince Eugène de Beauharnais**, HP
Eugène de Savoie M, mr, 1860, Moreau et Robert; flowers bright red, shaded, 10-12 cm., dbl., flat; some repeat
Eugène Desgaches – See **Desgaches**, B
Eugène d'Orléans HSem, lp, before 1829, Jacques; flowers delicate pink, 2 in., dbl., borne in small clusters; foliage oval, glabrous, glossy, leathery; prickles few, red, nearly straight; stems thick, reddish, creeping
Eugène E. Marlitt B, mr, 1900, Geschwind, R.; flowers bright carmine shaded scarlet, large, dbl.; few prickles; vigorous growth
Eugène Fürst HP, dr, 1875, Soupert & Notting; flowers crimson-red, shaded purple, large, dbl., globular; recurrent bloom; [Baron de Bonstetten × unknown]
Eugène Jacquet HWich, mr, 1916, Turbat; flowers cherry-red, dbl., borne in clusters; very early bloom; foliage bright green; vigorous, symmetrical growth; [Wichurana hybrid (red) × Multiflora hybrid (pink)]
Eugène Janvier HGal, dp; flowers dark pink, paling to lilac, medium, dbl.
Eugene Jardine N, w, 1898, Conard & Jones; flowers pure white, large, full, moderate fragrance
Eugène Maille HGal, mp, about 1825, Boutigny; flowers bright pink, very large, full
Eugène Picard HT, op, 1938, Sauvageot, H.; flowers light coppery-pink with red tints, large, very dbl.
Eugène Pirolle – See **Admiral de Rigny**, N
Eugène Transon LCl, or, 1926, Barbier; flowers orange and copper, reverse orange-red, shaded, borne in clusters; vigorous, climbing growth; [Mme Berard × Constance]
Eugène Vavin HP, mr, 1869, Duval; flowers shining cherry red, shaded scarlet, large, full
Eugène Verdier HP, m, 1863, Guillot fils; flowers rich dark violet, large, full; [Victor Verdier × unknown]
Eugène Verdier M, dp, 1872, Verdier, E.; flowers crimson or light red, center deeper, well-formed, very dbl.
Eugenia HT, rb, 1920, Collier; flowers coral-red to prawn-red, flecked or striped yellow, dbl.; [sport of Mme Edouard Herriot]
Eugénie Boullet – See **Mme Eugénie Boullet**, HT
Eugénie Bourgeois T, w, 1897, Bourgeois; flowers silky cream-white, center apricot, large, full; [Mme Bérard × unknown]
Eugénie Buatois Pol, 1904, Buatois
Eugénie Chamusseau C, dp
Eugénie de Guinoisseau – See **Eugénie Guinoisseau**, M
Eugénie Guinoisseau B, mp, 1860, Guinoisseau; flowers bright pink, shaded flesh white, medium, very full
Eugénie Guinoisseau M, mr, 1864, Bertrand-Guinoiseau; flowers reddish-cerise, changing to reddish-violet, 8-10 cm., dbl.; some repeat; foliage dark green, oval, pointed, finely dentate; prickles numerous, red; vigorous growth
Eugénie Guinoisseau × Nuits de Young M, dr, Dechant; flowers magenta red, brown tones in autumn, medium, dbl., cupped; recurrent; upright (5 ft.), strong growth; int. in 1938
Eugénie Jauvin – See **Mme Roussel**, T
Eugénie Lamesch Pol, yb, 1899, Lambert, P.; flowers ochre-yellow and bright yellow, shaded pink, dbl., borne in clusters, moderate fragrance; foliage glossy; dwarf, compact growth; [Aglaia × William Allen Richardson]
Eugénie Lebrun HP, dr, 1860, Fontaine; flowers amaranth red, shaded brown, large, full
Eugenio d'Ors HT, dr, 1946, Camprubi, C.; flowers oxblood-red, large, dbl.; [Sensation × Margaret McGredy]
Eugenio Fojo HT, mr, 1953, Dot, Pedro; bud pointed; flowers vermilion-red, well-formed, large, 35 petals; vigorous, bushy growth; [Texas Centennial × Carlos Fargas]
Eulalia HT, mp, 1934, Verschuren-Pechtold; flowers pink, lighter toward base, large, dbl.; vigorous growth; int. by H&S
Eulalia Berridge Pol, lp; flowers medium, dbl.
Eulalia de la Falconnière B, dr, 1854, Dorizy; flowers dark red, edges lighter, large, full
Eulalie Lebrun HGal, w, 1845, Vibert; flowers white, striped with rose and lilac, medium, dbl.; sometimes classed as C
Eumundi F, w, 1953, Ulrick, L.W.; flowers pure white, very dbl., cupped; foliage light green; vigorous, bushy growth; [Yvonne Rabier × Baby Alberic]
Euphémie B, lp, 1847, Vibert; flowers delicate rose, 7 cm., full
Euphoria S, ob, Interplant; flowers bright orange with yellow center and golden eye, 1½ in., semi-dbl., cupped, borne usually in clusters; free-flowering; foliage dense, medium green, glossy; low (6-12 in.), spreading (3-5 ft.)

growth; groundcover; int. in 1997

Euphrates S, pb, 1986, Harkness; flowers pale salmon red, deep pink eye, small, 5 petals, borne in small clusters; foliage small, variable form (usually long and narrow), ligh; prickly; low, spreading growth; [*Hulthemia persica* × seedling]

Euphrosine HCh, mp, 1826, Vibert

Euphrosine N, yb, before 1866; flowers light pink with yellow, large, full, cupped

Euphrosine l'Élégante C, dp, before 1811, Descemet; bud long; flowers dark rose pink, 2-3 in., borne in large clusters

Euphrosyne HMult, mp, 1895, Schmitt; flowers pure pink, 3-4 cm., single to semi-dbl., borne in large clusters, moderate fragrance; non-recurrent; very vigorous growth; [*R. multiflora* × Mignonette]

Eureka HT, mp, 1914, Hobbies; flowers bright rose

Eureka S, w, 1956, Wright, Percy H.; flowers pure white, small, semi-dbl., borne in clusters; intended for trial as a hardy understock; [probably Betty Bland × Ames 5]

Eureka F, ab; flowers golden, apricot yellow, 4 in., dbl., borne in clusters of 3-5, slight fragrance; good repeat; foliage glossy; growth to 3½ ft.; PP15712; int. by Kordes, 2003; AARS, 2003

Euro 92 F, dr, RvS-Melle; [Windekind × Patricia]; int. in 1989

Europa HT, mp, 1928, Keessen; flowers bright pink; [sport of Columbia]; int. by Nieuwesteeg

Europa F, mp, 1987, Kordes, W.; flowers medium, dbl.; foliage medium size, medium green, matte; bushy growth; PP6513; [(seedling × Banzai) × (Mercedes × Carol)]; int. in 1985

Europas Rosengarten F, mp, Hetzel; flowers medium, dbl.; int. in 1989

Europawelle Saar HT, op, Meilland; flowers salmon-pink, large, dbl.; int. in 1985

Europe 92 HT, mp, 1989, Delbard & Chabert; flowers pink magenta, long, large, 11 petals, slight fragrance; foliage bright; vigorous, bushy growth; [seedling × (Michèle Meilland × Karla)]; int. in 1988

Europe Sensation F, or

European Touch HT, ab, Von Koss; bud elongated, edged with pink; flowers dbl., high-centered, borne singly, no fragrance; foliage large, dark green, matte; long, straight stems; very tall (5-6 ft.), upright, vigorous growth; int. in 1997

Europeana F, dr, 1964, deRuiter; flowers dark velvety crimson, 3 in., 25-30 petals, rosette, borne in large, heavy clusters, slight tea fragrance; foliage bronze-green to dark green; vigorous growth; PP2540; [Ruth Leuwerik × Rosemary Rose]; int. by deRuiter, 1963; Gold Medal, The Hague, 1962, Gold Medal, Portland, 1970

Europeana, Climbing Cl F, dr, 1986, Burks, Joe J.; [sport of Europeana]; int. by Cooperative Rose Growers, 1987

Eurorose F, yb, 1974, Dickson, A.; flowers yellow-ochre, flushed fire-red, large, 25 petals, globular; [Zorina × Redgold]; int. in 1973

Eurorose – See **Eurorose 2000**, LCl

Eurorose 2000 LCl, pb, Croix, P.; int. by Croix, 2001

Eurosong HT, lp, 1986, Lens, Louis; flowers 38 petals, high-centered, borne singly or in three's, slight fragrance; foliage dark reddish-green; prickles large, brownish-red; upright growth; [(Queen Elizabeth × seedling) × Queen Elizabeth]; int. in 1984

Eurostar – See **Yellowstone**, F

Eurovision HT, dr, 1961, Delforge; flowers 4 in., 30 petals; foliage dark; vigorous, bushy growth; [Miss France × Rosita]

Euroway HT, mr, Hetzel; int. in 1993

Euryanthe S, mp

Eurydice HSet, pb, 1886, Geschwind, R.; flowers carmine flesh; [*R. setigera* × Louise Odier]

Eustace HT, w, Robinson; flowers large, ivory-cream with blush pink edges, high-centered; [Reve d'Or seedling]; int. by Vintage Gardens, 1989

Eustacia F, pb, 1999, McCann, Sean; flowers hand-painted with patches of pink and red, yellow center, 3 in., dbl., borne in small clusters; foliage medium size, medium green, glossy; numerous prickles; upright, medium (30 in.) growth; [(Copper Pot × Maxi) × Picasso]

Euterpe HMult, ly, 1937, Tantau; bud pointed; flowers semi-dbl., open, borne in medium clusters; foliage glossy; long stems; very vigorous, climbing growth; [(Ophelia × *R. multiflora*) × Florex]

Eutin F, dr, 1940, Kordes; bud globular, pointed; flowers glowing carmine-red, dbl., cupped, borne in clusters; foliage leathery, glossy, dark; vigorous growth; [Eva × Solarium]

Eutin, Climbing Cl F, dr, 1957, Lindquist; PP1531; [sport of Eutin]; int. by Howard Rose Co.

Eva HMsk, rb, 1933, Kordes; bud pointed; flowers carmine-red, center white, large, semi-dbl., borne in large clusters, moderate fragrance; intermittent bloom; very vigorous growth; [Robin Hood × J.C. Thornton]

Eva Corinne HSet, lp, about 1846, Pierce; bud reddish; flowers light flesh, 3-4 cm., dbl., globular, borne in clusters of 10-20; non-recurrent; foliage medium size, somewhat rugose; prickles purplish; growth very erect

Eva de Grossouvre HT, mp, 1908, Guillot; flowers salmon-pink, large, full, globular; [Mrs W. J. Grant × unknown]

Eva Eakins HT, or, 1926, McGredy; flowers scarlet-carmine, flushed orange, base bright yellow, small, dbl., high-centered; foliage leathery; bushy growth

Eva Gabor HT, dp, 1983, Olesen, Pernille & Mogens N.; flowers deep pink, large, 40 petals, moderate fragrance; foliage large, medium green, glossy; vigorous, upright, bushy growth; [seedling × seedling]; int. by Roses by Fred Edmunds, 1983

Eva Knott HT, ob, 1957, Mee; flowers coppery orange, well-formed, 35 petals; vigorous growth; [Ethel Sanday × Mrs Sam McGredy]

Eva Schubert – See **Frau Eva Schubert**, HWich

Eva Simone F, op, Michler, K. H.; flowers dbl.; int. in 1992

Eva Teschendorff Pol, w, 1923, Grunewald; flowers greenish-white, aging to pure white, medium, full, slight fragrance; [sport of Echo]; int. by Teschendorff

Eva Teschendorff, Climbing Cl Pol, w, 1926, Opdebeeck (also Teschendorff, 1932); flowers creamy white, small, full; [sport of Eva Teschendorff]

Evaline Pol, lp, 1920, Prosser; flowers light pink, edged brighter, petals quilled, small, dbl., borne in clusters, moderate fragrance; bushy growth; [Orléans Rose × Rayon d'Or]

Evangeline HWich, pb, 1906, Walsh; flowers rosy white, veined cameo-pink, 2 in., single, borne in large clusters, moderate fragrance; late seasonal bloom; foliage dark, leathery; long stems; very vigorous, climbimg (12-15 ft.) growth; [*R. wichurana* × Turner's Crimson Rambler]

Evangeline T, w, 1951, Krider Nursery; bud deep pink; flowers creamy white, edged blush-pink, medium, dbl.; almost thornless; vigorous, spreading growth; [sport of Mrs Dudley Cross]

Evangeline Bruce F, yb, 1971, Dickson, A.; flowers yellow, flushed pink, well-formed, 4½ in., 24 petals; foliage light; [Colour Wonder × Sea Pearl]

Evasion F, Hendricks; int. in 1972

Eve HT, ob, 1959, Gaujard; bud long, pointed; flowers coral-red shaded yellow, very large, dbl., moderate fragrance; foliage glossy; vigorous growth; int. by Gandy's Roses, 1959

Eve Allen HT, rb, 1964, Allen, E.M.; flowers crimson, reverse and base saffron-yellow, 5 in., 26 petals; foliage dark, glossy; vigorous growth; [Karl Herbst × Gay Crusader]; int. by Sanday

Eveka Min, pb, 2006, Hopper, Nancy; flowers pink/white blend, 2 in., full, borne mostly solitary; foliage medium green, matte; prickles ¼ in., reddish, few; growth upright, medium (16 in.); [pink seedling × unknown]; int. in 2006

Evelien F, lp, 1986, Interplant; flowers 35 petals, borne in clusters, slight fragrance; foliage medium size, medium green, semi-glossy; PP7368; [seedling × Fresh Pink]; int. in 1985

Evelina Min, lp, 1992, Mansuino, Dr. Andrea; flowers large, full, borne mostly singly, no fragrance; foliage medium size, medium green, semi-glossy; medium (100-150 cm.), bushy growth; [Rosa Maria × Seedling (Pink 078)]; int. in 1990

Eveline Turner HP, mp, 1876, Verdier, E.; flowers bright shining pink, very large, full

Evelyn HT, mp, 1918, Paul, W.; flowers salmon, shaded and edged rose, base yellow, imbricated, large, dbl.; RULED EXTINCT 1/92; [sport of Ophelia]; int. by Pierson

Evelyn S, ab, 1992, Austin, David; flowers very dbl., old-fashioned, rosette, borne in small clusters; foliage medium size, medium green, semi-glossy; some prickles; medium (110 cm.), upright, bushy growth; PP8680; [Graham Thomas × AUStamora]; int. by David Austin Roses, Ltd., 1991

Evelyn Min, dp, Agel

Evelyn Buchan HT, pb, 1959, Riethmuller; flowers pink tinted yellow, 3-4 in., 23 petals, high-centered; foliage leathery, dark; vigorous, upright growth; [Luis Brinas × Crimson Glory]

Evelyn Dauntessey HT, pb, 1909, McGredy; flowers salmon stained carmine-rose; moderately vigorous growth

Evelyn Ellice F, lp, 1966, Ellice; flowers light pink, becoming white, pointed, 3 in., borne in clusters; foliage light green; vigorous growth; [sport of Queen Elizabeth]

Evelyn Fison F, mr, 1962, McGredy, Sam IV; flowers scarlet, 3 in., dbl., borne in broad clusters; foliage dark, glossy; compact, bushy growth; PP2424; [Moulin Rouge × Korona]; int. by McGredy & Son, 1962; Gold Medal, NRS, 1963

Evelyn Grace F, ob, 1993, Horner, Heather M.; flowers orange/yellow bicolor, medium, dbl., borne in small clusters; foliage medium size, light green, glossy; some prickles; medium (90 cm.), compact growth; [Avocet × Remember Me]; int. by Horner, 1995

Evelyn Hough HT, lp

Evelyn Lauder – See **Miami Moon**, F

Evelyn May HT, dp, 1932, Edward; flowers vermilion-pink, 65 petals; free growth; [Lady Alice Stanley × Edith Part]

Evelyn May S, op, 2006, Beales, Peter; flowers yellow blend, reverse orange pink, 15 cm., dbl., borne in large clusters; foliage large, dark green, semi-glossy; prickles average, straight, moderate; growth upright, medium (1 m.); shrubs, hedging; [Elizabeth of Glamis × Arthur Bell]; int. by Peter Beales Roses, 2000

Evelyn Murland HT, pb, 1923, Dickson, A.; flowers salmon-pink and carmine, veined yellow, reverse veined pink, dbl.

Evelyn Redfern F, mr, 2003, Fleming, Joyce; flowers semi-dbl., 16-18 petals, borne in clusters of 3-12, moderate fragrance; recurrent; foliage medium size, medium green, matte, disease-resistant; prickles 3/16 in., light brown; growth medium (30 in.); [Morden Fireglow × Bonica]; int. by Hortico, Inc., 2002

Evelyn Rogers Min, mp, 1989, Williams, Ernest D.; flowers small, 34 petals, slight fragrance; foliage small, medium green, glossy; upright, bushy growth; [Tom Brown × Over the Rainbow]; int. in 1988

Evelyn Taylor F, ob

Evelyn Tebbutt F, ab, 2004, Paul Chessum Roses; flowers apricot-pink, reverse lighter, 6 cm., dbl., borne in small clusters, slight fragrance; foliage medium size, medium green, semi-glossy; prickles small, green, few; growth compact, bushy, medium (60 cm.); beds, borders, containers; [n/a × seedling]; int. by Love4Plants Ltd, 2004

Evelyn Thornton Pol, mp, 1919, Bees; flowers shell-pink deepening to salmon and lemon shaded orange, open, dbl.; foliage leathery, glossy, dark bronze; bushy growth; [Léonie Lamesch × Mrs W.H. Cutbush]

Evening Fire Min, rb, 1995, Frock, Marshall J.; flowers red, pink reverse, medium, dbl., borne mostly singly, moderate fragrance; foliage medium size, medium green, semi-glossy; some prickles; bushy growth; [Black Jade × Pierrine]

Evening Glow HT, r, 1960, Armbrust; bud long, pointed; flowers buff, large, 35 petals, moderate fragrance; foliage leathery; moderate growth; [Charlotte Armstrong × Narzisse]; int. by Langbecker, 1959

Evening Light – See **Tarde Gris**, HT

Evening Light S, pb, 2002, Warner, Chris; flowers light peach, pale pink reverse, 2 in., dbl., borne in small clusters, moderate fragrance; foliage small, medium green, glossy; prickles small, straight; growth spreading, tall (7 ft.); fences, walls, pillars; [Laura Ford × (Mary Sumner × Kiskadee)]; int. by Warner's Roses, 2003

Evening News HT, my, 1927, Letts; flowers apricot-yellow veined rose, base deep buttercup-yellow, open, dbl.; foliage glossy, rich green; vigorous, bushy growth; [sport of Mme Edouard Herriot]

Evening Queen HT, m, 1995, Davidson, Harvey D.; flowers slight red on edge of petals with aging, 3-3½ in., full, borne in small clusters, intense fragrance; foliage medium size, medium green, matte; medium (3 ft.), bushy growth; [Blue Ribbon × Great News]; int. by Hortico Roses, 1994

Evening Sentinel F, ob, Fryer, Gareth; int. in 1986

Evening Shadows Min, pb, 1990, Williams, Michael C.; bud pointed; flowers medium, 20 petals, high-centered, borne usually singly, slight fruity fragrance; foliage large, medium green, semi-glossy; prickles slight downward curve, small, red; growth bushy, medium; hips globular, light orange; [Tiki × Party Girl]; int. by The Rose Garden & Mini Rose Nursery, 1990

Evening Sky HT, ob, 1939, Moore, Ralph S.; flowers orange, tipped scarlet, base yellow, 2½-3 in., 6-8 ruffled petals; foliage bluish green; vigorous growth; [Talisman × unknown]

Evening Star HT, my, 1919, Morse; flowers golden yellow, shaded apricot, large, dbl.; bushy growth; [sport of Mme Edouard Herriot]

Evening Star F, w, 1973, Warriner, William A.; flowers white, base shading pale yellow, large, dbl., high-centered, slight fragrance; foliage large, dark, leathery; vigorous, upright, bushy growth; PP3432; [White Masterpiece × Saratoga]; int. by J&P, 1974; Gold Medal, Portland, 1977, Gold Medal, Belfast, 1977

Evening Star – See **Ichibanboshi**, Min

Evening Telegraph HT, dy, 1976, Haynes; [sport of Whisky Mac]

Evensong HT, op, 1963, Arnot; flowers rosy salmon, well-formed, 5 in., 25 petals; foliage dark; vigorous growth; [Ena Harkness × Sutter's Gold]; int. by Croll, 1963

Eventail HT, yb, 1989, Kono, Yoshito; bud ovoid; flowers light yellow to pink, medium, 50 petals, borne singly; foliage medium size, semi-glossy, slightly denticulated; prickles downward-pointed, reddish-purple; upright, tall growth; [Sonia × Miyabi]

Eventide HT, dr, 1948, Toogood; bud ovoid; flowers dark velvety red, open, medium, dbl.; foliage wrinkled, soft; moderate growth; [(Crimson Glory × unknown) × Rouge Mallerin]

Évêque de Nímes HP, mr, 1856, Plantier/Damaizin

Ever Ready LCl, mr, 1976, MacLeod; flowers bright crimson, 3 in., 32 petals; recurrent bloom; foliage large, medium green, matte; [Aloha × Étoile de Hollande]; int. by Christie Nursery, Ltd.

Everbloom Cl Pol, dp, 1939, Archer; flowers deep pink, single, borne in clusters; recurrent bloom; foliage glossy; growth to 3-6 ft. first year, 8-10 ft. in about 3 years; [Phyllis Bide × unknown]

Everblooming Dr W. Van Fleet – See **New Dawn**, LCl

Everblooming Jack Rose – See **Richmond**, HT

Everblooming Pillar No. 3 – See **White Cap**, Cl HT

Everblooming Pillar No. 12 – See **Eternal Flame**, LCl

Everblooming Pillar No. 73 – See **Scarlet Sensation**, LCl

Everblooming Pillar No. 82 – See **Show Garden**, LCl

Everblooming Pillar No. 83 – See **Salmon Arctic**, LCl

Everblooming Pillar No. 84 – See **Golden Arctic**, LCl

Everblooming Pillar No. 122 LCl, yb, 1954, Brownell; flowers light yellow and orange, 3½-4½ in., 90 petals, moderate fragrance; growth like a hybrid tea, followed by 4-5 ft. canes; PP1263; [seedling × Break o' Day, Climbing]

Everblooming Pillar No. 126 LCl, mp, 1955, Brownell; flowers pink, base yellow, 3½-4½ in., 35-50 petals, moderate fragrance; bushy, upright growth; PP1425; [seedling × Queen o' the Lakes]

Everblooming Pillar No. 214 LCl, my, 1954, Brownell; flowers amber-yellow, large, 75 petals; growth like a hybrid tea, followed by 4-5 ft. canes; PP1296; [seedling × Break o' Day, Climbing]

Everblooming Pillar No. 340 LCl, pb, 1957, Brownell; flowers pink and yellow, 4½-5 in., 35-40 petals, high-centered, moderate fragrance; growth like a hybrid tea, followed by longer canes.; PP1606; [Queen o' the Lakes × Scarlet Sensation]

Everdream HT, my, 1956, Motose; bud ovoid; flowers canary-yellow, 4-5 in., 35-40 petals; bushy growth; [Souv. de Claudius Pernet × Kaiserin Auguste Viktoria]

Everest HP, w, 1927, Easlea; flowers cream-white, center tinted green-lemon, very large, 38 petals, high-centered, moderate fragrance; foliage light; low, spreading growth; [Candeur Lyonnaise × Mme Caristie Martel]; Gold Medal, NRS, 1927

Everest Double Fragrance F, lp, 1980, Beales, Peter; bud pointed; flowers 25 petals, borne 3-7 per cluster; foliage dark, heavily veined; prickles large; tall, upright growth; [Dearest × Elizabeth of Glamis]; int. in 1979

Everglades F, op, 1999, Poulsen; flowers salmon-orange, 8-10 cm., semi-dbl. to dbl., cupped, very slight fragrance; foliage reddish green; bushy, tall (100-150 cm.) growth; int. by Poulsen Roser, 1996

Everglo Min, or, Laver, Keith G.; int. in 1998

Everglow F, ob

Evergold LCl, my, Kordes; flowers medium; foliage dark green, glossy; int. in 1966

Evergreen Gem HWich, w, 1899, Horvath; bud buff; flowers buff-yellow, 2-3 in., dbl., borne in clusters, moderate sweetbriar fragrance; foliage almost evergreen; vigorous, climbing or trailing growth; [*R. wichurana* × Maréchal Niel]; int. by W.A. Manda

Evergreen Gene HG, ly, 2006, Viraraghavan, M.S. Viru; flowers 5 in., full, high-centered, hybrid tea form, borne in small clusters; foliage large, medium green, semi-glossy; prickles large, pointing downward, grey, moderate; growth climbing, tall (12 ft.); [Carmosine × *R. gigantea*]; int. by Roses Unlimited, 2007

Evergreen Rose – See ***R. sempervirens*** (Linnaeus)

Everlasting Love F, mr, Grant, Doug; flowers large, scarlet, 2¾ in., dbl., borne in small clusters; foliage medium size, dark green, glossy, new growth is red; some prickles; medium (80-100 cm.), bushy growth; [Molly McGredy × Satchmo]; int. in 1998

Evermore – See **Carefree Delight**, S

Evert Regterschot F, mr, 1965, Buisman, G. A. H.; bud ovoid; flowers bright red, medium, semi-dbl.; foliage dark; [Korona × seedling]

Evert van Dyk HT, mp, 1931, Van Rossem; flowers rose-pink tinted salmon, large, dbl., high-centered; foliage dark; long stems; bushy growth; [Ophelia × Hill's America]; int. by H&S

Everything's Peachy Gr, pb, 2001, Byrnes, Robert L.; flowers pink/peach, medium pink reverse, large, dbl., borne mostly solitary, slight fragrance; foliage medium green; few prickles; growth upright, medium; [sport of Queen Elizabeth]; int. by Overbrooke Gardens, 2001

Evghenya F, op, 1985, Staikov, Prof. Dr. V.; flowers coral-orange, darker petal edges, base cream, large, 75 petals, borne in clusters of 3-12; foliage dark, glossy; vigorous growth; [Highlight × Masquerade]; int. by Kalaydjiev and Chorbadjiiski, 1975

Evian Cachat HT, mp, 1939, Chambard, C.; flowers bright pink, center copper salmon, very large, dbl., cupped; vigorous growth

Evita – See **Polarstern**, HT

Evita Min, w, 1985, Olesen, Pernille & Mogens N.; flowers white with touch of pale pink, small, 20 petals, borne in clusters, slight fragrance; foliage small, dark, glossy; bushy growth; [Mini-Poul × seedling]; int. by Poulsen, 1984

Evita Bezuidenhout HT, m, J&P; int. in 1995

Evodia HMult, lp, 1925, Bruder Alfons; flowers whitish pink, small, dbl., borne in medium clusters, moderate fragrance; nearly thornless

Evolution F, pb, Olij, Huibert; flowers white, edged pink, 4-5 in., high-centered; [Laminuette × Nicole]; int. in 1995

Evrard Ketten HT, m, 1920, Ketten Bros.; flowers bright unshaded carmine-purple, dbl.; [Farbenkonigin × Ruhm de Gartenwelt]

Évratin – See **Evratina**, A

Evratina A, dp, 1809, Bosc; flowers flesh tinted pale red, medium, dbl., borne in large clusters; foliage dark green, oblong, simply dentate; prickles few, straight, short

Ex Albo Inermis Violacea HGal, m, before 1814, Descemet; flowers lilac white

Exadelphé T, my, 1885, Nabonnand; flowers canary yellow, fading to creamy white, large, full, intense fragrance

Excalibur F, mr, 1967, Harkness, J.; flowers scarlet, 2½ in., 14 petals, borne in clusters, slight fragrance; foliage dark, glossy; bushy growth; [Vera Dalton × Woburn Abbey]

Excellence HT, mr; int. in 2004

Excellens Pol, pb, 1913, Levavasseur; flowers pink washed white, edged carmine, borne in small clusters; nearly thornless

Excellent S, mr, Tantau; int. by Rosen Tantau, 2003

Excellent Min, dy, Olesen; flowers dbl., borne mostly solitary, slight fragrance; foliage dark green, glossy; growth bushy, low (40-60 cm.)

Excellenz Kuntze S, ly, 1909, Lambert, P.; flowers creamy yellow, small, dbl., borne in large clusters; foliage dark, glossy; vigorous, upright growth; [Aglaia × Souv. de Catherine Guillot]

Excellenz M. Schmidt-Metzler HT, w, 1910, Lambert, P.; flowers large, dbl.; [Frau Karl Druschki × Franz Deegen]

Excellenz von Schubert Pol, dp, 1909, Lambert, P.; flowers dark carmine-rose, small, dbl., borne in clusters; late; foliage dark; vigorous growth; [Mme Norbert Levavasseur × Frau Karl Druschki]

Excelsa HWich, mr, 1909, Walsh; flowers intense crimson-maroon, tips of petals tinged scarlet, small, dbl., cupped, borne in clusters of 30-40; non-recurrent; foliage rich green, glossy; vigorous, climbing (12-18 ft.) growth; Gertrude M. Hubbard, ARS, 1914

Excelsa Superior – See **Super Excelsa**, LCl

Excelsior – See **Excellens**, Pol

Excelsior F, mp, 1959, Buisman, G. A. H.; flowers salmon, borne in clusters; foliage dark; vigorous, upright growth; [Pinocchio × Mrs Henri Daendels]

Exception – See **Märchenland**, F

Excite HT, dp, 2000, Giles, Diann; flowers deep pink, large, single, borne mostly singly, no fragrance; foliage small, medium green, semi-glossy; numerous prickles; spreading, medium growth; int. by Giles Rose Nursery, 2000

Excitement Gr, dy, 1986, Jelly, Robert G.; flowers 20 petals, high-centered, borne usually singly, moderate fragrance; foliage medium size, dark, semi-glossy; no prickles; medium, upright, bushy growth; hips medium, slightly pear-shaped, orange; PP4412; [Golden Fantasie × Coed]; int. by E.G. Hill Co., 1985

Exciting – See **Roter Stern**, HT

Exciting HT, pb; bud conical; flowers pink, mottled near edges, with lighter reverse, 4 in., 50-55 petals, high-centered, borne mostly singly; good repeat; foliage dark green, semi-glossy; prickles moderate; growth erect (5 ft.); PP14064; [Lorena × Laser]; greenhouse rose; int. by Meilland, 2002

Exciting S, lp, Harkness; flowers soft pastel pink to white, 3½ in., dbl., slight fruity/rose fragrance; foliage shiny, medium green; growth vigorous and spreading, 4-5 × 4-5 ft.; PPAF; int. by Heirloom Roses, 2005

Exhibitionist! Min, m, 2004, Jalbert, Brad; flowers mauve, petal edges darker in cool weather, 1½ in., very full, borne mostly solitary, slight fragrance; foliage medium size, dark green, glossy; prickles small, hooked, green, moderate; bushy, medium growth; containers, garden decoration, exhibition; [seedling × Black Jade]; int. by Select Roses, 2004

Exita HT, mr, 1962, Meilland; flowers pelargonium red, dbl., borne singly and in small clusters; numerous prickles

Exodus Gr, mp, 1979, Godin, M.; bud ovoid; flowers 3 in., 50-52 petals, cupped; foliage glossy, dark; [Kordes' Perfecta × Kalinka]; int. in 1974

Exotic – See **Sunset Celebration**, HT

Exotic HT, McGredy, Sam IV; int. in 1995

Exotic Beauty HT, op, 1990, Leon, Charles F., Sr.; bud rounded; flowers orange blend, reverse pink blend, large, dbl., high-centered, borne usually singly, slight fruity fragrance; foliage large, dark green, glossy; upright, bushy, medium growth; [Silver Jubilee (surmised) × seedling]; int. by Oregon Grown Roses, 1990

Exotic Treat – See **Phyllis Shackelford**, Min

Exotica HT, ob, Meilland; bud conical, large; flowers ochre and orange-yellow, 5-6 in., 36 petals, high-centered, borne mostly singly, no fragrance; good repeat; foliage medium green, semi-glossy; prickles medium; growth erect, tall; PP11731; [(Golden Emblem × Pareo) × (Lovely Girl × Marina)]; greenhouse rose; int. in 1999

Exploit LCl, dp, 1985, Meilland, Mrs. Marie-Louise; flowers deep pink, medium, 20 petals, borne in small clusters, no fragrance; foliage small, medium green, matte; very vigorous, spreading, climbing growth; [Fugue × Sparkling Scarlet]; int. in 1983

Explorer – See **Space Invader**, S

Explorer's Dream Min, op, 1992, Williams, Michael C.; flowers deep orange pink, just a touch of yellow at base of each petal, medium, dbl., no fragrance; foliage medium size, dark green, semi-glossy; some prickles; medium (50 cm.), upright growth; [Miniature seedling × Homecoming]; int. by The Rose Garden & Mini Rose Nursery

Explosion Border – See **Edmonton**, S

Expo 64 F, Tschanz, E.; int. in 1964

Exposé Min, dp, 2002, Denton, James A.; flowers full, borne mostly solitary, no fragrance; foliage medium size, medium green, semi-glossy; prickles medium, straight, moderate; growth upright, medium (35 cm.); garden decorative, exhibition; [Hot Tamale × Reiko]

Exposition de Brie – See **Maurice Bernardin**, HP

Exposition de Provins HP, mr, 1895, Cochet-Cochet; flowers velvety red, large, full; [Triomphe de l'Exposition × unknown]

Exposition de Toulouse HP, mr, 1873, Brassac; flowers bright cherry, shaded carmine

Express LCl, dp, VEG; flowers carmine-pink, 4 in., dbl., borne singly or in small clusters, slight fragrance; [Queen Elizabeth × Gurss an Heidelberg]

Expression HT, ob, Williams, J.B.; flowers unusual orange, reverse slightly darker, dbl., moderate fragrance; recurrent; growth to 4 ft.; int. by Hortico, Inc., 2006

Expressions HT, pb; int. by Certified/Co-Op., 2006

Exquisite HT, rb, 1899, Paul, W.; bud large, long; flowers bright crimson shaded magenta, large, full, globular

Exquisite HT, ly, 1918, Therkildsen; flowers creamy yellow, dbl.

Exquisite HMult, op, 1926, Praskac; flowers salmon pink, shaded red, very small, full; [Dorothy Perkins × Rubin]

Exquisite HT, lp, 1979, Leon, Charles F., Sr.; bud long, pointed; flowers 5½-6 in., 30 petals, high-centered, moderate fragrance; vigorous, upright growth; [Memoriam × ((Blanche Mallerin × Peace) × (Peace × Virgo))]

Extase HT, dr, 1956, Delforge; bud long, dark red; vigorous growth; [E.G. Hill × seedling]

Extase – See **Ecstasy**, HT

Extasis LCl, dr, 1963, Dot, Simon; flowers red, shaded darker, 5 petals, borne in clusters; vigorous growth; [Spectacular × Cocktail]

Extravaganza F, pb, 1974, Dawson, George; bud ovoid; flowers pink, base cream, medium, dbl.; foliage leathery; vigorous, bushy growth; [Stella × (Sabrina × Golden Giant)]; int. by Neil

Extravaganza HT, ab, Poulsen; bud long, pointed ovoid; flowers light apricot, 8 cm., 40 petals, high-centered, borne singly and in small clusters, slight floral fragrance; recurrent; prickles numerous, 9 mm., hooked downward; growth bushy, upright (100-150 cm.); PP15453; [seedling × Tivoli Gardens]; int. by Pousen Roser, 2003

Exuberance S, mr, Williams, J.B.; flowers bright red, semi-dbl. to dbl., rosette, moderate fragrance; recurrent; foliage reddish-green, matte; growth to 4 ft.; int. by Hortico, Inc., 2006

Eydie Min, w, 1982, Hooper, John C.; flowers white with pink blush, fading to white, small, 50 petals, borne in clusters, moderate tea fragrance; foliage medium green, purple, when young; prickles beige; vigorous, bushy growth; [Janna × seedling]; int. by E.M. Brown, 1981

Eye Appeal S, dr, 1992, Ilsink, Peter; flowers 2 in., 8 petals, cupped, borne singly, no fragrance; repeat bloom; foliage medium size, medium green, glossy; spreading, medium (40-60 cm.) growth; [Eyeopener × unknown]; int. by Interplant B.V., 1992

Eye Liner HT, dr, 1966, Armbrust; bud long, pointed; flowers blood red, medium, semi-dbl., high-centered; foliage dark, leathery; vigorous, upright growth; [Queen Elizabeth × Montezuma]; int. by Langbecker

Eye of the Dragon – See **Dragon's Eye**, HCh

Eye Paint F, rb, 1976, McGredy, Sam IV; bud ovoid; flowers bright red, whitish eye, gold stamens, 2½ in., 5-6 petals, slight fragrance; foliage small, dark; tall, bushy growth; PP3985; [seedling × Picasso]; int. in 1975; Gold Medal, Belfast, 1978, Gold Medal, Baden-Baden, 1974

Eyecatcher F, pb, 1977, Cants of Colchester, Ltd.; flowers pink flushed apricot, reverse silvery cream, 2½ in., 22 petals, moderate fragrance; foliage glossy, light; [Arthur Bell × Pernille Poulsen]; int. in 1976

Eyeopener S, mr, 1986, Interplant; flowers small, semi-dbl., no fragrance; foliage medium size, medium green, glossy; spreading growth; [(seedling × Eyepaint) × (seedling × Dortmund)]

Eyepaint – See **Eye Paint**, F

Eyriés HCh, m, about 1845, Calvert; flowers bright light purple, medium to large, full

Ezzy HMult, lp, Lowe; flowers single, borne in large clusters, moderate fragrance; non-recurrent; int. in 2001

F. Cambó HT, mr, 1933, Dot, Pedro; flowers carmine, large, dbl., cupped; foliage glossy; dwarf growth; [Li Bures × Florence L. Izzard]

F. Cuixart HT, rb, 1960, Dot, Simon; bud ovoid; flowers lincoln red, reverse fuchsine-red, open, large, 40 petals; foliage glossy, bronze; long stems; vigorous, compact growth; [Baccará × Golden Masterpiece]; int. as Francesca de Cuixart, P. Dot

F. Ferrer LCl, dr, 1940, Pahissa; bud long, pointed; flowers dark velvety red, open, large; somewhat recurrent bloom; foliage leathery; vigorous, climbing growth; int. by J&P

F. J. Grootendorst HRg, mr, 1915, de Goey; flowers bright red, edges serrated like a carnation, small, dbl., borne in clusters of up to 20, slight fragrance; recurrent bloom; foliage small, leathery, wrinkled, dark; growth vigorous, bushy (6 ft.); [*R. rugosa rubra* × Mme Norbert Levavasseur]; int. by F.J. Grootendorst

F. J. Lindheimer S, yb, 2006, Shoup, George Micheal; flowers dbl., borne in small clusters, moderate fragrance; very remontant; foliage medium size, medium green, matte, uniquely recurved; few prickles; growth upright, medium (3-4 ft.); containers, hedges; hardy to -20°F; [((Carefree Beauty × Bayse's Blueberry) × (Carefree Beauty × Bayse's Blueberry)) × Rise n Shine]; int. by Antique Rose Emporium, 2000

F. K. Druschkii – See **Frau Karl Druschki**, HP

F. Katom Gr, op, McGredy, Sam IV; int. in 1982

F. L. de Voogd HT, yb, 1920, Timmermans; flowers clear reddish-yellow, semi-dbl.; [Mme Mélanie Soupert × Mme Jenny Gillemot]

F. L. Segers T, pb, 1898, Ketten Bros.; bud long on strong peduncle; flowers carmine-scarlet with yellowish-pink, creamy white around the edge, large, very full, cupped, moderate fragrance; [Safrano × Adam]

F. M. Vokes HT, my, 1927, Hicks; flowers yellow, passing to cream, semi-dbl.; [Ophelia × unknown]

F. P. Merritt Cl HT, dr, 1951, Merritt; flowers bright fiery crimson, 5 in., 50-60 petals, high-centered; foliage glossy; very long stems; very vigorous, climbing (12 ft.) growth; [sport of Hoosier Beauty]

F. R. M. Undritz – See **Gen. John Pershing**, LCl

F. R. Patzer HT, pb, 1909, Dickson, A.; flowers creamy buff, reverse warm pink, large, dbl.; branching growth

F. W. Alesworth HT, dr, 1954, Robinson, H.; flowers deep crimson, well-shaped, large; foliage dark; vigorous growth; [Poinsettia × Crimson Glory]

F. W. Lowe HT, ab, 1936, Lowe; flowers rich orange-yellow, well-shaped; foliage glossy; vigorous growth

F. W. Mee – See **Fred W. Mee**, HT

Fab – See **Lady of Hertford**, F

Fab at Fifty F, dp, 2006, Paul Chessum Roses; flowers dbl., borne in small clusters; foliage medium size, dark green, matte; prickles large, long, yellow/pink, numerous; growth bushy, medium (2 ft.); bedding, borders, containers; [seedling × seedling]; int. by World of Roses, 2005

Fabergé F, pb, 1969, Boerner; bud ovoid; flowers light peach-pink, reverse tinted yellow, large, dbl., high-centered, slight fragrance; foliage dark, leathery; vigorous, dense, bushy growth; PP2886; [seedling × Zorina]; int. by J&P

Fabienne F, mp, 1958, Arles; flowers reddish-salmon, small, 35 petals; foliage clear green; bushy, low growth; [Orange Triumph × (Independence × Floradora)]; int. by Roses-France

Fabiola – See **Queen Fabiola**, Gr

Fabulous! F, w, 2000, Zary, Keith; bud pointed, ovoid buds; flowers pure white, 3-4 in., 25-30 petals, high-centered, borne in large clusters, slight sweet fragrance; recurrent; foliage dark green, glossy; prickels moderate; upright, bushy, vigorous (3-4 ft.) growth; PP12130; [Iceberg × Macrexy]; int. by J&P, 2001

Fabvier Ch, mr, 1832, Laffay, M.; flowers crimson-scarlet, often striped white, very showy, medium, semi-dbl.; recurrent bloom

Facade HT, mp, 1970, Fankhauser; flowers apricot-pink, very large, 60 petals, high-centered; foliage glossy, dark, leathery; vigorous, upright growth; [Elizabeth Fankhauser × Royal Highness]

Fackel HT, dr, 1937, Krause; flowers crimson-red, shaded blackish, very dbl., cupped; compact growth; [Vaterland × Barcelona]

Faïence HT, op, 1935, Van Rossem; flowers peach and apricot, reverse pure yellow, large, 45 petals, cupped; foliage leathery; vigorous, bushy growth; [Charles P. Kilham × Julien Potin]; int. by C-P, 1937

Faint Heart HT, w, 1980, Pavlick, Mike; flowers cream edged light pink, 25 petals, high-centered, borne 1-3 per cluster; foliage mid to dark, leathery, semi-glossy; prickles straight; medium, branching growth; [Hawaii × seedling]

Fair MinFl, mp, Olesen; flowers dbl., borne mostly solitary, slight fragrance; foliage dark green, glossy; growth bushy, low (40-60 cm.); PP10727; int. by Poulsen Roser, 1996

Fair Bianca S, w, 1983, Austin, David; flowers light yellow to white, very dbl., quartered, moderate fragrance; foliage medium size, light green, semi-glossy; upright, medium growth; hardy; int. by David Austin Roses, Ltd.

Fair Dinkum F, op, 1966, Small; flowers peach-salmon, 3-4 in., borne in clusters, moderate fragrance; foliage glossy; RULED EXTINCT 6/83 ARM; [Queen Elizabeth × Circus]

Fair Dinkum Min, pb, 1983, Bennett, Dee; flowers soft pink, petal margins darker, small, 25 petals, high-centered, slight fragrance; foliage small, medium green, semi-glossy; upright, bushy growth; PP5564; [seedling × Coral Treasure]; int. by Tiny Petals Nursery

Fair Eva Min, lp, 2003, McCann, Sean; flowers medium, semi-dbl., borne mostly solitary; foliage medium size, dark green, glossy; growth spreading, short; groundcover; [Kiss 'n' Tell × New Dawn]; int. by Ashdown Roses, 2003

Fair Genie Min, pb, 1989, Laver, Keith G.; bud pointed; flowers light orange in center with pink outer petals, reverse pink, 33 petals, high-centered, moderate fragrance; foliage small, medium green, glossy; prickles slender, straight, almost white, translucent; upright, bushy, low, strong growth; hips ovoid, orange; [Breezy × June Laver]; int. by Springwood Roses, 1990

Fair Lady HT, ab, 1959, Boerner; bud ovoid to pointed; flowers buff overcast pink, 4½ in., 50 petals, high-centered, intense fragrance; foliage glossy; vigorous, upright growth; PP1900; [Golden Masterpiece × Tawny Gold]; int. by J&P, 1959

Fair Lane Min, yb, 1980, Schwartz, Ernest W.; flowers near white flushed pink and yellow, 20 petals, high-centered, urn-shaped, borne 1-5 per cluster; foliage glossy, medium green, deeply serrated; prickles slanted downward; compact, bushy growth; PP4711; [Charlie McCarthy × seedling]; int. by Nor'East Min. Roses, 1981

Fair Maid HT, mp, 1940, Peirce; flowers bright rose to strawberry-pink, changing to deep pink, 4-5 in., 60-75 petals; foliage light green; vigorous, upright growth; [sport of Talisman]

Fair Marjorie Pol, lp, 1952, Armstrong, P.M.; bud ovoid, bright pink; flowers blush-pink, lighter in sun, medium, semi-dbl., cupped; vigorous, bushy growth; [Katharina Zeimet × unknown]

Fair Molly Pol, w, 1999, Moore, Ralph S.; flowers white blend, 1-1½ in., 6-14 petals, borne in small clusters; foliage small, medium green, semi-glossy; few prickles; bushy, spreading, medium (16-24 in.); landscape shrub growth; [(*R. polyantha nana* × unknown) × Fairy Moss]; int. by Sequoia Nursery, 1999

Fair Opal – See **Fire Opal**, F

Fair Play S, m, 1982, Interplant; flowers light violet, 18 petals, borne in large clusters; repeat bloom; foliage medium size, dark, matte; prickles dark green; groundcover; vigorous growth; [Yesterday × seedling]; int. in 1978

Fair Pol Min, Moore, R. E.; int. in 1985

Fair Princess S, mr, Williams, J. Benjamin; int. in 1999

Fairest Cape S, ab, Kordes; int. by Ludwig's Roses, 2003

Fairest of Fair Min, ly, 1982, Bennett, Dee; flowers medium yellow, 15-18 petals, high-centered, borne singly or 3-5 per cluster, slight tea fragrance; foliage small, medium green; very compact, low growth; [Sunbonnet × Rise 'n' Shine]; int. by Tiny Petals Nursery

Fairfield Blaze LCl, mr; int. by Sheridan Nurseries, 1962

Fairfield Pink Cluster HMult, lp, Lowe; flowers dbl., open, borne in large clusters, moderate fragrance; non-recurrent; int. by Ashdown Roses, 2003

Fairhope Min, ly, 1989, Taylor, Franklin "Pete" & Kay; bud pointed; flowers soft, light pastel yellow, aging same, color holds well, 16-28 petals, high-centered; foliage medium size, medium green, semi-glossy; prickles straight, medium, red; upright, bushy, medium growth; hips round, small, green; [Azure Sea × seedling]; int. by Taylor's Roses

Fairlie Rede HT, op, 1937, Clark, A.; flowers salmon, flushed fawn, large, dbl.; vigorous growth; [Mrs E. Willis × seedling]; int. by NRS Victoria

Fairlight F, op, 1964, Robinson, H.; flowers coppery salmon to flame, well-formed, large, dbl., borne in clusters; foliage coppery bronze; [Joybells × seedling]

Fairmount Memory S, pb, 2004, Starnes, John A, Jr.; flowers deep pink, reverse silvery pink, 4 in., very full, borne mostly solitary, intense fragrance; very remontant; foliage medium size, medium green, semi-glossy; prickles medium, claw-shaped; growth bushy, medium (5 ft.); very hardy; int. by John A. Starnes Jr., 2004

Fairqueen Min, ly, 2002, Denton, James A.; flowers full, borne mostly solitary, no fragrance; foliage medium size, medium green, semi-glossy; prickles medium, straight, moderate; growth upright, medium (40 cm.); garden decorative, exhibition; [Fairhope × Behold]

Fairy HMult, w, 1909, Paul, W.; flowers pure white, large, single; somewhat remontant

Fairy – See **The Fairy**, Pol

Fairy Castle – See **Dornröschenschloss Sababurg**, S

Fairy Changeling Pol, mp, 1980, Harkness; bud short, plump; flowers pink, pompon, medium, 22 petals, cupped, slight fragrance; foliage small, dark; recumbent, spreading growth; [The Fairy × Yesterday]; int. in 1981

Fairy Cluster F, mp, 1935, Archer; flowers rose-pink, single, borne in clusters; foliage glossy; long stems; very vigorous growth; [Dainty Bess × Ideal]

Fairy Crystal Pol, w, 1980, Harkness, R., & Co., Ltd.; bud squat; flowers 22 petals, cupped, borne several per cluster; foliage small, dark, glossy; prickles slender, dark; short, bushy growth; [The Fairy × Yesterday]

Fairy Damsel Pol, dr, 1980, Harkness, R., & Co., Ltd.; bud short, plump; flowers medium, 24 petals, cupped, borne in small clusters, slight fragrance; foliage small, dark green, glossy; prickles slender, dark; upright, spreading growth; [The Fairy × Yesterday]

Fairy Dance Pol, mr, Harkness; flowers small, medium red, dbl., borne in clusters; recurrent; vigorous, spreading (2 × 3 ft.) growth; int. in 1980

Fairy Dancer Pol, pb

Fairy Dancers HT, ab, 1969, Cocker; flowers buff-pink, small, dbl.; low, spreading growth; [Wendy Cussons × Diamond Jubilee]

Fairy Floss Min, mp, Hannemann, F.; [Sweet Chariot × seedling]; int. by The Rose Paradise, 1992

Fairy Frolic Pol, pb; flowers small, rosy pink with white reverse, very dbl.; hips numerous

Fairy Gold Min, dy, Fryer, Gareth; flowers golden-bronze, dbl.; recurrent; neat, bushy (15-18 in.) growth; int. in 1992

Fairy Hedge – See **Baby Jayne**, Cl Min

Fairy Lights – See **Niagara**, S

Fairy Like Pol, lp, 1980, Harkness; bud short, plump; flowers light rose-pink, small, 20 petals, cupped; foliage small, glossy; low, spreading growth; [The Fairy × Yesterday]

Fairy Magic Min, mp, 1979, Moore, Ralph S.; bud mossy, long, pointed; flowers semi-dbl., 10-15 petals, moderate fragrance; foliage small, glossy; bushy, upright growth; [Fairy Moss × unnamed min. moss seedling]; int. by Sequoia Nursery

Fairy Maid Pol, lp, 1980, Harkness; bud short, plump; flowers light rose-pink, medium, 20 petals, cupped; foliage glossy; low, bushy growth; [The Fairy × Yesterday]; int. in 1981

Fairy Moon – See **Warbler**, S

Fairy Moss Min, mp, 1969, Moore, Ralph S.; bud mossy; flowers semi-dbl.; foliage mini-moss, small, light green, leathery; vigorous, bushy, dwarf growth; PP3083; [(Pinocchio × William Lobb) × New Penny]; int. by Sequoia Nursery

Fairy Pompons Min, w, 1987, Travis, Louis R.; flowers flesh pink fading white, small, 45-60 petals, high-centered, borne usually singly, slight spicy fragrance; foliage small, medium green, matte; prickles straight, tan-brown; bushy, low growth; no fruit; [Fairy Moss × Fairy Moss]; int. in 1986

Fairy Prince Pol, mr, 1980, Harkness; bud short; flowers medium, 25 petals, cupped; foliage glossy; spreading growth; [The Fairy × Yesterday]; int. in 1981

Fairy Princess – See **Lilibet**, F

Fairy Princess Cl Min, lp, 1955, Moore, Ralph S.; bud pointed, salmon-apricot; flowers 1 in., very dbl., borne in clusters; foliage small, fern-like; growth to 2½ ft.; [Eblouissant × Zee]; int. by Sequoia Nursery

Fairy Queen T, yb, 1902, Paul, W; flowers fawn yellow, shaded cherry pink with cream white reflections, medium, full

Fairy Queen F, lp, 1972, Williams, J. Benjamin; bud ovoid; flowers bluish pink, center coral-pink, small, dbl., high-centered, moderate fragrance; foliage small, glossy, bronze; very vigorous, bushy growth; [The Fairy × Queen Elizabeth]

Fairy Queen Pol, mr, Vurens; flowers crimson red, 3 cm., dbl., rosette, borne in clusters, dense, no fragrance; recurrent; foliage dark green; PPAF; [sport of The Fairy]; int. in 1998

Fairy Red – See **Fairy Damsel**, Pol

Fairy Red 92 S, mr, Liebig; flowers scarlet, medium size, semi-dbl., borne in large clusters; recurrent; foliage dark green, glossy; bushy, spreading (12-20 in.) growth; int. in 1992

Fairy Ring Pol, mp, 1980, Harkness; bud short, plump; flowers rose-pink, 2 in., 20 petals, cupped; foliage glossy; low, bushy growth; [The Fairy × Yesterday]

Fairy Rose – See ***R. chinensis minima*** (Voss)

Fairy Rose – See **The Fairy**, Pol

Fairy Shell Min, mp; int. by Wheaton's Nursery, 2001

Fairy Snow Pol, w, 1979, Harkness; bud squat; flowers medium, 20-25 petals, cupped; low, bushy growth; [The Fairy × Yesterday]

Fairy Snow Pol, w, Holmes; int. in 1991

Fairy Tale S, lp, 1960, Thomson; bud ovoid; flowers open, small, dbl.; foliage dark, glossy; very vigorous, upright (6 ft.) growth; Ruled extinct, 3/93 ARM; [The Fairy × Goldilocks]

Fairy Tale Min, lp, J&P; flowers rosy pink, borne singly and in clusters; int. in 1994

Fairy-Tale Pol, dp, Keiren; flowers small, dbl., borne singly and in clusters; bushy, short growth; int. in 1995

Fairy Tale F, mp

Fairy Tale Queen – See **Bride's Dream**, HT

Fairy Tale Red F, mr

Fairyland Pol, lp, 1980, Harkness; bud short, fat; flowers medium, 24 petals, cupped; foliage glossy; spreading growth; [The Fairy × Yesterday]

Faith HT, my, 1998, Horner, Colin P.; flowers medium yellow, lighter reverse, 4 in., very dbl., borne mostly singly; foliage medium size, medium green, glossy; prickles moderate, medium, curved; upright, tall growth; [Golden Future × Solitaire]; int. by Warley Rose Gardens, Ltd., 2000

Faith HT, r, Grayco; [sport of Amatsu Otome]; int. in 2000

Faith Whittlesey HG, w, 2005, Viraraghavan, M.S. Viru; flowers white, varying to blush pink in cool weather, blush center, reverse white, 3½ in., dbl., borne mostly solitary; foliage medium size, medium green, semi-glossy; prickles small, triangular downpointed, dark grey, few; growth bushy, medium (2½ ft.); bedding; [Reve d'Or × ((Echo × *R. gigantea*) × Marie van Houtte)]; int. as Annapurna, Roses Unlimited, 2005

Faithful F, rb, 1964, Latham; flowers crimson edged white, becoming velvety crimson, well-shaped, semi-dbl.; foliage small, light green; vigorous growth; [Dusky Maiden × Tabarin]

Faithful F, mr, Harkness; flowers deep cherry red, dbl.; continuous bloom; bushy, compact (30 in.) growth; int. in 1998

Faithful Companion – See **Precious Child**, S

Faithful Friend HT, ab, Dickson; flowers of warm golden apricot; foliage rich, glossy; growth medium; int. in 2001

Faivre d'Arcier HT, mp, 1901, Schwartz; flowers carmine, edged lilac pink, large, full, globular, moderate fragrance

Faja Lobbi HT, mr, 1963, Leenders, J.; flowers bright red; vigorous growth; [Queen Elizabeth × Florence Mary Morse]

Fakir – See **Pigalle**, F

Fakir's Delight S, w, 2006, Moore, Ralph S.; bud mossy; flowers creamy white, reverse white, 2½-3 in., very full, borne in small clusters; recurrent; foliage medium size, medium green, glossy, new growth reddish; prickles medium, straight, green, numerous; growth upright, tall (6-8 ft.) spreading; shrub/climber; [(Little Darling × Lemon Delight) × (unnamed seedling × Out of Yesteryear)]; int. by Sequoia Nursery, 2006

Falbala HT, mp, 1948, Gaujard; bud long; flowers brilliant salmon; foliage glossy, dark; erect growth

Falcon F, Dot, Simon; int. in 1989

Falcon LCl, dr, Kordes; int. in 1998

Falkland HSpn, w, before 1930, possibly from Ireland; flowers pale pink to nearly white, medium, semi-dbl.; low, bushy growth

Fall Festival Min, rb, 1997, Laver, Keith G.; flowers tomato red with yellow stripes, medium, full, borne mostly singly, no fragrance; foliage medium size, dark green, semi-glossy; some prickles; upright, bushy, medium growth; PP11571; [seedling × Springwood Red Victor]; int. by Springwood Roses

Fall Splendor Min, yb, 1996, Williams, Ernest D.; flowers rich yellow with orange blush on edges, 1¼-1½ in., full, blooms borne mostly singly, moderate fragrance; foliage medium size, dark green, semi-glossy; some prickles; medium (16 in.), compact, bushy growth; [Rise 'n' Shine × Twilight Trail]; int. by Texas Mini Roses, 1996

Falling in Love HT, pb, 2006, Carruth, Tom; flowers medium to soft pink, reverse creamy pink, long-lasting, 11-13 cm., full, high-centered, borne mostly solitary, moderate rose and fruit fragrance; recurrent; foliage large, dark green, semi-glossy; prickles medium large, slightly hooked, greenish beige, numerous; growth upright, and bushy, medium (125-140 cm.); garden decoration; [Moonstone × Marilyn Monroe]; int. by Weeks Roses, 2007

False River Beauty Min, mp, 2000, Picard, Ancil; flowers medium pink, reverse white, 1¼-1½ in., full, borne mostly singly; foliage medium size, dark green, semi-glossy; few prickles; upright, spreading, tall (24-30 in.) growth; winter hardy; [sport of Over the Rainbow]; int. by Leo's Nursery, 2001

Falstaff S, dr, 2000, Austin, David; flowers dark crimson changing to rich purple, large, 105 petals, cupped, borne in small clusters; foliage medium size, medium green, semi-glossy; numerous prickles; vigorous, upright, bushy (3½ ft.) growth; PP13315; [seedling (red English shrub) × seedling (pink English shrub)]; int. by David Austin Roses, 1999

Fama HT, rb, 1942, Dot, Pedro; flowers amber and red, large, 25-30 petals, cupped; foliage soft, light green; short stems; vigorous, upright, bushy growth; int. by C-P

Fama F, dy, Cocker; int. in 1986

Fame – See **Fame Parade**, Min

Fame! Gr, dp, 1998, Zary, Dr. Keith W.; flowers deep shocking pink, almost light red, 5 in., 30-35 petals, high-centered, borne in small clusters; foliage large, dark green; shrubby, full bush, tall growth; PP11293; [Tournament of Roses × Zorina]; int. by Bear Creek Gardens, Inc., 1998

Fame Parade Min, dr, Poulsen; flowers dark red, medium, dbl., slight wild rose fragrance; foliage dark; growth narrow, bushy, 20-40 cm.; int. by Poulsen Roser, 1996

Family Life F, my, Harkness; flowers pure yellow; free-flowering; compact, medium growth; int. by R. Harkness & Co Ltd, 2003

Famosa HT, mp, 1964, Leenders, J.; flowers pink, well-formed; [Tallyho × Flamingo]

Famosa S, mr, Noack; int. by Noack's Rosen, 2003

Famous Cliff – See **Yaroslavna**, HT

Fan Fare '81 HT, ob, 1981, Byrum, Roy L.; bud short, pointed; flowers 23 petals, high-centered, borne singly, slight rose fragrance; foliage medium to large; prickles straight, short, broad-based; vigorous growth; PP4631; [Cotillion × Hoosier Gold]; int. by Joseph H. Hill, Co.

Fan Mail F, dy, 1974, Boerner; bud long, pointed; flowers open, medium, dbl., moderate fragrance; foliage large, leathery; very vigorous, bushy growth; [Spanish Sun × seedling]; int. by Spek

Fanal F, mr, 1946, Tantau; flowers large, 20 petals, borne in clusters of 10-15, moderate fragrance; foliage dark, glossy; upright growth; [(Johanna Tantau × Heidekind) × Hamburg]

Fancy HT, mr, 1928, Van Rossem; flowers peach shaded cherry-red, base yellow, open, semi-dbl.; [Souv. de Claudius Pernet × Gen. Smuts]

Fancy – See **Fancy Hit**, MinFl

Fancy F, ob; int. by Verschuren-Pechtold, 2001

Fancy Amazone HT, rb; PP11171

Fancy Beauty F, or; flowers orange-red, yellow reverse, semi-dbl.; int. by Hortico, 1999

Fancy Dancer MinFl, w, 2002, Bridges, Dennis; flowers white edged pink, 2¼ in., dbl., borne mostly solitary, no fragrance; foliage medium size, medium green, matte; prickles ¼ in., curved down, moderate; growth compact, medium (2½ ft.); PPAF; [Trickster × select pollen]; int. by Bridges' Roses, 2002

Fancy Free HT, pb, 1922, Clark, A.; flowers pink, center white, semi-dbl.; dwarf growth; [Gustav Grunerwald × seedling]; int. by NRS New South Wales

Fancy Hit MinFl, or, Poulsen; flowers orange-red, 5-8 cm., dbl., no fragrance; foliage dark; growth narrow, bushy, 40-60 cm.; int. by Poulsen Roser, 1994

Fancy Lace HT, mp, 1967, Patterson; bud ovoid; flowers pink tipped silver, large, dbl., high-centered, moderate fragrance; foliage glossy; very vigorous, upright growth; PP2989; [seedling × Queen Elizabeth]; int. by Patterson Roses

Fancy Lady Min, pb, 1991, Clements, John K.; flowers ivory white, edged bright pink and blushed pink, medium, very full, high-centered, borne mostly singly, no fragrance; foliage small, dark green, glossy; few prickles; tall (50 cm.), upright growth; [seedling × seedling]; int. by Heirloom Old Garden Roses, 1990

Fancy Pants Min, rb, 1987, King, Gene; flowers deep pink to golden yellow base, edged red, fading deeper pink, 40 petals, high-centered, slight spicy fragrance; foliage medium size, medium green, matte; prickles medium, light red, slightly crooked on end; upright, bushy, medium growth; fruit not observed; [Baby Katie × Rose Window]; int. by AGM Miniature Roses, 1987

Fancy Potluck Min, dr, 1998, Laver, Keith G.; flowers dark red, good substance, ½-1 in., very dbl., borne mostly singly; foliage small, dark green, matte; few prickles; low (15-20 cm.), compact growth; [seedling × Antique Gold]; int. by Springwood Roses, 1998

Fancy Princess – See **Otohime**, HT

Fancy Talk F, pb, 1965, Swim & Weeks; bud urn-shaped; flowers pink tinted orange, small, dbl., high-centered, borne in clusters, slight fragrance; foliage leathery; vigorous, bushy, low growth; PP2602; [Spartan × Garnette]; int. by Weeks Wholesale Rose Growers

Fancy That Min, pb, 1989, Jolly, Marie; bud pointed; flowers different shades of pink, reverse pink-yellow blend, medium, 68 petals, high-centered, slight spicy fragrance; foliage medium size, medium green, semi-glossy; no prickles; upright, spreading, medium, vigorous growth; hips globular, green-brown; [Rise 'n' Shine × Rainbow's End]; int. by Rosehill Farm

Fandango HT, mr, 1950, Swim, H.C.; bud ovoid, turkey-red, base yellow; flowers orange-red, 3½-4½ in., 16-25 petals, open, moderate fragrance; foliage leathery, glossy, dark; vigorous, upright, bushy growth; [Charlotte Armstrong × seedling]; int. by Armstrong Nursery

Fandango LCl, pb; flowers medium to light pink, 9 cm., semi-dbl., rosette, borne in small clusters; growth to 7 ft. and up; int. by Meilland, 1989

Fanely Revoil HT, or, 1962, Orard, Joseph; flowers cerise-red, reverse tinted orange, well-formed; long stems; [Michèle Meilland × seedling]

Fanette HT, rb, 1970, Laperrière; flowers red, reverse white, medium, 36 petals, high-centered, slight fragrance; foliage dark, glossy; vigorous, bushy growth; [Jeunesse × Souv. du President Plumecocq]; int. by EFR, 1966

Fanfan F, or, 1956, Gaujard; flowers coppery orange, small; foliage small; [Eternite × seedling]

Fanfare F, pb, 1956, Swim, H.C.; bud urn shaped; flowers orange and salmon to pink, open, 3-4 in., 20-30 petals, cupped, borne in large clusters, moderate spicy fragrance; foliage glossy, leathery; very vigorous, spreading growth; PP1385; [Fandango × Pinocchio]; int. by Armstrong Nursery; Gold Medal, Rome, 1955

Fanion – See **Puregold**, HT

Fanny A, pb, before 1848; flowers salmon blush, large, full

Fanny HT, mr, 1935, Lens; flowers bright red; vigorous growth; [Hadley × Mrs Henry Winnett]

Fanny Ardant HT, lp, Adam; flowers light pink with deeper center, full, low-centered; vigorous (80-100 cm.) growth; int. in 2004

Fanny Bias HGal, mp, before 1811, Descemet; flowers blush, center rosy, edges whitish, 3 in., full, moderate fragrance; erect, bushy growth

Fanny Blankers-Koen HT, ob, 1949, Verschuren-Pechtold; bud long, pointed; flowers orange-yellow, flushed and veined red, large, 16 petals; foliage glossy; very vigorous, upright, bushy growth; [Talisman × seedling]

Fanny Boydt T, w, before 1844, Burel, Adolphe; flowers white, center cream, medium, full

Fanny Bullivant HT, dr, 1941, Clark, A.; [sport of The Rajah]

Fanny Dupuis – See **Abricotée**, T

Fanny Elssler HGal, mp, 1835, Vibert; flowers bright pink with minute pale spots, very full, moderate fragrance

Fanny Oppenheimer HT, mr, 1923, McGredy; flowers brilliant cardinal, shaded gold

Fanny Parissot – See **Fanny Pavetot**, HGal

Fanny Pavetot HGal, mp, 1819; flowers large, very dbl., moderate fragrance

Fanny Rousseau A, lp, 1817, Vibert; flowers flesh pink, medium, semi-dbl.

Fanny-Sommesson A, lp, before 1826, Vibert; flowers light pink, fadeing to flesh white, large, very dbl.; nearly thornless; growth erect

Fanny's La France HT, dp; flowers large, deep pink, same as La France; recurrent; vigorous growth; may be sport of La France

Fano S, mp; flowers single

Fantaisie HT, r, 1948, Gaujard; flowers coppery-salmon, base yellow; foliage dark; vigorous growth

Fantan F, or, Gaujard; flowers soft tan overlaid on cream, small, dbl., slight fragrance; recurrent; int. in 1956

Fantan HT, r, 1959, Meilland, F.; bud urn-shaped; flowers burnt-orange to yellow-ochre, large, 48 petals, cupped, slight fragrance; foliage leathery; moderate growth; PP1913; [(Pigalle × Prelude) × (Pigalle × Prelude)]; int. by URS

Fantasi MinFl, w, 1986, King, Gene; flowers cream, reverse cream shaded deep pink, large, 50 petals, high-centered, slight fragrance; foliage medium size, dark, matte; prickles medium, hooked, brown; tall, upright growth; no fruit; int. by AGM Miniature Roses, 1985

Fantasia HT, my, 1943, Dickson, A.; bud long, pointed; flowers golden to lighter yellow, open, medium, 30-35 petals; foliage glossy; strong stems; vigorous, bushy, compact growth; RULED EXTINCT; [seedling × Lord Lonsdale]; int. by J&P

Fantasia, Climbing Cl HT, my, 1956, Mell

Fantasia HT, pb, 1974, Kordes; bud ovoid; flowers cherry pink with cream reverse, globular, borne in clusters of 3-5, moderate fragrance; foliage leathery; vigorous, well-branched, medium growth; [Silver Star × Tradition]; flora-tea; int. by Horstmann, 1977

Fantasia HT, ab, Kordes; int. by W. Kordes Söhne, 1998

Fantasia HT, dp

Fantasia Mondiale HT, ab, Kordes; int. by W. Kordes Söhne

Fantasque – See **Fantastique**, HT

Fantastique HT, yb, 1943, Meilland, F.; flowers yellow, heavily edged carmine, 2½-3 in., 38 petals, cupped, moderate spicy fragrance; foliage dark, leathery, glossy; vigorous, compact growth; [Ampere × (Charles P. Kilham × (Charles P. Kilham × Capucine Chambard))]; int. by C-P

Fantasy HT, rb, 1945, Wyant; bud long, pointed; flowers cerise, reverse yellow ashed pink, open, 4½ in., 9-11 petals; foliage leathery, glossy; slender stems; very vigorous, upright growth; RULED EXTINCT 1/86 ARM; [Soeur Thérèse × seedling]

Fantasy HT, w, J&P; flowers white, sometimes with slight pink tint, dbl., exhibition; recurrent; PP8646; int. in 1992

Fantasy – See **Fantasy Hit**, MinFl

Fantasy Min, pb; flowers large, cream edged cerise, semi-dbl.; medium growth

Fantasy Hit MinFl, dr, Poulsen; flowers dark red, 5-8 cm., semi-dbl., no fragrance; foliage dark; growth bushy, 40-60 cm.; int. by Poulsen Roser, 1993

Fantazia – See **Fantasia**, HT, 1974

Fantin-Latour C, lp, before 1900; flowers blush with a small yellow-green eye, dbl., flat to cupped, borne in clusters of 4-6, moderate fragrance; foliage dark green, broad, elliptical; prickles moderate; vigorous, bushy growth (5-6 ft.)

Far Side F, ob, 1989, Stoddard, Louis; bud ovoid, pointed; flowers orange-vermilion, yellow center, small, 5 petals, borne in sprays of up to 20, moderate spicy fragrance; foliage large, medium green, glossy, smooth; prickles straight, medium, stout, pink to brown; upright, spreading, tall growth; hips globular, medium, vermilion; [(Sunsprite × (Many Moons × Maigold)) × Eyepaint]; int. in 1990

Fara Shimbo M, m, 2007, Barden, Paul; flowers deep purple, reverse medium purple, 2½-3 in., semi-dbl., borne in small clusters; spring-blooming; foliage medium size, dark green, matte; prickles ¼ in., straight, brown, numerous; growth bushy, suckering, medium (3-5 ft.); very hardy; [Nuits de Young × Tuscany Superb]

Farah HT, yb, 1961, Gaujard; flowers coppery yellow, large, dbl.; foliage glossy; long stems; very vigorous, bushy growth; [Peace × Georges Chesnel]

Farandole F, mr, 1959, Meilland, Mrs. Marie-Louise; bud oval; flowers vermilion, open, medium, 25 petals, borne in large clusters; foliage leathery; vigorous, well branched growth (70-80 cm.); [(Goldilocks × Moulin Rouge) × (Goldilocks × Fashion)]; int. by Meilland, 2000; Gold Medal, Rome, 1959

Farandole F, or, Meilland; flowers Indian orange bordered red, borne in clusters; foliage dense, medium green; growth to 30 in.; int. in 2000

Farbenkönigin HT, mr, 1902, Hinner, W.; flowers bright carmine, overlaid with silvery gloss, deeper at base, large, dbl., moderate fragrance; [Grand-Duc Adolphe de Luxembourg × La France]

Farbenspiel F, rb, 1962, von Engelsen, A. J.; flowers pink edged red, dbl., intense fragrance; foliage dark; bushy, compact growth; [Pinocchio × Masquerade]; originally registered as Pol; int. by van Engelen

Farfadet F, or, 1955, Combe; flowers semi-dbl.; very upright growth; [Méphisto × Incendie]

Faria – See **Féria**, HT

Farida F, dp, 1941, Leenders, M.; flowers deep rose-pink, semi-dbl.; [seedling × Permanent Wave]

Farinet S, yb; int. in 2003

Farny Wurlitzer HT, mr, 1970, Cadey; bud long, pointed; flowers large, dbl., intense fragrance; foliage dark, glossy; vigorous, upright growth; [Poinsettia × Charlotte Armstrong]; int. by Ty-Tex Rose Nursery, 1968

Farouche – See **Paris Match**, HT

Farquhar HWich, mp, 1903, Dawson; flowers bright clear pink, carnation-like, resembling Lady Gay, 3 cm., dbl., borne in large clusters; late; foliage glossy; prickles long; vigorous, climbing growth; [*R. wichurana* × Crimson Rambler]; int. by Farquhar

Fasciculée – See **Comtesse de Chamoïs**, C

Fascinating HT, yb, 1960, Fisher, G.; bud long, pointed; flowers rose-opal suffused yellow, 4½ in., 25 petals, high-centered, moderate fragrance; foliage leathery, glossy, dark; upright, bushy growth; PP1945; [Peace × Orange Nassau]; int. by C-P, 1961

Fascination HT, pb, 1927, Chaplin Bros.; flowers rosy cerise, shaded yellow; foliage dark, glossy; vigorous growth; RULED EXTINCT 2/81

Fascination HT, op, 1981, Warriner, William A.; bud nearly globular; flowers orange and rose blend, 55 petals, high-centered, borne usually singly, no fragrance; foliage very large, semi-glossy; prickles long-based, hooked down; upright, heavy branching growth; PP4461; [seedling × Spellbinder]; int. by J&P, 1982; Gold Medal, NZ, 1976

Fascination – See **Miwaku**, HT

Fascination – See **Canyonlands**, F

Fashion F, pb, 1949, Boerner; bud ovoid, deep peach; flowers lively coral-peach, 3-3½ in., 23 petals, borne in clusters; vigorous, bushy growth; [Pinocchio × Crimson Glory]; int. by J&P; Gold Medal, Portland, 1949, Gold Medal, NRS, 1948, Gold Medal, Bagatelle, 1949, Gold Medal, ARS, 1954

Fashion, Climbing Cl F, pb, 1951, Boerner (also Mattock, 1955)

Fashion Min, mp, Poulsen; flowers dbl., moderate wild rose fragrance; foliage dark, glossy; growth bushy, low (20-40 cm.); not a duplicate with the rose of the same name from 1998; int. by Poulsen Roser, 1996

Fashion – See **Fashion Parade**, Min

Fashion S, dr, Poulsen; flowers dark red, 8-10 cm., dbl., no fragrance; foliage reddish green; growth narrow, bushy, 20-40 cm.; not synonymous with either of the other Poulsen Fashions; int. by Poulsen Roser, 2005

Fashion Doll F, mp, Bell, Laurie; flowers coral pink; free blooming; healthy, bushy, medium growth; int. by Bell Roses, 2001

Fashion Flame Min, op, 1977, Moore, Ralph S.; bud ovoid, pointed; flowers coral-orange, 1-1½ in., 35 petals, high-centered, slight fragrance; foliage large, leathery; bushy growth; PP4365; [Little Darling × Fire Princess]; int. by Sequoia Nursery

Fashion Hit – See **Fashion**, S

Fashion Parade – See **Fashion**, Min

Fashion Parade Min, mp, Poulsen; flowers light red or dark pink, less than 5 cm., dbl., slight fragrance; growth bushy, 20-40 cm.; PP11544; not synonymous with the 1996 Poulsen Fashion; int. by Poulsen Roser, 1998

Fashion Statement S, pb, John Clements; flowers white center blending to crisp pink toward the edges, 3 in., 8-12 petals, moderate sweet/honey fragrance; foliage dense; growth bushy, 3½ × 3 ft.; PPAF; int. by Heirloom Roses, 2005

Fashionette F, pb, 1959, Boerner; bud pointed to ovoid, coral; flowers pinkish coral, 3 in., 35-40 petals, cupped, borne in irregular clusters, moderate fragrance; foliage glossy; vigorous, upright growth; PP1563; [Goldilocks × Fashion]; int. by J&P, 1958

Fashionette, Climbing Cl F, pb, 1962, Noack, Werner

Fassadenzauber LCl, lp, Noack, Werner; int. by Noack's Rosen, 1997

Fastigiata – See **Comtesse de Chamoïs**, C

Fat 'n' Sassy Min, rb, 1986, Bennett, Dee; flowers white with a reddish border, reverse white, aging reddish blush, 28 petals, cupped, borne singly, slight fragrance; foliage medium size, medium green, semi-glossy; prickles small, reddish; medium, upright, bushy growth; hips globular, in., green-brown; PP6455; [Carrousel × Sheri Anne]; int. by Tiny Petals Nursery

Fat Tuesday Min, m, 1991, Taylor, Pete & Kay; flowers lavender with darker edges, blending to lighter center, reverse lighter, large, full, borne mostly singly, no fragrance; foliage medium size, medium green, semi-glossy; some prickles; tall (76 cm.), upright growth; [Azure Sea × Lavender Jewel]; int. by Taylor's Roses, 1992

Fata Morgana T, mp, 1893, Drögemüller; flowers silky pink, often shaded flesh pink, large, full; [Niphetos × Mme Lombard]

Fata Morgana F, ob, 1957, Kordes, R.; flowers orange-yellow, open, 2½ in., 28 petals, borne in large trusses; foliage leathery, glossy; vigorous, upright growth; [Masquerade × seedling]

Father Christmas Min, rb, 1996, Taylor, Franklin; flowers red with white base and white reverse, 1½ in., full, borne in small clusters; foliage small, dark green, semi-glossy; some prickles; low (18 in.), upright, bushy growth; [Party Girl × seedling]; int. by Taylor's Roses, 1997

Father David's Rose – See ***R. davidii*** (Crépin)

Father Hugo Rose – See ***R. hugonis*** (Hemsley)

Father Hugo's Rose – See ***R. hugonis*** (Hemsley)

Father's Day – See **Vatertag**, Pol

Fatima HT, ob, 1955, Gaujard; bud long, pointed; flowers orange, reverse bright golden yellow, very large; vigorous growth; [(Opera × unknown) × seedling]

Fatima '67 HT, Moreira da Silva, A.; int. in 1967

Fatime HGal, dp, before 1815, Descemet, M.; flowers carmine at center, tinted with mauve on the edges, with a central button, medium, very dbl., flat, quartered, borne singly or in pairs, slight fragrance; foliage medium green, elliptical, with 5-7 leaflets; Agathe group

Fatinitza HMult, pb, 1886, Geschwind; flowers varying light pink, sometimes striped white, 7 cm., semi-dbl., borne in medium clusters; a complex hybrid of Multiflora and Ayrshire

Fatinitza HT, op, Berger, W.; flowers yellowish salmon-pink, medium, dbl.; int. in 1956

Fausse Unique D, w, before 1818; flowers white, flesh center, large, full

Faust – See **Scarlano**, HSet

Faust – See **Dr Faust**, F

Faust, Climbing Cl F, yb, 1963, deRuiter

Favori F, op, 1986, Lens, Louis; flowers light salmon-pink, 3 in., 23 petals, urn-shaped, borne in clusters of 8-24, intense fragrance; foliage dark; prickles hooked, brownish-green; large, bushy growth; [seedling × seedling]; int. in 1980

Favorita HT, op, 1954, Boerner; bud ovoid, burnt-orange; flowers salmon overcast orange, 5½-6 in., 48 petals, moderate fragrance; foliage dark; vigorous growth; PP1340; [unnamed HT seedling × Serenade]; int. by Stark Bros., 1954; Gold Medal, Rome, 1952

Favorite – See **Favori**, F

Favorite Dream HT, pb, Twomey, Jerry; flowers medium, dbl., moderate musk fragrance; PP10155; [(Friendship × seedling) × (Emily Post × Royalty)]; int. in 1995

Favorite Purple – See **Belle de Stors**, HGal

Favourite – See **Favourite Hit**, MinFl

Favourite Hit MinFl, ab, Poulsen; bud broad based, pointed ovoid; flowers light peach, 5 cm., 20 petals, open cup, borne in small clusters, slight floral fragrance; recurrent; foliage dark green, glossy; prickles moderate, 5 mm., greyed-red, concave; bushy, compact (40-60 cm.) growth; PP15183; [Mini-Poul × seedling]; int. by Poulsen Roser, 2002

Favourite Rosamini Min, mp, deRuiter; int. in 1989

Fay S, pb, 1997, Robert, David; flowers medium, dbl., borne mostly singly; foliage medium size, light green, semi-glossy; few prickles; growth upright, medium (36 in.); [Cecile Brunner × Zéphirine Drouhin]

Fay Morris HT, mp, 2000, Poole, Lionel; flowers medium pink, 5½-6 in., very full, exhibition, borne mostly singly; repeats quickly; foliage large, dark green, glossy; few prickles; upright, bushy, very vigorous, tall (4 ft.) growth; [Gavotte × (Solitaire × Mischief)]; int. by David Lister Roses, 2001

Fayanne F, pb, 1953, Pinchbeck; flowers deep rose-pink, reverse lighter, 2 in., 55 petals, globular; foliage leathery; dwarf, bushy growth; [sport of Garnette]

Faye Reynolds Cl F, dp, 1992, Reynolds, Ted; flowers deep pink, 3-3½ in., full, borne in small clusters, moderate fragrance; foliage sage green, semi-glossy; some prickles; growth medium (6½ ft.); [Westerland × Gingersnap]; int. by Reynolds Roses

Fay's Folly HT, ob, Kordes; buds pointed, urn-shaped, warm tangerine orange; flowers warm tangerine orange fading to cream at the edges, dbl., no fragrance; recurrent; compact, dense, medium (4 ft.) growth; int. by Ludwig's Roses, 2002; Silver Medal, Durbanville, 2006

Fear Naught F, dp, 1969, Harkness, R.; flowers deep pink, dbl., slight fragrance; [Queen Elizabeth × Ena Harkness]; int. by J. L. Harkness, 1968

Fecirco HT, Ferrer, F.; int. in 1987

Federation LCl, op, 1938, Horvath; bud pointed; flowers rosy pink, orange undertone, large, 24-36 wavy petals, cupped; foliage leathery, glossy, dark; long, strong stems; very vigorous climbing (12-14 ft.) growth; [Mrs F. F. Prentiss × Director Rubió]; int. by Wayside Gardens Co.

Federico Casas HT, op, 1931, Dot, Pedro; flowers coppery pink and orange, open, very large, semi-dbl.; foliage dark; vigorous, bushy growth; [Unnamed variety × Eugene Barbier]; int. by C-P

Federico Casas, Climbing Cl HT, op, 1937, Stell; int. by Stell Rose Nursery

Federico Garcia Lorca HT, ab, Viveros Fco. Ferrer, S L; flowers 30 petals, globular; [Zambra × Susan Hamshire]

Fedra F, mr, 1963, Giacomasso; flowers brick-red, dbl.; vigorous growth; [(Fiamma × Independence) × seedling]; int. by Fratelli Giacomasso, 1958

Fedra S, ab, Barni; buds light pink; flowers soft apricot with outer petals lighter, dbl., rosette, borne in clusters; recurrent; growth to 4-5 ft.; int. by Rose Barni, 2005

Fedtschenkoana – See ***R. fedtschenkoana*** (Regel)

Fedugia – See **Marta Salvador**, HT

Fee F, or, 1963, Kordes, R.; flowers orange, large, dbl.; strong, wiry stems; moderate growth

Fee HT, lp, Martens; flowers pearly-pink; int. by Kordes, 1989

Fée Clochette Min, mp, Delbard; int. by Georges Delbard SA, 2002

Fée des Champs Pol, op, 1965, Dot; flowers salmon-orange, 20-25 petals; foliage bronze; low growth; [Queen Elizabeth × Zambra]; int. by Minier; Gold Medal, Bagatelle, 1965

Fée des Neiges – See **Iceberg**, F

Fée des Neiges, Climbing – See **Iceberg, Climbing**, Cl F

Fée Opale N, ly, 1899, Bruant; flowers light yellow with pearly white, large, full

Feeling HMsk, yb, 2000, Lens, Louis; flowers light yellow to white, reverse lighter, 2-2¼ in., semi-dbl., borne in large clusters, moderate fragrance; recurrent; foliage medium size, medium green, dull; prickles moderate; bushy, medium (4-5 ft.) growth; [Trier × Poesie]; int. by Louis Lens NV, 1992

Feeling F, lp, Barni, V.; int. in 1994

Féerie – See **The Fairy**, Pol

Féerie HT, ob, 1938, Gaujard; flowers coppery red, reverse orange-yellow, open, semi-dbl.; long stems; vigorous, erect growth

Feisty Min, mr, 2001, Zary; flowers medium, bold red, 2½ in., dbl., borne in small clusters, no fragrance; foliage small, dark green, glossy; prickles moderate; growth compact, low (2½ ft.); garden decorative; PP12994; [red miniature seedling × red miniature seedling]; int. by J&P, 2002

Felberg's Rosa Druschki HP, mp, 1929, Felberg-Leclerc; flowers bright rose-pink, large, 25 petals; [Frau Karl Druschki × Farbenkonigin]

Feliae Regis HT, pb, Delbard; int. by Ludwig's Roses, 2003

Felicia HMsk, pb, 1928, Pemberton; flowers pink fading to blush and partly white, large, branching panicles, semi-dbl., moderate musk fragrance; pillar or shrub growth; [Trier × Ophelia]

Felicia Teichmann HT, ob, Kordes; int. in 1991

Félicie HGal, m, 1820, Vibert; flowers deep magenta to violet, small, dbl., ranunculus-shaped, moderate fragrance; foliage small; Agathe group; foliage suggests it may be a hybrid China

Félicien David HP, m, 1872, Verdier, E.; flowers deep rose tinged with purple, large, very full

Felicitas S, dp, 2006; flowers carmine pink, 4 cm., single, borne in large clusters; foliage medium size, dark green, very glossy; bushy, spreading (3 × 5 ft.), arching growth; int. by W. Kordes' Söhne, 1998

Félicité Bohain M, dp, before 1866, from France; flowers vivid pink or bright rose, pronounced button eye, large, very full, globular to cupped, moderate fragrance

Félicité Bohan – See **Félicité Bohain**, M

Félicité et Perpétue – See **Félicité-Perpétue**, HSem

Félicité Hardy – See **Mme Hardy**, D

Félicité Parmentier A, lp, before 1841, Parmentier; flowers soft flesh-pink, aging to creamy white, petals reflexing, with a small yellow-green eye, very dbl., flat, intense fragrance; foliage gray-green, very dentate; prickles brown; vigorous, compact growth; according to François Joyaux, this rose should not be called simply 'Félicité', as it is listed in Parmentier's catalog as Félicité Parmentier

Félicité-Perpétue HSem, w, 1828, Jacques; flowers pale flesh changing to white, 3-4 cm., very dbl., globular, opening flat, borne in large clusters, strong musk fragrance; foliage almost evergreen; very vigorous growth; [thought to be *R. sempervirens* × a Noisette, or maybe Parson's Pink]; int. by Vibert, 1829

Felicity HT, mp, 1919, Clarke Bros.; flowers rose-pink suffused silvery, large, 50-60 petals; foliage dark; vigorous, branching growth; [Ophelia × Hoosier Beauty]

Felicity II – See **Buttons 'n' Bows**, Min

Felicity Kendal HT, op, 1986, Sealand Nurseries, Ltd.; flowers salmon-orange, large, 35 petals; foliage large; bushy growth; [Fragrant Cloud × Mildred Reynolds]; int. in 1985

Felidaé S, ab, Schultheis; flowers large, apricot center with cream outer petals, very full, moderate fragrance; foliage dark green, glossy, resistant; bushy (4 ft.) growth; int. by Rosen von Schultheis, 2002

Felix Brix HT, pb, 1921, Brix; flowers soft rose, suffused yellow, passing to salmon-rose, semi-dbl.; [Natalie Boettner × Old Gold]; int. by Teschendorff

Felix Dorizy B, dr, 1852, Dorizy; flowers dark scarlet, medium, full

Félix Généro HP, m, 1866, Damaizin

Felix Laporte HT, m, 1928, Buatois; flowers blackish velvety purple tinged garnet, dbl., cupped; foliage dark, leathery, glossy; vigorous, bushy growth; [Yves Druhen × Mme Edouard Herriot]

Felix Leclerc S, dp, Ag Canada; flowers bright pink with yellow stamens, semi-dbl., shallow cup to flat, borne in small clusters; tall growth; shrub or small climber; second in new Canadian Artist series; int. by Aubin Nurseries, 2007

Félix Mousset HP, m, 1884, Verdier, E.; flowers deep intense purplish pink, large, full; foliage rounded, dark green, regularly toothed; prickles unequal, short, straight, pink; growth upright

Fellemberg Ch, mr, before 1835, Fellemberg; bud crimson; flowers dark carmine, fading to mauve pink, 6 cm., 36 petals, cupped, borne in small clusters, moderate sweet fragrance; recurrent; foliage small, bluish-green; vigorous, spreading growth

Fellenberg – See **Fellemberg**, Ch

Fellini F, lp, Interplant; int. in 1996

Fellowship – See **Yu-Ai**, HT

Fellowship – See **De Greeff's Jubilee**, F

Fellowship – See **Livin' Easy**, F

Feloma – See **Yellow Coral**, F

Femina HT, lp, 1957, Poulsen, S.; flowers soft pink, large, dbl.; vigorous growth

Femina HT, op, 1963, Gaujard; bud long, pointed; flowers salmon-pink, large, dbl., moderate fragrance; foliage leathery; vigorous, upright growth; PP2586; [Fernand Arles × Mignonne]; int. by Ilgenfritz Nursery, 1966

Feminine Min, pb, Olesen; bud pointed ovoid; flowers medium pink, reverse darker, outer petals lighter, 1½ in., 30 petals, cupped, borne singly and in small clusters, very slight fragrance; recurrent; foliage dark green, glossy; prickles moderate, 6 mm., hooked downward; bushy, compact (30-40 cm.) growth; PP15473; [seedling × seedling]; container rose; int. by Poulsen Roser, 2003

Feminine Hit – See **Feminine**, Min

Femme HT, yb, 1983, Delbard, Georges; flowers ivory yellow, tinted pink, large, 28 petals, slight fragrance; foliage medium size, dark, glossy; prickles bronze-red; upright growth; [(Gloire de Rome × Bayadere) × (Queen Elizabeth × Provence)]; int. by Delbard Roses, 1970

Femme Actuelle – See **Auria**, HT

Femnet HT, dp, Pekmez, Paul; int. in 1993

Fen Queen F, lp, 1963, Sharman; flowers pale flesh, large, 25 petals; foliage light green; vigorous, upright growth; [Queen Elizabeth × Unknown Hybrid Tea]

Fen Zhuang Lou – See **Fun Jwan Lo**, S

Fénelon Ch, m, 1835, Laffay (possibly Desprez); flowers purple-violet, medium, full, globular

Fénelon HP, mp, 1852, Rousseau; flowers bright carmine, medium

Fenja HSpn, mp, Petersen; flowers bright pink, medium size, single; non-remontant; growth to 8 ft.; hips large, elongated, flask-shaped, orange-red; sometimes considered HMoy, or HDavidii; int. in 1965

Fennet HT, rb, Laperrière; buds ovoid; flowers red with white reverse, high-centered; int. by KSG Son Roses, 1985

Fennica – See **Invincible**, F

Ferdinand HP, mr, 1852, Bernède; flowers poppy red, shaded carmine, medium, full; [Géant des Batailles × unknown]

Ferdinand Batel HT, yb, 1896, Pernet-Ducher; flowers variable, from rosy flesh to nankeen orange, medium, dbl.

Ferdinand Chaffolte HP, mr, 1879, Pernet fils; flowers brilliant red, outer petals shaded violet, very large, very dbl., cupped, borne mostly solitary, moderate fragrance; foliage somber green; growth upright

Ferdinand de Buck HGal, mp, before 1842; flowers brilliant pink, medium, dbl.

Ferdinand de Lesseps – See **Maurice Bernardin**, HP

Ferdinand Deppe HP, m, 1852, Laffay

Ferdinand Jamin HP, mr, 1888, Lévêque; flowers vermilion-red, full; foliage dark glaucous green

Ferdinand Jamin HT, op, 1896, Pernet-Ducher; bud long, pointed; flowers carmine pink nuanced salmon, large, full, globular; foliage bronzy green

Ferdinand Lecomte HT, mp, 1909, Robichon; flowers China pink, center darker, large, full, moderate fragrance

Ferdinand Pichard HP, rb, 1921, Tanne; flowers streaked (striped) pink and scarlet, yellow stamens, 25 petals; recurrent bloom; vigorous, tall growth

Ferdinand Roussel HWich, m, 1902, Barbier; flowers purple/pink to light red, 3-4 cm., dbl., borne in medium clusters; foliage medium size, oval, glossy; prickles numerous, straight, long and narrow; [*R. wichurana* × Luciole]

Ferdinando Dukei HT, yb; flowers orange-yellow with red, large, semi-dbl.

Ferdin-Chaffolte – See **Ferdinand Chaffolte**, HP

Ferdy S, dp, 1984, Suzuki, Seizo; flowers deep pink, small, 20 petals, no fragrance; foliage medium size, medium green, matte; spreading (to 5 ft.) growth; groundcover; [unnamed climbing seedling × Petite Folie seedling]; int. by Keisei Rose Nursery

Fergie F, ob, 1987, Gandy, Douglas L.; flowers orange-buff and ginger with shell pink edges, 40 petals, hybrid tea form, borne in well-spaced clusters; foliage medium size, medium green, semi-glossy, disease-resistant; short, compact growth; frost-proof; [seedling × Copper Pot]; int. in 1988

Fergus Games S, op, Williams, J. Benjamin; flowers light salmon pink, dbl.; growth to 3 × 4 ft.; int. by Hortico Inc, 1999

Feria HT, op, 1970, Meilland; flowers coral suffused pink, large, dbl., globular, moderate fragrance; foliage leathery; upright growth; [(Grand Gala × Premier Bal) × Love Song]; int. by Meilland International, 1968

Féria HT, yb, Olij, Huibert; flowers pale yellow edged orange-red, dbl., high-centered; greenhouse rose; int. by Meilland Intl, 1996

Ferline HT, mr, Laperrière; int. in 1984

Fern Kemp HRg, lp, 1918, Kemp, J.A.; flowers delicate pink, 4 in., semi-dbl.; vigorous growth; hardy; [Conrad Ferdinand Meyer × Frau Karl Druschki]

Fern Roehrs LCl, mp, 1943, Graf; flowers same as parent but much more dbl.; [sport of Paul's Scarlet Climber]; int. by Roehrs

Fernand Arles HT, op, 1949, Gaujard; bud long, pointed; flowers orange-salmon shaded red, very large, dbl.; foliage bronze; very vigorous, bushy growth; [Mme Joseph Perraud × seedling]

Fernand Majorel F, Gaujard; int. in 1975

Fernand Point HT, rb, 1964, Orard, Joseph; flowers crimson-red, reverse flesh-pink, base yellow; foliage glossy; [Peace × seedling]

Fernand Rabier HWich, dr, 1918, Turbat; flowers pure deep scarlet, 3 cm., semi-dbl. to dbl., borne in clusters of 40-50, slight fragrance; vigorous, climbing or trailer growth; [Delight × unknown]

Fernand Tanne LCl, dy, 1920, Tanne; flowers deep yellow to cream-yellow, 7 cm., dbl., quartered, borne in clusters of 5-10, intense Tea fragrance; vigorous growth; int. by Turbat

Fernanda HT, (Brazil)

Fernande Krier HWich, pb, 1925, Walter, L.; flowers peach-pink, occasionally margined red, fading to white, medium, semi-dbl.; [sport of Excelsa]

Fernande Lumay HT, ab, 1922, Buatois; flowers apricot-nankeen-yellow, edged milk-white, dbl.; [Mrs Aaron Ward × seedling]

Fernandel – See **Mme Fernandel**, F

Ferniehurst HT, pb, 1912, Dickson; flowers coppery carnation pink, large, full, cupped, moderate fragrance

Fernielea HT, ab, 1926, Adam & Craigmile; flowers apricot, center deeper

Ferox A, w, before 1844; flowers flesh white, medium, very dbl.; foliage pointed, yellowish-green; prickles very numerous

Ferrin MinFl, mp, 2000, Tucker, Robbie; flowers medium pink, 7 cm., dbl., high-centered, borne singly or in small clusters; foliage medium size, medium green, dull; numerous prickles; upright, medium (20-24 in.) growth; [seedling × Figurine]; int. by Rosehill Nursery, 2001

Ferris Wheel Min, yb, 1984, Christensen, Jack E.; flowers yellow, turning pink, orange and red (striped), medium, 20 petals; foliage small, dark, semi-glossy; bushy growth; PP5703; [Golden Angel × Cricket]; int. by Armstrong Nursery

Ferrugineux du Luxembourg M, mr, before 1834, Hardy; flowers bright crimson red, medium, full, flat

Ferry Porsche HT, mr, 1976, W. Kordes Söhne; bud long, pointed; flowers 34 petals, high-centered, borne singly and in small clusters, slight fragrance; foliage large, dark, soft; vigorous, upright growth; [Tropicana × Americana]; int. in 1971

Fervid F, or, 1960, LeGrice; flowers scarlet-orange, 3 in., single, borne in clusters; foliage glossy, dark; vigorous, upright growth; [Pimpernell × Korona]

Festival HT, mr, 1943, Dixie Rose Nursery; flowers rich red, very dbl.; entirely prickle free; RULED EXTINCT, 8/93 ARM; [E.G. Hill × unknown]; int. by Krider Nursery, 1945

Festival, Climbing Cl HT, mr, 1945, Watkins, A.F.; flowers large, globular; free, intermittent bloom; foliage glossy; thornless; very vigorous, climbing growth; hardy in South; [sport of E.G. Hill]; int. by Dixie Rose Nursery

Festival MinFl, rb, Kordes; flowers crimson with silver reverse, borne singly and in clusters; compact (2 ft.) growth; int. in 1994

Festival – See **Matsuri**, LCl

Festival Beauty – See **Krasavitza Festivalia**, HT

Festival Fanfare S, pb, 1982, Ogilvie, W.D.; flowers dark orange-pink with paler stripes which become nearly white, 3 in., semi-dbl., borne in large clusters; tall, broad growth; [sport of Fred Loads]; int. in 1986

Festival Meidiland – See **Rote Woge**, S dbl.

Festival Music – See **Kagura**, HT

Festival Pink S, mp, 1991, Rupert, Kim L.; bud pointed; flowers clear medium pink, white petal base, golden stamens, medium, 5-7 cm. petals, borne in small and large clusters, slight fragrance; foliage medium size, bright green,glossy; numerous prickles; tall (4-5 ft.), bushy,spreading growth; [sport of Festival Fanfare]

Festival Queen HT, lp, 1969, Lindquist; bud long, pointed; flowers light pink, edged deeper, well-formed, high-centered, slight fragrance; foliage dark, leathery; upright, compact growth; int. by Roses by Edmunds, 1968

Festival Rouge F, dr, 1982, Delbard, Georges; flowers semi-dbl., well-formed, borne in clusters; foliage dark; [Walko × (Happiness × Sonia)]; int. by Delbard Roses

Festive Pol, dr, 1976, Jelly; bud short, pointed; flowers 3-3½ in., 30 petals, high-centered, slight sweetbriar fragrance; repeat bloom; foliage parsley-green; vigorous, upright growth; PP3914; [Baccará × seedling]; by E.G. Hill Co., 1975

Festive Jewel S, pb, 2006, Beales, Amanda; flowers full, borne in large clusters; foliage medium size, medium green, semi-glossy; prickles average, straight, few; growth bushy, medium (1½ m.); shrub, small climber, hedging; [Aloha × Comte de Chambord]; int. by Peter Beales Roses, 2004

Festivity F, ob, 1986, Lens, Louis; flowers orange, 3 in., 24 petals, borne in clusters of 3-24, slight fragrance; foliage dark; prickles hooked, green; bushy growth; [seedling × seedling]; int. in 1980

Fête des Mère, Climbing – See **Mothersday, Climbing**, Cl Pol

Fête des Mères – See **Mothersday**, Pol

Fête des Pères – See **Vatertag**, Pol

Fête des Pères, Climbing – See **Vatertag, Climbing**, Cl Pol

Fêtes Galantes HT, pb, Delbard; int. in 1994

Fétiche F, mr, 1962, Delforge; flowers coral-red, center white, open, 2 in., 12 petals, borne in clusters; foliage dark; moderate, bushy growth; [Philippe × Tabarin]

Feu Amoureux HGal, m, before 1811; bud round; flowers deep wine purple, large, dbl., no fragrance; foliage long, finely dentate, unequal in size; prickles numerous, broad-based, red

Feu d'Artifice – See **Fireworks, Climbing**, LCl

Feu d'Artifice – See **Feuerwerk**, S

Feu de Bengale F, lp, 1951, Gaujard, R.; flowers pearl-pink, large, dbl., cupped; foliage glossy; vigorous growth; [Orange Triumph × seedling]; int. by G. Truffaut

Feu de Buck – See **Ferdinand de Buck**, HGal

Feu de Camp – See **Lagerfeuer**, F

Feu de Joie F, mr, 1951, Gaujard, R.; flowers carmine-red, large, dbl., borne in clusters; foliage dark, glossy; vigorous growth; [Orange Triumph × seedling]; int. by G. Truffaut

Feu de Joie S, or, Croix; int. by Roses Paul Croix, 2005

Feu de Saint-Jean Pol, dr, 1951, Gaujard, R.; flowers blackish red, small, semi-dbl., borne in clusters; foliage dark, glossy; vigorous, bushy growth; [Orange Triumph × seedling]; int. by G. Truffaut

Feu de Vesta HGal, mr, before 1829, Coquerel; flowers velvety, light bright crimson, large, dbl.

Feu d'Enfer F, or, 1958, Gaujard, R.; flowers large, dbl.; upright, well branched growth; [Orange Triumph × seedling]; int. by G. Truffaut

Feu du Ciel Pol, ob, 1951, Gaujard, R.; flowers clear orange, small, semi-dbl., borne in clusters; foliage glossy; vigorous, bushy growth; [Orange Triumph × seedling]; int. by G. Truffaut

Feu Follet F, mp, 1953, Gaujard, R.; flowers salmon, cupped; vigorous growth

Feu Follet F, or, Dickson, Patrick; int. in 1989

Feu Joseph Looymans HT, ob, 1921, Looymans; flowers orange-yellow, large, dbl., cupped; foliage leathery; weak stems; vigorous growth; [Sunburst × Rayon d'Or]

Feu Joseph Looymans, Climbing Cl HT, ob, 1935, Western Rose Co.; flowers apricot, edged buff, 4½-5 in., semi-dbl., cupped

Feu Magique F, mr, 1956, Buyl Frères; flowers cherry-red, 18 petals; vigorous growth; [Independence × Signal Red]

Feu Pernet-Ducher HT, my, 1935, Mallerin, C.; flowers bright yellow, center apricot, large, dbl., moderate fruity fragrance; foliage leathery, dark; vigorous, branching growth; [Julien Potin × Margaret McGredy]; int. by A. Meilland; Gold Medal, Portland, 1936

Feu Rouge F, mr, 1959, Tantau, Math.; bud ovoid; flowers open, large, semi-dbl., slight fragrance; foliage glossy; vigorous growth; [Red Favorite × Fanal]; int. in 1956

Feudor HT, yb, 1963, Croix, P.; flowers golden yellow shaded vermilion; foliage bright green; vigorous growth; [Peace × Baccará]; int. by Minier

Feuerball HT, mr, 1965, Tantau, Math.; bud globular; flowers red lead color, well-formed, large, 25-30 petals; foliage glossy; very vigorous, bushy growth

Feuerfunken S, or, GPG Bad Langensalza; flowers large, dbl.; int. in 1979

Feuerland F, or, 1978, W. Kordes Söhne; bud ovoid; flowers 2½ in., 25 petals, cupped, slight fragrance; very vigorous, upright growth; [Kathe Duvigneau × Topsi]; int. by Dehner & Co., 1977

Feuermeer – See **Sea of Fire**, F

Feuerreiter F, mr, 1968, Haenchen, E.; bud long, pointed; flowers open, large, semi-dbl., borne in clusters; foliage dark, leathery; very vigorous, upright growth; [Alain × Oskar Scheerer]; int. by Teschendorff

Feuerschein F, mr, 1930, Krause; flowers brilliant red, not turning blue, dbl.; foliage dark; bushy growth; [sport of Lafayette]

Feuerschein, Climbing Cl F, mr, 1936, Krause

Feuersturm F, or, Verschuren; flowers medium

Feuertaufe Pol, GPG Bad Langensalza; flowers dbl.; int. in 1980

Feuerwerk S, ob, 1965, Tantau, Math.; flowers bright orange, semi-dbl., borne in clusters; foliage glossy; upright, bushy (to 5 ft.) growth; int. as Magneet, Buisman, 1964

Feuerzauber Ch, mr, 1913

Feuerzauber HT, or, 1974, Kordes, R.; flowers orange-red, reverse lighter, medium to large, dbl., high-centered; foliage dark, glossy; vigorous, upright growth; [Fragrant Cloud × seedling]

Feunon Rouge HGal, mr, before 1811; bud elongate; flowers medium, very dbl., moderate fragrance; foliage oval, very dentate, pointed; Agathe group

Feurio F, or, 1956, Kordes, R.; bud ovoid; flowers scarlet-red, 2½ in., 30 petals, cupped, borne in clusters; foliage glossy, light green; vigorous, low, bushy growth; [Rudolph Timm × Independence]; int. by J&P, 1957

Feurio, Climbing Cl F, or, 1963, Kordes

Fever F, dp, 1983, Pearce, C.A.; flowers deep pink, large, dbl., intense fragrance; foliage large, dark; upright growth; int. by Limes Rose Nursery, 1982

Fiaba HT, rb, 1963, Giacomasso; flowers bright red tipped yellow; foliage dark, glossy; very vigorous growth; [(Fiamma × Sovrana) × seedling]

Fiametta Min, dp; flowers sparkling pink; free-flowering

Fiametta F, dr, 1962, Leenders, J.; flowers velvety red, center yellow; moderate growth; [Karl Weinhausen × Goldilocks]

Fiamma F, or, 1948, Aicardi, D.; flowers vermilion, borne in clusters; vigorous growth; [Paul's Scarlet Climber × (Talisman × unknown)]; int. by Giacomasso; Gold Medal, Rome, 1951

Fiamma Nera HMult, w, about 1938, possibly from Yugoslavia; flowers white with a touch of yellow at center, 5 cm., semi-dbl., borne in clusters of 10-30

Fiammetta HG, ab, 1922, Nabonnand, P.; flowers warm amber-yellow, streaked yellow, single, intense fragrance; vigorous, climbing growth; [*R. gigantea* × Margaret Molyneux]

Fiançailles de la Princesse Stéphanie et de l'Archiduc Rodolphe N, ob, 1880, Levet; flowers orange salmon yellow, medium, full, borne in small clusters; foliage dark green; prickles long, hooked

Ficksburg F, ob, Delbard; flowers cream with petal edges turning salmon, then orange, dbl., no fragrance; recurrent; vigorous, medium to tall growth; int. in 1994; Gold Medal, Durbanville, 1992

Fiddler's Gold Min, dy, 1985, Williams, Ernest D.; flowers small, dbl.; foliage small, dark, glossy; bushy growth; [Tom Brown × Golden Angel]; int. by Mini-Roses

Fidélio F, ab, 1961, Horstmann; bud long, pointed, rosy red; flowers dbl., borne in large clusters; vigorous growth

Fidélio F, or, 1964, Meilland, Alain A.; bud long, pointed; flowers medium, 35 petals, high-centered; foliage leathery; vigorous, upright growth; [(Radar × Caprice) × Fire King]; int. by URS

Fidelity HT, mr, 1962, Abrams, Von; bud long, pointed; flowers large, dbl., high-centered; foliage glossy; tall growth; RULED EXTINCT 7/80 ARM; [Crimson Glory × Peace]

Fidelity – See **Scoop Jackson**, Gr

Fides HT, ly, Urban, J.; flowers large, dbl.; int. in 1970

Fidibus HT, rb, Kordes; flowers small, red with yellow stripes, dbl., high-centered; stems length 16 in; greenhouse rose; int. by W. Kordes Söhne, 2002

Fidji HT, yb; flowers striped; int. by Jan Spek Rozen, 2001

Field Marshal Cl Ch, mr, before 1910, Paul; flowers velvety blood-crimson

Field of Dreams F, mp, 2003, Umsawasdi, Dr. Theera & Chantana; flowers yellow eye, reverse pink, medium, semi-dbl., borne in small clusters; prickles average, curved; [Loving Touch × Peggy T]; int. by Certified Roses, 2005

Field Rose – See ***R. arvensis*** (Hudson)

Fieldfare S, rb, Delbard; flowers red with yellow eye, medium size, 10 petals; recurrent; foliage bronzy-green; vigorous (3 ft.) growth; int. in 1989

Fiery – See **Fiery Hit**, MinFl

Fiery Hit MinFl, ob, Poulsen; flowers orange and orange blend, 5-8 cm., semi-dbl., no fragrance; foliage reddish green; growth bushy, 40-60 cm.; PP12484

Fiery Star F, rb, Umsawasdi, Dr. Theera; flowers red with white eye, lighter reverse, medium, 6-14 petals, borne mostly singly, slight fragrance; foliage medium size, dark green, semi-glossy; no prickles; medium, bushy growth; [Libby × Impatient]; int. in 1995

Fiery Sunblaze – See **Cumba Meillandina**, Min

Fiery Sunsation – See **Red Ribbons**, S

Fiesta HT, rb, 1940, Hansen, C.B.; bud ovoid; flowers vermilion, splashed bright yellow, large, dbl.; foliage glossy, dark; vigorous, bushy, compact growth; [sport of The Queen Alexandra Rose]; int. by Armstrong Nursery

Fiesta – See **War Dance**, F

Fiesta – See **Fiesta Parade**, Min

Fiesta Brava Min, or, 1956, Dot, M.; flowers geranium-red, 14 petals, borne in clusters; foliage glossy; vigorous, upright, bushy growth; [Méphisto × Perla de Alcañada]; int. by Combe

Fiesta Charm F, Schloen, P.

Fiesta Clown Min, rb, 1994, Laver, Keith G.; flowers scarlet with orange-yellow reverse, bicolor, pointed, recurved, large, full, intense fragrance; foliage medium size, dark green, semi-glossy; some prickles; medium (24-30 cm.), upright growth; [(June Laver × seedling) × (Painted Doll × June Laver)]; int. by Springwood Roses, 1994

Fiesta Flame F, mr, 1978, Sanday, John; bud pointed; flowers intense scarlet, 3 in., 15 petals; low, bushy growth; [Sarabande × Ena Harkness]

Fiesta Flamenco S, mr, NIRP; int. in 2003

Fiesta Gold Min, yb, 1971, Moore, Ralph S.; bud long, pointed; flowers yellow orange, small, dbl., cupped, slight fragrance; foliage small, glossy, light, leathery; vigorous, dwarf, upright, bushy growth; PP3331; [Golden Glow × Magic Wand]; int. by Mini-Roses, 1970

Fiesta Parade Min, dp, Poulsen; bud pointed ovoid; flowers deep lavender-pink, medium, 55-65 petals, high-centered, borne in small clusters; prolific, very slight fragrance; recurrent; foliage dark green, glossy; prickles average, 3-4 mm., linear to hooked slightly downward; bushy, compact (25-35 cm.) growth; PP11509; [sport of Purple Parade]; int. by Poulsen Roser, 1999

Fiesta Ruby Min, mr, 1977, Moore, Ralph S.; bud ovoid, pointed; flowers 1 in., 40 petals, high-centered, slight fragrance; foliage dark; bushy, compact growth; PP4368; [Red Pinocchio × Little Chief]; int. by Sequoia Nursery

Fiesta Time Min, rb, 1983, Williams, Ernest D.; flowers yellow to orange to red, reverse yellow, small, dbl.; foliage small, dark, glossy; bushy growth; [Starburst × Over the Rainbow]; int. by Mini-Roses

Fièvre d'Or – See **Golden Giant**, HT

Fifi F, ab, 1993, Henson, R.W.; flowers cream pale peach, 3-3½ in., semi-dbl., borne in large clusters, intense fragrance; foliage large, dark green, glossy; numerous prickles; tall (100 cm.), upright growth; [Lichterloh × Liverpool Echo]; int. by Henson, 1993

Fifth Avenue HT, dp, 1948, Johnson, W.E.; bud large, ovoid; flowers grenadine-pink, dbl., high-centered; vigorous growth; [sport of Orange Nassau]

5th Avenue – See **Sutton Place**, Gr

Fifty Fifty F, ob; flowers striped; int. by Pépinières de la Saulaie, 2002

Figaro HT, dr, 1954, Lens; flowers velvety scarlet, 4½ in., 26 petals; vigorous growth; [(Crimson Glory × Grande Duchesse Charlotte) × New Yorker]

Figaro Panarosa – See **Madame Figaro**, S very dbl.

Figment F, m, 1998, Rawlins, R.; flowers purple, overlaid with bright magenta in fresh flower, dark magenta reverse, 4 in., very dbl., borne in small clusters; foliage medium size, medium green, semi-glossy; prickles moderate; upright, medium (2½ ft.) growth; [Len Turner × Remember Me]

Figurine HT, pb, 1952, Lens; flowers China pink, 25 petals; foliage bluish green; vigorous growth; RULED EXTINCT 11/91 ARM; [Soeur Thérèse × seedling]

Figurine Min, w, 1991, Benardella, Frank A.; buds delicately colored; flowers ivory white tinged pink, large, dbl., well-formed, borne mostly singly, some in small clusters; foliage medium size, dark green, matte; few prickles; long stems suitable for cutting; medium (40-50 cm.), upright, bushy growth; PP8020; [Rise 'n' Shine × Laguna]; int. by Weeks Roses, 1992; AOE, ARS, 1992

Fiji Gr, or, 1965, Schwartz, Ernest W.; bud ovoid; flowers bright orange-red, medium, dbl., cupped; vigorous, upright growth; [Queen Elizabeth × seedling]; int. by Wyant, 1964

Fil d'Ariane S, w, 2000, Lens, Louis; flowers pink and creamy white, reverse white, yellow stamens, 2-3 cm., semi-dbl., flat, borne in large clusters, intense fragrance; recurrent; foliage small, medium green, glossy; prickles moderate; low, spreading (8 in. × 3 ft.) growth; groundcover; [Running Maid × *R. multiflora nana*]; int. by Louis Lens NV, 1988

Fil des Saisons S, m, Lens; flowers deep lavender pink, yellow stamens, 4-5 cm., single, borne in large clusters, intense fragrance; recurrent; foliage small, clear green, glossy; low, spreading (16 × 32 in.) growth; int. by Louis Lens, 2004

Filagree Pillar LCl, dp, 1962, Riethmuller; bud ovoid; flowers Tyrian rose, heavily veined, reverse lighter, 50 petals; foliage glossy, bronze; strong stems; vigorous, upright (to 5 ft.) growth; [Titian × Sterling]; int. by Hazelwood Bros., 1962

Filipes Kiftsgate – See **Kiftsgate**, Misc OGR

Fillette F, mp, 1965, Lens; bud ovoid; flowers dbl., borne in clusters; foliage dark; [Circus × Papillon Rose]; int. by Spek

Filomena F, dy, 2007, Mallari, Hermes B.; flowers very full, 80+ petals, borne in small clusters; foliage medium size, dark green, glossy; prickles ½ cm., thin, triangular, tan, few; growth bushy, upright, compact; [sport of Korresia]

Fimbriata HRg, lp, 1891, Morlet; flowers medium, petals carnation-like, fringed & serrated, dbl., borne in clusters of 15-25, intense fragrance; foliage glossy above, glaucous beneath; growth compact (5 ft.); [*R. rugosa* × Mme Alfred Carrière]; int. by Morlet

Fimbriata à Pétales Frangés – See **Serratipetala**, Ch

Finale F, op, 1964, Kordes, R.; flowers salmon-rose, well-formed, large, 21 petals, borne in clusters; foliage light green; low, compact growth; [Nordlicht × Meteor]; int. by McGredy International

Financial Times Centenary S, dp, 1994, Austin, David; flowers deep pink, 3-3½ in., very dbl., borne in small clusters; foliage medium size, dark green, semi-glossy; some prickles; medium (43 in.), upright, bushy growth; PP8142; int. by David Austin Roses, Ltd., 1988

Fine Fare HT, or, 1978, Bees; bud pointed; flowers vermilion, rounded, 4 in., 40 petals; foliage dark; moderately vigorous, upright growth; [Fragrant Cloud × Mildred Reynolds]

Fine Gold HT, dy, 1982, Weeks, Michael W.J.; flowers deep golden yellow, 26 petals, high-centered, borne 1-3 per stem, moderate fragrance; foliage medium size, dark, glossy; branching, upright growth; [seedling × Hawaii sport]

Fine Touch Min, ab, 1986, Lyon; flowers pale apricot, deeper in center, large, 37 petals, high-centered, borne singly, slight fragrance; foliage medium size, medium green, matte; prickles few, reddish; medium, upright growth; hips globular, medium, orange; [Honey Hill × unknown]; int. by M.B. Farm Min. Roses, Inc.

Finesse Min, my, 1984, Hardgrove, Donald L.; flowers small, dbl., high-centered, borne 1-3 per stem, no fragrance; foliage small, medium green, semi-glossy; bushy, spreading growth; [Picnic × Rise 'n' Shine]; int. in 1983

Finest Hour Min, ob, 1996, Williams, Michael C.; flowers very bright orange with yellow at base, creamy orange yellow reverse, medium, very full, borne mostly singly, no fragrance; foliage medium size, medium green, semi-glossy; some prickles; upright, medium growth; [Glowry × unknown]; int. by The Mini Rose Garden, 1996

Fingerpaint Min, ob, 1990, Moore, Ralph S.; bud short, pointed; flowers orange blend, yellow base, with light yellow reverse, 12-14 petals, flat, no fragrance; foliage medium size, medium green, semi-glossy; prickles small, brownish,straight; bushy, spreading, low-medium growth; [Orangeade × Little Artist]; int. by Sequoia Nursery

Finkenrech F, mp, Michler, K. H.; flowers dbl.; int. in 1989

Finlandia Pol, op, 1969, Kraats; flowers orange-salmon; [sport of Greta Kluis]; int. by Longley

Finnstar – See **Finstar**, Min

Finstar Min, op, 1982, deRuiter, George; flowers orange-salmon, small, 20 petals; foliage small, medium green, semi-glossy; bushy growth; [Minuette × seedling]; int. by Fryer's Nursery, Ltd., 1979

Fintona HT, w, Brundrett; int. in 1997

Fiocco Bianco F, w, Barni, V.; flowers large, pure white, dbl., high-centered, borne in large clusters, moderate fragrance; growth to 2-3 ft.; int. by Rose Barni, 1988

Fiona F, mr, 1976, Kordes; bud long, pointed; flowers 3 in., 24 petals, high-centered; foliage wrinkled; vigorous, upright growth; RULED EXTINCT 9/82 ARM; [seedling × Prominent]

Fiona S, dr, 1983, Meilland, Mrs. Marie-Louise; flowers small, bright red, 20 petals, borne in clusters; recurrent; foliage small, dark, semi-glossy; spreading growth; [Sea Foam × Picasso]; int. by Meilland Et Cie, 1982

Fiona Ivin HT, dr, 2002, Poole, Lionel; flowers full, high-centered, borne mostly solitary; foliage dark green, semi-glossy; prickles medium, long, pointed, triangular, moderate; growth upright, bushy, medium (1 m.); garden, exhibition; [New Zealand × (Royal William × Gabi]; int. by David Lister Roses, 2004

Fiona Lynch F, w, 2003, Kenny, David; bud soft yellow; flowers creamy yellow-white, reverse creamy yellow, fading to white, 3 in., dbl., borne in small clusters; foliage medium size, light green, semi-glossy; prickles small, hooked, brown, moderate; growth bushy, 75 × 75 cm.; [(Aunty Lil × Rock'n Roll) × Kate Emily McCormack]; int. in 2004

Fiona Old – See **Fiona Parade**, Min

Fiona Parade Min, rb, Poulsen; flowers red blend, medium, dbl.; foliage dark; growth bushy, 20-40 cm.; PP11594; int. by Poulsen Roser, 1998

Fiona Ravenscroft HT, Tebbin, N.H.; int. in 1972

Fiona Stanley HT, ab; int. in 2005

Fiona's Affection F, pb, 2001, Rosenberg, Ronald; flowers large, full, borne mostly solitary, slight fragrance; foliage medium size, medium green, semi-glossy; prickles in., slightly curved, numerous; growth bushy, tall (4 ft.); [Honor × Affection]

Fiona's Delight HT, op, 2001, Rosenberg, Ronald J.; flowers large, medium orange-pink, large, full, borne mostly solitary, moderate fragrance; foliage medium size, medium green, semi-glossy; prickles medium, moderate;

growth upright, medium (3½ ft.); garden decorative; [Honor × Cherish]

Fiona's Honor HT, pb, 2005, Rosenberg, Ronald J; flowers full, borne mostly solitary, no fragrance; foliage medium size, dark green, semi-glossy; prickles few, in., slightly curved; growth upright, medium (2½ ft.); garden decoration; [sport of Honor]; int. by Rosenberg, Ronald J., 2006

Fiona's Wish HT, rb, Meilland; flowers cherry red, cream reverse, dbl., moderate fragrance; medium growth; int. in 2001

Fionia HWich, lp, 1985, Poulsen, D.T.; flowers light pink to rose, small, borne in clusters; foliage dark, glossy; vigorous growth; [Mme Norbert Levavasseur × Dorothy Perkins]; int. by Poulsen, 1914

Fiord – See **Amalia**, HT

Fiorella Gr, mp, 1985, Meilland, Mrs. Marie-Louise; flowers large, 35 petals; foliage medium size, dark, matte; upright growth; [(Queen Elizabeth × Nirvana) × (Tropicana × MEInaregi)]; int. by Meilland e Cie, 1981

Fiorella '82 – See **Fiorella**, Gr

Fiorona F, Mati

Fire 'n' Ice F, rb, 1987, Christensen, Jack & Carruth, Tom; flowers red, reverse white, fading purplish-red, medium, 40 petals, high-centered, borne mostly singly; foliage medium size, dark green, glossy, very attractive, pointed; upright, bushy, tall growth; no fruit; [Bluhwunder × Love]; int. by Armstrong Nursery, 1985

Fire and Peace HT, ob, Williams, J. B. ; bud deep red-orange; flowers orange-yellow with red edges, aging red, full, moderate fragrance; foliage dark, leathery, semi-glossy; int. by J. C. Bakker & Sons, 2005

Fire Bird – See **Oiseau de Feu**, F

Fire Bird F, rb, 1992, Strange, J.F.; flowers vermilion, pale yellow center, medium, 6-14 petals, borne in large clusters; foliage medium size, dark green, leathery; some prickles; medium (70 cm.), upright growth; [Avocet × Evelyn Fison]

Fire Chief HT, mr, 1942, Jacobus; bud long, pointed; flowers flame-red, large, 24-28 petals, high-centered; foliage glossy; very vigorous, bushy growth; [Crimson Glory × Ami Quinard]; int. by B&A

Fire Dance HT, mr, 1951, Verschuren; bud very long, ovoid; flowers brilliant velvety scarlet, 4-6 in., 25-35 petals, globular; foliage glossy, light green; upright, moderately vigorous growth; [(Ulrich Brunner Fils × Westfield Star) × (Chieftain × Better Times)]; int. by Totty

Fire Flame F, or, 1958, Morse; flowers scarlet, center orange, 4 in., single; moderate growth

Fire King F, or, 1959, Meilland; bud ovoid; flowers fiery scarlet, 2½ in., 48 petals, high-centered, borne in clusters, moderate musk fragrance; foliage dark, leathery; vigorous, upright, bushy growth; PP1758; [Moulin Rouge × Fashion]; int. by URS, 1958

Fire King HT, or, Meilland; flowers geranium red, dbl.; PP11748; greenhouse rose; int. by Meilland Intl, 1999

Fire Magic – See **Feuerzauber**, HT

Fire Meidiland S, mr, Meilland; bud conical, small; flowers fire engine red, 2½-3 in., 30 petals, cupped, opens flat, borne in small clusters; free-flowering; foliage medium size, dark green, glossy; prickles medium; growth mounding; groundcover; PP11583; [(Rote Max Graf × Fiona) × Red Meidiland]; int. in 1999

Fire Opal F, or, 1959, Boerner; bud ovoid; flowers reddish orange-scarlet, reverse lighter, medium, 20-25 petals, cupped, borne in clusters, moderate fragrance; foliage glossy; vigorous, open growth; [Goldilocks × unnamed orange Polyantha]; int. by J&P, 1954

Fire Pillar – See **Bischofsstadt Paderborn**, S

Fire Princess Min, or, 1969, Moore, Ralph S.; flowers small, dbl.; foliage small, glossy, leathery; vigorous, bushy growth; PP3084; [Baccará × Eleanor]; int. by Sequoia Nursery

Fire Queen F, dr, 1967, Von Abrams; bud ovoid; flowers bright red, medium, dbl., borne in clusters; foliage dark, glossy; vigorous, bushy growth; [Fusilier × (Carrousel × Queen o' the Lakes)]; int. by Peterson & Dering, 1963

Fire-Rider – See **Feuerreiter**, F

Fire Robe Gr, rb

Fire Signal – See **Signalfeuer**, F

Fire Sky HT, mr, 1952, Silva; bud long, pointed; flowers large, cupped; foliage dark, glossy; vigorous growth; [Gen. MacArthur × Étoile de Hollande]

Fire Star LCl, mr, Barni; flowers bright red, dbl., borne in clusters of 5-7, moderate fragrance; recurrent; rapid, tall (16-22 ft.) growth; int. by Rose Barni, after 1989

Fireball Pol, or, 1931, deRuiter; flowers glowing reddish-orange; foliage dark, glossy

Fireball HT, ob, Tantau; flowers salmon-orange to vermilion, large, dbl., well formed; int. in 1994

Firebeam F, rb, 1960, Fryers Nursery, Ltd.; flowers yellow, flame, orange and crimson, 2½ in., 14 petals, borne in clusters; foliage glossy; vigorous growth; [Masquerade × seedling]

Firebird F, ob, 1960, Watkins Roses; flowers bright orange, base golden yellow, 2½-3 in., 12-18 petals, borne in clusters; foliage glossy, light green; vigorous, upright growth; RULED EXTINCT 4/92; [Masquerade × Mme Henri Guillot]

Firebird HT, rb, Kordes; flowers bright red and yellow blend, medium, full, cupped, borne moslty singly; recurrent; stems long; florist rose; int. by W. Kordes Söhne, 2005

Firebrand HP, mr, 1874, Labruyère/Paul, W.; flowers bright crimson, sometimes shaded maroon, very large, full

Firebrand HT, or, 1938, Cant, B. R.; flowers bright scarlet; [sport of Flamingo]

Firebrand, Climbing Cl HT, or, 1953, Raffel; int. by Port Stockton Nursery

Fireburst F, or, 1993, Twomey, Jerry; flowers 3-3½ in., very dbl., borne mostly singly, slight fragrance; foliage medium size, medium green, semi-glossy; some prickles; medium (111 cm.), bushy growth; [Evening Star × seedling]; int. by DeVor Nurseries, Inc., 1993

Firecracker F, mr, 1956, Boerner; flowers scarlet, base yellow, 4½ in., 14 petals, borne in clusters, moderate fragrance; foliage leathery, light green; dwarf, bushy growth; PP1629; [(Pinocchio × unknown) × (Numa Fay × unknown)]; int. by McGredy, 1956

Firecracker S, mr, Lim, P, & Twomey, J.; flowers bright red, 3 in., single; recurrent; foliage medium green; growth compact (2 ft.), upright; PP15737; int. by Bailey Nurseries, 2004

Firecrest F, mr, 1964, LeGrice; flowers 3 in., 35 petals, borne in clusters; vigorous, low growth; PP2856; [(Cinnabar × Marjorie LeGrice) × Pimpernell]

Firecrest, Climbing Cl F, mr, 1969, LeGrice; int. by Hybridizers, Ltd., 1969

Firedance Min, rb, 2003, Bell, Judy; flowers red/yellow, reverse yellow/white, 1 in., full, borne in small clusters; foliage medium size, dark green, semi-glossy; prickles small, hooked; growth upright, medium (18 in.); garden, containers, exhibition; [Azure Sea × Rise 'n' Shine]; int. by Michigan Mini Roses, 2004

Firedragon HT, mr, 1923, Clark, A.; flowers fiery red, dbl.

Firefall Cl Min, dr, 1979, Moore, Ralph S.; bud short; flowers 1½ in., 43 petals, flat, borne in clusters; foliage small, glossy; trailing, arching growth; PP4717; [Dortmund × Little Chief]; int. by Roy Rumsey, 1980

Firefighter HT, dr, 2004, Orard, Pierre; flowers velvety dark red, reverse medium red, 4½ in., 40-45 petals, borne mostly solitary, intense fragrance; foliage small, semi-glossy; prickles smallish, straight, brown, few; growth upright, tall (60 in.); cutting, exhibition, garden decoration; [Lasting Love × Hidalgo]; int. by Edmunds' Roses, 2004

Fireflame F, mr, 1954, Boerner; bud ovoid; flowers carmine, 2½-3 in., 65-70 petals, borne in pyramidal clusters, moderate fragrance; vigorous growth; PP1379; [Chatter × Red Pinocchio]; int. by Stark Bros., 1954

Fireflash HT, yb, 1960, LeGrice; flowers golden yellow splashed scarlet, well-formed, 4½ in., 25-30 petals; foliage glossy; upright growth; [Marjorie LeGrice × seedling]; int. by Wayside Gardens Co.

Firefly – See **Holstein**, F

Firefly F, yb, 1978, Joliffe; bud slightly pointed; flowers medium yellow, large, 22 petals, cupped, slight fragrance; foliage dark; upright growth; [sport of Contempo]

Firefly Min, ob, 1986, McGredy, Sam IV; flowers small, 20 petals; foliage small, dark, glossy; bushy growth; [Mary Sumner × Ko's Yellow]; int. in 1985

Fireglow Pol, or, 1929, Wezelenburg; flowers brilliant vermilion-red, shaded orange, single, borne in clusters; dwarf, compact growth; [sport of Orange King]

Fireglow, Climbing Cl Pol, or, 1950, Guillot, M.

Firelight HT, or, 1971, Kordes, R.; flowers large, dbl., high-centered, moderate fragrance; foliage large, light, leathery; vigorous, upright growth; PP3078; [Detroiter × Orange Delbard]; int. by J&P

Fireside HT, yb, 1977, Lindquist; bud ovoid; flowers yellow, white, red, imbricated, 5½-6 in., 35 petals, slight fragrance; foliage large, glossy, dark; vigorous, bushy growth; PP4283; [Kordes' Perfecta × Belle Blonde]

Firestar – See **Fire Star**, LCl

Firestorm Min, or, 1991, Clements, John K.; flowers fiery oriental lacquer orange-red, medium, very full, high-centered, borne mostly singly, no fragrance; foliage small, medium green, semi-glossy; few prickles; medium (35 cm.), bushy, spreading growth; [seedling × seedling]; int. by Heirloom Old Garden Roses, 1991

Firestorm Min, mr, Pearce; int. in 2001

Firetail Cl Min, rb, Peden, G.H.

Fireworks, Climbing LCl, yb, 1935, Mallerin, C.; bud long, pointed, nasturtium-red; flowers yellow, tinted nasturtium-red, 4 in., semi-dbl., open, borne in clusters, slight fragrance; non-recurrent; foliage dark green, glossy; long stems; vigorous, climbing (over 8 ft.) growth; [*R. foetida* hybrid × Colette Clément]; int. as Feu d'Artifice, B&A, 1939

Fireworks – See **Feuerwerk**, S

Fireworks Min, rb, 1991, Saville, F. Harmon; flowers brilliant orange-yellow bicolor, 1½ in., 35 petals, high-centered, borne singly or in small clusters, slight fragrance; profuse; foliage medium size, dark green, semi-glossy; bushy, medium growth; PP8182; [(Rise 'n' Shine × Sheri Anne) × Rainbow's End]; int. by Nor'East Min. Roses, 1992

Fireworks MinFl, rb, Delbard; flowers red with white stripes and streaks, dbl.; int. by Bell Roses, 2005

Firlefanz S, yb, GPG Bad Langensalza; flowers golden yellow plus carmine-red, medium, dbl.; int. in 1968

Firmament HT, dr, 1978, Gaujard; flowers vermilion-crimson, large, dbl.; foliage bronze; [Chrysler Imperial × Credo]; int. in 1971

Firminio Huet HT, dr, 1909, Soupert & Notting; flowers fiery dark carmine red, large, full, globular; [American Beauty × Richmond]

First – See **First Hit**, Min

First Affair HT, w, J&P; int. in 1996

First Blush Pol, mp, 1967, Delbard-Chabert; flowers phlox-pink, 3 in., cupped, borne in clusters; intermittent bloom; foliage dull, light green; moderate growth; [Francais × Orléans Rose]; int. by Cuthbert, 1965

First Blush – See **Peter Mayle**, HT

First Born HT, pb, 1993, Gilmore, T.O.; flowers pink/peach, hold well for cutting, 47 petals, borne mostly singly; foliage medium size, dark green, glossy; some prickles; tall (80-90 cm.), upright growth; [Silver Jubilee × Tahiti]; int. by Gilmore, 1993

First Choice F, or, 1959, Morse; flowers fiery orange-scarlet, center yellow, in trusses, 5 in., 7 petals, moderate fragrance; tall, spreading growth; [Masquerade × Sultane]; int. by Morse & Sons, 1958

First Class – See **Class Act**, F

First Class Gr, w, Certified; flowers large, pure white; int. in 1993

First Class HT, ab; int. by Paul Chessum Roses, 2004

First Edition F, op, 1976, Delbard; bud ovoid, pointed; flowers luminous coral, shaded orange, 2-2½ in., 28 petals, slight tea fragrance; foliage glossy, light; upright growth; [(Zambra × (Orléans Rose × Goldilocks)) × ((Orange Triumph × unknown) × Floradora)]; int. by C-P

First Edition HT, or, Select; flowers 9 cm., 40 petals, pompon; greenhouse rose; int. by Terra Nigra BV, 2003

First Enterprise Gr, mr, Williams, J.B.; flowers large, deep pink to brilliant red, ruffled and quilled, very dbl., old fashioned; foliage clean; int. by Hortico, 2003

First Federal HT, pb, 1964, Boerner; bud ovoid; flowers geranium-pink tinted scarlet, 5-5½ in., 35-40 petals, high-centered, intense rose geranium fragrance; strong stems; vigorous, upright growth; PP2402; [(Radiance × Pageant) × Diamond Jubilee seedling]; int. by J&P, 1963

First Federal Gold HT, dy, 1967, Boerner; bud ovoid; flowers gold and yellow, large, dbl., high-centered, moderate fragrance; foliage glossy, leathery; vigorous, upright growth; PP2729; [Golden Masterpiece × unknown]; int. by J&P

First Federal's Renaissance HT, mp, 1979, Warriner, William A.; bud long, pointed; flowers medium pink, tinted lighter, 5-7 in., 23 petals, slight fragrance; very early bloom; foliage large; compact growth; PP4459; [unnamed variety × First Prize]; int. by J&P, 1980

First Flight HT, mr, 2001, Perry, Astor; flowers 4 in., 35 petals, borne mostly solitary, slight fragrance; foliage medium size, dark green, semi-glossy; prickles average, curved, moderate; growth upright (5 ft.); garden decorative; [seedling × seedling]; int. by Certified Roses Inc., 2003

First Gold HT, dy, Kordes; buds elongated, sharply pointed; flowers large, strong yellow, petals curl into points, dbl., high-centered, star-shaped, slight spicy fragrance; recurrent; foliage glossy green; no prickles on stems; stems long; vigorous, medium growth; int. as Isabel, W. Kordes Söhne; Trial Ground Certificate, Durbanville, 2006

First Hit Min, or, Poulsen; flowers bright orange-red, medium, dbl., slight wild rose fragrance; recurrent; foliage dark; growth bushy, 40-60 cm.; int. by Poulsen Roser, 1995

First Kiss F, pb, 1991, Warriner, William A.; flowers light pink, light yellow blend at base, large, dbl., slight fragrance; foliage medium size, medium green, matte; bushy, compact growth; PP7951; [Sun Flare × Simplicity]; int. by Bear Creek Gardens, 1991

First Lady HT, dp, 1961, Swim, H.C.; bud ovoid; flowers rose madder to phlox-pink, 3½-4½ in., 18-22 petals, cupped, slight fragrance; foliage leathery, dark, semi-glossy; very vigorous, upright growth; PP1893; [First Love × Roundelay]; int. by C.R. Burr, 1961

First Lady, Climbing Cl HT, dp, 1964, Burr, C.R.

First Lady S, mp, Tantau; flowers intense pink at center, outer petals lighter and tinted green, very full, old-fashioned, borne in clusters; foliage fresh green, resistant; strong, vigorous growth; int. by Rosen Tantau, 1997

First Lady HT, pb, Tantau; flowers deep pink with lighter reverse, 8 cm., very full, cupped; recurrent; vigorous (4-5 ft.), large, broad growth, arching canes; int. by Rosen Tantau, 2006

First Lady Nancy HT, yb, 1981, Swim, H.C. & Christensen, J.E.; bud ovoid, long, pointed; flowers light yellow tinged light pink, 36 petals, formal, spiraled, borne singly, slight tea fragrance; foliage semi-glossy, medium; prickles medium; medium, upright, bushy growth; [American Heritage × First Prize]; int. by Armstrong Nursery

First Light S, lp, 1998, Stanley/Marciel; bud pointed, dark candy pink; flowers light pink with purple stamens, 3½-4 in., 5-7 petals, borne in clusters, moderate spicy fragrance; foliage dark green; compact, low growth; PP11223; [Bonica × Ballerina]

First Love HT, lp, 1951, Swim, H.C.; bud long, pointed; flowers dbl., 25 petals; foliage leathery, light green; moderately bushy growth; [Charlotte Armstrong × Show Girl]; int. by Armstrong Nursery

First National Gold Min, dy, 1978, Saville, F. Harmon; bud pointed; flowers 1-1½ in., 38-42 petals, high-centered, slight fragrance; foliage small; compact, upright growth; [Rise 'n' Shine × Yellow Jewel]; int. by Flora World, 1976

First National Silver Min, w, 1978, Saville, F. Harmon; bud ovate; flowers very dbl., 50-55 petals, flat, slight fragrance; foliage small, very glossy; compact, spreading growth; [Charlie McCarthy × Little Chief]; int. by Flora World

First Offering F, dr, 1976, Viraraghavan, M.S. Viru; bud ovoid; flowers 2½ in., 15 petals, globular, open, moderate fragrance; profuse, very lasting bloom; foliage large, glossy, bronze, reddish brown when young; vigorous, dwarf, bushy growth; [seedling × Samba]; int. by K. S. G. Son, 1975

First Prize HT, pb, 1970, Boerner; bud long, pointed; flowers rose-pink, center blended with old ivory, 5½-6 in., 25-30 petals, high-centered, borne singly, moderate tea fragrance; foliage large, dark green, leathery; long, stout stems; vigorous, upright growth; PP2774; [(Enchantment × unknown) × Golden Masterpiece seedling]; int. by J&P; Gold Medal, ARS, 1971, Gertrude M. Hubbard, ARS, 1971

First Prize, Climbing Cl HT, pb, 1974, Reasoner; flowers magnolia pink, lighter at center, very large (up to 20 cm.), slight fragrance; very vigorous, climbing growth; PP3539; [sport of First Prize]; int. by J&P, 1976

First Red HT, dr, Pekmez, Paul; bud long, pointed; flowers cardinal red, 6 cm., 40 petals, high-centered, then flat, borne mostly singly, slight fragrance; recurrent; foliage medium green, leathery, glossy; prickles few, medium length, thin, straight, tan; growth vigorous (to 5 ft.); PP7749; [seedling × Korpek]; int. in 1988

First Rose Convention HT, dr, 1980, Hardikar, Dr. M.N.; bud globular; flowers dark crimson, 48 petals, cupped, borne singly, no fragrance; foliage red when young, turning dark green; prickles hooked, pale cream; vigorous, upright growth; [Flaming Peace × Helen Traubel]; int. by The Bombay Rose Society, 1978

Firstar HT, my, 1983; flowers large, semi-dbl., moderate fragrance; foliage medium size, medium green, glossy; bushy, spreading growth; [New Day × Oregold]; originally registered as Golden Anniversary; int. by J&P

Fisher & Holmes – See **Fisher Holmes**, HP

Fisher Holmes HP, dr, 1865, Verdier, E.; bud long, pointed; flowers deep red, well-formed, large, 30 petals; recurrent bloom; upright growth; [probably Maurice Bernardin seedling]

Fisherman's Friend S, dr, 1987, Austin, David; flowers deep crimson, reverse lighter, fading crimson-purple, large, very dbl., cupped, intense damask fragrance; repeat bloom; foliage medium size, dark green, semi-glossy; prickles broad, straight, large, red-brown; bushy growth; no fruit; [Lilian Austin × The Squire]

Fishpond Pebbles S, w, Kordes; flowers off-white, borne in tight clusters, no fragrance; foliage deep green, glossy; vigorous, speading (3 × 6 ft.) growth; int. by Ludwig's Roses, 2001

Fitzhugh's Diamond MinFl, yb, 2005, Wells, Verlie W.; flowers yellow base with pink & white edge, 1½ in., full, borne mostly solitary, no fragrance; foliage medium size, dark green, semi-glossy; prickles 1/16 in., hooked; growth upright, medium (3½ ft.); garden and show; [Wonderful × seedling]; int. by Wells MidSouth Roses, 2005

Five-Colored Rose – See **Fortune's Five-colored Rose**, T

Five-Roses Rose – See **Veterans' Honor**, HT

Flacon de Neige – See **Flocon de Neige**, Ch

Flag of the Union T, pb, before 1882, Hallock & Thorpe; [sport of Bon Silène]

Flair HT, op, 1951, Verschuren-Pechtold; bud ovoid; flowers coral-blush, 3½-4½ in., 30-35 petals, high-centered; vigorous growth; [Lady Sylvia × seedling]; int. by J&P

Flair HT, rb, 1989, Cummings, Peter E.; bud pointed; flowers medium red to dark red, reverse lighter, medium, dbl., high-centered, borne singly; foliage medium size, dark green, semi-glossy; prickles curved, hooked, reddish-brown, sparse; upright, medium growth; hips obovate, 1 in., green with red splotch; [Pristine × Ink Spots]; int. in 1991

Flair F, yb, Dickson, Patrick; int. in 1993; Gold Medal, Glasgow, 1995

Flair Min, op, Olesen; PP13109; not the same as Flair/Poulpar040, 2005; int. by Poulsen Roser, 2000

Flair – See **Flair Parade**, Min

Flair Parade – See **Flair**, Min

Flair Parade Min, mp, Poulsen; flowers medium pink, dbl., no fragrance; foliage dark; growth bushy, 20-40 cm.; not the same as Flair/Poulra003, 2000; int. by Poulsen Roser, 2005

Flamande – See **Agathe Incarnata**, HGal

Flambeau HT, mr, 1940, Nicolas; bud pointed; flowers crimson shaded scarlet, open, large, dbl.; foliage glossy; strong stems; vigorous, bushy, open growth; [Royal Red × Johanniszauber]; int. by J&P

Flambée F, or, 1954, Mallerin, C.; flowers medium, 25-30 petals, borne in clusters of 5-6; foliage reddish to bronze; upright, bushy growth; int. by EFR; Gold Medal, Bagatelle, 1952

Flambo HT, or, Kordes; int. in 1993

Flamboyance – See **Christopher Columbus**, HT

Flamboyant Pol, mr, 1931, Turbat; flowers bright scarlet, aging to crimson-carmine, large, dbl., borne in clusters; foliage glossy; dwarf growth

Flamboyant F, mr, Croix, P.; flowers bright red; vigorous growth; [Holstein × Incendie]

Flamboyante HGal, mr, before 1815, Descemet

Flamboyante HGal, m, about 1820, Godefroy; flowers bluish dark purple, center crimson, small to medium, full

Flamboyante B, mr, 1852, Vivant-Faivre; flowers bright crimson, medium, full

Flame HMult, op, 1912, Turner; flowers bright salmon-pink, semi-dbl., borne in large clusters; foliage dark, glossy; very vigorous, compact growth; [Crimson Rambler × unknown]

Flame Bouquet Min, or, 1999, Laver, Keith G.; flowers brilliant orange-red, very long lasting, 2½-3 in., full, borne mostly singly, no fragrance; foliage medium size, medium green, semi-glossy; few prickles; upright, medium (12 in.) growth; int. by Springwood Roses, 1999

Flame Dance – See **Flammentanz**, HEg

Flame Dancer F, ob, 1986, Harkness; flowers orange, red reverse, medium, dbl., cupped, moderate fragrance; foliage dense; prickles large; medium, bushy growth; [Orange Sensation × Alison Wheatcroft]; int. by Mason, 1976

Flame of Fantasy HT, rb, J&P; flowers medium, dark velvet red with silver reverse; recurrent; healthy, medium growth; int. in 2001

Flame of Fire HT, ob, 1917, McGredy; flowers orange-flame, open, large, dbl.; bushy growth; Gold Medal, NRS, 1916

Flame of Love HT, mr, 1950, Hieatt; flowers single

Flame of the East – See **Plamya Vostoka**, F

Flameburst F, dr, 1961, Brownell, H.C.; bud pointed; flowers crimson, center yellow, 2 in., single, borne in clusters, slight fragrance; foliage dark, glossy; very vigorous growth; PP2304; [Nearly Wild × unnamed Hybrid Tea seedling]

Flameche F, or

Flameglo Min, yb, 1982, Williams, Ernest D.; flowers deep yellow to orange-red, reverse deep yellow, small, dbl., slight fragrance; foliage small, dark, glossy; upright, bushy growth; PP5176; [Starburst × Over the Rainbow]; int. by Mini-Roses, 1981

Flamenco F, lp, 1960, McGredy, Sam IV; flowers light salmon-pink, large, 21 petals, borne in clusters; foliage dark; [Cinnabar × Spartan]; int. by McGredy & Son, 1960

Flamenco LCl, mp, Poulsen; flowers medium pink, 10-15 cm., 25 petals, old-fashioned, no fragrance; foliage dark; growth bushy, 200-300 cm.; PP12468; int. as Northern Lights, Poulsen Roser, 1998

Flamenco F, yb, Zary, Keith; int. by Bear Creek Gardens

Flamenco HT, yb; int. by K & M Nursery, 2004

Flamendr HT, dp, Urban, J.; flowers large, dbl.; int. in 1969

Flames 'n' Sparks HT, rb, Taschner; int. in 1995

Flametta Min, mp

Flamina F, my, 1964, Mondial Roses; bud pointed, flushed red; flowers golden yellow, large, dbl.; foliage clear green; very vigorous, upright, bushy growth; [(Faust × Peace) × seedling]

Flaminaire HT, ob, 1960, Dorieux; bud globular; flowers orange-flame, medium, semi-dbl.; foliage dark, glossy; vigorous, bushy growth; [Eclipse × Independence]; int. by Léon Pin, 1960

Flaming MinFl, ob, Olesen; flowers dbl., borne mostly solitary, slight fragrance; foliage dark green, glossy; growth bushy, low (40-60 cm.); PP14390; int. by Poulsen Roser, 2001

Flaming Arrow F, or, 1965, Schwartz, Ernest W.; bud long, pointed; flowers bright orange-red, medium, dbl.; foliage glossy; vigorous, upright growth; [Montezuma × Nadine]; int. by Wyant, 1965

Flaming Beauty HT, rb, 1979, Winchel, Joseph F.; flowers yellow and red-orange, 4 in., 35 petals, high-centered, slight fragrance; foliage matte, green; bushy growth; [First Prize × Piccadilly]; int. by Kimbrew-Walter Roses; Silver Medal, ARC TG, 1979

Flaming Heart F, pb, Umsawasdi, Dr. Theera; flowers creamy yellow with pink and reddish edge, medium, full, borne mostly solitary, slight fragrance; foliage medium size, dark green, semi-glossy; few prickles; medium, bushy, spreading growth; [Libby × seedling]; int. in 1995

Flaming June Pol, or, 1931, Cutbush; flowers bright orange-scarlet; vigorous growth

Flaming Peace HT, rb, 1965, McGredy, Sam IV; bud large, ovoid; flowers bright medium red, reverse straw-yellow veined red, large, dbl., high-centered, borne singly on long stems; foliage abundant, large, dark green, glossy, leathery; vigorous, full, rounded growth; PP2745; [sport of Peace]; int. by General Bionomics, 1966

Flaming Potluck Min, or, 1995, Laver, Keith G.; flowers flaming orange-scarlet, deeper center, medium, full, borne mostly singly; foliage medium size, dark green, semi-glossy; some prickles; medium (30-40 cm.), upright, bushy growth; int. by Springwood Roses, 1994

Flaming Rosamini Min, mr, deRuiter; int. in 1987

Flaming Ruby F, dr, 1963, Hennessey; flowers deep ruby-red, 3 in., 60 petals, borne in clusters; foliage dark, reddish green, small; vigorous growth; [((Eva × Eva) × Guinee) × Guinee]

Flaming Star S, dr, Barni, V.; flowers flaming red, semi-dbl., borne in clusters; recurrent; foliage dark green, abundant; spreading, low (2 ft.) growth; int. by Rose Barni, 1993

Flaming Sunset HT, ob, 1948, Eddie; flowers deep orange, reverse lighter; foliage light bronze; [sport of McGredy's Sunset]

Flaming Sunset, Climbing Cl HT, ob, 1956, Mattock

Flaming Torch F, op; int. in 1999

Flamingo HT, dp, 1929, Dickson, A.; flowers bright geranium-red to rosy cerise, dbl., high-centered, spiraled; vigorous growth; Gold Medal, NRS, 1927

Flamingo HRg, mp, 1956, Howard, F.H.; bud pointed; flowers rich pink, large, 5 petals, cupped, borne in clusters; recurrent bloom; foliage glossy, gray-green; vigorous (3 ft.) growth; [*R. rugosa* × White Wings]; int. by Wayside Gardens Co.

Flamingo F, mp, 1958, Buyl Frères; flowers rose; long, strong stems; very vigorous growth

Flamingo F, op, 1961, Horstmann; bud long, pointed; flowers deep scarlet-pink, open, 30 petals, borne in clusters; vigorous, upright growth

Flamingo HT, lp, 1979, Kordes, W.; bud large, long, pointed; flowers large, 24 petals, high-centered, borne singly, moderate fragrance; foliage matte, green; numerous prickles; vigorous, upright, bushy growth; PP5575; [seedling × Lady Like]; int. by Kordes, 1978

Flamingo HT, pb, 1985, Herholdt, J.A.; flowers light pink, silvery reverse, large, 35 petals, cupped, moderate fragrance; foliage medium green, semi-glossy; upright growth; [seedling × seedling]; int. in 1981

Flamingo MinFl, mp, Olesen; flowers dbl., 25-30 petals, borne mostly solitary, slight fragrance; foliage medium green, semi-glossy; growth bushy, low (40-60 cm.); int. by Poulsen Roser, 1999

Flamingo HT, mp, Kordes; int. by W. Kordes Söhne, 2002

Flamingo Meidiland S, mp, Meilland; flowers medium, semi-dbl., borne in clusters, no fragrance; modest growth; int. in 1990

Flamingo Queen Gr, dp, 1973, Chan; flowers deep pink; [sport of Queen Elizabeth]; int. by Canadian Ornamental Plant Foundation, 1972

Flammèche F, ob, 1959, Combe; flowers bright orange, medium, dbl., borne in clusters; bushy, vigorous (2 ft.) growth

Flammenmeer – See **Shalom**, F

Flammenrose HT, ob, 1921, Türke; bud striped orange and yellow; flowers bright orange-yellow, medium, 16 petals; [Mrs Joseph Hill × Mme Edouard Herriot]; int. by Kiese

Flammenspiel S, mp, 1975, Kordes; bud ovoid; flowers salmon-pink, dbl.; foliage large, leathery, dark; vigorous, upright growth; [Peer Gynt × seedling]; int. by Horstmann, 1974

Flammentanz HEg, mr, 1955, Kordes' Söhne, W.; flowers crimson, 9 cm., dbl., cupped, borne in clusters, moderate fragrance; non-recurrent; foliage dark, leathery, matte; very vigorous (10-15 ft.) growth; [*R. rubiginosa* hybrid × *R. kordesii*]; ADR, 1952

Flammentour S, mr, Meilland

Flammette – See **Crimson Gem**, Min

Flanders Field F, dp, 1991, Horner, Heather M.; bud ovoid; flowers light red aging slightly lighter, medium, semi-dbl., urn-shaped, loose, borne usually singly or in sprays of 5-9, slight fragrance; foliage medium size, medium green, semi-glossy; medium to tall, upright growth; [Prominent × Southampton]

Flandria Pol, mr, 1966, Delforge; bud ovoid; flowers open, semi-dbl.; foliage dark, glossy; bushy growth

Flapper F, lp, 1998, Bennett, Frank David; flowers light pink, slightly curled petals, 3 in., 5-7 petals, borne in small clusters; foliage medium size, dark green, semi-glossy; prickles few, medium sized, straight; compact, medium (5 ft.) growth; [sport of Permanent Wave]

Flash LCl, rb, 1938, Hatton; bud ovoid, yellow suffused scarlet; flowers orange-scarlet, reverse and center yellow, 4 in., dbl., cupped; long blooming season; foliage leathery, glossy, bronze; pillar (6-8 ft.), compact growth; [Rosella × Margaret McGredy]; int. by C-P; Gold Medal, Rome, 1939

Flash – See **Rosemary Gandy**, F

Flash S, lp, 1986, Lens, Louis; flowers 1½ in., 22 petals, borne in clusters of 3-50; foliage small, dark; prickles hooked, green; bushy, spreading growth; [*R. multiflora nana* × seedling]; int. in 1984

Flash F, ob, Barni; flowers brilliant coral-orange deepening to red-vermilion, 5-6 cm., dbl., high-centered, moderate fragrance; foliage medium size, bronze green; vigorous (2-3 ft.) growth; [Rita Levi Montalcini × seedling]; int. by Rose Barni, 2000

Flash Baccara HT, dp, Meilland; flowers hot fuchsia pink, full, high-centered; greenhouse rose; int. by Meilland Intl, 2004

Flash Meidiland S, dp, Meilland; flowers medium, strong deep pink, single, borne in clusters; bushy (3 ft.) growth; int. in 1993

Flashback HT, pb, Kordes; flowers pink and cream blend, large, full, high-centered, borne mostly singly; recurrent; stems long; florist rose; int. by W. Kordes Söhne, 2005

Flashdance HT, my, 1985, Olesen, Pernille & Mogens N.; flowers urn-shaped, large, dbl., borne singly, slight fragrance; foliage large, medium green, semi-glossy; upright growth; [Berolina × seedling]; int. by Poulsen Roser ApS, 1984

Flashdance LCl, dy, Poulsen; flowers deep yellow, small, 25 petals, slight wild rose fragrance; foliage dark; growth broad, bushy, 150-200 cm.; PP15502; int. by Poulsen Roser, 2002

Flashfire LCl, rb, 1992, Little, Lee W.; flowers brilliant coppery red-orange with yellow eye, 3-3½ in., 5 petals, borne in small clusters; foliage large, dark green, glossy, disease-resistant; some prickles; tall (210 cm.), upright, spreading growth; [Altissimo × Playboy]; int. by Oregon Miniature Roses, 1992

Flashlight F, or, 1976, LeGrice; flowers orange-scarlet, 3-3½ in., 28 petals, moderate fragrance; foliage large, bronze; tall growth; [Vesper × seedling]; int. in 1974

Flashlight S, or, Bell; flowers cerise-orange-red; free-flowering; spreading, groundcover growth; int. by Bell Roses, 2001

Flauce HT, rb

Flavescens – See **Parks' Yellow Tea-Scented China**, T

Flavescens HSpn, ly; flowers pale lemon, rounded; very hardy; int. by Prior to 1824

Flavia HGal, about 1810, Descemet

Flavia HCh, dr, about 1825, Laffay; flowers dark cherry red, medium, full

Flavia – See **Fleurette**, S

Flavien Budillon T, lp, 1885, Nabonnand; flowers pale flesh, large, globular, intense fragrance; very remontant

Fleet Street HT, dp, 1973, McGredy, Sam IV; flowers deep rose pink, well-formed, 6 in., 40 petals, intense fragrance; foliage large, dark, leathery; [Flaming Peace × Prima Ballerina]; int. by McGredy & Son, 1972

Fleetwood F, ob, 1990, Bridges, Dennis A.; bud pointed; flowers bright orange, reverse lighter, aging darker on outer petals, 32 petals, high-centered, slight fruity fragrance; foliage medium size, dark green, glossy; prickles straight, medium pink; bushy, medium, vigorous growth; [Little Darling × Orangeade]; int. by Bridges Roses, 1990

Flemington F, dp, 2007, Chapman, Bruce; flowers 7 cm., dbl., blooms borne in small clusters; foliage medium size, dark green, glossy; prickles small, hooked, brown, few; growth upright, medium (1¼ m.); garden decoration; [First Prize × Sexy Rexy]; int. by Ross Roses, 2007

Flemington Racecourse – See **Flemington**, F

Flesh-Coloured Noisette – See **Blush Noisette**, N

Flesh Taito F, ob, 1988, Kikuchi, Rikichi; flowers yellow at base to vermilion, reverse orange flushed with pink, 25-30 petals, cupped; foliage medium size, dark green, undulated; prickles ordinary, green; bushy, medium growth; [Masquerade × Matador]; int. in 1989

Fleur Cowles F, ly, 1972, Gregory; flowers cream, center buff, 3 in., 35 petals, moderate spicy fragrance; foliage glossy, dark; [Pink Parfait × unknown]

Fleur d'Amour S, ab, Austin, David; int. in 1998

Fleur de France HT, my, 1944, Gaujard; flowers capucine and yellow, medium, semi-dbl., globular; foliage glossy; vigorous, dwarf growth

Fleur de Peltier HGal, pb, 1824, Roseraie de l'Hay

Fleur de Vénus Ch, w, before 1813, Descemet; flowers flesh white, center light carmine, medium, full, globular; sometimes attributed to Laffay, 1835

Fleurette – See **Blush Boursault**, Bslt

Fleurette S, lp, 1982, Interplant; flowers 2 in., 5 petals, borne in clusters; repeat bloom; foliage medium green, glossy; prickles few, medium; vigorous (to 4 ft.) growth; groundcover; [Yesterday × seedling]; int. in 1978

Fleurop – See **Europa**, F

Fleurs de Pelletier HGal, dp, before 1842, Pelletier; flowers cherry edged slatey red, medium, very dbl.

Flicker F, ab

Fliegerheld Boelcke HT, my, 1920, Schmidt, J.C.; flowers nankeen yellow, shaded reddish-yellow; [Mme Caroline Testout × Sunburst]

Fliegerheld Öhring HT, or, 1919, Kiese; flowers red-orange, medium, dbl.

Flighty F, m, 1969, Trew, C.; bud cherry-red; flowers light mauve, medium, semi-dbl., borne in trusses; foliage dark; free growth; [Orangeade × Sterling Silver]; int. by Basildon Rose Gardens

Flimo F, lp, Poulsen; int. by Poulsen Roser, 1990

Flinders S, pb, 2001, Thomson, George L.; flowers ruffled, mid-pink, small to medium, very full, borne in large clusters, moderate fragrance; foliage medium size, dark green, glossy; prickles medium, hooked, moderate, brown; growth prostrate, medium (½ × 2 m.); groundcover; [Bonica × The Fairy]; int. by Ross Roses, 2001

Flip Flop Min, mp, 2003, Bridges, Dennis; flowers deep coral pink, reverse lighter, 1 in., full, borne in small clusters; foliage medium size, dark green, semi-glossy; prickles small, sharpe curved down, tan, moderate; growth bushy, slightly spreading, medium (20-24 in.); garden decoration; [sport of Ace of Diamonds]; int. by Bridges Roses, 2003

Flipper HT, or, 1978, Gaujard; bud long, pointed; flowers large; foliage large; [Tanagra × John S. Armstrong]; int. in 1973

Flirt F, mr, 1952, Brownell; bud pointed; flowers bright cherry-red, reverse yellow, medium, 35-40 petals, borne in clusters, moderate fragrance; foliage glossy, dark; vigorous, upright growth; [Pink Princess × Shades of Autumn]

Flirt F, mp, Kordes; flowers soft pink, medium, dbl., high-centered, borne mostly singly; recurrent; stems 14 in.; florist rose; int. by W. Kordes Söhne, 1990

Flirt F, dp, Koopmann; flowers bright, hot pink, semi-dbl., shallow cup, borne in large clusters; recurrent; foliage dark green, glossy; medium (100 cm.) growth; [sport of Sommerwind]; int. by W. Kordes Söhne, 2000

Flirt Kordana Min, mp, Kordes; flowers dbl., rosette; container rose; int. by W. Kordes Söhne, 2000

Flirtation HT, pb, 1953, Shepherd; bud pointed; flowers begonia-rose, reverse lemon to deep yellow, 5-6 in., 30 petals, high-centered, moderate fragrance; foliage dark, leathery; strong stems; vigorous, bushy, compact growth; PP1373; [Fiesta × Peace]; int. by Bosley Nursery

Flirtatious F, yb, 2005, Zary, Keith W.; flowers full, borne in large clusters, moderate fragrance; foliage medium size, dark green, glossy; prickles 7-10 mm., hooked downward, greyed-orange, moderate; growth upright, medium (1¼ m.); PP15335; [SunFlare × JACraw]; int. by Jackson & Perkins Wholesale, Inc., 2003

Flirting – See **Flirting Palace**, MinFl

Flirting Palace MinFl, mr, Olesen; bud pointed-ovoid with broadened base; flowers 2 in., full, shallow cup, borne in clusters, slight fragrance; recurrent; foliage dark green, glossy; prickles numerous, 8 mm., concave; bushy, compact (40-60 cm.) growth; PP15821; int. by Poulsen Roser, 2003

Floating Candle HT, ob, Williams, J. B.; flowers orange with peach and gold undertones at petal base, semi-dbl. to dbl., cupped to flat, moderate fragrance; recurrent; growth to 4 ft.; int. by Hortico, Inc., 2006

Floating Cloud – See **Ukigumo**, F

Flocon de Neige Ch, w, 1898, Lille; flowers pure white, small, very full, borne in large pyramidal clusters; recurrent; growth to 2 ft.; sometimes classed as Pol

Flon D, mr, 1845, Vibert; flowers bright red; very free bloom, occasionally repeated

Flor de Torino 61 HT, w, 1961, Moreira da Silva; flowers white edged violet-pink; [Monte Carlo × Michele Meilland]

Flora – See **Flore**, HSem

Flora HT, op, 1957, Maarse, G.; flowers pink tinted salmon, large, dbl.; vigorous, upright growth; [Independence × Charlotte Armstrong]

Flora Bama Min, rb, 1996, Taylor, Franklin; flowers medium red blending to cream center, cream reverse, large, full, borne mostly singly; foliage medium size, dark green, semi-glossy; few prickles; medium (24 in.), upright, spreading growth; [Party Girl × Poker Chip]; int. by Taylor's Roses, 1997

Flora Danica HT, ob, Poulsen Roser APS; flowers 10-15 cm., 25 petals, borne one to a stem, slight fragrance; foliage reddish green; growth bushy, 60-100 cm.; PP12465; int. by Poulsen Roser, 1996

Flora MacLeod LCl, lp, 1971, MacLeod; flowers pale rose-pink, 4½ in., 50 petals, intense fragrance; non-recurrent; foliage large, medium green, matte; vigorous growth; [New Dawn × Shot Silk, Climbing]

Flora McIvor HEg, pb, 1894, Penzance; flowers rosy pink, veined, white center, yellow stamens, small, single to semi-dbl.; summer bloom; foliage very fragrant (and flowers); vigorous growth; [*R. rubiginosa* × HP or B]; int. by Keynes, Williams & Co.

Flora Mitten – See **Miss Flora Mitten**, LCl

Flora Romantica – See **Mon Jardin et Ma Maison**, LCl

Florabelle F, op, 1964, Schwartz, Ernest W.; flowers soft salmon-pink, large, 33 petals, globular; foliage soft; vigorous, bushy growth; [Ma Perkins × seedling]; int. by Wyant

Floradora F, or, 1944, Tantau; bud globular; flowers cinnabar-red, 2 in., 25 petals, cupped, borne in sprays of 6-12, slight fragrance; foliage leathery, glossy; upright, bushy growth; [Baby Chateau × *R. roxburghii*]; int. by C-P

Floradora, Climbing Cl F, or, 1951, Shamburger, P.; int. by Shamburger Rose Nursery

Floral Choice F, ab, Fryer, Gareth; int. in 1982

Floral Dance Cl HT, or, 1955, Homan; flowers orange-cerise; very vigorous, climbing growth; [Souv de Mme Boullet, Climbing × Crimson Glory]; int. by Roseglen Nursery

Floral Fairy Tale F, ab, 2006, W. Kordes' Söhne; flowers soft apricot, fading to pink, 6-7 cm., full, old-fashioned, borne in trusses, moderate, sweetish fragrance; foliage medium size, dark green, dense; bushy, medium (70 cm.) growth; int. by NewFlora

Floralie T, w, 1838, Coquereau; flowers flesh white, medium, cupped

Floralies Valenciennoises LCl, mr, 1955, Dorieux; bud long, pointed; flowers currant-red, large, semi-dbl.; vigorous growth; [Matador × Soliel d'Orient]; int. by Pin

Floranje F, or; flowers 3 in., 23 petals, flat; foliage dense dark green; strong grower growth; [*R. fedtschenkoana* × Burghausen]; int. by RvS-Melle, 1990; Golden Rose of Courtrai, 1990

Floranne Min, my, 1996, Pratt, Florence; flowers medium yellow, fades in sun to white, color better in partial shade, large, single; foliage medium size, medium green, semi-glossy; some prickles; upright (30 cm.) growth; [sport of Crazy Dottie]

Flore HSem, m, about 1830, Jacques; bud crimson; flowers lilac-pink, center deeper, 6-7 cm., dbl., semi-globular, borne in small, loose clusters, moderate musk fragrance; seasonal bloom; [(*R. sempervirens* × *R. arvensis*) × Parson's Pink]; int. by Lévêque

Flore Berthelot Pol, my, 1921, Turbat; flowers clear lemon-yellow, passing to white, borne in clusters

Flore Magno – See **Foliacée**, C, before 1808

Flore Pallido – See **Vilmorin**, M

Flore Pleno – See **Plena**, A

Floréal Pol, pb, 1923, Turbat; flowers flesh and rose-pink, dbl.; [Orléans Rose × Yvonne Rabier]

Floréal HT, op, 1944, Gaujard; bud pointed; flowers coral-pink tinted yellow, medium, dbl., cupped; foliage dark, glossy; vigorous growth

Florence HT, lp, 1921, Paul, W.; flowers silvery pink

Florence HT, w, 1961, Dorieux; bud long; flowers pure white, large; int. by Pin

Florence F, lp, Kordes; int. in 1987

Florence Arthaud F, op, Adam; int. in 2003

Florence Chenoweth HT, yb, 1918, Chenoweth; flowers yellow, shaded coral-red; [sport of Mme Edouard Herriot]

Florence Delattre S, m, Guillot-Massad; flowers Parma violet with pale yellow center, full, rounded; growth to 5 ft.; int. by Roseraies Guillot, 1997

Florence Ducher B, mp, Ducher; flowers clear pink, large, dbl., pompon, moderate fragrance; recurrent; growth to 10 ft.; int. by Roseraies Fabien Ducher, 2005

Florence Edith Coulthwaite HT, ly, 1908, Dickson, A.; flowers deep cream, stippled with bright rose, large, dbl., moderate fragrance; foliage deep green, glossy

Florence Edna HT, lp, 1985, Owen, Fred; [sport of Princesse]

Florence Forrester HT, w, 1914, McGredy; flowers white tinged lemon, large, dbl.; Gold Medal, NRS, 1913

Florence Haswell Veitch Cl HT, dr, 1911, Paul, W.; flowers bright scarlet, shaded black, large, dbl.; vigorous growth; [Mme Emile Metz × Victor Hugo]

Florence L. Izzard HT, dy, 1923, McGredy; bud pointed; flowers bright deep golden yellow, large, dbl., high-centered; foliage dark, bronze, leathery, glossy; very vigorous, bushy growth

Florence Lorraine F, ab, 1974, Middlebrooks; bud ovoid; flowers dark apricot, large, very dbl., high-centered, moderate fragrance; foliage glossy, dark, leathery, wrinkled; very vigorous, upright, bushy growth; [Royal Highness × (Hawaii × Helen Traubel)]; int. by Ellesmere Nursery, 1973

Florence Lydia S, ab, 1999, Jones, L.J.; flowers apricot with tint of pink, fading to cream, 2 in., borne in large clusters; foliage medium size, medium green, glossy; prickles moderate; upright, tall (6 ft.) growth; [Burma Star × Admiral Rodney]

Florence Mary HT, dy, 1964, Morse; flowers deep yellow-ochre, well-formed, large; bushy growth; [sport of Doreen]

Florence Mary Morse F, mr, 1951, Kordes; flowers copper-scarlet, 3 in., 15 petals, borne in large trusses; foliage dark, glossy; [Baby Chateau × Magnifica]

Florence Mary Morse, Climbing Cl F, mr

Florence Mayer HT, w, 1998, Singer, Steven; flowers white and pink blend, reverse white, 4-6 in., very dbl., high-centered, borne mostly singly; foliage medium size, medium green, semi-glossy; prickles moderate, large, hooked downward; upright, tall growth; exhibition; [Great Scott × Headliner]; int. by Wisconsin Roses, 1998

Florence Nightingale S, w, 1990, Gandy, Douglas L.; bud pointed; flowers glowing white, flushed buff, reverse tinged pink, aging to white, 32 petals, moderate spicy fragrance; foliage medium size, medium green, semi-glossy; prickles very pointed, fawn; spreading, medium growth; hips rounded, green; [Morgengruss × seedling]; int. by Gandy Roses, Ltd., 1989

Florence Paul HP, mr, 1886, Paul, W.; flowers scarlet-crimson, shaded with rose, petals recurved, large, full

Florence Pemberton HT, w, 1903, Dickson, A.; flowers creamy white, suffused pink, large, dbl., high-centered; foliage rich green, leathery; vigorous growth

Florence Rambler HWich, lp

Florence Russ HT, Russ

Florentia HT, ob, 1941, Giacomasso; flowers deep orange, well-shaped, large; vigorous, bushy, compact growth; [Julien Potin × unnamed variety]; Gold Medal, Rome, 1940

Florentina F, pb, 1938, Leenders, M.; flowers hydrangea-pink, reverse rose-red, large, single; foliage leathery, dark; long stems; very vigorous growth; [seedling × Permanent Wave]

Florentina HT, dr, 1976, Kordes; bud large, long, pointed; flowers dark blood red, dbl., high-centered, moderate fragrance; foliage leathery, dark green; vigorous growth; [Liebeszauber × Brandenberg]; int. by Horstmann, 1973; ADR, 1974

Florescence F, ob; flowers dbl., high-centered, moderate fragrance; foliage glossy

Florescent Fuschia Gr, mr, 2001, Coiner, Jim; flowers medium red with white stripe on reverse, medium, dbl., borne in large clusters, no fragrance; foliage medium size, dark green, glossy; prickles small, angular, moderate; growth spreading, medium (40 in.); garden decorative; [seedling × seedling]; int. by Coiner Nursery, 2001

Florett F, op, GPG Bad Langensalza; flowers large, dbl.; int. in 1983

Florex HT, op, 1927, Geiger; bud pointed; flowers deep coral-salmon, suffused orange-carmine, large, dbl., high-centered; foliage leathery, glossy, dark; long stems; very vigorous growth; [Mme Butterfly × Premier]; int. by A.N. Pierson

Flori F, ob

Floriade Gr, ob, 1963, van der Schilden; bud urn shaped; flowers bright orange-scarlet, 4 in., dbl., high-centered to open; long, strong stems; vigorous growth; PP2109; [sport of Montezuma]; int. by Armstrong Nursery, 1963

Florian – See **Tender Night**, F

Florian, Climbing – See **Tender Night, Climbing**, Cl F

Floribunda Pol, lp, 1885, Dubreuil; flowers pale rose, medium, very dbl., borne in large clusters, moderate fragrance

Floricel HT, or, 1957, Dot, Pedro; bud pointed; flowers red and salmon, large, 25 petals, high-centered; foliage dark, glossy; strong stems; upright, compact growth; [Carito MacMahon × Luis Brinas]

Florida – See **Blush Boursault**, Bslt

Florida – See **Top Notch**, HT

Florida F, my, Select; int. by Terra Nigra, 2003

Florida International Min, ab, 1997, Fox, Tillie; flowers medium, 30-35 petals, high-centered, borne mostly singly; foliage medium size, medium green, semi-glossy; upright, spreading, medium to tall (1½-2 ft.) growth; exhibition; [Pierrine × (Loving Touch × seedling)]

Florida Red HT, mr, 1964, Hennessey; flowers rich red, 5 in., 60 petals; vigorous growth

Florida Sun F, my, 1997, Giles, Diann; flowers small, very dbl., borne in small clusters; foliage small, medium green, glossy; compact (2½-3ft.) growth; [Sun Flare × select pollen]; int. by Giles Rose Nursery

Florida von Scharbeutz F, ob, 1957, Kordes, R.; flowers orange-yellow shaded coppery, very large, dbl., high-centered, borne in large clusters; foliage dark, glossy; vigorous, bushy growth; [Golden Scepter × (Munchen × Peace)]

Florimel F, mp, 1959, Fryers Nursery, Ltd.; flowers silvery pink to deep rose-pink, well-formed, borne in clusters; foliage glossy; vigorous growth; [Pinocchio × seedling]; int. in 1958

Florinda Norman Thompson HT, pb, 1920, Dickson, A.; flowers delicate rose on lemon, base deeper, dbl.

Florine HT, Gaujard; int. in 1981

Florita MinFl, dp, Barni, V.; int. in 1994

Florizel HT, ab, RvS-Melle; flowers 36 petals, flat; growth strong

Floron HT, ab, 1948, Camprubi, C.; flowers Indian yellow-orange, inside lighter, very large, dbl., high-centered, slight fragrance; upright growth; [Comtesse Vandal × Pilar Landecho]

Florrie Joyce F, dp, Riethmuller; flowers cherry-pink, 43 petals, borne in large clusters; bushy growth; [Gartendirektor Otto Linne × Borderer]

Flossie F, mp, 1997, Horner, Colin P.; flowers small, dbl., borne in large clusters, moderate fragrance; foliage small, medium green, semi-glossy; some prickles; upright, medium (3 ft.) growth; [Coral Reef × (seedling × Lichtkonigin Lucia)]; int. by Warley Rose Gardens, Ltd.

Flower Basket – See **Hanakago**, F

Flower Basket Min, rb, 1995, McCann, Sean; flowers handpainted carmine red with pink stripes, fades to white with dark red, dbl., borne mostly singly, moderate fragrance; foliage small, medium green, semi-glossy; numerous prickles; bushy, very low growth; [Rose Gilardi × Ain't Misbehavin']; int. by Justice Miniature Roses, 1996

Flower Carpet S, dp, 1989, Noack, Werner; bud globular; flowers deep pink, reverse lighter, small, profuse, 15 petals, cupped, borne in sprays; foliage small, dark green, glossy, disease-resistant; prickles crooked, dark; vigorous, hardy, low, spreading growth; hips globular, small, light red; PP7282; [Immensee × Amanda]; int. by Pan-Am Northwest, Inc., 1990; Gold Medal, The Hague, 1990, Gold Medal, Glasgow, 1993

Flower Carpet Gold – See **Flower Carpet Yellow**, S

Flower Carpet Red – See **Heidefeuer**, F

Flower Carpet Yellow S, dy, Noack; flowers bright yellow, 1½ in., dbl., loose, borne in clusters, slight fragrance; good repeat; upright (2 ft.) growth; PP13869; int. in 2003

Flower Child Min, op, 1995, Horner, Heather M.; flowers salmon pink, medium, dbl.; foliage small, medium green, semi-glossy; compact, tall (40 cm.) growth; [Penelope Keith × Gold Bunny]; int. by Warley Rose Gardens, 1997

Flower Festival F, pb; int. by Burston Nurseries, 2006

Flower Garland – See **Guirlande Fleurie**, LCl

Flower Girl – See **Sea Pearl**, F

Flower Girl S, lp, 1999, Fryer, Gareth; bud short, ovoid; flowers soft pink fading to light pink centers, 1-1½ in., 8-15 petals, borne in very large clusters, slightly pendulous, slight apple fragrance; foliage medium size, light green, matte; few prickles; long, slender, arching stems; spreading, bushy, medium (4-5 ft.) growth; PP13268; [Amruda × Fairy Snow]; int. by Weeks Roses, 2000

Flower Haze – See **Hana-Gasumi**, F

Flower of Fairfield HMult, mr, 1909, Ludorf; flowers bright crimson red, 3 cm., semi-dbl., no fragrance; sometimes recurrent bloom; [sport of Crimson Rambler]; int. by H. Schultheis

Flower Parasol – See **Ehigasa**, F

Flower Power F, mp, Kordes; flowers clear salmon-pink, medium, open, borne in clusters, intense sweet fragrance; continuous bloom; foliage bronzy green, turning dark green, glossy; neat, vigorous, rounded-off (5-6 ft.) growth; int. in 1995

Flower Power MinFl, ob, Fryer, Gareth; flowers peachy-salmon, dbl., high-centered, moderate spicy fragrance; recurrent; upright (3 ft) growth; int. by Fryer's Roses, 1998

Flower Show – See **Ginger Rogers**, HT

Flower Show HT, rb, 1980, Bees; bud ovoid, pointed; flowers scarlet, yellow reverse, 25 petals, borne 3-4 per cluster, moderate fragrance; foliage mid-green, semi-matte; prickles dark red; vigorous, upright growth; [Fragrant Cloud × Tropicana]

Flower World HT, or, 1979, Warriner, William A.; bud pointed, oval; flowers 4 in., 20-30 petals, high-centered; foliage dark, leathery; tall growth; PP4576; [Baccará × South Seas]; int. by Flower World of America, 1980

Flower-Of-The-Month HT, mp, Lone Star Nursery; bud large, long, pointed; flowers full, 35-40 petals, borne mostly singly, moderate fragrance; foliage dark green, glossy; growth very vigorous, upright, compact (3 ft.); [sport of Etoile de Hollande]; int. by Michigan Bulb Company, 1963

Fluffly Ruffles – See **Fluffy Ruffles**, F

Fluffy Min, w, 1984, Interplant; flowers white, shaded creamy pink, small, 15 petals, borne in clusters; foliage dark, glossy; prickles few, medium; groundcover; spreading growth; [seedling × Nozomi]

Fluffy Cloud MinFl, w, 2007, Tolmasoff, Jan & William; flowers semi-dbl., borne in large clusters; foliage medium size, dark green, semi-glossy, disease-resistant; prickles small, dark red, moderate; growth bushy, short (20-24 in.); borders, containers, cutting; [unknown × unknown]; int. by Russian River Rose Company, 2004

Fluffy Ruffles F, pb, 1935, H&S; flowers silver-pink, reverse deeper rose, semi-dbl., cupped, borne in clusters; foliage leathery; vigorous growth; [Miss Rowena Thom × seedling]; int. by Dreer

Fluorescent F, mr, 1986, Delbard; flowers medium, 33 petals, cupped, no fragrance; glossy foliage; vigorous, bushy, branching growth; [Zambra × ((DELtorche × Tropicana) × (Alain × Souv. de J. Chabert))]; int. in 1977

Fluorette F, or, 1979, Lens, Louis; bud pointed; flowers salmon-orange, 3-3½ in., 22 petals, cupped, slight fragrance; vigorous, upright, bushy growth; [(Panache × Soprano) × Coloranja]; int. in 1971

Flush o' Dawn HT, lp, 1900, Walsh; flowers light pink changing to white, large, dbl.; vigorous, upright growth; [Margaret Dickson × Mme de Sombreuil]

Flushing Meadow HT, rb, Dorieux; int. in 1988

Flutterbye S, yb, 1999, Carruth, Tom; flowers multicolor yellow, coral, orange, tangerine, pink, 1½-2 in., 5-9 petals, borne in large clusters, moderate spice fragrance; foliage medium size, dark green, glossy; prickles moderate; very large, rounded, fountainous growth; PP9715; [Playboy × (*R. soulieana derivative* × Sunsprite)]; int. by Weeks Roses, 1996

Flying Colors Min, rb, 1983, Saville, F. Harmon; flowers red and yellow blend, aging to pink and white, micro-mini, semi-dbl., slight fragrance; foliage medium green, semi-glossy; upright, bushy growth; [(Yellow Jewel × Tamango) × Sheri Anne]; int. by Nor'East Min. Roses, 1983

Flying Colours LCl, dp, 1922, Clark, A.; flowers deep cherry pink, white at base, lighter reverse, large, single to semi-dbl.; foliage light, leathery, glossy; very vigorous, compact growth; ruled extinct ARA 1983; hybrid gigantea; int. by Hazlewood Bros.

Flying Doctor HT, or; int. by Carmel Rose Farm, 2005

Flying Tata HT, dr, 1984, Hardikar, Dr. M.N.; bud ovoid; flowers 45 petals, high-centered, borne singly, moderate fragrance; foliage medium size, dark, glossy; vigorous, upright growth; [Scarlet Knight × Cynosure]; int. in 1983

Foc de Tabara F, mr, Wagner, S.; bud small, ovoid; flowers velvety red, 33 petals, cupped, slight fragrance; foliage medium green, leathery, glossy; [Paprika × Coup de Foudre]; int. by Res. Stn. f. Horticulture, Cluj, 1970

Focus HMsk, lp, 1986, Lens, Louis; flowers small, 20 petals, borne in large clusters, intense fragrance; recurrent bloom; foliage small, dark; prickles hooked, brownish-green; spreading growth; [Marie Pavie × seedling]; int. by Louis Lens, 1984

Focus Gr, op, Noack, Werner; bud rounded, orange-red; flowers salmon-orange, 8-9 cm., dbl., high-centered; recurrent; foliage dark green, very glossy; upright, bushy (70 cm.) growth; int. by Noack's Rosen, 1997

Foggy Day Min, w, 2000, Justice, Jerry G.; flowers white, reverse ivory to white, medium size, dbl., high-centered, borne mostly singly, no fragrance; quick repeat; foliage small, medium green, semi-glossy; prickles moderate; compact, medium (14-18 in.) growth; [Kiss 'n' Tell × unknown]; int. by Justice Miniature Roses, 2000

Foliacée C, mp, before 1808, from Holland; sepals foliaceous, lanceolate; flowers light rose, very large, dbl., globular, borne mostly solitary; often showing proliferation

Foliacée C, dp, about 1810, Descemet; flowers very large, full, globular

Folie de Bonaparte D, mr, about 1810, from Belgium

Folie d'Espagne F, yb, 1965, Soenderhousen; flowers yellow, orange and scarlet, 2 in., 20 petals, flat, borne in clusters; foliage dark, glossy

Folies-Bergère HT, yb, 1948, Gaujard; flowers yellow shaded coppery, large, dbl.; foliage leathery, light green; very vigorous, erect growth; [Souv. de Claudius Pernet × seedling]

Folio Courtisane – See **Folle Courtisane**, HT

Folio Variegata – See **York and Lancaster**, D

Folk Dance Min, m, 1993, Bell, Judy G.; flowers medium, full, borne mostly singly, slight fragrance; foliage small, dark green, glossy; few prickles; bushy (41 cm.) growth; [Dale's Sunrise × Angel Face]; int. by Michigan Mini Roses, 1994

Folk Song S, pb, 1964, Von Abrams; flowers light pink, reverse darker, medium, dbl.; recurrent bloom; foliage glossy; vigorous (3-4 ft.), compact growth; int. by Edmunds Roses

Folkestone F, dr, 1936, Archer; flowers semi-dbl., borne in clusters; foliage dark; bushy, spreading growth

Folklore HT, ob, 1976, Kordes; bud long, pointed; flowers orange, reverse lighter, 4½ in., 44 petals, high-centered, intense fragrance; foliage glossy; very tall and vigorous, upright, bushy growth; [Fragrant Cloud × seedling]; int. by Barni, 1975

Folksinger S, yb, 1985, Buck, Dr. Griffith J.; flowers yellow flushed with dark peach, large, 28 petals, slightly cupped, borne in clusters of 1-15, moderate fragrance; repeat bloom; foliage leathery, glossy, coppery mid-green; prickles awl-like, tan; upright, bushy growth; hardy; [Carefree Beauty × Sunsprite]; int. by Iowa State University, 1984

Folle Courtisane HT, ly, Delbard, Georges; int. in 1996

Folletto F, or, Borgatti, G.; flowers semi-dbl.; int. in 1961

Fond Memories F, pb, McGredy; flowers pale pink, fading to white, edged with pink; medium growth; int. in 1999

Fond Memories Min, ob, Kirkam; flowers ginger-orange, fading to pale apricot, dainty, dbl.; recurrent; foliage glossy; growth to 18 in.; int. in 1999

Fond Thoughts – See **Dornröschenschloss Sababurg**, S

Fondant Cascade F, mp, 1996, Bees; flowers mid-pink fading to pale pink, bright yellow stamens, 1½ in., 26 petals, borne in large clusters, slight fragrance; foliage medium size, medium green, glossy; some prickles; spreading, medium (20 in.) growth; patio, containers; int. by L W Van Geest Farms, Ltd., 1995

Fondly F, lp, 1986, Jelly, Robert G.; flowers medium, 20 petals, high-centered, borne singly and in clusters of 2-4, moderate spicy fragrance; foliage medium size, dark, matte; prickles few, on peduncles; medium, upright growth; hips medium, ovoid, orange-red; PP4983; [seedling × seedling]; int. by E.G. Hill Co., 1985

Fontaine – See **Fountain**, HT

Fontaine Blue – See **Fontainebleu**, HT

Fontaine des Loups HMult, w, Louette, I.; flowers small, white, borne in large clusters, moderate fragrance; non-remontant; large, rambler-type (13-17 ft.) growth; [The Garland × unknown]; int. in 2000

Fontainebleu HT, dp, 1970, Delbard-Chabert; bud long, pointed; flowers magenta-pink, large, dbl., globular, slight fragrance; foliage dark, glossy, leathery; vigorous, bushy growth; [Dr. Albert Schweitzer × (Bayadere × Rome Glory)]

Fontana MinFl, ab, 2001, Bridges, Dennis; flowers 2¼ in., dbl., borne mostly solitary; foliage medium size, dark green, semi-glossy; prickles ¼ in., sharp, straight, moderate; growth upright, medium (3 ft.); garden decorative, exhibition, cutting; [Purple Dawn × select pollen]; int. by Bridges Roses, 2002

Fontanelle HT, my, 1927, E.G. Hill, Co.; flowers lemon-yellow, center gold, very large, dbl.; foliage leathery; vigorous growth; [Souv. de Claudius Pernet × Columbia]

Fontanelle, Climbing Cl HT, my, 1935, Johns

Fontenelle M, mp, 1849, Vibert

Fontenelle HP, mr, 1877, Moreau et Robert; flowers bright red, very large, dbl.; vigorous, growth

Foolish Pleasure MinFl, pb, 2003, Clemons, David; flowers medium to dark pink edge with white center, reverse white, 1½-2 in., full, borne mostly solitary, no fragrance; foliage medium size, dark green, glossy; prickles small, few; growth upright, tall (36-48 in.); exhibition and garden/decorative; [Lynn Anderson × select pollen]; int. by David E. Clemons, 2004

Fool's Gold Min, ob, 1984, Christensen, Jack E.; flowers gold, reverse bronze, well-formed, small, 20 petals, slight fragrance; foliage medium size, dark, semi-glossy; upright growth; [Cricket × Dr. A.J. Verhage]; int. by Armstrong Nursery

Footloose S, dp, 1998, Evers, Hans; Tantau; bud pointed ovoid; flowers 20-25 petals, high-centered, borne in large clusters, no fragrance; recurrent; foliage small, dark green, glossy; prickles moderate, straight; stems strong, 14-18 in.; growth spreading, bushy, medium (3½ ft.); PP11572; [seedling × Rosali 83]

For Ever Yours S, mp, Gear; flowers medium pink, dbl., cupped; low, spreading (80 × 80 cm.) growth; int. in 2001

For Keeps Gr, lp, Hortico; bud light pink; flowers delicate pink with almost-white outer petals, slight fragrance; foliage clean, disease-resistant; int. in 2003

For You – See **Para Ti**, Min

For You HT, mp, Teranishi; int. in 1997

For You F, w, 1999, Yasuda, Yuji; flowers white, deep pink on petal edge, 2½ in., 30 petals; foliage medium green; compact, low (75 cm.) growth; [Majorca × Sweet Memory]; Gold Medal, Japan Rose Club, 1996

For You Dad Min, op, 1995, Jones, Steve; flowers coral, petals reflex to form star, medium, 5 petals, borne mostly singly; foliage medium size, dark green, semi-glossy; some prickles; upright, tall growth; [Heartbreaker × seedling]

For You, With Love F, ob, Fryer; flowers soft orange, large, dbl., borne in clusters of several, moderate fragrance; good repeat; foliage dark green; neat, compact growth; int. by Fryer's Roses, 2004

Forbidden Min, m, 1994, Williams, Ernest D.; flowers medium lavender with dark lavender on edges, medium, full, moderate fragrance; foliage small, dark green, semi-glossy; few prickles; low (14-16 in.), bushy growth; [seedling × Twilight Trail]; int. by Texas Mini Roses, 1994

Fordham Rose HT, dr, 1990, Williams, J. Benjamin; bud pointed; flowers deep maroon-red with deep, black, velvety tones, dbl., urn-shaped, moderate fragrance; foliage large, dark green, semi-glossy, thick, disease-resistant; prickles few, ovoid, curved down, medium, tan; upright, medium growth; [Chrysler Imperial × Josephine Bruce]; int. by Fordham University, 1990

Forest Fire Min, or, 1985, Leon, Charles F., Sr.; flowers medium, dbl.; foliage medium size, medium to dark, semi-glossy; bushy growth; [(Sheri Anne × Starina) × ((Sheri Anne × Persian Princess) × Starina)]

Forest Queen F, dp; int. in 1997

Forever HT, dr, Armstrong; flowers non-fading crimson red, large; int. in 1978

Forever Amber F, ob, 1976, Bees; flowers golden amber, suffused fiery orange, 4 in., 15 petals, flat, intense fragrance; foliage dark, leathery; vigorous growth; [Arthur Bell × Elizabeth of Glamis]; int. in 1975

Forever Eve HT, m, 2002, Bossom, Bill; flowers medium, dbl., borne in small clusters, slight fragrance; foliage medium size, medium green, semi-glossy; prickles pointed, straight, moderate; growth upright, medium (3 ft.); garden decorative; [Silver Jubilee × News]

Forever Free S, w, 1997, Horner, Colin P.; flowers small, full, borne in large clusters; foliage small, medium green, glossy; some prickles; spreading, low (45 cm.) growth; [(Anna Ford × Little Darling) × Sea Foam]; int. by Ludwig's Roses

Forever Friends – See **Johann Strauss**, F

Forever Friends S, w, 2001, Horner, Colin P.; flowers creamy white, 7 cm., dbl., borne in small clusters, moderate fragrance; foliage medium size, dark green, glossy; prickles small, curved, few; growth spreading, medium (130 cm.); garden decorative; int. as The Matsukawa Rose, Keisi Roses, 2003

Forever, Michael Jon Gr, mp, 2001, Jerabek, Paul; flowers medium pink with lighter edge, medium, very full, borne in small clusters, moderate fragrance; foliage medium size, medium green, semi-glossy; prickles curved downwards, moderate; growth upright, medium (4 ft.); garden decorative, cutting; [unknown × unknown]; int. by Freedom Gardens, 2004

Forever Mine Min, ob, 1993, Rennie, Bruce F.; flowers medium, full, slight fragrance; foliage small, medium green, matte; some prickles; medium, bushy growth; [Hap Renshaw × Party Girl]; int. by Rennie Roses International, 1994

Forever Royal F, m, 2001, Cowlishaw, Frank R.; flowers dark purple, reverse lighter purple, 2 in., semi-dbl., borne in large clusters, slight fragrance; foliage medium size, dark green, glossy; prickles ¼ in., curved and hooked, few; growth upright, tall (3½ ft.); garden/decorative; [(International Herald Tribune × seedling) × seedling]; int. by Rearsby Roses, 2001

Forever Scarlet HT, pb, 1986, Epperson, Richard G.; flowers deep pink, reverse lighter, large, 80 petals, high-centered, borne singly, moderate spicy fragrance; prickles bright red; tall, upright growth; globular fruit; [Wini Edmunds × Mister Lincoln]; int. in 1976

Forever Yellow F, dy, Barni; flowers intense, clear, yellow gold; fast, continuous rebloom; compact (40-60 cm.) growth; int. by Rose Barni, 2004

Forever Young Min, pb, 1997, Bridges, Dennis A.; flowers full, 1½ in., very dbl., borne mostly singly; foliage medium size, dark green, semi-glossy; low (12-14 in.), compact growth; [Trickster × select pollen]; int. by Bridges Roses

Forever Young – See **Golden Girls**, F

Forever Young HT, yb, 2004, Burks, Larry; flowers full, borne mostly solitary; foliage medium size, medium green, semi-glossy; prickles average, recurved; growth upright, medium (60 in.); garden decorative; [Voodoo × unknown]; int. in 2004

Forever Yours HT, dr, 1964, Jelly; bud long, pointed; flowers cardinal-red, 4-5 in., 38 petals, high-centered, moderate spicy fragrance; vigorous, upright growth; PP2443; [Yuletide × seedling]; int. by E.G. Hill Co., 1964; John Cook Medal, ARS, 1969

Forever Zaidee HT, mr, 2002, Everitt, Derrick; flowers scarlet red, 10 cm., full, borne mostly solitary or small clusters, slight fragrance; foliage medium size, dark green, semi-glossy; prickles medium, hooked, moderate; growth upright, medium (80-100 cm.); garden decorative; [(L'Oreal Trophy × Edith Holden) × (Mary Sumner × (Silver Jubilee × L'Oreal Trophy))]

Forevermore Min, mr, 1986, Lyon; flowers large, 38 petals, high-centered, borne singly, intense spicy fragrance; foliage medium size, medium green, semi-glossy; prickles few, reddish, small; medium, upright growth; hips globular, medium, orange-red; [seedling × unknown]; int. by M.B. Farm Min. Roses, Inc.

Forez Rose F, mr, 1964, Croix, P.; flowers geranium-red, becoming old-rose, semi-dbl., borne in clusters; vigorous growth; [Sumatra × Antoine Noailly]

Forgotten Dreams HT, mr, 1981, Bracegirdle, Derek T.; bud pointed; flowers cardinal red, 24 petals, borne singly and in trusses of 3-5; foliage medium green, semi-glossy; prickles straight, red-brown; vigorous, bushy growth; [Fragrant Cloud × Teneriffe]; int. by Arthur Higgs Roses

Formby Favourite HT, or, Wright, R. & Sons; flowers orange-scarlet on golden yellow; [sport of McGredy's Sunset]; said to be identical with Flaming Sunset

Formby Show HT, mr, 1987, Dwight, Robert & Sons; flowers medium, full, slight fragrance; foliage medium size, dark green, semi-glossy; upright growth; [Fragrant Cloud × Elida]; int. in 1986

Formosa – See **Bourbon**, HGal

Fornarina HGal, dr, 1826, Vétillart; flowers blackish purple

Fornarina HGal, pb, 1841, Vibert; flowers deep rose, marbled white, medium, full, cupped

Fornarina M, mp, 1862, Moreau et Robert; flowers deep rose, 6-8 cm., full, rosette, flat; some repeat; dwarf growth

Forrest No. 14958 – See ***R. macrophylla glaucescens*** (Hillier)

Forrest No. 15309 – See ***R. macrophylla rubricaulis*** (Hillier)

Forst HT, or, 1937, Krause; flowers fiery scarlet red, well-formed, very large; vigorous growth; [Essence × Fritz Schrodter]

Forstmeisters Heim HSet, mp, 1887, Geschwind, R.; flowers dark pink, tinted purple, silvery pink at center, reverse lighter, medium, dbl., borne in medium clusters, no fragrance; [a Bourbon × a Boursault]

Forsythe HT, dp, 1970, Verbeek; flowers Venetian pink, carmine-rose, 4½-5 in., 45-50 petals, high-centered, intense fragrance; foliage glossy, dark, leathery; upright growth; [Miracle × Dr. A.J. Verhage]

Fort Knox HT, dy, 1956, Howard, A. P.; bud ovoid; flowers clear yellow, 3½-4½ in., 20 petals, intense fragrance; foliage dark, leathery; vigorous, upright, open growth; PP1525; [seedling × Ville de Paris]; int. by H&S, 1956

Fort Vancouver HT, mp, 1957, Swim, H.C.; bud long, pointed; flowers well-formed, 5-6 in., 42 petals, intense damask fragrance; foliage leathery; vigorous growth; [Charlotte Armstrong × Times Square]; int. by Peterson & Dering, 1956

Fortissima Cl Pol, dp, 2000, Lens, Louis; flowers 1 in., single, borne in large clusters, slight fragrance; recurrent; foliage small, dark green, glossy, disease-resistant; few prickles; climbing, upright, spreading, tall (150-250 cm.) growth; [(*R. adenocheata* × Ballerina) × Violet Hood]; int. by Louis Lens NV, 1994

Fortissimo S, mr, GPG Bad Langensalza; flowers large, dbl.; int. in 1974

Fortschritt F, yb, 1933, Kordes; flowers yellow-pink, open, large, semi-dbl., borne in clusters, slight fragrance; foliage glossy, light; vigorous, bushy growth; [Mrs Pierre S. duPont × Gloria Mundi]

Fortuna T, ab, 1902, Paul, W.; flowers apricot, outer petals lightly tinted red, large

Fortuna HT, mp, 1927, Pemberton; flowers rose-pink becoming lighter, many golden anthers, 25 petals, moderate fruity fragrance; dwarf, bushy growth; RULED EXTINCT 12/85; [Lady Pirrie × Nur Mahal]; Gold Medal, NRS, 1927

Fortuna HT, op, 1986, Kordes, W.; flowers medium salmon-pink, large, 30 petals, high-centered, borne singly, moderate fragrance; foliage medium size, medium green, semi-glossy; medium, upright growth; [Sonia × seedling]; int. in 1977

Fortuna F, lp, 2006; flowers soft salmon pink with white center, 4 cm., single, borne in large clusters; foliage small, dark green, glossy, dense; growth bushy, upright (50 cm.); int. by W. Kordes' Söhne, 2002

Fortune HT, yb, 1951, Watkins Roses; flowers gold shaded peach, 4 in., 60 petals; foliage glossy; vigorous growth; RULED EXTINCT 12/85; [sport of Phyllis Gold]

Fortuné Besson – See **Georg Arends**, HP

Fortune Cookie Min, ab, 1995, Saville, F. Harmon; flowers apricot blend, small, dbl., borne singly and in small clusters, no fragrance; foliage small, medium green, semi-glossy; no prickles; medium (16-18 in.), upright, compact growth; [Baby Katie × Mazurka]; int. by Nor'East Miniature Roses, 1996

Fortune Teller HT, m, 1993, Warriner, William A. & Zary, Keith W.; flowers deep mauve/purple, 3-3½ in., full, borne mostly singly, intense fragrance; foliage large, dark green, semi-glossy; some prickles; upright, spreading (150-160 cm.) growth; [seedling × Heirloom]; int. by Bear Creek Gardens, 1993

Fortuneana – See **Fortuniana**, Misc OGR

Fortunée Besson – See **Mme Fortuné Besson**, HP

Fortunella Min, op, Barni, V.; flowers orange pink, dbl.; recurrent; growth to 30-35 cm.; int. by Rose Barni, 1999

Fortune's Double Yellow Misc OGR, yb, 1845; flowers salmon-yellow, outside tinged red, 7-8 cm., dbl., loose, borne in small clusters, moderate sweet fragrance; non-recurrent; discovered in a garden in Ningpo, China, by Robert Fortune; similar to the Noisettes in certain characteristics

Fortune's Five-colored Rose T, w, 1844, Fortune; bud red-tinged; flowers creamy white tinged with pale blush, fading to white, large, dbl.; foliage light green; vigorous growth

Fortuniana Misc OGR, w, 1840; flowers blush white, 6 cm., dbl.; foliage dark green, glossy; prickles few, short, thick; climbing growth; [supposedly *R. banksiae* × *R. laevigata*]

Forty-niner HT, rb, 1949, Swim, H.C.; bud long, pointed; flowers medium red, reverse yellow, 3½-4 in., 33 petals; foliage leathery, glossy, dark; vigorous, upright, compact growth; [Contrast × Charlotte Armstrong]; int. by Armstrong Nursery; Gold Medal, Portland, 1947

Forty-niner, Climbing Cl HT, rb, 1952, Moffet; flowers crimson, reverse yellow, large; int. by Armstrong Nursery

Forum Pol, mr, 1969, Delforge; flowers bright red, open, large, dbl.; foliage light green, glossy; vigorous, upright growth; [Veronique × (Independence × unknown)]

Forum HT, my, McGredy; int. in 2001

Forward HT, my, 1962, LeGrice; flowers clear primrose-yellow, large, dbl.; upright growth; [Ethel Sanday × Peace]

Forward March HT, mp, 1934, Wolfe; bud pointed, bright old-rose; flowers bright rose-pink, becoming lighter, large, dbl.; foliage dark, bronze, leathery, glossy; long stems; very vigorous, bushy growth; [sport of Better Times]

Fosse Way HT, mp, 1980, Langdale, G.W.T.; bud long; flowers rose pink, paler reverse, 38 petals, high-centered, borne singly and several to a cluster; foliage matte, light green; prickles hooked; vigorous, tall, upright growth; [Colour Wonder × Prima Ballerina]

Foster's Melbourne Cup – See **Mount Hood**, HT

Foster's Wellington Cup – See **Mount Hood**, HT

Foucheaux HGal, mr, before 1846; flowers velvety carmine, medium, full

Foundation – See **Aphrodite**, HT

Founder's Dream S, my, Williams, J.B.; flowers bright yellow, medium, dbl., cabbage-like, moderate fragrance; recurrent; foliage dark green; growth to 4 ft.; int. by Hortico, Inc., 2005

Founder's Pride Min, pb, 1991, Williams, Michael C.; bud pointed; flowers deep pink, white center, mostly white reverse, aging deep pink to strawberry red, large, 24 petals, high-centered, borne mostly singly, slight spicy fragrance; foliage large, dark green, semi-glossy; upright growth; [seedling × Party Girl]; int. by The Rose Garden & Mini Rose Nursery, 1990

Fountain HT, mr, 1971, Tantau, Math.; flowers crimson, 5 in., 35 petals, cupped, intense fragrance; foliage dark, glossy; int. by Wheatcroft Bros., 1970; Gold Medal, RNRS, 1971, President's International Trophy, RNRS, 1971, ADR, 1971

Fountain of Beauty HT, ab, 1975, Golik; bud ovoid; flowers creamy to salmon, 3-4 in., 100 petals; foliage leathery; moderate growth; [seedling × Colour Wonder]; int. by Dynarose, 1974

Fountain Square HT, w, 1985, Humenick, Muriel F.; flowers clear white, 5-5½ in., 25-30 petals, high-centered, borne singly; foliage large, dark green, semi-glossy; tall growth; PP6805; [sport of Pristine]; int. by Fountain Square, Inc., 1986

Four Cheers HT, ob, 1989, Stoddard, Louis; bud ovoid; flowers soft orange with yellow center, medium, 30 petals, high-centered, urn-shaped, borne usually singly, slight fragrance; foliage medium size, medium green, glossy, smooth, leathery; prickles falcate, moderate, stout, maroon to ivory; spreading, medium growth; hips globular, medium, orange; [Daisy Mae × First Prize]

Four Inch Heels S, dr, 2003, Starnes, John A. Jr.; flowers burgundy, reverse magenta pink, 4 in., very full, borne mostly solitary, intense fragrance; early summer; foliage medium size, medium green, matte; prickles moderate, cat-claw, green to brown, moderate; growth upright, short; [Great Western × Othello]; int. by John A. Starnes Jr., 2003

Fourth of July LCl, rb, 1999, Carruth, Tom; flowers velvety red and white striped, ruffled, 4-4½ in., 10-16 petals, borne in medium to large clusters, moderate apple fragrance; reliable repeat; foliage large, deep green, glossy; prickles moderate; climbing, tall (10 ft.) growth; PP11518; [Roller Coaster × Altissimo]; int. by Weeks Roses, 1999

Fox-Trot – See **Augusta Luise**, S

Foxfire HT, mr, 1990, Stoddard, Louis; bud pointed; flowers 30 petals, high-centered, borne singly; foliage medium size, medium green, glossy; prickles straight, green; upright, tall growth; [seedling × First Prize]; int. in 1991

Foxi – See **Buffalo Gal**, HRg

Foxi Pavement – See **Buffalo Gal**, HRg

Foxtrot F, ob, 1997, Brown, Ted; flowers medium, single, borne mostly singly; foliage medium size, burgundy turning dark green, glossy; spreading, low (1ft.) growth; [Esprit × Stretch Johnson]

Foxy S, yb, Peden, R.

Foxy Lady Min, op, 1980, Christensen, Jack E.; bud ovoid, pointed; flowers salmon and creamy blend, imbricated, 1½ in., 25 petals; foliage small; tall, vigorous, bushy growth; PP4762; [Gingersnap × Magic Carrousel]; int. by Armstrong Nursery

Foxy Pavement – See **Buffalo Gal**, HRg

Fr. Lad. Rieger HT, mr, 1939, Böhm, J.; flowers large, dbl.

Fragezeichen HWich, mp, 1910, Böttner; flowers shining pink, 8 cm., 25 petals, globular, borne in small clusters, no fragrance; foliage large, glossy; vigorous growth; very hardy; [Dorothy Perkins × Marie Baumann]

Fragola HT, mr, Croix, P.; int. about 1980

Fragrance HT, dr, 1924, Chaplin Bros.; flowers deep crimson, high pointed, large, dbl.; vigorous growth; [Hoosier Beauty × George Dickson]

Fragrance HT, dp, 1965, Lammerts, Dr. Walter; bud long, pointed; flowers carmine to rose-madder, large, dbl., high-centered, intense fragrance; foliage bronze, leathery; vigorous, tall, compact growth; PP2493; [Charlotte Armstrong × Merry Widow]; int. by Germain's, 1964

Fragrant Air F, rb, 1977, Pearce, C.A.; flowers red changing to magenta-pink, 2½ in., 20 petals; foliage dark; int. by Limes Rose Nursery

Fragrant Alizée – See **Reflets de Saint Malo**, HT

Fragrant Apricot F, ab, 1998, Zary, Dr. Keith W.; bud pointed, oval, apricot blend; flowers light apricot, copper tinted, light coral reverse, 4 in., full, borne in large clusters, slight musk fragrance; foliage large, dark green, glossy; prickles moderate; compact, medium (3 ft.) growth; PP11485; [Impatient × Amber Queen]; int. by Bear Creek Gardens, Inc., 1999

Fragrant Beauty S, dp, 1950, Jacobus; bud ovoid; flowers carmine, large, 22 petals, cupped, intense spicy fragrance; profuse, repeated bloom; foliage glossy; very vigorous (4-5 ft.), upright, compact growth; [(Pharisaer × Conrad Ferdinand Meyer) × Crimson Glory]; int. by B&A

Fragrant Beauty HT, mr, Ghosh; flowers large, bright scarlet crimson, well formed, moderate fragrance; int. in 1980

Fragrant Bouquet HT, lp, 1922, H&S; flowers shell-pink, base yellow, large, 30-35 petals, intense fragrance

Fragrant Carpet Min, dp, 1997, Brown, Ted; flowers medium, dbl., borne in small clusters, intense fragrance; foliage medium size, dark green, semi-glossy; spreading (2 × 5 ft.)growth; [seedling × seedling]

Fragrant Charm HT, mr, 1973, Kordes, R.; bud ovoid; flowers rose-red, large, dbl., high-centered, intense fragrance; foliage light, soft; moderate, upright growth; [Prima Ballerina × Kaiserin Farah]; int. by McGredy & Son

Fragrant Charm 84 – See **Royal William**, HT

Fragrant Cloud HT, or, 1967, Tantau, Math.; bud ovoid; flowers coral-red becoming geranium-red, well-formed, 5 in., 28-35 petals, high-centered, borne mostly singly, intense damask-fruity-spicy-citrus-sharp fragrance; foliage dark, glossy; prickles moderate; vigorous, upright growth; PP2574; [seedling × Prima Ballerina]; int. by J&P, 1968; James Alexander Gamble Fragrance Medal, ARS, 1969, President's International Trophy, NRS, 1964, Hall of Fame, WFRS, 1981, Gold Medal, Portland, 1963

Fragrant Cloud, Climbing Cl HT, or, 1974, Collin, W.C.; flowers orange vermilion, large, strong fragrance; [sport of Fragrant Cloud]; int. by W.H. Collin & Sons

Fragrant Delight F, op, 1977, Wisbech Plant Co.; flowers light orange-salmon, reverse deeper, 3 in., 22 petals, intense fragrance; foliage glossy, reddish; [Chanelle × Whisky Mac]; int. in 1978; James Mason Medal, ARS, 1988, Gold Medal, ARS, 1988, Edland Fragrance Medal, ARS, 1976

Fragrant Dream HT, ab, 1989, Dickson, Patrick; flowers apricot blended orange, large, 20 petals, intense fragrance; foliage large, medium green, glossy; upright growth; [(Eurorose × Typhoon) × Bonfire]; int. by Dickson Nurseries, Ltd., 1989

Fragrant Fantasy HT, ab, 1992, Marciel, Stanley G. & Jeanne A.; flowers 3-3½ in., dbl., borne mostly singly, intense fragrance; foliage medium size, dark green, matte; few prickles; medium (3-4 ft.), upright growth; [unnamed seedling 80227-20 × unnamed seedling 82249-1]; int. by DeVor Nurseries, Inc.

Fragrant Glory HT, dp, 1950, Cobley; bud dark red; flowers deep cyclamen-pink, 6 in., 36 petals, high-centered; strong stems; vigorous growth; [Phyllis Gold × Crimson Glory]

Fragrant Gold HT, dy, 1983, Tantau, Math.; flowers large, semi-dbl., moderate fragrance; foliage medium size, dark, glossy; upright growth; int. in 1981

Fragrant Hour HT, op, 1973, McGredy, Sam IV; flowers bronze-pink, high-pointed, 4½ in., 35 petals, intense fragrance; foliage light; [Arthur Bell × (Spartan × Grand Gala)]; Gold Medal, Belfast, 1975

Fragrant Keepsake HT, yb, 2005, Zary, Keith W.; flowers yellow-pink blend, 12-13 cm., full, borne mostly solitary, intense fragrance; foliage large, dark green, glossy; prickles 8 mm., straight, greyed-green, few; growth upright, vigorous, medium (180 cm.); PP15773; [French Perfume × Sunbright]; int. by Jackson & Perkins Wholesale, Inc., 2004

Fragrant Lace HT, pb, 1998, Zary, Dr. Keith W.; flowers cream and lavender pink with cream and light yellow reverse, 5-5½ in., very dbl., borne mostly singly, intense fragrance; foliage large, dark green, glossy; prickles moderate; upright growth; PP11138; [seedling × Cherry Jubilee]; int. by Bear Creek Gardens, 1998

Fragrant Lady – See **Perfume Beauty**, HT

Fragrant Lady HT, mp, 1991, Perry, Anthony; bud ovoid; flowers medium, semi-dbl., cupped, urn-shaped, borne usually singly, intense fruity fragrance; foliage medium size, dark green, semi-glossy; upright, medium growth; [Queen Elizabeth × Broadway]; int. by Co-Operative Rose Growers, 1991

Fragrant Lavendar – See **Velvet Mist**, HT

Fragrant Lavender Simplicity S, m, 2007, Zary, Keith W.; flowers light lavender, 3½ in., full, borne in large clusters; foliage medium size, dark green, glossy; prickles 8-10 mm., hooked downward, greyed-orange, moderate; growth upright, tall (4-5 ft.); [seedling × seedling]; int. by Jackson & Perkins Wholesale, Inc., 2006

Fragrant Love HT, mr, 1981, Barni; bud globular, pointed; flowers medium purplish red, 45 petals, cupped, borne 1-3 per cluster, intense fragrance; foliage large, deep green, matte; prickles curved reddish; upright growth; [Chrysler Imperial × seedling]; int. by Rose Barni-Pistoia, 1979

Fragrant Masterpiece S, lp, Clements, John; flowers blush pink, 4-5 in., 100 petals, intense sweet, fruity/lilac/rose fragrance; blooms continuously; 4 × 3 ft. growth; resembles 'Maiden's Blush', but larger; int. by Heirloom, 2002

Fragrant Mauve HT, m, Dey, S. C.; flowers large, purple, intense fragrance; int. in 1999

Fragrant Memories – See **Sebastian Kneipp**, HT

Fragrant Memory – See **Jadis**, HT

Fragrant Minijet Min, my, Meilland

Fragrant Mist F, w, 1983, Smith, Edward; flowers well-formed, medium, 35 petals, intense fragrance; foliage medium size, medium green, matte; upright growth; [Elizabeth of Glamis × Jubilee Celebration]; int. in 1984

Fragrant Moon MinFl, my, Rickard, Vernon; flowers medium yellow, lighter at the petal edges, 3 in., semi-dbl., moderate fragrance; foliage dark green, glossy; upright, tall (36 in.) growth; int. by Almost Heaven Roses, 2005

Fragrant Morning Min, my, 1991, Rennie, Bruce F.; flowers small, full, borne mostly singly, intense fragrance; foliage small, light green, semi-glossy; upright (18 in.) growth; [Sunsprite × miniature seedling]; int. by Rennie Roses International, 1991

Fragrant Obsession Min, m, 1995, Rennie, Bruce F.; flowers 1½ in., dbl., borne mostly singly; foliage medium size, medium green, semi-glossy; few prickles; medium (18 in.), upright growth; [Lavonde × Blushing Blue]; int. by Rennie Roses International, 1995

Fragrant Pink Talisman HT, pb, 1938, Moore, Ralph S.; flowers pink shades, slightly larger than Talisman, 18 petals, intense fragrance; [Talisman × unknown]

Fragrant Plum Gr, m, 1990, Christensen, Jack E.; bud long, ovoid; flowers light lavender blushing purple, smoky edges, 4-4½ in., 20-25 petals, high-centered, borne singly and in large clusters, intense fruity fragrance; tall, upright growth; [Shocking Blue × (Blue Nile × (Ivory Tower × Angel Face))]; int. by Armstrong Nurseries, 1990

Fragrant Queen HT, op, Williams, J.B.; flowers coral pink, dbl., high-centered, intense fragrance; int. by Hortico, Inc., 1995

Fragrant Rhapsody HT, m, 1999, Zary, Dr. Keith W.; flowers light lavender blend, small, 20-40 petals, borne mostly singly, intense fragrance; foliage medium size, medium green, glossy; prickles moderate; upright, spreading, medium (4 ft.) growth; PP12072; [Intrigue × seedling]; int. by Bear Creek Gardens, Inc., 1999

Fragrant Star F, my, 1975, Northfield, G. H.; flowers 25-30 petals, borne in trusses; foliage medium size, medium green, matte; growth upright; [Masquerade × Golden Scepter]; int. in 1973

Fragrant Sunrise – See **Hawaiian Fragrant Sunrise**, HT

Fragrant Surprise – See **English Sonnet**, F

Fragrant Treasure – See **Koki**, HT

Fragrant Vision S, mr, 2006, Beales, Amanda; flowers plum red, 8 cm., full, borne in small clusters; foliage medium size, dark green, matte; prickles hooked, moderate; growth bushy, medium (1¼ m.); landscape, containers; [Roundelay × Crimson Glory]; int. by Peter Beales Roses, 2005

Fragrant Wave F, w, 2005, Zary, Keith W.; flowers 8-9 cm., dbl., borne in small clusters, moderate fragrance; foliage large, dark green, glossy; prickles 8-10 mm., hooked downward, greyed-yellow, few; upright, branching, tall (4 ft.) growth; PP16664; [seedling × Vie en Rose]; int. by Jackson & Perkins Wholesale, Inc., 2005

Fraîcheur – See **La Fraîcheur**, HWich

Fraîcheur HT, lp, 1942, Meilland, F.; bud long, pointed; flowers soft pink tinted pearl-white, medium, semi-dbl., cupped; foliage leathery, light green; vigorous, bushy growth; [Joanna Hill × unknown]; int. by A. Meilland

Franca F, pb, 1961, Moreira da Silva; flowers pink and yellow; [Confidence × seedling]

Français F, op, 1951, Mallerin, C.; flowers bright pink tinted orange, semi-dbl., borne in clusters; vigorous growth; [Holstein × Orange Triumph]; int. by EFR

France Bleu F, m, Adam; int. in 2004

France de Berville S, dp, Eve; flowers deep pink, single to semi-dbl., flat; non-recurrent; bushy, compact (5-6 ft.) growth; hips luminous red, already colored in July; int. by Andre Eve, 2001

France et Russie HT, dp, 1900, Bégault-Pigné; flowers carmine pink, edged silver, large, very full; [La France × unknown]

France Info S, yb, Delbard; flowers yellow, bordered with carmine, very full, moderate fruity, spicy fragrance; vigorous (80 cm.) growth; int. by Georges Delbard SA, 2002

France Inter HT, mr, 1969, Delbard; flowers magenta-red, ovoid, 4-5 in., 35-45 petals; [(Rome Glory × La Vaudoise) × Divine]; int. by Trioreau

France Libre HT, ob, 1991; flowers nasturtium orange and coppery, yellow and gold reverse, large, 25-30 petals, cupped, slight fragrance; foliage dark green, glossy; upright growth; [(Zambra × Orange Sensation) × (seedling × seedling)]; int. by Delbard & Chabert, 1990

Frances Ashton HT, mp, 1937, DePuy; bud pointed; flowers carmine, stamens wine-colored, large, 5 petals; foliage leathery; vigorous growth; [Lady Battersea × Hawlmark Crimson]; int. by Stocking

Frances Bloxam HP, op, 1892, Paul, G.; flowers salmon pink, medium, dbl.; sometimes classed as HCh

Frances E. Willard T, w, 1899, Good & Reese; flowers white with greenish tints, camellia-like, large, moderate fragrance; growth tall, almost climbing; [Marie Guillot × Coquette de Lyon]

Frances Gaunt HT, ab, 1918, Dickson, A.; flowers apricot to salmon-yellow, large, semi-dbl., cupped; foliage glossy; vigorous, branching growth; Gold Medal, Bagatelle, 1920

Frances Gaunt, Climbing Cl HT, ab, 1934, Cazzaniga, F. G.

Frances Louise Gr, ob, 2002, Everitt, Derrick; flowers rich salmon pink, cream reverse, medium, full, borne in small clusters, moderate fragrance; foliage medium size, medium green, semi-glossy; prickles medium, slightly hooked, moderate; growth upright, medium to tall (1 m.); garden decorative; [Golden Future × ((Mary Sumner × (L'Oreal Trophy × Edith Holden)) × ((Mary Sumner × (Korp × Southampton)) × Edith Holden))]

Frances Neale HT, mr, 1994, Kirkham, Gordon Wilson; flowers medium red, moderately large, 3-3½ in., dbl., borne in small clusters; foliage large, dark green, semi-glossy; few prickles; low, bushy growth; [Invincible × Red Dandy]; int. in 1995

Frances Perry F, w, 1995, Bossom, W.E.; flowers 7+ cm., full, borne in small clusters, moderate fragrance; foliage medium size, medium green, semi-glossy; some prickles; low, bushy growth; [Sexy Rexy × City of London]

Frances Phoebe HT, w, LeGrice; int. in 1979

Francesca HMsk, ab, 1922, Pemberton; flowers copper orange to apricot, medium, single to semi-dbl., borne in large sprays; recurrent bloom; foliage leathery; long stems; vigorous (5-6 ft.) growth; [Danaë × Sunburst]

Francesca de Cuixart – See **F. Cuixart**, HT

Francesch Matheu HT, ob, 1940, Dot, Pedro; bud long, pointed; flowers rich golden orange, large, dbl., cupped; foliage glossy, dark; strong stems; very vigorous, upright growth; [Luis Brinas × Catalonia]

Francesco Dona – See **Himmelsauge**, HSet

Francesco Ingegnoli HMult, rb, 1888, Bernaix; flowers bright carmine red, edged white, semi-dbl.

Francesco La Scola HT, or, 1934, Ketten Bros.; flowers bright orange-red, edged Nilsson pink, large, semi-dbl., slight fragrance; early; foliage holly-green; vigorous growth; [Hortulanus Budde × Cuba]

Francette Giraud F, op, 1961, Arles; flowers bright salmon-pink, dbl., borne in clusters; foliage dark; vigorous growth; [Aloha × (Gloire du Midi × Edith de Martinelli)]

Francfort Agathé HGal, lp, before 1827; bud large, flat; flowers pale pink mixed with white, inner petals concave, 3 in., dbl., flat; Agathe group

Francia HT, Dorieux, Francois; int. in 1982

Francie Simms HT, mp, 1926, Dickson, A.; flowers rose-pink, marked carmine, base buttercup yellow, dbl.

Francine HT, rb, 1961, Kriloff, Michel; bud pointed; flowers crimson, reverse silvery, 6 in., 30-35 petals; foliage glossy; vigorous, bushy growth; int. by Cramphorn's Nursery, 1961

Francine HMsk, w

Francine Austin S, w, 1994, Austin, David; flowers 1-½ in., very dbl., borne in large clusters; foliage small, medium green, semi-glossy; some prickles; groundcover; bushy, spreading (90 cm.) growth; PP8156; [Alister Stella Gray × Ballerina]; int. by David Austin Roses, Ltd., 1988

Francine Contier HT, my, 1979, Lens, Louis; bud long, pointed; flowers canary-yellow, 3½-4½ in., 40-45 petals, high-centered, slight fragrance; foliage glossy, dark; very vigorous growth; [Peer Gynt × Thalia]; int. in 1977

Francine Royneau F, dy, Guillot-Massad; flowers luminous yellow, single; growth to 1 m.; int. by Roseraies Guillot, 2003

Francis HMult, rb, 1908, Fauque et fils; flowers bright red, white center, fading to pale pink, 4-5 cm., single to semi-dbl., borne in clusters of 25-50; foliage large, dark green; [*R. wichurana rubra* × Turner's Crimson Rambler]; sometimes attributed to Barbier

Francis HWich, mp, 1933, Hauser; flowers rose-pink, dbl.; [*R. wichuraiana* hybrid × Crimson Rambler]

Francis B. Hayes B, mr, 1892, May; flowers scarlet

Francis Blaise S, pb, Guillot-Massad; flowers dark pink changing to bright yellow, full, cupped, moderate fragrance; int. by Roseraies Guillot, 2000

Francis Dubreuil T, dr, 1894, Dubreuil; bud long; flowers velvety crimson, medium, moderate sweet fragrance

Francis E. Lester HMsk, w, 1946, Lester Rose Gardens; flowers white edged pink, 2 in., single, borne in clusters of 25-30, strong fruity fragrance; infrequent repeat; very vigorous (8-10 ft.) growth; very hardy; [Kathleen × unknown]

Francis King HT, dy

Francis Moreau HT, ob

Francis Perry F, w; int. by Burston Nurseries, 2005

Francis Scott Key HT, pb, 1913, Cook, J.W.; flowers deep pink, reverse lighter, very large, dbl., high-centered; foliage dark, leathery, glossy; long, strong stems; very vigorous growth; [Radiance × seedling]

Francis Scott Key, Climbing Cl HT, pb

Francisca Krüger – See **Mlle Franziska Krüger**, T

Francisca Pries T, pb, 1888, Pries/Ketten Bros.; flowers pink striped salmon, medium, full, cupped, moderate fragrance; growth vigorous

Francisco Curbera HT, pb, 1923, Dot, Pedro; flowers salmon-pink and yellow, well-formed, very dbl.; vigorous growth

Francisque Barillot HP, mr, 1873, Damaizin; flowers cherry red with scarlet reflections, shaded darker, large, full, globular

Francita HT, dp, 1967, Dervaes, Dr Coninck; flowers light red, medium, very dbl., slight fragrance; foliage dark; [((Dame Edith Helen × Baccará) × Baccará) × Comtesse Vandal]

Francofurtensis – See ***R. × francofurtana*** (Muenchhausen), Misc OGR

François Allard HT, yb, 1927, Felberg-Leclerc; flowers creamy yellow, reverse salmon-pink, dbl.; [Mme Mélanie Soupert × Mme Segond Weber]

François Arago HP, dr, 1858, Trouillard; flowers velvety-maroon, shaded with fiery red, medium, dbl.; [sport of Géant des Batailles]

François Bollez – See **Mme François Bolley**, HT

François Coppée HP, dr, 1895, Lédéchaux; flowers dark crimson, large, dbl.; [Victor Verdier × unknown]

François Courtin HP, rb, 1873, Verdier, E.; flowers cherry purple, edged white, reverse pink

François Crousse Cl T, mr, 1900, Guillot, P.; flowers cerise-crimson shaded darker, 10 cm., dbl., globular, moderate fragrance; vigorous growth

François de Salignac M, mp, 1854, Robert; flowers amaranthe, shaded pink, large, full, rosette; vigorous growth

François Dubois HP, dp, 1866, Damaizin; flowers shining pink, aging to red, large, full

François Dubreuil – See **Francis Dubreuil**, T

François Fontaine HP, mr, 1867, Fontaine; flowers fiery red with vermilion, medium, full, globular

François Foucard HWich, my, 1900, Barbier; flowers lemon-yellow, fading to white, 5-6 cm., semi-dbl., quartered, borne in clusters, slight fragrance; very vigorous growth; [L'Idéal × *R. wichurana*]

François Foucquier HGal, dp, before 1885; flowers bright crimson, very large, full

Francois Gaujard HT, dr, Gaujard; flowers dark, velvety red; foliage glossy and healthy; int. in 2002

François Gaulain HP, dr, 1878, Schwartz; flowers deep purplish crimson, large, full; foliage dark green; nearly thornless; growth upright

François Guillot HWich, w, 1907, Barbier; bud long, yellowish-white; flowers milk-white, 8-10 cm., semi-dbl. to dbl., globular, borne singly or in small clusters; foliage dark green, glossy; vigorous (15-18 ft.) growth; [*R. wichurana* × Mme Laurette Messimy]

François Herincq HP, mr, 1878, Verdier, E.; flowers bright poppy red, medium, full, globular, moderate fragrance

François I – See **François Premier**, HP

François Juranville HWich, op, 1906, Barbier; flowers bright salmon-pink, base yellow, quite distinct, 7 cm., semi-dbl., borne in small clusters, moderate fruity fragrance; foliage small, dark green, glossy; very vigorous growth; [*R. wichurana* × Mme Laurette Messimy]

Francois Krige S, dr, Kordes; flowers crimson red, large, very full, quartered, no fragrance; recurrent; strong (5 ft.) growth; int. in 1993

François Lacharme HP, mr, 1861, Verdier

François Laplanche HT, w, 1934, Buatois; flowers flesh-white on yellow ground, veined and edged carmine, large, dbl., cupped; foliage leathery; bushy growth; [Mme Charles Detreaux × Mme Edouard Herriot]

François Levet HP, dp, 1880, Levet, A.; flowers cherry-rose, well-formed; very remontant; foliage light green; prickles short, straight; [Anna de Diesbach × unknown]

François Louvat HP, pb, 1861, Touvais; flowers carmine pink, shaded lilac pink, large, full, globular

François Michelon HP, m, 1871, Levet, A.; flowers deep rose tinged lilac, large, dbl., globular; foliage somewhat wrinkled; upright growth; [La Reine × unknown]

François Olin HP, dp, 1881, Ducher; flowers cerise red marbled with pure white, large, full, camellia-like, borne in small clusters; foliage dark green; numerous prickles; growth upright

François Poisson HWich, ly, 1902, Barbier; bud lemon yellow; flowers pale sulfur-yellow, center shaded orange, passing to white, 4-5 cm., dbl., borne in clusters; foliage dark green, glossy; prickles wide, red; growth upright, vigorous; [*R. wichurana* × William Allen Richardson]

François Premier HP, mr, 1859, Trouillard; [Géant des Batailles × unknown]

Francois Rabelais F, mr, 1998, Selection Meilland; flowers bright red, 2-2½ in., 41 petals, borne in small clusters, slight fragrance; foliage medium size, dark green, glossy; prickles moderate; bushy, medium (3 ft.) growth; [(Tchin-Tchin × Matthias Meilland) × Lilli Marlene]; int. by Conard-Pyle Co., 1996

François Treyve HP, mr, 1866, Liabaud

Françoise Blondeau HT, op, 1938, Mallerin, C.; flowers coral, large, dbl.; foliage dark; very vigorous growth; [Charles P. Kilham × Colette Clément]; int. by H. Guillot

Francoise Drion HMsk, mp, 2000, Lens, Louis; flowers deep pink reverse lighter, 3-4 cm., single, borne in large clusters; recurrent; foliage large, dark green, semi-glossy; few prickles; upright, tall (4-5 ft.) growth; [Ravel × Ballerina]; int. by Louis Lens NV, 1995

Frank Chapman HT, yb, 1937, Cant, F.; flowers yellowish-orange, medium, dbl.

Frank Leddy – See **Frans Leddy**, Pol

Frank Macmillan HT, dr, 1978, Scrivens; flowers crimson-red, 4 in., 26 petals; foliage semi-glossy; moderately vigorous, spreading growth; [Uncle Walter × (Ena Harkness × Fragrant Cloud)]

Frank Michael – See **Heimatmelodie**, F

Frank Naylor S, rb, 1977, Harkness; flowers dark red, yellowish eye, 1½ in., 5 petals, borne several together and in trusses, moderate musky fragrance; foliage small, plum shaded; [((Orange Sensation × Allgold) × ((Little Lady × Lilac Charm) × (Blue Moon × Magenta))) × (((Cläre Grammerstorf × Frühlingsmorgen) × (Little Lady × Lilac Charm)) × ((Blue Moon × Magenta) × (Cläre Grammerstorf × Frühlingsmorgen)))]; int. in 1978

Frank Neave HT, ly, 1928, Morse; flowers pale mustard-yellow, dbl.

Frank Penn HT, pb, 1971, Clayworth; bud long, pointed; flowers cerise, reverse pink, large, dbl.; foliage dark, leathery; very vigorous, upright growth; [Wendy Cussons × Lys Assia]; int. by F. Mason & Son

Frank Reader HT, my, 1927, Verschuren; flowers lemon-yellow, center apricot, fairly, large, dbl., high-centered; strong stems; vigorous growth; [Golden Ophelia × Souv. de H.A. Verschuren]; int. by Dreer

Frank Serpa Gr, op, 1960, Serpa; bud pointed; flowers pink tinted salmon, large, dbl., cupped; foliage leathery, glossy, dark; very vigorous growth; [Pres. Macia × unknown]

Frank W. Dunlop HT, dp, 1920, Dunlop; flowers deep bright rose-pink, large, 45 petals, high-centered; [Mrs Charles E. Russell × Mrs George Shawyer]; int. by Totty

Frank W. Dunlop, Climbing Cl HT, dp, 1933, Dixie Rose Nursery

Frankenland F, or, 1982, Tantau, Math.; bud medium, pointed; flowers brilliant scarlet, 23 petals, high-centered, borne in large clusters, no fragrance; foliage large, dark, semi-glossy; prickles straight, brown-red; bushy, low growth; int. by Tantau Roses, 1978

Frankfort Agathé HGal, dp; flowers cerise

Frankfurt – See ***R. × francofurtana*** (Muenchhausen), Misc OGR

Frankfurt HT, dr, 1909, Böttner; flowers large, full

Frankfurt am Main F, mr, 1963, Boerner; flowers blood-red shaded scarlet, well-formed, 2½-3 in., 25 petals, borne in clusters, slight fragrance; foliage dark; bushy, upright growth; int. by Kordes

Frankie F, pb, 2001, Hastings, Mr. and Mrs. Frank; flowers light mauve with pink edges, deep pink reverse, 4 in., single, borne mostly solitary, slight fragrance; foliage medium size, dark green, semi-glossy; prickles ¼ in., curved down, moderate; growth bushy, medium (4 ft.); garden decorative, exhibition; [Altissimo × unknown]; int. by Wisconsin Roses, 2005

Franklin HT, op, 1918, Pernet-Ducher; flowers salmon, shaded yellowish-salmon, dbl.

Franklin D. Roosevelt HT, mr, 1939, McClung; flowers bright red fading to rose-purple, medium, 26 petals, cupped; foliage glossy, dark; bush and semi-climbing growth; [sport of Betty Uprichard]

Franklin Engelmann F, dr, 1970, Dickson, A.; flowers bright scarlet, pointed, very large, 36 petals, borne in trusses; vigorous growth; [Heidelberg × (Detroiter × seedling)]

Frankly Scarlet F, mr, 2007, Zary, Keith W.; flowers light red, 4 in., dbl., blooms borne in small clusters; foliage medium size, dark green, glossy; prickles 6-8 mm., hooked downward, greyed-orange, moderate; growth compact, medium (3 ft.); [seedling × seedling]; int. by Jackson & Perkins Wholesale, Inc., 2008

Frans Hals S, mp, Williams, J. Benjamin; flowers soft pink, petals have some quilling, single to semi-dbl., flat, moderate fragrance; int. by Hortico Inc, 1997

Frans Leddy Pol, op, 1927, Kersbergen; flowers light orange-red, turning pink, small, dbl.; [sport of Kersbergen]; int. by Van Nes

Frans Post S, ob, J. B. Williams; int. by Hortico, Inc., 2005

Frantisek Valàsek Pol, dr, 1930, Valàsek; flowers small, dbl.

Frantonia Min, ob, Gönewein; flowers orange with yellow eye, semi-dbl., flat, moderate fragrance; recurrent; 30-35 cm. growth; [sport of Little Artist]; int. by Rosen Gönewein, 1996

Franz Deegen HT, my, 1901, Hinner, W.; flowers soft yellow to golden yellow, large, dbl.; [Kaiserin Auguste Viktoria × unknown]

Franz Degen Junion N, w, before 1900; [sport of Maréchal Niel]

Franz Grümmer HT, or, 1927, Maass; flowers coral-red, dbl.; [Mme Abel Chatenay × Château de Clos Vougeot]

Fraser McLay HT, mr, 1974, Dawson, George; bud ovoid; flowers glossy medium red, medium, dbl.; foliage glossy, leathery; bushy growth; [Grand Gala × Suspense]; int. by Neil

Fraser's Pink Musk N, lp, 1818, Fraser; flowers blush, medium, semi-dbl., cupped, borne in large clusters, intense fragrance

Frasquita F, op, Barni; int. by Rose Barni-Pistoia, 1982

Fratelli Ingegnoli HMult, pb, 1889, Bernaix; flowers pink with white

Fraternité F, pb, 1946, Leenders, M.; flowers Neyron rose, reverse pale lilac-rose, 3 in., 25 petals, globular, borne in clusters, slight fragrance; foliage bronze; vigorous growth; [Florentina × World's Fair]; int. by Longley

Fraternity F, m, Dey, S. C.; flowers purple with lilac stripes, borne in large trusses; recurrent; int. in 1987

Frau A. von Brauer HWich, lp, 1913, Lambert, P.; flowers white, aging to pink, 3-4 cm., very dbl., borne in clusters, moderate fragrance; [Farquhar × Schneewittchen]

Frau A. Weidling S, mp, 1930, Vogel, M.; flowers small, semi-dbl.

Frau Ada Rehfeld Pol, pb,]1914, Altmüller; flowers dark flesh pink, center golden, reverse darker, large, full

Frau Adolf Anders HT, 1937, Anders, Adolf

Frau Albert Fischer HWich, w, 1906, Weigand; flowers white with whitish pink, very large, full

Frau Albert Hochstrasser HWich, lp, 1908, Weigand, C.; bud golden yellow; flowers yellow, changing to white, 5-7 cm., dbl., borne in medium clusters, intense fragrance; intermittent repeat; foliage glossy; prickles numerous, very large

Frau Alexander Weiss Pol, yb, 1909, Lambert, P.; flowers light yellow with pink, small, dbl.; [Petite Léonie × Lutea Bicolore]

Frau Anna Lautz HT, mr, 1911, Kiese; flowers large, dbl.

Frau Anna Pasquay Pol, dp, 1909, Walter; flowers deep pink, small, dbl.; [Trier × Mme Norbert Levavasseur]

Frau Anny Beaufays F, mr, 1962, deRuiter; bud ovoid; flowers salmon-red, semi-dbl., borne in clusters; low growth; int. by Beaufays, 1962

Frau Astrid Späth F, dp, 1930, Späth; flowers clear carmine-rose, medium size, semi-dbl.; recurrent; [sport of Lafayette]; possibly synonymous with Direktor Rikala

Frau Astrid Späth, Climbing Cl F, dp, 1935, Lens

Frau Berta Gürtler HMult, lp, 1913, Gurtler; flowers light silky pink, dbl.; int. by P. Lambert

Frau Bertha Kiese HT, my, 1914, Kiese; flowers pure golden yellow, dbl.; [Kaiserin Auguste Viktoria × Undine]

Frau Berthe Kiese – See **Bertha Kiese**, HT

Frau Betty Hartmann HT, pb, 1901, Brauer; flowers flesh pink, aging to salmon with rose

Frau Bürgermeister Kirschstein HT, dp, 1906, Jacobs; flowers medium, semi-dbl.; [Luciole × Mrs W. J. Grant]

Frau Cecilie Walter Pol, ly, 1904, Lambert, P.; flowers small, dbl., intense fragrance; [Aglaia × Kleiner Alfred]

Frau Charlotte Gieseler Pol, dp, 1939, Vogel, M.; flowers medium, dbl.

Frau Dagmar Hartopp – See **Dagmar Hastrup**, HRg

Frau Dagmar Hastrup – See **Dagmar Hastrup**, HRg

Frau Dagmar Hastrup Geel – See **Topaz Jewel**, HRg

Frau Direktor Anni Hartmann HT, ly, 1933, Brada, Dr.; flowers medium, very dbl.

Frau Dr Erreth F, dy, 1915, Geduldig; flowers deep golden yellow, passing to white, dbl., borne in clusters; branching growth; [Gruss an Aachen × Mrs Aaron Ward]

Frau Dr Hooftmann Cl Pol, lp, 1935, Buisman, G. A. H.; flowers large, dbl.

Frau Dr Krüger HT, op, 1919, Kiese; flowers cream-salmon on golden ground; [Baronne Henriette de Loew × Mme Caroline Testout]

Frau Dr Schricker HCh, rb, 1927, Felberg-Leclerc; flowers fiery carmine and coppery-red, large, dbl., intense fragrance; dwarf growth; [Gruss an Teplitz × Souv. de Mme Eugene Verdier]; sometimes classed as B

Frau E. Weigand HT, yb, 1928, Weigand, C.; flowers canary-yellow, large, 70 petals, high-centered; foliage dark, leathery; strong stems; [Mme Caroline Testout × Souv. de Claudius Pernet]; int. by Weigand & H. Schultheis

Frau Eduard Bethge HT, dr, 1930, Felberg-Leclerc; flowers dark crimson and velvety blood-red, large, dbl.; foliage light; [Hadley × Admiral Ward]

Frau Elisabeth Balzer HT, w, 1933, Balzer; flowers white, base orange-yellow, reverse bright flesh-pink, pointed; vigorous growth; [sport of Mrs Henry Morse]

Frau Elisabeth Fisher HFt, dy, 1930, Fisher & Schulz; flowers medium, dbl.

Frau Elisabeth Münch Pol, mr, 1921, Münch & Haufe; flowers scarlet-cherry-red, with deeper reflexes; [sport of Orléans Rose]

Frau Elisabeth Sprenger HT, dy, 1937, Wirtz & Eicke; flowers medium, dbl.

Frau Elisabeth Weigand – See **Frau E. Weigand**, HT

Frau Elise Kreis Pol, mp, 1913, Kreis; flowers bright carmine, 5 cm., borne in large clusters; [seedling or sport of Annchen Muller]

Frau Emma Sasse HT, lp, 1908, Plog; flowers large, dbl.; [Mrs W. J. Grant × Paul Neyron]

Frau Emmy Hammann HT, yb, 1923, Weigand, C.; flowers reddish lemon-yellow shaded sunflower-yellow, dbl.; [Mme Caroline Testout × Mme Hoste]; int. by Hammann

Frau Ernst Fischer HT, op, 1909, Hinner

Frau Eva Schubert HWich, mp, 1937, Tepelmann; flowers small, semi-dbl., borne in tight clusters; remontant

Frau Felberg-Leclerc HT, my, 1921, Felberg-Leclerc; flowers pure golden yellow, medium, dbl., cupped, borne mostly solitary; foliage leathery, bronze-green; [sport of Louise Catherine Breslau]

Frau Felix Tonnar HT, mp, 1924, Leenders, M.; flowers bright rose, base coppery orange, semi-dbl.; [Mme Mélanie Soupert × Mme Annette Aynard]

Frau Fritz Pelzer HT, or, 1927, Leenders, M.; flowers reddish crimson-orange, dbl.; [Mme Edouard Herriot × Edward Mawley]

Frau Geheimrat Dr Staub Cl HT, dr, 1908, Lambert, P.; flowers large, dbl.; [Mrs W. J. Grant × Duke of Edinburgh]

Frau Geheimrat Späth S, lp, 1941, Tepelmann; flowers large, dbl.

Frau Geheimrat Von Boch T, w, 1898, Lambert; bud large, long; flowers cream, with carmine on reverse of outer petals, large, full, intense fragrance; [Princesse Alice de Monaco × Duchesse Marie Salviati]

Frau Georg von Simson HMult, mp, 1909, Walter; flowers rose, fading to white, 5-6 cm., semi-dbl., borne in large clusters, slight fragrance; non-recurrent; nearly thornless; vigorous growth; [Helene × Rosel Dach]

Frau H. Dentler HT, w, 1905, Dentler; flowers glossy porcelain white, striped pink, moderate fragrance; [Mme Caroline Testout × unknown]

Frau Hedwig Koschel Pol, w, 1921, Münch & Haufe; flowers white, slightly shaded yellow, edges tinted rose-pink, dbl.; [sport of Ellen Poulsen]

Frau Hedwig Wagner HT, mp, 1919, Krüger; flowers dbl.; [Enchantress × Mrs W.J. Grant]; int. by Kiese

Frau Helene Kühn HT, w, 1938, Vogel, M.; flowers medium, dbl.

Frau Helene Videnz HMult, lp, 1904, Lambert, P.; flowers salmon pink to medium, 3-4 cm., semi-dbl. to dbl., cupped, borne in medium to large clusters, moderate musky fragrance; few prickles; growth to 3 m.; [(Euphrosyne × Princesse Alice de Monaco) × Louis-Philippe]

Frau Hugo Lauster HT, dy, 1932, Lauster; flowers deep canary-yellow, edged lighter, well-formed, dbl.; vigorous growth; int. by Pfitzer & Dreer

Frau Ida Münch HT, ly, 1919, Beschnidt; flowers light golden yellow, center deeper, dbl.; [Frau Karl Druschki × Billard et Barré]

Frau J. Reiter HT, w, 1904, Welter; flowers pure white, sometimes with coppery tints, very large, very full, cupped; [Mlle Augustine Guinoisseau × (Viscountess Folkestone × Kaiserin Auguste Viktoria)]

Frau Jenny Wienke HT, mr, Berger, W.; flowers large, dbl.; int. in 1958

Frau Karl Brass HT, pb, 1913, Brass & Hartmann; flowers deep pink with butter yellow, center darker yellow, salmon reflections; [sport of Lyon Rose]

Frau Karl Druschki HP, w, 1901, Lambert, P.; bud pointed, tinged carmine-pink; flowers snow-white, center sometimes blush-pink, large, 35 petals, no fragrance; reliably remontant; foliage dark green; vigorous growth; [Merveille de Lyon × Mme Caroline Testout]

Frau Karl Druschki, Climbing Cl HP, w, 1906, Lawrenson; flowers dbl., slight fragrance; [sport of Frau Karl Druschki]

Frau Karl Smid – See **Mme Gustave Metz**, HT

Frau Käte Schmid HMult, mp, 1931, Vogel, M.; flowers bright pink, fading to silvery pink, darker reverse, 7 cm., semi-dbl., cupped, opening flat, borne in clusters of 5-10; foliage light green, glossy; [Fragezeichen × Tausendschön]

Frau Liesel Brauer HWich, mp, 1938, Thönges; flowers semi-dbl., cupped, borne in small to medium clusters, slight fragrance

Frau Lieselotte Weber Pol, 1938, Vogel, M.

Frau Lilla Rautenstrauch HT, w, 1902, Lambert; bud coppery orange; flowers creamy white, apricot-orange in center, large, very full, high-centered; [Mme Caroline Testout × Goldquelle]

Frau Lina Strassheim HMult, op, 1907, Strassheim; flowers reddish salmon-pink, fading to light pink, 3½ cm., semi-dbl., borne in clusters of 5-15; numerous prickles; [Crimson Rambler × unknown]

Frau Lita Rautenstrauch – See **Frau Lilla Rautenstrauch**, HT

Frau Luise Kiese HT, ly, 1921, Kiese; flowers ivory-yellow, sometimes clear yellow, very dbl.

Frau Luise Lindecke HT, dr, 1928, Lindecke; flowers deep claret-red, sometimes crimson, dbl.; [sport of Columbia]; int. by Lindecke & Kordes

Frau Margarete Oppenheim HT, rb, 1928, Felberg-Leclerc; flowers intense carmine-red shaded brick-red and yellow, semi-dbl.; [Hortulanus Budde × Souv. de Claudius Pernet]

Frau Maria Rüdt S, lp, Tagashira, Kazuso; flowers medium-large, dbl.; int. in 1994

Frau Marie Brockhues HT, w, 1913, Brass & Hartmann; flowers pure white, center tinted cherry red; [sport of Mme Segond Weber]

Frau Marie Bromme Pol, dr, 1928, Wirtz & Eicke; flowers bright dark red; [sport of Dr. Kater]

Frau Marie Weinbach HWich, w, 1906, Weigand, C.; flowers dbl., borne in medium clusters, moderate fragrance; foliage dark green, glossy

Frau Martha Schmidt HT, mr, 1923, Kiese; flowers carmine-red, dbl.; [Paula Clegg × Edward Mawley]

Frau Math. Noehl HT, my, 1913, Welter; flowers lemon-yellow, dbl.; [Kaiserin Auguste Viktoria × Mme Ravary]

Frau Mathilde Bätz HT, w, 1929, Felberg-Leclerc; flowers pure white, stamens yellow, dbl.; [seedling × Ophelia]

Frau Mélanie Niedieck HT, dy, 1916, Leenders, M.; flowers vivid lemon-yellow, dbl.; [Mme Jenny Gillemot × Prince de Bulgarie]

Frau Minka Rödiger HT, yb, Berger, W.; flowers yellow to light yellow with orange highlights, large, dbl.; int. in 1959

Frau O. Plegg B, dr, 1909, Nabonnand; flowers medium, dbl., intense fragrance

Frau Oberhofgärtner Schulze Pol, mp, 1909, Lambert, P.; flowers small, dbl.; [Euphrosyne × Mrs W. J. Grant]

Frau Oberhofgärtner Singer HT, pb, 1908, Lambert, P.; flowers soft pink edged white, large, very full, moderate fragrance; [Jules Margottin × Mme Eugenie Boullet]

Frau Oberpräsident von Grothe HT, op, 1920, Löbner; flowers rose-orange streaked carmine; [Richmond × Farbenkonigin]; int. by P. Lambert

Frau Peter Lambert HT, op, 1902, Welter; flowers pink shading to salmon, large, full, moderate fragrance; [(Kaiserin Auguste Viktoria × Mme Caroline Testout) × Mme Abel Chatenay]

Frau Philipp Siesmayer HT, yb, 1908, Lambert; flowers yellow, suffused with pink; [Mme Caroline Testout × Erzherzogin Marie Dorothea]

Frau Professor Baranov Pol, rb, 1947, Vogel, M.; flowers salmon-red, medium, semi-dbl.

Frau Professor Gnau HT, w, 1925, Kiese; flowers creamy white, large, semi-dbl.

Frau Professor Grischko S, mr, 1947, Vogel, M.; flowers medium, semi-dbl.

Frau Robert Türke HT, dr, 1928, Türke; flowers dark crimson, very dbl.; foliage dark, glossy; long stems; vigorous growth; [Hadley × Hugh Dickson]; int. by Teschendorff

Frau Rudolf Schmidt Pol, dr, 1919, Schmidt, R.; flowers dark ruby-red without objectionable blue shades; very dwarf growth; [sport of Jessie]

Frau Sophie Meyerholz S, mp, 1942, Vogel, M.; flowers medium, dbl.

Frau Therese Lang HT, dp, 1910, Welter; flowers large, very dbl.; [Mme Caroline Testout × Johanna Sebus]

Fräulein Oktavia Hesse HWich, ly, 1910, Hesse; flowers yellowish-white, center deeper, 6-7 cm., dbl., borne in small clusters, moderate fragrance; recurrent bloom; foliage glossy, light green; stems flexible, light green; vigorous, climbing growth; [*R. wichurana* × Kaiserin Auguste Viktoria]

Fraxinifolia – See **Turneps**, S

Frazier Annesley HT, dp, 1935, McGredy; bud pointed; flowers carmine, base golden yellow, dbl., high-centered; foliage glossy, bronze; very vigorous growth

Frechdachs Min, yb, Mehring, Bernhard F.; int. in 1998

Freckle Face S, pb, 1976, Buck, Dr. Griffith J.; bud ovoid; flowers light spirea-red, striped dark spirea, 3½-4 in., 23 petals, moderate clove fragrance; foliage coppery, leathery; bushy, spreading growth; [(Vera Dalton × Dornroschen) × ((World's Fair × Floradora) × Applejack)]; int. by Iowa State University, 1975

Freckle Face Min, pb, 2003, Wells, Verlie W.; flowers pink with speckles, reverse white, 1-1½ in., full, borne mostly solitary, slight fragrance; foliage medium size, dark green, semi-glossy; prickles ¼ in., hooked, moderate; growth upright, medium (18-24 in.); garden, exhibition; [seedling × seedling]; int. by Wells Mid-South Roses, 2002

Freckles S, pb, 1976, Buck, Dr. Griffith J.; bud ovoid, pointed to urn-shaped; flowers light scarlet, flushed yellow, 4-4½ in., 28 petals, cupped; foliage dark, coppery, leathery; upright, bushy growth; [Tickled Pink × Country Music]; int. by Iowa State University, 1975

Fred Birch HT, my, 1995, Poole, Lionel; int. by Battersby Roses, 1997

Fred Cramphorn HT, or, 1961, Kriloff, Michel; flowers rose-opal, fringed, 5-6 in., dbl., cupped; foliage dark, glossy; vigorous, upright, bushy growth; PP2258; [Peace × Baccará]; int. by Cramphorn's Nursery, 1961

Fred Edmunds HT, ob, 1943, Meilland, F.; bud long, pointed; flowers coppery orange, 5-5½ in., 25 petals, cupped, intense spicy fragrance; foliage leathery, glossy; bushy, open habit growth; [Duquesa de Peñaranda × Marie-Claire]; int. by C-P; Gold Medal, Portland, 1942

Fred Edmunds, Climbing Cl HT, ob, 1989, Weeks, O.L.; [sport of Fred Edmunds]; int. by Weeks Wholesale Rose Growers, 1977

Fred Fairbrother HT, dp, 1976, Sanday, John; flowers bright cerise, 4-5 in., 40 petals, moderate fragrance; foliage semi-glossy; [(Gavotte × Tropicana) × Fragrant Cloud]; int. in 1974

Fred Gibson HT, ab, 1966, Sanday, John; flowers apricot suffused gold, 5 in., 30 petals; foliage dark; tall, vigorous growth; [Gavotte × Buccaneer]

Fred Hollows Vision F, w; [sport of Mary McKillop]; int. by Stratford's Roses, 1996

Fred Howard HT, yb, 1952, Howard, F.H.; bud long; flowers golden orange shaded pink, 4 in., 55 petals, high-centered, slight fragrance; vigorous, upright growth; [Pearl Harbor × seedling]; int. by H&S

Fred Howard, Climbing Cl HT, yb, 1954, Howard, A.P.; PP1417; int. by H&S

Fred J. Harrison HT, mr, 1924, Dickson, A.; flowers cardinal-red shaded crimson, dbl.; Gold Medal, NRS, 1923

Fred Loads S, or, 1967, Holmes, R.A.; flowers vermilion-orange, 3 in., single, borne in clusters, moderate fragrance; foliage glossy; vigorous, tall growth; [Dorothy Wheatcroft × Orange Sensation]; int. by Fryer's Nursery, Ltd., 1968; Gold Medal, RNRS, 1967

Fred Owen HT, dy, 1985, Owen, Fred; [sport of Jan Guest]

Fred Streeter HMoy, dp, 1951, Jackman; flowers deep

cerise-pink, medium, single, borne in clusters (up to 3); upright, branching growth

Fred Streeter HT, my, 1955, Kordes; bud pointed; flowers clear yellow, 4 in., 48 petals, moderate fragrance; foliage dark; vigorous growth; [Luis Brinas × Golden Scepter]; int. by Wheatcroft Bros.

Fred W. Alesworth – See **F. W. Alesworth**, HT

Fred W. Mee HT, mr, 1960, Mee; flowers scarlet-cerise, 30 petals, high-centered, intense fragrance; vigorous, upright growth; [Karl Herbst × The Doctor]

Fred Walker HT, mp, 1935, McGredy; flowers glowing pink, base coppery orange, large, dbl., high-centered; foliage soft, light; vigorous growth

Fredagh of Bellinchamp – See **Swany River**, HT

Freddie Mercury HT, my, 1994, Stainthorpe, Eric; flowers medium, full, borne mostly singly, moderate fragrance; foliage large, dark green, glossy; some prickles; medium, bushy growth; [sport of Tina Turner]; int. by Battersby Roses, 1994

Freddy F, op, 1990, Pearce, C.A.; bud ovoid; flowers deep coral pink, aging paler, medium, 25 petals, urn-shaped, borne in sprays of 3-21, slight fragrance; foliage medium size, medium green, matte; prickles hooked, medium,red; bushy, even growth; rare fruit; [seedling × seedling]; int. by Rearsby Roses, Ltd., 1989

Fredensborg – See **Canyonlands**, F

Frédéric Bihorel HP, dr, 1865, Damaizin; flowers violet red, center carmine, large, full

Fréderic Chopin HT, ly, Zyla; flowers yellow-ivory, large, full, moderate fragrance; recurrent; growth to 4 ft.

Frédéric Lerr HT, pb, 1950, Sauvageot, H.; flowers carmine-red, reverse lighter, large, dbl., high-centered; foliage bronze; very vigorous growth; [Crimson Glory × (Mrs Pierre S. duPont × Signora)]; int. by Sauvageot

Frederic Mistral HT, lp, 1998, Selection Meilland; bud conical; flowers Venetian pink, reverse suffused rose, 4½ in., 40-45 petals, cupped, borne mostly singly, intense fragrance; good repeat; foliage large, dark green, semi-glossy; prickles moderate; upright, tall, 6 ft. growth; PP10004; [(Perfume Delight × Prima Ballerina) × The McCartney Rose]; int. by Conard-Pyle Co., 1995

Frederic Schneider II HP, dp, 1885, Ludovic; flowers deep pink with red, large, dbl.

Frédéric Soullier rb, 1854, Laffay, M.; flowers carmine-red with purple striping, large, dbl.

Frédéric II de Prusse HCh, m, 1847, Verdier, V.; flowers rich crimson-purple, medium, dbl., moderate fragrance; vigorous growth; sometimes classed as B

Frédéric Wood HP, mr, 1874, Verdier, E.; flowers shining cherry red, shaded poppy red, large, full

Frédéric Worth – See **Mme Charles Frédéric Worth**, HRg

Frederica HT, mr; flowers deep crimson, 5 in., 30 petals; foliage dark, glossy; vigorous growth; int. by About 1953 in England

Fredericia – See **Carmelita**, F

Frederick Keeling HT, op, 2001, Webster, Robert; flowers salmon pink, 4-5 in., very full, borne mostly solitary, moderate fragrance; foliage medium size, dark green, glossy; prickles 8 mm., hooked, moderate; growth bushy, medium (36 in.); bedding; [The Marquess of Bristol × Indian Summer]

Frederick R. M. Undritz – See **Gen. John Pershing**, LCl

Frederick S. Peck LCl, dp, 1938, Brownell; flowers deep grenadine-pink, center more yellow, 4 in., semi-dbl., borne in clusters of 2-8, moderate fragrance; foliage dark green, glossy; slightly arched stems; [Hybrid creeper × Mrs Arthur Curtiss James]

Frederick the Second – See **Frédéric II de Prusse**, HCh

Fredericksbergrosen F, dp, 1985, Poulsen, S.; flowers deep pink, medium, 5 petals, cupped, no fragrance; foliage medium size, medium green, semi-glossy; vigorous, bushy growth; [Orléans Rose × seedling]; int. by Poulsen's Roses, 1942

Frederico Cassio – See **Federico Casas**, HT

Frederik Mey F, op, Eve, A.; flowers coral-pink, dbl., high-centered, borne in clusters of 3-6; recurrent, better in fall; growth to 3 ft.; int. by Andre Eve, 1980

Frederiksborg F, op, Poulsen; flowers 8-10 cm., dbl., no fragrance; growth bushy, 100-150 cm.; PP12557; int. by Poulsen Roser, 1998

Frederyk Chopin – See **Fréderic Chopin**, HT

Fredica S, w, 1978, INRA; bud oval; flowers medium, 5 petals, cupped; thornless; very vigorous, bushy, upright growth; PP4463; [Indica Major × Multiflora Inermis]; used for understock; int. in 1974

Fredrik Hellstrand HRg, pb, 2005, Verghese-Borg, Helena; flowers dark pink at center, lighter towards edges, 8 cm., very full, borne in small clusters; foliage medium size, medium green, semi-glossy; prickles 4 mm., narrow, straight, green, moderate; growth bushy, medium (120 cm.); hedging, specimen; [Louis Bugnet × unknown]; int. in 2005

Free As Air Min, r, 1996, Mehring, Bernhard F.; flowers orange-red/russet with light orange pink reverse, 1½ in., 8-14 petals, no fragrance; foliage medium size, dark green, glossy; few prickles; compact, medium (35 cm.) growth; PPPVRO 5448;; [Anna Ford × Brown Velvet]; int. by Mehring, 1996

Free Gold HT, my, 1948, Brownell; bud long, pointed; flowers yellow, open, large, dbl., high-centered, moderate fragrance; foliage glossy; bushy, dwarf growth; RULED EXTINCT 5/83 ARM; [Pink Princess × Shades of Autumn]

Free Gold – See **Freegold**, Min

Free Spirit Min, ab, 1985, Strawn, Leslie E.; flowers small, 20 petals; foliage small, medium green, semi-glossy; upright growth; PP6188; [Prominent × Gold Pin]; int. by Pixie Treasures Min. Roses, 1984

Free Spirit F, op, Fryer; flowers salmon pink, dbl., globular, borne in clusters; free-flowering; foliage disease-resistant; bushy, speading growth; int. by Fryers Roses, 2006

Freedom LCl, w, 1918, Undritz; flowers white, center yellow, open, 4 in., 75 petals, high-centered, slight fragrance; foliage dark, bronze, glossy; long, strong stems; very vigorous, climbing growth; RULED EXTINCT 3/84 ARM; [Silver Moon × Kaiserin Auguste Viktoria]

Freedom HT, dy, 1984, Dickson, Patrick; flowers chrome yellow, large, 35 petals, high-centered, moderate fragrance; foliage medium size, medium green, glossy; bushy growth; [(Eurorose × Typhoon) × Bright Smile]; int. by Dickson Nurseries, Ltd.; Gold Medal, RNRS, 1983

Freedom USA – See **Spring Hill's Freedom**, S

Freedom's Ring LCl, rb, 1994, Dykstra, Dr. A. Michael; flowers red and white striped, small, semi-dbl., borne in small clusters; foliage medium size, medium green, matte; some prickles; medium, bushy, spreading growth; [Stars 'n' Stripes × Paradise]; int. by Certified Roses, Inc., 1994

Freegold Min, dy, 1983, McGredy, Sam IV; flowers deep yellow, gold reverse, small, 20 petals, high-centered, moderate fragrance; foliage small, light green, semi-glossy; upright growth; PP5850; [Seaspray × Dorola]

Freeleigh HT, my, 1956, LeGrice; flowers buttercup-yellow, well-shaped, small, dbl.; foliage glossy, light green; vigorous growth; [Kingcup × Golden Scepter]

Freemont HT, w, 1994, Bridges, Dennis A.; flowers near white blushed with salmon, 3-3½ in., very dbl., borne mostly singly; foliage large, dark green, semi-glossy; some prickles; tall, upright growth; [Thriller × Tiki]; int. by Bridges Roses, 1994

Freestar HT, or; int. in 2003

Fregate HT, lp, Delbard; flowers large, dbl.; int. in 1979

Freia HT, ab, 1936, Tantau; flowers sun-yellow tinted orange, base orange, open, large, dbl.; foliage leathery, glossy; vigorous, bushy growth; [Ville de Paris × Rev. F. Page-Roberts]

Freia S, lp, Barni; flowers 6-7 cm., semi-dbl., slight fragrance; foliage medium size, light green; growth to 4 ft.; [seedling × Rita Levi Montalcini]; int. by Rose Barni, 1999

Freiamt HT, mp, Huber; flowers rose-pink with tints of salmon, dbl., high-centered, moderate spicy fragrance; foliage matte; strong, upright (70 cm.) growth; int. by Richard Huber AG, 1995

Freiburg II HT, pb, 1917, Krüger; bud long, pointed; flowers silver-rose, reverse bright apricot-pink, large, dbl.; [Dr. G. Kruger × Frau Karl Drucshki]

Freiburg II, Climbing Cl HT, pb, 1958, Lindecke; int. by Kordes & Son, 1953

Freifrau Ida von Schubert HT, dr, 1912, Lambert, P.; flowers dark crimson-red, medium, dbl., moderate fragrance; [Oskar Cordel × Frau Peter Lambert]

Freifrau von Marschall HWich, mp, 1913, Lambert, P.; flowers fresh pink, 3-4 cm., dbl., borne in immense, loose clusters; mid-season bloom; nearly thornless; vigorous (8-12 ft.) growth; [Farquhar × Schneewittchen]

Freiheitsglocke – See **Liberty Bell**, HT

Freiherr von Marschall T, mr, 1903, Lambert, P.; bud pointed; flowers large, dbl.; foliage blood-red when young; vigorous growth; [Princesse Alice de Monaco × Rose d'Evian]

Freisinger Morgenröte S, ob, 2006; flowers orange with yellow reverse and pink edges, 7 cm., semi-dbl., high-centered, borne in large clusters; foliage deep green, glossy; growth wide, tall, 150 cm; int. by W. Kordes' Söhne, 1988

Freja S, mp, Carlsson-Nilsson; flowers pink to salmon, cupped, borne in large clusters; recurrent; vigorous (7-10 ft.) growth; int. in 2001

French Can Can HT, pb, 1956, Buyl Frères; bud well formed; flowers pink, reverse yellow, large, dbl.; vigorous, bushy growth

French Cancan – See **Tourbillon**, F, 1959

French Lace F, w, 1981, Warriner, William A.; bud pointed; flowers ivory, pastel apricot to white, 4½ in., 30-35 petals, high-centered, borne in small clusters, slight fruity fragrance; foliage small, dark; prickles small; bushy growth; PP4848; [Dr. A.J. Verhage × Bridal Pink]; int. by J&P, 1980; Gold Medal, Portland, 1984

French Liberty – See **Innovation Minijet**, Min

French Panarosa S, w, Delbard; int. by Ludwig's Roses, 2004

French Perfume HT, yb, 1993, Suzuki, Seizo; sepals very small, glandular, with soft prickles on reverse; flowers light yellow with rose pink picotee, 5-6½ in., 40-45 petals, borne mostly singly, intense fruity fragrance; foliage large, medium green, purple-red when new, semi-glossy; tall (110-150 cm.), upright, spreading growth; PP8476; [(Todoroki × Montana) × seedling]; int. by Bear Creek Gardens, 1993

French Rose – See ***R. gallica*** (Linnaeus)

French Vanilla Gr, w, 1987, Thomson, R.; flowers white and faint pink, fading white, medium, dbl., high-centered, borne usually singly, moderate fragrance; foliage medium size, dark green, matte; prickles few, moderate, brown; spreading growth; no fruit; [Araby × Royal Highness]; int. in 1984

French Vanilla HT, w; int. in 1999

Frénésie LCl, Combe, M.; flowers deep vermilion, reverse lighter, fading to orange, slight fragrance; int. in 1965

Frensham F, dr, 1946, Norman; flowers deep scarlet, 15 petals, borne in large trusses; vigorous growth; [floribunda seedling × Crimson Glory]; int. by Harkness, 1946;

Gold Medal, NRS, 1943, Gold Medal, ARS, 1955

Frensham, Climbing Cl F, dr, Bennett, J.A.; int. by Pedigree Nursery, 1958

Frensham's Companion F, dp, 1952, Morse; flowers cerise, loosely formed, medium, 18 petals, borne in trusses; very free growth; [sport of Frensham]

Frenzy F, rb, 1971, Meilland; flowers nasturtium-red, reverse yellow, rounded, 2 in., 25 petals, moderate fruity fragrance; foliage matte; vigorous, bushy growth; [(Sarabande × Dany Robin) × Zambra]; int. by URS, 1970

Frére Marie Pierre HP, mp, 1891, Bernaix; flowers China pink fading to blush, 11 cm., very dbl., cupped, borne mostly solitary; growth upright

Fresco F, ob, 1968, deRuiter; flowers orange, reverse golden yellow, well-formed, 3 in., slight fragrance; foliage dark, glossy; vigorous, bushy growth; [Metropole × Orange Sensation]

Fresh Cream HT, w, Kordes; flowers creamy white with hint of apricot in center, dbl., high-centered; strong, medium to tall growth; int. in 1991

Fresh Cream Min, w, Bell; bud slender, pointed buds; flowers creamy white, dbl., high-centered; tall growth; int. by Bell Roses, 1996

Fresh Hit Min, dp, Poulsen; flowers deep pink, large, no fragrance; foliage deep green; wiry stems; vigorous, dense, medium growth; int. in 1990

Fresh Pink Min, lp, 1963, Moore, Ralph S.; bud ovoid; flowers light pink tipped salmon, 25 petals, cupped, borne in clusters, slight fragrance; foliage leathery, glossy; vigorous, bushy growth; PP2525; [(*R. wichurana* × Floradora) × Little Buckaroo]; int. by Blue Ribbon Plant Co., 1962

Fresh Pink Min, mp, 1987, McGredy, Sam IV

Fresh Point LCl, pb, Barni; flowers cream changing to pink as they open and mature, 8 cm., 12-15 petals, borne in clusters; foliage medium to large, dark green; tall (8 ft and up) growth; [Altair × seedling]

Fresh Snow – See **Shin-Setsu**, LCl

Fresh Start Min, mp, 1986, Florac, Marilyn; flowers bright medium pink, dbl., globular, borne usually singly, no fragrance; foliage small, medium green, semi-glossy; prickles small, red; low, bushy growth; [Avandel × Little Chief]; int. by M.B. Farm Min. Roses, Inc.

Freshie – See **Sweetwaters**, HT

Freude – See **Cheer**, F

Freude HT, or, 1974, W. Kordes Söhne; flowers vermilion and gold blend, 4 in., dbl., high-centered; recurrent; foliage dark green, dense, leathery; vigorous, bushy, upright growth; [Fragrant Cloud × Peer Gynt]; int. by Mattock, 1975; ADR, 1975

Freudenfeuer Pol, mr, 1918, Kiese; flowers bright red; moderate growth

Freudentanz F, mr, 1975, Hetzel; bud pointed; flowers bright red, reverse flamed red, medium, intense fragrance; foliage glossy; vigorous, upright, bushy growth; [Fragrant Cloud × Goldmarie]; int. by GAWA, 1973

Freund Pilz HT, mr, 1930, Schildmann; flowers carmine-red, medium, dbl.

Freya S, pb, 1910, Geschwind, R.; flowers single to semi-dbl., borne in small clusters, no fragrance; hybrid canina

Freya HT, dp, 1956, Leenders, M.; flowers carmine-red, large, dbl.; vigorous growth; [seedling × Étoile de Hollande]

Friction Lights F, yb, 1987, Horner, Colin P.; flowers canary-yellow edged cherry-red, large, dbl.; foliage medium size, medium green, semi-glossy; upright growth; [Alexander × Champagne Cocktail]; int. by Battersby Roses, 1987

Friday's Child HT, mr, 1995, Horner, Colin P.; flowers 5 in., full, borne mostly singly, intense fragrance; foliage medium size, medium green, semi-glossy; tall (120 cm.), upright growth; [Spirit of Youth × seedling]; int. by Battersby Roses, 1997

Fridolin Min, yb; flowers yellow with orange edges, orange spreading down the petals as it ages, dbl., cupped, then open, borne in clusters; recurrent

Fridolin Bunnert T, mr, 1888, Bernaix; flowers carmine, shaded vermilion-amaranth, medium, full

Frieda Krause HT, or, 1935, Krause; flowers orange-scarlet-red, large, dbl., high-centered; foliage leathery, dark; very vigorous, bushy growth; [I Zingari × seedling]

Friedlanderiana HGal, mp; flowers bright rose-pink, single; non-recurrent; [*R. gallica* × *R. canina*]

Friedrich Albert Krupp – See **Friedrich Alfred Krupp**, HT

Friedrich Alfred Krupp HT, op, 1903, Welter; flowers yellowish salmon-pink, large, very dbl.

Friedrich Harms – See **Franz Deegen**, HT

Friedrich Heyer S, ob, 1956, Tantau, Math.; flowers bright orange, large, 10 petals, borne in large clusters, moderate fragrance; foliage dark, glossy, leathery; vigorous, upright growth

Friedrich Schwarz HT, dr, 1952, Kordes; flowers crimson, large, 30 petals, cupped; foliage dark; very tall, branching growth; [Poinsettia × (Crimson Glory × Lord Charlemont)]

Friedrich von Schiller HP, dr, 1881, Mietzsch; flowers crimson shaded with violet, medium, very full

Friedrich Wörlein F, dy, 1973, Kordes; bud globular; flowers golden yellow, large, dbl., moderate fragrance; foliage dark; vigorous, upright, bushy growth; [Clare Grammerstorf × Golden Masterpiece]; int. by Wörlein, 1963

Friedricharah – See **Friedrichsruh**, HT

Friedrichsruh HT, dr, 1908, Türke; flowers dark crimson, shaded black, turning blue, open, large, dbl.; foliage dark, glossy; bushy, open growth; [Princesse de Bearn × Francis Dubreuil]

Friend for Life F, pb, 1993, Cocker; flowers pink, medium, 6-14 petals, borne in large clusters; foliage medium size, dark green, glossy; some prickles; medium (2½ ft.), bushy, compact growth; [seedling × (Anne Cocker × Silver Jubilee)]; int. by James Cocker & Sons, 1994

Friend of Heart HT, pb, 1986, Hardikar, Dr. M.N.; flowers large, 30 petals, high-centered, borne singly, slight fragrance; foliage medium size, dark, glossy; prickles deep brown; upright growth; [(Festival Beauty × Scarlet Knight) × (Festival Beauty × Scarlet Knight)]; int. in 1985

Friend of Peace HT, yb, 1987, Hardikar, Dr. M.N.; flowers 20-22 petals, globular, intense fragrance; foliage large, dark green, glossy, leathery; prickles crescent, light brown; upright, open growth; [(Scarlet Knight × Festival Beauty) × Festival Beauty]; int. in 1986

Friendenspark Hiroshima F, dy, Niebourg ?; int. by Hiroshima Bara-en, 1998

Friends Forever S, dp, Lowe; flowers fuchsia pink, old fashioned, full, quartered; recurrent; hips disease resistant (6 ft) growth; int. in 2001

Friends of Benalla Gardens Pol, w, Sutherland; int. in 1996

Friendship HT, dp, 1937, Amling Co.; bud pointed; flowers dark red, semi-dbl., high-centered; foliage glossy; vigorous growth; RULED EXTINCT 9/77; [Templar × Talisman]

Friendship HT, dr, 1938, Dickson, A.; flowers bright strawberry-red, with bright scarlet undertone, very large, dbl.; very vigorous growth; RULED EXTINCT 9/77; Gold Medal, NRS, 1938

Friendship HT, dp, 1978, Lindquist; bud ovoid; flowers deep pink, 5½-6 in., 28 petals, cupped, intense fragrance; foliage large, dark; vigorous, upright growth; PP4284; [Fragrant Cloud × Miss All-American Beauty]; int. by C-P

Friendship Min, pb, 1985, Verschuren, Ted; bud ovoid; flowers pink and white blend, small, 5-6 petals, borne in sprays of 30-50, no fragrance; foliage medium size, light green, semi-glossy; groundcover; spreading, medium growth; very small fruit; [(Swany × Mozart) × Mozart]; int. by H.A. Verschuren, 1981

Friendship F, op, 2001, Horner, Colin P.; flowers orange/pink with light orange reverse, 4½ cm., semi-dbl., borne in large clusters, moderate fragrance; foliage small, medium green, glossy; prickles small, brown, slightly curved, few; growth bushy, medium (80 cm.); garden decorative; int. as Playmate, Ludwig's Roses, 2002

Friendship HT, rb, Meilland; flowers medium red, buttercup yellow reverse, dbl.; greenhouse rose; int. by Meilland Intl, 2004

Friesensöhne S, dy, 1983, Tantau, Math.; bud long, blunt top; flowers yellow-orange, 3½-4 in., 25-30 petals, high-centered, flattens, borne singly and in clusters, very slight fragrance; recurrent; foliage medium size, light, glossy; prickles numerous, long, straight, brown; stems short, strong; vigorous, upright growth; PP5706; [seedling × seedling]; int. by Tantau Roses, 1981

Friesia – See **Sunsprite**, F

Friesia, Climbing – See **Sunsprite, Climbing**, Cl F

Frigg S, m, 1969, Lundstad; flowers small, 15 petals, flat, borne in clusters; free, recurrent boom; foliage small, rich green; low growth; [Schneezwerg × *R. nitida*]

Frileuse Gr, mp, 1985, Poulsen, Niels D.; flowers large, dbl., urn-shaped, slight fragrance; foliage large, light green, glossy; tall, upright, bushy growth; [Queen Elizabeth × Baronesse Manon]; int. by Vilmorin-Andrieux, 1966

Frills HT, op, 1950, Moss; flowers deep salmon-pink becoming lighter, petals scalloped, large; compact, bushy growth

Frillseeker S, mr, George; flowers light red, petals frilled, borne in large clusters; long stems; tall growth; int. by Tasman Bay Roses, 2003

Frilly Dilly MinFl, lp, Cocker; flowers soft pink, medium, dahlia-like, borne in small clusters, no fragrance; compact, very low growth; int. in 1986

Frilly Dilly F, dp, 1987, Murray, Nola; flowers light magenta red, pointed, small, 25 petals, borne in sprays of 5-7, slight fragrance; foliage large, medium green, flat; prickles pointed, brown; upright growth; [Red Lion × Magenta]; int. in 1986

Frimousse F, op, 1959, Vilmorin-Andrieux; flowers orange-pink, base yellow, medium, single, borne in clusters; vigorous, very bushy growth; [Masquerade × unknown]

Friné HT, dr, 1961, Dot, Simon; flowers crimson suffused strawberry-red, well-formed, 35 petals; vigorous growth; [Lila Vidri × (Soraya × Vigoro)]

Frine S, mp, Barni, V.; int. in 1992

Fringette Min, dp, 1964, Moore, Ralph S.; flowers deep pink, white center, small, 25 petals; low (8 in.), compact growth; PP2718; [seedling × Magic Wand]; int. by Sequoia Nursery

Friquet T, mp, 1903, Croibier; flowers bright carmine, center petals streaked white, large, full

Frisco F, my, 1987, Kordes, W.; flowers medium, full, slight fragrance; foliage medium size, dark green, semi-glossy; mini-flora bushy growth; PP6695; [((New Day × Minigold) × Banzai) × Antique Silk]; int. in 1986

Frisco City F, dr; flowers dark cherry red with prominent yellow stamens; foliage glossy; strong, medium growth

Frisco Kordana Min, dy, Kordes; flowers deep yellow center, outer petals paler, full; container rose; int. by W. Kordes Söhne

Frisette F, or, 1964, Mondial Roses; flowers bright scarlet, open, semi-dbl., borne in clusters; growth vigorous, low to medium; [Unnamed seeding × Concerto]

Frisky HT, mr, 1960, Wyant; flowers velvety red, open, large, 50 petals, moderate fragrance; foliage dark, glossy; vigorous, bushy growth; [Charlotte Armstrong × Chrysler

Imperial]; int. by Landseadel, 1959

Frisson Frais HMsk, w, 2000, Lens, Louis; flowers light pink, reverse lighter, 1-1½ in., single to semi-dbl., borne in large clusters; recurrent; foliage medium green, semi-glossy, disease-resistant; prickles moderate; bushy, tall (120-150 cm.) growth; hedge; [Ravel × Rush]; int. by Louis Lens NV, 1991; Gold Medal, Madrid, 1991

Fritz Hegar Pol, dr, 1930, Schmitt-Eltville; flowers medium, semi-dbl.

Fritz Höger HT, dr, 1934, Kordes; bud pointed; flowers pure crimson, large, dbl., high-centered; foliage leathery, dark; very vigorous growth; [(Hadley × Comte G. de Rochemur) × Cathrine Kordes]

Fritz Maydt HT, w, 1925, Leenders, M.; flowers coppery flesh-white; [Mev. C. van Marwijk Kooy × Marquise de Sinéty]

Fritz Nobis S, pb, 1940, Kordes; bud long, pointed, light red; flowers white, reverse reddish salmon-pink, large, dbl., high-centered, borne in clusters, intense fragrance; non-recurrent; foliage glossy, leathery; vigorous growth; [Joanna Hill × Magnifica]

Fritz Reuter HMult, pb, 1913, Lambert; flowers carmine, yellow at center, violet pink towards edges, medium, full, moderate fragrance

Fritz Schrödter HT, dr, 1928, Mühle; flowers brilliant dark scarlet, large, dbl.; foliage bronze, soft; vigorous, bushy growth; [Hortulanus Budde × unknown]

Fritz Thiedemann HT, or, 1961, Tantau, Math.; bud pointed; flowers brick-red, well-shaped, 4 in., 36 petals, moderate fragrance; foliage dark; bushy growth; [(Horstmann's Jubilaumsrose × unknown) × Alpine Glow seedling]; int. by Wheatcroft Bros., 1960

Fritz Thiedemann, Climbing Cl HT, or, 1961, Kordes

Fritz Walter HT, or, Hetzel; int. in 1981

Fritzi Pol, mp, Hetzel; int. in 1994

Friuli HT, ab, 1933, Ingegnoli; flowers amber-yellow, large, cupped; vigorous growth

Frivole F, mr, 1958, Buyl Frères; flowers geranium-red, very dbl.; vigorous, low growth; [Independence × Country Girl]

Frivolité HT, or, 1956, Dot, Pedro; flowers scarlet shaded orange and salmon, large, 50 petals; vigorous, compact growth; [Peace × Catalonia]

Frivolous Min, mr, 1998, Williams, Ernest D.; flowers cherry red, with 8-10 broad petals, good substance, 1½ in., 8 petals, borne mostly singly, no fragrance; foliage medium size, semi-glossy; almost thornless; upright, medium (18 in.) growth; [Twilight Trail × seedling]; int. by Texas Mini Roses, 1997

Frivolous Pink HT, ab, 2001, Coiner, Jim; flowers pink with apricot, pink blend reverse, large, full, borne in small clusters, moderate fragrance; foliage medium size, medium green, semi-glossy; growth compact, medium (36 in.); garden decorative; PP15638; [seedling × seedling]

Frohsinn F, ab, 1961, Tantau, Math.; bud pointed; flowers apricot, cream and pink blend, large, 20 petals, cupped, borne in large clusters, slight fragrance; foliage glossy; vigorous, bushy growth; [Horstmann's Jubilaumsrose × Circus]

Frohsinn 82 – See **Joyfulness**, HT

Froissard – See **Mrs Standish**, HP, 1865

Frolic F, mp, 1953, Swim, H.C.; flowers bright pink, 2½ in., 21 petals, borne in large sprays; vigorous, bushy growth; [World's Fair × Pinocchio]; int. by Armstrong Nursery

Frolic F, pb, Dawson; int. in 1995

Frondeuse S, pb

Front 'n' Center Min, mr, 2002, Saville, John M.; flowers dbl., borne in small clusters; foliage medium size, medium green, matte; prickles 3/16 in., thin, angled down, few; growth upright, compact, medium (14-18 in.); garden, border, containers; [((Zorina × Baby Katie) × (Little Jackie × Rainbow's End)) × Lavender Jade]; drought resistant; int. by Nor' East Miniature Roses, 2002

Front Page – See **Conqueror's Gold**, F

Front Page HT, rb, 2000, Winchel, Joseph F.; flowers red with pink reverse, 5 in., 27-28 petals, high-centered, borne mostly singly, slight fragrance; recurrent; foliage large, dark green, semi-glossy; prickles moderate, dorsal, light yellow; compact, low (2-3 ft.) growth; PP12609; [Blue Nile × seedling]; int. by Coiner Nursery, 2000

Frontenac S, dp, 1992, Ogilvie, Ian S.; flowers dbl., borne in small clusters; foliage medium size, dark green, glossy; some prickles; medium (100 cm.), upright growth; very winter hardy; PP9210; [(((Queen Elizabeth × Arthur Bell) × (Simonet Red × Von Scharnhorst)) × ((*R.* × *kordesii* × (Red Dawn × Suzanne)) × ((Red Dawn × Suzanne) × (Red Dawn × Suzanne)))]; int. by Agriculture Canada, 1992

Frontier Twirl S, pb, 1985, Buck, Dr. Griffith J.; flowers pink-yellow blend, large, 25 petals, cupped, borne 1-8 per cluster, moderate fragrance; recurrent; foliage leathery, medium size, bronze green; prickles awl-like, tan; erect, bushy growth; hardy; [Sevilliana × Just Joey]; int. by Iowa State University, 1984

Frostfire Min, mr, 1963, Moore, Ralph S.; flowers red, sometimes flecked white, 1 in., 30 petals; foliage dark, glossy; bushy, compact (12-14 in.) growth; [((*R. wichurana* × Floradora) × seedling) × Little Buckaroo]; int. by Sequoia Nursery, 1963

Frosty Min, w, 1955, Moore, Ralph S.; bud ovoid, pale pink; flowers clear white, very small, 45 petals, borne in clusters of 3-10 or more, moderate honeysuckle fragrance; foliage glossy; vigorous (12-14 in.), compact, spreading growth; PP1412; [(*R. wichurana* × seedling) × (*R. wichurana* × seedling)]; int. by Sequoia Nursery, 1953

Frosty – See **Frosty Parade**, Min

Frosty Morning F, w, 1997, Horner, Colin P.; flowers white, cream at base, 3 in., dbl., borne in small clusters; foliage medium size, medium green, semi-glossy; prickles moderate; bushy, medium (100 cm.) growth; [Sexy Rexy × Princess Michael of Kent]; int. by Paul Chessum Roses

Frosty Paillette – See **Frosty Parade**, Min

Frosty Parade Min, w, Poulsen; flowers white, medium, slight wild rose fragrance; foliage dark; growth narrow, bushy, 20-40 cm.; PP10737; int. by Poulsen Roser, 1998

Frothy Min, w, 1992, McGredy, Sam IV

Froufrou HT, yb, 1955, Moulin-Epinay; flowers chamois-yellow, center carmine, large, very dbl.; vigorous, bushy growth; [Mme Joseph Perraud × Yvonne Plassat]

Frou-Frou HT, rb, 1957, Laperrière; flowers crimson, reverse carmine-pink, large, 25 petals; moderate growth; [Comtesse Vandal × seedling]; int. by EFR

Frou Frou HT, ob, Hiroshima; int. by Hiroshima Bara-en, 2001

Froy F, or, 1973, Lundstad; bud ovoid; flowers open, medium, semi-dbl., slight fragrance; foliage glossy, dark; bushy growth; [Traumland × Poulsen's Pink]; int. by Norges Landbruks-hogskole, 1972

Fru Dagmar Hartopp – See **Dagmar Hastrup**, HRg

Fru Dagmar Hastrup – See **Dagmar Hastrup**, HRg

Fru Gerda Helmuus HT, op, 1935, Poulsen, D.T.; flowers light orange-pink, large, semi-dbl.

Fru Inge Poulsen – See **Mrs Inge Poulsen**, F

Fru Johanne Poulsen HT, mp, 1924, Poulsen, S.; flowers bright pink, well-formed; vigorous growth; [Margrethe Moller × unknown]

Fru Julie Poulsen – See **Poulsen's Delight**, F

Fru Xenia Jacobsen HT, dr, 1925, Poulsen, S.; flowers deep red, well-shaped, dbl.; vigorous growth; [Étoile de France × Richmond]

Frühlingsanfang HSpn, w, 1950, Kordes; bud long, pointed; flowers ivory-white, 4 in., single; intermittent bloom; foliage leathery; very vigorous, bushy (9 ft.) growth; [Joanna Hill × *R. spinosissima altaica*]

Frühlingsduft HSpn, pb, 1949, Kordes; bud ovoid, golden yellow; flowers lemon-yellow with light pink, very large, dbl., high-centered, intense Marechal Niel fragrance; non-recurrent; foliage large, leathery; very vigorous, upright, bushy growth; [Joanna Hill × *R. spinosissima altaica*]

Frühlingsgold HSpn, my, 1937, Kordes; bud pointed, nasturtium-red; flowers creamy yellow, 3 in., single; non-recurrent; foliage large, light, soft, wrinkled; very vigorous, bushy growth; [Joanna Hill × *R. spinosissima hispida*]

Frühlingsmorgen HSpn, pb, 1940, Kordes; flowers cherry-pink at edges, center soft yellow, stamens maroon, medium, single; occasionally recurrent bloom; foliage dark; free growth (6 ft.); hips large, red; [(E.G. Hill × Cathrine Kordes) × *R. spinosissima altaica*]

Frühlingsschnee HSpn, w, 1956, Kordes; bud ovoid; flowers snow-white, very large, single, slight fragrance; foliage leathery, wrinkled, light green; very vigorous, upright growth; [Golden Glow × *R. spinosissima altaica*]

Frühlingsstunde HSpn, lp, 1942, Kordes; flowers whitish pink, medium, semi-dbl.

Frühlingstag HSpn, my, 1949, Kordes; bud ovoid; flowers golden yellow, large, semi-dbl., borne in small clusters, moderate fragrance; profuse non-recurrent bloom; foliage leathery; numerous prickles; growth to 5 ft.; [McGredy's Wonder × Fruhlingsgold]

Frühlingszauber HSpn, mp, 1940, Kordes; flowers pink, very large, single; non-recurrent; foliage dark; vigorous (7 ft.) growth; hips large, dark red; [(E.G. Hill × Cathrine Kordes) × *R. spinosissima altaica*]

Fruit Buffet F, yb

Fruité F, ob, Meilland, L.; flowers multiple shades of orange and red, medium, full, slight fruity fragrance; int. in 1984

Fruite HT, yb, Meilland; flowers striped; int. by Pep. de la Guerinais, 2003

Fruitee – See **Fruité**, F

Fryer's Orange HT, ab, 1934, Fryers Nursery, Ltd.; flowers orange-yellow; [sport of Mrs Sam McGredy]

Fuchsia HGal, m

Fuchsia Meidiland S, dp, 1994, Meilland, Alain A.; bud ovoid, small; flowers Bengal rose, medium, 15 petals, flat cup, borne in large clusters, slight fragrance; free-flowering; foliage medium size, light green, glossy; few prickles; low, spreading growth; PP8839; [Bordurella × Clair Matin]; int. by The Conard-Pyle Co., 1993

Fuchsia Meillandecor – See **Fuchsia Meidiland**, S

Fuchsia Minuetto Min, mp, 2000, Meilland International; flowers fuchsia pink, 2-3 cm., very full, borne in small clusters, no fragrance; foliage medium size, medium green, semi-glossy; prickles moderate; compact, medium (8-12 in.) growth; PP11571; int. by Conard-Pyle, 1999

Fuchsia Pink Castle – See **Berleburg**, F

Fuchsia Sunblaze MinFl, op, Meilland; int. in 2004

Fuchsine Guy F, m, 1930, Leenders, M.; flowers lilac-purple, open, large, semi-dbl., borne in clusters; foliage rich green; bushy growth; [sport of Lafayette]

Fuëgo F, or, 1964, Arles; bud pointed; flowers Chinese vermilion, medium, 30 petals, open, borne in clusters, slight fragrance; [Aloha × Gabychette]; int. by Roses-France

Fuego Negro – See **Carte Noir**, F

Fuggerstadt Augsburg F, or, 1985, Kordes, W.; flowers medium, semi-dbl.; foliage medium size, dark, glossy; upright, bushy growth; [Cordula × Topsi]; int. by Kordes Sons

Fugitive F, yb, 1969, Pal, Dr. B.P.; bud pointed; flowers apricot-yellow, becoming lighter, open, semi-dbl., borne in clusters; foliage glossy, bronze; vigorous, bushy growth; [Mrs Oakley Fisher × unknown]; int. by Indian

Agric. Research Inst., 1965

Fugue LCl, dr, 1959, Meilland, Mrs. Marie-Louise; bud globular; flowers medium, 30 petals, borne in small clusters; foliage leathery, glossy; vigorous growth; [Alain × Guinee]; int. by URS, 1958; Gold Medal, Madrid, 1958

Fujimai HT, m, 2006, Yasuda, Yuji; flowers full, borne mostly solitary; foliage medium size, dark green, matte; prickles medium, moderate; growth upright, medium (1 m.); cutting; garden; [Madame Violet × seedling]; int. in 2006

Fujimusume HT, dp, Keihan; int. by Keihan Gardening, 1999

Fujiyama Rose – See ***R. acicularis nipponensis*** (Koehne)

Fujiyama Rose – See **Akane Fuji**, HRg

Fujizakura Min, mp, 1997, Ohtsuki, Hironaka; flowers small, single; foliage small, medium green, semi-glossy; some prickles; spreading, low (20cm.) growth; [Azumino × Azumino]

Fukuyama HT, op, 1989, Tagashira, Kazuso; bud pointed; flowers salmon-pink, aging dark, large, 35 petals, high-centered, slight fragrance; foliage red aging dark green, matte, ovoid; prickles red to dark green; upright, tall growth; hips round, yellow-blend; [Pristine × Takao]; int. by Hiroshima Rose Nursery, 1988

Fulgens – See **Malton**, HCh

Fulgens HGal, dp, about 1830, Vibert; flowers delicate bright pink, medium, semi-dbl.

Fulgens HSpn, m; flowers lilac-pink, semi-dbl.; early bloom; growth to 3-4 ft.; hips glossy, black

Fulgorie HP, mp, before 1840, from Angers; flowers carmine pink, edged lilac, very large, full

Fulgurante HT, mr, J&P; flowers large, dbl.; foliage dark green, healthy; strong, upright (3 ft.) growth; int. by Sauvageot, 1977

Full Moon Min, ly, 1994, Sproul, James A.; flowers creamy light yellow, 1-1½ in., full, slight fragrance; foliage medium size, medium green, semi-glossy, disease-resistant; few prickles; medium (20 in.), spreading, rounded growth; [Avandel × Olympiad]

Full Sail HT, w, 1998, McGredy, Sam IV; flowers white, 4½ in., full, high-centered, borne mostly singly, intense fragrance; foliage large, dark green, glossy; few prickles; bushy, medium (110 cm.) growth; [sport of New Zealand]; int. by Edmunds' Roses, 1998

Fullcream HT, ly, 1960, LeGrice; flowers creamy yellow, well-formed, 5-7 in., 28 petals, intense honey fragrance; foliage glossy; vigorous, low growth; [Wellworth × Diamond Jubilee]; int. in 1959

Fullerton Centennial Min, or, 1987, Chaffin, Lauren M.; flowers orange-red with white base, bright, fading darker, medium, 20-25 petals, high-centered, borne singly or in sprays of 3-5, slight fragrance; foliage small, medium green, semi-glossy, disease-resistant; prickles needle-declining, sparse, light tan; upright, bushy, medium, neat, symmetrical growth; sometimes forms globular, medium-green hips; [Orange Honey × Rise 'n' Shine]; int. by Friends of the Fullerton Arboretum, 1987

Fulton MacKay HT, yb, 1989, Cocker, James; flowers large, 20 petals, moderate fragrance; foliage large, medium green, glossy; bushy growth; [Silver Jubilee × Jana]; int. by James Cocker & Sons, 1989; Golden Prize, Glasgow, 1992

Fulvia HT, dp, 1950, Gaujard; flowers pink tinted carmine, medium, dbl.; foliage leathery, light green; vigorous, bushy growth; [Mme Joseph Perraud × Mme Elie Dupraz]

Fun Min, dp, Poulsen Roser; flowers very small, dbl.; PP10628; int. in 1995

Fun Fair F, yb; int. by Burston Nurseries, 2006

Fun Jwan Lo S, w, before 1811; flowers white, center pale pink to medium, 6-7 cm., dbl., borne in clusters; very vigorous growth; not hardy; discovered in a garden in Pautung Fu, Chihli province, by Frank N. Meyer and sent to the U.S.D.A. for use as understock

Fun Sunsation – See **Carpet of Color**, S

Funchal HT, Moreira da Silva, A.

Funkenmariechen F, yb, 1975, Kordes; flowers yellow, red, dbl., globular, slight fragrance; foliage glossy; upright, bushy growth; [seedling × Samba]; int. by Horstmann, 1973

Funkuhr HT, yb, 1984, Kordes, W.; flowers yellow, petals edged medium red, aging red, large, 35 petals; foliage medium size, medium green, glossy; upright growth; [seedling × seedling]; int. by Kordes Sons

Funny Face Min, rb, 1982, Jolly, Betty J.; flowers white, petals edged red, aging red, medium, 35 petals, slight fragrance; foliage small, medium green, semi-glossy; upright, bushy growth; [Avandel × Zinger]; int. by Rosehill Farm

Funny Face S, pb, Lim, P, & Twomey, J.; flowers pink and white painted, 4 in., semi-dbl.; prolific; foliage very clean, disease-resistant.; compact, rounded, upright (3 ft.) growth; PP15753; int. by Bailey Nursery, 2004

Funny Girl Min, lp, 1982, Warriner, William A.; flowers small, 20 petals, slight fragrance; foliage small, medium green, matte; upright, bushy growth; PP5249; [Bridal Pink × Fire Princess]; int. by J&P, 1983

Funny Girl F, ob, Barni, V.; flowers orange/apricot/ocher, large, dbl., intense fragrance; growth to 60-80 cm.; int. as Funny Face, Rose Barni, 1998

Fur Elise S, pb, 2006, Rippetoe, Robert Neil; flowers semi-dbl., borne mostly solitary, strong old rose fragrance; foliage medium size, matte; prickles medium, slightly curved, tan, few; stems very short; growth spreading, medium (3 ft.); no hips; [Reveille Dijonnais × unknown]; int. by Robert Neil Rippetoe, 2006

Fure-Daiko – See **Piñata**, LCl

Furia HT, Combe, M.; int. in 1968

Furore HT, or, 1965, Verbeek; flowers scarlet, medium, very dbl.; foliage dark; [(Baccará × seedling) × Miracle]

Fürst Bismarck T, dy, 1886, Drögemüller; flowers golden yellow, large, very dbl., moderate fruity fragrance; [Gloire de Dijon × unknown (probably selfed)]

Fürst Leopold IV zu Schaumburg-Lippe HP, dr, 1918, Kiese; flowers large, dbl.

Fürst Niclot – See **Kaiser Wilhelm II**, HT

Fürstin Bismarck T, mr, 1887, Drögemüller; flowers China pink to cerise pink, fading lighter, large, very dbl.; [Gloire de Dijon × Comtesse d'Oxford]

Fürstin Bülow T, pb, 1908, Brauer; flowers yellow-pink with gold reflections, shaded violet, medium, full, moderate fragrance

Fürstin Hohenzollern – See **Fürstin Infantin von Hohenzollern**, T

Fürstin Infantin von Hohenzollern T, m, 1898, Brauer, P.; flowers purple rose, center yellowish-salmon, medium, dbl.; [Mlle la Comtesse de Leusse × Marie Van Houtte]

Fürstin Maria Hatzfeldt HT, dr, 1927, Boden; flowers bright dark red, dbl.; [Gen. MacArthur × seedling]

Fürstin von Hohenzollern Infantin – See **Fürstin Infantin von Hohenzollern**, T

Fürstin von Pless HRg, w, 1911, Lambert, P.; flowers white with lemon center, very large, full, cupped, borne mostly singly or in small clusters, moderate fragrance; foliage lush; upright, medium (5 ft.) growth; [Mme Caroline Testout × Conrad Ferdinand Meyer]

Furusato HT, mp, Keihan; int. by Keihan Gardening, 1970

Fushimi HT, pb, Keihan; flowers pink with a green edge; int. by Keihan Gardening, 1987

Fushimi, Climbing Cl HT, pb, Keihan; int. by Keihan Gardening, 1992

Fushino HT, lp, 1985, Ota, Kaichiro; flowers large, 45 petals, high-centered, no fragrance; foliage medium green; vigorous, spreading growth; [Utage × Ann Letts]; int. in 1980

Fusilier F, or, 1958, Morey, Dr. Dennison; bud globular; flowers orange-scarlet, 3-3½ in., 40 petals, borne in heavy clusters, slight fragrance; foliage dark, glossy, leathery; vigorous growth; PP1709; [Red Pinocchio × Floradora]; int. by J&P, 1957

Fusion T, yb, 1901, Croibier; flowers dark chamois-yellow, petals edged safron-yellow, medium to large, full; [Mme Eugene Verdier × unknown]

Futtaker Schlingrose HMult, dr, about 1900, Geschwind, R.; flowers velvety dark red, 4-5 cm., slight fragrance; foliage dark green, smooth; [De La Grifferaie × a HP or B]

Futura F, m, Kordes; int. in 1994

Future HT, mr, 1974, Warriner, W. A.; buds large, pointed; flowers vermilion, large, dbl, cupped, borne singly; foliage large, dark green, leathery; numerous prickles; growth very vigorous, upright, well-branched; [PP3569: seedling × seedling]; int. by J&P, 1975

Future Award HT, mr, J&P; int. in 1993

Fuxiana HT, Dot, Simon; int. in 1979

Fuyuume-no-ko Ch, mp

Fuzzy Navel – See **Winter Sunset**, S

Fuzzy Wuzzy Red M, mr, Moore, Ralph ; bud bright red, mossy buds; flowers bright red, 1½ in.; recurrent; foliage dark green, glossy; compact, low (18 in.) growth; [Scarlet Moss × Scarlet Moss]; int. by Sequoia Nursery, 2004

Fyfield Princess F, my, 1994, Shuttleworth, F.I.; flowers medium, dbl., borne in large clusters; foliage medium size, medium green, semi-glossy; numerous prickles; medium (4 ft.), upright growth; [sport of Southampton]; int. by F. Haynes & Partners, 1994

Fygi HT, dr, deRuiter; int. by deRuiter's New Roses

Fyvie Castle HT, pb, 1985, Cocker, Alexander M.; flowers light apricot, amber and pink blend, well-formed, large, 35 petals; foliage large, medium green, semi-glossy; upright growth; [(Sunblest × (Sabine × Dr. A.J. Verhage)) × Silver Jubilee]; int. by Cocker & Sons; Gold Star of the South Pacific, Palmerston North, NZ, 1985

G. Amédée Hammond HT, ab, 1915, Dickson, A.; flowers apricot-yellow on ivory yellow, dbl.; Gold Medal, NRS, 1913

G. F. Veronica HMult, ly, 1900, Demitrovisi; bud peachy pink; flowers creamy yellow, 3-4 cm., semi-dbl., borne in small to medium clusters, moderate fragrance

G. Forest-Colcombet – See **Mme G. Forest-Colcombet**, HT

G. H. Davison HT, mr, 1988, Davison, G.H.; flowers medium, well-defined red, large, 45 petals, high-centered, borne singly and in clusters of up to 3; foliage large, dark green, semi-glossy; prickles normal, large, red; upright growth; hips oval, large, green; [seedling × seedling]; int. by The Central Nursery, 1990

G. I. Joe HT, dp, 1943, Parmentier, J.; bud long, pointed; flowers rose-red to deep rose-pink, large, very dbl.; foliage leathery, dark; vigorous growth; [sport of Red Better Times]

G. K. Rose HT, rb, Chiplunkar; flowers crimson with white/cream reverse and base, large, full; int. in 1989

G. Nabonnand – See **Gilbert Nabonnand**, T

G. P. & J. Baker F, op, 1982, Harkness, R., & Co., Ltd.; flowers salmon orange, reverse lighter, 36 petals, flat, borne in clusters of 3-11, slight fragrance; foliage dark, glossy; numerous prickles; medium, bushy growth; [(Bobby Dazzler × seedling) × Marion Harkness]; int. in 1984

G. W. Peart HT, mr, 1948, Toogood; bud ovoid; flowers medium, very dbl.; foliage leathery, dark; moderate, bushy growth; [(Guineé × unknown) × Rouge Mallerin]

G. W. Watkins HT, lp, 1890, Williams, A.

Gaard um Titzebierg HMsk, pb, Lens; flowers bright, reddish-pink with white centers, fading to lilac pink, semi-dbl., shallow cup to flat, borne in clusters, moderate multiflora fragrance; recurrent; upright (4 ft.), arching growth; hips small, orange; int. by Louis Lens SA, 2006

Gabi Gr, or, 1988, Poole, Lionel; flowers very bright orange-red, fading to lighter orange, 24 petals, high-centered, moderate fragrance; foliage medium size, dark green, glossy; prickles fairly flat, small, dark brown; bushy, medium growth; hips rounded, small, light brown-green; [Pink Favorite × Red Dandy]

Gabina HGal, m, about 1845, Calvert; flowers light purple, medium, very full

Gabriel Fournier HP, dr, 1877, Levet; flowers dark cherry red, large, full, slight fragrance; [Jules Margottin × Victor Verdier]

Gabriel Lombart HT, w, 1932, Buatois; flowers flesh-white to cream-white, very large, dbl., cupped; vigorous, bushy growth; [Dr. A. Hermans × Rayon d'Or]

Gabriel Noyelle M, ab, 1933, Buatois; bud ovoid; flowers apricot, dbl., cupped; recurrent bloom; foliage leathery; very vigorous growth; [Salet × Souv de Mme Kreuger]

Gabriela Sabatini Min, or, 1992, Williams, J. Benjamin; flowers bright fire orange-red, medium, dbl., borne mostly singly, slight fragrance; foliage small, dark green, semi-glossy; few prickles; growth low (14-20 in.); [Marina × Pink Sweetheart]

Gabriella F, mr, 1977, Berggren; bud ovoid; flowers 3 in., 33 petals, cupped; foliage glossy; vigorous, bushy growth; PP4452; int. by W. Kordes Sons

Gabriella F, mr, Kordes; flowers dbl.

Gabrielle HCh, lp, before 1829, Coquerel; flowers flesh pink, edges lighter, large, full

Gabrielle – See **Gabriella**, F, 1977

Gabrielle – See **Gabi**, Gr

Gabrielle d'Estrées A, lp, 1819, Vibert; flowers flesh pink, becoming white, medium to large, full; foliage bullate, glaucous

Gabrielle Noyelle – See **Gabriel Noyelle**, M

Gabrielle Privat Pol, mp, 1931, Barthelemy-Privat; flowers brilliant carmine-pink, semi-dbl., borne in pyramidal corymbs of 30-50; continuous flowering; bushy (1 × 1 ft.) growth; int. by Turbat

Gabrielle Privat Rouge Pol, mr, Koopman; int. in 1940

Gabriel's Fire Min, rb, 1991, Bridges, Dennis A.; bud pointed; flowers creamy light yellow turning red, 2 in., 20-22 petals, high-centered, borne usually singly, intense fragrance; foliage medium size, medium green, semi-glossy; bushy, spreading, medium growth; [Sachet × unknown]; int. by Bridges Roses, 1991

Gaby Cover – See **Martha's Vineyard**, S

Gaby Morlay HT, ab, Dorieux; int. in 1994

Gabychette F, rb, 1960, Arles; bud ovoid; flowers reddish-salmon, base sulfur-yellow, reverse white to rosy white, dbl., high-centered; foliage glossy, light green; low growth; [Floradora × Pioupiou]; int. by Roses-France, 1960

Gaëtano Gonsoli – See **Gonsoli Gaëtano**, HP

Gaia MinFl, pb, Barni, V.; int. in 1993

Gaiata HT, yb, 1956, Moreira da Silva; flowers Indian yellow shaded pink; [Boudoir × Peace]

Gaiety HT, ob, 1926, E.G. Hill, Co.; bud pointed; flowers orange, Indian red and silver, large, dbl., cupped; foliage light, glossy; vigorous, branching growth; [Mme Butterfly × Souv. de Claudius Pernet]; int. by Hill Floral Products Co.

Gaiety HT, op, Archer; flowers salmon-pink flushed yellow; vigorous growth

Gaiezza HT, ob, 1940, Giacomasso; flowers orange touched red, center yellow; [Julien Potin × Mme G. Forest-Colcombet]

Gail MinFl, yb, 1986, Bennett, Dee; flowers golden yellow with orange blush on petal tips, orange spreading with age, large, 38 petals, high-centered, borne singly, moderate fragrance; foliage large, medium green, semi-glossy; prickles small reddish; medium, bushy, spreading growth; hips globular, in., light green; [Arizona × Orange Honey]; int. by Tiny Petals Nursery, 1986

Gail Borden HT, pb, 1958, Kordes; bud ovoid; flowers deep rose-pink, reverse overcast cream, 5½ in., 53 petals, high-centered, moderate fragrance; foliage dark, glossy, leathery; vigorous, upright growth; PP1618; [R.M.S. Queen Mary × Viktoria Adelheid]; int. by J&P, 1957; Gold Medal, NRS, 1957

Gail Borden, Climbing Cl HT, pb, 1960; flowers coral, fading to pink, reverse white, 5-6 in., very dbl., moderate fragrance; int. by J&P, 1960

Gaillarde Marbrée – See **Noire Couronnée**, HGal

Gainesville Garnet LCl, dr, 2006, John A. Starnes Jr.; flowers red, reverse magenta red, 4-5 in., very full, borne in small clusters; very remontant; foliage medium size, medium green, semi-glossy, disease-free; prickles medium, slightly curved, brown, moderate; growth upright, vigorous climber, tall (8-12 ft.); pillar/climber; [hybrid wichurana × unknown]; int. in 2006

Gainsborough Cl HT, lp, 1903, Good & Reese; flowers flesh-pink, almost white, large, dbl.; long stems; vigorous growth; [sport of Viscountess Folkestone]

Gala F, pb, 1975, Jelly; bud short, pointed; flowers light pink, 3-3½ in., 28-34 petals, high-centered, slight spicy fragrance; vigorous, upright, free growth; PP3774; [Seedling No. 19-64 ps × Seventeen]; int. by E.G. Hill Co., 1973

Gala Min, dp, 1999, Saville, F. Harmon; flowers 1½ in., dbl., borne mostly singly and in small clusters, loose sprays, no fragrance; foliage medium size, dark green, semi-glossy; prickles moderate; upright, spreading, medium (15-16 in.) growth; [High Jinks × seedling]; int. by Nor' East Miniature Roses, 2000

Gala Charles Aznavour F, lp, Meilland; flowers soft pink with lighter reverse, dbl., borne in small clusters of up to 7 blooms; continuous bloom; strong (60-70 cm.) growth; int. in 1997

Gala Day F, or, 1966, Watkins Roses; flowers vermilion-scarlet, pointed, 4 in.; foliage light green; free, upright growth; [Queen Elizabeth × Dickson's Flame]

Gala Gold Min, dy, 1993, Laver, Keith G.; flowers medium, full, borne mostly singly, no fragrance; foliage small, medium green, matte; some prickles; low (24-30 cm.), upright, bushy, compact growth; [Golden Promise × (June Laver × Tut's Treasure)]; int. by Springwood Roses, 1994

Gala Ribbon S, mr; flowers bright crimson red, spiraling, moderate fragrance; recurrent; strong growth, can be trained as medium climber

Gala Sunrise F, rb, 1997, Giles, Diann; flowers medium, very dbl., borne in small clusters; foliage medium size, dark green, dull; upright, medium (3½ ft.) growth; [Vera Dalton × Rainbow's End]; int. by Giles Rose Nursery

Galah HT, mp, 1956, Riethmuller; flowers carmine-pink, base lighter, large, semi-dbl., borne in clusters

Galahad HT, w, 1986, Kriloff, Michel; flowers very large, dbl., moderate anise fragrance; foliage medium green, semi-glossy; [Micaela × Lara]

Galatea HMsk, yb, 1914, Pemberton; flowers stone-color, edged pink, small rosette, borne in clusters; recurrent bloom

Galatea S, w, Barni; recurrent; spreading, low (16-20 in.) growth; int. by Rose Barni, 2004

Galatée HGal, lp, before 1828, Dubourg; flowers flesh pink, petals very thin, very dbl.

Galaty HT, or, 1979, Dot, Simon; flowers 4 in., 32 petals, cupped, intense fragrance; foliage dark; [Tropicana × Lola Montes]; int. in 1977

Galaxie Ch, w, 1827, Vétillard; flowers white, center cream, medium, full

Galaxy HWich, dp, 1906, Walsh; flowers bright carmine; vigorous growth

Galaxy Min, dr, 1980, Moore, Ralph S.; bud long, pointed; flowers deep velvety red, 23 petals, high-centered, borne 3, sometimes 5-10 per cluster; foliage small to medium; prickles slightly curved; vigorous, bushy, upright growth; PP4680; [Fairy Moss × Fairy Princess]; int. by Sequoia Nursery

Galaxy F, yb, Meilland; flowers ochre-yellow suffused with pastel red, medium, dbl., borne in small custers, moderate linseed oil fragrance; recurrent; foliage disease-resistant; growth to 70-80 cm.; int. in 1995

Galejade S, op, Reuter; int. in 1997

Galia HT, lp, 1966, Betzel; flowers light pink, center darker, large, very dbl.; foliage dark, leathery; very vigorous, upright growth; RULED EXTINCT; 4/81/ ARM

Galia HT, or, 1981, Meilland, Mrs. Marie-Louise; flowers 38 petals, cupped, borne singly, no fragrance; foliage matte, dense; vigorous growth; [Interview × Elegy]; int. by Meilland Et Cie, 1977

Galileo HT, mr, 1971, Meilland; flowers currant-red to cherry-red, 5 in., 30 petals, globular; foliage large, glossy; vigorous, upright growth; [Ma Fille × Love Song]

Galina HT, mr, Cocker; flowers large, dbl.; int. in 1979

Galina F, ab, VEG; flowers apricot and yellow, medium, dbl.

Galioca – See **Château de Chenonceaux**, HT

Gallagher F, rb, 1980, Murray, Nola; bud pointed; flowers cream, edged crimson, shapely, 2½ in., 41 petals, moderate fruity fragrance; foliage leathery; bushy growth

Gallande HSemp, mp, about 1830, Jacques; flowers dbl.

Gallant F, mr, 1968, Dickson, A.; flowers scarlet, 3-3½ in., dbl., borne in clusters; foliage glossy; [Tropicana × Barbecue]

Gallantry HT, pb, Delbard

Galleria HRg, mr, 1990, Weddle, Von C.; bud ovoid; flowers medium watermelon pink, reverse silvery pink, large, 13 petals, high-centered, borne in sprays of 3-5, moderate spicy, fruity fragrance; foliage large, dark green, glossy; prickles straight, medium, light green to pink; bushy, tall (8 ft.) growth; hips round, small, green-yellow; [The Duke × Hansa]; int. by Hortico Roses, 1990

Galleria Borghese HT, w, 1954, Giacomasso; flowers flesh streaked coral, very large; foliage glossy; strong stems; [Peace × Crimson Glory]

Galli-Curci HT, my, 1924, Kinsman; flowers golden yellow; [sport of Columbia]

Gallica Alba HGal, w, before 1811; bud elongate; flowers blush white, dbl., moderate fragrance; foliage pointed, medium size, finely dentate; prickles numerous, slender, straight

Gallica Alba Flore Plena HGal, w, before 1811; flowers white tinted pink, very dbl.

Gallica Grandiflora – See **Alika**, HGal

Gallica Macrantha Misc OGR, w, before 1750; flowers flushed rose at first, changing to nearly white; said to be a cross of *R. canina* and *R. gallica*, but more probably *R. gallica* × *R. alba*

Gallica Maheca – See **La Belle Sultane**, HGal

Gallica Vermilion HGal, about 1823, from Angers; flowers rose pink, very full

Gallicandy HGal, mp, 2003, Barden, Paul; flowers medium pink, reverse darker pink, 3-3½ in., full, borne in small clusters, moderate fragrance; Spring blooming only, over a three to six week period; foliage medium size, medium green, semi-glossy; prickles ¼-½ in., straight, brownish, moderate; growth spreading, thicket-forming, medium (5 ft.), somewhat wider; [Tuscany Superb × Othello]; int. in 2004

Gallique Nouvelle HGal, mp

Gallivarda HT, rb, 1978, W. Kordes Söhne; bud long, pointed; flowers red, yellow reverse, 4½ in., 34 petals, high-centered, slight fragrance; foliage glossy; vigorous, upright growth; [Colour Wonder × Wiener Charme]; int. by Willemse, 1977

Galsar – See **Gallivarda**, HT

Galway Bay LCl, op, 1966, McGredy, Sam IV; flowers salmon-pink, reverse darker, 3½-4 in., 20 petals, borne in small clusters; foliage medium green, glossy; vigorous (9-12 ft.) growth; [Gruss an Heidelberg × Queen Elizabeth]

Gambler HT, w, 1995, Gimer, Louis; flowers large, full, borne mostly singly; foliage large, medium green, semi-glossy; few prickles; tall (5 ft.), upright growth; [Grace de Monaco × seedling]; int. by Giles Rose Nursery, 1995

Gamin de Paris F, dr, 1964, Mondial Roses; flowers dark blood-red, large, dbl., borne in large clusters; vigorous, upright growth; [(Orange Triumph × Paprika) × seedling]

Gamine F, op, 1961, Kriloff, Michel; flowers salmon-pink, medium, dbl.; vigorous growth; [Eclipse × Baccará]; int. by Verbeek, 1961

Gamma HT, pb, 1978, Gaujard; bud pointed; flowers pink, suffused vermilion, intense fragrance; foliage large; [Jouvencelle × American Heritage]; int. in 1972

Gamon's Climbing Grolez – See **Mme Jules Grolez, Climbing**, Cl HT

Gamon's Thornless Misc OGR, mp; form of *R. canina*; used for understock

Gamusin HT, r, 1960, Dot, Pedro; flowers cinnamon to pale pink, 25 petals; vigorous, spreading growth; [Grey Pearl × (Lila Vidri × Prelude)]

Ganang – See **Crème Anglais**, LCl

Ganga HT, dy, 1970, Division of Vegetable Crops and Floriculture; flowers deep golden yellow, medium, dbl., high-centered, moderate tea fragrance; profuse, intermittent bloom; vigorous, upright growth; [Sabina × unknown]; int. by Indian Agric. Research Inst.

Ganges Mist S, w, 2005, Viraraghavan, M.S. Viru; flowers 3½-4 in., semi-dbl., borne in small clusters; foliage small, medium green, semi-glossy; prickles large, triangular pointing down, green, moderate; growth upright, medium (5 ft.); pillar; [Alliance × (Arthur Bell × (Little Darling × (*R. clinophylla* × *R. bracteata*)))]; int. by Roses Unlimited, 2005

Ganymed F, dr, 1976, Kordes; bud pointed; flowers 2½ in., 32 petals, cupped, slight fragrance; foliage glossy; vigorous, upright, bushy growth; [Europeana × seedling]; int. by Willemse, 1975

Gardejäger Gratzfeld Cl Pol, dp, 1940, Gratzfeld; flowers carmine-red, 6 cm., dbl., borne singly or in small clusters, slight fragrance; vigorous growth; [sport of Rödhätte]

Garden and Home S, ab, Delbard; buds round, pink; flowers apricot and gold in center, fading to light pink to white outer petals, full, cupped, borne in small clusters, moderate fruity, spicy fragrance; foliage deep green, slightly frilly; informal (4-5 ft.) growth; int. in 2001

Garden Art Grandma's Blessing – See **Grandma's Blessing**, S

Garden Art Last Tango – See **Last Tango**, S

Garden Art Macy's Pride – See **Macy's Pride**, S

Garden Art Orange Impressionist – See **Orange Impressionist**, S

Garden Beauty F, ab; int. in 2002

Garden Blanket S, dp, 1998, Walden, John K.; flowers dark pink, white at base, lighter reverse, 1-1½ in., single, borne in large clusters, slight fragrance; foliage small. dark green, glossy; prickles moderate; spreading, bushy, tall (3½ ft.) growth; PP11563; [Magic Carpet × Happy Trails]; int. by Bear Creek Gardens, Inc., 1998

Garden City – See **Letchworth Garden City**, F

Garden Club HT, Mansuino

Garden Delight F, dp, 1957, Norman; flowers deep rose-pink, rosette form, 3½-4 in., 34 petals, borne in clusters, moderate fragrance; vigorous, branching growth; int. by Harkness, 1956

Garden Gem HT, lp, 1930, Dingee & Conard; flowers satiny pink, dbl.; very vigorous growth; [Mrs E.T. Stotesbury × Hill's America]

Garden Glow HT, op, 1937, Cant, B. R.; flowers scarlet, base copper, dbl.; foliage glossy, bronze; very vigorous, bushy growth

Garden Jubilee Funny Face – See **Funny Face**, S

Garden Jubilee Golden Eye – See **Golden Eye**, S

Garden Jubilee Hot Wonder – See **Hot Wonder**, S

Garden Jubilee Sierra Skye – See **Sierra Skye**, HT

Garden Magic – See **Gartenzauber**, F, 1965

Garden News HT, dr, 1962, Verschuren; bud pointed; flowers dark crimson-scarlet, large, 32 petals; foliage dull, dark, leathery; strong stems; moderate growth; [New Yorker × Étoile de Hollande]; int. by Blaby Rose Gardens, 1962

Garden News – See **Flora Danica**, HT

Garden Party HT, w, 1960, Swim, H.C.; bud urn-shaped; flowers pale yellow to white, often tinged light pink, 4-5 in., 28 petals, high-centered, slight fragrance; foliage large, medium green, semi-glossy; vigorous, bushy, well-branched growth; PP1814; [Charlotte Armstrong × Peace]; int. by Armstrong Nursery, 1959; Gold Medal, Bagatelle, 1959

Garden Party, Climbing Cl HT, w, 1964, Itami Rose Nursery

Garden Party F, mr, Kordes; int. in 1999

Garden Path Mystic Fairy – See **Mystic Fairy**, S

Garden Path Pink Gnome – See **Pink Gnome**, S

Garden Path Sunrise Sunset – See **Sunrise Sunset**, S

Garden Pavilion Roos HT, op; flowers large, orange-vermilion, dbl., high-centered, borne mostly singly, no fragrance; recurrent; tall, vigorous growth; int. in 1998

Garden Pearl HT, w, Tejganga; int. in 1992

Garden Perfume HT, pb, Kordes; buds egg shaped; flowers blend of magenta and deep pink, large, long lasting, dbl., intense fragrance; int. in 1988

Garden Princess F, my, 1961, Leenders, J.; flowers yellow, becoming lighter, semi-dbl.; growth moderate; [Goldilocks × Lavender Pinocchio]

Garden Queen HT, op, 1960, Leenders, J.; flowers pink to salmon, 4 in., dbl.; vigorous growth; [Ambassadeur Nemry × Tawny Gold]

Garden State Gr, mp, 1965, Meilland, Alain A.; bud ovoid, pointed; flowers rose-pink, 3½-4 in., 42 petals, moderate fragrance; foliage leathery; vigorous, tall, bushy growth; PP2349; [(Happiness × Independence) × White Knight]; int. by C-P, 1965

Garden State II Gr, or, Williams, J. Benjamin; int. in 1997

Garden Sun LCl, ab, 2001, Meilland International; flowers 5 in., full, slight fragrance; foliage large, dark green, glossy; prickles moderate; growth climbing, tall (to 10 ft.); [Meipalsar × (Westerland × Circus)]; int. as Michka, Meilland Richardier, 1998

Garden Supreme F, ob, 1965, Jones; flowers orange blend shaded reddish, medium, 32 petals, borne in clusters; foliage leathery, bronze; low, vigorous growth; int. by Hennessey, 1958

Gardener's Joy S, ab, 2006, Beales, Amanda; flowers semi-dbl., borne in large clusters; foliage medium size, dark green, glossy; prickles average, straight, moderate; growth upright, medium (1½ m.); landscape, small climber; [Centennaire de Lourdes × Maigold]; int. by Peter Beales Roses, 2005

Gardeners' Sunday F, my, 1976, Harkness; flowers 3 in., 20 petals, moderate fragrance; foliage bright green; [(Pink Parfait × Masquerade) × Arthur Bell]; int. in 1975

Gardenia HT, w, 1898, Soupert & Notting; bud long; flowers gardenia white, large, full, moderate fragrance; [Comtesse Dusy × Mlle Hélène Cambier]

Gardenia HWich, w, 1899, Horvath/Manda, W.A.; bud pointed, yellow; flowers creamy white, center yellow, 6-7 cm., quartered, borne in small sprays; sparse repeat; foliage small, dark, glossy; short, strong stems; very vigorous growth; [*R. wichurana* × Perle des Jardins]

Gardeniaeflora HMult, w, 1901, Benary; flowers pure white, medium, semi-dbl., borne in large clusters; early bloom

Garden's Glory HMult, mp, 1905, Conard & Jones; flowers clear rose pink, large, dbl., borne in clusters; almost thornless; [Dawson × Clotilde Soupert]

Gardens of the World HT, pb, 1993, Christensen, Jack E.; bud small, ovoid; flowers magenta pink and cream blend, 3-3½ in., full, borne mostly singly, slight fragrance; foliage medium size, medium green, matte; few prickles; medium (120 cm.), upright growth; [Dame de Coeur × Sunbright]; int. by Bear Creek Gardens, 1991

Gardner's Pleasure – See **Gärtnerfreude**, S

Gareth Davies HT, mr, 1997, Poole, Lionel; flowers large, very dbl., borne mostly singly; foliage medium size, dark green, semi-glossy; upright, bushy, tall growth; [Crimson Glory × Loving Memory]

Garibaldi B, rb, 1860, Pradel; flowers cerise red, shaded with lilac, large, full

Garibaldi B, dp, Damaizin; flowers rosy lilac

Garisenda HWich, pb, 1911, Bonfiglio, A.; flowers clear rose-pink, tinted silvery, 6-7 cm., dbl., quartered, borne in clusters of 3-8; [*R. wichurana* × Souv. de la Malmaison]; sometimes sold as Souv de la Malmaison, Climbing

Garland's Gold F, ab, 2006, Horner; flowers apricot, reverse pink, 2 in., dbl., borne in small clusters; foliage medium size, light green, semi-glossy; prickles medium, straight, green, moderate; growth compact, short (2 ft.); garden decorative; [Phab Gold × Margaret Silverstein]; int. by LeGrice Roses, 2007

Garnet Climber HWich, mr, 1907, Van Fleet; [*R. wichurana* × Lucullus]

Garnet Crest T, pb, 2006, Viraraghavan, M.S. Viru; flowers up to 3½ in., full, borne in small clusters; foliage large, medium green, semi-glossy; prickles small, slender, point down, grey, few; growth bushy, tall (4 ft.); garden decorative; [mixed tea × *R. gigantea* seedling × unknown]; int. by Roses Unlimited, 2007

Garnet Striped Rose – See ***R. gallica versicolor*** (Linnaeus)

Garnette F, dr, 1951, Tantau; flowers garnet-red, base light lemon-yellow, small, 50 petals, slight fragrance; foliage leathery, dark; bushy growth; [(Rosenelfe × Eva) × Heros]; greenhouse rose; int. by J&P

Garnette – See **Carol Amling**, F

Garnette, Climbing Cl F, dr, 1954, Soria; PP1505; int. by Amling-DeVor Nursery

Garnette Apricot Pol, ab; free blooming; compact growth

Garnette Carol – See **Carol Amling**, F

Garnette Pink – See **Carol Amling**, F

Garnette Red – See **Garnette**, F

Garnette Rose Pol, dp

Garnette Supreme F, dp, 1954, Boerner; bud ovoid; flowers carmine, 2½-3 in., 35-40 petals, cupped, moderate fragrance; foliage glossy, bronze; vigorous, upright, compact growth; PP1318; [(Yellow Pinocchio × unknown) × Garnette]; int. by J&P

Garnette White Pol, w; flowers full; abundant bloom; very compact growth

Garnette Yellow Pol, my

Garnia F, dp, 1971, Butter; flowers deep pink, 4½ in., 48 petals, intense fragrance; foliage matte, green; moderately vigorous growth; [Lady Sylvia × Garnette]; int. by Wood End Gardens, 1970

Garo LCl, dr, 1987, Garelja, Anita; flowers blackish-red, large, 48 petals, high-centered, borne singly and in clusters of up to 5, slight fragrance; foliage red turning dark green, semi-glossy; prickles large, brown; upright growth; [Uncle Walter × seedling]; int. in 1978

Garry Brown F, mr, 1997, Mehring, Bernhard F.; flowers medium, dbl., borne in small clusters; foliage large, dark green, glossy; some prickles; upright, medium (26in.) growth; [Roger Lamberlin × Arthur Bell]; int. by Eurosa

Garry Paul Kirkman F, w, 2004, Paul Chessum Roses; flowers dbl., borne in small clusters, slight fragrance; foliage medium size, medium green, semi-glossy; growth compact, medium (80 cm.); beds, borders; [seedling × seedling]; int. by Love4Plants Ltd, 2004

Garry Woodward HT, or, 2000, Webster, Robert; flowers orange-red, medium, full, borne in small clusters; foliage medium size, medium green, semi-glossy; prickles moderate; compact, low (30 in.) growth; [Jeanette Talbot × The Marquess of Bristol]; int. by Handley Rose Nurseries, 2001

Gartenarchitekt Günther Schulze – See **The Pilgrim**, S

Gartenblut HT, dr, Noack, Werner; flowers 5 in., full; good repeat; growth to 80-100 cm.; int. by Noack Rosen, 1986

Gartendirektor Glocker F, or, 1957, Kordes; bud ovoid; flowers cinnabar-red, large, very dbl., borne in clusters; foliage glossy, leathery; vigorous, bushy growth; [Obergärtner Wiebicke × Independence]

Gartendirektor Hartrath HT, lp, 1911, Leenders; flowers light, satiny salmon pink

Gartendirektor Julius Schutze HT, pb, 1920, Kiese; flowers pale rosy pink and peach-blossom-pink, 4 in., full, moderate fragrance; [Mme Jules Gravereaux × Pharisaer]

Gärtendirektor Lauche – See **Éclair**, HP

Gartendirektor Nose HT, dr, 1930, Kordes; bud pointed; flowers dark crimson, large, dbl., high-centered; foliage dark, glossy; vigorous, bushy growth; [Royal Red × Templar]; int. by H&S

Gartendirektor Otto Linne S, dp, 1934, Lambert, P.; flowers dark carmine-pink, edged darker, base yellowish-white, medium, dbl., borne in clusters of up to 30; foliage leathery, light green; long strong stems; vigorous, bushy growth; [Robin Hood × Rudolph Kluis]

Gartenfee S, dp, Bergman; flowers deep rose-pink fading to soft pink, semi-dbl., borne in pyramidal clusters; recurrent; bushy growth; int. in 1987

Gartengold HT, dy, Noack, Werner; int. by Noack Rosen, 1984

Gartenstadt Liegnitz HMult, m, 1910, Lambert, P.; flowers violet/red, 5-6 cm., semi-dbl., borne in small to medium clusters; non-recurrent; [Frau Helene Videnz × Dr. Andry]

Gartenstolz F, op, 1945, Tantau; flowers rose tinted salmon, large, 8-10 petals, borne in clusters of 12-15; foliage leathery, light green; vigorous, upright, bushy growth; [Swantje × Hamburg]

Gartenstolz HT, op, Noack, Werner; int. in 1974

Gartenträume S, mp, Tantau; flowers medium pink with lilac tints, 4 in., full, cupped, borne in small clusters, intense fragrance; recurrent; foliage medium green; compact (90-140 cm.), bushy growth; int. by Rosen Tantau, 2006

Gartenzauber F, 1965, Kordes, R.; flowers blood-red, tinted cinnabar-red, well-formed, large; low growth; RULED EXTINCT 6/81 ARM; int. by Buisman, 1963

Gartenzauber F, mr, 1984, Kordes, W.; flowers large, 35 petals, high-centered; foliage medium size, dark, semi-glossy; upright growth; [(seedling × Tornado) × Chorus]; int. by Kordes Sons

Gartenzauber '84 – See **Gartenzauber**, F, 1984

Gärtnerfreude Pol, or, W. Kordes Söhne; flowers medium, dbl.; int. in 1965

Gärtnerfreude S, dr, 2006, W. Kordes' Söhne; flowers flower raspberry red, 3 cm., dbl., borne in small clusters, no fragrance; recurrent; foliage small, dark green, very glossy; vigorous (4 ft × 2 ft.) growth; int. by W. Kordes' Söhne, 1999

Garvey HT, pb, 1961, McGredy, Sam IV; flowers light geranium, reverse pale red, 6 in., 30 petals, globular; foliage dark, leathery; strong stems; vigorous, upright growth; [McGredy's Yellow × Karl Herbst]; int. by McGredy & Son, 1961

Gary Karr HT, ly, 2001, Burks, Larry; flowers 4 in., dbl., borne in small clusters, slight fragrance; foliage medium size, medium green, matte; prickles average, curved, few; growth medium (5 ft.); garden decorative; [seedling × (Gold Glow × unknown)]; int. by Certified Roses Inc., 2001

Gary Lineker F, ob, 1991, Pearce, C.A.; flowers luminous orange, yellow reverse, medium, single to semi-dbl., borne in small clusters, slight fragrance; foliage medium size, medium green, glossy; numerous prickles; medium (50-90 cm.), upright growth; [seedling × seedling]; int. by Rearsby Roses, Ltd., 1991

Gary Michael Min, my, 2004, Jalbert, Brad; flowers yellow, changing to buff or peach depending on weather, 1½ in., full, borne in small clusters, slight fragrance; foliage medium size, medium green, glossy; small, hooked, redish, no prickle; growth upright, medium (14 in.); containers, cutting; [Sandalwood × Sexy Rexy]; int. in 2003

Gary Player HT, ob, 1979, Herholdt, J.A.; flowers orange-vermilion, 4-4½ in., 35 petals, high-centered; foliage glossy, dark; vigorous growth; [Jolie Madame × seedling]; int. in 1978

Gary Wernett HT, op, 1986, French, Richard; flowers medium coral pink, large, petals wavy, dbl., high-centered to cupped, borne usually singly, moderate fragrance; foliage medium size, medium green, matte; prickles medium, triangular, light red; bushy growth; rare to full term fruit; [Helen Traubel × Helen Traubel]; int. in 1985

Gaspard Monge C, m, 1854, Robert; flowers light pink with lilac, 9-10 cm., dbl., globular, intense fragrance; some speculation that this may be a HCh, since the stems are too smooth for a centifolia

Gaspard Monge HP, mr, 1874, Moreau-Robert; flowers crimson, tinted lilac, large, full, globular

Gaston Bonnier HT, rb, 1910, Daniel/Laperrière; flowers silvery flesh-red, center dawn pink over ocher, large, full; [Antoine Rivoire × unknown]

Gaston Chandon Cl HT, pb, 1884, Schwartz; flowers light pink with coppery highlights, medium, dbl.; very remontant; [Gloire de Dijon × unknown]

Gaston Lenôtre – See **Greta**, F

Gaston Lesieur HWich, dp, 1915, Turbat; flowers carmine-pink, medium, dbl., flat, borne in clusters of 10-15

Gaston Lévêque HP, mr, 1878, Lévêque; flowers bright carmine to fiery vermilion, shaded brownish red, very large, full

Gateshead Festival HT, op, 1990, Thompson, Robert; flowers glowing orange flushed salmon with gold at base of petals, full, intense fragrance; foliage large, dark green, glossy; bushy growth; [Doris Tysterman × Silver Jubilee]; int. by Battersby Roses, 1989

Gaudi HT, Dot

Gaudia F, mp, 1946, Leenders, M.; flowers rose-pink, base gold and salmon, 4 in., 15 petals, borne in clusters; foliage bright green edged red; vigorous, tall growth; [Florentina × Talisman]; int. by Longley

Gaujard 985 HT, mr, Gaujard; flowers large, dbl.; int. in 1974

Gauntlet Min, dr, 1991, Bridges, Dennis A.; bud ovoid; flowers dark red, lighter reverse, lightens slightly with age, medium, 20-22 petals, high-centered, slight fragrance; foliage large, medium green, semi-glossy; spreading, medium growth; [Kitty Hawk × seedling]; int. by Bridges Roses, 1990

Gavá Cl HT, or, 1934, Munné, B.; flowers oriental red shaded rose-pink, base yellow, 3 in., dbl., cupped, intense fragrance; foliage leathery; very vigorous, climbing growth; [Souv. de Claudius Denoyel × Souv. de Claudius Pernet]; int. by Camprubi

Gaval – See **Atlantic**, Gr

Gavina HT, w, Dot; flowers pure white

Gavnø F, ob, 1989, Olesen, Pernille & Mogens N.; flowers orange, medium, 20 petals, no fragrance; foliage medium size, dark green, glossy; bushy growth; [seedling × Mary Sumner]; int. by Poulsen Roser ApS, 1988

Gavolda – See **Cri-Cri**, Min

Gavotte HT, pb, 1963, Sanday, John; flowers pink, reverse light yellow, 5 in., 45 petals; foliage dark; vigorous, upright growth; [Ethel Sanday × Lady Sylvia]

Gavroche F, ob, 1963, Robichon; flowers orange, center yellow, large; vigorous, bushy growth

Gavroche – See **Paprika**, LCl

Gay Crusader HT, rb, 1948, Robinson, H.; flowers red fading to pink, reverse deep yellow, large, high-centered; foliage dark; [Phyllis Gold × Catalonia]; int. by Baker's Nursery

Gay Dawn HT, op, 1956, Taylor, C.A.; bud pointed; flowers large, dbl., cupped, moderate spicy fragrance; foliage dark, semi-glossy; very vigorous, upright growth; [Eclipse × Mme Henri Guillot]; int. by California Nursery Co.

Gay Debutante HT, pb, 1960, Curtis, R.F.; flowers light pink, base yellow, very large, 40-45 petals, cupped, slight fragrance; foliage leathery, glossy; vigorous, upright growth; PP1750; [sport of Peace]; int. by C.R. Burr, 1961

Gay Dicky F, ob, 1956, Verschuren-Pechtold; flowers tangerine-orange; moderate growth; int. by Gandy Roses, Ltd.

Gay Gold HT, my, 1973, Lowe; flowers 5½ in., 30 petals; foliage glossy; [King's Ransom × Piccadilly]

Gay Gordons HT, yb, 1969, Cocker; flowers orange-yellow and red, dbl.; foliage dark, glossy; bushy, rather low growth; [Belle Blonde × Karl Herbst]

Gay Gypsy HT, dr, 1949, Crane; bud long, pointed; flowers oxblood-red shaded maroon, open, 4½-5 in., 15-20 petals, cupped; foliage leathery; vigorous, upright, bushy growth; [sport of Charles K. Douglas]; int. by Bosley Nursery

Gay Heart F, mp, 1951, Boerner; bud ovoid; flowers bright pink, large, 25 petals, high-centered, borne in large clusters; foliage leathery; vigorous, upright growth; [Joanna Hill × World's Fair]; int. by J&P

Gay Jewel Min, lp, 1959, Morey, Dr. Dennison; bud globular; flowers light rose-pink, ½ in., 35-40 petals, cupped, moderate fragrance; foliage glossy; compact (6-8 in.) growth; [Dick Koster × Tom Thumb]; int. by J&P, 1959

Gay Lady HT, mr, 1953, Swim, H.C.; bud ovoid; flowers currant-red, open, 3½-4½ in., 20-28 petals, moderate spicy fragrance; foliage dark, leathery, glossy; very vigorous, upright growth; [Charlotte Armstrong × Piccadilly]; int. by Breedlove Nursery

Gay Lyric HT, mp, 1971, Fankhauser; flowers rose-pink, large, very dbl., high-centered; foliage glossy, dark, leathery; vigorous, upright growth; [Royal Highness × Elizabeth Fankhauser]

Gay Maid F, or, 1969, Gregory; flowers red suffused orange-pink, 26 petals, globular, borne in trusses; foliage light green; very vigorous growth; [Masquerade × unknown]

Gay Mood LCl, dp, 1940, Lammerts, Dr. Walter; bud large, ovoid to urn shaped, rose-red; flowers deep rose-pink, open, dbl.; profuse, repeated bloom; foliage glossy, dark; very vigorous, climbing growth; [Joanna Hill × Sanguinaire]; int. by Armstrong Nursery

Gay Nineties Cl F, mr, 1955, Sima; bud ovoid; flowers rose-red, 2-2½ in., 65 petals, borne in clusters of 5-8, intense fragrance; foliage leathery, glossy; vigorous, pillar (8 ft.) growth; PP1354; [(New Dawn × Red Ripples) × Red Ripples]

Gay Paris HT, mr, 1962, Delbard-Chabert; bud long; flowers bright crimson, well-formed, large, dbl., moderate fragrance; foliage bright green; vigorous growth; [(Floradora × Barcelona) × (Charles Mallerin × Tonnerre)]; int. in 1960

Gay Princess F, lp, 1967, Boerner; bud ovoid; flowers blush-pink, large, dbl., cupped, borne in clusters, moderate fragrance; foliage leathery; vigorous, upright, bushy growth; PP2763; [Spartan × The Farmer's Wife]; int. by J&P

Gay Vista S, lp, 1957, Riethmuller; flowers cerise-pink with white eye, single, borne in large clusters; repeat bloom; growth to 3½ ft

Gayathri HT, dp, K&S; flowers rich rose pink, lasting, dbl., high-centered; recurrent; strong growth; int. by KSG Son Roses, 2004

Gaye Babe HWich, pb, 2000, Huxley, Ian; buds squat but pointed; flowers pale blush pink, reverse blush pink, prominent yellow stamens, 3 in., semi-dbl., cupped, borne in small clusters; remontant; foliage medium size, dark green, semi-glossy, disease-resistant; prickles moderate; rambling, spreading, medium (5 ft.) growth; [New Dawn × unknown]; int. by G & G Paulusz, 1994

Gayle F, w, J&P; PP11634; int. by Bear Creek, 2000

Gayness HT, Reithmuller; int. in 1955

Gaytime F, rb, 1966, Armstrong, D.L.; bud ovoid, pointed; flowers red and yellow, large, dbl., cupped, slight fragrance; foliage dark, glossy, leathery; vigorous, bushy, compact growth; PP2704; [seedling × Circus]; int. by Armstrong Nursery

Gazella HGal, dp, before 1906

Gazelle HGal, lp, before 1843; flowers delicate rose, large

G'Day – See **Madhatter**, Min

Ge Korsten HT, mr, (HERgeko)

Géant des Batailles HP, mr, 1846, Nérard; flowers deep fiery crimson, medium, 85 petals, intense fragrance; moderately vigorous growth; int. by Guillot Pere

Géant des Batailles a Fleurs Roses HP, dp, 1868, Carré; flowers large, full

Gebrüder Grimm F, ob, 2006; flowers dazzling orange and yellow, 7 cm., full, borne in small clusters; recurrent; foliage medium size, dark green, very glossy; vigorous, bushy, upright (70 cm.) growth; int. by W. Kordes' Söhne, 2002

Gedenke Mein HMult, w, 1912, Paul, J; flowers white, shaded flesh pink, semi-dbl.; [*R. arvensis* × Crimson Rambler]

Gedge's Glory HT, op, 1998, Webster, Robert; flowers pale orange, salmon pink reverse, 3-4 in., very dbl., borne mostly singly; foliage medium size, dark green, glossy; prickles moderate, medium, straight; low, compact growth; [Dave Hesswayon × Remember Me]

Gee Dee HT, mr, Dawson; int. in 1979

Gee Gee Min, ly, 1987, Benardella, Frank A.; flowers medium yellow, fading lighter, loose, small, 20-25 petals, cupped, borne usually singly, slight fruity fragrance; foliage medium size, light green, matte, edges toothed; prickles pointed, beige; upright, bushy, medium growth; no fruit; PP6783; [Rise 'n' Shine × Patricia]; int. by Kimbrew Walter Roses, 1987

Gee Whiz S, yb, 1985, Buck, Dr. Griffith J.; flowers yellow tinted orange-red, 23 petals, cupped, borne 1-10 per cluster, moderate sweet fragrance; repeat bloom; foliage medium size, leathery, dark olive green; prickles needle-like, brown; low, bushy, free-branching growth; hardy; [Gingersnap × Sevilliana]; int. by Iowa State University, 1984

Geheimrat Doctor Mittweg S, pb, 1909, Lambert, P.; flowers rose-red, center yellowish-white, large, borne in large clusters; recurrent bloom; foliage dark; vigorous, bushy growth; [Mme Norbert Levavasseur × Trier]

Geheimrat Duisberg – See **Golden Rapture**, HT

Geheimrat Duisberg, Climbing – See **Golden Rapture, Climbing**, Cl HT

Geheimrat Richard Willstätter HT, ab, 1931, Felberg-Leclerc; flowers apricot-yellow, veined carmine-red, stamens yellow, large, semi-dbl.; foliage bright, thick; vigorous growth; [Constance × Admiral Ward]

Geisha HMult, rb, 1913, Geschwind, R.; flowers scarlet crimson, with white streaks on center petals, 8-10 cm., full, cupped, borne in clusters; [De La Grifferaie × a HP or B]

Geisha HT, ob, 1920, Van Rossem; bud orange, marked coral-red; flowers golden yellow, sometimes striped red, medium to large, borne in small clusters, slight fragrance; foliage medium size, dark green, glossy; [sport of Mme Edouard Herriot]

Geisha F, mp, 1965, Tantau, Math.; bud long; flowers 2½-3 in., semi-dbl., borne in clusters of 1-3; foliage dark; growth bushy, medium; int. as Pink Elizabeth Arden, Wheatcroft Bros., 1964

Geisha F, ab, Tantau; flowers apricot-orange, 8 cm., dbl., cupped, borne in clusters, slight fragrance; free-flowering; foliage fresh green, durable; bushy (50-80 cm.), arching growth; int. by Rosen Tantau, 2006

Geisha Girl F, my, 1964, McGredy, Sam IV; flowers large, 25 petals, borne in clusters; foliage long, pointed; tall growth; [Gold Cup × McGredy's Yellow]; int. by McGredy

Gekko HT, my, Keisei; int. by Keisei Rose Nurseries, 1999

Gela Gnau HT, ab, 1926, Leenders, M.; flowers amber-yellow, reverse apricot, dbl.

Gela Tepelmann – See **Frau Eva Schubert**, HWich

Gelbe Dagmar Hastrup – See **Topaz Jewel**, HRg

Gelbe Florida von Scharbeutz F

Gelbe Holstein F, ly, 1951, Kordes; bud long, pointed; flowers yellow paling to lemon, 3 in., 20 petals, borne in large clusters; foliage glossy, light green; vigorous, upright, bushy growth; [(Eva × Viscountess Charlemont) × Sunmist]; int. by Wheatcroft Bros.

Gelbe Pharisäer HT, my, 1927, Hinner, W.; flowers clear yellow, center deeper; [Pharisaer × Mrs Aaron Ward]

Gelber Engel F, ly, 2006; flowers light yellow with golden stamens, 6 cm., dbl., borne in small clusters; foliage very dense, dark green, very glossy, disease-resistant; low, erect and bushy (80 × 60 cm.) growth; int. by W. Kordes' Söhne, 2002

Gelber Kobold MinFl, dy; int. in 1996

Gellert HMult, w, 1917, Lambert

Gelria F, Verbeek; int. in 1974

Geltendorf HT, ob, Croix; int. in 1971

Gem HT, mp, 1960, Walker; bud long, pointed; flowers deep soft pink, medium, semi-dbl., high-centered; foliage soft; vigorous, upright growth; [Ena Harkness × Mme Butterfly]

Gem of the Prairies HSet, dp, 1865, Burgess, A.;

flowers rosy red, occasionally blotched white, darker at center, 6-7 cm., full, flat, borne in large clusters; non-recurrent; vigorous growth; [Queen of the Prairies × Mme Laffay]

Gemini Pol, ob, 1967, Joseph H. Hill, Co.; bud pointed; flowers orange, small, dbl., high-centered, slight fragrance; foliage dark, glossy; vigorous, upright, bushy growth; PP2728; [seedling × Rumba]

Gemini HT, pb, 1999, Zary, Dr. Keith W.; bud pointed, ovoid; flowers cream, blushing coral pink, 4½-5 in., 25-30 petals, high-centered, borne usually singly, moderate sweet fragrance; foliage large, deep green, glossy; prickles moderate; long stems; upright, spreading, tall (5½ ft.) growth; PP11691; [Anne Morrow Lindbergh × New Year]; int. by Bear Creek Gardens, 2000; Silver Medal, Monza, 1999

Gemini HT, my, Burston; flowers clear yellow with thin pink petal edges, dbl., globular; foliage dark green, glossy; growth to 70 cm.; int. by Burston Nurseries, 2004

Gemma F, mp, Harkness; flowers bright mid-pink, medium, dbl., borne in large clusters, slight fragrance; free-flowering; foliage glossy, disease-resistant green; growth to 4 × 3 ft.; int. by Harkness Roses, 2003

Gemma Rouge S, dr; groundcover; spreading growth; int. by Willemse France, 2003

Gemstone HT, mp, 1978, J&B Roses; bud high-centered; flowers 4½-5 in., 28 petals, high-centered; foliage matte; vigorous, upright growth; [Helen Traubel × Swarthmore]; int. by Eastern Roses

Gen. John Pershing LCl, dp, 1917, Undritz; flowers large, 53 petals; vigorous, climbing growth; [Dr. W. Van Fleet × Mrs W.J. Grant]

Gene Boerner F, mp, 1968, Boerner; bud ovoid; flowers deep pink, medium, 35 petals, high-centered; foliage glossy; vigorous, upright growth; PP2885; [Ginger × (Ma Perkins × Garnette Supreme)]; int. by J&P

Gene Jones F, w, 2000, Williams, J. Benjamin; flowers ivory white, with pink washing, 2½-3 in., dbl., borne in small clusters; foliage medium size, medium green, semi-glossy, disease-resistant; few prickles; growth vigorous, bushy, medium (3½-4 ft.); [Handel × Stardance]; int. by J. B. Williams & Assoc.

Gene Sandberg HT, lp, 1996, Sheldon, John, Jennifer & Robyn; flowers light pink with a dark pink line around outer edge of each p, 4-6 in., full; foliage medium size, dark green, dull; prickles moderate; upright, medium (2-3 ft.) growth; [Touch of Elegance × First Prize]

Gene Tierney S, dy, Guillot-Massad; flowers amber yellow, full, cupped, borne in clusters, moderate myrrh fragrance; recurrent; tall growth; int. by Roseraies Guillot, 2000

Generaal Smuts HT, mr, 1922, Van Rossem; flowers cherry-red, shaded deep coral-red, dbl.; [Gen. MacArthur × Mme Edouard Herriot]

Generaal Snijders HT, dp, 1917, Leenders, M.; flowers deep carmine shaded coral-red, large, dbl., intense fragrance; [Mme Mélanie Soupert × George C. Waud]

Général Allard B, dp, 1835, Laffay, M.; flowers bright pink, medium, full, globular; growth branching, small

Général Appert HP, dr, 1884, Schwartz; flowers velvety blackish purple red, large, full; quite remontant; [Souv de William Wood × unknown]

Général Athalin – See **Athalin**, B

Général Baron Berge HP, mr, 1892, Pernet Père; flowers red, center occasionally striped white, large, 50 petals; erect, vigorous growth

General Barral HP, m, 1867, Damaizin; flowers violet pink, medium, full

Général Bedeau HP, pb, 1851, Margottin; flowers pink and red, large, dbl.

Général Bernard HP, pb, before 1845; flowers carmine, shaded dull violet, full, globular

Général Berthelot HT, dp, 1926, Walter, L.; flowers dark pink, slightly streaked white, dbl.; [J.B. Clark × Farbenkonigin]

General Browne HSpn, w, about 1860; flowers blush-white, fading pure white, quilled, dbl., moderate fragrance; foliage dark; twiggy, prickly growth

General Bülow HGal, mp, before 1845; flowers carmine, edges darker with violet tones, full

Général Canrobert B, mr, about 1860, Pradel; flowers shining crimson, large, full

General Cavaignac HP, mr, 1848, Foulard; flowers vary from deep red to pinky red depending upon weather, dbl.; slow to establish

Général Cavaignac HP, mr, 1849, Margottin; flowers shining cherry red, large, full

Général Clerc M, dr, 1845, Laffay, M.; flowers slaty purple-red, medium, full

Général D. Mertchansky T, mp, 1890, Nabonnand; flowers rosy flesh, petals somewhat imbricated, large, full; prickles moderate; stems reddish; growth very vigorous

Général Daumesnil HCh, m; flowers violet purple with lilac, full

Général de Castellane HP, mr, 1851, Guillot père

Général de la Martinière HP, rb, 1869, De Sansal; flowers wine red, center glossy crimson pink, outer petals lilac pink, very large, full

Général de Lamoricière HCh, m, before 1866; flowers lilac pink, medium, full

Général de Tartas – See **Général Tartas**, T

Général de Vaulgrenant HT, dp, 1926, Walter, L.; flowers rose-pink, very dbl.; [Mme Henriette Schissele × Mme Adele Gance]

Général Désaix HGal, dp, before 1829, Boutigny; flowers bright dark pink, edges lighter, medium, full

Général Désaix HP, mr, 1867, Moreau et Robert; flowers fiery red, shaded poppy, large, full

Général d'Hautpoul HP, mr, 1864, Verdier, E.; flowers bright scarlet, medium, dbl.

Général Dinot – See **Général Drouot**, M

General Domingos de Oliveira HT, ab, 1939, Moreira da Silva; flowers yellow-apricot tinted flesh-pink, large, dbl., cupped; foliage glossy; dwarf growth; [Frank Reader × Golden Gleam]

General Don HT, pb, 1919, Le Cornu; flowers strawberry tinted coppery, base golden yellow, dbl.; [Mme Mélanie Soupert × Louise Catherine Breslau]

Général Donadieu HGal, mr, before 1835; flowers purplish red, compact, very dbl.

Général Drouot M, m, 1847, Vibert; flowers grenadine-purple, becoming currant red, medium, dbl.; not very remontant; foliage dark, tinted brown; prickles numerous, flat at base, straight; vigorous growth

Général Duc d'Aumale HP, dr, 1875, Verdier, E.; flowers dark cerise red, large, dbl.

Général Fabvier – See **Fabvier**, Ch

Général Fetter HT, m, 1922, Walter, L.; flowers carmine-purple, glossy, very dbl.; [Jonkheer J.L. Mock × Luise Lilia]

Général Forey HP, dr, 1859, Moreau & Robert; flowers wine red, large, full, cupped; [Triomphe de l'Exposition × unknown]

Général Foy D, dp, 1825, Boutigny; flowers deep brilliant pink, lighter edges, small to medium, very dbl.

Général Foy HGal, mr, 1827, Pelletier; flowers ruby red, outer petals lighter, very large, full, flat, borne in small clusters

Général Foy HGal, pb, 1844, Vibert; flowers spotted

Général Galliéni T, rb, 1899, Nabonnand, G.; flowers coppery red, cupped, moderate fragrance; recurrent; vigorous growth; [Souv. de Therese Levet × Reine Emma des Pays-Bas]

General Gordon T, w, 1885, Bennett; flowers pure white, medium, dbl.

Général Grant HP, mr, 1869, Verdier, E.; flowers scarlet, shaded dark carmine, large, full

Général Guisan HT, dr, 1945, Heizmann, E.; flowers large, dbl.

Général Hoche B, mp; flowers bright pink, medium, very full, cupped

Général Hudelet HP, pb, 1852, Crousse; flowers light pink, center cherry red, large, full

General Jack – See **Général Jacqueminot**, HP

Général Jacqueminot HCh, dr, 1846, Laffay

Général Jacqueminot HP, rb, 1853, Roussel; bud scarlet-crimson; flowers dark red, whitish reverse, 27 petals, intense fragrance; recurrent bloom; foliage rich green; long, strong stems; vigorous, bushy growth; [probable seedling of Gloire des Rosomanes]

Général Kléber M, mp, 1856, Robert; bud well mossed; flowers pink tinted lilac, full, moderate fragrance; non-recurrent; foliage apple green; vigorous, upright (4 ft.) growth

Général Kléber HP, mr, 1872, Boyau; flowers bright red, shaded dark carmine, large, full; very remontant

General Korolkow – See **Eugène Fürst**, HP

Général Labutère Ch, mp

Général Lamarque – See **Lamarque**, N

General MacArthur HT, dp, 1905, E.G. Hill Co.; flowers rose-red, 20 petals, intense damask fragrance; foliage leathery

General MacArthur, Climbing Cl HT, dp, 1923, Dickson, H.; flowers bright carmine pink, large, semi-dbl.; [sport of General MacArthur]

Général Miloradowitsch HP, mr, 1869, Louvat or Lévêque; flowers red, shaded carmine, very large, full

Général Moreau HGal, m, before 1885, Moreau, F.; flowers purple pink, medium, full

Général Négrier HP, mp, 1851, Portemer; flowers bright pink, large, full

General Robert E. Lee T, my, 1896, Good & Reese; bud deep orange-yellow; flowers canary-yellow

Général Schablikine T, op, 1878, Nabonnand, G.; flowers deep pink with coppery overtones, full, flat; vigorous, medium (3 ft.) growth

Général Simpson HP, mp, 1854, Lacharme; flowers rose pink with lilac reflections, medium, full

Général Simpson HP, mp, 1857, Ducher; flowers bright carmine, medium, very full

General Snyders – See **Generaal Snijders**, HT

General Stefánik HP, m, 1933, Böhm, J.; flowers violet blue; [seedling or sport of La Brillante]; int. by J&P

General-Superior Arnold Janssen HT, dp, 1912, Leenders, M.; bud pointed; flowers deep rose-pink, veined darker, reverse much darker, large, dbl.; [Farbenkonigin × Gen. MacArthur]

General-Superior Arnold Janssen, Climbing Cl HT, dp, 1931, Böhm, J.; flowers deep rose-red, large, full; [sport of General-Superior Arnold Janssen]

Général Tartas T, dp, 1860, Bernède; flowers deep rose, large, dbl.

Général Testard HWich, rb, 1918, Pajotin-Chédane; flowers red, center white, 6 cm., semi-dbl., borne in large clusters; foliage small, glossy

Général Tétard – See **Général Testard**, HWich

General Th. Peschkoff HT, pb, 1909, Ketten, Gebrüder; flowers salmon red, fading to Hermosa pink, center yellow, very large, dbl., moderate fragrance; [Mme Ravary × Étoile de France]

General Vaidya HT, ab, More, Chandrakant; [sport of Freude]

Général Valazé T, w, before 1835, Dubourg; flowers flesh white, center brighter pink, large, full

General von Bothnia-Andreæ HP, mr, 1900, Verschuren; flowers carmine-red, very large, dbl.; [Victor Verdier × seedling]

General von Moltke HP, rb, 1873, Bell; flowers bright red, shaded scarlet orange, large, full; [Charles Léfèbvre × unknown]

Général Washington T, mr, 1855, Page

Général Washington HP, dr, 1860, Granger; flowers deep crimson, reflexes maroon, large, very dbl., flat, moderate fragrance; occasionally recurrent bloom; moderate growth; [sport of Triomphe de l'Exposition]

Générale Marie Raiewsky HP, pb, 1911, Ketten Bros.; flowers pink with dark yellow, large, dbl.; [Frau Karl Druschki × Fisher Holmes]

Generalin Isenbart HT, pb, 1915, Lambert, P.; flowers coppery-pink with dark yellow, large, dbl.; [Triumph × E. Veyrat Hermanos]

Generaloberst von Kluck HT, dp, 1917, Lambert, P.; flowers carmine-pink, large, dbl.; [Frau Geheimrat Dr. Staub × Germanica]

Generosa HT, mr, 1964, Mansuino, Q.; flowers crimson to spirea-red, small to medium, 35 petals, cupped; foliage small, dark; thin stems; PP2577; int. as Mansuino Rose, Carlton Rose Nurseries

Generosity HT, ob, 1983, Northfield, G.; flowers cream with orange center, large, 35 petals, moderate fragrance; foliage large, dark, matte; bushy growth; [Fred Gibson × Lady Elgin]

Genesis Min, m, 1991, Jolly, Marie; bud ovoid; flowers lavender, reverse white, 2 in., 45 petals, borne singly, moderate fragrance; foliage medium size, medium green, semi-glossy; upright growth; [Lavender Jade × Angel Face]; int. by Rosehill Farm, 1992

Genève HT, or, 1944, Meilland, F.; bud long; flowers salmon-carmine and capucine-red, high pointed, dbl.; vigorous growth; [Charles P. Kilham × Mme Joseph Perraud]

Genevieve Min, yb, 1983, Saville, F. Harmon; flowers yellow, streaked scarlet, scarlet increasing with age, small, 35 petals, moderate spicy fragrance; foliage medium size, medium green, semi-glossy; upright, bushy growth; [unnamed climbing miniature × unnamed miniature seedling]; int. by Nor'East Min. Roses, 1983

Genevieve – See **Colette**, LCl

Geneviève Genest – See **Mrs Sam McGredy, Climbing**, Cl HT

Geneviève le Goaster HT, w, 1923, Carrette; flowers white, center pale rose, base salmon-rose; int. by Richardier

Genevieve Rose S, ob, Peden, R.; int. in 1998

Génie de Châteaubriand HP, dr, 1852, Oudin; flowers bishop's violet, with scarlet reflections and tinted black violet, 4 in., rosette, borne in clusters of 2-4; foliage dark green above, silvery beneath, ovate, lightly serrated; prickles down-hooked, reddish when young, small; growth upright

Genius Mendel HT, mr, 1935, Böhm, J.; bud pointed; flowers light fiery red to pure red, large, dbl., high-centered; foliage glossy; bushy growth; [Mrs Henry Winnett × Sir David Davis]

Gensuar – See **Top of the Bill**, Min

Gentil – See **Les Trois Mages**, HGal

Gentil Bernard D, 1825, Bizard

Gentiliana – See **Polyantha Grandiflora**, HMult

Gentle F, op, 1960, Lens; flowers salmon-pink, well-formed, 2½-3 in., 26 petals, borne in clusters; vigorous, compact, bushy growth; [Independence × (Lady Sylvia × Fashion)]

Gentle Annie F, m, 2000, McCann, Sean; flowers purple, bright yellow stamens, large, semi-dbl., borne in very large clusters; foliage medium size, medium green, glossy; some prickles; upright, medium growth; [(News × International Herald Tribune) × Stolen Moment]; int. by Slattery Roses

Gentle Clown MinFl, pb, Harkness; int. in 1994

Gentle Cover – See **Natchez**, Min

Gentle Giant HT, pb, 2005, Carruth, Tom; flowers cerise pink with a yellow base, 12-14 cm., 30 petals, borne mostly solitary, slight fragrance; foliage large, light green, matte; prickles few, average, slightly hooked, beige; stems very long; growth upright, medium (120 to 150 cm.); garden decoration; [Rina Hugo × (seedling × O Sole Mio)]; int. by Edmunds Roses, 2006

Gentle Hermione S, lp, 2006; flowers very full, borne in small clusters; foliage medium size, dark green, matte; prickles medium, concave, curved inward, dark red, moderate; growth bushy, vigorous, medium (120 cm.); garden decorative; [seedling × seedling]; int. by David Austin Roses, Ltd., 2005

Gentle Kiss Min, ab, Harkness; int. in 1989

Gentle Lady HT, lp, 1975, Fuller; bud slender, long, pointed; flowers large, 35 petals, cupped, intense fragrance; foliage matte, dark, leathery; upright, bushy growth; [Tiffany × Michele Meilland]; int. by Wyant

Gentle Maid Min, m, Harkness; flowers small, full, borne in clusters; free-flowering; vase shaped, medium (2 ft.) growth; int. in 1988

Gentle Persuasion S, yb, 1985, Buck, Dr. Griffith J.; flowers yellow tinted orange, medium-large, 28 petals, cupped, borne 1-5 per cluster; repeat bloom; foliage large, leathery, semi-glossy, dark olive green; prickles awl-like, tan; vigorous, bushy, erect growth; hardy; [Carefree Beauty × Oregold]; int. by Iowa State University, 1984

Gentle Touch Min, lp, 1987, Dickson, Patrick; flowers moderately small, dbl., slight fragrance; foliage small, medium green, semi-glossy; patio; bushy growth; [(Liverpool Echo × Woman's Own) × Memento]; int. in 1986; Rose of the Year, 1986

Gentleman's Agreement MinFl, mr, 1998, Bridges, Dennis A.; bud long, slender; flowers medium red, excellent substance, 1-1½ in., full, high-centered, borne mostly singly, no fragrance; foliage large, medium green, semi-glossy; few prickles; tall, upright, bushy growth; Disease resistant; [Purple Dawn × select pollen]; int. by Bridges Roses, 1998

Genval HT, mp, 1963, Delforge; flowers cyclamen-pink; foliage bronze, dull; vigorous growth; [Rosita × Margaret]

Geoff Boycott F, w, 1976, McGredy, Sam IV; flowers large, 35 petals, slight fragrance; foliage dark; [Ice White × Tip-Top]; int. in 1974

Geoff Hamilton S, mp, 1998, Austin, David; flowers rounded, 3-4 in., 108 petals, borne in small clusters, moderate fragrance; foliage medium size, medium green, semi-glossy, good disease resistance; prickles moderate; sturdy, compact, upright, medium (4 ft.) growth; PP11421; [Heritage × seedling]; int. by David Austin Roses, Ltd., 1997

Geoffrey Henslow HT, mr, 1912, Dickson, A.; flowers very dbl.

Geordie Lad HT, r, 1989, Horner, Colin P.; bud ovoid, red; flowers mahogany-red, yellow at base, reverse lighter red, medium, dbl., cupped, moderate fruity fragrance; foliage medium size, medium green, matte; prickles small, light brown; upright, medium growth; hips ovoid, medium size; [Prominent × (Champagne Cocktail × Alpine Sunset)]; int. by Battersby Roses, 1990

Georg Ahrends – See **Georg Arends**, HP

Georg Arends HP, mp, 1910, Hinner, W.; flowers soft pink, large, 25 petals, intense fragrance; vigorous growth; [Frau Karl Druschki × La France]

Georg Geuder HT, op, 1931, Schmidt, I. C.; flowers dark salmon-pink, medium, dbl.

George Armer HT, dp, 1993, Bracegirdle, A.J.; flowers deep pink, medium, dbl., high-centered, borne mostly singly, slight fragrance; foliage medium size, bronze-red, matte; some prickles; medium (12 cm.), upright growth; [Gavotte × First Prize]; int. by Bracegirdle, 1993

George Baker HP, dp, 1881, Paul & Son; flowers cerise, very dbl.

George Burns F, yb, 1996, Carruth, Tom; flowers yellow striped irregularly with red, cream and pink, 3-3½ in., full, borne in small clusters, moderate fruit and citrus fragrance; foliage large, clean, dark green, glossy; numerous prickles; upright, compact, medium (3-3½ ft.) growth; PP10334; [Calico × Roller Coaster]; int. by Spring Hill Nurseries Co., 1997

George Burns Centennial – See **George Burns**, F

George C. Waud HT, mp, 1908, Dickson, A.; flowers rose, veined darker, 4½ in., dbl., high-centered, intense fragrance; bushy growth

George Dakin HT, pb, 1927, Burbage Nursery; flowers silvery pink, flushed apricot, reverse orange to apricot, dbl., high-centered; foliage glossy, bronze; vigorous, bushy growth; [Ophelia × Mrs Henry Morse]

George Dickson HT, mr, 1912, Dickson, A.; flowers large crimson, 36 petals, borne on weak stems, moderate fragrance; Gold Medal, NRS, 1911

George Dickson, Climbing Cl HT, mr, 1949, Woodward; [sport of George Dickson]

George Elger Pol, my, 1912, Turbat; bud small, golden yellow; flowers coppery yellow to clear yellow, very dbl., borne in large clusters; foliage small, dark, soft; bushy, dwarf growth

George Elliot HT, op, 1970, Wills; flowers shrimp-pink, 4-5 in., 35 petals; foliage bronze; [Highlight × Dorothy Peach]

George Fox HT, or, 1939, Savage Nursery; flowers orange-vermilion, medium, globular; foliage glossy; compact growth; [Charles P. Kilham × Lady Forteviot]

George Geary HT, yb, 1953, Geary; flowers golden yellow flushed vermilion, high pointed, 4 in.; foliage dark, bronze; vigorous growth; [Gwyneth Jones × seedling]; int. by Burbage Nursery

George Geuder HT, yb, 1931, Schmidt, J.C.; flowers salmon-pink and bright carmine on yellow ground; vigorous growth

George H. Mackereth HT, dr, 1924, Dickson, A.; flowers crimson shaded velvety maroon, dbl.

George Heers HT, pb, 1961, Langbecker; flowers rich pink, touched apricot and yellow

George Howarth HT, dp, 1928, Bees; flowers bright carmine, dbl.; [Gorgeous × The Queen Alexandra Rose]

George IV – See **Rivers' George IV**, HCh

George Laing Paul HT, mr, 1904, S&H; [Mme Caroline Testout × Fisher-Holmes]

George Peabody Ch, m, 1857, Pentland; flowers bright garnet-purple, large, full; [Joseph Paul × unknown]

George R. Hill HT, w, 1991, Varney, Eric; flowers 45 petals; foliage large, dark green; vigorous growth; [sport of Admiral Rodney]; int. by Battersby Roses, 1991

George Rimmer HT, dr, 2001, Poole, Lionel; flowers 5½ in., full, high-centered, borne mostly solitary, slight fragrance; foliage large, dark green, semi-glossy; prickles medium, hooked down, moderate; growth upright, bushy, medium (1 m.), vigorous; exhibition, bedding; [(Royal William × Gabi) × New Zealand]; int. by David Lister Roses, 2002

George Sand HP, mp, 1909, Roseraie de l'Hay; flowers flesh pink

George Sand – See **Lunelle**, HT

George Thomas HT, w, 1972, Ellick; flowers pure white, tinged pink, 6-8 in., 40 petals, moderate fragrance; foliage dark; vigorous growth; [Ena Harkness × Memoriam]; int. in 1975

George Vancouver S, mr, Ogilvie, Ian S.; flowers 24 petals, flat, borne singly and in clusters; good repeat; lush, disease-resistant foliage; open, arching (3 × 4 ft.) growth; PP10009; int. in 1994

George Will HRg, dp, 1939, Skinner; flowers deep pink, 3 in., dbl., flat, borne in clusters, moderate clove fragrance; all-summer bloom; foliage rugose; stems slender branches; growth to 3-4 ft.; [(*R. rugosa* × *R. acicularis*) × unknown]

Georgeous Min, mp, 1992, Ilsink, Peter; flowers 1¼ in., 6-8 petals, cupped, borne in sprays of 3-8; foliage small, dark green, glossy; bushy, low (30-40 cm.) growth; [Candy Rose × Eyeopener]; int. by Interplant B.V., 1990

Georges Cain HRg, dr, 1909, Gravereaux; flowers crimson with purple, large, dbl.; very vigorous growth; [Souv. de Pierre Notting × *R. rugosa*]

Georges Cassagne Gr, mr, Croix; int. by Roses Paul Croix, 1980

Georges Chesnel HT, dy, 1935, Pernet-Ducher; bud pointed; flowers deep golden yellow, veined copper, dbl.; foliage glossy; [(Julien Potin × unknown) × Étoile d'Or]; int. by Gaujard

George's Choice F, mr, 1978, Ellick; bud small, ovoid; flowers currant red, 35-40 petals, moderate fragrance; compact, bushy growth; [Evelyn Fison × Tabarin]; int. by Excelsior Roses, 1979

Georges Clemenceau HT, ob, 1919, Lévêque; flowers bright orange, shaded umber and carmine, large, very full; [sport of Mme Edouard Herriot]

Georges Cuvier B, dp, 1842, Souchet; flowers bright cerise, shaded pink, large, full, cupped; foliage very dark green; prickles straight, flattened at base; growth vigorous

Georges d'Amboise HP, mr, 1853, Boyau; flowers bright rose red, large, full, globular

Georges de Cadonel B, lp, 1904, Schwartz; flowers bright pink nuanced carmine on coppery ground, large, very full, globular, moderate fragrance; recurrent; foliage purplish green; short stems; arching growth; sometimes classed as Cl T

Georges de Cadoudal – See **Georges de Cadonel**, B

Georges Denjean S, ob, Guillot-Massad; int. by Roseraies Guillot, 2006

Georges Dubœuf – See **Lovers Lane**, HT

Georges Dupont B, mp, 1856, Lartay; flowers carmine

Georges Farber T, dr, 1889, Bernaix; bud longly oval, conical; flowers outer petals velvety purple, thick, veined and reticulated with fiery red, medium; foliage bright green; growth medium

Georges Hamonière HT, dr, 1937, Moulin; flowers medium, dbl.

Georges Moreau HP, mr, 1880, Moreau-Robert; flowers bright satiny red, tinted vermilion, very large, globular; nearly thornless; [Paul Neyron × unknown]

Georges Paquel HT, my, 1934, Leenders, M.; flowers saffron-yellow, large, dbl.; vigorous, bushy growth; [seedling × Souv. de Claudius Pernet]

Georges Paul HP, mr, 1863, Verdier, E.; flowers bright velvety red, 8-10 cm., full, borne in clusters of 6-8

Georges Perdoux HT, pb, 1927, Barbier; flowers reddish-pink tinted coppery red, dbl.

Georges Pernet Pol, mp, 1887, Pernet-Ducher; flowers bright peach-pink; [Mignonette × unknown]

George's Pride Min, ob, 2007, Mander, George; flowers orange blend, reverse dark yellow, 4-6 cm., full, high-centered, borne in small clusters; foliage medium size, dark green, glossy, disease-resistant; prickles ¼ in., needle-point, light brown, moderate; growth bushy, medium (40-50 cm.); garden, exhibition, containers; [sport of Glowing Amber]; int. by Select Roses, 2007

Georges Prince HP, mr, 1863, Verdier, E.; flowers bright red, shaded dark pink, medium, full

Georges Rousset HP, mr, 1893, Rousset; flowers light silky red, reverse pink, very large, full

Georges Schwartz T, my, 1899, Schwartz, Vve.; flowers canary-yellow; [Kaiserin Auguste Viktoria × Souv. de Mme Levet]

Georges Schwartz, Climbing Cl HT, my, 1917, Knight, G.

Georges Truffaut HT, dr, Dorieux; int. by Roseraies Dorieux, 1996

Georges Vibert HGal, rb, 1853, Robert; flowers purplish red, streaked carmine, small eye at center, medium to large, dbl., flat rosette, borne in clusters of 3, moderate fragrance; foliage medium green, small, elliptical; prickles moderate

Georgette Min, mp, 1981, Bennett, Dee; bud ovoid; flowers medium pink, veined darker, 30 petals, high-centered; foliage medium green, dense; prickles straight; upright, compact, bushy growth; [Electron × Little Chief]; int. by Tiny Petals Nursery

Georgette F, w, 1985, Interplant; flowers large, 35 petals, slight fragrance; foliage large, medium green, semi-glossy; upright growth; [seedling × Bordure Rose]; int. in 1983

Georgette F, mp, Kordes; int. by W. Kordes Söhne, 1995

Georgette and Valentine HT, w, 1911, Bernaix fils; flowers white, touched with flesh pink, aging to salmon pink, large, full, cupped

Georgeus Min, mp; int. in 1998

Georgia HT, ab, 1980, Weeks, O.L.; bud short, pointed; flowers peach-apricot blend, 5½-6 in., 53-55 petals, borne singly, moderate tea fragrance; foliage large, glossy, leathery; prickles long, hooked downward; tall, upright growth; PP4712; [Arizona × seedling]

Georgia Belle MinFl, op, 2000, Taylor, Pete & Kay; flowers orange pink, reverse lighter, 2 in., very full, exhibition, borne mostly singly; foliage medium size, dark green, glossy; prickles moderate; upright, bushy, tall (30 in.) growth; [unknown × Gitte]; int. by Taylor's Roses, 2000

Georgianna Doan HT, pb, 1942, Joseph H. Hill, Co.; bud long, pointed; flowers two-tone pink, medium, 25-30 petals, high-centered; foliage leathery, wrinkled, dark; vigorous, upright, much branched growth; [Ophelia × seedling]

Georgia's Life S, w, 2000, Horner, Colin P.; flowers white, reverse very pale cream, aging white, 8 cm., very full, borne in small clusters; foliage medium size, dark green, semi-glossy; prickles moderate; bushy, medium (4 ft.) growth; [Lichtkonigin Lucia × Bonica]; int. in 2002

Georgie Anderson F, ob, 1982, Anderson's Rose Nurseries; flowers shades of orange, medium, dbl.; foliage medium size, dark, semi-glossy; upright growth; [Elizabeth of Glamis × seedling]

Georgie Bee HT, rb, 2005, Smith, John T; flowers dark red with white reverse, petal edges darker, 6 in., very full, decorative, borne mostly solitary, no fragrance; foliage large, dark green, semi-glossy; prickles long, hooked downward, brown, moderate; growth upright (4-5 ft.); hedging; [Gemini × Donna Darling]; int. by same

Georgie Girl – See **Wishing**, F

Gerald Hardy HT, mr, 1936, Dickson, A.; bud pointed; flowers bright scarlet-red, spiral, large, dbl.; strong, erect stems; bushy growth

Geraldine HT, mp, 1924, Chaplin Bros.; flowers buff, shaded pink, dbl., moderate fragrance; RULED EXTINCT 11/82 ARM; [Antoine Rivoire × Marie Adélaide]

Geraldine F, ob, 1983, Pearce, C.A.; flowers orange, medium, 20 petals, slight fragrance; foliage medium size, light green, semi-glossy; upright growth; [seedling × seedling]; int. by Limes Rose Nursery, 1983

Geraldine Hicks HT, ab, 1950, Hicks; flowers bronze-yellow; [sport of William Moore]

Geranium HMoy, mr, 1938, Royal Hort. Soc.; flowers almost scarlet, 2 in., single, borne in clusters (up to 5) borne along length of laterals; non-recurrent; upright (8-10 ft.), compact growth; hips crimson

Geranium – See **Independence**, F

Geranium Primaplant Pol, mr, Vlaeminck; flowers medium, semi-dbl.; int. in 1964

Geranium Red F, or, 1947, Boerner; flowers bright geranium red, 4 in., 50 petals, globular, borne in clusters, intense geranium fragrance; foliage dark, glossy; bushy growth; [Crimson Glory × seedling]; int. by J&P

Gerard ter Borch S, dp, Williams, J. Benjamin; flowers dbl., moderate fragrance; free-flowering; int. by Hortico Inc, 1997

Gerbe de Roses HP, m, 1847, Laffay; flowers rosy lilac, medium, dbl., borne in small clusters; foliage dark green; prickles short, flattened; sometimes attributed to Vibert

Gerbe d'Or – See **Casino**, LCl

Gerbe Rose HWich, lp, 1904, Fauque; flowers delicate pink, 8 cm., dbl., cupped, borne in small clusters; some autumn repeat; foliage glossy, large, almost evergreen; nearly thornless; vigorous growth; [*R. wichurana* × Baroness Rothschild]; int. by Langue

Gerda Henkel HT, dr, 1964, Tantau, Math.; flowers deep blood-red, large, dbl.; foliage dark, leathery; strong stems; vigorous, upright growth; [New Yorker × Prima Ballerina]

Gerda Hnatyshyn HT, mp, 2004, Jalbert, Brad; flowers pure pink, 5 in., full, borne mostly solitary, intense fragrance; foliage medium size, dark green, very glossy, very thick; prickles large, dark, numerous; growth upright, medium (4 ft.); cut flower, garden rose; [Pristine × New Zealand]

Gerdo F, lp; PP4982; flora-tea; int. in 1986

Germaine HT, w, 1926, Chambard, C.; flowers creamy white, center salmon; [seedling × Sunburst]

Gérmaine Chenault HT, lp, 1910, Guillot; flowers cream-pink with darker edges, large, dbl.; [Killarney × Rosomane Gravereaux]

Germaine de Marest T, w, 1892, Guillot; flowers cream white, shaded salmon pink, large, full

Germaine Lacroix HMult, w, 1912, Dubreuil; [Crimson Rambler × unknown]

Germaine Laroulandie HT, yb, 1908, Chauvry; flowers yellow, shaded apricot and cream, large, full

Germaine Rossiaud HT, op, 1915, Chambard; flowers

salmon pink, aging to white, very large, full; [Antoine Rivoire × Mélanie Soupert]

Germain's Centennial HT, Lammerts; PP3203

Germanea HT, dp, 1929, Ravenberg; flowers deep shining rose-pink, well-formed, very large, dbl.; [sport of Columbia]

Germania – See **Gloire de Ducher**, HP

Germania – See **Charme**, HT

Germania-Africana HT, ob, Kordes; buds pointed; flowers cream and apricot in center, petal edges turning deep orange as they open, large, dbl., high-centered, intense fragrance; medium to tall growth; int. in 1992

Germanica HRg, mp, 1890, Müller; flowers rose pink, single

Germanica HRg, rb, 1900, Mueller, F.; flowers red violet, 3 in., full; hips large, round, with persistent spidery sepals, orange-red

Germiston Gold HT, dy, 1988, W. Kordes Söhne; flowers deep golden-yellow, large, petals slightly serrated and curly, 30-36 petals, borne singly and in clusters of 3, intense spicy fragrance; free-flowering; foliage medium green; prickles concave, brown; medium, well branched growth; [seedling × seedling]; int. by Ludwigs Roses Pty. Ltd., 1988

Germiston Gold, Climbing Cl HT, dy, Malanseuns; blooms freely all season; int. in 1992

Gero F, rb, Scholle, E.; flowers pink and red, medium, dbl.; int. in 1984

Gert Potgieter HT, 1968, Gowie; foliage light green; vigorous growth; int. by Gandy's Roses

Gertrud F, dr

Gertrud Huck HT, dp, 1932, Huck; bud pointed; flowers flamingo-red, large, dbl., cupped; foliage leathery, bronze; vigorous growth; [sport of Wilhelm Kordes]; int. by C-P

Gertrud Kiese HCh, mr, 1918, Kiese; flowers scarlet-vermilion, shaded dark red, medium, full; [Gruss an Teplitz × Cramoisi Supérieur]

Gertrud Schweitzer HT, ob, 1973, Kordes; bud long, pointed; flowers apricot-orange, large, dbl., cupped; foliage glossy, dark; [Colour Wonder × seedling]; int. by Horstmann

Gertrud Westphal F, or, 1951, Kordes; flowers orange-scarlet, 3 in., 5-7 petals; foliage glossy, dark reddish green; dwarf, bushy, much branched growth; [Baby Chateau × Obergärtner Wiebicke]

Gertrud Westphal, Climbing Cl F, or, 1961, Buisman, G. A. H.

Gertrude HT, lp, 1903, Dickson, A.; flowers flesh pink; [sport of Countess of Caledon]

Gertrude Bernard HGal, mr, 1827, Noisette

Gertrude Gregory HT, my, 1957, Gregory; flowers bright golden yellow; [sport of Lady Belper]

Gertrude Jekyll S, mp, Austin, David; PP7220; buds oval, pointed; flowers deep pink with yellow base, very full, slightly flattened cup, 11 cm., moderate old-rose fragrance, borne mostly singly; recurrent; foliage dark green, matte; growth tall (4 - 5 ft.), strong, shrubby; int. in 1986

Gertrude Raffel F, dp, 1957, Raffel; flowers pink, center rosy, well-formed, 2-3 in., 15-20 petals, borne in large clusters; foliage dark; vigorous, bushy growth; int. by Port Stockton Nursery, 1956

Gertrude Reutener F, dp, 1954, Leenders, M.; flowers crimson-pink; vigorous growth

Gertrude Shilling HT, dy, 1988, Poole, Lionel; flowers bright, deep yellow, aging paler, large, 52 petals, urn-shaped, decorative, moderate fruity fragrance; foliage large, medium green, matte; prickles broad, fairly flat, large, dark brown; upright, tall, vigorous, good basal growth; [Golden Splendour × Peer Gynt]; int. by Rearsby Roses, Ltd., 1989

Geschwind's Gilda HMult, dr, 1887, Geschwind, R.; bud round, small; flowers reddish-violet at center, pale pink at edges, 5-6 cm., very full, moderate fragrance; foliage pale green, rounded; [De La Grifferaie × a HP or B]

Geschwind's Gorgeous Cl HT, mr, 1916, Geschwind, R.; flowers light red, 3 in., semi-dbl., borne in small clusters

Geschwind's Most Beautiful – See **Geschwind's Schönste**, HMult

Geschwind's Nordlandrose HSet, lp, 1884, Geschwind, R.; flowers medium, very full, borne in clusters of 3-5, no fragrance; recurrent; [De La Grifferaie × a HP or B]; sometimes classed as HMult

Geschwind's Nordlandrose II HSet, mr, 1928, Geschwind, R.; flowers cherry red, lighter reverse, dbl., cupped, strong musk fragrance; foliage large, bright green; few prickles; sometimes classed as HMult

Geschwind's Northern Rose – See **Geschwind's Nordlandrose**, HSet

Geschwind's Orden HMult, m, 1886, Geschwind, R.; bud fat; flowers bright violet pink, white edges, medium, very full, cupped and quartered, borne in small clusters, moderate fragrance; non-recurrent; foliage slightly rugose; [*R. rugosa* × *R. multiflora* or *R. multiflora* cultivar]

Geschwind's Schönste HMult, mr, 1900, Geschwind, R.; flowers very bright crimson, 6 cm., full, cupped, borne in clusters of 6-10; non-recurrent; [De La Grifferaie × a HP or B]

Geschwind's Unermüdliche – See **Unermüdliche**, Ch

Geschwister Scholl Pol, w, GPG Bad Langensalza; flowers medium, dbl.; int. in 1974

Gessel HT, Pironti, N.

Gettysburg – See **Susan**, S

Gewohnliche Moss Rose – See **Communis**, M

Ghergana Gr, dr, 1985, Staikov, Prof. Dr. V.; flowers deep blackish-red, large, 55 petals, cupped, borne in clusters of 2-5, moderate tea fragrance; foliage dark; vigorous, upright growth; [Spectacular × seedling]; int. by Kalaydjiev and Chorbadjiiski, 1974

Ghislaine de Féligonde HMult, ly, 1916, Turbat; bud bright yellow/orange; flowers yellowish-white tinted flesh, small, dbl., cupped, borne in clusters of 10-20, moderate fragrance; some autumn repeat; few prickles; vigorous, climbing (8-10 ft.) growth; [Goldfinch × multiflora seedling]

Ghislaine Feuerwerk HMult, op, Ruf, Werner; flowers salmon pink with yellow base, small, dbl., cupped, borne in large clusters, slight tea fragrance; occasional repeat; prickles very few; vigorous, arching (180-250 cm.) growth; [sport of Ghislaine de Feligonde]

Ghita – See **Ghita Renaissance**, S

Ghita Renaissance S, mp, Olesen; bud urceolate; flowers medium pink, fading to pale pink on outer petals as it opens, 8 cm., 50 petals, cupped to flat, borne in clusters of 5-10, moderate fragrance; recurrent; foliage semi-glossy; prickles moderate, 5 mm., hooked downward, greyed-red; growth narrow, bushy (100-150 cm.); PP16541; [Clair Renaissance × seedling]; Perfume Cup, Lyon, 2006, Edland Medal, 2003

Gi Gi Min, pb, Benardella, Frank; int. in 1999

Giana F, dr

Gianlauro MinFl, Zandri, R.; int. in 1978

Giant of Battles – See **Géant des Batailles**, HP

Giant Pink S, pb, 2000, Lens, Louis; flowers deep pink, white center, reverse lighter, 2 in., single, borne in large clusters; recurrent; foliage medium green, glossy; prickles moderate; upright, medium (4-5 ft.) growth; [(*R. multiflora adenocheata* × Ballerina) × Rush]; int. by Louis Lens NV, 1990

Giant Samantha HT, mr; flowers large; [sport of Samantha]; int. by Ashdown Roses, 2005

Gibby HT, dp, 1977, Prof. F. Roses; bud ovoid, pointed; flowers carmine-pink, 4½ in., 50 petals, high-centered; foliage dull, dark, leathery; vigorous, upright, bushy growth; [sport of Christian Dior]; int. by Ludwigs Roses Pty. Ltd.

Gideon Lincecum S, w, 2006, Shoup, George Micheal; flowers single, borne in small clusters, moderate fragrance; remontant; foliage large, dark green, semi-glossy; few prickles; growth bushy, tall (4-6 ft.); hedging; hips large; [((Carefree Beauty × Basye's Blueberry) × self) × Mrs Oakely Fisher]; int. by Antique Rose Emporium, 2000

Gideux S, my; flowers soft yellow, large, dbl., cupped, slight fragrance; free-flowering; growth to 2 ft.; int. in 1998

Gidget Min, op, 1976, Moore, Ralph S.; bud pointed; flowers coral-pink to coral-red, 1 in., informal, slight fragrance; foliage small, glossy; vigorous, bushy growth; [(*R. wichurana* × Floradora) × Fire Princess]; int. by Sequoia Nursery, 1975

Giesebrecht – See **Bashful**, Pol

Gift Basket HT, rb, Delbard, Georges; flowers scarlet with yellow reverse, high-centered; int. in 1988

Gift of Grace HT, pb; int. in 2006

Gift of Life HT, yb, 1999, Harkness; flowers mid yellow-pink, reverse yellow, 4 in., full, borne mostly singly, moderate fragrance; foliage large, medium green, glossy; numerous prickles; bushy, medium (40 in.) growth; [Dr Darley × Elina]; int. by Harkness New Roses, 1996; Gold Medal, Belfast, 1999

Gigantea Blanc LCl, w, 1889, Colett; flowers golden white with yellow center, very large; sometimes classed as HGig

Gigantea Cooperi – See **Cooper's Burmese**, HG

Gigantesque T, lp, 1835, Hardy/Sylvain-Péan; flowers flesh pink, shaded with rose, 5 in., full; foliage glossy; prickles strong, few, reddish; growth horizontally spreading; probably extinct; [Parks' Yellow × unknown]

Gigantèsque T, dp, 1845, Odier; flowers deep pink

Giggles Min, pb, 1982, Lyon, Lyndon; bud pointed; flowers medium pink, white center, small, semi-dbl.; foliage small, medium green, semi-glossy; very small, upright, bushy growth; [seedling × seedling]; int. by L. Lyon Greenhouses

Giggles Min, mp, 1987, King, Gene; flowers light pink, reverse light to dark pink, fading to creamy pink, 18 petals, high-centered; foliage medium size, medium green, matte; prickles slightly crooked, white; upright, tall growth; hips oval, green; [Vera Dalton × Rose Window]; int. by AGM Miniature Roses

Gigi HT, mp, 1960, Verschuren; flowers rose-pink, reverse brighter, large, dbl., moderate fragrance; foliage light green; long, strong stems; vigorous growth; [The Doctor × seedling]; int. by Blaby Rose Gardens, 1959

Gigliola ; int. in 1969

Gigolette F, rb, 1953, Gaujard; bud ovoid; flowers yellow and red bicolor, medium, semi-dbl., borne in clusters; foliage leathery, light green; vigorous growth

Gil Blas HGal, pb, before 1843; flowers light pink, spotted, lighter at edges, large, dbl.; strong, upright (4-5 ft.) growth

Gil Blas HSpn, dp, before 1848; flowers light red

Gilbert Bécaud HT, yb, 1985, Meilland, Mme. Marie-Louise; flowers orange and yellow blend, large, 45 petals; foliage bronze, matte; upight growth; [(Peace

× Mrs John Laing) × Bettina]; int. by Meilland et Cie, 1979

Gilbert F. Levy F, mr, 1958, Combe; flowers currant-red, dbl.; very vigorous growth; [Moulin Rouge × Oiseau de Feu]

Gilbert Nabonnand T, op, 1888, Nabonnand; bud very long, clear rose; flowers pale rose shaded with yellow, large, semi-dbl., moderate fragrance

Gilberte Routurier T, w, 1908, Chauvry; flowers cream white, center coppery pink, base golden yellow, large, very full, moderate fragrance

Gilda HMult, m, 1887, Geschwind; flowers wine red, medium, full; strong, upright, overhanging (10 ft.) growth

Gilda HT, ab, 1936, Towill; bud long, pointed; flowers pure orange-yellow, large, dbl.; foliage leathery, dark; vigorous growth; RULED EXTINCT 3/87; [Souv. de Claudius Pernet × (Lady Hillingdon × Harry Kirk)]

Gilda F, lp, 1987, Pearce, C.A.; flowers pale shell pink, medium, dbl., intense fragrance; foliage medium size, medium green, matte; upright, spreading growth; [seedling × seedling]; int. by The Limes New Roses

Giliane F, mp, Sauvageot; flowers Neyron pink, petals ruffled, dbl., borne in large clusters; int. in 2004

Gillian HT, op, 1959, Verschuren; bud long, pointed; flowers soft coral-pink; foliage bronze; [Michèle Meilland × Mme Butterfly]; int. by Gandy Roses, Ltd., 1958

Gillian Dawn HT, mr, 1997, Robinson, Kenneth G.; flowers medium, very dbl., borne mostly singly; foliage medium size, medium green, semi-glossy; spreading, medium (24in.) growth

Gillian Levy F, yb, 2005, Rawlins, Ronnie; flowers yellow blend, reverse yellow and pink, 10 cm., full, borne in small clusters; foliage medium size, dark green, glossy; growth upright, medium (1 m.); garden; [Golden Future × (Baby Love × Silver Jubilee)]

Gilmore HT, ly, Select Roses, B.V.

Gilt Edged Cl Min, yb, Warner, Chris; int. in 1997

Gin Fizz HT, w, Meilland; int. in 1995

Gin no suzu – See **Silver Bell**, F

Gina F, dr, 1960, Kriloff, Michel; flowers velvety dark crimson, 6 petals, borne in large clusters, slight fragrance; foliage glossy; vigorous, upright growth; [Alain × Independence]; int. by Cramphorn's Nursery, 1960

Gina F, dr, Kordes; int. in 1978

Gina Kordana Min, mr, Kordes; flowers cherry red, full; container rose; int. by W. Kordes Söhne

Gina Lollobrigida HT, dy, 1997, Meilland International SA; flowers large, 70-90 petals, borne mostly singly, moderate fragrance; foliage medium size, medium green, semi-glossy; some prickles; upright, medium (5ft.) growth; PP7541; [Laura '81 × Tchin-Tchin]; int. by Conard-Pyle Co.

Gina Louise Min, op, 1987, Robinson, T.; flowers bright orange-pink, opening to bright yellow, gold anthers, 35 petals, high-centered, intense damask, fruity fragrance; foliage small, dark green, semi-glossy; prickles thin, red pointed down; bushy, low growth; hips globular, large, orange; [Orange Sensation × seedling]; int. in 1986

Gina's Rose S, rb, 2006, Moore, Ralph S.; flowers medium red, reverse light red, 2-2½ in., single, borne in small clusters; rapid repeat bloom; foliage medium size, medium green, semi-glossy; no prickles; growth spreading, medium (3-5 ft.); specimen, border, arching shrub; [Playboy × Basey's Legacy]; int. by Sequoia Nurs., 2006

Ginette HT, op, 1924, Buatois; flowers salmony maize-yellow, dbl.; [Paul Monnier × Souv. de Claudius Pernet]

Ginger F, or, 1962, Boerner; bud ovoid; flowers orange-vermilion, 4 in., 28 petals, cupped, borne in irregular clusters, moderate fragrance; foliage leathery; vigorous, compact, bushy growth; PP2293; [(Garnette × unknown) × Spartan]; int. by J&P, 1962

Ginger Hill HT, w, (HILcap); flowers white with blush pink center, petals crêped, dbl., high-centered; int. in 1999

Ginger Meggs F, ob, Tantau; int. in 1962

Ginger Rogers HT, op, 1969, McGredy, Sam IV; flowers salmon pink, dbl., loose, borne singly, moderate fragrance; foliage medium size, light green; [Super Star × Miss Ireland]

Ginger Syllabub LCl, ab, Harkness; flowers amber/ginger, large, 70 petals, intense fragrance; vigorous (10-12 ft.) growth; int. by Harkness, 2001

Ginger Toddler F, ob, Pearce; flowers ginger-orange, dbl., borne singly; free-flowering; compact, vigorous growth; int. in 1996

Gingerbread Man Min, ab, 1994, Poulsen Roser APS; flowers deep, long-lasting apricot amber, medium, full, quartered, borne in small clusters; foliage small, dark green, semi-glossy; some prickles; medium (40-45 cm.), upright, bushy, vigorous growth; PP9420; [seedling × Texas]; int. by Weeks Roses, 1995

Gingernut F, r, 1989, Cocker, James & Sons; flowers medium, 43 petals, moderate fragrance; foliage small, medium green, semi-glossy; patio; bushy growth; [(Sabine × Circus) × Darling Flame]; int. in 1989

Gingersnap F, ob, 1977, Delbard, G., & Chabert, A.; bud long, pointed; flowers pure orange, imbricated to ruffled, 4 in., 30-35 petals, borne in small clusters, slight fragrance; foliage dark green; vigorous, upright, bushy growth; PP4330; [(Zambra × (Orange Triumph × Floradora)) × (Jean de la Lune × (Spartan × Mandrina))]; int. by Armstrong Nursery

Gingia HT, w, 1984, Fumagalli, Niso; flowers large, 35 petals, intense fragrance; foliage large, light green, glossy; bushy growth; [seedling × seedling]

Ginny Min, rb, 1981, Bischoff, Francis J.; bud ovoid; flowers white edged medium red, yellow at hinge, yellow stamens, small, 45 petals, high-centered; foliage dark, leathery, reddish tinge on new growth; prickles straight red; upright, compact growth; PP5275; [Little Darling × Toy Clown]; int. by Kimbrew-Walter Roses

Ginny-Lou Min, mr, 1983, Robinson, Thomas, Ltd.; flowers bright medium red, dbl., borne in clusters; foliage small, dark, semi-glossy; bushy growth; [Dollie B. × seedling]; int. by Thomas Robinson, Ltd., 1984

Ginrei F, w, Keisei; int. by Keisei Rose Nurseries, 1990

Ginseikei F, w, Keisei; int. by Keisei Rose Nursery, 1997

Ginsky F, pb, 1983, Barker & Wood; flowers light salmon pink opening to pale pink to cream; [sport of Liverpool Echo]; int. by L.E.J. Wood

Ginza Komachi Cl Min, pb, 1985, Kono, Yoshito; bud globular; flowers deep pink, white eye, yellow stamens, small, 5 petals, borne in clusters, slight fragrance; foliage medium green, glossy; prickles numerous, hooked; vigorous growth; [Nozomi × seedling]

Gioia – See **Peace**, HT

Gioia, Climbing – See **Peace, Climbing**, Cl HT

Gioiello Min, my, 1985, Bartolomeo, Embriaco; flowers small, 20 petals, no fragrance; foliage small, dark, matte; [Zorina × Sole di San Remo]; int. in 1984

Gion Cl Min, pb, 1979, Onodera, Toru F.; bud rounded; flowers 1 in., 5 petals, flat; non-recurrent; foliage tiny, leathery; bushy, climbing growth; [Nozomi × seedling]; int. by S. Onodera

Giovane HT, op, 1970, Dot, Simon; bud pointed; flowers salmon-orange, large, 28 petals, high-centered, moderate fragrance; foliage glossy, bronze; dense growth; [Queen Elizabeth × Orient]; int. by Rosas Dot, 1965

Giovanezza HT, rb, 1933, Ingegnoli; flowers geranium-red, reverse cream-white, edged lighter; vigorous growth

Giovanni Paolo II HT, McEntire, J.; int. in 1984

Gipsy HT, dr, 1931, Van Rossem; flowers medium, dbl.

Gipsy Blood – See **Zigeunerblut**, Bslt

Gipsy Boy B, dr, 1909, Geschwind; flowers dark crimson-red shaded violet-purple, medium, moderate fragrance; non-recurrent; vigorous, angular (3-5 ft.) growth; int. as Zigeunerknabe, Lambert, P.

Gipsy Jewel Min, dp, Moore, Ralph S.; int. in 1975

Gipsy Lass HT, mr, 1932, Dickson, A.; flowers scarlet-crimson shaded blackish, dbl., globular; long, willowy stems; bushy growth

Gipsy Love HT, or, 1964, Delbard-Chabert; flowers orange-vermilion, 4 in., 25 petals; vigorous growth; [Chic Parisien × Fashion]; int. by Cuthbert

Gipsy Maid F, dp, 1955, LeGrice; flowers carmine-scarlet, base golden, single, borne in small clusters of 3 or more, moderate sweetbriar fragrance; foliage olive-green

Giranu Czecheti Pol, op, Madarsko; flowers medium, semi-dbl.; int. in 1955

Girasol HT, my, 1945, Dot, Pedro; bud oval; flowers sunflower-yellow, 25-30 petals; foliage dark, glossy; upright, compact growth; [Joanna Hill × Carito MacMahon]

Girija HT, dr, Friends Rosery; flowers crimson-red, high-centered; int. in 1989

Girl Friend – See **Podruga**, HT

Girl Guide HT, dr, Peden; int. by Otway Roses, 2002

Girl Guide F, op

Girl Scout F, my, 1961, Boerner; bud ovoid; flowers golden yellow, 3½-4 in., 50 petals, cupped, moderate fragrance; foliage leathery, glossy; vigorous, medium tall growth; PP2090; [Gold Cup × Pigmy Gold]; int. by J&P, 1960

Girlie Pol, dr, 1923, Wezelenburg; flowers bright scarlet-crimson; bushy growth; [sport of Orléans Rose]

Girlie Folies F, my, Meilland; flowers Egyptian yellow, dbl., borne in clusters; greenhouse rose; int. by Meilland Intl, 2004

Girls' Brigade F, or, 1993, Harkness; flowers vermilion, orange-red reverse, aging orange-red, 2 in., 28 petals; foliage small, dark green, glossy; bushy, low growth; [Sexy Rexy × Anna Ford]; int. by Harkness New Roses, Ltd., 1993

Girona HT, pb, 1936, Dot, Pedro; flowers soft red and yellow, well-formed, large, 30 petals, high-centered, intense damask fragrance; foliage bright green; vigorous, spreading growth; [Li Bures × Talisman]; int. by C-P, 1939

Gisborne 2000 HT, dy, Matthews; flowers strong yellow, dbl., moderate lemon fragrance; early to flower and repeats well; vigorous, strong, upright (1 m.) growth; int. by Matthews Nurseries, 2000

Giscard d'Estaing – See **Anne-Aymone Giscard d'Estaing**, F single

Gisela F, op, 1965, Verschuren, A.; flowers salmon-pink, base straw-yellow, 56 petals, borne in clusters; foliage dark, glossy, bronze; upright, bushy, compact growth; [Masquerade × Pinocchio]; originally registered as Pol; int. by van Engelen, 1963

Gisèle Alday HT, mp, 1933, Mallerin, C.; bud pointed; flowers bright rose-pink tinted flesh, large, semi-dbl., cupped; foliage glossy, dark; vigorous growth; [Mrs Pierre S. duPont × Lallita]; int. by H. Guillot

Gisella F, op, Barni; flowers coral rose, 5-6 cm., dbl., high-centered, slight fragrance; foliage medium to large, dark green; growth to 40-60 cm.; [Ambra × Venere]; int. by Rose Barni, 2003

Giselle HGal, mp, 1843, Vibert; flowers rose, spotted, medium

Giselle Min, dp, 1991, Justice, Jerry G.; bud small, pointed with medium green sepals; flowers pink outer edges with very light pink throat, reverse rosy pink with white midline, 1¼ in., 18 petals, urn-shaped, loose, borne usually singly, no fragrance; foliage small, dark green, glossy, disease-resistant; bushy, low growth; [Crazy Dottie × seedling]; int. by Justice Miniature Roses, 1992

Giselle Folies F, op, Meilland; flowers soft orange-pink, reverse darker, full, cupped, low-centered, borne in sprays; recurrent; florist rose; int. by Meilland Intl., 2005

Gisselfeld HT, dr, 1978, Poulsen, Niels D.; flowers 4-4½ in., 17-20 petals, moderate fragrance; foliage dark, leathery; upright growth; [(Tropicana × Champs-Elysees) × Furore]; int. by Poulsen, 1972

Gitane – See **Bright Wings**, HT

Gites de France LCl, dp, Meilland; flowers bengal pink, borne in large clusters; robust (7 ft.+) growth; int. in 1994

Gitta Grummer – See **Uwe Seeler**, F

Gitte HT, ab, 1979, W. Kordes Söhne; bud long, pointed; flowers apricot-pink blend, 4 in., 33 petals, high-centered, intense fragrance; foliage dark; vigorous, upright, bushy growth; [(Fragrant Cloud × Peer Gynt) × ((Dr. A.J. Verhage × Colour Wonder) × Zorina)]; int. by Horstmann

Giuletta B, lp, 1859, Laurentius; flowers white to light flesh pink, button center, medium, flat, borne in large clusters; foliage large, dark green; arching growth

Giuliana Borgatti HT, w, 1936, Borgatti, G.; flowers white, center shaded rose and salmon, very well-formed, large, dbl.; foliage dark ivy-green; vigorous growth; [Ophelia × Ville de Paris]

Giuseppe Motta HT, lp, 1936, Heizmann, E.; flowers large, semi-dbl.

Giuseppina Papandrea Min, pb, 1989, Papandrea, John T.; flowers cerise, reverse lighter; [sport of Petite Folie]

Giuseppina Saragat HT, w

Givaro F, w, Van Gampelaere, J.; [Graaf van Vlaanderen × Golden Wings]; int. by RvS-Melle, 2008

Give Life LCl, op, 2004, Horner, Colin P.; flowers orange-pink, reverse lighter, 4-5 in., full, borne in small clusters, moderate fragrance; foliage large, dark green, glossy; prickles large, straight; growth upright, tall (8-10 ft.); garden decorative; [Rabble Rouser × Pretty Lady]; int. by LeGrice Roses, 2006

Givenchy HT, rb, 1986, Christensen, Jack E.; flowers pink, blushed red, reverse pink, yellow base, 30 petals, high-centered, borne in sprays, intense spicy fragrance; foliage medium size, dark; prickles medium, brown, hooked; medium, upright, bushy growth; no fruit; [Gingersnap × Double Delight]; int. by Armstrong Nursery, 1985

Giverny HMult, w; int. by Roses d'Antan, 2003

Gizmo Min, ob, 1998, Carruth, Tom; flowers scarlet orange with white eye, long lasting, 1½-3 in., single, borne in small clusters, slight apple fragrance; foliage medium size, dark green, semi-glossy; prickles moderate, small; rounded, compact, medium (18 in.) growth; PP12327; [Carrot Top × Little Artist]; int. by Weeks Roses, 2000

Glacier F, w, 1952, Boerner; bud ovoid; flowers white, slightly overcast yellow, 4½ in., 28 petals, cupped; foliage glossy, dark; vigorous, upright growth; [unnamed white HT × Summer Snow]; int. by J&P

Glacier F, w, Poulsen; flowers 8-10 cm., dbl.; growth bushy, 100-150 cm.; int. by Poulsen Roser, 1996

Glacier Magic – See **Special Child**, F

Glad Eye Min, rb, 2003, McCann, Sean; flowers red with bright yellow eye, medium, semi-dbl., borne in small clusters; foliage medium size, medium green, glossy; growth compact, low-growing; [Crazy Dottie × seedling]

Glad Tidings F, dr, 1989, Tantau, R.; bud ovoid; flowers bright crimson, medium, 20 petals, cupped, borne in sprays, no fragrance; foliage medium size, medium green, semi-glossy; upright, medium (2 ft.) growth; [seedling × seedling]; int. by Wheatcroft Ltd., 1988; Rose of the Year, St. Albans, UK, 1989, Gold Medal, Durbanville, 1988

Gladiador Cl HT, dp, 1954, Dot, Pedro; bud pointed; flowers carmine, very large, dbl.; vigorous growth; [Texas Centennial × Guinée]

Gladiator LCl, mr, 1956, Malandrone, M.; bud ovoid; flowers rose-red, 4½-5 in., 35 petals, high-centered, moderate fragrance; foliage dark, leathery; vigorous (10-12 ft.) growth; PP1416; [Charlotte Armstrong × (Pink Delight × New Dawn)]; int. by J&P, 1955

Gladiator – See **Uncle Joe**, HT

Gladis – See **Gladys**, S

Gladness F, pb, 1959, Fletcher; bud pointed; flowers light pink edged darker, large, 25 petals, borne in clusters; foliage dark, glossy; upright growth; [Sunny Maid × Cinnabar]

Gladsome HMult, mp, 1937, Clark; flowers delicate light pink, white center, 3 cm., single, borne in large clusters; non-recurrent; growth tall hedge rose

Gladys S, mp, Adam; flowers bright pink, dbl., globular, to rosette; recurrent; low, spreading growth; int. by René Dessevre, 2004

Gladys Benskin HT, op, 1929, Dickson, A.; flowers rose-cerise, shaded orange, base deeper orange, large, dbl., high-centered; vigorous growth; int. by Dreer; Gold Medal, NRS, 1929

Gladys Harkness HT, op, 1900, Dickson, A.; flowers deep salmon pink, silvery pink reflections, very large, dbl., cupped, intense fragrance

Gladys Holland HT, lp, 1917, McGredy; flowers light pink, shaded buff, very large, dbl., moderate fragrance; Gold Medal, NRS, 1916

Gladys Moncrieff HT, yb, 1982, Jack, J.; flowers golden yellow to apricot, flushed rose red at petal tips; [sport of Granada]; int. by Girraween Nursery, 1981

Gladys Quine F, ob, 2005, Paul Chessum Roses; flowers dbl., borne in small clusters, slight fragrance; foliage medium size, dark green, semi-glossy; prickles medium, long, pink, moderate; growth bushy, medium (2 ft.); bedding, containers; [seedling × seedling]; int. by World of Roses, 2005

Gladys Saavedra HT, mp, 1922, Nabonnand, P.; flowers rosy peach-blossom-pink, dbl.; [Mme Abel Chatenay × Jonkheer J.L. Mock]

Gladys Tweedie HT, dr, 1950, Toogood; bud long, pointed; flowers crimson, 5 in., 30-35 petals, high-centered; foliage wrinkled; very vigorous, bushy growth; [Crimson Glory × William Orr]

Glaive HT, pb, 1951, Clark, A.; bud long, pointed; flowers cream, center tipped pink, small, 25 petals, high-centered; foliage glossy; vigorous, bushy, compact growth; int. by NRS Victoria

Glamis Castle S, w, 1994, Austin, David; flowers medium, very dbl., cupped, borne in small clusters, intense myrrh fragrance; foliage medium size, medium green, semi-glossy; numerous prickles; medium (100 cm.), bushy growth; PP8765; [Graham Thomas × Mary Rose]; int. by David Austin Roses, Ltd., 1992

Glamorgan F, op, 1994, Thompson, M.L.; flowers coral-salmon, medium, 14 petals, borne in large clusters; foliage medium size, red when young turning to medium green, glos; some prickles; low to medium (2½ ft.), upright, compact growth; [Old Master × Red Splendor]; int. by Haynes Roses, 1995

Glamorous Min, or, 1980, Williams, Ernest D.; bud pointed; flowers orange-red, base yellow, 1-1½ in., 35 petals, high-centered, slight fragrance; foliage small, glossy, bronze-green; bushy, spreading growth; [Starburst × Over the Rainbow]; int. by Mini-Roses, 1979

Glamour HT, op, 1939, Leenders, M.; bud long, ovoid; flowers salmon-pink, large, dbl.; vigorous growth; [Comtesse Vandal × Pres. Macia]; int. by T. Robinson, Ltd.

Glamour HT, mp, Poulsen; bud pointed ovoid, broad base; flowers 4 in., 26-30 petals, high-centered, borne mostly singly, moderate floral fragrance; recurrent; foliage dark green, glossy; prickles several, 6 mm., hooked downward; growth bushy (60-100 cm.); PP15383; [seedling × Sexy Rexy]; int. by Poulsen Roser, 2003

Glamour Girl HT, op, 1942, Joseph H. Hill, Co.; bud pointed, light jasper-red; flowers light salmon, open, 4-5 in., 45-50 petals; foliage dark, leathery; strong stems; very vigorous, upright, much branched growth; [Captain Glisson × Justine]

Glamour Girl MinFl, rb, Clements, John K.; flowers white with red edges that deepen and spread as it opens, single; growth to 18 in.; int. in 1992

Glamour Girl HT, yb, Ghosh; flowers deep yellow flushed red and pink with deeper veins, dbl.; int. in 1998

Glauque à Feuille de Pimprenelle – See **De Marienbourg**, HSpn

Glarona HT, w, 1922, Krüger; flowers creamy flesh, center rose, 4 in., borne singly or in small clusters; foliage broad, rounded; int. by Kiese

Glastonbury S, rb, 1981, Austin, David; bud globular; flowers dark crimson to deep purple, 55 petals, borne singly and in clusters of up to 5; repeat bloom; foliage medium green, sparse; prickles hooked, red; weak, spreading growth; [The Knight × seedling]; int. by David Austin Roses, Ltd., 1974

Glauca Nova S, lp; flowers pastel pink, single, cupped, moderate fragrance; growth to 150-200 cm.; very winter hardy

Gleam HRg, w, Erskine; int. in 1999

Gleaming F, dy, 1959, LeGrice; flowers deep lemon-yellow, 4 in., 6-8 petals, borne in trusses, intense fragrance; foliage dark; very free growth; [Goldilocks × Golden Scepter]; int. in 1958

Glee F, mp, Fleming; flowers 3 in., semi-dbl., borne in Clusters.; hardy to -40°F; int. by Hortico, 2004

Glen Almond HT, pb, 1972, Wallace; flowers pale orient pink, 3½-4 in., 30 petals; foliage glossy, leathery; free growth; [Pascali × Happy Event]

Glen Artney HT, dr, 1972, Wallace; flowers beet-root-purple, 3½-4 in., 40 petals, slight fragrance; vigorous growth; [Baccará × Sterling Silver]

Glen Myrie HT, ab, 2000, Giles, Diann; flowers apricot, medium, dbl., borne mostly singly; foliage medium size, medium green, glossy; few prickles; upright, medium growth; [sport of Lady Beauty]; int. by Giles Rose Nursery, 1999

Glenara LCl, dp, 1951, Clark, A.; bud long, pointed; flowers deep rosy pink, fading lighter, 9-10 cm., 18 petals; very remontant; foliage leathery; vigorous, upright bush or pillar growth; hybrid gigantea; int. by NRS Victoria

Glenara No. 14 Cl HT, pb, Clark, Alister

Glenda Marie F, w, 1999, Sitton, John; flowers white with shrimp pink edges, reverse darker, large, dbl., borne in small clusters, no fragrance; foliage medium dark green, glossy; prickles moderate; bushy, shrub-like, tall (5-6 ft.) growth; [sport of Hannah Gordon]; int. by Edmunds' Roses, 2000

Glendora – See **Joasine Hanet**, P

Glendora HT, ab, Kordes; flowers flower soft pink and honey yellow, with cream colored edges, 4 in., dbl., borne singly and in small clusters, intense fragrance; recurrent; foliage large, medium green, glossy; upright, vigorous (3 ft.) growth; [Harmonie × unknown]; int. in 1995

Glendore – See **Glendora**, HT

Glenfiddich F, dy, 1976, Cocker; flowers amber-gold, 4 in., 25 petals, moderate fragrance; foliage glossy, dark; [Arthur Bell × (Sabine × Circus)]

Glengarry F, or, 1969, Cocker; flowers vermilion, large, 32 petals; foliage semi-glossy; compact, bushy growth; [Evelyn Fison × Wendy Cussons]

Gleniti Gold HT, dy, 1983, Bone, John, & Son; flowers very deep yellow; [sport of Lady Mandeville]; int. by Trevor Griffiths Ltd., 1973

Glenn Dale HWich, ly, 1927, Van Fleet; bud small, lemon yellow; flowers lemon, fading to white, 7-8 cm., 40 petals, borne in clusters (to 20); foliage dark, leathery; vigorous (10 ft.) growth; [*R. wichurana* × possibly Isabella Sprunt]; int. by American Rose Society; Gold Medal, Portland, 1920

Glenora F, w

Glenshane S, mr, 1999, Dickson, Colin; flowers 1½ in., semi-dbl., borne in large clusters, no fragrance; foliage medium size, medium green, semi-glossy; few prickles; flori-shrub; spreading, bushy, medium (30 in.) growth; [seedling × Star Child]; int. in 1997

Glenys Stewart HT, dp, 1968, Kemp, M.L.; flowers deep rose-pink, dbl.; moderate bloom; moderate growth; [Montezuma × Pink Favorite]; int. by G. Stewart

Gletscher F, m, 1955, Kordes; bud ovoid; flowers pale lilac, large, dbl., high-centered, borne in large trusses; foliage glossy; vigorous, upright, bushy growth; [seedling × Lavender Pinocchio]

Gletscherfee S, w, Kordes; int. in 1991

Glimmer Min, rb, 1989, Bridges, Dennis A.; bud pointed; flowers bright, medium red, yellow at base, reverse slightly darker, 24 petals, high-centered, slight fragrance; foliage medium size, medium green, semi-glossy; prickles slightly downward pointed, medium, red; upright, medium growth; [Party Girl × seedling]; int. by Bridges Roses, 1989

Glitter – See **Kagayaki**, F

Glitter HT, w, Spek; flowers white with green tints on guard petals, 4 in., 30-35 petals, high-centered, borne mostly singly; recurrent; few prickles; stems long; int. by Jan Spek Rozen, 2005

Glitters Cl HT, mp, 1934, Smith, J.; bud pointed; flowers brilliant pink, base orange, open, very large, dbl., globular; recurrent bloom; foliage leathery; long stems; very vigorous growth; [Mrs W.J. Grant × Mrs Sam McGredy]

Gloaming HT, pb, 1935, Nicolas; bud pointed; flowers luminous pink suffused salmon, reverse lighter, open, very large, 36 petals; foliage leathery, dark; vigorous, bushy growth; [Charles P. Kilham × Mrs Pierre S. duPont]; int. by J&P

Global Beauty HT, dy, Tantau; flowers very large, dbl., intense fragrance; early bloomer; good repeat; healthy (3-4 ft.) growth; int. in 2003

Global Rose – See **Gletscherfee**, S

Global Rose F, pb, Kordes; flowers pink, with yellow and green shading, borne in large clusters, no fragrance; wide, compact growth; int. by Ludwig's Roses, 1999

Globe F, mr, 1956, Tantau, Math.; flowers blood-red, 2 in., 20 petals, cupped, borne in clusters; foliage dark; vigorous, bushy, compact growth; [Fanal × Red Favorite]

Globe Blanc – See **Globe White Hip**, C

Globe Hip – See **Globe White Hip**, C

Globe White Hip C, w, before 1826, Lee; flowers creamy white, medium, full, globular; growth erect

Globe Yellow HFt, my, before 1846, from Italy; flowers bright lemon yellow, large, full, globular

Globuleuse M, mp, 1825, Vibert; flowers bright carmine, aging to lilac-flesh, medium, full, globular

Gloira Dei-mutace HT, mr, Lorenc

Gloire d'Angers HP, m, 1846, Boyau; flowers bright, glowing medium purple, velvety

Gloire d'Angleterre – See **England's Glory**, HT

Gloire d'Antibes HT, dr, 1938, Mallerin, C.; flowers large, dbl.

Gloire de Bordeaux – See **Belle de Bordeaux**, T

Gloire de Bourg-la-Reine HP, mr, 1879, Margottin; flowers brilliant scarlet red, large, full

Gloire de Bruxelles HP, m, 1889, Soupert & Notting; flowers very dark, velvety crimson-purple, large, 60 petals; vigorous, upright growth; [Souv. de William Wood × Lord Macaulay]

Gloire de Charpennes Pol, mr, 1898, Lille; flowers carmine-red, small, dbl.

Gloire de Châtillon – See **Mme Masson**, HP

Gloire de Chédane-Guinoiseau HP, mr, 1907, Chedane-Pajotin; flowers bright crimson-red, well-formed, large, 40 petals, cupped, moderate fragrance; occasionally recurrent bloom; foliage dark, soft; vigorous growth; [Gloire de Ducher × unknown]

Gloire de Cibeins HT, or, 1958, Arles; flowers deep vermilion-red, well-formed, 30 petals; long stems; vigorous growth; [Mme Méha Sabatier × Léonce Colombier]; int. by Roses-France

Gloire de Colmar HGal, dr, before 1910

Gloire de Deventer T, ly, 1897, Soupert & Notting; flowers light yellow with pink tints, large, dbl.; [Devoniensis × Distinction]

Gloire de Dijon Cl T, op, 1853, Jacotot; flowers rich buff-pink shaded orange toward center, 10 cm., dbl., flat, moderate fragrance; very vigorous, climbing growth; [thought to be an unknown Tea, or possibly Desprez à Fleur Jaune × Souv. de la Malmaison]; Old Rose Hall of Fame, WFRS

Gloire de Dijon à Fleur Rouges – See **Reine Marie Henriette**, Cl T

Gloire de Ducher HP, dr, 1865, Ducher; flowers very large, dbl.; occasional recurrent bloom

Gloire de France HGal, lp, 1828, Bizard; flowers pale lilac pink, lighter at edges, very large, very dbl., flat, quartered, borne singly or in clusters of 2-3, intense fragrance; non-remontant; foliage soft, gray-green; bushy, low growth

Gloire de France HT, or, 1946, Gaujard; flowers orange-red variegated copper, well-formed, large, dbl.; vigorous growth; Gold Medal, Bagatelle, 1945

Gloire de Guérin HP, dp, 1833, Guérin; flowers deep carmine, medium, full, cupped; [Malton × unknown]

Gloire de Guilan D, lp, Hilling; flowers clear pink, center incurved, semi-dbl. to dbl., quartered, intense fragrance; spring bloom; foliage light green; prickles small, curved; sprawling shrub (4-5 ft.) growth; probably very old; re-introduced by Lindsay/Hilling in 1949

Gloire de Hollande HT, dr, 1918, Verschuren; flowers glowing blood-red, large, very full, moderate fragrance; [General MacArthur × Hadley]

Gloire de Hollande, Climbing Cl HT, dr; flowers large, dbl.

Gloire de la Brie HT, mr, Grandes Roseraies; bud long; flowers bright red, large

Gloire de l'Exposition de Bruxelles – See **Gloire de Bruxelles**, HP

Gloire de Libourne T, dy, 1887, Beauvillain; flowers dark canary yellow, shaded apricot, large, very full; [Perle de Lyon × unknown]

Gloire de Margottin HP, dr, 1887, Margottin; flowers large, 60 petals, globular; occasional recurrent bloom

Gloire de Mezel M, mp; flowers pale rose, very large

Gloire de Montplaisir HP, mr, 1866, Gonod; flowers bright red

Gloire de Paris – See **Anna de Diesbach**, HP

Gloire de Rome – See **Rome Glory**, HT

Gloire de Santenay HP, m, 1859, Ducher; flowers dark purple, large, full, globular; [Général Jacqueminot × unknown]

Gloire de Thalwitz – See **Ruhm von Thalwitz**, HP

Gloire de Toulouse HP, mr, 1883, Brassac; flowers shining red, petals edged carmine, very large, very full

Gloire de Vitry HP, mp, 1854, Masson; flowers bright pink, large, globular; [La Reine × unknown]

Gloire des Anciens S, pb, Interplant; int. in 1987

Gloire des Belges HT, dp, 1916, Chambard, C.; flowers vivid carmine

Gloire des Blanches T, w, 1904, Vigneron; flowers pure white, very large, full, globular; [Niphetos × Grossherzogin Mathilde]

Gloire des Brotteaux – See **Edouard Desfossés**, B

Gloire des Héllènes – See **La Nubienne**, HCh

Gloire des Lawranceanas Min, dr, 1837; flowers dark crimson; dwarf growth

Gloire des Mousseuses M, mp, 1852, Laffay; bud heavily mossed; flowers clear bright pink, center deeper, petals imbricated, large, dbl., borne in clusters; foliage light green; vigorous growth

Gloire des Mousseux – See **Gloire des Mousseuses**, M

Gloire des Perpetuelles – See **Flon**, D

Gloire des Polyantha Pol, mp, 1887, Guillot et Fils; flowers bright pink, well-shaped, small, dbl., borne in large clusters; dwarf (50 cm.) growth; [Mignonette × unknown]

Gloire des Rosomanes Ch, mr, 1825, Vibert; flowers glowing crimson, very large, semi-dbl., borne in large clusters, moderate fragrance; repeat bloom; vigorous growth; sometimes classed as B

Gloire d'Olivet B, lp, 1886, Vigneron; bud long; flowers delicate lilac-flesh, large, full, globular; prickles numerous, chestnut-colored

Gloire d'Orient M, dr, 1856, Béluze; flowers deep red, spotted, medium, full; some repeat

Gloire d'Orléans HP, mp, 1879, Boytard; flowers carmine pink, large, full

Gloire d'Orléans Pol, mr, 1912, Levavasseur; flowers small, dbl., borne in numerous terminal panicles; foliage dark green

Gloire du Beaujolais HT, Delbard, Georges; int. in 1990

Gloire du Bouchet HP, mr, 1885, de la Rocheterie/ Cochet; flowers crimson, slightly tinted purple, very large, full, cupped; foliage wide, sharply dentate; prickles numerous, small and medium; growth upright; grown from seeds collected by Pignard at Bouchet, the estate of Mons. de La Rocheterie

Gloire du Bourbonnais Pol, rb, 1988, Delbard-Chabert; flowers center cream, margin carmine, opening turns purple, large, 35-40 petals, no fragrance; foliage bright; good, dwarf growth; [(Milrose × Legion d'Honneur) × (Zambra × Sensation)]

Gloire du Midi Pol, or, 1932, deRuiter; flowers brilliant orange-scarlet, small, dbl., borne in clusters; good repeat; vigorous, compact (18 in.) growth; [sport of Gloria Mundi]; int. by J&P

Gloire du Midi Superior Pol, or, deRuiter; flowers like parent with more lasting color; [sport of Gloire du Midi]

Gloire du Sacré-Coeur HP, lp, 1864, Pernet; flowers flesh pink, shaded carmine, large, full

Gloire d'Un Enfant d'Hiram HP, mr, 1899, Vilin; flowers bright red; [Ulrich Brunner fils × unknown]

Gloire Lyonnaise HP, w, 1885, Guillot et Fils; flowers white with trace of yellow at center, very large, 84 petals, cupped; foliage leathery; very vigorous, bushy growth; not very hardy; [Baroness Rothschild × Mme Falcot]

Gloomy Fire – See **Düsterlohe**, S

Gloria HT, dr, 1922, Paul, W.; flowers brilliant scarlet-crimson, dbl.

Gloria F, m, 2000, Horner, Colin P.; flowers lavender mauve, reverse paler, 7-8 cm., full, borne in small clusters; foliage medium size, medium green, dull; few prickles; compact, low (2 ft.) growth; [((Over the Rainbow × Baby Faurax) × (Tassin × Harriny)) × Pretty Lady]; int. in 2002

Gloria – See **Gloria Palace**, MinFl

Gloria d'Autunno HT, 1952, Cazzaniga, F. G.

Gloria de Grado HT, mp, 1950, La Florida; flowers pink, tinted carmine, globular; foliage bright green; [Mari Dot × Comtesse Vandal]

Gloria Dei – See **Peace**, HT

Gloria Dei, Climbing – See **Peace, Climbing**, Cl HT

Gloria del Llobregat HT, or, 1940, Camprubi, C.; flowers strawberry-red to vermilion, large, dbl., cupped; foliage glossy; very vigorous growth; [Sensation × Margaret McGredy]

Gloria di Milano HT, Ingegnoli

Gloria di Roma – See **Rome Glory**, HT

Gloria di Roma, Climbing Cl HT, mr, Fineschi; flowers scarlet, very large; int. about 1990

Gloria di Venezia HT, Kordes, R.

Gloria Dot Min, Dot, Simon; int. in 1986

Gloria Ferrer HT, w, Viveros Fco. Ferrer, S L; flowers 30 petals, high-centered; [Zambra × Osiana]

Gloria Mundi Pol, or, 1929, deRuiter; flowers striking orange-scarlet, dbl., borne in clusters; foliage light, glossy; vigorous, bushy growth; [sport of Superb]; int. by Teschendorff

Gloria Mundi, Climbing Cl Pol, or, 1933, de Ruiter (Lens, 1934, Howard, 1943); flowers orange-scarlet, dbl., borne in large clusters, no fragrance

Gloria Mundi Superior Pol, or, deRuiter; flowers like parent with more lasting color; [sport of Gloria Mundi]

Gloria Nigrorum HGal, m, before 1845, Calvert; flowers dark violet-purple

Gloria Palace MinFl, lp, Olesen; bud broad based ovoid; flowers light pink, 5 cm., 80 petals, deep cup, borne mostly singly, slight fragrance; recurrent; foliage dark green, matte; prickles numerous, 6 mm., greyed-yellow, hooked downwards; bushy, upright (40-60 cm.) growth; PP15150; [Pernille Hit × seedling]; container plant; int. by Poulsen Roser, 2003

Gloria Solis HT, my, 1949, Giacomasso; flowers well-formed, 4-5 in.; foliage dark, glossy; vigorous growth; [Ville de Paris × Max Krause]

Gloriana HT, my, 1936, Hillock; flowers intense lemon-yellow in heat, deep gold with cerise markings, 35 petals, cupped; foliage leathery, glossy, dark; vigorous, compact growth; [Condesa de Sástago × Condesa de Sástago]

Gloriana – See **Gloriana 97**, Cl Min

Gloriana 97 Cl Min, m, 1997, Warner, Chris; flowers dbl., high-centered, borne in small clusters; foliage medium size, medium green, semi-glossy; upright, tall (7 ft.) growth; [Laura Ford × Big Purple]

Gloriette N, lp, 1836, Vibert; flowers flesh, brighter pink center, small, full; nearly thornless; possibly synonymous with either Centifolia or HGal of the same name

Gloriette C, lp, 1854, Robert; flowers flesh pink, 6-8 cm., full

Gloriette HGal, op, before 1885; flowers salmon pink, large, full

Gloriette S, op, Cocker; int. in 1979

Gloriette Min, rb

Glorified La France HT, lp, 1916, Cook, J.W.; flowers silvery pink, deeper than La France, 92 petals, slight fragrance; [Frau Karl Druschki × Mrs Charles E. Russell]

Gloriglo Min, ob, 1977, Williams, Ernest D.; bud pointed; flowers orange, yellow reverse, 1 in., 45 petals, high-centered, slight fragrance; foliage small, glossy, bronze; upright, bushy growth; PP4305; [seedling × Over the Rainbow]; int. by Mini-Roses, 1976; AOE, ARS, 1978

Glorimontana F, or, deRuiter; flowers medium, dbl.; int. in 1974

Glorio HT, mr, 1923, E.G. Hill, Co.; flowers scarlet-cerise, dbl.; [Premier × Primrose]; int. by Vestal

Gloriosa HT, w, 1920, Kiese; flowers ivory-white, base yellow; [Kaiserin Auguste Viktoria × Pharisaer]

Glorious F, dp, 1947, Duehrsen; bud pointed; flowers salmon scarlet, shaded orange, open, medium, large trusses, 15-17 petals; foliage leathery, dark; vigorous, upright growth; RULED EXTINCT 7/84 ARM; [(Betty Uprichard × Heidekind) × Heidekind]; int. by H&S

Glorious HT, ab, 1985, Leon, Charles F., Sr.; flowers medium pink tinted apricot, well-formed, large, 37 petals; foliage medium to large, medium green, semi-glossy; upright, bushy growth; [seedling × Mirato]

Glorious HT, my, Interplant; flowers clear medium yellow, dbl.; free-flowering; foliage medium green, glossy; strong, healthy (4-5 ft.) growth; int. in 2001

Glorious Easter HT, op, 1965, Howard, P.J.; bud ovoid; flowers salmon, medium, dbl., high-centered; foliage leathery; moderate, bushy growth; [seedling × Penelope]

Glorious Pernet HT, r, 1928, Myers & Samtmann; flowers copper, center orange; [sport of Souv. de Claudius Pernet]

Glorious Sunset Pol, rb, 1931, Allen; flowers bronze, suffused red, small, semi-dbl., borne in clusters; foliage small, thick; vigorous growth; [sport of Mariposa]

Glorius – See **Glorious**, HT

Glory HT, dy, 1993, Marciel, Stanley G. & Jeanne A.; flowers 3-3½ in., full, borne mostly singly, no fragrance; foliage large, dark green, semi-glossy; some prickles; tall (205 cm.), upright growth; [Capella × seedling]; int. by DeVor Nurseries, Inc., 1992

Glory Be Min, dy, 1994, Saville, F. Harmon; flowers small, dbl., borne singly or in small clusters, no fragrance; foliage small, dark green, semi-glossy; growth medium (16-20 in.), upright, bushy; PP9506; [Party Girl × Sonnenkind]; int. by Nor'East Min. Roses, 1995

Glory Days HT, mp, 1991, Warriner, William A.; flowers coral pink, large, full, moderate fragrance; foliage medium size, medium green, semi-glossy; growth tall, upright, bushy; PP7946; [seedling × Showstopper]; int. by Bear Creek Gardens, 1991

Glory of Battala Min, pb, Mandal, G.S.; flowers pink with white reverse; free-flowering; [sport of Don Don]; int. in 2004

Glory of California LCl, ly, 1935, Schoener; flowers large, dbl., moderate fragrance; hybrid gigantea

Glory of Ceylon F, op, 1967, Harkness, R.; flowers orange-yellow blended pink, 14 petals, borne in clusters, moderate fragrance; foliage dark, glossy; [Vera Dalton × Masquerade]

Glory of Cheshunt HP, dr, 1880, Paul & Son; flowers rich crimson, cupped; vigorous growth; [Charles Lefebvre × unknown]

Glory of Edsell – See **Glory of Edzell**, HSpn

Glory of Edzell HSpn, pb, before 1900; flowers bright cherry pink with a white eye, small, single, borne singly on short laterals; non-recurrent; foliage small, dull green, matte; prickles numerous, small; growth bushy, arching (to 6 ft.)

Glory of Hurst Pol, mr, 1921, Hicks; flowers cherry-red, semi-dbl., borne in clusters; foliage small, leathery, glossy, rich green; dwarf growth; [Orléans Rose × Jessie]

Glory of Mosses – See **Gloire des Mousseuses**, M

Glory of Paris – See **Anna de Diesbach**, HP

Glory of Rome – See **Rome Glory**, HT

Glory of Surrey HT, my, 1935, Ley; flowers golden yellow, semi-dbl.; fairly vigorous growth

Glory of Waltham HP, dr, 1865, Vigneron; flowers crimson, very large, very dbl.; vigorous, climbing or pillar growth; [Souv de Leveson-Gower × unknown]; int. by W. Paul

Glossy HT, pb, Select; flowers light pink with petal edges and veins darker pink, 4½ in., 30-40 petals, exhibition, borne mostly singly; stems 24-32 in; greenhouse rose; int. by Terra Nigra BV, 2003

Glossy Rose – See ***R. virginiana*** (Miller)

Glow In The Dark F, rb, Williams, J.B.; flowers deep rose with some white streaking in the middle of petals, aging to dark velvet, moderate fragrance; foliage large, dark, glossy; vigorous growth; int. by Hortico, 2003

Glow Worm HT, or, 1919, Easlea; flowers scarlet, suffused coppery orange, semi-dbl.

Glowing HT, my, Poulsen; flowers medium yellow, 8 cm., 30 petals, cupped, borne mostly singly, moderate fragrance; recurrent; foliage matte; prickles some, 8 mm., convex, greyed-yellow; narrow, upright, bushy (60-100 cm.) growth; PP15385; [seedling × The Lady]; int. by Poulsen Roser, 2003; Gold Medal, Buenos Aires, 2006, First Prize, Hradec Králové, 2006, First Prize, Barcelona, 2006

Glowing Abundance – See **Betty Harkness**, F

Glowing Achievement – See **Stadt Eltville**, F

Glowing Amber Min, rb, 1996, Mander, George; flowers scarlet red with deep yellow reverse and yellow center, 1½-2 in., full, borne mostly singly, slight fragrance; foliage medium size, dark green, glossy; some prickles; medium (40-50 cm.), bushy growth; [June Laver × Rubies 'n' Pearls]; int. by Select Roses, 1996

Glowing Carmine HT, dp, 1936, H&S; flowers carmine, large, dbl., globular; foliage leathery; vigorous, open growth; [Miss Rowena Thom × seedling]; int. by Dreer

Glowing Carpet – See **Ralph's Creeper**, S

Glowing Cushion S, mr, Ilsink; flowers single; int. by Interplant, 1996

Glowing Embers F, yb, 1982, Anderson's Rose Nurseries; flowers yellow, red reverse, medium, 35 petals, slight fragrance; foliage medium size, medium green, glossy; bushy growth; [Manx Queen × Daily Sketch]

Glowing Peace Gr, yb, 1999, Selection Meilland; flowers yellow and orange blend, medium, 35-40 petals, borne in small clusters, slight fragrance; foliage medium size, dark green, glossy; prickles moderate; upright, bushy, medium growth; [Sun King × Roxane]; int. by Conard-Pyle, 2001

Glowing Petals Min, op, 1996, Mander, George; flowers blend of salmon orange and pink, dark yellow reverse, 2-2½ in., full, no fragrance; foliage large, dark green, glossy; some prickles; medium (45-60 cm.), bushy growth; [June Laver × Rubies 'n' Pearls]; int. by Select Roses, 1996

Glowing Pink S, mp; flowers small, full, globular, to rosette, borne in clusters; compact (50 cm.) growth; int. by World of Roses, 2006

Glowing Ruby F, mr, J&P; int. by Matthews Nursery, 2001

Glowing Sunset HT, ob, 1933, Kordes; bud long, pointed; flowers orange shaded yellow and pink, very large, dbl., high-centered; foliage leathery, glossy, dark; vigorous growth; [Fontanelle × Julien Potin]; int. by Dreer

Glowing Velvet HT, dr, 1977, Pasley; flowers deep crimson to scarlet, 4 in., 25 petals, intense fragrance; bloom repeats quickly; foliage dark; int. in 1975

Glowing With Pride Min, ob, 2006, Hopper, Nancy; flowers velvety bright orange, reverse white, 2½ in., dbl., borne mostly solitary; foliage medium green, semi-glossy; prickles ¼ in., tan, few; growth bushy, short (10 in.); [Orange You Happy × seedling]; int. in 2006

Glowry Min, ob, 1989, King, Gene; bud pointed; flowers bright orange-yellow bicolor, medium, 24 petals, high-centered, borne singly; foliage small, medium green, matte; prickles straight, red; bushy, low growth; no fruit; [(Arthur Bell × Orange Honey) × Baby Diana]; int. by AGM Miniature Roses

Glücksburg S, yb, Jensen; flowers copper gold to whitish yellow; int. by Rosen Jensen, 1989

Glückskette S, dy; int. by Richard Huber AG, 2006

Glückskind HT, dp, 1935, Berger; flowers deep pink, well-formed, large

Glückskind F, dr, 1952, Leenders, M.; flowers dark crimson, medium, semi-dbl.; very vigorous growth

Glücksstern S, w, Schultheis; flowers clean white, large, very full, cupped, moderate fragrance; upright, bushy (4 × 4 ft.) growth; int. by Rosen von Schultheis, 2005

Glyndyfrdwy HT, mp, 1977, Ellick; flowers Neyron rose, 4-5 in., 35 petals, moderate fragrance; foliage large, light; very vigorous growth; [Gavotte × George Thomas]; int. by Excelsior Roses, 1978

Glynis Bryan Min, pb, 1997, Jones, L.J.; flowers medium, dbl., borne in large clusters, no fragrance; foliage small, medium green, semi-glossy; some prickles; growth spreading, tall; [Party Girl × Sheri Anne]

G'Mundi's Rose HT, mr, 2000, Rawlins, R.; flowers scarlet, reverse slightly darker, medium, full, borne in small clusters, no fragrance; foliage medium size, dark green, semi-glossy; prickles moderate; upright, low (30 in.) growth; [Kanagem × Florange]; int. in 1999

Gneisenau HMult, w, 1924, Lambert, P.; bud pale pink; flowers snow-white, stamens yellow, 8 cm., semi-dbl., cupped, borne in clusters of 5-15, moderate fragrance; non-recurrent; foliage dark; prickles numerous, large; growth to 5-6 ft.; [Schneelicht × (Killarney × Veilchenblau)]

Gnom F, op, Berger, W.; flowers salmon-orange and pink, medium, dbl.; int. in 1957

Gnome Pol, ly, 1936, Leenders, M.; flowers cream-yellow, large, dbl.; foliage leathery, light; short stems; bushy, dwarf growth; [seedling × Mev. Nathalie Nypels]

Gnome World F, op, J&P; flowers coral-salmon, semi-dbl., flat, borne in clusters, no fragrance; good rebloom; foliage brown-red on new growth; compact growth

Godavari HT, or, Kasturi; flowers vibrant vermilion; int. by KSG Son Roses, 1987

Goddess – See **Déesse**, HT

Godescalcus Vulf de Sapprothe S, lp, Scholle, E.; flowers small, semi-dbl.; int. in 1984

Godewind S, mr, Kordes; flowers single; int. in 1992

Godfrey Winn HT, m, 1968, Dot, Pedro; flowers purplish, dbl., globular, intense fragrance; free-flowering; int. by Wheatcroft & Sons

Godfrey's Red Petite HT, dr, 1969, Godfrey; flowers deep red, medium, 15 petals, slight fragrance; foliage dark; free growth; [Baccará × Audie Murphy]

Godstowe Girl HT, mr, Harkness; flowers clear red, dbl., high-centered; medium (3 ft.) growth; int. by R. Harkness & Co, 2001

Goedele HT, lp, RvS-Melle; int. in 1998

Goethe M, m, 1911, Lambert, P.; bud heavily mossed; flowers very dark crimson/magenta, with prominent yellow stamens, 4 cm., single to semi-dbl., open, moderate fragrance; non-recurrent; foliage blue-green, rough; numerous prickles; stems new wood bright red; very vigorous growth; [*R. multiflora* × a moss rose]; possibly Geschwind rather than Lambert

Going for Gold HT, my, 2004, Brown, Ted; flowers medium yellow, reverse medium yellow, 5 in., dbl., borne mostly solitary; foliage medium size, medium green, semi-glossy, red when new; prickles medium, hooked; growth upright, medium (4-5 ft.); garden decoration, exhibition; [seedling × seedling]; int. in 2005

Golconda HT, ly, 1970, Pal, Dr. B.P.; bud ovoid; flowers pale yellow, center deep apricot, large, dbl., cupped, intense fragrance; foliage leathery; moderate, bushy, compact growth; [Mme Charles Sauvage × unknown]; int. by Indian Agric. Research Inst., 1968

Gold – See **Kogane**, F

Gold 'n' Flame Min, rb, 1981, Williams, Ernest D.; bud long, pointed; flowers medium red, deep golden yellow reverse, 33 petals, cupped, borne singly, slight fragrance; foliage dark, glossy; prickles very thin, long, tan, curved down; upright, bushy growth; [seedling × Over the Rainbow]; int. by Mini-Roses, 1980

Gold 'n' Honey HT, yb, 1976, Leon, Charles F., Sr.; bud long, pointed; flowers yellow and peach, edged rose, 5-6 in., 28 petals, high-centered; vigorous, upright, bushy growth; [Helen Traubel × (seedling × Ulster Monarch)]; int. by Edmunds Roses

Gold Badge F, my, 1979, Paolino; bud conical, medium; flowers lemon-yellow, 3 in., 38 petals, cupped, borne in clusters, no fragrance; free-flowering; foliage dark green, semi-dull, leathery; prickles average, small; vigorous, bushy (70 cm.) growth; PP4625; [Poppy Flash × (Charleston × Allgold)]; int. by Meilland

Gold Badge, Climbing Cl F, my, Meilland; flowers citron yellow, dbl.; int. in 1991

Gold Blaze Min, yb, 1980, Lyon; bud ovoid, pointed; flowers yellow, dipped red, 23 petals, borne singly or several together, intense fragrance; foliage small, glossy, deep green; prickles tiny, straight; growth compact, upright; [seedling × seedling]; int. in 1979

Gold Blush LCl, ab, 2003, Starnes, John A. Jr.; flowers apricot-gold, reverse apricot-gold, 4 in., dbl., borne in small clusters, strong cinammon fragrance; very remontant; foliage medium size, medium green, semi-glossy; prickles ¼ in., straight and flat, dark brown, few; growth upright, wide climber, tall (6-10 ft.); pillar; [*R. moschata* × Abraham Darby]; int. by John A. Starnes Jr., 2003

Gold Britannia HT, my

Gold Bunny – See **Gold Badge**, F

Gold Bunny, Climbing – See **Gold Badge, Climbing**, Cl F

Gold Coast Gr, my, 1957, Robinson, H.; bud ovoid; flowers clear yellow, overcast buff-yellow, 4 in., 25-30 petals, cupped; foliage leathery, glossy; vigorous, upright growth; PP1790; [Pinocchio × Peace]; int. by J&P

Gold Coin Min, dy, 1967, Moore, Ralph S.; flowers buttercup-yellow, small, dbl., moderate fragrance; vigorous, bushy growth; PP2921; [Golden Glow × Magic Wand]; int. by Sequoia Nursery

Gold Cottage S, dy, Dickson; flowers golden yellow, borne in clusters; growth to 4-5 ft.; int. in 2004

Gold Cottage Ediparc – See **Gold Cottage**, S

Gold Country MinFl, my, 1986, McCann, Sean; flowers small, 20 petals, high-centered, borne singly, intense fragrance; foliage small, light green, semi-glossy; bushy growth; [Rise 'n' Shine × (Rise 'n' Shine × Casino)]; int. in 1987

Gold Crest – See **Golden Crest**, Cl HT

Gold Crown HT, dy, 1960, Kordes, R.; flowers golden yellow, well-formed, 5 in., 35 petals, moderate fragrance; foliage leathery, dark; vigorous, upright growth; [Peace × Golden Scepter]; int. by McGredy & Son, 1960

Gold Cup F, dy, 1958, Boerner; bud pointed; flowers golden yellow, 4 in., 28 petals, borne in clusters, moderate fragrance; foliage dark, glossy; bushy growth; PP1683; [(Goldilocks × unknown) × King Midas seedling]; int. by J&P, 1957

Gold Dame HT, dy, 1929, Dobbie; flowers deep golden yellow, semi-dbl.; foliage dark, glossy; vigorous, bushy growth

Gold Dollar HT, dy, 1970, Herholdt, J.A.; flowers large, 35 petals, slight fragrance; foliage glossy; vigorous growth; [seedling × Weiner Charme]; int. by Herholdt's Nursery, 1971

Gold Dot HT, my, 1963, Dot, Simon; flowers large, 25 petals; vigorous, upright growth; [Queen Elizabeth × Peace]

Gold Dust F, dy, Benny, David; flowers brilliant glowing golden yellow; foliage dark green, glossy; int. by Camp Hill Roses

Gold Fantasy Min, dy; int. in 1998

Gold Fever – See **Baby Sunrise**, Min

Gold Fever Min, my, 1990, Moore, Ralph S.; bud pointed; flowers medium yellow, aging lighter, 40-50 petals, high-centered, borne usually singly or in sprays of 3-5, moderate spicy fragrance; foliage medium size, medium green, semi-glossy; prickles slender, straight, medium to long, brownish; upright, bushy, medium growth; hips round, small, orange; [Sheri Anne × Gold Badge]; int. by Sequoia Nursery

Gold Fountain – See **Goldquelle 88**, F

Gold Glow HT, dy, 1960, Perry, Anthony; flowers bright yellow, 3½-4 in., 100 petals, moderate fragrance; foliage leathery, dark, glossy; vigorous, upright growth; PP2089; [Fred Howard × Sutter's Gold]; int. by C.R. Burr, 1959

Gold Glow, Climbing Cl HT, dy, 1964, Burr, C.R.

Gold Glow Bronze Sport HT, yb, Robinson; flowers amber-apricot to bronze; [sport of Gold Glow]; int. in 1986

Gold Heart – See **Burnaby**, HT

Gold Heart HT, dy, 1998, McGredy, Sam IV; flowers deep yellow, 4 in., dbl., borne in small clusters, moderate fragrance; foliage medium size, medium green, glossy; prickles moderate; upright, very tall, 160 cm. growth; PP10798; [Solitaire × Remember Me]; int. by McGredy, 1994

Gold Krone – See **Gold Crown**, HT

Gold Leaf F, dy, Tantau; int. in 1998

Gold Link Min, dy, Bell, Laurie; flowers rich golden yellow; free-flowering; medium growth; int. by Bell Roses

Gold Magic F, dy, 1991, Christensen, Jack E.; flowers golden yellow, medium, dbl., borne in large clusters; foliage medium size, dark green, glossy; bushy, medium growth; [Gold Badge × Friesensohne]; int. by Vaughan's Seed Co., 1991

Gold Magic Carpet – See **Aspen**, S

Gold Medal Gr, my, 1981, Christensen, Jack E.; bud ovoid, long, pointed; flowers deep golden yellow sometimes flushed orange, 4½-5 in., 30-35 petals, high-centered, borne mostly singly, slight fruity fragrance; foliage large, dark; tall, upright, bushy growth; PP5177; [Yellow Pages × (Granada × Garden Party)]; int. by Armstrong Nursery, 1982; Gold Star of the South Pacific, Palmerston North, NZ, 1983

Gold Mine HT, my, 1925, Joseph H. Hill, Co.; flowers Indian yellow paling toward edges, base deep orange, dbl., intense fragrance; ruled extinct, ARA 1985; [Golden Rule × Mrs Aaron Ward]; int. by J.H. Hill Co.

Gold Mine Min, dy, 1984, Laver, Keith G.; buds; flowers chrome yellow, small, 20 petals, no fragrance; foliage medium size, medium green, semi-glossy; bushy growth; [Rise 'n' Shine × yellow seedling]; int. in 1984

Gold Mist F, Swim, H. C.; PP1368

Gold Moon Min, dy, 1985, Verschuren, Ted; bud ovoid; flowers small, 15 petals, borne singly, slight fragrance; foliage medium size, medium green, glossy; no prickles; spreading, low growth; [(Aalsmeer Gold × seedling) × (Motrea × Golden Times)]; int. by H.A. Verschuren, 1984

Gold Nugget F, dy, 1972, Patterson; flowers bright yellow, medium, dbl., high-centered; foliage glossy, abundant; vigorous, upright growth; int. by Patterson Roses

Gold of Ophir – See **Fortune's Double Yellow**, Misc OGR

Gold Patio MinFl, dy; int. in 1997

Gold Pin Min, dy, 1976, Mattock; flowers bright golden yellow, 1 in., 18 petals, slight fragrance; foliage bronze; int. in 1974

Gold Pique Min, my, 1978, Lyon; bud pointed; flowers dbl., 36 petals, moderate fragrance; foliage small, dark; compact, bushy growth; [seedling × Yellow Jewel]; int. in 1977

Gold Reef F, dy, Poulsen; flowers deep yellow, 8-10 cm., dbl., borne one to a stem; foliage dark, glossy; growth bushy, 100-150 cm.; int. by Poulsen Roser, 1998

Gold Roje Min, dy; flowers intense yellow, 1-1½ in., dbl., rosette, slight fragrance; good rebloom; growth compact, moderately tall; from Japan

Gold Rush LCl, yb, 1941, Duehrsen; flowers gold, fading to lemon, 3 in., 24 petals, high-centered, borne in clusters, moderate fragrance; not dependably recurrent; foliage glossy, ivy-green; vigorous, climbing growth; int. by H&S

Gold Rush S, dy

Gold Spray F, my, 1971, Delforge; flowers medium, dbl.; foliage soft; moderate, bushy growth; [Philippe × Spek's Yellow]

Gold Star HT, yb, 1933, Vestal; bud pointed, orange; flowers golden yellow shaded orange, large, dbl.; foliage glossy, bronze, leathery; very vigorous growth; RULED EXTINCT 6/83 ARM; [Souv. de Claudius Pernet × Talisman]

Gold Star – See **Goldstern**, HKor

Gold Star – See **Goldstar**, HT

Gold Strike F, my, 1956, Swim, H.C.; bud urn shaped; flowers lemon-yellow, 2-2½ in., 30-35 petals, high-centered, borne in rounded clusters, moderate fragrance; foliage leathery; vigorous, bushy, compact growth; PP1435; [Goldilocks × Pinocchio]; int. by Armstrong Nursery, 1955

Gold Strike HT, dy, 1999, Schuurman, Frank B.; flowers 4½ in., full, borne in small clusters, slight fragrance; foliage large, dark green, glossy; prickles moderate; upright, tall growth; PP11752; [seedling × seedling]; int. by Franko Roses New Zealand, Ltd., 1997

Gold Sweetheart Min, my, 1985, Williams, J. Benjamin; flowers deep yellow, small, 35 petals, slight fragrance; foliage small, medium green, semi-glossy; upright, bushy growth; [Sunsprite × Rise 'n' Shine]; int. by J.B. Williams & Associates

Gold Symphonie Min, my, 1994, Meilland, Alain A.; flowers large, very dbl., borne mostly singly or in small clusters; foliage medium size, dark green, semi-glossy; some prickles; medium (40-50 cm.), bushy growth; [(Rise 'n' Shine × Yellow Meillandina) × Gold Badge]; int. by SNC Meilland & Cie, 1993

Gold Symphonie 2002 – See **Yellow Sunblaze 2004**, Min

Gold Top LCl, dy, 1976, Pearce; flowers golden yellow, 5½ in., 25 petals, moderate fragrance; foliage large, light matte green; free growth; int. by Limes Rose Nursery, 1978

Gold Topaz – See **Goldtopas**, F

Goldbay – See **Bayerngold**, F

Goldbeet F, dy, Noack, Werner; int. in 1974

Goldbonnet S, my, 1973, Harkness; flowers 4 in., 13 petals; foliage large, glossy; [(Ann Elizabeth × Allgold) × Golden Showers]

Goldbusch HEg, my, 1956, Kordes; bud long, pointed; flowers yellow, becoming lighter, large, semi-dbl., borne in clusters (up to 20); foliage leathery, glossy, light green; very vigorous, upright, bushy growth

Golddigger HT, dy, 1963, Verschuren, A.; flowers dark saffron-yellow, large, 50-55 petals, slight spicy fragrance; foliage glossy, bronze; upright growth; [Marcelle Gret × Dries Verschuren]; int. by Stassen

Golddorf Seppenrade S, dy, Scholle, E.; flowers light, clear yellow, tinted gold inside the petals, large, dbl., tulip-shaped, moderate fragrance; foliage deep green tinted olive green, glossy; int. in 1969

Golddust HT, my, 1963, Delforge; flowers golden yellow; foliage clear green; vigorous growth; [Brandywine × seedling]

Goldelse HT, ob, 1900, Hinner, W.; bud large; flowers golden orange, medium; [Kaiserin Auguste Viktoria × unknown]

Goldelse – See **Bowled Over**, F

Golden – See **Golden Hit**, MinFl

Golden Afternoon HT, ab, Pal, Dr. B.P.; flowers golden apricot-orange, moderate fragrance; int. in 1984

Golden Age HT, yb, 2004, Sheldon, John; flowers yellow, changing quickly to white, 3½-4½ in., full, borne mostly solitary, moderate fragrance; foliage medium size, medium green, matte; prickles medium, pointed, green, moderate; growth bushy, medium (3-5 ft.); [Spirit of Glasnost × Lanvin]; int. by Certified Roses, Inc., 2002

Golden Altai HSpn, ly, 1943, Wright, Percy H.; flowers cream to pale yellow, single; non-recurrent; very hardy; [*R. spinosissima altaica* × Harison's Yellow]

Golden Amazone HT, dy; flowers dbl., high-centered; PP12615; florist rose

Golden Angel Min, dy, 1975, Moore, Ralph S.; bud short, pointed; flowers 1 in., 65 petals, moderate fragrance; foliage matte; bushy, compact growth; PP4028; [Golden Glow × (Little Darling × Peachy White)]; int. by Sequoia Nursery

Golden Anniversary HT, dy, 1948, Mordigan Evergreen Nursery; bud ovoid; flowers 4½-5 in., 50-60 petals, high-centered; foliage leathery; vigorous, upright, bushy growth; RULED EXTINCT 9/82 ARM; [sport of Good News]; int. by C-P

Golden Anniversary – See **Firstar**, HT

Golden Anniversary MinFl, my; flowers golden yellow; growth to 2 ft.; int. in 1997

Golden Arch LCl, dy; flowers clear, deep yellow, large, dbl., borne in large clusters, no fragrance; stems supple, bending under weight of blooms; arching (7 × 10 ft.) growth, can be trained over arches; int. by Ludwig's Roses, 2000

Golden Arches Min, dy

Golden Arctic LCl, yb, 1954, Brownell; flowers yellow to orange, 3½-4 in., 38 petals, moderate fragrance; growth like a hybrid tea, followed by 4-5 ft. canes; PP1262; [seedling × Free Gold]

Golden Autumn HT, dy, Klimenko, V. N.; flowers large, dbl.; int. in 1955

Golden Bay S, yb, 1980, Murray, Nola; bud ovoid; flowers deep buff-yellow, shapely, large, 40 petals, slight fragrance; foliage large; spreading, bushy growth; [(Tropicana × Sabine) × Zitronenfalter]

Golden Bear Min, dy; int. by Keihan Gardening, 2002

Golden Beauty HT, ab, 1937, Van Rossem; bud very long; flowers orange buff-yellow, stamens golden, large, semi-dbl.; foliage clear green, glossy; vigorous, bushy growth

Golden Beauty Min, yb, 1992, Clements, John K.; flowers gold, edged copper and pink, medium, full, high-centered, borne mostly singly; foliage small, dark green, glossy; few prickles; medium (12-15 in.), bushy, spreading growth; [seedling × seedling]; int. by Heirloom Old Garden Roses, 1990

Golden Beryl Min, yb, 1995, Mander, George; flowers deep yellow brushed orange inside of petals, 1¾-2 in., dbl., borne singly and in small clusters; foliage medium size, medium green, glossy; few prickles; medium (35-40 cm.), bushy growth; [June Laver × Rubies 'n' Pearls]; int. by Select Roses, 1995

Golden Bettina HT, yb, Ruston, D.; [sport of Bettina]

Golden Biotech HT, yb, Shastri, Dr N.V.; flowers golden yellow with pink flush; int. in 1998

Golden Blush A, ab, Sievers; int. in 1988

Golden Border – See **Comtesse du Barry**, F

Golden Bounty S, my, 1999, Zary, Dr. Keith W.; flowers 2½ in., dbl., borne in large clusters, slight fragrance; foliage medium size, dark green, semi-glossy to glossy; few prickles; upright, arching, medium (3-4 ft.) growth; PP11849; [Sun Flare × seedling]; int. by Bear Creek Gardens, Inc., 2001

Golden Bouquet HT, dy, 1971, Gregory, C.; flowers deep yellow, large, 28 petals, high-centered, borne several together; foliage dark green, glossy

Golden Bouquet F, dy; flowers golden yellow; free-flowering; strong growth; int. by Certified Roses, 1999

Golden Boy HT, dy, 1964, McGredy, Sam IV; flowers

deep yellow, very, 5½ in., 35 petals, high-centered; foliage long, pointed; moderate growth; [Golden Masterpiece × Belle Blonde]; int. by Spek

Golden Buddha HBc, ob, 2005, Barden, Paul; flowers gold-orange, 3½ in., very full, borne in small clusters, intense fruity fragrance; generous rebloom in big flushes; foliage medium size, dark green, glossy; prickles ½ in., straight, green-tan, moderate; growth very compact, dense, short (2½ ft.); small shrub, containers; [June Laver × Out of Yesteryear]; int. in 2006

Golden Butterfly HT, ab, 1920, Therkildsen; flowers apricot-yellow, shaded carmine, dbl.; [Old Gold × unknown]

Golden Butterfly – See **Goudvlinder**, HT

Golden California HT, dy, 1966, Howard, P.J.; flowers golden, large, dbl., cupped; foliage bronze, leathery, glossy; tall, bushy growth; [sport of California]

Golden Cascade LCl, my, 1964, Morey, Dr. Dennison; bud ovoid; flowers chrome-yellow, 4½-5 in., 25-30 petals, cupped, moderate fruity fragrance; foliage leathery; vigorous (10-12 ft.) growth; PP2199; [(Capt. Thomas × Joanna Hill) × Lydia]; int. by J&P, 1962

Golden Celebration S, dy, 1993, Austin, David; flowers old fashioned, 3-3½ in., 55-75 petals, borne in small clusters, intense fragrance; foliage large, dark green, semi-glossy; some prickles; medium (120 cm.), bushy growth; PP8688; [Charles Austin × Abraham Darby]; int. by David Austin Roses, Ltd., 1992

Golden Century Cl Min, ob, 1977, Moore, Ralph S.; bud pointed; flowers cadmium-orange to nasturtium-red, 1½-2 in., 35 petals, intense fragrance; foliage glossy, leathery; moderate climber growth; [(*R. wichurana* × Floradora) × (Soeur Thérèse × unnamed miniature)]; int. by Sequoia Nursery, 1978

Golden Chain – See **Rêve d'Or**, N

Golden Chalice HT, dy, 1960, Boerner; bud ovoid; flowers clear yellow, open, 4 in., 40-45 petals, moderate fragrance; foliage glossy; vigorous, upright growth; PP1958; [(Starlite × Snow White) × Golden Masterpiece]; int. by J&P, 1959

Golden Charm HT, dy, 1933, Groshens & Morrison; [sport of Talisman]

Golden Charm, Climbing Cl HT, dy, 1948; int. by Krider Nursery

Golden Chateau HT, dy, Teranishi; int. in 1998

Golden Chersonese S, my, 1967, Allen, E.F.; flowers 1½-2 in., single, borne singly at each node; early; foliage with 7-9 leaflets; vigorous growth; [*R. ecae* × Canary Bird]

Golden Choice HT, my, 1967, Bardill Nursery; flowers lemon-yellow; [sport of My Choice]; int. by LeGrice Roses

Golden City HT, my, 1922, Lippiatt; bud golden yellow; flowers light buff; [Rayon d'Or × Frau Karl Druschki]

Golden Climber – See **Mrs Arthur Curtiss James**, LCl

Golden Coach Min, dy, 1991, Zipper, Herbert; flowers medium, very full, no fragrance; borne mostly singly; foliage small, dark green, semi-glossy; few prickles; medium (40 cm.), upright, compact growth; [Rise 'n' Shine × Pot O'Gold]; int. by Magic Moment Miniature Roses, 1992

Golden Colonel F, ob

Golden Comet HT, yb, 1937, Burbank; bud long, pointed; flowers yellow and pink, open, large, semi-dbl.; foliage dark, leathery; vigorous growth; int. by Stark Bros.

Golden Conquest – See **Toulouse Lautrec**, HT

Golden Coronet F, my, 1969, Morey, Dr. Dennison; flowers medium, dbl., high-centered, slight fragrance; foliage glossy, leathery; vigorous, compact growth; [(Lydia × Golden Scepter) × Isobel Harkness]; int. by General Bionomics

Golden Cover – See **Lexington**, S

Golden Crest Cl HT, my, 1948, Archer; flowers pure yellow, 3-4 in., dbl., moderate fragrance; good repeat; foliage glossy, dark; climbing (6 ft.) growth; pillars

Golden Curls F, yb, 2000, Hamilton, Noel; flowers gold fading to cream, medium, dbl., borne in small clusters, no fragrance; foliage medium size, medium green, semi-glossy, disease-resistant; prickles moderate; compact, medium (22 × 10 in.) growth; [seedling × seedling]; int. by Coming Up Roses, 2000

Golden Dance F, my, Barni, V.; flowers intense yellow, large, dbl., borne in clusters; free-flowering; vigorous (60-80 cm.) growth; int. in 1991

Golden Dawn HT, my, 1929, Grant; bud yellow, flushed pink; flowers well-formed, 45 petals; low, spreading growth; [Elegante × Ethel Somerset]; int. by Prior

Golden Dawn, Climbing Cl HT, my, 1935, Armstrong, J.A. (Knight, 1937, and Le Grice, 1947); bud deep yellow; flowers pale yellow, very full

Golden Day HT, my, 1931, Bentley; flowers bright golden yellow, center deeper, larger and fuller; vigorous growth; [sport of Independence Day]; int. by Harkness

Golden Days HT, dy, 1982, deRuiter, George; flowers large, 35 petals; foliage large, medium green, semi-glossy; bushy growth; [Peer Gynt × seedling]; int. by Fryer's Nursery, Ltd., 1980

Golden Delight F, my, 1956, LeGrice; flowers canary-yellow, 3 in., 58 petals; foliage dark, glossy; dwarf growth; [Goldilocks × Ellinor LeGrice]

Golden Delight, Climbing Cl F, my

Golden Diamond HT, dy, 1943, Verschuren; flowers large, 30 petals; foliage leathery, dark; strong stems; vigorous, upright, compact growth; int. by L.C. Lovett

Golden Dream HRg, my, 1932, Türke; bud pointed, streaked red; flowers pure yellow, large, dbl.; recurrent bloom; very vigorous (6½ ft.) growth; [Turke's Rugosa Sämling × Constance]; int. by J.C. Schmidt

Golden Drop HT, dy, 1939, Clark, A.; flowers rich yellow, small, semi-dbl., borne in clusters; tall growth; [Mme Mascuraud × seedling]

Golden Eagle Gr, dy, 2005, Carruth, Tom; flowers deep golden yellow, 7-10 cm., full, borne mostly solitary, slight fragrance; foliage medium size, medium green, semi-glossy; prickles average, slightly hooked, beige, moderate; growth upright, medium (125 to 130 cm.); garden decoration; [Brite Lites × Joshua Bradley]; int. by Spring Hill Nurseries, 1995

Golden Earing Min, dy, 1997, Williams, J. Benjamin; flowers large, mini flora, dbl., borne singly and in clusters; [Hershey Yellow × Copper Kittel]; int. by J. B. Williams & Assoc.

Golden Elegance HT, dy, Wagner, S.; bud long; flowers large, 30 petals, high-centered, borne singly or in clusters of 3-7, slight fragrance; foliage large, dark green, glossy; [sport of Ambassador]; int. by Res. Stn. f. Fruit Growing, Cluj, 1995

Golden Emblem HT, my, 1917, McGredy; bud yellow, splashed and shaded red; flowers canary-yellow, well-formed, large, dbl.; foliage dark, glossy, leathery; vigorous growth; [Mme Mélanie Soupert × Constance]; Gold Medal, NRS, 1915

Golden Emblem, Climbing Cl HT, my, 1927, Armstrong Nursery

Golden Emblem HT, dy, 1982, Warriner, William A.; flowers large, 20 petals; foliage large, medium green, glossy; upright growth; PP5121; [(Bridal Pink × Dr. A.J. Verhage) × (Golden Sun × South Seas)]; int. by J&P

Golden Empire HT, ob, 1957, Silva; flowers orange, dbl.; foliage leathery, glossy; [Orange Everglow × Golden Emblem]

Golden Evolution F, dy; int. by Verschuren–Pechtold, 1999

Golden Eye S, rb, Ping Lim, Ping; flowers bright red-orange with golden eye, 2 in., 7-10 petals, borne in clusters; foliage deep green; growth to 2-3½ ft.; PP16612; int. by Bailey Nursery, 2004

Golden Eye Cover – See **Sugarland Run**, S

Golden Fairy Pol, ly, 1889, Bennett; flowers clear buff, yellow and white; dwarf growth

Golden Fairy Tale HT, yb, 2006; flowers flower medium yellow, partly edged red, 12 cm., full, cupped, borne singly and in small clusters, moderate fragrance; recurrent; foliage dark green, semi-glossy, very disease-resistant; upright, medium (90 cm.) growth; int. as Sterntaler, W. Kordes' Söhne, 2004

Golden Fancy – See **Bowled Over**, F

Golden Fanfare S, my, 2007, Paul Chessum Roses; flowers single, borne mostly solitary; foliage medium size, medium green, semi-glossy; prickles small, sharp, green, moderate; growth bushy, medium (80 cm.); beds, borders, containers; [seedling × seedling]; int. by World of Roses, 2005

Golden Fantasie HT, my, 1972, Byrum; flowers large, semi-dbl., high-centered, intense fragrance; foliage large, dark, leathery; vigorous, upright, bushy growth; PP3272; [Dr. A.J. Verhage × Anniversary]; int. by J.H. Hill Co., 1971

Golden Fashion HT, dy, NIRP; int. by NIRP International, 2003

Golden Fiction F, my, 1958, Spek; free growth; [Yellow Pinocchio × Moonbeam]

Golden Fiesta S, my, Roman, G., and Wagner, S.; flowers intense lemon-yellow, medium to large, 30 petals, borne in clusters, moderate fragrance; foliage medium to large, light green, glossy; [Candy Rose × Allgold]; int. by Res. Stn. for Hort., 2000

Golden Fire – See **Sonnenkind**, Min

Golden Fish Min, dy; flowers deep yellow flushed with orange; int. in 1999

Golden Flame F, my, Laperrière

Golden Fleece F, my, 1956, Boerner; bud ovoid; flowers buff-yellow, 4½ in., 38 petals, cupped, borne in clusters (to 20), intense fragrance; foliage leathery; vigorous, bushy growth; PP1512; [Diamond Jubilee × Yellow Sweetheart]; int. by J&P, 1955; Gold Medal, Bagatelle, 1955

Golden Flipper F, dy

Golden Folies – See **Golden Mimi**, F

Golden Fox MinFl, dy, Warner, Chris; int. in 1997

Golden Friendship HT, my, Harkness; flowers golden amber with outer petals ivory, reverse flushed golden amber, dbl., exhibition; tall, erect growth; int. in 1992

Golden Frills HT, my, 1936, B&A; flowers rich golden yellow, dbl., cupped; foliage glossy, wrinkled; [sport of Feu Joseph Looymans]

Golden Future LCl, my, 1997, Horner, Colin P.; flowers medium yellow, reverse lighter, fading to lemon, 3-4 in., very dbl., borne in small clusters, moderate fragrance; foliage large, dark green, glossy; upright, medium (9-12 ft.) growth; [(Anytime × (Liverpool Echo × (Flamenco × *R. bella*))) × (Korressia × Kiskadee)]; int. by Paul Chessum Roses

Golden Galaxy F, my, J&P; PP10566; int. in 1997

Golden Gardens Min, my, 1989, Moore, Ralph S.; bud ovoid; flowers bright, clear medium yellow, reverse slightly lighter, 28 petals, cupped, informal, no fragrance; foliage medium size, medium green, semi-glossy; prickles slender, inclined downward, small, brownish; upright, medium growth; no fruit; [(Little Darling × Yellow Magic) × Gold Badge]; int. by Sequoia Nursery, 1989

Golden Garnette F, dy, 1960, Boerner; bud ovoid; flowers golden yellow, edged lighter, 3-4 in., 33 petals, cupped, borne in clusters, intense fruity fragrance; foliage leathery, dark, glossy; vigorous, upright, bushy growth; PP1898; [((Goldilocks × unknown) × seedling) × Tawny Gold]; int. by J&P, 1960

Golden Gate T, w, 1891, Dingee & Conard; bud pointed; flowers cream-white, anthers golden yellow, very large, dbl., cupped, moderate fragrance; foliage bright green; vigorous growth; [Safrano × Cornelie Koch]

Golden Gate HT, my, 1971, Warriner, William A.; bud ovoid; flowers large, dbl., high-centered, slight fragrance; foliage large, glossy; vigorous, upright, bushy growth; PP3080; [South Seas × King's Ransom]; int. by J&P, 1972

Golden Gate LCl, dy, Kordes; flowers golden yellow, changing to pure yellow, large, dbl., borne in clusters of 5 to 10, moderate fruity fragrance; recurrent; foliage large, dark green, matte, dense; bushy, upright (8 ft+) growth; int. by W. Kordes Söhne, 2005; Certificate of Merit, Paris, 2006, Silver Medal, Monza, 2006, Gold Medal, Rome, 2006, Gold Medal, Kortrijk, 2006

Golden Gate HT, dy, Kordes; flowers intense, lasting yellow, medium, dbl., high-centered, borne mostly singly; florist rose; int. by W. Kordes Söhne

Golden Gem HT, my, 1916, Towill; flowers golden yellow; [Lady Hillingdon × Harry Kirk]

Golden Giant HT, dy, 1965, Kordes, R.; flowers rich golden yellow, well-formed, 5 in., 45 petals, moderate fragrance; foliage dark; vigorous, tall growth; int. by A. Dickson; Gold Medal, NRS, 1960

Golden Giant, Climbing Cl HT, dy, 1970, Laveena Roses; [sport of Golden Giant]; int. in 1967

Golden Girl Gr, my, 1960, Meilland; bud pointed; flowers golden yellow, 4-4½ in., 45 petals, high-centered, moderate fragrance; foliage leathery, light green; upright, vigorous, bushy growth; PP1912; [(Joanna Hill × Eclipse) × Michele Meilland]; int. by C-P, 1959

Golden Girls – See **Golden Beauty**, Min

Golden Girls F, dy, Zary, Keith; buds pointed, amber-copper; flowers copper-yellow, petals ruffled, dbl., borne in large clusters; free-flowering; dark green, glossy foliage; medium to tall (5 ft.) growth; int. in 2000

Golden Glamour F, my, 1951, Boerner; bud pointed; flowers large, 25 petals, high-centered; foliage glossy; vigorous, upright, bushy growth; [Joanna Hill × (Mrs Pierre S. duPont × Amelia Earhart)]; int. by J&P

Golden Gleam HT, my, 1926, McGredy; flowers buttercup-yellow, outer petals streaked, 25 petals, slight fruity fragrance; foliage dark; int. by Beckwith

Golden Globe S, dy, John Clements; flowers large, sometimes quartered, golden yellow, 5 in., 100 petals, old-fashioned, slight fresh fragrance; PPAF; int. by Heirloom Roses, 2005

Golden Globe Min, dy

Golden Glory HT, dy, 1931, Dobbie; flowers deep golden yellow, large, dbl., intense fragrance

Golden Gloves F, dy, Bear Creek Gardens; int. by Bear Creek, 1991

Golden Glow HT, ab, 1918, Chaplin Bros.; flowers apricot, shaded bronzy orange; [sport of Mme Edouard Herriot]

Golden Glow HWich, my, 1937, Brownell; bud pointed; flowers dbl., high-centered, borne in small, moderate tea fragrance; non-recurrent; foliage large, dark green, glossy; very vigorous, climbing (20 ft.) growth; [Glenn Dale × (Mary Wallace × unknown)]

Golden Grand Gr, dy, Williams, J.B.; flowers golden, dbl., borne in large clusters; int. by Hortico, 2004

Golden Gruss an Aachen F, ob, 1935, Kordes; bud pointed, red; flowers golden orange, sometimes shaded reddish, very large, dbl., high-centered; foliage glossy; bushy growth; [Mme Butterfly × Gloria Mundi]

Golden Halo Min, my, 1991, Saville, F. Harmon; bud ovoid, pointed; flowers bright yellow, medium, 24-26 petals, cupped, borne mostly singly, slight fragrance; foliage medium size, medium green, semi-glossy; upright, bushy growth; PP7770; [Arthur Bell × Rainbow's End]; int. by Nor'East Min. Roses, 1991; AOE, ARS, 1991

Golden Hands MinFl, my, Chessum, Paul; int. in 1995

Golden Handshake Cl Min, dy, 1996, Warner, Chris; flowers clear bright yellow, small, dbl., borne in small clusters; foliage small, light green, glossy; few prickles; upright, bushy, tall growth; [Pam Ayres × Laura Ford]; int. by Warner's Roses, 1997; TGC, St. Albans, 1994

Golden Harvest HT, dy, 1943, Mallerin, C.; flowers clear yellow, 4½ in., 35 petals, high-centered; foliage leathery, glossy, bronze; vigorous growth; [McGredy's Ivory × seedling]; int. by C-P

Golden Haze HT, yb, 1965, Verschuren, H.A.M.; bud ovoid; flowers light golden yellow, large, dbl., moderate fragrance; foliage glossy; vigorous growth; PP2609; [Peace × Golden Rapture]; int. by J&P

Golden Heart – See **Burnaby**, HT

Golden Heart HT, dy, Tantau; int. in 1991

Golden Heritage HT, my, 1973, Herholdt, J.A.; flowers canary-yellow, pointed, large, 25 petals, moderate tea fragrance; bushy growth; [Golden Masterpiece × seedling]; int. in 1974

Golden Hit MinFl, dy, Poulsen; flowers deep yellow, 5-8 cm., semi-dbl., slight wild rose fragrance; foliage dark; growth bushy, 40-60 cm.; int. by Poulsen Roser, 1996

Golden Holstein F, dy, Kordes; flowers bright, clear yellow, wavy petals, semi-dbl., borne in large clusters; recurrent; foliage dark green, glossy; upright, medium to tall growth; int. in 1989

Golden Hope F, yb, 1998, Mehring, Bernhard F.; flowers yellow, pink edge, reverse amber with pink edge, 2¾ in., dbl., borne in small clusters; foliage large, medium green, semi-glossy; no prickles; upright, medium, 80 cm. growth; [Kronprinzessin Victoria von Schweden × Goldene Holstein]; int. by Henry Street Nurseries, 1998

Golden Horizon Min, my, 2006, Moore, Ralph S.; flowers 1½-2 in., full, borne in small clusters; foliage medium size, medium green, semi-glossy; prickles small, straight, green, few; growth compact, medium (15-18 in.); containers, borders, garden; [Cal Poly × Strawberry Ice]; int. by Sequoia Nurs., 2006

Golden Hour HT, ob, 1952, Howard, P.J.; bud ovoid; flowers golden yellow, reverse orange, 4-5 in., 45-55 petals, high-centered; foliage leathery, glossy; very vigorous, upright growth; [Los Angeles × California]

Golden Iceberg F, yb, 2006, Davidson, Harvey; flowers yellow and white, 8-9 cm., dbl., borne in large clusters; foliage medium size, medium green, semi-glossy, disease-resistant; few prickles; growth compact, medium (1 m.); garden; [Sun Flare × Sun Flare]; int. by Mea Nursery, 2006

Golden Ideal HT, dy, 1939, Lens; bud long, pointed; flowers brilliant chrome-yellow, large, dbl.; vigorous growth; [Roselandia × Joanna Hill]

Golden Jet – See **Goldschatz**, F

Golden Jewel HT, dy, 1960, Tantau, Math.; flowers golden yellow, 3 in., dbl., borne in clusters of up to 10, moderate fragrance; foliage dark, glossy; vigorous, bushy growth; [Goldilocks × Masquerade seedling]; int. by Wheatcroft Bros., 1959

Golden Jewel Min, dy, Tantau; flowers unfading golden yellow, dbl., high-centered; free blooming; foliage dark green, glossy; bushy, compact (18 in.) growth; int. as Bijou d'Or, Rosen Tantau, 1995

Golden Jubilee F, my, 1948, Jacobus; bud ovoid; flowers golden yellow, becoming buff and chrome, 3 in., dbl., borne in clusters; foliage glossy, dark; vigorous, bushy, compact growth; [(Mary Wallace × Talisman) × Mrs Pierre S. duPont]; int. by B&A

Golden Jubilee HT, my, Cocker, James; flowers 29 petals, high-centered, moderate tea fragrance; foliage large, matte green, glossy; prickles narrow, red-brown; [Peer Gynt × Gay Gordons]

Golden Julia HT, my, 1992, Rupert, Kim L.; bud long, pointed; flowers medium golden mustard, opening medium golden yellow, fading, 3-4 in., 18-22 petals, flat, slight fragrance; foliage medium size, medium green, matte; prickles few, yellow; stems green wood; growth medium (75-90 cm.), upright, bushy; [sport of Julia's Rose]

Golden King HRg, ly, 1935, Beckwith; flowers pale yellow, semi-dbl.; [sport of Dr. Eckener]

Golden Kiss HT, yb, Dickson; flowers golden yellow with pink edges, large, full, high-centered, borne singly and in clusters of up to 5; bushy, upright (3 ft.) growth; int. by Dickson Roses, 2003

Golden Lace F, dy, 1962, Von Abrams; bud pointed; flowers 3 in., 28 petals, high-centered, borne in clusters; foliage glossy; vigorous, upright growth; [Goldilocks × (Golden Scepter × Encore)]; int. by Peterson & Dering, 1962

Golden Lady HT, dy, McGredy; bud egg-shaped, large; flowers golden yellow, full, intense fragrance; foliage dark green, glossy; strong, upright (70 cm.) growth; int. in 2000

Golden Leader HT, ab, 1961, Leenders, J.; flowers apricot; [Tawny Gold × seedling]

Golden Leopard F, my, 1976, Takatori, Yoshiho; bud pointed; flowers daffodil-yellow, 2 in., 18-25 petals, high-centered; foliage glossy, leathery; low, compact growth; [Golden Slippers × unknown]; int. by Japan Rose Nursery

Golden Light LCl, ob, 1939, Nicolas; bud pointed; flowers orange-apricot to buff, edged pink, open, large, dbl.; foliage glossy, dark; strong stems; vigorous, climbing growth

Golden Lion HSet, my, 1944, Horvath; flowers clear golden yellow, open, cupped, borne in clusters; non-recurrent; foliage light, glossy; growth to 8-10 ft.

Golden Lustre HT, ab, 1964, Boerner; bud ovoid; flowers bronze-apricot overcast yellow, 5 in., 60-65 petals, cupped, moderate fragrance; foliage leathery; moderate growth; PP2442; [Kate Smith × Tanya]; int. by J&P, 1964

Golden Mme Segond Weber HT, op, 1923, Soupert & Notting; flowers salmon, center yellow, dbl.; [Mme Segond Weber × Primerose]

Golden Main HT, dy, 1933, Kordes; bud golden yellow striped red; flowers golden yellow, large, dbl., cupped; foliage glossy; very vigorous, bushy growth; [Fontanelle × Julien Potin]; int. by J&P

Golden Masterpiece HT, my, 1954, Boerner; bud long, pointed; flowers golden yellow, very large, 30-35 petals, high-centered, borne singly, moderate licorice fragrance; foliage very glossy; vigorous, upright growth; PP1284; [Mandalay × Golden Scepter]; int. by J&P

Golden Masterpiece, Climbing Cl HT, my, 1957, Valdrez; PP1660

Golden Medaillon – See **Limelight**, HT

Golden Medaillon HT, dy, 2006; bud long, deep yellow with a breath of copper; flowers deep yellow, tinted copper, 11 cm., full, high-centered, borne in airy clusters; foliage dark green, shiny, tough; bushy, upright (3 ft.) growth; int. by W. Kordes' Söhne, 1991; Gold Medal, Baden-Baden, 1991

Golden Medal – See **Gold Medal**, Gr

Golden Medallion HT, my, 1977, Permenter; bud long, pointed; flowers medium golden yellow, loosely imbricated, 7-8 in., 40-50 petals, slight fragrance; foliage large, light; upright growth; PP4086; [sport of Medallion]; int. by J&P, 1974

Golden Meillandina – See **Rise 'n' Shine**, Min

Golden Melody – See **Irene Churruca**, HT

Golden Memories HT, dy, 1965, Ravine; bud long, pointed, canary-yellow tinted coppery; flowers deep canary-yellow, to open, 5-6 in., 28-32 petals, high-centered, moderate spicy fragrance; foliage glossy; vigorous, upright growth; PP2205; [sport of Golden Rapture]; int. by Endres Floral Co.

Golden Memories F, dy, Kordes; flowers golden yellow, small, semi-dbl., borne in large trusses; recurrent; foliage glossy, disease-resistant; growth to 3 ft.; int. in 2004

Golden Midinette Cl Min, my; flowers clear yellow, borne in clusters on main branches and side stems, no fragrance; recurrent; arching, tall (5 ft.) growth; int. in 2000

Golden Mimi F, my, Meilland; flowers lemon yellow, edges brushed pink at times, dbl., borne in sprays; florist rose; int. by Meilland Intl, 1998

Golden Mist LCl, Bailey, Dorothy J.; PP4011

Golden Moments HT, dy, Fryer, Gareth; flowers soft golden-amber, full, high-centered, borne mostly singly, moderate fragrance; quick repeat; foliage mid-green, disease-resistant; long stems; rounded, medium (3 ft.) growth; int. by Fryer's Roses, 1991

Golden Monica HT, dy, Tantau; flowers golden yellow, dbl., high-centered, borne mostly singly; recurrent; stems long, almost thornless; healthy, tall growth; [sport of Monica]; int. in 1988

Golden Morning Min, dy, 2001, Bell, Judy G.; flowers bright golden yellow with bright yellow stamens, 1½ in., single, borne mostly solitary, no fragrance; foliage light green, matte; prickles small, straight, few; growth upright, medium; garden decorative, containers, exhibition; [Loving Touch × Party Girl]; int. by Michigan Mini Roses, 2002

Golden Moss M, my, 1932, Dot, Pedro; bud globular, peach-yellow, sepals well mossed; flowers tawny yellow, large, 37 petals, borne in clusters of 3-5, moderate fragrance; scanty bloom; no repeat; foliage almost rugose; vigorous growth; [Frau Karl Druschki × (Souv. de Claudius Pernet × Blanche Moreau)]; int. by C-P

Golden Mozart S, my, Verschuren; flowers lemon yellow; recurrent; upright, then arching (2½ ft.) growth; int. in 1986

Golden Mrs Sam McGredy – See **Golden Sam McGredy**, HT

Golden Nugget HT, my, Meilland; buds large, conical, lemon yellow; flowers intense, lasting yellow, 5½ in, 35 petals, cupped, borne mostly singly, no fragrance; good repeat; foliage dark green, glossy, disease-resistant; prickles moderate; erect (2-3 ft.) growth; PP9262; [Lovely Girl × (Emblem × Texas)]; int. in 1996

Golden Nugget Min, dy

Golden Nuggets – See **Yellow Fleurette**, S

Golden Oldie F, ab, 1998, McGredy, Sam IV; flowers apricot blend, 2¾ in., dbl., borne in large clusters; foliage medium size, dark green, semi-glossy; prickles moderate; bushy, low (50 cm.) growth; [Maiden Voyage × Orange Honey]; int. by McGredy, 1997

Golden Oldie HT, dy, Fryer; flowers golden yellow, 4 in., 40 petals, borne evenly on a neat bush; early to flower, quick to repeat; growth to 3½ × 3 ft.; int. by Fryer's Nursery, 2001

Golden Oldie S, dy, Kordes; int. in 2003

Golden Oldies – See **Golden Oldie**, HT

Golden Ophelia HT, my, 1918, Cant, B. R.; flowers golden yellow in center, paling slightly on outer petals, medium, dbl.; foliage glossy; vigorous growth; [Ophelia × Mrs Aaron Ward]; Gold Medal, NRS, 1918

Golden Ophelia, Climbing Cl HT, my, 1924, Hage; int. by Prior

Golden Opportunity Gr, dy, 1996, Perry, Anthony; bud urn-shaped; flowers golden yellow, light golden yellow, dbl., borne in small clusters, slight fragrance; foliage medium size, medium green, semi-glossy; some prickles; medium growth; [Broadway × Delta Gold]; int. by Certified Roses, Inc., 1995

Golden Orange Climber LCl, ob, 1937, Brownell; flowers orange to orange-scarlet, often overlaid golden yellow, 5 in., semi-dbl.; vigorous, climbing growth; [sport of Mrs Arthur Curtiss James]

Golden Oriole T, dy, 1905, Shepherd; flowers deep saffron-yellow, small, very dbl.

Golden Pamela HT, yb, 1969, Wheatley; bud ovoid; flowers yellow-apricot and pink, large, dbl., cupped; foliage large, glossy; vigorous, upright growth; [sport of Wellworth]

Golden Pavillion – See **Kinkaku**, HT

Golden Peace HT, my, 1970, LeGrice; flowers canary-yellow, large, 45 petals, high-centered, moderate fragrance; foliage dark, dull; very vigorous, tall growth; int. in 1961

Golden Pearl HT, my, 1967, Warmerdam; flowers large, single; foliage dark; free growth

Golden Penny LCl, yb, 1984, Cook, Sylven S.; flowers gold, reverse creamy, dbl., intense lemon fragrance; foliage medium size, medium green, semi-glossy; upright growth (7-8 ft.); [Queen Elizabeth × Scarlet Knight]; int. in 1981

Golden Penny Min, my

Golden Perfection Pol, my, 1937, Leenders, M.; flowers golden yellow, small, dbl.; bushy, dwarf growth

Golden Perfume F, my, 1960, Leenders, J.; flowers orange-yellow becoming golden yellow, large, 50 petals, borne in clusters, moderate fragrance; foliage dark, glossy, leathery; vigorous, bushy growth; [Goldilocks × Fashion]; int. by Brit. Hort. Co., 1958

Golden Pernet – See **Julien Potin**, HT

Golden Perraud HT, my, 1946, Lens; bud long, pointed, well formed; flowers brilliant golden yellow, large, dbl.; foliage glossy; vigorous growth; [sport of Mme Joseph Perraud]

Golden Pheasant F, ob, 1951, Kordes; flowers orange and gold, imbricated, 4 in., 40 petals; foliage glossy; low, compact growth; [Pres. Ferier × Dr. Debat]; int. by Wheatcroft Bros.

Golden Phoenix HT, my, 1986, Nakashima, Tosh; [sport of Bettina]; int. in 1985

Golden Piccolo – See **Texas**, Min

Golden Picture HT, yb, 1967, Handover, P.&R.; flowers light yellow tinged pink, medium; foliage leathery; upright growth; [(Picture × unknown) × Marcelle Gret]

Golden Pillar LCl, my, Meilland; flowers large, loose, golden yellow, non-fading, 4 in., 30-35 petals; foliage medium size, deep green, glossy; int. in 1999

Golden Pirrie HT, ly, 1921, Collin/Dobbie; flowers yellowish-white; [sport of Lady Pirrie]

Golden Pixie Min, my, 1985, Hardgrove, Donald L.; flowers medium golden yellow, medium, 60 petals; foliage small, medium green, semi-glossy; vigorous, upright, bushy growth; [Yellow Pages × Rise 'n' Shine]; int. by Rose World Originals

Golden Planet HT, yb, Teranishi; int. in 2004

Golden Plover – See **Aspen**, S

Golden Poly Pol, yb, 1931, Pahissa; flowers pure yellow, edged carmine, dbl., globular; dwarf growth; [Angèle Pernet × Orange King]

Golden Poly Pol, my, 1935, Leenders, M.; bud yellow with red lines; flowers golden yellow to yellowish-white, open, large, semi-dbl.; foliage light, glossy; bushy, dwarf growth

Golden Pride – See **Gold Coast**, Gr

Golden Prince HT, dy, 1970, Meilland, Mrs. Marie-Louise; buds medium, long pointed; flowers Indian yellow, medium, dbl, open, borne singly, slight fragrance; foliage dark green, glossy, disease-resistant; growth vigorous, upright, bushy, medium; PP2949; [(Monte Carlo × Bettina) × (Peace × Soraya)]; registrations published under both Golden Prince and Kabuki, ARA 1970; int. as Kabuki, URS

Golden Princess S, yb, 1985, Buck, Dr. Griffith J.; bud ovoid, pointed; flowers yellow, petals edged deep pink, large, 33 petals, cupped, borne singly and in clusters of up to 5, moderate fragrance; repeat bloom; foliage medium size, olive green, semi-glossy; prickles large, hooked, tan; upright, bushy growth; hardy; [Hawkeye Belle × (Roundelay × Country Music)]; int. by Iowa State University, 1984

Golden Promise F, dy, deRuiter; flowers bright yellow; free-flowering; large, bushy growth; blooms said to look much like Sunsprite; int. in 1972

Golden Promise Min, dy, 1992, Laver, Keith G.; flowers medium, full, borne mostly singly, no fragrance; foliage small, dark green, glossy; few prickles; low (30 cm.), bushy growth; [June Laver × Potluck Gold]; int. by Springwood Roses, 1993

Golden Pyramid LCl, my, 1939, Brownell; flowers large, semi-dbl.; free seasonal bloom; vigorous, pyramidal (to 5-6 ft.) growth

Golden Queen N, dy, 1902, Paul; flowers bright golden yellow

Golden Queen HT, my, 1937, Chambard, C.; bud gold, slightly marked carmine; flowers golden yellow, large, dbl.; foliage glossy; very vigorous, bushy growth

Golden Queen HT, ob, Kordes; int. in 1986; Gold Star of the South Pacific, Palmerston North, NZ, 1984

Golden Quill F, dy, Harkness; int. in 2002

Golden Rain F, my, 1951, Tantau; flowers golden yellow, well-formed, large, 20 petals, borne in clusters of 10-15; foliage glossy; upright, bushy growth; [Swantje × G. Bentheim]

Golden Rambler – See **Alister Stella Gray**, N

Golden Rambler – See **Easlea's Golden Rambler**, HWich

Golden Rapture HT, dy, 1933, Kordes; bud pointed; flowers golden yellow, very large, 40 petals; foliage glossy; vigorous growth; [Rapture × Julien Potin]; int. by H&S, 1934

Golden Rapture, Climbing Cl HT, dy, 1941, Swim, H.C. (also Knackfuss, 1954); flowers deep yellow, fading to lemon, 5 in.; int. by Armstrong Nursery

Golden Rapture No. 5 HT, my, Krieter; bud ovoid; flowers clear yellow, 5 in., 25 petals, high-centered, intense fragrance; foliage dark, leathery; vigorous growth; PP1413; [sport of Golden Rapture]; int. by A.N. Pierson

Golden Revelry HT, my, 1952, McGredy, Sam IV; flowers golden yellow, 21 petals, high-centered; foliage glossy, bright green; [Phyllis Gold × Blossom]

Golden Rider – See **Goldener Reiter**, F

Golden River LCl, dy

Golden Romance – See **Golden Main**, HT

Golden Rosamini Min, dy, Ilsink; int. in 1990

Golden Rose of China – See ***R. hugonis*** (Hemsley)

Golden Ruffels HT, my, 1954, Brownell; bud long, pointed; flowers golden yellow, medium, dbl., moderate fragrance; upright growth; [sport of Orange Ruffels]

Golden Rule HT, my, 1918, E.G. Hill, Co.; flowers clear yellow, dbl.; [(Ophelia × unknown) × Sunburst]

Golden Salmon Pol, ob, 1926, deRuiter; flowers pure orange, large, borne in huge trusses; vigorous, bushy growth; [sport of Superb]

Golden Salmon Improved – See **Golden Salmon Supérieur**, Pol

Golden Salmon Supérieur Pol, ob, 1929, deRuiter; flowers scarlet to orange, small, semi-dbl., borne in large clusters; good repeat; [sport of Golden Salmon]; int. by Sliedrecht & Co.

Golden Salute HT, dy, 1963, Boerner; bud ovoid; flowers golden yellow, 5-5½ in., 33 petals, cupped, moderate fragrance; foliage leathery, glossy; vigorous, moderately tall growth; PP2303; [(Diamond Jubilee × unknown) × Golden Masterpiece]; int. by J&P, 1963

Golden Sam McGredy HT, yb, 1935, Lens; flowers chrome-yellow, reverse salmon with chrome; [sport of Mrs Sam McGredy]

Golden Sástago HT, dy, 1938, Dot, Pedro; flowers clear yellow, large, dbl., globular; foliage soft; vigorous growth; [sport of Condesa de Sástago]; int. by C-P

Golden Scepter HT, dy, 1950, Verschuren-Pechtold; bud pointed; flowers deep yellow, 4½ in., 35 petals, high-centered, moderate fragrance; foliage leathery, glossy; vigorous, upright growth; [Golden Rapture × seedling]; int. by Spek

Golden Scepter, Climbing Cl HT, dy, 1956, Walters; [sport of Golden Scepter]

Golden Séverine HT, dy, 1929, Morse; flowers deep golden yellow

Golden Sheen F, my, 1966, Swim & Weeks; bud urn shaped; flowers yellow, edged lighter, dbl., high-centered, borne in clusters; foliage leathery; moderate, upright, bushy growth; PP2727; [Ophelia × Circus]; int. by Carlton Rose Nurseries

Golden Sheila F, my, Horner; int. in 2006

Golden Shot F, dy, 1976, Martin, J.; flowers golden yellow, 4 in., 24 petals, slight fragrance; foliage dark; [seedling × Allgold]; int. by Gandy Roses, Ltd., 1973

Golden Showers LCl, my, 1957, Lammerts, Dr. Walter; bud long, pointed; flowers daffodil-yellow, open quickly, loose, 4 in., 25-28 petals, high-centered, borne singly and in clusters, moderate sweet fragrance; recurrent bloom; foliage medium size, medium green, glossy; vigorous, pillar or climbing (6-10 ft.) growth; PP1557; [Charlotte Armstrong × Capt. Thomas]; int. by Germain's Seed & Plant Co., 1956; Gold Medal, Portland, 1957

Golden Signora HT, my, 1954, Lowe; flowers golden veined orange, large, 30 petals; foliage glossy; vigorous growth; [sport of Signora]

Golden Silence Min, yb, 1995, Rennie, Bruce F.; flowers 1½ in., dbl., borne mostly singly; foliage medium size, dark green, semi-glossy; some prickles; medium (15-18 in.), upright growth; int. by Rennie Roses International, 1995

Golden Slippers F, yb, 1961, Von Abrams; bud pointed; flowers yellow flushed vermilion, center golden yellow, 3 in., 23 petals, high-centered, borne in clusters, moderate fragrance; foliage leathery, glossy; vigorous, compact, low growth; PP2244; [Goldilocks × seedling]; int. by Peterson & Dering, 1961; Gold Medal, Portland, 1960

Golden Smiles F, my, Fryer; flowers golden-yellow, dbl., low-centered, borne in clusters; recurrent`; foliage dark green; bushy growth; int. by Fryers Roses, 2006

Golden Song Cl Min, yb, 1981, Williams, Ernest D.; bud long, pointed; flowers golden yellow, petals edged pink, 35 petals, high-centered, borne usually singly, moderate fragrance; foliage small, medium to dark, glossy; prickles long, thin, tan; upright (to about 5 ft.) growth; [Little Darling × Golden Angel]; int. by Mini-Roses, 1980

Golden Spire HT, dy, Kordes; flowers deep golden yellow, dbl., borne in grandiflora-like clusters, no fragrance; blooms early in spring and rapid repeat; upright stems; narrow, upright, tall (8 ft+) growth; int. in 1996

Golden Splendor HT, dy, 1965, Jones; bud long, pointed; flowers golden yellow, 5 in., 30 petals, high-centered; foliage glossy; vigorous, tall growth; int. by Hennessey, 1960

Golden Splendour HT, my, 1965, Kordes; flowers clear light yellow, large, 40 petals, moderate fragrance; [Buccaneer × Golden Sun]; int. by Wheatcroft Bros., 1962

Golden Spray HT, my, 1917, Dickson, H.; flowers clear lemon-yellow, huge mass of prominent anthers, semi-dbl., borne in long, arching sprays; Gold Medal, NRS, 1915

Golden Sprite F, dy, 1992, Marciel, Stanley G. & Jeanne A.; flowers 3-3½ in., dbl., borne mostly singly, slight fragrance; foliage medium size, dark green, matte; some prickles; medium, upright growth; [Golden Fantasie × Excitement]; int. by DeVor Nurseries, Inc.

Golden Star – See **Goldstern**, HKor

Golden Star HT, dy, 1976, Lowe; flowers full, 4-4½ in., 32 petals, slight fragrance; foliage dark; free growth; [sport of Whisky Mac]; int. in 1974

Golden Starlite – See **Sorraya**, HT dbl.

Golden State HT, dy, 1937, Meilland, F.; flowers golden yellow, large, dbl., cupped; foliage leathery, glossy; vigorous growth; [Souv. de Claudius Pernet × (Charles P. Kilham × seedling)]; int. by C-P, 1938; Gold Medal, Portland, 1937, Gold Medal, Bagatelle, 1937

Golden Summers – See **Funkuhr**, HT

Golden Sun HT, my, 1957, Kordes, R.; bud long, pointed; flowers golden yellow, 5 in., dbl., high-centered; foliage glossy; upright, bushy growth; [(Walter Bentley × Condesa de Sástago) × Golden Scepter]

Golden Sunblaze – See **Rise 'n' Shine**, Min

Golden Sunblaze Min, my, 1994, Selection Meilland; bud short, plump, ovoid; flowers bright golden yellow, like a zinnia, 1½ in., 40-45 petals, cupped, borne in small clusters; foliage medium size, dark green, glossy; few prickles; medium (15 in.), upright, bushy growth; PP8493; [(Rise 'n' Shine × Mark One) × Yellow Meillandina]; int. by The Conard-Pyle Co., 1993

Golden Sunburst HT, yb, 1969, Schneeberg; bud ovoid; flowers cadmium-orange and saffron-yellow, large, dbl., intense fragrance; foliage dark, glossy; vigorous, bushy growth; PP2708; [sport of Golden Wave]; int. by Carlton Rose Nurseries, 1967

Golden Sunset LCl, my, 1934, Burbank; flowers golden yellow, often tipped orange-red, large, dbl., cupped; foliage glossy; long stems; vigorous growth; int. by Stark Bros.

Golden Sunshine HT, my, 1964, Brownell, H.C.; bud pointed, ovoid, chrome-yellow splashed red; flowers canary-yellow, 5 in., 50 petals, high-centered; vigorous, upright growth; [Helen Hayes × Golden Masterpiece]; int. by Brownell Sub-Zero Roses, 1964

Golden Surprise F, my, 1979, Hamilton; [sport of Woburn Abbey]

Golden Symphony – See **Gold Symphonie**, Min

Golden Talisman HT, my, 1931, E.G. Hill, Co.; [sport of Talisman]

Golden Talisman, Climbing Cl HT, my, 1935, Elmer's Nursery; [sport of Talisman]

Golden Thoughts – See **McGredy's Orange**, HT

Golden Threshold HG, dy, 2005, Viraraghavan, M.S. Viru; flowers have distinctive red pollen, 4 in., single, borne mostly solitary; foliage large, medium green, glossy; prickles large, triangular; growth upright, tall; pillars, pergolas; [Golden Showers × Virgiant (Sirohi Sunrise)]; int. by Roses Unlimited, 2004

Golden Times F, Kordes, R.; PP4044

Golden Times HT, my, 1971, Cocker; flowers lemon-yellow, 4-5 in., 40 petals, slight fragrance; foliage glossy; [Fragrant Cloud × Golden Splendour]; int. by Wheatcroft & Sons, 1970

Golden Times F, my, 1985, Kordes, W.; flowers medium, dbl.; foliage medium size, dark, semi-glossy; bushy growth; [New Day × Minigold]

Golden Token Min, dy, 1993, Williams, Ernest D.; foliage small, medium green, glossy; medium (40 cm.), upright, bushy growth; [unknown × unknown]; int. by Mini Roses of Texas, 1993

Golden Topas Min, dy, 1995, Mander, George; flowers 1¾-2 in., dbl., borne in small clusters; foliage medium size, medium green, semi-glossy; some prickles; medium (35 cm.), bushy growth; [June Laver × Rubies 'n' Pearls]; int. by Oregon Miniagure Roses

Golden Touch – See **Sonnenschirm**, S

Golden Tower HT, dy, Tantau; flowers warm cream to dark yellow, sometimes with thin red petal edges, 14 cm., dbl., classic hybrid tea, borne mostly singly, moderate fragrance; recurrent; stems long; growth to 4-5 ft.; int. by Rosen Tantau, 2005

Golden Treasure F, my, 1966, Tantau, Math.; bud pointed; flowers golden yellow, large, dbl., borne in cluster (up to 30); foliage dark, glossy; bushy, upright growth; int. by Wheatcroft Bros., 1965

Golden Treasure, Climbing Cl F, my, 1977, Pearson; int. by Burston Nursery, 1976

Golden Tribute F, dy, Horner; flowers deep golden yellow, dbl., moderate fragrance; free-flowering; short to medium growth; int. in 1997

Golden Trust MinFl, yb; flowers yellow with light pink edge, 2 in., dbl., borne in large clusters, slight fragrance; free flowering all season; foliage mid-green, abundant; growth upright (2 × 1 ft.); int. by Harkness, 2001

Golden Tzigane HT, ob, 1961, Gregory; flowers orange; [sport of Tzigane]

Golden Unicorn S, yb, 1985, Buck, Dr. Griffith J.; flowers yellow, petals edged orange-red, large, 28 petals, cupped, borne 1-8 per cluster, moderate fragrance; repeat bloom; foliage dark olive green, leathery; prickles awl-like, tan; vigorous, upright, bushy, spreading growth; hardy; [Paloma Blanca × (Carefree Beauty × Antike)]; int. by Iowa State University, 1984

Golden Vale S, y, Sutherland, P; [Primula × unknown]; int. by Golden Vale Nursery, 2000

Golden Van Rossem HT, dy, 1937, Lens; flowers chrome yellow; [sport of Mev. G.A. van Rossem]

Golden Vandal HT, dy, 1935, Lens; flowers chrome yellow; [sport of Comtesse Vandal]

Golden Vision LCl, my, 1922, Clark, A.; flowers pale creamy yellow, fading nearly white, 7 cm., semi-dbl., moderate fragrance; [supposedly Maréchal Niel × *R. gigantea*]; int. by NRS Victoria

Golden Wave – See **Dr A. J. Verhage**, HT

Golden Wave Gr, dy, Williams, J.B.; flowers bright golden yellow, dbl., star shaped.; foliage dark green.; hardy to -20ºF; int. by Hortico, 2003

Golden Wedding HT, my, 1938, Krebs; bud pointed, yellow tinted crimson; flowers clear yellow, 5 in., dbl.; foliage leathery, dark; growth vigorous; [Souv. de H.A. Verschuren × yellow seedling]

Golden Wedding F, dy, Bear Creek Gardens; flowers deep golden yellow, large, dbl., high-centered, borne in clusters; free-flowering; foliage glossy, disease-resistant; growth vigorous, compact (3 ft.); int. in 1990

Golden Wedding Anniversary – See **Golden Wedding**, F

Golden Wedding Celebration F, my; flowers unfading yellow, dbl., high-centered, borne in masses of blooms, slight fragrance; foliage disease-resistant; tough (3 ft.) growth; int. in 2005

Golden West HT, my, 1936, Stocking; bud pointed; flowers golden yellow, open, large, semi-dbl.; foliage dark, leathery, glossy; vigorous, bushy, spreading growth; [sport of Duchess of York]

Golden Wings S, ly, 1953, Shepherd; bud long, pointed; flowers sulfur-yellow, prominent amber stamens, 4-5 in., single, slight fragrance; recurrent bloom; growth vigorous, bushy, to 4 ft.; very hardy; PP1419; [(*R. spinosissima* × unknown) × Soeur Thérèse]; int. by Bosley Nursery; Gold Medal, ARS, 1958

Golden Wishes – See **Sun Hit**, MinFl

Golden Wonder HT, ab, 1936, Gunn; flowers golden apricot suffused pink, globular; foliage olive-green; vigorous growth

Golden Wonder HT, yb, 1974, Gandy, Douglas L.; flowers lemon-yellow, edged red, 4-5 in., 36-40 petals, high-centered, moderate fragrance; foliage dark; [Miss Ireland × Princess]; int. by Morse Roses

Golden Wonders 99 HT, dy, 1999, Rawlins, R.; flowers large, dbl., borne in small clusters; foliage medium size, medium green, semi-glossy; prickles moderate; bushy (2½ ft.) growth; [(Gold Bunny × (Baby Love × seedling)) × Golden Celebration]

Golden Years F, my, 1989, Harkness, R., & Co., Ltd.; bud ovoid; flowers golden yellow, reverse some bronze tint, large, 46 petals, cupped, borne in sprays, slight fruity fragrance; foliage medium size, dark green, semi-glossy; prickles slightly curved, long, thin, greenish-red; bushy, medium growth; fruit not observed; [Sunblest × Amber Queen]; int. by R. Harkness & Co., Ltd., 1990; Hradec Golden Rose, 1989, Gold Medal, Orleans, 1990

Golden Zest S, my, 2005, Zary, Keith W.; flowers golden yellow, reverse golden yellow, 10 cm., very full, borne in small clusters, intense fragrance; foliage large, dark green, glossy; prickles 9-11 mm., hooked downward, greyed-orange, moderate; growth upright, branching, medium (120-130 cm.); PP16707; [Mirabella × Golden Celebration]; int. by Jackson & Perkins Wholesale, Inc., 2005

Goldendale HT, my, 1956, Grillo; bud long, pointed; flowers golden yellow, 5 in., 50 petals; [sport of Annabella]

Goldene Aue F, dy, GPG Bad Langensalza; flowers large, dbl.; int. in 1964

Goldene Druschki HP, my, 1936, Lambert, P.; bud pointed; flowers golden yellow, edged lighter turning creamy yellow in hot weather, cupped; foliage leathery, dark; very vigorous growth; [Frau Karl Druschki × Friedrich Harms]

Goldene Gruss an Aachen – See **Golden Gruss an Aachen**, F

Goldene Johanna Tantau F, my, 1945, Tantau; bud ovoid; flowers clear golden yellow, large, single, cupped, borne in clusters; foliage glossy, dark; compact, bushy growth; [Golden Rapture × (Johanna Tantau × Eugenie Lamesch)]

Goldene Sonne – See **Golden Sun**, HT

Goldener Adler F, my, 1967, Verschuren, A.; bud ovoid; flowers golden yellow, medium, semi-dbl., borne in clusters; foliage light green; [Allgold × seedling]; int. by van Engelen, 1965

Goldener Olymp LCl, dy, 1984, Kordes' Sohne, W.; flowers large, with wavy petals, 4-5 in., 20 petals, borne singly or in small clusters, moderate fragrance; occasional repeat; foliage large, medium green, matte; upright, bushy (to 7 ft.) growth; [seedling × Goldstern]; int. by Kordes Sons

Goldener Reiter F, my, 1970, Haenchen, E.; flowers golden yellow, large, 25 petals, cupped, intense fragrance; foliage dark; vigorous, upright growth; [Circus × Golden Giant]; int. by Teschendorff, 1969

Goldener Sommer 83 F, my, Noack, Werner; flowers large, dbl.; int. by Noack Rosen, 1983

Goldener Traum – See **Golden Dream**, HRg

Goldenes Herz HT, dy, 1974, Kordes; bud ovoid; flowers medium, dbl., cupped, moderate fragrance; foliage glossy, dark, leathery; vigorous, upright, bushy growth; [Dr. A.J. Verhage × seedling]; int. in 1975

Goldenes Mainz Pol, yb, 1927, Kröger; flowers orange yellow, large, semi-dbl., moderate fragrance

Goldenes Mainz – See **Golden Main**, HT

Goldenes Prag HT, GPG Bad Langensalza; flowers dbl.; int. in 1966

Goldenes Zweibrücken F, dy, Huber; flowers warm golden yellow; int. by Rosen Huber, 2005

Goldfächer – See **Minilights**, S

Goldfasan – See **Golden Pheasant**, F

Goldfassade LCl, my, Baum; flowers golden yellow, outer petals lighter and with pink tint, 4 in., dbl., intense fragrance; recurrent; foliage dark green, glossy; growth to 7-13 ft.; int. in 1967

Goldfever HT, dy; flowers golden yellow, large, 35-40 petals, borne mostly singly; recurrent; stems 16-24 in; florist rose; int. by Terra Nigra BV, 2004

Goldfinch HMult, ly, 1907, Paul; flowers yellow, aging white, 4 cm., semi-dbl., borne in clusters of up to 25; non-recurrent; foliage small, wrinkled, glossy; vigorous, climbing growth; [Helene × unknown]

Goldfinch S, my, Interplant; int. in 1994

Goldfinger F, dy, 1990, Pearce, C.A.; flowers medium, dbl., borne in small clusters, slight fragrance; foliage medium size, dark green, glossy; some prickles; low (40 cm.), compact growth; int. as William David, Rearsby Roses, 1990

Goldgleam F, my, 1965, LeGrice; flowers 3½-4 in., 18 petals, borne in small clusters, intense fragrance; foliage dark, glossy; growth moderate; PP2673; [Gleaming × Allgold]

Goldglow – See **Gold Glow**, HT

Goldie F, my, 1959, Boerner; bud ovoid; flowers golden yellow, edged lighter, 4 in., 25-30 petals, moderate fragrance; foliage leathery; vigorous, upright, bushy growth; PP1764; [Goldilocks × Pigmy Gold]; int. by J&P, 1958

Goldie HT, ly, 1988, McGredy, Sam IV; flowers pale yellow, large, full, intense fragrance; foliage large, medium green, glossy; upright growth; [seedling × Golden Gate]

Goldie Locks – See **Goldilocks**, F

Goldika HT, ob, Cocker; int. in 1986

Goldilocks F, my, 1945, Boerner; flowers deep yellow, fading to cream, large, 45 petals, globular, borne in clusters, moderate fragrance; foliage leathery, glossy; vigorous, bushy growth; [seedling × Doubloons]; int. by J&P; John Cook Medal, ARS, 1947

Goldilocks, Climbing Cl F, my, 1951, Caluya; int. by J&P

Goldilocks Min, my, 1999, Schuurman, Frank B.; flowers medium yellow, reverse light yellow, 1½ in., full, borne in large clusters, moderate fragrance; foliage large, medium green, glossy; prickles moderate; spreading, tall growth; [Scentasia × seedling]; int. by Franko Roses New Zealand, Ltd., 1998

Goldina – See **Goldstar**, HT

Goldjuwel – See **Golden Jewel**, HT

Goldjuwel – See **Golden Jewel**, Min

Goldkrone – See **Gold Crown**, HT

Goldlachs – See **Golden Salmon**, Pol

Goldlite Gr, dy, 1989, Marciel, Stanley G.; bud urn-shaped; flowers canary yellow, reverse buttercup yellow, aging without discoloration, dbl., slight musk fragrance; foliage medium size, dark green, semi-glossy; prickles declining, red; upright, tall growth; hips round, average, tangerine-orange; PP7462; [seedling × Excitement]; int. by DeVor Nurseries, Inc., 1987

Goldmarie F, dy, 1959, Kordes, R.; flowers orange-gold, very large, semi-dbl., borne in clusters, intense fragrance; foliage glossy; very vigorous, upright, bushy growth; ruled extinct ARA 1984; [Masquerade × Golden Main]; int. in 1958

Goldmarie F, dy, 1984, Kordes, W.; flowers deep yellow, red on reverse of outer petal, large, 35 petals, slight fragrance; foliage medium size, medium green, glossy; bushy growth; [((Arthur Bell × Zorina) × (Honeymoon × Dr. A.J. Verhage)) × (seedling × Sunsprite)]; int. by W. Kordes Söhne

Goldmarie, Climbing Cl F, yb, Martens; int. in 1998

Goldmarie Nirp – See **Goldmarie**, F, 1984

Goldmoss F, my, 1973, Moore, Ralph S.; bud long, pointed; flowers clear yellow, medium, dbl., intense fragrance; foliage light, leathery; vigorous, dwarf, bushy growth; PP3562; [Rumba × Moss hybrid]; int. by Sequoia Nursery

Goldpin Min, dy, Ilsink; int. in 1998

Goldpoint Min, my, 1984, Warriner, William A.; flowers small, 20 petals, slight fragrance; foliage small, light green, matte; growth upright, bushy; PP5645; [Rise 'n' Shine × (Faberge × Precilla)]; int. by J&P

Goldquelle T, ob, 1899, Lambert; [Kaiserin Auguste Viktoria × Mme Eugène Verdier]

Goldquelle S, my, 1965, Tantau, Math.; bud ovoid; flowers pure golden yellow, large, dbl., borne in clusters; recurrent bloom; foliage leathery; strong stems; upright (4 ft.) growth

Goldquelle 88 F, dy, Tantau, Math.; flowers golden yellow, medium, dbl.; quick repeat; foliage dark green, glossy; int. in 1988

Goldrausch – See **Golden Giant**, HT

Goldregen – See **Golden Rain**, F

Goldregen LCl, my, Noack; flowers lemon yellow, frilly, 4 in., dbl.; recurrent; foliage dark green, glossy; vigorous (7 ft.) growth; int. by Noack Rosen, 1985

Goldrush – See **Gold Rush**, LCl

Goldschatz – See **Golden Treasure**, F

Goldschatz F, dy, 1998, Rosen Tantau; flowers deep yellow, 4 in., dbl., borne in small clusters, slight fragrance; foliage large, medium green, glossy; prickles moderate; bushy, medium (70 cm.) growth; [seedling × seedling]; int. by Eurosa, 1996

Goldschmied F, dy, VEG (S) Baumschulen Dresden; flowers dbl., slight fragrance

Goldsmith – See **Helmut Schmidt**, HT

Goldstadt Pforzheim HT, dy, Hetzel; int. in 1998

Goldstar HT, dy, 1983, Cants of Colchester, Ltd.; flowers medium, 35 petals; foliage small, light green, matte; upright growth; [Yellow Pages × Dr. A.J. Verhage]; Gold Medal, The Hague, 1984

Goldstein F, ob, Cocker; int. in 1983

Goldstern HKor, my, 1966, Tantau, Math.; bud long, pointed; flowers golden yellow, 5 in., borne in clusters; recurrent bloom; foliage glossy; vigorous, bushy (7-8 ft.) growth

Goldstrike HT, yb, Perry, Astor; int. in 1997

Goldstück F, my, 1965, Verschuren, A.; flowers lemon-yellow, 40-55 petals, borne in clusters; foliage glossy, dark; vigorous, upright growth; [Goldilocks × seedling]; int. by van Engelen, 1963

Goldstück S, my, 1963, Tantau, Math.; bud long, pointed; flowers golden yellow, large, borne in clusters; abundant, non-recurrent bloom; vigorous, upright, bushy growth

Goldtopas F, my, 1963, Kordes, R.; bud ovoid; flowers amber-yellow, large, dbl., cupped, borne in clusters of up to 10; foliage glossy; vigorous, bushy growth; ADR, 1963

Goldy HT, dy, 1982, Kordes, W.; flowers large, 35 petals, moderate fragrance; foliage medium size, medium green, semi-glossy; upright, bushy growth; [Berolina × seedling]; int. by Kordes Söhne, 1981

Goldy HT, dy, Kordes; flowers golden yellow, medium, full, high-centered, borne mostly singly; stems 2 ft; florist rose.; int. by W. Kordes Söhne, 2003

Goldy Kordana Mini Brite Min, my, Kordes; bud long pointed, ovoid; flowers yellow, 1½ in., 35-40 petals, borne mostly singly, no fragrance; continuous; foliage small, glossy; prickles few, small, straight to hooked; vigorous, compact, upright (24 in.) growth; PP11188; [sport of Vanilla Kordana Mini Brite]; int. in 1997

Goldyla – See **Golden Holstein**, F

Golestan HT, or, 1979, Meilland, Mrs. Marie-Louise; bud tapering; flowers vermilion, small, 25 petals, high-centered; foliage glossy, dark; vigorous, upright growth; [(Tropicana × Tropicana) × ((seedling × Rouge Meilland) × Independence)]; int. by Meilland, 1975

Golf S, w, Wageningen; flowers clear white with yellow stamens, 1½ in., single, no fragrance; moderate (3 × 3 ft.) growth; int. in 1993

Golfe-Juan HP, mr, 1872, Nabonnand; flowers ruby red, very large, full

Goliath C, lp, 1829, Girardon; sepals non-foliaceous; flowers light rosy pink, touched with violet, large, very full, globular, borne in clusters of 2-3; foliage oblong, large; prickles very fine, numerous

Goliath HT, op, 1970, Wheatcroft; flowers salmon pink

Goliath – See **Gary Player**, HT

Golmain – See **Golden Main**, HT

Gomathi HT, mp, Kasturi; flowers flesh pink, edges darker, dbl., high-centered; int. by KSG Son Roses, 1987

Gomery HT, yb, DVP Melle; flowers 4½ in., 28 petals; foliage matte; strong grower growth; [Frederik Chopin × Mme Butterfly]; int. in 1999

Gondul F, mr, 1969, Lundstad; flowers cardinal-red, open, medium, 18 petals, borne in clusters; foliage dark, glossy; vigorous growth; [Lichterloh × Lumina]

Gone Fishin' Min, ob, 1992, Saville, F. Harmon; flowers bright orange, 1¼ in., 28-35 petals, cupped, borne singly and in sprays of 4-10; foliage medium size, dark green, glossy, very disease-resistant; bushy, medium growth; [Fairlane × Zorina]; int. by Nor'East Min. Roses, 1993

Gonsoli Gaëtano HP, mp, 1874, Pernet père; flowers satiny rose, large, dbl., borne in small clusters

Gonzalve HGal, mr, 1835, Vibert; flowers violet red, medium, full, globular

Good as Gold Cl Min, dy, 1994, Warner, Chris; flowers small, dbl., high-centered, borne in small clusters, moderate fragrance; foliage small, light green, semi-glossy; some prickles; tall (7 ft.), upright growth; [Anne Harkness × Laura Ford]; int. by Warner's Roses, 1995; Gold Star of the South Pacific, Palmerston North, NZ, 1996

Good Cheer HT, dp, 1937, Amling Co.; bud pointed; flowers cerise, open, dbl.; long, strong stems; very vigorous growth; [Talisman × Templar]

Good Companion F, mr, 1970, Dickson, A.; flowers rich red, large, 30 petals, flat, borne in trusses, moderate fragrance; foliage dark; vigorous growth; int. in 1961

Good Day Sunshine Min, dy, 1992, Taylor, Franklin "Pete" & Kay; flowers bright yellow, reverse same, large, very dbl., high-centered, borne mostly singly; foliage medium size, medium green, semi-glossy; few prickles; medium (60 cm.), upright, bushy, spreading growth; [Party Girl × Elina]; int. by Taylor's Roses, 1993

Good Golly F, ab; int. by Certified Roses, 2006

Good Life F, or, 1971, McGredy, Sam IV; flowers 2 in., 30 petals, high-centered, slight fragrance; free growth; [Elizabeth of Glamis × John Church]; int. by McGredy & Son, 1970

Good Life HT, op, Cocker; flowers copper salmon, tinged with orange, large, dbl., high-centered, moderate spicy fragrance; dark green, glossy foliage; growth vigorous, upright (4 × 3 ft.); [(Sabine × Circus) × Dr. A.J. Verhage]; int. in 2001

Good Live – See **Good Life**, HT

Good Luck – See **Sobhag**, F

Good Luck F, w, Burston; flowers apricot, shaded white, dbl., borne in clusters, moderate fragrance; recurrent; sturdy, low (2-2½ ft.) growth; int. in 1996

Good Morning HT, w, 1935, Kaucher; flowers white, reverse faintly tinged pink, very large, dbl.; foliage leathery; long, strong stems; very vigorous, bushy growth; [sport of Premier Supreme]; int. by Hill Crest Greenhouses

Good Morning – See **The Cheshire Regiment**, HT

Good Morning America Min, my, 1991, Saville, F. Harmon; bud ovoid, urn-shaped; flowers sunshine yellow, 1½ in., 55-60 petals, urn-shaped, borne mostly singly, moderate fruity fragrance; foliage medium size, dark green, semi-glossy; long stems; upright, bushy, tall growth; PP7761; [Fantasia × Rainbow's End]; int. by Nor'East Min. Roses, 1991; AOE, ARS, 1991

Good Morning Sunshine Min, dy, 1998, Bossom, W.E.; flowers golden yellow, 2½ in., very dbl., borne mostly singly; foliage small, dark green, semi-glossy; numerous prickles; low, compact growth; [Laura Ford × Forever Amber]

Good 'n Plenty S, pb, 2007, Zary, Keith W.; flowers raspberry pink with white eye, reverse medium pink, 2½ in., single, borne in small clusters; foliage small, dark green, glossy; prickles 4-6 mm., hooked downward, greyed-orange, few; growth compact, short (2 ½ ft.); [seedling × Footloose]; int. by Jackson & Perkins Wholesale, Inc., 2007

Good Neighbor HT, ob, 1960, Warriner, William A.; flowers burnt-orange, reverse golden, large, dbl., intense fragrance; foliage dark; vigorous, upright growth; [Fred Howard × seedling]; int. by H&S, 1958

Good News HT, pb, 1940, Meilland, F.; flowers silvery pink, center tinged apricot, 5-6 in., 50 petals, globular, moderate fragrance; vigorous, bushy growth; [(Radiance × Souv. de Claudius Pernet) × (Joanna Hill × Comtesse Vandal)]; int. by C-P

Good News F, my; int. by Warley Rose Gardens, 1992

Good News 95 F, mp, Chessum; int. in 1995

Good Ol' Summertime – See **Good Old Summertime**, S

Good Old Summertime S, ly, Clements, John K.; flowers soft, warm yellow, 4 in., 35 petals, intense spicy-myrrh fragrance; free-flowering; foliage mid-green; bushy (4 × 3½ ft.) growth; int. by Heirloom Roses, 1997

Good Show F, op, J&P; flowers bright salmon with yellow center, borne in clusters; medium growth; PP11262; int. in 1998

Good Times HT, pb, 1978, Williams, J. Benjamin; bud ovoid, pointed; flowers ivory to light pink with deep pink edging, 5-5½ in., 56 petals, cupped, slight fragrance; foliage large, glossy; compact, upright growth; [Pink Peace × Peace]; int. by Hershey Nursery, 1977

Good Vibes F, mp, 1999, Giles, Diann; flowers medium, dbl., borne in large clusters; foliage medium size, medium green, glossy; few prickles; compact, medium growth; [Sun Flare × Simplicity]; int. by Giles Rose Nursery, 1999

Good Wishes – See **Favourite Hit**, MinFl

Gooiland HT, mp, 1922, Van Rossem; flowers clear rose-pink, reverse dark coral-rose, dbl.; [(Sunburst × unknown) × Red-Letter Day]

Gooiland Beauty HT, ab, 1924, Van Rossem; flowers clear golden orange, open, large, semi-dbl.; foliage dark, leathery; vigorous, bushy growth; [Sunburst × Golden Emblem]; int. by Van Rossem & Prior; Gold Medal, Bagatelle, 1925

Gooiland Glory HT, or, 1925, Van Rossem; flowers cherry-red shaded coral-red, medium, semi-dbl.; [General MacArthur × Mme Edouard Herriot]; int. by Van Rossem & Prior

Goose Fair – See **Coral Meidiland**, S

Gooseberry Rose – See ***R. stellata*** (Wooton)

Gopika F, op, 1971, Singh, R. S.; flowers light salmon-pink, medium, dbl., globular, slight fragrance; foliage glossy; vigorous, bushy growth; [Marlena × Open pollination]; int. by K. S. Gopalsinamiengar & Son, 1969

Gordon Drake F, dp, 1956, Williams, G.A.; flowers cerise-pink, dbl., borne in large clusters; very vigorous growth; [sport of Eutin]

Gordon Eddie HT, ab, 1949, Eddie; flowers deep apricot, edged lighter, very large, 40 petals, high-centered; foliage leathery, glossy; very vigorous, bushy growth; [Royal Visit × Cynthia Brooke]; Gold Medal, NRS, 1950

Gordon Snell F, yb, Dickson; flowers pale yellow, flushed with pink and red, dbl., borne in clusters; compact growth; int. by Dickson Roses, 1999

Gordon's College F, op, 1992, James Cocker & Sons, Ltd.; flowers coral salmon, 3-3½ in., full, borne in large clusters, moderate fragrance; foliage large, dark green, glossy, purplish when young; some prickles; medium, upright growth; [Abbeyfield Rose × Roddy McMillan]

Gorgeous HT, op, 1915, Dickson, H.; flowers deep orange-yellow, veined copper, well-formed, large, dbl., moderate fragrance; foliage rich, green,soft; bushy, open growth; Gold Medal, NRS, 1913

Gorgeous HT, mp, 1956, Franc; flowers rose-pink, 5 in., 18-20 petals, high-centered; foliage leathery;

vigorous growth; [sport of Pink Delight]; int. by Carlton Rose Nurseries

Gorgeous George – See **Guy Laroche**, HT

Gosh S, lp, 2000, Cox, Roy; flowers light pink, reverse deep pink, 1½ in., single, borne in large clusters; foliage medium size, dark green, semi-glossy; few prickles; growth bushy, tall (4 ft.); [Mlle Cécile Brunner, Cl. × Ballerina]

Göteborg – See **Pink Robusta**, S

Gotenborgs Posten – See **Surrey**, S

Gotenhafen F, mp, 1940, Tantau; flowers pure bright rose, medium, 12-15 petals; vigorous, well branched growth; [Mev. Nathalie Nypels × Kardinal]

Gotha HT, op, 1932, Krause; flowers brownish yellow passing to apricot; [(Souv. de H.A. Verschuren × Sunset) × Mev. G.A. van Rossem]

Gotha IV – See **Gotha**, HT

Gottfried Keller HFt, ab, 1894, Müller, Dr. F.; flowers orange yellow to coppery pink, medium, single to semi-dbl., moderate fragrance; [(Mme Bérard × *R. foetida persiana*) × ((Pierre Notting × Mme Bérard) × *R. foetida persiana*)]

Goubault – See **Bon Silène**, T

Goudvlinder HT, ab, 1926, Van Rossem; flowers orange-yellow, small, 12 petals; foliage glossy, brownish red; vigorous, bushy growth; [Lady Hillingdon × Souv. de Claudius Pernet]

Goulburnian F, mp, 2005, Ryan, Max; flowers medium, semi-dbl., borne in small clusters, no fragrance; foliage medium size, medium green, glossy, leathery; prickles large, hooked, few; growth spreading, vigorous, medium (1 m.); garden decoration, exhibition; [Sparrieshoop × seedling]; semi-double; foliage leathery; vigorous; int. in 2002

Gourdault B, m, 1859, Guillot Père; flowers rich purple, medium to large, full

Gourmet Pheasant S, dp; flowers deep pink to light red, single, borne in clusters; recurrent; growth spreading, fast growing (2 × 8 ft.); groundcover; int. in 1995

Gourmet Popcorn Min, w, 1987, Desamero, Luis; flowers pure white, medium, semi-dbl.; foliage large, dark green, glossy; upright, bushy growth; PP6809; [sport of Popcorn]; int. by Wee Ones Miniature Roses, 1986

Governador Braga da Cruz HT, ly, 1954, Moreira da Silva; very vigorous growth; [Peace × seedling]

Governor Alfred E. Smith HT, yb, 1933, Denoyel, Vve.; flowers blend of buff, terra-cotta, gold and salmon, large, dbl., high-centered; foliage glossy; vigorous growth; [Souv. de F. Bohé seedling × seedling]; int. by J&P

Governor Mark Hatfield Gr, dr, 1962, Von Abrams; bud pointed; flowers rich red, large, 40 petals, high-centered, slight fragrance; foliage leathery; vigorous, upright growth; [Carrousel × Charles Mallerin]; int. by Peterson & Dering

Governor Phillip Cl HT, mr, 1939, Fitzhardinge; flowers ruby-red, flushed darker, open, large, very dbl.; foliage leathery, glossy, dark, bronze; long stems; vigorous, climbing growth; [(Ophelia × unknown) × Black Boy]; int. by Hazlewood Bros.

Governor Rosellini Gr, mr, 1959, Lindquist; flowers rose-red, 3-4 in., 30 petals, high-centered, moderate raspberry fragrance; foliage dark, leathery; vigorous, upright growth; PP1873; [Baby Chateau × Tiffany]; int. by Howard Rose Co., 1958

Governor's Lady Gloria HT, m, 1983, Christensen, Jack E.; flowers pastel mauve, well-formed, large, 35 petals, intense fragrance; foliage large, medium green, matte; growth upright, bushy; [Sweet Afton × Blue Nile]; int. by Armstrong Nursery

Gowan Brae S, pb, 2005, Cant, Heather; flowers very full, borne in small clusters, slight fragrance; foliage large, medium green, matte, dark red when new; prickles medium, pointed, few; growth upright, tall (1½ m.); landscape; [Leander × unknown]; int. in 2004

Gowirichs Traum Pol, dp

Gowrishankar HT, pb, Mandal, G.S.; flowers soft pink with violet tinge; free-flowering; [sport of Carmousine]; int. in 2004

Goya F, w, 1976, Bees; flowers cream, 30 petals, high-centered, borne in trusses; foliage dark green, heavy; vigorous growth; [Mildred Reynolds × Arthur Bell]

Graaf van Vlaanderen S, w, DVP Melle; [Mev. Nathalie Nypels × Yesterday]; int. in 1993

Graaff-Reinet HT, ab, 1988, W. Kordes Söhne; flowers apricot with orange on petal margin, large, 36 petals, borne in sprays, moderate fragrance; foliage dull, medium green; prickles concave, reddish-brown; compact, medium, well branched, free flowering growth; [seedling × seedling]; int. by Ludwigs Roses Pty. Ltd., 1988

Grace HRg, 1923, Saunders; flowers amber, center apricot, open, very dbl., moderate fragrance; foliage wrinkled; bushy (5-6 ft.) growth; RULED EXTINCT; [*R. rugosa* × Harison's Yellow]; int. by Central Exp. Farm

Grace S, ab, 2002, Austin, David; flowers apricot-yellow, fading to white, 7 cm., very dbl., rosette, borne in large clusters, intense fragrance; foliage medium size, light green, semi-glossy; prickles short, concave, brown/red, few; growth bushy, medium (120 cm.); garden decorative; [Sweet Juliet × yellow english-type shrub]; int. by David Austin Roses, Ltd., 2001

Grace Abounding F, w, 1968, Harkness; flowers ivory, semi-dbl., borne in trusses, moderate musk fragrance; foliage glossy; [Pink Parfait × Penelope]

Grace Amazing Min, my, 2003, Sproul, James A.; flowers yellow, reverse yellow, 1½-2 in., dbl., borne mostly solitary; foliage medium size, medium green, semi-glossy; prickles few, small; upright, medium (24-30 in.) growth; [Singin' in the Rain × Fairhope]; int. in 2003

Grace Darling T, w, 1885, Bennett; flowers cream-white shaded golden, large, dbl., globular; vigorous growth; sometimes classed as HT

Grace de Monaco HT, lp, 1958, Meilland, F.; flowers light rose-pink, well-formed, large, dbl., intense fragrance; foliage leathery; vigorous, bushy growth; [Peace × Michele Meilland]; int. by URS

Grace Donnelly HT, op, 1991, Horner, Colin P.; bud ovoid; flowers pink, orange, yellow striped, medium, dbl., urn-shaped, loose, borne singly or in sprays of 5-9, slight fruity fragrance; foliage medium size, medium green, semi-glossy; bushy, tall growth; [Alexander × (Southampton × ((New Penny × Little White Pet) × Stars 'n' Stripes))]; int. by Battersby Roses, 1992

Grace Haslam HT, ob, Fryers Nursery, Ltd.; flowers orange to carmine; [Scarlet Glory × Mrs Sam McGredy]

Grace Kelly – See **Princesse de Monaco**, HT

Grace Kimmins F, mr, 1972, Gobbee, W.D.; flowers crimson, 3 in., 28 petals; foliage glossy; vigorous, bushy growth; [Dainty Maid × Red Dandy]

Grace Molyneux HT, ab, 1909, Dickson, A.; flowers creamy apricot, center flesh, large, dbl.

Grace Moore HT, mr, 1948, Kordes; bud ovoid; flowers crimson-red, large, dbl., cupped; foliage leathery, dark olive-green; vigorous, bushy growth; [Kardinal × Crimson Glory]; int. by C-P

Grace Noll Crowell HT, pb, 1929, Vestal; flowers rose-pink, base slightly shaded cream, large, dbl., high-centered; foliage soft, light; vigorous, bushy growth

Grace Note S, pb, 1985, Buck, Dr. Griffith J.; bud ovoid, pointed; flowers medium pink, freckled red, imbricated, large, 38 petals, borne 3-8 per cluster, moderate fragrance; repeat bloom; foliage large, leathery, dark green; prickles awl-like, tan; vigorous, erect, bushy growth; hardy; [(Tiki × Marigold) × Freckle Face]; int. by Iowa State University, 1984

Grace Seward Min, w, 1991, Bennett, Dee; bud ovoid; flowers medium, 5 petals, moderate damask fragrance; good repeat; foliage medium size, medium green, semi-glossy; bushy, tall growth; PP8899; [Watercolor × seedling]; int. by Tiny Petals Nursery, 1990

Grace Sharington MinFl, mp, 2007, Mander, George; flowers medium pink, reverse light pink, 3½ in., full, borne in small clusters; foliage medium size, dark green, semi-glossy, disease-resistant; prickles ¼ in., needle-point, light brown, moderate; growth bushy, medium (30-36 in.); garden, exhibition, containers; [Hot Tamale × Rubies 'n' Pearls]; int. by Hortico, Inc., 2007

Grace Thomson HMult, rb, 1909, Paul, W.; flowers red over white, full

Grace Wayman Cl HT, mp, 1936, Wayman; flowers pink, very large, dbl.; foliage leathery; vigorous, climbing (10 ft.) growth

Grace Wood Min, my, 1993, Giles, Diann; flowers full, borne in small clusters, no fragrance; foliage small, medium green, matte; few prickles; medium, compact growth; [Sun Flare × Rise 'n' Shine]; int. by Giles Rose Nursery, 1992

Graceful S, ly, 1966, Smith, W.H.; flowers yellow fading to cream, well-formed, 4 in., dbl.; foliage glossy; vigorous, bushy growth; [Paul's Lemon Pillar × Marcelle Gret]

Graceland HT, my, 1988, Warriner, William A.; flowers medium yellow, aging lighter at margins, loose, medium, 30-35 petals, cupped, borne singly; foliage medium size, dark green, matte, smooth; prickles medium, reddish-green; upright growth; PP6069; [New Day × seedling]; int. by Bear Creek Gardens, 1989; Gold Medal, The Hague, 1988

Graceland MinFl, op, Kirkham, Gordon Wilson; int. in 1989

Gracie Allen F, pb, 1999, Carruth, Tom; flowers white with a pink heart, 4½ in., 25-30 petals, borne in small clusters, slight apple fragrance; foliage medium size, dark green, glossy; prickles moderate; upright, bushy, medium (3-4 ft.) growth; PP11103; [Crystalline × Regensberg]; int. by Weeks Roses, 1998

Gracie Fields HT, dy, 1937, Letts; flowers vivid buttercup-yellow, moderate sweetbriar fragrance; foliage glossy; vigorous growth

Gracieuse – See **Gracilis**, M

Gracilis M, dp, before 1829, Prévost; flowers deep pink, well mossed, large, dbl., globular; seasonal bloom; foliage large, glossy; vigorous growth; good as a standard

Gracilis Bslt, mr, 1830, Wood; flowers cherry shaded lilac-blush, medium, semi-dbl., cupped; foliage dark; prickles large, long; vigorous, slender, branching growth; apparently a cross between an early Boursault and *R. arvensis*

Gracilis HGal, w, before 1836, Vibert; flowers white, flesh center, full, flat

Gracilis HSet, mp, 1841, Prince Nursery; flowers pink to rose, very dbl., borne in clusters

Graciosa HT, w, 1957, Moreira da Silva; flowers white edged rose, well-formed; very vigorous growth; [Branca × Peace]

Graciosa LCl, w, Noack; flowers white with touch of pastel pink, 4 in., dbl., loose, intense fragrance; free-flowering; vigorous (10 ft.) growth; int. by Noack Rosen, 2002

Gracious Lady HT, pb, 1965, Robinson, H.; bud ovoid; flowers peach-pink, base apricot, large, dbl., high-centered, moderate fragrance; foliage glossy, dark; vigorous, bushy growth; PP2582; [((Peace × unknown) × Gail Borden) × Dorothy Peach seedling]; int. by J&P

Gracious Queen – See **Michelangelo**, HT

Gracious Queen HT, dy, 2001, Chessum, Paul; flowers medium, full, borne mostly solitary, moderate fragrance; foliage medium size, medium green, semi-glossy; prickles medium, hooked, few; growth compact, medium (90 cm.); beds, borders, containers; int. by Paul Chessum Roses, 2001

Graciously Pink S, mp; growth to 2 ft.; int. in 2003

Graduation Day MinFl, ab, 2004, Jalbert, Brad; flowers apricot, petals frilled, 2 in., very dbl., old-fashioned, borne in large clusters; foliage medium size, dark green, very glossy, reddish when new; prickles medium, slight hook, reddish, few; bushy, medium (20 in.), mounding growth; [Thelmas Glory × Sexy Rexy]; int. in 2000

Graeme Douglas HT, mp, 1995, McGredy, Sam IV; flowers 3 in., full; foliage large, medium green, semi-glossy; bushy (100 cm.) growth; [Silver Jubilee × (Harmonie × Auckland Metro)]; int. by McGredy Roses International, 1994

Graf Fritz Metternich HP, dr, 1896, Soupert & Notting; flowers velvety brownish red, shaded black, center cardinal red, large, full, intense fragrance; [Sultan of Zanzibar × Thomas Mills]

Graf Fritz Schwerin HT, mr, 1916, Lambert; flowers large, single; [General MacArthur × Goldelse]

Graf Fritz von Hochberg HT, op, 1905, Lambert, P.; buds almond shaped; flowers yellowish salmon pink, large, dbl., moderate fragrance; [Mme Caroline Testout × Goldquelle]

Graf Lennart HT, mr, 1994, Meilland; buds pointed, large; flowers dark ruby-red, 5-5½ in., full, cupped, borne singly and in small clusters, moderate fragrance; good repeat; foliage dark green, glossy; prickles numerous, medium; growth strong, well-branched, upright (2½ ft.); PP9253; [Fragrant Cloud × (Oklahoma × Royal William)]; registered as Gr; int. as Matilda, SNC Meilland Et Cie, 1993

Graf Silva Tarouca HT, dp, 1916, Lambert, P.; flowers carmine-red, very large, dbl.; very vigorous growth; [Étoile de France × Lady Mary Fitzwilliam]

Graf Zeppelin HMult, dp, 1910, Böhm; flowers light red to bright pink, aging lighter, medium, semi-dbl., borne in large clusters; very free bloom; vigorous (6-8 ft.) growth; [sport of Non Plus Ultra]

Gräfin Ada Bredow HMult, lp, 1909, Walter; flowers whitish pink, 2-2½ cm., semi-dbl., borne in large clusters; non-recurrent; [Thalia × Rösel Dach]

Gräfin Chotek HMult, lp, 1911, Kiese; bud peach pink; flowers luminous apple blossom pink; [Tausendschön × Mignonnette]

Grafin Esterhazy Ch, dp, Geschwind, R.

Gräfin Hardenberg S, dp, 1938, Vogel, M.; flowers carmine-pink, medium, semi-dbl.

Gräfin Marie Henriette Chotek HMult, mr, 1911, Lambert, P.; flowers bright red, medium, dbl., borne in very large clusters, moderate fragrance; non-recurrent; [Farquhar × Richmond]

Gräfin Minnie Schaffgotsch HT, w, 1928, Mühle; flowers cream-white, center pink, very dbl.; [Clio × unnamed Hybrid Tea]

Gräfin Sonja HT, pb, 2006; bud long, pointed, cherry pink; flowers cherry pink with a lighter center, opening silvery pink, long lasting, 10 cm., full, high-centered, borne mostly solitary, slight, soft fragrance; foliage large, dark green, glossy; well-branched, upright (2½ ft.) growth; int. by W. Kordes' Söhne, 1994

Grafton Pillar LCl, mr, 1960, Risley; bud globular; flowers bright red, small, dbl., borne in clusters, slight fragrance; free, recurrent boom; foliage wrinkled; moderate growth; [Second generation Skinner's Rambler × Gruss an Aachen]; int. in 1958

Graham HT, dr, 1961, Kriloff, Michel; flowers deep crimson-scarlet, large, 35-40 petals, high-centered; foliage glossy; long stems; vigorous, upright growth; [Eclipse × seedling]; int. by Cramphorn's Nursery, 1960

Graham Thomas S, dy, 1983, Austin, David; flowers rich deep yellow, medium, 35 petals, cupped, intense fragrance; recurrent bloom; foliage small, dark, glossy; bushy growth; [seedling × (Charles Austin × Iceberg seedling)]; int. by David Austin Roses, Ltd.

Grain de Beauté Min, mp; flowers small, semi-dbl., borne in clusters; free-flowering; compact, low (40-50 cm.) growth; int. by Meilland, 2004

Graines d'Or HT, ob, Dorieux; int. by Roseraies Dorieux, 2003

Gran Parada F, my, 1970, Dot, Simon; flowers yellow, becoming reddish, open, medium, 25 petals; foliage glossy; vigorous, upright, compact growth; [Gold Dot × (Queen Elizabeth × Zambra)]; int. by Rosas Dot, 1967

Granada HT, 1955, Delforge; flowers deep red, borne in clusters; [Opera × The Doctor]

Granada HT, rb, 1963, Lindquist; bud urn-shaped, medum; flowers multicolor with shades of rose Bengal, buttercup at base, reverse much lighter, 4-5 in., 18-25 petals, open, borne singly, moderate tea fragrance; foliage foliate leathery, slightly holly-like; vigorous, upright growth; PP2214; [Tiffany × Cavalcade]; int. by Howard Rose Co., 1963; James Alexander Gamble Fragrance Medal, ARS, 1968

Granada, Climbing Cl HT, rb, 1969, Swim & Weeks; flowers yellow at center, edged red, large, semi-dbl.; int. by Comley, 1964

Granada Sunset HT, ob, Rupert; flowers red, orange and apricot flecked with cascade of cream and pink, dbl., intense fragrance; [sport of Granada]; identical to Granada except for color; int. about 1997

Granadina Min, mr, 1956, Dot, Pedro; flowers oxblood-red, small, 30 petals, globular; foliage dark; low, upright growth; [Granate × Coralín]; int. by Kordes

Granat HT, dr, 1937, Krause; flowers blackish red, well-formed; very vigorous growth; [Barcelona × Château de Clos Vougeot]

Granate Min, dr, 1947, Dot, Pedro; flowers velvety oxblood-red, often streaked white, small; nearly thornless; growth short (6-8 in.); [Merveille des Rouges × Pompon de Paris]

Granatina HT, Cazzaniga, F. G.; int. in 1964

Grand S, dr, Poulsen; flowers dark red, 8-10 cm., dbl., no fragrance; foliage dark; growth bushy, 40-60 cm.; PP11610; int. by Poulsen Roser, 1998

Grand Age – See **Grand Siècle**, HT

Grand Amore HT, dr, Kordes; int. in 1968

Grand Amour HT, mr, 1956, Delbard-Chabert; flowers bright red, large

Grand Amour – See **True Love**, HT

Grand Apollon HGal, m, 1824, in Brussels; flowers violet, very large, full

Grand Bercam C, dp, before 1826, possibly Prévost; flowers medium to large, semi-dbl.

Grand Blue HT, m, Hiroshima; int. by Hiroshima Bara-en, 1996

Grand Canary HT, my, 1934, Lowman; flowers dbl., high-centered; foliage glossy; vigorous, compact growth; [sport of Token]; int. by U.S. Cut Flower Co.

Grand Canyon S, dy, 1951, Whisler; bud long, pointed, chrome-yellow; flowers yellow, salmon and copper, turning to crimson, open, medium; recurrent bloom; foliage glossy, bronze; very vigorous (6 ft.), arching growth; [Herrenhausen × Golden Rapture]; int. by Germain's

Grand Canyon F, op, Poulsen; bud pointed ovoid; flowers 2½-3 in., 18-22 petals, flat, borne singly or in small clusters, no fragrance; recurrent; foliage dark, glossy; prickles moderate, concave, slight downward curve; bushy, vigorous (100-150 cm.) growth; PP12902; [seedling × Sexy Rexy]; int. by Poulsen Roser, 1998

Grand Cels – See **Childling**, C

Grand Château – See **Taboo**, HT

Grand Condé – See **Rouge Formidable**, HGal

Grand Corneille – See **Cramoisi des Alpes**, HGal

Grand Cramoisi de Trianon – See **À Grand Cramoisi**, HGal

Grand Cramoisi de Vibert HGal, mr, about 1818, Vibert; flowers light crimson red, medium, full

Grand-Dauphin – See **Enfant de France**, HGal

Grand-Duc Adolphe de Luxembourg HT, rb, 1892, Soupert & Notting; flowers brick-red, reverse carmine, large, dbl.; weak stems; moderate growth; [Triomphe de la Terre des Roses × Mme Loeben Sels]

Grand-Duc Alexis HP, mr, 1892, Lévêque; flowers blood red, tinted purple and light vermilion, large, dbl.; foliage large

Grand Duc Héritier de Luxembourg – See **Mlle Franziska Krüger**, T

Grand-Duc Pierre de Russie T, pb, 1895, Perny/Cochet; flowers rose pink veined darker pink, aging to salmon, very large

Grand Duche HT, m, 1979, Godin, M.; bud ovoid; flowers 3-3½ in., 25 petals, cupped, slight fragrance; foliage dark; vigorous growth; [American Heritage × (seedling × Blue Girl)]; int. in 1973

Grand Duchess Hilda – See **Grossherzogin Mathilde**, T

Grand Duchess Victoria Melita – See **Grossherzogin Viktoria Melitta von Hessen**, HT

Grand Edouard – See **La Souveraine**, HP

Grand Finale HT, w, 1998, Zary, Dr. Keith W.; bud long, ovoid; flowers ivory white, 4-4½ in., very dbl., high-centered, borne singly, slight honeysuckle fragrance; foliage large, medium green, semi-glossy; prickles moderate; upright, medium (4 ft.) growth; PP11007; [Honor × Pristine]; int. by Bear Creek Gardens, Inc., 1998; Rose of the Year, J&P, 1998

Grand Gala HT, rb, 1954, Meilland, F.; bud globular; flowers rose-red, reverse white suffused pink, 4½-5 in., 45-60 petals, high-centered, slight fragrance; foliage leathery; vigorous, bushy growth; PP1489; [Peace × Independence]; int. by URS, 1954

Grand Gala, Climbing Cl HT, rb, 1961, Yamate; int. by Kakujitsuen

Grand Gala HT, mr, Meilland; bud conical, medium; flowers strawberry-red, 4 in., 40 petals, high-centered, borne mostly singly; good repeat bloom; foliage dark green, glossy; prickles few, small; growth erect, moderate (2-3 ft.); PP9309; [(Edith Piaf × Visa) × (Meiduitra × Madelon)]; florist rose; int. in 1995

Grand Hotel LCl, mr, 1972, McGredy, Sam IV; flowers scarlet, darker at petal tips, 4 in., dbl., high-centered, borne singly or in small clusters; repeat bloom; foliage dark green, glossy; ADR, 1977

Grand Huit – See **Lasting Love**, HT

Grand Huit, Climbing – See **Commandant Cousteau, Climbing**, Cl HT

Grand Impression HT, ab, 1998, Warriner, William A.; flowers yellow/peach/pink blend, apricot yellow reverse, 6 in., very dbl., borne in small clusters, slight fragrance; foliage large, dark green, semi glossy; few prickles; growth upright, tall (5 ft.); PP10273; [Spirit of Glasnost × Medallion]; int. by Bear Creek Gardens, Inc., 1999

Grand Ivory HT, w

Grand Lady HT, mp, 1968, Patterson; bud ovoid; flowers pink, center lighter, large, dbl., high-centered; foliage leathery; vigorous, upright, bushy growth; [Ma Perkins × Peace]; int. by Patterson Roses

Grand Marshall HT, mr, 1989, Christensen, Jack E.; bud ovoid, pointed; flowers large, 35 petals, high-centered, borne usually singly; foliage medium size, medium green, semi-glossy; prickles hooked, medium, red to brown; upright, bushy, medium growth; [Futura × Olympiad]; int. by Michigan Bulb Co., 1989

Grand Masterpiece HT, mr, 1978, Warriner, William A.; bud ovoid, pointed; flowers 5 in., dbl., high-centered; tall, upright growth; PP4767; [seedling × Tonight]; int. by J&P

Grand Mogul – See **Jean Soupert**, HP

Grand Mogul HT, w, 1970, Delbard-Chabert; flowers creamy white, large, 33 petals, high-centered, moderate fragrance; growth moderate; [Sultane × Chic Parisien]; int. by Cuthbert, 1965

Grand Monarche HGal, lp, before 1818, from Holland; flowers pale pink, shaded carmine-cerise, very large, full

Grand Napoléon HGal, m, 1809, Sevale & Haghen; flowers intense violet, large, very dbl.

Grand Nord HT, w, 1986, Delbard; flowers large, 28 petals, high-centered; vigorous, bushy growth; [((Queen Elizabeth × Provence) × (Virgo × Carina)) × ((Voeux de Bonheur × Virgo) × (Virgo × Peace))]; int. in 1974; Gold Medal, Rome, 1973, Gold Medal, Paris, 1970

Grand Occasion HT, pb, 1971, Delbard; flowers rosy coral shaded yellow, edged carmine, 3 in., 30 petals, intense fragrance; foliage glossy, light; vigorous growth; [Comtesse Vandal × Mme Henri Guillot]; int. by Laxton & Bunyard Nursery, 1970

Grand Opening Min, rb, 1991, Gruenbauer, Richard; bud ovoid; flowers orange-red showing yellow eye, red reverse, ages pale red, eye turns white, medium, 35 petals, high-centered, moderate fruity fragrance; foliage medium size, dark green, semi-glossy; upright, medium growth; [Poker Chip × Zinger]; int. by Flowers 'n' Friends Miniature Roses, 1993

Grand Opera HT, pb, 1964, Schwartz, Ernest W.; bud long, pointed; flowers cream edged pink, becoming pink, 4-5 in., 40 petals, high-centered, moderate fragrance; foliage leathery; vigorous, bushy growth; [Masquerade × Peace]; int. by Wyant, 1964

Grand Palace – See **Grand**, S

Grand Palais de Laeken HGal, lp, 1824; flowers bright light pink, medium, full; from Laeken, Holland

Grand Parcours – See **New Dawning**, LCl

Grand Parcours S, lp; groundcover; spreading growth; int. in 2002

Grand-Père Lottin HWich, op, 1918, Lottin; flowers salmony flesh-pink, center brighter, very dbl., borne in clusters; [Lady Godiva × Mrs W.H. Cutbush]

Grande Pompadour – See **Pourpre Charmant**, HGal

Grand Prix HT, op, 1970, Delbard-Chabert; flowers coral-pink shaded ochre, large, semi-dbl., slight fragrance; foliage glossy, leathery; vigorous, upright, bushy growth; [Chic Parisien × (Grande Premiere × (Sultane × Mme Joseph Perraud))]; int. in 1968; Gold Medal, Belgium, 1968

Grand Prix F, ab, Matthews; flowers apricot peach, full, OGR, intense fragrance; free-flowering; medium growth; int. in 1999

Grand Prix HT, dr, Select; flowers dark red, 4½ in., 35-40 petals, high-centered, borne mostly singly; recurrent; stem length 28-40 in; florist rose; int. by Terra Nigra BV

Grand Prize HT, rb, 1935, Kistler; flowers petals red, white and spotted, very large, dbl., cupped; foliage leathery; very vigorous growth; [sport of Red Radiance]

Grand Prize F, ly, 2005, Zary, Keith W.; flowers yellow-white, reverse yellow-white, 4 in., dbl., borne in small clusters, moderate fragrance; foliage large, dark green, glossy; prickles 8-10 mm., hooked downward, greyed orange, moderate; upright, branching and vigorous, medium (100 cm.) growth; PP14754; [Sunflare × Impatient]; int. by Jackson & Perkins Wholesale, Inc., 2003

Grand Romance HT, mp, 1991, Bridges, Dennis A.; bud ovoid; flowers medium pink, reverse slightly lighter, aging slightly lighter, medium, 50 petals, urn-shaped, borne singly, moderate fragrance; foliage medium size, dark green, semi-glossy; upright, medium growth; [Lady X × Wini Edmunds]; int. by Bridges Roses, 1990

Grand Siècle HT, pb, 1986, Delbard; flowers creamy pink blend, well-formed, large, 33 petals, cupped, slight fragrance; foliage large; vigorous, bushy, branching growth; [((Queen Elizabeth × Provence) × (Michele Meilland × Bayadere)) × ((Voeux de Bonheur × MEImet) × (Peace × Dr. Debat))]; int. in 1977

Grand Slam HT, mr, 1963, Armstrong, D.L. & Swim, H. C.; bud urn-shaped; flowers cherry to rose-red, 4 in., 28 petals, high-centered, slight fragrance; foliage leathery, dark, semi-glossy; vigorous, upright, spreading growth; PP2187; [Charlotte Armstrong × Montezuma]; int. by Armstrong Nursery, 1963

Grand Slam HT, my, Select Roses BV; florist rose; int. by Terra Nigra BV, 2003

Grand St. Francis – See **Lustre d'Église**, HGal

Grand Sultan – See **Le Grand Sultan**, HGal

Grand Sultan HGal, lp, before 1820, Descemet; flowers delicate flesh pink, large, very full; foliage light green

Grand Trianon HT, Truffaut, G.; int. in 1967

Grand Turban – See **Grand Sultan**, HGal

Grandad HT, dr; flowers dbl., cupped; foliage glossy; growth to 2 × 2 ft.; int. by Love4Plants Ltd, 2005

Grandchant – See **Chantilly**, HT

Grandchild Min, mp, 1987, Garelja, Anita; flowers clear, medium pink, small, 40 petals, high-centered, borne 3-15 per cluster, moderate sweet fragrance; foliage long, narrow, dense, reddish to medium green; prickles hooked, gray-brown; bushy, shrub-like, tall growth; [(Cécile Brunner × unknown) × (Cécile Brunner × unknown)]

Grand-Duc Henri F, op, Lens; flowers salmon-orange, full, borne in clusters; foliage dark green; growth to 60-80 cm.; int. by Louise Lens SA, 2002

Grande Agathe – See **Henriette**, HGal

Grande Agathe Nouvelle – See **Héloïse**, HGal

Grande Amore HT, dr, Kordes; int. in 1968

Grande Amore HT, mr, Kordes; bud pointed, red; flowers shining dark red, 4 in., full, high-centered, borne usually singly, moderate fragrance; recurrent; foliage medium size, dark green, slightly glossy; stems strong; growth bushy, well-branched, upright

Grande Bichonne HGal, mr, about 1815, Descemet

Grande Brique HGal, dp, before 1811; flowers dark wine pink, very large, dbl.

Grande Brune – See **Nouveau Monde**, HGal

Grande Centfeuilles de Hollande – See **Rose des Peintres**, C

Grande Classe – See **Lasting Love**, HT

Grande Cuisse de Nymphe – See **Great Maiden's Blush**, A

Grande Duchesse Charlotte HT, mr, 1942, Ketten Bros.; bud long, pointed; flowers tomato-red, shaded geranium-red, cactus form, 5-5½ in., 25 petals; foliage glossy, dark; vigorous, bushy growth; int. by C-P; Gold Medal, Rome, 1938, Gold Medal, Portland, 1941

Grande Duchesse de Luxembourg – See **Marie Adélaïde**, HT

Grande Duchesse Olga – See **Kaiserin Auguste Viktoria**, HT

Grande et Belle HGal, dp, before 1811; flowers deep purple pink; from Holland

Grande Henriette – See **L'Enchantresse**, HGal

Grande Maculée HGal, m, before 1829, Coquerel; flowers purple, large, semi-dbl.

Grande Parade – See **Gran Parada**, F

Grande Première HT, yb, 1959, Delbard-Chabert; bud long, pointed; flowers yellow edged pink, large, 38 petals; foliage bright green, glossy; upright, bushy growth; [Comtesse Vandal × Mme Henri Guillot]

Grande Premiere – See **Grand Occasion**, HT

Grande Renoncule Violette C, mp, before 1885; flowers dull pink, shading to violet, medium, dbl.

Grande Rouge F, dr, 1973, Tantau, Math.; bud ovoid; flowers medium, dbl.; foliage soft; upright, bushy growth; [unknown × unknown]; int. by Ahrens & Sieberz

Grande Sultane – See **Le Grand Sultan**, HGal

Grande Violette Claire HGal, m, about 1811; flowers pale violet, very large, semi-dbl.

Grande, Violette, et Belle – See **Roxelane**, HGal semi-dbl.

Grande Walzer HT, rb, 1981, Kordes, W.; bud ovoid; flowers deep orange-red, reverse deep yellow, 35 petals, cupped, borne singly, slight fragrance; foliage rather small, light green, glossy; prickles curved, light yellow; upright growth; int. by Rose Barni-Pistoia, 1978

Grandee Min, dr, 1985, McGredy, Sam IV; flowers gold stamens, medium, semi-dbl., moderate fragrance; foliage medium size, medium green, semi-glossy; upright growth; [Regensberg × Ko's Yellow]; int. by Oregon Miniature Roses, 1984

Grandessa – See **Messire Delbard**, Cl HT

Grandesse Royale – See **Grosse Mohnkopfs Rose**, S

Grandesse Royale – See **Great Royal**, HGal

Grandesse Royale – See **Lustre d'Église**, HGal

Grandeur HT, dp, 1954, Grillo; bud long, pointed; flowers cerise-red, 4 in., 70 petals, high-centered; foliage leathery; very vigorous, upright growth; [sport of Joyance]

Grandeur HT, Mallerin, C.; flowers vermilion-red, medium, 25 petals; moderate, bushy growth

Grandeur of Cheshunt HP, mr, 1883, Paul, G.; flowers bright carmine, tinted pink, very large, full; quite remontant

Grandeur Royale – See **Great Royal**, HGal

Grandezza HT, mp, 1962, Herholdt, J.A.; bud spiral, pointed; flowers peach-blossom-pink, well-formed, large, dbl.; moderate, bushy growth; [Monique × Radar]; int. by Herholdt's Nursery

Grandhotel – See **Dublin Bay**, LCl
Grandidentata – See **À Feuille de Chêne**, C
Grandidier HGal, m, 1826, Dubourg; flowers carmine-violet
Grandiflora – See **Alika**, HGal
Grandiflora II – See ***R. spinosissima altaica*** (Bean)
Grandioso HT, mr, 1961, Verbeek; flowers cherry-red, 5 in., 30-40 petals; foliage dark; [(Happiness × Satisfaction) × (Poinsettia × Happiness)]
Grandissima – See **Louis-Philippe**, HGal
Grandma F, mp; int. in 2005
Grandma F, my; flowers bright yellow, dbl., borne in clusters, moderate fragrance; recurrent; foliage dark green, glossy; growth to 80 cm.; int. by World of Roses, 2006
Grandma's Baby Min, lp, Wells, V.; flowers pale pink to white, medium, dbl., high-centered, borne mostly singly, very slight fragrance; recurrent; foliage medium size, medium green, matte; vigorous growth
Grandma's Blessing S, dp, Lim, Ping; flowers dusty pink, 3-4 in., 25-30 petals; foliage dark green; growth symmetrical, vase-shaped, small (18 in.); PP16993; int. by Bailey Nursery, 2004
Grandma's Girl Min, ab; int. in 2005
Grandma's Lace S, lp, 1994, Clements, John K.; flowers pale pink, medium, full, borne in clusters, moderate fragrance; foliage medium size, medium green, semi-glossy; medium, spreading growth; [Sexy Rexy × Trier]; int. by Heirloom Old Garden Roses
Grandma's Pink S, mp, 1991, Moore, Ralph S.; flowers medium, very full, borne in small clusters, no fragrance; foliage medium size, medium green, matte; medium, upright, bushy growth; [Shakespeare Festival × Marchioness of Londonderry]; int. by Sequoia Nursery, 1991
Grandma's Violet HT, m
Grandmaster HMsk, ab, 1954, Kordes; bud long, pointed; flowers apricot shaded lemon and pink, 10 petals, borne in clusters; recurrent bloom; foliage light green; bushy growth; [Sangerhausen × Sunmist]; int. by Morse; Gold Medal, NRS, 1951
Grandmaw's Girl Min, mp, 2003, Wells, Verlie W.; flowers light pink, reverse light pink, 1 1/4 in., dbl., borne mostly solitary; foliage medium size, dark green, semi-glossy; prickles 1/4 in., hooked, few; growth upright, tall (24-36 in.); garden, exhibition; [seedling × seedling]; int. by Wells Mid-South Roses, 2002
Grand'mère Jenny HT, yb, 1950, Meilland, F.; flowers apricot-yellow, edged and suffused pink, 4-4 1/2 in., 30 petals, high-centered; foliage dark, glossy; vigorous growth; [Peace × (Julien Potin × Sensation)]; int. by URS, 1950; Gold Medal, Rome, 1955, Gold Medal, NRS, 1950
Grand'mère Jenny, Climbing Cl HT, yb, 1959, Meilland, F.; flowers apricot yellow with light crimson tints, 12-13 cm.; int. by URS, 1958
Grandmom Schmidt T, pb, 2004, Delahanty, James; flowers light pink, reverse medium pink, 2-2 1/2 in., dbl., borne in small clusters, no fragrance; foliage medium size, light green, matte; prickles small, curved backwards, primarily on leaf stem, not canes; growth spreading, medium (4 ft.); specimen; [sport of Smith's Parish (Fortune's Five Color Rose)]; int. by James Delahanty, 2004
Grandpa Alex Min, w, 1995, Rennie, Bruce F.; flowers 1 1/2 in., full, borne in small clusters, moderate fragrance; foliage medium size, dark green, semi-glossy; few prickles; medium (15-18 in.), bushy growth; [Hap Renshaw × Summer Scent]; int. by Rennie Roses International, 1993
Grandpa Dan HT, pb, 1995, Sheldon, John & Robin; flowers pink blend, medium, full, borne mostly singly; foliage medium size, medium green, matte; upright, extremely vigorous, medium growth; [Pristine × Touch of Class]
Grandpa Dickson – See **Irish Gold**, HT
Grandpa Dickson, Climbing Cl HT, my; flowers large
Grandpa Ray HT, pb, 1995, Sheldon, John & Robin; flowers light pink blend, medium, full, borne mostly singly; foliage medium size, medium green, matte; upright, medium growth; [Pristine × Touch of Class]
Grandpa Toni HT, pb, 1995, Sheldon, John & Robin; flowers light pink blend, medium, full, borne mostly singly; foliage medium size, medium green, matte; upright, medium growth; [Pristine × Touch of Class]
Grandpa's Delight F, ob, 1984, Pawsey, Roger; flowers orange-red, yellow center and stamens, medium, semi-dbl.; foliage medium size, medium green, glossy; bushy growth; [Living Fire × seedling]; int. by Rearsby Roses, Ltd.
Grange Briar (strain of *R. canina*), lp; growth vigorous; once used as understock
Grange Colombe HT, w, 1912, Guillot, P.; bud pointed; flowers cream-white, center yellow, large, dbl., cupped; vigorous growth; [Mme Caroline Testout × Lady Ashtown]
Grannie's Bonnet – See **Sixth Sense**, F
Grannie's Rose S, my; flowers clear pink, semi-dbl., borne in clusters of 5-7; non-recurrent
Granny – See **Bossa Nova**, F
Granny Grimmetts HP, dr, Hilling; flowers dark purple-red, often streaked white, 3 in., semi-dbl. to dbl., borne singly and in small clusters, moderate fragrance; some autumn repeat; int. in 1955
Granny's Delight S, dp, Poulsen; int. in 2004
Granny's Favourite MinFl, op; flowers butterscotch; growth to 2 ft.
Grape Delight Min, m, 1999, Giles, Diann; flowers small, semi-dbl., borne in small clusters; foliage medium size, medium green, semi-glossy; numerous prickles; compact, low (1 1/2 ft.) growth; [Lavender Sweetheart × Herbie]; int. by Giles Rose Nursery, 1999
Grapeade Cl Min, m; int. in 1979
Gråsten – See **Glacier**, F
Gratia HT, w, 1934, Leenders, M.; bud pointed; flowers creamy white, large, semi-dbl., high-centered; foliage leathery, dark; vigorous growth; [seedling × Pius XI]
Gratitude HT, rb, 1962, Delbard-Chabert; bud ovoid; flowers reddish-orange, 3-3 1/2 in., 25-35 petals, slight fragrance; foliage leathery, dark, glossy; vigorous, upright, bushy growth; [Impeccable × Incendie]; int. in 1960
Gratulation F, GPG Bad Langensalza; int. in 1985
Graulhié HMult, w, before 1872, Van Houtte; flowers white, reverse light pink, very small, dbl., cupped
Graves de Vayres HMult, dr, Eve; flowers show shades of red, 8 cm., single to semi-dbl., flat; recurrent; broad (4-5 ft.), shrubby growth, or up to 10 ft. as aclimber; int. by Les Roses Anciennes de André Eve, 2000
Gravin D'Alcantara HT, dr, 1985, Rijksstation Voor Sierplantenteelt; flowers well-formed, 28 petals, cupped, borne singly and in clusters of up to 7; foliage matte, dark; prickles red; upright growth; [Montezuma × Forever Yours]; int. in 1982
Gravin Michel d'Ursel HMsk, ab, 2000, Lens, Louis; flowers salmon-pink with a touch of lavender-brown, reverse lighter, 4-6 cm., single, borne in small clusters, moderate fragrance; recurrent; foliage large, dark green, semi-glossy; few prickles; upright, bushy, medium (4-5 ft.) growth; [Lavender Pinocchio × (Ballerina × Echo)]; int. by Louis Lens NV, 1994
Grazia HT, op, 1941, Giacomasso; flowers salmon-pink, center darker, very large; foliage bright green; long stems; [Julien Potin × Mme G. Forest-Colcombet]
Graziella T, lp, 1893, Dubreuil
Graziella F, ob, 1962, Gaujard, R.; bud globular; flowers orange, open, medium, dbl., borne in clusters, slight fragrance; foliage glossy, light green; vigorous, bushy growth; [Feu Follet × seedling]; int. by G. Truffaut, 1960
Great Century – See **Grand Siècle**, HT
Great Day Min, dy, 1983, Williams, Ernest D.; bud long, pointed; flowers well-formed, small, 35 petals, moderate fragrance; foliage small, light green, glossy; bushy growth; PP5358; [(Little Darling × Gold Coin) × (Little Darling × Gold Coin)]; int. by Mini-Roses, 1982
Great Days HT, lp; buds pointed, elongated; flowers delicate pink, full; free-flowering from Japan
Great Double White – See **Alba Maxima**, A
Great Expectations HT, yb, 1988, Sealand Nurseries, Ltd.; flowers light pink, reverse light yellow, aging fading slightly, well-formed, 55 petals, high-centered; foliage medium size, medium green, semi-glossy, clean; prickles long, pointed, medium, red; upright growth; [Rosenella × Cassandra]
Great Expectations F, mp, 1993, J&P
Great Expectations F, ab, McGredy; flowers apricot-pink, sometimes with green at center, 4 in., 50 petals, borne one to a stem or in clusters of 5-6, moderate sweet fragrance; recurrent; foliage starts bronze red and finishes rich, glossy green; growth to 3 ft.; int. in 2001
Great Maiden's Blush A, w, before 1754; bud round; flowers white, tinged pink, petals slightly recurved, 3 in., dbl., globular, borne in clusters of 10-12, intense fragrance; foliage dark green, egg-shaped, pointed; prickles long, slightly hooked; growth branching, tall (5 ft.)
Great News F, m, 1976, LeGrice; flowers plum-purple, reverse silver, 4 in., 33 petals, intense fragrance; foliage large, olive-green; moderate growth; [Rose Gaujard × City of Hereford]; int. in 1973
Great Nord – See **Grand Nord**, HT
Great North – See **Grand Nord**, HT
Great North Eastern Rose F, w, Harkness; flowers pure white, medium, very dbl., borne in large clusters, strong sweet fragrance; repeats quickly; dark green, glossy foliage; vigorous, upright (3 ft × 1 ft.) growth; int. by Harkness Roses, 2001
Great Ormond Street F, my, Beales, Peter; flowers golden yellow, aging to creamy white, dbl., borne in clusters, moderate fragrance; foliage semi-glossy; growth to 2-3 ft.; int. in 1991
Great Phoebus LCl, ab, 1999, Hintlian, Nancy Sears; bud white, spherical; flowers opening to orange and yellow, with slight pink edge, 5 1/2 in., 41 petals, pompon, borne mostly singly; foliage large, dark green, semi-glossy; prickles moderate; upright, vigorous, medium (8 ft.) growth; [Abraham Darby × Breath of Life]
Great Royal HGal, lp, before 1813, from England; flowers light lilac-rose, globular, borne in clusters of 3-4; foliage thick, rugose; prickles unequal; possibly synonymous with Aimable Rouge
Great Scott HT, mp, 1991, Ballin, Don & Paula; peduncles slightly pubescent; flowers large, very full, high-centered; foliage large, medium green, matte; prickles light green with some red, large, hooked down; growth upright (4 ft.), bushy; exhibition; [sport of Cleo]
Great Splash Min, pb, Bell; flowers striped; int. by Bell Roses

Great Venture HT, yb, 1971, Dawson, George; bud long, pointed; flowers orange-yellow, flushed pink, medium, dbl., intense fragrance; foliage large, leathery; vigorous, upright growth; [Daily Sketch × Suspense]; int. by S. Brundrett & Son, 1970

Great Wall S, dp, Ping Lim; flowers blend of red and warm pink, 4 in., semi-dbl., shallow cup to flat; recurrent; foliage starts red and slowly turns to dark green; vigorous (3 ft.) growth; int. by Bailey Nurseries (Easy Elegance), 2005

Great Western B, m, 1840, Laffay, M.; flowers purplish maroon, large, dbl.; blooms mostly in early summer; vigorous growth

Greater Hastings HT, mp, 1957, Francis

Greatest Century – See **Grand Siècle**, HT

Greatheart HT, op, 1921, Rosenbluth; flowers pale flesh, shaded salmon, center deeper, dbl.; [sport of Mrs Walter Easlea]

Green Bubbles Min, w, 1979, Lyon; bud ovoid; flowers light green, 1 in., 12 petals, slight fragrance; foliage tiny; very compact, bushy growth; int. in 1978

Green Diamond Min, w, 1975, Moore, Ralph S.; bud pointed, dusty pink; flowers white to soft green, ½ in., 25 petals, cupped; foliage small, leathery; growth upright, bushy; [unnamed polyantha × Sheri Anne]; int. by Sequoia Nursery

Green Fire F, dy, 1959, Swim, H.C.; bud ovoid, pointed; flowers 3 in., 13 petals, flat, borne in clusters, slight fragrance; foliage semi-glossy; vigorous, bushy growth; PP1776; [Goldilocks × seedling]; int. by Armstrong Nursery, 1958

Green Ice Min, w, 1971, Moore, Ralph S.; bud pointed; flowers white to soft green, small, dbl.; foliage small, glossy, leathery; vigorous, dwarf, bushy growth; [(*R. wichurana* × Floradora) × Jet Trail]; int. by Sequoia Nursery

Green Light – See **Ryokkoh**, F

Green Planet HT, w, Spek; flowers yellow with a distinct green tone, dbl.; int. by Carlton, 2003

Green Rose Ch, w, before 1856, Bambridge & Harrison; flowers green, often touched with bronze, with narrow leaf-like petals, 1½-2 in., dbl.; recurrent bloom; medium, upright growth; [probably a sport of Parson's Pink China]; known to be in cultivation as early as 1743; some variations with slight red or pink coloration to some petals known to exist

Green Snake S, w, 1986, Lens, Louis; flowers pure white, small, 5 petals, borne in clusters of 3-24; non-recurrent; foliage small, spoon-shaped; prickles hooked, light brownish-green; groundcover; spreading growth; [*R. arvensis* × *R. wichurana*]; int. in 1985

Greenalls Glory F, w, Kirkham, Gordon Wilson; flowers silvery, delicate white with a pale blush center, reverse stark white, dbl.; recurrent; foliage glossy bronze; growth low, spreading (1½ × 2 ft.); int. in 1989

Greenmantle HEg, rb, 1895, Penzance; flowers bright rosy red, white eye, golden stamens, single; foliage richly fragrant; very vigorous, tall growth

Greensleeves F, w, 1980, Harkness; bud pointed, salmon-rose; flowers rosy-green and chartreuse, finishing creamy-mint with pick spots, large, 15 petals, flat; foliage dark green; vigorous, upright growth; [(Rudolph Timm × Arthur Bell) × ((((Pascali × Elizabeth of Glamis) × (Sabine × Violette Dot)) × ((Pascali × Elizabeth of Glamis) × (Sabine × Violette Dot))) × (Sabine × Violette Dot))]

Greer Garson HT, pb, 1943, Denoyel, Vve.; bud pointed; flowers begonia-rose, 5 in., 35 petals, high-centered; foliage leathery, dark; vigorous, tall, bushy growth; int. by J&P

Greet Koster Pol, op, 1933, Koster, D.A.; flowers deep pink, shaded salmon, globular, borne in small clusters; recurrent; [sport of Margo Koster]

Greetings HT, mr, 1965, Kordes, R.; bud ovoid; flowers pure red, 5½ in., 40 petals, high-centered, slight fragrance; foliage dark, glossy; vigorous, upright, bushy growth; int. by Wheatcroft Bros., 1964

Greetings S, m, 2005, Keith W. Zary; flowers red-purple with white reverse and yellow base, 2 in., semi-dbl., borne in large clusters; foliage small, dark green, glossy; prickles 6-7 mm., hooked downward, greyed orange, moderate; upright, branching, medium (4 ft.) growth; [Lavender Dream × Roller Coaster]; int. by Europe, 1999

Greetings from Alma-Aty – See **Privet iz Alma-Aty**, HT

Greetje Hennekens Pol, mr, Loose; flowers carmine-red, medium, semi-dbl.; int. in 1957

Greg Chappell HT, ab; buds deep golden; flowers rich apricot; growth short; int. in 1984

Greg Moore S, w, 1996, Horner, Colin P.; flowers cream tinged pink, 2 in., dbl., camellia-like, borne in large clusters; foliage small, grey green, dull; some prickles; medium (100 cm.), spreading growth; [Bonica × (Lichtkonigin Lucia × seedling)]

Grégor Mendel F, op, 1955, Maarse, G.; flowers coral-pink shaded yellow and carmine, dbl.; vigorous growth; [Pinocchio × unknown]

Gremlin S, mr, Kordes; flowers bright cherry-red, reverse cream and yellow; growth healthy, compact plant; int. in 2002

Grenadier HT, mr, 1930, Dickson, A.; flowers brilliant currant-red shaded scarlet, dbl., cupped; foliage rich green, leathery, glossy; vigorous, bushy growth

Grenadier – See **Fusilier**, F

Grenadine – See **Granadina**, Min

Grenadine – See **Caritas**, HT

Grenoble – See **Ville de Grenoble**, HT

Grenoble, Climbing Cl HT, mr, 1939, Western Rose Co.

Greta F, w, Briant; int. in 1995

Greta Fey HWich, lp, 1909, Strassheim; flowers creamy pink, small, semi-dbl., borne in clusters

Greta Kluis Pol, mr, 1916, Kluis & Koning; flowers carmine-red; [sport of Echo]

Greta Kluis Superior Pol, mr, 1928, Kluis; flowers deep carmine-red; [sport of Tausendschön]

Grete Bermbach HT, pb, 1925, Leenders Bros.; flowers silvery flesh, center rose, sometimes shaded yellow orange, dbl.; [Mrs Aaron Ward × Pharisaer]

Grete Schickendanz HT, Kordes, R.; int. in 1987

Grete Schreiber Pol, mp, 1916, Altmüller; flowers medium, full

Gretel Greul HT, mr, 1939, Greul; [sport of Rote Rapture]

Gretelein HFt, lp, 1933, Schmitt, K.; flowers large, semi-dbl.

Grethe Poulsen Pol, dp, 1928, Poulsen, S.; flowers light cherry-red, base yellow, semi-dbl.; early; dwarf, well branched growth; [Ellen Poulsen × Mme Laurette Messimy]

Gretta Min, dp, 1993, Spooner, Raymond A.; flowers deep pink, large, very dbl., borne mostly singly; foliage medium size, dark green, glossy; some prickles; bushy (44 cm.) growth; int. by Oregon Miniature Roses

Grevilii HMult, w, before 1828; flowers single

Grevillea – See **Grevilii**, HMult

Grevillia Rose – See **Seven Sisters**, HMult

Grevinde Rose Danneskjold Samsöe HT, dr, 1914, Poulsen, D.T.; bud dark velvety red; flowers scarlet

Grevinde Sylvia Knuth HWich, w, 1913, Poulsen, D.T.; bud yellow; flowers white, center yellow, 3 cm., semi-dbl., borne in clusters of 8-10; foliage narrow, glossy

Grey Dawn F, m, 1976, LeGrice; flowers gray, reverse flushed pink and gold, 3-4 in., 45 petals, moderate fragrance; foliage glossy; bushy growth; [Brownie × News]; int. in 1975

Grey Pearl HT, m, 1945, McGredy; bud ovoid; flowers lavender-gray, shaded olive and tan, 4-4½ in., 43 petals, high-centered, moderate fragrance; foliage glossy; vigorous growth; [(Mrs Charles Lamplough × seedling) × (Sir David Davis × Southport)]; int. by J&P

Grey Pearl, Climbing Cl HT, m, 1951, Caluya

Gribaldo Nicola T, w, 1891, Soupert & Notting; flowers white with touches of yellow, 11-12 cm., dbl., moderate fragrance; very remontant; foliage large, rounded; vigorous (8 ft × 6 ft.) growth; [Bouquet d'Or × La Sylphide]

Grido F, Pironti, N.; int. in 1972

Griff's Red S, mr, 2001, Buck, Dr. Griffith J.; bud clear ruby red; flowers clear ruby red, large, full, borne mostly solitary, moderate fragrance; foliage medium size, medium green, semi-glossy; prickles moderate; growth upright, medium (45-50 cm.); [Amiga Mia × Music Maker]; int. by Roses Unlimited, 2002

Grillodale HT, lp, 1926, Grillo; flowers light pink, center deeper, 4½ in., 50 petals; foliage dark; [sport of Mme Butterfly]

Grimaldi F, pb, Delbard; flowers deep pink striped and splashed with lighter pink and white, semi-dbl., loose, borne in clusters; int. by Georges Delbard SA, 1997

Grimbeert HT, Delforge, H.; int. in 1995

Grimm LCl, pb, 1932, Lambert, P.; flowers apple-blossom-pink, center white, stamens golden, edges fluted, single; non-recurrent; vigorous growth; [(Hiawatha × Altmarker) × (Mme Leon Pain × Marquise de Sinéty)]

Grimpant All Gold – See **Allgold, Climbing**, Cl F

Grimpant Allgold – See **Allgold, Climbing**, Cl F

Grimpant Baronne de Rothschild – See **Baronne Edmond de Rothschild, Climbing**, Cl HT

Grimpant Bettina – See **Bettina, Climbing**, Cl HT

Grimpant Carina – See **Carina, Climbing**, Cl HT

Grimpant Chrysler Imperial – See **Chrysler Imperial, Climbing**, Cl HT

Grimpant Clair Matin – See **Clair Matin**, LCl

Grimpant Comtesse Vandal – See **Comtesse Vandal, Climbing**, Cl HT

Grimpant Crimson Glory – See **Crimson Glory, Climbing**, Cl HT

Grimpant Danse des Sylphes – See **Danse des Sylphes**, LCl

Grimpant Delbard – See **Delbard's Orange Climber**, LCl

Grimpant Diablotin – See **Diablotin, Climbing**, Cl F

Grimpant Double Delight – See **Double Delight, Climbing**, Cl HT

Grimpant Ena Harkness – See **Ena Harkness, Climbing**, Cl HT

Grimpant Eric Tabarly – See **Eric Tabarly**, LCl

Grimpant Étoile de Hollande – See **Étoile de Hollande, Climbing**, Cl HT

Grimpant Exploit – See **Exploit**, LCl

Grimpant Grand'mère Jenny – See **Grand'mère Jenny, Climbing**, Cl HT

Grimpant Lilli Marleen – See **Lilli Marleen, Climbing**, Cl F

Grimpant Marie Claire – See **Marie Claire, Climbing**, Cl HT

Grimpant Michèle Meilland – See **Michèle Meilland, Climbing**, Cl HT

Grimpant Mrs Herbert Stevens – See **Mrs Herbert Stevens, Climbing**, Cl HT
Grimpant Opera – See **Opera, Climbing**, Cl HT
Grimpant Orange Meillandina – See **Orange Meillandina, Climbing**, Cl Min
Grimpant Papa Meilland – See **Papa Meilland, Climbing**, Cl HT
Grimpant Pierre de Ronsard – See **Pierre de Ronsard**, F
Grimpant Queen Elizabeth – See **Queen Elizabeth, Climbing**, Cl Gr
Grimpant Reine des Neiges – See **Frau Karl Druschki, Climbing**, Cl HP
Grimpant Rimosa – See **Gold Badge, Climbing**, Cl F
Grimpant Rose Gaujard – See **Rose Gaujard, Climbing**, Cl HT
Grimpant Rouge et Or – See **Redgold, Climbing**, Cl F, 1980
Grimpant Roxane – See **Roxane, Climbing**, Cl HT
Grimpant Sonia Meilland – See **Sonia, Climbing**, Cl Gr
Grimpant Soraya – See **Soraya, Climbing**, Cl HT
Grimpant Sutter's Gold – See **Sutter's Gold, Climbing**, Cl HT
Grimpant Tiffany – See **Tiffany, Climbing**, Cl HT
Grimpant Vendée Globe – See **Vendée Globe, Climbing**, Cl HT
Gripsholm – See **Viborg**, F
Grisbi – See **Sunlight**, HT, 1958
Grisbi, Climbing – See **Sunlight, Climbing**, Cl HT

Grisbi F, my, Meilland; bud conical; flowers yellow, petal edges turning white, 6-7 cm., 18-20 petals, cupped, borne usually singly, no fragrance; recurrent; foliage dark green, semi-matte; prickles average, small, tan; erect (4-5 ft.) growth; PP7313; [Sonia × Golden Times]; greenhouse rose; int. in 1989

Grisbi F, my, Richardier; flowers clear yellow, large, full, moderate anise fragrance; growth to 110-120 cm.; int. by Meilland Richardier, 1999

Griseldis LCl, mp, 1895, Geschwind, R.; flowers dark pink, darker at center, fading to light pink, 8-9 cm., semi-dbl., flat, borne in clusters of 1-6, no fragrance; some autumn repeat; [(*R. canina* × a Hybrid Tea) × (*R. canina* × a Bourbon)]

Griseldis F, w, Select Roses, B.V.

Grootendorst – See **F. J. Grootendorst**, HRg

Grootendorst Magenta HRg, m, Vidal; int. by Rosales Vidal

Grootendorst Pink – See **Pink Grootendorst**, HRg
Grootendorst Red – See **F. J. Grootendorst**, HRg

Grootendorst Supreme HRg, dr, 1936, Grootendorst, F.J.; flowers deeper crimson-red, small, full; [sport of F.J. Grootendorst]

Gros Choux d'Hollande C, lp, before 1820; flowers soft rose-pink, medium, dbl., intense fragrance; foliage doubly dentate; vigorous growth

Gros Pompon – See **Petite de Hollande**, C
Gros Provins Panaché – See **Provins Panaché**, B

Grosse Cerise HGal, mr, before 1810, Dupont

Grosse Hollande – See **Gros Choux d'Hollande**, C

Grosse Mohnkopfs Rose S, dp, before 1799, Schwarzkopf; flowers bright rose, 3 in., dbl.; foliage oval-acuminate, finely dentate, villose beneath; few prickles

Grossherzog Ernst Ludwig von Hesse Cl HT, mp, 1888, Müller, Dr. F.; flowers silvery carmine, very large, very dbl., intense fragrance; [Pierre Notting × Maréchal Niel]

Grossherzog Friedrich von Baden HT, mp, 1908, Lambert, P.; flowers carmine rose pink, medium, dbl., intense fragrance; [Mme Caroline Testout × Meta]

Grossherzog Wilhelm Ernst von Sachsen HT, dp, 1915, Welter; flowers bright scarlet with carmine rose, large, dbl., intense fragrance; [Mme Mélanie Soupert × Lyon Rose]

Grossherzogin Alexandra HT, w, 1904, Jacobs; flowers yellowish-white, large, full; [Mervielle de Lyon × Kaiserin Auguste Viktoria]

Grossherzogin Eleonore von Hessen HMult, m, 1907, Strassheim; flowers dark violet-red, fading to crimson, 3 cm., dbl., borne in small to medium clusters, no fragrance; [a Multiflora × Turner's Crimson Rambler]

Grossherzogin Feodora von Sachsen HT, w, 1914, Kiese; flowers creamy white, base deep yellow; [Frau Karl Druschki × Kaiserin Auguste Viktoria]

Grossherzogin Josefine Schararolle HT, lp, Lens, Louis; flowers medium-large, dbl.; int. in 1989

Grossherzogin Mathilde – See **Princesse Olympie**, HP

Grossherzogin Mathilde von Hessen T, w, 1861, Vogler; flowers white, tinged green, large, dbl.; [sport of Bougère]

Grossherzogin Viktoria Melitta von Hessen HT, w, 1897, Lambert; flowers cream with a yellow center, very large, full, borne mostly solitary; foliage large; [Safrano × Mme Caroline Testout]

Grossmütterchen HCh, mp, Weihrauch; flowers large, very dbl.; int. in 1983

Ground Zero HT, pb, 2002, Wells, Verlie W.; flowers white with pink edge, 3½-4½ in., full, borne mostly solitary, intense fragrance; foliage medium size, dark green, semi-glossy; prickles small, straight, moderate; growth upright, medium; garden decorative, exhibition; [seedling × Admiral Rodney]; int. by Wells' Midsouth Roses, 2002

Grouse – See **Immensee**, S
Grouse 2000 – See **Medeo**, S
Grove – See **Grove Cottage**, S

Grove Cottage S, dp, Poulsen; flowers deep pink to light red, less than 2 in., single, shallow cup, borne in clusters, very slight fragrance; recurrent; foliage dark green, glossy; flat, bushy (40-60 cm.) growth; int. by Poulsen Roser, 2004

Grugakind Pol, op; flowers small, dbl.

Grumpy Pol, mp, 1956, deRuiter; flowers pink, small, dbl., borne in long trusses; int. by Gregory & Willicher Baumschulen

Gruppenkönigin F, pb, 1935, Kordes, H.; flowers deep bicolor pink, very large, dbl.; foliage light, leathery; vigorous, bushy growth; [Gruss an Aachen × Mme Edouard Herriot]

Gruss an Aachen F, lp, 1909, Geduldig; bud orange-red and yellow; flowers flesh-pink fading to creamy white, 3-3½ in., 40-45 petals, borne in clusters, slight sweet fragrance; foliage rich green, leathery; slender stems, will nod; dwarf growth; [Frau Karl Druschki × Franz Deegen]

Gruss an Aachen, Climbing Cl F, lp, 1937, Kordes; flowers ivory-white, enriched with apricot-pink, large, full; [sport of Gruss an Aachen]

Gruss an Aachen Superior HT, lp, 1942, Leenders; flowers blush white, large, full; presumably a sport of Gurss an Aachen

Gruss an Angeln HT, mr, Clausen; int. in 1986

Gruss an Baden-Baden Cl Min, mr, Warner; flowers shining, warm ruby red; int. in 2000

Gruss an Bayern F, mr, 1973, Kordes, R.; flowers blood-red, medium, semi-dbl., globular, slight fragrance; foliage dark, leathery; vigorous, upright growth; [Messestadt Hannover × Hamburg]; int. by Kordes, 1971; ADR, 1973

Gruss an Berlin – See **Greetings**, HT

Gruss an Breinegg HMult, dp, 1925, Bruder Alfons; flowers light reddish-violet, fading almost white, small, single, borne in medium clusters

Gruss an Coburg HT, ab, 1927, Felberg-Leclerc; flowers apricot-yellow, reverse coppery pink, large, full, globular, intense fragrance; foliage bronze; vigorous growth; [Alice Kaempff × Souv. de Claudius Pernet]

Gruss an Dresden HT, mr, 1913, Türke; flowers fiery red; [Princesse de Bearn × unknown]; int. by Hoyer & Klemm

Gruss an Föhr HFt, yb, 1930, Riewers; flowers medium, semi-dbl.

Gruss an Freundorf HWich, dr, 1913, Praskac; flowers dark velvety crimson, center whitish, stamens bright yellow, 4-5 cm., semi-dbl., borne in clusters; foliage small, glossy; numerous prickles; [*R. wichurana rubra* × Crimson Rambler]; int. by Teschendorff

Gruss an Friedberg N, dy, 1902, Rogmanns; flowers pale yellow with golden center, medium to large, dbl., moderate fragrance; [sport of Duarte de Oliveira]

Gruss an Germershausen HMult, rb, 1926, Bruder Alfons; flowers crimson red, white center, 2-3 cm., single, borne in very large clusters; foliage medium green, somewhat glossy

Gruss an Hannover HMult, op, 1938, Lahmann; flowers orange pink, 6 cm., dbl.; vigorous, upright (10-13 ft.) growth

Gruss an Heidelberg – See **Heidelberg**, HKor

Gruss an Koblenz LCl, mr, 1963, Kordes, R.; flowers bright scarlet, 3 in., 20 petals, borne in clusters (up to 10); recurrent bloom; vigorous growth

Gruss an Lorrach F, Hetzel, K.; int. in 1983

Gruss an Maiengrun F, or

Gruss an Munchen F, Tantau, Math.; int. in 1962

Gruss an Naumburg HT, rb, 1928, Muller, J.F.; flowers medium, dbl.

Gruss an Oldenburg S, yb, Weihrauch; int. in 1995

Gruss an Rengsdorf S, mp, 1920, Boden-Kurtscheid; flowers medium, single; very hardy; hybrid canina

Gruss an Sangerhausen HT, mr, 1904, Müller, Dr. F.; flowers brilliant scarlet, center crimson, very large, dbl., moderate fragrance; [Pierre Notting × Safrano]

Gruss an Steinfurth F, my, 1961, Leenders, J.; flowers open, 21 petals, cupped, borne in large clusters (to 15); moderate growth; [Goldilocks × Masquerade]

Gruss an Stuttgart F, mr, 1976, Hetzel; bud ovoid; flowers velvety red, medium, dbl.; vigorous, bushy growth; [(Carina × seedling) × Sans Souci]

Gruss an Teplitz HCh, mr, 1894, Geschwind, R.; bud small, ovoid; flowers dark velvety scarlet, medium, 33 petals, borne on short, weak stems, intense spicy fragrance; recurrent bloom; foliage dark, young growth bronze-red; short, weak stems; vigorous (6 ft.), bushy growth; good for hedges; [((Sir Joseph Paxton × Fellenberg) × Papa Gontier) × Gloire des Rosomanes]; int. by P. Lambert; Old Rose Hall of Fame, WFRS

Gruss an Teplitz, Climbing Cl HCh, mr, 1911, Storrs & Harrison Co. (also Nonin, 1919); flowers crimson, 5-7 cm., cupped, borne in small clusters; [sport of Gurss an Teplitz]

Gruss an Weimar HP, pb, 1919, Kiese; flowers pink on yellowish ground, very large, full; [Frau Karl Druschki × Lyon Rose]

Gruss an Wörishofen – See **Bad Wörishofen**, F

Gruss an Zabern HMult, w, 1903, Lambert, P.; flowers full, borne in large clusters, intense spicy-sweet fragrance; numerous prickles; growth vigorous, climbing (4-5 m.); [Euphrosine × Mme Ocker Ferencz]

Gruss an Zweibrücken HT, mr, 1915, Lambert, P.;

flowers large, dbl.; [Charles Gater × Mme Caroline Testout]

Gruss aus Alma-aty HT, Sushkov, K. L.; int. in 1958

Gruss aus Pallien HP, rb, 1900, Welter; bud long; flowers bright fiery red with purple center, cupped, moderate fragrance; [Baronne Adolphe de Rothschild × Princesse de Béarn]

Gruss vom Westerwald HT, op, 1914, Kettenbeil; flowers medium, dbl.; [Mme Caroline Testout × Mme Ravary]

Gruss von Tannenhof HMult, w, 1913, Friedrich; flowers bright white, 3 cm., dbl., borne in large clusters

Guadalajara HT, my, 1986, McGredy, Sam IV; flowers large, 24 petals, high-centered, borne singly, moderate fragrance; foliage large, medium green, semi-glossy; prickles large, deltoid, red to brown; medium, upright growth; fruit never observed; PP6263; [New Day × Yellow Bird]; int. by Roses by Fred Edmunds, 1985

Guadalupe Volunteer HMsk, w, 2003, Hulse, Merrill; flowers very full, borne in large clusters, intense fragrance; foliage medium size, medium green, semi-glossy, 5-7 leaflets, disease-free; prickles 5/16 inches, falcate, reddish-brown, moderate; growth spreading, climbs when supported, tall (more than 30 ft.)

Guadalupe's Love HT, w, 1997, Price, Kathleen M.; flowers ruffled, medium, very dbl., borne mostly singly; foliage medium size, medium green, semi-glossy; upright, medium (2½ to 3ft.) growth; [sport of Bewitched]

Guardsman HT, or, 1937, Archer; flowers bright scarlet, base yellow, large, dbl.; foliage glossy; vigorous, compact growth; [seedling × Shot Silk]

Gudhem – See **Gudhemsrosen**, A

Gudhemsrosen A, w; flowers pure white, large, single, borne in early blooming; plentiful bloom; growth to 5 ft.; unknown origin and date

Guenille – See **Œillet**, C

Guernsey Gold Min, dy, 1992, Robinson, Thomas, Ltd.; flowers golden yellow, large, full, urn-shaped, borne in small clusters, slight fragrance; foliage small, medium green, semi-glossy; some prickles; low (30 cm.), upright, bushy growth; [Rise 'n' Shine × seedling]; int. by Thomas Robinson, Ltd., 1990

Guernsey Love Min, dr, 1986, Robinson, Thomas, Ltd.; flowers small, 35 petals, cupped, borne in sprays of 4-5, moderate fruity fragrance; foliage small, dark, glossy; prickles thin, red, curving downward; upright, bushy growth; hips globular, medium, orange-red; [Dollie B. × seedling]

Guerreiro Cl F, dr, Moreira da Silva; [seedling × Alain]

Guglielmo Betto S, dp; int. by Rose & Rose, 2001

Guglielmo Marconi HT, w, 1934, Giacomasso; flowers almost white, tinted flesh; [Ophelia × Elisabeth Faurax]

Guglielmo Marconi F, op, Harkness; int. in 1996

Guiding Spirit Min, dp, 1989, Harkness, R., & Co., Ltd.; bud ovoid; flowers deep pink, reverse lighter, medium, dbl., flat, borne is sprays of 3-9; foliage small, dark green, semi-glossy; prickles needle-like, very small; low, bushy growth; [(Blue Moon × seedling) × Little Prince]; int. by R. Harkness & Co., Ltd., 1989

Guido A. Zäch HT, rb, Huber; flowers bright red with golden-yellow reverse, full; int. by Richard Huber AG, 2005

Guildfordian HT, w; flowers pale cream; thornless; long stems; medium growth

Guillaume F, ob, Delbard; flowers bright orange with yellow reverse, dbl., cupped, borne in large clusters; recurrent; growth vigorous (3 ft.); int. by George Delbard SA, 1999

Guillaume Gillemot HP, dp, 1880, Schwartz; flowers carmine pink with pale silvery reflections, very large, full, globular

Guillaume Kaempff HT, dr, 1931, Felberg-Leclerc; flowers dark crimson-red, edged blackish, large, dbl.; foliage thick; vigorous growth; [Hadley × Admiral Ward]

Guillaume Tell HGal, lp, before 1835, from Angers; flowers bright light pink, large, full, globular

Guinea Gold HT, ab, 1945, Joseph H. Hill, Co.; bud long, pointed, buff-yellow; flowers apricot-yellow, open, dbl.; foliage dark, leathery; strong stems; vigorous, upright, much branched growth; [Joanna Hill × Golden Rapture]

Guinée Cl HT, dr, 1938, Mallerin, C.; bud pointed; flowers velvety blackish garnet, sometimes mottled scarlet, 3-3½ in., dbl., borne in small clusters, intense fragrance; occasional repeat; foliage leathery; growth to 6½-9 ft.; [Souv. de Claudius Denoyel × Ami Quinard]; int. by C-P

Guinevere HT, mp, 1967, Harkness; flowers 4½ in., 40 petals; foliage glossy; [Red Dandy × Peace]

Guinevere F, ab, 2001, Harkness New Roses Ltd.; flowers 8 cm., full, borne in large clusters; foliage large, dark green, glossy; growth spreading, medium (80 cm.); garden decorative; PP13184; [Harroony × Harwanted]; int. by J&P, 1997

Guinguette F, pb, 1958, Gaujard, R.; flowers pink edged darker, well-formed, cupped; vigorous growth; [Alain × Feu de Joie]; int. by Hémeray-Aubert

Guirlande d'Amour HMsk, w, 2000, Lens, Louis; flowers creamy white, nice stamens, 1 in., semi-dbl., borne in large clusters; recurrent bloom; foliage medium size, medium green, semi-glossy, disease-resistant; prickles moderate; upright, tall (180-200 cm.) growth; hedge, climber; [Seagull × (*R. multiflora nana* × Moonlight)]; int. by Louis Lens NV, 1993; Gold Medal, Madrid, 1991

Guirlande Diamand LCl, w; flowers small, single, borne in clusters; spring bloomer; foliage smooth, glossy; growth vigorous (4-6 m.) climbing, or used as groundcover; [unknown × unknown]; seedling found growing at nursery

Guirlande Fleurie LCl, mr, 1970, Robichon; bud ovoid; flowers bright red, large, semi-dbl., cupped, borne in large clusters; foliage leathery; very vigorous, climbing growth; [Valenciennes × Paul's Scarlet Climber]; int. by Ilgenfritz Nursery

Guiseppe Motta HT, pb, 1936, Heizmann, E.; bud long; flowers flesh-pink, reverse red and yellow, large, semi-dbl., intense fresh, fruity fragrance; recurrent; vigorous growth

Guitare F, ob, 1963, Gaujard; bud ovoid; flowers gold and orange-red blend, medium, dbl.; foliage light green, leathery; vigorous, bushy growth; [Vendome × Golden Slippers]; Gold Medal, Bagatelle, 1966

Guitare, Climbing Cl F, ob, Kasturi; flowers brilliant orange pink; [sport of Guitare]; int. by KSG Son Roses, 1974

Guizzo Rosso F, dr, Barni; flowers intense red, semi-dbl.; constant bloom; foliage glossy, healthy; moderate (80-100 cm.) growth; int. by Rose Barni, 2005

Gulab Angree Nashik – See **Rose City of Nashik**, HT

Gulab-E-Pal HT, m, 1986, Hardikar, Dr. M.N.; flowers mauve, blended with yellow, 70 petals, high-centered, borne singly, moderate fragrance; foliage medium size, light green; prickles brown; upright growth; [Festival Beauty × (Scarlet Knight × Festival Beauty)]; int. in 1985

Guldtop HSpn, dy; [*R. spinosissima* × unknown]

Gulf Breeze Min, pb, 1991, Taylor, Pete & Kay; flowers creamy getting darker pink toward edges, yellow base, large, very full, borne mostly singly, slight fragrance; foliage medium size, medium green, semi-glossy; some prickles; upright, medium (35 cm.), bushy growth; [Baby Katie × Poker Chip]; int. by Taylor's Roses, 1992

Gulgong Gold HT, yb

Gull Dagmar – See **Topaz Jewel**, HRg

Gulletta – See **Tapis Jaune**, Min

Gulliver's Glow S, mr, 1954, Gulliver; flowers bright red, small, dbl., borne in very large clusters; thornless; bushy growth; very hardy; [Hiawatha × (*R. maximowicziana pilosa* × Tausendschon)]; int. by Shenandoah Nursery

Gulnare HT, my, 1918, Poulsen, D.T.; flowers golden yellow

Gulzar HT, dr, 1971, IARI; buds medium, pointed; flowers deep magenta-red, satiny, dbl., high-centered, borne singly and several together; foliage medium size, light green, leathery; growth vigorous, bushy

Gumdrop Min, dr, 1982, Warriner, William A.; bud fat, pointed; flowers 25 petals, borne 3-12 per cluster; foliage small, semi-glossy; spreading growth; PP5152; [(San Fernando × Bridal Pink) × (Fire Princess × Mary DeVor)]; int. by J&P, 1981

Guna HRg, mr, Rieksta; flowers bright, light red, semi-dbl., loose, moderate fragrance; bushy, tall (4-5 ft. tall and wide) growth; winter hardy; int. in 1980

Gundy F, dp, 1967, Schloen, P.; bud ovoid; flowers deep rose-pink, semi-dbl., cupped, borne in clusters, slight fragrance; foliage dark; vigorous, upright growth; int. by Ellesmere Nursery, 1966

Gunnels Ros – See **Nirvana**, F

Gunner's Mate S, rb, Dickson; int. in 2000

Gunsei Cl F, pb, 1987, Kikuchi, Rikichi; flowers white flushed pink on fringe, 13-15 petals, cupped, borne in large clusters; foliage 7 leaflet, green; no prickles; vigorous, upright growth; [seedling × Summer Snow]; int. in 1988

Gunston Hall HT, mr, 1929, U.S. Dept. of Agric.; flowers scarlet-crimson; [seedling × Hoosier Beauty]; int. by C-P

Guo Se Tian Xiang Ch, mr

Gurney Benham HT, my, 1935, Cant, B. R.; flowers buttercup-yellow, large, dbl., cupped; foliage glossy, bronze; vigorous, bushy growth; [sport of Lady Forteviot]

Gurney Hill HT, mr, 1924, E.G. Hill, Co.; flowers pure red, dbl.

Gussie Min, pb, 1980, Lorenzen, Frederick; bud ovoid; flowers medium red, reverse pale pink and silver, 90 petals, high-centered, borne singly, slight fragrance; foliage green, leathery; few prickles; bushy, dwarf growth; [seedling × seedling]

Gustav Frahm F, mr, 1959, Kordes; flowers crimson-scarlet, 3 in., 25 petals, flat, borne in large clusters; foliage light, glossy; vigorous, upright growth; [Fanal × Ama]; int. by Timm

Gustav Grünerwald HT, pb, 1903, Lambert, P.; flowers carmine-pink, center yellow, large, full, cupped; [Safrano × Mme Caroline Testout]

Gustav Sobry HT, yb, 1902, Welter; flowers golden yellow and red, large; [Kaiserin Auguste Viktoria × Comte Chandon]

Gustave Bonnet N, w, 1864, Lacharme; flowers pure white, aging to whitish pink, shaded carmine, medium to large, full

Gustave Coraux HP, m, 1856, Robert

Gustave Courbet HT, dp, Sauvageot; flowers rose pink, 12 cm., dbl.; int. in 1992

Gustave Piganeau HP, mr, 1889, Pernet-Ducher; flowers bright carmine, very large, dbl., cupped; growth moderate

Gustave Règis HT, ly, 1890, Pernet-Ducher; flowers creamy yellow, large, semi-dbl.; [possibly a seedling of Mlle Blanche Durrschmidt]

Gustave Révilliod HP, mp, 1876, Schwartz; flowers pink, tinted dark red at center, purplish at edges, large, full; foliage medium size, thick, dark green, semi-glossy; prickles small, arched, green; [Victor Verdier × unknown]

Gustave Rousseau HP, m, 1862, Fargeton; flowers violet with fiery red edges, large, full

Gustave Thierry HP, dp, 1881, Oger; flowers bright cherry red fading to lilac pink, full, globular

Gustel Löbner HT, w, 1927, Löbner; flowers large, dbl.

Gustel Mayer Pol, mr, 1909, Lambert, P.; flowers light red, middle yellow, small, dbl.; [Turner's Crimson Rambler × (Mme Pierre Cochet × Dunkelrote Hermosa)]

Gute Besserung – See **Countess Celeste**, S

Gütersloh S, rb, Noack; flowers magenta tinted with crimson and white at the petal bases, dbl., cupped; arching growth; int. by Noack Roses, 1969

Gutersloh 85 S, mr

Guy de Maupassant F, mp, 1996, Meilland International SA; bud globular, large; flowers carmine pink, 3-3½ in., 90-100 petals, cupped, borne in clusters, intense green apple fragrance; good repeat; foliage large, dark green, glossy; prickles moderate; bushy, tall (70-90 cm.) growth; PP9613; [(Anne de Bretagne × Mrs John Laing) × Egeskov]; int. by The Conard-Pyle Co., 1995

Guy Fawkes F, yb, 1976, Cadle's Roses; flowers yellow center, reverse shading scarlet, large, 15 petals, intense fragrance; foliage glossy; [My Choice × Masquerade]; int. in 1975

Guy-Guy F, ab, 1966, Fankhauser; flowers apricot and pink, edged crimson, small, dbl.; foliage dark, glossy, leathery; low, compact growth; [(Circus × Circus) × (Circus × Circus)]

Guy Laroche HT, rb, 1986, Delbard, Georges; flowers brilliant red, silver reverse, large, 30 petals, high-centered, borne mostly singly; foliage medium size, medium green, matte; upright, bushy growth; [seedling × (Michele Meilland × Carla)]; int. by Armstrong Nursery, 1985

Guy Savoy S, rb, Delbard; flowers deep red striped with rosy white, moderate fruity, aromatic fragrance; vigorous growth; int. by Georges Delbard SA, 2002

Guyscliffe F, op, 1985, Lindner, Richard; flowers orange-salmon, 12 petals, cupped, borne 3-5 per cluster, intense fragrance; foliage light green; prickles light brown; tall, densely branched growth; int. by Ludwigs Roses Pty. Ltd., 1984

Gwen Fagan S, lp, Poulsen; flowers rose pink in the heart, with outer petals much lighter, large, full, quartered, borne in clusters, first on cane ends, then all along them; recurrent; upright, then arching (2 m.) growth; int. in 1992

Gwen Marie F, rb, 1964, Robins; flowers dark red, center light cream, open, large, semi-dbl.; foliage soft; tall growth; [Dainty Bess × unknown]

Gwen Mayor HT, ab, Cocker, Ann G.; flowers large, very dbl., borne mostly singly or in large clusters, moderate fragrance; foliage medium size, dark green, glossy; some prickles; bushy, upright, medium (2½ ft.)growth; [Silver Jubilee × Remember Me]; int. by James Cocker & Sons, 1997

Gwen Nash Cl HT, pb, 1920, Clark, A.; flowers rich pink, center white, 4-5 in., semi-dbl., cupped; reliable repeat; foliage glaucous, wrinkled; vigorous, climbing growth; [Rosy Morn × Scorcher]; int. by NRS New South Wales

Gwen Swane S, mp, 1988, McGredy, Sam IV; flowers medium, dbl.; foliage small, medium green, matte; spreading growth; [MACbroey × Snow Carpet]; int. by McGredy Roses International, 1988

Gwendoline Collins HT, mr, 1937, Clark, A.; flowers cerise shaded cherry, large, dbl., globular; vigorous, bushy growth; int. by NRS Victoria

Gwent – See **Aspen**, S

Gwyneth Pol, ly, 1923, Woosman; flowers pale yellow, tinted lemon, changing to nearly white, open, semi-dbl., moderate musk fragrance; foliage light, leathery; bushy growth; [(Trier × Rayon d'Or) × (Gottfried Keller × Entente Cordiale sport)]; int. by Easlea

Gwyneth HT, ly, 1928, Chaplin Bros.; flowers canary-yellow, without shading; [Willowmere × Mrs Wemyss Quin]

Gwyneth Jones HT, op, 1925, McGredy; bud pointed; flowers brilliant carmine-orange, medium, semi-dbl., open; foliage light, leathery; vigorous, bushy growth; Gold Medal, NRS, 1925

Gwynne Carr HT, lp, 1924, Dickson, A.; flowers silvery pink shaded lilac-rose, dbl.

Gwynne Carr, Climbing Cl HT, lp, 1934, Easlea

Gyldenorange F, ob, 1985, Poulsen, S.; flowers golden orange, fades to light yellow, large, dbl., no fragrance; foliage medium size, medium green, semi-glossy; medium growth; [Poulsen's Yellow × seedling]; int. by Poulsen, 1952

Gympie F, pb, 1953, Ulrick, L.W.; flowers white and pink, very dbl., borne in clusters; foliage light green; vigorous, bushy growth; [Yvonne Rabier × Tip-Top]

Gympie Beauty F, dr, 1962, Dunstan; flowers deep red, borne in clusters; int. by Langbecker

Gypsy HT, or, 1972, Swim & Weeks; bud ovoid; flowers fiery orange-red, large, dbl., slight fragrance; foliage large, glossy, leathery; vigorous, upright, bushy growth; PP3163; [((Happiness × Chrysler Imperial) × El Capitan) × Comanche]; int. by C-P

Gypsy – See **Kiboh**, F

Gypsy Bride Gr, w

Gypsy Carnival – See **Kiboh**, F

Gypsy Curiosa HT, ob, deRuiter

Gypsy Dancer S, yb, 1994, Dickson, Patrick; bud small, pointed; flowers hand-painted light yellow with orange and light yellow reverse, medium, 20 petals, borne in clusters, slight citrus fragrance; foliage medium size, dark green, glossy; few prickles; medium (100-110 cm.), bushy growth; PP8900; [Sweet Magic × Little Artist]; int. by Bear Creek Gardens, 1994

Gypsy Fire Min, or, 1982, Moore, Ralph S.; flowers small, semi-dbl., borne in clusters, no fragrance; foliage small, medium green, semi-glossy to glossy; upright, bushy growth; [(*R. wichurana* × Carolyn Dean) × Fire Princess]; int. by Moore Min. Roses, 1981

Gypsy Fire F, rb, Williams, J.B.; flowers red and white striped; dark, glossy foliage; growth upright; int. by Hortico Inc, 2003

Gypsy Jewel Min, dp, 1975, Moore, Ralph S.; flowers deep rose-pink, 1½ in., 50 petals, high-centered; foliage dark, leathery; vigorous growth; PP3940; [Little Darling × Little Buckaroo]; int. by Gregory & Son

Gypsy Jubilee Gr, yb

Gypsy Lady Gr, mp; flowers dbl., cup and saucer; int. by Hortico, Inc., 1995

Gypsy Lantern S, rb, Williams, J.B.; flowers red, pink and white stripes.; int. by Hortico Inc, 2003

Gypsy Lass – See **Gipsy Lass**, HT

Gypsy Leonidas HT, ob, Meilland; flowers orange-red, cream yellow reverse, dbl., high-centered; florist rose; int. by Meilland Intl, 2002

Gypsy Minijet – See **Gypsy Sunblaze**, Min

Gypsy Moth F, op, 1970, Tantau, Math.; flowers salmon, 35 petals, exhibition, borne in clusters; foliage glossy; int. by Wheatcroft & Sons, 1968

Gypsy Queen HMult, mr, 1929, Moore, Ralph S.; flowers crimson, small, dbl., borne in clusters; vigorous, climbing growth; [Crimson Rambler × unknown]

Gypsy Song HT, pb

Gypsy Sunblaze Min, rb, 1994, Meilland, Alain A.; flowers red/yellow bicolor, medium, dbl., borne mostly singly, no fragrance; foliage small, light green, matte; some prickles; growth medium, bushy; [(Bonfire Night × Zambra) × Tapis Jaune]; int. by The Conard-Pyle Co., 1993

Gypsy's Wine Cup F, mr, 1968, Austin, David; flowers deep crimson, borne in trusses; foliage dark; low, bushy growth; [Highlight × unknown]

Gyrene S, mr, 1987, James, John; flowers bright, medium red, large, dbl.; repeat bloom; foliage medium size, medium green, matte, disease-resistant; upright, bushy, branching, vigorous, hardy growth; [Arctic Glow × ((((Pink Hat × *R. arkansana*) × *R. arkansana*) × ((Pink Hat × *R. arkansana*) × *R. arkansana*)) × *R. arkansana*)]; int. by Historical Roses, 1987

Gzlaty Dech HT, ob, 1936, Böhm, J.; bud long, pointed; flowers orange-yellow, brown, red and gold shadings, large, semi-dbl., cupped; foliage glossy, light; vigorous growth; [Admiration × Talisman]

H. Armytage Moore HT, dp, 1908, Dickson

H. C. Andersen F, dr, 1987, Olesen, Pernille & Mogens N.; flowers large, semi-dbl., cupped, borne in sprays of 1-25, slight fragrance; foliage medium size, dark green, glossy; bushy, tall growth; PP6265; [Royal Occasion × seedling]; int. by Poulsen Roser ApS, 1979

H. C. Valeton HT, yb, 1926, Verschuren; flowers golden yellow overspread with rose, large; strong stems; vigorous growth; [Golden Ophelia × Aspirant Marcel Rouyer]

H. C. Young HT, op, 1934, Austin & McAslan; bud pointed; flowers shrimp-pink, deepening to salmon, base yellow; strong stems; vigorous growth

H. Chaubert HT, op, 1928, Barbier; flowers coppery salmon, open, semi-dbl., borne in clusters; foliage rich green, glossy; bushy growth; [Mrs Aaron Ward × seedling]

H. D. M. Barton HT, dr, 1917, Dickson, A.; flowers deep velvety crimson, large, dbl.; bushy growth

H. E. Richardson HT, mr, 1913, Dickson, A.; flowers dazzling crimson, large, dbl., high-centered; vigorous growth; Gold Medal, NRS, 1912

H. F. Alexander LCl, ab, 1952, Wilber; flowers very large, 30-40 petals; foliage glossy; very long stems; tall, climbing growth; [Duquesa de Peñaranda × Ruth Alexander]; int. by Buckley Nursery Co.

H. F. Eilers HT, mr, 1914, Lambert, P.; bud very long; flowers carmine and reddish terra-cotta, very large, dbl., borne mostly solitary, moderate fragrance; [Gustav Grünerwald × Luise Lilia]

H. G. Hastings – See **Harry G. Hastings**, HT

H. P. Pinkerton HT, mr, 1915, Dickson, H.; flowers glossy scarlet with velvety crimson, large, full

H. Plantagenet Comte d'Anjou T, mp, 1892, Tesnier; flowers brilliant China rose, with deeper shadings

H. V. Machin HT, dr, 1914, Dickson, A.; flowers very dark scarlet-crimson, very large, dbl., globular; foliage glaucous beech-green; Gold Medal, NRS, 1912

H. V. Machin, Climbing Cl HT, dr, 1919, Dickson, H. (also H&S, 1922); bud large; flowers crimson red, very large, full; [sport of H. V. Machin]

H. Vessey Machin – See **H. V. Machin**, HT

Haaksbergen F, my, 1961, Buisman, G. A. H.; flowers bright yellow, medium, semi-dbl., borne in clusters; foliage dark; moderate growth; [Mrs Pierre S. duPont × King Boreas]

Habanera S, dr, 1976, Buck, Dr. Griffith J.; bud ovoid, pointed; flowers dark cardinal-red edged lighter, shallow-cupped, 4-4½ in., 33 petals, cupped; repeat bloom; foliage leathery; upright, bushy growth; [(Vera Dalton × Dornroschen) × ((World's Fair × Floradora) × Applejack)]; int. by Iowa State University, 1975

Habitat for Humanity – See **Passionate**, HT

Habitat for Humanity 2003 F, ob; PP14803; int. by J&P, 2003

Habitat for Humanity 2004 S, ly, J&P; bud pointed, ovoid; flowers large, graceful, light yellow, 4 in., 50 petals, strong spicy fragrance; foliage semi-glossy, dark green; growth to 4 ft.; hardy; PPAF; int. by Jackson & Perkins, 2004

Habitat for Humanity Rose – See **Habitat for Humanity 2004**, S

Hacienda – See **Firefighter**, HT

Hackeburg HMult, pb, 1912, Kiese; flowers soft lilac-pink, center white, 4 cm., full, borne in very large clusters, slight fragrance; nearly thornless; vigorous, climbing growth; possibly a Tausendschön seedling

Hada del Amor F, mp

Hadden's Variety S, m, 1948, Hilling; flowers rosy purple, single, borne several together; non-recurrent; foliage small, gray-green; [*R. willmottiae* × unknown]; int. by Hilling

Haddington HGal, m; flowers dark purple/pink, small to medium, semi-dbl.

Hadley HT, mr, 1914, Montgomery Co.; flowers rich crimson, well-formed, very large, dbl.; foliage rich green; vigorous growth; [(Liberty × Richmond) × Gen. MacArthur]; int. by A.N. Pierson

Hadley, Climbing Cl HT, mr, 1927, Heizmann; flowers dark crimson, large, dbl.; [sport of Hadley]

Hadley Elatior HT, mr, 1927, Teschendorff; [sport of Hadley]

Haendel – See **Handel**, LCl

Hafiz HT, mp; flowers eglantine rose-salmon, carmine reverse, dbl.; growth ti 70-80 cm.; int. by Sauvageot, 1970

Hafnia F, op, Olesen; bud broad based ovoid; flowers medium orange-pink, 2½ in., 50 petals, open cup, borne in small clusters, very slight fragrance; recurrent; foliage dark green, glossy; prickles few, 4 mm., hooked downward, greyed-red; bushy, upright (60-100 cm.) growth; PP15875; [Fredericksborg × seedling]; int. by Poulsen Roser, 2003

Hagenbecks Tierpark – See **Gites de France**, LCl

Hagoromo LCl, op, 1973, Suzuki, Seizo; bud ovoid; flowers silvery coral-pink, 10-11 cm., dbl., high-centered, borne singly or in small clusters, moderate fragrance; free, intermittent bloom; foliage dark green, glossy; vigorous, climbing growth; [(Aztec × unknown) × New Dawn seedling]; int. by Keisei Rose Nursery, 1970

Haidee S, pb, 1953, Skinner; flowers clear pink, center cream, large, dbl., cupped; non-recurrent; foliage small, dark; sometimes very prickly; stems wood red; growth to 6 ft.; hips large, dark red; [*R. laxa* × *R. spinosissima* seedling]

Haiku F, my, 1987, Christensen, Jack & Carruth, Tom; flowers medium, 38 petals, high-centered, borne usually singly or in sprays of 2-3; foliage medium size, dark green, glossy; prickles normal, light green to tan; upright, bushy, medium growth; no fruit; [Bridal Pink × Sunspray]; int. by Armstrong Nursery, 1986

Haileybury HP, mr, 1896, Paul, G.; flowers crimson cerise, large, very full, moderate fragrance

Hailstorm S, w, 1999, Coiner, Jim; flowers 1 in., semi-dbl., borne in large clusters; foliage small, medium green, dull; prickles moderate; upright, tall (3 ft.) growth; PP13676; [seedling × seedling]; int. by Coiner Nursery, 2000

Hair Ornament – See **Kamikazari**, Min

Haïsha HT, yb, 1947, Meilland, F.; flowers gold, edges suffused carmine, 6 in., 60 petals; foliage leathery, glossy, dark; upright growth; [Peace × Fantastique]

Haitian Belle LCl, mp

Hakata Kanoko Min, rb, 1999, Yamazaki, Kazuko; flowers medium red with white eye, 3¾ in., 5 petals, borne in large clusters; foliage small, medium green, disease-resistant; bushy, very compact (6-10 in.) growth; int. by Takii & Co., Ltd, 1995

Hakeburg – See **Hackeburg**, HMult

Hakkoda HT, pb, 1986, Kodoya, Y.; flowers white, pink petal edges, large, 40 petals, high-centered, intense fragrance; foliage medium green, semi-glossy; prickles broad, curved downward; bushy growth; [Lady X × Izayoi]; int. by Kogura Rose Nursery, 1983

Hakucho HT, w, Keisei; int. by Keisei Rose Nurseries, 1989

Hakuhoh HT, w, 1999, Hayashi, Shunzo; bud pale cream, turning white; flowers 6 in., 40 petals, high-centered; foliage medium green; growth to 4½ ft.; [White Prince × Bridal Robe]; int. in 1989

Hakusyu HT, w, 1999, Ohtsuki, Hironaka; flowers white, center coral pink, 5½-6 in., full; foliage medium size, medium green; some prickles; upright, bushy, medium (4½-5 ft.) growth; [Sizunomai × Hoshizukuyo]; Bronze Medal, Japan Rose Concours, 1998

Hakuun F, w, 1978, Poulsen, Niels D.; bud small; flowers creamy white, patio, 2 in., 15 petals, slight fragrance; foliage light green; low, compact, bushy growth; [seedling × (Pinocchio × Pinocchio)]; int. by Poulsen

Hakuya HT, w, Keihan; int. by Keihan Gardening, 1971

Halali F, dp, 1959, Tantau, Math.; flowers deep pink, large, semi-dbl., borne in clusters; foliage leathery, dense; vigorous (5-6 ft.), spreading growth; [Marchenland × Peace]; int. in 1956

Halarious HT, Clark, A.; int. in 1935

Halcyon Days – See **Rosenprofessor Sieber**, F

Haleakala Min, m, 1996, Mander, George; flowers velvety dark ruby-purple inside with yellow center, 1¾-2 in., dbl.; foliage medium size, dark green, glossy; some prickles; medium (40-50 cm.), bushy growth; [Rubies 'n' Pearls × June Laver]; int. by Select Roses, 1996

Haleigh Joy HT, dp, Williams, J.B.; flowers solid pink, moderate fragrance; growth to 4 ft.; int. by Hortico, Inc., 2005

Half Time HT, rb, 1976, Weeks; bud pointed; flowers cherry-red, reverse yellow, 3½-4 in., 40 petals, moderate tea fragrance; foliage dark; upright growth; PP4007; [((Fandango × Roundelay) × (Happiness × Tiffany)) × Peace]; int. by Weeks Wholesale Rose Growers

Halka HT, lp, 1988, Bracegirdle, Derek T.; flowers white blush pink, reverse white-silver, large, 30 petals, high-centered, borne in sprays, moderate damask fragrance; foliage medium size, medium green, glossy; prickles straight, medium, red; upright, medium growth; [Red Queen × Peace]

Hall of Flowers Min, my, 1991, Moore, Ralph S.; bud pointed; flowers lemon yellow, aging slightly lighter, medium, dbl., high-centered, borne singly, slight fragrance; foliage medium size, medium green, semi-glossy; upright, bushy, medium growth; [Avandel × Gold Badge]; int. by Sequoia Nursery, 1991

Hallandsåsen HRg; probably from Sweden

Halle HT, ob, Fryer; flowers bright orange, gold reverse, large, dbl., borne both singly and in clusters, moderate fragrance; very free flowering; foliage resistant, dark green; growth medium; int. by Fryer's Roses, 2002

Hallelujah – See **Alleluia**, HT

Hallelujah! – See **Olbrich's Merry Red**, S

Halley's Comet F, mr, 1986, Rearsby Roses, Ltd.; flowers medium, 20 petals; foliage medium size, medium green, semi-glossy; [sport of Tip Top]

Hallmark HT, mr, 1966, Morey, Dennison H., Jr.; bud ovoid; flowers large, 28 petals, cupped, moderate fragrance; foliage glossy; PP2645; [Independence × Chrysler Imperial]; int. by J&P

Halloween HT, yb, 1969, Howard, A.P.; flowers deep yellow, tipped scarlet, large, 65 petals, intense fragrance; foliage glossy, dark, leathery; vigorous, upright growth; PP2523; [(Peace × Fred Howard) × seedling]; int. by Great Western Rose Co., 1962

Halloween HT, pb; int. by Carlton Rose Nurseries, 2002

Halo HT, w, 1957, Lens; bud ovoid, seafoam-green; flowers 4½-5 in., 25 petals, high-centered, moderate fragrance; foliage leathery; vigorous, upright growth; PP1530; [Lady Sylvia × (Virgo × White Briarcliff)]; int. by J&P, 1956

Halo Dolly Min, pb, 1992, Moore, Ralph S.; flowers

bicolor, reddish outside, pink inside with reddish-lavender, medium, semi-dbl., no fragrance; foliage medium size, medium green, semi-glossy; few prickles; medium (30-45 cm.), upright, bushy, rounded growth; [(Anytime × unknown) × (Anytime × Angel Face)]; int. by Sequoia Nursery, 1993

Halo Fire Min, rb, 1995, Moore, Ralph S.; flowers bright orange-red with darker red halo, 1½-2½ in., 8-10 petals, borne in small clusters; foliage small, medium green, matte; medium (35-45 cm.), upright, bushy growth; [Orangeade × seedling]; int. by Sequoia Nursery, 1996

Halo Glory Min, pb, 2004, Moore, Ralph S.; flowers light pink with darker pink to lavender base, reverse light pink to white, 1½-2 in., single, borne in small clusters, no fragrance; foliage medium size, medium green, semi-glossy; prickles small, straight, light green, few; growth compact, medium (1 ft.); containers, specimen, border; [un-named seedling (Gold Badge × (Anytime × Angel Face) × unknown]; int. by Sequoia Nurs., 2004

Halo Gold Min, yb, Ralph Moore; flowers single; int. by Sequoia Nursery, 2005

Halo Karol Min, pb, 1998, Moore, Ralph S.; flowers dark pink, lavendar base creates halo effect, 1-1½ in., 10 petals, borne singly, no fragrance; foliage medium size, medium green, semi-glossy; few prickles; bushy, compact growth; [(Anytime × Angel Face) × (Anytime × Angel Face)]; int. by Sequoia Nursery, 1998

Halo Rainbow Min, pb, 1994, Moore, Ralph S.; flowers pink edging with center of each petal creamy white and base pink, a picotee halo, large, 5 petals, borne in small clusters; foliage medium size, medium green, semi-glossy; no prickles; medium (28-35 cm.), bushy, spreading growth; [seedling × Make Believe]; int. by Sequoia Nursery, 1995

Halo Star Min, ob, 1992, Moore, Ralph S.; flowers reddish on outside, orange to pink on inside, reddish-lavender at base, medium, single, no fragrance; foliage small, medium green, matte; medium (35-40 cm.), upright, bushy growth; [(Anytime × Angel Face) × (Anytime × Angel Face)]; int. by Sequoia Nursery, 1993

Halo Sunrise Min, yb, Moore, Ralph; flowers bright yellow with a red halo at base of petals, 1-1½ in., 8-10 petals; fast repeat; growth to 12-18 in.; int. by Sequoia, 1997

Halo Sunset Min, ob, 2000, Moore, Ralph S.; flowers orange blend with reddish-pink center, large, 8-10 petals, borne in small clusters; foliage medium size, medium green, semi-glossy; few prickles; upright, bushy, medium (15-18 in.) growth; [seedling × Show 'n' Tell]; int. by Sequoia Nursery, 2000

Halo Sweetie Min, pb, 2002, Moore, Ralph S.; flowers single, borne in small clusters, no fragrance; foliage small, light green, matte; growth compact, medium (12-15 in.); containers, garden decorative, exhibition; [seedling × Halo Rainbow]; int. by Sequoia Nursery, 2002

Halo Today Min, op, 1994, Moore, Ralph S.; flowers have distinct pink/lavender area at base of each petal, large, 5-8 petals, no fragrance; foliage medium size, medium green, semi-glossy; no prickles; low (16-18 in.), upright, bushy growth; [(Anytime × Gold Badge) × (Anytime × Lavender Jewel)]; int. by Sequoia Nursery, 1994

Hambleden F, pb, 2000, Brown, Ted; flowers medium pink fading to yellow center, slightly deeper pink reverse, frilled outer, 4½ in., 8-14 petals, borne in small clusters, slight fragrance; foliage large, dark green, semi-glossy; prickles moderate; upright, medium (4½ ft.) growth; [Esprit × Night Light]

Hamburg S, dr, 1935, Kordes; bud pointed; flowers glowing crimson, very large, semi-dbl., borne in clusters; recurrent bloom; foliage large, leathery, glossy; vigorous growth; [Eva × Daily Mail Scented Rose]

Hamburg Girl – See **Hamburger Deern**, HT

Hamburger Deern HT, op, 2006; flowers flower salmon, reverse creamy yellow, 11 cm., full, high-centered, borne mostly solitary, moderate spicy fragrance; recurrent; foliage large, dark green, very glossy; vigorous, upright, medium growth; int. by W. Kordes' Söhne, 1997

Hamburger Phoenix HKor, mr, 1956, Kordes; bud long, pointed, bronze-black; flowers blood red, 7-8 cm., borne in small clusters; repeat bloom; foliage dark, glossy; vigorous, climbing or trailer growth; hips large, orange; [*R.* × *kordesii* × seedling]

Hamburger Phönix – See **Hamburger Phoenix**, HKor

Hamburg's Love F, dy, 1976, Timmerman's Roses; flowers 3 in., 28 petals, intense fragrance; foliage glossy; compact growth; [Fragrant Cloud × Manx Queen]; int. in 1974

Hamish HT, yb, 1980, Simpson, J.W.; bud ovoid; flowers 50 petals, high-centered; foliage medium green; prickles dark brown; vigorous, medium, upright to bushy growth; [Fairy Dancers × Diamond Jubilee]

Hamlet F, mr, Harkness; flowers rosy red to currant red, dbl., rosette, borne in clusters, moderate fragrance; foliage dark green, glossy, resistant; growth to 70-80 cm.; int. in 1999

Hammerberg S, m

Hammershus F, w, Poulsen; flowers white with light apricot in the heart, 8-10 cm., full, no fragrance; foliage dark green, glossy; bushy, medium (60-100 cm.) growth; int. by Poulsen Roser, 2001

Hampshire S, mr, Kordes; flowers bright scarlet with yellow stamens, single, borne in clusters, no fragrance; recurrent; low, spreading, groundcover (1 × 2 ft.) growth; int. in 1989

Hampshire – See **Knirps**, F

Hampton MinFl, w, Poulsen; flowers white, 8-10 cm., dbl., slight wild rose fragrance; foliage dark; growth broad, bushy, 40-60 cm.; PP10729; int. by Poulsen Roser, 1996

Hampton Palace – See **Hampton**, MinFl

Hana-Busa F, or, 1986, Suzuki, Seizo; bud ovoid; flowers 18 petals, flat, borne 6-10 per cluster; prickles straight; bushy growth; [Sarabande × (Rumba × Olympic Torch)]; int. by Keisei Rose Nursery, 1981

Hana-Gasumi F, w, 1986, Suzuki, Seizo; flowers soft white, aging pink, 13 petals, flat, borne 6-12 per cluster, moderate fragrance; foliage dark, semi-glossy; prickles small, hooked, slanted downward; bushy growth; [Europeana × (Myo-joh × Fidélio)]; int. by Keisei Rose Nursery, 1985

Hana-Gasumi, Climbing Cl F, w, Itamu; [sport of Hana-Gasumi]; int. by Keihan Gardening, after 1985

Hana-Kurenai HT, pb, 1986, Ohata, Hatsuo; bud ovoid; flowers light pink, flushed yellow, reverse deeper, 33 petals, high-centered, borne singly and in small clusters, slight fragrance; foliage medium size, medium green, glossy; prickles few, sickle-shaped; vigorous, upright growth; [Big Red × Star Queen]; int. in 1980

Hanabi – See **Fourth of July**, LCl

Hanae Mory HT, Delbard, Georges; int. in 1990

Hanagasa F, or, 1978, Suzuki, Seizo; bud globular; flowers vermilion, 4-4½ in., 23 petals, cupped; foliage large, light green; vigorous growth; [(Hawaii × seedling) × Miss Ireland]; int. by Keisei Rose Nursery, 1979

Hanaguruma HT, yb, 1977, Teranishi, K.; bud globular; flowers 6½-7 in., 58 petals, high-centered, slight fragrance; foliage light green; upright growth; [Kordes' Perfecta × (Kordes' Perfecta × American Heritage)]; int. by Itami Bara-en, 1974

Hanakagari HT, ob, Keisei; int. by Keisei Rose Nurseries, 1997

Hanakago F, or, 1973, Suzuki, Seizo; bud ovoid; flowers deep salmon-vermilion, medium, dbl., cupped, moderate fragrance; foliage glossy, dark; vigorous, bushy growth; [(Sarabande × unknown) × Rondo seedling]; int. by Keisei Rose Nursery, 1972

Hanami-Gawa Cl Min, op, 1986, Suzuki, Seizo; flowers soft salmon-pink, shaded orange, small, 23 petals, borne 6-10 per cluster, moderate fragrance; foliage dark, semi-glossy; prickles small, curved, slanted downward; vigorous, very bushy growth; [seedling × Petite Folie]; int. by Keisei Rose Nursery, 1986

Hanamori F, rb, 1977, Teranishi, K.; bud circular; flowers 2½ in., 20-25 petals, high-centered; foliage glossy, dark; bushy growth; [(Tropicana × Karl Herbst) × Lydia]; int. by Itami Bara-en

Hanatirusato Min, dp, 1999, Yamazaki, Kazuko; flowers brilliant rose, 1½ in., 70 petals, flat, borne 2-5 per cluster; foliage medium size, medium green; vigorous, bushy, compact (8 in.) growth; [seedling × Red Minimo]; int. by Takii & Co., Ltd., 1996

Hanayome HT, lp, Keihan; int. in 1970

Hanayoshino Min, mp; int. in 2001

Hanayuzen Min, dy, 1999, Yamazaki, Kzauko; flowers deep golden yellow, sometimes flushed orange, 1½ in., 45 petals, high-centered; foliage medium size, dark green; very vigorous, upright, bush, compact (12 in.) growth; [Himetatibana × Hanahotaru]; int. by Takii & Co., Ltd., 1996

Hand in Hand MinFl, or, Harkness; flowers small, dbl., borne in clusters, slight fragrance; free-flowering; bushy, shrubby (18 in.) growth; int. in 1994

Händel – See **Handel**, LCl

Handel LCl, rb, 1965, McGredy, Sam IV; flowers cream edged red, large, 22-30 petals, slight honey fragrance; recurrent bloom, on both old and new wood; foliage glossy, olive-green; climbing growth; [Columbine × Gruss an Heidelberg]; int. by McGredy; Gold Medal, Portland, 1975

Handel's Largo – See **Largo d'Haendel**, HT

Handout – See **Tranquility**, HT

Handsom Red HT, mr, 1954, Brownell; flowers spectrum-red, 4-5 in., 45 petals, high-centered, moderate fragrance; upright, bushy growth; [(Pink Princess × Mirandy) × Queen o' the Lakes]

Handy Andy HT, ab, 1965, McGredy, Sam IV; flowers apricot edged pink, 4 in.; free growth; [Kordes' Perfecta × Piccadilly]; int. by Geest Industries

Hanib – See **Cecilia 89**, F

Hanini Min, rb, 1995, Dykstra, Dr. A. Michael; flowers burgundy red stripes serrated by reddish-pink, white throat, 2 in., 5 petals, moderate fruity fragrance; foliage medium size, medium green, semi-glossy; medium (2 ft.), spreading (30in.) growth; PPRR; [Sarabande × Hurdy Gurdy]; int. by Justice Miniature Roses, 1995

Hanka HT, ly; flowers creamy yellow, very large, dbl.

Hanky Panky Min, ob, 1991, Bennett, Dee; flowers range from orange to golden peach as they open, large, full, borne mostly singly, moderate fruity fragrance; foliage small, medium green, semi-glossy, disease-resistant; some prickles; medium (40-60 cm.), bushy, spreading growth; [Deep Purple × Party Girl]; int. by Tiny Petals Nursery, 1992

Hanky Panky – See **City of Carlsbad**, F

Hannah Brown Min, dp, 2004, Brown, Ted; flowers deep pink, reverse deep pink, 1½ in., dbl., borne mostly solitary, moderate fragrance; foliage medium size, dark green, matte; prickles small, pointed; growth upright, medium (2 ft.); exhibition; garden decorative; [Luis Desamero × Shadow Dancer]; int. in 2005

Hannah Gordon F, pb, 1984, Kordes, W.; flowers white with deep pink to red petal edges, large, 20-25 petals, shallow cup to flat, borne singly and in clusters, slight fragrance; recurrent; foliage large, medium green, semi-glossy; strong, upright, tall, bushy growth; [seedling × Bordure]; int. by John Mattock, Ltd., 1983

Hannah Hansen HWich, m, Nobbs; int. in 1997

Hannah Hauxwell F, op, 1991, Battersby Roses; flowers deep salmon, small, full, slight fragrance; foliage small, medium green, matte; bushy growth; [seedling × seedling]

Hannah Rose Timings HT, dp, 2004, Poole, Lionel; flowers deep pink, reverse deep pink, 4½-5 in., full, borne mostly solitary; foliage medium size, dark green, semi-glossy; prickles medium, hooked; growth upright, bushy, medium (3 ft.); garden, bedding, borders; [Unnamed pink blend Seedling (Hazel Rose × Cardiff Bay) × Fiona Ivin]; int. in 2005

Hannah Ruby Min, rb, 2003, Zlesak, David C.; flowers dark red, reverse white blending to red edges, 1½ in., semi-dbl., borne in large clusters; foliage medium size, dark green, Semi-glossy; prickles moderate; growth spreading, medium; [MORIavmag × polyantha seedling]; int. by David C. Zlesak, 2004

Hanne HT, mr, 1959, Soenderhousen; flowers scarlet-crimson, medium to large, dbl., high-centered; foliage leathery; upright growth; [Ena Harkness × Peace]; int. by Hoersholm Nursery

Hanne Dänomik HT, mr; flowers large, dbl.

Hanneli Rupert HT, ob, Kordes; flowers deep coral-orange with cream-yellow reverse, dbl., high-centered, borne mostly singly; recurrent; straight stems; lush (5-6 ft.) growth; int. in 1995

Hannes – See **Rose Hannes**, HT

Hannover – See **Messestadt Hannover**, F

Hannover's Weisse S, w, Noack, Werner; flowers single; groundcover; spreading growth; int. by Noack Rosen, 1997

Hans HT, w, 1970, IARI; flowers open, large, semi-dbl.; foliage glossy, light; vigorous, upright growth; [Message × Virgo]; int. by Div. of Vegetable Crops & Flori.

Hans Berger HT, mr, Berger, W.; flowers carmine-red, large, dbl.; int. in 1958

Hans Billert HT, mr, 1928, Billert; flowers brilliant red, very dbl.; [Laurent Carle × Richmond]; int. by Teschendorff

Hans Christian Andersen – See **H. C. Andersen**, F

Hans Erni F, op, Meilland; bud small, pointed; flowers salmon-orange to salmon-pink, moderate fragrance; rounded (2 ft.) growth; int. in 1992

Hans Haubold HT, mp, 1942, Vogel, M.; flowers large, dbl.

Hans Mackart HP, rb, 1884, Verdier, E.; flowers bright deep geranium red, outer petals tinted carmine purple, dbl.

Hans Memling HT, op, Williams, J.B.; flowers salmon orange, dbl., moderate fragrance; foliage dark green; int. by Hortico, 2005

Hans Rathgeb HT, dp, Huber; flowers intense wine red, dbl.; int. in 2005

Hans Rosenthal – See **Révolution Française**, HT

Hans Schmid HWich, dp, 1934, Vogel, M.; flowers deep pink, rather well-formed to medium, 4-5 cm., dbl., globular, borne in medium clusters; foliage large; vigorous, climbing growth; [Fragezeichen × American Pillar]; int. by P. Lambert & Heinemann

Hansa HRg, mr, 1905, Schaum & Van Tol; flowers mauvy-red, large, dbl., intense clove-rose fragrance; recurrent bloom; short, weak stems; vigorous growth; hips large, red; hardy

Hansa-Park S, m, Kordes; flowers lavender-pink, 3-4 in., dbl., slight fragrance; free-flowering; vigorous (5-7 ft.) growth; int. in 1994

Hansaland HRg, dr, 2006; flowers bright, deep scarlet with yellow stamens, 7 cm., semi-dbl., cupped, borne singly and in small clusters; foliage reddish when young, turning light green, semi-glossy, rounded; bushy, upright (6 ft.) growth; int. by W. Kordes' Söhne, 1993

Hanseat S, mp, 1961, Tantau, Math.; flowers rose-pink, center lighter, medium, 5 petals, cupped; vigorous (6 ft.) growth

Hansen's Red Hedge S, mr

Hansestadt Bremen F, op, 1959, Kordes, R.; bud ovoid, crimson; flowers deep salmon and reddish-pink, large, 47 petals, borne in clusters (up to 10), moderate fragrance; foliage leathery; very vigorous, bushy growth; [Ama × Fanal]; int. in 1958

Hansestadt Lübeck F, mr, 1965, Kordes, R.; flowers large, dbl., slight fragrance; foliage dark; vigorous, tall growth; int. by McGredy

Hansette S, mr, 1938, Wright, Percy H.; flowers red, semi-dbl.; non-recurrent; [Hansa × *R. rubrifolia*]

Hanza Park – See **Hansa-Park**, S

Hap Renshaw Min, ab, 1991, Rennie, Bruce F.; flowers small, dbl., borne mostly singly, slight fragrance; foliage small, dark green, semi-glossy; upright growth; [Party Girl × Lavonde]; int. by Rennie Roses International, 1991

Happenstance HBc, ly, 1950, Buss; flowers pale yellow, small, short-lived, single; foliage small, dark green, glossy; prickles thorns large, hooked; growth low, prostrate ground cover; up to 15 ft.; [sport of Mermaid]

Happiness HT, mr, 1954, Meilland, F.; bud long, pointed; flowers 5-6 in., 38 petals, high-centered; upright, vigorous growth; [(Rome Glory × Tassin) × (Charles P. Kilham × (Charles P. Kilham × Capucine Chambard))]; int. by URS, 1949

Happiness, Climbing Cl HT, mr, 1954, Meilland, F.; int. by URS

Happy Pol, mr, 1957, deRuiter; flowers currant-red, very small, semi-dbl., borne in large trusses; foliage dark, glossy; vigorous, compact (12-15 in.) growth; [Robin Hood × Katharina Zeimet seedling]; int. by Gregory, 1954

Happy, Climbing Cl Pol, mr, 2000, Gordon, Barbara A. K.; flowers medium currant-red, 1-1¼ in., dbl., borne in large clusters, no fragrance; prolific; foliage medium size, medium to dark green, glossy; numerous prickles; vigorous, upright, tall (10-12 ft.) growth; [sport of Happy]; an earlier, non-registered, apparently identical, sport was introduced in Europe before the mid-1990's

Happy Anniversary – See **Heureux Anniversaire**, Gr

Happy Anniversary – See **Strawberry Ice**, F

Happy Anniversary HT, ob, Catt, Graeme Charles; flowers deep orange, full, exhibition, borne mostly singly, moderate fragrance; stems long, upright; [sport of Kardinal]; int. in 2000

Happy Anniversary F, pb, Chessum; flowers salmon pink, borne in clusters, moderate fragrance; recurrent; tall (1 m.) growth; int. in 2001

Happy Birthday HT, dp, 1964, Howard, P.J.; bud ovoid; flowers deep rose, large, 25 petals, high-centered, intense fragrance; foliage leathery; vigorous, upright growth; PP2281; [Peace × The Doctor]

Happy Birthday MinFl, w; flowers cream, borne in flushes, slight fragrance; good repeat; foliage light green, glossy; growth to 1-2 ft.; int. in 1997

Happy Butt HT, ab, 1995, Carlson, Wm.; flowers open apricot, 7+ cm., very full, borne mostly singly, moderate fragrance; foliage medium-size, medium green, semi-glossy; some prickles; upright, tall growth; [Nantucket × Medallion]

Happy Chappy S, yb; flowers medium size, semi-dbl.; continuous; int. by Jackson & Perkins, 2007

Happy Child S, my, 1994, Austin, David; flowers bright yellow, 3-3½ in., very dbl., borne in small clusters; foliage medium size, medium green, glossy; some prickles; medium (39 in.), bushy growth; PP9007; [seedling × Hero]; int. by David Austin Roses, Ltd., 1993

Happy Day HT, rb, 1980, Simpson, J.W.; bud pointed; flowers 30 petals, high-centered, borne singly, moderate fragrance; recurrent; foliage large, dark, semi-glossy; prickles brown; strong, upright, medium growth; [First Prize × Gypsy Moth]

Happy Day S, dp, Harkness; flowers 70 petals, cupped, old-fashioned; profuse; growth compact, bushy (2½ × 2½ ft.); PPAF; int. by Heirloom, 2004

Happy Days HT, or, 1932, Amling, M.C.; bud pointed; flowers geranium-red, open, large, dbl.; foliage dark; long stems; very vigorous growth; RULED EXTINCT 4/87; [sport of Briarcliff]; int. by Amling Bros.

Happy Days HT, dr, 1962, Herholdt, J.A.; bud pointed; flowers oxblood-red, 3-3½ in., dbl., high-centered; long stems; vigorous growth; RULED EXTINCT 4/87; [Exciting × Grand Gala]; int. by Herholdt's Nursery

Happy Days HT, pb, 1988, McGredy, Sam IV; flowers medium, dbl.; foliage medium size, medium green, matte; bushy growth; [(Unnamed Poulsen seedling × Picasso) × Paradise]; int. by McGredy Roses International, 1988

Happy Daze S, mp, Eagle; int. in 1995

Happy Event F, pb, 1964, Dickson, Patrick; flowers light chrome-yellow, flushed rose-opal, 3 in., 12 petals, borne in clusters; foliage glossy; growth moderate; [(Karl Herbst × Masquerade) × Rose Gaujard]; int. by A. Dickson

Happy Ever After F, pb, 1999, Dickson, Colin; flowers pale pink/lemon, revers pale pink, 2 in., semi-dbl., borne in large clusters; foliage medium size, light green, semi-glossy; prickles moderate; bushy (33 in.) growth; [The Fairy × seedling]; int. by Dickson Nurseries, Ltd., 1997

Happy Face Min, dp, 1991, Saville, F. Harmon; bud ovoid; flowers clear rosy pink, medium, 35-40 petals, cupped, borne usually singly or in sprays of 3-5, no fragrance; foliage medium size, dark green, glossy; bushy, medium, compact growth; [(Sheri Anne × Rise 'n' Shine) × Mountie]; int. by Nor'East Min. Roses, 1991

Happy Go Lucky Min, ob, 1987, Saville, F. Harmon; flowers brilliant orange-yellow blend, small, 17-24 petals, high-centered, borne usually singly, slight sweet fragrance; foliage small, dark green, semi-glossy; prickles long, thin pointed; bushy, medium growth; no fruit; PP6506; [Cheers × (Sheri Anne × (Yellow Jewel × Tamango))]; int. by Nor'East Min. Roses

Happy Go Lucky Gr, dr, 1999, Schuurman, Frank B.; flowers dark red, reverse medium red, 3 in., dbl., borne in large clusters; foliage medium size, medium green, semi-glossy; prickles moderate; spreading, medium (30-36 in.) growth; [Happy Days × Only Love]; int. by Franko Roses New Zealand, Ltd., 1998

Happy Hour Min, mr, 1984, Saville, F. Harmon; flowers bright medium red, yellow eye, small, 20 petals, moderate fragrance; foliage small, dark, glossy; bushy, spreading growth; PP5449; [(Tamango × Yellow Jewel) × Zinger]; int. by Nor'East Min. Roses, 1983

Happy Hour F, yb, Delbard; flowers blending of bright yellow, orange and red splashes; growth tall; int. by Bell Roses, 2003

Happy Hour HT, mr, Spek; flowers velvet red, 4 in., 35-40 petals, high-centered, borne mostly singly; recurrent; prickles moderate; stems long; florist rose; int. by Jan Spek Rozen, 2004

Happy Memories S, pb, 2006, Beales, Amanda; flowers small, full, borne in large clusters; foliage small, dark green, glossy; few prickles; growth bushy, short (60 cm.); containers, garden decoration; [Centenaire de Lourdes × Bonica]; flowers blended cherry red, pink and white; int. by Peter Beales Roses, 2001

Happy Minijet Min, mr, Meilland

Happy Red F, or, 1960, Leenders, J.; flowers bright brick-red, single, borne in clusters; foliage glossy; moderate growth; [Red Favorite × Cocorico]

Happy Retirement F, lp, 2000, Rosen Tantau; flowers soft pink, 5 in., dbl., borne in small clusters, slight fragrance; foliage large, medium green, glossy; prickles moderate; bushy, tall (3 ft.) growth; [seedling × seedling]; int. by Eurosa, 2000

Happy Talk F, mr, 1974, Weeks; flowers cherry-red, small, dbl., slight fragrance; foliage glossy, dark; vigorous, upright, bushy growth; PP3559; [Escort × Orange Garnet]; int. by O. L. Weeks, 1973

Happy Thought Min, op, 1978, Moore, Ralph S.; bud pointed; flowers pink blended with coral and yellow, 40 petals; foliage small, glossy; vigorous, bushy growth; PP4479; [(*R. wichurana* × Floradora) × Sheri Anne]; int. by Sequoia Nursery

Happy Thoughts Min, ob, 2006, White, Wendy R.; flowers dark yellow w/orange edges, reverse medium yellow, 2 in., semi-dbl., borne mostly solitary, slight fragrance; foliage medium size, dark green, matte, disease-resistant; prickles angled and curved downward, tan-brown, few; growth compact, short (10-12 in.); decorative garden perennial; [(Zorina × Baby Katie) × (June Laver × New Zealand)]; int. by Nor'East Miniature Roses, 2007

Happy Time Cl Min, rb, 1975, Moore, Ralph S.; bud short, pointed; flowers yellow overlaid red, 1 in., 35 petals, slight fragrance; foliage small, glossy, leathery; climbing growth; [(*R. wichurana* × Floradora) × (Golden Glow × Zee)]; int. by Sequoia Nursery, 1974

Happy Times MinFl, mp, Chessum, Paul; growth to 18 in.; int. by Paul Chessum Roses, 1995

Happy Trails Min, pb, 1992, Warriner, William A. & Zary, Keith W.; flowers pink with cream center, medium, very dbl., borne in small clusters, no fragrance; foliage small, medium to dark green, glossy; some prickles; low (20-30 cm.), groundcover, spreading 60-90 cm.across. growth; PP8719; [Immensee × Roller Coaster]; int. by Bear Creek Gardens, 1993

Happy Wanderer F, mr, 1972, McGredy, Sam IV; flowers scarlet, medium, slight fragrance; free-flowering; growth medium; [seedling × Marlene]; int. by McGredy, 1974

Happy Wanderer – See **Happy, Climbing**, Cl Pol

Happy Wedding Bells HT, w, 1970, Morey, Dr. Dennison; bud long, pointed; flowers large, 52 petals, high-centered, moderate spicy fragrance; foliage leathery; vigorous, upright growth; [White Swan × Virgo]; int. by Country Garden Nursery, 1966

Har Tabor HT, pb, Fischel; flowers dbl.; int. in 1972

Harbinger LCl, lp, 1923, Clark, A.; bud pointed; flowers soft pink, 12 cm., single; foliage light; vigorous, climbing growth; hybrid gigantea; int. by Hackett

Hardii – See **Hulthemia hardii**

Hardy Cherokee – See ***R. spinosissima altaica*** (Bean)

Hardy Musk Rose – See ***R. helenae*** (Rehder & Wilson)

Hardy Ottawa S, m; int. by Quebec Multiplants, 2003

Harewood – See **Satina**, S

Harfang des Neiges HRg, w; int. by Au Jardin de Jean-Pierre

Harglisser (withdrawn) – See **Sir Lancelot**, F

Haris HSpn, mp, Erskine; flowers semi-dbl. to dbl., cupped; non-remontant; growth tall grower; very hardy; [Harison's Yellow × unknown]; int. by Sheila Holmes

Harisonii – See **Harison's Yellow**, HFt

Harisonii No. 1 HFt, ly, before 1846, from England; flowers pale golden yellow, tinged with copper, medium, dbl., cupped

Harisonii No. 2 HFt, yb, before 1848; flowers buff, center reddish-salmon, medium, dbl., cupped

Harison's Hardy HSpn, ly, 1943, Wright, Percy H.; flowers cream, center tinted yellow, semi-dbl.; non-recurrent; very hardy; [*R. spinosissima altaica* × Harison's Yellow]

Harison's Lemon HSpn, ly, 1929, Hamblin; flowers clear lemon-yellow, semi-dbl., moderate fragrance; non-recurrent; bushy (5 ft.) growth; [Harison's Yellow × unknown]

Harison's Profuse HSpn; [Harison's Yellow × unknown]

Harison's Salmon HSpn, op, 1929, Hamblin; flowers salmon, medium, semi-dbl., globular, moderate fragrance; non-recurrent; foliage small, rich green; [Harison's Yellow × unknown]; sometimes classed as HFt

Harison's Yellow HFt, dy, about 1824, Harison; flowers bright yellow, yellow stamens, 2 in., semi-dbl., moderate fragrance; non-recurrent; growth upright (6 × 3 ft.); hips almost black, (28); [probably Persian Yellow × *R. spinosissima*]; int. about 1830

Harkness Marigold F, ob, 1986, Harkness, R., & Co., Ltd.; flowers well-formed, 35 petals, borne in clusters; foliage medium size, medium green, semi-glossy; upright growth; [Judy Garland × Anne Harkness]

Harlekijn F, yb

Harlekin LCl, pb, 2006; flowers cream white with clear red edging, 9 cm., full, borne in small clusters; foliage dark green, glossy; growth bushy, tall (250 cm.); int. by W. Kordes' Söhne, 1986

Harlekin – See **Harlequin**, HT

Harlequin HWich, pb, 1935, Cant, F.; flowers half pale pink and half dark red, small, borne in clusters; very vigorous, climbing growth; RULED EXTINCT 12/83; [sport of Excelsa]

Harlequin – See **Miss Liberté**, HT

Harlequin HT, m, 1998, Kordes, W.; flowers lavendar pink, white reverse, 4 in., full, borne mostly singly, slight fragrance; foliage medium size, dark green, glossy; few prickles; bushy, low (3 ft.) growth; PP11271; [Prima Ballerina × Peace]; int. by Bear Creek Gardens, 1998

Harlew F, Petersen, V.; int. in 1973

Harley – See **Paganini**, HMsk

Harlow HT, op, 1969, Cocker; flowers salmon, large, 29 petals; foliage glossy; [Fragrant Cloud × Melrose]

Harlow Carr F, mp, Kirkham, Gordon Wilson; int. in 1997

Harlow Carr S, mp, 2004; flowers very full, borne in small clusters, intense fragrance; foliage medium size, medium green, semi-glossy; prickles medium, concave curved inward; growth bushy, vigorous, branching, medium (125 cm.); garden decorative; [seedling (white English-type shrub) × Ausman]; int. by David Austin Roses, Ltd., 2004

Harm Saville MinFl, dr, 2004, Carruth, Tom & Bedard, Christian; flowers very deep red, 5-6 cm., dbl., borne mostly solitary; foliage medium size, dark green, semi-glossy; prickles small, almost straight; growth bushy, medium (60 to 80 cm.; garden decoration; [Santa Claus × Opening Night]; int. by Greenheart Farms, 2005; Award of Excellence, ARS, 2005

Harman F, Adam, M.; int. in 1991

Harman Inermis F, dp, Adam; relatively thornless; int. in 1991

Harmonia – See **Harmonia Sub Rosa**, HT

Harmonia Sub Rosa HT, pb, Dorieux; int. by Roseraies Dorieux, 2001

Harmonie S, pb, 1954, Kordes; bud ovoid, light red; flowers pink bicolor, large, borne in clusters; foliage leathery; very vigorous, upright growth; RULED EXTINCT 5/80; [*R. rubiginosa* hybrid × Peace]

Harmonie HT, op, 1980, Kordes, W.; bud long, pointed; flowers deep salmon, 20 petals, high-centered, intense fragrance; foliage slightly glossy; vigorous, upright, bushy growth; [Fragrant Cloud × Uwe Seeler]; int. by W. Kordes, 1981; Gold Medal, Baden-Baden, 1981

Harmonie HT, op, Kriloff

Harmonie 92 HT, ab, Vidal; int. in 1992

Harmonium Gr, op, Drummond; int. by Greenbelt Farm, 1993

Harmony Cl HP, ab, 1933, Nicolas; flowers apricot-pink, very large, semi-dbl., high-centered; foliage leathery, dark; strong stems; very vigorous, climbing growth; [Rosella × Rosella]; int. by C-P

Harmony – See **Harmonie**, HT

Harmony Min, lp, Olesen; flowers light pink, medium, dbl., no fragrance; foliage dark; growth bushy, 20-40 cm.; int. by Poulsen Roser, 1996

Harmony Parade – See **Harmony**, Min

Harold Ickes – See **Crepe Myrtle**, F

Harold Macmillan F, or, 1988, Harkness, R., & Co., Ltd.; flowers medium, 18 petals, cupped, borne in sprays of 3-7; foliage medium size, medium green, glossy, abundant; prickles broad, medium, green; bushy, medium growth; hips rounded, medium size, green; [Avocet × Remember Me]; int. by R. Harkness & Co., Ltd., 1989

Harper Adams F, my; flowers golden yellow with color that holds well, medium, very double, borne evenly in clusters of several together, moderate fragrance; begins early and continues through season; foliage bright green and dense, disease-resistant; growth compact, medium (4 × 2 ft.); int. by Fryers, 2002

Harpippin LCl, ob, 1984, Harkness; flowers pale salmon-red, yellow reverse, 22 petals, borne singly; foliage medium size, semi-glossy; upright (to 7 ft.) growth; [sport of Royal Dane]

Harriet Cl HT, my, 1931, Moore, Ralph S.; flowers golden yellow, edged paler, dbl.; recurrent bloom; foliage bronze; vigorous, climbing (12-15 ft.) growth; [sport of Golden Ophelia]

Harriet A. Easlea HT, rb, 1922, McGredy; flowers bright carmine, reverse golden yellow, dbl.

Harriet Elizabeth S, mp, 1987, James, John; flowers pure medium pink, large, full, borne singly and in clusters, intense fragrance; repeat bloom; foliage medium size, red aging dark green, leathery, disease-resistant; upright, bushy, vigorous, fully hardy growth; [Paula × (Micki × Northlander)]; int. by Historical Roses, 1987

Harriet Miller HT, pb, 1973, Brownell, H.C.; bud long, pointed; flowers pink, large, very dbl., globular, moderate fragrance; foliage large, glossy; very vigorous, bushy growth; PP3375; [Helen Hayes × Traviata]; int. by Stern's Nursery, 1972

Harriet Neese S, op, 1928, Conyers; flowers coral blended with yellow, base golden yellow, semi-dbl., slight fragrance; abundant non-recurrent bloom; growth bushy (to 4 ft.); [Ophelia × Harison's Yellow]

Harriet Nichola HT, pb, 2002, Poole, Lionel; flowers peach-pink, 5-5½ in., dbl., borne mostly solitary, moderate fragrance; foliage medium size, dark green, matte; prickles medium, lang, hooked downwards, moderate; growth bushy, medium (3 ft.); garden decorative, bedding; [Selfridges × Mischief]

Harriet Poulsen F, mp, 1912, Poulsen, D.T.; flowers apple-blossom-pink, single; vigorous growth; [Mme Norbert Levavasseur × Dorothy Perkins]

Harriet Shepherd Gr, mp, 1983, Shepherd, David; flowers medium, 35 petals, no fragrance; foliage medium size, medium green, holly-like; upright growth; [Queen Elizabeth × Queen Elizabeth]; int. in 1982

Harriet Sheppard HWich, m, Nobbs; int. in 1997

Harriny HT, mp, 1970, LeGrice; flowers clear pink, pointed, large, 40 petals, intense fragrance; foliage dark; [Pink Favorite × Lively]; int. in 1967

Harrison Weir HP, dr, 1880, Turner; [Charles Lefèbvre × Xavier Olibo]

Harry – See **Harry Wheatcroft**, HT

Harry Ashcroft F, op; int. by Love4Plants Ltd, 2005

Harry Campbell F, dp, 1976, Burnet; bud small, pointed; flowers cerise-pink shading to white, 2½ in., 45 petals, intense wild apple fragrance; foliage dark, leathery;

vigorous, bushy growth; int. by Benefield's Nursery, 1977

Harry Edland F, m, 1976, Harkness; flowers lilac-pink, 4 in., 26 petals, intense fragrance; foliage dark, glossy; [(Lilac Charm × Sterling Silver) × (Blue Moon × (Sterling Silver × Africa Star))]; int. in 1975; Edland Fragrance Medal, ARS, 1975

Harry G. Hastings HT, dr, 1965, Von Abrams; flowers large, dbl.; foliage leathery; vigorous growth; [Gov. Mark Hatfield × Helene Schoen]

Harry Kirk T, ly, 1907, Dickson, A.; bud pointed, very long; flowers light sulfur-yellow, dbl., open, moderate fragrance; foliage leathery; strong stems; vigrous, bushy growth

Harry Maasz S, rb, 1939, Kordes; bud long, pointed; flowers crimson, center white, very large, single, cupped; foliage large, leathery, wrinkled, dark; very vigorous, climbing growth; [Barcelona × Daisy Hill]; HMacrantha

Harry Oppenheimer HT, dy, Kordes; bud green-yellow, diamond shaped; flowers deep gold with green-yellow on guard petals, dbl., exhibition, borne mostly singly, slight fragrance; vigorous, medium growth; int. in 1996

Harry Wheatcroft HT, yb, 1973; flowers yellow striped red, reverse yellow, wide, dbl., moderate fragrance; bushy, vigorous, medium growth; [sport of Piccadilly]; int. by Wheatcroft & Sons, 1972

Harry Wheatcroft, Climbing Cl HT, yb, 1981, Mungia, Fred A., Sr.; bud pointed; flowers orange vermilion, striped and flecked yellow, large, 20-25 petals, cupped, borne singly with some side buds; foliage large, dark green, waxy; prickles flat, straight; PP4841; [sport of Caribia]; int. by Montebello Rose Co., Inc.

Hartina – See **Kammersanger Terkal**, F

Haru-Kaze LCl, op, 1986, Suzuki, Seizo; bud ovoid; flowers salmon yellow to orange-red, 33 petals, borne 6-8 per cluster; foliage dark, glossy; prickles small, curved, slanted downward; bushy, creeping growth; [Charleston × Dorothy Perkins]; int. by Keisei Rose Nursery, 1986

Harugasumi LCl, mp, Itami

Haruka F, dp, Hiroshima; int. by Hiroshima Bara-en, 2004

Harunomai F, mp, Keisei; int. by Keisei Rose Nurseries, 1994

Haruyo HT, w

Harvard HT, dr, 1926, Vestal; bud pointed; flowers deep crimson, open, very large, dbl.; foliage soft,bronze; long stems; [Hoosier Beauty × seedling]

Harvest Belle F, my; flowers bright, sunny yellow, borne several to a cluster; free-flowering; medium growth

Harvest Fayre F, ob, 1990, Dickson, Patrick; flowers medium, 15-24 petals, slight fragrance; foliage medium size, medium green, glossy; bushy growth; [seedling × Bright Smile]; int. by Dickson Nurseries, Ltd., 1990; Rose of the Year, 1990

Harvest Festival HT, ab, 1986, Law, M.J.; flowers light apricot-orange, reverse apricot flushed pink, 28 petals, urn-shaped, slight fragrance; foliage medium size, medium green, semi-glossy; prickles medium, reddish-brown; tall, bushy growth; hips globular, large, orange-yellow; [Blessings × Sunblest]; int. in 1980

Harvest Glow LCl, rb, 1941, Brownell; bud long, pointed, ovoid; flowers red to pink, reverse yellow, large, 60 petals, high-centered; foliage light green; long stems; vigorous, climbing growth; [Golden Glow × Mercedes Gallart]

Harvest Home HRg, mp, 1978, Rock, Mrs. W.E.; bud pointed; flowers mauve-pink, 4½ in., 14 petals, cupped, slight fragrance; abundant early bloom, then sporadic; foliage light green, wrinkled; bushy growth; [Scabrosa × unknown]; int. by Harkness, 1979

Harvest Moon HT, ly, 1938, Cant, B. R.; flowers cream, open, large, single, borne in clusters; foliage leathery, dark; long stems; vigorous, bushy, compact growth

Harvest Moon HT, my, 1976, Mason, A.L.; bud long, pointed; flowers 4-5 in., 35 petals; vigorous growth; [sport of Whisky]; int. by F. Mason

Harvest Moon F, dy, Clements; flowers deep yellow in heart, fading rapidly as petals open, dbl.; int. by Roses Unlimited, 2004

Harvest Song S, pb

Harvest Sun F, ob, 1997, Brown, Ted; flowers large, 8-14 petals, borne in large clusters (8-10), moderate fragrance; foliage medium size, dark green, glossy; growth upright, tall (4½ ft.); [Esprit × Mountbatten]

Harvest Time Cl HT, ab, 1939, Thomas; flowers apricot, reverse sometimes pinkish, open, very large, semi-dbl.; free, recurrent boom; foliage leathery, dark; very vigorous, climbing (15-20 ft.) long stems growth; [Sophie Thomas × Souv. de Claudius Pernet]; int. by Armstrong Nursery

Harvester HT, pb, 1976, Mayhew; flowers carmine, reverse silver, center lilac, 5 in., 35 petals, intense fragrance; foliage large, matte; [Wendy Cussons × Kordes' Perfecta]

Harwood F, dp, Harkness; flowers high-centered, borne in small clusters, intense fragrance; medium (3 ft.) growth; int. by R. Harkness & Co, 2002

Hasina HT, mr, Ghosh; flowers deep cherry red, shapely, dbl., high-centered; int. in 2001

Hassan F, mr, 1963, McGredy, Sam IV; flowers scarlet, 4 in., 28 petals; foliage glossy, light green; vigorous, upright growth; [Tivoli × Independence]; int. by Fisons Horticulture

Hassi-Messaoud LCl, or, 1961, Hémeray-Aubert; flowers garnet-red shaded orange, 2½-3 in., full, borne in small clusters; abundant, recurrent bloom

Hat Pin Min, m, 1987, Bennett, Dee; flowers pale lavender, small, 12-15 petals, urn-shaped, borne usually singly, moderate fruity fragrance; foliage small, medium green, semi-glossy; prickles straight, extremely small, pale yellow; micro-mini upright,bushy, low growth; hips globular, small, brown; PP6790; [Angel Face × Angelglo]; int. by Tiny Petals Nursery, 1986

Hat Trick HT, pb, 1992, Lienau, David W.; flowers pink, darker pink petal edges and reverse, natural recurve, 3-3½ in., very dbl.; foliage medium size, dark green, semi-glossy; few prickles on upper half of stems; medium (90-120 cm.), upright growth; [First Prize × seedling]; int. by Trophy Roses, Ltd., 1993

Hatakeyama HT, dp, 1995, Shimizu, Junji; flowers deep pink, large, full; foliage medium size, dark green, matte; some prickles; medium, upright growth; [Garden Party × Kolner Karneval]

Hatchell Brown Tea T, lp, Clark

Hatsu Kari – See **Hatsukari**, HT

Hatsukari HT, pb, 2005, Yasuda, Yuji; flowers pink blend, reverse light pink, 13 cm., full, borne mostly solitary; foliage medium size, dark green, matte; prickles medium; growth compact, short (100 cm.); cutting, containers; [Paradise × Colorama]; int. in 1994

Hatsukoi HT, w

Hatuzakura HT, ab, 1999, Teranishi, K.; flowers apricot-orange, 5½ in., 80 petals, hybrid tea, moderate fragrance; growth to 4 ft.; int. by Itami Rose Nursery, 1997

Hauff HMult, m, 1911, Lambert, P.; flowers reddish-violet, dbl., borne in clusters; recurrent when established; foliage dark, broad; vigorous, climbing growth; [Aimee Vibert × Crimson Rambler]

Hauraki F, or, 1994, McGredy, Sam IV; flowers medium, dbl.; foliage small, medium green, semi-glossy; patio; bushy (30 cm.) growth; [Trumpeter × Kapiti]; int. by McGredy Roses International, 1994; Rose of the Year, Auckland, NZ, 1998

Hauser HT, my, 1978, Gaujard; flowers yellow-cream, dbl.; vigorous growth; [Barbara × Guitare]; int. in 1975

Haute Pink HT, dp, 1987, Warriner, William A.; flowers rose pink fading little, loose, medium, 25-30 petals, cupped, borne singly; foliage medium size, medium green, matte; prickles long, narrow, red; upright, tall growth; no fruit; PP6653; [Bridal Pink × Grand Masterpiece]; int. by J&P

Havana HT, pb, 1950, Fisher, G.; flowers salmon-rose, reverse orange-yellow, 5-5½ in., 40 petals; foliage soft; vigorous, compact growth; [Peace × Orange Nassau]; int. by Arnold-Fisher Co.

Havana Min, dr, Poulsen; flowers dark red, medium, semi-dbl., no fragrance; growth bushy, 40-60 cm.; int. by Poulsen Roser, 2005

Havana Hit – See **Havana**, Min

Havering HMsk, mp, 1937, Bentall; flowers China-pink, large, borne in clusters of 4-5; vigorous growth

Havering Rambler HMult, mp, 1920, Pemberton; flowers almond-blossom-pink, 3-4 cm., dbl., rosette, borne in large clusters, slight fragrance; long stems; very vigorous growth; [sport of Turner's Crimson Rambler]

Havlickova Národni HP, rb, 1935, Böhm, J.; flowers dark red with white, medium, semi-dbl.

Hawa Mahal HT, op, 1977, Harkness; flowers salmon-pink, 5-6 in., 25 petals, moderate fragrance; foliage dark; [Fragrant Cloud × Kordes' Perfecta]; int. in 1976

Hawaii HT, or, 1960, Boerner; bud long, pointed; flowers orange-coral, 6 in., 33 petals, high-centered, intense fragrance; foliage leathery; vigorous, upright growth; PP1833; [Golden Masterpiece × seedling]; int. by J&P, 1960

Hawaii HT, op, J&P; greenhouse rose; int. by Bear Creek Gardens, 2001

Hawaiian Beauty HT, pb, 1993, Wyckoff, Gilbert R.; flowers have salmon pink outer petals, light pink inner petals, slightly darker reverse, 5-5½ in., very full, borne mostly singly, moderate fragrance; foliage medium size, medium green, semi-glossy; few prickles; medium (4½-5 ft.),bushy growth; [Thriller × Dothan]; int. by Wyckoff, 1994

Hawaiian Belle Min, pb, 1983, Dobbs, Annette E.; flowers medium pink, aging to pink blend, small, 35 petals, slight fragrance; foliage small, medium green, matte; bushy growth; [Pink Ribbon × Pink Ribbon]; int. in 1982

Hawaiian Delight F, op, 1970, deRuiter; flowers burnt-orange to pink, small, dbl., cupped, slight fragrance; recurrent; foliage dark, leathery; vigorous, bushy growth; PP2799; [Orange Sensation × Circus]; int. by Carlton Rose Nurseries, 1968

Hawaiian Duchess HT, op, 2002, Wyckoff, Gilbert R.; bud orange-pink with some red; flowers yellow and orange pink, 5½ in., full, borne mostly solitary, intense fragrance; foliage medium size, medium green, semi-glossy; prickles medium, moderate; growth upright, medium (5-6 ft.); garden decorative, exhibition; [Elsie Melton × Hawaiian King]; int. by Roses of Hawaii, 2002

Hawaiian Fragrance HT, or, 1994, Wyckoff, Gilbert R.; flowers coral, orange-red, similar to Fragrant Cloud, 5-6 in., full, borne mostly singly, intense fragrance; foliage large, medium green, semi-glossy; some prickles; tall (6+ ft.), upright growth; [Fragrant Cloud × Captain Harry Stebbings]; int. by Wyckoff, 1994

Hawaiian Fragrant Sunrise HT, pb, 2002, Wyckoff, Gilbert R.; flowers yellow with orange/pink, orange/pink reverse, 5-5½ in., full, borne mostly solitary; foliage medium size, medium green, semi-glossy; prickles medium, straight, moderate; growth upright, medium to tall (5-5½ ft.); garden decorative, exhibition; [Thriller × Hawaiian Queen Martha]; int. by Roses of Hawaii, 1998

Hawaiian King HT, lp, 1993, Wyckoff, Gilbert R.; flowers 3-3½ in., very dbl., borne mostly singly; foliage medium size, medium to dark green,semi-glossy; some prickles;

tall (5-6 ft.), upright growth; [Peggy Lee × Captain Harry Stebbings]; int. by Wyckoff, 1994

Hawaiian Lady HT, dp, 1993, Wyckoff, Gilbert R.; flowers deep pink, 3 in., very full, borne mostly singly, moderate fragrance; foliage medium size, medium green, semi-glossy; numerous prickles; medium (5 ft.), upright, bushy growth; [Peggy Lee × Captain Harry Stebbings]; int. by Wyckoff, 1994

Hawaiian Prince HT, mr, 2002, Wyckoff, Gilbert R.; flowers fading to light red, 5-6 in., dbl., borne mostly solitary, moderate fragrance; foliage medium size, medium green, semi-glossy; prickles medium, few; growth upright, medium to tall (5-6 ft.); garden decorative, exhibition; [Thriller × Captain Harry Stebbings]; int. by Roses of Hawaii, 1998

Hawaiian Princess HT, op, 2002, Wyckoff, Gilbert R.; flowers white with orange-pink, changing with weather, 5 in., full, borne mostly solitary, moderate fragrance; foliage medium size, medium green, semi-glossy; prickles medium, moderate; growth upright, medium (5 ft.); garden decorative, exhibition; [Elsie Melton × Hawaiian Queen Martha]; int. by Roses of Hawaii, 2002

Hawaiian Queen Martha HT, op, 1994, Wyckoff, Gilbert R.; flowers salmon, interspered with light pink on both petal surfaces, 5½-6 in., very dbl.; foliage medium size, medium green, semi-glossy; some prickles; medium (4 ft.), upright growth; [Kordes Perfecta × Dothan]; int. by Wyckoff, 1995

Hawaiian Sunrise Min, rb, 1982, Williams, Ernest D.; bud pointed; flowers red and yellow blend, 40 petals, high-centered, borne usually singly, slight fragrance; foliage small, dense, glossy, bronze; prickles thin, reddish; upright growth; [seedling × Over the Rainbow]; int. by Mini-Roses, 1981

Hawaiian Sunrise HT, op, Wyckoff, Gilbert R.; flowers yellow and orange-pink, reverse orange-pink, 5-5½ in., full, borne mostly solitary, intense fragrance; foliage medium size, medium green, semi-glossy; prickles medium, moderate; growth upright, tall (5 ft.); garden, exhibition; [Thriller × Hawaiian Queen Martha]; int. by Roses of Hawaii, 1998

Hawaiian Sunset HT, ob, 1962, Swim & Weeks; bud ovoid; flowers orange edged yellow, open, 4-5½ in., 45-50 petals, moderate fragrance; foliage leathery, glossy; vigorous, upright, well branched growth; PP2143; [Charlotte Armstrong × Signora]; int. by C.R. Burr, 1962

Hawaiian Thrill HT, pb, 1993, Wyckoff, Gilbert R.; flowers pink, white center, 5½ in., 23-25 petals, borne mostly singly, intense fragrance; foliage medium size, dark green, semi-glossy; some prickles; medium (4½-5 ft.), upright growth; [Fragrant Cloud × Thriller]; int. by Wyckoff, 1994

Hawkesbury Wonder S, mp; [Hebe's Lip × unknown]

Hawkeye Belle S, w, 1975, Buck, Dr. Griffith J.; bud ovoid, pointed; flowers white, tinted azalea-pink, 4-4½ in., 38 petals, high-centered, intense fragrance; foliage large, dark, leathery; vigorous, erect, bushy growth; [(Queen Elizabeth × Pizzicato) × Prairie Princess]; int. by Iowa State University

Hawlmark Crimson HT, mr, 1920, Dickson, A.; bud pointed; flowers crimson-scarlet, semi-dbl.; bushy growth

Hawlmark Scarlet HT, mr, 1923, Dickson, A.; flowers brilliant velvety scarlet-crimson; Gold Medal, NRS, 1920

Haydock Park F, mr, Fryer; flowers ruby red, dbl., classic hybrid tea, borne in clusters, moderate fragrance; recurrent; foliage dark green, disease-resistant; vigorous (100 cm.) growth; int. by Fryers Roses, 2006

Haylee Denise Min, ly, 2004, McConathy, George D.; flowers full, borne mostly solitary; foliage medium size, dark green, glossy; prickles moderate; growth bushy, medium (18-24 in.); [sport of Hot Tamale]; int. by George D. McConathy, 2004

Hayley Westenra – See **Augusta Luise**, S

Hazel Alexander HT, dr, 1933, Dicksons of Hawlmark; flowers deep red; [Ophelia × unknown]

Hazel Rose HT, lp, 1992, Poole, Lionel; flowers 3-3½ in., full, borne singly, slight fragrance; foliage medium size, dark green, semi-glossy; few prickles; medium (120 cm.), upright growth; [Queen Esther × Selfridges]

Hazel Woodland F, ab, 2005, Paul Chessum Roses; flowers apricot, 6 cm., semi-dbl., borne in small clusters, moderate fragrance; foliage medium size, dark green, glossy; spreading, medium growth; bedding, borders, containers; [seedling × seedling]; int. by Love4Plants Ltd, 2005

Hazeldean HSpn, my, 1948, Wright, Percy H.; flowers large, dbl., moderate fragrance; very hardy (to -60); [*R. spinosissima altaica* × Harison's Yellow]

Head of Rivers D, mp

Headleyensis S, ly, 1920, Warburg; flowers creamy yellow, single; foliage ferny; vigorous growth; [*R. hugonis* × *R. spinosissima altaica*]

Headline HT, yb, Dawson; flowers deep yellow blushed carmine, full; growth tall; int. in 1970

Headliner HT, pb, 1985, Warriner, William A.; flowers petals white, blending to deep pink at edges, large, 40 petals, high-centered, slight fragrance; foliage large, medium green, glossy; upright growth; PP5340; [Love × Color Magic]; int. by J&P, 1986

Healing Hands HT, yb, 1998, Poole, Lionel; flowers pale yellow, edged pink, 5½ in., very dbl., high-centered, borne mostly singly; foliage large, dark green, glossy; some prickles; upright, bushy, medium growth; [Gavotte × (Peer Gynt × Golden Splendour)]; int. by David Lister, Ltd., 1999

Heart 'n' Soul – See **Sans Souci**, Min

Heart 'n' Soul S, rb, 2001, Orard, Pierre; flowers white with red border, reverse same, 7-9 cm., dbl., borne in small clusters, slight fragrance; foliage medium size, dark green, glossy; prickles average, pointed, brown, moderate; stems new growth dark red; growth upright to spreading, medium (110-130 cm.); garden decorative; PP14500; [Tamango × Iceberg]; int. by Weeks Roses, 2001; Bronze Medal, Adelaide, 2006

Heart of England – See **Pink Silk**, HT

Heart of Gold HWich, rb, 1921, Hill, E. G.; flowers crimson, center white, large; [*R. wichurana* × *R. moyesii*]

Heart of Gold HMoy, rb, 1926, Van Fleet; flowers crimson, center white, stamens yellow, 4-5 cm., single, open, borne in clusters of 5-15, moderate fragrance; foliage rich green, glossy; vigorous (10 ft.) growth; [(*R. wichurana* × *R. setigera*) × *R. moyesii*]; int. by American Rose Society

Heart of Gold – See **Gold Heart**, HT

Heart O' Gold Gr, yb, 1999, Dykstra, Dr. A. Michael; flowers deep gold surrounded by cerise pink, 4-4½ in., 35-40 petals, high-centered, borne in large clusters, intense fruit and rose fragrance; foliage large, medium green, semi-glossy; prickles moderate; upright, tall (5-6 ft.) growth; PP10713; [Broadway × Gold Medal]; int. by Weeks Roses, 1997

Heart of Gold – See **Heart O' Gold**, Gr

Heart of Gold HT, ab, 2003, Cocker, A.G.; flowers ripe peach, reverse lighter, 3 in., full, borne mostly solitary; foliage large, dark green, glossy; prickles 9 mm., straight, moderate; growth upright, medium (30-36 in.); garden decorative; [Queen Charlotte × Shirley Spain]; int. by James Cocker & Sons, 2003; Winner - Hybrid Tea, Dublin, 2006

Heart of T. D. K. HT, op, 1985, Ogawa, Isamu; bud ovoid; flowers salmon-pink, large, 50 petals, borne singly, slight fragrance; foliage small, light green; prickles heavy hooked; vigorous, upright, tall growth; [Sunblest × Red Devil]; int. in 1983

Heart Throb F, yb, 1966, Fankhauser; bud urn shaped; flowers deep yellow, edges flushed pink, medium, very dbl., borne in clusters, intense fragrance; foliage dark, glossy; vigorous, bushy growth; RULED EXTINCT 4/82 ARM; [(Circus × Circus) × (Circus × Circus)]

Heart Throb – See **Paul Shirville**, HT

Heart Throb HT, mr, 1982, Leon, Charles F., Sr.; flowers 37 petals, high-centered, borne singly and several together, moderate damask fragrance; foliage medium to large, medium green, leathery; vigorous, bushy, tall growth; [Norita × ((((Norita × unnamed seedling) × Papa Meilland) × ((Norita × Unnamed seedling) × Papa Meilland)) × Papa Meilland)]

Heartache – See **Centenary**, F

Heartbeat F, op, 1971, Dickson, Patrick; flowers deep salmon-orange, 4½ in., 26 petals, globular, slight fragrance; foliage small, dull; very free growth; [(Castanet × Castanet) × (Cornelia × seedling)]; int. by A. Dickson & Sons, 1970

Heartbeat HT, mr, 1990, Bridges, Dennis A.; bud pointed; flowers medium red, darker outer petals, reverse lighter, medium, 45 petals, high-centered, borne usually singly, slight fruity fragrance; foliage medium size, medium green, semi-glossy; prickles straight, large, pink to yellow; upright growth; [Thriller × Wild Cherry]; int. by Bridges Roses, 1990

Heartbeat – See **Heartbeat 96**, F

Heartbeat 96 F, ab, 1997, Cocker, Ann G.; flowers medium, dbl.; foliage medium size, dark green, glossy; some prickles; upright, medium (2½ ft.) growth; int. by James Cocker & Sons

Heartbreaker Min, pb, 1989, Carruth, Tom; bud pointed; flowers deep pink with white base, small, dbl., high-centered, borne in sprays of 3-5; foliage small, dark green, glossy; prickles nearly straight, small, dark red-brown; upright, bushy, medium, vigorous growth; hips globular, small, dark orange; PP7588; [Crystalline × Magic Carrousel]; int. by Weeks Roses, 1990

Hearth Glow F, or, 1968, Von Abrams; bud ovoid; flowers brick-red, medium, dbl., borne in clusters; foliage soft, light green; vigorous, upright growth; [Red Pinocchio × (Carrousel × Queen o' the Lakes)]; int. by Peterson & Dering, 1963

Heartland Min, op, 1982, Saville, F. Harmon; bud short, pointed; flowers 38 petals, high-centered, borne in clusters; prickles long, thin; vigorous, upright growth; PP5045; [Sheri Anne × Watercolor]; int. by Nor'East Min. Roses

Heartland Lady Min, pb, 2000, Dickson, Jack; flowers dbl., borne mostly solitary, slight fragrance; foliage medium size, dark green, semi-glossy; prickles medium, pointed, straight, brown; growth compact, medium (16-20 in.); [seedling × Gene Boerner]; int. by Warren & Son Nursery, 2001

Heartlight MinFl, ob, 1985, King, Gene; flowers orange-yellow, reverse yellow, large, 16 petals, high-centered; foliage medium size, medium green, matte; prickles straight, light brown; upright, bushy, medium growth; [Golden Slippers × Rise 'n' Shine]; int. by AGM Miniature Roses

Hearts A'Fire Min, dr, 1996, Bridges, Dennis A.; flowers velvety, 1¼ in., single, borne mostly singly; foliage medium size, dark green, glossy, disease-resistant; prickles moderate; strong, upright growth; [Merrimac × seedling]; int. by Bridges Roses, 1996

Heart's Delight HT, op, 1933, Hart, L.P.; flowers apricot-coral-orange, veined red, large, very dbl., high-centered; foliage soft; vigorous, open growth; [sport of Mrs Beckwith]

Heart's Desire HT, dr, 1942, Howard, F.H.; bud long,

pointed; flowers crimson, 4½ in., 30 petals, high-centered, intense damask fragrance; foliage leathery, dark; vigorous, upright growth; [unnamed variety × Crimson Glory]; int. by H&S; Gold Medal, Portland, 1941

Heart's Desire, Climbing Cl HT, dr, 1945, Howard, F.H.; int. by H&S

Heartsong Mini Brite Min, dp, Walden, John; bud long, pointed, ovoid; flowers mauve pink, 2-2¼ in., 25-30 petals, borne in clusters of 3-5, slight fragrance; recurrent; foliage medium size, matte; prickles moderate, hooked downward; upright, medium (24 in.) growth; PP11144; [(seedling × Red Minimo) × Winsome]; int. by Bear Creek Gardens, 1998

Heartsounds Min, mp, 1998, Williams, Ernest D.; flowers clear medium pink, cream reverse, 1-1¼ in., 30-35 petals, borne mostly singly; foliage medium size, medium green, semi-glossy; few prickles; long stems; upright, bushy, medium (18 in.) growth; [Rise 'n' Shine × Twilight Trail]; int. by Texas Mini Roses, 1997

Heartstrings Min, mr, 1997, Brown, Ted; flowers large, opening to old-fashioned form, 41 petals, borne in small clusters; foliage medium size, dark green, dull; bushy, medium (16 in.)growth; [Esprit × seedling]

Heat Wave F, or, 1959, Swim, H.C.; bud urn-shaped; flowers orange-scarlet, 3½-4½ in., 30 petals, cupped, borne in clusters; foliage dark, semi-glossy, rounded; vigorous, upright, bushy growth; PP1786; [seedling × Roundelay]; int. by Armstrong Nursery, 1958

Heather – See **Silver Anniversary**, HT, 1991

Heather – See **Heather Cottage**, S

Heather Austin S, dp, 1997, Austin, David; flowers deep, dusky pink, 5-6 cm., 50 petals, borne in small clusters, moderate clove fragrance; foliage medium size, medium green, semi-glossy; some prickles; upright to bushy, medium (3x2½ ft.) growth; PP10618; int. by David Austin Roses, Ltd.

Heather Claire HT, ab, 1983, Allender, Robert William; bud long; flowers apricot-pink, 30 petals, borne singly, no fragrance; foliage dark, red reverse; prickles slightly hooked; medium growth; [Diamond Jubilee × Bonsoir]

Heather Cottage S, mr, Poulsen; flowers medium red, small, single, borne in clusters, very slight fragrance; recurrent; foliage dark green, glossy; broad, bushy (20-40 cm.) growth; int. by Poulsen Roser, 2005; Silver Medal, Baden-Baden, 2006, Certificate of Merit, Le Roeulx, 2006

Heather Elms HT, dr, Orard; flowers very dark red, stiff petals, dbl., high-centered, no fragrance; vigorous, tall growth; int. in 1999

Heather Honey HT, ab, 1989, Horner, Colin P.; bud ovoid, bronze; flowers apricot yellow, reverse apricot, medium, 25 petals, urn-shaped, borne usually singly, moderate fruity fragrance; foliage medium size, medium green, glossy; prickles small, greenish-brown; bushy, medium growth; hips globular, medium, yellow; [Silver Jubilee × (Honey Favorite × Southampton)]; int. by LeGrice Roses, 1990

Heather Jenkins HT, mp, 1970, Watson; bud globular; flowers pink, reverse darker, medium, dbl., high-centered, slight fragrance; foliage light green, wrinkled; moderate, upright, open growth; [Charlotte Armstrong × Ballet]; int. in 1968

Heather Leigh Min, mp, 1989, Taylor, Franklin "Pete" & Kay; bud pointed; flowers medium pink, reverse slightly darker, aging lighter, holds color well, 35-40 petals, high-centered, borne singly; foliage medium size, medium green, semi-glossy; prickles straight, small, reddish-brown; upright, bushy, medium growth; no fruit; [Azure Sea × unnamed Miniature seedling]; int. by Taylor's Roses

Heather Miranda HT, rb, 2001, Hiltner, Martin J.; flowers dark red, blending to white, 2½-3 in., dbl., borne mostly solitary, slight fragrance; foliage medium size, medium green, semi-glossy; prickles hooked downward; growth upright, bushy, medium (2½-3 ft.); garden decorative; [Lynn Anderson × Scentimental]

Heather Mist Min, m, 2001, Williams, Michael C.; flowers light to medium lavender, reverse same, 1½-2 in., full, borne mostly solitary, slight fragrance; foliage medium size, dark green, semi-glossy; prickles to ¼ in., straight, few; growth compact, medium (18-24 in.); garden decorative; [seedling × selected pollen]

Heather Muir (variety of *R. sericea*), w, 1957; flowers pure white, 3 in., single; blooms over a long period; foliage ferny; hips orange; int. by Sunningdale Nursery

Heather Paton HT, mr, 1934, Austin & McAslan; flowers carmine, center darker; vigorous growth

Heather Pudney HT, mp, Dawson; int. in 1995

Heather Sproul Min, mp, 2004, Sproul, James A.; buds long, tapered; flowers dbl., high-centered, borne in small clusters, slight fragrance; foliage medium size, dark green, semi-glossy, mildew-resistant; prickles medium; growth compact, medium (18 to 24 in.); borders, containers; [(Lynn Anderson × Tournament of Roses) × Hot Tamale]; int. in 2004

Heatherby S, op, Kordes; int. in 2004

Heaven HT, w, 1993, Warriner, William A.; flowers ivory or cream with a light pink blend, 3-3½ in., full, borne mostly singly, intense fragrance; foliage large, dark green, matte; some prickles; tall (150-160 cm.), upright, bushy growth; PP7943; [Honor × First Prize]; int. by Bear Creek Gardens, 1994

Heaven Bound F, mp, Williams, J. Benjamin; flowers bright pink, old-fashioned, ruffled, dbl.; compact (2½ ft.) growth; int. by Hortico, 1999

Heaven on Earth F, ab, Kordes; flowers thick petals, peach-apricot, large, dbl., cupped, slight spicy fragrance; foliage glossy, dark green; stems strong; growth compact (1½ × 2 m.); PP15253; int. as Avril Elizabeth Home, Ludwig's Roses, 2001

Heaven Scent F, op, 1970, Poulsen; flowers salmon, large, 30 petals, borne in trusses, intense fragrance; [Pernille Poulsen × Isabel de Ortiz]; int. by McGredy & Son, 1968

Heaven Scent – See **Memorial Day**, HT

Heaven Scent Pink Min, lp, 1996, Jalbert, Brad; flowers wide, 2 in., full, flat, intense fragrance; foliage medium size, medium green, dull, reddish; few prickles; upright, tall (24 in.) growth; [Rise 'n' Shine × Rosemary Harkness]; int. by Select Roses, 1997

Heavenly Days Min, op, 1988, Saville, F. Harmon; flowers glowing Indian-orange, reverse lemon yellow, flushed fire-red, 28-32 petals, cupped, no fragrance; foliage medium size, medium green, glossy, underside matte; bushy, medium, compact growth; PP6808; [seedling × (Sheri Anne × Glenfiddich)]; int. by Nor'East Min. Roses; AOE, ARS, 1988

Heavenly Fragrance HT, lp, 1963, Hennessey; flowers light pink, reverse darker, well-formed, 5 in., intense fragrance; moderate growth; [Tiffany × Mme Gregoire Staechelin]

Heavenly Gold – See **Gold Heart**, HT

Heavenly Pink HMsk, mp, 2000, Lens, Louis; flowers medium pink, reverse lighter, 3-4 cm., semi-dbl., borne in large clusters, slight fragrance; recurrent; foliage medium size, medium green, semi-glossy; prickles moderate; upright, medium (100 cm.) growth; [Seagull × seedling]; int. by Louis Lens NV, 1997; Bronze Certificate, The Hague, 2006

Heavenly Pink F, lp, Zary; PP11561; int. by Bear Creek Gardens, 2001

Heavenly Robe – See **Hagoromo**, LCl

Heavenly Rosalind S, pb, 1997, Austin, David; flowers wild-rose effect, medium, 5 petals, borne in small clusters; foliage medium size, dark green, dull, leathery; upright, bushy, medium growth; int. by David Austin Roses, 1995

Heavenly Scent S, mp, 1999, Hamilton, Noel; flowers cerise pink, lighter reverse, large, 58 petals, borne mostly singly and in small clusters, moderate fragrance; foliage medium size, dark green, glossy; prickles moderate; upright, compact, medium (5 ft.) growth; int. by Noel Berryman

Heavenly Vision Min, mp, 1996, Williams, Ernest D.; flowers clear, medium pink, 1½ in., dbl., borne mostly singly; foliage medium green, semi-glossy; few prickles; medium (16-18 in.), upright, bushy growth; [Angel Face × Tom Brown]; int. by Texas Mini Roses, 1996

Heavens Above MinFl, rb, 2003, Webster, Robert; flowers bright red, reverse pale red, 1½-2 in., full, borne in small clusters; foliage medium size, medium green, semi-glossy; prickles triangular; growth bushy, medium (24 in.); bedding, containers; [Little Jackie × (Anytime × Western Sun)]; int. in 2004

Hebe F, dp, 1941, Leenders, M.; flowers deep pink, reverse lighter

Hebe HT, op, 1949, Dickson, A.; flowers rosy salmon toned orange and apricot-yellow, high pointed, large, 27 petals; foliage glossy, bronze green; vigorous growth; Gold Medal, NRS, 1949

Hébé Ch, mp

Hebe Camargo HT, (Brazil)

Hebe's Lip HEg, w, before 1846, Lee; flowers creamy white, petals edged pink, wavy, semi-dbl., cupped, moderate fragrance; non-recurrent; vigorous, moderate growth; [thought to be *R.* × *damascena* × *R. rubiginosa* hybrid]; re-int. by W. Paul, 1912

Heckenfeuer F, mr, Kordes; int. in 1984

Heckengold F, dy, W. Kordes Söhne; flowers large, dbl.; int. in 1986

Heckenzauber – See **Sexy Rexy**, F

Hector HGal, m, before 1819, from Holland; flowers purple, faintly striped with white, small, dbl., pompon; sometimes attributed to Parmentier, about 1830. It is probable that more than one cultivar was grown under this name.

Hector Berlioz HT, or, Harkness; flowers red-orange, dbl., slight fragrance; medium (2-3 ft.) growth; int. in 1998

Hector Deane HT, rb, 1938, McGredy; bud pointed; flowers orange, carmine and salmon-pink, dbl., high-centered, intense fruity fragrance; foliage glossy, dark; vigorous, compact growth; [McGredy's Scarlet × Lesley Dudley]; int. by J&P

Hedda Hopper HT, mp, 1952, Howard, A.P.; bud ovoid; flowers light peach passing to pearly pink, 3½-4 in., 40 petals, globular; foliage coppery; very vigorous growth; [Radiance × seedling]; int. by H&S

Hede HT, my, 1934, Tantau; flowers pure sunflower-yellow, large, dbl.; foliage dark, leathery; strong stems; vigorous growth; [Prof. Gnau × Mev. G.A. van Rossem]

Hedgefire MinFl, mr, Kordes; very free flowering; sturdy, strong (18 in.) growth; int. in 1983

Hedgehog Rose – See ***R. rugosa*** (Thunberg)

Hedgerow Beauty HRg, m, Bell; flowers mauve pink, moderate fragrance; free-flowering; growth healthy, bushy plant; int. by Bell Roses, 2001

Hedgerow Bonny S, ly, Mann; int. by The Hedgerow Roses, 2003

Hedgerow Toby HMult, w, Mann; flowers pure white, single, borne in large clusters, moderate fragrance; foliage grey-green; climbing (20 ft.) growth; int. by The Hedgerow Rose, 2001

Hedwig Fulda Cl Pol, mr, 1934, Leenders Bros.; flowers clear vermilion-red, well-formed, large, dbl., borne in large clusters; foliage bright, dark; long strong stems; vigorous growth; [Orléans Rose × Farbenkonigin]

Hedwig Reicher HT, ly, 1912, Hinner, W.; flowers yellowish-white, darker center, large, very dbl., moderate fragrance

Heer HT, lp, 1971, Singh, R. S.; flowers rose-pink, medium, dbl., high-centered, slight fragrance; vigorous, upright growth; [Picture × unknown]; int. by Gopalsinamiengar, 1969

Hei Matisse HT, pb, Delbard; int. in 1995

Hei Matisse – See **Henri Matisse**, F

Hei W. Perron HT, or

Heian HT, op, Keihan; int. in 1979

Heidefee Pol, dp, Noack, Werner; int. in 1990

Heidefeuer F, dr, Noack, Werner; flowers bright red, 2 in., borne in clusters; free-flowering; upright (20-24 in.) growth; PP10084; int. by Noack Rosen, 1995

Heidegruss F, pb, 1937, Tantau; flowers salmon-flesh, base light yellow, large, very dbl., borne in clusters; foliage leathery; vigorous, bushy growth; [Heidekind × Ophelia]; int. by Münch & Haufe

Heidekind HRg, dp, 1931, Berger, V.; flowers brilliant pink shaded copper-red, large, dbl., borne in clusters; foliage thick, rugose; [Mev. Nathalie Nypels × *R. rugosa* hybrid]; int. by Münch & Haufe

Heidekind S, dr, 1985, Kordes, W.; flowers medium, 20 petals; foliage small, medium green, glossy; upright, bushy growth; [The Fairy × seedling]

Heidekönigin HWich, lp, 1985, Kordes, W.; flowers medium to dark pink, touched coral, 5-6 cm., 35 petals; foliage small, medium green, glossy; groundcover; spreading growth; [Zwerkönig '78 × (*R. wichurana* × unknown)]

Heidelberg HKor, mr, 1959, Kordes, R.; flowers bright crimson, reverse lighter, 4 in., 32 petals, high-centered, borne singly or in small clusters; foliage glossy, leathery; very vigorous, bushy growth; [Minna Kordes × Floradora]; int. in 1958

Heidelinde F, m, Kordes; int. in 1991

Heidemarie F, mr, 1945, Tantau; flowers carmine-red, large, 5-7 petals, borne in clusters of 4-6; foliage dark, leathery; vigorous, upright, bushy growth; [Hamburg × (Heros × Heidekind)]

Heidemarie Plücker HP, mp, 1940, Westphal; flowers large, very dbl.

Heidepark – See **Flamingo Meidiland**, S

Heideröslein LCl, yb, 1932, Lambert, P.; bud pointed, orange-red; flowers bright yellowish salmon-pink, base sulfur-yellow, 4-5 cm., single, flat, borne in clusters of 10-30, moderate fragrance; recurrent bloom; broad, bushy growth; [Chamisso × Amalie de Greiff]

Heideröslein Nozomi – See **Nozomi**, Cl Min

Heideschnee – See **Moon River**, S

Heidesommer F, w, 1985, Kordes, W.; flowers medium, 20 petals; foliage small, dark, glossy; upright, bushy growth; [The Fairy × seedling]

Heidetraum – See **Flower Carpet**, S

Heidezauber F, dr, 1936, Tantau; flowers large, very dbl., borne in clusters; foliage dark, leathery; bushy growth; [Heidekind × Johanniszauber]; int. by Münch & Haufe

Heidi Min, mp, 1977, Christensen, Jack E.; bud mossy; flowers clear medium pink, mini-moss, 1½ in., 35 petals, intense fragrance; foliage glossy; very vigorous, bushy growth; PP4355; [Fairy Moss × Iceberg]; int. by Armstrong Nursery, 1978

Heidi S, mp, Noack, Werner; int. in 1987

Heidi – See **Heidi Parade**, MinFl

Heidi-Ho Min, ab, 2006, Sawyer, Rosemary; flowers blended, apricot at edges, yellow at base, petals quilling on open blooms, up to 2 in., full, borne mostly solitary; foliage medium size, medium green, matte; prickles 3/16 in., straight, thin, moderate; growth upright, tall (to 28 in.); garden; exhibition; [sport of Rosemary's Dream]; int. in 2007

Heidi Jayne HT, dp, 1986, Esser; flowers bright deep pink, large, 32 petals, high-centered, borne mostly singly, moderate fragrance; recurrent; foliage large, light green, glossy; numerous prickles; medium, upright growth; [(Piccadilly × Queen Elizabeth) × (Fragrant Cloud × seedling)]; int. by Harkness

Heidi Kabel – See **Holsteinperle**, HT

Heidi Parade MinFl, mp, Poulsen; bud short, pointed ovoid; flowers salmon pink, 2-3 in., 25-35 petals, flat, borne mostly in small clusters, very slight fragrance; recurrent; foliage glossy; prickles very few, 2-3 mm., hooked downward, greyed-red; bushy, low (8-16 in.) growth; PP13275; [Charming Parade × Vanilla Kordana]; container plant; int. by Poulsen Roser, 2000

Heidi Rossin S, ly

Heietta T, m

Height of Fashion F, yb, 2003, McCann, Sean; flowers tan with apricot touches, medium, dbl., borne mostly solitary; foliage medium size, medium green; growth upright; [(Brandy × Royal Dane) × Tantalizing Mary]

Heiich Blanc LCl, w, Hetzel; int. in 1994

Heike HT, my, Kordes; bud green-yellow; flowers unfading, strong yellow, dbl., high-centered, slight fragrance; vigorous, medium growth; int. in 1993

Heimatlos S, mp, 1931, Lohrberg; bud pointed; flowers rose-pink, single, borne in clusters, intense fragrance; non-recurrent; short stems; vigorous (5-7 ft.), open habit growth; has endured -27; [(*R. canina* × *R. roxburghii*) × *R. canina*]

Heimatmelodie F, rb, Tantau; flowers red with white reverse; free-flowering; foliage dark green, glossy, healthy; growth to 2½ ft.; int. by Rosen Tantau, 2001

Hein Evers F, mr, 1959, Tantau, Math.; bud pointed; flowers bright blood-red, open, semi-dbl., borne in clusters, slight fragrance; foliage leathery; vigorous, upright growth; [Red Favorite × Fanal]; int. in 1957

Hein Evers, Climbing Cl F, mr, 1963, Kordes

Hein Mück S, dr, 1961, Tantau, Math.; flowers velvety blood-red, single, cupped, borne in clusters; vigorous (6 ft.) growth

Heine HMult, w, 1912, Lambert, P.; flowers white with dark reddish stamens, 2½-3 cm., dbl., borne in large clusters; remontant; [Trier × Frau Karl Druschki]

Heinfels – See **Super Sparkle**, LCl

Heinrich Blanc LCl, lp, Hetzel; flowers pale pink, fading to white, 2-2½ cm., very dbl., cabbage-shaped, borne in small clusters; int. in 1994

Heinrich Conrad Söth S, pb, 1919, Lambert, P.; flowers light rosy red, with white eye, 3 cm., single, borne in large pyramidal clusters, moderate fragrance; recurrent bloom; foliage large, glossy, dark; long, strong stems; very vigorous, bushy growth; [Geheimrat Dr. Mittweg × *R. foetida bicolor*]

Heinrich Eggers HT, op, 1928, Kordes; flowers orange-copper, often with lighter outer petals, dbl.; upright growth; [Mrs Charles E. Russell × Mrs Wemyss Quin]

Heinrich Karsch Pol, m, 1927, Leenders, M.; flowers violet-rose, small, semi-dbl., borne in clusters, moderate fragrance; free-flowering; upright, medium (2 ft.) growth; [Orléans Rose × Joan]

Heinrich Keller S, ly, 1894, Müller; flowers semi-dbl.

Heinrich Laurentius HP, rb, 1863, Verdier

Heinrich Münch HP, mp, 1911, Hinner, W.; flowers soft pink, very large, 50 petals, moderate fragrance; occasionally recurrent bloom; very vigorous growth; [Frau Karl Druschki × (Mme Caroline Testout × Mrs W.J. Grant)]; int. by Münch & Haufe

Heinrich Schultheis HP, lp, 1882, Bennett; flowers soft pink, well-formed, very large, dbl.; occasionally recurrent bloom; vigorous growth; [Mabel Morrison × E.Y. Teas]

Heinrich Siesmayer S, mr, McGredy; flowers fiery red; int. in 2002

Heinrich Wendland HT, mr, 1930, Kordes; flowers nasturtium-red, reverse deep golden yellow, very large, dbl., high-centered, intense fruity fragrance; foliage bronze, leathery, glossy; vigorous growth; [Charles P. Kilham × Mev. G.A. van Rossem]; int. by Dreer

Heinrich Wendland, Climbing Cl HT, mr, 1937, Stell; int. by Stell Rose Nursery

Heinsohn's Record S, lp, Heinsohn-Wedel

Heinz Erhardt F, mr, 1962, Kordes, R.; flowers 3 in., 25 petals, borne in clusters (up to 8); foliage coppery; vigorous, bushy growth; Gold Medal, Baden-Baden, 1961

Heinz Treffinger HT, mp, Hetzel; int. by Heinz Treffinger, 1998

Heinzelmännchen F, mr, 1983, Kordes, W.; flowers large, 35 petals; foliage medium size, medium green, glossy; bushy growth; [(Satchmo × seedling) × (Messestadt Hannover × Hamburg)]

Heiress HT, mp, 1959, Longsdon; bud pointed; flowers clear rose-pink, well-shaped, medium

Heirloom HT, m, 1971, Warriner, William A.; bud long, pointed; flowers deep lilac, medium, semi-dbl., intense fragrance; foliage leathery; vigorous, upright growth; PP3234; [seedling × seedling]; int. by J&P, 1972

Heirloom's Golden Rambler – See **Heirloom's Yellow Rambler**, HWich

Heirloom's Yellow Rambler HWich, my, Clements, John; flowers soft lemon yellow, 2 in., 15-20 petals, borne in clusters; foliage light green, holly-like; vigorous (10-12 ft.) growth

Heldengruss HT, dr, 1920, Kiese; flowers pure deep blood-red, dbl.; [Étoile de France × Baron Girod de l'Ain]

Helen HT, pb, 1930, Ferguson, W.; flowers salmon-pink, base shaded yellow, semi-dbl.; vigorous growth; RULED EXTINCT 11/91

Helen Min, mr, 1991, Bennett, Dee; flowers medium, full, high-centered, borne mostly singly, moderate fruity fragrance; foliage small, medium green, semi-glossy, disease-resistant; some prickles; long cutting stems; tall (60-80 cm.), upright, bushy growth; [Carrousel × Starina]; int. by Tiny Petals Nursery, 1992

Helen Allen HT, dr, 1976, Clayworth; flowers velvety red, 3½-4 in., 20 petals, moderate fragrance; upright growth; [Evelyn Fison × Vagabonde]; int. in 1975

Helen Antill Min, ab, 2005, Townson, S.; flowers apricot, 4-5 cm., full, borne in small clusters, slight fragrance; foliage large, medium green, semi-glossy; prickles average, pointed, few; growth bushy, medium (45 cm.); bedding, containers; [sport of Gem (MinFl)]; int. in 2002

Helen Bamber – See **St Clare**, S

Helen Bland S, mp, 1950, Wright, Percy H.; flowers rose-pink, center deeper, open, medium, semi-dbl., borne several together; profuse non-recurrent bloom; foliage soft; thornless; stems red-brown; vigorous (7-8 ft.), upright growth; [Betty Bland × *R. blanda*]

Helen Boehm Min, lp, 1982, Christensen, Jack E.; flowers soft pink, small, 20 petals, high-centered; foliage small, medium green, semi-glossy; upright, bushy growth; PP5397; [Foxy Lady × Deep Purple]; int. by Armstrong Nursery, 1983

Helen Chamberlain HT, yb, 1918, Easlea; flowers creamy yellow to orange-gold, paling on outer petals

Helen Davis HT, dr, 1925; flowers large, dbl.

Helen de Waal F, op, Kordes; flowers salmon-orange with yellow at the petal base, medium, dbl., high-centered, no fragrance; foliage glossy green, healthy; growth bushy, upright, tall; int. by Ludwig's Roses, 1999

Helen Fox HT, my, 1928, Buatois; bud pointed, indian

yellow; flowers golden yellow, dbl., cupped; foliage bronze; vigorous, bushy growth; [Mme Mélanie Soupert × Souv. de Claudius Pernet]; Gold Medal, Bagatelle, 1926

Helen Gambier – See **Mlle Hélène Gambier**, HT

Helen Good T, yb, 1907, Good & Reese; bud pointed; flowers delicate yellow suffused pink, edged deeper, dbl.; vigorous growth; [sport of Maman Cochet]

Helen Gould – See **Balduin**, HT

Helen Gould, Climbing Cl HT, pb, 1912, Good & Reese; [sport of Balduin]

Helen Hayes HT, yb, 1956, Brownell; bud long, pointed; flowers yellow splashed orange and pink, 4-5 in., 43 petals, high-centered, moderate fragrance; foliage glossy; very vigorous growth; PP1509; [(*R. wichuraiana* × unknown) × Sutter's Gold]

Helen Hoffmann HT, lp, 2004, Gareffa, N.; flowers solid light pink, 3-4 in., full, borne mostly solitary, moderate fragrance; continuous; foliage medium size, medium green, semi-glossy; prickles small, sharp; growth upright, short (2 ft.); container; exhibition; cutting; [seedling of unknown parentage]; int. in 2004

Helen Jane Burn HT, dp, 1999, Poole, Lionel; flowers high-pointed, classic form, 5½-6 in., full, borne mostly singly; foliage medium size, dark green, semi-glossy; some prickles; long stems; upright, bushy, medium (3 ft.) growth; [Blue Moon × seedling]

Helen Keller HP, dp, 1895, Dickson, A.; flowers rosy cerise, petals large, shell-shaped, full; very free bloom

Helen Keller HT, pb, Barni, V.; flowers soft pink suffused salmon-pink in heart, large, dbl., high-centered, slight fragrance; vigorous (3 ft.) growth; int. by Rose Barni, 1991

Helen Knight S, my, Knight; flowers canary yellow, 5 petals, no fragrance; non-recurrent; small foliage; vigorous (7 × 7 ft.) growth; seedling from *R. ecae*; int. in 1970

Helen Leenders S, mp, 1924, Leenders, M.; flowers hydrangea-pink, open, large, semi-dbl., borne in clusters; sometimes recurrent bloom; foliage large, rich green; very vigorous (5 ft.), bushy growth; [Orléans Rose × *R. foetida bicolor*]

Helen M. Greig HT, lp, Dobbie; flowers pastel pink; [Mrs A.R. Barraclough × Marmion]

Helen Margaret HT, w, 1997, Horner, Colin P.; flowers medium, dbl., borne in small clusters; foliage medium size, light green, glossy; growth compact, medium (80 cm.); [Champagne Cocktail × Alpine Sunset]; int. by Battersby Roses

Helen Mills – See **Reine Carola de Saxe**, HT

Helen Naudé HT, w, 1996, W. Kordes Söhne; flowers white flushed with pink, 4¾ in., very dbl.; foliage large, medium green, dull; prickles moderate; bushy, medium growth; int. by Ludwigs Roses Pty. Ltd., 1992

Helen of Troy HT, mp, 1956, Stevenson; flowers rose-pink, very dbl., slight spicy fragrance; vigorous, bushy growth; [Dame Edith Helen × Mrs Henry Morse]; int. by Waterer

Helen Paul HP, w, 1881, Lacharme; [Victor Verdier × Sombreuil]

Helen Rhodes F, pb, 2000, Rawlins, R.; flowers pale pink with fawn center, reverse primrose, large, very dbl., borne in small clusters, moderate fragrance; foliage medium size, dark green, semi-glossy; prickles 1 cm., triangular, few; growth upright, medium (3 ft.); [Sexy Rexy × Golden Celebration]

Helen Robinson HT, mp, Harkness; flowers medium pink in center, fading on outer petals, dbl., high-centered, moderate fragrance; recurrent; growth to 110 cm.; int. by R. Harkness & Co., 2006

Helen Suzman Rose F, lp

Helen Taft HT, 1913, Byrnes

Helen Taylor HT, pb, 1924, Pemberton; flowers rosy salmon, dbl.

Helen Traubel HT, pb, 1951, Swim, H.C.; bud long, pointed; flowers pink to apricot, 5-6 in., 23-30 petals, high-centered, borne singly, moderate fruity fragrance; foliage leathery, matte, green; stems weak necks; tall, vigorous growth; [Charlotte Armstrong × Glowing Sunset]; int. by Armstrong Nursery; Gold Medal, Rome, 1951

Helen Traubel, Climbing Cl HT, ab, 1974, Miller, Jack; bud long pointed; flowers pink to apricot, 5-6 in., 20-25 petals, high-centered; foliage leathery, dull green; [sport of Helen Traubel]; int. in 1970

Helen Vincent HP, mp, 1907, Dickson, A.; flowers carnation pink with lighter pink reflections, large, full

Helen Wild HT, op, 1959, Kemp, M.L.; flowers orange-pink veined rose-red, 5-6 in., 35 petals, high-centered; foliage light green; free growth; [Show Girl × Charlotte Armstrong]

Helena – See **Helena Renaissance**, S

Helena HT, mr, Strnad

Helena Johanna HT, mp, 2001, Palmer, Bobby J.; flowers medium pink with lighter pink reverse, 5 in., full, borne mostly solitary, slight fragrance; foliage medium size, dark green, glossy; prickles moderate; growth compact, medium (5 ft.); garden decorative, exhibition; [Kardinal × Gene Boerner]

Helena Renaissance S, lp, 1997, Olesen; flowers light pink, 10-15 cm., dbl., intense fragrance; foliage dark; growth bushy, 100-150 cm.; int. by Poulsen Roser, 1997

Helena Van Vliet Pol, lp, 1931, Kersbergen; flowers soft pink tinted salmon, borne in large trusses; vigorous growth; [sport of Salmonea]

Hélène HMult, pb, 1897, Lambert, P.; bud deep pink; flowers soft violet-rose, base yellowish-white, medium, semi-dbl., borne in clusters of 5-10; non-recurrent; nearly thornless; vigorous, climbing (12-15 ft.) growth; [Hybrid Tea × (Aglaia × Crimson Rambler)]

Helene HT, mp, Vecera, L.; flowers large, dbl.

Hélène Boulter HT, mr, 1902, Bernaix fils; flowers silky garnet

Hélène Dapples HT, mr, 1932, Heizmann, E.; bud pointed, dark; flowers glowing crimson-red; vigorous growth; [Mrs Henry Winnett × Lady Maureen Stewart]

Hélène de Gerlache HT, w, 2000, Lens, Louis; flowers white, champagne center, reverse lighter, 3 in., full, borne in small clusters, intense fragrance; recurrent; foliage medium size, light green, glossy; prickles moderate; upright, medium (70 cm.) growth; [(Pascali × Jour de Fete) × Vagabonde]; int. by Louis Lens N.V., 1982

Helène de Montbriand HT, mr, 1933, Schwartz, A.; flowers deep carmine-red, shaded vermilion, well-formed, large, globular; foliage glossy, dark; vigorous growth; [Reine Marie Henriette × Laurent Carle]

Hélène de Roumanie HT, rb, 1949, Meilland, F.; flowers red to pink, 5 in., 35 petals, urn-shaped; upright growth; [(Mme Joseph Perraud × seedling) × (seedling × Pres. Herbert Hoover)]; Gold Medal, NRS, 1950

Helene de Savoie HT, op, Kriloff; int. in 1995

Hélène Duché HT, lp, 1921, Buatois; flowers very large, dbl.

Hélène François HT, pb, 1923, Schwartz, A.; flowers salmon-pink shaded coppery red, center salmon-orange tinted, dbl.; [Mme Edouard Herriot × Viscountess Enfield]

Hélène Granger HMult, pb, 1910, Granger; flowers pink, center copper-yellow to medium, 4 cm., dbl., borne in clusters of 10-15, slight fragrance; foliage large; [Tea Rambler × Aglaia]

Hélène Guillot HT, pb, 1901, Guillot; flowers pink, tinted orange and yellow

Helene Leenders Pol, mp, Leenders, M.; flowers medium large, very dbl.; medium growth

Hélène Maréchal Cl Gr, w, 2000, Lens, Louis; flowers creamy white, 6 cm., dbl., borne in small clusters, moderate delicate fragrance; non-recurrent; foliage medium size, medium green, matte; prickles moderate; growth climbing, tall (6 m.); [*R. helenae* × Maréchal Niel]; int. by Louis Lens N.V., 1995

Hélène Puyravaud T, dy, 1893, Puyravaud; bud shaded carmine; flowers dark yellow, aging light yellow, large, full; [Pactole × Regulus]

Hélène Robinet HT, lp, 1928, Sauvageot, H.; flowers salmon-white, shaded rose, base yellow, dbl.; [Unnamed variety × Pres. Parmentier]; int. by F. Gillot

Helene Schoen HT, mr, 1963, Von Abrams; bud long, pointed; flowers 6 in., 60 petals, high-centered, slight fragrance; foliage leathery, glossy; vigorous, upright growth; [Multnomah × Charles Mallerin]; int. by Peterson & Dering, 1962

Hélène Vacaresco HT, pb, 1939, Chambard, C.; flowers salmon, shaded copper-carmine, large, cupped; foliage dark

Hélène Varabrègue HT, lp, 1958, Meilland, F.; bud pointed; flowers pale rose, very large, dbl., cupped; foliage leathery; strong stems; vigorous, bushy growth; [Lorraine × Michele Meilland]; int. by URS, 1953

Helene Videnz – See **Frau Helene Videnz**, HMult

Hélène Videnz Pol, pb, 1905, Lambert, P.; flowers salmon-pink, dbl., borne in clusters to 75; vigorous growth; [Euphrosyne × Louis Philippe]

Hélène Wattine HT, ly, 1910, Soupert & Notting; flowers light citron yellow; [Kaiserin Auguste Viktoria × Le Progrés]

Helenka HT, mp, Tesar

Helen's White Pol HMult, w, Diprose; int. by Mistydowns, 1993

Helga HT, dp, 1926, Weigand, C.; flowers deep pink to light red, dbl., high-centered, moderate fragrance; bushy (3-4 ft.) growth

Helga F, w, deRuiter; flowers white with pink markings on guard petals, large, semi-dbl., borne in clusters, moderate fragrance; int. in 1975

Helga Brichet S, lp, 2000; flowers single, borne mostly singly, moderate fragrance; foliage medium grey-green, dull; few prickles; bushy, tall (6 ft.) growth; [Complicata × Complicata]; int. by Nieuwesteeg Rose Nursery, 2001

Helgoland F, mr, 1936, Kordes; bud pointed, dark; flowers crimson to carmine, open, very large, semi-dbl., borne in clusters; foliage leathery, wrinkled, dark; vigorous, bushy growth; [Else Poulsen × Hybrid Tea seedling (dark crimson)]

Helgoland F, mr, 1976, Tantau, Math.; bud pointed; flowers copper-red, medium, semi-dbl., slight fragrance; foliage glossy, light; moderate, upright, bushy growth; int. by Horstmann, 1973

Héliodore Dober HGal, mr; flowers deep red edged crimson, quite large, ball-shaped

Helios HT, dy, 1935, Leenders, M.; flowers deep sunflower-yellow, open, semi-dbl.; foliage leathery, light; vigorous, bushy growth

Helklewei – See **Heinrich Blanc**, LCl

Hella Gr, dy, Guillot-Massad; flowers soft ocher yellow, slight fruity fragrance; moderate (3 ft.) growth; int. by Roseraies Guillot, 2004

Hellen Ann HT, Tantau, Math.; int. in 1989

Hello Min, mr, 1992, Cocker, James; flowers crimson with white eye, large, 6-14 petals, borne in large clusters; foliage medium size, medium green, semi-glossy; some prickles; patio; medium (50-80 cm.), bushy growth; [Darling Flame × seedling]; int. by James Cocker & Sons, 1990; Golden Prize, Glasgow, 1993

Hello HT, ob, Kriloff; int. in 1994

Hello F, mr, Meilland; flowers small, very dbl., borne in small clusters; growth to 50 cm.; int. by Meilland Richardier, 2002

Hello S, mr, Meilland; spreading, low (20 in.) growth

Hello There Min, w, 1987, Florac, Marilyn; flowers white, light yellow tints in center, good petal retention, small, 108 petals, cupped, borne usually singly, no fragrance; foliage small, medium green, matte; prickles tan, very few; bushy, low growth; [Care Deeply × Red Can Can]

Helma Min, Delforge, H.; int. in 1986

Helmut Kohl Rose HT, dr, Tantau, Math.; flowers very large, semi-dbl.; int. in 1996

Helmut Schmidt HT, my, 1980, Kordes, W.; bud large, long, pointed; flowers clear, even yellow, 4½-5 in., 30-40 petals, high-centered, borne 1-3 per cluster, moderate sweet tea fragrance; foliage dark green, matte; vigorous, upright, bushy growth; [New Day × seedling]; int. in 1979; Gold Medal, Geneva, 1979, Gold Medal, Belgium, 1979

Héloïse HGal, lp, 1816, Descemet; sepals long, viscous; flowers flesh pink nuanced purple, medium to large, full; prickles nearly thorness; Agathe group; probably re-introduced by Vibert around 1830, and sometimes attributed to him

Héloïse C, lp, 1818; flowers pale rose, small; growth compact

Héloïse HGal; Agathe group

Help the Aged HT, mp, 1987, Bracegirdle, A.J.; flowers clear pink, reverse slightly darker, satin two-tone effect, 23 petals, high-centered, intense damask fragrance; foliage medium size, light green, semi-glossy; prickles straight, brown, very few; bushy, medium growth; no fruit; [Mischief × Fragrant Cloud]; int. by Rosemary Roses, 1987

Helping Hand S, ob; int. in 2004

Helping Hands S, mr, Clements, John K.

Helpmekaar Roos HT, ab, Kordes; flowers deep apricot-cherry-brandy, large, full, moderate fragrance; foliage large, healthy; growth medium; int. in 1993

Helsingör – See **Elsinore**, F

Helvetia T, op, 1873, Ducher; flowers coppery salmon, tinged with fawn, large, full, globular

Helvetia HT, dp, 1911, Heizmann, E.; flowers large, dbl.; [Mme Caroline Testout × Farbenkonigin]

Helvétia – See **Mandalay**, HT

Helvetius HGal, rb, about 1830, Desprez; flowers red with lilac edges, large, dbl.

Hemaprova HT, ly, Ghosh; flowers cream to light yellow, large; int. by KSG Son Roses, 2001

Hemavathy F, op, Kasturi; flowers salmon-orange with brown overcast, deepening to smokey color; int. by KSG Son Roses, 1975

Hen Kauffmann F, mp, 1954, Leenders, M.; flowers rosy pink, dbl.; vigorous growth

Henderson – See **Triomphe de la Terre des Roses**, HP

Henkell Royal HT, mr, 1964, Kordes, R.; bud long; flowers blood-red, well-formed, large; vigorous, bushy growth; Gold Medal, Baden-Baden, 1964

Hennequin HGal, dr, about 1830, Desprez; flowers medium, full

Henri Barruet HWich, pb, 1918, Barbier; flowers coppery yellow, opening to pink and tinted white, 7-8 cm., dbl., borne in clusters of 8-15; vigorous, climbing (8 ft.) growth

Henri Brichard HT, w, 1891, Bonnaire; flowers bright carmine red shaded salmon pink, white reverse, large, very dbl.; foliage large, bronzy green; growth upright

Henri Caillaud LCl, Moreira da Silva, A.

Henri Coupé HP, mp, 1916, Barbier; flowers China pink, dbl., moderate fragrance; [Frau Karl Druschki × Gruss an Teplitz]

Henri Declinand LCl, mr, 1934, Mermet; flowers bright magenta-red, quite large, dbl.; foliage dark

Henri Foucquier HGal, mp, before 1842; flowers rose-pink, darker at center, large, dbl., moderate fragrance; not named for the jounalist/politician Henri Fouquier, but for a hybridizer named Foucquier

Henri Fouquier – See **Henri Foucquier**, HGal

Henri IV D, dp, before 1829, Trébucien; flowers rose pink, 4-5 in., full; foliage ovoid-oblong, pointed, serrate; prickles sparse, short, thick, unequal

Henri Lecoq B, dp, 1845, Lacharme

Henri Lecoq T, pb, 1871, Ducher; flowers pink, tinted yellow

Henri Lédéchaux HP, dp, 1868, Lédéchaux

Henri Linger LCl, yb, 1928, Barbier; flowers clear yellow-orange, open, semi-dbl.; foliage light, glossy; very vigorous, climbing growth; [*R. wichurana* × Benedicte Seguin]

Henri Mallerin – See **Rouge Mallerin**, HT

Henri Mallerin HT, yb, 1955, Mallerin, C.; bud ovoid; flowers empire-yellow suffused pink, large, 55-70 petals, slight fragrance; foliage leathery, glossy; bushy growth; PP1349; [Soeur Thérèse × Duquesa de Peñaranda]; int. by EFR

Henri Martin M, mr, 1862, Laffay, M.; bud sparsely mossed; flowers shining crimson, semi-dbl., borne in clusters of 3-8, slight fragrance

Henri Matisse F, pb, Delbard, Georges; flowers deep pink to medium red with white stripes, large, dbl., no fragrance; free-flowering; vigorous (50-100 cm.) growth; int. in 1996

Henri Pauthier HT, mr, 1933, Sauvageot, H.; flowers bright red, open, large, semi-dbl.; foliage glossy; bushy growth; [seedling × Edouard Mignot]; int. by C-P

Henri Puyravaud B, pb, 1893, Chauvry; flowers salmon pink, shaded carmine, base white, large, full; [Robusta × Imperatrice Eugénie]

Henri Quatre HGal, dp, 1821, Calvert; flowers bright purple pink, large, dbl.

Henri Salvador HT, w, Richardier; flowers cream, moderate fragrance; foliage semi-glossy; growth to 80-100 cm.; int. by Meilland Richardier, 1999

Henri IV HP, dr, 1862, Verdier, V. & C.; flowers bright purple red, shaded violet, large, full

Henri Ward-Beecher HP, m, 1874, Verdier, E.; flowers purple-violet, large, full

Henrietta HT, op, 1917, Merryweather; bud pointed, orange-crimson; flowers soft coral-salmon, open, semi-dbl., moderate fragrance; foliage dark; vigorous growth; [Alister Stella Gray × Andre Gamon]

Henrietta HT, ab, 1986, Olesen, Pernille & Mogens N.; flowers large, 25 petals, urn-shaped, borne singly, slight fruity fragrance; foliage large, dark, glossy; vigorous, upright, bushy growth; [seedling × (Pink Nordia × Sonny Boy)]; int. by Poulsen's Roses, 1984

Henrietta HT, yb, McGredy; int. in 2001

Henrietta de Snoy – See **Baronne Henriette de Snoy**, T

Henriette HGal, mr, before 1810, Dupont; flowers bright cherry red, large, full, borne in clusters of 8-10; Agathe group

Henriette – See **Bifera Italica**, HGal

Henriette HT, or, 1916, Dickson, A.; flowers coppery orange-red, large, dbl.

Henriette Ch, m; flowers violet, shaded purple, medium, semi-dbl.

Henriette Boulogne – See **Quatre Saisons d'Italie**, P

Henriette Campan A, m, before 1830; flowers purplish pink, 2½-3½ in., 70-80 petals; foliage very large, oval, pointed, dark green; prickles few, slender

Henriette Chandet HT, op, 1942, Mallerin, C.; bud oval; flowers orange-coral, large, dbl.; foliage glossy; vigorous, bushy growth; [Rochefort × La Parisienne]; int. by A. Meilland

Henriette Koster Pol, mr, 1939, Koster, D.A.; [sport of Dick Koster]

Henriette Pechtold HT, mr, 1946, Verschuren-Pechtold; bud long, pointed; flowers red, reverse salmon-red, large, dbl.; foliage soft; vigorous, bushy growth; [Briarcliff × Katharine Pechtold]

Henriette Petit HP, rb, 1879, Margottin père; flowers red and deep amaranth, large, full

Henros Cl F, dp, 1995, Henson, R.W.; flowers rose pink, medium, dbl., borne in small clusters; foliage medium size, medium green, glossy; some prickles; tall (250 cm.), climbing growth; [Glenfiddich × Lichterloh]

Henry A. Maynadier T, before 1920, Dingee & Conard

Henry Bennett T, pb, 1872, Levet; flowers light pink with deep sulphur yellow center, medium, full, intense fragrance

Henry Bennett HP, mr, 1875, Lacharme; flowers violet-crimson, medium, full; [Charles Lefebvre × unknown]

Henry Bierbauer S, pb, Williams, J.B.; flowers varying shades of pink, white and apricot, semi-dbl., flat, slight fragrance; recurrent; growth to 4 ft.; int. by Hortico, Inc., 2006

Henry Dunant HT, mr, Meilland; flowers bright red; int. in 2004

Henry Field HT, mr, 1948, Brownell; bud ovoid, long, pointed; flowers crimson-red, 5 in., 60 petals, high-centered, moderate fragrance; foliage glossy; vigorous, bushy growth; [Pink Princess × Crimson Glory]; int. by H. Field

Henry Fonda HT, dy, 1998, Christensen; bud pointed, ovoid; flowers deep yellow, pointed, 4½-5 in., 20-25 petals, high-centered, borne mostly singly; foliage medium size, dark green, glossy; tall growth; PP9390; int. by Bear Creek Gardens, 1996

Henry Ford HT, my, 1927, Deverman; flowers yellow edged salmon-orange, opening to lemon-yellow, semi-dbl.; [Mme Edouard Herriot × Golden Emblem]; int. by B&A

Henry Ford HT, mp, 1954, Howard, A.P.; bud long; flowers silvery pink, 4-5 in., 30 petals, high-centered, moderate fragrance; vigorous, upright growth; [Pink Dawn, Climbing × The Doctor]; int. by H&S

Henry Hudson HRg, w, 1977, Svedja, Felicitas; bud ovoid; flowers yellow stamens, 2½-3 in., 25 petals, intense fragrance; recurrent bloom; low, bushy growth; int. by Canada Dept. of Agric., 1976

Henry Irving Cl HP, dp, 1907, Conard & Jones; flowers light orange-red, medium, semi-dbl.; [unnamed HP × unnamed HMult]

Henry Kelsey HKor, mr, 1984, Svedja, Felicitas; flowers deep red fading to deep pink, 6-7 cm., 28 petals, borne in clusters of 9-18, moderate spicy fragrance; good repeat; foliage glossy; prickles moderate; trailing growth; remontant, very winter hardy; [*R.* × *kordesii* hybrid × seedling]

Henry King Stanford F, mr, 1975, Sheridan, V.V.; flowers semi-dbl., 15 petals; spreading growth; [Red Pinocchio × unknown]; int. in 1973

Henry Lawson HT, ob, Allender, Robert William; int. in 1999

Henry M. Stanley T, pb, 1891, Dingee & Conard; flowers deep rose, tinged with apricot yellow, bordered with carmine red, very full, moderate fragrance; [Mme Lombard × Comtesse Riza du Parc]

Henry Morse F, dr, 1959, Kordes; flowers deep blood-red shaded scarlet, 3 in., semi-dbl., borne in large trusses; free growth; int. by Morse, 1958

Henry Nevard HP, dr, 1924, Cant, F.; flowers crimson-scarlet, very large, 30 petals, cupped, intense fragrance; recurrent bloom; foliage dark, leathery; vigorous, bushy growth

Henry S. Badgery HT, Johnson

Henry V Ch, rb; flowers crimson, center white, cupped

Henry IV – See **Henri IV**, HP

Henry's Crimson China – See ***R. chinensis spontanea*** (Rehder & Wilson), Ch

Hens Verschuren HT, mr, 1948, Verschuren; bud long; flowers bright red, very large; [Mary Hart × seedling]

Her Majesty HP, mp, 1885, Bennett; flowers clear rose, with carmine reflexes toward center, very large, dbl.; occasionally recurrent bloom; very vigorous growth; [Mabel Morrison × Canari]

Her Majesty F, ab, 2001, Dickson, Colin; flowers apricot/peach/pink, paler reverse, predominately lemon yellow when young, s, 5 cm., very dbl., borne in small clusters, slight fragrance; foliage small, medium green, semi-glossy; prickles medium, moderate; growth bushy, low (70 × 95 cm.); garden decorative; [seedling × Interbronzi]; int. by Dickson Nurseries, 2001

Hera HT, mr, 1924, Van Rossem; flowers brilliant carmine shaded blood-red, 40 petals; [Gen. MacArthur × Luise Lilia]

Herald – See **De Ruiter's Herald**, Pol

Heraldo Cl HT, m, 1949, Dot, M.; bud long, pointed; flowers purple-pink, large, very dbl.; foliage leathery, dark; [Guineé × Texas Centennial]; int. by P. Dot

Herbalist – See **The Herbalist**, S

Herbemont's Musk Cluster N, w, Herbemont; flowers pure white, very large, dbl., borne in large clusters; recurrent bloom

Herbert Brunning HT, mr, 1940, Clark, A.; flowers brilliant red

Herbert Wilson F, w, 1967, Latham; flowers well-formed; foliage light green; [White Knight × The Optimist]

Herbie Min, m, 1987, Bennett, Dee; flowers rich mauve, outer petals deep mauve at margins, 25-30 petals, urn-shaped, slight fragrance; foliage medium size, medium green, semi-glossy; prickles slender, straight, average, reddish; upright, bushy, medium growth; hips globular, medium size, brown; PP6787; [Deep Purple × Dilly Dilly]; int. by Tiny Petals Nursery

Herbiz Min, op; int. in 1987

Herbstfeuer HEg, dr, 1961, Kordes; flowers large, semi-dbl., borne in clusters (up to 5), moderate fragrance; repeat bloom; vigorous (6 ft.) growth; hips large, pear-shaped, reddish-yellow; int. by Kern Rose Nursery

Hercules LCl, mp, 1938, Horvath; flowers Dame Edith Helen pink, over large, dbl., cupped; foliage large, glossy, dark; long stems; very vigorous, climbing growth; [Doubloons × Charles P. Kilham]; int. by Wayside Gardens Co.

Herero Gr, rb, 1985, Herholdt, J.A.; flowers yellow, reverse yellow with red overlay, spreading with age, semi-dbl., no fragrance; foliage large, dark, glossy; upright growth; [Angel Bells × Southern Sun]; int. in 1981

Here's Charlie HT, pb, 2006, Eddie Edwards; flowers full, high-centered, borne mostly solitary; foliage medium size, medium green; prickles small, moderate; growth upright, medium; exhibition; [Gemini × Fantasy]; int. in 2006

Here's Colette S, pb, 1999, Watson, Thomas L. & Glenda; flowers dark pink, white eye, reverse dark pink, 1½ in., single, borne in large clusters; foliage small, light green, dull; few prickles; spreading, low (3 ft.) growth; [seedling × Ballerina]

Here's Gert HT, mp, 2004, Edwards, Eddie & Phelps, Ethan; flowers full, exhibition, borne mostly solitary, moderate fragrance; foliage dark green, glossy; upright, tall (6 ft.) growth; exhibition; [Veteran's Honor × Hot Princess]; int. in 2005

Here's Ian Min, mr, 1996, Bell, Judy G.; flowers 1½ in., semi-dbl., borne mostly singly, no fragrance; foliage small, medium green, semi-glossy, disease-resistant; few prickles; small, compact, rounded growth; low (12 in winter hardy; [Dale's Sunrise × seedling]; int. by Michigan Mini Roses, 1997

Here's Sam HT, mp, 2004, Edwards, Eddie & Phelps, Ethan; flowers full, exhibition, borne mostly solitary, moderate fragrance; foliage large, dark green, glossy; growth upright, tall (6 ft.); exhibition; [Veteran's Honor × Hot Princess]; int. in 2005

Herfordia F, dp, Hempelmann; flowers medium, dbl.; int. in 1993

Herfsttooi HT, dr, 1919, Van Rossem; flowers dark crimson, medium, dbl., moderate fragrance; [General MacArthur × Leuchtfeuer]

Heriflor F, lp, Sauvageot; flowers dbl., borne in small clusters; int. in 1990

Heritage S, lp, 1985, Austin, David; flowers medium, full, cupped, intense fragrance; recurrent bloom; foliage small, dark, semi-glossy; upright, bushy growth; [seedling × (Iceberg × unknown)]; int. by David Austin Roses, Ltd., 1984

Herman Steyn HT, rb, Kordes; flowers carmine red with chrome yellow reverse, full, high-centered, slight fragrance; free-flowering; vigorous (2 m.) growth; int. in 1994

Hermance HP, lp, 1853, Robert; flowers flesh pink, large, full, globular

Hermance Louisa de la Rive T, w, 1882, Nabonnand; bud long; flowers white, with sometimes a pale pink center, large, full

Hermann Berger HT, or, GPG Bad Langensalza; flowers large, dbl.; int. in 1982

Hermann Eggers HT, or, 1930, Kordes; flowers deep orange-scarlet, very large, dbl., high-centered; foliage dark, leathery; very vigorous growth; [(Pink Pearl × Templar) × Florex]; int. by Dreer

Hermann Kegel M, m, 1849, Portemer fils; flowers reddish-violet, sometimes streaked crimson or lilac, medium, dbl., borne mostly solitary; freely remontant; foliage tinted reddish when young, oblong, dentate; growth vigorous, spreading

Hermann Kiese HT, yb, 1906, Geduldig; flowers yellow and pink, large, semi-dbl.

Hermann Lindecke HT, lp, 1929, Lindecke; flowers whitish pink, reverse salmon-pink large, dbl., high-centered; [sport of General-Superior Arnold Janssen]

Hermann Löns HT, dp, 1931, Tantau; flowers shining light red, large, single, cupped, borne in clusters; foliage glossy; vigorous growth; [Ulrich Brunner Fils × Red-Letter Day]

Hermann Neuhoff HT, mr, 1923, Neuhoff; flowers uniform blood-red, dbl.; [sport of General-Superior Arnold Janssen]; int. by Kordes

Hermann Robinow HT, op, 1918, Lambert, P.; flowers salmon-orange shaded salmon-rose and dark yellow, large, dbl.; vigorous growth; [Frau Karl Druschki × Lyon Rose]

Hermann Robinow, Climbing Cl HT, pb, 1934, Lambert, P.; flowers salmon pink, center orange, large, full, moderate fragrance; [sport of Hermann Robinow]

Hermann Schmidt LCl, dp, Hetzel; flowers crimson/cherry red, white center, 4-5 cm., semi-dbl., borne in medium to large clusters; reliable repeat; int. in 1986

Hermann Schönfeld HT, lp, 1925, Dechan; flowers large, dbl.

Hermann Teschendorff HT, rb, 1949, Berger, V.; bud ovoid; flowers copper-red, reverse old-gold, open, very large, dbl., cupped; foliage glossy, dark, bronze; very vigorous, upright growth; int. by Teschendorff

Hermelia Casas F, mp, 1956, Dot, Pedro; flowers pearly, reverse carmine, medium, 30 petals, borne in clusters of 3-6; moderate growth; [Méphisto × Perla de Alcañada]

Hermen Anglada HT, w, 1933, Dot, Pedro; bud very large; flowers white tinted pink, single; very vigorous growth

Hermes HT, dy, 1935, Teschendorff; flowers large, dbl.

Hermina S, pb, 1996, Buck, Dr. Griffith J.; flowers red with white reverse aging Neyron rose with white reverse, dbl., slight fragrance; good repeat; foliage medium size, dark green, semi-glossy; some prickles; upright, bushy, medium growth; hardy to 18-24; [((Tickled Pink × Prairie Princess) × Autumn Dusk) × ((Tickled Pink × (Carrousel × (Morning Stars × Suzanne))) × Maytime)]; int. by Kimbrew Walter Roses, 1997

Hermine Madèlé Pol, w, 1888, Soupert & Notting; flowers creamy white with yellowish reflections, center darker, small, full; [Mignonette × Marquise de Vivens]

Hermione HT, op, 1982, Gaujard, Jean; flowers deep salmon, large, 35 petals, moderate fragrance; foliage large, dark, glossy; upright, bushy growth; [Rose Gaujard × Colour Wonder]; int. by Roseraies Gaujard, 1981

Hermitage – See **Joachim du Bellay**, F

Hermosa Ch, lp, 1834 or before, Marcheseau; bud pointed; flowers light blush-pink, 35 petals, high-centered, moderate fragrance; recurrent bloom; foliage bluish green; small vigorous growth; sometimes classed as B; int. by Prior to 1837

Hermosa, Climbing – See **Setina**, Cl HCh

Hermosa, Climbing F, pb, 1997, Horner, Heather M.; flowers large, dbl., borne in small clusters; foliage medium size, semi-glossy; some prickles; upright, medium (80cm.) growth; [seedling × seedling]

Hero S, mp, 1983, Austin, David; flowers glistening medium pink, large, 20 petals, cupped, intense fragrance; foliage medium size, medium green, semi-glossy; spreading growth; [The Prioress × seedling]; int. by David Austin Roses, Ltd., 1982

Hérodiade N, yb, 1888, Brassac; flowers chamois yellow, center darker, tinted pink or carmine, medium to large, full; [Duarte de Oliveira × unknown]

Heroïca HT, dr, 1960, Lens; flowers deep velvety red, becoming lighter; vigorous growth; [Rome Glory × Independence]

Heroine HT, op, 1935, Krause; bud pointed; flowers salmon-shrimp-pink, large, dbl., high-centered; foliage leathery, dark; very vigorous, bushy growth; [Wilhelm Kordes × Mrs Atlee]

Héroïne de Vaucluse B, mp, 1863, Moreau et Robert; flowers velvety pink, sometimes washed with carmine, large, full, globular

Héroïque Commandant Marchand T, yb, 1900, Buatois; flowers nasturtium yellow, shaded fiery carmine, edges lighter, large, very full; [Laurette Messimy × Ma Capucine]

Heros HT, mr, 1933, Tantau; flowers very large, dbl., cupped; foliage leathery, dark; bushy growth; [Johanniszauber × Étoile de Hollande]

Herrenchiemsee – See **Berleburg**, F

Herrenhausen HMsk, ly, 1938, Kordes; bud ovoid, greenish yellow; flowers light yellow, fading white, red tints in sun, large, dbl., cupped, borne in clusters, moderate pansy fragrance; profuse, intermittent bloom; foliage leathery, glossy, light; long stems; vigorous, bushy growth; [Eva × Golden Rapture]

Herrin von Lieser HT, ly, 1907, Lambert, P.; flowers cream-yellow, center reddish-yellow; [Frau Karl Druschki × G. Schwartz]

Herself F, lp, 1965, Vincent; flowers 4 in., 18 petals, borne in clusters; free growth; [The Optimist × Moulin Rouge]; int. by Harkness

Hershey's Red HT, dr, Williams, J. Benjamin; int. in 1996

Hertfordshire S, dp, Kordes; flowers carmine-pink, yellow stamens, small, single, borne singly and in clusters, very slight fragrance; free-flowering; spreading, vigorous (1½ × 2½ ft.) growth; int. in 1991

Hertfordshire Glory F, yb, 1971, Harkness; flowers yellow, tinted red, large, 20 petals, slight fragrance; foliage glossy; [Isobel Harkness × Circus]

Hertogin van Brabant S, pb, DVP Melle; [seedling × Eclipse]; int. in 2000

Herz As HT, mr, 1963, Tantau, Math.; bud long, pointed; flowers pure blood-red, well-formed, large, dbl.; vigorous, upright growth

Herz As – See **Century Sunset**, HT

Herz As Typ II HT, mr, Tantau; flowers blood-red, slight fragrance; int. by Rosen Tantau, 2000

Herz-Dame – See **Dame de Coeur**, HT

Herz von Luzern F, op, Huber; flowers intense salmon color, large, graceful, 20-25 petals, slight fragrance; reddish early foliage; bushy, broad, medium (70 cm.) growth; int. by Richard Huber, 2001

Herzblättchen Pol, dp, 1889, Geschwind, R.; flowers carmine-pink, small, dbl.

Herzblut – See **Commonwealth**, F

Herzensgruss HT, dr, 1975, Hetzel, Karl; bud pointed; flowers dark velvety red, medium, dbl., intense fragrance; foliage glossy; vigorous, upright, bushy growth; [(Fragrant Cloud × Goldmarie) × Red American Beauty]; int. by GAWA, 1973

Herzog Friedrich II von Anhalt HT, lp, 1906, Welter; flowers soft pink; [Souv. du President Carnot × Mme Jules Grolez]

Herzog von Windsor – See **Duke of Windsor**, HT

Herzogin Frederike S, pb, Noack; flowers salmon-rose with yellow center, 2-2½ in., semi-dbl., borne in clusters; good repeat; growth to 5 ft.

Herzogin Marie-Antoinette von Mecklembourg HT, ob, 1910, Jacobs; bud long; flowers pure orange and golden yellow, large, full, moderate fragrance; foliage large

Herzogin Marie von Coburg-Gotha T, w, 1903, Welter; flowers pure white, aging to pale yellow, large; [Mme Carnot × Marie van Houtte]

Herzogin Viktoria Adelheid von Coburg-Gotha HT, op, 1905, Welter; flowers coppery carmine-pink, large, dbl.; [(Mme Jules Grolez × Kaiserin Auguste Viktoria) × Captain Hayward]

Herzogin von Calabrien HT, ly, 1914, Lambert, P.; bud long, pointed; flowers creamy white, with clear sulphur-yellow center, large, semi-dbl., moderate fragrance; [Frau Karl Druschki × (Hofgärtendirektor Graebener × Herrin von Lieser)]

Hessengruss HT, dp, 1928, Thönges; flowers deep pink, reverse carmine-rose, dbl.; [sport of Laurent Carle]

Hessenstar HT, or, 1975, Hetzel; bud ovoid; flowers orange-red to geranium-red, medium, 30-40 petals, moderate fragrance; moderate growth; [Baccará × Prima Ballerina]; int. by GAWA, 1973

Hessie Lowe HT, op, 1956, Lowe; flowers peach-pink, dbl., high-centered; foliage glossy; very vigorous growth

Hessoise HEg, mp, before 1811, Schwarzkopf; flowers bright rose, semi-dbl.; as many as 15 HEg hybrids may have been sold under this name

Hessoise Anémone – See **Zabeth**, HEg

Hessoise Pourpre Double HEg, m, before 1815, Descemet; flowers purple

Hester Prynne F, dr, Robinson; flowers deep, rich crimson, single, borne in clusters, slight fragrance; [Sarabande × unknown]; int. in 1993

Hestia F, Arles, F.

Heterophylla HRg, w, 1899, Cochet-Cochet; flowers semi-dbl., borne in clusters of 5-10; [*R. rugosa* × *R. foetida*]

Hettie LCl, w, 2004, Barden, Paul; flowers white, soft amber, reverse white, cream, 3½ in., very full, borne in large clusters, moderate green apple fragrance; remontant; foliage medium size, dark green, semi-glossy; prickles ½ in., curved, brown, moderate; lax, arching growth, medium (6-8 ft.); small climber, shrub; [Bonica 82 × Abraham Darby]; int. in 2004

Hetty Ann HT, pb, 2000, Poole, Lionel; flowers pink-peach, reverse pink, 4½ in., full, borne in small clusters, moderate fragrance; foliage medium size, medium green, glossy, weather-resistant; few prickles; upright, medium (2½ ft.) growth; [Selfridges × Seedling (pink HT)]; int. by David Lister Roses, 2001

Heure Mauve HT, m, 1965, Laperrière; flowers lilac-mauve tinted blush, well-formed, 5 in., 35 petals; foliage glossy, bright green; vigorous growth; [Simone × Prelude]; int. by EFR

Heureka HT, w, Urban, J.

Heureux Anniversaire Gr, op, 1960, Delbard-Chabert; bud urn-shaped; flowers salmon-orange, 3 in., 28 petals, slight spicy fragrance; foliage glossy; very vigorous, bushy growth; PP2079; [(Incendie × Chic Parisien) × (Floradora × Independence)]; originally registered as Pol; patent issued as Gr; int. by Stark Bros., 1963

Hewlet-Packard 2000 – See **HP 2000**, HT

Hexham Abbey F, op, 1976, Wood; flowers salmon-pink, base yellow turning copper, large, intense fragrance; foliage leathery; growth vigorous, low to medium, upright; [Fairlight × Arthur Bell]

Hey Paula HT, yb, 2007, Edwards, Eddie; flowers yellow with pink edging around outer petals, 4½-5 in., full, borne mostly solitary; foliage medium size, medium green, matte; prickles medium, straight, green, few; growth upright, medium; [unknown × unknown]; int. by Mills, James, 2007

Heywood S, ab, 1995, Kirkham, Gordon Wilson; flowers peach, medium, 6-14 petals, borne in large clusters; foliage medium size, medium green, matte; numerous prickles; tall, bushy growth; [Tynwald × Bright Smile]

Hi Min, yb, 2000, Moe, Mitchie; flowers yellow edged with pink, ½-¾ in., semi-dbl., high-centered, borne mostly solitary, slight fragrance; foliage small, dark green, semi-glossy; prickles very small, straight, few; growth compact, medium (12-14 in.); garden decorative, exhibition; [Klima × Stretch Johnson]; int. by Mitchie's Roses and More, 2001

Hi Min, lp, Strawn; flowers pale pink fading white, tiny, ½ in. or less, 5 petals; good repeat; bushy, very small (6-8 in.) growth; micro-mini

Hi-de-hi Min, mp, 1982, McGredy, Sam IV; flowers small, 20 petals, moderate fragrance; foliage small, dark, glossy; bushy growth; [Anytime × Gartendirektor Otto Linne]; int. in 1981

Hi Doll F, or, Dickson, Patrick; int. in 1995

Hi-Fi F, or, 1959, Gregory; flowers bright orange-scarlet, semi-dbl., borne in clusters; foliage glossy; [Independence × unknown]; int. in 1958

Hi Ho Cl Min, op, 1965, Moore, Ralph S.; flowers deep pink, small, dbl., borne in clusters; foliage glossy; vigorous, climbimg growth; PP2719; [Little Darling × Magic Wand]; int. by Sequoia Nursery, 1964

Hi, Neighbor! Gr, mr, 1981, Buck, Dr. Griffith J.; bud ovoid, pointed, crimson; flowers 40-45 petals, cupped, borne 1-6 per cluster, moderate sweet fragrance; continuous; foliage leathery, dark green, matte; prickles awl-like; bushy, erect growth; [(Queen Elizabeth × Prairie Princess) × Portrait]; int. by Iowa State University

Hi-Ohgi HT, or, 1986, Suzuki, Seizo; flowers deep orange-red, large, 28 petals, moderate fragrance; foliage dark, semi-glossy; prickles slanted downward; tall, upright growth; [San Francisco × (Montezuma × Peace)]; int. by Keisei Rose Nursery, 1981

Hi Society F, lp, 1999, Cocker, A.; flowers lilac pink, reverse lighter, 1 in., dbl., borne in large clusters; foliage small, light green, glossy; prickles moderate; upright, bushy, medium (2-2½ ft.) growth; [Conservation × ((Chanelle × Golden Masterpiece) × Adolf Horstmann)]; int. by James Cocker & Sons, 1999

Hi Teen – See **Designer's Choice**, Gr

Hiawatha HMult, rb, 1904, Walsh; flowers deep crimson, center white, anthers golden, small, single, cupped, borne in large clusters; foliage rich green, leathery, glossy; very vigorous, climbing (15-20 ft.) growth; [Crimson Rambler × Paul's Carmine Pillar]

Hiawatha Recurrent – See **Hiawatha Remontant**, Cl Pol

Hiawatha Remontant Cl Pol, op, 1931, Sauvageot, H.; flowers carmine suffused orange, white eye, 3 cm., borne in medium clusters; intermittent rebloom; foliage small, glossy; long stems; very vigorous, climbing growth; [Hiawatha × Mme Norbert Levavasseur]; sometimes classed as HMult; int. as Hiawatha Recurrent, C-P

Hibernica HSpn, lp, 1802; flowers varying shades of pink, 1 in., single, borne in clusters of 3; foliage glaucous green, with 5-7 leaflets; numerous prickles; growth compact, erect; hips sub-globose, bright red; probably *R. canina* × *R. spinosissima*; discovered by Templeton near Belfast

Hidalgo HT, mr, 1979, Meilland, Mrs. Marie-Louise; bud conical; flowers currant-red, very large, 30 petals, cupped; foliage matte, bronze; vigorous, upright growth; [((Queen Elizabeth × Karl Herbst) × (Lady X × Pharaon)) × (MEIcesar × Papa Meilland)]; int. by Meilland

Hidcote Gold HSpn, my, 1948, Hilling; flowers canary-yellow, single, borne several together; non-recurrent; foliage ferny; prickles very large, flattened, wing-like; thought by Graham Stuart Thomas to be *R. sericea pteracantha* × *R. hugonis*; int. by Hilling

Hidcote Yellow – See **Lawrence Johnston**, LCl

Hide and Seek F, op, Dickson; flowers coral-pink, metallic sheen to petals, borne in clusters; free-flowering; foliage reddish early, then medium green, glossy; low, rounded growth; int. by Dickson Roses, 2003

High Ambition MinFl, ab, 2006, Wells, Verlie W.; flowers light apricot, reverse lighter apricot, 1¾ in., full, borne mostly solitary; foliage medium size, medium green, semi-glossy; prickles ⅝ in., straight, moderate; growth upright, medium (36-45 in.); garden decorative, exhibition; [seedling × seedling]; int. by Wells MidSouth Roses, 2006

High Cloud Min, r, 1997, Bennett, Dee; flowers soft tan with yellow base, lighter reverse, 1½ in., full, borne singly or in small clusters, moderate fragrance; foliage medium size, medium green, glossy; bushy, tall (60-70 cm.) growth; [Lagerfeld × Ernie]; int. by Tiny Petals Nursery

High Esteem HT, pb, 1961, Von Abrams; bud pointed; flowers phlox-pink, reverse silvery, 6 in., 43 petals, high-centered, intense fruity fragrance; foliage leathery, light green; vigorous, upright, compact growth; PP2245; [(Charlotte Armstrong × Mme Henri Guillot) × (Multnomah × Charles Mallerin)]; int. by Peterson & Dering, 1961

High Fashion HT, dp, 1972, Patterson; bud ovoid; flowers deep pink, medium, dbl., high-centered; foliage glossy, soft; vigorous, upright growth; [Queen Elizabeth × Peace]; int. by Patterson Roses

High Five F, m, 1999, Schuurman, Frank B.; flowers 3¼ in., full, borne in large clusters, slight fragrance; foliage medium size, dark green, glossy; prickles moderate; spreading, medium (30-36 in.) growth; [Jacaranda × French Lace]; int. by Franko Roses New Zealand, 1997

High Flier LCl, mr, Fryer; flowers rich, blood red,

well-formed, dbl., moderate fragrance; repeats all season; foliage dark green; vigorous growth to 10-12 ft.; int. by Fryer's Roses, 2004

High Flight Min, w; int. by White Rose garden centers, 2001

High Flyer – See **Dynamite**, LCl

High Hope Min, or, 1985, Florac, Marilyn; flowers bright orange-red, small, 45 petals, cupped, borne singly and in clusters; foliage medium size, light, glossy; vigorous, upright growth; [Young Love × Little Chief]; int. by M.B. Farm Min. Roses, Inc., 1984

High Hopes LCl, mp, 1994, Harkness; flowers 32 petals, borne singly or in small clusters, moderate spicy fragrance; foliage medium size, medium green, semi-glossy; upright, tall, climbing growth; [Compassion × Congratulations]; int. by Harkness New Roses, Ltd., 1992

High Jinks Min, pb, 1992, Saville, F. Harmon; flowers 1½ in., 25-32 petals, high-centered, borne singly and in sprays of 4-30; foliage medium size, dark green, semi-glossy; upright, bushy, medium to tall growth; [Rise 'n' Shine × Sheri Anne]; int. by Nor'East Min. Roses, 1993

High Life Min, rb, 1996, McCann, Sean; flowers medium red with white at throat, reverse white with red, fading with age, 2½ in., full, high-centered; foliage large, medium green, dull; upright, tall (30 in.) growth; PPRR; [Lady in Red × Oriana]; int. by Justice Miniature Roses, 1997

High Noon Cl HT, my, 1946, Lammerts, Dr. Walter; flowers lemon-yellow, 3-4 in., 28 petals, loosely cupped, borne singly or in small clusters, moderate spicy fragrance; foliage leathery, glossy; upright, vigorous, climbing (8 ft.) growth; [Soeur Thérèse × Capt. Thomas]; int. by Armstrong Nursery

High Point Min, w, 1986, Molder, W.A.; [sport of Helen Boehm]; int. by Rose Acres

High Sheriff HT, or, 1992, Harkness, R., & Co., Ltd.; flowers medium, dbl., borne in small clusters; foliage large, dark green, glossy; few prickles; tall (95 cm.), upright growth; [seedling × Silver Jubilee]; int. by Harkness New Roses, Ltd.

High Society HT, mr, 1961, Kordes, R.; flowers bright red, 4 in., 30 petals, high-centered, slight fragrance; bushy growth; int. by A. Dickson, 1961

High Society LCl, dp, 2005, Zary, Keith W.; flowers full, borne in large clusters, intense fragrance; foliage large, dark green, glossy; prickles 7-9 mm., hooked downward, greyed-orange, moderate; growth spreading, vigorous, tall (4 m.); climber; PP16187; [Dynamite × America]; int. by Jackson & Perkins Wholesale, Inc., 2004

High Spirits Min, mr, 1984, Saville, F. Harmon; flowers small, 35 petals, high-centered, borne in sprays, slight fragrance; foliage small, dark, semi-glossy; upright growth; PP5450; [Sheri Anne × Tamango]; int. by Nor'East Min. Roses

High Stepper Cl Min, yb, 1983, Moore, Ralph S.; flowers yellow overlaid pink, reverse yellow, small, dbl.; foliage medium size, dark, semi-glossy; growth bushy, spreading (to 5 ft; needs support); [(Little Darling × Yellow Magic) × Magic Wand]; int. by Moore Min. Roses

High Style Min, mr, 1983, Lyon; flowers cardinal red, 35 petals, borne in clusters; foliage medium size, medium green, semi-glossy; upright, bushy growth; [seedling × seedling]

High Summer F, or, 1978, Dickson, Patrick; bud ovoid; flowers vermilion, 3 in., 26 petals, cupped; foliage large; bushy growth; [Zorina × Ernest H. Morse]; int. by Dickson Nurseries, Ltd.

High Tide Min, ob, 1986, McDaniel, Earl; flowers orange, yellow reverse, medium, 25 petals, cupped, borne usually singly; foliage small, dark, semi-glossy; few prickles; upright, bushy growth; [seedling × seedling]; int. by McDaniel's Min. Roses

High Time HT, pb, 1960, Swim, H.C.; bud urn-shaped; flowers claret-rose, reverse gold and pink, 4-5 in., 24 petals, high-centered, intense spicy fragrance; foliage dark, glossy; vigorous, upright growth; PP1809; [Charlotte Armstrong × Signora]; int. by Roseway Nursery, 1959

Highdownensis HMoy, mr, 1928, Stern, Sir Frederich; flowers bright medium red, fading to lighter centers, single, borne in clusters of 7-9; foliage dark, coppery; prickles colorful; vigorous, bushy (10 × 10 ft.) growth; hips orange-scarlet; [*R. moyesii* × unknown]

Highfield LCl, ly, 1979, Harkness; bud pointed; flowers primrose yellow, 39 petals, round, borne in clusters of 1-3, moderate sweet fragrance; good repeat; foliage dark green; prickles hooked; upright, free branching growth; [sport of Compassion]; int. in 1980

Highland Beauty F, mr, 1957, deRuiter; flowers rich red, 3 in., semi-dbl., borne in clusters, slight fragrance; foliage dark, glossy; vigorous growth; [Signal Red × Red Wonder]; int. by Easter Persley Nurs., 1956

Highland Charm F, op, 1957, deRuiter; flowers coral-salmon, large, semi-dbl., borne in large clusters, slight fragrance; foliage leathery; vigorous, bushy growth; [Duchess of Rutland × Fashion]; int. by Easter Persley Nurs., 1956

Highland Dancer F, rb

Highland Fling F, or, 1971, Anderson's Rose Nurseries; flowers orange-scarlet, veined black, 4-4½ in., 22 petals; foliage glossy; [Dearest × Elizabeth of Glamis]

Highland Glory F, mr, 1957, deRuiter; flowers crimson-red, 3 in., semi-dbl., borne in large clusters, slight fragrance; foliage coppery; vigorous growth; [Sidney Peabody × Floribunda seedling]; int. by Easter Persley Nurs., 1956

Highland Laddie Min, mr, 1990, Cocker, James & Sons; bud pointed; flowers scarlet red, medium, 19 petals, cupped, borne in sprays of 5-11, slight fragrance; foliage medium size, medium green, glossy; prickles medium, green; upright growth; hips urn-shaped, medium, brown; [National Trust × Dainty Dinah]; int. in 1989

Highland Lass Min, yb, 1991, Zipper, Herbert; flowers red and yellow with yellow reverse, medium, semi-dbl., borne in small clusters, no fragrance; foliage small, dark green, semi-glossy; few prickles; low (20 cm.), compact growth; [Rise 'n' Shine × High Spirits]; int. by Magic Moment Miniature Roses, 1992

Highland Mary T, 1908, Dingee & Conard

Highland Park HT, op, 1942, Mallerin, C.; bud tawny salmon; flowers salmon-pink, open, large, 35 petals; foliage leathery; vigorous, upright, bushy growth; [E.G. Hill × Mme Henri Guillot]; int. by C-P

Highland Wedding HT, w, 1971, MacLeod; flowers white, suffused blush, center light gold, 4½ in., 30 petals; foliage large, dark, semi-glossy; vigorous growth; [Virgo × Rose Gaujard]

Highlands Rose F, mp, 2000, McCann, Sean; flowers changing from rose pink to lilac with age, medium, semi-dbl., borne in small clusters, slight fragrance; foliage medium size, medium green (dark red when young), glossy; few prickles; growth upright; garden decorative; [Gentle Annie × Dainty Dora]

Highlight F, ob, 1957, Robinson, H.; flowers orange-scarlet, 2½ in., 24 petals, borne in large clusters; vigorous growth; [seedling × Independence]; int. by Victoria Nurs., 1957; Gold Medal, NRS, 1957

Hightae F, pb, 1988, Greenfield, Mrs. P.L.; flowers clear, medium pink outer petals, deeper in color at the heart, 45-50 petals, high-centered, intense fragrance; foliage small, bronze aging to medium green, glossy; prickles long, curved slightly downward, red; low, bushy, free-flowering growth; [Duet × Regensberg]; int. by Hightae Plant Nurs., 1988

Highveld Sun – See **Ralph's Creeper**, S

Highway Rose S, dp, Kordes; int. in 1984

Highway to the Capital – See **Miyako Oji**, HT

Higoromo HT, dr, 1999, Suzuki, Seizo; flowers deep red, 4-5 in., 30-35 petals, flat, slight fragrance; foliage dark green, semi-glossy; growth vigorous (4-5 ft.); [Duftzauber × (Josephine Bruce × seedling)]; int. by Keisei Rose Nurseries, 1990; Gold Medal, Japan Rose Club, 1990

Higth Parade F, pb

Hikari F, Suzuki, Seizo; int. in 1969

Hilda HT, pb, 1928, Cant, B. R.; flowers salmon-pink, reverse orange-carmine, very large, dbl., globular; foliage leathery; long stems; vigorous growth

Hilda Heinemann – See **Galileo**, HT

Hilda Murrell S, mp, 1986, Austin, David; flowers old rose form, large, full, flat, intense fragrance; few blooms after spring flush; foliage large, medium green, matte; strong, upright, bushy (4 ft.) growth; [seedling × (Parade × Chaucer)]; int. in 1984

Hilda Phillips HT, dy, 1948, Bees; flowers deep golden yellow, well-shaped, medium; foliage glossy, bronze; [Aureate seedling × Mrs Sam McGredy]

Hilda Rahn F, lp, 2002, Read, Allan; flowers full, borne in small clusters, intense fragrance; recurrent; foliage medium size, medium green, semi-glossy; prickles small, pointed, numerous; growth spreading, tall (10 ft.); garden; hardy; [Spring Song × unknown]; int. by Villa Rosa, 2004

Hilda Richardson HT, w, 1913, Dickson, A.; flowers milk white, flushed rosy lilac at tips, with prominent golden stamens, small to m, semi-dbl., intense geranium/primrose fragrance

Hilda Scott HT, my, 1955, Glassford; flowers butter-yellow, small; [Lady Hillingdon × unknown]; int. by Morse

Hilde Min, rb, 1999, Benardella, Frank A.; flowers white with red washing, reverse ivory, 1½-2 in., dbl., borne mostly singly, moderate fragrance; foliage medium size, dark green, glossy; few prickles; bushy, medium (12-18 in.) growth; PP14533; [Figurine × Kristin]

Hilde Apelt HT, ob, 1927, Leenders, M.; flowers saffron-yellow, dbl.; [seedling × Souv. de Claudius Pernet]

Hilde Steinert HT, rb, 1926, Leenders, M.; flowers coral-red, reverse reddish-salmon and old-gold, semi-dbl.

Hildegarde HT, ob, 1946, Boerner; bud long, pointed; flowers saffron-rose-pink, 5 in., 30-35 petals, high-centered; foliage leathery; very vigorous, upright growth; [sport of Briarcliff]; int. by J&P

Hildenbrandseck HRg, mp, 1909, Lambert, P.; flowers shining clear pink, single, borne in clusters; recurrent bloom; vigorous growth; [Atropurpurea × Frau Karl Druschki]

Hildeputchen HMult, m, 1922, Bruder Alfons; flowers violet-pink with white, 2-3 cm., single to semi-dbl., moderate fragrance

Hill – See **Hill Cottage**, S

Hill Cottage S, w, Poulsen; flowers white, small, semi-dbl., borne in clusters, no fragrance; foliage dark green, glossy; broad, bushy growth; int. by Poulsen Roser, 2004

Hill Crest HT, rb, 1948, Joseph H. Hill, Co.; bud short, pointed, oxblood-red; flowers carmine, 3½-4 in., 50-55

petals, high-centered; foliage leathery; very vigorous, upright, compact, tall growth

Hill Top HT, ab, 1942, Joseph H. Hill, Co.; bud long, pointed, light coral-red; flowers buff, 4-5 in., 28 petals, globular; foliage leathery, dark, wrinkled; vigorous, upright growth; [Joanna Hill × R.M.S. Queen Mary]; int. by Wayside Gardens Co., 1946

Hillary Min, yb

Hillary First Lady F, mr, Laperrière; flowers brilliant scarlet red, dbl.; int. in 1997

Hillcrest Pillar S, my, 1930, Hillcrest Gardens; flowers bright yellow, medium, semi-dbl.; pillar (6 ft.) growth; [*R. × harisonii* × unknown]

Hillier Rose HMoy, dr, 1920, Hillier; flowers deep red, 2 in., single; growth dense, to 9 ft.; [*R. moyesii* × *R. willmottiae*]

Hill's America HT, mp, 1921, E.G. Hill, Co.; flowers rose-pink, 44 petals; [Premier × Hoosier Beauty]; Gold Medal, NRS, 1924

Hill's Hillbilly F, mp, 1947; bud ovoid, red; flowers pink, open, 1-2 in., 5-6 petals, borne in clusters; foliage leathery, dark; vigorous, upright, bushy growth; [Juanita × Mrs R.M. Finch]; int. by Wayside Gardens Co.

Hill's Victory HT, rb, 1942, Joseph H. Hill, Co.; bud red; flowers rose-red to rose-pink, 5-6 in., 50-55 petals; foliage leathery, dark, wrinkled; long, strong stems; vigorous, upright, much branched growth; [Chieftain × Sweet Adeline]

Hilltop LCl, pb, Huxley, Ian; int. in 1989

Hilltop Rose – See ***R. collina*** (Jacquin), Misc OGR

Hiltig – See **Premier**

Hilton Edward HT, mp, 1994, Stibbard, Robert H.; flowers lavender pink, 3-3½ in., dbl., borne mostly singly, intense fragrance; foliage large, dark green, semi-glossy; some prickles; tall, upright growth; [Sweet Afton × News]; int. by Tallisker Nursery Enterprises, 1995

Himalayan Musk Rose – See ***R. brunonii*** (Lindley)

Himalayensis – See **Kaiserin des Nordens**, HRg

Himangini F, w, 1970, Indian Agri. Research Institute; bud ovoid; flowers ivory-white, center light buff, open, medium, dbl.; vigorous, bushy, compact growth; [Saratoga × unknown]; int. in 1968

Himatsuri HT, dr, 1977, Teranishi, K.; bud circular; flowers 3½-4 in., high-centered; foliage small; upright growth; [(Tropicana × Karl Herbst) × Mainauperle]; int. by Itami Bara-en, 1973

Hime Min, dp, 1999, Hirabayashi, Hiroshi; flowers bright purplish pink, 1½-2 in., 20-25 petals, flat; foliage dark green, semi-glossy; growth to 10 in.; [Ko's Yellow × seedling]; int. by Keisei Rose Nurseries, 1997; Gold Medal, Japan Rose Concours, 1997

Himmelsauge HSet, m, 1895, Geschwind, R.; flowers dark velvety purple-red, fading to medium pink, occaisionally striped with white, 4-6 cm., very dbl., borne in small to medium clusters; very fragrant; [*R. setigera* hybrid × *R. rugosa rubra plena*]

Himmelsstürmer HRg, pb, Wänninger, Franz; flowers carmine-pink with white, small, single; int. in 1990

Hinaarare F, lp, Keisei; int. by Keisei Rose Nurseries, 2001

Hinamatsuri F, mp

Hinemoa F, rb, 1963, Mason, P.G.; flowers buttercup-yellow shading to vermilion, 3-3½ in., 17-20 petals, cupped, borne in clusters; foliage bronze, leathery; upright, bushy growth; [Circus × unknown]

Hinrich Gaede HT, ob, 1931, Kordes; bud pointed, nasturtium-red; flowers orange-yellow tinted nasturtium-yellow, very large, dbl., high-centered, moderate fruity fragrance; foliage glossy, bronze; vigorous growth; [Lady Margaret Stewart × Charles P. Kilham]

Hinrich Gaede, Climbing Cl HT, ob, 1935, Armstrong, J.A.

Hipango F, yb, 1983, Murray, Nola; flowers deep yellow, petals edged orange, reverse yellow, shapely, large, 21 petals; foliage medium size, medium to light green; vigorous growth; [Smiley × Una Hawken]

Hipólito Lázaro LCl, dr, Pahissa; flowers carmine, large

Hippolyte HGal, m, Before 1842, Parmentier; flowers purple-violet, small button at center, medium, dbl., quartered, borne singly or in clusters of 2-3, slight fragrance; foliage light green, elliptical; almost thornless; growth vigorous, tall (6 ft.)

Hippolyte Abraham HT, mr, 1903, Abraham; flowers cherry red, shaded violet

Hippolyte Barreau HT, dr, 1894, Pernet-Ducher; [Comtesse de Labarthe × Louis van Houtte]

Hippolyte Flandrin HP, mp, 1895, Damaizin

Hippolyte Jamain B, m, 1856, Pradel; flowers purple, large, full

Hippolyte Jamain HP, mp, 1869, Faudon; flowers bright carmine pink, very large, full

Hippolyte Jamain HP, dp, 1874, Lacharme, F.; flowers carmine-red, well-formed, 38 petals, semi-globular, moderate fragrance; foliage red, when young; vigorous, erect growth; [Victor Verdier × unknown]

Hippolyte Jamain, Climbing Cl HP, m, 1887, Paul, G.; [sport of Hippolyte Jamain]

Hippy HT, yb, Delbard-Chabert; int. in 1971

Hiroshima HT, dp

Hiroshima Appeal HT, ob, Hiroshima; int. by Hiroshima Bara-en, 1985

Hiroshima Mind HT, ob, Harada; int. in 1995

Hiroshima no Kane HT, rb, Harada; int. in 1994

Hiroshima Requiem HT, dr, Hiroshima; int. by Hiroshima Bara-en, 1999

Hiroshima Spirit HT, yb, Harada, Toshiyuki; flowers dark yellow with red, large, dbl.; int. in 1991

Hiroshima's Children F, yb, 1985, Harkness, R., & Co., Ltd.; flowers light yellow, petals edged pink, large, 35 petals, high-centered, slight fragrance; foliage medium size, medium green, matte; bushy growth

His Majesty HT, dr, 1909, McGredy; flowers dark crimson shaded deeper, very large, dbl., high-centered; long, strong stems; very vigorous growth

Hisami HT, lp, 1988, Harada, Toshiyuki; flowers light cream, flushed crimson at tip, 50 petals, high-centered, borne usually singly, moderate fragrance; foliage medium size, dark green, matte; prickles downward curved, red to light green; upright, medium growth; [Kordes' Perfecta × Christian Dior]

Hispania HT, dr, 1938, Pahissa; bud pointed; flowers velvety red, open, overlarge, dbl.; foliage leathery; long, strong stems; very vigorous growth

Hispanica Moschata Simplex – See **Spanish Musk Rose**, HMsk

History HT, pb, Tantau; flowers deep pink with white reverse, large, slow opening, dbl., slight fragrance; foliage medium green; compact, upright growth; int. by Rosen Tantau, 2003

Hit Parade F, ob, 1962, Dickson, Patrick; flowers red, orange and gold, 4 in., 16 petals, borne in clusters; foliage dark; low growth; [(Independence × seedling) × Brownie]; int. by A. Dickson & Sons, 1962

Hjemmet-rosen – See **Chloe Renaissance**, S

Ho Hua Chiang Wei – See ***R. multiflora carnea*** (Thory)

Ho-Jun HT, pb, 1985, Suzuki, Seizo; flowers pink flushed rose-red, 28 petals, cupped, borne in clusters of 2-5, intense fragrance; foliage dark, semi-glossy; prickles large; compact growth; [Granada × Flaming Peace]; int. by Keisei Rose Nursery, 1984

Ho-No-o-no-nami LCl, or, 1968, Suzuki, Seizo; bud pointed; flowers orange-red, reverse lighter, to open, medium, dbl., high-centered, slight fragrance; foliage glossy, leathery; vigorous, climbing growth; PP3033; [Spectacular × Aztec]; int. by General Bionomics, 1968

Hoagy Carmichael HT, mr, 1990, McGredy, Sam IV; flowers large, full, moderate fragrance; foliage medium size, dark green, matte; upright, bushy growth; PP8001; [(Sir Harry Pilkington × Elegy) × Pounder Star]; int. by McGredy Roses International, 1990

Hobby F, op, 1959, Tantau, Math.; flowers coral-pink, large, dbl., borne in open clusters; foliage dark; upright, bushy growth; [Red Favorite × Kathe Duvigneau]; int. in 1955

Hobby Min, dp, Tantau; flowers strong pink, large, full, rosette; compact, rounded growth; int. by Rosen Tantau, 2001

Hobby Striped Sport F, ob; flowers red stripes against the orange- pink; [sport of Hobby]; int. by Vintage Gardens, 2003

Hochsommer F, dp, 1965, van Engelen, A. J.; flowers dbl., borne in clusters; foliage dark; low growth; [Queen Elizabeth × seedling]; int. by van Engelen, 1962

Hockey S, mr; flowers red with yellow stamens, small, semi-dbl., cupped to flat, borne in clusters; free-flowering; growth low, spreading, groundcover; int. by Belle Epoque, 2000

Hocus-Pocus Gr, or, 1975, Armstrong, D.L.; flowers 4-4½ in., 30 petals, cupped, slight fragrance; foliage large, dark; vigorous, upright growth; PP3972; [Fandango × Simon Bolivar]; int. by Armstrong Nursery

Hocus Pocus F, rb, Kordes; flowers deep red with irregular yellow stripes, small; stems 16 inches; int. by W. Kordes Söhne, 2001

Hocus Pocus Kordana Min, rb, Kordes; flowers red, orange and yellow stripes, dbl.; container rose; int. by W. Kordes Söhne

Hoddy Toddy Min, dr, 1990, King, Gene; bud pointed; flowers dark red, petals tipped darker, small, 28 petals, cupped, borne usually singly, no fragrance; foliage small, medium green, matte; prickles straight, very small, red; bushy, low growth; no fruit; [(Alain × Scamp) × Scamp]; int. by AGM Miniature Roses, 1989

Hoffman von Fallersleben LCl, rb, 1917, Lambert, P.; flowers salmon-red, shaded yellow and ochre, 4 cm., full, borne in clusters of 5-20; sometimes repeats; foliage glossy; vigorous, climbing growth; [Geheimrat Dr. Mittweg × Tip-Top]

Hoffnung HT, ob, Huber; int. in 1995

Hofgartendirektor Graebener HT, lp, 1899, Lambert, P.; flowers creamy pink, medium, dbl.; [Mme Caroline Testout × Antoinette Durieu]

Hofgärtner Kalb HCh, pb, 1913, Felberg-Leclerc; flowers bright carmine-rose, center yellow, outer petals shaded red, 35 petals, moderate fragrance; vigorous, bushy growth; [Souv. de Mme Eugène Verdier × Gruss an Teplitz]

Hoggar S, Lens, Louis

Hogg's Yellow – See **Harison's Yellow**, HFt

Hoh-Jun – See **Ho-Jun**, HT

Hohshun HT, dr, 1999, Ohkawara, Kiyoshi; flowers velvet deep red, 25-27 petals, high-centered; foliage dark green, half leathery; growth to 5 ft.; [Charles Mallerin × Mrs Nieminen]; int. by Nagashima Rose Nursery, 1971

Hoimashree HT, mr, Ghosh; flowers bright scarlet red, large; int. in 2001

Hojun – See **Ho-Jun**, HT

Hokey Pokey Min, ab, 1980, Saville, F. Harmon; bud long, pointed; flowers deep apricot, 28 petals, high-centered, borne singly, slight spicy fragrance; foliage finely serrated; prickles straight; compact, bushy growth; PP4642; [Rise 'n' Shine × Sheri Anne]; int. by Nor'East Min. Roses

Hokkaido HRg, mp; int. in 1988

Hoku-To HT, ly, 1986, Suzuki, Seizo; flowers soft buff yellow, 42 petals, high-centered, moderate fragrance;

foliage large, light green; vigorous, upright, spreading growth; [(Myoo-Jo × Chicago Peace) × King's Ransom]; int. by Keisei Rose Nursery, 1979

Holcombe Honey F, yb, 2001, Bracegirdle, A.J.; flowers medium, dbl., borne in small clusters; foliage medium size, dark green, semi-glossy; prickles medium, slightly hooked, moderate; growth upright, medium (4 ft.); [((Dusky Maiden × (Golden Autumn × Orangeade)) × (Chinatown × Picasso)]

Hold Slunci HP, ly, Blatnà; flowers medium, dbl.; int. in 1956

Hole in One F, pb, 1997, Horner, Colin P.; flowers small, dbl., borne in small clusters; foliage small, medium green,semi-glossy; some prickles; spreading, medium (90 cm.) growth; [((Southampton × New Penny) × (White Pet × Stars 'n' Stripes)) × ((Vester × seedling) × Edith Holden)]; int. by Paul Chessum Roses

Holiday F, my, 1948, Boerner; bud ovoid, orange-yellow flushed pink; flowers flame-pink, reverse clear yellow, 3-3½ in., semi-dbl., cupped, borne in clusters of 3-10, moderate clove fragrance; foliage glossy; vigorous, bushy, compact growth; ruled extinct ARA 1983; [McGredy's Pillar × Pinocchio]; int. by J&P

Holiday HT, mr, 1983, Strahle, B. Glen; flowers small, 35 petals, slight fragrance; foliage medium green; upright growth; [Cara Mia × Volare]; int. by Carlton Rose Nurseries, 1981

Holiday Cheer Min, dr, 1983, Moore, Ralph S.; flowers small, 35 petals, borne in clusters, no fragrance; foliage small, dark, matte; upright, bushy growth; [Red Pinocchio × Little Chief]; int. by Moore Min. Roses, 1982

Holland Double White Altai (form of *R. spinosissima altaica*), w; flowers dbl.; non-recurrent; int. by P.H. Wright

Hollandaise – See **Maheca**, Bslt

Holländerin – See **Red Favorite**, F

Hollandia HT, mr, 1930, Zijverden; flowers brick-red, shaded copper; [sport of Aspirant Marcel Rouyer]

Hollandia Pol, dr; flowers deep red, small, dbl., rosette

Hollandica C, dp, before 1695; flowers deep pink, veined darker, petals shell-shaped, very dbl., moderate fragrance; growth widely used as an understock, especially for tree roses; probably refers to multiple cultivars

Hollandica HRg, lp, about 1888; flowers single; nearly thornless; thought to have been raised by J. Spek; selected Dutch clone of *R. rugosa*, or perhaps a hybrid with Manettii, widely used as an understock, especially for tree roses

Hollands Rugosa HRg, mp; flowers medium, single

Hollie Roffey Min, mp, 1985, Harkness, R., & Co., Ltd.; flowers small, 35 petals, rosette, borne in clusters; foliage small, pointed, medium green, semi-glossy; spreading growth; [(Tip Top × (Manx Queen × Golden Masterpiece)) × Darling Flame]; int. in 1986

Holly Rochelle HT, dr, 1977, Graham; bud pointed; flowers velvety red, 4 in., 60-70 petals, high-centered, moderate fragrance; very vigorous, upright growth; PP3899; [Charlotte Armstrong × Scarlet Knight]; int. by South Forrest Rose Nursery, 1974

Hollybank F, mr, 1966, Hooney; flowers vermilion, 3-3½ in., globular; foliage coppery; upright growth; [Independence × United Nations]

Hollywood HT, rb, 1930, Scittine; bud pointed; flowers dark rose-red, veined darker, dbl., high-centered; foliage dark; long, strong stems; bushy growth; [sport of Premier]

Hollywood HT, w, Pouw; A. A.; bud ovate; sepals long, foliated; flowers white to yellow-white, petals reflex to points, 4-4½ in., 23 petals, exhibition, borne one to a stem, slight fragrance; recurrent; foliage abundant, medium green, semi-glossy; prickles few, none on top 16. in of stem; narrow, bushy (5 ft.) growth; PP10529; int. by deRuiter, 1998

Hollywood Beauty HT, dp, 1929, Pacific Rose Co.; flowers camellia-red, dbl.; [sport of Rose Marie]

Hollywood Star HT, ab, 2001, Sheldon, John; flowers medium, full, borne mostly solitary, slight fragrance; foliage medium size, medium green, semi-glossy; prickles average, recurved, few; growth upright, medium (5 ft.); garden decorative; [Summer Dream × Lanvin]; int. by Certified Roses Inc., 2002

Holoserica HGal, dr, before 1629; flowers deep purple speckled with violet, semi-dbl. to dbl.; foliage ovoid, saw-toothed; few prickles; Holoserica Duplex and Holoserica Multiplex are similar, with varying petalage

Holoserica Regalis HGal, m, before 1815, Schwarzkopf; flowers purple tending towards black, dbl., moderate fragrance; foliage oval, dentate; prickles short; stems long, slender

Holstein F, mr, 1939, Kordes; bud pointed, dark crimson; flowers clear crimson, 4 in., 6 petals, cupped, borne in immense clusters, slight fragrance; foliage leathery, dark, bronze; very vigorous, bushy growth; [Else Poulsen × Dance of Joy seedling]; int. by J&P; Gold Medal, Portland, 1939

Holstein, Climbing Cl F, mr, 1947, Kordes, P.

Holstein – See **Esprit**, S

Holsteinperle HT, op, 1987, Kordes, W.; flowers brilliant coral and salmon, open slowly, 4 in., dbl., high-centered, no fragrance; recurrent; foliage medium size, medium green, semi-glossy; bushy, vigorous, medium growth; [seedling × Flamingo]

Holstenrose HT, mr, 1937, Tantau; flowers scarlet-red, large, dbl., cupped; foliage glossy; vigorous, bushy growth; [Gen. MacArthur × Amulett]

Holstenstor F, op, Meilland; int. in 1990

Holstentor F, op, Meilland; flowers salmon-pink, large, dbl.; int. in 1990

Holt Hewitt HT, rb, 1925, Beckwith; flowers rich velvety crimson, flushed and edged scarlet, well-shaped; vigorous, bushy growth

Holtermann's Gold HT, my, Swane; int. in 1989

Holy Toledo Min, ab, 1979, Christensen, Jack E.; bud ovoid, pointed; flowers brilliant apricot-orange, reverse yellow-orange, imbricated, 1½-2 in., 28 petals; foliage small, glossy, dark; vigorous, bushy growth; PP4659; [Gingersnap × Magic Carrousel]; int. by Armstrong Nursery, 1978; AOE, ARS, 1980

Homage HT, pb, Pal, Dr. B.P.; bud cerise-red; flowers deep, warm pink with outer petals tinged lilac, large, dbl.; int. in 1986

Homage HT, m, Hiroshima; int. by Hiroshima Bara-en, 2005

Hombre Min, pb, 1983, Jolly, Nelson F.; flowers light apricot-pink, reverse light pink, small, dbl., high-centered; foliage small, medium green, semi-glossy; bushy growth; PP5552; [Humdinger × Rise 'n' Shine]; int. by Rosehill Farm, 1982; AOE, ARS, 1983

Home – See **Furusato**, HT

Home & Country HT, yb, 1982, Kriloff, Michel; flowers large, moderate fragrance; foliage medium green glossy; upright growth; [seedling × Peace]; int. as Comtesse d'Alcantara, Primavera, 1979

Home and Family HT, w, 2002, Carruth, Tom; flowers pure white, 10-12 cm., full, borne mostly solitary, slight fragrance; foliage large, dark green, glossy; prickles few, average, pointed, brownish-green; stems long; very upright, medium (120-140 cm.) growth; PP14356; [(Playboy × Lagerfeld) × New Zealand]; int. by Weeks Roses, 2002

Home & Garden F, lp, 2006; bud rounded, pink suffused greenish; flowers pure pink, aging softer, 8 cm., full, quartered, borne in large clusters, no fragrance; recurrent; foliage medium size, dark green, dense; bushy, upright (80 cm.) growth; int. by W. Kordes' Söhne, 2001

Home-Coming Min, mp, 1989, Williams, Michael C.; bud pointed; flowers medium pink with slightly darker petal edges, medium, 35 petals, high-centered; foliage medium size, medium green, semi-glossy; prickles straight, green; upright, tall growth; no fruit; PP7454; [Tiki × Party Girl]; int. by The Rose Garden & Mini Rose Nursery

Home of Time HT, r, 1998, Cocker, Ann G.; flowers cinnamon red with bronze shading, lighter reverse, 2 in., very dbl., borne mostly singly; foliage medium size, dark green, glossy; prickles moderate, medium, slightly hooked; upright, medium (2½ ft.) growth; [(Sabine × Circus) × Amber Queen]; int. by James Cocker & Sons, 1998

Home Run HT, pb, 1956, Motose; bud ovoid; flowers rose-bengal, 5 in., 40 petals, high-centered, moderate fragrance; foliage leathery; vigorous growth; PP1537; [sport of Pink Delight]

Home Run S, mr, 2004, Carruth, Tom; flowers bright velvet red, 6-8 cm., single, borne in small clusters, slight fragrance; foliage medium size, dark green, matte, very disease-resistant; prickles slightly hooked; growth compact, rounded, medium (70-90 cm.); garden decoration; [(City of San Francisco × Baby Love) × Knock Out]; int. by Weeks Roses, 2006

Home Sweet Home HT, mp, 1941, Wood & Ingram; flowers rich velvety pink, dbl., moderate damask fragrance; foliage glossy, dark; vigorous growth; int. by C-P

Home Sweet Home, Climbing Cl HT, mp; int. after 1941

Home Sweet Home – See **Coup de Coeur**, LCl

Homeland HT, pb, 1951, LeGrice; flowers Neyron rose, base tinted orange, well-formed, 5½-6 in., 50-60 petals; foliage leathery, dark; very free growth; [Hybrid Tea × Guinee]

Homeland HT, ab, Drummond; int. by Greenbelt Farm, 1992

Homenagem Egas Moniz HT, mp, 1959, Moreira da Silva; [Walter × Juno]

Homenagem Gago Coutinho HT, rb, 1959, Moreira da Silva; flowers crimson-red, reverse yellow; [Confidence × seedling]

Homenagem Pinto d'Azevedo HT, op, 1959, Moreira da Silva; flowers bright salmon-pink, dbl.; [Super-Congo × Independence]

Homère T, pb, 1858, Robert et Moreau; flowers pink, center flesh-white, dbl., cupped; vigorous, bushy growth; [possibly a seedling of 'David Pradel']

Home's Beauty – See **Olympic Glory**, HT

Home's Choice – See **Olympic Dream**, HT

Home's Pride – See **Firstar**, HT

Homestead HCh, dr

Homesteader Min, yb, Williams, J.B.; flowers yellow blend with orange heart, quilling petals, HT shaped, borne in masses of blooms; int. by Hortico, 2003

Hommage à Barbara S, dr, Delbard; flowers intense red, with tones of velvety black, large, full, cupped; recurrent; int. by Georges Delbard SA, 2005

Hommage d'Anjou HT, or, Minier; flowers coppery-red, large, dbl.; int. in 1965

Hondo HRg, dp; int. in 1988

Hondo HT, yb, 1990, Perry, Astor; flowers medium yellow with red-purple on tips, aging red-purple, large, 33 petals, moderate fragrance; foliage large, dark green, matte; upright growth; [Irish Gold × Las Vegas]

Honest Abe Min, dr, 1977, Christensen, Jack E.; bud mossy; flowers deep velvety crimson-red, mini-moss, 1½ in., 33 petals, slight tea fragrance; foliage glossy; vigorous, bushy growth; PP4356; [Fairy Moss × Rubinette]; int. by Armstrong Nursery, 1978

Honest Red HT, mr, 1991, Wambach, Alex A.; flowers

large, full, borne mostly singly, intense fragrance; foliage medium size, dark green, semi-glossy; tall, bushy growth; [seedling × Sea Pearl]

Honey F, my, 1955, Marsh; flowers coppery yellow, becoming lemon-yellow, small, semi-dbl.; [sport of Smiles]; int. by Marsh's Nursery

Honey HT, ab, Kordes; flowers honey colored, medium, dbl., cupped, borne mostly singly, moderate fragrance; recurrent; stems long; florist rose; int. by W. Kordes Söhne, 2005

Honey 'n' Spice Min, r, 1987, Williams, Ernest D.; flowers tan with red highlights, reverse deeper tan with more red, small, 45-49 petals, borne usually singly, moderate fresh honey fragrance; foliage small, medium green, semi-glossy; prickles few, short, thin, light tan; bushy, medium growth; no fruit; [Tom Brown × Over the Rainbow]; int. by Mini-Roses, 1986

Honey Bear – See **Bordure Nacrée**, Min

Honey Bear Min, ab, 1987, Chaffin, Lauren M.; flowers deep apricot, yellow base, reverse light apricot, aging cream, 50-55 petals, cupped; foliage small, medium green, semi-glossy, disease-resistant; prickles needle-like, straight, light tan; bushy, low compact growth; PP6844; [Rise 'n' Shine × Holy Toledo]; int. by Pixie Treasures Min. Roses

Honey Border – See **Palisades**, S

Honey Bouquet F, yb, 1999, Zary, Dr. Keith W.; bud pointed, ovoid; flowers light yellow, hint of pink, reverse light yellow, 4½-5 in., 35-40 petals, borne in small clusters, intense sweet fragrance; foliage medium size, dark green, semi-glossy; upright, spreading, medium (3½ ft.) growth; PP11882; [seedling × Amber Queen]; int. by Bear Creek Gardens, Inc., 1999

Honey Bun F, my, 1974, Ellis & Swim; bud ovoid; flowers medium, dbl., cupped, intense fragrance; foliage dark, leathery; very vigorous, upright, bushy growth; PP3518; [Gold Strike × Golden Garnette]; int. by Armstrong Nursery, 1973

Honey Bunch F, dy, 1971, Watkins Roses; flowers deep gold, shaded peach, long, pointed, 3 in., 20 petals; foliage light; moderate, upright growth; [Circus × Soraya]

Honey Bunch F, yb, 1990, Cocker, James & Sons; bud ovoid; flowers yellow with salmon-red, reverse yellow, aging honey-yellow, 45 petals, cupped, moderate fragrance; foliage small, dark green, glossy; prickles small, green; patio; bushy, low growth; hips round, small, green; [((Sabine × Circus) × Maxi) × Bright Smile]; int. in 1989

Honey Butter Min, ly, 1998, Chaffin, Lauren M.; flowers creamy yellow center, near white outer edges, 2-2½ in., very dbl., borne mostly singly; foliage medium size, medium size, semi-glossy; prickles few, small, straight; bushy, medium growth; [Deep Purple × Rainbow's End]; int. by Pixie Treasures Roses, 1998

Honey Child F, ab, Ilsink; flowers apricot orange, dbl., moderate fragrance; free-flowering; medium growth; int. in 1999

Honey Chile F, lp, 1963, Thomson; bud pointed; flowers dbl., cupped, borne in clusters, slight fragrance; foliage leathery; vigorous, upright, bushy growth; [Fashion × Queen Elizabeth]; int. by Tillotson, 1963

Honey Dew F, ab, Dickson; flowers golden apricot, wavy petals, medium; medium growth; int. in 1995

Honey Dijon Gr, r, 2003, Sproul, James; flowers golden tan, 10-12 cm., full, classic, borne in small clusters, intense fragrance; foliage medium size, dark green, glossy; prickles moderate, average, almost straight, brown; growth upright, vigorous, medium (120-140 cm.); garden decoration; [Stainless Steel × Singin' In The Rain]; int. by Weeks Roses, 2005

Honey Favorite HT, lp, 1962, Von Abrams; flowers light yellowish-pink, base yellow, slight fragrance; good repeat; [sport of Pink Favorite]; int. by Peterson & Dering, 1962

Honey Favourite – See **Honey Favorite**, HT

Honey Gold F, my, 1959, Boerner; bud ovoid; flowers maize-yellow overcast buff-yellow, 3-3½ in., 43 petals, moderate fragrance; foliage dark, glossy; vigorous, bushy growth; PP1535; [Yellow Pinocchio × Fashion]; int. by J&P, 1956

Honey Hill Min, ob, 1981, Lyon; bud ovoid, pointed; flowers orange, 48 petals, high-centered, borne singly or several together, moderate fragrance; foliage medium green, semi-glossy; prickles curved, light brown; vigorous, bushy, upright growth; [seedling × seedling]; int. in 1980

Honey Kordana Mini Brite Min, rb, Kordes, Wilhelm; bud long pointed, ovoid; flowers red with orange-yellow base, 1¾ in., 25-30 petals, borne mostly singly, no fragrance; free-flowering; foliage abundant, small, glossy; prickles few, small, straight; vigorous, compact, upright (18-20 in.) growth; PP11186; [(Joy × Korgiffer) × Mandarin]; int. by Bear Creek Gardens, 1997

Honey Mini-Delite Min, w, 1991, Clements, John K.; flowers honey cream, medium, full, borne in small clusters, no fragrance; foliage small, medium green, matte; few prickles; low (25 cm.), bushy, compact growth; [seedling × seedling]; int. by Heirloom Old Garden Roses, 1991

Honey Moss Min, ly, 1977, Sudol, Julia; bud mossy; flowers near white, toward honey, mini-moss, 1 in., 52 petals, flat, moderate fragrance; foliage dark, leathery; spreading growth; PP4354; [Fairy Moss × unknown]

Honey Perfume F, ab, 2005, Zary, Keith W. ; bud pointed, ovoid; flowers apricot-yellow, 10-12 cm., 30 petals, borne in large clusters, intense spicy fragrance; quick rebloom; foliage large, dark green, glossy; prickles 9-11 mm., straight, greyed-yellow, moderate; growth upright, branching, vigorous, compact, medium (110 cm.); [AROfres × Amber Queen]; int. by Jackson & Perkins Wholesale, Inc., 2004; AARS, 2004

Honey Rea HT, pb, 1973, Concord Floral Co.; bud ovoid; flowers pink, very large, semi-dbl., high-centered; foliage large, dark, leathery; very vigorous, bushy growth

Honeybee MinFl, ab, 2003, Zlesak, David C.; flowers very full, borne in small clusters, intense fragrance; foliage medium size, medium green, semi-glossy; prickles moderate; growth bushy, medium (28 in.); [Rise 'N Shine × induced tetraploid polyantha]; int. by David C. Zlesak, 2004

Honeycomb Min, ly, 1975, Moore, Ralph S.; flowers soft yellow to near white, 1½ in., 30 petals, high-centered, moderate fragrance; foliage small, glossy, light, leathery; dwarf, bushy growth; [(*R. wichurana* × Floradora) × Debbie]; int. by Sequoia Nursery, 1974

Honeycup HT, ab, Pouw; int. in 1990

Honeyflow F, pb, 1957, Riethmuller; flowers white edged pink, single, borne in very large clusters, moderate fragrance; foliage glossy; vigorous growth; [Spring Song × Gartendirektor Otto Linne]

Honeyglow F, yb, 1955, LeGrice; flowers lemon-yellow, reverse shaded orange, pointed, 2 in., semi-dbl., borne in clusters; foliage glossy; vigorous growth; [Goldilocks × Ellinor LeGrice]

Honeymilk Min, w, Tantau; flowers milk white with cream yellow center, dbl., borne in clusters; good repeat; compact (16-20 in.) growth; int. by Rosen Tantau, 2002

Honeymoon HT, ly, Benny, David; flowers creamy lemon yellow, silky texture, dbl., high-centered; medium to tall growth; int. by De Boer Roses, 2004

Honeymoon in England – See **Honigmond**, F

Honeypot S, my, 1969, Austin, David; flowers sulfur-yellow, 4 in., 40-50 petals, cupped; foliage dark, semi-glossy; vigorous growth; [Honigmond × Constance Spry]

Honeysweet S, op, 1985, Buck, Dr. Griffith J.; bud medium-large, ovoid, pointed; flowers yellow-red-orange blend, large, 28 petals, cupped, borne 1-8 per cluster; repeat bloom; foliage leathery, dark with copper tints; prickles awl-like, brown-tan; bushy, erect growth; hardy; [Serendipity × Wiener Charme]; int. by Iowa State University, 1984

Honeywood F, ab, Fryer; flowers orange-apricot, non-fading, small to medium, dbl., borne in large clusters, moderate fragrance; free-flowering; foliage dark green, disease-resistant; bushy, tall (3 ft.) growth; int. by Fryer's Roses, 2001

Hong-Kong HT, rb, 1962, Dot, Pedro; flowers citron-yellow edged currant-red, becoming red, dbl.; strong stems; bushy growth; [Soraya × (Henri Mallerin × Peace)]

Honigmond F, my, 1960, Kordes, R.; flowers canary-yellow, 40 petals, rosette, borne in clusters (up to 5); foliage dark, veined; vigorous, upright, bushy growth; [Clare Grammerstorf × Golden Scepter]; int. by A. Dickson

Honky Tonk Min, rb, 1996, Taylor, Franklin "Pete" & Kay; flowers red with darker edges, white reverse, large, dbl., borne mostly singly; foliage medium size, dark green, glossy; numerous prickles; medium (30 in.), upright, bushy growth; [Party Girl × seedling]; int. by Taylor's Roses, 1997

Honoho-No-Nami LCl, or, Suzuki; flowers semi-dbl.; [Danse du Feu × Aztec]; int. in 1968

Honoka F, w, Keisei; int. by Keisei Rose Nurseries, 2005

Honor HT, w, 1979, Warriner, William A.; bud ovoid, pointed; flowers loose, 5 in., 18-25 petals, borne singly or several together, slight fragrance; foliage large, dark green; upright growth; int. by J&P, 1980; Gold Medal, Portland, 1978

Honor Elizabeth – See **City Livery**, F full

Hon. A. Norton T, Williams, A.; [sport of Mme Lombard]

Hon. Charlotte Knollys HT, pb, 1926, Bees; flowers rose, edged lighter, center creamy yellow, dbl.; [Antoine Rivoire × Willowmere]; Gold Medal, NRS, 1926

Hon. Edith Gifford T, w, 1882, Guillot et Fils; flowers flesh-white tinted rose, large, dbl.; [Mme Falcot × Perle des Jardins]

Hon. George Bancroft HT, rb, 1879, Bennett; flowers red shaded violet-crimson, large, full, intense fragrance; almost thornless; moderate growth; [Mme de St. Joseph × Lord Macaulay]; rarely opens properly

Hon. Ina Bingham HP, mp, 1905, Dickson, A.; flowers pink, stamens golden yellow, large, 23 petals, cupped, intense fragrance; upright growth; sometimes classed as HT

Hon. Joan Acton HT, pb, 1950, Marshall, J.; flowers cream edged pink, pointed, very large, 90 petals; foliage bronze-green; hardy; [Mrs Sam McGredy × Golden Dawn]

Honorable Ken F, ob, 1993, Bracegirdle, Derek T.; flowers orange/yellow reverse, medium, full, borne in small clusters, moderate fragrance; foliage medium size, medium green, semi-glossy; some prickles; compact (100 cm.) growth; [John Lawrence × Zorina]; int. by Bracegirdle, 1994

Honorable Lady Lindsay – See **Hon. Lady Lindsay**, S

Hon. Lady Lindsay S, pb, 1939, Hansen, N.J.; flowers pink, reverse darker, 35 petals; recurrent bloom; foliage dark; bushy (3 × 3 ft.) growth; not dependably hardy; [New Dawn × Rev. F. Page-Roberts]; int. by B&A, 1938

Hon Mrs R. G. Grosvenor HT, w, 1916, Cant, B. R.; flowers porcelain white, center tinted orange-yellow, medium, full

Hon. Violet Douglas Pennant HT, pb, 1927, Bees; flowers blend of cream and rose, dbl.

Honore de Balzac HT, pb, 1998, Selection Meilland; bud globular, large; flowers light creamy yellow suffused with carmine, 4½-5½ in., 58 petals, borne 1-3 per stem, moderate peach-like fragrance; good repeat; foliage medium size, medium green, semi-glossy; prickles numerous, medium, reddish; upright, bushy, medium (3 ft.) growth; PP10477; [(Marion Foster × KORAv) × Lancome]; int. by Conard-Pyle Co., 1996

Honorine de Brabant B, pb; flowers pale lilac-pink, spotted and striped mauve and crimson, dbl., cupped; recurrent bloom; foliage light green; few prickles; vigorous (to 6 ft.) growth

Honorine Lady Lindsay – See **Hon. Lady Lindsay**, S

Honour – See **Honor**, HT

Honour Bright LCl, dr, 1950, Eacott; flowers brilliant crimson, medium, semi-dbl.; recurrent bloom; foliage bright green; very vigorous (4-6 ft.) growth; [(New Dawn × Allen Chandler) × (Mrs W.J. Grant, Climbing × Richmond, Climbing)]

Hoochie Koochie HT, m, 2000, Umsawasdi, Dr. Theera; flowers lavender, large, dbl., borne mostly singly, intense fragrance; foliage large, dark green, semi-glossy; few prickles; upright, tall growth; [Azure Sea × Mister Lincoln]; int. by Certified Roses, 2000

Hoosier Beauty HT, rb, 1915, Dorner; bud pointed; flowers glowing crimson shaded darker, large, dbl.; foliage sparse, rich green, glossy; bushy growth; [Richmond × Château de Clos Vougeot]; Gold Medal, NRS, 1915

Hoosier Beauty, Climbing Cl HT, rb, 1918, Western (also W.R. Gray, 1925); flowers crimson, large, full; [sport of Hoosier Beauty]

Hoosier Glory – See **Eutin**, F

Hoosier Gold F, dy, 1975, Byrum; bud ovoid; flowers 2½-3½ in., 30-35 petals, slight fragrance; vigorous growth; PP3544; [Lydia × Golden Wave]; int. by J.H. Hill Co., 1974

Hoosier Honey HT, my, 1955, Joseph H. Hill, Co.; bud ovoid; flowers amber-yellow, open, 4½-5 in., 45-50 petals, moderate fragrance; vigorous, upright, bushy growth; PP1336; [Anzac × Golden Rapture]

Hoosier Honey HT, dy, 1977, Byrum; bud long, pointed; flowers mimosa-yellow, 4-5 in., 25-30 petals, high-centered, intense fragrance; foliage dark, leathery; vigorous growth; PP4015; [Unnamed seedling No. 63-704 × Golden Fantasie]; int. by J.H. Hill Co., 1973

Hoosier Hysteria S, dr, 1981, Schwartz, Ernest W.; bud ovoid; flowers 45 petals, high-centered, borne singly or in sprays of 5-7; foliage dark, leathery; prickles very few, curved, dark green; vigorous, tall, upright growth; [Karl Herbst × Simone]; int. by Krider Nursery, 1979

Hoot 'n' Holler Min, rb, 1993, Moore, Ralph S.; flowers pleasing blend of red changing to lavender, large, semi-dbl., borne in small clusters, no fragrance; foliage medium size, medium green, matte; few prickles; upright, bushy growth; [Pink Petticoat × Make Believe]; int. by Sequoia Nursery, 1993

Hoot Owl Min, rb, 1990, Moore, Ralph S.; bud pointed; flowers red with white eye, small, 5 petals, borne usually singly or in sprays of 3-5, no fragrance; foliage small, medium green, semi-glossy; bushy, low growth; [Orangeade × Little Artist]; int. by Sequoia Nursery, 1991

Hope Min, w, 1985, Bridges, Dennis A.; flowers well-formed, small, 35 petals; foliage large, dark, glossy; bushy growth; [Rise 'n' Shine × Party Girl]; int. by Bridges Roses

Hope – See **Kiboh**, F

Hope – See **Hope 98**, F

Hope F, pb, Orard, P.; flowers white with lavender pink, dbl., slight fragrance; small to medium growth; int. in 2000

Hope S, w, 2001, Thomson, George L.; flowers cream to light pink, lighter reverse, medium, full, borne in small clusters, moderate fragrance; foliage medium size, medium green, semi-glossy; prickles medium, hooked, moderate; growth spreading, medium (4½-5½ ft.); garden decorative; [(Dove × unknown) × Ophelia]; int. by Ross Roses, 2001

Hope 98 F, mr, 1998, Cocker, Ann G.; flowers sparkling geranium red, lighter reverse, frilly petals, 1-1½ in., dbl., borne in large clusters; foliage small, medium size, glossy; prickles moderate, small, slightly hooked; compact, low, bushy growth; [Memento × Evelyn Fison]; int. by James Cocker & Sons, 1998

Hope And Joy Min, ob, 2007, Moore, Ralph S.; bud pale yellow; flowers orange-red, reverse light yellow, medium, 1½-2 in., dbl., borne in small clusters; foliage medium size, medium green, semi-glossy; prickles small, straight, reddish, few; growth bushy, medium (15 in.); containers, borders, garden decoration; [Show 'n' Tell × unknown]; int. by Sequoia Nurs., 2007

Hope for Humanity S, dr, 1996, Collicutt, L.M. & Davidson, C.G.; flowers deep, dark red, 1¾ in., dbl., borne in small clusters; foliage medium size, semi-glossy; prickles moderate; upright, low (56 cm.) growth; [(Prairie Princess × Morden Amorette) × (Morden Cardinette × K1)]; int. by Morden Research Center, 1995

Hopeful HT, lp, 1995, Sheldon, John & Robin; flowers medium, full, borne mostly singly; foliage medium size, medium green, matte; upright, medium growth; [Sheer Bliss × Elizabeth Taylor]

Hopie Girl HT, ly, 2003, Sheldon, John; flowers dbl., high-centered, borne mostly solitary; foliage medium size, medium green, matte; prickles medium, pointed; growth upright, medium, shrub; PPAF; [Polarstern × Lanvin]; int. by Certified Roses, Inc., 2004

Hopscotch Min, my, 1979, Christensen, Jack E.; bud ovoid, pointed; flowers golden yellow, imbricated, 1½ in., 28 petals; foliage small; vigorous, bushy growth; PP4664; [Gingersnap × Magic Carrousel]; int. by Armstrong Nursery

Horace McFarland HT, op, 1944, Mallerin, C.; bud mahogany-red; flowers coppery pink, 4½-5½ in., 43 petals, high-centered, moderate fruity fragrance; foliage leathery, dark; vigorous, bushy growth; [Mme Arthaud × seedling]; int. by A. Meilland, 1944

Horace Vernet HP, dr, 1866, Guillot et Fils; flowers deep scarlet-crimson, large, 40 petals, high-centered, intense fragrance; repeat bloom; moderate, erect growth; [Général Jacqueminot × unknown]

Horatio Nelson S, mp, 1998, Beales, Peter; flowers clear pink, outer petals lighter, 41-50 petals, cupped, then rosette, borne in small clusters; recurrent; foliage medium size, medium green, glossy; prickles moderate; compact (3 ft.) growth; [Centenaire de Lourdes × Aloha]; int. by Peter Beales Roses, 1997

Horatius Coclès HGal, mr, before 1828, Miellez; flowers large, full

Horden Hall LCl, w, 1928, Conyers; flowers pure white, with long yellow stamens, large, single; [*R. wichurana* × Frau Karl Druschki]

Horizon F, or, 1959, Tantau, Math.; bud pointed; flowers geranium-red, open, large, dbl., borne in large clusters, moderate fragrance; foliage leathery; vigorous, upright, bushy growth; [Crimson Glory × Cinnabar]; int. in 1956

Horizon 2000 HT, Delbard, Georges; int. in 1990

Horndon Pink HT, dp, 1963, Barter; flowers old-rose-pink, 4½ in., 60 petals; foliage dark; [Lady Elgin × Independence]

Horrido F, mr, 1963, Tantau, Math.; bud ovoid; flowers pure blood-red, dbl., cupped, borne in large clusters; foliage dark, glossy; bushy, low growth

Hørsholm By-Rose – See **Patio Princess**, S

Horstmann's Bergfeuer F, dr, 1954, Horstmann; flowers dark blood-red, well-formed, very large, dbl., borne in large clusters; moderate growth; [World's Fair × Independence]

Horstmann's Jubiläumsrose F, op, 1954, Tantau, Math.; flowers pink tinted peach, well-formed, large, dbl., borne in clusters of 10-12; foliage glossy, leathery; dwarf growth; [Golden Rain × Alpine Glow]; int. by Horstmann

Horstmann's Leuchtfeuer F, dr, 1954, Tantau, Math.; flowers blood-red, large, dbl., borne in large clusters; moderate growth; [Red Favorite × Karl Weinhausen]; int. by Horstmann

Horstmann's Rosenresli F, w, 1955, Kordes; flowers pure white, large, dbl., borne in clusters, moderate fragrance; bushy growth; [Rudolph Timm × Lavender Pinocchio]; int. by Horstmann

Horstmann's Schöne Brünette HT, or, 1955, Horstmann; flowers coppery brick-red, large, dbl.; strong stems; [Independence × Hens Verschuren]

Hortense de Beauharnais HGal, pb, 1834, Vibert; flowers rose edged rosy lilac, dbl.

Hortense Mignard HP, rb, 1873, Baltet; flowers shining cherry red, reverse flesh pink, full

Hortense Vernet M, w, 1861, Moreau et Robert; flowers white shaded rose, large, very dbl., flat, borne in clusters; some repeat; moderate growth

Hortensia – See **Great Royal**, HGal

Hortensia T, mp, 1870, Ducher; flowers pink with yellowish reflections, large, very full

Horticolor HT, yb, Laperrière; flowers Indian-yellow, edged with flame red on outer petals, dbl.; int. in 1989

Horticultor Vidal HT, op, 1952, Dot, Pedro; bud pointed; flowers salmon-pink, large, 35 petals; bushy growth; [Mme Butterfly × Federico Casas]

Hortiflora Pol, mp, 1976, Delforge, S.; bud oval; flowers dbl., 45 petals, slight fragrance; int. in 1974

Hortulanus Albert Fiet HT, ab, 1919, Leenders, M.; flowers apricot and lilac-rose, center coppery orange, dbl.; [Mme Mélanie Soupert × Mons. Paul Lédé]

Hortulanus Budde HT, mr, 1919, Verschuren; bud pointed; flowers dark velvet, shaded yellow at center, large, dbl., moderate fragrance; foliage dark; vigorous growth; [Gen. MacArthur × Mme Edouard Herriot]

Hortulanus Fiet HT, w, 1919, Verschuren; bud pointed; flowers deep and light cream, open, very large, dbl.; foliage sparse, glossy, dark; vigorous growth; [Cissie Easlea × Golden Star]

Hortus Tolosanus T, w, 1881, Brassac; flowers pure white, center light yellow, large, very full, moderate fragrance

Hoshikage HT, m, Hiroshima; int. by Hiroshima Bara-en, 2000

Hoshizukuyo HT, w, 1991, Ohtsuki, Hironaka; bud pointed; flowers ivory, large, 35-40 petals, high-centered, borne usually singly, intense fruity fragrance; foliage medium size, light green, semi-glossy; medium, upright growth; [(Izayoi × Sodori-Hime) × White Success]

Hospitality F, rb, 1997, Horner, Colin P.; flowers medium red, reverse gold, 7-8 cm., dbl., borne in small clusters, moderate fragrance; foliage medium size, medium green, glossy; prickles moderate; bushy, medium (100 cm.) growth; [(Champagne Cocktail × Alpine Sunset) × (Prominent × Southampton)]; int. by Paul Chessum Roses

Hostess F, op, 1960, Lens; flowers pink tinted salmon, open, large, semi-dbl., borne in clusters; vigorous, upright growth; [Papillon Rose × (Cinnabar × Alain)]

Hostess Gisela F, dp, 1975, Hetzel; bud ovoid; flowers medium, dbl., intense fragrance; foliage very glossy; vigorous, upright, bushy growth; [Sympathie × Dr. A.J. Verhage]; int. by GAWA, 1973

Hot – See **Hot Parade**, MinFl

Hot 'n' Spicy F, or, 1991, McGredy, Sam IV; flowers medium, semi-dbl., borne in small clusters; foliage medium size, dark green, glossy; bushy growth; PP8066; [Mary Sumner × Precious Platinum]; int. by Co-Operative Rose Growers, 1990

Hot 'n' Spicy, Climbing Cl F, or; PP16707; int. by Certified Roses, Inc., 2001

Hot Chile S, or, 1998, McGredy, Sam IV; flowers orange-red, 2¾ in., semi-dbl., borne in small clusters; foliage small, dark green, glossy; prickles moderate; spreading, low (30 cm.), bushy growth; [Trumpeter × Eyeopener]; int. by McGredy, Sam, 1995

Hot Chocolate F, r, Simpson; flowers sienna-red, 30 petals, moderate fragrance; foliage semi-glossy; int. in 1986; Gold Star of the South Pacific, Palmerston North, NZ, 1986

Hot Chocolate – See **Hot Cocoa**, F

Hot Cocoa F, r, 2001, Carruth, Tom; flowers smoky orange with deep rust reverse, 7-9 cm., full, cupped, borne in small clusters, moderate fragrance; foliage large, dark green, glossy; prickles numerous, assorted sizes, straight, light brown; growth bushy, rounded, medium (90-115 cm.); garden decoration; PP15155; [(Playboy × Altissimo) × Livin' Easy]; int. by Weeks Roses, 2003; AARS, 2003, Certificate of Merit, Belfast, 2006

Hot Diggity S, or, Delbard; int. by Certified Rose, Inc., 2002

Hot Fire S, mr, Interplant; int. in 1995

Hot Gossip Min, or, Zary, Dr. Keith; int. in 1997

Hot Gossip Min, or, 1998, Horner, Heather M.; flowers luminous orange-red, reverse matt orange, 1½ in., 8-14 petals, borne in small clusters; foliage medium size, medium green, dull; prickles moderate; compact, medium (50 cm.), dwarf-clustered growth; [Penelope Keith × (Prominent × Southampton)]; int. by Paul Chessum Rose Specialist, 1998

Hot Jazz HT, rb; bud Large, elegant and pointed.; flowers Opens slowly to golden rose with red edges. Good vase life.; int. by Carlton Rose Nurseries, 2002

Hot Lips Min, op, 1988, Bennett, Dee; flowers deep coral to orange, aging paler, medium, 25-30 petals, high-centered, borne usually singly, slight fruity fragrance; foliage medium size, medium green, semi-glossy; prickles hooked slightly downward, reddish; upright, bushy, tall growth; hips globular, green to yellow-brown; [Futura × Why Not]; int. by Tiny Petals Nursery

Hot Lips HT, or, Dickson

Hot Pants HT, or, 1980, Simpson, J.W.; bud high-pointed; flowers 48 petals, high-centered, borne usually 3 per cluster, no fragrance; foliage medium green; few prickles; spreading growth; [Gypsy Moth × Princesse]

Hot Parade MinFl, dp, Poulsen; flowers deep pink, 5-8 cm., dbl., no fragrance; foliage dark; growth bushy, 20-40 cm.; int. by Poulsen Roser, 2005

Hot Pewter HT, or, 1981, Harkness, R.; flowers brilliant orange-red, 41 petals, high-centered, borne usually singly; foliage large, mid-green, semi-glossy; prickles broad, dark; bushy growth; [Alec's Red × Red Dandy]; int. as Crucenia, F. Mason & Son, 1978

Hot Pink Folies F, dp, Meilland; int. by Australian Roses, 2004

Hot Pink Pastel – See **Pink Sweetheart**, F

Hot Point HT, mr, Barni, V.; flowers dark cherry red, long lasting, dbl., high-centered, no fragrance; good repeat; foliage dark green, disease-resistant; vigorous, tall growth; int. by Rose Barni, 1999

Hot Point Spire – See **Hot Point**, HT

Hot Poppy Min, or, 2001, Giles, Diann; flowers medium, dbl., borne mostly solitary, slight fragrance; foliage large, medium green, matte; prickles small, straight, few; growth upright, low; garden decorative, exhibition; [seedling × seedling]; int. by Giles Rose Nursery, 1999

Hot Princess HT, dp; flowers hot pink, medium, dbl., high-centered, borne mostly singly; recurrent; foliage large, dark green; int. by Tantau, 2000

Hot Romance HT, ob; flowers dbl., high-centered, no fragrance; int. by Certified Roses, Inc., 2002

Hot Shot Min, or, 1982, Bennett, Dee; flowers vibrant vermilion, medium, 28 petals, high-centered, slight fragrance; foliage small, medium green; upright, bushy growth; [Futura × Orange Honey]; int. by Tiny Petals Nursery; AOE, ARS, 1984

Hot Spot HT, dp, 1993, Strahle, B. Glen; flowers red pink, 3-3½ in., full, borne mostly singly, intense fragrance; foliage large, dark green, semi-glossy; some prickles; upright (90-100 cm.) growth; PP7995; [sport of Duchess]; int. by Carlton Rose Nurseries, 1990

Hot Stuff Min, mr, 1979, Lyon; bud pointed; flowers turkey-red, 1 in., 10 petals, slight fragrance; foliage tiny; very compact, bushy growth; int. in 1978

Hot Stuff Min, ob, McGredy; [sport of Pandemonium]; int. by Golden Fields Nursery, 2005

Hot Tamale Min, yb, 1993, Zary, Dr. Keith W.; flowers yellow-orange blend changing to yellow pink, finishing pink, large, full, high-centered, borne singly and in small clusters, slight fragrance; foliage small, dark green, semi-glossy; some prickles; low (36 cm.), bushy, compact growth; PP9015; int. by Bear Creek Gardens, Inc., 1994; AOE, ARS, 1994

Hot To Trot MinFl, or, 2006, Moe, Mitchie; flowers extremely vivid orange-red, reverse orange-red blend, 2½-2¾ in., dbl., high-centered, borne mostly solitary; foliage medium size, medium green, semi-glossy; prickles medium, straight, light tan, few; growth upright, tall (24-30 in.); [Klima × Freisinger Morgenrote]; int. by Mitchie's Roses and More, 2007

Hot Wonder S, mr, Lim, P, & Twomey, J.; flowers hot pink, flourescent, 3 in., 25 petals; flowers all season long.; foliage glossy green; growth short, upright (3 ft.) stature; PP15740; int. by Bailey Nurseries, 2004

Hotarugawa HT, my, 2005, Ohtsuki, Hiromaka; flowers full, borne mostly solitary, moderate fragrance; foliage medium size, medium green, glossy; prickles 7 mm., moderate; upright, medium (120 cm.) growth; garden; [Kamakura × Hoshizukuyo]; int. by Tayamaken Barakai

Hotel California HT, my, Orard; flowers yellow color lasts, opens fast in heat., 30 petals, high centered, slight. fragrance; foliage dark, shiny green, resistant.; stems strong; upright, slightly spreading (4-6 ft.) growth; int. by Edmunds Roses, 2001

Hotel Hershey Gr, or, 1976, Williams, J. Benjamin; bud long, pointed to urn-shaped; flowers salmon orange-red, 4-4½ in., dbl., high-centered, slight fragrance; foliage dark, leathery; upright growth; PP4138; [Queen Elizabeth × Comanche]; int. by Hershey Estates, 1977

Hotel Royal – See **Grand Hotel**, LCl

Hôtesse de France HT, dr, 1962, Hémeray-Aubert; flowers velvety deep red, medium, cupped; foliage bronze; [Soraya × seedling]

Hotline Min, mr, 1981, Christensen, Jack E.; bud ovoid, pointed, lightly mossed; flowers bright medium red, mini-moss, 22 petals, high-centered, borne usually singly, moderate moss fragrance; foliage medium green; prickles straight, thin; compact (12 in.) growth; PP5672; [Honest Abe × Trumpeter]; int. by Armstrong Nursery, 1984

Hotshot – See **Hot Shot**, Min

Hotspur F, or, 1963, McGredy, Sam IV; flowers orange-salmon, 3 in., 24 petals, high-centered, borne in clusters; [Independence × Spartan]; int. by McGredy & Son, 1962

House Beautiful MinFl, my, Harkness; flowers dbl., borne in clusters; free-flowering; moderate (2 ft.) growth; int. in 1995

House of York HT, w, Williams, J. Benjamin; flowers creamy white, large, high-centered, moderate fragrance; int. in 1998

Houston – See **Cathedral**, F

Houston HT, dy, 1980, Weeks, O.L.; bud ovoid; flowers deep bright yellow, 38 petals, high-centered, borne singly or 3-4 per cluster, moderate tea fragrance; foliage leathery, wrinkled, dark; prickles long, hooked downward; vigorous, upright growth; PP4687; [Summer Sunshine × seedling]

Houstonian Gr, dr, 1962, Patterson; bud ovoid; flowers 4 in., 35 petals; foliage leathery, glossy, bronze; vigorous, upright, tall growth; [Carrousel × seedling]; int. by Patterson Roses, 1962

Hovyn de Tronchère T, rb, 1899, Puyravaud; flowers red with orange depths, bordered silver; [Regulus × unknown]

Howard Florey F, ab, 1998, Thomson, George L.; flowers apricot, lighter reverse, 2 in., dbl., borne in small clusters; foliage medium size, medium green, semi-glossy; prickles moderate; bushy, medium (3½-4½ ft.) growth; [Seduction × Apricot Nectar]

Howard Jerabek S, mp, 1979, Jerabek, Paul E.; flowers pearl-pink, 100 petals, moderate apple-blossom fragrance; foliage large, glossy; vigorous growth

Howard Morrison HT, dr, 1983, McGredy, Sam IV; flowers large, 35 petals; foliage medium size, medium green, semi-glossy; upright, bushy growth; [seedling × seedling]; int. in 1982

HP 2000 HT, ab, Kordes; bud pointed, urn shaped; flowers deep peach-apricot, large, full, exhibition, intense fragrance; recurrent; growth vigorous, medium high, neat

Hubicka HT, pb, 1935, Böhm, J.; flowers alabaster-white, sometimes rosy, base yellow, very large, dbl.; foliage dark; bushy growth; [sport of Grete Bermbach]

Huckleberry HT, mr, Bell, Laurie; int. by Bell Roses, 2001

Hudson HT, mp, Mallerin, C.; flowers pale rose, well-shaped; foliage glossy

Hudson's Bay Rose – See ***R. blanda*** (Aiton)

Huette's Dainty Florrie Min, lp, 1980, Schwartz, Ernest W.; flowers 24 petals, moderate fragrance; foliage dark green edged dark red; prickles dark red; upright, bushy growth; [Sweet and Low × Mary Marshall]; int. by Men's Garden Club of Virginia, 1979

Hugh Dickson HP, mr, 1905, Dickson, H.; flowers very large, 38 petals, high-centered, intense fragrance; recurrent bloom; vigorous growth; [Lord Bacon × Gruss an Teplitz]

Hugh Ringold HT, Gregory, C.

Hugh Watson HP, op, 1905, Dickson, A.; flowers deep pink tinged salmon and silver-pink, very large, 24 petals, flat; vigorous growth

Hugo Maweroff HMult, dp, 1910, Soupert & Notting; flowers carmine-pink, edges lighter, white center, 5 cm., semi-dbl. to dbl., borne in medium clusters, slight fragrance; foliage large, light green; [Turner's Crimson Rambler × Mrs W. H. Cutbush]

Hugo Piller HT, ab, 1927, Leenders, M.; flowers flesh-white, center pale ecru; [sport of Ophelia]

Hugo Roller T, yb, 1907, Paul, W.; flowers lemon-yellow, edged and suffused crimson, well-formed, dbl.; foliage small, rich green; weak stems; compact, bushy growth

Hugo Roller, Climbing Cl T, yb, 1932, Rogers; [sport of Hugo Roller]

Hugo Schlösser HT, op, 1955, Kordes; bud long, pointed; flowers salmon-pink, very large, dbl., high-centered; foliage leathery; strong stems; very vigorous, upright, bushy growth; [World's Fair × Peace]

Hugonis – See ***R. hugonis*** (Hemsley)

Hugonis plena – See **Double Hugonis**, S dbl.

Hugs 'n' Kisses Min, pb, 1999, Walden, John K.; flowers

pink, white, reverse near white, 2½ in., dbl., borne in small to large clusters, moderate fragrance; foliage large, dark, grey-green, glossy; prickles moderate; compact, spreading, medium (16-18 in.) growth; PP12113; [Small Miracle × seedling]; int. by Bear Creek Gardens, Inc., 1999

Huguenot 300 F, ob, Delbard; flowers salmon-orange, dbl., high-centered, borne in large clusters, no fragrance; good repeat; new foliage red; vigorous, tall (4-5 ft.) growth; needs support in spring to hold up the large sprays.; int. in 1985

Hugues Aufray S, pb, Dorieux; int. in 1996

Huguette Min, op; flowers shrimp-pink shaded salmon

Huguette Despiney HWich, yb, 1911, Girin; flowers light buff-yellow, edged red, small, very dbl., borne in large clusters; vigorous growth; [sport of Marco]

Huguette Duflos HT, op, 1937, Lille; bud pointed, dark pink; flowers satiny pink, touched salmon, large, 30-40 petals; foliage dark; vigorous, bushy growth; [Betty Uprichard × seedling]

Huguette Vincent HT, op, 1921, Chambard, C.; flowers brilliant velvety geranium-red, semi-dbl.; [(Mrs Edward Powell × unknown) × Willowmere]

Hula Girl Min, ob, 1976, Williams, Ernest D.; bud long, pointed; flowers bright orange, 1 in., 45 petals, moderate fruity fragrance; foliage small, glossy, embossed; bushy growth; PP4091; [Miss Hillcrest × Mabel Dot]; int. by Mini-Roses; AOE, ARS, 1976

Hula Hoop HT, pb, 1960, Freud; flowers striped bright pink and red; RULED EXTINCT 11/90; int. by Horstmann

Hula Hoop F, pb, 1991, Moore, Ralph S.; bud pointed; flowers white with pink to red edge, aging less intense, 2½-3 in., 15 petals, flat, borne in sprays of 5-15, no fragrance; foliage medium size, medium green, matte; upright, medium growth; PP8201; [(Dortmund × seedling) × Self]; int. by Sequoia Nursery, 1991

Hulda C, dr, 1845, Vibert; flowers dark velvety purple, medium, dbl.

Hullabalou Min, yb, 1990, Stoddard, Louis; bud pointed; flowers light orange on yellow with yellow reverse, aging to dull yellow, 20 petals; foliage small, medium green when new, aging to maroon, semi-glossy; prickles straight, sparse, small, red; bushy, low growth; [Rise 'n' Shine × unknown]

Hulthemia berberifolia – See ***Hulthemia persica***

Hulthemia hardii ((Cels) Rowley) Sp, yb, 1832, Hardy; flowers yellow with the crimson eye of hulthemia, 2 in., 5 petals; foliage with 5-7 narrow leaflets; hips almost smooth, round; Simplicifoliae; [*Rosa clinophylla* × *Hulthemia persica*]; first described by Cels in 1836; int. by Hardy before 1836

Hulthemia persica ((Michaux) Bornmueller) Sp, yb; flowers buttercup-yellow with a scarlet-brown eye, 1 in., single; leaves simple, lacking stipules, bluish-green; hips prickly, round; Simplicifoliae, (14); brought from Iran to France in 1788; introduced to England in 1790 by Banks

Hulthemosa

Humanity MinFl, dr, Harkness; flowers medium, dbl., borne in abundant clusters, slight fragrance; good repeat; foliage dark green, glossy; rounded, medium (3 ft.) growth; int. in 1995

Humboldt HT, mp, 1922, E.G. Hill, Co.; flowers bright rose-pink, dbl., high-centered; foliage glossy, bronze; vigorous growth; [Ophelia × seedling]; int. by Cottage Gardens Co.

Humdinger Min, or, 1976, Schwartz, E. w.; buds pointed; flowers orange-red, medium, dbl, high-centered, borne singly and several together; foliage dark green, glossy, serrated; growth upright, bushy, branched; PP4294; int. by Nor'East Miniature Roses, 1975

Hume's Blush Tea-Scented China T, lp, 1809, Hume/ Banks/Colville; flowers pale pearly pink, fading to creamy white at the edges, 9-10 cm., semi-dbl. to dbl., borne singly or in groups of 2-3, on weak stems, intense fragrance; foliage deep green, ovate, with 3-5 leaflets, quite shiny, purplish when young; prickles sparse, hooked; stems green to brown; hips found, depressed, reddish-scarlet; [supposedly *R. chinensis* × *R. gigantea*]; int. by A. Hume

Hummingbird HT, ob, 1934, Scittine; bud pointed; flowers bronze-orange, 3 in., very dbl.; vigorous growth; [sport of Talisman]; int. by Lainson

Humoreske Min, lp, 1957, Spek; flowers white, tinged pink, small, dbl.; bushy, compact growth; [Midget × Pixie]; int. by McGredy

Humpty-Dumpty Min, lp, 1952, deVink; flowers soft carmine-pink, center deeper, very dbl., borne in clusters; growth to 6-8 in.; [(*R. multiflora nana* × Mrs Pierre S. duPont F2) × Tom Thumb]; int. by T. Robinson, Ltd.

Hundred-Leaved Blush C, lp, before 1759, from England

Hungaria F, mr

Hunslet Moss M, dp; bud heavily mossed; flowers large, deep pink cerise, full, intense fragrance; summer; growth to 3-5 ft.; said to have been grown for several generations by Humphrey Brook's ancestors; int. by re-introduced, 1984

Hunter HRg, mr, 1965, Mattock, R.H.; flowers bright crimson, 2½ in., 43 petals, borne in clusters, moderate sweet fragrance; recurrent bloom; foliage rugose, dark, glossy; vigorous (4-5 ft.) growth; [*R. rugosa rubra* × Independence]; originally registered as S; int. by Mattock, 1961

Hunter Pink HRg, mp; int. by Vintage Gardens, 2001

Hunter's Moon HT, my, 1951, McGredy, Sam IV; flowers 30 petals; foliage glossy, dark; very vigorous growth; [Condesa de Sástago × Gorgeous]

Huntingburg F, lp, Peters; flowers soft pink, large, semi-dbl.; [sport of Festival Fanfare]; int. in 1997

Huntington Brocade B, rb, Robinson; flowers deep crimson-mauve with pink pinstripes and ribbons of light crimson, large, full, globular, moderate fragrance; [sport of Variegata di Bologna]; int. in 1973

Huntington's Hero S, lp, Martin; flowers pale pink with yellow stamens, semi-dbl., slight fragrance; int. in 1995

Huntsman HT, rb, 1951, Robinson, H.; flowers spectrum-red, reverse yellow, 5½ in., 35-40 petals; foliage dark; [(The Queen Alexandra Rose × unknown) × Crimson Glory]; int. by J&P

Hurdy Gurdy Min, rb, 1987, McGredy, Sam IV; flowers dark red with white stripes, small, full, slight fragrance; foliage small, medium green, semi-glossy; mini-flora; upright growth; [Matangi × Stars 'n' Stripes]; int. in 1986

Huron S, lp, 1932, Central Exp. Farm; flowers white flushed pink, semi-dbl., moderate fragrance; non-recurrent; foliage leathery; vigorous (2½ ft.), compact, bushy growth; a good hedge rose; very hardy; [(*R. spinosissima* × Pythagoras) × *R. cinnamomea*]

Huron Sunset Min, ly, 1990, Rennie, Bruce F.; flowers small, full, borne in small clusters, no fragrance; foliage small, medium green, semi-glossy; bushy growth; [Party Girl × Golden Rule]; int. by Rennie Roses International, 1991

Hurra F, or, 1965, Tantau, Math.; bud pointed; flowers dbl., borne in clusters; foliage glossy; vigorous, bushy growth; int. by Buisman, 1964

Hurrikan Pol, mr, VEG; flowers large, dbl.

Hurst Charm LCl, pb, 1936, Hicks; flowers pink, slightly tinted mauve, large

Hurst Crimson Pol, dr, 1933, Hicks; flowers deep crimson, borne in large trusses; [sport of Ideal]

Hurst Delight LCl, w, 1936, Hicks; flowers clear pale cream; vigorous growth

Hurst Favourite LCl, w, 1936, Hicks; flowers pure ivory-white, very large, semi-dbl., borne in clusters; very vigorous, climbing growth

Hurst Gem Pol, ob, 1931, Hicks; flowers brilliant orange-scarlet, small, semi-dbl.; [sport of Orléans Rose]

Hurst Glory HT, ob, 1936, Hicks; flowers pale salmon-cerise, flushed yellow, well-shaped, large, dbl.; vigorous growth

Hurst Scarlet HT, dr, 1933, Hicks; flowers deep scarlet, large, dbl.

Husky F, w, Dickson; int. in 2003

Husmoderrose HSpn, mp; flowers medium pink, fading to white, full, cupped, moderate fruity fragrance; large (7 × 6 ft.) growth

Husnaa S, pb, Ludwig; flowers cream white, petal edges turning salmon-pink, large, dbl., loose, borne singly or in clusters, intense fragrance; free-flowering; wide spreading, medium growth; int. by Ludwig's Roses, 1999

Hutton Village HT, my, 1974, Deamer; flowers bright yellow; [sport of Whisky Mac]; int. by Warley Rose Gardens, 1973

Hviezdoslav – See **Hwiezdoslav**, HT

Hvissinge-Rose F, pb, 1943, Poulsen, S.; flowers pinkish with yellow, single, borne in clusters; vigorous growth; [Orléans Rose × seedling]

Hwiezdoslav HT, rb, 1936, Böhm, J.; flowers copper-red to orange-copper-red, large, dbl., cupped; foliage glossy; vigorous, bushy growth

Hybrida cum Bifera – See **Petite Lisette**, A

Hybride di Castello – See **Ibrido di Castello**, HBank

Hybride du Luxembourg S, dp, before 1841, Hardy; flowers deep pink, shaded blush, medium, full, borne in clusters

Hybride Stadtholder HCh, dp, before 1850; flowers deep pink, edged dark red

Hyde Hall S, pb, 2004; flowers very full, borne in small clusters; foliage large, medium green, matte; prickles medium, hooked downward; growth bushy, dense, vigorous, branching, tall (175 cm.); [seedling (white English-type shrub) × seedling (medium pink shrub)]; int. by David Austin Roses, Ltd., 2004

Hyde Park F, ab, Harkness; flowers light rose-salmon, dbl., borne in large clusters, moderate fresh fragrance; int. in 1999

Hylo F, mp, 1961, Cant, B. R.; flowers salmon-pink, 2-2½ in., 28 petals, borne in clusters; bushy growth; [sport of Highlight]

Hymenée T, ly, about 1820, Hardy; possibly Laffay

Hymenee S, Delbard-Chabert; int. in 1969

Hymne F, mp, 1965, Verbeek; bud short, pointed; flowers Neyron rose, large, 38-52 petals, borne in large clusters; foliage dark, glossy; vigorous growth; [Miracle × seedling]; int. in 1963

Hypacia C, pb, before 1844, Hardy; flowers bright rose-pink spotted white, center whitish, large, dbl., cupped, moderate damask fragrance

Hypathia – See **Hypacia**, C

Hypatia – See **Hypacia**, C

Hythe Cluster Pol, dp, 1935, Archer; flowers glowing deep pink, semi-dbl., cupped, borne in large clusters; foliage small, glossy, light; vigorous growth

I Have A Dream F, ob, 2005, Alberici, Marc; flowers yellow peach, reverse white cream, 10 cm., dbl., borne in small clusters, slight fragrance; foliage medium size, medium green, matte; prickles normal, numerous; growth bushy, medium (80 cm.); hedging; [Henri Matisse × Mutabilis]; int. in 2007

I Love You F, dp, 1981, Takatori, Yoshiho; flowers deep pink; [sport of Margaret Thatcher]; int. by Japan Rose Nursery, 1983

I Love You HT, mr, 1996, Bees of Chester; flowers bright red, large, full, borne mostly singly; foliage medium size, dark green, semi-glossy; some prickles; upright, medium growth; int. by L W Van Geest Farms, Ltd., 1995

I Promise Min, pb, 1986, Lyon; flowers pink, reverse pale yellow, medium, 28 petals, high-centered, borne usually singly, moderate spicy fragrance; foliage medium size, medium green, semi-glossy; prickles few, small; low, bushy growth; hips globular, very small, red-gold; [seedling × seedling]; int. by M.B. Farm Min. Roses, Inc.

I Zingari HT, ob, 1925, Pemberton; flowers orange-scarlet, 3 in., semi-dbl., borne in cmall clusters, no fragrance; foliage dark; stems claret

I. X. L. HMult, dp, 1925, Coolidge; flowers magenta with white center, 3-4 cm., dbl., borne in small clusters; thornless; very vigorous growth; [Tausendschön × Veilchenblau]

Ian Brinson HT, dr, 1945, Bees; flowers crimson, compact, 4-5 in., 30 petals; foliage dark; [Mrs J.J. Hedley-Willis × J.C. Thornton]

Ian Stuart F, dr, 2005, Paul Chessum Roses; flowers full, borne in small clusters, slight fragrance; foliage medium size, medium green, semi-glossy; prickles medium, sharp, pink, moderate; growth compact, medium (2½ ft.); bedding, containers; [seedling × seedling]; int. by World of Roses, 2005

Ian Thorpe – See **Estelle**, HT

Iberflora 95 HT, mr, Roses Noves Ferrer, S L; flowers 28 petals, high-centered; [FE-85138 × Dallas]

Ibica – See **Ibiza**, HT

Ibis F, ob, 1979, Godin, M.; bud ovoid; flowers orange, 14-16 petals; foliage dark; [Europeana × Orangeade]

Ibisco HRg, dp; flowers clear, deep pink, 5 petals, no fragrance; growth to 3-4 ft.

Ibiza HT, w, 1938, Dot, Pedro; flowers well-formed; erect growth; [Mme Butterfly × Frau Karl Druschki]

Ibrido di Castello HBank, ly, 1920, Ragionieri; flowers cream, fading to white, 4 cm., dbl., borne in small clusters, moderate tea and violets fragrance; [*R. banksiae lutescens* × Lamarque]

Ibu Tien Suharto HT, w; flowers white with apricot-pink blush in center, large, dbl., loose, intense fragrance; good repeat

Ice Angel Min, w, Zary, Dr. Keith W.; int. in 1997

Ice Breaker HT, lp, 1994, Bridges, Dennis A.; flowers medium, dbl., borne mostly singly; foliage medium size, medium green, semi-glossy; some prickles; tall, upright growth; [Thriller × Just Lucky]; int. by Bridges Roses, 1994

Ice Cascade S, w, Williams, J. Benjamin; flowers very dbl., borne in sprays; int. in 1999

Ice Cool – See **Blanche Colombe**, LCl

Ice Cream – See **Memoire**, HT

Ice Cream – See **Cherry Parfait**, Gr

Ice Crystal Min, w, 1991, Clements, John K.; flowers crystal white, micro-mini, very full, high-centered, borne in small clusters, no fragrance; foliage small, medium green, semi-glossy; some prickles; micro-mini; low (20 cm.), bushy, compact growth; [seedling × Baby Betsy McCall]; int. by Heirloom Old Garden Roses, 1989

Ice Fairy Pol, w, 1984, Sanday, John; bud small; flowers ice white, small, full, borne in large clusters, slight fragrance; recurrent; foliage small, light green, semi-glossy; spreading growth; [sport of The Fairy]; int. by Sanday Roses, Ltd.

Ice Flower HT, w, Teranishi; flowers green tint; int. by Itami Rose Garden, 2004

Ice Follies S, w, Williams, J. Benjamin; flowers white with delicate apricot tint in center, full, borne in large sprays, moderate unusual fragrance; foliage dark green; growth spreading, groundcover or can be trained as climber; int. by Hortico Inc., 1999

Ice Girl – See **Ice-Girl**, HT

Ice-Girl HT, w, Kordes; flowers snow white, medium, dbl., cupped, borne mostly singly, intense fragrance; free-flowering; foliage dark green; stems wiry, almost thornless; tall growth; int. by Treloar Roses

Ice Kordana Mini Brite Min, w, Kordes; bud short, pointed ovoid, greenish white; flowers clear white, 1¾ in., 55-60 petals, borne singly and in clusters of 3-5, no fragrance; foliage small, abundant, glossy; prickles moderate, short, straight; vigorous, branching, upright (18 in.) growth; PP11147; PP11147; [seedling × seedling]; by Bear Creek Gardens, 1998

Ice Maiden F, w, 1977, Garelja; bud pointed; flowers pure white, semi-formal, large, 15 petals, moderate fragrance; foliage narrow, glossy, light green; vigorous, upright growth; [Iceberg × Iceberg]

Ice Meidiland – See **Ice Meillandecor**, S

Ice Meillandecor S, w, Meilland; bud conical, small; flowers white, open flat, 2½-3 in., 21-30 petals, flattened pompon, borne in clusters, no fragrance; free-flowering; foliage medium size, medium green, glossy; prickles medium; compact, mounding, ground cover growth; hips 1 cm., orange-red to red; PP11577; [Katherina Zeimet × (Iceberg × White Meidiland)]; int. in 1996

Ice Princess Min, lp, 1983, Laver, Keith G.; flowers light pink, light yellow stamens, finishing white, medium, dbl.; foliage small, medium green, matte; [Unnamed pink seedling × Lemon Delight]

Ice Queen Min, w, 1991, Saville, F. Harmon; bud ovoid, pointed; flowers medium, 60 petals, high-centered, borne mostly singly or in sprays of 5-8, no fragrance; foliage medium size, dark green, semi-glossy; bushy, medium growth; PP7771; [sport of Cupcake]; int. by Nor'East Min. Roses, 1991

Ice Queen – See **Iceberg**, HT

Ice White F, w, 1966, McGredy, Sam IV; flowers 3 in., 25 petals, borne in clusters; foliage glossy; [Mme Léon Cuny × (Orange Sweetheart × Cinnabar)]; int. by McGredy; Gold Medal, Portland, 1970

Ice White, Climbing Cl F, w, McGredy, Sam IV; int. after 1966

Iceberg Cl Pol, w, 1910, Paul, G.; flowers pure white

Iceberg F, w, 1959, Kordes, R.; bud long, pointed; flowers pure white, 4 in., 20-25 petals, borne in clusters, moderate fragrance; good repeat; foliage light green, glossy; few prickles; vigorous, upright, bushy growth; [Robin Hood × Virgo]; int. by McGredy & Son, 1958; Gold Medal, Baden-Baden, 1958, Hall of Fame, WFRS, 1983, Gold Medal, NRS, 1958

Iceberg, Climbing Cl F, w, 1968, Cant, B. R.

Iceberg HT, w, Kordes; flowers white, large; foliage glossy, dark green; stems 28; PP14900; int. by W. Kordes Söhne, 2001

Iced Ginger F, ob, 1972, Dickson, A.; flowers inside of base strong orange to light orange, reverse deep pink with yellow base, 4½ in., 45 petals, borne in trusses, moderate fragrance; free-flowering; foliage light green, red veined, medium; [Anne Watkins × unknown]

Iced Parfait F, lp, 1985, Xavier, Sister M.; flowers pale pink, medium, 40 petals, urn-shaped, borne 6 per cluster, moderate fragrance; foliage light green; prickles straight, red; bushy, compact growth; [Pink Parfait × Iceberg]; int. in 1972

Iced Raspberry Min, rb, 2005, White, Wendy R; flowers dark and medium red, reverse white and red, 1¾ in., very full, borne mostly solitary, slight fragrance; foliage medium size, dark green, matte, disease-resistant; prickles moderate, ¼ in., fine point, angled down slightly; growth upright, compact, medium (15-20 in.); cutting, garden decoration; [Jilly Jewel × (Zorina × Baby Katie)]; int. by Nor'East Miniature Roses, 2006; Certificate of Merit, Rose Hills, 2006, AOE, ARS, 2006

Iced Tea Min, r, 2002, Moore, Ralph S.; flowers tan/russet, russet/peach reverse, 1-1½ in., single, borne mostly solitary, slight fragrance; foliage medium size, medium green, matte; growth upright, tall (18-24 in.); [Sequoia Ruby × Sequoia Ruby]; int. by Sequoia Nursery, 2001

Ice-Girl Panarosa – See **Ice-Girl**, HT

Iceland Queen HSet, w, 1935, Horvath; flowers creamy white, 7-9 cm., dbl.; vigorous growth; int. by Wyant

Ich hab Dich lieb – See **Redwood**, F

Ichalkaranji 100 HT, m, Chiplunkar; flowers lavender pink, outer petal edges and reverse darker, large, full; int. by Decospin, 1993

Ichi Boh Fun Pol, pb; from China

Ichibanboshi Min, ob, Keisei; int. in 1996

Ichiro Min, mr, 2002, Moe, Mitchie; flowers dbl., high-centered, borne mostly solitary, slight fragrance; foliage medium size, dark green, glossy; prickles small, straight, light tan, moderate; growth upright, medium (20-24 in.); garden decorative, exhibition; [Anne Hering × Miss Flippins]; int. by Mitchie's Roses 'n' More, 2002

ICI Golden Celebration Gr, dy, 1988, Pearce, C.A.; flowers golden yellow, large, full, moderate fragrance; foliage medium size, medium green, glossy, mildew resistant; bushy, healthy growth; [seedling × seedling]; int. by The Limes New Roses

Ico F, m, 1987, Patil, B.K.; flowers light purple, 60-70 petals, globular, slight fragrance; foliage dark green, glossy; prickles brownish-green curving downward; vigorous, upright, bushy growth; [sport of Deep Purple]; int. by K.S.G. Sons Roses, 1985

Ico Ambassador HT, my, Patil, B.K.; flowers light chrome yellow, dbl.; free-flowering; [sport of Ambassador]; int. by Icospin, 1988

Ico Beauty HT, pb, 1987, Patil, B.K.; flowers rose pink, reverse flushed white, medium, 25-30 petals, high-centered, slight fragrance; foliage glossy; prickles pale green curving downward; upright, bushy growth; [sport of Red Planet]; int. by K.S.G. Sons Roses, 1985

Ico Delight HT, w, Patil, B.K.; flowers pure white, large, full, high-centered; [sport of Eterna]; int. by Icospin, 1989

Ico Deluxe HT, pb, Patil, B.K.; flowers broad petals, lasting; free-flowering; [sport of Mistraline]; int. by Icospin, 1990

Ico Pearl F, pb, Patil, B.K.; flowers pink shaded apricot, full, borne in clusters; [sport of Dearest]; int. by Icospin, 1990

Ico Talk F, pb, Patil, B.K.; flowers light pink stripes on both sides of petals, borne singly and in clusters; free-flowering; [sport of Double Talk]; int. by Icospin, 1993

Ico Trimurthi HT, pb, Patil, B.K.; int. in 1989

Icy Tiding HT, w

Ida HMult, op, about 1890, Dawson; [Dawson × *R. multiflora*]

Ida HT, dp, 2003, Singer, Steve; flowers deep pink, reverse light pink, 12 cm., full, borne mostly solitary, moderate fragrance; foliage medium size, dark green, semi-glossy; prickles few, small; growth upright, medium (3-5 ft.); garden decorative; [Sheer Elegance × Great Scott]; int. by J.C. Bakker & Sons, Ltd., 2003

Ida Belle Min, m, 1990, Williams, Ernest D.; flowers lavender with blends of amber, very long-lasting, small, 33 petals, high-centered, intense fragrance; foliage small, medium green, glossy; bushy growth; PP7605; [(Tom Brown × (Rise 'n' Shine × Watercolor)) × Twilight Trail]; int. in 1989

Ida Elizabeth HT, mr, 1987, Welsh, Eric; flowers large, 30 petals, high-centered, borne singly, moderate fragrance; foliage matte; medium, bushy growth; [Red Lion × Mainauperle]; int. by Treloar Roses Pty. Ltd., 1987

Ida Eve Javior HT, w, 2003, Cockerham, John E.; flowers blushed light pink when newly-opened, 3 in., full, borne mostly solitary; foliage medium size, medium green, semi-glossy; prickles 3/8 in., blade-shaped; growth compact, vigorous, medium; garden decorative; [Savoy Hotel × open polinated]; int. in 2004

Ida Hoff HT, mp; flowers large, dbl.

Ida Klemm HMult, w, 1907, Walter, L.; flowers snow-white, 3½ cm., semi-dbl., borne in large clusters; foliage large, dark green, glossy; long, strong stems; vigorous growth; [sport of Crimson Rambler]

Ida McCracken HT, op, 1952, Norman; flowers salmon and coral, well-formed, 4 in., 25-30 petals; foliage leathery, dark; free growth; [Ethel Somerset × Mrs Sam McGredy]; int. by Harkness

Ida Red S, mr, 2006, Ponton, Ray; flowers full, borne mostly solitary and in small clusters; foliage medium size, medium green, semi-glossy; prickles medium, straight, moderate; growth upright, short (3 ft.); [Brass Band × Cameron Bohls]; int. in 2006

Ida Scholten HT, pb, 1933, Buisman, G. A. H.; flowers pink shaded carmine-red, very large, dbl.; foliage dark, leathery, glossy; bushy, dwarf, compact growth; [Capt. F.S. Harvey-Cant × Gen. MacArthur]

Ida Sisley B, dr; flowers violet-red, large, full

Ideal HT, mp, 1904, Becker; flowers carnation pink, very large, full; [sport of La France]

Ideal Pol, mr, 1921, Spek; flowers dark crimson scarlet; [sport of Miss Edith Cavell]

Ideal Home HT, pb, 1963, Laperrière; flowers carmine-pink, base white, well-formed, 5 in., 25-30 petals, moderate fragrance; vigorous, upright growth; [Monte Carlo × Tonnerre]; int. as Idylle, EFR

Idée Fixe F, or, 1986, Lens, Louis; flowers light orange-red, 2 in., 15 petals, borne in clusters of 3-18, slight fragrance; foliage small, dark; prickles hooked, light red; low, bushy growth; [seedling × (seedling × Floradora)]; int. in 1980

Idole HT, or

Idun F, mp, 1969, Lundstad; flowers Neyron rose, large, 41 petals, cupped, borne in clusters; foliage dark, glossy; bushy growth; [Schneewittchen × Fanal]

Idylle – See **Ideal Home**, HT

Iga 63 HT, pb, 1963, Moreira da Silva; flowers pink and red; [Confidence × seedling]

Iga 83 Munchen – See **Rose Iga**, F

Iga Erfurt F, op, GPG Bad Langensalza; flowers medium, semi-dbl.; int. in 1966

Igloo HT, w, 1969, Verbeek; bud ovoid; flowers medium, dbl.; foliage dark; [seedling × White Knight]

Igna HT, ob, Delbard; flowers orange-yellow with lighter reverse, medium, dbl., high-centered; cut flower trade

Ignasi Iglesias HT, mr, 1934, Dot, Pedro; flowers rose in early season, oriental red in summer, dbl., high-centered; foliage wrinkled; vigorous, bushy growth; [Angel Guimera × (Souv. de Claudius Pernet × Mme Butterfly)]

Ignis S, mr, 1934, Chotkové Rosarium; flowers fiery red, very large; non-recurrent; foliage leathery, dark; vigorous (3¼-6½ ft.) growth; int. by Böhm

Igor ; flowers carmine-white, medium, 36 petals; foliage dark; spreading growth

Ikaruga HT, yb, 1977, Ito; bud ovoid; flowers 6 in., 35 petals, high-centered, slight fragrance; vigorous, upright growth; [McGredy's Ivory × Garden Party]; int. in 1975

Ilam – See **Roseworld**, HT

Ilaria F, dp, 1962, Borgatti, G.; flowers coral-red, well-formed, semi-dbl.; foliage dark; [Cinnabar × Fashion]; int. by Sgaravatti

Ildiko F, mr, 1971, Institute of Ornamental Plant Growing; bud ovoid; flowers cherry-red, medium, semi-dbl., cupped; profuse, intermittent bloom; moderate, upright growth; [Mardi Gras × Paprika]

Île de France HWich, rb, 1922, Nonin; flowers bright scarlet, center white, 4-5 cm., semi-dbl., borne in medium to large clusters; foliage large, leathery, dark; numerous prickles; short, strong stems; very vigorous (15-20 ft.) growth; [American Pillar × unknown]

Ile de France – See **Adoration**, HT

Ile de France S, mr, Pekmez, Paul; int. in 1992

Ilicifolia – See **À Feuille de Chêne**, C

Ilios HT, dr; int. in 2002

Illinois Gr, or, 1969, Morey, Dr. Dennison; bud long, pointed; flowers large, 25 petals; foliage leathery; vigorous, bushy growth; [Soprano × Tropicana]; int. by Country Garden Nursery

Illisca HT, dp, Laperrière; flowers light cherry red, large, moderate fragrance; int. in 1974

Illos HT, m

Illumination F, dy, 1970, Dickson, Patrick; flowers deep sulfur-yellow, 3 in., 12 petals; foliage glossy, light; free growth; [Clare Grammerstorf × Happy Event]; int. by A. Dickson

Illumination F, ab, Pallek; int. in 1986

Illusion HKor, mr, 1961, Kordes, R.; flowers blood-red to cinnabar, 8-9 cm., dbl., borne in large clusters, moderate fragrance; foliage leathery, glossy, light green; vigorous growth

Illusion HT, my, 1961, Verbeek; flowers 50 petals; foliage glossy; vigorous growth; [Peace × seedling]

Illusion HT, pb, Kordes; bud very large; flowers white with deep pink petal edges brushed downward on the petals, large, full, exhibition, borne mostly singly, no fragrance; no prickles on stems; stems long, slender; growth vigorous, medium; int. by Ludwig's Roses, 2002

Illustre HGal, pb, before 1820, Descemet; flowers lilac-pink, sometimes shaded light purple, medium, full

Ilmenau S, mr, Hetzel; int. in 1992

Ilona HT, mr, 1974, Verbeek; flowers 4-4½ in., full; foliage glossy, leathery; bushy growth; PP3540; [Miracle × (Romantica × Edith Piaf)]; int. in 1973

Ilona Min, ab, 1999, Martin, Robert B., Jr.; flowers orange/apricot striped, reverse lighter, 1 in., single, borne in small clusters; foliage small, dark green, near rugose, disease-resistant; prickles moderate; compact, low (18-24 in.) growth; [Altissimo × Roller Coaster]

Ilse HT, pb, 2005, Edwards, Eddie & Phelps, Ethan; flowers full, borne mostly solitary, slight fragrance; foliage large, dark green, semi-glossy; few prickles; growth upright, tall (5-6 ft.); exhibition; [seedling × seedling]; int. in 2006

Ilse Haberland F, mp, 1956, Kordes; flowers crimson-pink, very large, dbl., high-centered, moderate fragrance; foliage glossy; vigorous, upright, bushy growth

Ilse Krohn HKor, w, 1958, Kordes; flowers pure white, 12-13 cm., very dbl., high-centered, borne in small clusters; non-recurrent; foliage large, glossy; very vigorous growth; [Golden Glow × *R.* × *kordesii*]; int. by Kordes & Son, 1957

Ilse Krohn Superior HKor, w, 1964, W. Kordes' Sohne; flowers pure white, buff at center, 12-13 cm., dbl., borne in small clusters, intense fragrance; remontant; foliage dark; vigorous (9 ft.) growth; [sport of Ilse Krohn]

Ilseta F, mp, 1985, Tantau, Math.; flowers medium, 35 petals; foliage medium size, medium green, matte; upright growth; PP5707; int. in 1983

Iluse HT, ob, Urban, J.; flowers salmon-orange and yellow, large, dbl.; int. in 1968

Image d'Epinal LCl, mr, Croix; growth to 7-10 ft.; int. by Roses Paul Croix, 1997

Imagination HT, ab, 1992, Winchel, Joseph F.; bud large, shapely; flowers apricot orange, yellow reverse, good distinct bicoloration, 3-3½ in., 26-30 petals, borne mostly singly; foliage large, clean, medium green, semi-glossy; some prickles; medium (100-130 cm.), attractive, compact, upright, bushy growth; PP8414; [Marmalade × seedling]; int. by Weeks Roses, 1993

Imagination – See **Countess Celeste**, S

Imagine S, ab, Clements, John; flowers soft apricot with brownish cast, 5 in., 36 petals, cup-and-saucer, moderate fragrance; recurrent; foliage dark green; vigorous, bushy (4 ft.) growth

Imagine HT, rb, Dorieux; int. by Roseraies Dorieux, 1992

Imagine Min, pb, 1995, Rennie, Bruce F.; flowers 1 in., full, borne in clusters; foliage small, medium green, semi-glossy; few prickles; low (12-15 in.), compact growth; [Forever Mine × Pink Sheri]; int. by Rennie Roses International, 1995

Imagine HT, w, Hiroshima; int. by Hiroshima Bara-en, 1999

Imatra F, pb, 1930, Poulsen, S.; flowers pink to white; [Orléans Rose × unknown]; int. by Olsson

Imbricata S, lp, 1869, Ducher; flowers delicate pink, large, full, cupped

Imbroglio Min, yb, Benardella, Frank A.; int. in 1990

Imma HT, lp; flowers high-centered, high-centered

Immaculada Galan F, w, 1970, LeGrice; flowers large, 60-70 petals, globular, borne in trusses; foliage small, blue-gray; very free growth; int. in 1968

Immensee S, lp, 1983, Kordes, W.; flowers light pink to near white, small, single; foliage small, dark, glossy; spreading (to 13 ft.) growth; groundcover; [The Fairy × (*R. wichurana* × unknown)]; int. in 1982; Gold Medal, RNRS, 1984

Immerblühender Crimson Rambler – See **Flower of Fairfield**, HMult

Immortal Juno S, dp, 1992, Austin, David; flowers deep pink, 3-3½ in., very dbl., borne in small clusters, intense fragrance; foliage medium size, medium green, semi-glossy; some prickles; tall (59 in.), upright growth; int. by David Austin Roses, Ltd., 1982

Imogen HT, w, 1915, Paul; flowers creamy white aging to light yellow with orange-yellow, large, full, moderate fragrance

Imogen F, Bidwell

Imogene Min, yb, 1985, Williams, Ernest D.; flowers yellow, marked red, well-formed, small, 45 petals; foliage small, dark, glossy; upright, bushy growth; [Little Darling × Over the Rainbow]; int. by Mini-Roses

Imp F, rb, 1971, Dawson, George; bud globular; flowers

red, reverse silver-pink, small, dbl.; foliage large, dark, leathery; bushy growth; [Daily Sketch × Impeccable]; int. by Brundrett, 1970

Impala F, op, 1977, Herholdt, J.A.; bud ovoid, pointed; flowers coppery, reverse orange, 2½-3 in., 30 petals, cupped; foliage bright green; bushy growth; [Zambra × seedling]; int. in 1972

Impala – See **Melinda**, HT

Impala F, ob, Kordes; flowers orange, medium, dbl., high-centered, borne mostly singly; recurrent; stems moderate; int. by W. Kordes Söhne, 2005

Impatient F, or, 1982, Warriner, William A.; flowers medium, orange-red, 4 in., 20-25 petals, borne in large clusters, slight fragrance; foliage medium size, light green, glossy; upright, bushy growth; PP5122; [America × seedling]; int. by J&P, 1984

Impeccable HT, dr, 1955, Delbard-Chabert; flowers deep velvety red, well-shaped, dbl.; foliage dark

Imperator – See **Crimson Wave**, F

Impératrice Charlotte HP, dp, 1867, Verdier, E.

Impératrice de Hollande – See **Roi des Pays-Bas**, D

Impératrice de Russie HGal, dp, about 1825, Péan; flowers large, very full

Impératrice Eugénie T, my, 1853, Pradel; flowers sulfur yellow, medium, very full

Impératrice Eugénie B, m, 1855, Plantier; flowers purple-pink

Impératrice Eugénie B, mp, 1855, Béluze; flowers silvery rose pink, medium, full; foliage dark green, glossy; prickles very sharp, hooked, purple-red

Impératrice Eugénie M, m, 1856, Guillot père; flowers lilac-pink, medium, dbl., moderate fragrance; some repeat; vigorous growth

Impératrice Eugénie HP, w, 1856, Avoux & Crozy; flowers white, center light pink, aging white, medium, full, globular

Impératrice Eugénie HP, w, 1856, Oger; bud spotted crimson; flowers delicately tinted at center with pink, aging to pure white, medium, full, globular; [Mme Récamier × unknown]

Imperatrice Farah HT, w, Delbard; flowers white with deep pink edges, petals form points, large, full, high-centered, slight fragrance; vigorous, upright (3 ft.) growth; int. in 1992

Impératrice Joséphine – See Empress Josephine

Impératrice Joséphine B, lp, 1842, Verdier, V.; flowers flesh pink, edges whitish, medium, very full, globular

Impératrice Joséphine HP, lp, 1852, Lartay; flowers flesh pink, shaded white, large, full

Impératrice Maria Alexandrina HP, w, 1862, Damaizin

Impératrice Maria Feodorowna HP, mp, 1892, Lévêque; flowers delicate pink, large, globular; foliage glaucous green

Impératrice Maria Féodorowna de Russie T, ly, 1883, Nabonnand; flowers canary yellow, fading to white, very large, imbricated, very full

Impératrice Rouge – See **Red Empress**, LCl

Imperial HT, rb, 1957, Moreira da Silva; flowers cardinal-red, reverse golden yellow, well-formed; [Geranium × Opera]

Imperial F, mr, Olesen, L. & M.; bud globular; flowers 8-10 cm., semi-dbl. to dbl., borne singly or in clusters of 3-4, slight wild rose fragrance; foliage medium size, medium to dark green, glossy; prickles moderate; growth bushy, 40-60 cm.; PP11151; [Christian IV × seedling]; int. by Poulsen Roser, 1996

Imperial Blaze – See **Demokracie**, LCl

Imperial Gold HT, my, 1962, Swim, H.C.; bud ovoid; flowers lemon-yellow to Indian yellow, 3½-4½ in., 30-35 petals, moderate fragrance; foliage leathery, dark, glossy; vigorous, upright growth; PP1894; [Charlotte Armstrong × Girona]; int. by C.R. Burr, 1962

Imperial Palace – See **Imperial**, F

Imperial Pink HT, mp, 1942, Coddington; [sport of Royal Beauty]

Imperial Potentate HT, mp, 1921, Clarke Bros.; flowers large, 45 petals, high-centered; foliage dark, leathery; vigorous growth; [Ophelia × Hoosier Beauty]; Gold Medal, Portland, 1921

Imperial Queen HT, mr, 1962, Lammerts, Dr. Walter; bud long, pointed; flowers cherry-red, 4½-5 in., 21 petals, cupped, moderate fragrance; foliage leathery, glossy; vigorous, compact growth; PP2121; [Queen Elizabeth × Chrysler Imperial]; int. by C.R. Burr, 1961

Imperial Rose B, dp

Impériale – See **Regina Dicta**, HGal

Imposant F, mp

Impress HT, rb, 1929, Dickson, A.; bud ovoid, cardinal-red, shaded orange; flowers salmon-cerise, tinted golden, very large, 40-45 petals; foliage dark, glossy; vigorous growth; int. by Liggit

Improved Cécile Brünner HG, op, 1948, Duehrsen; bud long, pointed; flowers salmon-pink, medium, 30 petals, high-centered, borne in clusters; foliage leathery, dull green; very vigorous, upright growth; [Dainty Bess × *R. gigantea*]; int. by H&S

Improved Lafayette F, mr, 1935, H&S; flowers semi-dbl.; foliage soft; vigorous, bushy growth; [E.G. Hill × seedling]; int. by Dreer

Improved Marquise Litta de Breteuil – See **C. W. Cowan**, HT

Improved Orléans Pol, mp, 1931, Green Norfolk Nurs.; [sport of Orléans]

Improved Peace HT, yb, 1959, Dean; bud ovoid; flowers yellow edged and flushed pink, large, dbl., high-centered; foliage leathery, wrinkled; very vigorous, bushy growth; [sport of Peace]

Improved Premier Bal HT, pb, Wheatcroft Bros.; flowers pale cream edged deep pink, large; foliage leathery; vigorous growth

Improved Prince Philip Gr, or, 1964, Leenders, J.; flowers well-formed; [Queen Elizabeth × Prince Philip]

Improved Princesse de Béarn – See **Mme Jean Everaerts**, HP

Improved Rainbow T, pb, about 1896, Burbank; flowers deep coral pink, striped and mottled with crimson, very large

Improved Universal Favorite HWich, mp, 1901, Manda, W.A.; flowers brilliant pink

Improved Verdun Pol, dp, 1946, Kluis; flowers vivid carmine-red, dbl., borne in clusters; foliage leathery; bushy growth; int. by Klyn

Impulse Min, op, 1986, Jolly, Marie; flowers salmon-pink, light yellow reverse, small, 38 petals, cupped; foliage small, medium green, semi-glossy; prickles long, brownish; medium, upright growth; fruit not observed; [Red Ace × Chris Jolly]; int. by Rosehill Farm

Impulse HT, mr, Barni, V.; flowers intense red, dbl., exhibition, no fragrance; growth to 3 ft.; int. by Rose Barni, 1990

In Appreciation HT, dp, Nieuwesteeg; flowers dbl., moderate fragrance; growth free branching

In Dreams HT, pb, 2004, Edwards, Eddie & Phelps, Ethan; flowers medium pink with yellow base, 5 in., full, high-centered, borne mostly solitary, moderate fragrance; recurrent; foliage medium size, dark green, glossy; prickles small, hooked; growth upright, medium, 5-6 ft.; [Veteran's Honor × Hot Princess]; int. in 2005

In the Mood Min, yb, 1989, McCann, Sean; flowers yellow streaked pink, small, 20 petals, slight fragrance; foliage small, medium green, semi-glossy; bushy growth; [Rise 'n' Shine × seedling]; int. in 1988

In the Mood HT, mr, 2005, Carruth, Tom; flowers bright clear red, 12-14 cm., full, borne mostly solitary, slight fragrance; recurrent; foliage large, dark green, semi-glossy; prickles moderate, average, slightly hooked, beige; growth upright, medium (120 to 150 cm.); garden decoration; [City of San Francisco × Olympiad]; int. by Weeks Roses, 2007

In the Mood HT, m, Hiroshima; int. by Hiroshima Bara-en, 2005

In the Pink F, mp, 1989, Ryan, C.; flowers medium, 60 petals, borne in sprays of 4-5, moderate musk fragrance; foliage greenish-red, glossy; prickles hooked, red; medium, bushy growth; [Baby Faurax × seedling]; int. by Melville Nursery, 1988

In the Pink F, pb, Limes New Roses; int. in 1994

Ina Min, w, 1994, Taylor, Franklin "Pete" & Kay; flowers white with pinkish edge, moderately good form, large, dbl., borne in clusters; foliage medium size, medium green, semi-glossy; few prickles; medium (30 in.), upright, bushy growth; [Party Girl × Fairhope]; int. by Taylor's Roses, 1993

Ina an' Mona S, ab, Jensen; int. in 1992

Inano HT, dy, 1986, Teranishi, K.; flowers urn-shaped, medium, 40 petals, borne singly, moderate fruity fragrance; foliage medium size, light green; prickles small, brown; medium, bushy growth; [Doreen × Goldilocks]; int. by Itami Rose Nursery, 1978

Inata F, op, 1967, deRuiter; flowers pink shaded salmon, open, semi-dbl., borne in trusses; vigorous growth; [sport of Valeta]

Inca Min, ob, Poulsen Roser; int. in 2000

Inca de Mallorca F, mr, 1958, Dot, Pedro; flowers strawberry-red, 20 petals; strong stems; compact growth; [Soller × Floradora]

Incandescent HT, mr, Wagner, S.; bud globular and short; flowers velvety bright red vermillion-red, dbl., slight fragrance; foliage large, reddish dark green, glossy; [Bond Street × Dame de Coeur]; int. by Res. Stn. f. Horticulture, Cluj, 1991

Incanto LCl, mp, Barni; flowers bright pink, golden stamens, single, flat, borne in clusters, slight fragrance; foliage dark green; vigorous (8-20 ft.) growth; int. by Rose Barni, 2006; Gold Medal, Barcelona, 2004, Gold Medal, Rome, 2004, Best Beautiful Italian Rose, Monza, 2005

Incarnata – See **My Lady Kensington**, C

Incarnata – See **Double Carnée**, HSpn

Incarnata Major – See **Great Maiden's Blush**, A

Incarnata Maxima – See **Celsiana**, D

Incarnate – See **Vilmorin**, M

Incense HT, dr, 1968, LeGrice; flowers deep red, pointed, dbl.; vigorous growth; [(Karl Herbst × New Yorker) × Konrad Adenauer]

Incense Indigo HT, m, 2005, Viraraghavan, M.S. Viru; flowers mauve, 5 in., full, borne mostly solitary, intense damask fragrance; foliage medium size, medium green, semi-glossy; prickles ¼ in., pointed; growth bushy, medium (3 ft.); garden decorative; [unknown × unknown]; int. by Roses Unlimited, 2004

Incense Rose – See ***R. primula*** (Boulenger)

Inch'Allah HT, pb, 1944, Meilland, F.; bud long; flowers bright pink, reverse flesh, stamens yellow, very large, semi-dbl.; vigorous growth; [Pres. Macia × Editor McFarland]

Inclination S, op, Williams, J. Benjamin; flowers salmon pink, dbl., moderate fragrance; recurrent; moderate (3 ft.) growth; int. by Hortico, Inc., 2006

Incognito Min, m, 1995, Bridges, Dennis A.; flowers mauve blend with yellow reverse, medium, dbl., borne mostly singly; foliage medium size, dark green, semi-glossy; few prickles; tall (30-34 in.), upright, bushy growth; PP9932;

[Jean Kenneally × Twilight Trail]; int. by Bridges Roses, 1995

Incomparable HGal, dp, before 1813; flowers deep pink, nuanced purple; from Holland

Incomparable HP, w, 1923, Giraud, A.; flowers rosy white, large

Incomparable d'Auteuil C, mp, before 1826, Laffay; flowers rose with carmine; non-remontant; growth to 5 ft.

Incredible S, yb, 1985, Buck, Dr. Griffith J.; bud ovoid, pointed; flowers yellow freckled and streaked with orange-red, large, 28 petals, urn-shaped, borne 1-10 per cluster, moderate fragrance; recurrent; foliage medium large, leathery, dark olive green, copper tinted when young; prickles awl-like, brown; vigorous, erect growth; hardy; [Gingersnap × Sevilliana]; int. by Iowa State University, 1984

Indéfectible Pol, mr, 1919, Turbat; flowers bright clear red, semi-dbl.; [Annchen Muller × unknown]

Independance du Luxembourg HT, w, Lens, Louis; flowers creamy white with orange and pink tones, large, dbl., intense fragrance; int. in 1960

Independence F, or, 1951, Kordes; bud urn-shaped; flowers pure scarlet, 4½ in., 35 petals, cupped, borne in clusters of up to 10, moderate fragrance; foliage glossy, dark; growth moderate; [(Baby Chateau × Crimson Glory) × (Baby Chateau × Crimson Glory)]; int. by J&P; Gold Medal, Portland, 1953, Gold Medal, NRS, 1950, Gold Medal, Bagatelle, 1943

Independence, Climbing Cl F, or, 1960, Balducci & Figli

Independence 76 F, mr, 1977, Byrum; bud short, pointed; flowers high-pointed, 3-4 in., 22 petals, moderate tea fragrance; vigorous, upright growth; PP3902; [Cotillion × Suspense]; int. by J.H. Hill Co., 1974

Independence Day HT, ab, 1919, Bees; bud pointed; flowers sunflower-gold, stained flame-color and orange-apricot, large, dbl., high-centered, intense fragrance; foliage leathery, glossy, dark; vigorous growth; [Mme Edouard Herriot × Souv. de Gustave Prat]; Gold Medal, NRS, 1919

Independence Day, Climbing Cl HT, ab, 1930, Brown, W.&J.; flowers red, orange yellow center, medium, very full; [sport of Independence Day]; int. by E. Murrell

Indian Baby S, my; flowers lemon yellow; free-flowering; graceful, trailing, groundcover growth

Indian Chief HT, rb, 1967, Gregory; flowers currant-red shaded orange, pointed, dbl.; foliage dark; very free growth; [Tropicana × unknown]

Indian Goddess Cl Min, pb, 1999, Sridharan, Dr. Lakshmi M.; flowers 2½ in., semi-dbl., borne singly and in small clusters; foliage dark green, semi-glossy, disease-resistant; few prickles; bushy, medium (4-5 ft.) growth; [Crazy Dottie × seedling]

Indian Gold F, yb, 1961, Von Abrams; bud ovoid, flushed red; flowers yellow flushed soft pink, large, 30-45 petals, high-centered, borne in clusters, moderate fragrance; foliage glossy, light green; short stems; upright, compact growth; [Goldilocks × seedling]; int. by Peterson & Dering, 1961

Indian Maid HT, ob, Padilla; bud long, pointed; flowers salmon, reverse bronze-yellow, dbl., high-centered; foliage glossy; vigorous growth; [(Talisman × unknown) × Souv. de Claudius Pernet]

Indian Meillandina – See **Carol-Jean**, Min

Indian Pink HT, pb, 1977, McDaniel, G. K.; flowers 5 in., 30-36 petals, globular; foliage leathery; very vigorous, upright, bushy growth; [seedling × Orange Tango]; int. by Carlton Rose Nurseries, 1971

Indian Princess – See **Princess of India**, HT

Indian Princess Min, r, 1982, Strawn, Leslie E.; flowers tan flushed orange, reverse burnt umber, shaded garnet-brown, 20 petals; foliage small, dark, semi-glossy; upright growth; [Yellow Jewel × Golden Cougar]; int. by Pixie Treasures Min. Roses

Indian Red HT, rb, 1948, Brownell; bud long, pointed; flowers red shaded deeper, large, dbl., high-centered, moderate fragrance; foliage small, glossy; vigorous, bushy, upright growth; hardy; [Pink Princess × Crimson Glory]

Indian Silk MinFl, ab, 2000, Lens, Louis; flowers apricot, 3-4 cm., full, borne in small clusters, moderate fragrance; recurrent; foliage medium size, light green, glossy; few prickles; bushy, medium (14 in.) growth; patio, containers; [Little Angel × Love Letter]; int. by Louis Lens NV, 1991

Indian Song HT, pb, 1971, Meilland; flowers rose, reverse gold, 5 in., 40 petals, high-centered; foliage glossy, dark; vigorous, upright growth; [(Radar × Karl Herbst) × Sabrina]; int. by L. Dol

Indian Summer Cl HT, ob, 1938, Duehrsen; bud pointed; flowers orange, streaked red, large, 25 petals; foliage dark bronze, leathery, glossy; very vigorous (12-18 ft.) growth; [Ednah Thomas × Autumn]; int. by H&S

Indian Summer Cl Min, op; int. by Harkness, 1991

Indian Summer HT, ob, Pearce; flowers creamy orange, dbl., high-centered, intense fragrance; good rebloom; foliage dark green, healthy; bushy, compact (2½ ft.) growth; int. in 1991

Indian Sunblaze – See **Carol-Jean**, Min

Indian Sunset HT, rb, Meilland; flowers vermilion-red, China yellow reverse, full, classic; cut flower rose; int. by Meilland Intl., 2004

Indian Warrior HT, dr

Indiana HGal, 1834, Vibert

Indiana M, mp, 1845, Vibert; flowers medium, very dbl., cupped

Indiana HT, pb, 1907, E.G. Hill, Co.; flowers bright pink, faintly suffused orange, dbl.; bushy growth; [Rosalind Orr English × Frau Karl Druschki]

Indiana HT, rb, Meilland, Marie Louise; bud large, ovoid, ruby red; sepals foliaceous; flowers rose-red, yellow at base, reverse lighter, white at base, 4¾-5¼ in., 34-38 petals, high-centered, borne mostly singly, but sometimes in small clusters, moderate tea fragrance; foliage medium size, medium green, leathery; prickles moderate, brown; growth bushy, branching; [(Happiness × Independence) × (Happiness × Charles Mallerin)]

Indianapolis HT, mp, 1971, Schloen, J.; flowers deep yellow-pink, medium, very dbl., cupped; foliage glossy, leathery; moderate, upright growth; [Coloranja × unknown]; int. by Ellesmere Nursery

Indica Alba Ch, lp, 1802; flowers very light blush; [sport of Old Blush]; discovered in an English garden

Indica Major – See **Fun Jwan Lo**, S

Indica Purpurea Ch, m, Chenault; flowers purple/pink, medium, single

Indigo P, m, before 1845, Laffay; flowers bluish violet, velvety, large, full, flat

Indigoletta LCl, m, Van de Laak; flowers dbl.; int. in 1981

Indira HT, pb, 1975, Hetzel; bud ovoid; flowers pink, reverse lighter, medium, slight fragrance; foliage soft; vigorous, upright, bushy growth; [Baccará × Prima Ballerina]; int. by GAWA, 1973

Indispensable LCl, mp, 1947, Klyn; bud globular; flowers pink, medium, dbl., high-centered, borne in clusters; foliage glossy; moderate, upright, pillar growth; [sport of Roserie]

Indra HMult, dp, 1937, Tantau; bud pointed; flowers rose-pink, 6-8 cm., semi-dbl., open, borne in small clusters; foliage greyish-green, glossy; long stems; very vigorous, climbing growth; [(Ophelia × *R. multiflora*) × Florex]

Indraman F, or, Chiplunkar; flowers bright fire-orange, non-fading, medium; int. in 1990

Indraneel HT, m, Mukherjee, K.P.; flowers lavender, large, moderate fragrance; int. in 1988

Indu HT, pb, Mandal, G.S.; flowers bright pink with gold reverse; free-flowering; [sport of Las Vegas]; int. in 2004

Indu Singhal Gr, pb, Singhal; flowers broad pink petals, marked and etched with white stripes; [sport of Queen Elizabeth]; int. in 1995

Indy 500 Gr, or, 1976, Williams, J. Benjamin; bud tapered; flowers brilliant orange-red, 4½-5 in., 32 petals, flat, intense fragrance; foliage large, glossy, dark, reddish; vigorous, upright growth; PP4361; [(Aztec × Queen Elizabeth seedling) × (Independence × Scarlet Knight seedling)]; int. by Krider Nursery

Inermis HSpn, mr, before 1824, Nestler/DeCandolle; flowers varying shades of red, single, borne mostly solitary; foliage ovate, simply dentate, glabrous; nearly thornless

Inermis Morletii – See **Morletii**, Bslt

Inermis Sub Albo Violacea – See **Bourbon**, HGal

Infanta Pilar HT, dp, 2001, Ferrer, Fco.; flowers dbl., borne mostly solitary, slight fragrance; foliage dark green, matte; [Zambra × Frisko]; int. by Viveros Fco. Ferrer, 1995

Infantania F, w, 1953, Heers; flowers snow-white, sometimes tinged green, small, dbl., borne in large clusters; [Baby Alberic × unknown]; int. by Langbecker

Infante Beatrice HT, ob, 1930, Guillot, M.; flowers orange-yellow, tinted reddish-gold, base golden, dbl.; vigorous growth; [Marie Adélaide × seedling]

Infante Maria Cristina HT, ob, 1930, Gaujard; bud pointed; flowers coppery, tinged carmine; foliage reddish bronze; vigorous growth

Infante Marie-Thérèse – See **Rosycola Panarosa**, F

Inferno HT, ob, 1983, Christensen, Jack E.; flowers well-formed, large, slight fragrance; foliage medium size, dark, semi-glossy; upright, bushy growth; PP5558; [Zorina × Yankee Doodle]; int. by Armstrong Nursery, 1982

Infidélité de Lisette – See **Mme Bureau**, HCh

Infinity HT, mp, 1995, Sheldon, John & Robin; flowers medium, full, borne mostly singly, slight fragramce fragrance; foliage medium size, medium green, matte; upright, tall growth; [Kordes' Perfecta × Prima Donna]

Ingar Olsson F, mr, 1931, Poulsen, S.; flowers brilliant cerise-red, semi-dbl., cupped, borne in clusters; foliage leathery; vigorous, rather compact growth; [Else Poulsen × Ophelia]

Inge Horstmann HT, rb, 1964, Tantau, Math.; bud long, red, reverse white tinged pink; flowers cherry-red, high-centered; long stems; vigorous, bushy growth

Inge Pein Pol, mr, 1939, Pein; flowers carmine-red, medium, semi-dbl.

Inge Schubert F, rb

Ingegnoli Prediletta – See **Zéphirine Drouhin**, B

Ingénieur Madèlé HP, dp, 1874, Moreau-Robert; flowers currant pink, very large, full

Ingénue HGal, w, 1833, Vibert; flowers white, buff center, medium, dbl., cupped; foliage pale green; growth branching

Ingenue S, lp, Eve; flowers soft pink, undulating petals, 5 petals; recurrent; growth to 4-5 ft.; int. by Andre Eve, 1972

Ingrata – See **Le Rire Niais**, C

Ingrid MinFl, rb, 2005, Mander, George; flowers very dark velvety red, reverse yellow, 3½-4 in., 25-30 petals, high-centered, borne in small clusters, moderate fragrance; foliage large, dark green, glossy; prickles numerous, ¼ to 5/16 in.es, needle point, brown; growth upright, tall (28 to 32 in.); garden decoration, containers, exhibition.; [Hot Tamale × Rubies 'n' Pearls]; int. by Select Roses, 2006

Ingrid Bergman HT, dr, 1984, Olesen; flowers large, clear bright red, 5 in., 35-40 petals, high-centered, borne singly, slight spice fragrance; foliage medium size, dark, semi-glossy; upright growth, vigorous, compact; PP6264; [seedling × seedling]; int. by John Mattock, Ltd, 1983; Rose Hall of Fame, WFRS, 2000, Golden Rose, The Hague, 1987, Gold Medal, Madrid, 1986, Gold Medal, Belfast, 1985

Ingrid Mander-Fuchs HT, pb, 2003, Mander, George; flowers pink/cream, 5 in., full, borne in small clusters; foliage large, dark green, glossy, disease-resistant; prickles in., pointed; growth upright, tall (4-5 ft.); garden, exhibition; [June Laver × Rubies 'n' Pearls]; int. by Select Roses, 2004

Ingrid Stenzig Pol, dp, 1951, Hassefras Bros.; flowers rose-pink, small, buttercup form, borne in large clusters; [sport of Orange Triumph]; int. by B&A

Ingrid Weibull – See **Showbiz**, F

Ingrid's Sister Elisabeth MinFl, pb, 2006, Mander, George; flowers dark pink, reverse cream, 3 in., very full, borne in large clusters; foliage medium size, dark green, glossy, disease-resistant; prickles 5/16 in., needle point, medium brown, moderate; growth upright, tall (30-36 in.); garden, containers, exhibition; [Hot Tamale × Rubies 'n' Pearls]; int. by Hortico, Inc.

Inigo Jones HP, pb, 1886, Paul, W.; flowers pink tinted purple, large, full, globular

Inisfree F, yb, 1964, Dickson, Patrick; flowers yellow, orange and pink, 22 petals, borne in clusters; vigorous, tall growth; [(Karl Herbst × Masquerade) × Circus]; int. by A. Dickson & Sons, 1964

Ink Spots HT, dr, 1985, Weeks, O.L.; flowers medium, 35 petals, slight fragrance; foliage large, dark, semi-glossy; upright, bushy, spreading growth; PP5855; [seedling × seedling]

Inka HT, op, 1978, Tantau, Math.; bud pointed; flowers salmon, large, dbl.; foliage large, glossy; upright, bushy growth

Inka HT, dy, Tantau

Inner Glow Min, rb, 1990, Chaffin, Lauren M.; bud ovoid; flowers red with golden yellow base, yellow reverse, red veining towards outer edges, 40 petals, high-centered; foliage medium size, medium green, semi-glossy; prickles hooked, tan; bushy, medium growth; hips round, medium green; [Ann Moore × Rainbow's End]; int. by Pixie Treasures Min. Roses, 1991

Inner Temple F, mr, 2000, Horner, Heather M.; flowers medium red, reverse paler, aging to deep pink, 7 cm., dbl., borne in large clusters, slight fragrance; foliage medium size, medium green, semi-glossy; prickles moderate; compact, medium (80 cm.) growth; [Honey Bunch × (Baby Love × unknown)]; int. by Warley Rose Gardens, 2002

Inner Wheel F, pb, 1984, Fryers Nursery, Ltd.; flowers carmine edged rose pink, large, 22 petals; foliage medium size, dark red, matte; bushy growth; [Pink Parfait × Picasso]

Innisfree – See **Inisfree**, F

Innocence HT, w, 1921, Chaplin Bros.; flowers stamens reddish, slightly waved, 5 in., 12 petals, borne in clusters, moderate fragrance; foliage dark; vigorous growth; supposedly *R.* × *hibernica* × a hybrid tea

Innocence, Climbing Cl HT, w, 1938, Armstrong, J.A.; int. by Armstrong Nursery

Innocence Min, w, 1997, Saville, F. Harmon; flowers medium, pure ivory white, 26-41 petals, borne mostly singly; foliage medium size, dark green, glossy; few prickles; upright, spreading, bushy, medium (30 in.) growth; PP10352; [SAVajinks × SAValite]; int. by Nor'East Miniature Roses

Innocence HT, w, Croix

Innocence 96 F, ab, 1997, Cocker, Ann G.; flowers small, 8-14 petals, borne in small clusters; foliage small, medium green, glossy; few prickles; bushy, low (2½ ft.) growth; [Clydebank Centenary × Ray of Sunshine]; int. by James Cocker & Sons

Innocencia F, w, 1987, Kordes, W.; flowers medium, full, no fragrance; foliage medium size, medium green, matte; bushy growth; [sport of Lorena]; int. in 1986

Innocencia F, w, 2006; flowers pure white, 5 cm., semi-dbl., flat, borne in clusters of 10-15; foliage dark green, very glossy; bushy, compact, upright (2 ft.) growth; int. by W. Kordes' Söhne, 2003; Silver Medal, Baden-Baden, 2002, Silver Medal, Le Roeulx, 2002, Golden Rose, Hradec Králové, 2006, Gold Medal, Rome, 2002

Innocent Blush Min, lp, 1990, Rennie, Bruce F.; bud ovoid; flowers pale blush pink, reverse white, aging white, medium, 40 petals, high-centered, borne usually singly and in sprays of 5-7, no fragrance; foliage medium size, medium green, matte; prickles straight, medium, yellow; upright, medium growth; fruit not observed; [Paul Shirville × Party Girl]; int. by Rennie Roses International, 1990

Innocente Pirola T, w, 1878, Ducher, Vve.; flowers clouded white, medium, full

Innovation F, Combe, M.; int. in 1973

Innovation Minijet Min, my, 1987, Meilland, Mrs. Marie-Louise; flowers medium, dbl., slight fragrance; foliage small, light green, glossy; bushy growth; PP6177; [(Rumba × Carol Jean) × (Zambra × Darling Flame)]; int. by SNC Meilland & Cie, 1987

Innoxa Femille HT, dr, 1981, Harkness, R.; flowers 50 petals, borne singly, sometimes 3 per cluster, slight fragrance; foliage large, semi-glossy; prickles dark; medium, bushy growth; [Red Planet × Eroica]; int. by Harkness, 1983

Inoa F, mr, 1958, Arles; flowers bright velvety red; vigorous growth; [Gruss an Teplitz × Pioupiou]; int. by Roses-France

Insel Mainau F, dr, 1959, Kordes, R.; bud ovoid; flowers deep crimson, large, dbl., borne in clusters of up to 5; foliage leathery, dark; low, compact growth; ADR, 1960

Insolite – See **Sweet Chariot**, Min

Inspecteur Jagourt F, m, 1932, Soupert & Notting; bud glowing red; flowers purplish pink to China-rose, large white stamens, large, 25-30 petals; foliage glossy; vigorous growth; [Mrs Henry Winnett × Eblouissant]

Inspector Rose HT, rb, 1969, Fryers Nursery, Ltd.; flowers maroon-red, reverse yellow, long, pointed, 35 petals; foliage coppery bronze-red; very free growth; [sport of Piccadilly]

Inspektor Blohm HMsk, w, 1942, Kordes; flowers medium, very dbl., borne in large corymbs, intense fragrance; recurrent bloom; foliage abundant, gray-green; vigorous, well-branched growth; [Joanna Hill × Eva]

Inspiration LCl, mp, 1946, Jacobus; flowers medium pink, fading to pale pink, 10-11 cm., semi-dbl., moderate fragrance; foliage large, dark green, glossy; moderate growth; [New Dawn × Crimson Glory]; int. by B&A

Inspiration HT, rb, Perry; flowers medium red blend, moderate fragrance; int. in 1991

Inspiration – See **Susan Jellicoe**, F

Inspiration HT, pb, Noack; flowers pink blended with yellow, 4 in., dbl., borne in clusters; growth to 70-80 cm.; int. by Noack Rosen, 2004

Inspiration HT, op; apparently never introduced into commerce, per J&P

Inspiration 2000 HT, pb, Horner; flowers pearly pink and cream, dbl.; growth vigorous; int. in 2002

Instigation S, dr, Williams, J. Benjamin; flowers dbl., classic hybrid tea, moderate fragrance; recurrent; foliage medium green, semi-glossy; medium (4 ft.) growth; int. by Hortico, Inc., 2006

Institut Lumière S, op, Guillot-Massad; flowers pink tinted orange, dbl., slight fragrance; foliage dark green; growth to 1 m.; int. by Roseraies Guillot, 2004

Institeuteur Sirdey HT, dy, 1905, Pernet-Ducher

Institutrice Moulins Ch, dp, 1893, Charreton

Insulinde HT, op, 1923, Leenders, M.; flowers pink and salmon, dbl.; [Ophelia × Jonkheer J.L. Mock]

Insulinde HT, yb, 1923, Van Rossem; flowers clear yellow shaded golden yellow, dbl.; [Mr Joh. M. Jolles × Melody]

Integrity – See **Savoy Hotel**, HT

Intel Min, m, Spooner, Raymond A.; int. in 1996

Intense Cover – See **Memphis**, S

Intensity HT, dr, 1908, Dingee & Conard; flowers very dark crimson scarlet, large, full, moderate fragrance; [Gruss an Teplitz × General MacArthur]

Interama F, dr, 1976, deRuiter; flowers 3 in., 18 petals; foliage large, glossy, dark; bushy growth; PP4018; [Kohima × (Europeana × Kimona)]

Interflora – See **Interview**, HT, 1970

Interfrico – See **Apricot Queen**, S

Interjada F, dp, 1986, Interplant; flowers deep pink, 35 petals, borne in sprays; foliage medium size, dark, semi-glossy; upright growth; [seedling × seedling]

Intermezzo HT, m, 1963, Dot, Pedro; bud ovoid; flowers deep lavender, large, 25 petals, moderate fragrance; foliage dark, glossy; moderately tall, compact growth; PP2430; [Grey Pearl × Lila Vidri]; int. by Minier

International Gold Min, my, 2004, Thomson, George L.; flowers gold, 2-3 cm., full, borne in small to large clusters, no fragrance; foliage medium size, medium green, semi-glossy; prickles small, straight; growth bushy, medium (20-30 cm.); garden decorative, containers; [Rise "n" Shine × Peace]; int. by Ross Roses, 2005

International Herald Tribune F, m, 1984, Harkness, R., & Co., Ltd.; flowers violet-purple, small, 20 petals, cupped, borne in trusses, moderate fragrance; foliage medium size, medium green, semi-glossy; low, bushy growth; [seedling × ((((Orange Sensation × Allgold) × *R. californica*) × ((Orange Sensation × Allgold) × *R. californica*)) × *R. californica*)]; Golden Rose, Geneva, 1983, Gold Medal, Tokyo, 1983, Gold Medal, Monza, 1984

Intersina HT, lp, 1985, Interplant; flowers large, 35 petals, no fragrance; foliage large, medium green, semi-glossy; upright growth; PP5836; [seedling × Red Success]; int. in 1984

Interview HT, dp, 1968, Meilland; flowers deep pink, large, 40 petals, high-centered; foliage leathery; vigorous, upright growth; [((Baccará × White Knight) × (Baccará × Jolie Madame)) × (Baccará × Paris-Match)]

Interview HT, or, 1970, Conard-Pyle; flowers light madder red, high-centered, borne singly, slight tea fragrance; foliage large, leathery; growth upright, vigorous; greenhouse

Intervilles LCl, mr, 1970, Robichon; bud ovoid; flowers semi-dbl., cupped, borne in small clusters, moderate fragrance; foliage dark, glossy; vigorous, climbing growth; [Etendard × unknown]; int. by Ilgenfritz Nursery, 1968

Interyassor HT, dr, Ilsink, Peter; PP15538

Inti HT, dy, deRuiter; int. by deRuiter Roses, 2005

Intimité HT, ob, 1956, Delforge; bud long; flowers golden orange shaded yellow and chamois, open, large, dbl.; foliage glossy, dark; vigorous, bushy growth; [Beauté × seedling]

Intrepid HT, dr, 1998, Perry, Astor; flowers dark velvety red, 4-4½ in., very dbl., high-centered, borne singly, moderate fragrance; foliage medium size, dark green, dull; prickles moderate; medium (5 ft.), upright growth; [Karl Herbst × Burgundy]; int. by Certified Roses Inc., 1999

Intrepid Red HT, mp, 2001, Coiner, Jim; flowers medium pink, white reverse, 3 in., full, borne in small clusters, no fragrance; foliage medium size, light green, matte; growth compact, medium (36 in.); garden decorative; PP15824; [seedling × seedling]; int. by Coiner Nursery, 2002

Intrépide LCl, or, Combe; int. in 1972

Intrigue – See **Lavaglut**, F

Intrigue F, m, 1982, Warriner, William A.; flowers reddish-purple, large, 20 petals; foliage medium size, dark, semi-glossy; PP5002; [White Masterpiece × Heirloom]; int. by J&P, 1984

Invention HT, dp, Patil, B.K.; flowers salmon and carmine; free-flowering; [sport of Ambossfunken]; int. by Icospin, 1988

Invertilis HSpn, mr; flowers carmine-red, medium-large, single

Invincible HGal, mr, before 1819, Miellez; flowers fiery red

Invincible F, dr, 1983, deRuiter; bud large; flowers large, 20 petals; foliage large, medium green, glossy; upright growth; [Rubella × National Trust]; int. by Fryer's Nursery, Ltd., 1982

Invitation HT, op, 1961, Swim & Weeks; bud long, pointed; flowers rich salmon-pink, base yellow, 4½ in., 30 petals, high-centered, intense spicy fragrance; foliage leathery, glossy; vigorous, compact, bushy growth; PP2018; [Charlotte Armstrong × Signora]; int. by C-P, 1961

Iobelle HT, pb, 1960, Buck, Dr. Griffith J.; bud ovoid; flowers ivory-white edged and overspread deep pink, large, high-centered, moderate fruity fragrance; foliage dark, glossy; vigorous, upright, compact growth; [Dean Collins × Peace]; int. by Iowa State University, 1962

Iode F, dr, 1974, Schloen, J.; bud ovoid; flowers large, semi-dbl., cupped; foliage glossy; vigorous, upright growth; [Lichterloh × Red Pinocchio]

Iolanthe HT, rb, 1940, Gaujard; flowers bright red, reverse yellow, large, semi-dbl.; vigorous growth

Ion Phillips HT, dy, 1934, Dickson, A.; flowers rich yellow, large, dbl.; vigorous growth

Iona Herdman HT, dy, 1914, McGredy; flowers brilliant yellow, dbl.; Gold Medal, NRS, 1913

Ione Min, ly, 1990, Jerabek, Paul E.; bud ovoid; flowers white with pale yellow center, medium, 50 petals, high-centered, borne singly and in small clusters; foliage medium size, medium green, semi-glossy; prickles very few, very small, light green; bushy, medium growth; fruit not observed; [seedling × seedling]

Ionian Rose – See **Lady Like**, HT

Iowa Belle – See **Iobelle**, HT

Ipitombi HT, ob, J&P; flowers deep salmon maturing to burnt orange, dbl., high-centered, slight fragrance; growth moderately vigorous, medium

Ipsilanté – See **Ypsilanti**, HGal

Iranja F, or, 1986, Lens, Louis; flowers orange-red, 2 in., 35 petals, borne in clusters of 3-24, no fragrance; foliage small, brilliant green; prickles hooked, red-green; low, bushy growth; [Little Angel × (Floradora × Angelina Louro)]; int. in 1984

Ireland Hampton HT, pb, 1934, Hillock; flowers flame-pink suffused gold, base gold, large, dbl., cupped, moderate spicy fragrance; foliage glossy; vigorous, compact growth; [Étoile de Feu × seedling]

Ireland Hampton, Climbing Cl HT, pb, 1936, Hillock

Irène HSpn, w, 1823, Vibert; flowers flesh white, 3-3½ in., dbl.

Irene F, pb, 1941, Leenders, M.; flowers rose-white, reverse pure white, semi-dbl.; [seedling × Permanent Wave]

Irene F, dp, Meilland; int. in 1983

Irene – See **Henri Salvador**, HT

Irene F, lp, Barni, Enrico; flowers clear, pearly pink, large, dbl., borne in clusters, slight fragrance; good repeat; foliage large, dark green; growth to 2 ft.; [seedling × Venere]; int. by Rose Barni, 2000

Irene F, ly, 2006, Paul Chessum Roses; flowers dbl., borne in small clusters; foliage medium size, dark green, semi-glossy; prickles large, sharp, pink, numerous; growth bushy, medium (24 in.); bedding, containers; [seedling × seedling]; int. by World of Roses, 2005

Irene au Danmark – See **Irene of Denmark**, F

Irène Bonnet Cl HT, mp, 1920, Nabonnand, C.; flowers hermosa pink, edges lighter, medium, dbl., moderate fragrance

Irene Churruca HT, ly, 1934, La Florida; bud pointed, yellow; flowers light buff, fading cream, well-formed, large; [Mme Butterfly × (Lady Hillingdon × Souv. de Claudius Pernet)]

Irene Curie HT, mr, 1952, San Remo Exp. Sta.; bud very long, pointed; flowers scarlet, large, 20 petals; foliage glossy; very vigorous, bushy growth; [seedling × Lawrence Johnston]

Irene Dean HT, pb, 2007, Horner; flowers pink/apricot, reverse pale pink, 2½ in., full, borne mostly solitary; foliage medium size, medium green, glossy; prickles medium, narrow, light green, moderate; growth compact, short (2½ ft.); garden decorative; [Tournament of Roses × Britannia]; int. by Warley Roses, 2008

Irene Jane HWich, m, Nobbs; int. in 1995

Irene Marie Cl Min, yb, 2006, Moore, Ralph S.; flowers yellow/orange, reverse yellow, 1½-2 in., single, borne in small clusters; recurrent; foliage medium size, medium green, semi-glossy; thornless; growth upright, tall (4-6 ft.); climber, free standing arching shrub; [(Little Darling × Yellow Magic) × Playboy]; int. by Sequoia Nurs., 2006

Irene of Denmark F, w, 1948, Poulsen, S.; bud pointed; flowers 3 in., 40 petals, cupped; foliage dark; vigorous, upright, bushy growth; [Orléans Rose × (Mme Plantier × Edina)]; int. by C-P, 1950

Irene of Denmark, Climbing Cl F, w, Ruston, D.; [sport of Irene of Denmark]

Irene Smith F, or, 1998, Bossom, W.E.; flowers coral with lighter reverse, 2¾ in., very dbl., borne in large clusters; foliage medium size, dark green, glossy; prickles moderate; bushy, medium growth; [Sexy Rexy × Eyepaint]

Irene Thompson HT, yb, 1921, McGredy; flowers deep ruddy gold shaded bronze or coppery, dbl.; Gold Medal, NRS, 1919

Irene Virag F, rb, 1999, Zipper, Herbert; flowers red, white eye, reverse streaked red and white, 2-2½ in., single, borne in small clusters; small, medium green, semi-glossy, new foliage mahogany red; prickles moderate; bushy, tall (3-4 ft.) growth; [seedling × Playboy]; int. by Island Roses, 1999

Irene von Danemark – See **Irene of Denmark**, F

Irène Watts Ch, w, 1896, Guillot, P.; bud soft apricot-orange, long; flowers creamy white with tints of apricot, dbl.; foliage dark green, margined with purple; [Mme Laurette Messimy × unknown]

Irene's Beauty Min, yb, 1999, Jolly, Betty J.; flowers very colorful, yellow blend, reverse med. yellow, aging to orange-red, 1½ in., dbl., borne in small clusters; foliage medium size, dark green, semi-glossy; few prickles; compact, low (1 ft.) growth; [Little Darling × Kristin]; int. by Langenbach, 1998

Irene's Choice HT, mp, 1977, Ellick; flowers azalea-pink, 4-5 in., 35-40 petals, slight fragrance; very free growth; [Karl Herbst × Blue Moon]; int. by Excelsior Roses, 1978

Irene's Delight HT, lp, 1982, Varney, E.; flowers large, dbl., high-centered; foliage medium size, dark, semi-glossy; upright growth; [Admiral Rodney × Red Lion]

Irene's Delight S, op, Lowe; flowers warm shades of orange to peach to apricot., single, borne in small clusters., moderate fragrance; once bloomer.; very cold hardy.; int. in 2001

Irene's Surprise F, ab, 1993, Kirkham, Gordon Wilson; flowers medium, dbl., high-centered, borne in small clusters; foliage medium size, medium green, semi-glossy; medium (2½ ft.), upright growth; int. by Kirkham, 1993

Irina F, dr, 1969, Grabczewski; flowers dark crimson-red, large, semi-dbl.; foliage soft, glossy; moderate, bushy growth

Iris HT, op, 2006, Cocker, A. G.; flowers coral pink, 2½ in., full, cupped, borne singly and in large clusters; recurrent; foliage large, dark green, glossy; prickles moderate, 9 mm., straight; growth upright, bushy, medium (2½-3 ft.); garden decoration; [Sheila's Perfume × Gordon's College]; int. by James Cocker & Sons, 2006

Iris HT, rb, Viveros Fco. Ferrer, S L; flowers 27 petals, high-centered; [Zambra × Jelcanodir]

Iris HSpn, w; flowers dbl.; foliage finely divided; dense, shrubby (3-4 ft.) growth; hips shining, black

Iris Foster HT, mp, 1998, Poole, Lionel; flowers medium pink, 6 in., very dbl., high-centered, borne mostly singly; foliage large, medium green, dull; some prickles; vigorous, upright, bushy, floriferous growth; [Gavotte × (Solitaire × Mischief)]

Iris Gee F, lp, Gee; flowers pale pink to apricot, fading to cream; growth tall; [sport of Liverpool Echo]; int. in 1987

Iris Hilda HT, mp, 2001, Hill, Ernest H.; flowers satin pink, lighter reverse, 4½-5 in., very full, borne mostly solitary, slight fragrance; foliage large, dark green, glossy; prickles moderate; growth upright, medium (3 ft.); exhibition; [Silver Jubilee × Red Devil]

Iris Patricia Green HT, mr, 1928, Pemberton; bud pointed; flowers cherry-red; foliage dark

Iris Squire F, mp, 1966, Bees; flowers soft rose, 4-5 in.; foliage dull; tall, vigorous growth; [seedling × Queen Elizabeth]

Iris Webb F, r, 1988, Warner, Chris; flowers tan, fading to slate gray, medium, dbl.; foliage medium size, dark green, semi-glossy; bushy growth; [Southampton × (Belinda × (Elizabeth of Glamis × (Galway Bay × Sutters Gold)))]; int. by LeGrice Roses, 1990

Irischer Regen – See **Irish Mist**, F

Irish Afterglow HT, ob, 1918, Dickson, A.; flowers very deep tangerine, passing to crushed strawberry; [sport of Irish Fireflame]

Irish Beauty Cl HT, w, 1900, Dickson; flowers pure white with yellow stamens, single, moderate fragrance

Irish Beauty – See **Elizabeth of Glamis**, F

Irish Brightness HT, mr, 1904, Dickson, A.; flowers velvety crimson shading pink at base of petals, medium, single

Irish Charity HT, rb, 1927, McGredy; bud intense fiery scarlet with golden sheen; flowers rosy scarlet, dbl.; int. by H&S

Irish Charm HT, ab, 1927, McGredy; bud pointed; flowers base golden apricot passing to blush-pink, dbl., high-centered; foliage dark, leathery; vigorous growth; int. by H&S

Irish Courage HT, op, 1927, McGredy; bud pointed; flowers soft shrimp-pink to salmon, dbl., high-centered; foliage rich green, leathery, glossy; vigorous growth

Irish Creme HT, w, 1999, Perry, Astor; flowers light beige, reverse same, 4 in., full, borne mostly singly, moderate fragrance; foliage medium size, medium green, dull; prickles moderate; upright, medium (5 ft.) growth; [Butterscotch × Mandelon]; int. by Certified Roses, 2000

Irish Elegance HT, ob, 1905, Dickson, A.; flowers bronze orange-scarlet, large, 5 petals, moderate fragrance; good repeat; vigorous growth

Irish Engineer HT, mr, 1904, Dickson, A.; flowers dazzling scarlet, large, single

Irish Eyes F, yb, 1975, Byrum; bud ovoid; flowers yellow edged red, 2½-3 in., 45 petals, high-centered, slight fragrance; vigorous growth; PP3631; [seedling × Gemini]; int. by J.H. Hill Co., 1974

Irish Eyes F, yb, 1999, Dickson, Patrick; flowers mid-yellow/red, reverse mid-red/yellow, 2½ in., full, borne in large clusters; foliage medium size, medium green, semi-glossy; prickles moderate; bushy (30 in.) growth; [Mr J. C. B. × Gypsy Dancer]; int. by Dickson Nurseries, Ltd., 2000

Irish Fireflame HT, ob, 1914, Dickson, A.; flowers orange to old-gold, veined crimson, anthers light fawn, 5 in., 5 petals, intense fragrance; foliage dark, glossy; compact, bushy growth; Gold Medal, NRS, 1912

Irish Fireflame, Climbing Cl HT, ob, 1916, Dickson, A.; flowers orange-yrllow and peach, large, single; [sport of Irish Fireflame]

Irish Glory HT, pb, 1900, Dickson, A.; flowers silvery pink, reverse crimson, large, 10 petals; very vigorous growth

Irish Gold HT, my, 1966, Dickson, A.; bud ovoid; flowers 7 in., 33 petals, high-centered, moderate fragrance; foliage dark, glossy, leathery; vigorous, upright, bushy growth; PP2769; [(Kordes' Perfecta × Governador Braga da Cruz) × Piccadilly]; int. by J&P; President's International Trophy, RNRS, 1965, Gold Medal, The Hague, 1966, Gold Medal, RNRS, 1965, Gold Medal, Portland, 1970

Irish Gold, Climbing Cl HT, Humphreys; int. in 1973

Irish Harmony HT, ly, 1904, Dickson, A.; flowers creamy white to saffron yellow

Irish Heartbreaker Cl Min, rb, 1990, McCann, Sean; flowers small, full, slight fragrance; foliage medium size, medium green, semi-glossy; upright growth; [Rise 'n' Shine × (Oonagh × Siobhan)]; int. in 1989

Irish Hope HT, dr, 1927, McGredy; bud pointed; flowers rosy crimson shaded maroon, large, dbl., high-centered; foliage dark, leathery; vigorous growth; int. by H&S

Irish Hope F, ly; flowers white, blushed lemon, frilled petal edges, 4 in., 50 petals, borne in clusters, intense honey/ lemon/clove fragrance; foliage dark green, healthy; tall (4-5 ft.) growth; int. by Harkness, 1998

Irish Lady Min, pb, 1991, Schmidt, Richard; flowers small, full, slight fragrance; foliage small, dark green, glossy; bushy growth; [sport of Kathy Robinson]; int. by Michigan Mini Roses, 1991

Irish Luck – See **St Patrick**, HT

Irish Marbled – See **Irish Rich Marbled**, HSpn

Irish Mist F, op, 1966, McGredy, Sam IV; flowers orange-salmon, well-formed, 4½ in., borne in clusters; foliage dark; dense growth; PP3068; [Orangeade × Mischief]; int. by McGredy

Irish Modesty HT, op, 1900, Dickson, A.; flowers light orange-pink, large, single

Irish Morn HT, pb, 1927, McGredy; flowers pink, center coral, dbl.; int. by Dreer

Irish Pride HT, rb, 1904, Dickson, A.; flowers red, coppery center, single

Irish Rich Marbled HSpn, rb; flowers rose to lilac-pink, flecked and marbled with lighter shading; hips shiny black

Irish Rose of India F, w, 2001, Kenny, David; flowers cream with soft yellow center, white reverse, medium, full, borne in small clusters, slight fragrance; foliage medium size, medium green, semi-glossy; prickles medium, hooked, few; growth bushy, medium; garden decorative; [(Mary Sumner × Kiskadee) × Spek's Centennial]

Irish Rover HT, op, 1970, McGredy, Sam IV; flowers salmon-pink, 4 in., 36 petals; foliage coppery, dark; vigorous growth; [Violet Carson × Tropicana]

Irish Simplicity – See **Simplicity**, HT

Irish Squire F, dp, Bees of Chester; flowers carmine-pink, large, dbl.; int. in 1966

Irish Star HT, mr, 1904, Dickson, A.; flowers rosy red, single

Irish Summer – See **Irish Mist**, F

Irish Sweetness HT, rb, 1927, McGredy; bud pointed; flowers crimson suffused scarlet, large, dbl., high-centered; foliage dark, leathery; vigorous growth; int. by H&S

Irish Wonder – See **Evelyn Fison**, F

Irma Ch, w, 1824, Laffay; flowers flesh white

Irma T, pb, 1835, Vibert; flowers medium pink with apricot

Irma S, lp, Carlsson-Nilsson; flowers full, cupped; bushy (6 ft.) growth

Irmela F, w, Hetzel, K.; int. in 1983

Iroquois S, lp, 1932, Central Exp. Farm; flowers flowers pale amaranth-pink, semi-dbl., moderate fragrance; non-recurrent; foliage leathery; vigorous, bushy, compact growth; [(*R. spinosissima* × Pythagoras) × *R. cinnamomea*]

Irresistible Min, w, 1990, Bennett, Dee; bud ovoid; flowers white with pale pink center, medium, greenish in shade, 43 petals, high-centered, borne singly and in small clusters, moderate spicy fragrance; foliage medium size, medium green, semi-glossy; prickles straight, yellow with red; upright, tall growth; hips globular, green to yellow-brown; PP7971; [Tiki × Brian Lee]; int. by Tiny Petals Nursery, 1989

Isa HT, lp, 1931, Evans, F.&L.; flowers light pinkish cream, well-shaped, dbl.; vigorous growth; [Abol × unknown]

Isa Carstens – See **It's Show Time**, HT

Isa Murdock HSpn, w, 1953, Skinner; flowers white, sometimes tinged with pink, dbl.; non-recurrent; foliage spinosissima type; numerous prickles; growth to 3 ft.; [*R. spinosissima altaica* × Double White]

Isabel – See **Isabel Renaissance**, S

Isabel – See **First Gold**, HT

Isabel de Ortiz HT, pb, 1962, Kordes, R.; flowers deep pink, reverse silvery, well-formed, 5 in., 38 petals, moderate fragrance; foliage dark, glossy; vigorous, upright growth; PP2449; [Peace × Kordes' Perfecta]; int. by W. Kordes Söhne, 1962; Gold Medal, NRS, 1962, Gold Medal, Madrid, 1961

Isabel Hit MinFl, dr, Poulsen; flowers dark red, 5-8 cm., dbl., no fragrance; foliage dark; growth bushy, 40-60 cm.; int. by Poulsen Roser, 1999

Isabel Llorach HP, yb, 1929, Dot, Pedro; flowers nankeen yellow, tinted red, semi-dbl.; [Frau Karl Druschki × Benedicte Seguin]

Isabel Ortiz – See **Isabel de Ortiz**, HT

Isabel Renaissance S, dr, Poulsen; flowers dark red, 4-6 in., dbl., moderate fragrance; foliage dark; bushy (3-5 ft.) growth; PP12825; int. by Poulsen Roser, 1995

Isabella HGal, dp, 1834

Isabella – See **Andenken an Alma de l'Aigle**, HMsk

Isabella HT, ob, 1964, Leenders, J.; flowers orange, star-shaped; [Queen Elizabeth × Pink Lustre]

Isabella – See **Isabel Renaissance**, S

Isabella Cara Min, w, 2003, McCann, Sean; flowers white with tones of light pink, medium, dbl., borne in small clusters; foliage medium size, dark green, glossy; growth spreading, low, some tall stems; [Kiss 'n' Tell × New Dawn]

Isabella Ducrot T, pb, Branchi; int. by Walter Branchi, 2001

Isabella Gray N, dy, 1857, Gray, Andrew; flowers golden yellow, more fragrant, but otherwise similar to parent; [Chromatella × unknown]

Isabella Rossellini HT, dr, Olesen; flowers intense dark red, medium, full, high-centered, borne singly and in clusters, very slight fragrance; recurrent; foliage dark green, glossy; strong, bushy growth; int. by Poulsen Roser, 2006

Isabella Skinner S, mp, probably Skinner; flowers pink, well-formed, dbl., slight fragrance; blooms on new wood all summer; bushy growth; [(*R. laxa* × Tea) × Floribunda]; int. before 1965

Isabella Sprunt T, my, 1865, Sprunt/Buchanan; flowers sulfur-yellow, dbl.; recurrent; medium growth; [sport of Safrano]; int. by Buchanan, 1865

Isabelle HGal, dr, before 1820, Descemet; flowers velvety purple red marbled violet purple, small to medium, very full; growth erect

Isabelle Autissier HT, pb, Adam; flowers shades of pink, yellow in heart, dbl., intense fragrance; foliage glossy, beginning red; upright (4-5 ft.) growth; int. in 2000

Isabelle de France HT, or, 1958, Mallerin, C.; bud pointed; flowers vermilion, large, dbl., high-centered, slight fragrance; vigorous, upright growth; [Peace × (Mme Joseph Perraud × Opera)]; int. by Hémeray-Aubert, 1957

Isabelle d'Orléans N, w, 1824, Vibert; flowers white, center straw yellow, large, full, semi-globular

Isabelle Mainoz S, dp, Guillot-Massad; growth to 5 ft.

Isabelle Milner HT, ly, 1908, Paul, W.; flowers ivory white tinted pink, large, dbl., moderate fragrance

Isabelle Nabonnand T, pb, 1875, Nabonnand, G.; flowers fawn-pink, darker at center, large, dbl.

Isabelle Renaissance – See **Isabel Renaissance**, S

Isabelle Sprungh – See **Isabella Sprunt**, T

Isabel's Jewel Min, ob, 1995, Rennie, Bruce F.; flowers 1¼ in., 6-14 petals, borne mostly singly; foliage medium size, medium green, glossy; some prickles; medium (15-18 in.), spreading, bushy growth; [Forever Mine × Fragrant Morning]; int. by Rennie Roses International, 1993

Isidore Malton – See **Mme Bravy**, T

Isarperle F, ab, Noack; flowers cream to salmon, dbl.; free-flowering; growth to 70-80 cm.; int. by Noack Rosen, 2005

Isella Min, lp, 1980, Bartolomeo, Embriaco; flowers small, 22 petals, cupped, borne singly and several together, no fragrance; foliage small, green; prickles pale pink; vigorous, compact, upright growth; [(Baccará × Generosa) × Miss Italia]; int. in 1973

Iséran LCl, or, Combe; flowers orange or light scarlet, medium to large, full, slight fragrance; int. in 1965

Isidingo LCl, op, Orard; bud green-yellow with pink edging; flowers coral, with deep gold in the heart, dbl., exhibition, borne mostly singly, slight fragrance; foliage glossy; tall (10 ft.) growth; int. by Ludwig's Roses, 1999

Isidore Ch, lp, from Angers; flowers flesh pink, medium, full

Isis N, w, 1853, Robert; flowers large, full, borne in small clusters; foliage dark green; prickles numerous, sturdy, hooked, flat

Isis F, w, 1973, Mattock; flowers ivory-white, 4-5 in., 40-45 petals; compact growth; [Vera Dalton × Shepherdess]

Isis – See **Karen Blixen**, HT

Iskara – See **Sparkling Scarlet**, Cl F

Iskra – See **Sparkling Scarlet**, Cl F

Iskra 82 LCl, mr

Island Cloud w; flowers small, single, borne in clusters, moderate fragrance; non-remontant; vigorous (20 × 8 ft.) growth; probably a HMult or HWich; int. in 2000

Island Dancer S, pb, Lim, Ping; flowers deep pink, reverse white, ruffled, 2 in., 18 petals, borne singly and in clusters; recurrent; low (2 ft.) growth; crown hardy to -30ºF; int. by Baileys Nursery (Easy Elegance), 2006

Island of Dreams F, dy, Spek; int. in 1995

Island of Fire – See **Red Ribbons**, S

Island Pearl lp; flowers pearly pink with slightly darker petal edges, single, borne in clusters, moderate fragrance; non-remontant; vigorous (15 × 12 ft.) growth; probably HMult or HWich; int. in 2000

Isle of Man – See **Manx Queen**, F

Isle of Roses Min, yb, 1993, Moore, Ralph S.; flowers large, full, borne in small clusters, no fragrance; foliage medium size, medium green, semi-glossy; few prickles; medium to tall (18-24 in.), upright,bushy growth; [Pink Petticoat × Gold Badge]; int. by Sequoia Nursery, 1994

Ismène D, lp, 1845, Vibert; flowers delicate carnation pink, large, full

Ismène M, lp, 1852, Robert; flowers flesh pink nuanced with lilac, 6 cm., full, rosette

Isobel HT, pb, 1916, McGredy; bud pointed; flowers light rose-pink, shaded apricot, large, 5 petals, cupped; foliage rich green, soft; Gold Medal, NRS, 1915

Isobel Champion – See **La Marseillaise**, HT

Isobel Derby HT, pb, 1992, Horner, Colin P.; flowers peach pink, reverse lighter pink, aging deeper pink, 5 in., dbl., urn-shaped, moderate fruity fragrance; foliage medium size, medium green, glossy; bushy, medium growth; [Champagne Cocktail × ((Honey Favorite × Dr. A.J. Verhage) × Pot 'o Gold)]; int. by Golden Fields Nursery, 1992

Isobel Harkness HT, dy, 1958, Norman; flowers bright yellow, 6 in., 32 petals, moderate fragrance; foliage dark, leathery, semi-glossy; vigorous, upright, bushy growth; PP1650; [McGredy's Yellow × Phyllis Gold]; int. by Armstrong Nursery, 1957

Isolde MinFl, pb, 1994, Bell, Judy G.; flowers light pink in center shading darker toward edges, small, full, slight fragrance; foliage medium size, medium green, matte; few prickles; upright, bushy (14-16 in.) growth; [Dale's Sunrise × Charmglo]; int. by Michigan Mini Roses, 1995

Isolde – See **Isolde Hit**, MinFl

Isolde Hit MinFl, rb, Poulsen; flowers red with white stripes, 5-8 cm., dbl., slight wild rose fragrance; foliage dark; growth bushy, 20-40 cm.; int. by Poulsen Roser, 2004

Isoline – See **Paul Dupuy**, HP

Ispahan D, mp, before 1832; flowers bright pink, medium, petals larger at the edges, dbl., borne in small clusters, intense fragrance; blooms over long season; foliage small, bluish-green, with 5-7 leaflets; prickles few, strong

Istropoliteana S, Chorvath, F.; int. in 1990

Ita Buttrose HT, op, Armstrong; flowers peach to orange, with burned edges, dbl., moderate fragrance; small growth; int. in 1984

Italia HT, pb, 1905, Berti; flowers carmine-pink, with silvery aurora red, very large, full

Italia HFt, yb, 1933, Aicardi; flowers golden yellow, reverse carmine red; [Julien Potin × unknown]

Italia HT, dr, 1959, Biga, Valentino; bud ovoid; flowers cardinal-red and cherry-red, to open, large, dbl., cupped, moderate fragrance; foliage leathery, dark; long, strong stems; bushy, upright growth; [Baccará × Poinsettia]

Italian Four-Seasons Rose – See **Quatre Saisons d'Italie**, P

Italian Pink S, mp, 1959, Leenders, J.; bud short, pointed; flowers begonia-pink, open, large, dbl., borne in clusters; foliage dark; vigorous, upright, well branched growth; [Cocorico × Yellow Holstein]

Italie Impériale HT, m, 1936, Capiago; flowers purplish garnet-red, large; vigorous growth

Italienisches Doerfchen F, or, 1967, Haenchen, E.; bud ovoid; flowers open, small, single, borne in clusters; foliage small, leathery; vigorous, bushy, low growth; [Highlight × unknown]; int. by Teschendorff

It's A Winner HT, yb, J & P; bud orange-yellow; flowers yellow with pink and apricot as it opens, large, dbl., high-centered, slight fragrance; foliage medium green, semi-glossy; tall (5-6 ft.) growth; int. in 2000

It's Magic – See **Great Expectations**, F

It's Show Time HT, ab, 1996, Moore, Ralph S.; flowers apricot blend, reverse slightly lighter, 4-4½ in., dbl., borne mostly singly; foliage medium size, dark green, semi-glossy; upright, medium (3-5 ft.) growth; PP10324; [Joycie × Bon Silene]; int. by Spring Hill Nurseries Co., 1997

ITV 50th Anniversary Coronation Street Rose – See **Mary Adrienne**, S

Ivan Meneve HT, dp, RvS-Melle; [Ingrid Bergman × Florex]; int. in 1996

Ivan Misson Pol, lp, 1922, Soupert & Notting; flowers small, dbl.; moderate (2 ft.) growth; [Jeanny Soupert × Katharina Zeimet]

Ivanhoe HT, rb, 1928, Easlea; bud pointed; flowers brilliant scarlet to rich crimson, large, dbl., high-centered; foliage glossy; vigorous growth

Ivany F, rb, 1985, Staikov, Prof. Dr. V.; flowers orange-yellow, shaded pink on petal edges, aging red, 50 petals, cupped, borne in clusters of 5-30; foliage dark, glossy; vigorous growth; [Masquerade × Rumba]; int. by Kalaydjiev and Chorbadjiiski, 1975

Iver Cottage HEg, lp, before 1846; flowers pale rose, single, cupped

Ivor Min, w, Olesen; int. in 2000

Ivor Hunter F, ab, Horner; int. in 2005

Ivora F, w, 1986, Interplant; flowers near white, 35 petals, borne in clusters; foliage medium size, light green, matte; upright growth; [AmRUda × seedling]

Ivor's Rose S, rb, 2006, Beales, Amanda; flowers medium red, reverse dark pink, 10 cm., very full, borne in large clusters; foliage light green, semi-glossy; prickles average, straight, few; growth upright, short (1 m.); garden decoration, hedging; [Bonica × Roundelay]; int. by Peter Beales Roses, 2004

Ivory T, w, 1901, Dingee & Conard; flowers ivory-white, large, dbl.; vigorous growth; [sport of Golden Gate]

Ivory Ann S, w, 1993, Jobson, Daniel J.; flowers creamy white, 3-3½ in., 5 petals, borne in small clusters; foliage large, medium green, glossy; medium, bushy, spreading growth; [Ivory Fashion × ((Valerie Jeanne × Eyepaint) × Twilight Trail)]; int. by Jobson, 1993

Ivory Beauty F, w, Kordes; bud pointed, urn-shaped; flowers cream-ivory, dbl., moderate fragrance; foliage dark green, glossy, healthy; well-rounded, medium (4-5 ft.) growth; int. in 1985

Ivory Buccaneer HT, w

Ivory Carpet S, w, 1995, Williams, J. Benjamin; flowers pure white, ½-1 in., very dbl., borne in small clusters; foliage small, dark green, glossy; some prickles; growth low (10-12 in.), spreading; [(Sea Foam × The Fairy) × Star Dance]; int. by J. Benjamin Williams & Associates, 1996

Ivory Castle LCl, w, 2007, Guest, M.; flowers ivory to cream, up to 4 in., full, borne in small clusters; foliage medium size, dark green, semi-glossy; prickles ½ in, hooked, moderate; growth upright, tall (up to 8 ft.); garden decoration; [Westerland × (Morgengruss × Baby Love)]; int. by Pococks Roses, 2008

Ivory Charm Cl F, w, 1968, Earing, Elsie A.; bud ovoid; flowers open, large, semi-dbl., intense fragrance; foliage glossy, leathery; vigorous, climbing growth; [sport of Ivory Fashion]

Ivory Fashion F, w, 1959, Boerner; bud ovoid; flowers ivory-white, well-formed, 4-4½ in., 17 petals, borne in clusters, moderate fragrance; foliage leathery; vigorous, upright growth; PP1688; [Sonata × Fashion]; int. by J&P, 1958

Ivory Fashion, Climbing Cl F, w, 1964, Williams, J. Benjamin; bud slender; flowers white, with crimson stamens, 4½-5 in.; PP2409

Ivory Festival Min, w, 1997, Laver, Keith G.; flowers large, very dbl., borne singly and in small clusters; foliage medium size, dark green, glossy; compact, bushy, medium growth; [seedling × Living Bouquet]; int. by Springwood Roses

Ivory Flush F, pb, 1996, Bees of Chester; flowers orange centered with pink blended edges, fading to pale pink, large, very dbl.; foliage medium size, light green, dull; some prickles; bushy, medium (26 in.) growth; int. by L W Van Geest Farms, Ltd., 1995

Ivory Grand Gr, w, Poulsen; flowers ivory white, large, dbl., high-centered; int. in 1996

Ivory Palace Min, w, 1991, Moore, Ralph S.; bud ovoid; flowers ivory white, white reverse, medium, very dbl., high-centered, borne in sprays of 3-8, slight fragrance; foliage medium size, medium green, semi-glossy; bushy, medium growth; [Sheri Anne × Pinocchio]; int. by Sequoia Nursery, 1991

Ivory Queen HT, w, 1954, Fletcher; bud ovoid; flowers ivory-cream, 5-6 in.; foliage dark, glossy; vigorous, bushy growth; [Edina × McGredy's Ivory]; int. by Tucker & Sons, 1954

Ivory Queen Gr, w, 1965, Delforge; flowers ivory; [sport of Queen Elizabeth]

Ivory Quill MinFl, w, Williams, J.B.; flowers ivory white, quilled, dbl.; int. by Hortico, 2003

Ivory Silk Min, w, Benardella, Frank; flowers pure white, large, dbl., hybrid tea; growth medium; int. by Bell Roses, 2001

Ivory Splendor Min, w, 1991, Gruenbauer, Richard; bud rounded; flowers white, pale yellow center, white reverse, aging white, large, 35 petals, high-centered, slight fruity fragrance; foliage medium size, medium green, matte; upright, tall growth; [Rise 'n' Shine × seedling]; int. by Flowers 'n' Friends Miniature Roses, 1993

Ivory Tip Top F, lp, 1977, Fryers Nursery, Ltd.; flowers ivory-pink, 2-2½ in., semi-dbl., slight fragrance; low, compact, bushy growth; [sport of Tip Top]; int. in 1976

Ivory Tower HT, w, 1977, Kordes, R.; bud very long, pointed; flowers ivory-white, shaded light pink and light yellow, 5½ in., 35 petals, high-centered, moderate fragrance; upright, bushy growth; PP4658; [Colour Wonder × King's Ransom]; int. by Armstrong Nursery, 1978

Ivory Triumph F, w, 1963, Von Abrams; bud pointed; flowers ivory, 3-4 in., 12 petals, open, borne in clusters; foliage leathery, light green; upright, compact growth; [Goldilocks × seedling]; int. by Peterson & Dering, 1961

Ivory Warrior S, w, 2006, Rippetoe, Robert Neil; flowers single, borne mostly solitary, moderate musky fragrance; foliage medium size, semi-glossy; prickles small to medium, slightly curved, tan, moderate; growth upright, 3 × 4 ft.; [Country Dancer × unknown]; int. in 2006

Ivresse HT, rb, 1958, Combe; flowers clear red, reverse silvery, large; vigorous growth; [Peace × Spectacular]; int. by Japan Rose Society

Ivy Alice HWich, op, 1927, Letts; flowers soft pink to blush-salmon, splashed carmine when fading, dbl., cupped, borne in very large clusters; foliage glossy, light; very vigorous, climbing (6 ft.) growth; [sport of Excelsa]

Ivy Evans HT, mr, 1926, Evans; flowers light cerise; [George C. Waud seedling × Gen. MacArthur]

Ivy May HT, pb, 1925, Beckwith; bud pointed; flowers rose-pink, base and edges amber, dbl.; foliage dark; vigorous growth; [sport of Mme Butterfly]

Iwara HMult, w; flowers single, borne in clusters of 5-15; [*R. multiflora* × *R. rugosa*]; described by Siebold in 1832

Izayoi HT, pb, Tanaka; int. in 1963

Izayoi bara – See ***R. roxburghii*** (Trattinnick)

Izu no Odoriko – See **Carte d'Or**, F

Izumi HT, m, 1999, Ohkawara, Kiyoshi; flowers lavender blended pale pink, 5-5½ in., 40 petals, high-centered; foliage bronze dark green; growth to 5 ft.; [(Intermezzo × Soir d'Automne) × (Intermesso × Soir d'Automne)]; int. by Komaba Rose Nursery, 1997

Izy HT, pb, 1997, Ballin, Don & Paula; flowers large, white stripes frequently appear, 5-6 in., 26-50 petals, borne mostly singly; foliage long, narrow, medium size, medium green semi-glossy; some prickles; upright, medium to tall growth; [sport of Sheer Bliss]

J

J. A. Escarpit HP, m, 1883, Bernède; flowers velvety purple, edged with cherry reflections, large, very full

J. A. Gomis HT, rb, 1933, Camprubi, C.; flowers crimson-red and yellow, medium, dbl., cupped; foliage dark, glossy; upright growth; [Sensation × Souv. de Claudius Pernet]

J. B. Clark HP, dr, 1905, Dickson, H.; flowers deep scarlet, shaded blackish crimson, large, 25 petals, high-centered; very prickly; vigorous (8-10 ft.), bushy, almost climbing growth; [Lord Bacon × Gruss an Teplitz]

J. B. Clark, Climbing Cl HT, mr, 1939, Vogel, M.; flowers carmine-red, very large, dbl.

J. B. M. Camm B, lp, 1900, Paul, G.; flowers light salmon pink,large, very dbl., moderate fragrance; [Mme Gabriel Luizet × Mrs. Paul]

J. B. Meilland HT, ob, 1941, Meilland, F.; flowers orange, reverse golden yellow, large, very dbl.; very vigorous growth; [Mme Joseph Perraud × (Charles P. Kilham × Margaret McGredy)]

J. B. Varonne T, dp, 1889, Guillot & fils; bud long; flowers deep pink, sometimes with a coppery yellow center, large, full

J. B. Waronne – See **J. B. Varonne**, T

J. Bienfait – See **Mr J. Bienfait**, HT

J. C. Hooper Min, rb, 2001, Hooper, J.C.; flowers white with burgundy red edges, reverse creamy white, 2 in., semi-dbl., borne in small clusters; foliage medium size, medium green, semi-glossy; prickles straight, moderate; growth bushy, medium; garden decorative, exhibition; [seedling × seedling]; int. by Wells Mid-South Roses, 2002

J. C. Thornton HT, mr, 1926, Bees; bud pointed; flowers glowing crimson-scarlet, dbl.; foliage light olive-green, glossy, leathery; vigorous, branching growth; [Kitchener of Khartoum × Red-Letter Day]; Gold Medal, NRS, 1928

J. F. Bailey HT, Williams, A.; [Frau Karl Druschki × unknown]

J. F. Barry HT, my, 1912, Piper; flowers light daffodil-yellow; [sport of Arthur R. Goodwin]

J. F. Müller F, dr, 1929, Muller, J.F.; flowers large; foliage dark; bushy, dwarf growth; [sport of Rodhatte]

J. F. Quadra – See **Quadra**, HKor

J. G. Glassford HT, dr, 1921, Dickson, H.; bud pointed; flowers deep crimson, very large, high-centered; very vigorous, branching growth

J. G. Mendel S, or, Urban, J.

J. G. Sandberg – See **Jonkheer G. Sandberg**, HT

J. H. Bruce HT, mr, 1937, Bees; flowers crimson-scarlet, over large, dbl., high-centered; foliage glossy; vigorous, bushy growth; [H.V. Machin × Marion Horton]; Gold Medal, NRS, 1936

J. H. Pemberton HT, mr, 1931, Bentall; flowers scarlet, moderate damask fragrance; vigorous growth

J. H. Pierneef F, or, Williams, J. Benjamin; flowers orange-red with white stripes and spots, semi-dbl., borne in clusters, no fragrance; upright, vigorous, tall growth; int. in 1994

J. H. Van Heyst HT, yb, 1936, Leenders, M.; bud pointed; flowers yellowish-flesh, reverse pink; vigorous growth; [Comtesse Vandal × Edith Nellie Perkins]

J. J. Audubon S, mr, 2005, Shoup, George Michael; flowers large, resembling a red Mutabilis, 3 in., single, borne mostly solitary, slight fragrance; remontant; foliage medium size, dark green, semi-glossy; prickles moderate; growth bushy, tall (6 ft.); hedging; [Carefree Beauty × Basye's Bluberry × Altissimo]; int. by Antique Rose Emporium, 1998

J. K. B. Roos HT, m, 1933, Leenders, M.; bud pointed; flowers pale reddish-lilac, shaded salmon-flesh, large, dbl.; very vigorous growth

J. K. Tyl LCl, mp, 1936, Brada, Dr.; flowers bright pink, cactus form; very free bloom; vigorous growth; int. by Böhm

J. M. López Picó HT, dr, 1947, Camprubi, C.; bud long, pointed; flowers crimson, large, dbl., high-centered; upright growth; [Editor McFarland × Comtesse Vandal]

J. M. López Picó, Climbing Cl HT, dr, 1954, Camprubi, C.

J. Michael Min, or, 1987, King, Gene; flowers orange-red, aging lighter, large, 18 petals, high-centered, borne usually singly, moderate fruity fragrance; foliage large, light green, matte; prickles straight, medium, white-green; mini-flora; upright, tall growth; [Poker Chip × Watercolor]; int. by AGM Miniature Roses

J. Michel HT, dy, 1930, Felberg-Leclerc; flowers dark golden yellow, large, dbl.; foliage leathery; vigorous growth; RULED EXTINCT 1/87; [seedling × The Queen Alexandra Rose]

J. N. Hart HT, dp, 1924, Chaplin Bros.; flowers rose-pink, dbl.; [George Dickson × Edith Cavell]

J. Otto Thilow HT, mp, 1927, Verschuren; bud pointed, well shaped; flowers rich glowing rose-pink, large, dbl., high-centered; very vigorous growth; [Hadley × Souv. de H.A. Verschuren]; int. by Dreer

J. Otto Thilow, Climbing Cl HT, mp, 1933, Howard Rose Co.

J. P. Connell S, my, 1987, Svedja, Felicitas; flowers pale, medium yellow at inner petals, yellow-white on upper petals, dbl., high-centered, borne 1-8 per cluster, intense tea fragrance; repeat bloom; foliage abundant, dark yellow-green, wide ovate, doubly serrate; no prickles; bushy, winter hardy growth; [Arthur Bell × Von Scharnhorst]; int. by Agriculture Canada, 1986

J. R. Byfield Cl HT, dr, 1941, Clark, A.; flowers deep red flowers with petals edged purple, slight fragrance; stems strong and long; [Sensation × unknown]

J. S. Baar HT, dr, 1934, Mikes Böhm, J.; flowers pure dark carmine-red, dbl.; foliage leathery; long, strong stems; vigorous, bushy growth; int. by Böhm

J. S. Fay HP, rb, 1905, Walsh; flowers dark crimson tipped scarlet, dbl.; vigorous growth; [Prince Camille de Rohan × Souv. de Pierre Notting]

J. W. Fargo (variety of *R. arkansana*), mp; flowers wild-rose-pink, borne in clusters; non-recurrent; well branched (20 in.) growth

Jacaby HT, or, 1985, Warriner, William A.; flowers large, slight fragrance; foliage large, medium green; upright, bushy growth; PP4649; [South Seas × Tonight]; int. by J&P, 1979

Jacage HT, yb, 1985, Warriner, William A.; flowers medium, 35 petals, slight fragrance; foliage medium size, dark, leathery; upright, bushy growth; PP4537; [seedling × Spellbinder]; int. by J&P, 1981

Jacal HT, or, 1985, Warriner, William A.; flowers large, 35 petals, no fragrance; foliage medium size, dark, semi-glossy; upright growth; PP5341; [Spellbinder × Futura]; int. by J&P, 1983

Jacalp HT, or, 1985, Warriner, William A.; flowers brick red, large, 50 petals, slight fragrance; foliage large, dark, leathery; upright growth; PP4541; [seedling × Medallion]; int. by J&P, 1980

Jacameer Warriner, W. A., Warriner, W. A.; PP4843

Jacaranda HT, mp, 1985, Kordes, W.; flowers mauve-pink, large, 35 petals, intense fragrance; foliage large, medium green; upright growth; PP6316; [(Mercedes × Emily Post) × seedling]

Jacfed HT, mp, 1993, Warriner, William A.; flowers 3-3½ in., very dbl., borne mostly singly; foliage large, medium green, semi-glossy; some prickles; tall (150-180 cm.), upright, spreading growth; [Grand Masterpiece × First Federal Renaissance]; int. by Bear Creek Gardens, 1992

Jacimp Warriner, W. A., Warriner, W. A.; PP4812

Jack Collier HT, ob, 1995, Horner, Colin P.; flowers orange blend, 4 in., dbl., borne mostly singly or in small clusters; foliage medium size, medium green, semi-glossy; tall (120 cm.), upright growth; [Marjorie May × Remember Me]; int. by Battersby Roses, 1997

Jack Dayson – See **Perfect Moment**, HT

Jack Folly HT, w, 1978, H. Buss Nurseries; bud ovoid; flowers cream color, opening, 5½ in., 40 petals, cupped; foliage dull, leathery; spreading growth; int. in 1976

Jack Frost F, w, 1962, Jelly; bud pointed; flowers white to creamy, sweetheart, medium, 42 petals, high-centered, moderate fragrance; foliage dark; vigorous, upright growth; PP2447; [Garnette × seedling]; int. by E.G. Hill Co., 1962

Jack Frost HT, w, Howard, A. P.; bud medium, conical, high-centered; flowers pure white, large, 25-30 petals, high-centered, borne mostly singly; foliage medium size, medium green; growth upright, branching, tall (5-6 ft.); hips ovoid to pear-shaped, dark green; PP2522; [Blanche Mallerin × Joseph Hill]

Jack Horner Min, mp, 1955, Robinson, T.; flowers bright pink, 50 petals; no prickles; growth to 4-8 in.; [Margo Koster × Tom Thumb]

Jack McCandless HT, rb, 1935, McGredy; bud long, pointed, carmine and yellow; flowers amber-yellow, veined red, dbl., high-centered; foliage small, glossy, dark

Jack of Hearts F, 1968, Waterhouse Nursery; flowers cardinal red, trusses, semi-dbl., cupped; free bloom; foliage dark, glossy; low, bushy growth

Jack O'Lantern Gr, yb, 1960, Swim & Weeks; bud ovoid; flowers gold and yellow blend, 4½ in., 25 petals, high-centered; foliage leathery; vigorous, tall, bushy growth; [Circus × Golden Scepter]

Jack Rose – See **Général Jacqueminot**, HP

Jack Rose – See ***R. maximowicziana jackii*** (Rehder)

Jack Wood F, dp, Fryer; flowers vibrant pink, dbl., slight fragrance; free-flowering; foliage dense, healthy, bright green; bushy, spreading, vigorous (2 ft.) growth; int. by Fryer's Roses, 2000

Jackie Min, ly, 1956, Moore, Ralph S.; flowers straw-yellow changing to white, 1½ in., 60 petals, high-centered, moderate fragrance; foliage glossy; vigorous, dwarf (12 in.), bushy, spreading growth; [Golden Glow × Zee]; int. by Sequoia Nursery, 1955

Jackie, Climbing Cl Min, ly, 1958, Moore, Ralph S.; flowers soft yellow to creamy white, 1-1½ in., 60 petals, moderate fragrance; foliage semi-glossy, leathery; growth to 10 ft.; [Golden Glow × Zee]; int. by Sequoia Nursery, 1957

Jackie Clark HT, dr, 1990, Wambach, Alex A.; bud pointed; flowers large, 35 petals, high-centered, borne singly; foliage medium size, dark green, matte, disease-resistant; prickles curved down, pink; vigorous, upright growth; [White Masterpiece × Red Planet]; int. by Alex A. Wambach, 1989

Jackman's White HT, w, Brookdale-Kingsway; flowers creamy white, very large, high-centered; vigorous growth; very hardy for this type; int. by Bosley Nursery, 1940

Jackpot Min, dy, 1985, Moore, Ralph S.; flowers small, dbl., moderate fragrance; foliage small, medium green, matte; vigorous, bushy, spreading growth; [Little Darling × Sunspray]; int. by Moore Min. Roses, 1985

Jackpot – See **Jackpot 99**, F

Jackpot 99 F, mr, 2000, Driscoll, William E.; flowers medium red, light yellow eye, medium, semi-dbl., borne in small clusters, no fragrance; foliage medium size, medium green, semi-glossy; numerous prickles; compact, medium (18-24 in.) growth; [Heathers Red × (Kiskadee × (Liverpool Echo × (Flamenco × *R. bella*)))]

Jack's Fantasy Min, yb, 1987, Bilson, Jack M., Jr. & Bilson, Jack M. III; flowers yellow blushed with orange-red from edge, reverse medium yellow, 21 petals, high-centered, slight fragrance; foliage medium size, medium green, semi-glossy; prickles few, beige slightly sloped downward; upright, bushy, medium growth; no fruit; [Little Darling × Over the Rainbow]

Jack's Wish HT, op, Kirkham; flowers salmon-orange, large, loose, borne singly and in small clusters; foliage starts dark copper, then dark green, glossy; medium growth; int. in 2001

Jackson Square Min, dr, 1995, Taylor, Pete & Kay; flowers dark red, medium, full, borne mostly singly; foliage medium size, medium green, semi-glossy; some prickles; upright, bushy, medium (30 in.) growth; [Jean Kenneally × Black Jade]; int. by Taylor's Roses, 1996

Jacky's Favorite S, pb, DVP Melle; foliage dark green, disease-resistant; [Melglory × Guirland d'Amour]; int. in 2000; Golden Rose of the Hague, 2004, Gold Medal, Dublin, 1999

Jaclow Warriner, W. A., Warriner, W. A.; PP4650

Jacnon HT, ob, 1985, Warriner, William A.; flowers medium, very dbl., slight fragrance; foliage large, medium green, matte; upright, bushy growth; PP5318; [Baccará × seedling]; int. by J&P

Jacob H. Pierneef – See **J. H. Pierneef**, F

Jacob van Ruysdael F, op, Williams, J. Benjamin; flowers peach orange, semi-dbl.; upright, compact growth; int. by Hortico Inc., 1997

Jacob's Ladder LCl, dr, 2003, Carruth, Tom; flowers clear red, 12-14 cm., 8-14 petals, borne in large clusters, slight fragrance; foliage extremely large, dark green, glossy; prickles moderate, large, almost straight, greenish brown; growth upright, free standing pillar, tall (170-200 cm.); garden decoration; PPAF; [Santa Claus × (*R. soulieana* derivative × Dortmund)]; int. by Edmunds Roses, 2003

Jacob's Robe LCl, yb, 2006, Carruth, Tom; flowers yellow, peach, pink stripe blushing all pink, reverse similar but with more yellow, 9-11 cm., dbl., borne in small clusters, moderate spice fragrance; foliage large, medium green, very glossy; prickles various, slightly hooked, brown, numerous; growth spreading, climbing, canes up to 250 cm. long, garden decoration; [Autumn Sunset × Playboy]; int. by Weeks Roses, 2008

Jacotte HWich, ab, 1920, Barbier; bud ovoid, orange and yellow; flowers deep coppery yellow, tinted coppery red, 3 in., semi-dbl., cupped, moderate fragrance; recurrent; foliage leathery, glossy, dark; long, strong stems; very vigorous, climbing growth; [*R. wichurana* × Arthur R. Goodwin]

Jacpetex – See **Flamenco**, F

Jacquard B, dp, 1842, Béluze; flowers carmine pink, medium, full

Jacqueline HEg, rb, 1923, Paul; flowers reddish-copper with yellow base, semi-dbl.; non-recurrent; growth moderate (3½ ft.); may be an older variety, reintroduced by Paul

Jacqueline – See **Baccará**, HT

Jacqueline HT, mr, 1961, Byrum, Roy L.; bud short, pointed; flowers turkey-red, 4-4½ in., 30 petals, high-centered, moderate fragrance; foliage glossy; vigorous, well-branched growth; PP2183; [Topper × seedling]; int. by J.H. Hill Co., 1962

Jacqueline F, ob, Kordes; int. in 1994

Jacqueline du Pré S, w, 1988, Harkness, R., & Co., Ltd.; flowers creamy blush to white, loose, large, 15 petals, cupped, borne singly or in sprays, moderate musk fragrance; recurrent; foliage medium size, dark green, glossy; prickles small, dark; tall, spreading growth; hips oval, medium size, green-orange; [Radox Bouquet × Maigold]; int. by R. Harkness & Co., Ltd., 1989; Gold Medal, LeRoeulx, 1988

Jacqueline Dufier HT, dr, 1957, Kemp, M.L.; flowers crimson shaded black, high pointed, 4 in., 25 petals; foliage bronze; vigorous growth; [Dicksons Red × Ena Harkness]

Jacqueline Humery HMsk, lp, 2000, Lens, Louis; flowers white, pink shade, reverse white, 6 cm., semi-dbl., borne in large clusters, moderate fragrance; recurrent; foliage medium size, dark green, semi-glossy; prickles moderate; bushy (80-120 cm.) growth; [(Serpent Vert × Tapis Volant) × (Robe Fleurie × Poesie)]; int. by Louis Lens NV, 1995

Jacqueline Nebout F, mp, Meilland; flowers silvery pink, dbl.; int. in 1989

Jacqueline Sternotte HT, rb, 1976, Select Delforge; bud ovoid; flowers red and white, 4½ in., 51 petals, moderate fragrance; int. in 1974

Jacquenetta – See **Jaquenetta**, S

Jacques Amyot N, m, 1844, Varangot; flowers lilac pink, 4 in., very dbl.; good repeat bloom; foliage dark green, regularly dentate; almost thornless; tall growth; sometimes classed as Po

Jacques Carroy Pol, m, 1929, Turbat; flowers carmine, slightly tinted purple, center velvety, borne in clusters

Jacques Carteau HT, ly, 1957, Privat; bud long; flowers creamy yellow, medium; foliage glossy; moderate growth

Jacques Cartier P, lp, 1868, Moreau-Robert; flowers clear rose, center darker, edges very pale, with a very small eye, 3½-4 in., 50 petals, quartered, borne singly and in small clusters, moderate fragrance; good repeat bloom; foliage medium green, matte; compact, low, branching growth

Jacques Cartier, Climbing Cl P, lp, Whartons; int. by Whartons Nurseries, 2002

Jacques Cartier Gr, or

Jacques Cartier Blanc P, w; flowers rosy-white; int. about 1870

Jacques Esterel HT, m, Croix; flowers silvery red, large, very dbl., moderate fragrance; growth to 75-85 cm.; int. by Sauvageot, 1973

Jacques Hackenburg HT, pb, 1919, Leenders, M.; flowers deep rose-pink and carmine, opening flesh-white, dbl.; [Jonkheer J.L. Mock × Marquise de Sinéty]

Jacques Laffitte HP, dp, 1846, Vibert; flowers carmine-pink, large, full

Jacques Latouche HT, pb, 1935, Mallerin, C.; flowers orange-pink in spring, red in summer, reverse yellow, very large, dbl., cupped; foliage glossy; vigorous growth; [Souv. de Claudius Pernet × Director Rubió]; int. by H. Guillot

Jacques Plantier HP, pb, 1872, Damaizin; flowers pink, aging to flesh white, large, full

Jacques Porcher HT, w, 1914, Guillot, P.; flowers white with tints of carmine, saffron and deep yellow, small, dbl., moderate fragrance

Jacques Prévert – See **Cardinal Song**, Gr

Jacques Proust Pol, m, 1904, Robichon; flowers violet-red, small, semi-dbl.

Jacques Vincent HT, rb, 1908, Soupert & Notting; flowers coral-red, center golden; vigorous growth; [Mme J.W. Budde × Souv. de Catherine Guillot]

Jacquie Williams Min, rb, 1997, Moore, Ralph S.; flowers medium, full, borne mostly singly, but some clusters; foliage medium size, medium green, semi-glossy; low to medium (30-45 cm.) growth; [(Yellow Jewel × Tamango) × Strawberry Ice]; int. by Sequoia Nursery, 1998

Jacquinot C, pb, before 1848; flowers deep rose, streaked with white, medium, dbl., flat; growth branching

Jacquot F, Dorieux, Francois; int. in 1973

Jacshel Warriner, W. A., Warriner, W. A.; PP4439

Jade – See **Cottage Maid**, S

Jade HT, ob, Richardier; flowers yellow suffused with orange, very dbl., cupped; growth to 80-100 cm.; int. by Meilland-Richardier, 1999

Jade HT, w, Tantau; flowers creamy white with green tint on outer petals, medium, dbl., exhibition; cut flower rose; int. by Rosen Tantau, 2000

Jadis HT, mp, 1974, Warriner, William A.; flowers large, dbl., high-centered, intense fragrance; foliage large, light, leathery; vigorous, upright, bushy growth; PP3423; [Chrysler Imperial × Virgo]; int. by J&P

Jaen HT, pb

Jägerbataillon (strain of *R. canina*), lp; almost thornless; growth once popular as an understock; int. by Klinken

Jaguar F, mr, Spek; PP4462; int. in 1977

Jake McIlroy HT, mp, Brundrett; int. in 1997

Jaltinskii Suvenir F, ly, Klimenko, V. N.; flowers large, dbl.; int. in 1956

Jam Session Min, op, 1986, Zipper, H.; flowers coral pink, yellow reverse, small, 20 petals, borne singly or in small clusters; foliage small, medium green, matte; upright growth; [Poker Chip × Anytime]; int. by Magic Moment Miniature Roses

Jamaica HT, mr, 1965, Lindquist; bud ovoid; flowers cherry-red, large, semi-dbl., cupped, moderate fragrance; foliage dark, glossy, leathery; vigorous, upright growth; PP2627; [(Charlotte Armstrong × Floradora) × Nocturne]; int. by Howard Rose Co.

Jambo HT, or, Kordes; flowers bright vermilion-orange, full, high-centered, borne singly and in clusters; cut flower rose; int. by W. Kordes Söhne, 2002

Jamboree F, rb, 1964, Gregory; flowers cherry-red, reverse lighter, 1½-2 in., 26 petals, flat, borne in clusters; foliage glossy, light green; free growth; [Masquerade × unknown]

James Appleby F, ob, 1963, Wood; flowers orange-scarlet flecked deep crimson, medium, semi-dbl., borne in clusters; vigorous growth; [sport of Orangeade]

James Biddle HT, mr, 1998, Williams, J. Benjamin; flowers burgundy red, reverse medium red, light silver edges, 4½-5 in., very dbl., high-centered, borne mostly singly; few prickles; [Pink Peace × Queen Elizabeth]; int. by J. Benjamin Williams & Associates, 1998

James Bond – See **James Bond 007**, HT

James Bond 007 HT, op, 1968, Tantau, Math.; flowers coral-pink, pointed; foliage glossy; bushy growth;

[unknown × Fragrant Cloud]; int. by Wheatcroft & Sons, 1966

James Bougault – See **James Bourgault**, HP

James Bourgault HP, w, 1887, Renaud-Guépet; flowers white, shaded rose; [sport of Auguste Mie]

James Brownlow HP, mp, 1890, Dickson, A.; flowers glossy pink, very large, full, moderate fragrance; [Marquise de Castellane × Paul Neyron]

James Dickson HP, pb, 1861, Verdier, E.; flowers carmine, shaded purple-violet, dbl.

James Ferris HT, w, 1927, Hall; flowers creamy white; vigorous growth

James Galway S, lp, 2001, Austin, David; flowers very full, borne in small clusters, moderate fragrance; foliage large, medium green, semi-glossy, disease-resistant; prickles medium, hooked downward, few; growth upright, tall (1¼ m.); garden decoration; PP13918; [AUSblush × seedling]; int. by David Austin Roses, Ltd., 2000

James Gibson HT, mr, 1928, McGredy; bud pointed; flowers crimson-scarlet, large, dbl., high-centered; foliage dark, leathery; vigorous, bushy growth; Gold Medal, NRS, 1929

James Mason HGal, mr, Beales, Peter; flowers bright crimson with golden anthers, large, semi-dbl., borne in clusters, profuse, moderate citrus fragrance; non-remontant; arching, spreading, vigorous (4 ft.) growth; int. by Peter Beales Roses, 1982

James Mitchell M, dp, 1861, Verdier, E.; flowers deep pink nuanced lilac, slaty, medium, dbl.; early bloom; very heavily mossed stems; int. by E. Verdier

James Pereire HT, pb, Meilland; flowers bengal pink, clear rose reverse, 24-26 petals, moderate fragrance; foliage semi-glossy; int. in 1995

James Rea HT, dp, 1930, McGredy; bud pointed; flowers rich carmine or rose-pink, very large, dbl., high-centered; foliage light, leathery; vigorous, bushy growth; Gold Medal, NRS, 1929

James Robert HT, m, 2001, Rawlins, R.; flowers mauve/pink, 2¼ in., full, borne mostly solitary, no fragrance; foliage medium size, dark green, semi-glossy; prickles 9 mm., triangular, moderate; growth compact, tall (42 in.); garden decorative; [Oranges 'n' Lemons × (Blue Moon × Jenny Duval)]

James Smile HT, pb, 1987, Rogin, Josip; flowers China-pink, reverse pink-yellow blend, loose, medium, semi-dbl., cupped, borne in sprays of 3, moderate spicy fragrance; foliage medium size, medium green, semi-glossy; prickles rare, small, brown; upright, medium growth; hips rounded, medium size, pink-red; [sport of Sea Pearl]

James Sprunt Cl Ch, mr, 1858, Sprunt; flowers carmine-red, velvety, medium, dbl.; [sport of Cramoisi Supérieur]; possibly synonymous with Cramoisi Supérieur, Climbing

James Veitch Laffay, dp, 1852, Laffay; flowers flower deep pink to bright carmine, large, full; [La Reine × unknown]

James Veitch M, m, 1865, Verdier, E.; flowers violet-slate shaded fiery red, large, dbl., borne in clusters of 3-8; some repeat; moderately vigorous growth

James Walley HT, ab, 1923, Easlea; flowers apricot and fiery salmon, large, dbl.; foliage olive-green, leathery; vigorous growth; [Ophelia × seedling]

James Weltch – See **James Veitch**, M

James Woodlock S, mr, 2004, Horner, Colin P.; flowers medium red, reverse darker, 2½ in., very full, borne in small clusters, no fragrance; foliage medium size, medium green, semi-glossy; prickles small, slightly curved; growth spreading, medium (4 ft.); garden; decorative; [seedling × seedling]; int. by Warley Roses, 2005

Jamestown Gr, op, Williams, J. Benjamin; flowers soft peach-pink, semi-dbl., moderate fragrance; upright growth; int. by Hortico Inc., 1999

Jamie Min, lp, 1992, Moglia, Thomas; flowers outer petals horizontal at exhibition stage, large, very dbl., high-centered, borne in small clusters; foliage medium size, medium green, semi-glossy; some prickles; medium (45-50 cm.), spreading growth; [Party Girl × Fairlane]; int. by Gloria Dei Nursery, 1993

Jamie Alexander S, rb, Hannemann, F.; [Ko's Yellow × Eyepaint]; int. by The Rose Paradise

Jamie's Love HT, mr, 1999, Giles, Diann; flowers medium, full, borne mostly singly; foliage medium size, dark green, dull; few prickles; upright, medium growth; [Vera Dalton × Special Merit]; int. by Giles Rose Nursery, 1999

Jan Abbing HT, rb, 1933, Tantau; bud pointed; flowers salmon-red shaded yellow, large, cupped; foliage leathery, dark; vigorous growth; [Columbia × Étoile de Hollande]

Jan and Rick Gr, w, 2000, Moe, Mitchie; flowers white with pale pink tint, 3-4 in., full, exhibition, borne in large clusters, intense fragrance; foliage medium size,dark green, semi-glossy; prickles moderate; upright, vigorous, tall (5-6 ft.) growth; [Pristine × City of London]; int. by Mitchie's Roses and More, 2000

Jan Böhm HP, mr, 1934, Svoboda; flowers velvety fiery red, 40 petals, moderate fragrance; recurrent bloom; vigorous growth; [Hugh Dickson × King George V]

Jan Guest HT, pb, 1976, Guest; flowers carmine-pink with yellow reverse, 4 in., 43 petals; foliage glossy; vigorous, upright growth; [Fragrant Cloud × Irish Gold]

Jan H. Meyer HT, mr, 1954, Leenders, M.; flowers cinnabar-red, well-formed, large; vigorous growth; [Tawny Gold × Gaudia]

Jan Hus HT, lp, 1933, Böhm, J.; flowers large, dbl.

Jan Spek F, dy, 1966, McGredy, Sam IV; flowers 3 in., 44 petals, flat, borne in clusters; foliage dark, glossy; [Clare Grammerstorf × Faust]; int. by McGredy; Gold Medal, The Hague, 1970, Gold Medal, Belfast, 1968

Jan Steen HT, mr, 1923, Spek; flowers brilliant scarlet-red, semi-dbl.; [Mev. Dora van Tets × Gruss an Dresden]

Jan Steen S, rb, Williams, J. Benjamin; bud high; flowers ivory and red striped, single; upright growth; int. by Hortico, Inc., 1997

Jan van Riebeeck HT, m, 1952, Leenders, M.; flowers carmine, large, dbl.; vigorous growth

Jan Vermeer F, m, Williams, J. Benjamin; flowers purple/burgundy blend, borne in sprays, intense fragrance; int. by Hortico Inc., 1997

Jan Wellum Min, dr, 1986, Fischer, C.&H.; flowers large, 20 petals, borne singly and in sprays of 3-5, slight fruity fragrance; foliage medium size, medium green, matte; prickles small, straight, near-white; spreading growth; small, globular fruit; [Unnamed Shrub × Dwarfking '78]; int. by Alpenflora Gardens

Jana – See **Janna**, Min

Jana HT, dy, Cocker; flowers large, dbl.; int. in 1976

Jana – See **Yardley English Rose**, HT double

Janal HT, dp, 1982, Dawson, George; bud pointed; flowers deep pink, 55 petals, high-centered, intense fragrance; foliage bronze-red to dark green; prickles hooked red; vigorous growth; [Charles Mallerin × (Duet × Kordes' Perfecta)]; int. by Rainbow Roses, 1978

Jane HSet, lp, about 1846, Pierce; flowers flesh to lilac-pink, medium, very dbl., borne in clusters of 25-30; foliage large, coarsely serrated

Jane HT, ob, 1957, Mee; flowers coppery orange suffused pink, well-formed, large, 24 petals, moderate fragrance; foliage dark; vigorous, upright growth; [Signora × Mrs Edward Laxton]; int. by Sanday, 1956

Jane Asher Min, mr, 1988, Pearce, C.A.; flowers scarlet, aging slightly paler, rounded, small, very dbl., borne in sprays, no fragrance; foliage small, medium green, semi-glossy; prickles straight, average, red; patio; bushy, low growth; [seedling × seedling]; int. by The Limes New Roses

Jane Bullock S, my, ARE; flowers yellow, 2 in., semi-dbl., borne in abundance, moderate fragrance; recurrent; growth small (3 ft.), cascading bush; int. by Antique Rose Emporium, 2004

Jane Carrel HT, yb, 1940, Gaujard; bud pointed; flowers yellow shaded orange, medium, dbl.; very vigorous, bushy growth

Jane Eyre LCl, mp, 1998, Mehring, Bernhard F.; flowers medium pink, 4½ in., dbl., borne in small clusters; foliage large, medium green, semi-glossy; prickles moderate; upright, climbing, medium (300cm.) growth; [Westfalenpark Dortmund × ((Anna Ford × Frank Naylor) × (Westerland × (Casino × Mermaid) × (Vesper × Picasso)))]; int. by Apuldram Roses, 1998

Jane Hardy – See **Jean Hardy**, N

Jane Isobella Linton T, pb, L'Hay

Jane Jackson F, ob, 1977, Jackson, J.R.; flowers strawberry-orange, dbl.; low, vigorous, bushy growth; [sport of Tip Top]

Jane Lathrop Stanford HT, dr

Jane Lazenby F, mp, 1960, McGredy, Sam IV; flowers rose-pink, large, 25 petals, flat, moderate fragrance; foliage dark; very vigorous, bushy growth; [Alain × Mme Henri Guillot]; int. by McGredy & Son, 1959

Jane Pauley HT, ob, 1992, Weddle, Von C.; flowers orange, reverse orange, aging orange pink, 6½ in., 35 petals, high-centered, borne singly, moderate fragrance; foliage large, medium green, semi-glossy; upright, medium growth; [Elizabeth Taylor × Fortuna]; int. by Hortico Roses, 1993

Jane Piekarski HT, w, 1994, Hoshall, Howard; flowers 3-3½ in., very dbl., borne mostly singly; foliage medium size, medium green, matte; numerous prickles; medium (24 in.), upright growth; [Honor × John F. Kennedy]

Jane Probyn HT, dp, 1979, Anderson, K.; flowers deep pink; [sport of Red Devil]; int. in 1978

Jane Rogers HT, ab, 1991, Mander, George; flowers large, full, borne mostly singly, sometimes in small clusters, slight fragrance; foliage medium size, medium green, semi-glossy; medium, spreading growth; [Fragrant Cloud × Diamond Jubilee]

Jane, Souvenir Du Barbicon F, dr, 2001, Horner, Colin P.; flowers very dark red, 8 cm., dbl., borne in small clusters, moderate fragrance; foliage medium size, dark green, glossy, reddish when young; prickles medium, brown, curved, moderate; growth upright, medium (1 m.); garden decorative; [(Anna Ford × (seedling × (Blessings × *R. moyesii fargesii*))) × (Wandering Minstrel × (Alexander × (Southampton × (seedling × Stars 'n' Stripes))))]

Jane Thornton HT, rb, Bees; flowers velvety crimson shaded maroon

Janet HT, ab, 1915, Dickson, A.; flowers golden fawn, shaded copper and rose, large, dbl., globular-cupped, moderate fragrance; Gold Medal, NRS, 1916

Janet S, pb, 2004; flowers very full, borne in small clusters, slight fragrance; foliage large, dark green, semi-glossy; prickles medium, deeply concave; growth bushy, broad, vigorous, medium (120 cm.); garden decorative; [Golden Celebration × seedling (medium pink English-type shrub)]; int. by David Austin Roses, Ltd., 2003

Janet A. Wood S, op, 2004, Jalbert, Brad; flowers orangey pink, reverse orange-pink, fading to pink, yellow eye, tiny, 1 in., single, borne in large clusters, slight fragrance; foliage small, medium green, semi-glossy; prickles small, hooked; growth bushy, medium (3-4 ft.); hedge, garden decoration; [Ana Ford × Ballerina]; int. in 1998

Janet Bebb F, ly, 1997, Meahring, Bernhard F.; flowers medium, dbl., borne in small clusters; foliage large, medium green, glossy; compact, medium (100cm.) growth; [Golden Holstein × Seafarer]; int. by Henry Street Nurseries

Janet Carnochan HT, w, Pallek; flowers white blend with faint mauve in center, dbl., exhibition, intense fragrance; recurrent; int. in 1996

Janet Frazer F, op, 1967, McGredy; flowers shrimp-pink and yellow, large, semi-dbl., borne in clusters, slight fragrance; foliage light green; [Mme Léon Cuny × (Orange Sweetheart × Cinnabar)]

Janet Greig F, ab, 2005, Paul Chessum Roses; flowers White, reverse Apricot, 3 cm., dbl., borne in large clusters, moderate fragrance; foliage medium size, medium green, semi-glossy; prickles medium, brown, few; growth bushy, medium; bedding, containers; [seedling × seedling]; int. by World of Roses, 2005

Janet Morrison Cl HT, dp, 1936, Clark, A.; flowers deep pink, 3-3½ in., semi-dbl., borne in small clusters, moderate fragrance; long stems; vigorous growth; [Black Boy × unknown]; int. by NRS Victoria

Janet's Pride – See **Clémentine**, HEg

Janette Murray HT, op, 1985, Bell, Ronald J.; flowers orange pink, large, 35 petals, borne singly; foliage large, medium green, semi-glossy; vigorous growth; [(Daily Sketch × unknown) × Montezuma]; int. by Brundrett & Sons

Janice Min, mp, 1972, Moore, Ralph S.; bud ovoid; flowers small, dbl.; foliage small, glossy, leathery; vigorous, dwarf, upright, bushy growth; [(*R. wichurana* × Floradora) × Eleanor]; int. by Sequoia Nursery, 1971

Janice Heyes HT, lp, Dawson; int. in 1986

Janice Kellogg F, dr, Meilland; flowers dark burgundy, large, very full, cupped, slight fragrance; recurrent; foliage dark green, semi-glossy; medium, bushy growth; int. in 2006

Janice Meredith HCh, dp, 1903, Hill, E. G.; flowers carmine pink, large, full, moderate fragrance; [Hermosa × La France]

Janice Tellian Min, op, 1979, Moore, Ralph S.; bud pointed; flowers light coral-pink, 1 in., 40 petals, high-centered, slight fragrance; foliage small; dwarf, bushy, compact growth; PP4657; [Fairy Moss × Fire Princess]; int. by Sequoia Nursery

Janida HT, rb, 1955, Robichon; bud long, pointed, blood-red veined maroon; flowers orange, dbl.; [Crimson Glory × Baby Chateau]

Janie Harrison F, mp, 2004, Horner, Colin P.; flowers pink, yellow center, reverse paler, 6 cm., semi-dbl., borne in small clusters, slight fragrance; foliage medium size, medium green, glossy; prickles small, curved; growth bushy, medium (80 cm.); garden decorative; [(Baby Love × Amber Queen) × Beverley-Ann]; int. by Warley Rose Gardens, 2005

Janina HT, ob, Tantau; flowers copper/salmon/orange with yellow reverse, dbl., high-centered, moderate fragrance; upright, medium growth; int. in 1974

Janine Astle F, mp, 1971, Hunt; flowers clear pink, 3 in., 22 petals, high-centered; foliage bluish green; vigorous, upright growth; [Charlotte Elizabeth × Grand Slam]

Janine Herholdt HT, ab, Herholdt; bud pointed, golden; flowers golden apricot fading to caramel-cream, semi-dbl., slight fragrance; recurrent; foliage glossy, healthy; easy, willing (5-6 ft.) growth; [sport of Johannesburg Sun]; int. by Ludwig's Roses, 1989

Janine Viaud-Bruant HT, mr, 1910, Viaud-Bruant; flowers crimson-purple-ruby, large, dbl., moderate fragrance; [Triomphe d'Orléans × Princesse de Béarn]

Janna Min, pb, 1970, Moore, Ralph S.; bud pointed; flowers pink, reverse white, small, dbl.; foliage leathery; dwarf, bushy growth; PP3245; [Little Darling × (Little Darling × (*R. wichurana* × Miniature seedling))]; int. by Sequoia Nursery

Janos Pol, or, VEG; flowers medium, dbl.

Jan's Wedding S, yb, 1993, Adams, Dr. Neil D.; flowers 2-2½ in., dbl., borne in large and medium clusters; foliage medium size, dark green, semi-glossy; some prickles; tall (6 ft.), bushy growth; winter hardy; [Dornroschen × Lichtkonigin Lucia]; int. by Rosehaven Nursery, 1993

Jan's Wedding Bouquet – See **Jan's Wedding**, S

Jantar HT, dr, 1966, Grabczewski; bud elongated; flowers dark crimson, shaded darker, large; vigorous, upright growth

Jantzen Girl Gr, mr, 1961, Von Abrams; bud ovoid; flowers 4-5 in., dbl., high-centered, borne in clusters, slight fragrance; foliage glossy; upright growth; PP2242; [Carrousel × (Chrysler Imperial × seedling)]; int. by Peterson & Dering, 1962

Japanese Rose – See ***R. rugosa*** (Thunberg)

Japonica – See **Mousseux du Japon**, M

Japonica Thornless (strain of *R. multiflora*); prickle-free; growth popular as an understock

Jaquenetta S, ab, Austin, David; flowers apricot-peach, large, dbl., cupped, borne singly and in clusters, slight fragrance; strong, tall (6 ft.) growth; int. in 1983

Jardin de Giverny HT, ob, Gillet; int. in 1992

Jardin de la Croix HMacr, op, 1901, L'Hay

Jardinero Ortiz HT, rb, Dot; flowers deep blackish crimson red, large, full; int. in 1969

Jardinier Ortiz – See **Jardinero Ortiz**, HT

Jardins d'Albertas F, lp, Guillot-Massad; [(*R. filipes* × Sanguinea) × (Artiste × Anne Laure)]

Jardins de Bagatelle HT, w, 1987, Meilland, Mrs. Marie-Louise; flowers large, creamy white tinted pink, very dbl., borne mostly solitary, intense fragrance; foliage large, medium green, semi-glossy; upright growth; [(Queen Elizabeth × Eleg) × MEIdragelac]; int. by SNC Meilland & Cie, 1987; Golden Rose, Geneva, 1984, Gold Medal, Genoa, 1987

Jardins de France – See **Passionate Kisses**, F

Jardins de l'Essonne S, lp, Delbard; flowers chamois-rose, lighter at edges, very dbl., rosette, moderate citron & herb fragrance; int. in 2000

Jardins de Valloires Pol, dp, Eve, A.; flowers full, rosette; good rebloom; foliage healthy, dark green; rounded (3 ft.) growth; int. by Andre Eve, 1994

Jardins de Viels Maisons S, mp, Guillot-Massad; int. in 1998

Jardins de Villandry HT, mp, Delbard, Georges; flowers very large, very dbl., cupped, intense rose-fruit fragrance; int. by Georges Delbard SA, 1995

Jardins et Loisirs S, ab; int. in 2001

Jaris Hudson Min, mp

Jarlina – See **Bellevue**, HT

Jarvis Brook HT, rb, 1928, Low; flowers carmine, reverse orange, dbl.

Jasena HT, dy, Urban, J.; flowers large, dbl.; int. in 1983

Jaslok HT, m, 1999, Chiplunkar, C. R.; flowers light mauve with dark mauve stripes, reverse lighter, 4-5 in., 41 petals, borne mostly singly; foliage large, medium green, semi-glossy; prickles moderate; compact, medium (2½-3½ ft.) growth; [sport of Blue Ocean]; int. by KSG's Roses, 1992

Jasmina LCl, pb, 2006; flowers violet and pink, 6-7 cm., very full, cupped, borne in large clusters, moderate sweetish fragrance; foliage medium size, semi-glossy; bushy, well-branched (200 cm.) growth; int. by W. Kordes' Söhne, 2004

Jasnaja Poljana HT, pb, Shtanko, E.E.; flowers salmon-pink with light yellow, large, very dbl.; int. in 1958

Jason HT, mp, 1999, Sheridan, John; flowers deep pink, reverse paler, medium, dbl., borne mostly singly; foliage medium size, dark green, dull; few prickles; upright (4 ft.) growth; [Silver Jubilee × (Redgold × Golden Slippers)]; TGC, RNRS, 1989

Jasper – See **Berleburg**, F

Jasper Crane HT, mr, Williams, J. B.; PP15680

Jaunatella HT, yb

Jaunâtre HSem, ly; flowers yellowish-white, moderate musk fragrance; probably a hybrid between *R. sempervirens* and a Noisette or Hybrid Musk

Jaunâtre Pleine Sp, my; flowers primrose yellow, dbl; [sport of *R. banksiae lutea*]

Jaune Ancien – See **Multiplex**, Misc OGR

Jaune Ancien – See ***R. hemisphaerica*** (Herrmann)

Jaune Bicolor S, yb, 1633; flowers yellow streaked red, medium, single; [sport of *R. foetida bicolor*]

Jaune de William – See **Williams' Double Yellow**, HFt

Jaune Desprez N, yb, about 1830, Desprez; flowers dull yellow to sulfur yellow, 6 cm., full, cupped, borne in small clusters, moderate fragrance; vigorous (to 20 ft.) growth; [Blush Noisette × Parks' Yellow Tea-scented China]

Jaune d'Italie HFt, ly, before 1846, from Italy; flowers pale straw yellow, darker center, dbl.

Jaune d'Or T, ob, Oger; flowers coppery yellow, large, dbl., globular

Jaune Double – See **Williams' Double Yellow**, HFt

Jaune of Smith – See **Smith's Yellow China**, T

Jaune Serin HBank, my; flowers canary yellow with gold, large, full; [sport of *R. banksiae lutea*]

Jaune Soufré – See **Sulphurea**, HSpn

Java F, ob, 1958, Mallerin, C.; bud ovoid; flowers orange-red, medium, 40-45 petals, borne in clusters of 4-5, slight fragrance; foliage bronze; vigorous, upright, bushy growth; [Francais × seedling]; int. by EFR, 1955; Gold Medal, Geneva, 1954

Jawahar HT, w, 1981, Division of Vegetable Crops and Floriculture; flowers creamy white, 47 petals, high-centered, borne 2-6 per cluster, intense fragrance; foliage light green, glossy; prickles straight, brown; vigorous, bushy growth; [Sweet Afton × Delhi Princess]; int. in 1980

Jawani HT, or, Pal, Dr. B.P.; flowers large, full; strong growth; int. in 1985

Jawarosa Mawa HT, or; flowers large, dbl.

Jay Jay HT, w, 1971, Kern, J. J.; flowers white, edged pink, very large, dbl., high-centered, slight fragrance; foliage large, dark, leathery; very vigorous, bushy growth; [sport of Peace]

Jayant HT, pb, Gokhale, Anand; flowers pink and white stripes on deep vermilion; [sport of Maharshi]; int. in 1998

Jayatsen HT, pb, K&S; flowers deep pink with reverse pure white, large, full, exhibition; int. by KSG Son Roses, 1998

Jaybo Min, rb, 1988, Bridges, Dennis A.; flowers very bright red, yellow at base, fading to pink, 22 petals, urn-shaped, slight fruity fragrance; foliage medium size, dark green, glossy; prickles long, pointed, pink; bushy, medium growth; [Rise 'n' Shine × seedling]; int. by Bridges Roses

Jaydon F, mr, 1998, Jellyman, J. S.; flowers velvety red, reverse dame, medium, dbl, borne in small clusters, slight fragrance; foliage medium size, medium green, semi-glossy; growth upright, compact, medium (2½ ft.); [seedling × (Tony Jacklin × Andrea)]

Jayne Austin S, my, 1993, Austin, David; flowers old fashioned, medium, 110-130 petals, borne in small clusters, intense fragrance; foliage medium size, dark green, semi-glossy; few prickles; medium (43 in.), upright growth; PP8682; [Graham Thomas × Tamora]; int. by David Austin Roses, Ltd., 1990

Jazz F, ob, 1960, deRuiter; flowers orange-yellow flushed crimson, 2 in., 26 petals, borne in clusters; foliage dark, glossy; vigorous growth; [Masquerade × seedling]; int. by Gregory & Son, 1960

Jazz – See **That's Jazz**, LCl

Jazz HT, ob, Tantau; int. by Rosen Tantau

Jazz Band Min, pb, Benardella, Frank; flowers pale pink with carmine red and coffee stripes, hybrid tea; medium growth

Jazz Club S, ab, Lowery/Robinson; flowers soft apricot shot with yellow and amber, semi-dbl., informal, slight fragrance; free-flowering; foliage bright green, glossy, disease-resistant; int. in 1995

Jazz Dancer Min, ob, 1999, McCann, Sean; flowers orange and yellow, reverse orange, 1¾ in., full, borne mostly singly; foliage medium size, dark green, glossy; prickles moderate; compact, medium (14-16 in.) growth; int. by Justice Miniature Roses, 1999

Jazz Fest F, mr, 1971, Armstrong, D.L.; bud long, pointed; flowers medium, semi-dbl., slight fragrance; foliage large, leathery; vigorous, upright, bushy growth; PP3323; [Pink Parfait × Garnette]; int. by Armstrong Nursery

Jazz Time Cl Min, dp, 1985, Williams, Ernest D.; flowers deep pink, small, 35 petals, borne in clusters; foliage small, dark, semi-glossy; upright, bushy (4-5 ft.) growth; [Little Darling × Little Chief]; int. by Mini-Roses, 1986

Jazzy Jewel Min, dr, 2000, Bell, Judy; flowers dark red with bright yellow eye, reverse light red, 2½ in., single, borne mostly singly, no fragrance; foliage medium size, dark green, semi-glossy; few prickles; growth bushy, medium (16 in.); [Rainbow's End × unknown]; int. by Michigan Miniature Roses, 2000

Jealous Joey – See **Grand Prix**, F

Jean F, pb, 2004, Cocker, A.G.; flowers peach pink, reverse lighter, 1½-2 in., semi-dbl., borne in large clusters; foliage small, medium green, glossy; prickles 6 mm., straight; growth compact, bushy, short (2 ft.); garden decorative, containers; [Claire Scotland × Pristine]; int. by James Cocker & Sons, 2004

Jean Adrien Mercer F, Dorieux, Francois; int. in 1991

Jean André T, yb, 1894, Pelletier; flowers orange-yellow with a darker center, medium, full, moderate fragrance; [William Allen Richardson × Ma Capucine]

Jean Armour F, ab; int. in 2005

Jean Bach Sisley Ch, pb, 1898, Dubreuil; flowers silvery rose, outer petals salmon-rose veined carmine, moderate fragrance; growth moderate

Jean Baker HT, w, 1998, Edwards, Eddie; flowers white, full, exhibition, borne mostly singly, intense fragrance; foliage medium size, dark green, glossy; few prickles; upright, medium to tall (4-5 ft.) growth; [Crystalline × Classic Touch]; int. in 1998

Jean-Baptiste HT, pb, Orard; int. in 2000

Jean-Baptiste Casati HP, dp, 1886, Schwartz; flowers carmine-pink, large, very dbl.

Jean Bart P, m, before 1836, Trébucien; flowers dbl., moderate fragrance

Jean Beeden F, yb, 2005, Paul Chessum Roses; flowers cream/yellow, reverse cream, 3 cm., semi-dbl., borne in small clusters, moderate fragrance; foliage medium size, medium green, matte; prickles medium, brown, moderate; growth bushy, medium (30 in.); bedding, containers; [seedling × seedling]; int. by World of Roses, 2005

Jean Bodin M, lp, 1848, Vibert; flowers light rose-pink, 6 cm., quartered; foliage dark green; prickles short, straight, numerous; vigorous growth

Jean Bostick HT, my, 1936, Bostick; flowers deep yellow, sometimes splotched red, large, 50 petals, globular; foliage leathery, glossy; very vigorous growth; [sport of Condesa de Sástago]

Jean Brosse HP, mp, 1867, Ducher; flowers full, spherical

Jean Brown HT, ly, 1930, Evans, F. David; flowers large, very dbl.

Jean Burion HT, mp, RvS-Melle; [Frederik Chopin × Waanrode]; int. in 1995

Jean C. N. Forestier HT, rb, 1919, Pernet-Ducher; flowers carmine, slightly tinted orange and yellow, very large, dbl.; foliage glossy, bronze; very vigorous growth; [seedling × Mme Edouard Herriot]; Gold Medal, Bagatelle, 1919

Jean Campbell HT, pb, 1964, Sanday, John; flowers blush-pink suffused apricot, well-formed, 4½ in., 28 petals; foliage dark; upright growth; [(Ethel Sanday × unknown) × Lady Sylvia]

Jean Cherpin HP, m, 1865, Liabaud; flowers purple/pink, very large, very dbl.

Jean Cote HT, yb, 1936, Gaujard; flowers old-gold, center deeper, very large, dbl.; foliage brilliant green; vigorous growth; int. by J&P

Jean Dalmais HP, dp, 1873, Ducher; flowers dark cherry pink, very large, full, spherical

Jean de la Lune F, dy, 1969, Delbard-Chabert; flowers dbl., cupped, borne in clusters; foliage matte; low growth; PP2995; [(Orléans Rose × Goldilocks) × (Fashion × Henri Mallerin seedling)]; also registered as Yelloglo in the same year; patent issued to Yelloglo; int. by Cuthbert

Jean Desprez N, rb, about 1820, Desprez; flowers crimson-pink, shaded coppery, medium, full

Jean Dorizy B, mp, 1850, Dorizy; flowers large, full

Jean du Tilleux HT, mp, 1981, Winchel, Joseph F.; bud long; flowers medium lavender pink, medium, 30 petals, high-centered, borne mostly singly, slight fragrance; recurrent; foliage deep green, waxy; prickles slightly hooked, red; medium, vigorous growth; [King of Hearts × Golden Masterpiece]; int. by Kimbrew-Walter Roses, 1980

Jean Ducher T, op, 1874, Ducher, Vve.; bud pale cream, occasionally streaked red; flowers salmon to peachy pink, 8-9 cm., semi-dbl. to dbl., globular, borne mostly solitary, moderate tea fragrance

Jean Galbraith S, ab, Nieuwesteeg, J.; flowers buff apricot fading to soft buff, large, to 50 petals, cupped, borne in small clusters, moderate fruity fragrance; recurrent; foliage medium green, shiny; vigorous, bushy growth; [sport of Abraham Darby]; int. in 1999

Jean Gaujard HT, mr, 1978, Gaujard; flowers brilliant red, 40 petals; vigorous growth; [Canasta × Rose Gaujard]; int. in 1977

Jean Giono HT, yb, 1998, Selection Meilland; bud globular, large; flowers sunny yellow, veined and edged in orange/apricot, 3-4 in., 110-120 petals, borne singly and in small clusters, slight fragrance; good repeat; foliage medium size, medium green, glossy; prickles numerous, large; upright, bushy, medium (90 cm.) growth; PP9979; [(Yakimour × Landora) × Graham Thomas]; int. as Outback Angel, Treloar Roses

Jean Girin HWich, pb, 1910, Girin; flowers bright rose-pink, base rosy white, yellow stamens, 3½-4 cm., dbl., no fragrance; profuse bloom, sometimes repeated in autumn; vigorous, climbing growth

Jean Goujon HP, mr, 1862, Margottin; flowers deep rose red, very large, full, cupped; nearly thornless

Jean Guichard HWich, pb, 1905, Barbier; bud bronzy crimson; flowers copper-pink, 7-8 cm., very dbl., flat, borne in small clusters; foliage dark green, glossy; stems flexible, coppery bronze to dark green; vigorous, climbing growth; [*R. wichurana* × Souv. de Catherine Guillot]

Jean Hardy N, yb, 1859, Hardy; flowers golden yellow with flesh pink

Jean Kathryn F, pb, 1973, Ellick; flowers Neyron rose, reverse white, 4 in., 45 petals; foliage light; very vigorous growth; [Memoriam × Gavotte]; int. by Excelsior Roses

Jean Kenneally Min, ab, 1984, Bennett, Dee; flowers pale to medium apricot, small, 22 petals, high-centered, borne mostly singly; foliage medium size, medium green, semi-glossy; long stems; upright, bushy, vigorous growth; PP5637; [Futura × Party Girl]; int. by Tiny Petals Nursery; AOE, ARS, 1986

Jean Lafitte HSet, mp, 1934, Horvath; bud pointed; flowers willowmere pink, darker at center, 7-8 cm., dbl., cupped, borne in tight clusters, moderate fragrance; foliage leathery; numerous prickles; growth very vigorous, climbing (8-10 ft.); very hardy; [(*R. setigera* × unknown) × Willowmere]; int. by J&P

Jean Lambert HP, mr, 1865, Verdier, E.; flowers fire-red, large, full

Jean Lambert HT, rb, 1903, Laperrière; flowers red with yellow base

Jean Lapeyre S, my, 1960, Gaujard; flowers well-formed; recurrent bloom; foliage bronze; vigorous, bushy growth

Jean Lelièvre HP, dr, 1879, Oger; flowers bright deep crimson, large, dbl., moderate fragrance

Jean l'Hoste HWich, rb, 1926, Congy; flowers rosy carmine, base flesh-white, 7 cm., dbl., borne in clusters of 50-100; foliage large, glossy; [Alexandre Girault × Gerbe Rose]; int. by Cochet-Cochet

Jean Liabaud HP, dr, 1875, Liabaud; flowers crimson-maroon, shaded scarlet, large, 60 petals; some recurrent bloom; vigorous growth; [Baron de Bonstetten × unknown]

Jean Lorthois HT, pb, 1879, Ducher, Vve.; flowers rose-pink, center darker, reverse silvery, well-formed, large; [Gloire de Dijon × unknown]

Jean MacArthur HT, mr, 1942, Joseph H. Hill, Co.; bud long, pointed, begonia-red; flowers 3½-4 in., 30-40 petals, high-centered; foliage leathery, wrinkled, dark; vigorous, upright growth; [Joanna Hill × California]

Jean Marc F, or, Croix; int. in 1975

Jean Marc Rosé F, Fineschi, G.; int. in 1995

Jean Marmoz – See **Jean Mermoz**, Pol

Jean Maycock HT, mr, 1999, Rawlins, R.; flowers crimson pink, reverse lighter, 3 in., full, borne in small clusters, slight fragrance; foliage medium size, medium green, semi-glossy; prickles moderate; compact, medium (36 in.) growth; [Sexy Rexy × Sharifa Asma]

Jean McGregor Reid HT, w, 1962, Sunter; flowers cream, large; foliage dark, glossy; vigorous growth; [sport of Peace]; int. by Ross & Son

Jean Mermoz Pol, mp, 1937, Chenault; flowers ruddy pink, imbricated, small, very dbl., borne in long clusters; foliage glossy, dark; vigorous growth; [*R. wichurana* × a hybrid tea]; int. by Hémeray-Aubert

Jean Monford – See **Jeanne de Montfort**, M

Jean Monnet F, mp, Pekmez, Paul; int. in 1988

Jean Morrison HT, or, Sutherland; int. in 1996

Jean Muraour F, w, 1935, Vogel, M.; flowers pure white, center light yellow, large; [sport of Gruss an Aachen]

Jean Noté HT, op, 1909, Pernet-Ducher; flowers light salmon-pink, large, dbl.

Jean Pernet T, my, 1867, Pernet père; flowers medium to large, full; prickles large, straight; growth upright; [Devoniensis × unknown]

Jean Piat HT, yb, Adam; flowers amber yellow, edged with orange-red, very large, dbl., high-centered; int. in 2003

Jean Rameau B, dp, 1918, Darclanne/Turbat; flowers iridescent rose, large, full; [sport of Mme Isaac Pereire]; int. by Turbat

Jean Renton HT, my, 1940, Clark, A.; vigorous growth

Jean Rex S, dr, 1999, Rex, Dr. Robert W.; flowers dark red (3 shades), center vein darkest, 4-4½ in., very dbl., borne in small clusters, intense fragrance; foliage medium size, dark green, matte; numerous prickles; bushy, very vigorous, strong, medium (4 ft.) growth; [sport of Prospero]; int. by Hortico, Inc., 1995

Jean Rose Min, pb, 1987, Bennett, Dee; flowers peach-pink with yellow base, reverse soft yellow, fading lighter, 20-25 petals; foliage medium size, medium green, semi-glossy; prickles few, slender, small, reddish; upright, medium growth; hips globular, medium size, brown; [Electron × Fairest of Fair]; int. by Tiny Petals Nursery

Jean Rosenkrantz HP, or, 1864, Portemer fils; flowers very bright coral-red, large, dbl.; [Victor Verdier × unknown]

Jean Sisley HT, m, 1879, Bennett; flowers lilac-rose, large, no fragrance; moderate growth; [Adam × Emilie Hausburg]; rarely opens properly; prone to mildew

Jean Soupert HP, dr, 1875, Lacharme, F.; flowers crimson-maroon, large, dbl.; [Charles Lefebvre × Souv. du Baron de Sémur]

Jean Thomson Harris F, op, 1976, Cocker; flowers salmon, shaded orange, 4 in., 30 petals; [(Fragrant Cloud × Heidelberg) × (Heidelberg × Kingcup)]

Jean Touvais HP, m, 1863, Touvais; flowers purple with carmine shades, large, full, spherical

Jean Webb HT, rb, 1966, Marks; flowers cochineal, reverse light bronze, 4 in.; foliage dark; vigorous growth; [sport of Bettina]

Jean-Baptiste Guillot HP, m, 1861, Verdier, E.; flowers violet, shaded with purple, very large, spherical

Jeanette Min, pb, 2001, Spooner, Ray; flowers 1¾ in., full, borne mostly solitary, no fragrance; foliage medium size, medium green, semi-glossy; prickles 1/16 in., few; growth bushy, compact, medium (14 in.); garden decorative; [Maurine Neuberger × seedling]; int. as Jeannette, Oregon Miniature Roses, 1997

Jeanette Heller – See **William R. Smith**, T

Jeanette Talbot F, op, 1998, Webster, Robert; flowers orange-pink, yellow at center, 2 in., dbl., borne in small clusters; foliage small, medium green, glossy; prickles moderate; compact, low (18 in.) growth; [(Robin Redbreast × Typhoon) × The Lady]; int. by Handley Rose Nurseries, 1998

Jeanie HT, w, 1959, Eddie; flowers cream to pink, 4-4½ in., 66 petals, high-centered; foliage dark; vigorous, spreading growth; [Condesa de Sástago × Mme Edmond Labbe]; int. by Wyant, 1958

Jeanie Williams Min, rb, 1965, Moore, Ralph S.; flowers orange-red, reverse yellow, small, dbl.; foliage leathery; vigorous, bushy growth; [Little Darling × Magic Wand]; int. by Sequoia Nursery

Jeanine Gr, op

Jeanine Defaucamberge Pol, pb, 1931, Turbat; flowers bright salmon-pink, passing to light pink, large, very dbl., peony-like; foliage slender; [sport of Merveille]

Jeanine Weber HT, ob, 1954, Leenders, M.; flowers orange, large; vigorous growth; [Soestdijk × Mary Hart]

Jean-Marc – See **Jean Marc**, F

Jeanne Buatois HT, w, 1902, Buatois; flowers pearly white, center light flesh pink, very large, moderate fragrance; [Merveille de Lyon × Mme Eugene Résal]

Jeanne Cabanis HT, rb, 1922, Guillot, P.; bud coral-red; flowers bright rose-carmine, reverse silvery, center coppery rose, dbl.

Jeanne Corboeuf HT, lp, 1902, Corboeuf; bud long; flowers satiny pink with carmine reflections on a yellow ground, very large, dbl., full, cupped; [Mme la Duchesse d'Auerstädt × Mme Jules Grolez]

Jeanne d'Arc A, w, 1818, Vibert; flowers creamy flesh fading to ivory-white, medium to large, dbl., cupped, borne in clusters, intense fragrance; foliage dark grey-green; prickles strong; dense bush (to 5 ft.) growth; [Elisa × unknown]

Jeanne d'Arc HP, w, 1847, Verdier, V.; flowers creamy white, dbl.; vigorous growth

Jeanne d'Arc T, my, 1870, Ducher; flowers full

Jeanne d'Arc N, w, 1882, Garçon/Margottin; flowers creamy white changing to pure white, 9-10 cm., full, moderate fragrance; [Gloire de Dijon × unknown]; sometimes classified as a T

Jeanne d'Arc Pol, w, 1909, Levavasseur; flowers pure milky white; [Mme Norbert Levavasseur × unknown]

Jeanne d'Arc – See **Jeanne d'Arc Parade**, MinFl

Jeanne d'Arc Parade MinFl, w, Poulsen; flowers white, 5-8 cm., dbl., no fragrance; foliage dark; growth broad, bushy, 20-40 cm.; PP15191; int. by Poulsen Roser, 2002

Jeanne de Montfort M, mp, 1853, Robert; bud heavily mossed, dark carmine; flowers clear pink, edged silver, semi-dbl., flat, borne in large clusters, moderate fragrance; foliage emerald-green; tall, vigorous growth

Jeanne Drivon Pol, w, 1883, Schwartz, J.; flowers white, faintly shaded pink, very dbl.

Jeanne Excoffier HT, pb, 1921, Buatois; bud large, long, pointed; flowers daybreak-pink, inside buff, large, dbl.; [Mme Philippe Rivoire × Mme Edouard Herriot]

Jeanne Gross HP, mp, 1871, Damaizin; flowers silky pink, large, full, cupped

Jeanne Guillot HP, mp, 1869, Liabaud; flowers pink with purple shades, very large, full

Jeanne Hachette HGal, dp, 1842, Vibert; flowers lilac rose, large, dbl., globular

Jeanne Hachette M, m, 1851, Robert; flowers slaty violet

Jeanne Hachette M, mp, 1851, Coquerel; flowers medium pink, edges lighter, large, full

Jeanne Hachette HP, dp, Oger; flowers carmine-rose

Jeanne Halphen HP, mp, 1878, Margottin; flowers large, full

Jeanne Hardy – See **Jean Hardy**, N

Jeanne Lajoie Cl Min, mp, 1976, Sima; bud long, pointed; flowers 1 in., 40 petals, high-centered, borne in small clusters and singly; foliage small, glossy, dark, embossed; upright, bushy growth; [(Casa Blanca × Independence) × Midget]; int. by Mini-Roses, 1975; AOE, ARS, 1977

Jeanne Lallemand LCl, pb, 1954, Buatois; flowers pink, reverse salmon-pink, large, 40-50 petals; very free, recurrent bloom; very vigorous growth; [Mrs Pierre S. duPont × George Dickson]

Jeanne Lassalle LCl, mp, 1936, Lassalle; flowers borne in clusters of 50-60; free, recurrent boom; foliage broad, light; long, stiff stems; vigorous (5 ft.) growth; int. by Vially

Jeanne Masson HP, lp, 1891, Liabaud; flowers whitish pink, medium, dbl., moderate fragrance

Jeanne Mermet Pol, w, 1909, Mermet; vigorous growth

Jeanne Moreau HT, w, Meilland; flowers pure white, full, high-centered, borne mostly singly, moderate fragrance; recurrent; moderate growth; int. in 2006

Jeanne Nicod HT, w, 1929, Schwartz, A.; flowers white, center tinted cream, dbl.

Jeanne Philippe – See **Mlle Jeanne Philippe**, T

Jeanne Richert HWich, w, 1929, Walter, L.; flowers cream, center red-brown, 4 cm., dbl., borne in large clusters, slight fragrance; foliage glossy; very vigorous, climbing growth; [Leontine Gervais × unknown]

Jeanne Saultier HT, pb, 1927, Laperrière; flowers salmon-rose, reverse reddish-pink, base yellow, dbl.; [Louise Catherine Breslau × Mme Edouard Herriot]

Jeanne Sury HP, dp, 1868, Faudon; flowers claret and crimson, very large, full, moderate fragrance

Jeannette HGal, dp, before 1815, Descemet, M.; flowers bright light red, fading light rose-pink, dbl.

Jeannette Min, pb, Spooner, Raymond A.; int. in 1997

Jeannie Deans HEg, dr, 1895, Penzance; flowers scarlet-crimson, medium to large, semi-dbl.; very free seasonal bloom; foliage fragrant; vigorous growth

Jeannie Dickson HP, pb, 1890, Dickson, A.; flowers rose-pink, edged silvery pink, large, 45 petals, high-centered; moderate bloom; vigorous growth

Jeannine Min, lp, 1992, Frock, Marshall J.; flowers light pink aging to white with a few red spots, similar to Royal Highness, 1½-1¾ in., 30 petals, high-centered; foliage medium size, medium green, semi-glossy; medium (40-50 cm.), upright growth; [Baby Katie × seedling]

Jeannine Gr, op

Jeannine Michelle Min, dy, 1989, Frock, Marshall J.; bud pointed; flowers deep gold-yellow, aging to pale yellow, medium, 30 petals, high-centered, borne usually singly, moderate fruity fragrance; foliage medium size, medium green, semi-glossy; prickles straight, tan; upright, bushy, medium, hardy growth; fruit not observed; [Rise 'n' Shine × seedling]

Jeanny Soupert Pol, w, 1913, Soupert & Notting; flowers soft flesh-white, borne in large clusters; moderately vigorous growth; [Mme Norbert Levavasseur × Petite Léonie]

Jean's Dream HT, pb, 1970, Ellick; flowers orient pink to azalea-pink, 6 in., 30 petals, high-centered; foliage large; vigorous, upright, bushy growth; [My Choice × (seedling × Memoriam)]

Jebsheim Mill S, lp, Williams, J. B.; flowers blush pink with ruffled petals, borne in clusters, slight fragrance; growth to 4 ft.; int. by Hortico, Inc., 2005

Jeep – See **Lucina**, F

Jeeper's Creeper S, w, 1993, W. Kordes Söhne; flowers medium, 6-14 petals, borne in large clusters; foliage medium size, dark green, semi-glossy; numerous prickles; low (40-50 cm.), spreading growth; PP8871; [Yesterday × Edelweiss]; int. by Bear Creek Gardens, 1994

Jeff Chait Min, rb, 2005, Zipper, Herbert; flowers velvety dark red, reverse silver, self-cleaning, 1-1½ in., very full, borne mostly solitary, no fragrance; foliage medium size, medium green, semi-glossy; prickles few, medium, downwards, green; growth bushy, medium (12-24 in.); garden decorative; [Big John × Charmglo]; int. by Cool Roses, 2006

Jeffrey HT, my, 1995, Sheldon, John & Robin; flowers medium, full, borne in small clusters; foliage medium size, light green, matte; upright, medium growth; [Polarstern × (Spirit of Glasnost × Lanvin)]

Jehoca – See **Jessika**, HT

Jelcanodir F, dy, 1976, Jelly; flowers aureolin-yellow, 2½-3 in., 30 petals; almost continuous bloom in glasshouse; vigorous, upright growth; [Undisseminated seedling 1-61-ys × Golden Garnette]; int. by Universal Plants

Jelena de Belder HBc, w, 2000, Lens, Louis; flowers single, borne in small clusters, moderate fragrance; recurrent; foliage yellow-green with bronze shadings, matte, evergreen; prickles moderate; growth bushy, medium (120-150 cm.); [*R. bracteata* × Schneezwerg]; int. by Louis Lens N.V., 1996

Jelfax – See **Cancan**, F

Jelico HT, or, 1974, Jelly; flowers vermilion, reverse crimson, 5 in., 35 petals, cupped, slight fragrance; foliage large, dark; [Baccará × (Forever Yours × seedling)]; int. by Universal Plants, 1973

Jelina HRg, dp, 1894, Kaufmann; flowers dark velvety carmine, large, dbl.; foliage elliptical, dark green, very stiff; [*R. rugosa rubra* × Perle de Lyon]

Jelly Bean Min, rb, 1982, Saville, F. Harmon; bud ovoid, pointed; flowers red-yellow blend, micro-mini, 20 petals, high-centered, borne 1-6 per cluster, moderate spicy fragrance; foliage small; no prickles; very compact, tiny growth; [seedling × Poker Chip]; int. by Nor'East Min. Roses, 1982

Jelona HMult, pb; flowers pink with white eye, single, borne in large clusters; foliage medium green

Jelrandoli F, rb, 1976, Jelly; flowers vermilion-red, base cardinal-red, 3-3½ in., 35 petals; foliage large; vigorous, upright growth; [San Francisco × Little Leaguer]; int. by Universal Plants

Jema HT, ab, 1982, Perry, Astor; bud ovoid; flowers large, 45 petals, borne singly, moderate fragrance; foliage medium size, light green; prickles small, triangular, straw; tall, vigorous growth; [Helen Traubel × Lolita]; int. by Perry Roses, 1982

Jemma Giblin F, my, 1995, Horner, Colin P.; flowers 2½ in., dbl., borne in small clusters, moderate fragrance; foliage medium size, medium green, semi-glossy; medium (50 cm.), bushy growth; [Gingernut × Amanda]; int. by Battersby Roses, 1997

Jemne Losos Interflora HT, op, Strnad

Jen HT, yb, 2001, Premeaux, John; flowers yellow and pink, ruffled edges on petals, 4 in., dbl., borne mostly solitary, slight fragrance; foliage medium size, medium green, semi-glossy; prickles moderate; growth spreading, tall; garden decorative, exhibition; [sport of Sorbet]; int. by Johnny Becnel Show Roses, 2001

Jenifer HT, 1954, Fletcher; flowers pale flesh pink, 4-5 in.; foliage dull green; vigorous growth; RULED EXTINCT 1/85 ARM; [(Mrs Henry Bowles × Phyllis Gold) × Edina.]; int. by Tucker, 1954

Jenna Rose S, w, 2005, Miladin, Suzanne; flowers white with pink stripes, 3½ in., very full, borne in small clusters, slight fragrance; foliage medium size, medium green, matte; prickles moderate, in., tan; growth bushy, medium; [sport of Mary Rose]

Jennie Anne Min, rb, 1987, King, Gene; flowers red, reverse yellow, fading light yellow with red edge, medium, 16 petals, high-centered, no fragrance; foliage medium size, medium green, matte; prickles straight, small, white; bushy, medium growth; oval fruit; [Gingersnap × Charmglo]; int. by AGM Miniature Roses, 1987

Jennie June HT, mr, 1990, Rosen Tantau; bud ovoid; flowers medium red, reverse lighter with some bluing, large, 50 petals, high-centered, borne usually singly, slight fragrance; foliage large, medium green, semi-glossy; prickles short, narrow, hooked down, red-green; upright, spreading, medium growth; [seedling × seedling]; int. by Bear Creek Gardens, 1990

Jennie Robinson Min, op, 1982, Robinson, Thomas, Ltd.; flowers orange flushed pink, patio, small, 35 petals, moderate fragrance; foliage small, dark, glossy; bushy growth; [Rumba × Darling Flame]; int. by Thomas Robinson, Ltd.

Jennie Sommer S, rb, 2001, Giles, Diann; flowers striped, large, semi-dbl., borne in small clusters, moderate fragrance; foliage medium size, light green, matte; prickles medium, straight, few; growth spreading, tall; garden decorative; [seedling × Scentimental]; int. by Giles Rose Nursery, 2001

Jennifer F, dp, 1959, Fryers Nursery, Ltd.; RULED EXTINCT 1/85 ARM; [Independence × Fashion]

Jennifer Min, pb, 1985, Benardella, Frank A.; flowers light pink, white reverse, small, 35 petals, high-centered, intense fragrance; foliage medium size, dark, semi-glossy; bushy, spreading growth; PP5857; [Party Girl × Laguna]; int. by Nor'East Min. Roses; AOE, ARS, 1985

Jennifer HT, op, Select; flowers coral, 4 in., 40-45 petals; foliage dark green; int. in 2003

Jennifer – See **Jennifer Hit**, MinFl

Jennifer-Betty Kenward HT, or, 1986, Sealand Nurseries, Ltd.; flowers medium, 35 petals, slight fragrance; foliage medium size, medium green, glossy; spreading growth; [Mildred Reynolds × Whisky Mac]; int. in 1985

Jennifer Clark HT, ob, 2003, Rawlins, R.; flowers orange apricot, medium, full, borne in small clusters; foliage medium size, dark green, semi-glossy; prickles 2 cm., triangular, moderate; growth upright, tall (38 in.); garden; [L'Oreal Trophy × (Fragrant Cloud × *R. bella*)]; int. in 2003

Jennifer Hart HT, dr, 1982, Swim, H.C. & Christensen, J.E.; bud ovoid, pointed; flowers 45 petals, high-centered, borne singly, slight tea fragrance; foliage medium size, medium green, semi-glossy; medium, upright, bushy growth; PP5219; [Pink Parfait × Yuletide]; int. by Armstrong Nursery, 1982

Jennifer Hit MinFl, dr, Olesen; bud pointed ovoid; flowers dark red, 5 cm., 43 petals, open cup, borne singly and in small clusters, very slight fragrance; free-flowering; foliage dark green, semi-glossy; prickles few, 3 mm., linear, greyed-orange; stems 14 cm; bushy (40-60 cm.) growth; PP15853; [sport of Valentina Hit]; int. by Poulsen Roser, 2003

Jennifer Jay HT, pb, 1977, Thomas, Dr. A.S.; flowers light to medium pink; [sport of Christian Dior]

Jennifer Joy Min, lp, 1985, Olesen, Pernille & Mogens N.; flowers 75 petals, borne in clusters, no fragrance; foliage light green; compact, low, bushy growth; [Mini-Poul × seedling]; int. by Ludwigs Roses Pty. Ltd., 1983

Jennifer Patiohit – See **Jennifer Hit**, MinFl

Jennifer's Rose HT, mr, Dawson; int. in 1997

Jennirene HT, pb, 2005, Felts, Stephen D; flowers dark pink, reverse light yellow, 4¼ in., full, borne mostly solitary, no fragrance; foliage medium size, dark green, glossy; prickles small, slightly diagonally slanted; growth upright, tall (5 ft.); exhibition; [sport of Brooks Red]; int. by Stephen D Felts, 2004

Jenny HCh, dr, before 1836; flowers fiery purple-crimson; Lawrenciana

Jenny – See **Jenny Duval**, HGal

Jenny Audio P, mp, before 1836, Audio; flowers bright pink, large, full

Jenny Brown HT, or, 1976, Parkes, Mrs M.H.; bud long, pointed; flowers salmon-pink, center paler, open, 4 in., 5 petals, intense fragrance; foliage glossy; very vigorous growth; [(Pink Favorite × Dorothy Peach) × Dainty Bess]; int. by Rumsey, 1974

Jenny Butchart HT, op, Hepworth, George; flowers deep orange pink fading to lighter pink, 30-35 petals, high-centered; foliage medium sized matte green; [Miss Canada × Fragrant Cloud]

Jenny Charlton HT, w, Simpson

Jenny Duval HGal, mp, before 1842; flowers rosy blush, tinted magenta and mauve, aging lilac-grey, medium, semi-dbl. to dbl., quartered, borne singly or in clusters of 2-3; foliage medium green, large, elliptical; prickles moderate; sometimes classed as HCh; possibly from Duval; the rose currently in commerce does not match early descriptions

Jenny Fair HT, mp, 1967, Gregory; flowers pink, globular; foliage dark; slender, upright growth; [Tropicana × unknown]

Jenny Gay B, w, 1865, Guillot; flowers flesh white with light pink tints, medium, full

Jenny Jones T, 1890, Williams, A.

Jenny Lind M, mp, 1845, Laffay, M.; bud abundantly mossed; flowers medium, dbl.

Jenny Lynn HT, pb

Jenny Reilly F, ob, 2002, Horner, Heather M.; flowers light orange, pale yellow reverse, 7 cm., dbl., borne mostly solitary, moderate fragrance; foliage medium size, medium green, glossy; prickles small, slightly curved, moderate; growth upright, medium (1 m.); garden decorative; [(Korp × Southampton) × Peacekeeper]

Jenny Wren F, ab, 1957, Ratcliffe; bud salmon-red; flowers creamy apricot, reverse pale salmon, small, dbl., borne in large clusters, intense fragrance; foliage dark; [Cécile Brunner × Fashion]

Jenny's Dream HT, dp, 1980, Beckett, Ian; bud large; flowers deep pink, 102 petals, classic, borne 5 per cluster, no fragrance; free-flowering; foliage large, medium green, glossy; vigorous, tall, upright growth; [sport of Red Devil]; int. in 1979

Jenny's Rose F, lp, Cants of Colchester, Ltd.; flowers soft pink with silver-white reverse, dbl., intense fragrance; foliage pale green, glossy; upright, medium growth; int. in 1996

Jens Munk HRg, mp, 1977, Svedja, Felicitas; bud ovoid; flowers yellow stamens, 3 in., 25 petals, intense fragrance; upright, bushy growth; [Schneezwerg × Frau Dagmar Hartopp]; int. by Canada Dept. of Agric., 1974

Jeppe Gold HT, yb, Kordes; int. in 2003

Jeri Jennings HMsk, yb, 2007, Barden, Paul; flowers yellow-orange, reverse paler yellow-orange, 1¾ in., very full, borne in large clusters; foliage medium size, medium green, semi-glossy; prickles ¼ in., curved, tan, few; bushy, arching growth habit, medium (4-7 ft.); specimen, containers; [Joycie × Trier]; int. in 2007

Jéricho – See **Bourbon**, HGal

Jericho HT, Dorieux, Francois; int. in 1971

Jerry Gr, pb, 1987, Jerabek, Paul E.; flowers white, flushing carmine red, reverse carmine, grading to white, dbl., cupped, intense sweet fragrance; foliage medium size, medium green, semi-glossy; prickles medium, red-brown, hooked downward; bushy, tall growth; small, rarely sets fruit; [seedling × seedling]; Silver Medal, ARC TG, 1986

Jerry Desmonde HT, mp, 1960, Norman; flowers rose-pink, reverse silvery, well-formed, 5 in., 50 petals; foliage dark, glossy; vigorous, upright growth; [Lord Rossmore × Karl Herbst]; int. by Harkness & Co., 1959

Jerry Lynn MinFl, ab, 2004, Tucker, Robbie; flowers light apricot, 2¼ in., full, borne mostly solitary, no fragrance; foliage medium green, semi-glossy; prickles no thorns on new growth, few on mature wood; growth bushy, medium (36 in.); exhibition, cutting, garden decoration; [Sam Trivitt × Memphis King]; int. by Rosemania, 2005

Jerry-O Min, mr, 1998, Saville, F. Harmon; flowers light ot medium red, 1½ in., 25 petals, high-centered, borne singly, intense fragrance; PP10630

Jersey – See **Jersey Beauty**, HWich

Jersey Beauty HWich, ly, 1899, Horvath/Manda, W.A.; flowers pale yellow, fading white, 6 cm., single, borne in clusters of 3-5, intense fragrance; non-recurrent; foliage dark green, glossy, evergreen; vigorous, climbing growth; [*R. wichurana* × Perle des Jardins]

Jersey Cream S, ly, Sutherland; int. in 1996

Jersey Gold Min, dy, Benardella, Frank; flowers clear yellow, dbl., high-centered; tall growth; int. in 1999

Jersey Queen HT, ob, 1920, Le Cornu; flowers flame-orange, edged rose, reverse lemon, dbl.; [Mme Mélanie Soupert × Queen Mary]; int. by Jersey Nursery

Jerusalem F, w, 1986, Holtzman, Arnold; flowers cream, large, 40 petals, high-centered, borne in sprays of 5-8, moderate fragrance; foliage medium size, light green, matte; upright, bushy growth; hips ovoid, small, green; [(Queen Elizabeth × seedling) × Moriah]; int. by Gandy Roses, Ltd., 1987

Jeslyn Min, ly, 2000, Bridges, Dennis A.; flowers light yellow, 2 in., dbl., exhibition, borne mostly singly, slight fragrance; foliage medium size, dark green, glossy; few prickles; stems long, straight; upright, vigorous, hardy, tall (26-30 in.) growth; [Fairhope × select pollen]; int. by Bridges Roses, 2001

Jesmond Dene F, op, 1976, Wood; flowers pastel salmon-pink, large, dbl., intense fragrance; vigorous, upright growth; [Arthur Bell × Betty May Wood]

Jessa Belle HT, pb

Jesse's Jewels HT, mp, 1996, Burks, Larry; flowers 6-14 petals, borne mostly singly; foliage medium size, medium green, dull; few prickles; upright, medium growth; [(unknown × Pink Apache Belle) × unknown]; int. by Certified Roses, Inc.

Jessica HWich, pb, 1910, Walsh; flowers cream-white, center light rose, 7-9 cm., semi-dbl., borne singly or in small clusters; foliage dark green, glossy; numerous prickles

Jessica – See **Jessika**, HT

Jessica S, mp, Clements, John; flowers soft pink becoming apricot-pink in the center, 4 in., 30 petals, deeply cupped., moderate fragrance; foliage deep green; growth bushy, compact (3½ ft. × 3 ft.); int. by Heirloom Roses, 2003

Jessica Lauren HRg, lp, Baskerville, Joanne; flowers blush pink, 4 in., single, moderate fragrance; blooms all summer; foliage crinkled, glossy; growth to 6 ft. tall and wide; hips large, orange-red; int. in 2000

Jessica Rose Min, pb, 2003, Moore, Ralph S.; flowers light to medium pink, reverse medium to dark pink, 1¼ in., full, borne in large clusters; foliage medium size, medium green, semi-glossy; prickles small, straight, brown, few; growth bushy, medium, (12 in.); containers, garden, borders; [Un-named seedling × Red Fairy]; int. by Sequoia Nurs., 2003

Jessie Pol, rb, 1909, Merryweather; flowers bright crimson, fading rose-pink, center white, 1½ in., semi-dbl.; foliage small, soft, glossy; bushy growth; [sport of Phyllis]

Jessie Anderson S, dp; flowers deep rose, well-formed, large, dbl.; blooms continuously on new wood; [(Old Crimson China × *R. canina*) × Souv. d'Alphonse Lavallee]

Jessie Brown Min, mp, 1978, Dobbs; bud mossy; flowers loosely formed, 1½ in., 15 petals; foliage small; bushy growth; [Fairy Moss × Fairy Moss]; int. by Small World Min. Roses

Jessie Clark LCl, mp, 1915, Clark, A.; flowers rosy pink, becoming lighter, 12 cm., single; non-recurrent; foliage dark, leathery; very vigorous growth; [*R. gigantea* × Mme Martignier]; int. by NRS Victoria

Jessie Mathews HT, yb, 1982, Bees; flowers light yellow, petals edged pink, medium, 35 petals; foliage medium size, light green, semi-glossy; bushy growth; [Ernest H. Morse × Rosenella]

Jessie Patricia F, ob, 2000, Bossom, Bill; flowers orange, reverse gold, 8 cm., semi-dbl., borne in small clusters, slight fragrance; foliage medium size, medium green, semi-glossy; few prickles; upright, medium (70 cm.) growth; [Sexy Rexy × Edith Holden]; int. in 2001

Jessie Segrave HT, rb, 1937, Mee; flowers scarlet on deep chrome base, with pencil markings on inside, dbl.; vigorous growth; int. by Beckwith

Jessika HT, op, 1974, Tantau, Math.; bud long, pointed; flowers peach-salmon, medium, dbl., moderate fragrance; free-flowering; vigorous, upright growth; [Colour Wonder × Piccadilly]; int. in 1971

Jet HT, dr, 1948, Brownell; bud long, pointed; flowers red to very dark red, large, dbl., moderate fragrance; foliage glossy, dark; vigorous, bushy, compact growth; [Pink Princess × Crimson Glory]

Jet Fire F, or, 1965, Schloen, J.; bud ovoid; flowers large, dbl., cupped, moderate spicy fragrance; foliage dark, glossy; vigorous, upright, bushy growth; [Sumatra × Fashion]; int. by Ellesmere Nursery, 1964

Jet Flame Min, m, 1986, Lens, Louis; flowers lavender-purple, small, 30 petals, rosette, borne in clusters, no fragrance; foliage very small, brilliant dark green; no prickles; bushy, spreading growth; [New Penny × Violet Hood]; int. in 1984; Gold Medal, Paris, 1984

Jet Flame Nirpaysage – See **Jet Flame**, Min

Jet Richards HT, rb, 2000, Poole, Lionel; flowers medium red, reverse light red, 5½ in, full, exhibition, borne mostly singly, slight fragrance; free-flowering; foliage large, dark green, semi-glossy; prickles moderate; bushy, medium (2½ ft.) growth; [(Silver Jubilee × Red Planet) × Gavotte]; int. by David Lister Roses, 2001

Jet Spray S, m, 1986, Lens, Louis; flowers purple-pink, small, 21 petals, rosette; foliage very small, dark; no prickles; growth bushy, spreading, low (60 cm.); [New Penny × seedling]; int. in 1984

Jet Trail Min, w, 1964, Moore, Ralph S.; bud pointed; flowers white, sometimes tinted pale green, small, 40 petals; bushy (12-14 in.) growth; PP2683; [Little Darling × Magic Wand]; int. by Sequoia Nursery

Jeune Fille – See **Brocade**, HT

Jeune Fille F, op, 1964, Gaujard; flowers bright salmon-pink, medium, dbl., borne in clusters; foliage leathery; very vigorous, bushy growth; [(Rose Gaujard × unknown) × Vendome]

Jeune France – See **Young France**, HT

Jeune Henry P, mr, before 1815, Descemet; flowers vivid rose/red, velvety, medium, full

Jeunesse HT, mp, 1959, Laperrière; flowers bright pink, dbl.; moderately bushy growth; [(Independence × Tonnerre) × Michele Meilland]; int. by EFR

Jeunesse Éternelle – See **Eternal Youth**, HT

Jewel HT, dr, 1938, Grillo; flowers velvety red, 5 in., 50 petals; [sport of Better Times]

Jewel Box Min, pb, 1984, Moore, Ralph S.; flowers light to deep pink blend, reverse lighter, small, 20 petals; foliage small, medium green, semi-glossy; bushy growth; PP5722; [Avandel × Old Master]; int. by Moore Min. Roses, 1983

Jewel's Delight Min, mp, 1990, Williams, Ernest D.; flowers small, 33 petals, moderate fragrance; foliage small, medium green, glossy; bushy growth; [Tom Brown × Twilight Trail]; int. in 1989

Jezebel HT, mp, 1964, Leenders, J.; flowers dbl.; strong stems; [Queen Elizabeth × Pink Lustre]

Jezebel – See **Jessa Belle**, HT

JFK – See **John F. Kennedy**, HT

Jian Min, mr, 1965, Williams, Ernest D.; bud ovoid; flowers medium red, reverse lighter, very small, dbl.; foliage narrow, leathery; very vigorous, bushy, dwarf growth; [Juliette × Oakington Ruby]; int. by Mini-Roses

Jigs F, or, 2001, Giles, Diann; flowers large, dbl., borne in small clusters, slight fragrance; foliage medium size, dark green, matte; prickles medium,slightly curved, few; growth upright, low; garden decorative; [Vera Dalton × Bing Crosby]; int. by Giles Rose Nursery, 1999

Jihoceske Slunce HT, w, 1937, Böhm, J.; flowers medium, dbl.

Jill F, mr, 1939, LeGrice; flowers cerise-scarlet, open, semi-dbl., borne in clusters; long stems; vigorous, bushy growth; [(Else Poulsen × seedling) × ((Seedling (single red) × Étoile de Hollande) × Daily Mail Scented Rose)]

Jill Carter F, yb, 1993, Sheridan, John; flowers yellow edged red, small, dbl., borne in small clusters, moderate fragrance; foliage small, dark green, semi-glossy; few prickles; medium, upright growth; [Sheila's Perfume × Darling Flame]; int. by Sheridan Nursery

Jill Dando S, rb, 2000, Beales, Peter; flowers red blend, reverse softer, 4 in., semi-dbl., very cupped, open, borne in small clusters, slight fragrance; foliage large, dark green, semi-glossy; prickles moderate; upright, medium (4 ft.) growth; [Armada × Maigold]; int. by Peter Beales Roses, 1999

Jill Darling HT, rb, 1937, Austin & McAslan; flowers rich cerise, reverse cinnamon-yellow; foliage glossy; vigorous growth

Jillian Louise Min, w, 1994, Fairweather, Mrs. P.H.; flowers white with light pink edge and center, large, full, borne in large clusters, slight fragrance; foliage medium size, medium green, semi-glossy; some prickles; medium to tall, upright growth; [sport of Magic Carrousel]

Jillian McGredy F, lp, 1998, McGredy, Sam IV; flowers light pink, large, dbl., borne in small clusters, moderate fragrance; foliage medium size, medium green, semi-glossy; prickles moderate; bushy, 120 cm. growth; [Sexy Rexy × Lagerfeld]

Jill's Rose F, op, Gandy; flowers soft salmon-pink, very large, dbl., borne in trusses, moderate musk fragrance; foliage pale green, disease-resistant; strong, bushy, medium growth; int. by Gandy's Roses, 1998

Jilly Cooper F, w, LeGrice; flowers cream, dbl., hybrid tea form, borne in clusters, moderate fragrance; free-flowering; vigorous, short growth; int. by Bill LeGrice Roses, 1998

Jilly Jewel Min, mp, 2003, Benardella, Frank; flowers light pink, flushed darker, reverse soft pink, medium, dbl., borne mostly solitary, moderate fragrance; foliage medium size, dark green, semi-glossy; prickles medium, thin, slight downward angle, moderate; growth upright, spreading, bushy, tall (30 in.); cutting, garden decorative; [Figurine × Kristen]; int. in 1996

Jim Bowie S, dp, Williams, J. Benjamin; flowers dark pink to light pink center, 4 in., semi-dbl., borne in sprays, intense fragrance; arching growth; hardy; int. by Hortico, Inc., 1996

Jim Dandy Min, rb, 1989, Benardella, Frank A.; bud pointed; flowers medium red, reverse yellow flushed red, aging lighter, medium, high-centered, slight spicy fragrance; foliage medium size, medium green, semi-glossy; no prickles; upright, bushy, medium growth; no fruit; PP7166; [Rise 'n' Shine × Marina]; int. by Nor'East Min. Roses, 1989; AOE, ARS, 1989

Jim Ingall HT, mr, 1998, Thomas, D.; flowers medium red, 4 in., very dbl., borne singly; foliage medium size, dark green, semi-glossy; prickles moderate; bushy, upright, 120-150 cm. growth; [Debbie Thomas × Maria Theresa]

Jim Larkin F, dr, 2000, Bossom, Bill; flowers small, semi-dbl., hydrangea-shaped, borne in large clusters, no fragrance; foliage medium size, medium green, glossy; few prickles; bushy, low (2½ ft) growth; [Red Ace × Ballerina]; int. in 2000

Jim Lounsbery S, or, 1995, Fleming, Joyce L.; flowers medium, 5-7 petals, borne in sprays of 5-25; foliage medium size, medium green, matte; upright (120-150 cm.), bushy growth; [Liverpool Echo × *R. virginiana*]; int. by Hortico Roses, 1994

Jim Pugh HT, pb, 2001, Horner, Calvin L.; flowers medium pink with yellow reverse, medium, dbl., borne mostly solitary, slight fragrance; foliage medium size, dark green, glossy; prickles medium, curved, brown, moderate; growth compact, medium (1 m.); garden decorative; [Silver Jubilee × Garden Party]; int. by Warley Rose Gardens, 2004

Jim Todd HT, rb, 1940, Mallerin, C.; flowers nasturtium-red, reverse touched yellow, large, semi-dbl., cupped; very vigorous, bushy growth; int. by A. Meilland

Jiminy Cricket F, op, 1955, Boerner; bud ovoid; flowers coral-orange to pink-coral, 3-4 in., 28 petals, cupped, borne in clusters, moderate rose geranium fragrance; foliage glossy; vigorous, upright, bushy growth; PP1346; [Goldilocks × Geranium Red]; int. by J&P, 1954

Jimmy Min, ob, Chandrakant; flowers lustrous orange with white base, compact, full; free-flowering; [sport of Don Don]; int. in 1993

Jimmy Greaves HT, m, 1971, Gandy, Douglas L.; flowers red-purple, reverse silver, 5 in., 55 petals, high-centered; foliage large; erect, bushy growth; [Dorothy Peach × Prima Ballerina]

Jimmy Savile F, ob, 1988, Pearce, C.A.; flowers coppery-orange, aging lighter, medium, 25-30 petals, cupped, loose, borne usually singly, moderate fruity fragrance; foliage medium size, medium green, matte; bushy, low growth; [seedling × seedling]; int. by Rearsby Roses, Ltd., 1988

Jindrich Hanus Böhm HRg, mr, 1937, Böhm; flowers large, full

Jingle Bells Min, dr, 1998, Zary, Dr. Keith W.; bud short, pointed ovoid; flowers dark red, light red reverse, 2 in., 30 petals, high-centered, borne in clusters, slight fragrance; recurrent; foliage medium size, dark green, semi-glossy; prickles moderate, short, straight; stems short, strong; bushy, medium (2 ft.) growth; border; PP9325; [seedling × seedling]; int. by Bear Creek Gardens, Inc., 1997; AOE, ARS, 1995

Jingles F, mp, 1956, Boerner; bud ovoid; flowers pink overcast deep rose-pink, to open, 2½-3 in., 35-40 petals, cupped, moderate fragrance; foliage leathery, glossy; vigorous, upright, bushy growth; PP1570; [Goldilocks × Garnette]; int. by J&P

Jisraela Amira HT, Nevo, Motke; int. in 1980

Jitka F, yb, Urban, J.

Jitka F, Strnad

Jitrenka HWich, lp, 1933, Mikes-Böhm, J.; flowers rich pink, fading to pale pink, white at base of petals, 4 cm., semi-dbl., borne in medium clusters

Jitrenka Pol, dy, Urban, J.; flowers medium, semi-dbl.; int. in 1978

Jitterbug Min, ob, 1992, Warriner, William A.; flowers orange, slightly lighter on reverse, heavy petal substance, large, dbl., nicely formed, open, borne in small clusters; foliage medium size, dark green, glossy; some prickles; tall (60-75 cm.), upright, bushy growth; PP8766; [Caribe × Impatient]; int. by Bear Creek Gardens, 1993

Jive LCl, mr, Poulsen; bud pointed ovoid; flowers 25 petals, open cup, borne in large clusters, slight floral fragrance; recurrent; foliage dark green, glossy; prickles few, 8 mm., hooked downward, greyed-orange; bushy (150-200 cm.) growth; PP15411; [seedling × Poulket]; int. by Poulsen Roser, 2003; Gold Medal, Buenos Aires, 2006

Jkvr D. Baroness von Ittersum – See **Baronesse von Ittersum**, HMult

Jo Min, op, 2001, Moe, Mitchie; flowers light russet, reverse orange pink, 1-1½ in., dbl., borne mostly singly, slight fragrance; foliage medium size, dark green, glossy; prickles small, hooked down, light tan, moderate; growth spreading, medium (18-24 in.), exhibition, garden; [Violet Mist × mixed yellow pollen]; repeats quickly, lots of blooms; int. by Mitchie's Roses and More, 2002

Jo-Jo Min, dy, Interplant; int. in 1988

Jo McMath F, ly, 2001, Driscoll, W.E.; flowers medium, very full, borne in small clusters, slight fragrance; foliage medium size, medium green, semi-glossy; prickles 1 cm., triangular, moderate; growth compact, medium (3-3½ ft.); garden decorative; [Anne Harkness × Robin Redbreast]; int. in 2001

Joachim du Bellay HP, mr, 1882, Moreau-Robert; flowers vermilion red, tinted flame, large, full; foliage dark green

Joachim du Bellay F, m, Sauvageot; bud globular; flowers deep lilac-pink center, pale lilac-pink to white edges, full, cupped; recurrent; moderate growth; int. by René Dessevre, 2004

Joan HMsk, ob, 1919, Pemberton; bud peach; flowers copper, semi-dbl., borne in clusters; [Trier × Perle des Jeannes]

Joan Alder HT, pb, 1950, Moss; bud long; flowers salmon-pink tinted mauve; foliage dark; very vigorous growth

Joan Anderson – See **Else Poulsen**, F

Joan Austin Min, pb, 1981, Moore, Ralph S.; bud pointed; flowers light to medium pink, white stripes, 38 petals, high-centered, borne singly, sometimes 3 or more per cluster, intense fragrance; foliage small, medium green, semi-glossy to matte; very bushy, compact growth; [Avandel × seedling]; int. by Moore Min. Roses

Joan Ball Min, mp, 1986, Robinson, Thomas, Ltd.; flowers small, 30 petals, high-centered, borne in sprays of 3-6, moderate fruity fragrance; foliage small, dark, glossy; prickles short, thin, red-brown; upright, bushy growth; [Orange Sensation × seedling]

Joan Beales S, dr, 2006, Beales, Amanda; flowers semi-dbl., borne in large clusters; foliage medium size, dark green, matte; prickles average, straight, moderate; growth upright, medium (1-1½ m.); containers, hedges; [Henry Kelsey × Souvenir du Docteur Jamain]; int. by Peter Beales Roses, 2004

Joan Bell HT, dp, 1985, Bell, John C.; flowers light crimson, large, dbl.; [sport of Portland Trailblazer]; same as parent except for color

Joan Brickhill – See **Golden Fantasie**, HT

Joan Cant HT, pb, 1929, Cant, B. R.; bud pointed; flowers salmon-pink, reverse brighter, very large, dbl.; foliage light, leathery; vigorous, bushy growth

Joan Davis HT, ab, 1927, Allen; flowers salmon-apricot shaded cerise-pink, base yellow, dbl.; [Ophelia × unknown]

Joan Elizabeth HT, yb, 1949, Fletcher; bud long, pointed; flowers golden yellow, reverse flushed pink, well-formed, 5 in., 30 petals; foliage dark, glossy; vigorous growth; int. by Tucker

Joan F. Mills HT, mr, 2000, Jellyman, J.S.; flowers medium red, reverse light red, 3 in., semi-dbl., borne in small clusters, slight fragrance; foliage medium size, dark green, glossy; few prickles; bushy, medium (2½ ft.) growth; [Minnie Pearl × seedling]

Joan Fittall HT, yb, 1946, Moss; bud long, pointed; flowers bronze and gold fading to pink, open, medium, semi-dbl.; foliage leathery; vigorous, bushy growth; [Luis Brinas × unknown]; int. by F. Mason

Joan Fontaine S, w, Clements, John K.; bud soft, flesh pink; flowers creamy white with touch of amber in center, 4½ in., 140 petals, quartered, moderate licorice fragrance; foliage deep green; growth to 4-5 ft.; int. by Heirloom Roses, 1996

Joan Frueh HT, lp, 1924, Frueh; flowers shell-pink, dbl.; [Ophelia × General-Superior Arnold Janssen]

Joan Howarth HT, pb, 1924, Bees; flowers shell-pink shaded carmine, very large, dbl.; [Lyon Rose × Mme Abel Chatenay]

Joan Knight Cl HT, dr, 1928, Knight, J.; vigorous growth

Joan Kruger S, w, Kordes; bud globular, slightly pointed; flowers white with touches of ivory and pink in the center, very full, quartered, borne in clusters, basals produce candelabras, no fragrance; growth tall and vigorous; int. in 1997

Joan Longer S, w, 1991, Williams, J. Benjamin; bud pointed; flowers blush pink opening to ivory with a hint of coral pink in center, medium, semi-dbl., cupped, borne in sprays of 5-9, moderate damask fragrance; foliage large, dark green, semi-glossy; upright, bushy, tall growth; [Queen Elizabeth × Ivory Fashion, Climbing]; int. by The Scott Arboretum of Swarthmore College, 1991

Joan Margaret Derrick Pol, dr, 1953, Derrick; flowers carmine-red, small, 15 petals; vigorous growth; [sport of Golden Salmon]

Joan Ollis HT, dp, 2000, Poole, Lionel; flowers 4½ in., full, exhibition, classic, borne mostly singly, slight fragrance; free-flowering; foliage medium size, dark red turning medium green, semi-glossy; prickles moderate; vigorous, bushy, medium (1 m.) growth; [(Selfridges × Mischief) × Gavotte]; int. by David Lister Roses, 2001

Joan Ross HP, pb, 1933, Nicolas; bud pointed; flowers blush, reverse light pink, very large, dbl.; profuse, non-recurrent bloom; vigorous growth; [Frau Karl Druschki × Paul Neyron]

Joanie F, ab, 2003, Rawlins, R.; flowers full, borne in small clusters; foliage medium size, medium green, semi-glossy; prickles triangular; growth upright, medium (36 in.); garden; [World Peace 2000 × (Laura Ford × Sharifa Asma)]

Joanna Bridge HT, yb, 1916, Hicks; flowers canary-yellow shaded strawberry, semi-dbl., borne on large trusses; vigorous growth

Joanna Elise F, w, 2005, Rawlins, R.; flowers semi-dbl., borne in large clusters, slight fragrance; foliage medium size, dark green, glossy; upright, tall (120 cm.) growth; garden; [Pretty Lady × Crazy For You]

Joanna Hill HT, ly, 1928, J.H. Hill Co.; bud long, pointed; flowers creamy yellow, base flushed orange, large, 48 petals; foliage leathery; vigorous growth;

[Mme Butterfly × Miss Amelia Gude]

Joanna Hill, Climbing Cl HT, ly, 1935, Howard Rose Co.

Joanna Lumley HT, ab, 1994, Poole, Lionel; flowers 3-3½ in., full, borne singly, slight fragrance; foliage medium size, dark green, glossy; some prickles; upright (100 cm.) growth; [Chicago Peace × Joanne]; int. by F. Haynes & Partners, 1995

Joanna Troutman HT, ob, 1929, Vestal; bud pointed; flowers orange-yellow, open, semi-dbl.; foliage bronze, glossy; [Mme Alexandre Dreux × unknown]

Joanne HT, op, 1985, Poole, Lionel; flowers medium shrimp pink, large, 43 petals, high-centered, borne singly; foliage large, dark, semi-glossy; prickles large, dark brown; medium, upright growth; hips large, globular, orange; [Courvoisier × Princesse]

Joanne S, pb, Mekdeci; flowers two-toned blush pink, borne in floriferous; growth tall; int. by Hortico, 2001

Joannes Ginet HT, pb, 1929, Gaujard; flowers white, tinted cream, edged oriental red; [sport of The Queen Alexandra Rose]

Joanne's Wedding Min, pb, 2003, Denton, James A; flowers deep pink, reverse white, medium, full, borne mostly solitary, no fragrance; foliage medium size, medium green, semi-glossy; prickles medium, down curved, dark brown, moderate; growth upright, medium (20 in.), garden decorative, exhibition; [Fairhope × Kristin]; int. by James A Denton, 2004

Joan's Desire – See **Audrey Hepburn**, HT

Joao Moreira da Silva HT, my, 1959, Moreira da Silva; [Mme Marie Curie × Dr. Manuel Alves de Castro]

Joao Pereira da Rosa HT, rb, 1936, Moreira da Silva; flowers brilliant red shading orange and yellow, large, dbl., cupped; foliage light, soft; vigorous growth; [Angèle Pernet × Mme Méha Sabatier]

Joaquin Aldrufeu HT, m, 1897, Aldrufeu; flowers garnet-purple, reverse violet to magenta, dbl.; foliage light green; moderate growth

Joaquin Mir HT, dy, 1940, Dot, Pedro; flowers golden yellow, large, dbl., cupped; foliage glossy, dark; upright growth; [Mrs Pierre S. duPont × Senora Gari]

Joaquina Munoz HT, Dot, Simon; int. in 1980

Joasine Hanet P, m, 1846, Vibert; flowers deep rose tinged with violet, 5-6 cm., dbl., quartered, moderate fragrance; heavy bloomer; very hardy; roses sold as Amanda Patenaude in the U.S. in recent years are almost certainly Joasine Hanet

Jocelyn F, r, 1970, LeGrice; flowers mahogany aging purplish-brown, 3 in., dbl.

Jocelyne Pardo – See **Jonise**, F

Jockey – See **Horrido**, F

Jodrell Bank HT, pb, 1967, Dale, F.; flowers light pink, reverse rose-pink; [sport of Charles F. Warren]

Joe Grey – See **The Abbottsford Rose**, S

Joe-Joe Min, ob, 1985, King, Gene; flowers orange-yellow, reverse yellow, 25 petals, cupped, borne singly; foliage medium size, dark, matte; prickles straight, light yellow to brown; bushy, spreading growth; [seedling × Rise 'n' Shine]; int. by AGM Miniature Roses

Joe Longthorne HT, op, 1995, Poole, Lionel; flowers orange pink, 3-3½ in., full, borne singly, intense fragrance; foliage medium size, dark green, matte; some prickles; medium (100 cm.), upright growth; [Gavotte × Pot of Gold]; int. by Battersby Roses, 1995

Joe Roscoe HT, mp, 1972, Wright & Son; flowers rose-red, 6 in., 62 petals, moderate fragrance; [Karl Herbst × Tzigane]; int. by Halsall Lane Nurs.

Joëlle HT, w, 1986, Kriloff, Michel; flowers white, aging light pink, well-formed, dbl.; foliage glossy; [seedling × seedling]; int. by Sauvageot, 1977

Joëlle Marouani S, dy, Guillot-Massad; flowers yellow with a whitish tinge on the petal tips, large, 60 petals, borne singly and in clusters, moderate fruity fragrance; foliage dark green; growth to 4 ft.; int. by Roseraies Guillot, 2001

Joe's Little Red Creeper S, mr; flowers single; groundcover; spreading growth; PPAF; int. by Certified Nurseries, 2001

Joe's Red Creeper – See **Joe's Little Red Creeper**, S single

Joey's S, ab, Poulsen; flowers apricot blend, 8-10 cm., full, slight wild rose fragrance; foliage dark; stems bushy, 40-60 cm; PP11598; int. by Poulsen Roser, 1997

Joey's Palace – See **Joey's**, S

Jofitali F, rb, 1976, DeWitte; flowers rose-bengal, center cardinal-red; PP4083; [sport of Sonia]; int. by Meilland & Cie

Jogan HT, ab, Bansal, O.P.; flowers pale apricot, dbl., high-centered; int. in 1988

Johan Ludwig Lumberg HT, dr, 1905, Björ-Lindberg; flowers dark cherry red

Johann Strauss F, pb, 1994, Meilland, Alain A.; flowers orient pink slightly suffused with aureolin yellow, 3-5 in., 100 petals, cupped, borne in clusters of 3-7, slight sweet fragrance; foliage medium size, dark green, semi-glossy; few prickles; low (50-60 cm.), bushy, compact growth; PP9998; [Flamingo × (Pink Wonder × Tip Top)]; int. as Sweet Sonata, SNC Meilland & Cie, 1993

Johanna Ofman HT, dp, 1962, Ofman; flowers carmine-pink, large, dbl.; [sport of Pink Sensation]

Johanna Röpcke – See **Johanna Röpke**, HWich

Johanna Röpke HWich, op, 1931, Tantau; bud pointed; flowers salmon-pink, resembling Ophelia but smaller, 7-9 cm., dbl., cupped, borne in small clusters, moderate fragrance; foliage dark, bronze-green; thornless; very vigorous, climbing growth; [Dorothy Perkins × Ophelia]

Johanna Sebus Cl HT, pb, 1894, Müller; flowers cherry pink with yellow at base, very large, full, strong heliotrope fragrance

Johanna Tantau Pol, w, 1928, Tantau; flowers white, center pinkish yellow, large, dbl., borne in clusters; foliage dark, leathery; bushy, dwarf growth; [Dorothy Perkins × Ophelia]

Johanna Tantau, Climbing Cl Pol, lp; flowers medium, semi-dbl.

Johanna Thuillard S, lp, Huber; flowers dbl., cupped; int. by Richard Huber AG, 2006

Johannes Boettner F, mr, 1943, Kordes; flowers light crimson, very large, dbl., high-centered, borne in clusters; vigorous, bushy, compact growth; [(Baby Chateau × unknown) × Else Poulsen]

Johannes Rau S, yb, Noack; flowers dark yellow with soft pink on outer petals, 4 in., full; free-flowering; spreading (4 × 5 ft.) growth; int. by Rosen Noack, 2002

Johannes Schultheis S, mp, Schultheis; flowers silvery rose, deeper in center, medium, dbl., cupped, borne in clusters, moderate fragrance; good repeat; foliage delicate, medium green, glossy; vigorous (5 × 5 ft.) growth; int. by Rosen von Schultheis, 2000

Johannes Wesselhöft HT, my, 1899, Welter & Hinner; bud long; flowers sulphur yellow, aging to light yellow, large, full; [Kaiserin Auguste Viktoria × (William Francis Bennett × Comtesse de Frigneuse)]

Johannes XXIII HT, w

Johannesburg Centennial HT, dy

Johannesburg Garden Club – See **Cape Cod**, S

Johannesburg Sun HT, dy, 1988, W. Kordes Söhne; flowers deep golden yellow, large, 22 petals, borne singly, moderate fragrance; foliage glossy, deep green; prickles concave, brown; tall, upright growth; [seedling × seedling]; int. by Ludwigs Roses Pty. Ltd., 1988

Johannisfeuer HT, mr, 1910, Türke; flowers red, yellow center, large, dbl., cupped; [(Princesse de Béarn × Deutschland) × *R. foetida bicolor*]

Johannisfeuer S, mr, Tantau; flowers blood red, semi-dbl., borne in sprays; foliage large, dark green; bushy, upright, strong (4½ ft.) growth; int. in 1988

Johannisröschen HSpn, ly; flowers full; good repeat; growth to 5 ft.; very winter hardy

Johanniszauber HT, dr, 1926, Tantau; bud pointed; flowers dark velvety blood-red, very dbl.; vigorous growth; [Château de Clos Vougeot × seedling]

Johasine Hanet – See **Joasine Hanet**, P

John A. Allison Gr, lp, 1974, Golik; bud ovoid; flowers large, very dbl., slight fragrance; very vigorous, upright growth; [Queen Elizabeth × Montezuma]; int. by J. Schloen, 1973

John A. Macdonald Gr, dr, Delbard

John A. Weall LCl, dr; flowers velvet red, dbl., borne in clusters, slight fragrance; foliage medium green; growth vigorous; int. in 1994

John Abrams F, op, 1977, Sanday, John; flowers vermilion and salmon, 3 in., 15 petals; [Vera Dalton × Sarabande]; int. in 1976

John Allen Sp, lp, 1944; recurrent bloom; growth to 18 in.; collected in southern Saskatchewan; a form of *R. suffulta*; int. by P.H. Wright

John Andrews HT, dr, Williams, J. Benjamin; flowers large, moderate fragrance; foliage disease-resistant; growth to 5 ft.; int. by Hortico Inc., 1997

John Boy Min, yb, 2006, Tucker, Robbie; flowers yellow with light pink edge, ¾ in., full, borne in large clusters; foliage medium green, semi-glossy; prickles ¼-½ in., straight, pointed slightly down, green to brown; growth compact, medium (to 36 in.); exhibition, cut flower, landscape; [Cal Poly × Little Tommy Tucker]; int. by Rosemania

John Bradshaw Min, dp, 1986, Harkness; flowers light rose red, 24 petals, rosette, flat, star-shaped, borne in clusters, slight fragrance; foliage small, semi-glossy; low, bushy growth; [seedling × Esther's Baby]; int. by White Rose Nurseries, Ltd., 1985

John Bright HP, mr, 1878, Paul & Son; flowers bright crimson, medium, round, globular

John Burton HWich, mp, 1903, Hoopes & Thomas; flowers very full; [*R. wichurana* × Safrano]

John C. M. Mensing HT, mp, 1924, Eveleens; flowers deep bright rose-pink, open, large, dbl.; vigorous growth; [sport of Ophelia]

John Cabot HKor, mr, 1978, Svedja, Felicitas; bud ovoid; flowers fuschia tinted red, opens flat, 2½ in., 40 petals, borne in clusters, moderate fragrance; foliage yellow-green; vigorous, upright, medium growth; [*R. × kordesii* × seedling]; int. by Canada Dept. of Agric.

John Cant S, dp, 1895, Cant, B. R.; flowers carmine-pink, small, semi-dbl.; sometimes classed as HEg

John Church F, or, 1964, McGredy, Sam IV; flowers orange-scarlet, well-formed, large, 30 petals, borne in clusters; vigorous growth; [Ma Perkins × Red Favorite]; int. by McGredy

John Clare S, dp, 1997, Austin, David; flowers deep pink to light crimson, medium, 110-130 petals, borne in small clusters; foliage medium size, dark green, semi-glossy; few prickles; upright, medium (4 ft.) growth; [Wife of Bath × seedling]; int. by David Austin Roses, 1994

John Cook HT, pb, 1917, Krüger; bud dark pink; flowers La France pink, reverse very dark, dbl., moderate fragrance; [La France × unknown]; int. by Ketten Bros

John Cramphorn F, or, Kriloff; flowers large, dbl.; int. in 1980

John Cranston M, m, 1861, Verdier, E.; flowers crimson, shaded purple, expanded, medium, dbl.; some repeat; vigorous growth

John Cronin HT, dp, 1935, Clark, A.; flowers deep pink, large, dbl., globular; vigorous growth; int. by NRS Victoria

John Crou – See **John Grow**, M

John Cuff HT, pb, 1909, Dickson, A.; flowers deep carmine pink with yellow at base of each petal, large, full

John Davis HKor, mp, 1986, Svedja, Felicitas; flowers medium pink, yellow at base, large, 40 petals, borne in clusters of up to 17, intense spicy fragrance; recurrent bloom; foliage glossy, leathery; prickles straight; trailing growth; [*R.* × *kordesii* × (Red Dawn × Suzanne)]; int. by Agriculture Canada

John Davison HT, dr, 1919, McGredy; flowers rich velvety crimson, dbl.

John Dijkstra F, dr, 1965, Buisman, G. A. H.; bud ovoid; flowers medium, semi-dbl., borne in clusters; foliage dark; [Olala × Paprika]

John Donne S, mp

John Downie HT, ob, 1921, Dobbie; flowers salmon; [sport of Lyon Rose]

John E. Sleath HT, rb, 1937, Mee; flowers carmine-red, suffused vermilion-orange; vigorous growth; int. by Beckwith

John Edward Reed HT, dy, 1950, Reed; bud long, pointed; flowers buttercup-yellow, 5½-6 in., 32 petals; vigorous, upright growth; [sport of Talisman]

John F. Kennedy HT, w, 1965, Boerner; bud ovoid, tinted greenish; flowers 5-5½ in., 48 petals, high-centered, moderate fragrance; foliage leathery; vigorous growth; PP2441; [seedling × White Queen]; int. by J&P

John Franklin S, mr, 1980, Svedja, Felicitas; bud ovoid; flowers vibrant red, large, 25 petals, borne in clusters, floriferous; foliage rounded; prickles yellow-green with purple hues; upright, bushy growth (3-4 ft.); [Lilli Marleen × seedling]; int. by Agriculture Canada

John Fraser M, rb, 1861, Lévêque; flowers bright red, shaded crimson and purple, 10-12 cm., dbl.; remontant; prickles reddish; shy growth

John Gibb F, ab, Cocker; flowers soft apricot-gold, dbl., cupped, slight fragrance; recurrent; foliage dark green, glossy; upright (2½-3 ft.) growth; int. by James Cocker & Sons, 2005

John Gould Veitch HP, mr, 1864, Lévêque; flowers brilliant red, large, full

John Greenwood F, mr, 1976, Lea; flowers bright red, 2½ in., 25 petals; foliage large, dark; vigorous, free growth; [Marlena × Fragrant Cloud]

John Grier HP, dp, 1865, Verdier, E.; flowers rose pink, reverse silver, large, full

John Grooms LCl, pb, Beales, Peter; flowers salmon pink, fading to medium pink, medium, dbl.; recurrent; relatively thornless; dense (10 ft.) growth; int. by Peter Beales Roses, 1993

John Grow M, mp, 1859, Laffay, M.; flowers violet crimson red, shaded deep purple, large, full

John H. Ellis HT, dp, 1948, McGredy; flowers deep rose-pink, well-formed, large, 48 petals; free, bushy growth

John Hackling Min, mr, 2001, Jellyman, J.S.; flowers variable red and white striping, 2 in., single, borne in small clusters; foliage small, dark green, glossy; prickles 6 mm., curved, few; growth compact, medium (10 in.); bedding, containers; [Imbroglio × Beverley Stoop]

John Harris HT, pb, Dawson; int. in 1995

John Hart HT, mp, 1922, Hicks; flowers cherry-pink, dbl.

John Henry HT, mr, 1925, Beckwith; bud rosy scarlet; flowers rich pink

John Hopper HP, pb, 1862, Ward; flowers bright rose edged lilac, center carmine, large, 70 petals, semi-globular, intense fragrance; occasionally recurrent bloom; vigorous, upright, bushy growth; [Jules Margottin × Mme Vidot]

John Hughes F, ab, 1987, Sanday, John; flowers soft apricot, medium, 6-14 petals, slight fragrance; foliage medium size, dark green, glossy; bushy growth; [City of Gloucester × Bristol Post]; int. in 1986

John Jambor Min, m, 2005, Jalbert, Brad; flowers full, borne mostly solitary, slight fragrance; foliage medium size, medium green, semi-glossy; prickles small, hooked, green, numerous; growth upright, medium (14 in.); [seedling × rainbows end]; petals turn pink at the edges in cool weather; int. in 2005

John-John F, my, 1999, Carruth, Tom; flowers bright yellow, 3-3½ in., dbl., borne in small clusters; foliage medium size, light green, dull; prickles moderate; upright, bushy, medium (3-4 ft.) growth; PP13106; [(seedling × Sunsprite) × (Old Master × Texas)]; int. by Weeks Roses, 2000

John Keats – See **Colette**, LCl

John Kemp HWich, w

John Keynes HP, dr, 1864, Verdier, E.; flowers red shaded maroon, 48 petals, intense fragrance; vigorous growth

John Kidman HT, my, 1969, Fankhauser; bud ovoid; flowers lemon-yellow, very large, dbl., camellia-like; foliage leathery; vigorous, tall, compact growth; [Radar × Allgold]

John Laing HP, dr, 1872, Verdier; flowers velvety crimson-maroon, small to medium, dbl.

John Lawrence F, my, 1991, Bracegirdle, Derek T.; bud pointed; flowers canary yellow, fading as it ages, medium, 18 petals, flat, borne in sprays of 5-7, moderate spicy fragrance; foliage medium size, glossy; medium, upright growth; [seedling × Sunsprite]; int. by D. T. Bracegirdle, 1990

John Leese – See **Peach Surprise**, HT

John McCarthy Min, lp, 2003, McCarthy, John; flowers light pink, reverse medium pink, 6 cm., dbl., borne mostly solitary, no fragrance; foliage medium size, dark green, glossy, with ruffled edges; prickles 7 mm., triangular, numerous; growth upright, bushy, medium (20 in.); garden decorative; [Savoy Hotel × Polar Star]; int. by Battersby Roses, 1999

John McNabb HRg, mp, 1932, Skinner; flowers dbl.; profuse midseason bloom, sometimes continuing later; [*R. rugosa kamtchatica* × *R. beggeriana*]

John Moore HT, yb, 1939, Gaujard; flowers buff shaded gold, well-shaped, very large, 47 petals, high-centered; foliage dark

John Morley HT, dp, 1945, Duehrsen; bud long, pointed; flowers glowing pink, very large, dbl., high-centered; foliage dark, leathery; vigorous, bushy growth; [Joanna Hill × J.C. Thornton]; int. by California Roses

John Owen Min, yb, 2004, Jellyman, J.S.; flowers yellow-cream, reverse pink, medium, dbl., borne in small clusters; foliage medium size, medium green, semi-glossy; prickles 5-6 mm., curved; growth upright, compact, medium (30-38 cm.); containers; patio; [Cider Cup × (Ibroglio × Beverley Stoop)]

John-Paul II HT, ob, 1985, J&P; bud blunt top; flowers dbl., 35-40 petals, borne mostly singly, no fragrance; recurrent; foliage medium size, dark, semi-glossy, resistant to powdery mildew; prickles numerous, hooked downward; upright growth; PP5639; [Apricot Parfait × Futura]; int. by McConnell Nurs., Inc., 1984

John Phillip Sousa S, rb

John Ruskin HT, mp, 1903, Dickson, A.; flowers bright rosy carmine, very large, full, moderate fragrance

John Ruskin – See **Ruskin**, HRg

John Russell HT, dr, 1924, Dobbie; flowers glowing crimson flushed deeper, well-shaped, large, very dbl.; vigorous growth; Gold Medal, Bagatelle, 1924

John Russell, Climbing Cl HT, dr, 1930, Ketten Bros.

John S. Armstrong Gr, dr, 1961, Swim, H.C.; bud ovoid to urn-shaped; flowers 3½-4 in., 40 petals, high-centered, slight fragrance; foliage leathery, semi-glossy, dark; tall, bushy growth; PP2056; [Charlotte Armstrong × seedling]; int. by Armstrong Nursery, 1961

John S. Bloomfield HT, ab, 1964, Fankhauser; bud ovoid; flowers deep apricot flushed pink, open, large, dbl.; compact growth; [Ma Perkins × Burnaby]

John Saul HP, mr, 1878, Ducher; flowers red, reverse carmine, very full, spherical

John Snowball HT, w

John Square Cl HT, dy, 1937, Square; flowers sunflower-yellow, center deeper, very large, dbl., cupped; foliage glossy, dark; vigorous, climbing (6-8 ft in season) growth; [sport of Souv. de Claudius Pernet]

John Stuart Mill HP, mr, 1875, Turner; flowers rosy crimson, large, dbl.; [Beauty of Waltham × unknown]

John Wallace Pol, dr, 1941, Kluis; flowers deep red, open, large, dbl.; foliage large, leathery, glossy; bushy growth; [sport of Marianne Kluis Superior]; int. by Klyn

John Waterer HT, dr, 1970, McGredy, Sam IV; flowers 4 in., 44 petals, high-centered, moderate fragrance; [King of Hearts × Hanne]; int. by McGredy

John Weitch – See **John Gould Veitch**, HP

John Willan – See **Princess Charming**, HT

Johnnie Walker HT, ab, 1983, Fryers Nursery, Ltd.; flowers buff apricot, well-formed, large, 20 petals; foliage medium size, medium green, matte; vigorous, bushy growth; [Sunblest × (Arthur Bell × Belle Blonde)]

Johnny Becnel HT, ob, 2004, Edwards, Eddie; flowers coral and white, 5 in., full, high-centered, borne mostly solitary, intense fragrance; foliage medium size, dark green, glossy; growth upright, medium (5-6 ft.); exhibition; [Gemini × Crystalline]; int. by Johnny Becnel Show Roses

John's Rose S, ob, 1995, Mekdeci, John; flowers brilliant orange to fluorescent pink, 3-3½ in., dbl., borne in small clusters, no fragrance; free-flowering; foliage large, dark green, glossy; some prickles; tall, upright growth; [((Tropicana × Queen of the Lakes) × seedling) × Golden Wings]; int. by Hortico Roses, 1995

Joia F, yb, 1962, Moreira da Silva; flowers yellow shaded carmine; [seedling × Virgo]

Joie – See **Joie de Vivre**, HT

Joie de Vivre HT, pb, 1949, Gaujard; flowers pink, base gold, well-shaped, very large, dbl.; foliage bronze green; moderately vigorous growth; int. by Wheatcroft Bros.

Joker HT, ob, 1958, Lens; flowers orange-red, reverse lighter; foliage glossy; [Peace × Karl Herbst]

Jolanda HT, dp, 1959, Malandrone; bud long, pointed; flowers rose, cupped; vigorous, upright, bushy growth

Jolanda – See **Jolanda Hit**, MinFl

Jolanda d'Aragon – See **Yolande d'Aragon**, P

Jolanda Hit MinFl, w, Olesen; bud short, pointed ovoid; flowers white with green shading, 5 cm., 75-85 petals, borne mostly singly, no fragrance; recurrent; foliage dark green, semi-glossy; prickles numerous, 4 mm., linear; narrow, bushy (20-40 cm.) growth; PP14742; [Patricia Kordana × seedling]; container plant; int. by Poulsen Roser, 2002

Jolene Min, w, Buchanan; [sport of Pink Petticoat]

Joli Coeur F, dr, 1963, Gaujard; bud globular; flowers dark crimson, medium, dbl.; foliage dark; symmetrical growth; [Rose Gaujard × (seedling × Josephine Bruce)]

Joli Mome HT, Ducher, Ch.; int. in 1969

Joli Tambour – See **Gebrüder Grimm**, F

Jolie Comtoise F, op, Sauvageot; flowers shrimp-pink and salmon, large, very dbl., borne in small clusters; int. by Sauvageto, 1973

Jolie Demoiselle Pol, lp

Jolie Madame HT, or, 1959, Meilland, F.; bud ovoid; flowers vermilion-red, 4-4½ in., 65 petals, cupped, slight fragrance; foliage leathery, glossy; vigorous, upright, bushy growth; PP1700; [(Independence × Happiness) × Better Times]; int. by URS, 1958

Jolie Môme – See **Sunset Celebration**, HT

Jolie Princesse F, pb, 1955, Gaujard; flowers pink, shaded ochre, dbl., borne in large trusses, moderate fragrance; foliage leathery, bronze; very vigorous, bushy growth; [Peace × Independence]

Jolie Rose HT, Mondial Roses; int. in 1967

Jolie Rose Pierret – See **Agathe Incarnata**, HGal

Jolisquare S, mp, Adam; int. in 1998

Jollity Jane Pol, m, 1993, Jobson, Daniel J.; flowers lilac-cream blend, medium, very dbl., borne in large clusters, slight fragrance; foliage small, medium green, glossy; few prickles; tall, upright, bushy growth; [Valerie Jeanne × Yesterday]; int. by Jobson, 1993

Jolly Pol, m, 1934, Leenders, M.; flowers carmine-purple, center white, single, borne in clusters; foliage sparse, dark; dwarf growth; [Miss Edith Cavell × Tip-Top]

Jolly – See **Lustige**, HT

Jolly HT, ab; int. by Greenbelt Farms

Jolly Cupido Min, rb, deRuiter; PP9734; int. in 1992

Jolly Dance HKor, ob; [sport of Leverkusen]; possibly from Kordes

Jolly Good F, pb, 1975, Fuller; bud ovoid; flowers salmon-pink, large, 55 petals, moderate fragrance; foliage glossy, dark leathery; bushy, compact growth; [Cupid's Charm × Lucky Piece]; int. by Wyant, 1973

Jolly Good MinFl, op, 2000, Lens, Louis; flowers orange pink, reverse lighter, 3-4 cm., dbl., borne in small clusters, moderate fragrance; foliage medium size, medium green, matte; few prickles; growth bushy, medium (35 cm.); [(Little Angel × Elizabeth of Glamis) × Pernille Poulsen]; int. by Louis Lens, 1991

Jolly Joker F, w

Jolly Roger F, or, 1973, Armstrong, D.L.; bud ovoid, pointed; flowers bright reddish-orange, medium, semi-dbl., cupped; foliage wrinkled; growth moderate, bushy; [Spartan × Angelique]; int. by Armstrong Nursery

Joly Rose Primaplant HT, mp, Vlaeminck; flowers medium to large, dbl.; int. in 1963

Jonathan F, mr, Asami; int. in 1988

Jone Asher MinFl, Pearce, C.A.; int. in 1987

Jonetsu HT, mr, 1978, Suzuki, Seizo; bud pointed; flowers dark scarlet, 4½-6 in., 30-35 petals, high-centered; foliage dark, leathery; vigorous growth; [(Kagayaki × Prima Ballerina) × Kagayaki]; int. by Keisei Rose Nursery

Jonise F, dy, Barni; flowers yellow-ocher, outer petals turning lighter, dbl., borne in clusters, moderate fragrance; foliage glossy; vigorous, bushy (3 ft.) growth

Jonkheer G. Sandberg HT, my, 1936, Buisman, G. A. H.; flowers clear yellow, dbl.; foliage dark, leathery; vigorous growth; [Christine × Mrs Wemyss Quin]; int. by Armstrong Nursery, 1941

Jonkheer J. L. Mock HT, pb, 1910, Leenders, M.; bud pointed; flowers silvery rose-white, reverse carmine-pink, bluing slightly, dbl., high-centered; foliage dark, leathery; vigorous growth; [((Mme Caroline Testout × Mme Abel Chatenay) × Farbenkonigin) × unknown]; Gold Medal, Bagatelle, 1911

Jonkheer J. L. Mock, Climbing Cl HT, pb, 1923, Timmermans; flowers whitish pink, large, full; [sport of Johkheer J. L. Mock]

Jonkheer Mr G. Ruys de Beerenbrouck HT, ob, 1919, Timmermans; flowers pure orange-yellow fading clear yellow, large, dbl.; vigorous growth; [Mme Mélanie Soupert × Joseph Hill]

Jonkheer Ruis de Beerenbrouck – See **Jonkheer Mr G. Ruys de Beerenbrouck**, HT

Jonquille F, dy, 1982, Delbard, Georges; flowers large, 35 petals; foliage medium size, medium green, matte; bushy growth; [(Peace × Marcelle Gret) × (Velizy × Jean de la Lune)]; int. by Pepinieres et Roseraies

Jorianda HT, m, Erica Intl.; flowers pinkish-mauve to crimson red, dbl., moderate fragrance; recurrent

Jorja Julianna HT, ob, 2003, Webster, Robert; flowers pale orange, 4 in., full, borne mostly solitary; foliage medium size, medium green, glossy; prickles 6 mm., slightly hooked; growth bushy, medium (30 in.); bedding; [(Indian Summer × ((Matangi × Memorium) × Gold Bunny)) × ((Daily Sketch × Eye Paint) × Freedom)]; int. in 2004

Joro HT, ob, RvS-Melle; flowers pastel orange, dbl., high-centered; int. in 1979

José Bonifacio T, pb, 1910, Amaury Fonseca; flowers salmon with rose, medium, full

José Carreras HT, w, Olesen, Pernille & Mogens N.; flowers 15 cm., 25 petals, borne one to a stem, slight fragrance; growth bushy, 100-150 cm.; int. by Poulsen Roser, 1998; Golden Rose, Hradec Kralove, Czech Republic, 1999

José Carreras – See **Monsoon**, HT

Josef Angendohr F, dp, 1985, Angendohr, Hans-Werner; flowers deep pink; [sport of Dame de Coeur]; int. by Baumschulen Angendohr, 1982

Josef Peter HT, m, 1929, Ketten Bros.; flowers pale blush, reverse mauve-rose, dbl.; [Ruth × Frank W. Dunlop]

Josef Rothmund – See **Joseph Rothmund**, HEg

Josef Strnad HT, rb, 1932, Böhm, J.; flowers dark red, with traces of yellow, orange and rose, very large, dbl., cupped; foliage leathery, glossy, dark, bronze; very vigorous, bushy, branching growth; [Aspirant Marcel Rouyer × Toison d'Or]; int. by J&P, 1934

Josefa HT, Laperriere, J.; int. in 1982

Josefina de Salgado HT, dp, 1963, Dot, Simon; flowers bright pink, large, 30 petals; somewhat weak stems; very vigorous growth; [Queen Elizabeth × Peace]

Joseph Arles Cl HT, rb, 1964, Arles; flowers vermilion-red, reverse silvery white; foliage leathery; vigorous, climbing growth; [Aloha × Gabychette]; int. by Roses-France

Joseph Baud HT, yb, 1919, Gillot, F.; flowers golden yellow and orange-yellow, very large, dbl., intense fragrance; [Rayon d'Or × seedling]

Joseph Bernacchi N, w, 1878, Ducher; flowers cream white with yellow tints, slightly pink at center, full; very remontant

Joseph Billard HWich, mr, 1906, Barbier; flowers carmine-red, yellow at center, reverse lighter, 7-9 cm., single, borne in small clusters, moderate musk fragrance; foliage dark green, large, glossy; [*R. wichurana* × Mme Eugène Résal]

Joseph Chappaz – See **Mons Joseph Chappaz**, HP

Joseph Courbis HT, pb, 1958, Arles; flowers carthamus-pink to orange-red, 48 petals; foliage dark, glossy; vigorous, upright growth; [Margaret McGredy × Emma Wright]; int. by Roses-France

Joseph Durand HP, m, 1863, Ledéchaux; flowers slatey dark crimson, shaded velvety violet, large, full

Joseph F. Lamb S, dr, 1989, Buck, Dr. Griffith J.; bud ovoid, pointed; flowers dark red, reverse lighter, aging darker, loose, medium, 23 petals, cupped, moderate fruity fragrance; foliage medium size, medium green, semi-glossy; prickles awl-like, small, tan toreddish brown; upright, bushy, low, winter hardy growth; hips yellow-orange; [Prairie Star × ((Dornroschen × Peace × Music Maker) × (Music Maker × Topsi))]

Joseph Fiala HP, rb, 1863, Verdier, E.; flowers large, full

Joseph Gourdeau – See **Joseph Gourdon**, B

Joseph Gourdon B, pb, 1851, Robert; flowers dark flesh pink to incarnate red, 6-7 cm., full, globular; sometimes classed as HP

Joseph Guy – See **Lafayette**, F

Joseph Guy, Climbing Cl F, dp, 1928, Nonin; flowers dark scarlet-pink; [sport of Lafayette]

Joseph Guy Pol, dp, 1930, Feldmann; flowers carmine-pink, medium, semi-dbl.

Joseph Guy Pol, mp, 1950, Westhus; flowers large, semi-dbl.

Joseph Hill HT, pb, 1903, Pernet-Ducher; bud pointed; flowers pink shaded salmon, reverse coppery pink, dbl.; [Mme Eugénie Boullet × unknown]

Joseph Klimes HT, dr, Urban, J.; flowers large, very dbl.; int. in 1985

Joseph Lamy HWich, w, 1906, Barbier; flowers porcelain white, tinted pink, large, semi-dbl.; [*R. wichurana* × Mme Laurette Messimy]

Joseph Liger HWich, yb, 1909, Barbier; bud dark pink; flowers canary-yellow, edged and washed light pink, reverse cream-white, 7-10 cm., full, borne in small clusters; foliage glossy; vigorous, climbing growth; [*R. wichurana* × Irene Watts]

Joseph Lowe HT, op; flowers salmon-pink; [sport of Mrs W.J. Grant]

Joseph Métral T, rb, 1888, Bernaix; bud ovoid; sepals reddish; flowers magenta red, aging to cherry with purple tints, petals undulate and creped, very dbl., slightly flattened

Joseph Paquet T, pb, 1905, Ketten Bros.; bud very long; flowers rose pink, with light yellow petal base, large, full, moderate fragrance; [G. Nabonnand × Margherita di Simone]

Joseph Pernet d'Annemasse HT, op, 1934, Pernet-Ducher; bud pointed; flowers salmon, dbl.; foliage glossy, dark, bronze; very vigorous growth; int. by Gaujard

Joseph Rothmund HEg, ob, 1940, Kordes; bud small, ovoid, orange-red; flowers light red with pinkish yellow, very dbl., borne in clusters; profuse, non-recurrent bloom; foliage bronze, leathery; very vigorous growth; [Joanna Hill × Magnifica]

Joseph Sauvageot HT, ob, Sauvageot; flowers luminous orange, full; int. in 1989

Joséphina HGal, lp, before 1813, possibly Savoureux; flowers spotted, medium, dbl.

Joséphine – See **Buffon**, P

Joséphine HGal, mp, before 1829, Boutigny; flowers medium, semi-dbl.

Joséphine M, dp, before 1846; flowers deep rose pink, medium, dbl., globular

Josephine Min, w, 1969, Moore, Ralph S.; flowers

white or soft pink, micro-mini, small, dbl.; foliage small, glossy; dwarf, bushy growth; [(*R. wichurana* × Carolyn Dean) × Jet Trail]; int. by Sequoia Nursery

Joséphine A, lp

Joséphine HGal, dp, before 1825, Boutigny; flowers semi-dbl.

Joséphine Baker – See **Velvet Flame**, HT

Josephine Baker, Climbing Cl HT, dr, Orard; flowers rich crimson, 4 in., intense fragrance; int. in 1983

Josephine Bruce HT, dr, 1949, Bees; flowers crimson, 5-6 in., 24 petals, slight fragrance; foliage dark; vigorous, branching growth; PP1294; [Crimson Glory × Madge Whipp]; int. by Totty, 1953

Josephine Bruce, Climbing Cl HT, dr, Ross; flowers dark crimson, large; possibly introduced about 1952; int. in 1968

Josephine Carmody S, lp, 1995, Collins, Frank E. Jr.; flowers light pink, medium sized, dbl., borne in small clusters; foliage small, dark green, glossy; numerous prickles; growth bushy, medium (36 in.); [sport of Sea Foam]

Josephine Clermont B, mp, 1857, Guillot

Joséphine de Beauharnais HP, lp, 1865, Guillot fils; flowers delicate pink, reverse silvery, very large, full

Joséphine de Salgado – See **Josefina de Salgado**, HT

Josephine Elizabeth S, m, Peden, R.; int. in 1999

Joséphine Guyet B, dr, 1873, Touvais; flowers deep red, medium, full, globular; recurrent bloom

Josephine Lédéchaux HP, ob, 1855, Lédéchaux

Josephine Maille HGal, mp, about 1825, Boutigny; flowers bright pink, large

Josephine Malton Ch, ab, about 1830, Guérin; flowers cream with apricot-orange, large, full

Joséphine Maltot – See **Mme Bravy**, T

Joséphine Marot HT, lp, 1894, Bonnaire; flowers white washed pink, large, full

Joséphine Morel Pol, dp, 1892, Alégatière; flowers carmine-pink, small, dbl.

Joséphine Parmentier HGal, mp, about 1840, Parmentier; flowers medium, full

Josephine Ritter HMult, mp, before 1900, Geschwind, R.; flowers rich pink, aging to silvery pink, 7 cm., dbl., quartered, quilled, moderate damask/musk fragrance; foliage dark green, large; numerous prickles

Josephine Spiecker HT, ob, 1939, Verschuren-Pechtold; flowers deep orange to yellow, very dbl., globular; foliage glossy, dark bronze; vigorous, bushy growth; int. by Bentley

Josephine Thomas HT, ob, 1924, H&S; flowers orange-salmon to cream-flesh, very dbl., high-centered; foliage leathery; vigorous, bushy growth; int. by Dreer

Josephine Vestal HT, lp, 1923, E.G. Hill, Co.; flowers soft pink, dbl., high-centered; very vigorous, bushy growth; [Ophelia × seedling]; int. by Vestal

Josephine Wheatcroft – See **Rosina**, Min

Joseph's Coat LCl, rb, 1964, Armstrong, D.L. & Swim, H. C.; flowers yellow and red, 3 in., 23-28 petals, borne in clusters; recurrent bloom; foliage dark, glossy; vigorous, pillar growth; PP2488; [Buccaneer × Circus]; patent issued as Cl F; int. by Armstrong Nursery, 1963; Gold Medal, Bagatelle, 1964

Josh Min, dy, 1999, Bennett, Dee; flowers 1-1½ in., full, borne singly and in small clusters, slight fragrance; foliage medium size, medium green, semi-glossy; prickles moderate; upright, bushy, medium (2-3 ft.) growth; [Futura × Rise 'n' Shine]; int. by Tiny Petals, 2000

Josh Alonso Min, op, 2006, Alonso, Peter G., Jr.; flowers orange/pink blend, reverse yellow, 2-3 in., full, high-centered, borne mostly solitary; foliage medium size, dark green, semi-glossy; prickles average, sharp, green to brown, numerous; growth upright, tall (36-48 in.); [sport of Bee's Knees]; int. in 2007

Joshua Min, pb, 1990, Moglia, Thomas; bud pointed; flowers clear, deep pink with yellow at base, reverse lighter to white, 20 petals, high-centered, slight fragrance; foliage medium size, medium green, semi-glossy; prickles hooked, small, red; long stems; upright, medium growth; fruit not observed; [Loving Touch × Rainbow's End]; int. by Gloria Dei Nursery, 1989

Joshua Bradley HT, yb, 1998, Christensen, Jack E.; flowers deep gold, bronze reverse, strong substance, 3-3½ in., dbl., borne mostly singly; foliage medium size, dark green, dull; prickles moderate, medium, hooked; upright, medium growth; [(Gingersnap × Brandy) × Caramel Creme]; int. by Armstrong Garden Centers, 1999

Josi S, ly, 2007, Pawlikowski, Martin & Elaine; flowers large, 4-5 in., very full, borne mostly solitary; foliage medium size, dark green, semi-glossy; prickles small, pointed, green, few; growth bushy, medium (4 × 4 ft.); landscape; [English Garden]; int. by Cool Roses, 2007

Josie Whitney F, yb, Harkness; flowers yellow with red edges, dbl., borne in clusters, slight fragrance; growth to 3 ft.; int. by R. Harkness & Co., 2001

Jospice F, mr, 2004, Thomas William Yates; flowers red, reverse red, medium, single, borne in small clusters; foliage medium size, dark green, matte; prickles small; growth upright, tall; [Birthday Girl × Apricot Nectar]

Josyane S, m, Lens, Louis; flowers violet-red, small, dbl.; int. in 1980

Josysigal HT, mr, 1976, Delforge; flowers large, 60 petals, cupped, intense fragrance; int. in 1975

Jour de Fête HT, w, Lens; flowers pure white with touch of pink in heart, large, full, slight fragrance; growth to 3 ft.; int. by Louis Lens SA, 1968

Jour des Pères – See **Vatertag**, Pol

Jour d'Eté HT, mr, 1964, Combe; bud very long; flowers bright red, open; vigorous growth; [Coup de Foudre × Berthe Mallerin]; int. by Vilmorin-Andrieux

Journey's End HT, ob, 1978, Gandy, Douglas L.; flowers Indian orange, pointed, 6 in., 37 petals; foliage large, glossy; vigorous, upright growth; [Doreen × Vienna Charm]

Jouvencelle HT, pb, 1978, Gaujard; flowers salmon-pink suffused red, 50 petals; foliage reddish; [Prima Ballerina × Helen Traubel]; int. in 1969

Jove F, or, 1968, Harkness; flowers scarlet, semi-dbl., borne in clusters; foliage glossy; low growth; [Vera Dalton × Paprika]

Jovita F, or, 1986, Harkness; flowers borne in large clusters, slight fragrance; foliage bright green; medium, bushy growth; [Jove × Tip Top]; int. by Hauser, 1975

Jovita Pérez HT, ob, 1929, Munné, B.; flowers coppery salmon, shaded coral, dbl., cupped; foliage soft, dark; long, strong stems; vigorous, compact growth; [Mme Butterfly × Souv. de Claudius Pernet]

Joy HT, pb, 1929, Beckwith; bud tangerine-red; flowers rose-pink suffused tangerine, base yellow, dbl., high-centered; foliage leathery; vigorous, branching growth

Joy – See **Yorokobi**, Pol

Joy F, dp, 1986, Interplant; flowers deep pink, 35 petals, borne in clusters, no fragrance; foliage medium size, medium green, semi-glossy; upright growth; [Amruda × seedling]; int. in 1985

Joy Min, mp, Olesen; int. in 1997

Joy Min, pb, 2007, Clemons, David E.; flowers white with pink edge, reverse white, 1-1½ in., dbl., borne singly and in sprays; foliage medium size, medium green, matte, disease-resistant; prickles average, angled down, bottom curved, tan, moderate; growth spreading, tall (24-28 in.); garden decoration, exhibition; [Silverhill × Kristin]; int. in 2008; AOE, ARS, 2008

Joy Bells – See **Joybells**, F

Joy Button Min, ab, Taschner; flowers soft apricot on cream yellow base, dbl., no fragrance; free-flowering; stems long, thin; neat, vigorous, medium growth; int. by Ludwig's Roses, 1993

Joy In The Morning Min, ab, 2006, Hopper, Nancy; flowers single, borne mostly solitary; foliage medium size, medium green, matte; prickles ½ in., few; growth upright, medium (15 in.); [seedling × seedling]; int. in 2006

Joy O'Brien Gr, op, 1969, Verschuren; flowers pink shaded orange-salmon, large, dbl.; foliage dark; vigorous growth; [Queen Elizabeth × seedling]; int. by Stassen

Joy of Health F, mp, Harkness; flowers soft peachy salmon; modest growth; Australian nurseries call it a HT; int. in 1996

Joy of Life – See **Maxim**, HT

Joy Owens HT, mr, 1976, McGredy, Sam IV; bud ovoid; flowers 4 in., high-centered; foliage very dark; moderate, bushy growth; [Electron × Pharaoh]; int. by McGredy Roses International, 1977

Joy Pagram HT, lp, Dawson; int. in 1995

Joy Parfait F, lp, 1966, McIlroy; [sport of Pink Parfait]

Joy Poynter HT, Matthews; int. by Matthews Nurseries, 2002

Joyance HT, mr, 1939, Grillo; flowers velvety red, 4 in., 50 petals, camellia-like; foliage leathery, dark; very vigorous, upright growth; [sport of Regina Elena]

Joybells F, mp, 1961, Robinson, H.; flowers rich pink, large, 30 petals, camellia-like, borne in clusters; [seedling × Fashion]

Joybells HT, ab, Kordes; flowers cream apricot with greenish guard petals, full, high-centered, no fragrance; free-flowering; healthy, vigorous, medium growth; int. in 1988

Joyce HT, dr, 1953, Cant, F.; flowers dark velvety crimson, pointed, medium, 24 petals; foliage leathery; vigorous growth; [George Dickson × Étoile de Hollande]

Joyce MinFl, lp, Williams, J.B.; flowers Ivory pink., single, borne in masses of blooms, moderate fragrance; int. by Hortico, 2001

Joyce HT, dy; int. by Jan Spek Rozen, 2001

Joyce Barden S, ly, 1999, Barden, Paul; flowers 4 in., full, borne in small clusters, intense fragrance; foliage medium size, dark green, dull, light green when new; moderate, outer shoots mostly thornless; upright, spreading, medium (5-6 ft.) growth; [Sweet Juliet × Souv de la Malmaison]

Joyce Claire F, dp, 1965, Tonkin; bud globular; flowers deep pink, open, small, dbl.; foliage glossy; very vigorous, upright growth; [Queen Elizabeth × unknown]

Joyce Edmonds F, op, Nieuwesteeg, J.; flowers large, dbl., cupped, borne in small clusters, no fragrance; recurrent; int. in 1992

Joyce Fairey Cl HT, dp, 1929, Clark, A.; flowers soft red; pillar growth; int. by NRS Victoria

Joyce Hunt ; [Scented Bouquet × Stella]

Joyce Lomax – See **Satan**, HT

Joyce Longley HT, ob, 1970, Court; flowers in sunset shades; [sport of Opera]; int. by Thanet Roses, 1958

Joyce Mary HT, pb, 2003, Heath, William; flowers pink blush, outer petals creamy white, reverse cream, 4-5 in., full, borne mostly solitary; foliage medium size, medium green, semi-glossy; prickles medium, triangular, light, moderate; growth upright, medium; garden, exhibition; [Silver Jubilee × Pristine]; int. by C&J Jones - Golden Fields Nursery, 2004

Joyce Northfield HT, ob, 1977, Northfield; flowers deep orange, high-pointed, 3-4 in., dbl.; foliage dark; vigorous, upright growth; [Fred Gibson × Vienna Charm]

Joyce Riley F, ob, 1979, Wood; bud well formed; flowers vermilion, yellow-salmon, 2½ in., 25 petals, slight fragrance; foliage dark, leathery; vigorous, upright growth; [Paddy McGredy × Arthur Bell]

Joyce Robinson HT, op, 1945, Selwood; flowers peach-pink, high-centered; foliage dark, leathery; vigorous, bushy growth; [sport of Rose Berkley]; int. by Rosecraft Nursery

Joyce's Rose HT, pb, Johnstone; int. in 2004

Joycie Min, ob, 1988, Moore, Ralph S.; flowers orange-apricot, reverse lighter, small, dbl., high-centered, borne singly or in small clusters, moderate fruity fragrance; foliage small, medium green, semi-glossy; prickles slender, small, brown; bushy, medium growth; hips globular, orange; PP7055; [(Little Darling × Yellow Magic) × Gold Badge]; int. by Sequoia Nursery

Joyena Pillar LCl, m, 1969, Mason, P.G.; flowers spirea-red, reverse Tyrian purple, high-centered, borne in small clusters, moderate fragrance; foliage dark, bronze, leathery; vigorous growth; [Blossomtime × unknown]; int. by Mason, 1964

Joyeux Anniversaire HT, mr; int. by Pépinières de la Saulaie, 2005

Joyeux Noël HT, or, 1960, Delbard-Chabert; bud long, pointed; flowers well-formed, medium, 30-35 petals; foliage bronze, leathery; vigorous, bushy growth; [(Floradora × Independence) × (La Vaudoise × Léonce Colombier)]

Joyful HT, pb, 1931, Vestal; bud pointed; flowers pink, reverse streaked red, base red and orange; vigorous growth

Joyful Jubilee S, dp; flowers strong pink, small, dbl., rosette, borne in clusters; free-flowering; foliage shiny, dark green; fast-growing, groundcover (24 × 36 in.) growth; int. by Northwest Horticulture, 2005

Joyful Singer S, mr, Clements, John; flowers scarlet red, 3 in., 30 petals, borne in clusters of 6-8 blooms; growth large shrub or low climber; int. by Heirloom Roses, 2002

Joyfulness F, ab, 1965, Tantau, M.; flowers dbl, borne in clusters; foliage large, dark green, glossy; int. by Wheatcroft Bros., 1963

Joyfulness HT, ab, 1985, Tantau, Math.; flowers apricot and orange blend, large, 35 petals, borne singly and in clusters; foliage large, dark, glossy

Joyfulness, Climbing Cl HT, ob, Ruston, D.; flowers large, high-centered, moderate fragrance; recurrent; growth strong; [sport of Joyfulness]; int. in 1988

Joyous F, pb, 1939, deRuiter; flowers rose-pink, reverse slightly darker; vigorous, bushy growth; [sport of Else Poulsen]; int. by J&P

Joyous Cavalier HT, mr, 1926, Archer; bud pointed; flowers brilliant red, open, large, 25-30 petals; foliage dark, glossy; very vigorous growth; [Red-Letter Day × Clarice Goodacre]

Joyous Moment Min, ab, J&P

Joyride Min, mp, 1995, Rennie, Bruce F.; flowers 2¾ in., very dbl., borne mostly singly; foliage large, medium green, semi-glossy; few prickles; tall (24 in.), upright growth; [seedling × Innocent Blush]; int. by Rennie Roses International, 1994

Juan Maragall HT, mr, 1960, Dot, Simon; flowers bright strawberry-red, large, 35 petals; long, strong stems; vigorous, compact growth; [Chrysler Imperial × Buccaneer]

Juan Pich HT, m, 1921, Leenders, M.; flowers purplish wine-red, dbl.

Juan Quevedo HT, ly, 1921, Leenders, M.; flowers cream-yellow, dbl.; [Entente Cordiale × My Maryland]

Juana de Darder HT, yb, 1947, Munné, M.; flowers deep yellow shaded salmon, cupped; foliage bright green; strong stems; vigorous growth; [Souv. de Claudius Pernet × (Sensation × Souv. de Claudius Pernet)]

Juane Adam F, my, Adam, M.; int. in 1997

Juanita HGal, pb, 1836, Vibert; flowers pink edged paler, medium, dbl.

Juanita C, pb, 1855, Robert; flowers pink spotted white, 5-7 cm.

Jubilaire de Masaryk – See **Masarykova Jubilejni**, HT

Jubilant F, lp, 1967, Dickson, A.; flowers flesh pink, 2½ in., borne in clusters; foliage glossy; [Dearest × Circus]

Jubilation F, lp, 1995, J&P

Jubilation F, or; int. by Certified Roses, 2006

Jubiläumsrose HT, w, 1910, Schmidt, I. C.; flowers creamy white, large, semi-dbl.

Jubiläumsrose HFt, mp, 1929, Schmidt, I. C.; flowers large, dbl.

Jubilé du Prince de Monaco – See **Cherry Parfait**, Gr

Jubilé Loubert HMult, mp, Loubert; flowers semi-dbl., borne in large clusters, slight fragrance; vigorous, tall (7-10 ft.) growth; int. by Roses Loubert, 1998

Jubilee HP, m, 1897, Walsh; flowers purple, shaded maroon, large, dbl.; some recurrent bloom; moderate growth; [Victor Hugo × Prince Camille de Rohan]

Jubilee HT, w, 1930, Allen; bud pointed; flowers cream, tinged salmon-pink and Indian yellow, center coral-pink, dbl., high-centered; vigorous growth; [Paul's Lemon Pillar × Aspirant Marcel Rouyer]

Jubilee – See **Masarykova Jubilejni**, HT

Jubilee F, ab, Olesen; bud pointed ovoid; flowers apricot, 5 cm., 55-60 petals, cupped, borne in corymbs, slight fruity fragrance; recurrent; foliage dark green, glossy; prickles moderate, hooked downward; bushy, upright (5 ft.) growth; PP16552; [Atlantis Palace × seedling]; int. by Poulsen Roser, 2004

Jubilee HRg, m; flowers deep purplish-red, 3 in., single, borne mostly singly; recurrent; foliage dark green, glossy, disease-resistant; vigorous (4-5 ft.) growth; hips large, round, red; imported from Russia

Jubilee 150 – See **Pigalle**, F

Jubilee Celebration F, pb, 1977, Smith, E.; flowers pink shaded salmon, 4 in., 20 petals; foliage matte, green; growth moderate; [Elizabeth of Glamis × Prima Ballerina]; int. by Wheatcroft, 1977

Jubilee Celebration S, pb, 2004; flowers pink blend & light yellow, reverse pink blend, 8-9 cm., very full, borne in small clusters, intense fruity fragrance; foliage medium size, dark green, semi-glossy; prickles medium, deeply concave; growth bushy, broad, vigorous (120 cm.); garden decorative; [Ausgold × seedling (medium yellow English-type shrub)]; int. by David Austin Roses, Ltd., 2002; Certificate of Merit, Adelaide, 2006

Jubilee Sunset Min, ob, 1991, Taylor, Pete & Kay; flowers bright vivid orange, yellow eye, reverse creamy yellow, bright yellow stamens, large, dbl., borne mostly singly, slight fragrance; foliage medium size, medium green, semi-glossy; some prickles; low (40 cm.), upright, bushy growth; [Baby Katie × Poker Chip]; int. by Taylor's Roses, 1992

Jubilejnaja HT, pb, 1940, Kosteckij; flowers rose pink with dark yellow, medium, semi-dbl.

Jubilejni HT, m, Urban, J.

Jubileum 110 HT, dp, Urban, J.

Jude the Obscure S, my, 1997, Austin, David; flowers large, 55-70 petals, globular, borne singly or in small clusters, intense fragrance; foliage medium size, medium green, semi-glossy; some prickles; bushy, medium growth; PP10757; [Abraham Darby × Windrush]; int. as England's Rose, Rosen Jensen, 1995

Judi Dench – See **Red Velvet**, F

Judie Darling Cl Min, pb, 1979, Sudol, Julia; flowers marbled pink, reflexed, 1-1½ in., 45-50 petals; vigorous, climbing growth

Judit F, yb, Wagner, S.; flowers 35 petals, cupped, slight fragrance; foliage large, dark green, leathery, glossy; [(Frankfurt am Main × Maria Callas) × Dr Faust]; int. by Res. Stn. f. Fruit growing, Cluj, 1997

Judith HT, rb, 1938, LeGrice; flowers glowing cerise, reverse golden yellow, dbl., globular, intense fruity fragrance; foliage glossy, bronze; vigorous, bushy growth

Judith Ann HT, dp, 1998, Schamel. Al; flowers deep pink with medium reverse and silvery sheen, 6-7 in., 41 petals, borne singly, candelabras in summer; foliage medium size, dark green, glossy; prickles moderate; growth upright, medium (4-5 ft.); [sport of Red Devil]; int. by Edmunds Roses, 1998

Judith Black HT, dr, 1930, Clark, A.; bud pointed; flowers rich dark red flushed fiery red, dbl., globular; foliage soft; dwarf growth; int. by Hazlewood Bros.

Judith I. B. Hall HT, pb, 1953, Balcombe Nursery; flowers pink, base orange, 5 in., 32 petals; very vigorous growth; [Crimson Glory × Sterling]

Judy HT, mr, 1940, Grillo; flowers cerise-red, 4 in., 55 petals; [sport of Jewel]

Judy HT, my, Tantau; int. in 1997

Judy Finnigan HT, op, 1999, Poole, Lionel; flowers orange/peach, 4-4½ in., full, high-centered, borne in small clusters, moderate fragrance; foliage medium size, medium green, semi-glossy, very rain-resistant; almost thornless; upright, tall (4 ft.) growth; [Hazel Rose × Joe Longthorne]; int. by David Lister, Ltd., 2000

Judy Fischer Min, mp, 1968, Moore, Ralph S.; bud pointed; flowers rose-pink, small, dbl.; foliage dark, bronze, leathery; vigorous, bushy, low growth; PP3137; [Little Darling × Magic Wand]; int. by Sequoia Nursery; AOE, ARS, 1975

Judy Garland F, yb, 1977, Harkness; flowers yellow, petals edged orange-red, medium-large, 35 petals, borne singly and in small clusters; foliage semi-glossy; medium, bushy growth; [((Tropicana × Circus) × (Sabine × Circus)) × Pineapple Poll]; int. in 1978

Judy Hart HT, mp, 1959, Motose; bud ovoid; flowers 4-5 in., 30-40 petals, intense fragrance; foliage leathery; vigorous, bushy growth; PP1715; [Pink Delight × (Senator × Florex)]; int. by G.B. Hart, 1958

Judy Robertson Min, my, 1998, Warner, A.J.; flowers medium yellow, 2 in., 80 petals, high-centered, borne singly and in small clusters; foliage medium size, medium green, semi-glossy; no prickles; long, thin stems; growth upright, bushy (3 ft.); [Little Darling × Rise 'n' Shine]

Judy Shaw F, ab, 2000, Shaw, Dr. John A.; bud apricot; flowers deep apricot, reverse light apricot, 6½ cm., very full, cupped, borne in small clusters, slight fragrance; foliage medium size, medium green, semi-glossy, reddish when young; prickles moderate; upright, medium (100 cm.) growth; [Etoile de Hollande × Rise 'n' Shine]

Judy's Song HT, lp, 2007, Courage, Ray; flowers full, blooms borne mostly solitary; foliage medium size, dark green, semi-glossy; prickles medium, hooked, brown, few; growth bushy, medium (1¼ m.); garden decoration; [Aotearoa × Auckland Metro]; int. by Ross Roses, 2007

Jugoslavie HT, w, 1936, Böhm, J.; flowers large, dbl.

Juillet S, rb, Briant; int. in 1989

Jujnoberejnaia F, dr, 1955, Klimenko, V. N.; flowers velvety red, well-shaped, medium; [Independence × Vaterland]

JuJu Min, rb, 1996, Bischoff, Francis J.; flowers dark red with a little white at base, slow opening, medium, full, exhibition, borne in small clusters, no fragrance; foliage medium size, dark green, glossy; few prickles; upright, bushy, medium growth; [Little Darling × Black Jade]; int. by Kimbrew Walter Roses, 1997

Jules LCl, dr, 1997, Jerabek, Paul E.; flowers dark to medium red, velvety, 2½ in., 41 petals, borne in small clusters, moderate fragrance; foliage medium size, light green turning medium green, sem-glossy; spreading, medium growth; [seedling × seedling]

Jules Barigny HP, mr, 1886, Verdier, E.; flowers carmine red with paler reverse, large, dbl., intense fragrance; foliage oval-rounded, irregularly toothed; prickles few, straight, large, pink; growth erect

Jules Bire HP, dp, 1887, Bire; flowers carmine, shaded lilac pink, very large, full; [Général Jacqueminot × Paul Neyron]

Jules Bourgeois HP, dr, 1867, Ledéchaux; flowers velvety dark red, dbl.

Jules Bourquin T, yb, 1893, Chauvry; flowers chrome yellow, reverse tinted lilac, edges whitish, very large, full; [Gloire de Dijon × unknown]

Jules Calot HP, pb, 1866, Verdier, E.; flowers carmine, white edges, large, full

Jules Chrétien HP, mp, 1869, Damaizin; flowers large, full

Jules Chrétien HP, mr, 1878, Schwartz; flowers poppy red, tinged with purple, reverse tinted violet, large, full; foliage very large, glossy; prickles whitish; growth upright

Jules Closen HWich, dr, 1935, Opdebeeck; flowers darker and more, dbl.; [sport of Excelsa]

Jules d'Asnières Pol, w, 1900, d'Asnières

Jules Finger T, rb, 1879, Ducher, Vve.; flowers vivid red fading light red, shaded silvery, very large, dbl.; vigorous growth; [Catherine Mermet × Mme de Tartas]

Jules Gaujard HT, ob, 1928, Pernet-Ducher; flowers bright orange-red flushed carmine, very large, cupped; foliage bright green; very vigorous growth; [Jean C.N. Forestier × seedling]; int. by Gaujard

Jules Girodit HT, op, 1900, Buatois; flowers light orange-pink, large, dbl.

Jules Jamain Ch, mp; flowers small to medium, full

Jules Jürgensen B, m, 1879, Schwartz; flowers purple-crimson, large, full, moderate fragrance

Jules Lavay HP, mp, 1864, Damaizin; flowers medium carmine pink, large, full

Jules Lesourd P, mr, 1863, Robert & Moreau; flowers light red, medium, full, globular

Jules Levacher HWich, lp, 1908, Barbier; bud globular; flowers creamy light rose pink, 3-4 cm., semi-dbl.; foliage small, dark green; [*R. wichurana* × Mme Laurette Messimy]

Jules Margottin HP, mp, 1853, Margottin; flowers carmine-rose, large, 90 petals, flat, slight fragrance; occasionally recurrent; numerous prickles; vigorous growth; very hardy; [probably La Reine seedling]

Jules Margottin, Climbing Cl HP, mr, 1874, Cranston; bud round; flowers red with purple tints, 10-11 cm., dbl., flat, borne singly or in small clusters, intense fragrance; numerous prickles; [sport of Jules Margottin]

Jules Roussingihol HP, mr, 1864, de Sansal; flowers bright carmine-red, large, full; [Général Jacqueminot × unknown]

Jules Seurre HP, mr, 1869, Liabaud, I.; flowers carmine red, tinted blue, large, full; [Victor Verdier × unknown]

Jules Tabart HT, pb, 1920, Barbier; flowers silvery salmon-pink, center coppery coral-pink, dbl.; [seedling × Mme Edouard Herriot]

Jules Toussaint HT, dr, 1900, Bonnaire; flowers dark brownish red, base of petals citron yellow, reverse silvery, very large, dbl., moderate fragrance

Jules Verne HT, yb, Adam; int. in 2000

Juleschke – See **Julischka**, F

Juli de Sala Gr, or, Roses Noves Ferrer, S L; flowers 30 petals, high-centered; [FE-85143 × MT-86173]

Julia – See **Julia Renaissance**, S

Julia – See **Pascal Sevran**, HT

Julia HT, ob, Pekmez; flowers orange, apricot-silver reverse, dbl.

Julia Cl Min, ob; flowers orange with yellow base, 2 in., semi-dbl., borne singly and in clusters; foliage large; growth tall

Julia Ann Bostick Pol, pb, 1935, Bostick; flowers apple-blossom-pink, base white, small, single, cupped; dwarf growth; [sport of Ideal]

Julia Bartet HT, yb, 1920, Schwartz, A.; flowers dark canary-yellow, fading pale straw-yellow, dbl.; [Lyon Rose × Georges Schwartz]

Julia Child F, my, 2005, Carruth, Tom; flowers butter gold, 8-10 cm., full, cupped, old-fashioned, borne in small clusters, intense sweet licorice fragrance; free-flowering; foliage medium size, medium green, very glossy; prickles medium, straight; growth compact, medium (65-80 cm.); garden decoration; [(Voodoo × *R. soulieanna* derivative) × Summerwine × Top Notch]; int. by Weeks Roses, 2006; Certificate of Merit, Rose Hills, 2006

Julia Clements F, mr, 1958; flowers bright red, 3 in., single, borne in clusters; foliage dark, glossy; very vigorous growth; int. by Wheatcroft Bros., 1957

Julia Countess of Dartrey HT, pb, 1927, Hall; flowers rose pink with golden yellow, very large, dbl.

Julia Dymonier HP, lp, 1880, Gonod; flowers light pink, sometimes striped flesh pink, large, full

Julia Faye F, m, 2001, Certified Roses, Inc.; flowers lavender purple, mauve reverse, 2¾ in., dbl., borne in small clusters, moderate fragrance; foliage medium size, dark green, matte; prickles average, curved, moderate; growth compact, bushy; garden decorative; [seedling × seedling]; int. by Certified Roses Inc., 2001

Julia Ferran – See **Lady Trent**, HT

Julia Fontaine B, lp, 1879, Fontaine; flowers bright flesh pink, medium, full

Julia Mannering HEg, lp, 1895, Penzance; flowers pearly pink, yellow stamens, semi-dbl., borne along the cane, moderate fragrance; summer bloom; vigorous growth

Julia Renaissance S, lp, Olesen; flowers light pink, 10-15 cm., full, moderate fragrance; foliage dark; growth bushy, 100-150 cm.; int. by Poulsen Roser, 1996

Julia Touvais HP, lp, 1868, Touvais; flowers flesh pink, large, full

Julia, Countess of Dartrey HT, rb, 1927, Hall; bud pointed; flowers Tyrian rose, base yellow, very large, dbl., high-centered; foliage dark, leathery, glossy; very vigorous growth; int. by McGredy; Gold Medal, NRS, 1925

Juliana-Roos Pol, op, 1920, den Ouden; flowers pale salmon; [sport of Orléans Rose]

Juliane HT, r, McGredy; flowers light coffee-brown, dbl.; int. in 2000

Juliane

Julia's Kiss HT, lp, 2001, Poole, Lionel; flowers cream/pink, 5-6 in., full, high-centered, borne mostly solitary, slight fragrance; foliage large, dark green, semi-glossy; prickles medium, long, narrow, few; stems very strong, vigorous; growth upright, bushy, medium (1 m.); exhibition, bedding, borders; [(Hazel Rose × Cardiff Bay) × (Hazel Rose × Silver Jubilee)]; int. by David Lister Roses, 2003

Julia's Rose HT, r, 1978, Wisbech Plant Co.; bud long, pointed; flowers parchment and copper shades, pointed, 2½ in., 22 petals, slight fragrance; foliage reddish; upright growth; [Blue Moon × Dr. A.J. Verhage]; int. in 1980; Gold Medal, Baden-Baden, 1983

Julia's Rose, Climbing Cl HT, r, St. Kilda's; [sport of Julia's Rose]; int. in 1994

Julia's Secret HT, r, Martin; flowers amber-fawn tinged lavender-pink, moderate fragrance; free-flowering; vigorous growth; int. in 2003

Julie HT, dr, 1973, Kordes, R.; bud ovoid; flowers large, dbl., cupped, intense fragrance; foliage dark, soft; upright growth; [seedling × Red American Beauty]; int. by Kordes, 1970

Julie – See **Julie Parade**, MinFl

Julie Andrews F, op, Fryer, Gareth; flowers coral-salmon with lighter reverse, full, high-centered, moderate fragrance; recurrent; bushy (3 × 3 ft.) growth; int. in 1992

Julie Ann Min, or, 1984, Saville, F. Harmon; flowers brilliant vermillion orange, 1-1½ in., 20 petals, high-centered, borne mostly singly; foliage small, medium green, semi-glossy; prickles moderate; upright, bushy growth; PP5415; [Zorina × Poker Chip]; int. by Nor'East Min. Roses; AOE, ARS, 1984

Julie Anne Ashmore HT, yb, 1986, Owen, Fred; flowers deep yellow, suffused with pink throughout; [sport of Peace]; int. in 1985

Julie Cussons F, ob, Fryer, Gareth; flowers bright orange-salmon, dbl., slight fragrance; moderate (80 cm.) growth; int. in 1988

Julie de Fontenelle B, dp, 1855, Portemer; flowers dark carmine pink, shaded violet, full

Julie de Krüdner – See **Julie Krüdner**, P

Julie de Loynes B, lp, 1835, Desprez; flowers flesh pink, full

Julie de Mersan M, mp, 1854, Thomas; flowers rose shaded blush, striped white, full, borne in small clusters

Julie de Mersent – See **Julie de Mersan**, M

Julie Delbard F, ab, 1986, Delbard; flowers apricot with yellow and orange hues, large, 28 petals, hybrid tea, no fragrance; vigorous, bushy growth; [(Zambra × (Orange Triumph × Floradora)) × ((Orléans Rose × Goldilocks) × (Bettina × Henri Mallerin))]; int. in 1976; Gold Medal, Madrid, 1976

Julie d'Étanges HGal, m, 1834, Vibert; flowers rosy lilac, edged blush, large, dbl., cupped; erect, vigorous growth

Julie Dupont HP, mp, 1841, Dupont; flowers bright pink, center carmine, large, full

Julie Evans – See **Our Julie**, F

Julie Krüdner P, lp, 1847, Laffay; flowers pale flesh pink, medium, full

Julie Link Min, op, 2004, Moore, Ralph S.; flowers peachy pink, reverse pink, 2 in., full, borne mostly solitary, moderate fragrance; foliage medium size, medium green, semi-glossy; prickles small, straight; growth upright, bushy, tall (24-30 in.); specimen, pot, hedge, cutting; [seedling (Halo seedling) × seedling (Queen Elizabeth × striped seedling)]; int. by Sequoia Nurs., 2005

Julie Lynne Zipper S, lp, 2003, Zipper, Herbert;

flowers light pink, reverse dark pink, 2-2½ in., dbl., borne in small clusters, no fragrance; foliage small, dark green, semi-glossy, resistant to mildew; growth bushy, 3-4 ft.; [Maytime × Charmglo]; int. as Summer Fantasy, Island Roses, 1999

Julie Mansais T, w, 1834, Mansais; flowers rich creamy white, large, full

Julie Newmar HT, yb, 2003, Carruth, Tom; flowers soft gold blushing deep pink, reverse soft gold, ruffled, 12-14 cm., full, borne mostly solitary, intense fragrance; foliage medium size, light green, matte; prickles moderate, average, almost straight, light greenish brown; growth upright, slightly spreading, medium (120-150 cm.); garden decoration; PP17175; [Livin' Easy × St. Patrick]; int. by Armstrong Garden Centers, 2004

Julie Parade MinFl, lp, Poulsen; flowers light pink, 5-8 cm., dbl., moderate fragrance; foliage dark; growth bushy, 20-40 cm.; PP14941; int. by Poulsen Roser, 2001

Julie Sharp F, w, 1976, Sharp; flowers white, pink edge maturing to scarlet, large, 25-30 petals, cupped; foliage matte green; vigorous, upright growth; [sport of Evelyn Fison]

Julie Sisley B, pb; flowers bright pink, shaded lilac-violet, large, full

Julie Strahl HT, rb, 1928, Leenders Bros.; flowers nasturtium-red, passing to golden yellow, dbl.; [Lady Greenall × Gorgeous]

Julie Y HT, or, Harkness; flowers bright, non-fading, dbl., high-centered, slight fragrance; growth to 3 ft.; int. by R. Harkness & Co., 1994

Julie Youell – See **Julie Y**, HT

Julien Potin HT, ly, 1927, Pernet-Ducher; bud golden, pointed; flowers primrose-yellow, large, dbl., high-centered; foliage bright green; vigorous growth; [Souv. de Claudius Pernet × seedling]; int. by Dreer; Gold Medal, Portland, 1929

Julien Potin, Climbing Cl HT, dy, 1935, Bostick; flowers yellow, with a blush; [sport of Julien Potin]

Julien Renouard – See **Portland Rose Festival**, HT

Julienne HT, mp, 1940, Grillo; flowers silvery pink; [sport of Jewel]

Julie's Choice Min, ly, 1991, Rennie, Bruce F.; flowers small, full, borne in small clusters, slight fragrance; foliage small, medium green, glossy; bushy growth; [seedling × seedling]; originally registered as pink blend; int. by Rennie Roses International, 1991

Juliet HP, pb, 1910, Paul, W.; bud globular, golden yellow; flowers rich rosy red to deep rose, reverse old-gold, large, dbl.; occasionally recurrent bloom; foliage curiously curled; vigorous growth; [Captain Hayward × Soleil d'Or]

Juliet Ann Min, ly, Harkness; flowers primrose yellow, dbl., rosette; int. in 1990

Juliet Staunton Clark HT, w, 1933, Robichon; flowers white, center blush-white, turning white, large, very dbl.; [sport of Juliet]

Juliet Williamson Ayr, mp

Julietta HT, mp, Orard; int. in 2000

Juliette – See **La Belle Sultane**, HGal

Juliette HGal, mr, before 1828, Miellez; flowers carmine-pink at the center, striped violet pink at the edges, medium, dbl., flat; growth upright

Juliette Min, mr; flowers brilliant crimson-scarlet, 30 petals; foliage bright red in fall; vigorous (10-12 in.) growth; int. by Lamb Nursery

Juliette E. van Beuningen HT, dp, 1937, Buisman, G. A. H.; bud pointed; flowers bright pink, open, very large, semi-dbl.; foliage leathery, dark; [Dame Edith Helen × Mrs Sam McGredy]

Juliette Gréco S, dy; flowers large, very dbl., quartered, intense herbal fragrance; recurrent; medium growth; int. by Delbard, 1999

Julischka F, mr, 1974, Tantau, Math.; bud long, pointed; flowers bright red, medium, semi-dbl.; foliage glossy, bronze; int. by Horstmann; Gold Star of the South Pacific, Palmerston North, NZ, 1976

Julius Fabianics de Misefa T, mr, 1902, Geschwind, R.; flowers crimson, full

Julius Finger HT, op, 1879, Lacharme; flowers salmon pink, large, full; [Victor Verdier × Mlle de Sombreuil]

Julius Gofferje HT, pb, 1930, Schmidt, J.C.; flowers peach-pink on yellow ground, dbl.; foliage bright green; vigorous growth

Julklap S, op, 1940, Krause; flowers light salmon-pink, large, semi-dbl.

July Glory HWich, dp, 1932, Chaplin Bros.; flowers rich rose-pink, 3 cm., dbl., borne in large clusters; foliage dark green, glossy; vigorous growth

Jumpin' Jack – See **Gnome World**, F

Jumping Jack Flash Min, yb, 1992, Taylor, Franklin "Pete" & Kay; flowers yellow edged with deep pink to red, cream reverse, tipped with deep pink, large, dbl., high-centered; foliage medium size, medium green, semi-glossy; few prickles; medium (42 cm.), upright, bushy growth; [Party Girl × Poker Chip]; int. by Taylor's Roses, 1993

June HT, pb, 1937, Archer; bud pointed; flowers shell-pink, center darker, well-shaped; vigorous growth

June Aberdeen F, ob, 1977, Cocker; flowers salmon, 2½ in., 20 petals; foliage dark; [Anne Cocker × (Sabine × Circus)]

June Anne Noisette, mp, 2004, Robert Neil Rippetoe; flowers medium pink, fading to light pink, 1 in., very full, borne in small clusters, intense fragrance; foliage medium size, medium green; prickles ¼ in., sickle-shaped; growth spreading, tall (8-10 ft.); pillar, climber; [Champney's Pink Cluster × Katherine Zeimet]; int. in 2004

June Boyd HT, rb, 1924, McGredy; flowers salmon-carmine, base yellow, opening to bright peach-blossom, dbl.

June Bride Gr, w, 1957, Shepherd; bud pointed, greenish white tipped pink; flowers creamy white, 4 in., 30 petals, high-centered, borne in clusters of 3-7, moderate fragrance; foliage leathery, crinkled; vigorous, upright growth; PP1770; [(Mme Butterfly × New Dawn) × Crimson Glory]; int. by Bosley Nursery, 1957

June Bug Min, ob, 1994, Chaffin, Lauren M.; flowers bright medium orange, slightly lighter reverse, yellow base, 1½ in., full, borne mostly singly, slight fragrance; foliage medium size, dark green, semi-glossy; some prickles; medium (12 in.), bushy, compact growth; [(Prominent × Orange Honey) × Ann Moore]; int. by Pixie Treasures Min. Roses, 1994

June Flame HT, ob, 1949, Fletcher; bud small, tight; flowers bright orange-flame shaded copper; very early bloom; int. by Tucker

June Laver Min, dy, 1988, Laver, Keith G.; flowers dark yellow, aging cream, large, 20-25 petals, high-centered, borne usually singly or in small sprays, no fragrance; foliage large, dark green, matte; prickles small, short, green; bushy, medium, compact growth; hips rounded, light orange-red; PP6859; [Helmut Schmidt × Gold Mine]; int. by Springwood Roses, 1985

June Moon – See **June Morn**, LCl

June Morn LCl, rb, 1939, Nicolas; bud ovoid; flowers carmine-red, reverse touched gold, 5 in., dbl., high-centered; some recurrent bloom; vigorous, climbing (8 ft.) growth; [Mme Gregoire Staechelin × Souv. de Claudius Pernet, Climbing]; sometimes classed as HMult; int. by J&P

June Opie F, ab, 1959, Kordes; flowers apricot shaded salmon-pink, 3 in., semi-dbl., borne on trusses, slight fragrance; foliage leathery; very free, upright growth; [Masquerade × seedling]; int. by Morse, 1958

June Park HT, dp, 1959, Park; flowers rose-pink, 4½-5 in., 40 petals, intense fragrance; foliage dark; vigorous, spreading growth; [Peace × Crimson Glory]; int. by Sanday Roses, 1958; Gold Medal, NRS, 1959

June Patricia HT, lp, 1966, Lees, H.; flowers silvery pink, 3 in., dbl., moderate fragrance; foliage dark, glossy; moderate growth; [Peace × Ena Harkness]

June Time Min, lp, 1963, Moore, Ralph S.; flowers light pink, reverse darker, small, 75 petals, borne in clusters; foliage glossy; bushy, compact (10-12 in.) growth; PP2563; [(*R. wichurana* × Floradora) × ((Étoile Luisante × unknown) × (Red Ripples × Zee))]; int. by Sequoia Nursery, 1963

June Way HT, mp, 1976, Atkiss; flowers 4-5 in., 33 petals, cupped, slight fragrance; foliage glossy; spreading growth; [Pink Favorite × Chrysler Imperial]; int. by Wyant, 1977

June Wedding HT, w, 1977, Graham; bud pointed; flowers white, tinted yellow, 4 in., 27 petals, high-centered; foliage glossy, dark; upright growth; [sport of Bewitched]; int. by South Forrest Rose Nursery

June Whitfield HT, ob, Harkness, R.; flowers dbl.; int. in 1995

Juneen HT, my, 1969, Mason, P.G.; flowers high-centered, slight fragrance; compact growth; [Burnaby × Burnaby seedling]; int. by Mason, 1967

June's Delight F, w, 2000, Tucker, Dr. Kenneth; flowers full, high-centered, borne mostly singly, slight fragrance; foliage medium size, medium green, semi-glossy; few prickles; compact, medium growth; [sport of Sweet Inspiration]

June's Joy F, pb, Benardella, Frank; flowers ivory blushed pink, dbl., exhibition, borne in clusters and individual blooms, no fragrance; good repeat; stems short; compact, dense growth; int. in 2000

Junior HT, St Zila; int. in 1973

Junior Bridesmaid F, mp, 1962, Jelly; bud short, pointed; flowers sweetheart, 2 in., 35 petals, slight fragrance; foliage leathery; vigorous, upright growth; PP2446; [Stoplite × Lovelight]; int. by E.G. Hill Co., 1962

Junior Geisha F, or, Keisei

Junior Gilbert HT, or, 1954, Mallerin, C.; flowers cupped, cupped; vigorous growth; int. by EFR

Junior Miss F, pb, 1943, Duehrsen; bud well formed; flowers pink and yellow, medium, semi-dbl., high-centered, borne in clusters; foliage glossy; vigorous, bushy growth; [Joanna Hill × Heidekind]; int. by California Roses

Junior Miss – See **America's Junior Miss**, F

Junior Prom F, dr, 1962, Jelly; bud ovoid; flowers crimson, open, 1½-2 in., 30-45 petals; vigorous, upright growth; [Orange Sweetheart × Lovelight]; int. by E.G. Hill Co., 1962

Junior Van Fleet S, lp, 1923, Kemp, J.A.; flowers flesh-pink, dbl.; non-recurrent; [Dr. W. Van Fleet × Frau Karl Druschki]

Juno C, lp, before 1832; flowers blush pink, with a small center eye, large, very dbl., globular, quartered, strong fragrance; foliage bright green; arching growth; possibly synonymous with the HCh of this name from Laffay

Juno HCh, lp, 1847, Laffay, M.; flowers pale rose, very large, dbl., globular

Juno HT, mp, 1950, Swim, H.C.; bud ovoid; flowers soft

medium pink, large, 30 petals, high-centered; foliage bright, leathery, wrinkled, glossy; moderate upright, bushy growth; [Duquesa de Peñaranda × Charlotte Armstrong]; int. by Armstrong Nursery

Juno Rose – See **Petite Junon de Hollande**, C

Junon HGal, dp, before 1811, Dupont; flowers deep crimson pink, often plumed white, edges lighter, large, full, slight fragrance

Junon – See **Surpasse Tout**, HGal

Junon HT, or, 1979, Gaujard; bud full; flowers dbl., 45 petals; foliage large, brownish; bushy growth; [Tanagra × Dora]; int. in 1978

Junon Argentée – See **Petite Junon de Hollande**, C

Junonis – See **Junon**, HGal

Jupiter HP, lp, 1900, Williams, A.; [Prince Camille de Rohan × unknown]

Jupiter S, pb, GPG Bad Langensalza; flowers ivory with pale to strong pink edges, large, dbl.; recurrent; upright, arching (4 ft.) growth; int. in 1987

Jupiter HT, pb

Jupiter Sp; flowers bright pink, dbl.; foliage finely divided; dense, shrubby (3-4 ft.) growth; hips shining, black

Jupon Rose F, op, 1986, Lens, Louis; flowers light salmon pink, 28 petals, cupped, borne in clusters of 3-24, slight fragrance; foliage dark; prickles hooked, reddish-green; upright, bushy growth; [Little Angel × Pernille Poulsen]; int. in 1982

Jura – See **Berliner Luft**, F

Jurassic Pink HKor, mp

Jurie Els HT, yb, Orard; flowers yellow with pink edging as exposed to sun, dbl., high-centered, borne mostly singly, no fragrance; stems medium long; growth medium; int. by Ludwig's Roses, 2001

Just Brilliant F, yb, 2007, Ross, Andrew; flowers 8 cm., full, blooms borne in small clusters; foliage medium size, dark green, matte; prickles medium, hooked, brown, few; growth compact, medium (1¼ m.); garden decoration; [Gina Lollobrigida × Friesia]; int. by Ross Roses, 2007

Just Buddy Min, ly, 1985, King, Gene; flowers mini-flora, large, 45 petals, high-centered, borne singly; foliage medium size, light green, matte; prickles straight, light brown; medium upright, bushy growth; no hips; [New Day × Rise 'n' Shine]; int. by AGM Miniature Roses, 1986

Just Dreamy HT, yb, 1999, Perry, Astor; flowers yellow-gold, reverse apricot gold, 3½-4 in., dbl., borne mostly singly, slight fragrance; foliage medium size, medium green, semi-glossy; few prickles; upright, bushy, medium growth; [Folklore × Golden Gate]; int. by Certified Roses, 2000

Just For Fun HT, lp, 1996, Strickland, Frank A.; flowers light pink, outer petals sometimes white with inner petals lighter, 6 in., very dbl.; foliage medium size, medium green, dull; prickles moderate; very long stems, upright, medium (4-5 ft.) growth; [Secret Love × First Prize]

Just For You Min, dp, 1991, Moore, Ralph S.; bud pointed; flowers dark pink to light red, lighter reverse, aging lighter, medium, 35 petals, high-centered, borne singly or in sprays of 3-5, slight fragrance; foliage medium size, medium green, semi-glossy; bushy, medium growth; [Orangeade × Rainbow's End]; int. by Sequoia Nursery, 1991; AOE, ARS, 1991

Just Happy – See **Shine On**, Min

Just Jennie – See **Just Jenny**, Min

Just Jenny Min, ab; flowers soft peachy-apricot, dbl., moderate fragrance; int. in 1993

Just Joanna HT, m, 2000, Williams, J. Benjamin; flowers lavender pink & ivory blend, lavender pink with deep lavender reverse, 4½-5 in., very full, high-centered, borne mostly solitary, moderate fragrance; foliage large, dark green, glossy; prickles moderate; growth upright, medium (3½-4 ft.); garden, cutting, exhibition; [Kordes' Perfecta × Lady X]; int. as Lavender Lady, Hortico, 1996

Just Joey HT, ob, 1972, Cants of Colchester, Ltd.; flowers buff-orange, 5 in., 30 petals, classic, intense fragrance; foliage glossy, leathery; growth moderate; [Fragrant Cloud × Dr. A.J. Verhage]; James Mason Medal, RNRS, 1986, Hall of Fame, WFRS, 1994, Gold Medal, RNRS, 1986

Just Judy HT, lp, 1992, Poole, Lionel; flowers medium, full, borne mostly singly, slight fragrance; foliage medium size, dark green, semi-glossy; some prickles; upright growth; [Mischief × Simba]

Just Lucky HT, w, 1985, Bridges, Dennis A.; flowers well-formed, large, 35 petals, intense fragrance; foliage medium size, dark, glossy; bushy growth; [Typhoo Tea × Pascali]; int. by Bridges Roses, 1985

Just Magic Min, pb, 1990, Robinson, Thomas, Ltd.; bud rounded; flowers cream to deep pink, reverse cream tinged pink, aging often strongly, 21 petals, cupped, moderate damask fragrance; foliage small, dark green, glossy; prickles very thin, pointed, red aging brown; upright, bushy, medium growth; hips spheroid, orange; [(Parkdirektor Riggers × New Penny) × ((((Parkdirektor Riggers × New Penny) × unnamed seedling) × ((Parkdirektor Riggers × New Penny) × unnamed seedling)) × seedling)]

Just Peachy HT, op, 1997, Giles, Diann; flowers small, dbl., borne mostly singly; foliage medium size, dark green, glossy; upright, medium growth; [Vera Dalton × select pollen]; int. by Giles Rose Nursery

Just Peachy HT, pb, 2006, Ballin, Don; flowers peach pink, reverse lighter, yellow petal hinge, 3½-4 in., full, borne mostly solitary; foliage medium size, medium green, semi-glossy; prickles large, slighly curved, light green, moderate; growth upright, tall (6-7 ft.); exhibition; [sport of European Touch]; int. in 2007

Just Reward Cl HT, ob, 1994, Guest, M.M.; flowers orange, 3-3½ in., dbl., borne mostly singly; foliage medium size, medium green, glossy; some prickles; tall (6-8 ft.), upright growth; [Basildon Bond × Alexander]; int. by F. Haynes & Partners, 1994

Just Simon – See **Simply Irresistible**, HT

Just William Min, op, 1999, Driscoll, W.E.; flowers salmon pink, reverse pale rose, 2½ in., full, no fragrance; foliage medium size, light green, semi-glossy; few prickles; upright, tall (40 in.) growth; [Perestroika × Pink Petticoat]

Justa Little Goofy F, or, 1992, Rennie, Bruce F.; flowers medium, full, borne mostly singly, moderate fragrance; foliage medium size, medium green, semi-glossy; some prickles; medium, bushy growth; [seedling × seedling]; int. by Rennie Roses International

Justin HT, mr, Kordes; flowers clear red, large, dbl., exhibition, borne mostly singly, no fragrance; foliage healthy, disease-resistant; growth medium; int. by Ludwig's Roses, 1997

Justina HT, mp

Justine C, m, 1822, Vibert; flowers pale lilac-pink, medium, very dbl.

Justine B, dp, 1845, Rousseau; flowers dark pink mixed with carmine, full

Justine HT, ly, 1935, Joseph H. Hill, Co.; bud orange; flowers creamy yellow, base dark orange, reverse almost white, large, 30-35 petals; foliage dark, leathery; vigorous growth; [Joanna Hill × Sweet Adeline]

Justine S, mp, Jerabek; int. by Freedom Gardens, 2005

Justine Mee Liff Gr, mp, 2004, Jerabek, Paul; flowers light pink, reverse medium pink, 4½ in., very full, borne singly and in small clusters, moderate fragrance; foliage medium size, semi-glossy; prickles 3/16 in., straight; growth spreading, medium; [unknown × unknown]; int. by Freedom Gardens, 2005

Justine Ramet C, m, 1845, Vibert; flowers purplish-rose, medium, dbl.

Justine Silva – See **Rita Sammons**, Pol

Justino Henriques HT, yb, 1926, deFreitas; flowers yellow tinted orange, stamens carmine, dbl.; [sport of Louise Catherine Breslau]; int. by P. Guillot

Justizrat Dr Hessert HT, pb, 1919, Lambert, P.; bud carmine-red; flowers salmon-pink shaded red and yellow, dbl.; [Gen. MacArthur × Tip-Top]

Jutland F, lp, Poulsen; flowers light pink, 8-10 cm., 25 petals; foliage dark, glossy; growth bushy, 100-150 cm.; int. by Poulsen Roser, 1995

Jutlandia HWich, mp, 1913, Poulsen, D.T.; flowers dbl.; vigorous growth; [Mme Norbert Levavasseur × Dorothy Perkins]

Jutta Pol, lp, Rupprecht-Radke; flowers large, dbl.; int. in 1964

Jutta Pol, mr, Scholle, E.; flowers medium, semi-dbl.; int. in 1970

Jutul F, dp, 1983, Lundstad, Arne; flowers deep pink, small, 14 petals, cupped, borne in clusters of 7-9, slight fragrance; foliage dark, glossy; prickles curved, red-brown; vigorous growth; [New Dawn × Moulin Rouge]; int. by Agricultural University of Norway

Juwel HT, ly, 1911, Hinner, W.; flowers lemon-white, large, dbl., moderate fragrance

Juwena F, ob, Tantau; int. in 1978

Juwena F, dy, Tantau; int. by Rosen Tantau, 2003

Jwala F, or, K&S; free-flowering; strong, vigorous growth; int. by KSG Son Roses, 2003

K S G Centenary HT, yb, K&S; int. by KSG Sons Roses, 1995

K S R HT, Keisei Rose Nurseries, Inc.; int. in 1987

K. A. Viktoria – See **Kaiserin Auguste Viktoria**, HT

K. of K. – See **Kitchener of Khartoum**, HT

K. T. – See **Kev**, Min

K. T. Marshall – See **Katherine T. Marshall**, HT

Kabuki, Climbing Cl HT, my, Vidal; int. after 1968

Kabuki – See **Golden Prince**, HT

Kabuki HT, dy, Meilland

Kagaribi HT, yb, Oshima; flowers striped; int. in 1970

Kagayaki F, rb, 1973, Suzuki, Seizo; flowers brilliant scarlet and yellow, large, dbl., high-centered, slight fragrance; foliage glossy, dark; vigorous, upright growth; [((Aztec × unknown) × (Spectacular × Aztec)) × Cover Girl seedling]; int. by Keisei Rose Nursery, 1970

Kagayaku Seishin HT, my, Hiroshima; int. by Hiroshima Bara-en, 1997

Kagerou F, w, Hiroshima; flowers green-grey; int. by Hiroshima Bara-en, 2004

Kagura HT, rb, Hiroshima; int. by Hiroshima Bara-en, 1998

Kagura

Kaguya-Fuji HT, w, 2003, Matsumoto, Masayuki; flowers full, borne in large clusters; foliage medium size, dark green, glossy; few prickles; growth upright, medium (150 cm.); [seedling × seedling]

Kaguyahime HT, my, Keisei; int. by Keisei Rose Nurseries, 1998

Kaguyama HT, w, Tanaka; int. in 1974

Kaikoura Min, ob, 1978, McGredy, Sam IV; flowers orange, patio, medium, 27 petals; foliage glossy, dark; vigorous, bushy growth; [Anytime × Matangi]

Kaileen F, ob, 1991, Nakashima, Tosh; flowers bright orange, yellow reverse, medium, full, borne in small clusters, slight fragrance; foliage medium size, dark green, glossy; some prickles, light green to yellow; upright (6 ft.) growth; [sport of Marina]; int. by Bear Creek Gardens, 1992

Kaimai Sunset LCl, r, 2004, Somerfield, Rob; flowers light russet, reverse dark russet, medium, dbl., borne in small clusters, no fragrance; foliage medium size, dark green, glossy; prickles medium, slightly downfacing, few; growth bushy, tall (3 m.), climbing; [School Girl × Hot Chocolate]; int. in 2002

Kaina HT, pb, G&L; int. in 1985

Kaiser Friedrich T, pb, 1890, Drögemüller; flowers silky China pink, center golden yellow, shaded cherry red, large, full, moderate fragrance; [Gloire de Dijon × Countess of Oxford]

Kaiser Wilhelm der Siegreiche T, pb, 1889, Drögemüller; flowers exterior petals yellowish-white, interior brilliant deep yellow with carmine pink, 10 cm., very dbl., borne singly or in small clusters, moderate fragrance; [Mme Bérard × Perle des Jardins]

Kaiser Wilhelm I HP, m, 1878, Ruschpler; flowers purple/pink, large, dbl., moderate fragrance; foliage dark green, grayish-green underneath; nearly thornless

Kaiser Wilhelm II HT, mr, 1909, Welter; bud conical, long; flowers fiery red with poppy reflections, large, semi-dbl., moderate fragrance

Kaiserin Auguste Viktoria HT, w, 1891, Lambert, P.; bud long, pointed; flowers snowy white, center tinted lemon, well-formed, 100 petals, intense fragrance; foliage rich green, soft, very disease-resistant; growth moderate; [Coquette de Lyon × Lady Mary Fitzwilliam]; parentage also given as Perle des Jardins × Belle Lyonnaise

Kaiserin Auguste Viktoria, Climbing Cl HT, w, 1897, Dickson, A. (also De Voecht & De Wilde, 1898); flowers cream-white, very large, dbl.; [sport of Kaiserin Auguste Viktoria]

Kaiserin des Nordens HRg, m, 1879; flowers purple violet, large, dbl.; possibly synonymous with Taïcoun

Kaiserin Farah HT, dr, W. Kordes Söhne; flowers very large, very dbl.; int. in 1965

Kaiserin Farah – See **Imperatrice Farah**, HT

Kaiserin Friedrich T, pb, 1890, Drögemüller; flowers golden yellow on pink, large, very dbl.; [Gloire de Dijon × Perle des Jardins]

Kaiserin Goldifolia HT, w, 1909, Conard & Jones; flowers identical to Kaiserin Auguste Viktoria; foliage bright golden yellow; [sport of Kaiserin Auguste Viktoria]

Kaiserin Zita HT, lp

Kaiteri Gold ClMin, dy, Warner; flowers soft golden-yellow, fading paler, dbl.; free-flowering; moderately vigorous (6 ft.) growth; int. by Tasman Bay Roses, 2003

Kaitlyn S, dp, Williams, J.B.; flowers very deep reddish-pink, semi-dbl., globular; growth spreading; int. by Hortico, 2003

Kaitlyn Ainsley HRg, m, Baskerville, Joanne; flowers mauve-pink, large, semi-dbl., intense fragrance; recurrent; foliage medium green, disease-resistant; tidy (4 ft.) growth; [Dagmar Hastrup × Roseraie de l'Haÿ]; int. in 1998

Kaj Munk – See **Best of Friends**, HT

Kakadu S, w, Peden, R.; int. in 2000

Kakayan Pol (?), w; flowers single; int. before 1867

Kakwa HSpn, w, Wallace, John A.; flowers creamy white, moderate fragrance; some repeat; arching, open growth, much suckering; open pollination of *R. spinosissima hispida*; int. by Ag. Canada - Beaverlodge, 1973

Kala Agneta – See **Agnes und Bertha**, HMult

Kaladi HT, op, K&S; flowers salmon with yellow base and reverse, aging to deeper tones of apricot-orange-red, dbl.; int. by KSG Son Roses, 1998

Kalahari HT, op, 1971, McGredy, Sam IV; flowers salmon-pink, high-pointed, 4 in., 25 petals; foliage glossy, dark; [Uncle Walter × (Hamburger Phoenix × Danse de Feu)]

Kalavalla F, mp, 1935, Poulsen, S.; flowers dbl., borne in large clusters; vigorous growth; [Else Poulsen × seedling]

Kaleidoscope F, ob, 1970, Fryer, Gareth; flowers orange and yellow, 3 in., 28 petals, slight fragrance; foliage glossy; [Circus × Redgold]; int. by Fryer's Nursery, Ltd., 1972

Kaleidoscope S, m, 1998, Walden, John K.; flowers tan mauve blend, reverse yellow mauve blend, 3 in., full, borne in large clusters, slight fruity fragrance; foliage dark green, glossy; numerous prickles; spreading, bushy, 3½ ft. growth; hedging; PP11690; [Pink Pollyanna × Rainbow's End]; int. by Bear Creek Gardens, Inc., 1999; AARS, 1999

Kalinka – See **Pink Wonder**, F

Kalinka, Climbing – See **Pink Wonder, Climbing**, Cl F

Kalmar – See **Lazy Days**, F

Kalmia HWich, w, 1911, Walsh; flowers white, upper half of petals tinged pink, single, borne in clusters; foliage dark, glossy; vigorous, climbing growth

Kalyana HT, ob, Kasturi; flowers rich salmon with creamy yellow base and reverse, large; int. by KSG Son Roses, 1995

Kamakura HT, my, 2004, Hironaka Ohtsuki; flowers medium yellow, reverse medium yellow, 14 cm., full, borne mostly solitary; foliage medium size, medium green, semi-glossy; no prickles; growth upright, 100-150 cm.; cutting exhibition; [Kabuki × Kewai]; int. by Komaba Rose Garden, 2003

Kamaladevi Chattopadhayay HT, op, Pal, Dr. B.P.; int. in 1989

Kamalakantha HT, or, Deby's; flowers orange-red with clear, distinct white stripes; [sport of La Marseillaise]; int. in 2005

Kambala HT, my, Swane; int. in 1988

Kamchatka Rose – See ***R. amblyotis*** (Meyer)

Kamchin HT, mp, 1974, Kammeraad; flowers Neyron rose, outside rose, 4-5 in., 45 petals, cupped, slight fragrance; foliage dull, dark; vigorous growth; [sport of Carina]; int. by Meilland, 1972

Kameleon HT, yb, de Groot; Henk C. A.; flowers yellow-cream at center, greenish-hued outer petals, 10-12 cm., 42 petals, no fragrance; prickles moderate; stems long; PP15796; int. by DeRuiter, 2004

Kamelia HT, mr, Urban, J.; flowers large, dbl.; int. in 1969

Kamikazari Min, mp, Yoshida; int. in 1996

Kamion Min, or, 1988, Schoen-Jones, Helen; flowers bright orange-red, reverse matte finish, clear, golden stamens, 12 petals, high-centered; foliage large, dark green, glossy; prickles curved, small, reddish; upright, tall, sturdy growth; hips oval, large, light orange; [Starina × seedling]; int. by Justice Miniature Roses, 1988

Kammersanger Karl Terkal – See **Kammersanger Terkal**, F

Kammersanger Terkal F, ob, 1974, Tantau, Math.; bud small, globular; flowers pure orange, medium, dbl., slight fragrance; foliage glossy; dwarf, bushy growth; int. by Ahrens & Sieberz, 1971

Kammersingerin Perra S

Kamo HT, w, Keihan; int. by Keihan Gardening, 1978

Kampai HT, dr, 1985, Suzuki, Seizo; flowers deep red, 48 petals, high-centered, borne singly and in small clusters, moderate fragrance; foliage medium size, dark; upright growth; [(Yu-ai × (Happiness × American Beauty)) × Pharoah]; int. as Kanpai, Keisei Rose Nursery, 1985; Gold Medal, Rome, 1983

Kamtchatica S, dr, about 1800; sepals entire; flowers velvety purple-carmine, medium, single; hips rounded, glabrous, reddish-brown; from Siberia, discovered by Ventenat; now thought to be a hybrid of *R. davurica* × *R. rugosa*; int. as *R. rugosa kamtchatica*, ca. 1770

Kana HT, dr, 1985, Ota, Kaichiro; flowers large, 38 petals, high-centered, borne singly and in small clusters, no fragrance; foliage medium green; prickles small, slanted downward; tall, bushy growth; [Ginger Rogers × Chiyo]; int. in 1982

Kanaal F, op, RvS-Melle; int. in 1998

Kanak F, yb, Sunil Jolly; flowers pale yellow with petal edges blended pale pink; growth medium; [sport of Charisma]; int. in 1988

Kanakangi HT, ab, 1970, Pal, Dr. B.P.; bud globular; flowers gold and apricot, open, medium, semi-dbl., intense fragrance; foliage leathery; moderate, bushy, open growth; [Mme Charles Sauvage × unknown]; int. by Indian Agric. Research Inst., 1968

Kanarie HT, dy, 1919, Verschuren; flowers clear dark yellow, dbl.; [Golden Star × Melody]

Kanchani 2003 HT, my, K&S; bud pointed, ovoid; flowers non-fading yellow, well-formed, dbl.; int. by KSG Son Roses, 2003

Kanchi HT, dp, Viraraghavan, M.S.; flowers hues of magenta, cerise, and purple, lighter reverse, dbl.; int. in 1976

Kanegem F, or, 1985, Rijksstation Voor Sierplantenteelt; flowers large, 42 petals, high-centered to cupped, borne 1-7 per cluster; foliage dark, glossy; upright growth; [Ludwigshafen am Rhein × Satchmo]; int. in 1982; Gold Medal, Lyon, 1982

Kanon HT, op, Keisei; int. by Keisei Rose Nurseries, 2004

Kanpai – See **Kampai**, HT

Kansas City HT, dp, 1903, Conard & Jones

Kanten HWich, m, 1910, Barbier; flowers lilac pink

Kantha Selvon F, ob, 1999, Everitt, Derrick; flowers light orange, reverse cream yellow, 3-3½ in., full, borne singly and in small clusters, slight fragrance; foliage medium size, medium green, glossy; prickles moderate; upright, medium (2½ ft.) growth; [Pot O'Gold × (Mary Sumner × (Glenfiddich × (Arthur Bell × Maigold)))]; TGC, RNRS, 1997

Kanva HT, op, Kasturi; flowers salmon pink, large, dbl., high-centered, moderate fragrance; int. in 1974

Kanyakumari LCl, op, 2006, Viraraghavan, M.S. Viru; flowers orange salmon, reverse orange salmon, 20-25 cm., single, borne mostly solitary; prickles small, triangular, pointed downward, reddish brown, moderate; growth climbing (12 ft.); pillar, trellis. arch; [Montezuma × seedling]; int. by KSG Sons, 1979

Kapai F, or, 1976, McGredy, Sam IV; flowers large, 30 petals, intense fragrance; foliage small; low, bushy growth; [Madame Bollinger × Tombola]; int. in 1977

Kapiti F, mp, 1991, McGredy, Sam IV; flowers medium, semi-dbl., slight fragrance; foliage medium size, medium green, semi-glossy; spreading growth (to 60 cm.); [Sexy Rexy × Eyeopener]; int. by McGredy Roses International, 1992

Kara Min, mp, 1973, Moore, Ralph S.; bud long, mossy; flowers light to medium pink, micro-mini, mini-moss, small, single; foliage small, soft; vigorous, dwarf, bushy growth; [Fairy Moss × Fairy Moss]; int. by Sequoia Nursery, 1972

Kardinal HT, dr, 1934, Krause; flowers scarlet-red, sometimes tipped blackish, large, cupped; vigorous, compact, bushy growth; [(Château de Clos Vougeot × unknown) × seedling]

Kardinal HT, mr, 1986, Kordes, W.; flowers large, bright red, 4½-5 in., 30-35 petals, high-centered, borne singly, long vase life, slight fragrance; foliage medium size, dark, semi-glossy; upright growth, medium; PP5846; [seedling × Flamingo]; int. in 1985

Kardinal, Climbing Cl HT, mr, Knight, J.; [sport of Kardinal]; int. in 1999

Kardinal 85 – See **Kardinal**, HT, 1986

Kardinal Kordana Min, dr, Kordes; flowers full; container rose; int. by W. Kordes Söhne

Kardinal Piffl HT, ob, 1925, Leenders Bros.; flowers red-orange, reverse golden yellow, very large, dbl.; foliage good; [(Mme Edouard Herriot × Rayon d'Or) × Mme Charles Lutaud]; Gold Medal, Bagatelle, 1926

Kardinal Schulte HT, mr, 1926, Leenders Bros.; flowers brilliant scarlet-red, dbl.; [(Jonkheer J.L. Mock × Radiance) × Commandeur Jules Gravereaux]

Kardinal Schulte, Climbing Cl HT, mr; flowers large, dbl.; [sport of Kardinal Schulte]

Kardinal's Flame HT, or

Karel Hynek Mácha HT, dr, 1936, Brada, Dr.; flowers velvety red, well-shaped; int. by Böhm

Karel IV HT, mr, 1935, Brada, Dr.; flowers large, dbl.

Karen F, my, 1961, Borgatti, G.; flowers straw-yellow shaded ochre-yellow, 3 in., 30-35 petals; bushy growth; [Goldilocks × Fashion]; int. by Sgaravatti

Karen HT, yb, deVor; int. in 1989

Karen F, op, Keisei; int. by Keisei Rose Nurseries, 1995

Karen S, w; flowers creamy white flecked red, well-shaped, very dbl.; non-recurrent; bushy, erect (5 ft.) growth; [*R. primula* × *R. spinosissima* cultivar]

Karen Blixen HT, w, 1994, Poulsen Roser APS; flowers 3-3½ in., very dbl., borne in small clusters; foliage large, medium green, glossy; some prickles; medium (60-80 cm.), upright growth; PP9274; int. by DeVor Nursery, 1994

Karen Julie HT, or, Allender, Robert William; flowers flame orange, dbl., high-centered, slight fragrance; free-flowering; medium growth; [Alexander × Weinerwold]; int. in 1979

Karen Maria HT, yb, 1972, Gates; flowers cream and yellow, flushed pink, 4 in., 40 petals, intense fragrance; foliage glossy, dark; free growth; [sport of Kordes' Perfecta]

Karen Poulsen F, mr, 1932, Poulsen, S.; flowers scarlet, single, borne in huge trusses; vigorous growth; [Kirsten Poulsen × Vesuvius]; int. by J&P, 1933; Gold Medal, Portland, 1935, Gold Medal, NRS, 1933

Karen Poulsen, Climbing Cl F, mr, Roger; [sport of Karen Poulsen]

Karen Rudall F, pb, 2000, Rawlins, R.; flowers light pink with orange center, reverse light yellow, 3 in., full, borne in large clusters, moderate fragrance; foliage medium size, medium green, semi-glossy; prickles 1 cm., triangular, moderate; growth upright, medium (3 ft.); garden decorative; [Laura Ford × Golden Celebration]

Karenina Min, op; int. in 1999

Karen's Cream HT, Neil, J.; [sport of Shocking Blue]

Karen's Pink Lace F, mp, 1998, Prevatt, Clarence; flowers medium pink, creamy reverse at base, 41 petals, borne mostly singly; foliage medium size, medium green, dull; prickles moderate, medium size; bushy, medium (3-4 ft.) growth; [sport of French Lace]; int. by Giles Rose Nursery, 1998

Karina – See **Karina Parade**, Min

Karina Eloise F, dr, 2004, Paul Chessum Roses; flowers deep red, reverse lighter red, 5 cm., dbl., borne in small clusters; foliage medium size, dark green, semi-glossy; prickles small, dark green, moderate; growth compact, medium (75 cm.); bedding, containers; int. by Love4Plants Ltd, 2004

Karina Parade Min, mr, Olesen; bud pointed ovoid; flowers medium red, 3½ cm.-less than 5 cm., 30 petals, rosette, borne singly, slight floral fragrance; recurrent; foliage dark green, glossy; prickles moderate, straight; growth bushy, 20-40 cm.; PP16148; [Patricia Kordana Mini Brite × seedling]; int. by Poulsen Roser, 2003

Karine Pol, mp, Knopf, Ruth; flowers bright pink with bright yellow stamens, single, slight fragrance; good repeat; seedling that appeared in Knopf's garden in South Carolina; int. in 1992

Karine Sauvageot F, op, Sauvageot; flowers rose-peach and salmon, single, borne in small clusters, moderate fragrance; int. in 1989

Karkulka F, Urban, J.; int. in 1986

Karkulka HT, mr, Strnad

Karl Diehl S, dy, Schultheis; flowers gold-yellow, wavy petals, semi-dbl., borne in clusters; recurrent; foliage light green; strong (5-7 ft.) growth; int. by Rosen von Schultheis, 1997

Karl Fischer S, or, Hetzel; int. in 1976

Karl Förster HSpn, w, 1931, Kordes; bud pointed; flowers snow-white, very large, semi-dbl. to dbl., high-centered; borne intermittently throughout the summer; foliage wrinkled, light; vigorous (7 ft.) growth; [*R. spinosissima altaica* × Frau Karl Druschki]

Karl Heinz Hanisch – See **Jardins de Bagatelle**, HT

Karl Herbst HT, mr, 1950, Kordes; flowers dull dark scarlet, well-shaped, large, 60 petals, intense fragrance; vigorous growth; [Independence × Peace]; Gold Medal, NRS, 1950

Karl Herbst, Climbing Cl HT, mr; [sport of Karl Herbst]; int. about 1980

Karl Höchst F, dp, Hetzel; flowers carmine-pink, large, dbl.; int. in 1983

Karl Mayer HT, Hetzel, K.; int. in 1970

Karl Schneider HMult, lp, 1934, Vogel, M.; flowers salmon pink, 9 cm., semi-dbl., flat, borne singly or in small clusters, moderate fragrance; [(Fragezeichen × American Pillar) × Professor C. S. Sargent]

Karl Weinhausen F, dr, 1942, Tantau; flowers dark red tinted salmon, large, 20 petals, rosette, borne in clusters; vigorous, upright growth; [Baby Chateau × (Heidekind × Ingar Olsson)]

Karla – See **Raven**, S

Karlea HT, pb, 1965, O'Brien; flowers pink and salmon, base yellow, dbl.; foliage glossy; vigorous, upright growth

Karlian HT, mr, 1991, Alde, Robert O.; flowers medium, full, borne mostly singly, intense fragrance; foliage medium size, medium green, semi-glossy; medium, upright, compact growth; [Pristine × Burgund]

Karlsruhe HKor, dp, 1958, Kordes; bud ovoid; flowers deep rose-pink, 12-14 cm., very dbl., cupped; repeat bloom; foliage dark green, glossy; vigorous, climbing growth; [*R.* × *kordesii* × seedling]; int. by Kordes & Son, 1957

Karma – See **Pounder Star**, HT

Karneol Rose HT, op, Rupprecht-Radke; flowers dark salmon-pink, large, dbl.; int. in 1964

Karolina F, mr, Hempelmann; flowers carmine-red, medium, very dbl.; int. in 1994

Karoline Reiber Pol, mr, Hetzel; flowers carmine-red, small, dbl.; int. in 1991

Karoline Svetla Pol, lp, 1937, Brada, Dr.; flowers medium, semi-dbl.

Karol's Rose Min, mp

Karolyn – See **Coralin**, Min

Karoo F, or, 1988, Poulsen Roser APS; flowers orange-red, aging watermelon-pink, medium, 32 petals, borne in sprays, no fragrance; good repeat; foliage medium size, medium green, very hardy; prickles concave, yellow-brown; neat, medium, densely branched growth; [seedling × seedling]; int. by Ludwigs Roses Pty. Ltd., 1988

Karoo HT, lp, Elton Farm Nursery; flowers bright pink, large, high-centered; vigorous growth; RULED EXTINCT 2/88

Kasachstanskaia Jubilejnaja HT, dr, Sushkov & Besschetnova; flowers large, very dbl.; int. in 1958

Kasbah HT, dp, 1977, Takatori, Yoshiho; bud pointed; flowers dark pink, reverse lighter, large, 80-110 petals, cupped, moderate fragrance; foliage leathery; upright growth; [seedling × Tropicana]; int. by Japan Rose Nursery

Kasbek HT, w, VEG; flowers medium to large, semi-dbl.

Kashmir Cl F, m, 1973, Thomson; bud ovoid; flowers clear mauve, medium, dbl.; foliage glossy, leathery; vigorous, climbing growth; [Magenta × Royal Tan]

Kassel HEg, or, 1958, Kordes, R.; bud ovoid; flowers orange-scarlet, large, semi-dbl., borne in clusters of up to 10, moderate fragrance; recurrent bloom; foliage dark, glossy; vigorous growth; not dependably hardy; [Hamburg × Scarlet Else]; int. by Kordes & Son, 1956

Kasteel Van Ooidonk F, lp, RvS-Melle; flowers 10 petals, flat; foliage matte; [Melglory × seedling]; int. in 1995

Kasturi Rangan HT, m, Agarwal; flowers dusky mauve with yellow base, dbl., high-centered, moderate fragrance; int. in 1983

Kasumi HT, op, Keisei; int. by Keisei Rose Nurseries, 1998

Kasya no Sato HT, pb, Hiroshima; int. by Hiroshima Bara-en, 2001

Kätchen Meiner Pol, op, 1914, Altmüller; flowers carmine pink with salmon, center darker, large

Kätchen von Heilbronn Pol, dr, 1922, Kiese; flowers very dark red, small, dbl.; [Freudenfeuer × unnamed variety]

Kate HRg, Rieksta, Dr. Dz.

Käte Beyer Pol, op, 1947, Vogel, M.; flowers salmon-pink, medium, dbl.

Kate Edwards HT, m, 1965, Edwards; flowers magenta; [sport of Condessa de Mayalde]

Kate Emily McCormack F, rb, 1999, Kenny, David; flowers red, pink to white edges,handpainted with white eye, reverse silver, 3 in., 8-14 petals, borne in large clusters; foliage large, dark green, glossy; numerous prickles; spreading, bushy, tall (4 ft.) growth; [((Mary Sumner × Kiskadee) × Bassino) × Little Artist]

Käte Felberg HT, pb, 1930, Felberg-Leclerc; bud pointed; flowers creamy white, reverse violet-rose, large, dbl.; vigorous growth; [seedling × Mrs Wemyss Quin]

Kate Hausburg HP, lp, 1863, Granger; flowers very large, full

Kate Moulton, Climbing Cl HT, pb, 1928, Opdebeeck; [sport of Miss Kate Moulton]

Kate Mull HT, op, 1934, Easlea; flowers crushed strawberry and coppery rose, very dbl.

Kate Rainbow HT, pb, 1935, Beckwith; flowers blend of glowing pinks and gold, well-formed, very large, dbl.; foliage glossy, leathery; very vigorous growth

Käte Schmid HMult, dp, 1931, Vogel, R., Jr.; flowers deep rose-pink, very large, dbl., borne in clusters; foliage light; long stems; very vigorous, climbing growth; [Fragezeichen × Tausendschon]; int. by Kordes

Kate Sheppard F, mp, Sherwood; flowers clear, warm pink, dbl., high-centered, borne in clusters; free-flowering; medium growth; int. in 1994; Best NZ-Bred Rose, Hamilton, NZ, 2006

Kate Smith HT, pb, 1954, Boerner; bud ovoid; flowers apricot overcast grenadine-pink, 4½-5 in., 35-40 petals, high-centered, intense fragrance; foliage glossy; vigorous growth; PP1317; [(Break o' Day × Golden Rapture) × Ballet]; int. by J&P

Katelyn Ann F, mp, 1992, Williams, Michael C.; bud small, ovoid; flowers deep pink, reverse pale pink with hint of yellow, aging paler, 2½ in., 60 petals, cupped, borne singly and in small clusters, intense fruity fragrance; foliage medium size, dark green, glossy; prickles moderate, grayish-green; medium, upright (3-3½ ft.) growth; PP8968; [unknown × unknown]; int. by Roses Unlimited, 1992

Katerina HP, mr, Kosteckij; flowers large, very dbl.; int. in 1955

Katerina Lou F, pb, 2005, Johnson, Kenneth E.; flowers pink blend with white stripes, pronounced stamens, 3 cm., dbl., borne in large clusters, slight fragrance; foliage medium size, medium green, semi-glossy; prickles 1¼ cm., acuminate; growth bushy, tall (3½ ft.); exhibition; [sport of Vera Daulton]

Kateryna S, mp, Clements, John K.; flowers soft, shell pink, delicate, 2½ in., 12 petals, borne in large clusters, moderate rose/honey fragrance; recurrent; foliage dark green, glossy; compact (3 ft × 3½ ft.) growth; PPAF; int. by Heirloom Roses, 1996

Kate's Delight Min, op, Benardella, Frank; flowers bright coral, fading to pink, dbl., high-centered; int. in 1999

Kate's Rose Pol, m, Cox, Mrs K.; [Baby Faurax × unknown]; int. in 1988

Katharina Kündgen S, mp, Michler, K. H.; flowers dbl.; int. in 1996

Katharina Sophia F, lp, Karwecki; int. in 1991

Katharina Zeimet Pol, w, 1901, Lambert, P.; flowers pure white, small, dbl., borne in clusters of 25-50, moderate fragrance; foliage small, rich green; short stems; dwarf, bushy growth; [Étoile de Mai × Marie Pavie]

Katharine Pechtold HT, ob, 1934, Verschuren-Pechtold; bud old-gold and bronzy orange; flowers coppery orange, flushed rose and gold, semi-dbl., moderate clove pink fragrance; foliage leathery; vigorous, bushy growth; [Roselandia × Charles P. Kilham]; int. by Dreer

Katharine Worsley F, mr, 1962; flowers bright oriental red, large, 28 petals, borne in large, well-spaced clusters; moderate, bushy growth; int. by Waterhouse Nursery, 1962

Käthchen F, mr, Hetzel; flowers large, dbl.; int. in 1985

Käthe Duvigneau S, mr, 1942, Tantau; flowers glistening red tinted salmon, large, 15 petals, borne in clusters of 12-15, slight fragrance; foliage leathery, glossy, bright green; vigorous, upright growth; [Baby Chateau × *R. roxburghii*]

Käthe von Saalfeld HT, yb, 1914, Elbel; flowers orange yellow, large, very full, moderate fragrance

Katherine Cook HT, mr, 1927, Cook, J.W.; flowers cherry-red, dbl.; [Crusader × seedling]

Katherine Harbour HT, mp, 1974, Meyer, Harry; bud ovoid; flowers pink, tinted apricot, open, large, dbl., moderate fragrance; foliage glossy; vigorous, upright growth; [Queen Elizabeth × Comtesse Vandal]; int. by Aloe Vera Nurs., 1973

Katherine Helen F, dr, 2004, Horner, Colin P.; flowers dark red, reverse black red, 6 cm., dbl., borne in small clusters; foliage medium size, medium green, semi-glossy; prickles medium, straight; growth compact, medium (80 cm.); garden decorative; [(Phantom × Seedling) × Golden Future]; int. by Warley Rose Gardens, 2006

Katherine Loker F, my, 1978, Swim, H.C. & Christensen, J.E.; bud pointed; flowers medium golden yellow, imbricated, large, 28 petals, high-centered; upright, spreading growth; PP4666; [Zorina × Dr. A.J. Verhage]; int. by Armstrong Nursery, 1979

Katherine Mansfield – See **Charles de Gaulle**, HT

Katherine McCarty Min, yb, 1991, Gruenbauer, Richard; bud ovoid; flowers yellow center, then white, with coral edges, coral spreads with age, medium, 60 petals, high-centered, moderate damask fragrance; foliage medium size, dark green, matte; bushy, medium growth; [Poker Chip × Rise 'n' Shine]; int. by Flowers 'n' Friends Miniature Roses, 1993

Katherine McGredy HT, McGredy, Sam IV; int. in 1997

Katherine Mock HT, my, 1943, Mock; [sport of President Herbert Hoover]

Katherine T. Marshall HT, mp, 1943, Boerner; flowers deep rose-pink, flushed yellow, 5 in., 22 petals, cupped, slight spicy fragrance; foliage leathery; vigorous, upright growth; [seedling × Chieftain]; int. by J&P

Kathleen HMult, pb, 1907, Paul, W.; flowers soft rose with white eye, small, single, borne in large clusters; [Turner's Crimson Rambler × Félicité et Perpétue]

Kathleen HMsk, lp, 1922, Pemberton; flowers blush-pink, small, single, borne in large clusters; recurrent bloom; vigorous (6 ft.) growth; [Daphne × Perle des Jardins]

Kathleen HT, lp, 1934, Dickson, A.; bud very long; flowers light yellowish-salmon, large; vigorous, free branching growth

Kathleen Ferrier F, op, 1952, Buisman, G. A. H.; flowers deep salmon-pink, 2½ in., 18 petals, borne in small clusters, moderate fragrance; foliage dark, glossy; vigorous, upright growth; [Gartenstolz × Shot Silk]

Kathleen Ferrier, Climbing Cl F, op; [sport of Kathleen Ferrier]

Kathleen Harrop B, lp, 1919, Dickson, A.; flowers soft shell-pink, semi-dbl., moderate fragrance; good repeat; foliage gray-green; prickles almost none; shrubby (10 × 6 ft.) growth; [sport of Zephirine Drouhin]

Kathleen Jane S, mp, 1997, Horner, Colin P.; flowers medium, 41 petals, borne in large clusters; foliage medium size, light green, glossy; growth spreading, medium (4 ft.); [Bonica × Leverkusen]; int. by Paul Chessum Roses

Kathleen Jermyn HT, or, 1988, LeGrice, E.B.; flowers medium, dbl., urn-shaped, loose, borne usually singly, slight fragrance; foliage large, dark green, semi-glossy; growth bushy, medium; [Royal Dane × Alexander]; int. by E.B. LeGrice Roses, Ltd.

Kathleen Joyce F, lp, 1970, McGredy, Sam IV; flowers soft pink, 4 in., 30 petals, high-centered; [Paddy McGredy × Ice White]

Kathleen Kaye HT, mp, 1959, Kemp, M.L.; flowers rich rose-pink, 5 in., 60 petals; foliage dark; vigorous growth; [Directeur Guerin × Mirandy]

Kathleen Kellehan S, rb, 1999, Laving, Peter; flowers 4 in., full, borne in large clusters, intense fragrance; foliage medium size, medium green, semi-glossy; prickles moderate; upright, medium (4 ft.) growth; [Lilian Austin × Oklahoma]

Kathleen Kennedy HT, op, 1939, Dickson, A.; flowers light salmon-carmine, shaded orange, well-formed, large; strong stems; vigorous growth

Kathleen King HT, dp, 1930, Marriott; flowers carmine-pink, well-formed, large, high-centered; vigorous growth

Kathleen Kirkham F, pb, 1985, Kirkham, Gordon Wilson; flowers variable, pink, apricot, peach and yellow, medium, semi-dbl., moderate fragrance; foliage medium size, medium green, semi-glossy; upright growth; [Manx Queen × seedling]

Kathleen Mills HT, pb, 1934, LeGrice; bud long, pointed; flowers pale pink tinted silvery, reverse deep pink, large, semi-dbl.; foliage leathery; vigorous growth

Kathleen Nash HT, mr, 1944, Spera; bud urn shaped; flowers bright cerise, 4 in., 28 petals, globular; foliage leathery, dark; vigorous growth; [sport of Pink Delight]; int. by Rose Farms Corp

Kathleen O'Rourke HT, op, 1976, Dickson, Patrick; flowers soft orange-pink, 4 in., 38 petals, high-centered; foliage large, matte; [Fragrant Cloud × Red Planet]; int. by A. Dickson

Kathleen Peden HT, dr, 1959, Peden, G.H.; bud long pointed; flowers crimson, large, dbl., high-centered; foliage leathery, dark; very vigorous, upright growth; [Crimson Glory × Charles Mallerin]

Kathleen Rumble Min, lp, 1994, Wells, Verlie W.; flowers pale pink, dbl., borne mostly singly, slight fragrance; foliage medium size, dark green, glossy; some prickles; medium (6 cm.), upright growth; [seedling × Miss Pearl]; int. by Wells Midsouth Roses, 1994

Kathleen Wiggin Cl HP, w, 1932, Wiggin; bud long pointed, opening one at a time on each cluster; flowers white, sometimes tinged pink, large, very dbl., borne in clusters; foliage glossy, heavy; long stems; vigorous, climbing (12-15 ft.) growth; [Frau Karl Druschki × unknown]

Kathleen's Rose – See **Kathleen Kirkham**, F

Kathrinerl S, rb, Weihrauch, Jürgen; flowers mottled, hand painted, semi-dbl., flat, no fragrance; good spring flush, scattered later bloom; medium growth; [Gruss an Teplitz × Bonica Meidiland]; int. by Vintage Gardens, 1992?

Kathryn S, ab, 1986, Eggeman, H.W.; bud copper; flowers apricot, aging to buff, copper stamens, 4-5 in., 25 petals, open, moderate fruity fragrance; foliage semi-glossy; vigorous growth; [Wind Chimes × Yellow HT]

Kathryn Bailey F, w, 1992, Bailey, Dr. Edwin; flowers medium, full, slight fragrance; foliage light green, glossy; some prickles; medium tall, upright growth; [sport of Gene Boerner]; int. by Bailey's Plant Farm, 1993

Kathryn Gram F, ab, 1945, Moore, Ralph S.; bud urn shaped; flowers large; bushy, low growth; [Talisman × unknown]; int. by Sequoia Nursery

Kathryn McGredy HT, mp, 1998, McGredy, Sam IV; flowers 4½ in., dbl., borne mostly singly; foliage medium size, medium green, glossy; prickles slight; bushy, moderate (110 cm.) growth; [City of Auckland × Lady Rose]; int. by McGredy, Sam, 1996

Kathryn Morley S, lp, 1995, Austin, David; flowers pale pink, 3-3½ in., very dbl., cupped, borne in small clusters, moderate fragrance; foliage medium size, dark green, glosssy; numerous prickles; tall (5-6 ft.), bushy growth; PP8814; [Mary Rose × Chaucer]; int. by David Austin Roses, Ltd., 1990

Kathy Min, mr, 1970, Moore, Ralph S.; bud pointed; flowers small, dbl., moderate fragrance; foliage small, leathery; moderate, dwarf, bushy growth; PP3246; [Little Darling × Magic Wand]; int. by Sequoia Nursery

Kathy Fiscus F, mp, 1950, Duehrsen; bud ovoid; flowers deep flesh-pink, open, medium, 45 petals, borne in clusters; foliage leathery; very vigorous, upright, bushy growth; [seedling × Baby Chateau]; int. by Elmer Roses Co.

Kathy Reid HRg, m, Sandbrook; int. in 1987

Kathy Robinson Min, pb, 1975, Williams, Ernest D.; flowers pink, creamy reverse, 1 in., 26 petals, high-centered, slight fragrance; foliage small, glossy, dark, embossed; upright, bushy growth; PP3860; [Little Darling × Over the Rainbow]; int. by Mini-Roses, 1974

Katie LCl, mp, 1960, O'Neal; bud long, pointed; flowers reverse darker, large, 17 petals, cupped, intense fragrance; recurrent bloom; foliage glossy; vigorous growth; [New Dawn × Crimson Glory]; int. by Wyant, 1959

Katie Crocker F, or, Burrows, Steven; int. in 1995

Katiroy F, ob, 2001, Everitt, Derrick; flowers pale tangerine with red edging, medium, dbl., borne in small clusters, slight fragrance; foliage medium size, medium green, semi-glossy; prickles medium, straight, moderate; growth compact, low to medium (2-3½ ft.); [(*R. virginiana* × (Mary Sumner × Typhoon)) × Remember Me]

Katkoff HP, mr, 1887, Moreau-Robert; flowers cerise red with carmine, tinted currant red, large, full; foliage glossy; [Charles Lefebvre × unknown]

Katrin HT, op, GPG Bad Langensalza; flowers salmon-pink, large, dbl.; int. in 1972

Katrin Kron S, ab, Huber; flowers dbl., borne singly and in clusters, moderate tea rose fragrance; foliage dark green, glossy; growth to 3-5 ft.; int. by Richard Huber AG, 2002

Katrina HT, op, 1965, Samtmann, Charles; bud pointed; flowers orange-scarlet, medium, dbl., cupped, slight fragrance; foliage glossy, leathery; bushy, vigorous growth; PP2545; [sport of Baccará]; int. by C-P, 1964

Katy Girl S, lp, 2000, Ponton, Ray; flowers semi-dbl., borne mostly singly, slight fragrance; quick repeat; foliage medium size, medium green, disease-resistant; few prickles; bushy, tall (6 ft.) growth; landscape, short climber; [Carefree Beauty × unknown]; int. in 2000

Katy Lampkin Min, mp, 1993, Taylor, Franklin; flowers medium pink, cream base, medium, dbl., borne singly and in small clusters, slight fragrance; foliage small, medium green, semi-glossy; few prickles; low (18 in.), compact growth; [Winsome × Admiral Rodney]; int. by Taylor's Roses, 1993

Katy Mae F, w, Pagowski; flowers semi-dbl.; good bloomer; [sport of Regensberg]; int. in 2002

Katy Road Pink – See **Carefree Beauty**, S

Kauff – See **Kauth**, (strain of *R. canina*)

Kauth (strain of *R. canina*), lp; growth sometimes used as understock

Kavita F, pb, 1972, IARI; buds small, pointed; flowers orient-pink with light yellow base, medium, dbl, open, borne in clusters; foliage medium size, soft; growth vigorous, compact, bushy (90 cm.); [Margaret Spaull × unknown]

Kawkasskaja HGal, m; bud thick, spherical; flowers magenta to lilac-red, large, very full, dish-shaped, borne in clusters, moderate fragrance; medium strong (5 ft.) growth

Kay F, or, 1971, Delforge; bud ovoid; flowers vermilion, large, dbl., cupped; foliage large, bronze; vigorous, upright growth; [Queen Elizabeth × Numero Un]

Kay Ann HT, rb, 2000, Williams, J. Benjamin; flowers red and yellow blend, large, full, borne mostly singly or in small clusters, moderate fragrance; repeats well; foliage large, dark green, semi-glossy, disease-resistant; few prickles; strong, compact, upright (3½-4 ft.) growth; [Peace × Canadian Sunset]; int. by J.B. Williams & Assoc., 2000

Kay Barnard HT, lp, 1974, Dingle; bud long, pointed; flowers pale pink, high-centered; upright growth; [South Seas × Queen Elizabeth]

Kay Denise Min, pb, 1995, Bennett, Dee; flowers soft creamy pink, pink blush margins, full, high-centered, borne mostly singly, moderate fragrance; foliage small, medium green, semi-glossy; some prickles; upright, bushy, tall growth; PP10946; [Tiki × My Delight]; int. by Tiny Petals Nursery, 1995

Kayla Min, pb, 1994, Moore, Ralph S.; flowers 2-3½ in., dbl., borne mostly singly, but some in small clusters; foliage large, medium green, semi-glossy; few prickles; tall (45-55 cm.), upright, bushy growth; [Sheri Ann × Violette]; int. by Sequoia Nursery, 1995

Kaylee Rose MinFl, lp, 2001, Kuze, Hugo; flowers small, very full, borne in large clusters, no fragrance; foliage medium size, medium green, matte; prickles in., straight, moderate; growth bushy, medium; garden decorative; [sport of Red Flush]

Kayli Joy Min, yb, 2004, Brown, Ted; flowers light yellow/pink edging, reverse light yellow, 1½ in., dbl., borne mostly solitary; foliage medium size, dark green, matte; prickles small, pointed; growth upright, medium (2 ft.); exhibition; garden decorative; [Luis Desamero × Hot Tamale]; int. by Ted Brown, 2005

Kazaguruma F, mr, Keisei; int. by Keisei Rose Nurseries, 2000

Kazanlik D, dp, before 1700; flowers deep pink, aging to lighter pink, medium, 30 petals, loose, intense fragrance; foliage soft, light green; growth spindly, tall (2 m.); introduced from Bulgaria by Dr. Dieck about 1900; often assumed to be the same as Trigintipetala

Kde Domov Muj HMult, dp, 1935, Böhm, J.; flowers carmine-pink, lighter at center, 4 cm., semi-dbl. to dbl., borne in clusters of 10-20, slight fragrance

Kean HGal, m, before 1843; flowers velvety purple, scarlet crimson center, medium to large, full; growth branching, vigorous; possibly from Laffay or Godefroy; first reference in Verdier's 1843 catalog

Kebu mr; int. by Belle Epoque

Keely Min, or, 1989, Bridges, Dennis A.; bud pointed; flowers bright, orange-red, reverse slightly darker, aging color fading, 20 petals, high-centered; foliage medium size, medium green, semi-glossy; prickles straight, pointed, medium, red; bushy, medium growth; [Party Girl × seedling]; int. by Bridges Roses, 1989

Keep in Touch F, mr, Harkness; flowers bright red, semi-dbl., borne in clusters; recurrent; compact, low (2½ ft.) growth; int. by Robert Harkness & Co, 1999

Keep Smiling HT, dy, Fryer; flowers bright, unfading yellow, dbl., moderate fragrance; free-flowering; strong, vigorous (4 ft.) growth; int. by Fryer's Roses, 2004

Keepit HT, lp, Dawson; int. in 1988

Keepsake HT, dr, 1941, Clark, A.; flowers deep red; RULED EXTINCT 7/81; [Anne Leygues × unknown]

Keepsake HT, pb, 1981, W. Kordes Söhne; bud ovoid; flowers deep pink blended with lighter pink shades, reflexed, large, 40 petals, exhibition, moderate fragrance; foliage dark; prickles large, stout; vigorous, bushy growth; int. by John Mattock, Ltd.; Gold Medal, Portland, 1987

Kees Knoppers Pol, w, 1930, Leenders, M.; flowers flesh-white, open, large, semi-dbl., borne in clusters; foliage rich green; vigorous, bushy growth; [sport of Mev. Nathalie Nypels]

Keewatin HRg, w, 2002, Olsen, Paul G.; flowers large, semi-dbl., borne in small clusters, moderate fragrance; foliage medium size, gray-green, matte; prickles moderate; upright, tall (150 cm.) growth; [Henry Hudson × Henry Hudson]; int. by Brentwood Bay Nurseries, 2002

Kegon HT, mr, 1979, Onodera, Toru F.; bud pointed; flowers deep red, 5 in., 30 petals, high-centered; foliage leathery; tall growth; [Gruss an Berlin × Christian Dior]; int. by S. Onodera, 1976

Kei Min, lp, 1980, Lyon, Lyndon; bud ovoid, pointed; flowers 33 petals, borne 1-3 per cluster; foliage tiny, dark; prickles straight; very compact, bushy growth; [seedling × seedling]; int. in 1979

Keimateo – See **Alliance**, HT

Keith Harder HT, m, Harder, K.

Keith Kirsten F, or, Tantau; int. in 1990

Keithie F, rb

Keith's Delight HRg, yb, 2004, Moore, Ralph S.; flowers pale yellow to white, reverse pale yellow, 3 in., full, borne in small clusters; recurrent; foliage medium size, medium green, glossy; prickles small, hooked; growth upright, tall (5-6 ft.); low climber, free standing shrub; hips orange; [seedling (Little Darling × Yellow Jewel) × Rugelda]; int. by Sequoia Nurs., 2005

Kelleriis-Rose – See **Poulsen's Supreme**, F

Kelli Ann Min, w, 1982, Dobbs, Annette E.; flowers small, 35 petals, slight fragrance; foliage small, medium green, matte; bushy growth; [Patricia Scranton × (Patricia Scranton × Fairy Moss)]; int. in 1981

Kelly Country LCl, pb, Sutherland; int. in 1997

Kelly-Leigh Min, yb, 1984, Stephens, Paddy; flowers white and gold, medium, semi-dbl., no fragrance; foliage medium size, medium green, glossy; bushy growth; [Ko's Yellow × seedling]; int. in 1981

Kelly Reynolds HT, pb, 1999, Reynolds, Ted; flowers apricot peach pink blend, large, full, high-centered, borne mostly singly, slight fragrance; foliage large, medium green, glossy; few prickles; upright, medium growth; [Perfume Delight × seedling]; int. by Ted Reynolds Roses International, 1999

Kempton Park – See **Loulou de Cacharel**, F

Ken Davis HT, pb, 1998, Davis, Ken; flowers light pink with darker edges, medium size, dbl., borne mostly singly; foliage medium size, light green, dull; prickles medium; upright, medium (4 ft.) growth; [sport of Bride's Dream]; int. by Giles Rose Nursery, 1995

Ken n Norma – See **Kennorma**, HT

Kenmore HT, dy, 1971, Macara; flowers deep yellow, 4½ in., 36 petals; foliage glossy; [Jane Lazenby × Golden Delight]; int. by Sanday Roses

Kenneth Vincent Orpe Taylor F, ab, 2005, Paul Chessum Roses; flowers dbl., borne in small clusters, slight fragrance; foliage large, medium green, semi-glossy; prickles large, sharp, yellow, few; growth bushy, tall (36 in.); bedding, containers; [seedling × seedling]; int. by World of Roses, 2005

Kennorma HT, mp, 2002, Horner, Colin P.; flowers medium pink, lighter reverse, 11 cm., full, borne mostly solitary, intense fragrance; foliage medium size, medium green, semi-glossy; prickles medium, curved, moderate; growth bushy, medium (1 m.); garden decorative, exhibition; [Prima Ballerina × Memoriam]; int. by Battersby Roses, 2003

Kenny's Rose HT, mr, 1996, Giles, Kenneth; flowers 3-3½ in., full, borne mostly singly, moderate fragrance; foliage medium size, dark green, semi-glossy; some prickles; medium, spreading, sprawling growth; [Swarthmore × Mister Lincoln]; int. by Giles Rose Nursery, 1995

Kenora Duet F, ab, 1977, Tresise; bud long, pointed; flowers salmon-pink, open, medium, semi-dbl., slight fragrance; foliage glossy; vigorous, bushy growth; [sport of Duet]

Kensington F, dr, Olesen; bud pointed ovoid; flowers 40-45 petals, open cup, borne in small clusters, slight fragrance; recurrent; foliage dark green, semi-glossy; prickles numerous, 6 mm., hooked downward, greyed-purple; vigorous, upright to bushy (60-100 cm.) growth; PP15288; [seedling × Redwood]; int. by Poulsen Roser, 2002

Kent S, w, 1988, Olesen; bud ovate; flowers clear white, bright yellow stamens, 1½ in., 10-15 petals, flat, borne singly and in clusters, very slight fragrance; free-flowering; foliage medium green, semi-glossy; prickles some, 6 mm., hooked downward, brown; growth arching, compact, spreading, low (60-100 cm.); hips few, small ; PP10648; int. as White Cover, Poulsen Roser, 1991

Kentfield Pol, mp, 1922, Diener; flowers soft cameo-pink to deeper pink, small, dbl.; [Cécile Brunner × seedling]

Kentucky HT, w, Select; int. about 1995

Kentucky Derby HT, dr, 1972, Armstrong, D.L.; flowers large, dbl., high-centered, slight fragrance; foliage large, glossy, leathery; vigorous, upright, bushy growth; PP3303; [John S. Armstrong × Grand Slam]; int. by Armstrong Nursery

Kerfany F, dp; int. by Reuter Frères, 2005

Kerry Anne Min, ab, 2000, Bossom, Bill; flowers dbl., borne in small clusters; foliage small, dark green, semi-glossy; prickles moderate; growth upright, medium (3 ft.); containers; [Laura Ford × English Miss]

Kerry Gold F, yb, 1967, Dickson, A.; flowers canary-yellow, outer petals veined red, 3 in., globular, borne in clusters; foliage dark; [Circus × Allgold]

Kerry MacNeil F, mr, 1967, Vincent; flowers bright vermilion; free growth; [Orangeade × Anna Wheatcroft]

Kerryman F, pb, 1971, McGredy, Sam IV; flowers salmon and pink, 4½ in., 24 petals, high-centered; [Paddy McGredy × (Mme Leon Cuny × Columbine)]; int. by McGredy

Kersbergen Pol, mr, 1927, Kersbergen; flowers bright currant-red, very small, full, borne in clusters; free-flowering; [sport of Miss Edith Cavell]

Kesri F, or, 1971, Singh; bud ovoid; flowers orient orange, small, dbl., open, slight fragrance; foliage leathery; vigorous growth; [Orangeade, Climbing × unknown]; int. by Gopalsinamiengar, 1969

Kessi S, mp, Schultheis; flowers bright carmine rose, dbl., borne in clusters; free-flowering; spreading, low (2 ft.) growth; int. by Rosen von Schultheis, 2000

Kessy HT, yb, Tantau; flowers peach-yellow with reddish hues, full, high-centered, borne singly and in clusters; good repeat; prickles moderate; stems upright, strong; int. by Rosen Tantau, 2001

Kessy F, my

Ketje HT, mr, 1938, Lens; bud pointed; flowers brilliant red mixed dark pink, well-formed, very dbl.; foliage bronze; very vigorous growth; [Mrs Sam McGredy × E.G. Hill]

Kev Min, dy, 1991, Taylor, Pete & Kay; flowers medium, full, borne mostly singly, no fragrance; foliage medium size, medium green, semi-glossy; medium, upright growth; [Azure Sea × Party Girl]; int. by Taylor's Roses, 1991

Kevin HT, dp, Twomey, Jerry; int. in 1997

Kew Beauty HT, dr, 1918, Therkildsen; flowers crimson, dbl.

Kew Rambler HMult, mp, 1913, Royal Botanic Gardens, Kew; flowers pink, center paler, 4 cm., single, borne in large clusters, moderate fragrance; foliage gray-green; growth to 15 ft.; [*R. soulieana* × Hiawatha]

Kewai HT, yb, 1997, Ohtsuki, Hironaka; flowers yellow with orange-yellow center, 5 in., full; foliage medium size, medium green, semi-glossy; few prickles; upright, bushy, medium (6 ft.) growth; [Izayoi × Golden Emblem]; int. in 1997

Key Largo HT, op, 2001, Zary; bud pointed, ovoid; flowers clear coral, 4-5 cm., 30 petals, borne mostly solitary, slight citrus fragrance; foliage medium size, dark green, glossy; prickles moderate; growth upright, tall (5 ft.); garden decorative; PP13296; [Touch of Class × unnamed yellow hybrid tea seedling]; int. by J&P, 2001

Key Rock Rose Misc OGR, yb

Key West S, dp, Poulsen; flowers deep pink, 8-10 cm., semi-dbl., no fragrance; foliage dark; growth broad, bushy, 60-100 cm.; PP13450; int. by Poulsen Roser, 2000

Keystone LCl, dy, 1904, Dingee & Conard; flowers deep lemon-yellow

Ki Ki Paquel F, or, 1960, Moreira da Silva; flowers bright brick color; [Super-Congo × Independence]

Kia Ora F, or, 1962, Mason, P.G.; flowers orange-scarlet, large, 35 petals; foliage glossy, dark; vigorous, bushy, compact growth; [Independence × Independence]

Kia Ora Gr, mp, 1999, Schuurman, Frank B.; flowers 4 in., borne in large clusters; foliage medium green, glossy; few prickles; bushy, medium growth; [Innocendi × Firefly]; int. by Franko Roses New Zealand, Ltd., 1994

Kiboh F, rb, 1986, Suzuki, Seizo; flowers orange-red, reverse yellowish, large, 50 petals, high-centered, borne in clusters of 3; foliage dark, semi-glossy; prickles slanted downward; vigorous, upright growth; PP7139; [Liberty Bell × Kagayaki]; int. by Keisei Rose Nursery; Gold Medal, The Hague, 1985

Kibune HT, rb, Keisei; flowers deep red with yellow base, large, exhibition

Kickapoo HT, rb, 1990, Stoddard, Louis; bud ovoid; flowers yellow, outer petals red, white reverse aging to light red blend, 20 petals; foliage medium size, medium green, dull; prickles straight, green aging to tan; bushy, medium, slightly spreading growth; hips round, green to light yellow; [(Daisy Mae × First Prize) × seedling]

Kickoff HT, mr, Teranishi; int. by Itami Rose Garden, 2005

Kiddy Pol, mr, 1967, Delforge; bud pointed; flowers dark red, becoming brighter, medium, single, cupped; abundant, recurrent bloom; foliage glossy; vigorous, upright growth; [Mme Dieudonne × seedling]

Kidwai – See **Kidway**, HT

Kidway HT, mp, 1933, Pernet-Ducher; bud long, pointed; flowers salmon-rose, lower half of petals golden yellow, large, semi-dbl.; foliage leathery, dark, bronze, glossy; very vigorous, bushy growth; int. as Kidwai, Dreer

Kieran Ross Clark Gr, mr, 1999, Horner, Colin P.; flowers bright scarlet red, reverse paler, 3 in., dbl., borne in small clusters; foliage medium size, dark green, glossy; prickles moderate; upright, tall (4 ft.) growth; [(Anytime × (Liverpool Echo × (Flamenco × Rosa Bella))) × Remember Me]

Kieran's Rose MinFl, yb, 2006, Aguilar, Sergio; flowers yellow red edges, reverse white, 1½ in., single, borne mostly solitary; foliage large, medium green, glossy, disease-resistant; prickles small, hooked downward, few; growth upright, medium (24-30 in.); small specimen; border; cut flower; [Elizabeth Taylor × Playboy]; int. by Orange County Rose Society, 2006

Kiese S, mr, 1910, Kiese; flowers bright red, medium, single to semi-dbl.; [Général Jacqueminot × *R. canina*]

Kiese's Unterlage – See **Kiese**, S

Kiftsgate Sp, w, 1954; flowers creamy white, 5 petals, borne in large clusters, moderate fragrance; very vigorous, sprawling growth; *R. filipes* form; int. by E. Murrell

Kiftsgate Violett S, m; flowers whitish-violet, small, single, shallow cup, borne in large clusters, moderate fragrance; non-remontant; strong (8-10 m.) growth

Kiftsgate × Violet Hood S, m, Lens; flowers violet, small, heavy spring bloom; once bloomer; tall (to 10 ft.) growth; possibly the same as Kiftsgate Violett (above)

Kika HT, ly, 1993, Ortega, Carlos; flowers 3-3½ in., dbl., borne mostly singly; foliage medium size, dark green, semi-glossy; no prickles; medium (150 cm.), upright growth; [JACice × seedling]; int. by Aebi Nursery, 1993

Kiki HT, Dorieux, Francois; int. in 1972

Kiki F, ab, Select; flowers 9 cm., 30-35 petals, high-centered, borne mostly singly; stems 20-28 in; cut flower rose; int. by Terra Nigra BV, 2003

Kiki Paquel Gr, Moreira da Silva, A.; int. in 1960

Kiki Rose – See **Caterpillar**, S

Kiko HT, lp, J&P; int. in 1994

Kilbreda Centenary HT, mr, 2007, Chapman, Bruce; flowers 9 cm., dbl., blooms borne singly and in small clusters; foliage large, dark green, semi-glossy; prickles medium, hooked, brown, few; growth compact, medium (1¼ m.); garden decoration; [Kardinal × Aotearoa]; int. by Ross Roses, 2005

Kilimanjaro HT, w, 1977, Herholdt, J.A.; bud pointed; flowers pure white, 4½-5 in., 35-38 petals; foliage rich green; vigorous growth; [seedling × Pascali]

Kilkea Castle S, pb, McCann, Sean; recurrent; int. by Ashdown Roses, 2004

Killarney HT, mp, 1898, Dickson, A.; bud long, pointed; flowers bright medium pink, loose, large, dbl.; foliage bronze; [Mrs W.J. Grant × Charles J. Grahame]

Killarney, Climbing Cl HT, mp, 1908, Reinberg; [sport of Killarney]

Killarney Brilliant HT, dp, 1914, Dickson, A.; bud long, pointed; flowers brilliant pink to rosy carmine, open, dbl.; foliage rich green, soft; [sport of Killarney]

Killarney Double Pink HT, mp, 1935, Vestal; flowers sparkling shell-pink; [sport of Killarney Double White]

Killarney Double White HT, w, 1912, Budlong; flowers snowy white; [sport of Killarney]; int. by A.N. Pierson

Killarney Double White, Climbing Cl HT, w, 1935, Howard Rose Co.

Killarney Queen HT, dp, 1912, Budlong; flowers Tyrian rose, brighter than killarney; [sport of Killarney]

Kilmore Rose HRg, dp, 2003, Collins, Leon; flowers dbl., borne in small clusters; foliage medium size, dark green, glossy; prickles small, hooked downwards; growth bushy, medium (4 ft.); hedging, specimen; [*R. rugosa alba* × unknown]; int. by Leon Collins, 2003

Kilwinning HSpn, w, Wright, Percy H.; foliage fern like; [*R. spinosissima altaica* × Hansen's Yellow]

Kilworth Gold HT, dy, 1977, Gandy, Douglas L.; flowers golden yellow, 28 petals, borne singly and several together, moderate fragrance; free-flowering; foliage large, dark green; bushy growth; [sport of Whisky Mac]

Kilworth Pride F, dr, 1955, deRuiter; flowers semi-dbl., borne in clusters; foliage bronze; dwarf, bushy growth; [Better Times × Floribunda seedling]; int. by Gandy Roses, Ltd.

Kim Pol, mp, 1956, Buyl Frères; flowers geranium-rose, small, borne in clusters; vigorous growth; [Independence × Salmon Perfection]

Kim F, my, 1971, Harkness; flowers 3 in., 28 petals; foliage small, light green, matte; dwarf growth; [(Orange Sensation × Allgold) × Elizabeth of Glamis]; int. in 1973

Kim Peters MinFl, mp, 2006, Paul Chessum Roses; flowers 4 cm., full, borne mostly solitary, intense fragrance; foliage medium size, dark green, semi-glossy; prickles large, sharp, yellow, moderate; growth bushy, medium (24 in.); bedding, containers; [seedling ×

seedling]; int. by World of Roses, 2005

Kim Rupert Min, rb, 2003, Moore, Ralph S.; bud moderate, balsam scented mossing; flowers red/light yellow stripes, reverse red and yellow, 2 in., dbl., borne in small clusters; foliage medium size, medium green, semi-glossy; prickles straight; growth upright, tall (16-24 in.); containers, raised beds, borders; [Golden Angel × (Dortmund × striped moss seedling)]; int. by The Uncommon Rose, 2003

Kimberley S, dp, Poulsen; flowers deep pink, 8-10 cm., dbl., slight fragrance; foliage dark; growth bushy, 20-40 cm.; PP15621; int. by Poulsen Roser, 2002

Kimberley Anne HT, w, 1984, Evans, F. David; flowers large, 35 petals, intense fragrance; foliage medium size, medium green, matte; upright growth; [Virgo × Secret Love]; Bronze Medal, ARC TG, 1985

Kimberley Hit – See **Kimberley**, S

Kimberly Min, ab, 1986, Williams, Michael C.; flowers 24 petals, high-centered, urn-shaped, borne usually singly, moderate fruity fragrance; foliage medium size, medium green, semi-glossy; no prickles; upright, medium growth; hips globular, small, orange; [Party Girl × Sheri Anne]; int. by The Rose Garden & Mini Rose Nursery

Kimbo F, Pineau; int. in 1977

Kimmy F, rb, Laperriere, L.; flowers brilliant red tinted red-orange, dbl.; growth to 60-70 cm.; int. in 1975

Kimono F, pb, 1962, deRuiter; flowers salmon-pink, 3 in., 30 petals, borne in broad clusters, moderate fragrance; vigorous, bushy growth; [Cocorico × Frau Anny Beaufays]; int. by Horstmann

Kimono, Climbing Cl F, pb; [sport of Kimono]; int. after 1961

Kim's Cream F, w, 1991, Rupert, Kim L.; bud ovoid, pointed; flowers cream with coffee and gold tints, opening cream, tint remains in cool weather, 3-3½ in., full, flat, borne in small clusters, intense spicy fragrance; foliage leathery, medium size, medium green, semi-glossy; some prickles; low (45-50 cm.), bushy, compact, vigorous growth; [Lavender Pinocchio × Lavender Pinocchio]

Kind Regards F, mr, 1956, Kordes; flowers crimson-red, very large, dbl., borne in clusters; free-flowering; vigorous, bushy growth

Kind Regards F, mr, Pearce; int. in 1995

Kindness HT, dp, Certified; flowers high-centered, slight fragrance; int. in 1994

King Alexander I – See **Roi Alexandre**, HT

King Arthur F, op, 1967, Harkness; flowers salmon-pink, large, dbl., borne in clusters; foliage glossy; [Pink Parfait × Highlight]

King Arthur – See **English Sonnet**, F

King Boreas F, my, 1941, Brownell; flowers pure yellow shading to nearly white, recurved, medium, 100 petals, moderate fragrance; vigorous growth; [Golden Glow × unknown]

King Crimson S, dr, 1991, Warriner, William A.; flowers large, semi-dbl., no fragrance; foliage large, dark green, semi-glossy; tall, upright, bushy growth; [Razzle Dazzle × seedling]; int. by Bear Creek Gardens, 1991

King David HP, 1910, California Rose Co.; [sport of Vick's Caprice]

King David – See **Ashram**, HT

King Edward HT, dr, Laver; flowers dbl., high-centered, no fragrance; good repeat; vigorous, medium (3 ft.) growth; int. by Ludwig's Roses, 2002

King George IV – See **Rivers' George IV**, HCh

King George V HP, dr, 1912, Dickson, H.; flowers crimson, large, 40 petals, high-centered; sparse, intermittent bloom; strong stems; very vigorous, open growth

King George's Memorial – See **Památnik Krále Jiríhо**, HT

King Henry S, dp, Genesis

King Hey S, dr

King J. HRg, w, 1996, Fleming, Joyce L.; flowers yellow stamens, dbl., borne in small clusters, intense spicy fragrance; good repeat; foliage dark green, glossy, very healthy, disease/insect resistant; numerous prickles; growth bushy, medium; hardy to -10ºF; [*R. rugosa alba* × Assiniboine]; int. by Hortico Roses, 1989

King Midas LCl, my, 1942, Nicolas; bud long, pointed; flowers clear yellow, 4-5 in., 20 petals, cupped, borne in clusters of 4-6; repeat bloom; foliage large, leathery, dark; vigorous, climbing or pillar (8-10 ft.) growth; int. by J&P

King o' Kings HT, mr, 1973, Anderson's Rose Nurseries; flowers 6 in., 35-40 petals, high-centered; foliage dark; [My Love × Duftwolke]

King of Hearts HT, mr, 1968, McGredy, Sam IV; bud long, pointed; flowers medium, dbl., high-centered; foliage dark, leathery; vigorous, bushy growth; PP3091; [Karl Herbst × Ethel Sanday]; int. by Edmunds Roses

King of Scotland – See **King of Scots**, HSpn

King of Scots HSpn, dp, 1803, Brown, R.; flowers deep rosy purple-pink to red, pale reverse, medium, semi-dbl.; profuse, early bloom; foliage finely divided; dense, shrubby (3-4 ft.) growth; hips glossy, black

King of Siam HT, mr, 1912, Bräuer; flowers large, full; [Mme Victor Verdier × Safrano]

King of Sweden – See **Oscar II, Roi de Suéde**, HP

King of the Prairies HSet, mr, 1843, Feast; flowers bright red

King Richard S, m, Genesis

King Tut Bailey, Dorothy J.; PP4396

King Tut Min, dy, 1989, Laver, Keith G.; bud pointed; flowers rich, deep yellow, reverse medium yellow, small, 45 petals, high-centered, borne singly; foliage small, dark green, disease-resistant; prickles curved down, light brown; upright, low, compact growth; hips ovoid, orange-red; [June Laver × Genevieve]; int. by Springwood Roses

King Tut – See **Laura Ford**, Cl Min

King William S, dp, Genesis

Kingaroy HT, dr, 1980, Perry, Astor; bud long, pointed; flowers 30 petals, urn-shaped, borne singly, slight fruity fragrance; foliage medium size, matte; prickles small; medium growth; [seedling × Red Lion]; int. in 1981

Kingcup HT, my, 1953, LeGrice; flowers buttercup-yellow, well-formed, 4 in., 40 petals, intense fruity fragrance; foliage dark, glossy; very free growth; [Mrs Sam McGredy × Ellinor LeGrice]

Kingdon Ward No. 3505 Sp, dp; a form of *R. pendulina oxyodon*

Kingdon Ward No. 6101 Sp, w; a form of *R. pendulina oxyodon* with cream-colored flowers and fern-like foliage

Kingi F, pb, 1983, Murray, Nola; flowers yellow flushed rose pink, large, 35 petals; foliage dense, dark; prickles large, red; bushy growth; [Liverpool Echo × Una Hawken]

King's Acre HP, rb, 1864, Cranston; flowers dusty scarlet, reverse flesh pink, large, full

King's Macce HT, ab, Fryer; flowers yellow-apricot blend, beautifully formed, dbl., strong fragrance; repeats well; foliage dark green; upright (3 ft.) growth; int. by Fryer's Roses, 2003; Silver Certificate, The Hague, 2006

King's Mountain Min, dy, 2004, Bridges, Dennis; flowers 1¼ in., dbl., borne mostly solitary, slight fragrance; foliage medium size, medium green, semi-glossy; prickles ¼ in., curved slightly downward; growth compact, medium (26-30 in.); container, garden, cutting, exhibition; [Doris Morgan × select pollen]; int. by Bridges Roses, 2005

King's Ransom HT, dy, 1961, Morey, Dr. Dennison; bud ovoid; flowers clear golden yellow, 5-6 in., 38 petals, high-centered, moderate fragrance; foliage leathery, glossy; vigorous, upright growth; PP2103; [Golden Masterpiece × Lydia]; int. by J&P, 1961

King's Row S, yb, 1965, Whisler; flowers yellow becoming rose-red, medium, dbl., borne in clusters, moderate fragrance; foliage bronze, leathery; vigorous (4 ft.), compact growth; PP2593; [Easter Parade × Herrenhausen]; int. by Germain's

King's Treasure F, my, Williams, J. Benjamin; int. in 1995

Kingsmead Heritage F, w, Kordes; flowers cream-ivory, dbl., no fragrance; good repeat; vigorous growth; int. in 1996

Kingswood College F, mr, Kordes; int. in 1990

Kinistino S, dp, Erskine; flowers single; [Aurora × Leafland Glow]; int. by Sheila Holmes

Kinkaku HT, dy, 1986, Okamoto, K.; flowers golden yellow, large, 38 petals, high-centered, usually borne singly; foliage medium size, light green; prickles brown; medium, bushy growth; [seedling × Peace]; int. by K. Hirakata Nursery, 1975

Kinsmen HT, rb, Delbard; flowers white with red edges, dbl., moderate fragrance; recurrent; medium (4 ft.) growth

Kinugasa HT, lp, 1986, Shibata, T.; flowers large, 45 petals, exhibition, borne usually singly, moderate fruity fragrance; foliage medium size, light green; prickles brown, hooked; medium, bushy growth; [Michèle Meilland × (Michelle Meilland × Anne Letts)]; int. by K. Hirakata Nursery, 1984

Kiora F, mr, 1989, Cattermole, R.F.; bud pointed; flowers light vermillion shading to darker petal edges, small, dbl., flat; foliage dark green, shiny, veined; upright, bushy growth; [Liverpool Echo × John Church]; int. by South Pacific Rose Nursery

Kir Royal LCl, pb, Meilland; flowers dark pink at opening, lighter at edges, speckled with crimson, medium, dbl., slight fragrance; int. in 1995

Kirang HT, pb, Tejganga; int. in 1995

Kirari F, yb, Keisei; int. by Keisei Rose Nurseries, 2004

Kiri HT, dp, Matthews; int. in 1994

Kirkcaldie – See **Carmel Sunset**, HT

Kirsch, Climbing – See **Vintage Wine**, Cl HT

Kirsch Cover – See **Petaluma**, S

Kirsi HT, rb, 1967, Palmer, H.E.; flowers cream-white edged pink, becoming red over white, large, dbl.; very vigorous growth; PP2706; [sport of Rose Gaujard]; int. by Edmunds Roses

Kirsten HT, lp, Poulsen; int. in 1985

Kirsten Klein HMsk, mp, Scarman; flowers single; int. in 1995

Kirsten Poulsen F, mr, 1924, Poulsen, S.; flowers bright scarlet, single, borne in clusters; foliage leathery; vigorous growth; [Orléans Rose × Red Star]

Kirsten Poulsen Improved F, mr, 1938, Radmore; flowers scarlet, single, borne on trusses; free bloom; foliage dark; free growth

Kirsty HT, dp, 2004, Paul Chessum Roses; flowers fuchsia pink, 8 cm., full, cupped, borne mostly solitary, moderate fragrance; recurrent; foliage medium size, medium green, semi-glossy; prickles medium size, medium green, moderate; growth compact, bushy, medium (80 cm.); beds, borders, containers; [unknown × seedling]; int. by Love4Plants Ltd, 2004

Kirsty Jane F, or, 1980, Simpson, J.W.; bud ovoid; flowers fluted, 28 petals, borne 3-10 per cluster, no fragrance; foliage medium size, glossy; prickles straight brown; bushy, vigorous growth; [(Orangeade × unknown) × Megiddo]

Kiska Rose – See ***R. rugosa*** (Thunberg)

Kiskadee F, my, 1973, McGredy, Sam IV; flowers bright yellow, large, 25 petals, high-centered; foliage dark; [Arthur Bell × Cynthia Brooke]

Kisme F, pb, Raffel; flowers soft, warm pink, deepening

with age, large, very full, borne in clusters, moderate fragrance; good repeat; int. about 1960

Kismet HT, my, 1930, Nicolas; flowers clear yellow, center deeper, large, dbl., cupped; foliage light, glossy; [sport of Talisman]; int. by J&P

Kismet MinFl, yb, 2005, Tucker, Robbie; flowers yellow with red edging, reverse yellow and red, up to 2 in., dbl., high-centered, borne in small clusters; foliage medium size, dark green, glossy; prickles few, 1/4 to 1/2 in., slightly curved downward, brown; growth compact, medium (to 30 in.); exhibition, cut flower, garden; [Cal Poly × Soroptimist International]; int. by Rosemania, 2005

Kiss Min, ob, 1980, Lyon, Lyndon; bud ovoid, pointed; flowers Indian orange, reverse lighter, 28 petals, high-centered, borne in clusters of 1-3, moderate fruity fragrance; foliage small, medium green; prickles straight; growth strong, upright; [seedling × seedling]; int. by Dreer, 1979

Kiss F, op; flowers salmon-pink, small, dbl., high-centered, slight fragrance; growth vigorous, medium (18 in.); int. by Kordes, 1988

Kiss 'n' Tell Min, ab, 1985, McCann, Sean; flowers small, 35 petals, flat, slight fragrance; foliage small, medium green, semi-glossy; bushy growth; [Rise 'n' Shine × (Sally Mac × New Penny)]; int. in 1989

Kiss Kordana Min, dr, Kordes; flowers dbl.; container rose; int. by W. Kordes Söhne

Kiss Kordana Mini Brite Min, op, Kordes; PP11363; int. by Johnny Becnel Show Roses

Kiss Me Gr, mp, Lim, Ping; flowers clear pink, 4 in., 20-25 petals, loose, borne in clusters, intense fragrance; recurrent; foliage disease-resistant; low (2-3 ft.) growth; int. by Bailey Nurseries, 2006

Kiss Me Quick Min, lp, 2000, McCann, Sean; flowers light pink, reverse pink salmon, fades slowly, 2 in., full, borne mostly singly, slight fragrance; quick repeat; foliage medium size, medium green, semi-glossy; upright, medium (18-22 in.) growth; [Kiss 'n' Tell × Lady in Red]; int. by Justice Mini Roses, 2000

Kiss of Fire F, rb, Gaujard; flowers pale yellow with red edges, dbl., borne in clusters, moderate fragrance; int. in 1960

Kiss of Fire HT, yb, Laveena Roses; int. in 1969

Kiss the Bride Min, w, 1986, McCann, Sean; flowers small, 20 petals, borne singly and in clusters of 4-6, moderate spicy fragrance; foliage medium size, medium green, semi-glossy; bushy growth; [Rise 'n' Shine × White Bouquet]; int. in 1987

Kissin' Cousin S, op, 1978, Buck, Dr. Griffith J.; bud ovoid, pointed; flowers pink to coral-pink, 4-5 in., 28 petals, high-centered; foliage large, dark, leathery; vigorous, upright, spreading growth; [((Ophelia × Prairie Princess) × Tiki) × ((Corbeille Royale × American Heritage) × Hawkeye Belle)]; int. by Iowa State University

Kitana HRg, m, 1927, Hansen, N.E.; flowers deep lavender-pink, large, semi-dbl., intense fragrance; non-recurrent; hips profuse, red; very hardy; [Tetonkaha × Rose Apples]

Kitano HT, w, Keihan; int. by Keihan Gardening, 1985

Kitayama HT, w, Keihan; int. by Keihan Gardening, 1994

Kitchener of Khartoum HT, mr, 1917, Dickson, A.; flowers dazzling velvety scarlet, 3 in., 10 petals; vigorous, branching growth; Gold Medal, NRS, 1916

Kitty Pol, mr, 1925, Koster; flowers carmine-red, small, dbl.

Kitty Bice LCl, mp, 1932, Fitzhardinge; [Ophelia, Climbing × Lady Waterlow]

Kitty Cleo F, yb; int. by Ashdowne, 2003

Kitty Hawk Min, pb, 1986, Bridges, Dennis A.; flowers deep pink, reverse lighter pink, 29 petals, high-centered, borne mostly singly; foliage large, medium green, semi-glossy; prickles medium, long, red; medium, upright growth; [Watercolor × unknown]; int. by Bridges Roses, 1986

Kitty Kingsbury HT, mp, 1930, Evans; flowers shell-pink; vigorous growth; [Abol × Abol]

Kitty Kininmonth HG, dp, 1922, Clark, A.; flowers deep pink, lighter reverse, golden stamens, 12 cm., semi-dbl., cupped; some recurrent bloom; foliage dark, wrinkled; few prickles; vigorous, climbing growth; [seedling × *R. gigantea*]; int. by Hackett

Kitty-Lew Min, yb, 2001, Hough, Robin; flowers yellow with pink edges, reverse lighter, 1 1/4 in., single, borne mostly solitary, slight fragrance; foliage medium size, medium green, semi-glossy; prickles long, straight, moderate; growth compact, medium (18 in.); [Phyllis Shackelford × Oriental Simplex]; int. in 2001

Kitty's Rose S, lp, 2006, Beales, Amanda; flowers 8 cm., dbl., borne in large clusters; foliage small; prickles average, hooked, few; growth bushy, short (60 cm.); landscape, containers; [Centenaire de Lourdes × City of London]; int. by Peter Beales Roses, 2003

Kiwi HT, w, 1989, Cattermole, R.F.; bud pointed; flowers creamy pink opening to creamy white, reflexed, pointed, medium, dbl.; foliage dark green, shiny; prickles needle-like, red to light brown; tall, upright growth; [Judith Morton × (Pascali × Blue Moon)]; int. by South Pacific Rose Nursery

Kiwi – See **Hot Cocoa**, F

Kiwi Belle F, pb, 1984, Cattermole, R.F.; flowers tan apricot to pink in cool weather, light pink in hot summer, large, 40 petals, globular, borne in clusters of 3-5, intense spicy fragrance; foliage bronze green when young, turning light green; prickles brown; upright, spreading growth; [Silent Night × Irish Mist]

Kiwi Charm HT, pb, 1972, Lindquist; bud ovoid; flowers creamy yellow, edged pink, large, semi-dbl., high-centered, moderate fragrance; foliage glossy, leathery; vigorous, bushy growth; [Kordes' Perfecta × Champagne]; int. by Bell Roses, Ltd.

Kiwi Delight HT, yb, 1984, Cattermole, R.F.; flowers golden yellow, petals edged deep pink, aging pink overall, large, 40 petals, globular, intense fragrance; foliage bronze green turning dark green, glossy; prickles gray-brown, very small and large; upright, bushy growth; [Peace × (Peer Gynt × Irish Mist)]

Kiwi Enterprise HT, yb, 2000, Cattermole, R.F.; flowers full, high-centered, borne mostly singly, slight fragrance; foliage medium size, light green, glossy; nearly thornless; growth compact, medium (4 ft.); [Royden × Irish Gold]; int. by Sharalea Gardens, 2001

Kiwi Gold HT, yb, 1983, Cattermole, R.F.; bud pointed; flowers light yellow, reverse edges of petals flushed pink, 22 petals, high-centered, intense fragrance; foliage light green, glossy; prickles very few, light brown; upright growth; [(Pink Parfait × Pink Parfait) × Waipounamu]; int. in 1984

Kiwi Queen HT, yb, 1984, Cattermole, R.F.; flowers yellow, shaded orange and pink, large, 44 petals, high-centered, slight fragrance; foliage medium green; prickles light brown; upright, spreading growth; [Peer Gynt × Command Performance]

Kiwi Reds HT, mr, 2000, Cattermole, R.F.; flowers very large, borne in small clusters, moderate fragrance; foliage large, medium to dark green, glossy; prickles few, on basal shoots only; growth upright, tall (up to 6 ft.); [Kiwi Gold × Prima Ballerina]; int. by Sharalea Gardens, 2001

Kiwi Sunrise Min, ob, 1993, McGredy, Sam IV; flowers florescent orange with yellow eye, light yellow to white accents, light yellow reverse, 2 in., dbl., borne in small clusters, moderate spicy fragrance; foliage medium size, dark green, glossy; few prickles; medium (24-30 in.), bushy growth; [Orange Honey × Pandemonium]; int. by Justice Miniature Roses, 1994

Kiwiana F, dp, 2002, Jones, Diana; flowers cerise pink, medium pink reverse, 7 cm., full, borne in large clusters, slight fragrance; foliage medium size, medium green, semi-glossy; prickles average, triangular, moderate; growth compact, short (80 cm.); garden decorative; [seedling × Dublin Bay]

Kiyosumi HT, m, 1979, Onodera, Toru F.; bud slender; flowers clear light purplish blue, 3 in., 25 petals, high-centered; foliage light green, leathery; upright growth; [seedling × Sterling Silver]; int. by S. Onodera

Klassy Lady Min, pb, 2006, Klassy, Diana; flowers deep pink, reverse white, 2 in., dbl., borne mostly solitary; foliage medium size, dark green, semi-glossy; prickles 3/16 in., hooked downward, deep pink, moderate; growth bushy, tall (20-24 in.); [sport of Miss Flippins]; int. in 2007

Klaus Groth – See **Claus Groth**, HSpn

Klaus Störtebeker HT, mr, 1965, Kordes, R.; flowers well-formed, 5 in., 40 petals; foliage dark; low, bushy growth; int. by Buisman, 1964

Klein Tausendschön HMult, mp, 1916, Kiese; [Tausendschön × unknown]

Kleine Ballerina Pol, Noack, Werner; int. in 1998

Kleine Dortmund F, rb, Noack, Werner; flowers carmine-scarlet with white eye, small, borne in large clusters, no fragrance; good repeat; foliage glossy; bushy, spreading growth; int. in 1992

Kleine Dortmunderin – See **Kleine Dortmund**, F

Kleine Echo Pol, mp, 1925, Kiese; flowers small, semi-dbl.

Kleine Eva Pol, mp, Hetzel, Karl; recurrent; low (12 in.) growth; int. in 1995

Kleine Leo HT, mr, 1921, Timmermans; flowers brilliant red shaded dark red, dbl.; [Farbenkonigin × Gen. MacArthur]

Kleine Regina Min, dr, Hetzel; int. in 1983

Kleine Renate Min, pb, J&P; int. in 1993

Kleine Rösel HWich, m, 1929, Vogel, M.; flowers dark violet-pink, reverse lighter, 4 cm., single, borne in flat clusters, no fragrance; foliage glossy; numerous prickles

Kleiner Alfred Pol, or, 1904, Lambert, P.; bud garnet-red; flowers well-formed, medium; foliage glossy; dwarf growth; [Anna-Maria de Montravel × Shirley Hibberd]

Kleiner Liebling Pol, mp, 1895, Schmidt, J. C.; flowers carmine rose, medium, cupped, borne in very large clusters; [Polyantha Grandiflora × Fellemberg]

Kleopatra – See **Cleopatra**, HT

Kleopatra HT, rb, 2006; bud large, round, pointed; flowers wine red with brass colored reverse, 11 cm., very full, high-centered, borne mostly solitary, moderate fragrance; foliage reddish at first, then large, dark green, shiny; erect, upright, vigorous, bushy growth with many canes, to 3 ft.; int. by W. Kordes' Söhne, 1994

Klerksdorp Horizon HT, rb, 1988, W. Kordes Söhne; flowers tomato-red, reverse golden yellow, large, 32 petals, borne 1-3 per cluster, no fragrance; foliage medium green, large; prickles concave, reddish-brown; upright, medium, free-flowering growth; [seedling × seedling]; int. by Ludwigs Roses Pty. Ltd., 1988

Kletternde Ruby Cl Pol, mr, 1946, Kordes; bud globular; flowers scarlet, small, dbl., borne in clusters; foliage dark, wrinkled; very vigorous, trailing growth; [sport of Ruby]

Klima Cl Min, dy, 1993, Saville, F. Harmon; flowers medium, semi-dbl., no fragrance; foliage small, medium green, semi-glossy; few prickles; tall (4-5 ft.), upright, climbing growth; PP8411; [Ferris Wheel × Golden Jubilee]; int. by Nor'East Min. Roses, 1993

Klimentina HT, mp, Klimenko, V. N.; flowers pink with silvery reverse, large, dbl.; int. in 1955

Klondyke HWich, my, 1911, Paul; flowers soft yellow, center deeper, passing to ivory-white, large, dbl.; very vigorous, climbing growth

Klondyke HT, my, 1934, LeGrice; flowers clear golden yellow; [sport of Lady Forteviot]

Klostertaler Power S, ob, Schultheis; flowers bright orange, wavy petals, dbl., borne in clusters, slight fragrance; foliage dark green, glossy; dense, bushy (5 × 5 ft.) growth; int. by Rosen von Schultheis, 2000

Kluis Orange – See **Klyn's Orange**, Pol

Kluis Scarlet F, mr, 1931, Kluis, R.; flowers brilliant red; very free growth; [sport of Lafayette]

Klyn's Orange Pol, or, Kluis; flowers orange-scarlet, small, dbl., borne in dense clusters; foliage light green; dwarf growth

Klyn's Yellow HT, my, 1948, Klyn; bud pointed; flowers clear yellow, open, large, dbl.; foliage glossy; very vigorous, compact growth; [McGredy's Yellow × unknown]

Knezna Libuse HT, op, Cerveny

Knick Knack Min, ob, 2000, Justice, Jerry G.; flowers peachy white, reverse pale orange, fading to white with gold edges, 1½ cm., semi-dbl., flat, borne mostly singly, slight fragrance; foliage medium size, medium green, semi-glossy; prickles moderate; growth upright, medium (18-22 in.); [Baby Diana × unknown]; int. by Justice Mini Roses, 2000

Knirps F, dp, 2006; flowers full, rosette, borne in small clusters; foliage small, dark green, very glossy; growth spreading, short (30 cm.); int. by W. Kordes' Söhne, 1997; Gold Medal, Baden-Baden

Knock Out S, rb, 1999, Radler, William; flowers medium, light red to deep pink, 2½ in., single, borne in small clusters, slight tea fragrance; foliage large, medium green, semi-glossy, very resistant to blackspot; prickles moderate; bushy, rounded, medium (3 ft.) growth; PP11836; [((Carefree Beauty × ((Tampico × Applejack) × Playboy)) × self) × (Razzle Dazzle × (Deep Purple × (Faberge × Eddie's Crimson)))]; int. by Conard-Pyle, 2000; AARS, 2000, ARS Members' Choice, 2004 Trial Ground Certificate, Durbanville, 2006

Knockout – See **Knock Out**, S

Knocktopher Lady Min, pb, 2001, McCann, Sean; flowers striped peach/cream, fading to linen, small, semi-dbl., borne in small clusters, slight fragrance; foliage small, light green, matte; some prickles; growth upright; garden decorative; [Dreamcoat × Dreamcatcher]

Ko-Choh F, ob, 1986, Suzuki, Seizo; flowers orange, reverse yellow shaded orange, small, 45 petals, high-centered, borne 3-5 per cluster, moderate fragrance; foliage dark, semi-glossy; prickles small; low, compact growth; [(Rumba × Olympic Torch) × Allgold]; int. by Keisei Rose Nursery, 1983

Koa Min, op, 1979, Rovinski & Meredith; bud ovoid; flowers coral-pink, 1 in., 44 petals, high-centered, slight fragrance; tall, open, leggy growth; [Persian Princess × Gene Boerner]; int. by Kingsdown Nursery, 1978

Koai HT, mr; int. in 1970

Koala LCl, w, Meilland; int. in 1993

Koba HT, or, 1979, Meilland, Mrs. Marie-Louise; flowers scarlet, medium, 40 petals, cupped; foliage dark; very vigorous, upright growth; [((seedling × Rouge Meilland) × Independence) × Queen Elizabeth]; int. by Meilland

Koba – See **Veronèse**, HT full

Kobé HG, lp, about 1900, Busby; flowers light flesh pink, large

København – See **Copenhagen**, Cl HT

Kobold F, op, McGredy, Sam IV; flowers large, semi-dbl.; int. in 1981

Kogane F, my, Keisei; int. by Keisei Rose Nurseries, 1993

Koh-I-Noor HT, pb, 1973, Ellick; flowers white, center deep pink, 5 in., 60 petals; foliage glossy, dark; vigorous growth; [(Memoriam × Peace) × My Choice]; int. by Excelsior Roses

Koha HT, rb, 1984, Cattermole, R.F.; flowers medium red, reverse lighter, large, 32 petals, high-centered, slight fragrance; foliage light, glossy, veined; prickles brown; upright, branching growth; [Silent Night × (Josephine Bruce × Irish Mist)]

Koharu-Biyori F, lp, 1999, Yasuda, Yuji; flowers pale pink, 2 in., 5 petals; foliage medium green; growth to 2½ ft.; [Hanagasumi × seedling]; int. in 1994; Gold Medal, Japan Rose Concours, 1993

Kohima F, rb, 1972, Ellick; flowers fire-red to orange, reverse cream, 4 in., 45-50 petals; vigorous growth; [Orange Sensation × Mischief]; int. by Excelsior Roses

Kohsai – See **Mikado**, HT

Koigokoro HT, dp, Keisei; int. by Keisei Rose Nurseries, 1992

Koigoromo HT, w, Hiroshima; int. by Hiroshima Bara-en

Kojack – See **Miss Blanche**, HT

Kojo – See **Sweet Dreams**, HT

Kojo no Tsuki LCl, dy, 1977, Teranishi, K.; bud circular; flowers deep yellow, 4½-5 in., 35 petals, high-centered, slight fragrance; foliage light; vigorous, climbing growth; [(Souv. de Jacques Verschuren × Thais) × Amarillo]; int. by Itami Bara-en, 1975

Koka HT, ly, Keihan; int. by Keihan Gardening, 1996

Koki HT, op, Keisei

KoKo Min, yb, 1983, Meredith, E.A. & Rovinski, M.E.; bud globular; flowers pale yellow, aging orange-red on petal edges, 55 petals, borne mostly singly, moderate fragrance; foliage medium size, medium green, matte; prickles thin, triangular, light brown; low, bushy growth; int. by Casa de Rosa Domingo

Koksijde F, pb, RvS-Melle; flowers 19 petals, flat; foliage matte; strong growth

Kokulinsky's Unterlage (strain of *R. canina*), lp; foliage susceptible to rust; growth once used as understock; used in Europe as an understock; int. as Kokulensky

Kokyu HT, w, Itami; flowers ivory with pink blush, shapely; growth medium; int. in 1990

Kolbe's Diamond HT, lp, Ludwig; [sport of Andrea Stelzer]; int. by Ludwig's Roses, 2003

Koldinghus F, dp, 1978, Poulsen, Niels D.; flowers deep rose, open, 2-2½ in., 23 petals, slight fragrance; foliage dark, glossy; upright growth; [Pernille Poulsen × seedling]; int. by Poulsen, 1968

Kolgian S, lp, Kolster; Peter Rudolf; flowers single; PP16042

Kolibre F, mr, 1946, Leenders, M.; bud long, pointed; flowers 3 in., 20 petals, borne in small trusses; foliage bronze; moderately vigorous growth; [Mev. Nathalie Nypels × seedling]; int. by Longley

Kolkhoznitsa HT, m, 1957, Sushkov & Besschetnova; flowers lilac-pink, large, 45 petals; foliage dark; very vigorous, compact growth; [Peace × Mirandy]

Köln am Rhein HKor, op, 1958, Kordes; flowers deep salmon-pink, 10-12 cm., semi-dbl., borne in large clusters, moderate fragrance; recurrent bloom; foliage dark, glossy; vigorous, climbing growth; [*R.* × *kordesii* × Golden Glow]; int. by Kordes & Son, 1956

Kölner Karneval, Climbing Cl HT, m, Kyle; flowers 12-15 cm.; PP4088; int. in 1977

Kölner Karneval – HT, m, 1965, Kordes, R.; flowers silvery lilac-lavender, 5½ in., 35-40 petals, high-centered, borne singly, moderate lightly fruity fragrance; foliage large, deep green; vigorous, bushy growth; int. by Wheatcroft Bros., 1964; Gold Medal, Rome, 1964

Komala '89 HT, pb, K&S; bud ovoid; flowers rosy pink with almond, large, dbl.; int. by KSG Son Roses, 1989

Kombination F, VEG; int. in 1982

Komet HT, mr, VEG; flowers vermilion red, medium to large, dbl.

Komfort F, mp, 1967, Tantau, Math.; flowers salmon-pink, large, semi-dbl., borne in clusters (to 20); foliage glossy; very vigorous, bushy growth

Kommerzienrat W. Rautenstrauch HFt, mp, 1909, Lambert, P.; flowers pure salmon-pink, center yellow, reverse lighter, 5-6 cm., semi-dbl., open, borne in small clusters, slight licorice fragrance; some repeat; nearly thornless; [Léonie Lamesch × *R. foetida bicolor*]

Kommodore F, mr, 1959, Tantau, Math.; flowers blood-red, well-formed, large, dbl., borne in clusters; vigorous, low growth

Kommodore, Climbing Cl F, mr; [sport of Kommodore]; int. after 1959

Kon-Tiki F, mr, 1971, Institute of Ornamental Plant Growing; bud ovoid; flowers bright red, large, semi-dbl., cupped; foliage glossy, dark; vigorous, upright growth; [Aztec × Paprika]

Konfetti HT, pb, 1965, Tantau, Math.; bud globular; flowers claret-rose, reverse light cream, well-formed, 5 in., 40-45 petals; foliage dark, leathery; strong stems; bushy, upright growth

Konfetti – See **Tantau's Konfetti**, HT

Kong Frederik den IX – See **Peach Surprise**, HT

König Friedrich II von Dänemark, Climbing Cl HP, dr, 1840, Vogel; [sport of König Friedrich II von Dänemark]

König Friedrich II von Dänemark HP, dr; flowers deep red, medium, dbl.

König Laurin HT, w, 1910, Türke; flowers whitish pink, large, dbl., moderate fragrance; [Mme Caroline Testout × White Maman Cochet]

König Ludwig-Rose S, mp, Tantau; flowers large, dbl.; int. in 1994

König von Sachsen HGal, mp, 1878, Ruschpler; foliage light green, deeply serrated; numerous prickles; stems strong; growth vigorous

Königen HWich, mp; flowers small, dbl.

Königin Beatrix HT, ob, 1983, Kordes, W.; flowers orange, large, 35 petals, high-centered; foliage medium size, medium green, semi-glossy; upright, bushy growth; [seedling × Patricia]

Königin Carola – See **Königin Carola von Sachsen**, HT

Königin Carola von Sachsen HT, pb, 1904, Türke; bud pointed; flowers satiny rose-pink, reverse silvery white, very large, dbl.; foliage dark, leathery; vigorous growth; [Mme Caroline Testout × Viscountess Folkestone]

Königin der Rosen – See **Colour Wonder**, HT, 1964

Königin Emma HT, lp, 1903, Verschuren; flowers fleshy white with rosy center, large, dbl.; [Kaiserin Auguste Viktoria × seedling]

Königin Juliana F, 1948, Buisman, G. A. H.

Königin Kunigunde F, mp, Tantau; flowers soft pink fading to white, dbl., rosette, borne in clusters; int. by Rosen Tantau, 2002

Königin Luise HT, w, 1927, Weigand, C.; flowers very large, dbl., high-centered; foliage dark, leathery, glossy; vigorous, bushy growth; [Frau Karl Druschki × Sunburst]

Königin Margrethe – See **Queen Margrethe**, S

Königin Maria Therese HT, dp, 1916, Lambert, P.; flowers carmine-pink, very large, very dbl.; [Frau Karl Druschki × Luise Lilia]

Königin Viktoria von Schweden HT, yb, 1919, Ries; flowers light saffron-yellow, aging to pale salmon-pink, dbl.; [Mme Segond Weber × Mrs Joseph Hill]; int. by Teschendorff

Königin von Blatna – See **Blatenskà Kràlovna**, HWich

Königin von Dänemark A, mp, 1816, Booth; flowers flesh-pink, center darker, petals recurved, with a very small center eye, medium, very dbl., quartered, flat, borne in clusters, intense fragrance; non-recurrent; foliage dark bluish-green, with 5-7 toothed, elliptical leaflets; prickles numerous, hooked; vigorous growth; [probably *R. alba* × Damask hybrid]

Königin Wilhelmine Pol, dp, 1925, Koster; flowers carmine-pink, medium, full; [sport of Orléans Rose]

Koniginrosa – See **Regina Dicta**, HGal

Konigliche Hoheit – See **Royal Highness**, HT

Königlicht Hoheit – See **Royal Highness**, HT

Königsberg HT, mr, 1940, Weigand, L.; flowers scarlet-red; [Mrs Henry Winnett × Marechal Petain]; int. by Teschendorff

Koningin Astrid HT, mr, 1935, Leenders, M.; bud long, pointed, nasturtium-red; flowers reddish-apricot and bronze, very large, dbl.; foliage dark, bronze; vigorous growth

Koningin Juliana F, mp, 1948, Buisman, G. A. H.; flowers salmon-pink becoming light yellow with salmon, large, dbl., borne in clusters; blooms late; foliage glossy; [Poulsen's Pink × Mrs Pierre S. duPont]

Koningin Wilhelmina HT, pb, 1904, Verschuren; flowers rose pink with coppery salmon, dahlia-like

Konoe HT, ob, Keihan; int. by Keihan Gardening, 1989

Konrad Adenauer – See **Konrad Adenauer Rose**, HT

Konrad Adenauer Rose HT, dr, 1955, Tantau, Math.; bud globular; flowers blood-red, 4 in., 35 petals, cupped, intense fragrance; foliage light green, glossy; vigorous, upright growth; PP1452; [Crimson Glory × Hens Verschuren]; int. by J&P, 1955

Konrad Glocker F, dr, 1965, Kordes, R.; flowers 3 in., dbl.; foliage dark; vigorous, bushy, low growth; int. by Buisman, 1964

Konrad Henkel HT, mr, 1983, Kordes, W.; flowers large, 35 petals, high-centered, moderate fragrance; foliage large, medium green, semi-glossy; upright, bushy growth; [seedling × Red Planet]

Konrad Thönges HFt, op, 1929, Thönges; flowers salmon-orange/pink, large, semi-dbl.

Kontiki HT, rb; int. by deRuiter

Kontrast HT, rb, Hchen; int. in 1981

Kooiana Butterscotch HT, my, Gibson, P.; [sport of Golden Times]; int. by Sunrise Flowers, Int., 1995

Kooiana Daybreak HT, ab; flowers delicate cream-pink, fading with age, borne mostly singly; tall growth; int. in 1995

Kooiana Moonlight HT, ly, Gibson, P.; [sport of Gerdo]; int. by Sunrise Flowers, Int., 1995

Kooiana Watermelon HT, Gibson, P.; [sport of Kooiana Daybreak]; int. by Sunrise Flowers, Int., 1995

Kookaburra – See **Vogelpark Walsrode**, S

Koopmanns Sport von Else Poulsen Pol, mr, 1940, Koopmann; flowers medium, semi-dbl.

Kooshti-Bok F, or, 1997, Jellyman, J.S.; flowers medium, single, borne in small clusters; foliage medium size, dark green, semi-glossy; growth upright, spreading, medium to tall (3½-4ft.); [(Tony Jacklin × seedling) × (Tony Jacklin × Andrea)]; int. by F. Haynes & Partners

Kootenay HT, lp, 1917, Dickson, A.; flowers primrose-color, tinged yellow, large, full, moderate fragrance

Köpenicker Sommer F, dy, Rupprecht-Radke; flowers medium-large, dbl.; int. in 1968

Koppies HT, lp, 1980, Perry, Astor; bud ovoid; flowers 35 petals, high-centered, borne usually singly, moderate fruity fragrance; foliage medium size, matte; prickles short, recurved; vigorous, tall growth; [Tropicana × Wendy Cussons]; int. in 1981

Koralie S, lp

Koralle F, mr, 1942, Koopman; flowers light red; [sport of Else Poulsen]; int. by Tantau

Koralle F, op, Harkness; int. in 1991

Korallovyj Sjurpriz F, op, Klimenko, V. N.; flowers luminous coral-red, large, dbl.; int. in 1966

Korbasta HT, my, Kordes; flowers golden yellow that can have orange tints, large, 30-35 petals, exhibition, borne mostly singly, slight fragrance; stems short; moderate growth; may not be from Kordes, in spite of the name

Korbel Bicolor Pink – See **Mrs Henry Morse**, HT

Korcarill Min, mp, Kordes, T-H; PP15716; [Korlusma × Korkleiva]

Kordana Vanilla Min, w, Kordes; flowers white with a greenish tint; int. by Ludwig's Roses, 2003

Kordes' Brillant S, ob, 1983, Kordes, W.; flowers orange, large, 35 petals; foliage medium size, medium green, glossy; upright, bushy growth; [(Sympathie × unknown) × seedling]

Kordes' Gärtnerfreude – See **Gärtnerfreude**, Pol

Kordes' Harmonie – See **Harmonie**, S

Kordes' Magenta – See **Magenta**, F

Kordes' Perfecta HT, pb, 1959, Kordes; bud urn-shaped; flowers cream tipped and then flushed crimson, suffused yellow, 4½-5 in., 68 petals, high-centered, intense fragrance; foliage dark, leathery, glossy; vigorous, upright growth; PP1604; [Golden Scepter × Karl Herbst]; int. by A. Dickson, 1957; President's International Trophy, NRS, 1957, Gold Medal, Portland, 1958, Gold Medal, NRS, 1957

Kordes' Perfecta, Climbing Cl HT, pb, 1962, Japan Rose Soc.; bud pointed; flowers creamy pink, edged crimson, large, borne in small clusters, intense fragrance; [sport of Kordes' Perfecta]

Kordes' Perfecta Superior – See **Perfecta Superior**, HT

Kordes' Rose Aloha – See **Aloha**, HT

Kordes' Rose Anabel – See **Anabell**, F

Kordes' Rose Angelique – See **Ankori**, HT

Kordes' Rose Bella Rosa – See **Bella Rosa**, F

Kordes' Rose Champagner – See **Antique Silk**, F

Kordes' Rose Delicia – See **Elegant Beauty**, HT

Kordes' Rose Esmeralda – See **Keepsake**, HT, 1981

Kordes' Rose Flamingo – See **Flamingo**, HT

Kordes' Rose Florentina – See **Florentina**, HT

Kordes' Rose Gabriella – See **Gabriella**, F dbl.

Kordes' Rose Holstein – See **Esprit**, S

Kordes' Rose Immensee – See **Immensee**, S

Kordes' Rose Julie – See **Julie**, HT

Kordes Rose Kardinal – See **Kardinal**, HT, 1986

Kordes' Rose Lady Rose – See **Lady Rose**, HT

Kordes' Rose Pasadena – See **Pasadena**, HT, 1982

Kordes' Rose Patricia – See **Patricia**, F

Kordes' Rose Repandia – See **Repandia**, S

Kordes' Rose Robusta – See **Robusta**, S

Kordes' Rose Sylt – See **Sylt**, HKor

Kordes' Rose Sylvia – See **Congratulations**, HT

Kordes' Rose Weisse Immensee – See **Weisse Immensee**, S

Kordes' Rose Westfalenpark – See **Westfalenpark**, S

Kordes' Silver Star – See **Silver Star**, HT

Kordes' Sondermeldung – See **Independence**, F

Kordes' Sondermeldung, Climbing – See **Independence, Climbing**, Cl F

Kordesii – See ***R. × kordesii*** (Wulff), HKor

Kore S, pb, Urban, J.; flowers yellowish-pink, with russet tints, large, dbl., intense fragrance; good repeat; vigorous (6 × 5 ft.) growth; int. in 1980

Korglolev Min, mp, Kordes; PP15717; [Korengir × Korfrauma]

Körner HMsk, yb, 1914, Lambert, P.; bud reddish; flowers orange-yellow tinted salmon, dbl., borne in clusters; [Trier × Eugenie Lamesch]

Koro HT, mr, 1984, Cattermole, R.F.; flowers scarlet, large, 32 petals, high-centered, intense fruity fragrance; foliage medium green; prickles reddish; upright growth; [(Pink Parfait × unknown) × Red Planet]

Korona F, or, 1955, Kordes; flowers orange-scarlet, 2½ in., 20 petals, borne in large trusses; vigorous, upright growth; int. by Morse; Gold Medal, NRS, 1954

Korona, Climbing Cl F, or, 1957, Kordes; [sport of Korona]

Korona S, ab, Unmuth; flowers amber yellow, borne singly and in clusters; upright, branching (7 ft.) growth; int. about 2000

Koronam HT, w, Kordes; int. in 1994

Koronet HT, ob, 1941, Mallerin, C.; bud globular, lemon shaded orange; flowers orange, reverse deep primrose, 4½ in., 40-50 petals, high-centered; foliage dark, glossy, leathery; vigorous, upright, bushy, open growth; [Julien Potin × Bright Wings]; int. by A. Meilland

Korovo HT, mp, 1931, Leenders, M.; bud pointed; flowers peach-blossom-pink and coppery old-rose, large, 30 petals; foliage thick; vigorous growth; [Mrs T. Hillas × Étoile de Hollande]

Korrigan F, lp, 1978, Poulsen, Niels D.; bud globular; flowers dbl., 25 petals, slight fragrance; foliage glossy, dark, leathery; vigorous, bushy growth; [seedling × (Orléans Rose × Eden Rose)]; int. by Poulsen, 1972

Ko's Yellow Min, yb, 1978, McGredy, Sam IV; flowers yellow, edges marked red, fading to cream, classic form, medium, 39 petals; foliage dark, glossy; bushy growth; PP4385; [(New Penny × Banbridge) × (Border Flame × Manx Queen)]; int. by McGredy Roses International

Kosai HT, or, Keisei; flowers bright red, reverse orange blend, full

Kosmos F, dr, VEG; flowers medium, dbl.

Koster Blanc – See **Blanche Neige**, Pol

Koster's Orléans Pol, mr, 1920, Koster, M.; flowers brilliant scarlet-red; [sport of Orléans Rose]

Koster's Triumph Pol, or, 1920, Koster; flowers small, dbl.

Kostior Arteka F, or, 1955, Klimenko, V. N.; flowers coral-red tinted orange, large; [Independence × unknown]

Koto HT, dy, 1973, Suzuki, Seizo; bud ovoid; flowers pure deep yellow, large, dbl., high-centered, moderate fragrance; foliage glossy, dark, leathery; vigorous, upright growth; [Lydia seedling × (Peace × unknown)]; int. by Keisei Rose Nursery, 1972

Kotobuki HT, yb, 1991, Ogura Rose Nurseries; bud pointed; flowers creamy to creamy yellow, creamy yellow reverse with light pink at fringe, large, 30-35 petals, high-centered, borne usually singly, slight fragrance; foliage dark green, glossy; medium growth; [sport of Souma]

Kotobuki HT, rb, Hiroshima; int. by Hiroshima Bara-en, 2000

Kotohogi Cl Min, dp, 2003, Tsuyoshi Ishii; flowers single, borne in small clusters; foliage small, medium green, semi-glossy; prickles sharp, numerous; growth spreading, short (100 cm.); groundcover; [Azumino × seedling]

Kotone F, ab, Keisei; int. by Keisei Rose Nurseries, 2002

Koukaku LCl, my, Hiroshima; int. by Hiroshima Bara-en, 1998

Kouzan HT, dr, 2004, Matsumoto, Masayuki; flowers dark red, 12 cm., full, borne mostly solitary, moderate fragrance; foliage large, medium green, semi-glossy; prickles medium; growth upright, tall (200 cm.); exhibition; [seedling × seedling]

Kovalam HT, w, 1979, Viraraghavan, M.S. Viru; bud globular; flowers cream-white, 4 in., 20-25 petals, cupped, intense fragrance; foliage wrinkled; moderate, bushy growth; [(Amberlight × Traumland) × Western Sun]; int. by KSG Roses, 1976

Kovsie Roos S, m, Taschner, Ludwig; flowers lilac-crimson, dbl., cupped, intense fragrance; recurrent; stems long; vigorous, tall growth; int. by Ludwig's Roses, 2005

Koyo F, rb, 1989, Kikuchi, Rikichi; bud ovoid; flowers vermilion, reverse orange-yellow, small, 17-20 petals, cupped, borne in large sprays; foliage dark green, glossy; prickles ordinary; spreading growth; [Masquerade × Matador]; int. in 1990

Koyuki – See **Snow Infant**, Min

Koza HRg, dp, 1927, Hansen, N.E.; flowers deep pink, medium, semi-dbl.; vigorous (over 7 ft.) growth; extremely hardy; [(*R. rugosa* × La France) × La Mélusine]

Krakow HT, dr, Grabczewski; bud ovate; flowers very dbl.

Kralj Alexander I HT, dr, 1935, Böhm, J.; flowers velvety blood-red, reflexes fiery red, very large, dbl.; vigorous growth; [Capt. Kilbee Stuart × Jan Bohm]

Kralj Petar II HT, pb, 1936, Brada, Dr.; flowers salmon-pink, reverse carmine, with coppery sheen

Kralj Tomislav HT, mr, 1931, Leenders, M.; bud long, pointed; flowers solferino-red, open, very large, dbl., high-centered; vigorous growth; [Dora Stober × Étoile de Hollande]

Kraljica Marija HT, ly, 1935, Brada, Dr.; flowers creamy yellow to creamy white, large, dbl.; [Frau Karl Druschki × Golden Ophelia]; int. by Böhm

Kranenburg F, dp, 1965, Verschuren, A.; flowers very dark pink, 32 petals, borne in clusters; foliage glossy, dark; bushy growth; [Pinocchio × Ma Perkins]; int. by van Engelen, 1963

Krasavitza Festivalia HT, yb, 1955, Klimenko, V. N.; flowers yellow edged raspberry-red, medium, 28 petals; foliage glossy, light green; spreading growth; [(Peace × Crimson Glory) × Poinsettia]

Krasavitza Festivalia, Climbing Cl HT, yb, Vidal; [sport of Krasavitza Festivalia]; int. after 1955

Krásná Azurea – See **General Stefánik**, HP

Krásná Uslavanka HT, ob, 1930, Böhm, J.; flowers orange-rose, reverse dark orange-yellow; very vigorous, bushy growth; [Mrs Beckwith × Arthur Cook]

Krasnaia Moskva HT, dr, 1955, Klimenko, V. N.; flowers dark velvety red, medium; [Peace × Crimson Glory]

Krasni Mak-Sin F, dr, Klimenko, V. N.; flowers dark, velvety red, medium, dbl.; int. in 1975

Krasnokamenka F, mr, 1955, Klimenko, V. N.; flowers crimson-red, medium, 12 petals; foliage dark, glossy; upright growth; [Independence × Kirsten Poulsen]

Krasnyi Mak F, mr, 1955, Klimenko, V. N.; flowers scarlet, medium, 26 petals; foliage glossy, light green; short stems; upright growth; [Independence × Kirsten Poulsen]

Krause Macrantha S, pb, Krause; flowers medium pink outer half of petals with lighter center, semi-dbl.; foliage dark green; HMacrantha

Krause's Rote Joseph Guy – See **Feuerschein**, F

Kretly HGal, m, 1842, Bardou; flowers velvety lilac-violet, marbled purple-garnet, medium, full

Krimhilde T, yb, 1893, Drögemüller; flowers chamois yellow, aging to carmine, center coppery golden yellow, medium to large, full, moderate fragrance; [Mme Bérard × Perle des Jardins]

Krioga F, lp, 1986, Kriloff, Michel; flowers 35 petals, borne in clusters; foliage dense; bushy growth; [seedling × Orange Garnet]

Krishna's Peach T, ab, 2006, Viraraghavan, M.S. Viru; flowers 4 in., full, high-centered, hybrid tea form, borne mostly solitary; foliage medium size, medium green, semi-glossy; prickles small, triangular, brown, few; growth spreading, medium (4 ft.); garden decorative; [Safrano × (mixed Tea × *R. gigantea*)]; int. by Roses Unlimited, 2007

Kristall F, w, GPG Bad Langensalza; int. in 1979

Kristi HT, mp, 1976, Swim, H.C. & Ellis, A.E.; bud ovoid, pointed; flowers clear medium pink, 5 in., 45 petals, moderate spicy fragrance; foliage large; vigorous, upright growth; [White Satin × Bewitched]; int. by Armstrong Nursery

Kristian IV – See **Mariandel**, F

Kristin Min, rb, 1992, Benardella, Frank A.; flowers white/red bicolor, do not open beyond 1/2 open stage, 1½ in., 27-30 petals, high-centered, borne singly, no fragrance; foliage large, dark green, semi-glossy; upright, bushy, medium growth; PP8603; [Buttons × Tinseltown]; int. by Nor'East Min. Roses, 1993; AOE, ARS, 1993

Kristina av Tunsberg F, or, 1973, Lundstad; bud long, pointed; flowers large, very dbl., high-centered, slight fragrance; foliage glossy, dark; vigorous, bushy growth; [Charleston × Toni Lander]; int. by Norges Landbruks-hogskole, 1972

Kristo Pienaar HT, yb, Herholdt; int. in 1990

Kronborg – See **Redwood**, F

Kronborg Castle – See **Redwood**, F

Kronenbourg – See **Flaming Peace**, HT

Kronenbourg, Climbing Cl HT, rb, Kasturi; flowers bicolor red and yellow; int. by KSG Son Roses, 1973

Kronjuwel F, mr, Noack, Werner; flowers 6 cm., semi-dbl. to dbl., borne in clusters; good repeat; low to medium (2 ft.) growth; int. by Noack Rosen, 1997

Kronos HT, dy, Tantau; flowers large, full, high-centered, borne mostly singly; stems long; greenhouse rose; int. by Rosen Tantau, 2002

Kronprincessin Victoria – See **Kronprinzessin Viktoria von Preussen**, B

Kronprinsesse Ingrid – See **Kronprinzessin Ingrid**, F

Kronprinsesse Mary S, w, Olesen; bud urceolate; flowers white with yellow shading in center, 5 cm., 130 petals, cupped, borne in large clusters, moderate fragrance; recurrent; foliage dark green, glossy; prickles numerous, 10 mm., hooked downward, greyed-orange; upright to bushy (60-100 cm.) growth; PP16991; [seedling × Clair Renaissance]; int. by Poulsen Roser, 2004

Kronprinzessin Cecilie HT, lp, 1907, Kiese; flowers large, very dbl.; [Mme Caroline Testout × Mrs W. J. Grant]

Kronprinzessin Ingrid F, mp, 1936, Poulsen, S.; bud long, pointed; flowers deep rose-pink, open, semi-dbl.; foliage dark; vigorous growth; [Else Poulsen × Dainty Bess]; int. by C-P, 1942

Kronprinzessin Victoria HT, mr, Hetzel, K.; flowers dbl., moderate apple fragrance; moderate (4 ft.) growth; int. in 1986

Kronprinzessin Viktoria – See **Kronprinzessin Viktoria von Preussen**, B

Kronprinzessin Viktoria von Preussen B, w, 1887, Volvert; flowers milk-white, center tinted yellow; free-flowering; growth compact; [sport of Souv. de la Malmaison]

Krymchanka F, m, Klimenko, V. N.; flowers dark purple-red, medium, dbl.; int. in 1955

Krymskaja Notsch HT, dr, Klimenko, V. N.; flowers large, dbl.; int. in 1955

Kühnhilda S, mp, Weihrauch; flowers medium, single; int. in 1983

Kukolinsky – See **Kokulinsky's Unterlage**, (strain of *R. canina*)

Kulu Belle HT, dp, 1974, Pal, Dr. B. P.; buds medium, long pointed; flowers deep pink, medium to large, full, high-centered, borne singly; foliage medium size, leathery; growth vigorous, bushy (75 cm.); int. by K. S. G. & Son, 1972

Kum Kum HT, lp, Muckerjee, K.P.; flowers delicate pink, large, lasting, moderate fragrance; free-flowering; int. in 1994

Kumaradhara F, pb, K&S; flowers salmon with silvery white reverse; int. by KSG Son Roses, 1988

Kumari F, mp, Kasturi; flowers high-centered; [White Junior Miss × unknown]; int. by KSG Son Roses, 1982

Kumbaya F, my, 1981, Sanday, John; bud pointed; flowers bright medium yellow, 22 petals, borne up to 15 per cluster; foliage deep green; prickles slightly hooked, red; low, bushy growth; [Chatterbox × Allgold]; int. by Sanday Roses, Ltd.

Kumiko HT, dp, Reuter; int. by Reuter Frères, 1997

Kumkum F, or, 1974, Pal, Dr. B. P.; buds small, pointed; flowers vivid orange-scarlet, medium, semi-dbl., open, borne in clusters; foliage medium size, glossy; growth vigorous, open, upright (115 cm.); int. by K. S. G. Son, 1971

Kunigunde F, 1960, Horstmann; flowers pink, large, 35 petals, high-centered; vigorous growth

Kupferkönigin HT, dy, 2006; bud large, pointed; flowers copper-yellow, 11 cm., very full, high-centered, borne mostly solitary, slight fragrance; recurrent; foliage medium size, dark green, glossy; upright, medium (80 cm.) growth; int. by W. Kordes' Söhne, 1996

Kurama HT, mr, Keihan; int. by Keihan Gardening, 1977

Kurenai F, dp, Keisei; int. by Keisei Rose Nurseries, 2004

Kurenai Seishin HT, ob, Hiroshima; int. by Hiroshima Bara-en, 2000

Kurocho F, dr, Keisei; int. by Keisei Rose Nurseries, 2005

Kuroshinju HT, dr, Suzuki, Seizo; int. in 1988

Kurstadt Baden HT, pb, Tantau, Math.; flowers pink and red, large, dbl.; int. in 1966

Kurt Scholz HT, mr, 1934, Kordes; bud pointed; flowers blood-red with some crimson, very large, dbl., high-centered; foliage leathery; vigorous, bushy growth; [Cathrine Kordes × W.E. Chaplin]

Kushali Gr, mp, Solanki-Tejganga; free-flowering; stems long; [sport of Prima Donna]; int. in 1996

Kusum F, lp, Padhye; flowers pale pink, long lasting, borne in clusters; [sport of Fusilier]; int. in 1978

Kutno Pol, m, 1965, Wituszynski, B.; flowers lavender-pink, dbl.; growth low; [Margo Koster × unknown]

Kwinana F, rb, 1962, Riethmuller; bud ovoid; flowers crimson overlaid carmine, single, open, borne in clusters, moderate fragrance; foliage leathery; strong stems; vigorous, tall growth; [Orange Triumph × unknown]; int. by Hazelwood Bros., 1962

Kynast HT, mr, 1917, Krüger; flowers amaranth-red, large, full; [Dr G. Krüger × unknown]

Kyo-Maiko F, op, 1973, Suzuki, Seizo; bud ovoid; flowers deep bright salmon-orange, small, dbl., cupped, slight fragrance; foliage small, glossy, light; moderate, dwarf, bushy growth; [(Sarabande × unknown) × Ruby Lips seedling]; int. by Keisei Rose Nursery, 1974

Kyogoku HT, pb; int. in 1989

Kyoto – See **Koto**, HT

Kyoto 1200 – See **Arashiyama**, HT

Kyria F, lp, 1976, Royon; flowers full, 4 in., 25-30 petals, high-centered; PP4017; [sport of Sweet Promise]; int. as Pitica, Universal Plants

Kyson Cl HT, mr, 1940, Eacott; flowers bright red, open, very large, single, borne in clusters; recurrent bloom; foliage leathery, glossy, dark; short, strong stems; very vigorous, climbing (7 ft. or more) growth; [New Dawn × Allen Chandler]; int. by R. MurrellL. D. Braithwaite – See **Leonard Dudley Braithwaite**, S

L. E. Longley HT, mr, 1949, Longley, L.E.; flowers open, large to medium, semi-dbl.; foliage glossy, dark, bronze; very vigorous, bushy growth; [Pink Princess × Crimson Glory]; int. by Univ. of Minn.

L. G. Harris HT, Gregory, C.; int. in 1972

L. J. de Hoog HT, mr, 1934, Leenders Bros.; flowers scarlet-red, well-formed, large, dbl.; vigorous, bushy growth; [Hadley × Hawlmark Scarlet]

L. R. May HT, dr, 1935, Chaplin Bros.; flowers scarlet-crimson, paling to silvery pink, base orange, well-formed; vigorous growth

La Bamba S, my, Dickson; flowers pale yellow, semi-dbl., open, borne in open clusters; low, spreading groundcover growth; int. by Dickson Roses, 2003

La Baraka HT, or

La Bella HT, dr, 1975, Kordes; bud large, ovoid; flowers dbl., globular, slight fragrance; foliage glossy, dark; very vigorous, upright growth; [Liebeszauber × Herz As]; int. by Horstmann, 1976

La Belle HT, pb, Kordes; flowers light pink, green tint on outer petals, medium, full, cupped, borne mostly singly; recurrent; thornless; stems medium to long; florist rose; int. by W. Kordes Söhne, 2005

La Belle Alsacienne S, dp, 2002, Eve; flowers velvety pink-crimson with purplish reflections, dbl., tangled OGR form, intense fragrance; vigorous (5 ft.) growth; int. by Le Roses Anciennes de André Eve, 2001

La Belle Augusta – See **Belle Auguste**, D

La Belle Distinguée HEg, mr, about 1820; flowers bright crimson, small, dbl.; non-recurrent; foliage dainty, fragrant; compact (3-4 ft.) growth

La Belle Inconnue S, mp

La Belle Irisée HT, ob, 1943, Gaujard; bud ovoid, coppery; flowers clear orange-yellow, medium, dbl., globular; foliage leathery; dwarf growth; [Mme Joseph Perraud × seedling]

La Belle Marie T, dp, 1856, Raynaud; flowers pink, veined darker, reverse deep rose, center incurved, medium, moderate fruity fragrance; foliage smooth, pointed; vigorous, tall growth; [Old Blush × Mme Laurette Messimy]; int. by Tillotson

La Belle Mathilde HSpn, w, 1816, Descemet; flowers white, washed pink, 3-3½ in., semi-dbl., moderate fragrance; foliage very close-set, simply serrate

La Belle Ninon – See **Belle Ninon**, HGal

La Belle Sultane HGal, dr, Before 1801; flowers velvety deep crimson-purple, becoming violet, base white, with prominent yellow stamens, medium, 10-12 petals, flat, borne solitary or in cluster of 2-3; early summer; foliage thick, medium green, round; prickles numerous, brown, slightly recurved, small; from Holland, distributed by Dupont; int. in ca. 1795

La Belle Suzanne T, lp; flowers light pink suffused white; foliage smooth, pointed; vigorous, tall growth; [Old Blush × Mme Laurette Messimy]; int. by Tillotson

La Belle Villageoise – See **Panachée Pleine**, HGal

La Biche N, w, 1832, Trouillet; flowers white, center flesh, 7-9 cm., very dbl., cupped, borne in large clusters, strong damask/Tea fragrance; very remontant; foliage dark

La Biche – See **Mlle de Sombreuil**, T

La Bien Aimé – See **Bien-Aimée**, HGal

La Bitta S, dy; groundcover; int. by Arena Roses, 2005

La Blancheur – See **Sodori-Himé**, HT

La Bonne Geneviève – See **Bonne Geneviève**, HCh

La Bonne Maison HMsk, w, Masquelier, Odile; flowers white with pink blush, single, borne in large clusters, intense fragrance; recurrent; vigorous (6 ft.) growth; [Francis E. Lester × *R. multiflora nana*]; int. in 1997

La Boule d'Or T, dy, 1860, Margottin; flowers golden yellow, very large, full, globular

La Brillante – See **Général Jacqueminot**, HP

La Brillante HP, mr, 1861, Verdier, V.; flowers bright crimson, well-formed, large, dbl.; numerous prickles; growth upright

La Brunajeune – See **La Brunoyenne**, HP

La Brunoyenne HP, rb, 1908, Bourgeois; flowers velvety red with flame, center lighter madder red, large, very full, cupped

La Caille M, mp, 1857, Robert et Moreau; flowers bright rose-pink, nuanced violet, full, flat

La Canada Min, dp

La Canadienne HT, ob, 1967, Morey, Dr. Dennison; bud long, pointed; flowers orange to shrimp and cream, large, semi-dbl.; foliage dark, bronze, glossy; vigorous, bushy growth; [Royal Sunset × Sierra Sunset]; int. by General Bionomics

La Centfeuilles Prolifère Foliacée – See **Prolifera de Redouté**, C

La Champagne HT, ob, 1919, Barbier; bud long, pointed; flowers light coppery red, base yellow, edged light pink, large, 25 petals, globular; foliage rich green, leathery; vigorous growth

La Chinoise – See **Fortuniana**, Misc OGR

La Cicogne HT, mp, 1903, Corboeuf

La Cocarde – See **Majestueuse**, HGal

La Cocarde – See **L'Évêque**, HGal

La Coquette – See **Celsiana**, D

La Coquette de Lyon – See **Coquette de Lyon**, T

La Coquette de Marly-le-Roy B, w, 1863, Cagneux; flowers white, shaded pink

La Couronne Tendre HGal, lp; flowers flesh-pink, small, dbl.

La Croix d'Honneur – See **Croix d'Honneur**, HCh

La Delphinie – See **Delphinie**, M

La Désirée HGal, about 1810, Descemet

La Desirée HCh, mp, before 1848; flowers very small, full; Lawrenciana

La Detroite HT, lp, 1904, Hopp & Lemke; flowers flesh-pink, shading to deep rose, large, dbl., intense fragrance; [Mme Caroline Testout × Bridesmaid]

La Diaphane M, lp, 1848, Laffay; flowers blush rose, large, very dbl., rosette

La Digittaire – See **Childling**, C

La Divinité – See **Damas Violacé**, D

La Duchesse HGal, mp, 1838

La Duchesse de Morny HP, mp, 1863, Verdier, E.; flowers tender rose-pink, reverse pale pink, nuanced silver, large, dbl., globular, cupped; very remontant; foliage dark above, pale beneath, oval, pointed; prickles unequal

La Esmeralda – See **Esmeralda**, HP

La Favorita HT, or

La Favorite HGal, mr, about 1815, Descemet

La Favorite HT, mp, 1900, Schwartz; flowers blush white washed cream, large, dbl., cupped; [Mme Caroline Testout × Reine Emma des Pays-Bas]

La Félicité D, pb, before 1810, Dupont; flowers light blush pink, speckled with white, large, semi-dbl.

La Fiamma HWich, ob, 1909, Walsh; flowers flame red, 3 cm., single, borne in very large clusters; foliage small, glossy; vigorous, climbing (15 ft.) growth

La Fiancée d'Abydos T, w; flowers white, tinted with coppery carmine pink, full

La Florida HT, mp, 1932, La Florida; flowers salmon, well-formed; foliage glossy; strong stems; very vigorous growth

La Florifère B, dp, 1846, Bougère; flowers dark carmine pink,shaded silky pink, medium, full

La Florifère B, mp, 1865, Soupert; flowers glowing carmine

La Follette Cl T, mp, about 1910, Busby; bud long, pointed; flowers pink and carmine, 13 cm., dbl., moderate fragrance; vigorous (to 20 ft .); half-hardy; [*R. gigantea* × unknown]

La Fontaine HP, mr, 1845, Vibert; flowers bright garnet, medium, full

La Fontaine M, lp, 1852, Robert; flowers delicate pink, shaded deep pink, 5-7 cm., full, flat

La Fontaine HP, mp, 1855, Guinoisseau; flowers bright pink, large, full

La Fontaine F, my, 1961, Meilland, Mrs. Marie-Louise; bud pointed, ovoid; flowers barium-yellow, 3½-4 in., 20-25 petals, high-centered to cupped, borne in clusters; foliage leathery, dark; vigorous, bushy growth; PP2040; [Mme Charles Sauvage × Fashion]; int. by C-P, 1961

La Fraîcheur HWich, mp, 1921, Turbat; flowers dark pink with lighter edges, 4 cm., dbl., borne in clusters of 15-20, slight fragrance; non-recurrent; foliage small, dark green

La France HT, lp, 1867, Guillot et Fils; bud long, pointed; flowers silvery pink, reverse bright pink, large, petals slightly waved, 60 petals, intense fragrance; vigorous, short (2-3 ft.) growth; [Mme Bravy × Mme Victor Verdier]; considered to be one of the first Hybrid Teas introduced, and the prototype of the class; reported parentage is probably not correct

La France, Climbing Cl HT, lp, 1893, Henderson, P.; flowers rich peach pink, large, dbl.; [sport of La France]

La France de '89 HT, rb, 1889, Moreau et Robert; bud long, pointed; flowers bright red, sometimes striped white, 3-3½ in., dbl., borne in small clusters; good repeat; very vigorous growth; [Reine Marie Henriette × La France]

La France Striped HT, pb, 1956, Hennessey; flowers deep pink to red, and white to blush; [sport of La France]

La France Victorieuse HT, dp, 1919, Gravereaux; flowers silvery carmine-pink, inside tinted yellow, very large, dbl., moderate fragrance; int. by M. Guillot

La Garçonne – See **Nostalgie**, HT

La Giralda HT, mp, 1926, Dot, Pedro; [Frau Karl Druschki × Mme Edouard Herriot]

La Globuleuse HP, dp, 1862, Crousse; flowers silky dark pink

La Gloire des Jardins HGal, m, before 1815, Descemet; flowers carmine pink, tinted violet, large, dbl.

La Gloire des Laurencias HCh, dr, before 1829, Miellez; flowers dark crimson purple, small, full, flat; Lawrenciana

La Glorieuse – See **Illustre**, HGal

La Gracieuse – See **Célina**, M

La Grand Obscurité – See **Passe-Velours**, HGal

La Grande Belgique – See **Blush Belgiques**, A

La Grande Junon – See **Minerve**, HGal

La Grande Parade S, mr; flowers small, single, borne in clusters; free-flowering

La Grande Violette – See **Roxelane**, HGal semi-dbl.

La Grandeur T, m, 1878, Nabonnand; flowers violet-pink, very large, full; very remontant

La Grandeur HT, my, 1894, Pernet-Ducher; flowers medium yellow, edges lighter and tinted pink, sometimes striped, very large, dbl.

La Joconde HT, my, 1920, Croibier; flowers pure golden yellow; RULED EXTINCT 2/88; [sport of Arthur R. Goodwin]

La Joconde HT, or, 1988, Delbard & Chabert; flowers well-shaped, large, 40 petals; upright, vigorous growth; [(Tropicana × (Rome Glory × Impeccable)) × (Spartan × MElger)]

La Jolie HT, mr, 1956, Buyl Frères; bud long, pointed; flowers geranium-red, 30-35 petals; very vigorous growth; [Independence × Hens Verschuren]

La Jolla HT, pb, 1954, Swim, H.C.; bud long, pointed; flowers soft pink veined deeper, center cream and gold, 5 in., 65 petals, high-centered; foliage dark, glossy; upright growth; [Charlotte Armstrong × Contrast]; int. by Armstrong Nursery

La Jonquille T, my, 1871, Ducher; flowers medium, semi-dbl.; [Lamarque × unknown]

La Julie HGal, before 1815, Descemet

La Laponne HCh, mp, before 1829; flowers violety-pink, very small, flat; Lawrenciana

La Liliputienne HCh, dp, before 1829, Miellez; flowers deep violet pink, very small, full; Lawrenciana

La Louise C, m, before 1810, Dupont; flowers fleshy mauve-pink, semi-dbl.

La Louise HGal, dr, about 1840, Parmentier; flowers red, shaded purple, full

La Luna HT, ly, Kordes; flowers lemon-yellow, dbl., high-centered, borne singly, occasionally two or three per stem; stems long, near thornless; int. in 1999

La Lune T, ly, 1878, Nabonnand; flowers creamy yellow, center darker, semi-dbl., globular

La Maculée HGal, pb, before 1815, Dupont; flowers rose pink with carmine striping, medium, semi-dbl.

La Madelon de Paris F, lp, 1962, Robichon; flowers bright pink, well-formed, medium, dbl., borne in clusters of 6-8; vigorous growth; [Cécile Brunner × seedling]

La Magnifique – See **Pourpre Charmant**, HGal

La Maréchale Pétain HT, mr, 1927, Sauvageot, H.; flowers carmine, dbl.; [Col. Leclerc × Château de Clos Vougeot]; int. by F. Gillot

La Marne Pol, pb, 1915, Barbier; flowers blush white, edged vivid pink, single, borne in large, loose clusters; vigorous growth; [Mme Norbert Levavasseur × Comtesse du Cayla]

La Marseillaise HT, dr, 1986, Delbard; bud large, ovoid; flowers well-formed, large, 40 petals; vigorous, bushy growth; [((Gloire de Rome × Impeccable) × (Rouge Meilland × Soraya)) × (MElsar × Walko)]; int. in 1976

La Marylene F, dr

La Mascotte Cl HT, dy, 1933, Schwartz, A.; flowers deep saffron-yellow, passing to straw-yellow, slightly tinted salmon, dbl.; foliage dark, glossy; [Reine Marie Henriette × Laurent Carle]

La Mélusine HRg, dp, 1906, Späth; flowers pinkish red, large, dbl., borne in large clusters, intense fragrance; very vigorous growth

La Mère de St Louis – See **Mère de St Louis**, HP

La Mère Gigogne HGal, before 1815, Descemet

La Mère Gigogne Ch, dp, about 1830, Vibert; flowers dark pink, aging to purple, medium, very full

La Mère Gigogne C, lp, about 1830, Vibert; flowers light pink, medium, full

La Merveille HGal, before 1820, Descemet

La Mexique – See **Le Mexique**, HWich

La Mie au Roy HT, yb, 1927, Bernaix, P.; flowers yellow, salmon and copper large, dbl., globular, moderate fragrance; [Duchess of Wellington × Pax Labor]

La Mienne – See **Flon**, D

La Minuette – See **Minuette**, F

La Moderne P, lp, before 1820; flowers blush, large, semi-dbl.; prickles feeble

La Mortola Sp, w, 1970, Hanbury; flowers yellowish-white, 3 in., 5 petals, borne in trusses, intense fragrance; foliage downy gray-green; very vigorous, climbing growth; form of *R. brunonii*; int. by Sunningdale Nursery, 1954

La Motte Sanguine – See **Lamotte Sanguin**, HP

La Mouche HCh, dp, before 1830, Miellez; flowers cerise, very small, full; Lawrenciana

La Nankeen T, yb, 1871, Ducher; bud deep orange yellow at base, white at point; flowers coppery-yellow, outer petals lighter, large, full; foliage light green, smooth, oval-pointed; prickles reddish brown, upright, flattened; stems thin and reflexing, pale green

La Nantaise HP, dr, 1885, Boisselot; flowers intense red darkened by deeper tints, large, full, cupped, borne singly and in small clusters; foliage dark green; prickles hooked, medium; growth erect; [Général Jacqueminot × unknown]

La Napolitaine – See **Charles X**, HGal

La Napolitaine – See **Ulysse**, HGal

La Nationale HGal, pb, before 1836; flowers pink and red, striped and marbled with purplish crimson, medium, dbl.

La Négresse – See **Superbe en Brun**, HGal

La Négresse D, dr, 1842, Vibert; flowers very deep crimson-purple, medium, full, flat; growth branching, small

La Neige HGal, w, 1853, Robert; flowers white with green pip, full, flat rosette; foliage dark green; growth vigorous

La Neige M, w, 1905, Moranville; flowers pure white, medium, dbl.; foliage turns purple; vigorous growth; [Blanche Moreau × unknown]

La Nina HGal, about 1810, Descemet

La Nina F, pb, Richardier; int. in 1998

La Noble Fleur HGal, about 1810, Descemet

La Noblesse C, lp, 1856, Pastoret; flowers soft pink with carmine center, somewhat silvery, large, dbl., borne singly or in clusters of 2-3, intense fragrance; later bloom than most centifolias; foliage light gray-green; bushy growth; int. by Soupert & Notting

La Nuancée T, w, 1875, Guillot; flowers white, copper at base, edges tinted salmon, medium, full

La Nubienne HCh, m, 1825, Laffay; flowers deep velvety purple, medium, full, globular

La Paloma F, w, 1959, Tantau, Math.; flowers creamy white, well-formed, dbl., borne in clusters of up to 30; foliage dark, glossy; [Yellow Rambler × Goldene Johanna Tantau]

La Paloma HT, w, 1973, Swim & Weeks; buds medium, long-pointed to urn-shaped; flowers large, dbl, high-centered, borne mostly singly; foliage dark green, leathery; growth vigorous, upright (4½-5 ft.); PP2853; [Mount Shasta × White Knight]; int. by O. L. Weeks, 1968

La Paloma 85 – See **The Dove**, F

La Panachée – See ***R. gallica versicolor*** (Linnaeus)

La Pâquerette – See **Pâquerette**, Pol, 1875

La Parfaite HT, op, 1956, Buyl Frères; bud pointed; flowers bright salmon-pink, large, 40-50 petals; vigorous, bushy growth; [R.M.S. Queen Mary × Lady Sylvia]

La Parfumee HT, or

La Parisienne HT, or, 1937, Mallerin, C.; bud long, pointed, deep coral-red; flowers orange-coral, open, very large, semi-dbl.; foliage glossy, dark; very vigorous growth; [Lucy Nicolas × Charles P. Kilham]; int. by C-P

La Parisienne HT, ab, 1999, Schuurman, Frank B.; flowers 4½ in., full, borne mostly singly; foliage large, dark green, glossy; prickles moderate; upright, tall growth; [Kia Ora × Texas]; int. by Franko Roses New Zealand, Ltd., 1996

La Passionata – See **Betsy Ross**, HT, 1970

La Passionata HT, Barni, V.; int. in 1987

La Passionata HT, rb, Delbard; flowers red and orange mixed, large, dbl.; good repeat; vigorous (50-100 cm.) growth; int. by Georges Delbard SA, 1997

La Perie – See **La Perle**, HWich

La Perla F, lp, Kordes; int. in 1994

La Perle HWich, ly, 1905, Fauque; flowers pale yellow to white, 7 cm., full, borne in small clusters, moderate fragrance; foliage dark green, glossy; [*R. wichurana* × Mme Hoste]

La Petite Min, lp, 2002, Umsawasdi, Dr. Theera & Chantana; flowers medium, full, borne in small clusters; foliage medium size, medium green, glossy; prickles average, curved, moderate; growth upright, medium; garden decorative; [Loving Touch × Hansa]; int. by Certified Roses, Inc., 2002

La Petite Duchesse – See **La Belle Distinguée**, HEg

La Peyrouse HP, dr, 1854, Robert

La Phocéenne HP, dp, 1862, Geoffre; flowers shining, velvety carmine, large, full

La Pinta F, mr, Richardier; int. in 1998

La Pivoine HP, mr, 1862, Moreau & Robert; flowers poppy red

La Plus Belle des Ponctuées HGal, pb, before 1929; flowers deep rose, spotted pale rose, flat; probably much older than the stated date

La Plus Élégante – See **Cramoisie Triomphante**, HGal

La Poilu – See **Cumberland Belle**, Cl M

La Pologne HT, or, 1938, Chambard, C.; flowers orange-carmine, very large, cupped; foliage bronze; vigorous growth

La Prédestinée – See **Illustre**, HGal

La Presumida – See **Presumida**, Min

La Princesse Vera T, w, 1877, Nabonnand; flowers white with a coppery base, large, very full; few prickles

La Promise HT, mr, 1956, Buyl Frères; bud long, pointed; flowers brick-red, semi-dbl.; tall growth; [seedling × Betty Uprichard]

La Proserpine HMult, op, 1897, Ketten; flowers peach, yellow center, edge fading to white, medium, dbl., moderate fragrance; [Georges Schwartz × Duchesse Marie Salviati]

La Provence HGal, dr, before 1819; flowers velvety crimson, 4 in.

La Pucelle HGal, m, before 1811, Dubourg; bud pointed; flowers bright purple pink, small, dbl., pompon; foliage small, light green, finely dentate

La Pucelle – See **Pucelle de Lille**, HGal

La Pudeur B, w, about 1835, Laffay; flowers flesh white, small, full; perhaps synonymous with La Pudeur from de Fauw

La Pudeur B, w, 1853, de Fauw; flowers white with pink, large, full; possibly synonymous with La Pudeur from Laffay

La Pyramidale – See **Porcelaine**, HGal

La Quintinie HCh, m, before 1848; flowers dark lilac pink, very large, cupped

La Quintinie B, dp, 1853, Thomas; flowers dark carmine, aging to poppy red, full

La Ramée F, dr, 1949, Meilland, F.; flowers crimson, 13 petals, borne in clusters; foliage dark, bronze; vigorous growth; [Holstein × Alain]

La Reine HP, mp, 1842, Laffay, M.; flowers glossy rose-pink, large, 78 petals, cupped, moderate fragrance; vigorous growth; [possibly a seedling of William Jesse]

La Reine d'Angleterre – See **Reine d'Angleterre**, T

La Reine de Hamburg P, mp

La Reine de la Pape – See **Reine de la Pape**, HP
La Reine de Provence – See **Reine des Centfeuilles**, C
La Reine Victoria – See **Reine Victoria**, B
La Remarquable A, w, before 1833; flowers medium, full, cupped
La Revenante HGal, mp, 1825, Miellez; flowers cerise, dbl., loose
La Roche aux Fees HT, yb, Adam, M.; int. in 1997
La Rochefoucauld-Liancourt HGal, pb, 1825, Coquerel; flowers light pink, center brighter, shaded and marbled purple, very large, very full
La Rose – See **Guy de Maupassant**, F
La Rose Bordeaux S, mp, Guillot-Massad; flowers pale pink, deeper in center, full, borne in clusters, moderate fragrance; foliage medium size, medium green; vigorous (4 ft.) growth; int. by Roseraies Guillot, 2001
La Rose de Mme Raymond Poincaré – See **Mme Raymond Poincaré**, HT
La Rose de York – See **White Rose of York**, A
La Rose Romantica – See **Guy de Maupassant**, F
La Rose Tatouée – See **The Rose Tatoo**, HT
La Rosée Pol, w, 1920, Turbat; flowers sulfur-white, passing to pure white, then to soft pink
La Rosée – See **Doctor F. Debat**, HT
La Rosiere HP, 1861, Verdier, E.
La Rosière, Climbing – See **Prince Camille de Rohan**, HP
La Rosière HP, dr, 1875, Damaizin; bud long; flowers maroon crimson, shaded with black, medium, dbl., cupped
La Rossa F, mr, Barni, V.; flowers unfading red, 10 petals, open, borne in clusters; good repeat; compact (40-60 cm.) growth; int. by Rose Barni, 1999
La Roxelane HGal, m, 1828, Vibert
La Royale – See **Great Maiden's Blush**, A
La Royale – See **Plena**, A
La Royale de Mulhouse F, ly, Sauvageot; flowers light yellow, darker towards center, petals ruffled, dbl.; int. in 2003
La Rubanée HGal, pb, before 1832, possibly Vibert; flowers rose pink, striped with white and violet, 8 cm., very dbl., early bloomer, moderate fragrance; foliage large, deep green; numerous prickles; open (6 ft.) growth; int. by Vibert
La Sanguine – See **Sanguinea**, Ch
La Saumonée HCh, op, 1877, Margottin fils; flowers salmony pink, large, full, cupped; sometimes reblooming in autumn
La Scala HT, rb, 1965, Lindquist; flowers reddish-orange, large, dbl., cupped, intense fragrance; foliage leathery; upright, open growth; [(Mme Henri Guillot × Mirandy) × Peace]; int. by Ansaloni, 1964; Gold Medal, Rome, 1961
La Séduisante – See **Great Maiden's Blush**, A
La Serenissima HT, (Italia)
La Sevillana F, or, 1978, Meilland, Mrs. Marie-Louise; bud conical; flowers vermilion, 8 cm., 10-15 petals, borne in clusters of 5-20, no fragrance; recurrent; foliage bronze, leathery; vigorous, bushy (3 ft.) growth; PP6384; [((MEIbrim × Jolie Madame) × (Zambra × Zambra)) × ((Tropicana × Tropicana) × (Poppy Flash × Rusticana))]; int. by Meilland, 1982; ADR, 1979
La Sevillana, Climbing Cl F, or, Meilland; [sport of La Sevillana]; int. in 1997
La Sirène HP, m, 1867, Soupert & Notting; flowers dark reddish-purple
La Soleil F, or, 1961, Mallerin, C.; flowers bright vermilion, 3 in., 29 petals, borne in clusters; foliage clear green; dwarf, bushy growth; int. by EFR
La Somme HT, or, 1919, Barbier; bud large, ovoid; flowers deep coral-red tinted copper, turning salmon, large, semi-dbl., open, cupped, moderate fragrance; foliage medium size, leathery, dark green, glossy; [Mme Caroline Testout × Rayon d'Or]
La Souveraine HP, mp, 1874, Verdier, E.; flowers shining carmine pink, reverse silvery, very large, full, moderate melon fragrance
La Stupenda HT, pb, 1966, Taylor, L.R.; bud long, pointed; flowers pink, reverse darker, large, very dbl.; foliage glossy; upright, bushy growth; [Aztec × First Love]
La Superba Gr, Mansuino; int. in 1970
La Surprise A, w, 1823, Poilpré; flowers medium, very dbl.; nearly thornless
La Sylphide T, ly, 1838, Vibert; probably extinct
La Sylphide T, m, 1842, Boyau; flowers pink tinted lavender, deeper in fall, semi-dbl.; tall growth
La Syrène – See **La Sirène**, HP
La Syrène HP, mr, 1874, Touvais; flowers light cherry red, large, full
La Temponaise HT, rb, Reuter; int. by Reuter Frères, 2000
La Tendresse HGal, m, before 1820, Dupont; flowers pale violet pink
La Tendresse HP, mp, 1864, Oger; flowers hydrangea pink, large, full
La Tosca HT, pb, 1901, Schwartz, Vve.; flowers shell-pink, center and reverse darker, 4 in., dbl., moderate fragrance; foliage rich green, leathery; vigorous, bushy growth; [Josephine Marot × Luciole]
La Toulousaine HP, lp, 1877, Brassac; flowers flesh pink, aging to carmine, medium, full
La Tour d'Argent – See **Guy Laroche**, HT
La Tour d'Auvergne HGal, rb, 1842, Vibert; flowers deep rosy crimson, flecked carmine, incurved, large, dbl.
La Transparente – See **Unique Carnée**, C
La Très Haute – See **Aigle Brun**, HGal
La Triomphante – See **Illustre**, HGal
La Tulipe T, w, 1868, Ducher; flowers creamy white, tinted with pale carmine, large, semi-dbl.
La Vaillante Bergère HP, dp, 1847, Cherpin; flowers medium, full
La Vanoise Parc National – See **Rosanna**, LCl
La Variable – See **Childling**, C
La Vaudoise HT, mr, 1946, Heizmann, E.; bud oval; flowers blood-red touched brilliant scarlet, medium, dbl.; foliage leathery; vigorous, bushy growth; int. by A. Meilland
La Vendômoise HT, pb, 1907, Moullière; flowers pink and red, large, dbl.; [Mrs W. J. Grant × Marie d'Orléans]
La Vénissiane F, ly, Guillot-Massad; flowers yellow fading quickly to white with pink dots, large, slight fragrance; foliage dark green, glossy; solid (80 cm.) growth; int. by Roseraies Guillot, 2001
La Vie HT, dr, 1931, Groshens; flowers crimson to scarlet, base orange to carmine, fading to red; [sport of Talisman]
La Vie en Rose – See **Vie en Rose**, F
La Vierzionnaise HP, lp, 1893, André; sepals foliaceous; flowers light lilac pink, shaded darker pink, borne in small clusters; prickles red, hooked; growth upright
La Villageoise – See **Panachée Pleine**, HGal
La Ville de Bruxelles D, mp, 1836, Vibert; sepals long, leafy; flowers pink tinted salmon, center incurved, with a small center eye, medium, very dbl., quartered, cupped, strong fragrance; non-remontant; foliage glossy, light green, elongated; tall (5 ft.) growth; *R. centifolia* may have been one parent
La Ville de Londres HGal, dp, before 1844, Vibert; flowers deep rose pink, very large, full, cupped
La Virginale – See **Great Maiden's Blush**, A
La Virginale – See **Beauté Virginale**, D
La Volumineuse P, lp, before 1835; flowers rosy flesh, large
La Volupté HGal, dp, before 1828, Bizard; flowers bright glowing deep pink, large, full
La Voulzie F, dr, 1953, Robichon; flowers garnet-red, very large, semi-dbl., borne in clusters; very vigorous growth; [Brise Parfumee × Alain]
Labareda F, mr, Moreira da Silva; flowers bright red
L'Abbandonata – See **Lauré Davoust**, HMult
L'Abondance HP, mr, 1864, Verdier, E.
L'Abondance N, w, 1877, Moreau et Robert; bud slightly pink; flowers flesh-pink, opening to pure white, 5-6 cm., full, borne in large clusters; good repeat; foliage glossy; growth semi-climbing (8 ft.)
Labrador Rose – See ***R. blanda*** (Aiton)
Lac Blanc – See **Weisse Immensee**, S
Lac La Nonne HRg, dp, 1950, Bugnet; bud pointed, deep red; flowers very deep pink, 2-3 in., semi-dbl., moderate fragrance; foliage light; growth vigorous (7-8 ft.); hardy; [*R. rugosa plena* × *R. acicularis*]; int. by P.H. Wright
Lac Majeau HRg, w, Bugnet; flowers large, semi-dbl.; recurrent; few prickles; upright, bushy (5 ft.) growth; int. before 1984
Lac Rose – See **Immensee**, S
Lace Cascade LCl, w, 1992, Warriner, William A.; bud pointed, ovoid; flowers icy white, floriferous, 3-3½ in., full, borne in small and large clusters, moderate sweet fragrance; foliage large, medium green to dark green,semi-glossy; some prickles; growth tall (150-160 cm.), upright, spreading; PP8689; [Iceberg × Prairie Fire]; int. by Bear Creek Gardens
Lacépède HP, dp, 1865, Vibert; flowers light red, aging to dark pink, large, full
Lachs Pol, or, 1943, Kordes; flowers glowing orange-red; [sport of Dick Koster]
Lacination S, mp, Twomey, Jerry; int. in 1997
Lacre F, mr, 1963, Moreira da Silva; flowers bright red, loose, semi-dbl.; [Concerto × seedling]
Lacteola – See **White Provence**, C
Lada HT, dp, Urban, J.
Ladakh Rose Ch, lp, before 1936; flowers light pink, aging to dark pink, large; from India
Laddie HT, or, 1926, McGredy; flowers deep carmine, flushed orange and scarlet, base orange; bushy growth; int. by Beckwith
Ladera S, ob; int. by Spring Hill Nurseries, 2003
Ladies Choice HT, pb, 1969, Anderson's Rose Nurseries; flowers cerise, reverse silvery, high pointed, large, dbl.; foliage light green; free growth; [Liberty Bell × Prima Ballerina]
Ladies' Choice, Climbing Cl HT, pb, 1976, Anderson's Rose Nurseries; flowers cerise, reverse silvery, high-pointed, large, dbl., intense fragrance; foliage light green; [sport of Ladies' Choice]; int. in 1975
Ladies Home Journal HT, m, 1998, Winchel, Joseph F.; flowers pinkish mauve, medium, 8-14 petals, borne mostly singly; foliage medium size, medium green, semi-glossy; few prickles; upright, medium (4½-5 ft.) growth; [unknown × unknown]; int. by Certified Roses, 1998
Ladies In Waiting S, ab; PP14334; int. by J&P, 2003
Ladies' View Min, yb, 1991, McCann, Sean; flowers small, dbl., slight fragrance; foliage small, medium green, semi-glossy; bushy growth; [You 'n' Me × Amber Queen]

L'Admirable – See **Admirable**, HGal

L'Admiration Ch, mp, 1856, Robert; flowers medium, single

Lady HT, mp, 1984, Weeks, O.L.; flowers medium, 35 petals, high-centered, slight fragrance; foliage large, medium green, matte to semi-glossy; upright, compact growth; [Song of Paris × Royal Highness]

Lady – See **Lady Parade**, MinFl

Lady Aberdeen – See **Awareness**, HT

Lady Alice Stanley HT, pb, 1909, McGredy; bud pointed; flowers pale flesh-pink, reverse coral-rose, large, 75 petals; foliage rich green, leathery; branching growth

Lady Anderson HT, pb, 1920, Hall; flowers coral pink to flesh pink and yellow, dbl.

Lady Angela S, mp, 2003, Monteith, Joan; flowers medium, full, borne in large clusters, intense fragrance; foliage medium green, matte; growth upright, tall; [Heritage × Westerland]; int. by Joan Monteith

Lady Ann Min, mp, 1961, Moore, Ralph S.; bud pointed; flowers rose-pink, 1¾ in., 42 petals, cupped; foliage leathery, glossy, dark; vigorous, bushy, low growth; [(*R. wichurana* × Floradora) × Little Buckaroo]; int. by Sequoia Nursery, 1961

Lady Ann Kidwell Pol, dp, 1948, Krebs; bud pointed; flowers deep pink, medium, dbl., star-shaped; foliage glossy; vigorous, upright growth; [Cécile Brunner × unknown]; int. by Marsh's Nursery

Lady Arthur Hill HP, lp, 1889, Dickson; flowers lilac-pink, large, full

Lady Ashtown HT, pb, 1904, Dickson, A.; bud pointed; flowers carmine-pink, base yellow, large, 43 petals, high-centered; foliage rich green, soft; vigorous, bushy growth; [Mrs W.J. Grant × unknown]

Lady Ashtown, Climbing Cl HT, pb, 1909, Bradley; [sport of Lady Ashtown]

Lady Baillie HSpn, ly, before 1848, Lee; flowers pale sulfur-yellow, semi-dbl.; profuse, early bloom; foliage finely divided; dense, shrubby (3-4 ft.) growth; hips glossy, black

Lady Banks Rose – See ***R. banksiae*** (Aiton)

Lady Barbara LCl, ob, 1985, Warner, Chris; flowers tangerine, reverse yellow, medium, 20 petals, high-centered, moderate fragrance; foliage medium size, medium green, semi-glossy; upright growth; [Red Planet × (Elizabeth of Glamis × (Galway Bay × Sutter's Gold))]; int. in 1987

Lady Barbara Bossom F, lp, 1997, Bossom, W.E.; flowers frilly, 4 in., very dbl., borne in small clusters; foliage medium size, light green, glossy; some prickles; upright, tall (90cm.) growth; [Savoy Hotel × Pearl Drift]

Lady Barham HT, op, 1911, Dickson; flowers fleshy coral-pink, shaded orange pink, very large, full

Lady Barnby HT, pb, 1930, Dickson, A.; bud pointed; flowers glowing pink, shaded red, large, dbl., high-centered; foliage rich green, leathery; bushy, low growth

Lady Barnett HT, dr, 1958, Verschuren; flowers crimson, reverse darker, high-centered, moderate fragrance; vigorous, upright growth; int. by Blaby Rose Gardens, 1957

Lady Battersea HT, pb, 1901, Paul; flowers cherry-blossom, base orange, dbl.; [Mme Abel Chatenay × Liberty]

Lady Be Good Min, mp, 1990, McCann, Sean; flowers dbl.; foliage small, medium green, semi-glossy; bushy growth; [Kiss 'n' Tell × (Irish Mist × Matangi)]; int. in 1991

Lady Beatty HT, lp, 1918, Chaplin Bros.; flowers blush-pink, well-formed; vigorous growth

Lady Beauty HT, pb, 1985, Kono, Yoshito; bud ovoid; flowers light pink flushed yellow, reverse deeper, large, 33 petals, high-centered, slight fragrance; foliage medium size, medium green, glossy; prickles few, sickle-shaped; vigorous, upright growth; [Lady × Princess Takamatsu]; int. in 1984

Lady Belper HT, ob, 1948, Verschuren; flowers bronze-orange shaded light orange, semi-globular, 4 in., 38 petals, high-centered, borne mostly singly, moderate fragrance; foliage glossy, dark; vigorous growth; [Mev. G.A. van Rossem × seedling]; int. by Gregory

Lady Betty HT, ab, 1930, Bees; bud pointed; flowers apricot-pink, veined red, semi-dbl., high-centered; [Sunburst × Mrs Aaron Ward]

Lady Beverley F, lp, Owens; flowers clear pink; [sport of Independence]; int. in 1958

Lady Bird F, yb, 1966, Joseph H. Hill, Co.; flowers yellow shaded red at edge, small, dbl., borne in clusters; foliage leathery; vigorous, bushy growth; PP2626; [seedling × Rumba]

Lady Bird HT, yb; int. by Richard Huber AG, 2006

Lady Bird Johnson HT, or, 1970, Curtis, E.C.; bud long, pointed; flowers medium, dbl., moderate fragrance; vigorous, upright growth; [Montezuma × Hawaii]; int. by Texas Rose Research Foundation, 1971

Lady Bissett HT, ob, 1928, Lilley; flowers bright orange, reverse apricot

Lady Blanche LCl, w, 1913, Walsh; flowers snow-white, dbl., borne in large clusters; free bloom, sometimes repeated in fall; very vigorous, climbing growth

Lady Bountiful LCl, mr, 1938, Tait; flowers scarlet-rose, center white, open, large, single, borne in clusters; foliage leathery, dark; very vigorous, climbing or trailing growth; [American Pillar × unknown]; int. by B&A

Lady Braye HT, dp, 1960, Verschuren; flowers deep rose-pink, long, pointed; foliage dark; int. by Gandy Roses, Ltd.

Lady Bren Min, mp, 2004, Smith, Joe and Landers, Brenda; flowers med pink, reverse white, medium, dbl., borne mostly solitary; foliage medium size, dark green, glossy; prickles ¼ in.; growth upright, medium; [sport of Miss Flippins]; int. in 2005

Lady Brisbane – See **Cramoisi Supérieur**, Ch

Lady Brisbane, Climbing – See **Cramoisi Supérieur, Climbing**, Cl Ch

Lady Cahn HT, ab, 1937, Gaujard; bud long, pointed; flowers rich apricot-yellow, veined darker, large, 40-50 petals; long, strong stems; vigorous growth

Lady Canada HT, mp, 1927, Dale; flowers bright rose, dbl.; [Mme Butterfly × Premier]

Lady Carolina S, lp, 1990, Jeremias, Lephon L.; bud ovoid; flowers blush pink, same reverse, aging to white, decorative, small, 35-40 petals; repeat bloom; foliage average, dark, glossy; prickles small, hooked, reddish-brown; bushy, spreading, hedge-type, medium growth; hips round, very red, very small; [sport of Lady Gay]

Lady Castlereagh T, yb, 1888, Dickson, A.; flowers rosy yellow, well-formed; vigorous growth

Lady Catherine HT, or, 1976, Von Koss; bud urn shaped; flowers 3½-4 in., 32-45 petals, high-centered; foliage leathery; vigorous, upright, compact growth; [Montezuma × Rubaiyat]; int. by Kern Rose Nursery

Lady Catherine Rose HT, dp, 1912, Bide; [Antoine Rivoire × La Fraîcheur]

Lady Cecily Gibson – See **Cecily Gibson**, F

Lady Charles Townshend HT, ob, 1931, Daniels Bros.; flowers orange, overlaid salmon, large, dbl., globular; vigorous, bushy growth; [The Queen Alexandra Rose × Shot Silk]

Lady Charmion HT, mr, 1923, Bees; flowers bright cherry-carmine, dbl.; [Lyon Rose × Gen. MacArthur]

Lady Clanmorris HT, w, 1900, Dickson, A.; flowers creamy white with pale rose center, edged with deep rose, very large

Lady Clonbrock N, lp; flowers light pink, medium, dbl., borne in large clusters; introduced by Smith, 1903, but is possibly an older variety

Lady Coventry HT, m, 1913, Smith of Downley

Lady Craig HT, ly, 1922, Dickson, H.; flowers cream-yellow, center apricot-yellow, well-formed, large, dbl.; vigorous, free branching growth

Lady Cromwell HT, dr, 1956, Verschuren; flowers crimson, base gold, large, dbl.; foliage bronze; vigorous growth; int. by Gandy Roses, Ltd.

Lady Cunliffe Owen HT, pb, 1932, Ley; flowers salmon and cream, base yellow, flushed carmine-rose, outer petals reflexed, dbl., high-centered; foliage leathery; vigorous growth; [sport of Mrs A.R. Barraclough]

Lady Curzon HRg, mp, 1901, Turner; flowers delicate pale pink, golden anthers, large, single, moderate fragrance; prickles very numerous; arching stems; vigorous growth; [*R. macrantha* × *R. rugosa rubra*]

Lady Dallas Brooks HT, mp, 1955, Downes; [sport of Peace]

Lady Dartmouth HT, pb, 1909, Bermaix fils

Lady Dawson Bates HT, yb, 1939, McGredy; flowers golden yellow, flushed pink, opening, high-centered; vigorous growth

Lady de Bathe HT, w, 1911, Cant, B.; flowers creamy white, center shaded peach-rose with yellow, large, full

Lady Di HT, lp, Huber; bud pointed; flowers soft pink, 25-29 petals, high-centered, slight fragrance; good repeat; upright, strong (80 cm.) growth; int. by Richard Huber AG, 1982

Lady Diana HT, lp, 1986, Hoy, Lowel L.; flowers 37 petals, high-centered, borne in sprays of 3-4; foliage medium size, medium green, matte; prickles short, hooked; tall, upright growth; hips ovoid, orange; PP5360; [Sonia × Caress]; int. by Joseph H. Hill, Co., 1983

Lady Diana – See **Her Majesty**, F

Lady Dixon HT, ab, 1919, Dickson, A.; flowers rich apricot, flushed salmon-pink, dbl.

Lady Dixon-Hartland HT, pb, 1923, Cant, B. R.; flowers centers deep salmon, outer petals pale pink, high-centered; vigorous growth

Lady Donaldson – See **Mary Donaldson**, HT

Lady Dorothea T, pb, 1898, Dunlop; flowers yellow over pink; [sport of Sunset]

Lady Downe HT, my, 1911, Paul, W.; flowers medium to large, full, moderate fragrance

Lady Dumas HT, pb, White, T.H.

Lady Duncan HRg, pb, 1900, Dawson; flowers rich glowing pink, center and stamens yellow, 3 in., single, borne in small clusters; non-recurrent; foliage glossy; trailing (6 ft.) growth; [*R. wichurana* × *R. rugosa*]; int. by Eastern Nursery

Lady Dunleath HT, w, 1913, Dickson, A.; flowers ivory-white edged yellow, small, dbl.

Lady Dunmore HSpn, lp, before 1906, from England

Lady Edgeworth David HT, mp, 1939, Fitzhardinge; bud long, pointed; flowers Malmaison rose shaded soft pink, large, dbl., open, moderate fragrance; foliage glossy; vigorous growth; [seedling × Betty Uprichard]; int. by Hazlewood Bros.

Lady Edine HSpn, w, before 1906, from Scotland

Lady Eleanore Cl HT, yb, 1923, Dreer; flowers light yellow-cream splashed rose, center golden to copper; [Gruss an Teplitz × Barbara]

Lady Elgin HT, yb, 1957, Meilland, F.; bud ovoid with

conspicuous neck; flowers buff-yellow washed pink, large, 40 petals, cupped, borne singly, moderate fragrance; recurrent; foliage dark, leathery; stems medium; vigorous, upright, bushy growth; PP1469; [Mme Kriloff × (Peace × Geneve)]; int. by URS, 1954

Lady Elphinstone HT, yb, 1921, Dobbie; bud long, pointed; flowers Indian yellow to clear rose, very large, semi-dbl.; foliage dark green, glossy; [sport of Mme Edouard Herriot]

Lady Elsie May S, op, 2001, Noack, Reinhard; flowers semi-dbl., with 1-3 petaloids in center, 3-4 in., 10-11 petals, borne in clusters and large sprays, moderate rose fragrance; continuous; foliage dark green, glossy; prickles medium, hooked downward, green when young, few; growth upright, dense, bushy (3 ft.); landscape; disease-resistant; PP15763; [Repandia × Gruss an Angeln]; int. by Angelica Nurseries, 2002; AARS, 2005

Lady Emily Peel N, w, 1862, Lacharme, F.; flowers white, tinged with blush, large, full; [Mlle Blanche Lafitte × Sapho]; sometimes classed as B

Lady Emma Hamilton S, ob, 2006; bud dark red with dashes of orange; flowers tangerine orange, reverse yellow-orange, 8½ cm., very full, cupped, borne in small clusters; recurrent; foliage medium size, medium green, matte; prickles medium, deeply concave, dark red, moderate; growth bushy, vigorous, medium (120 cm.); garden decoration; [seedling × seedling]; int. by David Austin Roses, Ltd., 2005

Lady English HT, or, 1934, Cant, B. R.; flowers bright cerise, center orange, open, very large, dbl.; foliage glossy, bronze; long stems; vigorous growth

Lady E'owyn MinFl, pb, 2000, Tucker, Robbie; flowers white with crimson petal edges, sometimes green tinge on outer petals, full, high-centered, no fragrance; foliage medium size, medium green, matte; some prickles; growth bushy, medium (24 in.); [seedling × Lynn Anderson]; int. by Rosehill Nursery, 2001

Lady Ethel S, ab, Sutherland, P; int. by Golden Vale Nursery, 1998

Lady Eve Min, op, 1979, Rovinski & Meredith; bud globular; flowers creamy white, edged coral-pink, 1½-2 in., 40 petals, high-centered, slight fragrance; vigorous, upright, tall, spreading growth; [Neue Revue × Sheri Anne]; int. by Casa de Rosa Domingo, 1978

Lady Eve Price – See **Caprice**, HT, 1948

Lady Eve Price, Climbing – See **Caprice, Climbing**, Cl HT

Lady Evelyn Guinness HT, mp, 1932, Evans; [sport of Ophelia]

Lady Fairbairn HT, mp, 1929, Clark, A.; flowers bright pink, 40 petals; vigorous, upright growth; [Mme Abel Chatenay × seedling]; int. by NRS New South Wales

Lady Faire HT, mp, 1907, Bentley; flowers salmon-pink; [sport of Mrs W.J. Grant]

Lady Fairfax HT, ob, 1930, Cant, F.; flowers rose and orange-cerise, flushed orange to yellow, well-formed; foliage light green; long stems; vigorous growth

Lady Florence Stronge HT, lp, 1925, McGredy; bud pointed; flowers pale flesh, base pink and gold, very large, dbl., high-centered; foliage leathery, glossy; vigorous, bushy growth

Lady Fordwich HP, pb, 1838, Laffay; flowers bright carmine, shaded garnet-purple, fading to bluish pink, medium, full, cupped

Lady Forteviot HT, yb, 1926, Cant, B. R.; flowers golden yellow to deep apricot, large, dbl., high-centered; foliage bronze, glossy; vigorous, bushy growth; Gold Medal, NRS, 1927

Lady Forteviot, Climbing Cl HT, yb, 1935, Howard Rose Co.; flowers golden-yellow to apricot, reverse darker; [sport of Lady Forteviot]

Lady Fraser HT, mr, 1941, Clark, A.; flowers rich red; [War Paint × unknown]

Lady Frost HT, dp, 1935, Bees; flowers deep rose, very large, dbl.; foliage leathery; vigorous, bushy growth; [Lady Alice Stanley × Dr. Herbert Hawkesworth]

Lady Gay HWich, op, 1905, Walsh; flowers cherry pink fading to blush white, small, dbl., borne in clusters, no fragrance; foliage small, dark, glossy; vigorous, climbing (12-20 ft.) growth; [*R. wichurana* × Bardou Job]

Lady Gay HMult, mr, 1905, Geschwind; [Crimson Rambler × unknown]

Lady Genevieve HP, mr

Lady Georgia HT, pb, 1974, Curtis, E.C.; flowers pink, base blending to ivory, medium, dbl., moderate fragrance; foliage dark, leathery; very vigorous, bushy growth; [Miss Hillcrest × Peace]; int. by Kimbrew, 1973

Lady Glencora – See **Orange Juice**, F

Lady Godiva HWich, lp, 1908, Paul, G; flowers cameo-pink, small, dbl., borne in clusters, moderate fragrance; [sport of Dorothy Perkins]

Lady Gowrie Cl HT, my, 1938, Fitzhardinge; bud long, pointed; flowers maize and champagne-yellow, large, very dbl.; intermittent bloom; foliage leathery, glossy, dark; long stems; very vigorous, climbing growth; [Sunburst, Climbing × Rev. F. Page-Roberts]; int. by Hazlewood Bros.

Lady Grade HT, or, 1983, Gregory, C.; flowers vermilion, large, 35 petals, moderate fragrance; foliage large, medium green, semi-glossy; bushy growth; [Tropicana × seedling]; int. in 1982

Lady Greenall HT, yb, 1911, Dickson, A.; flowers saffron-yellow, edges tinted shell-pink, dbl.

Lady Greenall, Climbing Cl HT, yb, 1923, Lippiatt; [sport of Lady Greenall]

Lady Gwendoline Colvin Cl HT, pb, 1918, Chaplin Bros.; flowers apricot-salmon, shaded chrome-yellow, outer petals stained carmine, dbl.; growth to 6-10 ft.

Lady Hailsham HT, or, 1951, Knight's Nursery; bud pointed; flowers orange flushed red, 3 in., 30 petals; foliage glossy; vigorous growth; [sport of McGredy's Sunset]

Lady Hamilton HSpn, w; flowers creamy white, occasionally tinted rose, large, semi-dbl.; profuse, non-recurrent bloom; dwarf growth

Lady Harriet HT, op, 1992, Williams, J. Benjamin; flowers coral and peach blend, deep orange washings on petals, long, 3-3½ in., full, intense fragrance; foliage large, dark green, semi-glossy; few prickles; tall (4-5 ft.), upright, bushy growth; [Carla × Sonia]; int. in 1993

Lady Heirloom S, mp, Clements, John; int. by Heirloom Roses, 2005

Lady Helen HT, mp, 1971, McTeer, Gilbert; flowers soft clear pink, pointed, 5 in., 30 petals, intense fragrance; foliage glossy, dark; bushy growth; [Margaret × (McGredy's Ivory × Peace)]; int. by Waterhouse Nursery, 1970

Lady Helen Maglona HT, dr, 1926, Dickson, A.; bud pointed; flowers bright crimson-red to scarlet-red, center deeper, very large, dbl., high-centered; foliage leathery; vigorous, bushy growth; Gold Medal, NRS, 1926

Lady Helen Stewart HP, dr, 1887, Dickson, A.; flowers bright crimson shaded scarlet, dbl.; vigorous growth

Lady Henry Grosvenor HT, lp, 1892, Bennett; flowers flesh pink, large, full, globular

Lady Hillingdon T, yb, 1910, Lowe & Shawyer; bud long, pointed; flowers deep apricot-yellow, semi-dbl.; foliage bronze; bushy growth; sometimes as hardy as a Hybrid Tea; [Papa Gontier × Mme Hoste]

Lady Hillingdon, Climbing Cl T, yb, 1917, Hicks; bud long; flowers apricot-yellow, large, dbl., loose; foliage purplish; prickles moderate; growth rampant (20 ft.); [sport of Lady Hillingdon]

Lady Hiroshima HT, ob, Hiroshima; int. by Hiroshima Bara-en, 1996

Lady Hudson HT, ab, 1930, Chaplin Bros.; flowers deep apricot, large, dbl.; vigorous growth

Lady Huntingfield HT, my, 1937, Clark, A.; flowers rich golden yellow, reverse lighter, large, dbl., globular; long stems; vigorous, bushy growth; [Busybody × unknown]; int. by NRS Victoria

Lady Iliffe HT, mr, 1976, Gandy, Douglas L.; flowers Tyrian rose, 5 in., 38 petals, intense fragrance; free-flowering; foliage large, olive-green; [Saul × Wendy Cussons]

Lady in Red Min, rb, 1989, McCann, Sean; flowers red with touch of white at base of petals, small, dbl.; foliage small, medium green, semi-glossy; bushy growth; [Rise 'n' Shine × Siobhan]; int. in 1988

Lady in Red – See **Veterans' Honor**, HT

Lady In Waiting S, op, Harkness; flowers unusual copper salmon color, 4½ in., 80 petals, cupped, moderate sweet clove fragrance; recurrent; foliage medium green; growth bushy (3½ ft.); int. by Heirloom, 2003

Lady Inchiquin HT, or, 1922, Dickson, A.; flowers orange-vermilion, large, very dbl., high-centered; foliage leathery, rich glossy green; very vigorous, bushy growth; Gold Medal, NRS, 1920

Lady Jane HT, dy, 1992, Poole, Lionel; flowers 3-3½ in., full, borne mostly singly; foliage medium size, medium green, semi-glossy; some prickles; medium (75 cm.), upright growth; [Dorothe × Helmut Schimdt]; int. in 1993

Lady Jane HT, pb, Tantau; int. by Australian Roses, 2004

Lady Jane Grey – See **Sue Hipkin**, HT

Lady Jennifer Green MinFl, w, 2006, Paul Chessum Roses; flowers 4 cm., single, borne mostly solitary, no fragrance; prickles large, sharp, yellow, few; growth to 18 in; beds, borders, containers; [seedling × seedling]; int. by World of Roses, 2005

Lady Joan HT, w, 2001, Twomey, Jerry; flowers 10 cm., very full, borne mostly solitary, moderate fragrance; foliage large, medium green, matte; prickles 6 mm., straight, moderate; growth upright, medium-tall (1¼ m.); garden decorative, greenhouse; [Bahia × Marina]; int. by Jerry Twomey Roses, 2001

Lady Johnstone HG, dp, 1922, Nabonnand, P.; bud yellow; flowers reddish-pink, turning lilac-rose, stamens yellow, large, single, moderate fragrance; vigorous, climbing growth; [*R. gigantea* × Beauté Lyonnaise]; hybrid gigantea

Lady Kathleen Grade – See **Lady Grade**, HT

Lady Kathryn Min, m, 1990, Jolly, Marie; bud pointed; flowers lavender, aging brown, medium, 22 petals, high-centered, urn-shaped, borne usually singly, moderate damask fragrance; foliage medium size, medium green, semi-glossy, disease-resistant; upright, medium, vigorous growth; hips round, green-brown; [Lavender Jade × Angel Face]; int. by Rosehill Farm, 1991

Lady Lauder HT, yb, 1931, Morse; flowers deep canary-yellow, reverse flushed crimson, dbl., cupped; foliage thick, light; long stems; very vigorous growth

Lady Lavender HT, m, 1993, Weeks, O.L.; flowers 3-3½ in., full, borne mostly singly, moderate fragrance; foliage medium size, dark green, glossy; some prickles;

bushy (40-48 in.) growth; [(Paradise × seedling) × Swarthmore]; int. by Estrella Rose Company, 1993

Lady Layton HT, my, 1932, Layton; bud long, pointed; flowers light sunflower-yellow, deepening as it opens, large; vigorous growth; [sport of Joanna Hill]

Lady Le-Ru HT, mp, 1965, Lothrop; bud round; flowers deep pink, 3½-4 in., 50 petals, cupped, moderate fragrance; free, non-recurrent bloom; thornless; long stems; growth moderate, open (2½ ft.); hardy; PP2241; [*R. rugosa* hybrid × unknown Hybrid Tea]

Lady Leconfield HT, w, 1939, Burbage Nursery; bud long, pointed, cream, flushed pink; flowers cream-white, 25-30 petals, cupped; foliage leathery; vigorous, bushy growth; int. by C-P

Lady Leslie HT, rb, 1929, McGredy; flowers rosy scarlet to scarlet-carmine suffused saffron-yellow, large, dbl., high-centered; foliage dark, leathery, glossy; vigorous growth

Lady Liberty HT, w, 1987, deVor, Tom; flowers clear white, yellow at base, large, 35 petals, high-centered, borne usually singly or in small clusters; foliage medium size, medium green, semi-glossy; prickles straight, medium, light yellow; extremely long stems; upright, profuse growth; hips globular, medium size, medium green; PP6142; [sport of Lady Diana]

Lady Like HT, ob, 1973, Tantau, Math.; bud globular; flowers dark orange, large, dbl.; vigorous, upright growth; [seedling × Tropicana]; int. by Ahrens & Sieberz, 1971

Lady Like HT, pb, Tantau; flowers deep pink, yellow base, large, 30 petals, low-centered, intense fragrance; free-flowering; foliage deep green, glossy; stems long; upright, medium (3 ft.) growth; int. in 1989

Lady Lilford HT, my, 1930, Gregory; flowers clear yellow, center deep golden yellow; foliage rich green, glossy; vigorous, bushy, branching, compact growth; [sport of Independence Day]

Lady Loch HT, 1885, Johnson; [sport of Aspasia]

Lady Lou HT, ob, 1948, Brownell; bud long, pointed; flowers coral-peach, large to medium, 50 petals, high-centered, moderate fragrance; foliage glossy, light; vigorous, dwarf growth; [Pink Princess × Shades of Autumn]

Lady Love – See **Ribbon Rose**, Min

Lady Luck HT, pb, 1957, Miller, A.J.; bud long, pointed; flowers blends of pale to rich pink, 4-4½ in., 38 petals, high-centered, intense damask fragrance; foliage dark, leathery; vigorous, upright, bushy growth; PP1579; [Tom Breneman × Show Girl]; int. by Elmer Roses Co., 1956

Lady MacGregor HT, 1911, Williams, A.; [Boule de Neige × a Tea]

Lady MacRobert F, ab, 1993, Cocker; flowers light apricot, medium, dbl., borne in large clusters; foliage medium size, light green, semi-glossy; some prickles; medium (2½ ft.), upright, compact growth; [Clydebank Centenary × seedling]; int. by James Cocker & Sons, 1993

Lady Madeleine F, ob, 1993, Everitt, Derrick; flowers tangerine, paler reverse, medium, dbl., borne singly and in small clusters; foliage medium size, medium green, semi-glossy; some prickles; medium (30 cm.), upright growth; [(Pristine × Edith Holden) × (L'Oreal Trophy × Edith Holden)]

Lady Mandeville HT, my, 1941, McGredy; flowers yellow, flushed amber, well-formed, 5 in., 35 petals, slight fruity fragrance; foliage dark, bronze; branching, moderate growth; [seedling × Mrs Sam McGredy]; int. by J&P

Lady Mann HT, pb, 1940, Clark, A.; flowers rosy salmon, large, dbl., cupped, borne in small clusters, moderate tea fragrance; recurrent; foliage large, glossy; [Lorraine Lee × unknown]

Lady Margaret Boscawen HT, mp, 1911, Dickson, A.; flowers soft shell pink on fawn, large, dbl., intense fragrance

Lady Margaret Stewart HT, ob, 1926, Dickson, A.; bud long, pointed; flowers golden yellow shaded and streaked orange and red, very large, dbl., high-centered; foliage sage-green, leathery; vigorous, bushy growth; Gold Medal, NRS, 1926, Gold Medal, Bagatelle, 1928

Lady Marine HT, or, 1981, DeLashmutt; flowers dark orange-red, 53 petals, high-centered, urn-shaped, borne 1-3 per cluster; foliage dark, leathery; prickles medium, reddish; medium growth; [seedling × Tropicana]; int. by Roseway Nursery

Lady Mars T, 1909, California Rose Co.; [sport of Gloire de Dijon]

Lady Martha Bruce HT, mp, 1925, Ferguson, W.; flowers pink, outer petals tinged peach-blossom-pink

Lady Mary HT, mr, 1999, Teranishi, K.; flowers crimson red, 40 petals, high-centered; foliage medium green; growth to 3 ft.; [Princess Mikasa × seedling]; int. by Itami Rose Nursery, 1990

Lady Mary Corry T, dy, 1900, Dickson, A.; flowers deep golden yellow, large, moderate tea fragrance; growth vigorous, erect, branching

Lady Mary Elizabeth HT, dp, 1927, Dickson, A.; bud pointed; flowers brilliant carmine-pink, large, dbl., high-centered; vigorous, bushy growth

Lady Mary Fitzwilliam HT, lp, 1882, Bennett; flowers flesh-color, large, full, globular, intense fragrance; weak growth; [Devoniensis × Victor Verdier]

Lady Mary Ward HT, ob, 1913, McGredy; flowers orange, shaded deeper, dbl.; Gold Medal, NRS, 1912

Lady Maureen Stewart HT, dr, 1920, Dickson, A.; flowers velvety blackish scarlet-cerise, reflex orange-maroon, dbl.

Lady Mavis Pilkington HT, ob, Kordes; flowers orange with yellow; medium growth; int. in 1992

Lady Maysie Robinson HT, pb, 1957, Kordes; flowers deep pink, center white, large, 22 petals, cupped, moderate fragrance; foliage dark, glossy; vigorous, upright, bushy growth; [seedling × Peace]; int. by Wheatcroft Bros., 1955

Lady Medallist HT, lp, 1912, Clark, A.; flowers pink with lighter reverse, large, high-centered; foliage dark green; growth vigorous, early summer climber

Lady Meilland HT, op, Meilland; flowers orange-mandarine, dbl.; int. by Sauvageot, 1986; Gold Medal, Durbanville, 1982, Gold Star of the South Pacific, Palmerston North, NZ, 1982

Lady Meillandina – See **Lady Sunblaze**, Min

Lady Miller HT, dr, 1940, Clark, A.; flowers dark-red, well-formed

Lady Mitchell HT, mr, 1990, Harkness, R., & Co., Ltd.; bud pointed; flowers deep rose-red, reverse to rose-red, paling with age, 50 petals, cupped; foliage medium size, medium green, semi-glossy; prickles slightly declining, medium, green; bushy, low to medium growth; [Dr. Darley × Silver Jubilee]; int. by R. Harkness & Co., Ltd., 1991

Lady Mond HT, w, 1920, Paul, W.; flowers deep cream, outer petals shaded rose

Lady Moss F, ab, 2004, Moore, Ralph S.; flowers apricot, reverse white, 3 in., semi-dbl., borne in small clusters, moderate fragrance; recurrent; foliage medium size, medium green, semi-glossy; prickles small, straight; growth upright, tall (4 ft.); specimen, cutting; [Fairy Moss × Gabriel Noyelle]; int. by Sequoia Nurs., 2005

Lady Moyra Beauclerc HT, mr, 1901, Dickson, A.; flowers carmine-red, large, dbl.

Lady Moyra Cavendish HT, mr, 1939, McGredy; bud long, pointed; flowers bright strawberry-red, flushed crimson, dbl., high-centered; foliage glossy, dark; bushy growth

Lady Nutting HT, mp, 1938, Wheatcroft Bros.; flowers soft salmon-pink, large, high-centered; foliage leathery, dark; vigorous growth

Lady of Hertford F, pb, 1997, Bossom, W.E.; flowers semi-dbl., 8-14 petals, borne in small clusters, slight fragrance; foliage small, medium green, glossy; few prickles; upright, tall (120 cm.) growth; [Conversation × Pearl Drift]

Lady of Megginch S, dp, 2006; flowers very full, borne in small clusters; foliage medium size, dark green, matte; prickles small, concave, curved inward, light green, moderate; growth bushy, vigorous, medium (120 cm.); garden decorative; [seedling × seedling]; int. by David Austin Roses, Ltd., 2006

Lady of Sky HT, or, 1976, Gregory; flowers 35 petals, high-centered; foliage dark; vigorous, upright growth; [Queen Elizabeth × unknown]; int. in 1974

Lady of Stifford F, or, 1982, Warley Rose Gardens; [sport of Matador]; int. in 1981

Lady of the Dawn F, lp, 1984, Interplant; flowers large, ruffled, soft cream edged with pink, semi-dbl., borne in large clusters, moderate fruity fragrance; foliage large, medium green, matte, leathery; upright growth, arching, 4 ft.; PP6068; [INTerdress × Stadt den Helder]

Lady of the Mist S, ob, Harkness; flowers soft violet-pink at the edges, shading to cream and then coppery buff at center, 4-5 in., 100 petals, quartered; foliage rich green; growth upright, strong growing; large shrub or small climber; PPAF; int. by Heirloom, 2002

Lady Overtoun HP, op, 1907, Dickson; flowers salmon-flesh

Lady Parade MinFl, mp, Olesen; bud long, broad based; flowers 5 cm., 35-45 petals, cupped, to flat, borne mostly singly, no fragrance; recurrent; foliage matte; vigorous, bushy (20-40 cm.) growth; PP15506; [Isabel Hit × Patricia Kordana Mini Brite]; container plant; int. by Poulsen Roser, 2001

Lady Penelope LCl, op, 1998, Warner, Chris; flowers salmon pink, pink reverse, 2½-3 in., full, pompon, borne in small clusters; repeats well; foliage medium size, medium green, glossy; few prickles; spreading, medium (8 ft.) growth; [Laura Ford × Royal Baby]; int. by Bransford Garden Plants, 1998

Lady Penzance HEg, op, 1894, Penzance; flowers coppery salmon-pink with yellow center and yellow stamens, 1 in., single, slightly cupped; summer bloom; foliage dark; stems drooping; very vigorous growth; [*R. rubiginosa* × *R. foetida bicolor*]; int. by Penzance

Lady Phelia S, pb, 2004, Thomson, George L.; flowers copper pink, reverse lighter, 8-10 cm., very full, borne in small clusters; foliage small, light green, semi-glossy; prickles small, hooked; growth bushy, medium (3-4½ ft.); garden decorative; [(Abraham Darby × Anna Oliver) × Mrs Mary Thomson]; int. by Ross Roses, 2004

Lady Pirrie HT, ab, 1910, Dickson, H.; bud pointed; flowers apricot-yellow, reverse coppery, large, dbl.; vigorous, bushy growth; Gold Medal, NRS, 1909

Lady Pirrie, Climbing Cl HT, ab, 1938; [sport of Lady Pirrie]; int. by Unknown

Lady Plymouth T, w, 1914, Dickson, A.; bud long, pointed; flowers deep ivory-cream, very faintly flushed, large, dbl.; foliage rich green, leathery; vigorous, bushy growth, with numerous canes; Gold Medal, NRS, 1913

Lady Quartus Ewart HT, w, 1904, Dickson, H.; flowers pure white, large, full

Lady Rachel F, w, Cants of Colchester, Ltd.; flowers soft cream, dbl., borne singly and in clusters, slight fragrance; foliage dark green, glossy; growth upright, compact; int. by Cants of Colchester, 1990

Lady Rachel Verney HT, mp, 1935, Bees; flowers rose, base lemon, large, dbl., cupped; foliage glossy, bronze; vigorous, bushy growth; [Annie Laurie × Lord Charlemont]

Lady Reading Pol, mr, 1921, Van Kleef; flowers clear red, rosette, slight fragrance; good repeat; [sport of Ellen Poulsen]

Lady Reay HT, dp, 1911, Dickson or Cant; flowers dark pink, petals edged pearly white, moderate fragrance

Lady Rhodes HT, dp, 1934, Clark, A.

Lady Roberts T, ab, 1902, Cant, F.; flowers rich reddish-apricot, base coppery red, edges shaded orange, dbl., moderate fragrance; vigorous, tall growth; [sport of Anna Olivier]

Lady Romsey F, w, Beales, Peter; flowers creamy white, suffused pink and yellow, dbl., moderate sweet fragrance; free-flowering; foliage dark green, leathery; int. in 1985

Lady Rose HT, op, 1978, W. Kordes Söhne; bud long, pointed; flowers salmon-orange, 5 in., 34 petals, high-centered, borne singly and in clusters, moderate fragrance; recurrent; foliage large, dense, glossy; vigorous, upright, bushy (3 ft.) growth; [seedling × Traumerei]; Gold Medal, Belfast, 1981

Lady Rose, Climbing Cl HT, or, Orard; [sport of Lady Rose]; int. in 1993

Lady Rossmore HT, mr, 1907, Campbell Hall; flowers reddish-crimson with claret shading, medium, dbl.

Lady Roundway HT, ab, 1923, Cant, B. R.; flowers bright apricot-orange, fading to creamy buff, open, semi-dbl.; vigorous, but stubby growth; Gold Medal, NRS, 1923

Lady Russon – See **Orange Delbard**, HT

Lady Sackville – See **Night**, HT

Lady Sackville HT, w, 1933, Cant, B. R.; bud pointed; flowers pure white, very large, dbl., high-centered; foliage leathery, bronze; very vigorous growth

Lady Seton HT, lp, 1966, McGredy, Sam IV; flowers 4½ in., 35 petals; vigorous, tall growth; [Ma Perkins × Mischief]; int. by McGredy

Lady Sheffield HP, mp, 1881, Postans; flowers glowing cherry pink, aging to bluish pink, large, full, globular; [François Michelon × unknown]

Lady Somers HT, lp, 1930, Clark, A.; flowers fresh pink, tinted flesh, dbl.; foliage wrinkled, light; bushy growth; [Comte G. de Rochemur × Scorcher]; int. by NRS Victoria

Lady Sonia S, my, 1961, Mattock; flowers golden yellow, 4-4½ in., 20 petals; foliage dark; vigorous, upright, branching growth; [Grandmaster × Doreen]

Lady Stanley B, dp, 1849, Dubos; flowers large, full

Lady Stanley T, m, 1886, Nabonnand; bud long; flowers lilac over a yellow base, edged darker purple, very large, dbl., globular, moderate fragrance

Lady Stuart HCh, lp, 1851, Portemer fils; flowers flesh pink to blush, darker at center, large, very full, globular; foliage leaflets 5-7

Lady Sunblaze Min, lp, 1987, Meilland, Mrs. Marie-Louise; bud plump, pointed; flowers pale orient pink to light coral pink, 1½ in., 40 petals, high-centered, borne singly, no fragrance; foliage small, dark green, glossy; bushy growth; PP6170; [(Fashion × Zambra) × Belle Meillandina]

Lady Sunshine HT, my, 1965, Lens; bud ovoid; flowers large, very dbl.; foliage dark; [Belle Étoile × (Michele Meilland × Tawny Gold)]; int. by Spek

Lady Susan Birch HT, ab, 1934, Cant, B. R.; bud pointed; flowers large, dbl., high-centered; foliage glossy, dark; vigorous, bushy growth

Lady Suzanne HT, w, 1985, Bridges, Dennis A.; flowers creamy white, large, 32 petals, high-centered; foliage large, dark, glossy; bushy growth; [Lady X × Flaming Beauty]; int. by Bridges Roses

Lady Sydney Eardley-Wilmot HT, mp, 1925, Chaplin Bros.; flowers coppery reddish-salmon, tinted fawn and apricot, semi-dbl.

Lady Sylvia HT, lp, 1926, Stevens, W.; flowers flesh-pink, deeper in center, dbl., moderate fragrance; moderate (3 ft.) growth; [sport of Ophelia]

Lady Sylvia, Climbing Cl HT, pb, 1933, Stevens, W.; flowers pink, cream and apricot, large, full, moderate fragrance; moderate (10 ft.) growth; [sport of Lady Sylvia]; int. by Low

Lady Taylor F, or, 1982, Smith, Edward; flowers vermilion, medium, 35 petals; foliage medium size, medium green, matte; bushy growth; [Elizabeth of Glamis × Topsi]; int. as Smitling, C. Gregory & Sons, 1983

Lady Tervueren Pol, mr, 1969, Buisman, G. A. H.; flowers medium to small, dbl.; foliage dark; [Allotria × seedling]

Lady Trent HT, ob, 1940, Dot, Pedro; flowers coppery orange, large, 46 petals, high-centered; foliage dark, glossy; vigorous growth; [Rosieriste Gaston Leveque × Federico Casas]; int. by Wheatcroft Bros.

Lady Ursula HT, pb, 1908, Dickson, A.; flowers pink fading lighter, reverse cameo-pink, base lemon, large, very dbl., high-centered; foliage dark, leathery, glossy; vigorous, bushy growth

Lady Venables Vernon HT, lp, 1922, Jersey Nursery; flowers soft flesh-color, overlaid blush; [Mrs Amy Hammond × Sir Alexander N. Rochfort]

Lady Vera HT, pb, 1975, Smith, R.W.; flowers silvery pink, reverse rose-pink, dbl.; vigorous growth; [Royal Highness × Christian Dior]; int. by Brundrett, 1974

Lady Verey HT, mp, 1922, Hicks; flowers rose-pink, dbl.

Lady Violet Astor HT, dp, 1933, Cant, B. R.; flowers deep rose-pink, over large, dbl., high-centered; foliage leathery; vigorous growth

Lady Wakefield HT, ab, 1926, Cant, B. R.; bud pale orange; flowers bright apricot, fading to pink, moderate fragrance; foliage dark green; strong (80-100 cm.) growth

Lady Warrender – See **Clara Sylvain**, T

Lady Waterlow Cl HT, pb, 1903, Nabonnand, P.& C.; bud red; flowers salmon-pink edged carmine, 11 cm., dbl., moderate fragrance; vigorous (8-10 ft.) growth; [La France de '89 × Mme Marie Lavalley]

Lady Wenlock HT, lp, 1904, Bernaix, P.; flowers China-pink tinted apricot, large, dbl.

Lady White D, w, 1901, Turner; flowers white, striped red, large, semi-dbl.; [*R. macrantha* × *R.* × *damascena*]

Lady Willingdon HT, lp, 1928, Dale; flowers very light pink, large, dbl.; foliage rich green, glossy; vigorous growth; [Ophelia × Premier]

Lady Woodward HT, lp, 1960, Riethmuller; bud long, pointed; flowers pink veined, large, dbl., high-centered, moderate fragrance; foliage dark, glossy; vigorous, upright, bushy growth; [Heinrich Wendland × Elli Knab]; int. in 1959

Lady Worthington Evans HT, dr, 1926, Dickson, A.; bud pointed; flowers deep crimson shaded blackish, semi-dbl., high-centered; foliage bronze, leathery; vigorous, bushy growth; Gold Medal, NRS, 1926

Lady X HT, m, 1968, Meilland, Mrs. Marie-Louise; bud long, pointed; flowers large, dbl., high-centered; foliage leathery; vigorous, upright growth; PP2691; [seedling × Simone]; int. by C-P, 1966; Gold Medal, Portland, 1968

Lady X, Climbing Cl HT, m, 1970, Ruston (also Takatori, 1976); [sport of Lady X]; int. by Japan Rose Nursery, 1975

Lady Yvonne F, lp, 1999, Bossom, W.E.; flowers large, dbl., borne in small clusters; foliage medium size, medium green, semi-glossy; prickles moderate; medium (3 ft.) growth; [Southampton × seedling]

Lady Zia HT, or, 1960, Park; flowers light orange-scarlet, well-formed, 5-6 in., 50 petals, moderate fragrance; foliage dark, glossy; vigorous growth; [Peace × Independence]; int. by Harkness & Co., 1959; Gold Medal, NRS, 1959

Lady Zoë Brougham T, my, 1886, Nabonnand; bud elongated; flowers bright chamois yellow, darker at petal edges, large, imbricated, full; [Isabelle Nabonnand × unknown]

Ladybird HT, my, Tantau; int. by Rosen Tantau, 2003

Ladybug Min, mr, 1992, Moore, Ralph S.; flowers medium, semi-dbl., borne in small clusters; fast repeat; foliage small, medium green, semi-glossy; few prickles; low (30-40 cm.), bushy, compact growth; [Sheri Anne × Cherry Magic]; int. by Sequoia Nursery, 1993

Ladybug F, rb, 2001, Meilland International; flowers red with white dots, 2½ in., semi-dbl., borne in small clusters, no fragrance; foliage medium size, dark green, semi-glossy; prickles moderate; growth bushy, low (3 ft.); PP13757; [(Tamango × Evelyn Fisson) × Glad Tidings]; int. by The Conard-Pyle Co., 2001

Ladylove HT, mp, 1926, McGredy; flowers light rose-pink fading hydrangea-pink, flushed apricot, well-formed, dbl.; foliage dark; very vigorous growth; [Ophelia × seedling]; int. by Beckwith

Laelia HP, mp, 1857, Avoux & Crozy; flowers very large; possibly synonymous with Louis Peyronny

Laetitia – See **La Volupté**, HGal

Laetitia Pujol HT, pb, Tantau; int. by Jardiland, 2006

Lafayette F, dp, 1924, Nonin; flowers bright cherry-crimson, large, semi-dbl., cupped, borne in clusters (up to 40); foliage rich green, glossy; vigorous, bushy growth; [Rodhatte × Richmond]; int. by H&S

Lafayette, Climbing – See **Auguste Kordes**, Cl F

Lafayette S, ab, Olesen; bud globular; flowers light apricot, 8 cm., 61 petals, open cup, borne mostly singly, slight fragrance; recurrent; foliage dark green, semi-glossy; thornless; stems 6 in.; growth vigorous, compact (20-40 cm.); PP16354; [sport of Tiffany Hit]; int. by Poulsen Roser, 2003

Lafayette Hit – See **Lafayette**, S

Lafayette Patio Hit – See **Lafayette**, S

Laffay Ch, mr, about 1825, Laffay; flowers bright cerise red, full; probably extinct

Lafollette – See **La Follette**, Cl T

Laforcade HP, mr, 1889, Lévêque; flowers carmine red, very large, cupped; foliage dark green; growth upright

L'Africaine LCl, dr, 1953, Mallerin, C.; flowers garnet shaded coppery, 4 in., dbl., borne mostly solitary; abundant early bloom, not recurrent; strong stems; very vigorous growth; [Guineé × Crimson Glory]; int. by EFR

Lafter HT, yb, 1948, Brownell; bud pointed; flowers salmon-yellow, 4 in., 23 petals, moderate fragrance; vigorous, upright, branching growth; [(V for Victory × (Général Jacqueminot × Dr. W. Van Fleet)) × Pink Princess]

Lagerfeld Gr, m, 1983, Christensen, Jack E.; flowers

silvery lavender, 4-5 in., 30 petals, high-centered, borne in sprays of 5-15, intense fragrance; foliage medium size, medium green, matte; prickles medium, light brown, hooked downward; tall, upright, bushy growth; hips large, globular, orange; [Blue Nile × (Ivory Tower × Angel Face)]; int. by Armstrong Nursery, 1986

Lagerfeuer F, mr, 1959, Tantau, Math.; bud pointed; flowers velvety scarlet, large, dbl., borne in clusters; foliage leathery, dark; vigorous, upright growth; [Red Favorite × Kathe Duvigneau]; int. in 1958

Lago Maggiore S, m, Kordes; int. in 2003

Lagoon F, m, 1970, Harkness; flowers lilac, reverse darker, gold stamens, 2½ in., 7 petals, moderate fragrance; foliage glossy; hips large, abundant, colorful; [Lilac Charm × Sterling Silver]

Laguna HT, or, 1975, Kordes; bud large, long, pointed; flowers dbl., cupped, moderate fragrance; foliage glossy; vigorous, upright growth; [Hawaii × Orange Delbard]; int. by Horstmann, 1974

Laguna S, ab, 1999, Poulsen; flowers apricot blend with tones of other hues, 8-10 cm., full, no fragrance; foliage dark, glossy; growth bushy, 40-60 cm.; PP11608; int. by Poulsen Roser, 1998

Laguna LCl, dp, 2006; bud round, magenta; flowers strong pink, 10 cm., very full, borne in clusters of 6-8, very strong, fruity fragrance; recurrent; foliage medium size, dark green, glossy, dense; bushy, erect, climbing (8 ft.) growth; int. by W. Kordes' Söhne, 2004

Laguna Palace – See **Laguna**, S

Lahar F, my, IARI; flowers mimosa yellow with tinge of pink; recurrent; int. in 1991

Laila F, ob, 1968, Abdullah; flowers bright orange, well-formed, dbl., borne on trusses; foliage glossy; vigorous growth; [Orangeade × unknown]

L'Aimable Beauté HGal

L'Aimant – See **Victorian Spice**, F

L'Aimont – See **Victorian Spice**, F

Lake – See **Lake Cottage**, S

Lake Como F, m, 1968, Harkness; flowers lilac, semi-dbl., borne in tursses; [Lilac Charm × Sterling Silver]

Lake Cottage S, lp, Olesen; bud ovate, deep pink; flowers light pink, small, 6-7 petals, almost flat, borne in small clusters, no fragrance; recurrent; foliage dark green, glossy; prickles numerous, 10 mm., hooked; low (40-60 cm.), spreading growth; hips 15 × 13 mm., greyed-orange; PP16550; [Diamond Head × seedling]; int. by Poulsen Roser, 2004

Lake Kayoichou F, m, Hiroshima; int. by Hiroshima Bara-en, 2002

Lake Street S, dp; flowers very full, moderate fragrance; medium (3 ft.) growth; int. by Brentwood Bay Nursery, 2003

Lakeland HT, lp, 1976, Fryer, Gareth; flowers soft shell-pink, 5-6 in., 36 petals; [Fragrant Cloud × Queen Elizabeth]; int. by Fryer's Nursery, Ltd.

Lakeland Princess – See **Vintage Wine**, Cl HT

Lakeland's Pride – See **Double Feature**, Gr

Lal HT, pb, 1933, Easlea; bud long, pointed; flowers deep salmon pink, suffused yellow; foliage dark; vigorous growth; [Commonwealth × Florence L. Izzard]

Lal, Climbing Cl HT, mp, 1937, Vogel, M.; flowers very large, dbl.; [sport of Lal]

L'Alcazar – See **Elfe**, LCl

Lalima HT, mr, 1983, Pal, Dr. B.P.; flowers large, 50 petals, high-centered, borne singly, intense fragrance; foliage large; vigorous, upright growth; [Picture × Jour d'Ete]; int. by K.S.G. Son's Roses, 1978

Lallita HT, mp, 1929, Mallerin, C.; flowers rose, very large, dbl.; foliage rich green, leathery; long, strong stems; [Pres. Briand × unknown]

Lamarque N, w, 1830, Maréchal; flowers pure white, center lemon-yellow, 7-8 cm., dbl., flat, quartered, borne in small clusters, intense fragrance; prickles few, straight, thin; vigorous, climbing growth, with long, trailing shoots; [Blush Noisette × Parks' Yellow Tea-scented China]

Lamarque Jaune N, ly, 1869, Ducher; flowers light yellow, center golden yellow, medium, full

Lamartine B, mr, 1842, Guillot; flowers red, shaded light violet, medium, full

Lamartine HP, dp, 1890, Dubreuil; flowers velvety dark carmine, shaded violet over amaranth, medium, full, cupped

Lamartine HT, op, 1943, Meilland, F.; flowers pearly pink shaded orange, dbl.

Lamb Chop S, pb, Peden, R.; int. in 1997

Lambada HT, op, Kordes; bud long, pointed, ovoid; flowers bright salmon orange, 4 in., 30-35 petals, high-centered, borne singly, slight fragrance; recurrent; foliage large. leathery; prickles few, short, hooked downward; stems 20-24 in.; growth vigorous, upright, branching (5 ft.); PP9116; [Frisco × seedling]; greenhouse rose; int. in 1992

Lambert F, m, Poulsen; flowers lavender and purple, 4-6 in., full, slight fragrance; foliage dark green, glossy; growth bushy, 60-100 cm.; PP15643; int. by Poulsen Roser, 2002

Lambert Closse S, mp, 1994, Ogilvie, Ian S.; flowers 3-3½ in., 53 petals, borne mostly singly, slight fragrance; foliage medium size, light green, glossy; some prickles; medium (85 cm.), upright growth; PP9978; [Arthur Bell × John Davis]; int. by Agriculture Canada, 1994

L'Ami E. Daumont HP, mr, 1903, Vilin; bud conical, very large; flowers carmine-red, reverse silvery, large, very dbl.; foliage delicate green; few prickles

L'Ami Maubray HP, rb, 1890, Mercier; flowers light red, shaded delicate violet, borne mostly singly or in small clusters; [Xavier Olibo × unknown]

L'Ami Noël HP, mr, 1886, Chauvry; flowers bright velvety red

Lamia HT, or, 1918, Easlea; bud rich apricot; flowers intense reddish-orange, semi-dbl.; vigorous growth; Gold Medal, NRS, 1918

Laminuette – See **Minuette**, F

L'Amitié D, lp, before 1813, Stegerhoek/Dupont; flowers flesh pink, sometimes spotted white, large, semi-dbl.

Lamoon F, w, Umsawasdi, Dr. Theera; flowers creamy white with greenish tint and pink edge, medium, 6-14 petals, borne in clusters, slight fragrance; foliage medium size, medium green, semi-glossy; few prickles; medium, upright, bushy growth; [Simplicity × Sweet Vivien]; int. in 1995

Lamotte Sanguin HP, mr, 1869, Vigneron; sepals leaf-like; flowers bright carmine red, 4 in., full, widely cupped, borne singly and in small clusters; foliage thick, quite rugose, somber green; prickles numerous, reddish brown, straight, strong

Lampion F, or, 1959, Tantau, Math.; bud pointed; flowers blood-red shaded orange, large, 5 petals, open, borne in large clusters; foliage dark, leathery, glossy; dwarf, bushy growth; [Fanal × Kathe Duvigneau]; int. in 1957

Lampion HT, op, Tantau; int. by Australian Roses, 2004

Lamplighter Cl HT, dy, 1948, Duehrsen; flowers blend similar to talisman and autumn, large, dbl., globular; foliage leathery; very vigorous, climbing (10-15 ft.) growth; [Talisman × Gold Rush]; int. by California Roses

Lamplighter HT, pb, 1950, McGredy, Sam IV; flowers salmon-rose, reverse gold, very large, 37 petals, high-centered; foliage bronze; vigorous growth; [Sam McGredy × seedling]

Lamplighter HT, yb, 1959, Joseph H. Hill, Co.; bud long, pointed; flowers mimosa-yellow, 4-4½ in., 55-60 petals, high-centered; foliage dark, semi-glossy, leathery; strong stems; vigorous, upright growth; [Peace × Yellow Perfection]

Lampo F, Cazzaniga, F. G.; int. in 1958

Lamrhowitch – See **Oyster Pearl**, HT

Lancashire HT, mr, 1950, Wright, R. & Sons; flowers fiery red; [Christopher Stone × seedling]

Lancashire – See **Gärtnerfreude**, S

Lancashire Lass HT, mr, 1939, Archer; bud well shaped, crimson; flowers scarlet-cerise, semi-dbl.; foliage glossy, dark; vigorous growth

Lancashire Life F, or, 1984, deRuiter, George; flowers scarlet, semi-dbl., borne in clusters; foliage medium size, medium green, semi-glossy; bushy growth; [Robert Stolz × Diablotin]; int. by Fryer's Nursery, Ltd.

Lancaster Cl HT, mr, 1962, Hicks, S.J.; bud ovoid; flowers medium rose-red, 5 in., 35-40 petals, high-centered, intense fragrance; foliage leathery, dark; vigorous growth; PP1892; [sport of President Eisenhower]; int. by C-P, 1962

Lancastrian HT, mr, 1965, Gregory; flowers crimson-scarlet, 3½-4 in., 40 petals; foliage light green, glossy; vigorous, upright growth; [Ena Harkness × unknown]

Lance Hird HT, mp, 1973, Wood; flowers deep pink, reverse lighter, 4 in., 20-30 petals; free growth; [seedling × Greetings]; int. by Wood Roses

Lancier HT, dr, 1959, Mallerin, C.; flowers crimson-red; [Karl Herbst × seedling]; int. by Vilmorin-Andrieux

Lancôme HT, dp, 1986, Delbard; flowers deep pink, large, 28 petals, high-centered; vigorous, upright, bushy growth; [(Dr. Albert Schweitzer × (Michele Meilland × Bayadere)) × (MElmet × Present Filial)]; int. in 1973

Land Brandenburg – See **Bossa Nova**, F

Land of the Long White Cloud – See **Full Sail**, HT

Lander Gold Min, my, 1986, Williams, Michael C.; flowers 36 petals, high-centered, borne usually singly, moderate fruity fragrance; foliage medium size, medium green, semi-glossy; prickles very few, small, straight; medium, bushy growth; no fruit; [Rise 'n' Shine × Little Jackie]; int. by The Rose Garden & Mini Rose Nursery

Landmark S, pb, 2005, Shoup, George Michael; flowers dbl., borne mostly solitary, moderate fragrance; remontant; foliage medium size, dark green, semi-glossy; prickles moderate; growth bushy, medium (3-4 ft.); hedging; [Carefree Beauty × Basye's Blueberry]; int. by Antique Rose Emporium, 1995

Landora – See **Sunblest**, HT

Landora, Climbing – See **Clinora**, Cl HT

Landour Cl HT, w, 1979, Takur; bud oval; flowers 6-6½ in., very dbl., high-centered, moderate fruity fragrance; intermittent bloom; foliage large, glossy, dark, leathery; upright growth; [Peace, Climbing × Peace, Climbing]; int. by Doon Valley Roses, 1978

Landrover HRg, mr; int. in 1995

Landscape Splendor HWich, w, Clements, John K.; rambler growth; int. in 1996

Landwirtschaftsrat Hubert Schilling Pol, or, Pieper; flowers medium, semi-dbl.; int. in 1964

Lane – See **Laneii**, M

Lane M, lp, 1860, Robert; flowers blush pink, lightly shaded with carmine, large, full

Laneii M, mr, 1846, Laffay, M.; bud large, globular, well-mossed; flowers rosy crimson, occasionally tinted purple, large, dbl., globular; foliage large, bright green,

5 leaflets; robust growth; [a Moss rose × *R. gallica*]; int. into England by Lane & Son, ca. 1846

Lane's Moss – See **Laneii**, M

Lang Havey – See **Unconditional Love**, Min

Langdale Chase F, ab, Fryer, Gareth; int. in 1990

Langenhoven LCl, mp, Kordes; int. by Ludwig's Roses, 2003

Langford HSet, dp, about 1940, Preston; flowers dark pink to nearly red, dbl., borne in medium clusters; non-recurrent, late; foliage large, dark; needs protection in cold areas; [*R. setigera* × Aennchen Müller]; int. by Central Exp. Farm

Langford Light Min, w, 1985, Sealand Nurseries, Ltd.; flowers bright yellow stamens, small, semi-dbl.; foliage medium size, dark, matte; bushy growth; [Ballerina × Little Flirt]; int. in 1984

Langley HT, dy, 1942, Eacott; bud streaked red; flowers clear deep yellow, edges flushed old-gold, 4-5 in., 50 petals; foliage bronze, dark; [Mrs Sam McGredy × Phyllis Gold]; int. by Ley

Langley Gem HMoy, dp, 1939, Eacott; flowers scarlet-cerise, single, open, borne in clusters; recurrent; foliage leathery, bronze; strong stems; vigorous growth; [Karen Poulsen × *R. moyesii*]; int. by R. Murrell

Lansezeur M, dp, before 1846, Panaget; flowers deep crimson, veined with lilac, medium, dbl., cupped; possibly synonymous with Panaget

Lantern – See **Octoberfest**, Gr

Lanvin HT, ly, 1986, Christensen, Jack E.; flowers 30 petals, high-centered, borne in sprays of 3-5, moderate fragrance; foliage medium size, dark green tinted red, semi-glossy; prickles medium, straight, light brown to red; medium, upright bushy growth; no fruit; [seedling × Katherine Loker]; int. by Armstrong Nursery, 1985

Lapponia F, op, 1978, Tantau, Math.; bud broadly ovoid; flowers medium salmon-pink, 25 petals; bushy, upright growth

Laque de Chine HMsk, mr, Lens, Louis; once blooming; int. in 1991; Gold Medal, Baden-Baden, 1991

Lara HT, op, 1971, Kriloff, Michel; flowers salmon-carmine, well-formed, large, 38 petals; foliage dark, glossy; vigorous, tall growth; PP3011; [Tropicana × Romantica]; int. by Cramphorn's Nursery, 1967

Larado Min, mr, 1991, Spooner, Raymond A.; flowers bright, clear red with small white eye in center, micro-mini, semi-dbl., borne singly, no fragrance; foliage small, medium green, semi-glossy; micro-mini; low (15 cm.), bushy growth; [Tobo Yellow × seedling]; int. by Oregon Miniature Roses, 1992

L'Archévêque – See **Pourpre Charmant**, HGal

Large Double Two-Coloured – See **King of Scots**, HSpn

Large Provence – See ***R. centifolia batavica*** (Clusius), C

L'Argentee HT, rb

Largo d'Haendel HT, dp, 1947, Mallerin, C.; flowers reddish-apricot to salmon-carmine; int. by URS

Larini HT, rb, Olij; flowers medium red, reverse cream edged red, dbl., high-centered; cut flower rose; int. by Meilland Intl., 1998

L'Arioste N, lp, 1859, Moreau-Robert; flowers delicate pink

Larissa F, mr, 1987, Kordes, W.; flowers medium, full, no fragrance; foliage small, medium green, semi-glossy; spreading growth; [(seedling × Marina) × Rumba]

Lark – See **Alouette**, Pol

L'Arlésienne – See **Fred Edmunds**, HT

Larry Burnett HSpn, w, 1925, Skinner; flowers blush-white, center deeper, large, semi-dbl., cupped, intense fragrance; profuse bloom; foliage small, rich green, soft; short stems; dwarf, bushy, spreading growth; very hardy; [*R. acicularis* × *R. spinosissima*]

Larry Daniels HP, lp, Liggett, Thomas; flowers 2-3 in., very full; recurrent; int. by Liggett's Rose Nursery, 2000

Larry's Surprize Min, dy, 1991, Rennie, Bruce F.; flowers small, semi-dbl., borne mostly singly; foliage small, light green, matte; bushy (15 in.) growth; [Golden Rule × Rise 'n' Shine]; int. by Rennie Roses International, 1991

Las Casas – See **Las-Cases**, B

Las-Cases B, dp, 1828, Vibert; flowers purplish-pink, large, full, flat; non-remontant

Las Vegas HT, pb, 1956, Whisler, Milton; bud long, pointed; flowers salmon-pink, reverse darker, 5 in., 25-30 petals, high-centered; foliage leathery; vigorous, bushy growth; PP1486; RULED EXTINCE 6/80; [Charlotte Armstrong × Mission Bells]; int. by Germain's, 1957

Las Vegas HT, ob, 1980, Kordes, W.; bud large, pointed; flowers deep orange, reverse lighter, 26 petals, borne 1-3 per cluster, moderate fragrance; foliage green, slightly glossy; prickles brown; vigorous, upright, bushy growth; PP4798; [Ludwigshafen am Rhein × Feuerzauber]; int. in 1981; Gold Medal, Portland, 1988, Gold Medal, Genoa, 1985

Laser Gr, dp, Keisei; bud medium, conical; flowers rose bengal, 9 cm., 31 petals, elongated, borne usually singly; recurrent; foliage dark green; prickles numerous, average size, pinkish-green; growth upright (4 ft.); PP7739; [(Sonia × seedling) × seedling]

Laser Beam – See **Funkuhr**, HT

Laska F, lp, Dräger; flowers soft pink, medium, semi-dbl.; free-flowering; growth low (40-60 cm.); int. in 1990

Lasker HT, pb, 1980, Perry, Astor; bud very long; flowers very dbl., high-centered, borne singly, moderate fragrance; foliage glossy; prickles curved; tall growth; [South Seas × Oregold]; int. in 1981

Lassie HT, pb, 1946, Tuttle Bros. Nursery; bud long, pointed; flowers shell-pink, base canary-yellow, dbl., high-centered; foliage leathery; vigorous, compact growth; [sport of Picture]

Last Tango S, mr, Ping Lim; flowers clear red with ruffled edges, 2½-3 in., 20-30 petals; excellent repeat; growth mounded habit with blooms distributed evenly over the plant, 1½-4 ft.; PP16505; int. by Bailey Nurseries, 2004

Lasting Beauty S, mp; flowers medium, semi-dbl., cupped, borne in clusters; once-bloomer; int. in 1998

Lasting Impression Min, pb, 1998, Williams, Michael C.; flowers medium pink with darker pink edges, 1½ in., dbl., borne mostly singly; foliage medium size, dark green, semi-glossy; thornless; growth compact, medium (20 in.); [seedling × select pollen]; int. by The Mini Rose Garden, 1998

Lasting Love HT, dr, Adam, M.; flowers velvety red, dbl., moderate fragrance; PPAF; Fragrance Award, Hamilton, NZ, 2006

Lasting Peace Gr, ob, Meilland; bud conical; flowers brick red, 3½-4 in., 33 petals, cupped, borne 2-5 per stem; free-flowering; foliage medium size, medium green, glossy, dense; numerous prickles; growth semi-erect, compact (3 ft.); PP10544; [(Tropicana × First Edition) × Catherine Deneuve]; int. in 1997

Latan HT, 1978, Williams, J. Benjamin; bud long; flowers light lavender-tan, 4½-5½ in., 43 petals, high-centered, intense fragrance; foliage leathery; upright, bushy growth; [Lady X × Bronze Masterpiece]; int. by J.B. Williams & Associates

Lathom Chapel F, w, 1973, Ellick; flowers buff-cream, blended to white, 4 in., 20-25 petals; vigorous growth; [Orange Sensation × Sutter's Gold]; int. by Excelsior Roses

Lathom Park F, dp, 1972, Ellick; flowers carmine, 4 in., very dbl.; foliage glossy, light; vigorous growth; [Orange Sensation × Ballet]

Lathom Sunrise F, ob, 1973, Ellick; flowers orange-flame, 4 in., 25-30 petals; vigorous growth; [(Orange Sensation × Ballet) × Sutter's Gold]

Lathom Sunset HT, ob, 1973, Ellick; flowers orange-yellow, pink and red, 4½ in., 20-25 petals; vigorous growth; [Karl Herbst × Mischief]

Lathom Twilight HT, m, 1973, Ellick; flowers deep purple to Indian lake, 5 in., 28-30 petals; foliage dark; vigorous growth; [Karl Herbst × Mischief]; int. by Excelsior Roses

Latin Gypsy Curiosa HT, yb

Latina – See **Kent**, S

Latone – See **Lane**, M

Latte Min, m, 1995, Justice, Jerry G.; flowers russet with lavender edge, 1½ in., 56 petals, borne singly, moderate spicy fragrance; foliage medium size, medium green, semi-glossy; medium, bushy growth; [Twilight Trail × seedling]; int. by Justice Miniature Roses, 1995

Laughing Cavalier M, rb, 2001, McCann, Sean; flowers red with white stripes, large, semi-dbl., borne mostly solitary, slight fragrance; foliage medium size, dark green, glossy; numerous prickles; growth upright, medium; garden decorative; [(Rose Gilardi × Ferdinand Pichard) × (Rose Gilardi × William Lobb)]

Laughter Lines F, pb, 1987, Dickson, Patrick; flowers large, semi-dbl.; foliage small, medium green, semi-glossy; bushy growth; [(Pyecolour × Sunday Times) × Eyepaint]; Gold Medal, RNRS, 1984

Laura C, mp, before 1836; flowers hydrangea pink, large, full, cupped, borne in clusters of 10-12

Laura HT, op, 1968, Meilland, Mrs. Marie-Louise; flowers coral-pink, large, dbl., high-centered, moderate fragrance; foliage leathery; vigorous, upright, bushy growth; PP2986; [((Happiness × Independence) × Better Times) × (Baccará × White Knight)]; int. by C-P, 1969

Laura – See **Laura '81**, HT

Laura MinFl, rb, 2001, Giles, Diann; flowers medium, full, borne in small clusters, no fragrance; foliage medium size, medium green, matte; prickles mixed size, straight, numerous; growth upright, tall; garden decorative, exhibition; [seedling × seedling]; int. by Giles Rose Nursery, 2001

Laura S, pb, Clements, John; flowers creamy apricot and pink center shades to cream with a lipstick red picotee edge, 4 in., 70 petals; foliage light green, matte; moderate (3 × 3 ft.) growth; PPAF; int. by Heirloom Roses, 2002

Laura '81 HT, or, 1985, Meilland, Mrs. Marie-Louise; flowers orange-red, lighter reverse, large, 30 petals; foliage small, dark, semi-glossy; medium growth; [(Pharaoh × Colour Wonder) × ((Suspense × Suspense) × King's Ransom)]; int. as Natilda, Meilland Et Cie, 1981; Gold Medal, Japan, 1981

Laura-Alexander S, yb, Matthews; flowers lemon tinged pink, golden stamens, large, semi-dbl., borne in clusters, moderate lemon scented fragrance; good repeat; foliage glossy; vigorous, upright, bushy (3 ft.) growth; int. by Matthews Nurseries, 2001

Laura Anne HT, op, 1992, Cocker, James; flowers pink flushed orange, 3-3½ in., full, borne in large clusters, moderate fragrance; foliage large, medium green, glossy; some prickles; growth bushy (75 cm.); [((Sabine × Circus) × Maxi) × Harriny]; int. by James Cocker & Sons, 1990

Laura Ashley Cl Min, m, 1990, Warner, Chris; bud pointed; flowers lilac-mauve pink, reverse pink, aging same, loose, small, single, moderate fruity fragrance; foliage small, medium green, semi-glossy; prickles hooked, small, brown; spreading, low growth; hips oval, small, red; [Marjorie Fair × Nozomi]; int. by R. Harkness & Co., Ltd., 1990

Laura Bush F, or, 2007, Zary, Keith W.; flowers smoky orange, reverse orange, 4 in., dbl., blooms borne in large clusters; foliage medium size, dark green, glossy; prickles 8-10 mm., hooked downward, greyed-orange, numerous; growth upright, medium (3 ft.); [Sorbet Bouquet × Outrageous]; int. by Jackson & Perkins Wholesale, Inc., 2008

Laura Chantal Min, pb, 1997, Thomson, George L.; flowers varying shades of pink, dark reverse, full, borne in small clusters, intense fragrance; foliage medium size, medium green, semi glossy; upright, medium (30 in.) growth; [Avandel × Madam President]

Laura Clements S, dp, Clements, John K.; flowers warm pink, 4 in., 80 petals, rosette, moderate fragrance; recurrent; upright (4 ft.) growth; int. by Heirloom Roses, 1999

Laura Ford Cl Min, my, 1990, Warner, Chris; bud pointed; flowers medium yellow, reverse lighter yellow, aging pink, 2 in., 22 petals, high-centered, borne in small clusters, slight fruity fragrance; foliage small, light green, glossy; prickles straight, small, infrequent, light brown; upright, bushy, tall growth (7 ft.); round, large, average fruit; PP9012; [Anna Ford × (Elizabeth of Glamis × (Galway Bay × Sutter's Gold))]; int. in 1990

Laura Jane HT, lp, Gandy; flowers soft pink, large, dbl.; foliage dark green, dense; sturdy, upright, medium growth; int. by Gandy's Roses, 1990

Laura Louisa HKor, dp, Riches; flowers deep cerise pink to salmon, dbl., loose, moderate fragrance; recurrent; growth vigorous (10-12 ft.); [sport of Leverkusen]; int. by Peter Beales Roses, 1996

Laura Louise – See **Laura Louisa**, HKor

Laura Louise Cl Min, pb, Peden; int. in 1998

Laura Rose Elliott HT, dp, 1995, Thomas, D.; flowers deep pink with light reverse, 4-4¾ in., very dbl., borne mostly singly; foliage medium size, medium green, dull; numerous prickles; medium (60-70 cm.), upright growth; [Gavotte × City of Gloucester]

Laura Towill HT, yb, 1929, Towill; flowers copper-yellow, becoming copper-pink, semi-dbl.; [Phantom × Buttercup]

Laura's Laughter Min, pb, 2000, McCann, Sean; flowers dusty pink, reverse silvery pink, 1½ in., full, borne mostly singly, slight fragrance; foliage medium size, medium green, semi-glossy; prickles moderate; growth bushy, medium (22-26 in.); [Kiss Me Quick × Kristin]; int. by Justice Miniature Roses

Laura's Red Koster Pol, mr; int. in 1992

Laure – See **Laura**, C

Laure Brémont T, m, 1884, Guillot; flowers light grenadine-purple, shaded darker, large, very full

Laure Charton F, or, Guillot

Lauré Davoust HMult, lp, 1846, Laffay, M.; flowers clear pink, fading to flesh, then white, small, dbl., cupped, quartered, borne in clusters; non-recurrent; foliage dark green; very susceptible to winter injury; [*R. sempervirens* × a Noisette]

Laure de Broglie Ch, w, 1910, Dubreuil; bud very long; flowers blush ivory-white, full; growth shrubby, branching, robust; [Baronne Piston de St.-Cyr × G. Nabonnand]

Laure de Fénelon T, mr, 1884, Nabonnand; flowers glowing silky red, large, dbl.

Laure Dubourg B, mr, 1850, Pradel; flowers fire-red, large, full

Laure Fontaine T, w, 1867, Fontaine; flowers cream white, center brighter, large, full

Laure Gravereaux HRg, mp, 1901, L'Hay

Lauré Soupert HMult, ly, 1927, Soupert & Notting; flowers yellowish-white to pure white, 3 cm., dbl., borne in clusters of 80, intense fragrance; recurrent bloom; foliage small, glossy; strong stems; vigorous, climbing or trailing growth; [Tausendschön × George Elger]; int. by Notting

Laure Wattinne HT, mp, 1902, Soupert & Notting; flowers bright pink, center more intense, large, dbl., moderate fragrance; [Marie Baumann × Mme Caroline Testout]

Laureate F, m, 1990, Jobson, Daniel J.; bud pointed; flowers lavender with pink highlights, aging lighter, medium, dbl., high-centered, urn-shaped, slight fruity fragrance; foliage medium size,dark green, glossy, disease-resistant; prickles straight, medium, red; growth upright, bushy, medium; fruit not observed; winter-hardy; [Baby Talk × Angel Face]

Laurel Louise MinFl, ab, Clements, John; flowers deep apricot, dbl., high-centered; foliage dark green, leathery; growth medium; int. by John's Miniatures, 1999

Laurelle F, m, 1966, Harris, J.R.; flowers lavender-pink, base veined lemon, dbl., borne in clusters; foliage glossy; vigorous, bushy growth; [Rumba × Lavender Princess]; int. by Paulen Park Nursery

Lauren Pol, m, Rupert, Kim; flowers small, borne in clusters, slight fragrance; recurrent; graceful (5 ft.) growth; [seedling × Baby Faurax]

Lauren Amy HT, or, Dawson; int. in 1995

Lauren Elizabeth HT, m, 1991, Ortega, Carlos; flowers mauve blend, large, full, borne mostly singly, intense fragrance; foliage large, dark green, matte; tall, upright growth; [Moonlight × seedling]

Laurence Allen HP, mp, 1896, Cooling; flowers carnation pink, shaded lighter pink, large, full

Laurence Olivier – See **Wapiti**, F

Laurent S, yb, Poulsen; flowers yellow blend, 8-10 cm., dbl., slight wild rose fragrance; foliage dark; growth bushy, 40-60 cm.; int. by Poulsen Roser, 2000

Laurent Carle HT, mr, 1907, Pernet-Ducher; flowers brilliant velvety carmine, large, dbl., open, intense fragrance; foliage rich green, soft; bushy growth

Laurent Carle, Climbing Cl HT, mr, 1923, Rosen, L.P. (also Mermet, 1924); flowers deep carmine, aging to blood-red, large, full; [sport of Laurent Carle]

Laurent de Rillé HP, mr, 1885, Lévêque; flowers bright light cerise red, large, dbl., moderate fragrance; foliage glaucous green

Laurent Descourt HP, m, 1862, Liabaud; flowers velvety purple, medium, full, cupped

Laurent Heister P, mr, 1859, Robert et Moreau; flowers carmine red-purple, 7-9 cm.; very remontant

Laurent Hit – See **Laurent**, S

Laurette T, lp, 1853, Robert; flowers salmony flesh, 3 in., dbl.; few prickles

Laurette HRg, lp, 1999, Hortico; flowers medium, dbl., moderate fragrance; recurrent; int. by Hortico Inc., 1999

Laurie HT, lp, 1970, Scott, D.H.; flowers creamy pale pink, tipped salmon, 5 in., 28 petals; foliage matte green; vigorous growth; [sport of Princesse]

Lauriston HT, rb; int. by S. Brundrett & Sons, 2001

Lausitz S, mp, Berger, W.; flowers medium, semi-dbl.; int. in 1959

Lava Flow – See **Lavaglut**, F

Lava Gold F, ob, Williams, J. Benjamin; flowers bright orange yellow, red overlay, deepens to copper orange, semi-dbl., borne in large clusters, intense fragrance; int. by Hortico Inc., 1999

Lavaglow – See **Lavaglut**, F

Lavaglut F, dr, 1979, W. Kordes Söhne; flowers 2½ in., 24 petals, globular, borne in clusters; foliage glossy; vigorous, upright, bushy growth; [Gruss an Bayern × seedling]; int. by Dehner & Co.

Lavalette D, dp, 1823, Vibert; flowers lilac-rose, medium, full; foliage wide, elliptical; prickles red, short, unequal, sparse, intermixed with red bristles

Lavalette HGal, m, about 1840, Cartier/Prévost; flowers light lilac pink, medium, full

Lavalier Min, dp, 1989, Laver, Keith G.; bud pointed; flowers deep mauve-pink, reverse medium pink, small, 50 petals, cupped, borne singly; foliage small, medium green, matte, disease-resistant; prickles straight, small,light brown; upright, bushy, low, prolific growth; hips round, red; [Loving Touch × (Honest Abe × seedling)]; int. by Springwood Roses

Lavaluck Min, dp, 1989, Laver, Keith G.; bud pointed; flowers vivid, deep cherry pink, aging fuchsia, small, 28 petals, urn-shaped; foliage small, medium green, matte, long sepals, disease resistant; no prickles; bushy, low growth; hips ovoid, orange-red; [Blueblood × Julie Ann]; int. by Springwood Roses

Lavamaze Min, lp, 1989, Laver, Keith G.; bud ovoid; flowers light pink with deeper center, reverse light pink, small, 80 petals, high-centered; foliage small, medium green to red, disease-resistant; prickles straight, narrow, red; bushy, low growth; hips round, orange-red; [Loving Touch × Potluck]; int. by Springwood Roses

Lavande F, m, Rennie, Bruce F.; flowers shades of lavender, small, dbl., borne mostly singly, moderate fragrance; good repeat; florist rose; int. before 1994

Lavbound Min, op, 1989, Laver, Keith G.; bud pointed; flowers coral to orange-pink, outer petals pink-apricot, reverse pink, 53 petals, high-centered; foliage medium size, medium green, semi-glossy, disease-resistant; upright, bushy, low, prolific growth; [June Laver × Black Jade]; int. by Springwood Roses

Lavbrun Min, ob, 1995, Laver, Keith G.; flowers orange, full, borne mostly singly, no fragrance; foliage medium size, medium green, semi-glossy; some prickles; bushy, medium growth; [seedling × Apricot Doll]; int. by Springwood Roses, 1995

Laveena HT, yb, 1969, Laveena Roses; bud long, pointed; flowers yellow tinged pinkish, large, dbl., high-centered; foliage glossy; vigorous, upright, compact growth; [Kiss of Fire × unknown]

Lavendale Min, m, 1990, Jolly, Marie; bud pointed; flowers deep lavender, medium, very dbl., high-centered, borne singly, intense fragrance; foliage medium size, medium green, semi-glossy; no prickles; growth upright, bushy, medium, vigorous; hips round, greenish-brown; [Lavender Jade × Angel Face]; int. by Rosehill Farm, 1990

Lavender HT, m; int. by Howerton Rose Nursery

Lavender Beauty F, m, K & S; flowers lavender mauve, borne singly and small clusters, slight fragrance; int. by KSG Son Roses, 1999

Lavender Bird HT, m, 1964, Herholdt, J.A.; bud long, spiral, pointed; flowers lavender-pink, well-formed, large, dbl., moderate lavender fragrance; vigorous growth; int. by Herholdt's Nursery

Lavender Blue HT, m, 1982, Leon, Charles F., Sr.; flowers lavender, darker edges, large, dbl., high-centered; foliage medium size, dark, semi-glossy; upright, bushy growth; [Silver Star × Kolner Karneval]

Lavender Charm HT, m, 1964, Boerner; flowers

Persian lilac, 4½-5 in., 45-50 petals, cupped, intense fragrance; foliage dark, leathery; vigorous, bushy growth; PP2421; [Brownie × Sterling Silver]; int. by J&P, 1964

Lavender Cover – See **Cambridge**, S

Lavender Crystal Min, m; flowers cool mauve, deeper in center, 2 in., very full, slight spicy fragrance; recurrent; growth to 16-20 in.; int. in 1985

Lavender Delight Min, m, 1993, Moore, Ralph S.; flowers medium, semi-dbl., borne in small clusters; foliage medium size, medium green, semi-glossy; few prickles; medium, upright, bushy growth; [Orangeade × Cherry Magic]; int. by Sequoia Nursery, 1994

Lavender Dream S, m, 1984, Interplant; bud long; flowers deep lilac pink, 1½ in., 11-15 petals, flat, borne in large clusters, no fragrance; repeat bloom; foliage medium size, light green, matte, narrow; prickles few, medium; bushy, arching, 5 ft., growth; PP5916; [Yesterday × Nastarana]; ADR, 1987

Lavender Duet HT, m, Zary; int. by Bear Creek Gardens, 1999

Lavender Floorshow S, m, Harkness; flowers lavender, 2½-3½ in., 12 petals, intense expensive perfume fragrance; free-flowering; low, spreading (2 × 3 ft.) growth; int. by Heirloom, 2002

Lavender Folies F, m, Meilland; bud globular, small; flowers violet-purple, 2½ in., 100 petals, dome-shaped, borne mostly singly or in small clusters; recurrent; foliage dark green, semi-glossy; prickles both short and long; growth bushy (70 cm.); PP14017; [Debut × (Dreamer × Lavender Meillandina)]; florist rose; int. by Meilland Intl., 2004

Lavender Friendship S, m, Verschuren; flowers deep lavender to purple, white eye, small, semi-dbl., borne in trusses, slight fragrance; good repeat; spreading (2½ ft.) growth; int. in 1984

Lavender Garnette F, m, 1960, Boerner; bud globular; flowers lavender, open, medium, 35-45 petals, moderate fragrance; foliage leathery; vigorous, bushy growth; [(Grey Pearl × unknown) × Garnette]; int. by J&P, 1959

Lavender Girl F, m, 1958, Meilland, F.; flowers rosy purple, reverse magenta, changing to lavender, large, 35-42 petals, cupped, moderate spicy fragrance; dwarf, bushy growth; PP1672; [Fantastique × (Ampere × (Charles P. Kilham × Capucine Chambard))]; int. by C-P, 1957

Lavender Jade Min, m, 1987, Benardella, Frank A.; flowers lavender-white bicolor-mauve blend, large, 32-35 petals, high-centered, borne usually singly, intense damask fragrance; foliage medium size, dark green, semi-glossy; prickles short, straight; growth upright, tall; PP6517; [Rise 'n' Shine × Laguna]; int. by Nor'East Min. Roses, 1987

Lavender Jewel Min, m, 1978, Moore, Ralph S.; bud pointed; flowers clear lavender-mauve, 1 in., 38 petals, high-centered; foliage dark; compact, bushy growth; PP4480; [Little Chief × Angel Face]; int. by Sequoia Nursery

Lavender Joy S, m, Interplant

Lavender Kordana Min, m, Kordes; flowers lavender, full; container rose

Lavender Lace Min, m, 1968, Moore, Ralph S.; flowers lavender, small, dbl., high-centered, moderate fragrance; foliage small, glossy; vigorous, bushy dwarf growth; PP2991; [Ellen Poulsen × Debbie]; int. by Sequoia Nursery; AOE, ARS, 1975

Lavender Lace, Climbing Cl Min, m, 1971, Rumsey, R.H.

Lavender Lace F, m, 2005, Zary, Keith W.; flowers light lavender, reverse light lavender, 7-9 cm., full, borne in small clusters, moderate fragrance; foliage large, dark green, glossy; prickles 9-10 mm., straight, greyed-red, few; growth upright, vigorous, medium (80 cm.); PP14760; [seedling × Herbie]; int. by Jackson & Perkins Wholesale, Inc., 2004

Lavender Lady F, m, 1956, LeGrice; flowers pastel mauve, large, semi-dbl., borne in clusters; vigorous, upright growth; [seedling × Lavender Pinocchio]

Lavender Lady – See **Just Joanna**, HT

Lavender Lassie HMsk, m, 1960, Kordes; flowers lilac-pink, 3 in., dbl., borne in large clusters, intense fragrance; very vigorous, tall growth; [Hamburg × Mme Norbert Levavasseur]; int. by Morse, 1960

Lavender Love F, m, 1964, Daugherty; flowers lavender, medium; low growth; [Fashion × Floradora]; int. by Wyant

Lavender Mascara HT, m, Meilland; bud conical, large; flowers light cyclamen pink to mauve, 4 in., 40 petals, high-centered, borne mostly singly; recurrent; foliage semi-glossy, dense; stems medium; growth narrow, bushy (5 ft.); PP14275; [(Sterling Silver × Peace) × Meigormon]; florist rose; int. by Meilland Intl., 2003

Lavender Meillandina – See **Lavender Sunblaze**, Min

Lavender Midinette Min, m, Moore; flowers purple lavender, yellow stamens, pompon, borne in dense clusters, moderate fragrance; recurrent; willowy, arching (5 ft.) growth

Lavender Mist LCl, m, 1981, Christensen, Jack E.; bud ovoid; flowers 35 petals, borne mostly 3 per cluster, slight tea fragrance; foliage large; prickles medium, hooked downward; vigorous growth; long arching canes; [Angel Face × Allspice]; int. by Armstrong Nursery

Lavender Mist – See **Violet Mist**, MinFl

Lavender Pearl HT, m, 1977, Shaw; flowers lavender, center shading to pearl, large, very dbl., moderate lemon fragrance; foliage small; moderate, bushy growth; [Blue Moon × Grandpa Dickson]

Lavender Pearl F, m, Williams, J.B.; flowers lavender pink, small; int. by Hortico, Inc., 2004

Lavender Pinocchio F, m, 1948, Boerner; bud ovoid, light chocolate-olive-brown; flowers pink-lavender, 3-3½ in., 28 petals, borne in clusters, moderate fragrance; vigorous, bushy, compact growth; [Pinocchio × Grey Pearl]; int. by J&P

Lavender Princess F, m, 1960, Boerner; bud ovoid; flowers lavender, lightly overcast purplish lilac, 3½-4 in., 25 petals, open, borne in large clusters, moderate fruity fragrance; foliage leathery; vigorous, upright growth; PP1905; [(World's Fair × unknown) × (Lavender Pinocchio × unknown)]; int. by J&P, 1959

Lavender Queen HT, m, 1951, Raffel; bud pointed, touched red; flowers pinkish, lavender, 5-6 in., 20-35 petals, cupped; vigorous growth; int. by Port Stockton Nursery

Lavender Simplex Min, m, 1985, Williams, Ernest D.; flowers lavender, purple stamens, small, single, borne usually singly, moderate fragrance; recurrent; foliage small, dark, semi-glossy; growth upright, bushy; [Angel Face × Yellow Jewel]; int. by Mini-Roses, 1984

Lavender Spoon Min, m, 1995, Spooner, Raymond A.; flowers large, 5 petals, borne in sprays of 3-7; foliage small, dark green, semi-glossy; some prickles; growth medium (12-14 in.), bushy; [(Black Jade × Blue Peter) × seedling]; int. by Oregon Miniature Roses, 1995

Lavender Star Min, m, 1989, Williams, Ernest D.; flowers mauve blended lavender-tan, small, 5 petals, intense fragrance; foliage small, dark green, semi-glossy; upright, bushy, dense growth; [seedling × Lavender Simplex]

Lavender Sunblaze Min, m, Meilland; bud conical; flowers lavender-mauve, 1-1½ in., 25-30 petals, cupped, borne singly and in small clusters; good repeat; foliage small, deep green, glossy; prickles few, small; bushy, compact, medium (18 in.) growth; PP11025; [(Prelude × Blue Peter) × Lavender Jewel]; int. in 1999

Lavender Sweetheart Min, m, 1985, Williams, J. Benjamin; flowers deep blue lavender, small, 20 petals, high-centered, borne mostly singly, intense fragrance; foliage small, dark, semi-glossy; bushy growth; [Double Feature × unnamed Min seedling]; int. by J.B. Williams & Associates

Lavender Symphony Min, m; int. in 2004

Lavendula F, m, 1965, Kordes, R.; flowers lavender, 4 in., borne in clusters, intense fragrance; foliage dark; [(Magenta × (F)) × Sterling Silver]; int. by McGredy & Son

L'Avenir – See **Avenir**, B

L'Avenir – See **Avenir**, HWich

Lavgold Min, dy, 1987, Laver, Keith; flowers deep, strong yellow, reverse slightly lighter, fading creamy, small, 20 petals, high-centered, borne singly; foliage small, medium green, matte; prickles light beige, finely pointed, set at right angles; growth upright, bushy, low, compact; fruit ovoid, orange-yellow; [Loving Touch × Gold Mine]; int. by Springwood Min. Roses, 1986

Lavina HT, mp, 1962, Reynolds, W.H.; flowers buff-pink, large, 60 petals, high-centered; foliage dark, leathery; vigorous growth; [Queen Elizabeth × Anne Letts]

Lavina HT, dp, Strnad

Lavinia – See **Lawinia**, LCl

Lavinia Harrison HT, mp, 1988, Harrison, G.; flowers shell pink with light undertones, large, 30-35 petals, borne in sprays of 1-3; foliage red to light green, aging dark green; prickles pyramidal, red-brown; vigorous growth; [Duet × seedling]

Lavlemo Min, my, 1989, Laver, Keith G.; bud ovoid; flowers lemon yellow, deeper in center, medium, 28 petals, high-centered, borne usually singly; foliage small, medium green, matte; prickles beige; upright, bushy, medium growth; hips ovoid, green; [Dorola × Genevieve]

Lavlinger – See **Living Bouquet**, Min

Lavlow Min, ob, 1991, Laver, Keith G.; flowers orange yellow, small, full, borne in small clusters, no fragrance; foliage small, medium green, semi-glossy; few prickles; low, compact growth; [(Painted Doll × June Laver) × Potluck Yellow]; int. by Springwood Roses, 1991

Lavonda – See **Lavande**, F

Lavsho Min, lp, 1984, Laver, Keith G.; flowers small, 20 petals, borne in large clusters; foliage small, light green, glossy; spreading growth; [Mighty Mouse × Fairy Rose]

Lavsno Min, w, 1985, Laver, Keith G.; flowers dbl., no fragrance; foliage small, medium green, matte; upright, bushy growth; [Ice Princess × Sue Lawley]

Lawinia LCl, mp, 1983, Tantau, Math.; flowers translucent pink, darker at center, 4 in., 20 petals, cupped, moderate fragrance; foliage large, medium green, semi-glossy; spreading (to 8 ft.) growth; int. in 1980

Lawrence Johnston LCl, my, 1923, Pernet-Ducher; flowers large, semi-dbl., borne in clusters, moderate fragrance; repeat bloom; very vigorous, climbing (to 30 ft.) growth; [Mme Eugene Verdier × *R. foetida persiana*]

Lawrence Johnston HT, yb, 1946, San Remo Exp. Sta.; bud pointed; flowers yellow edged red and salmon, large, semi-dbl.; foliage light green; vigorous, upright, bushy growth; [Souv. de Denier van der Gon × Brazier]; Gold Medal, Rome, 1954

Lawrence of Arabia HT, yb, 1938, Dickson, A.; flowers Indian yellow, flushed coppery rose, large, dbl.; vigorous, bushy growth

Lawrence of Arabia – See **English Sonnet**, F

Laxton's Monthly Rambler – See **Monthly Rambler**, HWich

Laxton's Pink Delight – See **Pink Delight**, Pol

Laxton's Standard HT, mp, 1926, Laxton Bros.; flowers clear cerise-pink

Lays N, lp, about 1860, Guillot; flowers flesh pink, shaded white, medium, full, moderate fragrance

Lays T, my, 1863, Damaizin; flowers sulfur-yellow, medium

Lazy Days F, ab, Poulsen; flowers apricot blend, 8-10 cm., 25 petals, no fragrance; foliage dark; growth bushy, 60-100 cm.; int. by Poulsen Roser, 1999

Lazy Daze Min, m, 1991, Taylor, Pete & Kay; flowers light lavender, reverse slightly darker, white base, large, very full, bloom sometimes quarters, borne mostly singly; foliage small, medium green, semi-glossy; some prickles; low (30 cm.), compact growth; [Azure Sea × seedling]; int. by Taylor's Roses, 1992

Lazy Susan – See **Hertfordshire**, S

Le Baron de Rothschild – See **Baron de Rothschild**, HP

Le Bengale à Bouquets – See **Slater's Crimson China**, Ch

Le Bienheureaux de la Salle – See **Mme Isaac Periere**, B

Le Bourguignon Pol, yb, 1901, Buatois; flowers light egg-yolk yellow, edged carmine, medium, full; [Étoile de Mai × Mme Chédane Guinoisseau or Lauretty Messimy]

Le Camée B, m, 1845, Béluze; flowers bluish pink, center darker, medium, full, cupped

Le Chamois F, mr, 1954, Combe, M.; flowers crimson, medium, semi-dbl., borne in small clusters

Le Cid HRg, mr, 1908, Vigneron; flowers dazzling crimson, large, semi-dbl., borne mostly solitary; vigorous growth; [Conrad Ferdinand Meyer × Belle Poitevine]

Le Cid F, rb, Dorieux; flowers fire red with white reverse, semi-dbl., borne in clusters; recurrent; vigorous (80-110 cm.) growth; int. in 1996

Le Droit Humain HMult, pb, 1907, Vilin; bud pale crimson; flowers pink with darker carmine-pink, 6-7 cm., very dbl., borne in small clusters, slight fragrance

Le Flambeau T, dr, 1907, Chédane-Guinoisseau & Pajotin; flowers dark red, center fiery, medium, dbl.; [sport of Mons Tillier]

Le Géant HP, dp, 1863, Bruant; flowers dark pink, shaded violet, large, full

Le Grand Dauphin – See **Enfant de France**, HGal

Le Grand Huit – See **Lasting Love**, HT

Le Grand Huit, Climbing – See **Commandant Cousteau, Climbing**, Cl HT

Le Grand Sultan HGal, m, before 1815, Descemet; flowers purplish crimson, large, very dbl.; growth branching

Le Grand Triomphe – See **Nouvelle Pivoine**, HGal

Le Grande Capitain B, dr; bud fat, pink; flowers deep crimson, flushing purple, very dbl., quartered, slight fragrance; good repeat

Le Gras St Germain – See **Mme Legras de St Germain**, A

Le Havre HP, mr, 1870, Eude; flowers vermilion, imbricated, large; vigorous growth

Le Jacobin – See **Marcel Bourgouin**, HGal

Le Jeune Roi Dauphin – See **Enfant de France**, HGal

Le Lobèrde M, mp; flowers medium, very dbl.

Le Loiret Pol, mp, 1920, Turbat; flowers very brilliant pink to salmon-rose, borne in clusters of 10-15

Le Majestueuse – See **Majestueuse**, HGal

Le Masquerade en Villefranche F, pb, 2006, Kenny, David; flowers pink to light apricot, reverse pink, 3 in., dbl., borne in small clusters; foliage medium size, light green, glossy; prickles small, pointed, brown, moderate; growth bushy, upright, medium (3 ft.); [Nice 'n' Easy × Rock'n Roll × Aunty Lil]; int. in 2007

Le Météore HCh, mr, before 1846, Thierry; flowers carmine, nuanced purple, very large, dbl., borne in large clusters

Le Mexique HWich, lp, 1912, Schwartz, A.; flowers pale silvery rose, reverse lighter, medium, semi-dbl., borne in clusters; some autumn repeat; foliage glossy; vigorous, climbing growth; [Dorothy Perkins × Marie Pavie]

Le Mont Blanc T, ly, 1870, Ducher; flowers light yellowish-white, full

Le Nankin T, yb, 1871, Ducher; flowers yellow shaded coppery, well-formed

Le Pactole T, ly, before 1841, Miellez; flowers pale yellow, large, dbl.; [Lamarque × Yellow Tea]

Le Pérou HGal, dr, before 1826, Gossard/Parmentier; flowers velvety cerise with very deep grenadine reflections, medium, full

Le Petit Orange Pol, ob, Adam

Le Phoenix HGal, mp, 1843, Vibert; flowers medium carmine-pink, large, very dbl.

Le Pink Min, lp, 1986, Warriner, William A.; flowers crowded, small, very dbl., cupped, borne in sprays of 3-20, slight damask fragrance; foliage small, light green, matte; prickles long, thin, numerous on pecuncle; very dense, bushy, upright, medium growth; PP6011; [seedling × Watercolor]; int. by J&P

Le Poilu – See **Cumberland Belle**, Cl M

Le Poilu HWich, mp, 1915, Barbier; flowers satiny rose, turning to lilac-rose, silvery reverse to medium, 5-6 cm., borne in clusters of 8-15; stems covered with numerous hairs or small thorns; [Wichmoss × Moussue de Japon]

Le Ponceau Pol, dr, 1912, Hémeray-Aubert; flowers deep garnet-red, small, semi-dbl.; [Gruss an Teplitz × Mme Norbert Levavasseur]

Le Président – See ***R. rubrifolia*** (Villars)

Le Prince de Galles P, dp, before 1826; flowers light red or deep pink, large, full; foliage large, dark green, sharply dentate; few prickles

Le Progrès HT, my, 1903, Pernet-Ducher; bud ovoid golden yellow; flowers nankeen yellow, aging lighter, very large, full, cupped; very vigorous growth

Le Rêve LCl, ly, 1923, Pernet-Ducher; bud pointed; flowers pale yellow, large, semi-dbl., moderate fragrance; foliage rich green, glossy; vigorous, climbing growth; [Souv de Mme Eugene Verdier × *R. foetida persiana*]

Le Rhône HP, mr, 1862, Guillot; flowers velvety vermilion, medium to large, full

Le Rigide HMult, mp, 1920, Turbat; flowers Neyron pink, semi-dbl., borne in clusters of 25-30; vigorous growth

Le Rire Niais C, mp, before 1810, Dupont; flowers pink tinted lilac, medium, with a small center button, full, quartered, moderate unpleasant fragrance; foliage medium green, pointed; few prickles

Le Roi de Siam – See **Roi de Siam**, Cl T

Le Roitelet B, mp, 1869, Soupert & Notting; flowers silky pink, small, dbl.

Le Rosier Aurore Poniatowska – See **Celestial**, A

Le Rosier de Philippe Noisette – See ***R. × noisettiana*** (Thory), N

Le Rosier du Jardin ou Cecile S, op; flowers striped

Le Rosier Evêque HGal, m, before 1790; flowers dark violet-red to magenta, petals recurved, medium, very dbl., flat, strong fragrance; foliage pointed, bright green; from Holland

Le Rosier Pompon Blanc – See **Rose de Meaux White**, C

Le Rouge et Le Noir HT, dr, Delbard; flowers dark red with black tones, large, dbl., high-centered, intense rose and vanilla fragrance; recurrent; foliage dark green, glossy; int. in 1973

Le Royal-Époux – See **Royal Époux**, HP

Le Soleil T, my, 1891, Dubreuil; flowers silky glowing yellow, very large, very full, semi-globular

Le Triomphe – See **Majestueuse**, HGal

Le Triomphe – See **Aimable Rouge**, HGal, 1819-1820

Le Triomphe de Saintes HP, mr, 1885, Derouet; flowers scarlet, large, very full, round, slight fragrance; remontant; growth to 4 ft.

Le Vésuve Ch, pb, 1825, Laffay, M.; flowers carmine shading to pink, large, very dbl.; vigorous growth

Le Vésuve, Climbing Cl Ch, mp, 1904, Guillot; flowers variable, from pink to red, large, full; [sport of Le Vésuve]

Le Vingt-Neuf Juillet HCh, dr, before 1836; flowers crimson-purple, shaded with scarlet, large, full

Léa HGal, dp, about 1825, Vétillart; flowers bright rose-pink, large, full, cupped; abundant early bloom

Lea F, dr, Urban, J.

Lea Ann Gr, w, 1976, Patterson; bud long, pointed; flowers clear white, 4 in., 25-30 petals, high-centered; foliage soft; vigorous growth; [Queen Elizabeth × Ivory Fashion]; int. by Patterson Roses

Leader HT, mr, 1924, E.G. Hill, Co.; [sport of Premier]

Leading Lady HT, lp, 1935, Dickson, A.; flowers flesh-pink, flushed peach-blossom, large, dbl., high-centered; foliage deep green, leathery; vigorous, bushy growth; RULED EXTINCT 1/85; Gold Medal, NRS, 1934

Leading Lady HT, mp, 1985, Warriner, William A.; flowers large, 35 petals; foliage large, light green, matte; upright growth; PP5859; [seedling × seedling]; int. by J&P

Leading Lady MinFl, w, 2006, Benardella, Frank; flowers white with pink, reverse white, long-lasting, 2¾-3 in., dbl., borne mostly solitary; foliage medium size, medium green, glossy, disease-resistant; prickles moderate, ¼ in., angled and curved down, medium orange-brown; growth upright, well branched, medium (3 × 2 ft.); cutting, garden decoration; [seedling × Timeless (dp)]; int. by Nor'East Miniature Roses/ Greenheart Farms, Inc., 2007; Award of Excellence, ARS, 2007

Leafy-Proliferous Cabbage Rose – See **Prolifera de Redouté**, C

League of Nations HT, m, 1929, Leenders, M.; flowers reddish-lilac, shaded salmon-pink, semi-dbl.; [Frau Felix Tonnar × Solliden]

Leah Pol, mr, Holzman; int. in 1970

Leah June HT, pb, 2007, Greenwood, Chris; flowers medium pink, reverse creamy white, 4-5 in., full, borne mostly solitary; foliage medium green, semi-glossy; prickles ¼ in., slightly hooked downward, green, moderate; growth upright, medium; cutting, exhibition, garden; [Stainless Steel × Rosie O'Donnell]; int. in 2007

Lealand Jewel S, dp, 1963, Erskine; flowers deep pink, fading quickly, semi-dbl.; [Athabasca × unknown]

Leana HT, w; flowers apricot cream, dbl., exhibition, no fragrance; recurrent; vigorous, tall growth; [sport of Esther Geldenhuys]; int. in 1993

Leander S, ab, 1983, Austin, David; flowers small, very dbl., flat, borne in clusters; foliage medium size, medium green, semi-glossy; spreading growth; [Charles Austin × seedling]; int. by David Austin Roses, Ltd., 1982

Leandra HT, ab, Tantau; flowers cream, white, and apricot tones, large, full, high-centered, borne mostly singly; good repeat; foliage medium green; prickles moderate; stems long; growth strong, vigorous; florist rose; int. by Rosen Tantau, 2004

LeAnn Rimes HT, pb, 1999, Harkness; flowers rose pink edged ivory yellow, reverse cream, 5 in., full, high-centered, borne mostly singly, intense citrus and rose fragrance; foliage large, dark green, glossy; prickles moderate; upright, tall (4½ ft.) growth; [Dr Darley × Sweetheart]; int. by Harkness New Roses, 1997

LeAnn Rimes, Climbing Cl HT, pb, 2007, Brown, Ted; flowers medium, full, borne mostly solitary; prickles moderate; growth climbing, tall (15 ft.); [sport of LeAnn Rimes]; int. in 2007

Leaping Salmon LCl, op, 1984, Pearce, C.A.; flowers salmon pink, 5 in., 20 petals, moderate fragrance; foliage large, medium green, semi-glossy; upright (to 8-10 ft.) growth; PP7196; [((Vesper × Aloha) × (Paddy McGredy × Maigold)) × Prima Ballerina]; int. by Limes Rose Nursery, 1986

Leatherleaf Rose – See ***R. coriifolia*** (Fries)

Lebensfreude HT, or, GPG Bad Langensalza; flowers large, dbl.; int. in 1979

L'Eblouissante HP, mp, 1852, Touvais; flowers bright carmine, very large, full

L'Eblouissante M, mr, 1853, Robert; flowers fiery red, becoming scarlet, medium, full

L'Eblouissante de La Queue HGal, dr, about 1820, Noisette; flowers dark velvety crimson, large, very dbl.

Lecocq-Dumesnil HP, mr, 1882, Verdier, E.; flowers carmine-red, very large, very dbl., moderate fragrance; foliage dark green, deep irregular serration; prickles numerous, unequal, short, very pointed; stems reddish

Léda D, w, 1826, Deschiens; bud long; flowers white to blush, edged crimson, medium, dbl., flat, with central rosette, moderate fragrance; sometimes recurrent bloom; foliage dark green, large; compact (3 ft.) growth; hardy

Leda S, lp, 1960, Skinner; flowers pale pink, shallow, cupped, borne in clusters of 4-5; foliage dark; bushy (5 ft.) growth; hips large, apple-like, red

Ledonneau-Leblanc HGal, w, before 1834; flowers large, full

Ledreborg F, w, Poulsen; flowers 5-8 cm., 25 petals, no fragrance; foliage dark; growth bushy, 60-100 cm.; PP15484; int. by Poulsen Roser, 2001

Ledreborg Castle – See **Ledreborg**, F

Lée – See **Léa**, HGal

Leea Rubra C, lp, before 1906; flowers pink, center darker, medium, dbl., moderate fragrance

Leeds Castle S, m, 1998, Tantau; flowers carmine purple, reverse medium pink, 1½ in., single, borne in large clusters, no fragrance; foliage medium size, dark green, glossy; prickles moderate; spreading, low (30-40 cm.) growth; groundcover; int. by Eurosa, 1998

Leela HT, rb, Shastri, Dr. N. V.; flowers blend of red, white and yellow, large, full; strong growth; int. in 1999

Leenders' Bergfeuer F, mr, 1959, Leenders, J.; bud long; flowers scarlet, large, semi-dbl.; foliage dark, glossy; [Independence × Fashion]

Leenders' Flamingo F, ob, 1960, Leenders, J.; bud ovoid; flowers bright coral-peach, open, large, semi-dbl., borne in clusters; vigorous, bushy growth; [Cocorico × Ma Perkins]

Leenders' Pink F, mp, 1959, Leenders, J.; flowers bright pink, large, dbl., borne in heavy clusters; foliage dark, leathery, glossy; [Goldilocks × Mrs Inge Poulsen]

Leerder's Harlequin – See **The Jester**, Gr

Leersum 700 F, ob, 1985, Interplant; flowers light orange-yellow, medium, semi-dbl., borne in clusters, slight fragrance; foliage medium size, light green, matte; prickles numerous, small; upright growth; [Lichtkonigin Lucia × Marlena]; int. in 1979

Lee's Crimson Perpetual – See **Rose du Roi**, P

Lee's Duchess – See **La Belle Distinguée**, HEg

Legacy HT, pb, 1963, Hamilton; flowers rose-pink streaked white, large, dbl.; foliage leathery; moderate growth; [sport of Mrs Bryce Allan]; int. by Junior Legacy Club, 1963

Legacy HT, mr, 1993, J&P

Legacy Jubilee HT, yb, 1974, Dawson, George; bud long, pointed; flowers yellow, edged red, large, dbl.; foliage large, glossy; vigorous, upright growth; [Great Venture × Fred Streeter]; int. by Neil

Legend HT, mr, 1992, Warriner, William A.; flowers 3-3½ in., very dbl., high-centered, borne mostly singly; foliage medium size, dark green, semi-glossy; prickles very small, on peduncle; tall (120-140 cm.), upright, bushy growth; PP6092; [Grand Masterpiece × seedling]; int. by Bear Creek Gardens

Legendary HT, lp, 1962, Von Abrams; bud long, pointed; flowers soft pink, 5½ in., 55 petals, high-centered, moderate fragrance; foliage leathery; vigorous, upright growth; int. by Peterson & Dering, 1962

Legion HT, dp, 1920, Towill; flowers deep cerise-red, dbl.; [(Milady × unknown) × Hadley]

Légion d'Honneur F, mr, 1986, Delbard; flowers well-formed, medium, 55 petals, cupped; low, bushy growth; [(Souv. de J. Chabert × (Walko × Souv. de J. Chabert)) × ((Tamango × Gay Paris) × (Zambra × Jean de la Lune))]; int. in 1974; Gold Medal, Geneva, 1974

Leicester Abbey HT, mr, 1987, Greensitt, J.A.; flowers large, very dbl., moderate fragrance; foliage large, dark green, glossy; bushy growth; [(Gavotte × E.H. Morse seedling) × Erotika]; int. by Nostell Priory Rose Gardens, 1981

Leigh Ann Min, pb, 1987, Jolly, Marie; flowers pink, reverse cream, yellow center, fading to light pink, medium, 34 petals, high-centered; foliage medium size, medium green, semi-glossy; prickles bayonet-shaped, pinkish brown; upright, medium, vigorous growth; hips round, red-orange; [Poker Chip × Rise 'n' Shine]; int. by Rosehill Farm, 1987

Leigh-Lo HT, mp, 1980, Harkness; bud pointed; flowers rose-bengal, large, 42 petals, urn-shaped; foliage large; vigorous, upright growth; [Elizabeth Harkness × Red Devil]; int. in 1981

Leila – See **Léda**, D

Leila Min, ob, 1995, Berg, David H.; flowers light orange with yellow reverse, 1½ in., full, borne mostly singly, slight fragrance; foliage medium size, medium green, semi-glossy; some prickles; medium (15 in.), upright growth; [Arizona Sunset × June Laver]

Leila Francis HT, pb, 1948, Francis; bud ovoid; flowers two-toned pink, large, dbl., high-centered; foliage leathery; vigorous, bushy growth; [Earl Haig × Crimson Glory]; int. by F. Mason

Leila Verde F, m

Leipzig HMsk, or, 1939, Kordes; flowers orange-scarlet, open, semi-dbl., borne in clusters; recurrent bloom; foliage leathery, glossy, wrinkled; long, strong stems; vigorous, bushy growth; [Eva × Mermaid]

Leitrim Glory HT, dy, 1976, Hughes; flowers deep yellow, 5 in., 28-30 petals; foliage bronze, matte green; [sport of Whisky Mac]

Lele HT, dr, 1939, San Remo Exp. Sta.; bud pointed; flowers dark red, veined, very large, 30 petals; foliage bright green; strong stems; very vigorous growth; [Marquise d'Andigne × President Herbert Hoover]

L'Élégante – See **Élégante**, HP

Lelia Laird Min, ob, 1980, Bennett, Dee; bud long, pointed; flowers orange-red with yellow eye and reverse, 38 petals, high-centered, borne 1-4 per cluster, moderate tea fragrance; foliage medium green with red edging; prickles long, thin, red; upright growth; [Contempo × Sheri Anne]; int. by Tiny Petals Nursery, 1979

Lemania HT, dr, 1937, Heizmann, E.; bud almost black; flowers velvety blackish red, well-formed, very large, dbl.; vigorous growth; int. by A. Meilland

Lemesle – See **Le Vésuve**, Ch

Lemon HSpn, w, from Scotland; flowers yellowish-white

Lemon Beauty HT, w, 1932, Cant, B. R.; flowers creamy white, quickly fading to paper-white, base lemon-yellow, moderate fruity fragrance; foliage light

Lemon Bells – See **Yellow Simplicity**, S

Lemon Blush A, ly, Sievers; flowers pastel yellow, full, cupped, intense fragrance; growth large (6 × 6 ft.); int. in 1988

Lemon Bouquet Min, my, 1999, Laver, Keith G.; flowers medium yellow, reverse light yellow, 2-2½ in., full, high-centered, borne mostly singly, slight fragrance; foliage medium size, dark green, glossy; no prickles; growth upright, medium (12-15 in.); int. by Springwood Roses, 1999

Lemon Chiffon HT, my, 1955, Swim, H.C.; bud long, pointed; flowers lemon-yellow, to open, 3-4 in., very dbl., high-centered, intense spicy fragrance; compact, bushy growth; PP1241; RULED EXTINCT 9/86; [Soeur Thérèse × Golden Dawn]; int. by Arp Nursery Co., 1954

Lemon Couture S, ly; flowers bright yellow, slight fragrance; low (50 cm.) growth; int. by Paul Chessum Roses, 2003

Lemon Delight Min, my, 1978, Moore, Ralph S.; bud mossy, long, pointed; flowers mini-moss, 1½ in., 10 petals; bushy, upright growth; PP4447; [Fairy Moss × Goldmoss]; int. by Sequoia Nursery

Lemon Diana HT, ly, Tantau; flowers lemon yellow, dbl., moderate fragrance; foliage medium green; few prickles; growth strong, upright; int. in 2002

Lemon Dream HT, ly, Kordes; flowers delicate, light yellow, outer petals fading to white, dbl., high-centered; PP11357; [sport of Dream]; int. in 1997

Lemon Drop Min, ly, 1954, Moore, Ralph S.; flowers ¾ in., dbl.; foliage very small; very prickly; growth dwarf (6 in.); [(*R. wichurana* × Floradora) × Zee]; int. by Sequoia Nursery

Lemon Drop Min, my, 1999, Carruth, Tom; flowers clear yellow, 1-1½ in., full, borne in small clusters, slight fragrance; foliage medium size, light green, semi-glossy; few prickles; upright, compact, medium (20-24 in.) growth; PP14555; [Gingerbread Man × seedling]; int. by Weeks Roses, 1999

Lemon Elegance HT, my, 1965, Jones; bud long, pointed; flowers lemon-yellow, well-shaped, 4½-5 in., 38 petals, moderate fragrance; foliage leathery; vigorous, tall growth; int. by Hennessey, 1960

Lemon Flower Circus F, my, Kordes; flowers lemon yellow, 3.5 in., 20 petals, cupped, borne mostly in clusters, slight sweet fragrance; recurrent; low (25-30 in.), wide growth; int. by Wayside Gardens, 2007

Lemon Fluff Min, my, 1985, Curtis, Thad; flowers small, 20 petals, high-centered, borne singly and in clusters; foliage small, medium green, matte; upright, bushy growth; [(seedling × Rise 'n' Shine) × Summer Butter]; int. by Hortico Roses, 1986

Lemon Gems Min, my, 1999, Walden, John K.; flowers rich, deep yellow, 2½-2¾ in., full, cupped, borne mostly singly; recurrent; foliage medium size, dark green, glossy; prickles moderate; upright, spreading, low (18-20 in.) growth; PP12112; [seedling × Small Miracle]; int. by Bear Creek Gardens, 1999; Award of Excellence, ARS, 2000

Lemon Glow HT, my, 1963, Schwartz, Ernest W.; bud long, pointed; flowers lemon-yellow, 6-7 in., 55 petals, high-centered, moderate fragrance; foliage soft; vigorous, upright growth; [Sunlight × Golden Masterpiece]; int. by Wyant, 1963

Lemon Honey F, ly, Dickson, Patrick; flowers lemon yellow with paler margins; growth medium; int. in 1986

Lemon Ice HT, my, 1960, Kern, J. J.; bud pointed; flowers lemon-yellow, 4 in., 65 petals; foliage leathery, dark; vigorous, bushy, compact growth; [sport of Leonard Barron]

Lemon Ice Min, ly, Hannemann, F.; [Oz Gold × Lemon Delight]; int. by The Rose Paradise

Lemon Light LCl, ly

Lemon Meringue Min, my, 1996, Justice, Jerry G.; flowers medium yellow, with white to ivory tips, reverse becomes lighter, petals highly reflexed, 1 in., full; foliage medium size, dark green, dull; nearly thornless; growth compact (16-20 in.); PPRR; [Rise 'n' Shine × seedling]; int. by Justice Miniature Roses, 1997

Lemon Meringue S, ly, 2003, Radler, William; flowers clear light yellow, 11-13 cm., dbl., borne in large clusters, intense spicy fragrance; foliage large, dark green, glossy, clean; prickles numerous, average, almost straight, brown; growth spreading, near climbing, tall (over 200 cm.); garden decoration; [sport of Autumn Sunset]; int. by Weeks Roses, 2005

Lemon Mist Min, w, 1991, Gruenbauer, Richard; bud ovoid; flowers white with yellow center, aging white, medium, 50 petals, high-centered, slight fruity fragrance; foliage medium size, medium green, matte; upright growth; [Rise 'n' Shine × seedling]; int. by Flowers 'n' Friends Miniature Roses, 1993

Lemon Ophelia HT, my, 1922, Leenders, M.; flowers lemon-yellow, dbl.; [sport of Ophelia]

Lemon Pearl Min, ly, 1998, Williams, Michael C.; flowers light yellow, 1-1½ in., 41 petals, borne mostly singly; foliage medium size, light green, matte; prickles few, small, straight; compact, medium (22 in.) growth; [seedling × select pollen]; int. by The Mini Rose Garden, 1998

Lemon Pearls HBc, my, 2003, Moore, Ralph S.; flowers yellow, reverse light yellow, 2 in., full, borne mostly solitary, moderate fragrance; foliage medium size, medium green, glossy; prickles small, hooked, brown, few; growth spreading, medium (24 in.); landscape, pots, specimen; [un-named seedling × Out of Yesteryear]; int. by Sequoia Nurs., 2003

Lemon Pillar – See **Paul's Lemon Pillar**, Cl HT

Lemon Queen Cl HT, w, 1912, Hobbies; flowers creamy white, large, dbl.; [Frau Karl Druschki × Mme Ravary]

Lemon Rosamini Min, ly

Lemon Sherbet HT, ly, 1975, Kern, J. J.; bud ovoid; flowers white, center light yellow, 4 in., 35 petals, high-centered; foliage large, leathery; upright growth; [sport of Florence]; int. in 1973

Lemon Spice HT, ly, 1966, Armstrong, D.L., & Swim, H. C.; bud long, pointed; flowers 5½ in., 30-35 petals, high-centered to cupped, borne mostly singly, intense fragrance; recurrent; foliage dark, leathery; vigorous, spreading growth; PP2836; [Helen Traubel × seedling]; int. by Armstrong Nursery

Lemon Surprise F, my, 1980, Slack; flowers lemon, 12 petals, moderate spicy fragrance; foliage glossy; low, upright growth; [Allgold × Elizabeth of Glamis]; int. in 1978

Lemon Swirl Min, ly, 1992, Rennie, Bruce F.; flowers large, dbl., borne in small clusters; foliage medium size, light green, glossy; few prickles; growth tall, upright; [seedling × Sunsprite]; int. by Rennie Roses International

Lemon Time HT, my, Kasturi; flowers lemon yellow with green tinge, large, dbl.; int. by KSG Son, 1989

Lemon Twist Min, dy, 1989, Jacobs, Betty A.; bud pointed; flowers medium, 25 petals, high-centered, borne usually singly and in sprays of up to 3, slight tea fragrance; foliage medium size, medium green, glossy; prickles slightly declining, long, red to brown; bushy, medium growth; PP7450; [Gold Badge × Great Day]; int. by Four Seasons Rose Nursery

Lemon Up Min, yb, 2006, Hopper, Nancy; flowers light yellow, edged pink, reverse light yellow, 2½ in., single, borne mostly solitary; foliage medium size, medium green, semi-glossy; prickles ½ in., brown, few; growth bushy, medium (14-15 in.); [yellow seedling × yellow seedling]; int. in 2006

Lemon Yellow F, my, 1977, Gandy, Douglas L.; flowers lemon-yellow, 2 in., 21 petals; foliage dark; bushy growth; [Orange Sensation × King's Ransom]

Lemon Zen N, ly, 2006, Starnes, John A., Jr.; flowers 3 in., single, borne in large clusters, intense cinnamon fragrance; foliage medium size, medium green, matte; prickles medium, claw-shaped, moderate; growth upright, tall (8 ft.), pillar; [*R. moschata* × Graham Thomas]; int. in 2004

Lemon Zest S, my, 2001, Zary, Keith; bud pointed, ovoid; flowers 3½-4 in., 40-50 petals, old-fashioned, borne in small clusters, moderate citrus fragrance; foliage medium size, dark green, glossy; prickles moderate; growth compact, medium (3½ ft.); garden decorative; PP13342; [Jacyim × yellow shrub seedling]; int. by J&P, 2002

Lemonade F, w, 1976, Haynes Roses; flowers cream, 4½ in., 25 petals; foliage matte; [sport of Nancy West]; int. in 1974

Lemonade F, w, Kordes; flowers white, tinged green, medium, dbl., borne mostly singly; good repeat; florist rose; int. by W. Kordes Söhne, 2002

Len Gallagher Min, rb, 2004, Jalbert, Brad; flowers mottled red with white stripes, reverse red with white stripes, 1½ in., full, borne in small clusters; foliage medium size, medium green, semi-glossy; prickles medium, green, moderate; growth upright, tall (16-18 in.); garden; [Sachet × Pin Stripe]; int. in 2002

Len Mace HT, ly, 2003, Poole, Lionel; flowers cream tinged pink, 5 in., full, borne mostly solitary; foliage small, medium green, matte; prickles medium, triangular, moderate; growth upright, medium (36 in.); garden, exhibition; [Tom Foster × (Joanna Lumley × Pedrus Aquarius)]; int. by David Lister Roses, 2005

Len Turner F, rb, 1984, Dickson, Patrick; flowers ivory petals flushed and edged carmine, large, 35 petals; foliage medium size, medium green, glossy; bushy, very compact growth; [Electron × Eyepaint]

Lena T, ab, 1906, Dickson, A.; flowers apricot, edged yellow, borne in large clusters

Lena HT, or, deRuiter; int. in 1981

Lena HT, ab, Dickson; int. by Hortico Inc., 2004

Léna Turner HP, rb, 1869, Verdier, E.; flowers deep carmine, brightened at center with flame, shaded with violet, large, full; foliage dark green; prickles reddish

L'Enchantresse HGal, mp, before 1824, François; flowers clear pink, fading with age, large, dbl.

L'Enfant de France – See **Enfant de France**, HGal

L'Enfant du Mont Carmel HP, dp, 1851, Cherpin; flowers dark pink, shaded purple, large, full

L'Enfant Trouvé – See **Enfant Trouvé**, T

Leni Neuss HT, pb, 1933, Leenders, M.; bud pointed; flowers hydrangea-pink, reverse reddish old-rose, very large, dbl.; very vigorous, bushy growth; [Lilly Jung × Baronesse M. van Tuyll van Serooskerken]; int. by C-P

Lenidora S, Lens, Louis; int. in 1990

Lenka F, ly, Vecera, L.

Lens Pink – See **Dentelle de Malines**, S

Lenzburger Duft HT, mr, Schaiber; flowers cardinal red, shaded violet; int. in 1985

Leo F, mp, Burston; flowers solid pink, dbl., cupped, borne in clusters; recurrent; foliage dark green, glossy; growth medium (80 cm.); int. by Burston Nurseries, 2004

Leo Ferre HT, rb, Adam; int. by Roseraies Barth, 2006; Certificate, Lyon, 2006, Crystal Rose of the Parc Floral, Orléans, 2006

Léon Chenault HT, pb, 1931, Pernet-Ducher; flowers carmine-rose shaded salmon, base deeper, very large, dbl.; foliage dark; very vigorous growth; int. by Gaujard

Léon de Bruyn T, ly, 1895, Soupert & Notting; flowers light yellow with darker center, large, full, moderate fragrance

Léon Delaville HP, dr, 1885, Verdier, E.; flowers dark red strongly shaded carmine, tinted violet crimson, large, full; foliage dark green

Léon Lecomte D, dp, about 1854; flowers warm pink, fading paler, darker veins, large, full, moderate fragrance

Léon Oursel B, dp, 1847, Oger; flowers large, full

Léon Renault HP, mr, 1878, Lédéchaux; flowers cherry-red, reverse tinted carmine, very large, very dbl.

Léon Robichon HP, w, 1901, Robichon; flowers large, dbl.

Léon Say HP, rb, 1882, Lévêque; flowers bright red shaded brown, light pink, and lilac pink, very large, moderate centifolia fragrance; foliage large, thick, glaucous green

Léon XIII T, w, 1892, Soupert & Notting; flowers white, with shades of straw yellow, center ochre, large, full; foliage large; growth vigorous; [Anna Olivier × Earl of Eldon]

Leona F, mp, Noack; flowers 2 in., semi-dbl., borne in clusters; good repeat; growth to 2 ft.; int. by Rosen Noack, 2004

Leonard Barron HT, op, 1931, Nicolas; bud pointed; flowers salmon-copper and shell-pink, very large, dbl., moderate fragrance; foliage leathery; bushy growth; [Schoener's Nutkana × Souv. de Mme Boullet]; int. by C-P; David Fuerstenberg Prize, ARS, 1933

Leonard Cheshire HT, mr; int. by Ross Roses

Leonard Dudley Braithwaite S, dr, 1993, Austin, David; flowers bright red, 3-3½ in., very dbl., informal, borne in small clusters, intense fragrance; foliage medium size, dark green, semi-glossy; some prickles; growth medium (110 cm.), bushy; PP8154; [Mary Rose × The Squire]; int. by David Austin Roses, Ltd., 1988

Leonardo de Vinci F, lp, 1994, Meilland, Alain A.; bud globular, large; flowers bengal pink, 3½-4 in., 75-80 petals, borne in small clusters; free-flowering; foliage medium size, dark green, glossy; some prickles; bushy (70-110 cm.) growth; PP9980; [Sommerwind × (Milrose × Rosamunde)]; int. by SNC Meilland & Cie, 1993

Léonce Colombier HT, mr, 1943, Meilland, F.; bud oval; flowers brilliant geranium-red, stamens yellow, medium, dbl., cupped; foliage leathery; very vigorous, bushy growth; [Charles P. Kilham × (Charles P. Kilham × Capucine Chambard)]; int. by A. Meilland

Leonidas HT, rb, Meilland; bud conical, medium; flowers red-orange with creamy yellow reverse, 5 in., dbl., high-centered, borne mostly singly; recurrent; foliage medium green, semi-glossy; prickles moderate; erect growth; PP9997; [Hello × Mme. A. Meilland]; int. in 1995

Leonie F, mp, 1964, Leenders, J.; flowers dbl.; vigorous growth; [Queen Elizabeth × Circus]

Leonie – See **Leonie Parade**, MinFl

Léonie Lambert HP, lp, 1913, Lambert, P.; flowers silver-pink, shaded yellow and flesh, well-shaped, large, moderate fragrance; very vigorous growth; [Frau Karl Druschki × Prince de Bulgarie]

Léonie Lamesch Pol, ob, 1899, Lambert, P.; flowers light coppery red, center yellow, edges flecked darker, semi-dbl.; foliage rich green, soft; vigorous, bushy growth; [Aglaia × Kleiner Alfred]

Léonie Lartay HP, mr, 1860, Lartay; flowers bright scarlet, large, full

Léonie Osterrieth T, w, 1892, Soupert & Notting; flowers porcelain white with very light yellow center, large, full, borne in large clusters, moderate fragrance; [Sylphide × Mme Bravy]

Leonie Parade MinFl, mr, Olesen; bud pointed ovoid; flowers medium red, 2 in., 13-15 petals, cupped, borne mostly singly, slight fragrance; recurrent; foliage dark green, matte; prickles some, 3 mm., yellow-green, hooked downward; bushy, compact (20-40 cm.) growth; PP15573; [sport of Heidi Parade]; int. by Poulsen Roser, 2001

Léonor de March HT, dr, 1958, Camprubi, C.; bud long, pointed; flowers deep blood-red, large, dbl., moderate fragrance; foliage glossy; upright growth; [J.M. Lopez Pico × Poinsettia]; int. in 1956; Gold Medal, Rome, 1958

Léonora HT, mr, 1921, Paul, W.; flowers brilliant velvety red, center brighter, dbl.

Leonorah F, ob, 2003, Rawlins, R.; flowers medium, semi-dbl., borne in small clusters; foliage medium size, medium green, semi-glossy; prickles triangular; growth compact, medium (30 in.); garden decoration; [Laura Ford × Heritage]

Leonore Annenberg HT, pb, 2004, Williams, J. Benjamin; flowers medium pink, reverse deeper, 4½-5 in., full, borne mostly solitary, moderate fragrance; foliage large, dark green, semi-glossy; prickles medium, curved downward; growth upright, tall (3½ -4 ft.); garden, exhibition, cutting; [First Prize × Love]

Léontine Contenot HT, yb, 1935, Ketten Bros.; bud pointed; flowers sunflower-yellow bordered pink and yellow, large, 45-50 petals, high-centered; foliage quaker green; vigorous growth; [Joanna Hill × Souv. de Claudius Pernet]

Léontine Gervais HWich, ab, 1903, Barbier; bud coppery red; flowers salmon-orange and yellow, 5 cm., semi-dbl., borne in clusters of 3-10, moderate fragrance; non-recurrent; foliage dark, glossy; very vigorous, climbing growth; [*R. wichurana* × Souv. de Catherine Guillot]

Léopold Hausburg HP, pb, 1863, Granger; flowers carmine, shaded purple to dark garnet, large, full

Léopold I HP, dr, 1863, Van Asche; flowers deep red, well-formed, large, dbl.; [Général Jacqueminot × unknown]

Léopold I, Roi des Belges – See **Léopold I**, HP

Leopold II HP, lp, 1868, Margottin; flowers light pink, shaded salmon, very large, full, cupped

Léopold Lambotte HT, mr, 1944, Meilland, F.; bud long, pointed; flowers scarlet-red; very tall growth; [Grenoble × National Flower Guild]

Léopold Premier – See **Léopold I**, HP

Leopold Ritter HMult, mr, 1900, Geschwind, R.; flowers brilliant velvety red, aging to purplish crimson, medium, semi-dbl., borne in small clusters; somewhat recurrent; foliage large; numerous prickles

Léopoldine P, lp, 1826, Toutain; flowers flesh pink, tinted violet

Léopoldine M, lp, 1850, Robert; flowers bright flesh pink, medium, full

Léopoldine d'Orléans HSem, w, 1828, Jacques; flowers white, shaded rose, medium, dbl.

Leora Stewart HT, op, Wilber; long continued bloom

Leotilde Minguez HT, rb, 1961, Dot, Pedro; flowers carmine, shaded vermilion and yellow, large, 30 petals; upright growth; [Pres. Herbert Hoover × Vicky Marfa]

Leprechaun F, yb, 1972, Adams, M.R.; bud ovoid; flowers red, reverse yellow, small, dbl., globular, moderate fragrance; foliage glossy; growth moderate, upright; [(Easter Parade × Masquerade) × Little Darling]

L'Ermite Ch, about 1826, from Angers

Lerna F, rb; int. by Willemse France, 2004

Les Amis de Lille HT, pb, 1928, Ketten Bros.; bud lincoln red on pale buff ground; flowers pale buff, edges and reverse suffused salmon-pink; [Golden Emblem × Pres. Bouche]

Les Amis de Troyes HT, mp, 1935, Vially; flowers China-pink, passing to carmine-pink, base ochre-yellow, well-formed, dbl.; vigorous growth; [Feu Joseph Looymans × seedling]

Les Amoureux de Peynet F, dp, Meilland; flowers rose-carmine, medium, dbl., borne in large clusters; good repeat; foliage dark green, matte; growth to 50 cm.; int. in 1992; Rose of the Century, Lyon, 1992, Gold Medal, Bagatelle, 1991

Les Quatre Saisons S, mp; flowers very dbl., pompon; int. by Meilland, 2003

Les Rosati HFt, rb, 1906, Gravereaux; bud dark pink; flowers bright carmine, center yellow, medium, full

Les Sables d'Olonne HT, ob, Dorieux; int. by Roseraies Dorieux, 2001

Les Saisons d'Italie HGal, mr; flowers carmine-red, medium, very dbl.

Les Sjulin Gr, pb, 1981, Buck, Dr. Griffith J.; flowers coral pink, reverse light red, 28 petals, urn-shaped to imbricated, moderate old rose fragrance; foliage medium size, dark olive green, leathery; prickles awl-like; erect, bushy growth; [Country Dancer × ((Dornroschen × Peace) × Pink Peace)]; int. by Iowa State University

Les Sylphides HT, op, 1960, Watkins Roses; flowers pink shading to yellow and orange, well-shaped; foliage reddish; long stems; very vigorous growth; [sport of Margaret]

Les Trois Mages HGal, mp, 1823, Gentil; flowers medium, very full, borne in clusters of 3; sometimes classed as a D

Lesbos LCl, op, Peden, R.

Leschenault's Rose – See ***R. leschenaultii*** (Wight & Arnott)

Lesdain HT, ob, RvS-Melle; [Roklea × Candia]; int. in 1989

Lesja Jean HT, lp, 1990, Weddle, Von C.; bud pointed; flowers large, 37 petals, high-centered, borne usually singly; foliage medium size, medium green, semi-glossy; prickles medium, light; upright, medium growth; [seedling × seedling]; int. in 1989

Lesja Ukrajinka HT, lp, Lempickij; flowers medium, dbl.; int. in 1964

Lesley Anne Min, op, 1987, Fryer, Gareth; flowers pale peach-pink, pale yellow base, fading slightly paler, large, 45 petals, cupped; foliage medium size, light green, matte; prickles thin, small, pointed, light brown; upright growth; hips oval, orange-red; [seedling × seedling]

Lesley Dudley HT, op, 1932, McGredy; flowers warm carmine-pink shaded orange, well-shaped, large, dbl.; foliage dark; vigorous, bushy growth; Gold Medal, NRS, 1931

Lesley Johns – See **Leslie Johns**, HT

Leslie Min, mp, 1997, Bennett, Dee; flowers 1¼ in., dbl., borne in small clusters; foliage medium size, medium green, semi-glossy; bushy (40-50 cm.), tall growth; [Deep Purple × Jean Kenneally]; int. by Tiny Petals Nursery, 1997

Leslie Dudley – See **Lesley Dudley**, HT

Leslie Evans HT, dr, 1927, Evans; flowers rich dark velvety crimson, semi-dbl.; vigorous growth; [J.B. Clark × Red-Letter Day]; int. by Beckwith

Leslie G. Harris HT, mr, 1970, Gregory; flowers crimson-scarlet, pointed, 4 in., 27 petals; moderate growth

Leslie Holland HT, dr, 1911, Dickson, H.; flowers deep velvety crimson, large, dbl.; Gold Medal, NRS, 1909

Leslie Johns HT, dp, 1973, Gregory; flowers Persian rose, 5-6 in., 32 petals, high-centered, moderate fragrance; foliage dark, glossy; [Soraya × unknown]; int. in 1972

Leslie Pidgeon HT, ob, 1922, Dickson, H.; flowers orange-buff, suffused terra-cotta, semi-dbl.

Leslie Wheal F, yb, 1978, Buss; bud ovoid; flowers cream-yellow, 1½ in., 25-35 petals, cupped; foliage light green; compact growth; [sport of Zorina]; int. by H. Buss Nursery

Leslie's Dream HT, mr, 1984, Dickson, Colin; flowers signal red, 7+ cm., full, borne mostly solitary, slight fragrance; foliage medium size, dark green, glossy; numerous prickles; growth upright, tall (1 m.); garden decoration; [Bonfire × Typhoon]

L'Esperance HP, pb, 1871, Lartay (or Fontaine); flowers light carmine, changing to rose with cherry red, large, dbl., flat

Lessing HMsk, rb, 1914, Lambert, P.; flowers reddish-rose streaked white, center citron-yellow, small, dbl.; foliage large, light; [Trier × Entente Cordiale]

Lest We Forget F, mr, Matthews; flowers vibrant red, borne in clusters; repeats well; shrubby, compact (80 cm.) growth; int. by Matthews Nurseries, 2000

Lestra Hibberd HT, dy, 1935, Joseph H. Hill, Co.; bud dark yellow; flowers amber-yellow to orange-yellow, large, dbl.; foliage leathery; strong stems; vigorous, compact growth; [Joanna Hill × Sweet Adeline]

Lesueur P, m, 1853, Robert; flowers violety red pink, 7-9 cm., full, cupped, borne in clusters; foliage dark green

Let Freedom Ring HT, mr, 2005, Earman, Ernest; flowers light strawberry red, 10-13 cm., dbl., high-centered, borne mostly solitary, no fragrance; foliage medium size, medium green, matte; prickles average, straight; stems long; growth upright, tall (160-190 cm.); garden decoration; [Prima Donna × Touch of Class]; int. by Weeks Roses, 2006

Letchworth Centenary S, mp, Harkness; flowers 2½ in., very dbl., borne in large, abundant clusters, moderate fragrance; continuous bloom; foliage glossy, light green; growth mounded, 2 × 2 ft.; bedding, borders; int. by R. Harkness & Co., 2004

Letchworth Garden City F, op, 1978, Harkness;

flowers medium salmon-pink, 2½ in., 20 petals, moderate spicy fragrance; foliage medium green, semi-glossy; vigorous, bushy growth; [(Sabine × Pineapple Poll) × (Circus × Mischief)]; int. in 1972; Gold Medal, Monza, 1978

L'Étincelante HP, mr, 1891, Vigneron; flowers bright red, somewhat velvety within, large, full, cupped

Letitia HT, dr, 1949, Bees; bud long, pointed; flowers crimson, 5-6 in., 35 petals; foliage dark; very vigorous growth; [Crimson Glory × Southport]

Letizia Gr, Cazzaniga, F. G.; int. in 1962

Letizia HT, w, Kordes; flowers creamy white, large, dbl., high-centered, moderate sweet tea rose fragrance; foliage large, deep green; strong, well-branched, compact (2½-3 ft.) growth; int. in 1996

Letizia Bianca HBanksiae, w, Mansuino; flowers pure white, 1½ in., dbl., high-centered, borne mostly solitary, slight fragrance; foliage small, medium green, semi-glossy; growth upright, small (24 in.); int. in 1963

Letkis – See **John Dijkstra**, F

L'Etna Ch, mp, 1825, Laffay, M.; flowers pink, becoming brighter, medium, very dbl.

Letty Coles T, w, 1876, Coles/Keynes; flowers white, center pink; [sport of Mme Mélanie Willermoz]

Leuchtfeuer HCh, mr, 1909, Türke; flowers bright red, large, full, moderate fragrance; [Gruss an Teplitz × Cramoisi Superieur]; sometimes classed as B

Leuchtstern HMult, pb, Kiese; flowers deep rose pink, center white, 3-4 cm., single, borne in clusters of 10-30; growth to 8-10 ft.; [Daniel Lacombe × Crimson Rambler]; int. by Schmidt, 1899

Leventina HT, op, Huber; int. in 1984

L'Évêque HGal, m, before 1790; bud round; flowers deep violet, slightly striped, ticked with small white spots, 2 in., dbl., borne mostly solitary, moderate fragrance; foliage ovate, deeply toothed; prickles brown, hooked, massed at the leaf joints

Leverkusen HKor, ly, 1956, Kordes; bud long, pointed; flowers clear lemon yellow, crinkly petals, dbl., borne in small clusters; recurrent bloom; foliage small, medium green, glossy; vigorous, creeper or pillar (to 8 ft.) growth; [*R.* × *kordesii* × Golden Glow]

Leverson-Gower – See **Leweson-Gower**, B

Leveson-Gower – See **Leweson-Gower**, B

Levianthan ; [Great Venture × Fritz Thiedemann]

Leweson-Gower B, op, 1845, Béluze; flowers rose shaded salmon, very large, dbl., cupped

Lewiston HT, my, 1982, Perry, Astor; flowers pointed, large, very dbl., high-centered, borne singly, intense fruity fragrance; foliage large, glossy; vigorous, tall growth; [Red Lion × King's Ransom]

Lexie Pol, Miers, A.

Lexington S, my; flowers medium yellow, fading lighter, 5-8 cm., dbl., pompon, borne in clusters, slight wild rose fragrance; recurrent; foliage dark green, glossy; broad, bushy (60-100 cm.) growth; hips none; int. as Yellow Cover, Poulsen, 1993

Lexus Min, mp, Benardella, Frank; int. by Australian Roses, 2004

Lexy S, mp, Clements, John; flowers old-fashioned, English style, 3 in., 70 petals, borne in clusters of 12-15, slight fragrance; foliage dark green, glossy; vigorous (5-6 ft.) growth; int. by Heirloom, 2000

Ley's Perpetual Cl HT, ly, 1936, Ley; bud apricot yellow; flowers pale yellow, fading to buff/cream, 4 in., dbl., cupped, moderate fragrance; vigorous, climbing (to 15 ft.) growth; int. in 1936

Lheritieranea – See **Boursault Rose**, Bslt

Li Burés HT, rb, 1929, Dot, Pedro; flowers rose-red and yellow mixed (very variable), dbl., cupped; very vigorous, bushy growth; [Château de Clos Vougeot × Souv. de Claudius Pernet]; int. by C-P

Li Schluter HT, Moreira da Silva, A.

Li-Ying HCh, w, Dening; bud creamy pink; flowers white with yellow stamens, small, semi-dbl., shallow cup, borne in sprays; modest (2 ft.) growth; [*R. chinensis minima* × unknown]; int. by Brentwood Bay Nurseries, 2007

Lia HT, pb, 1909, Ketten; flowers rosy scarlet, reverse crimson-pink, base of petals Indian yellow, medium to large, full; [Farbenkönigin × Mme Ravary]

Lia Min, or

Liaison – See **Pete Musser**, F

Liane LCl, ob, Cocker; flowers salmon pink, fading to pinkish-yellow, 5 in., high-centered, borne mostly solitary; foliage dark green, glossy; int. in 1989

Liane des Champs dp; flowers clear pink, semi-dbl. to dbl.; once bloomer; foliage glossy; vigorous (10 m.) growth; [chance seedling]

Lianne Reynolds F, lp, 1996, Reynolds, Ted; flowers light pink, china-porcelain appearance, full, borne in small clusters, no fragrance; foliage small, medium green, glossy; some prickles; compact, medium growth; [Gloire de Dijon × Hot Pewter]; int. by Ted Reynolds Roses International, 1997

Libby Min, rb, 1979, Rovinski & Meredith; bud ovoid; flowers white, edged red, 1-1½ in., 20 petals, high-centered, then flat; foliage glossy; upright, compact growth; PP4597; [Overture × Perla de Alcanada]; int. by Casa de Rosa Domingo, 1978

Libby's Gold HT, yb, 1977, Carpenter; bud long, slender; flowers 5 in., very dbl.; foliage dark; upright, compact growth; [sport of Apollo]

Liberté F, dr, 1946, Leenders, M.; flowers brilliant crimson-red, large, dbl.; [Florentina × seedling]

Liberty HT, dr, 1900, Dickson, A.; flowers brilliant velvety crimson, large, dbl., intense fragrance; foliage dark; vigorous growth; [Mrs W.J. Grant × Charles J. Grahame]

Liberty, Climbing Cl HT, dr, 1908, May; flowers velvety crimson; [sport of Liberty]

Liberty – See **Liberty Parade**, MinFl

Liberty Bell HT, rb, 1968, Kordes, R.; flowers claret-rose, reverse light cream, 5 in., 50 petals, globular, moderate fragrance; foliage leathery; vigorous growth; [Detroiter × Kordes' Perfecta]; int. by McGredy, 1963

Liberty Bell MinFl, rb, 2003, Benardella, Frank; flowers dark red with white eye, reverse white, large, full, borne mostly solitary; foliage medium size, dark green, semi-glossy; prickles ¼- in., curved slightly down; growth upright, bushy, tall; exhibition, cutting, garden decoration; int. by Nor East Miniature Roses, 2003

Liberty Miss Min, pb, 1997, Zipper, Herbert; flowers medium, 8-14 petals, borne mostly singly; foliage medium size, medium green, semi-glossy; few prickles; bushy, medium (12-18 in.) growth; [seedling × Cupcake]; int. by Island Roses

Liberty Parade MinFl, ob, Poulsen; flowers orange in heart with paler outer petals, 5-8 cm., dbl., slight wild rose fragrance; foliage dark; growth bushy, 20-40 cm.; PP13103; int. by Poulsen Roser, 2000

Libia HT, w, 1934, Borgatti, G.; flowers milk-white, center creamy yellow, large, very dbl.; vigorous growth

Libra Min, dp, Burston; int. by Burston Nurseries, 2004

Librarian F, m, Kaneko; int. by Hiroshima Bara-en, 2002

Libre Ingenue S, w, Delbard; int. in 1996

Libretto HT, dp, 1967, Verschuren, A.; bud ovoid; flowers pink-red, medium, dbl., borne in clusters; foliage dark; [Elli Knab × seedling]; int. by van Engelen, 1966

Libretto LCl, w

Lichfield Angel S, w, 2006; flowers white, reverse light yellow, 8½ cm., very full, borne in small clusters; foliage medium size, dark green, semi-glossy; prickles medium, concave, curved inward, medium red, few; growth bushy, vigorous, medium (120 cm.); garden decorative; [seedling × seedling]; int. by David Austin Roses, Ltd., 2006

Lichtblick S, yb, VEG; flowers yellow and pink, large, dbl.; int. in 1972

Lichterloh HMsk, mr, 1959, Tantau, Math.; bud ovoid; flowers velvety blood-red, semi-dbl., borne in clusters; foliage leathery, dark, glossy; vigorous, upright (3 ft.) growth; [Red Favorite × New Dawn]; int. in 1955

Lichtkönigin Lucia S, my, 1985, Kordes, W.; flowers 18 petals, cupped, borne 3-5 per cluster, moderate fragrance; foliage medium size, dark, glossy; bushy, tall growth; [Zitronenfalter × Clare Grammerstorf]; int. in 1966; ADR, 1968

Licorice Twist HT, dy, deVor; int. in 1995

Lída Baarová HT, mp, 1934, Böhm, J.; bud pointed; flowers rosy salmon, large, dbl., cupped; foliage glossy; vigorous, bushy growth; [Ophelia × unknown]

Lida O Min, my, 1997, Bischoff, Francis J.; flowers very dbl., borne in small clusters; foliage medium size, medium green, semi-glossy; medium (23 cm.) compact growth; [Party Girl × Miss Dovie]

Lida Paar – See **Lída Baarová**, HT

L'Idéal N, mr, 1887, Nabonnand, G.; flowers geranium to turkey-red, base Indian yellow, semi-dbl.; vigorous, climbing growth

Lidice F, or, Wheatcroft; flowers large, dbl.; int. in 1961

Lidka HT, mr, Urban, J.

Lidka Böhm – See **Lidka Böhmova**, HT

Lidka Böhmova HT, mp, 1929, Böhm, J.; flowers salmon-pink, tips veined reddish, base golden yellow, large, dbl.; foliage soft, bronze; very vigorous, bushy growth; [sport of Una Wallace]

Lido di Roma HT, yb, 1970, Delbard-Chabert; bud long, pointed; flowers deep yellow, shaded red, large, dbl., high-centered; foliage glossy, leathery; vigorous, upright, bushy growth; [(Chic Parisien × Michele Meilland) × (Sultane × Mme Joseph Perraud)]; Gold Medal, Japan, 1968

Lie de Vin HGal, dr, before 1815, Descemet; flowers wine red

Liebesbote HT, dr, 1935, Weigand, C.; bud pointed; flowers velvety dark red, very large, dbl., high-centered; foliage soft; very vigorous, bushy growth; [Hadley × Miss C.E. van Rossem]; int. by Pfitzer

Liebeserklärung HT, mr, Horstmann; flowers large, dbl.; int. in 1968

Liebesglut – See **Crimson King**, HT

Liebeslied – See **Love Song**, HT

Liebeslied F, lp, Noack, Werner; flowers soft pastel pink, 3 in., 30 petals, cupped to flat, borne in clusters, slight fragrance; recurrent; foliage glossy; growth medium; int. by Noack Rosen, 1990

Liebestraum – See **Red Queen**, HT, 1968

Liebeszauber HT, mr, 1959, Kordes; flowers velvety red, large, cupped; foliage dark; vigorous, upright growth; [Detroiter × Crimson King]

Liebeszauber HT, dr, 2006, W. Kordes' Söhne; bud large, oval, dark red; flowers brilliant deep red, 11 cm., very full, high-centered, borne mostly solitary; foliage reddish, turning dark green, leathery; large, spreading (4-6 ft.) growth; int. as Crimson Spire, Ludwig's Roses; Fragrance Award, The Hague, 1994

Lied – See **Bouquet**, F

Lien Budde – See **Caroline Budde**, HMult

Liesbeth Canneman F, dy, Interplant; int. in 1997

Liesbeth van Engelen HT, w, 1960, Verschuren, A.; flowers creamy white edged lilac-pink, dbl.; foliage dark, glossy; upright growth; [Briarcliff × seedling]; int. by van Engelen

Liésis – See **Céline Forestier**, N

Lieutenant Chauré HT, dr, 1909, Pernet-Ducher; flowers velvety crimson-red, shaded garnet, very large, dbl., cupped; foliage rich green, leathery; vigorous, bushy growth; [Liberty × Étoile de France]

Lieutenant Colonel A. Fairrie HT, my, 1930, Bees; bud pointed; flowers primrose, base deep yellow large, dbl., high-centered, moderate apple fragrance; [Rev. F. Page-Roberts × Mme Ravary]

Lieutenant Colonel Desmaires F, ob, 1967, Boerner; bud ovoid; flowers orange and yellow, dbl., borne in clusters; foliage leathery; vigorous, low growth; [Rondo × Fashion seedling]; int. by J&P

Lieve Louise S, pb, Lens; bud slim; flowers pink on the outer half of the petals, with white in the center, single to semi-dbl., flat, borne in large clusters, slight fragrance; free-flowering; growth to 4 ft.; int. by Louis Lens SA, 2002

Lieven Gevaert HT, mr, 1976, Delforge; bud ovoid; flowers dbl., 30 petals, moderate fragrance; foliage dark; int. in 1974

Liewe Heksie S, r, Ludwig; int. by Ludwig's Roses, 2003

Liezl de Swardt HT, ab; int. by Ludwig's Roses, 2003

Life Begins at 40 MinFl, w, 2001, Horner, Colin P.; flowers cream, white reverse, small, dbl., borne in large clusters, slight fragrance; foliage small, medium green, glossy; prickles small, curved, moderate; growth compact, low (50 cm.); garden decorative; [Laura Ford × (Robin Redbreast × Lichtkonigin Lucia)]; int. by Paul Chessum Roses, 2002

Life Lines Cl Min, or, 2004, Sproul, James A.; flowers orange-red striped white, reverse lighter, 1½-2 in., semi-dbl., borne in large clusters, no fragrance; foliage medium size, medium green, semi-glossy, mildew-resistant; prickles medium, curved downward; growth upright, tall (60 to 72 in.); trellis, pillar; [Roller Coaster × Hot Tamale]; AOE, ARS, 2005

Lifeboat Jubilee HT, mr, 1974, Sanday, John; flowers scarlet, shaded crimson, 4 in., 20 petals, high-centered; [Karl Herbst × (Karl Herbst × Crimson Glory)]

Lifestyle Min, pb, 1992, Moore, Ralph S.; flowers large, color holds well, dbl., borne mostly singly; foliage medium size, medium green, semi-glossy; few prickles; medium (35-45 cm.), upright, bushy, rounded growth; [Little Darling × Rainbow's End]; int. by Sequoia Nursery, 1993

Lifestyle F, lp, Bell, Laurie; flowers dusky, soft pink, old-fashioned, moderate fragrance; medium growth; int. by Bell Roses

Lifirane HT, mp, 1976, Zwemstra; flowers Neyron rose, 3 in., 20-25 petals, high-centered; foliage dull; vigorous, upright growth; PP4034; [sport of Sweet Promise]; int. by Meilland

Liga HRg, lp, Rieksta; flowers soft pink in center, fading to white on outer petals, large, dbl., loose, moderate fragrance; recurrent; growth 3-5 ft. tall and wide

Light MinFl, my, Poulsen; flowers medium yellow, 5-8 cm., dbl., no fragrance; growth bushy, 20-40 cm.; PP13425; int. by Poulsen Roser, 2000

Light Editor McFarland HT, lp, 1950, Thomasville Nursery; [sport of Editor McFarland]

Light of Day F, my, 2006; flowers full, borne in singly and in clusters; foliage large, medium green, matte, disease-resistant; prickles deltoid with concave upper and, dark reddish-brown; growth upright, full and rounded, medium (32-38 in.); garden decoration; very hardy; [Cal Poly × Sunsprite]; int. by Nor'East Miniature Roses

Light Orlando HT, pb; flowers light pink with light yellow reverse, pointed petals, large, dbl., high-centered; foliage glossy; stems long; [sport of Orlando]; int. by Carlton Roses, 2004

Light Touch S, pb, 1997, Weatherly, Lilia; flowers medium, dbl., borne in large clusters; foliage medium size, light green, very glossy; growth bushy, tall (2 m.); [Cousin Essie × Open Pollination]; int. by Prophyl Pty. Ltd.

Lighten Up Min, ly, 2000, Bridges, Dennis A.; flowers 1½ in., full, borne mostly singly; foliage medium size, medium green, semi-glossy; upright, bushy (26-30 in.) growth; [Loving Touch × select pollen]; int. by Bridges Roses, 2001

Lights of Broadway Min, rb, 1993, Saville, F. Harmon; flowers yellow with broad red edge, yellow reverse, medium, very dbl., borne mostly singly, no fragrance; foliage medium size, medium green, semi-glossy; some prickles; medium (16-20 in.), upright, bushy growth; PP8918; [(Tamango × Yellow Jewel) × Party Girl]; int. by Nor'East Min. Roses, 1994

Ligia HT, Moreira da Silva, A.

Ligne d'Arenberg HT, w, 1903, Soupert & Notting; [Souv du President Carnot × Golden Gate]

Lijang Rose HGig, mp; flowers pink with shades of apricot and bronze, large, dbl., borne mostly singly, pendulous, moderate fragrance

Lijnbaanroos F, ly, 1961, Buisman, G. A. H.; bud yellow; flowers creamy yellow, semi-dbl., borne in clusters; foliage dark; vigorous, upright growth; [Schneewittchen × Koningin Juliana]

Li'l Alleluia Min, rb, 1991, King, Gene; flowers wine to silver with yellow base, small, dbl., borne mostly singly, moderate fragrance; foliage medium size, medium green, matte; upright, tall growth; [((B.C. × Scamp) × Tamango) × Magic Carrousel]; int. by AGM Miniature Roses

Lil' Rebel Min, mr, 2003, Sproul, James A.; flowers red, reverse red, 1½-2 in., 5-7 petals, borne in small clusters, no fragrance; foliage small, medium green, matte; few prickles; growth upright, tall (30-36 in.); bedding; ['Anytime' × 'Santa Claus']; int. in 2003

Li'l Rip Min, w, 1992, Moglia, Thomas; flowers white with yellow center, medium, full, borne in small clusters; foliage small, medium green, matte; few prickles; medium (35-45 cm.), narrow, upright growth; [Loving Touch × Cupcake]; int. by Gloria Dei Nursery, 1993

Li'l Touch Min, ab, 1992, Moglia, Thomas; flowers apricot, yellow stamens showing, moderately open, medium, dbl.; foliage medium size, medium green, matte; some prickles; medium (40-50 cm.), upright growth; [Loving Touch × Prima Donna]; int. by Gloria Dei Nursery, 1993

Lila Pol, Miers, A.

Lila Banks S, m, 2003, Rippetoe, Robert Neil; flowers light mauve, reverse deeper mauve, 2 in., single, borne mostly solitary; good repeat; foliage medium size, medium green, semi-glossy, puckered, banksia-like; prickles small, straight, brown, few; growth compact, short (2 ft.); specimen, hedge, bedding; [Lilac Charm × (Rosa banksiae alba-plena × Old Blush)]; int. by Robert Neil Rippetoe

Lila Queen of Bermuda HT, m, Strnad, J.; flowers lilac-pink, large, dbl.; int. in 1970

Lila Tan HT, m, 1961, Dot, Pedro; flowers violet-cobalt, medium, 30 petals; vigorous, spreading growth; [Grey Pearl × Simone]

Lila Vidri HT, m, 1959, Dot, Simon; bud pointed; flowers lilac, 30 petals, exhibition, moderate fragrance; stems strong; upright, compact growth; [(seedling × Prelude) × Rosa de Friera]; int. in 1958

Lila Zwerg Min, m, Hetzel; int. in 1998

Lilac Airs HT, lp, 1988, Sanday, John; flowers soft lilac pink, yellow at base, reverse silver at base, large, 36 petals, exhibition, intense damask fragrance; foliage large, medium green, semi-glossy; prickles long, fairly straight, medium brown, matte; bushy, tall, strong growth; [Fred Gibson × Whisky Mac]; int. by John Sanday Roses, Ltd., 1988

Lilac Belle HT, m, Bell, Laurie; bud long, elegant; flowers soft lilac, dbl., well-formed, moderate fragrance; stems long; tall growth; int. by Bell Roses

Lilac Castle – See **Lambert**, F

Lilac Charm F, m, 1962, LeGrice; bud pointed; flowers pastel mauve, anthers golden, filaments red, 4 in., 5-8 petals, flat, borne in clusters, moderate fragrance; foliage dark; upright, compact growth; PP2189; int. by Roseland Nurs., 1961; Gold Medal, NRS, 1931

Lilac Chrysler Imperial HT, m, Strnad

Lilac Dawn F, m, 1964, Swim, H. C.; bud pointed; flowers lavender-pink to lilac, 2½ in., 43 petals, borne in clusters, moderate lilac fragrance; foliage leathery, light green; vigorous, bushy growth; PP2225; [Lavender Pinocchio × Frolic]; int. by Armstrong Nursery, 1964

Lilac Dream F, m; int. in 2005

Lilac Joseph Guy

Lilac Magic Carpet S, m; groundcover; int. by Swane's Roses

Lilac Minimo Min, m; possibly hybridized by Dawson; int. in 1997

Lilac Mystery – See **Plum Dandy**, Min

Lilac Mystery S, m; int. in 1994

Lilac Queen Elizabeth Gr, m

Lilac Rose HT, lp, 1964, Sanday, John; flowers soft silver pink with lilac shading, 5 in., 30 petals, moderate fragrance; foliage dark; vigorous, upright growth; [Karl Herbst × Chrysler Imperial]; int. in 1962

Lilac Rose S, pb, 1994, Austin, David; flowers lilac pink, 3-3½ in., very dbl., borne in small clusters; foliage medium size, medium green, semi-glossy; some prickles; upright (90 cm.) growth; PP8837; [seedling × Hero]; int. by David Austin Roses, Ltd., 1990

Lilac Snow HT, w, 1985, Williams, H.; flowers white, strong lilac tinge to inside petals; [sport of Admiral Rodney]; int. by P. Loaney

Lilac Time Min, m, 1955, Moore, Ralph S.; flowers lilac-pink to light red, becoming lilac tinted, small, dbl.; dwarf (10 in.) growth; [Violette × Zee]; int. by Sequoia Nursery

Lilac Time HT, m, 1956, McGredy, Sam IV; flowers lilac, large, 33 petals, high-centered, moderate fragrance; foliage light green; growth moderate; [Golden Dawn × Luis Brinas]

Lilet Dot F, Dot, Simon; int. in 1987

Lilette Mallerin HT, m, 1937, Mallerin, C.; bud pointed, yellow; flowers mauve-red to mauve pink, deepening in cooler weather, reverse yellow, dbl., cupped; foliage glossy; vigorous growth; [Charles P. Kilham × *R. foetida bicolor* seedling]; int. by A. Meilland

Lilette Mallerin Improved HT, m, 1942, J&P; bud pointed; flowers mauve-red, reverse yellow, large, 25 petals, high-centered; foliage bronze, glossy; vigorous, upright, bushy growth; [sport of Lilette Mallerin]

Lili Dieck HRg, mr, 1899, Dieck; medium (5 ft.) growth; int. in 1899

Lili Marlene – See **Lilli Marlene**, F

Lilian HT, dy, 1931, Cant, B. R.; flowers golden yellow, very large, dbl., cupped; foliage bronze, glossy; vigorous, bushy growth; RULED EXTINCT 12/85

Lilian Austin S, pb, 1981, Austin, David; bud globular; flowers 33 petals, flat, borne 1-5 per cluster, moderate fragrance; foliage glossy, dark; prickles hooked, brown; spreading growth; [Aloha × The Yeoman]; int. by David Austin Roses, 1973

Lilian Baylis F, ly, Harkness, R.; flowers yellow in center, fading white on outer petals, full, rosette; good repeat; int. by Harkness, 1996

Lilian Bootle HT, dp, 1972, Bootle; flowers cerise, 4½-5 in., 35 petals, high-centered, moderate fragrance; foliage matte green; compact, bushy growth; [Margaret × Seedling (red)]

Lilian Doris HT, mr, 2002, Poole, Lionel; flowers full, borne mostly solitary; foliage medium size, medium green, semi-glossy; prickles medium, hooked down, moderate; growth upright, bushy, medium (1 m.); garden, exhibition; [Raewyn Henry × Red Planet]; int. in 2004

Lilian Harvey HT, or, 2000, Poole, Lionel; flowers very bright orange-red, large, borne in small clusters, slight fragrance; foliage medium size, dark green, semi-glossy; prickles moderate; growth bushy, medium (3 ft.); [Adrienne Berman × Corso]; int. by David Lister Roses, 2001

Lilian Nordica HT, w, 1898, Walsh; flowers large, dbl.; vigorous growth; [Margaret Dickson × Mme Hoste]

Liliana HT, pb, 1956, Camprubi, C.; flowers soft pink, reverse carmine; RULED EXTINCT 12/85; [Edith Krause × Fashion]; Gold Medal, Geneva, 1956

Liliana Gr, w, 1986, Staikov, Prof. Dr. V.; flowers large, 50 petals; foliage light green, leathery; vigorous, tall, upright growth; [Queen Elizabeth × seedling]; int. by Kalaydjiev and Chorbadjiiski, 1977

Liliana – See **Clair Renaissance**, S

Liliana LCl, dr; flowers strong red, borne in clusters; recurrent; foliage dark green, glossy; stems reddish; climbing (8 ft.) growth; int. by Delbard, 2002

Lilibet F, lp, 1953, Lindquist; bud ovoid; flowers 2½-3½ in., 30 petals, borne in clusters, moderate spicy fragrance; foliage glossy; low, bushy growth; [Floradora × Pinocchio]; int. by Howard Rose Co.

Lill Lindfors – See **Egeskov**, F

Lillebror Min, mr, 1978, Hubner; flowers dbl.; dwarf, bushy growth; int. by O. Baum

Lilli Dieck HRg, mr, 1899, Dieck; [*R. rugosa* × *R. gallica*]

Lilli Marleen – See **Lilli Marlene**, F

Lilli Marleen, Climbing Cl F, mr, 1983, Pekmez, Paul

Lilli Marlene F, mr, 1960, Kordes, R.; bud ovoid; flowers 3 in., 25 petals, cupped, moderate fragrance; foliage leathery; vigorous growth; [(Our Princess × Rudolph Timm) × Ama]; int. by McGredy & Son, 1959; Golden Rose, The Hague, 1966, ADR, 1960

Lilli von Posern HT, mp, 1910, Kiese; flowers large, dbl.; [Mme Caroline Testout × Oberbürgermeister Dr. Troendlin]

Lillian Min, pb, 1958, deVink; flowers rose pink, white center, small, semi-dbl.; very dwarf growth; [Ellen Poulsen × Tom Thumb]; int. by de Vink, 1958

Lillian F, ob, Williams, J. Benjamin; flowers soft orange, borne in clusters; recurrent; [Rose Parade × Zorina]; int. by Hortico, Inc., 1997

Lillian French HT, pb, 1985, French, Richard; flowers light to medium pink, reverse deep pink, large, 50-120 petals, quartered, borne in clusters of 1-5, moderate fragrance; foliage medium size, medium green, semi-glossy; prickles large, pointed downward; growth upright, bushy; [Miss Hillcrest × Bishop Darlington]

Lillian Gibson S, mp, 1938, Hansen, N.E.; flowers rose-pink, 3 in., very dbl., intense fragrance; non-recurrent; vigorous growth; very hardy; [*R. blanda* × Red Star]

Lillian Gish F, ly, 1985, French, Richard; flowers very pale yellow, large, 35 petals, borne singly and in small clusters; foliage medium size, medium green, semi-glossy; prickles few, straight; upright growth; [Queen Elizabeth × Allgold]

Lillian Gomez-Mena Cl HT, pb, 1927, Chambard, C.; flowers salmon-cream, reverse carmine, dbl.

Lillian Moore HT, yb, 1917, Dickson, H.; flowers white, shaded yellow over pink, medium, full, moderate fragrance

Lillie Bell HT, dp, 1979, Williams, J. Benjamin; bud ovoid to pointed; flowers deep pink to cerise-red, ruffled, 4½-5 in., 34 petals; foliage large; upright growth; [Pink Peace × Miss All-American Beauty]; int. by Central Mississippi Rose Soc.

Lillie Dawber HT, dr, 1952, Kordes; flowers scarlet overlaid crimson, 5 in., 25 petals, cupped; foliage dark; free growth

Lilliput Cl Pol, mr, 1897, Paul, G.; flowers carmine-red, small, dbl.

Lilly Jung HT, dy, 1925, Leenders, M.; bud large, ovoid; flowers golden yellow, large, dbl., moderate fragrance

Lily Bertschinger F, w, Hauser; int. in 1980

Lily de Gerlache HT, dp, 1971, Institute of Ornamental Plant Growing; bud long, pointed; flowers rose-red, large, dbl., cupped; foliage glossy, bronze, leathery; growth moderate, upright, bushy; [Kordes' Perfecta × Prima Ballerina]

Lily Freeman S, mp, 1998, Huxley, Ian; flowers 5¼ in., single, flat, borne in small clusters, moderate fragrance; foliage small, medium green, dull; numerous prickles; bushy, medium tall growth; [Schneezwerg × Schneezwerg]

Lily Kemp HT, dp, 1928, Morse; flowers deep cherry-cerise, dbl.; [Mme Butterfly × Capt. Ronald Clerk]

Lily Mertschersky N, m, 1878, Nabonnand; flowers violet-red, fading to mauve-pink, 5 cm., very full, borne in clusters of up to 10, no fragrance

Lily Pons HT, ly, 1939, Brownell; flowers yellow center, shading to white outer petals, large, 50 petals, high-centered, moderate fragrance; foliage glossy; [Glenn Dale × Stargold]

Lily the Pink HT, lp, 1992, Scrivens, Len; flowers 3-3½ in., very dbl., borne mostly singly; foliage medium size, medium green, semi-glossy; some prickles; tall (100 cm.), upright growth; [seedling × seedling]

Lily van Oost HT, mp, 1938, Verschuren-Pechtold; flowers very large, dbl.

Lily White HT, w, 1950, Hartgerink; bud ovoid; flowers 4½ in., very dbl., high-centered; foliage glossy; vigorous, upright growth; [sport of Starlite]; int. by J&P

Limbo HT, my, Kordes; bud large, pointed; flowers yellow with greenish tint, large, full, high-centered, borne mostly singly; free-flowering; stems long; growth vigorous; florist rose; int. by W. Kordes Söhne, 1999

Limburgia HT, rb, 1921, Leenders, M.; flowers glowing deep carmine, reverse lilac-white, dbl.

Lime Kiln HWich, w; int. in 1970

Lime Sublime F, w, 2004, Dickson, Colin; flowers pastel chartreuse-white, long-lasting, 7-9 cm., dbl., borne in small clusters; prolific, slight fragrance; foliage medium size, dark green, glossy; prickles small, almost straight, brown, moderate; growth upright, vigorous, medium (120-140 cm.); garden decoration; [Sexy Rexy × Dawn Chorus]; int. by Weeks Roses, 2005

Limeburners Bay Min, ob; flowers deep apricot with orange tonings, moderate fragrance; medium growth

Limelight F, r, 1960, Morse; flowers vermilion splashed golden, semi-dbl., borne in clusters; vigorous growth; RULED EXTINCT 5/85; [sport of Enterprise]; int. in 1959

Limelight HT, ly, 1985, Kordes, W.; flowers large, 35 petals, high-centered, intense fragrance; foliage medium size, dark, semi-glossy; upright, bushy, spreading growth; [Peach Melba × seedling]

Limelight – See **St Patrick**, HT

Limerick MinFl, rb, 1991, Zipper, Herbert; flowers red with white reverse, medium, dbl., high-centered, borne in small clusters; foliage medium size, dark green, glossy; few prickles; medium (40 cm.), spreading growth; [Tamango × Jennifer]; int. by Magic Moment Miniature Roses, 1992

Limited Edition HT, mr, 1984, J&P; flowers large, dbl., no fragrance; foliage medium size, medium green, semi-glossy; upright growth; PP5037; [seedling × seedling]; int. by McConnell Nurs., Inc.

Limoges F, w, Poulsen; flowers 8-10 cm., 25 petals, no fragrance; foliage dark; growth bushy, 60-100 cm.; PP15549; int. by Poulsen Roser, 2003

Limona HT, ly, Kordes; flowers cream yellow, large, dbl., high-centered, intense fragrance; stems long; PP11393; florist rose; int. by W. Kordes Söhne, 1997

Lina Pol, lp, 1930, Vogel, M.; flowers creamy light pink, medium, dbl.

Lina – See **Lina Renaissance**, S

Lina Renaissance S, w, Poulsen; flowers white, 10-15 cm., dbl., moderate fragrance; foliage dark; growth bushy, 100-150 cm.; PP15695; int. by Poulsen Roser, 2002

Lina Schmidt-Michel HT, yb, 1906, Lambert, P.; flowers yellowish-pink, large, semi-dbl.; [Mme Abel Chatenay × Kleiner Alfred]

Lina Vogel HFt, ob, 1936, Vogel, M.; flowers orange with golden and light yellow shades, medium, single

Linburn Light F, mp, Andersons; flowers dbl., high-centered, moderate fragrance; int. in 1986

Lincelle HGal, m, 1826, Dubourg; flowers violet, center darker, edges more red, medium, very full

Lincoln Cathedral HT, ob, 1986, Langdale, G.W.T.; flowers outer petals pink, inner ones orange, yellow reverse, large, 28 petals; foliage medium size, medium green glossy; prickles numerous, reddish; bushy growth; [Silver Jubilee × Royal Dane]; int. in 1985; Gold Medal, RNRS, 1985

Lincolnshire Poacher HT, yb, 1992, Langdale, G.W.T.; flowers yellow flushed apricot and pink, 3-3½ in., full, borne mostly singly; foliage medium size, medium green, semi-glossy; some prickles; medium (80-100 cm.), bushy growth; [Silver Jubilee × Woman and Home]; int. in 1993

Linda HT, yb, 1997, Bracegirdle, A.J.; flowers medium, very dbl., borne in small clusters; foliage medium size, medium green, semi-glossy; upright, medium (3½ ft.) growth; [Champion × (Pink Favourite × Golden Autumn)]

Linda – See **Linda Parade**, MinFl

Linda Min, mr, 2005, Paul Chessum Roses; flowers semi-dbl., borne in large clusters, slight fragrance; foliage medium size, dark green, glossy; prickles moderate, small, sharp, pink; growth bushy, medium (2 ft.); bedding, borders, containers; [seedling × seedling]; int. by Love4Plants Ltd, 2005

Linda Ann Gr, mp, 1996, Dobbs, Annette E.; flowers medium pink, deeper pink than parents, more petals than parent, full; foliage medium size, medium green, semi-glossy; prickles moderate; upright, tall growth; [Queen Elizabeth × Katherine T. Marshall]

Linda Buford Min, ly, 1993, Bennett, Dee; flowers soft light yellow, medium, full, borne mostly singly; foliage small, medium green, semi-glossy; some prickles;

medium, bushy growth; [Irish Gold × Jean Kenneally]; int. by Tiny Petals Nursery, 1994

Linda Campbell HRg, mr, 1991, Moore, Ralph S.; bud pointed; flowers medium red, slightly lighter reverse, aging medium red, medium, 25 petals, cupped, borne in sprays of 5-25; fast repeat; foliage large, dark green, semi-glossy; growth upright, bushy, medium; PP8199; [Anytime × Rugosa Magnifica]; int. by Wayside Gardens Co., 1991

Linda Christine F, pb, 1980, Taylor, W.J.; flowers cerise, silver reverse; [sport of Molly McGredy]

Linda Guest HT, ab, 1984, Guest, M.M.; flowers large, 20 petals, high-centered; foliage medium size, medium green, matte; bushy growth; [(((Golden Jewel × Mischief) × Red Planet) × Valencia]

Linda Lou F, ob, 1987, Harvey, R.E.; flowers orange-yellow-red, medium, 30 petals, high-centered, borne in sprays of 1-8; foliage medium size, dark green; medium growth; [Golden Slippers × Roman Holiday]; int. by Kimbrew Walter Roses, 1988; Silver Medal, ARC TG, 1987

Linda Mary F, dr, 1996, Bossom, W.E.; flowers dark red, silver reverse, 3¼ in., dbl., borne in small clusters; foliage medium size, dark green, semi-glossy; few prickles; bushy, medium (70 cm.) growth; [Guineé × Glad Tidings]

Linda Parade MinFl, mp, Olesen; bud pointed ovoid; flowers medium pink, reverse slightly darker, 5 cm., 31 petals, cupped, borne singly or in pairs, slight fragrance; recurrent; foliage dark green, matte; prickles few, 4-5 mm., linear, greyed-yellow; compact, bushy (20-40 cm.) growth; PP15017; [sport of Heidi Parade]; int. by Poulsen Roser, 2003

Linda Porter HT, op, 1957, Dot, Pedro; bud ovoid; flowers salmon-pink, 5-6 in., 55 petals, globular, intense fragrance; foliage leathery; vigorous, upright growth; PP1507; [Senateur Potie × Poinsettia]; int. by B&A, 1957

Linda Radja – See **Lindaraja**, HT

Linda Sue Min, my, 2001, Giles, Diann; flowers medium, dbl., borne mostly solitary, no fragrance; foliage medium size, dark green, matte; growth upright, medium; garden decorative; [Rise 'n' Shine × Early Ray]; int. by Giles Rose Nursery, 2001

Linda Thomson F, dp, 1996, Thomson, George L.; flowers dark dusky pink, ruffled edge, reverse darker, large, dbl., borne in large clusters, moderate fragrance; foliage medium size, dark green, glossy; bushy, medium growth; [Fidelio × Showbiz]

Linda Vista F, de Ruiter, G.; int. in 1974

Lindaraja HT, r

Linda's Choice HT, m, Thomson

Linda's Lipstick F, mr, 1998, Sheridan, John; flowers scarlet red, white reverse, hand painted, 3 in., 8-14 petals, borne in large clusters; foliage medium size, dark green, semi-glossy; prickles moderated, pointed; upright, tall growth; [seedling × Picasso]

Lindbergh Pol, mr, 1927, Croibier; flowers bright geranium-red; [sport of Orléans Rose]

Lindee Pol

L'Indéfrisible – See **Permanent Wave**, F

Linden Heath S, mp

Linderhof S, mp, 2006; flowers brilliant pink with yellow stamens, 8 cm., single, borne in small clusters; foliage medium size, dark green, very glossy; vigorous (6 ft.) growth, canes arch over and down; int. by W. Kordes' Söhne, 1999

Lindsay's Rose Min, w, 2003, Barden, Paul; flowers white, light yellow, reverse white, light yellow, 1½ in., very full, borne in large clusters; foliage medium size, dark green, semi-glossy; prickles in., straight, reddish, moderate; growth bushy, medium (12-18 in.); exhibition, cutting, specimen; [(Poker Chip × Poker Chip) × Loving Touch]; int. in 2002

Lindsey HT, op, 1973, Watkins Roses; flowers salmon-pink, shaded copper, pointed, 3-4 in., moderate fragrance; foliage large; free growth; [sport of Whisky Mac]

Linette Pol, dp, 1922, Turbat; bud reddish apricot; flowers shrimp-carmine-pink, passing to soft rose-pink, large

L'Infante d'Espagne – See **Cramoisie Éblouissante**, HGal

L'Ingenue C, w, 1848, Vibert; flowers pure white with a green center pip, 8-9 cm., full, rosette; [from Globe Hip]

Linneanhall Beauty Ayr, lp, before 1866; flowers light pink, fading to white, very full

L'Innocence HT, w, 1897, Pernet-Ducher; flowers large, full, globular; foliage bronze green; prickles small, few; [seedling × Mme Caroline Testout]

Linville Min, w, 1990, Bridges, Dennis A.; bud pointed; flowers light pink, aging white, large, 28 petals, high-centered, borne usually singly, slight fruity fragrance; foliage medium size, medium green, semi-glossy; prickles straight, medium, deep pink; upright, medium growth; PP7737; [seedling × seedling]; int. by Bridges Roses, 1990

Liolà HT, w, 1958, Giacomasso; flowers ivory edged crimson, dbl.; very vigorous growth; [Peace × (Baiser × Marguerite Chambard)]

Liolà F, w, Barni; flowers creamy white with pink edges, aging ivory suffused lavender pink, single, borne in clusters; free-flowering; healthy (60-80 cm.) growth; int. by Rose Barni, 2004

Lion des Combats HP, mr, 1850, Lartay; flowers reddish-violet, often shaded with scarlet, large, dbl.

Lionel Barrymore F, my, 1956, Silva; bud urn shaped; flowers yellow, center deeper, 3-3½ in., very dbl., cupped, intense fragrance; foliage dark; strong stems; bushy growth; PP1574; [Duchess of Atholl × Orange Everglow]; int. by Booy Rose Nursery

Lionheart Min, r, 1998, Williams, Ernest D.; flowers russet with coral edge, deep yellow reverse, 1¼ in., 25 petals, borne mostly singly; foliage medium size, dark green, semi-glossy; prickles moderate; upright, bushy, medium growth; [seedling × Twilight Trail]; int. by Texas Mini Roses, 1997

Lionheart HT, mr; flowers coral-red, intense fragrance; growth to 3 ft.; int. by Paul Chessum Roses, 2004

Lion's Fairy Tale – See **Lions-Rose**, F

Lions International HT, dy, Fryer, Gareth; flowers golden yellow, dbl., high-centered, moderate spicy fragrance; good repeat; foliage dark green, glossy; vigorous, compact (3 ft.) growth; int. by Fryer's Roses, 1998

Lions-Rose F, w, 2006; flowers cream-white, opening tinted apricot and pink, center darker, 8 cm., full, borne in clusters of 3-5, slight fragrance; foliage medium size, green, shiny, dense; compact, medium (60 cm.) growth; int. by W. Kordes' Söhne, 2002

Liopearl – See **Bill Heath**, HT

Liparfum HT, m, RVS; flowers mauve blend; recurrent; int. in 1999

Lippe-Detmold HT, mp, Noack, Werner; int. in 1985

Lipsiana Pol, 1952, Cazzaniga, F. G.

Lipstick F, rb, 1940, Verschuren; flowers deep cerise shaded salmon, 2 in., semi-dbl., cupped, borne in clusters; foliage glossy, dark; vigorous (3 ft.), bushy growth; int. by Dreer

Lipstick HT, rb; int. by K & M Nursery, 2004

Lipstick 'n' Lace Min, rb, 1991, Clements, John K.; flowers cream, shaded lipstick red, large, full, high-centered, borne in small clusters, moderate fragrance; foliage medium size, medium green, matte; no prickles; medium (30 cm.), upright, compact growth; [seedling × seedling]; int. by Heirloom Old Garden Roses, 1992

Lisa F, Zandri, R.; int. in 1988

Lisa – See **Lisa Maree**, HT

Lisa HSpn, w, Sutherland, P; [Single Cherry × Primula]; int. by Golden Vale Nursery, 1996

Lisa F, dy, Noack; flowers golden yellow, 2½ in., full, loose, borne in clusters; recurrent; growth to 70 cm.; int. by Noack Rosen, 2004

Lisa F, op, Kirkham; foliage large, dark green, semi-glossy; short to medium growth; int. by C&K Jones, 2005

Lisa Ann HT, dr, 2003, Rawlins, R.; flowers dark red, reverse gold, medium, very full, borne mostly solitary; foliage medium size, dark green, glossy; prickles triangular; growth compact, medium (39 in.); garden decoration; [Solitaire × Ingrid Bergman]

Lisa Colfax F, ob, 1976, Parkes, Mrs M.H.; bud ovoid; flowers vermilion, overlaid brown, medium, dbl., high-centered, intense fragrance; foliage leathery; very vigorous growth; [Mignonne × Sherry]; int. by Rumsey, 1975

Lisa Kent HT, dp, Dawson; correct name may be Lisa Kerr; int. in 1995

Lisa Maree HT, dp, 1989, Cowper, Mrs. Maree; flowers deep pink, reverse lighter, exhibition; good repeat; growth vigorous; [sport of Esther Geldenhuys]; int. by Cherry Wood's Nursery, 1989

Lisa Michelle HT, ab, 2006, Murray, Jean; flowers apricot, reverse mauve, medium, full, borne mostly solitary; foliage medium green, semi-glossy; prickles small, red, few; growth compact, medium; [seedling × seedling]; int. in 2006

Lisbeth Prim HT, or, 1934, Felberg-Leclerc; flowers coppery red, fading lighter, large, dbl.; vigorous growth; [Hadley × Lady Inchiquin]

Lisbeth Stellmacher Pol, or, 1919, Lambert, P.; bud coppery orange-red; flowers coppery red with golden yellow, striped pink, small, dbl.; [Aglaia × Marie van Houtte]

Lisbeth von Kamecke HMult, lp, 1910, Kiese; flowers light violet pink, 3 cm., semi-dbl., borne in large clusters; foliage small; [Veilchenblau × Katharina Zeimet]

Lisboa HT, dr, 1953, Moreira da Silva; flowers red shaded darker, large; very vigorous growth; [Barcelona × Crimson Glory]

Lisboa de 1947 HT, mr, 1947, Moreira da Silva, A.; flowers bright red, dbl., moderate fragrance; recurrent; foliage medium green, matte; medium growth

Lise Chiavassa HT, mr, 1931, Buatois; flowers carmine, very large, dbl., cupped; foliage glossy; vigorous growth; [Mme Philippe Rivoire × Yves Druhen]

Lise Palais – See **Opal**, HT

Liselle HT, ob, 1982, deRuiter, George; flowers orange-peach, well-formed, large, 35 petals; foliage large, dark, semi-glossy; bushy growth; [Whisky Mac × Matador]; int. by Fryer's Nursery, Ltd., 1980

Liselotte Hollweg F, mr; int. in 1962

Lisette HT, ly, Select Roses, B.V.

Lisette de Béranger HP, mp, 1867, Moreau, F./Guillot fils; flowers flesh pink, fading to almost white, medium, full, globular, borne in clusters; recurrent; vigorous (4 ft.) growth

Lisima HT, mr, Gaujard

Lissy Horstmann HT, mr, 1943, Tantau; flowers

brilliant scarlet-crimson, large, 28 petals, cupped; foliage leathery; vigorous growth; [Hadley × Heros]; int. by C-P

Literary Giant HT, pb; re-introduced by Heirloom Roses in 1991

Little Amigo Min, mr, 1983, Bennett, Dee; flowers small, 35 petals, high-centered, no fragrance; foliage small, medium green, semi-glossy; upright growth; [Futura × Orange Honey]; int. by Tiny Petals Nursery

Little Amy Min, yb, 2004; flowers yellow blend, reverse red blend, 4 cm., dbl., borne in large clusters; foliage small, medium green, semi-glossy; prickles small; growth bushy, short (25 cm.); garden decoration, exhibition; [sport of Amber Sunset]; int. by Battersby Roses, 2004

Little Angel F, mr, 1961, Verschuren; flowers salmon becoming scarlet, 30 petals, borne in large clusters; foliage dark, glossy; moderate growth; int. by Blaby Rose Gardens, 1961

Little Angel Min, op, Lens; int. by Louis Lens, 1974

Little Artist Min, rb, 1983, McGredy, Sam IV; bud small, pointed; flowers open with hand-painted marks becoming solid medium red, off-white in base half, 1¼ in., semi-dbl., flat, borne mostly in clusters; recurrent; foliage small, medium green, semi-glossy; prickles profuse; upright, bushy (12-14 in.) growth; [Eyepaint × Ko's Yellow]

Little Awesome Beauty Min, r, Taschner, Ludwig; flowers brownish, reverse greenish-yellow, dbl., cupped, moderate fragrance; recurrent; stems thin, wiry; vigorous, upright, tall growth; int. by Ludwig's Roses, 2005

Little Ballerina Min, pb, 1988, Curtis, Thad; flowers white flushed pink, medium, 34-40 petals, high-centered, urn-shaped, borne singly; foliage medium size, medium green, semi-glossy; no prickles; growth bushy, medium; no fruit; [Little Darling × Little Pioneer]; int. by Oregon Miniature Roses, 1988

Little Beauty F, mp, 1935, Howard, F.H.; flowers bright cerise-pink, fading to pink, small, very dbl.; foliage leathery; vigorous, bushy growth; [E.G. Hill seedling × Polyantha]; int. by Dreer

Little Betty S, lp, 1940, Wright, Percy H.; flowers soft pink, small; non-recurrent; growth to 3 ft.; [Betty Bland × *R. nitida*]

Little Bit o' Sunshine – See **Bit o' Sunshine**, Min

Little Bo-Peep – See **Natchez**, Min

Little Boy Pol

Little Breeze Min, ob, 1981, McCann, Sean; bud long, slender; flowers orange-red, fading to pink, loose, 17 petals, borne singly; foliage large, dark, glossy; prickles straight, gray; vigorous growth; [Anytime × Elizabeth of Glamis]

Little Bridesmaid HT, lp, Archer; flowers shrimp-pink, well-shaped

Little Brother Min, mr, 1998, Chaffin, Lauren M.; flowers medium red, 2 in., full, borne mostly singly, slight fragrance; foliage medium size, medium green, semi-glossy; compact, medium growth; [Pink Petticoat × Happy Hour]; int. by Pixie Treasures Roses, 1998

Little Buckaroo Min, mr, 1957, Moore, Ralph S.; flowers bright red, small, 23 petals, moderate fresh apple fragrance; foliage bronze, glossy, leathery; growth to 14-16 in.; PP1726; [(*R. wichurana* × Floradora) × (Oakington Ruby × Floradora)]; int. by Sequoia Nursery, 1956

Little Butterfly S, pb, Rupert; flowers light pink, darker pink reverse, small, single, borne in large clusters, moderate fragrance; int. by Ashdown Roses, 2002

Little Cameo F, pb, 1982, Strahle, Robert; bud medium, pointed; flowers pink blend with cream outer petals, 26 petals, borne mostly singly; foliage medium green, leathery; prickles straight, short, red; vigorous, upright growth; PP5381; [Lara × seedling]; int. by Carlton Rose Nurseries, 1981

Little Carol Min, dp, 1990, Bennett, Dee; bud ovoid; flowers deep magenta-pink, reverse slightly lighter, medium, 38 petals, high-centered, borne singly, slight spicy fragrance; foliage medium size, dark green, semi-glossy, disease-resistant; prickles hooked slightly downward, red, few; upright, tall growth; hips globular, green-brown; PP7970; [Sonia × Jean Kenneally]; int. by Tiny Petals Nursery, 1989

Little Chameleon Min, pb, 1977, Lyon; bud pointed; flowers rose-pink to red, 1½ in., 30 petals; upright growth; [Little Amy × unknown]

Little Chap – See **Knirps**, F

Little Charm Min, mp, 1984, Lyon, Lyndon; flowers small, semi-dbl.; foliage small, medium green, semi-glossy; upright, bushy growth; [seedling × seedling]

Little Chief Min, dp, 1972, Moore, Ralph S.; bud long, pointed; flowers small, semi-dbl.; foliage small, glossy, leathery; growth moderate, dwarf, bushy; [Cotton Candy × Magic Wand]; int. by Sequoia Nursery

Little Compton Creeper HWich, dp, 1938, Brownell; flowers deep rose-pink, white at center, 6-7 cm., single, borne in small clusters; non-recurrent; foliage small, dark green, glossy; hips yellow-oragne

Little Crimson Min, dr, 1994, Saville, F. Harmon; flowers small, dbl., borne mostly singly, no fragrance; foliage small, dark green, semi-glossy; few prickles; medium (16-20 in.), upright, bushy growth; [Teddy Bear × (Zorina × Baby Katie)]; int. by Nor'East Min. Roses, 1995

Little Curt Min, dr, 1973, Moore, Ralph S.; bud long, pointed; flowers deep velvety red, medium, semi-dbl.; foliage dark, leathery; vigorous, upright, bushy growth; [Unnamed red Cl F × Westmont]; int. by Sequoia Nursery, 1971

Little Darling F, yb, 1957, Duehrsen; bud ovoid; flowers blend of yellow and soft salmon-pink, well-formed, 2½ in., 27 petals, moderate spicy fragrance; foliage dark, glossy, leathery; very vigorous, spreading growth; PP1581; [Capt. Thomas × (Baby Chateau × Fashion)]; int. by Elmer Roses Co., 1956; Gold Medal, Portland, 1958, David Fuerstenberg Prize, ARS, 1964

Little Darling F, w; int. by Burston Nurseries, 2003

Little Deb MinFl, or, 2002, Williams, J. Ben; flowers bright, velvety orange, reverse dull orange-red, 1-1½ in., semi-dbl., borne in small clusters; foliage small, dark green, semi-glossy; prickles insignificant; growth compact, short (12-14 in.); containers, edging, borders; [Scarlet Sunblaze × Orange Sunblaze]; int. by Certified Roses, Inc., 2003

Little Devil – See **Diablotin**, F

Little Devil, Climbing – See **Diablotin, Climbing**, Cl F

Little Diamond Min, or, 1999, Schuurman, Frank B.; flowers 1 in., full, borne in small clusters, no fragrance; foliage medium size, dark green, glossy; few prickles; upright, medium (12-18 in.) growth; [Sexy Rexy × Firefly]; int. by Franko Roses New Zealand, Ltd., 1993

Little Diane – See **Fairy Tale**, Min

Little Dickens Min, ob, 1979, Schwartz, Ernest W.; bud ovoid; flowers orange-red and yellow, small, 25 petals, cupped; foliage small; compact growth; PP4693; [(Ma Perkins × Sheri Anne) × Over the Rainbow]; int. by Nor'East Min. Roses

Little Dorrit Pol, mp, 1930, Reeves; flowers glowing pink; growth to 2 ft.; [sport of Coral Cluster]

Little Dorrit, Climbing Cl Pol, mp, 1935, Letts

Little Dot Pol, lp, 1889, Bennett; flowers soft pink, flaked deeper on the outer petals, borne in clusters; very dwarf growth

Little Embers F, rb, 1988, McFarland, John; flowers cerise to yellow, reverse yellow with cerise on tips, aging, 25 petals, high-centered; foliage medium size, medium green, matte; prickles long, narrow, small, light green; upright, low growth; no fruit; [Rise 'n' Shine × Prominent]

Little Emma Min, my, 2004, Moore, Ralph S.; flowers dbl., borne in small clusters, slight fragrance; foliage small, medium green, semi-glossy; prickles small, hooked; growth compact, short (12-15 in.); pot, low hedge, border planting; [(Little Darling × Yellow Jewel) × Clytemnestra]; int. by Sequoia Nurs., 2005

Little Eskimo Min, w, 1981, Moore, Ralph S.; bud long, pointed; flowers near white, 55 petals, borne 3-7 per cluster, sometimes singly; foliage small, semi-glossy, leathery; prickles long, slender; vigorous, bushy, upright growth; [(*R. wichurana* × Floradora) × Jet Trail]; int. by Moore Min. Roses

Little Esperanza F, mr, 2005, le Fevre, Ivan James; flowers bright red, reverse misty red, 2 in., semi-dbl., borne in large clusters, no fragrance; foliage medium size, dark green, matte; prickles small, straight; growth bushy, medium (4 ft.); specimen, hedging; [unknown × unknown]

Little Fire – See **Ogoniok**, F

Little Fireball Min, or, 1968, Moore, Ralph S.; bud ovoid; flowers bright coral-red, small, dbl.; foliage small, glossy; bushy, compact, low growth; [(*R. wichurana* × Floradora) × New Penny]; int. by Sequoia Nursery

Little Flame Min, ob, 1998, Walden, John K.; flowers brilliant orange, 2 in., dbl., borne in large clusters, no fragrance; foliage medium size, dark green, semi-glossy; prickles moderate, straight; growth compact, tall (3 ft.); borders; PP11632; [New Year × seedling]; int. by Bear Creek Gardens, Inc., 1998; AOE, ARS, 1999

Little Flirt Min, rb, 1961, Moore, Ralph S.; bud pointed; flowers orange-red, reverse yellow, 1½ in., 42 petals, moderate fragrance; foliage light green; vigorous, bushy (12-14 in.) growth; PP2287; [(*R. wichurana* × Floradora) × (Golden Glow × Zee)]; int. by Sequoia Nursery, 1961

Little Gem M, dp, 1880, Paul, W.; bud heavily mossed; flowers bright deep pink, small, dbl., borne in clusters, intense fragrance; dwarf, compact growth

Little Gem Pol, lp, about 1898, Alderton

Little Gem – See **Patio Gem**, Min

Little Gigi S, pb, 1998, Delbard; bud yellow; flowers pink with pale yellow in heart, semi-dbl., borne in clusters; vigorous, shrubby (3 ft.) growth

Little Girl Cl Min, op, 1974, Moore, Ralph S.; bud long, pointed; flowers coral-salmon-pink, medium, dbl.; foliage glossy; bushy, climbing growth; [Little Darling × Westmont]; int. by Sequoia Nursery, 1973

Little Green Snake S, w, Lens, Louis; recurrent; spreading, low (12 in.) growth; int. in 1996

Little Guy Min, mr, 1986, Moore, Ralph S.; flowers medium red, reverse lighter, small, semi-dbl., borne in clusters of 3-7, no fragrance; foliage small, medium green, semi-glossy; low, bushy growth; no fruit; [Magic Wand × Violette]; int. in 1980

Little Huzzy Min, rb, 1991, Bennett, Dee; flowers white with striping of pink to medium red over most upper surfaces of petals, large, full, high-centered, borne mostly singly, moderate fragrance; foliage small, medium green, semi-glossy, disease-resistant; some prickles; stems long; growth tall (60-80 cm.), upright; [Futura × Pucker Up]; int. by Tiny Petals Nursery, 1992

Little Jackie Min, ob, 1982, Saville, F. Harmon; flowers light orange-red, yellow reverse, small, 20 petals; foliage medium size, medium green, semi-glossy; vigorous growth; [(Prominent × Sheri Anne) × Glenfiddich]; int. by Nor'East Min. Roses; AOE, ARS, 1984

Little Jewel Min, dp, 1980, Cocker, James; flowers deep pink, 34 petals, borne 6-12 per cluster; foliage small, glossy, dark; prickles straight; growth low, compact; containers; [Wee Man × Belinda]

Little Jewel Min, ob, 1999, Schuurman, Frank B.; flowers 1½-2 in., dbl., borne in small clusters, slight fragrance; foliage small, medium green, semi-glossy; prickles few, small; growth upright; [Innocenti × Firefly]; int. by Franko Roses New Zealand, Ltd., 1991

Little Joe HT, dr, 1921, Looymans; flowers crimson-red, single; [Red-Letter Day × H.V. Machin]; int. by Prior

Little John Min, rb, 1959, Mason, F.; bud pointed; flowers scarlet, center white, medium, semi-dbl., high-centered, borne in clusters; foliage soft; vigorous, bushy (12-15 in.) growth; [sport of Baby Masquerade]

Little Joker Min, pb, 1958, Spek; flowers rose-pink, center cream, well-shaped; bushy growth

Little Juan Min, mr, 1966, Williams, Ernest D.; flowers medium red, reverse lighter, small, dbl.; foliage small, leathery; vigorous, dwarf growth; [Juliette × seedling]; int. by Mini-Roses

Little Juliet HT, yb, 1924, Looymans; flowers apricot and peach on yellow ground, dbl.; [(F.J. Looymans × unknown) × unknown]; int. by Prior

Little Lady Pol, w, 1967, Harkness; flowers blush to ice-white, small, 70 petals; dwarf growth; [Schneewittchen × Baby Faurax]

Little Leaguer F, dr, 1962, Jelly; bud ovoid; flowers 2-2½ in., 28-40 petals, cupped; vigorous, upright growth; PP2623; [(Garnette × unknown) × Yuletide]; int. by E.G. Hill Co., 1962

Little Lemmy Min, my, Kordes; flowers lemon yellow; int. by W. Kordes Söhne, 1988

Little Len MinFl, ab, Hatfield & Buckley; int. in 1987

Little Lighthouse Min, rb, 1991, Clements, John K.; flowers bright red with yellow to white eye, medium, single, high-centered, borne in small clusters, no fragrance; foliage small, medium green, semi-glossy; some prickles; low (18 cm.), bushy, spreading, compact growth; groundcover; [Robin Red Breast × Little Artist]; int. by Heirloom Old Garden Roses, 1992

Little Linda Min, ly, 1977, Schwartz, Ernest W.; bud high-pointed; flowers micro-mini, 1 in., 17 petals, high-centered; compact growth; PP4264; [(Gold Coin × unknown) × seedling]; int. by Nor'East Min. Roses, 1976

Little Liza Min, mp, 1976, Saville, F. Harmon; bud mossy; flowers rose-pink, ½-1 in., 15 petals; low, very compact growth; [Fairy Moss × Fairy Moss]; int. by Nor'East Min. Roses

Little Love Min, mp, 1977, Lyon; bud pointed; flowers rose-pink, open, 1½ in., 25-30 petals; foliage tiny; very low, compact growth; [Little Amy × seedling]; int. by L. Lyon Greenhouses

Little Lucy Min, rb, 2002, Hough, Robin; bud yellow; flowers bright velvety red with yellow eye, reverse yellow, 1¼-1½ in., single, borne usually solitary, slight fragrance; foliage medium size, medium green, semi-glossy; prickles medium, straight, moderate; growth compact, medium (18 in.); [Phyllis Shackelford × Oriental Simplex]

Little Lutea LCl, my; int. in 1990

Little Mabel Min, mr, de Ruiter; int. in 1991

Little Magician Min, yb, 1990, Williams, J. Benjamin; bud ovoid; flowers light yellow with orange-red blend, loose, small, 32 petals, high-centered, borne usually singly, slight damask fragrance; foliage small, medium green, semi-glossy; no prickles; growth low; winter hardy; [Circus × Magic Carrousel]; int. by White Rose Nurseries, Ltd., 1990

Little Marvel Min, or, 1988, deRuiter, George; flowers bright orange-scarlet, small, 6-14 petals; foliage small, medium green, semi-glossy; bushy growth; PP7572; [seedling × seedling]; int. by Fryer's Nursery, Ltd.

Little Meg Pol, w, 1917, Easlea; flowers milk white, reverse shaded carmine, small, semi-dbl.; [Shower of Gold × Jersey Beauty]

Little Meghan Min, dy, 1993, Spooner, Raymond A.; flowers bright yellow, medium, dbl., borne mostly singly; foliage small, light green, matte; no prickles; growth low, compact; [Good Morning America × seedling]; int. by Oregon Miniature Roses, 1994

Little Melody Min, pb, 1980, Strawn, Leslie E.; bud globular; flowers soft peach-yellow blend, 38 petals, high-centered, moderate fragrance; foliage medium green; prickles light brown, curved downward; compact, bushy growth; [Neue Revue × Sheri Anne]; int. by Tiny Petals Nursery, 1979

Little Mermaid Cl Min, ly, 1995, Moore, Ralph S.; flowers medium, 5 petals, borne in small clusters, no fragrance; foliage small, medium green, semi-glossy; some prickles; growth bushy, spreading; [sport of Mermaid]; int. by Sequoia Nursery, 1995

Little Mike Min, dr, 1967, Moore, Ralph S.; bud ovoid; flowers deep red, small, dbl., high-centered; foliage dark, glossy, leathery; vigorous, dwarf growth; PP2988; [((*R. wichurana* × Floradora) × seedling) × Little Buckaroo]; int. by Sequoia Nursery

Little Mischief S, pb, Ping Lim; flowers deep pink with white eye, fading as they mature, 1 in., 19-24 petals, cupped; always in bloom; foliage medium green, semi-glossy; growth to 1½-2 ft.; PP17196; int. by Bailey Nurseries, 2004

Little Mischief Garden Path – See **Little Mischief**, S

Little Miss Muffet Cl Min, ly, Olesen; flowers soft yellow, tiny, dbl., borne in clusters; foliage dark green; groundcover; spreading growth; int. in 1995

Little Miss Muffett F, pb, 1940, LeGrice; bud pointed, cerise; flowers bright rose-pink, reverse deeper, open, large, semi-dbl., borne in clusters; strong stems; vigorous, bushy growth; [Else Poulsen × Étoile de Hollande]; int. by C-P

Little Miss Springtime Min, rb, Williams, J.B.; flowers ivory white with deep pink edges, scarlet-purple when fully open, high-centered; growth to 6 in.; int. by Hortico Inc., 2001

Little Muff Min, w, 2000, Horner, Heather M.; flowers cream edged pink, reverse cream, 3½ cm., dbl., high-centered, borne in small clusters, moderate fragrance; foliage medium size, medium green, semi-glossy; few prickles; growth bushy, medium (40 cm.); [Luis Desamero × (Prominent × Southampton)]; int. by Battersby Roses, 2001

Little Nell HT, yb, 1933, Archer; flowers deep cream, center apricot, reverse primrose, well-shaped; foliage glossy, dark; vigorous growth

Little Nugget Min, my, 1992, Schuurman, Frank B.; flowers golden yellow, 1½ in., dbl., slight fragrance; foliage small, medium green, semi-glossy; bushy growth; [Lorena × Firefly]; int. by Riverland Nurseries, Ltd., 1991

Little One S, rb, 1988, Sanday, John; flowers red with white eye, 5 petals, borne in sprays of 12-20; repeat bloom; foliage medium size, medium green, glossy; prickles average, light brown; bushy, low growth; [(Sarabande × seedling) × Circus]; int. by John Sanday Roses, Ltd.

Little Opal Min, lp, 1992, Schuurman, Frank B.; flowers medium, dbl.; foliage small, medium green, glossy; upright growth; [White Dream × Dicky Bird]; int. by Riverland Nurseries, Ltd., 1991; Rose of the Year, Auckland, NZ, 1992

Little Paradise Min, m, 1988, Carruth, Tom; flowers deep lavender, blushing purple, reverse deep lavender, aging lighter, 20 petals, high-centered, slight fragrance; foliage small, dark green, semi-glossy, disease-resistant; prickles nearly straight, small, yellow-brown; upright, medium, vigorous, abundant growth; no fruit; PP7580; [Shocking Blue × Helen Boehm]; int. by Weeks Roses, 1991

Little Peaces Min, yb, 1985, Bennett, Dee; flowers yellow, edged pink, medium, 33 petals, high-centered; foliage medium size, medium green, semi-glossy; compact, bushy growth; [Electron × Fairest of Fair]; int. by Tiny Petals Nursery

Little Pearl Min, lp, 1992, Schuurman, Frank B.; flowers medium, full; foliage small, medium green, glossy; few prickles; medium (50 cm.), upright growth; [Innocent × MACfrabro]; int. by Riverland Nurseries, Ltd.

Little Pete Min, or; int. by Hand Rose Farms, 2006

Little Pim Min, mr, 1986, Lens, Louis; flowers small, 24 petals, rosette, borne in clusters of 3-32, no fragrance; foliage dark; prickles hooked, greenish-brown; bushy growth; [Unnamed Miniature seedling × Ruth Leuwerick]; int. in 1984

Little Pink F, pb, 1965, Castleberry; flowers pink, center creamy pink, small, very dbl., high-centered; foliage glossy; vigorous, compact growth; [Little Darling × unknown]

Little Pink Hedge F, pb; flowers clear pink, semi-dbl. to dbl., borne in clusters, no fragrance; good rebloom; foliage glossy; medium (3 ft.) growth; int. in 1992

Little Pinkie Min, mp, 2000, Moore, Ralph S.; flowers dbl., borne in small clusters, no fragrance; foliage small, medium green, semi-glossy; thornless; growth small, bushy, compact (8-12 in.); micro-mini; [Anytime × Renae]; int. by Sequoia Nurs.

Little Pioneer Min, mr, 1985, Curtis, Thad; flowers gold stamens, small, 35 petals, high-centered, borne singly and in clusters, moderate fragrance; foliage small to medium size, medium green, matte; upright, bushy growth; [(Rise 'n' Shine × Summer Butter) × Sheri Anne]; int. by Hortico Roses, 1986

Little Pooh Min, or, 1980, Fong, William P.; bud slim, pointed; flowers 5-6 petals, flat, borne 5-6 per cluster, moderate fragrance; foliage heavy, thick; prickles triangular; upright growth; [Anytime × seedling]

Little Prancer Cl HT, mr, 1996, Thurman, Robert R.; flowers red, lighter reverse, 3 in., dbl., borne mostly singly, moderate fragrance; foliage medium size, medium green striped with red, dull; prickles moderate; upright, tall (7-9 ft.) growth; [Don Juan × Joseph's Coat]; int. by Thurman's Nursery

Little Prince Min, or, 1983, Cocker, James; flowers orange-red, yellow eye, small, semi-dbl.; foliage medium size, medium green, semi-glossy; growth upright, bushy; containers, patio; [Darling Flame × (National Trust × Wee Man)]; int. by Cocker & Sons, 1983

Little Princess Pol, ob, 1937, Knight, G.; flowers pale salmon-coral, well-formed, dbl.; vigorous, bushy growth; int. by Beckwith

Little Princess – See **Pixie**, Min

Little Princess F, mp, Sodano, J.; flowers rose-pink, reverse lighter, 2 in., 50-75 petals, cupped, moderate fragrance; long stems; vigorous growth; PP1364; [sport of Garnette]; int. in 1955

Little Purple F, m

Little Rambler Cl Min, lp, 1994, Warner, Chris; flowers pale pink, 1½ in., full, borne in large clusters, intense fragrance; foliage small, dark green, semi-glossy; few prickles; tall (7 × 7 ft.), bushy, spreading growth; [(Mlle Cecile Brunner × Baby Faurax) × (Marjorie Fair × Nozomi)]; int. by Warner's Roses, 1995

Little Rascal Min, mr, 1981, Jolly, Betty J.; flowers medium red, shading to yellow at base, reverse lighter, 34 petals, high-centered; foliage tiny, light green; prickles slightly hooked; compact, bushy growth; [Sheri Anne × Rise 'n' Shine]; int. by Rosehill Farm

Little Rascal F, dp, Pearce; int. in 1998

Little Red Min, or, 1979, Lens, Louis; bud ovoid; flowers red-orange, 1½ in., 18-22 petals, pompon; foliage glossy; compact growth; [New Penny × Coloranja]; int. by Spek, 1975

Little Red Min, mr, Tantau; flowers bright red, borne in clusters; free-flowering; growth to 12-16 in.; int. in 2004

Little Red Devil Min, mr, 1980, Christensen, Jack E.; bud ovoid, pointed; flowers imbricated, 1½ in., 44 petals, borne 1-8 per cluster; foliage small, semi-glossy, irregularly serrated; prickles small, narrow; vigorous, bushy, fairly tall growth; [Gingersnap × Magic Carrousel]; int. by Armstrong Nursery

Little Red Hedge F, mr, Kordes; bud small, pointed; flowers carmine-red, firm, lasting, dbl., borne in clusters on tall flowering spikes; free-flowering; foliage deep green, very glossy; basals to 24 inches, short, rigid individual stems; upright (24-32 in.) growth; Gold Medal, Durbanville, 1983

Little Red Monkey F, mr, 1954, Ratcliffe; flowers bright red, short stiff petals, very dbl., borne singly and in sprays; bushy growth; [Donald Prior × seedling]

Little Ruby MinFl, dr, Williams, J.B.; flowers deep crimson, with bright yellow stamens., single; int. by Hortico, 2003

Little Russel Min, mr, 1982, Robinson, Thomas, Ltd.; flowers small, 20 petals; foliage small, dark, glossy; bushy growth; [Marlena × New Penny]; int. by T. Robinson, Ltd., 1983

Little Sapphire Min, mp, 1999, Schuurman, Frank B.; flowers medium pink, reverse light pink, 2½-3 in., dbl., borne in small clusters; foliage medium size, medium green, semi-glossy; prickles moderate; bushy, medium (16-20 in.) growth; [White Dream × seedling]; int. by Franko Roses New Zealand, Ltd., 1993

Little Scotch Min, ly, 1959, Moore, Ralph S.; bud long; flowers straw-yellow to white, 1½ in., 55 petals, moderate fragrance; foliage leathery; vigorous, bushy (12 in.) growth; PP1952; [Golden Glow × Zee]; int. by Sequoia Nursery, 1958

Little Showoff Cl Min, yb, 1960, Moore, Ralph S.; bud pointed; flowers bright yellow, sometimes tinted red, 1-1½ in., 30 petals, high-centered, moderate fragrance; upright (to 4 ft.) growth; PP2176; [Golden Glow × Zee]; int. by Sequoia Nursery, 1960

Little Shrimp F, lp, 1986, Lens, Louis; flowers light shrimp-pink, rosette, 2 in., very dbl., borne in clusters of 3-24; foliage small; prickles hooked, brownish-red; bushy growth; [Little Angel × (Little Angel × Spartan)]; int. in 1984

Little Silver – See **Eloquence**, F

Little Sir Echo Min, mp, 1977, Schwartz, Ernest W.; bud long, pointed; flowers 1-1½ in., 48 petals, high-centered; foliage matte, green; compact, upright growth; [Ma Perkins × Baby Betsy McCall]; int. by Nor'East Min. Roses

Little Sir Echo, Climbing Cl Min, mp, 1985, Watterberg, Leah; [sport of Little Sir Echo]

Little Sister Min, mp, 1995, Chaffin, Lauren M.; flowers large, 40-60 petals, borne mostly singly, occasional side buds, slight fragrance; foliage medium size, medium green, semi-glossy; few prickles; growth medium (30 cm.), bushy; [Gene Boerner × Crissy]; int. by Pixie Treasures Miniature Rose Nursery, 1996

Little Sister Min, lp, 2004, Moore, Ralph S.; flowers 1 in., semi-dbl., borne in small clusters; abundant bloom; foliage small, medium green; no prickles; growth compact (8-12 in.); containers, borders, cutting; [sport of Little Pinkie]; int. by Sequoia Nurs., 2004

Little Sizzler Min, mr, 1989, Warriner, William A.; bud ovoid, pointed; flowers large, 38 petals, cupped, borne usually singly and in sprays of 16-20; foliage large, dark green, semi-glossy; prickles hooked downward, reddish-brown; bushy, medium growth; PP6091; [seedling × Funny Girl]; int. by Bear Creek Gardens, 1989

Little Slam Min, dr, 1990, King, Gene; flowers small, dbl., borne mostly singly, no fragrance; foliage small, medium green, semi-glossy; bushy, low growth; [((B.C. × Scamp) × Red Ace) × Scamp]; int. by AGM Miniature Roses, 1990

Little Smiles Min, yb, 1979, Lyon; bud ovoid; flowers chinese yellow vermilion, 1 in., 12 petals, moderate spicy fragrance; compact growth; [Q17a × Redgold]; int. in 1978

Little Squirt Min, dy, 1984, Bennett, Dee; flowers micro-mini, very small, 14 petals, high-centered; foliage small, medium green, semi-glossy; upright, compact growth; int. by Tiny Petals Nursery, 1983

Little Star Rose – See **Soroptimist International**, Min

Little Starburst Min, yb, 1991, Williams, J. Benjamin; flowers orange-red washing on golden yellow, small, full, borne mostly singly and in small clusters, slight fragrance; foliage small, medium green, semi-glossy; low, bushy growth; PP6821; [Prominent × Rise 'n' Shine]

Little Stephen HT, mp, 1971, Sanday, John; flowers glowing pink, 3 in., very dbl., high-centered; foliage matte; upright growth; [Gavotte × seedling]

Little Stripes Min, yb, 1999, Sheridan, John; flowers yellow with orange stripes, reverse yellow, 2 in., dbl., borne in small clusters; foliage medium size, semi-glossy; few prickles; patio; compact, low (18 in.) growth; [Summer Tan × seedling]

Little Sunset Min, pb, 1967, Kordes; flowers salmon-pink on yellow, star-shaped, borne in clusters; foliage small, light green; [seedling × Tom Thumb]

Little Sunshine Pol, my, 1915, Cumming/Pierson; flowers creamy yellow, varying to deep golden yellow, occasionally flecked crimson, 1½-2 in., dbl.; dwarf growth; [*R. multiflora nana* × Soleil d'Or]; int. by A.N. Pierson

Little 't' Min, w, 1989, Travis, Louis R.; bud pointed; flowers white tinged pale pink, reverse white, small, dbl., cupped, borne in sprays; foliage small, medium green, matte; no prickles; growth bushy; no fruit; [Cinderella × seedling]

Little Tease Min, pb, 1989, Zipper, Herbert; flowers yellow to cream at base, suffused with clear pink, darker at edges, high-centered, no fragrance; foliage small, medium green, semi-glossy; bushy, compact growth; [High Spirits × Charmglo]; int. by Magic Moment Miniature Roses, 1989

Little Tiger Min, rb, 1989, Moore, Ralph S.; bud short, pointed; flowers red, yellow and white stripes of varying patterns, reverse with more yellow, very dbl., high-centered, no fragrance; foliage small, medium green, matte; prickles average, slender, inclined downward, brown; bushy, low, rounded growth; [Golden Angel × Pinstripe]; int. by Sequoia Nursery

Little Tommy Tucker Min, my, 1998, Tucker, Robbie; flowers medium yellow, reverse lighter, long-lasting, 1½-1¾ in., dbl., high-centered, borne in small clusters, no fragrance; foliage medium size, dark green, glossy; prickles few, small to medium, slightly hooked downward; upright, low (14-20 in.) growth; PP12360; [Rise 'n' Shine × Captivation]; int. by Nor'East Miniature Roses, 1999; AOE, ARS, 1999

Little Tyke Min, pb, 1986, Rennie, Bruce F.; flowers medium pink, white reverse, loose, 25 petals, borne singly; foliage small, medium green, matte; prickles small, reddish; small, bushy, very compact growth; small fruit; [Julie Ann × Red Love]; int. by Rennie Roses International

Little Vegas Min, mr, 1985, Spooner, Raymond A.; flowers small, 20 petals, high-centered; foliage small, medium green, semi-glossy; growth bushy; [(Rise 'n' Shine × Prominent) × red seedling]; int. by Oregon Miniature Roses, 1984

Little Wallace F, pb, 1952, Beall; bud very long; flowers light pink, center yellow, 25 petals, high-centered, borne in clusters; foliage leathery, dark; vigorous growth; PP1116; [sport of Elfe]; int. by Beall Greenhouse Co.

Little Wendy Min, w, 2004, Pullen, Sarah Mary; flowers white, reverse white, 1½-2 in., single, borne in small clusters, intense fragrance; foliage small, dark green, semi-glossy; prickles few, small, downward, green; growth bushy, short (12-15 in.); [June Laver × Winter Magic]; int. by Sarah Mary Pullen, 2004

Little White Lies Min, w, 2000, McCann, Sean; flowers white with bright yellow stamens, 1¼ in., single, borne in small clusters, no fragrance; foliage small, medium green, semi-glossy; numerous prickles; growth spreading, low (8-10 in. × 2 ft.); [Kent × Cliffs of Dover]; int. by Justice Miniature Roses, 2001

Little White Pet – See **White Pet**, Pol

Little White Pet, Climbing – See **White Pet, Climbing**, Cl Pol

Little White Spray Min, w, Lens, Louis; flowers small, 5 petals, borne in clusters; foliage small; growth dwarf; small gardens; int. by Louis Lens SA, 1991

Little White Star Pol, w, 2007, Tolmasoff, Jan & William; flowers pearly white, 1 in., single, borne in large clusters; foliage medium size, medium green, semi-glossy; prickles medium, red, moderate; growth bushy, short (20-24 in.); borders, containers, low hedge; hips numerous; [seedling × seedling]; int. by Russian River Rose Company, 2004

Little Wings Min, ly, Smith; buds light yellow; flowers light yellow, fading quickly to white, yellow stamens, small, single, flat, no fragrance; recurrent; foliage dark green, matte; rounded, medium (2 ft.) growth; int. about 1990

Little Woman Min, pb, 1987, Dickson, Patrick; flowers soft pink with deeper edges, dbl., classic, moderate fragrance; foliage small, medium green, semi-glossy; patio; tall, bushy growth; [Memento × (Liverpool Echo × Woman's Own)]; int. in 1986

Little Wonder F, or, 1979, Huber; bud pointed; flowers 3½-4 in., 22-28 petals, moderate spicy fragrance; foliage small; upright to spreading growth; [Duftwolke × Ena Harkness]; int. in 1975

Little Woods Rose – See ***R. gymnocarpa*** (Nuttall)

Little Wren Min, mp, 2004, Smith, Redmond; flowers pink, medium, full, borne in small clusters, slight fragrance; foliage medium size, medium green, glossy; prickles to ¼ in., recurved; growth upright, short (15 × 12 in.); patio rose; [sport of Little Buckaroo]; int. in 2003

Littlest Angel Min, my, 1976, Schwartz, Ernest W.; bud short, pointed; flowers medium to deep yellow, micro-mini, ½ in., 28 petals, high-centered; foliage small; low, compact, bushy growth; PP4168; [(Gold Coin × unknown) × unnamed Miniature seedling]; int. by Nor'East Min. Roses, 1975

Littlest Spartan Min, rb, 1992, Gruenbauer, Richard; flowers medium red and yellow, 1 in., 22-30 petals, borne mostly singly, no fragrance; foliage medium size, medium green, semi-glossy; some prickles; growth low (20-30 cm.),upright, bushy; [Red Ace × seedling]; int. by Flowers 'n' Friends Miniature Roses

Liv Tyler – See **Comtesse de Provence**, HT

Live Wire Min, dp, 1988, Saville, F. Harmon; flowers deep cardinal red-pink, reverse darker, aging lighter, loose, 27-30 petals, cupped, no fragrance; foliage small, medium green, semi-glossy; prickles thin, straight, dark gray-purple; micro-mini; bushy, low, compact growth; no fruit; PP6811; [(Rise 'n' Shine × Sheri Anne) × Rainbow's End]; int. by Nor'East Min. Roses

Lively HT, dp, 1960, LeGrice; flowers rose pink, 4-6 in., 32 petals, intense fragrance; foliage dark, glossy; vigorous, compact, low growth; PP2061; [Wellworth × Ena Harkness]; int. in 1959

Lively Lady F, or, 1969, Cocker; flowers vermilion, large, dbl.; foliage dark, glossy; [Elizabeth of Glamis × Tropicana]

Liverpool – See **Liverpool Echo**, F

Liverpool Daily Post – See **Raven**, S

Liverpool Echo F, op, 1971, McGredy, Sam IV; flowers salmon, 4 in., 23 petals, high-centered; foliage light; tall growth; [(Little Darling × Goldilocks) × Munchen]; int. by McGredy; Gold Medal, Portland, 1979

Liverpool Remembers HT, or, 1992, Fryer, Gareth; flowers vermilion, 3-3½ in., full, borne mostly singly; foliage medium size, medium green, glossy; numerous prickles; tall (240 cm.), upright growth; PP7989; [Corso × seedling]; int. by Roses by Fred Edmunds, 1991

Liverton Lady Cl HT, mp, 1978, Warner; flowers 3-4 in., 16-20 petals; foliage small, glossy; tall, climbing growth; [Bantry Bay × Sympathie]; int. by Bradley Nursery

Livia HT, mp, Meilland; bud ovoid, fairly short; flowers Venetian pink, 4½ in., 25 petals, borne mostly singly, no fragrance; good repeat; foliage medium size, matte, leathery; stems long; erect (5-6 ft.) growth; [seedling × Golden Garnette seedling]; int. by Meilland Intl., 1984

Livin' Easy F, ob, 1992, Harkness; bud ovoid, short; flowers frilly, orange-apricot, 4-4½ in., 25-30 petals, borne in clusters, moderate sweet and citrus fragrance; foliage medium size, medium green, semi-glossy; rounded, medium growth; PP9161; [Southampton × Remember Me]; Gold Medal, RNRS, 1990

Living HT, rb, 1958, Lammerts, Dr. Walter; flowers reddish-orange, reverse copper streaked red, 5-6 in., 24 petals, high-centered, moderate spicy fragrance; foliage leathery, semi-glossy; vigorous growth; PP1463; [Charlotte Armstrong × Grande Duchesse Charlotte]; int. by Consolidated Nursery, 1956

Living Bouquet Min, ly, 1991, Laver, Keith G.; bud ovoid; flowers medium, 40-50 petals, flat, borne in sprays of 3-5, no fragrance; recurrent; foliage medium size, light green, semi-glossy; bushy, compact, semi-upright growth; PP9159; [Loving Touch × (Dorola × Genevieve)]; int. by Springwood Miniature Roses, 1991

Living Coral HT, op, 1975, Golik; bud ovoid; flowers soft coral-pink, 5 in., 28 petals, high-centered, moderate fruity fragrance; foliage glossy; moderate growth; [Queen of Bermuda × Tropicana]; int. by Dynarose, 1974

Living Fire F, ob, 1973, Gregory; flowers orange, suffused orange-red, 2½ in., 33 petals, rosette, moderate fragrance; foliage dark; [Tropicana × seedling]

Living Well S, mp; int. in 1999

Liz F, w, Meilland; int. in 1995

Liz McGrath – See **Brandy Snap**, HT

Liza MinFl, mr, Barni, V.; int. in 1993

Lizabeth's Lullabye HT, yb, 1991, Robbins, William C.; flowers yellow with pink tips, large, 35-40 petals, moderate fragrance; foliage large, dark green, glossy; upright, tall growth; [Queen Elizabeth × Song of Paris]

Lizzie Ann Min, lp, 2000, Stewart, Betty C.; flowers silvery light pink, 1½ in., full, high-centered, borne mostly singly, slight fragrance; foliage medium size, medium green, semi-glossy; few prickles; growth compact, medium (2 ft.); [sport of Winsome]

Lizzie Molk S, pb, 1984, Rusnock, Ann M.; flowers light pink, white center, 20 petals, borne in clusters, intense fragrance; does not repeat; foliage medium size, blue-green, glossy; spreading growth

Ljuba Rizzoli HT, dr, 1981, Dot, Simon; bud pointed; flowers 25 petals, cupped, borne singly, intense fragrance; foliage large, dark, matte; prickles purple-green; upright, bushy growth; int. by Rose Barni-Pistoia, 1978

Lleida HT, rb, 1936, Dot, Pedro; flowers bright red, reverse yellow; very vigorous growth; [Edouard Renard × Condesa de Sástago]; int. by A. Meilland

Llorver – See **Verdi**, HT

Lloyd Center Supreme Gr, pb, 1990, Twomey, Jerry; bud pointed; flowers light pink with yellow base, reverse dark pink blending to yellow, large, 25 petals, high-centered, borne in sprays of 4-7, moderate fruity fragrance; foliage medium size, dark green, glossy; upright, bushy, medium growth; PP7979; [Brion × seedling]; int. by DeVor Nurseries, Inc., 1990

Lloyds of London F, ob, Cants of Colchester, Ltd.; int. in 1991

Lloyds Supreme HT, mp, Twomey, Jerry; [Brion × Silver Jubilee]

Loads of Pink F, mp, 1991, Fiamingo, Joe; flowers medium, semi-dbl., borne in large clusters, moderate fragrance; foliage medium green, semi-glossy, disease-resistant; some prickles; growth tall, upright, very vigorous; [sport of Fred Loads]

Loan Hulse M, dr, 2003, Barden, Paul; buds heavily mossed; flowers dark crimson-red, reverse medium crimson-red, 3 in., dbl., borne in small clusters; foliage medium size, dark green, semi-glossy; prickles in., straight, some hooked, tan and green, numerous; growth upright, medium (3-4 ft.); feature shrub, back of border; [Scarlet Moss × The Prince]

Lobo HT, rb, 1988, Perry, Astor; flowers red-purple, reverse white, large, full, high-centered, intense fragrance; foliage large, dark green, matte; upright growth; [Kordes' Perfecta × Gavotte]; int. in 1989

L'Obscurité HGal, m, before 1820, Van Eeden; flowers purple aging to velvety brown, medium, dbl.

L'Obscurité M, dr, 1848, Lacharme, F.; flowers dark garnet-crimson, large, dbl.

Locarno Pol, or, 1926, deRuiter; flowers large, borne in huge clusters; vigorous, bushy growth; [sport of Orléans Rose]

Loch Lomond HSpn, 1945, Wright, Percy; [*R. spinossima altaica* × Harison's Yellow]

Lochinvar S, lp, 2005; flowers light pink, reverse light pink, 6 cm., very full, borne in small clusters, intense fragrance; foliage medium size, medium green, semi-glossy; prickles medium, deeply concave; growth bushy, branching, short (70 cm.); garden decorative; [seedling (light yellow species type) × seedling (light pink species type)]; int. by David Austin Roses, Ltd., 2002

Locomotion HT, yb, 1965, Verschuren, H.A.M.; flowers salmon tinted peach, becoming citron-yellow; foliage dark, leathery; vigorous, bushy growth; [R.M.S. Queen Mary × Lady Sylvia]; int. by Ravensberg

Lod. Lavki HT, w, Lens; flowers white, apricot tones in center, dbl., cup and saucer, moderate fragrance; recurrent; foliage dark green; int. by Louis Lens SA, 2005

Lodestar HT, pb, 1953, Boerner; bud ovoid to globular; flowers buff-pink, center peach, 4½-5 in., 35-40 petals, intense spicy fragrance; foliage leathery; bushy growth; PP1251; [(Diamond Jubilee × unknown) × Serenade]; int. by J&P

Lodewijk Opdebeek HT, dr, 1921, Leenders, M.; flowers oxblood-red, reverse rose, dbl.; [Jonkheer J.L. Mock × Mev. Dora van Tets]

Lodovico F, Cazzaniga, F. G.; int. in 1960

Lœlia – See **Louise Peyronny**, HP

Loeta Liggett HT, pb, 1985, Liggett, Myron T.; flowers light pink, darker pink reverse, often with salmon center; [sport of Duet]; int. in 1984

Lohengrin HT, lp, 1903, Kiese; flowers silvery pink, large, dbl.; [Mme Caroline Testout × Mrs W. J. Grant]

Lois Min, mp, 1985, Bennett, Dee; flowers medium lilac pink, medium, dbl., high-centered; foliage medium size, medium green, semi-glossy; upright, bushy growth; PP6140; [Deep Purple × Plum Duffy]; int. by Tiny Petals Nursery

Lois Crouse HT, lp, 1937, Moore, Ralph S.; bud pointed; flowers light pink, suffused salmon, large, dbl., peony-like; foliage dark; vigorous, bushy growth; [Mme Butterfly × unknown]; int. by Brooks & Son

Lois Holin HT, pb, 2002, McCall, Sharan; flowers white with fuchsia edging & veining, 6 in., very dbl., borne mostly solitary, intense fragrance; foliage medium size, medium green, semi-glossy; prickles ¼ in., slanting down, moderate; growth upright, medium (4½ ft.); garden decorative, exhibition; [Elsie Melton × Michele Meilland]

Lois Maney LCl, op, 1953, Maney; flowers salmon-pink, 4-5 in., dbl.; abundant, non-recurrent bloom; foliage leathery; very vigorous (25 ft.) growth; [*R. maximowicziana pilosa* × Templar]; int. by Iowa State College

Lois Wilson HT, pb; flowers medium pink with yellow in heart, large, dbl.; good repeat; stems long; strong, upright growth; int. in 1998

Lola – See **Olivia**, HT

Lola de Porcioles HT, Camprubi, C.

Lola Montes HT, mr, Dot; int. in 1969

Lola Vendrell HT, pb, 1958, Bofill; flowers soft pink streaked deeper, well-formed, large, full, moderate fragrance; foliage glossy; long stems; vigorous growth; [Serafina Longa × Mme Kriloff]; int. by Roses Torre Blanca, 1957

Lolette Dupain Cl Pol, pb, 1918, Lottin; flowers yellowish-rose, reverse silvery rose, dbl., borne in clusters; sometimes recurrent bloom; vigorous growth; [Casimir Moulle × Mme Norbert Levavasseur]

Loli Creus HT, dp, 1953, Dot, Pedro; flowers carmine, well-formed, large; foliage glossy; strong stems; very vigorous growth; [Cynthia × Manuelita]

Lolita HT, w, 1937, Croibier; flowers white, center cream, overlarge, dbl., globular; foliage leathery; vigorous growth; [Frau Karl Druschki × unnamed Hybrid Tea]

Lolita HT, ab, 1976, Kordes, R.; flowers golden bronze, 5 in., 28 petals, moderate fragrance; [Colour Wonder × seedling]; int. by Dicksons of Hawlmark, 1973; ADR, 1973

Lolita, Climbing Cl HT, ab; int. after 1973

Lolita Lempicka – See **Peter Mayle**, HT

Lolita Lempicka, Climbing – See **Peter Mayle, Climbing**, LCl

Lollipop Min, mr, 1960, Moore, Ralph S.; flowers bright red, 1-1½ in., 35 petals; foliage glossy; vigorous (14 in.), bushy growth; PP2080; [(*R. wichurana* × Floradora) × Little Buckaroo]; int. by Sequoia Nursery, 1959

Lollo HT, rb, 1949, San Remo Exp. Sta.; bud pointed; flowers purplish red, reverse crimson-carmine, well-formed, 32-36 petals; foliage dark; strong stems; vigorous, bushy growth; [Lele × Crimson Glory]

Lolly Pop – See **Lollypop**, HT

Lollypop HT, op, Kordes; flowers salmon, large, dbl., high-centered, borne mostly singly; recurrent; florist rose; int. by W. Kordes Söhne, 2001

Lolo HT, rb, 2000, Cooper, Ralph D.; flowers cherry red, reverse silver white, 4-5 in., full, high-centered, borne mostly singly, slight fragrance; foliage medium size, dark green, semi-glossy; prickles moderate; growth spreading, medium (5-6 ft.); [seedling × seedling]; int. by Cecil Godman's Show Roses, 2001

London Pride HT, op, 1954, Ratcliffe; flowers deep salmon-pink shaded coral, high-centered; upright growth

London Starlets HT, ob, 1959, Maarse, G.; flowers orange to orange-red, well-shaped, large, 50 petals; long, strong stems; vigorous growth; [Mission Bells × Jiminy Cricket seedling]

London Town HT, op, 1955, Letts; flowers salmon-pink, base buff, well-formed, medium, moderate fruity fragrance; vigorous growth; [Peace × Charles Gregory]

Lone Star HT, mr, 1925, Buller; flowers velvety cardinal-red, large, semi-dbl.; vigorous, upright growth; [Étoile de France × unknown]; int. by Hillje

Lone Star State HT, pb, 1943, Collins; flowers darker than parent, irregularly striped white; [sport of Texas Centennial]

Lonesome Dove HWich, w, 2006, Thomson, George L.; flowers 4 cm., very full, borne in small clusters; summer flowering, with some autumn repeat; foliage medium size, glossy, evergreen; prickles medium, hooked, brown, numerous; growth rambling, tall (20 m.) climber; [(seedling × May Queen) × seedling]

Lonette Chenault Pol, lp, 1925, Chenault; flowers creamy rose pink, medium, dbl.

Long Island HT, rb, 1996, Castillo, Angel; flowers creamy white with red edge, 4 in., full, borne mostly singly, moderate fragrance; foliage medium size, light green, semi-glossy; upright, tall (3-4 ft.) growth; [Tiki × Color Magic]; int. by Z&B Own Root Roses, 1998

Long John Silver HSet, w, 1934, Horvath; bud pointed; flowers silvery white, 11 cm., dbl., cupped, borne in large clusters, moderate fragrance; occasional repeat; foliage large, leathery; growth vigorous, climbing; [(*R. setigera* × unknown) × Sunburst]; int. by J&P

Long Tall Sally S, w, 1999, Carruth, Tom; flowers buff white, 3-3½ in., single, borne in large clusters, moderate fragrance; foliage large, dark green, semi-glossy; prickles moderate; upright, very vertical, tall (5-7 ft.) growth; PP14041; [All That Jazz × *R. soulieana* derivative]; int. by Weeks Roses, 1999

Long White Cloud – See **Full Sail**, HT

Longchamp F, mr, 1962, Laperrière; flowers bright red cerise, medium, semi-dbl., borne in clusters; foliage glossy; vigorous, symmetrical growth; int. by EFR, 1960

Longchamp 80 S, Laperrière; int. in 1980

Longford S, dp, before 1938, Preston; flowers carmine-pink to medium, 3½ cm., dbl., borne in clusters of 5-10, no fragrance; [*R. helenae* × a gallica]

Longleat – See **Wanaka**, Min

Longwood LCl, mp, 1914, Wintzer; flowers semi-dbl.; [American Pillar × seedling]

Longworth Rambler LCl, mr, 1880, Liabaud; flowers light crimson, semi-dbl.; vigorous growth; possibly the same as Deschamps

Looking Good HT, pb, 2004, Wells, Verlie W.; flowers large, very full, borne in small clusters, slight fragrance; foliage medium size, medium green, semi-glossy; prickles ¼ in., hooked; growth upright, medium; exhibition; [seedling × mixed hybrid tea pollen]; int. by Wells Mid-South Roses, 2004

Looks Like Fun Min, pb, 1997, McCann, Sean; flowers medium, 41 petals, borne mostly singly, moderate fragrance; foliage medium size, medium green, semi-glossy; spreading, bushy, medium (16 in.)growth; [Lady in Red × (Rose Gilardi × seedling)]; int. by Justice Miniature Roses

Looping LCl, ob, 1979, Meilland, Mrs. Marie-Louise; bud conical; flowers orange-coral, medium, 40 petals, cupped; spring bloom; foliage dark; vigorous, climbing growth; [((Zambra × Danse des Sylphes) × Cocktail) × Royal Gold]; int. by Meilland, 1977

Lord Allenby HT, dr, 1923, Dickson, A.; flowers bright crimson, very large, dbl., high-centered; foliage rich green, leathery; dwarf, sturdy growth

Lord Bacon HP, dr, 1883, Paul & Son; flowers deep crimson shaded scarlet, large, dbl., globular; vigorous growth

Lord Baden-Powell HT, ob, 1937, Leenders, M.; bud orange striped red; flowers saffron-yellow, large, very dbl.; vigorous, bushy, compact growth

Lord Beaconsfield HP, dr, 1878, Christy; flowers blackish crimson, large, full, globular

Lord Byron – See **Polka**, LCl

Lord Calvert HT, dr, 1919, Cook, J.W.; flowers dark velvety red, dbl.; [Radiance × Hoosier Beauty]

Lord Castlereagh HT, dr, 1927, Dickson, A.; bud pointed; flowers dark blackish crimson, open, semi-dbl.; foliage dark, leathery; vigorous, bushy growth

Lord Charlemont HT, dr, 1922, McGredy; bud long, pointed; flowers clear deep crimson, well-shaped, large, dbl., high-centered; foliage dark, leathery; bushy growth

Lord Charlemont, Climbing Cl HT, dr, 1932, Hurcombe; [sport of Lord Charlemont]

Lord Chelmsford HT, mr, Williams, H.

Lord Clyde HP, dr, 1863, Paul & Son; flowers bright crimson, well-formed, large

Lord Don S, rb; flowers rich red, large, semi-dbl., cupped, slight fragrance; recurrent; robust, bushy growth; hips small, round, red; int. in 1993

Lord Eldon – See **Earl of Eldon**, N

Lord Fairfax HT, dp, 1925, Gray, W.R.; flowers cherry-rose-pink, moderate fragrance; foliage leathery; long stems

Lord Frederick Cavendish HP, mr, 1884, Frettingham; flowers bright scarlet

Lord Gold HT, dy, Delbard; flowers well-formed, dbl.; stems long, strong; growth medium; int. in 1980

Lord Herbert HP, dp, 1864, Paul, W.

Lord Houghton of Sowerby HT, op, 1990, Harkness, R., & Co., Ltd.; bud pointed; flowers warm, reddish, salmon-pink, reverse deeper, large, high-centered, borne singly, slight spicy fragrance; foliage large, dark green, glossy; prickles broad based, large, reddish; upright, medium growth; fruit not observed; [Silver Jubilee × Basildon Bond]

Lord Kitchener HT, dp, 1918, Chaplin Bros.; flowers bright carmine-rose, dbl.

Lord Lambourne HT, yb, 1925, McGredy; bud pointed; flowers buttercup-yellow, edged carmine-scarlet, very large, dbl., high-centered; foliage light, leathery, glossy; very vigorous, bushy growth

Lord Lonsdale HT, ab, 1933, Dickson, A.; bud pointed; flowers deepest orange-yellow, large, dbl., high-centered; foliage glossy, light; vigorous, bushy growth; int. by H&S; Gold Medal, NRS, 1931

Lord Louie – See **Mountbatten**, F

Lord Louis HT, dp, 1981, Gregory, C.; bud pointed; flowers light crimson, 30 petals, borne several together, moderate fragrance; foliage mid-green, glossy; vigorous growth; [Pink Favorite × seedling]; int. by C. Gregory & Sons, 1982

Lord Macaulay HP, dr, 1863, Paul, W.; flowers crimson, large, full, nearly globular

Lord Mountbatten – See **Mountbatten**, F

Lord Napier HP, dp, 1874, Paul, W.

Lord Palmerston HP, mr, 1857, Margottin; flowers rose red, medium, full

Lord Penzance HEg, yb, 1894, Penzance; flowers soft rosy yellow, paler at base, yellow stamens, small, single, 1 in., borne in small clusters, moderate fragrance; summer bloom; foliage small, dark, fragrant; very vigorous growth; [*R. rubiginosa* × Harison's Yellow]

Lord Raglan HP, dr, 1854, Guillot Père; flowers bright velvety crimson, very large, very dbl.; [Geant des Batailles × unknown]

Lord Robbie HT, w; flowers ivory white with apricot buff shading; stems long

Lord Rossmore HT, w, 1930, Hall; flowers creamy white shaded rose toward edge, large, dbl., high-centered; foliage dark olive-green, leathery; vigorous growth; int. by McGredy; Gold Medal, NRS, 1928

Lord Scarman HGal, pb, Scarman; int. in 1996

Lord Stair HT, dr, 1930, Smith, T.; bud pointed; flowers velvety crimson-scarlet, large, dbl., high-centered; foliage dark, leathery; very vigorous, bushy growth

Lord Worthington HT, mp, 1928, Dickson, A.; flowers medium, dbl.

Lordly Oberon S, lp, 1983, Austin, David; flowers large, very dbl., cupped; foliage large, medium green, matte; upright growth; [Chaucer × seedling]; int. by David Austin Roses, Ltd., 1982

L'Oréal Trophy HT, ob, 1980, Harkness, R., & Co., Ltd.; flowers orange; [sport of Alexander]; int. in 1981; Gold Medal, Bagatelle, 1984, Golden Rose, Courtrai, 1986, Gold Medal, Belfast, 1984

Loredo – See **Flower Carpet Yellow**, S

Loree F, w, 1969, Pal, Dr. B.P.; bud long, pointed; flowers white tinted pink, small, dbl., cupped; foliage leathery; vigorous, bushy, compact growth; [Frolic × unknown]; int. by K. S. G. Son

Lorelei S, ab, 1947, Fisher, R.C.; bud ovoid; flowers peach-pink, center yellow, 3-4 in., semi-dbl., intense fragrance; non-recurrent; foliage leathery, dark; vigorous, upright growth; [Joanna Hill × Harison's Yellow]

Lorelei S, mp, Poulsen; bud pointed ovoid; flowers 5 cm., 25 petals, reflexed open cup, borne in clusters, slight fragrance; recurrent; foliage dark green, semi-glossy; prickles numerous, 5 mm., hooked downward, greyed-red; bushy (80 cm.) growth; PP15748; [seedling × seedling]; int. by Poulsen Roser, 2003

Loreley Pol, lp, 1913, Kiese; flowers creamy rose pink, medium, dbl.

Loreley 82 HT, dr, Noack, Werner; int. in 1982

Lorena F, mp, 1984, Kordes, W.; flowers medium salmon-pink, flora-tea, large, 35 petals, high-centered; foliage medium size, medium green, semi-glossy; upright growth; PP5679; [Angelique × seedling]; int. in 1983

Lorena Kordana Min, dp, Kordes; flowers dbl., high-centered; int. by W. Kordes Söhne

Lorenz Schwamborn Pol, mr, Schmid, P.; flowers medium, semi-dbl.; int. in 1960

Lorenzo Pahissa HT, op, 1941, Pahissa; flowers coral, 5-6 in., dbl., borne mostly solitary, moderate fragrance; good repeat; foliage abundant; very vigorous, upright growth; [seedling × Mari Dot]; Gold Medal, Bagatelle, 1941

Loreto Gold S, yb, 2007, Ross, Andrew; flowers 8 cm., full, blooms borne mostly solitary; foliage medium size, dark green, glossy; prickles medium, hooked, brown, moderate; growth upright, tall (1¾ m.); garden decoration; [Gina Lollobrigida × Friesia]; int. by Ross Roses, 2007

Loretta F, mp, 1987, Kordes, W.; flowers medium, full, no fragrance; foliage medium size, medium green, matte; flora-tea, bushy growth; PP7479; [sport of Lorena]; int. in 1986

Loretta F, dp, Kordes; flowers rich pink, fading slightly as they open, full, cupped, borne mostly singly; recurrent; stems moderately long; florist rose; int. in 2005

Loretto LCl, pb, 1922, Clark, A.; flowers reddish, center white, semi-dbl., borne in clusters; few prickles; vigorous, climbing growth; [Jersey Beauty × seedling]; int. by Brundrett

Lori LCl, or, 2007, Jerabek, Paul; flowers orange-red, reverse slighlty lighter, 3¼ in., 50 petals, borne in small clusters; foliage medium size, medium green, semi-glossy; prickles ¼ in., triangular red, moderate; growth upright, medium; garden decorative; [unknown × unknown]; int. by Freedom Gardens, 2007

Lori Ann F, yb, 1991, Schneider, Peter; flowers bright amber yellow, flushed orange and pink, reverse yellow, large, 20 petals, cupped, loose, borne usually singly or in sprays of 3-5, moderate fruity fragrance; foliage medium size, medium green, semi-glossy, slightly elongated and narrow; slightly spreading, medium growth; [Judy Garland × Sutter's Gold]; int. by Peter Schneider, 1990

Lori Nan Min, dp, 1965, Moore, Ralph S.; bud globular; flowers rose-red, small, dbl.; foliage glossy, leathery; moderate growth; [(*R. wichurana* × Floradora) × (seedling × Zee)]; int. by Sequoia Nursery

L'Orientale HGal, m, before 1829, Coquerel; flowers light purple, edges lighter, medium, very full

L'Orléanaise Bslt, lp, 1899, Vigneron; flowers very light pink, darker at center, 7-8 cm., very full, sometimes quartered, borne singly or in small clusters; foliage glaucous; thornless; [Mme de Sancy de Parabère × Blush Boursault]

Lorna HT, op, 1936, Cant, B. R.; bud pointed; flowers salmon, dbl., high-centered; foliage leathery, glossy, light; vigorous, bushy growth

Lorna F, dp, 2003, Cocker, A.G.; flowers rich rose pink, 3 in., dbl., borne in large clusters; foliage medium size, dark green, glossy; prickles 9 mm., straight, moderate; growth bushy, medium (2½ ft.); garden decorative; [Ginger Nut × Memento]; int. in 2003

Lorna Anderson HT, mr, 1940, Clark, A.; flowers well-formed

Lorna Clare F, ab, 2000, Rawlins, R.; flowers apricot-orange, 3 in., full, borne in small clusters, moderate fragrance; foliage medium size, light green, matte; prickles 1 cm., triangular, moderate; growth compact, low (24 in.); garden decorative; [(Laura Ford × Goldbusch) × (Baby Love × Amber Queen)]

Lorna Doone B, mr, 1894, Paul, W.; flowers magenta carmine, shaded with scarlet, large, full, globular

Lorna Doone F, mr, 1971, Harkness; flowers 4 in., 24 petals; foliage dark, glossy; [Red Dandy × Lilli Marleen]; int. by J. L. Harkness, 1970

Lorna May F, rb, 1959, deRuiter; flowers crimson-red, center white trusses, 2 in., single; foliage light green; vigorous growth; [Poulsen's Pink × Kathe Duvigneau]; int. by Blaby Rose Gardens, 1958

Lorraine HT, op, 1945, Meilland, F.; flowers salmon-carmine touched red, large, dbl.; vigorous growth; [Peace × Mme Mallerin]

Lorraine S, mp; int. in 1992

Lorraine Lee T, pb, 1924, Clark, A.; bud pointed; flowers rosy apricot-pink, dbl., cupped, moderate fragrance; foliage rich green, leathery, glossy; vigorous growth; [Jessie Clark × Capitaine Millet]; int. by Hackett

Lorraine Lee, Climbing Cl T, pb, 1932, McKay; bud pointed; flowers golden apricot-pink, darker reverse, semi-dbl.; [sport of Lorraine Lee]

Lorraine Stebbings Min, w, 1985, Morey, Dr. Dennison; flowers small, 23 petals, borne singly, slight honey fragrance; foliage small, glossy; upright, bushy growth; [Cinderella × Popcorn]

Los Angeles HT, op, 1916, Howard, F.H.; bud pointed; flowers coral-pink, base gold, large, dbl.; foliage leathery; vigorous, spreading growth; [Mme Segond Weber × Lyon Rose]; int. by H&S; Gold Medal, Bagatelle, 1918

Los Angeles, Climbing Cl HT, pb, 1925, H&S; flowers light orange pink, yellow center, very large, full; [sport of Los Angeles]

Los Angeles Beautiful Gr, yb, 1967, Lammerts, Dr. Walter; flowers yellow blended with coral and scarlet, medium, dbl., high-centered; foliage dark, leathery; vigorous, upright, compact growth; PP2876; [Queen Elizabeth × Rumba]; int. by Germain's

Los Angeles Frost HT, lp, Robinson; flowers soft ivory to ivory-pink, pale apricot at petal base, moderate fragrance; recurrent; foliage dark green; growth moderate to tall; int. in 1989

Los Tejas HT, mr, 1968, Patterson; bud globular; flowers large, dbl., high-centered, moderate fragrance; foliage leathery; vigorous, upright growth; PP3073; [Chrysler Imperial × Happiness]; int. by Patterson Roses

Lost in Paradise Min, m, Spooner, Raymond A.; int. in 1997

Lotte Günthart HT, mr, 1964, Armstrong, D.L.; bud ovoid; flowers bright red, large, 90 petals, peony-like; foliage leathery; tall, upright, bushy growth; PP2585; [Queen Elizabeth × Bravo]; int. by Armstrong Nursery

Lottie Forster Pol, mr, Matthews, W.J.

Lottum Abundance – See **St Piers**, F

Lou-Celina S, dr, 1984, James, John; flowers large, 50 petals, moderate fragrance; repeat bloom; foliage medium size, dark red-green, semi-glossy; upright growth; [(Venture × ((Cecilia × China Belle) × Suzanne)) × (Paula × Soeur Kristin)]; int. in 1979

L'Ouche HCh, pb, 1901, Buatois; flowers rose shaded yellow, large, full, cupped, moderate peppery-tea fragrance; growth upright, large

Louis Baldwin – See **Louise Baldwin**, HT

Louis Barbier HFt, ob, 1909, Barbier; flowers coppery orange with dark yellow striping, 7 cm., semi-dbl., borne in small clusters; [Mme Bérard × *R. foetida bicolor*]

Louis Barlet T, w, 1876, Ducher, Vve.; flowers flesh white with salmon

Louis Béluze B, mp, about 1840, Béluze; flowers bright pink, medium, full

Louis Bernard HT, or, Croix; int. in 1969

Louis Bourgoin HT, lp, 1921, Gillot, F.; flowers flesh-pink passing to silvery pink, dbl.; [Jonkheer J.L. Mock × Frau Karl Druschki]

Louis Brassac HP, mp, 1872, Brassac; flowers silky pink, reverse silver, large, full

Louis Bruyère Cl HT, dp, 1941, Buatois; flowers deep cerise pink, reverse and center lighter, 3-4 in., dbl., flat

Louis Bulliat HP, mp, 1867, Gonod; flowers carmine

Louis Calla HP, m, 1885, Verdier, E.; flowers purple/pink, large, dbl.

Louis Cazas D, lp, about 1850; flowers medium, very full, moderate fragrance

Louis Chaix B, mr, 1857, Lacharme; flowers bright red, shaded carmine, large, full; [Géant des Batailles × unknown]

Louis Charlin HP, pb, 1871, Damaizin; flowers bright pink, center red, very large, full

Louis Clapot HT, dp, 1906, Bidaud; flowers dark carmine with violet reflections, large, full, cupped

Louis Corbie HP, mr, 1871, Corbie; flowers bright crimson, large, full

Louis de Funes HT, ob, 1987, Meilland, Mrs. Marie-Louise; flowers orange capucine reverse cadmium yellow, large, dbl.; foliage medium size, dark green, glossy; upright, strong growth; [(Ambassador × Whisky Mac) × (Arthur Bell × Kabuki)]; int. in 1983; Gold Medal, Monza, 1983, Gold Medal, Geneva, 1983

Louis Donadine HP, dr, 1887, Gonod; flowers deep velvety maroon, nuanced flame, very large, full; very remontant; foliage dark green; growth upright; [Duhamel-Dumonceau × unknown]

Louis d'Or HT, Dorieux; int. in 1965

Louis Doré HP, mr, 1879, Fontaine; flowers shining cherry red, shaded purple, large to very large, full

Louis' Double Rush S, pb, Lens; bud red; flowers medium pink with white eye, 2-3 in., loose, borne in clusters, slight fragrance; foliage dark green, glossy; growth to 4 ft.; int. by Louis Lens SA, 2001

Louis Faurax HT, ob, 1941, Gaujard; flowers coppery-salmon with dark yellow, large, dbl.

Louis Faure – See **Lucie Faure**, T

Louis Gimard M, mp, 1877, Pernet père; flowers bright pink, very large, dbl.; prickles very bristly, moss-like; long stems; vigorous growth

Louis Gulino HP, dr, 1859, Guillot; flowers purple-red, shaded pink, medium, full

Louis J. Appell, Jr. HT, w, 2003, Carruth, Tom; buds long, elegant; flowers pure white, 12-14 cm., full, borne in small clusters, slight fragrance; foliage large, dark green, semi-glossy; prickles moderate, average, almost straight, greenish brown; growth upright, compact (100-120 cm.); garden decoration; [Moonstone × Sunset Celebration]; int. by Susquehanna Pfaltzgraff, 2004

Louis Joliet – See **Louis Jolliet**, HKor

Louis Jolliet HKor, mp, 1991, Svejda, Felicitas & Ogilvie, Ian S.; flowers 6-7 cm., full, borne in large clusters, slight fragrance; foliage medium size, medium green, semi-glossy; spreading, low growth; PP9222; [(*R.* × *kordesii* × O.P. Max Graf) × (*R.* × *kordesii* × (Red Dawn × Suzanne × Champlain))]; int. by Agriculture Canada, 1990

Louis Kahle HT, mr, 1922, Kiese; flowers bright cherry-red; [Lieutenant Chaure × Étoile de France]

Louis Lévêque – See **Erzherzog Franz Ferdinand**, T

Louis Lille HP, mr, 1887, Dubreuil; flowers bright red with light flame, very large, full, cupped; foliage dark green

Louis Mon Ami Ayr, pb, Louette; flowers magenta/lilac with white eye, dbl., pompon, borne in clusters, slight fragrance; non-remontant; foliage glossy; flexible, climbing growth; [*R. arvensis* 'Plena' × unknown]; int. by Louis Lens SA, 2001

Louis Noisette HP, mp, 1865, Ducher; flowers carmine pink, large, full, borne in small clusters

Louis Pajotin HT, op, 1940, Mallerin, C.; flowers coral, stamens yellow, large, very dbl.; long, stiff stems; very vigorous growth; [Souv. de Claudius Pernet × Margaret McGredy]; int. by Meilland, A.

Louis Pajotin, Climbing Cl HT, op, 1959, Pajotin-Chédane; [sport of Louis Pajotin]

Louis-Philippe Ch, rb, 1834, Guérin; flowers dark crimson with edges of center petals blush, aging crimson, dbl., globular; bushy growth

Louis-Philippe HGal, m, before 1835; flowers rosy crimson, sometimes purplish, aging to violet, very large, dbl., cupped, quartered; foliage medium green, rounded; prickles moderate; moderate, branching growth; possibly from Hardy, 1824

Louis-Philippe B, dr, 1835, Miellez; flowers purplish rose, center pinkish, large, very dbl., cupped

Louis-Philippe, Climbing Cl Ch, rb, before 1955; flowers deep red; [sport of Louis-Philippe]

Louis Philippe Albert d'Orléans – See **Louis Philippe d'Orléans**, HP

Louis-Philippe d'Angers – See **Louis-Philippe**, Ch

Louis Philippe d'Orléans HP, mr, 1884, Verdier, E.; flowers cerise red, tinted purplish scarlet grenadine, large, full; foliage large, rounded, somber green; prickles unequal, short, hooked; growth upright

Louis-Philippe I P, dr, 1832, Duval, C.; flowers crimson shaded with purple and violet, very large, full, intense fragrance; probably extinct

Louis Puyravaud N, my, 1896, Puyravaud; flowers canary yellow, aging to light yellow, large, full; [Rêve d'Or × unknown]

Louis' Rambler HMult, w, Lens, Louis; bud yellow, pointed; flowers white, sometimes with yellow flush, large, single, flat, borne in panicles of 7-48, intense musk fragrance; non-remontant; prickles spines on pedicels; growth strong climber to 20 ft.; hips yellow-orange with black tip; [*R. brunonii* × *R. multiflora adenocheata*]; int. in 1997

Louis Ricard HP, m, 1902, Boutigny, P.; flowers velvety dark purple, shaded vermilion, very large, full

Louis Richard – See **Helvetia**, T

Louis Riel S, w, 1996, Zubrowski, Stanley; flowers 5 petals; foliage medium size, purplish-green, dull; numerous prickles; bushy, tall growth; [*R. rubrifolia* × *R. spinosissima altaica*]

Louis Rödiger LCl, ob, 1935, Kordes; bud pointed; flowers orange shaded yellow and red, open, very large, semi-dbl., moderate fruity fragrance; foliage leathery, wrinkled, dark; prickles numerous, large; very vigorous, climbing trailing growth; [Daisy Hill × (Charles P. Kilham × Mev. G.A. van Rossem)]

Louis Rollet HP, dr, 1886, Gonod; flowers purplish red, large, full; very remontant; foliage large; prickles large, red

Louis Sauvage HWich, m, 1914, Turbat; flowers purple/red, 3 cm., dbl., flat, borne in clusters of 5-15, no fragrance; foliage medium green; numerous prickles

Louis van Houtte HP, dp, 1863, Granger; flowers shining carmine pink, shaded velvety dark red, edges fire-red, reverse lighter, full

Louis van Houtte HP, dr, 1869, Lacharme, F.; flowers crimson-maroon, well-formed, large, 40 petals, intense fragrance; some recurrent bloom; [Général Jacqueminot × unknown]

Louis van Tyle HGal, m, before 1846; flowers light crimson, shaded black or purple, small, semi-dbl.

Louis Walter HT, ab, 1938, Mallerin, C.; flowers golden orange-yellow, large, dbl.; foliage clear green, glossy; vigorous growth; [(Mrs Pierre S. duPont × unknown) × Charles P. Kilham]

Louis XII HGal, m, before 1829, Coquerel; flowers lilac pink, becoming violet red, medium, full, cupped

Louis XIV HGal, m, 1824, Hardy; flowers light lilac pink, large, full

Louis XIV HP, dr, 1859, Guillot et Fils; flowers dark crimson, medium, 25 petals, intense fragrance; foliage sparse; moderate growth; [Général Jacqueminot × unknown]; sometimes classed as Ch

Louis XVI – See **Achille**, HGal

Louis XVIII Ch, m, 1827, Mauget; flowers bright purple

Louisa Jane HT, pb, 1976, Ross, A., & Son; flowers center soft white, shading to deep pink, full, high-centered; growth medium; [sport of Baronne Edmond de Rothschild]; int. by A. Ross & Son, 1975

Louisa Jane Morris LCl, dr, 1997, Bossom, W.E.; flowers frilly, medium, dbl.; foliage medium size, medium green, semi-glossy; some prickles; climbing (15 ft.) growth; [Admiral Rodney × Evelyn Fison]

Louisa Schultheis HT, op, 1925, Schultheis, A.; flowers pink and salmon, center darker, 32-36 petals; [Golden Ophelia × Ruhm von Steinfurth]

Louisa Stone – See **Guinevere**, F

Louise – See **La Louise**, C

Louise – See **La Louise**, HGal

Louise HT, mp, 1924, Prince; bud pointed; flowers rose-pink shaded cerise, large, dbl.; foliage dark, leathery; vigorous growth; [Isobel × unnamed variety]

Louise S, dy, 2004, Zilligen, George D.; flowers golden yellow, blushing pink on petal ends, fading to bright yellow, small, semi-dbl., borne mostly solitary, moderate fragrance; foliage medium size, medium green, semi-glossy; spreading growth; bedding, borders; [Golden Celebration × unknown]; int. by George D. Zilligen

Louise Abdy F, mp, 1964, Abdy, S.; flowers pink, base yellow, 4 in., 6 petals, moderate fragrance; foliage dark; vigorous growth; [Donald Prior × McGredy's Yellow]

Louise Aimé P, 1845, Aimé

Louise Baldwin HT, ob, 1919, McGredy; bud pointed; flowers rich orange, tinted soft apricot, dbl., high-centered; vigorous growth

Louise Barbier – See **Louis Barbier**, HFt

Louise Béluze B, dp, about 1840, Béluze; flowers dark carmine, medium, full

Louise Bugnet HRg, w, Bugnet, George; bud red; flowers white with hint of pink, dbl.; foliage tough; almost thornless; growth medium (4 ft.); int. before 1960

Louise Carique – See **Mme Louise Carique**, HP

Louise Catherine Breslau HT, op, 1912, Pernet-Ducher; flowers shrimp-pink shaded reddish coppery orange, reverse chrome-yellow, very large, dbl., moderate fragrance; foliage dark, bronze, leathery; bushy growth; [unnamed variety × (Soleil d'Or × unknown)]

Louise Catherine Breslau, Climbing Cl HT, op, 1917, Kordes; flowers copper orange-red, large, very full, flat; [sport of Louise Catherine Breslau]

Louise Clements S, ob, Clements, John K.; flowers intense copper, 4 in., 70 petals, old-fashioned, borne in clusters, moderate fruity fragrance; free-flowering; foliage bronze-green; stems reddish; medium (3½ ft.) growth; int. by Heirloom Roses, 1996

Louise Cretté HP, w, 1915, Chambard, C.; flowers snow-white, center creamy white, well-formed, 6-7 in., 55 petals, high-centered, moderate fragrance; foliage dark; vigorous, bushy growth; [Frau Karl Druschki × Kaiserin Auguste Viktoria, Climbing]

Louise Criner HT, w, 1919, Chambard, C.; flowers snow-white, center creamy, dbl.; few prickles; [Louise Cretté × unknown]

Louise Damaizin HP, mp, 1864, Damaizin; flowers fresh pink, medium, full

Louise d'Arzens N, w, 1861, Lacharme, F.; flowers creamy white, small, full, cupped; [probably Mlle Blanche Laffitte × Sapho (DP)]; sometimes classed as B

Louise d'Autriche HP, m; flowers violet, large, full; [sport of La Reine]

Louise de Savoie T, ly, 1854, Ducher; flowers pale canary yellow, very large, full

Louise de Vilmorin HT, ab, 1944, Gaujard; bud ovoid; flowers orange-yellow, overlarge, very dbl.; foliage glossy, dark; dwarf growth

Louise Estes HT, pb, 1991, Winchel, Joseph F.; bud pointed; flowers pink blend, reverse white, aging medium pink, 4 in., 35 petals, high-centered, borne usually singly, moderate fruity fragrance; quick repeat; foliage medium size, medium green, matte, disease-resistant; upright, medium growth; [seedling × Miss Canada]; int. by Coiner Nursery, 1992; Silver Medal, ARC TG, 1991

Louise Gardner HT, yb, 1988, McGredy, Sam IV; flowers large, dbl.; foliage medium size, medium green, matte; upright, bushy growth; [Freude × (Sunblest × unknown)]; int. by McGredy Roses International, 1988

Louise Gaujard HT, op, 1941, Gaujard; flowers coppery pink shaded coral, open, very large, very dbl., cupped; foliage light green; vigorous, upright growth; [Mme Joseph Perraud × seedling]

Louise Hopkins HMult, lp, 1923, Hopkins; flowers white, center shell-pink, 200-225 petals; non-recurrent; vigorous, climbing (20 ft. or more) growth; [sport of Trier]

Louise Joly HT, or, 1922, Buatois; flowers coral-red, shaded shrimp-pink, large, dbl., cupped, borne mostly solitary, moderate fragrance; foliage glossy; few prickles; growth upright, bushy; [Mme Edouard Herriot × seedling]

Louise Krause HT, ob, 1930, Krause; flowers reddish-orange, passing to golden yellow, large, dbl.; foliage dark, glossy; vigorous, bushy growth; [Mrs Beckwith × Souv. de H.A. Verschuren]

Louise le Cardonnel HT, yb, 1939, Mallerin, C.; bud globular; flowers yellow tinted coral, very large, dbl.; stiff stems; very vigorous growth; [seedling × Mev. G.A. van Rossem]; int. by Meilland, A.

Louise Lilia – See **Luise Lilia**, HT

Louise Mack Min, dr, 1992, Jerabek, Paul E.; flowers 1¼ in., 30 petals, high-centered, borne usually singly; foliage medium size, dark green, semi-glossy; medium, spreading growth; [unknown × unknown]; int. in 1984

Louise Magnan HP, w, 1855, Fontaine; flowers pure white, medium, dbl.

Louise Margottin B, lp, 1862, Margottin; flowers silky light pink, medium, full

Louise Méhul HGal, pb, Parmentier; flowers light red, spotted white, large, flat

Louise Odier B, dp, 1851, Margottin; flowers bright rose-pink, well-formed, dbl., cupped; foliage medium green, matte; prickles very few; tall growth

Louise Park HT, mr, 2005, Williams, J. Benjamin; flowers bright red, 3 in., dbl., cupped, ruffled, borne mostly solitary, moderate fragrance; free-flowering; foliage small, medium green, glossy; prickles moderate, in., downturned; growth upright, medium; garden decorative; winter hardy; [Pete Musser × Peggy

Rockerfeller]; originally named Firefighter; int. in 2003

Louise Pernot HT, lp, 1903, Robichon; flowers delicate silvery pink, salmon at center, large, dbl.

Louise Peyronny HP, dp, 1844, Lacharme, F.; flowers deep pink shaded carmine, very large, dbl., moderate fragrance; moderate growth; [supposedly a seedling of La Reine]; possibly synonymous with Laelia

Louise Pigné T, mp, 1905, Pigné; flowers China-pink, base buff-yellow, petals crinkled, very large, very dbl.; very vigorous growth; [Mme Eugene Resal × Mme Lombard]

Louise Pommery F, ab, Sauvageot; flowers apricot with carmine tints at edges, dbl.; int. in 2002

Louise Simplex – See **La Louise**, C

Louise Verger M, lp, 1860, Robert et Moreau; flowers bright pink, lighter at edges, 8-9 cm., dbl., cupped

Louise Walter Pol, pb, 1909, Walter, L.; flowers white and flesh-pink, open, dbl.; foliage small, rich green; very dwarf growth; [Tausendschön × Rosel Dach]; int. by P. Lambert

Louise Weiss F, ly, Pekmez; int. by Roseraies Barth, 2006

Louise Wood HP, mp, 1869, Verdier, E.; flowers shining pink, large, dbl.

Louisiana HT, w, 1975, Weeks, O. L.; flowers creamy white, 3-4 in., 38 petals, high-centered; foliage dark, leathery; upright growth; PP3719; [seedling × seedling]; int. in 1974

Louisiana, Climbing Cl HT, w, Weeks; PP4797; [sport of Louisiana]; int. in 1985

Louisiana HT, op, Kordes; int. in 1992

Louisiana Lady Min, yb, 1997, Taylor, Franklin; flowers medium, full, borne mostly singly; foliage medium size, medium green, semi-glossy; upright, bushy, medium (24 in.) growth; [seedling × seedling]; int. by Taylor's Roses

Louisiana Purchase HT, dp, 1955, Swim, H.C.; bud long, pointed; flowers rich cerise, 4-5 in., 20-25 petals, cupped, intense damask fragrance; foliage dark, leathery; very vigorous, upright growth; [Charlotte Armstrong × Piccaninny]; int. by Stark Bros., 1954

Louisville Lady HT, pb, 1986, Weddle, Von C.; flowers bright pink, silver reverse, medium, 35 petals, high-centered; foliage medium size, dark, semi-glossy; bushy growth; [Osiria × seedling]

Louisville Lady MinFl, dp, 2003, Wells, Verlie W.; flowers deep pink, reverse lighter, long-lasting, 2 in., full, high-centered, borne mostly solitary, slight fragrance; foliage large, dark green, glossy; prickles 1/4 in., hooked; growth spreading, bushy, tall (36 in.); garden, exhibition; [seedling × seedling]; int. by Wells MidSouth Roses, 2002

Louita F, rb

Louksor – See **Louqsor**, HT

Loulou de Cacharel F, rb, Dorieux; int. by Roseraies Dorieux, 2000

Louqsor HT, ab, 1970, Delbard-Chabert; flowers golden coral with base yellow, medium, dbl., globular, borne singly and several together; foliage medium size, glossy; vigorous, bushy growth; [Dr. Albert Schweitzer × Provence]; int. by Pepinieres G. Delbard, 1967

Lourdes HT, dy, 1960, Brownell, W. D.; bud ovoid; flowers golden yellow, 4-5 in., 35-50 petals, moderate fragrance; foliage leathery, glossy, dark; vigorous growth; hardy for the class; [V for Victory × (New Dawn sport × Copper Glow sport)]; int. by Stern's Nursery, 1959

Lourdes Arroyo HT, yb, Viveros Fco. Ferrer, S L; flowers 26 petals, high-centered; [Zambra × Inedita]

Louvre HT, ab, 1970, Delbard-Chabert; bud long, pointed; flowers rosy apricot, medium, dbl.; foliage bronze, glossy; moderate, upright growth; [Souv. de J. Chabert × (Walko × Souv. de J. Chabert)]; int. by Pepinieres G. Delbard, 1967

Lovable HT, lp, 1979, Leon, Charles F., Sr.; bud long, pointed; flowers 4½-6 in., 30 petals, high-centered; vigorous, upright, bushy growth; [(Helen Traubel × Michele Meilland) × ((Blanche Mallerin × Peace) × (Peace × Virgo))]

Lovace – See **Sheila Sorensen**, HT

Lovania S, or, 1979, Lens, Louis; bud ovoid; flowers bright red-orange, 1½ in., 18-22 petals, pompon, moderate fruity fragrance; recurrent bloom; foliage dark; vigorous, upright, climbing growth; [Robin Hood × (New Penny × Coloranja)]; int. in 1978

Love Cl HT, or, 1935, Mallerin, Berthe; flowers scarlet, medium to large, semi-dbl., moderate fragrance; occasional repeat; foliage dark; long stems; vigorous, climbing (6½-10 ft.), bushy growth; declared extinct, ARA 1979; [Hadley × Ami Quinard]; int. by H. Guillot

Love Gr, rb, 1979, Warriner, William A.; bud short, pointed; flowers bright scarlet red, reverse silvery white, large, 35 petals, high-centered, borne mostly singly, slight rose fragrance; foliage dark green, glossy, new growth is red; long stems; upright growth; PP4437; [unknown × Redgold]; int. by J&P, 1980; Gold Medal, Portland, 1980

Love Affair HT, dr, 1972, Jelly; bud short pointed; flowers brilliant red, large, very dbl., high-centered, moderate fragrance; foliage large, dark, leathery; vigorous, upright growth; [red seedling × Forever Yours]; int. by E.G. Hill Co., 1970

Love 'n' Kisses – See **S. W. A. L. K.**, Cl Min

Love and Peace HT, yb, 2001, Twomey, Jerry, and Lim, Ping; flowers golden yellow with pink edge, 5 in., full, high-centered, borne mostly solitary, slight fragrance; foliage medium size, dark green, glossy, disease-resistant; prickles moderate; growth upright, medium (4-5 ft.), garden, cutting; PP14731; [seedling × Peace]; int. by Bailey Nurseries, Inc., 2002; AARS, 2002

Love And Peace Min, rb, 2007, Moore, Ralph S.; bud mossy; flowers red and lavender striped, reverse red, medium, 1½ in., dbl., borne in small clusters; foliage medium size, medium green, semi-glossy; prickles small, straight, green, numerous; growth bushy, medium (15 in.); containers, border, specimens; [seedling × striped seedling]; int. by Sequoia Nurs., 2007

Love Bug Min, ob, 1987, Bridges, Dennis A.; flowers orange, white base, reverse orange, veining to white base, fades slightly, 14 petals, high-centered; foliage medium size, medium green, semi-glossy; prickles short, small, pink, hooked slightly downward; growth bushy, medium; [Heartland × seedling]

Love Call HT, pb, 1990, Bridges, Dennis A.; bud ovoid; flowers deep pink, lighter at base, reverse light pink, large, 50 petals, high-centered, borne singly, moderate damask fragrance; recurrent; foliage medium size, dark green, glossy; prickles pointed slightly downward, medium, light green; growth upright, tall; [Lady X × Wini Edmunds]; int. by Bridges Roses, 1990

Love Dove Min, w, 1982, Lyon, Lyndon; flowers near white, medium, 35 petals, high-centered; foliage medium size, medium green, semi-glossy; low growth; [seedling × seedling]

Love in Bloom Min, m, 1994, Bell, Judy G.; flowers mauve to tan with bright yellow stamens, medium, single, borne in small clusters, slight fragrance; foliage medium size, dark green, semi-glossy; few prickles; bushy, spreading (10-12 in.) growth; [Angel Face × unknown]; int. by Michigan Mini Roses, 1995

Love Knot Cl Min, mr, 1999, Warner, Chris; flowers crimson, reverse light red, 2½ in., dbl., borne in small clusters; foliage small, medium green, glossy; few prickles; upright, tall (6 ft.) growth; [Laura Ford × Ingrid Bergman]; int. by Warner's Roses, 2000

Love Letter F, w, 1979, Lens, Louis; flowers creamy white, 3-3½ in., 30-35 petals, cupped, intense fragrance; foliage glossy, dark; vigorous, bushy, upright growth; [Pink Parfait × Rosenelfe]; int. in 1977

Love Me Min, w, 1994, Walsh, Richard Bruce; flowers creamy white, pink edge, medium, dbl., borne in small clusters; foliage small, medium green, matte; few prickles; low, upright growth; [Magic Carrousel × Old Master]; int. by Fradee Nursery, 1992

Love Me Do HT, w, Benny; flowers ivory white, opening with a peach center, dbl; foliage glossy; int. by Camp Hill Roses

Love Me Tender HT, m; flowers light lavender, cream pink petal edges, moderate fragrance; int. by Certified, 2002

Love Note MinFl, pb, 1990, Zipper, Herbert; flowers deep pink, light red going to cream at base, reverse deep pink, 35 petals, high-centered; foliage large, medium green, semi-glossy; prickles straight, small, light brown; bushy, tall growth; hips round, medium, orange; [Tamango × Cupcake]; int. by Magic Moment Miniature Roses, 1991

Love Potion F, m, 1993, Christensen, Jack E.; flowers deep clear lavender, 3-3½ in., full, borne in small clusters, intense raspberry fragrance; foliage medium size, dark green, glossy; some prickles; medium (90-100 cm.), upright, spreading growth; PP9172; [seedling × Dilly Dilly]; int. by Bear Creek Gardens, 1994

Love Song HT, pb, 1956, Fisher, E. G.; bud ovoid; flowers Neyron rose, reverse yellow, 4½-5 in., 45 petals, cupped, intense fragrance; foliage dark, glossy; vigorous, upright growth; PP1360; [Peace × Orange Nassau]; int. by C-P

Love Story HT, ob, 1974, Tantau, Math.; bud ovoid; flowers orange, large, dbl., cupped; int. by Horstmann, 1972

Love Surprise – See **William Shakespeare 2000**, S

Love Token F, mp, 1965, Gregory; flowers peach-pink, well-formed, 2 in., 28 petals; foliage dark, glossy; vigorous growth; int. in 1963

Love Torch Min, rb, 1992, Williams, Ernest D.; bud long, pointed; flowers red, orange and yellow blend, holds color well, heavy substance, medium, full; foliage small, dark green, glossy; some prickles; low (30 cm.), upright, bushy growth; hardy; [Starburst × Over the Rainbow]

Love 'Ya Dad Min, mr, 1996, Bennett, Dee; flowers do not fade, 1½ in., full, high-centered, borne mostly singly, intense fragrance; foliage medium size, dark green, semi-glossy, disease-resistant; prickles moderate; stems long; growth upright, bushy, tall (70-80 cm.), vigorous; [Carrousel × Big John]; int. by Tiny Petals Nursery, 1997

Love You S, mp, 1999, Nemko, Martin; flowers ¾-1 in., borne in large clusters; foliage medium size, medium green, glossy; prickles moderate; bushy, low (2 ft.) growth; int. by Bailey Nurseries, 1999

Lovebird MinFl, mp, Cowlishaw, Frank; int. in 1998

Loveglo Min, op, 1983, Williams, Ernest D.; flowers light coral pink and cream, small, dbl., high-centered; foliage small, dark, glossy; bushy growth; PP5677; [Little Darling × Over the Rainbow]; int. by Mini-Roses

Loveliest HT, lp, 1956, Leon, Charles F., Sr.; bud ovoid; flowers clear rose-pink, large, dbl., high-centered; foliage leathery, light green; vigorous, upright growth; [Charlotte Armstrong × Juno]

Lovelight F, mp, 1960, Jelly; bud short, pointed;

flowers large, 33 petals, high-centered; vigorous, upright growth; PP1887; [Garnette × seedling]; originally registered as Pol; int. by E.G. Hill Co., 1959

Loveliness HWich, lp, 1933, Chaplin Bros.; flowers pale pink, white spot at base, round, large, dbl., borne in large clusters; foliage small, light green, glossy; vigorous, climbing growth

Lovely HT, dp, 1936, H&S; bud pointed; flowers carmine-pink, large, semi-dbl., high-centered, moderate violet fragrance; foliage soft; vigorous, compact growth; int. by Dreer

Lovely – See **Karen**, F

Lovely Amazone HT, ab, Pouw; bud ovate; flowers dbl., high-centered, star-shaped, borne mostly singly, slight fragrance; free-flowering; foliage glossy, abundant; prickles moderate; growth vigorous, narrow, upright (6 ft.); PP10914; [seedling × seedling]; greenhouse rose; int. by Panorama Roses NV, 1997

Lovely Blue Min, m, Keisei; int. in 1990

Lovely Bride – See **Lovely Meilland**, S

Lovely Child S, ab, 2006; flowers apricot to yellow, outer petals fading near white, medium, full, cupped, borne mostly solitary, moderate fragrance; recurrent; foliage small, medium green; no prickles; growth upright, short; [sport of Tamora]; int. by Roses Unlimited, 2006

Lovely Dream HT, dp; PP10769

Lovely Fairy Pol, dp, Spek, Hette; bud small; flowers 3-3½ cm., 21-36 petals, cupped, borne in clusters of 11-42; free-flowering; foliage medium size, leathery, semi-glossy; few prickles; stems 10-12 in; growth compact, spreading; PP10701; [sport of The Fairy]; int. in 1990

Lovely Fairy – See **Tornerose**, F

Lovely Girl HT, ob; flowers ochre and orange-yellow, dbl., high-centered; foliage matte; growth to 90-100 cm.; PP11731; [((seedling × Jelfax) × Meigerium) × seedling]; greenhouse rose; int. by Meilland, 1984

Lovely Green F, w, Meilland; flowers creamy white with green tint, full, high-centered; florist rose; int. by Meilland Intl., 2002

Lovely Jubilee HT, m, Interplant; int. in 1992

Lovely Lady HT, mr, 1934, Asmus; bud long, pointed; flowers pure rose-red, large, very dbl., high-centered, intense fragrance; foliage leathery; long, strong stems; growth very vigorous, open; RULED EXTINCT 10/86; [sport of Better Times]

Lovely Lady HT, mp, 1984, Dickson, Patrick; flowers large, 35 petals, moderate fragrance; foliage medium size, mid-green, glossy; bushy growth; [Silver Jubilee × (Eurorose × Anabell)]; Gold Medal, Belfast, 1988

Lovely Lady HMsk, mp; int. by Heirloom, 2004

Lovely Lorrie Min, mp, Moore; flowers soft pink turning lighter as it opens, 1½ in., dbl., borne singly and in small clusters; recurrent; moderate (12-16 in.) growth; int. in 1998

Lovely Louise F, ab; int. in 1990

Lovely Lynda HT, my, 2005, Wells, Verlie W.; flowers light to medium yellow, 4½-5 in., full, borne mostly solitary; foliage medium size, dark green, semi-glossy; prickles moderate, ½ in., straight; growth upright, bushy, medium (4 ft.); garden decorative, exhibition; [seedling × seedling]; int. by Wells MidSouth Roses, 2005

Lovely Meidiland – See **Lovely Meilland**, S

Lovely Meilland S, lp, Meilland; flowers clear rose pink, medium, dbl., borne in large clusters; growth to 60-80 cm.; int. as Lovely Bride, Wharton's

Lovely Red HT, dr, Meilland; flowers deep, velvety red, dbl., high-centered, borne mostly singly; recurrent; florist rose; int. by Meilland Intl., 1998

Lovely Rosamini Min, lp

Lovely Ruffles F, pb; int. in 2002

Lovely Symphonie Min, mp, Meilland; flowers rose pink, dbl., borne in small clusters; growth to 40-45 cm.

Loverly F, ab, 1984, Stoddard, Louis; flowers medium, semi-dbl., moderate fragrance; foliage medium size, medium green, semi-glossy; bushy growth; [Restless Native × Apricot Nectar]; int. in 1986; Silver Medal, ARC TG, 1985

Lovers Lane HT, mr, 2001, Zary, Keith; bud pointed, ovoid; flowers thick velvety petals, classic hybrid tea form; lighter, silvery reverse., 4½-5 in., 35 petals, borne mostly solitary, slight sweet fragrance; foliage large, dark green, semi-glossy; prickles moderate; stems tall, straight; growth upright, tall (5-6 ft.); garden decorative; PP13317; [Jacpico × Poulman]; int. by J&P, 2002

Lovers' Meeting HT, ob, 1980, Gandy, O.L.; bud pointed; flowers bright orange, 25 petals, high-centered, borne singly and in clusters, moderate fragrance; foliage bronze; prickles short; strong, upright growth; [seedling × Egyptian Treasure]

Lovers Only Min, rb, 1990, McCann, Sean; sepals are fancy; flowers cherry red, with straw-yellow bicolor, reverse fades to cream, dbl.; foliage medium size, medium green, glossy; prickles pubescent on peduncle; upright, compact growth; [Rise 'n' Shine × Siobhan]; int. in 1989

Love's Gift S, rb, 2001, Thomson, George L.; flowers creamy yellow with cherry red edges, 3½-5 in., semi-dbl., borne in small clusters, slight fragrance; foliage medium size, dark green, glossy; prickles medium, hooked, numerous; growth upright, tall (5½-6.5 ft.); garden decorative; [Hannah Gordon × Tomone]; int. by Ross Roses, 2001

Love's Promise – See **Graf Lennart**, HT

Love's Song – See **Rosenresli**, S

Love's Spring – See **Singin' in the Rain**, F

Lovesong S, lp, Clements, John; flowers elegant shade of pink, 4 in., 28 petals, globular, borne in clusters of 5-8, intense grapefruit and tea fragrance; foliage dark green; growth upright (4-5 ft.); PPAF; int. by Heirloom, 2004

Lovestruck F, pb, 2007, Zary, Keith W.; flowers pink white handpaint, reverse light pink, 4 in., dbl., blooms borne in small clusters; foliage medium size, dark green, glossy; prickles 6-8 mm., hooked downward, greyed-orange, moderate; growth compact, medium (3½ ft.); [Sorbet Bouquet × Pure Poetry]; int. by Jackson & Perkins Wholesale, Inc., 2008

Loving HT, pb, J&P; int. in 1994

Loving Heart – See **Koigokoro**, HT

Loving Memory HT, mr, 1983, Kordes, W.; flowers large, dbl., high-centered; foliage medium green, semi-glossy; upright, bushy growth; [seedling × Red Planet seedling]; int. in 1981

Loving Son HT, w, 1994, Mengel, Russell R.; flowers 4-7 cm., very dbl., borne mostly singly, moderate fragrance; good rebloom; foliage medium size, medium green, semi-glossy; some prickles; medium, bushy growth; [Honor × Captain Harry Stebbings]; int. by Mengel, 1994

Loving Touch Min, ab, 1983, Jolly, Nelson F.; flowers deep apricot, 25 petals, high-centered, borne usually singly, slight fragrance; foliage medium size, medium green, semi-glossy; bushy, spreading growth; globular fruit; PP5835; [Rise 'n' Shine × Angel Darling]; int. by Rosehill Farm, 1982; AOE, ARS, 1985

Loving Wishes – See **Fiery Hit**, MinFl

Lovita HT, mr, 1967, Meilland; bud ovoid; flowers bright red, large, dbl.; foliage dark; vigorous, upright growth; PP2598; [Baccará × (Independence × Peace)]; int. by Moerheim, 1965

Lovita – See **Kiboh**, F

Lovita F, ab; flowers brown apricot deepening as it opens, dbl., classic; int. in 1989

Lowburn Rose Misc OGR, dp

Lowea berberifolia – See ***Hulthemia persica***

Lowel Allen S, op, Williams, J. Benjamin; flowers soft salmon-pink, single, slight fragrance; recurrent; medium (4 ft.) growth; int. by Hortico, Inc., 2005

Lowell Thomas HT, dy, 1943, Mallerin, C.; bud long, pointed; flowers rich yellow, 4-4½ in., 38 petals, high-centered; foliage leathery; vigorous, upright, bushy, compact growth; [Mme Mélanie Soupert × Nonin]; int. by C-P, 1943; Gold Medal, Portland, 1944

Lowell Thomas, Climbing Cl HT, dy, 1955, Armstrong, J.A.; PP1448; [sport of Lowell Thomas]; int. by Armstrong Nursery, 1954

Lowe's Eglantine HEg, dp, Lowe; flowers semi-dbl., flat, borne in huge spring flush, no fragrance; intermittent repeat; foliage not fragrant; growth to 20 ft.; groundcover or climber on low fence; int. in 2001

Loyal Friend MinFl, w, Gardner; int. by Freedom Gardens, 2001

Loyal Rosarian HT, mr, 1990, Leon, Charles F., Sr.; bud ovoid; flowers medium red becoming darker red as it ages, large, 36-42 petals, high-centered, borne usually singly; foliage medium size, leathery, green; upright, bushy, tall growth; large fruit, germinates rapidly; [Red Planet × Red Devil]; int. by Oregon Grown Roses, 1990

Loyal Vassal MinFl, ob, 2007, Wells, Verlie W.; flowers medium orange, reverse yellow and darker orange, 1½-1¾ in., full, borne mostly solitary; foliage medium size, dark green, semi-glossy; prickles in., straight, moderate; growth upright, tall; garden decoration, exhibition; [seedling × seedling]; int. by Wells MidSouth Roses, 2007

Loyalist – See **Great Maiden's Blush**, A

Loyalist Dream Gr, w

Luarca HT, Dot, Simon

Lübeck – See **Hansestadt Lübeck**, F

Lübecker Rotspon – See **Glad Tidings**, F

Luberon – See **Buffalo Gal**, HRg

Lubov Chevtsova HT, lp, 1956, Sushkov, K. L.; flowers light pink, base tinted orange, large (5 in); foliage glossy; strong stems; upright growth; [Cathrine Kordes × Peace]

Lubra HT, dr, 1938, Fitzhardinge; bud long, pointed; flowers dark crimson, dbl., high-centered; foliage leathery, dark; vigorous growth; [(Ophelia, Climbing × unknown) × Black Boy]; int. by Hazlewood Bros.

Luc Steeno HT, mp, RvS-Melle; int. in 1997

Luc Varenne F, mr, 1959, Delforge; bud oval; flowers scarlet, open, medium, semi-dbl., borne in clusters; foliage dark, glossy; vigorous, bushy growth; [Alain × Montrouge]

Luce di Todi HT, dr, 1998, Williams, J. Benjamin; flowers dark velvet red, 5 in.-5½ in., 26-41 petals, high-centered, borne singly, intense fragrance; foliage large, dark green, semi-glossy; few prickles; tall (4-5 ft.), upright, growth; [Mister Lincoln × Miss All-American Beauty]; int. by J. Benjamin Williams & Associates, 2000

Lucens Erecta HLong, lp, 1921, Paul, W.; flowers almost white, small to medium, semi-dbl.; non-recurrent; foliage dark green, glossy

Lucetta S, ab, 1992, Austin, David; flowers pale peach, 5¼ in., semi-dbl. to dbl., borne in small clusters, moderate fragrance; foliage medium size, medium green, semi-glossy; some prickles; medium (47 in.), spreading growth; int. by David Austin Roses, Ltd., 1983

Lucette HWich, pb, 1910, Guillot; flowers medium pink,

base white, center yellow, medium, full

Luchian F, mr, Palocsay, R. and Wagner, S.; bud globular; flowers large, velvety vermillion red, 35 petals, slight fragrance; [Paprika × Coup de Foudre]; int. by Res. Stn. f. Horticulture, Cluj, 1972

Lucia – See **Lichtkönigin Lucia**, S

Lucia Cotarelo Min, op, Viveros Fco. Ferrer, S L; flowers 15 petals, rosette; [M Litigan × Scarlet Meilladina]

Lucia Zuloaga HT, rb, 1932, Dot, Pedro; flowers velvety brownish scarlet with a golden undertone, open, very large, semi-dbl., moderate fruity fragrance; foliage glossy, dark; [Duquesa de Peñaranda × F. Cambo]; int. by C-P, 1934

Lucie Duplessis M, lp, 1854, Robert; flowers rosy white, 2½ in., full, rosette

Lucie Faure T, w, 1898, Nabonnand; flowers ivory white, flesh/salmon centers, large, full, borne mostly solitary; [Mme Léon Février × Niphetos]

Lucie Fernand-David HT, w, 1924, Chambard, C.; flowers white, center slightly tinted cream, dbl.

Lucie Hallouin T, w, 1902, Corboeuf-Marsault; flowers white, center tinted garnet; [Mme Charles × Mme Hoste]

Lucie Marie HT, yb, 1930, Dickson, A.; bud pointed; flowers buttercup-yellow veined apricot-orange and shaded salmon-cerise, dbl., high-centered; foliage dark, leathery, glossy; vigorous, compact, bushy growth

Lucie Nicolas Meyer HT, dp, 1922, Gillot, F.; flowers dark pink, edged lighter, dbl.; [Jonkheer J.L. Mock × seedling]

Lucie Petzka Pol, dr, 1953, Petzka; flowers medium, dbl.

Lucien Chaurè HT, lp, 1913, Soupert & Notting; flowers flesh pink with light cream pink, very large, dbl.; [Mme Abel Chatenay × Pié X]

Lucien de Lemos HT, lp, 1905, Lambert, P.; flowers carnation pink, large, dbl., globular, moderate fragrance; [Princesse Alice de Monaco × Mme Caroline Testout]

Lucien Duranthon HP, mr, 1894, Bonnaire; flowers pure carmine red, large, dbl.; thornless; growth upright

Lucie's Dream Min, my, 1995, Meilland, Alain A.; flowers large, very dbl., borne in small clusters, moderate lemony fragrance; foliage medium size, medium green, semi-glossy; some prickles; medium (25-30 cm.), bushy growth; [(Yellow Pages × Gold Badge) × Lemon Delight]; int. by SNC Meilland & Cie, 1994

Lucifer Pol, or, 1931, Easlea; flowers small, dbl.

Lucile HWich, lp, 1911, Walsh; flowers flesh-pink, base tinged rosy salmon, dbl., borne in clusters; foliage large, rich green, glossy; vigorous, climbing growth

Lucile Barker HT, ab, 1922, Hicks; bud pointed; flowers apricot-yellow, semi-dbl., high-centered; foliage bronze; vigorous growth

Lucile Dubourg HGal, m, 1826, Dubourg; flowers velvety violet-purple

Lucile Duplessis HGal, dp, 1836, Vibert; flowers deep pink, spotted with white, medium, full

Lucile Hill HT, dp, 1939, Joseph H. Hill, Co.; bud long, pointed, rose-red; flowers spinel-pink, very large, dbl.; foliage leathery; long stems; very vigorous, compact growth; [(Senior × De Luxe) × Sweet Adeline]

Lucile Rand HT, pb, 1930, Pernet-Ducher; bud pointed; flowers brilliant carmine, shaded yellow and orange, very large, dbl.; very vigorous, semi-climbing, bushy growth; int. by Gaujard

Lucile Supreme HT, dp, 1941, Joseph H. Hill, Co.; flowers rose-red, 6 in., 25-35 petals; [sport of Lucile Hill]

Lucilla F, ab, 1992, Stainthorpe, Eric; flowers small, semi-dbl., borne in small clusters; foliage small, medium green, semi-glossy; some prickles; low (35 cm.), compact growth; [sport of Conservation]; int. by Battersby Roses, 1993

Lucille – See **Lucile Duplessis**, HGal

Lucille Ball HT, ab, 1991, Christensen, Jack E.; flowers apricot, amber blend, good petal substance, 2¾ in., full, borne mostly singly, moderate fragrance; foliage medium size, medium green, semi-glossy; some prickles; tall (145-160 cm.), upright, bushy growth; [Hello Dolly × seedling]; int. by Bear Creek Gardens, 1993

Lucille McWherter Min, pb, 1997, Wells, Verlie W.; flowers medium, pink blend, 8-14 petals; foliage medium size, dark green, glossy; upright, medium (18-24in.) growth; [seedling × seedling]; int. by Wells Mid-South Roses

Lucille Ross LCl, w, 1940, Ross; flowers white, center golden, open, semi-dbl.; vigorous, climbing (20-40 ft.) growth; [sport of Dr. W. Van Fleet]; int. by Roselawn Gardens

Lucina F, m; int. by Melville Nurseries, 2005

Lucinda HT, dp, 1927, Heacock; [sport of Columbia]

Lucinde S, dy, Kordes; flowers bright yellow, aging lighter, 3-4 in., dbl., borne singly or in small clusters, moderate fragrance; int. in 1988

Luciole T, dp, 1886, Guillot et Fils; bud long; flowers carmine-rose, base coppery yellow, large, intense fragrance; [Safrano à Fleurs Rouges × unknown]

Luciole HWich, rb, 1923, Nonin; flowers bright scarlet, center white, small, single, borne in large clusters; vigorous, climbing growth; [Hiawatha × unknown]

Lucious HT, mr, 1995, Sheldon, John & Robin; flowers intense medium red, dbl., borne mostly singly; foliage medium size, dark green, semi-glossy; upright growth

Lucky F, dr, 1962, Leenders, J.; flowers deep velvety red, 3 in., 13 petals; [Goldilocks × Independence]

Lucky Beauty HT, pb, 1971, Fuller; bud ovoid; flowers pink, yellow reverse, large, 90 petals, high-centered, moderate fragrance; vigorous, upright, bushy growth; [Kordes' Perfecta × Lucky Piece]; int. by Wyant, 1970

Lucky Charm F, yb, 1961, Robinson, H.; flowers bright yellow tipped red, 3½-4 in., 18 petals, borne in clusters of 6-10; foliage glossy; vigorous growth; int. by Lowe

Lucky Charm Min, yb, 1990, Moore, Ralph S.; bud ovoid; flowers yellow, reverse tinting red, aging to pink to red, lightly striped, small, 50-60 petals, high-centered, borne in sprays of 3-5, no fragrance; foliage small, medium green, matte; prickles straight, small, brown; bushy, spreading, low growth; no fruit; [Rumba × Pinstripe]; int. by Sequoia Nursery, 1989

Lucky Choice HT, w, 1985, Ota, Kaichiro; flowers creamy white, flushed light pink in center, large, 35 petals, high-centered, borne 1-3 per stem; foliage large, medium green; prickles few, small, slender; upright growth; [American Heritage × Sodori-Hime]

Lucky Duck Min, rb, Dickson; int. in 2001

Lucky Four F, dy, Hiroshima; flowers bluish-yellow; int. by Hiroshima Bara-en, 2002

Lucky Kordana Mega Brite Min, op, Kordes; int. by Bear Creek Gardens, 2000

Lucky Lady Gr, lp, 1966, Armstrong, D.L. & Swim, H. C.; bud long, pointed; flowers light pink, reverse darker, large, 28 petals, high-centered; foliage dark, glossy; vigorous, upright growth; PP2829; [Charlotte Armstrong × Cherry Glow]; int. by Armstrong Nursery

Lucky Lucy Min, m, 2004, Moe, Mitchie; flowers mauve, reverse mauve, ½ in, full, high-centered, borne mostly solitary, moderate fragrance; free-flowering; foliage small, medium green, semi-glossy; prickles small, straight; growth compact, medium (18-20 in.); exhibition, garden decoration; [Vista × Elegant Beauty]; int. by Mitchie's Roses and More, 2005

Lucky Me MinFl, dp, 2003, Eagle, B & D; flowers reverse deep pink with white base, 5-5½ cm., full, borne in small clusters, no fragrance; good repeat; foliage dark green, semi-glossy, disease-resistant; prickles small, straight; growth bushy, medium (40-50 cm.); garden, cutting; [Heidi × seedling]; int. by Southern Cross Nurseries, 1993

Lucky Piece HT, pb, 1962, Gordon, Winifred; flowers copper, pink and gold blend, full, bowl-shaped, moderate fragrance; growth strong and stout; PP1948; [sport of Peace]; int. by Wyant, 1962

Lucky Star HT, yb, 1936, Armacost; flowers golden yellow, suffused flame-scarlet; [sport of Souvenir]; int. by Armacost & Royston

Lucky Star F, mp, Zary; PPAF; int. by Bear Creek Gardens, 2000

Lucrèce – See **Majestueuse**, HGal

Lucrèce HCh, lp, about 1830, Laffay; flowers bright light pink, medium, full

Lucrèce A, lp, 1847, Vibert; flowers pale rose, center deeper rose, 8-9 cm., dbl., globular; nearly thornless

Lucrèce T, op, 1866, Oger; flowers salmon pink, aging to dark pink, large, full, cupped

Lucretia F, mr

Lucullus Ch, dr, 1854, Guinoisseau-Flon; flowers velvety black purple, medium, very dbl.; probably extinct

Lucy Cl HT, dp, 1935, Williams, A. H.; flowers brilliant carmine, large; foliage glossy; growth very vigorous, climbing

Lucy Min, ob, Barni, V.; flowers intense orange with yellow tints, dbl., high-centered; growth to 35-40 cm.; int. by Rose Barni, 1992

Lucy Min, mp, Moore, Ralph S.; flowers bright pink, 1-1½ in., semi-dbl., flat; free-flowering; foliage medium green, semi-glossy; growth compact (8-12 in.); int. by Sequoia Nursery, 1997

Lucy F, ob, Kirkham, S.; flowers bright orange with yellow reverse, dbl., borne in clusters, slight fragrance; good repeat; foliage bright, glossy; growth compact, upright; int. by C&K Jones, 2001

Lucy Ashton HEg, w, 1894, Penzance; flowers pure white, edged pink, medium, single; mid-spring bloom, non-recurrent; foliage dark, fragrant; vigorous growth

Lucy Bertram HEg, rb, 1895, Penzance; flowers dark shining crimson, center white, single; mid-spring, non-recurrent; foliage dark, fragrant; very vigorous growth

Lucy Constable HT, pb, 1924, Lilley; flowers silver pink, reverse deep salmon pink

Lucy Cramphorn HT, or, 1960, Kriloff, Michel; flowers signal-red, well-formed, 5 in., very dbl.; foliage glossy; vigorous, upright growth; [Peace × Baccará]; int. by Cramphorn's Nursery, 1960

Lucy Cramphorn, Climbing – See **Maryse Kriloff, Climbing**, Cl HT

Lucy Locket F, mp, 2004, Horner, Colin P.; flowers medium pink, reverse lighter, 7 cm., dbl., borne in small clusters, moderate fragrance; foliage medium size, medium green, glossy; prickles small, curved; growth compact, short (60 cm.); garden decorative; [Tournament of Roses × seedling]; int. by Warley Rose Gardens, 2006

Lucy Marguerite HT, yb, 1977, Ellick; flowers buttercup-yellow, diffused red, 4 in., 35-40 petals, moderate fragrance; foliage small, glossy, dark; [Val De Mosa × Denise-Anne]; int. by Excelsior Roses, 1978

Lucy Nicolas HT, r, 1935, Mallerin, C.; bud pointed; flowers coppery salmon, large, dbl., high-centered; foliage glossy, bronze; very vigorous growth; [Odette

Foussier × Cécile Walter]; int. by C-P

Lucy Thomas Cl HP, mp, 1924, Nabonnand, P.; flowers pink, center brighter, semi-dbl.; rarely recurrent bloom; [Ulrich Brunner Fils × Georg Arends]

Lucyle HT, mp, 1933, Vestal; flowers glowing pink, very large, dbl.; foliage leathery, dark; vigorous, bushy growth

Ludek Pik HP, mr, 1933, Böhm, J.; flowers large, very dbl.

Ludlow Castle – See **England's Rose**, S

Ludmilla HT, m, 1970, Laperrière; bud ovoid; flowers medium, semi-dbl.; foliage glossy; vigorous, upright growth; [(Peace × Independence) × Heure Mauve]; int. by EFR, 1968

Ludovic Létaud HP, dp, 1849, Cherpin or Ducher; flowers medium, full

Ludovicus HGal, m, about 1845, Calvert; flowers violet-purple

Ludsponelle – See **Anne Colle**, HT

Ludvik Vecera LCl, mr, Vecera, L.; flowers vermilion, 3 in., dbl., borne in large clusters, moderate fragrance; int. in 1981

Ludwig Möller HP, ab, 1915, Kiese; flowers bright amber-yellow, fading white, large, full; [Frau Karl Druschki × Marechal Niel seedling]

Ludwig Oppenheimer HT, dr, 1932, Leenders Bros.; bud pointed; flowers crimson-scarlet, large, dbl.; foliage dark; vigorous growth; [Villa Pia × Capitaine Georges Dessirier]

Ludwigshafen – See **Ludwigshafen am Rhein**, F

Ludwigshafen am Rhein F, dp, 1976, Kordes; bud ovoid; flowers deep pink, flora-tea, 4 in., 45 petals, high-centered, moderate fragrance; foliage soft; vigorous, upright, bushy growth; [seedling × Pink Puff]; int. in 1975; ADR, 1973

Luis Brinas HT, ob, 1934, Dot, Pedro; bud long, pointed; flowers rose-orange, large, dbl., cupped; foliage soft; vigorous growth; [Mme Butterfly × Federico Casas]; int. by C-P; Gold Medal, Portland, 1934, Gold Medal, Bagatelle, 1932

Luis Desamero Min, ly, 1989, Bennett, Dee; bud ovoid; flowers pastel yellow, medium, 28 petals, high-centered, borne usually singly and in sprays of 3-5, slight fruity fragrance; foliage medium size, medium green, semi-glossy; prickles straight and tapering, pale yellow, reddish base; upright, bushy, tall growth; hips globular, green-yellow-orange; PP7496; [Tiki × Baby Katie]; int. by Tiny Petals Nursery, 1988

Luisa HT, w, Tantau; flowers creamy white, pink blush on petals as they age, full; int. by Richard Huber AG, 2004

Luisa Fernanda da Silva HT, rb, 1946, Dot, Pedro; flowers reddish, passing to purplish and then yellowish-red, base yellow; foliage dark, glossy; vigorous growth

Luisa Fernanda de Silva – See **Luisa Fernanda da Silva**, HT

Luisa Stone S, Harkness, R.; int. in 1997

Luise Kiese – See **Frau Luise Kiese**, HT

Luise Kühnel HT, dy, 1937, Kühnel; flowers medium, dbl.

Luise Lilia HT, dr, 1912, Lambert, P.; flowers deep crimson, large, full, intense fragrance; moderate growth; [General MacArthur × Frau Peter Lambert]

Luisella Angelini HT, Dot, Simon; int. in 1980

Lullaby Pol, w, 1953, Shepherd; bud ovoid; flowers white, center flushed pink, 1½-2 in., 75 petals, cupped, borne in loose clusters; foliage dark, leathery; vigorous, bushy, compact growth; PP1495; [(*R. soulieana* × Mrs Joseph Hiess) × Mlle Cécile Brunner]; int. by Bosley Nursery

Lullaby F, dp, 1957, Bishop; flowers rich rose-pink, 3 in., semi-dbl., flat, camellia-like, borne in clusters (to 28); vigorous growth; int. by Baker's Nursery

Lulu HT, op, 1919, Easlea; bud very long, pointed, deep orange-red; flowers salmon-pink, large, 8 petals; foliage glossy; bushy, compact growth

Lulu F, ob, 1973, Kordes; flowers orange-pink, medium, dbl., high-centered; foliage glossy, dark, bronze; vigorous, upright, bushy growth; [Zorina × seedling]

Lulu HT, rb, Kordes; flowers cream, pink and red, medium, full, high-centered, borne singly and in sprays; int. by W. Kordes Söhne, 2002

Luluette Min, mp, 1986, Fischer, C.&H.; flowers small, single, borne singly and in small sprays; foliage small, medium green, semi-glossy; prickles small, straight, red; low, compact, tiny growth; [Fairy Moss × Fairy Moss]; int. by Alpenflora Gardens

Lumen HT, ob; flowers coral, tinted red, with yellow at base of petals, large, 35-40 petals, high-centered, moderate fragrance; foliage matte; int. by Sauvageot, 1973

Lumen HT, ab; flowers amber yellow, paler reverse, dbl.; recurrent; int. by Sauvageot, 1990

Lumière HT, yb, 1944, Mallerin, C.; flowers golden yellow suffused capucine-red, large; foliage dark, leathery; vigorous growth; int. by A. Meilland

Lumina F, or, 1955, Tantau, Math.; flowers orange-scarlet, 2½ in., 25 petals, rosette, borne in large tursses; foliage dark; vigorous growth; [Fanal × Alpine Glow]

Luminator Pol, dr, 1938, Smith, J.; flowers scarlet-crimson; vigorous growth; [sport of Lady Reading]; int. by Eddie

Luminion F, or, 1976, Kordes; bud globular; flowers 3 in., 34 petals, cupped, moderate fragrance; foliage glossy, dark; vigorous, upright, bushy growth; [Hurra × Peer Gynt]; int. by Frankreich, 1975

Luminosa HT, or, 1964, Mondial Roses; bud long, pointed; flowers vermilion, large, 52 petals, high-centered; foliage dark, glossy; strong stems; vigorous, upright, bushy growth

Luminosity HT, my, Williams, J. Ben; flowers dbl., some fragrance; growth to 4 ft.; int. by Hortico, Inc., 2005

Luminous Pol, or, 1932, deRuiter; flowers brilliant scarlet tinted orange, small, dbl., cupped; foliage small, light, wrinkled; dwarf growth; [sport of Gloria Mundi]; int. by J&P

Lum's Double White HT, w, 1930, Lum; flowers pure white, overlarge, semi-dbl., high-centered; foliage dark, leathery; vigorous growth; [sport of Killarney Double White]; int. by Totty

Luna HT, ly, 1918, Poulsen, S.; bud pointed; flowers pale yellow, large, dbl., high-centered; foliage dark; strong stems; very vigorous, bushy growth; [Harry Kirk × Sunburst]

Luna Park LCl, or, 1964, Croix, P.; flowers red shaded orange, large; recurrent bloom; vigorous, climbing growth; [Gladiator × seedling]

Luna Rossa HT, Delbard-Chabert

Lunds Jubiläum – See **Baby Blaze**, F

Lunelle HT, lp, 1955, Meilland, F.; buds apricot; flowers pale pink, very large, 50 petals, high-centered, intense fragrance; vigorous growth; [Young France × Signora]

Lupe's Buttons HMsk, w, 2006, Hulse, Merrill; bud apricot; flowers ivory, 1¾ in., single, borne in very large panicles, very mild fragrance; foliage medium size, medium green, semi-glossy; prickles small, dilated, brown, few; growth bushy, bushy with tall basal breaks, tall (3 ft.); landscape, fences; [unknown]; int. by Merrill Hulse, 2008

Lupo Kordana Min, dp, Kordes; flowers full; int. by W. Kordes Söhne

Luray F, mr, 1962, Masek, R. J.; flowers rose-red, 2-3 in., 40-45 petals, moderate fragrance; foliage leathery, glossy; vigorous, bushy growth; PP2088; [sport of Patty's Pink]; patent issued as Pol; int. by Carlton Rose Nurseries, 1958

Lusambo – See **Red Rock**, HT

Lusambo F, rb, Meilland; int. in 1998

Luscious HT, pb, Perry, Astor; flowers blend of magenta and amber, dbl., moderate fragrance; growth vigorous; int. in 2003

Luscious Lucy MinFl, m, 2004, Tucker, Robbie; flowers cream/yellow center reddish/mauve edges, reverse white and mauve, 2 in., dbl., borne mostly solitary, no fragrance; foliage dark green, semi-glossy; prickles few, tiny, straight; growth bushy, medium (30 in.); exhibition, cutting, garden; [Sam Trivitt × seedling]; int. by Rosemania, 2005

Lusiadas – See **Céline Forestier**, N

Lusitania HG, 1905, Cayeux; [Souv de Mme Léonie Viennot × unknown]

Lustige HT, rb, 1973, Kordes; bud ovoid; flowers copper-red, reverse yellow, large, dbl., cupped; foliage large, glossy, leathery; vigorous, upright growth; [Peace × Brandenburg]

Lustre HT, mp, 1926, E.G. Hill, Co.; flowers rose-pink, large, semi-dbl.; [Ophelia × Hoosier Beauty]; int. by Amling Bros.

Lustre d'Église HGal, mp, before 1790; flowers medium pink with lighter reverse, small, dbl., intense fragrance; from Holland

Lustrous – See **Celebrity**, HT, 1945

Lustrous Spirit – See **Kagayaku Seishin**, HT

Lutea – See ***R. banksiae lutea*** (Rehder)

Lutea Flora T, my, 1874, Touvais; flowers brilliant yellow, fading to white, large, full

Lutea Flore Pleno – See **Multiplex**, Misc OGR

Lutea Plena – See **Sulphurea**, HSpn

Lutea Simplex – See ***R. banksiae lutescens*** (Voss)

Luteola HFt, ly, before 1821; bud round; flowers pale yellow, single; repeats in autumn; foliage ovate, pointed, ribbed, dark green; prickles numerous, unequal

Lutescens Flavescens – See **Parks' Yellow Tea-Scented China**, T

Lutescens Simplex – See ***R. banksiae lutescens*** (Voss)

Lutetia HT, yb, 1961, deRuiter; flowers coppery yellow, medium, 28 petals; vigorous, upright growth; [The Optimist × Tudor]

Luther Russell F, op, 1956, Morse; flowers salmon, semi-dbl., borne several together; foliage olive-green; [sport of Korona]

Lutin – See **Rosey Gem**, Min

Lutin S, pb, Meilland; flowers bengal-rose, white eye, medium, semi-dbl., cupped, then flat, borne in clusters, moderate sharp fragrance; recurrent; foliage light green, glossy; upright (3-4 ft.) growth; int. in 1984

Luv Ya HT, lp, 1998, Muha, Julius; flowers soft apricot-pink, 4-4½ in., very dbl., borne mostly singly; foliage medium size, medium green, semi-glossy; prickles moderate; upright, 3-5 ft. growth; int. by Hortico, 1998

Luvvie Min, pb, 1980, Bennett, Dee; bud ovoid; flowers soft to deep coral pink, micro-mini, very small, 38 petals, high-centered; foliage small, deep green with red peduncle and petiole; prickles straight, thin, red; low, bushy growth; [Little Darling × Over the Rainbow]; int. by Tiny Petals Nursery, 1979

Luxembourg – See **Ferrugineux du Luxembourg**, M

Luxembourg – See **Pourpre du Luxembourg**, M
Luxembourg – See **Marie Adélaïde**, HT
Luxembourg, Climbing Cl HT, op, 1932, Wight; flowers pinkish orange, base deep yellow; very vigorous, climbing growth; [sport of Marie Adélaide]
Luxembourg – See **Fanny Blankers-Koen**, HT
Luxor HT, rb; flowers red with white reverse, 14 cm., 50 petals, high-centered, borne mostly singly, no fragrance; recurrent; prickles medium; stems long; florist rose; int. by deRuiter, 2004
Luxor HT, mp
Luxury HT, rb, 1968, Patterson; flowers light red, reverse white, large, dbl., high-centered; foliage soft; moderate growth; [seedling × Suspense]; int. by Patterson Roses
Lybelle LCl, mp, Noack, Werner; flowers large, dbl., borne in small clusters; int. in 1984
Lybie HT, yb, 1999, Hiltner, Martin; flowers yellow blend, reverse medium yellow, 4 in., dbl., borne in small clusters; foliage medium size, dark green, semi-glossy; few prickles; upright, medium (3 ft.) growth; [Lynn Anderson × ((Carefree Beauty × Picasso) × seedling)]
Lycoris HGal, pb, 1835, Vibert; flowers light rosy red spotted white, large, dbl., flat; sometimes classes as M
Lyda Rose S, w, Lettunich, Kleine; flowers white, edges brushed lavender pink, 2 in., 5 petals, borne in clusters, intense spicy fragrance; good repeat; growth spreading (4 × 4 ft.); [Francis E. Lester × unknown]; int. in 1994
Lydia HT, op, 1933, Verschuren; bud pointed; flowers bright orange-rose, large, very dbl.; foliage glossy; vigorous, bushy growth; [Briarcliff × Florex]; int. by H&S
Lydia HT, dy, 1949, Robinson, H.; bud long, pointed; flowers intense saffron-yellow, medium, very dbl., high-centered; foliage dark, leathery, glossy; vigorous, bushy growth; [Phyllis Gold × seedling]; int. by Baker's Nursery
Lydia S, ob, 1973, Kordes; bud ovoid; flowers deep orange, reverse yellow, medium, semi-dbl., cupped; foliage glossy, dark, leathery; very vigorous, upright, climbing growth; [seedling × Circus]
Lydia F, lp, Ilsink; int. in 1995
Lydia HT, op, Croix; int. by Roses Paul Croix
Lydia Grimm HT, ly, 1907, Geduldig; flowers large, dbl.; [(Général Jacqueminot × Mme Caroline Testout) × Kaiserin Auguste Viktoria]
Lydia Kordana Min, mp, Kordes; flowers strong pink, dbl., high-centered; int. by W. Kordes Söhne
Lydia Morris S, m
Lydie F, ob, Harkness; int. in 1993
Lykkefund LCl, w, 1930, Olsen; bud small, pink; flowers cream color, small, semi-dbl., borne in clusters of 10-20, intense fragrance; foliage small, dark, glossy; nearly thornless; vigorous growth; [seedling from *R. helenae*, Barbier's form, possibly crossed with Zéphirine Drouhin]
Lyle Barbour HT, Watt, Mrs B.; int. in 1970
Lyn Keppler S, lp, Taschner, Ludwig; int. by Ludwig's Roses, 2003
Lynda HT, Mondial Roses; int. in 1970
Lynda Hurst HT, mp, 1938, Clark, A.; flowers large, dbl.; vigorous growth; [Mme Abel Chatenay × seedling]; int. by NRS Victoria
Lyndarajha HT, Dorieux; int. in 1982
Lynette HT, w, 1985, Kordes, R.; bud long, pointed; flowers cream blended with coral pink, well-formed, large, dbl., borne singly or in clusters of up to 5, no fragrance; foliage dark; prickles straight, brown; tall, upright growth; [Clivia × MEItakilor]; int. by Ludwigs Roses Pty. Ltd., 1983
Lynette Joseph HT, mr, 2004, Poole, Lionel; flowers medium red, reverse medium red, 5 in., full, borne mostly solitary; foliage medium size, dark green, semi-glossy; prickles medium, triangular; growth bushy, vigorous, tall (45 in.); garden decoration, exhibition; [Naomi Rebecca × Adrienne Berman]; int. in 2005
Lynn Anderson HT, pb, 1993, Winchel, Joseph F.; flowers white edged deep pink, 5-5½ in., full, high-centered, borne mostly singly; foliage very large, medium green, matte; few prickles; tall (170-180 cm.), upright, bushy growth; PP9389; [seedling × Gold Medal]; int. by Weeks Roses, 1995
Lynn Anne Min, ob, 1980, Saville, F. Harmon; bud short, pointed; flowers orange-yellow blend, 38 petals, high-centered, borne singly and in large sprays, moderate fragrance; foliage medium; prickles long, thin; vigorous, upright, compact growth; PP4699; [Rise 'n' Shine × Sheri Anne]; int. by Nor'East Min. Roses, 1981
Lynne Elizabeth S, pb, 1999, Byrnes, Robert; flowers light pink, reverse medium pink, 4 in., dbl., borne mostly singly; foliage medium size, medium green, semi-glossy, disease-resistant; few prickles; spreading, bushy, medium (4½ ft.) growth; winter hardy; [Carefree Beauty × Carefree Beauty]; int. by Overbrooke Gardens, 1999
Lynne Gold Min, my, 1983, Moore, Ralph S.; flowers micro-mini, small, 20 petals; foliage small, medium green, semi-glossy; bushy, spreading growth; PP5742; [Ellen Poulsen × Yellow Jewel]; int. by Moore Min. Roses
Lynne's Gold F, yb, 2001, Everitt, Derrick; flowers deep yellow, red edgings to petals, medium, dbl., borne in small clusters, slight fragrance; foliage medium size, dark green, glossy; prickles medium, hooked, moderate; growth upright, bushy, medium (3-3½ ft.); garden decorative; [(Mary Sumner × (L'Oreal Trophy × Edith Holden)) × (Mary Sumner × ((Southampton × Korp) × Edith Holden))]
Lynnie S, mp, Rupert; flowers saturated dark pink fading to hot pink, semi-dbl., borne in clusters, slight fragrance; recurrent; prickles few to none; growth to 3 ft.; int. by Ashdown Roses, 2002
Lynn's Jubilee HT, pb, 2001, Hiltner, Martin J.; flowers light pink, aging to dark pink, 3½-4 in., dbl., high-centered, borne mostly solitary; foliage medium size, medium green, glossy; prickles -½ in., curved down, numerous; growth upright, medium (2½-3 ft.); garden decorative, exhibition; [Lynn Anderson × Silver Jubilee]
Lynn's Saint HT, w, 2002, Hiltner, Martin; flowers large, fading to solid white, 3½-4½ in., full, borne mostly solitary; foliage medium size, medium green, semi-glossy; prickles hooked down, moderate; growth upright, medium (3-4 ft.); decorative, exhibition; [Lynn Anderson × St. Patrick]; int. in 2003
Lyon Rambler HMult, dp, 1909, Dubreuil; flowers bright rose-pink, flushed carmine, medium, semi-dbl., borne in rounded clusters; foliage dark green, glossy; [Crimson Rambler × unknown]
Lyon Rose HT, op, 1907, Pernet-Ducher; flowers shrimp-pink, center coral-red shaded yellow, large, 44 petals; [Mme Mélanie Soupert × (Soleil d'Or × unknown)]; Gold Medal, Bagatelle, 1909
Lyon Rose, Climbing Cl HT, op, 1924, Ketten Bros.; flowers copper pink, illumined by yellow-gold; [sport of Lyon Rose]
Lyonfarbige Druschki HP, yb, 1928, Rosarium Sangerhausen; flowers yellowish-pink, large, dbl.; [Frau Karl Druschki × Lyon Rose]
Lyonnais HP, mp, 1872, Lacharme, F.; flowers large, dbl.; [Victor Verdier × unknown]
Lyre de Flore – See **Beauté Insurmontable**, HGal
Lyric S, mp, 1951, deRuiter; bud ovoid; flowers rose-pink, 28 petals, cupped, borne in large clusters, moderate fragrance; foliage leathery; vigorous (4 ft.), upright growth; good for hedge and border; [Sangerhausen × seedling]; int. by J&P
Lyrical F, pb, 1990, Jobson, Daniel J.; bud pointed; flowers salmon pink shading to cream at base, medium, 11 petals, flat, borne in sprays of 5-7, moderate spicy fragrance; foliage medium size, dark green, glossy, disease-resistant; prickles hooked downward, red; upright, bushy, low, winter-hardy growth; fruit not observed; [Snow White × Yesterday]; int. in 1989
Lys Assia F, mr, 1959, Kordes, R.; flowers deep orange-scarlet, 4 in., 20 petals, high-centered, borne in small clusters; foliage glossy; vigorous, upright, bushy growth; [Spartan × Hens Verschuren]; int. in 1958
Lysa HT, lp, RvS-Melle; [Windekind × Melglory]; int. in 1989
Lysbeth-Victoria F, lp, 1977, Harkness; flowers light shell-pink, 4½ in., 11 petals; foliage matte; growth moderate; [Pink Parfait × Nevada]; int. in 1978

M

M Boncenne – See **Mons Bonçenne**, HP

M. A. Keessen Pol, dp, 1923, Keessen; flowers darker; [sport of Ellen Poulsen]

M. A. Willett HT, op, 1960, Kernovske, V.R.; bud globular; flowers pink to salmon-pink, base coppery, large, dbl., moderate fragrance; foliage leathery; moderate, upright growth; [Picture × Tahiti]; int. by Langbecker, 1959

M. B. HT, rb, 1941, Brownell; flowers red shading to pink, overlaid orange and yellow, open, large, 25 petals; long stems; vigorous, compact, upright growth; [Dr. W. Van Fleet hybrid × Frau Karl Druschki hybrid]

M. Bunel – See **Mons Bunel**, HT

M. Geier HT, dp, 1929, Felberg-Leclerc; flowers fiery dark carmine, shaded darker, dbl.; [Augustus Hartmann × Admiral Ward]

M. H. Graire – See **Lady Zoë Brougham**, T

M. H. Walsh HP, mr, 1905, Dickson, A.; flowers carmine-red, large, dbl.

M. Kockel Pol, lp, 1926, Kockel; flowers small, dbl.

M. S. Hershey HT, dr, 1941, Coddington; bud long, pointed; flowers velvety crimson, 4-4½ in., 33 petals, cupped; bushy growth; [seedling × E.G. Hill]; int. by C-P

M.T. Ruby Sunday HT, dr, 2005, Poole, Lionel; flowers deep red, 4 in., full, borne in small clusters, moderate fragrance; foliage medium size, dark green, semi-glossy; prickles moderate, medium, slightly hooked, dark brown; growth bushy, medium (30 in.); garden decoration, beds, borders; [Raewyn Henry × Red Planet]; int. in 2006

Ma Capucine T, yb, 1871, Levet; bud pointed, small; flowers bronzy yellow, shaded red, fading to white, medium, dbl.; [Ophirie × *R. foetida*]

Ma Cherie HT, op, Teranishi; int. by Itami Rose Garden, 2002

Ma Fiancée HT, dr, 1922, Van Rossem; flowers dark crimson, often nearly black, dbl.; [(Gen. MacArthur × unknown) × Red-Letter Day]

Ma Fille HT, ob, 1962, Mallerin, C.; flowers orange, large, 45 petals; foliage glossy; vigorous, bushy, symmetrical growth; [Berthe Mallerin × seedling]; int. by EFR, 1960

Ma Mie HT, yb, 1955, Laperrière; flowers yellow, edge tinted pink, well-formed, very large, 50 petals; foliage bright green; very vigorous, upright growth; [Peace × seedling]; int. by EFR

Ma Pâquerette – See **Pâquerette**, Pol, 1875

Ma Perkins F, pb, 1952, Boerner; bud ovoid; flowers sparkling salmon shell-pink, large, 25 petals, cupped, moderate fragrance; foliage rich green, glossy; vigorous, bushy growth; [Red Radiance × Fashion]; int. by J&P

Ma Petite Andrée Pol, dr, 1898, Chauvry; flowers deep carmine red, large, dbl.

Ma Pivoine du Roi HGal, dp, 1810, Descemet; flowers bright pink, aging to red, shaded lighter, large, full

Ma Ponctuée M, pb, 1857, Guillot père; flowers rose, spotted white, medium, dbl.; recurrent bloom; moderate growth

Ma Ponctuée Semi-Double M, rb, 1850, Moreau & Robert; flowers red, striped, semi-dbl.

Ma Surprise S, w, 1872, Guillot et Fils; flowers white tinged salmon, large, dbl.; [probably *R. roxburghii* × *R. odorata*]

Ma Tulipe HT, mr, 1899, Bonnaire; flowers carmine-red, large, semi-dbl.

Maaike HT, pb

Maaseik HMsk, pb, 2000, Lens, Louis; flowers light pink, reverse white, yellow stamens, 4-5 cm., single, borne in large clusters, moderate fragrance; foliage large, bronze-green, semi-glossy; prickles moderate; growth spreading, medium (1-1½ m.); [(*R. multiflora adenocheata* × Ballerina) × Kathleen]; int. by Louis Lens N.V., 1994

Maaseik 750 – See **Maaseik**, HMsk

Mab Grimwade HT, yb, 1937, Clark, A.; flowers rich chrome, shaded yellow, center apricot, dbl.; [Souv. de Gustave Prat × unknown]; int. by NRS Victoria

Mabel Dot Min, or, 1966, Dot; flowers rose-coral, small, dbl., borne in clusters; foliage small, bronze; [Orient × Perla de Alcanada]; int. by Minier

Mabel Drew HT, w, 1911, Dickson, A.; flowers deep cream, center canary-yellow, dbl., borne in clusters; Gold Medal, NRS, 1910, Gold Medal, Bagatelle, 1913

Mabel Francis HT, my, 1943, Bees; flowers rose-pink, 5 in., 35-40 petals, moderate fragrance; foliage light green; free growth; [Leading Lady × Southport]

Mabel Jackson HT, ab, 1924, Easlea; flowers apricot and pink, dbl.; [Edith Part × Queen Mary]

Mabel Lynas HT, dr, 1926, McGredy; bud pointed; flowers crimson-scarlet, base yellow, large, dbl.; foliage glossy; strong stems; very vigorous, bushy growth; Gold Medal, NRS, 1924

Mabel Morrison HP, w, 1878, Broughton; flowers flesh-white, becoming pure white, sometimes tinged pink in autumn, 30 petals, cupped; seasonal bloom; stout, erect growth; [sport of Baronne Adolphe de Rothschild]

Mabel Morse HT, my, 1922, McGredy; bud pointed; flowers bright golden yellow, well-shaped, large, dbl.; foliage dark, bronze; bushy growth; Gold Medal, NRS, 1921

Mabel Morse, Climbing Cl HT, my, 1931, Moulden

Mabel Morse, Climbing Cl HT, my, 1932, Ley

Mabel Prentice HT, mp, 1923, Lippiatt; flowers clear rose-pink

Mabel Stewart LCl, dr, 1942, Clark; bud almost black; flowers velvety crimson, semi-single

Mabel Turner HT, pb, 1923, Dickson, H.; bud pointed; flowers blush, center and reverse rosy carmine, very large, high-centered; foliage olive-green; vigorous growth

Mabella – See **New Day**, HT

Mabella Kordana Min, my, Kordes; flowers full, exhibition; recurrent; int. by W. Kordes Söhne

Mabelle Stearns S, mp, 1938, Horvath; flowers peach-pink with silvery reflex, 55 petals, blooms in clusters, intense fragrance; recurrent bloom; foliage small, glossy, dark; to 2 ft., spreading (6-8 ft.) growth; hardy; [Mrs F.F. Prentiss × Souv. de Georges Pernet]; int. by Wayside Gardens Co.

Mable Dot Min, op, 1967, Dot; bud small, ovoid; flowers rose-coral, small, very dbl., open, borne several together and in clusters; foliage small, bright bronze green; no prickles; [Orient × Perle d'Alcanada]; int. by Minier, 1966

Mable Ringling F, mr, 2002, Mallory

Macabo – See **Astrid Lindgren**, S

Macartney Rose – See ***R. bracteata*** (Wendland)

Macbeth HT, dr, 1921, Bees; bud pointed; flowers deep crimson, shaded darker, large, dbl., high-centered; foliage dark, bronze; vigorous, bushy, compact growth; [Richmond × Admiral Ward]

MacFarlane's Own F, pb, Williams, J. Benjamin; flowers deep pink, ivory reverse, large, semi-dbl., flat, mass bloomer; int. by Hortico Inc., 1999

MacGregor's Damask – See **Joasine Hanet**, P

Macha Méril HT, rb, Adam; flowers red with white reverse, full, high-centered, intense fruity fragrance; int. in 2004; Plus Belle Rose de France, 2005

Machana Min, my, McGredy, Sam IV; int. in 1983

Macho Man HT, m, 1999, Perry, Astor; flowers lavender, medium, dbl., borne mostly singly, moderate fragrance; foliage medium size, medium green, dull; few prickles; bushy growth; int. by Certified Roses, 2000

Macmillan Nurse S, w, 1998, Beales, Peter; flowers white, 41-50 petals, borne in large clusters; foliage medium size, dark green, glossy; prickles moderate; compact, 3 ft growth; [Bonica × Maigold]; int. by Peter Beales Roses, 1998

Macrantha Rubicunda HGal, mr, before 1877; flowers light red, large, very dbl.

Macrophylla Scandens – See **Scandens**, Ayr

Macspice Min, m, 1983, McGredy, Sam IV; flowers small, semi-dbl.; foliage small, medium green, semi-glossy; spreading growth; [Anytime × Gartendirektor Otto Linne]

Maculata HSpn, w, before 1770; flowers blush white marbled with pink, small, semi-dbl.

Maculata – See **La Maculée**, HGal

Macy's Pride S, w, Lim; P. and Twomey; J.; bud lemon yellow, slim; flowers creamy white with a hint of pink as they age, 4-5 in., 22 petals, borne mostly in clusters of 3; recurrent; foliage red-trimmed, aging to semi-glossy, medium green.; prickles ½- ¾ cm., grey-purple; upright, bushy (5 ft.) growth; PP15574; [Graham Thomas × Carefree Beauty]; int. by Bailey Nurseries, 2003

Mada – See **Spectacular**, LCl

Madam President F, pb, 1976, McGredy, Sam IV; bud long, pointed; flowers blend of pink shades, 4 in., 70 petals, hybrid tea, slight fragrance; bushy growth; [seedling × Handel]; int. by Avenue Nursery, 1975

Madam Speaker – See **Bolchoï**, HT

Mme A. Bouchayer HT, op, 1927, Siret-Pernet; flowers shrimp-pink, base Indian yellow

Mme A. Chatain HT, 1940, Mallerin, C.

Mme A. Étienne T, dp, 1886, Bernaix; bud long; sepals long, pointed; flowers rosy pink with lighter center, large, full

Mme A. Galland HT, pb, 1928, Mallerin, C.; flowers rose-pink, shaded shrimp-pink, dbl.; [Pharisaer × (Constance × Unnamed Hybrid Tea)]; int. by Laperrière

Mme A. Labbey HP, pb, before 1885; flowers pink and lilac, medium or small, full

Mme A. Lerche HT, mp, 1928, Bernaix, P.; flowers China-rose shaded carmine, reverse silvery rose, dbl.; [Mme L. Hot × Mrs Henry Winnett]

Mme A. Meilland – See **Peace**, HT

Mme A. Meilland, Climbing – See **Peace, Climbing**, Cl HT

Mme A. Roure HT, yb, 1932, Lens; flowers brilliant chrome-yellow shaded salmon, to amaranth-red, dbl.; [Wilhelm Kordes × Mev. G.A. van Rossem]

Mme A. Schwaller HT, mp, 1886, Bernaix; flowers large, full

Mme Abel Chatenay HT, pb, 1895, Pernet-Ducher; bud pointed; flowers pale pink, center deeper, reverse carmine-pink, 3 in., dbl.; foliage bronze when young; [Dr. Grill × Victor Verdier]

Mme Abel Chatenay, Climbing Cl HT, pb, 1917, Page; flowers pale silvery pink, reverse dark salmon, 10-12 cm., full; [sport of Mme Abel Chatenay]; int. by Easlea

Mme Achille Fould T, yb, 1903, Lévêque; flowers yellow, shaded carmine rose and salmon, very large, dbl., globular

Mme Achille Villey HT, or, 1939, Colombier; flowers coral-red, tinted yellow, dbl.; foliage dark; very vigorous

Whisper HT, w, Dickson, 2003 *(photo: Dickson Nurseries Ltd.)*

Bicentenaire de Guillot S, dp, Roses Guillot, 2004

(photo: Roseraie Guillot)

Dany Hahn S, w, Roses Guillot, 2006

(photo: Roseraie Guillot)

Desiree S, pb, Clements, 2004

Kateryna S, mp, Clements, 1996

Louise Clements S, ob, Clements, 1996

Morning Has Broken S, my, Clements, 1996

Mardi Gras F, pb, Zary, 2007

(photo: Jackson & Perkins)

Pope John Paul II HT, w, Zary, 2007 *(photo: Jackson & Perkins)*

Veterans' Honor HT, mr, Zary, 1999

(photo: Jackson & Perkins)

Good 'n' Plenty S, pb, Zary, 2007 *(photo: Jackson & Perkins)*

Happy Chappy S, yb, Zary, 2007 *(photo: Jackson & Perkins)*

Snowcone S, w, Zary, 2007 *(photo: Jackson & Perkins)*

Spring Fever S, w, Zary, 2007 *(photo: Jackson & Perkins)*

Gebrüder Grimm F, ob, 2006 *(photo: W. Kordes Söhne)*

Lions-Rose F, w, 2006 *(photo: W. Kordes Söhne)*

Caramel Antike F, ab, 2005 *(photo: W. Kordes Söhne)*

Laguna LCL, dp, 2006 *(photo: W. Kordes Söhne)*

Iced Raspberry Min, rb, White, 2005 *(photo: Nor'East/Greenheart Farms)*

Mother Lode Min, yb, White, 2006 *(photo: Nor'East/Greenheart Farms)*

Pam Tillis MinFl, ab, Saville, 2004 *(photo: Nor'East/Greenheart Farms)*

Teddy Bear Min, r, Saville, 1990 *(photo: Nor'East/Greenheart Farms)*

Amazing Grace '07 HT, w, Chapman, 2007 *(photo: Ross Roses)*

Community Banquet HT, lp, Bell, 2007 *(photo: Ross Roses)*

Howard Florey F, ab, Thomson, 1998 *(photo: Ross Roses)*

Loreto Gold S, yb, Ross, 2007 *(photo: Ross Roses)*

Falling In Love HT, pb, Carruth, 2006 *(photo: Weeks Roses)*

Cicely P. Marks S, lp, Williams, 2007 *(photo: J. B. Williams & Assoc.)*

Expression HT, ob, Williams, 2006 *(photo: J. B. Williams & Assoc.)*

Double Feature Gr, m, Williams, 1976 *(photo: Cliff Orent)*

Misty Veil S, mp, Williams, 1999 *(photo: J. B. Williams & Assoc.)*

Alba Maxima A, w, before 1867

Alba Semi-Plena A, w, before 1754

Blanche de Belgique A, w, before 1848

Félicité Parmentier A, lp, Parmentier, before 1841

Amédée de Langlois B, m, Vigneron, 1872

Boule de Neige B, w, Lacharme, 1867

Mrs. Paul B, lp, Paul, 1891

Queen of Bedders B, dp, Noble, 1876

Blanchefleur C, w, Vibert, 1835

Centifolia Minima (Rouletii), Ch, mp, 1815

Fantin-Latour C, lp, origin unknown

Foliacée C, mp, from Holland, before 1808

La Noblesse C, mp, Pastoret, 1856

Reine des Centfeuilles C, mp, from Belgium, 1824

Belle di Monza Ch, mr, Villaresi/Noisette, about 1825

Bengale Animée Ch, mp, from England, before 1817

Green Rose Ch, w, Bambridge & Harrison, 1856

Hermosa Ch, lp, Marcheseau, 1834 or before

Le Vésuve Ch, pb, Laffay, 1825

Old Blush Ch, mp, 1751, introduced by Parsons

Celsiana D, lp, from Holland, before 1817

Coralie D, lp, before 1848

Léda D, w, Deschiens, 1826

Mme Zoëtmans D, w, Marest, 1830

Sheila's Perfume F, yb, Sheridan, 1982

(photo: Rich Baer)

Dainty Maid F, pb, LeGrice, 1940 *(photo: Marily Young)*

Pleasure F, mp, Warriner, 1989 *(photo: Jim Linman)*

Sexy Rexy F, mp, McGredy, 1985 *(photo: Jim Hockstaff)*

Playgirl F, mp, Moore, 1986 *(photo: Rich Baer)*

Playboy F, rb, Cocker, 1976 *(photo: Rich Baer)*

Blueberry Hill F, m, Carruth, 1999 *(photo: Rich Baer)*

French Lace F, w, Warriner, 1981 *(photo: Greg Sohrweide)*

Blairii #2 HCh, lp, Blair, 1845

Brennus HCh, dp, Laffay, 1830

De Candolle HCh, m, Calvert, about 1845

Gruss an Teplitz HCh, mr, Geschwind, 1894

Hofgärtner Kalb HCh, pb, Felberg-Leclerc, 1913

L'Ouche HCh, pb, Buatois, 1901

Antonine d'Ormois HGal, lp, Vibert, 1835

Belle Biblis HGal, m, Descemet, 1815

Ombrée Parfait HGal, m, Vibert, 1823

Tricolore de Flandres HGal, pb, 1846

Alain Blanchard HGal, m, Vibert, 1839

Buff Beauty HMsk, ab, Bentall, 1939

Cornelia HMsk, pb, Pemberton, 1925

Erfurt HMsk, pb, Kordes, 1939

Kathleen HMsk, lp, Pemberton, 1922

Nur Mahal HMsk, mr, Pemberton, 1923

Vanity HMsk, dp, Pemberton, 1920

Apple Blossom HMult, lp, Dawson, 1890

Veilchenblau HMult, m, Schmidt, 1909

Perle vom Wienerwald HMult, pb, Praskac, 1913

Enfant de France HP, lp, Lartay, 1860

Amedée Philibert HP, m, Lévêque, 1879

Baron Girod de l'Ain HP, rb, Reverchon, 1897

Bicolore Incomparable HP, pb, Touvais, 1861

Charles Lefèbvre HP, dr, Lacharme, 1861

Comte de Paris HP, dp, Verdier, 1864

Comtesse Henrietta Combes HP, pb, Schwartz, 1881

Duc de Marlborough HP, dr, Lévêque, 1884

Duchesse d'Ossuna HP, dp, Jamain, 1877

Archiduchesse Elisabeth d'Autriche HP, mp, Moreau et Robert, 1881

Mlle Berthe Lévêque HP, lp, Céchet père, 1865

Bessie Johnson HP, lp, Curtis, 1873

Champion of the World HP, mp, Woodhouse, 1894

Charlemagne HP, dp, Dorisy, 1836

Clio HP, lp, Paul, 1894

Eugène Verdier HP, m, Guillot fils, 1863

François Levet HP, dp, Levet, 1880

Général Stefanik HP, m, Böhm, 1933

Henri Coupé HP, mp, Barbier, 1916

Mme Alfred de Rougemont HP, lp, Lacharme, 1862

Mme Louis Lévêque HP, dp, Lévêque, 1873

Albert Edward S (HSpn), ly, Hillier, 1970

Double Pink HSpn, mp, from Scotland

William's Double Yellow HFt/HSpn, my, Williams, before 1819

Robbie Burns S (HSpn), lp, Austin, 1987

Single Red HSpn, rb, origin unknown

Stanwell Perpetual HSpn, w, Lee, before 1836

Marilyn Monroe HT, ab, Carruth, 2001 *(photo: Jim Linman)*

Signature HT, pb, Warriner, 1998 *(photo: Tom Foster)*

Commonwealth Glory HT, ab, Harkness, 1998 *(photo: Rich Baer)*

Dame de Coeur HT, mr, Lens, 1959

Louise Estes HT, pb, Winchel, 1991 *(photo: Rich Baer)*

St. Patrick HT, yb, Strickland, 1999 *(photo: Ron Shaw)*

Bride's Dream HT, lp, Kordes, 1985 *(photo: Rich Baer)*

Coral Fiesta HT, or, Dot, 1983 *(photo: Rich Baer)*

Kardinal HT, mr, Kordes, 1986 *(photo: Rich Baer)*

Keepsake HT, pb, Kordes, 1981 *(photo: Rich Baer)*

Crystalline HT, w, Christensen & Carruth, 1987 *(photo: Rich Baer)*

Dainty Bess HT, lp, Archer, 1925 *(photo: Rich Baer)*

Dolly Parton HT, or, Winchel, 1985 *(photo: Rich Baer)*

Dublin HT, mr, Perry, 1983 *(photo: Rich Baer)*

Elina HT, ly, Dickson, 1984 *(photo: Rich Baer)*

Folklore HT, ob, Kordes, 1976 *(photo: Rich Baer)*

Fragrant Cloud HT, or, Tantau, 1967 *(photo: Rich Baer)*

Hot Princess HT, dp, Tantau, 2000 *(photo: Rich Baer)*

Joyfulness HT, ab, Tantau, 1985 *(photo: Rich Baer)*

Lady X HT, m, Meilland, 1968 *(photo: Rich Baer)*

Stephens' Big Purple HT, m, Stephens, 1986 *(photo: Rich Baer)*

White Masterpiece HT, w, Boerner, 1969 *(photo: Rich Baer)*

Pristine HT, w, Warriner, 1977 *(photo: Rich Baer)*

Rina Hugo HT, dp, Dorieux, 1993 *(photo: Rich Baer)*

Sheer Bliss, w, Warriner, 1985 HT *(photo: Rich Baer)*

Sheer Elegance HT, op, Twomey, 1990 *(photo: Rich Baer)*

Touch of Class HT, op, Kriloff, 1985 *(photo: Rich Baer)*

Tropicana HT, or, Tantau, 1960 *(photo: Rich Baer)*

Lady Godiva HWich, lp, Paul, 1908

Auguste Gervais HWich

Excelsa HWich, ab, Barbier, 1918

Fragazeichen HWich, mp, Böttner, 1910

François Guillot HWich, w, Barbier, 1907

Fraulein Oktavia Hess HWich, ly, Hesse, 1910

Greta Fey HWich, lp, Strassheim, 1909

High Hopes LCl, mp, Harkness, 1994

Aschermittwoch LCl, w, Kordes, 1955

Hoffman von Falersleben LCl, rb, Lambert 1917

Lady Waterlow Cl HT, pb, Nabonnand, 1903

Mme Gregoire Staechelin LCl, pb, Dot, 1927

Shirpa LCl, op, Eve, 1976

Source d'Or LCl, yb, Turbat, 1913

My Sunshine Min, my, Bennett, 1986 *(photo: Susan McCarthy)*

Bees Kness Min, yb, Zary, 1998 *(photo: Robert Sutherland)*

Fairhope Min, ly, Taylor, 1989 *(photo: David Bossert)*

Child's Play Min, pb, Saville, 1991 *(photo: Nancy Baldwin)*

Emily Louise Min, dy, Harkness, 1990 *(photo: Rich Baer)*

Candy Cane Cl Min, pb, Moore, 1959

Dorothy Rose Min, or, Jones, 1998 *(photo: Steve Jones)*

Miss Flippins Min, mr, Tucker, 1997 *(photo: David Bossert)*

Hot Tamale Min, yb, Zary, 1993 *(photo: Tom Foster)*

Communis M, mp, before 1720

Crested Moss C, mp, Kirche/Roblin/Vibert, 1827

Goethe M, m, Lambert, 1911

Nuits de Young M, dr, Laffay, 1845

À Longs Pédoncle M, lp, Robert, 1854

Arthur Young M, m, Portemer fils, 1863

Duchesse de Verneuil M, pb, Portemer fils, 1856

Général Kléber M, mp, Robert, 1856

James Mitchell M, dp, Verdier, 1861

Le Loberd M, mp, origin unknown

Alister Stella Gray N, ly, Gray, 1894

Lamarque N, w, Maréchal, 1830

Duchesse d'Auerstädt N, my, Bernaix, 1888

Bouquet d'Or N, yb, Ducher, 1872

Céline Forestier N, ly, Trouillard, 1842

Chromatella N, ly, Coquereau, 1843

Jaune Desprez N, yb, Desprez, about 1830

Souv de Mme l'Advocat N, op, Veysset, 1899

William Allen Richardson N, yb, Ducher, 1878

Bernard P, op, 1836

Delambre P, dp, Moreau et Robert, 1863

Marbrée P, rb, Moreau et Robert, 1858

Marie de St. Jean P, w, Damaizin, 1869

Panachée de Lyon P, pb, Dubreuil, 1895

Quatre Saisons d'Italie P, dp, Dupont, before 1815

Relax S, or, Meilland, 1979

Cantabrigiensis S, ly, Cambridge Botanic Garden, 1935

Carminetta S, lp, Central Exp. Farm, 1923

Distant Drums S, m, Buck, 1985

Golden Wings S, ly, Shepherd, 1953

Abbotswood S, mp, Hilling, 1954

Agnes HRg, my, Saunders, 1900

Jens Munk HRg, mp, Svedja, 1977

Lady Penzance HEg, op, Penzance, 1894

Moje Hammarberg HRg, m, Hammarberg, 1931

Othello S, mr, Austin, 1991

R. albertii (Regel) Sp, w, 1877

R. banksiae banksiae (Aiton) Sp, w, 1807

R. banksiae lutescens (Voss) Sp, my, about 1816

R. bracteata (Wendland) Sp, w, 1793

R. britzensis (Koehne) Sp, lp, 1901

R. californica plena (Rehder) Sp, mp, 1894

R. corymbifera (Borkhausen) Sp, w, 1838

R. farreri persetosa (Stapf) Sp, mp, before 1900

R. fedtschenkoana (Regel) Sp, w, 1876

R. gallica officinalis (Thory) Sp, dp, before 1600

R. giraldii (Crépin) Sp, pb, 1867

R. hemsleyana (Täckholm) Sp, lp, 1904

R. horrida (Fischer) Sp, w, 1796

R. laevigata (Michaux) Sp, w, 1803

R. macounii (Greene) Sp, lp, before 1826

R. roxburghii (Trattinnick) Sp, mp, before 1814

R. rubiginosa (Linnaeus) Sp, lp, before 1551

R. sericea pteracantha (Franchet) Sp, w, 1890

Archiduc Joseph T, pb, Nabonnand, 1892

Catherine Mermet T, lp, Guillot et Fils, 1869

Clementina Carbonieri T, yb, Bonfiglio, 1913

Francis Dubreuil T, dr, Dubreuil, 1894

Général Schablikine T, op, Nabonnand, 1878

Grace Darling T, w, Bennett, 1885

Isabelle Nabonnand T, pb, nabonnand, 1875

Marie van Houtte T, pb, Ducher, 1871

Mme Antoine Mari T, pb, Mari, 1901

Mme de Tartas T, lp, Bernède, 1859

Papa Gontier T, pb, Nabonnand, 1883

Safrano T, ab, Beauregard, 1839

growth; [Charles P. Kilham × Mrs Aaron Ward]

Mme Ada Carmody T, w, 1898, Paul, W.; bud very long; flowers ivory white bordered with pink tints, center lightish yellow, large, full

Mme Adélaïde Côte HP, mr, 1882, Schmitt; flowers shining crimson with fire red, fading to dark brownish red, large, full, strong sweet fragrance; foliage dark green, glossy; growth compact, shrubby; [Senateur Vaisse × unknown]

Mme Adélaïde Ristori B, dp, 1861, Pradel; flowers cerise and fawn, full

Mme Adolphe Dahair – See **Mme Adolphe Dohair**, T

Mme Adolphe Dohair T, ly, 1900, Puyravaud; flowers white and cream, satiny, large, dbl., cupped, moderate fragrance; [Général Schablikine × Mlle Lazarine Poizeau]

Mme Adolphe Lafont HT, ab, 1921, Croibier; flowers deep apricot-red tinted buff, semi-dbl.; [sport of Joseph Hill]

Mme Adolphe Loiseau HT, lp, 1897, Buatois; flowers rosy flesh pink, aging to creamy white, very large, very full; nearly thornless; [Merveille de Lyon × Kaiserin Auguste Viktoria]

Mme Agathe Nabonnand T, lp, 1886, Nabonnand, G.; flowers rosy flesh tinted amber, petals shell-like, very large

Mme Albert Barbier HT, ob, 1925, Barbier; flowers salmon, tinted nankeen yellow, center darker, large, 50 petals, cupped; recurrent bloom; vigorous, bushy growth; [Frau Karl Druschki × unknown]; int. by Dreer

Mme Albert Bernardin T, w, 1904, Mari; flowers white, shaded with carmine, center yellow, medium, full; prickles small; [Comtesse de Frigneuse × Marie Van Houtte]

Mme Albert Gilles HT, op, 1934, Guillot, H.; flowers light coral-pink, very large, very dbl.; [Unnamed variety × Jean C.N. Forestier]; int. by Mallerin

Mme Alboni M, lp, 1850, Verdier, V.; flowers flesh pink, medium, full

Mme Alégatière Pol, dp, 1888, Alégatière; flowers carmine-pink, medium, dbl.; [Polyantha Alba Plena × Jules Margottin]

Mme Alexandre HT, rb, 1926, Walter, L.; flowers crimson-vermilion-red, shaded velvety purple, dbl.

Mme Alexandre Bernaix HT, pb, 1877, Guillot; flowers shining dark pink with China pink, edged white, large, full, globular, moderate fragrance; [La France × unknown]

Mme Alexandre Charvet HT, or, 1943, Meilland, F.; bud long, pointed; flowers orange-red, edged lilac, medium, dbl., cupped; foliage leathery; moderate growth; [Charles P. Kilham × (Charles P. Kilham × Mme Joseph Perraud)]; int. by A. Meilland

Mme Alexandre Dreux HT, my, 1921, Soupert & Notting; bud pointed; flowers golden yellow, large, dbl.; [Rayon d'Or × Primerose]

Mme Alexandre Jullien HP, lp, 1882, Vigneron; bud elongated; flowers light, satiny pink, large, full; quite remontant; foliage light green; numerous prickles; growth upright; [Elisabeth Vigneron × unknown]

Mme Alexandre Pommery HP, mp

Mme Alfred Carrière N, w, 1879, Schwartz, J.; bud pearly pink; flowers pale pinkish white, 10 cm., dbl., globular, borne in small clusters, intense fragrance; recurrent bloom; vigorous, climbing growth; Old Rose Hall of Fame, WFRS

Mme Alfred de Rougemont HP, lp, 1862, Lacharme, F.; flowers white tinted pink, medium, full, cupped, borne in small clusters, moderate fragrance; foliage light green; vigorous growth; [Mlle Blanche Lafitte × Sapho]; sometimes classed as B

Mme Alfred Digeon HT, my, 1911, Puyravaud; flowers lemon yellow tinted chamois, medium to large, slight fragrance; nearly thornless

Mme Alfred Leveau – See **Alfred Leveau**, HP

Mme Alfred Ponnier HT, w, 1920, Bernaix, P.

Mme Alfred Sabatier HT, rb, 1904, Bernaix; flowers satiny peach-red, fading when open, large; foliage dark green

Mme Alfred Schisselé HT, m, 1930, Leenders, M.; flowers lilac-white, center coppery orange, large, dbl.; foliage bronze; [Frau Felix Tonnar × Angèle Pernet]

Mme Alice Dureau HP, lp, 1867, Vigneron; flowers lilac pink, large, full

Mme Alice Garnier HWich, pb, 1906, Fauque; flowers bright rose, center yellow to light pink, 3-4 cm., full, borne in medium clusters, intense sweet fragrance; some autumn repeat; foliage dark, glossy; [*R. wichurana* × Mme Charles]

Mme Alphonse Lavallée – See **Marie Baumann**, HP

Mme Alphonse Seux HP, mp, 1887, Liabaud; flowers delicate pink, very large, full; foliage glaucous green; growth upright; [Victor Verdier × unknown]

Mme Alvarez del Campo HRg, pb, 1903, Gravereaux; flowers rosy flesh, tinted salmon, large, semi-dbl.; prickles few for its type, straight

Mme Amadieu T, pb, 1880, Pernet; flowers shining carmine-pink, centers white shaded carmine, very large, dbl., strong fragrance

Mme Amandinoli T, lp, 1881, Brassac; flowers flesh pink

Mme Ambroise Triollet HP, op, 1869, Moreau & Robert; flowers pink over salmon, large, full

Mme Ambroise Verschaffelt HP, dp, 1865, Verdier, E.; flowers deep pink, large, full

Mme Amélie Baltet HP, lp, 1878, Verdier, E.; flowers satiny delicate pink, silvery, large, full, cupped; foliage light green, rounded, regularly dentate; prickles few, short, slightly recurved, yellowish

Mme Anatole Leroy HP, lp, 1892, Levet

Mme Ancelot HRg, lp, 1901, Gravereaux & Müller; flowers whitish pink, large, full, moderate fragrance; prickles numerous, small, straight, unequal

Mme André Charmet HT, mp, 1921, Croibier; flowers carnation-pink, dbl.; [Mme Mélanie Soupert × Mme Maurice de Luze]

Mme André de Halloy HT, ob, 1929, Ketten Bros.; flowers orange, reverse salmon-pink, very dbl.; [Gloire de Hollande × Benedicte Seguin]

Mme André Dulin HT, op, 1959, Gaujard; flowers bright coppery pink, large, dbl.; vigorous, bushy growth; [Opera × Ville de Gand]

Mme André Duron HT, mr, 1887, Bonnaire; flowers clear light red, very large; growth upright

Mme André Gillier HT, rb, 1934, Reymond; bud pointed; flowers coppery red, shaded yellow, semi-dbl., cupped; [Padre × seedling]; int. by Vially

Mme André Leroy HP, mp, 1864, Trouillard; flowers salmon-rose, large, dbl.; vigorous growth

Mme André Saint HP, w, 1926, Barbier; flowers milk-white to pure white, center clear chamois, dbl.; prickles few thorns; stocky growth; [Frau Karl Druschki × Benedicte Seguin]

Mme Angèle Dispott HP, mr, 1879, Dauvesse; flowers fiery red, medium, full

Mme Angèle Favre HT, op, 1888, Perny; flowers pink and salmon

Mme Angèle Jacquier T, pb, 1879, Guillot; flowers bright pink, tinted coppery yellow, edged lighter, reverse dark pink, large, full; [Mme Damaizin × unknown]

Mme Angèle Jacquier T, pb, 1890, Veysset; flowers pink, striped

Mme Angélina B, my, 1844, Chanet; flowers nankeen yellow, center creamy, tinted salmon, medium, very full

Mme Angélique Veysset HT, pb, 1890, Veysset; flowers pink, striped with bright red, large, dbl.; recurrent; [sport of La France]

Mme Anna Bugnet HP, lp, 1866, Gonod; flowers large, full

Mme Anna de Besobrasoff HP, w, 1877, Nabonnand; flowers flesh white, striped pink, edged white, center tinted carmine, large, full, moderate fragrance

Mme Anna de Besobrasoff HP, mr, 1878, Gonod; flowers bright cherry red, aging to purple, large, full; [Charles Lefèbvre × unknown]

Mme Anna Moreau HP, lp, 1883, Moreau & Robert; flowers light pink, center lighter, edges and reverse white, very large, very full

Mme Anne Béluze B, mp, about 1840, Béluze; flowers bright pink aging to flesh pink, medium

Mme Annette Aynard HT, w, 1919, Leenders, M.; flowers milk-white edged pink, passing to amber-yellow, dbl.; [Mme Caroline Testout × Prince de Bulgarie]

Mme Anth. Kluis Pol, op, 1924, Kluis; flowers salmon-pink tinted orange, large, semi-dbl., borne in clusters; int. by Kluis & Koning

Mme Antoine Mari T, pb, 1901, Mari, A.; flowers rosy flesh, shaded lilac and rose, large, dbl.

Mme Antoine Montagne HT, lp, 1930, Richardier; flowers flesh-pink, with reflexes of old ivory

Mme Antoine Rébé T, rb, 1900, Laperrière; bud long; flowers bright red; [Alphonse Karr × Princesse de Sagan]

Mme Antoine Rivoire HP, lp, 1894, Liabaud; flowers delicate frosty pink with carmine reflections, very large, cupped; foliage light green; growth compact, erect

Mme Antonin Charvet HWich, lp, 1912, Girin; flowers silvery pink, edges lighter, large

Mme Antony Choquens T, pb, 1900, Bernais fils; flowers flesh pink, reverse apricot gold, large, full

Mme Apolline Foulon HP, pb, 1882, Vigneron; flowers light salmon, reverse touched with lilac, large, full; very remontant; few prickles; growth upright

Mme Armand Souzy HT, rb, 1945, Meilland, F.; flowers geranium-red and saffron-yellow, very large; [Charles P. Kilham × (Charles P. Kilham × Margaret McGredy)]

Mme Arsène Bonneau HP, mr, 1871, Bonnaire; flowers cherry red with white reflections

Mme Arthaud HT, ob, 1938, Mallerin, C.; flowers deep orange, large, very dbl.; vigorous growth; [Charles P. Kilham × (Kitchener of Khartoum × Mari Dot)]

Mme Arthur Oger Cl B, mp, 1899, Oger; flowers brilliant pink, very large, dbl.; very vigorous, climbing growth; [Mme Isaac Pereire × unknown]

Mme Arthur Robichon Pol, dp, 1912, Robichon; flowers carmine-pink, small, dbl.; [Mme Norbert Levavasseur × Mrs W. H. Cutbush]

Mme Aude B, m, 1839, Desprez; flowers lilac pink, large, full, globular

Mme Audot A, lp, 1844, Verdier, V.; flowers pale flesh, medium, full, cupped; growth branching

Mme Auguste Chatain HT, op, 1940, Mallerin, C.; bud very long; flowers coral-salmon, well-formed, large, dbl.; very vigorous growth; int. by A. Meilland; Gold Medal, Bagatelle, 1939

Mme Auguste Choutet LCl, ob, 1901, Godard; flowers orange-yellow, 7-9 cm., semi-dbl., borne in small clusters, intense tea fragrance; [William Allen Richardson × Kaiserin Auguste Viktoria]

Mme Auguste Nonin HWich, dp, 1914, Nonin; flowers deep shell-pink, center white, small, semi-dbl., cupped, borne in clusters of 20-30; foliage large, glossy; very vigorous, climbing (15-20 ft.), open growth; [Dorothy Perkins × Blush Rambler]

Mme Auguste Perrin N, lp, 1878, Schwartz; flowers pearly pink, reverse whitish to medium, 7 cm., very full, moderate damask fragrance; foliage olive green

Mme Auguste Rodrigues B, mp, 1897, Chauvry; flowers frosty pink, reverse silvery, 9 cm., very full, globular, borne in small clusters, moderate fragrance; non-recurrent; [Souv de Nemours × Max Singer]; sometimes classed as HMult

Mme Auguste Sommereau HT, lp, 1892, Corboeuf-Marsault; flowers flesh pink, aging white, large, full, globular, moderate fragrance

Mme Auguste van Geert HP, pb, 1861, Robichon; flowers deep rosy-pink, striped white, medium, full

Mme Augustine Hammond HT, mp, 1897, Vigneron; flowers clear satin-rose, lighter at edges, very large, dbl., globular; foliage light green

Mme Autrand HT, ob, 1922, Leenders, M.; flowers coppery orange, dbl.; [Mme Caroline Testout × Prince de Bulgarie]

Mme Azélie Imbert T, yb, 1870, Levet, F.; flowers yellow, tinted with salmon, large, full; [Mme Falcot × unknown]

Mme Badin T, pb, 1897, Croibier; flowers bright carmine pink, shaded violet, center coppery yellow, medium, full

Mme Ballu HRg, m, 1904, Gravereaux; flowers violet-pink, medium, semi-dbl.; foliage not rugose; prickles large, nearly straight, reddish

Mme Bardou Job HT, ly, 1913, Dubreuil; flowers canary-yellow, center chrome-yellow, large, semi-dbl., cupped; [Prince de Bulgarie × unknown]

Mme Barillet-Deschamps T, w, 1853, Bernède; flowers white, shaded yellow, large, full

Mme Barriot HP, dp, 1867, Damaizin; flowers carmine pink, large, full

Mme Barthélemy Levet T, ly, 1879, Levet, A.; flowers canary-yellow, large, full; foliage brilliant green; growth vigorous; [Gloire de Dijon × unknown]

Mme Baulot HP, mp, 1885, Lévêque; flowers bright pink nuanced carmine, large, dbl.; foliage glaucous green

Mme Bégault-Pigné HP, dp, 1906, Bégault-Pigné; flowers very large, full, moderate fragrance

Mme Bellenden Kerr HP, w, 1866, Guillot père

Mme Bellon HP, mp, 1871, Pernet père; flowers cerise pink, very large, full

Mme Bento Vidal HT, mr, about 1910, Cotrim; flowers velvety crimson, large, full; [sport of Étincelante]

Mme Bérard Cl T, ob, 1870, Levet, F.; bud long; flowers salmon-yellow shaded salmon-rose, 10-11 cm., dbl., cupped, moderate fragrance; [Mme Falcot × Gloire de Dijon]

Mme Berkeley T, pb, 1898, Bernaix fils; flowers salmon-pink, cerise and gold, moderate fragrance; recurrent

Mme Bernard T, yb, 1875, Levet; flowers copppery yellow, aging to flesh pink, large, full; [Mme Falcot × unknown]

Mme Bernède T, pb, 1856, Bernède; flowers coppery pink, large, full

Mme Bernutz HP, mp, 1873, Jamain; flowers satiny pink, very large, full, cupped

Mme Bertha Mackart HP, mp, 1883, Verdier, E.; flowers bright carmine pink, reverse silvery, very large, full, cupped, globular; foliage oblong, dark green, regularly and deeply toothed; prickles long, straight, unequal, very sharp; growth upright

Mme Berthe de Forge HT, op, 1935, Chambard, C.; flowers orange-coral, tinted coppery salmon, very large, cupped; foliage bronze

Mme Berthe Fontaine HP, mp, 1898, Buatois; flowers bright pink, very large, very full, moderate fragrance; [Luciole × Cl. Jaquet]

Mme Bessemer HT, op, 1898, Conard & Jones; flowers peachy-pink, large, very full

Mme Betty Hendlé HP, dr, 1892, Boutigny, P.; flowers velvety red, shaded darker, large, full; [Mme Victor Verdier × Abel Carrière]

Mme Bijou HP, dr, 1886, Chauvry; flowers velvety red, shaded chestnut brown, reverse marbled violet, large, full

Mme Blachet T, mp, 1859, Boyau

Mme Blondel HT, mp, 1899, Veysset; flowers bright pink with silvery edge, very large, dbl., moderate fragrance; [La France de '89 × unknown]

Mme Blytha Pearkes HT, ab, 1970, Blakeney; flowers light apricot flushed yellow and pink, medium, dbl.; bushy, compact growth; [Karl Herbst × Lady Hillingdon]; int. by Eddie

Mme Boll HP, dp, 1843, Boll, Daniel; flowers carmine-rose, large; recurrent bloom; foliage 5 leaflets per leaf; vigorous growth; two parentages given: HP × Belle Fabert, or Baronne Prévost × Portlandica; int. by Boyau, 1859

Mme Bollaert HT, rb, 1938, Chambard, C.; bud long, coppery red; flowers carmine, shaded nasturtium-red, very large, dbl., cupped; strong stems; very vigorous, bushy growth; [Ami F. Mayery × seedling]

Madame Bollinger F, op, 1973, McGredy, Sam IV; flowers deep orange-salmon, 3 in., 25 petals, high-centered; free growth; [(Little Darling × Goldilocks) × Bobbie Lucas]; int. by McGredy & Son, 1972

Mme Bollinger F, rb, McGredy, Sam IV; flowers coppery red with dark yellow, medium, semi-dbl.; int. in 1972

Mme Bonnet-Aymard T, w, 1874, Pernet; flowers pure white, center yellow, medium, full

Mme Bonnet des Claustres T, w, 1891, Reboul; flowers creme, center light yellow, very large, full

Mme Bonnin HP, op, 1877, Cochet; flowers bright silvery-salmon pink, large, very full; foliage dark green; few prickles

Mme Bory d'Arnex HT, op, 1907, Soupert & Notting; flowers coral-red, center flesh, large; [Laure Wattine × Antoine Rivoire]

Mme Boutin – See **Christina Nilsson**, HP

Mme Bovary S, m, Delbard; flowers mauve pink with lighter reverse, large, dbl., rounded, intense floral and fruity fragrance; growth to 50-100 cm.; int. by Georges Delbard SA, 2002

Mme Bravy T, w, 1846, Guillot Père; flowers creamy white shaded blush, dbl.

Mme Bréon Ch, dp, 1841, Verdier, V.; flowers carmine pink, shaded scarlet-salmon, large, full

Mme Briançon HP, rb, 1862, Fontaine; flowers carmine, shaded scarlet, large, full

Mme Brosse HP, mr, 1886, Brosse; flowers poppy red, large, full

Mme Bruel – See **Mme François Bruel**, HP

Mme Brunner N, ly, 1890, Brunner; flowers pale yellow; [sport of Aimée Vibert]

Mme Bruno Coquatrix Gr, or, Pineau

Mme Bruny HP, m, 1858, Avoux & Crozy; flowers flesh-white, shaded lilac, large, full, globular

Mme Bureau HCh, w, before 1846; flowers white, centers straw yellow, large, very full, moderate fragrance

Mme Butterfly HT, lp, 1918, Hill, E.G.; flowers light creamy pink, tinted gold, well-formed, 30 petals; growth vigorous, well branched; [sport of Ophelia]

Mme Butterfly, Climbing Cl HT, lp, 1926, Smith, E.P.; flowers yellowish-pink, large, full; [sport of Mme Butterfly]

Mme Byrne N, w, 1840, Buist; flowers cream color, center rose, large, dbl.; [Lamarque × unknown]

Mme C. Chambard HT, lp, 1911, Chambard, C.; flowers rosy flesh-pink, shaded salmon, base yellow, very large, 72 petals, moderate fragrance; [Frau Karl Druschki × Prince de Bulgarie, or Lady Ashtown]

Mme C. Liger – See **Mme C. Ligier**, T

Mme C. Ligier T, pb, 1900, Berland; bud round, very large; flowers pink with darker red, large, very dbl., intense fragrance

Mme C. P. Strassheim T, my, 1897, Soupert & Notting; flowers yellowish-white to sulphur-yellow, large, full, intense fragrance; foliage coppery-red, glossy; growth vigorous; [Mlle Adèle Jougant × Mme la Princesse de Bessaraba de Brancovan]

Mme C. Richardier HT, my, 1924, Richardier; flowers yellow, passing to clear yellow, dbl.

Mme Cadeau-Ramey HT, op, 1896, Pernet-Ducher; flowers deep flesh pink, center shaded yellow, edged carmine pink, large, full, moderate fragrance

Mme Caillat HP, mr, 1861, Verdier, E.; flowers shining cherry red, large, full

Mme Calot B, dp, 1850, Miellez

Mme Camille T, lp, 1871, Guillot et Fils; flowers aurora-pink, veined, with white reflections, well-formed, large, dbl.

Mme Camille Laurens HT, or, 1956, Dorieux; flowers crimson-red tinted orange, well-formed; foliage bright green; strong stems; [Peace × Happiness]; int. by Pin

Mme Campbell d'Islay – See **Triomphe de Valenciennes**, HP

Mme Caradori-Allan HMult, lp, 1843, Feast; flowers shining light pink, medium, dbl

Mme Caristie Martel HT, ly, 1916, Pernet-Ducher; flowers pure sulfur-yellow, center deeper, 5-6 in., full, globular; Gold Medal, Bagatelle, 1917

Mme Carle HT, mr, 1888, Bernaix; flowers bright cherry red, edged carmine pink, medium, full

Mme Carnot N, yb, 1889, Moreau et Robert; flowers golden yellow tinged orange, center darker, large, very dbl., globular; vigorous, climbing growth; [William Allen Richardson × unknown]

Mme Caro T, yb, 1880, Levet; flowers salmon-yellow, medium, very full; foliage dark green, purplish beneath; growth weak; [Gloire de Dijon × unknown]

Mme Caroline Küster N, yb, 1872, Pernet; flowers yellow and orange blend, medium, dbl.; [Le Pactole × unknown]

Mme Caroline Schmitt N, yb, 1878, Schmitt; flowers salmon-yellow, medium to large, dbl.; recurrent bloom; [Solfaterre × unknown]

Mme Caroline Testout HT, mp, 1890, Pernet-Ducher; bud pointed; flowers bright satiny rose, center darker, edged soft carmine-pink, very large, dbl., moderate fragrance; foliage rich green, soft; vigorous, bushy growth; [Mme de Tartas × Lady Mary Fitzwilliam]

Mme Caroline Testout, Climbing Cl HT, mp, 1901, Chauvry; flowers satin pink with a deeper center, large, dbl., moderate fragrance; [sport of Mme Caroline Testout]

Mme Carré D, w, before 1885; flowers flesh white, medium, full

Mme Casimir Moullé – See **Casimir Moullé**, HWich

Mme Catherine Fontaine T, dp, 1892, Liabaud; flowers dark rose pink over cream, streaked darker pink, semi-dbl.; [Marie van Houtte × unknown]

Mme Ceccaldi HT, op, 1938, Chambard, C.; bud long; flowers salmon-carmine-pink, shaded vermilion, very large, dbl.; strong stems; very vigorous growth; [Soeur Thérèse × seedling]

Mme Cécile Berthod T, dy, 1871, Guillot; flowers sulfur-gold, reverse yellowish-white, medium to large, very full, slight fragrance

Mme Cécile Brünner – See **Mlle Cécile Brünner**, Pol

Mme Cécile Brünner, Climbing – See **Mlle Cécile Brünner, Climbing**, Cl Pol

Mme Cécile Morand HP, dr, 1890, Corboeuf; flowers deep carmine red, reverse slightly silvery, large, very full

Mme Cécile Piètre HP, mr, 1909, Denis; flowers rose red, shaded vermilion, large, full

Mme Céline Noirey T, lp, 1868, Guillot et Fils; flowers soft pink, reverse purple, large, very dbl.

Mme Céline Touvais HP, mp, 1859, Touvais; flowers bright pink, dbl., peony-shape

Mme Céphalie Laurent HP, mp, 1894, Boutigny, P.

Mme César Brunier HP, mp, 1887, Bernaix, A.; bud oval, long; flowers China pink, satiny, center petals muddled, very dbl., moderate centifolia fragrance; prickles numerous, unequal; growth upright

Mme Chaban Delmas HT, mr, 1957, Privat; flowers bright red, well-formed, large; foliage bright green

Mme Chabanne Cl T, yb, 1896, Liabaud; flowers canary yellow, outermost petals cream white, medium to large, full, cupped

Mme Chamouton-Murgue HT, op, 1925, Chambard, C.; flowers orange-carmine, shaded vermilion, very large, dbl., cupped; foliage dark; vigorous, erect, branching growth; [seedling × Mrs Edward Powell]

Mme Charles T, yb, 1864, Damaizin; flowers yellow, center salmon, large, full, semi-globular; [Mme Damaizin × unknown]

Mme Charles Allizon HT, w, 1928, Schwartz, A.; flowers rosy white, edges tinted yellow, dbl.; [Mme Vittoria Gagniere × Lady Pirrie]

Mme Charles Baltet B, lp, 1865, Verdier, E.; flowers delicate pink, large, very full, borne in clusters of 4-6; [Louise Odier × unknown]

Mme Charles Boutmy HT, lp, 1892, Vigneron; flowers light flesh pink, very large, full, cupped

Mme Charles Chapelet – See **Mme Charles Crapelet**, HP

Mme Charles Crapelet HP, pb, 1859, Fontaine; flowers cerise, frosted and veined with lilac, large, full, moderate fragrance; foliage large, rugose; prickles numerous, small, unequal

Mme Charles Damé HP, lp, 1904, Damé; flowers fresh light pink, large, full

Mme Charles de Lapisse – See **Charles de Lapisse**, HT

Mme Charles de Luze HT, w, 1903, Pernet-Ducher; flowers flesh white, center chamois-yellow, very large, full, globular, moderate fragrance

Mme Charles Détreaux B, mr, 1895, Vigneron; flowers bright carmine-red, large

Mme Charles Druschki – See **Frau Karl Druschki**, HP

Mme Charles Dubreuil HT, pb, 1911, Guillot, P.; flowers salmon-rose, reverse shaded carmine, dbl.; [sport of Pharisaer]

Mme Charles Frédéric Worth HRg, dp, 1889, Schwartz, Vve.; flowers rosy carmine, fading, large, semi-dbl., borne in large clusters, moderate fragrance; profuse early bloom, but sparse in summer and fall; foliage glossy, rugose; vigorous growth

Mme Charles Guillaud HT, op, 1943, Mallerin, C.; flowers orange-pink with fiery tints

Mme Charles Guillot HT, pb, 1943, Mallerin, C.; flowers carmine-pink and orange, large, dbl.

Mme Charles Haas HT, w, 1930, Ketten Bros.; flowers amber-white, tinted flesh-white, large, 60-70 petals, high-centered, moderate fragrance; foliage leathery; vigorous, free branching growth; [Mme Abel Chatenay × Golden Emblem]

Mme Charles Joly HT, op, 1942, Chambard, C.; flowers bright salmon shaded coppery yellow

Mme Charles Lejeune HWich, lp, 1924, Vandevelde; flowers soft pink, 7-8 cm., full, borne in small clusters, moderate fragrance; foliage glossy; [Dr W. Van Fleet × La Perle]

Mme Charles Levet T, op, 1870, Levet; flowers salmon pink

Mme Charles Lutaud HT, yb, 1912, Pernet-Ducher; flowers chrome-yellow, blending to rosy scarlet at edge, dbl.; [seedling × Marquise de Sinéty]; Gold Medal, Bagatelle, 1913

Mme Charles Lutaud, Climbing Cl HT, yb, 1922, Guillot, P.

Mme Charles Magny HT, rb, 1941, Gaujard; flowers coppery red and golden yellow, very large, very dbl., cupped; vigorous, bushy growth; [Mme Joseph Perraud × seedling]

Mme Charles Mallerin HT, ob, 1939, Mallerin, C.; flowers orange-salmon, large, dbl., cupped; foliage leathery, dark; vigorous growth; [Lucy Nicolas × Brazier]; int. by C-P

Mme Charles Meurice HP, dr, 1878, Meurice; flowers velvety dark red, well-formed, large, dbl.; bushy growth

Mme Charles Monnier HT, op, 1901, Monnier/Pernet-Ducher; flowers flesh pink, center orange with golden salmon, very large, very full, globular

Mme Charles Montigny HP, mr, 1900, Corboeuf-Marsault; flowers blackish red, nuanced flame, large, full; [Prince Camille de Rohan × Éclair]

Mme Charles Rouveure HT, dy, 1946, Mallerin, C.; flowers 4-5 in., 36 petals, moderate fruity fragrance; foliage dark; free growth; int. by A. Meilland

Mme Charles Roy HP, mp, 1862; flowers rose pink, edges silky

Mme Charles Salleron M, mr, 1867, Fontaine; flowers carmine shaded fiery red, large, full; some repeat

Mme Charles Sauvage HT, yb, 1949, Mallerin, C.; flowers yellow tinted saffron, center orange-yellow, well-shaped, 5 in., 30 petals; bushy growth; [Julien Potin × Orange Nassau]; int. by URS

Mme Charles Singer T, dp, 1916, Nabonnand, C.; flowers garnet, becoming dark velvety purple-garnet, large, dbl.; vigorous growth

Mme Charles Truffaut HP, lp, 1878, Verdier, E.; flowers satiny rose, large; foliage light green, oblong, regularly dentate; prickles straight, pointed; growth vigorous, upright

Mme Charles Verdier HP, mp, 1863, Lacharme; flowers rosy pink, large, full, globular, moderate fragrance

Mme Charles Wood HP, mr, 1861, Verdier, E.; flowers fiery scarlet, large, 45 petals; moderate growth

Mme Charles Yojerot HMult, mr, 1933, Thebault-Lebreton; flowers large, single

Mme Charlet T, yb, 1856, Corbie; flowers nankeen yellow, center salmon pink, large, semi-dbl.

Mme Chaté HP, rb, 1871, Fontaine; flowers cherry red, blended with white, large, full

Mme Chatelaine de Lullier HT, Meilland, L.; int. in 1987

Mme Chauvel HP, dp, 1855, Chauvel; flowers dark pink, aging to flesh pink, reverse light pink, large, full

Mme Chauvry N, yb, 1886, Bonnaire; flowers nankeen yellow, shaded copper-yellow, reverse China pink, 4½ in., full; foliage large, glossy, dark green; [Mme Bérard × William Allen Richardson]; sometimes classed as T

Mme Chavaret T, yb, 1872, Levet; flowers apricot with nankeen-yellow, shaded salmon and white, large, very full, globular, moderate fragrance; [Mme Damaizin × unknown]

Mme Chédane-Guinoisseau T, ly, 1880, Lévêque; bud pointed; flowers sulphur yellow, large, full; foliage glossy; [seedling or sport of Safrano]

Mme Cheine Duguy HT, pb, 1929, Schwartz, A.; flowers cerise-red, shaded scarlet, dbl.

Mme Chevalier B, mp, 1886, Pernet père; flowers bright pink, large, dbl.; growth upright

Mme Chiang Kai-shek HT, ly, 1942, Duehrsen; bud long, pointed; flowers lemon yellow, turning lighter, 5-5½ in., 27 petals, exhibition, moderate fragrance; foliage leathery, glossy, dark; vigorous, upright, compact growth; [Joanna Hill × Sir Henry Segrave]; int. by H&S

Mme Chirard HP, mp, 1867, Pernet père; flowers rose, tinged with vermilion, large, full, globular, moderate fragrance

Mme Claire Jaubert T, yb, 1887, Nabonnand; flowers brick yellow, shaded to rose pink, imbricated, very large, semi-dbl.

Mme Clara d'Arcis HT, pb, 1931, Gaujard; flowers brilliant rose-pink, base yellow, large, dbl., moderate spicy fragrance; foliage dark, leathery; [Julien Potin × seedling]; int. by C-P

Mme Claude Olivier HT, op, 1939, Mallerin, C.; bud long, pointed; flowers coral, tinted nasturtium-yellow, very large, dbl., high-centered; foliage leathery; strong stems; very vigorous, bushy growth; [Soeur Thérèse × *R. foetida bicolor* seedling]; int. by A. Meilland

Mme Clémence Beauregard M, mp, 1851, Laffay; flowers crimson, shaded lilac, large, dbl.

Mme Clémence Joigneaux HP, pb, 1861, Liabaud; flowers pink and red, very large, dbl.; foliage large, dark green, regularly serrated; numerous prickles; growth upright

Mme Clémence Marchix T, rb, 1899, Bernaix, P.; bud deep cherry red, ovoid; flowers crimson and rose, cupped

Mme Clément Massier N, mp, 1884, Nabonnand; flowers bright pink, petal edges lighter, medium to large, very full

Mme Clert HP, op, 1868, Gonod; flowers salmon-rose, large, full

Mme Clorinde Leblond HP, dr, 1870, Dauvesse; flowers velvety garnet, medium, dbl.

Mme Clothilde Perrault B, dp, 1863, Vigneron; flowers dark pink, becoming light red, medium to large, full

Mme Cochet-Cochet HT, op, 1934, Mallerin, C.; bud very long; flowers coppery rose-pink, tinted coral, large, 30 petals, cupped, moderate fragrance; foliage glossy; vigorous growth; [Mrs Pierre S. duPont × Cécile Walter]; int. by C-P; Gold Medal, Bagatelle, 1932

Mme Colette Martinet HT, yb, 1915, Pernet-Ducher; flowers old-gold shaded orange-yellow, dbl.

Mme Collet B, lp, 1864, Liabaud; flowers whitish pink, medium

Mme Collet HP, pb, 1864, Liabaud; flowers dark carmine-pink with salmon, large, full

Mme Comtesse B, lp, 1857, Margottin; flowers bright flesh pink, medium, full

Mme Constans HWich, lp, 1902, Gravereaux; flowers medium pink, aging to light pink, 6 cm., very dbl., borne in small clusters, no fragrance; foliage light green

Mme Constant David HP, mr, 1909, Boutigny; bud long; flowers grenadine red with velvety vermilion, 5 in., full; foliage dark green; prickles long

Mme Constant Soupert T, yb, 1905, Soupert & Notting; bud long, pointed, upright, deep golden yellow; flowers yellow shaded peach, large, very full; foliage dark green, deeply serrated; [Souv. de Pierre Notting × Duchesse Marie Salviati]

Mme Consuelo Brignone HT, w, Croix, D.; flowers silky white with pink blush, slight fragrance; recurrent; foliage disease-resistant; robust growth; int. by Roseraie Paul Croix, 2006

Mme Corboeuf HT, mr, 1895, Corboeuf; flowers

velvety scarlet, large, semi-dbl.; [Reine Marie Henriette × General Jacqueminot]

Mme Cordier HP, m, 1903, Leroy; flowers bright lilac-pink, large, dbl.

Mme Cornélissen B, lp, 1865, Cornélissen; flowers white with blush-pink and yellow center, large, very dbl., moderate fragrance; [sport of Souv de la Malmaison]

Mme Couibes HT, ab, 1938, Meilland, F.; flowers salmon, center apricot, edged lighter, passing to golden coral, dbl.; foliage fresh green; long stems; vigorous, bushy growth; [Charles P. Kilham × Rochefort]

Mme Cousin B, dp, 1849, Margottin; flowers silky dark pink, large, full

Mme Couturier-Mention – See **Cramoisi Supérieur, Climbing**, Cl Ch

Mme Crespin HP, m, 1862, Damaizin; flowers rose shaded violet

Mme Creux T, op, 1890, Godard; flowers light salmon-pink, 13-15 cm., dbl., moderate tea fragrance

Mme Creyton HP, rb, 1868, Gonod; flowers crimson, shaded rose pink, large, full

Mme Croibier – See **Mme J. B. Croibier**, HT

Mme Crombez T, op, 1888, Nabonnand, G.; flowers rosy buff tinted bronze, well-formed, very large, dbl., moderate fragrance

Mme Crosy – See **Mme Crozy**, HP

Mme Crozy HP, mp, 1881, Levet; flowers rose pink, large; foliage dark green; prickles very pointed

Mme Cunisset Carnot HT, op, 1900, Buatois; bud very long; flowers salmony carnation pink, medium, borne mostly solitary

Mme Cusin T, rb, 1881, Guillot et Fils; flowers crimson, center yellowish-white, well-formed, medium, dbl.; foliage light green, small

Mme Dailleux HT, pb, 1901, Buatois; flowers salmon pink with dark yellow, large, dbl.; [Victor Verdier × Dr. Grill]

Mme Damaizin T, w, 1858, Damaizin; flowers creamy white shaded salmon, poorly formed, very large, dbl.; [probably Caroline × Safrano]

Mme Damême HP, pb, 1842, Cochet; flowers lilac pink, shaded bright pink, large, full

Mme d'Arblay HMult, w, about 1835, Wells or Waldstein; flowers soft flesh changing to white, 2½-3 cm., semi-dbl., cupped, borne in large conical clusters, moderate musk fragrance; [*R. moschata* × *R. multiflora*]

Mme Daurel HP, rb, 1884, Bernède; flowers red, tinted violet, large, full, cupped

Mme David T, lp, 1895, Pernet Père; flowers pale flesh, center darker, medium, very dbl., flat, moderate fragrance

Mme de Beauvoire HT, lp, 1922, Schwartz, A.; flowers pinkish white, center pale pink, dbl.; [Mme Vittoria Gagniere × Lady Ashtown]

Mme de Cambacérès – See **Duchesse de Cambacérès**, HP

Mme de Canrobert HP, m, 1862, Liabaud; flowers bluish-lilac, large, full

Mme de Canrobert HP, mr, 1868, Gonichon; flowers shining crimson, medium, very full

Mme de Carbuccia HT, mr, 1941, Kriloff; bud long, pointed; flowers bright crimson-red, medium, dbl.; foliage leathery; very vigorous, upright growth; [Admiral Ward × Mme Méha Sabatier]; int. by A. Meilland

Mme de Chalonges – See **Le Pactole**, T

Mme de Knorr – See **Mme Knorr**, P

Mme de la Boulaye HP, op, 1877, Liabaud; flowers salmon pink, centers bright pink, large, full, cupped

Mme de la Rôchelambert M, m, 1851, Robert; flowers dark reddish-purple, 7-8 cm., dbl., globular; moderate growth

Mme de Lamoricière HP, pb, 1849, Portemer; flowers bright pink, reverse white, medium, full

Mme de Loeben-Sels HT, w, 1879, Soupert & Notting; flowers silvery white, nuanced salmon/dawn/gold, large, very full, flat

Mme de Loisy T, op, 1901, Buatois; flowers salmon pink, shaded carmine, large, full

Mme de Plantamour HRg, m; int. before 1900

Mme de Pompadour HT, rb, 1945, Gaujard; flowers coppery red and bright yellow, medium, dbl., globular, borne on short stems; foliage dark, glossy; vigorous, bushy growth

Mme de Ridder HP, dr, 1871, Margottin; flowers dark shaded crimson, touched with violet, large, full, globular, moderate fragrance

Mme de Rohan – See **Mme Bureau**, HCh

Mme de St Fulgent HP, dr, 1872, Gautreau; flowers velvety slate-red, medium, full

Mme de St Joseph T, lp, 1846; flowers fawn shaded salmon, large, dbl., intense fragrance; moderate growth

Mme de Sancy de Parabère – See **Mme Sancy de Parabère**, Bslt

Mme de Sansal P, mr, about 1850, de Sansal; flowers cherry red

Mme de Selve HP, mr, 1886, Bernède; flowers bright red with lilac reflections, very large; [Monsieur Fillion × unknown]

Mme de Sertot – See **Mme Bravy**, T

Mme de Serval HP, rb, 1854, Desprez; flowers cherry red, shaded salmon, medium, full

Mme de Sévigné B, pb, 1874, Moreau et Robert; flowers bright rose in center, edges lighter, large, dbl., borne in small clusters; vigorous growth

Mme de Sevigne S, lp, Delbard; int. in 1998

Mme de Sombreuil – See **Mlle de Sombreuil**, T

Mme de Soubeyran – See **Mme Soubeyran**, HP

Mme de Staël M, lp, 1857, Robert & Moreau; flowers flesh pink, 2-2½ in., full, cupped; some repeat

Mme de Stella – See **Louise Odier**, B

Mme de Tartas T, lp, 1859, Bernède; flowers flush-pink, mixed with pale yellow, large, dbl., cupped; vigorous, sprawling growth

Mme de Thartas – See **Mme de Tartas**, T

Mme de Tressan HGal, mp, 1822, Sommesson; flowers flesh pink, large, full; sometimes classed as D

Mme de Trotter HP, pb, 1854, Granger; flowers pink and red, medium, dbl.

Mme de Vatry T, dp, 1855, Guérin; flowers deep pink, center lighter, large, dbl.; recurrent bloom; vigorous growth

Mme de Villars M, mp, 1847, Béluze; flowers delicate pink, spotted; some repeat

Mme de Ville-Mareuil HP, w, 1853, Carré; flowers flesh white, large, full

Mme de Vitry – See **Mme de Vatry**, T

Mme de Watteville T, yb, 1883, Guillot et Fils; flowers lemon edged pink, large, dbl.

Mme Delaunay HT, Privat, J.; int. in 1963

Madame Delbard – See **Mme Georges Delbard**, HT, 1985

Mme Dellevaux HP, mp, 1883, Besson; flowers silky pink

Mme Delville HP, pb, 1890, Schwartz; flowers shining velvet-pink, edges lighter, reverse silvery, large, full

Mme d'Enfert B, lp, 1904, Vilin; flowers pale blushing flesh white, pinker towards center, full; growth upright; [Mme Ernst Calvat × Duchesse d'Auerstädt]

Mme Denis T, w, 1853, Guillot; flowers white shaded salmon, medium to large, very full

Mme Denis T, w, 1872, Gonod; flowers white, center sulfur-yellow, large, full

Mme Denise Cassegrain – See **Denise Cassegrain**, Pol

Mme Denise Cassegrain Misc OGR, w

Mme Denise Gallois HT, pb, 1941, Sauvageot, H.; flowers salmon shaded yellow, deeper reverse

Mme Derepas-Matrat T, dy, 1897, Buatois; bud large; flowers sulphur-yellow, center darker, dbl., borne mostly solitary; nearly thornless; growth vigorous; [Mme Hoste × Marie Van Houtte]

Mme Derouet HP, w, 1885, Derouet; flowers white, center rose, reverse lilac, large, full, globular

Mme Derreult-Douville HP, mp, 1863, Lévêque; flowers silky rose, becoming light red, edges silky white, large, full

Mme Desbordes T, pb, 1903, Corboeuf-Marsault; flowers pink with golden reflections, large, full, moderate fragrance; [Cérès × Louis Guillaud]

Mme Désir Vincent T, yb, 1898, Marqueton; flowers dark chrome yellow, salmon at base, reverse shaded pink-violet, large, full; [Souv de Mme Levet × unknown]

Mme Desirée Bruneau HT, mp, 1907, Moublot

Mme Desirée Giraud HP, pb, 1854, Van Houtte; flowers blush-white, striped rose; [sport of Baronne Prévost]

Mme Deslongchamps N, w, 1850, Lévêque; flowers white, shaded carmine-pink, medium, full

Mme Desmars HT, yb, 1929, Mallerin, C.; bud long; flowers golden yellow, tinted nasturtium-red, very large, dbl., high-centered; foliage glossy; vigorous, bushy growth; [Ophelia × Constance]; int. by H. Guillot, 1932

Mme Desmary HT, yb, 1950, Moulin-Epinay; flowers ochre-yellow tinted orange, 30-35 petals; foliage bright green; vigorous growth; [Aspirant Marcel Rouyer × Emma Wright]; int. by Vilmorin-Andrieux

Mme Desprez B, mp, 1831, Desprez; flowers rosy lilac, large, dbl., cupped, borne in large clusters; foliage dark green; [Rose Edouard × unknown]

Mme Desprez Ch, w, about 1835, Desprez; flowers white tinged with lemon, large, very dbl., cupped, borne in small clusters, moderate fragrance; probably extinct

Mme Devacourt – See **Mme Devoucoux**, T

Mme Devacoux – See **Mme Devoucoux**, T

Mme Devert HP, pb, 1876, Pernet; flowers flesh pink, center dark pink, very large, full, globular; [Victor Verdier × unknown]

Mme Devoucoux T, my, 1874, Ducher, Vve.; flowers bright yellow, well-formed, dbl.

Mme d'Hébray – See **Unique Panachée**, C

Mme Didkowsky HT, rb, 1943, Mallerin, C.; flowers fiery red, reverse golden yellow; int. by A. Meilland

Mme Dieudonné HT, rb, 1950, Meilland, F.; flowers rose-red, reverse gold, 4-5 in., 30 petals, slender, tulip-shaped, moderate fragrance; recurrent; foliage dark, glossy; vigorous growth; [(Mme Joseph Perraud × Brazier) × (Charles P. Kilham × Capucine Chambard)]

Mme Dieudonné, Climbing Cl HT, rb, 1960, Anderson

Mme Dimitriu Pol, mp, 1970, Delbard-Chabert; bud globular; flowers pink tinted lighter, large, dbl., borne in clusters of 5-10; foliage bronze, glossy; vigorous, bushy growth; [Chic Parisien × Provence]; int. in 1967; Gold Medal, Rome, 1967, Gold Medal, Geneva, 1967

Mme Dr Jütté T, yb, 1872, Levet; flowers salmon, orange and copper, intense fragrance; [Ophirie × unknown]

Mme Domage HP, mr, 1853, Margottin; flowers crimson

Mme Doré B, lp, 1863, Fontaine; flowers large, dbl., moderate fragrance; medium growth

Mme Driout Cl T, pb, 1902, Thirat, J.; flowers bright rose, striped carmine, large, dbl.; very vigorous, climbing growth; [sport of Reine Marie Henriette]

Mme Dubarry HGal, mp, before 1866; flowers bright shining carmine, medium, full

Mme Dubois HP, mr, 1866, Fontaine; flowers vermilion

Mme Dubost B, lp, 1890, Pernet Père; flowers flesh, center rose, medium, full, borne in small clusters; growth upright

Mme Dubroca T, pb, 1882, Nabonnand, G.; flowers salmon shaded carmine, large, dbl.

Mme Dubuisson HP, mp, 1861, Baudry; flowers carmine, large, full

Mme Ducamp HP, m, 1863, Fontaine; flowers bright garnet-purple, aging to currant, large, full

Mme Ducher HP, mr, 1851, Cordier/Ducher; flowers cherry red

Mme Ducher T, ly, 1869, Ducher; flowers medium, full; [Gloire de Dijon × unknown]

Mme Ducher HP, rb, 1880, Levet; flowers cherry red, petals edged dark purple, center petals whitish, very large, full

Mme Durand T, dy, 1890, Moreau & Robert; flowers coppery dark yellow, large, full, globular

Mme Durand T, w, 1903, Croibier; flowers white, center salmon pink, lrage, full

Mme Dustour HP, pb, 1869, Pernet; flowers carmine-pink, centers white, very large, full

Mme E. A. Nolte Pol, ly, 1892, Bernaix; flowers light nankeen yellow, passing to white

Mme E. Rocque HMult, m, 1918, Lottin; flowers violet, sometimes striped white, passing to amethyst, very dbl.; [Veilchenblau × Reine des Violettes]

Mme E. Souffrain N, yb, 1897, Chauvry; bud large, ovoid; flowers golden yellow tinged with salmon and pink, large, very full; foliage glossy; nearly thornless; [Rêve d'Or × Duarte de Oliveira]

Mme E. Terracol HT, yb, 1940, Meilland, F.; bud globular; flowers pure yellow, base orange, very large, dbl.; foliage leathery; very vigorous, upright growth; [Julien Potin × Soeur Thérèse]; int. by A. Meilland

Mme Edmée Cocteau Cl HT, lp, 1903, Margottin fils; flowers delicate pink, very large; [Captain Christy × unknown]

Mme Edmée Metz HT, pb, 1901, Soupert & Notting; flowers rosy carmine shaded salmon, dbl.; [Mme Caroline Testout × Ferdinand Jamin]

Mme Edmond Corpus B, w, 1903, Boutigny, P.; flowers pure white, reverse fresh pink

Mme Edmond Fabre HP, mp, 1884, Verdier, E.; flowers large, dbl.

Mme Edmond Gillet HT, yb, 1921, Pernet-Ducher; flowers reddish nankeen yellow, slightly shaded carmine at tips, dbl.; [Mme Edmond Rostand × Marquise de Sinéty]

Mme Edmond Labbé HT, rb, 1938, Mallerin, C.; bud pointed; flowers orange-red, reverse golden yellow, large, dbl.; long stems; very vigorous growth; [Souv. de Claudius Pernet × unnamed Hybrid Tea seedling]; int. by A. Meilland; Gold Medal, Bagatelle, 1938

Mme Edmond LaPorte B, pb, 1893, Boutigny; flowers silvery white within, fresh pink without, very large, semi-globular; foliage dark green, glossy

Mme Edmond Raynal HT, ly, 1927, Sauvageot, H.; flowers yellowish-cream, center salmon, dbl.; int. by F. Guillot

Mme Edmond Rostand HT, pb, 1912, Pernet-Ducher; flowers pale flesh, center shaded salmon and reddish orange-yellow, very large, dbl., moderate fragrance; [unnamed variety × Prince de Bulgarie]

Mme Edouard Estaunié HT, yb, 1936, Buatois; bud long; flowers nankeen yellow, center reddish, edges and reverse flesh-pink, dbl.; long stems; very vigorous growth; [Seabird × Souv. de Claudius Pernet]

Mme Edouard Helfenbein T, yb, 1893, Guillot; flowers chamois yellow with carmine and China pink reflections, large, full

Mme Édouard Herriot HT, ob, 1913, Pernet-Ducher; bud pointed; flowers coral-red shaded yellow and bright rosy scarlet, passing to rose pink, large, semi-dbl., moderate fragrance; foliage bronze, glossy; vigorous, spreading, branching growth; [Mme Caroline Testout × a Pernetiana]; Gold Medal, NRS, 1913

Mme Édouard Herriot, Climbing Cl HT, ob, 1921, Ketten Bros.; flowers copper yellow red, large, semi-dbl., moderate fragrance; [sport of Mme Edouard Herriot]

Mme Edouard Michel HP, dp, 1886, Verdier, E.; flowers clear deep pink, very large, full; foliage delicate green, irregularly toothed; prickles unequal, straight; growth upright

Mme Édouard Ory M, dp, 1854, Robert; sepals foliaceous; flowers bright carmine-pink, 6-8 cm., dbl., globular, moderate fragrance; very remontant; foliage dark green, oval

Mme Elie Dupraz HT, mr, 1948, Gaujard; bud large; flowers brilliant red, medium, dbl., high-centered; foliage dark, glossy; very vigorous, bushy growth

Mme Elie Lambert T, w, 1890, Lambert, E.; flowers creamy white, faintly tinted with pale yellow, bordered with soft rose, very large, very full, cupped, globular; [Anna Olivier × Souv de Paul Neyron]

Mme Elisa de Vilmorin HP, mr, 1864, Lévêque; flowers dark carmine, large, 30 petals; sparse bloom; upright, bushy growth; sometimes considered to be one of the earliest Hybrid Teas

Mme Elisa Jaenisch HP, rb, 1870, Soupert & Notting; flowers cherry red with bluish tints, shaded violet and flame-red, large, full

Mme Elisa Tasson HP, mr, 1879, Lévêque; flowers scarlet cerise, very large, full, globular; foliage glossy

Mme Elise de Chénier B, dp, 1857, Touvais; flowers deep pink, medium, full

Mme Eliza de Vilmorin – See **Mme Elisa de Vilmorin**, HP

Mme Emain HP, m, 1862, Pernet; flowers purple, shaded slate, large, full

Mme Emile Daloz HT, pb, 1934, Sauvageot, H.; flowers satiny purplish pink, reverse bright rose-pink, very large, dbl., globular; foliage leathery, glossy; very vigorous, bushy growth; [Frau Karl Druschki × Souv. de Georges Pernet]; int. by Sauvageot

Mme Emile Mayen HT, ly, 1924, Chambard, C.; flowers sulfur-yellow passing to cream, dbl.

Mme Emile Metz HT, lp, 1893, Soupert & Notting; [Mme de Loeben-Sels × La Tulipe]

Mme Emile Sénéclauze HT, mp, Croix, P.; int. by Croix, 1966

Mme Emile Thierrard HT, yb, 1919, Turbat; flowers chamois-yellow and pink, stamens pure yellow, dbl.; [Mrs Aaron Ward × Joseph Hill]

Mme Emilie Boyau HP, lp, 1864, Boyau; flowers flesh pink, aging darker

Mme Emilie Charrin – See **Mme Emilie Charron**, T

Mme Emilie Charron T, mp, 1895, Perrier; flowers China-pink, large, cupped; very vigorous growth

Mme Émilie Dupuy – See **Émilie Dupuy**, Cl T

Mme Emilie Lafon HT, mr, 1905, Moranville; flowers cerise red, large, dbl.; [La France de 89 × unknown]

Mme Emilie van der Goes HT, op, 1925, Verschuren; bud pointed, orange-yellow and rosy shadings; flowers more pink than bud, large, semi-dbl.; foliage bronze, leathery; bushy growth; [Columbia × Irish Fireflame]

Mme Emma Combey HP, mp, 1872, Cordier/Gonod; flowers carmine

Mme Emma Dampierre HP, mp, 1842, Desprez; flowers bluish pink, shaded crimson, medium, full

Mme Ernest Calvat B, mp, 1888, Schwartz, Vve.; flowers pink shaded darker, very large, semi-dbl.; [sport of Mme Isaac Pereire]

Mme Ernest Charles HT, or, 1933, Buatois; bud large, long; flowers coral-red, reverse shrimp-red, dbl., cupped; foliage leathery, glossy, bronze; vigorous, bushy growth; [Mme Edmond Rostand × Severine]

Mme Ernest Dréolle HP, m, 1861, Grujoire; flowers lilac pink

Mme Ernest Levavasseur HP, mr, 1900, Vigneron; flowers carmine-red, very large, very dbl.; [Mme Isaac Pereire × Ulrich Brunner]

Mme Ernest Perrin T, op, 1900, Schwartz; flowers light orange-pink, very large, dbl.

Mme Ernest Piard HT, dp, 1888, Bonnaire; flowers carmine-pink, very large, dbl.

Mme Ernest Picard – See **Mme Ernest Piard**, HT

Mme Ernestine Verdier T, pb, 1894, Perny/Aschery; flowers mauve-rose, shaded salmon, medium, very large, very full; numerous prickles; growth upright

Mme Ernst Calvat – See **Mme Ernest Calvat**, B

Mme Errera T, ob, 1899, Soupert & Notting; flowers salmon yellow, sometimes cerise, large, full, intense fragrance; [Mme Lombard × Luciole]

Mme Etienne T, mp, 1887, Bernaix, A.; flowers rose, well-formed; vigorous growth

Mme Étienne Levet HP, mr, 1878, Levet; flowers carmine-red, large, dbl., moderate fragrance; [Antonine Verdier × unknown]

Mme Eugène Appert HP, op, 1866, Trouillard; flowers salmon pink, large, full

Mme Eugene Boullet – See **Mme Eugénie Boullet**, HT

Mme Eugene Cavaignac – See **Baron Heckeren de Wassenaer**, HP

Mme Eugène Chambeyran HP, pb, 1878, Gonod; flowers deep pink, shaded aurora pink, large, full, globular; [Victor Verdier × unknown]

Mme Eugène Mallet N, yb, 1875, Nabonnand, G.; flowers pink and yellow, dbl.; moderate, climbing growth

Mme Eugène Marlitt – See **Eugène E. Marlitt**, B

Mme Eugène Moreau HT, my, 1925, Richardier; flowers dbl.; vigorous growth

Mme Eugène Picard HT, my, 1932, Gillot, F.; bud medium, oval, carmine-red; flowers medium, semi-dbl., high-centered, borne in small clusters, moderate fragrance; foliage medium size, dark green, leathery; [sport of Ariel]; int. by C-P

Mme Eugène Résal Ch, pb, 1894, Guillot, P.; bud pointed; flowers bright pink shaded reddish-orange, base yellow, broad, dbl.; [Mme Laurette Messimy × unknown]

Mme Eugène Sudreau HP, dp, 1857, Bernède

Mme Eugène Verdier HP, mp, 1859, Guillot; flowers bright shining pink, very large, full, globular, moderate fragrance; [Louise Peyrony × unknown]

Mme Eugène Verdier HP, lp, 1875, Verdier, E.; flowers silvery pink, large, dbl., globular, moderate fragrance; vigorous growth; [Gloire de Dijon × possibly Mme Barthélemy Levet]

Mme Eugène Verdier N, my, 1882, Levet; flowers varying from golden yellow to canary, to straw, large, moderate fragrance; foliage dark green; few prickles; [Gloire de Dijon × Mme Barthélemy Levet]; sometimes classified as a T

Mme Eugénie Boullet HT, pb, 1897, Pernet-Ducher; flowers pink tinted yellow

Mme Eugénie Bréon B, my, 1847, Belet

Mme Eugénie Frémy HP, dp, 1885, Verdier, E.; flowers carmine-pink, large, very dbl.

Mme Eugénie Savary HP, w, 1875, Gonod; flowers flesh white, reverse brighter pink, large, full

Mme Falcot T, my, 1858, Guillot et Fils; flowers nankeen yellow passing to clear yellow, darker at center, 7 cm., dbl., borne mostly solitary, moderate tea fragrance; [Safrano × unknown]

Mme Fanny de Forest N, lp, 1882, Schwartz; flowers pure white, very large, dbl.; foliage dark green; growth upright; sometimes classed as B

Mme Fanny Pauwels T, yb, 1885, Soupert, C.; flowers bright yellow, darker towards center, sometimes reddish-gold, medium, full

Mme Farfouillon HP, op, 1869, Liabaud; flowers silky pink with salmon and chamois

Mme Faurax-Lille HT, mr, 1933, Reymond; bud pointed; flowers bright vermilion-red passing to geranium-red, large, dbl.; [Cuba × Sir David Davis]; int. by Vially

Mme Fearnley Sander HT, m, 1921, Ketten Bros.; flowers carmine, deepening to purple, base yellow, dbl.; [Gen. MacArthur × Rayon d'Or]

Mme Félix Boulanger N, 1910, Boulanger

Mme Félix Faivre HT, lp, 1901, Buatois; flowers silky light pink

Mme Ferdinand Jamin – See **American Beauty**, HP

Mme Fernand Gentin HT, op, 1939, Mallerin, C.; bud long, pointed; flowers copper shaded coral, large, semi-dbl., cupped; vigorous growth; [seedling × Brazier]; int. by A. Meilland

Mme Fernand Gregh HT, yb, 1955, Robichon; flowers canary-yellow shaded coppery, large; foliage glossy; vigorous growth; [Padre × Madeleine Pacaud]

Mme Fernandel F, dp, Meilland; flowers rose-purple, medium, dbl.; int. in 1989

Mme Ferray – See **Bernard**, P

Mme Fey-Pranard P, 1869, Cherpin

Madame Figaro S, lp, Delbard; flowers very dbl., cupped, moderate rose-citron fragrance; int. in 2000

Mme Fillion HP, op, 1865, Gonod; flowers salmon-pink, large, dbl.; [Mme Domage × unknown]

Mme Florentin Laurent HP, dp, 1870, Granger; flowers shining cherry pink, large, very full

Mme Florentin Laurent T, w, 1906, Bidaud; flowers white with cream reflections, large, full

Mme Fojo HT, ob, 1937, Dot, Pedro; flowers orange, well-formed, large; strong stems; vigorous growth; int. by H. Guillot

Mme Fontaine – See **Prince Albert**, B

Mme Forest HT, mp, 1928, Walter, L.; [Lieutenant Chaure × Mrs George Shawyer]

Mme Fortuné Besson HP, lp, 1881, Besson; flowers delicate flesh pink, very large, very full; [Jules Margottin × unknown]

Mme Foureau N, dy, 1913, Viaud-Bruant; flowers yellowish-salmon, medium, dbl.; [Rêve d'Or × unknown]

Mme Fraculy HT, dy, 1929, Siret-Pernet; flowers deep golden yellow, dbl.; foliage dark, glossy; long, strong stems; vigorous growth; [Ophelia × Constance]

Mme Francis Buchner HP, lp, 1884, Lévêque; flowers very light pink, darker towards center, large, full; foliage glossy

Mme Francisque Favre Pol, 1915, Dubreuil

Mme Franck Augis HT, ob, 1969, Laperrière; bud ovoid; flowers clear orange, medium, dbl., high-centered; foliage glossy; vigorous, bushy growth; [Magicienne × seedling]; int. by EFR

Mme François Bolley HT, op, 1934, Gillot, F.; bud shrimp-pink; flowers salmon, base orange, large, very dbl., moderate fragrance

Mme François Bollez HT, op, 1934, Gillot, F.; flowers coral-pink, center brighter, tinted orange, very large, dbl.; foliage dark, bronze; very vigorous growth

Mme François Brassac T, rb, 1883, Nabonnand; bud very large; flowers bright bronze-red, tinted with coppery yellow, large, very dbl.

Mme François Bruel HP, mp, 1882, Levet; flowers carmine-rose; very remontant; foliage light green; few prickles; [Victor Verdier × Comtesse d'Oxford]

Mme François Graindorge Pol, pb, 1922, Grandes Roseraies; flowers dark reddish-pink shaded magenta, base tinged lilac, large; vigorous growth

Mme François Hot HT, pb, 1928, Schwartz, A.; flowers salmon shaded coppery rose, edged lighter, base salmon-yellow; [Lady Pirrie × Mme de Bauvoire]

Mme François Janain T, ob, 1872, Levet; flowers dark orange, becoming golden yellow, center coppery, medium, full, moderate fragrance

Mme François Pittet B, w, 1878, Lacharme, F.; flowers small to medium, very dbl., globular; [Mlle Blanche Laffitte × unknown]; sometimes classed as N

Mme François Royet HMult, mr, 1914, Royet; flowers bright red, 6-7 cm., cupped, borne in small clusters, moderate fragrance; foliage large, deeply dentate; numerous prickles; [Crimson Rambler × Général Jacqueminot]

Mme Frank Augis HT, Laperrière; int. in 1969

Mme Frédéric Daupias T, yb, 1899, Chauvry; flowers siena-yellow, center apricot, edges tinted violet-pink, large, full; [Charles de Legrady × unknown]

Mme Frédéric Daupias HT, pb, 1899, Soupert & Notting; flowers dark flesh pink, marbled silvery white, very large, full; [Léonie Osterrieth × Belle Siebrecht]

Mme Frédéric Weiss Pol, rb, 1892, Bernaix; flowers carmine, shaded magenta, sometimes striped white

Mme Freemann HP, w, 1862, Guillot; flowers creme, medium, full; sometimes classified as N

Mme Freemann T, w, 1874, Nabonnand; flowers pure white, large, full

Mme Frémion HP, mr, 1853, Margottin; flowers bright cherry, medium, full

Mme Fresnoy HP, mr, 1865, Pernet; flowers shining crimson, becoming carmine pink, large, full

Mme Furtado B, dp, 1852, Bélot-Défougères; flowers dark pink, shaded poppy red, large, full

Mme Furtado HP, dp, 1860, Verdier, V.; flowers shining carmine pink, very large, very full

Mme Furtado-Heine HP, pb, 1887, Lévêque; flowers bright glowing pink, shaded carmine-lilac, large, full, globular

Mme G. Cossard – See **Mme Clément Massier**, N

Mme G. Forest-Colcombet HT, dp, 1928, Mallerin, C.; flowers deep carmine, strongly tinted scarlet; [sport of Hadley]; int. by Grandes Roseraies

Mme G. Hekkens HT, dr, 1929, Faassen-Hekkens; flowers velvety dark red (nearly as dark as Chateau de Clos Vougeot), single; foliage glossy; [Gloire de Holland × Hawlmark Crimson]

Mme Gabriel Hanra HT, rb, 1929, Ketten Bros.; flowers strawberry-red, shaded carmine-purple, dbl.; [The Adjutant × Kitchener of Khartoum]

Mme Gabriel Luizet HP, lp, 1877, Liabaud; flowers light silvery pink, edged lighter, large, 34 petals, cupped, moderate fragrance; non-recurrent; vigorous growth; [sport of Jules Margottin]

Mme Gadel HP, m, 1872, Pernet; flowers lilac pink, large, full

Mme Gaillard B, mp, 1866, Pradel; flowers carmine-pink, medium

Mme Gaillard T, op, 1871, Ducher; flowers salmon yellow, large, full

Mme Galli-Marié HCh, mp, 1876, Verdier, E; flowers medium, full, borne in small clusters

Mme Gamon T, ab, 1905, Gamon; bud long; flowers apricot on golden yellow, large, full; growth vigorous, bushy

Mme Gaston Allard T, w, 1893, Cailleau; flowers cream white, medium

Mme Gaston Anouilh N, w, 1899, Chauvry; bud tinged pink; flowers white tinted canary, medium to large, dbl., intense fragrance; nearly thornless

Mme Gaston Doumergue Pol, lp, 1934, Levavasseur; flowers soft salmon; [probably a sport of Gloria Mundi]

Mme Gaston Mestreit Pol, lp, 1922, Soupert & Notting; flowers very soft flesh-white, borne in clusters; [Jeanny Soupert × Katharina Zeimet]

Mme Gaston Nocton Pol, w, 1928, Soupert & Notting; flowers white, center flesh-pink, opening pure white, borne in clusters; dwarf growth; [Amaury Fonseca × Jeanny Soupert]

Mme George Paul HP, mr, 1886, Verdier, E.; flowers crimson, shaded dark pink, large, full

Mme Georges Bénard HT, dp, 1900, Corboeuf; flowers carmine-pink with silvery reverse, large, dbl.

Mme Georges Brédif HT, rb, 1955, Privat; flowers red mottled garnet, well-formed; strong stems

Mme Georges Bruant HRg, w, 1887, Bruant; bud pointed; flowers waxy white, large, semi-dbl., loose, borne in clusters, moderate fragrance; recurrent bloom; [*R. rugosa alba* × Mlle de Sombreuil]

Mme Georges Clenet HT, Godin, M.; int. in 1980

Mme Georges Cozon HT, pb, 1929, Laperrière; flowers shrimp-pink, reverse yellow; [Mme Charles Lutaud × unnamed Hybrid Tea seedling]

Mme Georges Delbard HT, or, 1959, Delbard-Chabert; flowers bright red suffused orange, 5 in., 35-45 petals; foliage dull green; long, strong stems; very vigorous growth; RULED EXTINCT 4/85; [Impeccable × Mme Robert Joffet]

Mme Georges Delbard HT, dr, 1985, Delbard, Georges; flowers large, 40 petals, exhibition, no fragrance; foliage large, medium green, semi-glossy; upright growth; PP4391; [(Tropicana × Samourai) × (Tropicana × (Rome Glory × Impeccable))]; int. by Roseraies Delbard, 1980

Mme Georges Desse HP, pb, 1897, Desse/Duprat

Mme Georges Droin HT, op, 1930, Gaujard, Jules; flowers orange-shrimp-pink; foliage bronze; very vigorous growth

Mme Georges Halphen T, op, 1899, Lévêque; flowers salmon pink, shaded yellow, large

Mme Georges Landard HT, lp, 1925, Walter, L.; flowers rose-red, large, full, borne mostly solitary, moderate fragrance; foliage glossy; [Mme Abel Chatenay × Lyon Rose]; int. by Lamesch

Mme Georges Paul HP, mr, 1886, Verdier, E.; flowers crimson, shaded dark pink, large, full

Mme Georges Petit HT, mr, 1928, Ketten Bros.; bud pointed; flowers bright purple-red to velvety crimson-red, large, dbl., high-centered; very vigorous growth; [Gen. MacArthur × Mme Edouard Herriot]

Mme Georges Renoard HT, dy, 1988, Delbard-Chabert; flowers long, large, 35-40 petals, moderate fragrance; foliage clear, matte; upright, vigorous growth; [(Peace × Marcelle Gret) × (Legion d'Honneur × unknown)]

Mme Georges Schwartz HP, mp, 1871, Schwartz; flowers rose pink with soft lavender shading, fading to frosty pink, large, full

Mme Georges Vibert HP, mp, 1879, Moreau-Robert; flowers delicate pink, veined bright pink, center carmine, very large, full, borne in small clusters; foliage dark green

Mme Ghys HMult, m, 1912, Ghys; flowers lilac-rose, borne in clusters; growth to 6-10 ft.; [Crimson Rambler × unknown]; int. by Decault

Madame Gilberte Dubois HT, op, RvS-Melle; flowers 30 petals, flat; foliage dense, luxurious; [Silver Jubilee × Mountbatten]; int. in 1990

Mme Gilberte Janaud F, mp, 1957, Privat; flowers bright pink tinted salmon, very dbl.; dwarf growth

Mme Gillen – See **Mrs M. J. Gillon**, HT

Mme Gillet Lafond HT, pb, 1930, Leenders, M.; flowers salmon-white, center old-rose, large, semi-dbl.; foliage light, leathery; vigorous growth; [Frau Felix Tonnar × Angèle Pernet]

Mme Gina Demoustier HT, mr, 1920, Laperrière; flowers pure garnet-red, dbl.; [Étoile de France × unnamed variety]

Mme Gonod HP, mp, 1867, Moreau & Robert; flowers silky pink, large, full

Mme Grandin-Monville HP, rb, 1875, Verdier, E.; flowers crimson, edged bright pink, large, full, borne in small clusters

Mme Grégoire Staechelin LCl, pb, 1927, Dot, Pedro; bud brushed deep maroon; flowers delicate pink, reverse stained crimson, ruffled, 5 in., semi-dbl., moderate fragrance; non-recurrent; foliage heavy, large, dark, glossy; vigorous (13-14 ft.) growth; hips pear-shaped, pinkish-orange, large; [Frau Karl Druschki × Château de Clos Vougeot]; int. by C-P, 1929; Gold Medal, Bagatelle, 1927, John Cook Medal, ARS, 1929

Mme Grondier HP, op, 1867, Gonod; flowers salmon pink, large, full, globular

Mme Guimet HT, dp, 1942, Laperrière; flowers large, dbl.

Mme Gustave Bonnet – See **Zéphirine Drouhin**, B

Mme Gustave Fintelmann HP, mp, 1853, Baumann; flowers large, full

Mme Gustave Henry T, op, 1899, Buatois; flowers bright coppery pink, very large

Mme Gustave Metz HT, lp, 1906, Lamesch; flowers creamy white, going to pink, very large, dbl.; [(Mme Caroline Testout × Viscountess Folkestone) × unknown]

Mme Gustave Soupert HT, pb, 1928, Soupert & Notting; flowers purplish pink, center brighter, reverse silvery carmine, dbl.; [Augustus Hartmann × Souv. de Georges Pernet]

Mme H. de Potworoska T, dp, 1899, Bernaix; flowers amaranthe, shaded azalea pink with lighter reflections, medium, dbl.

Mme H. Heinemann – See **Galileo**, HT

Mme Hardon HP, mp, 1897, Cochet, P.; flowers bright pink and carmine

Mme Hardy D, w, 1832, Hardy; bud large, round, pink outside; sepals long, foliaceous at top; flowers pure white, occasionally tinged flesh-pink, petals incurved at center, green pip, 8 cm., very dbl., cupped, opening flat, borne in small clusters, intense fragrance; foliage medium green, slightly pubescent underneath, regularly dentate, large; prickles numerous, uneven; stems light green; growth erect, vigorous; Old Rose Hall of Fame, WFRS

Mme Hardy du Thé – See **Clotilde Soupert**, Pol

Mme Haussmann – See **Baronne Haussmann**, HP

Mme Hébert – See **Président de Sèze**, HGal

Mme Hector Jacquin HP, pb, 1853, Fontaine; flowers flower pink, shaded lilac, large, full

Mme Hector Leuillot HT, yb, 1903, Pernet-Ducher; bud pointed; flowers golden yellow on carmine ground, dbl.

Mme Hélène Dapples HT, mr, 1932, Heizmann, E.; flowers large, semi-dbl.

Mme Hélène Duché HT, pb, 1921, Buatois; flowers soft rose with silvery reflexes, edged carmine, dbl.; [Mme Caroline Testout × Reine Emma des Pays-Bas]

Mme Hélène Parmentier HT, or, 1935, Sauvageot, H.; bud long; flowers clear nasturtium-red, shaded orange, passing to pink, semi-dbl., cupped; foliage glossy, wrinkled, bronze; long stems; vigorous, bushy growth; [seedling × Angèle Pernet]

Mme Helfenbein B, m, 1852, Guillot; flowers lilac pink, large, full

Mme Helmut Kohl – See **Anne Laure**, S

Mme Hélye HP, mp, 1862; flowers carmine-lilac, large, full

Mme Henri Berger T, mp, 1901, Bonnaire; flowers China pink, very large, full, moderate fragrance

Mme Henri Bonnet HT, pb, 1948, Boerner; bud ovoid; flowers deep salmon-pink suffused golden orange, large, dbl., high-centered; foliage leathery; vigorous, upright, compact growth; [Elite × seedling]; int. by J&P

Mme Henri Fontaine HT, lp, 1914, Guillot; flowers creamy pink with yellow base, large, dbl., moderate fragrance; [Pharisäer × unknown]

Mme Henri Graire T, pb, 1895, Lévêque; flowers pink, tinted bronze and chamois yellow, center deep peach, large, full; foliage dark green; growth vigorous

Mme Henri Gravereaux HRg, pb, 1904, Gravereaux; bud large, protrusive, reddish; flowers cream, with salmony pink center, large, dbl., cupped, borne mostly solitary; foliage not rugose; prickles sparse, small, upright; [Marie Zahn × Conrad Ferdinand Meyer]

Mme Henri Gravereaux HT, yb, 1926, Barbier; flowers coppery yellow tinted bronze-yellow, veined orange, dbl.; [Mrs Aaron Ward × seedling]

Mme Henri Grimm HT, lp, 1934, Buatois; bud long; flowers pinkish white tinged carmine, edged crimson, base yellow, dbl., high-centered; foliage leathery, dark; vigorous, bushy growth; [Mme Charles Detreaux × Mme Edouard Herriot]

Mme Henri Guillot HT, rb, 1938, Mallerin, C.; flowers orange-coral-red, large, 25 petals; foliage glossy; vigorous, bushy growth; [Rochefort × *R. foetida bicolor* seedling]; int. by C-P; Gold Medal, Bagatelle, 1936, Gold Medal, Portland, 1939

Mme Henri Guillot, Climbing Cl HT, rb, 1942, Meilland, F. (also van Barneveld, 1947); flowers crimson-coral, 5-6 in., semi-dbl.

Mme Henri Laforest HT, my, 1942, Gaujard; bud pointed; flowers golden yellow, very large, semi-dbl.; foliage glossy; very vigorous, upright growth

Mme Henri Lustre HT, rb, 1924, Buatois; flowers purplish garnet tinted currant-red, very large, dbl., high-centered; foliage leathery; very vigorous, bushy growth; [Mme Edouard Herriot × Yves Druhen]

Mme Henri Paté HT, ly, 1929, Pernet-Ducher; bud pointed; flowers sulfur-yellow, very large, semi-dbl.; foliage bronze; very vigorous, bushy growth; [Souv. de Claudius Pernet × seedling]; int. by Gaujard

Mme Henri Pelley HT, ly, 1928, Richardier; flowers transparent cream-yellow

Mme Henri Pereire HP, mr, 1887, Vilin; flowers crimson-red

Mme Henri Perrin HP, pb, 1892, Widow Schwartz; flowers bright carmine lilac pink, somtimes striped white, large; foliage bullate

Mme Henri Queuille HT, op, 1928, Pernet-Ducher; bud long, pointed; flowers bright shrimp-pink, center deeper, reverse coppery gold, large, semi-dbl., moderate fragrance; foliage bronze; very vigorous growth; int. by Gaujard

Mme Henri Thiebaut HT, op, 1931, Chambard, C.; bud pointed; flowers salmon-coral base coral-orange, very large, dbl.; foliage bright green; strong stems; vigorous growth

Mme Henriette C, pb; flowers lilac pink, edged whitish pink, very large, full

Mme Henriette Thomson HT, op, 1909, Bruant; flowers orange-pink, edged carmine

Mme Hérivaux – See **Mme Charles Crapelet**, HP

Mme Hermann N, op, 1861, Avoux / Crozy; flowers salmon pink with flesh white, medium, full

Mme Hermann Haefliger S, dr, 1951, Hauser; flowers velvety scarlet-crimson, yellow petal base, large, slight fragrance; some repeat; foliage dark; vigorous growth; [*R. foetida bicolor* seedling × Charles P. Kilham]

Mme Hermann Stenger HP, mp, 1864, Gonod; flowers shining pink, medium

Mme Herriot Panachée HT, yb, 1921, Cassegrain; flowers coral and golden yellow; [sport of Mme Edouard Herriot]

Mme Hersilie Ortgies HP, lp, 1868, Soupert & Notting; flowers pink and pinkish lilac, medium, full

Mme Hide HT, pb, 1997, Ohta, Kaichiro; flowers blush edged pink, large, dbl.; foliage large, medium green, matte; some prickles; compact (1½ m.) growth

Mme Hippolyte Dumas HT, pb, 1924, Guillot, P.; flowers flesh tinted salmon-pink, base yellow, dbl.

Mme Hippolyte Jamain T, yb, 1869, Guillot; flowers yellowish-white, center coppery, large, full, globular

Mme Hippolyte Jamain HP, w, 1871, Garçon; flowers lightly blushing white, 4½ in., very full, cupped, borne singly or in small clusters; foliage light green, slightly glaucous, finely dentate; prickles numerous, slender, reddish

Mme Hoche M, lp, 1859, Moreau & Robert; flowers whitish pink, medium, full

Mme Honoré Defresne Cl T, my, 1886, Levet, F.; flowers golden yellow, large, dbl.; vigorous growth; [Mme Falcot × unknown]

Mme Hortense de Montefiori B, op, 1900, Bernaix; flowers light salmon-flesh, brighter at edges, semi-dbl., moderate fragrance

Mme Hoste HP, w, 1865, Gonod

Mme Hoste T, w, 1887, Guillot et Fils; flowers yellowish-white, imbricated, large, globular; vigorous growth; [Victor Pulliat × unknown]

Mme Huguette Despiney – See **Huguette Despiney**, HWich

Mme Hunnebel HP, mp, 1873, Fontaine; flowers China pink, shaded darmine, very large, full

Mme Isaac Periere B, dp, 1881, Garçon; flowers deep rose-pink shaded purple, large, dbl.; vigorous growth

Mme J. B. Croibier HT, op, 1935, Gaujard; flowers bright salmon, open, very large, dbl.; foliage leathery; very vigorous growth; [seedling × Mme Nicolas Aussel]; Gold Medal, Rome, 1936

Mme J. Bonnaire-Pierre – See **Mme Joseph Bonnaire**, HT

Mme J. Bonnaire Pierre HP, 1892, Bonnaire

Mme J. M. Fructus HT, pb, 1935, Chambard, C.; flowers satiny carmine, shaded salmon, base yellow, well-formed, dbl., cupped; foliage dark; very vigorous growth

Mme J. M. Gonod HP, dr, 1875, Gonod; flowers dark crimson, center flame red, very large, full

Mme J. P. Soupert HT, w, 1900, Soupert & Notting; flowers white with a yellow glow, very large, very dbl., moderate fragrance; [Mme Caroline Testout × Mlle Alice Furon]

Mme J. Phillips – See **Mlle Jeanne Philippe**, T

Mme J. W. Büdde HT, dp, 1906, Soupert & Notting; flowers bright carmine

Mme Jacques Charreton T, ab, 1897, Bonnaire; bud long, oval; flowers outer petals milky white, center coppery salmon, large, full; growth vigorous

Mme Jacques Privat HT, mr, 1959, Privat, J.; bud long; flowers red; foliage glossy; vigorous growth

Mme Jacquier HP, m, 1869, Guillot; flowers violet-pink, very large, full

Mme James Gross HP, mp, 1864, Baumann; flowers bright carmine-pink, large, full

Mme Jard B, mr, 1857, Guillot; flowers cherry red, medium

Mme Jean Bonnet T, pb, 1903, Godard; flowers very light pink, almost white, medium, full

Mme Jean Croibier – See **Mme J. B. Croibier**, HT

Mme Jean Demeshayne HT, op, 1934, Nicolas; flowers yellowish salmon-pink, large, very dbl.

Mme Jean Dupuy T, yb, 1902, Lambert, P.; bud long, pointed; flowers golden yellow washed pink, large, dbl.; vigorous growth

Mme Jean Everaerts HP, dr, 1907, Geduldig; flowers dark flame red, large, dbl., moderate fragrance; [Eugene Furst × (Mme Eugene Verdier × Johannes Wesselhoft)]

Mme Jean Favre HT, pb, 1900, Godard; bud long, deep carmine; flowers light carmine with bluish reflections, large; [La France de 89 × Xavier Olibo]

Mme Jean Gaujard HT, yb, 1938, Gaujard; bud long, pointed; flowers creamy yellow, reverse shaded orange and carmine-pink, very large, dbl.; foliage leathery, light; very vigorous, bushy growth; [Julien Potin × seedling]; int. by J&P

Mme Jean Paquel HT, ly, 1934, Walter, L.; bud long, pointed; flowers yellow, passing to cream; foliage glossy; [Alice Stern × Lilly Jung]; int. by Amis des Roses

Mme Jean Raty HT, w, 1932, Ketten Bros.; bud pointed; flowers amber-white, edges tinted peach-blossom, well-formed, large, dbl.; [Mme Abel Chatenay × seedling]

Mme Jean Sisley Ch, w, 1885, Dubreuil; flowers matte white with pink reflections, medium, full, cupped, moderate fragrance; [Ducher × Sombreuil]

Mme Jeanne Bouvet HP, lp, 1887, Bernède; flowers silvery light pink, medium; [Jules Margottin × unknown]

Mme Jeanne Philippe – See **Mlle Jeanne Philippe**, T

Mme Jeannine Joubert B, dp, 1877, Margottin fils; flowers bright cerise-carmine, medium, full

Mme Jenny HMult, mp, 1925, Nonin; flowers satiny rose, fading to silvery pink, 4 cm., dbl., cupped, borne in clusters of 5-15, moderate fragrance; foliage dark green; vigorous, climbing growth; [Dorothy Perkins × unknown]

Mme Jenny Gillemot HT, ly, 1905, Pernet-Ducher; bud pointed; flowers light saffron-yellow, large, dbl., high-centered; [Lady Mary Fitzwilliam × Honourable Edith Gifford]

Mme Joannes Beurrier HT, op, 1942, Gaujard; bud pointed; flowers bright orange-pink, reddish reflections, very large, very dbl.; foliage glossy, bronze; very vigorous, bushy growth

Mme John Twombley HP, dr, 1882, Schwartz; flowers bright currant red, large, full; [Alfred Colomb × unknown]

Mme Jolibois HP, pb, 1879, Verdier, E.; flowers bright lilac-carmine-pink, edged silvery white, medium to large, full

Mme Joly B, mp, 1859, Oger; flowers rose pink with carmine

Mme Joseph Bonnaire HT, pb, 1891, Bonnaire; bud very large; flowers China pink, reverse silvery, very large, very full; [Adam × Paul Neyron]

Mme Joseph Bouvet HP, w, 1886, Bernède; flowers flesh white

Mme Joseph Combet HT, pb, 1894, Bonnaire; flowers pink with yellow and white, large, very dbl.

Mme Joseph Desbois HT, w, 1886, Guillot & fils; flowers flesh white, delicate salmon pink center, 6 in., full; [Baronne Adolphe de Rothschild × Mme Falcot]

Mme Joseph Godier T, pb, 1887, Pernet-Ducher; flowers China pink, center carmine, shaded coppery yellow, large, very full, moderate fragrance; [Souv de Marie Détry × unknown]

Mme Joseph Halphen T, pb, 1858, Margottin; flowers yellow-pink, medium, full

Mme Joseph Jullien HT, pb, 1938, Chambard, C.; flowers coppery carmine, very large, dbl., cupped; foliage slightly bronze; [Ami F. Mayery × seedling]

Mme Joseph Métral – See **Souv de Mme Joseph Métral**, Cl HT

Mme Joseph Perraud HT, yb, 1934, Gaujard; flowers yellow, center deeply tinted coppery, large, 33 petals, moderate fragrance; foliage glossy; [Julien Potin × seedling]; Gold Medal, Bagatelle, 1934

Mme Joseph Perraud, Climbing Cl HT, yb, 1945, Marsh's Nursery

Mme Joseph Schwartz T, w, 1880, Schwartz, J.; flowers white washed flesh-pink, medium, dbl.; vigorous growth; [probably a sport of Duchesse de Brabant]

Mme Joséphine Guyet – See **Joséphine Guyet**, B

Mme Joséphine Mühle – See **Safrano à Fleurs Rouges**, T

Mme Jules Barandou HT, dp, 1900, Bonnaire; flowers dark China pink, very large

Mme Jules Bouché HT, w, 1911, Croibier; bud pointed; flowers white, center shaded primrose or pale blush, large, 34 petals, moderate fragrance; tall growth; [Pharisaer × seedling]

Mme Jules Bouché, Climbing Cl HT, w, 1938, Bigot; flowers white, flesh center, 5 in., intense fragrance

Mme Jules Cambon T, pb, 1888, Bernaix; flowers pint, edged carmine, with magenta shading, yellow at center

Mme Jules Finger HT, lp, 1893, Guillot; flowers creamy white nuanced salmon pink at center, aging to pure white, very large, full, globular

Mme Jules Fontaine-Lamarche HT, mr, 1936, Soupert & Notting; flowers velvety scarlet-red, large, dbl.; [Sensation × E.G. Hill]

Mme Jules Franke N, w, 1887, Nabonnand; flowers white, fading to yellowish, medium, very full

Mme Jules Gouchault Pol, op, 1913, Turbat; flowers bright pink, tinted coral and orange, dbl., cupped, borne in clusters; bushy growth; [Maman Turbat × George Elger]; int. by Teschendorff

Mme Jules Gravereaux Cl T, ab, 1901, Soupert & Notting; bud very long, pointed; flowers flesh, shaded peach or yellow, 10 cm., very dbl.; recurrent bloom; foliage large, dark, glossy; to 3-4 ft., bushy growth; [Reve d'Or × Viscountess Folkestone]

Mme Jules Grévy HT, pb, 1881, Schwartz; flowers salmon-white within, bright carmine-pink outer, medim to large, full; [Triomphe de l'Exposition × Mme Falcot]

Mme Jules Grolez HT, mp, 1896, Guillot, P.; bud long, pointed; flowers bright china-rose, dbl., high-centered; bushy growth; [Triomphe de l'Exposition × Mme Falcot]

Mme Jules Grolez, Climbing Cl HT, mp, 1911, Gamon (also Dingee & Conard, 1920); flowers glowing China pink with coppery carmine reflections, large, dbl., moderate fragrance; [sport of Mme Jules Grolez]

Mme Jules Guérin HT, ly, 1931, Gaujard; flowers deep cream, very large, dbl.; foliage bronze

Mme Jules Margottin T, pb, 1871, Levet; flowers light pink, base yellow, center darker red, medium to large, full, moderate fragrance

Mme Jules Siegfried T, w, 1894, Nabonnand; flowers creme white, shaded flesh, center darker, very large, dbl; [Rêve d'Or × Baronne Henriette de Loew]

Mme Jules Thibaud Pol, op; flowers coral-pink, dbl., slight fragrance; good repeat; foliage bronzy; moderate (3 ft.) growth; [sport of Mlle Cécile Brunner]; according to some, color is peachy pink, definitely lighter than coral pink; sometimes classed as China

Mme Jules Walthery HT, my, 1924, Allen; flowers outer petals becoming white

Mme Julia Daran HP, dr, 1861, Touvais; flowers violet-crimson, very large, full, cupped

Mme Julie Gonod – See **Mme J. M. Gonod**, HP

Mme Julie Lasseu N, dp, 1881, Nabonnand; flowers large, very full, cupped

Mme Julie Weidmann HT, op, 1881, Soupert & Notting; flowers silvery salmon pink with carmine and ocher, reverse silky violet, very large, full; [Antoine Verdier × unknown]

Mme Julien Potin HRg, lp, 1913, Gravereaux; flowers pure flesh-pink, large, dbl., flat; recurrent bloom; foliage very leathery; vigorous growth; [Germanica × Gloire de Dijon]; int. by Cochet-Cochet

Mme Juliette – See **Juliette E. van Beuningen**, HT

Mme Juliette Guillot F, dp, Guillot; flowers magenta-pink, dbl., cupped; free-flowering; vigorous (80 cm.) growth; int. by Roseraies Guillot, 1984

Mme Just-Détrey B, dp, 1869, Just-Détrey; flowers velvety carmine, reverse lighter, large, full

Mme Kahn HT, ly, 1939, Colombier; flowers canary-yellow, reverse slightly reddish; vigorous growth; [Charles P. Kilham × Ville de Paris]

Mme Karen Shadish F, mp, 1999, Chaney, William; flowers 2-3 in., dbl., borne in small clusters; foliage small, medium green, semi-glossy; prickles moderate; upright, medium (2-3 ft.) growth; [Pink Petticoat × Mary Rose]

Mme Kastler HT, mr, 1934, Walter, L.; bud long, pointed; flowers large, dbl.; very vigorous growth; [Mme Adele Gance × Mme Caroline Testout]; int. by Amis des Roses

Mme Knorr P, mp, 1855, Verdier, V.; flowers strong pink in center, outer petals fade, full, moderate fragrance

Mme Kriloff HT, yb, 1944, Meilland, F.; flowers clear saffron-yellow, veined reddish-orange, large, dbl., globular; foliage leathery; vigorous, bushy growth; [Peace × Signora]; int. by A. Meilland; Gold Medal, NRS, 1948, Gold Medal, Bagatelle, 1944

Mme L. Cuny – See **Mme Léon Cuny**, HT

Mme L. Dieudonné – See **Mme Dieudonné**, HT

Mme L. Faucheron HT, w, 1911, Croibier; flowers cream white with light sulfur yellow reflections, large to very large, full, moderate fragrance

Mme L. Hot HT, pb, 1926, Bernaix, P.; flowers reddish-salmon, shaded salmon-rose and chrome-yellow, dbl.; [Gorgeous × Rosomane Narcisse Thomas]

Mme L. Ladoire F, op

Mme L. Laperriere HT, 1951, Laperrière

Mme la Baronne Berge T, pb, 1892, Pernet père; flowers cream and yellow, edged bright pink, medium to large, full, intense fragrance

Mme la Baronne de Brezetz HT, dp, 1903, Chauvry; flowers dark porcelain pink, center cream, reverse carmine pink, very large, full

Mme la Baronne de Rothschild – See **Baroness Rothschild**, HP

Mme la Colonelle Desmaires F, dr, 1969, Delforge; flowers large, dbl.; foliage soft, bronze; moderate growth; [Mercator × Alain]

Mme la Comtesse de Camondo HP, mr, 1880, Lévêque; flowers carmine red, tinged brown, very large, full

Mme la Comtesse de Caserta – See **Comtesse de Caserta**, T

Mme la Comtesse de Jaucourt HP, mp, 1866, Desmazures père; flowers pink, shaded salmon at center, edges pale and silvery, very full; foliage light green; [Triomphe de l'Exposition × unknown]

Mme la Duchesse d'Auerstädt – See **Duchesse d'Auerstädt**, N

Mme la Duchesse de Vallombrosa – See **Duchesse de Vallombrosa**, T

Mme la Générale Ardouin HT, rb, 1927, Chambard, C.; flowers coppery carmine shaded chrome-yellow, dbl.

Mme la Générale Decaen HP, mp, 1869, Gautreau; flowers bright pink, center flesh pink, large, full

Mme la Générale Paul de Benoist Cl T, op, 1901, Berland; flowers salmon-pink, very large, very dbl.; [Mme Chauvry × unknown]; sometimes classed as N

Mme la Princesse de Bessaraba de Brancovan T, pb, 1900, Bernaix, A.; flowers flesh-pink, shaded copper, medium, dbl.

Mme l'Abbey C, mp, before 1846; flowers brilliant rose pink, large, full, cupped

Mme Lacharme HT, w, 1872, Lacharme; flowers white, very pale blush center, large, cupped; [Jules Margottin × Mlle de Sombreuil]

Mme Lacoste HP, dp, 1856, Bernède; flowers medium, full

Mme Laffay HP, mr, 1839, Laffay, M.; flowers bright crimson, dbl.; very vigorous growth; [Général Allard × unknown]

Mme Lajotte HT, pb, Gaujard; flowers bright salmon, reverse yellow, large, dbl.; very vigorous, bushy growth; [Rome Glory × Marie-Rose Toussaint]

Mme Lambard – See **Mme Lombard**, T

Mme Lambert D, mr, before 1848; flowers very large, full

Mme Landeau M, rb, 1873, Moreau et Robert; flowers light red with white striping and spotting, medium, dbl.; some repeat

Mme Lanquetin HT, ab, Ofman; flowers apricot; int. by Pin

Mme Lartay T, lp, 1856, Lartay; flowers light pink, edged whitish pink, very large

Mme Lauras HT, mr, 1958, Gaujard; flowers bright red, medium, dbl.; foliage leathery; very vigorous growth; [Rome Glory × (Mme Elie Dupraz × unknown)]; int. in 1956

Mme Laure Dupont HCh, dp, 1906, Schwartz; flowers bright carmine, shaded silvery rose, reverse silvery pink; [Hermosa × Louis van Houtte]

Mme Laurent HP, dp, 1870, Granger; flowers shining cherry pink, large, very full

Mme Laurent Simons T, op, 1894, Lévêque; bud long; flowers coppery-pink, large, very dbl., moderate fragrance; foliage glossy; growth vigorous

Mme Laurette Messimy Ch, dp, 1887, Guillot et Fils; bud long; flowers rose-pink, base shaded yellow, large, dbl.; vigorous growth; [(Rival de Pæstum × Mme Falcot) × Mme Falcot]

Mme Lauriol de Barny B, lp, 1868, Trouillard; flowers silvery pink, large, dbl., quartered, moderate fruity fragrance; rarely repeats; growth to 5-6 ft.

Mme le Guelinel HT, mr, 1959, Gaujard, R.; flowers large; [Mme Kriloff × Marrakech]; int. by G. Truffaut

Mme Lecomte HT, op, 1901, Buatois; flowers salmon pink, large, full

Mme Lecomte-Bouquet HP, dr, 1884, Singer; flowers garnet, shaded chestnut, large, full

Mme Lefebvre HP, mp, 1885, Moreau et Robert; flowers delicate satiny pink, center brighter, large, dbl., cupped, borne in small clusters; foliage glossy

Mme Lefèvre – See **Mme Lefebvre**, HP

Mme Lefrançois HP, op, 1870, Oger; flowers bright flesh-pink, large, full; [Comtesse de Chabrillant × unknown]

Mme Legrand M, pb, 1863, Fontaine; flowers pink and red, large, dbl.; some repeat

Mme Legras de St Germain A, w, before 1846; sepals long; flowers ivory-white, center rich cream, with a small central eye, large, very dbl., flat-cupped, borne in clusters, moderate fragrance; non-recurrent; foliage light gray-green; few prickles; vigorous (6-7 ft.) growth

Mme Lelièvre de la Place HP, mr, 1882, Verdier; flowers bright currant-red, shaded white along the edges, large, full, slight fragrance

Mme Lemelles – See **Mme Lemesle**, HP

Mme Lemerle – See **Mme Lemesle**, HP

Mme Lemesle HP, m, 1890, Moreau et Robert; flowers purple/violet, medium, dbl., globular; foliage dark green; prickles recurved

Mme Léon Constantin Cl T, pb, 1907, Bonnaire; bud long; flowers satiny pink with a light salmon interior, 10 cm., full, moderate fragrance

Mme Léon Cuny HT, mr, 1955, Gaujard; bud long, pointed; flowers bright red, veined purple, very large, dbl., high-centered; foliage dark, bronze; upright growth; [Peace × seedling]

Mme Léon de St Jean T, m, 1875, Levet; flowers light lilac, center lilac tinted salmon, very large, full; [Mme Falcot × Mme Damaizin]

Mme Léon Février T, pb, 1884, Nabonnand, G.; flowers silvery rose shaded crimson, well-formed, dbl., intense fragrance; growth vigorous

Mme Léon Guinotte HT, pb, 1924, Verschuren; flowers glistening pink shaded yellow; [Mme Edouard Herriot × Old Gold]

Mme Léon Halkin HP, mr, 1886, Lévêque; flowers bright crimson red, nuanced purple, large, full, globular

Mme Léon Pain HT, pb, 1904, Guillot, P.; bud pointed; flowers silvery flesh-pink, center orange-yellow, reverse salmon-pink, large, 45 petals, moderate fragrance; vigorous, bushy growth; [Mme Caroline Testout × Souv. de Catherine Guillot]

Mme Léon Pin HT, ob, 1958, Gaujard; flowers soft orange, medium, dbl.; foliage dark, leathery; upright growth; [Louise de Vilmorin × Capucine seedling]; int. in 1954

Mme Léon Simon HT, pb, 1909, Lambert, P.; flowers dark pink with cream, large, dbl.; [Marie van Houtte × Mme Caroline Testout]

Mme Léon Troussier HT, op, 1941, Mallerin, C.; flowers coral, base golden yellow; int. by A. Meilland

Mme Léon Volterra HT, mp, 1958, Leenders, M.; flowers salmon-pink, well-shaped, dbl.; vigorous growth; [Ambassadeur Nemry × Tawny Gold]; Gold Medal, Bagatelle, 1957

Mme Léonce Colombier HT, ly, 1926, Richardier; flowers center straw-yellow passing to white, reverse light rose, dbl.

Mme Léonie Lamesch – See **Léonie Lamesch**, Pol

Mme Léopold Dupuy HT, mp, 1912, Robichon; flowers carmine pink nuanced purple, large, dbl., intense fragrance; [La France de '89 × Mme Ernst Calvat]

Mme Léopold Moreau HP, mr, 1882, Vigneron; flowers varnished red, large, dbl; [Souv de Charles Montaut × unknown]

Mme Létuvée de Colnet B, lp, 1887, Vigneron; flowers lilac pink, edges silvery, very large, full; foliage dark green; growth upright; [Mme Dubost × unknown]

Mme Levet Cl T, yb, 1870, Levet; flowers yellow, tinted violet, reverse salmon-yellow, shaded rose pink, large, very full, cupped; [Gloire de Dijon × unknown]

Mme Liabaud HP, w, 1858, Lacharme, F.; flowers white with flesh center, medium, dbl.; delicate growth habit

Mme Lierval HP, pb, 1868, Fontaine; flowers delicate pink mixed with bright crimson, large, full

Mme Lilienthal HP, dp, 1878, Liabaud; flowers rose red with salmon tints, large, full

Mme Line Renaud HT, mr, 1956, Mondial Roses; flowers velvety red; foliage bright green; [Crimson Glory × seedling]

Mme Loeben de Sels – See **Mme Loeben Sels**, HT

Mme Loeben Sels HT, w, 1879, Soupert & Notting; flowers silvery white shaded rose, large, dbl., flat; moderate growth

Mme Loiseleur – See **Adèle Pavié**, N

Mme Lombard T, op, 1878, Lacharme, F.; flowers rosy salmon, center darker, sometimes rosy flesh, large, very dbl.; vigorous growth; [Mme de Tartas × unknown]

Mme Louis Armand HT, pb, Croix; int. in 1974

Mme Louis Blanchet N, m, 1894, Godard; flowers lilac pink, marbled

Mme Louis Donadine HP, w, 1878, Gonod; flowers flesh white, center darker, large, full; [sport of Countess of Oxford]

Mme Louis Gaillard T, w, 1892, Liabaud; flowers white, shaded yellow, large, full; [Mme Bérard × unknown]

Mme Louis Gravier T, op, 1896, Gamon; flowers salmon with orange-yellow, edged pink, aging coppery apricot, large, full, moderate fragrance

Mme Louis Henry N, w, 1879, Ducher; flowers white, slightly yellowish in center, 7 cm., full, borne in small clusters; foliage light green; prickles numerous, short, reddish

Mme Louis Ladoire F, Arles, F.

Mme Louis Laperrière HT, mr, 1951, Laperrière; flowers rich scarlet, well-formed, medium, 48 petals, intense fragrance; foliage dark; upright, bushy growth; [Crimson Glory × seedling]; int. by EFR; Gold Medal, Bagatelle, 1950

Mme Louis Laurans T, dr, 1894, Bonnaire; flowers dark red, shaded fiery magenta, very large, full, moderate fragrance

Mme Louis Lens HT, 1932

Mme Louis Lens, Climbing Cl HT, w, 1935, Lens; [sport of White Briarcliff]

Mme Louis Lévêque HP, dp, 1873, Lévêque; flowers carmine-rose, very large, dbl., globular, slight fragrance; moderate growth; [Jules Margottin × unknown]

Mme Louis Lévêque T, yb, 1892, Lévêque; flowers yellow washed pink, dbl.; moderate growth

Mme Louis Lévêque M, mp, 1898, Lévêque; flowers brilliant salmon-pink, large, full, globular, moderate fragrance; sometimes blooms in fall; upright, vigorous (4 ft.) growth

Mme Louis Poncet T, pb, 1899, Guillot; flowers nasturtium-red, base coppery China pink, large, full, moderate fragrance

Mme Louis Pradel HT, ob, 1970, Laperrière; flowers clear orange, medium, dbl., high-centered; foliage bronze, glossy, leathery; vigorous, upright growth; [Magicienne × seedling]; int. by EFR, 1967

Mme Louis Puyravaud T, mp, 1906, Puyravaud; flowers satiny China pink with darker reflections, large, dbl., moderate fragrance; [Souv de Mme Détrey × unknown]

Mme Louis Ricard B, lp, 1892, Duboc; flowers pale pink, brighter around center, petals reflexed, large, full, moderate fragrance; foliage oval; prickles few, straight; [possibly a seedling of Baron G. B. Gonella]

Mme Louis Ricard HP, mp, 1904, Boutigny, P.

Mme Louis Ricard, Climbing Cl HP, mp, 1904, Boutigny; flowers bright pink, large, borne in small clusters; [sport of Mme Louis Ricard]

Mme Louisa Cointreau HT, mr, 1957, Robichon; flowers garnet-red, dbl.; vigorous growth; [Crimson Glory × Symbole]

Mme Louise Carique HP, mp, 1859, Fontaine; flowers bright carmine, medium, full

Mme Louise Collet M, dp, 1840, Vibert; flowers bright, shining deep pink, large, full

Mme Louise Guillot F, Guillot, M.; int. in 1955

Mme Louise Mulson T, yb, 1897, Lévêque; flowers silvery white with sulfer yellow, shaded chrome over pink, large, full

Mme Louise Piron HP, lp, 1903, Piron-Medard; flowers large, full, moderate fragrance; remontant; upright (4 ft.) growth; [La Reine × Ulrich Brunner fils]

Mme Louise Seydoux HP, lp, 1856, Fontaine; flowers light silky pink, very large, full

Mme Louise Trémeau HT, op, 1931, Mallerin, C.; flowers pink, shaded nasturtium-red, center brighter, open, large, dbl., cupped; vigorous growth; [(Frau Karl Druschki × Mme Edouard Herriot) × (Mrs Edward Powell × *R. foetida bicolor*)]; int. by C-P

Mme Louise Vigneron HP, lp, 1882, Vigneron; bud elongated; flowers light pink, center darker, large, full; quite remontant; foliage light green; prickles fairly numerous, brown; growth upright; [Elisabeth Vigneron × unknown]

Mme Lucien Baltet HT, pb, 1911, Pernet'Ducher; flowers flesh pink, shaded coppery yellow, petals edged carmine, very large, full, globular

Mme Lucien Chauré HP, mr, 1884, Vigneron; flowers bright cerise red, 5 in., full, globular, borne mostly solitary; quite remontant; foliage dark green; prickles numerous, chestnut; growth upright

Mme Lucien Duranthon T, w, 1898, Bonnaire; flowers cream white, tinted coppery and salmon at center, large, cupped

Mme Lucien Perrier HT, rb, 1938, Gaujard; bud long; flowers coppery red, lighter on opening, open, very large, dbl.; foliage glossy, dark; vigorous growth

Mme Lucien Picard HT, w, 1910, Croibier; bud ovoid; flowers white with salmon tints, large, full; [Mme Abel Chatenay × unknown]

Mme Lucien Villeminot HRg, lp, 1901, Gravereaux & Müuller; flowers pale pink, large, dbl., globular, moderate fragrance; vigorous growth; [Conrad Ferdinand Meyer × Belle Poitevine]

Mme Luizet B, pb, 1867, Liabaud; flowers carmine, shaded salmon, large, full

Mme Lureau-Escalaïs HP, mp, 1886, Verdier, E.; flowers delicate pink, large, dbl.; [Victor Verdier × unknown]

Mme Macker HP, lp, 1863, Damaizin; flowers large, full

Mme Madeleine Margat T, w, 1900, Perny; flowers white, edged cherry red

Mme Mallerin HT, rb, 1924, Chambard, C.; flowers crimson-scarlet shaded vermilion; [Mrs Edward Powell × seedling]

Mme Mantel – See **Mme Montel**, HP

Mme Marcel Astic F, Orard, Joseph; int. in 1978

Mme Marcel Delauney HT, pb, 1916, Leenders, M.; flowers pale pink or soft rose, shaded hydrangea-pink, large, dbl., moderate fragrance; Gold Medal, Bagatelle, 1915

Mme Marcel Fauneau HP, mr, 1886, Vigneron; flowers carmine-red, large, dbl.; [Alexis Lepère × unknown]

Mme Marchal B, w, 1858, de Fauw; flowers flesh white, edges lighter, medium, full

Mme Margottin T, yb, 1866, Guillot et Fils; flowers lemon-yellow, peach center, edges white, large, dbl., slightly globular; growth vigorous

Mme Marguerite Lagières HT, w, 1955, Privat; flowers cream, base golden yellow, very large, dbl.; foliage glossy; strong stems; vigorous growth

Mme Marguerite Marsault HP, m, 1894, Corboeuf; flowers reddish-violet, large, dbl.

Mme Marie Accary – See **Marie Accary**, N

Mme Marie Berton – See **Marie Berton**, T

Mme Marie Bianchi HP, m, 1881, Guillot; flowers lilac pink, centers brighter, reverse white, medium to large, full, globular; [Victor Verdier × Virginale]

Mme Marie Brémond T, m, 1866, Guillot; flowers light purple, shaded dark red, medium to large, full

Mme Marie Cirodde HP, dp, 1867, Verdier, E.; flowers deep pink, large, full

Mme Marie Closon – See **Mlle Marie Closon**, HP

Mme Marie Croibier HT, dp, 1901, Croibier; bud long; flowers deep China pink, very large, dbl.; [Mme Caroline Testout × unknown]

Mme Marie Curie HT, dy, 1943, Gaujard; flowers clear yellow, 5 in., 25 petals, high-centered; foliage leathery, dark; vigorous, bushy, compact growth; int. by J&P

Mme Marie Dubourg B, lp, 1851, Pradel; flowers light pink, medium, full

Mme Marie Eberlin HT, w, 1923, Walter, A.; flowers cream, passing to white, base light yellow, dbl.; [Comtesse Melanie de Pourtales × Capt. Christy]; int. by Bacher

Mme Marie Finger – See **Mlle Eugénie Verdier**, HP

Mme Marie Finger HP, op, 1872, Lacharme; flowers salmon pink

Mme Marie Lavalley HT, pb, 1881, Nabonnand, G.; flowers bright rose tinted white, semi-dbl.; few prickles

Mme Marie Legrange HP, mr, 1882, Liabaud; flowers brilliant carmine, very large, full; [Sénateur Vaïsse × unknown]

Mme Marie Moreau – See **Mlle Marie Moreau**, T

Mme Marie Rady – See **Mlle Marie Rady**, HP

Mme Marie Röderer HP, dp, 1881, Lévêque; flowers cherry pink; [Jules Margottin × unknown]

Mme Marie Van Houtte HP, lp, about 1870, van Houtte; flowers delicate, satiny pink, large, full

Mme Marius Côte HP, dp, 1872, Guillot; flowers fresh dark pink with light red, reverse lighter, very large, very full, cupped

Mme Marius Dévigne HT, pb, 1930, Reymond; bud long; flowers salmon-pink, reverse vivid carmine, large, globular

Mme Martha Ancey – See **Marthe Ancey**, HT

Mme Marthe d'Halloy HP, mp, 1881, Lévêque; flowers carmine cerise pink, large, full; very remontant; foliage glaucous green

Mme Marthe Dubourg T, w, 1890, Bernaix; flowers white, washed violet-carmine with a blush border, aging to pale yellow washed blush, large, full

Mme Martignier Cl T, m, 1903, Dubreuil; flowers red tinted purplish, on yellow ground, medium, cupped; [a Tea × a Noisette]

Mme Martin de Bessé HP, w, 1866, Bernardin; flowers white, shaded light pink, large, full, cupped

Mme Massicault HP, lp, 1884, Schwartz; flowers fleshy pink-white with silvery highlights, medium to large, very dbl., borne mostly solitary; foliage large, dark green, glossy; prickles few, short, slightly hooked; growth straight, erect

Mme Masson HP, dr, 1856, Masson; flowers pure crimson-rose, very large, very full, moderate fragrance; free bloom during long season; vigorous, compact growth

Mme Massot B, w, 1856, Lacharme, F.; flowers white, center flesh, medium, full; sometimes classified as N

Mme Maurice Baudot HT, ob, 1941, Gaujard; flowers bright orange, medium, semi-dbl., high-centered; foliage dark; very vigorous, bushy growth; [Mme Joseph Perraud × seedling]

Mme Maurice Capron HT, ab, 1914, Guillot, P.; flowers deep apricot-yellow tinted salmon

Mme Maurice Cazin HT, rb, 1931, Schwartz, A.; bud pointed; flowers dark scarlet, reverse clear reddish-crimson, large, dbl.; [Gen. MacArthur × Hadley]

Mme Maurice de Luze HT, pb, 1907, Pernet-Ducher; flowers rose-pink, center carmine, reverse paler, large, full, cupped, moderate sweet fragrance; [Mme Abel Chatenay × Eugene Fürst]

Mme Maurice Fenaille HT, lp, 1904, Boutigny, P.; flowers very light pink, nearly white, large, full

Mme Maurice Genevoix F, op, Hémeray-Aubert; int. in 1966

Mme Maurice Kuppenheim T, ab, 1877, Ducher, Vve.; flowers salmon-yellow tinged with pink, large, dbl.

Mme Maurice Rafin HT, mp, 1913, Bernaix fils; flowers clear pink, carmine center, large, full, moderate fragrance

Mme Maurice Rivoire HP, lp, 1876, Gonod; flowers deep flesh, exterior petals white, medium, full

Mme Maurin – See **Mme Denis**, T, 1853

Mme Maxime Bonnet B, mr, 1861, Pradel; flowers cherry-carmine

Mme Maxime de la Rocheterie HP, mp, 1880, Granger; flowers flesh pink, medium to large, full; [sport of Victor Verdier]

Mme Méha Sabatier HT, rb, 1916, Pernet-Ducher; flowers deep red, with white stripes in some petals, large, dbl.; [seedling × Château de Clos Vougeot]

Mme Mélanie Soupert HT, yb, 1905, Pernet-Ducher; bud pointed; flowers salmon yellow, suffused pink and carmine, large, semi-dbl., moderate fragrance; vigorous growth

Mme Mélanie Soupert, Climbing Cl HT, op, 1914, Burrell; flowers dawn pink, becoming salmon pink, very large, dbl.; [sport of Mme Mélanie Soupert]

Mme Mélanie Vigneron HP, m, 1882, Vigneron; flowers lilac pink, reverse silver, large, very full; [Elisabeth Vigneron × unknown]

Mme Mélanie Willermoz T, w, 1849, Lacharme, F.; flowers white tinted salmon pink at center, shaded cream, large, dbl, semi-globular, moderate fragrance; good repeat; growth compact

Mme Melon du Thé – See **Clotilde Soupert**, Pol

Mme Mercier de Molin HT, rb, 1921, Schwartz, A.; flowers fiery red, tinted crimson, edges slightly tinged rose-pink, dbl.; [Comte G. de Rochemur × Liberty]

Mme Michel Dufay HMoy, rb, 1932, Sauvageot, H.; flowers maroon, reverse purplish garnet, large, dbl., cupped; occaisionally recurrent; foliage dark; very vigorous, upright, bushy growth; [George Dickson × *R. moyesii*]

Mme Millerand HT, w, 1926, Walter, L.; flowers rosy white, shaded salmon, dbl.; [Pharisaer × Mme Henriette Schissele]

Mme Miniver HT, ob, 1947, Vilmorin-Andrieux; bud pointed; flowers orange-red tinted apricot, base yellow, large, dbl.; vigorous growth; [Joanna Hill × Charles P. Kilham]

Mme Miolan Carvalho N, dy, 1876, Chédane-Guinoisseau; flowers dark sulfur-yellow, large, full, moderate fragrance; [Chromatella × unknown]; sometimes attributed to Lévêque

Mme Moisans LCl, mp, 1955, Robichon; flowers hortensia-pink, dbl.; recurrent bloom; foliage glossy; [Lady Sylvia × seedling]; int. by Pin

Mme Montel HP, lp, 1880, Liabaud; flowers delicate rose pink, very large, dbl.; [La Reine × unknown]

Mme Montet – See **Mme Montel**, HP

Mme Morand Andrée HT, dr, 1957, Privat; flowers blackish red, very large; foliage dark; vigorous growth

Mme Moreau HP, mr, 1864, Moreau; flowers bright red, tinged violet, 4½-5½ in., very dbl., globular, borne mostly solitary; foliage dark green; [Victor Verdier × unknown]; int. by Gonod

Mme Moreau M, pb, 1872, Moreau et Robert; flowers vermilion, edged and striped white, large, dbl.; some repeat; upright, broad (5 × 5 ft.) growth

Mme Moreau T, yb, 1889, Moreau & Robert; flowers coppery yellow, center darker, reverse pink with apricot-yellow, very large, full; [Mme Falcot × Mme Bérard]

Mme Moser HT, pb, 1889, Vigneron; flowers pink to rosy white, large, dbl.

Mme Mouseur-Fontaine HT, yb, 1931, Soupert & Notting; bud pointed; flowers sulfur-yellow, center saffron-yellow, large, dbl.; [Sunburst × Primerose]

Mme Mulson T, pb, 1895, Bernaix; flowers silky yellow, shaded salmon pink, center canary yellow with copper red, large, full

Mme Nabonnand T, w, 1877, Nabonnand; flowers flesh white shaded pink; growth tall, not exceptionally vigorous

Mme Nachury HP, mp, 1873, Damaizin; flowers silky pink, very large, full, cupped; [La Reine × unknown]

Mme Neige – See **Youki San**, HT

Mme Nérard B, pb, 1838, Nérard; flowers delicate blush pink, large, full, flat; [Rose Edouard × unknown]

Mme Neumann – See **Hermosa**, Ch

Mme Nicolas Aussel HT, ob, 1930, Pernet-Ducher; bud pointed; flowers salmon shaded carmine and ochre, large, dbl.; foliage dark; vigorous growth; int. by Gaujard

Mme Nicolas Boudler HT, pb, 1934, Boudler; bud round; flowers rose, reverse shaded yellow, large, dbl.; [Souv. de Georges Pernet × Gloire de Dijon]

Mme Nicolas Koechlin C, mp, about 1860, Baumann

Mme Nobécourt B, lp, 1893, Moreau et Robert; bud very large and long; flowers light satiny pink very large, dbl., cupped, borne in small clusters, intense fragrance; foliage light green; [Mme Isaac Pereire × unknown]

Mme Noël HT, rb, 1939, Chambard, C.; flowers vermilion-red, reverse carmine-yellow, very large, dbl., cupped; foliage dark; vigorous growth

Mme Noël le Mire HT, rb, 1934, Sauvageot, H.; flowers brilliant crimson-red with yellow reflections, semi-dbl., cupped, borne in clusters; strong stems; dwarf growth; [George Dawson × Dance of Joy]

Mme Noman HP, w, 1867, Guillot père; flowers pure white, small, full, globular; foliage somewhat cimpled; prickles numerous, small; [Mme Récamier × unknown]

Mme Norbert Levavasseur Pol, mr, 1903, Levavasseur; flowers crimson-red, center lighter, bluing badly, small, semi-dbl., cupped, borne in large clusters; foliage glossy, dark; bushy, dwarf growth; [Crimson Rambler × Gloire des Polyantha]

Mme Norman HP, w, 1867, Guillot; flowers medium, dbl.

Mme Ocker Ferencz T, yb, 1892, Bernaix, A.; bud long, washed with violet pink; flowers canary and carmine, large, full

Mme Ofman HT, or, 1958, Ofman; bud long, pointed; flowers large, very dbl., high-centered, moderate fragrance; foliage dark, glossy; strong stems; vigorous, upright, bushy growth; int. in 1954

Mme Olga T, w, 1889, Lévêque; flowers white, finely and delicately shaded yellow, large, full; foliage dark green; growth vigorous

Mme Olympe Téretschenko B, w, 1882, Lévêque; flowers white with light blush, large, full, cupped; [sport of Louise Odier]

Mme Orève HT, ob, 1926, Chambard, M.; flowers rose-salmon, center coppery salmon

Mme Oswald de Kerchove HP, pb, 1879, Schwartz; bud oval; flowers white to coppery yellow at center, medium, very full, borne in clusters of 3-5; foliage medium green; prickles short, horizontal, unequal; [Mme Falcot × (Mme Recamier × unknown)]

Mme P. Doithier HT, pb, 1920, Chambard, M.; flowers glossy pink, shaded shrimp-pink

Mme P. Euler – See **Mme Pierre Euler**, HT

Mme P. Olivier – See **Shining Star**, HT

Mme Paquel HT, my, 1945, Mallerin, C.; flowers chrome-yellow, well-formed, dbl.; foliage wood and reddish; int. by A. Meilland

Mme Paul Bouju HT, ob, 1930, Chambard, C.; bud long, pointed; flowers carmine-orange, very large, cupped; foliage bronze

Mme Paul Duringe HT, mp, 1934, Chambard, C.; flowers deep coral, large; very vigorous growth

Mme Paul Euler – See **Mme Pierre Euler**, HT

Mme Paul Gravereaux HRg, mr, 1901, L'Hay

Mme Paul Lacoutière HT, op, 1897, Buatois; flowers coppery-pink, large, semi-dbl.; [Ma Capucine × Baronne Adolphe de Rothschild]

Mme Paul Marchandeau HT, w, 1928, Barbaras; flowers white, base deep yellow, dbl.

Mme Paul Marmy T, yb, 1884, Marmy; bud large, globular, cream; flowers very light yellow at center, pale pink at edges, medium to large, full, borne mostly solitary; foliage thick, glossy; numerous prickles; [Gloire de Dijon × unknown]

Mme Paul Olivier HT, op, 1902, Pernet-Ducher; flowers salmon pink, shaded carmine, large, full, globular, moderate fragrance; [Mme Eugene Boullet × Mme Cadeau-Ramey]

Mme Paul Ollivary HT, dp, 1924, Schwartz, A.; bud pointed; flowers coppery salmon, reverse shaded yellow, nearly large, single; [Mme Mélanie Soupert × Emma Wright]

Mme Paul Parmentier HT, ob, 1919, Gillot, F.; flowers salmon-yellow shaded flesh, copper and daybreak-pink, dbl.; [Le Progres × Lyon Rose]

Mme Paul Rottier F, rb, 1957, Buisman, G. A. H.; flowers red shaded orange, borne in large clusters; moderate growth

Mme Paul Varin-Bernier T, pb, 1906, Soupert & Notting; bud dark yellow; flowers various shades of melon, large, dbl.; foliage dark green; [Mme C. P. Strassheim × Mme Dr. Jütté]

Mme Paula Guisez – See **Heat Wave**, F

Mme Paule Massad S, ab, Guillot-Massad; flowers soft blend of apricot, pink and yellow, outer petals white, large, very full, borne in clusters of 3-5, slight fragrance; recurrent; moderate (4-5 ft.) growth; int. by Roses Guillot, 1997

Mme Pauline Labonté T, op, 1852, Pradel; flowers salmon-pink, large, dbl.; vigorous growth

Mme Pauline Vilot HP, mr, 1859, Marest

Mme Pelisson T, ly, 1891, Brosse; flowers light citron, white reverse, medium, dbl.; growth vigorous, compact

Mme Pellissier – See **Mme Pelisson**, T

Mme Pernet-Ducher HT, dy, 1891, Pernet-Ducher; flowers canary yellow, outer petals washed carmine, fading to creamy white, large, very dbl., moderate fragrance; [unnamed Tea × Victor Verdier]

Mme Petit HP, dr, 1900, Corboeuf; flowers velvety carmine shaded purple, striped with one white line, borne in small clusters; [Charles Lefebvre × Pride of Reigate]

Mme Ph. Tsirnana – See **Mme Tsiranana**, HT

Mme Phélip HP, lp, 1852, Lacharme; flowers light pink, edges brighter, large, full

Mme Philbert Boutigny HP, mp, 1913, Boutigny, P.; flowers bright, clear rose pink, full; [Ulrich Brunner fils × Paul Neyron]

Mme Philémon Cochet T, lp, 1887, Cochet, S.; bud large, truncated; flowers extremely light pink, often marked with blotches of light salmon pink, medium to large, very dbl., slightly cupped, borne mostly solitary, moderate fragrance; foliage bright green, purplish underneath; prickles triangular, few; growth upright; [Sylphide × unknown]

Mme Philémon Plantamour – See **Mme Philippe Plantamour**, HRg

Mme Philippe Kuntz T, pb, 1889, Bernaix; flowers cerise red fading to delicate blush pink toward center, large, full, cupped, moderate fragrance; foliage brilliant green

Mme Philippe Plantamour HRg, mr, about 1900; flowers flame red, large, semi-dbl.

Mme Philippe Rivoire HT, ab, 1908, Pernet-Ducher; flowers apricot-yellow, center nankeen yellow, reverse red, large, dbl., globular; vigorous growth

Mme Pierre Cochet N, yb, 1891, Cochet, S.; flowers saffron-yellow, shaded scarlet, center apricot, dbl.; vigorous, climbing growth; [Reve d'Or × unknown]

Mme Pierre Euler HT, rb, 1907, Guillot, P.; flowers silvery vermilion-pink, large, dbl., moderate fragrance; [Antoine Rivoire × Killarney]

Mme Pierre Forestier HT, ob, 1933, Chambard, C.; flowers orange, shaded shrimp-carmine to satiny China-pink, very large, cupped

Mme Pierre Guillot T, ob, 1888, Guillot & fils; flowers coppery orange yellow grading to a lighter shade at top, bordered with carmine, full, borne mostly solitary

Mme Pierre Guillot HT, 1928, Guillot

Mme Pierre Koechlin HT, op, 1934, Sauvageot, H.; flowers salmon-pink, very large, dbl., high-centered; [seedling × The Queen Alexandra Rose]; int. by C-P

Mme Pierre Margery HP, mp, 1881, Liabaud; flowers cerise pink, large, full; freely remontant; [Jules Margottin × unknown]

Mme Pierre Oger B, pb, 1878, Oger; flowers blush, reverse tinged rosy lilac, medium size, dbl., cupped, moderate sweet fragrance; good repeat; upright (5 ft.) growth; [sport of Reine Victoria]; int. by C. Verdier

Mme Pierre Perny T, ly, 1880, Nabonnand; bud elongated; flowers saffron yellow, large, semi-dbl.; nearly thornless

Mme Pierre Place HP, mp, 1854, Margottin; flowers bright pink, medium, full

Mme Pierre S. duPont – See **Mrs Pierre S. duPont**, HT

Mme Pierre S. duPont, Climbing – See **Mrs Pierre S. duPont, Climbing**, Cl HT

Mme Pierson HP, lp, 1860, Fontaine; flowers light pink, aging to light red with silvery tintes, large, full

Mme Pirrie – See **Lady Pirrie**, HT

Mme Pizay HT, op, 1920, Chambard, C.; flowers light salmon; [Unnamed variety × Mme Mélanie Soupert]

Mme Pizay, Climbing Cl HT, op, 1920, Chambard, C.; flowers light salmon-pink, reverse darker, 4 in., dbl.

Mme Plantamour – See **Mme Philippe Plantamour**, HRg

Mme Plantier A, w, 1835, Plantier; sepals long; flowers creamy white changing to pure white, green pip, 6-7 cm., very dbl., flat, borne in clusters of 10-20, moderate fragrance; non-recurrent; foliage small, light gray-green; almost thornless; vigorous, spreading,bushy (about 5 ft.) growth; [thought to be *R. alba* × *R. moschata*]; sometimes classed as hybrid N, HCh, or D

Mme Platz M, dp, 1864, Moreau et Robert; flowers carmine-pink, 7-9 cm., dbl., flat, intense fragrance; freely remontant

Mme Plumecocq HT, dy, 1931, Lens; flowers golden yellow, center brighter; [Roselandia × Ville de Paris]

Mme Plumecocq HT, pb, 1954, Gaujard; flowers bright pink, reverse silvery, very large, dbl., high-centered; foliage bronze; vigorous, upright growth; [Peace × seedling]

Mme Poincaré – See **Mme Raymond Poincaré**, HT

Mme Portier Durel HWich, w, 1910, Portier-Durel; flowers pure white, 3 cm., rosette, borne in medium clusters, slight fragrance

Madame President – See **Madam President**, F

Mme Prévost HP, w, 1900, Corboeuf; flowers white, tinted salmon pink

Mme Prosper Laugier HP, mr, 1875, Verdier, E.; flowers carmine-red, large, dbl., moderate fragrance; foliage dark green, irregularly dentate; prickles numerous, short, thick, brown; [John Hopper × unknown]

Mme Prudhomme HP, mr, 1872, Moreau & Robert; flowers bright cherry red, center flame red, large, full

Mme Puissant HP, mr, 1861, Moreau & Robert; flowers light cherry, edges shaded crimson, large, full

Mme Pulliat HP, pb, 1866, Ducher; flowers dark pink, shaded purple, medium to large, full, globular

Mme Rambaux HP, dp, 1881, Rambaux; bud conical; flowers carmine pink, paler on reverse, very large, very full, moderate fragrance; foliage dark green above, glaucescent beneath

Mme Raoul Fauran HT, m, 1934, Sauvageot, H.; flowers carmine shaded velvety purple, reverse light purple, very large, semi-dbl., cupped; foliage leathery, dark; vigorous, bushy growth

Mme Rathswell – See **Mme Therese Roswell**, T

Mme Ravary HT, ob, 1899, Pernet-Ducher; bud long, golden yellow, conical; flowers orange-yellow, large, dbl., cupped, moderate fragrance; foliage brownish-green; prickles strong; vigorous, bushy growth

Mme Raymond Chevalier-Appert HT, rb, 1917, Guillot, P.; flowers cerise-red, edged lighter, dbl., intense fragrance; robust (5 ft.) growth; [Gen. MacArthur × Richmond]

Mme Raymond Chevalier-Appert, Climbing Cl HT, rb, after 1917

Mme Raymond Gaujard – See **Olympiad**, HT, 1931

Mme Raymond Poincaré HT, pb, 1919, Gravereaux; flowers pale pink and salmon, center yellow, large, dbl.; [Antoine Rivoire × Ophelia]; int. by Kieffer & Sons; Gold Medal, Bagatelle, 1915

Mme Récamier HP, w, 1853, Lacharme; flowers flesh white, passing to pure white, medium, dbl., borne in small clusters

Mme Remond T, yb, 1882, Lambert, E.; flowers pale sulphur yellow, broadly margined with bright red, medium, full, moderate fragrance; nearly thornless; growth vigorous; [Comtesse de Labarthe × Anna Olivier]

Mme Rémond T, yb, Lambert, E.; flowers sulfur-yellow, edged red, very dbl.

Mme Renahy HP, dp, 1889, Guillot et Fils; flowers carmine, center brighter, reverse delicate pink, large, full, globular

Mme Renard HP, op, 1872, Moreau et Robert; flowers salmon-pink, very large, dbl.; [Jules Margottin × unknown]

Mme René André HT, lp, 1906; flowers large, dbl.

Mme René Cassin HT, pb, 1964, Delbard-Chabert; flowers cyclamen-pink, reverse silvery, 5 in., 24 petals, high-centered, moderate fragrance; foliage dark, glossy; vigorous, upright growth; [Mme Armand Souzy × Impeccable]; Gold Medal, Lyon, 1962, Gold Medal, Bagatelle, 1962

Mme René Collette HT, pb, 1909, Gamon; flowers yellowish-pink with red, large, dbl.; [Mlle Anna Charron × Kaiserin Auguste Viktoria]

Mme René Coty HT, rb, 1958, Meilland, F.; bud globular; flowers Persian red, reverse yellow, very large, dbl., moderate fragrance; foliage glossy, leathery; long, strong stems; vigorous, upright growth; [Peace × Brazil]; int. by URS, 1955; Gold Medal, Bagatelle, 1954

Mme René Gérard T, yb, 1897, Guillot; flowers dark coppery yellow, shaded nasturtium red, large, full

Mme René Gravereaux HRg, lp, 1902, Gravereaux; flowers lilac pink with light violet, base tinted yellow, very large; [Conrad Ferdinand Meyer × Safrano]

Mme René Lefèvre HT, yb, 1938, Robichon; bud long, pointed, sulphur-yellow, edged cerise; flowers golden yellow, flushed carmine, open, large, semi-dbl.; foliage leathery, bronze; [Elizabeth of York × Mme Henri Pate]

Mme René Truchot HT, 1952, Orard, Joseph

Mme Renée Baltet B, dr, 1865, Verdier; flowers fiery carmine-purple, large, full

Mme Renée Oberthür HT, w, 1908, Vigneron; flowers procelain white, with occasional salmon tints at center, large, dbl., moderate fragrance; foliage dark green; [Mme Caroline Testout × unknown]

Mme Renshy – See **Mme Renahy**, HP

Mme Retornaz T, yb, 1867, Guillot; flowers yellow with copper tings, large, full

Mme Rival – See **Auguste Mie**, HP

Mme Rival HP, lp, 1866, Gonod; flowers light silky pink, large, full, slight fragrance

Mme Rival Verne HP, pb, 1874, Liabaud; flowers carmine pink over salmon pink, large, full

Mme Rivers HP, mp, 1850, Guillot; flowers flesh pink, medium, full, globular

Mme Robert HT, yb, 1917, Chambard, C.; flowers nankeen yellow with chamois reflexes, dbl.

Mme Robert Fortin HT, m, 1935, Buatois; flowers carmine-purple, large, dbl., cupped; very vigorous growth; [Mme Caroline Testout × Yves Druhen]

Mme Robert Joffet F, rb, 1956, Delbard-Chabert; flowers salmon to geranium, reverse carmine-pink, well-formed, large, semi-dbl.

Mme Robert Martin HT, pb, 1943, Meilland, F.; bud long, pointed; flowers pink, center coral, very large, very dbl.; foliage leathery; vigorous, bushy growth; [Charles P. Kilham × Mme Joseph Perraud]; int. by A. Meilland

Mme Robert Perrier HT, ob, Orard, Joseph; flowers coppery, stamens saffron, large, semi-dbl.

Mme Roberte Huet HT, rb, 1960, Hémeray-Aubert; flowers velvety scarlet, reverse raspberry-red, base gold, dbl.; foliage glossy, slightly bronze; strong stems; vigorous growth

Mme Rochefontaine HP, pb; flowers rosy flesh to clear pink, large, dbl.

Mme Rocher HP, dr, 1878, Cochet, S.; flowers bright pink, with the inside of the petals darker, 5-5½ in., very full; numerous prickles; growth upright

Mme Rodolphe Arnaud HT, pb, 1911, Perdriolle; flowers dark pink, shaded yellow, with shrimp pink tints, moderate fragrance; [Lyon Rose × Mme Segond Weber]

Mme Roger HP, lp, 1877, Moreau-Robert; flowers delicate pink, nearly white, large, full

Mme Roger Douine HT, rb, 1926, Reymond; flowers crimson, shaded scarlet, dbl.; [Souv. de Claudius Denoyel × Mme Edouard Herriot]

Mme Roger Verlomme HT, pb, 1951, Mallerin, C.; flowers ochre edged flesh-pink, very large, very dbl.; very vigorous growth; Gold Medal, Geneva, 1951

Mme Roland HP, pb, 1869, Roland; flowers flesh pink with salmon shades, large, full

Mme Rolland HGal, dp, before 1835, Girardon

Mme Rolland HP, dp, 1867, Moreau & Robert; flowers very large, full; [Victor Verdier × unknown]

Mme Rosa Monnet HP, dp, 1885, Monnet; flowers light crimson, large, cupped, moderate sweet fragrance; good repeat

Mme Rose Caron HP, mp, 1898, Lévêque; flowers monotone pink, nuanced carmine at center, large; foliage light green

Mme Rose Chéri mp, 1850, Laffay, M.; flowers delicate pink, medium, dbl.; foliage blackish green

Mme Rose Romarin T, rb, 1888, Nabonnand; bud tall, pointed; flowers light coppery red with salmon, large, full, moderate fragrance; [Papillon × Chromatella]

Mme Roudillon HP, mr, 1903, Vigneron; flowers bright carmine red, very large, very full, intense fragrance; foliage dark green; [Mme Isaac Pereire × Mme Ernest Levavasseur]

Mme Roussel T, w, 1830, Desprez; flowers white, center flesh pink, large

Mme Rousset HP, lp, 1864, Guillot; flowers light silvery pink, large, full, cupped

Mme Royet LCl, m

Mme Rozain-Boucharlat T, yb, 1894, Liabaud; flowers chamois yellow, shaded pink, large, full, globular

Mme Ruau HFt, pb, 1909, Gravereaux; flowers orange/pink with dark yellow, large, dbl.; [Pharisäer × Les Rosati]

Mme S. Croza HT, ab, 1935, Laperrière; bud long; flowers flesh-pink, very large, dbl., high-centered; foliage leathery; long stems; vigorous growth; [Sunburst × unknown]

Mme S. Mottet N, my, 1899, Cochet-Cochet; bud pink; [William Allen Richardson × unknown]

Mme Sachi HT, w, Meilland; int. by Keisei, 1984

Mme Sancy de Parabère Bslt, mp, 1874, Bonnet; flowers bright violet-rose, 5 in., semi-dbl. to dbl., peony-shaped, borne in clusters of 3-5, moderate clove fragrance; very early, non-recurrent bloom; thornless; growth to 7 ft.; very hardy; cross between a Boursault and a form of *R. centifolia*; int. by Jamin, 1874

Mme Saportas HGal, dp; flowers bright rosy red, large, dbl.

Mme Savary HRg, dr, 1901, L'Hay; flowers red-violet

Mme Schmitt HP, mp, 1854, Schmitt; flowers rosy pink, shaded carmine, reverse silvery white, 12-15 cm., full; few prickles; growth upright

Mme Schmitt HT, ab, 1922, Schwartz, A.; flowers salmon-pink, shaded peach-blossom-pink, dbl.

Mme Schultz N, yb, 1856, Béluze; flowers pale yellow, center darker, medium, dbl., intense fragrance; vigorous growth

Mme Schwaller HT, mp, 1886, Bernaix, A.; flowers large; vigorous growth

Mme Scipion Cochet HP, rb, 1872, Desmazures/Cochet; flowers shining cherry pink edged soft pink and white, center petals wrinkled, dbl., cupped; vigorous growth

Mme Scipion Cochet T, pb, 1886, Bernaix, A.; flowers pale pink to white, center yellow, large, dbl., cupped, moderate fragrance; vigorous growth; [Anna Olivier × Duchesse de Brabant]

Mme Segond Weber HT, op, 1907, Soupert & Notting; bud ovoid, pointed; flowers clear salmon-pink, very large, dbl., cupped, moderate fragrance; long, strong stems; bushy growth; [Antoine Rivoire × Souv. de Victor Hugo]; Gold Medal, Bagatelle, 1909

Mme Segond Weber, Climbing Cl HT, op, 1911, Ardagh (also Reymond, 1929); flowers salmon pink, very large, full; [sport of Mme Segond Weber]

Madame Seneclause HT, lp

Madame Shizuko HT, mp, Hiroshima; int. by Hiroshima Bara-en, 1998

Mme Simon Delaux T, yb, 1891, Degressy; flowers yellow, shaded copper

Mme Soëtmans – See **Mme Zoëtmans**, D

Mme Soledad de Ampuera de Leguizamon HT, pb, 1928, Soupert & Notting; flowers hydrangea-pink, reverse carmine-rose, dbl.; [General-Superior Arnold Janssen × Mrs E.G. Hill]

Mme Solvay LCl, dp, Eve, A.; flowers crimson, flecked white at base, medium, semi-dbl., borne in large clusters, moderate fragrance; int. in 1992

Mme Sophie Charlotte A, lp, Weihrauch; int. in 1986

Mme Sophie Froppot HP, mp, 1876, Levet; flowers pale satin rose, large, dbl., cupped; foliage nearly thornless; [Victor Verdier × unknown]

Mme Sophie Stern HP, dp, 1887, Lévêque; flowers brilliant light bright rose, with metallic reflections, very large, dbl., globular

Mme Sophie Tropot – See **Mme Sophie Froppot**, HP

Mme Soubeyran HP, dp, 1872, Gonod; flowers bright rose, small, full

Mme Souchet B, pb, 1843, Souchet; flowers bluish rose pink, edges lighter, large, very full

Mme Soupert M, mr, 1851, Robert; bud well mossed; flowers cerise red, medium, full, rosette, borne in small clusters

Mme Soupert HP, w, 1863, Portemer; flowers flesh white, medium, full

Mme Soupert HP, w, 1864, Pernet; flowers pure white, medium, full; perhaps the same as Mme Soupert from Portemer, 1863

Mme Souveton P, pb, 1874, Pernet père; flowers delicate pink, medium, full, cupped

Mme Spotti HT, m, 1955, Privat; flowers pink striped mauve, very dbl.; foliage glossy; very vigorous growth

Mme Standish HP, mp, 1860, Trouillard; flowers bright pink, medium, full

Mme Steffen HT, w, 1900, Buatois; flowers flesh white, large, full; [Irene Watts × Mavourneen]

Mme Steinbach HT, pb, 1934, Caron, B.; bud very long; flowers coppery pink tinted coral, very large, dbl.; [Mrs Pierre S. duPont × Cécile Walter]

Mme Stolz D, ly, before 1848; flowers pale straw yellow, medium to large, full, cupped, moderate fragrance; foliage light green

Mme Suzanne Hervé HP, dr, 1936, Hervé; bud very long, pointed; flowers velvety red, heavily streaked maroon; vigorous growth; [Baron Girod de l'Ain × unknown]; int. by Vially

Mme Taft Pol, dp, 1909, Levavasseur; flowers ruby-pink medium, dbl., borne in clusters; vigorous, bushy growth; [Crimson Rambler × Mme Norbert Levavasseur]

Mme Taha Hussein HT, rb, 1939, Colombier; flowers Indian red, reverse darker, semi-dbl.; vigorous growth; [Charles P. Kilham × Betty Uprichard]

Mme Teresa Estaban – See **Coral Fiesta**, HT

Mme Th. Cattier T, my, 1900, Bénard; flowers canary yellow, medium, very full

Mme Théobald Sernin HP, mr, 1877, Brassac; flowers currant-red nuanced carmine, large, full

Mme Théodore Cornet HP, mr, 1899, Bénard; flowers currant red

Mme Théodore Delacourt HT, mp, 1913, Pernet-Ducher; bud long, rosy-scarlet; flowers reddish-salmon nuanced light yellow, large, very dbl., globular; foliage bronzy reddish green; prickles unequal, protrusive, few

Mme Théodore Vernes HP, mp, 1891, Lévêque; flowers bright pink with lighter edges, large, full; foliage dark green

Mme Thérèse Deschamps T, pb, 1888, Nabonnand; bud crimson; flowers very bright pink, striped on the upper surface with carmine, reverse whitish, large, semi-dbl., borne in small clusters; foliage thick, matte bronze-green; prickles few, small; growth erect

Mme Thérèse Levet – See **Mlle Thérèse Levet**, HP

Mme Therese Roswell T, dp, 1906, California Nursery Co.; bud carmine; flowers rose pink with deeper shadings, small; nearly thornless

Mme Thévenot HP, dr, 1878, Jamain, H.; flowers bright red, large, very dbl.

Mme Thibaut HP, lp, 1889, Lévêque; flowers delicate satiny pink nuanced carmine pink, dbl., camellia-like; foliage bright green

Mme Thiers B, pb, 1873, Pradel; flowers pink, center brighter, edged violet, medium, full

Mme Tiret HRg, mr, 1901, Gravereaux & Müller; flowers bright red, with silvery pink exterior, large, semi-dbl., cupped, borne mostly solitary; foliage large, light green, slightly dentate; prickles small, straight; stems reddish; [(Pierre Notting × Cardinal Patrizzi) × Germanica]

Mme Tixier – See **Souv d'un Ami**, T

Mme Tony Baboud HT, my, 1895, Godard; flowers medium golden yellow, large, semi-dbl.

Mme Tressan – See **Mme de Tressan**, HGal

Mme Trifle N, yb, 1869, Levet; flowers deep yellow, center salmon yellow with copper, 9-10 cm., very dbl., cupped, moderate fragrance; good repeat; foliage large; tall, vigorous, climbing growth; [Gloire de Dijon × unknown]

Mme Trotter – See **Mme de Trotter**, HP

Mme Trottier HT, yb, 1937, Leenders, M.; flowers yellowish-flesh, large, very dbl.; vigorous, bushy growth

Mme Trudeaux HP, dp, 1850, Boll; flowers shining dark pink, aging lighter pink, medium to large, full

Mme Tsiranana HT, mr, Croix; int. in 1971

Mme V. Morrell – See **V. Viviand-Morel**, T

Mme Vachez B, lp, 1864, Ducher; flowers whitish pink, very large

Mme Valembourg HP, m, 1863, Oger; flowers shining purple, shaded violet, large, full

Mme Van de Voorde HT, mr, 1928, Mallerin, C.; bud pointed; flowers brilliant scarlet, large, semi-dbl., cupped; very vigorous growth; [Mme Méha Sabatier × Kitchener of Khartoum]; int. by C-P

Mme van Houtte HP, dp, 1857, Margottin; flowers dark pink, aging to flesh pink

Mme Vannier HT, or, Orard, Joseph; flowers coppery red, large, dbl., cupped

Madame Verbelen HT, dr, 1976, Delforge; flowers dbl., 65 petals, cupped, intense fragrance; int. in 1973

Mme Verdier HP, w, 1840, Verdier, V.; sepals very long; flowers pale flesh; foliage gray-green

Mme Verlot HP, mp, 1876, Verdier, E.; flowers velvety pink, very large, very full, slightly cupped

Mme Vermorel T, yb, 1901, Mari/Jupeau; flowers dark coppery yellow with bronze center, medium, dbl.

Mme Verrier-Cachet HP, mr, 1895, Chédane-Guinoisseau; flowers carmine-red, very large, dbl.

Mme Veuve Alexandre Pommery HP, lp, 1882, Lévêque; flowers delicate pink, nuanced bright pink within, petal edges very light pink, very large; foliage large, dark green

Mme Veuve Alexis Pommery – See **Mme Veuve Alexandre Pommery**, HP

Mme Veuve Ménier HT, lp, 1891, Schwartz; flowers pale light rose, nuanced dawn gold and carmine, large, very full; foliage glaucous green; stems tinted purple; [Camoëns × unknown]

Mme Vibert HP, dp, about 1835, Vibert; flowers deep rose pink, edges carmine, medium, full

Mme Victor Bozzola HT, mp, 1935, Soupert, C.; bud pointed; flowers bright coral-pink, well-formed, large; [Kardinal Piffl × Mme Edouard Herriot]

Mme Victor Caillet T, pb, 1891, Bernaix; flowers peony pink with carmine and salmon, fading to white, large, dbl., cupped

Mme Victor Lottin HWich, rb, 1921, Lottin; flowers dark red, shaded crimson; vigorous, climbing growth

Mme Victor Morlot T, m, 1906, Chauvry; flowers violet-pink, base lighter, large, full; [Marquise de Vivens × Mme Caro]

Mme Victor Rault HT, w, 1920, Croibier; flowers white tinted salmon, center yellow, dbl.; [Mme Mélanie Soupert × Lyon Rose]

Mme Victor Verdier HP, mr, 1863, Verdier, E.; flowers clear light crimson, large, 75 petals, flat, intense fragrance; seasonal bloom; vigorous growth; [Senateur Vaisse × unknown]

Mme Victor Wibaut HP, op, 1870, David; flowers salmon pink, medium, full

Mme Vidot HP, ab, 1854, Couturier; sepals long, acuminate; flowers flesh-white, large, full; foliage smooth, light green, oval-elliptical; prickles unequal, nearly straight, very sharp; int. by E. Verdier

Mme Viger HT, lp, 1901, Jupeau; flowers creamy pink, very large, dbl.; [Heinrich Schultheis × G. Nabonnand]

Mme Vigneron HP, op, 1858, Vigneron; flowers peach-pink, large, full

Mme Villate HT, ob, 1936, Walter, L.; flowers orange with yellow, dbl.; foliage glossy; [Korovo × seedling]

Mme Ville HGal, mp, before 1885; flowers carmine pink, medium, full

Mme Vincent Auriol HT, yb, 1951, Caron, B.; bud long; flowers golden coral, large, dbl., peony-like; foliage glossy; vigorous growth; [Trylon × seedling]; int. by URS; Gold Medal, Bagatelle, 1948

Madame Violet HT, m, 1986, Teranishi, K.; flowers lavender, 45 petals, high-centered, borne singly, no fragrance; foliage medium size, medium green, semi-glossy; prickles medium, reddish light-green; tall, upright growth; PP6315; int. by Itama Rose Nursery, 1981

Madame Violet, Climbing Cl HT, m, 1999; flowers pale violet, 5½ in., 45 petals, high-centered, no fragrance; growth to 9-12 ft.; int. by Itami Rose Nursery, 1992

Mme Virgilio Pirola HT, mr, 1939, Lens; bud long, pointed; flowers very bright red, dbl.; foliage dark; vigorous, bushy growth; [Charles P. Kilham × Étoile de Hollande]; Gold Medal, Bagatelle, 1939

Mme Visseaux HT, op, 1936, Mallerin, C.; bud long; flowers orange-pink, base yellow, 4-5 in., dbl.; [Odette Foussier × Elvira Aramayo]; int. by C-P

Mme Vittoria Gagnière HT, w, 1909, Schwartz, Vve.; flowers white tinted pink; [Anna Chartron × Mrs W.J. Grant]

Mme Viviand-Morel Ayr, dp, 1882, Schwartz; flowers carmine pink tinted cerise, reverse violet-white, medium, full, borne in clusters; foliage reddish green; [*R. arvensis* × Cheshunt Hybrid]

Mme Viviand-Morel HP, mr, 1887, Bernaix; flowers carmine red with cherry-garnet shades, very large, dbl.

Mme Von Boch – See **Frau Geheimrat Von Boch**, T

Mme von Siemens T, mp, 1895, Nabonnand; bud long; flowers flesh pink, very large, full

Mme W. Baumann HT, rb; flowers clear satin red-orange, large, dbl., high-centered; growth to 60-70 cm.; int. by Sauvageot, 1973

Mme W. C. Whitney – See **Mrs W. C. Whitney**, HT

Mme Wagram, Comtesse de Turenne T, pb, 1894, Bernaix, A.; flowers bright satiny rose suffused with darker rose, very large, full, moderate fragrance; vigorous growth; sometimes classed as HT

Mme Walter Baumann HT, rb, 1934, Reymond; bud long; flowers carmine, base yellow, open, dbl.; [Mlle Franziska Kruger × Gwynne Carr]; int. by Vially

Mme Welche T, yb, 1878, Widow Ducher; bud pointed; flowers coppery orange-yellow within, outer petals pale yellow, large, full, globular, intense fragrance; growth vigorous

Mme Willermoz – See **Mme Mélanie Willermoz**, T

Mme William T, ly, 1856, Lartay; flowers straw yellow

Mme William Paul HP, m, 1862, Verdier, E.; flowers

violet-purple, edged bright crimson, aging to flesh pink, medium to large, full

Mme William Paul M, dp, 1869, Moreau et Robert; flowers bright rose, large, dbl., cupped; recurrent bloom

Mme William Wood HP, pb, 1876, Verdier, E.; flowers carmine pink, centers bright red, edges lighter, large, very full

Mme York HP, dr, 1881, Moreau et Robert; flowers vermilion red shaded carmine and nuanced blackish purple, large, dbl., intense fragrance; foliage dark green

Mme Yves Latieule HT, my, 1949, Meilland, F.; flowers primrose-yellow, 5 in., 70 petals; foliage glossy, dark; vigorous growth; [Mme Joseph Perraud × Léonce Colombier]; Gold Medal, NRS, 1950

Mme Yvette Gayraud HT, ob, Wisbech Plant Co.

Mme Yvonne Chaverot HT, op, Orard, Joseph; flowers rose-salmon, with yellow reverse, large, dbl; foliage glossy, disease-resistant; int. in 1976

Mme Zélia Bourgeois Pol, w, 1906, Vilin; flowers pure white, full, moderate fragrance; [Bouquet de Neige × Miniature]

Mme Zoëtmans D, w, 1830, Marest; flowers pale flesh, tinged with buff, medium, with a small green eye at center, very dbl., cupped, early bloomer, moderate fragrance; non-recurrent; foliage medium green, with 5-7 leaflets; few prickles; bushy, vigorous (5 ft.) growth

Mme Zoutmann – See **Mme Zoëtmans**, D

Madames de Villeparisis M, pb, Morley, Dr B.; [sport of Henri Martin]

Mmes Soeurs Chevandier HP, dr, 1864, Pernet; flowers slatey-wine red, medium

Mlle Anna Vigier T, yb, 1901, Puyravaud; flowers golden, shaded pink, with salmon tints, medium to large, full, moderate fragrance; [General Schablikine × Mlle Lazarine Poizeau]

Madcap F, mr, 1956, Kordes; bud urn-shaped; flowers scarlet-red, 4½ in., 20-25 petals, cupped, moderate fragrance; foliage leathery; bushy growth; PP1363; [Independence × Crimson King]; int. by Stark Bros., 1955

Madcap HT, rb, 1955, Ratcliffe; bud dark red; flowers flame-scarlet striped yellow, or orange without stripe; [sport of Grand Duchesse Charlotte]

Maddalena HT, op, 1934, San Remo Exp. Sta.; bud pointed to ovoid; flowers salmon-pink, reverse begonia-rose, very large, 30-32 petals, cupped; foliage light green, glossy, leathery; long stems; very vigorous, upright, bushy growth; [Julien Potin × J.C. Thornton]

Maddalena Scalarandis Ch, dp, 1901, Scalarandis; flowers dark, rich rose with touches of scarlet and crimson, large; probably extinct

Madeleine HT, ly, Kordes; greenhouse rose; int. by W. Kordes Söhne, before 2005

Madeleine, Climbing Cl HT, ly; int. by Wagner's Rose Nursery, 2005

Madeleine MinFl, yb, 2005, Guillebeau, Ray; flowers yellow, edged pink or red depending on weather, reverse yellow, 1½ in., dbl., borne mostly solitary, no fragrance; foliage medium size, dark green, matte; prickles medium length, straight, slight downward angle, lt. green; bushy, medium (24-30 in.) growth; exhibition, garden decoration; [Fairhope × unknown]; int. by Guillebeau, Ray, 2005

Madeleine d'Aoust T, lp, 1889, Bernaix; flowers light flesh pink, aging white, large, full

Madeleine de Garnier des Garets T, pb, 1900, Buatois; flowers dark coppery pink, very large, full

Madeleine de Vauzelle – See **Mlle Madeleine de Vauzelles**, B

Madeleine Faivre HT, lp, 1902, Buatois; flowers pinkish white, yellow center, large, very dbl.

Madeleine Gaillard HT, w, 1908, Bernaix; flowers white and cream, large, cupped

Madeleine Guillaumez T, w, 1892, Bonnaire; flowers white with salmony center, medium, globular; growth vigorous, upright; [unnamed Tea × Mlle de Sombreuil]

Madeleine Lemaire HWich, op, 1923, Nonin; bud medium, long-pointed; flowers bright salmon-pink, 5-6 cm., semi-dbl., cupped, slight fragrance; [Mrs F.W. Flight × unknown]

Madeleine Lemoine HG, w, before 1930, Franchetti; flowers cream-white, large, single to semi-dbl., moderate fragrance; [*R. gigantea* × *R. moschata*]

Madeleine Monod HT, op, 1939, Chambard, C.; bud long; flowers salmon-carmine, very large, dbl.; foliage bronze; vigorous growth

Madeleine Nonin – See **Mlle Madeleine Nonin**, HP

Madeleine Orosdy Pol, mp, 1912, Gravereaux

Madeleine Pacaud HT, op, 1922, Chambard, C.; flowers silvery rose, tinted salmon

Madeleine Rivoire HT, lp, Orard; int. in 1988

Madeleine Seltzer HMult, ly, 1926, Walter, L.; flowers pale lemon, fading white, 5-6 cm., full, borne in large clusters; non-recurrent; foliage large; few prickles; vigorous growth; [Tausendschön × Mrs Aaron Ward]

Madeleine Selzer – See **Madeleine Seltzer**, HMult

Madeleine Weidert HMult, mp, 1928, Walter, L.; flowers rose-pink; [Tausendschön × Rosel Dach]

Madeline HEg, w, before 1910, possibly Prévost; flowers creamy white edged pink, semi-dbl.; much confusion exists between this an a HCh of the same name

Madeline Correy HT, dp, 1971, Watson; bud globular; flowers cerise, medium, dbl., moderate lemon fragrance; foliage glossy, dark; moderate growth; [Minnie Watson × Sterling Silver]

Madeline Spezzano MinFl, mp, 1985, Bennett, Dee; flowers medium, 45 petals, high-centered; foliage large, medium green, semi-glossy; upright, bushy growth; PP6132; [Sonia × Beauty Secret]; int. by Tiny Petals Nursery

Madeline's Choice S, ab, Erskine; flowers pale yellow and pink, single, moderate fragrance; non-remontant, long blooming season

Madelon HT, or, 1983, deRuiter, George; flowers medium, 20 petals; foliage medium size, medium green, semi-glossy; upright growth; PP5820; [Varlon × MEIgenon]; int. by Fryer's Nursery, Ltd., 1981

Madelon de Paris F, Robichon, M.; int. in 1961

Madelon Friquet HGal, pb, 1842, Vibert; flowers rosy pink, spotted lighter, medium, very full; growth branching

Madelyn Lang Cl Min, dp, 1975, Williams, Ernest D.; bud slightly ovoid; flowers deep pink, 1 in., very dbl.; foliage small, glossy, dark, embossed; upright growth; [Little Darling × Little Chief]; int. by Mini-Roses, 1974

Mademoiselle F, dp, 1950, Boerner; bud ovoid; flowers rose-red, large, 50-60 petals; very vigorous, branching growth; [Goldilocks × Marionette]; int. by J&P

Mademoiselle HT, mp, Meilland

Mlle Adèle Jougant Cl T, my, 1862, Lédéchaux; flowers clear yellow, medium, dbl.; foliage small, light yellowish-green; [Mlle de Sombreuil × unknown]

Mlle Adèle Launay HP, dp, 1863, Boyau; flowers bright dark pink, large, full

Mlle Adelina Viviand-Morel N, ab, 1890, Bernaix; flowers apricot-yellow, shaded golden, with flesh pink reflections, medium to large, dbl., globular

Mlle Alice Furon HT, ly, 1896, Pernet-Ducher; flowers yellowish-white, large, full, globular; [Lady Mary Fitzwilliam × Mme Chedane-Guinoisseau]

Mlle Alice Leroi M, m, 1842, Vibert; flowers light violet-pink, medium, dbl.

Mlle Alice Leroy M, lp, 1856, Trouillard; flowers delicate pink, medium, full; some repeat

Mlle Alice Marchand B, lp, 1891, Vigneron; flowers delicate pink, shading to blush white, large, full

Mlle Alice Morhange HP, dp, 1879, Bernède; flowers velvety carmine, large, full, globular

Mlle Alice Rousseau Pol, lp, 1903, Vilin; flowers small, dbl.

Mlle Amélie Halphen HP, mp, 1864, Margottin; flowers bright carmine pink, very full

Mlle Andrée Dourthe N, mp, 1903, Chauvry; flowers silky procelain pink, becoming silvery pink, striped white, reverse lilac, large, full; [Triomphe de la Duchère × unknown]

Mlle Andrée Worth B, lp, 1890, Lévêque; flowers light pinkish white, sometimes washed with carmine, large, full; quite remontant; foliage glaucous green

Mlle Angeline Seringe HP, mp, 1852, Bernède; flowers bright pink, large, full

Mlle Anna Charron T, yb, 1896, Widow Schwartz; bud very long; flowers cream-yellow, washed lilac-rose, large, full, borne mostly solitary; foliage somber green edged purple; growth vigorous; [Kaiserin Auguste Viktoria × Luciole]

Mlle Anna Chartron – See **Mlle Anna Charron**, T

Mlle Annette Murat T, my, 1884, Levet; flowers citron yellow, medium, full; [Gloire de Dijon × unknown]

Mlle Annie Wood HP, mr, 1866, Verdier, E.; flowers clear red, 3½-4 in., dbl., moderate fragrance; recurrent bloom; foliage dark green; prickles strong, straight; stems reddish

Mlle Antonia Decarly T, dy, 1873, Levet; flowers dark canary yellow, full

Mlle Antonine Veysset T, yb, 1874, Veysset; flowers yellow, shaded red

Mlle Argentine Cramon HT, w, 1915, Chambard; flowers white, center tinted salmon-rose, very large, full

Mlle Aristide N, ly, 1857, Robert; flowers straw yellow, centers reddish or shaded pink, large, full

Mlle Aristide M, dp, 1858, Laffay; flowers velvety carmine with very dark crimson, medium, full, globular

Mlle Augustine Guinoisseau – See **Augustine Guinoiseau**, HT

Mlle Bep van Rossem HT, my, 1926, Van Rossem; flowers deep canary-yellow, dbl.; [seedling × Souv. de Claudius Pernet]

Mlle Berger B, lp, 1884, Pernet père; flowers delicate pink, orange, full; quite remontant; growth upright

Mlle Bertha Ludi Pol, w, 1891, Pernet-Ducher; flowers white with carmine pink, becoming flesh white, full; [Mignonnette × Jules Margottin]

Mlle Berthe Chanu HP, dp, 1867, Fontaine; flowers bright carmine, large, full

Mlle Berthe Clavel B, w, 1892, Chauvry; flowers white, center pink over yellow base, reverse tinted violet, large, full; [sport of Souv de la Malmaison]

Mlle Berthe Lévêque HP, lp, 1865, Céchet père; flowers flesh white, changing to pink, small; foliage large, rough; growth upright

Mlle Berthe Levet HP, mp, 1865, Cochet; flowers large, full

Mlle Blanche Durrschmidt T, lp, 1878, Guillot fils; flowers flesh pink, aging to white, medium, dbl., borne mostly singly and small clusters; foliage glossy; prickles hooked, few; [Mme Falcot × unknown]

Mlle Blanche Laffitte B, lp, 1851, Pradel; flowers whitish-rose, medium, dbl., borne in clusters, moderate fragrance; repeats in autumn; vigorous growth

Mlle Blanche Martignat T, yb, 1902, Gamon; flowers salmon, shaded with dawn-pink, creped, intense fragrance; [possibly a seedling of Marie Van Houtte]

Mlle Blanche Rebatel – See **Blanche Rebatel**, Pol

Mlle Bonnaire HP, w, 1859, Pernet père; flowers white, center sometimes pink, dbl.; growth moderate

Mlle Brigitte Viollet HT, m, 1878, Levet; flowers silvery-rose, tinged with violet, large, full, borne in small clusters; [Antonine Verdier × unknown]

Mlle C. Riguet – See **Caroline Riguet**, B

Mlle Camille de Rochetaillée Pol, w, 1886, Bernaix; flowers white, shaded carmine, medium, full, moderate fragrance

Mlle Cécile Brünner Pol, lp, 1880, Ducher, Vve.; bud long, pointed; flowers bright pink on yellow ground, small, dbl., borne in clusters, moderate fragrance; foliage sparse, soft, dark, 3-5 leaflets; prickles very few; growth like a tea, dwarf; [a climbing Polyantha × Mme de Tartas]; int. by Pernet-Ducher; Old Rose Hall of Fame, WFRS

Mlle Cécile Brünner, Climbing Cl Pol, lp, 1894, Hosp (also Ardagh, 1904); flowers soft, light pink, fading in sun, 2 in., borne in very large clusters, intense fragrance; good repeat; [sport of Mlle Cécile Brunner]

Mlle Charlotte de la Trémoille HP, lp, 1877, Chédane-Guinoisseau; flowers very large, full, globular

Mlle Christine de Noué T, rb, 1890, Guillot; flowers deep rosy crimson, sometimes shaded with salmon-rose

Mlle Christine de Noué T, rb, 1890, Guillot & fils; flowers carmine shaded salmon, petals imbricated, large, full, moderate fragrance

Mlle Claire Andruejol HT, lp, 1920, Schwartz, A.; flowers pale pink tinted carmine, dbl.; [Comte G. de Rochemur × Mme Maurice de Luze]

Mlle Claire Jacquier – See **Claire Jacquier**, N

Mlle Claire Truffaut B, lp, 1887, Verdier, E.; flowers silvery pink medium, dbl.; prickles hooked, pinkish

Mlle Clarisse Juranville HT, lp, 1903, Corboeuf; [sport of Mme Caroline Testout]

Mlle Claudine Perreau – See **Mlle Claudine Perreault**, T

Mlle Claudine Perreault T, mp, 1885, Lambert, E.; flowers rose flesh, center darker, very large, dbl.; free bloom; [Souv d'Un Ami × unknown]

Mlle Danielle Dumur HT, lp, 1910, Laroulandie; flowers delicate pink, fading to silvery pink, large, dbl., moderate fragrance; [sport of Mme Caroline Testout]

Mlle de Dinant F, w, 1979, Lens, Louis; bud globular; flowers creamy white, open, 3-3½ in., 22 petals, intense fruity fragrance; foliage light green; vigorous, spreading growth; [Purpurine × Lavender Pinocchio]; int. in 1966

Mlle de la Vallette HCh, rb, 1910, Schwartz; flowers coppery red over gold base, reverse ruby red, medium, very full, moderate fragrance; [Mme Eugène Résal × Aurore]

Mlle de Labarthe – See **Duchesse de Brabant**, T

Mlle de Morlaincourt HT, pb, 1934, Walter, L.; flowers pink and yellow; [Cécile Walter × Korovo]; int. by Amis des Roses

Mlle de Neux HT, dp, 1901, Berland; flowers carmine-pink, medium, dbl.; [Mme Caroline Testout × unknown]

Mlle de Sombreuil T, w, 1850, Robert; flowers creamy white, often tinted pink, well-formed, large, dbl.; vigorous growth; [reputed to be a seedling of Parks' Yellow]; incorrectly called La Biche by some nurseries.

Mlle Denise de Reverseau – See **Cornelia Cook**, T

Mlle Eglantine Guillot F, op, Guillot; flowers orange pink, dbl., open, borne in clusters; growth to 2 ft.; int. by Roseraies Guillot, 1987

Mlle Eléonore Grier HP, dp, 1876, Verdier, E.; flowers large, full

Mlle Elisabeth de la Rocheterie HP, lp, 1881, Vigneron; flowers delicate flesh pink, reverse silvery, very large, full; quite remontant; foliage dark green; prickles numerous, chestnut brown; growth upright

Mlle Elisabeth Marcel N, yb, 1901, Berland; flowers coppery yellow, with metallic pink, reverse China pink, aging whitish pink; [Ophirie × unknown]

Mlle Elise Chabrier – See **Mlle Louise Chabrier**, HP

Mlle Emain B, w, 1861, Pernet; flowers white with light pink center, large, full

Mlle Emélie Verdier HP, mp, 1875, Verdier, E.; flowers carmine pink, large, full, moderate fragrance

Mlle Emélie Verdier, Climbing Cl HP, lp, 1878, Paul, G.; [sport of Mlle Emélie Verdier]

Mlle Emilienne Moreau HT, yb, 1920, Verschuren; flowers dark yellow and creamy pink, medium, semi-dbl.

Mlle Emma Hall HP, op, 1876, Liabaud; flowers shining carmine and salmon pink, revers lighter, large, full, globular; [Souv de la Reine d'Angleterre × unknown]

Mlle Emma Vercellone T, rb, 1901, Schwartz; bud long; flowers bright coppery red, golden yellow at base, fading to coppery salmon pink, large, full; foliage purple red; [Chamoïs × Mme Laurette Messimy]

Mlle Eugénie Savary – See **Mme Eugénie Savary**, HP

Mlle Eugénie Verdier HP, mp, 1869, Guillot et Fils; flowers clear silvery pink, reverse silvery white, large, very dbl.; vigorous, upright growth; [Victor Verdier × unknown]

Mlle Eugénie Verdier M, mr, 1872, Schwartz

Mlle Favart B, lp, 1869, Lévêque; flowers light satiny pink, lightly edged white, medium, full

Mlle Félicité Trouillot B, mp, 1861, Verdier, E.; flowers bright pink, medium, semi-dbl.

Mlle Fernande de la Forest HP, pb, 1872, Damaizin; flowers deep pink, reverse white, large, full

Mlle Fernande Dupuy Pol, dp, 1899, Vigneron; flowers carmine-pink, small, dbl.

Mlle Franziska Krüger T, op, 1879, Nabonnand, G.; flowers coppery yellow and pink, center often green, large, very dbl., moderate fragrance; weak stems; hardy for this class; [Catherine Mermet × Gén. Schablikine]

Mlle Gabrielle de Peyronny HP, mr, 1863, Lacharme; flowers fiery red, nuanced violet towards center

Mlle Gabrielle Touvais HP, dp

Mlle Geneviève Godard T, yb, 1889, Godard; flowers yellow with pink and orange, medium, dbl.

Mlle Germaine Caillot HT, op, 1887, Pernet-Ducher; bud long; flowers salmon flesh pink, brighter at center, white at edge, very large, full, borne mostly solitary; foliage dark green; prickles few, nearly straight; growth upright; [Baronne Adolphe de Rothschild × Mme Falcot]

Mlle Germaine Trochon HT, pb, 1893, Pernet-Ducher; flowers salmon pink, aging to yellow-pink, center orange-nankeen, edges pink, large, full, globular, moderate fragrance; [Victor Verdier × Mme Eugene Verdier]

Mlle Godard HP, mp, 1857, Ducher

Mlle Grévy – See **Mlle Jules Grévy**, HP

Mlle Guiomar Cotrim T, yb, about 1908, Fontes; flowers light yellow, edges carmine, large, full, moderate fragrance; [Marie Budlow × unknown]

Mlle Hélène Croissandeau HP, mp, 1882, Vigneron; bud very elongated; flowers velvety pink, center brighter, very large; quite remontant; foliage dark green; few prickles; growth upright; [Victor Verdier × unknown]

Mlle Hélène Gambier HT, op, 1895, Pernet-Ducher; flowers salmon-pink to coppery rose, large, dbl.

Mlle Hélène Michel HP, dr, 1883, Vigneron; flowers deep red, center brighter, outer petals velvety, large, full; foliage light green; prickles numerous, chestnut brown

Mlle Henriette HP, mp, 1857, Lartay; flowers bright pink

Mlle Henriette de Beauveau T, my, 1887, Lacharme

Mlle Henriette Martin HT, w, 1936, Reymond; flowers white, shaded ivory, edges lightly tinted pale pink; int. by Vially

Mlle Honorine Duboc HP, dp, 1894, Duboc; flowers bright wine-pink, very large, dbl., borne mostly solitary; foliage brownish green

Mlle Hortense Blanchette B, w, 1860, Damaizin; flowers white touched with pink

Mlle Irene Hennessy HT, or, 1923, Guillot, P.; flowers bright vermilion-orange, dbl.; [George C. Waud × seedling]

Mademoiselle Jacqueline Pol, dp, Weihrauch; int. in 1985

Mlle Jacquiline Bouvet HP, dr, 1884, Bernède; flowers dark fiery red, medium to large; [Aviateur Duvivier × unknown]

Mlle Jeanne Guillaumez T, dp, 1889, Bonnaire; bud long, dark rose; flowers brick red with salmon, dark yellow at base, large, full; foliage evergreen

Mlle Jeanne Lenail Pol, mr, 1924, Schwartz, A.; flowers bright ruby-red shaded carmine, large, dbl.; [Mrs W.H. Cutbush × Mme Taft]

Mlle Jeanne Marix HP, m, 1866, Liabaud; flowers garnet purple, often marbled, large, full

Mlle Jeanne Philippe T, yb, 1898, Godard; flowers nankeen yellow with chamois reflections, base ocher, edged carmine, very large, full

Mlle Jenny Gay – See **Jenny Gay**, B

Mlle Joséphine Burland Pol, w, 1886, Bernaix; flowers pure white, aging to light pink. large, very dbl., borne mostly solitary

Mlle Joséphine Guyet – See **Joséphine Guyet**, B

Mlle Joséphine Guyot – See **Joséphine Guyet**, B

Mlle Jules Grévy HP, dr, 1879, Gautreau; flowers velvety dark red, large, full; quite remontant; [Duhamel-Dumonceau × unknown]

Mlle Julie Dymonier – See **Julia Dymonier**, HP

Mlle Julie Péréard HP, mp, 1872, Pernet; flowers bright pink, very large, full; [Jules Margottin × unknown]

Mlle Juliette Doucet T, yb, 1881, Bernède; flowers cream yellow, washed with vermilion, large, full

Mlle Juliette Halphen HP, lp, 1869, Margottin; flowers light pink, aging flesh white, large, full, globular

Mlle la Comtesse de Leusse T, pb, 1878, Nabonnand; bud bright pink; flowers delicate pink with saffron at center

Mlle Lazarine Poizeau T, ob, 1876, Levet; flowers orange-yellow, medium, full; foliage glossy, reddish when young; few prickles

Mlle Lenari la Granada HT, Dot, Simon; int. in 1982

Mlle Léonie Giessen HP, lp, 1876, Lacharme; flowers pink washed white, large, full, centifolia-like; prickles long, recurved; growth bushy

Mlle Léonie Persin HP, lp, 1861, Fontaine; flowers frosty, silvery pink, large

Mlle Loïde de Falloux HP, w, 1864, Trouillard or Boyeau; flowers white with light pink shades

Mlle Louise Boyer HP, dp, 1881, Bernède; flowers silky dark pink, very large, full; [Jules Margottin × unknown]

Mlle Louise Chabrier HP, lp, 1867, Gautreau/Cochet; flowers delicate pink, edged satiny blush white, large, dbl.

Mlle Lucie Chauvin T, op, 1893, Moreau & Robert; flowers salmon yellow, shaded apricot, very large, full, globular

Mlle Madeleine de Vauzelles B, lp, 1881, Vigneron; flowers delicate pink, center brighter, large, full; quite remontant; foliage light green; few prickles; growth upright

Mlle Madeleine Delaroche T, lp, 1890, Corboeuf;

flowers flesh pink, large, very full; [Mlle Mathilde Lenaerts × unknown]

Mlle Madeleine Marot N, w, 1902, Corboeuf-Marsault; flowers cream white, sometimes edged pink, large, full; [Rêve d'Or × Dr A. Carlès]

Mlle Madeleine Nonin HP, op, 1866, Ducher; flowers pink with some salmon, medium, full, globular

Mlle Malvine Lartay HP, mr, about 1855, Lartay; flowers flame red, center violet, medium, full

Mlle Marcelle Gaugin Pol, lp, 1910, Corboeuf; flowers creamy pink, small, dbl.

Mlle Marguérite Appert HT, mr, 1896, Vigneron; flowers bright velvety red, very large, full, globular

Mlle Marguerite Dombrain – See **Marguerite d'Ombrain**, HP

Mlle Marie Achard HP, lp, 1896, Liabaud; flowers delicate frosty pink, very large, cupped; foliage dark green; growth upright

Mlle Marie Arnaud T, my, 1872, Levet; flowers canary yellow, aging to white,large, full, moderate fragrance

Mlle Marie Chauvet HP, dp, 1881, Besson; flowers deep rose pink, center darker, fading lighter, very large, very full; [Baronne Adolphe de Rothschild × unknown]

Mlle Marie Closon HP, lp, 1882, Verdier, E.; flowers delicate pink, edged in white, medium to large, very full; foliage elongated, dark green; prickles very numerous, unequal, upright, brown; growth upright

Mlle Marie Cointet HP, mp, 1872, Guillot; flowers bright pink, silky, shaded whitish pink, large, full

Mlle Marie Dauvesse HP, mp, 1859, Vigneron; flowers bright light pink, medium, full

Mlle Marie de la Villeboisnet HP, lp, 1864, Trouillard; flowers bright, delicate pink, large, full

Mlle Marie Drivon B, pb, 1887, Schwartz; flowers pink shaded with peach, sometimes marbled or spotted with carmine, medium, very dbl., borne in clusters; [Apolline × unknown]

Mlle Marie Gaze N, pb, 1892, Godard; flowers yellowish-pink with dark yellow, 7 cm., dbl., moderate tea fragrance; stems weak

Mlle Marie Gonod HP, lp, 1871, Gonod; flowers flesh white, aging pure white, large, full; [Mme Laffay × unknown]

Mlle Marie Halphen HP, mp; flowers shining carmine-pink, large, full

Mlle Marie-Louise Bourgeoise M, w, 1891, Corboeuf; flowers white, yellow center, large, full; some repeat

Mlle Marie-Louise Oger T, w, 1895, Lévêque; flowers milk white, very lightly shaded with yellow, very large; foliage dark green

Mlle Marie Magat HP, mr, 1889, Liabaud; flowers carmine-red, large, dbl.

Mlle Marie Mascuraud HT, w, 1909, Bernaix, P.; flowers white tinted flesh

Mlle Marie Moreau T, w, 1879, Nabonnand, G.; flowers silver-white flushed crimson, well-formed

Mlle Marie Page N, lp, 1894, Corboeuf; flowers glossy light pink, large, full

Mlle Marie Rady HP, mr, 1865, Fontaine; flowers vermilion-red shaded with crimson, large, very full, globular; foliage glossy; prickles numerous, red

Mlle Marie Thérèse Coumer B, mp, 1867, Liabaud; flowers bright, glowing pink, center lighter, large, full

Mlle Marie Thérèse de la Devansaye B, w, 1895, Chédane-Guinoisseau; flowers large, full

Mlle Marie van Houtte – See **Marie van Houtte**, T

Mlle Marie Verdier HP, mp, 1883, Verdier, E.; flowers bright silky pink, very large, full, moderate fragrance

Mlle Marie Villeboisnet – See **Mlle Marie de la Villeboisnet**, HP

Mlle Marthe Cahuzac Pol, ly, 1901, Ketten Bros.; bud long, pointed; flowers yellowish-white, center silky yellow, passing to whitish pink, medium, full, flat; [Mignonette × Safrano]

Mlle Marthe Carron HWich, w, 1931, Mermet; flowers white, slightly tinted pink on opening, borne in clusters of 40-50; vigorous growth; [*R. wichurana* × *R. wichurana*]

Mlle Marthe Moisset HT, my, 1935, Ducroz; flowers chrome-yellow on ochre ground, very large, cupped; foliage glossy, dark; vigorous, erect, bushy growth; [Mme Henri Queuille × seedling]

Mlle Mathilde Lenaerts T, lp, 1880, Levet; flowers bright pink, silvered white, large, dbl., quartered, moderate fragrance; [Gloire de Dijon × unknown]

Mlle Maurand HP, lp; flowers pale flesh

Mlle Pauline Bersez HT, w, 1900, Pernet-Ducher; flowers white with cream-yellow center, large, full, globular

Mlle Portier HP, dp, 1864, Guillot; flowers bluish pink, medium

Mlle Rachel T, w, 1860, Damaizin; flowers greenish white, tinted with sulfur yellow, very large, full

Mlle Renée Denis HP, w, 1906, Chédane-Guinoisseau; flowers white with light pink wash, dbl.; [Margaret Dickson × Paul Neyron]

Mlle Rosa Bonheur – See **Rosa Bonheur**, M

Mlle Simone Beaumez HT, w, 1907, Pernet-Ducher; flowers flesh-white, center sometimes tinted saffron-yellow, dbl.

Mlle Sontag HGal, dp; flowers deep pink, reverse pale blush

Mlle Sophie de la Villeboisnet HP, mp, 1867, Touvais; flowers medium to large, full

Mlle Stella Mallerin HT, w, 1926, Chambard, C.; bud pointed; flowers white, center slightly shaded cream, very large, dbl., cupped

Mlle Suzanne Bidard Pol, op, 1913, Vigneron; bud very long, salmon; flowers light coppery salmon, bases lighter, stamens golden, medium, full, borne in clusters; [Georges Pernet × Perle d'Or]

Mlle Suzanne Blanchet T, mp, 1885, Nabonnand; flowers flesh pink, imbricated, large, very full, cupped, intense fragrance

Mlle Suzanne-Marie Rodocanachi – See **Suzanne-Marie Rodocanachi**, HP

Mlle Thérèse Appert HP, lp, 1855, Trouillard; flowers light pink, shaded darker, large, full

Mlle Thérèse Levet HP, mp, 1864, Levet; flowers light carmine-rose, large, very dbl., moderate fragrance; [Jules Margottin × unknown]

Mlle Victoire Hélye HP, pb, 1878, Verdier, E.; flowers fresh pink, edges whitish, medium to large, full

Mlle Yvette Bouquil F, yb, 1955, Privat; flowers yellow edged orange; bushy growth

Mlle Yvonne Gravier T, yb, 1894, Bernaix; flowers cream yellow, shaded canary yellow, reverse pink, large, full, moderate fragrance

Mademoiselle's Bouquet – See **French Perfume**, HT

Madeo F, w, Kordes; int. in 1991

Madette HT, op, 1922, Guillot, P.; bud medium, long, pointed, nasturtium-red; flowers coppery orange-pink, medium, full

Madge Elliott HT, lp, 1966, Darvall; flowers light pink, center shaded apricot, medium, dbl.; foliage dark, leathery; very vigorous, upright growth; [Queen Elizabeth × unknown]; int. by Knight, 1964

Madge Prior F, pb, 1934, Prior; flowers brilliant claret, white eye, single, borne in large clusters; foliage dark; vigorous growth

Madge Taylor HT, dp, 1930, Clark, A.; flowers deep pink, large, dbl., globular; foliage light; vigorous growth; [(Rhea Reid × unknown) × unknown]; int. by Hazlewood Bros.

Madge Whipp HT, or, 1936, Bees; flowers bright scarlet, dbl.; foliage leathery; vigorous, bushy growth; [Lady Charmion × J.C. Thornton]

Madge Wildfire HT, or, 1932, Dobbie; bud pointed; flowers Indian red, very large, very dbl., high-centered; foliage leathery; vigorous growth; Gold Medal, NRS, 1933

Madhatter Min, my, 1988, Bennett, Dee; flowers medium yellow, aging paler, medium, 25-30 petals, high-centered, borne usually singly or in sprays of 3-5, moderate damask fragrance; foliage medium size, medium green, semi-glossy; prickles hooked slightly downward, reddish; bushy, medium growth; hips globular, green-brown; [Autumn × Avandel]; int. by Tiny Petals Nursery

Madhosh HT, rb, 1976, IARI; bud globular; flowers deep magenta-red, streaked mauve and white, 4½ in., 45 petals; foliage leathery; vigorous, bushy, compact growth; [sport of Gulzar]; int. in 1975

Madhumati HT, mp, 1983, Pal, Dr. B.P.; flowers large, 55 petals, high-centered, borne singly, intense fragrance; foliage medium size, medium green, smooth; prickles brown; vigorous, upright, bushy growth; [General MacArthur × seedling]; int. by IARI, 1973

Madhura F, yb, 1980, Pal, Dr. B.P.; bud pointed; flowers 70 petals, high-centered, borne 3-6 per cluster, moderate fragrance; foliage glossy; vigorous, upright, bushy growth; [Kiss of Fire × Goudvlinder]; int. by K.S.G. Son's Roses, 1979

Mädi Pol, or, GPG Bad Langensalza; flowers medium-large, semi-dbl.; int. in 1969

Madiba HT, m, Kordes; bud deep maroon-pink; flowers deep lilac with overtones of beige, large, dbl., high-centered, moderate fragrance; foliage large, dark green; thornless; stems strong; growth vigorous, tall; int. in 1996

Madison T, w, 1912, Brant-Hentz; flowers pure white; [Perle des Jaunes × (The Bride × Meteor)]

Madison S, mp, Poulsen; bud pointed, ovoid; flowers 5-8 cm., 20-25 petals, cupped, borne in large clusters, slight wild rose fragrance; recurrent; foliage dark; prickles moderate; growth broad, bushy, 60-100 cm.; PP12519; [seedling × Dorus Rijkers]; int. as Bayernland Cover, Poulsen Roser, 1996

Madison Min, pb, 2000, Giles, Diann; flowers medium, high-centered, borne mostly singly, slight fragrance; foliage small, dark green, semi-glossy; numerous prickles; growth upright, low; [seedling × seedling]; int. by Giles Rose Nursery

Madison HT, mp, Tantau; int. in 2005

Madlenka F, mp, Vecera, L.

Madness at Corsica – See **Napoléon**, Ch

Madoka F, rb, 1977, Teranishi, K.; flowers 2-2½ in., 25 petals, high-centered; foliage glossy, dark; upright growth; [(Zambra × Peace) × Cherry Brandy]; int. by Itami Bara-en, 1975

Madoka HT, yb, Hiroshima; int. by Hiroshima Bara-en, 1996

Madona HT, pb, Meilland; bud long; flowers coral-peach, reverse amber blush, moderate fragrance; recurrent; int. in 1992

Madonna HT, w, 1908, Cook, J.W.; [Mlle Alice Furon × Marie van Houtte]

Madonna – See **Madona**, HT

Madonna MinFl, ab, Poulsen; flowers apricot blend, 5-8 cm., dbl., slight wild rose fragrance; foliage dark; growth bushy, 40-60 cm.; PP14971; int. by Poulsen Roser, 2001

Madonna Hit – See **Madonna**, MinFl

Madras HT, pb, 1980, Warriner, William A.; bud ovoid;

flowers rose with yellow and light pink reverse, 48 petals, borne singly, moderate fragrance; foliage large, leathery; prickles hooked downward; medium, spreading growth; PP4460; [seedling × seedling]; int. by J&P, 1981

Madraz – See **Knock Out**, S

Madrigal HT, dp, 1950, Gaujard; bud long, pointed; flowers brilliant salmon-pink flushed coppery, very large, dbl., moderate spicy fragrance; vigorous growth; [((Mme Joseph Perraud × unknown) × seedling) × ((Mme Joseph Perraud × unknown) × *R. foetida bicolor*)]

Madrigal S, dr; flowers deep, rich red, ruffled, 4 in., 50 petals, borne in clusters, intense rose/berry fragrance; recurrent; growth vigorous; int. by Harkness, 1998

Mady Cl HT, ly, 1925, Gemen & Bourg; flowers creamy white, with ruffled petals, 4 in., dbl., borne mostly solitary

Mae Dean S, pb, ARE; flowers medium pink with lighter reverse, slight fragrance; growth tall (3-5 ft.); int. by Antique Rose Emporium, 2004

Maestro HT, dr, 1957, Delforge; bud oval; flowers deep velvety red, open, large, dbl.; foliage dark, glossy; vigorous, bushy growth; RULED EXTINCT 2/81; [Crimson Glory × Charles Mallerin]

Maestro HT, rb, 1981, McGredy, Sam IV; bud ovoid; flowers medium red, painted white, reverse lighter red and white, 28 petals; foliage olive green, matte; prickles narrow, red; upright, bushy growth; [(Picasso × unknown) × seedling]; int. in 1980

Mafalda di Savoia F, op, Barni, V.; int. by Rose Barni, 1999

Magali HT, dp, 1952, Mallerin, C.; flowers carmine, open, medium, 35-40 petals; foliage abundant, leathery; very vigorous, upright, bushy growth; [Charles P. Kilham × Brazier]; int. by Meilland-Richardier

Magali F, mp, Meilland, Alain A.; flowers rose pink, large, dbl.; int. in 1986

Magali Bonnefon HT, pb, 1916, Nabonnand; flowers pink, reverse bright salmon-pink, semi-dbl.; [sport of Mme Abel Chatenay]

Magaliesburg Roos – See **Mary Pope**, HT

Maganwilare HT, pb, Huber; flowers full, moderate spicy fragrance; foliage coppery colored; bushy, compact (50-60 cm.) growth; int. by Richard Huber AG, 1995

Magda HT, r; flowers tan apricot, large, very full, moderate fragrance; growth strong, bushy; int. by Ludwig's Roses, 2000

Magda Wichmann HMult, pb, 1910, Kiese; flowers pink over cream-white, medium, very full; remontant

Magdalena HT, ob, Adam; flowers bright orange, reverse yellow, dbl., cupped, moderate fragrance; recurrent; compact (90-100 cm.) growth; int. by Pepinieres Gueranais, 2005

Magdalena de Nubiola HT, op, 1932, Dot, Pedro; flowers salmon-rose, semi-dbl.; [Li Bures × Mari Dot]; int. by C-P

Magdeburg HT, VEG; int. in 1988

Magdeleine Beauvillain T, ly, 1887, Beauvillain

Magenta Pol, m, 1916, Barbier; flowers violet-red, semi-dbl.; dwarf growth

Magenta HT, mr, 1934, Leenders, M.; bud pointed; flowers crimson-carmine, large, dbl.; foliage glossy, dark; vigorous, bushy growth

Magenta F, m, 1956; bud ovoid; flowers rosy magenta to soft deep mauve, large, dbl., borne in large clusters, intense fragrance; foliage dark, leathery; vigorous, upright, bushy growth; [Yellow Floribunda × Lavender Pinocchio]; int. by Kordes, 1954

Magenta Diadem F, m, Tantau; int. by Rosen Tantau, 1994

Magenta Floorshow S, m, Harkness; flowers deep reddish-purple, large, dbl., moderate fragrance; spreading (3½ × 4 ft.) growth; int. by R. Harkness & Co., 1999

Magenta Mystique Min, m, 2004, Benardella, Frank A.; flowers mauve & magenta, reverse mauve, 1¾-2 in., very full, borne singly and in small clusters, moderate fragrance; foliage medium size, dark green, glossy; prickles in., triangular; apex hooked down; growth upright, well branched, medium (18-24 in.); garden decoration, exhibition; [seedling × Kristin]; int. by Nor'East Miniature Roses, 2005

Maggie HT, w, Nieuwesteeg; flowers white with soft lemon in center, very full, moderate fragrance; recurrent; growth to 4 ft.; int. by Nieuwesteeg Rose Nursery, 2004

Maggie Barry HT, pb, 1995, McGredy, Sam IV; bud pointed; flowers salmon edged orange, 4 in., full, borne mostly singly; foliage large, light green, matte; prickles profuse, wing shaped, curved downward; bushy (100 cm.) growth; PP10938; [Louise Gardner × West Coast]; int. by McGredy Roses International, 1993

Maggie Tabberer – See **Tchaikovski**, Gr

Magia Nera HT, dr; flowers very dark, velvety red, dbl., high-centered, no fragrance; recurrent; growth to 3 ft.

Magic HT, pb, 1954, Grillo; bud globular; flowers silver-pink, open, 5½ in., 75 petals; foliage leathery; very vigorous, upright growth; RULED EXTINCT 11/88; [sport of Thornless Beauty]

Magic HT, mr, 1989, Strahle, Robert; bud pointed; flowers medium, 24 petals, high-centered, borne usually singly; foliage medium size, medium green, matte; prickles slender, straight, medium, light green; upright, tall growth; hips pear shaped, medium, orange; [Volare × Tonight]; int. by Carlton Rose Nurseries, 1987

Magic – See **Great Expectations**, F

Magic – See **Magic Hit**, MinFl

Magic Baby F, pb, 1997, Giles, Diann; flowers medium, very dbl., borne mostly singly, no fragrance; foliage medium size, medium green, dull; growth upright, medium (3½ ft.); int. by Giles Rose Nursery

Magic Beauty HT, yb, 2000, Williams, J. Benjamin; flowers bright golden yellow aging to blend of yellow and purple-red, 4½-5 in., dbl., borne mostly solitary, intense fragrance; foliage large, dark green, glossy; prickles medium, curved down, few; growth upright, tall (4½-5 ft.); PP12655; [Love × Gold Medal]; int. by Conklin Rose Co., 2000

Magic Blanket S, w, 1999, Evers, Hans & Rosen Tantau; flowers creamy white, blushed light pink, 2½ in., 12-21 petals, flat, borne in large clusters, self cleaning, slight sweet fragrance; foliage medium size, dark green, glossy; prickles moderate; growth spreading, mounding, medium (to 3 ft.); groundcover; int. as Schneekönigin, Rosen Tantau, 1992

Magic Carpet LCl, yb, 1941, Brownell; flowers yellow, splashed orange, scarlet and rose, 9 cm., semi-dbl., borne in clusters, intense sweet fragrance; foliage small, dark green, glossy; strong stems; vigorous, climbing or trailing growth; [Coral Creeper × Stargold]

Magic Carpet S, m, Zary, Keith & Warriner, William; flowers lavender, 2 in., 12 petals, flat, borne in clusters, intense spicy fragrance; free-flowering; foliage medium size, dark green, glossy; prickles numerous, medium, hooked downward; growth spreading, low (18 in.); groundcover; PP9324; int. in 1992

Magic Carrousel Min, rb, 1973, Moore, Ralph S.; flowers petals white, edged red, small, dbl., high-centered; foliage small, glossy, leathery; vigorous, bushy growth; PP3601; [Little Darling × Westmont]; int. by Sequoia Nursery, 1972; AOE, ARS, 1975, Miniature Rose Hall of Fame, ARS, 1999

Magic Carrousel, Climbing Cl Min, rb; int. after 1972

Magic Charm HT, mp, 1966, Aufill; flowers medium, dbl., high-centered; vigorous growth; [Mount Shasta × Granada]

Magic Day – See **Barnard's Magic Day**, F

Magic Dragon Cl Min, dr, 1973, Moore, Ralph S.; bud short, pointed; flowers small, dbl.; foliage leathery; very vigorous, upright growth; [((*R. wichurana* × Floradora) × seedling) × Little Buckaroo]; int. by Sequoia Nursery, 1969

Magic East S, pb, 1998, Viraraghavan, M.S. Viru; flowers white with pink and white splashes, creamy yellow eye, 5 in., dbl., borne singly and in clusters, slight fragrance; foliage medium size, blue green, matte; prickles moderate, medium; bushy, medium growth; [Honor × Priyatama]; int. by Hortico, 1995

Magic Fire F, or, 1970, Laperrière; bud pointed; flowers bright orange-red, small, semi-dbl., high-centered; foliage glossy; vigorous, bushy growth; int. by EFR, 1967

Magic Fire F, ob, Laperrière; flowers scarlet-orange, dbl.; int. in 1983

Magic Fire – See **Zambra 93**, F

Magic Fire 83 – See **Magic Fire**, F

Magic Forez HT, Croix; int. in 1970

Magic Hit MinFl, rb, Poulsen; flowers red with yellow and orange reverse, 5 cm., full, hybrid tea, very slight fragrance; recurrent; foliage dark green, glossy; bushy (2 ft.) growth; int. by Poulsen Roser, 2001

Magic Lantern Gr, ob, 1995, Royon, René; flowers copper-orange-gold, large, full, borne in small clusters, slight fragrance; foliage medium green, semi-glossy; some prickles; upright, bushy (150 cm.) growth; PP8861; [sport of Gold Medal]; int. by Bear Creek Gardens, Inc., 1994

Magic Medley HT, pb, 1997, Viraraghavan, M.S. Viru; flowers pink with dark red markings, white reverse, 6 in., full, borne mostly singly; foliage large, medium green, dull; bushy, medium (3 ft.) growth; [Pristine × Priyatama]; int. by Hortico, 1995

Magic Meidiland S, mp, 1994, Meilland, Alain A.; flowers red purple, lighter centers, medium, dbl., flat, borne in small clusters, no fragrance; foliage small, dark green, glossy; some prickles; medium to low, spreading, growth; groundcover; PP9469; [*R. sempervirens* × (Milrose × Bonica)]; int. by SNC Meilland & Cie, 1992

Magic Meillandecor – See **Magic Meidiland**, S

Magic Mikado F, mr, Tantau; flowers bright red, borne in clusters; florist rose; int. by Rosen Tantau

Magic Mist Min, mr, 1981, Williams, Ernest D.; bud pointed; flowers medium red, veined darker, 47 petals, high-centered, borne usually singly, moderate fragrance; foliage small, medium to dark green, glossy; prickles thin, tan; bushy, spreading growth; [Tom Brown × Little Chief]; int. by Mini-Roses, 1980

Magic Moment HT, mr, 1964, Buyl Frères; bud pointed; flowers scarlet to geranium-red, large, dbl., high-centered, moderate fragrance; int. by Cuthbert

Magic Moment Min, pb, 2004, Jones, Mark W.; flowers pink, base yellow, reverse fringe pink, 2 in., full, borne mostly solitary, slight fragrance; foliage medium size, medium green, semi-glossy; prickles slightly hooked downward; growth upright, medium (18-24 in.); garden; exhibition; [sport of MARbutter]

Magic Moments F, pb, 2007, Courage, Ray; flowers semi-dbl., blooms borne in small clusters; foliage medium size, dark green, semi-glossy; prickles small, hooked, brown, few; growth bushy, medium (1¼ m.); garden decoration; [Friesia × Michelle Meilland]; int. by Ross Roses, 2007

Magic Moon Gr, ob, 1970, Schwartz, Ernest W.; bud

ovoid; flowers deep salmon, reverse silver, medium, very dbl.; foliage large, leathery; vigorous, upright growth; [Little Darling × Golden Scepter]; int. by Wyant

Magic Mountain F, yb, 1971, Armstrong, D.L.; bud ovoid; flowers large, dbl., high-centered; foliage glossy, dark, leathery; vigorous, bushy growth; PP3315; [Circus × Texan]; int. by Armstrong Nursery, 1973

Magic Red F, mr, 1942, Kordes; flowers large, 45 petals, globular, borne in clusters; foliage leathery, glossy; vigorous, bushy growth; [Henri Panthier × Dance of Joy]; int. by J&P

Magic Silver HT, m, Kordes; int. in 1998

Magic Splendor Min, dr, 1983, Lyon, Lyndon; flowers small, 35 petals, borne in clusters; foliage medium size, medium green, semi-glossy; upright, bushy growth; [Baby Betsy McCall × seedling]

Magic Sunblaze Min, rb, Schwartz; int. in 1984

Magic Sunset F, ob, Tantau; flowers deep copper, dbl.; growth small; int. in 1995

Magic Touch HT, lp, 1975, Golik; bud ovoid; flowers soft pink, 5 in., 32 petals, high-centered, moderate fragrance; foliage glossy; moderate growth; [Tropicana × Queen of Bermuda]; int. by Dynarose, 1974

Magic Wand Cl Min, dp, 1958, Moore, Ralph S.; flowers light red, 1 in., 20 petals, borne in clusters; foliage small, dark; arching (to 4 ft.) growth; hips orange; [Eblouissant × Zee]; int. by Sequoia Nursery, 1957

Magician Min, m, 1993, Williams, Ernest D.; flowers mauve with deeper petal edges, large, very dbl., borne mostly singly, intense fragrance; foliage small, medium green, semi-glossy; few prickles; medium (45 cm.), upright, bushy growth; [seedling × Twilight Trail]; int. by Mini Roses of Texas, 1993

Magicienne HT, or, 1957, Laperrière; flowers geranium-red, well-formed, 30 petals; foliage bronze; dwarf, bushy growth; [Comtesse Vandal × (Peace × Independence)]; int. by EFR

Magicienne 78 HT, ob, Laperrière; flowers dbl.; int. in 1978

Magie de Feu – See **Feuerzauber**, HT

Magie des Jardins – See **Gartenzauber**, F, 1965

Magie d'Orient HMsk, dp, 2000, Lens, Louis; flowers deep pink, white center, reverse paler, 1-1½ in., single, borne in large clusters; recurrent; foliage large, medium green, semi-glossy, disease-resistant; prickles moderate; spreading, medium (100-120 cm.) growth; [(*R. multiflora adenocheata* × Ballerina) × Puccini]; int. by Louis Lens N.V., 1991

Magitta HT, mr, 1983, Tantau, Math.; flowers large, 20 petals; foliage medium size, medium green, semi-glossy; upright growth; int. in 1981

Magma HT, or, Kordes; flowers bright orange-red with yellow at the petal base, dbl., high-centered, borne mostly singly; recurrent; stems medium; florist rose; int. by W. Kordes Söhne, 1998

Magna Charta HP, mp, 1876, Paul, W.; flowers bright pink, suffused carmine, very large, dbl., globular; some recurrent bloom; foliage thick, rich green; vigorous, compact growth

Magnafrano HT, mr, 1900, Van Fleet; flowers rich crimson-rose, large, dbl.; [Magna Charta × Safrano]; int. by Conard & Jones

Magneet – See **Feuerwerk**, S

Magnet F, mr, VEG; flowers luminous red, large, dbl.

Magnifica HRg, dr, 1907, Van Fleet; bud carmine; flowers deep blood red, 4-5 in., full; [*R. rugosa* × Victor Hugo]

Magnifica HEg, mr, 1918, Hesse; flowers light red, large, 10 petals; [Lucy Ashton × Lucy Ashton]

Magnificence HT, op, 1954, Gaujard; flowers salmon-pink tinted yellow, large, dbl., high-centered; foliage dark; vigorous, bushy growth; [Peace × unknown]; int. by McGredy

Magnificent Perfume S, lp, Clements, John; flowers soft pink shading to apricot at their center, 4-5 cm., 50 petals, heavy sweet and fresh fragrance; foliage rich, green; vigorous (4 × 3½ ft.) growth; PPAF; int. by Heirloom Roses, 2003

Magnifique Pol, lp, 1928, deRuiter; flowers clear pink, open, large, semi-dbl., cupped, borne in clusters; foliage rich green, glossy; vigorous growth; [sport of Orléans Rose]; int. by Sliedrecht & Co.

Magnolia Kordana Min, lp, Kordes; flowers cream-pink, dbl.; recurrent; int. by W. Kordes Söhne

Magnolia Rose – See **Devoniensis**, T

Magnolia Rose, Climbing – See **Devoniensis, Climbing**, Cl T

Magnolia Springs Min, w, 1999, Taylor, Franklin "Pete" & Kay; flowers white with pink edge, greenish guard petals, 2 in., 41 petals, borne in large clusters; foliage medium size, medium green, semi-glossy; few prickles; upright, bushy, medium (18 in.) growth; int. by Taylor's Roses, 1998

Magnolija HP, w, 1940, Kosteckij; flowers creamy white, large, dbl.

Magnum HT, dr; bud conical, large; flowers 4 in., 30-35 petals, high-centered, borne mostly singly, no fragrance; good repeat; foliage medium green, semi-glossy; prickles numerous, medium; erect (5 ft.) growth; PP16493; [Mahalia × (Challenger × Meigormon)]; int. by Meilland, 1998

Magrana F, or, 1954, Dot, Pedro; flowers well-formed, dbl.; vigorous growth; [Méphisto × Alain]

Mahadev F, or, 1976, Viraraghavan, M.S. Viru; bud long, pointed; flowers open, 1½ in., 20 petals; foliage glossy; vigorous, tall, bushy growth; [seedling × (unknown × unknown)]; int. by K. S. G. Son, 1975

Mahaeca – See **La Belle Sultane**, HGal

Mahaeca de Dupont – See **Charles de Mills**, HGal

Mahagona HT, pb, 1956, Kordes; bud pointed; flowers dull orange-scarlet, open, very large; foliage leathery, wrinkled; very vigorous, upright, bushy growth; [Golden Rapture × Hens Verschuren]; int. by McGredy

Mahaja HT, dp, 1936, Carbaugh; bud long, pointed; flowers deep rose-pink, center rose-red, base yellow, 4 in., dbl., high-centered; foliage glossy; long stems; vigorous growth; [sport of Rose Hill]; int. by Johnstown Greenhouses

Mahalaxmi HT, yb, Patil, B.K.; int. in 1988

Mahalia HT, mr

Maharajah HP, mr, 1904, Cant, B. R.; flowers velvety crimson, golden anthers, large, semi-dbl., borne in clusters, moderate fragrance; foliage dark, bronze, leathery

Maharani HT, pb; int. in 1996

Maharishi HT, or, Tejganga; flowers vermilion orange, dbl., high-centered; recurrent; [sport of Kardinal]; int. by Tejanga Roses, 1995

Maheca Bslt, m, about 1815, Noisette; flowers purple crimson, nuanced light violet, medium, semi-dbl., borne in corymbs

Maheca Nova – See **Aigle Noir**, HGal

Maheck à Fleurs Simples – See **Holoserica**, HGal

Maheka – See **Purpurea**, (*R. roxburghii* hybrid)

Mahina HT, ab, 1952, Meilland, F.; flowers reddish-apricot, reverse golden yellow, large, 35 petals; foliage leathery; very vigorous, bushy growth; [Peace × Fred Edmunds]; Gold Medal, Bagatelle, 1952

Mahogany – See **Mahagona**, HT

Mai Tai Min, op, 2001, Zary, Keith; bud pointed, ovoid; flowers coral and yellow buds opening to a dusty orange, finishing in pink., 2 in., 20 petals, borne in small clusters, slight fresh fragrance; foliage medium size, dark green, glossy; prickles moderate; growth upright, compact, medium (2½ ft.); PP12993; [seedling × seedling]; int. by J&P, 2002

Maia HT, Barni, V.; int. in 1986

Maid Marian HT, pb, 1920, Therkildsen; flowers carmine-rose, reverse silvery pink, dbl.

Maid Marion HWich, w, 1909, Walsh; flowers white, tipped pink, center filled with yellow stamens, slightly incurved, single; foliage large, glossy; vigorous growth

Maid Marion HMsk, w, 1930, Pemberton; flowers white, opening blush, semi-dbl., borne in very large clusters; vigorous (3-4 ft.) growth; int. by Bentall

Maid Marion – See **Red Imp**, Min

Maid of Gold Cl HT, my, 1936, Raffel; bud globular, reddish; flowers golden yellow, large, very dbl.; profuse, intermittent bloom; foliage glossy; vigorous, climbing (12 ft.), compact growth; [Golden Emblem, Climbing × unknown]; int. by Port Stockton Nursery

Maid of Honour T, mp, 1899, Hofmeister; flowers soft rose pink to flesh-pink, large, full; [sport of Catherine Mermet]

Maid of Honour F, op, 1951, Kordes; bud long, pointed; flowers salmon-pink, open, large, single, borne in trusses; foliage leathery, glossy, light green; vigorous, upright growth; RULED EXTINCT 1/86; [Crimson Glory × Holstein]; int. by Morse

Maid of Honour HT, yb, 1986, Weddle, Von C.; flowers yellow, light pink center, large, dbl., borne singly and in small clusters, moderate fragrance; foliage large, dark, semi-glossy; tall, upright growth; [Folklore × seedling]; int. by Hortico Roses, 1984

Maid of Kent HT, op, 1929, Archer; flowers soft salmon-pink; [Ophelia × Mrs W.J. Grant]

Maid of Kent LCl, lp, Rumwood; delicate pink flowers, small, borne in clusters, slight fragrance; foliage dark, glossy; growth to 10 ft.; int. by Rumwood Nurseries, 2000

Maid of Orleans F, ob, 1976, Ellick; flowers orange-flame blend, 4 in., very dbl.; foliage glossy, dark; very free growth; [Val De Mosa × Tropicana]; int. in 1977

Maid of the Valley – See **Unique Panachée**, C

Maiden Voyage F, pb, 1992, McGredy, Sam IV; flowers medium, dbl., borne in small clusters; foliage medium size, medium green, glossy; medium (3½'), bushy growth; [Sexy Rexy × New Year]; int. by Cooperative Rose Growers, 1992

Maiden's Blush – See **Great Maiden's Blush**, A

Maiden's Blush A, w, 1802, Dumont de Courset; flowers whitish rose, medium, dbl., cupped, moderate fragrance; growth erect; probably a clone from the Royal Botanic Gardens, Kew

Maiden's Blush – See **Héloïse**, C

Maiden's Blush – See **William R. Smith**, T

Maiden's Blush Sweet Briar – See **Manning's Blush**, HEg

Maidi HT, pb

Maids of Jubilee Min, pb, 1989, Taylor, Franklin "Pete" & Kay; bud pointed; flowers bright deep pink with cream base in center, reverse cream and pink blend, 25-30 petals, high-centered; foliage medium size, dark green, semi-glossy; prickles yellowish-green; upright, bushy, medium growth; [Azure Sea × unnamed Miniature seedling]; int. by Taylor's Roses

Maidstone S, my, Kordes; groundcover; spreading growth; int. by Mattock's Roses, 2001

Maidy Min, rb, 1984, Kordes, W.; flowers medium, 20 petals; foliage small, medium green, semi-glossy; bushy growth; [Regensberg × seedling]

Maigold S, dy, 1953, Kordes; flowers bronze-yellow, 4 in., 14 petals, cupped, borne singly or in small clusters, intense fragrance; non-recurrent; foliage glossy;

numerous prickles; bushy (5 ft.), pillar or shrub growth; [Poulsen's Pink × Fruhlingstag]

Maiko – See **Kyo-Maiko**, F

Mainak HT, dp, Ghosh; flowers deep rose pink, very large, dbl.; good repeat; int. in 2003

Mainauduft – See **Peter Mayle**, HT

Mainaufeuer – See **Red Ribbons**, S

Mainauperle HT, dr, 1973, Kordes, R.; bud ovoid; flowers large, dbl., high-centered, intense fragrance; foliage large, dark, leathery; vigorous, upright, bushy growth; [seedling × Americana]; int. by Kordes & Son, 1969; ADR, 1966

Mainz HT, my, 1930, Leenders Bros.; flowers citron-yellow, very large, dbl., moderate fragrance; vigorous growth; [sport of Kardinal Piffl]

Mainzer Fastnacht – See **Blue Moon**, HT

Mainzer Fastnacht, Climbing – See **Blue Moon, Climbing**, Cl HT

Mainzer Rad – See **Mainzer Wappen**, S

Mainzer Wappen S, or, 1963, Kordes, R.; bud pointed; flowers red, tinted orange, large, 25 petals, borne in clusters of up to 20, moderate fragrance; foliage dark; bushy, upright (5 ft.) growth

Maiogi HT, op, Keihan; int. by Keihan Gardening, 1988

Mairöschen – See ***R. majalis*** (Herrmann) dbl.

Maisie HT, op, 1926, Dickson, A.; flowers salmon-orange and pink, medium, semi-dbl.

Maisie Gowie HT, ?, 1968, Gowie; foliage dark, leathery; bushy growth; int. by Gandy's Roses

Maison Pernet-Ducher HT, my, 1934, Pernet-Ducher; bud pointed; flowers golden yellow, veined copper, large, dbl.; foliage glossy, dark; very vigorous, bushy growth; int. by Gaujard

Maitland White T, w; flowers dbl., moderate fragrance; recurrent; growth medium; discovered in Bermuda.

Maiwunder S, ly, Kordes; int. in 1966

Maizières F, mr, RvS-Melle; flowers 29 petals, flat; foliage dense dark green; [seedling × Ernest H. Morse]; int. in 1993

Maja F, mr, 1960, deRuiter; flowers cinnabar-red, 30 petals, cupped, borne in broad clusters; vigorous, bushy growth; [Independence × Signal Red]; int. by Horstmann

Maja Mauser – See **Cara Mia**, HT

Maja Mauser F, or, 1978, Poulsen, Niels D.; flowers dark orange-red, 4 in., 20 petals; foliage glossy, dark; bushy, upright growth; [Evelyn Fison × seedling]; int. by Poulsen, 1970

Maja Oetker – See **Coronation Gold**, F

Majestade HT, w, 1957, Moreira da Silva; flowers cream-white, base deep yellow, well-formed; very vigorous growth; [Mme Marie Curie × Peace]

Majesté HT, op, 1970, Dorieux; bud oval; flowers salmon, large, dbl., moderate fragrance; foliage glossy, leathery; very vigorous, upright growth; [Radar × Eclipse]; int. by Vilmorin, 1966

Majestic HT, or, 1955, Gaujard; bud long, purplish; flowers cinnabar-red, open, large, dbl.; vigorous growth; [Peace × seedling]

Majestic HT, lp, Poulsen; flowers light pink, 10-15 cm., 25 petals, borne one to a stem, no fragrance; foliage dark, glossy; growth bushy, 60-100 cm.; PP15600; int. by Poulsen Roser, 2002

Majestic S, lp, Clements, John; flowers silvery pink, 6-7 in., 24 petals, moderate sweet, fresh fragrance; foliage large, bluish green; growth vigorous; large shrub or small climber.; PPAF; int. by Heirloom, 2004

Majestic Kiwi HT, rb, 2000, Cattermole, R.R.; flowers medium red, reverse yellow, 4½-5 in., full, borne singly or in small clusters, moderate fragrance; foliage medium size, light green, glossy; prickles moderate, aging light brown; growth upright, tall (5-6 ft.); [Royden × Chivalry]; int. by Sharalea Gardens, 2001

Majestic Sunrise HT, my, Courage; flowers large, dbl., moderate fragrance; medium growth; charity rose for multiple schlerosis; int. by Ross Roses, 2002

Majestueuse HGal, lp, before 1790, from Holland; bud red; flowers pale rose, 3 in., full, moderate fragrance; Agathe group

Majeure – See **Tanya**, HT

Maji – See **Magic Moment**, Min

Majken S, Thor; int. in 1974

Majolika F, lp, Tantau; bud creamy ivory; flowers small, dbl., borne in small, tight clusters, moderate fragrance; free-flowering; stems slender; growth medium; int. in 1988

Major – See **Alector Cramoisi**, HGal

Major Frank Hayes HT, dr, 1934, Bees; flowers crimson, center darker, very large, dbl., high-centered; foliage leathery, dark; vigorous growth; [Joan Howarth × J.C. Thornton]

Major Multiplex – See **Rose des Peintres**, C

Major Shelley HT, mr, 1939, Howard, F.H.; bud pointed; flowers rich crimson-scarlet, 5-6 in., 35 petals, high-centered; foliage leathery, dark; very vigorous, bushy growth; [Mrs J.D. Eisele × Crimson Glory]; int. by H&S

Majorca HT, mr, 1938, Dot, Pedro; flowers scarlet, large, dbl., cupped; foliage glossy, bronze; vigorous, bushy growth; [Aribau × Angels Mateu]; int. by C-P, 1941

Majorca HT, op, 1958, Buyl Frères; bud short, thick; flowers rose-salmon, 52 petals; moderate growth

Majorette Gr, lp, 1960, Carlton Rose Nurs.; bud medium, ovoid; flowers soft powder pink, medium, dbl., borne in clusters; foliage dark green, glossy, disease-resistant; growth very vigorous, upright; int. in 1958

Majorette HT, op, 1970, Meilland; bud pointed; flowers coppery salmon, large, dbl., high-centered; foliage dark, leathery; vigorous, upright growth; [Zambra × Fred Edmunds]; int. by URS, 1967; Gold Medal, Bagatelle, 1966

Majorette MinFl, mr, 1987, Meilland, Mrs. Marie-Louise; flowers medium cardinal-red, medium, dbl., no fragrance; foliage small, medium green, semi-glossy; growth bushy; [Magic Carrousel × (Grumpy × Scarletta)]; int. in 1985

Majorica – See **Majorca**, HT, 1938

Majuna HT, yb, 2000, Makosch, Joachim; flowers light yellow, reverse light pink, medium, full, borne in large clusters, moderate fragrance; foliage large, dark green, semi-glossy; prickles moderate; growth upright, tall (4 ft.); [sport of Broadway]; int. in 1999

Make A Wish Min, pb, 1996, Mehring, Bernhard F.; flowers salmon pink, light pink reverse, 2 in., very dbl., borne in large clusters, moderate fragrance; foliage medium size, dark green, glossy; prickles moderate; growth bushy, medium (35 cm.); [Robin Redbreast × Amber Queen]; int. by Henry Street Nurseries, 1996

Make Believe Min, m, 1986, Moore, Ralph S.; flowers mauve and white blend, reverse red-purple, 10 petals, borne in sprays, no fragrance; foliage medium size, dark, semi-glossy; prickles very few, hooked, dark brown; upright, bushy growth; hips small, globular, orange; [Anytime × Angel Face]; int. by Moore Min. Roses, 1980

Make Mine Sherry Min, rb

Make-Up – See **Denise Grey**, S

Making Memories Min, mp, 2003, Taylor, Franklin & Kay Taylor; flowers medium pink, reverse lighter, 2 in., dbl., borne mostly solitary; foliage medium size, dark green, Semi-glossy; prickles small, straight, brown, few; growth upright, medium (3 ft.); garden/decorative; [Mobile Jubilee × Gitte]; int. in 2003

Mala Rubinstein HT, mp, 1971, Dickson, A.; flowers 5½ in., 45 petals, high-centered, moderate fragrance; foliage large, matte; [Sea Pearl × Colour Wonder]; Gold Medal, Belfast, 1973, Edland Fragrance Medal, ARS, 1972

Malaga Cl HT, dp, 1971, McGredy, Sam IV; flowers reddish-pink, 4½ in., 36 petals, high-centered, borne in small clusters, intense fragrance; foliage glossy, dark; [(Hamburger Phoenix × Danse de Feu) × Copenhagen]; originally registered as LCl

Malaguena S, mp, 1976, Buck, Dr. Griffith J.; bud ovoid, long, pointed; flowers 4½ in., 28 petals, cupped; foliage large, dark, leathery; erect, bushy growth; [Tickled Pink × Country Music]; int. by Iowa State University

Malahat HT, rb, 1988, Betts, John; flowers scarlet, reverse white, fading slightly, medium, very dbl., high-centered, borne usually singly, intense fragrance; foliage medium size, red-brown to dark green, glossy; bushy, vigorous growth; hips round, medium, brown; [Pristine × Shockling Blue]; int. by Wisbech Plant Co., 1988

Malak HT, pb, Mahendrakumar C. Shah; flowers ivory and pale pink blend, large, full, high-centered; [sport of Admiral Rodney]; int. in 1988

Malakarsiddha HT, lp, Patil, B.K.; flowers porcelain pink, large, high-centered, slight fragrance; [sport of Century Two]; int. by Icospin, 1987

Mälar-Ros HT, dr, 1932, Kordes; bud pointed; flowers glowing ruby-red indoors, dark blood-red with crimson outdoors, dbl., high-centered; very vigorous, bushy growth; [Hadley × Fragrance]

Malcolm HT, dp, 1977, Ellick; flowers carmine, 4-5 in., 35-40 petals; foliage large, glossy, dark; vigorous, free growth; [Hector Deane × Chopin]; int. by Excelsior Roses, 1979

Malcolm Sargent HT, mr, 1987, Harkness, R., & Co., Ltd.; flowers shining, bright crimson, medium, 25 petals, urn shaped, loose, borne usually singly, slight spicy fragrance; foliage medium size, dark green, glossy; prickles pointed, narrow, small, reddish-green; bushy, medium growth; hips rounded, medium, green; [Herbstfeuer × Trumpeter]; int. in 1988; Gold Medal, Belfast, 1990

Malcolm Scott F, mr, 2000, Brown, Ted; flowers large, full, borne in small clusters, slight fragrance; foliage large, dark green, semi-glossy; few prickles; growth upright, medium (3 ft.); [Esprit × Rosana]

Maleica F, w, Tantau; flowers soft, creamy with apricot tints; growth compact, upright, medium; int. in 1988

Maleica HT, yb, Tantau; flowers gold and yellow, slight fragrance; int. by Rosen Tantau, 2003

Malek-Adel HGal, lp; flowers soft pink, dotted white, large

Malene HT, Laperrière; int. in 1980

Malesherbes HGal, m, 1834, Vibert; flowers red, nuanced purple, spotted with white, very large, very full

Malia Min, mp, 1992, Mansuino, Dr. Domenico; flowers medium, very dbl., borne singly, no fragrance; highly recurrent bloom; foliage small, medium green, semi-glossy; some prickles; bushy (100-150 cm.) growth; [(Pink 1172) × Rosa Maria]; int. in 1988

Malibu F, or, 1960, Morey, Dr. Dennison; bud pointed, ovoid; flowers coral-orange-red, becoming lighter, 4-4½ in., 35 petals, high-centered, intense fragrance; foliage leathery; vigorous, bushy, upright growth; PP1962; [Charlotte Armstrong × Independence]; int. by J&P, 1959

Malibu Lake Shady Pink HT, dp; int. in 1994

Malicorne – See **Beverly Hills**, HT

Malicorne F, dr, Delbard; flowers dark, velvety red, 3 in., dbl., cupped, borne in clusters, slight fragrance; free-flowering; foliage bronzy green, glossy; medium (2-3 ft.) growth; int. by George Delbard SA, 2006; Certificate of Merit, Rome, 2002

Malin Jaune Delbard S, dy, Delbard; int. by Georges Delbard SA, 2002

Malin Rose Delbard S, mp, Delbard; int. by Georges Delbard SA, 2002

Malin Rouge Delbard S, mr, Delbard; int. by Georges Delbard SA, 2002

Malindall F, mr, Noack, Werner; int. in 1996

Malindi F, mr, Noack, Werner; flowers medium, semi-dbl.; int. in 1974

Malinovka F, dp, 1956, Sushkov, K. L.; flowers raspberry-red, medium; [Staatsprasident Pats × Independence]

Malkarsiddha HT, lp, 1989, Patil, B.K.; [sport of Century Two]; int. by K.S.G. Son's Roses, 1987

Mallory Marie F, pb, 2000, Schramm, Dwayne; flowers light pink, reverse medium pink, medium, semi-dbl., borne in small clusters, no fragrance; foliage medium size, medium green, semi-glossy; few prickles; growth upright, medium (2-3 ft.); [Gene Boerner × Dainty Bess]

Malmaison Rose – See **Leweson-Gower**, B

Malmaison Rouge B, dr, 1882, Gonod; flowers velvety dark red, medium, full, cupped; [sport of Souv de la Malmaison]

Malmesbury HT, my, 1980, Sanday, John; bud pointed; flowers 23 petals, borne singly and several together; foliage medium green; prickles slightly hooked; compact, bushy growth; [Vera Dalton × Parasol]

Malton HCh, mr, about 1830, Guérin; flowers bright crimson, paler reverse, 7-8 cm., full, borne in small clusters, intense tea fragrance; foliage dark, small

Malva F, m, 1935, Leenders, M.; flowers mauve, center white, open, large, semi-dbl.; foliage large, glossy, light; very vigorous, bushy growth

Malva Rambler HMult, m, 1908, Puyravaud; flowers violet pink, fading lighter, 3 cm., semi-dbl.; non-recurrent

Malvena HT, lp, Dawson, George

Malvern Hills LCl, yb, 2001, Austin, David; flowers 4¾-6 cm., full, borne in large clusters; foliage medium size, medium green, semi-glossy, disease-resistant; prickles medium, deeply concave, few; growth upright, sprawling, tall (3 m.); garden, decorative; [seedling × seedling]; int. by David Austin Roses, Ltd., 2000

Malverns – See **Heidelinde**, F

Malvina – See **Bourbon**, HGal

Malvina C, lp, 1841, Verdier, V.; flowers pale pink, edged lighter, well-formed, large, very dbl., borne in clusters; sometimes classed as M

Malwa 94 HT, pb, Gokhale, J. & A.; flowers broad pink petals with white stripes, moderate fragrance; [sport of Eiffel Tower]; int. in 1994

Mama – See **Maman**, HT

Mama HT, dr, Wänninger, Franz; flowers large, very dbl.; int. in 1991

Mama de Meyer HT, w, 1931, Lens; flowers cream, center salmon, well-formed, large, dbl.; vigorous growth; [Duchess of Wellington × Aspirant Marcel Rouyer]

Mama Lamesch HT, op, 1922, Lambert, P.; flowers orange-rose, center deeper, reverse reddish-rose, dbl.; [Frau Oberprasident von Grothe × Mme Edouard Herriot]

Mama Looymans HT, dp, 1910, Leenders, M.; flowers carmine-pink, medium, semi-dbl.; [Gruss an Teplitz × Hortensia]

Mama Mia MinFl, mp, 1986, Zipper, H.; flowers miniflora, dbl., high-centered, borne singly or in clusters of 3; foliage medium size, medium green, matte; growth upright, bushy; [Sheri Anne × Sparrieshoop]; int. by Magic Moment Miniature Roses

Mama Pechtold HT, 1938, Pechtold; bud long, pointed; flowers rosy salmon, dbl.; foliage bronze; long, strong stems; vigorous growth; [Katherine Pechtold × Briarcliff]; int. by op

Mamaia Pol, or, GPG Bad Langensalza; flowers semi-dbl.; int. in 1972

Maman HT, or, 1963, Delbard-Chabert; flowers orange-vermilion, well-formed, 4-5 in., 30-40 petals; foliage bright green; bushy growth; [(Rome Glory × La Vaudoise) × Impeccable]; int. by Laxton & Bunyard, 1970; Gold Medal, Geneva, 1962

Maman Chérie HT, pb, 1982, Delbard, Georges; flowers dbl., borne in clusters; [Gay Paris × (Baccará × Impeccable)]

Maman Cochet T, pb, 1893, Cochet, P.; bud pointed; flowers pale pink, center deeper, base lemon-yellow, 4 in., dbl., high-centered, moderate fragrance; foliage dark, leathery; vigorous, bushy growth; [Marie van Houtte × Mme Lombard]

Maman Cochet, Climbing Cl T, pb, 1909, Upton (also Lee-Concord, 1909, H&S, 1915); flowers shades of pink and cream, darker at center, 10 cm., moderate fragrance; [sport of Maman Cochet]

Maman Dental HT, mp, 1921, Dental; flowers pure rose-pink; [sport of Mme Caroline Testout]

Maman Geneviève F, or, 1960, Hémeray-Aubert; flowers red tinted orange; bushy growth

Maman Levavasseur Pol, dp, 1907, Levavasseur; flowers bright crimson-pink, dbl.; [sport of Mme Norbert Levavasseur]

Maman Loiseau T, yb, 1899, Buatois; flowers sulfur-yellow, center peach pink, edges cream yellow, large

Maman Lyly HT, lp, 1911, Soupert & Notting; bud long, oval; flowers pale coral pink, large, semi-dbl., cupped, moderate fragrance; recurrent; [Mme Mélanie Soupert × Mrs Peter Blair]

Maman Pineau HT, dr, 1979, Godin, M.; bud pointed; flowers dark red-purple, 3-3½ in., 26-28 petals, cupped; foliage bronze; vigorous growth; [Maryse Kriloff × Uncle Walter]; int. in 1976

Maman Turbat Pol, pb, 1911, Turbat; flowers China-rose shaded lilac, reverse almost white, large, semi-dbl., borne in clusters of 5-10; foliage dark, soft; bushy growth; [Mme Norbert Levavasseur × Katharina Zeimet]

Mambo Gr, mr, 1970, Swim, H. C.; bud ovoid; flowers currant-red to cardinal-red, medium, dbl., high-centered; foliage dark, leathery; vigorous, tall, bushy growth; [Charlotte Armstrong × seedling]; int. by Armstrong Nurs., 1968

Mambo F, op, 1971, Tantau, Math.; bud ovoid; flowers salmon-pink, medium, dbl.; dwarf, bushy growth; [Tropicana × Zorina]

Mambo F, ob, Tantau; flowers orange, yellow and red on tips, small, dbl., borne in sprays; recurrent; greenhouse rose; int. by Rosen Tantau, 1998; Trial Ground Certificate, Durbanville, 2006

Mambo No. 5 F, yb, Tantau; flowers yellow with edges turning red, small, dbl., borne in sprays; recurrent; greenhouse rose; int. by Rosen Tantau, 2002

Mamie HT, pb, 1902, Dickson, A.; flowers pink and red, large, dbl., moderate fragrance

Mamie, Climbing Cl HT, mr, 1938, Vogel; flowers rose red, large, full, moderate fragrance; [sport of Mamie]

Mamie Serpa F, w, 1955, Serpa; bud ovoid, creamy; flowers open, 2½ in., 50 petals; foliage dark, soft; vigorous, bushy, compact growth; [Goldilocks × Snowbird]

Mamille HT, my, 1976, Kordes; bud long, pointed; flowers 4½ in., 35 petals, high-centered; foliage soft; vigorous, upright growth; [Peer Gynt × Valencia]; int. by Vilmorin

Mamina HWich, dp, Scheiber; flowers intense rose-pink, large, full, quartered; foliage matte green; strong, tall (10 ft.) growth

Mamita HT, mr, 1958, Robichon; flowers garnet-red, large; vigorous growth; [Dickson's Red × seedling]

Mamy Blue HT, m, 1985, Delbard, Georges; flowers large, 35 petals, high-centered; foliage medium size, dark; few prickles; bushy growth; [((Holstein × Bayadère) × (Prelude × St. Exupery)) × unnamed seedling.]; int. by Pepinieres et Roseraies, 1984

Mamy Laperrière HT, rb, Laperrière; flowers blended vermilion, edges deepen with age, high-centered; int. in 1991

Mana F, yb, 1989, Cattermole, R.F.; flowers creamy yellow, edges flushed pink, large, dbl., high-centered; foliage medium green, glossy, veined; prickles light brown; upright growth; [Liverpool Echo × Arthur Bell]; int. by South Pacific Rose Nursery

Mana Böhm – See **Mána Böhmová**, HMult

Mána Böhmová HMult, w, 1925, Böhm, J.; flowers greenish white, medium, full, globular, borne in clusters; foliage large, light green, soft; nearly thornless; [sport of Tausendschön]

Manaia HT, ob, 1999, Schuurman, Frank B.; flowers orange, reverse apricot, 4½-5 in., dbl., borne mostly singly; foliage large, medium green, semi-glossy; prickles moderate; bushy, tall (3½-4 ft.) growth; int. by Franko Roses New Zealand, Ltd., 1994

Manapouri F, mp, 1994, McGredy, Sam IV; flowers medium, dbl., slight fragrance; foliage medium size, medium green, semi-glossy; bushy (35 cm.) growth; [Trinity × Moody Blues]; int. by McGredy Roses International, 1994

Manas HT, ob, Londe & Gokhale; flowers salmon with stripes and blotches of white and red, dbl.; int. in 1997

Manasi F, lp, IARI; flowers light pink, deeper at the margins, small, dbl., borne in small and large clusters; [Frolic × unknown]; int. in 1991

Manchu Rose – See ***R. xanthina*** (Lindley)

Mandalay HT, my, 1942, Mallerin, C.; flowers clear yellow, open, 6 in., very dbl.; foliage leathery; long stems; very vigorous, upright growth; [Soeur Thérèse × Feu Joseph Looymans]; int. by J&P

Mandalay – See **Mandalay Victory**, S

Mandalay Victory S, my, Poulsen; flowers medium yellow, 8-10 cm., 25 petals, moderate fragrance; foliage dark; growth bushy, 20-40 cm.; int. by Poulsen Roser, 2002

Mandarin HT, my, 1946, Robichon; flowers golden yellow; foliage glossy; vigorous growth; [Betty Uprichard × Ville de Paris]

Mandarin F, mr, 1951, Boerner; bud ovoid; flowers mandarin-red, 3-4 in., 18 petals, high-centered, borne in large clusters, moderate fragrance; foliage leathery, glossy; vigorous (3½-4 ft.), upright growth; [Lilette Mallerin × Red F seedling]; int. by J&P

Mandarin Min, ab, 2006; flowers salmon pink and mandarin orange-yellow with lighter center, 4 cm., full, borne in small clusters; foliage tiny, light green, glossy; growth compact, short (25 cm.); int. by W. Kordes' Söhne, 1987

Mandarin Delight Min, ob, 1990, Jacobs, Betty A.; bud pointed; flowers soft, light mandarin orange, reverse lighter, aging peach in cooler weather, dbl., high-centered; foliage medium size, medium green, semi-glossy; prickles needle, medium, red to tan; bushy, medium growth; no fruit; [Party Girl × Gingersnap]; int. by Four Seasons Rose Nursery, 1989

Mandarin Silk MinFl, ob, 2005, Denton, James A; flowers orange, reverse medium yellow, medium, full, borne mostly solitary, no fragrance; foliage medium size, medium green, semi-glossy; prickles few, medium, downturning, red-brown; growth upright, tall (30in.); exhibition, garden decoration; [Hot Tamale × June Laver]; int. by James A Denton

Mandarin Sunblaze Min, ab, 2003, Meilland International; bud elongated, medium; flowers apricot blend, reverse light yellow, 5-7 cm., 66 petals, cupped, borne in small clusters, no fragrance; free-flowering; foliage large, medium green, semi-glossy; prickles moderate; growth bushy, tall (2 ft.); garden decoration, containers; PP13291; [(Mark One × Teddy Bear) × Leonidas]; int. by The Conard-Pyle Company, 2003

Mandarine – See **Mandrina**, F

Mandarine Symphonie – See **Mandarin Sunblaze**, Min

Manda's Pink Roamer – See **Pink Roamer**, HWich

Manda's Triumph HWich, w, 1899, Horvath; flowers pure white, 2 in., very dbl., borne in clusters of 10-12; some autumn repeat; very vigorous growth; [*R. wichurana* × Paquerette]; int. by W.A. Manda

Mander #1 – See **Mander's Nutkana**, S

Mander's Nutkana S, dr, 2006, Mander, George; flowers red/crimson, reverse light red, 4-5 in., full, borne in small clusters; non-rem,ontant; foliage medium size, medium green, semi-glossy; prickles 1/4- in., needle-point, light brown, few; growth bushy, tall (7-8 ft.); garden; hips brightly colored; [Shades of Pink × *R. nutkana*]; int. in 2000

Mander's Orange Dream Min, ob, 2006, Mander, George; flowers dark burnt orange, reverse lighter orange, 2 in., full, high-centered, borne in small clusters; recurrent; foliage medium size, dark green, glossy; prickles moderate, -1/4 in.es, needle point, light brown; growth compact, medium (20-24 in.); garden, containers, exhibition; [June Laver × Rubies 'n' Pearls]; int. by Hortico, Inc., 2006

Mandrina F, or, 1964, deRuiter; flowers 2½-3 in., 30 petals, borne in clusters; foliage dark; vigorous, bushy growth; [Moulin Rouge × Frau Anny Beaufays]; int. by Carlton Rose Nurseries

Mandryka S, or, Mekdeci-Olsen; flowers medium red with orange, borne in clusters, moderate fragrance; int. in 1992

Mandy F, ly, 1963, Robinson, H.; flowers creamy yellow to soft peach, large, dbl.; foliage coppery; very free growth; [Pinocchio × Sweet Repose]

Mandy HT, dr, Kordes; int. in 1987

Mandy Jo HT, pb, 1970, Abrahams; flowers pale biscuit, flushed light pink, 4½ in., 22 petals; foliage very glossy, bright green; vigorous growth; [sport of Pink Favorite]

Mandy Kordana Min, mr, Kordes; flowers dbl.; recurrent; int. by W. Kordes Söhne

Mandy Singleton HT, pb, Dawson; int. in 1995

Maneca HT, lp, 1929, Pernet-Ducher; flowers dbl.; int. by Gaujard

Manette HGal, rb, before 1820, Lecoffé; flowers violet, slatey edges, medium, very dbl., cupped; vigorous, upright growth; possibly synonymous with Nanette; int. in 1820

Manette HGal, dp, about 1835, Prévost; flowers dark pink, aging to red, edges lighter, medium, full

Manettii N, lp, 1835, Manetti, Dr.; flowers violet-rose, 2 in., single, borne in large clusters, no fragrance; foliage extremely susceptible to blackspot; stems red shoots; vigorous shrub growth; probably a cross of Blush Noisette × Slater's Crimson China; used as an understock by Thomas Rivers in 1850; int. by Rivers, 1835, from S. Manetti, Monza Bot. Gdn., It

Mango HT, ob, Dorieux; flowers melon-orange with yellow center, large, dbl.; int. in 1988

Mango HT, yb, J&P; int. in 1994

Mango Blush S, ab; int. in 1999

Mango Tango MinFl, ab, 2000, Giles, Diann; flowers medium, dbl., borne mostly singly, no fragrance; foliage medium size, medium green, semi-glossy; few prickles; growth upright, medium; [New Year × miniature seedling]; int. by Giles Rose Nursery, 2000

Manhattan HT, or, 1936, Asmus; bud urn shaped; flowers jasper-red to coral-red, base yellow, very large, dbl., cupped; very vigorous growth; [sport of Souvenir]

Manhattan – See **Charming Cover**, S

Manhatten Blue HT, m

Manifesto HT, op, 1920, McGredy; flowers flesh-pink, tinged salmon, dbl.

Manilla HT, Kordes, R.

Manille HT, yb, 1951, Mallerin, C.; flowers golden yellow edged red, very large, 40-50 petals, globular; foliage leathery, bronze; vigorous, upright growth; [Pierre × Lumiere]; int. by Vilmorin-Andrieux

Manille HT, my, Kordes; flowers chrome yellow, aging to canary, large, dbl.; growth to 60-70 cm.

Manipur Magic HG, ly, 2005, Viraraghavan, M.S. Viru; flowers up to 5 in., full, borne in small clusters; will repeat when established; foliage large, light green, semi-glossy; prickles small, triangular, down curving, grey, moderate; growth climbing, tall (to 20 ft); [Reve d'Or × Rosa Gigantea]; int. by Roses Unlimited, 2005

Manipuri – See **Alister's Gift**, HG

Manit HT, dr, 1991, Umsawasdi, Dr. Theera; flowers medium, semi-dbl., borne mostly singly, no fragrance; foliage medium size, medium green, matte; upright, bushy, tall (5-6 ft.) growth; [seedling × Olympiad]

Manita LCl, mp, 2006; flowers pink with white-yellow center, 9 cm., semi-dbl., borne in small clusters; foliage large; growth spreading, tall (250 cm.); int. by W. Kordes' Söhne, 1996

Manitoba Centennial Rose – See **Cuthbert Grant**, S

Manitou HT, rb, 1957, Swim, H.C.; flowers coppery red, reverse golden yellow, well-formed, very large, dbl.; upright, bushy growth; int. by Kordes

Manja – See **Six Flags**, Gr

Manja Mourier – See **Six Flags**, Gr

Manjana F, op, 1969, deRuiter; flowers salmon-pink-apricot, high-centered; free growth; [Orange Sensation × (Pink Parfait × Lavender Pinocchio)]

Manlissa LCl, dp, 1991, Mander, George; flowers large, dbl., borne in small clusters, intense fragrance; foliage medium size, dark green, glossy; tall, upright, bushy growth; [Morgengruss × Whisky Mac]

Manmariam – See **Mariam Ismailjee**, MinFl

Manmatha F, m, Pal, Dr. B.P.; flowers smoky pink to silvery mauve, small, dbl.; a smaller version of Paradise; int. in 1989

Mannequin F, mp, 1961, Lens; vigorous, upright growth; [(Peace × Cinnabar) × Fashion]

Mannheim S, dr, 1959, Kordes, R.; flowers crimson, large, dbl., borne in clusters; recurrent bloom; upright (3 ft.), bushy growth; [Rudolph Timm × Fanal]; int. in 1958

Manning's Blush HEg, w, before 1819, Manning; flowers white faintly flushed pink, very small, dbl.; foliage fragrant (apple); growth to 4-5 ft.

Mannington Lavender m

Mannington Mauve Rambler Misc OGR, m, 2007, Walpole, Lord; flowers small, dbl., borne in large clusters; foliage small, medium green, matte; numerous prickles; growth spreading, bushy, tall (5 m.), rambling; [The Garland × unknown]; discovered by Lord Walpole on grounds of Mannington Hall; int. by Peter Beales Roses, 2001

Manola – See **Fred Cramphorn**, HT

Manon HT, ab, 1924, Bernaix, P.; flowers yellow mixed with apricot, semi-dbl.; [Christine × Mrs Farmer]

Manora HT, mr, Tantau; int. in 1992

Manosque HT, mr, 1958, Buyl Frères; flowers well-formed, intense fragrance; moderately vigorous growth

Manou Gr, Meilland, L.; int. in 1979

Manou Meilland HT, m, 1979, Meilland, Mrs. Marie-Louise; bud conical; flowers mauve-pink, medium, 50 petals, cupped; foliage glossy, dark; vigorous, bushy growth; [(Baronne Edmond de Rothschild × Baronne Edmond de Rothschild) × (Ma Fille × Love Song)]; int. by Meilland & Co SNC; Gold Star of the South Pacific, Palmerston North, NZ, 1980

Manou Meilland, Climbing Cl HT, dp, Meilland; [sport of Manou Meilland]; int. in 1997

Manprincess HT, lp, 1991, Mander, George; flowers large, very full, borne mostly singly, slight fragrance; foliage medium size, light green, semi-glossy; tall, upright growth; [(Tiffany × Pascali) × Super Sun]

Manpurple HT, m, 1991, Mander, George; flowers purple/cream bicolor, large, dbl., borne mostly singly; foliage medium size, dark green, glossy; medium, bushy growth; [Mount Shasta × Super Sun]

Mansais T, pb, 1838, Mansais; flowers pink with yellow shades, verylarge, full

Mansopas Cl F, op, 1991, Mander, George; flowers medium pink shaded coral and cream, medium, full, borne in small clusters, slight fragrance; foliage medium size, dark green, glossy; tall, upright, bushy growth; [Shades of Pink × Pascali]

Mansuino Rose HT, mr, 1964, Mansuino, Q.; flowers crimson to spirea-red, small to medium, 35 petals, cupped; foliage small, dark; thin stems; PP2577; int. by Carlton Rose Nurseries

Manteau de Jeanne d'Arc B, lp, about 1840, Béluze; flowers flesh pink, fading to white, medium, very full

Manteau d'Évêque HGal, m, before 1819; flowers violet, slightly striped, somtimes spotted white, medium, semi-dbl.

Manteau d'Évêque HP, m, 1853, Moulins; flowers purple, becoming amaranth-voilet, large, full

Manteau d'Évêque HCh, dr, in Angers; flowers velvety dark red, large, full

Manteau Pourpre – See **Rouge Formidable**, HGal

Manteau Pourpre HGal, m, before 1811; flowers bright carmine-purple, underside silvery, very large petals, semi-dbl.; foliage long, deeply toothed, bright green

Manteau Rouge – See **Rouge Formidable**, HGal

Manteau Rouge – See **Manteau Pourpre**, HGal

Manteau Royal HGal, dr, before 1820, Descemet; flowers fiery crimson to Roman purple, medium, very full

Manteo Min, mp, 1993, Bridges, Dennis A.; flowers medium, dbl., borne mostly singly; foliage small, medium green, semi-glossy; some prickles; tall (55-60 cm.), upright, bushy growth; [Rise 'n' Shine × seedling]; int. by Bridges Roses, 1993

Manu Mukerji HT, my, 1972, Friends Rosery; [sport of Fragrant Cloud]

Manuel Canovas S, w, Guillot-Massad; flowers white with yellow highlights, full, borne in clusters, moderate fragrance; recurrent; vigorous (1 m.) growth; int. by Roses Guillot, 1995

Manuel P. Azevedo HT, mr, 1911, Soupert & Notting; flowers carmine-red, large, dbl.; [Étoile de France × Ulrich Brunner fils]

Manuel Pinto de Azevedo HT, pb, 1958, Moreira da Silva; flowers deep rose-pink, reverse lighter, 4 in., 48 petals, moderate fragrance; foliage dark, glossy, leathery; vigorous, upright growth; [seedling × Peace]; int. by McGredy & Son, 1957

Manuela HT, mp, 1970, Tantau, Math.; flowers large, 30 petals, high-centered, moderate fragrance; foliage glossy; vigorous, upright, bushy growth; int. by Wheatcroft & Sons, 1969

Manuelita HT, or, 1947, Dot, Pedro; flowers large; very vigorous growth; [Cynthia × Vive la France]

Manureva F, lp, Sauvageot; flowers pale rose, darker at center, semi-dbl.; int. in 1997

Manx Queen F, ob, 1963, Dickson, Patrick; flowers rich gold flushed bronze red, medium, 18 petals, borne in large clusters, moderate fragrance; foliage dark; bushy, compact growth; [Shepherd's Delight × Circus]; int. by A. Dickson & Sons, 1963

Many Happy Returns – See **Prima**, S

Many Moons F, my, 1984, Stoddard, Louis; flowers deep yellow to light yellow, large, 35 petals, moderate fragrance; foliage medium size, medium green, matte; upright, bushy, tall, arching growth; [Chinatown × Maigold]

Many Summers HT, ob, 1976, Fryer, Gareth; flowers orange-copper, 6 in., 30 petals, intense fragrance; vigorous growth; [Arthur Bell × Belle Blonde]; int. by Fryer's Nursery, Ltd., 1975

Many Thanks Min, ab, Geytenbeek; [sport of Mary Marshall]; int. in 1976

Manyo F, ab, Keisei; int. in 1988

Mao HT, rb, Takatori; int. by Takatori Roses

Maori Doll Min, yb, 1977, Bell Roses; bud pointed, somewhat ovoid; flowers straw yellow in heat, azalea pink overlaying yellow in cool weather, 50 petals, borne in clusters, moderate fragrance; free-flowering; foliage medium green, glossy; growth bushy, upright; [sport of Yellow Doll]; int. by Sequoia Nursery, 1977

Maori Lullaby F, pb, 1963, Mason, P.G.; flowers carmine-rose, base light yellow to white, 3-3½ in., 10-12 petals, borne in clusters; foliage bronze, leathery; bushy, low, compact growth; [Traumland × seedling]

Maori Moon F, pb, 1976, Clayworth; bud pointed; flowers pink, center cream, large, 10 petals, cupped; foliage light, aging darker; upright, compact, bushy growth; [Bengali × (Pink Parfait × King Boreas)]; int. in 1974

Maorilander HT, mr, 1956, Mason, P.; bud ovoid, pointed; flowers crimson, lighter reverse, large, dbl., high-centered; foliage bronze, leathery; bushy growth; [Crimson Glory × Peace]

Maoz II Pol, pb, Motke Nevo; flowers dbl., slight fragrance

Marama HT, w, 1980, Simpson, J.W.; bud pointed; flowers 45 petals, high-centered, intense fragrance; foliage large, medium green, semi-glossy; prickles dark brown; bushy, medium growth; [Lady Helen × seedling]

Maranta F, yb, 1974, Tantau, Math.; bud globular; flowers yellow, red, medium, semi-dbl.; foliage soft; upright, bushy growth; int. by Ahrens & Sieberz

Marathon F, op, 1956, Mondial Roses; flowers salmon-rose, 4 in., semi-dbl., borne in clusters; moderate, compact growth; [Fashion × Hybrid Tea seedling]

Marbled – See **Marmorea**, HGal

Marbled Gallica HGal, m, Scarman; int. by Roses du Temps Passé, 2000

Marbrée – See **Marmorea**, HGal

Marbrée P, rb, 1858, Robert et Moreau; flowers strawberry red marbled white, large, semi-dbl. to dbl., very slight fragrance

Marbrée d'Enghien HSpn, w, about 1830, Parmentier; flowers cream white marbled with med, medium, dbl.; foliage small, oval, closely-set; prickles numerous, unequal, narrow, straight

Marbrée d'Enghien M, m, about 1850, Robert; flowers purple-violet, striped and marbled with pink

Marc Guillot F, dr, 1958, Mallerin, C.; bud ovoid; flowers dark scarlet-red, medium, 25-35 petals, cupped; foliage dull green, leathery; vigorous, upright growth; [Happiness × Demain]; int. by EFR, 1955

Marc-Antoine Charpentier S, yb, Guillot-Massad; flowers yellow, fading through vanilla to creamy white as they open, full, cupped, opening flat, borne in clusters, slight tea fragrance; recurrent; arching, dome-shaped (2 m.) growth

Marcel Boivin HT, op, 1954, Buatois; flowers coral-pink, base yellow, very large, 50-60 petals; vigorous growth; [Souv. de Claudius Pernet × Château de Clos Vougeot]

Marcel Bourgouin HGal, m, 1898, Corboeuf-Marsault; flowers velvety, rich scarlet-purple, mottled violet; int. by Corboeuf, 1899

Marcel Grammont HP, dr, 1868, Vigneron; flowers dark brownish-red, large, full, globular

Marcel Pagnol – See **Graf Lennart**, HT

Marcel Pajotin F, Kriloff, Michel; int. in 1976

Marcel Turbat LCl, Moreira da Silva, A.

Marcelin Roda T, w, 1872, Ducher; flowers white with yellow base, large, very full

Marceline HT, rb, 1928, Buatois; flowers crimson, edge and reverse violet-rose, dbl., slight fragrance; recurrent; [Frau Karl Druschki × Yves Druhen]

Marcella HP, w, 1865, Liabaud

Marcella HT, op, 1913, Paul, W.; bud yellow; flowers salmon flesh, large, full, borne mostly solitary

Marcella Baldge – See **Souv de Marcelle Balage**, HT

Marcelle Auclair F, or, 1970, Robichon; flowers medium, semi-dbl., high-centered, borne in clusters of 5-8, intense fragrance; foliage glossy, leathery; vigorous, upright growth; [Soleil de Lyon × seedling]; int. by Ilgenfritz Nursery, 1964

Marcelle Gret HT, my, 1947, Meilland, F.; bud long, pointed; flowers saffron-yellow, 6 in., 28 petals; foliage dark; vigorous growth; [Peace × Prinses Beatrix]; Gold Medal, Geneva, 1948

Marcelle Gret, Climbing Cl HT, my, 1957, Frères, Brenier

Marcelle Marchand HT, mp, Adam; int. by Pépinières de la Guerinais, 2002

Marcelle Petit F, op, 1958, Arles; flowers glowing salmon-pink; foliage glossy; vigorous growth; [Pinocchio × Independence]; int. by Roses-France

Marcellin Champagnat – See **Caroline de Monaco**, HT

Märchen Pol, lp, 1927, Kiese; flowers light rose pink with white, small, single

Marchen Hiroko HT, lp, Kitagawa; [sport of Bride's Dream]; int. in 2002

Märchenkönigin – See **Bride's Dream**, HT

Märchenland F, ob, 1951, Tantau; flowers bright rose tinted salmon, large, 18 petals, blooms in clusters of 40, moderate fragrance; foliage dark; vigorous, upright growth; [Swantje × Hamburg]

Märchentag HT, lp, 1929, von Württemberg, Herzogin Elsa; flowers creamy pink, large, dbl.

Marchesa Boccella HP, lp, 1842, Desprez; flowers delicate pink, edges almost blush, compact, large; petals smaller than other HP's, dbl., moderate fragrance; recurrent; stiff, erect stems; growth dwarf, robust habit

Marchioness of Downshire HP, pb, 1894, Dickson, A.; flowers glossy carnation pink, shaded light red, aging to ivory-white, large, full

Marchioness of Dufferin HP, mp, 1891, Dickson, A.; flowers very large, dbl.

Marchioness of Exeter HP, lp, 1877, Laxton; flowers pale pink, tinted with cherry pink, petals recurved, semi-globular, moderate fragrance; [Jules Margottin × unknown]

Marchioness of Linlithgow HT, dr, 1929, Dobbie; flowers deep blackish crimson, open, large, dbl.; foliage soft, bronze; vigorous growth; Gold Medal, NRS, 1930

Marchioness of Londonderry HP, lp, 1893, Dickson, A.; flowers pale pink, very large, 50 petals, high-centered, moderate fragrance; very vigorous growth; [probably a seedling of Baronne Adolphe de Rothschild]

Marchioness of Lorne HP, pb, 1889, Paul, W.; flowers rich rosy pink shaded darker, large, dbl., cupped; vigorous growth

Marchioness of Ormonde HT, ly, 1918, Dickson, H.; flowers clear wheat-straw color, center deep honey-yellow, dbl.

Marchioness of Salisbury HT, dr, 1890, Pernet père; flowers velvety intense red, medium, dbl.; foliage thick, dark green; prickles prominent, numerous; growth upright

Marchioness of Waterford HT, pb, 1910, Dickson, H.; flowers dark silvery pink, edges lighter, reverse glossy salmon pink, large, full, globular

Marcia HT, op, 1952, Raffel; flowers pink to coral, base yellow, well-shaped, large; foliage glossy; vigorous, upright growth; [Étoile de Hollande × Raffel's Yellow]; int. by Port Stockton Nursery

Marcia Coolidge HT, pb, 1927, Coolidge; flowers very light pink, reverse darker, stamens dark crimson, semi-dbl.; [Gen. MacArthur × unknown]

Marcia Gandy HT, rb, 1959, Verschuren; flowers crimson to rose-red, reverse rose-opal, intense fragrance; vigorous growth; int. by Gandy Roses, Ltd., 1957

Marcia Stanhope HT, w, 1922, Lilley; flowers pure white, large, 25 petals, globular; foliage leathery; [Frau Karl Druschki × unknown]; Gold Medal, NRS, 1924

Marco HWich, w, 1905, Guillot, P.; bud buff; flowers white, center coppery, aging to reddish orange-yellow, 6-7 cm., full, borne in clusters; foliage glossy, purplish; growth to 10 ft.; [*R. wichurana* × Souv. de Catherine Guillot]

Marco Polo HT, lp, 1971, Fankhauser; flowers soft dawn-pink, large, dbl., high-centered; foliage glossy; vigorous, upright growth; [Memoriam × Elizabeth Fankhauser]

Marco Polo HT, my, 1994, Meilland, Alain A.; bud conical, large; flowers lemon yellow, lighter at the edges, 3-3½ in., 35 petals, cupped, borne mostly singly or in small clusters, moderate fragrance; good repeat; foliage medium green, semi-glossy; prickles numerous, medium, pink; tall, upright growth; PP9042; [Ambassador × (Sunbright × Oregold)]; int. by SNC Meilland & Cie, 1992

Mardi Gras HT, dr, 1953, Jordan, G.L.; bud ovoid; flowers deep velvety red, 5 in., 33 petals, high-centered; foliage leathery; vigorous, upright, bushy growth; [Crimson Glory × Poinsettia]; int. by J&P; Gold Medal, Baden-Baden, 1953

Mardi Gras, Climbing Cl HT, dr, 1956, Kordes

Mardi Gras F, pb, 2007, Zary, Keith W.; flowers pink orange yellow blend, 4 in., dbl., blooms borne in small clusters; foliage medium size, dark green, semi-glossy; prickles 6-8 mm., hooked downward, greyed-orange, moderate; growth upright, medium (4 ft.); [Arofres × Singin' in the Rain]; int. by Jackson & Perkins Wholesale, Inc., 2008

Mardonius HP, m, 1845, Béluze; flowers bluish pink, medium, full

Maréchal Bazaine HP, dp, 1864, de Fauw; flowers dark carmine-pink, medium

Maréchal Bugeaud T, pb, 1843; flowers lilac pink, shaded chamois, large, full

Marechal Carmona HT, op, Moreira da Silva; flowers salmon-pink with reddish tones

Maréchal Davoust M, mp, 1853, Robert; flowers bright rose, large, full, cupped

Maréchal de Canrobert HP, pb, 1863, Pernet; flowers bright pink with red, shaded purple, very large, dbl

Maréchal de Canrobert HP, pb, 1885, Lévêque; flowers light cherry, shaded carmine-purple, large, full, globular

Maréchal de Villars B, dp; flowers deep rose shaded violet, cupped

Maréchal du Palais B, lp, 1846, Béluze; flowers rosy blush, large, full, cupped

Maréchal Foch Pol, dp, 1918, Levavasseur; flowers cherry-red to pink, semi-dbl., open, borne in compact clusters, moderate fragrance; vigorous, bushy growth; [sport of Orléans Rose]

Maréchal Forey HP, mr, 1862, Margottin; flowers bright crimson with velvety violet, large, cupped

Maréchal Forey HP, mp, 1863, Pradel; flowers large, full

Maréchal Le Clerc – See **Touch of Class**, HT

Maréchal Lyautey HT, dr, 1931, Croibier; flowers deep red, large, very dbl., high-centered; foliage thick, dark, bronze; very vigorous, bushy growth; [Hadley × Laurent Carle]

Maréchal Mortier – See **Deuil du Maréchal Mortier**, HCh

Maréchal Niel N, my, 1864, Pradel; bud long, pointed; flowers golden yellow, large, dbl., intense fragrance; foliage large, light green; weak stems; very vigorous, climbing growth; [Chromatella × unknown (possibly Isabella Gray)]

Maréchal Niel a Feuilles Panachées T, cy, 1895, Dienemann; foliage striped with yellow; [sport of Maréchal Niel]

Maréchal Pétain HT, yb, 1926, Reymond; flowers soft pink on yellow ground

Maréchal Robert T, yb, 1875, Widow Ducher; flowers yellow, blushing slightly along edges, very large, full, globular

Maréchal Stalin HT, mr, Mélichar; flowers carmine-red, large, dbl.; int. in 1965

Maréchal Suchet HP, mr, 1863, Guillot; flowers crimson, shaded chestnut, large, full; possibly synonymous with one of the same name from Damaizin, 1877

Maréchal Vaillant – See **Pourpre d'Orléans**, HP

Marella HT, pb, 1961, Meilland, Mrs. Marie-Louise; bud globular; flowers pink-red, large, 35 petals; foliage glossy, leathery; vigorous growth; [(Happiness × Independence) × Better Times]; int. by URS

Marella 2002 HT, ob, Meilland; flowers orange center, outer petals lighter, dbl., high-centered; florist rose; int. by Meilland Intl., 2004

Maren S, mr, 1988, Gimpel, W.F.; flowers deep scarlet red with velvet overtones, large, full; foliage large, dark green, semi-glossy, leathery, disease-resistant; growth upright, spreading, vigorous, free-standing; [Red Fountain × Red Fountain]; int. by J.B. Williams & Associates, 1989

Mareva – See **Appleblossom**, S

Marfa HT, w, Shtanko, E.E.; flowers dbl.; int. in 1975

Marfil HT, w, 1962, Dot, Pedro; flowers ivory-white, large; strong stems; tall growth; [White Knight × Angelis]

Marga HRg, lp, Rieksta; flowers medium, semi-dbl.; int. in 1979

Marga Weil HT, or, 1938, Weil; flowers salmon-red, large, dbl.

Margalit HT, op, 2002, Poole, Lionel; flowers salmon pink, pale pink/cream reverse, 5 in., full, borne mostly solitary, moderate fragrance; foliage large, dark green, semi-glossy; prickles medium, hooked, moderate; growth upright, bushy, vigorous, medium (1 m.); garden decorative, cutting; [Joanne × Pot of Gold]

Margaret HT, lp, 1909, Paul, W.; flowers light carnation pink, large, full

Margaret HT, pb, 1954, Dickson, A.; flowers bright pink, reverse silvery pink, well-shaped, 70 petals, moderate fragrance; vigorous growth; [(May Wettern × unknown) × Souv. de Denier van der Gon]; Gold Medal, NRS, 1954

Margaret Amos HT, dp, 1952, McGredy, Sam IV; flowers strawberry-red, large, 25 petals, high-centered; foliage dark reddish green; very free growth; [McGredy's Scarlet × unknown]

Margaret Anderson LCl, w, 1931, Thomas; flowers centers deep cream, outer petals cream-flesh, very large, dbl.; recurrent bloom; foliage thick, leathery; very vigorous, climbing growth; int. by H&S

Margaret Ann Silverstein F, ob, 2001, Horner, Colin P.; flowers orange, pale orange reverse, very wavy petals, semi-dbl., borne in small clusters, moderate fragrance; foliage medium size, medium green, semi-glossy; prickles small, curved, few; growth spreading, medium (80 cm.); garden decorative; [((Baby Love × Golden Future) × L'Oreal Trophy) × L'Oreal Trophy]; int. by Paul Chessum Roses, 2003

Margaret Anne HT, pb, Matthews, W.J.; int. in 1977

Margaret Anne Baxter HT, w, 1927, Smith, T.; bud pointed; flowers white, sometimes tinted flesh, large, 88 petals; foliage thick, leathery, glossy, bronze; vigorous, bushy growth; [Harry Kirk × unknown]; Gold Medal, NRS, 1927

Margaret Belle Houston HT, dr, 1929, Vestal; flowers velvety crimson, very large, dbl.; foliage light, leathery

Margaret Browning S, lp; int. in 2001

Margaret Bushby S, pb, 2000, Weatherly, Lilia; flowers deep pink opening paler, fading to almost white, yellow base, 5-6 cm., full, borne in small clusters, slight fragrance; foliage medium size, dark green, semi-glossy; prickles moderate; growth spreading, medium (5 ft.); [*R. macrantha* × unknown]; int. by Prophyl Pty, Ltd., 1999

Margaret Chase Smith HT, dr, 1966, Brownell, H.C.; bud long, pointed; flowers large, dbl., moderate fragrance; vigorous, upright growth; PP2959; [Red Duchess × Queen Elizabeth]

Margaret Chessum F, dp, 2000, Bossom, Bill; flowers deep pink, white reverse, no fragrance; foliage light green, semi-glossy; growth bushy, medium (3½ ft.); [Sexy Rexy × Eyepaint]; int. by Chessum, 2000

Margaret Clara HT, ab, 1999, Jones, L.J.; flowers 2 in., full, borne mostly singly, moderate fragrance; foliage medium size, dark green, glossy, impervious to rain; prickles moderate; upright, medium (3½ ft.) growth; [Solitaire × (Alexander × Remember Me)]

Margaret Daintry F, dr, 1988, Horner, Colin P.; flowers crimson-scarlet, large, dbl., borne singly and in clusters; foliage medium size, dark green, glossy; bushy growth; [Red Planet × (Blessings × (Parkdirektor Riggers × Honey Favorite))]; int. by Rosemary Roses, 1988

Margaret Denton MinFl, rb, 2003, Denton, James A.; flowers red/orange, reverse yellow/orange, 2½-3 in., full, borne mostly solitary, no fragrance; foliage medium size, dark green, glossy; prickles small, straight, brown, few; stems long; growth compact, medium (24 in.); patio, exhibition; [June Laver × Glowing Amber]; int. by James A Denton, 2003

Margaret Dickson HP, w, 1891, Dickson, A.; flowers white, center pale flesh, well-formed, large, 65 petals, cupped; occasionally recurrent bloom; foliage dark; vigorous growth; [Lady Mary Fitzwilliam × Merveille de Lyon]

Margaret Dickson Hamill HT, yb, 1915, Dickson, A.; flowers straw-yellow, flushed salmon, petals shell-shaped, large, dbl.; foliage dark, leathery; bushy growth; Gold Medal, NRS, 1914, Gold Medal, Bagatelle, 1917

Margaret Egerton HT, dp, 1931, Chaplin Bros.; flowers rosy cerise passing to carmine, base yellow, well-formed; vigorous growth

Margaret Elbogen Pol, w, 1936, Brada, Dr.; flowers pinkish white; very vigorous growth; int. by Böhm

Margaret Fleming HRg, mp, 1995, Fleming, Joyce L.; flowers very clear pink, no lavender tones, small, semi-dbl., borne up to 5 per cluster, no fragrance; foliage medium to large, medium green, semi-glossy, somewhat; bushy (to 120 cm.) growth; [*R. rugosa alba* × Masquerade]; int. by Hortico Roses, 1994

Margaret H S, my, 2001, Moe, Mitchie; flowers medium yellow, light yellow reverse, 2½-3 in., single, borne in small clusters, moderate fragrance; fast repeat; foliage medium size, medium green, semi-glossy; prickles medium, slightly hooked, few; growth upright, tall (5-6 ft.), vigorous; garden decorative; [Pristine × City of London]; int. by Mitchie's Roses and More, 2001

Margaret Hall HT, pb, 2003, Horner, Colin P.; flowers medium pink/peach, reverse paler, 12 cm., full, borne in small clusters, moderate fragrance; foliage medium size, dark green, glossy; prickles medium, curved, moderate; growth compact, medium (1 m.); garden decorative; [Wandering Minstrel × Silver Anniversary]; int. by Battersby Roses, 2003

Margaret Haywood HP, lp, 1890, Haywood; flowers full; [sport of Mme Clémence Joigneaux]

Margaret Herbert HT, lp, 1956, Harrison

Margaret Horton HT, ab, 1921, Hicks; bud pointed; flowers apricot-yellow, open, large, dbl., high-centered; foliage leathery, glossy, light; vigorous growth

Margaret Isabel HT, w, 1984, Summerell, B.L.; flowers oyster white, cream center, delicately flushed pink petal edges, 45 petals, high-centered, intense fragrance; prickles red-brown; upright growth; [Strawberry Ice × Redgold]; int. in 1983

Margaret Isobel Hayes – See **International Herald Tribune**, F

Margaret Jean Min, dp, 1978, Dobbs, Annette E.; bud ovoid; flowers deep pink, very dbl., borne 4-8 per cluster; foliage small, dark; prickles very few; bushy, vigorous growth; [Fairy Moss × Fairy Moss]; int. by Small World Min. Roses

Margaret Jean S, pb, 2006, Ponton, Ray; flowers deep pink, reverse light pink, 2-3 in., dbl., borne mostly solitary; foliage medium green, semi-glossy; prickles medium, straight, moderate; growth upright, short (2 ft.); [Carefree Beauty × Scentimental]; int. in 2006

Margaret Laver Min, w, 2001, Laver, Keith G.; flowers luminous cream, 1-1½ in., full, borne mostly solitary, moderate fragrance; foliage medium size, light green, matte; prickles ¼ in., straight, few; growth bushy, medium (10-12 in.); garden decorative, containers; [seedling × seedling]; int. by Springwood Roses, 1998

Margaret Law F, ob, 1981, McTeer, Gilbert; flowers luminous orange, pink on outer petals, 25 petals, high-centered, borne 3-23 per cluster; foliage dark, glossy; prickles hooked, red; vigorous growth; [Princess Michiko × Gold Gleam]; int. by Bridgemere Nursery

Margaret Lucas F, w, 2001, Kenny, David; flowers white with pink edge, 3 in., semi-dbl., borne in large clusters, slight fragrance; foliage small, medium green, semi-glossy; prickles small, straight, moderate; growth upright, tall; garden decorative; [Bonica × Solitaire]

Margaret M. Wylie HT, pb, 1921, Dickson, H.; flowers flesh, edges heavily flushed deep rosy pink, dbl.; Gold Medal, NRS, 1920

Margaret McDowell HT, mr, 1992, McCann, Sean; flowers medium, full; foliage medium size, medium green, semi-glossy; some prickles; growth medium (36; [(Ruby Wedding × (Seedling × Oonagh)) × (seedling × Oonagh)]

Margaret McGredy HT, or, 1927, McGredy; flowers orange-scarlet, large, 35 petals, high-centered, moderate fragrance; foliage light, leathery, glossy; vigorous growth; Gold Medal, NRS, 1925

Margaret McGredy, Climbing Cl HT, or, 1936, Dixie Rose Nursery

Margaret Mercer HT, yb, 1977, Mercer; flowers pale yellow, edged light pink, 4½ in., 53-65 petals; foliage glossy, dark; vigorous growth; [Pink Favorite × Peace]

Margaret Merril F, w, 1977, Harkness; flowers blush white, 4 in., 28 petals, high-centered, borne singly and several together, intense fragrance; free-flowering; foliage medium green with slight grayish tint; growth vigorous, rounded (3 ft.); [(Rudolph Timm × Dedication) × Pascali]; James Mason Medal, RNRS, 1990, Gold Star of the South Pacific, Palmerston North, NZ, 1982, Gold Medal, Rome, 1978, Gold Medal, Monza, 1978

Margaret Molyneux HT, my, 1909, Dickson, A.; flowers canary-yellow

Margaret Moore Jacobs HT, mp, 1968, Fuller; bud ovoid; flowers large, dbl., cupped; foliage glossy; vigorous, bushy growth; [Tiffany × Pink Masterpiece]; int. by Wyant

Margaret O HT, w, 1995, Ortega, Carlos; flowers medium, very dbl., borne mostly singly; foliage medium size, dark green, matte; some prickles; tall (180 cm.), upright growth; [Pristine × Lauren Elizabeth]; int. by Aebi Nursery, 1995

Margaret Roberts F, dp, 1976, Wood; flowers cerise, large, 20-25 petals; foliage small, dark; moderate, free growth; [Elizabeth of Glamis × Wendy Cussons]

Margaret Ruth HT, w, 1969, Taylor, L.R.; flowers creamy white, center pale pink, large, dbl., high-centered; intermittent bloom; foliage glossy, leathery; vigorous, upright, bushy growth; [Anne Letts × Christian Dior]

Margaret Sharpe T, mp

Margaret Spaull HT, ob, 1928, Cant, B. R.; flowers variable orange and lilac, dbl.; [Ophelia × seedling]

Margaret Telfer Min, w, 1992, McCann, Sean; flowers large, dbl., borne in small clusters; foliage small, medium green, semi-glossy; some prickles; low (14 in.), upright growth; [Kiss the Bride × Margaret Merril]

Margaret Thatcher – See **Flamingo**, HT

Margaret Thatcher F, rb, 1981, Takatori, Yoshiho & Sunao; flowers striped red and white; [sport of Bridal Pink]; growth habit and other characteristics same as Bridal Pink; int. by Japan Rose Nursery, 1983

Margaret Trudeau – See **Sweepstakes**, HT

Margaret Turnbull Cl HT, yb, 1931, Clark, A.; flowers soft pink on amber ground, 4½ in., dbl., cupped; recurrent; foliage wrinkled, light; vigorous, pillar growth; int. by NRS New South Wales

Margaret van Rossem HT, op, 1946, Van Rossem; flowers coppery salmon, center old-gold; moderate growth

Margaret von Hessen HT, Hetzel, K.; int. in 1973

Margaret Wasserfall HT, w, Kordes; int. in 1994

Margaret Watson HT, pb; flowers pink and white, large, dbl., high-centered

Margarete Fuchs HT, m, Mander, George; flowers mauve pink, lighter reverse, 5½ in, 28-30 petals, high-centered, intense fragrance; recurrent; foliage mildew resistant; growth to 3 ft.; int. by Hortico Inc., 2006

Margarete Gnau HT, ob, 1930, Krause; flowers creamy white on orange ground, very large, dbl., high-centered; foliage leathery; very vigorous growth; [Mrs Charles Lamplough × Souv. de H.A. Verschuren]

Margarete Herbst Pol, dr, 1934, Herbst; flowers dark blood-red, dbl.; late bloom; recurrent; foliage ruby-red when young; vigorous, bushy growth

Margarete Krüger HT, or; flowers salmon-red, large, semi-dbl.

Margaretha Adelheid S, mr, Drummond; int. by Greenbelt Farm, 2000

Margaretha Mühle HT, pb, 1925, Mühle; flowers clear satiny pink with silvery reflex, dbl.; [Mme Caroline Testout × Mrs W.J. Grant]; int. by F.J. Grootendorst

Margarethe van de Mandere F, dp, 1952, Leenders, M.; flowers raspberry-red, large, single; very vigorous growth

Margaret's Choice Gr, or, 1999, Tough, Ian Murray; flowers orange-vermillion, reverse whitish, stiff petals, 4½ in., full, borne mostly singly, moderate fragrance; foliage medium size, dark green, semi-glossy; prickles moderate; upright, tall (3-5 ft.) growth

Margaret's World F, or, Kirkham, Gordon Wilson; int. in 1995

Margarita N, yb, 1868, Guillot; flowers shining yellow, edges white, shaded pink, medium, full

Margarita Riera HT, op, 1924, Dot, Pedro; flowers brilliant rose-salmon, base yellow, dbl.; [Mme Ravary × Mme Edouard Herriot]

Margat Jeune HCh, mr, before 1850; flowers crimson, center lighter garnet, large, full

Marge S, pb, 1999, Jerabek, Paul E.; flowers med. pink, creamy white at base, deep pink splotches on outer petals, 3 in., full, borne mostly singly, moderate fragrance; foliage medium size, medium green, dull; prickles moderate; spreading, medium to tall (5 ft.) growth

Margherita Croze HT, m, 1914, Ketten Bros.; flowers carmine-purple changing to purple-rose, base shaded deep rose, large, dbl., moderate fragrance; [Étoile de France × Earl of Warwick]

Margherita di Simone T, yb, 1898, Guillot, P.; bud elegant, carmine orange yellow; flowers bright pink to carmine, shaded with deep yellow, reverse orange-yellow, large, full

Margie Cl Min, rb, 1999, Martin, Robert B., Jr.; flowers dark red with white eye, reverse lighter, 2 in., dbl., borne in small clusters, slight fragrance; foliage medium size, dark green, semi-glossy; prickles moderate; growth upright, climbing (5-7 ft.); shade tolerant; [Roller Coaster × Roller Coaster]

Margie Burns HT, mp, 1970; flowers rose-pink, reverse Tyrian rose, large, dbl., high-centered, moderate fragrance; foliage leathery; very vigorous, upright, bushy growth; int. by Carrigg

Margina – See **White Fairy**, Pol

Margined Hip – See **Hebe's Lip**, HEg

Margit HT, op, Kordes; flowers peach salmon, large, dbl., high-centered, borne mostly singly; stems long; growth vigorous, tall; int. in 1999

Margo Koster Pol, ob, 1931, Koster, D.A.; flowers coral, small, 25-30 petals, globular, cupped, borne in clusters, slight fragrance; recurrent; growth medium, mounded; [sport of Dick Koster]

Margo Koster, Climbing Cl Pol, ob, 1962, Golie; flowers coral-orange, semi-dbl. to dbl., borne in large clusters, no fragrance; PP2291; [sport of Margo Koster]; int. by Crombie Nursery, 1962

Margo Koster Superior Pol, ob, 1956, Koster, D.A.; flowers deep salmon-pink; [sport of Dick Koster]

Margo's Baby Pol, yb, 1988, Partain, Joe L.; flowers creamy ivory, salmon edges, aging dark edge, small, 30 petals, cupped, no fragrance; foliage small, medium green, glossy; prickles few, medium, light green; upright, bushy, low, vigorous growth; winter hardy; [sport of Margo Koster]; int. in 1995

Margo's Sister Pol, lp, 1954, Ratcliffe; flowers shell pink; [sport of Margo Koster]

Margot Amos HT, op; bud high, pointed; flowers coral-pink flushed strawberry, large; foliage glossy, bronze

Margot Anstiss HT, lp, 1947, Norman; flowers glossy satin-pink, 6 in., 40-45 petals; vigorous, branching growth; int. by Harkness

Margot Asquith HT, mr, 1934, Prince; flowers shining cerise-red, well-formed; very vigorous growth; [Betty Uprichard × Kitchener of Khartoum]

Margot Fonteyn HT, op, 1964, McGredy, Sam IV; flowers salmon-orange, 4 in., very dbl.; very free growth; [Independence × Ma Perkins]; int. by Fisons Horticulture

Margraten F, mr, 1949, Leenders, M.; flowers currant-red, 3-4 in., 16 petals, flat, borne in trusses; foliage light green; vigorous, bushy growth; [Donald Prior × World's Fair]

Margrethe Möller HT, dp, 1914, Poulsen, D.T.; flowers deep cerise-rose, well-formed, dbl.; stems weak necks; [Lady Mary Fitzwilliam × seedling]

Margriet Hermans HT, yb, RvS-Melle; [Frederik Chopin × seedling]; int. in 1993

Marguerite T, dp, 1869, Guillot; flowers deep pink, aging to light red, medium, full

Marguerite Amidieu de Clos HT, my, 1926, Ketten Bros.; flowers buttercup-yellow, dbl.; [Souv. de Claudius Pernet × Golden Emblem]

Marguerite Anne F, lp, 1997, Cocker, Ann G.; flowers medium, full, borne in large clusters, moderate fragrance; foliage medium size, dark green, glossy; bushy, broad, medium (2½ ft.) growth; [Anisley Dickson × Roddy McMillan]

Marguérite Appert – See **Mlle Marguérite Appert**, HT

Marguerite Bonnet B, w, 1864, Liabaud; flowers flesh white, medium

Marguerite Brassac HP, dr, 1874, Brassac; flowers purplish crimson, large, full; perhaps the same as Mme F. Brassac

Marguerite Carels Cl HP, mp, 1922, Nabonnand; bud pointed, large; flowers Neyron pink, center darker, 5 in., dbl., moderate fruity fragrance; recurrent bloom; vigorous, climbing growth; [Frau Karl Druschki × General MacArthur]

Marguerite Chambard HT, or, 1928, Chambard, C.; bud pointed; flowers geranium-red to vermilion, very large, high-centered; foliage dark; very vigorous, bushy growth

Marguérite d'Anjou Ch, mp, 1827, Guérin; flowers small to medium

Marguérite d'Anjou HP, m, 1847, Boyau; flowers silky lilac pink, medium to large, full

Marguérite d'Anjou HP, rb, 1862, Trouillard; flowers red over white, small

Marguérite d'Anjou B, mp, 1864, Moreau-Robert; flowers silky, soft pink

Marguerite d'Autricho HT, dr, Dorieux

Marguerite de Fénelon T, pb, 1884, Nabonnand; flowers pink, shaded sulfur-yellow, large, semi-dbl.

Marguerite de Flandre C, dr, before 1862; flowers slatey deep red, full

Marguerite de Flandre D, lp, before 1885; flowers flesh pink, large, full

Marguerite de Roman HP, w, 1882, Schwartz; flowers flesh white with flesh pink center, very large, full, moderate fragrance; recurrent; foliage light green; growth upright, strong

Marguerite de St Amand HP, mp, 1864, De Sansal; [Jules Margottin × unknown]

Marguerite Defforey HT, Orard, Joseph; int. in 1973

Marguerite Desrayaux N, mp, 1906, Nabonnand; flowers peachy pink and white, 9-10 cm., semi-dbl., borne in small clusters; foliage large; nearly thornless; [Mme Alfred Carrière × Mme Marie Lavalley]

Marguerite d'Ombrain HP, mp, 1865, Verdier, E.; flowers very large, very full

Marguerite Dubourg B, mp, 1854, Pradel; flowers bright pink, large, full

Marguerite Gigandet T, yb, 1902, Nabonnand; bud coppery yellow; flowers reddish-coppery yellow, aging to golden yellow, very large, very full; [Mlle Franziska

Kruger × Reine Emma des Pays-Bas]

Marguerite Guillard HP, w, 1915, Chambard, C.; flowers stamens yellow, 20 petals, flat; [sport of Frau Karl Druschki]

Marguerite Guillot HT, ly, 1902, Guillot; flowers cream colored, fading to pure white, very large, dbl., globular, moderate fragrance; [Mme Caroline Testout × unknown]

Marguerite Heitzmann HT, or, 1930, Buatois; flowers salmon-pink, stamens golden yellow, very large, dbl., cupped; foliage leathery; very vigorous growth; [Frau Karl Druschki × Mme Edouard Herriot]

Marguerite Hilling HMoy, mp, 1965, Hilling; flowers large, single, moderate fragrance; recurrent; foliage grey-green; growth open, arching; [sport of Nevada]; int. in 1959

Marguerite Jaffelin T, pb, 1902, Buatois; flowers China pink, shaded yellow, petal edges bright carmine, large, dbl.

Marguerite Jamain HP, lp, 1873, Jamain, H.; flowers flesh pink, large, very dbl.

Marguerite Ketten T, yb, 1897, Ketten Bros.; bud elegant; flowers yellowish peach red, petal edges tinted pink, large, full, moderate fragrance; growth vigorous, medium; [Mme Caro × Georges Farber]

Marguerite Lartay – See **Impératrice Eugénie**, B

Marguerite Lartay B, m, 1873, Lartay; flowers purple-pink, aging to light red, large, full, globular

Marguerite Lecureaux HP, rb, 1853, Cherpin; flowers bright red, striped white, medium, full

Marguerite Moulin HT, pb, 1938, Moulin; flowers lilac-pink, center salmon, large, very dbl., cupped; vigorous, bushy growth; [(Mme Edouard Herriot × Mrs Aaron Ward) × Mme Caroline Testout]; int. by Hamonière

Marguerite Rose Pol, mp, 1905, Robichon; flowers medium, dbl., borne in clusters

Marguerite Rose F, pb, Laperriere; flowers medium pink with white eye and reverse, petals notched like a daisy, single, shallow cup to flat, borne in clusters; low to medium (2 ft.) growth; int. by Roseraie Laperriere, 2006

Margy Pol, mr, 1936, Sauvageot, H.; flowers brilliant red, open, semi-dbl., moderate spicy fragrance; foliage small, soft; bushy growth; int. by C-P

Mari Carolyn HT, m, 1999, Sproul, James A.; flowers 4-5 in., dbl., borne mostly singly; foliage medium size, medium green, semi-glossy; few prickles; bushy, medium (5 ft.) growth; [Heirloom × Chrysler Imperial]; int. by Roses By Design, 1999

Mari Dot HT, ab, 1927, Dot, Pedro; flowers bright salmon to salmon-pink, base yellow, borne in clusters; foliage glossy; long, strong stems; very vigorous growth; [O. Junyent × Jean C.N. Forestier]; int. by C-P

Maria F, or, 1963, Gregory; flowers orange-scarlet, 3 in., 10 petals, borne in clusters; foliage very large, dark, leathery; vigorous, upright growth; [seedling × Border Beauty]

Maria HT, rb, 1986, Staikov, Prof. Dr. V.; flowers red, yellow reverse, large, 60 petals, borne singly, moderate tea fragrance; foliage dark, glossy; vigorous growth; [Rina Herholdt × seedling]; int. by Kalaydjiev and Chorbadjiiski, 1974

Maria – See **Maria Renaissance**, S

Maria Antonia Camprubi HT, mp, 1956, Munné, M.; flowers soft carmine, well-formed, large; vigorous growth; [Peace × Rosa Munne]

Maria Burnett Min, yb, 1980, Dobbs, Annette; bud globular; flowers light yellow, edged pink, small, 70 petals, globular; foliage light green; low growth; [Little Darling × Patricia Scranton]; int. by Miniature Plant Kingdom

Maria Callas – See **Miss All-American Beauty**, HT

Maria Callas, Climbing – See **Miss All-American Beauty, Climbing**, Cl HT

Maria Carta HT, Zandri, R.; int. in 1976

Maria Chavarri de Salazar HT, lp, 1935, Dot, Pedro; flowers large, dbl.

Maria Cinta HT, op, 1970, Dot, Simon; bud long, pointed; flowers coral, large, 28 petals, moderate fragrance; foliage glossy, bronze; low, compact growth; [Duet × (Soraya × Chrysler Imperial)]; int. by Minier, 1967

Maria Cristina T, ob, 1895, Aldrufeu, Joaquin; flowers bright orange'yellow, tinted carmine, medium to large, full, globular

Maria de Mello HT, dr, 1935, Ketten Bros.; bud pointed; flowers bright velvety carmine-purple, large, 40-45 petals, cupped; foliage bronze Quaker green; vigorous, branching growth; [Mme Gabriel Hanra × Mrs John Bell]

Maria Delforge Pol, mp, 1959, Delforge; bud oval; flowers pink, rosette form, medium, dbl., borne in clusters; foliage glossy; vigorous, bushy, low growth; [Orange Triumph × Ma Perkins]

Maria Georgiana F, mp, Horner; int. by Warley Rose Gardens, 2005

Maria Graebner S, mp, about 1900; buds with leafy bracts; flowers bright rose pink, small, single, slight fragrance; a few borne all summer; foliage orange and red in fall; growth to 5 ft.; hips subglobose, red; [*R. palustris* × *R. virginiana*]

Maria Guarro HT, dp, 1935, Dot, Pedro; bud pointed; flowers pink in spring, blood-red in summer, large, very dbl., high-centered; foliage glossy, dark; very vigorous growth; [Château de Clos Vougeot × Li Bures]

Maria Hofker HT, my, Interplant; int. in 1993

Maria Isabel HT, mr, Camprubi, C.; flowers deep strawberry-red, base yellow, high-centered; foliage dark; vigorous growth

Maria Iurato Cl F, dp, 2002, Gareffa, N.; flowers full, borne in large clusters, moderate fragrance; foliage medium size, medium green, semi-glossy; prickles variable, sharp, numerous; growth climbing, tall (to 15 ft.); very hardy; [unknown × unknown]; int. in 1991

Maria Leonida HBc, w, 1829, Lemoyne; flowers white, nuanced straw yellow, tinged rose at center, 6-8 cm., full, flat, quartered, intense tea fragrance; foliage small, dark green, glossy; prickles moderate; often confused with Alba Odorata; possibly *R. bracteata* × *R. laevigata*, or *R. bracteata* × Tea

Maria Liesa HMult, dp, 1925, Bruder Alfons; flowers carmine-pink, white center, prominent yellow stamens, 2½-3 cm., single, borne in very large clusters; foliage dark green; nearly thornless

Maria Lisa HWich, pb, 1936, Liabaud; flowers clear rose, center white, stamens yellow, open, small, single; profuse, non-recurrent bloom; foliage dark, leathery; very vigorous, climbing or trailing growth

Maria Maass HT, w, 1927, Maass; flowers very large, very dbl.

Maria Mathilda F, w, 1986, Lens, Louis; flowers white, shaded pink, small, 24 petals, borne in clusters of 3-24, intense fragrance; foliage very dark, glossy; prickles hooked, brownish-red; growth upright, bushy (100 cm.); [Unnamed Min seedling × (New Penny × Jour de Fete)]; int. in 1980; Rose d'or a La Haye, 1981, Golden Rose, The Hague, 1981

Maria McGredy HT, pb, 1998, McGredy, Sam IV; flowers pink blend, 4½ in., full, borne mostly singly, slight fragrance; foliage large, medium green, semi-glossy; prickles moderate; bushy, tall (120 cm.) growth; [Freude × Remember Me]; int. by McGredy, 1997

Maria Peral HT, yb, 1941, Dot, Pedro; flowers yellow suffused red, large, dbl.; very vigorous growth

Maria Reid HT, dp, 1924, Ferguson, W.; flowers dark rose-pink tinted peach, base yellow, dbl.; [Mme Caroline Testout × George C. Waud]

Maria Renaissance S, dp, Olesen; bud broad based pointed ovoid; flowers deep pink to light red, white vertical line bisects reverse of petals, 8 cm., 50 petals, deep cup, borne in clusters of 5-9, moderate floral perfume fragrance; recurrent; foliage matte; upright to bushy (100-150 cm.) growth; PP15620; [seedling × Radox Bouquet]; int. by Poulsen Roser, 2002

Maria Serrat HT, op, 1946, Munné, M.; flowers salmon-pink, base yellow, reverse deep yellow; [Mrs Pierre S. duPont × Baronesa de Ovilar]

Maria Shriver Gr, w, Dorieux; flowers large, pure white, 40 petals, borne in neat clusters, strong citrus fragrance; foliage polished, dark green; stems long; growth tall (4-5 ft.) and stately; PPAF; int. by Edmunds' Roses, 2005

Maria Star T, op, 1913, Pery-Gravereaux; flowers salmon-gold; [Mme Gustave Henry × Mme Jules Gravereaux]

Maria Stern HT, ob, 1969, Brownell, H.C.; bud pointed; flowers orange, large, 43 petals, globular, moderate fragrance; vigorous, upright growth; PP2960; [Tip Toes × Queen Elizabeth]; int. by Stern's Nursery

Maria Teresa S, lp, 1986, Lens, Louis; flowers 28 petals, cupped, borne in clusters of 32, intense fragrance; recurrent bloom; foliage light green; prickles hooked, brownish-green; bushy growth; [seedling × *R. macrantha*]; int. in 1984

Maria Teresa de Esteban – See **Coral Fiesta**, HT

Maria Theresa HP, lp, 1872, Ducher; flowers light pink, medium to large, very full, globular

Maria-Theresa HT, ab, Fryer, Gareth; int. in 1994

Mariaeburgensis – See **De Marienbourg**, HSpn

Mariah Carey LCl, w, 2003, Horner, Colin P.; flowers cream edged pink, reverse white, 9 cm., dbl., borne in small clusters, moderate fragrance; foliage medium size, medium green, semi-glossy; prickles medium, curved, moderate; growth upright, medium (2 m.); garden decorative; [Tynwald × Rhapsody in Blue]; int. by Warley Roses, 2004

Mariale HT, ab, 1956, de Boer; flowers orange-yellow, semi-dbl.; vigorous growth; [sport of Souv. de Jacques Verschuren]

Mariam Ismailjee MinFl, rb, 2006, Mander, George; flowers medium red, reverse cream, 2½ in., single, borne mostly solitary; prickles 5/16 in., needle point, dark brown, few; growth to 30-36 in.; garden decorative, exhibition, containers; [Hot Tamale × Rubies "n" Pearls]; disease-resistant; int. by Select Roses, 2007

Marian Anderson HT, dp, 1964, Lammerts, Dr. Walter; flowers deep pink, large, semi-dbl., high-centered, moderate spicy fragrance; foliage glossy; vigorous, tall, compact growth; PP2526; [Queen Elizabeth × Merry Widow]; int. by Germain's, 1964

Marian Colthorpe HT, op, 1946, Wheatcroft Bros.; flowers coral shaded lemon and pink

Mariana HT, ob, Kordes; flowers orange developing pink on the edges, medium to large, dbl., high-centered, borne mostly singly; stems long; greenhouse rose; int. in 2003

Mariandel F, mr, 1987, Kordes, W.; bud pointed, dark red; flowers scarlet crimson-red, 7 cm., dbl., shallow cup, borne in clusters, slight fragrance; recurrent; foliage medium size, dark green, semi-glossy, disease-resistant; bushy (2 ft.) growth; [Tornado × Redgold]; int. by John Mattock, Ltd, 1985; President's International Trophy, RNRS, 1982, Golden Rose, The Hague, 1990

Mariandel 92 F, rb, Hannemann, F.; [Ko's Yellow × Eyepaint]

Marianna Rolfs Cl HT, lp, 1926, Walter, L.; flowers silvery pink, semi-dbl.

Marianne HT, yb, 1933, Krause; flowers mixture of copper-yellow, pink and red, large, high-centered; vigorous, bushy growth; [Sybil × Sunstar]

Marianne F, rb, Meilland; flowers rose-scarlet, edged cerise, semi-dbl.; int. in 1993

Marianne – See **Marianne Hit**, MinFl

Marianne HGal, ab, 2004, Barden, Paul; flowers apricot/gold, reverse pale apricot, 3½ in., very full, borne in small clusters, intense fragrance; spring-blooming, non-recurrent; foliage medium size, dark green, glossy; prickles ½ in., curved; growth upright, arching, tall (5-7 ft.); specimen, small climber; [Duchesse de Montebello × Abraham Darby]; int. in 2005

Marianne Busse T, dr, 1901, Brauer; flowers medium

Marianne Hit MinFl, my, Poulsen; flowers medium yellow, 5-8 cm., semi-dbl., slight wild rose fragrance; foliage dark; growth bushy, 40-60 cm.; PP14990; int. by Poulsen Roser, 2001

Marianne Kluis Pol, mr, 1942, W. Kordes Söhne; flowers carmine-red, small, dbl.

Marianne Kluis Superior Pol, mr, 1930, Kluis & Koning; flowers deep violet-red; [sport of Greta Kluis Superior]

Marianne Pfitzer HT, lp, 1902, Jacobs; flowers flesh, with a deep pink and reddish sheen, very large, dbl.; [Kaiserin Auguste Viktoria × unknown]

Marianne Powell HT, dr, 1987, Powell, G.; flowers large, 50 petals, moderate fragrance; foliage large, dark green, glossy; upright growth; [Kerryman × Red Dandy]; int. in 1986

Marianne Tudor HT, mr, Fryer, Gareth; flowers bright red, large; growth strong, vigorous; int. in 1993

Marianne Wolff S, mp, 2003, Wolff, Stefan; flowers 2½ in., full, borne mostly solitary; remontant; foliage medium size, medium green, semi-glossy, disease-resistant; few prickles; growth upright, medium (3-4 ft.); hardy to -30ºF; [Winnipeg Parks × unknown]; int. by Stefan Wolff

Mariano Vergara T, mr, 1896, Aldrufeu; flowers magenta-red with vermilion reflections, large, dbl.; vigorous growth

Mariatheresia F, mp, Tantau; flowers full, quartered, borne in clusters, slight fragrance; recurrent; foliage dark green, glossy; growth strong, bushy; int. by Rosen Tantau, 2004

Maribel – See **Fulton MacKay**, HT

Maribell HT, rb, 1988, Gressard, J.; flowers carmine red, reverse silver white, large, 40-45 petals; upright, vigorous growth; [(Sea Pearl × Zorina) × Lovita]; int. by Delbard Roses, 1988

Marica HT, mp, 1964, Mondial Roses; flowers bright pink, large, dbl.; strong stems; vigorous, symmetrical growth

Marica Cl Min, pb, 1989, Kono, Yoshito; flowers pink, reverse white; [sport of Ginza Komachi]

Marichu Zayas HT, lp, 1906, Soupert & Notting; bud long; flowers light strawberry, large, full; [(Mrs W. J. Grant × unknown) × unknown]

Marie HT, w, 1995, Sheldon, John & Robin; flowers medium, full, borne mostly singly; foliage medium size, medium green, matte; upright, medium growth

Marie Accary N, pb, 1872, Guillot et Fils; flowers white tinted pink and yellow, fading to white, small, full, borne in small clusters

Marie Adélaïde HT, yb, 1912, Soupert & Notting; bud pointed; flowers coppery yellow, center deeper, large, dbl., high-centered; foliage bronze, soft; vigorous, spreading growth; [Mme J.W. Budde × Lyon Rose]

Marie-Antoinette HGal, m, 1829, Vibert; flowers lilac-rose, large, dbl.

Marie Antoinette HT, mp, 1968, Armstrong, D.L.; bud long, pointed; flowers pink, reverse darker, large, dbl., cupped; foliage dark, glossy; very vigorous, upright growth; PP2928; [Queen Elizabeth × Chrysler Imperial]; int. by Armstrong Nursery

Marie Antoinette F, w, Tantau; flowers ivory, dbl., cupped, borne in clusters, intense spicy fragrance; recurrent; low (2 ft.) growth; int. by Rosen Tantau, 2004

Marie Antoinette Rety HT, Orard; int. in 1983

Marie-Antoinette Rety HT, op

Marie Baumann HP, mr, 1863, Baumann; flowers carmine-red, large, 55 petals, globular, moderate fragrance; foliage dark; vigorous growth; [Alfred Colomb × unknown]

Marie Beaumann – See **Marie Baumann**, HP

Marie Berton T, ly, 1875, Levet; flowers straw yellow fading to cream, very large, full; [Gloire de Dijon × unknown]; sometimes classed as N

Marie Boissée HP, w, 1864, Oger; flowers blush-white, aging to pure white, large, full, cupped

Marie Boyer HP, dp, 1858, Lartay

Marie Brissonet Pol, lp, 1913, Turbat; flowers flesh-rose, borne in pyramidal clusters of 75-100

Marie Bugnet HRg, w, 1965, Bugnet; bud long, pointed; flowers snow white, 3 in., dbl., intense fragrance; recurrent bloom; foliage light green, rugose; vigorous (3 ft.), bushy, compact growth; [(Therese Bugnet × seedling) × F.J. Grootendorst]; int. by Skinner, 1959

Marie Bülow N, pb, 1903, Welter; bud long, pointed; flowers China rose, changing to carmine and pure yellow, large, full; [Maréchal Niel × Luciole]

Marie Casant – See **Marytje Cazant**, Pol

Marie-Chantal F, mp, 1959, Gaujard; flowers bright pink, open, large, semi-dbl.; foliage glossy; vigorous, bushy growth; [Peace × Fernand Arles]

Marie Chargé N, yb, 1853, Desponds; flowers golden yellow, shaded carmine pink, medium, full

Marie Christina MinFl, lp; int. in 1988

Marie Claire HT, or, 1938, Meilland, F.; bud deep orange-red; flowers golden coral-red, passing to orange-yellow, large, dbl.; foliage bronze, glossy; strong stems; very vigorous, cmpact growth; [(Charles P. Kilham × Duquesa de Peñaranda) × (Charles P. Kilham × Margaret McGredy)]

Marie Claire, Climbing Cl HT, or, 1944, Meilland, F.

Marie Curie F, ob, Meilland; flowers orange with yellow base and pale pink edges, 30-35 petals, high-centered, borne in clusters, moderate clove fragrance; recurrent; foliage dark green; growth to 60-70 cm.; int. in 1996

Marie Daly Pol, mp; bud long, pointed; flowers dbl., borne in small clusters, moderate sweet musk fragrance; good repeat; foliage large, rich green; few prickles; growth compact, bushy; [sport of Marie Pavie]; EarthKind; int. by Antique Rose Emporium, 1999

Marie de Blois M, mp, 1852, Moreau et Robert; flowers pink tinted lighter, 9-10 cm., full

Marie de Bourgogne A, pb, before 1844, Vibert; flowers rose, spotted white, medium, very dbl.

Marie de Bourgogne M, mp, 1853, Robert; flowers bright rose, 2½ in., dbl., globular/cupped, borne in clusters of 5-6; some repeat

Marie de Saint Jean P, w, 1869, Damaizin; flowers white, edged with carmine red, 6 cm., dbl., borne mostly solitary, intense fragrance; foliage glaucous green, rounded; prickles small, moderate; stems medium-sized, thin; growth vigorous, upright

Marie Dermar N, ly, 1889, Geschwind, R.; flowers cream and flesh, 5 cm., dbl., borne in small clusters, moderate fragrance; numerous prickles; [Louise d'Arzens × unknown]

Marie Desfossés B, mp, 1850, Desfossés; flowers dark flesh pink, large, full

Marie Dietrich HWich, yb, 1928, Walter, L.; bud small, crimson; flowers yellowish-red, passing to white to medium, 4-5 cm., semi-dbl., borne in clusters of 10-20, moderate fragrance; foliage glossy; [Leontine Gervais × Eugenie Lamesch]

Marie d'Orléans Bslt, lp, 1825, Boutigny; flowers flesh pink, fading to white

Marie d'Orléans T, mp, 1883, Nabonnand, G.; flowers bright pink shaded darker, large, dbl., flat; vigorous growth

Marie Dougherty F, dr, 1977, Linscott; bud long, slender; flowers large, 5 petals, slight tea fragrance; foliage glossy; moderate, bushy growth; [Sarabande × Sarabande]; int. in 1972

Marie Ducher T, lp, 1869, Ducher; flowers large, full, moderate fragrance

Marie Duleau B, w, about 1850, Desfossés; flowers flesh white, medium, full

Marie Dutour F, op, 1962, Arles; flowers reddish-salmon, well-formed, large; [Aloha × (Gloire du Midi × Edith de Martinelli)]; int. by Roses France

Marie Eads Pol, mr, 1991, Eads, C.E.; bud rounded; flowers medium red with blue overtones, reverse light red, small, 25 petals, borne in sprays of 10-25, no fragrance; repeat bloom; foliage medium size, medium green, semi-glossy with fringed stipules; bushy, low growth; [Baby Faurax × Verdun]

Marie Elizabeth F, yb, 1965, McGredy, Sam IV; flowers yellow shaded rose-pink, 3 in., 28 petals, flat; foliage dark, heavily veined; vigorous growth; [Clare Grammerstorf × Cavalcade]; int. by McGredy

Marie Faist HT, op, 1925, Berger, V.; flowers shell-pink tinted salmon, center darker, with orange, dbl.; [Mme Edmond Rostand × Mrs T. Hillas]; int. by Faist

Marie Finger – See **Mlle Eugénie Verdier**, HP

Marie-France HT, my, 1957, Dorieux; bud apricot shaded orange; flowers pure yellow, large, semi-dbl.; very vigorous growth; [Feu Pernet-Ducher × Léonce Colombier]; int. by Pin

Marie-Francoise Saignes HT, mr

Marie Girard HT, lp, 1898, Buatois; flowers flesh white nuanced yellowish-salmon, dbl., cupped, moderate fragrance; foliage large, dark green

Marie Gouchault HWich, mr, 1927, Turbat; flowers clear red passing to brilliant salmon-rose, reverse lighter, 4 cm., dbl., borne in clusters of 30-40, no fragrance; sometimes recurrent bloom; foliage medium green, glossy; nearly thornless; very vigorous growth

Marie Greene HT, mr, 1941, Clark, A.; flowers rich red

Marie Guillot T, w, 1874, Guillot et Fils; flowers white, tinged yellow, large, dbl.; strong stems; vigorous growth

Marie Guillot, Climbing Cl T, w, 1898, Dingee & Conard; flowers yellowish-white, extra large, full, moderate fragrance; [sport of Marie Guillot]

Marie Henriette Gräfin Chotek – See **Gräfin Marie Henriette Chotek**, HMult

Marie Henry HT, ly, 1900, Buatois; flowers white, lightly tinted canary yellow, large, dbl., moderate fragrance; [Irene Watts × Beauté Lyonnaise]

Marie Isakoff HT, yb, 1901, Dubreuil; flowers apricot yellow fading to pale canary, large, full; [Mme Caroline Testout × unknown]

Marie-Jeanne Pol, w, 1913, Turbat; flowers pale blush-cream, fading to white, 4 cm., dbl., round, borne in clusters of 20; remontant; no prickles; growth to 2-3 ft.

Marie Jeannette Min, yb, 2000, Fletcher, Ira R.; flowers light yellow to white, sometimes touch of light pink, medium, dbl., borne singly and in small clusters, slight fragrance; foliage medium size, medium green, matte; prickles moderate; growth upright, tall (to 120 cm.); [sport of Irresistible]; int. in 2001

Marie Joly B, lp, 1860, Oger; flowers light flesh pink, medium, full

Marie Laforet HT, w, Dorieux; int. by Roseraies Dorieux, 1997

Marie Lambert T, w, 1886, Lambert, E.; flowers pure white, semi-dbl. to dbl., loose; recurrent; growth low, compact; [sport of Mme Bravy]

Marie Larpin B, lp, 1867, Guillot; flowers light pink, tinted white, medium, full

Marie Lavalley – See **Mme Marie Lavalley**, HT

Marie Lavier HT, yb, 1935, Buatois; bud brownish yellow; flowers reddish nankeen yellow to salmon-yellow, rather large, dbl.; vigorous, bushy growth; [Souv. de Claudius Pernet × Mme Edouard Herriot]

Marie Lecomte T, my, 1885, Singer; flowers butter yellow, tinted dark carmine, very large, full

Marie Leczinska HP, lp, 1847, Béluze; flowers flesh pink, center bright pink, medium, full

Marie Leczinska M, dp, 1865, Moreau-Robert; flowers full, globular; some repeat

Marie Leonida – See **Maria Leonida**, HBc

Marie-Louise D, dp, around 1811; flowers mauve-pink, very large, very dbl., quartered, intense fragrance; foliage medium green, elliptical; few prickles; bushy, shrubby (about 4 ft.) growth; cultivated at Malmaison; possibly from Prévost

Marie Louise Marcenot HT, op, 1900, Buatois; flowers salmon pink with copper and saffron tints, large, full; [Victor Verdier × Dr Grill]

Marie-Louise Mathian HT, ly, 1912, Fugier; flowers cream white, with a salmon tint at the center, large, dbl., intense fragrance

Marie Louise Pernet HP, dp, 1876, Pernet père; flowers deep rose, large, full, cupped

Marie-Louise Poncet HT, op, 1929, Gaujard; flowers coppery rose to pale coppery pink, reverse carmine-salmon

Marie Louise Puyravaud T, my, 1896, Puyravaud; flowers citron yellow, striped canary yellow, edged peach, reverse white, large, full; [Mlle Lazarine Poizeau × unknown]

Marie-Louise Sondaz HT, w, 1970, Gaujard; flowers cream shaded red, very large, dbl., moderate fragrance; foliage dark; very vigorous, upright growth; [Rose Gaujard × Peace]; int. in 1967

Marie-Louise Velge F, lp, RvS-Melle; flowers light pink suffused white, 4 in., 20 petals, flat, borne in clusters, slight fragrance; recurrent; foliage dense dark green; int. in 1997; Gold Medal, Baden-Baden, 1997, Golden Rose, Geneva, 1997, Gold Medal, The Hague, 1996

Marie-Luise Marjan HT, w, 2006; bud pointed, bright apricot; flowers cream white with a touch of pink and apricot, fading to clean white, 11 cm., dbl, high-centered, borne mostly solitary, moderate sweet/spicy fragrance; foliage first reddish, then dark green, leathery, glossy; upright, medium (120 cm.) growth; int. by W. Kordes' Söhne, 1999

Marie Lünnemann HT, my, 1920, Timmermans; flowers clear pink, dbl.; [Pharisaer × Laurent Carle]

Marie Maass HT, w, 1928, Maass; flowers pure white to ivory-white, very large, dbl.; vigorous, bushy growth; [Kaiserin Auguste Viktoria × Marechal Niel]

Marie Menudel HP, op, 1927, Barbier; flowers rose-pink, tinted salmon, large, dbl.

Marie Nordlinger M, lp, Morley, Dr B.; [Henri Martin × unknown]; int. in 1988

Marie Palit HT, pb, Datt, Braham; flowers white with deep pink edges, dbl.; int. in 1988

Marie Paré B, lp, 1880, Paré/Jamain; flowers light flesh, center brighter, medium, full; [Mistress Bosanquet × unknown]

Marie Pavic – See **Marie Pavié**, Pol

Marie Pavié Pol, w, 1888, Allégatière; flowers white, center flesh, 2 in., dbl., borne in clusters; foliage large, rich green; no prickles; vigorous, bushy growth

Marie Pavié, Climbing Cl Pol, lp, 1904, Bénard; flowers whitish pink, center darker, medium, full, rosette; [sport of Marie Pavié]

Marie Perrachon HP, m, 1864, Ducher; flowers violet-purple, medium

Marie Pochin – See **Mary Pochin**, HP

Marie Portemer HP, m, 1857, Portemer; flowers purple, large, full

Marie Rady – See **Mlle Marie Rady**, HP

Marie Robert P, m, 1850, Robert et Moreau; flowers lilac-pink, medium, dbl.

Marie Robert N, pb, 1893, Cochet; flowers bright rose marbled with salmon and apricot, large, full, no fragrance; [Isabella Gray × unknown]

Marie Roland T, lp, 1870, Roland; flowers flesh pink, edges lighter, large, semi-dbl.

Marie-Rose Pol, mp, 1930, Truffaut, T.A.; flowers ruddy pink, large, dbl., carnation-like, borne in clusters of 30; foliage glossy; very vigorous growth; [sport of Marie-Jeanne]; int. by Turbat

Marie-Rose, Climbing Cl Pol, dp; flowers dbl.

Marie-Rose Besson HT, lp, 1939, Mallerin, C.; bud long, pointed, yellow, tinted coral; flowers light pink, tinted coral-orange, large, dbl.; foliage glossy; long stems; vigorous growth; [Souv. de Claudius Pernet × seedling]; int. by A. Meilland

Marie-Rose Toussaint HT, lp, 1946, Gaujard; flowers satiny pink, very large; foliage dark, leathery; strong stems; vigorous, bushy growth

Marie Schmitt HT, lp, 1910, Schmitt; flowers large, dbl.; [sport of Mme Caroline Testout]

Marie Segond T, pb, 1902, Nabonnand; bud elongated, coppery tinted carmine; flowers pink tinted flame, medium, full; [Mme la Comtesse de Leusse × Mlle Lazarine Poizeau]

Marie Shields Min, mp, 1988, Moore, Ralph S.; flowers medium pink, reverse pink veined white, small, very dbl., high-centered, borne usually in sprays or clusters; foliage small, medium green, semi-glossy; prickles slightly hooked, small, brown; bushy, medium growth; [Avandel × (Rumba × Unnamed Floribunda mossed seedling)]; int. by Sequoia Nursery

Marie Sisley T, yb, 1868, Guillot fils; flowers pale yellow, broadly margined with bright rose, large, full, globular

Marie Soleau T, mp, 1895, Nabonnand; flowers slivery pink, large, full; [Mlle Suzanne Blanchet × unknown]

Marie Stuart HGal, dp, 1820, Dubourg; flowers crimson pink, large, full

Marie Teresa Bordas HT, mp, 1958, Bordas; bud ovoid; flowers rose-pink, very large, very dbl., high-centered, moderate fragrance; foliage dark, glossy; very vigorous, upright, bushy growth; [Sensation × Peace]; int. in 1956

Marie-Thérèse HWich, dp, 1917, Turbat

Marie Thérèse Dubourg N, dy, 1888, Godard; flowers deep coppery golden yellow

Marie Treusz HMult, m, 1909, Walter

Marie Tudor HGal, dp, before 1835; flowers slaty violet-red

Marie van Houtte T, pb, 1871, Ducher; flowers deep cream, tinged pink, base buff-yellow, large, very dbl., high-centered; foliage rich green, leathery; vigorous, bushy, sprawling growth; [Mme de Tartas × Mme Falcot]

Marie van Houtte, Climbing Cl T, pb, 1936, Thomasville Nursery; flowers creamy, pink-tinged yellow; [sport of Marie Van Houtte]

Marie Verbrugh F, op, 1954, Leenders, M.; flowers yellow-salmon, reverse coral, well-formed, large, dbl.; bushy growth; [Ambassadeur Nemry × Souv. de Claudius Pernet]

Marie Verdier – See **Mlle Marie Verdier**, HP

Marie-Victoria Benoît M, mp, 1905, Puyravaud; flowers satiny pink, very large, cupped, moderate fragrance; foliage dark green; prickles small, short, reddish; [Eugénie Guinoisseau × unknown]

Marie-Victorin HKor, pb, 1999, Agriculture et Agroalimentaire Canada; flowers medium pink-yellow, reverse pink-yellow, 3 in., full, borne in small clusters; foliage medium size, light green, semi-glossy; few prickles; arching, medium (1½ m.) growth; PP11650; [Arthur Bell × (*R.* × *kordesii* × Max Graf O.P.)]

Marie Victorin S, op, L'Assomption; flowers 38 petals, flat

Marie Young HT, or; flowers brilliant orange-red, well-formed

Marie Zahn HT, lp, 1887, Müller, Dr. F.; bud long, pointed; flowers light pink, yellow at center, large, full, cupped; foliage light green; [(Reine des Ile-Bourbons × Maréchal Niel) × (Pierre Notting × Safrano)]

Marie-Caroline F, dp, Adam; flowers bright pink, large, full, cupped, then flat, borne in clusters; recurrent; squat, vigorous (2-3 ft.) growth; int. by Pepinieres Guerinais, 2006

Mariechen S, mp, Schultheis; flowers bright pink, dbl., loose, borne in clusters; recurrent; foliage dark green, glossy; growth upright, bushy (60-100 cm.); very winter hardy; does well in shady, windy conditions.; int. by Rosen von Schultheis, 2000

Mariee S, ab, 2007, Iwata, Masaaki; flowers single, borne in large clusters; foliage medium size, light green, glossy; prickles 1 cm., few; growth spreading, shrub, medium (130 cm.); cutting, containers, garden decorat; [Graham Thomas × Iceberg]; int. by Same, 2008

Marieken F, ab, RvS-Melle; int. in 1987

Marielle F, mp, 1964, deRuiter; flowers deep rosy pink, 4 in., 25 petals, borne in large clusters, moderate fragrance; foliage dark; vigorous growth; [Independence × F seedling]

Marietta F, yb, 1985, Tantau, Math.; flowers gold, yellow and orange, medium, 20 petals, no fragrance; foliage medium green, glossy; upright growth

Marietta de Besobrasoff T, pb, 1879, Nabonnand; flowers bright pink, shaded carmine, center darker, underlaid with copper, reverse lighter, medium, full, moderate fragrance

Marietta Silva Tarouca HMult, mp, 1925, Tarouca/Zeman; flowers bright rose, white center, large, semi-dbl., borne in small clusters, slight fragrance; foliage rich green; very vigorous, climbing growth; [Colibri × Crimson Rambler]

Marigold HT, op, 1955, Lens; bud long, pointed; flowers salmon-yellow lightly washed pink, 6 in., 52 petals, high-centered; foliage leathery, glossy, bright green; vigorous, upright growth; [Peace × Mme Joseph Perraud]

Marijke Koopman HT, mp, 1980, Fryer, Gareth; bud long, pointed; flowers 25 petals, borne singly and 3-5 per cluster, moderate fragrance; foliage dark, leathery; prickles red; vigorous, medium-tall, upright growth; int. by Fryer's Nursery, Ltd., 1979; Gold Medal, The Hague, 1978

Mariko HT, ly, 1992, Marciel, Stanley G. & Jeanne A.; flowers 3-3½ in., full, borne mostly singly, moderate fragrance; foliage large, dark green, semi-glossy; some prickles; tall (210 cm.), upright growth; [seedling × seedling]; int. by DeVor Nurseries, Inc.

Marilena HT, w; flowers white with pink tones in center, 9 cm., 30-35 petals, borne mostly singly; recurrent; stems 50-70 cm; florist rose; int. by Terra Nigra BV, 2004

Marilyn HT, ab, 1955, Fletcher; bud long, pointed; flowers apricot-pink veined red, intense fragrance; foliage dull, green; vigorous growth; [May Wettern × Phyllis Gold]; int. by Tucker, 1954

Marilyn Min, lp, 1958, Dot, M.; flowers light pink, base purplish, small, 60 petals, borne in clusters; very compact growth; [Perla de Montserrat × Bambino]; int. in 1955

Marilyn Gowie F, ?, 1968, Gowie; flowers borne in trusses; foliage bronze; bushy growth; int. by Gandy's Roses

Marilyn Monroe HT, ab, 2001, Carruth, Tom; bud greenish; flowers soft apricot, 10-12 cm., full, high-centered, borne mostly solitary, no fragrance; foliage medium size, medium green, semi-glossy; prickles moderate, assorted sizes, almost straight, light brown; growth upright to spreading, medium (110-125 cm.); garden decoration; PP14398; [Sunset Celebration × Saint Patrick]

Marilyn Ross Min, my, 2000, Jellyman, J.S.; flowers medium, single, borne in small clusters, moderate fragrance; foliage medium size, dark green, semi-glossy; few prickles; growth bushy, medium (15 in.); patio, containers; [Baby Love × (Priscilla Burton × (Tony Jacklin × Andrea))]

Marilyn Wellan Min, lp, 1999, Moe, Mitchie; flowers apricot-pink, reverse lighter, 1-2 in., dbl., high-centered; foliage medium size, dark green, semi-glossy; few prickles; upright, tall (18 in.) growth; [Sheri Anne × Wistful]; int. by Mitchie's Roses & More, 1999

Marilyn Wellan HT, mr, 2005, Edwards, Eddie & Phelps, Ethan; flowers medium to dark pink in hot weather; red in cool weather, 5 in., dbl., borne mostly solitary, moderate fragrance; foliage large, dark green, glossy; few prickles; upright, tall (5-6 ft.) growth; exhibition; [Veteran's Honor × Hot Princess]; int. in 2006

Marimba F, mp, 1965, Dekkers; [sport of Garnette]; int. by Verbeek

Marime Min, mr, 1992, Moore, Ralph S.; flowers excellent medium red, good form, large, semi-dbl., borne mostly singly, no fragrance; foliage medium size, medium green, semi-glossy; few prickles; medium (35-45 cm.), upright, bushy growth; [Anytime × Happy Hour]; int. by Sequoia Nursery

Marina F, ob, 1975, Kordes; bud long, pointed; flowers orange, base yellow, dbl., moderate fragrance; foliage glossy, dark, leathery; vigorous, upright growth; PP3789; [Colour Wonder × seedling]; int. in 1974

Marina, Climbing Cl F, ob, Teranishi; int. by Itami Rose Garden, 1997

Marina Fontcuberta HT, dp, 1924, Dot, Pedro; flowers brilliant carmine, center rose-carmine, dbl.; [Entente Cordiale × Laurent Carle]

Marina Marini HT, dr, Barni, V.; flowers velvet red, dbl., high-centered, borne mostly singly, moderate fragrance; recurrent; stems long, reddish; growth vigorous, erect; int. by Rose Barni, 1992

Marinette S, mp, 1997, Austin, David; bud pointed; flowers lighten with age, large, semi-dbl., flat, borne singly or in small clusters, slight myrrh fragrance; foliage medium size, medium green, semi-glossy; prickles few to some; bushy, medium growth; [Lucetta × Red Coat]; int. by David Austin Roses, Ltd.

Mario Clemente HT, Moreira da Silva, A.

Mario Lanza HT, yb, 1999, Horner, Calvin; flowers medium yellow, edged red, reverse paler yellow, 5 in., full, borne mostly singly, moderate fragrance; foliage medium size, dark green, glossy; prickles moderate; bushy, medium (3 ft.) growth; [Elina × Remember Me]; int. by Warley Rose Gardens, 2000

Mariolina S, Embriaco, B.; int. in 1989

Marion F, op, 1956, deRuiter, G.; flowers pink tinted salmon, medium, dbl., high-centered, moderate fragrance; foliage first reddish, then light green; bushy (2 ft.) growth; [Duchess of Rutland × Fashion]

Marion Brunell T, 1917, Brunell; [sport of Reine Marie Henriette]

Marion Cran HT, or, 1927, McGredy; bud buttercup-yellow, flushed cerise; flowers scarlet veined orange and yellow, dbl., high-centered; foliage bronze, leathery, glossy; very vigorous, bushy growth

Marion Dingee HT, dr, 1889, Cook, J.W.; flowers crimson; [((Comtesse de Caserta × Général Jacqueminot) × Marechal Niel) × (Pierre Notting × Safrano)]

Marion Foster – See **Fiorella**, Gr

Marion Harkness HT, yb, 1978, Harkness; flowers canary-yellow, flushed orange-red, large, 24 petals; bushy growth; [((Manx Queen × Prima Ballerina) × (Chanelle × Piccadilly)) × Piccadilly]; int. in 1979

Marion Hess HT, dr, Hetzel; int. in 1981

Marion Horton HT, my, 1929, Bees; flowers primrose-yellow; [Gorgeous × Sunstar]

Marion Lawrie HT, mp, 1976, Lawrie; flowers pink, base gold, 4 in., 75 petals; foliage dark, leathery; [sport of Kordes' Perfecta]

Marion Manifold – See **Miss Marion Manifold**, Cl HT

Marion R. Hall HT, dp, Balcombe Nursery; flowers bright cerise-red, well-formed, 5 in., 20 petals; vigorous growth; [Crimson Glory × Sterling]

Marion Rich HT, yb, 1997, Skinner, A.W.; flowers medium, dbl., borne mostly singly; foliage medium size, dark green, glossy; upright, medium (3-3½ ft.) growth; [Solitaire × Remember Me]

Marionette F, w, 1944, deVor, Paul F.; bud cream-yellow; flowers dbl., 25-30 petals, borne in clusters; vigorous, bushy growth; [sport of Pinocchio]; int. by J&P

Mariposa Pol, or, 1927, Allen; flowers deeper orange-red; [sport of Orange King]

Mariposa Gem S, rb, 1995, Moore, Ralph S.; flowers red with yellow reverse and white eye, 2½ in., semi-dbl., flat, borne in clusters of 5-20; foliage medium size, medium green, semi-glossy; few prickles; growth upright, bushy, spreading (3-5 ft.), with arching canes; [Little Darling × Magic Wand]; int. by Sequoia Nursery, 1995

Mariquita D, pb, 1860, Moreau & Robert; flowers flesh pink with lilac pink, large, full

Marisa HT, mp, 1996, Ortega, Carlos; flowers medium pink, lighter pink reverse, 5 in., dbl., high-centered, urn-shaped; foliage medium size, dark green, semi-glossy; prickles moderate; upright, tall (5 ft.) growth; [sport of Paris d'Yves St. Laurent]; int. by Aebi Nursery, 1996

Mariska F, dr; int. in 1995

Marista HT, rb, 1985, Staikov, Prof. Dr. V.; flowers medium red, whitish reverse, large, 75 petals, borne singly, moderate tea fragrance; foliage dark, glossy; upright growth; [Sarah Arnot × Rina Herholdt]; int. by Kalaydjiev and Chorbadjiiski, 1975

Maristella HT, 1952, Giacomasso

Marita F, ob, 1970, Mattock; flowers copper-orange, heavily veined yellow, medium, 30-40 petals, borne in trusses; foliage coppery; growth very free, straggly; [Masquerade × Serenade]; int. in 1961

Marita Lindner Min, lp, 2006, Desamero, Luis; flowers full, borne in small clusters; foliage small, medium green, semi-glossy; prickles small, straight and tapering, reddish, moderate; growth bushy, medium (24 in.); [Jilly Jewel × Luis Desamero]; int. in 2006

Maritim HT, m, Tantau; int. by Rosen Tantau, 2001

Maritime Bristol HT, ob, 1983, Sanday, John; flowers tangerine, large, 35 petals; foliage medium size, dark, semi-glossy; upright, bushy growth; [City of Gloucester × seedling]; int. by Sanday Roses, Ltd.

Maritime Heir S, dp, 1987, James, John; flowers lavender pink, petals tight and frilled, carnation-like, large, 40 petals, intense fragrance; occasionally recurrent bloom; foliage small, light green, disease-resistant; prickles fine; upright, bushy, very hardy growth; [Therese Bugnet × *R. nitida*]; int. in 1986

Marjan HT, ob, Select Roses, B.V.

Marjolaine F, ab, Sauvageot; flowers ochre and vanilla-yellow, large, dbl., moderate fragrance; recurrent; int. in 2002

Marjolin HGal, dr, 1829, Hardy/Roeser; flowers dark crimson-purple, inclining to violet, 5 in., very full, cupped, borne in clusters of 2-3; foliage light green, semi-glossy

Marjolin du Luxembourg Ch, pb, about 1830, Desprez; flowers carmine-pink, shaded dark crimson, very large, very full

Marjoline HT, rb, 1949, Meilland, F.; flowers cardinal-red, reverse Indian yellow, 6 in., very dbl., cupped; vigorous, upright growth; [Boudoir × Léonce Colombier]

Marjorie HT, w, 1895, Dickson, A.; flowers white with pink, large, dbl.

Marjorie Anderson F, mp, 1973, Dickson, Patrick; flowers 5½ in., 26 petals; foliage very large, matte; [Fragrant Cloud × Sea Pearl]; int. by Dicksons of Hawlmark

Marjorie Atherton HT, my, 1977, Bell, Ronald J.; bud ovoid, large; flowers lemon yellow, large, dbl., high-centered, borne singly, moderate fragrance; good repeat; foliage light green, leathery; stems strong; vigorous, upright, bushy, tall growth; [Mt. Shasta × Peace]; int. by Brundrett

Marjorie Bulkeley HT, yb, 1921, Dickson, H.; flowers buff, flushed rose-pink, passing to silvery pink, dbl.; Gold Medal, NRS, 1920

Marjorie Chase HT, ab, Kordes; int. in 1996

Marjorie Conn F, lp, 1981, Berry, Howard; bud ovoid; flowers 14 petals, borne in clusters of 5-7; foliage dark; prickles brown, hooked down; bushy growth; [Bon Bon × seedling]

Marjorie Ellick F, w, 1977, Ellick; flowers rowanberry, 4-6 in., 95 petals; foliage glossy, light; very vigorous, free growth; [(Spion-Kop × Ena Harkness) × (Sam Ferris × Karl Herbst)]; int. by Excelsior Roses, 1978

Marjorie Fair S, rb, 1977, Harkness; flowers medium red, white eye, 1 in., 5 petals, borne in very large clusters; free-flowering; foliage small, light green, semi-glossy; dense, bushy growth; [Ballerina × Baby Faurax]; int. in 1978; Gold Medal, Rome, 1977, Gold Medal, Baden-Baden, 1979

Marjorie Foster HWich, dr, 1934, Burbage Nursery; flowers deep blood-red, small, dbl.; vigorous growth

Marjorie LeGrice HT, ob, 1949, LeGrice; flowers orange and yellow, pointed, 5 in., 30 petals; foliage glossy; vigorous growth; [Mrs Sam McGredy × President Plumecocq]

Marjorie LeGrice, Climbing Cl HT, ob, 1959, Tantau, Math.; [sport of Marjorie Legrice]; int. in 1956

Marjorie Marshall S, ab, Harkness; flowers apricot, dbl., borne in small clusters, slight fragrance; good repeat; shrubby, medium (3 ft.) growth; int. in 1996

Marjorie May F, op, 1993, Horner, Heather M.; flowers orange/pink blend, 3-3½ in., full, borne in small clusters; foliage medium size, medium green, semi-glossy; some prickles; medium (100 cm.), upright growth; [Playgroup × Peer Gynt]; int. by Horner, 1995

Marjorie Proops HT, dr, 1969, Harkness; flowers crimson, dbl., high-centered; [Red Dandy × Ena Harkness]

Marjorie Reid HT, pb, 1997, Jellyman, J.S.; flowers small, dbl.; foliage small, dark green, glossy; low (25

cm.) growth; [seedling × Wee Barbie]

Marjorie W. Lester HMsk, lp; flowers soft pink with a lavender tinge; [Kathleen × unknown]

Marjory Palmer Pol, mp, 1936, Clark, A.; flowers rich pink, full, borne in clusters, intense fragrance; bushy, compact growth; [Jersey Beauty × unknown]; int. by NRS Victoria

Mark One Min, or, 1982, Saville, F. Harmon; flowers brilliant orange-red, 43 petals, cupped, borne singly and in clusters of up to 10, moderate spicy fragrance; foliage very glossy; prickles long, thin, soft on peduncles; compact, bushy growth; PP5044; [Sheri Anne × Glenfiddich]; int. by Nor'East Min. Roses

Mark Sullivan HT, op, 1942, Mallerin, C.; flowers gold flushed and veined rose, 4-4½ in., 33 petals, high-centered, moderate fragrance; foliage dark, leathery, glossy; vigorous, upright. growth; [Luis Brinas × Brazier]; int. by C-P

Mark Sullivan, Climbing Cl HT, ob

Mark Twain HT, dp, 1902, Hill, E. G.; bud pointed; flowers satiny rose-red, large, full, open

Mark Twain Gr, lp, Huber; flowers silvery pink, full, borne singly and in clusters, moderate fragrance; recurrent; foliage matte green; growth strong, broad, 80-100 cm.; int. by Rosen Huber, 2001

Markgräfin Wilhelmine F, lp, Tantau; flowers large, dbl.; int. in 1995

Markham Maiden Gr, w; bud large, full, plump; flowers white with blush pink or buttery cream in the center, full, tea rose, borne in clusters, moderate fragrance; recurrent; int. by J. C. Bakker Nurseries, 2003

Marlena F, mr, 1965, Kordes, R.; flowers crimson scarlet, small, 18 petals, flat, borne in clusters; free-flowering; low, compact bushy growth; PP2700; [Gertrud Westphal × Lilli Marleen]; int. by McGredy, 1964; Gold Medal, Belfast, 1966, Gold Medal, Baden-Baden, 1962, ADR, 1964

Marlena – See **Red Queen**, HT

Marlene Castronovo HT, mp, 2000, Webster, Robert; flowers medium, very full, borne mostly singly, no fragrance; foliage medium size, medium green, glossy; prickles moderate; growth upright, medium (36 in.); [City of London × Fragrant Hour]

Marlène Jobert Gr, pb, Guillot-Massad; bud small, pointed; flowers bright pink, reverse yellow, very full, borne in clusters; foliage matte; growth dwarf; int. by Roses Guillot, 2001

Marlies F, or

Marlon's Day HT, w, 2005, Wright, Fred; flowers white with pink edge, white reverse, large, full, borne mostly solitary, no fragrance; foliage large, dark green, semi-glossy; prickles angled down; growth upright, medium; garden decorative, exhibition; [sport of Moonstone]

Marlyn HT, mp, Tantau; int. in 1997

Marlyse HT, pb; int. in 1985

Marmalade HT, ob, 1976, Swim, H.C. & Ellis, A.E.; bud long, pointed; flowers bright orange, reverse deep yellow, 5 in., 30 petals, intense tea fragrance; foliage large, glossy, dark; upright growth; PP4243; [Arlene Francis × Bewitched]; int. by Armstrong Nursery

Marmalade Mist HT, op, 1990, Lammerts, Dr. Walter; bud pointed; flowers medium salmon pink, with lighter salmon pink reverse, 25 petals, cupped, slight fruity fragrance; foliage large, dark green, semi-glossy; prickles deep plum and brown; upright, medium growth; PP7549; int. by DeVor Nurseries, Inc., 1990

Marmalade Skies F, ob, 1999, Selection Meilland; bud conical, large; flowers dbl., flat, cupped, borne in large clusters, slight fragrance; foliage medium size, dark green, glossy; prickles moderate, large; bushy, medium (3-4 ft.) growth; hips round, 2 mm. orange-red; PP12579; [(Tamango × Parador) × Patricia]; int. by Conard-Pyle, 2001

Marmion HT, pb, 1934, Dobbie; flowers pale rose flushed orange, reverse salmon-pink, dbl.; vigorous, branching growth

Marmorata – See **Maculata**, HSpn

Marmorea HGal, rb, before 1754; flowers pale red, tinted bluish, with lighter marbling, medium, semi-dbl.; sometimes considered to be a form of *R. gallica officinalis*

Marnie Louise HT, w, 2004, Thomson, George L.; flowers cream bordered red, reverse cream, 14 cm., full, borne mostly solitary, moderate fragrance; foliage medium size, dark green, glossy; prickles medium, hooked; growth compact, medium (4-5 ft.); garden decorative; [Pascali × Frances Phoebe × Ophelia]; int. by Ross Roses, 2004

Marondo S, mp, Kordes; recurrent; growth to 5 ft.; int. in 1991

Marovilla F, or; int. in 1992

Marques de Narros HT, ob, 1951, La Florida; flowers salmon-pink, pointed; thornless

Marquesa de Aguilar HT, mr, 1958, Bofill; bud ovoid; flowers cardinal-red to begonia pink, large, 60 petals, high-centered, moderate fragrance; foliage glossy; vigorous growth; [Comtesse Vandal × Caprice]; int. by Torre Blanca, 1954

Marquesa de Bolarque HT, my, 1945, Camprubi, C.; bud long, pointed; flowers lemon-yellow, large, dbl., high-centered; foliage dark, glossy; vigorous growth; [Shot Silk × Julien Potin]

Marquesa de Casa Valdés HT, or, 1958, Dot, Pedro; bud pointed; flowers scarlet-red slightly shaded orange, large, 35-40 petals, high-centered, moderate fragrance; foliage dark; very vigorous, compact growth; [Peace × Poinsettia]; int. in 1955

Marquesa de Goicoerrotea HT, ab, 1947, Dot, Pedro; flowers amber-yellow, well-formed; upright growth; [Eclipse × Joanna Hill]

Marquesa de Urquijo – See **Pilar Landecho**, HT

Marquesa de Urquijo, Climbing – See **Pilar Landecho, Climbing**, Cl HT

Marquesa del Vadillo HT, pb, 1945, Dot, Pedro; flowers Neyron pink, reverse silvery pink, open, 5 in.; foliage glossy, dark; upright growth; [Girona × Condesa de Sástago]

Marquis d'Ailsa – See **Dr Marx**, HP

Marquis d'Alex HP, m, 1880, Brassac; flowers purple, center bright carmine, large, full

Marquis de Bouillé HT, dp, 1904, Schwartz; flowers light red tinted pale pink, very large, very full; foliage glaucous green

Marquis de Salisbury HP, mr, 1880, Paul, G.

Marquise Adèle de Murinais HP, mp, 1873, Schwartz; flowers silvery pink, aging to dark pink, large, full; [Mme Laffay × unknown]

Marquise Boccella – See **Marchesa Boccella**, HP

Marquise d'Alex T, w, 1880, Brassac; flowers white, center light yellow, large, very full

Marquise d'Andigné HT, dr, 1927, Leenders Bros.; flowers velvety scarlet-crimson, dbl.; [(Lieutenant Chaure × George C. Waud) × Laurent Carle]

Marquise de Balbiano B, m, 1855, Lacharme, F.; flowers pink, tinged with lilac, medium, full, cupped

Marquise de Barbentane HT, ab, 1928, Fugier; flowers apricot-yellow, shaded orange and sunflower-yellow, dbl.; [Mrs Farmer × Severine]

Marquise de Castellane HP, dp, 1869, Pernet père; flowers dark rose-pink, well-formed, large, dbl., moderate fragrance; moderate growth; [Jules Margottin × unknown]

Marquise de Chaponnay T, yb, 1897, Bernaix; flowers butter yellow, edges tinted salmon, large, full

Marquise de Chavaudon HP, pb, 1853, Carré; flowers medium pink, center petals white-edged, large, full

Marquise de Forton T, yb, 1889, Charreton; flowers saffron yellow, center carmine pink, medium, cupped

Marquise de Foucault T, w, 1860, Margottin; flowers white, center cream, large, dbl.

Marquise de Ganay HT, mp, 1910, Guillot, P.; bud very large; flowers silvery rose, very large, dbl., cupped, moderate fragrance; foliage dark green; [Liberty × La France]

Marquise de Gibot HP, lp, 1868, De Sansal; flowers pale rose, large, full, globular; foliage dark green

Marquise de la Rochejacquelein S, ab, Guillot-Massad; flowers bright apricot, fading to white, 8 cm., full, cupped, slight fragrance; foliage glossy; growth to 1 m.; int. by Roseraies Guillot, 2006

Marquise de Marat HP, lp, 1855, Ducher; flowers large, full

Marquise de Mortemart HP, w, 1868, Liabaud; flowers blush-white, center pale flesh, large, full, cupped; [Jules Margottin × unknown]

Marquise de Querhoënt T, pb, 1901, Godard; flowers coppery pink with golden yellow at base of petals, medium, full; growth medium, bushy; [G. Nabonnand × Mme Laurette Messimy]

Marquise de Salisbury lp, 1888, Lévêque

Marquise de Salisbury HT, mr, 1891, Pernet père; flowers bright velvety crimson, medium to large, dbl.; foliage thick, dark green

Marquise de Sinéty HT, yb, 1906, Pernet-Ducher; flowers golden yellow, shaded bronzy red, dbl.; Gold Medal, Bagatelle, 1907

Marquise de Sinéty, Climbing Cl HT, yb, 1912, Griffon

Marquise de Verdun HP, mp, 1868, Oger; flowers bright carmine pink, large, full, globular

Marquise de Vivens T, dp, 1886, Dubreuil; flowers carmine, base yellowish, large, dbl.

Marquise d'Hautpoul HT, pb, 1915, Hicks; flowers bright pink, shaded cream, moderate fragrance

Marquise d'Ivry HT, dp, before 1866; flowers dark pink with lilac tints, very large, full

Marquise Jeanne de la Chataigneraye HT, w, 1902, Soupert & Notting; flowers silky white with pink tints, center yellowish, large, full, moderate fragrance; [Souv de President Carnot × Mme Jules Grolez]

Marquise Litta de Bréteuil HT, mr, 1893, Pernet-Ducher; flowers carmine pink, center vermilion red, 5 in., very full, cupped

Marquise Spinola S, mp, Guillot-Massad; int. in 1996

Marquisette Ch, op, 1872, Ducher; flowers pink with salmon

Marr Pol, op; flowers coral overcast orange, 1 in., cupped, borne in clusters; thornless; growth rangy (10-12 in.)

Marraine – See **Anne Laure**, S

Marrakech HT, dr, 1945, Meilland, F.; flowers oxblood-red shaded bright scarlet, well-formed, very large, dbl.; upright, vigorous growth; [Rome Glory × Tassin]

Marriotta Min, dp, 1990, McGredy, Sam IV; flowers deep pink, small, 20 petals, blooms with side buds and sprays; foliage small, medium green, semi-glossy, resistant to blackspot; bushy growth; PP9413; [Seaspray × Little Artist]; int. by McGredy Roses International, 1989

Marry Me Min, mp, 1999, Dickson, Patrick; flowers 2 in., full, borne in small clusters; foliage medium size, dark green, glossy; prickles moderate; growth upright, medium (28 in.); containers, patio; [seedling × Cider Cup]; int. by Dickson Nurseries, Ltd., 1998

Mars HT, op, 1927, Chaplin Bros.; flowers deep coral

Marselisborg – See **Yellowstone**, F

Marsh – See **Marsh Cottage**, S

Marsh Cottage S, dp, Olesen; bud ovate, red; flowers deep pink, small, single, almost flat, borne in clusters of 5-11, no fragrance; recurrent; foliage dark green, semi-glossy; prickles numerous, 8 mm., hooked downward; flat, bushy (40-60 cm.) growth; hips rounded to somewhat elliptical, greyed-orange; PP16941; [seedling × Diamond Head]; int. by Poulsen Roser, 2005

Marshall P. Wilder HP, dr, 1885, Ellwanger & Barry; flowers bright deep red, large, 45 petals, globular, intense fragrance; vigorous, tall growth; [Général Jacqueminot × unknown]

Marsyanka HT, dp; flowers carmine-pink, medium, semi-dbl.; int. in 1958

Marta Min, or, 1983, Dobbs; flowers small, 20 petals; foliage small, light green, matte; upright growth; [Persian Princess × Anytime]; int. by Small World Min. Roses

Marta Salvador HT, Ferrer, F.

Martha Pol, pb, 1906, Lambert, P.; flowers coppery rose, dbl., borne in clusters of 7-20; dwarf growth; [Thalia × Mme Laurette Messimy]

Martha B, pb, 1912, Knudson; flowers pale coral, dbl., borne in clusters of 1-5, moderate fragrance; prickles few thorns; tall, climbing growth; [sport of Zéphirine Drouhin]

Martha Allen Gr, ab, Williams, J. Benjamin; flowers apricot-pink with silvery overlay, dbl., moderate fragrance; recurrent; growth to 4 ft.; int. by Hortico, Inc., 2005

Martha Bugnet HRg, mr, 1959, Bugnet; bud long, pointed; flowers purplish red, open, large, semi-dbl.; abundant, recurrent bloom; foliage dark rugosa type; weak stems; vigorous, bushy (5-6 ft.) tall and broad growth; very large fruit; [((*R. rugosa kamtchatica* × *R. amblyotis*) × *R. rugosa plena*) × F.J. Grootendorst]

Martha Drew HT, w, 1919, McGredy; flowers creamy white, center rose, large, dbl., moderate fragrance; Gold Medal, NRS, 1919

Martha Ford HMult, ab, Nobbs; int. in 1987

Martha Keller Pol, lp, 1912, Walter; flowers medium, very dbl.

Martha Kordes F, dp, 1941, Kordes; flowers light capucine-red, becoming pink, open, medium, semi-dbl., borne in clusters; vigorous, upright growth; [Hedwig Fulda × Holstein]

Martha Lambert Pol, rb, 1939, Lambert, P.; flowers brilliant scarlet with small yellow eye, small, single, borne in clusters, slight fragrance; recurrent bloom; foliage glossy; stems strong; vigorous, bushy growth; [Frans Leddy × Paul's Scarlet Climber]; int. by C-P

Martha Rice F, dp, 1970, Raffel, Frank c.; buds pointed; flowers light red to rose-pink with some gold at base, medium, dbl, open, borne singly, several together and in clusters; foliage medium size, soft; growth vigorous, upright, bushy; [Tropicana × Sweet Vivien]; int. by Port Stockton Nurs.

Martha Washington S, mp, before 1900; hybrid roxburghii

Martha's Choice HT, dp, 1977, Bailey; bud high-centered; flowers deep pink, 5 in., 37 petals; [Gavotte × Prima Ballerina]

Martha's Vineyard S, dp, 1995, Olesen, Pernille & Mogens N.; flowers hot pink, blending to white at center, 2-4 in., dbl., borne in small clusters; foliage small, light green, semi-glossy; few prickles; spreading (36 in.) growth, tall, vigorous; PP9664; int. by Young's American Rose Nursery, 1995

Marthe Ancey HT, w, 1932, Schwartz, A.; flowers cream, tinted salmon-pink, center with straw-yellow reflections, dbl.; vigorous growth; [Souv. de Claudius Pernet × Mme Mélanie Soupert]

Marthe Cahuzac Pol, ly, 1902, Ketten, Gebrüder; flowers medium, dbl.

Martian Glow F, mr, 1972, Gandy, Douglas L.; flowers red, reverse lighter, 1½ in., 10 petals, borne in clusters; foliage semi-glossy, medium green; vigorous, spreading growth; [Joseph's Coat × Dorothy Wheatcroft]

Martian Sunrise S, or, 1980, Taylor, Thomas E.; bud ovoid; flowers 43 petals, high-centered, urn-shaped, borne singly or in small clusters; repeats well; foliage light to medium green, semi-glossy; prickles semi-hooked; upright, bushy growth; [Paddy McGredy × Heidelberg]

Martin des Senteurs F, ab, Adam; flowers soft chamois with salmon tints, medium, dbl., open, borne mostly in clusters, intense fragrance; foliage large, glossy; bushy (3-4 ft.) growth; int. in 2000

Martin Faassen HT, dp, 1965, Verbeek; bud ovoid; flowers pink-red, medium, dbl., borne in clusters; foliage dark; [Baccará × seedling]

Martin Frobisher HRg, lp, 1970, Svedja, Felicitas; bud ovoid; flowers light pink, center darker, medium, dbl., intense fragrance; foliage light green; vigorous, tall growth; [Schneezwerg × unknown]; int. by Canada Dept. of Agric., 1968

Martin Liebau HP, mp, 1930, Kiese; flowers large, dbl.

Martin Martin HT, w, 1985, McCann, Sean; flowers cream, petals tipped red, large, high-centered; foliage large, dark, semi-glossy; upright growth; [Jimmy Greaves × Irish Gold]

Martina HT, w, Noack, Werner; int. in 1989

Martina – See **Martina Hit**, MinFl

Martina F, yb, Urban, J.

Martina Hit MinFl, dr, Poulsen; flowers dark red, 5-8 cm., semi-dbl., no fragrance; growth bushy, 40-60 cm.; PP11538; int. by Poulsen Roser, 1998

Martine Guillot S, w, Guillot-Massad; flowers creamy white, sometimes blushed pink, full, globular, borne in clusters, intense fragrance; recurrent; foliage medium size, medium green, glossy; vigorous, tall (8-10 ft.) growth; int. by Roses Guillot, 1996

Martine Hémeray F, or, 1958, Gaujard, R.; flowers China-red, well-formed, dbl.; foliage leathery; [(Orange Triumph × Mme Edouard Herriot) × seedling]; int. by Hémeray-Aubert

Martinez – See **Blue Bell**, HT

Martini HT, Delforge; int. in 1967

Martinique – See **Martinique Hit**, MinFl

Martinique Hit MinFl, ab, Poulsen; flowers apricot blend, 5-8 cm., dbl., no fragrance; foliage reddish green; growth bushy, 20-40 cm.; int. by Poulsen Roser, 2004

Martone Min, pb, 1990, Bridges, Dennis A.; bud pointed; flowers medium pink, lighter at base, reverse light pink, medium, 30 petals, high-centered, slight damask fragrance; foliage medium size, medium green, semi-glossy; prickles straight, medium, deep pink; upright, medium growth; [Queen City × seedling]; int. by Bridges Roses, 1990

Marty F, mr, 1991, Pearce, C.A.; flowers dusty red, medium, very full, hybrid tea form, borne in small clusters; foliage small, medium green, semi-glossy; few prickles; low (40-60 cm.), bushy growth; [seedling × Sweetheart]; int. by Rearsby Roses, Ltd., 1991

Marty's Triumph Min, op, 1985, Bischoff, Francis J.; flowers bright coral pink, white reverse, small, 28 petals, high-centered, borne singly; foliage medium size, dark, semi-glossy; prickles pale green, straight; upright, bushy growth; PP6099; [Little Darling × seedling]

Marushka HT, dy, 1985, Staikov, Prof. Dr. V.; flowers 35 petals, high-centered, borne 1-3 per stem; foliage dark, leathery, glossy; vigorous, bushy growth; [Kabuki × seedling]; int. by Kalaydjiev and Chorbadjiiski, 1984

Marvel HT, dp, Zary, Keith; PPAF; int. by Bear Creek Gardens, 1999

Marvelle – See **Tropical Sunset**, HT

Marvie Min, mr, 1995, Giles, Diann; flowers medium red, small, full, borne mostly singly; foliage small, medium green, semi-glossy; some prickles; medium, upright growth; [Winsome × seedling]; int. by Giles Rose Nursery, 1995

Marvin Lassalle S, my, Gilet; int. in 2005; Gold Medal, Barcelona, 2004

Marvlous HT, mr, 1937, Cant, B. R.; flowers crimson, open, large, dbl.; foliage leathery; very vigorous growth

Marx HSpn, my, about 1825, Cartier; flowers sulfur yellow, small, full, moderate fragrance

Mary HT, ob, 1931, Bentall; flowers buff and orange; vigorous growth

Mary Pol, op, 1947, Qualm; flowers orange-cerise, borne in small clusters; vigorous growth; [sport of Orange Triumph]; int. by Spek

Mary Adair Min, ab, 1966, Moore, Ralph S.; flowers buffy apricot, small, dbl., moderate fragrance; foliage light green, soft; vigorous, bushy, dwarf growth; PP2910; [Golden Glow × Zee]; int. by Sequoia Nursery

Mary Adrienne S, op, 2001, Carruth, Tom; flowers coral pink, deepening in cool weather, 5-7 cm., semi-dbl., borne in large clusters, somewhat pendulous, slight fragrance; foliage light green, matte; prickles moderate, small, nearly straight, light brown; growth bushy, medium (80-100 cm.); garden decorative; [Sweet Chariot × Trumpeter]; int. by Weeks Roses, 2002

Mary 'n' John MinFl, my, 2000, McCann, Sean; flowers medium, dbl., borne in small clusters, slight fragrance; foliage medium size, medium green, semi-glossy; some prickles; growth bushy, medium; garden decorative; [Rise 'n' Shine × Amy Rebecca]

Mary Ann F, dp, 1959, Restani; bud ovoid; flowers rose-red, 2 in., 60-78 petals, high-centered; foliage dark; upright growth; PP1794; [sport of Garnette]

Mary Ann HT, m, 2005, Edwards, Eddie & Phelps, Ethan; flowers mauve with plum overtones in cool weather, 5-6 in., full, borne mostly solitary, intense fragrance; foliage large, dark green, glossy; few prickles; upright, tall (5-6 ft.) growth; exhibition; [seedling × Barbra Streisand]; int. by Johnny Becnel Show Roses, 2006

Mary Barnard F, op, 1978, Sanday, John; bud ovoid; flowers deep salmon-pink, large, 18 petals; foliage dark; low, vigorous growth; [(Karl Herbst × Sarabande) × Ernest H. Morse]

Mary Beaufort HT, lp, 1969, Sanday, John; flowers light peach-pink, well-shaped, small; compact, low growth; [Gavotte × (Ethel Sanday × Crimson Glory)]

Mary Bell Min, w, 1987, Bell, Charles E., Jr.; flowers small, full, moderate fragrance; foliage medium size, medium green, semi-glossy, disease-resistant; bushy, hardy growth; [Cherish × Rise 'n' Shine]; int. by Kimbrew Walter Roses, 1987

Mary Bennett HP, dp, 1885, Bennett; flowers cherry pink, large, full; [Baronne Adolphe de Rothschilde × unknown]

Mary Bostock HT, lp, 1952, Clark, A.; flowers shell-pink tinted white, 60 petals; strong stems; vigorous growth

Mary Bradby HT, op, 1999, Byrnes, Robert; flowers unusual orange and russet, reverse salmon, ruffled petals, 3 in., dbl., borne mostly singly; foliage medium size, dark green, semi-glossy, disease-resistant; few prickles; upright, medium (5 ft.) growth; hardy; [Queen Elizabeth × Taboo]; int. by Overbrooke Gardens, 1999

Mary Bruni Pol, lp, 1914, Gratama; flowers light creamy rose pink, small, dbl.

Mary Burke Min, op, Hannemann, F.; int. by The Rose Paradise

Mary C HT, pb, 2005, Smith, John T.; flowers medium pink, reverse white, 4½-5 in., full, high-centered, borne mostly solitary; foliage medium size, dark green, semi-glossy; prickles long, straight, light red, moderate; growth compact, medium (3½-4 ft.); hedging, exhibition; [Gemini × Donna Darling]; int. by same, 2007

Mary Campbell F, ob, 1992, Horner, Heather M.; flowers orange, medium, 6-14 petals, borne in small clusters; foliage medium size, medium green, semi-glossy; some prickles; medium (80 cm.), bushy growth; [Lovers Meeting × Amber Queen]; int. in 1993

Mary Carver HT, lp, 1950, Chick; bud globular; flowers shell-pink, 5 in., 80 petals, cupped; foliage leathery, light green; vigorous, upright growth; [sport of Red Radiance]

Mary Casant – See **Marytje Cazant**, Pol

Mary Cave F, Harkness; int. in 1993

Mary Clark Min, lp, 1982, Hooper, John C.; flowers medium, 55 petals; foliage mid-green; prickles straight, light yellow; [Janna × Gene Boerner]; int. in 1981

Mary Clay HT, dr, 1951, Kordes; flowers blood-red, 6 in., 40-45 petals; foliage very heavy, dark; very free growth; [Kardinal × Crimson Glory]; int. by Morse

Mary Conn S, mp, Williams, J.B.; growth to 3 ft.; int. by Hortico, Inc., 2005

Mary Corelly HP, op, 1901, Prince; flowers dark salmon-pink, medium, dbl.

Mary Cullen S, dr, 2001, Kenny, David; flowers old-fashioned, 5 in., full, quartered, borne in small clusters, slight fragrance; foliage large, dark green, glossy; prickles large, slightly hooked, numerous; growth spreading, tall (5 ft.); garden decorative; [Laura Ford × Phantom]

Mary Delahunty HT, dr, 1991, Bell, Ronald J.; bud pointed; flowers large, 35-40 petals, borne usually singly, moderate damask fragrance; foliage dark green, glossy; bushy, tall growth; [(Daily Sketch × Impeccable) × Red Planet]; int. by Treloar Roses Pty. Ltd., 1990

Mary DeVor F, mr, 1970, Lammerts, Dr. Walter; flowers cardinal-red, sweetheart, medium, 35 petals, moderate fragrance; foliage leathery; vigorous, upright growth; PP2838; [Christian Dior × Rumba]; int. by Amling-DeVor Nursery, 1967

Mary Donaldson HT, mp, 1984, Cants of Colchester, Ltd.; flowers medium salmon-pink, medium, dbl., high-centered, intense fragrance; foliage large, dark, glossy; upright growth; [Kathleen O'Rourke × seedling]

Mary Dutton HT, op, 1949, Bees; bud long, pointed; flowers salmon-pink, 6 in., very dbl.; foliage glossy; very vigorous growth; [Crimson Glory × Mrs Sam McGredy]

Mary E. Thomas HT, dp, 2002, Thomas, D.; flowers medium, very full, borne mostly solitary, slight fragrance; foliage medium size, dark green, semi-glossy; prickles moderate; growth upright, medium; exhibition; [Selfridges × Red Devil]

Mary Edith Min, w, 1991, Taylor, Pete & Kay; flowers white, tipped with pink edges, flower turns darker pink tints with age, medium, full, borne mostly singly, moderate fragrance; foliage medium size, medium green, semi-glossy; low, upright, bushy growth; [Azure Sea × seedling]; int. by Taylor's Roses, 1991

Mary Egerton F, rb, 1983, Lea, R.F.G.; flowers white, petals edged orange-red, spreading with age, reverse white, 35 petals; foliage large, dark, glossy; upright, bushy growth; [Fragrant Cloud × Prominent]

Mary Elizabeth Min, lp, 1983, Dobbs; flowers small, 29 petals; foliage small, light green, matte; bushy growth; [Fairy Moss × Fairy Moss]; int. by Small World Min. Roses

Mary Fleming F, mp, 1995, Fleming, Joyce L.; bud opening to very pale pink; flowers medium, 6-14 petals, borne 2-15 per cluster; foliage medium size, medium green, matte; bushy (90-100 cm.), spreading growth; [Marchenland × Golden Salmon Superieur]; int. by Hortico Roses, 1994

Mary Gammon – See **Mary Gamon**, Min

Mary Gamon Min, op, Fryer, Gareth; flowers salmon orange, dbl., borne mostly in clusters; good repeat; neat, bushy (15 in.) growth; int. in 1993

Mary Greer – See **Kootenay**, HT

Mary Guthrie Pol, mp, 1929, Clark, A.; flowers rich pink, small, single, borne in large clusters, moderate fragrance; foliage light; bushy (2½ ft.) growth; [Jersey Beauty × Scorcher]; int. by NRS Victoria

Mary Hart HT, mr, 1931, Hart, G.B.; [sport of Talisman]

Mary Hart, Climbing Cl HT, mr, 1937, Western Rose Co. (also Meilland, 1942)

Mary Hayley Bell S, mp, Kordes; flowers semi-dbl.; growth to 3-4 ft.; winter hardy

Mary Haywood Min, mp, 1958, Moore, Ralph S.; flowers bright pink, base white, 1 in., 50 petals, moderate fragrance; foliage glossy; very compact (10 in.), bushy growth; PP1766; [(*R. wichurana* × Floradora) × Oakington Ruby]; int. by Sequoia Nursery, 1957

Mary Helen Tanner HT, dp, 1932, Tanner; flowers carmine, stems white or pinkish; [sport of Templar]

Mary Hicks HMult, dr, 1927, Hicks; flowers deep scarlet, 3-3½ cm., semi-dbl., moderate fragrance; foliage light; vigorous, climbing growth

Mary Hilda Law HT, dp, 1995, Kirkham, Gordon Wilson; flowers deep pink, 3-3½ in., dbl.; foliage large, dark green, semi-glossy; medium, upright growth; [Lady Helen × Fragrant Cloud]; int. by Kirkham, 1997

Mary Hill HT, w, 1916, E.G. Hill, Co.; flowers cream, center deep orange, dbl.; [Ophelia × Sunburst]

Mary Hill Min, pb, 1990, Moore, Ralph S.; bud pointed; flowers medium pink, yellow reverse, aging lighter, medium, 30-35 petals, high-centered, moderate fruity fragrance; foliage medium size, medium green, semi-glossy; prickles slender, straight, small, brownish; upright, bushy, medium growth; PP7994; [Little Darling × Golden Angel]; int. by Sequoia Nursery

Mary Jean HT, ab, 1990, Harkness, R., & Co., Ltd.; bud ovoid to pointed; flowers large, 37 petals, cupped, borne usually singly, moderate sweet fragrance; foliage medium to large, oval, medium green, semi-glossy; prickles slightly decurved, medium, green; bushy, medium growth; [Dr. Darley × Amber Queen]; int. by R. Harkness & Co., Ltd., 1991

Mary Jo HT, my, 1959, Joseph H. Hill, Co.; bud short, pointed; flowers maize-yellow, large, 30-35 petals, high-centered; foliage leathery; strong stems; vigorous, upright, bushy growth; PP1504; [seedling × Orange Delight]; int. in 1958

Mary Johnston HT, lp, 1997, Wambach, Alex A.; flowers light pink, 4 in., full, borne mostly singly, slight fragrance; foliage medium size, dark green, semi glossy; medium (4½ ft.) growth; [Elizabeth Taylor × Touch of Class]; int. by Certified Roses, Inc.

Mary Kate Min, dp, 1977, Dobbs; bud mossy; flowers light red, 1 in., 29 petals, flat; foliage dark, soft; vigorous, upright growth; [Fairy Moss × Fairy Moss]; int. by Small World Min. Roses

Mary Kay Min, lp, 1984, Williams, Ernest D.; flowers small, 35 petals; foliage small, dark, glossy; upright, bushy growth; PP5631; [Tom Brown × Over the Rainbow]; int. by Mini-Roses

Mary Kittel HT, dr, 1976, Harvey, R.E.; bud pointed; flowers 5 in., 35 petals, high-centered, intense fragrance; foliage large, glossy; vigorous growth; [(Chrysler Imperial × Night 'n' Day) × Night 'n' Day]; int. by Kimbrew-Walter Roses, 1975

Mary L. Evans HRg, dp, 1936, Wright, Percy H.; flowers deep wild-rose-pink; non-recurrent; growth very similar to Tekonkaha but more spreading; [Hansa × *R. macounii*]

Mary Lawrance's Shell Rose Ch, mr, 1799; flowers dusky rose-crimson with small green pointel in center of bloom, full; stems light, slender

Mary Lee Johnson Richards HT, lp

Mary Louise MinFl, m, 1996, Buster, Larry S.; flowers red lavender, lighter lavender reverse, full, borne mostly singly, moderate fragrance; foliage medium green, dull; prickles moderate; upright, tall growth; [Lady X × Winsome]; int. by Kimbrew Walter Roses, 1996

Mary Louise HT, pb, 1996, Taylor, Thomas E.; flowers light pink, reverse medium pink, 5 in., dbl., form similar to First Prize, borne mostly singly; foliage medium size, medium green, glossy, similar to Honey Favorite; prickles moderate; compact, bushy, medium (3-4 ft.) growth; [Honey Favorite × First Prize]; int. in 2000

Mary Lovett HWich, w, 1915, Van Fleet; flowers snow-white, 7-8 cm., dbl., borne in clusters of 10-20, moderate fragrance; some repeat bloom; vigorous, climbing (to 10-12 ft.) growth; [*R. wichurana* × Kaiserin Auguste Viktoria]; int. by J.T. Lovett

Mary Lynn HT, dr, 1988, Rennie, Bruce F.; flowers maroon red, reverse lighter, aging darker, medium, 15 petals, high-centered, borne usually singly, intense damask fragrance; foliage medium size, medium green, semi-glossy; prickles hooked, medium, red-brown; upright, tall growth; hips oblong, medium, yellow; [(Electron × Watercolor) × Lavonde]; int. by Rennie Roses International, 1988

Mary Lyon Gr, w, 1988, Williams, J. Benjamin; flowers pure chalk white, medium, full, intense fragrance; foliage large, dark green, semi-glossy, thick; upright, hardy growth; [(Mount Shasta × Sonia) × (White Masterpiece × Ivory Fashion)]

Mary McKillop HT, pb, Swane; flowers shell pink, edged rose pink, dbl., high-centered, borne singly or in clusters of 2 or 3, slight fragrance; free-flowering; foliage dense; growth medium; int. in 1989

Mary Magdalene S, pb, 1998, Austin, David; flowers soft pink shaded apricot, 4 in., 100-110 petals, borne in small clusters, intense myrrh fragrance; foliage medium size, medium green, dull; prickles moderate; spreading, medium (3 ft.) growth; [seedling × seedling]; int. by David Austin Roses, Ltd., 1998

Mary Malva HT, lp, 1979, Lens, Louis; bud long, pointed; flowers 3½-4½ in., 18-24 petals, high-centered, moderate spicy fragrance; foliage dark, leathery; upright growth; [(Pascali × Charlotte Armstrong) × Lilac Charm]; int. in 1971

Mary Mangano Min, op, 1989, Papandrea, John T.; flowers deep coral pink; [sport of Petite Folie]

Mary Manners HRg, w, Leicester; flowers creamy white, sometimes with pink blush on petal edges, slight fragrance; recurrent; possibly a sport of Sarah van Fleet; int. in 1970

Mary Margaret Min, op, 1993, Taylor, Franklin; flowers coral pink, creamy yellow base, medium, full, borne mostly singly; foliage medium size, medium green, semi-glossy; few prickles; low (18 in.), spreading growth; [Party Girl × Watercolor]; int. by Taylor's Roses, 1993

Mary Margaret McBride HT, mp, 1942, Nicolas; bud long, pointed; flowers salmon-pink, 4-5 in., 42 petals, high-centered; foliage dark, leathery, glossy; vigorous, upright, bushy growth; [Sunkist × Olympiad]; int. by J&P; David Fuerstenberg Prize, ARS, 1945

Mary Marques HT, or, 1958, Bofill; bud long, pointed; flowers orange-red tinted yellow, medium, very dbl., high-centered; upright growth; [Mediterranea × Suzanne Balitrand]; int. by Torre Blanca, 1955

Mary Marshall Min, ob, 1971, Moore, Ralph S.; bud long, pointed; flowers orange, base yellow, small, dbl., cupped, moderate fragrance; foliage small, leathery; vigorous, dwarf, bushy growth; PP3346; [Little Darling × Fairy Princess]; int. by Sequoia Nursery, 1970; AOE, ARS, 1975

Mary Marshall, Climbing Cl Min, ob, 1983, Williams, Ernest D.; int. by Mini-Roses, 1982

Mary Mathis Min, lp, 2005, Singer, Judith A; flowers light pink with green eye, reverse medium pink, 1 in., full, borne mostly solitary, slight fragrance; foliage small, medium green; prickles small, moderate; bushy growth; [Bonica × seedling]

Mary Maud Min, mp, 1999, Giles, Diann; flowers medium, dbl., borne in small clusters; foliage medium size, medium green, semi-glossy; prickles moderate; upright, medium growth; [Little Darling × unknown]; int. by Giles Rose Nursery, 1999

Mary May F, rb, 1999, Sheridan, John; flowers red on white, reverse white, 3 in., dbl., borne in small clusters; foliage small, dark green, semi-glossy; prickles moderate; bushy (2 ft.) growth; [Daily Sketch × (Cream Peach × unknown)]; TGC, RNRS, 1988

Mary McHutchin Cl Pol, mr, 1935, Cant, B. R.; flowers crimson, semi-dbl., cupped, borne in clusters; foliage large, leathery; vigorous, climbing (6-8 ft.) growth

Mary Merryweather HT, dy, 1925, Merryweather; bud pointed; flowers deep golden yellow, semi-dbl., cupped; foliage glossy; vigorous, bushy growth; [Marquise de Sinéty × Lady Hillingdon]

Mary Mine Gr, op, 1972, Harkness, R.; flowers salmon-pink to light rose, large, 27 petals; [Queen Elizabeth × Buccaneer]; int. by J. L. Harkness, 1971

Mary Monro HT, pb, 1921, Pemberton; flowers carmine-pink, flushed saffron-yellow, dbl.

Mary Mulligan HT, or, 1944, Mallerin, C.; bud long, pointed; flowers flame, dbl., cupped; vigorous growth; int. by A. Meilland

Mary Murray HT, ab, 1930, Prior; flowers deep apricot-yellow becoming lighter, 30 petals; foliage glossy, bronze; vigorous growth

Mary Nish HT, w, 1928, Pacific Rose Co.; flowers white, center tinted shell-pink, very large, dbl., moderate fragrance; foliage rich green, soft, glossy; vigorous, bushy growth; [sport of Radiance]

Mary of Penola HT, pb, 1999, Thomson, George L.; flowers dark pink, reverse darker, 6 in., 41 petals, borne mostly singly; foliage medium size, medium green, glossy; prickles moderate; upright, medium (3-3½ ft.) growth; [Maria Callas × Elina]

Mary Pauline HT, w, 1998, McCrury, Curtis; flowers palest pink, dbl., high-centered, borne mostly singly; foliage large, medium green, semi-glossy; some prickles; upright, tall growth; [Queen Elizabeth × Chablis]

Mary Pickford HT, ab, 1923, H&S; bud pointed, orange-yellow; flowers pale yellow, center deeper, large, dbl.; foliage bronze; vigorous, bushy growth; [(Grange Colombe × unknown) × Souv. de Claudius Pernet]

Mary Pilkington F, pb, 1993, Everitt, Derrick; flowers peach, quickly paling to light pink, creamy yellow reverse, medium, dbl., moderate fragrance; foliage medium size, dark green, semi-glossy; some prickles; tall (80-90 cm.), bushy growth; [Mary Sumner × Remember Me]

Mary Pochin HP, mr, 1881, Pochin; flowers bright red tinted velvety crimson, medium

Mary Pope F, yb, 1965, Sanday, John; flowers golden yellow suffused pink, edged darker, 3 in., 25 petals, borne in clusters; foliage glossy, dark; vigorous growth; [seedling × Independence]

Mary Pope HT, m, Kordes; int. in 1993

Mary Poppins HT, mp, 1967, Morey, Dr. Dennison; [sport of Hallmark]; int. by General Bionomics

Mary, Queen of Scots HSpn, pb; flowers lavender-pink with a white eye, single

Mary Rand HT, w, 1965, Latham; flowers cream, edged rose-pink, well-formed, large; foliage glossy, light green; vigorous growth; [Caprice × Scandale]

Mary Ratcliffe HT, pb, 1958, Ratcliffe; flowers soft pink, reverse darker

Mary Robertson Pol, mr, 1969, Buisman, G. A. H.; bud ovoid; flowers medium, dbl.; foliage dark; [Paprika × seedling]

Mary Rose S, mp, 1983, Austin, David; flowers large, very dbl., cupped; recurrent bloom; foliage medium size, medium-green, matte; upright, bushy growth; [seedling × The Friar]; int. by David Austin Roses, Ltd.

Mary Russell HT, mr, 1940, Clark, A.; flowers well-formed, large

Mary Sampere de Guanabara F, Moreira da Silva, A.

Mary Sheffield F, mr, 1987, Bracegirdle, Derek T.; flowers medium, dbl., moderate fragrance; foliage small, medium green, glossy; spreading growth; [Doris Tysterman × Admiral Rodney]

Mary Summers F, ob, 2004, Horner, Colin P.; flowers orange, reverse lighter, 9 cm., dbl., borne mostly solitary, moderate fragrance; foliage medium size, dark green, glossy; prickles medium, curved; growth upright, tall (120 cm.); garden decorative; [Golden Future × Fellowship]; int. by Warley Rose Gardens, 2006

Mary Sumner F, or, 1976, McGredy, Sam IV; flowers semi-dbl., 15 petals; tall, upright growth; [seedling × seedling]; int. by McGredy Roses International

Mary Swindells F, op, 1995, Kenny, David; flowers salmon pink, medium, full, borne in small clusters; foliage medium size, dark green, glossy; numerous prickles; tall, upright, bushy growth; [(Mary Sumner × Kiskadee) × (Mary Sumner × Regensberg)]; int. in 1990

Mary Taylor HT, lp, Taylor, L.R.; int. in 1966

Mary Thomson S, pb, Thomson, G.A.

Mary Toomey Min, yb, 2001, McCann, Sean; flowers yellow-apricot, small, semi-dbl., borne in small clusters; foliage small, medium green, semi-glossy; growth compact, short; [seedling × You 'n' Me]

Mary Wallace HWich, mp, 1924, Van Fleet; bud long, pointed; flowers warm rose pink, 8 cm., semi-dbl., cupped, moderate fragrance; seasonal bloom; foliage large, thick, glossy; vigorous, climbing (8-12 ft.) growth; [*R. wichurana* × a pink Hybrid Tea]; int. by American Rose Society

Mary Warm Cl Min, or; int. in 1997

Mary Warren Cl HT, mp, 1931, Clark, A.; flowers pink, open, large, semi-dbl.; recurrent bloom; foliage soft, large, dark; vigorous, pillar growth; [Mrs Frank Guthrie × Scorcher]; int. by NRS New South Wales

Mary Washington N, w; flowers white tinted pink, fading to white, medium, dbl., borne in clusters of 7-11, moderate fragrance; very vigorous growth; first evidenced in documents dated in 1891, but may be much older; sometimes classed as HSet; int. by Registered by Frank L. Ross, Nashville, Tenn

Mary Webb S, ab, 1986, Austin, David; flowers very large, dbl., cupped, intense fragrance; foliage large, light green, matte; bushy growth; [seedling × Chinatown]; int. in 1984

Mary Wheatcroft HT, ob, 1945, Robinson, H.; bud high-pointed; flowers deep copper; foliage bronze; [Mrs Sam McGredy × Princess Marina]; int. by Wheatcroft Bros.

Mary Wise HT, rb, 1982, Herholdt, J.A.; flowers medium red and gold with red reverse, large, 40 petals, no fragrance; foliage medium green, semi-glossy; bushy growth; [Madelaine × (seedling × Apogee)]

Mary Woodcock HMsk, mp, Stydd; int. in 1989

Mary, Countess of Ilchester HT, mp, 1909, Dickson, A.; flowers deep rose-pink, open, large, dbl.; foliage rich green, leathery, glossy; very vigorous, bushy growth

Marybeth Min, m, 1994, Williams, Ernest D.; flowers pastel mauve, very dbl., high-centered, borne mostly singly, moderate fragrance; foliage small, medium green, semi-glossy; few prickles; medium (18-20 in.), upright growth; [seedling × Twilight Trail]; int. by Texas Mini Roses, 1994

Marycka Magdanová Pol, dr, 1938, Böhm, J.; flowers small, semi-dbl.

Maryellen Min, pb, 1981, Lemrow, Dr. Maynard W.; flowers deep pink, yellow center, 5 petals, borne 3 or more per cluster; foliage small, deep green; prickles triangle-shaped; upright growth; [Darling Flame × seedling]

Maryke-Marika F, ob, 1975, Kordes; bud medium, ovoid; flowers orange, base yellow, dbl., globular; foliage glossy; vigorous, upright growth; [Colour Wonder × Zorina]; int. in 1973

Marylea Johnson Richards HT, ab, 1992, Williams, J. Benjamin; flowers light pink with peach tones, medium, full, borne mostly singly and in small clusters, intense fragrance; foliage medium size, dark green, semi-glossy; few prickles; medium (3-4 ft.), upright, bushy growth; [Royal Highness × Command Performance]

Marylène HT, mp, 1965, Gaujard; bud long, pointed; flowers pearl-pink, medium, dbl.; foliage dark, glossy; upright growth; [Mignonne × Queen Elizabeth]

Marylene S, ob; flowers orange; free-flowering; moderate (3 ft.) growth

Marylka Min, Wituszynski, B.; int. in 1967

Mary's Delight HT, pb, Kordes; bud long, pointed; flowers deep pink blend, dbl., high-centered, intense fragrance; recurrent; growth vigorous; int. by Ludwig's Roses, 1999

Mary's Favorite F, dp, 1994, Hemphill, William J.; flowers deep pink, 3-3½ in., dbl., borne in small clusters; foliage large, medium green, semi-glossy, disease-resistant; few prickles; medium (48-54 in.), upright, compact growth; [Pink Favorite × unknown]

Mary's Memory F, pb, 2003, Roszko, Terry; flowers medium pink, reverse white, 2½-3 in., very full, borne in small clusters, moderate fragrance; foliage medium size, dark green, semi-glossy; prickles in., typical, pink, few; growth bushy, medium; bedding, specimen; [Gold Marie × Morden Blush]; int. by Terry Roszko, 2005

Mary's Pink HT, mp, 1952, Spanbauer; bud long, pointed; flowers Neyron rose, 4-4½ in., 32 petals; foliage leathery; vigorous, compact, bushy growth; [sport of Better Times]

Mary's Pleasure - The Mary Woods Rose MinFl, dp, 2006, Paul Chessum Roses; flowers 3 cm., dbl., borne in small clusters; foliage medium size, light green, semi-glossy; prickles small, sharp, pink, few; growth compact, medium (12 in.); garden decorative, containers; [seedling × seedling]; int. by World of Roses, 2005

Mary's Pride LCl, rb, 2005, Jerabek, Paul E.; flowers dark red, reverse red shaded silver, 3 in., dbl., borne in small clusters, slight fragrance; foliage medium size, medium green, semi-glossy; prickles moderate, 7/16 in., triangular; upright, short growth; [unknown × unknown]; int. by Freedom Gardens, 2008

Marysa Pol, w, 1936, Brada, Dr.; flowers pure white, moderate lily-of-the-valley fragrance; vigorous growth; int. by Böhm

Maryse Kriloff – See **Lucy Cramphorn**, HT

Maryse Kriloff, Climbing Cl HT, or, Kriloff; flowers large, dbl.; int. in 1984

Marytje Cazant Pol, ab, 1927, van Nes; bud globular; flowers coral-pink, borne in large clusters; dwarf growth; [sport of Jessie]

Masako – See **Eglantyne Jebb**, S

Masarykova Jubilejni HT, dr, 1931, Böhm, J.; flowers velvety red shaded black, very large, single; foliage dark, glossy; vigorous growth; [sport of Blanta]

Masaryk's Jubilee – See **Masarykova Jubilejni**, HT

Masaryk's Jubileums-Rose – See **Masarykova Jubilejni**, HT

Masayuki HT, w, Keisei; int. by Keisei Rose Nurseries, 1992

Mascara HT, m, Meilland; bud conical, medium; flowers bengal pink, 25 petals, high-centered, borne mostly singly, no fragrance; recurrent; foliage medium size, leathery; prickles average, medium, tan; growth upright (4 ft.); PP8342; florist rose; int. by Meilland Intl., 1992

Mascotte HT, mp, 1951, Meilland, F.; bud pointed; flowers hermosa pink, 4 in., dbl.; foliage dark; vigorous growth; [Michèle Meilland × Pres. Herbert Hoover]

Mascotte '77 HT, yb, 1977, Paolino; flowers yellow, edged cardinal-red, 4½ in., 40 petals; foliage glossy; vigorous growth; [(MEIrendal × (Rim × Peace)) × Peace]; int. by URS; Gold Medal, Belfast, 1979

Masked Ball HT, pb, 1968, Schwartz, Ernest W.; bud globular; flowers scarlet and gold, large, dbl., moderate fragrance; foliage dark, glossy; vigorous, bushy growth; [Masquerade × Peace]; int. by Wyant, 1966

Masquerade F, rb, 1949, Boerner; bud small, ovoid, yellow; flowers bright yellow turning salmon-pink and then dark red, 2½ in., 17 petals, borne in clusters of 10-25; foliage leathery, dark; vigorous, bushy, compact growth; [Goldilocks × Holiday]; int. by J&P; Gold Medal, NRS, 1952

Masquerade, Climbing Cl F, rb, 1958, Dillian; int. by Gregory

Masquerade HT, pb, Kordes; flowers bright pink with white eye and reverse, dbl., high-centered, slight fragrance; growth to 3-4 ft.; int. in 2006

Massabielle HT, w, 1958, Guillot, M.; flowers well-formed, large; upright growth

Massara F, Sauvageot; int. in 1995

Massey University – See **Pride of Scotland**, HT

Master David HT, pb, 1949, Cox; flowers pink, reverse carmine, pointed, 4 in., 25 petals; almost thornless; vigorous growth

Master Hugh S, dp, 1970, Mason, L.M.; flowers rich rose-pink, 2½-3 in., 5 petals, borne in clusters; [*R. macrophylla* × unknown]; int. by Sunningdale Nursery

Master John Cl HT, or, 1944, Duehrsen; flowers fiery orange-red, base gold, large, dbl., globular, intense fragrance; profuse spring bloom, then scattered until fall; foliage glossy, dark; very vigorous, climbing growth; [Ednah Thomas × Golden Rapture]; int. by California Roses

Masterpiece HP, mp, 1880, Paul, W.; flowers carmine pink, very large, full, globular; [Beauty of Waltham × unknown]

Matador HT, dr, 1935, Van Rossem; bud long, pointed; flowers scarlet-crimson, shaded darker, large, very dbl., cupped; foliage leathery, dark; vigorous, bushy growth; [(Charles P. Kilham × unknown) × Étoile de Hollande]; int. by J&P; Gold Medal, Portland, 1940

Matador, Climbing Cl HT, dr, 1938, Western Rose Co.

Matador F, ob, 1972, Kordes, R.; bud ovoid; flowers light scarlet and orange, reverse gold, medium, dbl., high-centered; foliage large, dark, leathery; vigorous growth; PP3229; [Konigin der Rosen × Zorina]; int. by J&P, 1972

Matador – See **Rosy Carpet**, S

Matangi F, rb, 1975, McGredy, Sam IV; bud ovoid; flowers orange-red, silver eye and reverse, large, 30 petals; foliage small; bushy growth; [seedling × Picasso]; int. by McGredy Roses Int., 1974; President's International Trophy, RNRS, 1974, Gold Medal, Rome, 1974, Gold Medal, Portland, 1982, Gold Medal, Belfast, 1976

Matangi, Climbing Cl F, ob, Chiplunkar; int. in 1985

Matawhero Magic – See **Top Notch**, HT

Matchball HMsk, w, 2000, Lens, Louis; flowers white, pink shade, reverse white, 1½ in., single, borne in large clusters, moderate fragrance; recurrent bloom; foliage medium size, medium green, semi-glossy, disease-resistant; prickles moderate; growth bushy, medium (80-100 cm.); hedge, border; [*R. multiflora adenocheata* × Kathleen]; int. by Louis Lens N.V., 1990; Gold Medal, Baden-Baden, 1991

Matchless HT, dp, 1926, Duckham-Pierson Co.; flowers cerise-pink, dbl.; upright, bushy growth; [sport of Premier]

Mateo's Silk Butterflies Ch, mp, Lettunich; flowers medium pink fading almost to white, single, slight fragrance; free-flowering; growth upright (4 ft.); int. in 1992

Mater Casta S

Mateus Rose HT, pb, 1973, Winship; flowers peach, reverse pale pink, 4 in., 20 petals; [Pink Parfait × Mme Butterfly]

Mathé Altéry – See **Dresden**, HT

Matherin Regnier HP, lp, 1855, Lévêque; flowers medium, full

Mathilde – See **Niphetos**, T

Mathilde Bernard HP, m, 1860, Bernède; flowers velvety purple, full

Mathilde Jesse P, dp, 1847, Laffay; flowers flame pink

Mathilde Kärger Pol, dp, 1929, Kärger; flowers carmine-pink, medium, dbl.

Mati Bradová HT, dp, 1934, Brada, Dr.; flowers dark rose-pink, sometimes almost carmine, very large, dbl.; foliage glossy, dark; very vigorous, bushy growth; [Gorgeous × Gen. MacArthur]; int. by Böhm

Matilda F, pb, 1988, Meilland, Alain A.; bud oval, small; flowers light yellow, edged and suffused pink, 9-10 cm., 15-20 petals, flat, borne in clusters of 1-7, no fragrance; foliage medium size, dark green, semi-glossy; prickles moderate, large, tan; upright, low, compact, proliferous growth; PP7667; [Coppelia 76 × Nirvana]; int. by SNC Meilland & Cie; Gold Medal, Courtrai, 1987, Gold Medal, Bagatelle, 1987

Matilda – See **Graf Lennart**, HT

Matilda, Climbing – See **Seduction, Climbing**, Cl F

Matilda HT, my, Meilland; flowers dbl., high-centered, borne mostly singly; florist rose; int. by Meilland Intl., 2004

Matilda Campbell HT, dp, 1952, Campbell; bud ovoid; flowers bengal rose, 5-6½ in., very dbl., high-centered, intense fragrance; foliage glossy; vigorous, bushy growth; PP1274

Matilda Jones F, ab, 2007, Dawson, John F.; flowers dbl., borne in small clusters; foliage medium size, medium green, semi-glossy; prickles average, hooked, numerous; growth bushy, medium (3 ft.); [Laura Ford × Fulton Mackay]; int. by David E Lister, 2008

Matka Vlast HWich, pb, 1934, Böhm; flowers pink, striped red and white, small, full; [sport of Dorothy Perkins]

Matson Modesty HT, lp, 1946, Prosser; flowers pale pink, 4 in., 60 petals; vigorous growth; [Mrs Sam McGredy × Heinrich Wendland]

Matsuo-Hime HT, lp, 1999, Shimizu, Junji; flowers pale pink, 5½ in., 31-33 petals, high-centered; foliage medium green; growth to 4½ ft.; [Hatakeyama × Yonina]; int. in 1991; Silver Medal, Japan Rose Concours, 1995

Matsuri LCl, rb, Keisei; flowers striped; int. by Keisei Rose Nurseries, 1994

Matterhorn HT, w, 1965, Armstrong, D.L. & Swim, H. C.; flowers medium to large, dbl., high-centered; foliage leathery; very tall, upright growth; PP2688; [Buccaneer × Cherry Glow]; int. by Armstrong Nursery; Gold Medal, Portland, 1964

Matthew Duckett HT, or, 1999, Jones, L.J.; flowers 2 in., dbl., borne mostly singly; foliage medium size, medium green, bronze when new, semi-glossy; few prickles; upright, tall growth; [Solitaire × (Alexander × Remember Me)]

Matthew's Surprise T, lp, 1889, Matthews, H.

Matthias Meilland F, mr, 1988, Meilland, Mrs. Marie-Louise; flowers large, dbl., no fragrance; foliage medium size, dark green, glossy, disease-resistant; upright, floriferous growth; [(Mme Charles Sauvage × Fashion) × (Poppy Flash × Parador)]; int. by SNC Meilland & Cie, 1985

Mattie Eloise S, w, 2003, Nicholls, Deborah; flowers pale lavender, reverse light lavender, 4 in., full, borne mostly solitary, intense lavender fragrance; foliage medium size, medium green, semi-glossy; prickles ¼ in., needle, green/brown, moderate; growth compact, medium (3 ft.); [Blue Girl × Blue Moon]; int. by Deborah Nicholls, 2002

Mattinata HT, Voightlander

Matty HT, dp, 1994, Marciel, Stanley G. & Jeanne A.; flowers deep pink, 3-3½ in., dbl., borne mostly singly; foliage large, medium green, matte; some prickles; tall (97 cm.), upright growth; [(Happiness × seedling) × (Emily Post × Visa)]; int. by Sakai Brothers Rose Co., 1993

Maturity HT, mp, 1974, LeGrice; flowers rose-pink, pointed, 7 in., 50 petals; foliage large, dark; free growth; [Duftwolke × Lively]; int. in 1973

Maud HT, pb, 1921, Paul, W.; flowers salmon-pink

Maud Alston – See **Mrs Alston's Rose**, Pol

Maud Betterton HT, mp, 1965, Gregory; flowers rose-pink, medium, dbl.; vigorous growth; int. by Gregory & Son, 1958

Maud Cole F, m, 1968, Harkness; flowers mauve-purple, dbl.; foliage dark, glossy; [Lilac Charm × Africa Star]

Maud Cuming HT, op, 1923, Dickson, A.; bud pointed; flowers coral-pink, shaded peach and orange, very large, dbl., high-centered; foliage dark, glossy; vigorous, bushy growth

Maud Dawson HT, or, 1915, Dickson, A.; flowers orange-red, large, dbl., intense fragrance

Maud E. Gladstone Pol, pb, 1926, Bees; bud pointed; flowers malmaison pink, shaded coral and chrome-yellow, small, dbl., globular; foliage rich green, leathery, glossy; vigorous, bushy growth; [Orléans Rose × Edward VII]

Maud Little T, mp, 1891, Dingee & Conard; flowers full

Maud Nash HT, mr, 1942, Clark, A.; flowers rich red with fire; upright growth

Maud Nunn F, ly, 1989, Driscoll, W.E.; bud pointed; flowers creamy yellow, aging paler lemon yellow, loose, small, 16 petals, high-centered; foliage medium green, semi-glossy; prickles green; bushy, medium growth; [Rise 'n' Shine × Rise 'n' Shine]; int. in 1988

Maude Elizabeth S, mr, 2006, Beales, Amanda; flowers 8 cm., single, borne in large clusters; foliage medium size, dark green, semi-glossy; prickles average, straight, numerous; growth compact, spreading, bushy, short (60 cm.); landscape, containers; [Robin Redbreast × Cuthbert Grant]; int. by Peter Beales Roses, 2000

Maude Sumner F, ob; int. in 1994

Mauget M, dp, 1840, Prévost; flowers medium, full

Mauna Loa HT, mr, 1937, H&S; flowers bright red, large, dbl.; foliage heavy

Maupertuis M, mp, 1868, Moreau et Robert; bud very mossy; flowers rosy-pink, medium, full; some repeat

Maure de Venise – See **Othello Maure de Venise**, HCh

Maureen Elizabeth HT, ab, 2005, Webster, Robert; flowers pale apricot, 5 in., full, borne in small clusters, moderate fragrance; foliage medium size, dark green, glossy; prickles moderate, 10 mm., triangular; growth upright, medium (42 in.); garden; [Samantha Barker × Golden Future]; int. in 2006

Maureen Hendzel HT, dp, 1974, Concord Floral Co.; buds medium, ovoid; flowers deep pink, large, very dbl., cupped, borne singly, strong spicy fragrance; foliage medium size, glossy; few prickles; growth vigorous, upright (4-6 ft.); [sport of Forever Yours]; int. in 1973

Maureen Lipman Min, pb, Cowlishaw, Frank

Maureen MacNeil F, op, 1967, Vincent; flowers salmon, borne in clusters; moderate growth; [Anna Wheatcroft × Orangeade]

Maureen Thompson HT, dr, 1949, Cant, B. R.; bud pointed; flowers 3 in., 35 petals; foliage leathery; very vigorous growth; int. by Bosley Nursery

Maurice – See **McGredy's Triumph**, HT

Maurice S, mr, Williams, J.B.; int. by Hortico, Inc., 2005

Maurice Bernardin HP, mr, 1861, Granger; bud vermilion; flowers bright crimson, moderately large, dbl., borne in clusters, intense fragrance; vigorous growth; [Général Jacqueminot × unknown]; probably re-introduced by Verdier in 1869 as Ferdinand de Lesseps

Maurice Chevalier HT, mr, 1959, Delbard-Chabert; bud long; flowers rich red shaded garnet, large, 25 petals; foliage glossy; vigorous growth; [Incendie × (Floradora seedling × Independence)]

Maurice Lepelletier HP, dr, 1868, Moreau et Robert; flowers vermilion red

Maurice Noyelle HT, 1951, Buatois

Maurice Perrault HP, dr, 1869, Vigneron; flowers glowing dark cherry red, large, full

Maurice Rouvier T, pb, 1890, Nabonnand; bud long; flowers delicate pink, lightly veined red, pale on outer edge, very large, very full; foliage light green; prickles medium

Maurice Utrillo F, rb, Delbard; flowers red with white stripes, dbl., moderate earthy fragrance; growth to 80 cm.; int. in 2003

Maurice Vilmorin HP, rb, 1868, Lédéchaux; flowers garnet-crimson to purple-maroon, dbl.; profuse bloom, sometimes repeated

Mauricette Sistau Pol, w, 1925, Turbat; flowers pure white to rosy white, large, dbl., borne in clusters of 25-50; thornless

Maurine – See **Bangsbo**, F

Maurine Neuberger Min, mr, 1989, Spooner, Raymond A.; bud pointed; flowers medium, 30 petals, high-centered, borne singly, moderate fragrance; foliage medium size, medium green, matte; prickles needle-like, light brown; upright, medium growth; hips ovoid, light green; PP7772; [(Prominent × Zinger) × Centerpiece]; int. by Oregon Miniature Roses

Mauve – See **Bourbon**, HGal

Mauve Mallerin – See **Simone**, HT, 1958

Mauve Melodee HT, m, 1963, Raffell; bud long, pointed, purple; flowers rose-mauve, 4½-5 in., dbl., moderate fragrance; foliage dark, leathery; vigorous, upright growth; [Sterling Silver × seedling]; int. by Port Stockton Nursery

Maverick Min, rb, 1995, Laver, Keith G.; flowers red with white stripes and patches, large, dbl., high-centered, borne mostly singly; free-flowering; foliage medium size, medium green, dull; some prickles; upright, bushy, medium growth; [Striped Pet × Apricot Doll]; int. by Springwood Roses, 1995

Maverick – See **Mavrik**, HT

Mavis Ballinger HT, mr, 2001, Horner, Colin P.; flowers medium red, paler reverse, 8 cm., dbl., borne mostly solitary, moderate fragrance; foliage medium size, dark green, semi-glossy; prickles small, curved, moderate; growth compact, medium (90 cm.); garden decorative; [Coral Reef × Isobel Derby]

Mavis Campbell HT, dp, 1942, Clark, A.; bud long, deep pink; vigorous, tall growth

Mavourneen HT, lp, 1895, Dickson, A.; flowers pale silvery pink

Mavourneen S, rb, 1985, Buck, Dr. Griffith J.; bud medium-large, ovoid, pointed; flowers medium red, white reverse, large, 23 petals, borne in clusters of 1-10; repeat bloom; foliage large, leathery, semi-glossy, dark; prickles awl-like, tan; erect, bushy growth; [(Tickled Pink × Prairie Princess) × El Catala]; int. by Iowa State University, 1984

Mavrik HT, pb, 2000, Edwards, Eddie; flowers pink, reverse white, 5-6 in., full, high-centered, borne mostly singly, slight fragrance; foliage large, dark green, glossy; few prickles; growth upright, tall (5-6 ft.); [Louise Estes × Signature]; int. by Johnny Becnel Show Roses

Mawson F, w, 2001, Thomson, George L.; flowers medium, full, borne in large clusters, moderate fragrance; foliage medium size, dark gren, glossy; prickles medium, hooked; growth compact, medium (1 m.); garden decorative; [(Iceberg × unknown) × (Francis Phoebe × unknown)]; int. by Ross Roses, 2002

Max Colwell Min, or, 1975, Moore, Ralph S.; bud long, pointed; flowers orange-red to red, 1½ in., 25 petals; foliage leathery; bushy, spreading growth; PP3963; [red floribunda seedling × (Little Darling × miniature seedling)]; int. by Sequoia Nursery

Max Graf HRg, pb, 1919, Bowditch; flowers bright pink, petals somewhat crinkled, prominent golden stamens, 7-8 cm., single, borne in small clusters, slight musky fragrance; non-recurrent; foliage glossy, rugose, small; prickles numerous, reddish-brown; vigorous, bushy, trailing growth; groundcover; hardy; [*R. rugosa* × *R. wichurana*]

Max Haufe HEg, lp, 1939, Kordes; bud long, pointed, dark pink; flowers large, semi-dbl.; seasonal bloom; foliage large, leathery, light; somewhat arching, very vigorous (5-7 ft.), trailing growth; [Joanna Hill × *R. rubiginosa*]

Max Hesdörffer HT, dp, 1903, Jacobs; flowers deep rose, bordered with silvery rose, large, dbl., moderate fragrance; [Kaiserin Auguste Viktoria × unknown]

Max Krause HT, yb, 1930, Krause; flowers reddish-orange, opening golden yellow, very large, dbl.; foliage dark, glossy; vigorous growth; [Mrs Beckwith × Souv. de H.A. Verschuren]; int. by J&P

Max Krause, Climbing Cl HT, yb, 1940, Moreira da Silva; flowers buff yellow, reverse apricot, large

Max Krause Superior HT, op, 1940, Heizmann, E.; flowers coppery pink, very large, very dbl.

Max Schmeling F, or, 1973, Tantau, Math.; bud ovoid; flowers large, dbl.; foliage large, glossy; upright, bushy growth; [unknown × unknown]; int. by Ahrens & Sieberz

Max Singer – See **Rosiériste Max Singer**, HMult

Max Vogel HT, op, 1929, Leenders, M.; flowers coppery orange, large, very dbl.; foliage bronze; [Fritz Maydt × Lilly Jung]

Maxi F, rb, 1971, McGredy, Sam IV; flowers red, white eye, 3 in., 12 petals; free growth; [(Evelyn Fison × (Tantau's Triumph × *R. macrophylla coryana*)) × (Hamburger Phoenix × Danse de Feu)]; int. by McGredy

Maxi Vita F, op, 2006, W. Kordes' Söhne; flowers orange pink with yellow-orange petal base, 5 cm., semi-dbl., borne in large clusters, no fragrance; foliage medium size, fresh green, semi-glossy; compact, moderate, 60-70 cm. growth; int. by W. Kordes' Söhne, 2001

Maxim F, op, 1965, Tantau, Math.; bud ovoid; flowers salmon-pink, large, dbl., borne in broad clusters; foliage leathery; vigorous, bushy growth; int. by Buisman, 1963

Maxim HT, rb, Tantau; flowers cream white flushed carmine, deepens with age, dbl., high-centered, moderate fragrance; growth strong, vigorous; int. in 1993

Maxima – See **Majestueuse**, HGal

Maxima – See **Goliath**, C

Maxima – See **Alba Maxima**, A

Maxima – See **Regina**, C

Maxima – See **Maxima Hit**, MinFl

Maxima Hit MinFl, ob, Olesen; bud pointed ovoid; flowers orange and orange blend, 5 cm., 60-70 petals, hybrid tea, borne singly, very slight fragrance; recurrent; foliage dark green, matte; prickles some, 5 mm., linear; narrow, bushy (20-40 cm.) growth; PP15044; [Mandy Kordana × Vanilla Kordana]; int. by Poulsen Roser, 2002

Maxima Multiplex – See **Rose des Peintres**, C

Maxima Multiplex A, w, before 1829, possibly Prévost; sepals foliaceous; flowers white, slightly yellow at center, large

Maxime – See **Maxim**, HT

Maxime Buatois Pol, yb, 1900, Buatois; flowers fiery copper-yellow, aging to carmine pink, medium, full; [Étoile de Mai × Laurette Messimy]

Maxime Corbon HWich, rb, 1918, Barbier; flowers dark coppery red turning apricot-yellow, 6-7 cm., dbl., borne in small clusters, moderate fragrance; abundant seasonal bloom; foliage rich green, glossy, leathery; vigorous, climbing and trailing growth (8-18 ft.); [*R. wichurana* × Léonie Lamesch]

Maxime de la Rocheterie HP, dr, 1871, Vigneron; flowers velvety blackish purple red, large, full

Maximin Chabuel HT, op, 1943, Mallerin, C.; int. by A. Meilland

Maxine F, rb, 1957, Silva; bud globular, creamy pink; flowers camellia-red becoming maroon flecked pink and white, rosette, 37-40 petals, flat, moderate fragrance; foliage leathery, glossy; very vigorous, low, bushy growth; PP1879; [Pinocchio × Crimson Glory]; int. by Booy Rose Nursery

Maxine S, dp, Williams, J. Benjamin; bud cherry red; flowers single to semi-dbl.; growth prostrate; int. by Hortico Inc., 1999

Maxine's Sister S, dp, Williams, J.B.; bud cherry red; flowers dark red, single to semi-dbl.; growth prostrate; int. by Hortico, 2000

Maxistar HT, or, 1979, Huber; bud round; flowers 5½-6 in., 70-80 petals; foliage dark, leathery; vigorous, upright growth; [Duftwolke × Pharaon]; int. in 1975

May Alexandra Lippiat HT, dp, 1909, Lippiat; flowers dark pink

May Banks T, ly, 1938, Banks; flowers lemon-yellow; [sport of Lady Hillingdon]

May Graham F, ab, 1996, Kenny, David; flowers coppery apricot, fading to pink, medium, 26 petals, borne in small clusters, slight fragrance; foliage medium size, medium green, glossy; numerous prickles; medium (3½ ft.), bushy growth; [Prominent × Kiskadee]

May Kenyon Slaney HT, dp, 1911, Dickson, A.; flowers dark pink, lighter at base, large, full, moderate fragrance

May Lawlor HT, w, 1993, Kirkham, Gordon Wilson; flowers cream and pink, 2¾-3 in., dbl., borne mostly singly, intense fragrance; foliage large, dark green, semi-glossy; numerous prickles; tall, upright growth; [Morgengruss × Mary Sumner]

May Lyon HT, mp, 1983, Cocker, James; flowers large,

35 petals; foliage large, medium green, glossy; bushy growth; [((Anne Cocker × Arthur Bell) × National Trust) × Silver Jubilee]; int. by Cocker & Sons, 1983

May Martin HT, ly, 1918, Martin & Forbes Co.; flowers pure canary-yellow, center darker, semi-dbl.; [sport of Ophelia]

May Miller HT, op, 1911, E.G. Hill, Co.; flowers coppery pink, large, dbl., moderate sweet fragrance; recurrent; [seedling × Paul Neyron]

May Queen HWich, lp, 1898, Van Fleet; bud light red; flowers lilac-pink, 7-8 cm., semi-dbl., flat, borne in small to medium clusters, intense fruity fragrance; occasional repeat; foliage glossy, rounded; vigorous, climbing or groundcover growth; [*R. wichurana* × Mrs DeGraw]

May Quennell HP, mr, 1878, Postans; flowers fiery crimson, petal edges shaded magenta and carmine, large, very full

May Rivers T, w, 1890, Rivers; flowers cream white, center citron yellow, large, full

May Robinson F, op; flowers bright salmon-pink

May Taylor HT, dp, 1966, Taylor, L.R.; flowers deep rose-pink, large, dbl., high-centered; foliage soft; vigorous, bushy growth; [Tassin × Ballet]

May Turner HP, op, 1874, Verdier, E.; flowers light salmon pink, reverse darker, very large, full, moderate fragrance

May Wettern HT, mp, 1928, Dickson, A.; bud pointed; flowers rosy pink, large, dbl., high-centered; foliage rich green, leathery; vigorous, bushy growth; Gold Medal, NRS, 1928

May Woolley F, ab, 1976, Wood; flowers bronze-apricot to peach, 2½-3 in., 25-25 petals, cupped; foliage small, glossy; moderate, free growth; [Fairlight × Arthur Bell]

Maya F, or, 1986, Kriloff, Michel; flowers borne in clusters; foliage dense, bright; low growth; [Zorina × Lara]

Maya Kordana Min, ab, Kordes; flowers copper-yellow, full; growth compact; [sport of Vanilla Kordana]; container rose; int. by NewFlora, 2005

Maya Lee HT, or, 1992, Jerabek, Paul E.; flowers 3-3½ in., 50 petals, borne mostly singly; foliage medium size, medium green, semi-glossy; numerous prickles; long stems; medium (100+ cm.), upright growth; [unknown × unknown]

Maybe Baby Min, pb, 2000, Giles, Diann; flowers medium, dbl., high-centered, borne in small clusters, no fragrance; foliage medium size, medium green, matte; few prickles; growth upright, medium; int. by Giles Rose Nursery

Maybelle Stearns – See **Mabelle Stearns**, S

Mayday F, lp, 1959, Boerner; bud ovoid; flowers white overcast pink, 3 in., 25-30 petals, cupped, borne in clusters, moderate fragrance; foliage rich green, leathery; vigorous, bushy growth; PP1625; [((Pinocchio × unknown) × Unnamed Hybrid Tea) × Fashion]; int. by J&P, 1956

Mayet HT, mr, 1958, Dot, Pedro; flowers crimson-red passing to Neyron pink, base yellow, well-formed, 30 petals, intense fragrance; foliage olive-green; vigorous growth; [Condesa de Sástago × Mme Henri Guillot]; int. in 1951

Mayfair HT, dp, 1935, Bentall; flowers deep pink, well-formed, large; foliage bronze; very vigorous growth

Mayflower T, w, 1910, Hill, E. G.; flowers cream white, edges shaded pink, large

Mayflower HT, pb, 1960, Gregory; flowers light cerise, reverse silvery pink, 4 in., 30 petals, intense fragrance; foliage glossy; vigorous growth; [Eden Rose × unknown]; int. in 1958

Maylina Cl HT, w, 1916, Gersdorff; flowers silvery white, reverse Killarney pink to shell-pink, very large, dbl., cupped, moderate spicy fragrance; abundant, intermittent bloom; foliage large, soft; growth vigorous, climbing (15 ft.); [white climber × Killarney]

Mayor Baker HT, or, 1928, Thomas; flowers terra-cotta to scarlet, base light orange, semi-dbl.; vigorous growth; [Mons. Paul Lédé × Hadley]

Mayor Cermák HT, dr, 1932, Böhm, J.; flowers very dark red, shaded purple, large; vigorous, branching growth; [Mrs Henry Winnett × Vaterland]; int. by J&P, 1934

Mayor of Casterbridge S, lp, 1997, Austin, David; flowers very dbl., 90 petals, old-fashioned, borne in small clusters; foliage medium size, light green, leathery; some prickles; upright, medium (3½ × 2½ ft.) growth; int. by David Austin Roses, Ltd.

Maysa HT

Maytime LCl, lp, 1953, Maney; bud red; flowers flesh-pink, reverse rose-pink, 5-6 in., single, borne in clusters of 5; profuse, non-recurrent bloom; foliage leathery; vigorous growth; [*R. maximowicziana pilosa* × Betty Uprichard]; int. by Iowa State College

Maytime S, pb, 1975, Buck, Dr. Griffith J.; bud ovoid, pointed; flowers carmine-rose, base yellow, shallowly-cupped, 3½-4 in., single, cupped, moderate fragrance; repeat bloom; foliage dark, leathery; upright, bushy growth; [Elegance × Prairie Princess]; int. by Iowa State University

Maywonder Pol, or, Grootendorst; int. in 1968

Maywood HT, mr, 1924, Joseph H. Hill, Co.; flowers bright red, dbl.; [Charles K. Douglas × (Killarney × Ophelia)]; int. by Amling Bros.

Maywood Red HT, mr, 1923, E.G. Hill, Co.; [Premier × seedling]; int. by J.H. Hill Co.

Mazeppa HGal, rb, before 1841; flowers red, edged and marbled with white, medium, dbl.

Mazowsze HT, dp, 1966, Grabczewski; bud oblong; flowers deep pink edged lighter, dbl.; foliage leathery; very vigorous growth; [Marella × unknown]

Mazurka F, mp, 1965, Verbeek; bud ovoid; flowers pink, medium, dbl., borne in clusters; foliage dark

Mazurka F, mp, Meilland; flowers dbl., borne in clusters; int. in 1995

Mazzini HT, w, 1925, Easlea; flowers blush-white suffused pink, dbl.; [Mme Butterfly × Gladys Holland]

McCallun House T, ly

McCartney Rose – See **The McCartney Rose**, HT

McGredy's Coral HT, op, 1936, McGredy; flowers coral-pink, overlaid salmon, shaded copper, large, high-centered; foliage dark cedar-green; very vigorous, branching growth

McGredy's Gem HT, lp, 1933, McGredy; bud pointed; flowers creamy pink, base yellow, deepening to rose-pink edges, full, cupped, slight fragrance; very vigorous growth

McGredy's Ivory HT, w, 1930, McGredy; bud long, pointed; flowers creamy white, base yellow, large, 28 petals, high-centered, moderate damask fragrance; foliage dark, leathery, glossy; vigorous growth; [Mrs Charles Lamplough × Mabel Morse]; int. by Dreer; Gold Medal, NRS, 1928

McGredy's Ivory, Climbing Cl HT, w, 1939, Raffel; int. by Port Stockton Nursery

McGredy's Orange HT, ob, 1936, McGredy; flowers deep Indian yellow, reverse orange, flushed salmon, dbl., high-centered; foliage dark, bronze; vigorous growth; [sport of Mrs Sam McGredy]

McGredy's Peach HT, op, 1933, McGredy; bud pointed; flowers creamy yellow, washed salmon, very large, cupped; foliage glossy, dark; vigorous growth; Gold Medal, NRS, 1932

McGredy's Perfection HT, lp, 1936, McGredy; flowers large, dbl.

McGredy's Pillar HT, or, 1935, McGredy; flowers terra-cotta

McGredy's Pink HT, lp, 1936, McGredy; flowers bright rose, outer petals pearly cream and pink, base saffron; foliage dark; vigorous, branching growth; int. by J&P

McGredy's Pride HT, op, 1936, McGredy; bud long, pointed; flowers orange and salmon-pink, flushed saffron-yellow, reverse yellow, dbl.; [Angèle Pernet × Mrs Charles Lamplough]; int. by J&P; Gold Medal, NRS, 1936

McGredy's Salmon HT, ab, 1940, McGredy; bud pointed; flowers apricot-salmon, dbl.; foliage dark, wrinkled; strong stems; vigorous, compact growth; [Mrs Henry Morse × seedling]; int. by J&P

McGredy's Scarlet HT, mr, 1930, McGredy; flowers medium, 35 petals, high-centered; foliage leathery, glossy; vigorous growth

McGredy's Sunset HT, ob, 1936, McGredy; bud long, pointed; flowers chrome-yellow shading to scarlet, reverse clear buttercup-yellow, 40 petals, globular, moderate fragrance; foliage glossy, bronze; vigorous growth; [Margaret McGredy × Mabel Morse]; int. by J&P

McGredy's Sunset, Climbing Cl HT, ob, 1957, Shamburger, P.; PP1633

McGredy's Triumph HT, dp, 1934, McGredy; flowers soft rose flushed orange, very large, dbl., high-centered; foliage dark reddish bronze, glossy; strong stems; vigorous, branching growth; [Admiration × seedling]; int. by J&P; Gold Medal, NRS, 1932

McGredy's Triumph, Climbing Cl HT, dp, 1948, Simmonds Nursery

McGredy's Wonder HT, ob, 1934, McGredy; flowers coppery orange, flushed orange-red, reverse orange-red, large, semi-dbl., cupped, moderate fruity fragrance; foliage glossy, olive-green; vigorous growth

McGredy's Yellow HT, my, 1933, McGredy; bud long, pointed; flowers bright buttercup-yellow, large, 30 petals, cupped; foliage glossy, bronze; vigorous growth; [Mrs Charles Lamplough × (The Queen Alexandra Rose × J.B. Clark)]; Gold Medal, Portland, 1956, Gold Medal, NRS, 1930

McGredy's Yellow, Climbing Cl HT, my, 1937, Western Rose Co.

McMillan's Pink – See **Affirm**, HT

McMillan's Yellow HT, my

Me Darling F, pb, 1971, Anderson's Rose Nurseries; flowers cream suffused pink, 3½-4 in., 37 petals, high-centered; foliage glossy, light; [Evelyn Fison × Dearest]

Me-Gami HT, op, 1985, Suzuki, Seizo; flowers medium salmon-pink, large, 33 petals, high-centered, moderate fragrance; foliage dark, leathery; upright growth; [seedling × Fragrant Cloud]; int. by Keisei Rose Nursery, 1984

Me Too F, lp, 1998, Muha, Julius; flowers pink-purple, white eye, white reverse, ½-1½ in., 8-14 petals; foliage small, light green, dull; prickles moderate; upright, medium growth; [MACkaukaup × Nickelodeon]; int. by Garden Jules, 1999

Meadow – See **Meadow Cottage**, S

Meadow Cottage S, my, Olesen; bud ovate; flowers medium yellow, small, semi-dbl., open cup to flat, borne usually in clusters of 7, slight fragrance; recurrent; foliage dark green, semi-glossy; prickles numerous, 9 mm., hooked downward, yellow-green; low (40 cm.), spreading growth; PP16303; [Diamond Head × seedling]; int. by Poulsen Roser, 2004; Certificate of Merit, Belfast, 2006

Meadow Dancer Min, lp, 1991, Gruenbauer, Richard; bud ovoid; flowers medium, 45 petals, cupped, no fragrance; foliage medium size, medium green, semi-glossy; spreading, tall growth; [sport of Judy Fischer]; int. by Flowers 'n' Friends Miniature Roses, 1990

Meadow Fresh Min, ab, Bell; flowers soft pink and buff apricot; free-flowering; growth medium

Meadow Rose – See ***R. blanda*** (Aiton)

Meadow Ruby S, mr, 1982, James, John; flowers large, very dbl., high-centered, borne singly, moderate fragrance; repeat bloom; foliage leathery; prickles long, red; vigorous, upright growth; [Prairie Princess × (Queen Elizabeth × Borealis)]; int. in 1978

Mécène HGal, pb, 1845, Vibert; flowers white, striped with rose and light pink, compact, medium, dbl.; prickles shoots very smooth; erect, moderate growth

Mecertsar – See **Concerto, Climbing**, Cl F

MeChabaku F, mp, Poulsen; flowers dbl., cupped, borne in clusters; recurrent; stems short; growth tall (2 m.); int. by Ludwig's Roses, 2000

Mechak HT, dr, 1983, Pal, Dr. B.P.; flowers very large, 20 petals, high-centered, no fragrance; foliage medium size, dark, smooth; prickles brown; upright growth; [Samourai × seedling]; int. by Arand Roses, 1979

Mechliniae S, lp; flowers very similar to *R. rubrifolia*; foliage touched with mauve

Mechtilde von Neuerburg HEg, mp, 1920, Boden-Kurtscheid; flowers pure pink, 1 in., semi-dbl., borne in corymbs; foliage typical sweetbriar; vigorous (10 × 10 ft.) growth; hips large, crimson; very hardy

Mecklenburg LCl, lp, Lützow; int. by Gartenbau Lützow, 1999

Meda HSet, op, 1942, Horvath; flowers shrimp-pink, open, imbricated, 3½-4 in., 40-60 petals, intense fragrance; foliage large, leathery; long stems; very vigorous, climbing (10-12 ft.) growth; [(*R. setigera* × Mme Butterfly) × Golden Dawn]; int. by Wayside Gardens Co.

Medal of Honor – See **American Spirit**, HT

Medallion HT, ab, 1972, Warriner, William A.; bud long, pointed; flowers light apricot, very large, dbl., moderate fragrance; foliage large, leathery; vigorous, upright growth; PP2997; [South Seas × King's Ransom]; int. by J&P, 1973; Gold Medal, Portland, 1972

Medea T, ly, 1890, Paul, W.; flowers lemon yellow with silk-yellow center, large, very full

Medeo F, w, Kordes; flowers cream; growth vigorous, medium, healthy; [sport of Kiss]; int. in 1991

Medeo S, w, 2006; flowers white, blushed pink, 3 cm., single, flat, borne in large clusters; foliage small, dark green, glossy; moderate, low, spreading (60 × 80 cm.) growth; groundcover; int. by W. Kordes' Söhne, 2003

Medialis HT, mr, Hetzel; int. in 1993

Mediator HT, op, 1949, Totty; flowers coral-pink shading to salmon base, medium, 45 petals, high-centered; foliage soft, dark green; vigorous, bushy growth

Medima – See **Victor Borge**, HT

Medina HT, w, 1918; [sport of Sunburst]; int. by White Bros., 1923

Mediterranea HT, pb, 1943, Dot, Pedro; flowers carmine with yellow, passing to pink with white markings, 5 in., very dbl., high-centered; upright growth; [sport of Signora]

Medley HT, lp, 1962, Boerner; bud pointed; flowers bright salmon-pink, reverse flushed yellow, 5-5½ in., 35-40 petals, cupped, moderate fragrance; foliage leathery; vigorous, upright growth; PP2200; [HT seedling × Pageant]; int. by J&P, 1962

Medley Pink Min, mp, Noack; flowers 6 cm., dbl., borne in clusters; recurrent; growth to 10-14 in.; int. by Noack Rosen, 2003

Medley Red Min, mr, Noack; flowers 6 cm., dbl., cupped, borne in clusters; recurrent; growth to 10-14 in.; int. by Noack Rosen, 2003

Medley Soft Pink Min, lp, Noack; flowers 6 cm., dbl., borne in clusters; recurrent; growth to 10-14 in.

Medusa S, m, Noack, Werner; flowers lavender-pink, 2 in., dbl., borne in clusters; good repeat; bushy (80-100 cm.) growth; int. by Noack Rosen, 1996

Méduse HT, m, 1981, Gaujard, Jean; flowers lavender red, 35 petals, moderate fragrance; foliage large, dark, semi-glossy; upright growth; [Chenonceaux × Tropicana]; int. by Roseraies Gaujard, 1980

Meduse – See **Simone Merieux**, HT

Mee Maw MinFl, pb, 2006, Sproul, James A.; flowers reverse lighter, 2 in., dbl., high-centered, borne in small clusters; foliage medium size, medium green, semi-glossy, resistant to powdery mildew; prickles medium, few; growth bushy, medium (24-36 in.); [(Lynn Anderson × Tournament of Roses) × Hot Tamale]; int. in 2006

Meera Min, pb, 2001, Siddiqui, Tariq; flowers medium pink with darker edges, large, high-centered, borne mostly solitary, slight fragrance; foliage medium size, medium green, matte; prickles moderate; growth upright, tall (24 in.); garden decorative, exhibition; [Irresistible × select pollen]

Meerzicht Glory – See **Orange Delight**, HT

Meg Cl HT, ab, 1954, Gosset; flowers salmon-apricot, stamens red, 5½ in., 10 petals, borne in large clusters, moderate fragrance; recurrent bloom; foliage dark, glossy; vigorous growth; [probably Paul's Lemon Pillar × Mme Butterfly.]; int. by Harkness; Gold Medal, NRS, 1954

Meg Merrilies HEg, dp, 1894, Penzance; flowers rosy crimson, center white, small, single to semi-dbl., moderate fragrance; summer bloom; foliage very fragrant; very vigorous (10 ft.) growth; [*R. rubiginosa* × HP or B]; int. by Keynes, Williams & Co.

Megami – See **Me-Gami**, HT

Megan HT, pb, 1981, Adams, Dr. Neil D.; bud pointed; flowers white with pink petal edges, high-centered, borne 3-5 per cluster; foliage medium green, glossy; prickles broad, slightly hooked; upright, strong growth; [Daily Sketch × seedling]; Bronze Medal, ARC TG, 1981

Megan Dolan HT, mp, 1989, Marciel, Stanley G.; bud urn-shaped; flowers small, sweetheart, 18 petals, cupped, borne singly, slight spicy fragrance; foliage medium size, dark green; prickles declining, copper brown with olive green tinges; upright, tall growth; PP7520; [Angel × Independence '76]; int. by DeVor Nurseries, Inc.

Megan Louise HT, pb, 1981, Erich Welsh Roses; bud ovoid; flowers silvery pink, deep pink petal edges, large, 48 petals, high-centered, borne in clusters of 1-5, intense fragrance; foliage matte, green, tough; prickles red-brown; short, bushy growth; [Red Lion × Silver Lining]; int. by Australian Rose Society & Roy Rumsey Ltd., 1983

Megan's Melody HT, mr, 2003, Harris, Peter G.; flowers medium red, reverse lighter, medium to large, dbl., high-centered, borne mostly solitary, strong fragrance; foliage large, dark green, semi-glossy; prickles large, hooked, moderate; growth upright, tall (4-7 ft.); garden decorative, exhibition; [Granada × Karl Herbst]; int. by Ashdown Roses, 2004

Megastar HT, or, 1981, Sohne, W. Kordes; bud globular; flowers very dbl., cupped, borne singly, intense fruity fragrance; foliage light green; prickles curved yellow-brown; int. by Rose Barni-Pistoia, 1978

Megastar '04 HT, mr; flowers cardinal red, slow opening, 12 cm., dbl., high-centered, moderate fragrance; recurrent; growth strong, medium (80-110 cm.); int. by Rose Barni, 2005

Megenaris F, rb, Olesen; flowers red with tones of yellow and orange, 8-10 cm., dbl., borne in small clusters, slight fragrance; foliage dark, glossy; growth bushy, medium (60-100 cm.); int. by Poulsen Roser, 1998

Meggie Min, lp

Meghan's Arrival F, mr, 1995, Bull, Derek Gordon; flowers small, full, borne in large clusters; foliage medium size, light green, glossy; some prickles; upright, bushy, medium (1 m.) growth; [Doris Tysterman × unknown]; int. in 1986

Meghdoot HT, w, 1974, Pal, Dr. B. P.; buds large, long pointed; flowers large, dbl, cupped, borne singly; foliage medium size, leathery; numerous prickles; growth very vigorous, upright (170 cm.); int. by IARI, 1972

Megiddo F, or, 1971, Gandy, Douglas L.; flowers bright orange-red, 4½ in., 25 petals, borne in clusters, slight fragrance; recurrent; foliage large, olive-green, glossy; upright growth; [Coup de Foudre × S'Agaro]; int. by Gandy's Roses, Ltd., 1970; Trial Ground Cert., RNRS, Silver Medal, Germany

Meher HT, mp, 1998, Pavri, Nadir J.; flowers medium pink, lighter reverse, 3-3½ in., full, high-centered, borne mostly singly, moderate fragrance; free-flowering; foliage medium size, medium green, semi-glossy; prickles numerous small and large; growth upright, tall (5 ft.); [American Heritage × Paradise]

Méhul HGal, m, 1826, Cartier; flowers carmine-violet, large, very full

Méhul B, mp, 1846, Guillot; flowers carmine

Mei S, lp, Komatsu; int. by Komatsu Garden

Meiburgana HT, mr, 1981, Meilland, Mrs. Marie-Louise; flowers large, dbl.; foliage medium size, dark, semi-glossy; upright growth; [((seedling × Independence) × Suspense) × (((Alain × Mutabilis) × Caprice) × Pharaoh)]; int. as Miriana, Meilland Et Cie, 1982

Meidiland Alba – See **Alba Meidiland**, S

Meidirapo HT, dr, 1976, Paolino; flowers red to purple, 3½-4 in., 25 petals, cupped; vigorous growth; [(Queen Elizabeth × (Peace × Michele Meilland)) × (Baccará × seedling)]; int. by Meilland

Meifluney Min, dp, 1984, Meilland, Mrs. Marie-Louise; flowers deep pink, medium, dbl.; foliage medium size, medium green, matte; bushy growth; [(Alain × Fashion) × (Rumba × (Zambra × Cinderella))]; int. by Meilland Et Cie

Meigerium HT, or, 1976, Paolino; flowers light vermilion-red, 4-4½ in., 35 petals; foliage glossy; very vigorous growth; PP3803; [(Romantica × Tropicana) × ((Show Girl × Baccará) × Romantica)]; int. by URS

Mei-li HCh, pb, Dening; bud dark pink; flowers light pink, dbl., borne in sprays; growth to 2 × 2 ft.; [*R. chinensis minima* × unknown]; int. by Brentwood Bay Nurseries, 2007

Meilland Decor Arlequin – See **Decor Arlequin**, S

Meilland Decor Rose – See **Anne de Bretagne**, S

Meilland Rosiga 83 – See **Rose Iga**, F

Meillandina Min, mr, 1976, Paolino; bud globular, medium; flowers currant-red, then imbricated, 1½-1¾ in., 30-35 petals, cupped, then flat, borne in clusters, no fragrance; foliage yellow-green, matte; vigorous, bushy (16-20 in.) growth; [Rumba × (Dany Robin × Fire King)]; int. by URS

Mein München F, yb, Cocker; flowers yellow and red, large, dbl.; int. in 1987

Mein Rubin HT, dr, 1986, Teranishi, K.; flowers urn-shaped, well-formed, 35 petals, borne usually singly; foliage medium size, medium green, semi-glossy; prickles medium, lavender; medium, bushy growth; [(Helene Schoen × Charles Mallerin) × (Helene Schoen × Charles Mallerin)]; int. by Itami Rose Nursery, 1984

Mein Schöner Garten S, mp, 2006, W. Kordes' Söhne; flowers soft pink with a breath of salmon, center lighter, 9 cm., dbl., borne in small clusters, slight fruity, fresh fragrance; foliage medium size, dark green, very glossy; growth compact, medium (120 cm.); int. by W. Kordes' Söhne, 1997

Meinartemi F, Meilland

Meindeert Hobbema S, rb, Williams, J. Benjamin; flowers red, striped ivory and pink, semi-dbl.; landscape shrub; int. by Hortico Inc., 1997

Meine Oma – See **Bossa Nova**, F

Meinustrel F, Meilland

Meirinlor HT, my, 1976, Paolino; flowers 4 in., 15-18 petals; foliage dark; [Golden Garnette × ((Golden Garnette × Bettina) × Dr. A.J. Verhage)]; int. by URS

Meisogrel – See **White MiniJet**, Min double

Meisterstück F, mr, 1940, Kordes; bud ovoid; flowers velvety crimson, large, dbl., cupped, borne in clusters; foliage dark, glossy; upright, bushy growth; [Holstein × Kardinal]

Meitoflapo F, mp, 1985, Meilland, Mrs. Marie-Louise; flowers large, 29 petals, no fragrance; foliage small, dark, semi-glossy; [(Jack Frost × (Zambra × (Baccará × White Knight))) × ((Zambra × (Baccará × White Knight)) × seedling)]; int. by Meilland Et Cie, 1980

Meiwonder Pol, mr, 1965, Grootendorst, F.J.; bud globular; flowers small, dbl., borne in clusters; [sport of Marianne Kluis Superior]

Mel Hulse M, m, 2001, Barden, Paul; bud moderately mossed and scented of balsam; flowers dark crimson/mauve, medium crimson/magenta reverse, large, full, borne in large clusters, slight fragrance; medium size, medium green, young leaves bright green, semi-glossy; prickles 1/4-1/2 in., straight, red and straw color, numerous; growth bushy, medium (2-3 ft tall × 2-3 ft. wide); specimen, containers; [Scarlet Moss × The Prince]

Mel Lippincott Gr, rb, Williams, J. B.; flowers burgundy red with ivory-pink striping, borne in clusters; int. by Hortico, 1998

Mel Rince Min; int. by Keihan Gardening, 2000

Melanie S, dr, 1946, Wright, Percy H.; flowers deep red, semi-dbl.; non-recurrent; foliage reddish; hardy (to about -15); [*R. rubrifolia* × Gruss an Teplitz]

Melanie HT, dp, 1958, Combe; bud long; flowers carmine-pink, dbl.; vigorous growth; [Sterling × Mme Auguste Chatain]; int. by Japan Rose Society

Melanie Min, op, 1989, McGredy, Sam IV; bud ovoid; flowers light salmon-pink, reverse lighter, small, 23 petals, cupped, borne in sprays of 20-25; foliage small, medium green, semi-glossy; prickles straight, red-brown; bushy, low growth; [Seaspray × Wanaka]; int. by Sealand Nursery, 1989

Mélanie Cornu HP, m, 1841, Cornu; flowers bright reddish-violet, large, full

Mélanie de Montjoie HSem, w, before 1829, Jacques; flowers pure white, large, full, flat, borne in corymbs; foliage widely-set, small, lanceolate, glossy; prickles few, equal, straight, thin; stems smooth, tinted reddish; vigorous growth

Mélanie Lemarié – See **Hermosa**, Ch

Mélanie Soupert T, w, 1881, Nabonnand, G.; flowers pure white, large, very full; [Gloire de Dijon × unknown]

Mélanie Waldor HGal, 1836, Vibert

Mélanie Waldor M, m, 1865, Moreau et Robert; flowers lilac pink, white center, medium, flat; some repeat

Mélanie Willermoz – See **Mme Mélanie Willermoz**, T

Melany – See **Amie Renaissance**, S

Melba F, yb, 1963, Sanday, John; flowers soft cream and peach, well-formed, small, dbl., borne in clusters; foliage light green; spreading growth; [Masquerade × (Independence × unknown)]

Melba – See **Times Past**, LCl

Melba Jean Min, dp, 2001, Giles, Diann; flowers small, dbl., borne in small clusters, slight fragrance; foliage small, dark green, matte; prickles large, straight, few; growth upright, low; garden decorative, exhibition; [seedling × seedling]; int. by Giles Rose Nursery, 2001

Melchior Salet – See **Salet**, M

Meleagris – See **Pintade**, HGal

Meletta Min, ob, 2000, Giles, Diann; flowers apricot, medium, dbl., high-centered, borne mostly singly, slight fragrance; foliage medium size, dark green, semi-glossy; growth compact, medium; int. by Giles Rose Nursery

Melflor F, lp, RvS-Melle; int. in 1988

Melglory F, mr, 1985, Rijksstation Voor Sierplantenteelt; flowers large, 23 petals, borne in clusters of 4-16, no fragrance; foliage dark, matte; upright growth; [Lilli Marleen × Patricia]; int. in 1982

Melgold HT, dy, 1985, Rijksstation Voor Sierplantenteelt; flowers large, 62 petals, cupped, borne singly and in small clusters, no fragrance; foliage dark, matte; prickles reddish-green; upright growth; [Sunblest × Souv. de Jacques Verschuren]; int. in 1980

Meli-Melo HT, rb, Orard; flowers clear red, white reverse, striped yellow, slight fragrance; growth medium, vigorous; int. in 1998

Melica HT, op, Hicl

Melik El Adel – See **Malek-Adel**, HGal

Melina – See **Sir Harry Pilkington**, HT

Melinda HT, rb, 1983, deRuiter, George; flowers scarlet, gold reverse, large, 35 petals, moderate fragrance; foliage medium size, dark, glossy; upright growth; [Whisky Mac × Criterion]; int. by Fryer's Nursery, Ltd., 1980

Melinda Claire Min, m, 1990, Taylor, Thomas E.; bud pointed; flowers reddish-magenta, yellow stamens, small to medium, 15 petals, high-centered, borne usually singly; foliage medium size, medium green, semi-glossy; prickles curved downward, small, widely spaced, brownish; hips globular, medium, orange; [Charmglo × Charmglo]; int. by Michigan Mini Roses, 1990

Melinda Gainsford – See **Anne Morrow Lindbergh**, HT

Melinda Marie F, lp, 1977, Linscott; bud ovoid; flowers clear light pink, 3 in., 20-25 petals, flat; foliage dark, leathery; bushy growth; [Sarabande × Sarabande]; int. in 1972

Mélisande HT, lp, 1964, Mondial Roses; bud long; flowers soft pink, reverse darker, well-formed, large, dbl.; foliage dark; long, strong stems; vigorous, symmetrical growth

Melissa HT, mp, 1977, McDaniel, Earl; flowers 4 in., 27-32 petals, globular; foliage leathery; very vigorous, upright, bushy growth; PP4082; [seedling × seedling]; int. by Carlton Rose Nurseries, 1975

Melissa Min, rb, Martin, J.; int. in 1985

Melissa F, lp, Noack, Werner; int. in 1996

Mélissa HT, dy, Sauvageot; flowers chrome yellow, tinted at center with salmon, dbl.; int. in 2003

Melissa Joyce – See **Silver Phantom**, Min

Melissa McCartney F, dp, 1991, Troyer, Ray & Pat; bud ovoid; flowers hold color well, do not fade, 5 in., 36 petals, high-centered, borne usually singly; foliage medium size, dark green, glossy, slight red tinge to new growth; growth bushy, low (70 cm.); [sport of Cherish]

Melita HWich, mp, 1934, Easlea; flowers carnation-pink, 5-6 cm., dbl., borne in small to medium clusters; non-recurrent; foliage glossy, light; vigorous, climbing growth; [sport of Thelma]; Gold Medal, NRS, 1933

Melle Fischer Pol, mp, 1914, Pfitzer; flowers small, dbl.

Mellow HT, ab, Dawson; int. in 1995

Mellow Glow HT, pb, 1990, Bridges, Dennis A.; bud ovoid; flowers medium pink, reverse creamy yellow, medium, 52 petals, high-centered, borne usually singly, intense damask fragrance; foliage medium size, medium green, semi-glossy; prickles pointed slightly downward, large, yellow; bushy growth; [Thriller × Wild Cherry]; int. by Bridges Roses, 1990

Mellow Yellow HT, my, 1968, Waterhouse Nursery; flowers sunflower-yellow, edged pink, urn-shaped; free growth; [sport of Piccadilly]

Mellow Yellow HT, dy, 2000, Carruth, Tom; bud pointed to slightly ovoid; flowers solid yellow, 10-12 cm., 39-44 petals, cupped, borne mostly singly or in clusters of 2 or 3, moderate fruity fragrance; good repeat; foliage medium size, dark green, semi-glossy; prickles moderate; growth upright, vigorous, bushy, medium (110-150 cm.); PP14401; [O Sole Mio × Midas Touch]; int. by Weeks Roses, 2002

Mellow Yellow F, yb, 2004, Cocker, A.G.; flowers golden, reverse lighter, 2½-3 in., full, borne in large clusters, moderate fragrance; foliage large, medium green, glossy; prickles 6 mm., straight; growth upright, tall (2½-3 ft.); garden decorative; [Princess Alice × (Sunblest × Fyvie Castle)]; int. by James Cocker & Sons, 2004

Melmore Terrace HSem, w

Melo-melo-day Cl F, mp, 1955, Motose; bud ovoid; flowers cameo-pink, 2-2½ in., very dbl., cupped, moderate fragrance; climbing (10-15 ft.) growth; PP1428; [sport of Demure]

Melodie F, mr, Noack, Werner; int. in 1980

Mélodie HT, ly, Dickson; flowers creamy pale lemon with white, well-formed, dbl.; good repeat; growth to 90-100 cm.; int. in 1999

Melodie Parfumée – See **Melody Parfumée**, Gr

Melodie Parfumée, Climbing Cl HT, m; [sport of Melodie Parfumee]; int. in 2004

Melody HT, yb, 1911, Scott/Dickson; flowers intense saffron yellow bordered spring yellow, medium to large, very dbl.; foliage dark violet green

Melody HT, pb, 1946, Lammerts, Dr. Walter; bud urn-shaped; flowers deep pink, edged lighter, large, 35 petals; low, bushy growth; [Joanna Hill × Miss C.E. van Rossem]; int. by Armstrong Nursery

Melody HT, lp, Kordes; bud long, pointed ovoid; flowers 4½ in., 30-35 petals, high-centered, borne mostly singly, slight fragrance; good repeat; foliage large, dark green; prickles numerous, medium, hooked downward; stems long, strong; growth vigorous, upright; PP7509; [Lorena × Emily Post]; int. in 1991

Melody – See **Melody Hit**, MinFl

Melody Hit MinFl, dp, Poulsen; flowers deep pink, 5-8 cm., dbl., no fragrance; growth narrow, bushy, 40-60 cm.; PP11514; int. by Poulsen Roser, 1998

Melody Lane Min, m, 1991, Williams, Michael C.; flowers small, full, borne in small clusters, no fragrance; foliage small, medium green, semi-glossy; low (6 cm.) growth; [Lavender Jewel × Party Girl]; int. by The Rose Garden & Mini Rose Nursery, 1992

Melody Maker F, or, 1990, Dickson, Patrick; flowers light vermillion with silver reverse, large, full, high-centered, borne in clusters; foliage medium size, dark green, semi-glossy; bushy growth; [Anisley Dickson × Wishing]; int. by Dickson Nurseries, Ltd., 1991; Rose of the Year, 1991

Melody Marshall Min, ly, 1993, Moore, Ralph S.; flowers large, dbl., borne mostly singly; foliage medium size, medium green, semi-glossy; no prickles; medium (25-35 cm.), upright, bushy growth; [sport of Mary Marshall]; int. by Sequoia Nursery, 1989

Melody Parfumée Gr, m, 1998, Dorieux, Francois; bud long, pointed ovoid; flowers dark lavender-plum, lighter reverse, 4½ in., 25-30 petals, high-centered, borne in large clusters, intense damask fragrance; recurrent; foliage medium size, dark green, semi-glossy; prickles moderate, straight; stems strong, 14-18 in; bushy, upright, 5 ft. growth; PP11014; [Dioressence × Stephens' Big Purple]; int. by Bear Creek Gardens, Inc., 1995

Melody Queen HT, pb, Ghosh, Mr. and Mrs. S.; bud conical; flowers white with pink glow, large; int. in 1998

Melonda HT, ob, J&P; flowers yellowish salmon-orange, very large, dbl.; int. in 1974

Melpink F, lp, RvS-Melle; [Centurion × Patricia]; int. in 1983

Melrose HT, rb, 1963, Dickson, A.; flowers creamy white flushed cherry-red, large, 35 petals; foliage dark, leathery; vigorous, bushy growth; [Silver Lining × E.G. Hill]

Melrose F, dp, RvS-Melle; flowers 3 in., 24 petals, borne in large clusters, intense fragrance; growth to 2 ft.; [Melflor × Melglory]; int. in 1992; Gold Medal, Durbanville, 1994, Gold Medal, Orléans, Gold Medal, Geneve, 1990

Melvena HT, op, 1972, Dawson, George; bud ovoid; flowers salmon-pink, medium, dbl., moderate fragrance; foliage leathery; vigorous, upright growth; [Daily Sketch × Impeccable]

Melvin F, rb, 1981, Jerabek, Paul E.; bud pointed; flowers ivory, flushed red, aging darker red, 30 petals, high-centered, borne in clusters of up to 11; foliage medium green; prickles triangular, hooked; medium, dense growth; [seedling × seedling]; Bronze Medal, ARC TG, 1980

Mémé Buy HT, or, 1935, Chambard, C.; flowers coppery coral-red, lightly streaked golden yellow, large, very dbl., cupped; foliage bronze; very vigorous growth

Mémée Arles HT, dr, 1955, Arles; flowers deep red tinted vermilion; foliage glaucous green; [Peace × Emma Wright]; int. by Roses-France

Mémée Azy HT, pb, 1921, Gillot, F.; flowers pink shaded carmine, bordered whitish, stamens orange-yellow, dbl.; [Étoile de France × Le Progres]

Mémée Chanteur F, dr, 1961, Arles; bud ovoid; flowers deep crimson, large, dbl., cupped, borne in clusters; foliage dark, leathery; vigorous, upright growth; [Karl Herbst × Pioupiou]; int. by Roses-France, 1959

Memento F, rb, 1978, Dickson, Patrick; bud globular; flowers salmon-red, 3 in., 22 petals, cupped, borne in clusters; free-flowering; foliage sage green; bushy growth; [Bangor × Anabell]; int. by Dickson Nurseries, Ltd.; Gold Medal, Belfast, 1980

Memoire HT, w, 2006; flowers pure white shaded cream, 11 cm., full, high-centered, borne mostly solitary, moderate tea fragrance; foliage large, dark green, glossy; growth upright, medium (70 cm.); int. by W. Kordes' Söhne, 1992

Memorial Day HT, mp, 2002, Carruth, Tom; bud globular to somewhat ovoid; flowers pink with orchid wash, reverse slightly darker, 12-14 cm., 28-52 petals, old-fashioned, borne mostly solitary, intense old rose fragrance; good repeat; foliage large, medium green, matte; prickles few, medium-small, slightly hooked, brownish-green; stems very well foliated, strong, medium to long; growth upright to somewhat spreading, medium (110-130 cm.); garden decorative; hips moderately obovate, somewhat flat at the top ; PP16572; [Blueberry Hill × New Zealand]; int. by Weeks Roses, 2002; AARS, 2004

Memorial Rose – See ***R. wichurana*** (Crépin)

Memoriam HT, lp, 1961, Von Abrams; bud long, pointed; flowers pastel pink to nearly white, 6 in., 55 petals, high-centered, moderate fragrance; foliage dark, leathery; moderately tall growth; PP2280; [(Blanche Mallerin × Peace) × (Peace × Frau Karl Druschki)]; int. by Peterson & Dering, 1961; Gold Medal, Portland, 1960

Memories HT, dy, 1979, Byrum; bud short, pointed, ovoid; flowers empire-yellow, 2½-3 in., 25-30 petals, high-centered, intense tea fragrance; continuous bloom in greenhouse; foliage large, glossy; vigorous, upright, bushy growth; PP4407; [Spanish Sun × Hoosier Gold]; int. by J.H. Hill Co., 1977

Memories S, mp, Clements, John K.; flowers warm pink, large, very full, moderate fragrance; free-flowering; foliage rich green; slightly spreading (4 × 3 ft.) growth; int. by Heirloom Roses, 1996

Memories Min, pb, 2000, Hamilton, Noel; flowers light pink, base lemon, reverse lighter, medium, full, high-centered, borne in small clusters, no fragrance; foliage medium size, medium green, glossy; few prickles; growth compact, medium (11 in.); [seedling × seedling]; int. by Coming Up Roses

Memory HT, pb, 1932, Cant, B. R.; bud pointed; flowers light pink to deeper pink, base yellow, very large, dbl., high-centered; foliage rich green, leathery; vigorous, compact growth; int. by J&P; Gold Medal, NRS, 1932

Memory – See **Memoire**, HT

Memory – See **Memory Hit**, MinFl

Memory HT, dp, Kordes; flowers bright magenta pink, medium, dbl., high-centered, borne mostly singly; int. by W. Kordes Söhne, 2001

Memory Bells – See **Newport**, S

Memory Hit MinFl, ob, Poulsen; flowers orange and orange blend, 5-8 cm., dbl., slight wild rose fragrance; foliage dark; growth bushy, 20-40 cm.; int. by Poulsen Roser, 2000

Memory Lane Min, lp, 1974, Moore, Ralph S.; bud ovoid; flowers rose-pink, small, very dbl.; foliage leathery; vigorous, dwarf, bushy growth; [(Pinocchio × William Lobb) × Little Chief]; int. by Sequoia Nursery, 1973

Memory Lane – See **Berleburg**, F

Memory Lane F, ab, 1994, Pearce, C.A.; flowers apricot-pink, 3-3½ in., full, borne in small clusters; foliage large, dark green, semi-glossy; some prickles; upright (60 cm.) growth; [Carol Ann × seedling]; int. by The Limes New Roses, 1995

Memory of D. M. Roy HT, w, Ghosh

Memphis S, mr, Poulsen; flowers bright red, fading as they mature, small, semi-dbl., slight wild rose fragrance; foliage dark, glossy; broad, bushy (60-100 cm.) growth; PP15111; int. as Intense Cover, Poulsen Roser, 2002

Memphis HT, dp, Select Roses, B.V.

Memphis Blues MinFl, m, 2005, Wells, Verlie W.; flowers mauve to red, reverse light mauve, 1½ in., dbl., borne mostly solitary; foliage medium size, dark green, glossy; prickles few, in., hooked; growth spreading, medium (2-3 ft.); exhibition, garden decorative; [seedling × Memphis Magic]; int. by Wells Mid-South Roses, 2005

Memphis Cajun MinFl, m, 2006, Wells, Verlie W.; flowers light mauve, reverse darker, 1¾ in., full, borne in small clusters; foliage medium size, dark green, glossy; prickles in., hooked, moderate; growth upright, medium (2½ ft.); garden, exhibition; [seedling × seedling]; int. by Verlie W. Wells, 2006

Memphis Heritage Gr, pb, 1969, Patterson; bud long, pointed; flowers pink blended with gold, large, dbl., high-centered, moderate fragrance; very vigorous, compact growth; PP3113; [Queen Elizabeth × Happiness]; int. by Patterson Roses

Memphis King MinFl, dr, 2002, Wells, Verlie W.; flowers bright, dark red, reverse red with orange base, medium, full, high-centered, borne singly and in small clusters, slight fragrance; foliage medium size, medium green, semi-glossy; prickles moderate, ¼ to ½ in., hooked; growth upright, medium; exhibition; [seedling × seedling]; int. by Wells' Midsouth Roses, 2003

Memphis Magic MinFl, dr, 2005, Wells, Verlie W.; flowers dark red / almost black, reverse red, 2½ in., dbl., borne in small clusters; foliage medium size, medium green, semi-glossy; prickles ½ in., hooked; upright, medium growth; garden decorative, exhibition; [seedling × Black Magic]; int. by Wells Mid-South Roses, 2004

Memphis Music MinFl, rb, 2006, Wells, Verlie W.; flowers dark red and yellow stripes, reverse yellow and red, 1½ in., dbl., borne mostly solitary; foliage medium size, medium green, semi-glossy; prickles few, in., straight; growth upright, medium (24-30 in.); show and garden; [sport of Memphis Magic]; int. by Verlie W. Wells / Wells Midsouth Roses, 2006

Memphis Queen Min, w, 1997, Wells, Verlie W.; flowers medium, very full, borne mostly singly, slight fragrance; foliage medium size, dark green, glossy; upright, medium (60 cm.) growth; PP11645; [Miss Pearl × Pacesetter]; int. by Wells Mid-South Roses, 1997

Ménage A, w, 1847, Vibert; flowers flesh, 6 cm., dbl., cupped

Ménage M, mp, 1858, Robert & Moreau; flowers bright carmine pink, 7-9 cm., full, flat

Menaka Durga Roy HT, dr, 1996, Driscoll, W.E.; flowers deep red, full, borne mostly singly, moderate fragrance; foliage medium size, medium green, lighter underside, semi-glossy; few prickles; upright, tall (3 ft.) growth; [(Silver Jubilee × (Red Planet × Blessings)) × (Parkdirector Riggers × Honey Favorite)]

Mendel F, mr, 1946, Leenders, M.; bud pointed; flowers cherry-red, 4 in., 15 petals, borne in trusses; foliage reddish green; vigorous, bushy growth; [Florentina × seedling]; int. by Longley

Mendocino Delight HWich, w, Demits; once-bloomer; growth to 20 ft.; int. in 1988

Menine HT, mr, Laperrière; flowers carmine red, moderate fragrance; int. in 1977

Menja HMsk, mp, Petersen; flowers medium pink when opening, fading quickly to pale pink, small, single, cupped, borne in medium clusters, slight fragrance; foliage light green; growth to 4-5 ft.; int. by Petersen, 1960

Mennie d'Agnin F, mr, 1962, Orard, Joseph; flowers vermilion-red, large; [Independence × Fashion]

Menoux B, lp, 1845, Lacharme; flowers light carmine pink, large, full

Menoux HMult, dp, 1848, Jobert; flowers pink, with a bluing edge, medium, full, borne in large clusters; [Laure Davoust × unknown]

Mentor S, mp, 1960, Wyant; bud globular; flowers light pink, reverse darker, medium, dbl., intense fragrance; recurrent bloom; foliage dark, glossy; very vigorous (6 ft.), bushy, upright growth; [Tallyho × New Dawn]; int. in 1959

Menuett HT, ob, Hill, S. H.; flowers orange and yellow, large, dbl.; int. in 1961

Menuett HT, yb, GPG Bad Langensalza; flowers dark yellow with carmine pink, large, dbl.; int. in 1988

Menut Min, dp, 1958, Dot, Simon; flowers carmine, small, 20 petals; abundant, intermittent bloom; dwarf, bushy, compact growth; [Rouletii × Perla de Alcanada]; int. in 1956

Méphisto F, or, 1951, Mallerin, C.; flowers geranium-red, medium, semi-dbl., borne in clusters; foliage leathery; vigorous, upright, bushy growth; [Francais × seedling]; int. by EFR

Mephisto Pol, or, GPG Bad Langensalza; flowers large, semi-dbl.; int. in 1985

Mercator HT, dr, 1962, Delforge; flowers deep red, large, dbl.; foliage dark; [Chrysler Imperial × Tango]

Mercedes HGal, lp, 1847, Vibert; flowers white and lilac, changing to pale pink, large, dbl., moderate fragrance; spring flowering; growth to 3-5 ft.

Mercedes HMult, lp, 1886, Geschwind; flowers pale lilac pink, medium; sometimes classified as HSet

Mercedes HRg, lp, 1900, Guillot, P.; flowers delicate

carnation pink on a white ground, outer petals white, large, full; very hardy

Mercedes F, or, 1975, Kordes, R.; bud ovoid; flowers bright scarlet, medium, 33 petals, high-centered; foliage large, leathery; PP3724; [Anabell × seedling]; greenhouse rose; int. by J&P, 1974

Mercedes, Climbing Cl F, or, Ruston, D.; [sport of Mercedes]; int. in 1982

Mercedes Gallart Cl HT, dp, 1932, Munné, B.; flowers deep pink, base yellow, very large, dbl.; recurrent bloom; foliage glossy; very vigorous, climbing growth; [Souv. de Claudius Denoyel × Souv. de Claudius Pernet]; int. by J&P

Mercedes Juncadella HT, op, 1933, Munné, B.; flowers salmon-orange; [Frau Karl Druschki × Angèle Pernet]

Mercedes Kordana Min, or, Kordes; flowers dbl., high-centered; recurrent; int. by W. Kordes Söhne

Mercedes Mendoza HT, or, 1962, Dot, Simon; flowers large, 30 petals; foliage glossy; vigorous growth; [Asturias × Grand'mere Jenny]

Mercedia HT, or, Kordes; greenhouse rose; int. by W. Kordes Söhne, 2002

Merci F, mr, 1972, Warriner, William A.; bud ovoid, long, pointed; flowers medium, dbl.; foliage dark, leathery; vigorous growth; int. by J&P, 1971

Merci F, mr, Kordes; flowers velvety red, small to medium, full, high-centered, flat top, borne mostly singly; free-flowering; stems moderate; florist rose; int. by W. Kordes Söhne, 2005

Mercurius LCl, op, 1940, Horvath; flowers light coral-pink, large, semi-dbl., cupped, borne in clusters; profuse seasonal bloom; foliage glossy; vigorous, climbing growth; [(Doubloons × Damask) × Clio]; int. by Wayside Gardens Co.

Mercury F, or, 1967, Sanday, John; flowers orange-scarlet edged mahogany, borne in clusters; foliage dark; low, bushy growth; [Independence × Paprika]

Mercury HT, mr, Kordes; flowers bright red, large, full, high-centered; foliage dark green, glossy; int. by Karl Zundel, 2005

Mercy HT, dr, Simpson

Mère de la Patrie – See **Moeder des Vaderlands**, F

Mère de St Louis HP, w, 1851, Lacharme; flowers waxy flesh-white aging to delicate pink, medium, dbl.

Mère Gigogne – See **Prolifera de Redouté**, C

Meredith LCl, lp, 1983, Thomson, Richard; flowers light pink to almost white, large, 20 petals, high-centered, moderate fragrance; repeat blooming; foliage large, dark, semi-glossy; long stems; upright (to 12 ft.) growth; [(Charlotte Armstrong × New Dawn) × Araby]; int. in 1984

Meredith HT, lp, 2002, Carruth, Tom; flowers very pastel pink, 10-12 cm., full, borne mostly solitary, intense fragrance; foliage large, dark green, glossy; prickles moderate, average, straight, light brown; growth upright, medium (90-110 cm.); garden decorative; [Karen Blixen × New Zealand]; int. by Weeks Roses, 2002

Meredith Anne Min, pb, 1984, Bennett, Dee; flowers salmon-pink, soft pink reverse, 23 petals, high-centered, borne in clusters; prickles brown to pale yellow; vigorous growth; [Sonia × Tea Party]; int. by Tiny Petals Nursery, 1983

Meredith Bohls S, mp, 2003, Ponton, Ray; flowers medium, full, borne in small clusters, slight fragrance; foliage medium size, medium green, semi-glossy; prickles medium, straight, moderate; spreading, medium (3-4 ft.) growth; [Brass Band × Lichterloh]; int. by Peaceful Habitations, 2003

Meredith Hughes Min, op, 1984, Dobbs, Annette E.; flowers medium coral pink, medium, dbl., high-centered; foliage medium size, medium green, glossy; bushy growth; [Anne Scranton × Patricia Scranton]

Merengue – See **Merengue Parade**, Min

Merengue – See **Dacapo**, LCl

Merengue Parade Min, yb, Poulsen; flowers yellow blend, medium, dbl., no fragrance; growth bushy, 20-40 cm.; int. by Poulsen Roser, 2003

Merete Stenbock HCh, w; flowers creamy white, suffused with rose-brown, dbl.; borne in small clusters; foliage dark green; vigorous (80 cm.) growth; int. by Walter Branchi, 1996

Mériame de Rothschild T, dp, 1897, Cochet; flowers carmine pink, edged silver, center darker, reverse shaded dark red, dbl.

Meridian HT, mr, VEG; flowers luminous red, very large, dbl.

Meridiana HT, op, Barni, V.; flowers vermilion-orange, full, intense fragrance; recurrent; growth to 90-110 cm.; int. by Rose Barni, 1994

Meriggio S, op, 1998, Barni, V.; flowers coral, edges darker, 15-20 petals, high-centered; growth to 130-150 cm.

Merindah HMult, mp, Sutherland; int. in 1994

Merindah Red HMult, mr, Sutherland; int. in 1995

Meringue Kisses Min, ab, 2003, Taylor, Pete & Kay; flowers apricot with yellow base, 1½ in., full, borne in small clusters, slight fragrance; foliage small, dark green, semi-glossy; prickles small, straight, brown; growth compact, medium (2 ft.); garden decorative; [unknown × unknown]; int. by Taylors Roses, 2003

Merit F, mp, 1952, Domilla; bud short, pointed; flowers brilliant rose, reverse lighter, base white, 1½-2 in., 50-90 petals, flat, borne in clusters; foliage leathery, dark; very vigorous, bushy growth; [sport of Garnette]; int. by Twin Nursery

Merit Min, ob, 1989, Spooner, Raymond A.; bud pointed; flowers brilliant orange, yellow base, reverse yellow, small, 17 petals, high-centered; foliage small, dark green, semi-glossy; prickles needle-like, brown; bushy, low growth; no fruit; [(Prominent × Zinger) × unnamed Miniature seedling]; int. by Oregon Miniature Roses

Merle Blanc S, lp, 1986, Lens, Louis; flowers blush pink, 2 in., 22 petals, borne in clusters of 3-22, intense fragrance; recurrent bloom; foliage dark; prickles hooked, brownish-green; tall, spreading growth; [Ballerina × Surf Rider]; int. in 1985

Merlin F, pb, 1967, Harkness; flowers yellow, pink and red, 2½ in., dbl., borne in clusters; foliage glossy; [Pink Parfait × Circus]

Merlin S, lp, Poulsen; int. in 1991

Merlot Min, rb, 2001, Benardella, Frank; flowers dark red, white washed reverse, 2 in., dbl., borne mostly singly or in small clusters, slight fragrance; foliage large, dark green, semi-glossy; prickles ¼ in., angled down, few; growth upright, medium (24-30 in.); exhibition, specimen, containers, cutting; PP16483; [Kristin × seedling]; int. by Nor' East Miniature Roses, 2002; Award of Excellence, ARS, 2002

Mermaid HBc, ly, 1918, Paul, W.; flowers creamy yellow, amber stamens, 5-6 in., 5 petals; dependably recurrent; foliage dark, glossy; vigorous, climbing, pillar or trailer (6-9 ft.) growth; tender in cold regions; [*R. bracteata* × double yellow Tea rose]; Gold Medal, NRS, 1917

Mermaid – See **Mermaid Palace**, Min

Mermaid Palace Min, or, Poulsen; flowers orange-red, 5 cm., dbl., no fragrance; foliage dark; growth bushy, 40-60 cm.; PP15570; int. by Poulsen Roser, 2003

Mernieuw – See **Romeo**

Merrie f, ab, 1994, Jellyman, J.S.; flowers apricot, pale pink, dbl., 30 petals, borne 6-20 per cluster; foliage medium size, dark green, semi-glossy; medium, upright, bushy growth; [Minnie Pearl × seedling]

Merrie England HP, pb, 1897, Harkness; flowers crimson pink, striped silvery; [sport of Heinrich Schultheis]

Merrie Miss HT, mp, 1975, Fuller; bud long, ovoid; flowers soft rose-pink, 4 in., 60 petals, high-centered, intense fragrance; foliage dark, matte; upright, bushy growth; [Pink Favorite × Margaret]; int. by Wyant

Merrimac Min, dr, 1989, King, Gene; bud pointed; flowers deeper at tips, medium, 18 petals, high-centered, borne usually singly and in sprays, slight fruity fragrance; foliage medium size, medium green, matte; prickles straight, small, red; upright, medium growth; hips ovoid, ornage; [(Alain × Scamp) × Lilli Marleen]; int. by AGM Miniature Roses, 1989

Merriment Min, yb, 1986, Bridges, Dennis A.; flowers bright yellow tipped red, reverse yellow edged red, 8 petals; foliage large, medium green, semi-glossy; prickles medium, long, pink; tall, upright growth; [Rise 'n' Shine × unknown]

Merry Christmas Min, mr, 1977, Lyon; bud pointed; flowers currant-red, open, 2 in., 5 petals; foliage dark; upright, compact, branching growth; [Red Can Can × unknown]; int. by L. Lyon Greenhouses

Merry England HP, mr, 1897, Harkness; flowers satiny light red, shaded carmine, 50 petals, intense fragrance; vigorous growth

Merry-Go-Round HT, op, 1950, Fisher, G.; bud pointed, becoming urn shaped, orange; flowers orange and pink blend, 5 in., 25 petals; foliage dark, leathery; tall, compact growth; [Talisman × R.M.S. Queen Mary]; int. by Arnold-Fisher Co.

Merry Go Round F, w; int. by Burston Nurseries, 2006

Merry Go Round F, rb; flowers green-white with thick petal edging of deep carmine, full, rosette, borne mostly in clusters; recurrent; healthy, vigorous, medium growth

Merry Heart Gr, rb, 1960, Swim, H.C.; bud ovoid; flowers Orient red, 3½-4 in., 30 petals, high-centered, borne in small clusters; foliage glossy, dark; vigorous, upright growth; PP1846; [El Capitan × seedling]; int. by C.R. Burr, 1960

Merry Widow Gr, dr, 1958, Lammerts, Dr. Walter; bud long, pointed; flowers velvety crimson, 6 in., 23 petals, cupped, intense spicy fragrance; foliage dark, glossy; vigorous growth; PP1711; [Mirandy × Grande Duchesse Charlotte]; int. by Germain's, 1957

Merryglo Min, m, 1995, Williams, Ernest D.; flowers medium lavender, 1¼ in., full, borne mostly singly, intense fragrance; foliage medium size, medium green, semi-glossy; some prickles; medium (18 in.), bushy growth; [seedling × Twilight Trail]; int. by Texas Mini Roses, 1995

Merryweather's Crimson HT, mr, 1958, Merryweather; flowers bright crimson, well-formed; strong stems; vigorous, bushy growth

Mers du Sud – See **South Seas**, HT

Merveille – See **Tausendschön**, HMult

Merveille d'Anjou HP, m, 1867, Touvais; flowers bright garnet-purple, very large, full

Merveille de Gien – See **Cesar E. Chavez**, HT

Merveille de la Brie HWich, mr; flowers scarlet red, white eye, 3-4 cm., semi-dbl., borne in medium clusters; once-blooming

Merveille de l'Univers HGal, rb, before 1827, from Belgium; flowers carmine, edged lilac, large, very full

Merveille de Lyon HP, w, 1882, Pernet Père; flowers pure white, tinted satiny rose, 4 in., dbl., cupped, borne mostly solitary; some recurrent bloom; foliage light green; prickles numerous, upright; vigorous growth; [Baronne Adolphe de Rothschild × Safrano]

Merveille des Blanches HP, w, 1894, Pernet; flowers medium-large, dbl.

Merveille des Jaunes Pol, yb, 1920, Turbat; flowers bright coppery golden yellow, dbl., borne in clusters; dwarf growth

Merveille des Polyanthas Pol, w, 1909, Mermet; flowers white, aging to lilac pink; foliage light green

Merveille des Rouges Pol, rb, 1911, Dubreuil; flowers deep velvety crimson, center whitish, semi-dbl., cupped, borne in large clusters; dwarf growth

Merveille du Monde – See **Roi des Pays-Bas**, D

Merveilleuse HT, Dot, Simon

Mervelle HT, McGredy, Sam IV; int. in 1995

Meryl Jane Gaskin HT, pb, 1948, Mee; flowers shell-pink edged deeper pink, well-formed, 5-6 in., 48 petals; free, branching growth; [sport of Rose Berkeley]; int. by Fryer's Nursery, Ltd.

Message – See **White Knight**, HT

Message, Climbing – See **White Knight, Climbing**, Cl HT

Message 91 HT, my, Meilland; flowers clear Naples yellow, full, high-centered; cut flower variety; int. by Meilland Intl., 1991

Messagere – See **Bettie Herholdt**, HT

Messara F, ab; flowers creamy vanilla with touches of rose, deepens with age, very dbl., hybrid tea, borne in clusters; growth compact; int. by Sauvageot, 1997

Messestadt Hannover F, mr, 1965, Kordes, R.; flowers large, dbl., borne in clusters; foliage light green, glossy; moderate growth; int. by Buisman, 1964

Messidor HT, dy

Messire LCl, mr, 1963, Laperrière; flowers bright scarlet red, 3 in., 10-15 petals, borne singly or in small clusters; profuse, repeated bloom; foliage bronze; moderately vigorous growth; [seedling × Spectacular]; int. by EFR

Messire Delbard Cl HT, dr, 1986, Delbard; flowers deep crimson red, well-formed, large, 38 petals, borne in small clusters; foliage large; vigorous (to 9 ft.) growth; [(Danse du Feu × Guinee) × ((Tenor × Fugue) × (Delbard's Orange Climber × Gloire de Dijon))]; int. in 1976

Meta T, rb, 1898, Dickson, A.; flowers strawberry red touched with saffron yellow

Metallina HT, r, Kordes; flowers metallic silver, opening to pale mauve; greenhouse rose; int. by W. Kordes Söhne, 1999

Metanoia LCl, ob; flowers semi-dbl.; growth to 10 ft.

Meteor HT, mr, 1887, Bennett; flowers crimson-carmine, open, dbl.; recurrent bloom; foliage small, soft; prickles few thorns; dwarf growth

Meteor N, dp, 1887, Geschwind, R.; flowers deep rose tinted carmine-purple, 7 cm., dbl., moderate fragrance; good repeat; vigorous growth

Meteor, Climbing Cl HT, mr, 1901, Dingee & Conard

Meteor F, or, 1959, Kordes, R.; flowers orange-scarlet, 3 in., 40 petals, cupped, borne in clusters (up to 10); foliage light green; vigorous, bushy, low growth; patio; [Feurio × Gertrud Westphal]; int. by A. Dickson; ADR, 1960

Meteor Shower F, mp, J&P; PP11736

Meteor Sparks Min, ob; int. by Hortico, Inc., 2004

Metis S, mp, 1975, Harp; bud ovoid; flowers soft rose, 2½-3 in., 35 petals, flat; spring bloom; foliage small, glossy; [*R. nitida* × Therese Bugnet]; int. by Morden Exp. Farm, 1967

Métro – See **Auckland Metro**, HT

Metropole HT, mp, 1961, deRuiter; flowers 4-6 in., 45 petals, globular; foliage matte, green; vigorous growth; [Sidney Peabody × Peace]; int. by Blaby Rose Gardens

Metset – See **Christian**, F

Mette – See **Mette Parade**, MinFl

Mette Parade MinFl, w, Poulsen; flowers white, 5-8 cm., full, no fragrance; recurrent; bushy (20-40 cm.) growth; int. by Poulsen Roser, 2004

Mevrouw A. del Court van Krimpen HT, lp, 1917, Leenders, M.; flowers flesh-white and pale pink, tinted copper, large, dbl., moderate fragrance; [seedling × Prince de Bulgarie]

Mevrouw A. H. de Beaufort HT, pb, 1934, Van Rossem; flowers clear salmon-pink, large, dbl.; foliage bronze, glossy; vigorous growth; [Morgenglans × Gooiland Beauty]

Mevrouw Amélie Müller HT, yb, 1927, Verschuren; flowers old-gold, shaded orange, dbl., moderate fragrance; growth to 3 ft.; [Golden Ophelia × Golden Emblem]

Mevrouw Boreel van Hogelander HT, w, 1918, Leenders, M.; flowers flesh-white shaded carmine and pink, medium, dbl., intense fragrance; [Mme Leon Pain × Mme Antoine Mari]

Mevrouw C. van Marwijk Kooy HT, w, 1921, Leenders, M.; flowers white, center Indian yellow, sometimes coppery orange, large, dbl., moderate fragrance; [Mme Caroline Testout × Mrs Aaron Ward]

Mevrouw D. A. Koster Pol, mr, 1934, Koster, D.A.; flowers bright red; [sport of Dick Koster]

Mevrouw Daendels – See **Mrs Henri Daendels**, HT

Mevrouw Dr L. Crobach HT, pb, 1928, Leenders, M.; flowers carmine, base salmon, dbl.; [Pink Pearl × Red Star]

Mevrouw Dora van Tets HT, mr, 1913, Leenders, M.; flowers velvety deep crimson, medium, dbl., moderate fragrance; [Farbenkonigin × Gen. MacArthur]; Gold Medal, Bagatelle, 1914

Mevrouw G. A. van Rossem HT, ob, 1929, Van Rossem; flowers orange and apricot on golden yellow, veined red, reverse often dark bronze, large, dbl., intense fragrance; foliage very large, dark, bronze, leathery; vigorous, upright growth; [Souv. de Claudius Pernet × Gorgeous]; int. by C-P

Mevrouw G. A. van Rossem, Climbing Cl HT, ob, 1937, Gaujard; flowers dark orange yellow, large, full; [sport of Mevrouw G. A. van Rossem]

Mevrouw G. de Jonge van Zwynsbergen HT, pb, 1923, Leenders, M.; flowers pale flesh, center flesh-pink and salmon, dbl.; [Mme Mélanie Soupert × George C. Waud]

Mevrouw H. Cremer HT, mr, 1932, Buisman, G. A. H.; flowers large, dbl.

Mevrouw Henri Daendels HT, op, 1931, Buisman, G. A. H.; flowers light salmon, large, very dbl.

Mevrouw L. C. van Gendt HT, ab, 1925, Van Rossem; flowers salmon-apricot on yellow ground, dbl.; [seedling × Golden Emblem]

Mevrouw Lala Philips HT, or, 1931, Leenders Bros.; flowers brilliant orange-toned shrimp-red, well-formed, large, dbl.; foliage dark; vigorous growth; [sport of Elvira Aramayo]

Mevrouw M. J. Gillon – See **Mrs M. J. Gillon**, HT

Mevrouw Nathalie Nypels Pol, mp, 1919, Leenders, M.; flowers rose-pink, medium, semi-dbl.; dwarf, spreading growth; [Orléans Rose × (Comtesse du Cayla × Jaune Bicolore)]

Mevrouw S. van den Bergh, Jr. – See **Mrs Vandenbergh**, HT

Mevrouw Smits Gompertz HT, op, 1917, Leenders, M.; flowers yellowish-salmon and coppery orange shaded lilac, medium, dbl., intense fragrance; [Lady Wenlock × (Mme J.W. Budde × Souv. de Catherine Guillot)]

Mevrouw van Straaten van Nes – See **Permanent Wave**, F

Mevrouw Welmoet van Heexk HT, dp, 1933, Buisman, G. A. H.; flowers carmine-red, well-formed; foliage dark; vigorous, bushy growth

Mexica Aurantia – See **Tricolore**, HGal

Mexicali Rose F, yb, 1957, Whisler; bud short, pointed, yellow suffused red; flowers deep yellow turning deep rose-pink, then cerise-red, open, 3 in., 65-70 petals, slight spicy fragrance; foliage dark; vigorous, upright growth; PP1496; [((Herrenhausen × unknown) × Golden Rapture) × Easter Parade]; int. by Germain's, 1956

Mexican Festival S, dp, Dickson, Patrick; flowers single; int. in 1996

Mexicana HT, rb, 1966, Boerner; bud ovoid; flowers red, reverse silvery, large, 33 petals, high-centered, moderate fragrance; foliage dark, glossy, leathery; vigorous, upright growth; PP2636; [Kordes' Perfecta × seedling]; int. by J&P

Mexico HP, m, 1863, Bruant; flowers velvety purple, shaded black, large, full

Mexico F, or, 1944, Krause; bud globular, deep carmine; flowers deep scarlet, suffused orange, 4 in., 18 petals, cupped, borne in clusters; foliage leathery; strong stems; vigorous, bushy growth; [Baby Chateau × Helgoland]; int. by J&P

Mexico Min, rb

Meyerbeer HP, dr, 1867, Verdier; flowers purple red, tinted flame, petals wavy, very large, full

Mhairi's Wedding HT, w, 1983, MacLeod, Major C.A.; flowers 35 petals, flat; foliage large, dark, matte; upright growth; [Dalvey × Virgo]; int. by Christie Nursery, Ltd.

Mia HT, lp, Urban, J.

Mia-Lucy Rose F, pb, 2004, Horner, Colin P.; flowers pink-apricot, reverse paler, 4 in., full, borne in small clusters, moderate fragrance; foliage medium size, dark green, glossy; prickles medium, slightly curved; growth bushy, tall (4 ft.); garden decorative; [((Robin Redbreast × Lichtkonigin Lucia) × Flower Carpet) × Golden Future]; int. by LeGrice Roses, 2007

Mia Maid HT, mp, 1953, Swim, H.C.; bud ovoid; flowers phlox-pink, open, 3½-4 in., 40-50 petals; foliage leathery, glossy; upright, compact growth; [Charlotte Armstrong × Signora]; int. by Mt. Arbor Nursery

Mia Snock HT, ly, 1925, Leenders, M.; flowers lemon-yellow, dbl.; [Mrs T. Hillas × Mrs Wemyss Quin]

Miami HT, yb, 1953, Meilland, F.; flowers orange, veined, reverse yellow, long, pointed, 5 in., 25 petals; foliage dark; very vigorous, branching growth; [Mme Joseph Perraud × Fred Edmunds]; int. by C-P

Miami Holiday Min, rb, 1977, Williams, Ernest D.; bud pointed; flowers red, reverse yellow, 1-1½ in., 60 petals, moderate fragrance; foliage small, glossy; upright, bushy growth; [seedling × Over the Rainbow]; int. by Mini-Roses, 1976

Miami Moon F, op, 2000, Carruth, Tom; flowers shrimp or seashell pink, ruffled, 10-13 cm., 30-35 petals, borne in small clusters, slight spice fragrance; foliage large, medium green, semi-glossy, clean; prickles numerous, variable in length, straight; growth upright, compact, rounded, medium (80-110 cm.); garden decorative; PP13509; [(Voodoo × *R. soulieana* seedling) × Impatient]; int. by Weeks, 2002

Miami Playa HT, Dot

Mic Mac – See **Mio Mac**, F

Micaela M, lp, 1864, Moreau et Robert; flowers blush, compact, medium, very dbl.; erect growth

Micaëla HT, or, 1986, Kriloff, Michel; flowers orange-red, fading to dark carmine red, borne in clusters; vigorous growth; [Manola × seedling]

Michael F, or

Michael Bates' Moss – See **Princesse Adélaide**, M

Michael Crawford – See **Victor Borge**, HT

Michael Fish F, mp, Kirkham; flowers mid-pink with yellow stamens, semi-dbl. to dbl., borne up to 12 per stem, moderate sweet fragrance; foliage medium green, glossy; growth to 30 in.; int. by C&K Jones, 2001

Michael Flatley F, ob, 2003, Kenny, David; flowers deep peach, reverse orange-salmon, 2½ in., dbl., borne in large clusters, moderate fragrance; foliage small, medium green, matte; prickles small, pointed, few; growth upright, medium (3 ft.); garden; [Benita × (Mary Sumner × Kiskadee)]; int. in 2002

Michael Jon Halvorson HT, lp, 1999, Adams, Dr. Neil D.; flowers 3 in., dbl., borne in small clusters; foliage medium size, medium green, semi-glossy; prickles moderate; spreading, tall (6 ft.) growth

Michael Leek F, or, 1995, Fleming, Joyce L.; flowers bright orange-red, medium, 5-8 petals; borne 2-8 per cluster; foliage medium size, dark green, glossy; bushy (75-90 cm.) growth; [Liverpool Echo × Traumerei]; int. by Hortico Roses, 1994

Michael Saunders HT, pb, 1879, Bennett; flowers deep pink and coppery red, well-formed, medium, very dbl., moderate fragrance; moderate growth; [Adam × Mme Victor Verdier]

Michaelhouse Centenary HT, mr, Meilland; int. in 1995

Michal F, rb, Neeman; flowers dbl., slight fragrance

Michal Kowal F, pb, 2003, Rawlins, R.; flowers pink with white stripe, medium, single, borne in small clusters, no fragrance; foliage medium size, medium green, semi-glossy; prickles 1½ cm., scimitar-shaped, numerous; growth compact, medium (32 in.); garden decoration; [Golden Future × Crazy For You]

Michel-Ange HP, dp, 1863, Oger; flowers bright grenadine, large, full

Michel Bonnet – See **Catherine Guillot**, B

Michel Bras S, mp, Delbard; flowers semi-dbl., cupped, borne in clusters of up to 40-50, intense fragrance; medium growth; int. by Georges Delbard, 2002

Michel Cholet Min, ab, 2000, Jacobs, Betty; flowers dark rich apricot, medium to large, dbl. to full, high-centered, borne singly or in small clusters, slight fragrance; foliage medium size, dark green, semi-glossy; few prickles; growth upright, bushy, medium (2½ ft.); [Prima Donna × San Jose Sunshine]; int. by Roses By Design, 2001; AOE, ARS, 2001

Michel Hidalgo – See **Hidalgo**, HT

Michel Joye Min, yb, Guillot-Massad; int. in 2000

Michel Lis le Jardinier HT, mr, Meilland; flowers luminous red, large, 45-50 petals, high-centered; int. in 1987

Michel Strogoff HP, dr, 1882, Barault; flowers slatey violet red, shaded crimson, medium, full; few prickles; growth upright

Michelangelo F, rb, 1998, McGredy, Sam IV; flowers striped and splotched red, orange, cream and yellow, 4 in., dbl., spiral, borne in small clusters, slight fragrance; recurrent; foliage medium size, medium green, matte; prickles moderate; tall (120 cm.), bushy growth; [Louise Gardner × (Auckland Metro × Stars 'n' Stripes seedling)]; int. by McGredy, 1995

Michelangelo HT, my, Meilland; flowers mimosa-yellow, medium, 42-45 petals, cupped, slight fragrance; free-flowering; foliage semi-glossy; growth to 110-130 cm.; int. by Meilland Richardier, 1997

Michèle F, op, 1970, deRuiter; flowers deep salmon-pink, large, 25 petals; foliage light green; bushy growth; [seedling × Orange Sensation]; int. in 1968

Michele Bross F, Dorieux; int. in 1975

Michele Lemming F, yb, 2001, Horner, Heather M.; flowers yellow edged with red, paler reverse, 7 cm., dbl., borne in small clusters, moderate fragrance; foliage medium size, medium green, semi-glossy; prickles small, curved, few; growth upright, medium (1 m.); garden decorative; [(Korp × Southampton) × Solitaire]

Michèle Meilland HT, lp, 1945, Meilland, F.; flowers light pink shaded lilac, center salmon, large, dbl., high-centered, moderate fragrance; vigorous, upright (3 ft.) growth; [Joanna Hill × Peace]

Michèle Meilland, Climbing Cl HT, lp, 1951, Meilland, F.; bud pearly pink; flowers dbl., intense fragrance

Michèle Torr – See **Honor**, HT

Micheline HT, dp, 1953, de Basso, Mata; flowers deep salmon-pink, base darker, 30-35 petals; foliage dark; [Edouard Renard × Luis Brinas]

Micheline HT, dp, Guillot; free-flowering; foliage green, healthy; growth to 4 ft.; int. by Roseraies Guillot, 1985

Michelle F, rb; int. in 1998

Michelle Chetcuti HT, mr, Kirkham; flowers bright red, aging to soft scarlet, medium, dbl., high-centered; recurrent; foliage large, plum when young, mature green, matte; medium growth; int. by C & K Jones, 2005

Michelle Claire MinFl, op, 2001, Horner, Heather M.; flowers orange/salmon, paler reverse, 4 cm., dbl., borne in large clusters, slight fragrance; foliage small, light green, glossy; prickles small, straight, moderate; growth compact, medium (40 cm.); garden decorative; [Sunseeker × Fellowship]; int. by Bill LeGrice Roses

Michelle d'Hoop F, w, DVP Melle; [Melglory × Porcelaine de Chine]; int. in 1998; Gold Medal, Monza, 1999

Michelle Joy HT, op, Bear Creek Gardens

Michelle Wright – See **Pensioners Voice**, F

Michigan HT, pb, 1948, Mallerin, C.; flowers salmon-carmine, reverse Indian yellow, very large, dbl.; bushy growth; [Mme Joseph Perraud × Vive la France]; int. by URS

Michigan Perpetual – See **Perpetual Michigan**, HSet

Michigan Rose – See ***R. setigera*** (Michaux)

Michka – See **Garden Sun**, LCl

Mick Micheyl Gr

Mickael – See **Michael**, F

Micki HT, or, 1982, James, John; flowers light tangerine, 36 petals, high-centered; foliage dark, glossy, leathery; prickles small, brown; vigorous, upright growth; [Fragrant Cloud × Tropicana]; int. in 1979

Micky HT, op, 1951, Houghton, D.; bud long, pointed; flowers coral-pink, 9 petals; foliage leathery; prickles few thorns; very vigorous, upright, bushy growth; [Lulu × Vesuvius]; int. by Elmer Roses Co.

Micky Cl Min, mr, Warner, Chris; int. in 1995

Micmac S, w, Central Exp. Farm; flowers borne in clusters; non-recurrent; foliage deep purplish red; open habit (4 ft.) growth; hardy; [*R. rubrifolia* × *R. rugosa*]

Micro White Min, w, 2001, Weeks, Michael; flowers ½ in., semi-dbl., borne in small clusters, moderate fragrance; foliage small, medium green, semi-glossy; prickles small, pointed, few; growth bushy, low (5 in.); garden decorative, containers; [Weesnowflake × unknown]

Micrugosa – See ***R. × micrugosa*** (Henkel), S

Micrugosa Alba S, w, about 1910, Hurst, C. C.; flowers white, otherwise similar to micrugosa, single; blooms for many months; foliage compound; arching, colonizing growth; [Microgosa × unknown]; possibly *R. roxburghii* × *R. rugosa*

Micurin LCl, mr, 1936, Böhm, J.; flowers bright red, very large, semi-dbl., globular, borne in large clusters; abundant seasonal bloom; foliage dark, soft; vigorous, climbing growth

Midas – See **Dorothe**, HT

Midas Touch HT, dy, 1992, Christensen, Jack E.; bud urn-shaped; flowers bright, non-fading yellow, 3½-4 in., dbl., high-centered, borne mostly singly, moderate musk fragrance; foliage large, medium green, matte; prickles small on peduncle; tall (150-160 cm.), upright, bushy growth; PP8706; [Brandy × Friesensohne]; int. by Bear Creek Gardens, 1994

Middleborough Football Club F, mr, 1997, Horner, Heather M.; flowers large, dbl., borne in small clusters; foliage medium size, reddish bronze, glossy; some prickles; upright, medium (60 cm.) growth; [Alpha × (Old Master × Southampton)]; int. by Battersby Roses

Middlesbrough Pride HT, pb, 1987, Greensitt, J.A.; flowers medium, full, moderate fragrance; foliage medium size, medium green, semi-glossy; bushy growth; [Prima Ballerina × E.H. Morse]; int. by Nostell Priory Rose Gardens, 1984

Middlesex County – See **Capel Manor College**, F

Middo F, Laperrière; int. in 1971

Midget Min, mr, 1941, deVink; bud pink; flowers carmine-red, micro-mini, ½ in., 20 petals; foliage fern-like; dwarf growth; [Ellen Poulsen × Tom Thumb]; int. by C-P

Midget Gem S, ly, Dickson, Patrick; flowers yellow, fading white, 2 in., 5-8 petals, flat, borne in conical clusters, slight fragrance; growth to 50 cm.; int. in 1994

Midi HT, op

Midinette HT, mp, 1962, Delforge; flowers cyclamen-pink, well-formed, dbl.; vigorous growth; [Pink Spiral × seedling]

Midjet Min, 1941, deVink, J.

Midnapur Delight HT, w, Pushpanjali; flowers white with red edge, dbl.; compact growth; int. in 1997

Midnight HT, dr, 1957, Swim, H.C.; bud urn shaped; flowers currant-red to cardinal-red, 3½-4½ in., 23-30 petals, high-centered, intense fragrance; foliage dark, glossy; long, strong stems; vigorous, compact growth; PP1542; [Gay Lady × Texas Centennial]; int. by Armstrong Nursery, 1956

Midnight Blue S, m, 2003, Carruth, Tom; flowers deep velvety purple, reverse slightly lighter, 6-8 cm., dbl., borne in large clusters, intense clove fragrance; foliage medium size, light green, semi-glossy; prickles moderate, small, almost straight, light brown; growth compact, bushy, short (60-80 cm.); garden decoration; [(Sweet Chariot × Blue Nile) × Stephen's Big Purple × (International Herald Tribune × *R. soulieanna* derivative) × (Sweet Chariot × Blue Nile)]; int. by Weeks Roses, 2004; Gold Medal, Rose Hills, 2006

Midnight Magic HT, dr, 1985, Williams, J. Benjamin; flowers large, 35 petals, high-centered; foliage large, dark, semi-glossy; [(Chrysler Imperial × Mister Lincoln) × (Christian Dior × Josephine Bruce)]; int. by Hortico, Inc., 1986

Midnight Rambler Cl Min, rb, 1993, Taylor, Franklin "Pete" & Kay; flowers red with white eye, large, 6-14 petals, borne in small clusters; foliage medium size, medium green, semi-glossy; some prickles; medium (30 in.), spreading growth; [Party Girl × Andrea]; int. by Taylor's Roses, 1993

Midnight Rendezvous Min, dr, 1985, Hardgrove, Donald L.; flowers small, 27 petals; foliage small, dark, semi-glossy; bushy growth; [Scarlet King × Big John]; int. by Rose World Originals

Midnight Sun HT, dr, 1921, Grant; flowers deep crimson flushed velvety black, semi-dbl.; [Star of Queensland × Red-Letter Day]; int. by Kershaw, 1921

Midnite Sun HT, yb, 1955, Brownell; flowers buttercup-yellow edged red, becoming lighter, 5 in., very dbl., moderate fragrance; bushy growth; [Sutter's Gold × (*R. wichurana* × unknown)]

Midsummer HT, mp, 1947, Prosser; flowers 4-5 in., 20 petals, high-centered, moderate fruity fragrance; foliage leathery, dark; [Heinrich Wendland × Lady Sylvia]

Midsummer Night's Dream – See **Pat James**, F

Midsummer Night's Dream – See **A Midsummer Nights Dream**, Gr

Midwest Living Min, ob, 1991, King, Gene; bud

globular; flowers orange, slight ruffle to petal edges, good substance, holding well, large, full, borne singly or in small clusters, slight fragrance; foliage medium size, medium green, semi-glossy; few prickles; bushy, spreading, medium (18 in.), healthy, vigorous growth; [Evelyn Fison × Party Girl]; int. by Michigan Mini Roses, 1992

Mie Min, mr, 1980, Lyon; bud long, pointed; flowers 18 petals, cupped, borne several together; foliage very tiny, medium green; prickles tiny, curved; very compact growth; [Red Can Can × seedling]; int. in 1979

Miellez Ch, w; flowers cream, fading to pure white, medium, full

Mien de Jonge F, mr, 1969, Verschuren, A.; bud ovoid; flowers scarlet, large, semi-dbl., cupped; vigorous, bushy growth; [Sumatra × seedling]; int. by Stassen

Mier y Teran S, pb, 2005, Shoup, George Michael; flowers very full, borne mostly solitary, moderate fragrance; remontant; foliage large, medium green, glossy; few prickles; growth bushy, tall (6-8 ft.); hedging; [seedling from China × unkown]; int. by Antique Rose Emporium, 1998

Mies Bouwman F, op, 1978, Buisman, G. A. H.; bud round; flowers salmon-reverse yellow; foliage glossy, dark; vigorous, bushy growth; [Lijnbaanroos × seedling]; int. in 1973

Mieszko Pol, lp, 1966, Grabczewski; flowers pale pink, small; foliage small, light green; low growth

Mieze Pol, ob, 1909, Lambert, P.; flowers orange-yellow, borne in small clusters; vigorous growth; very hardy; [Petite Léonie × *R. foetida bicolor*]

Mieze Schwalbe Pol, mr, 1927, Lohse & Schubert; flowers rose-red; [sport of Frau Rudolf Schmidt]

Mighty Moe Min, ob, 1999, Moe, Mitchie; flowers orange, reverse lighter, micro-mini, ½ in., semi-dbl., high-centered, slight fragrance; foliage small, medium green, dull; few prickles; compact, medium (12 in.) growth; [Luis Desamero × seedling]; int. by Mitchie's Roses & More, 1999

Mighty Mouse F, ob, 1981, McGredy, Sam IV; bud small, short ovoid to globular; flowers bright orange, white eye, 2-2½ in., 10-14 petals, flat, then loosely cupped, borne 20 per cluster; free-flowering; foliage dark, very long, pointed; prickles slightly hooked, red; tall, spreading growth; hips orange-red; PP5036; [Anytime × Eyepaint]; int. in 1980

Mignard HP, mp, 1858, Baltet; flowers silky pink

Mignardise Pol, mr, 1971, Delforge; bud ovoid; flowers open, large, single; foliage large, leathery; vigorous, upright growth; [Luc Varenne × seedling]

Mignon – See **Mlle Cécile Brünner**, Pol

Mignon, Climbing – See **Mlle Cécile Brünner, Climbing**, Cl Pol

Mignon Pol, ly, 1904, Mille-Toussaint; flowers flesh yellow fading to white; [Mme Laurette Messimy × Marie Pavie]

Mignonette Pol, lp, 1881, Guillot et Fils; flowers rose, sometimes blush white bordered with wine-red spots, 1 in., dbl., borne in short, full panicles of 50, resembling the Chinas; foliage dark green above, reddish beneath, glossy, 5-7 leaflets; prickles hooked, red; stems branches dark red; very dwarf, bushy growth; [double-flowered multiflora × probably China or Tea]

Mignonne HT, 1962, Gaujard; bud long, pointed; flowers bright salmon-pink, large, 80 petals, moderate fragrance; foliage leathery; very vigorous growth; PP2456; [Mme Butterfly × Fernand Arles]; int. by Ilgenfritz Nursery, 1966

Miguel Aldrufeu – See **Linda Porter**, HT

Mijayima F, dy, Tagashira, Kazuso; flowers large, dbl.; int. in 1992

Mikado HRg, dr, 1888, Morlet; flowers deep red, large, full

Mikado Cl HT, mr, 1913, Kiese; flowers large, semi-dbl.

Mikado Ch, dy, 1929, Dobbie; flowers deep golden yellow; vigorous growth; RULED EXTINCT 2/87

Mikado F, dy, Guillot; flowers old yellow gold, semi-dbl., moderate fragrance; foliage healthy, beginning red; growth to 80 cm.; int. by Roseriaes Guillot, 1972

Mikado HT, rb, 1987, Suzuki, Seizo; flowers brilliant luminous light scarlet, suffused with yellow at base, fading darker, medium, 30-35 petals, high-centered, borne usually singly; foliage medium size, medium green, glossy; prickles slightly recurved, medium green, tinged purple; upright, tall growth; hips rounded, dull orange-red; PP6470; [Fragrant Cloud × Kagayaki]; int. by C-P, 1987

Mikado F, mp, Tantau; flowers bright pink, borne in clusters; florist rose; int. by Rosen Tantau

Mikäel – See **Michael**, F

Mikagura HT, dp, 1999, Hayashi, Shunzo; flowers bright velvet red, 30 petals, high-centered; foliage medium green; growth to 4½ ft.; [Christian Dior × seedling]; int. in 1992; Bronze Medal, Japan Rose Concours, 1995

Mikayla Paige F, w; flowers creamy white, dbl., high-centered, moderate fragrance; medium growth; int. by De Boer Roses, 2005

Mike Peterson MinFl, ly, 2000, Moe, Mitchie; flowers dbl., high-centered, borne mostly singly, slight fragrance; foliage medium size, medium green, semi-glossy; few prickles; growth upright, tall (20-24 in.); [Tracey Wickham × select pollen]; int. by Mitchie's Roses and More

Mike Sheppard HT, mr, 2001, Poole, Lionel; flowers 6 in., full, high-centered, borne mostly solitary, slight fragrance; foliage large, dark green, semi-glossy; prickles medium, wide, angular, moderate; growth upright, bushy, vigorous (1 m.); exhibition, beds, borders; [(Royal William × Gabi) × (Hazel Rose × Silver Jubilee)]; int. by David Lister Roses, 2003

Mike Thompson HT, mr, 1997, Thompson, Mike; flowers large, full, borne mostly singly, slight fragrance; foliage large, dark green, semi-glossy; some prickles; medium, bushy growth; [(Silver Jubilee × seedling) × (Red Planet × Pharaoh)]; int. by John Sheridan

Mike's Old-Fashioned Pink S, lp, 1999, Lowe, Malcolm; flowers 2½ in., full, borne in small clusters; foliage large, dark green, semi-glossy; prickles moderate; bushy, medium (4 ft.) growth; [Heritage × William Baffin]; int. by Ashdown Roses, 2001

Mikheil F, m; flowers light mauve blending to darker edges, medium, dbl., borne singly or in clusters, moderate fragrance; int. in 1998

Mikulás Ales HT, lp, 1936, Bojan; flowers rosy salmon-white; very vigorous growth

Miky Tea HT, pb, 1999, Sheridan, John; flowers pink blend, reverse cream, 4 in., 8-14 petals, borne in small clusters; foliage medium size, light green, semi-glossy; few prickles; upright, low (2 ft.) growth; [Cream Peach × Double Delight]

Mil Lamp HT, w, 1991, Colclasure, C.E.; flowers white with pink border, medium, dbl., intense fragrance; foliage medium size, medium green, semi-glossy; bushy growth; [sport of Admiral Rodney]

Milady HT, dp, 1914, Towill; flowers deep pink, large, dbl., high-centered, moderate fragrance; foliage small, soft; dwarf, sparse bloom. growth; [J. B. Clark × Richmond]; int. by A.N. Pierson

Milagros de Fontcuberta HT, m, 1968, Dot, Simon; bud pointed; flowers violet-mauve, medium, 50 petals; upright, compact growth; [(Sterling Silver × Intermezzo) × (Sterling Silver × Simone)]; int. by Rosas Dot

Milan F, rb, 1986, Jerabek, Paul E.; flowers red, silver or yellow reverse, medium, 28 petals; foliage medium size, medium green, semi-glossy; upright, bushy growth; [seedling × seedling]

Milano HWich, op, 1923, Ingegnoli; bud very long, pointed; flowers nasturtium-pink on Indian yellow ground, dbl., borne in large clusters; foliage glossy; vigorous, climbing (10 ft.) growth

Mildewfree Else Poulsen F, pb, 1937, Poulsen, S.; flowers pink slightly tinged yellow, medium, single; [Else Poulsen × Dainty Bess]

Mildred Cant HT, mr, 1935, Cant, B. R.; bud pointed; flowers bright crimson, very large, dbl., high-centered; foliage leathery; vigorous, open growth

Mildred Grant HT, w, 1901, Dickson, A.; flowers silvery white, tinted pink at edge, dbl., high-centered; very large, vigorous growth; [Niphetos × Mme Mélanie Willermoz]; Gold Medal, NRS, 1898

Mildred Reynolds F, mr, 1966, Dorieux; flowers cardinal-red, 3 in., cupped, borne in large, compact clusters; foliage glossy; [Peace × seedling]; int. by Bees

Mildred Scheel – See **Deep Secret**, HT, 1977

Milena HT, mp, Vecera, L.; int. in 1971

Milestone HT, rb, 1984, Warriner, William A.; flowers medium red, silvery red reverse, opening to coral-pink, dbl., cupped; foliage large, medium green, semi-glossy; upright growth; [Sunfire × Spellbinder]; int. by J&P, 1985

Milevsko S, mp, Vecera, L.; flowers medium, yellow stamens, semi-dbl. to dbl., cupped; heavy spring flush, scattered repeat bloom; bushy, branching (5 ft.) growth; int. in 1980

Mili de Vega HT, Moreira da Silva, A.

Milkana HT, rb, 1985, Staikov, Prof. Dr. V.; flowers brick-red, outer petals shaded pink, large, 50 petals; foliage dark, glossy; vigorous, upright, tall growth; [Tallyho × Spartan]; int. by Kalaydjiev and Chorbadjiiski, 1974

Milkmaid N, w, 1925, Clark, A.; flowers white tinted fawn, 5 cm., semi-dbl., borne in medium clusters, moderate fragrance; foliage dark green; stems slender; very vigorous, climbing growth; [Crépuscule × unknown]; int. by Brundrett

Milky Way HWich, w, 1900, Walsh; flowers pure white, tips lightly tinged pink, stamens yellow, very large, semi-dbl.; seasonal bloom; foliage glossy; vigorous, climbing growth; RULED EXTINCT 9/86

Milky Way – See **Amanogawa**, F

Milky Way HT, w, 1992, Ilsink, Peter; flowers white with hint of pink on reverse/edge, 4 in., 20 petals, urn-shaped, borne in sprays of up to 10, slight fragrance; foliage large, dark green, glossy; upright, medium (100-120 cm.) growth; [Esmeralda × True Love]; int. by Interplant B.V., 1991

Milky Way Min, w, Keihan; int. by Keihan Gardening, 2005

Milkyway Gr, w, 1987, Ohlson, John; flowers yellow stamens, loose, medium, 21 petals, cupped, borne singly, slight fruity fragrance; foliage small, medium green, semi-glossy; prickles straight, small, greenish-yellow; spreading, medium growth; [seedling × seedling]; int. in 1982

Mill Beauty – See **Miller's Climber**, Ayr

Mille – See **Rose Mille**, A

Mille et Une Nuits HT, ob, Dorieux; flowers orange in center, outer petals fading as it opens, dbl.; int. by Roseraies Dorieux, 2001

Milledgeville (natural variation of *R. setigera*), mp, 1842; flowers carmine

Millefleurs Min, ob; flowers bright orange, dbl., cupped, borne in clusters

Millenium LCl, lp, Schultheis; bud spherical; flowers mother of pearl pink, full, cupped, moderate fragrance; recurrent; foliage dark green, glossy; growth rapid, tall (10-13 ft.); int. by Rosen von Schultheis, 2000

Millennium HT, mr, 1997, Perry, Astor; flowers large, full, borne mostly singly; foliage medium size, medium green, semi-glossy; upright, medium (5ft. 6 in.) growth; [Fire Magic × Precious Platinum]; int. by Certified Roses, Inc.

Millennium – See **Everlasting Love**, F

Millennium – See **Weight Watcher Success**, HT

Millennium Memories F, lp; int. by Roses du Temps Passe, 2001

Miller-Hayes HP, mr, 1873, Verdier, E.; flowers crimson red with brighter center, nuanced poppy, dbl., moderate fragrance; [Charles Lefebvre × unknown]

Miller's Climber Ayr, dp, before 1838; flowers purple pink, large, semi-dbl.; foliage large; sometimes listed as a HSet, or a setigera × arvensis cross; some say origin is England, but the U.S. is more likely

Millgrove HMult, lp; int. in 1998

Millicent HMult, dp, 1914, Paul, W.

Millicent S, mp, Central Exp. Farm; flowers light coral-red fading to flesh-pink, reverse yellowish; non-recurrent; foliage dark green veined red-brown; medium-tall growth; hips flattened, globe shape, light red; hardy

Millie Pol, rb, 1937, Russ; flowers light cherry-red, base yellow, borne in clusters; foliage dark; strong stems

Millie – See **Ghita Renaissance**, S

Millie Perkins HT, mr, 1960, Maarse, G.; flowers velvety red, well-formed, large, dbl.; long, strong stems; vigorous growth; [Ena Harkness × Chrysler Imperial]

Millie Walters Min, op, 1984, Moore, Ralph S.; bud small, long, pointed; flowers deep coral pink, 1½ in., 45 petals, high-centered, borne singly and in clusters of 3-5; good repeat; foliage small, medium green, matte; prickles medium to long, straight; stems slender, wiry; growth upright, bushy (14-18 in.); PP5741; [Little Darling × Galaxy]; int. by Moore Min. Roses, 1984

Millier-Hayes – See **Miller-Hayes**, HP

Millionaire F, dp, Pearce; int. by James Cocker & Sons, 1998

Mills and Boon F, mr, Gandy; flowers bright red, borne in clusters; foliage deep green; bushy, compact growth; int. by Gandy's Roses Ltd., 2002

Mill's Beauty – See **Miller's Climber**, Ayr

Milord F, dr, 1961, Gaujard; flowers large, dbl., borne in clusters; foliage dark; vigorous growth; [Opera × Ville de Gand]

Milord HT, mr, 1962, McGredy, Sam IV; flowers crimson-scarlet, well-formed, 5-6 in., 35 petals; foliage dark; upright growth; [Rubaiyat × Karl Herbst]; int. by McGredy & Son, 1962

Milou F, dr, 1964, Mondial Roses; flowers dark vermilion-red, medium, semi-dbl.; vigorous, low growth

Milrose F, mp, 1970, Delbard-Chabert; flowers rose pink, semi-dbl., cupped, borne in clusters of 5-15; foliage light green, glossy; vigorous, bushy growth; [Orléans Rose × (Francais × Lafayette)]; originally registered as Pol; int. in 1965; Gold Medal, Baden-Baden, 1964

Milva F, m, 1985, Tantau, Math.; flowers medium, 35 petals; foliage medium size, medium green, semi-glossy; upright growth; int. in 1983

Milva HT, ob, Tantau; flowers apricot, edges copper-colored, large, long lasting, dbl.; foliage full and green; growth to 60-70 cm.; int. by Rosen Tantau, 2002

Mimi Min, mp, 1963, Meilland, Alain; bud ovoid; flowers 1-1½ in., 33 petals, cupped, borne in clusters; foliage leathery; vigorous, bushy (14 in.) growth; [Moulin Rouge × (Fashion × Perla de Montserrat)]; int. by C-P, 1963

Mimi Coertse Gr, mp, 1963, Herholdt, J.A.; bud pointed; flowers bright rose-pink, 4 in., dbl., high-centered; foliage glossy; upright growth; [Queen Elizabeth × Constantia]; int. by Herholdt's Nursery

Mimi Eden Min, pb, Meilland; flowers pink with white reverse, full, urn-shaped, borne in clusters; PP14194; cut flower rose; int. by Meilland Intl., 2002

Mimi Mathy F, pb, Dorieux; flowers white brushed with pink, semi-dbl.; int. by Roseraies Dorieux, 2000

Mimi Pearl F, w

Mimi Pink F, lp, 1984, Jelly, Robert G.; flowers light pink, reverse darker, sweetheart, large, 35 petals, no fragrance; foliage medium size, dark, semi-glossy; upright growth; PP5636; [seedling × Misty Pink]; int. as Mimi Rose, Universal Plants, 1980

Mimi Pinson Pol, dp, 1919, Barbier; flowers clear crimson, passing to purplish rose and then to Neyron purple

Mimi Rose – See **Mimi Pink**, F

Mimollet F, lp, 1977, Ota, Kaichiro; bud pointed; flowers bright light pink, 3-4 in., very dbl., high-centered; foliage glossy; upright growth; [(Queen Elizabeth × Ethel Sanday) × Zambra]; int. in 1975

Mimosa Cocktail HT, ob, 2003, Taylor, Pete & Kay Taylor; flowers soft tangerine with yellow base, ruffled, 4 in., full, decorative, borne mostly solitary, intense fragrance; foliage medium size, medium green, semi-glossy; prickles medium, slight hook, brown, moderate; upright, medium (4 ft.) growth, garden/decorative/cut blooms; [unknown × unknown]; int. by Taylor, Franklin & Kay Taylor, 2003

Min Jurgensen HT, w, 1974, Bauer; flowers center buff, aging to pink edges, medium, dbl.; foliage dark, soft; very vigorous, upright growth; [sport of Pascali]; int. by Trenallyn Nursery, 1973

Minden – See **Sunday Press**, HT

Mindor F, yb, 1976, Station Exp. de Roses; flowers deep yellow, slightly flushed orange, 3 in., 30-60 petals, urn-shaped; foliage dark; vigorous, low growth; [Dr. Faust × Mme Lucky]

Minerette Min, lp, 1982, Interplant; flowers small, semi-dbl., borne in clusters; free-flowering; foliage small, medium green, glossy; prickles numerous, small; bushy growth; [(Marlena × unknown) × seedling]; Gold Medal, Baden-Baden, 1984

Miners Cottage Misc OGR, dp

Minerve HGal, dp, before 1811, Miellez; flowers very deep pink

Minerve HP, mr, 1868, Gonod; flowers crimson, shaded velvety fire-red, large, full

Minerve HP, dp, 1869, Jamain; flowers medium, full

Minerve HT, yb, 1947, Meilland, F.; flowers chrome-yellow shaded red, high pointed, 36 petals; foliage thick, dark; vigorous, branching growth; [Peace × Prinses Beatrix]

Minette C, lp, 1819, Vibert; flowers pink edged blush white, small, full; foliage elliptical, light green; sometimes classed as A

Ming Toy F, dp, 1947, Krebs; bud globular; flowers deep rose-pink, loose trusses, 2 in., 50 petals; foliage leathery, dark; vigorous, upright, bushy growth; int. by H&S

Minha Mulher HT, Moreira da Silva, A.; int. in 1969

Mini Eden – See **Mimi Eden**, Min

Mini Jet – See **Minijet**, Min

Mini Love Min, pb; flowers single; int. by Jan Spek, 2002

Mini Magic Min, rb, 1988, Williams, Michael C.; flowers white with red edges, reverse more red color, small, 35 petals, cupped; foliage small, medium green, semi-glossy; prickles straight, light green; slightly spreading, low growth; [Baby Katie × Watercolor.]; int. by The Rose Garden & Mini Rose Nursery

Mini Magic Min, yb, Walsh; int. in 1998

Mini Mercedes Min, mr

Mini Metro – See **Finstar**, Min

Mini Nicole Min, pb; flowers white with carmine edges, high-centered; free-flowering; rugged, medium to tall growth; holds half open stage for a long time

Mini Pink Melodies Min, mp, 1991, Spooner, Raymond A.; flowers small, dbl.; foliage small, medium green, semi-glossy; bushy growth; [seedling × seedling]

Mini-Poul Min, pb, 1985, Poulsen, Niels D.; flowers yellow and deep pink blend, small, 25 petals, no fragrance; foliage small, dark, glossy; compact growth; [Darling Flame × seedling]; int. by D.T. Poulsen, 1978

Mini Tango Min, pb, 2001, Williams, Michael C.; flowers deep pink, with halo at base of petals, medium, dbl., borne mostly solitary, no fragrance; foliage medium size, dark green, semi-glossy; prickles few, ¼ in., straight; growth upright, tall (23 in.); garden decorative, exhibition, containers; [seedling × select pollen]; int. by The Mini Rose Garden, 2002

Miniature Pol, lp, 1884, Alégatière; flowers pink, becoming yellowish-white, very small, very dbl.; moderate growth

Miniature, Climbing Cl Pol, lp, 1908, Lambert; flowers whitish pink, very small, very full

Miniature Moss M, lp, before 1838, Rivers; flowers light crimson, small, semi-dbl.; [Rivers' Single Crimson Moss × unknown]

Minigold F, my, 1970, Tantau, Math.; flowers pointed, 2½ in., 35 petals, moderate fragrance; foliage glossy, dark; PP3103; [Whisky Mac × Zorina]

Minijet Min, mp, 1977, Paolino, Mrs M. L.; int. in 1977

Minilights S, my, 1987, Dickson, Patrick; flowers small, single to semi-dbl., flat, borne in small clusters; quick repeat; foliage small, dark green, glossy; spreading, compact growth; [White Spray × Bright Smile]; int. in 1988

Minirosa Min, pb, VEG; flowers bright pink with white eye, small, semi-dbl., flat, borne in clusters, slight fragrance; free-flowering; bushy, compact (40 cm.) growth; int. in 1976

Minirot Min, m, VEG; flowers purple/pink with cream reverse, small, semi-dbl.

Minisa HRg, mr, 1927, Hansen, N.E.; flowers deep crimson, medium, 17 petals, intense fragrance; bloom repeats; very hardy; [*R. rugosa* × Prince Camille de Rohan]

Minister Afritsch F, or, 1973, Tantau, Math.; flowers large, dbl.; vigorous, bushy growth; [seedling × Signalfeuer]; int. by Starkl, 1964

Minister Luns F, dp, 1968, Wijnhoven; bud ovoid; flowers pink-red, medium, semi-dbl.; foliage dark; [Marchenland × Florence Mary Morse]

Minister Rasín – See **Ministre des Finances Rasín**, HT

Ministre des Finances Rasín HT, dp, 1930, Böhm, J.; bud long; flowers carmine-rose, large, dbl.; vigorous growth; [Mme Maurice de Luze × Hadley]

Mink F, ob, 1959, Boerner; bud globular; flowers orange-pink, 2½ in., 75-80 petals, flat, borne in pyramidal clusters, moderate fragrance; strong stems; vigorous, upright growth; PP1513; [(Pinocchio × unknown) × Garnette]; int. by J&P, 1955

Minna HEg, w, 1895, Penzance; flowers white, tinted blush-lilac, large, semi-dbl.; very vigorous growth

Minna F, mp, 1930, Kordes; flowers rosy pink, large, dbl., borne in clusters; foliage rich green, leathery; bushy, dwarf growth; [sport of Gruss an Aachen]

Minna Kordes – See **World's Fair**, F

Minna Lerche Lerchenborg – See **Majorette**, HT

Minnehaha HWich, lp, 1905, Walsh; flowers pink fading white, small, dbl., borne in large clusters; non-recurrent;

foliage small, glossy, dark; climbing (15-20 ft.) growth; [*R. wichurana* × Paul Neyron]

Minnelli MinFl, ab, Olesen; bud ovate; flowers apricot, outer petals fading lighter, 2½ in., 40-50 petals, cupped, borne usually singly, slight wild rose fragrance; recurrent; foliage dark green, semi-glossy; prickles few, 4 mm., linear; growth compact, upright, bushy (8-16 in.); [seedling × Patricia Kordana Mini Brite]; int. by Poulsen Roser, 2003

Minnelli Patiohit – See **Minnelli**, MinFl

Minnie Min, rb, 1978, Williams, Ernest D.; bud long, pointed; flowers red and yellow blend, 1 in., very dbl., high-centered, moderate fragrance; foliage small, glossy; upright growth; [Starburst × Over the Rainbow]; int. by Mini-Roses, 1977

Minnie Dawson HMult, w, 1896, Dawson; flowers pure white, borne in very large clusters; [Dawson × *R. multiflora*]

Minnie Francis T, dp, 1905, Griffing Nursery; flowers deep pink, open; vigorous growth

Minnie Marcus HT, pb, 1983, Rodgers, Shafner R.; flowers large, 35 petals; foliage large, dark, glossy; upright growth; [Queen Elizabeth × Windsounds]; int. by Neiman-Marcus, 1984

Minnie Mouse – See **Roller Coaster**, Min

Minnie Pearl Min, pb, 1983, Saville, F. Harmon; flowers light pink, reverse darker, yellow base, 25 petals, high-centered, borne mostly singly; foliage small, medium green, semi-glossy; few prickles; thin, wiry stems; upright growth; PP5097; [(Little Darling × Tiki) × Party Girl]; int. by Nor'East Min. Roses, 1982

Minnie Pearl White Min, w, Lee; [sport of Minnie Pearl]; int. in 1993

Minnie Saunders HT, mr, 1921, Hicks; flowers bright red, single; vigorous growth

Minnie Watson HT, op, 1965, Watson; bud globular; flowers semi-dbl.; foliage glossy; compact, bushy growth; [Dickson's Flame × Dickson's Flame]

Minor – See **Petite de Hollande**, C

Minor – See **Pompone Jaune**, Misc OGR

Minor – See **Gracilis**, M

Minor Details Min, pb, 2002, White, Wendy R.; flowers white edged deep pink, reverse magenta, 1 -1¼ in., dbl., borne in small clusters; foliage small, dark green, semi-glossy; growth upright, compact, short (12-16 in.); containers, border, garden; [Vista × Cal Poly]; drought resistant; int. by Nor" East Miniature Roses, 2002

Minori HT, ob, Hiroshima; int. by Hiroshima Bara-en, 2002

Minou F, Moreira da Silva, A.

Minouchette LCl, lp, Croix; flowers medium, dbl., borne in small clusters, slight fragrance; free-flowering; foliage clear green, disease-resistant; vigorous growth; int. in 1971

Minstrel F, mr, 1967, Sanday, John; flowers scarlet, 2½ in., single to semi-dbl., borne in clusters; foliage dark, glossy; very free growth; [Independence × Paprika]

Mint Julep HT, w, 1983, Christensen, Jack E.; flowers pale green and pink blend, large, 35 petals; foliage medium size, medium green, semi-glossy; upright growth; [White Masterpiece × Queen Elizabeth]; int. by Armstrong Nursery, 1983

Minuet HT, my, 1930, Thompson's, J.H., Sons; flowers open,large, semi-dbl.; foliage leathery; vigorous growth; [sport of Joanna Hill]

Minuette F, rb, 1969, Lammerts, Dr. Walter; bud ovoid, pointed; flowers with heart-shaped, ivory-white petals, tipped red, medium, dbl.; foliage glossy, dark green; bushy, branching, strong (2 ft.) growth; PP3162; [Peace × Rumba]; int. by DeVor Nurseries, Inc.

Minuette, Climbing Cl F, w, Kato; flowers white, edged crimson; int. in 1974

Minuette – See **Darling Flame**, Min

Minuetto – See **Darling Flame**, Min

Minx – See **Mink**, F

Mio Mac F, dy, 1976, Tantau, Math.; bud ovoid; flowers coppery yellow, medium, dbl.; foliage glossy; growth moderate, upright, bushy; int. by Horstmann, 1973

Miomac – See **Mio Mac**, F

Mirabella F, my, 1994, Zary, Dr. Keith W.; flowers very dbl., borne singly and in small clusters, intense fragrance; foliage medium size, dark green, glossy; some prickles; medium (80-100 cm.), upright,bushy growth; PP9657; [Sunsprite × Silver Jubilee]; int. by Bear Creek Gardens, 1994

Mirabile – See **Mirabilis**, T

Mirabilia F, Cazzaniga, F. G.; int. in 1960

Mirabilis – See **Admirable**, HGal

Mirabilis T, ab, about 1845, Boyau; flowers apricot yellow, shaded aurora pink, medium, full

Miracle F, op, 1961, Verbeek; flowers soft coral, 3 in., 16-35 petals, high-centered, borne in large trusses; foliage glossy; vigorous growth; PP1863; [seedling × Fashion]; int. by Ilgenfritz Nursery, 1961; Gold Medal, Bagatelle, 1958

Miracle HT, ob, Pouw; bud medium, ovate; sepals short; flowers orange-yellow, again to salmon-orange to orange, 3-4 in., 33 petals, high-centered, star-shaped, borne singly, slight fragrance; good repeat; foliage medium size, matte; prickles few, concave; growth vigorous, narrow, bushy (5 ft.); PP10907; [seedling × seedling]; greenhouse rose; int. by De Ruiter, 1997

Miragaia HT, pb, 1958, Moreira da Silva; flowers lilac-pink; [Peace × Coimbra]

Mirage Gr, op, 1966, Gaujard; bud ovoid; flowers bright salmon shaded red, medium, dbl.; foliage dark; very vigorous, bushy growth; [Peace × Circus]

Mirakel F, yb, VEG; flowers dark yellow with orange and red, medium, dbl.

Miralba – See **Miralda**, HCh

Miralda HCh, m, about 1825, Laffay; flowers dark crimson-purple, nearly black, striped carmine, small, very dbl.; prickles very small; vigorous, branching growth; perhaps Vibert, rather than Laffay

Miramar – See **Almirante Américo Tomás**, HT

Miramar F, or, 1956, Gaujard; bud globular; flowers cinnabar shaded coppery, large; foliage dark; very vigorous growth; [(Opera × unknown) × seedling]

Miramare HT, yb, Keisei; int. by Keisei Rose Nurseries, 2002

Miranda P, mp, 1869, de Sansal; flowers satiny pink, with a small center button, large, 8 cm., semi-dbl., moderate fragrance; recurrent; growth upright, medium

Miranda – See **Belfast Belle**, HT

Miranda Jane F, op, 1973, Cocker; flowers salmon, 4 in., 20 petals, high-centered, moderate fragrance; [Orange Sensation × Red Dandy]; int. in 1972

Mirandolina Min, w, Interplant; flowers pure white, 4-5 cm., dbl.; recurrent; foliage dark green; compact (10 in.) growth; int. in 1989

Mirandy HT, dr, 1945, Lammerts, Dr. Walter; flowers garnet-red, aging darker, 5-6 in., 45 petals, globular, intense damask fragrance; foliage leathery; vigorous, upright, bushy growth; [Night × Charlotte Armstrong]; int. by Armstrong Nursery

Mirandy, Climbing Cl HT, dr, 1961, Moore

Mirato HT, mp, 1974, Tantau, Math.; bud ovoid; flowers pink to salmon, dbl., intense fragrance; foliage large, glossy; upright, bushy growth; [unknown × unknown]

Mirato – See **Footloose**, S

Mireille HT, mr, 1952, Gaujard; flowers coppery crimson-red, 4 in., 26 petals, moderate fragrance; foliage rich green; vigorous growth; [Opera × seedling]

Mireille Mathieu F, or, 1973; bud ovoid; flowers large, 27 petals, high-centered; foliage soft; vigorous, upright, bushy growth; [Fragrant Cloud × Peer Gynt]; int. by Kordes, 1972

Mireille Mathieu F, or, Kordes; flowers brilliant orange-red, full, slight fragrance; int. in 1988

Mirela F, pb, Wagner, S.; flowers intense pink with yellow, medium to large, 50 petals, borne in clusters, slight fragrance; foliage medium size, dark green, glossy; [Castanet × Carillon]; int. by Res. Stn. for Hort., 2003

Mirella HT, pb, Barni, V.; int. in 1986

Miriam HT, my, 1919, Pemberton; flowers nasturtium-yellow, dbl., globular; Gold Medal, NRS, 1919

Miriam HT, yb, 1989, McGredy, Sam IV; flowers golden yellow edged pink, medium, 20 petals; free-flowering; foliage medium size, dark green, semi-glossy; vigorous, bushy growth; [Sexy Rexy × Yabadabadoo]; int. in 1990

Miriam's Climber LCl, op, 1950, Rosen, H.R.; bud ovoid, apricot-pink; flowers peach-pink, lighter at tip, large, dbl., borne in clusters; foliage dark, soft; very vigorous, climbing (25 ft.) growth; [seedling × Edith Nellie Perkins]

Miriam's White (found) – See **Sleigh Bells, Climbing**, Cl HT

Miriana HT, yb, 1983, Meilland, Mrs. Marie-Louise; PP5046; [sport of Meibiranda]

Miriana HT, mr, 1981, Meilland, Mme. Marie-Louise; flowers large, dbl.; foliage medium size, dark, semi-glossy; growth upright; [((seedling × Independence) × Suspense) × (((Alain × Mutabilis) × Caprice) × Pharoah)]; int. by Pépinières Jarrige, 1999

Miroir de Perfection B, mp, 1846, Armand, Étienne; flowers rose pink, shaded violet, medium, full

Mirza F, ob, 1976, Kordes; bud ovoid; flowers 4 in., 35 petals, cupped, moderate fragrance; foliage glossy; vigorous, upright, bushy growth; [Zorina × Samba]; int. by Willemse, 1974

Mischief HT, op, 1961, McGredy, Sam IV; flowers salmon-pink, 4 in., 28 petals, moderate fragrance; foliage light green; vigorous, upright growth; [Peace × Spartan]; int. by McGredy & Son, 1961; President's International Trophy, NRS, 1961, Gold Medal, Portland, 1965, Gold Medal, NRS, 1961

Miss Aalsmeer F, Spek, J.; PP3051

Miss Ada F, lp, 1998, Pawlikowski, Martin & Elaine; flowers light pink, darker edges, reverse darker pink, 2-4 in., single, borne singly and in small clusters; foliage medium size, medium green, semi-glossy; prickles few, brown; upright, bushy, medium growth; [sport of Playgirl]; int. by Giles Ramblin' Roses, 1998

Miss Agnes C. Sherman T, rb, 1901, Nabonnand; flowers rose, salmon and red; [Paul Nabonnand × Catherine Mermet]

Miss Alice S, lp, 2001, Austin, David; flowers 7-8½ cm., very full, borne mostly solitary, moderate fragrance; foliage small, light green, matte, disease-resistant; prickles medium, hooked downward, numerous; growth compact, medium (1 m.); garden decorative; [Mary Rose × seedling]; int. by David Austin Roses, Ltd., 2000

Miss Alice Min, m, 2000, Moe, Mitchie; flowers full, high-centered, borne mostly singly, moderate fragrance; foliage medium size, dark green, glossy; few prickles; growth upright, medium (15-18 in.); [Vista × unknown]; int. by Mitchie's Roses and More

Miss Alice de Rothschild T, ly, 1910, Dickson, A.; flowers light canary-yellow, center deeper, dbl.

Miss All-American Beauty HT, dp, 1965, Meilland, Mrs. Marie-Louise; bud ovoid, large; flowers large, 55 petals, cupped, borne usually singly, intense fragrance; recurrent; foliage leathery; vigorous, bushy growth; PP2625; [Chrysler Imperial × Karl Herbst]; int. as Maria Callas, Wheatcroft Bros, 1965; Gold Medal, Portland, 1966

Miss All-American Beauty, Climbing Cl HT, dp, 1969, Meilland; [sport of Miss All-American Beauty]; int. by URS

Miss All-American Dream HT, dp, 1997, Williams, J. Benjamin; flowers large, deep pink, 5½-6 in., very dbl., borne mostly singly, intense fragrance; foliage large, dark green, semi-glossy; prickles moderate; upright, bushy, tall growth; [Miss All-American Beauty × Bride's Dream]; int. by J. Benjamin Williams & Associates, 1996; ARS Patron Rose, ARS, 1996

Miss All Australian Beauty HT, dp, 1969, Armbrust; bud ovoid; flowers light red, reverse darker, medium, dbl.; upright growth; [Aztec × Impeccable]; int. by Langbecker

Miss Amber HT, or, 2001, Coiner, Jim; flowers yellow/orange blend, 6 in., dbl., high-centered, borne mostly solitary, no fragrance; foliage medium green, matte; prickles -¼ in., wide, curved; growth bushy, medium (48 in.); garden decorative; PP16157; [seedling × seedling]

Miss Amelia Gude HT, dy, 1921, Lemon; flowers deep yellow center shading to cream, 35-40 petals; foliage dark; vigorous growth; [Columbia × Sunburst]

Miss America HT, pb, 1938, Nicolas; flowers light pink, flushed salmon and gold, 6 in., 65 petals; foliage dark, leathery; vigorous growth; [Joanna Hill × S.M. Gustave V]; int. by J&P

Miss Annamarie Bally HT, or, 1926, Easlea; flowers reddish-copper, reverse suffused whitish fawn; [Aspirant Marcel Rouyer × Lamia]

Miss Annie Crawford – See **Annie Crawford**, HP

Miss Ashley HT, w, 2001, Coiner, Jim; flowers 6 in., dbl., borne mostly solitary; foliage medium size, light green, matte; prickles small, few; growth bushy, medium (48 in.); garden decorative; [seedling × seedling]

Miss Australia HT, mp, 1933, Knight, G.; flowers pink, center salmon, very large, 50 petals, globular; foliage thick; very vigorous, bushy growth; [Dame Edith Helen × Mme Segond Weber]

Miss Behavin' F, dp, 2000, Zary, Keith; bud short, pointed ovoid; flowers deep pink, reverse cream pink, yellow at petal base, 4 in., 25-30 petals, high-centered, borne in small clusters, slight apple fragrance; foliage large, dark green, glossy; prickles moderate, hooked downward; upright, medium (3½ ft.) growth; PP12129; [Tournament of Roses × red floribunda seedling]; int. by Bear Creek Gardens, 2001

Miss Blanche HT, w, 1981, Warriner, William A.; bud long; flowers 38 petals, urn-shaped to high-centered, borne usually singly, very slight fragrance; foliage large, dark, leathery; prickles straight, reddish; upright growth; [Evening Star × Coquette]; int. as Kojack, Spek, 1980

Miss Bloomsalot S, op, 2006, Ponton, Ray; flowers 2 in., single, borne in small clusters; recurrent; foliage medium size, dark green, glossy, disease-resistant; prickles medium, straight, moderate; growth upright, medium (4 ft.); [(Paloma Blanca × Hippolyte) × Baby Love]; int. in 2006

Miss Brenda HT, m, 2006, Popwell, Larry G., Sr.; flowers mauve, reverse lighter, large, single, borne mostly solitary; foliage medium size, dark green, glossy; prickles medium, straight, light tan, moderate; growth upright, 4-5 ft.; [Queen Elizabeth × Love]; int. in 2006

Miss Brisbane HT, lp, 1955, Ulrick, L.W.; flowers shell-pink, medium, dbl., cupped, moderate fragrance; foliage light green; vigorous growth; [unknown × The Doctor]

Miss C. E. Bernays HT, 1905, Williams, A.; [Mme Lombard × unknown]

Miss C. E. van Rossem HT, mr, 1919, Verschuren; bud long, pointed; flowers crimson-scarlet shaded carmine and black, open, medium to small, semi-dbl., cupped; foliage leathery, bronze, dark; vigorous, bushy growth; [Leuchtfeuer × Red-Letter Day]

Miss California HT, dp, 1933, Smith, J.; flowers deep glowing pink; [sport of Dame Edith Helen]

Miss Canada – See **Pacific Beauty**, HT

Miss Caroline T, pb, 1997, Knopf, Ruth; flowers medium, 50-60 petals, borne in small clusters; foliage medium size, medium green, semi-glossy; bushy, medium (4-5ft.) growth; [sport of Duchesse de Brabant]; int. by Vintage Gardens, 2000

Miss Charleston Min, m, 2003, Williams, Michael C.; flowers medium mauve, reverse darker, 2½ in., dbl., borne mostly solitary, no fragrance; foliage medium size, light green, semi-glossy; prickles ¼ in., slightly curved down, moderate; growth upright, tall (25-30 in.), garden, exhibition; [seedling × select pollen]; int. by The Mini Rose Garden, 2003

Miss Clipper HT, pb, 1942, Lammerts, Dr. Walter; bud long, pointed to ovoid; flowers pale salmon-pink shaded yellow, 3½-4 in., 25-30 petals, high-centered, moderate spicy fragrance; foliage glossy, light; strong stems; vigorous, upright, bushy growth; [Angèle Pernet × Pres. Herbert Hoover]; int. by Armstrong Nursery

Miss Conner HT, ly, 1920, Dickson, A.; flowers canary-yellow on lemon-yellow, dbl.

Miss Cynthia Forde HT, dp, 1909, Dickson, A.; flowers deep brilliant rose-pink, reverse lighter, large, dbl., moderate fragrance; long stems; vigorous, bushy growth; Gold Medal, NRS, 1909

Miss Daisy Min, dy, 1991, Warriner, William A.; bud short, pointed ovoid; flowers full, 30-35 petals, high-centered, borne singly and several together; foliage small, dark green, glossy; prickles medium, hooked slightly downward; stems short, strong; vigorous, low, bushy growth; [seedling × Sun Flare]; int. by Bear Creek Gardens, 1991

Miss Delightful F, my, 1966, Sanday, John; flowers bright yellow, 3 in., 30 petals, rosette, borne in heavy clusters; foliage glossy; vigorous, upright growth; [(Masquerade × seedling) × Golden Scepter]

Miss Dior S, ab, Harkness; flowers pearl ivory with apricot shading, 4 in., full, high-centered, slight sweet fragrance; recurrent; foliage medium green; bushy (4 ft.) growth; int. in 1998

Miss Dovey Min, ab, 1985, King, Gene; flowers deep apricot, 21 petals, high-centered, borne usually singly; foliage medium size, medium green, semi-glossy; prickles straight, reddish-brown; upright, bushy growth; sets hips; [Anne Harkness × Rise 'n' Shine]; int. by AGM Miniature Roses

Miss Edith Cavell Pol, dr, 1917, deRuiter; flowers scarlet-crimson overlaid velvety crimson, small, semi-dbl., flat, borne in large clusters; low (2 ft.), bushy growth; [sport of Orléans Rose]; int. by Spek

Miss Edith Gifford – See **Hon. Edith Gifford**, T

Miss Elvis HT, ob, 2000, Edwards, Eddie; flowers full, high-centered, borne mostly singly, slight fragrance; foliage medium size, medium green, semi-glossy; few prickles; growth upright, medium (4½ ft.); [seedling × seedling]; int. by Johnny Becnel Show Roses, 2002

Miss Emily HT, dp, 2001, Hiltner, Martin J.; flowers 3-3½ in., very full, borne mostly solitary; foliage medium size, medium green, semi-glossy; prickles ¼ in., straight, numerous; growth upright, bushy, medium (3-3½ ft.); exhibition; [Lynn Anderson × seedling]

Miss England HT, w, 1936, Cant, B. R.; flowers creamy, very large, dbl.; foliage leathery, dark; vigorous, compact growth

Miss Ethel Brownlow – See **Ethel Brownlow**, T

Miss Ethel Richardson HP, w, 1897, Dickson, A.; flowers white tinged pink, very large, dbl.

Miss Evelyn Davey T, 1905, Williams, A.; [Souv de S.A. Prince × Niphetos]

Miss Finland F, ob

Miss Flippins Min, mr, 1997, Tucker, Robbie; flowers medium red, deep pink reverse, 1½ in., dbl., high-centered, borne mostly singly or in small clusters of up to 4, no fragrance; foliage medium size, dark green, glossy; prickles moderate, hooked downward; stems strong; bushy, medium (2 ft.) growth; PP10601; [Elizabeth Taylor × Kristin]; int. by Bridges Roses, 1997

Miss Flora Mitten LCl, lp, 1913, Lawrenson; flowers soft pink, stamens yellow, 3 in., single, borne in small clusters, moderate fragrance; vigorous growth; [*R. wichurana* × *R. canina*]

Miss France Gr, or, 1955, Gaujard; flowers bright scarlet, large, dbl., globular; foliage bronze; vigorous growth; [Peace × Independence]

Miss Frotter HSpn, lp, before 1906, from Scotland

Miss G. Mesman Cl Pol, mr, 1910, Mesman; flowers purplish red, borne in small clusters; [sport of Mme Norbert Levavasseur]

Miss G. Radcliffe HT, 1900, Williams, A.; [Pharisaer × unknown]

Miss Georgie HT, ab, 1981, Warriner, William A.; flowers 35 petals, borne usually singly, moderate fragrance; foliage large, semi-glossy; prickles long; upright, compact growth; [South Seas × seedling]; int. by J&P, 1976

Miss Glegg N, w, 1835, Vibert; flowers white, center salmon, small, full

Miss Gunnell HSet, lp, about 1846, Pierce; flowers pale pink, with a tinge of buff, medium, dbl., cupped, borne in clusters of 25-30; foliage large, undulated, partially rugose

Miss Harp – See **Oregold**, HT

Miss Hassard HP, lp, 1874, Turner; flowers delicate flesh pink, large, full, loose, moderate fragrance; prickles numerous, large; [Marguerite de St Amand × unknown]

Miss Havisham Min, pb, 2003, Burrows, Steven; flowers lavender pink, reverse warm cream, medium, dbl., borne in small clusters, slight fragrance; foliage medium size, dark green, glossy; prickles small, few; growth bushy, medium (18 in.); containers, patio; [Lavender Jewel × Sheri Anne × Richard Buckley]; int. by Burrows, Steven, 2003

Miss Hawaii HT, w, 1976, Payne; flowers creamy white, 5½-6 in., 30-35 petals, high-centered; foliage leathery; very vigorous growth; [sport of Hawaii]; int. by Lone Star Nursery

Miss Helyett HWich, pb, 1909, Fauque; bud coral, rounded; flowers bright carmine-pink, center yellowish salmon-pink, 8-9 cm., dbl., open, borne singly or in small clusters; foliage large, dark green, glossy; vigorous, climbing (10-12 ft.) growth; [*R. wichurana* × Ernest Metz]

Miss Henriette Tersteeg HT, pb, 1922, Van Rossem; flowers flesh and salmon-pink, dbl.; [(Mme Abel Chatenay × unknown) × Mrs Joseph Hill]

Miss Heylett – See **Miss Helyett**, HWich

Miss Hillcrest HT, or, 1969, Curtis, E.C.; flowers large, dbl., high-centered, intense fruity fragrance; foliage glossy; vigorous, tall growth; PP3027; [Peace × Hawaii]; int. by Kimbrew

Miss Hillcrest S, op, 1993, Poulsen

Miss Hiroshima HT, lp, Hiroshima; int. by Hiroshima Bara-en, 1983

Miss House HP, w, 1838, House; flowers satin white

Miss Huntington HT, ob, 1972, Patterson; bud ovoid; flowers bright orange, large, dbl., high-centered, moderate fragrance; foliage leathery; vigorous, upright growth; [Ma Perkins × San Francisco]; int. by Patterson Roses, 1971

Miss Ingram HP, w, 1867, Ingram; flowers white, shaded light flesh pink, center darker pink, large, full, globular

Miss Ireland HT, or, 1961, McGredy, Sam IV; flowers orange-red, yellow reverse, 5 in., 37 petals; foliage dark; vigorous, bushy growth; [Tzigane × Independence]; int. by McGredy & Son, 1961

Miss Italia S, Mansuino; int. in 1963

Miss Jekyll Ayr, lp, before 1934, from England; flowers light rose pink, medium, dbl.

Miss Joan Cl HT, op, 1943, Duehrsen; flowers copper-bronze and salmon-pink, large, dbl., globular; foliage dark, glossy; very vigorous, climbing growth; [Ednah Thomas × Golden Dawn]; int. by California Roses

Miss Kate Moulton HT, pb, 1906, Monson; flowers rosy pink shaded rosy salmon, large, dbl.; [Mme Caroline Testout × (La France × Mrs W.J. Grant)]; int. by Minneapolis Floral Co.

Miss Kate Sessions Cl HT, pb, 1953, Hieatt; flowers deep rose-pink on white base, reverse shell-pink, open, large, dbl., moderate fragrance; profuse, intermittent bloom; foliage light green, leathery; moderate, climbing growth; [Heart of Gold × Ednah Thomas]

Miss Katherine G. Warren T, mr, 1895, Bernaix; flowers carmine, shaded garnet, aging China pink, medium, full

Miss Kitty HT, w, 2007, Belendez, Kitty; flowers 4½ in., very full, blooms borne mostly solitary; foliage medium size, dark green, semi-glossy; prickles in., triangular, curved downward, pinkish-beige, few; growth upright, tall (6 ft.); [sport of Cajun Moon]; int. by Kitty Belendez, 2007

Miss Koganei Cl Min, rb, 1986, Asano, S.; flowers medium red, white eye, yellow stamens, 7-10 petals, cupped; foliage small; few prickles; vigorous (to 3 ft.) growth; [Nozomi × unknown]; int. in 1985

Miss Lakeland Min, dp, 2004, Barnes, Fred; flowers deep pink, reverse medium pink, 1½ in., dbl., borne in large clusters, slight fragrance; foliage small, medium green, glossy, healthy; prickles ¼ in., slight hooked; growth vigorous, bushy, medium (15 in.), exhibition; garden; [Minnie Pearl × unknown]; int. by C&K Jones, 2004

Miss Lawrance's Rose – See ***R. chinensis minima*** (Voss)

Miss Leslie HT, w, 1998, Garrett, Troy O.; flowers white with light pink edges, very dbl., high-centered, borne mostly singly; foliage medium size, medium green, semi-glossy; prickles moderate; upright, tall growth; [sport of Rina Hugo]

Miss Liberté HT, ob, 1984, Christensen, Jack E.; bud medium to large, pointed, ovoid; flowers coral-orange to dusty deep red, well-formed, 4½-5½ in., 35 petals, high-centered, borne usually singly, sometimes 2 or 3 in cluster; foliage large, dark, semi-glossy; prickles straight to hooked slightly downward; upright, bushy, medium growth; PP6151; [(Camelot × First Prize) × Gingersnap]; int. by Armstrong Nursery

Miss Liberty LCl, mp, 1959, Boerner; bud ovoid; flowers Tyrian rose, 9-10 cm., 15-20 petals, cupped, borne singly or in small clusters, moderate fragrance; repeat bloom; foliage dark, leathery; numerous prickles; strong stems; vigorous, climbing (10-12 ft.) growth; PP1529; [New Dawn × Minna Kordes]; int. by Stuart, 1956

Miss Liberty – See **Miss Liberté**, HT

Miss Lillian S, pb, 2005, Shoup, George Michael; flowers semi-dbl., borne in small clusters, moderate fragrance; remontant; foliage large, dark green, semi-glossy; few prickles; growth spreading, tall (6-8 ft.); hedging; [(Buff Beauty × Heritage) × Heritage]; int. by Antique Rose Emporium, 2004

Miss Lolita Armour HT, or, 1919, Howard, F.H.; flowers deep coral-red suffused coppery red, base yellow, very large, dbl., cupped; int. by H&S; Gold Medal, Bagatelle, 1921

Miss Lolita Armour, Climbing Cl HT, or, H&S

Miss Lorraine Gr, mp, 2002, Eve, André; flowers dbl., borne in small clusters, slight fragrance; foliage medium size, medium green, semi-glossy; prickles moderate; growth upright, medium (80 cm.); [seedling × Versailles]; int. in 2001

Miss Lowe – See **Miss Lowe's Variety**, Ch

Miss Lowe's Variety Ch, mr, 1887, Lowe; flowers bright red, single; recurrent bloom; dwarf growth; possibly a sport of Slater's Crimson China

Miss Luann Min, ob, 2000, Close, Clarence; flowers dark orange, 1½ in., dbl., borne in small clusters; growth medium (20-24 in.); [sport of Pink Meidiland]; int. by Justice Miniature Roses, 2001

Miss M. J. F. Gostling Pol, Williams, A.; [Miss Pollock × unknown]

Miss M. J. Spencer HT, my, 1920, Dickson, H.; flowers clear bright golden yellow, dbl.

Miss M. Robertson Pol, 1902, Williams, A.; [Mlle Cécile Brünner × unknown]

Miss Maine 1999 S, dp, 1999, Law, Stephen; flowers deep pink, reverse medium pink, 2 in., full, borne in small clusters, slight fragrance; foliage small, medium green, semi-glossy; numerous prickles; bushy, medium (4 ft.) growth; hardy to -30ºF; [sport of Henry Kelsey]

Miss Maine 2000 S, lp, 2001, Law, Stephen; flowers light pink with white center, 3 in., single, borne in small clusters, slight fragrance; continuous bloom; foliage medium size, dark green, semi-glossy; prickles average, numerous; growth spreading, medium (3-4 ft.); garden decoration, hedge; very hardy; [Henry Kelsey × open pollination]

Miss Marion Manifold Cl HT, mr, 1913, Adamson; flowers velvety scarlet, shaded crimson, large, dbl., globular, moderate fragrance; foliage large, leathery; vigorous, climbing (12 ft.) growth; int. by Brundrett

Miss Marston T, pb, 1889, Pries/Ketten Bros.; flowers yellowish-white, bordered very deep pink, center yellow/peach/red, large, full, moderate violet fragrance; growth bushy

Miss Mary HT, dp, 1996, Miller, Carol; flowers deep pink, 3-3½ in., full, no fragrance; foliage large, medium green, matte; few prickles; tall (5 ft.), upright growth; [sport of Big Ben]; int. by Giles Rose Nursery, 1995

Miss May Marriott HT, ab, 1917, Robinson, T.; flowers glowing apricot to orange-red, large, semi-dbl.; [sport of Mme Edouard Herriot]

Miss May Paul T, m, 1880, Levet; flowers lilac white, reverse red, large, full, globular to cupped, moderate fragrance; [Mme Thérèse Genevay × unknown]

Miss May Thurlowe T, Williams, A.

Miss Mayne HT, Williams, A.; [Marie van Houtte × General Jacqueminot]

Miss Megan Min, mp, 2004, Rickard, Vernon; flowers dbl., borne mostly solitary, slight fragrance; foliage medium size, dark green, glossy; prickles angled down, red, moderate; growth spreading, tall (36 in.); exhibition; garden; [Fairhope × Ruby]; int. by Almost Heaven Roses, 2004

Miss Melanie Min, pb, 2003, Denton, James A; flowers medium pink and white, reverse white, 1½ in., full, borne mostly solitary, no fragrance; foliage medium size, dark green, glossy; prickles medium, down-curved, light brown, few; growth compact, medium (18 in.); garden decoration, exhibition; [Hot Tamale × Kristin]; int. by James A Denton, 2004

Miss Middleton F, op, 1965, Hill, A.; flowers coral-pink, 2½-3 in., 20 petals, cupped, borne in small clusters; foliage light green; low, bushy growth; [Independence × Masquerade]

Miss M'liss F, mp, 1960, Jelly; bud short pointed; flowers phlox-pink, 2½-3 in., 25-30 petals, high-centered; very vigorous, upright growth; PP1888; [Garnette × Garnette seedling]; int. by E.G. Hill Co., 1958

Miss Modesto HT, my, 1934, Brooks, L.L.; flowers pure yellow, very large, dbl., high-centered; [sport of Rev. F. Page-Roberts]; int. by Brooks & Son

Miss Muffett Min, mp, 1955, Robinson, T.; bud rather mossy; flowers apple-blossom-pink, compact growth, 4-6 in., 80 petals; [Baby Bunting × Tom Thumb]

Miss Muriel Jamison – See **Muriel Jamison**, T

Miss Murine F, dp, 1937, Fitzgerald; flowers deep pink, base yellow, small, dbl.; upright, bushy growth; [seedling × Cécile Brunner]

Miss N. Robertson Pol, Williams, A.; [Mlle Cécile Brünner × unknown]

Miss Newell F, m, 2006, Rawlins, Ronnie; flowers mauve, 2½ in., full, borne mostly solitary; foliage medium size, dark green, semi-glossy; prickles ½ in., triangular, few; growth upright, medium (30 in.); garden decoration; [Len Turner × Old Port]; int. in 2006

Miss P. Williams Pol, Williams, A.; [Perle d'Or × unknown]

Miss Pam Ayres – See **Bonanza**, S

Miss Paula Min, pb, 2004, Carman, Howard; flowers medium pink blend, reverse white, 2 in., dbl., borne mostly solitary, no fragrance; foliage medium size, dark green, glossy; growth upright, medium; exhibition, garden, cutting; [sport of Miss Flippins]; int. by Howard Carman, 2006

Miss Pearl Min, lp, 1991, Hooper, John C.; flowers large, dbl., borne mostly singly, intense spicy fragrance; foliage medium size, medium green, matte; few prickles; tall (80 cm.), upright growth; [Gene Boerner × Pacesetter]; int. by AGM Miniature Roses

Miss Perfect Min, lp, 1989, Warriner, William A.; bud ovoid, pointed; flowers light pink to near white at edge, reverse lighter, medium, very dbl., cupped; foliage medium size, medium green, semi-glossy; prickles straight to slightly hooked downward, light yellow; spreading, low growth; PP7650; [Over the Rainbow × Lavender Lace]; int. by Bear Creek Gardens

Miss Personality F, pb, 1973, Sherwood; bud ovoid; flowers cerise-pink, white eye, open, medium, semi-dbl.; foliage small, dark, leathery; vigorous, bushy growth; [Pink Parfait × (Ophelia × Parkdirektor Riggers)]; int. by F. Mason, 1972

Miss Pollock P, 1906, Williams, A.

Miss Poole HP, mp, 1875, Turner; flowers bright silvery pink, large, full; [Victor Verdier × unknown]

Miss Pretty HT, ob, Keisei; PP13438; int. in 2004

Miss Prissy HT, w, Wells; flowers white with pink tint on petal edges; int. in 1995

Miss Rainbow HT, rb; int. by K & M Nursery, 2004

Miss Reus HT, op, Dot; flowers salmon orange to vermilion

Miss Rita F, lp, Robertson; int. about 1986

Miss Rose Gr, Dorieux

Miss Rose Hill HT, 1913, Williams, A.

Miss Rowena Thom HT, pb, 1927, H&S; flowers fiery rose and rosy mauve, center washed gold, 6 in., 50 petals, intense fragrance; vigorous growth; [Radiance × Los Angeles]

Miss Rowena Thom, Climbing Cl HT, pb, 1937, van Barneveld; int. by California Roses

Miss Schweiz HT, dr, Tantau; flowers very dark red, large, dbl.; foliage glossy; healthy (60-80 cm.) growth; int. in 1996

Miss Smithson HSpn, m, 1827, Dagonnet; flowers violet-purple

Miss Stewart Clark HT, dy, 1916, Dickson, A.; flowers golden yellow, shaded citron and chrome yellow, medium, full, globular, moderate fragrance

Miss Talmadge HT, dy, 1927, Pacific Rose Co.; flowers dbl.; [sport of Constance]

Miss Universe HT, rb, 1956, Gaujard; bud long, pointed; flowers orange-red, reverse tinted copper, large; foliage dark; vigorous growth; [(Peace × seedling) × seedling]

Miss Universe, Climbing Cl HT, rb; int. after 1956

Miss Wenn T, mp, 1890, Guillot & fils; flowers large, full

Miss Willmott T, rb, 1899, Paul, G.; flowers coppery red; [L'Ideal × unknown]

Miss Willmott HT, ly, 1917, McGredy; bud large; flowers soft sulfur-cream, edges flushed pale pink, large, dbl., cupped, moderate fragrance; vigorous growth; Gold Medal, NRS, 1916

Miss Windsor HT, mr, 1967, Heron; flowers medium, dbl., high-centered; foliage light green, leathery; very vigorous, upright growth; [sport of Tropicana]

Miss Winifred Denham T, Williams, A.; [Marie van Houtte × unknown]

Missing You F, w, 2000, Horner, Calvin; bud cream; flowers white, reverse cream, 7 cm., dbl., borne in small clusters, moderate fragrance; foliage medium size, medium green, glossy; few prickles; growth bushy, medium (80-90 cm.); [Sweet Magic × Golden Future]; int. by Warley Roses, 2002

Mission Bells HT, pb, 1949, Morris; bud long, pointed; flowers vermilion-pink, 5 in., 43 petals, high-centered, moderate fragrance; foliage dark, soft; vigorous, bushy growth; [Mrs Sam McGredy × Malar-Ros]; int. by Germain's

Mission Supreme HT, ab, 1981, Sanday, John; bud pointed; flowers pale peach pink to apricot, 30 petals, borne singly; foliage deep green; prickles straight, red-brown; vigorous, bushy, medium growth; [City of Glouchester × seedling]

Mississippi – See **Mme Charles Sauvage**, HT

Mississippi HT, dr, 1976, Williams, J. Benjamin; bud pointed; flowers deep red, 4½-5 in., 38 petals, moderate damask fragrance; foliage dark; upright growth; [Charlotte Armstrong × Mister Lincoln]; int. by Kimbrew-Walter, 1976

Mississippi Rainbow HT, yb, 1977, Graham; flowers full, 4 in., 41 petals; foliage thick, glossy; upright growth; int. by South Forrest Rose Nursery

Missy Min, mr, 1979, Lyon; bud pointed; flowers cardinal-red, 1½ in., 22 petals; foliage small; compact, bushy growth; [seedling × seedling]; int. in 1978

Missy Eleanor S, pb, 1999, Watson, Thomas L, & Glenda; flowers light pink, yellow eye, reverse medium pink, 2½ in., single, borne in large clusters; foliage medium size, light green, glossy; prickles moderate; bushy, medium (4-6 ft.) growth; [Anna Ford × Ballerina]

Mistee Min, ly, 1979, Moore, Ralph S.; bud long, pointed; flowers white, tinted yellow, 1½ in., 28 petals, flat, moderate fragrance; foliage small; bushy, upright growth; PP4618; [Little Darling × Peachy White]; int. by Sequoia Nursery

Mister America LCl, dr, 1971, Zombory; flowers blood-red, very large, dbl., high-centered, moderate fragrance; abundant bloom; foliage leathery; very vigorous, climbing growth; [(Paul's Scarlet Climber × Golden Climber) × Pinocchio]; int. by General Bionomics, 1974

Mr Bluebird Min, m, 1960, Moore, Ralph S.; bud ovoid; flowers lavender-blue, 1¼ in., 15 petals; foliage dark; compact, bushy (10-14 in.) growth; [Old Blush × Old Blush]; int. by Sequoia Nursery, 1960

Mr Chips HT, yb, 1970, Dickson, A.; flowers yellow and orange, large, dbl., high-centered; foliage glossy; [Irish Gold × Miss Ireland]

Mr E. E. Greenwell F, op, 1979, Harkness; flowers rosy salmon, 3 in., 18 petals, flat; vigorous, bushy, spreading growth; [Jove × City of Leeds]; int. in 1978

Mr Ernest Holmes – See **Big Pink**, HT

Mr Faithful F, mp, 1968, Harkness; flowers dbl., borne in trusses; [Pink Parfait × Pink Parfait]

Mr Feast's No. 1 – See **Queen of the Prairies**, HSet

Mr Gladstone HP, mp, 1866, Paul, G.; flowers medium, full

Mr J. Bienfait HT, mr, 1923, Van Rossem; flowers brick-red; [Mme Leon Pain × Red-Letter Day]

Mr J. C. B. S, dy, Dickson, Patrick; flowers small, single to semi-dbl., flat, open, borne in small clusters; foliage small, medium green, semi-glossy; growth spreading (groundcover), small; int. in 1993

Mr Joh. M. Jolles HT, ly, 1920, Van Rossem; flowers clear creamy yellow, shaded apricot and golden yellow, dbl.; [Frau Karl Druschki × Mrs Joseph Hill]

Mr John Laing HP, mp, 1887, Bennett; flowers silky pink

Mr Leigh F, mp

Mr Lenard MinFl, mp, 2007, Wells, Verlie W.; flowers reverse slightly lighter, 2¼ in., full, borne mostly solitary; foliage medium size, dark green, semi-glossy; prickles ¼ in., straight, brown, few; growth upright, medium (36-40 in.); exhibition; [seedling × seedling]; int. by Wells MidSouth Roses, 2007

Mister Lincoln HT, dr, 1965, Swim & Weeks; bud urn-shaped; flowers 4½-6 in., 35 petals, high-centered to cupped, intense fragrance; foliage leathery, dark green, matte; vigorous, tall growth; PP2370; [Chrysler Imperial × Charles Mallerin]; int. by C-P, 1965

Mister Lincoln, Climbing Cl HT, dr, 1976, Ram; int. in 1974

Mr McCawber F, w, 1989, White, James J.; bud pointed, white flushed pink; flowers medium, 15-17 petals, high-centered, borne in sprays of 8-10; foliage medium size, medium green, semi-glossy, disease-resistant; prickles hooked, light brown; upright, bushy, tall, prolific growth; hips globular, orange; [(French Lace × Simplex) × (Pristine × White Angel)]; int. in 1988

Mister Otis Min, mr, 1985, Curtis, Thad; flowers small, 35 petals, high-centered, borne singly, no fragrance; foliage small, medium green, matte; upright, bushy growth; [Rise 'n' Shine × Fire Princess]; int. by Hortico Roses, 1986

Mr Pat HT, dr, 1966, Patterson; bud globular; flowers large, dbl., high-centered, intense spicy fragrance; foliage leathery; compact growth; PP2881; [Red Jacket × Mirandy]; int. by Patterson Roses

Mister Sam Min, yb, 2003, Guillebeau, Ray; flowers light yellow with pink, varying to dark pink with light yellow, reverse light yellow, 2 in., very full, borne mostly solitary, no fragrance; foliage medium size, medium green, semi-glossy; prickles average, curving down, brown, moderate; growth bushy, medium; garden decoration, exhibition; [Dora Delle × unknown]; int. by Cool Roses, 2005

Mister Softee HT, w, 1964, Morton's Rose Nursery; flowers creamy white edged pink, open, 4½ in., very dbl.; foliage glossy, dark; very free growth

Mr Standfast HT, w, 1968, Harkness; flowers cream, large, dbl.; foliage glossy; [Dr. A.J. Verhage × Kordes' Perfecta]

Mr Tall HT, op, 1958, Wyant; bud long, pointed; flowers salmon-pink, open, 4 in., 7 petals, intense cinnamon fragrance; foliage dark, leathery; vigorous, upright growth; [Vogue × Grande Duchesse Charlotte]; int. by Wyant Nurs., 1957

Misterre HT, pb

Mistica HT, m, 1967, Dot; bud ovoid; flowers lilac, very large, dbl., cupped, intense fragrance; foliage dark; vigorous growth; [Sterling Silver × Intermezzo]; int. by Minier, 1966

Mistigri – See **Molde**, F dbl.

Mistigri Min, dp, Dickson; flowers fuchsia, dbl., slight fragrance; growth to 50-60 cm.; int. in 2001

Mistral – See **Mistral Parade**, MinFl

Mistral S, ab, Barni; flowers deep apricot, outer petals fade, full, high-centered; growth to 4-5 ft.; int. by Rose Barni, 2004

Mistral Parade MinFl, dy, Poulsen; flowers deep yellow, 5-8 cm., full, moderate fragrance; foliage dark, glossy; bushy (20-40 cm.) growth; int. by Poulsen Roser, 2000

Mistraline HT, op, Laperrière; flowers rose-salmon, silver reverse, large, dbl., high-centered; int. by Sauvageot, 1986

Mrs A. Glen Kidston – See **Mrs Glen Kidston**, HT

Mrs A. Gordon Cl T, 1916, Fell, J.B.

Mrs A. Hudig – See **Flaming June**, Pol

Mrs A. J. Allen HT, pb, 1930, Allen; flowers rich pink, base lemon-yellow, tipped almost white, large, dbl.; [Richmond × Souv. de Mme Boullet]

Mrs A. J. Wylie – See **Margaret M. Wylie**, HT

Mrs A. Kingsmill S (HLaev), lp, 1911, Paul, G.; flowers pale pink, reverse soft rose, single; growth dwarf; [Anemone × unknown]

Mrs A. M. Kirker HP, mr, 1906, Dickson, H.; flowers glossy cherry red, very large, full, moderate fragrance

Mrs A. R. Barraclough HT, mp, 1926, McGredy; bud long, pointed; flowers bright carmine pink, large, dbl., high-centered; vigorous growth

Mrs A. R. Barraclough, Climbing Cl HT, mp, 1935, Fryers Nursery, Ltd.

Mrs A. W. Atkinson HT, w, 1918, Chaplin Bros.; flowers ivory-white, dbl.

Mrs Aaron Ward HT, yb, 1907, Pernet-Ducher; bud long, pointed; flowers yellow, occasionally washed salmon (quite variable), dbl., high-centered; dwarf, compact growth

Mrs Aaron Ward, Climbing Cl HT, yb, 1922, Dickson; flowers Indian yellow, nuanced salmon, very large, full, moderate fragrance; [sport of Mrs Aaron Ward]

Mrs Albert Nash HT, dr, 1929, Clark, A.; buds small; flowers deep black red, medium, dbl., loose, moderate fragrance; recurrent; growth to 1 m.; int. by NRS Victoria

Mrs Alfred Tate HT, rb, 1909, McGredy; flowers coppery red shaded fawn, base shaded ochre

Mrs Alfred West HT, op, 1922, Cant, F.; flowers salmon-pink, dbl.

Mrs Alice Broomhall T, yb, 1910, Schwartz, A.; bud long; flowers salmon apricot, tinted coppery orange yellow, fading to pale pink, large, dbl.; [Dr. Grill × G. Nabonnand]

Mrs Allen Chandler B, w, 1903, Chandler; [Mrs Paul × unknown]

Mrs Alston's Rose Pol, dp, about 1940, Clark; flowers reddish-pink with lighter eye, semi-dbl., borne in large trusses

Mrs Ambrose Ricardo HT, yb, 1914, McGredy; flowers deep honey-yellow, overlaid brighter yellow, very large, dbl., moderate fragrance

Mrs Amy Hammond HT, pb, 1911, McGredy; flowers cream and amber, sometimes flushed pink, base apricot, large, dbl., moderate fragrance; [Mme Abel Chatenay × unknown]; Gold Medal, NRS, 1910

Mrs Andrew Carnegie HT, w, 1913, Cocker; flowers white, center lightly tinted lemon-yellow, very large, dbl.; recurrent; [Niphetos × Frau Karl Druschki]; Gold Medal, NRS, 1912

Mrs Anne Dakin LCl, pb, 1973, Holmes, R.; flowers salmon-pink, reverse cream, large, dbl.; foliage glossy;

moderate, climbing growth; int. by Albrighton Roses, 1972

Mrs Annie Beaufays – See **Frau Anny Beaufays**, F

Mrs Anthony Spalding HT, or, 1934, McGredy; flowers strawberry-red flushed orange, reverse shaded orange, dbl.; vigorous growth

Mrs Anthony Waterer HRg, dr, 1898, Waterer; flowers deep crimson-carmine, large, semi-dbl., intense fragrance; free-flowering; growth vigorous, spreading, 3-4 ft.; hardy; [*R. rugosa* × Général Jacqueminot]

Mrs Archie Gray HT, ly, 1914, Dickson, H.; flowers deep creamy yellow, opening light canary-yellow, large; Gold Medal, NRS, 1913

Mrs Arnold Burr HT, w, 1945, Burr, A.; flowers pure white, large, very dbl., high-centered; foliage glossy; vigorous, upright growth; [Peace × unknown]

Mrs Arthur Bide HT, 1914, Bide

Mrs Arthur Curtiss James LCl, my, 1933, Brownell; bud long, pointed; flowers golden yellow, 10-12 cm., 18 petals, borne mostly solitary, moderate fragrance; non-recurrent; foliage dark green, glossy; prickles large; vigorous, climbing growth; [Mary Wallace × unknown]; int. by J&P

Mrs Arthur E. Coxhead HT, dr, 1911, McGredy; flowers claret-red, shaded brighter red, dbl.

Mrs Arthur Johnson HT, yb, 1920, McGredy; flowers rich orange-yellow to chrome-yellow

Mrs Arthur Moore HT, 1911, Moore, A.K.; [Victor Hugo × C.J. Graham]

Mrs Arthur Munt HT, yb, 1910, Dickson, A.; flowers dark creamy yellow with peach reflections, large, full

Mrs Arthur Robert Waddell HT, op, 1909, Pernet-Ducher; bud long, pointed; flowers reddish-salmon, reverse garnet-red, large, semi-dbl., open, slight apricot fragrance; vigorous growth

Mrs Atlee HT, op, 1926, Chaplin Bros.; flowers silvery pink, shaded soft salmon

Mrs B. L. Rose T, yb, 1902, Bernais fils; flowers coppery aurora yellow, shaded flesh, edges silvery rose-amaranth, medium, full, moderate fragrance

Mrs B. R. Cant T, mp, 1901, Cant, B. R.; flowers silvery rose, base suffused buff, reverse deep rose, dbl., cupped, moderate fragrance; vigorous growth

Mrs B. R. Cant, Climbing Cl T, mp, 1960, Hjort; flowers rose-red to silvery pink; growth to 10-12 ft.; [sport of Mrs B. R. Cant]

Mrs B. Story T, pb, 1905, Williams, A.; [Mme Lombard × unknown]

Mrs B. T. Galloway HT, 1918, Byrnes

Mrs Baker HP, mr, 1876, Turner; flowers bright carmine shaded crimson, very large, full, globular, slight fragrance; stems bushy, shrubby (3 ft.) growth; [Victor Verdier × unknown]

Mrs Bayard Thayer HT, pb, 1915, Waban Conservatories; flowers clear silvery pink, reverse deep rose; [sport of Mrs Charles E. Russell]

Mrs Beatty HT, my, 1926, Cant, B. R.; flowers Marechal Niel yellow, moderate fragrance; foliage bronze; vigorous growth; Gold Medal, NRS, 1925

Mrs Beckwith HT, my, 1922, Pernet-Ducher; bud long, pointed; flowers buttercup-yellow, edged lighter, open, semi-dbl.; vigorous growth; Gold Medal, NRS, 1923

Mrs Belmont Tiffany HT, yb, 1918, Budlong; flowers golden yellow, base apricot-orange; [sport of Sunburst]; int. by A.N. Pierson

Mrs Benjamin R. Cant – See **Mrs B. R. Cant**, T

Mrs Bertram J. Walker HT, dp, 1915, Dickson, H.; flowers bright cerise-pink, large, dbl.; Gold Medal, NRS, 1914

Mrs Billy Crick LCl, mp, Scarman; int. in 1995

Mrs Blamire Young HT, op, 1932, Young; flowers salmon pink, slightly more petals than parent; [sport of Una Wallace]

Mistress Bosanquet B, lp, 1832, Laffay, M.; flowers rosy flesh. large, very dbl., cupped; vigorous growth

Mrs Bosanquet – See **Mistress Bosanquet**, B

Mrs Breedlove HT, pb, 1947, Breedlove; bud ovoid; flowers pink, base yellow, very large, very dbl.; foliage leathery, glossy, dark; vigorous, bushy growth; [sport of Golden Dawn]; int. by Breedlove Nursery

Mrs Brook E. Lee HT, 1918, Byrnes

Mrs Brownell HT, rb, 1942, Brownell; flowers red to pink and coppery orange, medium, semi-dbl., moderate spicy fragrance

Mrs Bryce Allan HT, dp, 1916, Dickson, A.; flowers rose-pink, very dbl.; Gold Medal, NRS, 1916

Mrs Bullen HT, rb, 1917, Pernet-Ducher; flowers crimson, shaded yellow, passing to carmine, large, dbl.

Mrs C. E. Bernays – See **Miss C. E. Bernays**, HT

Mrs C. E. Prell HT, rb, 1938, Fitzhardinge; bud long, pointed; flowers dark cerise, reverse pink, stamens golden, very large, dbl.; long stems; very vigorous growth; [Gustav Grunerwald × Betty Uprichard]; int. by Hazlewood Bros.

Mrs C. E. Salmon HT, mp, 1917, Cant, F.; flowers single

Mrs C. J. Bell – See **Mrs Charles J. Bell**, HT

Mrs C. L. Fitzgerald F, pb, 1937, Fitzgerald; bud pointed; flowers deep pink, base apricot-yellow, small, dbl.; foliage glossy; upright growth; [seedling × Cécile Brunner]

Mrs C. V. Haworth HT, ab, 1919, Dickson, A.; flowers cinnamon-apricot, passing to buff, large, semi-dbl., intense fragrance; [Mrs Wemyss Quin × Hugh Dickson]

Mrs C. V. Haworth, Climbing Cl HT, ab, 1932, Cant, F.; flowers dark apricot with pink, large, semi-dbl.; [sport of Mrs C. V. Haworth]

Mrs C. W. Dunbar-Buller HT, dp, 1919, Dickson, A.; flowers deep rosy carmine, large, dbl.

Mrs C. W. Edwards HT, rb, 1924, McGredy; bud pointed; flowers crimson-carmine, base yellow, reverse veined yellow, over large, dbl., high-centered; foliage dark, glossy; long stems; very vigorous growth

Mrs C. W. Thompson HMult, dp, 1920, U.S. Dept. of Agric.; flowers deep pink, quilled, small, dbl., borne in clusters; good seasonal bloom; vigorous, climbing growth; int. by Storrs & Harrison Co.

Mrs Calvin Coolidge HT, yb, 1924, U.S. Cut Flower Co.; bud long, pointed; flowers golden yellow, deepening to rich orange, semi-dbl.; [sport of Ophelia]; int. by F.R. Pierson

Mrs Campbell Hall T, ab, 1914, Hall/Dickson; flowers soft creamy buff, edged or suffused rose, center warm salmon, high-centered, intense fragrance; foliage leathery, dark; vigorous growth; int. by A. Dickson

Mrs Caroline Swailes HP, lp, 1884, Swailes; flowers light flesh pink to flesh white, large, full; [Eugénie Verdier × unknown]

Mrs Cecily McMullen Cl F, dp, 1995, Bossom, W.E.; flowers salmon pink, 2¾ in., very dbl., borne in small clusters; foliage large, medium green, semi-glossy; few prickles; tall, spreading (10 × 10 ft.), climbing growth; [English Miss × Summer Wine]

Mrs Chaplin HT, pb, 1918, Chaplin Bros.; flowers creamy pink, base shaded yellow

Mrs Charles Bell – See **Mrs Charles J. Bell**, HT

Mrs Charles Custis Harrison HT, m, 1910, Dickson, A.; flowers purple/pink, large, dbl.

Mrs Charles E. Allan HT, ly, 1911, Dickson, H.; bud large, globular; flowers ocher yellow, aging to light yellow, medium to large, very full

Mrs Charles E. F. Gersdorff – See **Maylina**, Cl HT

Mrs Charles E. Pearson HT, ob, 1913, McGredy; bud pointed; flowers orange-apricot, flushed fawn and yellow, large, globular to flat, slight fragrance; Gold Medal, NRS, 1912

Mrs Charles E. Russell HT, dp, 1914, Montgomery, A.; bud long, pointed; flowers rosy carmine, large, dbl., globular; foliage leathery; long stems; vigorous growth; [Mme Caroline Testout × (Mme Abel Chatenay × Marquise Litta de Breteuil)]; int. by Waban Conservatories

Mrs Charles E. Shea HT, rb, 1917, McGredy; flowers shrimp pink, shaded scarlet, petals edges shaded dark red

Mrs Charles H. Rigg HT, my, 1946, McGredy; bud long, pointed; flowers lemon-yellow, large, dbl.; vigorous growth

Mrs Charles Hunter HT, dp, 1912, Paul, W.; flowers carmine-pink, large, dbl.

Mrs Charles J. Bell HT, op, 1915, Bell, Mrs. C.J.; flowers shell-pink, shaded soft salmon, large, dbl.; [sport of Radiance]; int. by A.N. Pierson

Mrs Charles J. Bell, Climbing Cl HT, op, 1929, Thomasville Nursery

Mrs Charles Lamplough HT, ly, 1920, McGredy; flowers pale lemon-yellow, very large, dbl.; vigorous growth; [Frau Karl Druschki × unknown]; Gold Medal, NRS, 1919

Mrs Charles Reed HT, w, 1914, Hicks; flowers pale cream, tinted deep peach, base soft golden yellow, dbl.

Mrs Charles Steward HT, mp, 1960, Verschuren; flowers bright pink, large, dbl., intense fragrance; foliage dark; vigorous growth; int. by Gandy Roses, Ltd., 1959

Mrs Charles Tennant HT, yb, 1936, Cant, F.; flowers clear primrose, shaded rich canary-yellow; foliage bronze; vigorous growth

Mrs Charlotte Guilfoyle HT, 1885, Johnson; [M. Berard × unknown]

Mrs Claude Aveling HT, rb, 1929, Bees; flowers scarlet-cerise, tinted orange, base buttercup-yellow, anther, semi-dbl., moderate fruity fragrance; [The Queen Alexandra Rose × Gorgeous]

Mrs Clement Yatman HT, dr, 1927, Hicks; flowers deep crimson, dbl.

Mrs Cleveland – See **Général Jacqueminot**, HP

Mrs Cocker HP, mp, 1899, Cocker; flowers carnation pink, becoming bluish red, large, full, globular, intense fragrance; [Mrs John Laing × Mabel Morrison]

Mrs Colville HSpn, m; flowers bright crimson-purple, white eye, single; foliage dark; arching, vigorous (4 ft.) growth; [probably *R. spinosissima* × *R. pendulina*]

Mrs Conway Jones HT, w, 1904, Dickson, A.; flowers velvety cream white, center tinted salmon pink, very large, very full, moderate fragrance

Mrs Cornwallis-West HT, w, 1911, Dickson, A.; flowers white, center blush, very large, imbricated, globular; vigorous growth; Gold Medal, NRS, 1910

Mrs Courtney Page HT, ob, 1922, McGredy; bud long, pointed; flowers orange-cerise, shaded carmine, very large, dbl., high-centered; strong stems; Gold Medal, NRS, 1922

Mrs Cripps HP, mp, before 1845, Laffay; flowers delicate rose pink, with a deeper center, large, dbl.

Mrs Curnock Sawday HT, mp, 1920, Hicks; flowers satiny pink, dbl.

Mrs Cynthia Forde – See **Miss Cynthia Forde**, HT

Mrs D. A. Koster Pol, 1934, Koster, D.A.

Mrs Dan Prosser HT, rb, 1946, Prosser; flowers red shaded gold, 5½ in., 60 petals, high-centered; foliage glossy, dark red when young; [Mrs Sam McGredy × Heinrich Wendland]

Mrs David Baillie HT, dp, 1912, Dickson, H.; flowers carmine, penciled deeper, dbl.

Mrs David Jardine HT, mp, 1908, Dickson, A.; flowers

bright rosy pink, shading in the outer petals to salmon pink, very large, full

Mrs David McKee HT, ly, 1904, Dickson, A.; flowers creamy yellow, well-formed, large, full, moderate fragrance; dwarf, compact growth; [Frau Karl Druschki × Kaiserin Auguste Viktoria]

Mrs de Graw – See **Champion of the World**, HP

Mrs DeGraw B, op, 1885, Burgess; flowers bright coral pink, borne in small clusters

Mrs d'Ombrain HP, dr, 1862, Trouillard; flowers red, shaded black

Mrs Doreen Pike HRg, mp, 1994, Austin, David; flowers medium, very dbl., borne in large clusters; foliage small, light green, semi-glossy; numerous prickles; medium (35 in.), bushy, spreading, compact growth; [Martin Frobisher × Roseraie de l'Hay]; int. by David Austin Roses, Ltd., 1993

Mrs Douglas Copeland HT, mp, 1945, Clark, A.; flowers dbl.; vigorous growth

Mrs Dudley Cross T, yb, 1908, Paul, W.; flowers pale yellow, tinted in autumn with crimson, dbl.; vigorous growth

Mrs Dudley Fulton Pol, w, 1931, Thomas; flowers silver-white, large, single, borne in large clusters; dwarf growth; [Dorothy Howarth × Perle d'Or]; int. by Armstrong Nursery

Mrs Dunlop Best – See **Cleveland II**, HT

Mrs Dunlop-Best HT, ab, 1916, Hicks; bud long, pointed; flowers reddish-apricot, base coppery yellow, large, 28 petals, moderate fragrance; foliage leathery, bronze, glossy; vigorous growth

Mrs Dunlop-Best, Climbing Cl HT, ab, 1933, Rosen, L.P.

Mrs E. Alford HT, lp, 1913, Lowe; flowers silvery pink, large, dbl., high-centered

Mrs E. Claxton HT, pb, 1928, Cant, F.; flowers light pink, shaded salmon and carmine

Mrs E. G. Hill HT, w, 1906, Soupert & Notting; flowers alabaster-white, reverse rose-coral, well-shaped, large, dbl.; vigorous growth; [Mme Caroline Testout × Liberty]

Mrs E. Gallagher HT, dr, 1924, McGredy; flowers dark crimson

Mrs E. J. Hudson HT, mp, 1923, Lilley; flowers bright pink, dbl., globular; [Mrs W.J. Grant × unknown]

Mrs E. J. Manners HT, dr, 1938, Burbage Nursery; flowers deep velvety crimson, becoming darker, well-shaped; long, strong stems; vigorous, branching growth

Mrs E. M. Gibson HT, dr, 1940, Clark, A.; [Countess of Stradbrooke × unknown]

Mrs E. M. Gilmer HT, mr, 1927, Cook, J.W.; [seedling × Crusader]

Mrs E. T. Stotesbury HT, pb, 1918, Towill; flowers light cream-pink, reverse dark pink, very dbl.; [(Joseph Hill × My Maryland) × Milady]

Mrs E. Townsend – See **Mrs Edward Townshend**, HT

Mrs E. W. Sterling HT, mp, 1916, Cook, J.W.; flowers rose-pink; [Antoine Rivoire × unnamed pink seedling]

Mrs E. Willis HT, op, 1923, Poulsen; flowers light salmon-pink, large, dbl.

Mrs E. Willis, Climbing Cl HT, lp, 1948, Wilson

Mrs E. Willis HT, lp, Weightman; flowers semi-dbl.; growth moderate; [Mme Segond Weber × unknown]

Mrs E. Wood HT, yb, 1934, Dickson, A.; bud very long; flowers light buff-yellow, tinted yellowish-salmon, becoming cream-yellow; vigorous growth

Mrs Edith Stanley HT, w, 1919, Easlea; flowers creamy white, shaded Indian yellow

Mrs Edward J. Holland HT, op, 1909, McGredy; flowers salmon-rose, large; moderately vigorous growth; Gold Medal, NRS, 1909

Mrs Edward Laxton HT, ob, 1935, Laxton Bros.; flowers flaming orange and old-rose, large, very dbl., high-centered; foliage leathery, dark; very vigorous growth; [Mrs Henry Bowles × Shot Silk]

Mrs Edward Mawley T, pb, 1899, Dickson, A.; flowers bright rich pink, shading to rose or flesh, very large, full, moderate fragrance

Mrs Edward Powell HT, dr, 1911, Bernaix, P.; flowers velvety crimson, large, dbl., globular, moderate fragrance

Mrs Edward Townshend HT, pb, 1911, Guillot; flowers soft rosy fawn, orange carmine reverse, large, full; [Mme Laurette Messimy × Mme Léon Pain]

Mrs Elisha Hicks HT, w, 1919, Hicks; flowers flesh, nearly white, dbl.; [Frau Karl Druschki × Mme Gabriel Luizet]

Mistress Elliot HP, m, 1841, Laffay; flowers purplish pink, silky, large, full, cupped, borne in clusters of 3-4; prickles short, pointed, reddish

Mrs Erskine Pembroke Thom HT, my, 1926, Howard, F.H.; bud long, pointed; flowers clear yellow, well-formed, large, 40 petals, moderate fragrance; vigorous growth; [Grange Colombe × Souv. de Claudius Pernet]; int. by H&S

Mrs Erskine Pembroke Thom, Climbing Cl HT, my, 1933, Dixie Rose Nursery

Mrs Eveline Gandy HT, dr, 1965, Verschuren; flowers dark velvety crimson-scarlet, well-formed, large, 50 petals, high-centered, intense fragrance; bushy, healthy growth; int. by Gandy Roses, Ltd., 1959

Mrs F. F. Prentiss HSet, lp, 1925, Horvath; flowers pale pink, 7-9 cm., dbl., borne in clusters of 5-10, moderate musky fragrance; vigorous, climbing growth; extremely hardy; [(*R. setigera* × *R. wichurana*) × Lady Alice Stanley]

Mrs F. J. Jackson HT, mr, 1933, LeGrice; bud pointed; flowers cerise, dbl.; foliage leathery, bronze; vigorous growth

Mrs F. J. Knight HT, mr, 1928, Knight, J.; flowers velvety scarlet; [sport of Lord Charlemont]

Mrs F. Millar HT, lp, 1904, Williams, A.

Mrs F. R. Pierson HT, dr, 1926, Pierson, F.R.; bud pointed; flowers crimson, shaded scarlet, very large, dbl.; [sport of Premier]

Mrs F. W. Flight HMult, dp, 1905, Flight/Cutbush; flowers rose-pink, fading to light pink, 4 cm., semi-dbl., open, borne in large clusters; non-recurrent; foliage large, rich green, soft; pillar (6-8ft.) growth; [Crimson Rambler × The Garland]

Mrs F. W. Sanford HP, lp, 1898, Curtis; flowers pink tinged white, moderate fragrance; good repeat; [sport of Mrs John Laing]

Mrs F. W. Woodroffe T, lp, 1904, Williams, A.

Mrs Farmer HT, yb, 1918, Pernet-Ducher; bud pointed; flowers yellow, reverse reddish-apricot, dbl.

Mrs Foley-Hobbs T, pb, 1910, Dickson, A.; flowers soft ivory-white, edges tinged clear pink, dbl., moderate fragrance; vigorous, upright growth

Mrs Forde HT, pb, 1913, Dickson, A.; flowers carmine-rose on soft rose-pink, base chrome-yellow, large, dbl., moderate fragrance; Gold Medal, NRS, 1913

Mrs Francis King HT, ly, 1934, Nicolas; flowers cream-white shaded straw-yellow, large, 80 petals, high-centered; foliage leathery; vigorous, bushy growth; [Lady Lilford × Leonard Barron]; int. by J&P

Mrs Frank Bray HT, yb, 1912, Dickson, A.; flowers dark coppery yellow, aging to pink, large, full, moderate fragrance

Mrs Frank Cant HP, mp, 1898, Cant, F.; flowers carnation pink, base darker, reverse silvery white, large, very full; [Mme Gabriel Luizet × Baronne Nathalie de Rothschild]

Mrs Frank Guthrie HT, lp, 1923, Clark, A.; flowers deep flesh in autumn, pale in summer, semi-dbl.; foliage dark, leathery; [(*R. gigantea* × unknown) × unknown]; int. by Hazelwood Bros.

Mrs Frank J. Usher HT, yb, 1920, Dobbie; flowers rich yellow, edged rosy carmine, very dbl.; stems weak; [Queen Mary × unnamed variety]

Mrs Frank Schramm HT, pb, 1934, Schramm; flowers bright glowing rose-pink, reverse slightly lighter, dbl.; foliage leathery, dark; very large, long stems; very vigorous growth; [sport of Briarcliff]

Mrs Frank Serpa Pol, dp, 1954, Serpa; flowers deep pink, borne in clusters; dwarf (18 in.) growth; [Rouletii × China Doll]; int. by Port Stockton Nursery

Mrs Frank Verdon HT, my, 1935, Bees; flowers creamy yellow, very large, dbl.; foliage leathery, dark; vigorous growth; [Joan Horton × Marion Horton]

Mrs Frank Workman HT, dp, 1911, Dickson, H.; flowers bright rose-pink

Mrs Franklin D. Roosevelt HT, dy, 1933, Traendly & Schenck; bud long, pointed; flowers golden yellow, large, dbl., globular; foliage glossy; very vigorous growth; [sport of Talisman]

Mrs Franklin Dennison HT, w, 1915, McGredy; bud long, pointed; flowers porcelain-white, veiled primrose-yellow, base ochre, very large, dbl., high-centered

Mrs Fred Cook HT, ob, 1920, Easlea; flowers light terra-cotta, edged silvery white, dbl.

Mrs Fred Danks HT, m, 1951, Clark, A.; bud long, pointed; flowers pink tinted lilac, large, 15 petals; foliage leathery; very vigorous, upright, pillar growth; int. by NRS Victoria

Mrs Fred H. Howard HT, ob, 1926, Dobbie; flowers orange-apricot edged straw-yellow, dbl.

Mrs Fred L. Lainson HT, pb, 1934, Scittine; bud long, pointed; flowers deep pink, almost red, base yellow and bronze, reverse orange, dbl.; foliage leathery, glossy, bronze; vigorous growth; [sport of Talisman]; int. by Lainson

Mrs Fred Poulsom HT, mp, 1920, Therkildsen; flowers vivid pink; prickles thorny; vigorous growth; [Edith Part × unnamed variety]

Mrs Fred Searl HT, pb, 1917, Dickson, A.; flowers fawny shell-pink, reflex silvery carmine-rose, deeper at edges, large, full, globular, moderate fragrance

Mrs Fred Straker HT, yb, 1910, Dickson, A.; flowers light orange-yellow, medium, dbl.

Mrs Frederick Lee S, pb, Williams, J.B.; flowers cherry pink with ivory center, 5 petals, borne usually in clusters, slight fragrance; growth to 5 ft.; int. by Hortico, Inc., 2005

Mrs Frederick W. Vanderbilt HT, or, 1912, McGredy; flowers deep orange-red, shaded apricot, large, dbl., pointed, moderate musky, tea fragrance; Gold Medal, NRS, 1913

Mrs G. A. van Rossem – See **Mevrouw G. A. van Rossem**, HT

Mrs G. A. van Rossem, Climbing – See **Mevrouw G. A. van Rossem, Climbing**, Cl HT

Mrs G. A. Wheatcroft HT, pb, 1926, Wheatcroft Bros.; flowers coppery pink to silver-rose at tips, reverse soft salmon-pink, dbl.; [sport of Lady Pirrie]

Mrs G. M. Smith HT, dr, 1935, Bees; bud long, pointed; flowers deep crimson, dbl., cupped; vigorous growth; [Red-Letter Day × Mrs J.J. Hedley-Willis]

Mrs G. Payne T, lp, 1911, Williams, A.

Mrs G. W. Kershaw HT, mp, 1906, Dickson, A.; flowers shining carnation pink, very large, full

Mrs George B. Easlea HT, dp, 1939, Easlea; flowers sparkling carmine-pink, well-formed, very large, high-centered; strong stems

Mrs George C. Thomas HMsk, op, 1925, Thomas;

flowers salmon-pink, center orange, 2-2½ in., semi-dbl.; repeat bloom; climbing growth to 10ft.; [Mme Caroline Testout, Climbing × Moonlight]; int. by B&A

Mrs George Dickson HP, mp, 1884, Bennett; flowers brilliant satiny pink, large, dbl.; [Mme Clémence Joigneaux × unknown]

Mrs George Geary HT, ob, 1929, Burbage Nursery; bud pointed; flowers orange-cerise, shaded cardinal, very large, 35-40 petals, high-centered; vigorous growth; [Red-Letter Day × Mrs Wemyss Quin]

Mrs George Gordon HT, mr, 1915, Dickson; flowers glossy rose red, edged silvery pink, base yellowish-pink, large, full

Mrs George Marriott HT, w, 1918, McGredy; bud long, pointed; flowers deep cream and pearl, suffused rose, very large, dbl., high-centered; Gold Medal, NRS, 1917

Mrs George Preston HT, lp, 1910, Dickson, A.; flowers silvery pink, very large, full, globular

Mrs George Shawyer HT, pb, 1911, Lowe & Shawyer; flowers rosy pink, reverse pale pink, very large, dbl.; [Mme Hoste × Joseph Lowe]

Mrs George Shawyer, Climbing Cl HT, pb, 1918, Lindquist, E.J.

Mrs Georgia Chobe HT, lp, 1937, H&S; bud long; flowers large, dbl., high-centered; foliage leathery, light; vigorous growth; [Miss Rowena Thom × Renault]

Mrs Glen Kidston HT, dp, 1916, Dickson; flowers carmine-pink, large, full, moderate fragrance

Mrs Gordon Sloan HT, op, 1912, Dickson, A.; flowers bright coppery salmon pink, center flesh white, edged cream white, large, full

Mrs Graham Hart Cl T, lp, 1900, Williams, A.

Mrs H. Cobden Turner HT, rb, 1948, Mee; flowers cherry-cerise flushed orange, base yellow, 3-4 in., 26 petals; foliage glossy; moderately vigorous growth; [Ophelia × seedling]; int. by Fryer's Nursery, Ltd.

Mrs H. D. Greene HT, rb, 1918, Easlea; flowers reddish-bronze, becoming flame and coppery pink; [sport of Joseph Hill]

Mrs H. G. Johnstone HT, pb, 1930, Bees; bud long; flowers rose-pink, base and edges rose, very large, dbl., high-centered; vigorous growth; [Mme Caroline Testout × Mrs George Shawyer]

Mrs H. J. Hedley-Willis HT, dr, 1930, Bees of Chester; flowers medium, semi-dbl.

Mrs H. L. Wettern HT, mp, 1922, McGredy; flowers vivid pink, dbl.

Mrs H. M. Eddie HT, w, 1932, Eddie; flowers creamy white, passing to purest white, 5-6 in., 40-45 petals, high-centered; foliage dark, leathery, glossy; vigorous, bushy growth; [Mrs Charles Lamplough × Mev. G.A. van Rossem]

Mrs H. M. Eddie, Climbing Cl HT, w, 1944, Eddie

Mrs H. P. Abbot T, lp, 1901, Williams, A.; [Mme Lombard × unknown]

Mrs H. R. Darlington HT, ly, 1919, McGredy; bud long, pointed; flowers clear creamy yellow, well-formed, balling in wet weather; long stems; vigorous growth; Gold Medal, NRS, 1919

Mrs Harkness – See **Paul's Early Blush**, HP

Mrs Harkness HP, pb, 1894, Harkness; flowers white striped pink; [sport of Heinrich Schultheis]

Mrs Harold Alston Cl HT, mp, 1940, Clark, A.; flowers dbl.; good repeat; [Sunny South × unknown]

Mrs Harold Bibby HT, pb, 1936, Bees; flowers soft pink veined red, outer petals silvery pink; foliage dark

Mrs Harold Brocklebank HT, w, 1907, Dickson, A.; flowers creamy white, center buff, base soft yellow, dbl.

Mrs Harold Brookes HT, mr, 1931, Clark, A.; flowers very bright red, large, dbl., cupped, moderate fragrance; foliage light; vigorous, bushy growth; [Frau Oberhofgartner Singer × Firebrand]; int. by NRS Victoria

Mrs Harry Turner HP, mr, 1880, Turner; flowers shining scarlet-crimson, shaded chestnut, large, full, globular; [Charles Lefèbvre × Alfred de Rougemont]

Mrs Harvey Thomas HT, pb, 1905, Bernaix fils; flowers carmine with coppery red reflections, large, full, cupped, moderate fragrance

Mrs Henri Daendels HT, ab, 1931, Buisman, G. A. H.; flowers apricot shaded orange, reverse violet-pink, large, very dbl.; foliage bronze; strong stems; very vigorous growth; [Mrs Henry Bowles × Rev. F. Page-Roberts]

Mrs Henri Daendels, Climbing Cl HT, ab, 1950, Buisman, G. A. H.

Mrs Henry Balfour HT, pb, 1918, McGredy; flowers ivory-white, base primrose, edge penciled rose, like a picotee

Mrs Henry Bowles HT, mp, 1921, Chaplin Bros.; flowers rosy-pink, flushed salmon, well-formed, large, 50 petals, high-centered; foliage dark, glossy; vigorous growth; [Lady Pirrie × Gorgeous]

Mrs Henry Bowles, Climbing Cl HT, mp, 1929, Dobbie; flowers pink, peach at base, very large

Mrs Henry Morse HT, pb, 1919, McGredy; bud long, pointed; flowers cream, tinted rose, marked and veined red, large, dbl., high-centered; dwarf growth; [Mme Abel Chatenay × Lady Pirrie]; Gold Medal, NRS, 1919

Mrs Henry Morse, Climbing Cl HT, pb, 1929, Chaplin Bros.; flowers yellowish-pink, very large, full; [sport of Mrs Henry Morse]

Mrs Henry Winnett HT, dr, 1917, Dunlop; bud long, pointed; flowers deep rich red, large, dbl., high-centered; foliage leathery; vigorous growth; [Mrs Charles E. Russell × Mrs George Shawyer]

Mrs Henry Winnett, Climbing Cl HT, dr, 1930, Bernaix, P.; flowers large, full, moderate fragrance; [sport of Mrs Henry Winnett]

Mrs Herbert Carter HT, ab, 1934, Cant, F.; flowers apricot-yellow, center deeper, veined bronze, dbl., moderate fragrance; vigorous growth

Mrs Herbert Dowsett HT, pb, 1928, Easlea; flowers several shades deeper, otherwise similar to parent; [sport of Los Angeles]

Mrs Herbert Hawksworth T, r, 1912, Dickson, A.; flowers ecru on milk-white, dbl.

Mrs Herbert Hoover HT, mr, 1928, Coddington; bud long, pointed; flowers rich velvety red, dbl.; foliage dark, leathery; vigorous growth; [Ophelia × Hoosier Beauty]

Mrs Herbert Nash HT, dr, 1925, Chaplin Bros.; flowers scarlet-crimson shaded deep crimson, overlarge; long, strong stems; vigorous growth

Mrs Herbert Stevens HT, w, 1910, McGredy; bud long, pointed; flowers white tinged with soft pink, dbl., high-centered, moderate fragrance; foliage light; vigorous, bushy growth; [Frau Karl Druschki × Niphetos]

Mrs Herbert Stevens, Climbing Cl HT, w, 1922, Pernet-Ducher; bud large, pure white; flowers semi-dbl., intense fragrance; foliage large; growth to 12 ft.; [sport of Mrs Herbert Stevens]

Mrs Hilton Brooks HT, yb, 1929, Cant, F.; flowers saffron-yellow, base deeper, suffused pink and carmine, dbl., moderate fragrance

Mrs Hornby Lewis HT, ob, 1921, Hicks; flowers orange-yellow, very dbl.; [Gorgeous × Mme Mélanie Soupert]

Mrs Hovey HSet, w, 1850, Pierce; flowers blush to almost white, large, full; foliage dark green; [*R. setigera* × unknown]

Mrs Hubert Taylor T, pb, 1910, Dickson, A.; flowers shell pink, edges with ivory white; susceptible to mildew

Mrs Hugh Dettmann Cl HT, ab, 1930, Clark, A.; flowers bright apricot-yellow, dbl.; non-recurrent; climbing growth; pillars; int. by NRS Victoria

Mrs Hugh Dickson HT, yb, 1915, Dickson, H.; flowers deep cream, heavily suffused orange and apricot, large, 44 petals; Gold Medal, NRS, 1916

Mrs Inge Poulsen F, pb, 1949, Poulsen, S.; flowers pink with a yellow center, open, medium, semi-dbl.; foliage light, matte; vigorous, compact (80 cm.) growth; [Poulsen's Pink × seedling]; int. by Poulsen, 1949

Mrs Iris Clow F, lp, 1993, Harkness; flowers blush pink, light pink reverse, paling to near white, loose, 28 petals, cupped, moderate spicy fragrance; foliage large, dark green, glossy; upright, medium growth; [Memento × Princess Alice]; int. by Harkness New Roses, Ltd., 1994

Mrs Isabel Milner – See **Isabelle Milner**, HT

Mrs J. Berners HP, dp, 1866, Ward; flowers magenta pink, small

Mrs J. C. Ainsworth HT, mp, 1918, Clarke Bros.; flowers rose-pink, very dbl.; [sport of Mrs Charles E. Russell]

Mrs J. C. Manifold HP, lp, 1915, Adamson; [Prince Camille de Rohan × unknown]

Mrs J. D. Eisele HT, pb, 1933, Howard, F.H.; bud long, pointed; flowers brilliant cherry-pink, center shaded scarlet, very large, dbl.; vigorous growth; [Premier Supreme × McGredy's Scarlet]; int. by H&S

Mrs J. D. Russell HT, dr, 1930, Bees; flowers deep crimson, center maroon, almost black in certain lights, dbl., cupped; [Prince Camille de Rohan × Mrs Aaron Ward]

Mrs J. F. Redly HT, lp; flowers pale flesh-pink, center tinted salmon, large, very dbl.; lightly repeats in late summer.; vigorous growth

Mrs J. Heath HT, yb, 1924, McGredy; flowers maize-yellow, tinted peach-red, center yellow, dbl.

Mrs J. J. Hedley-Willis HT, dr, 1929, Bees; bud pointed; flowers dark crimson, center almost plum-black, dbl., high-centered; [Admiral Ward × Richmond]

Mrs J. Pierpont Morgan T, dp, 1895, May; flowers bright cerise or rose pink, large, very dbl.; [sport of Mme Cusin]

Mrs J. T. McIntosh HT, ab, 1935, McIntosh; flowers creamy apricot, center deeper apricot, base golden yellow, dbl.; vigorous growth; int. by Brundrett

Mrs J. Wylie HT, lp, 1923, Dickson, H.; flowers silvery blush-pink

Mrs James Craig HT, op, 1909, Dickson, H.; flowers salmon pink, petal edges peach, large, full

Mrs James Garner HT, ab, 1931, Cant, F.; flowers buff, base orange

Mrs James Lynas HT, pb, 1914, Dickson, H.; flowers pearly pink, reverse and edges flushed rosy peach, dbl.; Gold Medal, NRS, 1913

Mrs James Shearer HT, w, 1923, Ferguson, W.; flowers pure white, base yellow, large, dbl., high-centered; [seedling × Mme Colette Martinet]

Mrs James White HT, w, 1911, Dickson, H.; flowers muddy whitish-pink, medium, full

Mrs James Williamson HT, mp, 1922, Dickson, H.; flowers clear pink, dbl.

Mrs James Wilson T, yb, 1889, Dickson, A.; flowers deep lemon yellow, edged pink, very large, full, moderate fragrance; growth upright, vigorous

Mrs Jeannette G. Leeds HT, rb, 1942, Joseph H. Hill, Co.; bud globular, jasper-red and apricot-buff; flowers venetian pink, 5-6 in., 50-60 petals; foliage dark, leathery; very vigorous, upright growth; [Joanna Hill × R.M.S. Queen Mary]

Mrs Jennie Deverman HT, pb, 1933, Deverman; flowers cerise edged silvery, base tinted gold; [sport of Pres. Herbert Hoover]

Mrs Jessie Fremont T, w, 1891, Dingee & Conard; flowers white, aging to deep flesh pink, sometimes shaded with coppery red, medium; [Duchesse de Brabant × unknown]

Mrs Joan Lewis S, m, 2000, Lewis, Victor; flowers mauve-pink, reverse light pink, 11-12 cm., very full, borne mostly singly; foliage large, light green, matte; numerous prickles; growth spreading, tall (2 m.)

Mrs John Bateman HT, dp, 1905, Dickson, A.; flowers dark China pink, base tinted yellow, very full

Mrs John Bell HT, dr, 1928, Bell, Judy G.; bud long; flowers carmine, large, dbl., cupped; int. by Dobbie

Mrs John Cook HT, w, 1920, Cook, J.W.; bud long, pointed; flowers white, suffused soft pink, deepening in cool weather, large, dbl., cupped; [Ophelia × seedling]; int. by A.N. Pierson

Mrs John Foster HT, dr, 1915, Hicks; flowers rich vermilion, large, dbl., moderate fragrance

Mrs John Inglis HT, dr, 1920, McGredy; flowers rich crimson, dbl.

Mrs John K. Allan HT, lp, 1920, Dickson, H.; flowers soft rosy pink, reverse darker, dbl.; Gold Medal, NRS, 1920

Mrs John Laing HP, mp, 1887, Bennett; bud pointed; flowers soft pink, large, 45 petals, moderate fragrance; recurrent bloom; foliage light; vigorous, rather dwarf growth; [Francois Michelon × unknown]

Mrs John McLaren HP, dp, 1905, California Nursery Co.; flowers deep silvery pink

Mrs John McNabb S, w, 1941, Skinner; bud with very long sepals; flowers very dbl.; non-recurrent; foliage large, dark, slightly rugose, prickly underneath; few prickles; growth to 5 ft.; [*R. beggeriana* × *R. rugosa*]

Mrs John Taylor T, mp, 1887, Bennett; flowers silky pink

Mrs Jones – See **Centenaire de Lourdes**, F

Mrs Joseph H. Welch HT, mp, 1911, McGredy; flowers brilliant rose-pink, large, dbl.; vigorous growth; Gold Medal, NRS, 1910

Mrs Joseph H. Welch, Climbing Cl HT, mp, 1922, Perkins, H.S.

Mrs Joseph Hiess Pol, lp, 1943, Shepherd; flowers Mary Wallace pink, base white, 40 petals, cupped, borne in clusters of 3-16; foliage leathery; strong stems; growth vigorous, upright, bushy, compact; [Roserie × unknown]; int. by Klyn

Mrs Jowitt HP, rb, 1880, Cranston; flowers glossy crimson, shaded salmon red, very large, full, globular

Mrs K. B. Sharma HT, w, Pal, Dr. B.P.; buds long; flowers flower petals very large, slight fragrance; int. in 1989

Mrs L. B. Coddington HT, mp, 1931, Coddington; bud long, pointed; flowers large, dbl.; foliage leathery; vigorous growth; [Templar × Souv. de Claudius Pernet]

Mrs L. B. Copeland F, pb, 1934, Fitzgerald; flowers salmon-pink, veined, base yellow, small, dbl., globular; foliage dark, glossy; vigorous growth; [seedling × Cécile Brunner]

Mrs Laing HP, mp, 1872, Verdier, E.; flowers bright carmine pink, medium, full

Mrs Laing HP, mp, 1882, Cranston; flowers carmine pink

Mrs Laxton HP, mp, 1875, Laxton; flowers bright crimson-pink, very large, very full, moderate fragrance

Mrs Leela Subhedar – See **Leela**, HT

Mrs Leonard Petrie HT, yb, 1911, Dickson, A.; flowers sulfur-yellow, reverse petal edges with wine red reflections, large, full, moderate fragrance

Mrs Leslie Moss Cl HT, dp, 1944, Moss; flowers carmine-pink, medium, semi-dbl.; foliage leathery; vigorous, climbing growth; int. by Mason, F.

Mrs Lincoln HT, dr, Williams, J. Benjamin; flowers large dark red with velvet texture, slight fragrance; growth strong, upright plant; int. by Hortico, 1997

Mrs Littleton Dewhurst HWich, w, 1912, Pearson; flowers small, semi-dbl., borne in large, loose trusses; [sport of Lady Gay]

Mrs Lovell Swisher HT, pb, 1926, Howard, F.H.; bud pointed; flowers salmon-pink, edged flesh, well-formed, dbl., moderate fragrance; foliage bronze; very vigorous growth; [seedling × Souv. de Claudius Pernet]; int. by H&S

Mrs Lovell Swisher, Climbing Cl HT, pb, 1930, H&S

Mrs Luther Burbank HT, mp, 1954, Swim, H.C.; bud long, pointed; flowers rose-pink, 4-4½ in., 34 petals, cupped, intense spicy fragrance; foliage leathery; vigorous growth; [Christopher Stone × Charlotte Armstrong]; int. by Stark Bros., 1954

Mrs M. H. Horvath HT, ly, 1940, Horvath; bud long, pointed; flowers pale yellow, open, large, 40 petals; foliage glossy; long stems; very vigorous, upright growth; [(Mme Butterfly × ?) × Souv. de Claudius Pernet]; int. by Wayside Gardens Co.

Mrs M. H. Walsh HWich, w, 1913, Walsh; flowers pure snow-white, small, dbl., borne in clusters; foliage large, glossy; very vigorous, trailing growth

Mrs M. J. Gillon HT, dr, 1976, Rijksstation Voor Sierplantenteelt; bud ovoid; flowers red-purple, 4 in., 37 petals, globular, moderate fragrance; foliage glossy, dark; upright growth; [Super Star × Prima Ballerina]; int. in 1974

Mrs Mabel V. Socha HT, my, 1935, H&S; bud pointed; flowers pure lemon-yellow, dbl.; long, strong stems; [seedling × Souv. de Claudius Pernet]

Mrs MacDonald's Rose HRg, dp, Reid; non-recurrent; apparently *R. rugosa plena* × *R. acicularis*; int. by P.H. Wright

Mrs MacKellar HT, my, 1915, Dickson, A.; flowers deep citron or pure canary, passing to primrose, large, dbl., high-centered, moderate fragrance

Mrs Mary D. Ward HT, pb, 1927, Ward, F.B.; flowers shell-pink and gold, reverse ivory-white; [Double Ophelia × Souv. de Claudius Pernet]

Mrs Mary Thomson S, pb, 1996, Thomson, George L.; flowers lilac pink, cream center, prominent gold stamens, reverse slightly lighter, 5½-6½ in., 8-14 petals, borne in large clusters, intense fragrance; foliage medium size, medium green, dull; few prickles; spreading, medium (5 × 4 ft.) growth; [Dapple Dawn × Ophelia]

Mrs Matso's Moss M, dr

Mrs Matthews HT, dp, 1923, Matthews, W.J.

Mrs Maud Alston – See **Mrs Alston's Rose**, Pol

Mrs Maud Dawson – See **Maud Dawson**, HT

Mrs Mavis Watson MinFl, ly, 2005, Paul Chessum Roses; flowers dbl., borne in large clusters; foliage medium size, dark green, semi-glossy; prickles medium, medium, pink, moderate; growth bushy, medium (24 in.); bedding, containers; [seedling × seedling]; int. by World of Roses, 2005

Mrs Maynard Sinton HT, pb, 1909, McGredy; flowers silvery white suffused pink, very large; moderately vigorous growth; Gold Medal, NRS, 1909

Mrs Mina Lindell Sp, lp, 1927; flowers 10-12 petals; non-recurrent; growth to 4 ft.; hardy; a form of *R. macounii*, found in S. Dakota; int. by N.E. Hansen

Mrs Miniver HT, mr, 1944, Chambard, C.; flowers scarlet-crimson, reverse slightly darker, 5½-6 in., 20 petals, cupped; foliage soft; vigorous, upright, bushy, compact growth; int. by J&P

Mrs Mona Hunting HT, yb, 1916, Dickson, H.; bud long, pointed, deep chamois yellow; flowers pure fawn, medium, dbl.

Mrs Moorfield Storey HT, lp, 1915, Waban Conservatories; flowers shell-pink, center deeper, large, dbl.; [(Gen. MacArthur × unknown) × Joseph Hill]

Mrs Moyna HT, 1913, Dickson

Mrs Muir MacKean HT, dr, 1912, McGredy; flowers carmine-crimson, large, high-centered; vigorous growth

Mrs Murray Allison HT, pb, 1925, Prior; flowers rose-pink, base carmine, dbl.

Mrs Myles Kennedy T, pb, 1906, Dickson, A.; flowers silvery white tinted buff, center and reverse pink, large, dbl.; vigorous growth

Mrs Nancy Cannon HMsk, m, 2004, Clyde W. Cannon; flowers mauve, reverse light mauve, 1 in., single, borne in clusters of 15-20, no fragrance; continuous; foliage medium size, medium green, matte; prickles 3/16 in., slightly curve, few; growth bushy, short; border, containers; [sport of Ballerina]; int. in 2003

Mrs Nieminen HT, rb, 1954, Buyl Frères; flowers blood-red shaded scarlet, well-formed, large, very dbl.; bushy, compact growth; [Hens Verschuren × Poinsettia]

Mrs Norman Watson Cl HT, dp, 1930, Clark, A.; flowers deep cherry-pink, lighter at edges, 5 in., borne mostly solitary; growth very vigorous; pillar; [Radiance × Gwen Hash]; int. by Geelong Hort. Soc.

Mrs Norris M. Agnew HT, ob, 1934, Bees; bud pointed; flowers orange-cerise, large, dbl.; foliage leathery, light; very vigorous growth; [J.C. Thornton × Florence L. Izzard]

Mrs O. G. Orpen HGal, dp, 1906, Orpen; flowers glowing carnation pink, center lighter, large

Mrs Oakley Fisher HT, dy, 1921, Cant, B. R.; flowers deep orange-yellow, very large, single, borne in clusters, moderate fragrance; foliage dark, bronze, glossy; vigorous growth

Mrs Octavia Hill – See **Octavia Hill**, F

Mrs Olive Sackett F, mr, 1931, Wirtz & Eicke; flowers bright red, well-formed, 2-2½ in., semi-dbl.; foliage bronze in autumn; vigorous growth; [sport of Else Poulsen]; int. by Spath

Mrs Oliver Ames T, pb, 1898, Montgomery, R.; flowers delicate pink, edged deep pink, nearly white at base, ruffled, full; growth compact, bushy; [sport of Mme Cusin]

Mrs Oliver Ames HT, my, 1941, Verschuren; bud long, pointed; flowers lemon-yellow, 3½-4 in., 63 petals, globular; foliage leathery; long stems; vigorous growth; [Max Krause × Julien Potin]; int. by Dreer

Mrs Oliver Mee HT, rb, 1948, Mee; flowers scarlet shaded gold, 5-6 in., 35 petals, high-centered; foliage glossy, bronze; very vigorous growth; [Mrs Charles Lamplough × Edith Mary Mee]; int. by Fryer's Nursery, Ltd.

Mrs Opie T, op, 1877, Bell; flowers glowing salmon pink, medium to large, full

Mrs Oswald Lewis HT, yb, 1936, Cant, F.; flowers soft canary-yellow, outer petals edged flame, well-formed, dbl.; long stems; vigorous growth; Gold Medal, Bagatelle, 1935

Mrs Oswald Smeaton HT, pb, 1932, Easlea; flowers ivory-cream, center and petal tips pink, very large, 50-60 petals; long stems; vigorous growth

Mrs P. H. Coats HT, w, 1909, Dickson, H.; flowers cream white, large, full

Mrs Pat Pol, lp, 1928, Lilley; flowers Chatenay pink, small, dbl., moderate fragrance

Mrs Paul B, lp, 1891, Paul & Son; flowers blush-white shaded rosy peach, large, moderate Damask fragrance; recurrent; stout, upright, modest growth; [Mme Isaac Pereire × unknown]

Mrs Paul Goudie HT, yb, 1932, McGredy; flowers deep buttercup-yellow, edged carmine-scarlet, very large, dbl., moderate fruity fragrance

Mrs Paul Hvid B, w

Mrs Paul J. Howard Cl HT, rb, 1938, Howard, F.H.; bud long, pointed; flowers brilliant crimson, reverse flame-red, 5 in., 30 petals, moderate spicy fragrance; foliage large, bronze,leathery; long stems; very vigorous, climbing (12-15 ft.) growth; [Miss Rowena Thom × Paul's Lemon Pillar]; int. by H&S

Mrs Paul M. Pierson HT, pb, 1930, Pierson, P.M.; bud long, pointed; flowers soft pink, reverse brighter, very large, dbl., high-centered; [sport of Premier]

Mrs Paul R. Bosley HT, my, 1941, Bosley Nursery; flowers apricot-yellow; [sport of Mme Joseph Perraud]

Mrs Percy V. Pennybacker HT, pb, 1929, Vestal; flowers peach-pink shaded silver, dbl., cupped; [Mme Butterfly × unknown]

Mrs Peter Blair HT, yb, 1906, Dickson, A.; flowers lemon-chrome, center golden yellow, well-formed, large; Gold Medal, NRS, 1906

Mrs Philip Russell HT, dr, 1927, Clark, A.; bud long, pointed; flowers dark red, shaded black, semi-dbl.; foliage glaucous green; vigorous, semi-climbing growth; pillar or large bush; [Hadley × Red Letter Day]; int. by Hackett

Mrs Pierce HSet, mp, 1850, Pierce; flowers rose pink, well-formed

Mrs Pierre S. duPont HT, my, 1929, Mallerin, C.; bud long, pointed, reddish gold; flowers golden yellow, becoming lighter, 40 petals, moderate fruity fragrance; foliage rich green; moderate growth; [(Ophelia × Rayon d'Or) × ((Ophelia × Constance) × Souv. de Claudius Pernet)]; int. by C-P; Gold Medal, Bagatelle, 1929

Mrs Pierre S. duPont, Climbing Cl HT, my, 1933, Hillock; flowers yellow on an ochre ground, large, full, moderate fragrance; [sport of Mrs Pierre S. Dupont]

Mrs Potter Palmer HT, op, 1909, Breitmeyer; flowers salmon red, edged silvery pink, reverse darker, medium to large, full

Mrs Prentiss Nichols HT, dp, 1923, Scott, R.; flowers brilliant deep pink, dbl.; [Ophelia × seedling]

Mistress Quickly S, mp, 1997, Austin, David; flowers petals informally arranged, small, 90-100 petals, borne in very large clusters; foliage small to medium size, medium green, semi-glossy; few prickles; bushy, medium growth; disease resistant; PP10617; [Blush Noisette × Martin Frobisher]; int. by David Austin Roses, Ltd., 1998

Mrs R. B. McLennan HT, pb, 1924, Easlea; flowers satiny rose suffused yellow, very dbl.; [George C. Waud × Mme Caristie Martel]

Mrs R. B. Moloney HT, mr, 1925, McGredy; flowers brilliant carmine-red, dbl.

Mrs R. C. Bell HT, mr, 1920, Clark, A.; flowers bright red; [Gen. MacArthur × Château de Clos Vougeot]

Mrs R. D. McClure HT, op, 1913, Dickson, H.; flowers salmon-pink, very large, dbl.

Mrs R. G. Sharman-Crawford HP, pb, 1894, Dickson, A.; flowers rosy pink, outer petals tinted flesh, large, 75 petals, cupped, moderate fragrance; good repeat; vigorous growth; general appearance and recurrent bloom suggest that it is a descendent of Victor Verdier

Mrs R. M. Finch Pol, mp, 1923, Finch; flowers rosy pink, becoming lighter, medium, dbl., borne in large clusters; bushy growth; [Orléans Rose × unknown]

Mrs R. M. Finch, Climbing Cl Pol, mp

Mrs R. M. King HT, ab, 1927, Harrison, A.; [Mme Abel Chatenay × W.R. Smith]

Mrs Ramon de Escofet HT, dr, 1919, Easlea; flowers flame-crimson, large, dbl.

Mrs Redford HT, ab, 1919, McGredy; flowers bright apricot-orange, medium, semi-dbl., intense fragrance; foliage dark green, glossy, holly-like; Gold Medal, NRS, 1917

Mrs Reynolds Hole T, pb, 1900, Nabonnand, P.&C.; flowers carmine shaded purple rose, reverse carmine, large, dbl.; [Archiduc Joseph × André Schwartz]

Mrs Richard Draper HT, mp, 1912, Dickson, H.; flowers glossy carmine pink, center lighter silvery flesh pink, very large, full

Mrs Richard Turnbull LCl, w, 1945, Clark, A.; bud yellow; flowers cream, handsome stamens, 14 cm., single; hybrid gigantea

Mrs Richards F, pb, 1968, Harkness; flowers pink tinged apricot, single, borne in trusses; foliage dark, glossy; [Ann Elizabeth × Circus]

Mrs Robert Bacon HT, ab, 1934, Bertanzel; flowers golden apricot shading to coral, base yellow, large, very dbl., cupped; [sport of Talisman]

Mrs Robert Garrett HT, mp, 1900, Cook, J.W.; flowers shell pink, center deeper, medium, dbl.; [Comtesse de Caserta × Mme Eugene Verdier]

Mrs Robert Mitchell HT, pb, 1926, Jersey Nursery; flowers salmon-rose, overlaid coppery pink, very large, full; foliage glossy; [St. Helena × Mrs Redford]

Mrs Robert Peary – See **Kaiserin Auguste Viktoria, Climbing**, Cl HT

Mrs Robinson F, pb, 2005, Orent, Clifford; flowers white center with pink outers, 2-3 in., single, borne in small clusters, moderate fragrance; foliage small, dark green, glossy; bushy, short (18-24 in.) growth; [seedling × seedling]; int. by Ashdown Roses Ltd, 2006

Mrs Rosalie Wrinch LCl, lp, 1915, Brown, W.&J.; flowers shell-pink, large, semi-dbl.; vigorous, pillar (5-8 ft.) growth; [Frau Karl Druschki × Hugh Dickson]

Mrs Roy Green HT, dr, 1940, Clark, A.; flowers very large; long stems

Mrs Rumsey HP, mp, 1899, Rumsey; flowers rosey pink; [sport of Mrs George Dickson]

Mrs Russell Grimwade T, mp, 1938, Grimwade; flowers fuchsia-pink; [sport of Lorraine Lee]

Mrs S. K. Rindge HT, yb, 1919, H&S; bud long, pointed; flowers deep golden yellow, suffused soft pink with age, over large, semi-dbl., cupped; long stems; [Rayon d'Or × Frau Karl Druschki]

Mrs S. Paton HT, ob, 1928, McGredy; bud long, pointed; flowers orange-carmine, base orange, large, dbl.

Mrs S. Peters HT, dp; flowers rich pink, dbl., high-centered, moderate fragrance

Mrs S. T. Wright T, ob, 1914, Dickson, A.; flowers old gold, center suffused rose-pink on orange, dbl.; [sport of Harry Kirk]

Mrs S. W. Burgess HT, ab, 1925, Burgess, S.W.; flowers apricot-yellow, base deeper, dbl.; [Mme Mélanie Soupert × Joseph Hill]

Mrs Sam McGredy HT, op, 1929, McGredy; bud pointed; flowers scarlet-copper-orange, reverse heavily flushed red, large, 40 petals, high-centered, moderate fragrance; foliage glossy, reddish bronze; vigorous growth; [(Donald Macdonald × Golden Emblem) × (seedling × The Queen Alexandra Rose)]; Gold Medal, Portland, 1956, Gold Medal, NRS, 1929

Mrs Sam McGredy, Climbing Cl HT, op, 1937, Buisman, G. A. H.; flowers copper orange-red, large, full, moderate fragrance; [sport of Mrs Sam McGredy]

Mrs Sam Ross HT, ly, 1912, Dickson, H.; flowers pale straw to light chamois-yellow, buff reverse, very large, full, cupped; foliage dark green

Mrs Spencer Browne HT, mp, 1928, Harrison, A.

Mrs Standish HP, mr, 1853, Cherpin; flowers scarlet, striped

Mrs Standish – See **Mme Standish**, HP

Mrs Standish HP, mp, 1865, Liabaud; flowers bright pink, large, full

Mrs Stewart Clark HT, mp, 1906, Dickson, A.; flowers bright cerise pink to brilliant rose, large, dbl., moderate fragrance; foliage glossy; [Rubens × Tom Wood]

Mrs T. B. Doxford HT, rb, 1932, Dickson, A.; bud pointed; flowers salmon-carmine to peach-blossom-pink, reverse old-rose, large, dbl., high-centered

Mrs T. Hillas HT, my, 1913, Pernet-Ducher; flowers pure chrome-yellow, dbl.

Mrs T. J. English HT, ab, 1922, English; flowers apricot and amber, tinted salmon-flesh, heavily veined

Mrs Talbot O'Farrell HT, rb, 1926, McGredy; bud small to medium, long, pointed; flowers cerise flushed bronze, reverse old-gold, medium, dbl., moderate fragrance; foliage small, dark bronzy green, leathery, glossy; few prickles; growth upright, bushy

Mrs Theodore Roosevelt HT, lp, 1903, E.G. Hill, Co.; flowers cream white with a pink center, very large, dbl., moderate fragrance; vigorous, bushy growth; [La France × unknown]

Mrs Theodore Salvesen HT, op, 1922, Dobbie; flowers salmon-pink

Mrs Theonville van Berkel HT, pb, 1935, Buisman, G. A. H.; bud long, pointed; flowers pink, reverse flushed yellow, large, dbl., high-centered; foliage leathery, dark; vigorous growth; [Briarcliff × Mrs Sam McGredy]

Mrs Tom Henderson Pol, dp

Mrs Tom Paul HT, yb, 1920, Dickson, H.; flowers saffron-yellow, suffused pink, dbl.

Mrs Tom Smith HT, mr, 1924, Smith, T.; flowers glowing cerise, dbl.

Mrs Tom Whitehead HT, ab, 1938, Whitehead; flowers cream, center apricot-orange, outer petals veined, very large, dbl., high-centered; very vigorous growth; [Mrs Charles Lamplough × seedling]; int. by Beckwith

Mrs Treseder T, ly, 1889, Paul, G.; flowers citron yellow

Mrs Tresham Gilbey HT, op, 1923, Chaplin Bros.; bud pointed; flowers coral-rose shaded salmon, very large, dbl.; [Waltham Flame × Edith Cavell]; Gold Medal, NRS, 1923

Mrs Tresham Gilbey, Climbing Cl HT, op, 1938, Vogel, M.; flowers light salmon-pink, very large, dbl., moderate fragrance

Mrs U. M. Rose HT, dp, 1931, Vestal; bud long, pointed; flowers cerise-pink, semi-dbl., cupped

Mrs V.A.Treloar – See **Bridget Mary**, S

Mrs van Beresteyn-Frowein HT, op, 1935, Buisman, G. A. H.; flowers salmon, large, very dbl.; foliage leathery, light; vigorous growth; [Souv. de Claudius Pernet × Mrs Henry Bowles]

Mrs Van Nes – See **Permanent Wave**, F

Mrs Vandenbergh HT, mr, 1938, Buisman, G. A. H.; flowers bright red, semi-dbl., high-centered; foliage dark; strong stems; vigorous growth; [E.G. Hill × Étoile de Hollande]

Mrs Veitch HP, mp, 1872, Verdier, E.; flowers carmine pink, medium, full, slight fragrance

Mrs Verschuren – See ***R. M. S. Queen Mary***, HT

Mrs W. A. Lindsay HT, pb, 1920, Dickson, H.; flowers peach-pink, center golden yellow, dbl.

Mrs W. A. Taylor HT, 1918, Byrnes

Mrs W. C. Whitney HT, lp, 1894, May; bud long; flowers flesh-pink, large, intense fragrance; [Mme Ferdinand Jamin × Souv d'Un Ami]

Mrs W. E. Nickerson HT, pb, 1927, McGredy; bud pointed; flowers silvery pink deeply shaded old-gold and salmon, large, dbl.; int. by Dreer

Mrs W. Ewart T, pb, 1909, Williams, A.; [Souv de Catherine Guillot × unknown]

Mrs W. H. Cutbush Pol, mp, 1907, Levavasseur; flowers rich pink, variable, with light and dark pink blooms in one cluster, dbl., rosette; [sport of Mme Norbert Levavasseur]

Mrs W. H. Cutbush, Climbing Cl Pol, mp, 1911, Paling; flowers rich pink, variable, with light and dark pink blooms in one cluster; foliage light green; growth strong, upright (6 ft.); [sport of Mrs W. H. Cutbush]

Mrs W. J. Grant HT, lp, 1895, Dickson, A.; bud long, pointed; flowers light pink fading purplish, dbl.; [La France × Lady Mary Fitzwilliam]

Mrs W. J. Grant, Climbing Cl HT, lp, 1899, E.G. Hill, Co.; flowers large, full; [sport of Mrs W. J. Grant]

Mrs W. R. Groves HT, dr, 1941, Clark, A.; flowers deep red; foliage good

Mrs Wakefield Christie-Miller HT, pb, 1909, McGredy; flowers blush, shaded salmon, reverse vermilion-rose, very large, dbl.; foliage light, leathery; dwarf growth

Mrs Wallace H. Rowe HT, m, 1912, McGredy; flowers bright sweet-pea mauve, large, full, high-centered; vigorous growth

Mrs Walter Brace HT, dp, 1939, Beckwith; flowers vivid cerise-rose-pink, slightly larger; [sport of Picture]

Mrs Walter Burns F, mp, 1978, Harkness; bud ovoid; flowers patio size, 2½ in., very dbl., flat; foliage fragrant (musky), medium size, matte, dark; compact, bushy growth; [(((Queen Elizabeth × Escapade × Escapade) × (Orangeade × Lilac Charm) × (Sterling Silver × Africa Star))) × (Cläre Grammerstorf × Fruhlingsmorgen)]

Mrs Walter Easlea HT, dr, 1910, Dickson, A.; flowers glowing crimson-carmine, deepening to intense crimson-orange, large, dbl., moderate fragrance

Mrs Walter Jones HT, rb, 1930, Cant, B. R.; flowers brilliant coral-red, shaded orange, dbl.

Mrs Walter T. Sumner HT, dp, 1920, Clarke Bros.; flowers carmine to deep rose-pink, large, 12-18 petals; [Ophelia × Hadley]

Mrs Walter T. Sumner, Climbing Cl HT, dp, 1932, Hazlewood Bros.

Mrs Ward HP, mp, 1866, Ward; flowers bright pink, center crimson, large, full

Mrs Warren E. Lenon HT, dr, 1924, E.G. Hill, Co.; bud long, pointed; flowers crimson, large, dbl., globular; vigorous growth; [Hoosier Beauty × Premier]; int. by Vestal

Mrs Warren G. Harding HT, dp, 1923, Pierson, A.N.; [sport of Columbia]

Mrs Wemyss Quin HT, dy, 1914, Dickson, A.; flowers intense lemon-chrome, washed with maddery orange, medium, dbl., moderate fragrance; foliage dark, glossy; bushy, branching growth; [Harry Kirk × unknown]; Gold Medal, Bagatelle, 1916

Mrs Whitman Cross Cl HT, ob, 1943, Cross, C.W.; bud long, pointed; flowers orange-apricot, overlaid pinkish, reverse sometimes striped, semi-dbl.; foliage glossy, soft; growth to 8-9 ft. as climber or pillar, upright; [Nanjemoy × Marion Cran]; int. by B&A

Mrs Wilfred Lloyd HT, dp, 1911, Dickson, A.; flowers fiery pink, large, full, globular

Mrs William C. Egan HT, lp, 1922, H&S; bud long, pointed; flowers soft pink, 35 petals, moderate fragrance

Mrs William C. Egan, Climbing Cl HT, lp, 1933, Howard Rose Co.

Mrs William Fife HT, pb, 1926, Dobbie; flowers soft rose-pink, flushed blush-pink, dbl.

Mrs William G. Koning Pol, w, 1917, Kluis & Koning; flowers pure white, open, dbl., borne in clusters; vigorous, bushy growth; [sport of Louise Walter]

Mrs William Paul – See **Mme William Paul**, M

Mrs William R. Hearst HT, dp, 1915, Pierson, A.N.; flowers clear dark pink; [sport of My Maryland]

Mrs William Sargent HT, ab, 1923, Dickson, H.; flowers apricot and peach, edges flushed rose-pink, dbl.

Mrs William Sprott HT, my, 1938, McGredy; bud long, pointed; flowers large, dbl.; foliage glossy, bronze; vigorous, compact growth; [Portadown Glory × Mrs Sam McGredy]

Mrs William Watson HP, m, 1890, Dickson, A.; flowers purple-pink, large, full, globular; [Mme Vidot × Merveille de Lyon]

Misty HT, w, 1975, Armstrong, D.L.; bud ovoid, pointed; flowers creamy white, 4 in., 35 petals, cupped to formal, moderate tea fragrance; foliage large, leathery; vigorous, upright growth; PP3983; [Mount Shasta × Matterhorn]; int. by Armstrong Nursery, 1976

Misty HT, lp, Zary; PPAF; int. by Bear Creek Gardens, 1999

Misty Min, mp, Olesen; bud pointed ovoid; flowers medium pink, outer petals fading lighter, medium, 30 petals, shallow cup, borne in large clusters, no fragrance; recurrent; foliage semi-glossy; prickles moderate, 8 mm., hooked downward; bushy (40-60 cm.), vigorous growth; PP15252; [sport of Pink Hit]; int. in 2002

Misty HT, m, Kordes; flowers small, moderate fragrance; stems short; cut flower trade; int. by Australian Roses, 2003

Misty Dawn Min, w, 1979, Schwartz, Ernest W.; bud ovoid, pointed; flowers pure white, 1 in., 33 petals, cupped; foliage small, dark; vigorous, compact, spreading growth; PP4630; [Charlie McCarthy × seedling]; int. by Nor'East Min. Roses

Misty Delight HT, mp, 1990, Christensen, Jack E.; flowers full, borne mostly singly; foliage large, dark green, glossy; upright growth; [Blue Wonder × seedling]; int. by Vaughan's Seed Co., 1991

Misty Eyed MinFl, w, 2003, McCann, Sean; flowers white with suggestions of gray, medium, dbl., borne in small clusters, slight fragrance; foliage medium size, medium green, semi-glossy; growth spreading, medium; garden decorative; [Jennifer × seedling]; int. by Ashdown Roses, 2005

Misty Gold F, my, 1954, Boerner; bud ovoid, pointed; flowers empire-yellow, 3½-4 in., 45-50 petals, cupped, moderate fragrance; foliage glossy; vigorous growth; PP1380; [floribunda seedling × floribunda seedling]; int. by Stark Bros., 1954

Misty Hit – See **Misty**, Min

Misty Moonlight LCl, lp, 2004, Graham, Susan Brandt; flowers light pink fading to white, petals ruffled, 3 in., 50-80 petals, old-fashioned, borne in small and large clusters, slight fragrance; foliage large, medium green, semi-glossy; prickles medium, straight; growth spreading, climbs if trained, tall (10-12 ft.); pillar; [sport of Dream Weaver]; int. by Susan Brandt Graham, 2006

Misty Morn HT, ly, 1949, McGredy; flowers pale lemon-yellow, pointed, large, 45 petals; foliage dark; [seedling × Mrs Charles Lamplough]

Misty Morning MinFl, m, 1995, Bell, Judy G.; flowers lavender shaded yellow/tan, small, full, borne mostly singly; foliage medium size, medium green, matte; few prickles; tall (18 in.), upright, bushy growth; [Dale's Sunrise × Angel Face]; int. by Michigan Miniature Roses, 1996

Misty Pink F, mp, 1973, Swim & Weeks; PP2945; int. by Carlton Rose Nurs., 1971

Misty Twilight HT, mp, 2004, Ballin, Don; flowers medium, 24-26 petals, borne mostly solitary, no fragrance; foliage medium size, medium green, semi-glossy; prickles medium, curved, moderate; growth compact to slightly spreading, medium; [sport of Rina Hugo]; int. by Edmunds Roses, 2003

Misty Veil S, mp, Williams, J. Benjamin; flowers delicate pink, large, single, cupped to flat; free-flowering; int. by Hortico, Inc., 1999

Mitcheltonii S, mp, 1967, Armbrust; flowers pink, small, single; profuse spring bloom; foliage small, leathery; thornless; very vigorous, climbing growth; [*R. multiflora* × I.X.L.]

Mitchie's Gold Min, dy, 2000, Moe, Mitchie; flowers dbl., high-centered, borne mostly singly, slight fragrance; foliage medium size, medium green, semi-glossy; few prickles; growth upright, medium (15-18 in.); [Vista × select pollen]; int. by Mitchie's Roses and More, 2001

Mitsouko HT, yb, 1983, Delbard, Georges; flowers yellow, petals edged red, large, 50 petals, moderate fruity fragrance; foliage medium size, clear green; prickles bronze-red; dense, bushy growth; [(Michèle Meilland × Chic Parisien) × Peace]; int. in 1970

Mitzi HT, yb, 1956, Meilland, F.; flowers pearly tints flushed mauve-rose, well-formed, 35 petals; foliage dark; strong stems; upright, bushy growth; [(Peace × Mme Joseph Perraud) × (Mrs Pierre S. duPont × MrsJohn Laing)]; int. by URS; Gold Medal, Rome, 1956

Mitzi HT, my, Meilland; flowers dbl.; int. in 1981

Mitzi 81 – See **Mitzi**, HT dbl.

Miwaku HT, w, Suzuki, Seizo; int. in 1988

Mix 'n' Match S, mp, 1999, Warner, Chris; bud short, furled; flowers pastel pearl pink with golden boss of stamens, 1½-2 in., 10-15 petals, borne in large clusters; foliage medium size, dark green, quilted; medium, rounded, slight spreading growth; [Seaspray × (Rosa sinowilsonii × Marjorie Fair)]

Mixed Emotions Min, rb, Jalbert; flowers striped; int. in 2003

Mixed Marriage F, pb, Ruston, D.; [sport of Bridal Pink]; int. in 1987

Miyabi HT, w, 1977, Teranishi, K.; bud ovoid; flowers near white, 4-4½ in., 30 petals, high-centered; upright growth; [(Amatsu-Otome × Samba) × (Kordes' Perfecta × American Heritage)]; int. by Itami Bara-en, 1976

Miyagino Cl Min, pb, 1979, Onodera, Toru F.; bud rounded; flowers light pink, small, 5 petals, flat; scattered rebloom; foliage tiny; [Nozomi × seedling]; int. by S. Onodera, 1978

Miyako Oji HT, pb, Keihan; int. by Keihan Gardening, 1988

Miyoshino Min, mp; int. by Keihan Gardening, 2001

Ms Amanda Coombes S, or, 2006, Laurie Newman; flowers deep scarlet, reverse red, 2½ in., single, borne in small clusters; foliage large, dark green, glossy; prickles medium, red/brown, moderate; growth bushy, tall, pillar; very healthy and vigorous; [China Sunrise × Vesper]; int. by Reliable Roses, 2007

Ms Linda HT, rb, 2006, Premeaux John W.; flowers red, sometimes with darker edges, reverse pink, 4½ in., full, borne mostly solitary; foliage medium size, medium green, semi-glossy; prickles average, straight, red, moderate; growth upright, medium; [Elizabeth Taylor × Hot Princess]; int. in 2006

Ms Mary Min, yb, 1999, Bennett, Dee; flowers pale yellow/apricot, reverse pale yellow, 1 in., full, borne mostly singly, moderate fragrance; foliage medium size, medium green, semi-glossy; prickles moderate; compact, bushy, low (18-24 in.) growth; [Deep Purple × Fairest of Fair]; int. by Tiny Petals, 1999

Ms Wendy Poulier S, pb, 2006, Newman, Laurie; flowers pink, reverse salmon, 3 in., single, borne in large clusters, no fragrance; foliage large, dark green, semi-glossy; prickles medium, brown, few; growth upright, tall (6 ft.), pillar; [Parador × unknown]; int. by Reliable Roses, 2006

Mizar S, dy, Barni, V.; flowers gold-yellow, unfading, 6-7 cm., semi-dbl., borne in clusters; growth to 4-5 ft.; int. by Rose Barni, 1999

Mlada F, yb, Urban, J.; flowers yellow and red, medium, dbl.; int. in 1983

Mme Baptiste Desportes – See **Baptiste Desportes**, HP

Mme Figaro HT, dp, Lens, Louis; int. by Lens, 1954

Mme Selzer – See **Madeleine Seltzer**, HMult

Mme Thérèse Meyer S, mr, Huber; flowers cherry red, 6 in., single, flat, intense fragrance; vigorous (5-6 ft.) growth; int. by Richard Huber AG, 2005

Mo Mama F, ab, 2001, Hough, Robin; flowers peach blend, lighter reverse, 2-2¼ in., full, exhibition, borne mostly solitary, slight fragrance; foliage medium size, medium green, semi-glossy; prickles small, straight, very few; growth upright, tall (24 to 30 in.); [Joyfulness × Linville]; int. in 2001

Moana Min, mp, 1978, McGredy, Sam IV; flowers rose-pink, small, 35 petals; foliage glossy, dark; [seedling × New Penny]

Mobile Jubilee Min, op, 1994, Taylor, Franklin; flowers light salmon blending to darker edges, yellow base, large, full; foliage medium size, medium green, semi-glossy; some prickles; tall (90 cm.), upright, bushy growth; [Party Girl × Gitte]; int. by Taylor's Roses, 1994

Möckel Rose HT, dr, Huber; flowers flower dark wine red; int. by Richard Huber AG, 2005

Mockin' Bird S, rb; flowers striped.; int. by Certified Roses, 2001

Mock's Rosa Druschki Cl HP, mp, before 1935, Mock; flowers rose pink, fading lighter, 3½-4 in., dbl.; foliage glossy

Model of Perfection F, ob, 1977, Dickson, A.; bud globular; flowers yellow, pink and orange, large, 28 petals; free-flowering; small growth; [Zorina × Arthur Bell]

Modèle de Perfection B, mp, 1859, Guillot; flowers bright silky pink, medium, full; [Louise Odier × unknown]

Modern Art HT, rb, 1985, Olesen, Pernille & Mogens N.; bud medium, pointed; flowers scarlet, reverse silvery with red wash, 3½-4 in., 25 petals, high-centered, borne singly and several together in large sprays; foliage medium size, dark, matte; upright, bushy (4 ft.) growth; hips small ; PP5646; [seedling × seedling]; int. by D.T. Poulsen, 1983; Gold Medal, Rome, 1984

Modern Crusader S, dr, Kordes; flowers burgundy red, large, dbl., open cup; recurrent; vigorous, tall growth; int. by Ludwig's Roses, 2005

Modern Magic F, ob, 2001, Christensen, Jack; flowers orange with red stripes, 4 in., dbl., borne in small clusters, no fragrance; foliage medium size, medium green, glossy; prickles moderate; growth compact, medium (4 ft.); PP14936; [Voodoo × Tiger Tail]; int. by Star Roses, 2001

Modern Miss F, pb, Benny; flowers medium pink with amber glow in center, dbl., high-centered, spiral; medium growth; int. by De Boer Roses, 2005

Modern Times HT, rb, 1956, Verbeek; flowers red, striped pink; [sport of Better Times]; int. by Minier

Modesty HT, pb, 1916, McGredy; bud pointed; flowers white, center rose-pink, large, dbl., high-centered; Gold Medal, NRS, 1915

Moeder des Vaderlands F, mr, 1958, Leenders, M.; flowers bright vermilion-red; strong stems; vigorous growth; [Ambassadeur Nemry × Cinnabar]; int. as Mother's Country, Leenders & Co., 1957

Moejo-netsu Min, dp, 1998, Moe, Mitchie; flowers magenta pink, 1-1½ in., dbl., high-centered, borne mostly singly, slight fragrance; foliage medium size, dark green, semi-glossy; no prickles; upright, tall (18 in.) growth; [Klima × Seedling (mauve)]; int. by Mitchie's Roses & More, 1999

Mogador P, dp, after 1810, Descemet; flowers carmine, shaded purple, medium, full; [sport of Rose du Roi]

Mohak HT, ob, Chiplunkar; int. in 1993

Mohawk S, m, Central Exp. Farm; flowers brighter than aster-purple, center white, single; profuse, non-recurrent bloom; foliage dull green; rounded, dwarf growth; hardy; [*R. rubrifolia* × *R. rugosa*]

Mohican HT, mr, 1937, J.H. Thompson's Sons; bud long, pointed; flowers cherry-red, large, dbl.; foliage leathery, glossy, dark; long stems; very vigorous growth; [Unnamed variety × Briarcliff]

Mohican F, mr, Thompson's, J.H., Sons; flowers dark rose-red; PP2123; [sport of Garnette]; int. in 1961

Mohini F, ob, 1970, Division of Vegetable Crops and Floriculture; bud long, pointed; flowers chocolate-brown, base tinged yellow, medium, full; foliage glossy, dark; moderate, bushy growth; [Sea Pearl × Shola]

Mohykan HT, dr, Strnad

Moiret T, yb, 1843, Moiret; flowers whitish yellow, shaded pink and chamois, large, full

Moïse HGal, m, 1828, Parmentier; flowers rosy-carmine, shaded purplish slate, expanded, large, dbl.; moderate upright growth

Moja Mesta S, mp, Lempickji; growth to 10 ft.; int. in 1956

Mojave HT, ob, 1954, Swim, H.C.; bud long; flowers apricot-orange tinted red, prominently veined, 4-4½ in., 25 petals, high-centered, moderate fragrance; foliage glossy; vigorous, upright growth; [Charlotte Armstrong × Signora]; int. by Armstrong Nursery; Gold Medal, Geneva, 1953, Gold Medal, Bagatelle, 1953

Mojave, Climbing Cl HT, ob, 1964, Trimper, K.; [sport of Mojave]; int. by Ruston

Moje Hammarberg HRg, m, 1931, Hammarberg; flowers reddish-violet, large, dbl., intense fragrance; recurrent bloom; short, weak stems; vigorous growth; hips large, red; hardy; int. by Stockholm Stads Gatukontor

Moksha HT, op; flowers large

Molde F, or, 1964, Tantau, Math.; flowers dbl., borne in clusters; foliage dark, glossy; bushy, low, compact. growth; Gold Medal, Baden-Baden, 1964

Molineux S, dy, 1994, Austin, David; bud pointed ovoid and globular; flowers 7 cm., 110-120 petals, rosette, borne in clusters, slight fragrance; recurrent; foliage large, leathery; prickles few, medium, hooked downward; vigorous (3 ft.) growth; PP9524; [Graham Thomas × seedling]; Gold Medal, Durbanville, 1993

Molitor HT, or, 1982, Gaujard, Jean; flowers deep orange-red, large, 35 petals, moderate fragrance; foliage medium size, dark, semi-glossy; [Junon × Tanagra]; int. in 1980

Mollie Claire Min, w, 1989, King, Gene; bud pointed; flowers white, pink edge blushing toward center, reverse white tipped, 28 petals, high-centered; foliage small, medium green, matte; prickles crooked,very few, white to brown; bushy, low growth; no fruit; [(Evelyn Fison × Magic Mist) × Baby Diana]; int. by AGM Miniature Roses

Molly Min, mp, 2006, Bridges, Dennis A.; flowers medium pink, reverse slightly lighter, 1½ in., full, borne mostly solitary; foliage medium size, dark green, semi-glossy; prickles moderate, ¼ in., straight, tan; growth compact, medium (22-24 in.); garden decoration, containers, exhibition, cutting; [Sam Trivett × select pollen]; int. by Bridges Roses, 2006

Molly Abdy HT, rb, 1956, Abdy; bud pointed; flowers deep scarlet to lighter red, medium, dbl., moderate fragrance; vigorous growth; [Southport × unknown]; int. by Shepperson

Molly Beckley F, pb, 1997, Jellyman, J.S.; flowers small, 8-14 petals, slight fragrance; foliage small, dark green, glossy; growth spreading, low (1½ ft.); [(Tony Jacklin × Andrea) × Wee Barbie]

Molly Bishop HT, op, 1951, Robinson, H.; bud long, pointed; flowers large, dbl., high-centered; foliage leathery, rich green; vigorous growth

Molly Bligh HT, pb, 1917, Dickson, A.; flowers deep pink, base deep orange, large, full, moderate fragrance

Molly Darragh HT, pb, 1930, McGredy; bud pointed; flowers bright old-rose, base orange-yellow, very large, dbl., high-centered, moderate fragrance

Molly Doyle F, pb, 1965, Barter; flowers old-rose-pink, base silvery white, 5 in., 6 petals, intense fragrance; foliage light green; low, bushy growth; [Étoile de Hollande × Queen Elizabeth]

Molly Kirby F, or, 1984, Wilson, George D.; flowers vermilion; [sport of Matangi]; int. in 1980

Molly Lloyd Lee F, ab, 2003, Rawlins, R.; flowers full, borne in small clusters, slight fragrance; foliage medium size, medium green, semi-glossy; prickles triangular; growth upright, medium (40 in.), garden; [Golden Future × (Baby Love × Amber Queen)]

Molly McGredy F, rb, 1969, McGredy, Sam IV; flowers medium red, reverse silver, well-formed, large, 35 petals, borne in trusses; foliage dark, glossy; PP3111; [Paddy McGredy × (Mme Leon Cuny × Columbine)]; int. by McGredy; Gold Medal, Portland, 1971, President's International Trophy, RNRS, 1968, Gold Medal, RNRS, 1968, Gold Medal, Belfast, 1971

Molly Sharman-Crawford T, w, 1908, Dickson, A.; bud long, pointed; flowers greenish white, becoming whiter, very dbl., high-centered, moderate fragrance; foliage sparse, rich green; bushy growth

Mollycita Min, dp, 2001, Hough, Robin; flowers deep hot pink with bright yellow stamens, 1½-1¾ in., single, borne mostly solitary, no fragrance; foliage medium size, medium green, semi-glossy; prickles medium, straight, moderate; growth upright, medium (18 in.); [June Laver × After Midnight]; int. in 2001

Molodost HT, lp, 1956, Sushkov, K. L.; flowers 5 in., 37 petals; foliage dark; strong stems; vigorous, upright growth; [Staatsprasident Pats × Cathrine Kordes]

Molodost Mira HT, mr, 1955, Klimenko, V. N.; flowers coral-red, well-formed, large, 50 petals; foliage dark; vigorous, well branched growth; [Peace × (Crimson Glory × Poinsettia)]

Moments S, op, Williams, J.B.; flowers single; recurrent; growth to 4 ft.; int. by Hortico, Inc., 2005

Momo HT, dp, 1988, Ota, Kaichiro; flowers deep pink, large, 35-40 petals, borne usually singly; foliage medium size, dark green; prickles pointed, straight; hips medium, copper; [(Picnic × Kordes' Perfecta) × Christian Dior]

Momo LCl, dr, Noack, Werner; flowers cherry crimson, 1½ in., very dbl., borne in very large clusters; foliage small, dark green, glossy; growth to 8 ft.; int. by Noack Rosen, 1995

Momoka HT, ob, Keisei; int. by Keisei Rose Nurseries, 2004

Momoyama HT, op, Keihan; int. by Keihan Gardening, 1981

Momozono F, mp, Hiroshima; int. by Hiroshima Bara-en, 1990

Mom's Fancy Min, lp, 1995, Rennie, Bruce F.; flowers slight moss on buds, 1¼ in., dbl., borne in large clusters; foliage small, medium green, semi-glossy; some prickles; low (12-15 in.), compact growth; [Pink Sheri × Hap Renshaw]; int. by Rennie Roses International, 1994

Mom's Rose HT, pb, 2003, Winchel, Joe; flowers smoky pink with pastel shading, large, 35 petals, classic hybrid tea, borne mostly solitary, slight fruity fragrance; recurrent; foliage medium size, medium green, semi-glossy; prickles average, curved; growth upright, medium (5 ft.); exhibition, garden decoration; [seedling × seedling]; int. by Certified Roses, Inc, 2003

Momy F, dp

Mon Ami Min, mr, Justice; int. by Justice Miniatures, 2001

Mon Amour Cl HT, pb, 1967, Coggiatti, Stelvio; bud ovoid; flowers phlox-pink, reverse silver-rose, large, dbl., cupped, moderate fragrance; profuse, intermittent bloom; foliage dark, leathery; very vigorous growth; [Peace, Climbing × Caprice]

Mon Cheri HT, rb, 1981, Christensen, Jack E.; bud ovoid, pointed; flowers medium pink, suffusing to near yellow at base, aging to dark, 38 petals, slight spicy fragrance; foliage semi-glossy, medium green; prickles short; upright, medium growth; PP5156; [(White Satin × Bewitched) × Double Delight]; int. by Armstrong Nursery

Mon Cherie F, mp, Spek; flowers medium pink, outer petals fading lighter, 6 cm., 60-65 petals, cupped, borne in clusters; recurrent; prickles moderate; stems medium; int. by Jan Spek Rozen, 2005

Mon Jardin et Ma Maison LCl, w, Meilland; flowers large, slight fragrance; free-flowering; foliage glossy; strong (7 ft.) growth; int. by Meilland Richardier, 1998

Mon Pays Gr, w, 1983, Gailloux, Gilles; flowers large, dbl.; foliage medium to large, medium green, glossy; upright growth; [Iceberg × Peace]

Mon Petit Min, dp, 1947, Dot, Pedro; flowers light red, 80 petals; foliage pointed; dwarf, compact growth; [Merveille des Rouges × Pompon de Paris]; int. by URS

Mon Trésor HGal, m, about 1845, Calvert; flowers light purple, medium, full

Mon Tresor – See **Red Imp**, Min

Mona F, mr, 1958, Kordes, R.; flowers light crimson, center lighter, 2 in., dbl., high-centered, borne in large clusters; foliage light green; vigorous, upright, bushy growth; [Rudolph Timm × Fanal]; int. by Dehner & Co., 1957

Mona Lisa LCl, pb, 1956, Malandrone; bud ovoid; flowers warm pink overcast cameo-pink, 4-4½ in., 35-40 petals, cupped, borne singly or in small clusters, intense fragrance; free, recurrent boom; foliage dark, leathery; vigorous growth; bushy pillar or climbing (8-10 ft.); PP1459; [Mrs Sam McGredy × (Mrs Sam McGredy × (seedling × Capt. Thomas))]; int. by Armstrong Nursery

Mona Lisa – See **Australian Gold**, F

Mona Lisa HT, lp, Kordes; flowers porcelain pink, 35-40 petals, high-centered, borne singly; recurrent; stems long; [sport of Eliza]; florist rose; int. by W. Kordes Söhne, 2005

Mona Rosette F, pb, 1963, Manski; bud ovoid; flowers pink and white striped, medium, dbl., cupped, borne in clusters; foliage dark, leathery; bushy, low growth; [sport of Pink Rosette]; int. by Paulen Park Nursery, 1963

Mona Ruth Min, mp, 1960, Moore, Ralph S.; flowers 1-1½ in., 30 petals; foliage leathery; vigorous (12-14 in.), bushy growth; PP2081; [((Soeur Thérèse × Skyrocket) × (seedling × Red Ripples)) × Zee]; int. by Sequoia Nursery, 1959

Monarch HT, mp, 1926, Dobbie; bud pointed; flowers silvery pink, very large, dbl., high-centered

Mönch F, mp, 1959, Tantau; flowers pink, large, dbl., borne in large corymbs; foliage dark, leathery; vigorous, upright growth; [Karl Weinhausen × unknown]; int. in 1952

Moncton HRg, lp, 1978, Svedja, Felicitas; bud ovoid; flowers dbl., 20 petals, intense fragrance; foliage gray-green; upright, bushy growth; [Schneezwerg × *R. chinensis*]; int. by Canada Dept. of Agric., 1977

Monday's Child Min, m, 1995, Bell, Judy G.; flowers lavender and white, small, dbl., borne in small clusters, no fragrance; foliage medium size, medium green, glossy; few prickles; medium (16 in.), upright, bushy growth; [Dale's Sunrise × Angel Face]; int. by Michigan Miniature Roses, 1996

Mondial Pink HT, pb, 1967, Hendrickx; flowers pink, base yellow, medium, high-centered; foliage glossy; int. by DeConinck-Dervaes, 1965

Mondiale HT, op, 2006; bud high-centered, darker on top; flowers salmon-pink, outer petals lighter, 10 cm., full, borne mostly solitary; foliage large, reddish, dense; well-branched, vigorous, upright (80 cm.) growth; int. by W. Kordes' Söhne, 1993

Mondorf-les-Bains HT, r, Lens; flowers bright yellow, turning cream as it fades to white, 7 cm., semi-dbl., shallow cup to flat, borne in clusters, slight fragrance; recurrent; foliage dark green; growth to 40-45 cm.; int. by Louis Lens SA, 2006

Mondovision HT, dp, 1969, Delbard, G.; flowers cyclamen-pink, 4-5 in., 35-45 petals, moderate fragrance; [Dr. Albert Schweitzer × (Bayadere × Mme Rene Cassin)]; int. by Pepinieres G. Delbard, 1969

Monet HT, m, Great Western; flowers smoky-mauve, large, quartered, flat, moderate tea-damask fragrance; int. in 1996

Monet – See **Grand Impression**, HT

Moneta F, pb, 1969, Freytag; bud ovoid; flowers pinkish red, small, very dbl.; foliage dark; [sport of Garnette]; int. by Santhof

Monette HWich, w, 1921, Hémeray-Aubert; flowers small, very dbl., borne in clusters; vigorous, climbing growth; [*R. wichurana* × Yvonne Rabier]

Monette Pol, rb, 1922, Turbat; flowers fiery red, passing to rose, with many white streaks, borne in clusters of 60-100; [Phyllis × seedling]

Money For Nothing Min, ab, 2003, Taylor, Franklin (Pete) & Kay Taylor; flowers full, high-centered, borne mostly solitary, moderate fragrance; foliage medium size, medium green, semi-glossy; prickles small, slight hook, brown, few; growth bushy, medium (3 ft.); exhibition, garden decorative, cutting; [unknown × unknown]; int. by Taylor Roses, 2003

Mongioia Gr, Mansuino; int. in 1966

Monica A, lp, before 1838; flowers delicate pink, medium, full; possibly synonymous with Monique

Monica – See **Columbine Parade**, MinFl

Monica Astmann F, or; flowers light orange, large, dbl.

Monica Mary HT, dy, 2003, Rawlins, R.; flowers lemon yellow, medium, full, borne in small clusters, moderate fragrance; foliage medium size, medium green, semi-glossy; prickles 1 cm., triangular, moderate; growth upright, medium (33 in.); garden; [(Laura Ford × Goldbusch) × (Baby Love × Amber Queen)]

Monica Mitchell – See **Monica Mary**, HT

Monika HT, pb, 1985, Tantau, Math.; flowers medium, 35 petals; foliage medium size, dark, glossy; upright growth

Monique A, lp, 1828, Prévost; flowers medium, 60-80 petals, globular; foliage ovoid, acuminate, simply serrate; few prickles

Monique HT, op, 1949, Paolino; flowers medium salmon-pink, well-shaped, large, 25 petals; vigorous, upright growth; [Lady Sylvia × seedling]; int. by URS; Gold Medal, NRS, 1950

Monique van Honsebrouck Gr, Delforge, H.

Monna Lisa HT, w; flowers ivory white, large

Monna Lisa, Climbing Cl HT, w; flowers ivory white, large

Monplaisir HGal, m, about 1845, Calvert; flowers purple

Monroe St. Yellow Tea – See **Étoile de Lyon**, T

Monseigneur Fournier HP, mr, 1876, Lalande; flowers brilliant light red, very large, full

Monseigneur Touchet T, w, 1895, Corboeuf-Marsault; flowers cream white, large, full; [Niphetos × Mme Chédane-Guinoisseau]

Mons A. Maille B, pb, 1889, Moreau & Robert; flowers shining carmine, shaded dark red, very large, full, borne in small clusters; foliage dark green; prickles recurved

Mons Aimé Colcombet T, mp, 1891, Bernaix; flowers bright carmine, center rose pink with flesh pink, medium

Mons Albert Dureau – See **Albert Dureau**, HP

Mons Alexandre Pelletier B, mp, 1879, Duval, H.; flowers velvety pink, medium, full

Mons Alfred Daney M, dp, 1886, Bernède; flowers dark pink with silvery reflections, very large, full

Mons Alfred Leveau – See **Alfred Leveau**, HP

Mons Barillet-Deschamps HP, mp, 1867, Vigneron; flowers bright carmine, medium to large, full, globular; [Comte Bobrinsky × unknown]

Mons Barthélemy Levet HP, mp, 1878, Levet; flowers bright pink, large, full; [Victor Verdier × unknown]

Mons Bonçenne HP, dr, 1864, Liabaud; flowers deep crimson, medium, full, moderate fragrance; moderate growth; [Général Jacqueminot × Géant des Batailles]

Mons Bunel HT, pb, 1899, Pernet-Ducher; flowers rosy peach, shaded with yellow, edged with bright rose, very large, full, somewhat flat

Mons Chaix d'Est-Ange HP, mr, 1866, Lévêque; flowers bright scarlet-vermilion, large, full

Mons Charles de Lapisse – See **Charles de Lapisse**, HT

Mons Charles de Thézillat T, yb, 1888, Nabonnand; flowers creamy yellow, centers chamois, very large, full, globular

Mons Chédane-Guinoisseau HRg, lp, 1895, Chédane-Guinoisseau; flowers very large, dbl.

Mons Cordeau B, dp, 1892, Moreau et Robert; flowers deep red with violet, very dbl., globular, intense fragrance; prickles very thorny

Mons Cordier HP, mr, 1871, Gonod; flowers scarlet, very large, full, flat; [Géant des Batailles × unknown]

Mons de Montigny HP, dp, 1855, Paillet; flowers carmine-pink, large, dbl.

Mons de Morand HP, rb, 1891, Schwartz, J.; flowers bright crimson cerise nuanced bluish lilac purple, large, full; [sport of Général Jacqueminot]

Mons de Pontbriand HP, dr, 1864, Damaizin; flowers brownish-crimson, shaded dark carmine, medium to large

Mons Désir N, dr, 1888, Pernet père; flowers crimson red, darkened with violet, 8 cm., full; [Gloire de Dijon × unknown (possibly Généeral Jacqueminot)]

Mons Dorier T, dp, 1897, Croibier; flowers bright pink, aging to crimson, large, full

Mons Dubost B, op, 1864, Vigneron; flowers very light salmon

Mons E. Y. Teas – See **E. Y. Teas**, HP

Mons Edg. Blanchard – See **Edgar Blanchard**, HT

Mons Edouard Detaille HP, m, 1893, Gouchault; flowers purple/pink, large, dbl.

Mons Edouard Littaye T, pb, 1891, Bernaix; bud large, long; flowers rosey carmine, tinted light pink, often shaded with violet pink, full

Mons Édouard Ory HP, mr, 1864, Moreau & Robert; flowers vermilion, large, full

Mons Émile Lelong HP, mp, 1887, Bire; flowers rose pink, shaded lilac, globular; [Général Jacqueminot × unknown]

Mons Ernest Dupré HP, mr, 1904, Boutigny; bud long; flowers bright carmine red, nuanced deep carmine, velvety, large, dbl., camellia-like

Mons Étienne Dupuis – See **Mons Étienne Dupuy**, HP

Mons Étienne Dupuy HP, lp, 1873, Levet; flowers pale satin and rosy pink, reverse silvery, large, full; [Victor Verdier × Anna de Diesbach]

Mons Eugène Delaire HP, mr, 1879, Vigneron; flowers velvety red illuminated with bright flame, large, full, borne singly or in small clusters; prickles chestnut brown; growth upright

Mons Fillion HP, mp, 1876, Gonod/Lévêque; flowers carmine-rose, center brighter, large, full

Mons Fontaine HT, w, 1932, Soupert & Notting; flowers pure white, large, full, slight fragrance

Mons Fournier – See **Monseigneur Fournier**, HP

Mons Fraissenon HT, dp, 1911, Gamon; bud long; flowers deep frosty pink, large, dbl., moderate fragrance; [Lady Ashtown × unknown]

Mons Francisque Rive HP, mr, 1883, Schwartz, J.; flowers cerise red nuanced carmine, petals concave, reverse glaucescent, large, full; very remontant

Mons Frédéric Daupias T, w, 1898, Chauvry; flowers silvery cream white, shaded carmine pink, center darker, very large, very full, moderate fragrance

Mons Furtado T, ly, 1867, Laffay; flowers light sulfur-yellow, large, very full

Mons Georges Cain – See **Georges Cain**, HRg

Mons Georges de Cadoudal – See **Georges de Cadonel**, B

Mons Guillaume Popie HP, mr, 1894, Corboeuf; flowers bright red, large, full

Mons Gustave Bienvêtu HRg, pb, 1906, Gravereaux; flowers bright salmony pink with darker reflections, large, dbl., borne mostly solitary; prickles relatively few, straight or slightly hooked; [(Pierre Notting × Safrano) × Conrad Ferdinand Meyer]

Mons Hélye HRg, lp, 1900, Morlet; flowers creamy pink, medium, semi-dbl.

Mons Hippolyte Marchand HP, rb, 1881, Vigneron; flowers light red, edges carmine-lilac, very large, full

Mons Hoste HP, mr, 1884, Liabaud; flowers velvety crimson red, large, dbl.; foliage thick, dark green

Mons Jacobs HP, mp; flowers carmine pink, large, full, globular

Mons Jard B, m, before 1866; flowers dark garnet-purple, large, full

Mons Jean France HP, m, 1866, Levet; flowers dark purple

Mons Joseph Chappaz HP, m, 1882, Schmitt; flowers violet-pink, large, dbl., globular; [sport of Jules Margottin]

Mons Joseph Hill – See **Joseph Hill**, HT

Mons Journaix HP, mr, 1868, Marest; flowers scarlet, nuanced darker, large, full; very remontant

Mons Journaux – See **Mons Journaix**, HP

Mons Jules Deroudilhe HP, m, 1886, Liabaud; flowers purple/pink, medium, dbl.

Mons Jules Lemaître HP, dp, 1890, Vigneron; flowers carmine-pink with lighter reverse, very large, dbl.; [Mme Isaac Pereire × unknown]

Mons Jules Maquinant HP, mr, 1882, Vigneron; flowers light red, center brighter, large, dbl.; [Jules Margottin × unknown]

Mons Jules Monges HP, mp, 1881, Guillot fils; flowers carmine pink, very large, full, cupped; foliage light green; growth upright; [Souv de la Reine d'Angleterre × unknown]

Mons Just-Détrey HP, mp, 1883, Just-Détrey; flowers shining carmine, medium to large, full

Mons Lauriol de Barney HP, dr, 1866, Trouillard; flowers currant red, shaded purple, large, full

Mons le Capitaine Louis Frère HP, dr, 1883, Vigneron; flowers velvety crimson, large; freely remontant; prickles small, chestnut brown, numerous; growth upright

Mons le Chevalier Angelo Ferrario – See **Chevalier Angelo Ferrario**, T

Mons le Préfet Limbourg HP, dr, 1878, Margottin fils; flowers velvety crimson, tinged with violet, large, dbl.; [Pierre Notting × unknown]

Mons Claude Levet – See **Claude Levet**, HP

Mons Louis Ligier HP, dr, 1899, Berland; flowers dark red aging to bring carmine, reverse silvery, very large, full, globular

Mons Louis Ricard HP, mr, 1899, Boutigny, P.; flowers currant red, large, full; [Simon St. Jean × Abel Carrière]

Mons Mathieu Baron HP, dr, 1886, Schwartz; flowers dark violet-red, large, dbl.

Mons Moreau HP, m, 1864, Guillot; flowers purple, medium, full

Mons Moreau HP, mp, 1885, Vigneron; flowers shining pink, petals edges silvery, large, full, globular

Mons Morlet HRg, dp, 1900, Morlet; flowers deep carmine

Mons Nomann HP, lp, 1866, Laffay or Guillot; flowers light pink, edged white, large, full; [Jules Margottin × unknown]

Mons Paul Lédé HT, pb, 1902, Pernet-Ducher; flowers carmine-pink, shaded yellow, large, dbl., cupped

Mons Paul Lédé, Climbing Cl HT, pb, 1913, Low; flowers carmine pink and dawn yellow, large, full; [sport of Mons Paul Lédé]

Mons Pélisson – See **Pélisson**, M

Mons Pierre Migron T, yb, 1898, Chauvry; flowers chamois yellow, petals edged dark pink, streaked China pink, large, full

Mons Pierson HP, mr, 1864, Fontaine; flowers amaranth and crimson, large, full

Mons Plaisançon HP, dp, 1866, Ducher; flowers dark carmine, large, full

Mons Rosier T, pb, 1887, Nabonnand; flowers rose and yellow, 9-10 cm., full, cupped; [Mlle Mathilde Lenaerts × unknown]

Mons Seringe HP, m, 1856, Guillot; flowers purple, aging brown, medium; [Géant des Batailles × unknown]

Mons Thiers HP, mr, 1866, Trouillard; flowers shining red, large, full

Mons Tillier T, op, 1891, Bernaix, A.; flowers rosy flesh, shaded salmon-rose and purple-rose, fairly large, dbl., cupped; recurrent; vigorous growth

Mons Van Eeden – See **L'Obscurité**, HGal

Monsieur Victor Verdier – See **Victor Verdier**, HP

Mons Woolfield HP, mp, 1868, Guillot; flowers bright pink, large, full, globular

Monsoon HT, w, Poulsen; flowers 10-15 cm., 25 petals, borne in clusters of 2 or 3, no fragrance; foliage dark, glossy; growth bushy, 60-100 cm.; PP13300; int. by Poulsen, 2001

Monstrueuse – See **Bullata**, C

Monstrueux D, lp, before 1830; flowers pale pink, large, full, globular

Mont-à-camp HT, yb, 1928, Delobel; flowers pure yellow, reverse shaded orange, very large, dbl.; vigorous, upright growth

Mont Blanc HRg, w, Baum; flowers semi-dbl. to dbl., moderate fragrance; recurrent; growth to 3 ft.; hips numerous, plump, orange-red; very hardy; int. in 1986

Mont d'Or T, w, 1863, Ducher; flowers white, shaded light carmine-purple, aging to tan, large, full

Mont Hamel LCl, mp, 1937, Constantin; flowers semi-dbl., globular, borne in clusters; foliage glossy; very vigorous, climbing growth

Mont Rosa T, yb, 1872, Ducher; flowers dawn gold with flesh pink, medium, full

Montagny – See **Flaminaire**, HT

Montagut HT, Dot, Simon; int. in 1991

Montalembert HGal, m, 1852, Moreau-Robert; flowers dark violet, plumed and often spotted with white and crimson, large, full, globular

Montana – See **Royal Occasion**, F

Montana Min, dr, 2001, Saville, F. Harmon; flowers dark red, medium red reverse, 1½ in., dbl., borne mostly solitary, slight fragrance; foliage medium size, dark green, disease-resistant; prickles 3/16 in., thin, tapered, slightly curved, moderate; growth upright, compact, medium (18-22 in.); garden decorative, containers; [Lavender Jade × Red Minimo]; int. by Nor'East Miniature Roses, 2001

Montauban HT, dr, Croix; flowers large, 50 petals, moderate fragrance; free-flowering; foliage large, disease-resistant; int. by Roses Paul Croix

Montauban de Bretagne F, w, Adam

Montblanc – See **Mont Blanc**, HRg semi-dbl. to dbl.

Monte Carlo HT, ob, 1949, Meilland, F.; flowers Indian yellow suffused russet-orange, well-shaped, 5 in., 45 petals; foliage glossy; vigorous growth; [Peace × seedling]; int. by URS; Gold Medal, NRS, 1950

Monte Carlo Country Club HT, rb, Adam; flowers bright red, reverse pale yellow suffused red, dbl., high-centered; medium growth; int. in 2006

Monte Cassino HRg, dr, Baum; flowers medium, semi-dbl., borne in clusters, moderate fragrance; recurrent; growth to 3 ft.; hips plump, orange-red; int. in 1987

Monte Cristo HP, dr, 1861, Fontaine; flowers large, 50 petals, globular; low growth

Monte Cristo S, mr, 2002, Eve, André; flowers strawberry red, semi-dbl., borne in small clusters; foliage medium green, semi-glossy; prickles moderate; growth upright, tall (100-120 cm.); int. by Les Roses Anciennes de André Eve, 2001

Monte Igueldo HT, dr, 1944, La Florida; flowers velvety dark red, well-formed, open; upright, open habit growth; [Étoile de Hollande × Majorca]

Monte Nevoso HT, 1929, Cazzaniga, F. G.

Monte Rosa HRg, mp, Baum; flowers large, semi-dbl., moderate fragrance; growth to 3 ft.; numerous hips; int. in 1984

Monte Toro HT, pb, 1962, Dot, Simon; flowers strawberry-pink shaded red, large, dbl.; [Berthe Mallerin × Grand'mere Jenny]

Montearioso HG, about 1920, Franchetti; [*R. gigantea* × *R. moschata*]

Montebello HP, mr, 1859, Fontaine; flowers medium, full

Montecito HG, w, 1930, Franchetti; flowers white to blush, 6 in., 5 petals; foliage medium green, disease-resistant; vigorous, climbing (to 50 ft.) growth; [*R. gigantea* × *R. moschata*]

Monterey HT, rb, 1933, Lester Rose Gardens; flowers light gold flushed rose, veined and edged crimson, reverse lighter, dbl., moderate fruity fragrance; [sport of The Queen Alexandra Rose]

Monterosa HT, pb, 1958, Giacomasso; flowers deep rose, edged lighter, full, peony-like; very vigorous growth; [Elettra × Superba]; int. in 1952; Gold Medal, Rome, 1952

Montesquieu HT, pb, 1959, Dot, Simon; flowers deep rose shaded crimson, 45 petals, high-centered; strong stems; very vigorous growth; [Loli Creus × Tahiti]

Montesuma Rosice HT, Strnad

Montézuma HGal, m, before 1830, Coquerel; flowers lilac pink, edges paler, large, full, semi-globular; nearly thornless

Montezuma Gr, op, 1956, Swim, H.C.; bud urn-shaped; flowers 3½-4 in., 36 petals, high-centered; foliage leathery, semi-glossy; very vigorous, compact growth; PP1383; [Fandango × Floradora]; int. by Armstrong Nursery, 1955; Gold Medal, Portland, 1957, Gold Medal, NRS, 1956, Gold Medal, Geneva, 1955

Montezuma, Climbing Cl HT, op, Langbecker; [sport of Montezuma]; int. in 1970

Monthly Rambler HWich, dr, 1926, Laxton Bros.; flowers brilliant crimson-red, 5-6 cm., semi-dbl., borne in large clusters, moderate fragrance; some autumn repeat; [*R. wichurana* × Old Crimson China]

Monthly Rose – See **Old Blush**, Ch

Monthyon – See **Crignon de Montigny**, HGal

Monticello S, mp, Olesen; bud short, pointed ovoid; flowers medium pink, reverse lighter, ruffled, 5 cm., 10-15 petals, shallow cup, borne in clusters of 2-7, slight fruity fragrance; free-flowering; foliage dark; prickles moderate, 8 mm., concave; broad, bushy (60-100 cm.) growth; PP12125; [seedling × seedling]; int. as Sweet Cover, Poulsen, 1999

Montigny – See **Crignon de Montigny**, HGal

Montigny-le-Tilleul S, dr, RvS-Melle; flowers 60 petals, flat; foliage dense dark green; [Frederik Chopin × Florex]; int. in 1990

Montijo F, dr, 1954, Dot, Pedro; bud ovoid; flowers crimson-red, medium, very dbl.; very vigorous growth; [Méphisto × Magrana]

Montmartre F, m, 1955, Gaujard; bud ovoid; flowers bright purplish red, large, dbl.; foliage dark, bronze; very vigorous growth; [Peace × seedling]

Montparnasse, Climbing Cl HT, ab, 1986, Kodoya, Y.; flowers large, 34 petals, high-centered; foliage coppery green, leathery, semi-glossy; bushy, vigorous growth; [sport of Montparnasse]; int. by Ogura Rose Nursery, 1980

Montrea F, mr, 1970, Mosselman & Terreehorst; buds ovoid; flowers light red, small, very dbl., borne in clusters; foliage dark green; [Coronet × unknown]

Montreal HT, pb, 1981, Gaujard, Jean; bud long; flowers cream and pink blend, large, 45 petals, high-centered, moderate fragrance; foliage large, dark; prickles green; [Americana × Dora]; int. in 1979

Montresor – See **Red Imp**, Min

Montrosa – See **Mont Rosa**, T

Montrose HT, dp, 1916, Cook, J.W.; flowers deep pink; [Unnamed red seedling × Laurent Carle]

Montrose Min, mp, 1994, Taylor, Franklin; flowers with bright yellow stamens, large, dbl., borne in large clusters, moderate fragrance; foliage medium size, dark green, semi-glossy; some prickles; medium (60 cm.), upright, bushy growth; [Party Girl × Andrea]; int. by Taylor's Roses, 1994

Montrouge F, rb, 1958, Gaujard; flowers clear red, center tinted copper, medium, semi-dbl.; foliage glossy; vigorous, bushy growth; [Peace × Alain seedling]; int. in 1956

Montseny HT, op, 1944, Dot, Pedro; flowers salmon-pink, well-formed, very dbl., high-centered; foliage glossy; upright growth; [Mme Butterfly × Jean C.N. Forestier]

Montserrat HT, op, 1958, Camprubi, C.; flowers orange-salmon-pink, large, dbl., cupped, moderate fragrance; foliage dark, glossy; very vigorous, upright growth; [Comtesse Vandal × Angels Mateu]; int. in 1954

Montuna HP, 1928, Luke, E.R.; [Prince Camille de Rohan × unknown]

Monty's White – See **White Ensign**, HT

Monument HT, mr, Urban, J.; flowers large, dbl.; int. in 1969

Monumental HT, dr, Weeks, O.L.; int. by Certified Roses Inc., 2005

Monviso HT, pb, 1958, Giacomasso; bud pointed; flowers white streaked pink, large, dbl.; strong stems; [Julien Potin × Monterosa]; int. in 1955

Monymusk HMsk, my, 1954, Ratcliffe; flowers clear yellow, large, semi-dbl.; recurrent bloom; vigorous (3-4 ft.) growth; [Pax × Phyllis Gold]

Monyna HT, ob, Delbard; buds elongated, apricot with green overlay; flowers cream with coral-orange edges, flowing toward the center, large, high-centered, spiral, borne mostly singly; stems strong, upright; growth vigorous; int. by Ludwig's Roses, 2003

Monza HT, Leenders; int. in 1965

Mood Music Min, op, 1977, Moore, Ralph S.; bud mossy; flowers orange to orange-pink, mini-moss, 1 in., 45 petals, flat to rounded; foliage small; upright, bushy growth; PP4254; [Fairy Moss × Goldmoss]; int. by Sequoia Nursery

Moody Blues F, m, 1998, McGredy, Sam IV; flowers mauve, 2¾ in., full, moderate fragrance; foliage large, medium green, semi-glossy; bushy, medium (100 cm.) growth; [Sexy Rexy × Blue Nile]; int. by McGredy, 1991

Moody Dream F, m, McGredy, Sam IV; flowers lavender mauve, borne in clusters; good repeat; medium to tall growth; int. in 1996

Moon Adventure HT, my, Kordes; buds pointed; flowers clear yellow, dbl., high-centered; free-flowering; stems long; growth tall, strong, vigorous; int. by Ludwig's Roses, 1999

Moon Glow LCl, pb, 1937, Brownell; flowers creamy primrose, center soft yellow, 3 in., 60-75 petals, moderate fragrance; strong stems; vigorous growth; [Glenn Dale × Mrs Arthur Curtiss James]

Moon Magic – See **Jean de la Lune**, F dbl.

Moon Maiden F, ly, 1970, Mattock; flowers creamy yellow, 3½-4 in., 55 petals; foliage dark; [Fred Streeter × Allgold]

Moon Mist Min, w, 1985, Strawn, Leslie E.; flowers ivory tinged pale pink, well-formed, small, 20 petals, moderate fragrance; foliage small, medium green, semi-glossy; bushy growth; [The Optimist × Darling Flame]; int. by Pixie Treasures Min. Roses

Moon Over the Castle Ruins – See **Kojo no Tsuki**, LCl

Moon River S, w, 1998, Kordes, W.; flowers white, 2 in., single, borne in large clusters, slight fragrance; foliage medium size, dark green, glossy; prickles moderate; medium tall groundcover (2½ ft.), spreading growth; PP10637; [Yesterday × (Sea Foam × Red Max Graf)]; int. by Bear Creek Gardens, 1996

Moon River Min, m, Benardella, Frank A.; flowers lavender and silvery blue, hybrid tea, moderate fragrance; good repeat; int. in 1997

Moon Shadow HT, m, 1998, Warriner, William A.; bud long, pointed, oval; flowers medium lavendar, 4½-5 in., 35 petals, borne in small clusters, intense sweet pea fragrance; foliage medium size, dark green, semi glossy; few prickles; upright, tall, bushy (4½ ft.) growth; PP9538; int. by Bear Creek Gardens, Inc., 1996

Moon Shadow Min, m, Benardella, Frank; flowers lavender and silvery blue, moderate fragrance; free-flowering; medium growth; int. by Bell Roses

Moon Star HT, or, 2003, Atherton, Kyle B.; flowers scarlet orange, reverse silvery, 4 in., full, borne mostly solitary, moderate fragrance; foliage medium size, dark green, semi-glossy; prickles small to medium, curved down, moderate; growth upright, medium (3 ft.); ornamental; [sport of Killarney]; int. by Moonstar Roses, 2003

Moonbeam HT, dy, 1950, Robinson, H.; flowers deep golden yellow, large, high-centered; foliage dark, glossy; RULED EXTINCT 4/92; [seedling × McGredy's Yellow]; int. by Baker's Nursery

Moonbeam, Climbing Cl HT, dy, 1955, Kordes

Moonbeam S, ab, 1992, Austin, David; flowers apricot yellow, medium, semi-dbl., borne in small clusters, intense fragrance; foliage medium size, light green, semi-glossy; some prickles; medium (39 in.), bushy growth; int. by David Austin Roses, Ltd., 1983

MoonBerry HT, dp, Dorieux; flowers deep pink, 4-6 in., 40-45 petals, intense sweet fragrance; foliage dark green, glossy; growth tall (3-5 ft.); PPAF; int. by Edmunds' Roses, 2005

Moondance – See **Paul Ricard**, HT

Moondance F, w, 2007, Zary, Keith W.; flowers full, blooms borne in large clusters; foliage medium size, dark green, glossy; prickles 8-10 mm., straight, greyed-orange, few; growth upright, tall (5 ft.); [Hartanna × Iceberg]; int. by Jackson & Perkins Wholesale, Inc., 2007; AARS, 2007

Moondance Masquerade MinFl, w, 2005, Jalbert, Brad; flowers white, sometimes with a cream-green hue, 1 in., full, borne mostly solitary, slight fragrance; foliage medium size, medium green, semi-glossy; prickles medium, pointed, green, moderate; growth upright, tall (2 ft.); [Auntie Louise × Marilyn Monroe]; int. in 2006

Moondrops HT, op, 1965, Delforge; bud ovoid; flowers rose-amaranth shaded salmon, open, single, intense spicy fragrance; vigorous growth; [Sunny Boy × seedling]

Moondrops 85 HT, m, Delforge; flowers violet mauve with pink shadings, classical, moderate fragrance; int. in 1985

Moonglow S, w, 2004, Guest, M.; flowers white to pink, reverse white, 3 in., full, borne in large clusters, moderate fragrance; foliage medium size, dark green, glossy; prickles up to ½ in., hooked; growth spreading, medium (30 in.), groundcover; [(Morgengruss × Baby Love) × Flower Carpet]; int. by Pococks Roses, 2006

Moonlight HMsk, ly, 1913, Pemberton; flowers lemon-white, prominent yellow stamens, single, borne in small clusters, moderate fragrance; repeat bloom; foliage dark, glossy; vigorous (4-5 ft.) bushy growth; [Trier × Sulphurea]; Gold Medal, NRS, 1913

Moonlight HT, w, 1985, Warriner, William A.; flowers medium, 35 petals, no fragrance; foliage large, medium green, matte; upright growth; PP5743; [Coquette × seedling]; greenhouse rose; int. by J&P, 1984

Moonlight – See **Tsukiakari**, HT

Moonlight – See **Gekko**, HT

Moonlight LCl, yb, 2006, W. Kordes' Söhne; flowers copper yellow, fading lighter, 12 cm., semi-dbl., borne in clusters of 4-6; foliage large, dark green, very glossy; vigorous, tall (2 m.) growth; int. by W. Kordes Söhne, 2004

Moonlight MinFl, ly, Olesen; flowers dbl., 25-30 petals, borne mostly solitary, moderate wild rose fragrance; foliage medium green, semi-glossy; growth narrow, bushy, low (40-60 cm.); PP13658

Moonlight and Roses Min, m, 1998, Bridges, Dennis A.; flowers light lavender with rosy edges, with darker lavender and lavender overlay, 2-2½ in., full, high-centered, borne mostly singly; foliage medium size, dark green, glossy; some prickles; bushy, upright growth; PP11531; [seedling × select pollen]; int. by Bridges Roses, 1998

Moonlight Bay F, w, 1995, Rennie, Bruce F.; flowers 3¼ in., very dbl., borne mostly singly; foliage small, light green, semi-glossy; some prickles; medium (3 ft.), upright growth; [(Paul Shirville × Lavonde) × Party Girl]; int. by Rennie Roses International, 1991

Moonlight Dreamer Min, m, 2002, Moe, Mitchie; flowers petals quill to star-shaped, obvious stamens, 1½-2 in., single, borne mostly solitary, slight fragrance; foliage medium size, dark green, semi-glossy; prickles small, straight, light tan, few; growth upright, medium (18-20 in.); garden decorative, exhibition; [Anne Hering × Miss Flippins]; int. by Mitchie's Roses 'n' More, 2002

Moonlight Fragrance LCl, ly

Moonlight Lady Min, w, 1985, Eagle, Barry & Dawn; flowers creamy white, center buff pink, small, 52 petals, high-centered, borne singly and in small clusters; foliage medium size, dark, semi-glossy; prickles narrow, red; upright growth; [Pink Petticoat × Pink Petticoat]; int. by Southern Cross Nursery, 1986

Moonlight Lady HT, my, J&P; int. in 1995

Moonlight Magic HT, m, 1991, Burks, Larry; flowers lavender, medium, dbl., borne mostly singly, slight fragrance; foliage medium size, medium green, matte; medium, bushy growth; [seedling × seedling]; int. by Co-Operative Rose Growers, 1991

Moonlight Mist HT, w, 1965, Armbrust; bud pointed; flowers ivory-white, very large, dbl.; very vigorous growth; [Buccaneer × Golden Harvest]; int. by Langbecker

Moonlight Niagara HT, or, 1987, Rogin, Josip; flowers orange, reverse pale orange, loose, medium, 60 petals, high-centered, star-shaped, borne singly, moderate spicy fragrance; foliage large, dark green, matte; prickles semi-thick, medium, brown-red; growth upright, tall; hips rounded, medium, orange-red; [sport of Red Queen]

Moonlight Panarosa S, yb, Kordes; flowers light yellow with pink and apricot tones, outer petals fade, large, full, borne in large clusters, slight fragrance; arching growth; int. by Ludwig's Roses, 2004

Moonlight Scentsation MinFl, w, 2004, White, Wendy R.; flowers very pale lavender, near white, 2½-2-¾ in., very full, borne mostly solitary, intense fragrance; foliage small, medium green, matte; prickles ¼ in. long, acute triangular; growth upright, medium (3-3½ ft.); garden decoration, cutting; [Admirable × Pacific Serenade]; int. by NorEast Miniature Roses, 2005

Moonlight Serenade – See **Pfälzer Gold**, HT

Moonlight Serenade HT, yb, 1994, Ohata, Hatsuo; flowers yellow with red fringe, 3-3½ in., full, moderate fragrance; foliage large, medium green, semi-glossy; numerous prickles; medium (120 cm.), spreading growth; [Garden Party × Jana]; Gold Medal, JRC, 1991

Moonlight Sonata HT, ab, 1966, Boerner; bud ovoid; flowers large, dbl., cupped, moderate fragrance; foliage dark, glossy; vigorous, upright, bushy growth; PP2652; [(Diamond Jubilee × unknown) × (Goldilocks × Orange Nassau)]; int. by J&P

Moonlight Sonata F, w, 2003, Greenwood, Chris; flowers full, borne mostly solitary, intense fragrance; foliage medium size, medium green, matte; prickles medium, straight or slightly hooked, greenish; bushy (4-5 ft.) growth; [Sheila's Perfume × Silverado]; int. in 2003

Moonraker F, ly, 1968, Harkness; flowers pale yellow to white, large, dbl., borne in clusters; foliage light green; [Pink Parfait × Highlight]

Moonrise HT, ly, 1997, McMillan, Thomas G.; flowers medium, full, cupped, borne mostly singly, no fragrance; foliage medium size, medium green, semi-glossy; upright, low (2 ft.) growth; [(Lady X × Antigua) × Midas Touch]

Moonshine Cl HT, w, before 1920; flowers single; foliage blue-green, glossy

Moonsprite F, ly, 1956, Swim, H.C.; bud ovoid; flowers creamy white, center pale gold, 2-2½ in., 80 petals, cupped, blooms in clusters, intense fragrance; foliage leathery, semi-glossy; dwarf, bushy growth; PP1450; [Sutter's Gold × Ondine]; int. by Armstrong Nursery, 1956; Gold Medal, Rome, 1956, Gold Medal, Baden-Baden, 1955

Moonstone HT, w, 1998, Carruth, Tom; flowers ivory white with a fine, delicate pink edging, 4½-5 in., full, high-centered, borne singly, slight fragrance; recurrent; foliage large, medium green, dull; prickles moderate; upright, medium (120-160 cm.) growth; PP11384; [Crystalline × Lynn Anderson]; int. by Weeks Roses, 1998

Moonstruck F, w, J&P; PP10931; int. in 1997

Moonwalker S, ob, 2005, Valentic, Dzejna; flowers coral-orange, reverse coral, 4 in., full, borne mostly solitary, moderate fragrance; intermittent bloom; foliage medium size, medium green, semi-glossy; prickles small, moderate; growth upright, medium (5-7 ft.); hedging, specimen; [Kon 35-02 × (Camelot × Kon 13)]; int. in 2006

Moore's Classic Perpetual S, dp, 1999, Moore, Ralph S.; flowers 3 in., 41 petals, borne in small clusters, moderate fragrance; foliage medium size, medium green, semi-glossy; few prickles; growth bushy, compact (16-24 in.); [Anytime × Paul Neyron]; a dwarf hybrid perpetual; int. by Sequoia Nursery, 1998

Moore's Odorata w, Moore, Ralph S.; flowers white with pale pink centers, small, dbl.; a form of Odorata 22449

Moore's Pink Perpetual S, pb, 1999, Moore, Ralph S.; flowers pink blend, 3-3½ in., very dbl., borne in small clusters, moderate fragrance; foliage medium size, medium green, semi-glossy; numerous prickles; dwarf hybrid perpetual, bushy, compact (16-24 in.) growth; [seedling × Paul Neyron]; int. by Sequoia Nursery, 1998

Moore's Striped Rugosa HRg, rb, 2004, Ralph S. Moore; flowers red/white stripes, reverse red, 4 in., full, borne in small clusters, moderate fragrance; recurrent; foliage medium size, dark green, matte; prickles medium, straight; growth bushy, medium (4 ft.); hedge, specimen; [striped seedling (Golden Angel × 44st) × Rugosa Magnifica]; int. by Sequoia Nursery, 2005

Moore's Yellow Min, my

Moose Range HRg, mr, 1944, Wright, Percy H.; [Hansa × Mary L. Evans]

Morabito S, ab, Guillot; int. by Roses Guillot, 1997

Morag Ross MinFl, yb, 2001, Horner, Heather M.; flowers peach/yellow, pale yellow reverse, 3½ cm., dbl., borne in large clusters, moderate fragrance; foliage medium size, medium green, glossy; prickles small, curved, moderate; growth compact, medium (60 cm.); garden decorative; [Sunseeker × Fellowship]

Morava HT, Strnad; int. in 1970

Morden Amorette S, dp, 1977, Marshall, H.H.; bud pointed; flowers carmine, 3 in., 28 petals; foliage dark; compact growth; [(Independence × (Donald Prior × *R. arkansana*)) × (Fire King × (J.W. Fargo × Assiniboine))]; hybrid suffulta; int. by Agriculture Canada

Morden Belle S, mp, Ag. Canada; flowers dusky pink, full; free-flowering; foliage medium size, dark green, glossy; bushy (3 × 3 ft.) growth; very hardy to -40ºF; Parkland series; int. in 2005

Morden Blush S, lp, 1988, Collicutt, L.M. & Marshall, H.H.; flowers light pink, fading to ivory, small, flat, 51 petals, flat, borne in sprays of 1-5; repeat bloom; foliage medium size, medium green, matte; prickles straight; bushy, low (3-4 ft.) growth; hardy; PP8054; [(Prairie Princess × Morden Amorette) × (Prairie Princess × (White Bouquet × (*R. arkansana* × Assiniboine)))]; int. by Agriculture Canada

Morden Cardinette S, mr, 1980, Marshall, H.H.; bud ovoid; flowers cardinal red, 25 petals, cupped, borne singly or in clusters of up to 15; foliage 7 leaflets, globulous, dark; bushy, low growth; hardy; int. by Agriculture Canada

Morden Centennial S, mp, 1980, Marshall, H.H.; bud ovoid; flowers medium-pink, shapely, 40 petals, borne 1-15 per cluster; repeat bloom; foliage 7 leaflets, dark, slightly glossy; prickles slightly recurved; typical shrub growth, 3-4 ft.; [Prairie Princess × (White Bouquet × (J.W. Fargo × Assiniboine))]; int. by Agriculture Canada

Morden Fireglow S, or, 1990, Collicutt, L.M. & Marshall, H.H.; bud pointed; flowers brilliant red-orange, reverse red, loose, 3 in., 28 petals, cupped, borne in sprays; repeat bloom; foliage medium size, medium green, matte; prickles slight downward curve, tan; growth bushy, low (4 ft.); globular, reflexed calyx fruit; PP8060; [seedling × Morden Cardinette]; int. by Agriculture Canada, 1990

Morden Magic F, rb; int. by Moffet Nursery & Garden Shop, 2006

Morden Ruby S, pb, 1977, Marshall, H.H.; bud ovoid; flowers 2½-3½ in., very dbl.; heavy bloom; vigorous, irregular growth; [Fire King × (J.W. Fargo × Assiniboine)]; hybrid suffulta; int. by Agriculture Canada

Morden 6910 HWich, mr; flowers bright red, single, borne in clusters of 5-10, slight fragrance; spring bloom; vigorous (20+ ft.) growth

Morden Snow Beauty – See **Morden Snowbeauty**, S

Morden Snowbeauty S, w, 1998, Davidson, C.G. & Colicutt, L.M.; flowers semi-dbl., 8-14 petals, borne in small clusters, slight fragrance; foliage medium size, medium green, semi-glossy; prickles small; compact, low growth; PP11730; [(Prairie Princess × Morden Amorette) × (Mount Shasta × (Adelaide Hoodless × *R. arkansana*))]; int. by Agriculture & Agri-Food Canada, 1997

Morden Sunrise S, yb, Davidson, C.G.; bud orange-yellow, pointed; flowers dark orange with yellow base, opening to light orange with bright yellow, 3 in., 12 petals, borne in clusters, moderate fragrance; foliage dark green, glossy; upright (70 cm.), open growth; PP13969; int. in 1999

More Vale Pride Gr, mp, 1957, Ulrick, L.W.; [Ma Perkins × Overloon]

Moreau T, w, 1825, Foulard; flowers greenish white, center flesh pink shaded red, large, very full

Morena Min, op, Cocker; int. in 1983

Morena Min, mp, 2000, Cattermole, R.F.; flowers very full, borne in small clusters, no fragrance; foliage medium size, very dark blue-green, glossy; growth upright, bushy, tall (3 ft.); int. by Sharalea Gardens, 2001

Morey's Pink S, mp, Morey; flowers medium pink, aging lighter, full, borne in clusters; int. in 1994

Morey's Salmon HT, pb, 1953, Morey, Dr. Dennison; growth to 3 ft.

Morga HRg, mp; flowers dbl., borne in clusters

Morgan Gilet S, mp, Gilet; int. by Les Rosiers du Berry, 2005

Morgenglans HT, op, 1916, Van Rossem; bud coppery orange; flowers salmon-flesh, medium, semi-dbl.

Morgengruss HKor, op, 1962, Kordes, R.; bud ovoid; flowers light pink tinted orange-yellow, 8-9 cm., dbl., borne in small clusters, intense fragrance; foliage glossy, light green; very vigorous (13-14 ft.), bushy growth

Morgenluft F, pb, 1965, Verschuren, A.; flowers dark pink, reverse lighter, 55-60 petals, borne in clusters; foliage dark buff-green; upright, bushy growth; [La France × seedling]; int. by van Engelen, 1963

Morgenrot Cl HT, dr, 1903, Lambert; flowers dark carmine red, white eye, large, single

Morgenrot S, rb, 1986, Kordes, W.; flowers medium, 5 petals; foliage small, dark, matte; bushy growth; [(Marlena × Europeana) × ((Tropicana × Carina) × (Clare Grammerstorf × Fruhlingsmorgen))]; int. in 1985

Morgenröte HT, mp, 1951, Burkhard; RULED EXTINCT 12/85

Morgensen – See **Morgensonne**, F

Morgensonne F, my, 1954, Kordes; bud ovoid; flowers golden yellow, very large, moderate fragrance; foliage glossy, light green; very vigorous, upright, bushy growth

Morgensonne 88 LCl, ly, 2006, W. Kordes' Söhne; flowers rich yellow, fading quickly to cream, 10 cm., dbl., borne mostly solitary; foliage dark green, glossy; growth compact, tall (300 cm.); int. by W. Kordes" Söhne, 1988

Morgenster HT, ob, 1916, Nyvelt; flowers coppery orange, large, semi-dbl.

Morgenstern S, ly, Liebig; int. in 1989

Morgentau HT, w, 1908, Hinner; flowers very large, full, moderate fragrance

Moriah HT, ob, 1984, Holtzman, Arnold; flowers creamy yellow, orange reverse, large, 35 petals, intense fragrance; foliage large, dark, matte; bushy growth; [Fragrant Cloud × seedling]; int. by Gandy Roses, Ltd., 1983

Morinaye F, rb

Morletii Bslt, lp, 1883; flowers blush pink, 4-5 cm., semi-dbl., borne in small clusters; prickles branches plum-colored, without thorns; growth to 5 ft.; very hardy; rediscovered and put in commerce by Morlet; often confused with Mme Sancy de Parabère

Morning Blush – See **Duquesa de Peñaranda**, HT

Morning Blush A, ly, Sievers; flowers pure white edged strawberry red, 3-4 in., full; profuse spring bloom with occasional repeat; few prickles; growth center upright (4-5 ft.), outer canes spreading; int. in 1988

Morning Cloud – See **Asagumo**, HT

Morning Dawn LCl, lp, 1955, Boerner; flowers silvery rose flushed salmon, 5 in., 63 petals, high-centered, borne singly or in small clusters, moderate spicy fragrance; foliage dark, glossy, leathery; vigorous, pillar (6-8 ft.) growth; PP1447; [(New Dawn × unknown) × R.M.S. Queen Mary]; int. by J&P, 1955

Morning Fog HT, pb

Morning Glory – See **McGredy's Orange**, HT

Morning Glory Cl HT, rb, 1937, Beckwith; flowers carmine, reverse sulfur-yellow stained carmine, well-formed, dbl.; very vigorous, compact growth; [sport of Portadown Sally]

Morning Glow T, op, 1902, Paul, W.; flowers bright crimson pink tinted orange and maroon, large, full

Morning Glow Min, ly, 1999, Jolly, Betty J.; flowers light yellow, slight blushing on top surface in cool weather, 1¼ in., dbl., high-centered, borne mostly singly, no fragrance; foliage large, medium green, semi-glossy; few prickles; upright, tall (24 in.) growth; [Tidewater × Kristin]; int. by Langenbach, 1998

Morning Greeting – See **Morgengruss**, HKor

Morning Has Broken S, my, Clements, John K.; flowers rich yellow aging gradually to soft yellow, 3½ in., 15 petals, moderate honey/sweet fragrance; recurrent; foliage disease-resistant; growth to 4 ft.; [Graham Thomas × Gold Badge]; int. by Heirloom Roses, 1996

Morning in Moscow – See **Utro Moskvy**, HT

Morning Jewel LCl, mp, 1968, Cocker; flowers rich pink, lighter reverse, white towards petal bases, 8-9 cm., semi-dbl., flat, borne in small clusters, moderate fragrance; recurrent bloom; foliage glossy; [New Dawn × Red Dandy]; ADR, 1975

Morning Joy HT, ab, 1968, Williamson; flowers creamy amber, reverse flushed coppery pink, well-formed, dbl.; foliage light green; vigorous, upright growth; [sport of Mischief]

Morning Light LCl, pb, Harkness; flowers creamy pink, high-centered, borne in large clusters, slight fragrance; int. in 1994

Morning Mist HT, m, 1950, Fisher, G.; flowers lavender tinted gray, large, 15-20 petals, high-centered; moderately vigorous, upright growth; int. by Arnold-Fisher Co.

Morning Mist S, pb, 1997, Austin, David; flowers coppery red, 4 in., 5 petals, borne in small clusters; foliage large, light green, leathery; prickles moderate; attractive, shrubby, spreading, tall (4½x4ft.) growth; int. by David Austin Roses, Ltd., 1996

Morning Mist 96 – See **Morning Mist**, S

Morning Red – See **Morgenrot**, Cl HT

Morning Red – See **Morgenrot**, S

Morning-Red – See **Morgengruss**, HKor

Morning Skies Min, ab, 1997, Giles, Diann; flowers medium, very dbl., borne mostly singly; foliage medium size, medium green, dull; upright, low (1½ ft.) growth; [Little Darling × Rainbow's End]; int. by Giles Rose Nursery

Morning Song Min, ob, 1996, Williams, Ernest D.; flowers orange with yellow base, 1¼ in., full, borne mostly singly; foliage medium size, medium green, semi-glossy; some prickles; medium (16-18 in.), upright, bushy growth; [Sue Jo × Twilight Trail]; int. by Texas Mini Roses, 1996

Morning Star S, yb; int. in 1998

Morning Stars S, w, 1949, Jacobus; bud ovoid; flowers dbl., cupped, borne in clusters, moderate fragrance; free, recurrent boom; foliage glossy; upright, bushy, compact growth; [(New Dawn × Autumn Bouquet) × (New Dawn × Inspiration)]; int. by B&A

Morning Sun – See **Morgensonne**, F

Morning Sun HT, my, Christensen, Jack E.; free-flowering; prickles very few; int. in 1983

Morocco HT, mr, 1961, Von Abrams; bud pointed; flowers velvety red, 5 in., 30 petals, high-centered; foliage glossy; vigorous, upright growth; [Carrousel × Charles Mallerin]; int. by Peterson & Dering, 1961

Morongo S, dr, Peden, G.H.

Morpho F, Leenders

Morris F, or, Williams, J.B.; int. by Hortico, Inc., 2005

Morsdag – See **Mothersday**, Pol

Morsdag Alba Pol, w; low (40 cm) growth

Morsdag Red Pol, mr

Mort de Virginie HGal, m, 1824, in Brussels; flowers dark violet, large

Mortimer Sackler S, lp, 2004; flowers very full, borne in small clusters, moderate fragrance; foliage large, dark green, semi-glossy; prickles medium, concave; growth upright, vigorous, branching, tall (5 ft.); garden decorative; [Lillian Austin × seedling (apricot English-type shrub)]; int. by David Austin Roses, Ltd., 2002

Mosaik F, rb, VEG; flowers red with dark yellow, medium, dbl.; int. in 1978

Mosaïque F, yb, 1960, Lens; flowers light yellowish-pink, becoming red, open, semi-dbl.; foliage light green; low, bushy growth; [(Alain × Cinnabar) × Circus]

Mosaïque S, op, Croix; flowers soft orange and salmon tones; flowers generously; foliage disease-resistant; int. by Roseraies Paul Croix, 2002

Moschata Grandiflora HMult, w, 1866, Bernaix, A.; flowers prominent golden stamens, large, single, intense fragrance; very vigorous growth; [*R. moschata* × *R. multiflora*]

Moschata Himalayica – See **Paul's Himalayan Musk Rambler**, HMsk

Moscow Morn – See **Utro Moskvy**, HT

Mosel HMult, m, 1920, Lambert, P.; flowers bluish violet, center reddish-violet, medium, dbl.; sometimes recurrent bloom; [Mme Norbert Levavasseur × Trier]

Moselblümchen HCh, dp, 1889, Lambert

Mosella Pol, w, 1895, Lambert & Reitner; flowers cream white, medium, borne in large clusters; [Mignonette × (Mme Falcot × Shirley Hibberd)]

Mosella, Climbing Cl Pol, yb, 1909, Conard & Jones; flowers golden yellow and cream, borne in small clusters; [sport of Mosella]

Mosellied HMsk, m, 1932, Lambert, P.; flowers purplish red, center white, stamens golden yellow, medium, single, intense fragrance; non-recurrent; foliage dark; vigorous (about 6½ ft.), broad growth; [(Geheimrat Dr. Mittweg × Tip-Top) × (Chamisso × Parkzierde)]

Moss Magic Min, mp, 1977, Sudol, Julia; bud cupped, mossy; flowers medium to dark pink, circular, 1 in., 48 petals, flat; profuse bloom, repeating well; foliage dark; spreading growth; [Fairy Moss × unknown]

Moss Provence Rose – See **Communis**, M

Moss Rose – See **Communis**, M

Mossman S, mp, 1954, Skinner; flowers heavily mossed, pale dusty pink, 2½ in., very dbl.; vigorous (4 ft.) growth; [(*R. acicularis* × *R. rugosa*) × a Moss rose]

Mossy de Meaux – See **Mossy Rose de Meaux**, M

Mossy Gem Min, mp, 1984, Kelly, Martin; bud small, mossy; flowers medium pink, outer petals fading, small, dbl.; foliage medium size, dark, semi-glossy; bushy growth; [Heidi × Violette]

Mossy Rose de Meaux M, mp, about 1813, from England; flowers blush, peach center, small, full, cupped, borne in clusters of 2-3; foliage ovate, pointed, small; prickles red, straight, small, very numerous and dense; growth dwarf (1 ft.); hybridizer possibly Sweet; sport of Rose de Meaux or Pompon de Mai

Mossy Sweetbriar – See **Manning's Blush**, HEg

Most Unusual Day F, pb, 1999, Moore, Ralph S.; flowers 1½-2½ in., dbl., borne in small clusters, no fragrance; foliage medium size, medium green, semi-glossy; few prickles; medium (16-24 in.), upright, bushy growth; [Show 'n' Tell × Blastoff]; int. by Sequoia Nursery, 1999

Moth S, m, Austin, David; flowers pale grey-pink fading to nearly white, yellow stamens, large, semi-dbl., flat, intense myrrh fragrance; recurrent; low (1 ft.), spreading (1½ ft.) growth; hips rounded; int. in 1983

Mother HT, pb, 1939, Cant, B. R.; flowers white edged bright pink; [sport of Memory]

Mother and Baby HT, dr, 1988, Sanday, John; flowers dark red with a velvet sheen, some black marking, reverse deep red-matte, medium, 48 petals, quartered, flat, borne usually singly, sometimes in sprays; foliage medium size, medium green, semi-glossy; prickles barbed, light brown; low growth; [Bristol × (Lilac Rose × (Magenta × Magenta × Crimson Glory))]; int. by John Sanday Roses, Ltd.

Mother Lode Min, yb, 2006, White, Wendy R.; flowers golden yellow, reverse light orange or orange/yellow blend, 1¾-2 in., dbl. to full, borne in small clusters; foliage small, medium green, matte; prickles few, 3/32-3/16 in., straight; attenuate, crimson; growth bushy, mounded, short, (10-14 × 16-22 in.); containers, garden; [Light of Day × Sachet]; int. by Nor'East Miniature Roses/ Greenheart Farms, Inc., 2007

Mother Marie Pol, w, 1954, Podesta; flowers white, center green, 1½-2 in., very dbl., flat, borne in clusters; foliage light green; PP1243; [sport of Garnette]

Mother Mary McKillop – See **Mary McKillop**, HT

Mother Theresa HT, w, IARI; flowers white with pink tones, lasting, high-centered; stems long; int. in 1994

Mother's Country – See **Moeder des Vaderlands**, F

Mother's Day HT, w, 1937, Knight, G.; flowers white, at times shaded pink, very large; very vigorous growth

Mothers Day – See **Mothersday**, Pol

Mother's Day Orange Sport Pol, ob, 1958, Klyn; flowers orange-yellow; [sport of Mothersday]

Mother's Heart S, m, Thomson; flowers lavender, double, moderate fragrance; recurrent; Named for MOPS (Mothers of Pre-Schoolers); int. by Ross Roses, 2002

Mothers Joy S, mp; flowers soft pink, dbl., high-centered, borne usually in clusters, intense fragrance; foliage medium green, glossy; growth to 3 ft.

Mother's Love Min, pb, 1989, Bennett, Dee; bud ovoid; flowers pastel pink, blending to soft yellow at base, medium, 23 petals, high-centered, slight fruity fragrance; foliage medium size, medium green, semi-glossy; prickles straight, tapering, reddish; upright, bushy, medium growth; hips globular, green-yellow-brown; PP7484; [Futura × Party Girl]; int. by Tiny Petals Nursery, 1988

Mother's Love HT, pb; flowers soft white with a shell pink center, large, very full, borne singly and in clusters, intense sweet fragrance; good repeat; foliage dark green; stems long, strong; vigorous, upright (5 ft.) growth; int. in 1999

Mother's Love HT, mr; int. by K & M Nursery, 2004

Mother's Rose HT, op, 2001, Zary, Keith; bud creamy coral, long, pointed, ovoid.; flowers deep coral and pink, 5 in., 30 petals, high-centered, borne mostly solitary, slight light and fresh fragrance; continuous; foliage medium size, dark green, semi-glossy; prickles moderate; growth upright, tall (6 ft.); garden decorative; PP13087; [Olympiad × HT seedling]; int. by J&P, 2002

Mother's Value HT, mr, Kordes; buds sharply pointed; flowers clear carmine-red, large, dbl., high-centered, borne mostly singly; tall growth; int. in 1989

Mothersday Pol, dr, 1949, Grootendorst, F.J.; flowers medium, dbl., globular, borne in clusters of up to 20; foliage glossy, small; dwarf growth; containers, forcing; [sport of Dick Koster]

Mothersday, Climbing Cl Pol, dr, 1956, Kordes

Motiv HT, mp, VEG; flowers large, dbl.; int. in 1983

Motrea F, mr, 1968, Mosselman & Terreehorst; bud ovoid; flowers light red, small, very dbl.; foliage dark; [sport of Coronet]

Mottled Moss – See **Prolifère**, M

Motylek HT, w, 1954, Shtanko, I.; flowers cream, base yellow, medium, 40-45 petals, high-centered; moderate growth with thin, strong shoots; [Freiburg II × Golden Dawn]

Moulin Rouge F, mr, 1952, Meilland, F.; flowers 2 in., 20-25 petals, cupped, borne in clusters; foliage glossy; upright, very bushy growth; PP1298; [Alain × Orange Triumph]; int. by URS; Gold Medal, Geneva, 1952, President's International Trophy, NRS, 1952, Gold Medal, NRS, 1952

Moulin Rouge, Climbing Cl F, mr, 1958, Hendrick; int. by URS, 1957

Mouna HT, mr

Mount Everest S, mp; flowers crimson with a white eye and soft yellow stamens, large, slight fragrance; heavy spring bloom and scattered repeat; hips bottle-shaped; hybrid of *R. pendulina*

Mount Hobben HT, mr, 1985, Ota, Kaichiro; flowers bright scarlet, large, 30 petals, high-centered, borne 1-3 per stem, no fragrance; foliage medium green; prickles numerous, small; tall, upright growth; [Fragrant Charm × Christian Dior]

Mount Homan HT, ab, 1985, Ota, Kaichiro; bud ovoid; flowers large, petals quilled, dbl., high-centered, borne 1-3 per stem; foliage dark, semi-glossy; prickles large; tall, upright, bushy growth; [Ginger Rogers × Sunblest]; int. in 1984

Mt Hood – See **Mount Hood**, HT

Mount Hood HT, w, 1989, McGredy, Sam IV; bud medium, ovoid; flowers creamy white, medium, 40-48 petals, borne in sprays of 6-10, moderate old rose fragrance; foliage large, medium green, semi-glossy; prickles medium, curved downward, wide at base; bushy growth; PP9095; [Sexy Rexy × Pot O'Gold]; int. as Foster's Wellington Cup, McGredy Roses International, 1991; Gold Star of the South Pacific, Palmerston North, NZ, 1991, AARS, 1996

Mount Nelson F, w, J&P; flowers white with pink edges, semi-dbl., borne in clusters; free-flowering; vigorous, short growth; int. in 1998

Mt Rai HT, w, 1988, Ota, Kaichiro; flowers white, pale cream at center, aging pale pink at edges, 42 petals, high-centered, urn-shaped; foliage dark green, semi-glossy; prickles medium, downward-shaped, slightly dented, green; bushy, medium growth; hips medium, yellow-green; [(Golden Scepter × Narcissus) × Ginger Rogers]

Mt St Helens Gr, dp, 1982, Northwest Rose Growers; bud long, pointed; flowers deep pink, 35 petals, urn-shaped, borne singly and in small clusters, slight spicy fragrance; foliage dark, leathery; prickles bronze; growth to 4-5 ft.; [seedling × Queen Elizabeth]; int. in 1981

Mount Shasta Gr, w, 1962, Swim & Weeks; bud long, pointed; flowers 4½-5 in., dbl., cupped, moderate fragrance; foliage leathery, gray-green; vigorous, upright growth; PP2132; [Queen Elizabeth × Blanche Mallerin]; int. by C-P, 1963

Mount Shasta, Climbing Cl Gr, w, Knight, G.; flowers white, tinted yellow at center, 5-6 in., cupped; [sport of Mount Shasta]; int. in 1968

Mt Tara HT, or, 1988, Ota, Kaichiro; flowers large, 35 petals, high-centered, borne usually singly; foliage dark green, semi-glossy; prickles medium, downward-shaped, slightly dented, green; bushy, medium growth; hips medium, yellow-green; [Ginger Rogers × Fragrant Charm]

Mount Temple F, my, 2001, Kenny, David; flowers bright lemon yellow, full, high-centered, borne in large clusters; foliage medium size, dark green (purple when young), semi-glossy; prickles large, pointed, moderate; growth upright, bushy, medium (3½ ft.); garden decorative; [Golden Wedding × Bright Smile]

Mountain Haze F, m, 1967, Morey, Dr. Dennison; flowers lavender, reverse silver, medium, 55-60 petals, high-centered; foliage dark, leathery; vigorous, low, spreading growth; [Amy Vanderbilt × Lilac Time]; int. by General Bionomics

Mountain Mist S, m, 1990, Jobson, Daniel J.; bud pointed; flowers purple-lavender shading to white at base, small, 5 petals, flat, borne in sprays of 10-35, intense multiflora, vanilla fragrance; foliage small, light green, semi-glossy; prickles very few, red; spreading, medium (4 × 6 ft.), prolific growth; hips globular, red; [Yesterday × Yesterday]

Mountain Music S, pb, 1985, Buck, Dr. Griffith J.; flowers pink and yellow blend, medium, 23 petals, cupped, borne 5-15 per cluster, moderate fragrance; repeat bloom; foliage leathery, semi-glossy; prickles awl-like, tan; vigorous, erect, bushy growth; hardy; [Sevilla × Tom Brown]; int. by Iowa State University, 1984

Mountain Rose – See ***R. woodsii*** (Lindley)

Mountain Side S

Mountain Snow HWich, w, 1986, Austin, David; flowers dbl., 20 petals, borne in large clusters; foliage large, dark, semi-glossy; vigorous (to 20 ft.) growth; int. in 1985

Mountaineer HT, op, 1963, Wyant; bud long, pointed, orange-red; flowers orange-pink, reverse creamy yellow, 5 in., 35 petals, high-centered; foliage glossy; vigorous growth; [Mrs Sam McGredy × Crimson Glory]

Mountbatten F, my, 1980, Harkness, R., & Co., Ltd.; flowers large, 45 petals, cupped, borne singly or several together, moderate fragrance; foliage large, leathery, glossy; prickles numerous, large; upright, dense growth; [Peer Gynt × ((Anne Cocker × Arthur Bell) × Southampton)]; int. in 1982; Golden Rose, The Hague, 1986, Rose of the Year, 1982, Gold Medal, Orleans, 1982, Gold Medal, Courtrai, 1986

Mountie Min, mr, 1984, Laver, Keith G.; bud medium, globular; flowers unusually stable red color, 1¼-1½ in., 35 petals, cupped, becoming flat, borne mostly singly, no fragrance; recurrent; foliage small, dark, semi-glossy; prickles medium, long, thin, straight, pointed; compact, upright (12-15 in.), bushy growth; hips none ; PP6054; [Party Girl × Dwarfking '78]; int. by Springwood Roses, 1985

Mountjoy (natural variation of *R. setigera*), lp; flowers blush, center darker

Mourne Gold HT, yb, 1981, Kane Brothers; flowers deep yellow, pink flush; [sport of Whisky Mac]; int. in 1980

Mouse Min, pb, 1999, McCann, Sean; flowers pink yellow at base, changes to red-pink, 1 in., dbl., borne in small clusters; foliage small, medium green, semi-glossy; few prickles; bushy, medium (18 in.) growth; [Portland Dawn × Siobhan]

Mousha HT, lp, 1976, Kordes; bud long, pointed; flowers 4 in., 24 petals, high-centered; foliage glossy, dark; vigorous, upright growth; [Königin der Rosen × King's Ransom]; int. by Willemse, 1974

Mousha S, yb; flowers striped; int. by Hortico (not Hortico, Inc.), 2002

Mousseau Ancien – See **Communis**, M

Mousseline – See **Alfred de Dalmas**, M

Mousseline M, w, 1881, Moreau-Robert; flowers blush white, medium to large, full, moderate fragrance; recurrent; prickles numerous, very fine; growth upright

Mousseuse Blanche – See **Shailer's White Moss**, M

Mousseuse Blanche Nouvelle – See **White Bath**, M

Mousseux Anémone – See **Anémone**, M

Mousseux du Japon M, m, before 1906; bud and stems heavily mossed; flowers purplish rose, quickly fading to lavender, many stamens, semi-dbl.; growth moderate; in actuality, a mutation of the rugosa group, not from the Centifolias

Moussu du Japon – See **Mousseux du Japon**, M

Moussue des Quatre Saison Blanc ; flowers medium, dbl.

Moussue Partout – See **Zoé**, M

Moustique Min, w, Dickson; int. in 2003

Movement LCl, ob, Williams, J. Benjamin; flowers clear orange, yellow eye and stamens, single, shallow cup, moderate fragrance; recurrent; growth to 6 ft.; int. by Hortico, Inc., 2006

Movie Star HT, op, Tantau; int. in 1995

Moxie S, dp, 2001, Zary, Keith; flowers large, full, borne in large clusters, moderate fragrance; foliage medium size, dark green, glossy; prickles moderate; growth bushy, medium (4 ft.); garden decorative; PP13319; [La Marne × Matangi]; int. by J&P, 2002

Moyse – See **Moïse**, HGal

Mozart HMsk, pb, 1937, Lambert, P.; flowers deep pink with large white eye, small, single, borne in clusters, moderate fragrance; repeat bloom; vigorous, trailing or bushy growth; [Robin Hood × Rote Pharisaer]

Mr Joseph Cyril Bamford – See **Mr J. C. B.**, S

Mridula HT, w, 1976, IARI; bud long, pointed; flowers white, center soft pink, large, 35 petals, high-centered, moderate fragrance; foliage large, light, soft; very vigorous, upright, compact growth; [Queen Elizabeth × (Sir Henry Segrave × unknown)]; int. in 1975

Mrigasira HT, w, Kasturi & Sriram; flowers cream with pale pink at petal edges, dbl., well formed; free-flowering; int. by KSG Son, 2004

Mrinalini HT, mp, 1972, IARI; bud long, pointed; flowers phlox pink, very large, dbl., high-centered, borne singly, moderate fragrance; foliage medium size, medium green, soft; vigorous, bushy growth; [Pink Parfait × Christian Dior]; int. in 1975

Mu Lan HT, ob, 2003, Edwards, Eddie; flowers coral, 5½ in., full, borne mostly solitary, slight fragrance; foliage medium size, dark green, semi-glossy; growth upright, medium (5½ ft.); high-centered, exhibition; [Gemini × Fantasy]; int. by Johnny Becnel Show Roses, 2003

Muave Pol, m, 1915, Turbat

Mucaba HT, pb, 1962, Moreira da Silva; flowers pink stained carmine; [Marechal Carmona × Suzon Lotthe]

Muchacha F, or, 1979, Meilland, Mrs. Marie-Louise; bud conical; flowers brilliant vermilion, shallowly-cupped, medium, 12 petals, cupped; foliage dark; very vigorous, semi-shrub growth; [(Frenzy × Frenzy) × (Sangria × Sangria)]; int. by Meilland & Co SNC, 1977; Golden Rose, The Hague, 1976

Mudgee Red HT, mr, Dot

Muffy LCl, op, Bell, Laurie; flowers bright coral pink with yellow stamens, borne in large clusters; free-flowering; int. by Bell Roses, 2001

Mühle Hermsdorf HWich, w, 1928, Dechant; flowers pure white, 5 cm., dbl., borne in large clusters; nearly thornless; [*R. wichurana* × Gruss an Zabern]

Muhme Löffler HT, dr, 1940, Krause; flowers large, dbl.

MuLan – See **Mu Lan**, HT

Mulbarton LCl, mr, 1965, Hooney; flowers 4½ in., dbl.; foliage coppery; vigorous growth; [Paul's Lemon Pillar × (Ena Harkness × Richmond)]

Mulbry Rose – See **Bowled Over**, F

Mullard Jubilee – See **Electron**, HT

Mullem HT, rb, RvS-Melle; flowers 4 in., 29 petals, cupped, intense fragrance; foliage dense dark green; [Mme A. Meilland × Melglory]; int. in 1996

Multiflora – See **Red Damask**, D

Multiflora – See **Œillet**, C

Multiflora – See **Royale**, HGal

Multiflora Japonica – See ***R. multiflora*** (Thunberg ex Murray)

Multiflora Nana Perpétuelle Pol, lp, 1893, Lille; flowers small, single

Multiflore de Vaumarcus N, lp, 1875, Menet; flowers soft pink, medium, very dbl., borne in large clusters; good repeat

Multiflore Tricolore – See **Tricolore**, HMult

Multiplex Misc OGR, my, before 1629; bud large, round; flowers sulphur yellow, very large, very dbl., globular, no fragrance; foliage oval, dentate, pale green, small; prickles numerous, strong, hooked

Multiplex – See **Admirable**, HGal

Multnomah HT, rb, 1948, Swim, H.C.; bud long, pointed; flowers carmine, base gold, open, 4-5 in., 18-22 petals; foliage glossy, dark; vigorous, upright, compact growth; hardy in Pacific Northwest; [Contrast × Charlotte Armstrong]; int. by Peterson & Dering

Mum in a Million – See **Ghita Renaissance**, S

Mum Mum Min, w, 1986, McDaniel, Earl; flowers pure white, small, 55 petals, cupped, borne in clusters of 3-25; foliage light green, semi-glossy; prickles short, curved, light green; low, upright, bushy, spreading growth; [seedling × seedling]; int. by McDaniel's Min. Roses

München HMsk, dr, 1940, Kordes; bud long, pointed; flowers scarlet-crimson, large, semi-dbl., borne in clusters; repeat bloom; foliage dark, glossy; very vigorous, trailing growth; [Eva × Reveil Dijonnais]

Munchen 83 – See **Rose Iga**, F

München Kindl – See **Dicky**, F

Münchener Fasching S, mr, 1963, Kordes, R.; bud ovoid; flowers bright red, 30 petals, borne in large clusters (up to 40); foliage dark, glossy; vigorous, bushy (6-6½ ft.) growth

Munchkin Min, pb, 1987, Bridges, Dennis A.; flowers pink edging, white center, reverse slight pink edged on white, 22 petals, high-centered; foliage medium size, medium green, semi-glossy; prickles short, pointed, small, tan; bushy, low growth; [Watercolor × seedling]

Munchner Herz F, ab, Cocker; int. in 1990

Münchner Kindl – See **Dicky**, F

Munot Gr, or, Huber, Richard; bud pointed, oblong; flowers dbl., high-centered, borne singly and in clusters, moderate spicy fragrance; new foliage reddish, turning to green; upright (70 cm.) growth; int. by Richard Huber AG, 1983

Munro's Improved Premier HT, dp, 1927, Munro

Munster S, pb, 1959, Kordes; flowers soft pink shaded deeper, large, 28 petals, high-centered, borne in trusses; foliage light green; int. by McGredy, 1958

Münsterland S, pb, Noack, Werner; flowers light pink, deeper in center, 4 in., dbl., borne in clusters; free-flowering; growth to 6 ft.; int. in 1986

Mur-Ray HT, pb, 1936, Murray; flowers darker pink, tinged salmon; [sport of Briarcliff]

Murasaki no Sono F, m, 1985, Kobayashi, Moriji; flowers silver lilac, 13 petals, flat, borne singly and in small clusters; foliage light green; prickles slanted downward; vigorous, tall growth; [Tasogare × seedling]

Murasakisuisho Min, m; int. in 1984

Muraskino HT, m, Keihan; int. by Keihan Gardening, 1992

Murdina Lowe F, pb, 2004; flowers pink blend, 2 in., dbl., borne in small clusters, slight fragrance; foliage light green, semi-glossy; growth upright, medium (2½ ft.); garden; [Elsie Warren × Tina Turner]; int. by Battersby Roses, 2005

Muria HT, op, 1979, McGredy, Sam IV; bud long, pointed; flowers salmon-orange, 4 in., 40 petals, high-centered; foliage light green; bushy growth; [Miss Ireland × Tropicana]; int. by Spek, 1966

Muriel HT, dr, 1929, Archer; bud long, pointed; flowers brilliant velvety scarlet, semi-dbl.; strong stems

Muriel HBc, lp, 1990, Moore, Ralph S.; bud ovoid; flowers light to medium pink, aging slightly lighter, large, 15 petals, flat, borne singly and in sprays of 3-5; foliage large, medium green, semi-glossy; prickles sharp, pointed, average, brown; spreading, tall growth; hips short, oval, large, prickly, orange; [*R. bracteata* × Guinee]; int. by Sequoia Nursery

Muriel F, mp, 1992, Harkness, R., & Co., Ltd.; flowers small, dbl., borne in large clusters, slight fragrance; foliage small, medium green, semi-glossy; few prickles; low (30 cm.), bushy growth; patio; [Liverpool Echo × seedling]; int. by Harkness New Roses, Ltd., 1991

Muriel Armitage HT, dp, 1972, Ellick; flowers deep rose-pink, 5 in., 60-70 petals; foliage large, glossy, dark; vigorous, upright growth; [(Orange Sensation × Ballet) × Mischief]; int. by Excelsior Roses

Muriel Dickson HT, ob, 1915, Dickson, H.; flowers reddish-copper; Gold Medal, NRS, 1913

Muriel Grahame T, yb, 1898, Dickson, A.; flowers light canary yellow, tipped with rosy pink, very large, full; [sport of Catherine Mermet]

Muriel Humenick S, ly, 2002, Moore, Ralph S.; flowers dbl., borne mostly solitary; foliage medium size, light green, matte; prickles small, straight, green, few; bushy, tall (5-6 ft.) growth; [Golden Angel × Honorine de Brabant]; int. by Sequoia Nurs., 2002

Muriel Jamison T, ob, 1910, Dickson, H.; flowers dark orange, becoming cadmium yellow, large

Muriel Moore HT, w, 1916, Moore, F.M.; [sport of My Maryland]

Muriel O'Leary HT, pb, 1980, Murray, Nola; bud long; flowers light and deep pink, well-formed, 3 in., 27 petals; foliage large, glossy; vigorous, upright growth; [Honey Favorite × Rose Gaujard]

Muriel Pasquill HT, pb, 1927, Pasquill; flowers strawberry-pink, reverse golden yellow, semi-dbl.; [sport of Padre]

Muriel Robin HT, m, Orard; flowers magenta, dbl., cupped, intense fruity fragrance; medium growth; int. in 2006

Muriel Wilson T, ly, 1923, Hall; flowers rich lemon-cream, dbl.; int. by Prince; Gold Medal, NRS, 1921

Murillo HP, m, 1862, Fontaine; flowers velvety violet-purple, reverse amaranth, medium to large, dbl

Murmure LCl, dr, Croix; flowers scarlet, medium, dbl., borne in small clusters; [Luna Park × Moulin Rouge]; int. in 1971

Murphy's Law HT, mp, 1982, McCann, Sean; flowers medium pink, lighter reverse, large, 35 petals; foliage medium size, dark, matte; bushy growth; [Fragrant Cloud × (Prima Ballerina × Gavotte)]; int. in 1983

Murray Hill HT, my, 1939, Coddington; [sport of Joanna Hill]

Musashino HT, op, 1989, Takahashi, Takeshi; bud ovoid; flowers orange-pink, changing to pink, large, 35 petals, high-centered, urn-shaped, borne usually singly; foliage medium green, oblong, semi-glossy; few prickles; upright, medium growth; [Garden Party × Daimonji]

Muscade d'Alexandrie – See ***R. moschata*** (Herrmann)

Muscade Rouge – See **Evratina**, A

Muscosa Japonica – See **Mousseux du Japon**, M

Muscosa Rubra – See **Old Red Moss**, M

Muscosa Simplex M, mp, 1807; flowers single; native to the Caucasus Mountains and in France; discovered by Shailer

Musette F, dr, 1936, Tantau; flowers glowing light crimson, open, large, single, borne in clusters; foliage leathery, wrinkled, dark; strong stems; bushy growth; [Ingar Olsson × Johanniszauber]

Music F, rb, Asami, Hitoshi; flowers 7 cm.; int. by Keihan Gardening, 1986

Music, Climbing Cl F, rb; [sport of Music]; int. after 1986

Music Maker S, lp, 1972, Buck, Dr. Griffith J.; flowers medium, dbl., high-centered, moderate fragrance; foliage glossy, light, leathery; vigorous, dwarf, upright, bushy growth; int. by Iowa State University, 1973

Music Man Min, ob, 1997, Brown, Ted; flowers medium, dbl., borne mostly singly; foliage medium size, medium green, semi-glossy; upright, tall (20-24in.)growth; [Esprit × seedling]

Musicale Gr, rb, 1964, Buck, Dr. Griffith J.; bud long, pointed; flowers straw-yellow changing to cherry red, small, dbl.; foliage glossy, bronze; moderate, bushy growth; [(Bravo × Nellie E. Hillock) × Iobelle]; int. by Iowa State University

Musician S, rb, 1953, Wright, Percy H.; flowers bicolor, nearer red than yellow, with gray tones, 20 petals, borne in small clusters; non-recurrent; foliage modified rugose; hardy to -50F; [Hansa × Hazeldean]

Musikantenland F, mp, Hetzel; int. in 1993

Musimara LCl, mr

Musk Rose – See ***R. moschata*** (Herrmann)

Musketeer – See **Boulie's Dream**, S

Musketeer HMsk, w, Lester Rose Gardens; flowers stamens bright yellow, semi-dbl.; spring bloom; vigorous (20-25 ft.) growth

Muskoka Moonlight HT, w, 1999, Lougheed, Larry; flowers near white, medium, full; foliage medium size, medium green, glossy; some prickles; vigorous, spreading, tall growth; very hardy; [Pristine × Lichtkönigin Lucia]; int. by Lougheed Hybrid Roses, 1998

Muso HT, op, Keisei; int. by Keisei Rose Nurseries, 1999

Musquée Sans Soucis S, w, Louette; flowers white, single, borne in large clusters; recurrent; growth to over 2 m.; hips small, borne in large clusters, orange; int. in 2003

Mustang HT, or, 1965, Lens; bud ovoid; flowers large

to medium, dbl., high-centered; foliage dark, leathery; vigorous, bushy growth; PP2657; [Fandango × (Independence × Papillon Rose)]; int. by McHutchison & Co., 1964

Mutabilis – See **White Provence**, C

Mutabilis – See **Cocarde**, A

Mutabilis Ch, yb, before 1894; flowers sulfur-yellow, changing to orange, red and finally crimson, 7 cm., single, borne in small clusters; foliage bronze-green; prickles large; possibly a sport of *R. chinensis spontanea*

Mutabilis Variegata – See **Unique Panachée**, C

Mutace Caramba HT

Mutter Brada HT, ab, 1934, Brada, Dr.; flowers apricot-yellow and red, varying; vigorous growth; [Lady Craig × Freifrau Ida von Schubert]

Mutter Brada II HT, dp, 1934, Brada, Dr.; flowers large, dbl., intense fragrance; upright (80 cm.) growth

Mutter Brada III HT, lp, 1934, Brada, Dr.; flowers large, dbl.

Muttergruss F, dr

Muttertag – See **Mothersday**, Pol

Muttertag, Climbing – See **Mothersday, Climbing**, Cl Pol

My Angel F, dp, 1987, Pencil, Paul S.; flowers deep pink, medium, dbl., borne singly or in sprays of 6-10; foliage medium size, medium green, matte; upright, hardy growth; [Pink Parfait × Roman Holiday]; int. in 1988

My Baby Min, dp, 1967, Quackenbush; bud ovoid; flowers deep pink, small, very dbl., cupped; foliage small, glossy, dark; moderate, dwarf growth; [Cinderella × *R. rouletti*]

My Beauty HT, lp; int. by Jac. Verschuren-Pechtold, 1999

My Best Friend Min, pb, 2002, Moore, Ralph S.; bud mauve to red; flowers light pink, mauve/pink reverse, 1-1½ in., semi-dbl., borne in small clusters, slight fragrance; foliage medium size, dark green; prickles small, straight, green; growth spreading, medium (15-18 in.); containers, garden decorative; [Sugar Plum × striped seedling]; int. by Sequoia Nursery, 2002

My Blue Heaven – See **Blue Heaven**, HT

My Choice HT, pb, 1959, LeGrice; flowers pink, reverse pale yellow, 4½-5 in., 33 petals, intense damask fragrance; foliage leathery; vigorous, upright growth; PP1769; [Wellworth × Ena Harkness]; int. in 1958; Gold Medal, Portland, 1961, Gold Medal, NRS, 1958

My Dad – See **Connie Crook**, F

My Delight Min, lp, 1984, Bennett, Dee; flowers small, 30 petals, high-centered; foliage medium size, medium green, semi-glossy; upright, spreading growth; [Futura × Avandel]; int. by Tiny Petals Nursery, 1983

My Dream HT, dp, 1969, Winchel, Joseph F.; bud long, pointed; flowers deep pink, medium, dbl., high-centered; foliage glossy; upright growth; [Pink Favorite × Karl Herbst]; int. by General Bionomics, 1970

My Estelle F, pb, Kordes; flowers deep salmon with cream-golden reverse, semi-dbl. to dbl., borne in clusters, slight fragrance; good repeat; growth medium; int. by Ludwig's Roses, 1998

My Everything F, or, 2006, Cocker, A. G.; flowers salmon vermilion, reverse lighter, 2½ in., dbl., cupped, borne in large clusters, slight fragrance; foliage medium size, medium green, glossy; prickles moderate, 9 mm., straight; growth bushy, medium (2½ ft.); garden decoration; [Fyvie Castle × Beautiful Britain]; int. by James Cocker & Sons, 2006

My Fair Lady F, pb, 1959, Wheatcroft Bros.; flowers rose-pink, reverse darker, large, semi-dbl., borne in large clusters; foliage glossy; tall growth

My Fancy F, or, 1971, Meilland; flowers Dutch vermilion, imbricated, 3 in., 25-30 petals; foliage dull, dark; vigorous, upright, bushy growth; [(Dany Robin × Fire King) × Rumba]; int. by URS, 1970

My Fifi S, w, Delbard; flowers single; int. in 1998

My Friend F, lp, 1956, Motose; bud ovoid; flowers apple-blossom-pink, 2½ in., 30 petals, flat; dwarf, bushy growth; PP1460; [(Garnette × unknown) × Summer Snow sport]

My Gail F, ly, 2006, Rawlins, Ronnie; flowers primrose, reverse primrose, 2½ in., full, borne in small clusters, moderate fragrance; foliage medium size, dark green, semi-glossy; prickles ½ in., triangular, few; growth upright (33 in.); garden decoration; [Laura Ford × Goldbusch × Crazy For You]

My Gal Gale F, lp, 1958, Marsh; flowers soft pink, very dbl., borne in clusters; dwarf growth; [Pinocchio × Morning Star]; int. by Marsh's Nursery

My George HT, mr, 2002, McCall, Sharan; flowers large, petals reflexing, 6 in., full, high-centered, borne mostly solitary, moderate fragrance; foliage medium size, dark green, semi-glossy; prickles ¼ to ½ in., hooked downwards, moderate; growth upright, tall (5 ft.); garden decorative, exhibition; [Dorothy Anne × Dara]

My Gina S, mp, 1972, Shortland; [sport of Dorothy Wheatcroft]

My Girl F, op, 1964, deRuiter; flowers deep salmon, large, 30 petals, cupped to open, borne in clusters; foliage dark; vigorous growth; [Dacapo × Floribunda seedling]; int. by Gregory; Gold Medal, The Hague, 1963

My Girl HT, mp, McGredy; flowers satin pink with hint of lavender, dbl.; low to medium growth; int. by De Boer Roses, 1999

My Grandad F, ab, 2002, Bossom, Bill; flowers dbl., borne in small clusters, slight fragrance; foliage medium size, medium green, semi-glossy; prickles ¼ in., triangular, moderate; growth upright, medium (2½ ft.); garden decorative, containers; [seedling × seedling]

My Grandma F, mp, 2002, Bossom, Bill; flowers very full, borne in small clusters, slight fragrance; foliage medium size, dark green, glossy; prickles in., slender, slightly curved, moderate; growth upright, tall (3½ ft.); garden decorative, containers; [Sexy Rexy × (Kathlene's Rose × seedling)]

My Granny – See **Bossa Nova**, F

My Guy F, or, 1987, Milner, William; flowers bright orange-red, fading darker, medium, 13 petals, cupped, borne in sprays of 7-20, moderate fragrance; foliage medium size, medium green, semi-glossy; prickles medium, light brown, slightly hooked; bushy, medium growth; hips round, medium, light green; [Rosalynn Carter × Dorothy Wheatcroft]; int. in 1979

My Hero S, mr, Bailey; bud red; flowers red, fading to deep pink as they mature, 3½ in., 23 petals; produced continuously; foliage satiny, light green; mounded (3 ft.) growth; PP15400; int. by Bailey Nurseries, 2003

My Honey Min, ob, 1991, Justice, Jerry G.; bud pointed; flowers orange with light yellow accent at base, acquiring a pinkish cast with age, medium, dbl., urn-shaped, loose, borne singly, no fragrance; foliage medium size, dark green, semi-glossy; spreading, medium growth; [sport of Orange Honey]; int. by Justice Miniature Roses, 1991

My Inspiration F, w, 2004, Sawyer, Rosemary; flowers white with pink edges, reverse white, 4 in., full, borne mostly solitary, with some clusters in warm weather, moderate fragrance; foliage medium size, medium green, matte; growth compact, medium; exhibition, garden decoration; [sport of Sweet Inspiration]; int. by Rosemary Sawyer

My Inspiration MinFl, w, 2007, Wells, Verlie W.; flowers white with pink edge, reverse creamy white, 2½-3 in., full, borne mostly solitary; foliage medium size, dark green, semi-glossy; prickles in., hooked, few; growth upright, medium (3 ft.); exhibition; [seedling × Soroptimist International]; int. by Wells MidSouth Roses, 2007

My Jeannie F, ob, 2004, Horner,Colin P.; flowers orange, reverse slightly darker, 1½ in., dbl., borne in large clusters, slight fragrance; foliage small, medium green, semi-glossy; prickles small, slightly curved; growth compact, medium (2½ ft.); garden/decorative; [(seedling × Flower Carpet) × Playmate]; int. by Warley Rose Gardens Ltd. (Warley Roses), 2006

My Joy HT, mp, 1976, Wood; flowers fuchsia pink, dbl., high-centered, moderate fragrance; [sport of Red Devil]

My Kim F, dr, 2000, Horres, Marietta; flowers dark blue-red, white center, reverse dark red, 2¾ in., very full, borne in large clusters, slight fragrance; foliage medium size, mahogany red, turning dark green, glossy; prickles moderate; growth spreading, bushy, medium (3-3½ ft.); [sport of Europeana]; int. by Roses Unlimited

My Lady HT, ab, 1957, Robinson, H.; bud pointed; flowers apricot flushed gold, 5 in., 46 petals, high-centered, moderate fragrance; foliage dark, leathery; very vigorous, bushy growth; [seedling × Peace]; int. by Victoria Nurs., 1956

My Lady Kensington C, lp, before 1819; bud round; flowers flesh pink, exterior petals washed white, 4½ in.; foliage large

My Little Boy Min, my, Burrows, Steven; int. in 1982

My Love HT, dr, 1960, Anderson, P & J; flowers deep red, large, 45 petals, high-centered, intense fragrance; foliage dark; vigorous growth; [Bayadere × Ena Harkness]

My Love, Climbing Cl HT, dr

My Love LCl, pb, 1996, Coggiatti, Stelvio; flowers phlox pink, reverse coral pink, cream pink at base, 4½ in., full, borne mostly singly, moderate fragrance; foliage medium size, dark green, semi-glossy to glossy; few prickles; growth spreading, tall (300 cm.); [Caprice × Peace, Climbing]; int. by Curbishley's Roses, 1996

My Lucky Starr HT, mr, 1987, Evans, F. David; flowers large, full, no fragrance; foliage large, dark green, semi-glossy, leathery; spreading growth; [Secret Love × Karl Herbst]

My Maryland HT, pb, 1908, Cook, J.W.; flowers bright salmon-pink, edged paler, large, dbl.; vigorous growth; [Madonna × Enchanter]

My Maryland, Climbing Cl HT, op, 1915, Dingee & Conard; [sport of My Maryland]

My Mum F, pb, 2000, Webster, Robert; flowers ivory, shaded red and pink, reverse ivory with red edge, medium, full, borne in large clusters; foliage medium size, dark green, glossy; prickles moderate; growth compact, low; [Robin Red Breast × Regensberg]; int. by Burston Nurseries

My Ouma – See **Bossa Nova**, F

My Own Min, rb, 1984, Cook, Sylven S.; flowers red, yellow center, small, 5 petals, moderate fragrance; foliage medium size, medium green, semi-glossy; [(Scarlet Knight × Soeur Therese) × Willie Winkie]; int. in 1977

My Pink HT, pb, 2001, Bryan Epstein; flowers petals pink with white edge, reverse lighter, 2½ in., very full, high-centered, borne mostly solitary, slight fragrance; foliage medium size, dark green, semi-glossy; growth upright, tall (6-7 ft.); garden decorative, exhibition; [Duchess × First Prize]

My Pleasure Min, pb, 1987, King, Gene; flowers lavender pink, reverse light pink, fading lighter pink, medium, 45 petals, high-centered, moderate fruity fragrance; foliage medium size, dark green, matte; prickles straight, white with brown tips; upright, medium growth; hips oval, medium green; [Lavender Pinocchio × seedling]; int. by AGM Miniature Roses, 1987

My Prayer HT, op, 1953, H&S; bud long, pointed; flowers peach-pink, 5 in., 25-30 petals, high-centered; foliage leathery; vigorous, upright growth; [seedling × The Doctor]

My Pretty Garden – See **Mein Schöner Garten**, S

My Sister Min, w, 2003, Eagle, B & D; flowers very pure white, long-lasting when cut, 4-5 cm., full, borne in small clusters, intense fragrance; foliage medium size, medium green, semi-glossy; prickles small, straight; growth bushy, medium (40-50 cm.); garden, cutting; [Winter Magic × seedling]; int. by Southern Cross Nurseries, 1999

My Stars S, pb, 2004, Moore, Ralph S.; flowers pink, reverse white, 3 in., single, borne in small clusters, slight fragrance; recurrent; foliage medium size, medium green, glossy; thornless; stems turn reddish bronze in autumn; growth bushy, medium (3 ft.); specimen, containers, garden decoration; [Playboy × Basye's Legacy]; int. by Sequoia Nurs., 2005

My Sunshine Min, my, 1986, Bennett, Dee; flowers medium yellow, aging soft orange, bright yellow stamens, single, flat, borne singly and in small clusters, moderate fragrance; foliage medium size, medium green, semi-glossy; prickles small, reddish-brown; medium, upright, bushy growth; hips globular, 1/2 in., green; PP6453; [Sunsprite × Fool's Gold]; int. by Tiny Petals Nursery

My Sweet Girl F, m, 2001, Bossom, Bill; flowers large, dbl., borne mostly solitary, moderate fragrance; foliage medium size, dark green, semi-glossy; prickles 5/16 in., pointed, moderate; growth upright, bushy, medium (2½ ft.); garden decorative; [Purple Splendour × Sexy Rexy]

My Sweetie – See **Caliente**, Min

My Valentine Min, dr, 1975, Moore, Ralph S.; flowers deep red, 1 in., 65 petals, high-centered; foliage small, glossy, tinted bronze; vigorous, bushy growth; PP3935; [Little Chief × Little Curt]; int. by Sequoia Nursery

My Valentine – See **Grande Amore**, HT

My Way HT, w, Simpson; int. in 1988

My Wife Kathryn HT, ob, 2005, Wells, Verlie W.; flowers orange blend, reverse yellow blend, 4½ in., full, borne in small clusters, moderate fragrance; foliage medium size, dark green, semi-glossy; prickles moderate, ½ in., hooked; growth upright, bushy, medium (4-5 ft.); garden decorative, exhibition; [seedling × Rosie O'Donnell]; int. by Wells MidSouth Roses, 2005

My Wild Irish Rose S, pb, 2004, McCann, Sean; flowers pink, reverse apricot, 2 in., single, borne in small clusters, moderate fragrance; foliage medium size, dark green, glossy; prickles medium, hooked, red/brown, moderate; growth spreading, medium, lax (to 7 ft.); hedge; [seedling × seedling.]; int. in 2004

Myfanwy Welbourne HT, pb, 1999, Poole, Lionel; flowers 4½ in., full, borne mostly singly, intense fragrance; foliage medium size, dark green, semi-glossy; prickles moderate; upright, bushy, medium (3 ft.) growth; [(Hazel Rose × Cardiff Bay) × Darling Jenny]; int. by David Lister Roses, 2000

Myra LCl, w, 1926, Wilber; flowers creamy white, very large, dbl., borne in clusters of 2-3; foliage dark, bronze; vigorous, climbing growth; RULED EXTINCT 1/92; [Dr. W. Van Fleet × Lady Roberts]

Myra HT, pb, 1992, Stainthorpe, Avril E.; flowers medium, dbl., borne in small clusters; foliage medium size, dark green, glossy; numerous prickles; medium (75 cm.), bushy growth; [Matangi × Mood Music]; sometimes classed as a floribunda, but registered as HT; int. by Battersby Roses, 1990

Myra Stegmann Gr, op, Ludwig's Roses; flowers salmon-apricot, softening on the petal edges, dbl., high-centered; free-flowering; stately, medium to tall growth; int. in 1991

Myriam HT, lp, 1992, Cocker, James; flowers 3-3½ in., very dbl., borne mostly singly; foliage large, medium green, semi-glossy; some prickles; medium (75 cm.), upright growth; [Typhoo Tea × Grandpa Dickson]; int. by James Cocker & Sons, 1990

Myrianthes Renoncule HSem, pb; flowers pale peach, large, dbl.; free bloom; not dependably hardy

Myrna Courage HT, dr, 2007, Courage, Ray; flowers 9 cm., full, blooms borne mostly solitary; foliage medium size, dark green, glossy; prickles medium, hooked, brown, few; growth upright, medium (1¼ m.); garden decoration; [(Charles Mallerin × Chrysler Imperial) × (Chrysler Imperial × Mister Lincoln)]; int. by Ross Roses, 2007

Myrna's Dream HT, ab, Kordes; flowers light apricot, medium, full, high-centered, borne mostly singly; PP11388; cut flower rose; int. by W. Kordes Söhne, 1998

Myrniong HT, pb, Bell, Ronald J.; int. in 1994

Myrrh-Scented Rose – See **Splendens**, Ayr

Mystelle HT, dy, deRuiter; flowers yellow shaded green; int. by deRuiter's New Roses Intl., 2001

Mystère T, pb, 1877, Nabonnand; flowers pink, veined and marbled darker, very large, full, cupped

Mystère HT, dp, 1978, Gaujard; bud long; flowers scarlet pink, 45 petals; RULED EXTINCT 10/86; [Premiere Ballerine × Femina seedling]; int. in 1969

Mysterious Min, m, 1995, Williams, Ernest; flowers full, borne mostly singly, moderate fragrance; foliage medium size, medium green, semi-glossy; some prickles; upright (16-18 in.), bushy growth; [seedling × Twilight Trail]; int. by Texas Mini Roses, 1995

Mysterium F, yb, 1966, Kordes, R.; bud long, pointed; flowers golden yellow striped scarlet, 3 in., 25 petals, borne in clusters (up to 20); foliage glossy; bushy, spreading, low growth; [Masquerade × Kordes' Perfecta]; int. by Wheatcroft Bros., 1963

Mystery HT, rb, 1985, Herholdt, J.A.; flowers light orange-red, edged amber, golden reverse, large, 35 petals; foliage large, medium green semi-glossy; bushy growth; [(seedling × Southern Sun) × Southern Sun]

Mystery Min, lp, Poulsen; flowers light pink, medium, dbl., no fragrance; foliage dark; growth bushy, 20-40 cm.; int. by Poulsen Roser, 1996

Mystic S, dp, Olesen; flowers deep pink, 8-10 cm., 14 petals, no fragrance; growth broad, bushy, 60-100 cm.; PP12511; int. as Supreme Cover, Poulsen Roser, 1996

Mystic HT, w, Tantau, M.; flowers creamy white, large, 30-35 petals; healthy, vigorous growth; int. by Maclean, 1998

Mystic HT, m, Dot; flowers deep lavender, well-formed; free-flowering

Mystic Beauty B, lp, 2003, Patterson, William; flowers large, full, borne in small clusters, intense fragrance; foliage medium size, medium green, matte; prickles curved; growth compact, medium (3½ ft.); specimen; [sport of Kronprincessin Viktoria]; int. by Roses Unlimited, 2002

Mystic Fairy S, mr, Bailey; flowers rich red with pink tones, 3 in., 27 petals, borne in large clusters; blooms continuously; foliage glossy red giving way to dark green.; growth compact (3 ft.), vigorous; hardy to -30ºF; PP16131; int. by Bailey Nurseries, 2004

Mystic Gem HT, dp, 1960, Armbrust; bud long, pointed; flowers reddish-pink, large to medium, dbl., high-centered; foliage leathery; vigorous, upright growth; [Rod Stillman × Bravo]; int. by Langbecker, 1959

Mystic Mauve – See **Lavender Mist**, LCl

Mystic Meidiland S, yb, 1998, Selection Meilland; flowers coppery peach fading to butter cream yellow, 1-1½ in., semi-dbl., borne in small clusters, no fragrance; foliage medium size, dark green, semi-glossy; prickles moderate; compact, medium (3 ft.) growth; PP11044; int. by Conard-Pyle Co., 1997

Mystique HT, mr, 1989, Marciel, Stanley G.; bud pointed, slender, tapering; flowers bright red, sweetheart, large, 28 petals, cupped, borne singly, intense musk fragrance; foliage large, medium green, semi-glossy; prickles declining, pale red with tinges of green; upright, tall growth; [Samantha × Royalty]; int. by DeVor Nurseries, Inc.

Mystique F, ob, Kirkham; flowers rustic orange, aging reddish-pink, yellow stamens, dbl., borne usually in clusters of 7-12, occasionally singly; good repeat; foliage young shoots plum red, maturing medium green, glossy; growth to 3-3½ ft.; int. by C&K Jones, 1999

Mystique HT, mp, Kordes; flowers dusty pink with soft mauve tints, moderate fragrance; stems short to medium; greenhouse rose; int. by Australian Roses, 2001

Mystique HT, mp, Neil, J.; [sport of Mysty]

Mysty HT, Neil, J.; [sport of Shocking Blue]

Mysty Blue – See **Mysty**, HT

Mythos HT, w, Tantau; flowers creamy white with greenish tones, full, high-centered; int. by Richard Huber AG, 2004; Members' Choice, Monza, 2006

N-Joy HT, pb, Spek; flowers white with deep pink edges, lighter pink spreading down petals, 4 in., 55-60 petals, high-centered; numerous prickles; stems moderately long; int. by Jan Spek Rozen, 2005

N S J Pink Moss M, dp

N. L. Chrestensen Pol, or, GPG Bad Langensalza; flowers medium, semi-dbl.; int. in 1968

Naarden Red HT, rb, 1932, Van Rossem; bud pointed; flowers crimson-red shaded orange, large, dbl., high-centered; [Étoile de Hollande × Charles P. Kilham]

Naas Botha F, pb, Tantau; int. in 1990

Nabab F, Delbard; int. in 1959

Nacha Pobeda HT, dr, Costetske; flowers dark velvety red

Nachsommer LCl, mp, Wänninger, Franz; flowers coral pink, large, dbl., borne in clusters; foliage glossy; int. in 1990

Nachtfalter HT, dr, Baum, Oswald; flowers large, dbl.; int. in 1971

Nadia HT, dr, 1956, Delforge; foliage light green; [Mme G. Forest-Colcombet × seedling]

Nadia – See **Nadia Renaissance**, S

Nadia Renaissance S, dr, Olesen; bud broad based, ovoid; flowers dark red, 8-10 cm., 40-60 petals, cupped rosette, borne in clusters, moderate floral perfume fragrance; recurrent; foliage dark green, semi-glossy; prickles few, 5 mm., hooked downward; upright to bushy (100-150 cm.) growth; PP15197; [seedling × Queen Margrethe]; int. by Poulsen Roser, 2002

Nadine F, dr, 1962, Schwartz, Ernest W.; bud long, pointed; flowers maroon-red, 3 in., 38 petals, cupped; foliage bronze, soft; vigorous, bushy growth; [Red Pinocchio × seedling]; int. by Wyant, 1962

Nadine HT, ob, Croix; flowers delicate orange, 40 petals; int. by Roseraies Paul Croix

Nadine de Karadec Ch, w, 1852, Dorisy; flowers white, shaded light flesh pink, medium, full

Nadine Faye HCh, mp, 1847, Bélot-Défougères; flowers bright carmine, medium, very full

Nadja HT, mr, Rupprecht-Radke; flowers large, dbl.; int. in 1964

Naga Belle HT, dp, 2006, Viraraghavan, M.S. Viru; flowers 5 in., full, high-centered, hybrid tea form, borne mostly solitary; foliage large, blue-green, glossy; prickles medium, triangular, slender, pointed, dark brown, numerous; growth bushy, tall (5 ft.); garden decorative, hedge, exhibition; [Carefree Beauty × (Carmosine × *R. gigantea*)]; int. by Roses Umlimited, 2006

Naheglut – See **That's Jazz**, LCl

Nahéma LCl, lp, Delbard; flowers very dbl., cupped, moderate fruit and citrus fragrance; growth to 100 cm.; int. by Georges Delbard SA, 1998; Silver Medal, Fragrance, Gifu, 2006

Naia F, Gaujard

Nain – See **Rosier d'Amour**, HGal

Nain – See **De Chartres**, HCh

Naina HT, op, Kordes; flowers light salmon with almost brown center, medium; free-flowering; foliage full green, healthy; few prickles; int. in 1998

Nair HFt, or, 1936, Chambard; flowers vermilion red, reverse yellow, semi-dbl.; recurrent; growth to 6 ft.; [*R. foetida bicolor* × *R. wichurana* seedling]

Naïr HFt, yb, 1936, Chambard, C.; bud long, yellow and carmine; flowers vermilion-red, reverse yellow, stamens yellow, large, semi-dbl.; recurrent bloom; vigorous, bushy growth; [*R. foetida bicolor* × (*R. wichurana* × unknown)]

Naissance de Vénus – See **Königin von Dänemark**, A

Nambour F, w, 1953, Ulrick, L.W.; flowers white flushed pink, medium, very dbl., borne in clusters; foliage bronze; very vigorous growth; [Yvonne Rabier × Mrs Tom Henderson]

Nämenlose Schöne T, w, 1886, Deegen; flowers white tinted blush, well-formed, large

Namib Sunrise Min, yb, 1985, Moore, Ralph S.; flowers yellow blended with coral pink, 64 petals, borne in clusters of 15; foliage light; prickles straight, light brown; dense growth; [Rumba × Yellow Jewel]; int. by Ludwigs Roses Pty. Ltd., 1984

Nan Anderson F, op, 1970, Anderson's Rose Nurseries; flowers deep pink, coral sheen, 2½-3 in., 30 petals; foliage glossy, dark; low, bushy growth

Nan Mac HT, m, Ludwig, Heike; flowers blend of brown, mauve and lilac, high-centered, moderate fragrance; quick repeat; growth medium; int. by Ludwig's Roses, 2004

Nan Poole Min, pb, 1983, Meredith, E.A. & Rovinski, M.E.; bud globular; flowers yellow and pink blend, giving an overall coral-pink effect, 25 petals, high-centered; foliage small, dark, semi-glossy; prickles thin; low, spreading growth; [seedling × Libby]; int. by Casa de Rosa Domingo

Nana Mouskouri F, w, 1976, Dickson, A.; flowers well-formed, 2½ in., 30 petals, borne usually in clusters, moderate fragrance; growth shrubby; [Redgold × Iced Ginger]; int. in 1975

Nanako Rose Pol, pb; flowers can be pink or white; int. before 1867

Nana's Rose Min, m, 2004, Jalbert, Brad; flowers reddish-purple, striped white, reverse white-purple, ½ in., full, borne in small clusters, slight fragrance; foliage small, medium green, semi-glossy; prickles small, green, numerous; growth compact, bushy, dense, short (under 12 in.); containers, garden decoration; [Fairy Moss × Hurdy Gurdy]; int. in 2000

Nance Christy HT, op, 1906, Cant, B. R.; flowers salmon pink, large, semi-dbl.

Nancy HT, dr, 1930, Ferguson, W.; flowers bright scarlet-crimson, semi-dbl.

Nancy HWich, lp, 1932, Williams; flowers semi-dbl., moderate fragrance

Nancy HT, my, 1934, Mallerin, C.; flowers chamois-yellow, semi-dbl., cupped; [Mrs T. Hillas × Souv. de Claudius Pernet]; int. by H. Guillot

Nancy F, or, Croix, Paul; flowers intense orange-red; free-flowering; foliage glossy, healthy; dedicated to the town of Nancy, France; int. by Roseraies Paul Croix, 1982

Nancy – See **Nancy Renaissance**, S

Nancy F, mr; flowers bright red, very small, single; foliage very glossy

Nancy Bennett F, m, 1998, Bossom, W.E.; flowers lavender pink, 2¾ in., dbl., borne in small clusters; foliage large, dark green, semi-glossy; prickles moderate; tall, spreading growth; [City of London × Paprika]

Nancy Bergh F, pb, 1968, Fankhauser; bud ovoid; flowers pink, reverse silver-pink, open, large, semi-dbl.; foliage dark, glossy, leathery; vigorous, open growth; [Independence × Impeccable]; int. by A. Ross & Son

Nancy Clare Min, w, 1995, Justice, Jerry G.; flowers nearly pure white with pink accent at outer edge, 1¾-2 in., 18-20 petals, borne mostly singly, moderate spicy fragrance; recurrent; foliage medium size, light green, semi-glossy; medium (32 in.), upright growth; [Jennifer × seedling]; int. by Justice Miniature Roses, 1995

Nancy Elizabeth HT, w, 1947, Mason, F.; bud long, pointed; flowers cream, large, dbl., high-centered; foliage glossy; vigorous, upright growth; [Korovo × Florinda Norman Thompson]

Nancy Gardiner F, op, Kordes; flowers soft coral salmon, dbl., borne singly and in clusters, slight fragrance; good repeat; thornless; neat, medium growth; int. in 1994

Nancy Hall Min, pb, 1973, Moore, Ralph S.; buds small, long pointed; flowers pink with some yellow or apricot undertones, small, dbl., high-centered, borne singly and several together, moderate fragrance; continuous; foliage small, soft, light green; bushy, dwarf (10 in.) growth; [sport of Mary Adair]; int. by Mini-Roses, 1972

Nancy Hayward LCl, mr, 1937, Clark, A.; flowers rich bright cerise, large, single; very vigorous, climbing growth; [Jessie Clark × unknown]; hybrid gigantea; int. by NRS Victoria

Nancy Jean Min, ab, 2004, Rickard, Vernon; flowers apricot, reverse apricot blend, 1¾ in., dbl., borne mostly solitary, no fragrance; foliage large, dark green, glossy; prickles angled down, red, moderate; growth upright, tall (36 in.); exhibition; [Fairhope × Michael Chelot]; int. by Almost Heaven Roses, 2004

Nancy Lee HT, dp, 1879, Bennett; flowers deep pink, small, intense fragrance; dwarf, slender, weak growth; [Mme Bravy × Edward Morren]; susceptible to mildew

Nancy Pretty HWich, pb, 1917, MacLellan; flowers pink, reverse lighter, small, dbl., borne in clusters; [Dorothy Perkins × Ellen Poulsen]

Nancy Reagan HT, or, 1967, Morey, Dr. Dennison; flowers orange-scarlet, 5-5½ in., 28 petals, high-centered; foliage dark, bronze, glossy, leathery; vigorous, tall growth; [Orange Delight × Hawaii]; int. by General Bionomics

Nancy Reagan HT, ab, 2005, Zary, Keith W.; flowers full, 30 petals, borne mostly solitary, moderate fragrance; foliage large, dark green, glossy; prickles 5-6 mm., hooked downward, greyed-orange, moderate; growth upright, branching, medium (150 cm.) bush; PP15115; [Tournament of Roses × seedling]; int. by Jackson & Perkins Wholesale, Inc., 2004

Nancy Renaissance S, rb, Poulsen; flowers red, striped and painted yellow, 10-15 cm., semi-dbl., moderate fragrance; foliage dark; growth bushy, 100-150 cm.; PP12267; int. by Poulsen Roser, 1998

Nancy Shaw HT, lp, 1992, Wilke, William; flowers medium, full, borne mostly singly; foliage medium size, medium green, semi-glossy; some prickles; upright, bushy, tall (4 ft.) growth; [Peggy Lee × unknown]

Nancy Steen F, pb, 1976, Sherwood; flowers blush pink, center pale cream, 3½ in., 30 petals, flat, moderate fragrance; foliage glossy, dark, bronze, leathery; [Pink Parfait × (Ophelia × Parkdirektor Riggers)]; int. by F. Mason

Nancy West F, yb, 1970, Haynes; flowers medium yellow, suffused peach; [sport of Elizabeth of Glamis]

Nancy Wilson HT, mp, 1940, Clark, A.

Nancy Wilson, Climbing Cl HT, mp, 1959, Campton; int. by Hazlewood Bros.

Nancy's Keepsake HT, lp, 1995, Grierson, Mrs. Nancy; flowers pale pink, medium, full, borne mostly singly; foliage medium size, medium green, glossy; some prickles; medium (2½ ft.), upright growth; [sport of Keepsake]; int. by Battersby Roses, 1995

Nanda HT, mp, 1959, Sartore; bud ovoid to urn shaped, claret-red; flowers light rose, large; vigorous growth; [Dame Edith Helen × Eternal Youth]

Nandini HT, pb, 1984, Pal, Dr. B.P.; bud long, pointed; flowers pink with creamy white reverse, 46 petals, high-centered, borne singly, intense fragrance; foliage large, medium green, leathery; prickles brown-gray, hooked; compact growth; [Kiss of Fire × unknown]; int. by Laveena Roses, 1983

Nanette HGal, pb, before 1848; flowers rosy crimson, marbled with purple, medium, very dbl., cupped; growth erect; possibly synonymous with Manette from Ecoffay

Nanette HWich, w, 1926, Hicks; flowers creamy white to medium, 5-6 cm., semi-dbl. to dbl., flat, borne in large clusters, strong musky fragrance; foliage small, glossy

Nanjemoy Cl HT, mp, 1937, Cross, C.W.; bud long, pointed; flowers pink, open, large, semi-dbl.; free, intermittent bloom; foliage dark; strong stems; vigorous, climbing growth; [Mme Gregoire Staechelin × Bloomfield Comet]

Nankin HSpn, w, before 1818, Descemet; flowers flesh-colored, percepibly yellowish, pink at center, medium, single; prickles numerous, uneven, bristly; hips globular or flattened, nearly black

Nankin – See **Mme Yves Latieule**, HT

Nankin Double HSpn, pb, 1827, Vibert; flowers flesh pink, tinted yellowish, dbl.

Nano Nagle HT, dr, 1997, Xavier, Sister M.; flowers medium, very dbl., borne mostly singly; foliage medium size, medium green, semi-glossy; medium (114 cm.) upright growth; [Papa Meilland × Northern Lights]

Nantucket HT, ab, 1973, Kern, J. J.; flowers peach apricot, large, dbl., high-centered; foliage leathery; vigorous, upright growth; [sport of Chantré]; int. in 1972

Naomi HT, ob, 1926, Pemberton; flowers coppery buff, dbl.; RULED EXTINCT 1/88

Naomi HT, dr, 1988, Poole, Lionel; flowers dark red, shaded very dark in center, fading to red-purple, 32 petals, high-centered; foliage large, dark green, semi-glossy; prickles flat, medium, medium green; tall, spreading, upright growth; [Red Lion × seedling]

Naomi HT, pb; int. in 1998

Naomi F, mp, Takatori; int. by Takatori Roses

Naomi Rebecca HT, pb, 1996, Poole, Lionel; flowers deep pink, reverse pale pink, large, full, borne mostly singly; foliage large, dark green, dull; some prickles; upright, bushy, tall growth; [Solitaire × Gavotte]

Napa Valley S, mr, 1995, Olesen, Pernille & Mogens N.; flowers bright red, 2 in., semi-dbl., borne in clusters; foliage small, dark green, glossy; low (36 in.), spreading growth; PP9554; int. by DeVor Nurseries, Inc., 1995

Napoléon HGal, 1814; possibly from Holland, or by Dupont

Napoléon Ch, pb, about 1835, Laffay; flowers pale blush pink, tinted with crimson, large, dbl., cupped

Napoléon HGal, m, 1846, Hardy; flowers bright rose, shaded purple, very large, dbl.; erect, vigorous growth

Napoléon III B, mp, 1852, Bacot; flowers carmine

Napoléon III HP, rb, 1866, Verdier, E.; flowers very bright scarlet and deep slatey violet, large, full

Naranga HT, ob, Tantau; flowers deep orange, lighter reverse, large, dbl., high-centered, borne mostly singly, moderate fragrance; stems length 60-80 cm.; greenhouse rose; int. by Rosen Tantau, 1998

Narcisse T, my, 1859, Avoux & Crozy; flowers large, dbl.

Narcisse de Salvandy HGal, mp, 1843, Parmentier/Van Houtte; flowers deep rose-pink, prominent yellow stamens, large, flat, borne in clusters; large, spreading growth; int. by Van Houtte

Narcisse Gravereaux HRg, mr, 1901, L'Hay; flowers blood red

Nardy N, dy, 1888, Nabonnand; flowers coppery yellow, occasionally tinted pink, very large, very full, globular; foliage bronzy green; [Gloire de Dijon × unknown]

Nardy Frères HP, m, 1865, Ducher; flowers violet-pink, tinted slate, very large, full, globular; [Mme Boll × unknown]

Narita Korinkaku HT, dy, 1979, Kikuchi, Rikichi; bud pointed; flowers light orange, 5-6 in., 35-40 petals, high-centered, intense fragrance; foliage glossy, dark; upright growth; [Burnaby × Montparnasse]

Narmada F, pb, Kasturi; flowers pink with darker edges

Narmada Lahari HT, pb, 1980, Hardikar, Dr. M.N.; bud ovoid; flowers 90 petals, borne singly, moderate fragrance; foliage small, green; prickles beak-shaped; bushy, dwarf growth; [sport of Shree Dayananda]; int. in 1979

Narragansett S, mp, Schneider; int. by Freedom Gardens, 2005

Narre Fragrance HT, ob, 1942, Brundrett; flowers golden orange; [sport of Portadown Fragrance]

Narre Peace HT, yb, 1960, Brundrett; [sport of Peace]

Narrow Water N, lp, 1883, Daisy Hill Nursery; flowers very pale pink, almost white, 1½-2 in., single to semi-dbl., borne in cluster of 6-12, slight fragrance; repeats reliably

Nartaki Pol, m, Kasturi; flowers deep lavender with yellow stamens; int. by KSG Son, 1977

Narvik HT, op, 1960, Robichon; bud long, pointed; flowers salmon-pink to coppery, large, dbl.; foliage leathery; long, strong stems; vigorous growth; [seedling × Praline]

Narzisse HT, my, 1942, Krause; bud long, pointed; flowers apricot to maize-yellow, large, 23 petals, high-centered, moderate fragrance; foliage dark, leathery; vigorous, upright growth; [Golden Rapture × Golden Glory]; int. by C-P

Nascapee S, w, 1946, Preston; flowers open, 5 petals; free, recurrent boom; tall, vigorous growth; hardy; [(Ross Rambler × (*R. rugosa* × *R. eglanteria*)) × unknown]; int. by Central Exp. Farm

Nase Národni HP, m, 1935, Böhm, J.; flowers purple/pink with white, medium, dbl.

Naseby Rose HGal, m

Nashira – See **Jutland**, F

Nashville S, rb, Poulsen; flowers red with modest stripes, 5-8 cm., dbl., very slight fragrance; foliage dark, glossy; bushy, medium (60-100 cm.) growth; hips none; PP12491; int. as Candy Cover, Poulsen, 1996

Nastarana N, w, 1879, Paul; flowers white tinged pink, 2 in., semi-dbl., blooms in clusters on new wood; recurrent bloom; very vigorous growth; [probably an early *R. chinensis* × *R. moschata* hybrid]

Natacha – See **Cara Mia**, HT

Natal Briar ; understock for greenhouse roses

Natali F, dr, 1973, Tantau, Math.; bud ovoid; flowers small, semi-dbl.; foliage glossy; dwarf, upright growth; RULED EXTINCT 4/85; [unknown × unknown]; int. by Horstmann

Natali F, mp, 1985, Tantau, Math.; flowers large, 20 petals, high-centered; recurrent; foliage medium size, medium green, matte; int. in 1981

Natalie Pol, ob, GPG Bad Langensalza; flowers orange to orange-red, with dark yellow, medium, semi-dbl.; int. in 1972

Natalie Ann F, m, 2003, Rawlins, R.; flowers palest lavender, medium, semi-dbl., borne in small clusters, slight fragrance; foliage medium size, dark green, glossy; prickles 2 cm., triangular; growth upright, medium (36 in.); garden; [Odyssey × (Golden Future × Mary Rose)]; int. in 2003

Natalie Böttner HT, my, 1909, Boettner; flowers sulfur-yellow, passing to cream-yellow, tinted flesh, large, dbl.; [Frau Karl Druschki × Goldelse]

Natalie Ward F, mp, 1976, Thomas, R.; bud long, pointed; flowers pink, base yellow, 2-2½ in., 20 petals; bloom repeats quickly; foliage light; bushy growth; [Pink Parfait × unknown]; int. by Pattullo's Nursery, 1975

Natalka HT, lp, Costetske

Natascha – See **Malcolm Sargent**, HT

Natasha F, my, 1985, Staikov, Prof. Dr. V.; flowers lemon yellow, fading white, large, 135 petals, borne in clusters of 7-13; foliage dark, glossy; bushy growth; [Highlight × Masquerade]; int. by Kalaydjiev and Chorbadjiiski, 1974

Natasha Maria LCl, or, 1995, Fleming, Joyce L.; flowers bright, intense, vibrant orange-red, yellow base, medium, semi-dbl., borne 2-5 per cluster, moderate fragrance; foliage medium size, dark green, glossy; growth to 60-80 cm.; [Wilfrid H. Perron × Golden Olymp]; int. by Hortico Roses, 1994

Natasha Monet HT, m, 1993, Pawlikowski, Martin & Elaine; flowers very light lavender, large, full, borne mostly singly; foliage medium size, medium green, semi-glossy; some prickles; tall, upright, bushy growth; [sport of Crystalline]

Natasja – See **Natasja Hit**, MinFl

Natasja Hit MinFl, lp, Poulsen; flowers light pink, 5-8 cm., semi-dbl., no fragrance; foliage dark; growth bushy, 40-60 cm.; int. by Poulsen Roser, 2005

Natchez Min, mp, 1994, Olesen, Pernille & Mogens N.; flowers small, full, borne in small clusters; foliage small, dark green; few prickles; low (65 cm.), compact growth; patio; PP9273; int. as Little Bo-Peep, DeVor Nurseries, Inc., 1994; President's International Trophy, RNRS, 1991

Nathalie Ch, mr, about 1835, Laffay; flowers cherry pink, aging to light lilac, small to medium, full

Nathalie M, dp, 1849, Vibert; flowers dark pink, medium, full

Nathalie Daniel B, pb, 1845, Verdier, V.; flowers light peach pink, medium, very full, cupped

Nathalie Nypels – See **Mevrouw Nathalie Nypels**, Pol

Natilda – See **Laura '81**, HT

National Beauty HT, mr, 1983, Burks, Joe J.; [sport of The Alamo]; int. by J.B. Roses, Inc.

National Emblem HT, dr, 1915, McGredy; flowers velvety dark crimson, edged vermilion, dbl., high-centered

National Flower Guild HT, mr, 1927, Mallerin, C.; flowers pure scarlet-red, large, dbl.; long stems; very vigorous growth; [(Capt. F. Bald × Kitchener of Khartoum) × Mme Van de Voorde]; int. by C-P, 1930

National Radio – See **Centenary**, F

National Trust HT, dr, 1970, McGredy, Sam IV; flowers bright red, 4 in., 53 petals, classic; [Evelyn Fison × King of Hearts]; int. by McGredy

National Velvet HT, dr, 1988, Burks, Larry; flowers dark, deep velvet red, medium, 35 petals, urn-shaped, borne usually singly; foliage large, medium green, semi-glossy; prickles recurved, average, dark; upright, tall growth; hips globular, average, orange; PP7236; [Poinsettia × National Beauty]; int. by Co-Operative Rose Growers, 1990

Nationale Tricolore – See **La Nationale**, HGal

Native Wedding S, lp, 1980, Stoddard, Louis; bud short, pointed; flowers 14 petals, cupped, borne singly; repeat bloom; foliage broad, waved, medium green, semi-glossy, 5-7 leaflet; prickles straight; upright, medium growth; [Restless Native × (Mount Shasta × *R. suffulta*)]

Nativity S, ab, Williams, J. Benjamin; flowers very soft apricot and pink, fading to almost white, single, flat, slight fragrance; recurrent; growth to 3 ft.; int. by Hortico, Inc., 2006

Natural Beauty HT, pb, 1999, Scrivens, Len; flowers pink/apricot blend, reverse pink blend, 3 in., full, rosette, borne in small clusters, intense fragrance; foliage medium size, medium green, semi-glossy; few prickles; compact, medium (3 ft.) growth; [Pretty Lady × Silver Jubilee]; int. by John Tooby & Co., Ltd., 1998

Nature's Wonder MinFl, pb, 2007, Wells, Verlie W.; flowers deep pink, reverse creamy white, 1½ in., dbl., borne mostly solitary; foliage medium size, dark green, semi-glossy; prickles ¼ in., straight, few; growth upright, medium (3½ ft.); exhibition, garden decoration; [seedling × seedling]; int. by Wells MidSouth Roses, 2007

Naughty But Nice Min, ab, 1991, Bennett, Dee; bud ovoid; flowers soft apricot, medium, 20-25 petals, high-centered, slight damask fragrance; foliage medium size, medium green, semi-glossy; bushy, tall growth; [Futura × Why Not]; int. by Tiny Petals Nursery, 1990

Naughty Nancy F, pb, 1970, Cants of Colchester, Ltd.; flowers cream to red, 2 in., 12 petals; foliage dull, matte green; moderate growth

Naughty Patricia Min, pb, 1989, Bilson, Jack M., Jr. & Bilson, Jack M. III; flowers medium pink, edges blush, outer petals quill, large, 29 petals, high-centered, borne usually singly and in clusters of 3-5, slight fruity fragrance; foliage large, medium green, matte; prickles slight downward slope, reddish-tan; upright, tall growth; hips globular, medium, green blotched with orange-red; [Rise 'n' Shine × Redgold]

Nautilus F, op, 1960, deRuiter; flowers coral-salmon, open, 30 petals, borne in clusters; vigorous growth; [Signal Red × Fashion]

Nav-Sadabahar F, pb, 1981, Division of Vegetable Crops and Floriculture; bud pointed; flowers deep pink striped white, 20 petals, borne in clusters of 15, no fragrance; foliage medium size, green; prickles straight, pink to brown; medium, spreading, bushy growth; [sport of Sadabahar]; int. in 1980

Navajo HT, dp, 1959, Malandrone; bud long, pointed; flowers dark red to rose-red, 4½-5 in., 35-40 petals, high-centered, intense fragrance; foliage leathery; vigorous, upright growth; [Hortulanus Budde × E.G. Hill]; int. by J&P

Navarro Rambler LCl, pb

Navarro Ridge N, lp

Navid F, or, 1985, Payne, A.J.; flowers patio, medium, semi-dbl.; foliage medium size, medium green, semi-glossy; bushy growth; [Roydon Hall × Trumpeter]

Navigator LCl, mp, 1925, Verhalen; bud globular; flowers radiance pink, large, 25 petals, cupped; foliage soft; long stems; very vigorous, climbing growth; [*R. soulieana* × Radiance]; int. by Verhalen Nursery Co., 1943

Navneet F, w, 1973, IARI; buds medium, pointed; flowers cream-white, large, semi-dbl., open, borne singly and several together; foliage large, green, soft; growth vigorous, bushy; [Prelude × Africa Star]; int. in 1971

Nayika HT, pb, 1976, Pal, Dr. B.P.; bud pointed; flowers delft-rose, reverse and base darker, 4 in., 45 petals, high-centered, slight tea fragrance; foliage leathery; moderate, upright, bushy growth; int. by Anand Roses, 1975

Nazneen HT, lp, 1970, Pal, Dr. B.P.; bud ovoid; flowers very soft pink, large, very dbl., high-centered, moderate fragrance; foliage light green, glossy; vigorous, upright growth; [Queen Elizabeth × unknown]; int. by K. S. G. Son, 1969

Nazr-e-Nazar HT, mp, 1970, Singh, Raja Surendra; bud pointed; flowers light pink edges flushed darker, large, dbl., high-centered; foliage leathery; vigorous, upright, compact growth; [Clovelly × unknown]

NDR 1 - Radio Niedersachsen – See **Centenary**, F

Ne Plus Ultra N, w; flowers creamy white

Néala HGal, dp, 1822, Vibert; flowers deep rose edged lighter, medium, dbl.

Near You Min, w, 1990, McCann, Sean; flowers medium, dbl.; foliage small, medium green, semi-glossy; spreading growth; [Rise 'n' Shine × (Elina × Royal Gold)]

Nearly Black HT, dr; may be Dame de Coeur

Nearly Wild F, pb, 1941, Brownell; bud small, long, pointed; flowers rose-pink, white eye, 5 petals, moderate sweet fragrance; bushy (2-3 ft.) growth; [Dr. W. Van Fleet × Leuchtstern]

Nearly Wild, Climbing Cl F, mp, 1962, Burks; int. by Co-Operative Rose Growers, 1962

Nearly Wild Gallica HGal, dp

Nébuleuse F, dr, 1978, Gaujard; flowers deep crimson, medium, dbl.; vigorous growth; [Ritz × Lilli Marleen]; int. in 1971

Nec Plus Ultra HGal, mp, about 1810, Descemet; flowers large, full

Nedbank Rose F, dy, Delbard; buds golden; flowers golden yellow with flecks of pink and tones of salmon, semi-dbl., slight fragrance; free-flowering; growth medium; int. by Ludwig's Roses, 1997

Nederland HT, dr, 1919, Verschuren; flowers deep glowing red, very large, 60 petals; [General-Superior Arnold Janssen × George C. Waud]

Neela HT, m, K&S; flowers pale lavender with a tinge of pink, petal edges deeper lavender; [sport of Paradise]; int. by KSG Son, 1989

Neelakanti F, m, Chiplunkar; flowers deep purple mauve, deepening with age, rosette, borne singly and in small clusters; int. by Decospin, 1993

Neelambari F, dr, 1976, IARI; flowers deep red, large, 35 petals; foliage dark, glossy; vigorous, compact, bushy growth; [Blue Moon × Africa Star]; int. in 1975

Neena HT, lp, Bulsara; [sport of Queen Elizabeth]; int. in 1990

Neervelt Cl HT, mr, 1910, Verschuren; flowers carmine-red, lighter reverse, aging to purple, 9 cm., dbl., borne mostly solitary, moderate fragrance; reliable repeat; [Gloire de Dijon × Princesse de Béarn]

Nefertiti HT, my, 1997, Viraraghavan, M.S. Viru; flowers amber yellow, 6 in., dbl., high-centered, borne mostly singly, slight fragrance; foliage large, medium green, semi glossy; upright, medium (3 ft.) growth; [Julien Potin × First Prize]; int. by KSG Sons, 1985

Négretienne – See **Subnigra**, HGal

Negrette – See **Subnigra**, HGal

Negridte F, dr, Urban, J.; flowers medium, dbl.; int. in 1972

Nehru Centenary HT, dr, 1990, IARI; bud pointed; flowers dark red, reverse deeper, large, 60 petals, high-centered, borne singly; foliage very large, dark green, dense; prickles hooked, brown; tall, upright growth; [Christian Dior × Avon]; int. in 1989

Neige – See **White Provence**, C

Neige d'Avril HMult, w, 1908, Robichon; flowers pure white, stamens yellow, 4-5 cm., semi-dbl., borne in large pyramidal clusters; early, non-recurrent; foliage light green; thornless; very vigorous, climbing (to 8 ft.) growth; *R. wichurana* is one parent

Neige de Printemps HMsk, w, Lens, Louis; int. in 1991

Neige d'Eté HMsk, w, 2000, Lens, Louis; flowers creamy white, 1-1½ in., semi-dbl., borne in large clusters; recurrent; foliage medium size, light green, semi-glossy, disease-resistant; few prickles; upright, medium (120-150 cm.) growth; hedge, border, cut flower; [*R. multiflora adenocheata* × Ballerina]; int. by Louis Lens N.V., 1991

Neige d'Été – See **Magic Blanket**, S

Neige Parfum HT, w, 1942, Mallerin, C.; flowers white, sometimes tinted cream, large, dbl., intense fragrance; foliage leathery; vigorous growth; [Joanna Hill × (White Ophelia × seedling)]; int. by A. Meilland

Neige Rose LCl, pb, 1955, Delbard-Chabert; flowers center deep pink, becoming lighter at petal edges, large, borne in small clusters; very vigorous growth

Neiges d'Été Min, w, 1984, Gailloux, Gilles; flowers small, 37 petals; foliage medium size, medium green, glossy; upright growth; [Unnamed Baby Masquerade × Baby Masquerade seedling]; int. by Gilles Gailloux, 1985

Neisse S, pb, Berger, W.; flowers yellowish-pink, medium, dbl.; int. in 1959

Nejenka F, m, 1955, Klimenko, V. N.; flowers purplish pink, large, 57 petals; foliage dark, glossy; upright growth

Nelie Niel HT, w

Nelkenrose – See **F. J. Grootendorst**, HRg

Nell Gwyn HT, or, 1968, Cobley; flowers orange-copper, globular; upright growth; [sport of Tzigane]; int. by Blaby Rose Gardens

Nella Martinetti HT, op, Meilland; flowers salmon pink with lighter reverse, dbl., high-centered, intense fragrance; upright (80 cm.) growth; int. in 1990

Nellie Charlton HT, mp, 1923, Lilley; flowers silvery pink, reverse salmon-pink, dbl.; [Mme Abel Chatenay × unknown]

Nellie Deaser F, ab, 2001, Kenny, David; flowers old-fashioned, apricot blend fading to cream, 3 in., very full, borne in large clusters; foliage medium size, dark green (red when young), matte; prickles large, hooked, moderate; growth upright, bushy, tall (4 ft.); garden decorative; [Sexy Rexy × Wiggy]

Nellie E. Hillock HT, mp, 1934, Hillock; flowers silvery pink, base deep gold, reverse old-rose, 60 petals, cupped, peony, moderate fragrance; foliage leathery, dark; low, spreading growth; [Golden Dawn × seedling]

Nellie E. Hillock, Climbing Cl HT, mp, 1948, Buck, Dr. Griffith J.; int. by Lester Rose Gardens

Nellie Maud Powell HT, yb, 1977, Powell; flowers yellow edged red, 4-5 in., 75-80 petals; foliage glossy; vigorous growth; [Columbine × Kordes' Perfecta]

Nellie Parker HT, w, 1916, Dickson, H.; flowers creamy white, center darker, well-shaped, large, dbl.; vigorous, upright growth; Gold Medal, NRS, 1916

Nelly Custis HSet, w, 1934, Conard-Pyle; flowers small, dbl., borne in clusters of 7-9, moderate fragrance; vigorous, upright growth

Nelly Johnstone T, mp, 1906, Paul, G.; bud long; flowers pure rose pink often shot with light pale violet on the outside, large, full, moderate fragrance; [Mme Berkeley × unknown]

Nelly Verschuren HT, my, 1918, Verschuren; flowers clear yellow, large, intense fragrance; [seedling × Duchess of Wellington]

Nelson Girls HT, ab, Warner; flowers apricot, classic hybrid tea; free-flowering; 125th Ann. of Nelson College for Girls; int. by Tasman Bay Roses, 2006; Certificate of Merit, Palmerston, NZ, 2006

Nelson's Pride S, w, 2006, Beales, Amanda; flowers dbl., borne mostly solitary; foliage medium size, dark green, semi-glossy; prickles medium, curved downwards, moderate; growth bushy, short (1 m.); landscape, containers; [Bonica × Maigold]; int. by Peter Beales Roses, 2005

Némésis Ch, dr, 1836, Bizard; flowers purplish crimson, dbl., pompon; dwarf growth

Nemesis MinFl, rb, 2004, Tucker, Robbie; flowers red, reverse red with yellow tones, small, dbl., borne mostly solitary, no fragrance; foliage medium green, matte; prickles medium, straight; upright, medium growth; exhibition, cutting, garden; [seedling × Soroptimist International]; int. by Rosemania, 2005

Nemo S, w, Noack; flowers clear white with yellow stamens, 4 cm., single, cupped, borne in clusters; low, bushy (80-100 cm.) growth; int. by Noack Rosen, 2002

Nénette Leydier Pol, mr, 1924, Richardier; flowers crimson-scarlet, base lighter

Nenikujaku F, pb, 1986, Kikuchi, Rikichi; flowers pink, blended with yellow and red, 15 petals, cupped, borne in clusters, moderate fragrance; vigorous growth; [Masquerade × Matador]; int. in 1984

Nenita F, w, 1962, Moreira da Silva, A.; flowers large, 22 petals, moderate fragrance; foliage light green; vigorous, low growth; [seedling × Virgo]

Neon HT, mr, 1936, Nicolas; flowers crimson-scarlet, large, very dbl.; vigorous, branching growth; int. by Beckwith

Neon F, ob, 1970, Waterhouse Nursery; flowers intense orange, 2 in., 26 petals; compact growth

Neon HT, op, Kordes; flowers deep salmon pink, 4 in., 30-35 petals, high-centered; good repeat; stems strong; growth to 6 ft.; PP11273; originally a greenhouse rose; int. in 1993

Neon F, dp, 2006, W. Kordes' Söhne; bud small, rounded; flowers crimson pink, white at base of petals, yellow stamens, 5 cm., semi-dbl., shallow cupped, borne in small clusters; foliage medium size, reddish, turnin dark green, very glossy, disease-resistant; wide, bushy (60 cm.) growth; possibly synonymous with Neon, HT (above); int. by W. Kordes' Söhne, 2001

Neon Cowboy Min, rb, 2001, Carruth, Tom; flowers red with yellow eye, 3-4 cm., single, borne in small clusters, slight fragrance; foliage small, dark green, glossy; prickles moderate, small, straight, light brown; growth compact, short (28-38 cm.); garden decoration; PP15256; [Emily Louise × (Playboy × Little Artist)]; int. by Weeks Roses, 2001

Neon Lights F, dp, 1991, Warriner, William A.; flowers hot magenta pink, large, dbl., borne in small clusters, moderate fragrance; foliage medium size, medium green, semi-glossy; medium, bushy growth; PP8692; [Intrigue × Impatient]; int. by Bear Creek Gardens, 1992

Néphis HSpn, dp, 1825, Dagonnet

Neptune HSpn, dr, before 1848; flowers deep crimson, medium, full

Neptune HT, m, 2003, Carruth, Tom; flowers blended lavender, reverse blended lavender sometimes edged purple, 11-14 cm., full, borne mostly solitary, intense fragrance; foliage large, medium green, semi-glossy; prickles average, almost straight, brown, none; growth upright, medium (90 to 120 cm.); garden decoration; [(Blueberry Hill × Stephen's Big Purple) × Blue Nile]; int. by Weeks Roses, 2004

Neptunia HT, pb, 1998, Poole, Lionel; flowers pink blending to white, classic, 6 in., very dbl., high-centered, borne mostly singly; foliage large, dark green, semi-glossy; some prickles; upright, medium growth; [(Precious Platinum × Silver Jubilee) × seedling]

Nerene HT, yb, Malanseuns

Nerissa HT, ly, 1912, Paul, W.; bud short, sharply pointed; flowers cream-yellow, shaded white, very large, dbl., high-centered

Nero – See **Néron**, HGal

Néron HGal, rb, 1841, Laffay, M.; flowers crimson, blotched and marbled violet; growth to 4 ft.

Nerone HT, Cazzaniga, F. G.

Nerrière HBc, w, before 1847, Vibert; flowers cream with a darker center, large, full, cupped

Nervi HT, Mansuino

Nescapee LCl; derivative of Ross Rambler

Nessie LCl, lp, Rupert, Kim; bud apricot and gold; flowers blush pink, 2 in., dbl., borne in clusters, intense spicy, sweet fragrance; spring flowering; stems long; growth to 20 ft.; [sport of Montecito]; int. by Ashdown, 2001

Nest Rose – See **Electric Blanket**, F

Nesta Burnett Snowdon Min, my, 2004, Jellyman, J.S.; flowers semi-dbl., borne in small clusters, moderate fragrance; foliage medium green, glossy; prickles 9-10 mm., curved, few; growth bushy, medium (2½-3 ft.); garden; decorative; [Remember Me × Marylin Robb]

Nestor HGal, mr, 1834, Vibert; flowers crimson, edges tinted lilac, medium, dbl., quartered, borne in clusters of 2-3; foliage light green, oval; numerous prickles; very vigorous growth

Nestor Bolderdijk HT, pb, 1938, Leenders, M.; bud long, pointed; flowers pale ecru, reverse yellowish-salmon, base golden, very large, dbl.; foliage glossy; vigorous growth; [Comtesse Vandal × Pres. Macia]

Netravathy F, mp, Kasturi; flowers pink, deepening with age, borne in compact trusses; int. by KSG Son, 1975

Netsujo HT, dr, Keisei; int. by Keisei Rose Nurseries, 1993

Netujoh HT, dr, 1999, Hirabayashi, Hiroshi; flowers deep red, 4-5 in., 30-35 petals, high-centered; foliage dark green, semi-glossy; upright (3-4 ft.) growth; int. by Keisei Rose Nurseries, Inc., 1993; Gold Medal, Japan Rose Concours, 1993

Neue Revue HT, rb, 1975; flowers yellow-white, touched dark red, well-formed, 4½ in., 30 petals, intense fragrance; foliage leathery; prickles many large; upright growth; [Colour Wonder × unknown]; int. by Kordes, 1962; ADR, 1969

Neues Europa – See **Nouvelle Europe**, F

Neus HT, w, Viveros Fco. Ferrer, S L; flowers 25 petals, high-centered; [Shocking Blue × Carta Blanca]

Neutron (form of *R. rugosa*), m, 1985, Lundstad, Arne; flowers purple, shallow-cupped, 3 in., 10 petals, cupped, borne singly or in small clusters, intense fragrance; repeat bloom; foliage thick, rugose, shining,dark; prickles straight, gray; upright, dense growth; [*R. rugosa* × unknown]; grown from irradiated seed; int. by Agricultural University of Norway, 1984

Nevada HMoy, w, 1927, Dot, Pedro; bud ovoid, pink or apricot; flowers white, reverse sometimes splashed carmine, on strong stems, 4 in., single; may repeat; vigorous (7 ft.), shrubby growth; [La Giralda × *R. moyesii*]

Never Forgotten HT, mr, 1997, Sealand Nurseries, Ltd.; flowers medium, very dbl., borne in small clusters, moderate fragrance; foliage medium size, dark green; some prickles; growth compact, medium (2-2½ ft.); int. by Gregory Roses

Nevertheless F, rb, 1993, Henson, R.W.; flowers orange/red/yellow blend, medium, full, borne in small clusters, moderate fragrance; foliage large, medium green, matte; few prickles; tall (100 cm.), upright growth; [(Silver Jubilee × Trumpeter) × Gold Medal]; int. by Henson, 1993

Neville Chamberlain HT, ob, 1940, Lens; bud ovoid; flowers salmon, center orange, 4 in., 26 petals, high-centered; foliage bronze; vigorous, tall growth; [Charles P. Kilham × Mrs Sam McGredy]; int. by J&P; Gold Medal, Portland, 1941

Neville Gibson HT, mp, 1982, Harkness, R., & Co., Ltd.; flowers large, 40 petals, high-centered; foliage large, medium green, semi-glossy; medium, upright growth; [Red Planet × (Carina × Pascali)]; int. in 1983; Golden Rose, Geneva, 1980

Nevis Moss M, mp

New Adventure Min, w, 1989, Moore, Ralph S.; bud pointed; flowers creamy white, medium, 25 petals, flat, borne singly and in sprays of 3-5, no fragrance; foliage small, medium green, matte; prickles short, pointed, brownish-gray; upright, bushy, medium growth; hips globular, orange; [Sheri Anne × Safrano]; int. by Sequoia Nursery

New Age – See **Purple Heart**, F

New Antique Min, lp, 1997, Brown, Ted; flowers large, very dbl., borne in small clusters; foliage medium size, dark green, semi-glossy; growth bushy, tall (30 in.)

New Arrival MinFl, or, Chessum; flowers coral-red, yellow stamens, slight fragrance; foliage neat, medium green; bushy (18 in.) growth; int. in 1998

New Ave Maria – See **Ave Maria**, HT

New Ballerina HT, lp, Kordes; flowers full, high-centered; int. by Treloar Roses, 2004

New Ballet – See **Ballet**, HT

New Beginning Min, ob, 1988, Saville, F. Harmon; flowers bright orange-yellow bicolor, decorative, medium, 40-50 petals, borne usually singly, no fragrance; foliage medium size, medium green, semi-glossy; prickles very few; bushy, compact (16-20 in.) growth; no fruit; PP6707; [Zorina × seedling]; int. by Nor'East Min. Roses, 1989

New Blaze – See **Demokracie**, LCl

New Blush HG, pb, 2005, Viraraghavan, M.S. Viru; flowers medium pink, deep pink in center, 3 in., full, borne mostly solitary; foliage medium size, medium green, semi-glossy; prickles few, slender, small, ¼ in., straight, light brown; growth spreading, short (1½ ft.); specimen; [Old Blush × (unknown Tea × *R. gigantea*) seedling]; int. by Roses Unlimited, 2005

New Blush Hip – See **Blush Hip**, A

New Carousel – See **Carousel**, HT

New Castle Min, rb, 1983, Bridges, Dennis A.; flowers red, white reverse, small, 20 petals, no fragrance; foliage medium size, dark, semi-glossy; upright growth; [Watercolor × seedling]; int. in 1984

New Century HRg, pb, 1900, Van Fleet; flowers flesh-pink, center light red, edges creamy, 3-4 in., dbl., moderate fragrance; intermittent rebloom; foliage wrinkled, light, tough; vigorous (4-5 ft.), bushy growth; [*R. rugosa alba* × Clotilde Soupert]; int. by Conard & Jones

New Columbia HT, mp, 1924, E.G. Hill, Co.; flowers true pink, deepening to glowing pink; [sport of Columbia]

New Cork LCl, ob

New Daily Mail F, dr, 1972, Tantau, Math.; bud globular; flowers large, semi-dbl.; vigorous, upright, bushy growth; [Letkis × Walzertraum]

New Daily Mail, Climbing Cl F, dr, 1989, Patil, B.K.; [sport of New Daily Mail]; int. by K.S.G. Son's Roses, 1987

New Dawn LCl, lp, 1930, Dreer/Somerset Rose Nursery; flowers same as parent, 35-40 petals, borne singly and in clusters, moderate sweet fragrance; recurrent; foliage medium size, dark green; climbing to 20 ft. growth; PP1; [sport of Dr. W. Van Fleet]; int. by Somerset Rose Nursery, 1930; Rose Hall of Fame, WFRS, 1997

New Dawn Rouge – See **Étendard**, HWich

New Dawn White LCl, w, Schultheis; flowers dbl., looser than New Dawn; foliage dark green, glossy; bushy, vigorous (3-5 m.) growth; int. by Rosen von Schultheis, 2000

New Dawning LCl, lp, Horner; flowers medium, shallow cup; free-flowering; foliage deep green, glossy, healthy; long, strong growth; int. by Ludwig's Roses, 2001

New Day HT, my, 1973, Kordes, R.; bud ovoid, pointed; flowers mimosa-yellow, 4-5 in., 30 petals, cupped, intense fragrance; foliage large, light; upright growth; PP3228; [Arlene Francis × Roselandia]; int. by J&P

New Debbie F, ob; good repeat; growth to 3 ft.; int. by Appalachian Rose, 2001

New Design HT, yb, Tantau; flowers medium yellow with outer petals fading and showing pink wash, large, dbl., high-centered, borne mostly singly; good production; stems 70-90 cm; growth upright; greenhouse rose; int. by Rosen Tantau, 2001

New Duet – See **Duett**, HT

New Emely HT, lp; int. in 2001

New Era – See **Rosie O'Donnell**, HT

New Europe – See **Nouvelle Europe**, F

New Face S, yb, 1982, Interplant; flowers yellow edged pink, small, 5 petals, borne in large clusters; repeat bloom; foliage medium size, medium green, semi-glossy; numerous prickles; upright growth

New Fashion – See **Patio Princess**, S

New Fashion HT, rb; flowers bright yellow heart and reverse with bright red petal edges on face; int. by Carlton Roses, 2002

New Gold Min, dy, 1977, Lyon; bud long, pointed; flowers buttercup-yellow, open, 2-2½ in., 20 petals; foliage small, very dark; vigorous, upright growth; [Yellow Jewel × Allgold]; int. by L. Lyon Greenhouses

New Hampshire Min, yb, Benardella, Frank; flowers golden yellow, flushed apricot to red, dbl., cupped; medium growth; int. by Treloar Roses, 2002

New Haven Queen HT, ob, 1939, Grillo; bud pointed; flowers tangerine, large, 40 petals; foliage leathery; vigorous growth; [sport of Token]

New Hope Min, w, 1989, Bridges, Dennis A.; bud pointed; flowers creamy white, slight pink edge, medium, high-centered, borne usually singly; foliage medium size, dark green, semi-glossy; prickles straight, pointed, medium, medium red; bushy, medium growth; [Party Girl × seedling]; int. by Bridges Roses, 1989

New Horizon F, ob, Dickson, Patrick; int. in 1991; Gold Medal, Belfast, 1993

New Horizons – See **Fragrant Lace**, HT

New Iceberg – See **Iceberg**, HT

New Imagine HT, m, Dorieux; flowers striped; int. by Roseraies Dorieux, 2005

New Kleopatra – See **Kleopatra**, HT

New Look F, rb, 1963, Gaujard; flowers maroon, reverse silver, 3 in., 50 petals, borne in clusters, moderate fragrance; foliage glossy, coppery; vigorous, bushy growth; [(Charles Gregory × unknown) × (Orange Triumph × unknown)]; int. by Gandy's Roses, Ltd., 1962

New Look F, ob; int. by Pépinières de la Saulaie, 2003

New Love HT, rb, 1970, Morey, Dennison; flowers cardinal-red, reverse golden yellow, large, dbl., high-centered; foliage glossy, bronze; vigorous, bushy growth; [South Seas × Coronado]; int. by Country Garden Nursery, 1968

New Maiden's Blush – See **Königin von Dänemark**, A

New Mexico HT, mr, 1967, Aufill; flowers medium, dbl., high-centered; foliage bronze, leathery; very vigorous growth; [Mount Shasta × Granada]

New Moonlight HT, my, 1935, Elmer's Nursery; flowers very large, dbl.; foliage glossy; long stems; very vigorous growth; [Sun Gold × Joseph Hill]

New Orange Min, ob

New Orleans HT, yb, 1966, Tate; bud ovoid; flowers yellow, veined light red, large, dbl., globular, moderate fragrance; foliage glossy; vigorous, upright growth; PP2787; RULED EXTINCT 2/87; [sport of Peace]

New Orleans Min, mr, 1987, King, Gene; flowers medium to dark red toward base, non-fading, reverse medium red, medium, 32 petals, cupped, borne singly or in sprays of 3-5, slight spicy fragrance; foliage medium size, medium green, matte; prickles straight, small, red; bushy, spreading, medium growth; hips oval, small, green; [Evelyn Fison × Magic Mist]; int. by AGM Miniature Roses, 1987

New Orleans S, dp, John Clements; flowers hot raspberry-pink, shaded plum-purple, 5 in., 40 petals, quartered, borne one to a stem and in clusters of three to five, intense fragrance; growth vigorous, upright, well foliaged, 4 × 3½ ft.; PPAF; int. by Heirloom Roses, 2005

New Orleans Lady Min, mp, 2003, Taylor, Pete & Kay; flowers medium pink with yellow base, reverse lighter, 1½ in., full, borne mostly solitary, no fragrance; foliage medium size, medium green, semi-glossy; prickles medium, straight, brown, moderate; growth upright, medium (2 ft.); exhibition/garden/cut blooms; [unknown × unknown]; int. by Taylor's Roses, 2003

New Orleans Lady HT, mp, 2004, Edwards, Eddie & Phelps, Ethan; flowers full, borne mostly solitary, slight fragrance; foliage large, dark green, glossy; prickles hooked; growth upright, tall (5-6 ft.); exhibition; [unknown × unknown]; int. by Johnny Becnel Show Roses, 2005

New Peace HT, yb, 1988, Christensen, Jack E.; flowers yellow-cream with bright red margins aging larger red margin, 48-52 petals, high-centered; foliage medium size, medium green, matte; prickles pointed, small, dark tan; upright, medium growth; [Gingersnap × Young Quinn]; int. by Michigan Bulb Co., 1988

New Penny Min, or, 1962, Moore, Ralph S.; bud short, pointed; flowers orange-red to coral-pink, 1½ in., 20 petals; foliage leathery, glossy; bushy, dwarf (10 in.) growth; [(*R. wichurana* × Floradora) × seedling]; int. by Sequoia Nursery, 1962

New Planet HT, MP, 1930, Cleveland Cut-Flower Co.; flowers bright rose-pink, center light pink, dbl.; [sport of Premier]

New Polyantha Pol, lp, Scarman?; int. by Rose du Temps Passé, 2001

New Pristine – See **Helen Naudé**, HT

New Red Pet – See **Red Pet**, Ch

New Rouge Meilland – See **Rouge Meilland**, HT

New Scotland Yard LCl, mr, 2004, Paul Chessum Roses; flowers semi-dbl., borne in small clusters, slight fragrance; foliage medium size, medium green, semi-glossy; prickles small; growth vigorous (10 ft.); climber; [seedling × seedling]; int. by Love4Plants Ltd, 2004

New Star HT, my, Keisei Rose Nurseries, Inc.; int. by Keisei Rose Nurseries, 1987

New Style HT, mr, 1965, Meilland, Alain A.; bud oval; flowers crimson flushed brighter, large, 25 petals; foliage leathery, glossy; long stems; very vigorous, bushy growth; [(Happiness × Independence) × Peace]; int. by URS

New Wave HT, m, Teranishi; int. in 2000

New White Moss – See **White Bath**, M

New William Shakespeare – See **William Shakespeare 2000**, S

New World F, rb, 1945, Jacobus; flowers velvety red and crimson, reverse lighter, dbl.; foliage soft, glossy; bushy growth; [Crimson Glory × Château de Clos Vougeot]; int. by B&A

New Year Gr, ob, 1983, McGredy, Sam IV; flowers orange and gold blend, medium, 20 petals; foliage large, dark, glossy; upright growth; PP5428; [Mary Sumner × seedling]

New Year, Climbing Cl Gr, ob, 1995, Burks, Joe J.; flowers spanish orange, medium, semi-dbl., borne in small clusters, slight fragrance; foliage medium size, medium green, glossy; some prickles; spreading, tall growth; [sport of New Year]; int. by Certified Roses, Inc., 1995

New Yorker HT, mr, 1947, Boerner; flowers velvety bright scarlet, 4-4½ in., 35 petals, high-centered, moderate fruity fragrance; vigorous, bushy growth; [Flambeau × seedling]; int. by J&P

New Yorker, Climbing Cl HT, mr, 1951, Boerner

New Zealand HT, lp, 1989, McGredy, Sam IV; flowers large, soft creamy pink, 4½-5 in., 34 petals, high-centered, borne singly, intense honeysuckle fragrance; foliage large, medium green, semi-glossy; upright, medium growth; PP8279; [Harmonie × Auckland Metro]; Rose of the Year, Auckland, NZ, 1990, Gold Medal, Portland, USA, 1995

New Zealand, Climbing Cl HT, lp; int. by Regan Nursery, 2000

Newbury Angel Min, yb, 1993, Barrett, F.H.; flowers open yellow turning to pale orange, medium, full, borne in large clusters, no fragrance; foliage small, medium green, matte; some prickles; low (40 cm.), bushy growth; [Freegold × Orange Honey]; int. by Hills Nurseries, 1993

Newcomer – See **Novitchkova**, HT

Newly Wed – See **Blossom Blanket**, S

Newport S, mp, 1994, Olesen; bud small, round to slightly ovoid; flowers pink, old fashioned, 3 in., very full, pompon, borne usually in large clusters, slight fragrance; foliage medium size, medium green, glossy; some prickles; compact, bushy growth; PP9261; int. by DeVor Nurseries, Inc., 1994

Newport Fairy HWich, pb, 1908, Gardner; flowers very deep rosy pink, white eye, golden stamens, 3 cm., single, borne in clusters of 15-20; foliage medium green, glossy; [*R. wichurana* × Crimson Rambler]; int. by Roehrs

Newport Rambler – See **Newport Fairy**, HWich

Newry pink – See **Paulii Rosea**, HRg

News F, m, 1968, LeGrice; flowers red-purple, semi-dbl., borne in trusses, moderate fragrance; foliage olive-green, glossy; [Lilac Charm × Tuscany Superb]; int. by Roseland Nurs., 1968; Gold Medal, RNRS, 1970

News Review – See **Neue Revue**, HT

Newsace HT, ab, 1963, Wyant; bud ovoid; flowers light apricot, center darker, 4 in., 70 petals, moderate fragrance; foliage glossy; strong stems; vigorous, upright growth; [Horace McFarland × Good News]; int. by Wyant Nurs., 1961

Newsgate HT, op, 1964, Verbeek; flowers rose and persimmon-orange, base yellow, reverse darker, 4 in., 50-58 petals; foliage dark, glossy; vigorous growth;

[Paulien Verbeek × (Jolie Madame × Baccará)]

Newton F, or, 2004, Horner, Colin P.; flowers orange/edged red, reverse yellow, small, dbl., borne in small clusters, moderate fragrance; foliage small, medium green, semi-glossy; prickles small, curved; growth compact, short (60 cm.); garden decorative; [Gold Pin × Easy Going]; int. by Unknown at this stage

Ngarla P, lp, 1955, Riethmuller

NH NH #1 – See **Ezzy**, HMult

Niagara HT, mr, 1952, Davis; bud long, pointed; flowers bright red, dbl., high-centered, intense fruity fragrance; [Crimson Glory × seedling]; int. by Garden Town Nursery

Niagara S, w, Poulsen; bud blush pink; flowers pearl white, small, full, flat, borne usually in clusters, slight wild rose fragrance; foliage dark green, glossy; compact, spreading (1 × 2½ ft.) growth; int. as Snow Cover, Poulsen Roser, 1996; Rose of the Year, Auckland, NZ, 1996

Niagara Blossom Min, pb, 2001, Laver, Keith G.; flowers 2 in., full, borne in small clusters, slight fragrance; foliage medium size, medium green, semi-glossy; growth upright, tall (9-11 in.); garden decorative, containers; [seedling × Lavlinger]; int. by Niagara Under Glass, 2001

Niagara Mist HT, pb, 1968, Davis; bud ovoid; flowers light pink, base yellow, large, dbl., high-centered; foliage glossy; vigorous, upright growth; [Tiffany × Mrs A.R. Barraclough]; int. by Wyant

Niagara Moonlight Min, w, 2001, Laver, Keith G.; flowers 2 in., very full, borne in small clusters, slight fragrance; foliage medium size, medium green, semi-glossy; prickles 1/8 in., straight, light brown, few; growth bushy, medium (7-9 in.); garden decorative, containers; int. by Niagara Under Glass, 2001

Niagara Pride – See **Dolce Vita**, HT

Niagara Sunrise Min, dy, 2001, Aalbers, Jamie; flowers 1½-2 in., full, borne mostly solitary, no fragrance; foliage medium size, medium green, semi-glossy; prickles ¼ in., straight, numerous; growth upright, medium (8-10 in.); garden decorative, containers; [seedling × Lavjune]; int. by Niagara Under Glass, 2001

Niagara Sunshine HT, dy, 1969, Davis; flowers chrome-yellow, large, dbl., globular; foliage glossy, light green; vigorous, upright growth; int. by Wyant

Niagara Wildfire Min, dr, 2001, Laver, Keith G.; flowers 1-1½ in., full, borne mostly solitary, no fragrance; foliage small, dark green, glossy; prickles 3/8 in., straight, reddish, moderate; growth bushy, medium (8-10 in.); garden decorative, containers; [seedling × seedling]; int. by Niagara Under Glass, 2001

Niagara Winter Min, w, 2001, Laver, Keith G.; flowers 2 in., very full, borne in small clusters, no fragrance; foliage medium size, dark green, glossy; growth upright, medium (8-10 in.); garden decorative, containers; [seedling × seedling]; int. by Niagara Under Glass, 2001

Nic-Noc Min, mr, 1985, Poulsen, Niels D.; flowers medium red, lighter reverse, 20 petals, cupped, borne in clusters; foliage small, dark, semi-glossy; spreading growth; [Anytime × Gruss an Bayern]; int. by D.T. Poulsen, 1978

Niccolo Paganini F, mr, Meilland; flowers small, compact, velvety red, dbl., high-centered, borne in large clusters, slight fragrance; growth to 70-90 cm.; int. in 1991

Nice 'n' Easy S, ab, 2003, Horner, Colin P.; flowers buff/apricot, reverse apricot, 5-6 cm., semi-dbl., borne in large clusters; foliage medium size, medium green, disease-resistant; prickles small, straight, few; growth spreading, medium (50-60 cm.); garden, decorative; PP15982; [Baby Love × Flower Carpet]; int. as Apricot Garland, Taschner

Nice Day Cl Min, op, 1992, Warner, Chris; flowers salmon pink, medium, dbl., moderate fragrance; foliage small, bronze turning medium green, glossy; few prickles; upright (200 cm.), bushy, climbing growth; [Seaspray × Warm Welcome]; int. by Warner's Roses, 1993

Nicholas Sweetbriar (strain of *R. rubiginosa*), lp, Nicholas; foliage fragrant; prickles very thorny; growth to 6-8 ft.; hips abundant, red; int. by Univ. of Neb., 1959

Nickelodeon Min, rb, 1989, McGredy, Sam IV; flowers small, semi-dbl.; foliage small, dark green, semi-glossy; bushy growth; patio; [Roller Coaster × (Freude × ((Anytime × Eyepaint) × Stars 'n' Stripes))]

Nicky F, or, 1970, Institute of Ornamental Plant Growing; bud medium, pointed; flowers large, semi-dbl., cupped, borne in clusters, no fragrance; foliage medium size, light green, sparse, leathery; vigorous, upright, bushy growth; [Cyclamen × Fire King]

Nicola F, dp, 1981, Gandy, Douglas L.; flowers deep rose pink, 8 petals, borne 6-10 per cluster; prickles green; bushy growth; [seedling × seedling]; int. by Gandy Roses, Ltd., 1980

Nicola – See **Nicola Parade**, MinFl

Nicola Parade MinFl, pb, Poulsen; flowers medium pink striped and painted with white, 5-8 cm., dbl., no fragrance; foliage dark; growth bushy, 20-40 cm.; int. by Poulsen Roser, 2004

Nicolas S, mr, L'Assomption; flowers bright red, 3 in., 18 petals, flat, no fragrance; good repeat; foliage disease-resistant; compact growth; hardy; int. in 1996

Nicolas Hulot HT, my; flowers primrose yellow, dbl., high-centered; free-flowering; growth to 90-100 cm.; int. by Meilland, 2004

Nicolas Koechlin HGal, m, about 1860, Baumann; flowers dark purple

Nicolas Rolland B, mp, 1846, Dorisy; flowers bright carmine, medium, full

Nicole HT, yb, 1931, Gaujard; bud long, pointed; flowers yellow, center coppery, shaded carmine; very vigorous growth; RULED EXTINCT 11/80; int. by C-P

Nicole, Climbing Cl HT, yb, 1933, Kordes

Nicole F, w, 1985, Kordes, W.; flowers white with soft pink petal edges, large, 30-35 petals, high-centered to cupped, borne singly and in clusters, slight fragrance; recurrent; foliage large, dark, semi-glossy; moderate, upright growth; [seedling × Bordure Rose]; int. in 1984

Nicole HT, rb, Kordes; flowers deep red with cream white reverse, large, dbl., high-centered, borne mostly singly; florist rose; int. in 1998

Nicole Carol Miller Gr, m, 2004, Meilland International; flowers light lavender, 10-12 cm., dbl., borne in small clusters, intense fragrance; foliage medium green, semi-glossy; growth upright, medium (to 6 ft); garden; PPAF; [Charles de Gaulle × (Shocking Blue × Sterling Silver)]; int. by The Conard-Pyle Company, 2004

Nicole Debrosse HT, dr, 1962, Croix, P.; flowers dark red, shaded scarlet; vigorous growth; [seedling × Baccará]; int. by Minier

Nicole Kordana Min, rb, Kordes; flowers red, cream reverse, dbl., globular; int. by W. Kordes Söhne

Nicole Marie MinFl, ly, 2002, LeBlanc, Albert; flowers light yellow to white, reverse white, 1¾-2¼ in., full, borne in small clusters, no fragrance; foliage medium size, medium green, semi-glossy; prickles 3/8 in., hooked, red to tan, moderate; growth spreading, tall (24-30 in.); garden, exhibition; [Little Darling × Linville]; petals have pink edges in warm weather; int. in 2002

Nicole Mioulane S, ab, Guillot-Massad; bud globular; flowers apricot/amber/yellow, medium, full, cupped, borne mostly singly, slight fragrance; growth to 4 ft.; int. by Roseraies Guillot, 2005

Nicole Morris F, dp, 2005, Paul Chessum Roses; flowers pure deep pink, 6 cm., dbl., borne in small clusters, slight fragrance; foliage medium size, medium green, semi-glossy; prickles small; bushy, medium growth; bedding, borders, containers; [seedling × seedling]; int. by Love4Plants Ltd, 2005

Nicoletta HT, mp, 1969, deRuiter; bud ovoid; flowers pink, medium, dbl.; foliage dark; [sport of Carla]

Nicolette HT, ab, Taschner; flowers soft apricot buff, dbl., high-centered; free-flowering; tall growth; [sport of Esther Geldenhuys]; int. by Ludwig's Roses, 1995

Nicolina Min, pb, 1991, Zipper, Herbert; bud ovoid; flowers coral pink shading to white, reverse pink edge, shading to creamy white, 1¼ in., 25 petals, cupped, borne usually singly, slight fragrance; foliage small, dark green, semi-glossy; upright, bushy, tall growth; [(Dandy Lyon × Razzle Dazzle) × Pink Petticoat]; int. by Magic Moment Miniature Roses, 1992

Nicoline – See **Nicoline Parade**, MinFl

Nicoline Parade MinFl, or, Poulsen; flowers orange-red, 5-8 cm., dbl., no fragrance; foliage dark; growth bushy, 20-40 cm.; PP13108; int. by Poulsen Roser, 2000

Nida Senff Pol, mp, 1946, Kersbergen; flowers soft rosy pink, borne in large clusters

Nigel Hawthorne S, pb, 1990, Harkness, R., & Co., Ltd.; bud pointed; flowers pale salmon-rose, deep scarlet eye at base, reverse same, 5 petals, cupped, slight spicy fragrance; foliage medium size, medium green, semi-glossy; prickles thin, narrow, variable, dark to light; spreading, low growth; hips plump, small, green, infrequent; [*H. persica* × Harvest Home]; int. in 1989

Nigel Quiney F, w, 2001, Sheridan, John; flowers cream flushed deep pink with cream reverse, handpainted, large, semi-dbl., borne in small clusters, moderate fragrance; foliage medium size, medium green, glossy; prickles small, pointed, moderate; growth compact, low (2 ft.); [Little Darling × Old Master]

Nigger Boy HT, dr, 1933, Knight, G.; bud long, pointed; flowers very dark velvety blackish maroon, 56 petals, high-centered; foliage thick, glossy, bronze; low, compact growth; [Hadley × Yves Druhen]

Night HT, dr, 1930, McGredy; bud long, pointed; flowers deepest blackish crimson, shaded maroon, dbl., high-centered, intense fragrance; foliage dark, glossy; bushy growth

Night, Climbing Cl HT, dr, 1936, Armstrong, J.A.; int. by Armstrong Nursery

Night 'n' Day HT, dr, 1968, Swim & Weeks; bud pointed; flowers large, dbl., moderate fragrance; foliage dark, leathery; vigorous, tall, bushy growth; PP2655; [(World's Fair × Chrysler Imperial) × Happiness]

Night Fire Min, dr, 1982, Lyon, Lyndon; flowers deep red, petals often edged black, small, 20 petals; foliage medium size, dark,semi-glossy; upright, bushy growth; [seedling × seedling]

Night Flight – See **Vol de Nuit**, HT

Night Lady Min, rb, 1983, Meredith, E.A. & Rovinski, M.E.; flowers red, white reverse, medium, 36 petals, high-centered, borne singly; foliage medium size, dark, semi-glossy; upright growth; [seedling × Libby]; int. by Casa de Rosa Domingo

Night Life S, op, 2000, Brown, Ted; flowers orange pink, reverse lighter, 3½ in., dbl., borne in small clusters, slight fragrance; foliage medium size, medium green, semi-glossy; few prickles; upright, medium (5-6 ft.) growth; [Esprit × seedling]

Night Light LCl, dy, 1985, Poulsen, Niels D.; flowers deep yellow with red on some petal edges, aging to crimson, 8-10 cm., 27 petals, borne in medium clusters, moderate fragrance; foliage large, dark, reddish green, glossy; prickles large, dark red; bushy growth, 150-200 cm.; [Westerland × Pastorale]; int. by D.T. Poulsen, 1980

Night Music MinFl, mp, 1989, Zipper, Herbert; flowers deep pink, medium, dbl., borne singly and in sprays, intense fragrance; foliage large, medium green, semi-glossy; upright growth; [Tamango × Pink Petticoat]; int. by Magic Moment Miniature Roses, 1989

Night of the Midnight Sun – See **Hakuya**, HT

Night Out F, pb, 2004, Bridges, Dennis A.; flowers deep pink with a little white at base of petals, reverse slightly lighter, 3½ in., dbl., high-centered, borne mostly solitary, slight fragrance; foliage medium size, dark green, semi-glossy, disease-resistant; prickles ¼ in., pointed, curving downward; growth upright, medium (3½ ft.); garden, exhibition, cut flower; [Signature × Doris Morgan]; int. by Bridges Roses, 2005

Night Owl LCl, m, 2005, Carruth, Tom; flowers deep wine red, bright yellow stamens, 9-11 cm., single, borne in large clusters, moderate fragrance; foliage large, medium grayish-green, semi-glossy; prickles few, average, pointed, beige; growth spreading, long (to 200 cm.) climbing canes; garden decoration; PPAF; [(International Herald Tribune × Rosa soulieana derivative) × (Sweet Chariot × Blue Nile) × Rosy Outlook]; int. by Weeks Roses, 2007

Night Sky F, rb, Dickson; flowers carmine red, striped, and with an ivory/pale yellow center, 6 petals, shallow cup, borne in clusters of 5-19, moderate fragrance; free-flowering; foliage large, dark green with hint of bronze, glossy; upright to bushy, slightly taller than average growth; int. by Dickson Roses, 2004

Night Song S, dr, 1985, Buck, Dr. Griffith J.; flowers large, 33 petals, borne singly and in clusters of up to 10, moderate fragrance; repeat bloom; foliage medium-large, dark bronze green, semi-glossy; prickles awl-like, tan; compact, erect, bushy growth; hardy; [(Rosali × Music Maker) × Meisterstuck]; int. by Iowa State University, 1984

Night Star F, m, J&P; PP10450; int. in 1997

Night Time HT, dr, 1976, Weeks; bud long, pointed; flowers dark black-red, 39 petals, high-centered, intense fragrance; foliage dark, leathery; vigorous growth; PP3924; [Forty-niner × Oklahoma]; int. in 1975

Nighthawk Min, mr, 1989, Hardgrove, Donald L.; bud globular, pointed; flowers medium, 22 petals, high-centered, then flat, borne singly and in sprays of 3-5, intense damask fragrance; foliage medium size, medium green; prickles straight, slanted down, medium, reddish-brown; upright, bushy, medium growth; PP7417; [Quinella × Poker Chip]; int. by Nor'East Min. Roses, 1989; AOE, ARS, 1989

Nightingale HT, pb, 1970, Herholdt, J.A.; flowers rich rose-red, blended lighter, large, 25 petals, high-centered; moderate growth; [Rina Herholdt × Tiffany]; int. by Herholdt's Nursery

Nightmoss M, m, 2001, Barden, Paul; flowers deep royal purple, medium purple reverse, yellow stamens, large, full, flat, borne in small clusters, intense earthy, smoky rose scent fragrance; spring only; foliage medium size, dark green, matte; prickles ¼ in., straight, needle-shaped, brown; growth spreading, arching, medium (5 ft.); specimen, back of border; [Nuits de Young × Tuscany Superb]; int. by The Uncommon Rose, 2001

Nightmoss #1; See **Fara Shimbo**

Night's Musk LCl, w; possibly Demits, 1986; HFilipes

Nigra HCh, m, before 1835; flowers very dark purple, reverse nearly black, very small, full; Lawrenciana

Nigrette – See **Subnigra**, HGal

Nigrette HT, dr, 1934, Krause; flowers blackish maroon or plum color, varying with season and weather, medium, dbl., open; bushy growth; [Château de Clos Vougeot × Lord Castlereagh]; int. by C-P

Nigritella F, dr, 1953, Cazzaniga, F. G.; flowers red shaded darker, dbl.; dwarf, bushy growth

Nigritiana – See **Superbe en Brun**, HGal

Nigrorum HGal, m, about 1845, Calvert; flowers velvety dark purple-violet, small, full

Nikita F, mr, 1993, Ilsink, G.P.; flowers small, dbl., borne in sprays; foliage medium size, medium green, glossy; some prickles; medium (45 cm.), bushy growth; int. by Interplant B.V., 1988

Nikitskaja Rosowaja HP, mp, 1937, Kosteckij; flowers medium, very dbl.

Nikki F, ob, 1982, Bracegirdle, A.J.; flowers vermilion, white eye and reverse, medium, semi-dbl., no fragrance; foliage medium size, medium green, semi-glossy; bushy growth; [Dusky Maiden × Eyepaint]; int. in 1981

Nil Bleu – See **Blue Nile**, HT

Nil Desperandum HT, ob, 1977, Ellick; flowers Indian orange, 4 in., 25-30 petals; foliage large, light matte green; very vigorous growth; [Gavotte × Montezuma]; int. by Excelsior Roses, 1979

Niles Cochet T, rb, 1906, California Nursery Co.; flowers cherry-red on outer petals, lighter within; [sport of Maman Cochet]

Nilima HT, m, Ghosh, Mr and Mrs S.; flowers silvery mauve, large, high-centered; int. in 2001

Nilsson Guy F, dp, 1930, Leenders, M.; flowers deep rose-pink, open, large, semi-dbl., borne in clusters; [sport of Lafayette]

Nimble S, pb, 1995, Jobson, Daniel J.; flowers hand-painted birght pink, stippling to white center, white reverse, 4 in., 6-14 petals, borne in small and large clusters; foliage medium size, medium green, dull; some prickles; medium (5 × 5 ft.), upright, bushy growth; [(Valerie Jeanne × Eyepaint) × Twilight Trail]

Nimbus F, m, 1990, LeGrice, E.B. Roses; bud pointed; flowers lilac-gray, medium, very dbl., cupped, borne in sprays; foliage medium size, medium green, semi-glossy; bushy, medium growth; [Grey Dawn × seedling]; int. in 1989

Nimes F, rb, 1978, Gaujard; flowers vermilion, reverse gold, dbl.; [Pampa × Piccadilly]; int. in 1970

Nina T, lp, 1825, Vibert; flowers light lilac pink, large, full, globular

Nina S, dr, 2000, Mehring, B.F.; flowers semi-dbl., borne in large clusters, slight fragrance; foliage medium size, dark green, glossy; prickles moderate; bushy, medium (90-100 cm.) growth; [(Iceberg × Anytime) × Eyeopener]; int. by Eurosa

Nina Marshall HT, dp, 1967, Golik; flowers cerise, base gold, semi-dbl., cupped; foliage glossy; moderate growth; [Serenade × Queen o' the Lakes]; int. by Ellesmere Nursery, 1966

Nina Nadine F, yb, Kirkham; bud lemon edged cherry pink; flowers cream with pink blush on petal edges, full; foliage dark green, glossy; vigorous (4 ft.) growth; int. by C&K Jones, 2002

Nina Poulsen F, mr, 1940, Poulsen, S.; flowers clear red, semi-dbl.; [Grethe Poulsen × Hybrid Tea (red)]; int. by Poulsen

Nina Rosa HT, op, 1946, Robichon; flowers coppery pink shaded yellow, very large, dbl.; [Frank Reader × Condesa de Sástago]

Nina Weibull F, dr, 1965, Poulsen, S.; flowers dbl., 25 petals, no fragrance; foliage dark; compact, bushy (100-150 cm.) growth; [Fanal × Masquerade]; int. by D. T. Poulsen, 1961

Nina Weibull, Climbing Cl F, dr

Nine-Eleven HT, mr, 2002, Wells, Verlie W.; flowers velvety dark red, 4 in., very full, borne mostly solitary, no fragrance; foliage medium size, dark green, semi-glossy; prickles few, hooked; growth upright, medium (4 ft.); exhibition, garden; [Alec's Red × (First Prize × unknown)]; int. by Wells Mid-South Roses, 2002

1997 Traditional Home HT, pb, 1997, Wambach, Catherine; flowers light pale pink with ivory shading, full, slight fragrance; foliage medium size, dark green, dull; medium (5 ft.) growth; [Bobby Charlton × Touch of Class]; int. by Certified Roses, Inc.

Ninetta F, dp, 1985, Tantau, Math.; flowers deep pink, medium, 20 petals; foliage medium green, semi-glossy; upright growth

Ninetta Min, ab, Tantau; int. by Ets Orard, 2006

Ninette M, mr, 1857, Robert & Moreau; flowers bright cherry red, 4-5 cm., full

Ninety-Niner – See **Rosie O'Donnell**, HT

Ninfea HT, Borgatti, G.; int. in 1957

Nini T, mp, 1825, Barrier

Ninie Vandevelde Pol, mp, 1924, Vandevelde; flowers salmon

Ninon Vallin HT, ab, 1936, Gaujard; flowers apricot, reverse fresh yellow, large, dbl.; foliage bright green; very vigorous growth

Niobe F, w, 1942, J&P; flowers white, center sometimes flushed light pink; [sport of Rosenelfe]

Nioumiya Min, w, 1999, Yamazaki, Kazuko; flowers ivory white, 1½ in., 35 petals, high-centered, borne 2-5 per cluster; foliage medium size, dark green; vigorous, bushy, compact (10 in.) growth; [seedling × Hatuzakura]; int. by Takii & Co., 1995

Niphetos T, w, 1841 or before, Bougère; bud pointed; flowers large, globular, intense fragrance

Niphetos, Climbing Cl T, w, 1889, Keynes, Williams & Co.; bud pale pink; flowers pure whiter than bush form, 9-10 cm., globular, intense fragrance; [sport of Niphetos]

Nipper S, mr, Harkness, R.; flowers velvet red; low, spreading growth; int. by R. Harkness & Co., 1997

Nippy HT, yb, 1932, Cant, B. R.; flowers canary-yellow, reverse splashed red, moderate fruity fragrance; foliage dark

Niramol Min, ab, 1991, Umsawasdi, Dr. Theera; flowers medium, dbl., borne mostly singly, no fragrance; foliage medium size, medium green, semi-glossy; medium, bushy growth; [Loving Touch × seedling]

Nirpette Pink & White Min, pb; int. in 1997

Nirvana F, lp, 1979, Meilland, Mrs. Marie-Louise; bud ovoid; flowers large, 20 petals, cupped; foliage glossy; bushy growth; [(Pink Wonder × Kalinka) × Centenaire de Lourdes]; int. by Meilland & Co SNC, 1977; Gold Medal, Geneva, 1975

Nirvana HT, lp, Meilland; flowers dbl., high-centered, borne mostly singly; int. by Meilland Intl., 2004

Nisette F, dp, 1967, van't Kruis; flowers pink-red, globular, borne in trusses; foliage small, dark; moderate growth; [sport of Garnette]; int. by DeRuiters Nieuwe Rozen B.V.

Nishiki F, yb, Keisei; int. by Keisei Rose Nurseries, 2000

Nishiki-E F, ob, 1986, Suzuki, Seizo; flowers orange-yellow, 38 petals, high-centered, borne 2-5 per stem; foliage dark, semi-glossy; prickles small slanted downward; upright growth; [(Sarabande × Amanogawa) × Kagayaki]; int. by Keisei Rose Nursery, 1981

Nisida C, lp, 1822, Vibert

Nisida HGal, mr, 1827, Noisette

Nisida T, pb, 1840, Goubault; flowers pink, shaded fawn, medium, full, very fragrance

Niso Fumagalli F, w, Barni; flowers pure white, large, full, cupped, borne in clusters, slight fragrance; recurrent; medium (60-80 cm.) growth; int. by Rose Barni, 2006

Nita Min, ab, 1986, McDaniel, Earl; flowers apricot, lighter apricot reverse, 55 petals, high-centered, borne singly; foliage medium size, dark, semi-glossy; prickles few, light green; medium, upright, bushy growth; [seedling × unknown Miniature]; int. by McDaniel's Min. Roses, 1987

Nita Weldon T, w, 1908, Dickson, A.; flowers ivory-white edged light pink

Nitouche F, pb, 1978, Poulsen, Niels D.; flowers silvery, deep salmon pink reverse, 4 in., 25 petals, borne 3-5 per cluster; recurrent; foliage glossy, dark; bushy, upright growth; [seedling × Whisky Mac]; int. by Poulsen, 1974

Nivaida HT, ab; int. in 1997

Nivea – See **White Provence**, C

Nivea – See ***R. laevigata*** (Michaux)

Nivea – See **Aimée Vibert**, N

Nivea HT, w, 1949, Dot, Pedro; bud long, pointed; flowers medium, dbl., high-centered; foliage sparse; dwarf growth; [Nuria de Recolons × Blanche Mallerin]

Nivescens HT, lp; flowers medium, semi-dbl.

No Worries Min, yb, White, W. R.; bud pointed, yellow with orange tips; flowers orange and yellow with gold stamens, 1½ in., semi-dbl., borne in small, open clusters; growth micro-mini (12-15 in.); PPRR; int. by Nor-East Miniroses, 2005

Noack's Uberraschung HT, yb, Noack, Werner; flowers caramel colored, 12 cm., dbl., high-centered; good repeat; int. by Noack Rosen, 1985

Noacres – See **Crescendo**, F

Noah HT, ob, 1985, Nevo, Motke; flowers orange; [sport of Dr. A.J. Verhage]; int. by Maoz Haim Rose Nursery, 1976

Noawild – See **Wildfang**, S

Nobilia S, mp, Roman, G., and Wagner, S.; flowers medium to large, 40 petals, high-centered, borne in clusters, slight fragrance; foliage medium to large, medium green, glossy; [Rosabunda × Dr Faust]; int. by Res. Stn. for Hort., 1998

Nobility HT, lp, 1961, Boerner; bud ovoid; flowers ivory lightly overcast pink, center deeper, 5-5½ in., 35-40 petals, high-centered, moderate fragrance; foliage leathery; vigorous, upright growth; PP2093; [(Peace × unknown) × Peace]; int. by J&P, 1961

Nobilo's Chardonnay HT, my, 1985, McGredy, Sam IV; flowers orange yellow, large, 35 petals; foliage small, light green, glossy; bushy growth; [Freude × (Wienerwald × Benson & Hedges Gold)]; int. in 1984

Noble – See **Noble Hit**, MinFl

Noble Antony S, mr, 1997, Austin, David; flowers deep magenta, deeply domed, outer petals recurve, large, 85-90 petals, borne singly or in small clusters, moderate fragrance; foliage medium size, dark green, semi-glossy; some prickles; bushy, medium, growth; PP10779; [seedling × seedling]; int. by David Austin Roses, Ltd., 1995

Noble Hit MinFl, mr, Poulsen; flowers medium red, 5-8 cm., dbl., no fragrance; growth bushy, 40-60 cm.; PP10728; int. by Poulsen Roser, 1998

Noblesse HT, pb, 1917, McGredy; flowers apricot primrose-yellow, outer edges flushed deep pearl pink, medium, dbl.; name released, MR 8

Noblesse HT, or, 1969, Spek or Lens; flowers very large, 28 petals; foliage glossy; moderate growth; PP3227; [Coloranja × Coloranja]; int. by A. Dickson

Noblesse HT, op, Tantau; greenhouse rose; int. by Rosen Tantau, 1989

Noces d'Or – See **Golden Wedding**, F

Nocturne HT, dr, 1947, Swim, H.C.; bud long, pointed; flowers 4½ in., 24 petals, cupped, moderate spicy fragrance; foliage leathery, dark; vigorous, upright, bushy growth; [Charlotte Armstrong × Night]; int. by Armstrong Nursery

Nocturne, Climbing Cl HT, dr, 1956, Armstrong, J.A.; int. by Armstrong Nursery

Nocturne F, dr, Archer; flowers dbl.; moderate growth

Noëlla Nabonnand Cl T, dr, 1901, Nabonnand, G.; bud tall; flowers velvety crimson-red, much lighter reverse, 15-16 cm., semi-dbl., loose, moderate fragrance; [Reine Marie Henriette × Bardou Job]

Noella Virebent Cl T, lp, 1922, Nabonnand, P.; flowers flesh-pink, center brighter, semi-dbl., moderate fragrance; foliage dark, glossy; prickles few thorns; very vigorous growth; [*R. gigantea* × Archiduc Joseph]

Noelle Marie Min, ab, Eagle, Barry; flowers soft apricot with peach tonings; tall growth; [Pink Petticoat × unknown]; int. in 1990

Noémie HCh, m, about 1820, Hardy; flowers violet pink, large, very full

Noémie D, dp, 1845, Vibert; flowers deep rose, slightly spotted, large, full

Noémie HP, lp, 1845, Aubert; flowers bright flesh pink, full, cupped

Noémie HT, mr, 1850, Foulard; flowers red, marble light pink, large, full

Nogawa HT, w, 1989, Takahashi, Takeshi; bud ovoid; flowers cream, fringed with pink, large, 30 petals, high-centered, borne usually singly; foliage medium size, dark green, semi-glossy; prickles almost right-angled to stem; bushy, tall growth; [Garden Party × Kordes' Perfecta]

Noire – See **Hector**, HGal

Noire Couronnée HGal, dr, before 1810, Dupont; sepals short, pointed; flowers velvety, purple-violet marbled crimson, medium to large, very dbl.; foliage narrow, wavy

Noire de Holland – See **Subnigra**, HGal

Noire Pourpre Panachée – See **Ombre Panachée**, HGal

Noisette Ayez – See **Spectabilis**, HSem

Noisette de l'Inde – See ***R. × noisettiana*** (Thory), N

Noisette Desprez – See **Jaune Desprez**, N

Noisette Jaune – See **Smith's Yellow China**, T

Noisette Moschata N, w, 1873, Schwartz; flowers blush white

Noisette Rose – See ***R. × noisettiana*** (Thory), N

Nokomis HWich, dp, 1918, Walsh; flowers dark rose-pink, larger than Lady Gay or Dorothy Perkins, dbl., borne in clusters of 5-30, intense fragrance; foliage light, glossy; vigorous, climbing growth; [*R. wichurana* × Comte Raimbaud]

Nola Emily HT, mp, Allender, Robert William; [sport of Peter Benjamin]

Nolhelen F, w, 2004, Nolan, Gordon, D.; flowers very full, borne in small clusters, moderate fragrance; foliage medium size, dark green, semi-glossy; prickles small, straight; growth bushy, medium (100 cm.); garden display; cutting; [Bonica × Angel Face]

Nolpeg MinFl, m, 2004, Nolan, Gordon D.; flowers full, borne in small clusters, no fragrance; foliage medium size, medium green, semi-glossy; prickles small, straight; growth upright, medium (90 cm.); garden display; [Jean Kenneally × Angel Face]

Nolsue MinFl, pb, 2004, Nolan, Gordon D.; flowers light pink, reverse medium pink, 5 cm., dbl., borne in small clusters, slight fragrance; foliage medium size, dark green, matte; prickles small, straight; growth bushy, medium (75 cm.); garden display; [Jean Kenneally × Angel Face]

Non Plus Ultra HMult, dr, 1904, Weigand, C.; flowers semi-dbl., borne in large clusters; none; vigorous growth; [Crimson Rambler × Mlle Blanche Rebatel]

Nona HT, op, 1924, Easlea; bud long, tapering, flame and orange; flowers flame and pink, medium, semi-dbl., moderate fragrance; foliage medium size, leathery; [Mme Edouard Herriot × Constance]

Nonin HT, yb, 1938, Mallerin, C.; flowers golden yellow, tinted coral-orange, very large, dbl.; foliage glossy; vigorous growth; [Souv. de Claudius Pernet × seedling]; int. by A. Meilland

Nonino F, mr; int. in 1997

Noon Sunshine Min, ly, 2006, Hopper, Nancy; flowers semi-dbl., borne mostly solitary; foliage medium size, medium green, matte; prickles $^{1}/_{8}$ in., tan, moderate; growth bushy, medium (13 in.); [sport of Tobo]; int. in 2006

Nora Min, yb, 1997, Berg, David H.; flowers medium, dbl., borne mostly singly; foliage medium size, medium green, dull; upright, tall (15-18in.) growth; [Rainbow's End × Leila]

Nora Cunningham Cl HT, lp, 1920, Clark, A.; flowers flesh-pink, center paler, large, semi-dbl., cupped; free bloom, sometimes recurrent; foliage wrinkled, light; vigorous growth, long stems; climbing; [Gustav Grunerwald × unknown]; int. as Nora Cuningham, Hackett

Nora Henslow HT, dp, 1925, Evans; flowers crimson-cerise, single; [Mme Mélanie Soupert × Gen. MacArthur]; int. by Beckwith

Nora Hooker F, mr, 1971, Hooker, W. J.; flowers 4 in., 22 petals; free growth; [sport of Queen Elizabeth]; int. by Harkness, 1970

Nora Johnson HMoy, dp, 1957; flowers cerise, small; hips small, bright; [believed to be *R. willmottiae* × *R. moyesii*]; int. by Sunningdale Nursery

Nora Power Cl HT, ab, Dearing

Nora Pugh F, mp, 2005, Paul Chessum Roses; flowers dbl., borne mostly solitary, intense fragrance; foliage medium size, medium green, semi-glossy; prickles moderate, medium, green; growth compact, medium (18 in.); beds, borders and tubs; [seedling × seedling]; int. by Love4Plants Ltd, 2004

Norah Cruickshank HT, op

Norah Gabbattass F, mp, 2000, Driscoll, William E.; flowers medium pink, center lighter, reverse lighter, large, full, borne in small clusters, slight fragrance; foliage medium size, medium green, glossy; prickles moderate; growth upright, tall (120 cm.); [((Minnie Pearl × Flower Carpet) × (Mountbatten × (Angelina × *R. bella*))) × (Kiskadee × (Liverpool Echo × (Flamenco × *R. bella*)))]

Norah Longley Pol, ob, 1948, Longley; flowers flame-orange, borne in trusses; foliage bright green; vigorous, branching growth; [sport of Cameo]

Nordfeuer F, mr, Noack, Werner; int. in 1986

Nordhausen S, dp, 1940, Krause; flowers carmine-pink, large, semi-dbl.

Nordia F, or, 1967, Poulsen, N. D.; flowers medium, dbl.; PP2850; int. by McGredy & Son

Nordic Chant HT, mp, 1976, Golik; bud long, pointed; flowers salmon-pink, 4½ in., 40 petals, high-centered, moderate spicy fragrance; foliage glossy, light;

vigorous growth; [Tropicana × Queen of Bermuda]; int. by Dynarose, 1974

Nordina – See **Cascade**, LCl

Nordlandrose – See **Geschwind's Nordlandrose**, HSet

Nordlicht HT, or, 1910, Kiese; flowers coppery red, large, semi-dbl.; [Mme Caroline Testout × Luciole]

Nordlicht – See **Northlight**, F

Nordstern F, Kordes, R.; int. in 1964

Noreen Mackey HT, my, 2001, Everitt, Derrick; flowers chrome yellow, 10-12 cm., full, borne mostly solitary, slight fragrance; foliage small, medium green, glossy; prickles medium, hooked, moderate; growth upright, medium (90 cm.); [Silver Jubilee × (Arthur Bell × Maigold)]

Norfolk S, my, Poulsen; flowers dbl., moderate fragrance; low, spreading (60 × 100 cm.) growth; int. in 1990

Norfolk Harmony HT, dp, 1940, LeGrice; bud long, pointed; flowers rosy cerise, large, dbl., high-centered; foliage glossy, dark; very vigorous, tall growth; [Comtesse Vandal × Mrs Sam McGredy]

Norida F, dp, 1967, Poulsen; flowers light crimson-scarlet, medium, dbl.; [(Pinocchio × Pinocchio) × Elsinore]; greenhouse rose; int. by DeVor Nursery

Norita HT, dr, 1973, Combe; flowers very deep red, large, dbl., high-centered, moderate fragrance; foliage dark, leathery; vigorous, bushy growth; [Charles Mallerin × seedling]; int. by Kern Rose Nursery, 1971

Norma HT, lp, 1904, Dingee & Conard; flowers glossy light pink, very large, very full, moderate fragrance

Norma HT, mr, 1978, Gaujard; flowers brilliant red, large, 50 petals; [Clio × Credo]; int. in 1976

Norma Bennett F, dr, 1958, Bennett, H.; flowers crimson; [Florence Mary Morse × Border Queen]; int. by Waikato Rose Soc.

Norma Major HT, mp; flowers dbl., high-centered; int. about 1998

Norma Margaret Min, pb, 1990, Frock, Marshall J.; bud pointed; flowers pink, blending with copper shading, reverse white with pink, 30 petals, high-centered, moderate fragrance; foliage medium size, medium green, semi-glossy; prickles straight, medium, brown; upright, medium growth; fruit not observed; [Baby Katie × seedling]

Norman HT, mr, 1934, Dickson, A.; flowers well-formed, borne in bright scarlet-red; vigorous growth

Norman Hartnell HT, mr, 1964, Kordes, R.; flowers crimson-red, well-formed, large, 21 petals; foliage dark; very vigorous growth; [Ballet × Detroiter]; int. by Wheatcroft Bros.

Norman Lambert HT, ob, 1926, McGredy; bud long, pointed; flowers deep salmon-orange, suffused bronze and yellow, base lighter, large, dbl., high-centered; Gold Medal, NRS, 1924

Norman Rogers HT, dp, 1933, Chaplin Bros.; flowers deep rose-pink, base yellow, large

Normandica – See **Petite de Hollande**, C

Normandie HWich, mp, 1929, Nonin; flowers salmon-pink, aging lighter, 4 cm., dbl., borne in medium clusters, no fragrance; vigorous growth

Normandie – See **Laura Ford**, Cl Min

Norris Pratt HT, my, 1964, Buisman, G. A. H.; flowers bright yellow, large; foliage leathery; growth moderate; [Mrs Pierre S. duPont × Marcelle Gret]

Norrköping HT, mr, 1961, Poulsen, S.; bud pointed; flowers scarlet, reverse darker; long stems; very vigorous growth; [Karl Herbst × (Baccará × Golden Sun)]

Norseman F, mp, 1963, Von Abrams; flowers pink, medium, dbl.; foliage soft; vigorous, upright growth; [Unnamed seedling × Pinocchio]

North Star HT, lp, 1964, Golik; bud ovoid; flowers light silvery pink, 6 in., 60 petals; foliage glossy; vigorous, medium growth; [Marcia Stanhope × Peace]; int. by Ellesmere Nursery

Northamptonshire S, w, Mattock; flowers flesh pink and white; dainty, dense, groundcover (1½ × 3 ft.) growth; int. in 1990

Northern Cherokee Rose – See ***R. spinosissima altaica*** (Bean)

Northern Dancer HT, ob, 1965, Schloen; bud ovoid; flowers orange-yellow, edges flushed pink, large, dbl.; foliage dark, glossy, leathery; vigorous, tall, compact growth; [sport of Tzigane]; int. by Ellesmere Nursery

Northern Encore S, lp, Lim, Ping; flowers light pink, single, borne in clusters, slight fragrance; repeats well; foliage light green; stems reddish tone; growth upright (5-8 ft.) tall and wide; very winter hardy; int. by Bailey Nurseries, 2004

Northern Gold – See **Radiant Gold**, HT

Northern Gold HT, my; flowers non-fading golden yellow, large; possibly from Delbard, about 1999

Northern Light HWich, lp, 1898, van Fleet; flowers whitish pink, large, single

Northern Lights HT, yb, 1969, Cocker; flowers lemon-cream, tinted pink, 5 in., 50 petals; [Fragrant Cloud × Kingcup]

Northern Lights S, mp, Noack, Werner; int. in 1997

Northern Lights – See **Flamenco**, LCl

Northern Prairie Rose – See ***R. blanda*** (Aiton)

Northern Sensation S, dp, Lim, Ping; int. in 2006

Northern States HSpn, w, 1952, Shepherd; bud long, pointed; flowers white tinged pink and yellow, open, large, 5 petals; profuse, non-recurrent bloom; foliage leathery; bushy, compact (2½ ft.) growth; makes a good hedge; hardy; [*R. spinosissima* × Irish Charm]; int. by Kern Rose Nursery

Northern Yellow HGal, yb, Sievers; int. in 1977

Northland – See **Sweet Gesture**, F

Northlander S, mp, 1985, James, John; flowers 4 in., 5 petals, borne singly and in clusters of 3; repeat bloom; foliage medium size, dark, matte; vigorous, upright (to 8 ft.) growth; [Baronne Prevost × ((((Magnifica × Joanna Hill) × (Blanche Mallerin × *R. laxa*)) × ((Magnifica × Joanna Hill) × (Blanche Mallerin × *R. laxa*))) × (Blanche Mallerin × *R. laxa*))]

Northlight F, or, 1958, Kordes, R.; flowers deep cinnabar-red, large, dbl., high-centered, borne in small clusters; foliage leathery; very vigorous, low, bushy growth; [Bergfeuer × Gertrud Westphal]; int. as Nordlicht, R. Schmidt, 1957

Northumberland W. I. HT, ab, 1988, Thompson, Robert; flowers deep apricot, reverse lighter, medium, full; foliage large, dark green, glossy; bushy growth; [Silver Jubilee × Doris Tysterman]; int. by Battersby Roses, 1988

Norwich Castle F, ob, 1980, Beales, Peter; flowers copper orange, 30 petals, borne 3-5 per cluster, slight fruity fragrance; foliage medium green, shiny, smooth; prickles wedged; vigorous, upright growth; [(Whisky Mac × Arthur Bell) × seedling]; int. in 1976

Norwich Cathedral HT, my, 1997, Beales, Peter; flowers full, borne mostly singly, intense fragrance; foliage medium size, medium green, leathery, semi-glossy; some prickles; upright, low (3 ft.)growth; [sport of Diamond Jubilee]; int. by Peter Beales Roses, 1996

Norwich Cerise HT, mr, 1962, Morse; flowers cerise, 4-5 in., 25-30 petals; vigorous growth; [sport of Bettina]

Norwich Gold S, ob, 1965, Kordes; bud well-formed; flowers yellow shaded orange, large, 55 petals, moderate fragrance; vigorous, upright growth; int. by Morse, 1962

Norwich Pink HKor, dp, 1965, Kordes; flowers bright cerise, 4 in., 16 petals, moderate fragrance; foliage dark green, glossy; vigorous, pillar, well-branched growth; int. by Morse, 1962

Norwich Salmon HKor, op, 1965, Kordes; flowers salmon-pink, 6-7 cm., 30 petals, borne in medium clusters, moderate fragrance; foliage dark green, thick, glossy; vigorous, pillar, well-branched growth; int. by Morse, 1962

Norwich Sweetheart Min, mr, 2002, Berg, David; flowers medium, dbl., borne mostly solitary, moderate fragrance; foliage medium size, medium green, matte; growth upright, medium; garden, exhibition; [Radiant × Jilly Jewel]; int. in 2002

Norwich Union F, my, 1976, Beales, Peter; flowers bright yellow, changing to lemon as they age, 3 in., cupped, intense fragrance; foliage glossy, leathery; compact growth; [Arthur Bell × (seedling × Allgold)]; int. by Intwood Nurs., 1975

Nossa Senhora de Fátima HT, rb, Moreira da Silva; flowers deep red, reverse golden yellow

Nostalgia Min, mp, 1990, Saville, F. Harmon; bud ovoid; flowers medium pink, reverse lighter, aging lighter, medium, 38 petals, cupped, quartered, borne usually singly and in sprays of 3-5, no fragrance; foliage medium size, medium green, semi-glossy; prickles thin, straight, medium, gray-purple to brown; spreading, low growth; fruit not observed; PP7418; [Rita × (Rise 'n' Shine × Sheri Anne)]; int. by Nor'East Min. Roses, 1990

Nostalgica S, m, Roman, G., and Wagner, S.; flowers mauve-pink, medium, 35 petals, globular, borne in clusters, very strong sweet fragrance; semi-recurrent; foliage large, dark green, glossy, very healthy; [Vigorosa × Angela]; int. by Res. Stn. for Hort., 1998

Nostalgie HT, rb, Tantau; flowers cream white with cherry red edges, dbl.; foliage leathery, glossy, reddish; int. by Rosen Tantau, 1995

Nostalgie HRg, dp, Delbard, Georges; int. by Georges Delbard SA, 2003

Notaire Bonnefond HP, m, 1868, Liabaud; flowers velvety purple, very large, full

Notre Dame LCl, dp, Peden, R.; int. in 1997

Notre Dame de Fourvière HP, lp, 1861, Ducher

Notre Pere F, mr, Croix, Paul; flowers bright red, borne mostly in clusters; foliage disease-resistant; compact growth; int. by Roseraie Paul Croix, 1982

Nottingham HT, yb, 1938, Robinson, H.; flowers clear yellow, center tinted orange; vigorous growth; int. by Wheatcroft Bros.

Nottingham F, dy, Gandy; flowers golden yellow, large, borne in trusses, slight fragrance; foliage olive green, disease-resistant; strong, bushy growth; int. by Gandy's Roses, 2002

Nottingham Forest F, mr, 1971, deRuiter; flowers large, 28 petals; foliage dark; moderate, bushy growth; [Metropole × Diamant]; int. by Geo. deRuiter

Nottingham's Pride S, my; int. by Vilmorin, 2000

Notturno HT, dr, 1983; flowers dark purplish red, 35 petals, intense fragrance; foliage large, dark; prickles reddish, hooked; upright, bushy growth; [Papa Meilland × seedling]; int. by Rose Barni-Pistoia, 1981

Nouveau Intelligible HGal, m, before 1811; bud round, inflated; flowers deep violet, 3 in., very dbl.; foliage small, oval, very bullate

Nouveau Monde HGal, m, before 1811; bud large, round; flowers purple violet, dark and velvety, petals thick, very dbl.; foliage oval, dark green, largely dentate; nearly thornless

Nouveau Petite Serment C, m, before 1811; flowers deep purple, lightening from center to edge, small, very dbl., moderate fragrance; foliage oval, deeply and finely dentate; prickles numerous, hooked, red

Nouveau Rouge HGal, dr, before 1811; bud round, nearly glabrous; flowers sparkling purple red, very dbl., moderate fragrance; foliage nearly round, finely dentate, medium green

Nouveau Triomphe – See **Duc de Chartres**, D

Nouveau Vulcain HGal, m, before 1843; flowers dark purple, medium, very dbl.

Nouvelle Duchesse d'Orléans HGal, w; flowers flesh white, center touched violet, large, full

Nouvelle Etoile HT, yb, 1966, Delbard-Chabert; flowers creamy yellow, edged carmine-red, well-shaped, 40-48 petals; free growth; [Chic Parisien × Provence]; int. by Cuthbert

Nouvelle Europe F, or, 1964, Gaujard; flowers bright cinnabar orange, 3 in., dbl., high-centered, borne in small clusters, slight fragrance; free-flowering; foliage dark green; vigorous, bushy growth; hardy; [Miss France × Vendome]; ADR, 1964

Nouvelle Europe, Climbing Cl F, or; tall (2-4 m.), vigorous growth; int. after 1964

Nouvelle Gagnée HGal, mp, before 1813, Miellez

Nouvelle Héloïse – See **Héloïse**, HGal

Nouvelle Pivoine HGal, m, before 1818, Lille; flowers violet tinted, center vivid red, large

Nouvelle Transparente HGal, dp, 1835, Miellez; flowers rosy crimson, large, dbl.

Nova F, or, 1969, Harkness, R.; flowers semi-dbl., borne in clusters; foliage dark, glossy; [Anne Elizabeth × Paprika]; int. by J. L. Harkness, 1967

Nova Min, lp, Poulsen; flowers light pink, medium, dbl., no fragrance; foliage dark; growth bushy, 40-60 cm.; PP10082; int. as Avon, Poulsen Roser, 1996

Nova Coelestis – See **Celestial**, A

Nova Hit – See **Nova**, Min

Nova Incarnata – See **Elisa**, A

Nova Lux HT, yb, 1955, Aicardi, D.; flowers chrome-yellow with red reflections; foliage glossy; very vigorous growth; [Julien Potin × Sensation]; int. by Giacomasso

Nova Red Min, mr, 1964, Moore, Ralph S.; bud pointed; flowers crimson, small, 10 petals, borne in clusters; low (12 in.) growth; [seedling × Little Buckaroo]; int. by Sequoia Nursery

Nova Zembla HRg, w, 1907, Ruys/Mees; flowers light pink to white, large, dbl., moderate fragrance; good repeat; vigorous, erect (6 ft.) growth; [sport of Conrad Ferdinand Meyer]

Novaia F, rb, Orard; flowers flushed bright red, heart yellow, reverse silver, dbl., slight fragrance; free-flowering; growth to 90-100 cm.; int. in 1997

Novelty HT, ob, 2002, Weeks, O.L.; flowers orange/yellow with gold, orange blend reverse, 4 in., full, borne mostly solitary, moderate fragrance; foliage medium size, medium green, matte; prickles average, curved, few; growth upright, medium (5 ft.); garden decorative; [First Prize × Arizona]; int. by Certified Roses, Inc., 2002

November Rain HT, m, Urban, J.

Novitchkova HT, ob, Novitchkov; flowers orange-yellow, medium; foliage dark, leathery; low growth

Noweta F, mr, 1960, Boerner; bud ovoid; flowers rose-red, medium, dbl., borne in clusters; foliage leathery; vigorous, upright, bushy growth; [Spice × Garnette seedling]; int. by J&P, 1960

Nozomi Cl Min, lp, 1968, Onodera, Toru F.; flowers pearl-pink, single, flat, borne in trusses; foliage small, glossy; trailing growth; [Fairy Princess × Sweet Fairy]

Nu Gold Min, my; flowers bright yellow

Nuage Blanc – See **Weisse Wolke**, S

Nuage Parfumé – See **Fragrant Cloud**, HT

Nuage Parfumé, Climbing – See **Fragrant Cloud, Climbing**, Cl HT

Nuance Min, or, 1992, White, Al; flowers medium, full, borne mostly singly; foliage small, medium green, matte; few prickles; medium, upright growth; [sport of Pierrine]; int. by Giles Rose Nursery, 1991

Nuance HT, op, J&P; int. in 1993

Nuancée de Bleu – See **Celestial**, A

Nubia – See **Hot Cocoa**, F

Nubian LCl, dr, 1937, B&A; flowers dark velvety red, 4 in., dbl., high-centered; sometimes recurrent bloom; foliage large, leathery; vigorous (6-8 ft.) growth

Nubienne – See **La Nubienne**, HCh

Nubya F, ob; flowers dark orange to brownish orange; int. by Richard Huber AG, 2006

Nucarina HT, mr

Nugget F, my, 1974, Warriner, William A.; bud ovoid; flowers small, very dbl., high-centered; foliage large, glossy, dark; vigorous growth; [Yellow Pinocchio × seedling]; int. by J&P, 1973

Nuggets HT, dy, 1941, Joseph H. Hill, Co.; bud short, pointed, buff-yellow; flowers pale orange-yellow, open, 2-3 in., 15-20 petals; foliage small, dark, leathery; [Joanna Hill × seedling]

Nuit de Chine S, m, Tantau; int. in 2005

Nuit d'Èté – See **Marianne Tudor**, HT

Nuit d'Orient – See **Stephens' Big Purple**, HT

Nuits de Velours F, rb; int. by Willemse France, 2002

Nuits de Young M, dr, 1845, Laffay, M.; bud well mossed; flowers reddish-purple shading to dusky violet-maroon, medium, very dbl., moderate fragrance; non-recurrent; upright, medium (3 ft.) growth

Numa Fay HT, op, 1938, Richard; flowers salmon-pink, edged pale pink, well-formed, large, dbl.; vigorous growth; int. by A. Meilland

No. 15/2000 S, mp, Adam; int. by Pépinières de la Guerinais, 2002

Numéro Un HT, or, 1963, Mallerin, C.; flowers scarlet-red passing to vermilion-red, 5 in., 35-40 petals, globular; foliage bronze, glossy; growth vigorous, bushy, symmetrical; int. by EFR

Nuntius Pacelli HT, w, 1929, Leenders Bros.; flowers white, center cream, large, dbl.; [Mrs David McKee × British Queen]; int. by C-P

Nuntius Schioppa HT, my, 1931, Leenders Bros.; flowers golden yellow, sometimes washed peach-blossom-pink; [sport of Los Angeles]

Nur Mahal HMsk, mr, 1923, Pemberton; flowers bright crimson, medium, semi-dbl., borne in clusters, moderate musk fragrance; recurrent bloom; foliage small; strong stems; vigorous bush or pillar growth; [Château de Clos Vougeot × Hybrid Musk seedling]

Nuria de Recolona – See **Nuria de Recolons**, HP

Nuria de Recolons HP, w, 1933, Dot, Pedro; flowers well-formed, on a very short peduncle, very dbl.; foliage dense; [Canigo × Frau Karl Druschki]

Nurjehan HT, dp, 1981, Division of Vegetable Crops and Floriculture; bud long, pointed; flowers deep pink, 50 petals, high-centered, borne singly, intense fragrance; foliage medium size, dark green, coppery when young; prickles straight; medium, spreading growth; [Sweet Afton × Crimson Glory]; int. in 1980

Nurse Cavell – See **Miss Edith Cavell**, Pol

Nurse Donna Min, pb, 2003, Moore, Ralph S.; flowers dark pink, reverse white/lt pink, 1½ in., dbl., borne in small clusters, slight fragrance; foliage medium size, medium green; prickles small, straight, green, few; growth spreading, medium (15 in.); containers, garden, borders; [Pink Petticoat × Rainbow's End]; int. by Sequoia Nurs., 2003

Nurse Masako HT, lp, Kadoya

Nurse Tracey Davies F, dy, Fryer; flowers golden yellow, dbl., cupped, borne in clusters; recurrent; foliage dark green, disease-resistant; compact, low (50 cm.) growth; int. by Fryers Roses, 2006

Nursing Centenary – See **Crystalline**, HT

Nutka Rose – See ***R. nutkana*** (Presl)

Nutkhut F, or, 1970, Pal, Dr. B.P.; bud long, pointed; flowers coral-red, small, very dbl., globular; foliage leathery; very vigorous, bushy, open growth; [Rumba × Cocorico]; int. by K. S. G. Son, 1969

Nutneyron S, mp, Schoener; flowers semi-dbl.; occasionally repeats sparingly; growth to 4 ft.; [Paul Neyron × *R. nutkana*]

Nutzwedel F, mr, 1937, Schmidt, K.; flowers light crimson; [sport of Else Poulsen]; int. by Kordes

Nymph F, op, 1953, Dickson, A.; flowers coral-salmon, 3 in., 30 petals, borne in trusses; foliage dark, glossy; very free growth; [Fashion × seedling]

Nymphaea Alba HT, w, 1889, Drögemüller; flowers glossy satin-white, medium, dbl.; [Mlle Eugene Verdier × Gloire de Dijon]

Nymphe LCl, w, 1910, Türke; flowers white, center pale yellow, 6 cm., full, borne in small clusters, moderate fragrance; [Mignonette × Maréchal Niel]

Nymphe Egeria HMult, mp, 1892, Geschwind, R.; flowers deep pink, aging to pure pink, 4-5 cm., dbl., globular, borne in small clusters; supposedly a hybrid multiflora, but bearing more resemblance to *R. canina* (perhaps crossed with a Bourbon)

Nymphe Naine Émue – See **Maiden's Blush**, A

Nymphe Tepla HMult, dp, 1886, Geschwind, R.; flowers carmine pink, fading lighter, 6-7 cm., very dbl., cupped, opening loosely, borne in medium clusters; numerous prickles; [De la Grifferaie × unknown]; sometimes classified as HSet

Nymphenburg HMsk, op, 1954, Kordes; flowers salmon-pink shaded orange, very large, semi-dbl., flat, borne in clusters, moderate fragrance; recurrent bloom; foliage large, glossy; upright growth; [Sangerhausen × Sunmist]; int. by Morse

Nypels Perfection Pol, pb, 1930, Leenders, M.; flowers hydrangea-pink, shaded deep pink, large, semi-dbl., borne in clusters; vigorous, bushy growth; [sport of Mevrouw Nathalie Nypels]

Nyveldt's White HRg, w, 1965, Nyveldt; flowers snow-white, large, single; hips orange-red; [(*R. rugosa rubra* × *R. cinnamomea*) × *R. nitida*]; int. in 1958

O Sole Mio HT, my, 1985, Delbard, Georges; flowers bright, well-formed, large, 35 petals, borne singly and in clusters of 2 or 3, slight fresh fragrance; foliage medium size, medium green, glossy; growth to over 100 cm.; [(Peace × Marcelle Gret) × Velizy seedling]; int. by Georges Delbard SA, 1984

O. Junyent HT, mr, 1924, Dot, Pedro; bud large, ovoid; flowers coral-red, base yellow, large, semi-dbl., borne in small clusters; foliage large, dark green, glossy; numerous prickles; [Frau Karl Druschki × Mme Edouard Herriot]

O. L. Weeks HT, dr, Weeks, O.; flowers deep red, 40 petals; stems strong; int. in 2006

Oakington Ruby Min, mr, 1933, Bloom; bud deep crimson; flowers ruby-crimson, white-eye, 1-1½ in., dbl.; dwarf (1 ft or less) growth; [sport of Rouletii]

Oakley HT, pb, 1937, Fairhead; flowers bright rose, base deep red, tipped flesh-pink, large; vigorous growth

Oakmont HP, pb, 1893, May; flowers deep pink, reverse lighter, borne in clusters; recurrent bloom

Oamaston Pride HT, yb, 1954, C.W.S. Ltd. Hort. Dept.; flowers buttercup-yellow suffused deep carnation-pink, large, dbl.; foliage dark, glossy; very vigorous growth; [sport of Haisha]; int. by Co-op. Wholesale Soc., 1954

Oasis – See **Rose Bengal**, HT

Oasis Sunset – See **Manaia**, HT

Obbo HT; [sport of Alfred Colomb]

Obélisque LCl, op, 1970, Delbard-Chabert; flowers coppery orange-pink, medium, semi-dbl., globular, borne in large clusters; abundant, intermittent bloom; foliage bronze, glossy; vigorous, climbing growth; [Spectacular × (Orange Triumph × Floradora)]; int. by Laxton & Bunyard, 1967; Gold Medal, Geneva, 1967

Oberbürgermeister Boock Pol, dr, GPG Bad Langensalza; flowers medium, dbl.; good repeat; upright (50 cm.), branching growth; int. in 1964

Oberbürgermeister Dr Külb HT, op, 1931, Nauheimer; flowers flame-colored, passing to salmon; [sport of Roselandia]

Oberbürgermeister Dr Troendlin HT, lp, 1904, Kaiser; flowers delicate flesh pink, large, very dbl.; [sport of Mme Caroline Testout]

Oberbürgermeister Heimerich HP, mp, 1929, Weigand, C.; flowers fresh rose, some petals with reverse lighter, dbl.; [Frau Karl Druschki × Souv. de Claudius Pernet]

Obergärtner Burgner HT, mr, 1934, Burgner; flowers medium, semi-dbl.

Obergärtner Wiebicke F, mr, 1950, Kordes; bud long, pointed; flowers light red, open, very large, semi-dbl., borne in clusters; foliage glossy, light green; vigorous, bushy growth; [Johannes Boetnner × Magnifica]

Oberhofgärtner A. Singer HP, mr, 1904, Lambert, H.; flowers carmine, center darker, 40 petals; dwarf, compact growth; [Mme Caroline Testout × Marie Baumann]

Oberhofgärtner Terks HT, pb, 1902, Welter; flowers flesh pink, muddled with carmine, tinted salmon-nankeen-yellow, very large, very full, moderate fragrance; [Belle Siebrecht × La France]

Oberlehrer L. Burkhardt HT, dp, 1939, Burkhardt; flowers carmine-pink, large, dbl.

Oberleutnant Immelmann HT, lp, 1916, Henniger; flowers soft yellowish-pink, center deeper, petals incurved, globular

Oberon F, ab, 1955, Dickson, A.; flowers salmon-apricot, 2-2½ in., 38 petals, borne in trusses; bushy growth; [Nymph × seedling]

Obsession HT, dr, 1990, Marciel, Stanley G.; bud high-centered, pointed; flowers currant red, large, 42 petals, cupped, imbricated, borne singly, moderate fragrance; free-flowering; foliage medium size, medium green, semi-glossy; prickles wing-shaped, reddish tinge; stems strong, upright; upright, tall (200 cm.) growth; hips pear-shaped, green; PP7902; [seedling × seedling]; greenhouse rose; int. by DeVor Nurseries, Inc.

Ocarina – See **Angela Rippon**, Min

Occhi di Fata F, pb, Barni; flowers open white, then turn deep pink in sun, semi-dbl., borne in very large clusters, slight fragrance; compact, upright (2 ft.) growth; int. by Rose Barni, 2005

Ocean Song HT, w, Tantau; greenhouse rose; int. by Australian Roses, 2004

Ocean Spray – See **Humdinger**

Oceana – See **Osiana**, HT

Océane S, rb, Guillot-Massad; int. by Roseraies Guillot, 2000

Ocho HT, ab, Suzuki, Seizo; flowers full, high-centered; int. in 1983

Ocooch Mountain Rose S, mp, 1980, Hall, William W.; bud small, pointed; flowers 5 petals, borne 3-4 per cluster, intense spicy fragrance; foliage having 9 leaflets, small, slightly rugose, medium green; prickles straight, fine; arching growth; int. in 1981

Octandre T, pb

Octavia Hill F, mp, 1993, Harkness; flowers 3¼ in., 75 petals, borne in sprays of 3-5, moderate damask fragrance; foliage medium size, dark green, semi-glossy; medium, bushy growth; [Armada × Compassion]; int. by Harkness New Roses, Ltd., 1994

Octavie HGal, dp, about 1810, Descemet; flowers dark pink, edges lighter; possibly re-introduced by Vibert about 1835

Octavie HGal, lp, before 1829, Coquerel; flowers light pink, edged blush, open, medium, dbl.; vigorous, branching growth

Octavie N, m, 1845, Vibert; flowers bright velvety purple-pink, medium, full, moderate fragrance

Octavie Fontaine B, w, 1858, Fontaine; flowers white, shaded light flesh pink, medium, full

Octet S, m, 1979, Rowley; bud narrow, pointed; flowers pale purple, 3 in., 5 petals; prolific bloom in summer only; foliage gray-green; extrememly vigorous growth; [*R. rudiuscula* × *R. subglauca*]; int. by Royal National Rose Soc., 1977

October HT, ob, 1980, Weeks, O.L.; bud long, pointed; flowers rich salmon orange, 30 petals, high-centered, borne singly and 2-3 per cluster, moderate fragrance; foliage leathery, dark; prickles long, hooked; tall, upright growth; PP4708; [seedling × seedling]

October Moon F, ab, 2005, Barden, Paul; flowers apricot-orange, reverse lighter apricot, 3 in., very full, borne in small clusters; foliage medium size, medium green, semi-glossy; prickles ½ in., curved, green/tan, moderate; growth bushy, somewhat upright but very full, medium (3-4 ft.); [Rise 'N' Shine × It's Showtime]; int. by The Uncommon Rose, 2006

Octoberfest Gr, ob, 1998, McGredy, Sam IV; bud long, pointed; flowers blended autmnal colors, cream through gold to red-orange, 5-5½ in., dbl., high-centered, borne in small clusters, slight fruity fragrance; foliage large, dark green, glossy; prickles moderate; reddish new growth, tall, upright (6 ft.) growth; [Louis Gardner × New Zealand]; int. by Weeks Roses, 1999

Oddball F, rb, 1998, Horner, Colin P.; flowers crimson stripes on buff brown, fading to red stripes on pink, 2½ in., 8-14 petals, borne in small clusters; foliage medium size, medium green, dull; prickles moderate; spreading growth; [(Lichterloh × (Tall Story × Southampton)) × (New Penny × White Pet)]; int. by Paul Chessum Rose Specialist, 1998

Odense By-Rose – See **Cottage Maid**, S

Odense City – See **Cottage Maid**, S

Odeon HT, op, 1979, Gaujard; bud globular; flowers coral-pink, 3 in., 50 petals, globular, moderate fragrance; foliage large, dark; vigorous growth; [(Chateau de Chenonceaux × Mignonne) × Americana]; int. by Roseraies Gaujard, 1977

Oderic Vital HP, lp, 1858, Oger; flowers delicate silvery-rose pink, large, full; [sport of Baronne Prévost]

Odessa Min, m, 1998, Williams, Michael C.; flowers 1½ in., full, high-centered, borne mostly singly, no fragrance; foliage medium size, dark green, matte; prickles few, small; upright, tall (30 in.) growth; [Jean Kenneally × select pollen]; int. by The Mini Rose Garden, 1998

Odette F, mp, GPG Bad Langensalza; flowers medium, dbl.; int. in 1972

Odette Chène HT, mp, 1940, Colombier; flowers pink, base coral; vigorous growth; [Richmond, Climbing × Charles P. Kilham]

Odette Foussier HT, mp, 1924, Chambard, C.; flowers salmon-pink, inside chrome on yellow ground, dbl.

Odette Foussier, Climbing Cl HT, mp, 1929, Chambard, C.

Odette Joyeux LCl, op, 1959, Robichon; bud globular, coral-orange; flowers pink to lilac-pink, large, dbl., cupped; abundant, recurrent bloom; foliage leathery, glossy; very vigorous growth; [Lady Sylvia × unknown]

Odile Masquelier S, lp, Guillot-Massad; int. by Roses Guillot, 2005

Odine – See **Ondine**, HT

Odorata – See **Hume's Blush Tea-Scented China**, T

Odorata HT, pb, 1928, Van Rossem; flowers carmine-pink, reverse white edged pink, base golden yellow, dbl.; [Sunburst × Ma Fiancee]

Odorata 22449 – See **Fun Jwan Lo**, S

Odyssée F, or, 1981, Gaujard, Jean; flowers well-formed, 25 petals, borne 3-5 per cluster, moderate fragrance; foliage dark; prickles small, brown; [Pampa × seedling]; int. in 1979

Odyssey F, m, 2001, Cowlishaw; flowers mauve with prominent yellow stamens, 3 in., single, borne in large clusters, intense fragrance; foliage medium size, light green, glossy; prickles medium, pointed, moderate; growth bushy, medium (30 in.); garden decorative; [Summer Wine × seedling]; int. by Rearsby Roses Ltd., 2001

Œillet C, lp, 1789, Poilpré; flowers bright pink, sometimes variegated, small, petals small and lacinated, dbl., borne in clusters of 3-6, moderate fragrance; foliage ovate, toothed; prickles numerous, unequal, reddish, slightly recurved; vigorous growth

Œillet de Saint-Arquey – See **Serratipetala**, Ch

Œillet Double HGal, m, about 1835, Prévost; flowers lilac pink, striped

Œillet Flamand HGal, pb, 1845, Parmentier or Vibert; flowers pale pink striped white and brighter pink, medium, very dbl., flat, intense fragrance; foliage medium green, oval; very vigorous growth

Œillet Panachée M, pb, 1888, Verdier, C.; flowers pale pink striped deep pink, petals quilled, small, full, flat, moderate fragrance

Œillet Parfait HGal, pb, 1841, Foulard; flowers blush, striped lilac and dark red, medium, dbl., flat; dwarf growth; sometimes classed as Damask; possibly a Gallica × Damask hybrid

Oekonomierat Echtermeyer HT, dp, 1913, Lambert, P.; flowers deep carmine, shaded lighter, very large, dbl., moderate fragrance; [Rose Benary × unknown]

Officinalis – See ***R. gallica officinalis*** (Thory)

Offley Rose – See ***R. gallica officinalis*** (Thory)

Offrandé HT, Gaujard; int. in 1982

Offranville F, dp, Eve, A.; int. in 1993

Ognewaja HT, mr, 1937, Kosteckij; flowers medium, dbl.

Ogni Jalty F, mr, Klimenko, V. N.; flowers medium, dbl.; int. in 1955

Ogoniok F, ob, 1955, Sushkov, K. L.; flowers fiery orange edged darker, medium

Oh-Choh HT, yb, 1986, Suzuki, Seizo; flowers yellow tinted rose, aging red, large, 38 petals, high-centered, moderate fragrance; foliage dark, semi-glossy; prickles small, slanted downward; upright growth; [(Rumba × Olympic Torch) × Wisbech Gold]; int. by Keisei Rose Nursery, 1983

Oh Darlin Min, ab, 1995, Rennie, Bruce F.; flowers 1¼ in., 6-14 petals, borne mostly singly; foliage small, dark green, glossy; few prickles; low (10-12 in.), compact growth; [Pink Sheri × Hap Renshaw]; int. by Rennie Roses International, 1992

Oh La La – See **Olala**, F

Oh My God – See **Lynn Anderson**, HT

Oh My Stars Min, ly, 1996, Bough, Melvin; flowers medium, full, high-centered, borne mostly singly; foliage medium size, medium green, dull; prickles moderate; upright, tall (2-2½ ft.) growth; [sport of Giggles]; int. by Giles Rose Nursery

Oharame HT, w; int. in 1974

Ohio S, mr, 1949, Shepherd; flowers bright red, semi-dbl.; recurrent bloom; growth to 4 ft.; hardy; [*R. soulieana* × Gruss an Teplitz seedling]

Ohio Belle LCl, lp, 1975, Jerabek, Paul E.; bud globular; flowers dbl., 53 petals; repeat bloom; foliage glossy, dark; tall (15-20 ft.) growth; [New Dawn × unknown]; int. by Wyant, 1974

Ohl HGal, m, before 1839; flowers violet-purple, center bright red, large, dbl.; vigorous growth; int. by Hardy

Ohlala – See **Olala**, F

Ohshima Rose HT, or, 1992, Cocker, James; flowers medium, full, borne mostly singly, moderate fragrance; foliage medium size, medium green, matte; some prickles; tall (1 m.), upright growth; [(National Trust × Alexander) × Red Planet]; int. by James Cocker & Sons, 1991

Oil Painting – See **Aburae**, HT

Oirase HT, mr, 1977, Ito; bud ovoid; flowers 5½ in., 24 petals, high-centered, moderate fragrance; below-average bloom continuity; foliage glossy, dark; vigorous, upright growth; [Red Lion × Christian Dior]; int. in 1973

Oiseau Bleu HT, m, 1978, Poulsen, Niels D.; flowers mauve-rose, 4-4½ in., 30 petals, intense fragrance; foliage large, glossy, dark; vigorous growth; int. by Vilmorin-Andrieux, 1970

Oiseau de Feu F, mr, 1956, Mallerin, C.; flowers scarlet-red, 2 in., 35 petals, cupped, borne in clusters; bushy growth; [Chant Indou × Peace]

Ojibway LCl, w, 1946, Preston; bud pointed; flowers 3 in., 12-15 petals, borne in clusters; free, non-recurrent bloom; foliage dark; vigorous, spreading growth; hardy; [Ross Rambler × ((*R. rugosa* × *R. eglanteria*) × unknown)]; int. by Central Exp. Farm

Okaga HRg, dp, 1927, Hansen, N.E.; flowers deep pink, semi-dbl.; non-recurrent; low, bushy growth; very hardy; [Alika × Tetonkaha]

Okaku LCl, my, Hiroshima

Oklahoma HT, dr, 1964, Swim & Weeks; bud ovoid, long, pointed; flowers very dark red, 4-5½ in., 48 petals, high-centered, intense fragrance; foliage leathery, dark, matte; vigorous, bushy growth; PP2326; [Chrysler Imperial × Charles Mallerin]; int. by Weeks Wholesale Rose Growers; Gold Medal, Japan, 1963

Oklahoma, Climbing Cl HT, dr, 1968, Swim & Weeks (also Ross, 1972); PP2649; patent issued to Swim & Weeks; int. by Weeks Wholesale Rose Growers

Okresni Heitman Cubr HT, mp, 1933, Böhm, J.; flowers large, dbl.

Oksana HT, pb, 2001, Singer, Steven; flowers yellow, color blends into base of petals, 4-5 in., full, borne mostly solitary, intense fragrance; foliage medium size, medium green, semi-glossy; prickles moderate, medium, slightly downturned; growth upright, medium (4-5 ft.); garden, cutting; [Great Scott × Lanvin]; int. by Wisconsin Roses, 1995

Okuyoshino Min, w; int. in 2001

Olala F, mr, 1959, Tantau, Math.; bud pointed; flowers blood-red, center lighter, large, semi-dbl., borne in clusters of up to 25; foliage leathery, dark, glossy; vigorous, bushy, upright growth; [Fanal × Crimson Glory]; int. in 1956; Gold Medal, Baden-Baden, 1955

Olave Baden-Powell HT, mr, 1974, Cobley, A.; flowers scarlet, 5 in., dbl., borne singly; free-flowering; foliage dark, leathery; very free growth; hardy; int. by Harry Wheatcroft Gardening, 1972

Olavus M, lp, 1932, Nielsen; flowers salmon-pink, medium, semi-dbl.; [Cristata or Blanche Moreau × Mme Edouard Herriot]

Olbrich's Merry Red S, mr, 2000, Radler, William J.; flowers large, semi-dbl., borne in small clusters, slight fragrance; foliage medium size, medium green, matte, blackspot-resistant; prickles moderate; growth upright, tall; hedge; very hardy; [Carefree Beauty × ((((Fairy Moss × First Prize) × unknown) × (Lucky Lady × Eddie's Crimson)) × G48)]

Old Baylor S, w, 2005, Shoup, George Michael; flowers semi-dbl., borne in small clusters, slight fragrance; remontant; foliage medium size, dark green, semi-glossy; numerous prickles; growth bushy, medium (3-4 ft.); hedging; [(Carefree Beauty × Basye's Blueberry) × Heritage]; int. by Antique Rose Emporium, 1996

Old Black – See **Nuits de Young**, M

Old Blush Ch, mp, 1751, Parsons; flowers two-tone pink, semi-dbl., borne in loose sprays; dependably recurrent; vigorous, upright growth; int. by Int. into Sweden in 1751; Old Rose Hall of Fame, WFRS

Old Blush, Climbing Cl Ch, mp; flowers bright to medium pink, medium, semi-dbl. to dbl., moderate tea fragrance; [sport of Parsons' Pink]

Old Blush Single Ch, pb

Old Charleston S, w, Poulsen; flowers white, small, dbl., slight wild rose fragrance; foliage dark green, glossy; broad, bushy (40-60 cm.) growth; hips none; PP12623; int. as Bright Cover, Poulsen Roser, 1998

Old Country Charm Min, pb, 1996, Williams, Michael C.; flowers medium to dark pink with salmon, full, borne mostly singly, no fragrance; foliage medium size, dark green, dull; upright, medium growth; [seedling × unknown]; int. by The Mini Rose Garden, 1996

Old Crimson – See **Slater's Crimson China**, Ch

Old Crimson China – See **Slater's Crimson China**, Ch

Old Danish LCl, mp

Old Faithful HT, dy, 1991, Warriner, William A.; flowers large, full, moderate fragrance; foliage large, dark green, semi-glossy; upright, bushy growth; PP6445; [Sunbright × Medallion]; int. by Bear Creek Gardens, 1991

Old Fashion Red HT, mr, 1947, Brownell; flowers spectrum-red fading blush, large, very dbl., high-centered, moderate fragrance; foliage glossy; vigorous, bushy growth; [Pink Princess × Crimson Glory]

Old Fashioned Girl Min, w, 1992, Bennett, Dee; flowers soft lavender to white, large, full, old-fashioned form, intense fragrance; foliage small, medium green, semi-glossy; some prickles; medium (60-80 cm.), bushy growth; [Blue Ribbon × unnamed Miniature seedling]; int. by Tiny Petals Nursery, 1993

Old Fashioned Lady S, w

Old Fashioned Romance S, dp, 2001, Byrnes, Robert L.; flowers large, full, borne in small clusters, no fragrance; foliage medium green, semi-glossy; prickles moderate; growth bushy, tall; [Illusion × Illusion]; int. by Overbrooke Gardens, 2001

Old Flame F, ob, Dickson, Patrick; int. in 1987

Old Glory – See **Gloire de Dijon**, Cl T

Old Glory HT, mp, 1940, Hausermann; flowers clear brilliant pink, large, dbl.; RULED EXTINCT 2/88; [sport of Briarcliff]

Old Glory Min, mr, 1988, Benardella, Frank A.; flowers bright post office red, aging blood-red to crimson, 1½-2 in., 23-25 petals, high-centered, borne singly and in small clusters; foliage medium size, medium green, semi-glossy; prickles long, thin, curved downward, gray-red; upright, tall, vigorous growth; PP5658; [Rise 'n' Shine × Harmonie]; int. by Nor'East Min. Roses, 1988; AOE, ARS, 1988

Old Glory HT, mr, Devor; int. in 1995

Old Gold HT, or, 1913, McGredy; flowers vivid reddish-orange, shaded coppery red and apricot, medium, 10 petals, borne mostly solitry, moderate fragrance; foliage dark coppery green; short stems; Gold Medal, NRS, 1912

Old John F, ob, 1999, Dickson, Colin; flowers mid-orange, reverse orange-red, 2½ in., dbl., borne in large clusters, moderate fragrance; foliage medium size, dark green, glossy; prickles moderate; upright, medium (40 in.) growth; [Sunseeker × New Horizon]; int. by Dickson Nurseries, Ltd, 1999

Old Lavender Ayr, m

Old Lilac – See **Lilac Rose**, S

Old Man Bailey HT, pb, 2002, Hiltner, Martin; flowers deep pink, white eye, reverse light yellow, opening to lavender and white, 3½-4 in., semi-dbl., high-centered, borne mostly solitary; foliage medium size, medium green, semi-glossy; prickles straight, numerous; growth upright, medium (2½-5 ft.); garden, cut flower; [Lynn Anderson × Royal Amethyst]; int. in 2003

Old Master F, rb, 1975, McGredy, Sam IV; flowers carmine, white eye and reverse, 4½ in., 15 petals;

foliage semi-glossy, medium green; vigorous, bushy growth; [(Maxi × Evelyn Fison) × (Orange Sweetheart × Fruhlingsmorgen)]; int. by McGredy Roses Int., 1973

Old of Days HT, mp

Old Pink Daily – See **Old Blush**, Ch

Old Pink Monthly – See **Old Blush**, Ch

Old Pink Moss – See **Communis**, M

Old Port F, m, 1990, McGredy, Sam IV; flowers medium, full, moderate fragrance; foliage medium size, medium green, matte; bushy growth; PP10698; [((Anytime × Eyepaint) × Purple Splendour) × Big Purple]; int. by McGredy Roses International, 1991

Old Red HCh, mr

Old Red Boursault Bslt, mr; flowers pale red, boursault type, poorly formed, semi-dbl., borne in large clusters; hips nearly round; probably the original, typical form of *R. lheritieranea*

Old Red Moss M, mr; flowers carmine-red, medium, very dbl., moderate fragrance; heavy bloom; non-recurrent; vigorous (5 ft.) growth

Old Red Pet – See **Lucullus**, Ch

Old Smokey F, Murley, J.J.; int. in 1976

Old Smoothie HT, mr, 1970, Weeks; flowers large, very dbl., high-centered; foliage large, glossy, leathery; largely thornless; vigorous, upright growth; PP3098; [Night 'n' Day × ((First Love × unknown) × (Queen Elizabeth × Chrysler Imperial))]

Old Spanish Rose – See **Russelliana**, HMult

Old Spice – See **Spiced Coffee**, HT

Old Stone School Misc OGR, mp

Old Time – See **Oldtimer**, HT

Old Time Fragrance Gr, dp; flowers deep pinkish red, very strong, thick petals, large, dbl., intense fragrance; growth to 3-4 ft.; int. by Hortico, 2003

Old Tuscan – See **Tuscany**, HGal

Old Velvet Moss – See **William Lobb**, M

Old Velvet Rose – See **Tuscany**, HGal

Old White Moss – See **Shailer's White Moss**, M

Old Yella Min, dy, Benardella, Frank; bud golden yellow; flowers buttercup yellow with splashings of red on petal edges; tall growth; [sport of Old Glory]; int. by Treloar Roses, 1999

Old Yellow HSpn, ly; bud yellow, rounded; flowers quickly turn white, full, cupped, borne in clusters along the canes; vigorous (1½ m.) growth; hardy

Old Yellow Scotch HSpn, dy; flowers golden yellow, small, dbl., moderate fragrance; foliage small, fern-like; prickles numerous, needle-like; compact (4 ft.) growth

Old Yellow St. Albans – See **Old Yellow**, HSpn

Old Yellow Tea – See **Parks' Yellow Tea-Scented China**, T

Oldcastle HT, mp, 1985, LeMire, Walter; flowers large, 55 petals, high-centered, borne singly; foliage large, dark, glossy; medium, upright growth; [Queen Elizabeth × Charlotte Armstrong]; int. by Roses by Walter LeMire

Olde English F, dp, 1976, Orard, Joseph; flowers light red, 3-4 in., 30-35 petals; foliage glossy, bronze; free growth; [(Floradora × Independence) × Siren]; int. by Harry Wheatcroft Gardening, 1974

Olde Fragrance – See **Duftrausch**, HT

Olde Lace HT, ly, 1993, Davidson, Harvey D.; flowers 3-3½ in., very dbl.; foliage large, dark green, glossy; some prickles; medium (3-4 ft.), bushy growth; [Pink Favorite × (Polly × Peace)]; int. by C & L Valley Rose Co., 1994

Olde Romance HT, mp, 1993, Davidson, Harvey D.; flowers light pink, 7 cm., very full, borne mostly singly; foliage large, dark green, glossy; some prickles; growth tall (5-6 ft.), upright; [Smooth Sailing × Promise]; int. by C & L Valley Rose co., 1994

Olde Romance HT, mp, 1996, Davidson, Harvey; flowers peach pink, lighter reverse, 9 cm., very full, old-fashioned, quartered, flat, borne mostly singly, moderate fragrance; foliage medium size, medium green, glossy; prickles moderate; growth bushy, medium (1 m.); [Shining Ruby × (Smooth Sailing × Futura)]; int. by L. E. Cooke Co., 1996

Olde Romeo HT, dr, 1993, Davidson, Harvey D.; bud ovoid; flowers ruffled, 3-4 in., 38-40 petals, globular, opening flat, borne mostly singly, intense old rose fragrance; foliage medium size, medium green, matte; prickles numerous, straight, downward pointing; medium (4 ft.), upright growth; PP9404; [Smooth Sailing × (Old Smoothie × ((Polly × Peace) × Simon Bolivar))]; int. by C & L Valley Rose Co., 1994

Olde Sweetheart HT, lp, 1996, Davidson, Harvey D.; flowers light pink, with large, raspberry-colored stamens, large, single; foliage medium size, medium green, glossy; prickles moderate; upright, medium (100 cm.) growth; [Smooth Sailing × Red Planet]; int. by L E Cooke Co., 1997

Olde Tango HT, ob, 1996, Davidson, Harvey D.; flowers orange, old fashioned, 3¼-3½ in., very dbl., flat, borne mostly singly, moderate pine fragrance; foliage medium size, medium green, glossy; prickles moderate; bushy (80-90 cm.) growth; [Shining Ruby × The World]; int. by L E Cooke Co., 1996

Olden Days Pol, mr, 1989, Vash, Ernest J.; flowers small, 10 petals, borne in sprays of 36; foliage small, light green, ellipical, slightly serrated, ma; prickles brown; bushy, compact growth; [sport of Unnamed pink Polyantha Paul Carpel]; int. by Historical Roses, 1987

Oldtimer HT, ob, 1969, Kordes, R.; flowers bronze, long, pointed, dbl., high-centered; good repeat; vigorous (4-5 ft.) growth; PP2999; int. by McGredy & Son

Olé Gr, or, 1964, Armstrong, D.L.; bud well-shaped; flowers medium, 50 petals, high-centered to cupped, moderate fragrance; foliage glossy; vigorous growth; PP2474; [Roundelay × El Capitan]; int. by Armstrong Nursery, 1964

Olé, Climbing Cl Gr, or, 1982, Haight, George S. & Swim, H.C.; [sport of Olé]; int. by Armstrong Nursery

Oleander Rose S, op, 1983, Interplant; flowers salmon-pink, small, 7 petals, borne in large clusters; repeat bloom; foliage medium size, medium green, semi-glossy; prickles very few, small; upright growth; [Liverpool Echo × seedling]

Olegario Junyent – See **O. Junyent**, HT

Oleifolia HGal, dp, 1900, Dieck; flowers large, very full; growth tall

Olga HT, Delforge; int. in 1988

Olga HT, Mansuino

Olga Marix B, lp, 1873, Schwartz; flowers flesh, changing to pure white, medium, full

Olga Rippon F, m, 1992, Horner, Colin P.; flowers purple/mauve, loose, 2½ in., dbl., borne in sprays of 5-9, slight spicy fragrance; foliage medium size, medium green, semi-glossy; bushy, low growth; [Sexy Rexy × ((INTermezzo × Baby Faurax) × (Tassin × seedling))]

Olga Tschechowa HT, ly, Cocker; flowers creamy yellow, very large, very dbl.; int. in 1978

Olijprin – See **Rendez-vous**, HT

Olive S, mr, 1982, Harkness, R., & Co., Ltd.; flowers large, 36 petals, cupped, borne in clusters, moderate spicy fragrance; foliage large, dark, glossy; prickles dark; branching growth; [((Vera Dalton × Highlight) × seedling) × Dublin Bay]

Olive Cook HT, w, 1934, Cant, F.; flowers white, base faintly tinged lemon-yellow, large, high-centered; foliage glossy; vigorous growth

Olive Elsie F, mr, Bossom, W.E.; flowers medium red, lighter reverse, 3 in., very full, borne in small clusters; foliage medium size, light green, semi-glossy; prickles moderate; medium (2½ ft.) growth; [Sexy Rexy × Wonder of Woolies]; int. in 1999

Olive Elsie F, lp, 2000, Bossom, Bill; flowers 80 petals, borne in small clusters, moderate fragrance; foliage foliate large, medium green, semi-glossy; prickles moderate; upright, medium (3½ ft.) growth; [Sexy Rexy × Wonder of Woolies]

Olive McKenzie HT, yb, 1971, Dawson, George; bud long, pointed; flowers orange-yellow, marked red, large, dbl., moderate fragrance; foliage large, dark; vigorous, upright, bushy growth; [Daily Sketch × Manitou]; int. by Brundrett

Olive Moore HT, lp, 1927, Allen; flowers pale rose-pink, reflexed silver-pink

Olive Percival HT, rb, 1948, Howard, P.J.; bud long, pointed; flowers intense cherry-red, base gold, 3½-4 in., 14-20 petals, cupped; foliage leathery, bronze; very vigorous, upright, free branching growth; [California × Eternal Youth]

Olive Taylor Min, rb, 1989, Pearce, C.A.; flowers vermillion red with yellow eye, small, 20 petals; foliage medium size, dark green, glossy; bushy growth; [seedling × seedling]; int. by The Limes New Roses, 1988

Olive Whittaker HT, op, 1920, Easlea; flowers rich coppery rose to cerise and salmon

Oliver Delhomme HP, mr, 1861, Verdier, V.; flowers carmine-red, medium, dbl.

Oliver Mee HT, mp, 1927, Dickson, S.; flowers deep salmon tinted fawn, becoming deep salmon-pink, large, dbl., high-centered

Oliver Orange Min, ob, 2000, Giles, Diann; flowers orange, reverse blending white, medium, full, borne mostly singly, no fragrance; foliage medium size, medium green, matte; few prickles; growth spreading, medium; [seedling × seedling]; int. by Giles Rose Nursery

Oliver Twist Min, w, 1996, Burrows, Steven; flowers creamy white, 1 in., dbl., borne in large clusters; foliage medium size, dark green, glossy; some prickles; tall (45-60 cm.), upright, spreading, bushy growth; [Sheri Anne × Richard Buckley]; int. by Burrows Roses, 1996

Olivers HT, m, 1965, Oliver, H.; flowers purple to pink, medium, semi-dbl., moderate fragrance; [Pres. Herbert Hoover × unknown]

Olivet HMult, mr, 1892, Vigneron; flowers light red, center slightly darker, 10-11 cm., full, flat; foliage dark green; growth tall (4 m.); [De la Grifferaie × Mme Baron Veillard]

Olivia HT, mr, Tantau

Olivier Belhomme HP, mr, 1861, Verdier, V. & C.; flowers fiery purplish red, medium, full

Olivier Métra HP, mr, 1885, Verdier, E.; flowers bright cerise red, large, very full; foliage dark green, irregularly dentate; prickles numerous, very long, recurved; growth upright

Olivier Roellinger S, pb, Delbard; flowers yellow heart with pink flush on petals, semi-dbl., cupped, open, borne usually in clusters, moderate fruity fragrance; free-flowering; vigorous (5 ft.) growth; int. by Georges Delbard SA, 2003

Ollie HT, mr, 1982, James, John; bud globular, pointed; flowers 45 petals, borne singly; foliage large, leathery, rounded; prickles red brown; vigorous, tall growth; [(Pink Garnette × Pink Hat) × ((Frau Karl Druschki × McGredy'sYellow) × (Baronne Prevost × Gruss an Teplitz))]; int. in 1974

Olwyn HT, mp, 1946, Bird; bud long, pointed; flowers pink, medium, high-centered; foliage leathery; vigorous, bushy growth; int. by F. Mason

Olympe D, dr, 1843, Vibert; flowers crimson purple, medium, full

Olympe HT, Gaujard; int. in 1974

Olympe Frécinay T, w, 1861, Damaizin; flowers white, becoming yellow

Olympia HT, mr, 1935, Tantau; flowers bright red, large, dbl.; long, strong stems; vigorous growth; [Johanniszauber × Hadley]

Olympia HT, my, 1955, Delforge; bud bright yellow, well formed; bushy, semi-upright growth; [Eclipse × seedling]

Olympiad HT, rb, 1931, Pernet-Ducher; bud long, pointed; flowers blood-red, shaded copper and yellow, large, dbl.; RULED EXTINCT 11/82; int. by Gaujard; Gold Medal, Bagatelle, 1930

Olympiad, Climbing Cl HT, rb, 1938, Raffel; int. by Port Stockton Nursery

Olympiad HT, mr, 1983, McGredy, Sam IV; flowers brilliant medium red, non-fading, 4½-5 in., 30-35 petals, high-centered, borne mostly singly; foliage large, medium green, matte; upright, bushy growth, vigorous; PP5519; [Red Planet × Pharaoh]; int. by Armstrong Nursery, 1984; Gold Medal, Portland, 1985

Olympic – See **Olympic Palace**, F

Olympic Champion HT, yb, 1995, Pugh, D. J.; flowers yellow/pink blend, medium, very dbl.; foliage medium size, dark green, semi-glossy; some prickles; medium (70 cm.), bushy growth; [sport of Champion]; int. by Pugh, 1995

Olympic Charm HT, lp, 1965, Barter; flowers silvery, reverse bright pink, well-formed, large, 65 petals, intense fragrance; foliage dark, glossy; [Grand'mere Jenny × Claude]

Olympic Dream HT, pb, 1984, J&P; flowers large, 35 petals; foliage large, dark, semi-glossy; upright growth; PP5842; [seedling × seedling]; int. by McConnell Nurs., Inc.

Olympic Fire – See **Olympisches Feuer 92**, F

Olympic Flame F, or, 1962, Brett; bud pointed; flowers orange-vermilion, 3 in., 8 petals, borne in clusters; foliage glossy, bright green; vigorous, upright, bushy growth

Olympic Glory HT, dr, 1984, J&P; flowers medium, 35 petals; foliage large, medium green, glossy; upright growth; [seedling × seedling]; int. by McConnell Nurs., Inc.

Olympic Gold Min, ly, 1983, Jolly, Nelson F.; flowers large, 31 petals, high-centered; foliage medium size, medium green, semi-glossy; upright, bushy growth; [Rise 'n' Shine × Bonny]; int. by Rosehill Farm

Olympic Gold – See **Goldener Olymp**, LCl

Olympic Palace F, ob, Olesen; bud pointed; flowers orange to golden bronze, 3 in., 25-30 petals, cupped, borne mostly singly, slight spice fragrance; free-flowering; foliage dark green, glossy; prickles few, 5-6 mm., yellow-green; narrow, bushy (40-60 cm.) growth; PP16744; [seedling × seedling]; int. by Poulsen Roser, 2001

Olympic Spirit – See **Firstar**, HT

Olympic Spirit F, ob, 1988, Pearce, C.A.; flowers orange, reverse yellow, aging orange-brown, medium, semi-dbl., cupped, borne in sprays of 4-5, slight fruity fragrance; foliage small, dark green, glossy; prickles pointed, medium, red; bushy, low growth; [seedling × seedling]; int. by Rearsby Roses, Ltd., 1988

Olympic Star HT, mp, 1959, Trebbin; flowers cerise-pink; vigorous growth; [sport of Picture]

Olympic Torch HT, rb, 1968, Suzuki, Seizo; bud long, pointed; flowers white and red, becoming all red, medium, dbl., high-centered; foliage glossy, bronze, leathery; vigorous growth; PP2968; [Rose Gaujard × Crimson Glory]; int. by General Bionomics, Inc., 1966; Gold Star of the South Pacific, Palmerston North, NZ, 1970

Olympic Torch, Climbing – See **Seika, Climbing**, Cl HT

Olympic Triumph F, rb, 1973, Dickson, Patrick; flowers red and yellow, 4½ in., dbl., globular; foliage sage green; upright growth; [Shiralee × Apricot Nectar]; int. by Dicksons of Hawlmark

Olympisches Feuer F, ob, 1973, Tantau, Math.; bud ovoid; flowers orange, medium, dbl.; upright growth; [Ahoi × Signalfeuer]; int. by Dehner & Co., 1971

Olympisches Feuer 92 F, or, Tantau; flowers bright, full, borne in clusters; recurrent; int. by Rosen Tantau, 1992

Olympus S, rb, Barni, V.; int. by Rose Barni, 1998

Olysko – See **Yellow River**, F

Olytel – See **Super Disco**, F

Omar Khayyám D, lp, 1894, Simpson/Kew; flowers clear pink, center incurved, small, with a small center eye, very full, quartered, moderate fragrance; foliage small, downy; numerous prickles; dense, prickly growth (to 3 ft.)

Omar Pacha B, mr, 1863, Pradel; flowers bright cherry, large, full; recurrent bloom; growth vigorous, upright

Omara HT, lp, Tantau; flowers fresh soft pink; int. by Richard Huber, 2004

Ombre Panachée HGal, m, before 1811; bud round; flowers dark velvety purple, petals folding back, 4 in., dbl.; foliage long, regularly dentate

Ombre Superbe HGal, m, before 1811; flowers dark black-purple, large, dbl., flat; foliage dark green, nearly ovoid, pointed; prickles moderate; from Holland

Ombrée Parfaite HGal, m, 1823, Vibert; flowers variable, light pink to deep purple, often in the same flower, dbl.

Ombretta S, Embriaco, B.; int. in 1991

Omega – See **Emily Post**, HT

Omer-Pacha – See **Omar Pacha**, B

Omi Oswald HMsk, ly, 2000, Lens, Louis; flowers light yellow to cream white, reverse white, 4-5 cm., single, borne in large clusters, slight fragrance; foliage medium size, medium green, semi-glossy; prickles moderate; growth upright, medium (120 cm.); [Ravel × Bright Smile]; int. by Louis Lens N.V., 1988

Omni S, yb, Lens, Louis; int. in 1988

Omphale HGal, lp, 1820, Vibert; different from the Omphale of 1839

Omphale HGal, mp, 1839, Vibert, J. P.; flowers rosy pink, sometimes spotted with white, large, very dbl., cupped; growth erect

Omul S, dy, GPG Bad Langensalza; flowers dark golden yellow, large, dbl.; int. in 1974

On Fire S, pb, Peden, R.; int. in 1999

Once Touched – See **Artistry**, HT

Onda Rose S, mp

Ondella HT, or, 1979, Meilland, Mrs. Marie-Louise; bud conical; flowers vermilion, large, 33 petals; foliage dark; vigorous, upright growth; [(Elegy × Arturo Toscanini) × (Peace × Demain)]; int. by Meilland & Co SNC

Ondella F, dr, Meilland; flowers medium, borne in clusters; free-flowering; groundcover; spreading growth; int. in 1994

Ondina F, m, 2005, Kobayashi, Moriji; flowers semi-dbl., borne in small clusters, intense fragrance; foliage medium size, light green, matte; prickles medium; growth compact, medium (140 cm.); cutting, garden; [seedling × seedling]

Ondine HT, w, 1936, Ketten Bros.; bud pointed; flowers creamy white, slightly tinted pink, high pointed, large, 20-25 petals; foliage dark gray-green; long, strong stems; very vigorous growth; [Louise Criner × Souv. de Claudius Pernet]

O'Neal's Bequest S, yb, 1986, O'Neal, Conrad; flowers yellow with pink petal edges, medium, semi-dbl.; foliage large, medium green, glossy; upright growth; int. by Paul Jerabek

O'Neal's White LCl, w, 1961, O'Neal; flowers large; vigorous growth; [Blossomtime × New Dawn]; int. by Wyant

Onex HGal, dr, Vintage Gardens; flowers crimson violet, yellow stamens, small, semi-dbl., slight fragrance; foliage emerald green, tinted bronze; many, fine, needle-like prickles; int. by Rosen von Schultheis

Onguiculata Cariophillata – See **Œillet**, C

Onkaparinga S, ab, 1997, Thomson, George L.; flowers apricot-pink, reverse lighter, ages pink, 4-5 in., 41 petals, borne in small clusters, intense myrrh fragrance; foliage medium size, medium green, semi-glossy; spreading growth; [Cymbaline × Troilus]; int. in 1999

Onkel Svend F, rb, 1985, Poulsen, Niels D.; flowers medium red and silvery red blend, 23 petals, borne in sprays, moderate spicy fragrance; foliage medium size, dark, matte; low, bushy, spreading growth; [Sonia × Ernest H. Morse]; int. by D.T. Poulsen, 1978

Only Love HT, dr, 1986, Interplant; flowers large, 35 petals; foliage medium size, dark, semi-glossy; upright growth; PP6698; [seedling × Caramba]

Only You HT, dp, 1971, Vahldiek-Bissingen; flowers rose-carmine, 4½-5 in., dbl., high-centered, borne singly, slight fragrance; good repeat; foliage medium size, leathery; very vigorous, dense growth; [sport of Carina]; int. by URS, Meilland, 1970

Ontario Celebration Min, or, 1984, Laver, Keith G.; flowers small, 35 petals, moderate fragrance; foliage small, deep reddish green, semi-glossy; spreading, compact growth; [Nic-Noc × (Party Girl × Queen of the Dwarfs)]; int. in 1983

Onterama – See **Interama**, F

Onyx Flamboyant HT, lp, 1967, Delbard-Chabert; flowers peach to shell-pink, 4 in., high-centered; foliage serrated; vigorous, bushy growth; [Sultane × Queen Elizabeth]; int. by Cuthbert, 1965

Oodnadatta Pol, pb, Sutherland; int. by Golden Vale Nursery, 2000

Oonagh HT, mr, 1990, McCann, Sean; flowers large, full; foliage medium size, medium green, semi-glossy; very spreading growth; [Matangi × Gavotte]

Ooo! Baby! Min, rb, 2000, Bennett, Dee; flowers full, high-centered, borne mostly singly, moderate fragrance; foliage medium size, medium green, matte; few prickles; growth bushy, medium (18-24 in.); [Shocking Blue × Jean Kenneally]; int. by Tiny Petals Nursery, 2001

Oor Wullie Min, mp, 1978, Anderson's Rose Nurseries; flowers salmon-pink, medium, 24 petals;

foliage glossy, leathery; free growth; [sport of New Penny]

Opa Pötschke – See **Precious Platinum**, HT

Opal HT, mp, 1934, Gaujard; flowers salmon to opal, 5½ in., 45 petals, high-centered; vigorous growth; [Julien Potin × *R. foetida bicolor* seedling]; int. by J&P, 1941

Opal Brünner Cl F, lp, about 1948, Marshall, O.C.; bud very small; flowers blush-pink to pale rose, dbl., borne in large clusters, slight musk fragrance; tall (10 ft.), pillar growth

Opal Gold HT, ab, 1936, Bate; flowers apricot, changing to pink; [sport of Joanna Hill]

Opal Jewel Min, mp, 1962, Morey, Dr. Dennison; bud ovoid; flowers pink, center darker, 1 in., 45 petals; foliage leathery; vigorous, compact (8-10 in.) growth; PP2292; [Mothersday × Rosy Jewel]; int. by J&P, 1962

Opal of Arz HT, ob, 1938, Brownell; flowers variable orange shades, dbl., moderate fragrance; [(sport of Mary Wallace) × unknown]

Opalia – See **White Flower Carpet**, F

Opaline HT, pb, 1922, Lippiatt; flowers pale pink, shaded carmine and old-gold; [Louise Catherine Breslau × Frau Karl Druschki]

Opaline Cl HT, pb, Clause; flowers apricot-pink, lighter at edges, moderate fragrance; foliage large, dark green; int. in 1982

Open Arms Cl Pol, lp, 1995, Warner, Chris; bud peach; flowers shell pink, small, semi-dbl., borne in large clusters, moderate fragrance; foliage small, dark green, glossy; few prickles; spreading, medium growth; PPAF; [Mary Sumner × Laura Ashley]; int. by Warner's Roses; Certificate of Merit, St. Albans, 1993

Open d'Australie HT, yb, Dorieux; int. in 1990

Open Field – See **Heritage**, S

Open Secret F, ab, 1987, Weeks, Michael W.J.; flowers peach to salmon-pink, sometimes flecked darker, shading to white, 5 petals; foliage medium size, medium green, semi-glossy; bushy, tall growth; [sport of Eyepaint]

Opening Act Min, dr, 1993, Jalbert, Brad; flowers medium, single, borne in small clusters, no fragrance; foliage medium size, dark green, glossy; some prickles; medium (30-35 cm.), upright growth; [Anytime × Black Jade]; int. by Select Roses, 1994

Opening Night HT, dr, 1998, Zary, Dr. Keith W.; bud ovoid, pointed; flowers bright, deep red, 4½ in., 25-30 petals, high-centered, borne singly, slight fruity fragrance; foliage medium size, dark green, semi glossy; prickles moderate, straight; upright, tall, slightly spreading growth; PP11265; [Olympiad × Ingrid Bergman]; int. by Bear Creek Gardens, Inc., 1998

Opéra HT, rb, 1950, Gaujard; bud long, pointed; flowers light scarlet-red, base yellow, 6 in., dbl.; foliage leathery, light green; vigorous, erect growth; [La Belle Irisee × seedling]; int. by J&P; Gold Medal, NRS, 1949

Opera, Climbing Cl HT, rb, 1956, Armbrust

Operetta Bailey, Dorothy J., Bailey, Dorothy J.; PP4429

Operettenrose HT, lp

Ophelia HT, lp, 1912, Paul, W.; bud long, pointed; flowers salmon-flesh, center tinted light yellow, 28 petals, moderate fragrance; foliage leathery; vigorous growth; seed parent probably Antoine Rivoire; pollen parent either Mme Caroline Testout, Pharisäer, or Prince de Bulgarie; int. by E. G. Hill, 1914

Ophelia, Climbing Cl HT, lp, 1920, Dickson, A.; flowers soft salmon pink, large, dbl., flat; [sport of Ophelia]

Ophelia Queen, Climbing Cl HT, lp, 1923, Westbury Rose Co.; [sport of Ophelia]

Ophelia Supreme HT, lp, 1917, Dailledouze Bros.; flowers light rose-pink, center darker; [sport of Ophelia]

Ophie O HT, lp, 2001, Adlong, Paula; flowers medium, full, borne mostly singly, slight fragrance; [Crystilline × Elizabeth Taylor]

Ophir HMsk, my, about 1835, Laffay; flowers nankeen yellow, small, full

Ophirie N, op, 1841, Goubault; flowers reddish-copper, reverse rosy and fawn, very dbl., cupped; vigorous growth

Opium! HT, dr, Schreurs; int. by Yates Botanicals, 2002

Oporto HT, dr, 1930, Allen; flowers port-wine-red, petals very leathery, dbl.; [Château de Clos Vougeot × Betty Uprichard]

Optima Orange Min, or, Pouw, A.; flowers very dbl., 40-50 petals, no fragrance; growth low (8-12 in.); containers; PP10820; [seedling × seedling]; int. by De Ruiter's Nieuwe Rosen B.V., 1997

Opulence HT, w, J&P; bud long, pointed ovoid; flowers full, 30-35 petals, high-centered, borne mostly singly and in small clusters, moderate fragrance; good repeat; foliage large, medium green, leathery; prickles medium, 3/8 in., hooked slightly downwards; vigorous growth; PP10667; [Crystalline × Osiana]; greenhouse rose; int. in 1997

Opus Pol, or, VEG; flowers medium to large, semi-dbl.

Or Hatabor HT, dy, Fischel; int. in 1989

Ora Kelly Min, op, Moore, Ralph; flowers peach pink with a light halo, 1½-2 in., 5-10 petals, borne singly and in small clusters; recurrent; vigorous, healthy (18 in.) growth; int. by Sequoia Nursery, 2001

Ora Kingsley S, dr, Clements, John K.; flowers deep velvet crimson, 3 in., 67 petals, borne in clusters; free-flowering; foliage dark green, dense; compact (3½ ft.) growth; PPAF; int. by Heirloom Roses, 1999

Oracle HT, or, Select; int. by Terra Nigra BV, 2003

Oradour F, dr, 1955, Mallerin, C.; flowers dbl.; [Happiness × Demain]; int. by EFR

Orafe HT, pb; int. in 1997

Orana Gold – See **Louise Gardner**, HT

Orange Ace HT, or, Roman, G., and Wagner, S.; flowers deep orange-red, medium to large, 25 petals, slight fragrance; foliage medium size, glossy, healthy; [Rosabunda × Galia]; int. by Res. Stn. for Hort., 1999

Orange Adam F, ob, Adam, M.; int. in 1993

Orange Appeal Min, or, 1995, Rennie, Bruce F.; flowers 2¾ in., very dbl., borne mostly singly; foliage large, medium green, semi-glossy; some prickles; tall (24 in.), spreading, bushy growth; [Justa Little Goofy × seedling]; int. by Rennie Roses International, 1992

Orange Baby – See **Ceres**, Min

Orange Babyflor – See **Ceres**, Min

Orange Beauty Cl F, op, 1961, Raffel; flowers orange to salmon, medium, dbl., high-centered, borne in clusters; foliage glossy; vigorous (6-8 ft.) growth; [Little Darling × Gertrude Raffel]; int. by Port Stockton Nursery, 1961

Orange Beauty Min, ob

Orange Blossom S, w, McLeod, J.; [*R. brunonii* × unknown]; int. in 1990

Orange Blossom Special Cl Min, ob, 1990, Warriner, William A.; bud ovoid, sepals serrated; flowers coral-orange, edges darker, reverse lighter coral pink, small, 55+ petals, high-centered, borne in sprays of 3-9; foliage small, dark green, semi-glossy; prickles straight to hooked down, reddish-green; upright, bushy, tall growth; [Zorina × Andrea]; int. by Bear Creek Gardens, 1990

Orange Bouquet F, ob, 1972, Northfield; flowers coppery orange, turning pink, 2½ in., 25 petals, rosette; foliage dark; upright, free growth; [Masquerade × Paris-Match]

Orange Bunny F, or, 1981, Meilland, Mrs. Marie-Louise; bud pointed; flowers orange-red, reverse darker, 13 petals, cupped, borne singly and in clusters of up to 25; foliage bronze, matte, very dense; bushy growth; [Scherzo × (Sarabande × Frenzy)]; int. by Meilland Et Cie, 1979

Orange Butterfly S, or, Williams, J. Benjamin; flowers orange-red with prominent yellow stamens and eye, single, mass blooming; int. by Hortico, Inc., 1997

Orange Cascade Cl Min, ob, 1979, Moore, Ralph S.; bud pointed; flowers yellow-orange, 1 in., 20 petals, moderate fragrance; foliage small, fern-like; slender, willowy growth; PP4596; [unnamed yellow seedling × Magic Wand]; int. by Sequoia Nursery

Orange Chalice S, ob, Williams, J.B.; flowers delicate light orange, single; foliage dark green and glossy; growth shrub that can be trained as a climber; int. by Hortico, 2003

Orange Charm Min, or, 1983, Williams, Ernest D.; flowers well-formed, small, dbl.; foliage small, medium green, glossy; bushy growth; [Starburst × Over the Rainbow]; int. by Mini-Roses, 1982

Orange Chateau – See **Hatuzakura**, HT

Orange Cheer Pol, ob, 1937, Letts; flowers clear orange, almost, dbl.; vigorous growth

Orange-Cherry Up Min, or, 2006, Hopper, Nancy; flowers full, borne mostly solitary; foliage medium size, medium green, semi-glossy; prickles 1/8 in., brown, few; growth bushy, short (10-12 in.); [orange seedling × Ralph Moore]; int. in 2006

Orange Chiffon F, ob, 1966, Mease; flowers orange-salmon, reverse silvery orange, medium, dbl., cupped; foliage dark, leathery; vigorous, bushy growth; [Little Darling × Goldmarie]; int. by Wyant

Orange Class Min, ob

Orange Classic Min, ob, Spooner; flowers clear orange, dbl., high-centered, moderate fruity fragrance; recurrent; medium growth; int. by Heirloom Roses, 2006

Orange Cluster S, or, Williams, J. Benjamin; flowers orange-red with ivory reverse, medium, dbl., open cup, borne in large clusters, slight fragrance; recurrent; foliage small, medium green; growth to 3 ft.

Orange Combe HT, ob, 1956, Combe; flowers orange, very dbl., globular; vigorous, upright growth; [Charlotte Armstrong × seedling]; int. by Delbard

Orange Cup F, or, 1969, Pal, Dr. B.P.; bud pointed; flowers orange-scarlet, open, medium, single, borne in clusters, intense fragrance; foliage dark, glossy; vigorous, compact growth; [Cocorico × unknown]; int. by Indian Agric. Research Inst., 1965

Orange Darling Cl Min, ob, 1979, Sudol, Julia; flowers orange, 1½ in., 32 petals; foliage dark, leathery; climbing or pillar growth

Orange Dawn F, ob, 1973, Ellick; flowers orange, tinted vermilion, 4 in., 30-35 petals; foliage glossy, dark; vigorous growth; [Orange Sensation × Sutter's Gold]; int. by Excelsior Roses

Orange Delbard HT, or, 1959, Delbard-Chabert; flowers bright orange, well-formed, large, dbl.; strong stems; vigorous growth; [Impeccable × Mme Robert Joffet]

Orange Delight HT, ob, 1950, Verschuren-Pechtold; bud urn shaped; flowers orange, reverse veined red, 5½-6 in., 30 petals, cupped; foliage glossy, dark; vigorous, tall growth; int. by J&P

Orange Delight, Climbing Cl HT, ob, 1957, Verschuren-Pechtold

Orange d'Éte F, rb, Dorieux; int. in 1997

Orange Dot HT, ob, 1963, Dot, Pedro; bud long; flowers carthamus-red, large, 50 petals; bushy growth; [Chrysler Imperial × Soraya]

Orange Drop Min, ob, 1988, Bridges, Dennis A.; flowers soft orange, white at base, reverse soft orange edging veining, 20 petals, high-centered; foliage medium size, medium green, semi-glossy; prickles long, very pointed, medium, light green; bushy, medium, vigorous growth; [Heartland × seedling]; int. by Bridges Roses

Orange Elf Cl Min, ob, 1960, Moore, Ralph S.; bud pointed; flowers orange, fading lighter, small, 25 petals; vigorous, climbing growth; trailer or ground-cover; [Golden Glow × Zee]; int. by Sequoia Nursery, 1959

Orange Elizabeth of Glamis F, ob, 1976, Thames Valley Rose Growers; flowers orange-flame, 3 in., 30 petals, intense fragrance; foliage glossy; compact, bushy growth; [sport of Elizabeth of Glamis]; int. in 1974

Orange Everglow LCl, ob, 1942, Brownell; flowers orange slightly shaded red and yellow, semi-dbl.; [sport of Copper Glow]

Orange Festival HT, op, 1961, Leenders, J.; flowers pink to coral-orange, small; [Souv. de Jacques Verschuren × Serenade]

Orange Fire Min, op, 1975, Moore, Ralph S.; bud short, pointed; flowers orange, pink, carmine, rose, 1 in., 40 petals; foliage very glossy, leathery; upright growth; PP3876; [(*R. wichurana* × Floradora) × Fire Princess]; int. by Sequoia Nursery

Orange Fire F, ob, 1992, Ilsink, Peter; flowers very bright orange, 3¼ in., 15-20 petals, urn-shaped, borne in sprays of 7-12, slight fragrance; foliage large, medium green, matte; upright growth; [Orange Wave × seedling]; int. by Pekmez, 1987

Orange Flame HT, or, 1963, Meilland, Mrs. Marie-Louise; bud ovoid, pointed; flowers 4½-5 in., 33 petals, high-centered, moderate fragrance; foliage leathery, glossy; vigorous growth; PP2141; [Monte Carlo × Radar]; int. by C-P, 1962

Orange Flame F, ob, Williams, J. Benjamin; flowers brilliant orange and yellow blend; growth to 3 ft.; border/container; int. in 1983

Orange Flame HT, ob; PP11036; int. in 1999

Orange Flame Min, or; flowers flame orange; free-flowering

Orange Flare F, ob

Orange Floorshow S, or, Harkness; flowers orange with yellow stamens, semi-dbl., flat, borne in clusters, moderate fragrance; low, spreading (60 × 80 cm.) growth; int. by R. Harkness & Co., 1999

Orange Frenzy Min, ob, 2002, Moore, Ralph S.; flowers dbl., borne mostly solitary, slight fragrance; foliage medium size, medium green, glossy; prickles small, straight, green; growth upright, tall (18-24 in.); containers, garden decorative, cutting; [Avandel × Golden Salmon]; int. by Sequoia Nursery, 2002

Orange Garnet F, or, 1965, Swim & Weeks; bud ovoid; flowers small, dbl.; foliage dark, leathery; vigorous, upright, bushy growth; PP2710; [(Garnette × Circus) × Spartan]

Orange Glory HT, ob, 1936, Leenders, M.; flowers orange, open, large, semi-dbl.; foliage leathery, light; vigorous growth; [seedling × Charles P. Kilham]

Orange Glow Pol, ob, 1936, Verschuren; flowers bright golden orange, borne in large trusses; int. by Dreer

Orange Goliath HT, op, 1978, Gandy, Douglas L.; bud long, pointed; flowers copper-orange, 8 in., 26 petals, moderate fragrance; foliage matte, green; vigorous growth; [Beauté × Serenade]; int. in 1975

Orange Honey Min, ob, 1979, Moore, Ralph S.; bud pointed; flowers orange-yellow, 1½ in., 23 petals, high-centered to cupped, moderate fruity fragrance; foliage matte, green; bushy, spreading growth; PP4496; [Rumba × Over the Rainbow]; int. by Sequoia Nursery

Orange Ice F, or, 1963, Thomson, R.; bud ovoid; flowers light orange-red, 3 in., 25 petals, cupped, borne in clusters; foliage leathery, dark; vigorous, upright, bushy growth; [Fashion × Sumatra]; int. by Tillotson, 1963

Orange Ice F, ob, Williams, J. Benjamin; flowers orange with ivory streaks, semi-dbl.; int. by Hortico, 1999

Orange Ilseta F, ob, 1985, Tantau, Math.; flowers orange; [sport of Ilseta]

Orange Impressionist S, ob, Lim, P, & Twomey, J.; flowers orange, 3½ in., 25 petals; free-flowering; foliage medium green; upright, compact (3 ft.) growth; hardy; PP15738; int. by Bailey Nurseries, 2004

Orange Jade Min, or, 1991, Cole, Catherine W.; flowers medium, full, borne mostly singly, slight fragrance; foliage medium size, dark green, semi-glossy; upright, medium growth; [sport of Black Jade]; int. by East Tennessee Miniature Roses, 1990

Orange Juice F, ob, 1986, Christensen, Jack E.; flowers clear orange, 33 petals, high-centered, borne in sprays of 3-5; prickles long, red; medium, upright, bushy growth; hips ovoid, medium, orange-red; [Katherine Loker × Gingersnap]; int. by Michigan Bulb Co.

Orange Juwel Min, op, 2006; flowers salmon orange, 3 cm., full, borne in small clusters; foliage medium size, dark green; bushy, short (30 cm.) growth; int. by W. Kordes' Söhne, 1987

Orange Kardinal – See **Maharishi**, HT

Orange Killarney – See **Duchess of Wellington**, HT

Orange King Pol, ob, 1922, Cutbush; flowers light coral-red, fading greenish, ¾ in., dbl., open, borne in clusters; foliage glossy, dark; bushy, dwarf growth; [sport of Orléans Rose]

Orange Kordana Min, or, Kordes; containers; int. by W. Kordes Söhne, mid 1990s

Orange Kordana Min, ob, Kordes; flowers bright orange, dbl.; recurrent; growth compact; containers; int. by NewFlora, 2005

Orange Korona F, or, 1961, Morse; flowers orange-scarlet, well-formed, 4 in., 20 petals, borne in clusters; foliage olive-green; vigorous, upright growth; [Bergfeuer × Independence]; int. by Morse & Sons, 1959

Orange Koster Pol, or

Orange Love Min, pb, 1987, Williams, Ernest D.; flowers orange, reverse deeper orange to dark red, fading lighter, 45 petals, high-centered; foliage small, dark green, semi-glossy; prickles very few, short, light tan; upright, bushy, medium growth; no fruit; PP6546; [Tom Brown × Over the Rainbow]; int. by Mini-Roses, 1986

Orange Marmalade Min, ob, 1991, Williams, J. Benjamin; flowers bronze with yellow blend, small, full, borne mostly singly and in small clusters, moderate fragrance; foliage medium size, light green, matte; low, upright, bushy growth; PP6820; [Gingersnap × Orange Honey]

Orange Marvel Pol, op, 1928, Van der Vis; flowers salmon-orange; [sport of Miss Edith Cavell]

Orange Masterpiece F, or, 1970, deRuiter; flowers small, dbl., borne in trusses; foliage dark; bushy growth; [seedling × Orange Sensation]

Orange Meillandina – See **Orange Sunblaze**, Min

Orange Meillandina, Climbing Cl Min, or, 1987, Meilland, Mrs. Marie-Louise; bud small, conical; flowers bright vermilion red, 2 in., 40 petals, cupped, then flat, borne singly or in clusters of 2 or 3, no fragrance; free-flowering; foliage small, medium green, matte; vigorous, upright (5 ft.) growth; PP6817; [sport of Orange Meillandina]; int. in 1986

Orange Mikado F, ob, Tantau

Orange Mini-Wonder – See **Potluck Orange**, Min

Orange Minijet – See **Potluck Orange**, Min

Orange Miss Edith Cavell Pol, ob; flowers medium, full; free-flowering; bushy (50 cm.) growth; int. in 1998

Orange Mist F, ob, 1959, Boerner; flowers orange-salmon to yellow-orange, 4 in., dbl., moderate fragrance; dwarf, bushy growth; PP1757; [Ma Perkins × seedling]; int. by J&P, 1955

Orange Morsdag Pol, ob, 1958, Grootendorst, F.J.; flowers deep orange, dbl., cupped, borne in clusters, slight fragrance; good repeat; upright, low growth; hardy; [sport of Muttertag]; int. by F.J. Grootendorst & Sons, 1956

Orange Mothersday – See **Orange Morsdag**, Pol

Orange Muttertag – See **Orange Morsdag**, Pol

Orange Muttertag – See **Vatertag**, Pol

Orange Nassau HT, ob, 1941, Verschuren; bud long, pointed; flowers two-toned coppery orange, reverse yellow, dbl., cupped; foliage leathery; [Mev. G.A. van Rossem × seedling]; int. by Dreer

Orange Nymph F, or, 1960, Tulp; flowers medium, dbl., borne in small clusters; [sport of Nymph]; int. by G. Maarse

Orange Paillette – See **Absolute Hit**, MinFl

Orange Parfait HT, ob, 1982, Weeks, O.L.; bud ovoid, pointed; flowers orange, yellow reverse, large, 45 petals, high-centered, borne singly, slight tea fragrance; foliage medium to large, bronze green, leathery; prickles long, narrow, hooked downward, reddish at base; vigorous growth; int. by Weeks Wholesale Rose Growers

Orange Parfait Min, ob, Moore; flowers flower clean, soft orange, 1-1½ in., 18 -24 petals, high-centered, no fragrance; recurrent; medium (12-18 in.) growth; int. by Sequoia Nursery, 1998

Orange Passion HT, ob, 1999, Zary, Dr. Keith W.; flowers coral-orange, reverse lighter, 4½-5 in., full, borne mostly singly; foliage large, dark green; prickles moderate; upright growth; PP9330; [Anne Morrow Lindbergh × Angelique]; int. by Bear Creek Gardens, Inc., 1999

Orange Passion F, ob, Dorieux; flowers bright, deep orange, dbl., high-centered, borne in clusters, slight fragrance; good repeat; foliage bronze green; growth to 80-100 cm.; int. by Rose Barni, 2005

Orange Pastel Min, ob, 1997, Williams, J. Benjamin; flowers medium, bright orange-red, reverse dull, 2½-3 in., dbl., borne in small clusters, slight fragrance; foliage medium size, dark green, semi-glossy; few prickles; growth compact, low (12-18in.); [Red Sunblaze × Orange Sunblaze]; int. by Paramount Roses, 1997

Orange Patio Wonder Min, ob, 2004, Jalbert,

Brad; flowers orange, reverse light orange, 1½ in., very full, borne in large clusters, slight fragrance; foliage medium size, medium green, glossy; prickles moderate, small, green; upright, medium (14-16 in.) growth; [Orange Honey × Sexy Rexy]; int. in 1999

Orange Perfection Pol, or, 1927, Spek; [sport of Ideal]

Orange P'ins – See **Gizmo**, Min

Orange Pixie Min, or, 1978, Moore, Ralph S.; bud ovoid, pointed; flowers bright orange-red, 1 in., 48 petals, high-centered; foliage small, glossy, leathery; bushy, compact, upright growth; PP4484; [Little Chief × Fire Princess]; int. by Sequoia Nursery

Orange Queen Pol, op, 1923, van Nes; flowers salmon-orange; [sport of Orléans Rose]

Orange Queen Elizabeth Gr, ob

Orange Rapture HT, op, 1935, Schmidt, K.; bud long, pointed; flowers orange with pink, large, dbl., high-centered; [sport of Rapture]; int. by Kordes

Orange Red Supreme F, or, 1959, Boerner; bud ovoid; flowers open, 2½-3 in., 18-24 petals, borne in clusters, moderate fragrance; foliage glossy, wrinkled; bushy growth; [Spice × Garnette seedling]; int. as Orange-Red Supreme, J&P, 1958

Orange Rosamini Min, or, 1988, deRuiter, George; flowers semi-dbl.; medium growth; PP6236; [seedling × Red Rosamini]; int. by DeRuiters Nieuwe Rozen B.V.

Orange Rosette Pol, or, 1941, deRuiter; flowers scarlet-orange, 1-1¼ in., 30 petals, borne in clusters; vigorous, compact growth; [sport of Gloire du Midi]; int. by J&P

Orange Ruffels HT, ob, 1952, Brownell; bud long, pointed; flowers orange to saffron-yellow, petals frilled, 4-5 in., 40 petals, high-centered, moderate fragrance; foliage dark, glossy; vigorous, compact growth; [(Dr. W. Van Fleet × Général Jacqueminot) × Lafter]

Orange Rumba F, ob, 1962, Zieger; flowers orange; PP2111; [sport of Rumba]; int. by C-P

Orange Sauvageot F, ob, Sauvageot; flowers shining orange, dbl.; foliage matte; int. in 1987

Orange Scepter HT, yb, 1953, Verschuren-Pechtold; flowers orange-yellow with dark golden yellow, large, dbl.

Orange Schoon HT, ob, 1938, Lens; flowers pure orange; [sport of Katharine Pechtold]

Orange Seabreeze MinFl, op, Williams, J. Benjamin; int. in 1996

Orange Sensation F, or, 1961, deRuiter; flowers 3 in., 24 petals, borne in clusters; foliage dark; vigorous, bushy growth; int. by Gregory & Son, 1961; Golden Rose, The Hague, 1968, Gold Medal, NRS, 1961

Orange Sensation, Climbing Cl F, or; [sport of Orange Sensation]

Orange Sherbert Min, ob, 1985, Lyon; flowers orange, small, 35 petals, cupped, borne singly; foliage medium size, medium green, matte; upright growth; [Dandy Lyon × unknown]; int. by M.B. Farm Min. Roses, Inc.

Orange Silk – See **Apricot Silk**, HT

Orange Silk F, or, 1968, McGredy, Sam IV; flowers orange-vermilion, large, dbl., shallow-cupped, borne in large clusters; good repeat; foliage dark, glossy; vigorous, compact growth; [Orangeade × (Ma Perkins × Independence)]; int. by Gregory

Orange Slippers – See **Golden Slippers**, F

Orange Smoke F, ob, 1964, Hennessey; flowers orange, with blue haze in cool weather, 3-4 in.; very vigorous growth; [Orange Ruffels × (Eva × Guinee)]

Orange Sovereign Pol, ob

Orange Sparkle F, ob, 1985, Kordes, R.; flowers bright orange, yellow stamens, semi-dbl., borne in small clusters, moderate fragrance; foliage very glossy; prickles straight, brown; tall, bushy growth; [(Colour Wonder × Zorina) × Uwe Seeler]; int. by Ludwigs Roses Pty. Ltd., 1984

Orange Sparks HT, ob, 1969, Vasishth; flowers orange-vermilion blend, striped gold, medium, dbl.; foliage glossy, bronze; vigorous, bushy growth; [sport of Cherry Brandy]

Orange Special F, or, 1958, deRuiter; flowers orange-scarlet, 1½ in., 30-35 petals, cupped, borne in large trusses; dwarf, bushy growth; [sport of Salmon Perfection]; int. by Blaby Rose Gardens, 1957

Orange Spice Min, ob, 1980, Lyon; bud ovoid, pointed; flowers orange, deeper on petal edges, 23 petals, cupped, borne singly or several together, moderate fragrance; foliage small, medium green; prickles recurved; bushy, upright growth; [seedling × seedling]

Orange Spice Min, ob, 1985, Eagle, Barry & Dawn; flowers orange, yellow reverse, small, 25 petals, borne singly and in small clusters; foliage small, medium green; prickles very few; short, compact, very bushy growth; [Over the Rainbow × Over the Rainbow]; int. by Southern Cross Nursery

Orange Splash F, ob, 1991, Christensen, Jack E.; flowers bright orange to orange-red with white and lighter orange stripes and flecks, 3-3½ in., dbl., borne in small clusters, moderate fragrance; foliage large, dark green, glossy; some prickles; medium (75-90 cm.), upright, bushy growth; [seedling × seedling]; int. by Bear Creek Gardens, 1992

Orange Splendor F, ob, Select Roses, B.V.; int. in 1998

Orange Star Min, ob, 1987, Williams, Ernest D.; bud short, pointed; flowers orange, reverse orange with yellow at base, non-fading, 1½ in., 35 petals, high-centered, borne usually singly, intense damask fragrance; foliage small, medium green, semi-glossy; prickles few, tan, dilated at base, hooked slightly downward; stems thin, wiry; bushy, upright, medium growth; PP6893; [Tom Brown × unnamed miniature seedling]; int. by Mini-Roses

Orange Starina Min, ob, 1982, Graff, Roy; bud pointed; flowers light orange, 30 petals, high-centered, borne mostly singly, moderate fragrance; foliage small; abundant growth; [sport of Starina]; int. by Mini Roses, 1981

Orange Sunblaze Min, or, 1982, Meilland, Mrs. Marie-Louise; flowers non-fading deep orange, 1½-2 in., 40 petals, cupped, borne 1-3 per cluster; foliage small, light green, matte; prickles straw-brown; upright, bushy (15 in.) growth; drops spent blooms; PP4682; [Parador × (Baby Bettina × Duchess of Windsor)]; int. by C-P, 1981

Orange Sunblaze, Climbing – See **Orange Meillandina, Climbing**, Cl Min

Orange Sunset Min, ob, 1996, Mander, George; flowers salmon-orange inside, some yellow stripes, orange-yellow reverse, 1½-2 in., full; foliage medium size, dark green, glossy; some prickles; medium (40-50 cm.), bushy growth; [June Laver × Rubies 'n' Pearls]; int. by Select Roses, 1996

Orange Sunshine Min, ob, 1968, Moore, Ralph S.; flowers orange; [sport of Bit o' Sunshine]; int. by Sequoia Nursery

Orange Supreme HT, ob

Orange Surprise F, ob; int. in 1998

Orange Sweetheart F, op, 1952, Boerner; bud ovoid; flowers 3-3½ in., 20-25 petals, cupped, slight fruity fragrance; foliage dark; upright, bushy growth; [(Pinocchio × unknown) × Fashion]; int. by J&P

Orange Symphonie Min, or, 1994, Meilland, Alain A.; flowers orange vermilion, large, full, borne mostly singly or in small clusters, no fragrance; foliage medium size, dark green, semi-glossy; some prickles; low (35-45 cm.), bushy growth; [(Baby Bettina × Anytime) × Meteor]; int. by SNC Meilland & Cie, 1993

Orange Tango HT, or, 1973, McDaniel, G. K.; flowers large, very dbl., high-centered; foliage bronze; vigorous growth; PP3407; [from unnamed seedlings]; int. by Carlton Rose Nurseries, 1972

Orange Thérèse HT, ob, 1943, Howard Rose Co.; flowers orange-yellow; [sport of Soeur Thérèse]

Orange Thor S, ob, Pedersen, Thor; flowers orange with touch of yellow, 5-10 petals, slight fragrance; free-flowering; growth to 2-3 ft.; int. in 1976

Orange Time Min, ob, Bell, Laurie; flowers bright orange, borne in large clusters; good repeat; short growth; int. by Bell Roses

Orange Treasure HT, ob; int. by InterState Nurseries, 2001

Orange Triumph Pol, mr, 1937, Kordes; flowers small, semi-dbl., cupped, borne in clusters; foliage glossy; compact, bushy growth; [Eva (HMsk) × Solarium]; int. by Dreer; Gold Medal, NRS, 1937

Orange Triumph, Climbing Cl Pol, mr, 1945, Leenders, M.; flowers salmon orange-red, 2 in., semi-dbl., borne in medium to large clusters, no fragrance; [sport of Orange Triumph]; int. by Koopmann, 1948

Orange Triumph Improved Pol, or, 1960, Cant, F.; flowers orange, dbl., borne in large clusters; [sport of Orange Triumph]

Orange Triumph Superba Pol, ob, 1953, Maarse, J.D.; flowers clear orange; [sport of Orange Triumph]

Orange Twist Min, ob, 1986, Moore, Ralph S.; flowers tannish-orange; [sport of Sungold]; same as parent except for color; int. by Moore Min. Roses, 1985

Orange Unique HT, ob, Pouw ; bud medium, ovate; flowers medium orange with yellow at base, reverse rose pink, 3-4 in., 24 petals, star-shaped, borne mostly singly, slight fragrance; good repeat; foliage small to medium size, semi-glossy; few prickles; long stems; growth vigorous, narrow, tall (6 ft.); PP10674; [seedling × seedling]; int. by deRuiter, 1996

Orange Van Gogh F, ob, Williams, J.B.; flowers orange with white stripes and splashes, semi-dbl., cupped, borne in clusters; int. by Hortico, 2002

Orange Velvet LCl, or, 1987, Williams, J. Benjamin; flowers bright orange-red with dark velvet overlay, reverse orange-red to orange pink, fading to orange-pink, with dark velvet overlay on inside petals, large, 37 petals, high-centered, borne singly and in sprays of 3-5, moderate damask fragrance; foliage large, dark green, glossy, dark-waxed; upright, tall, vigorous growth; hips medium, rounded, medium bright orange; PP6596; [Tropicana, Climbing × Swarthmore]; int. in 1977

Orange Vilmoria – See **Uwe Seeler**, F

Orange Vilmorin – See **Uwe Seeler**, F

Orange Wave F, ob; int. by Hortico, 2001

Orange Waves S, ob, Clements, John; flowers velvety true orange painted with scarlet toward the petal edges, 3½-4 in., 12-18 petals, slight clove fragrance; growth 3½ ft. tall and wide; PPAF; int. by Heirloom Roses, 2005

Orange You Happy Min, ob, 2006, Hopper, Nancy; flowers orange, reverse white, 2½ in., dbl., borne mostly solitary; foliage medium size, medium green, semi-glossy; prickles 1/4 in., yellow, few; growth bushy, medium (13-14 in.); [orange seedling × orange seedling]; int. in 2006

Orange Zest Min, or, 1994, Laver, Keith G.; flowers medium, very dbl., borne mostly singly; foliage small, dark green, semi-glossy; few prickles; upright, bushy (25 cm.) growth; [seedling × Painted Doll]; int. by Springwood Roses, 1994

Orangeade F, or, 1960, McGredy, Sam IV; flowers bright scarlet orange, wide, semi-dbl., borne in clusters; foliage dark; very vigorous, bushy growth; hips large, ribbed, orange; [Orange Sweetheart × Independence]; int. by McGredy & Son, 1959; Gold Medal, Portland, 1965, Gold Medal, NRS, 1959

Orangeade, Climbing Cl F, or, 1964, Waterhouse Nursery

Oranges 'n' Lemons S, ob, 1994, McGredy, Sam IV; flowers striking orange and yellow striped, 3-3½ in., full, borne in small clusters, slight fruity fragrance; foliage medium to large, dark red when new, turning dark green; some prickles; tall, spreading, very vigorous growth; PP9191; [New Year × (Freude × seedling)]; int. by Weeks Roses, 1995

Orangextra F, ob; int. by Roseraies Dorieux, 2001

Orangina F, or, 1983, Orard, Joseph; [sport of Royal Occasion]; int. by Paul Pekmez

Oraniën F, or, 1962, Verschuren, A.; flowers orange-red, sometimes lined yellow, base light yellow, large, 42 petals; foliage dark; upright, compact, symmetrical growth; [Highlight × seedling]; int. by van Engelen

Oranzova Garnette F, or, Strnad

Orapent – See **Côte Jardins**, F

Oratam D, pb, 1939, Jacobus; bud globular; flowers pink edged copper-pink, base and reverse yellow, large, dbl., intense damask fragrance; non-recurrent; foliage leathery, dark, matte, yellow-green; bushy, tall (5-6 ft.) growth; [*R.* × *damascena* × Souv. de Claudius Pernet]; int. by B&A

Oratia Maid F, lp, Garelja, Anita; int. in 1986

Oratorio – See **Spellbinder**, HT

Orchard's Pride HT, pb, 2006, Coiner, Jim; flowers dbl., borne mostly solitary; foliage medium size, light green, matte; prickles ½ in., triangle, light green, moderate; growth upright, medium (4½ ft.); garden; [seedling × seedling]; int. by Coiner Nursery, 2006

Orchid Jubilee Cl Min, m, 1992, Moore, Ralph S.; flowers mauve blend, holds color well in heat, large, dbl., borne in small clusters, no fragrance; profuse repeat bloom; foliage medium size, medium green, matte; few prickles; tall (2 m.), upright, climbing growth; [(Little Darling × Yellow Magic) × Make Believe]; int. by Sequoia Nursery, 1993

Orchid Lace Min, m, Benardella, Frank A.; flowers lilac to lavender, well formed, moderate fragrance; free-flowering; bushy growth; int. in 1995

Orchid Masterpiece HT, m, 1961, Boerner; bud ovoid, deep orchid; flowers lavender-orchid, large, 68 petals, moderate fruity fragrance; foliage leathery, dark; vigorous growth; PP2039; [Golden Masterpiece × Grey Pearl seedling]; int. by J&P, 1960

Orchid Masterpiece, Climbing Cl HT, m, Buckner, G.; PP3566; [sport of Orchid Masterpiece]

Orchid Melody HT, m, Benardella, Frank; flowers dark lilac, paling to light lilac as they open, dbl.; foliage glossy; int. by Bell Roses, 2003

Orderic Vital – See **Oderic Vital**, HP

Oregold HT, dy, 1970, Tantau, Math.; flowers dbl., high-centered, borne mostly singly; foliage large, glossy, dark; vigorous, upright, bushy growth; PP3415; [Piccadilly × Colour Wonder]; int. as Silhouette, Wheatcroft Bros., 1970

Oregon Centennial HT, mr, 1959, Von Abrams; bud pointed; flowers rose-red, 4-5 in., 30-35 petals, high-centered to cupped, moderate fruity fragrance; foliage dark; long, strong stems; vigorous, upright, bushy growth; PP1914; [Charles Mallerin × (Charles Mallerin × Chrysler Imperial)]; int. by Peterson & Dering, 1959

Oregon Ophelia HT, mp, 1921, Clarke Bros.; flowers salmon, edged pink, base yellow, dbl.; [sport of Ophelia]

Oregon Rainbow Min, yb, 1991, Clements, John K.; bud high-pointed; flowers golden yellow, shaded and edged red, medium, full, high-centered, no fragrance; foliage small, dark green, semi-glossy; medium (40 cm.), bushy growth; [seedling × seedling]; int. by Heirloom Old Garden Roses, 1991

Oregon Trail S, op, Clements, John; flowers deep pink, amber and bronze blended together, 5 in., 40+ petals, old fashioned; foliage deep green with a bluish tone; vigorous (4½ × 3½ ft.) growth; PPAF; int. by Heirloom, 2004

Oreseed – See **Valerie Howard**, HT

Oreste Sgaravatti HT, Sgaravatti, A.

Orfeo LCl, dr, Leenders, J.; flowers bright crimson, fading to cerise, 4 in., full, borne in clusters, moderate fragrance; [Curly Pink × Guinée]; int. in 1963

Organdi HT, dr

Orgeuil de Lyon HP, mr, 1886, Besson; flowers velvety poppy crimson, highlighted vermilion, medium, dbl.; nearly thornless

Oriana HT, rb, 1970, Tantau, Math.; flowers cherry-red, reverse white, 5 in., 38 petals; foliage glossy, dark; int. by Wheatcroft & Sons

Oribe HT, r, Hiroshima; int. by Hiroshima Bara-en, 1995

Orient HT, dr, 1959, Dot, Simon; bud pointed; flowers crimson becoming vermilion, reverse vermilion with yellow base, 22 petals; [Queen of Bermuda × Henri Mallerin]

Orient Express HT, or, 1978, Wheatcroft; flowers deep orange-red, reverse lighter, 4-5 in., 40 petals, intense fragrance; foliage bronze; vigorous growth; [Sunblest × seedling]

Orient Express – See **Love and Peace**, HT

Orient Silk HT, my, 1996, Viraraghavan, M.S. Viru; bud golden; flowers large, clear yellow with darker centers, 5 in., full, borne mostly singly, moderate fragrance; foliage large, medium green, semi-glossy; no prickles; upright, medium (3 ft.) growth; [Mme Charles Sauvage × seedling]; int. as Ahimsa, Hortico Roses, 1996

Orient Spice HT, m, 1996, Viraraghavan, M.S.; flowers pinkish lilac, 5 in., full, borne mostly singly, intense fragrance; foliage large, medium green, semi-glossy; prickles moderate; bushy, medium growth; [Violaine × Margaret Merrill]; int. by Anand Roses, 1984

Oriental S, op, Poulsen; flowers 8-10 cm., semi-dbl., no fragrance; foliage dark; growth bushy, 40-60 cm.; PP11622; int. in 1999

Oriental Charm HT, or, 1961, Duehrsen; bud globular; flowers 3-4 in., 11 petals; foliage leathery, glossy, dark; vigorous, upright, bushy growth; PP2106; [(Charlotte Armstrong × Gruss an Teplitz) × (Mme Butterfly × Floradora)]; int. by Elmer Roses Co., 1960

Oriental Dawn – See **Asagumo**, HT

Oriental Emporer Cl Min, or, deRuiter (?); flowers lacquer orange-red; free flowering; 7-8 ft. growth; [sport of Minimo]; int. by Heirloom Roses, 1999

Oriental Glamour F, mr, 1972, Gandy, Douglas L.; flowers orient red, 4-5 in., 15 petals, high-centered; foliage bronze; free growth; [Coup de Foudre × Tropicana]

Oriental Palace – See **Oriental**, S

Oriental Queen Ch, or, 1926, McGredy; flowers brilliant orange-scarlet, base yellow, fading to vivid carmine, 26 petals; foliage dark; prickles few thorns; int. by Beckwith

Oriental Simplex Min, or, 1987, Williams, Ernest D.; flowers bright orange-red, reverse creamy yellow, aging deeper, non-fading, small, 5 petals, flat, borne usually singly, no fragrance; foliage small, medium green, glossy; prickles tan, declining, dilated at base; upright, bushy, medium growth; hips none observed; [(Starburst × Over the Rainbow) × Little Chief]; int. by Mini-Roses

Oriental Staer HT, op, 2006, Yasuda, Yuji; flowers full, borne mostly solitary; foliage medium size, medium green, matte; prickles medium, numerous; growth upright, medium (1 m.); garden decorative, cutting; [seedling × Laura]; int. in 2006

Orientale Cl HT, op, 1946, Robichon; flowers coral, becoming old-rose, 5 in., dbl., borne mostly solitary, moderate fragrance; free, recurrent boom; foliage glossy; very vigorous growth; not dependably hardy; [George Dickson × Mrs Pierre S. duPont]

Oriflamme D, rb, 1819, Bozérian; flowers red, marbled

Oriflamme HMult, pb, 1914, Paul, G.; flowers deep rose-pink, suffused coppery gold, 2½ in., semi-dbl. to dbl., borne in small clusters, moderate fragrance; foliage dark green, glossy; vigorous, climbing growth

Oriflamme de St Louis HP, dp, 1858, Baudry & Hamel; flowers brilliant rose-crimson, very large, full; [Général Jacqueminot × unknown]

Origami F, pb, 1987, Christensen, Jack & Carruth, Tom; flowers clear, soft pink, outstanding form, medium, 25 petals, high-centered, borne usually singly, moderate spicy fragrance; foliage medium size, medium green, semi-glossy; prickles normal, light green-tan; upright, bushy, medium growth; [Coquette × Zorina]; int. by Armstrong Nursery, 1986

Orihime HT, pb, 1986, Itami Rose Nursery; flowers light pink flushed rose pink, reverse pearly light pink; [sport of Confidence]; int. in 1983

O'Rilla HT, r, 1996, Sheldon, John, Jennifer & Robyn; flowers 5-7 in., full, high-centered, borne mostly singly, slight fragrance; foliage medium size, dark green, semi-glossy; prickles moderate; upright, medium (3-4 ft.) growth; [Lanvin × First Prize]

Orimanda HT, dr, 1976, Kordes; bud long, pointed; flowers large, 27 petals, high-centered; foliage glossy, dark; vigorous, upright, bushy growth; [Duftwolke × seedling]; int. by Willemse, 1975

Orinda HSpn, ly, 1922, Central Exp. Farm; flowers deep cream to amber, medium, dbl.; profuse, non-recurrent bloom; foliage soft, dark; vigorous (5 ft.), bushy growth; [Harison's Yellow × unknown]

Oriola – See **Maiden Voyage**, F

Oriole HMult, ly, 1912, Lambert, P.; bud yellowish-pink; flowers creamy yellowish-white, small, dbl., rounded, borne in large tight clusters, moderate fragrance; foliage dark green, glossy; vigorous, climbing growth; [Aglaia × unknown]

Orion F, mr, 1968, Harkness; flowers scarlet, medium, dbl.; foliage glossy; [Pink Parfait × Red Dandy]

Orion Gr, ob, Williams, J.B.; flowers orange-yellow, borne in large clusters, moderate fragrance; growth to 5 ft.; int. by Hortico, Inc., 2004

Orione HT, ob

Orlando HT, pb, Ilsink; bud pointed; flowers medium pink with darker pink edges, 20-24 petals, high-centered, 11-12 cm., borne mostly singly, no fragrance; foliage large, dark green, glossy; PP9706; int. in 1995

Orlando Sport – See **Light Orlando**, HT

Orlando Sunshine Min, pb, 1992, Williams, Michael C.; flowers pink and yellow blend, large, dbl., borne mostly singly; foliage large, medium green, semi-glossy; some prickles; medium (18-24 in.), bushy growth; [seedling × unnamed miniature seedling]; int. by The Mini Rose Garden

Orléans Improved Pol, mp, 1931, Norfolk Nursery; flowers vivid rose-pink; [sport of Orléans Rose]

Orléans Rose Pol, rb, 1909, Levavasseur; flowers vivid rosy crimson, center white, semi-dbl.; repeat bloom; foliage glossy; vigorous, bushy growth; [Mme Norbert Levavasseur × unknown]

Orléans Rose, Climbing Cl Pol, rb, 1913, Levavasseur

Orléans Simmgen Pol, dr, 1925, Simmgen

Ormiston Roy S, dy, 1953, Doorenbos; flowers large, single; non-recurrent; bushy (3 ft.) growth; [*R. spinosissima* × *R. xanthina*]

Ornella Muti HT, pb

Ornement de Carafe – See **Ornement de Parade**, HGal

Ornement de la Nature HGal, m, before 1813; flowers deep lilac-rose, large, full, slight fragrance; from Holland

Ornement de Parade HGal, dp, before 1811, from Holland; flowers varying from deep pink to violet-purple, 3 in., semi-dbl., moderate fragrance; foliage oval, deeply toothed; nearly thornless

Ornement des Bosquets HSem, dp, 1860, Jamain, H.; flowers dark pink, aging to lilac pink, 5 cm., dbl., borne in clusters of 10-15; foliage small, glaucous; sometimes classed as Bslt

Ornement du Luxembourg HP, m, 1840, Hardy; flowers violet/red, small, dbl.

Orphée de Lille – See **Marie-Louise**, D

Orpheline de Juillet HGal, m, before 1836, Parmentier or Vibert; flowers crimson-purple, base of petals fiery red with occasional striping, very dbl.; erect, moderate growth; int. by Prior to 1837

Orphèse – See **Orphise**, HGal

Orpheus HT, op, 1965, Verschuren, A.; flowers salmon-orange, medium, 35-40 petals; foliage glossy, dark; long stems; vigorous growth; [Montezuma × seedling]; int. by Stassen, 1963

Orphise HGal, m, before 1826, Vibert; flowers purple crimson, large, full

Orpington Gem HT, or, 1953, Buckwell; bud long, pointed; flowers coppery orange shaded gold, 3 in., 32 petals; foliage dark, leathery; vigorous growth; [Princess Marina × Alamein]

Orpington Jewel HT, op, 1953, Buckwell; bud very long; flowers coral-pink shaded coppery, base orange, 3 in., 30 petals; foliage dark, leathery; vigorous growth; [Princess Marina × Picture]

Orsola Spinola – See **Marquise Spinola**, S

Osahachi Min, w; int. in 1997

Oscar S, pb, Hauser; int. in 1994

Oscar Chauvry N, mp, 1900, Chauvry; flowers deep China pink on golden ground, purple reverse, 8-10 cm., dbl., borne in small, tight, clusters, moderate fragrance; numerous prickles; [Elise Heymann × unknown]

Oscar II, Roi de Suéde HP, mr, 1889, Soupert & Notting; bud long; flowers carmine-vermilion with silvery reflections, large, very dbl., moderate fragrance

Oscar Leclerc M, dr, 1853, Robert; flowers red, tinged with violet, spotted with white, 2-2½ in., full; some repeat; foliage dark green; growth upright

Oshun S, ab, 2004, Barden, Paul; flowers apricot-orange, reverse lighter apricot, 4 in., very full, borne in small clusters, intense rose and citrus fragrance; foliage medium size, dark green, glossy, very disease-resistant; prickles ½ in., hooked, brown, moderate; growth bushy, medium (4 to 7 ft.); specimen, middle border, small climber; [Abraham Darby × Abraham Darby]; holds its color well in hot weather; int. in 2004

Osiana HT, ab, Tantau; bud large, pointed ovoid; flowers pastel cream, slightly darker in the center, 5-6 in., 30 -35 petals, high-centered, borne mostly singly, moderate fragrance; good repeat; foliage large, long, dark green, leathery; prickles few, medium (¼ in.), hooked downward; stems long, strong; vigorous, upright, branching growth; PP7660; [seedling × seedling]; int. by Rosen Tantau, 1988

Osiria HT, rb, 1979, Kordes, W.; bud long, pointed; flowers dark red, white reverse, 4½ in., 50 petals, high-centered, intense fragrance; short stems; vigorous, upright, bushy growth; [Snowfire × seedling]; int. by Willemse, 1978

Osjen HT, dp; flowers carmine-pink, medium, dbl.

Oskar Cordel – See **Oskar Kordel**, HP

Oskar Kordel HP, mp, 1897, Lambert, P.; flowers carmine, large, 40 petals, cupped, moderate fragrance; vigorous, compact growth; [Merveille de Lyon × Andre Schwartz]

Oskar Scheerer S, dr, 1961, Kordes, R.; flowers velvety dark red, large, dbl., borne in large clusters; vigorous (6 ft.), well-branched growth

Osmunda Pol, dr, 1923, Holland (?); flowers dark carmine; [sport of Jessie]

Ostara F, mr, 1964, deRuiter; flowers bright red, medium, dbl., borne in clusters; foliage dark; [Highlight × Valeta]

Ostrava S, mr, Vecera, L.

Oswald Sieper HT, w, 1933, Krause; bud long, pointed; flowers creamy white, very large, dbl., high-centered; foliage glossy; vigorous growth; [Mrs Charles Lamplough × Ville de Paris]; int. by C-P

Otago Min, or, 1978, McGredy, Sam IV; flowers medium, 35 petals, high-centered; bushy growth; [Anytime × Minuette]; int. by McGredy Roses International

Othello HT, dr, 1911, Paul; flowers dark maroon red, large, full; [unrecorded × Gustav Grünerwald]

Othello F, or, 1961, Leenders, J.; flowers light orange-red, 2½ in., 22 petals, cupped; [Ma Perkins × Cocorico]

Othello HT, mr, 1965, Verschuren, A.; flowers velvety bright red, large, 48-60 petals, moderate fragrance; foliage dark; vigorous, upright, bushy growth; [New Yorker × seedling]; int. by Stassen, 1964

Othello S, mr, 1991, Austin, David; bud medium, broad with flat top; flowers clear red, fading to purple-red, 4-5 in., 78 petals, cupped, borne usually singly, intense old rose fragrance; recurrent; foliage dark green, semi-glossy; prickles many large thorns; vigorous, bushy growth; PP7212; [Lilian Austin × The Squire]; int. by David Austin Roses, Ltd., 1989

Othello Maure de Venise HCh, m, before 1828, from Angers; flowers dark violet with garnet purple, medium, full

Otohime HT, or, 1977, Keisei Rose Nurseries, Inc.; bud pointed; flowers 6-6½ in., 58 petals, high-centered, moderate fragrance; foliage large, glossy, dark; vigorous growth; [(Hawaii × Tropicana) × (Tropicana × Peace)]

Otome Pink HT, pb, 1967, Rumsey, R.H.; flowers salmon-pink, reverse buff-yellow; [sport of Amatsu Otome]

Otto Krause HT, dy, 1931, Weigand, C.; flowers coppery yellow, large, dbl., high-centered; foliage soft, glossy, bronze,dark; vigorous growth; [Mme Caroline Testout × Souv. de Claudius Pernet]

Otto Miller HT, mr, 1968, Morey, Dr. Dennison; bud long, pointed; flowers deep red, 6 in., dbl., high-centered; foliage glossy, leathery; vigorous, upright growth; [(Chrysler Imperial × Independence) × (Mrs Charles Russell × Happiness)]; int. by General Bionomics

Otto von Bismarck HT, mp, 1908, Kiese; flowers large, dbl.; [Mme Caroline Testout × La France]

Oudtshoorn Joy HT, ob, Kordes; bud egg-shaped; flowers vermilion, large, long-lasting, dbl., high-centered, borne singly and in clusters, slight fragrance; free-flowering; vigorous, medium to tall growth; int. in 1988

Oui Min, dr, 2005, Barden, Paul; flowers deep red, reverse medium pink-red, ½ in., semi-dbl., borne in small clusters, no fragrance; foliage small, dark green, semi-glossy; prickles 1/16 in., straight; growth compact, very bushy, short, 8 in; specimen, containers; [Oakington Ruby × Little Chief]; int. in 2006

Ouma Smuts F, ly, 1950, Leenders, M.; flowers straw-yellow shaded rosy flesh; [Egalite × Vanessa]

Our Allies Pol, lp, 1915, Matthews, W.J.

Our Annie HT, op, 1937, Letts; flowers vivid orange-cerise, large, dbl., globular; foliage glossy; very vigorous growth

Our Baby Min, pb, 2002, Bossom, Bill; flowers very full, borne in small clusters, intense fragrance; foliage small, medium green, matte; prickles very small, very few; growth upright, medium (2 ft.); garden decorative, containers; [seedling × seedling]

Our Beth S, lp, 2006, Beales, Amanda; flowers full, borne in small clusters; foliage medium green, semi-glossy; prickles average, hooked, moderate; growth bushy, medium (4 ft.); landscape, containers; [Louise Odier × English Miss]; int. by Peter Beales Roses, 2006

Our Bob HT, mr, 1928, Dawes; flowers velvety red, center golden

Our Copper Queen – See **Kupferkönigin**, HT

Our Coral Pearl Min, op, 1991, Osburn, Dr. William; flowers coral-salmon-pink, petals quill, large, full, borne mostly singly; foliage medium size, medium green, semi-glossy; prickles few, tan, straight and sharp; medium growth; [sport of Minnie Pearl]

Our Daughter MinFl, mp, 2001, Bossom, Bill; flowers 2¼ in., very full, rosette, borne in small clusters, intense fragrance; foliage small, dark green, semi-glossy; prickles ¼ in., hooked down, moderate; growth compact, low (20 in.); garden decorative, containers; [Sexy Rexy × Suffolk]

Our Diana HT, mp, 1998, Twomey, Jerry; flowers pink, reverse medium pink, 5 in., dbl., borne singly, drops clean; foliage medium size, medium green, semi-glossy; some prickles; bushy, medium growth

Our Esther – See **Esther**, HT

Our Freedom HT, rb, Diby; flowers red with white stripes and splashes; [sport of Mon Cheri]; int. in 2005

Our George Min, ab, Kirkham, Gordon; flowers

apricot-orange, golden yellow in summer heat, dbl., cupped; recurrent; foliage dense; stems long; medium (18-24 in.), speading growth; int. in 1999

Our Hilda F, dp, Bees

Our Indira HT, w, Viraraghavan, M.S.; bud long, pointed; flowers ivory, edged lilac, moderate fragrance; int. in 1998

Our Jane HT, yb, 2001, Horner, Colin P.; flowers yellow tinged red, pale yellow reverse, 7 cm., dbl., borne mostly solitary, moderate fragrance; foliage medium size, medium green, glossy; prickles few, small, curved; stems flexible, upright; growth upright, tall (130 cm.); garden decorative; [Tynwald × (Baby Love × Amber Queen)]; int. by Warley Rose Gardens, 2003

Our Joy F, pb, 1997, Horner, Heather M.; flowers candy pink, silver reverse, 3 in., dbl., borne in small clusters; foliage medium size, semi-glossy; prickles moderate; upright (80 cm.) growth; [seedling × seedling]; int. by Battersby Roses, 1997

Our Jubilee HT, ob, 1986, Cocker, James & Sons; flowers medium, 20 petals; foliage medium size, medium green, semi-glossy; upright growth; [Yellow Pages × Silver Jubilee]

Our Julie F, dp, 2003, Rawlins, R.; flowers light primrose red, reverse primrose, medium, single, borne in small clusters, slight fragrance; foliage light green, semi-glossy; prickles 1½ cm., hooked; growth compact, short (24 in.); garden; [Sunset Boulevard × LF × BQ/S]; int. in 2004

Our Lady F, mr, 1956, Leenders, M.; flowers carmine; vigorous growth; [seedling × Soestdijk]

Our Lady of Guadalupe F, pb, 2000, Zary, Keith; flowers light pink, reverse medium pink, 8-9 cm., 25 petals, borne in small clusters, moderate fragrance; foliage medium size, dark green, glossy; prickles moderate; growth upright, medium (80-90 cm.); [Jacsedi × Jacsim]; int. as Shining Hope, Bear Creek Gardens, 2001

Our Little Secret Min, w, 2002, Umsawasdi, Dr. Theera & Chantana; flowers white with pink edge, medium, full, borne in small clusters, no fragrance; foliage medium size, dark green, glossy; prickles average, curved, moderate; growth upright, medium (24 in.); garden decorative; [Loving Touch × Rainbow's End]; int. by Certified Roses, Inc., 2002

Our Love HT, yb, 1984, Anderson's Rose Nurseries; flowers yellow-orange; [sport of Doris Tysterman]

Our Molly S, mr, 1994, Dickson, Colin; flowers currant red with a silvery white eye, medium, 5 petals, borne in large clusters, no fragrance; foliage medium size, medium green; some prickles; tall (90 cm.), spreading growth; hips orange; int. as Bright Eyes, Treloar Roses; Gold Medal, Glasgow, 1996

Our Pearl LCl, pb, 1993, Jerabek, Paul E.; flowers white with pink edges, medium, 13-18 petals, semi-dbl. to double, borne in small clusters; foliage medium size, medium green, matte; some prickles; medium (7 ft.), bushy, spreading growth; Bronze Medal, ARC TG, 1993

Our Princess F, dr, 1949, Robinson, H.; flowers deep velvety crimson, semi-dbl., borne in large trusses; foliage glossy, dark; vigorous growth; [Donald Prior × Orange Triumph]; int. by Baker's Nursery

Our Rodeo F, rb, Kordes; int. in 1997

Our Rosamond HT, pb, 1982, Bell, Ronald J.; flowers silver and pink blend, large, 35 petals, high-centered, borne singly; foliage medium size, medium green, glossy; upright growth; [(Daily Sketch × unknown) × Red Planet]; int. by Treloar Roses Pty. Ltd., 1983

Our Rosy Carpet – See **Palmengarten Frankfurt**, S

Our Sacha – See **Sacha**, HT

Our Shirley HT, w, 1989, Wilson, George D.; bud pointed; flowers medium, 28 petals, borne singly; foliage small, medium size, dark green; prickles long, slender, red; medium, upright growth; [Judith Morton × Sylvia]

Our Son MinFl, mr, 2001, Bossom, Bill; flowers 2 in., dbl., borne in small clusters, moderate fragrance; foliage small, dark green, semi-glossy; prickles ¼ in., moderate; growth compact, bushy (20 in.); garden decorative, containers; [Sexy Rexy × Suffolk]

Our Sweet Ann F, op, 1976, Horsfield; flowers warm pink, with orange glow, 3½-4 in., 28 petals, intense fragrance; foliage dark, leathery; vigorous, upright growth; [Queen Elizabeth × Elizabeth of Glamis]; int. by Pot House Mill Farm

Our Terry MinFl, dr, 2001, Webster, Robert; flowers 3 in., full, borne mostly solitary; foliage medium size, dark green, glossy; prickles 10 mm., hooked, moderate; growth compact, medium (24 in.); bedding; [Sealady × Poulvue]; int. by Handley Rose Nurseries, 2003

Our Town Min, mp, 1986, Zipper, H.; flowers small, semi-dbl., borne in small sprays; foliage small, medium green, semi-glossy; spreading growth; [Maytime × Sheri Anne]; int. by Magic Moment Miniature Roses

Our Vanilla – See **Vanilla**, F

Our Victory – See **Nacha Pobeda**, HT

Out of Africa HT, ob, Kordes; flowers bronze, apricot and orange, 4 in., dbl., high-centered, moderate nutty, tea fragrance; free-flowering; growth to 3½ ft.; int. in 1997

Out of Canada HT, pb, Williams, J. Benjamin; flowers peach and ivory blend, yellow stamens, dbl., intense fragrance; foliage dark green; int. by Hortico Inc., 1998

Out of India HG, mr, 2005, Viraraghavan, M.S. Viru; flowers medium red, changing to purple, 4 in., dbl., borne in small clusters; foliage large, semi-glossy; prickles few, small, straight, grey; growth bushy, medium (4 ft.); garden decorative; [Carefree Beauty × (Bonica × Sirohi Sunrise)]; int. by Roses Unlimited, 2006

Out of the Night S, w, 2006, Moore, Ralph S.; flowers full, borne in small clusters; foliage medium size, medium green, semi-glossy; prickles small, hooked, brown, moderate; growth compact (2-2½ ft.); containers, borders; [Yellow Jewel × Out of Yesteryear]; int. by Sequoia Nurs., 2006

Out of Yesteryear S, w, 1999, Moore, Ralph S.; flowers white blend, 3 in., very dbl., borne in large clusters, moderate fragrance; foliage medium size, dark green, glossy; numerous prickles; upright, spreading (4-6 ft.) growth; [Golden Angel × Muriel]; int. by Sequoia Nursery, 1999

Outback Angel – See **Jean Giono**, HT

Outrageous F, ob, 1999, Zary, Dr. Keith W.; bud pointed, ovoid; flowers soft orange tinged with yellow, 3½-4 in., 25-30 petals, high-centered, borne in small clusters, moderate lemon fragrance; foliage medium size, dark green, dull; prickles moderate; bushy, medium (3½ ft.) growth; PP12073; [Summer Fashion × seedling]; int. by Bear Creek Gardens, Inc., 1999

Outsider F, mr, 1959, Tantau, Math.; bud ovoid; flowers bright blood-red, open, medium, semi-dbl., borne in clusters; foliage glossy; vigorous, upright growth; [Fanal × Red Favorite]; int. in 1956

Outta the Blue S, m, 2000, Carruth, Tom; flowers magenta, reverse magenta and yellow, aging to blue lavender, 9-11 cm., full, old-fashioned, borne in small clusters; foliage medium size, medium green, matte; prickles moderate; upright, bushy, medium (120-140 cm.) growth; PP13449; [Stephen's Big Purple × (International Herald Tribune × *R. soulieana* derivitive)]; int. by Weeks Roses, 2001

Ovation HT, or, 1978, Weeks; bud ovoid; flowers 4-4½ in., 25 petals, high-centered; foliage dark, leathery; vigorous, upright growth; [First Prize × seedling]; int. in 1977

Over the Rainbow Min, rb, 1972, Moore, Ralph S.; flowers red, yellow reverse, small, dbl., high-centered; foliage leathery; vigorous, bushy growth; [Little Darling × Westmont]; int. by Mini-Roses; AOE, ARS, 1975

Over the Rainbow, Climbing Cl Min, rb, 1975, Rumsey, R.H.; [sport of Over the Rainbow]; int. in 1974

Overloon F, dp, 1949, Leenders, M.; flowers rosy pink, medium, dbl.; vigorous growth; [Irene × Hebe]

Overnight Scentsation MinFl, mp, 1997, Saville, F. Harmon; flowers large, very dbl., borne mostly singly, intense fragrance; foliage medium size, medium to dark green, semi-glossy; upright, medium (2 ft.) growth; PP11303; [Taxi × Lavender Jade]; int. by Nor'East Miniature Roses

Overton on Dee HT, pb, 1976, Ellick; flowers pink, reverse cream, 4½ in., 40 petals; [(Ballet × Gavotte) × Orange Sensation]

Overture F, m, 1960, LeGrice; flowers lilac-lavender, well-formed, 3-3½ in., 18 petals; foliage dark; vigorous, low growth; [(seedling × Lavender Pinocchio) × Prelude]

Ovid HSet, mp, 1890, Geschwind, R.; flowers flesh and velvety pink, large, full, flat, borne in clusters of 3-5; non-recurrent

Owen's Pride F, mp, Kirkham, Gordon Wilson; int. in 1968

Oxbow Min, or, 1997, Berg, David H.; flowers medium, dbl., borne mostly singly; foliage medium size, medium green, dull; compact, medium (12-15in.) growth; [Luis Desamero × Rainbow's End]

Oxfam HT, pb, 1976, Cobley; flowers deep pink, shaded lilac, 5 in., 40 petals, intense fragrance; foliage dark; upright growth; [Fragrant Cloud × Blue Moon]; int. by Harry Wheatcroft Gardening, 1973

Oxford HT, yb, 1930, Prince; flowers deep warm peach, tipped orange-gold, well-shaped, large

Oxford – See **Victorian Spice**, F

Oxfordshire – See **Baby Blanket**, S

Oyster Pearl HT, lp; flowers pale cream-pink with hint of deeper pink in center, dbl., high-centered, borne singly, intense fragrance; vigorous, tall growth; [sport of Bewitched]

Oz Baby Min, yb, Hannemann, F.; [Poker Chip × Oz Gold]; int. by The Rose Paradise

Oz Gold Min, yb, McGredy, Sam IV; flowers deep yellow with orange reverse, dbl.; int. in 1981

P. G. Wodehouse HT, dr, Poulsen; flowers dark red, 8-10 cm., full, cupped, slight fragrance; foliage dark green, glossy; bushy, tall (100-150 cm.) growth; hips none; int. by Poulsen Roser, 2000

P. H. Kulkarni HT, pb, 2005, Shastri, N.V.; flowers full, borne mostly solitary, slight fragrance; foliage medium size, medium green, matte; prickles medium, straight; growth upright, medium (38 in.); rose bed, exhibition; [Headliner × Ariana]; int. by N.V.Shastri, 2001

P. J.'s Pride Min, rb, 1996, Bell, Judy G.; bud medium, pointed; flowers white with bright pink to red edging shading down petals to white, 1 in., high-centered, borne in small clusters, no fragrance; foliage medium size, dark green, dull; some prickles; medium, upright growth; [American Rose Centennial × unknown]; int. by Michigan Mini Roses, 1997

P. L. Baudet HT, lp, 1915, Lourens; flowers large, dbl.; [Veluwezoom × Le Progrès]

P. M. Leenders – See **President Macia**, HT

Pablo Diez HT, Moreira da Silva, A.

Pace Setter – See **Pacesetter**, Min

Pacemaker HT, dp, 1980, Harkness; bud pointed; flowers deep pink, 4 in., 40 petals, borne singly or in clusters of 3, intense fragrance; foliage large, semi-glossy; prickles large, broad, dark; vigorous, upright, bushy growth; [Red Planet × Wendy Cussons]; int. in 1981; Gold Medal, Belfast, 1983

Pacesetter Min, w, 1979, Schwartz, Ernest W.; bud long, pointed; flowers pure white, 1½ in., 46 petals, high-centered, borne singly and in small clusters, moderate fragrance; foliage dark, matte; few prickles; vigorous, compact growth; PP4513; [Ma Perkins × Magic Carrousel]; int. by Nor'East Min. Roses; AOE, ARS, 1981

Pachinko F, or, 1999, Schuurman, Frank B.; flowers 3 in., semi-dbl., borne in large clusters; foliage medium size, dark green, glossy; prickles moderate; spreading, medium (30-36 in.) growth; [Alexander × Golden Emblem]; int. by Franko Roses New Zealand, Ltd., 1997

Pacific HT, lp, 1927, Pacific Rose Co.; flowers soft pink, semi-dbl.; [sport of Los Angeles]

Pacific F, mr, 1958, Gaujard; flowers bright red, semi-dbl.; foliage bright green; [Alain × Chanteclerc]

Pacific HT, lp, Heers, C W; [Catherine Kordes × Rose Marie]

Pacific Beauty HT, pb, 1963, Blakeney, F.; bud ovoid; flowers rose-madder, reverse silver, large, dbl., high-centered; foliage glossy, leathery; vigorous, upright, spreading growth; [Peace × Karl Herbst]; int. by Eddie, 1962

Pacific Belle HT, mp, 1989, Cattermole, R.F.; bud pointed; flowers light pink, reverse deeper pink, reflexed, pointed, medium, 31 petals; foliage light green, veined, glossy; prickles pointed, light brown; bushy, branching, upright growth; [(Peer Gynt × unknown) × Josephine Bruce]

Pacific Blue HT, m; flowers lavender, large, full, high-centered, borne mostly singly; PP14410; greenhouse rose; int. by Tantau, 2002

Pacific Darling Min, pb, 1991, Sudol, Julia; flowers large, semi-dbl., borne in large clusters, slight fragrance; foliage large, dark green, glossy; low, upright, bushy, compact growth; [Winifred Coulter × seedling]

Pacific Princess HT, mp, 1989, Cattermole, R.F.; bud tapering; flowers medium, 56 petals, globular, borne usually singly and in sprays of 3-4; foliage dark green, semi-glossy, veined; upright, branching growth; [Pink Parfait × Red Planet]; int. by South Pacific Rose Nursery, 1988

Pacific Serenade Min, dy, 1997, Saville, F. Harmon; flowers bright yellow, medium, dbl., cupped, borne mostly singly, moderate fragrance; foliage medium size, medium green, semi-glossy; no prickles; upright, compact, spreading, bushy, vigorous growth; PP11810; [Cal Poly × New Zealand]; int. by Nor'East Miniature Roses

Pacific Sunset HT, pb, 1978, Fong; bud deep pointed; flowers pink to orange-scarlet, 5 in., semi-dbl., high-centered; foliage dark; upright growth; [Mme Henri Guillot × California]; int. by United Rose Growers, 1977

Pacific Triumph Pol, mp, 1949, Heers; flowers salmon-pink, intense fragrance; growth like parent; [sport of Orange Triumph]; int. by Pacific Nursery

Pacifica F, ab, 1983, Warriner, William A.; flowers medium, 35 petals; foliage medium size, light green, matte; upright, bushy growth; PP5261; [Mercedes × Marina]; int. by J&P

Paco Rabanne F, dy, Adam; int. by Pépinières de la Guerinais, 2003

Pacoima HT, lp, 1927, Pacific Rose Co.; flowers flesh tinted yellow, dbl.; [sport of William F. Dreer]

Pacsix Min, mp, Jauchen; Dan; PP15657

Paddy McGredy F, mp, 1962, McGredy, Sam IV; bud ovoid; flowers deep rose-pink, 4 in., 33 petals, cupped, borne in clusters, moderate fragrance; foliage leathery; vigorous, bushy growth; PP2327; [Spartan × Tzigane]; int. by J&P, 1962; Gold Medal, NRS, 1961

Paddy 'n' Elizabeth S, ob, 2006, McCann, Sean; flowers orange-yellow-pink blend, reverse orange fading to light yellow, 2 in., single, borne in small clusters; foliage medium green, matte; prickles medium, hooked, light, moderate; growth bushy (36 in.); garden; [Joseph's Coat × Kiss 'n' Tell]; int. in 2007

Paddy Stephens HT, ob, 1991, McGredy, Sam IV; flowers large, dbl., slight fragrance; foliage large, dark green, red when young; bushy (100 cm.) growth; [Solitaire × (({[(Tombola × (Elizabeth of Glamis × (Circus × Golden Fleece))) × (Mary Sumner] × Unknown}))]; int. by McGredy Roses International, 1991

Paddywack Min, pb, 1993, Williams, Ernest D.; flowers medium, full, borne mostly singly; foliage small, medium green, semi-glossy; few prickles; medium (50 cm.), upright, compact growth; [Tom Brown × Over the Rainbow]; int. by Mini Roses of Texas, 1993

Paderborn – See **Bischofsstadt Paderborn**, S

Padmavathi '95 HT, pb, Kasturi & Sriram; flowers creamy white with pink petal edges, large; [sport of Uncle Joe]; int. by KSG Son, 1995

Padre HT, rb, 1921, Cant, B. R.; flowers bright coppery scarlet, flushed yellow, large, semi-dbl., cupped, moderate fruity fragrance; foliage small, sparse, dark green; vigorous growth

Padre Américo HT, mr, 1956, Moreira da Silva; flowers carmine-red; [Crimson Glory × Peace]

Padre Cruz HT, w, 1956, Moreira da Silva; flowers rosy white edged ruby; [Branca × Peace]

Padre Mañanet HT, dr, 1958, Dot, Pedro; flowers bright purple-garnet, reverse crimson-red, large, 30 petals, high-centered, moderate fragrance; strong stems; upright growth; [Charles Mallerin × (Satan × Mirandy)]; int. in 1957

Pæonia HP, dr, 1855, Lacharme, F.; flowers crimson, large, dbl.

Pæonia HP, dp, 1914, Geduldig; flowers large, full; [Frau Karl Druschki × (Ulrich Brunner fils × Mrs John Laing)]

Paeonia HT, m, Strnad

Paeonienrose HGal, mp; flowers peony pink, full, quartered, slight fragrance; 4 × 4 ft. growth

Pagan Beauty F, pb, 1965, Verschuren; flowers bright vermilion, reverse salmon-pink, 4-5 in., 42 petals, globular; foliage dark, leathery; vigorous growth; [Montezuma × seedling]; int. by Blaby Rose Gardens

Paganini HMsk, dr, 2000, Lens; flowers dark red, 3 cm., single, borne in large clusters, slight fragrance; recurrent; foliage medium size, dark green, glossy; prickles moderate; bushy, medium (80-100 cm.) growth; hips in autumn; [Running Maid × *R. multiflora nana*]; int. by Louis Lens NV, 1989

Paganini – See **Niccolo Paganini**, F

Paganini HT, pb, Meilland; flowers light pink, reverse darker, full, high-centered, borne mostly singly; cut flower trade; int. by Meilland Intl., 1999

Pageant HT, rb, 1953, Boerner; bud ovoid; flowers red, reverse yellow, 4½-5 in., 35-40 petals, high-centered, moderate fragrance; foliage leathery; vigorous, upright growth; PP1252; [Unnamed Hybrid Tea seedling × (Orange Nassau × unknown)]; int. by J&P

Pagliacci Gr, yb, 1969, Von Abrams; bud pointed; flowers yellow, becoming cerise, medium, semi-dbl.; foliage glossy, bronze; vigorous, upright growth; int. by Edmunds Roses

Pagoda S, dr, 1995, Jobson, Daniel J.; flowers dark velvet red with showy gold stamens, small, 5 petals, borne in large clusters; foliage medium size, medium green, semi-glossy; no prickles; low (3 × 6 ft.), spreading, bushy growth; [Anytime × Mountain Mist]

Pahadi Dhun HT, m, Pal, Dr. B.P.; int. in 1981

Paharan F, lp, 1974, Pal, Dr. B. P.; buds medium, pointed; flowers shell-pink, medium, semi-dbl., open, borne singly and several together; foliage small, bronzy, glossy; stems reddish; growth moderate, bushy, open (45 cm.); [Anna Wheatcroft × unknown]; int. by K. S. G. Son, 1971

Pailine HT, ob, Melle; flowers yellow with pink edges; [Lorena × Kardinal]; int. in 1989

Paint Box F, yb, 1963, Dickson, Patrick; bud ovoid; flowers red and golden yellow, becoming deep red, 3 in., semi-dbl., flat, borne in clusters; foliage dark; vigorous, upright growth; [seedling × St. Pauli]; int. by A. Dickson

Paint-Pot Min, or, 1983, Robinson, Thomas, Ltd.; flowers medium, 24 petals, intense fragrance; foliage small, medium green, semi-glossy; bushy growth; [seedling × Darling Flame]; int. by T. Robinson, Ltd.

Paint the Town S, mr, Lim, Ping; flowers bright red, 3½ in., dbl., cupped, borne in clusters; free-flowering; foliage dark green, glossy, disease-resistant; mounding (2-3 ft.), spreading growth; int. by Bailey (Easy Elegance), 2005

Paintbrush Min, ly, 1975, Moore, Ralph S.; bud mossy; flowers soft yellow to white, mini-moss, 1½ in., 8-10 petals; foliage small, glossy, leathery; vigorous, upright, bushy growth; [Fairy Moss × Goldmoss]; int. by Sequoia Nursery

Painted Damask – See **Léda**, D

Painted Desert HT, op, 1965, Lone Star Rose Nursery; bud long, pointed; flowers pink and copper, open, dbl.; foliage leathery; vigorous, upright growth; [sport of Talisman]

Painted Desert Gr, or, 1998, McGredy, Sam IV; flowers orange-red, 4 in., dbl., borne in small clusters, slight fragrance; foliage large, medium green, bushy growth;

prickles moderate; growth upright, bushy (110 cm.); PP10697; [Louise Gardner × Mme. Delbard]; int. by McGredy, Sam, 1997

Painted Doll Min, ob, 1984, Laver, Keith G.; flowers orange, reverse yellow, small, 35 petals; foliage small, light green, matte; bushy growth; [Party Girl × Dwarfking '78]

Painted Lady HT, mp, 1931, Ward, F.B.; bud long, pointed; flowers bright cerise, base old-gold, large, 42 petals; [(Crusader × Premier) × Julien Potin]

Painted Lady HT, yb, 1980, Herholdt, J.A.; bud pointed; flowers cream and gold, red tipped, 4 in., dbl.; foliage glossy, bronze; bushy growth

Painted Melody HT, yb, Kasturi & Sriran; int. in 1993

Painted Moon HT, rb, 1990, Dickson, Patrick; flowers large, 40 petals, cupped; foliage medium size, medium green, semi-glossy; upright, bushy, stocky growth; [Bonfire × Silver Jubilee]; int. by Dickson Nurseries, Ltd., 1990; Gold Medal, Belfast, 1992

Painted Spain Min, ob, 1995, Jobson, Daniel J.; flowers handpainted orange stippled with white, white reverse, medium, dbl., borne in small clusters; foliage medium size, medium green, semi-glossy; numerous prickles; tall (3 ft.), almost climbing, upright growth; [Rise 'n' Shine × (Queen Elizabeth × Eyepaint)]

Painted Star – See **Mighty Mouse**, F

Painter's Palette Min, rb, 1985, Moore, Ralph S.; bud mossy; flowers creamy white, striped deep pink to deep red, 72 petals, borne 3-5 per cluster; foliage deep green; prickles needle straight, brown; shrubby growth; int. by Ludwigs Roses Pty. Ltd., 1984

Painter's Touch Min, ob, 1998, Laver, Keith G.; flowers luminous orange blend, 1½-3 in., very dbl., borne mostly singly; foliage large, medium green, matte; prickles moderate; bushy, medium tall growth; [seedling × Antique Gold]; int. by Springwood Roses, 1998

Paisley Anniversary F, dr, 1987, Anderson's Rose Nurseries; flowers medium, dbl.; foliage medium size, dark green, glossy; upright growth; [Michele × Smiling Through]

Pakeh HT, ly, Dawson; int. in 1980

Pal HT, ob

Palacky HT, ob, 1936, Böhm, J.; flowers orange-yellow, open, large, single; foliage glossy; vigorous growth; [Mme Mélanie Soupert × Sunburst]

Paladin F, or, 1960, deRuiter; flowers open, 2½ in., semi-dbl., borne in clusters; moderate growth; [Signal Red × Fashion]

Palais de Laeken – See **Grand Palais de Laeken**, HGal

Palais de Papes HT, dr, Dorieux; flowers intense, unfading deep crimson, medium, dbl., turbinate, moderate fragrance; recurrent; foliage dark green, glossy, disease-resistant; moderate growth; int. by Roseraies Dorieux, 2006

Palais Royal – See **White Eden**, LCl

Palais Royale LCl, w, Meilland; flowers 100 petals, cupped, borne singly and in small clusters, slight fragrance; recurrent; foliage dark green, glossy; strong (200 cm.and more) growth; int. by Meilland Richardier, 2006

Palatino F, mr, 1956, Buyl Frères; flowers dbl.; very vigorous growth

Palatino Min, rb, Dickson; int. in 2004

Pale-Flowered – See **Vilmorin**, M

Pale Hands HT, ab, 1969, Pal, Dr. B.P.; bud pointed; flowers ivory-white to buff and peach, very large, dbl., moderate fragrance; foliage leathery; vigorous, upright growth; [McGredy's Ivory × unknown]; int. by Indian Agric. Research Inst., 1965

Pale Moon HT, my, 1967, Patterson; flowers large, dbl., high-centered, moderate fragrance; foliage glossy; vigorous, compact growth; PP2984; [Ma Perkins × Peace]; int. by Patterson Roses

Pale Rouge Panaché – See **Belle Aimable**, HGal

Pâle Rouge Superbe – See **Bouquet Charmant**, HGal

Paleface Gr, w, 1960, Lindquist; bud ovoid; flowers nearly white, base naples yellow, 3-5 in., dbl., high-centered; foliage leathery, semi-glossy; vigorous, upright growth; PP1971; [Joanna Hill × seedling]; int. by Howard Rose Co., 1959

Palestro HP, rb, 1859, Boyau; flowers lilac red

Palette F, yb, 1960, Leenders, J.; bud ovoid; flowers yellow to salmon-pink and then red, dbl., borne in clusters; foliage glossy; compact growth; [Masquerade × High Noon]

Palisades S, mp, Olesen; bud ovate; flowers soft medium pink, 5 cm., 14 petals, open cup, borne in clusters of 3-6, no fragrance; recurrent; foliage dark green, glossy; prickles numerous, pointed, brown; upright to bushy (60-100 cm.) growth; PP16466; [seedling × seedling]; int. by Poulsen Roser, 2004; Silver Medal, Kortrijk, 2006

Palissade Rose – See **Heidekönigin**, HWich

Paljas HT, pb

Pallas HGal, m, before 1811, Miellez; bud round; flowers purple, large, full, moderate fragrance; foliage long, dark green; prickles numerous, flexible, brown

Pallas HT, dr, 1976, Murray & Hawken; flowers garnet-red, reverse paler, 40 petals, high-centered, intense spicy fragrance; foliage large, dull, dark; tall growth; [Chrysler Imperial × Shannon]; int. by Kennedy-Rasmussens, 1975

Pallas Min, lp, 1990, Harkness, R., & Co., Ltd.; bud ovoid; flowers light buff pink, paling to buff white, rosette, medium, 60 petals, rosette, borne in sprays of 5-17, no fragrance; foliage small, medium green, semi-glossy, pointed, plentiful; prickles narrow, small, dark green; bushy, spreading, low growth; fruit not a noticeable feature; [Clarissa × New Penny]; int. in 1989

Pallasii – See ***R. spinosissima altaica*** (Bean)

Pallida Ch, mp, 1789, Kerr; flowers clear rose

Pallida HFt, ly, 1824, Souchet; flowers light sulphur yellow, medium, single; numerous prickles; [*R. foetida bicolor* × unknown]

Pallida HSet, lp, 1843, Feast; flowers very pale blush, almost white, dbl.

Pallidior – See **Agathe Incarnata**, HGal

Palm Springs F, rb, 1965, Duehrsen; bud ovoid; flowers oriental red to light bronze, center yellowish-pink, 50 petals, intense fragrance; foliage bronze; vigorous, upright growth; PP2466; [Oriental Charm × Circus]; int. by Elmer Roses Co.

Palm Springs S, mr, 2006, Rippetoe, Robert, Neil; flowers heat-resistant, long-lasting, 2-2½ in., single, borne mostly solitary; foliage medium size, dark green, glossy; prickles medium-large, slightly curved, tan, moderate p; growth bushy, 3 ft.; hedge, shrub, bedding; [Dortmund × unknown]

Palmengarten Frankfurt S, dp, 2006; flowers rose pink, 4 cm., dbl., cupped/pompon, borne in small clusters; foliage fresh green, glossy; spreading, medium (70 cm.) growth; int. by W. Kordes' Söhne, 1988

Palmetto Sunrise Min, ob, 1992, Williams, Michael C.; flowers orange with a yellow base, yellow reverse, opening orange, large, 20-25 petals, high-centered, borne mostly singly, no fragrance; foliage medium size, medium green, semi-glossy; prickles ¼ in., straight; growth vigorous, upright (50 cm.); hips round, 1/2 in.; PP9252; [Orange Honey × miniature seedling]; int. by The Rose Garden & Mini Rose Nursery, 1993; AOE, ARS, 1993

Palmira Bastos HT, Moreira da Silva, A.

Palmira Feijas HG, pb, 1905, Cayeux

Palmyre P, lp, 1817, Vibert; flowers pale pink, shaded lilac, medium, full; often repeats; probably extinct

Palmyre D, lp, 1844, Laffay

Palo Alto T, ab, 1898, Conard & Jones; flowers chamois rose, tinged at center with golden-yellow and creamy white, large, full

Palocsay Rudolf HT, ob, Palocsay, R.; bud long; flowers well-shaped suitable for glasshouse as cut flower, 30 petals, high-centered, moderate fragrance; leaves medium size, medium green, glossy; growth semi-vigorous upright; [(Charles P Kilham × *R. harisonii*) × Ville de Paris]; int. by Res. Stn. f. Horticulture, Cluj, 1955

Paloma – See **La Paloma**, HT

Paloma HT, w; flowers full, 30-40 petals, high-centered, borne mostly singly; stems long; cut flower trade; int. by Terra Nigra BV, 2002

Paloma Blanca S, w, 1985, Buck, Dr. Griffith J.; flowers ivory-white, medium, 35 petals, cupped, borne in clusters of 3-10, moderate fragrance; repeat bloom; foliage leathery, dark olive green; prickles awl-like, tan; erect, spreading, bushy, compact growth; hardy; [Vera Dalton × ((((Pink Princess × Lillian Gibson) × (Florence Mary Morse × (Josef Rothmund × *R. laxa*)) × ((Pink Princess × Lillian Gibson) × (Florence Mary Morse × (Josef Rothmund × *R. laxa*))) × (Florence Mary Morse × (Josef Rothmund × *R. laxa*)))]; int. by Iowa State University, 1984

Paloma Falcó HT, op, 1930, Dot, Pedro; flowers coral-salmon, dbl.; [Li Bures × Château de Clos Vougeot]; int. by C-P

Palpitation F, mr, Kunieda; int. in 1995

PALS Niagara S, mr, 2004, Fleming, Joyce L.; flowers medium red, reverse slightly lighter, 3 in., full, borne in large clusters, no fragrance; foliage medium size, dark green, semi-glossy, disease-resistant; prickles 4 mm., D-shaped; stems sturdy; upright, tall (5 ft.) growth; back of border; hedging; hardy to -30°F; [Red Hot × breeding line 83, issued by Ag Canada]; int. by Hortico, Inc., 2004

Pam F, yb, 1965, Annabel; bud ovoid; flowers yellow edged red, becoming deep red, small, semi-dbl., cupped; moderate, bushy growth; [Masquerade × unknown]; int. in 1962

Pam Golding – See **Honey Perfume**, F

Pam Tillis MinFl, ab, 2004, Saville, F. Harmon; flowers pastel pink and yellow blend, reverse lighter yellow and pink blend, 2½-3 in., very full, old-fashioned, borne mostly solitary, slight fragrance; foliage small, medium green, semi-glossy, very disease-resistant; prickles ¼ in., sharply acuminate; growth upright, as wide as tall (26-32 in.); garden decorative; [Cal Poly × New Zealand]; int. by Nor East Miniature Roses, 2004

Památnik Komenského LCl, mp, 1936, Bojan; flowers salmon-pink, medium, moderate fragrance; free early bloom; vigorous, climbing growth; int. by Böhm

Památnik Krále Jirího HT, dr, 1936, Böhm, J.; bud pointed; flowers deep crimson, marked velvety purple, large, dbl.; foliage glossy, dark; vigorous growth; [Gorgeous × Gen. MacArthur]

Pamela HT, yb, 1924, Therkildsen; flowers canary-yellow and bright blush-pink shaded deep carmine, dbl.

Pamela – See **Frisco**, F

Pamela HT, ob, Tantau; flowers copper-orange, outer petals fading and developing red-orange edges, full; int. by Rosen Tantau, 2003

Pamela Min, pb, Olesen; flowers dbl., 25-30 petals, slight fragrance; foliage dark green, glossy; growth bushy, low (40-60 cm.)

Pamela Ann HT, mr, Tudor; int. in 1998

Pamela Jane Taylor HT, w, 2004, Webster, Robert; flowers ivory, 4 in., very full, borne in small clusters, moderate fragrance; foliage medium size, dark green, glossy; prickles 10 mm., straight; growth bushy, medium (30 in.); bedding; [Samantha Barker × Golden Future]; int. by To be arranged, 2004

Pamela Joy S, yb, Hannemann, F.; [Oz Gold × Eye Paint]; int. by The Rose Paradise

Pamela Louise Webb F, ly, 2004, Paul Chessum Roses; flowers semi-dbl., borne in large clusters, slight fragrance; foliage small, light green, semi-glossy; prickles small; growth compact, short (50 cm.); bedding, borders, containers; [seedling × seedling]; int. by Love4Plants Ltd, 2004

Pamela Travers HT, mp, 1966, Morey, Dr. Dennison; flowers large, dbl.; foliage leathery; vigorous, upright growth; [Pink Favorite × Queen Elizabeth]; int. by General Bionomics, 1966

Pamela's Choice HT, my, 1966, Bardill Nursery; flowers golden yellow, 4½ in.; foliage bronze; [sport of Piccadilly]

Pamina HT, dp, Liebig; int. in 1991

Pampa F, mr, 1978, Gaujard; bud pointed; flowers brilliant vermilion-red, dbl.; foliage dark; [Colisee × Atlantic]; int. in 1971

Pampa HT, dy, K&S; flowers large, full; int. by KSG Son, 1988

Pam's Passion HT, ob, 1999, Giles, Diann; flowers medium, full, borne mostly singly; foliage dark green, semi-glossy; few prickles; upright, medium growth; [Vera Dalton × unknown]; int. by Giles Rose Nursery, 1999

Pan America HT, ob, 1941, Boerner; flowers deep orange suffused tawny yellow, becoming light gold, open, 5½ in., 30-40 petals; foliage glossy, bronze; long stems; vigorous, upright, bushy, open, growth; [Heinrich Wendland × Max Krause]; int. by J&P

Panaché – See ***R. gallica versicolor*** (Linnaeus)

Panaché Gr, mp, 1959, Lens; flowers light salmon-pink, well-formed, large; vigorous growth; [Rubin × Cinnabar]

Panache – See **Carrot Top**, Min

Panache Min, pb, 2003, Eagle, B & D; flowers pink/lavender/tan, prominent stamens, 5 cm., semi-dbl., borne mostly solitary, intense fragrance; foliage medium size, medium green, matte; prickles small, straight; growth bushy, medium (35-40 cm.); garden; [sport of Sachet]; int. by Southern Cross Nurseries, 1995

Panachée M, w, around 1818, Shailer; bud with moss arranged in longitudinal bands; flowers pure white plumed light pink, medium, semi-dbl.; thornless; [sport of Old White Moss or White Bath]

Panachée D, pb, about 1820, Godefroy (possibly Girardon); flowers white variegated with pink, medium, dbl.

Panacheé à Fleurs Doubles HGal, pb, 1839, Viert; flowers rose pink with violet striping, medium, dbl.

Panachée a Fleurs Plaines HGal, m, 1839, Vibert

Panachée d'Angers – See **Commandant Beaurepaire**, HP

Panachée de Bordeaux – See **Coquette Bordelaise**, HP

Panachée de Lyon P, pb, 1895, Dubreuil; flowers pink, variegated crimson, medium, dbl., intense fragrance; recurrent; upright, medium growth; [sport of Rose du Roi]

Panachée d'Orléans HP, pb, 1854, Dauvesse; flowers blush-white striped deep rose, full, borne in clusters of 5-7; [sport of Duchesse d'Orléans]

Panachée Double – See **La Rubanée**, HGal

Panachée Double – See **Panachée Pleine**, HGal

Panachée Langroise HP, rb, 1873, Rimancourt; flowers bright cherry red, plumed deep carmine, large, full; [sport of Jules Margottin]

Panachée Pleine HGal, pb, 1839, Vibert; flowers violet-purple, strongly striped with white, small, petals recurved, green center, dbl., cupped, slight fragrance; foliage light green, elliptical

Panachée Pleine M, w, before 1844, possibly Robert; flowers white or flesh, sometimes plumed pink, medium, full, cupped; [possibly a sport of White Bath]

Panachée Pleine a Petales Etroites – See **Panachée Pleine**, M

Panachée Superbe – See **Beauté Insurmontable**, HGal

Panachée Superbe HGal, dr, before 1811, from Holland; flowers velvety purple red, lighter reverse, some petals folding back to give the striped, full, moderate fragrance

Panaget M, rb, before 1844; flowers purple striped and spotted with red, medium, semi-dbl.; possibly synonymous with Lansezeur

Panama HT, lp, 1913, Cook, J.W.; flowers flesh edged lighter, dbl.; [Frau Karl Druschki × unnamed seedling (pink)]

Paname LCl, mp, 1959, Delbard-Chabert; flowers bright pink, reverse apricot tinted salmon, large, dbl., borne mostly solitary; free, recurrent boom; long, strong stems; well branched growth; [Spectacular × unknown]

Pancha Ganga HT, pb, Patil, B.K.; flowers dbl., high-centered; int. in 1993

Panchaganga – See **Pancha Ganga**, HT dbl.

Panchu F, mr, 1970, Pal, Dr. B.P.; bud globular; flowers ruby-red, open, medium, semi-dbl.; foliage leathery; very vigorous, upright, compact growth; int. by Indian Agric. Research Inst., 1966

Pand565 HT, pb, de Groot; Henk C. A.; PP15533

Panda Meidiland S, w; bud ovoid; flowers bright white, 6-7 cm., 5-7 petals, flat saucer, borne usually in clusters of 3-5, slight fragrance; free-flowering; foliage dark green, glossy, disease-resistant; prickles 1 cm.; growth low (40-60 cm.), spreading (70-120 cm.); no hips; PP15487; [Fiona × The Fairy]; int. by Meilland, 2003

Pandemonium F, yb, 1988, McGredy, Sam IV; flowers yellow and red stripes, full; foliage small, medium green, glossy; patio; bushy growth; [New Year × ((Anytime × Eyepaint) × Stars 'n' Stripes)]

Pandora HT, my, 1947, Barké; bud ovoid; flowers cream to deep yellow, 5 in., 35-55 petals, high-centered; foliage dark, semi-glossy; very vigorous, tall growth; [Golden Rapture × R.M.S. Queen Mary]; int. by Arnold-Fisher Co.

Pandora Min, w, 1990, Harkness, R., & Co., Ltd.; bud ovoid; flowers ivory, medium, 100 petals, rosette, borne in sprays of 3-15, slight fragrance; foliage small, medium green, semi-glossy; prickles thin, small, reddish; bushy, spreading, low, compact growth; fruit not a noticeable feature; [Clarissa × Darling Flame]; int. in 1989

Paneera HT, w, 1984, Fumagalli, Niso; flowers large, 35 petals, moderate fragrance; foliage medium size, dark, glossy; upright growth; [seedling × seedling]; int. in 1983

Pania HT, lp, 1968, McGredy, Sam IV; flowers pure pink, well-formed; foliage leathery; strong, bushy growth; [Paddy McGredy × (Kordes' Perfecta × Montezuma)]; Gold Star of the South Pacific, Palmerston North, NZ, 1969

Paniculé – See **Reversa**, Bslt

Panochre – See **Peach Calypso**, HT

Panorama HT, mp, 1943, McGredy; flowers rose-pink, reverse silvery pink, 5 in., 30 petals, cupped, moderate fragrance; foliage glossy; vigorous, upright, compact growth; [Mrs A.R. Barraclough × seedling]; int. by J&P

Panorama – See **Panorama Holiday**, F

Panorama Holiday F, mp, 1973, Gregory; flowers rose, pointed, large, 34 petals; foliage glossy, dark; [Queen Elizabeth × seedling]

Panthea – See **Women's Institute**, HT

Pantheon – See **Leslie's Dream**, HT

Panthere Rose – See **Pink Panther**, HT

Pantomime F, dp, 1965, McGredy, Sam IV; flowers deep pink, 4 in., 30 petals, high-centered, borne in clusters, moderate fruity fragrance; [Ma Perkins × Karl Herbst]; int. by McGredy

Paola HT, mr, 1983, Tantau, Math.; flowers large, 20 petals, high-centered, moderate fragrance; foliage large, dark, matte; int. in 1981

Papa Falcon Min, w, 2001, Ferrer, Fco.; flowers very dbl., borne mostly solitary, no fragrance; foliage medium green; [FE-84113 × Orange M]

Papa Gontier T, pb, 1883, Nabonnand, G.; bud long, pointed; flowers bright pink, reverse carmine-red, large, semi-dbl.; intermittent bloom; foliage rich green; vigorous, bushy growth; [Duchess of Edinburgh × unknown]

Papa Gontier, Climbing Cl T, pb, 1898, Hosp (also Vigneron/Chevrier, 1904, and Chase & Co; flowers intense pink, shaded yellow twards center, reverse purplish-red, dbl.; [sport of Papa Gontier]

Papa Gouchault HMult, dr, 1922, Turbat; bud long, pointed; flowers pure crimson-red, 3 cm., dbl., open, borne in clusters of 10-20; foliage large, glossy; few prickles; long stems; very vigorous, climbing growth; [Rubin × unknown]

Papa Hémeray Ch, rb, 1912, Hémeray-Aubert; flowers red, center white, single, borne in clusters; very vigorous growth; [Hiawatha × Parsons' Pink China]

Papa Hendrickx HT, or, 1964, Mondial Roses; bud long, pointed; flowers vermilion-orange, large, 45-50 petals, high-centered; foliage bronze; very vigorous, upright growth; [(Jolie Madame × *R. rugosa rubra*) × seedling]

Papa Joao XXIII HT, lp, 1963, Moreira da Silva; flowers pearl-pink; [Plaisir de France × La Jolla]

Papa Klein HT, or, 1934, Ketten Bros.; flowers reddish coppery orange, passing to salmon-pink, imbricated, dbl.; foliage cedar-green; very vigorous growth; [Margaret Spaull × Norman Lambert]

Papa Lambert HT, mp, 1899, Lambert, P.; flowers vivid pink, darker outside, large, dbl., cupped, borne mostly solitary, intense fragrance; [(White Lady × Marie Baumann) × Oskar Cordel]

Papa Leo F, dy, Vidal; int. by Rosales Vidal

Papa Meilland HT, dr, 1963, Meilland, Alain A.; bud pointed; flowers dark velvety crimson, large, 35 petals, high-centered, intense fragrance; foliage leathery, glossy, olive-green; vigorous, upright growth; [Chrysler Imperial × Charles Mallerin]; int. by URS; James Alexander Gamble Fragrance Medal, ARS, 1974, Hall of

Fame, WFRS, 1988, Gold Medal, Baden-Baden, 1962

Papa Meilland, Climbing Cl HT, dr, 1971, Stratford (also Meilland, 1976); flowers velvety red, 4-5 in., borne mostly solitary, intense fragrance; int. by Rumsey

Papa Pirosha HT, my, Bulsara; flowers greenish yellow; stems long; [sport of Yankee Doodle]; int. in 1990

Papa Reiter HT, lp, 1900, Hinner; flowers cream tinted pink; [sport of Mme Caroline Testout]

Papa Rouillard HWich, mr, 1923, Turbat; flowers bright carmine, reverse lighter, 3-4 cm., dbl., borne in long clusters of 15-25; abundant seasonal bloom; foliage rich green, glossy; thornless; long stems; very vigorous, climbing growth; [Leontine Grevais × seedling]

Papa Schneider HT, dr, 1961, Kriloff, Michel; flowers dark red-purple, large, dbl.; foliage glossy; vigorous, upright growth; [Crimson Glory × seedling]

Papagayo HT, rb, Kordes; flowers medium red, striped yellow, medium, full, high-centered, borne mostly singly; recurrent; stems long (70 cm); greenhouse rose; int. by W. Kordes Söhne, 2003

Papagena – See **Oranges 'n' Lemons**, S

Papageno HT, rb, 1990, McGredy, Sam IV; flowers deep rose red with cream stripes, large, dbl.; foliage large, light green, matte; upright growth; [Freude × ((Anytime × Eyepaint) × Stars 'n' Stripes)]; int. by McGredy Roses International, 1989

Papaverina Major – See **Grosse Mohnkopfs Rose**, S

Paper Anniversary Min, w; flowers creamy white, dbl., cupped, borne mostly in clusters, slight fragrance; foliage glossy; growth to 24 in.; int. in 2003

Paper Doll Min, ab, 1992, Zary, Dr. Keith W.; flowers light apricot with a hint of pale pink fading to light amber, then white, large, dbl., borne in small clusters, no fragrance; foliage small, dark greeen, glossy; some prickles; low (45-60 cm.), upright growth; [Fiddler's Gold × Sequoia Gold]; int. by Bear Creek Gardens

Papi Delbard LCl, ab, Delbard; flowers apricot, base darker, lighter reverse, 5 in., very dbl., cupped, borne mostly solitary, strong fruity fragrance; int. in 1995

Papilio HT, Aicardi, D.; int. in 1955

Papillon Ch, mr, about 1826, Dubourg

Papillon T, op, 1881, Nabonnand; flowers coppery salmon rose, 6 cm., semi-dbl., borne in medium clusters, slight fragrance

Papillon HT, my, Tantau; flowers yellow with red on outer petals, large, dbl., high-centered, borne mostly singly, slight fragrance; recurrent; foliage large, glossy; prickles moderate; stems strong, long; growth upright, strong, fast growing; florist rose; int. in 1997

Papillon Rose F, mp, 1956, Lens; flowers pink tinted salmon, dbl., high-centered, borne in clusters, intense fragrance; vigorous, bushy growth; [White Briarcliff × (Lady Sylvia × Fashion)]

Papoose Cl Min, w, 1956, Moore, Ralph S.; bud pointed; flowers 1 in., single, borne in clusters; foliage small, fern-like, semi-glossy; vigorous, spreading (to 3-4 ft.) growth; trailer or groundcover; [*R. wichurana* × Zee]; int. by Sequoia Nursery, 1955

Paprika F, or, 1959, Tantau, Math.; bud long, pointed; flowers brick red, semi-dbl., borne in large clusters; foliage leathery, glossy, olive-green; vigorous, upright growth; [Marchenland × Red Favorite]; int. in 1958; Gold Medal, NRS, 1959, Golden Rose, The Hague, 1961

Paprika LCl, or, Meilland International SA; bud oblong; flowers vermilion, reverse lighter, 3 in., single, flat cup, borne in small clusters, no fragrance; free-flowering; foliage large, dark green, semi-glossy; prickles numerous, medium to large; growth spreading, tall (8+ ft.); PP9537; [(Centenaire de Lourdes × Picasso) × Sparkling Scarlet]; int. in 1992

Papst Johannes XXIII HT, w, Brauner; flowers large, dbl.; int. in 1963

Papworth Hospital Rose F, dr; flowers semi-dbl., flat cup, borne in clusters, slight fragrance; good repeat; growth to 90 cm.; int. by World of Roses, 2005

Pâquerette Pol, w, 1875, Guillot et Fils; flowers pure white, with imbricated petals, 1 in., very dbl., cupped, borne in broad clusters of up to 40; foliage glossy, with 5-7 leaflets; prickles very few; stems bright green; dwarf (12-15 in.), bushy growth; seedling of a seedling of *R. multiflora polyantha*, blooms much like a Noisette, claimed to be the first polyantha

Pâquerette Pol, w, Guillot et Fils; flowers white, tinged with clear pink, very dbl., globular, borne in pyramidal clusters, moderate fragrance; good repeat; Beales form

Paquita HGal, m, before 1841; flowers violet, medium to large, full

Para Ti Min, w, 1949, Dot, Pedro; flowers white, base tinted yellow, semi-dbl.; foliage glossy; very bushy (6-8 in.) growth; [Eduardo Toda × Pompon de Paris]; int. by A. Meilland, 1946

Parade LCl, dp, 1953, Boerner; bud ovoid; flowers deep rose-pink, lighter reverse, medium to large, 33 petals, cupped, moderate fragrance; foliage dark green, glossy; vigorous growth; PP1253; [(New Dawn × unknown) × World's Fair, Climbing]; int. by J&P

Parade Marshal F, mr, 1975, Byrum; flowers full, 2-2½ in., 25-30 petals, high-centered; vigorous growth; [Little Leaguer × Gemini]; int. by J.H. Hill Co., 1974

Paradis HT, mr, 1944, Gaujard; bud pointed; flowers clear red, medium, dbl., cupped; foliage glossy; vigorous growth

Paradise HWich, pb, 1907, Walsh; flowers rose-pink, center white, tips of petals notched, 6-7 cm., single, borne in large clusters; non-recurrent; foliage glossy; vigorous, climbing (10-15 ft.) growth; RULED EXTINCT 1/79

Paradise HT, m, 1979, Weeks; bud long, pointed; flowers silvery lavender shading to ruby-red at edge, well-formed, 3½-4½ in., 22-28 petals, high-centered, borne singly and in clusters, moderate rose with slight musk fragrance; recurrent; foliage large, glossy, dark green, waxy; prickles several, long, hooked downward, brown; upright growth; hips oblong, very smooth, yellow-green; PP4552; [Swarthmore × seedling]; int. by C-P, 1978; Gold Medal, Portland, 1979

Paradise, Climbing Cl HT, m, Weeks; PP4796; [sport of Paradise]; like its parent except for climbing habit and blooming on laterals from climbing canes; int. in 1985

Paradise Min, ob; flowers orange with a yellow heart, semi-dbl., shallow cup; free-flowering; vigorous, tall (3 ft.) growth; int. by Greenhead Nursery, 2005

Paradisea – See **Garden Perfume**, HT

Parador HT, yb, 1978, Paolino; flowers chrome-yellow, 4½ in., 30 petals, cupped; vigorous growth; [((Zambra × Suspense) × King's Ransom) × (Kabuki × Dr. A.J. Verhage)]; int. as Tchin-Tchin, URS

Parador – See **Tchin-Tchin**, F

Paraglider S, ob, 1985, Buck, Dr. Griffith J.; bud ovoid, pointed; flowers light pink, reverse orange-red, medium-large, 28 petals, cupped, borne in clusters of 1-10; recurrent; foliage medium size, dark green tinted copper, leathery; prickles awl-like, tan; vigorous, bushy, spreading growth; hardy; [(Country Dancer × Carefree Beauty) × Alexander]; int. by Iowa State University, 1984

Paragon HT, mp, 1964, Macres, T.; bud large, long, pointed; flowers brilliant cerise, 5½ in, 36-50 petals, high-centered, borne mostly singly; foliage dark green, leathery; few prickles; growth very vigorous, erect tall; [sport of Better Times]; int. by Paragon Greenhouses, 1963

Paragon – See **Patricia Neal**, HT

Paragon Min, mr, 1983, McGredy, Sam IV; flowers 35 petals, moderate fragrance; foliage small, dark, glossy; bushy growth; [Ko's Yellow × Little Artist]; int. in 1982

Parallel Dreams HT, w, Drummond; int. by Greenbelt Farm, 1994

Paramount HT, ab, 1950, Swim, H.C.; bud long, pointed; flowers orange-salmon-buff, becoming, 4-5 in., 30 petals, high-centered; foliage glossy; very vigorous, upright, bushy growth; [Charlotte Armstrong × Glowing Sunset]; int. by Paramount Nursery

Parapluie de Neige LCl, w

Parasol HT, dy, 1964, Sanday, John; flowers rich yellow, 5 in., 28 petals; foliage dark; compact growth; [Peace × Ethel Sanday seedling]

Paray F, mr

Parc des Princes HT, rb, Dorieux; int. in 1990

Pardinas Bonet HT, yb, 1931, Dot, Pedro; bud large, oval; flowers deep yellow, reverse red, large, dbl., globular, intense fragrance; foliage medium glossy; few prickles; [La Giralda × Souv. de Claudius Pernet]; int. by C-P

Paree Pink Pol, mp

Paree Red – See **Mothersday**, Pol

Paree Salmon – See **Vatertag**, Pol

Paree White – See **Sneprinsesse**, Pol

Parel van Aalsmeer – See **Perle von Aalsmeer**, HT

Pareo F, ob, 1986, Meilland; flowers exotic orange-mandarine and citron-yellow, dbl.

Pareo HT, ob, Suzuki. Seizo; bud large, conical; flowers light tangerine orange, reverse Chinese yellow, edges suffused tangerine orange, 4 in., 30-38 petals, high-centered, borne usually singly, no fragrance; good repeat; foliage dark green, semi-glossy; few prickles; upright (4-5 ft.) growth; PP8024; [(Elmera × Capella) × Keivlanox]; cut flower trade; int. in 1991

Parfait F, rb, 1976, Knight, C.; bud small, pointed, ovoid; flowers white with yellow base and red edges, spreading down the petals as they open, 3-3½ in., 30-48 petals, globular, borne singly and in clusters of 2-4, slight mild cinnamon fragrance; good repeat; foliage large, leathery, glossy; prickles grayed-orange, 10-13 mm.; compact, upright (4-6 ft.), branching, vigorous growth; hips fertile, round, orange-red; PP4046; [sport of Minuette]; int. by DeVor Nurseries, Inc., 1975

Parfait Delight F, pb; flowers watermelon pink with ivory reverse; free-flowering; medium growth

Parfum d'Armor HT, mp, Adam, M.; int. in 1992

Parfum de Franche Comté HT, op, Sauvageot; flowers rose and coral, large, dbl.

Parfum de la Neige HT, w, 1939, Mallerin, C.; flowers large, dbl.

Parfum de l'Hay – See **Rose à Parfum de l'Hay**, HRg

Parfum de Liberté – See **Memorial Day**, HT

Parfum d'Ispahan – See **Ispahan**, D

Parfum Liffreen F, m, Adam; int. in 1995

Parfum Rose HT, dp, Orard; int. by Vilmorin, 2000

Paris Pol, mr, 1929, deRuiter; flowers bright red; vigorous growth

Paris de Yves St Laurent HT, dp, 1995, Meilland; bud conical, large; flowers deep pink, 5 in., 32-35 petals, high-centered, borne mostly singly, slight fragrance; good repeat; foliage large, dark green, glossy; prickles moderate; upright (5 ft.) growth; PP8619; [sport of Silva]; int. by The Conard-Pyle Co., 1992

Paris-Match HT, dp, 1958, Meilland, F.; flowers carmine to rose, center darker, dbl.; foliage leathery; vigorous growth; [Independence × Grand'mere Jenny]; int. by URS, 1957; Gold Medal, Bagatelle, 1956

Paris Match HT, mr, Richardier; flowers rose red, large, full, high-centered, heavy rebloom in autumn, intense fragrance; vigorous, moderate (80-100 cm.) growth; int. by Meilland-Richardier, 2004

Paris Pink – See **Givenchy**, HT

Paris Red – See **Rouge de Paris**, F

Paris Superior Pol, mr, deRuiter; flowers have more lasting color than parent; [sport of Paris]

Paris 2000 HT, dp, 1986, Delbard; flowers deep pink, large, 28 petals, cupped, no fragrance; vigorous, upright, bushy growth; [(DELtorche × (Sultane × Mme Joseph Perraud)) × (Queen Elizabeth × Provence)]; int. in 1974

Paris 2000 S, mp, Delbard; flowers pink/soft lavender, yellow stamens and white eye when fully open, semi-dbl., shallow cup, borne in clusters, moderate fragrance; free-flowering; vigorous, short to medium growth; int. by Paris Two Thousand, 2001

Pariser Charme HT, mp, 1965, Tantau, Math.; bud ovoid; flowers pink, well-formed, 5 in., 28 petals, borne in clusters of up to 10, intense fragrance; foliage dark, glossy; vigorous, upright growth; ADR, 1966

Parish Life Gr, or, 1999, Wilson, George D.; flowers orange, red edged, reverse orange, fades to light pink, 4 in., full, borne mostly singly, slight fragrance; foliage medium size, medium green, semi-glossy; few prickles; upright, tall (5 ft.) growth; [Piccadilly × Marijke Koopman]; int. by Holy Family Catholic Church, 2000

Park Avenue HT, dr, 1962, Jelly; bud ovoid; flowers cardinal-red, 3-4 in., 38-48 petals, open, moderate fragrance; foliage leathery, dark; vigorous, upright growth; [Yuletide × San Fernando]; greenhouse rose; int. by E.G. Hill Co.

Park Jewell – See **Parkjuwel**, S

Park Place F, rb, Christensen, Jack E.; flowers white and ruby red blend, cupped; int. in 1987

Park Place HT, m, 2004, Edwards, Eddie; flowers mauve & white, reverse lighter, 5 in., full, high-centered, borne mostly solitary, moderate fragrance; foliage large, dark green, glossy; upright, medium (5-6 ft.) growth; exhibition; [Crystalline × Barbra Streisand]; int. by Cool Roses, 2004

Park Royal F, ob, 1967, Eddie, J.H.; bud ovoid; flowers coral-pink, center white, reverse silver, medium, dbl., open; foliage light green; vigorous, upright growth; [Tropicana × Shepherd's Delight]; int. by Sheridan Nursery

Park Wilhelmshöhe HGal, dp, 2006; flowers carmine pink, 10 cm., full, borne in small clusters; non-recurrent; foliage deep green, glossy; growth bushy, tall (180 cm.); int. by W. Kordes' Söhne, 1987

Parkay – See **Dorola**, Min

Parkdirektor Riggers HKor, dr, 1958, Kordes, R.; bud long, pointed; flowers velvety crimson, occasionally flecked white, 5-6 cm., semi-dbl., borne in very large clusters; recurrent bloom; foliage dark, glossy, leathery; very vigorous, climbing growth; [*R.* × *kordesii* × Our Princess]; int. by Kordes & Son, 1957; ADR, 1960

Parkfeuer HFt, or, 1906, Lambert, P.; flowers bright scarlet, medium, single to semi-dbl., borne in small clusters; non-recurrent; thornless; vigorous (6-8 ft.) growth; [*R. foetida bicolor* × unknown]

Parkjewel – See **Parkjuwel**, S

Parkjuwel S, mr, 1956, Kordes; bud ovoid; flowers very large, very dbl., cupped, intense fragrance; non-recurrent; foliage leathery, wrinkled, light green; vigorous (4 ft.), bushy growth; [Independence × Red Moss]; int. by Morse Roses, 1950

Parklane HT, my, 1961, Jelly; bud ovoid; flowers canary-yellow, 4½-5 in., 25-35 petals, high-centered; foliage glossy; vigorous, upright growth; [Peace × Dawn]; int. by E.G. Hill Co., 1961

Parkprinzessin HT, mp

Parkrose S, dr, Elvinge, H.; flowers large, dbl.

Parks' Yellow Tea-Scented China T, my, 1824, Parks; flowers bright yellow, dbl.; the rose in commerce today under this name is, most likely, not correct; int. by England in 1824

Parkside Rose S, dp; flowers deep pink, single; vigorous (6 ft.) growth

Parkstone Pride S, Delforge

Parkstown's Pride HT, pb, Tantau; int. in 1990

Parkstrauchrose S, rb, Scholle, E.; flowers dark red with golden yellow, small to medium, semi-dbl.; int. in 1975

Parkwood Scarlet F, mr, Kordes; flowers scarlet red, semi-dbl.; foliage dark green, leathery; medium growth; int. in 1995

Parkzauber M, dr, 1958, Kordes; bud long, pointed; flowers dark crimson, large, dbl., moderate fragrance; non-recurrent; foliage dark, leathery; very vigorous (4 ft.), upright, bushy growth; [Independence × Nuits de Young]; int. by Kordes & Son, 1956

Parkzierde B, dr, 1909, Geschwind; flowers scarlet crimson, petals shell-shaped, dbl., moderate fragrance; non-recurrent; foliage dark green; long stems; very vigorous (2 m.) growth; int. by Lambert, P.

Parly 2 HT, lp; flowers large, dbl.

Parme – See **Simone**, HT, 1958

Parmelia HT, mr, 1957, Lennard; bud long, pointed; flowers flamingo-red, 5-5½ in., 24-30 petals, high-centered; foliage dark, glossy, leathery; very vigorous, upright, compact growth; [sport of Mme Chiang Kai-shek]

Parmentier M, mp, 1847, Robert/Vibert; flowers dbl., cupped

Parmentier HP, dp, 1860, Guillot et Fils; flowers medium to deep pink with silvery whitish reverse; growth to 5 ft.

Parnassine HRg, m, 1825, Noisette, E.; flowers light violet, dbl., borne in clusters of 3-5; foliage elongate; prickles straight, unequal; growth erect

Parole HT, dp, 2006; bud large; flowers deep pink with a breath of purple, 14 cm., very full, high-centered, borne mostly solitary, intense fragrance; foliage large, green,shiny; upright, medium (80 cm.) growth; int. by W. Kordes' Söhne, 2001

Parsifal F, op, 1968, deRuiter; flowers coral-salmon, well-shaped, 34 petals; vigorous, bushy growth; [Dacapo × Ballade]

Pársla HRg, w, Reikstra; flowers clean white, medium, semi-dbl., cupped, slight fragrance; recurrent; bushy (4 ft.), broad growth; hardy; originated in Latvia; int. in 1980

Parsons' Pink China – See **Old Blush**, Ch

Parsons' Pink China, Climbing – See **Old Blush, Climbing**, Cl Ch

Parthenon HT, pb, 1970, Delbard-Chabert; flowers carmine-pink, reverse soft yellow, large, dbl., cupped, moderate fragrance; recurrent; foliage bronze, glossy; vigorous, upright, bushy growth; [Chic Parisien × (Bayadere × Rome Glory)]; int. in 1967

Partridge – See **Weisse Immensee**, S

Party Doll F, ab, 1960, Boerner; bud ovoid; flowers pink, 2½ in., 40 petals, cupped, moderate fragrance; foliage leathery, glossy; vigorous, bushy growth; [(Goldilocks × unknown) × Fashion]; int. by J&P, 1959

Party Dress HT, ab, 1961, Robinson, H.; flowers deep apricot shaded buff-peach, 5 in., 25 petals, high-centered; foliage glossy; vigorous, bushy, compact growth; [Gay Crusader × seedling]; int. by Lowe

Party Girl Min, yb, 1979, Saville, F. Harmon; bud long, pointed; flowers soft apricot-yellow, 1-1½ in., 23 petals, high-centered, borne mostly singly, moderate spicy fragrance; compact, bushy growth; PP4598; [Rise 'n' Shine × Sheri Anne]; int. by Nor'East Min. Roses; Miniature Rose Hall of Fame, ARS, 1999, AOE, ARS, 1981

Party Girl's Daughter Min, pb, 2005, Wells, Verlie W.; flowers pink and yellow, reverse yellow, 1 in., dbl., borne in small clusters; foliage small, dark green, semi-glossy; prickles moderate, ¼ in., straight; growth compact, upright, medium (1½-2 ft.); garden decoration, exhibition; [Party Girl × select pollen]; int. by Wells Mid-South Roses, 2005

Party Lights Min, op, 2007, Zary, Keith W.; flowers coral-orange, reverse cream, 2 in., dbl., blooms borne in small clusters; foliage medium size, dark green, glossy; prickles 6-8 mm., hooked downward, greyed-orange, few; growth upright, medium (12-18 in.); [seedling × Jingle Bells]; int. by Jackson & Perkins Wholesale, Inc., 2006

Party Line Min, op, 1992, Moglia, Thomas; flowers coral, medium, dbl., borne in clusters of 6 or more on basal canes; foliage small, medium green, matte; few prickles; medium (45-50cm.), compact growth; [Party Girl × Fairlane]; int. by Gloria Dei Nursery, 1993

Party Pink F, mp, 1958, Raffel; flowers bright pink, 1-1½ in., 30-50 petals, borne in clusters, moderate fragrance; moderate growth; [seedling × (Pinocchio × unknown)]; int. by Port Stockton Nursery, 1957

Party Popcorn Min, w, 1993, Laver, Keith G.; flowers medium, full, borne mostly singly; foliage small, medium green, matte; few prickles; medium (20-25 cm.), bushy growth; [(June Laver × Painted Doll) × Popcorn]; int. by Springwood Consultants, Ltd., 1993

Party Time HT, yb, 1987, Weeks, O.L.; flowers lemon yellow with pink overlay, reverse lemon yellow, large, 45 petals, cupped, borne singly, moderate fruity fragrance; foliage medium size, medium green, semi-glossy; prickles medium, reddish, hooked downwards; upright, medium growth; PP6457; [Perfume Delight × Half Time]; int. in 1986

Party Trick F, dp, 1999, Dickson, Colin; flowers cerise pink, 2 in., single, borne in small clusters; foliage small, medium green, glossy; prickles moderate; compact, low (18 in.) growth; [Robin Redbreast × seedling]; int. by Dickson Nurseries, Ltd., 1999

Partyglo Min, yb, 1985, Williams, Ernest D.; bud long, pointed; flowers yellow with pink petal edges, yellow reverse, 1½ in., 35 petals, high-centered, borne usually singly; recurrent; foliage small, dark green, semi-glossy; prickles average, slender, hooked downward, tan; stems slender, wiry; growth bushy, upright to slightly spreading; few hips; PP5880; [Little Darling × Over the Rainbow]; int. by Mini-Roses, 1984

Parure HT, dp, 1967, Delbard-Chabert; flowers carmine-rose, 5 in., cupped; foliage serrated; tall to medium growth; [Michèle Meilland × Chic Parisien]; int. by Cuthbert, 1965

Parure des Vierges D, w, before 1810; flowers medium, dbl.; foliage rounded, light green

Parure d'Or LCl, yb, 1970, Delbard-Chabert; flowers golden yellow edged orange, medium, semi-dbl., borne in small clusters; repeat bloom; foliage dark, glossy; vigorous, climbing growth; [(Queen Elizabeth × Provence) × (Sultane × Mme Joseph Perraud)]; int. in 1968; Gold Medal, Bagatelle, 1968

Parviflora – See **Burgundian Rose**, HGal

Parvifolia – See **Burgundian Rose**, HGal

Parvula Nobis HMult, m, 1866, Cochet; flowers light

lilac pink, aging white, very small, full

Parwana F, yb, 1975, Pal, Dr. B.P.; bud pointed; flowers golden yellow, edged plum-red, open, 3 in., 37 petals, cupped; foliage glossy, dark; vigorous growth; [unknown × unknown]; int. in 1974

Pas de Deux LCl, my, Poulsen; flowers medium yellow, fading to white, 8-10 cm., dbl., slight wild rose fragrance; foliage dark green, glossy; bushy (150-200 cm.) growth; int. by Poulsen Roser, 2000

Pasadena HT, yb, 1927, Coolidge; flowers golden yellow, edged flame, dbl.; RULED EXTINCT 1/82; [sport of The Queen Alexandra Rose]

Pasadena HT, or, 1982, Kordes, W.; flowers large, lasting, 35 petals, high-centered, no fragrance; foliage large, medium green, matte; upright growth; [Mercedes × (Sweet Promise × (Miss Ireland × Zorina))]; int. in 1981

Pasadena Star F, w, 2001, Martin, Robert B., Jr.; flowers ivory with light pink edging and yellow at base, 4 in., full, high-centered, borne mostly solitary, no fragrance; foliage medium size, medium green, semi-glossy; prickles medium, downward pointed, brown; growth upright, medium (36 in.); exhibition; [Anne Morrow Lindbergh × Glowing Amber]; int. by Wisconsin Roses, 2001

Pasadena Tournament F, mr, 1942, Krebs; bud long, pointed; flowers velvety red, small, 36 petals, cupped, moderate fragrance; foliage bronze; long stems; very vigorous, bushy growth; [Cécile Brunner × seedling]; int. by Marsh's Nursery

Pasadena Tournament, Climbing Cl F, mr, 1945, Marsh's Nursery; [sport of Pasadena Tournament]

Pascal Sevran HT, rb, Adam; flowers white with red edges that spread down the petals as it opens, full, high-centered, borne mostly singly, moderate fragrance; foliage dark green, glossy, disease-resistant; moderate (3 ft.) growth; int. in 2002

Pascali HT, w, 1963, Lens; flowers creamy white, medium, 30 petals, high-centered, borne singly and in small clusters, slight fragrance; good repeat; foliage large, dark green; vigorous, upright, bushy growth; PP2592; [Queen Elizabeth × White Butterfly]; int. by A. Dickson, 1963; Gold Medal, Portland, 1967, Hall of Fame, WFRS, 1991, Gold Medal, The Hague, 1963

Pascali, Climbing Cl HT, w, 1978, Anderson's Rose Nurseries; [sport of Pascali]

Pascaline Min, w, 1986, Lens, Louis; flowers long lasting, 35 petals, high-centered, borne singly or in clusters, no fragrance; foliage dark gray-green; prickles slightly hooked, brownish-red; upright, bushy growth; [Unnamed Miniature seedling × (New Penny × Jour de Fete)]; int. in 1984

Pascha HT, mr, Kordes; flowers bright red, medium, full, borne mostly singly; greenhouse rose; int. by W. Kordes Söhne, 2001

Pashmina HT, mp, Kordes; flowers soft pink, medium, full, high-centered, borne mostly singly; good repeat; greenhouse rose; int. by W. Kordes Söhne, 2003

Pasita HT, dr, 1985, Kordes, R.; flowers bright dark red, flora-tea, 25 petals, borne singly; foliage glossy; prickles straight, light brown; medium-high, densely branched growth; [Mercedes × seedling]; int. by Ludwigs Roses Pty. Ltd., 1982

Paso Doble F, or, 1976, Paolino; flowers geranium-red, 3 in., 9 petals; vigorous growth; int. by URS

Passaya HT, w

Passe-Princesse HGal, mp, before 1813, Prévost; flowers light lilac-rose, very large, full

Passe-Velours HGal, m, before 1820, Descemet; flowers dark violet-purple, medium, dbl.

Passion HT, mr, 1955, Gaujard; bud long, pointed; flowers scarlet-cerise, 4 in., 36 petals, moderate fragrance; foliage dark; very vigorous, bushy growth; [Peace × Alain]

Passion – See **Paradise**, HT

Passion – See **Showy Pavement**, HRg

Passion – See **Netsujo**, HT

Passion de J. Renoard HT, m

Passion Rose – See **Manhattan**, HT

Passionate HT, mr, 2001, Zary, Keith; bud pointed, ovoid; flowers bright red, ruffled, 5 in., 25-30 petals, high-centered, borne mostly solitary, slight light, sweet fragrance; recurrent; foliage medium size, dark green, glossy; prickles moderate; growth upright, tall (5 ft.); garden decorative; PP13332; [Poulman × HT seedling]; int. as Habitat for Humanity, J&P, 2002

Passionate Kisses F, mp, 2001, Meilland International; flowers bright salmon-pink, 3 in., semi-dbl., borne in large clusters, slight fragrance; foliage medium size, medium green, semi-glossy; prickles small, few; growth bushy, tall (4-5 ft.); hedges, landscape; PPAF; [Celine Delbard × Laura]

Passion's Flame Min, dp, 1995, Rennie, Bruce F.; flowers deep pink, 1½ in., 6-14 petals, borne in small clusters; foliage medium size, medium green, semi-glossy; some prickles; tall (18-24 in.), spreading growth; int. by Rennie Roses International, 1993

Passoa HT, ob, Select; flowers flowes soft orange, 4 in., 30-40 petals, high-centered, borne mostly singly; recurrent; foliage dark green; stems long; florist rose; int. by Terra Nigra BV, 2005

Passport Cl HT, dr, 1940, Clark, A.; flowers well-formed; vigorous growth

Pastel HT, ab, 1961, Von Abrams; bud long, pointed; flowers creamy yellow and soft pink, 5 in., 25 petals, high-centered; foliage glossy, wrinkled; strong stems; vigorous, upright growth; [(Sutter's Gold × seedling) × Fred Edmunds]; int. by Peterson & Dering, 1961

Pastel Delight HT, lp, Kasturi; flowers delicate pastel pink, dbl., high-centered; int. by KSG Son, 1984

Pastel Princess HT, pb

Pastel Tower HT, Ruston, D.; [sport of Eiffel Tower]

Pastelina F, w, 1992, Schuurman, Frank B.; flowers near white, medium, full; foliage medium size, medium green, glossy; upright growth; [White Dream × Freegold]; int. by Riverland Nurseries, Ltd., 1991

Pastella F, pb, Tantau; flowers medium pink in center, outer petals creamy white, 8 cm., full, cupped, borne mostly in clusters, moderate fragrance; recurrent; compact (60-80 cm.), bushy growth; int. by Rosen Tantau, 2005; Certificate, Lyon, 2006

Pasteur HT, pb, 1978, Gaujard; bud long; flowers brilliant pink, flushed red, dbl.; upright growth; [Firmament × Femina]; int. in 1973

Pastorale S, pb, 1986, Poulsen, Niels D.; flowers deep pink, yellow reverse, large, 25 petals, urn-shaped, borne in sprays; foliage large, leathery, dark, glossy; prickles dark green; very vigorous, upright, bushy growth; [seedling × Royal Dane]; int. in 1970

Pastorella HT, 1953, Meilland, F.

Pastourelle HT, op, 1952, Robichon; flowers salmon-pink, very large; very free bloom; RULED EXTINCT 12/85; [Comtesse Vandal × Étoile d'Or]; Gold Medal, Rome, 1953

Pastourelle – See **Pastorale**, S

Pasture Rose – See ***R. carolina*** (Linnaeus)

Pat Austin S, ob, 1997, Austin, David; bud pointed, ovoid; flowers bright copper inside, paler outside, 3½-4½ in., 50 petals, borne in small clusters, moderate fragrance; foliage large, dark green, glossy; prickles some, long to medium, slighty hooked downward; branching, rounded, medium growth; PP9527; [Graham Thomas × Abraham Darby]; int. by David Austin Roses, Ltd.

Pat James F, ob, Harkness; flowers soft rosy copper, dbl., high-centered, borne singly and in clusters; int. in 1991

Pat Nixon F, dr, 1973, Meilland, Marie Louise; bud ovoid; flowers large, dbl., moderate fragrance; foliage large, glossy, dark; vigorous, upright, bushy growth; PP3546; [Tamango × (Fire King × Banzai)]; int. by Stuart & Co., 1972

Pat Phoenix HT, yb, 1964, Latham; flowers cream to yellow, flushed pink, base yellow, 4½-5 in., 40 petals; foliage dark, leathery; very vigorous growth; [(Wellworth × Clarice Goodacre) × Peace]

Pat Stewart HT, dp, 1977, Stewart, G.; flowers cerise to deep rose-pink, 5-5½ in., 26 petals; foliage dark; vigorous, upright growth; [Red Devil × Honey Favorite]

Patchwork HT, rb, Bailey, Dorothy J.; PP4012

Patchwork, Climbing Conklin, H. A., Conklin, H. A.; PP4441

Patchwork Quilt Min, ob, 1991, Jolly, Marie; bud ovoid; flowers orange-yellow-pink blend, aging light orange, medium, 60 petals, urn-shaped, borne usually singly, slight fragrance; foliage small, medium green, matte; upright, bushy, medium growth; [Rise 'n' Shine × Dandy Lyon]; int. by Rosehill Farm, 1991

Pathfinder S, or, 1995, Warner, Chris & Barbara; flowers vermillion, yellow eye, small, semi-dbl., borne in large clusters, slight fragrance; foliage small, medium green, glossy; few prickles; spreading, low growth; patio, groundcover; [(Little Darling × Anna Ford) × Eyeopener]; int. by Warner's Roses, 1996; TGC, St. Albans, 1994, Breeders Choice, 1996

Patience HT, ob, 1927, McGredy; bud pointed; flowers scarlet-carmine shaded orange and orange-scarlet, large, dbl., high-centered; Gold Medal, NRS, 1926

Patience, Climbing Cl HT, ob, 1935, Shamburger, C.S.

Patience Strong HT, mr, 1969, Trew, C.; flowers crimson-scarlet, pointed, large, dbl.; foliage dull, gray-green; free growth; [Basildon Belle × Red Dandy]; int. by Basildon Rose Gardens

Patina HT, w, Tantau; flowers creamy white with pink and green tones, dbl., borne mostly singly; florist rose; int. by Rosen Tantau, 1997

Patio Charm Cl Min, ab, Warner, Chris; flowers delicate, soft apricot; vigorous, upright growth; int. in 1994

Patio Cloud – See **Fluffy**, Min

Patio Dance MinFl, rb, 1985, Williams, J. Benjamin; flowers medium red, white reverse, small, 20 petals, high-centered; foliage medium size, dark, glossy; strong, low, bushy growth; [Winifred Coulter × White Gem]

Patio Delight F, op

Patio Flame – See **Apricot Medinette**, Min

Patio Gem Min, op, 1992, Schuurman, Frank B.; flowers moderately patio, medium, dbl., moderate fragrance; foliage small, medium green, matte; spreading growth; [Sexy Rexy × Firefly]; int. by Riverland Nurseries, Ltd., 1991

Patio Gold MinFl, my, 1985, Williams, J. Benjamin; flowers small, dbl.; foliage medium size, dark, semi-glossy; low, compact, bushy growth; [Patio Patty × Rise 'n' Shine]

Patio Honey Cl Min, ly, Warner, Chris; int. in 1995; Gold Star of the South Pacific, Palmerston North, NZ, 1995

Patio Jewel MinFl, m, 1976, Williams, J. Benjamin; bud pointed; flowers purple to clear amethyst, open, 2½ in., 5-7 petals; foliage leathery; very vigorous growth; [Europeana × Angel Face]; int. in 1975

Patio Jewel – See **Little Sizzler**, Min

Patio Orange MinFl, or, Harkness

Patio Patty MinFl, yb, 1976, Williams, J. Benjamin; bud pointed; flowers yellow, washed peach and orange, 2 in., 16 petals, globular, intense fragrance; foliage small, reddish-green; PP4360; [(Circus × The Optimist) × (Little Darling × Starina)]

Patio Pearl MinFl, pb, 1976, Williams, J. Benjamin; flowers light pearl-pink, base deeper, 1-1½ in., 18-20 petals, high-centered; foliage small, glossy, dark; vigorous growth; [Fairy Queen × The Optimist]; int. in 1975

Patio Pearl MinFl, lp, Olesen; flowers soft creamy pink, large, open; low, compact growth; int. in 1990

Patio Pearl, Climbing Cl MinFl, lp; bud pointed; flowers soft pink, open quickly, cupped, slight fragrance; growth to 2 m.; int. after 1990

Patio Prince – See **Crimson Medinette**, Min

Patio Princess S, op, Olesen; flowers blend of orange, pink and apricot, 8-10 cm., dbl., little to no fragrance; foliage reddish green; broad, bushy (100-150 cm.) growth; int. as Hørsholm By-Rose, Poulsen Roser, 1990

Patio Queen – See **Nice Day**, Cl Min

Patio Ribbon MinFl, dr, 1976, Williams, J. Benjamin; bud ovoid; flowers velvety bright dark scarlet, 2½-3 in., 16 petals, cupped, moderate fragrance; foliage dark; strong growth; [Europeana × Red Favorite]; int. in 1975

Patio Snow MinFl, w, 1985, Williams, J. Benjamin; flowers small, 35 petals, moderate fragrance; foliage small, medium green, semi-glossy; groundcover; very compact, spreading growth; [Sea Foam × Charlie McCarthy]

Patrice HT, w, 1985, Bartolomeo, Embriaco; flowers large, 25 petals, high-centered; foliage medium size, dark, semi-glossy; upright, bushy growth; [(Baccará × Generosa) × Zecchino d'Oro]

Patricia HT, mr, 1932, Chaplin Bros.; flowers carmine flecked pink, base orange-yellow; foliage glossy, dark; vigorous growth

Patricia F, ab, 1972, Fermor, E. R.; flowers apricot, base shaded gold; [sport of Elizabeth of Glamis]; int. by Fermor, 1972; Gold Medal, Orleans, 1979

Patricia Anne HT, dp, 1965, Buzza; flowers deep pink, reverse silvery pink, 4-5 in., moderate fragrance; foliage dark, glossy; vigorous growth; [sport of Kordes' Perfecta]

Patricia Beucher HMsk, m, Lens; flowers dark purplish pink, fading toward cream, 2 in., single, borne in large, pyramidal trusses of up to 50 or more; foliage red brown when young, changing to dark green; vigorous (150-200 cm.), arching growth; hips none; [Trier × Mutabilis]; int. by Lens Roses, 2001

Patricia C. Oppmann F, w, 1981, Jerabek, Paul E.; bud pointed; flowers very light yellow, 43 petals, cupped, borne singly and in clusters of up to 7; foliage medium green, glossy; prickles slightly hooked; vigorous, upright, dense growth; [seedling × seedling]; Bronze Medal, ARC TG, 1984

Patricia Dawn HT, or, 1998, Austin, M.L.; flowers orange-red, lighter reverse, 4 in., very dbl., high-centered, borne singly, moderate fragrance; foliage medium size, medium green, dull; prickles moderate; upright, medium growth; [sport of unknown]

Patricia Eileen Adams HT, mp, 2000, Kenny, David; flowers salmon pink, reverse lighter, 4 in., dbl., borne in small clusters, moderate fragrance; foliage medium size, dark green, glossy; prickles moderate; growth bushy, medium (2½ ft.); [(Avocet × (Prominent × Kiskadee)) × New Zealand]

Patricia Harknett HT, dp, 1961, Harknett, A. & P.; flowers deep pink, 4 in., 23 petals, moderate fragrance; foliage bronze-red; vigorous growth; [sport of Lady Sylvia]

Patricia Hyde F, mp, 1969, Harkness; flowers medium, semi-dbl.; [Ann Elizabeth × Red Dandy]

Patricia Kent S, ly, Harkness; flowers yellow with outer petals fading white, full, cupped, moderate fragrance; growth to 4 ft.; int. by Wharton's Nurseries, 2004

Patricia Kordana Mini Brite Min, lp, Kordes; PP11242; int. by Bear Creek Gardens, 2000

Patricia Lewis HT, dp, Kordes; bud pointed; flowers strong, deep pink to red, full, high-centered, borne usually singly; good repeat; foliage dark green, glossy; stems long, strong; vigorous, tall growth; int. by Ludwig's Roses, 2001

Patricia Macoun LCl, w, 1945, Preston; flowers small, dbl., loose, borne in clusters of 15-25, moderate fragrance; non-recurrent; foliage dark, glossy; hardy; [*R. helenae* × unknown]

Patricia Miller HT, w, 1977, Miller, J.; bud ovoid; flowers pure white, open, large, semi-dbl.; foliage leathery; vigorous, bushy growth; [sport of Queen Elizabeth × sport of Queen Elizabeth]; int. by Treloar Roses Pty. Ltd., 1978

Patricia Neal HT, mr, 1970, Macres; flowers bright cerise, large, dbl., high-centered; foliage dark, leathery; vigorous, tall growth; [sport of Better Times]; int. by Paragon Greenhouses, 1968

Patricia Piesse HT, lp, 1971, Fankhauser; flowers luminous light pink, medium, 50-60 petals, high-centered; foliage glossy; vigorous, upright growth; [Elizabeth Fankhauser × Memoriam]

Patricia Scranton Cl Min, yb, 1977, Dobbs; bud pointed; flowers light yellow, streaked red, 1½ in., 17 petals; foliage glossy, dark, soft; [Fairy Moss × Fairy Moss]; int. by Small World Min. Roses

Patricia Watkins F, lp, 1947, Watkins Roses; flowers bright pink, medium, 5 petals, borne in trusses; foliage dark; vigorous growth; [sport of Karen Poulsen]

Patricia Weston LCl, lp, 1992, Reynolds, Ted; flowers 3-3½ in., full, borne in small clusters, moderate fragrance; foliage large, dark green, glossy; some prickles; medium (2 m.), upright growth; [Westerland × Perfume Delight]; int. by Reynolds Roses

Patricia Willats S, op, 1973, Bottle, A. W.; flowers peach pink, 3 in., full, borne singly and in trusses; foliage small, light green, matte; growth upright 5-6 ft.; [Golden Showers × Hamburger Phoenix]

Patrician HT, mr, 1976, Warriner, William A.; bud ovoid, pointed; flowers cardinal red, 4-5 in., 28 petals, high-centered, intense fragrance; foliage large, dark; very upright growth; PP4043; [Fragrant Cloud × Proud Land]; int. by J&P, 1977

Patrick Anderson HT, dp, 1938, McGredy; bud long, pointed; flowers deep rose-pink, large, dbl., high-centered; foliage leathery; vigorous growth; [John Henry × Portadown Fragrance]; int. by J&P

Patrick Rudden's Rose HT, r, 2000, Rawlins, R.; flowers russet, 4 in., very full, borne mostly singly, no fragrance; foliage medium size, dark green, semi-glossy; prickles moderate; upright, medium (27 in.) growth; [Kanagem × Fellowship]

Patrick Vincent HT, dr, 1967, Vincent; flowers crimson; foliage dark; free growth; [Mirandy × F.W. Alesworth]

Patriot HT, pb, 1973, Meilland; buds large, long pointed; flowers pale pink to cream with petal margins shaded through pin to red, large, dbl, high-centered, borne mostly singly; foliage medium size, dark green, leathery, disease-resistant; growth vigorous, upright, bushy; int. by C-P, 1975

Patriot HT, dr, 1991, Warriner, William A.; flowers large, full, borne mostly singly, slight fragrance; foliage large, dark green, semi-glossy to glossy; upright (5 ft.), spreading growth; [Showstopper × Mister Lincoln]; int. by Bear Creek Gardens

Patriot Flame – See **Scudbuster**, Min

Patriot Kordana Min, rb, Kordes; flowers red and white striped, small, dbl., cupped, borne in clusters; recurrent; compact growth; int. by NewFlora, 2005

Patriot Song Min, dr, 2003, Moore, Ralph S.; flowers semi-dbl., borne mostly solitary, slight fragrance; foliage medium size, medium green; prickles small, straight, light green, few; growth upright, tall (18 in.); garden, landscape, hedge; [seedling (Sheri Anne × Dortmund) × Orangeade]; int. by Sequoia Nurs., 2003

Patriot's Dream MinFl, rb, 2000, Williams, Michael C.; flowers medium red, reverse white, medium, full, high-centered, borne mostly singly, slight fragrance; foliage medium size, dark green, semi-glossy; few prickles; upright, tall growth; [seedling × selected pollen]; int. by The Mini Rose Garden

Pat's Choice HT, or, Kordes; flowers coral vermilion, large, full, high-centered, borne in large candelabras, slight fragrance; good repeat; vigorous, medium to tall growth; int. in 1996

Pat's Delight S, mr, 1987, Williams, J. Benjamin; flowers crimson to light scarlet, loose, 16 petals, cupped, borne in sprays of 5-7; foliage large, dark green, glossy; prickles light green, curving downwards; upright, strong, good branching growth; [Queen Elizabeth × Chrysler Imperial]

Patsy HT, w, 1930, Dickson, H.; bud pointed; flowers pure white, open, very large, dbl., cupped; int. by Morse

Patsy Cline HT, m, 1983, Christensen, Jack E.; flowers light lavender, petals edged ruby lavender, large, 35 petals, high-centered, intense fragrance; foliage medium size, dark, matte; upright, bushy growth; PP5556; [Angel Face × Double Delight]; int. by Armstrong Nursery

Patte de Velours S, rb, Meilland; flowers red with white at base, medium, dbl., borne in small clusters; growth to 60-120 cm.; int. by Meilland Richardier, 2000

Patti Quarles HT, pb, 2005, Edwards, Eddie & Phelps, Ethan; flowers 4-5 in., full, borne mostly solitary, slight fragrance; foliage dark green, semi-glossy; prickles moderate; growth upright, medium (4-5 ft.); garden; exhibition; [seedling × Barbra Streisand]; int. in 2006

Patty Cakes Min, dy, 2005, Moe, Mitchie; flowers dbl., high-centered, borne mostly solitary, moderate fragrance; foliage small, medium green, matte; prickles few, small, straight, light brown; growth upright, short (15-18 in.), micro-mini; exhibition, garden; [Snow Bunny × Mighty Moe]; int. by Nor'East Miniature Roses, 2006

Patty Lou Min, pb, 1955, Moore, Ralph S.; bud ovoid; flowers rose pink, reverse silvery pink, 1 in., 55 petals, moderate fragrance; foliage small; dwarf (10-12 in.), bushy growth; PP1335; [Oakington Ruby × Oakington Ruby]; int. by Sequoia Nursery, 1953

Patty Sue Min, mp, 1985, Bennett, Dee; flowers medium, 35 petals, high-centered; foliage medium size, medium green, matte; vigorous, upright growth; [Little Darling × Little Chief]; int. by Tiny Petals Nursery

Patty's Pink F, lp, 1960, Spanbauer; bud long, pointed; flowers rose-opal, reverse camellia-rose, 2½ in., 40-45 petals, high-centered; foliage leathery, glossy; very vigorous, upright, compact growth; PP1860; [(Cécile Brunner × Mrs R.M. Finch) × (Cécile Brunner × Mrs R.M. Finch)]

Patty's Red F, mr, 1968, Paulen Park Nursery; flowers

cherry-red; [sport of Patty's Pink]

Paul Bigot HWich, dp, 1924, Turbat; flowers bright rose, shaded vermilion, borne in clusters of 5-10; vigorous, climbing growth

Paul Bocuse S, ab, Guillot-Massad; bud round, apricot; flowers apricot, fading pink, full, cupped, moderate fruity fragrance; free-flowering; vigorous (5 ft.) growth; int. by Roseraies Guillot, 1997

Paul Bouclainville HT, yb, 1930, Buatois; flowers carmine on yellow ground, reverse pinkish white tinted yellow, semi-dbl., cupped; very vigorous growth; [Mme Charles Detreaux × Mme Edouard Herriot]

Paul Buatois Cl HT, dr, 1931, Buatois; flowers velvety red, base yellow passing to purplish carmine, very large, dbl., cupped; foliage leathery; very vigorous, climbing growth; [Marie Baumann × Mme Edouard Herriot]

Paul Bunyan Gr, dr, 1961, Von Abrams; bud long, pointed; flowers deep red, 5 in., 55 petals, high-centered; foliage leathery; very vigorous, upright growth; [Charles Mallerin × Carrousel]; int. by Peterson & Dering, 1961

Paul Cezanne HT, yb, J&P; flowers striped yellow and deep coral-orange, medium, dbl., loose, borne in clusters, moderate fragrance; stems short; medium growth; int. in 1992

Paul Cottingham S, dy, 2006, Paul Chessum Roses; flowers dbl., borne mostly solitary, intense fragrance; foliage medium size, light green, semi-glossy; prickles medium, thin, pink, few; growth upright, medium (36 in.); beds, borders, containers; [seedling × seedling]; int. by World of Roses, 2005

Paul Crampel Pol, or, 1930, Kersbergen; flowers deep orange-scarlet, brighter and larger than Gloria Mundi, but not as double, borne in large clusters

Paul Crampel, Climbing Cl Pol, or, 1934, Vially (also Appleton, 1934; Tantau, 1937); [sport of Paul Crampel]

Paul Dauvesse HMult, my, 1933, Barbier; bud long, golden yellow; flowers bright canary-yellow, large, dbl., borne in clusters of 4-8; vigorous, climbing growth

Paul de Fontainne – See **Deuil de Paul Fontaine**, M

Paul de la Meilleraye HP, mr, 1863, Guillot; flowers carmine-red with lighter reverse, very large, dbl.

Paul de Zutter HT, ab, Van Gampelaere, J.; [Kanegem × Graham Thomas]; int. by RvS-Melle, 2008

Paul Délépine Pol, mp, 1933, Délépine; flowers brilliant rose-pink, dbl., globular, borne in clusters; foliage leathery, glossy; vigorous growth; [Yvonne Rabier × Dorothy Perkins]; int. by Pajotin-Chédane

Paul Dupuy HP, mr, 1852, Dupuy-Jamain; flowers crimson-scarlet, shaded velvety dark violet, large, full

Paul Duvivier HT, mr, 1932, Laperrière; flowers carmine, base yellow, dbl.; [Constance × Pax Labor]

Paul Ecke, Jr. S, ob, 2004, Carruth, Tom; flowers bright orange with a broad smoky edge, reverse deep orange, 2-3 in., single, borne in large, showy clusters, no fragrance; foliage medium size, dark green, semi-glossy, disease-resistant; prickles average, straight; growth spreading, medium (130 to 150 cm.); garden decoration; PPAF; [(Playboy × Altissimo) × Santa Claus × (International Herald Tribune × *R. soulieana* derivative)]; int. by Armstrong Garden Centers, Inc., 2005

Paul et Virginie B, m, 1847, Oger; flowers light lilac, mixed with flesh pink, large, full

Paul Fontaine HP, m, 1852, Fontaine; flowers lilac pink, medium, full

Paul Fromont – See **Boudoir**, HT

Paul Gauguin HT, m, J&P; flowers deep reddish-mauve with pink and white stripes, dbl., cupped, borne in clusters; foliage dark green; short to medium growth; int. in 1992

Paul Gold HT, my, Poulsen; flowers buttercup yellow, large, dbl., high-centered; int. in 1998

Paul Harris HT, dy, 1993, Weeks, O.L.; flowers 3-3½ in., full, borne mostly singly; foliage medium size, medium green, matte; some prickles; medium (40-48 in.), bushy growth; [(Summer Sunshine × Georgia) × seedling]; int. by Estrella Rose Company, 1993

Paul Holtge – See **Grace Moore**, HT

Paul Jamain – See **Charles Lefèbvre**, HP

Paul Jamain HP, dr, 1878, Jamain; flowers bright dark red, large, full

Paul Jerabek LCl, pb, 2007, Jerabek, Paul; flowers cream shading to pink, reverse white, 3 in., dbl., borne in large clusters; foliage large, dark green, semi-glossy; prickles moderate, medium to large, awl-like, green to brown; growth upright, tall (5-7 ft.); pillars, arbors, trellises; hardy; [unknown × unknown]; int. by Freedom Gardens, 2006

Paul Kadolozigue HMult, mp, 1912, Lambert, P.; flowers crimson, fading to lilac pink, 3½-4 cm., dbl., borne in clusters of 10-20, moderate damask and musk fragrance; foliage light green; few prickles

Paul Krampel – See **Paul Crampel**, Pol

Paul Krüger – See **Niphetos, Climbing**, Cl T

Paul Lafont HT, ly, 1920, Guillot, P.; flowers golden yellow to white tinted yellow, dbl.; low to medium growth; [Mme Maurice Capron × seedling]

Paul Lédé – See **Mons Paul Lédé**, HT

Paul Lédé, Climbing – See **Mons Paul Lédé, Climbing**, Cl HT

Paul Lucchini HT, dr, 1931, Buatois; flowers purplish garnet, shaded velvety red, dbl., cupped; foliage bronze, leathery; vigorous growth; [Rhea Reid × Yves Druhen]

Paul Marot HT, mp, 1893, Bonnaire; bud ovoid; flowers China pink, large, full; [Baronne Adolphe de Rothschild × Souv de Victor Hugo]

Paul McCartney – See **The McCartney Rose**, HT

Paul Meunier HT, yb, 1902, Buatois; bud elongated; flowers light yellow shaded salmon, very large, full; foliage bronzy green

Paul Monnier – See **Paul Meunier**, HT

Paul Nabonnand T, mp, 1877, Nabonnand, G.; flowers satiny rose, large, dbl., cupped; vigorous growth

Paul Neyron HP, mp, 1869, Levet, A.; flowers clear pink to rose-pink, tinted lilac, 6 in., 50 petals, cupped, good repeat, moderate fragrance; occasionally recurrent bloom; foliage large, rich green; vigorous growth; [Victor Verdier × Anna de Diesbach]

Paul Neyron Panachée – See **Coquette Bordelaise**, HP

Paul Noël HWich, pb, 1913, Tanne; bud salmon-orange-pink, with yellow base; flowers old rose and pale yellow, fading to medium pink, 2-3 in., very full, borne in clusters of 4-6, moderate fragrance; intermittent repeat; foliage small, dark green; vigorous, climbing growth; [*R. wichurana* × Mons. Tillier]

Paul Perras HP, lp, 1870, Levet; flowers pale rose, compact, large, very dbl.; sets many hips; sometimes classed as B

Paul Ploton HWich, mr, 1910, Barbier; flowers bright crimson red, reverse lighter, 3 cm., dbl., rosette, borne in clusters of 10-12; foliage dark; [*R. wichurana* × Mme Norbert Levavasseur]

Paul Potter S, rb, Williams, J. Benjamin; flowers bright red with ivory stripes, ruffled, dbl., borne in sprays, moderate fragrance; recurrent; compact, upright growth; int. by Hortico, 1997

Paul Red Star – See **P. G. Wodehouse**, HT

Paul Revere HT, mr, 1940, Roland; flowers carmine, opening scarlet-crimson, 4-5 in., 24-30 petals, cupped; vigorous, upright growth; [sport of Talisman]

Paul Ricard HT, yb, 1994, Meilland, Alain A.; bud ovoid, large; flowers amber yellow, 4 in., 40-44 petals, cupped, borne usually singly, intense anise fragrance; free-flowering; foliage large, medium green, matte; prickles numerous, medium, light tan; tall (110-120 cm.), upright growth; PP9001; [(Hidalgo × Mischief) × Ambassador]; int. by SNC Meilland & Cie, 1990; Gold Medal, Rome, 1991

Paul Ricault C, mp, 1845, Portemer fils; flowers rose-pink, large, dbl., quartered, intense fragrance; growth to 5 ft.; sometimes classed as B

Paul Richard – See **Paul Ricard**, HT

Paul Shirville HT, op, 1981, Harkness, R., & Co., Ltd.; flowers light salmon-pink, medium-large, 30 petals, high-centered, borne singly and in clusters of 3, moderate sweet fragrance; foliage large, dark, semi-glossy; prickles large, reddish; medium, bushy growth; [Compassion × Mischief]; int. in 1983; Edland Fragrance Medal, ARS, 1982

Paul Transon HWich, op, 1900, Barbier; bud dark pink; flowers pale salmon, darker at center, aging to lighter pink, 6 cm., dbl., borne in clusters of 3-5; foliage dark green, glossy; short, strong stems; growth to 10 ft.; [L'Idéal × *R. wichurana*]

Paul Verdier HP, dp, 1866, Verdier, C.; flowers bright rose, cupped, borne on laterals from longer canes, moderate fragrance; good repeat

Paul Vogel HT, mp, 1932, Vogel, M.; flowers medium, dbl.

Paula T, ly, 1908, Paul, G.; flowers straw yellow, center ocher yellow, very large, semi-dbl.; [Marechal Niel × Gilbert Nabonnand]

Paula Gr, or, 1980, James, John; flowers dusty salmon; [radiation induced sport of Queen Elizabeth]

Paula Anne Creasey F, rb, 1999, Dobbs, Annette E.; flowers 2/3 medium red, lower white, reverse light pink, 2½ in., 26 petals, borne in small clusters; foliage medium size, medium green, dull; prickles moderate; compact, low (2½ ft.) growth; [Tamango × Anne Scranton]; int. in 1998

Paula Clegg HT, mr, 1912, Kiese; flowers bright scarlet; [Kaiserin Auguste Viktoria × *R. foetida bicolor*]

Paula Louise F, yb, 2000; flowers light yellow, reverse medium yellow, medium, dbl., slight fragrance; foliage medium size, dark green, semi-glossy; prickles moderate; growth bushy, medium (60 cm.); [Matangi × Mood Music]; int. by Battersby Roses, 2001

Paula Mayer HT, pb, 1929, Leenders Bros.; flowers silvery carmine-pink, reverse yellowish-pink, semi-dbl.; [Mme Edmee Metz × Betty Uprichard]

Paula Meidinger HT, lp, 1923, Meidinger; flowers large, dbl.

Paula Nunn F, dy, 2001, Horner, Colin P.; flowers deep yellow, paler reverse, 8 cm., dbl., borne in large clusters, moderate fragrance; foliage medium size, medium green, semi-glossy; prickles moderate, medium, slightly curved; growth upright, tall (120 cm.); garden decorative; [(seedling × Ann Harkness) × Freedom]

Paula Scholle S, mp, Scholle, E.; flowers medium, semi-dbl.; int. in 1975

Paula Scholle II F, op, Scholle, E.; flowers large, dbl.; int. in 1980

Paula Vapelle HSpn, w, Louette; flowers 8 cm., dbl., rosette, moderate fragrance; free-flowering; foliage bluish green; vigorous (5 ft.) growth; hardy; [Stanwell Perpetual × unknown]; int. in about 1990

Paule Delavey Pol, ly, 1957, Privat; flowers creamy yellow; vigorous, bushy growth

Paulette F, ly, 1934, Buatois; flowers saffron-yellow to yellowish-white, very dbl., cupped, borne in clusters;

foliage leathery, glossy; vigorous growth; [Leontine Gervais × Paul Monnier]

Paulette HT, dp, 1946, Meilland, F.; flowers bright rosy scarlet, center tinted salmon, well-formed, large, very dbl.; foliage rich green; tall growth; [Peace × Signora]

Paulette Bentall HMult, m, 1916, Bentall; flowers purple/pink, small, semi-dbl., borne in very large clusters

Paulette Buffet HT, lp, 1921, Gillot, F.; flowers pale flesh-pink, reverse silvery pink, dbl.; [Jonkheer J.L. Mock × seedling]

Paulette Coquelet HT, mr, 1947, Mallerin, C.; bud long; flowers salmon-red tinted bright coral, large, dbl.; very vigorous growth; [seedling × Daniel]; int. by URS

Paulien Verbeek HT, ob, 1959, Verbeek; flowers orange-yellow, large, 55 petals; very vigorous growth; int. in 1958

Paulii HRg, w, 1903, Paul, G.; flowers pure white with bright yellow stamens, 2½ in., single, borne in small clusters; prostrate shrub growth; [*R. rugosa alba* × *R. wichurana*]

Paulii Rosea HRg, pb, 1904, Smith; flowers medium pink, white eye, yellow stamens, single; [sport of Paulii]

Pauline Min, w, 2004, Fletcher, Ira; flowers pure white, 1-1½ in., dbl., high-centered, borne mostly solitary, slight fragrance; good repeat; foliage small, light green, semi-glossy; growth compact, short (12-18 in.); garden decoration, containers, exhibition; [Fairhope × June Laver]; int. by Tiny Petals Nursery, Inc., 2004

Pauline Bonaparte – See **Mistress Bosanquet**, B

Pauline Dawson HWich, dp, 1916, Dawson; flowers deep pink, large, single; vigorous, climbing growth; int. by Eastern Nursery

Pauline Lancezeur HP, dr, 1854, Lancezeur; flowers crimson shaded violet, large, dbl.; recurrent bloom

Pauline Lansezeur – See **Pauline Lancezeur**, HP

Pauline Plantier T, w, 1841, Plantier; flowers medium, full

Pauliska HP, lp, 1856, Avoux & Crozy; flowers flesh white, large, full, moderate fragrance

Paul's Carmine Pillar HMult, mr, 1895, Paul; bud long, pointed; flowers carmine-red, open, 8-10 cm., single, borne in clusters of 5-20; very early bloom; foliage rich green; vigorous growth; [Gloire de Margottin × unknown]; sometimes classed as HCh or HGal

Paul's Double Musk S, w

Paul's Early Blush HP, lp, 1893, Paul; flowers blush, large, dbl., recurrent, intense fragrance; upright, low (2 ft.) growth; [sport of Heinrich Schultheis]; blooms earlier than other HPs

Paul's Himalayan Musk Rambler HMsk, lp, 1899, Earle/Paul; flowers blush-lilac-pink, fading to white, yellow stamens, 3 cm., dbl., borne in clusters, strong musk fragrance; thread-like stems; growth to 30 ft.; [*R. brunonii* × unknown]

Paul's Himalayica Alba Magna Sp, w, 1899, Paul; flowers semi-dbl., borne in huge, rhododendron-like clusters; form of *R. brunonii*

Paul's Himalayica Double Pink Sp, lp, 1899, Paul, G.; flowers semi-dbl., borne in large clusters; form of *R. brunonii*

Paul's Lemon Pillar Cl HT, ly, 1915, Paul; bud pale lemon-yellow; flowers pale sulfur-yellow to almost white, 12-13 cm., dbl., high-centered, intense fragrance; non-recurrent; foliage large; long, strong stems; vigorous growth; not dependably hardy; [Frau Karl Druschki × Maréchal Niel]; Gold Medal, NRS, 1915

Paul's Perpetual White – See **Paul's Single White**, N

Paul's Pink HT, lp, 1979, deVor, Paul F.; flowers soft pink, small, 28 petals, intense fragrance; vigorous growth; PP4613; [Snowsong Supreme × Pink Puff]; int. by DeVor Nurseries, Inc., 1978

Paul's Scarlet Climber LCl, mr, 1916, Paul, W.; flowers vivid scarlet, shaded bright crimson, 6-7 cm., semi-dbl., borne in large clusters; sometimes slightly recurrent; vigorous, climbing or pillar growth; very hardy; [Paul's Carmine Pillar × Reve d'Or]; Gold Medal, NRS, 1915, Gold Medal, Bagatelle, 1918

Paul's Single White N, w, 1883, Paul; flowers pure white, single, borne singly or in small clusters; foliage light green; vigorous growth; sometimes classed as Cl HP

Paul's Single White Perpetual – See **Paul's Single White**, N

Paul's Tree Climber HMsk, w, 1916, Paul, G.; flowers blush white, small, dbl.; hybrid of *R. brunonii* or *R. himalayica*

Paulspride LCl, yb, 1996, Jerabek, Paul E.; flowers yellow with pink edge changing to mostly pink, reverse medium yellow, 3½ in., full, borne in small clusters, moderate fragrance; foliage medium size, medium green, semi-glossy; few prickles; growth spreading, medium (8 ft.)

Pavane HT, Herholdt, J.A.; int. in 1969

Pavarotti – See **Leslie's Dream**, HT

Pavarotti HT, pb, deRuiter; bud medium, ovate; flowers medium pink, reverse somewhat lighter, 6 in., 25 petals, high-centered, borne mostly singly; good repeat; foliage medium size, medium green, semi-glossy; prickles medium, hooked downward, tan; vigorous, narrow, bushy (6 ft.) growth; hips funnel-shaped ; PP8631; [sport of Vivaldi]; greenhouse rose; int. by de Ruiter, 1993

Pavillon de Prégny N, m, 1863, Guillot père; bud small; flowers light violet-pink, 10-11 cm., full, globular, moderate fragrance; foliage small

Pavot – See **Grosse Mohnkopfs Rose**, S

Paw Maw Gr, m, 1994, Jerabek, Paul E.; flowers mauve turning red at edges of petals, large, 25-30 petals, borne singly or in clusters of up to 5, moderate fragrance; foliage large, medium green, semi-glossy; some prickles; tall, upright growth; [unknown × unknown]

Paws S, mp, 1999, Beales, Peter; flowers 4 in., very dbl., borne mostly singly, intense fragrance; foliage medium size, medium green, dull; numerous prickles; bushy, medium (2½ × 2 ft.) growth; [Silver Jubilee × Constance Spry]; int. by Peter Beales Roses, 1999

Pax HMsk, w, 1918, Pemberton; flowers pure white, prominent golden anthers, 3-4 in., semi-dbl., borne in clusters, intense fragrance; recurrent bloom; foliage large, leathery, dark green; long, strong stems; vigorous (4 ft.), bushy growth; [Trier × Sunburst]; Gold Medal, NRS, 1918

Pax F, w, 1946, Leenders, M.; flowers white tinted greenish, large, semi-dbl.; [Irene × Mme Alexandre Dreux]

Pax Amanda S, lp, 1937, Hansen, N.E.; flowers light pink, turning to white, 17 petals, borne in clusters; free, non-recurrent bloom; thornless; vigorous (7 ft.), growth; very hardy; [Frau Georg von Simson × *R. blanda*]

Pax Apollo S, dp, 1938, Hansen, N.E.; flowers deep pink, 14 petals, borne in large clusters; non-recurrent; thornless; vigorous (7 ft.), growth; very hardy; [*R. sempervirens* × *R. blanda*]

Pax Iola S, lp, 1938, Hansen, N.E.; flowers clear shell-pink, passing to nearly white, large, 25 petals, borne in large clusters; non-recurent bloom; thorness; vigorous, pillar, growth; very hardy; [Anci Bohmova × *R. blanda*]

Pax Labor HT, yb, 1918, Chambard, C.; flowers pale golden yellow, slightly shaded coppery carmine, large, dbl., globular; foliage dark bronzy green; vigorous growth; [sport of Beauté de Lyon]

Pax Labor, Climbing Cl HT, yb, 1929, Gaujard

Paxton – See **Sir Joseph Paxton**, B

Payable – See **Anusheh**, F

Paysagiste Faure-Laurent HT, ob, 1947, Gaujard; flowers orange, reverse orange-yellow, large, dbl.; foliage glossy, dark; vigorous growth

Paz Vila HT, mr, 1931, Munné, B.; flowers large, dbl.; foliage glossy; vigorous growth; [Jovita Perez × Jean C.N. Forestier]

Pea-Fruited Rose – See ***R. pisocarpa*** (Grav)

Peace T, ly, 1902, Piper

Peace HT, yb, 1945, Meilland, F.; flowers golden yellow edged rose-pink, 6 in., 43 petals, high-centered to cupped, slight fragrance; foliage large, very dark, leathery, glossy; very vigorous, tall, bushy growth; [((George Dickson × Souv. de Claudius Pernet) × Joanna Hill) × (Charles P. Kilham × Margaret McGredy)]; int. by C-P, 1945; Gold Medal, Portland, 1944, Hall of Fame, WFRS, 1976, Golden Rose, The Hague, 1965, Gold Medal Certificate, ARS, 1947

Peace, Climbing Cl HT, yb, 1950, Brandy (also Kordes, 1951); [sport of Peace]; int. by C-P

Peace S, dy, Poulsen; flowers deep yellow, 8-10 cm., semi-dbl., no fragrance; foliage dark; growth bushy, 40-60 cm.; PP12885; int. by Poulsen Roser, 2000

Peace Maker F, ob, Tagashira, Kazuso; flowers borne in clusters; int. in 1990

Peace Meillandina – See **Lady Sunblaze**, Min

Peace of Vereeniging – See **Kleopatra**, HT

Peace Palace – See **Peace**, S

Peace Sunblaze – See **Lady Sunblaze**, Min

Peaceful HT, pb, 1956, Boerner; bud globular; flowers deep coral rose pink, reverse lighter, 5½-6 in., 50 petals, cupped, moderate fragrance; foliage leathery; vigorous, upright growth; PP1599; [seedling × Peace]; int. by J&P, 1956

Peaceful Habitations S, mp, 2001, Ponton, Ray; flowers show some striping with age, medium, semi-dbl., borne mostly solitary, moderate fragrance; foliage medium size, medium green, matte; prickles medium, straight, moderate; growth upright, medium; garden decorative; [Folksinger × Lichterloh]; int. by Peaceful Habitations Rose Garden, 2000

Peacekeeper F, pb, 1994, Harkness; flowers orange/pink blend, yellowing with age, 3½ in., 30 petals, borne 7-10 per cluster, slight spicy fragrance; foliage medium size, light green, glossy; bushy, medium growth; [Dame of Sark × Bright Smile]; int. as United Nations Rose, Harkness New Roses, Ltd., 1996

Peaceport HT, op, 1960, Rokos; flowers deep orange-pink with yellow base and thin white outer edge, moderate fragrance; PP1282; [sport of Peace]; similar to it parent, Peace, in all respects but color and fragrance; int. by Wyant, 1960

Peaceport, Climbing Cl HT, op

Peach Min, ab, Poulsen; int. in 1998

Peach – See **Peach Parade**, MinFl

Peach Beauty HT, pb, 1970, Boerner; bud ovoid; flowers peach-pink, large, dbl.; foliage large, leathery; vigorous, bushy growth; [Ma Perkins × Polynesian Sunset]; int. by Thomasville Nursery

Peach Blossom – See **Egeria**, HP

Peach Blossom T, op, 1890, Dingee & Conard; flowers golden rose or peach blossom

Peach Blossom F, dp, 1932, Chaplin Bros.; bud orange-red; flowers soft carmine-rose, medium, semi-dbl., borne in clusters of 6-12; vigorous growth

Peach Blossom S, lp, 1994, Austin, David; flowers blush

pink, medium, semi-dbl., borne in large clusters, slight fragrance; foliage medium size, medium green, semi-glossy; some prickles; bushy, spreading (4 ft.) growth; [The Prioress × Mary Rose]; int. by David Austin Roses, Ltd., 1990

Peach Brandy Min, ab, 1979, Schwartz, Ernest W.; bud pointed; flowers small, 23 petals, high-centered, moderate fragrance; compact, bushy growth; int. by Bountiful Ridge Nursery, 1978

Peach Calypso HT, dy, de Ruiter; int. by deRuiter's New Roses Intl.

Peach Candy Min, ab, 1995, Moore, Ralph S.; flowers soft peach, small, dbl., borne in small clusters, slight fragrance; foliage small, light green, matte; few prickles; medium (24-30 cm.), upright, bushy growth; [Sheri Anne × Topaz Jewel]; int. by Sequoia Nursery, 1996

Peach Castle – See **Countess Celeste**, S

Peach Clementine Min, ab, Tantau; flowers creamy peach, large, full, cupped; free-flowering; growth to 40 cm.; int. by Rosen Tantau, 2002

Peach Delight MinFl, ab, 2001, Saville, F. Harmon; bud pale apricot; flowers deep peach, 2 in., very full, borne mostly solitary, intense fragrance; foliage medium size, dark green, semi-glossy; prickles 1/4 in., hooked down, numerous; growth upright, spreading, bushy, medium (20-26 in.); garden decorative; [Sequoia Gold × Harmony]; int. by Nor'East Miniature Roses, 2001

Peach Dream F, op, 1996, Bees of Chester; bud opening to peach orange center with pink edging; flowers 2½ in., dbl., high-centered, borne in small clusters; foliage medium size, dark green, glossy; few prickles; upright, medium (26 in.) growth; patio; int. by L W Van Geest Farms, Ltd., 1995

Peach Elite Min, ab, 1986, Lyon; flowers peach, to loose form, large, 26 petals, high-centered, borne singly; foliage large, medium green, matte; prickles small; upright growth; hips globular, medium, orange-red; [Dandy Lyon × unknown]; int. by M.B. Farm Min. Roses, Inc.

Peach Festival Min, op, 1997, Laver, Keith G.; flowers medium, very dbl., borne mostly singly, slight fragrance; foliage medium size, medium green, glossy; few prickles; upright, bushy, medium growth; [seedling × Painted Doll]; int. by Springwood Roses

Peach Fragrance – See **Momoka**, HT

Peach Fuzz Min, ab, 1990, Carruth, Tom; bud pointed, moss; flowers apricot blend fading to pastel, medium, 22 petals, high-centered, borne singly or in small clusters, intense moss fragrance; foliage medium size, dark green, glossy; prickles straight, yellow brown; bushy, rounded, full, medium growth; [Fairy Moss × New Year]; int. by Weeks Wholesale Rose Growers, 1990

Peach Garden – See **Momozono**, F

Peach Glow F, pb, 1960, Boerner; bud ovoid; flowers golden coral, base pink, 3 in., 30 petals, cupped, moderate spicy fragrance; foliage leathery; vigorous, upright, compact growth; PP1999; [Goldilocks × Fashion]; int. by J&P, 1960

Peach Kordana Min, ab, Kordes; bud pointed ovoid; flowers apricot, yellow, peach and pink, 5 cm., 20-24 petals, high-centered, borne mostly singly, slight fragrance; recurrent; foliage dark green, glossy; prickles few, thin, small, green-white; upright (16 in.), bushy growth; PP15612; [Amber Kordana × Golden Gate]; int. by W. Kordes Söhne, 2005

Peach-Leaved Rose – See ***R. chinensis longifolia*** (Voss) single

Peach Meillandina – See **Pêche Meillandina**, Min

Peach Melba HT, yb, 1960, Dicksons of Hawlmark; flowers yellow marked flame and pink; vigorous growth; [Golden Scepter × Hazel Alexander]

Peach Melba – See **Gitte**, HT

Peach Mikado F, ab, Tantau; flowers peachy apricot, borne in clusters; florist rose; int. by Rosen Tantau

Peach Mountain – See **Momoyama**, HT

Peach Nature S, ab; flowers yellow-apricot in center, pink on edges, medium, single; free-flowering; int. by Verschuren-Pechtold, 1999

Peach Parade MinFl, ab, Poulsen; flowers apricot blend, 5-8 cm., dbl., no fragrance; foliage dark; growth bushy, 20-40 cm.; int. by Poulsen Roser, 2000

Peach Parfait HT, op, 1993, Strahle, B. Glen; flowers pink coral, medium, full, borne mostly singly; foliage medium size, medium green, semi-glossy; few prickles; medium (70-100 cm.), upright growth; [Indian Pink × Melissa]; int. by Carlton Rose Nurseries, 1992

Peach Pastel MinFl, ab, Williams, J.B.; int. by Hortico, 2003

Peach Princess – See **Corina**, HT

Peach Schnapps S, ab; flowers amber-peach, semi-dbl., flat, borne mostly singly; foliage glossy, disease-resistant; compact, upright growth; hardy; int. by J.C. Bakker & Sons, 2000

Peach Sherbet F, pb, 1999, Teranishi, K.; flowers salmon pink, 4 in., 30 petals, high-centered, slight fragrance; [Sonia × seedling]; int. by Itami Rose Nursery, 1996

Peach Silk LCl, op, Clements, John; flowers soft peach pink, 4-5 in., 24+ petals, slight fragrance; abundant; growth vigorous to 8-10 ft.; PPAF; int. by Heirloom Roses, 2004

Peach Silks Min, ab, 1991, Clements, John K.; flowers rich peach, medium, dbl., borne in small clusters, no fragrance; foliage small, dark green, glossy; few prickles; tall (50 cm.), upright growth; [seedling × seedling]; int. by Heirloom Old Garden Roses, 1991

Peach Spire HT, ob, Kordes; flowers soft peach with a deeper shade of orange, large, full, high-centered, borne mostly singly; good repeat; neat, upright, very tall growth; int. by Ludwig's Roses, 1994

Peach Sunblaze – See **Pêche Meillandina**, Min

Peach Sunsation S, ab, Kordes; flowers tinted peach, small, dbl., borne in large clusters; low (18-24 in.), spreading growth; groundcover, hanging basket; int. in 1997

Peach Surprise HT, yb, 1994, Poulsen Roser APS; flowers peach and cream, large, full, borne mostly singly, moderate fragrance; foliage large, dark green, glossy; numerous prickles; spreading (80-100 cm.) growth; [sport of Freude]; int. by Cants of Colchester Ltd., 1995

Peach Treat HT, pb, 1968, Fuller; bud ovoid; flowers peach-pink, large, very dbl.; foliage leathery; vigorous, bushy growth; [Beauté × Kordes' Perfecta]; int. by Wyant

Peach Waterfall Min, lp, 2000, Meilland International; flowers light scarlet pink, reverse light carmine pink, 2½-3½ cm., very full, borne in small clusters, slight fragrance; foliage medium size, dark green, semi-glossy; prickles moderate; spreading, low (20-30 cm.) growth; PP10489; [(Meiplarzon × Meitrisical) × Katharina Zeimet]; int. by Conard-Pyle Co.

Peachblow HT, lp, 1942, Coddington; bud long, pointed; flowers large, dbl.; foliage glossy; vigorous growth; [Mme Butterfly × Yellow seedling]; int. by C-P

Peaches – See **Bouquet Vanille**, S

Peaches and Cream HT, ob, 1936, H&S; flowers salmon shaded gold and rose-pink, very dbl.; bushy growth; RULED EXTINCT 4/77; [seedling × Miss Rowena Thom]; int. by Dreer

Peaches 'n' Cream Min, pb, 1977, Woolcock; bud tapering; flowers light peach-pink blend, 1 in., 52 petals, high-centered, slight fragrance; foliage dark; upright, spreading growth; PP4278; [Little Darling × Magic Wand]; int. by Pixie Treasures Min. Roses, 1976; AOE, ARS, 1977

Peaches 'n' Cream HT, pb, J&P; int. in 1998

Peachy Min, pb, 1964, Moore, Ralph S.; flowers pink tinted yellow, small, 50 petals; foliage light green, soft; vigorous, bushy (12 in.) growth; [Golden Glow × Zee]; int. by Sequoia Nursery

Peachy – See **Nobilo's Chardonnay**, HT

Peachy Cheeks F, ob, 2006, Martin, Robert B., Jr.; flowers cream with peach edges, 3 in., full, borne mostly solitary; foliage medium size, medium green, semi-glossy; prickles medium, slightly hooked, brown, few; growth upright, vigorous, medium (36 in.); exhibition, garden; [Anne Morrow Lindbergh × Bolivar]; int. in 2006

Peachy Creeper – See **Euphoria**, S

Peachy Keen Min, ab, 1979, Bennett, Dee; bud long, pointed; flowers soft apricot-pink, 1 in., 18-20 petals; bushy, spreading growth; PP4769; [Little Darling × Sheri Anne]; int. by Tiny Petals Nursery

Peachy Pink HT, pb, 2006, Wells, Verlie W.; flowers pink, reverse lighter, 4 in., dbl., borne mostly solitary; foliage medium size, medium green, semi-glossy; prickles 3/16 in., straight, moderate; growth upright, medium (4 ft.); garden decorative, exhibition; [seedling × seedling]; int. by Wells MidSouth Roses, 2006

Peachy Pink Magic Carpet – See **Mystic**, S

Peachy Queen Min, ab, 2003, Denton, James A.; flowers apricot/pink, reverse apricot, 1¾ in., dbl., borne mostly solitary, no fragrance; foliage medium size, medium green, semi-glossy; prickles small, straight, light brown; growth bushy, medium (20-24 in.); garden decoration, containers; [June Laver × Reiko]; int. by James A Denton, 2003

Peachy White Min, w, 1976, Moore, Ralph S.; bud long, pointed; flowers near white, often tinted pink, 1½ in., 18 petals, moderate fragrance; foliage leathery; upright, bushy growth; [Little Darling × Red Germain]; int. by Nor'East Min. Roses; AOE, ARS, 1976

Peacock HT, op, 1985, LeMire, Walter; bud ovoid, pointed; flowers orange-coral, reverse cream, 5½ in., dbl., high-centered, borne usually singly, moderate spicy fragrance; foliage large, dark, semi-glossy; vigorous, upright, bushy growth; hips large, globular, orange-red; [Red Queen × Red Queen]; int. by Roses by Walter LeMire

Peak Performance HT, dr, 1991, Burks, Larry; flowers large, full, borne mostly singly; foliage medium size, dark green, matte; tall, bushy, spreading growth; [seedling × seedling]; int. by Co-Operative Rose Growers, 1991

Peanut Butter & Jelly – See **Chipmunk**, Min

Pearhip Rose – See ***R. pyrifera*** (Rydberg)

Pearl HT, lp, 1879, Bennett; flowers flesh pink, shaded carmine, medium, very dbl., moderate Bourbon fragrance; slender, weak growth; [Adam × Comtesse de Serenye]

Pearl HMult, w, 1915, Turner; flowers whitish pink, 2 in., single, borne in large clusters

Pearl HT, w, 1933, Bentall; flowers white, shaded pink

Pearl – See **Jilly Jewel**, Min

Pearl HT, w, 1999, Winchel, Joseph F.; flowers pearl white, 4½-5 in., dbl., borne mostly singly, slight fragrance; foliage large, dark green, glossy; prickles moderate; upright, bushy, medium (4-5 ft.) growth; PP13115; [unknown × unknown]; int. by Weeks Roses, 1999

Pearl – See **Bremer Stadtmusikanten**, S

Pearl P, Matthews, D.W.

Pearl Min, w, Olesen; flowers dbl., 25-30 petals, borne mostly solitary, slight fragrance; foliage dark green, glossy; growth bushy, low (40-60 cm.); PP11641

Pearl Abundance – See **The Soham Rose**, F

Pearl Anniversary MinFl, lp, Chessum, Paul; flowers delicate pearl pink, full, cupped, borne in clusters of 3-5, no fragrance; good repeat; foliage medium green, matte; compact (18 in.), bushy growth; int. in 1995

Pearl Chatsworth – See **Pearl Mirato**, S

Pearl Costin HT, yb, 1959, Reithmuller; bud long, pointed; flowers light yellow, center pink, large, semi-dbl., cupped; foliage leathery, wrinkled; vigorous, upright, bushy growth; [Elli Knab × Amy Johnson]

Pearl Dawn Min, mp, 1976, Saville, F. Harmon; bud short, pointed; flowers micro-mini, 1 in., 38 petals; very compact, bushy growth; [(Cécile Brunner × Perla de Montserrat) × Perla de Montserrat]; int. by Nor'East Min. Roses, 1975

Pearl Drift S, w, 1980, LeGrice; flowers white flushed pink, 18 petals, borne in small clusters; foliage glossy, reddish to dark green; prickles small, light brown; vigorous, compact, spreading growth; [Mermaid × New Dawn]; int. in 1981

Pearl Drift, Climbing – See **E. B. LeGrice**, LCl

Pearl Essence HT, lp, 2000, Zary, Keith; bud long, pointed ovoid; flowers large, 30-35 petals, high-centered, borne mostly singly, moderate sweet fragrance; free-flowering; foliage medium size, dark green, glossy; prickles moderate, hooked downward; stems strong; vigorous, upright, medium (5 ft.) growth; PP12127; [Sterling Silver × Honor]; int. by Bear Creek Gardens, 2001

Pearl Harbor HT, pb, 1943, Howard, F.H.; bud long, pointed; flowers light pink, reverse China-rose, 3-3½ in., 45 petals, high-centered, intense fragrance; foliage leathery, dark; very vigorous, upright growth; [Unnamed variety × Miss Rowena Thom]; int. by H&S

Pearl Kordana Min, w, Kordes; flowers cream white, dbl., high-centered; int. by W. Kordes Söhne

Pearl Meidiland S, lp, 1989, Meilland, Alain A.; bud ovoid; flowers light ochre pink, aging white, 2½ in., 28-32 petals, flat cup, borne in sprays of 3-15, no fragrance; good repeat bloom; foliage medium size, dark green, glossy; prickles small, reddish-brown; spreading, low growth; hips globular, small dish, reddish; PP6807; [(Sea Foam × MEIsecaso) × Sea Foam]; int. by The Conard-Pyle Co., 1989

Pearl Mirato S, lp, Tantau; bud pointed ovoid; flowers light pink, fading white, 2 in., 25-28 petals, high-centered, to pompon, borne in clusters of 7-15; starts late, then free flowering; foliage medium green, leathery, disease-resistant; prickles 4 mm., hooked downward, dark brown; low (50-60 cm.), spreading growth; groundcover; hips none ; PP12851; [sport of Footloose]; int. by Rosen Tantau, 2002

Pearl Nature S, lp; int. in 2001

Pearl of Baltimore HT, lp, 1925, Cook, J.W.; flowers shell-pink, center deeper, very dbl.; [Ophelia × Glorified La France]

Pearl of Bedfordview – See **Matilda**, F

Pearl of Canada – See **Perla de Alcañada**, Min

Pearl of Joy Gr, ab, J&P; flowers between light apricot and pearl pink; free-flowering; bushy, medium growth; int. in 1994

Pearl Palace – See **Pearl**, Min

Pearl Queen HWich, w, 1901, Van Fleet; flowers pearly white, finely tinted with deep rose, large, very dbl.

Pearl Rivers T, w, 1890, Dingee & Conard; bud peachy-red; flowers ivory-white, tinted and bordered light pink, intense fragrance; [Devoniensis × Mme de Watteville]

Pearl S. Buck HT, yb, 1940, Kordes; bud long, pointed, deep orange; flowers golden yellow suffused apricot, 4½ in., 45 petals; foliage leathery, dark; long stems; vigorous, bushy growth; [Joanna Hill × Étoile d'Or]; int. by J&P

Pearl Sanford Min, pb, 2007, Sproul, James A.; flowers creamy white with pink edging, 1½ in., dbl., high-centered, borne in small clusters; foliage medium size, dark green, semi-glossy; prickles small, few; growth compact, short (16-20 in.); borders, containers; hips numerous; [(Chipmunk × Heather Sproul) × [(Singin' in the Rain × Roller Coaster) × Tropical Twist]]; int. in 2007

Pearl Sevillana S, w, 1996, Meilland International SA; bud conical; flowers white edged light pink, 6 cm., 18 petals, cupped, borne in clusters of 6-15, very slight fragrance; recurrent; foliage medium size, dark green, dull; prickles very few, small to medium, pinkish to brown; bushy, medium (4-5 ft.) growth; hips small, many, decorative, orange with black eye; PP9536; [(Bonica × Pascali) × Edelweiss]; int. by The Conard-Pyle Co., 1996

Pearl Wilson Kissel HT, dp, 1954, Kissel and Motose; flowers bright red, 4½ in., 30-40 petals; foliage leathery; vigorous, bushy growth; [Red Columbia × Chrysler Imperial]

Pearl Wishes – See **Snow Hit**, MinFl

Pearlie Mae Gr, ab, 1981, Buck, Dr. Griffith J.; bud ovoid, pointed; flowers yellow blended with pink, reverse pink, 35 petals, cupped, borne singly and in clusters of up to 8, moderate fragrance; foliage leathery, semi-glossy, dark olive green, tinted copper; prickles awl-shaped; erect, bushy growth; [Music Maker × (Queen Elizabeth × Country Music)]; int. by Iowa State University

Pearls F, w, 2001, Rawlins, R.; flowers small, semi-dbl., borne in small clusters, moderate fragrance; foliage small, medium green, semi-glossy; prickles small, moderate; growth upright, low (60 cm.); garden decorative; [Laura Ford × Margaret Merrill]; int. by Pocock's Roses, 2001

Pearly Gates LCl, mp, 1999, Meyer, Lawrence; flowers pastel pearl pink, 5 in., very dbl., borne in small clusters on old and new wood, intense spicy fragrance; foliage large, medium green, dull; few prickles; climbing, tall (9-12 ft.) growth; PP10640; [sport of America]; int. by Weeks Roses, 1999

Pearly King S, w, Genesis

Pearly Peace HT, lp, 1959, Fryers Nursery, Ltd.; flowers soft pearl-pink; [sport of Peace]

Pearly Queen F, lp, 1963; flowers well-formed, 4 in., 22 petals, moderate fragrance; vigorous growth; [sport of Queen Elizabeth]; int. by North Hill Nursery, 1963

Pearly Shell HT, pb, 1972, Sherwood; flowers shell pink, center cream, large, 30 petals, high-centered; foliage glossy; vigorous, upright growth; [Pink Parfait × Michele Meilland]

Pearly Shores HT, ab, (EUGhien)

Pearly White LCl, w, 1942, Brownell; bud long, pointed; flowers white tinted pearl, open quickly, 21 petals; long, strong stems; vigorous, climbing (to 20 ft.), upright growth; [Glenn Dale × Mrs Arthur Curtiss James self seedling]

Pearly Wonder HRg, lp, Williams, J.B.; flowers very soft pink, dbl., globular, borne in clusters; int. by Hortico, 2004

Peat Fire Flame HT, op, 1985, MacLeod, Major C.A.; flowers pale orange, reverse salmon-pink, medium, 20 petals; foliage medium size, medium green, glossy; upright growth; [Red Planet × Bonnie Anne]

Peaudouce – See **Elina**, HT

Pebble Beach S, mp, Poulsen; flowers initially deep pink, fading quickly to medium pink, 2-3 in., dbl., loose, borne in clusters, no fragrance; foliage dark green, glossy; low (40-60 cm.), bushy growth; int. as Easy Cover, Poulsen Roser, 1996

Pebble Mill F, rb, 1973, Gregory; flowers magenta, reverse spirea-red, large, 28 petals, flat; foliage dark; [Paddy McGredy × seedling]

Peccato di Giola – See **Joyfulness**, HT

Pêche Meillandina Min, ab, Meilland; bud conical, small; flowers azalea pink tinted orange-buff, 2 in., 30-34 petals, cupped, borne mostly singly or in pairs, slight fragrance; recurrent; foliage medium green, semi-dull; few prickles; growth short, bushy; PP8000; [Pink Meillandina × (Frenzy × Ann Moore)]; int. by Meilland Intl., 1991

Pechtold's Flame – See **Tudor**, HT

Pechtold's Triumph F, dr, 1961, Verschuren-Pechtold; flowers oxblood-red, medium, semi-dbl., borne in large clusters; [Red Favorite × Frensham]

Pedrálbes HT, my, 1931, Camprubi, C.; flowers butter yellow, shaded gold, 5 in., 30 petals; foliage dark, glossy; very vigorous growth; [Frau Karl Druschki × Souv. de Mme Boullet]; int. by J&P

Pedro Costa HT, yb, 1889, da Costa; flowers yellow, with red and orange

Pedro Veyrat HT, ab, 1933, Dot, Pedro; bud long, pointed; flowers large, dbl., cupped; [Li Bures × Benedicte Seguin]; int. by C-P

Pedrus Aquarius HT, w, 1999, Poole, Lionel; flowers white/ivory, 6 in., full, borne mostly singly, slight fragrance; foliage medium size, dark green, glossy; prickles moderate; upright, bushy, medium (3 ft.) growth; [Solitaire × Joe Longthorne]; int. by David Lister Roses, 1999

Peek a Boo – See **Brass Ring**, Min

Peep-Eye Cl Min, mr, 1992, Williams, Ernest D.; flowers very distinct shade of medium red, medium, 25 petals, borne in large clusters; foliage small, dark green, glossy; some prickles; tall (4 ft.), upright, bushy growth; hardy (both heat & cold); [Red Delight × seedling]

Peep o' Day F, op, 1972, Harkness; flowers salmon, shaded orange, large, 28 petals; foliage dark; [(Pink Parfait × Highlight) × Orion]; int. by Mason, 1973

Peeping Tom S, dp, 1968, MacLeod; flowers deep pink, pointed, large, dbl.; recurrent bloom; foliage medium size, medium green, matte; vigorous, tall growth; [Kordes' Perfecta × Parade]

Peer Gynt HT, yb, 1970, Kordes, R.; flowers yellow, outer petals edged red, large, 50 petals, slight fragrance; vigorous, bushy growth; [Colour Wonder × Golden Giant]; int. by McGredy & Son, 1968; Gold Medal, Belfast, 1970

Peerless HT, mr, 1935, Joseph H. Hill, Co.; bud long, pointed; flowers bright velvety scarlet-carmine, large, 38-40 petals; [sport of Better Times]

Pegasus S, ly, 1997, Austin, David; flowers large, camelia-like, 110 petals, borne in small clusters, intense rich tea-rose fragrance; foliage large, dark green, semi-glossy, leathery; few prickles; bushy, branching, medium growth; PP9705; [Graham Thomas × Pascali]; int. by David Austin Roses, 1995

Peggy HT, my, 1905, Dickson, A.; flowers safron yellow, becoming primrose, semi-dbl.

Peggy HT, dp, 1934, Bees; bud long, pointed; flowers deep rose, dbl., high-centered; foliage glossy, light; vigorous growth; [Ophelia × Red-Letter Day]

Peggy A. Smith HT, pb, 1936, Smith, A.; flowers pink with yellow tints, medium, dbl.

Peggy Ann Landon LCl, ob, 1938, Brownell; flowers yellow-orange, becoming lighter, 3½-5 in., dbl., high-centered, moderate fragrance; foliage large, leathery, glossy, dark; long, strong stems; very vigorous, climbing (15-25 ft.) growth; [Glenn Dale × ((seedling × seedling) × Mary Wallace)]

Peggy Astbury HT, ab, 1920, Easlea; flowers soft amber to light yellow

Peggy Bell HT, ab, 1929, Clark, A.; flowers peach-buff pink, copper reverse, large, full, moderate tea myrrh fragrance; good repeat; vigorous, very tall (10-12 ft.) growth; int. by NRS New South Wales

Peggy England HT, ab, 1923, Lilley; flowers cream-apricot, sometimes tinted carmine

Peggy Gordon Gr, r, McGredy; flowers shades of apricot brown, reverse russet, dbl., high-centered, borne in large candelabras of up to 25; good repeat; foliage deep bronze, very glossy; stems medium; neat, medium high growth, many basals; int. by Ludwig's Roses, 2002

Peggy Grant Min, lp, 1954, Moore, Ralph S.; flowers shell-pink, small, 25 petals; foliage light green; dwarf (5-6 in.), bushy growth; [(Robinette × Mons. Tillier) × Zee]; int. by Sequoia Nursery

Peggy Jane Min, lp, 1986, Utz, Peggy L.; flowers light pink, with lighter petal edges and base; PP5999; [sport of Starina]; int. by Nor'East Min. Roses

Peggy Joan Reynolds S, mp, 1992, Reynolds, Ted; flowers 1½ in., 5 petals, borne in small clusters; very remontant, almost perpetual; foliage medium size, light green, semi-glossy, disease-resistant; few prickles; upright (150 cm.) growth; very hardy; [possibly HCh × *R. gigantea*]

Peggy Lee HT, lp, 1983, Feigel, John R.; flowers pale pink; PP5467; [sport of Century Two]; same description as Century Two, except for color; int. by Armstrong Nursery, 1982

Peggy M S, pb, 1996, Jerabek, Paul E.; flowers pink gradually turning white on outer petals, reverse yellow, 2½-3 in., 75 petals; foliage medium size, light green, glossy; numerous prickles; upright, medium (5 ft.) growth

Peggy Netherthorpe HT, mp, 1976, Delbard; flowers 5 in., 35 petals; foliage light; [(Voeux de Bonheur × Chic Parisien) × (Michele Meilland × Mme Joseph Perraud)]; int. by Harry Wheatcroft Gardening, 1974

Peggy Newton F, my, 1959, Boerner; flowers primrose-yellow, 2½-3 in., 40-50 petals, globular, borne in clusters; foliage small, leathery, glossy; dwarf, spreading growth; PP1682; [Golden Glow × Goldilocks]; int. by Stuart, 1957

Peggy Rockefeller HT, dr, 1992, Williams, J. Benjamin; flowers bright crimson to cherry red with dark, smoky red on edge of petals, 40 petals, moderate spicy fragrance; foliage large, dark green, semi-glossy; few prickles; upright, bushy, medium growth; [Queen Elizabeth × Swarthmore]; int. by New York Botanical Garden, 1991

Peggy 'T' Min, mr, 1988, King, Gene; flowers medium red with white, circular base, reverse white, 5 petals; foliage medium size, medium green, matte; prickles straight with hook, white; bushy, medium growth; no fruit; [Poker Chip × Rise 'n' Shine]; int. by AGM Miniature Roses

Peggy's Delight Min, pb, 1983, Williams, Ernest D.; bud medium to long, slender; flowers deep pink, white base and reverse, 1½ in., 45 -50 petals, high-centered, borne usually singly, slight fragrance; good repeat; foliage small, dark, semi-glossy; prickles few, slender, hooked downward, tan; stems slender, wiry; dwarf, bushy, upright growth; hips none ; PP5357; [Little Darling × Over the Rainbow]; int. by Mini-Roses, 1982

Peintre Renoir HT, mp, 1925, Roseraie de St. Jean; flowers large, dbl.

Pekali HT, ob, 1985, Pekmez, Paul; flowers orange, large, 35 petals, no fragrance; foliage large, glossy; upright growth; [seedling × Marina]

Pekamecel F, or, 1985, Pekmez, Paul; flowers 20 petals; foliage dark; upright growth; [seedling × seedling]; int. in 1984

Pekgold HT, dy, 1985, Pekmez, Paul; flowers medium, moderate fragrance; foliage dark, glossy; upright growth; [seedling × seedling]; int. in 1984

Peklican HT, dy, 1985, Pekmez, Paul; flowers large, 35 petals, moderate fragrance; foliage medium size, light green, matte; bushy growth; [seedling × Bellona]; int. in 1984

Pelé LCl, w, 1980, Benardella, Frank A.; bud ovoid; flowers pale pink, fading to pearly pink, 6 in., 35 petals, borne mostly solitary, slight soft, fruity fragrance; repeat bloom; foliage medium green; prickles triangular, hooked; upright growth with long canes; [seedling × seedling]; Bronze Medal, ARC TG, 1980

Pélisson M, dr, 1849, Vibert; flowers velvety red, turning purple, 6 cm., full, rosette

Pelletier HGal, lp, about 1825, Pelletier; flowers pale pink, medium, full

Pellion HT, w, Keisei; greenhouse rose; int. by Australian Roses, 2004

Pellonia T, w, 1874, Touvais; flowers creme, center white with light pink, large, very full, globular

Pelton Lonnen HT, my, 1977, Wood; flowers pure yellow, 28-30 petals, cupped, moderate fragrance; foliage light; bushy, compact growth; [sport of Whisky Mac]; int. in 1975

Pemberton's White Rambler HMult, w, 1914, Pemberton; flowers dbl., rosette, borne in large clusters, strong musky fragrance; non-recurrent; foliage glossy; prickles large

Pembridge HT, ob, 1934, Stevens, E.; flowers richer, deeper orange-yellow; [sport of Roselandia]

Pénélope D, dp, 1818, Vibert; flowers deep grenadine-rose, large, very dbl., globular; foliage edges tinged with red

Penelope T, rb, 1906, Williams, J.; flowers dark red, center creamy white, medium, full, high pointed, moderate fragrance; recurrent; growth to 4 ft.

Penelope HMsk, lp, 1924, Pemberton; flowers shell-pink fading to white, center lemon, semi-dbl., borne in clusters, moderate fragrance; recurrent bloom; foliage dark green; shrubby growth; [Ophelia × William Allen Richardson]; Gold Medal, NRS, 1925

Penelope, Climbing Cl T, rb, 1932, Rosen, L.P.

Pénélope HT, op, 1985, Gaujard, Jean; flowers medium salmon pink, well-formed, large, 35 petals, moderate fragrance; foliage large, medium green, semi-glossy; upright growth; [Americana × Chenonceaux]; int. by Roseraies Gaujard, 1980

Penelope Keith – See **Freegold**, Min

Penelope Mayo – See **Duchesse de Caylus**, HP

Penelope Plummer F, dp, 1970, Beales, Peter; bud orange; flowers vivid flamingo-pink, 4 in., 16 petals, flat; foliage dark green; moderate growth; [Anna Wheatcroft × Dearest]; int. by Intwood Lane Nursery, 1970

Penkala Slavoljub HT, ab, 1995, Rogin, Josip; flowers apricot-orange striped, medium, full, borne mostly singly; foliage medium size, dark green, semi-glossy; few prickles; medium (100 cm.), bushy growth; [sport of Ambassador]; int. by Rogin, 1995

Pennant LCl, mp, 1941, Clark, A.; flowers begonia-pink, dbl., moderate fragrance; profuse, non-recurrent bloom; [Flying Colours × Lorraine Lee]; hybrid gigantea

Pennies from Heaven Cl Min, r, 2006, Carruth, Tom; flowers smoky lavender-brown and orange blend, reverse similar but slightly lighter, 3-5 cm., semi-dbl., borne in small clusters; foliage small, dark green, glossy; prickles moderate, small, straight, beige; growth spreading, climbing, canes up to 150 cm. long; garden decoration; PPAF; [What a Peach × Easy Going]; int. by Nor'East Miniature Roses, Inc., 2007

Pennsylvania HT, pb, 1934, Neuner; bud long, pointed; flowers salmon-pink, center apricot, outer petals striped dark pink, semi-dbl., high-centered; [sport of Joanna Hill]

Pennsylvanian HT, ob, 1953, Ohlhus; bud pointed; flowers apricot-orange, 4-5 in., 25-30 petals; upright, bushy growth; [Luna × (Mrs Pierre S. duPont × Mrs Sam McGredy)]; int. by C-P

Penny F, rb, 1973, Sanday, John; flowers strawberry-red, base orange, rosette form, 2 in., 17 petals; dwarf growth; [Sarabande × Circus]

Penny Annie Min, lp, 1984, Bischoff, Francis J.; flowers small, 35 petals, high-centered, no fragrance; foliage medium size, medium green, matte; bushy growth; [Little Darling × seedling]

Penny Ante Min, yb, 2003, Cochran, L.C.; flowers yellow, reverse orange-tinted, 1½ in., full, borne in small clusters, no fragrance; foliage large, medium green, matte; prickles straight; upright, medium (24-30 in.) growth; [Poker Chip × open pollinated]; int. by Duane L. Coyier, 2003

Penny Candy Min, ob, 1982, Saville, F. Harmon; bud small, ovate, long pointed; flowers orange with yellow heart, yellow reverse, 1 in., 25-30 petals, cupped, borne singly or several together, slight fragrance; foliage small, glossy; prickles few, small, long, thin; tiny, compact growth; PP5031; [Rise 'n' Shine × Sheri Anne]; int. by Nor'East Min. Roses, 1981

Penny Coelen – See **Regatta**, HT, 1994

Penny Heyns F, ly, Tantau; int. in 1997

Penny Lane Min, lp, 1992, Taylor, Franklin; flowers cream base blending to light pink, medium, full, high-centered, no fragrance; foliage small, medium green, semi-glossy; few prickles; medium (38 cm.), upright, bushy growth; [Party Girl × Maids of Jubilee]; int. by Taylor's Roses, 1993

Penny Lane LCl, ab, Harkness; flowers apricot buff, pearly tones in hot weather, 4 in., 40 petals, borne singly and in clusters, moderate green apple fragrance; recurrent; growth to 8-10 ft.; int. in 1998

Pensioners Voice F, ab, Fryer, Gareth; flowers orange apricot with shades of pink, large, dbl., high-centered, borne in clusters, moderate fragrance; free-flowering; vigorous, upright (3 ft.) growth; int. in 1989

Penthouse – See **West Coast**, HT

Penthouse HT, mp, 1988, McGredy, Sam IV; flowers large, dbl., moderate fragrance; foliage large, medium green, matte; bushy growth; [seedling × Ferry Porsche]

Peon – See **Tom Thumb**, Min

Peony Blanc HRg, w, Johnson, M.; flowers large, mound of petaloids in the center, very full, rosette, intense sweet fragrance; good repeat; numerous prickles; vigorous, tall (6 ft.) growth; hips insignificant; [unknown × unknown]; int. in 2002

Peony of Fragrance HP, mp, 1933, Pahissa; flowers pink, peony-like, large; recurrent bloom

People F, dr, 1957, Tantau, Math.; flowers crimson shaded pink, large, 26 petals, flat, borne in large trusses; foliage light green; vigorous, bushy growth; [Cinnabar × (Kathe Duvigneau × Cinnabar)]; int. by Wheatcroft Bros., 1956; Gold Medal, NRS, 1955

People's Princess – See **Tickled Pink**, HT

Pepe HT, rb, 1961, deRuiter; flowers flame, base and reverse gold, 4 in., dbl.; foliage dark, glossy; vigorous growth; [Amor × Sutter's Gold]; int. by Blaby Rose Gardens, 1961

Pepino F, lp, Tantau; int. by Rosen Tantau, 1987

Pépita HGal, pb, about 1850, Moreau; flowers soft rosy pink striped white

Pepita Min, dp, 1987, Kordes, W.; flowers deep pink, small, full, no fragrance; foliage small, medium green, semi-glossy; spreading growth; [LENpi × (Mercedes × Garnette)]; int. in 1985

Pepita Min, dp, 2006; flowers full, borne in small clusters; foliage small, dark green, very glossy; growth bushy, medium (50 cm.); int. by W. Kordes' Söhne, 2004

Pepita F, pb, Kordes; flowers rich pink, lighter reverse, outer petals take on green tint, small, full, cupped, borne in sprays; good repeat; florist rose; int. by W. Kordes Söhne, 2006

Pepita Kordana Min, w, Kordes; flowers white with pink blush on reverse, dbl., urn-shaped; compact growth; container rose; int. by NewFlora, 2005

Pépite – See **Souv de J. Chabert**, F

Pepper Pot F, pb, 1973, Fryers Nursery, Ltd.; flowers rose-pink to red, splashed yellow, 3 in., 24 petals, high-centered; foliage light; free growth; [Circus × seedling]

Peppermint F, rb, 1965, Boerner; bud ovoid; flowers red, reverse cream, medium, dbl., cupped; foliage leathery; vigorous, bushy growth; PP2549; [Jingles × Jingles]; int. by J&P, 1964

Peppermint HT, r, Kordes; flowers russet with green tint on outer petals; greenhouse rose; int. by W. Kordes Söhne, 2002

Peppermint LCl, rb; flowers striped

Peppermint Candy Min, w, 1991, Williams, J. Benjamin; flowers ivory with red blend, medium, full, borne mostly singly, intense fragrance; foliage small, dark green, glossy; medium (12-18 in.), upright, bushy growth; PP6819; [Rose Parade × Easter Morning]

Peppermint Delight LCl, rb

Peppermint Ice F, w, 1992, Bossom, W.E.; flowers creamy greenish white, 3¼ in., 10 petals, cupped, borne singly and in sprays of 3-5; foliage medium size, medium green, semi-glossy; upright, medium growth; [Anne Harkness × Greensleeves]; int. by E.B. LeGrice Roses, Ltd., 1991

Peppermint Kordana Min, w, Kordes; flowers cream with a greenish tint, full, high-centered; int. by W. Kordes Söhne

Peppermint Patty Min, rb, 1990, Gruenbauer, Richard; bud pointed; flowers white with red edging, same reverse, aging darker red, 33 petals, urn-shaped, slight fruity fragrance; foliage medium size, medium green, semi-glossy; prickles straight, very few, tan; very hardy, upright growth; hips oblong, orange; [Libby × Libby]; int. by Richard Gruenbauer

Peppermint Stick Min, pb, J&P

Peppermint Stripe Min, rb, 1991, Spooner, Raymond A.; flowers small, dbl., intense fragrance; foliage small, medium green, semi-glossy; bushy growth; [Roller Coaster × seedling]

Peppermint Swirl HT, rb, 1989, Marciel, Stanley G.; bud slender, tapering; flowers currant red, aging discolors slightly, large, 30 petals, cupped, slight spicy fragrance; foliage medium size, dark green, semi-glossy; prickles declining, copper brown; upright, tall growth; PP7612; [seedling × seedling]; int. by DeVor Nurseries, Inc.

Peppermint Twist F, rb, 1992, Christensen, Jack E.; sepals have glandular structures on back; flowers red/white/pink striped, large, very full, flat to slightly cupped, borne in small clusters; foliage large, medium green, semi-glossy; some prickles on peduncle; medium (90-110 cm.), upright, bushy growth; [Pinstripe × Maestro]; int. by Bear Creek Gardens, 1992

Pepperoni S, or, Poulsen; int. in 1994

Per Chance Min, op, 1985, Florac, Marilyn; flowers orange-red fading bright pink, small, 5 petals, borne singly and in small clusters, moderate fragrance; foliage small, dark, matte; bushy growth; [Red Can Can × Care Deeply]; int. by M.B. Farm Min. Roses, Inc.

Perce Neige S, lp, Pekmez, Paul; int. in 1991

Perception – See **LeAnn Rimes**, HT

Perchè Si? HT, rb, 1958, Giacomasso; flowers carmine-red, reverse silvery white, well-formed; foliage dark, glossy; very vigorous growth; [Peace × Crimson Glory]; int. in 1956

Percussion F, rb, 1990, Zipper, Herbert; bud ovoid; flowers dark red with touch of yellow at base, reverse white at base, 25 petals, high-centered, moderate sweet fragrance; foliage medium size, medium green, semi-glossy; prickles very small, tan; mini-flora; upright, tall growth; [Sheri Anne × Deep Purple]; int. by Magic Moment Miniature Roses, 1990

Percy Izzard HT, yb, 1936, Robinson, H.; flowers maize-yellow, reverse buff flushed warm rose, large, dbl., high-centered; foliage leathery; vigorous growth; [May Wettern × Barbara Richards]; int. by Wheatcroft Bros.

Percy Pilcher F, op, 1961, Verschuren; flowers salmon-orange, large, dbl., borne in large clusters

Percy Thrower HT, mp, 1964, Lens; flowers rose-pink, well-formed, 4-5 in., 28 petals, moderate fragrance; foliage glossy; vigorous, tall growth; [La Jolla × Karl Herbst]; int. by C. W. Gregory, 1964

Percy Thrower, Climbing Cl HT, mp, Stoneham; [sport of Percy Thrower]; int. in 1978

Perdita S, ab, 1992, Austin, David; flowers blush apricot, large, very full, borne in small clusters, intense fragrance; foliage medium size, medium green, semi-glossy; some prickles; medium (100 cm.), bushy growth; [The Friar × (seedling × Iceberg)]; int. by David Austin Roses, Ltd., 1983; Edland Fragrance Medal, ARS, 1984

Perdita F, lp, Bidwell

Perennial Blue LCl, m, Mehring; flowers deep magenta with lilac tones, base of petals white, small, semi-dbl., cupped, borne in large clusters, moderate sweet fragrance; recurrent; foliage medium green, semi-glossy; growth to 8-10 ft.; int. in 2004; Silver Medal, Baden-Baden, 2006, German Rose Society Prize, Baden-Baden, 2006

Perennial Blush LCl, lp; flowers blush pink, fading quickly to white, small, semi-dbl., shallow cup, borne in large clusters; vigorous growth; int. by Pococks Roses, 2007

Perestroika – See **Sonnenkind**, Min

Perfect – See **Perfect Hit**, MinFl

Perfect Day – See **Hammershus**, F

Perfect Hit MinFl, dp, Poulsen; bud short, pointed ovoid; flowers deep salmon pink, 2 in., 30-35 petals, high-centered, then flat, borne singly or in small clusters, no fragrance; foliage small, glossy; prickles moderate, short, straight; stems short and strong; bushy, low (40-60 cm.) growth; PP10083; [seedling × Ruiforto]; int. by Poulsen Roser, 1996

Perfect Moment HT, rb, 1990, W. Kordes Söhne; bud pointed; flowers red on outer half of petals, yellow on inner, reverse yellow, 4-4½ in., 30-35 petals, high-centered, borne singly and in small clusters; foliage medium size, medium green, semi-glossy; prickles broad at base, narrowing, hooked down, red to brown; upright, bushy, medium growth; PP8007; [New Day × seedling]; int. by Bear Creek Gardens, 1991

Perfect Paillette – See **Perfect Hit**, MinFl

Perfect Peace – See **Dorothy Goodwin**, HT

Perfect Potluck Min, dy, 1992, Laver, Keith G.; flowers golden yellow, medium, dbl., borne in small clusters; foliage medium size, dark green, glossy; few prickles; low (30 cm.), compact growth; [Showbound × (Party Girl × June Laver)]; int. by Springwood Roses

Perfecta Pol, dr, 1920, Spek; flowers scarlet-crimson under glass, dark crimson in the open, large, dbl.; vigorous growth; [Ellen Poulsen × Merveille des Rouges]

Perfecta – See **Kordes' Perfecta**, HT

Perfecta Superior HT, mp, 1965, Kordes; flowers bright pink; [sport of Kordes' Perfecta]; int. by Wheatcroft Bros., 1964

Perfection HT, mp, 1925, Stielow Bros.; [sport of Columbia]

Perfection Pol, op, 1932, Prior; flowers softer coral-pink; [sport of Marytje Cazant]

Perfection F, pb, 1957, Ulrick, L.W.; flowers pink turning red, reverse white; [Masquerade × Masquerade]

Perfection Min, dp, Benardella, Frank; flowers dusky, deep cerise pink, large, dbl., high-centered, moderate fruity fragrance; medium growth; int. in 1999

Perfection de Lyon HP, pb, 1868, Ducher; flowers pink, reverse lilac, very large, full

Perfection de Montplaisir T, 1871, Levet, A.; flowers clear lemon, medium, full, moderate fragrance; [Canari × unknown]

Perfection des Blanches N, w, 1873, Schwartz, J.; flowers medium, dbl., borne in corymbs; vigorous growth

Perfection Orange – See **South Orange Perfection**, HWich

Perfectly Red HT, dr, 1999, Zary, Dr. Keith W.; bud pointed, ovoid; flowers velvety red, 4-4½ in., 25-30 petals, high-centered, borne mostly singly, slight sweet apple fragrance; recurrent; foliage medium size, dark green, semi-glossy; prickles moderate; upright (5 ft.) growth; PP11715; [seedling × Love]; int. as Topsy, Ludwig's Roses

Perfeita F, or, Moreira da Silva; flowers orange and carmine; [Cocorico × Vogue]

Perfume HT, dr, 1929, Marriott; bud long, pointed; flowers velvety, fiery deep crimson, 15 petals; vigorous growth; int. by Beckwith

Perfume HT, lp, Spek; int. in 1995

Perfume Beauty HT, mp, 1991, Meilland, Alain A.; bud conical; flowers rose bengal, medium, very dbl., cupped, borne singly, moderate fragrance; foliage large, dark green; upright, tall growth; PP7819; [Princess Margaret of England × (Carina × Silvia)]; int. by The Conard-Pyle Co., 1990

Perfume de Multiflore HT, m, 1935, Pahissa; flowers purple/pink, large, dbl.

Perfume Delight HT, mp, 1973, Swim & Weeks; bud long, pointed; flowers large, 26-35 petals, high-centered, borne mostly singly, intense fragrance; free-flowering; foliage large, leathery, glossy; prickles short to medium, hooked downward, brown; stems long, strong; vigorous, upright, bushy growth; PP3282; [Peace × ((Happiness × Chrysler Imperial) × El Capitan)]; int. by C-P

Perfume Perfection – See **Cotillion**, F, 1999

Perfume Simplex Min, yb

Perfume Tiger F, rb, 1999, Winchel, Joseph F.; flowers dark red and white striped, 1¾ in., 41 petals, borne in large clusters, intense fragrance; foliage medium size, medium green, semi-glossy; prickles moderate; spreading, medium (27 in.) growth; PP12630; [Roller Coaster × seedling]; int. by Coiner Nursery, 2000

Perfumed Bride HT, pb, Bell; int. in 1994

Perfumella HT, mp, Meilland; bud medium, conical; flowers 5 in., 45 petals, high-centered, borne 1-3 per stem, intense fragrance; good repeat; foliage medium to large, dark green, glossy; prickles numerous, medium, reddish to brown; vigorous, erect (5 ft.) growth; PP10565; [Noblesse × Silver Anniversary]; florist rose; int. in 1999

Pergolèse P, m, 1860, Robert et Moreau; flowers bright purplish crimson, shading to lilac, medium, very dbl., moderate fragrance; occasionally recurrent bloom; often classed as HP

Péricles D, dp, before 1826, Vibert; flowers purple-pink, marbled, medium, dbl.

Péricles HCh, lp, before 1830, Laffay

Perigord – See **Laura Ashley**, Cl Min

Perky Min, dp, 1959, Moore, Ralph S.; bud pointed; flowers 1 in., dbl., intense fragrance; foliage glossy; very bushy (12 in.), compact growth; [(*R. wichurana* × Floradora) × Oakington Ruby]; int. by Sequoia Nursery, 1958

Perl-Ilseta F, w, 1985, Tantau, Math.; flowers pearly white; [sport of Ilseta]; int. in 1984

Perla de Alcañada Min, dp, 1944, Dot, Pedro; bud small, ovoid; flowers carmine, 18 petals; foliage dark, glossy; dwarf, very compact (6-10 in.) growth; [Perle des Rouges × Rouletti]; int. by A. Meilland

Perla de Alcañada, Climbing Cl Min, dp, Dot, Pedro

Perla de Montserrat Min, pb, 1945, Dot, Pedro; bud small; flowers hermosa pink edged pearl, 18 petals, borne in clusters; dwarf, very compact growth; [Cécile Brunner × Rouletti]; int. by A. Meilland

Perla d'Oriolo S, Embriaco, B.; int. in 1992

Perla Rosa Min, mp, 1946, Dot, Pedro; bud well-formed; flowers bright pink, very full; very compact (6-8 in.) growth; [Perle des Rouges × Rouletti]

Perla Rosa, Climbing Cl Min, mp, 1947, Dot, Pedro

Perla Transilvaniei F, pb, Roman, G., and Wagner, S.; flowers mauvish-pink, small, 30 petals, borne in clusters, slight fragrance; foliage small to medium, dark green, glossy, healthy; [Rusticana × Lavender Dream]; int. by Res. Stn. for Hort., 2004

Perle Pol, lp, 1913, Kiese; flowers delicate pink, borne in clusters of 40

Perle Pol, w, 1920, Easlea

Perle Angevine Pol, lp, 1920, Délépine; flowers pale rose, small, dbl., borne in clusters; prickles few thorns; [Jeanne d'Arc × Mrs W.H. Cutbush]

Perle Blanche HT, w, 1985, Delbard, Georges; flowers large, 35 petals, no fragrance; foliage medium size, medium green, semi-glossy; upright, bushy growth; [(Virgo × Peace) × (Goldilocks × Virgo)]; int. in 1981

Perle d'Amour B, lp, Weihrauch

Perle d'Angers B, lp, 1879, Moreau et Robert; flowers delicate frosty flesh-pink, nearly white, large, very full, borne in small clusters

Perle d'Anjou Min, mp

Perle de Alcañada – See **Perla de Alcañada**, Min

Perle de Feu T, yb, 1893, Dubreuil; flowers yellow with copper-red and purplish tints, medium, dbl.; [Mme Falcot × Claire Carnot]

Perle de France A, w, 1824, Dematra; flowers medium, full

Perle de l'Orient HGal, rb, before 1811, Schwarzkopf; bud round; flowers purple red with edges nuanced violet

Perle de Lyon T, dy, 1872, Ducher; flowers apricot yellow, large, dbl.

Perle de Weissenstein – See **Perle von Weissenstein**, HGal

Perle des Blanches N, w, 1872, Lacharme, F.; bud hard, round, slightly pinkish; flowers creamy-white, aging to pure white, 5-7 cm., full, globular, borne in large clusters; growth tall; [Mlle Blanche Laffitte × Sapho (DP)]

Perle des Jardins T, ly, 1874, Levet, F.; flowers straw-yellow, large, dbl., globular, intense fragrance; foliage dark green; slender growth; [sport of Mme Falcot seedling]

Perle des Jardins, Climbing Cl T, ly, 1890, Henderson, J.; flowers golden-yellow, fading to very light yellow, very large, very full, cupped, intense fragrance; foliage dark green; [sport of Perle des Jardins]

Perle des Jaunes T, dy, 1903, Reymond; flowers golden yellow tinted salmon, large, dbl., moderate fragrance

Perle des Neiges HMult, w, 1902, Dubreuil; flowers medium, semi-dbl., borne in corymbs of 25-30

Perle des Panachées – See **La Rubanée**, HGal

Perle des Panachées HGal, m, 1845, Vibert; flowers white striped with lilac and violet or rose, small, dbl., borne in clusters of 3-8, moderate fragrance; foliage medium green, pointed, usually with 3 leaflets; possibly also has a synonym of Panachée Double

Perle des Rouges Pol, dr, 1896, Dubreuil; flowers velvety crimson

Perle d'Or Pol, yb, 1875, Rambaux; flowers golden pink, very dbl., borne in clusters, intense fragrance; foliage rich green, soft; growth to 3 ft.; [Polyantha alba plena × Mme Falcot]; int. by Dubreuil

Perle d'Or, Climbing Cl Pol, yb; flowers deep yellow, opening lemon-yellow; [sport of Perle d'Or]

Perle d'Or Yellow – See **Ravensworth**, Pol

Perle du Lac – See **Perle du Lac Annecy**, HT

Perle du Lac Annecy HT, dr, Dorieux; int. in 1992

Perle Meillandécor – See **Pearl Meidiland**, S

Perle Noire HT, dr, 1986, Delbard; flowers velvety dark red, well-formed, large, 38 petals; vigorous, bushy growth; [((Impeccable × Papa Meilland) × (Gloire de Rome × Impeccable)) × ((Charles Mallerin × Gay Paris) × (Rouge Meilland × Soraya))]; int. in 1975

Perle Orléanaise Pol, dp, 1913, Duveau; flowers carmine-pink, medium, dbl.; [Mme Norbert Levavasseur × Frau Cecilie Walter]

Perle vom Wienerwald HMult, pb, 1913, Praskac; flowers carmine-rose, reverse soft rose-pink, 2 in., semi-dbl., borne in medium to large clusters; foliage medium green; nearly thornless; vigorous, climbing growth; [Helene × Crimson Rambler]; int. by Teschendorff

Perle von Aalsmeer HT, dr, 1941, Verschuren; flowers deep red; [sport of Better Times]

Perle von Britz HMult, lp, 1910, Kiese; flowers pearly pink, fading to white, 3 cm., semi-dbl., borne in clusters of 30-50; [Tausendschön × unknown]

Perle von Godesburg HT, ly, 1902, Schneider; flowers cream, shaded lemon, large, full, moderate fragrance; [sport of Kaiserin Auguste Viktoria]

Perle von Heidelberg HT, lp, 1905, Scheurer; flowers silvery pink, reverse lilac pink, very large, full, intense fragrance; vigorous growth; [sport of La France]

Perle von Heidelberg, Climbing Cl HT, lp; int. in 1906

Perle von Hohenstein Pol, lp, 1923, Kiese; flowers carmine-red, small, semi-dbl., borne in clusters; [Freudenfeuer × seedling]

Perle von Remagen HT, lp, 1959, Burkhard; bud pointed; flowers soft pink, reverse tinted creamy white, large, dbl., high-centered, moderate fragrance; foliage glossy, leathery; long stems; vigorous, upright growth; [R.M.S. Queen Mary × Peace]; int. by Kordes, 1957

Perle von Weissenstein HGal, m, 1773, Schwartzkopf; flowers brownish, center purple, medium, dbl.; foliage dark green, finely dentate; prickles very small, straight, brown

Perlmutt-Prinzessin S, lp, Wänninger, Franz; flowers small, very dbl.; int. in 1990

Permanent Wave F, mr, 1932, Leenders, M.; flowers bright carmine, petals wavy, large, semi-dbl., borne in clusters; foliage glossy, dark green; vigorous, bushy growth; [sport of Else Poulsen]; int. by J&P, 1935; Gold Medal, Rome, 1934, Gold Medal, Bagatelle, 1933

Permeate Peace HT, pb, Dawson; int. in 1990

Permoser HT, yb, Institut für Obstbau Dresden Pillnitz; flowers light yellow with carmine edges, large, dbl.

Pernetiana ; int. by Pernet-Ducher

Pernille – See **Pernille Hit**, MinFl

Pernille Hit MinFl, pb, Olesen; bud pointed ovoid; flowers soft pink, overlaid with pale greenish-yellow, reverse slightly darker, 5-7½ cm., 16-19 petals, classic hybrid tea, borne mostly singly, slight wild rose fragrance; recurrent; foliage dark green, glossy; prickles few, 4-5 mm., linear, greyed-yellow; vigorous, bushy (40-60 cm.) growth; PP13301; [seedling × seedling]; int. by Poulsen Roser, 1998

Pernille Poulsen F, mp, 1965, Poulsen, Niels D.; flowers large, 18 petals, borne in clusters, moderate fragrance; foliage pointed, light green; [Ma Perkins × Columbine]; int. by McGredy & Son, 1965

Pernille Poulsen, Climbing Cl F, mp, 1985, Poulsen, Niels D.; [sport of Pernille Poulsen]; int. by Vilmorin-Andrieux, 1980

Pero d'Alenquer F, dr, Moreira da Silva; flowers dark velvety red, center lighter; [seedling × Alain]

Pérou de Gossard – See **Le Pérou**, HGal

Perpetual Michigan HSet, m, 1843, Feast; flowers rosy pink, changing to purple, large, full, globular, borne in large clusters; not remontant, but having a long bloom period

Perpetual Pink – See **Perpetual Michigan**, HSet

Perpetual Red S, mr, 1955, Gaujard; flowers bright red, open, medium, semi-dbl.; recurrent bloom; foliage abundant; very vigorous growth; [Gruss an Teplitz × seedling]

Perpetual Red Moss – See **Perpétuelle Mauget**, M

Perpetual Scotch HSpn, lp, 1819, from Scotland; flowers pale flesh pink, medium to large, dbl., flat, moderate fragrance; quite remontant

Perpetual Thalia – See **Thalia Remontant**, HMult

Perpetual White Moss – See **Quatre Saisons Blanc Mousseux**, M

Perpetually Yours LCl, my, Harkness; flowers creamy lemon yellow, large, 70 petals, slight fragrance; recurrent; foliage glossy, light green; growth shrubby climber to 8 ft., medium vigor; int. by R. Harkness & Co., 1999

Perpétuelle P, 1827, Vibert

Perpétuelle d'Anjou D, lp, before 1845; flowers whitish pink, petals edged lighter

Perpétuelle de Neuilly HP, mp, 1834, Verdier, V.; flowers lilac-pink, medium, full, cupped, globular; growth erect; [Athalin × unknown]

Perpétuelle de St Ouen – See **De Tous Mois**, HMsk

Perpétuelle Mauget M, mp, 1844, Mauget; flowers rose pink, 8-10 cm., full, cupped; very remontant; foliage light green, medium

Perpétuelle Sapho – See **Sapho**, P

Perroquet LCl, dy, 1957, Robichon; flowers large; foliage glossy; vigorous growth

Perroquet F, rb, 1960, Lens; flowers red, reverse yellow, becoming dark red, well-formed; foliage bronze; vigorous growth; [Peace × (Cinnabar × Circus)]

Persane HT, Dorieux; int. in 1984

Persepolis HT, dy, 1986, Kriloff, Michel; flowers 25

petals, intense tea fragrance; foliage clear green, glossy; [seedling × seedling]

Persian Autumn S, ab, 2004, Moore, Ralph S.; flowers orange/apricot with red eye, reverse orange/apricot streaked with red, 2½ in., single, borne in small clusters, slight fragrance; recurrent; foliage medium size, medium green, semi-glossy; prickles medium, hooked; growth spreading, vigorous, arching canes, tall (4-5 ft.); specimen; [Tigris × Seedling (Anytime × Gold Badge)]; hybrid Hulthemia; int. by Sequoia Nurs., 2005

Persian Carpet – See **Persian Delight**, F

Persian Delight F, rb, 1995, Fleming, Joyce L.; flowers rich crimson with yellow base of petal and reverse, medium, 10 petals, slight fragrance; foliage medium size, dark green, glossy; upright (up to 70 cm.) growth; [Masquerade × Traumerei]; int. as Persian Carpet, Hortico Roses, 1994

Persian Flame S, rb, 2007, Moore, Ralph S.; buds appear yellow; flowers Chinese red with a deep red eye, reverse yellow, large, 2½ in., single, borne in small clusters; foliage medium size, light green, matte; prickles medium, hooked, brown, moderate; growth spreading, medium (3-5 ft.); specimens hedge; [Tigris × Playboy]; Hulthemia hybrid; int. by Sequoia Nurs., 2007

Persian Light S, yb, 2006, Moore, Ralph S.; flowers medium yellow with a distinct red splotch at center, reverse light yellow, 2½ in., semi-dbl., borne in small clusters; some repeat; foliage small, medium green, matte; small, straight, brown, many prick; growth spreading, medium (3-5 ft.); arching shrub, specimen; [Tigris × un-named yellow mini]; Hulthemia hybrid; int. by Sequoia Nurs., 2006

Persian Musk Rose – See **Nastarana**, N

Persian Peach S, yb, 2007, Moore, Ralph S.; flowers peachy-yellow with red eye, reverse yellow, medium, 2½ in., semi-dbl., blooms borne mostly solitary; foliage medium size, matte; prickles medium, straight, tan to brown, numerous; growth upright, 3-5 ft.; [Cal Poly × *Hulthemia persica* seedling]; int. by Sequoia Nurs., 2007

Persian Princess Min, or, 1970, Moore, Ralph S.; bud small, pointed; flowers coral-red, small, 25 petals, high-centered to cupped, borne singly and in sprays of 4-6, slight fragrance; free-flowering; foliage medium small, semi-glossy, leathery; prickles medium, slender, hooked slightly downward; vigorous, bushy, dwarf (12-14 in.) growth; PP3161; [Baccará × Eleanor]; int. by Sequoia Nursery

Persian Sunset S, ob, 2006, Moore, Ralph S.; bud yellow; flowers pink/orange/red with a distinct red blotch at center, reverse yellow, 2-2½ in., semi-dbl., borne in small clusters; foliage medium size, medium green, matte; prickles small, straight, green, moderate; growth spreading, medium (3-5 ft.); [Tigris × seedling]; Hulthemia hybrid; int. by Sequoia Nurs., 2006

Persian Yellow – See ***R. foetida persiana*** (Rehder)

Persicifolia – See **À Feuilles de Pêcher**, A

Persistence LCl, mp, 2000, Brown, Ted; flowers dbl., borne in small clusters; foliage medium size, dark green, semi-glossy; prickles moderate; growth upright, climbing, tall (9 ft.); [Esprit × Meg]

Personality HT, yb, 1960, Morey, Dr. Dennison; bud large, ovoid; flowers golden yellow splashed red, 4½ in., 35-40 petals, open, borne singly, intense very sweet fragrance; recurrent; foliage large, leathery, glossy; prickles ordinary, medium length, hooked downward; vigorous, upright growth; hips none ; PP2097; [Peace × Sutter's Gold]; int. by J&P, 1960

Persuader HT, mp, 1960, Eacott; flowers bright pink, large, 30 petals, high-centered; vigorous growth; [Golden Scepter × Southport]

Persuasion F, lp, 1972, Sanday, John; flowers pale blush-pink, base orange, large, 30 petals, high-centered; foliage glossy; [Vera Dalton × Tropicana]

Persue de Gossart C, dp; flowers velvety cerise, with garnet reflexes, dbl.

Petal Pushers S, lp, 2007, Zary, Keith W.; bud pointed, ovoid; flowers soft pink with lighter pastel edges, 3 in., very full, pompon, blooms borne in small clusters; recurrent; foliage medium size, dark green, glossy; prickles few, 6-8 mm., hooked downward, greyed-orange; stems 12-14 in.; growth spreading, medium (3 ft.); groundcover; PPAF; [seedling × Footloose]; int. by Jackson & Perkins Wholesale, Inc., 2006

Petaluma S, rb, Poulsen; flowers medium red, fading as they open to medium pink on upper side, 5-8 cm., semi-dbl., flat, very slight fragrance; recurrent; foliage dark green, glossy; broad, bushy (60-100 cm.) growth; int. as Kirsch Cover, Poulsen Roser, 2004

Pete Musser F, or, 2000, Williams, J. Benjamin; flowers orange-red, non-fading, large, full, high-centered, borne mostly singly, moderate fragrance; foliage large, dark green, glossy; few prickles; upright, tall (3½-4 ft.) growth; [Olympiad × Mister Lincoln]; int. by J. B. Williams & Assoc., 2000

Pete Paul HT, mp, 2000, Warner, A.J.; flowers very full, high-centered, borne mostly singly, slight fragrance; foliage dark green, glossy; prickles moderate; very vigorous, upright, bushy, tall (5-6 ft.) growth; [sport of Swarthmore]

Peter Beales S, mr, Clements, John; flowers crimson-red with pronounced golden eye, 3 in., 5-8 petals, moderate sweet, honey fragrance; free-flowering; foliage dark green; rounded and densely foliaged (4 × 3½ ft.) growth; PPAF; int. by Heirloom, 2000

Peter Benjamin HT, ab, 1981, Allender, Robert William; bud long; flowers light apricot-pink, 40 petals, rounded, borne 2-3 per cluster, moderate fragrance; free-flowering; foliage small to medium size, light green; prickles red; medium-tall growth; [Benjamin Franklin × Peter Frankenfeld]; int. in 1978

Peter Cottontail MinFl, w, 2004, Martin, Robert B., Jr.; flowers dbl., high-centered, borne mostly solitary, slight fragrance; foliage medium size, medium green, semi-glossy, disease-resistant; prickles medium, pointed, on main canes only; bristles on rachis; bushy, tall (3 ft.,) growth; borders, small gardens, cutting; [Anne Morrow Lindbergh × Fairhope]; int. by Rosemania, 2004

Peter Cottrell – See **Sunny Abundance**, F

Peter Frankenfeld HT, dp, 1966, Kordes, R.; flowers rose-pink, well-shaped, large, dbl., high-centered; good repeat; foliage medium green, leathery, disease-resistant; rugged (4-5 ft.), spreading growth; flower size diminished noticeably in warmer climates; int. by A. Dickson

Peter Frankenfeld, Climbing Cl HT, dp, 1976, Welsh, E.; [sport of Peter Frankenfeld]; int. by Allen, L. C., 1975

Peter Goldman HT, yb, 1987, Dickson, Patrick; flowers medium, full; foliage medium size, medium green, glossy; bushy growth; [Silver Jubilee × Bright Smile]

Peter John HMsk, op, 2000, Jerabek, Paul E.; flowers light pink, yellow at base, 4 in., full, borne in small clusters, moderate fragrance; foliage medium size, light green turning dark green, semi-glossy; prickles moderate; spreading, medium (5-6 ft.) growth; int. by Freedom Gardens

Peter Lambert HWich, dp, 1936, Vogel, M.; flowers carmine-pink, 6 cm., dbl., globular, borne in small to medium clusters, no fragrance; foliage very glossy; prickles numerous, long

Peter Lawson HP, dr, 1862, Thomas; flowers deep scarlet shaded purple

Peter Long HT, or

Peter Mac Gold Jewel – See **Golden Jewel**, Min

Peter Mayle HT, dp, 2003, Meilland International; bud conical; flowers rose magenta, 4-5 in., 55 petals, cupped, borne mostly solitary, intense fruity and acidulous fragrance; good repeat; foliage dark green, glossy; bushy (4 ft.) growth; PP11660; [(Miss All-American Beauty × Papa Meilland) × Susan Hampshire]; int. as Lolita Lempicka, Meilland, 2002

Peter Mayle, Climbing LCl, dp; int. in 2005

Peter Nay HT, mr, 1959, Verschuren; flowers scarlet, large, dbl., intense fragrance; foliage leathery; long stems; very vigorous growth; [The Doctor × New Yorker]; int. by Blaby Rose Gardens, 1958

Peter Pan HT, dr, 1935, Knight, G.; flowers dark crimson, large; vigorous growth

Peter Pan – See **Presumida**, Min

Peter Pan F, mr, 1999, Schuurman, Frank B.; flowers 2 in., full, borne in large clusters and sprays, no fragrance; foliage medium size, dark green, glossy; prickles moderate; upright, medium growth; PP10937; [Pink Delight × seedling]; int. by Franko Roses New Zealand, Ltd., 1993

Peter Pan Min, mr, 1997, Warner, Chris; flowers bright red, dull red reverse; foliage small, medium green, glossy; bushy, low (10-12 cm.) growth; [Eyeopener × seedling]; int. by Wharton's Nursery

Peter Piper HT, or, 1969, Waterhouse Nursery; flowers Chinese orange, large, semi-dbl., urn-shaped; bushy growth; [sport of Piccadilly]

Peter Rosegger HMult, op, 1914, Lambert, P.; bud coral; flowers coral-pink, fading to white, 5-6 cm., dbl., rosette, borne in clusters of 5-15, strong musk fragrance; repeat bloom; foliage dark green; vigorous, climbing growth; [Geheimrat Dr. Mittweg × Tip-Top]

Peter Turvey HT, rb, 2003, Poole, Lionel; flowers red, reverse red/peach blend, 4½ in., full, borne mostly solitary, slight fragrance; foliage large, dark green, semi-glossy; prickles large, triangular; upright, bushy, medium (36 in.) growth; garden, exhibition; [Mike Thompson × (Royal William × Gabi)]; int. in 2004

Peter Wessel – See **Glad Tidings**, F

Peter's Briarcliff HT, mp, 1940, J&P; flowers true unshaded rose-pink, long pointed, well-formed; foliage dark; vigorous, free growth

Pétillante – See **Roter Champagner**, HT

Petit Ange – See **Little Angel**, Min

Petit Bonheur LCl, mp, Adam; int. in 2001

Petit Canard Min, ly, 1986, Lens, Louis; flowers small, 20 petals, high-centered, borne in clusters of 12-22; foliage small; prickles few, green; bushy growth; [Rosina × (Le Vesuve × Belle Étoile)]; int. in 1984; Gold Medal, Paris, 1984

Petit Constant Pol, mr, 1899, Soupert & Notting; flowers nasturtium-red, small, dbl.; vigorous growth; [Mignonette × Luciole]

Petit Four Min, mp, 1982, Ilsink; flowers large, semi-dbl., borne in clusters, moderate fragrance; foliage small, medium green, glossy; prickles numerous, small; bushy growth; [(Marlena × unknown) × seedling]; int. by J&P, 1986

Petit François F, or, 1957, Dorieux; flowers semi-dbl.; foliage glossy; very dwarf growth; [Alain × (Brazier × Léonce Colombier)]; int. by Pin

Petit Jean HT, ob, 1926, Vestal; flowers deep orange-buff, shaded to yellow, edged peach-pink, large, dbl., moderate fragrance; [White Killarney × Sunburst]

Petit Louis HWich, op, 1912, Nonin; flowers shrimp-pink, 3½ cm., very dbl., borne in medium clusters;

foliage small; vigorous, climbing growth; [Dorothy Perkins × unknown]

Petit Marquis – See **Esprit**, S

Petit Poucet F, mr, 1955, Combe; flowers bright red, center tinted yellow, petals wavy, single; dwarf growth; [Cocorico × seedling]

Petit Prince Pol, mr, 1956, Laperrière; flowers geranium-red, borne in clusters of 8-10; very dwarf growth; int. by EFR

Petit Quatre Saisons D, dp, Noël; flowers deep pink, small, dbl.; growth dwarf

Petit Rat de l'Opéra HMsk, pb, 2000, Lens, Louis; flowers deep pink, reverse lighter, 2 cm., single, borne in large clusters, slight fragrance; recurrent; foliage large, medium green, semi-glossy; few prickles; upright, medium (60-90 cm.) growth; [(*R. multiflora adenocheata* × Ballerina) × Ballerina]; int. by Louis Lens N.V., 1990

Petit René HWich, mr, 1925, Nonin; bud small, globular; flowers brilliant red, 3½ cm., very dbl., borne in small to medium clusters, intense fragrance; non-recurrent; vigorous, climbing growth

Petit St François C, m, about 1850, Robert; flowers bluish-pink with purple-violet, full, globular; dwarf Centifolia

Petit St. François – See **Pompon de Saint-François**, C

Petit Sam F, dp, Adam

Petit Serpent S, w, 2000, Lens, Louis; flowers white, shaded pink, reverse white, 2 cm., single, borne in large clusters, moderate fragrance; non-recurrent; foliage small, dark green, glossy; prickles moderate; spreading, low (10 × 80 cm.) growth; groundcover, containers; hips red; [Green Snake × (*R. multiflora* × unknown)]; int. by Louis Lens N.V., 1994

Petit Trianon F, lp, Meilland; flowers clear Neyron pink, 34-37 petals, cupped, borne in clusters, slight fragrance; recurrent; foliage dark green; growth to 60-70 cm.; int. by Meilland Richardier, 2005

Petit Vermilion HGal, mr, about 1823, from Angers

Petite – See **Patty Lou**, Min

Petite Agathe – See **Sommesson**, HGal

Petite Aimée HGal, before 1814, Descemet

Petite Anglaise – See **Maiden's Blush**, A

Petite Carrousel Min, w, 1985, Michelis, Dorothy; flowers ivory, coral pink petal edges, small, borne singly and in clusters, slight fragrance; foliage small, dark, semi-glossy; upright, tiny growth; [Thought to be Magic Carrousel × unknown]

Petite Chalons – See **Burgundian Rose**, HGal

Petite de Hollande C, mp, before 1791; flowers rose pink, small, dbl., borne in small clusters, moderate fragrance; foliage ovoid, pointed, serrated; prickles small, sharp, slightly hooked; short (18 in.) growth; from Holland

Petite de Terre Franche HMsk, pb, Louette; flowers light rosy pink dotted with carmine, fading to white, 3-4 cm., semi-dbl., pompon, borne in large clusters, slight fragrance; free-flowering; canes up to 2½ m. long, spreading growth; int. in 1996

Petite Écossaise HSpn, lp, before 1826, Vibert or Prévost; flowers flesh, small, semi-dbl.; non-recurrent; moderate growth

Petite Ernestre – See **Petite Junon de Hollande**, C

Petite Évêque HGal, before 1815, Descemet

Petite Folie Min, ob, 1970, Meilland; flowers vermilion, reverse carmine, small, dbl., globular, borne in trusses, slight fruity fragrance; foliage leathery; vigorous growth; [(Dany Robin × Fire King) × (Cricri × Perla de Montserrat)]; int. by URS; Gold Medal, Japan, 1969

Petite Francoise Pol, lp, 1915, Gravereaux

Petite Fredaine MinFl, op, 2000, Lens, Louis; flowers orange pink, reverse lighter, 3-4 cm., dbl., borne in small clusters, moderate fragrance; foliage medium size, medium green, semi-glossy; few prickles; growth bushy, medium (35-40 cm.); [(Little Angel × unknown) × Little Angel]; int. by Louis Lens N.V., 1991

Petite Frolic Min, yb, Taschner, Ludwig; bud orange-red; flowers yellow base with varying orange and red markings over the petals, single, shallow cup to flat; free-flowering; compact growth; int. by Ludwig's Roses, 2005

Petite Hessoise HEg, mp, about 1810, Redouté/Lahaye; bud pointed; flowers bright rose, small, semi-dbl.; foliage large, light green, round; prickles protrusive, strong

Petite Hollande – See **Petite de Hollande**, C

Petite Jeanne HWich, mr, 1912, Nonin; flowers currant-red; [Dorothy Perkins × unknown]

Petite Junon de Hollande C, lp, before 1820, from Holland; flowers small, full; Petite Ernestre may be a separate cultivar (D) from Descemet

Petite Léonie Pol, w, 1893, Soupert & Notting; flowers pinkish white, small; [Mignonette × Duke of Connaught]

Petite Lisette A, dp, 1817, Vibert; flowers rich rose, with a small center eye to medium, 1 in., full, pompon, borne in small clusters, slight fragrance; non-remontant; foliage matte, pointed, grayish-green, toothed, small; few prickles; growth to 3-4 ft.; sometimes classified as C or D, but listed by Vibert as A; probably a hybrid of an Alba and a Damask Perpetual

Petite Louise – See **Belle Mignonne**, HGal

Petite Louise LCl, op; flowers salmon-pink

Petite Marcelle Pol, w, 1910, Dubreuil; flowers snow white, small, borne in clusters of 5-10; foliage dark green

Petite Michelle Min, pb, J&P; int. in 1993

Petite Odette HWich, lp, 1923, Nonin; flowers very dbl., borne in clusters; vigorous, climbing growth; [Lady Godiva × seedling]

Petite Orléanaise HGal, mp, before 1843; flowers strong pink, with a small central eye, small, dbl., flat, rosette at center, borne in clusters of 2-6, slight fragrance; vigorous, almost climbing. growth; sometimes classed as C; documented in Vibert's catalog of 1843

Petite Penny F, w, 1988, McGredy, Sam IV; flowers small, semi-dbl., moderate fragrance; foliage small, medium green, semi-glossy; bushy growth; [(Crépuscule × seedling) × Royal Occasion]; int. by McGredy Roses International, 1988

Petite Perfection Min, rb, 1999, Walden, John K.; bud long, ovoid; flowers bright red/yellow, reverse deep yellow, 2¼-2½ in., 25 petals, high-centered, borne singly and in small clusters, slight tea fragrance; foliage medium size, dark green, glossy; prickles moderate; upright, compact, medium (16-22 in.) growth; patio mini; PP12049; [seedling × seedling]; int. by Bear Creek Gardens, Inc., 1999

Petite Perle d'Or Min, ab, 2007, Rippetoe, Robert Neil; flowers ¾ in., dbl., borne in small clusters; foliage small, medium green, semi-glossy; no prickle; growth bushy, dense, twiggy, short (12 in.); border hedge, containers; [Perle d'Or × Cinderella]; int. in 2006

Petite Provins – See **Rosier d'Amour**, HGal

Petite Red Scotch – See **Double Dark Marbled**, HSpn

Petite Reine – See **Queenie**, F

Petite Renoncule Violette – See **Félicie**, HGal

Petite Rosamund C, lp, 2003, Boutin, Fred; flowers streaked lavender-pink on white, reverse fainter streaks of lavender-pink, 1¾ in., very full, borne mostly solitary, no fragrance; foliage small, medium green, matte; prickles very small, in., thin, slightly recurved, light brown; growth upright, compact, short (24 in.); specimen or hedge; [Burgundian Rose (Parvifolia, Pompon de Bourgogne) × Ferdinand Pichard]; very similar in character and size to Pompon de Bourgogne; int. in 2003

Petite Violette HGal, m, before 1815, Descemet; flowers violet, small

Petito F, yb, Agel

Petra F, mr, 1975, Kordes; bud medium, globular; flowers blood-red, dbl.; foliage dark, leathery; moderate, bushy growth; [seedling × Taora]; int. by Dehner & Co., 1974

Petra F, mp, Roman, G., and Wagner, S.; flowers pure pink, small, 40 petals, rosette, borne in clusters, slight fragrance; foliage medium size, medium green, glossy; practically thornless; [Bonica '82 × Rosabunda]; int. by Res. Stn. for Hort., 2004

Petrine HT, ob, 1921, Therkildsen; flowers coral-red, shaded chrome-yellow, dbl.; [Old Gold × Mme Edouard Herriot]

Petro F, w

Petrol HT, r, Spek; flowers deep brownish red, 4 in., 55-60 petals, high-centered, borne mostly singly; recurrent; numerous prickles; stems moderately long; int. by Jan Spek Rozen, 2005

Petronella HT, rb, 1980, MacLeod, Major C.A.; flowers pointed, 49 petals, borne singly; foliage dark, glossy; prickles straight, red; compact growth; [Gail Borden × (Dalvey × Fragrant Cloud)]; int. by Christie Nursery, Ltd.

Pétronille – See **Beauté Superbe Agathée**, HGal

Petticoat Min, w, 1982, Warriner, William A.; bud short; flowers white tinted pink, 55 petals; foliage dark, small, pointed; very compact, spreading growth; PP5039; [Bon Bon × Lemon Delight]; int. by J&P, 1981

Petticoat F, w, 2006; flowers cream white with soft apricot coloured center, 6-7 cm., full, borne in small clusters; growth compact, medium (70 cm.); int. by W. Kordes' Söhne, 2004; Silver Medal, Kortrijk, 2006

Petticoat Fairy Tale – See **Petticoat**, F

Petticoat Lane Min, pb, 1985, Eagle, Barry & Dawn; flowers medium pink, deeper in center, light pink reverse, small, 28 petals, high-centered; foliage small, dark, semi-glossy; upright, very small growth; [Pink Petticoat × Pink Petticoat]; int. by Southern Cross Nursery, 1986

Petula Clark HT, mr, 1963, Lens; flowers clear red, well-formed, dbl., high-centered; foliage bronze; vigorous, bushy growth; [Purpurine × Lavender Pinocchio]

Petula Clark, Climbing Cl HT, mr, 1979, Lens; int. in 1967

Pfaffstädt HP, ly, 1929, von Württemberg, Herzogin Elsa; flowers yellowish-white, large, dbl., moderate fragrance

Pfälzer Gold HT, dy, 1983, Tantau, Math.; flowers large, 20 petals, no fragrance; int. in 1981

Pfander's Canina (strain of *R. canina*), lp; int. by Pfander, prior to 1954

Pfuss Pfree F, mp, 1989, Stoddard, Louis; bud ovoid, pointed; flowers light pink, reverse medium pink, small, 25 petals, cupped, borne in sprays of 4-6; foliage medium size, medium green, very glossy, black-spot resistant; prickles straight, tan-brown; spreading growth; hips round, deep orange; [Sea Foam × (unnamed Restless Native seedling × Europeana)]

Phab Gold F, dy, Fryer, Gareth; flowers vibrant gold, full, high-centered, borne in clusters, moderate fragrance; recurrent; foliage bright green, disease-resistant; low (45 cm.) growth; int. in 1998

Phaenomen HT, op, 1934, Chotkové Rosarium; flowers

slightly rosy salmon, reverse light rosy red, very large, dbl.; foliage dark; very vigorous growth; int. by Böhm

Phaloé HGal, mp, about 1845, Calvert; flowers bright pink, shaded lilac, medium to large, very full

Phaloé N, yb, 1846, Vibert; flowers light yellow, shaded dawn pink, large, full

Phantasy HT, lp, 1927, Dunlop; flowers medium light pink, base yellow, dbl.; [Lady Alice Stanley × Royal]

Phantom HT, ob, 1920, Towill; flowers coppery yellow, center lighter, semi-dbl.; RULED EXTINCT 4/92; [(Joseph Hill × (My Maryland × Unknown)) × Lady Hillingdon]

Phantom S, mr, 1992, McGredy, Sam IV; flowers scarlet red, large, semi-dbl., slight fragrance; foliage large, medium green, semi-glossy; spreading (80 cm.) growth; [Pandemonium × Eyeopener]; int. by McGredy Roses International

Pharaoh HT, or, 1970, Meilland, Mrs. Marie-Louise; bud ovoid; flowers bright orange-red, 5 in., dbl., high-centered, moderate fragrance; foliage dark, glossy, leathery; vigorous, upright growth; PP2859; [(Happiness × Independence) × Suspense]; int. by URS, 1967; Gold Medal, The Hague, 1967, Gold Medal, Madrid, 1967, Gold Medal, Geneva, 1967, Gold Medal, Belfast, 1969

Pharaon B, mr, before 1889, Bernède; flowers velvety red

Pharaon – See **Pharaoh**, HT

Phare LCl, or, 1961, Delbard-Chabert; flowers bright orange-red, 3 in., 33 petals, borne in small clusters; foliage glossy, dark green; vigorous (to 10 ft.) growth; [Spectacular × (Floradora × seedling)]

Pharericus HGal, dp, about 1829, Calvert; flowers dark pink to light red, large, full

Pharisäer HT, op, 1903, Hinner, W.; bud long, pointed; flowers rosy white, shaded salmon, dbl., high-centered, moderate fragrance; foliage bronze; long, weak stems; vigorous growth; [Mrs W.J. Grant × unknown]

Pheasant – See **Heidekönigin**, HWich

Pheidippides F, mr, 1977, Ellick; flowers currant-red, 4 in., 35 petals; foliage light green; moderately vigorous, low growth; [Sam Ferris × Chopin]; int. by Excelsior Roses, 1979

Phelan's Flag HCh, rb, 1952, Phelan; bud ovoid, greenish white flushed purplish red; flowers red when newly opened, changing to pink, then white with a red eye, 2½-3 in., 75-100 petals, quartered, intense fragrance; semi-recurrent bloom; foliage dark; vigorous (6 ft. or more) growth, with tendency to climb

Phénice HGal, dp, 1843, Vibert; flowers reddish-rose, spotted, medium, dbl.

Phenomène LCl, w, Delbard; flowers cream, fading white, medium, semi-dbl., borne in small clusters, moderate apple fragrance; int. in 1989

Phenomenon – See **Phaenomen**, HT

Philadelphia – See **Philadelphia Rambler**, HMult

Philadelphia HT, yb, 2001, Thomson, George L.; flowers lemon yellow, 2 in., full, borne mostly solitary, moderate fragrance; foliage medium size, dark green, glossy; prickles medium, hooked; growth upright, medium (4½-5½ ft.); garden decorative; [Francis Phoebe × Ophelia]; int. by Ross Roses, 2001

Philadelphia Rambler HMult, dr, 1904, Van Fleet; flowers scarlet-crimson, center lighter, 4 cm., dbl., borne in large clusters, no fragrance; midseason bloom; numerous prickles; vigorous, climbing growth; [Crimson Rambler × Victor Hugo]; int. by Conard & Jones

Philadelphica HBank, w; flowers cream white, single; [sport of *R. banksiae lutea*]

Philatelie HT, rb, McGredy; flowers red and white striped, dbl., high-centered, borne singly and in clusters; foliage dark green; compact (70-80 cm.) growth; int. by Rosen-Union, 2000

Philémon Ch, m, 1821, Cochet or Vibert; flowers dark purple, becoming lilac pink, medium, dbl.

Philémon N, m, about 1835, Laffay; flowers lilac, striped purple, small, full

Philémon – See **Philémon Cochet**, B

Philémon Cochet B, dp, 1895, Cochet, Sc.; flowers deep bright pink, very large, very full, somewhat globular, borne mostly solitary; foliage dark green; prickles slightly recurved, reddish; growth semi-climbing

Philibert Boutigny HP, mp; flowers silvery rose, very large; vigorous growth

Philip Harvey F, ob, 1972, Harkness; flowers salmon-red, shaded orange, 5 in., 25 petals, moderate fragrance; foliage glossy, dark; [Fragrant Cloud × Circus]

Philipp Melanchthon F, dr, Hetzel; int. in 1994

Philipp Paulig HP, dr, 1908, Lambert; flowers large, full, moderate fragrance; [Captain Hayward × Baronne Adolphe de Rothschild]

Philippe F, op, 1959, Delforge; bud oval; flowers peach-salmon, open, medium, 15 petals, borne in clusters; foliage glossy; moderate growth; [Cognac × Fashion]

Philippe Bardet HP, mr, 1874, Moreau-Robert; flowers red nuanced carmine, very large, full, borne in small clusters

Philippe Noiret – See **Glowing Peace**, Gr

Philippe Pétain HT, dp, 1940, Nabonnand, C.; flowers velvety carmine with coppery reflections, not turning blue, cupped; foliage bright chive-green

Philippe Rivoire HT, op, 1941, Gaujard; flowers large, dbl.

Philippine Lambert HMult, op, 1903, Lambert; flowers bright salmon and peach, darker center, borne in clusters; [(Euphrosyne × Safrano) × Dr. Grill]; sometimes classed as Pol

Phillipa – See **Julia Renaissance**, S

Phillipp Paulig HP, dr, 1908, Lambert, P.; flowers large, dbl.

Philomèle N, lp, 1844, Vibert; flowers flesh pink

Philomene C, m, Hardy; growth to 4 ft.

Philomène Crozy HP, m, 1857, Avoux; flowers lilac pink

Philomène Pollaert HT, or, 1925, Pollaert; flowers crimson tinted orange, dbl.; [(Gen. MacArthur × unknown) × Old Gold]

Phil's Chromatella N, dy

Phil's Hot Pink Perpetual Damask D, mp

Phloxy F, rb

Phoebe HT, w, 1922, Cant, B. R.; flowers cream-white, sometime pure white, dbl.; [Ophelia × Verna Mackay]; Gold Medal, NRS, 1921

Phoebe Min, lp, 1990, Harkness, R., & Co., Ltd.; bud pointed; flowers pale rose pink, aging very little, rosette, medium, very dbl., slight fragrance; foliage small, medium green, semi-glossy; prickles needle-like, long, decurved, small, dark green; bushy, low growth; fruit not a noticeable feature; [Clarissa × (seedling × Mozart)]; int. in 1989

Phoebe's Choice Min, pb, 1987, Bilson, Jack M., Jr. & Bilson, Jack M. III; flowers pink, edges yellow, pink softens, white edges, dbl., high-centered; foliage medium size, medium green, glossy; prickles reddish-green, sloped downwards; upright, bushy growth; hips round, light orange and green; [Little Darling × Over the Rainbow]

Phoebe's Frilled Pink – See **Fimbriata**, HRg

Phoebus HGal, mp, 1818

Phoebus HP, mp, 1837; flowers bright pink, shading lighter, large, dbl.; bushy growth

Phoebus D, m, before 1848; flowers lilac blush, centers rosy crimson, large, full; growth erect

Phoenix – See **Beauté Insurmontable**, HGal

Phoenix HT, dp, 1973, Armstrong, D.L.; flowers light cerise, large, dbl., high-centered, moderate fragrance; foliage large, glossy, leathery; vigorous, upright growth; [Manitou × Grand Slam]; int. by Armstrong Nursery

Phoenix Min, rb, 1990, Harkness, R., & Co., Ltd.; bud urn-shaped; flowers blood red, with yellow base, aging orange-carm, dbl., slight fragrance; foliage small, medium green, semi-glossy, pointed; prickles narrow, recurved, small, green; bushy, low growth; fruit not a noticeable feature; [Clarissa × (Wee Man × (Southampton × Darling Flame))]; int. in 1989

Phoenix First F, dr, 1959, Kernovske, V.R.; bud ovoid; flowers dark red shaded black, small, very dbl., borne in clusters; foliage leathery; bushy growth; [Our Princess × Pompon Beauty]; int. by Langbecker, 1959

Photogenic S, w, 1999, Jerabek, Paul E.; flowers white with pink edge, reverse white with narrow pink edge, 2½-3 in., 10 petals, borne in small clusters, moderate fragrance; foliage large, medium green, semi-glossy; upright, tall (10 ft.) growth; int. by Freedom Gardens, 1998

Phyllis Pol, mr, 1908, Merryweather; flowers bright red, small, dbl., borne in large clusters; recurrent bloom; [Mme Norbert Levavasseur × unknown]

Phyllis Bide Cl Pol, yb, 1923, Bide; flowers pale gold, shaded pink, 3 cm., semi-dbl., borne in large clusters, slight fragrance; dependably recurrent; growth to 6-10 ft.; [Perle d'Or × Gloire de Dijon]; Gold Medal, NRS, 1924

Phyllis Burden HT, op, 1935, Cant, B. R.; bud long, pointed; flowers shrimp-pink and orange, large, dbl.; foliage glossy, light; very vigorous growth

Phyllis Diller Gr, dy, 2005, Carruth, Tom; flowers very deep pure yellow, long lasting, 11-13 cm., dbl., borne in small clusters; foliage large, dark green, glossy; prickles average, straight; growth bushy, medium (100-130 cm.); garden decoration; [John-John × seedling]; int. by Armstrong Garden Centers, Inc., 2006

Phyllis Gold HT, my, 1935, Robinson, H.; flowers butter-yellow, edged lighter, dbl., high-centered; foliage rich olive-green; very vigorous, branching growth; [Lady Florence Stronge × Julien Potin]; int. by Wheatcroft Bros.; Gold Medal, NRS, 1933

Phyllis Gold, Climbing Cl HT, my, 1949, Fryers Nursery, Ltd.

Phyllis Lucas HT, ob, 1961, Wheatcroft Bros.; flowers orange shaded bronze, well-shaped; [sport of Bettina]

Phyllis McDonald HT, dp; int. in 1998

Phyllis Poyser HT, op, 1969, Fankhauser; bud long, pointed; flowers orange-pink, large, 50 petals, high-centered, intense spicy fragrance; foliage light green, soft, elongated; vigorous, compact, bushy growth; [Golden Sun × Spartan]

Phyllis Shackelford Min, ob, 1987, Moore, Ralph S.; flowers orange, fading pink, small, 20 petals, high-centered, borne usually singly, moderate fruity fragrance; foliage small, medium green, semi-glossy; prickles few, medium, brownish, slightly hooked downwards; upright, bushy, medium growth; hips rounded, medium, orange; [Anytime × Gold Badge]

Phynelia HT, mr, 1928, Reeves; flowers crimson-cerise, borne in clusters

Pia Berghout Pol, mp, 1967, Buisman, G. A. H.; flowers pink, medium, dbl., borne in clusters; foliage dark; [Saskia × seedling]

Piacenza – See **Sara**, HT

Pia-Nissimo HT, w, Keisei; flowers dbl., high-centered, slight fragrance; int. in 1996

Piano HT, mr, Tantau; int. in 1998

Pic-Nic – See **Picnic**, F

Picador F, mr, 1964, Verschuren, A.; flowers cherry-red, dbl., borne in clusters; foliage glossy, dark; upright, compact growth; [sport of Oranien]; int. by van Engelen

Picaninni Min, ob, Wright; flowers bright orange with yellow reverse, dbl., high-centered, moderate fragrance; free-flowering; vigorous, tall growth; int. in 1991

Picante HT, ob, Weeks; flowers iridescent orange; foliage dark green; medium to tall growth; PPAF; int. in 2005

Picardy HT, dp, 1967, Trew, C.; flowers rose-bengal, globular; foliage dark, glossy; free growth; [Rose Gaujard × Bayadere]; int. by Willik Bros.

Picasso F, pb, 1971, McGredy, Sam IV; flowers deep pink, petal edges lighter, white eye and reverse, 3 in., 18 petals; foliage small; PP3351; [Marlena × (Evelyn Fison × (Frulingsmorgen × Orange Sweetheart))]; int. by McGredy; Gold Star of the South Pacific, Palmerston North, NZ, 1971, Gold Medal, Belfast, 1973

Picayune Ch, lp, before 1843; flowers light pink to white, small, dbl., borne in clusters

Piccadilly HT, rb, 1960, McGredy, Sam IV; flowers scarlet, base and reverse gold, 4½-5 in., 28 petals, high-centered; foliage dark, glossy; vigorous, upright, branching growth; [McGredy's Yellow × Karl Herbst]; int. by McGredy & Son, 1960; Gold Medal, Rome, 1960, Gold Medal, Madrid, 1960

Piccadilly, Climbing Cl HT, rb, 1973, Minzen, 1963; Sutton, 1973; flowers scarlet at base, reverse gold, 1½-3 in., 25-30 petals; [sport of Piccadilly]; 1963 version was never introduced into commerce

Piccadilly Sunset HT, ob, 1971, Goodwin; flowers orange flushed apricot, reverse gold, high pointed, 4-5 in., 34 petals; foliage glossy, dark; moderate, upright growth; [sport of Piccadilly]; int. by The Valley Nursery, 1970

Piccaninny HT, dr, 1941, Lammerts, Dr. Walter; bud long, pointed; flowers stamens yellow, large, 5-6 petals; foliage dark, glossy; vigorous growth; [Night × Sanguinaire]; int. by Armstrong Nursery

Picciola Ina Pol, op, 1937, Giacomasso; flowers pure salmon, borne in clusters of 10-50; vigorous, bushy growth

Piccola Es S, lp, 1984, Fumagalli, Niso; flowers medium, 20 petals; foliage medium size, medium green, semi-glossy; bushy growth; [seedling × seedling]; int. in 1983

Piccolo F, dr, 1959, Tantau, Math.; bud ovoid; flowers velvety dark red, open, dbl., borne in clusters; foliage dark, leathery, glossy; moderate, bushy growth; RULED EXTINCT 4/85; [Red Favorite × Kathe Duvigneau]; int. in 1957

Piccolo F, or, 1985, Tantau, Math.; flowers medium, 20 petals, no fragrance; foliage large, dark green, glossy; upright growth; int. in 1983

Piccolo Pete S, mr, 1985, Buck, Dr. Griffith J.; flowers 4 in., 7-10 petals, flat, borne 1-10 per cluster, moderate fragrance; repeat bloom; foliage large, leathery, dark olive green; prickles slightly hooked, tan; upright, bushy growth; hardy; [Carefree Beauty × ((((Peace × Dornroschen) × Country Music) × ((Peace × Dornroschen) × Country Music)) × Country Music)]; int. by Iowa State University, 1984

Pick Me Up HT, mr, 1941, Clark, A.; flowers well-shaped

Pickering Baby Faurax Pol

Pickering Red HP (found) – See **Star of Waltham**, HP

Pickwick Min, w, 1998, Burrows, Steven; flowers cream and white, medium, dbl., borne in small clusters; foliage medium size, medium green, semi-glossy; prickles moderate; compact, bushy, medium growth; [Buttons × Richard Buckley]; int. by Burrows Roses, 1998

Picnic F, or, 1975, Warriner, William A.; bud short, pointed; flowers shrimp-red, petal base yellow, 3-3½ in., 70 petals, high-centered, borne singly and in flat clusters, slight fragrance; foliage medium size, leathery; prickles medium, long, straight, brown; vigorous, upright, branching growth; PP3829; [South Seas × seedling]; int. by J&P, 1976

Pico HT, rb, 1962, Buyl Frères; bud pointed; flowers salmon-red and canary-yellow, dbl.; foliage glossy; bushy growth

Picobello F, or; int. in 1998

Picotee F, rb, 1960, Raffel; flowers white, edged red, 2½-3½ in., 24 petals, cupped to flat, borne in clusters, slight fragrance; foliage dark green, glossy; vigorous, upright, bushy growth; [Little Darling × Gertrude Raffel]; int. by Port Stockton Nursery, 1961

Picotee Min, rb, 2003, Benardella, Frank; flowers white with red edges, reverse white, 1½ in., 20-25 petals, borne singly and in small clusters; foliage small, medium green, semi-glossy; prickles 3/16-7/16 in., trianglular, sometimes hooked down; growth upright, bushy, medium (18-24 in.); exhibition, cut flower, decorative; PP16817; [seedling × Ruby]; int. by Nor East Miniature Roses, Inc., 2004; Award of Excellence, ARS, 2004

Picpa HT, Dorieux; int. in 1974

Picture HT, lp, 1932, McGredy; flowers 34 petals, high-centered, slight fragrance; foliage glossy, dark green; vigorous growth

Picture, Climbing Cl HT, lp, 1942, Swim, H.C.; flowers pale pink, darker at center, reverse creamy, high-centered; [sport of Picture]; int. by Armstrong Nursery

Picture Book F, ob, 2002, Burrows, Steven; flowers bright orange, reverse soft orange with medium yellow, medium, full, borne in small clusters, moderate fragrance; foliage medium size, medium green, semi-glossy; prickles small to medium, moderate; growth bushy, medium (3½ ft.); garden decorative; [Buck's Fizz × Bright Smile]; int. by Burrows' Roses, 2002

Picture of Health S, ab, Harkness; flowers blush white with pale apricot center, large, very full, borne in compact trusses; vigorous growth; int. by R. Harkness & Co., 1999

Picture Page HT, lp, 1953, Jordan, B.L.; flowers peach-pink shading to flesh-pink, base yellow, well-formed, 4 in., 23-25 reflexed petals; foliage dark; very free growth; [Picture × Mme Butterfly]

Picture Perfect – See **Elsie Melton**, HT

Picture Perfect MinFl, pb, 2007, Wells, Verlie W.; flowers medium pink with yellow base, reverse creamy white with yellow base, 3 in., full, borne mostly solitary; foliage medium size, dark green, semi-glossy; prickles ¼ in., straight, few; growth upright, medium (3 ft.); exhibition, garden decorative; [seedling × seedling]; int. by Wells MidSouth Roses, 2007

Picturesque HT, lp, 1950, Eddie; bud long; flowers pale pink with pronounced red veining, large, 30-35 petals, high-centered; foliage leathery; vigorous, upright, bushy growth; [Mrs H.M. Eddie × Mrs Sam McGredy]

Pie IX – See **Pius IX**, HP

Pie X HT, w, 1905, Hildebrand; flowers cream white aging to delicate pink, center darker, large, very full, cupped, moderate fragrance; [Kaiserin Auguste Viktoria × Mrs W. J. Grant]

Piece d'Or S, dy

Pied Piper F, mr, 1969, Lindquist; flowers small, dbl., globular; foliage leathery; moderate, low growth; PP3069; [Garnette × Moulin Rouge]; int. by Howard Rose Co.

Piera Rose S, ob, Harkness; flowers soft orange, full, cupped, moderate fragrance; growth to 100 cm.; int. by R. Harkness & Co., 2005

Pierette HRg, dp, Uhl, J.; flowers semi-dbl. to dbl., moderate fragrance; recurrent; low (30 in.), spreading growth; hardy; int. in 1987

Pierette Pavement – See **Pierette**, HRg semi-dbl. to dbl.

Pierre HT, yb, 1945, Mallerin, C.; bud large, ovoid; flowers deep golden yellow edged red, very dbl.; foliage glossy; vigorous, upright, bushy growth; [Soeur Thérèse × Lumiere]; int. by A. Meilland

Pierre HT, ab

Pierre Aguetant HT, my, 1938, Gaujard; bud long, pointed; flowers chamois-yellow, open, very large, dbl.; foliage leathery; vigorous growth

Pierre B HT, ab, Bell, Ronald J.; flowers soft apricot, long lasting when cut; medium growth; [sport of Dr A.J. Verhage]

Pierre Bredy HT, rb, 1958, Arles; flowers currant-red, reverse silvery; foliage dark; low growth; [Peace × Scheherazade]; int. by Roses-France

Pierre Caro HP, dr, 1879, Levet; flowers dark red, fading lighter, medium to large, dbl., intense fragrance; foliage dark green; growth upright

Pierre Cormier Pol, or, 1926, Turbat; flowers brilliant scarlet-red, center lighter, borne in clusters; dwarf growth

Pierre Cuillerat HT, w, 1900, Buatois; flowers flesh white, very large, full

Pierre de Ronsard LCl, pb, Sauvageot; bud globular; flowers cream white suffused with carmine pink, 4½-5 in., 40-55 petals, hollow cup, borne in clusters, slight fragrance; recurrent; foliage medium size, deep green, semi-glossy; spreading, climbing growth; [(Danse des Sylphes × Handel) × Pink Wonder, Climbing]; int. in 1985; Rose Hall of Fame, WFRS, 2006

Pierre de St Cyr B, lp, 1838, Plantier; flowers glossy pale pink, large, very dbl., cupped; vigorous growth

Pierre Dupont HP, dr, 1861, Clément; flowers glowing dark red, medium

Pierre Durand HP, mp, 1881, Pernet; flowers bright pink, large, dbl.

Pierre Gagnaire S, ab, Delbard; bud small, orange; flowers cream, with tones of orange and pink fading to white, single, borne in large clusters, moderate floral, fruity fragrance; good repeat; foliage olive green, glossy; vigorous (5 ft.) growth; int. by Georges Delbard SA, 2003

Pierre Gaujard HT, rb, 1944, Gaujard; bud pointed; flowers fiery shades, very large, dbl.; foliage glossy; vigorous growth

Pierre Guillot HT, rb, 1879, Guillot; flowers red with white, large, dbl.; [Mme Falcot × unnamed HP]

Pierre Notting HP, dr, 1863, Portemer fils; flowers large, 42 petals, globular, moderate fragrance; not often recurrent; upright growth; [Alfred Colomb × unknown]

Pierre Seletzky HP, dr, 1872, Levet; flowers fiery dark purple with slatey tints, large, full

Pierre Troisgros HT, pb, Dorieux; flowers soft pink in center, fading toward white with brighter pink edges on opening, large, dbl., high-centered, borne mostly singly, moderate fragrance; good repeat; stems short; growth medium (3 ft.); int. in 1991

Pierre Wattinne HT, dp, 1901, Soupert & Notting; flowers cherry pink nuanced salmon yellow, large, dbl., moderate fragrance; [Papa Gontier × seedling]

Pierrette HT, rb, 1931, Tantau; flowers blackish red streaked white, passing to steel-blue, small, very dbl., cupped; foliage small; short stems; dwarf growth; [sport of Felix Laporte]

Pierrette HT, or, 1945, Tantau; flowers bright copper red, flecked brighter, large, 25 petals; upright, bushy growth; [sport of Texas Centennial]

Pierrine Min, op, 1988, Williams, Michael C.; flowers medium pink, reverse slightly lighter, medium, 40 petals, high-centered, borne singly, slight damask fragrance; foliage medium size, medium green, semi-glossy serrated edges; prickles curved down slightly, light green; upright, medium growth; hips round, green-orange-yellow; [Tiki × Party Girl]; int. by The Rose Garden & Mini Rose Nursery

Pierrot F, rb, 1979, Lens, Louis; bud ovoid; flowers white marked red, becoming red, 2½ in., 30 petals, cupped, moderate spicy fragrance; foliage leathery; vigorous, compact growth; [Poupee × Fillette]; int. in 1971

Pierson's Pink HT, dp, 1950, Pierson, A.N.; bud long, pointed; flowers rose-pink, 5 in., 32 petals, high-centered; very vigorous, upright growth; [sport of Better Times]

Piet Retief F, dr, 1950, Leenders, M.; flowers dark morocco-red; [Irene × Donald Prior]

Piet Saverys F, ob, 1955, Buyl Frères; flowers orange, semi-dbl.; bushy growth; [Independence × Border King]

Pietermaritzburg Rose S, lp; flowers translucent pink with yellow stamens, single, shallow cup, moderate fragrance; foliage dark green, disease-resistant; stately, tall growth

Pietro Tione HT, rb, 1907, Fugier-Bonnaire; flowers brick red, shaded orange-yellow, large, full

Pigalle HT, m, 1955, Meilland, F.; flowers reddish-violet, 4 in., dbl.; foliage bronze; bushy growth; [Fantastique × Boudoir]; int. by Wheatcroft Bros., 1951

Pigalle F, ob, 1985, Meilland, Mrs. Marie-Louise; flowers yellow blended with orange and orange-red, large, 40 petals, no fragrance; foliage medium size, medium green, semi-glossy; bushy growth; [Frenzy × ((Zambra × Suspense) × King's Ransom)]; int. by Meilland Et Cie, 1983

Pigalle HT, ob, Keisei; flowers tangerine orange, full, high-centered, borne mostly singly; florist rose; int. by Meilland Intl., 2004

Pigalle, Climbing Cl HT, m; int. by Roses-France

Pigmy Gold F, dy, 1953, Boerner; bud ovoid; flowers golden yellow, small, dbl.; foliage dark, glossy; dwarf growth; int. by J&P

Pigmy Lavender F, m, 1961, Boerner; bud ovoid; flowers lavender tinted pink, 2 in., 30-35 petals, cupped, moderate fragrance; foliage leathery, dark; short, strong stems; vigorous, dwarf growth; PP2195; [(Lavender Pinocchio × unknown) × unnamed Hybrid Tea seedling]; int. by J&P, 1961

Pigmy Red F, dr, 1953, Boerner; bud ovoid; flowers deep red, white eye, small, dbl., borne in clusters, moderate fragrance; foliage glossy; dwarf growth; PP1319; [Chatter × Red Pinocchio]; int. by J&P

Pihca – See **Kyria**, F

Pike's Peak S, pb, 1940, Gunter; bud long, pointed; flowers light bright red, center yellow, fading white, large, 13 petals, borne in clusters of up to 17; non-recurrent; foliage light, wrinkled; very vigorous (6 ft.), bushy growth; [*R. acicularis* × Hollywood]; int. by B&A

Pilar de Arburua HT, op, Camprubi, C.; flowers salmon, large, dbl., high-centered; foliage dark reddish green; free growth; [Comtesse Vandal × Fashion]

Pilar Dot Min, op, 1964, Dot, Pedro; flowers coral, well-formed, small; vigorous, well-branched growth; [Orient × Perla de Alcanada]

Pilar Landecho HT, ob, 1940, Camprubi, C.; bud long, pointed; flowers yellow, reverse dark coral-orange, large, dbl., high-centered; foliage dark, leathery; vigorous growth; [(Sensation × Julien Potin) × Feu Joseph Looymans]; int. by A. Meilland; Gold Medal, Bagatelle, 1938

Pilar Landecho, Climbing Cl HT, ob, 1954, Folgado, Comes; bud marked with red; [sport of Pilar Landecho]

Pilarín Vilella HT, or, 1936, Dot, Pedro; flowers lacquer-red, large, dbl., cupped; foliage dark; vigorous growth; [Mrs Pierre S. duPont × Lucia Zuloaga]

Pilgrim HT, pb, 1920, Montgomery Co.; bud long, pointed; flowers silvery pink reverse clear rose-pink, large, dbl., high-centered; foliage leathery, rich green; vigorous, bushy growth; int. by A.N. Pierson

Pilgrim HT, dr, 1970, Armstrong, D.L.; bud ovoid; flowers large, dbl., cupped; foliage dark, leathery; vigorous, upright, bushy growth; [seedling × Chrysler Imperial]; int. by Armstrong Nursery

Pílina Mata HT, ob, 1934, Munné, B.; flowers orange-yellow; [Souv. de Claudius Pernet × Los Angeles]

Pillar Box F, or, 1987, Warner, Chris; flowers vivid vermillion, medium, dbl.; foliage medium size, medium green, semi-glossy; upright growth; [Alexander × (Galway Bay × Elizabeth of Glamis)]; int. in 1986

Pillar of Fire Cl F, or, 1963, Shamburger, P.; bud short, ovoid; flowers coral-red, 2-2½ in., 33 petals, cupped, borne in clusters; foliage leathery, matte; vigorous growth; PP2329; [sport of Floradora, Climbing]; originally registered as LCl; int. by C-P, 1963

Pillar of Gold – See **E. Veyrat Hermanos**, Cl T

Pillar Stratford Cl HT, lp, 1946, Watkins, A.F.; flowers silvery pink, base deeper, large, very dbl.; vigorous, upright (8 ft.) growth; [sport of Stratford]; int. by Krider Nursery

Pillnitzer Marcellina Pol, dr, Institut für Obstbau Dresden Pillnitz; flowers semi-dbl.

Pillow Fight S, w, 1999, Carruth, Tom; flowers bright white, 1½-2 in., dbl., rosette, borne in large clusters, intense honey and rose fragrance; floriferous; foliage medium size, dark green, glossy; few prickles; rounded, bushy, medium (30-36 in.) growth; PP13113; [Pink Pollyanna × Gourmet Popcorn]; int. by Weeks Roses, 2000

Pillow Talk F, m, 1980, Weeks, O.L.; bud short, ovoid; flowers reddish-lavender, 28 petals, high-centered, borne singly or several together, moderate tea fragrance; foliage medium size, thin, leathery, dark; prickles long, hooked downward; low to medium, rounded growth; PP4714; [Plain Talk × Angel Face]

Pilona pb, 1965, Hendrickx; bud ovoid; flowers pink with white, medium, very dbl., borne in clusters; foliage dark green

Pilurett F, or, Schmadlak, Dr.; flowers medium, semi-dbl.; int. in 1966

Pimbonson LCl, mp, 1953, Muraour; flowers cerise pink, semi-dbl.

Pimlico – See **Pimlico '81**, F

Pimlico '81 F, mr, 1984, Meilland, Mrs. Marie-Louise; flowers deep scarlet, gold stamens, large, 35 petals, no fragrance; foliage large, dark green, glossy; bushy growth; [(Tamango × Fidélio) × (Charleston × Lilli Marleen)]; int. by Meilland Et Cie, 1980; Gold Medal, Belfast, 1983

Pimpant F, or, 1963, Laperrière; flowers bright orange-red, 25-30 petals, borne in clusters of 7-8; moderate, bushy growth; [seedling × Soleil]; int. by EFR

Pimpernel F, or, 1954, LeGrice; flowers turkey-red, open, semi-dbl., borne in clusters; foliage dark; [seedling × (Poulsen's Pink × Golden Dawn)]

Pimpernel Rose – See ***R. spinosissima*** (Linnaeus)

Pimprenelle S, dy, Delbard; flowers sunny yellow, fading lighter, single to semi-dbl., cupped to flat, borne in clusters; free-flowering; vigorous (2-3 ft.) growth; int. by George Delbard SA, 1997

Pin-up F, dp, 1959, Fletcher; flowers deep China-rose, medium, 16-18 wavy petals, borne in clusters; foliage light green; low, bushy growth; [Else Poulsen × unknown]

Piña Colada Min, ly, 2005, Alonso, Peter G., Jr.; flowers creamy light yellow, 2½ in., full, high-centered, borne mostly solitary, slight fragrance; foliage medium size, medium green, matte; prickles few, small, pointed, reddish brown; growth upright, tall (3 to 4 ft.); exhibition; [Olympic Gold × Olympic Gold]; int. by Peter G. Alonso Jr., 2005

Pinafore Pol, ly, 1960, Swim, H.C.; flowers pale yellow to white, tinged pink, 1½-2 in., single, flat, borne in large, rounded clsuters; foliage glossy; low, bushy, compact growth; PP1810; [China Doll × Mrs Dudley Fulton]; int. by Roseway Nursery, 1959

Pinal Pol, mr, Institut für Obstbau Dresden Pillnitz; flowers medium, single

Piñata LCl, yb, 1973, Suzuki, Seizo; bud short, ovoid, vermilion; flowers yellow with vermilion overlay, changing to vermilion over most of petal, 3 in., 25-30 petals, borne in clusters, moderate fragrance; foliage large, glossy, dark; vigorous, climbing growth; PP3996; [((Goldilocks × unknown) × Sarabande) × (Golden Giant × unknown))]; int. as Fure-Daiko, Keisei Rose Nursery, 1974

Pinchu Quiye HT, w; flowers pure white; free-flowering; almost thornless; vigorous growth

Pincushion S, mp, Kordes; flowers strong pink, fading lighter, small, full, rosette, borne in large clusters, slight fragrance; free-flowering; low (12 in.), spreading growth; int. in 1992

Pine-Scented Rose – See ***R. glutinosa*** (Sibthorp & Smith)

Pineapple Poll F, ob, 1970, Cocker; flowers orange-yellow, flushed red, 2½ in., 30 petals; foliage glossy; [Orange Sensation × Circus]

Pinehurst Min, pb, 1988, Bridges, Dennis A.; flowers light pink, fading lighter at base, reverse light pink to cream, 60 petals, moderate fruity fragrance; foliage medium size, dark green, semi-glossy; prickles straight, medium, pink; bushy, medium, vigorous, neat growth; [Rise 'n' Shine × seedling]; int. by Bridges Roses

Pingan F, w, 1980, Fong, William P.; bud ovoid, pointed; flowers white with pink petal edges, 13 petals, borne 4-6 per cluster; foliage large, leathery; prickles long; upright growth; [seedling × (Ivory Fashion × Little Darling)]; int. by Del Rose Nursery

Pink – See **Pink Hit**, Min

Pink – See **Pink Parade**, Min

Pink Min, mp, Poulsen; int. in 1998

Pink-A-Boo F, mp, 1961, Boerner; bud ovoid; flowers 3-3½ in., 33 petals, borne in large clusters, moderate fragrance; foliage leathery; vigorous, upright growth; PP2149; [Spartan × Pink Garnette]; int. by J&P, 1961

Pink-a-ling Min, w, 1989, Zipper, Herbert; flowers white edged deep pink, small, dbl., borne singly and in sprays; foliage medium size, dark green, glossy; upright growth; [Tamango × Avandel]; int. by Magic Moment Miniature Roses, 1989

Pink Above All – See **Star Performer**, Cl Min

Pink Abundance F, mp; flowers deep coral-salmon pink. long lasting, 4 in., 60 petals, slight sweet pear and mint fragrance; foliage glossy, dense; bushy, compact (3½ ft.) growth; PPAF; int. by Harkness, 1999

Pink Agatha – See **Agathe Incarnata**, HGal

Pink Alain F, mp; int. by Belle Epoque, 2001

Pink Alicia HT, mp, 1968, Dale, F.; flowers pink, pointed; spreading growth; [Duftwolke × Gavotte]

Pink American Beauty – See **Queen of Edgely**, HP

Pink American Beauty – See **Mrs Charles E. Russell**, HT

Pink 'n' Pretty Min, pb, Wells, Whit; int. by Wells Midsouth Roses, 2006

Pink Angel Min, mp, 1982, Hunton, Claude B.; [sport of Starina]

Pink Angel – See **Angel Pink**, Cl Min

Pink Angel HT, mp, Parkes, Mrs M.H.

Pink Anne F, mp, 1951, Cant, B. R.; flowers borne in trusses; [sport of Anne Poulsen]

Pink Arctic – See **Show Garden**, LCl

Pink Avalanche S, mp, 1988, Williams, J. Benjamin; flowers coral pink to medium red, small, dbl., borne in sprays of 20-30; foliage medium size, medium green, glossy; spreading, compact growth; [Sea Foam × The Fairy]; int. in 1989

Pink Babyflor Min, dp, Tantau; int. by Rosen Tantau, 1993

Pink Bassino F, mp, 2006; flowers apple blossom pink with white base and yellow stamens, 4 cm., single, cupped, borne in small clusters; foliage medium size, moss green, very glossy; growth bushy, medium (50 cm.); int. by W. Kordes' Söhne, 1995

Pink Beauty HT, mp, 1919, Cook, J.W.; flowers clear pink, large, semi-dbl., cupped; [Ophelia × My Maryland]

Pink Bedder HT, mp, 1920, Paul, W.; flowers rose-pink, center yellow, borne in clusters

Pink Belle HT, dp, 1975, Harkness; flowers deep rose pink, large, 28 petals, moderate fragrance; foliage dark; RULED EXTINCT 11/83; [Fragrant Cloud × Elizabeth of Glamis]; int. by Morse Roses, 1973

Pink Bells Min, dp, 1984, Poulsen Roser APS; flowers deep pink, small, 35 petals; foliage small, medium green, semi-glossy; groundcover; spreading growth; [Mini-Poul × Temple Bells]; int. by John Mattock, Ltd, 1983

Pink Bianca S, pb; int. by Roses Unlimited, 2006

Pink Blush HT, lp, 1975, Warriner, William A.; bud long, pointed; flowers 4-5 in., 30 petals, cupped; foliage large, leathery; very free growth; PP3729; [Bridal Pink × seedling]; int. by J&P, 1974

Pink Bountiful F, mp, 1945, Joseph H. Hill, Co.; bud short, pointed; flowers 3 in., 55 petals, borne in clusters, moderate fragrance; foliage dark, leathery; vigorous, upright, much-branched growth; [Juanita × Mrs R.M. Finch]; int. by J.H. Hill Co.

Pink Bounty Min, mp, 1985, Williams, Ernest D.; flowers small, 35 petals, high-centered; foliage small, medium green, semi-glossy; very dense, bushy growth; [Tom Brown × Over the Rainbow]; int. by Mini-Roses, 1984

Pink Bouquet F, mp, 1954, Brownell; flowers China-rose pink, slightly tinted yellow, to ovoid, 3-4 in., 60-75 petals, high-centered, moderate fragrance; foliage leathery; upright, open, compact growth; PP1371; RULED EXTINCT 11/90; [Curly Pink × Free Gold]

Pink Bouquet Min, lp, 1991, Laver, Keith G.; bud pointed; flowers white to luminous blush pink, white reverse, aging white, medium, 50-60 petals, flat, borne in sprays of 1-3, no fragrance; foliage small, dark green, matte; bushy, spreading, low growth; [Loving Touch × Ontario Celebration]; int. by Springwood Roses, 1991

Pink Bouquet HWich, pb, Treasure

Pink Bourbon – See **Mme Ernest Calvat**, B

Pink Bowie S, pb, Williams, J.B.; flowers pink and ivory, single, borne in clusters, slight fragrance; free-flowering; upright (4 ft.) growth; int. by Hortico, 2003

Pink Brocade F, lp, 1977, Bees; flowers very full, 3 in., 70 petals; foliage glossy; small, compact growth; [Spartan × Lilli Marlene]

Pink Bunting Min, mp, 1993, Taylor, Franklin; flowers pink, creamy yellow base blending to pink edges around petals, medium, dbl., no fragrance; foliage small, dark green, semi-glossy; few prickles; low (12 in.), spreading, compact growth; int. by Taylor's Roses, 1993

Pink Butterfly HT, dp, 1926, Brown, A.C.; flowers bright cerise, base light buff; [sport of Mme Butterfly]

Pink Butterfly S, pb, Williams, J.B.; flowers pink and ivory, single, borne in large clusters; free-flowering; foliage dark green; int. by Hortico, 2003

Pink Button Min, mp, Kordes; bud pointed; flowers clear pink with a touch of coral, dbl., high-centered; good repeat; neat, medium growth; int. in 1990

Pink Calypso HT, lp; florist rose; int. by de Ruiter

Pink Cameo Cl Min, mp, 1954, Moore, Ralph S.; flowers rose-pink, center darker, 1¼ in., 23 petals, borne in clusters of up to 20; foliage small, glossy, rich green; growth to 3-5 ft.; PP1451; [(Soeur Thérèse × Skyrocket) × Zee]; int. by Sequoia Nursery

Pink Candy HT, pb, Thomas; [sport of Candy Stripe]; int. before 1992

Pink Cardinal Hume S, mp, Rupert, Kim L.; flowers small, dbl., loose, borne in clusters, slight fragrance; recurrent; small (under 3 ft.), tidy growth; int. in 1998

Pink Carpet Min, mp, 1983, Williams, Ernest D.; flowers small, dbl., borne in large clusters, no fragrance; foliage small, light to medium green, glossy; low, spreading (to 6 ft.) growth; hanging baskets; PP5606; [Red Cascade × Red Cascade]; int. by Mini-Roses

Pink Carrousel Min, mp; flowers clear, strong pink; [sport of Magic Carrousel]; grows like its parent, Magic Carrousel; int. by Ludwig's Roses, 2000

Pink Cascade Pol, lp, 1945, Lammerts, Dr. Walter; flowers la france pink, small, very dbl., borne in clusters; foliage glossy; vigorous, bushy growth; RULED EXTINCT 12/81; [Mrs Dudley Fulton × Tom Thumb]; int. by Univ. of Calif.

Pink Cascade Cl Min, mp, 1982, Moore, Ralph S.; flowers small, 35 petals; foliage small, medium green, matte to semi-glossy; spreading (5-7 ft; similar to Red Cascade) growth; [(*R. wichurana* × Floradora) × Magic Dragon]; int. by Moore Min. Roses, 1981

Pink Cavalcade F, pb, 1959, Shamburger, C.S.; flowers deep pink, reverse light yellow to white, 2½-3 in., 28-32 petals, cupped, borne in pyramidal clusters, moderate fragrance; foliage leathery, glossy, bronze; vigorous, bushy growth; PP1456; [sport of Cavalcade]; int. by Stuart, 1955

Pink Cavalier S, mp, Courage, R.; flowers full, pompon, moderate fragrance; long flowering season; Australian patent 54257/01; int. by Ross Roses, 2001

Pink Cécile Brunner Pol, dp, 1918, Western Rose Co.; flowers rose-pink; [sport of Mlle Cécile Brunner]

Pink Chalice S, pb, Williams, J.B.; flowers light pink blend, single to semi-dbl., borne in clusters on upright canes, slight fragrance; vigorous, spreading growth, can be trained as a climber.; int. by Hortico, 2000

Pink Chameleon Pol, pb, 1945, Lammerts, Dr. Walter; bud rose-red; flowers Venetian pink, darkening to purple, open, small, single, borne in clusters; abundant, recurrent bloom; foliage dark, glossy; very vigorous, bushy growth; [Mrs Dudley Fulton × Mutabilis]; int. by Univ. of Calif.

Pink Champagne HT, mp, 1956, Jelly; bud long, pointed; flowers 5-6 in., 32-48 petals, high-centered, moderate fragrance; foliage leathery; vigorous, bushy growth; PP1375; [seedling × Pink Bountiful]; int. by E.G. Hill Co.

Pink Champagne S, mp, Clements, John K.; int. in 1995

Pink Champagne Min, pb; flowers shades of pink, slight fragrance; growth to 50 cm.; hanging basket; int. by Paul Chessum Roses, 2003

Pink Charles Austin S, pb, Austin, David; int. by David Austin, 1992

Pink Charm F, dp, 1938, Kordes; flowers deep clear pink, very dbl.; foliage leathery; short stems; bushy growth; int. by Dreer

Pink Charm – See **Penthouse**, HT

Pink Charmer Min, mp, 1984, Lyon, Lyndon; flowers medium, 20 petals; foliage small, medium green, semi-glossy; upright, bushy growth; [Baby Betsy McCall × seedling]

Pink Charming HT, lp, 1953, Leenders, M.; flowers pale pink, loosely formed, 5½ in., 36 petals; vigorous growth

Pink Chateau HT, w, 1999, Teranishi, K.; flowers white, center soft pink, 5 in., 35 petals, high-centered; growth to 4½ ft.; [(Sheer Bliss × seedling) × seedling]; int. by Itami Rose Nursery, 1997

Pink Cherokee – See **Anemone**, S

Pink Cherub Min, lp, 1981, Moore, Ralph S.; bud ovoid; flowers medium to light pink, often lighter at tips, 43 petals; foliage small, medium green, matte; prickles straight, small; compact, very bushy growth; [Fairy Moss × Fairy Moss]; int. by Moore Min. Roses, 1980

Pink Chiffon F, lp, 1958, Boerner; bud ovoid; flowers 3½-4 in., 53 petals, cupped to flat, intense fragrance; foliage glossy; vigorous, bushy growth; PP1564; [Fashion × Fantasia]; int. by J&P, 1956

Pink Chiffon, Climbing Cl F, lp; int. after 1956

Pink Chimo S, mp, 1992, Ilsink, Peter; flowers 1-1½ in., 5 petals, cupped, borne singly; repeat bloom; foliage medium size, medium green, semi-glossy; spreading, low (30 cm.) growth; [seedling × Immensee]; int. by Interplant B.V., 1989

Pink Christian Dior HT, dp, 1966, Chang, Chi-Shiang; bud ovoid; flowers light red and deep pink, large, dbl., high-centered; foliage glossy; very vigorous, upright growth; [sport of Christian Dior]

Pink Cloud LCl, mp, 1952, Boerner; bud ovoid; flowers rich pink, large, 28 petals, cupped, borne in clusters of 5-20, moderate fragrance; recurrent bloom; foliage glossy; vigorous, climbing (6-8 ft.) growth; [New Dawn × (New Dawn × unknown)]; int. by J&P

Pink Clouds Cl Min, dp, 1956, Moore, Ralph S.; flowers deep rose pink, small to medium, single, borne in clusters; foliage dark, glossy; vigorous (5-8 ft.) growth; [Oakington Ruby × *R. multiflora*]; int. by Sequoia Nursery

Pink Cluster F, op, 1938, Morse; flowers salmon-pink, shaded gold, borne in clusters

Pink Coctail HT, pb, 1965, Barter; flowers light pink, reverse darker, 5 in., 38 petals; foliage dark, glossy; very free growth; [Queen Elizabeth × Claude]

Pink Confection B, mp, 2007, Rippetoe, Robert Neil; flowers 2 in., very full, borne mostly solitary; foliage medium green, matte; prickles small, sickle, tan, moderate; growth compact, short (18 in.); containers, short hedges; [Louise Odier × unknown]; int. by Robert Neil Rippetoe, 2006

Pink Cottage – See **Mix 'n' Match**, S

Pink Cover – See **Essex**, S

Pink Crinoline HT, pb, Kordes; flowers deep pink on inside, silvery pink on reverse, large, full, globular, borne singly and in candelabras, slight fragrance; recurrent; foliage deep green; stems firm, wiry; vigorous, medium high growth; int. by Ludwig's Roses, 1999

Pink Crumble Bar HT, mp, Thomson, G.A.; [sport of Crumble Bar]

Pink Crystal HT, m, Wathen; flowers light lavender pink, 30-35 petals, high-centered, borne usually singly, moderate sweet fragrance; foliage medium size, medium green, semi-glossy; upright, bushy growth; PP9289; [sport of Crystalline]; grows much like its parent; int. by Weeks Roses, 1998

Pink Curtain LCl, dp, Kordes; flowers deep, clear pink, borne on cane tips and side stems, intense sweet fragrance; recurrent; vigorous, arching growth; int. in 1994

Pink Cushion Pol, mp

Pink Danyland S, dp

Pink Dawn HT, mp, 1935, H&S; bud long, pointed; flowers large, 60 petals, high-centered, intense fragrance; foliage soft; vigorous growth; [Joanna Hill × seedling]; int. by Dreer

Pink Dawn, Climbing Cl HT, mp, 1941, H&S

Pink Delight Pol, dp, 1922, Laxton Bros.; flowers rose-pink, single

Pink Delight HT, op, 1936, Kordes; bud long, pointed; flowers deep salmon-pink, large, dbl., high-centered, intense fragrance; foliage leathery, light green; vigorous growth; [Senator × Florex]; int. by J&P

Pink Delight Min, lp, 2000, Lens, Louis; flowers light pink, reverse lighter, 3-4 cm., full, borne in small clusters, moderate fragrance; recurrent; foliage medium size, medium green, matte; thornless; bushy, medium (35 cm.) growth; [(Le Vesuve × (*R. rouletii* × (New Penny × Rosenelfe))) × Cecile Brunner]; int. by Louis Lens N.V., 1982

Pink Devil HT, mp

Pink Diadem F, dp, Tantau; int. in 1994

Pink Diamond HT, lp, 1942, Howard, F.H.; bud long pointed; flowers shell-pink, base yellow, 3½-4 in., 38 petals, cupped; foliage leathery; vigorous, upright growth; int. by Diamond State Nursery

Pink Diane F, dp, 1959, Sodano, A.; bud ovoid; flowers deep rose-pink, 3½-4 in., 50-55 petals, cupped, intense fruity fragrance; foliage leathery, glossy, dark; vigorous, upright growth; [sport of Rosenelfe]

Pink Diddy Min, mp, 1991, King, Gene; bud pointed; flowers medium, 28 petals, cupped, slight fruity fragrance; foliage small, medium green, semi-glossy; bushy, spreading, low growth; [((B.C. × Scamp) × Miss Dovey) × Tudelum]; int. by AGM Miniature Roses, 1990

Pink Diëlma HT, mp, 1969, Tas; bud ovoid; flowers pink, medium, very dbl.; foliage dark; [sport of Furore]

Pink Don Juan LCl, mp, 1996, Nelson, Brian; flowers medium, semi-dbl., borne in small clusters, slight fragrance; foliage medium size, medium green, semi-glossy; some prickles; tall, upright, spreading, climbing growth; [sport of Don Juan]; int. by Certified Roses, Inc., 1997

Pink Dream HT, pb, 1951, McGredy, Sam IV; flowers pink, inside rosy white, 6-7 in., 45 petals, high-centered; foliage dark; vigorous growth; [Mrs Sam McGredy × R.M.S. Queen Mary]

Pink Dream Min, mp, Moore, Ralph; flowers cherry pink., 1-1½ in., dbl., borne in small clusters; free-flowering; foliage healthy and attractive; short (12 in.), compact and neat growth; int. by Sequoia Nursery, 2001

Pink Drift – See **Caterpillar**, S

Pink Druschki HT, mp, 1949, Longley; flowers bright pink, well-formed, 5 in., 27 petals; very vigorous growth

Pink Duchess HT, dp, 1960, Boerner; bud ovoid; flowers rose-red, 5-6 in., 38 petals, cupped, moderate fragrance; foliage glossy; vigorous, upright, bushy growth; PP1834; [(Peace × unknown) × seedling]; int. by J&P, 1959

Pink Elegance HT, lp, 1960, Hoefer, P.; bud long, pointed; flowers bright pink, medium, dbl., high-centered; foliage glossy; very vigorous growth; [White Butterfly × Baccará]; int. by Carlton Rose Nurseries, 1960

Pink Elf Min, pb, 1983, Moore, Ralph S.; flowers medium pink, blended with yellow, small, semi-dbl., no fragrance; foliage small, medium green, matte to semi-glossy; upright, bushy growth; [Ellen Poulsen × Fire Princess]; int. by Moore Min. Roses

Pink Elizabeth Arden – See **Geisha**, F

Pink Emely – See **Emely Vigorosa**, F

Pink Emperor HT, mp, 1965, Jones; flowers clear pink, 4-5 in., 50-60 petals; foliage glossy; vigorous, bushy growth; [Peace × Crimson Glory]; int. by Hennessey, 1958

Pink Empress HT, mp, 1991, Davidson, Harvey D.; flowers clean medium pink, large, 32-36 petals, high-centered, borne usually singly or sprays of 1-3, moderate fruity fragrance; foliage medium size, medium green, glossy; bushy, medium growth; [Smooth Sailing × Medallion]; int. by Hortico Roses, 1991

Pink Euphoria S, mp; flowers single, borne in sprays; recurrent; int. in 1999

Pink Eutin F, mp, 1962, Lindquist; bud pointed, globular; flowers fuchsine pink, 1½-2 in., 25-35 petals, cupped, borne in clusters; recurrent; foliage large, semi-glossy; prickles few, medium, sepia brown; growth vigorous, bushy, somewhat spreading; PP2269; [sport of Eutin]; int. by Howard Rose Co., 1962

Pink Fairy Pol, mp; flowers 10-20 petals; bushy (2-3 ft.) growth; [sport of The Fairy]; grows much like The Fairy

Pink Fantasy HT, mp, K&S; flowers glowing pink, non-fading; free-flowering; [sport of Mme Denise Gallois]; int. by KSG Son, 1995

Pink Fantasy S, dp; flowers open deep pink, fade to medium pink, 3 in., full, pompon, borne in clusters; free-flowering; foliage disease-resistant; low (2-3 ft.), spreading (5 ft.) groundcover growth

Pink Favorite HT, mp, 1956, Von Abrams; bud pointed; flowers Neyron rose, 3-4 in., 25 petals, loosely cupped, slight fragrance; foliage very glossy, bright green; vigorous, upright, bushy growth; PP1523; [Juno × (Georg Arends × New Dawn)]; int. by Peterson & Dering; Gold Medal, Portland, 1957

Pink Favourite – See **Pink Favorite**, HT

Pink Festival – See **Pink Bouquet**, Min

Pink Fire F, mp, Ilsink; int. in 1995

Pink Fizz LCl, lp, Poulsen; bud medium pink; flowers light pink with yellow stamens, 8-10 cm., dbl., cupped, borne in clusters, no fragrance; recurrent; foliage reddish green; bushy, tall (150-200 cm.) growth; hips none; int. as Bournonville, Poulsen Roser, 2000

Pink Flair F, mp, 1966, Swim & Weeks; bud urn shaped; flowers small, dbl.; foliage leathery; vigorous, bushy growth; PP2724; [Verona × Escort]; int. by Carlton Rose Nurseries

Pink Flamingo HT, pb, 1958, Kern, J. J.; flowers rose-pink tinted lighter, 2½-3½ in., 50 petals, intense fragrance; foliage dark, leathery; dwarf, bushy growth; [sport of Golden Dawn]; int. by Kern Rose Nursery, 1957

Pink Floradora F, op, 1951, Shamburger, P.; bud ovoid; flowers shrimp-pink, 3 in., 35-40 petals, cupped; foliage glossy, light green; bushy growth; [sport of Floradora]

Pink Flower Carpet – See **Flower Carpet**, S

Pink Flurries F, lp; int. in 1999

Pink Formal S, pb, 1978, Williams, J. Benjamin; bud pointed; flowers bright coral-pink, loosely-ruffled, 3½-4 in., 23 petals; foliage leathery; vigorous, upright growth; [(Queen Elizabeth × Gladiator) × (Aztec × Little Darling)]; int. by Krider Nursery

Pink Fountain LCl, dp, LeGrice; int. in 1990

Pink Fragrance HT, mp, 1957, deRuiter; bud long, pointed; flowers rose-pink, open, 4½-5 in., 78-85 petals, borne in pyramidal clusters, moderate spicy fragrance; foliage glossy, leathery; very vigorous, bushy, upright growth; PP1493; [(Orange Triumph × Golden Rapture) × Peace]; int. by Ilgenfritz Nursery, 1956

Pink Frau Karl Druschki HP, mp, 1910, California Rose Co.; [sport of Frau Karl Druschki]

Pink French Lace F, lp, 2000, Roses Unlimited (also Takefuji, 2005); flowers 4½ in., full, high-centered, borne in small clusters, slight fragrance; foliage medium size, dark green, semi-glossy; few prickles; growth bushy, medium; [sport of French Lace]; int. by Roses Unlimited, 2001

Pink Friendship S, mp, Verschuren; int. by Verschuren, 1986

Pink Frills F, lp, 1954, Carlton Rose Nursery; [sport of Garnette]

Pink Fringe – See **Pink Fire**, F

Pink Frost HT, mp, 1954, Swim, H.C.; bud ovoid; flowers rose, 4-5 in., 38-45 petals, high-centered, intense fragrance; foliage glossy, leathery; vigorous, bushy growth; PP1269; [Charlotte Armstrong × Texas Centennial]; int. by Arp Nursery Co., 1954

Pink Frostfire Min, lp, 1968, Moore, Ralph S.; [sport of Frostfire]; int. by Sequoia Nursery

Pink Frosting HT, mp, 1992, Rennie, Bruce F.; flowers 3-3½ in., full, borne mostly singly, intense fragrance; foliage large, medium green, matte; some prickles; tall, upright growth; [seedling × Prima Ballerina]; int. by Rennie Roses International

Pink Garland S, mp, 1935, Skinner; flowers clear pink, open, 3-3½ in., semi-dbl.; non-recurrent; upright (3 ft.) growth; [*R. blanda* × *R. spinosissima* cultivar]

Pink Garnette F, dp, 1950, Schneeberg (also Boerner, 1951); flowers Tyrian rose; [sport of Garnette]

Pink Garnette Supreme F, mp, 1959, Perkins, C.H.; flowers rose-pink, 2½ in., 35-40 petals, cupped, borne in clusters, moderate fragrance; foliage glossy, leathery; vigorous, upright growth; PP1642; [sport of Garnette Supreme]; int. by J&P, 1957

Pink Gem HT, lp, 1949, Fletcher; bud long, pointed; flowers pearl-pink, 4-5 in., 30 petals, flat; foliage bluish green; vigorous, tall growth; int. by Tucker

Pink Gem Min, lp, 1974, Meilland; bud ovoid; flowers rose-pink, medium, dbl.; foliage soft; moderate, upright, bushy growth; [sport of Scarlet Gem]; int. by C-P

Pink Gemini F, pb, Zary, Keith; bud long, pointed ovoid; flowers 35 petals, high-centered, borne in clusters of 5-7; good repeat; foliage medium size, leathery, glossy; prickles medium, hooked downward; stems medium, strong; vigorous, upright (4½ ft.), branching growth; PP11140; [(Jacpray × Party Girl) × Jacanne]; greenhouse rose; int. by Bear Creek Gardens, 1998

Pink Gift Pol, lp; recurrent; growth to 3-4 ft.; int. in 1999

Pink Gin HT, mp; flowers medium, dbl.

Pink Glory HT, mp, 1960, Boerner; bud long, pointed; flowers clear pink, 5 in., 25 petals, high-centered, intense fragrance; foliage leathery; vigorous, upright growth; PP1998; [(Ernie Pyle × unknown) × Peace]; int. by J&P, 1960

Pink Glow HT, lp, 1951, Boerner; bud globular; flowers rose-pink, 5-5½ in., 40 petals, cupped; foliage leathery, glossy; vigorous, upright growth; [((Schoener's Nutkana × seedling) × Mrs Pierre S. duPont) × Home Sweet Home]; int. by J&P

Pink Gnome S, pb; bud pink; flowers light pink with white centers, 3/4 in., 5 petals, cupped; free-flowering; foliage medium green, disease-resistant; growth compact (12 in.), with tight, round habit; PP16602; int. by Bailey Nurseries, 2004

Pink Golden Dawn HT, mp, 1938, Bostick; flowers large, dbl.; [sport of Golden Dawn]

Pink Gown HT, lp, 1971, Sanday, John; flowers light clear pink, 4 in., 20 petals; foliage matte green; tall, very free growth; [Vera Dalton × Tropicana]

Pink Grootendorst HRg, mp, 1923, Grootendorst, F.J.; flowers clear pink, carnation style petal edges, very dbl., borne in small clusters, slight fragrance; free-flowering; foliage medium size, dark green, rugose; tall growth; [sport of F.J. Grootendorst]

Pink Gruss an Aachen F, op, 1929, Kluis & Koning; flowers light salmon pink, very full; [sport of Gruss an Aachen]

Pink Hadley HT, mp, 1928, Knight, G.; flowers clear rose pink; [sport of Hadley]

Pink Hat F, pb, 1980, James, John; bud pointed; flowers light pink, center deep pink, 24 petals, high-centered, borne singly of 3-7 per cluster; foliage red turning dark green, glossy; prickles red; vigorous, upright, bushy growth

Pink Haze F, pb, 1973, Khanna, K. R., & Lata, P.; buds medium, long pointed; flowers pink with yellow centers, large, semi-dbl., open, borne several together and in clusters; foliage medium size, green, soft; few prickles; growth very vigorous, bushy; [Pink Parfait × Edward Mawley]; int. by National Botanic Gardens

Pink Haze S, mp, Tantau; groundcover; spreading growth; int. in 1999

Pink Heather Min, lp, 1960, Moore, Ralph S.; flowers lavender-pink to white, very small, 45 petals, borne in clusters; foliage very small, glossy; vigorous (10-12 in.), bushy growth; PP2082; [(*R. wichurana* × Floradora) × (Violette × Zee)]; int. by Sequoia Nursery, 1959

Pink Hedge HRg, mp, Nyveldt; flowers bright pink, medium, single to semi-dbl., flat, borne in clusters; good repeat; foliage small, bronze; low, spreading growth; hips red; [(*R. rugosa rubra* × *R. cinnamomea*) × *R. nitida*]; int. in 1956

Pink Hedge F, dp, Interplant; int. in 1996

Pink Heidelberg HKor, mp

Pink Hit Min, mp, 1988, Olesen, Pernille & Mogens N.; flowers small, 6-14 petals; foliage small, medium green, semi-glossy; bushy, compact, even, abundant growth; [seedling × seedling]; int. by Poulsen Roser ApS, 1986

Pink Hit Min, mp, Poulsen; flowers medium pink, 2 in., dbl., cupped, borne in clusters, no fragrance; recurrent; foliage dark green, glossy; bushy (40-60 cm.) growth; int. by Poulsen Roser, 1996

Pink Honey Min, mp, 1988, Bridges, Dennis A.; flowers medium honey-pink, yellow at base, reverse light yellow at base, 20 petals, high-centered, slight fruity fragrance; foliage large, medium green, semi-glossy; prickles long, pointed, medium, pink; bushy, tall growth; [Summer Spice × seedling]; int. by Bridges Roses

Pink Ice F, w, 1984, Anderson's Rose Nurseries; flowers white with deep pink petal edges, medium, 20 petals, no fragrance; foliage medium size, light green, semi-glossy; bushy (2 ft.) growth; [seedling × Iceberg]

Pink Ice F, pb; flowers striped; int. by Burston Nurseries, 2006

Pink Iceberg F, pb, Weatherly, Lilia; flowers light to medium pink blend, darkens in cool weather, 3 in., 35 petals, borne singly and in sprays of 3-4, slight fragrance; recurrent; foliage large, light green, glossy; prickles few, thin, curved downward, tan; growth upright, rounded, medium; PP9600; [sport of Iceberg]; int. by Swane's Nursery, 1995

Pink Ilseta Gr, Tantau; int. in 1986

Pink Jacqueline HT

Pink Jenny HT, mp, 1961, Ruston, D.; flowers rose-pink; [sport of Grand'mere Jenny]

Pink Jewel F, mp, 1940, Kordes; flowers arbutus-pink, center camellia-pink, semi-dbl., cupped; foliage leathery; vigorous growth; [Crimson Glory × Holstein]; int. by Dreer

Pink Jewel HT, mp, de Ruiter; int. by deRuiter's New Roses Intl.

Pink Jonathan F, mp, Asami; int. in 1997

Pink Joy Min, dp, 1958, Moore, Ralph S.; flowers deep pink, well-shaped, 1 in., 30 petals, moderate sweet violet fragrance; dwarf (12in.), bushy growth; PP1378; [Oakington Ruby × Oakington Ruby]; int. by Sequoia Nursery, 1953

Pink Kardinal HT, dp, Stratford; [sport of Kardinal]; RAFT Rose of the Year, Australia, 1995

Pink Karen Poulsen F, mp, 1936, Poulsen, S.; [sport of Karen Poulsen]

Pink Key HT, mp, 1920, Pierson, F.R.; [sport of Francis Scott Key]

Pink Kiss Min, lp, 1987, Williams, Ernest D.; flowers light pink, non-fading, small, 40-45 petals, high-centered, borne singly or in sprays; foliage small, medium green, semi-glossy; prickles tan-red, dilated at base; bushy, medium growth; [Tom Brown × Anita Charles]; int. by Mini-Roses

Pink Knock Out S, mp, Radler, W. ; bud cherry red.; flowers medium pink., single; foliage blackspot resistant; growth to 3 × 3 ft.; PP15070; [sport of Knock Out]; int. in 2004

Pink Koster Pol, mp, Koster, D.A.; flowers dbl., cupped, slight fragrance; growth under 3 ft.; [sport of Margo Koster]; int. after 1931

Pink La Sevillana F, mp, 1984, Meilland, Mrs. Marie-Louise; bud conical; flowers carmine pink, 8 cm., 10-15 petals, cupped, then flat, borne in clusters of 5-20, no fragrance; recurrent; foliage bronzed green, leathery; bushy, spreading (3 ft.) growth; PP7117; [sport of La Sevillana]; int. by Meilland Et Cie, 1983; Gold Medal, Durbanville, 1986, Gold Medal, Baden-Baden, 1985

Pink Lace F, pb, 1961, Watkins Roses; flowers light pink, becoming darker and then red, medium (2-2 1/2 in.), 20 petals, flat; foliage dark; vigorous growth; [The Optimist × Korona]

Pink Lady HT, mp, 1947, Wiltgen; bud urn-shaped; flowers soft pink, reverse darker, large, semi-dbl.; medium, vigorous growth; [sport of Pink Delight]; int. by Premier Rose Gardens

Pink Lafayette F, mp, 1925, Griffin; flowers clear rose-pink; [sport of Lafayette]

Pink Lamesch Pol, lp, Hiroshima; [sport of Léonie Lamesch]; int. by Hiroshima Bara-en, 2001

Pink LD S, dp, 2003, Jennings, George; flowers very full, borne mostly solitary; foliage medium size, medium green, matte; prickles small, straight, reddish-brown, moderate; growth upright, medium (4 1/2-5 1/2 ft.); garden, decorative; [sport of Leonard Dudley Braithwaite]; int. in 2002

Pink Léda D, mp, before 1827; flowers flesh pink to carmine lilac, fading to pale pink; [sport of Leda, or vice-versa]

Pink Lemonade HT, yb, 1983, Christensen, Jack E.; flowers yellow turning bright pink, well-formed, large, 35 petals, moderate fragrance; foliage large, medium green, semi-glossy; upright, bushy growth; [Friendship × Rosy Cheeks]; int. by Armstrong Nursery, 1986

Pink Licorice HT, pb, 1995, Sheldon, John & Robin; flowers pink blend, medium, full, borne mostly singly, slight licorice fragrance; foliage medium size, medium green, matte; upright, medium growth; [Osiria × Elegant Beauty]

Pink Lorraine HT, w, 1973, Williams, J. Benjamin; flowers pink, paling to white, base cream, 4 1/2 in., 40 petals; foliage matte green; vigorous, upright growth; [Milord × Farah]

Pink Love HT, mp; int. in 1998

Pink Lustre HT, lp, 1958, Verschuren; bud ovoid; flowers 5 in., 48 petals, high-centered, intense fragrance; foliage dark, glossy, leathery; vigorous, upright growth; PP1641; [Peace × Dame Edith Helen]; int. by J&P, 1957

Pink Macartney Rose HBc, lp

Pink Mme Plantier – See **Garden's Glory**, HMult

Pink Magic HT, dp, 1952, Joseph H. Hill, Co.; bud long, pointed, spinel-red; flowers phlox-pink, 4-6 in., 40-45 petals; foliage leathery; vigorous, upright growth; [Better Times × Snow White]

Pink Magic HMsk, pb, 2000, Lens, Louis; flowers single, borne in large clusters, slight fragrance; recurrent; foliage large, medium green, semi-glossy; prickles moderate; upright, arching, medium (4-5 ft.) growth; [(*R. multiflora adenocheata* × Ballerina) × Kathleen]; int. by Louis Lens N.V., 1990

Pink Magic – See **Randilla Rose**, Min

Pink Magic Carpet S, pb, McGredy, Sam IV; flowers open pink, then fade to white, semi-dbl., borne in clusters at tips and on laterals; recurrent; spreading, arching growth; int. in 1994

Pink Maiden F, mp, 1965, Boerner; bud ovoid; flowers large, dbl., borne in clusters, slight fragrance; foliage dark; [(Spartan × unknown) × Queen Elizabeth]; int. by Spek

Pink Majesty F, mp, 2003, McMillan, Thomas; flowers large, with scalloped petal edges, 4 1/2 in., dbl., pointed center, borne in small clusters, no fragrance; foliage medium green, semi-glossy; prickles small, needle-shaped, moderate; growth compact, medium (2 ft.); garden decorative; [Lagerfeld × Love Potion]; int. by Wisconsin Roses, 2004

Pink Maman Cochet, Climbing Cl T, mp, 1915, Conard & Jones

Pink Mandy Min, mp, 1975, Moore, Ralph S.; bud globular, small; flowers medium pink blending into white near base, 1 in., 40-50 petals, borne usually in clusters of 3-5; recurrent; foliage small, medium green, very glossy, leathery; prickles numerous, medium, curved downward, brown; growth low, bushy, spreading; PP3869; [Ellen Poulsen × Little Chief]; int. by Sequoia Nursery, 1974

Pink Margaret Thatcher F, pb, Takatori; flowers striped; int. by Takatori Roses

Pink Marina Min, dp, Kordes; flowers strong pink, dbl., high-centered; part of Kordana series; int. by W. Kordes Söhne

Pink Marvel F, dp, 1960, deRuiter; flowers spirea-red, 2 1/2 in., 45-55 petals, flat, borne in clusters; foliage leathery; bushy, compact growth; PP1763; [Rosemary Rose × (Cécile Brunner × Floribunda seedling)]; int. by C-P, 1960

Pink Masquerade S, op, Simonet; flowers 5 petals; [Suzanne × Red Dawn]

Pink Masterpiece HT, pb, 1962, Boerner; bud ovoid, pointed; flowers La France pink, tinted shrimp-pink, 6 in., 38 petals, high-centered, borne mostly singly, moderate fragrance; foliage leathery; vigorous, upright growth; PP2294; [(Serenade × unknown) × Kate Smith]; int. by J&P, 1962

Pink Meidiland S, pb, 1985, Meilland, Mrs. Marie-Louise; bud conical; flowers deep pink with white eye, reverse whitish suffused red, 3 in., 5 petals, flat, borne in large clusters, no fragrance; good repeat; foliage small, medium green, semi-glossy; bushy, arching (5 ft.) growth; PP5956; [Anne de Bretagne × Nirvana]; int. by Meilland & Son, 1983; ADR, 1987

Pink Meillandina Min, mp, 1982, Meilland, Mrs. Marie-Louise; PP4961; [sport of Orange Sunblaze]; int. by Meilland Et Cie, 1980

Pink Melody HT, op, K&S; flowers pale salmon-pink; good repeat; [sport of Pasadena]; int. in 1993

Pink Meringue S, lp, 1999, Bennett, Frank David; flowers large, 41 petals, borne in small clusters; foliage medium size, medium green, semi-glossy; numerous prickles; upright, tall (6 ft.) growth; [sport of Mary Rose]

Pink Mermaid LCl, mp, 1940; flowers soft pink, large, single, very heavy first bloom flush, moderate fragrance; good repeat; growth tall (15-20 ft.), climbing; int. in about 1960

Pink Meteor F, mp, 1964, Timmerman's Roses; [sport of Meteor]

Pink Midinette S, mp, Pearce; flowers small, borne in clusters all along canes, moderate sweet fragrance; growth strong (to 10 ft.), arching; int. by Ludwig's Roses, 1996

Pink Millie Min, mp, 2003, Wathen, E.N.; flowers full, high-centered, borne mostly solitary, slight fragrance; foliage medium size, medium green, semi-glossy; prickles moderate; growth medium (12-14 in.); exhibition; [sport of Millie Walters]

Pink Mini-Wonder Min, mp, 1990, Selection Meilland; bud rounded; flowers light rose bengal, reverse pale rose bengal, aging pale rose, 39-42 petals, cupped; foliage medium green, semi-glossy; prickles small, very few, green, aging tan; bushy, medium growth; PP7361; [(Anytime × Parador) × Mogral]; int. by Meilland, 1987

Pink Minijet Min, mp, Meilland

Pink Minimo Min, mp

Pink Mist HT, mp, 1959, Joseph H. Hill, Co.; bud pointed, ovoid; flowers phlox-pink, becoming darker, 4-5 in., 25-35 petals, high-centered, intense fragrance; foliage dark, leathery; vigorous, bushy growth; PP1774; [sport of Red Better Times]

Pink Mist S, op

Pink Montezuma Gr, lp, 1964, Williams, J. Benjamin; flowers light pink, reverse blush-pink, large, dbl., high-centered; foliage dark, leathery; vigorous, bushy growth; [sport of Montezuma]

Pink Mothersday Pol, mp

Pink Mystery S, do, 2000, Lens, Louis; flowers deep pink to purple, reverse lighter, 7-8 cm., single, borne in small clusters; recurrent; foliage medium size, dark green, matte; numerous prickles; growth upright, medium (80-120 cm.); [*R. stellata mirifica* × (*R. bracteata* × *R. nutkana*)]; int. by Louis Lens N.V., 1997

Pink 'n' White Min, pb

Pink Nature S, mp; int. in 1999

Pink Nevada – See **Marguerite Hilling**, HMoy

Pink Nevada HMoy, lp, 1985, Sanday, John; flowers pale lilac pink; [sport of Nevada]

Pink Nymph F, mp, 1959, Koster, D.A.; flowers clear pink; [sport of Nymph]

Pink Nymph Min, mp; flowers dbl.; [sport of *R. chinensis minima*]

Pink Ocean Cl HT, lp, 1985, Verschuren; flowers salmon pink, fading to pale pink, large, 20 petals, intense fragrance; foliage medium size, medium green semi-glossy; upright (to 7 ft.) growth; [Pink Showers × Alexander]; int. by H.A. Verschuren, 1980

Pink Oklahoma HT, dp; int. by Golden Vale Nursery, 1999

Pink Olympiad HT, mp, Humenick, Muriel F.; int. in 1995

Pink Ophelia HT, mp, 1916, Breitmeyer; flowers rose-pink; [sport of Ophelia]

Pink Ophelia – See **John C. M. Mensing**, HT

Pink Osiana HT, lp, Tantau; bud long, pointed ovoid; flowers light pink with slightly darker center, 5-6 in., 30 -35 petals, high-centered, borne mostly singly, moderate fragrance; recurrent; foliage large, leathery; prickles few, 1/4 in., hooked downward; stems long, strong; vigorous, upright, branching, tall growth; PP10799; [sport of Osiana]; int. by Rosen Tantau, 1997

Pink Pagode Min, lp, Poulsen; flowers light pink, medium, dbl., no fragrance; foliage dark; cascading growth, hanging basket type; PP13452; int. by Poulsen Roser, 2000

Pink Panoramic – See **Pink Chimo**, S

Pink Panther HT, pb, 1983, Meilland, Mrs. Marie-Louise; flowers silvery pink, edged deep pink, large, dbl., no fragrance; foliage medium size, semi-glossy; upright growth; [MEIgurami × MEInaregi]; int. by Meilland Et Cie, 1981; Gold Medal, The Hague, 1981

Pink Parade Min, pb, Poulsen; flowers pink blend, medium, dbl., slight wild rose fragrance; foliage dark; growth narrow, bushy, 20-40 cm.; int. by Poulsen Roser, 1996

Pink Parasol HT, mp, 1950, Fisher, G.; bud long, pointed; flowers clear pink, 6 in., 25-30 petals; foliage leathery, dark; very vigorous growth; [Rapture × Rome Glory]; int. by Arnold-Fisher Co.

Pink Parfait Gr, pb, 1960, Swim, H.C.; bud ovoid to urn-shaped; flowers outer petals medium pink, center blended pale orange, 3½-4 in., 23 petals, high-centered to cupped, slight fragrance; foliage leathery, semi-glossy; vigorous, upright, bushy growth; PP1904; [First Love × Pinocchio]; int. by Armstrong Nursery, 1960; Gold Medal, Baden-Baden, 1959, Gold Medal, Portland, 1959, Gold Medal, NRS, 1962

Pink Passion Min, pb, 1979, Schwartz, Ernest W.; bud pointed; flowers shell-pink and ivory, 1½ in., 26 petals, high-centered, moderate fragrance; upright, bushy growth; [Sweet and Low × unknown]; int. by Bountiful Ridge Nursery, 1978

Pink Passion S, mp; int. by Kelly Nurseries, 2004

Pink Patio MinFl, lp; int. in 1997

Pink Patio Wonder Min, mp, 2004, Jalbert, Brad; flowers very full, borne in small clusters, slight fragrance; foliage very dark green, very glossy; prickles small, green, numerous; growth bushy, medium (14 in.); containers, garden decoration; [seedling 68-91 × Sexy Rexy]; int. in 1999

Pink Pavement HRg, op, Baum; flowers salmon pink, semi-dbl., moderate fragrance; recurrent; foliage dark green, disease-resistant; compact, spreading (2½ ft.) growth; int. in 1991

Pink Peace HT, mp, 1959, Meilland, F.; bud medium, ovoid; flowers dusty pink, 4½-6 in., 58 petals, cupped, borne mostly singly, intense tea fragrance; free-flowering; foliage leathery; stems long, strong; vigorous, tall, bushy growth; PP1759; [(Peace × Monique) × (Peace × Mrs John Laing)]; int. by URS; Gold Medal, Geneva, 1959, Gold Medal, Rome, 1959

Pink Peace, Climbing Cl HT, mp, 1970, Meilland; [sport of Pink Peace]; int. by URS, 1968

Pink Pearl HWich, op, 1901, Manda; bud crimson; flowers salmony pink, often darker at center, 6-7 cm., dbl., borne in small clusters; [*R. wichurana* × Meteor]

Pink Pearl Cl HT, op, 1913, Hobbies; flowers pink shaded salmon, single; [Irish Elegance × Una]

Pink Pearl HT, mp, 1924, Leenders, M.; flowers Neyron pink, base salmon, dbl.; long stems; vigorous growth; [Ophelia × (Gen. MacArthur × Marie van Houtte)]

Pink Pearl, Climbing Cl HT, mp, 1933, Dixie Rose Nursery

Pink Pearl – See **Fee**, HT

Pink Perfection HT, mp, 1927, Ward, F.B.; flowers clear rose-pink, 45 petals; [Premier × Baroness Rothschild]

Pink Perfection HT, mp; int. in 1998

Pink Perfekta HT, pb, 1962, Ross, A.; flowers deep pink, often edged red; [sport of Kordes' Perfecta]; int. by A. Ross & Son, 1962

Pink Perfume HT, op, Robinson, H.; int. in 1955

Pink Perpétué LCl, mp, 1965, Gregory; flowers bright rose-pink, medium, 32 petals, globular, borne in clusters, moderate fragrance; recurrent bloom; foliage glossy, light green; vigorous growth; [Spectacular × New Dawn]

Pink Pet Ch, mp, 1928, Lilley; flowers bright pink, fading lighter, dbl., pompon, borne in clusters, slight fragrance; recurrent; moderate (3 ft.) growth

Pink Pet, Climbing Cl Ch, mp; flowers bright pink, fading lighter, medium, dbl., pompon, borne in large clusters; recurrent; growth to 5-10 ft.; [sport of Pink Pet]

Pink Petticoat Min, pb, 1979, Strawn; bud pointed; flowers creamy white, edged coral-pink, 1½-2 in., 33 petals, high-centered, rounded, borne singly, slight sweet fragrance; recurrent; foliage glossy, dark; prickles very few, needle shape, declining, light tan; stems upright, slender; tall, vigorous, upright growth; hips globular, form readily ; PP4636; [Neue Revue × Sheri Anne]; int. by Pixie Treasures Min. Roses; AOE, ARS, 1980

Pink Picotee Min, pb, 1990, King, Gene; flowers white to cream with dark pink picotee edge, small, full, borne mostly singly, no fragrance; foliage medium size, light green, matte; upright, spreading, medium growth; [(Vera Dalton × Fancy Pants) × Magic Carrousel]; int. by AGM Miniature Roses

Pink Pillar LCl, mp, 1940, Brownell; flowers clear medium pink, small, dbl., slight fragrance; good repeat; hardy

Pink Pin's Min, mp, Interplant; int. by Pep. Jacques Briant, 2003

Pink Pirouette MinFl, mp, Harkness; flowers rosy pink, dbl., high-centered, moderate fragrance; good rebloom; growth to 50 cm.; int. by R. Harkness & Co., 1998

Pink Pixie – See **Pixie Rose**, Min

Pink Pollyanna S, mp, 1990, Warriner, William A.; bud ovoid; flowers medium pink, reverse slightly darker, aging lighter, small, dbl., high-centered, moderate fruity fragrance; repeat bloom; foliage small, medium green, glossy; prickles small, straight, red to brown; growth upright, bushy, medium; [Zorina × Heidi]; int. by Bear Creek Gardens, 1990

Pink Poodle Min, pb, 1991, Moore, Ralph S.; flowers pink changing to lighter pink to white, medium, very full, borne in small clusters, moderate fragrance; foliage small, medium green, matte; few prickles; low (26-30 cm.), upright growth; [(Little Darling × Yellow Magic) × Old Blush]; typical china characteristics; int. by Sequoia Nursery, 1992

Pink Popcorn S, lp, 1991, Williams, J. Benjamin; flowers light pink to coral, small, semi-dbl., borne in large clusters in small, grape-like sprays, slight fragrance; foliage small, medium green, matte, disease-resistant; few prickles; low (12-18 in.), compact, bushy growth; [*R. chinensis minima* × (Sea Foam × The Fairy)]

Pink Porcelain Min, lp, 1983, Bennett, Dee; flowers small, 23 petals, high-centered, borne singly and in clusters; foliage small, medium green, semi-glossy; upright growth; [Futura × Avandel]; int. by Tiny Petals Nursery

Pink Posy Min, m, 1983, Cocker, James; flowers lilac, small, dbl., moderate fragrance; foliage dark, matte; bushy growth; [Trier × New Penny]; int. by Cocker & Sons

Pink Posy Ch, dp; flowers deep pink, fading to lighter lavender pink, single, flat, borne in clusters; good repeat; growth to 3-4 ft.; forms hip readily; [*R. chinensis minima* × unknown]; int. by Countryside Roses, 2003

Pink Powder Puff F, mp, 1970, Pal, Dr. B.P.; bud ovoid; flowers soft pink, open, medium, dbl.; foliage leathery; vigorous, upright, compact growth; int. by Indian Agric. Research Inst., 1965

Pink Powderpuff HBc, lp, 1991, Moore, Ralph S.; bud pointed; flowers light pink, aging slightly lighter, old garden rose type, large, 100 petals, high-centered, loose, borne heavily in the spring, intense damask fragrance; repeat bloom; foliage large, medium green, semi-glossy; tall, spreading, climbing growth; [Lulu × Muriel]; int. by Sequoia Nursery, 1990

Pink Prelude HG, mp, 2005, Viraraghavan, M.S. Viru; flowers up to 5 in., full, camellia-like, borne mostly solitary; foliage large, medium green, glossy, disease-resistant; prickles large, triangular, grey brown, numerous; growth upright, tall; pillar or hedge; [Eterna × Sirohi Sunrise]; int. by Roses Unlimited, 2005

Pink Pride HT, lp, 1959, Fletcher; flowers silvery pink, 5-6 in., 30-35 petals, high-centered; foliage light green; free growth; [May Wettern × Peace]

Pink Princess HT, pb, 1939, Brownell; flowers deep rose pink to yellowish, large, dbl., high-centered, intense fragrance; foliage dark, leathery, glossy; vigorous, bushy growth; [(Dr. W. Van Fleet × Général Jacqueminot) × Break o' Day]

Pink Princess Min, mp

Pink Profusion HSet, pb, 1938, Horvath; flowers pale flesh-pink, reverse deep coral-rose, small, 80 petals, globular, borne in clusters; non-recurrent; foliage large, glossy; long, strong stems; very vigorous growth; [Mrs F.F. Prentiss × Lady Alice Stanley]; int. by Wayside Gardens Co.

Pink Profusion F, op, Kordes; flowers clear, intense coral pink, medium, 20 petals, cupped, borne in clusters, slight sweet fragrance; free-flowering; foliage glossy; stems short; bushy (2-3 ft.), vigorous growth; int. by Ludwig's Roses, 2001

Pink Promises HT, dp, 2005, Smith, John T; flowers deep pink, reverse lighter pink, 4-4½ in., dbl., borne mostly solitary, no fragrance; foliage large, medium green, semi-glossy, disease-resistant; prickles short, straight, brown, numerous; growth compact, medium (3-3½ ft.); landscape, garden decoration; [Crystalline × Veterans' Honor]; int. by same, 2007

Pink Prophyta HT, mp, de Ruiter; PP10532; florist rose; int. by de Ruiter's New Roses

Pink Prosperity HMsk, lp, 1931, Bentall; flowers medium, dbl., borne in large trusses, moderate musk fragrance; very vigorous growth

Pink Puff F, lp, 1965, Boerner; bud medium, ovoid; flowers soft pink, 3½-4 in., 25-30 petals, cupped, borne singly and several together, moderate fruity (russet apple) fragrance; free-flowering; foliage medium size, dark green, leathery; prickles medium, short, hooked downward; stems long, strong; growth vigorous, upright; no hips; PP2634; [(Pinocchio × unknown) × (Red Pinocchio × Garnette)]; int. by J&P

Pink Quill Min, mp, 1992, Weeks, Michael W.J.; flowers medium bright pink, medium, semi-dbl., borne in large clusters, moderate fragrance; foliage medium size, dark green, bronze when young, semi-glossy; some prickles; tall (25 cm.), spreading growth; [Mr Bluebird × unknown]

Pink Radiance – See **Radiance**, HT

Pink Radiance, Climbing – See **Radiance, Climbing**, Cl HT

Pink Rambler – See **Euphrosyne**, HMult

Pink Reflection Min, pb

Pink Revelation F, lp, 1980, Schramm, D.; flowers small, cupped, borne in clusters of 3-12, slight fragrance; recurrent; foliage light green; prickles very few; growth bushy; [sport of Summer Snow]

Pink Rhapsody LCl, op, 1973, Ellick; flowers deep vermilion-pink, 4 in., 35-40 petals; very vigorous growth; [(Heidelberg × Bonn) × Pink Parfait]

Pink Rhythm Min, op, 1991, Jolly, Marie; bud pointed; flowers coral pink, white center, medium pink reverse, aging light pink, 18 petals, high-centered, loose, borne usually singly, moderate fruity fragrance; foliage medium size, medium green, matte; upright, spreading, medium growth; [Party Girl × Fashion Flame]; int. by Rosehill Farm, 1991

Pink Ribbon Min, lp, 1966, Moore, Ralph S.; flowers soft pink, small, dbl.; foliage glossy, light green; vigorous, bushy, dwarf growth; [(*R. wichurana* × Floradora) × Magic Wand]; int. by Sequoia Nursery

Pink Ribbon – See **Clos Fleuri Rose**, F

Pink Ribbon – See **Clos Fleuri Rose No. 2**, F

Pink Ripples F, lp, 1956, Sanders, H.T.; flowers pink, open, 2½-3 in., 15-20 wavy petals, borne in clusters; very vigorous, upright, compact growth; [sport of Red Ripples]

Pink River – See **Mary Rose**, S

Pink Roadrunner HRg, mp, Uhl; flowers 2 in., semi-dbl. to dbl., cupped, intense rugosa fragrance; recurrent; foliage dark green, leathery, disease-resistant; vigorous, bushy (18-24 in.), spreading growth; int. by W. Kordes Söhne, 2003

Pink Roamer HWich, pb, 1897, Horvath; flowers pink, center white, fading to pale mauve pink, 3 cm., single, borne in medium clusters, moderate fragrance; foliage small; vigorous growth; [*R. wichurana* × Cramoisi Supérieur]; int. by W.A. Manda

Pink Robin S, mp, 2000, Lens, Louis; flowers dbl., borne in large clusters, moderate fragrance; non-recurrent; foliage small, yellow and red to medium green, matte; few prickles; stems red; growth bushy, tall (200 cm.); [*R. helenae* × Robin Hood]; int. by Louis Lens N.V., 1992

Pink Robin – See **Pink Licorice**, HT

Pink Robusta S, mp, 1987, Kordes, W.; flowers large, semi-dbl.; foliage large, dark green, glossy; bushy, spreading growth; [(Zitronenfalter × Grammerstorf, Climbing) × Robusta]; int. in 1986

Pink Rocket S, pb, 1949, Longley, L.E.; bud ovoid; flowers deep pink suffused copper, open, large, single to semi-dbl.; profuse, non-recurrent bloom; foliage glossy, bronze, dark; very vigorous, upright growth; hardy; [Skyrocket × unknown]; int. by Univ. of Minn.

Pink Rosette F, lp, 1948, Krebs; bud small, ovoid; flowers soft pink, 2 in., 50 petals, cupped, rosette, borne in clusters, slight fragrance; foliage leathery, dark; growth vigorous, dwarf, bushy; int. by H&S

Pink Roundelay HT, mp, Taylor, L.R.; [sport of Roundelay]; int. in 1968

Pink Rover Cl HT, lp, 1891, Paul, W.; bud long; flowers pale pink, deeper in center, borne mostly solitary, moderate fragrance

Pink Royal HT, mp, 1928, Vestal; flowers glowing pink, dbl.; [Columbia × Mme Butterfly]

Pink Ruby HT, mp, 1966, Anstiss; flowers high pointed, 4-4½ in.; foliage light green; vigorous growth; [sport of Rubaiyat]

Pink Ruffles F, mp, 1976, Ellis; bud pointed; flowers rose-pink, ruffled, 3 in., 5-7 petals, slight tea fragrance; foliage very glossy, dark; very bushy growth; [(Frolic × Frolic) × Pinafore]; int. by Mansion Nursery, 1977

Pink Ruffles HT, dp, Williams, J. Benjamin; flowers strong pink, ruffled, 4 in., full, moderate fragrance; int. in 1996

Pink Sachet HT, dp, Shinoda, D. S. & Umeda, G. Y.; PP3959

Pink Sandy Min, pb, 1991, King, Gene; flowers light pink to light apricot center, aging deep pink edges, small, full, borne mostly singly, slight fragrance; foliage small, medium green, matte; bushy, low growth; [(Vera Dalton × Rainbow's End) × Fancy Pants]; int. by AGM Miniature Roses

Pink Sarabande F, mp, Keihan; int. by Keihan Gardening, 1981

Pink Satin F, mp, 1945, Cross, Mrs. C.W.; bud large; flowers clean rose-pink, showy stamens, open, semi-dbl., cupped; foliage soft,light green; very vigorous, bushy, compact growth; [Indiana × William F. Dreer]; int. by B&A

Pink Satin F, lp, 1975, Warriner, William A.; bud ovoid; flowers 4-5 in., 30-35 petals, high-centered; foliage large; vigorous, very free growth; PP3825; [seedling × Bridal Pink]; int. by J&P, 1974

Pink Scotch HSpn, mp

Pink Secret Min, mp, 1982, Robinson, Thomas, Ltd.; [sport of Beauty Secret]; int. by T. Robinson, Ltd.

Pink Seduction HT, dp, Meilland; int. in 2003

Pink Semi (form of *R. laxa*), lp; flowers resemble *R. blanda*

Pink Sensation HT, mp, Bos, Henry; bud urn-shaped; flowers deeper pink in center, lighter on outer petals, 3½-4 in., 30 petals, high-centered, cupped, borne singly, intense fragrance; free-flowering; foliage large, dark green, glossy; stems long, strong; vigorous (5-6 ft.) growth; PP1584; [sport of Pink Delight]; int. in 1958

Pink Shadow Min, dp, 1978, Williams, Ernest D.; bud plump, pointed; flowers dusty pink, reverse darker, 1 in., 52 petals, moderate fragrance; foliage glossy; growth bushy, spreading; [Over the Rainbow × Over the Rainbow]; int. by Mini-Roses, 1977

Pink Sheri Min, lp, 1985, Rennie, Bruce F.; [sport of Sheri Anne]

Pink Showers Pol, mp, Ramson; int. in 1968

Pink Showers Cl HT, lp, 1978, Verschuren, Ted; flowers satin pink, large, dbl., loose, borne in small clusters; good repeat; vigorous, tall, climbing growth; [Carla × Golden Showers]; int. by Verschuren, 1974

Pink Silk HT, mp, 1972, Gregory; flowers carmine-rose, 4 in., 42 petals, high-centered, borne singly and sometimes in small clusters, moderate fragrance; medium growth; [Pink Parfait × seedling]; int. by Gregory Roses; Gold Star of the South Pacific, Palmerston North, NZ, 1974

Pink Simplicity – See **Simplicity**, F

Pink Skyliner LCl, mp, Cowlishaw; flowers soft pink, small, semi-dbl. to dbl., cupped, borne in clusters; recurrent; vigorous (8 ft.) growth; int. by C & K Jones, 2003

Pink Snow Cl F, pb, 1981, Reed, Harry, Jr. (also Hanneman, 1987); flowers light pink shading to white in center, deeper on edges of petals; [sport of Summer Snow, Climbing]

Pink Soupert Pol, mp, 1896, Dingee & Conard; flowers

glossy rose red, shaded violet, small to medium, full, cupped, borne in clusters; vigorous growth; [Clotilde Soupert × Lucullus]

Pink Spectacle S, mp, Kordes; flowers clear pink, full, high-centered; stems medium; vigorous (6 ft. high & wide) growth; int. in 1995

Pink Spice HT, lp, 1962, Von Abrams; bud long, pointed; flowers light pink flushed yellow, 5 in., 30 petals, high-centered; foliage leathery, light green; vigorous, upright growth; int. by Peterson & Dering, 1962

Pink Spiral HT, dp, 1953, McGredy, Sam IV; flowers deep China-rose-pink, 4 in., dbl., high-centered; foliage cedar-green; growth very vigorous

Pink Spire HT, mp

Pink Splendour HT, mp, 1951, McGredy, Sam IV; flowers rose-pink, 6-7 in., 48 petals; foliage dark; very free growth; [Sam McGredy × Crimson Glory]

Pink Spray S, dp, 2000, Lens, Louis; flowers deep pink, white center, reverse deep pink, 2 cm., single, borne in large clusters, slight fragrance; non-recurrent; foliage small, dark green, glossy, disease-resistant; prickles moderate; growth spreading (60 cm.); groundcover; [*R. wichurana yakachinensis* × seedling of *R. multifora adenocheata*]; int. by Louis Lens NV, 1980

Pink Star S, mp, 1982, Interplant; flowers medium, semi-dbl., borne in clusters; foliage medium size, light green, semi-glossy; spreading growth; [Yesterday × seedling]; int. in 1978

Pink Starina Min, pb, Asami; int. in 1975

Pink Starina, Climbing Cl Min, pb; int. after 1975

Pink Stream LCl, mp, Teranishi; int. by Itami Rose Garden, 2003

Pink Strike Min, lp, Laver, Keith G.; int. in 1998

Pink Sublime HMsk, pb

Pink Summer Snow, Climbing – See **Pink Snow**, Cl F

Pink Summer Snow F, lp; [sport of Summer Snow]; similar to Summer Snow except for flower color.

Pink Sunblaze – See **Pink Meillandina**, Min

Pink Super Bouquet – See **Sanjith**, F

Pink Supreme HT, lp, 1964, deRuiter; flowers 4-5 in., 23 petals; foliage light green; vigorous, upright, well-branched growth; [Amor × Peace]; Gold Medal, Geneva, 1965, Gold Medal, Belfast, 1967

Pink Surprise S, dp, Ottawa; int. in 1975

Pink Surprise Min, mp, 1980, Lyon; bud ovoid, pointed; flowers 48 petals, borne singly or several together; foliage tiny, medium green; prickles curved; compact, bushy growth; [seedling × seedling]; int. in 1979

Pink Surprise HBc, lp, 2000, Lens, Louis; flowers light pink, nearly white, reverse white, red stamens, 10-11 cm., single, borne in small clusters, moderate fragrance; recurrent; foliage large, medium green, glossy, evergreen; numerous prickles; bushy, tall (1¾-2 m.) growth; [*R. bracteata* × La Rosee]; int. by Lous Lens N.V., 1987

Pink Swany S, mp, Meilland; flowers strong pink, small, full, rosette, borne in clusters; recurrent; growth mounding (50 cm.); int. in 2004

Pink Sweetheart F, mp, 1985, Williams, J. Benjamin; flowers medium coral pink, well-formed, 2-2½ in., dbl., borne singly, moderate fragrance; foliage medium size, medium green, semi-glossy; prickles moderate; upright, dwarf growth; [(Carla × Sonia) × (Circus × Ma Perkins)]; int. by Paramount Roses, 1985

Pink Sweetie Pol, lp, 2007, Tolmasoff, Jan & William; flowers semi-dbl., borne in large clusters, intense sweet fragrance; foliage medium size, medium green, semi-glossy, disease-free; prickles medium, greenish red, moderate; growth bushy, short (20-24 in.); borders, containers, low hedge; [unknown × unknown]; int. by Russian River Rose Company, 2004

Pink Symphony Min, lp, 1987, Meilland, Mrs. Marie-Louise; bud oval, small; flowers light cardinal pink, unfading, 1½-2 in., 26 petals, flat, borne singly and in small clusters; good repeat; foliage medium size, dark green, glossy, disease-resistant; prickles small; vigorous, bushy (18 in.) growth; PP7277; [Darling Flame × Air France]; Gold Medal, Glasgow, 1992

Pink Talisman HT, op, 1943, Howard Rose Co.; flowers orange to pink with pink predominating, large; upright growth; [sport of Talisman]

Pink Tapestry F, dp, Williams, J. Benjamin; flowers fluorescent pink; free-flowering; compact growth; int. in 1997

Pink The Fairy Pol, dp; flowers very deep pink; [sport of The Fairy]; int. in 1985

Pink Tiara Min, mp; flowers bright pink, yellow stamens, semi-dbl., shallow cup; foliage dark green; growth to 20 × 20 in.; int. in 2003

Pink Tingle Min, mp, 1979, Lyon; bud ovoid; flowers dawn-pink, to recurved, 1 in., 20 petals, cupped; foliage tiny; compact growth; int. in 1978

Pink Toddler – See **Dr McAlpine**, F

Pink Topaz Min, pb, 2000, Mander, George; flowers dark pink with red tips, pink-cream blend reverse, 2½-3 in., full, high-centered, borne mostly solitary, no fragrance; foliage medium size, dark green, glossy; prickles 5/16 in., needlepoint, few; growth upright, tall (20-24 in.); garden, containers, exhibition; [Hot Tamale × Rubies 'n' Pearls]; int. by Select Roses, 2001

Pink Torch S, mp, 1986, Interplant; flowers small, single, borne in large, pyramidal sprays; good repeat; foliage medium size, medium green, glossy; upright (to 4 ft.) growth; [(Mozart × seedling) × (seedling × Eyepaint)]; int. in 1987

Pink Traumland F, mp, Tantau; flowers luminous pink, medium-large, dbl.; int. by Rosen Tantau, 1996

Pink Traviata HT, dp, Meilland; bud globular; flowers hot pink, 3 in., very full, shallow cup, borne in clusters of 2-5, very slight fragrance; recurrent; foliage dark green, semi-glossy; prickles very numerous, large; growth tall (4 ft.), upright; PP16890; [sport of Traviata]; int. by Meilland Star Roses, 2006

Pink Treasure HT, mp, 1995, Davidson, Harvey D.; flowers 4½ in., full, borne mostly singly, moderate fragrance; foliage large, medium green, semi-glossy; some prickles; upright, medium (110 cm.) growth; [Smooth Sailing × Red Planet]; int. by Hortico Roses, 1995

Pink Treasure S, mp, Williams, J.B.; flowers 3 in., dbl.; int. by Hortico, 2004

Pink Triumph – See **Ingrid Stenzig**, Pol

Pink Triumph Min, mp, 1983, Jolly, Nelson F.; flowers small, 48 petals, borne usually singly; foliage small, medium green, semi-glossy; upright, bushy growth; [Operetta × Bonny]; int. by Rosehill Farm

Pink Twist Min, pb, 2007, Moore, Ralph S.; flowers dark pink, petals quilled, revealing white reverse, medium, 1½ in., dbl., borne in large clusters; foliage medium size, medium green, semi-glossy; prickles small, straight, brown, few; growth upright, tall (24 in.); hedging, containers; [Doris Bennett × Doris Bennett]; int. by Sequoia Nurs., 2007

Pink Twister S, mp

Pink Vogue F, mp, 1962, Kelleher, Mrs J.; bud pointed; flowers pink, medium, semi-dbl., borne in clusters, moderate fragrance; moderate, upright growth; [sport of Vogue]; int. by Hazlewood Bros., 1960

Pink Wave F, mp, 1984, Mattock, John, Ltd.; flowers soft medium pink, medium, semi-dbl., moderate fragrance; foliage medium size, medium green, semi-glossy; groundcover; spreading growth; [Moon Maiden × Eyepaint]; int. in 1983

Pink Wedding LCl, lp; [sport of Wedding Day]; int. by Rose du Temps Passé, 2000

Pink Wings HT, lp

Pink Winks Min, mp, 1987, Florac, Marilyn; flowers small, 13 petals, urn-shaped, borne usually singly, no fragrance; foliage small, medium green, matte; bushy, low growth; [Baby Betsy McCall × Red Can Can]

Pink Wonder F, lp, 1971, Meilland; flowers imbricated, 3 in., 28 petals, intense fragrance; foliage large, glossy, leathery; vigorous, upright growth; [Zambra × (Sarabande × (Goldilocks × Fashion))]; int. by URS, 1970; Gold Medal, Madrid, 1969, Gold Medal, Belfast, 1972

Pink Wonder, Climbing Cl F, lp, 1979, Meilland, Mrs. Marie-Louise; [sport of Pink Wonder]; int. by Meilland & Co SNC, 1976

Pinkces LCl, yb, 1962, Schmalz & Limpert; bud pointed; flowers light yellow to pink, open, 3½-4 in., 30 petals, moderate fragrance; abundant, non-recurrent bloom; foliage leathery; vigorous, tall, compact growth; PP2268; [sport of Doubloons]

Pinkerton HT, mp, 1949, Eacott; bud long, pointed; flowers pink shaded deeper, 4 in., 30 petals; foliage light green; vigorous growth

Pinkie Pol, mp, 1947, Swim, H.C.; flowers Neyron rose, 1¾-2½ in., 16 petals, cupped, borne in large trusses; soft, glossy, mostly 7 leaflet leaves; dwarf, bushy growth; [sport of China Doll]; int. by Armstrong Nursery

Pinkie, Climbing Cl Pol, mp, 1952, Dering; flowers rose-pink, fading to pale pink, 1¾-2½ in., semi-dbl., cupped, borne in large clusters; foliage glossy; thornless; [sport of Pinkie]; int. by Armstrong Nursery

Pink-n-Pretty Min, pb, 2007, Wells, Verlie W.; flowers medium pink, reverse dark pink, 2 in., dbl., borne mostly solitary or in sm; foliage medium size, medium green, semi-glossy; prickles ¼ in., straight, few; growth upright, medium (2½ ft.); exhibition, garden decorative; [seedling × seedling]; int. by Wells MidSouth Roses, 2007

Pinky – See **Rebekah**, HT

Pinky Rugostar HRg, lp, Meilland; flowers single; int. in 1996

Pinnacle F, rb, 2004, Benardella, Frank; flowers scarlet red, reverse silver, 2 in., semi-dbl., borne in small clusters, slight fragrance; foliage medium size, medium green, semi-glossy; prickles small, recurved; compact, medium growth; garden; [Ivory Beauty × Kristen]; int. by Burks, Larry, 2004

Pinnatifide S, mp, before 1828; wild form found in the French Pyrenees

Pinocchio F, op, 1940, Kordes; flowers pink suffused salmon, edged deeper, 2 in., 30 petals, cupped, borne in long sprays, moderate fruity fragrance; foliage leathery; vigorous, bushy growth; [Eva × Golden Rapture]; int. by J&P, 1942; Gold Medal, Portland, 1942

Pinocchio, Climbing Cl F, pb, 1951, Parmentier, J.; good rebloom; [sport of Pinocchio]; int. by J&P

Pinocchio Min, ob, Delbard; int. in 1998

Pinocchio Min, m, 1999, Schuurman, Frank B.; flowers magenta, 2-2½ in., dbl., borne in large clusters, no fragrance; foliage large, dark green, semi-glossy; prickles moderate; upright, medium growth; patio; [Tinkerbell × Chess]; int. by Franko Roses New Zealand, Ltd., 1998

Pinson LCl, my, 1909, Barbier; flowers chamois-yellow, tinted rosy white, very large, semi-dbl., borne in clusters; early; vigorous, climbing growth; [*R. wichurana* × Souv. de Catherine Guillot]

Pinstripe Min, rb, 1985, Moore, Ralph S.; flowers red with white stripes, well-formed, small, 35 petals; foliage small, medium green, semi-glossy; low, mounded growth; [Pinocchio × seedling]; int. by Armstrong Nursery, 1986

Pinta HT, w, 1976, Beales, Peter; flowers creamy white, large, 23 petals, moderate sweetbriar fragrance; foliage dark, matte; [Ena Harkness × Pascali]; int. by Intwood Lane Nurs., 1973

Pintade HGal, mp, before 1817, Loiseleur-Deslongchamps; flowers pink, spotted white

Pinwheel Min, pb, 1977, Moore, Ralph S.; flowers pink and yellow blend; [sport of Jeanie Williams]; int. by Sequoia Nursery, 1979

Pinwheel – See **Kazaguruma**, F

Pione F, m, Hiroshima; int. by Hiroshima Bara-en, 2000

Pioneer HT, mr, 1971, LeGrice; flowers very full, 4 in., 50 petals, intense fragrance; foliage small, dark; very free growth; int. by Roseland Nurs., 1970

Pioneer Spirit LCl, mp, 2005, Shoup, George Michael; flowers very full, borne in small clusters, moderate fragrance; foliage large, dark green, semi-glossy; numerous prickles; growth mannerly climber, tall (8 ft.); climber/pillar; [((Seafoam × Himilayan Musk) × Carefree Beauty) × Crimson Glory]; int. by Antique Rose Emporium, 1996

Pionerka F, ob, 1955, Sushkov, K. L.; flowers reddish-orange, medium; vigorous growth

Pioupiou F, mr, 1958, Arles; flowers cerise-red, large; very vigorous, bushy, low growth; [Alain × (Alain × seedling)]; int. by Roses-France

Pip Min, mr, 1978, Lyon; bud pointed; flowers small, 12-15 petals, cupped; foliage tiny; very compact, bushy growth; RULED EXTINCT 7/90; [N74 × seedling]

Pip HT, w, 1991, Stoddard, Louis; bud ovoid; flowers white rimmed pink, white reverse, aging same, medium, 30 petals, high-centered, borne singly, slight fragrance; foliage medium size, light to medium green, matte; bushy, medium growth; [(Poker Chip × Helmut Schmidt) × (Rise 'n' Shine × Granada × Handel)]

Pipe Dreams S, mp, 1985, Buck, Dr. Griffith J.; flowers medium pink, reverse darker, 5 in., 28 petals, cupped, borne 5-10 per cluster, intense clove fragrance; repeat bloom; foliage leathery, medium olive green; prickles awl-shaped, red-brown; bushy, compact, upright growth; hardy; Countryman × ((Meisterstuck × Prairie Princess) × (Tickled Pink × Prairie Princess)); int. by Iowa State University, 1984

Pipi Min, dp, Hiroshima; int. by Hiroshima Bara-en, 1998

Pippa's Song S, mp, 1985, Buck, Dr. Griffith J.; flowers imbricated, 3 in., borne 3-10 per cluster; repeat bloom; foliage medium size, leathery, dark olive green; prickles awl-shaped, tan; shrubby, erect, bushy growth; hardy; [Prairie Princess × (Queen Elizabeth × (Morning Stars × Morning Stars × Suzanne))]; int. by Iowa State University, 1984

Pippy MinFl, pb, Barni, V.; flowers medium pink with darker pink to red edges, dbl., high-centered, moderate fragrance; growth to 40-45 cm.; int. by Rose Barni, 1995

Pipsqueak Min, m, 1986, Dobbs; flowers pinkish mauve, quilled, small, 40 petals, flat, borne in sprays of 5-20; foliage small, light green, matte; prickles very small, brown, hooked downward; bushy, spreading growth; no fruit; [Blue Mist × Snow Magic]; int. by Port Stockton Nursery

Pirate Gold F, dy, 1973, deRuiter; flowers dbl., globular; foliage glossy, leathery; vigorous, upright growth; [Golden Wave × seedling]; int. by Carlton Rose Nurseries, 1972

Pirbright F, mp, 1948, Norman; flowers semi-dbl., borne in trusses; foliage dark; vigorous growth

PiRo 3 S, lp, Stritzke; flowers deep rose pink, single, borne in clusters; once-blooming; foliage glossy; few prickles; growth to 6 ft.; hips oblong, 3 in. long, very high in vitamin C ; hardy; [*R. dumalis* × *R. pendulina salaevensis*]; bred to produce hips that contain very high levels of vitamin C; selection from Institute for Horticulture, Dresden-Pillnitz; int. in 1995

Piroja HT, m, 1999, Chiplunkar, C. R.; flowers deep mauve, medium, full, high-centered, borne in small clusters, moderate fragrance; foliage medium size, medium green, semi-glossy; few prickles; upright, medium (3-3½ ft.) growth; [Blue Moon × Heirloom]; int. by KSG's Roses, 1992

Pirol Pol, dy, Tantau; flowers small, dbl.; int. by Rosen Tantau, 1994

Pirol HT, dy, Tantau; florist rose; int. by Rosen Tantau, 2002

Piron-Médard HP, mp, 1906, Piron-Médard; bud long; flowers satin pink, large, dbl.; foliage nearly thornless; growth upright

Pironia – See **Centenaire du Vesinet**, Gr

Pironti Arabian HT, Pironti, N.

Pironti Blithe F, Pironti, N.; int. in 1970

Pironti Critow Cl HT, Pironti, N.

Pironti Konrad Gr, Pironti; int. in 1971

Pironti Tornedos F, Pironti; int. in 1971

Pirontina LCl, mp, Pironti; flowers small, dbl., cupped, slight fragrance; recurrent; vigorous (10-12 ft.) growth; hips none; hardy; int. in 1975

Pirosa – See **PiRo 3**, S

Piroschka HT, mp, 1972, Tantau, Math.; bud long, pointed; flowers large, dbl.; moderate, upright growth; [Fragrant Cloud × Dr. A.J. Verhage]

Pirouette F, pb, 1968, Fankhauser; flowers pink tinged orange-red, open, medium, dbl.; [Ma Perkins × Radar]; int. by A. Ross & Son

Pirouette S, dr, 2000, Lens, Louis; flowers dark red, white center, reverse dark red, 7 cm., single, borne in small clusters, slight fragrance; recurrent; foliage medium size, medium green, semi-glossy; prickles moderate; upright, medium (4-5 ft.) growth; [Wilhelm × Picasso]; int. by Louis Lens N.V., 1983

Pirouette – See **Kristin**, Min

Pirouette LCl, pb, Poulsen; flowers pink blend with touch of apricot in center, small, full, shallow cup, slight wild rose fragrance; recurrent; broad, bushy (150-200 cm.) growth; hips none ; PP15106; int. by Poulsen Roser, 2002

Pisces Fl, mp, Burston; flowers soft pink, large, dbl., cupped; foliage glossy; upright (30 in.) growth; int. by Burston Nurseries, 2004

Pisen HT, op, Brabec

Pismi HT, rb, 1972, Pecollo; bud ovoid; flowers solferino-purple to spirea-red, large, dbl., cupped; foliage large, dark, leathery; vigorous, upright bushy growth; [Dame Edith Helen × Rote Rapture]

Pissardii – See **Nastarana**, N

Pitica – See **Kyria**, F

Pitord HP, rb, 1867, Lacharme; flowers fiery red, center velvety violet, large, full

Pitstop HT, dr, Select; flowers velvety dark red, 4 in., 30-35 petals, high-centered, borne mostly singly; recurrent; foliage dark green; stems long

Pittsburgh HP, lp, 1929, Schoener; flowers flesh-pink, base yellow, very large, 25 petals, globular; foliage leathery; long stems; very vigorous growth; [((*R. gigantea* × unknown) × Frau Karl Druschki) × Mrs John Laing]; int. by B&A

Pius the Ninth – See **Pius IX**, HP

Pius IX HP, mp, 1849, Vibert; flowers violet-rose, large, very dbl., flat, intense fragrance; vigorous growth

Pius XI HT, w, 1925, Leenders, M.; bud long, pointed; flowers cream-white, center cream-yellow, very large, dbl.; [Ophelia × seedling]

Pivoine – See **Bourbon**, HGal

Pivoine – See **Lustre d'Église**, HGal

Pivoine de Lille – See **Nouvelle Pivoine**, HGal

Pivoine des Hollandais – See **Great Royal**, HGal

Pixie Min, w, 1940, deVink; flowers white, center light pink, small, 55 petals; foliage very small, soft; short stems; dwarf, compact growth; [Ellen Poulsen × Tom Thumb]; int. by C-P

Pixie, Climbing Cl Min, w, 1964, Ruston, D.

Pixie Delight Min, w, 1982, Williams, J. Benjamin; flowers dbl.; foliage small, dark, semi-glossy; upright growth; PP5270; [Ma Perkins × Easter Morning]; int. by C-P, 1981

Pixie Dust Min, yb, 2003, Denton, James A.; flowers light yellow/pink, reverse light yellow, medium, full, borne mostly solitary, no fragrance; foliage medium green, semi-glossy; prickles small, straight, light brown, moderate; growth bushy, medium (18-20 in.); garden decoration, exhibition; [Hot Tamale × Amber Sunset]; int. by James A Denton, 2003

Pixie Gold Min, my, 1961, Dot, Pedro; flowers mimosa-yellow, 1-1½ in., 11 petals; foliage very small, thin, dark; bushy growth; PP2091; [Perla de Montserrat × (Rosina × Eduardo Toda)]; int. by C-P, 1961

Pixie Hat F, mr, Kordes; flowers bright red with yellow stamens, single, shallow cup, borne in large clusters; recurrent; growth medium, with many basals; int. in 1993

Pixie Hedge – See **Baby Jayne**, Cl Min

Pixie Pearl Min, w, about 1910; flowers pearly white, small, very dbl., borne in clusters; vigorous, compact growth; int. by Lamb Nursery

Pixie Rose Min, dp, 1961, Dot, Pedro; flowers 43 petals, high-centered to cupped, borne in irregular clusters; foliage very small, dark; dwarf, much-branched growth; PP2095; [Perla de Montserrat × Coralín]; int. by C-P, 1961

Pizzazz Min, rb, 1991, Jolly, Marie; bud ovoid; flowers various yellows, pink hues, aging to orange-red, 1½ in., 50 petals, borne usually singly or in sprays of 2-3, slight fragrance; foliage medium size, medium green, semi-glossy; upright, spreading, medium growth; [Orange Honey × Loving Touch]; int. by Rosehill Farm, 1992

Pizzazz Min, rb, 2003, White, Wendy R.; flowers medium red, reverse medium yellow, 2-2½ in., dbl., borne mostly solitary, moderate fragrance; recurrent; foliage large, dark green, glossy, disease-resistant; prickles straight, flat, triangular, few; growth upright, compact, medium (16-24 in.); container, decorative; pp15870; [Sachet × Pierrine]; int. by Nor' East Miniature Roses, 2003

Pizzicato S, lp, 1964, Buck, Dr. Griffith J.; bud ovoid, long, pointed; flowers light salmon-rose, 3-4 in., 40 petals, cupped, moderate fragrance; foliage leathery, bronze; vigorous, upright (3-4 ft.), bushy. growth; [Florence Mary Morse × (Josef Rothmund × *R. laxa*)]; int. by Iowa State University, 1962

Placet S, w, 1981, Bevan, Mrs. Ruth M.; bud small, ovoid; flowers 5 petals, borne 40 or more per cluster; all summer bloom; foliage soft green, 7 leaflet; bushy growth

Placida HT, mr, 1959, Cayzer; bud ovoid; flowers crimson, large, dbl.; foliage glossy, dark; vigorous, bushy, compact growth; [Crimson Glory × Una Wallace]

Placidie A, mp, 1820, Prévost/Vibert; flowers bright

pink, medium, semi-dbl.; foliage small, narrow, deep green; nearly thornless; stems slender; growth vertical; [sport of Great Maiden's Blush]

Placido Domingo – See **Velvet Ruby**, HT

Plain Talk F, mr, 1965, Swim & Weeks; bud long-pointed; flowers bright, clear red, 2½-2¾ in., 25-30 petals, borne in flat to rounded clusters of 3 or more, slight fragrance; free-flowering; foliage large, dark green, leathery; prickles few, straight, grayish-brown; growth vigorous, bushy, low; PP2538; [Spartan × Garnette]; int. by Weeks Wholesale Rose Growers

Plaisante F, mp, 1957, Riethmuller; flowers bright pink, base and reverse lighter, semi-dbl.; low growth; [Borderer × seedling]

Plaisanterie HMsk, pb, 2000, Lens, Louis; bud orange; flowers yellow, aging to pink and dark pink, reverse lighter, 4 cm., semi-dbl., borne in large clusters, slight fragrance; foliage dark green, semi-glossy; few prickles; upright (4-5 ft.) growth; [Trier × Mutabilis]; int. by Louis Lens N.V., 1996

Plaisir de France HT, dp, 1952, Gaujard; flowers bright deep coppery pink, 6 in., 35 petals; foliage glossy, dark; vigorous growth; [Peace × seedling]

Plameny HT, mr, Urban, J.; flowers large, dbl.; int. in 1970

Plamya Vostoka F, or, Klimenko, V. N.; flowers fiery red tinted darker, medium, 30 petals; medium growth; [Independence × Kirsten Poulsen]; int. in 1955

Planten un Blomen – See **Cherrio**, F, 1948

Plate Bonde Seedling Pol, mp; recurrent; growth to 2-3 ft.

Platinum Lady Min, m, 1989, Laver, Keith G.; bud pointed; flowers light lavender, reverse white, very slow to open, 21 petals, high-centered, borne singly, no fragrance; foliage small, dark green, young edged in red, semi-glossy; prickles slender; upright, bushy, medium growth; hips ovoid, orange; [unnamed seedling (lavender) × Lavender Jade]; int. by Springwood Roses, 1989

Plato HSpn, mr, about 1850, Vibert; flowers clear red, dbl.; non-recurrent; foliage finely divided; dense, shrubby (3-4 ft.) growth; hips glossy, black

Platyphylla – See **Seven Sisters**, HMult

Play Girl F, or; int. by Bear Creek Gardens, 2002

Play Rose – See **Deborah**, S dbl.

Playboy F, rb, 1976, Cocker; flowers scarlet, gold eye, large, single, flat to slightly cupped, borne singly and in clusters, slight apple fragrance; recurrent; foliage glossy, dark green; growth moderate (3-4 ft.); [City of Leeds × (Chanelle × Piccadilly)]; Gold Medal, Portland, 1989

Player HT, pb, 1999, Schuurman, Frank B.; flowers 4½-5 in., dbl., borne mostly singly; foliage large, dark green, glossy; numerous prickles; upright, tall (4½-5 ft.) growth; [Raspberry Ice × Karen]; int. by Franko Roses New Zealand, Ltd., 1993

Playfair F, w, 1991, Wilke, William; flowers medium, single, borne in small clusters, slight fragrance; foliage medium size, medium green, semi-glossy; medium growth; [Playgirl × seedling]

Playful HT, ab, 1970, Watson; flowers light apricot, edged pink; [sport of Mischief]

Playful F, mp, 2003, Wilke, William; flowers pink, reverse deeper pink, golden stamens, 3 in., single, borne in large clusters, slight fragrance; foliage medium size, dark green, glossy; prickles ¼ in., straight out, no hook, brown; upright, medium growth; containers, bedding; [sport of Playgirl]

Playfulness F, mp, Williams, J.B.; recurrent; int. by Hortico, 2004

Playgirl F, mp, 1986, Moore, Ralph S.; bud long pointed, slender; flowers pink with yellow stamens, wavy petal edges, 3½ in., 5-7 petals, flat to slightly cupped, borne singly and in sprays; recurrent; foliage medium size, medium green, semi-glossy; prickles few, straight, brown; growth upright, bushy; PP6468; [Playboy × Angel Face]; int. by Moore Min. Roses

Playgirl, Climbing Cl F, mp, 1993, Moore, Ralph S.; flowers 3-3½ in., 5-7 petals, borne in small clusters; foliage medium size, medium green, semi-glossy; tall (2-3 m.), upright, spreading, climbing growth; [sport of Playgirl]; int. by Sequoia Nursery, 1995

Playgold Min, ob, 1997, Moore, Ralph S.; flowers small, semi-dbl., borne in small clusters; foliage small, medium size, green, glossy; low (12-18 in.) growth; [Playgold × Sequoia Gold]; int. by Sequoia Nurs.; Award of Excellence, ARS, 1998

Playgroup Rose F, yb, 1986, Horner, Heather M.; flowers yellow, petals edged red, reverse pale yellow, 25 petals, cupped, borne in sprays, moderate fragrance; foliage medium size, light green, glossy; prickles large, light brown; medium, bushy growth; hips small, globular, orange; [Prominent × Southampton]

Playmate F, rb, 1987, Fonda, Henry; flowers vivid scarlet, yellow center, large, 5 petals, borne usually singly; foliage medium size, dark green, glossy; upright, bushy growth; [Playboy × seedling]; int. by Wee Ones Miniature Roses, 1986

Playmate – See **Friendship**, F

Playmate S, ab, Williams, J.B.; recurrent; low (2 ft.), spreading (3 ft.) growth; int. by Hortico, Inc., 2003

Playpretty S, op, 2000, Cockerham, John E.; flowers orange pink, reverse deep pink, large, semi-dbl., borne mostly singly, slight fragrance; foliage medium size, medium green,matte; few prickles; upright, low (2-3 ft.) growth

Playrose HT, dp, Ferrer; florist rose; int. by Meilland Intl., 2004

Playtime F, or, 1990, Moore, Ralph S.; bud pointed; flowers vibrant orange-red, aging slightly darker, medium, 5 petals, flat, borne singly and in sprays of 3-5; foliage medium size, dark green, semi-glossy; prickles straight, slightly hooked, medium, light brown; upright, bushy, medium growth; hips round, medium, orange-red; [Playboy × Old Master]; int. by Sequoia Nursery, 1990

Playtime – See **Rosalina**, S

Pleasant Valley – See **Plaisanterie**, HMsk

Pleasantly Pink Min, mp, 1992, Laver, Keith G.; flowers clear pink, large, very dbl., borne in small clusters; foliage medium size, medium green, matte; some prickles; medium (30-35 cm.), bushy growth; [(June Laver × Rosamini Red) × (Dwarfking × Julie Ann)]; int. by Springwood Roses

Pleasure F, mp, 1989, Warriner, William A.; bud ovoid, pointed; flowers coral pink, reverse lighter, large, 33 petals, cupped, borne in sprays of 3-7; foliage medium size, dark green, semi-glossy; prickles slightly hooked downward, reddish-brown; low, compact growth; globular fruit; PP7480; [(Merci × Faberge) × Intrigue]; int. by Bear Creek Gardens, 1990; All-American Rose, AARS, 1990

Pleasure! HT, w, Schreurs; int. by Yates Botanicals, 2002

Plein Ciel HT, mp, 1967, Hendrickx, Adolf; bud pointed; flowers large, dbl., high-centered, moderate fragrance; foliage dark, glossy; vigorous, well branched growth; [seedling × Golden Rapture]; int. in 1965

Plein Soleil F, or, Laperrière; flowers bright red-orange, dbl.; growth short (2 ft.); int. in 1991

Pleine de Grâce S, w, 1985, Lens, Louis; flowers creamy white, 4-5 cm., 5 petals, borne in clusters of 20-50, intense fragrance; non-recurrent; foliage yellowish-green; bushy, spreading growth; [Ballerina × *R. filipes*]; int. by Louis Lens NV, 1983

Pleins Feux 92 Pol, rb, Dorieux; flowers bright red, reverse lighter, semi-dbl., flat, borne in clusters; int. by Dorieux, 1992; Rose of the Century, Lyon, 1990, Gold Medal, Madrid, 1990

Plena A, w, before 1770; bud slightly pink; flowers washed nankeen in center, single to semi-dbl., borne in large clusters; foliage ovoid, pointed, dentate, dark green; prickles reddish, shield-shaped

Plena HSem, lp, before 1830, Laffay, M.; flowers flesh-tinted, dbl.

Plenissima – See **Double Hugonis**, S dbl.

Plentiful F, dp, 1961, LeGrice; bud globular; flowers 3-4 in., 75 petals, flat, quartered, borne in large clusters, slight fragrance; good repeat; foliage light green; vigorous, bushy growth; int. by Roseland Nurs., 1961

Plisiedame F, ab, Kordes; int. in 1990

Plnokvety Super Star HT, or, Strnad

Plomin F, pb, 1951, Tantau; flowers golden peach, fading thru peach/blush pink to white, large, semi-dbl., borne in large clusters, intense fragrance; foliage leathery; bushy, dwarf growth; [(Johanna Tantau × Karen Poulsen) × Stammler]

Plonia – See **Pæonia**, HP

Pluie de Feu LCl, or, 1964, Mondial Roses; flowers bright scarlet, semi-dbl., borne in clusters; vigorous growth

Plukovnik Svec HT, dr, 1935, Böhm, J.; bud long (over 3 in.), pointed; flowers blood-red, large, semi-dbl.; foliage small; vigorous, bushy growth; [Pres. Jac. Smits × Kitchener of Khartoum]

Plum Brandy Min, m; flowers plum/purple/pink, small, full, rosette, slight fragrance; growth low (10-14 in.)

Plum Cake HT, dr, 1987, Murray, Nola; flowers deep plum red, pointed, 27 petals, borne in sprays of 3-7; almost everblooming; foliage medium size, dark green, glossy; prickles pointed, brown; bushy growth; [(Chanelle × Sabine) × Pompadour]; int. in 1986

Plum Crazy HT, m, 1985, Christensen, Jack E.; flowers deep lavender, well-formed, large, 35 petals, moderate fragrance; foliage medium size, dark, matte; bushy growth; [(Ivory Tower × Angel Face) × Blue Nile]; int. by Armstrong Nursery

Plum Dandy Min, m, 1991, Warriner, William A.; bud ovoid, pointed, short; flowers medium lavender, lighter near petal base, fades to light lavender with age, 2-2½ in., 35 petals, cupped, borne several together in pyramidal clusters, moderate fruity fragrance; good repeat; foliage medium size, medium green, semi-glossy; prickles medium, medium size, hooked slightly downward; stems short, strong; bushy, spreading, medium growth; PP8402; [seedling × Angel Face]; int. by Bear Creek Gardens/Jackson & Perkins, 1991

Plum Duffy Min, m, 1978, Bennett, Dee; bud ovoid; flowers deep plum, 1½ in., 25 petals, high-centered, slight fragrance; foliage dark; growth compact; [Magic Carrousel × Magic Carrousel]; int. by Tiny Petals Nursery

Plum Frost S, m, 2007, Zary, Keith W.; flowers smoky purple, reverse lavender, 3½ in., semi-dbl., borne in small clusters; foliage medium size, dark green, glossy; prickles 8-10 mm., hooked downward, greyed-orange, moderate; growth upright, medium (4 ft.); hedge, in mixed perennial beds; [seedling × Perfume Perfection (formerly Cotillion)]; int. by Jackson & Perkins Wholesale, Inc., 2007

Plum Pudding Min, m, 1985, Williams, J. Benjamin; flowers blue-lavender washed red and purple, small, 35 petals, moderate fragrance; foliage small, dark, semi-glossy; upright, bushy growth; [Angel Face × unnamed lavender seedling]

Plums 'n' Cream F, rb, 2001, Weeks, Michael; flowers plum red, cream reverse, 2½ in., dbl., borne in small clusters, moderate fragrance; foliage large, dark green, glossy; prickles large, pointed, numerous; growth spreading, medium (3 ft.); garden decorative; [Picasso × unknown]

Pluto C, dr, before 1799; flowers very dark red

Pluto – See **Hurdy Gurdy**, Min

Pluton HGal, m, 1843, Vibert; flowers very deep blackish purple, medium, full

Plzen HT, dr, 1930, Böhm, J.; bud very long; flowers dark blood-red, very large, semi-dbl.; very vigorous growth; [Étoile de Hollande × Macbeth]

Pobjeditel HT, dp, 1940, Kosteckij; flowers large, dbl.

Poblet HT, ob, Dot; flowers bright vermilion, long lasting

Pocahontas – See **Kay Ann**, HT

Poco Min, pb, 1987, Bridges, Dennis A.; flowers pink, white center, fades slightly, medium, 29 petals, urn-shaped, borne usually singly; foliage medium size, medium green, semi-glossy; prickles medium, light green, pointed downwards; growth bushy, medium; [Heartland × seedling]

Podruga HT, mp, 1939, Costetske; flowers bright pink, base dark red, oval, irregular shape; low, rather weak growth; [Vaterland × Mme Edouard Herriot]

Poëma Cl Pol, mp, 1933, Brada, Dr.; flowers bright pink, passing to La France pink, 4-5 cm., semi-dbl., borne in clusters of 10-20; recurrent bloom; foliage bright, dark; vigorous (5-10 ft.) growth; [Tausendschön × Farbenkonigin]; int. by Böhm

Poema HT, dr; int. by Pep. Jacques Briant, 2004

Poeme! HT, lp, Schreurs; int. by Yates Botanical, 2002

Poente F, ob, Moreira da Silva; flowers orange and carmine; [Pinocchio × Goldilocks]

Poesie – See **Promise**, HT

Poesie HMsk, pb, 1986, Lens, Louis; flowers white shaded pink, 2 in., 20 petals, borne in clusters of 5-32, intense fragrance; foliage large, leathery, dark; prickles hooked, light brown; bushy, spreading growth; [Ballerina × Moonlight]; int. in 1982

Poesie – See **Tournament of Roses**, Gr

Poesie S, w; groundcover; int. in 1997

Poète Jean du Clos HT, op, 1919, Gillot, F.; flowers pink, shaded salmon, dbl.; [Le Progres × Lyon Rose]

Poetry Min, rb, 1991, Zipper, Herbert; bud pointed; flowers red with white at base, white reverse with some red at edges, medium, 30 petals, high-centered, borne usually singly, slight fragrance; foliage small, medium green, semi-glossy; bushy, low growth; [Libby × Deep Purple]; int. by Magic Moment Miniature Roses, 1991

Poetry HT, lp, Kordes; flowers delicate pink, large, very full, high-centered, borne mostly singly, intense fragrance; good repeat; foliage fresh green; stems long, strong; int. by W. Kordes Söhne, 2002

Poetry in Motion – See **Gift of Life**, HT

Poetry Kordana Min, lp, Kordes; flowers silvery pink, full, high-centered; int. by W. Kordes Söhne, 2005

Pohadka Maje HT, mr, Certek

Poiana HT, dy, GPG Bad Langensalza; flowers large, dbl.; int. in 1972

Poinsettia HT, mr, 1938, H&S; bud long, pointed; flowers bright scarlet, large, 28 petals, moderate spicy fragrance; recurrent; foliage glossy; growth vigorous, compact; [(Mrs J.D. Eisele × Vaterland) × J.C. Thorton]; int. by Dreer; Gold Medal, Portland, 1940

Poinsettia, Climbing Cl HT, mr, 1950, Thompson, D.L.; int. by Rosemont Nursery Co.

Point Clear Min, w, 1991, Taylor, Pete & Kay; flowers white, light yellow base, medium, full, borne mostly singly, slight fragrance; foliage small, medium green, semi-glossy; some prickles; low (40 cm.), upright growth; [Azure Sea × Party Girl]; int. by Taylor's Roses, 1992

Point de Avignon F, or

Point du Jour – See **Goldstar**, HT

Pointsfield HT, ab, 1977, Simpson, J. W.; buds high pointed; flowers dbl, high-centered, borne singly and in small clusters; foliage glossy, reddish green; growth vigorous, medium tall; [Bonsoir × Percy Thrower]; int. by McKenzie, 1977

Poise S, lp, Williams, J. Benjamin; flowers soft, creamy pink, darker center, semi-dbl., cupped, moderate fragrance; recurrent; foliage dark green, semi-glossy; low (2 ft.), spreading growth

Poison! HT, dp, Schreurs; int. by Yates Botanicals, 2002

Poiteau HP, dp, 1855, Robert; flowers large, full

Poker HT, dp, 1985, Verschuren, Ted; flowers large, 11 petals, cupped, borne in sprays of 6-8, intense fragrance; foliage medium size, medium green, semi-glossy; bushy, medium growth; rounded fruit; [Red Planet × Sonia]; int. by H.A. Verschuren

Poker HT, w, Meilland; flowers creamy white, dbl., high-centered, borne mostly solitary, moderate fragrance; vigorous (90-100 cm.) growth; int. in 1998

Poker Chip Min, rb, 1979, Saville, F. Harmon; bud pointed; flowers red with yellow reverse, medium, 28 petals, high-centered, intense fragrance; foliage glossy, dark; vigorous, compact growth; large fruit; PP4582; [Sheri Anne × (Yellow Jewel × (Tamango × Unknown))]; int. by Nor'East Min. Roses

Pokornyana S, lp, before 1916; sepals appendaged; flowers 1¾ in.; foliage leaflets doubly serrate; [*R. canina* × *R. glauca*]; from Hungary

Pol Robson F, dr, Klimenko, V. N.; flowers medium, very dbl.; int. in 1955

Polar Bear HP, w, 1934, Nicolas; flowers white tinted blush, becoming pure white, large, very dbl., globular, intense fragrance; recurrent bloom; foliage large, leathery, wrinkled; vigorous, bushy growth; [Schoener's Nutkana × New Century]; int. by J&P

Polar Cap MinFl, w, 2004, Brown, Ted; flowers white, green tinge, reverse white, 2¼ in., dbl., borne mostly solitary, slight fragrance; foliage medium size, dark green, matte; prickles very small, pointed; growth upright, tall (30 in.); exhibition; [Luis Desamero × Radiant (Min)]; int. in 2005

Polar Spire – See **Polarstern**, HT

Polar Star – See **Polarstern**, HT

Polar Sun – See **Polarsonne**, HRg

Polareis – See **Ritausma**, HRg

Polaris HSet, w, 1939, Horvath; flowers pure snow-white, open, dbl., borne in clusters, intense fragrance; profuse, non-recurrent bloom; foliage glossy, light; very vigorous, climbing (12-15 ft.) growth; [(*R. setigera* × *R. wichurana*) × *R. foetida bicolor*]; int. by Wayside Gardens Co.

Polaris Min, mp, Olesen; int. in 2000

Polarsonne HRg, mp, Strobel; flowers medium, dbl., slight fragrance; growth to 2 ft.; int. in 1991

Polarstern HT, w, 1983, Tantau, Math.; flowers pale yellow to white, medium, 35 petals, high-centered, slight fragrance; good repeat; foliage medium size, medium green, matte; bushy growth; int. in 1982; Rose of the Year, 1985

Pôle Nord HT, w, 1944, Mallerin, C.; bud long, pointed; flowers pure white, base tinted greenish; vigorous growth; int. by A. Meilland

Pole Position HT, mr, Select; flowers 4½ in., 35-40 petals, high-centered, borne mostly singly; good repeat; stems long, straight; florist rose; int. by Terra Nigra BV, 2003

Polestar – See **Polstjärnan**, LCl

Poliarchus S, w, Central Exp. Farm; flowers cream flushed salmon, fading rapidly; non-recurrent; spreading shrub (4 ft.) growth; hardy; [seedling × *R. × harisonii*]

Polichinelle Min, yb, Delbard; flowers yellow with red stripes, small, semi-dbl.; free-flowering; stems vigorous (2 ft.) growth; int. by Georges Delbard SA, 2000

Polina HT, dp, 1985, Staikov, Prof. Dr. V.; flowers deep pink, large, 38 petals; foliage dark, leathery; bushy growth; [Mistica × Chenon]; int. by Kalaydjiev and Chorbadjiiski, 1984

Polisiedame – See **Plisiedame**, F

Polka F, mp, 1960, Meilland, Mrs. Marie-Louise; bud ovoid; flowers 3-3½ in., 42 petals, high-centered, borne in clusters, moderate fragrance; foliage leathery; vigorous, bushy growth; PP1939; [Moulin Rouge × Fashion]; int. by C-P, 1960

Polka LCl, ab, 1996, Meilland International SA; bud ovoid, large; flowers ivory yellow, 3½-4 in., 90-100 petals, quartered, borne singly and in small clusters, moderate fragrance; good repeat; foliage large, medium green, semi-glossy; few prickles on young stems, numerous on adult wood; upright, climbing, tall (12 ft.) growth; PP9233; [(MEIpalsar × Golden Showers) × Lichtkonigin Lucia]; int. by The Conard-Pyle Co., 1991

Polka 91 – See **Polka**, LCl

Polka Dot Min, w, 1956, Moore, Ralph S.; flowers ivory white, small, dbl.; foliage dark, leathery; vigorous, dwarf (10 in.), bushy growth; [Golden Glow × Zee]; int. by Sequoia Nursery

Polka Time S, op, 1985, Buck, Dr. Griffith J.; bud ovoid, pointed; flowers salmon tinted yellow, veined pink, petals imbricated, 5 in., 38 petals, cupped, borne in clusters of 1-10, moderate fragrance; repeat bloom; foliage dark, leathery; prickles awl-like, tan; growth low, bushy, compact; hardy; [Bonfire Night × Countryman]; int. by Iowa State University, 1984

Pollentia HT, dp, 1942, Dot, Pedro; bud large, long pointed; flowers satiny strawberry-red, 40 petals, high-centered; foliage dark, glossy; upright, compact growth

Polleriana – See **Pollmeriana**, (strain of *R. canina*)

Polliniana Misc OGR, w, 1820; flowers white to pale pink, occasionally tinted rose, large, borne singly or in pairs; long stems; [*R. arvensis* × *R. gallica*]

Pollmeriana (strain of *R. canina*), lp; almost thornless; very vigorous growth; [De la Grifferaie × *R. canina*]; used for understock; int. by Pollmer

Polluce S, mr, Barni, V.; int. in 1987

Pollux – See **Polluce**, S

Polly HT, w, 1927, Beckwith; bud long, pointed; flowers cream, center tinted pink or light orange, fading white, large, 38 petals, high-centered, intense fragrance; [(Ophelia × unknown) × Mme Colette Martinet]

Polly Flinders Min, w, 1954, Robinson, T.; flowers cream tinted copper-orange, 1 in., 30 petals; foliage veined red; [Little Princess × Fashion]

Polly Perkins HT, op, 1969, Gregory; flowers orange-cerise, pointed, moderate fragrance; foliage dark; very free growth; int. by C. Gregory & Son, 1967

Polly Sunshine Pol, my, 1999, Moore, Ralph S.; flowers 2-3 in., full, borne in small clusters; foliage medium size, medium green, glossy; few prickles; bushy (16-24 in.) growth; [Golden Angel × seedling]; int. by Sequoia Nursery, 1999

Polo HT, w, Tantau; int. in 1997

Polo Club HT, yb, 1987, Christensen, Jack E.; flowers yellow bordered red, fading cream with pink edges, dbl., high-centered; foliage medium size, dark green, semi-glossy; prickles straight, small, few, greenish to light brown; upright, bushy, tall growth; fruit not observed; PP6758; [Gingersnap × Young Quinn]; int. by Armstrong Nursery, 1986

Polo Queen HT, pb, 2003, Hayes, Cal; flowers pale pink at the base of each petal blending to a very dark pink on the margin, 4-5 in., full, borne mostly solitary; foliage large, dark green, semi-glossy; upright, tall (4-5 ft.) growth; [sport of Cajun Moon]; int. by Cal Hayes

Polonaise HT, mr, 1961, Von Abrams; flowers bright red, ruffled petals, 6 in., 40-50 petals, high-centered, moderate fragrance; foliage glossy; growth vigorous, upright, compact; [Carrousel × (Chrysler Imperial × seedling)]; int. by Peterson & Dering, 1962

Polonaise S, dp, 1985, Buck, Dr. Griffith J.; bud ovoid, pointed; flowers deep pink, imbricated, 3 in., 43 petals, borne 5-10 per cluster; repeat bloom; foliage leathery, dark green with reddish veination; prickles awl-like, red-brown; dwarf, upright, bushy growth; hardy; [San Francisco × Prairie Princess]; int. by Iowa State University, 1984

Polstjärnan LCl, w, 1937, Wasastjerna; flowers pure white, very small, borne in clusters; non-recurrent; very vigorous (to 18 ft.) growth; very hardy

Poly Peace F, yb, 1960, Leenders, J.; flowers golden yellow edged rose-pink, large, semi-dbl., high-centered; foliage dark, glossy; strong stems; very vigorous, tall, bushy growth; [Masquerade × Peace]; int. by Brit. Hort. Co., 1959

Poly Prim F, dy, 1953, Eddie; flowers well-shaped, 3 in., 70 petals, borne in clusters; foliage dark, glossy; very vigorous, bushy growth; [Goldilocks × Golden Rapture]; Gold Medal, NRS, 1954

Polyana S, dp, 1925, Skinner; [*R. rugosa* × Polyantha]

Polyantha – See ***R. multiflora*** (Thunberg ex Murray)

Polyantha Grandiflora HMult, w, 1886, Bernaix; flowers pure white, medium, single to semi-dbl., flat, borne in large clusters; not recurrent; foliage large, light to medium green, glossy; probably *R. multiflora* hybrid × *R. moschata* hybrid; int. in 1886

Polyantha Simplex – See ***R. multiflora*** (Thunberg ex Murray)

Polybag Joshi HT, lp, 1999, Chiplunkar, C. R.; flowers light pale pink, reverse deeper, 4-5 in., very dbl., borne mostly singly, moderate fragrance; foliage large, medium green, dull, leathery; numerous prickles; spreading, medium (3-4 ft.) growth; [First Prize × (First Prize × Perfume Delight)]; int. by KSG's Roses, 1995

Polygold F, dy, 1983, Tantau, Math.; flowers medium, semi-dbl., no fragrance; foliage medium size, light green, glossy; bushy growth; int. in 1978

Polynesian Pearl Gr, lp, 1977, Takatori, Yoshiho; bud ovoid; flowers shell-pink, 2 in., 35-59 petals, high-centered, moderate fruity fragrance; foliage leathery; upright growth; [Floribunda × Tropicana]; int. by Japan Rose Nursery

Polynesian Sunset HT, op, 1965, Boerner; bud long; flowers coral-orange, 6 in., dbl., high-centered, moderate fruity fragrance; foliage leathery; vigorous, bushy growth; PP2530; [(Diamond Jubilee × unknown) × Hawaii]; int. by J&P

Pom-Pom HWich, 1910, USDA; [Crimson Rambler × *R. wichurana*]

Pommifère à Fleur Double – See **Duplex**, Misc OGR

Pomona – See **Niagara**, S

Pomona F, ob, Fryer, Gareth; flowers dusky peach, dbl., high-centered, borne in well-spaced clusters, slight fragrance; good repeat; neat, even, medium (2 ft.) growth; int. by Fryer's Roses, 1994

Pompadour HT, dp, 1978, Murray, Nola; bud pointed; flowers deep pink, 5½ in., 43 petals, high-centered, intense fruity fragrance; foliage dark, glossy; bushy, compact growth; [Molly McGredy × Prima Ballerina]; int. by Rasmussen's, 1979

Pompadour Red F, dp, 1951, deRuiter; bud globular; flowers rose-red, large, 30-35 petals, cupped, moderate fruity fragrance; vigorous growth; [Orange Triumph × Anne Poulsen]; int. by J&P

Pompeii HT, rb, Bailey, Dorothy J.; bud large, ovoid; flowers velvety red with yellow reverse, 4½-5½ in., 30-32 petals, high-centered, borne usually singly, moderate damask fragrance; free-flowering; foliage large, leathery; prickles very few, flat, medium; growth vigorous, upright (4 ft.); hips globular; PP4430; [Grand Gala × Peace]; int. by San Joaquin Rose Co., 1980

Pompon HGal, dr, 1835, Joly; flowers brilliant crimson

Pompon – See **Pompon Panachée**, HGal

Pompon Bazard A, lp, before 1835, Bazard; flowers flesh pink, edges lighter, full

Pompon Beauty F, or, 1949, deRuiter; flowers scarlet, very dbl., borne in large trusses; vigorous growth; [Polyantha seedling × Hybrid Tea seedling]; int. by Spek; Gold Medal, NRS, 1950

Pompon Blanc C, w, before 1811; bud round; flowers small, very dbl., moderate fragrance; foliage oval, doubly dentate; nearly thornless; possibly synonymous with De Meaux White

Pompon Blanc HSpn, w, before 1817, Descemet; flowers very large, full, borne mostly solitary; foliage round, or rounded-ovate, deeply dentate, bright green; prickles uneven, straight; hips globose, bright red maturing to black

Pompon Blanc Parfait A, lp, 1876, Verdier, E.; flowers blush-white, small, dbl., pompon, borne in clusters, intense fragrance; occasional rebloom in autumn; prickles very few; compact, upright (4 ft.) growth; int. in 1876

Pompon Commun – See ***R. × centifolia pomponia*** (Lindley), C

Pompon de Bourgogne – See **Burgundian Rose**, HGal

Pompon de Bourgogne à Fleurs Blanches HGal, w, 1827, Mauget; flowers pure white, flesh at center, very small, very dbl., cupped

Pompon de Bretagne S, dp, Adam; growth low; groundcover; int. in 1997

Pompon de Kingston C, lp, before 1817; flowers flesh pink, very small, full

Pompon de Lyon Pol, mp, 1912, Dubreuil; flowers bright carmine pink, small, cupped

Pompon de Meaux – See ***R. × centifolia pomponia*** (Lindley), C

Pompon de Panachée – See **Pompon Panachée**, HGal

Pompon de Paris Ch, mp, 1839; bud very pointed; flowers bright pink, very small, dbl.

Pompon de Paris, Climbing Cl Ch, mp, about 1839; flowers bright pink, button-like, 3-4 cm., dbl., borne in small clusters, slight fragrance; scattered rebloom; foliage small, greyish-green; tall and arching, wiry canes, twiggy growth; [sport of Pompon de Paris]

Pompon de St. Francis – See **Pompon de Saint-François**, C

Pompon de Saint-François C, dp, about 1850, Robert; flowers deep violet-pink, small, dbl., globular; low, bushy growth

Pompon des Dames – See **Petite de Hollande**, C

Pompon des Princes – See **Ispahan**, D

Pompon Diadem F, mp, Tantau; int. in 1984

Pompon Moss – See **Mossy Rose de Meaux**, M

Pompon Mousseux – See **Mossy Rose de Meaux**, M

Pompon Panachée HGal, w, 1857, Robert et Moreau; flowers cream to white, striped light pink, well-formed, dbl., flat; foliage very small; wiry, erect growth

Pompon Perpetual – See **Bernard**, P

Pompon Perpétuel M, lp, 1849, Vibert; flowers delicate pink, 4-5 cm., full, rosette; sometimes repeats; sometimes classed as C or P

Pompon Robert – See **Pompon Panachée**, HGal

Pompon Rose – See ***R. × centifolia pomponia*** (Lindley), C

Pompon Rouge F, mr, 1971, Delforge; bud ovoid; flowers brilliant red, medium, very dbl.; foliage soft; dwarf, bushy growth; [Reverence × Miracle]

Pompon Spong – See **Spong**, C

Pompon Varin C, mp, before 1819; flowers pink, darker in center, small, semi-dbl.; foliage oval-rounded

Pompone Jaune Misc OGR, my, before 1806; flowers sulphur yellow, small, very dbl., globular; foliage small, close-set; nearly thornless; growth dwarf (2 ft.); [sport of *R. hemisphaerica*]; from France

Pomponella F, dp, Kordes; bud small, rounded; flowers 4 cm., dbl., globular, borne in clusters of 5-7, slight fragrance; recurrent; foliage dark green, dense, semi-glossy; vigorous, upright (80 cm.) growth; int. by W. Kordes Söhne, 2006; Certificate, Lyon, 2006

Pomponia Muscosa – See **Mossy Rose de Meaux**, M

Poncet – See **Dan Poncet**, S

Poncheau-Capiaumont HCh, dr; flowers borne in clusters of 3; foliage curiously stiff, thick, deeply veined

Ponctué HP, pb, before 1845, Laffay; flowers rose pink, spotted with lilac and white, medium, dbl., flat

Ponctuée – See **Belle Herminie**, HGal

Ponctuée M, pb, 1829, Hébert

Ponctuée M, pb, 1846, Laffay; flowers rose, spotted with white, large, very dbl.

Ponctuée – See **Ma Ponctuée**, M

Ponderosa F, or, 1973, Kordes, R.; bud globular; flowers red-orange, medium, dbl., cupped; foliage leathery; vigorous, dwarf, bushy growth; [seedling × Marlena]; int. by Kordes, 1970; ADR, 1971

Ponderosa – See **Flower Power**, F

Ponderosa HT, ab, Kordes; flowers creamy apricot, outer petals adding pink tone, medium, full, high-centered, borne mostly singly; good repeat; [sport of Sioux]; florist rose; int. by W. Kordes Söhne, 2002

Poniatowsky HEg, lp, 1821, Cartier; flowers flesh pink, medium, semi-dbl.

Pont d'Avignon F, or, Dot; flowers vermilion, non-fading, reflexed petals

Pontbriant HT, mp, 1948, Gaujard; flowers bright pink, very large, dbl.; foliage leathery; vigorous growth; [Mme Joseph Perraud × Kidwai]

Pontcarral HT, dp, 1943, Meilland, F.; bud long, pointed; flowers strawberry-red, reverse dull yellow, medium, semi-dbl., cupped; foliage leathery; moderate, bushy growth; [Charles P. Kilham × (Charles P. Kilham × Margaret McGredy)]; int. by A. Meilland

Ponte d'Arrabida HT, op, 1963, Moreira da Silva; flowers salmon-pink veined deep pink; [Grand'mere Jenny × seedling]

Ponte Rosa LCl, mr

Ponte Salazar F, Moreira da Silva, A.

Pontevedra HT, Moreira da Silva, A.; int. in 1969

Pony HGal, dr, before 1828, Deschiens; flowers cark crimson

Pooh Bear S, ab, Kordes; flowers deep apricot, outer petals fading to near white, medium, full, cupped, borne in small clusters, slight fragrance; free-flowering;

foliage dark green, glossy; neat, compact, short growth; int. by Ludwig's Roses, 2003

Poopsie MinFl, w, 2003, Greenwood, Chris; flowers white with light pink picotee edging, 1-2 in., full, borne in small clusters, no fragrance; foliage medium green, matte; prickles small, straight, greenish red, moderate; upright, tall (3-4 ft.) growth; [Stainless Steel × Lynn Anderson]

Poornima HT, ly, 1983, Pal, Dr. B.P.; bud long, pointed; flowers large, 46 petals, high-centered, borne singly, moderate fragrance; foliage medium size, medium green, smooth; bushy, tall growth; [Fernand Arles × seedling]; int. by K.S.G. Son's Roses, 1971

Pop Warner HT, pb, 2000, Edwards, Eddie; flowers pink and white, 4-5 in., full, high-centered, borne mostly singly, slight fragrance; foliage medium green, semi-glossy; few prickles; growth upright, medium (4-5 ft.); [Crystalline × Fantasy]; int. by Johnny Becnel Show Roses, 2001

Popcorn Min, w, 1976, Morey, Dr. Dennison; bud ovoid; flowers pure white, 1 in., 13 petals, moderate honey fragrance; foliage glossy; upright growth; [Katharina Zeimet × Diamond Jewel]; int. by Pixie Treasures Min. Roses, 1975

Pope D, dr, before 1844, Laffay; flowers crimson and purple, centers sometimes fiery, very large, full; growth branching

Pope John Paul II HT, w, 2007, Zary, Keith W.; flowers full, blooms borne mostly solitary; foliage medium size, dark green, glossy; prickles 8-10 mm., hooked downward, greyed-orange, moderate; growth upright, tall (5 ft.); [Secret × Fragrant Lace]; int. by Jackson & Perkins Wholesale, Inc., 2007; Fragrance Award, Rose Hills, 2006

Pope Pius IX – See **Pius IX**, HP

Pope Pius XI – See **Pius XI**, HT

Poppet F, mp, 1978, Bees; flowers large, 60 petals, cupped; foliage light green, matte; upright growth; [Spartan × Arthur Bell]; int. in 1979

Poppi John S, ab, 2005, Paul Chessum Roses; flowers dbl., borne in small clusters, slight fragrance; foliage medium size, dark green, semi-glossy; prickles large, red, numerous; growth upright, medium (4 ft.); bedding, containers; [seedling × seedling]; int. by World of Roses, 2005

Popping White Min, w, 1977, Lyon; bud ovoid; flowers 1 in., 12 petals; vigorous, compact growth

Poppius HSpn, mp, Steinberg; flowers deep pink, fading to lilac pink, semi-dbl., cupped, slight fragrance; few prickles; growth medium (3-4 ft.); hardy

Poppy HT, op, 1939, Archer; flowers coral-pink, passing to shell-pink, petals serrated, dbl.; vigorous growth

Poppy F, or, 1960, Soenderhousen; flowers scarlet, 2-2½ in., semi-dbl., open, borne in clusters; very vigorous growth; [Cocorico × Geranium Red]; int. by Hoersholm Nursery

Poppy Flash F, or, 1972, Meilland; flowers vermilion, 3 in., 20 petals, slight fruity fragrance; vigorous, bushy growth; [(Dany Robin × Fire King) × (Alain × Mutabilis)]; Gold Medal, Rome, 1972, Gold Medal, Geneva, 1970

Poppy Flash, Climbing Cl F, or, 1976, Paolino; [sport of Poppy Flash]; int. by URS, 1975

Poppy Rose – See **Grosse Mohnkopfs Rose**, S

Pops Min, dp, 1984, Bennett, Dee; flowers deep pink, small, 20 petals, high-centered; foliage medium size, medium green, semi-glossy; bushy growth; [Sheri Anne × Little Girl]; int. by Tiny Petals Nursery, 1983

Popsy S, op, Peden, G.H.

Popular – See **Popular Palace**, Min

Popular Palace Min, ob, Poulsen; flowers orange and orange blend, 5 cm., dbl., no fragrance; foliage dark; growth broad, bushy, 40-60 cm.; int. by Poulsen Roser, 2005

Porcelain – See **Flamingo**, HT

Porcelain F, lp, 1984, Gobbee, W.D.; flowers shell pink over cream, medium, semi-dbl.; foliage small, dark, semi-glossy; upright, bushy growth; [Dainty Maid × ((Tropicana × Anna Wheatcroft) × (Tropicana × Anna Wheatcroft))]

Porcelain Bouquet – See **Porcelina**, HT

Porcelain Panarosa S, lp, Kordes; flowers pale pink, center darker, full, high-centered; recurrent; very tall growth; int. by Ludwig's Roses, 2005

Porcelain Princess Min, pb, 1990, Gruenbauer, Richard; bud rounded; flowers cream with pale pink edging, aging light pink, medium, 35 petals, high-centered, borne in sprays of 2-3; foliage medium size, dark green, semi-glossy; prickles straight, tan; bushy, medium growth; hips oblong, orange-red; [Libby × seedling]; int. by Richard Gruenbauer

Porcelaine HGal, lp, before 1815, Descemet; flowers light pink, aging white, large, semi-dbl.

Porcelaine de Bayeux S, lp, Adam; groundcover; spreading growth; int. by Pepinieres Guerinais, 2006

Porcelaine de Chine Ayr, lp, 2000, Lens, Louis; flowers pale pink to white, reverse lighter, 1½ in., semi-dbl., borne in large clusters; recurrent; foliage medium size, dark green, semi-glossy; thornless; upright, tall (4-5 ft.) growth; hedge, climber; [*R. arvensis* × *R. chinensis minima*]; int. by Louis Lens N.V., 1996

Porcelaine Royale HGal, m, about 1840, Miellez; flowers lilac, marbled, small, full

Porcelina HT, w, 1985, Interplant; flowers cream with pink tint, 30 petals, borne singly or in small clusters, moderate fragrance; foliage large, dark, glossy; few prickles; upright growth; PP5648; [seedling × Golden Times]; int. in 1983

Porcia – See **Rouge Formidable**, HGal

Porsalino – See **H. C. Andersen**, F

Port St John HT, Herholdt; int. in 1974

Porta Nigra HT, dr, Meilland; flowers large, dbl., moderate fragrance; int. in 1992

Porta Westfalica F, dr

Portadown HT, dr, 1928, McGredy; bud long, pointed; flowers velvety deep crimson, large, dbl., high-centered; vigorous, bushy growth; Gold Medal, NRS, 1929

Portadown Bedder HT, op, 1929, McGredy; bud long, pointed; flowers scarlet-cerise on orange ground, reverse orange-yellow flush, dbl., high-centered; foliage glossy, dark; vigorous, bushy growth

Portadown Crimson HT, dr, 1928, McGredy; flowers dark crimson, globular, moderate fragrance

Portadown Fragrance HT, op, 1931, McGredy; bud long, pointed; flowers brilliant orange-salmon-pink, flushed orange-scarlet, dbl., high-centered, intense fragrance; foliage thick, bronze; low, sprawling growth; Gold Medal, NRS, 1928

Portadown Glory HT, my, 1932, McGredy; flowers clear canary-yellow, well-formed, large, dbl.; foliage glossy, bright; vigorous growth; Gold Medal, NRS, 1933

Portadown Glow – See **Portadown Yellow**, HT

Portadown Ivory – See **McGredy's Ivory**, HT

Portadown Sally HT, mr, 1931, McGredy; bud long, pointed; flowers crimson-carmine, base yellow, reverse sulfur-yellow, semi-dbl., high-centered; foliage thick, glossy; vigorous growth

Portadown Scarlet HT, mr, 1927, McGredy; flowers scarlet

Portadown Yellow HT, my, 1927, McGredy; flowers chrome yellow, shaded golden yellow, medium, very dbl., moderate fragrance

Portail Rouge LCl, mr, Combe, C.; flowers crimson, 4 in., moderate fragrance; int. in 1973

Portchester Pink HT, dp, 1979, Poole, K. E.; flowers deep rose-pink, intense fragrance; [sport of Red Devil]

Porthos F, or, Laperrière; int. in 1971

Porthos, Climbing Cl F, or, Laperrière; [sport of Porthos]; int. in 1976

Portia HT, lp, 1910, Paul, W.; flowers pale rose, center yellow, large, full

Portia HT, mr, 1921, Bees; flowers nasturtium-red, paling to pink, dbl.; [Bridesmaid × Sunburst]

Portland HT, dp, 1958, Lowe; flowers rose-madder, large, dbl.; foliage dark, glossy; vigorous, symmetrical growth; int. by Wm. Lowe & Son, 1958

Portland Blanc P, w, 1836, Vibert; flowers medium, full, flat

Portland Crimson Monthly Rose – See **Duchess of Portland**, P

Portland Dawn Min, pb, 1989, McCann, Sean; flowers veined pink and bronze, small, 20 petals; foliage small, medium green, semi-glossy; bushy growth; [Rise 'n' Shine × (Copper Pot × Maxi)]; int. in 1988

Portland from Glendora – See **Joasine Hanet**, P

Portland Pink F, dp, 1957, Murrel, E.; flowers glowing deep pink; [sport of Pinocchio]

Portland Pourpre P, dp, about 1830, Prévost; flowers deep bright crimson, medium, semi-dbl.

Portland Rose – See **Duchess of Portland**, P

Portland Rose Festival HT, rb, 1992, Dorieux, Francois; bud large, ovoid; flowers strawberry red, white reverse, 5 in., 40 petals, high-centered, borne singly, moderate spicy fragrance; foliage large, dark green, glossy; prickles numerous, scattered, slighty recurved; growth tall (5 ft.), upright; PP8278; [Osiria × Pharaon]; int. by Roses by Fred Edmunds, 1992

Portland Trailblazer HT, dr, 1976, Dickson, A.; bud pointed, ovoid; flowers crimson, 5½ in., 20-30 petals, high-centered, borne singly, slight fragrance; foliage large, matte, brittle; prickles few, short, hooked downward, brown; growth vigorous, very upright; PP4222; [Ernest H. Morse × Red Planet]; int. as Big Chief, Dickson & Sons, 1975

Portlandia LCl, pb, Clements, John; flowers golden apricot center shading to pink and cream, 3½-4 in., 80 petals, borne in good size clusters, moderate fruity fragrance; foliage dark green, leathery; stems long; growth climbing (8-10 ft.); PPAF; int. by Heirloom, 2002

Portmeirion S, dp, 2000, Austin, David; flowers very full, shallow cupped, borne singly or in small clusters, strong old rose fragrance; foliage medium size, dark green, semi-glossy, disease-resistant; numerous prickles; spreading, low (3 ft.) growth; [Ausblush × seedling (pink English shrub)]; int. by David Austin Roses, Ltd., 1999

Porto HT, dr, 1934, Mallerin, C.; flowers deep garnet tinted bright scarlet, large, dbl.; foliage leathery; vigorous growth; [Capt. F. Bald × Mrs Edward Powell]

Porto Fino Min, w, Adam; flowers white with thin, bright fuchsia pink edges, full; free-flowering; growth to 10-12 in.; int. by Pepinieres Guerinais, 2006

Portofino F, rb, 1964, Delforge; flowers red, reverse deep yellow; low growth; [Miramar × seedling]

Portrait HT, pb, 1971, Meyer, C.; bud ovoid; flowers medium pink and light pink blend, medium, dbl., high-centered, moderate fragrance; good repeat; foliage glossy, dark; growth upright, bushy; PP3097; [Pink Parfait × Pink Peace]; int. by C-P; AARS, 1972

Portrait of Jenny F, dr, 1951, Hope; flowers crimson, 2 in., 30 petals, borne in trusses; foliage dark; vigorous, bushy growth; [Donald Prior × unknown]

Portuense HP, m, 1890, da Costa; flowers purple

Portugal Pink HT, dp, 1959, Mondial Roses; bud globular; flowers deep pink, large, dbl., cupped; foliage leathery; vigorous, upright growth; [Independence × seedling]

Post Office F, rb, J&P; int. in 1997

Postillion S, my, 2006; bud copper yellow; flowers shining yellow, 10 cm., dbl., shallow cupped, borne in small clusters; foliage medium size, dark green, glossy; vigorous, upright (5 ft.) growth; int. by W. Kordes' Söhne, 1998

Postillon HT, ab, 1962, Verbeek; flowers coppery yellow, large, dbl.; foliage glossy; moderate growth; [Peace × seedling]

Posy F, pb, 1951, LeGrice; flowers clear pink, reverse deeper, 3 in., 30 petals, borne in large clusters; foliage dark; dwarf growth; [Rosenelfe × Dusky Maiden]

Pot Black Min, dr, 1984, Pearce, C.A.; flowers small, dbl., no fragrance; foliage small, medium green, matte; bushy growth; [seedling × seedling]; int. by Limes Rose Nursery, 1985

Pot o' Gold HT, my, 1980, Dickson, Patrick; bud pointed; flowers golden yellow, 32 petals, high-centered, open flat, borne singly and in clusters, intense sweet fragrance; recurrent; foliage mid-green with strong purple veins; prickles brown; bushy, medium growth; [Eurorose × Whisky Mac]

Potager du Dauphin HRg, mp, 1899, Gravereaux

Potch Pearl HT, pb, Herholdt; bud large, pointed, egg shaped; flowers carmine pink with white base, dbl., high-centered, slight fragrance; foliage dark green; medium growth

Potifar HT, ab, 1985, Poulsen, Niels D.; flowers pale peachy orange, large, 25 petals, urn-shaped, borne usually singly, slight fragrance; foliage large, leathery, dark green, matte; bushy growth; [Royal Dane × Pjerrot]; int. by A. Grumer, 1979

Potluck Min, dr, 1984, Laver, Keith G.; flowers small, 20 petals; foliage small, medium green, glossy; compact, bushy, tiny growth; [Dwarfking '78 × Little Liza]

Potluck Blue Min, m, 1995, Laver, Keith G.; flowers lavender, reverse white, dbl., semi-dbl., borne mostly singly; foliage medium size, medium green, semi-glossy; some prickles; upright, bushy, medium growth; [Blue Ice × seedling]; int. by Springwood Roses, 1995

Potluck Cream Min, ly, 1988, Laver, Keith G.; flowers light yellow center, cream edges, reverse cream with yellow, 30 petals, high-centered, no fragrance; foliage medium size, medium green, matte; prickles slender, brown; bushy, low, very free-flowering growth; no fruit; [Cornsilk × seedling]; int. by Springwood Roses, 1988

Potluck Crimson Min, dr, 1997, Laver, Keith G.; flowers medium, 41 petals, borne mostly singly and in small clusters; foliage medium size, medium green, semi-glossy; few prickles; compact, low growth; [June Laver × Springwood Red Victor]; int. by Springwood Roses

Potluck Frosty Min, w

Potluck Gold Min, my, 1991, Laver, Keith G.; flowers small, 20 petals, flat, borne in sprays of 3-5, no fragrance; foliage small, medium green, semi-glossy; bushy, low, very dwarf growth; [Dorola × Julie Ann]; int. by Springwood Roses, 1990

Potluck Orange Min, or, 1989, Laver, Keith G.; bud ovoid; flowers intense, dark orange, compact, small, 24 petals, borne in sprays; foliage small, medium green, matte; prickles straight, pointed, light brown; bushy, low, symmetrical growth; PP7326; [Julie Ann × Potluck]

Potluck Pink Min, mp, 1992, Laver, Keith G.; flowers rose pink, 1½ in., full, borne mostly singly; foliage small, medium green, matte; few prickles; low (25-30 cm.), compact growth; [June Laver × Julie Ann]; int. by Springwood Roses

Potluck Purple Min, dr, 1992, Laver, Keith G.; flowers fuchsia, 1½ in., dbl., borne in small clusters; foliage small, medium green, matte; few prickles; micro-mini; low (25-30 cm.), compact growth; [(June Laver × Painted Doll) × Springwood Purple]; int. by Springwood Roses

Potluck Red Min, dr, 1989, Laver, Keith G.; bud pointed; flowers deep red, compact, small, 35 petals, borne singly, no fragrance; foliage small, dark green, young edged in red, matte; no prickles; upright, low growth; hips globular, orange-red; [Breezy × June Laver]; int. by Springwood Roses, 1989

Potluck White Min, w, 1985, Laver, Keith G.; flowers 35 petals; foliage small, light green, glossy; spreading growth; [Baby Katie × Mountie]

Potluck Yellow Min, my, 1984, Laver, Keith G.; flowers 20 petals, no fragrance; foliage small, medium green, semi-glossy; bushy growth; [Rise 'n' Shine × Lemon Delight]; int. as Yellow Minijet, Australian Roses

Potter & Moore S, mp, Austin, David; flowers soft rose pink to lilac-pink, large, very full, cupped, moderate fragrance; free-flowering; low (3½ ft.) growth; [Wife of Bath × seedling]; int. in 1988

Potton Heritage HT, rb, 1986, Harkness; flowers plum red, reverse straw-yellow, large, 32 petals, high-centered, moderate fragrance; foliage large, dark, glossy; bushy, branching growth; [Precious Platinum × Dr. A.J. Verhage]; int. in 1987

Poulbright F, or, Poulsen; int. in 1985

Poulidor S, yb, Adam; int. by Pep. de la Guerinais, 2003

Poully F, Poulsen; int. in 1991

Poulsen's Bedder F, lp, 1948, Poulsen, S.; flowers clear pink, 3 in., semi-dbl., borne in trusses; foliage bronze; vigorous, upright growth; [Orléans Rose × Talisman]; int. by McGredy, 1948

Poulsen's Copper F, op, 1940, Poulsen, S.; flowers rose-pink to orange, base yellow, 3-3½ in., 25-35 petals, cupped, borne in clusters, slight spicy fragrance; foliage small, light green; vigorous growth; [Grethe Poulsen × Souv. de Claudius Pernet]; int. by C-P, 1940

Poulsen's Crimson F, dr, 1985, Poulsen, S.; flowers 6 petals, borne in clusters; foliage medium size, dark, matte; vigorous, bushy growth; [Orange Triumph × (Betty Uprichard × Johanniszauber)]; int. by McGredy, 1950

Poulsen's Delight F, lp, 1948, Poulsen, S.; flowers apple-blossom-pink, 5-7 petals, borne in trusses; foliage dark, glossy; vigorous, upright growth; [Else Poulsen × seedling]; int. by McGredy

Poulsen's Fairy F, lp, 1940, Poulsen, S.; flowers light pink with amber-pink stamens, single, borne in large clusters; free-flowering; very vigorous, tall growth; [Orléans Rose × Dainty Bess]; int. by Poulsen

Poulsen's Grupperose – See **Poulsen's Bedder**, F

Poulsen's Jubilaeumsrose Min, yb, 1985, Poulsen, Niels D.; flowers deep pink and yellow blend, 28 petals, borne in clusters; foliage dark, glossy; upright growth; [Darling Flame × seedling]; int. in 1978

Poulsen's Park Rose S, lp, 1953, Poulsen; flowers silvery pink, well-shaped, 4-5 in., dbl., borne in trusses; vigorous (6 × 6 ft.) growth; [Great Western × Karen Poulsen]

Poulsen's Peach F, ab, 1985, Poulsen, S.; flowers peach, large, semi-dbl., cupped, borne in clusters; foliage medium size, medium green, semi-glossy; growth medium, bushy; int. in 1948

Poulsen's Pearl F, lp, 1949, Poulsen, S.; flowers pearly pink, 5 petals, borne in trusses; foliage light green; vigorous growth; [Else Poulsen × seedling]; int. by Poulsen's Roses, 1948

Poulsen's Pink F, lp, 1939; flowers soft pink with yellow base, semi-dbl., cupped, borne in clusters, slight fragrance; foliage glossy, light green; vigorous growth; [Golden Salmon × Yellow HT]; int. by Poulsen, 1942

Poulsen's Scarlet F, dp, 1941, Poulsen, S.; flowers bright rose, 2½ in., 30 petals, borne in clusters; bushy growth; [D.T. Poulsen × Red HT]

Poulsen's Supreme F, mp, 1945, Poulsen, S.; flowers 3 in., semi-dbl., borne in trusses; foliage light green; very free growth; [Poulsen's Pink × seedling]; int. by McGredy, 1953

Poulsen's Yellow F, my, 1938, Poulsen, S.; bud ovoid; flowers semi-dbl., borne in clusters, intense fragrance; foliage glossy; [Mrs W.H. Cutbush × Gottfried Keller]; int. by C-P, 1939; Gold Medal, NRS, 1937

Poultimes F, my, Poulsen; int. in 1993

Pounder Star HT, mr, 1978, McGredy, Sam IV; bud long, pointed; flowers currant red, non-fading, 4 in., 20-24 petals, high-centered, borne mostly singly, moderate old rose to spicy fragrance; recurrent; foliage large, dark green, glossy; prickles small, curved; growth upright, vigorous, medium (4½ ft.); hips small, long, ovoid, green with reddish tone; PP4694; [John Waterer × Kalahari]; int. by Roses by Fred Edmunds, 1982

Poupée F, lp, 1979, Lens; flowers flesh-pink, 3-3½ in., 25-30 petals, cupped; foliage glossy; vigorous, upright growth; int. in 1965

Pour Toi – See **Para Ti**, Min

Pour Vous Madame F, dp, 1961, Gaujard; flowers rose-red, reverse lighter, open, 4 in., 25 petals; foliage dark; vigorous growth; int. by Gandy Roses, Ltd., 1961

Pourpre – See **Rubra**, M

Pourpre Ch, m, 1827, Vibert; flowers deep purple-red, small, 5-8 petals, borne in clusters; growth to 2 ft.

Pourpre Ancien Misc OGR, m, about 1829; flowers purple, sometimes striped with white, large, very full; foliage small, glossy

Pourpre Ardoisée – See **Charles de Mills**, HGal

Pourpre Brillant HGal, m, before 1815, Descemet; flowers glossy purple

Pourpre Brun HCh, dr, before 1844; flowers purplish crimson, very small, full; Lawrenciana

Pourpre Charmant HGal, m, before 1811; flowers deep velvety purple-pink, 3-4 in., very dbl., moderate sweet fragrance

Pourpre Cramoisi – See **Rouge Formidable**, HGal

Pourpre d'Orléans HP, m, 1861, Dauvesse; flowers bright garnet purple, large, full; sometimes attributed to Viennot or Lecomte/Jamain

Pourpre Double – See **Lustre d'Église**, HGal

Pourpre du Luxembourg M, m, 1848, Hardy; flowers deep crimson, shaded with purple, medium, dbl., moderate fragrance; scattered rebloom; growth to 5 ft.

Pourpre d'Yèbles Ch, m, 1830, Desprez; flowers dark purple

Pourpre Favorite – See **Belle de Stors**, HGal

Pourpre Foncé HGal, m, before 1815, Descemet; flowers dark purple, small

Pourpre Marbrée HGal, m, before 1821, perhaps Paillard; flowers violet purple, marbled, small, very full

Pourpre Noir – See **Ombre Superbe**, HGal

Pourpre Rouge – See **Temple d'Apollon**, HGal

Pourpre Violet M, m, before 1862; flowers violet purple, medium, full

Poustinia F, ab, Orye; flowers yellow-apricot in center and cream white on outer petals, large, dbl., pompon, intense fragrance; growth to 80 cm.; int. in 1994

Powder Puff F, lp, 1962, Mason, A.L.; flowers creamy

light pink, becoming darker, open, medium, dbl., slight fragrance; foliage glossy; bushy growth; [Masquerade × Masquerade seedling]; int. by F. Mason, 1959

Poyntzfield HT, ab, 1977, Simpson, J.W.; flowers 5 in., 35 petals; foliage glossy, reddish-green; vigorous growth; [Bonsoir × Percy Thrower]

Pozdrav Prohunice S, mp, Schmidt; int. in 1915

Poznan HT, dr, 1966, Grabczewski; bud ovoid; flowers vivid dark crimson, well-formed, large, dbl.; vigorous growth

Praecox (form of *R. sericea*), w

Prairie HT, dy, Kordes; flowers soft yellow, medium, full, high-centered, borne mostly singly; good repeat; [Sioux × unknown]; florist rose; int. by W. Kordes Söhne, 2003

Prairie Belle – See **Queen of the Prairies**, HSet

Prairie Breeze S, m, 1979, Buck, Dr. Griffith J.; bud ovoid, pointed; flowers Tyrian purple, 4½ in., 25 petals, cupped, moderate spicy fragrance; repeat bloom; foliage olive-green, leathery; upright, bushy, spreading growth; [Dornroschen × (Josef Rothmund × *R. laxa*)]; int. by Iowa State University, 1978

Prairie Celebration S, dp, Ag Canada; flowers single, slight fragrance; vigorous (4 ft.) growth; winter hardy; one of the Parkland series

Prairie Charm S, op, 1959, Morden Exp. Farm; flowers bright salmon-coral, semi-dbl.; free, non-recurrent bloom; foliage light green; growth to 4 ft., arching; hardy on prairies; [Prairie Youth × Prairie Wren]

Prairie Clogger S, mr, 1985, Buck, Dr. Griffith J.; bud medium-small, ovoid, pointed; flowers 2½ in., 8-10 petals, shallow-cupped to flat, borne 1-10 per cluster, moderate fragrance; repeat bloom; foliage leathery, dark olive green; prickles awl-like, tan; vigorous, erect, bushy growth; [Carefree Beauty × (Marlena × Pippa's Song)]; int. by Iowa State University, 1984

Prairie Dawn S, mp, 1959, Morden Exp. Farm; flowers glowing pink, 2-2½ in., dbl.; repeat bloom on current season's wood; foliage dark, glossy; upright (5 ft.) growth; hardy on prairies; [Prairie Youth × (Ross Rambler × (Dr. W. Van Fleet × *R. spinosissima altaica*))]

Prairie Fire S, mr, 1962, Phillips, R. A.; bud pointed; flowers bright red, base white, 2½-3 in., 9 petals, borne in clusters of 35-50, moderate fragrance; recurrent; foliage glossy, dark; long stems; very vigorous, tall growth; [Red Rocket × *R. arkansana*]; int. by Wyant Nurs., 1960

Prairie Flower S, rb, 1975, Buck, Dr. Griffith J.; bud ovoid, pointed; flowers cardinal-red, center white, 2-3 in., 7 petals, flat, slight old rose fragrance; repeat bloom; foliage dark, leathery; erect, bushy growth; [Rose of Tralee × (Queen Elizabeth × (Morning Stars × Suzanne))]; int. by Iowa State University, 1975

Prairie Harvest S, ly, 1985, Buck, Dr. Griffith J.; flowers medium yellow, petals imbricated, 4-5 in., 43 petals, borne singly and in clusters of up to 15, moderate fragrance; repeat bloom; foliage leathery, glossy, medium size, dark; prickles awl-like, tan; growth upright, bushy; hardy; [Carefree Beauty × Sunsprite]; int. by Iowa State University, 1984

Prairie Heritage S, op, 1978, Buck, Dr. Griffith J.; bud ovoid, pointed; flowers peach to coral-pink, 4-5 in., 50 petals, cupped; repeat bloom; foliage dark, leathery; vigorous, upright, spreading, bushy growth; [(Vera Dalton × Prairie Princess) × (Apricot Nectar × Prairie Princess)]; int. by Iowa State University

Prairie Joy S, mp, 1990, Collicutt, Lynn M.; flowers medium pink, aging to light pink, medium, 30-40 petals, cupped, borne singly or in sprays of 2-6, slight fragrance; sparse repeat bloom; foliage medium size, medium green, matte, very disease-resistant; growth tall, bushy; [Prairie Princess × Morden Cardinette]; int. by Agriculture Canada, 1990

Prairie Lass S, pb, 1978, Buck, Dr. Griffith J.; bud ovoid, pointed; flowers claret-rose to rose-red, large, 28 petals, moderate spicy fragrance; repeat bloom; foliage dark, leathery; vigorous, upright, spreading, bushy growth; [(Hawkeye Belle × Vera Dalton) × (Dornroschen × (World's Fair × World's Fair × Applejack))]; int. by Iowa State University, 1978

Prairie Maid S, w, 1959, Morden Exp. Farm; flowers cream, 25 petals; intermittent bloom; compact (4 ft.) growth; hardy on prairies; [(Ophelia × Turkes Rugosa Samling) × *R. spinosissima altaica*]

Prairie Moon LCl, ly, 1953, Maney; bud ovoid, deep yellow; flowers creamy yellow, large, 30-35 petals, borne in clusters of 4-5; abundant, non-recurrent bloom; foliage glossy, dark, leathery; vigorous, climbing (15 ft.) growth; [*R. maximowicziana pilosa* × Autumn]; int. by Iowa State College

Prairie Peace HSpn, yb, Erskine; flowers yellow and pink, sometimes peach, semi-dbl. to dbl., cupped, moderate fragrance; recurrent, two crops of blooms per year; [Beauty of Leafland × Hazeldean]

Prairie Pinkie S, op, 1958, Skinner; flowers deep coral-pink, dbl., intense fragrance; midsummer bloom; foliage like *R. spinossissima*; growth upright (2½ ft.), bushy

Prairie Princess S, op, 1971, Buck, Dr. Griffith J.; bud ovoid, long, pointed; flowers light coral-pink, large, semi-dbl.; repeat bloom; foliage large, dark, leathery; vigorous, upright growth; [Carrousel × (Morning Stars × Suzanne)]; int. by Iowa State University, 1972

Prairie Red Min, rb, 1981, Lyon; flowers red-yellow blend, 18 petals, borne singly or several together, moderate fragrance; foliage tiny, medium green; prickles brownish, curved downward; growth bushy, upright; [seedling × seedling]; int. in 1980

Prairie Rose – See ***R. setigera*** (Michaux)

Prairie Sailor HSpn, yb, 1946, Morden Exp. Farm; flowers golden yellow deeply edged bright red, single; profuse, non-recurrent bloom; vigorous (6 ft.) growth; hardy on prairies

Prairie Schooner Min, rb, 1986, King, Gene; flowers red, reverse yellow edged red, 22 petals, high-centered, borne singly and in sprays; foliage small, dark, matte; prickles straight, brown; upright growth; no fruit; PP6748; [Vera Dalton × Sheri Anne]; int. by AGM Miniature Roses

Prairie Squire S, mp, 1985, Buck, Dr. Griffith J.; flowers 4-5 in., 20 petals, cupped, borne singly and in clusters of up to 10, slight fragrance; repeat bloom; foliage leathery, dark green, tinted copper; prickles awl-like, tan; vigorous, erect, bushy, spreading growth; hardy; [Countryman × Carefree Beauty]; int. by Iowa State University, 1984

Prairie Star S, w, 1975, Buck, Dr. Griffith J.; bud ovoid, pointed; flowers pale chrome-yellow, tinted pink, 3½-4 in., 54 petals, cupped, moderate green apple fragrance; repeat bloom; foliage dark, leathery; vigorous, erect, bushy growth; [Tickled Pink × Prairie Princess]; int. by Iowa State University, 1975

Prairie Sunrise S, ab, 1997, Buck, Dr. Griffith J.; flowers golden apricot yellow, 4 in., 50+ petals, borne in small clusters, intense fragrance; foliage large, medium green, glossy; glossy, compact, bushy, medium growth; [Friesia × Freckle Face]; int. by Sam Kedem Nursery

Prairie Sunset S, pb, 1985, Buck, Dr. Griffith J.; flowers deep pink, reverse yellow, 4 in., 38 petals, urn-shaped, borne 5-10 per cluster, moderate fragrance; repeat bloom; foliage moderately large, leathery, dark; prickles tan; erect, bushy, slightly spreading growth; hardy; [Bonfire Night × (Music Maker × Athlone)]; int. by Iowa State University, 1984

Prairie Valor S, mr, 1985, Buck, Dr. Griffith J.; flowers 4-5 in., 38 petals, cupped, borne 3-5 per cluster, moderate damask fragrance; repeat bloom; foliage leathery, dark; prickles awl-like, brown; upright, bushy growth; hardy; [((Dornroschen × (Josef Rothmund × *R. laxa*)) × Rose du Roi a Fleurs Pourpres) × (Music Maker × Topsi)]; int. by Iowa State University, 1984

Prairie Wren S, mp, 1946, Morden Exp. Farm; flowers rich pink, large, semi-dbl.; heavy, non-recurrent bloom; very hardy

Prairie Youth S, op, 1948, Morden Exp. Farm; flowers pure salmon-pink, semi-dbl., borne in clusters, slight fragrance; repeat bloom; vigorous (6 ft.) growth; completely hardy on prairies; [((Ross Rambler × Dr. W. Van Fleet) × *R. suffulta*) × ((Dr. W. Van Fleet × Turkes Rugosa Samling) × *R. spinosissima altaica*)]

Praise of Jiro F, or, 1959, Kordes, R.; bud ovoid; flowers large, 30 petals, borne in clusters; foliage leathery; vigorous, upright, bushy growth; [Korona × Spartan]

Praline HT, dr, 1955, Robichon; flowers carmine-purple to crimson; foliage glossy; [Camelia × seedling]

Pranabandajee HT, dr, Pushpanjali; flowers deep crimson, large, full; vigorous growth; int. in 1999

Präsent F, ab, 1969, Haenchen, E.; flowers yellow-orange, reverse yellow, large, 27 petals, high-centered; foliage dark, glossy, leathery; vigorous, upright, bushy growth; [Highlight × Allgold]; int. by Teschendorff

Präsident Dr H. C. Schröder – See **President H. C. Schroder**, HT

Präsident Hindenburg Pol, mr, 1927, Bom; flowers carmine to deep red, base white, dbl.; [Greta Kluis × unknown]; int. by P. Lambert

Praterstern HT, yb

Prato Rosso Min, Motta; int. in 1984

Prattigosa HRg, mp, 1953, Kordes; bud long, pointed, red; flowers pink, overlarge, single; foliage leathery, light green; vigorous (3½ ft.), upright, bushy growth; [*R. prattii* × *R. rugosa alba*]

Pray Gr, Delforge; int. in 1987

Précieuse – See **Prolifère**, HGal

Precilla HT, dy, 1973, Kordes; bud ovoid; flowers deep golden yellow, medium, dbl., cupped, moderate fragrance; foliage dark, leathery; vigorous, upright growth; PP3726; [Peer Gynt × seedling]

Preciosa HT, pb, Meilland; flowers pink and yellow, large, dbl.; int. in 1972

Precious HT, pb, 1985, Dawson, Charles P.; flowers blend of light, medium and deep pink, reverse medium pink, l, 35 petals, high-centered, moderate fragrance; foliage medium size, medium green, semi-glossy; prickles very few; upright, bushy growth; [(Briarcliff × (Carla × Unknown)) × Pink Parfait]; int. in 1987

Precious Anya F, m, 2004, Horner, Colin P.; flowers cerise/purple, reverse lighter, 6 cm., semi-dbl., borne in small clusters, slight fragrance; foliage medium size, dark green, semi-glossy; prickles medium, curved; compact, medium (80 cm.) growth; garden decorative; [seedling × Pretty Lady]; int. by Warley Rose Gardens, 2006

Precious Child S, my, 1999, Gear, Ian Robert; flowers medium, dbl., borne in small clusters; foliage medium size, dark green, semi-glossy; prickles moderate; spreading (4 ft.) growth; [Hokey Pokey × Patio Princess]

Precious Dream HBc, pb, 2002, Moore, Ralph S.; flowers pink/apricot, reverse pink/yellow, 2-2½ in., full, borne in small clusters; foliage medium size, medium green, semi-glossy; prickles small, pointed, green, few;

bushy, medium (2-3 ft.) growth; containers, specimen; int. by Sequoia Nurs., 2002

Precious Gift F, dp, 1997, Jellyman, J.S.; flowers medium, dbl., borne in small clusters; foliage medium size, medium green, semi-glossy; few prickles; upright, bushy, medium (20cm.) growth; [Silver Jubilee × seedling]; int. by Pocock's Nurseries

Precious Lady HT, w, 2003, Rawlins, R.; flowers medium, very full, borne mostly solitary, slight fragrance; foliage medium size, dark green, semi-glossy; prickles 2 cm., triangular, few; upright, medium (39 in.) growth; garden; [Solitaire × Silver Anniversary]

Precious Michelle – See **Auckland Metro**, HT

Precious Moments Min, my, 1982, Lyon; flowers medium, 35 petals, moderate fragrance; free-flowering; foliage medium size, medium green, semi-glossy; extremely short, upright, bushy growth; [Dandy Lyon × seedling]

Precious Moments F, ob; flowers yellow-orange, edges turning pink, full, high-centered, moderate fragrance; growth to 3 ft.; int. by Greenhead Nursery

Precious Pet S, mp, Matthews; int. by Matthews Nurseries, 2001

Precious Platinum HT, mr, 1976, Dicksons of Hawlmark; flowers cardinal-red, medium to large, 35 petals, high-centered, borne mostly singly, slight fragrance; good repeat; foliage dark green, glossy, leathery; stems long, strong; vigorous, upright (4 ft.) growth; [Red Planet × Franklin Englemann]; int. in 1974

Precision S, dr, Williams, J. Ben; flowers semi-dbl., slight fragrance; recurrent; growth to 4 ft.; int. by Hortico, Inc., 2005

Précoce M, dp, 1843, Vibert; flowers rosy red, sometimes spotted at the edge, medium, dbl.; very early bloom

Prediction HT, mp, 1975, Golik; flowers luminous pink, 4 in., 35 petals, high-centered; foliage leathery; moderate growth; [Queen of Bermuda × Golden Giant]; int. by Dynarose, 1974

Preference – See **Princesse de Monaco**, HT

Préférence HT, mr, Meilland; bud large, conical, elongated; flowers strawberry red, reverse cardinal red, 4 in., 40-45 petals, high-centered, cupped, borne mostly singly; good repeat; foliage dark green, matte; prickles numerous, tan; growth erect (4-5 ft.); PP7383; [Visa × Royalty]; florist rose; int. by Meilland Intl., 1998

Preference F, mr, Meilland International; bud ovoid; flowers deep scarlet red, 3 in., 20-25 petals, borne singly and in clusters of up to 6, very slight fragrance; free-flowering; foliage dense, dark green, semi-glossy; numerous prickles; growth compact (3-4 ft.), bushy; PP15878; [(Tamango × Korona) × Pharaon]; int. by Meilland, 2004

Préfet Limbourg – See **Mons le Préfet Limbourg**, HP

Préfet Monteil T, my, 1901, Bernaix fils; flowers canary yellow, shaded sulfur yellow, aging to coppery carmine, large, full

Prekrasnaja Rossijanka HT, mr, Klimenko, V. N.; flowers large, dbl.; int. in 1966

Prelud F, mr, Urban, J.

Prélude HT, m, 1958, Meilland, F.; bud medium, stubby; flowers lilac-mauve, well-formed, medium, 25 petals, borne singly or several together, moderate fragrance; free-flowering; foliage dense, soft; strong stems; vigorous, bushy growth; [Fantastique × (Ampere × (Charles P. Kilham × Capucine Chambard))]; int. by URS, 1954

Prélude HT, m, Keisei; flowers lavender pink, dbl., high-centered, borne mostly singly; good repeat; florist rose

Preludium F, ab, Hannemann, F.; [Poker Chip × unknown]; int. by The Rose Paradise

Prema F, pb, 1970, Division of Vegetable Crops and Floriculture; flowers soft pink, petals edged deep pink, medium, dbl., high-centered; foliage leathery; vigorous, upright growth; [Sea Pearl × Shola]

Prémice des Charpennes B, m, 1845, Cherpin; flowers lilac pink, edges white, medium, full, globular

Premier HT, mr, 1918, E.G. Hill, Co.; bud long, pointed; flowers dark velvety rose-rev, veined darker, reverse lighter, open, dbl.; foliage rich green, leathery; vigorous growth; [(Ophelia × Mrs Charles E. Russell) × unknown]

Premier, Climbing Cl HT, mr, 1927, Vestal

Premier Jelly, R. G.; PP4408

Premier Amour – See **First Love**, HT

Premier Bal HT, w, 1950, Meilland, F.; flowers ivory edged carmine, 30-40 petals, cupped; NOW DISCARDED; [Fantastique × Caprice]

Premier Bal HT, w, 1955, Meilland, F.; flowers ivory edged cyclamen-rose, picotee effect, large, 45 petals, intense fragrance; recurrent; vigorous, bushy growth; [(Fantastique × Caprice) × Peace]; int. by URS

Premier Bal HT, pb, Richardier; flowers deep pink with silvery pink reverse, dbl., high-centered; good repeat; growth to 80-100 cm.; int. by Meilland Richardier, 1999

Premier Essai S, w, 1866, Geschwind; flowers flesh white, center carminy, medium, full; [*R. roxburghii* × Reine de la Lombardie]

Premier Supreme HT, dp, 1927, Zieger; bud long, pointed; flowers deep rose-pink, almost scarlet, very large, dbl., high-centered; foliage dark, leathery; long stems; very vigorous growth; [sport of Premier]

Première Ballerine – See **Prima Ballerina**, HT

Présence HT, lp, 1983, Delbard, Georges; flowers pink, lighter reverse, large, 38 petals, slight fruity fragrance; foliage medium size, medium green, matte; upright, bushy growth; [Dr. Albert Schweitzer × (Michele Meilland × Bayadere)]; int. by G. Delbard, 1970

Present – See **Präsent**, F

Présent Filial HT, pb, 1956, Delbard-Chabert; bud long; flowers old rose tinted coppery yellow, center salmon-pink, reverse, 85 petals; foliage dense; [Verschuren's Pink × seedling]

Preservation F, mr, 1995, Bossom, W.E.; flowers bright red, large, very full, borne in small clusters, slight fragrance; foliage medium size, medium green, glossy; some prickles; medium, upright growth; [Silver Jubilee × Paprika]

Preservation S, lp

President – See **Adam**, T

President HSet, dp, about 1846, Pierce; flowers reddish-pink, small, very dbl., borne in clusters of 15-20; foliage medium size, rugose, deeply serrated; prickles puplish red

President Armand Zinsch HT, dy, Delbard; flowers bright, large, dbl., high-centered, intense rose, lemon and raspberry fragrance; free-flowering; growth vigorous, medium; int. by Georges Delbard SA, 1998

Président Blondeau N, w, 1909, Denis; flowers pure white

President Boone HT, dr, 1936, Howard, F.H.; bud long, pointed; flowers scarlet-crimson, large, dbl., globular; foliage leathery; stems sometimes weak; vigorous growth; [seedling × Miss Rowena Thom]; int. by H&S

Président Bouché HT, or, 1917, Pernet-Ducher; flowers coral-red, shaded carmine, large to medium, full; vigorous growth; [seedling × Lyon Rose]

Président Bray HT, op, 1954, Privat; flowers salmon-pink veined pink; strong stems; vigorous growth

Président Briand HP, op, 1929, Mallerin, C.; flowers pink suffused salmon, overlarge, dbl., globular, moderate fragrance; recurrent; foliage wrinkled; strong stems; vigorous, compact growth; [((Frau Karl Druschki × unknown) × Lyon Rose) × (Frau Karl Druschki × Willowmere)]; int. by C-P

Président Carnot HP, mr, 1891, Degressy; flowers bright reddish-pink, nuanced carmine, large, full; foliage dark green, bullate; nearly thornless

Président Charles Hain – See **Amelia Earhart**, HT

Président Chaussé – See **Mark Sullivan**, HT

Président Chérioux HT, rb, 1923, Pernet-Ducher; flowers red and salmon-pink, shaded yellow, dbl.; Gold Medal, Bagatelle, 1923

President Cleveland – See **Frances E. Willard**, T

Président Cochet-Cochet HT, dr, 1937, Mallerin, C.; flowers deep garnet-red, tinted scarlet, very large, dbl.; foliage leathery; very vigorous growth; [Grenoble × seedling]

President Coolidge HSet, dr, 1925, Horvath; flowers glowing crimson, dbl.; very hardy; [(*R. setigera* × *R. wichurana*) × Château de Clos Vougeot]

President Cosnier HT, mp, Orard; int. in 1994

Président de la Rochterie B, m, 1891, Vigneron; flowers dark purple/red, very large, dbl.; [sport of Baron G. B. Gonella]

Président de Sèze HGal, m, 1828, Hébert, Mme.; flowers magenta center, paler at edges, small eye at center, very dbl., cupped, then convex, borne in clusters of 2-3, moderate to strong fragrance; non-remontant; foliage medium size, rounded; prickles moderate, hooked

Président Deville HT, mr, 1929, Leenders, M.; flowers dbl.; [Fritz Maydt × Mme J.W. Budde]; Gold Medal, Bagatelle, 1929

Président d'Olbecque – See **Louis-Philippe**, Ch

Président Duhem Pol, mr, 1930, Reymond; flowers bright red, dbl.; foliage dark; vigorous growth

Président Dutailly HGal, m, 1888, Dubreuil; bud globular; flowers reddish-purple, dbl., cupped, borne in small clusters, intense fragrance; foliage matte; prickles numerous, small; stems strong, erect

President Eisenhower HT, mr, 1953, Joseph H. Hill, Co.; bud ovoid; flowers rose-red, 4-5 in., 35-40 petals, high-centered to open, intense fragrance; foliage dark, leathery; vigorous, bushy growth; [sport of unnamed seedling (Captivator × Red Delicious)]; int. by C-P

President F. A. des Tombe HT, ab, 1925, Van Rossem; flowers apricot on golden yellow ground, reverse peach, dbl.; [Mr Joh. M. Jolles × Golden Emblem]

Président Férier HT, op, 1938, Gaujard; flowers reddish coppery pink, base tinted yellow, very dbl.; foliage bright green; very vigorous growth

President Franklin D. Roosevelt HT, or, 1933, Traendly & Schenck; flowers velvety scarlet, large, 35-40 petals; [sport of Templar]; int. by S. Reynolds

President Gaupin HT, dr

Président Gausen B, mr, 1862, Pradel; flowers bright carmine red, large, full

Président Georges Feuillet LCl, yb, 1954, Vially; flowers sulfur-yellow edged vermilion, reverse saffron, semi-dbl.

President H. C. Schroder HT, mr, 1970, Kordes, R.; flowers velvety deep red, large, dbl.; strong stems; [New Yorker × seedling]

President Heidar Aliyev HT, rb, 1998, Cocker, Ann G.; flowers vibrant salmon red, lighter reverse, 2-2½ in., 41 petals, borne singly or in large clusters; foliage large, dark green, glossy; prickles moderate, medium, slightly hooked; upright, medium growth; [Silver Jubilee × Remember Me]; int. by James Cocker & Sons, 1999

Président Henri Queuille HT, mr, 1952, Gaujard;

flowers carmine-red, very large, dbl.; very vigorous, upright growth; [Rome Glory × seedling]

President Herbert Hoover HT, pb, 1930, Coddington; bud long, pointed; flowers orange, rose and gold, reverse lighter, large, 25 petals, moderate spicy fragrance; recurrent; foliage leathery; vigorous, tall growth; [Sensation × Souv. de Claudius Pernet]; int. by Totty; John Cook Medal, ARS, 1935, Gertrude M. Hubbard, ARS, 1934

President Herbert Hoover, Climbing Cl HT, pb, 1931, Dixie Rose Nursery (also Cant, B. R., 1937); flowers pink, tinted cream and apricot, large; [sport of Herbert Hoover]

President Hoover, Climbing – See **President Herbert Hoover, Climbing**, Cl HT

Président J. B. Croibier HT, ob, 1940, Colombier; bud well shaped, pure orange; flowers dark orange, reverse yellow; foliage light green; very vigorous growth; [Mrs Pierre S. duPont × Talisman]

President Jac. Smits HT, dr, 1928, Verschuren; bud long, pointed; flowers brilliant dark red, large, semi-dbl.; foliage bronze, leathery; very vigorous growth; [Étoile de Hollande × Kitchener of Khartoum]; int. by Dreer

President Jacob Smith – See **President Jac. Smits**, HT

President John F. Kennedy – See **John F. Kennedy**, HT

President Kekkonen F, or, de Ruiter, G.; flowers medium, single; free-flowering; hardy; int. in 1983

President L. Senghor – See **Président Léopold Senghor**, HT

Président Léon de St Jean HP, mr, 1875, Lacharme; flowers crimson, shaded velvety flame red, large, full; [Charles Lefèbvre × unknown]

Président Léopold Senghor HT, dr, 1979, Meilland, Mrs. Marie-Louise; bud conical; flowers velvety red, large, 25 petals, cupped, pointed; abundant; foliage glossy, dark; vigorous, bushy growth; int. by Meilland & Co SNC

President Leopold Senghor, Climbing Cl HT, dr, Meilland; flowers deep velvety crimson, 5-6 in., borne mostly solitary; int. in 1982

Président Lincoln HP, dr, 1862, Granger; flowers dark red shaded crimson, large, dbl., slight fragrance; recurrent; growth to 5 ft.

President Macia HT, lp, 1933, Leenders, M.; flowers light pink, darker veining, 6 in., 25 petals; foliage dark; vigorous, bushy growth; [(Ophelia × Gloire de Hollande) × (Ophelia × Sensation)]

President MacKinley HP, mp, 1900, Charltons; flowers carnation pink

Président Magnaud Ch, dr, 1916, Nabonnand, C.; flowers small, semi-dbl.

Président Menoux HP, lp, 1854, Guillot; flowers silky light pink, reverse lighter, large, full

Président Morel Journel HT, rb, 1934, Chambard, C.; flowers scarlet, reverse yellow, large, cupped; foliage bronze; vigorous growth; [Mrs Edward Powell × *R. foetida bicolor* hybrid]

Président Nomblot – See **Horace McFarland**, HT

Président Pacaud HT, yb, 1946, Sauvageot, H.; flowers ochre-yellow shaded dark carmine-red and copper, well-formed, dbl.; foliage glossy; [Mme Joseph Perraud × seedling]; int. by Sauvageot

Président Parmentier HT, ab, 1926, Sauvageot, H.; flowers apricot-pink, dbl.; [Col. Leclerc × Le Progres]; int. by Cochet-Cochet

President Pats – See **Staatspräsident Päts**, HT

Président Paul Martin HT, my, 1942, Moulin-Epinay; flowers purplish carmine-red, large, semi-dbl.; vigorous growth; [Charles K. Douglas × Souv. de Georges Pernet]; int. by Hamonière

Président Paulmier Pol, dr, 1932, Turbat; flowers pure blood-red, passing to garnet, well-formed, very dbl., borne in clusters; dwarf growth

Président Plumecocq HT, yb, 1931, Gaujard; flowers coppery buff and deep salmon, large, 34 petals, cupped, moderate fruity fragrance; int. by C-P

Président Poincaré HT, 1920, Grandes Roseraies; flowers reddish-magenta, center crimson, shaded yellow, reverse brighter, dbl.

Président Rodolphe Burghes HP, mr, 1886, Bire; flowers bright rose red, shaded lilac, medium, full; [Jules Margottin × Jean Bart]

Président Schlachter HP, m, 1877, Verdier, E.; flowers purple/violet, large, dbl.

Président Seize F, dp, 1958, Delbard-Chabert; bud long; flowers light red becoming darker, 4 in., 10-15 petals; foliage dark; strong stems; upright growth

Président Sénélar HP, dr, 1883, Schwartz; flowers dark cerise ved, velvety, fading to purple, large, full

President Smith – See **William R. Smith**, T

President Sono HT, ly, 1978, Kikuchi, Rikichi; bud pointed; flowers cream-yellow, 45-50 petals, high-centered, intense fragrance; foliage dark; very large (5-6 in.) upright growth; [Burnaby × Montparnasse]; int. in 1972

President Souzy F, mp, 1985, Pekmez, Paul; flowers 20 petals, moderate fragrance; upright growth; [Emily Post × seedling]; int. in 1984

President Taft – See **Leuchtfeuer**, HCh

Président Thiers HP, mr, 1871, Lacharme; flowers fiery red, very large, full, globular; [Victor Verdier × unknown]

Président Van Oost HT, my, 1934, Lens; flowers golden yellow, edged deeper, large, dbl.; foliage glossy; long, strong stems; vigorous growth; [Souv. de Claudius Pernet × Ville de Paris]

President Viard HT, mr

Président Vignet HT, dr, 1911, Pernet-Ducher; flowers deep carmine-red, large, full, slight fragrance; strong, bushy (3-5 ft.) growth

Président Vignet, Climbing Cl HT, dr, 1942, Vogel, M.; flowers large, full, slight fragrance; recurrent; strong, upright (8 ft.) growth; [sport of Président Vignet]

President W. H. Taft HT, op, 1908, McCullough; bud long, pointed; flowers salmon-pink, large, dbl., high-centered; foliage glossy; long, strong stems; vigorous growth

Président Willermoz HP, mp, 1867, Ducher; flowers birght rose, full, globular

President Wilson HT, op, 1918, Easlea; flowers shrimp-pink, large, dbl.

President Wilson S, yb, Orard; int. in 1999

President Wm. R. Smith – See **William R. Smith**, T

Presidente HT, or, Croix; flowers large, 60 petals; free-flowering; vigorous growth; int. by Roseraies Paul Croix

Presidente Carmona HT, dr, 1937, Moreira da Silva; flowers blackish crimson, shaded salmon, large, dbl., cupped; foliage soft; vigorous, bushy growth; [Hortulanus Budde × Château de Clos Vougeot]

Presidente Craveiro Lopes HT, rb, 1958, Moreira da Silva; flowers cherry, reverse yellow, medium, 33 petals, moderate fragrance; foliage dark; strong stems; very vigorous, upright growth; [Sirena × Peace]; int. by McGredy & Son, 1955

Presidential Gr, lp, 1960, Lammerts, Dr. Walter; bud long, pointed; flowers light crimson, reverse China-rose, 5½ in., dbl., cupped; foliage leathery, glossy; vigorous, tall growth; [Charlotte Armstrong × (Charlotte Armstrong × Floradora)]; int. by Germain's, 1960

Presque Bleu HGal, dr, about 1815, Descemet

Presque Partout M, dp, before 1850; flowers rose, medium, dbl., cupped; vigorous growth

Press and Journal HT, op, Cocker; int. in 1997

Pressin HT, Dorieux; int. in 1975

Prestance HT, Dorieux; int. in 1985

Prestatyn Rover HT, op, 1929, Lavender; flowers salmon-pink, reverse darker, dbl.; [Alfred Colomb × Mrs Wemyss Quin]

Prestige HEg, mr, 1958, Kordes, R.; flowers light crimson, large, semi-dbl., open, borne in clusters, slight fragrance; recurrent bloom; foliage dense, dark green, glossy; vigorous, bushy growth; hardy, tips freeze; [Rudolph Timm × Fanal]; int. by Morse, 1957

Prestige de Bellegarde F, mr, Eve, A.; flowers pure red, 8 cm., semi-dbl., borne in clusters; good repeat; foliage dense, disease-resistant; growth to 2-3 ft.; int. by Le Roses Anciennes Andre Eve, 1974

Prestige de Lyon – See **Regatta**, HT, 1994

Prestige de Seine-et-Marne F, yb, Eve, A.; flowers soft yellow and chamois, fading as it opens, 3 in., semi-dbl., borne in large, broad clusters; good repeat; foliage dense, glossy; growth to 70-100 cm.; int. by Le Roses Anciennes de Andre Eve, 1992

Presumida Min, yb, 1948, Dot, Pedro; flowers pumpkin-yellow to white, center yellowish, small, dbl.; dwarf growth; [Eduardo Toda × Pompon de Paris]

Pretoria HT, or, 1953, Moro; bud long; flowers copper-red to orange, large; very vigorous growth; Gold Medal, Rome, 1953

Pretoria HT, dp, Kordes; bud long, pointed; flowers deep reddish-pink, maturing to carmine, dbl., high-centered, borne mostly singly, slight fragrance; blooms early, good repeat; well-balanced, medium growth; int. by Ludwig's Roses, 1992

Pretoria Boys Centenary HT, mr, Kordes; flowers bright red, medium, dbl., high-centered, borne mostly singly; free-flowering; vigorous, medium growth; int. by Ludwig's Roses, 2001

Pretty Min, or, Poulsen; flowers orange-red, medium, dbl., no fragrance; foliage dark; growth bushy, 20-40 cm.; int. by Poulsen Roser, 1996

Pretty 'n' Pink HT, mp, 2000, Palmer, Bobby J.; flowers medium pink, reverse light pink, 5½ in., very full, borne mostly singly; foliage large, dark green, glossy; prickles moderate; upright, tall (5-7 ft.) growth; [Miss All-American Beauty × Rebekah]; int. in 2001

Pretty 'n' Single Min, dp, 1990, Umsawasdi, Dr. Theera; flowers deep pink, small, 5 petals; foliage medium size, dark green, semi-glossy; upright, bushy, tall growth; [Nymphenburg × Libby]; int. by Theera Umsawasdi, 1986

Pretty Baby Min, pb, 1982, Jolly, Betty J.; flowers light pink, reverse creamy yellow, medium, 35 petals, high-centered; foliage small, medium green, semi-glossy; bushy, spreading growth; [Baby Katie × unnamed Miniature seedling]; int. by Rosehill Farm

Pretty Belinda HT, ab, Tantau; int. by Australian Roses, 2004

Pretty Bride HT, mp, Keisei; flowers soft pink, dbl., high-centered, borne mostly singly; good repeat; florist rose; int. in 2004

Pretty Celine Min, pb, 1995, Rennie, Bruce F.; flowers 1¼ in., dbl., borne mostly singly; foliage medium size, medium green, semi-glossy; some prickles; medium (15 in.), upright, bushy growth; [Strawberry Delight × Strawberry Delight]; int. by Rennie Roses International, 1994

Pretty Cupido Min, mp, de Ruiter; bud ovate; flowers bright pink, 1-1½ in., 25 petals, rosette, borne in small clusters; good repeat; prickles sparse, 5 mm.; PP10819; [seedling × seedling]; int. by Greenheart Farms

Pretty Fairy S, dp; groundcover; spreading growth; int.

by Pep. des Pigeats, 2003

Pretty Girl – See **Miss France**, Gr

Pretty Girl HT, w, Meilland; flowers ivory white, dbl., high-centered, borne mostly singly; good repeat; florist rose; int. by Meilland Intl., 1998

Pretty in Pink S, lp, 1999, Dickson, Colin; flowers pale pink, 2 in., very dbl., rosette, borne in small clusters, moderate fragrance; foliage medium size, medium green, glossy; few prickles; groundcover; low (24 in.), spreading (4-5 ft.) growth; [seedling × Grouse]; int. by Dickson Nurseries Ltd., 1994

Pretty Jennifer S, w, 2000, Belcher, Kenneth A.; flowers cream, reverse lighter, medium, very full, borne in small clusters; foliage medium size, dark green, semi-glossy; few prickles; growth upright, tall (4-5 ft.); [sport of Ausjess]

Pretty Jessica S, dp, 1992, Austin, David; flowers medium, very full, cupped, borne in small clusters, intense old rose fragrance; free-flowering; foliage medium size, dark green, semi-glossy; some prickles; low (65 cm.), bushy growth; [Wife of Bath × seedling]; int. by David Austin Roses, Ltd., 1983

Pretty Lady F, lp, 1997, Scrivens, Len; flowers semi-dbl., 8-14 petals; foliage medium size, dark green, semi-glossy; numerous prickles; medium (4ft.) growth; [(seedling × (*R. davidii elongata* × seedling)) × ((Troika × Alpine Sunset) × Freedom)]; int. by Warner's Roses; Best Established Rose, Glasgow, 2006

Pretty Little Thing Min, dp, 2000, Bell, Judy; flowers dbl., high-centered, borne mostly singly, slight fragrance; foliage medium size, medium green, matte; prickles moderate; upright, compact, medium (16 in.) growth; [Jean Kenneally × Poker Chip]; int. by Michigan Mini Roses

Pretty Penny Min, ob, 1994, Moore, Ralph S.; flowers large, semi-dbl., borne mostly singly or in small clusters, no fragrance; foliage medium size, medium green, matte; no prickles; medium (28-34 cm.), bushy, spreading, compact growth; [seedling × seedling]; int. by Sequoia Nursery, 1995

Pretty Pink LCl, dp, 1968, Patterson; flowers deep pink, open, medium, dbl.; recurrent bloom; foliage glossy; very vigorous, climbing growth; [New Dawn × Spartan]; int. by Patterson Roses

Pretty Pink HMsk, pb, 2000, Lens, Louis; flowers single, borne in large clusters, moderate fragrance; recurrent; foliage large, medium green, semi-glossy; prickles moderate; bushy, medium (4-5 ft.) growth; [*R. multiflora adenocheata* × Ballerina]; int. by Louis Lens N.V., 1992

Pretty Pink HWich, dp, Barni, V.; flowers bright carmine pink, 5-6 cm., semi-dbl., borne in small clusters, moderate fragrance; foliage small, glossy; growth vigorous, tall; int. by Rose Barni, 1992

Pretty Please Min, lp, 1986, Epperson, Richard G.; flowers small, 25 petals, urn-shaped, borne usually singly, no fragrance; foliage medium size, light green, semi-glossy; prickles very thin, long, straight, light red; medium, bushy growth; [Bride's White × unnamed Miniature seedling]; int. in 1985

Pretty Polly – See **Pink Symphony**, Min

Pretty Poly Pol, mr, 1954, Bishop; flowers cherry-red, flat, camellia-like, borne in clusters; vigorous, upright growth; [Mme Butterfly × Our Princess]; int. by Baker's Nursery, 1954

Pretty Princess HT, dp, Meilland; flowers fuchsia pink, dbl., high-centered, borne mostly singly; good repeat; florist rose; int. by Meilland Intl., 2002

Pretty Tiny Min, w, 1995, Rennie, Bruce F.; flowers 1 in., dbl., borne in small clusters; foliage small, medium green, semi-glossy; few prickles; low (8-10 in.), compact growth; int. by Rennie Roses International, 1995

Pretty Woman Min, pb, 1991, Williams, Ernest D.; flowers pink with yellow and orange, deeper at edges, aging darker, good substance, small, full, high-centered, borne mostly singly, moderate fragrance; foliage small, medium green, glossy; few prickles; low (30 cm.), bushy growth; [Tom Brown × Over the Rainbow]; int. by Mini-Roses, 1992

Pretty Woman HT, lp, Ferrer; flowers soft pink, small to medium, dbl., high-centered; florist rose; int. by Meilland-Star, 1999

Preussen HT, dr, 1920, Löbner; flowers glowing dark blood-red, dbl.; [Farbenkonigin × Richmond]; int. by Kordes

Préval P, lp, about 1821, Prévost; flowers blush pink, large, full, moderate fragrance

Prevalent F, Verbeek

Preview HT, w, Meilland

Prevue S, w, 1984, James, John; flowers medium, semi-dbl., no fragrance; foliage medium size, medium green, semi-glossy; bushy growth; [(Tausendschon × (Perle d'Or × Old China)) × Safrano]; originally registered as Pol; int. in 1978

Preyasi HT, dp, IARI; bud pointed; flowers flower fuchsia pink, large, intense fragrance; abundant bloomer; stems long; int. in 1991

Preziosa – See **Indian Song**, HT

Prickly Rose – See ***R. acicularis*** (Lindley)

Pride HT, dr; flowers full, 30-35 petals, high-centered, borne usually singly; good repeat; florist rose; int. by Terra Nigra BV, 2004

Pride 'n' Joy Min, ob, 1991, Warriner, William A.; bud ovoid, pointed; appendages on all sepals; flowers bright, medium orange, reverse orange and cream, fades to salmon pink, 2 in., 30-35 petals, high-centered, borne singly and several together in pyramid shape, moderate fruity fragrance; recurrent; foliage medium size, dark green, semi-glossy; prickles medium, short, hooked slightly downward; bushy, spreading, medium growth; PP8578; [Chattem Centennial × Prominent]; int. by Bear Creek Gardens, 1992

Pride Meidiland – See **Cherry Meidiland**, S

Pride of Canada HT, dp, 1981, Collins; bud long, ovoid; flowers deep pink, 34 petals, high-centered, borne in pairs; foliage dark; prickles small, brown; tall growth; [Ena Harkness × Charlotte Armstrong]; int. by Pan American Bulb Co.

Pride of Daylesford Hmult, dp, Huxley, Ian

Pride of England HT, mr, Harkness; flowers velvety crimson red, 5 in., 30 petals, high-centered, borne mostly singly, slight fragrance; good repeat; vigorous, medium (4 ft.) growth; int. in 1998

Pride of Hurst Pol, op, 1926, Hicks; flowers coral-pink, small, very dbl., borne in clusters; [sport of Coral Cluster]

Pride of Ichalkaranji HT, yb, Patil, B.K.; int. in 1989

Pride of Leicester HT, pb, 1960, Verschuren; flowers rose-pink, base yellow, large, dbl., high-centered; foliage light green; vigorous growth; [R.M.S. Queen Mary × seedling]; int. by Blaby Rose Gardens, 1960

Pride of Lille – See **Triomphe de Lille**, D

Pride of Maldon F, ob, 1990, Harkness, R., & Co., Ltd.; bud pointed; flowers bright reddish-orange, light orange-yellow reverse, darkening, 10 petals, cupped; foliage medium size, dark green, glossy; prickles straight or slightly curved, medium to small, green; bushy, medium growth; [Southampton × Wandering Minstrel]; int. by R. Harkness & Co., Ltd., 1991

Pride of Midnapur HT, rb, Mandal, G.S.; flowers blackish red with distinctive pink stripes and streaks; free-flowering; vigorous growth; [sport of Carmousine]; int. in 2004

Pride of Mountbarker HT, ab, 1996, Thomson, George L.; flowers peach cream tinted rose edge, apricot center, lighter reverse, full, moderate fragrance; foliage small, medium green, semi-glossy; prickles moderate; upright, medium (5 × 2 ft.) growth; [Gold Medal × Sylvia]

Pride of Nagpur HT, dr, Datt, Braham; flowers dark, dusky red, large, moderate sweet fragrance; int. in 1983

Pride of New Castle HT, dr, 1930, E.G. Hill, Co.; flowers deep velvety crimson, large, dbl.; vigorous, bushy growth; [Hoosier × Beauty unnamed seedling]; int. by Heller Bros.

Pride of Newark F, lp, 1968, Morey, Dr. Dennison; flowers shell-pink, 4 in., dbl., cupped, intense fragrance; foliage glossy, bronze, leathery; very vigorous, upright, compact growth; [Joanna Hill × The Fairy]; int. by General Bionomics, 1966

Pride of Oakland F, mp, 1977, Lindquist; bud pointed; flowers 2½ in., 26 petals, rosette, moderate spicy fragrance; upright, spreading growth; [Pinocchio × China Doll]; int. by Howard of Hemet, 1976

Pride of Pacific F, op, 1957, Silva; flowers salmon-pink, dbl., borne in clusters of 4-7; symmetrical growth; [Pinocchio × Maxine]

Pride of Park F, ob

Pride of Reigate HP, rb, 1884, Brown, J.; flowers carmine, striped and mottled white and soft pink, dbl.; recurrent; upright (4 ft.), bushy growth; [sport of Comtesse d'Oxford]

Pride of Reigate, Climbing Cl HP, rb, 1941, Vogel, M.; flowers red with pink or white striping, 10-12 cm., dbl., moderate fragrance; occasional repeat; [sport of Pride of Reigate]

Pride of Runcorn HT, Williams, A.

Pride of Scotland HT, dp, McGredy; flowers deep pink, changing to salmon pink as they age, dbl., slight fragrance; good repeat; foliage large, medium green, matte; upright (3½-4 ft.), bushy growth; int. in 2003

Pride of Sunnybank Gr, mp, 1957, Ulrick, L.W.; [Ma Perkins × Charlotte Armstrong]

Pride of the Valley – See **Mrs F. W. Sanford**, HP

Pride of Tryon S, ab, Lowe, Malcolm; flowers with apricot, peach and pink tones, dbl., borne in small clusters, slight fragrance; repeat bloom; growth low, prostrate, groundcover; int. in 2002

Pride of Waltham HP, mp, 1881, Paul, W.; flowers silvery rose, large, dbl.; vigorous growth; [sport of Comtesse d'Oxford]

Pride of Wansbeck HT, dp, 1987, Greensitt, J.A.; flowers light red, medium, 26-49 petals, moderate fragrance; foliage medium size, medium green, semi-glossy; bushy growth; [Christian Dior × seedling]; int. by Nostell Priory Rose Gardens, 1979

Pride of Washington HSet, m, 1849, Pierce; flowers rosy violet, medium, very dbl., cupped, borne in clusters of 10-20; foliage medium size, slightly serrated

Pridwin HT, m, Kordes; flowers mauve maroon, large, dbl., high-centered to globular, borne mostly singly, intense fragrance; recurrent; stems strong, sturdy; medium to tall growth; int. by Ludwig's Roses, 1999

Prima S, pb, 1988, Harkness, R., & Co., Ltd.; flowers blush white, reverse blush pink, aging blush to white, large, 18 petals, cupped, moderate fruity fragrance; repeat bloom; foliage medium size, medium green, semi-glossy; prickles straight, small, red; spreading, medium growth; hips round, medium, red; [Herbstfeuer × Pearl Drift]; int. by R. Harkness & Co., Ltd., 1990; Gold Medal, Geneva, 1987

Prima Min, mp, Olesen

Prima Ballerina – See **Solistka Baleta**, HT

Prima Ballerina HT, dp, 1959, Tantau, Math.; bud long, pointed; flowers cherry-pink, medium to large, 20 petals, high-centered, intense fragrance; recurrent; foliage leathery, light green; upright (3 ft.) growth; [unknown × Peace]; int. in 1957

Prima Donna – See **Mme Pierre Euler**, HT

Prima Donna HT, mp, 1944, Dickson, A.; bud pointed; flowers rich deep salmon-pink tinted buff, 5 in., 45 petals, high-centered; foliage glossy; vigorous, upright, open growth; RULED EXTINCT 1/85; [Heinrich Wendland × seedling]; int. by J&P

Prima Donna Gr, dp, 1985, Shirakawa, Takeshi; bud pointed; flowers deep fuchsia pink, large, 27 petals, high-centered, slight fragrance; foliage large, medium green, semi-glossy; prickles greyed-orange, hooked slightly downward; vigorous (6 ft.), bushy, spreading growth; [(seedling × Happiness) × Prominent]; int. by Tosh Nakashima, 1983; Gold Medal, Portland, 1992

Prima Donna HT, pb, J&P; flowers creamy yellow with pink edges, gradually covering the petals, dbl., high-centered, intense fragrance; free-flowering; upright (3 ft.) growth; int. by Rose Barni, 2000

Primaballerina – See **Prima Ballerina**, HT

Primarosa HT, dp, 1950, Giacomasso; bud long; flowers carmine, base yellow, streaked orange, very large; strong stems

Primavera HT, op, 1936, Aicardi, D.; flowers salmon-pink, well-formed, dbl., moderate musk fragrance; vigorous growth; [Julien Potin × Sensation]; int. by Robichon

Prime Time Min, my, 1985, Hardgrove, Donald & Mary; flowers medium, 35 petals, high-centered; foliage small, medium green, semi-glossy; upright, bushy growth; [Picnic × Rise 'n' Shine]; int. by Rose World Originals, 1984

Primerose HT, my, 1913, Soupert & Notting; flowers melon-yellow, deeper in autumn, shaded apricot, dbl.; [Mme Mélanie Soupert × Mrs Peter Blair]

Primrose Queen HT, my; originally a J&P test rose, but not introduced by them; before 1980

Primerose Sistau Pol, pb, 1925, Turbat; flowers carmine, shaded yellow, medium, cupped, borne in clusters of 5-6; prickles few thorns; half-dwarf growth

Primevère HWich, yb, 1929, Barbier; flowers primrose-yellow to canary-yellow, 7 cm., dbl., borne in small clusters; non-recurrent; foliage dark green, glossy; long stems; very vigorous, climbing and trailer growth; [*R. wichurana* × Constance]; int. by Dreer, 1930

Primo Passo S, ly, Barni, V.; flowers creamy yellow, golden stamens, medium, semi-dbl., cupped to flat, borne in large clusters, slight fragrance; good repeat; rapid, arching (70-90 cm.) growth; int. in 1995

Primo Premio HT, pb, 1964, Giacomasso; flowers rose suffused yellow, well-formed, medium

Primo Sole HT, my, Barni, V.; flowers unusual yellow, slow opening, full, slight fragrance; good repeat; strong (70-90 cm.) growth; int. by Rose Barni, 1987

Primrose T, ly, 1908, Dingee & Conard

Primrose – See **Primevère**, HWich

Primrose Bedder F, my, 1957, Kordes; flowers primrose-yellow, dbl., borne in large trusses; foliage light green; int. by Morse, 1956

Primrose Pet Pol, Williams, A.

Primrose Pirrie HT, my, 1920, Dobbie; [sport of Lady Pirrie]

Primrose Queen Ch, ly, before 1918, Lippiat; flowers medium, full; [sport of Arethusa]

Primrose Sistau Pol, op; flowers coral pink, small, dbl., pompon, borne in clusters; recurrent; growth to 2 ft.; int. in 1925

Primula Pol, pb, 1900, Soupert & Notting; flowers carmine pink with white eye, small, dbl.; [Mignonette × unknown]

Primula HT, Aicardi; int. in 1956

Prince S, rb, Poulsen; bud ovoid to globular; flowers 8-10 cm., 60+ petals, borne singly and in small clusters, no fragrance; foliage dark, glossy; prickles moderate, 1/4 in., straight, greyed-orange; vigorous, compact, bushy (2 ft.) growth; hips none observed ; PP11626; [Dalli Dalli × seedling]; int. by Poulsen Roser, 1998

Prince A. de Wagram HP, m, 1891, Cochet; bud globular; flowers bright purple, aging carmine, large, very full

Prince Abricot – See **Gingersnap**, F

Prince Albert HP, rb, 1837, Laffay, M.; flowers carmine-rose changing to dark, velvety crimson, large, globular; [Gloire des Rosomanes × a damask perpetual]

Prince Albert – See **Souv de la Reine des Belges**, HP

Prince Albert B, mr, 1852, Fontaine/Paul; flowers brilliant crimson-scarlet, medium, full, borne in small clusters; nearly thornless; [Comice de Seine-et-Marne × unknown]

Prince Albert – See **Bangsbo**, F

Prince Antoine d'Arenberg HGal, about 1830, Parmentier

Prince Arthur HP, mr, 1875, Cant, B. R.; flowers deep crimson, medium, 55 petals, intense fragrance; vigorous growth; [Général Jacqueminot × unknown]

Prince Bernhard HT, mr, 1937, Van Rossem; bud pointed; flowers shining red, shaded strawberry-red, well-formed, large, dbl.; foliage dark; vigorous growth; [(sport of Matador × unknown)]; int. by J&P, 1941; Gold Medal, Bagatelle, 1937

Prince Camille de Rohan HP, dr, 1861, Verdier, E.; flowers very deep velvety crimson-maroon, well-formed, large, 100 petals, cupped, intense fragrance; rarely repeats; rather weak stems; vigorous, upright growth; [possibly Général Jacqueminot × Geant des Batailles]

Prince Charles B, dp, 1842, Hardy; flowers deep red-purple, fading to lavender, veined magenta, base of petals near white, semi-dbl., loose, intense fragrance; non-recurrent; foliage large, dark; prickles very few; growth vigorous (to 5 ft.); sometimes classed as Ch

Prince Charles Gr, dr; flowers deep, royal red, dbl., high-centered; vigorous, tall growth; int. in 1992

Prince Charles d'Arenberg HP, mp, 1888, Soupert & Notting; flowers silky carmine pink, silvery reflections, center bright pink, very large, full, cupped; [Dupuy Jamain × Mme Sévigné]

Prince Charles du Luxembourg Ch, dp; flowers bright carmine, cupped

Prince Charlie HT, op, 1932, Dobbie; bud long, pointed; flowers coral-pink, overlaid salmon, base orange, large, dbl., cupped; foliage leathery, bronze tinted; vigorous, bushy growth

Prince Charming HT, rb, 1916, Dickson, H.; flowers reddish-copper, base bright gold, medium, full

Prince Charming Min, mr, 1953, deVink; flowers bright crimson, 1 in., dbl.; foliage tinted red; dwarf (8-12 in.) growth; [Ellen Poulsen × Tom Thumb]; int. by T. Robinson, Ltd.

Prince Charming S, lp, 1958, Skinner; flowers pale blush-pink, dbl.; prolonged bloom; upright (2½ ft.), bushy growth

Prince Damask HT, dr, 1954, LeGrice; flowers maroon, medium, 30 petals; foliage small, dark; [Guineé × unknown]

Prince d'Arenberg – See **Duc d'Arenberg**, HGal

Prince de Beïra HP, mr, 1888, Verdier, E.; flowers vermilion-red, shaded lighter, glossy red, large, full

Prince de Bulgarie HT, lp, 1900, Pernet-Ducher; bud long, pointed; flowers silvery flesh, center deeper, shaded salmon and saffron-yellow, dbl., cupped, moderate fragrance; foliage bright green; vigorous growth

Prince de Galles P, rb, before 1826, Blinière; flowers red, aging violet pink, large, full

Prince de Joinville HP, mr, 1867, Paul, W.; flowers bright carmine-crimson, medium, dbl.

Prince de Monaco – See **Modern Art**, HT

Prince de Monaco – See **Cherry Parfait**, Gr

Prince de Porcia HP, dr, 1865, Verdier, E.; flowers deep scarlet-vermilion, 10 cm., dbl.

Prince de Vaudémont – See **Princesse de Vaudémont**, M, 1854

Prince Englebert Charles d'Arenberg HT, or, 1909, Soupert & Notting; flowers scarlet shaded purple, very large, dbl., moderate fragrance; [Étoile de France × Richmond]

Prince Eugène – See **Eugène de Beauharnais**, Ch

Prince Eugène de Beauharnais HP, dr, 1864, Moreau et Robert

Prince Félix de Luxembourg HT, mr, 1930, Ketten Bros.; flowers carmine-red, shaded purplish, large, 30-35 petals, moderate fragrance; foliage dark; very vigorous, bushy growth; [Gen. MacArthur × George C. Waud]

Prince Frédéric – See **Prince Frederick**, HGal

Prince Frederick HGal, mr, about 1840, Parmentier; flowers bright red, large, very dbl.

Prince Henri F, mr, 1954, Reuter, A.; flowers large, dbl.

Prince Henri des Pays-Bas HP, mp, 1862, Soupert; flowers bright carmine, reverse lilac, medium, full

Prince Henri d'Orléans HP, dp, 1886, Verdier, E.; flowers light carmine cerise red, large, dbl., cupped; foliage dark green, deeply serrated; prickles numerous, unequal, thing and sharp, slightly hooked; growth erect

Prince Henry F, mp, 1926, Easlea; bud long, pointed; flowers bright pink, passing to blush-pink, borne in clusters of 18-20; [St. Helena × seedling]

Prince Igor – See **Frenzy**, F

Prince Igor, Climbing Cl F, ob, Meilland; int. in 1985

Prince Jean de Luxembourg Pol, w, 1926, Soupert & Notting; flowers pure white, very small, dbl., borne in immense clusters of 100-150; moderately dwarf growth; [Jeanny Soupert × Miniature]

Prince Klaus – See **Rosalynn Carter**, Gr

Prince Klaus F, ob; flowers salmon-red, large, dbl.; int. by Sauvageot, 1986

Prince Meillandina Min, dr, 1988, Meilland, Alain A.; bud oval, small; flowers dark currant-red, 1½-2 in., 20-22 petals, cupped, borne singly and in clusters, no fragrance; free-flowering; foliage medium size, dark green, semi-glossy; bushy, branching (15 in.) growth; PP7021; [Parador × Mogral]; int. by SNC Meilland & Cie

Prince Napoléon B, pb, 1864, Pernet; flowers bright rose, very large, very full, moderate fragrance; recurrent; upright (4-5 ft.) growth

Prince Noir HP, m, 1854, Boyau; flowers dark velvety crimson-purple, full, cupped, intense sweet fragrance; free-flowering; moderate (4-5 ft.) growth

Prince of Denmark HT, mp, 1964, McGredy, Sam IV; flowers rose-pink, 4 in., dbl.; free growth; [Queen Elizabeth × Independence]; int. by Fisons Horticulture

Prince of Orange HT, ob, Williams, J. B.; flowers dusky orange-salmon, high-centered; int. by Hortico, 1998

Prince of Peace HT, yb, 1985, J&P; flowers yellow edged with pink, medium, 35 petals; foliage medium size, medium green, glossy; upright growth; PP5901; [Bridal Pink × unknown]; int. by McConnell Nurs., Inc.

Prince of Peace HT, pb, 2005, Murray, Jean; flowers medium, semi-dbl., borne mostly solitary; recurrent; foliage medium size, dark green; prickles moderate; upright, tall growth; [Peace × Love]

Prince of Wales HT, mr, 1921, Easlea; bud long, pointed; flowers brilliant cherry-scarlet, semi-dbl.

Prince Orange F, op

Prince Palace – See **Prince**, S

Prince Philip – See **Tudor Prince**, Gr

Prince Prosper d'Arenberg T, op, 1880, Soupert & Notting; flowers reddish-salmon with flesh pink, reverse carmine, medium, full; [Mme Bérard × unknown]

Prince Regent S, m, Genesis

Prince Stirbey HP, dp, 1871, Schwartz; flowers flesh pink, 3½-4 in., full, flat

Prince Sunblaze – See **Prince Meillandina**, Min

Prince Tango Pol, or, 1970, Delbard-Chabert; bud pointed; flowers mandarin color, open, small, semi-dbl.; foliage bronze, glossy; moderate, bushy growth; [(Orléans Rose × Goldilocks) × ((Orange Triumph × unknown) × Floradora)]; Gold Medal, Madrid, 1968

Prince Theodore Bonney HT, 1898, Dingee & Conard; [Bon Silène × W. F. Bennett]

Prince Waldemar HP, rb, 1885, Verdier, E.; flowers bright carmine cerise, bordered whitish, large, full, cupped; foliage large, delicate green

Prince Wasiltchikoff – See **Duchess of Edinburgh**, T

Prince Yugala HT, dr, 1923, Cant, F.; bud long, pointed; flowers deep velvety maroon, dbl.

Princeps LCl, mr, 1942, Clark, A.; flowers deep crimson, reverse lighter, medium to large, dbl., cupped, slight fragrance; may repeat in hot climates; pillar (10 ft.) growth

Prince's Trust – See **The Prince's Trust**, LCl

Princes van Oranje Cl Pol, or, 1933, Sliedrecht; flowers blazing red and orange, borne in large clusters; [sport of Gloria Mundi]; int. as Princess van Orange, J&P

Princesa Carmen de Borbon F, Dot, Simon; int. in 1979

Princesa Sofia HT, Dot, Simon; int. in 1972

Princesita – See **Pixie**, Min

Princess HT, or, 1965, Laperrière; flowers geranium-red, 4-5 in., 45 petals, globular; vigorous, upright growth; [(Peace × Magicienne) × (Independence × Radar)]; int. by EFR

Princess F, w, 1993, Ilsink, G.P.; flowers medium, full, borne in large clusters; foliage medium size, dark green, glossy; some prickles; tall to medium (60 cm.), upright growth; [Pink Delight × seedling]; int. by Interplant B.V., 1989

Princess – See **Hime**, Min

Princess Aiko F, mp, Keisei; int. by Keisei Rose Nurseries, 2002

Princess Alexandra F, yb, 1970, Cobley; flowers creamy yellow suffused carmine-pink, medium, 30-35 petals, borne in trusses, moderate fragrance; foliage dark, glossy; very vigorous growth; [Masquerade × seedling]; int. by Blaby, 1962

Princess Alexandra S, dp, Olesen, P. & M.; flowers 4 in., 20-30 petals, shallow cup, borne 1-4 per stem, intense spicy fragrance; free-flowering; foliage medium size, dark green, glossy; prickles moderate, ¼ in., hooked downward, yellow-green; growth moderate (3-4 ft.), upright to bushy; PP12999; [Margaret Merril × seedling]; int. by Poulsen Roser, 1997

Princess Alice M, m, 1853, Paul, A.; bud globular; flowers violet-rose, not very mossy, small, full, borne in small clusters; non-recurrent; stems long, covered with moss with citrus scent; [Pourpre du Luxembourg × unknown]

Princess Alice F, my, 1985, Harkness, R., & Co., Ltd.; bud medium, pointed to ovoid; flowers butter yellow, ruffled, 4-4½ in., 28-32 petals, cupped, borne in large clusters, slight fruity fragrance; free-flowering; foliage medium size, medium green, semi-glossy; prickles few, long, almost straight; bushy, upright, medium to tall growth; disease resistant; PP6953; [Judy Garland × Anne Harkness]; Gold Medal, Dublin, 1984

Princess Angela HT, lp, 1991, Alde, Robert O.; flowers large, very full, borne mostly singly, slight fragrance; foliage medium size, dark green, semi-glossy; tall, upright, bushy growth; [Pristine × Granada]

Princess Angeline HT, mp, 1945, Swim, H.C.; flowers pink, becoming open, 4½-5½ in., 35-50 petals, cupped, intense damask fragrance; foliage leathery; vigorous, tall growth; [Charlotte Armstrong × Times Square]; int. by Peterson & Dering

Princess Beatrix T, yb, 1887, Bennett; flowers dark golden yellow, reverse lighter, edged pink, large, full, moderate fragrance

Princess Bonnie T, dr, 1896, Dingee & Conard; bud long; flowers vivid crimson, large, semi-dbl., intense fragrance; [Bon Silène × William Francis Bennett]

Princess Charming HT, mp, 2001, Fryer, Gareth; flowers satin pink, 12-15 cm., full, high-centered, borne mostly solitary; foliage large, medium green, semi-glossy; prickles moderate; growth bushy, tall (110 cm.); garden decorative; int. by Fryer's Nurseries, Ltd., 2002

Princess Chichibu F, pb, 1971, Harkness; flowers two-toned pink, 2½-3 in., 30 petals, borne several together, slight fragrance; free-flowering; foliage glossy, dark green; hardy; [(Vera Dalton × Highlight) × Merlin]

Princess des Roses – See **Principessa delle Rose**, HT

Princess Diana HT, op, Noack; flowers coral, salmon and pink blend, dbl., high-centered; recurrent; int. in 1981

Princess Elizabeth HT, ob, 1927, Wheatcroft Bros.; flowers orange-gold, striped with dark cherry red, large, full, some fragrance; [sport of The Queen Alexandra Rose]

Princess Elizabeth of Greece HT, my, 1926, Chaplin Bros.; flowers golden yellow shaded terra-cotta, well-shaped, high-centered

Princess Ena Pol, mp, 1906, May, H. B.

Princess Fair HT, ab, 1965, Morey, D.; flowers light apricot, large, dbl., cupped, moderate fragrance; foliage glossy; vigorous, upright growth; [Queen Elizabeth × (Crimson Glory, Climbing × Happiness)]; int. by J&P, 1964

Princess Fukuyma HT, ly, Hiroshima; int. by Hiroshima Bara-en, 1991

Princess Grace – See **Princesse de Monaco**, HT

Princess Louise HP, w, 1869, Laxton/Paul; flowers blush, medium, globular; vigorous growth; [Mme Vidot × Virginal]; int. by G. Paul

Princess Margaret – See **Prinsesse Margrethe**, HT

Princess Margaret of England HT, mp, 1970, Meilland, Mrs. Marie-Louise; flowers phlox-pink, large, dbl., high-centered, borne mostly singly, slight tea fragrance; free-flowering; foliage abundant, large, leathery; growth vigorous, upright; [Queen Elizabeth × (Peace × Michele Meilland)]; int. by URS, 1968; Gold Medal, Portland, 1977

Princess Margaret of England, Climbing Cl HT, mp, 1970, Meilland; bud long; flowers medium pink, fading to silvery pink, borne mostly solitary; [sport of Princess Margaret of England]; int. by URS

Princess Margaret Rose HT, pb, 1933, Cant, B. R.; bud long, pointed; flowers glowing pink suffused orange, large, dbl., cupped; foliage leathery; vigorous growth; [Unnamed seedling of Los Angeles parentage × seedling]

Princess Marianna S, w, 1999, Poulsen Roser APS; flowers ivory white, old-fashioned form, 2½-3 in., very dbl., borne in small clusters, moderate fragrance; foliage medium size, dark green, glossy; prickles moderate; compact, bushy, rounded, low (20-24 in.) growth; PP10638; [seedling × Queen Margrethe]; int. by Weeks Roses, 1998

Princess Marina HT, ab, 1938, Robinson, H.; flowers apricot, shaded salmon and copper, well-shaped, dbl.; stiff stems; vigorous growth; int. by Port Stockton Nursery

Princess Mary of Cambridge HP, lp, 1867, Paul, G.; flowers flesh pink, large, full; [Duchess of Sutherland × Jules Margottin]

Princess May HT, lp, 1893, Paul, W.; flowers very light pink, slightly darker reverse, 10 cm., dbl., globular, borne singly or in small clusters, moderate fragrance; remontant; [Gloire de Dijon × unknown]

Princess Michael of Kent F, my, 1980, Harkness, R., & Co., Ltd.; flowers large, 38 petals, high-centered, borne singly or in clusters of 2-3, moderate fragrance; foliage medium large, mid-green, glossy; prickles short, thick, red; growth low (2 ft.), bushy; [Manx Queen × Alexander]; int. in 1981

Princess Michiko F, ob, 1966, Dickson, A.; flowers coppery orange, yellow eye, 3 in., 15 petals, cupped, borne in clusters; foliage glossy; bushy growth; [Circus × Spartan]

Princess Michiko, Climbing Cl F, ob, Keisei; [sport of Princess Michiko]; int. by Keisei Rose Nurseries, 1977

Princess Mikasa HT, dp, 1986, Teranishi, K.; flowers deep pink, 45 petals, urn-shaped, borne singly, no fragrance; foliage large, medium green, semi-glossy; prickles small, light green; tall, bushy growth; [(Red Lion × Samantha) × (Red Lion × Samantha)]; int. by Itami Rose Nursery, 1983

Princess Nagako HT, rb, 1922, Pemberton; flowers fiery red, shaded yellow, small, semi-dbl.

Princess Nobuko HT, mp, 2001, Cocker, A.G.; flowers medium pink, reverse lighter pink, 2½ in., dbl., high-centered, borne mostly solitary, moderate fragrance; foliage large, medium green, semi-glossy; prickles 9 mm., straight, moderate; upright, tall (3 ft.) growth; garden, decorative; [Pristine × National Trust]; int. by James Cocker & Sons, 2002

Princess of Holland HT, op, Williams, J. B.; flowers dusky orange-salmon, reverse lighter, dbl., high-centered, moderate fragrance; recurrent; int. by Hortico, Inc., 1998

Princess of India HT, rb, 1983, Pal, Dr. B.P.; flowers outer petals deep red, inner petals carmine, large, 35 petals, high-centered, intense fragrance; foliage medium to large, dark, smooth; prickles brown to gray; upright, bushy growth; [Tropicana × Granada]; int. by K.S.G. Son's Roses, 1980

Princess of Monaco – See **Princesse de Monaco**, HT

Princess of Nassau – See **Princesse de Nassau**, N

Princess of Orange – See **Princess of Holland**, HT

Princess of Wales HP, mr, 1864, Paul, W.; flowers vivid crimson

Princess of Wales HP, lp, 1871, Laxton; flowers light pink center with outer petals fading to white, full, cupped, borne in clusters, intense fragrance; frequent flowering; growth medium (4-5 ft.)

Princess of Wales T, yb, 1882, Bennett; bud long,

pointed; flowers exterior petals pink yellow, center deep waxy yellow, medium, dbl., cupped; [Adam × Elise Sauvage]

Princess of Wales F, w, Harkness; flowers clear white, yellow stamens, medium, 25-30 petals, open, borne in clusters, slight fragrance; good repeat; foliage dark green, glossy; stems upright, medium (2-2½ ft.); int. by R. Harkness & Co., 1997

Princess Pearl F, w, 1960, Beldam Bridge Nursery; flowers white center blush, 3 in., 40 petals, borne in clusters; foliage leathery, dark; moderate growth; [sport of Carol Amling]

Princess Rose Blossom S, pb, Kordes; flowers combination of cream, white and shades of coral, large, deeply cupped to globular, borne singly and in clusters, slight fragrance; growth to 4 ft.; int. by Ludwig's Roses, 2003

Princess Royal HT, mp, 1935, Dickson, A.; flowers rose-pink to hydrangea-pink, petals shell-shaped, very large; foliage dark, glossy; vigorous growth; RULED EXTINCT 4/92

Princess Royal HT, ab, 1992, Dickson, Colin; flowers apricot center, outer petals fading lighter, large, full, borne mostly singly, slight fragrance; foliage large, medium green, semi-glossy; numerous prickles; stems very stiff; medium (3 ft.), bushy growth; [Tequila Sunrise × seedling]; int. by Dickson Nurseries, Ltd.

Princess Takamatsu HT, pb, 1977, Kono, Yoshito; bud globular; flowers 6 in., 50 petals, high-centered; vigorous, upright growth; [Bonsoir × Christian Dior]; int. in 1974

Princess van Orange – See **Princes van Oranje**, Cl Pol

Princess Victoria HT, or, 1920, McGredy; flowers glowing scarlet-crimson shaded orange, passing to carmine, b, dbl.; Gold Medal, NRS, 1920

Princess White F, w, 1957, Boerner; bud pointed; flowers medium, dbl., flat, moderate fragrance; foliage leathery; strong stems; vigorous,upright, bushy growth; PP1540; [unnamed orange seedling × Demure]; int. by J&P, 1956

Princesse HGal, dp, 1824, Hardy

Princesse Adélaide M, lp, 1845, Laffay, M.; flowers pale carmine pink, medium to large, dbl., moderate fragrance; non-recurrent; foliage dark, often variegated; vigorous growth

Princesse Adélaïde d'Orléans – See **Adélaïde d'Orléans**, HSem

Princesse Alexandra – See **Princess Alexandra**, S

Princesse Alice de Monaco T, yb, 1893, Weber; flowers cream-yellow edged pink

Princesse Alix de Ligne HT, mp, RvS-Melle; [Korland × seedling]; int. in 1993

Princesse Amédée de Broglie HP, lp, 1885, Lévêque; flowers light pink, silvery towards center, reverse blush, large, full, globular; very remontant; foliage large, dark green

Princesse Amédée de Broglie HT, or, 1936, Mallerin, C.; bud very long, fiery red; flowers nasturtium-red, deeper in autumn, well-formed, large; foliage dark, glossy; vigorous growth; [(Charles P. Kilham × unknown) × Colette Clément]; int. by Meilland; Gold Medal, Bagatelle, 1935

Princesse Amélie M, m, 1851, Robert; flowers lilac-carmine, large, dbl.

Princesse Amélie d'Orléans HP, lp, 1884, Lévêque; flowers silky flesh pink, very large, full, globular

Princesse Bacchiochi M, mp, 1866, Moreau et Robert; flowers raspberry pink, buttoned eye, medium, dbl., cupped, loose, moderate fragrance; non-remontant

Princesse Béatrice – See **Prinses Béatrix**, HT

Princesse Blanche d'Orléans HP, dp, 1877, Verdier, E.; flowers dark carmine pink, shaded purple-violet, medium, full

Princesse Charles d'Arenberg HP, pb, 1877, Soupert; flowers silvery lilac rose, center darker carmine, large, full; [Dupuy Jamain × Mme de Sévigné]

Princesse Charlotte de la Trémoille – See **Mlle Charlotte de la Trémoille**, HP

Princesse Christine von Salm – See **Baron Girod de l'Ain**, HP

Princesse de Bassaraba de Brancovan – See **Mme la Princesse de Bessaraba de Brancovan**, T

Princesse de Béarn HP, mr, 1885, Lévêque; flowers velvety poppy-red, large, dbl., globular; vigorous growth; [Duc de Cazes × unknown]

Princesse de Galles – See **Princess of Wales**, F

Princesse de Joinville B, mp, 1840, Poncet; flowers bright pink, medium; sometimes classed as HP

Princesse de Lamballe A, w, before 1830, Miellez; sepals long; flowers milky white, sometimes tinted flesh, medium, very dbl., borne in clusters of 6-10, moderate fragrance; foliage gray-green; growth vigorous, compact, branching

Princesse de Metternich HP, mp, 1871, de Sansal; flowers bright, shining pink, large, full

Princesse de Monaco HT, w, 1982, Meilland, Mrs. Marie-Louise; bud large, oblong; flowers cream, edged pink, large, 35 petals, cupped, borne usually singly, slight fragrance; good repeat; foliage large, dark green, glossy; prickles moderate, large; growth upright, low, bushy; PP5067; [Ambassador × Peace]; int. by Meilland Et Cie, 1981

Princesse de Monaco, Climbing Cl HT, w; [sport of Princesse de Monaco]; int. in 1985

Princesse de Naples HP, lp, 1897, Gaëtano, Bonfiglioli & Figlio; flowers silvery pink on ground of cream, reverse lilac, very large, full; foliage light green

Princesse de Nassau N, ly, 1835, Laffay, M.; bud yellowish, tinted pink; flowers creamy yellow, fading to cream, 5-7 cm., very dbl., cupped, borne in large clusters, moderate musk fragrance; growth with crossing branches; sometimes classed as HMsk

Princesse de Nassau HGal, dp, about 1840, Miellez

Princesse de Parme M, mp, Morley, Dr B.; [William Lobb × unknown]; int. in 1988

Princesse de Portugal HGal, mp, before 1828, Pelletier; flowers bright cerise pink, very large, full; sometimes classes as D

Princesse de Sagan Ch, dr, 1887, Dubreuil; flowers crimson shaded with purple, medium, dbl., cupped; vigorous growth

Princesse de Vaudémont M, lp, about 1825, Vibert; bud globular, large; flowers medium, dbl., peony-like, moderate fragrance

Princesse de Vaudémont M, lp, 1854, Robert; flowers full, globular

Princesse de Venosa T, w, 1895, Dubreuil; bud long, ovoid; flowers white tinted blush and yellow

Princesse d'Orange – See **Princes van Oranje**, Cl Pol

Princesse d'Orient HT, Poulsen

Princesse Éléonore HGal, mr, before 1826, Miellez; flowers crimson red, large, dbl.; nearly thornless

Princesse Étienne de Croy T, m, 1898, Ketten Bros.; flowers violet rose, dbl.; [Comtesse de Labarthe × Mme Eugène Verdier]

Princesse Ghika T, mr, 1922, Nabonnand, P.; flowers brilliant red with dark reflexes, large, dbl.; [Gén. Schablikine × Papa Gontier]

Princesse Hélène HP, dp, 1837, Laffay; flowers rosy purple, medium, very dbl., globular; growth erect

Princesse Hélène d'Orléans HP, mp, 1886, Verdier, E.; flowers fresh, brilliant pink, large, full, cupped; foliage dark green, irregularly dentate; prickles numerous, strong, fairly straight; growth erect

Princesse Henri des Pays-Bas HP, w, 1868, Soupert; flowers white, tinted silvery pink and flesh, large, full

Princesse Hohenzollern T, rb, 1886, Nabonnand; flowers peach-red to crimson, well-formed, very large, dbl.

Princesse Ita HT, yb, 1943, Meilland, F.; bud oval; flowers Indian yellow edged red, open, medium, semi-dbl.; foliage leathery; vigorous, bushy growth; [Julien Potin × Charles P. Kilham]; int. by A. Meilland

Princesse Jaune HT, my, 1945, Fessel; flowers citron-yellow, large, dbl.; int. by A. Meilland

Princesse Joséphine-Charlotte Pol, op, 1945, Lens; flowers bright pink suffused apricot-salmon, small, semi-dbl., cupped, slight fragrance; very vigorous, bushy growth; [sport of Orange Triumph]

Princesse Joséphine de Flandres Pol, pb, 1888, Soupert & Notting; flowers blush pink on a ground of salmon; growth to 80 cm.; [Mignonette × Marquise de Vivens]

Princesse Josephine de Hohenzollern D, mp, 1840, Baumann; flowers medium, full

Princesse Julie d'Arenberg T, yb, 1885, Soupert & Notting; flowers yellow, shaded dark yellow, center canary, large, very full, cupped

Princesse Lamballe – See **Princesse de Lamballe**, A

Princesse Liliane HT, mr, 1954, Buyl Frères; flowers blood-red, 5 in., 25-30 petals; foliage dark; vigorous, upright growth; [Happiness × Hens Verschuren]; int. by Morse

Princesse Lise Troubezkoi HP, lp, 1878, Lévêque; flowers delicate pink, bordered white, medium, full

Princesse Louise HSem, w, 1829, Jacques; bud crimson; flowers creamy white, back petals shaded with rose, 2-2½ in., dbl., cupped, borne in clusters of 3-20; foliage dark green, smooth, sharply and regularly toothed; prickles numerous, strong, straight; [*R. sempervirens* × Parson's Pink]

Princesse Louise Cl HT, m, 1924, Nabonnand, P.; bud long, pointed; flowers rich purple, center tinted brilliant garnet, large, semi-dbl.; vigorous, climbing growth; [La France de '89 × Victor Hugo]

Princesse Louise d'Orléans HP, mp, 1886, Verdier, E.; flowers glowing, silky pink, silvery edges, large, full

Princesse Louise-Victoria HP, op, 1872, Knight; flowers dark carmine-pink, shaded peach, medium to large

Princesse Margaret d'Angleterre – See **Princess Margaret of England**, HT

Princesse Margaret d'Angleterre, Climbing – See **Princess Margaret of England, Climbing**, Cl HT

Princesse Margaretha Pol, lp, 1985, Poulsen, S.; flowers pale pink, dbl., borne in clusters, no fragrance; foliage medium size, medium green, semi-glossy; medium, bushy growth; int. in 1932

Princesse Marguerite d'Orléans HP, dp, 1888, Verdier, E.; flowers deep pink, shaded darker pink, large to very large, full

Princesse Marguerite d'Orléans T, lp, 1890, Nabonnand; flowers light pink, center carmine, reverse silvery, very large, full; [Papa Gontier × Isabelle Nabonnand]

Princesse Marie HSem, mp, 1829, Jacques; flowers bright pink, fading to pale pink, medium, full, flat, quartered, borne in clusters of 3-12; non-remontant; foliage oval, pointed, sharply dentate; prickles moderate; int. by Vibert

Princesse Marie Adelaide de Luxembourg Pol, w, 1895, Soupert & Notting; flowers white with pink tones, full, borne in clusters; foliage dark green, glossy;

growth to 2 ft.; [Mignonette × unknown]

Princesse Marie-Astrid HT, mp, 1964, Mondial Roses; bud globular; flowers deep rose to camellia-pink, large, dbl.; moderate, bushy growth; [(Mme Edouard Herriot × *R. rugosa rubra*) × La Jolie]

Princesse Marie-Christine HT, dr, 1955, Buyl Frères; bud ovoid to long; flowers blood-red, 25-30 petals; vigorous, bushy growth; [Poinsettia × Ena Harkness]

Princesse Marie Clotilde Napoléon Pol, w, 1924, Opdebeeck; flowers white shaded pink, base pale yellow, large, dbl.; vigorous growth

Princesse Marie Dagmar – See **Socrate**, T

Princesse Marie Dagmar T, 1919, Lévêque

Princesse Marie Dolgorouky HP, lp, 1878, Gonod; flowers light pink, often striped with white, very large, dbl.; [Anna de Diesbach × unknown]

Princesse Marie d'Orléans HP, mp, 1885, Verdier; flowers bright cerise pink shaded silvery, large, full; foliage light green, glossy; growth upright

Princesse Marie José Pol, w, 1924, Opdebeeck; flowers white shaded rose, base yellow, large, dbl.; vigorous growth

Princesse Marie José HT, or, 1925, Klettenberg-Londes; bud long, pointed; flowers orange-scarlet, dbl., moderate fruity fragrance; int. by F.J. Grootendorst

Princesse Olympie HP, w, 1858, Béluze; flowers greenish white

Princesse Paola HT, mp, 1967, Hendrickx; bud cerise-pink; flowers bright pink, 5 in., dbl., high-centered, intense fragrance; foliage glossy; vigorous growth

Princesse Queen Pol, pb

Princesse Radziwill HP, mp, 1883, Lévêque; flowers carmine pink shaded bright crimson, large, full; foliage light green

Princesse Royale M, mp, 1846, Portemer; bud well mossed; flowers rosy flesh, 5-6 cm., dbl., globular, borne in clusters; foliage dark green, oval, pointed, much serrated; prickles short, saffron; [Ponctuée × Tuscany]

Princesse Sophie de Bavière F, lp, RvS-Melle; [Melglory × seedling]; int. in 1996

Princesse Stéphanie – See **Fiançailles de la Princesse Stéphanie et de l'Archiduc Rodolphe**, N

Princesse Stéphanie T, op, 1880, Levet, A.; flowers salmon-yellow, large, dbl.; very vigorous growth; [Gloire de Dijon × unknown]

Princesse Stéphanie de Belgique HT, dp, 1929, Soupert & Notting; bud long, pointed; flowers carmine, center deeper, dbl.; [Gen. MacArthur × seedling]; int. by C. Soupert

Princesse Vera Orbelioni HT, op, 1909, Schwartz; flowers light salmon-pink, large, dbl.; [Kaiserin Auguste Viktoria × Sénateur Saint-Romme]

Princesse Verona S, mp, 1985, Buck, Dr. Griffith J.; flowers Neyron rose, 4 in., 30 petals, cupped, high-centered, borne singly and in clusters of up to 15, slight honey clove fragrance; repeat bloom; foliage leathery, dark olive green; prickles awl-like, tan; upright (4 ft.), bushy, compact growth; hardy; [Verona × Prairie Princess]; int. by Iowa State University, 1984

Princesse Wilhelmine des Pays-Bas Pol, w, 1886, Soupert & Notting; flowers bright white, greenish at center, small to medium, full, moderate fragrance; [Mignonette × Mme Damaizin]

Princesse Yvonne Ghika HT, w, 1927, Mühle; flowers white, center salmon, dbl.; [Stadtrat Glaser × unknown]

Principal A. H. Pirie HT, mp, 1910, Bernaix fils; flowers silvery pink, medium, very full, moderate fragrance

Principe da Beïra HP, m, 1890, da Costa; flowers purple

Principe de Napoli HT, my, 1937, Aicardi Bros.; bud long; flowers large, dbl.; foliage clear green; vigorous growth

Principe de Piemonte HT, dr, 1929, Giacomasso; flowers crimson-red, large; [Mrs Edward Powell × Gen. MacArthur]

Principessa delle Rose HT, mr, 1953, Aicardi, D.; bud long, pointed; flowers lilac-rose, large, 30-40 petals, cupped, moderate fragrance; very vigorous, upright growth; PP1355; [Julien Potin × Sensation]; int. by V. Asseretto

Principessa di Napoli T, lp, 1898, Brauer/Ketten Bros.; bud long; flowers pale rose, base of petals cream, large, full, borne mostly solitary, moderate Maréchal Niel fragrance; [Duc de Magenta × Safrano]

Prins Claus – See **Rosalynn Carter**, Gr

Prins Hamlet HT, lp, 1927, Mohr; bud long, pointed; flowers light pink, base yellow, open, large, semi-dbl., high-centered; foliage light, leathery; vigorous, bushy growth; [sport of Ophelia]

Prins Willem-Alexander F, ob, 1973, Verschuren; flowers coral-vermilion, 2-3 in., single, borne in trusses, slight fragrance; free-flowering; foliage dark green, red when young; growth bushy, large; [Tropicana × Europeana]; int. by de Ruiter New Roses, Ltd., 1972

Prinses Astrid HT, yb, DVP Melle; [Australian Gold × Princesse Alix de Ligne]; int. in 2000

Prinses Béatrix HT, ob, 1940, Busiman; bud long, pointed; flowers terra-cotta, shaded light apricot, large, dbl., cupped, intense fruity fragrance; foliage leathery, bronze; vigorous, bushy growth; [Heinrich Wendland × Max Krause]; int. by Morse

Prinses Christina F, mr, 1945, Buisman, G. A. H.; bud large; flowers clear carmine-red, dbl., borne in clusters; very vigorous growth; [Lafayette × Donald Prior]

Prinses Juliana HT, dr, 1918, Leenders, M.; bud long, pointed; flowers deep crimson-red, shaded darker, dbl.; foliage dark; vigorous growth; [Gen. MacArthur × Marie van Houtte]

Prinses Mathilde F, r, DVP Melle; flowers large, dbl, moderate soft fragrance; [Melglory × Marchenland]; int. in 2004

Prinses van Oranje, Climbing – See **Gloria Mundi, Climbing**, Cl Pol

Prinsesse Astrid af Norge F, ob, 1958, Poulsen, S.; flowers bright orange, semi-dbl.; vigorous, upright growth; [Pinocchio × Pinocchio]

Prinsesse Benedikte S, yb, Poulsen; flowers yellow blend, 10-15 cm., 25 petals, slight fragrance; foliage dark; growth narrow, bushy (20-40 cm); int. by Poulsen Roser, 2005

Prinsesse Margrethe HT, op, Poulsen, S.; flowers dark salmon-orange, dbl., slight fragrance; free-flowering; strong stems; growth vigorous, upright; [Queen Elizabeth × (Independence × Golden Scepter)]; int. in 1963

Printemps HT, pb, 1948, Mallerin, C.; bud long; flowers old-rose tinted light red, reverse yellow, 4 in., dbl.; foliage glossy, dark; very vigorous growth; [Trylon × Brazier]; int. by URS

Printemps Fleuri HMult, m, 1922, Turbat; flowers bright purple passing to carmine-pink, stamens yellow, 3 cm., semi-dbl., borne in clusters of 5-15; [Étoile Luisante × unknown]

Prinz Hamlet HT, lp, 1927, Mohr; flowers large, dbl.

Prinz Hirzeprinzchen HMult, m, 1912, Geschwind, R.; flowers purple-red, striped white, lighter reverse, 5-6 cm., semi-dbl., borne in clusters of up to 20, moderate fragrance

Prinz Max zu Schaumburg-Lippe HT, op, 1934, von Würtemberg, Herzogin Elsa; flowers salmon-pink, large, dbl., intense fragrance; vigorous growth; [Frau Karl Druschki × Lyon Rose]

Prinzessin Bathildis zu Schaumburg-Lippe HT, ly, 1929, von Württemberg, Herzogin Elsa; flowers yellowish-white, very large, dbl.; sometimes classed as HP

Prinzessin Elsa zu Schaumburg-Lippe – See **Prinzessin Bathildis zu Schaumburg-Lippe**, HT

Prinzessin Hildegard – See **Prinzessin Hildegard von Bayern**, HT

Prinzessin Hildegard von Bayern HT, my, 1917, Lambert, P.; flowers bright yellow, fading to cream-yellow, large, dbl., moderate fragrance; [Frau Karl Druschki × Friedrich Harms]

Prinzessin Irrlieb F, mr, 1963, Kordes, R.; flowers velvety bright red, dbl., borne in large clusters; moderate, symmetrical growth

Prinzessin Leontine Fürstenberg T, my, 1908, Chalupecky; flowers large, full; [sport of Mme Lombard]

Prinzessin Ludwig von Bayern HMult, mp, 1911, Brög; flowers bright pink, lighter reverse, 3½ cm., dbl., borne in medium clusters, no fragrance; [Turner's Crimson Rambler × unknown]

Prinzessin M. von Arenberg HT, w, 1928, Leenders, M.; flowers rosy white, shaded pale rose-pink, dbl., cupped, intense fragrance; [Ophelia × Los Angeles]

Prinzessin Maria Teresa F, lp, Lens, Louis; flowers medium, dbl.; int. in 1982

Prinzessin Marie HT, lp, 1907, Lindemann; flowers large, full; [Mme Caroline Testout × Mme Mélanie Willermoz]

Prinzessin Tatiana Wasiltchikoff HT, lp, 1941, Spath; flowers flesh-pink, dbl.; long stems; upright growth

Prinzessin von Battenberg T, w, 1912, Brauer; flowers white, aging to flesh pink

Prior M. Oberthau HMult, dp, 1923, Bruder Alfons; flowers rose red, white center, 3½ cm., dbl., flat, borne in medium clusters, slight fragrance; non-recurrent; few prickles

Priory Pride HT, mp, 1987, Greensitt, J.A.; flowers medium, full, moderate fragrance; foliage medium size, medium green, semi-glossy; bushy growth; [Pink Peace × Chicago Peace]; int. by Nostell Priory Rose Gardens, 1981

Priory Rose HT, mp, 1987, Greensitt, J.A.; flowers medium, full, intense fragrance; foliage medium size, medium green, semi-glossy; upright growth; [seedling × seedling]; int. by Nostell Priory Rose Gardens, 1976

Priscilla – See **Marie Lambert**, T

Priscilla HT, mp, 1922, Montgomery Co.; bud long, pointed; flowers pink, outer petals rose-pink, very large, dbl., cupped; foliage leathery, glossy; vigorous growth; [seedling × Ophelia]; int. by A.N. Pierson

Priscilla Burton F, rb, 1977, McGredy, Sam IV; flowers deep carmine pink and white blend (with variable combinations), 2½ in., 10 petals, borne in trusses, moderate fragrance; free-flowering; foliage glossy, dark green; free, hardy growth; [Old Master × seedling]; int. by Mattock; President's International Trophy, RNRS, 1976

Prissy Missy Min, mp, 1965, Williams, Ernest D.; flowers medium pink, reverse lighter, small, very dbl., moderate spicy fragrance; vigorous, bushy, dwarf growth; [Spring Song × seedling]; int. by Mini-Roses

Pristine HT, w, 1977, Warriner, William A.; bud long, pointed ovoid; flowers near white, shaded light pink, imbricated, 5-6 in., 28-35 petals, high-centered, borne singly or several together, slight fragrance; good repeat; foliage very large, dark green, semi-glossy; prickles numerous, medium, hooked downward, brown; stems medium, strong; vigorous, upright growth; PP3997;

[White Masterpiece × First Prize]; int. by J&P, 1978; Gold Medal, Portland, 1979, Edland Fragrance Medal, ARS, 1979

Pristine, Climbing Cl HT, w; int. after 1978

Pristine Pavement HRg, w, Baum; flowers pure white, semi-dbl., moderate fragrance; foliage glossy; compact, mounding (3 ft.) growth; int. in 1990

Prithi Rani HT, pb, Ghosh, Mr. & Mrs. S.; flowers porcelain pink with deep center, reverse pinkish white, dbl.; strong growth; int. in 2001

Priti Pol, lp, Kasturi; flowers pink to white, globular; prolific; [sport of Margo Koster]; int. by KSG Son, 1971

Priub HT, ly, 1990, Umsawasdi, Dr. Theera; flowers yellowish-cream turning to pure white, large, 5 petals; foliage medium size, medium green, semi-glossy; numerous prickles; vigorous, upright, tall growth; [seedling × seedling]; int. by Theera Umsawasdi, 1986

Prive Gr, mp

Privet iz Alma-Aty HT, op, 1958, Sushkov & Besschetnova; flowers pink tinted orange, large, 60 petals; foliage dark, glossy; very vigorous growth; [Independence × Peace]

Priyadarshini HT, pb, IARI; flowers rhodamine pink with darker edges; free-flowering; dedicated to late Mrs. Indira Gandhi; int. in 1988

Priyatama HT, pb, 1984, Viraraghavan, M.S. Viru; bud ovoid; flowers deep pink, paler edges and reverse, medium, 35 petals, high-centered, borne singly; foliage glossy, slightly wrinkled; prickles red; growth bushy; [Inge Horstmann × Picasso]; int. by K.S.G. Son's Roses, 1981

Probuzeni – See **Awakening**, LCl

Prodaná Nevesta S, w, 1934, Brada, Dr.; flowers snow-white, center tinted yellow, borne in large clusters; non-recurrent; foliage light, glossy; vigorous growth; int. by Böhm

Prodigieuse HT, ob, Croix; flowers orange with silver reverse, large, 65 petals; good repeat; foliage dark green, disease-resistant; int. by Roseraies Paul Croix, 1969

Professeur Bérard HT, dp, 1930, Laperrière; flowers bright purple-carmine, base yellow, petals laciniated, dbl.; foliage leathery, dark; very vigorous growth; [Hadley × The Queen Alexandra Rose]

Professeur Christian Cabrol HMsk, pb, Lefebvre; flowers carmine with white center, small, single, borne in clusters of 8-10; free-flowering; growth compact (3 ft.), vigorous; named for professor of cardiac surgery.; int. in 1993

Professeur Déaux HT, ly, 1935, Pernet-Ducher; flowers light yellow streaked chamois, dbl.; foliage glossy, dark, bronze; long stems; very vigorous growth; int. by Gaujard

Prof Émile Perrot D, mp, 1931; flowers light pink, medium, dbl.; brought from Persia by Prof. Perrot; may be synonymous with Ispahan, Kazanlik, or Trigintipetala; int. by Turbat

Professeur Ganiviat T, pb, 1890, Perrier; flowers salmon carmine, shaded carmine purple, large, very dbl., high-centered; growth to 1 m.

Professeur Jean Bernard HT, dr, 1990, Delbard & Chabert; bud cupped; flowers very large, 25-30 petals; foliage dark green, abundant; bushy growth; [(Charles Mallerin × Divine) × (Tropicana × (Rome Glory × Impeccable))]; int. in 1989

Professeur Jolibois HP, dr, 1888, Verdier, E.; flowers dark red, magenta, carmine and flame, large, full, globular

Professeur Jules Courtois HP, mr, 1886, Bire; flowers glowing red, shaded lilac, medium, dbl.; [Général Jacqueminot × unknown]

Professeur Maxime Cornu HP, mr, 1885, Lévêque; flowers cerise red, very large, full, some fragrance; recurrent; foliage lanceolate, glaucous green

Prof. Alfred Dufour F, mr, 1970, Cazzaniga, F. G.; flowers bright red, medium, semi-dbl.; foliage light green; compact growth; [Paprika × Coup de Foudre]; int. in 1961

Professor Baranov HT, yb, 1947, Vogel, M.; flowers large, dbl.

Prof. Bento Carqueja HT, op, 1936, Moreira da Silva; bud long, pointed; flowers pink and salmon, shaded coral-red, large, dbl., high-centered; foliage soft; vigorous growth; [Ophelia × Mme Edouard Herriot]

Professor Boesman F, mp, RvS-Melle; flowers dbl.; [Melflor × Melglory]; int. in 1992; Gold Medal, Courtrai, 1991

Professor Borza HT, or, 1940, Ambrosi; flowers medium, dbl.

Prof C. S. Sargent HWich, my, 1903, Farrell; flowers yellow, center deeper, fading to cream, 2½ in., dbl., borne in small clusters, moderate fragrance; early bloom; foliage small, ornamental; vigorous growth; [*R. wichurana* × Souv. d'Auguste Metral]

Prof Chris Barnard HT, mr, 1972, Fisher, P.; flowers blood-red, pointed, 4 in., 40 petals; foliage glossy; upright growth; [Ena Harkness × Karl Herbst]; int. by Eden Rose Nursery, 1970

Prof. Costa Leite HT, my, 1955, Moreira da Silva; very vigorous growth; [Peace × Julien Potin]

Professor Dr Hans Molisch Cl HT, mp, 1923, Mühle; flowers silvery pink, medium to large, very dbl., borne in small clusters; numerous prickles

Professor Dr Kurth HT, mr, Schmid, P.; flowers large, dbl.; int. in 1960

Prof. Dr von Beck HT, pb, 1927, Ries; flowers bright rose-pink, reverse carmine-red, dbl.; [Mme Abel Chatenay × Farbenkonigin]

Professor Erich Maurer Cl HT, mp, 1939, Tepelmann; flowers dark pink, lighter at center, 5-6 in., semi-dbl. to dbl.

Professor Fred Ziady HT, my, 1987, Kordes, R.; flowers clear medium yellow, 43 petals, high-centered, star-shaped, borne usually singly, moderate fragrance; foliage medium green; prickles straight, dark brown; growth medium, sturdy; [Lusambo × Deep Secret]; int. by Ludwigs Roses Pty. Ltd., 1985; Trial Ground Certificate, Durbanville, 2006

Professor Gnau HT, w, 1928, Tantau; bud long, pointed; flowers creamy white; [Oskar Cordel × seedling]

Professor Ibrahim LCl, mp, 1937, Krause; flowers rose-pink, base yellow, large, borne in clusters of 4-5; very vigorous, climbng (over 13 ft.) growth; [Daisy Hill × Talisman]

Professor Knöll HT, mr, Berger, W.; flowers very large, very dbl.; int. in 1964

Prof. Leite Pinto HT, mr, 1960, Moreira da Silva; flowers cherry-red, center ochre; [Buccaneer × La Jolla]

Prof M. C. Nath HT, dp, 2005, Shastri, N.V.; flowers deep mauve pink, 11 cm., dbl., borne mostly solitary, moderate fragrance; free-flowering; foliage medium size, medium green, matte; prickles medium, elongated, gray, moderate; compact, medium (35 in.) growth; [Jadis × Swarthmore]; int. by N.V.Shastri, 1998

Prof Madhab Chandra Nath – See **Prof M. C. Nath**, HT

Prof. N. E. Hansen HRg, dr, 1892, Budd; flowers rich velvety red

Prof O. L. Kunz S, mp, Hetzel; int. in 1980

Professor Panalla HT, Dot, Simon; int. in 1988

Prof Reynaldo Santos HT, Moreira da Silva, A.

Professor Schmeil HFt, yb, 1925, Kröger; flowers light orange-yellow, large, semi-dbl.

Profil HT, op, VEG; flowers coral pink, large, dbl.; int. in 1985

Profile Gr, op, 1988, McGredy, Sam IV; flowers orange blend, large, full; foliage large, medium green, semi-glossy; upright growth; [Freude × ((Arthur Bell × unknown) × Sunsong)]; int. by McGredy Roses International, 1988

Profondo Rosso F, dr, Kordes; flowers very dark red, semi-dbl.; upright (60-70 cm.), compact, strong growth; int. by Rose Barni

Profumo Romano HT, Zandri, R.

Profusion HT, dp, 1939, Dickson, A.; bud long, pointed; flowers carmine, base orange-yellow, dbl.; vigorous growth

Profusion HT, op, 1944, Meilland, F.; bud very long; flowers orange-salmon and carmine; foliage glossy; [Mme Henri Guillot × Signora]

Progress HT, pb, 1890, Drögemüller; flowers shining carmine, shaded yellow, large, dbl., moderate fragrance; [Mme Bérard × Marie van Houtte]

Progress – See **Fortschritt**, F

Prohadka Maje HT

Prolet S, pb, 1985, Staikov, Prof. Dr. V.; flowers brick, shaded deep pink, medium, 85 petals; non-recurrent; foliage light green; vigorous, upright, branching growth; [General Stefanik × Bonn]; int. by Kalaydjiev and Chorbadjiiski, 1975

Prolifera – See **Childling**, C

Prolifera de Redouté C, mp, before 1824; sepals long, fringed; flowers rose pink, large; new buds often protrude from the center, full, rosette, intense fragrance; non-remontant; growth to 6 ft.; probably synonymous with King of Holland

Prolifère – See **Childling**, C

Prolifère HGal, lp, before 1804, Dupont (?); flowers medium size, delicate pink, petals shell-shaped, very dbl.; prickles light brown; Agathe group; very subject to proliferation

Prolifère M, dp, before 1826, Philippe; flowers deep-rose, too full to open well at times, large, cupped; vigorous growth

Prolific – See **Gracilis**, M

Prom Date Min, dp, 1989, Moore, Ralph S.; bud short, pointed; flowers deep pink, aging lighter, medium, 38 petals, globular, borne singly, no fragrance; profuse; foliage medium size, medium green, matte; prickles straight, pointed, medium, gray to brown; upright, bushy, medium growth; hips globular, orange; [Sheri Anne × (seedling × Fairy Moss)]; int. by Sequoia Nursery

Prom Night MinFl, pb, 1987, Zipper, Herbert; flowers creamy yellow, shading to pink with deep pink flushing the edges, very dbl.; foliage large, medium green, matte; upright, bushy, candelabra-formed growth; [Poker Chip × Libby]; int. by Magic Moment Miniature Roses

Promenade Min, dr, 1985, Lyon; flowers very dark red, informal, ruffled, small, 35 petals, borne singly; foliage medium size, dark, matte; bushy growth; [Red Can Can × seedling]; int. by M.B. Farm Min. Roses, Inc.

Promethean S, rb, 1985, James, John; flowers medium red, reverse darker, white eye, medium, 12 petals; repeat bloom; foliage medium size, light green, smooth, matte; bushy growth; [(Blanche Mallerin × Pink Hat) × *R. multibracteata*]

Promethée D, m, about 1835, Vibert

Prominent Gr, or, 1971, Kordes, R.; bud long, pointed; flowers large, 33 petals, cupped; free-flowering; foliage matte; upright growth; PP3380; [Zorina × Colour Wonder]; int. by McGredy & Son, 1970; Gold Medal, Portland, 1975

Promise HMult, op, 1929, Cant, F.; flowers salmon-pink, stamens bright yellow, single, borne in large clusters, moderate fragrance; non-recurrent; foliage almost evergreen; vigorous, climbing growth; [sport of Mme Eugène Résal]

Promise HT, lp, 1974, Warriner, William A.; bud ovoid, pointed; flowers camellia pink, 4½-5 in., 40-45 petals, high-centered, borne usually singly; good repeat; foliage large, glossy; prickles medium, hooked downward; stems long, strong; vigorous growth; PP3492; [South Seas × Peace]; int. by J&P, 1976; Gold Medal, Bagatelle, 1976

Promise Me HT, w, 1971, Jelly; flowers 4 in., 45 petals, high-centered, slight sweetbriar fragrance; foliage matte, dark, leathery; vigorous, upright growth; PP3167; [Snowsong Supreme × seedling]; int. by E.G. Hill Co., 1969

Promotion F, mp, 1966, Verbeek; bud ovoid; flowers pink, medium, dbl., borne in clusters; foliage dark; [seedling × Miracle]

Prophecy Min, mr, 1998, Williams, Ernest D.; flowers rose red, heat stable, 1-1¼ in., very dbl., high-centered, borne mostly singly; foliage medium size, medium green, semi-glossy; prickles moderate; upright, bushy, medium (18 in.) growth; [Red Delight × Twilight Trail]; int. by Texas Mini Roses, 1997

Prophyta HT, ab, de Ruiter, G.

Prose – See **Burgundy Iceberg**, F

Proserpine HGal, m, 1835, Prévost; flowers velvety black-purple, shaded bronze, medium, full

Proserpine B, m, 1841, Mondeville/Verdier, V.; bud round; flowers crimson to purplish crimson, variable, medium, full, borne in clusters of 3-4; foliage dark green; prickles hooked, red; the cultivar sold in the U.S. as Meteor may be the same as this

Prosper Laugier HP, mr, 1883, Verdier, E.; flowers scarlet-red, large, 30 petals, cupped, moderate fragrance; recurrent bloom; growth tall (5 ft.)

Prosperity HMsk, w, 1919, Pemberton; bud creamy white flushed pale pink; flowers ivory white, small to medium, semi-dbl., rosette, borne in very large clusters, moderate fragrance; recurrent bloom; foliage glossy; vigorous, pillar (6-8 ft.) growth; [Marie-Jeanne × Perle des Jardins]

Prospero S, dr, 1983, Austin, David; flowers large, full, flat, rosette, intense fragrance; good repeat; foliage medium size, dark green, matte; weak, upright (3 ft.) growth; PP9008; [The Knight × seedling]; int. by David Austin Roses, 1982

Proteiformis HRg, w, 1894; flowers semi-dbl., borne in clusters; foliage variable; [*R. rugosa alba* × unknown]

Proud Bride S, ab, Austin, David; int. in 1992

Proud Heritage Min, dr, 1986, Jolly, Nelson F.; flowers patio, large, 28 petals, high-centered, borne in sprays of 2-3; foliage medium size, medium green, matte; prickles light green to brown, hooked downward; upright, bushy growth; hips globular, orange; PP6561; [Red Beauty × Big John]; int. by Rosehill Farm

Proud Land HT, dr, 1969, Morey, Dennison; bud urn-shaped, large; flowers deep red, large, very full, cupped, borne singly and several together, moderate tea fragrance; free-flowering; foliage large, dark green, leathery; prickles medium; stems long, strong; growth vigorous, upright; PP2737; [Chrysler Imperial × seedling]; int. by J&P

Proud Mary Gr, or, 1991, Twomey, Jerry; bud pointed; flowers scarlet red, medium, 19-21 petals, moderate damask fragrance; foliage medium size, dark green, semi-glossy; upright, bushy, medium growth; PP7981; [(Sarabande × Marina) × Royalty]; int. by DeVor Nurseries, Inc., 1991

Proud Titania S, w, 1983, Austin, David; flowers white with apricot blush, large, 35 petals, flat, rosette, intense fragrance; recurrent; foliage small, medium green, semi-glossy; growth upright, medium; [seedling × seedling]

Provence HT, ob, 1945, Paolino; flowers orange, tinted copper and pink, well-formed; int. by A. Meilland

Provence HT, w, Dorieux; int. by Roses Dorieux, 1996

Provence Bergsoe C, mp

Provence Moss – See **Unique Moss**, M

Provence Pink C, mp, 1759

Providence MinFl, my, 2003, Tucker, Robbie; flowers non-fading, 1½ -2¼ in., full, borne in small clusters, no fragrance; foliage medium green, glossy; prickles small ¼ in., straight to slightly turned, light red to brown; growth bushy, medium (30 in.); exhibition, cut flower, garden decorative; [Cal Poly × Kristin]; int. by Rosemania, 2003

Province d'Anjou F, mr, Croix; flowers luminous red; int. in 1967; Certificate of Merit, Geneva-Saverne

Provincialis Hybrida – See **Spong**, C

Provins Ancien HGal, lp, before 1906, Cochet, P.

Provins Blanc – See **Fausse Unique**, D

Provins Double – See **L'Évêque**, HGal

Provins Marbré – See **Marmorea**, HGal

Provins Panaché – See ***R. gallica versicolor*** (Linnaeus)

Provins Panaché B, pb, about 1860, Fontaine; flowers light pink, striped deep pink, dbl., cupped, borne in clusters, intense fragrance; recurrent; foliage bluish-green; upright (6 ft.), narrow growth; sometimes classed as P

Provins Renoncule HGal, mp, before 1810, Cartier/Dupont; flowers clear purple-pink, lighter at edges, green pip center, very dbl., moderate fragrance; foliage oval, edged pink, finely dentate; prickles small, straight, numerous, brown

Provins Renonculée – See **Provins Renoncule**, HGal

Provins Rose – See ***R. gallica*** (Linnaeus)

Prudence Cl HT, op, 1938, Fitzhardinge; flowers salmon-pink, large, semi-dbl., cupped; recurrent bloom; very vigorous, climbing (10 ft.) growth; [Warrawee × Souv. de Claudius Pernet]; int. by Hazlewood Bros.

Prudence Besson HP, mp, 1865, Lacharme; flowers cerise pink to carmine red, very large, dbl., flat

Prudence Elizabeth HT, w, 2007, Jacobs, Mrs. Margaret; flowers 12 cm., dbl., borne mostly solitary; foliage large, medium green, semi-glossy; prickles medium, regular, maroon, moderate; growth upright, tall (1½ m.); garden decoration; [Mount Shasta × (Elizabeth Arden × Crimson Glory)]; int. by Laurie Newman, 2008

Prudhoe Peach HT, ab, 1971, Wood; flowers apricot-peach, 25 petals; foliage glossy, dark, leathery; free growth; [sport of Piccadilly]; int. by Homedale Nursery, 1970

Pruhonice S, mp, Vecera, L.; flowers light coral-pink, golden stamens, large, semi-dbl., flat, slight fragrance; recurrent; foliage pewter-green, matte; flowers can be double in fall; int. by Pruhonice, 1973

Prunella Stack HT, ab, 2000, Jellyman, J.S.; flowers apricot, reverse deep pink, 3 in., dbl., borne in small clusters, slight fragrance; foliage medium size, dark green, glossy; few prickles; growth upright, low (2 ft.); patio, containers; [Cider Cup × Don Charlton]

Psyche HMult, mp, 1899, Paul, W.; flowers medium pink, paler reverse to medium, 5 cm., dbl., borne in clusters of 15-25; tall (4-5 m.) growth; [Turner's Crimson Rambler × Golden Fairy]

Pteragonis S, ly, 1937, Krause; flowers creamy yellow, medium, single, moderate fragrance; prickles pinkish-red

P'tit Pacha F, rb, 1965, Combe; bud pointed; flowers geranium-red edged dark red, large, semi-dbl.; moderate growth; [seedling × Coup de Foudre]; Gold Medal, Madrid, 1963

PTMR HT, Kurowski, L.; int. in 1975

Pu Tâo Hóng Ch, mr

Puanani F, lp, 1997, Belendez, Kitty; flowers medium, single, borne in small clusters; foliage medium size, medium green, semi-glossy; bushy, medium (3 ft.) growth; [sport of Playgirl]

Pubescens – See **Manning's Blush**, HEg

Puccini HT, rb, 1968, Ellick; flowers red, veined yellow, 4-6 in., 26-33 petals; foliage large, light; very vigorous growth; [Opera × Teenager]

Puccini HMsk, lp, 2000, Lens, Louis; flowers medium pink, white center, 2 cm., single, borne in large clusters, slight fragrance; foliage medium size, medium green, semi-glossy; prickles moderate; growth upright, medium (60-80 cm.); hips globular, red; [(*R. luciae* × unknown) × (Ballerina × Robin Hood)]; int. by Louis Lens N.V., 1984; Grand Rose du Siecle, Lyon, 1985

Puccini's Daughter F, ob, 1972, Ellick; flowers orange-flame, reverse streaked yellow, 4 in., 20-25 petals; foliage glossy, dark; very vigorous, upright growth; [(Puccini × Peace) × Orange Sensation]; int. by Excelsior Roses

Pucelle de Lille HGal, pb, before 1828, Miellez; flowers deep purple-red, fading quickly to pink, medium to large, full, borne in clusters

Puck HT, mr, 1921, Bees; bud long, pointed; flowers cherry-crimson, dbl.; [Lyon Rose × Gen. MacArthur]

Puck F, or, 1960, Leenders, J.; bud globular; flowers cinnabar-red, large, dbl., cupped; foliage leathery; moderate growth; [Pour Toi × Margaret McGredy]

Puck Pulling Cl Min, lp, 1997, Pulling-Smith, Mrs. Pam; flowers small, single, borne in large clusters; foliage medium size, medium green, semi-glossy; spreading, tall (8 ft.) growth; [seedling × seedling]

Pucker Up Min, or, 1984, Bennett, Dee; bud small; flowers bright, velvety orient-red with some darker shadowing, 1-1½ in., 20-25 petals, urn-shaped, borne usually singly, slight fragrance; good repeat; foliage medium size, medium green, semi-glossy; prickles small, slender, straight, reddish; upright, bushy growth; PP5407; [Futura × Avandel]; int. by Tiny Petals Nursery, 1983

Pudsey Bear HT, dy, Chessum, Paul; int. in 1996

Puerta del Sol Cl HT, my, 1986, Delbard; flowers medium golden yellow, large, 28 petals, borne in small clusters, slight fragrance; foliage deep green, glossy; vigorous, climbing (to 9 ft.) growth; [(Queen Elizabeth × Provence) × (Michele Meilland × Bayadere)]; int. in 1971

Puerto del Sol – See **Guillaume**, F

Puerto Rico F, ob, 1974, Delbard; flowers orange, reverse blended with yellow, medium, dbl., cupped, borne in large clusters, slight spicy fragrance; good repeat; foliage small to medium size, bronze, leathery, semi-glossy; prickles medium, hooked downward, brown; vigorous, bushy growth; PP3519; [Zambra × (Orange Triumph × Floradora)]; int. by Armstrong Nursery

Puerto Rico Shell Pink Noisette N, lp

Pullman Orient Express – See **Love and Peace**, HT

Pulmonaire – See **La Maculée**, HGal

Pulsar HT, mr; flowers bright red, dbl., high-centered, no fragrance; growth to 3 ft.

Pumila – See **Rosier d'Amour**, HGal

Pumila Ch, w, about 1806, Colville; flowers star-like, small to medium

Pumila Min, dp; bud long, pointed; flowers bright pink to red, dbl.; good repeat; almost thornless; dwarf (8-10 in.) growth

Pumila Alba N, w, 1847, Hardy; flowers pure white, very small, cupped; foliage dark green

Pumpkin Frost Min, r, 1995, Williams, Ernest; flowers russet, 1-1¼ in., dbl., borne in small clusters; foliage medium size, dark green, semi-glossy; some prickles; low (12 in.), compact growth; [seedling × Twilight Trail]; int. by Texas Mini Roses, 1995

Punch F, dp, 1960, Delforge; flowers raspberry-red, open, medium, semi-dbl., borne in clusters; foliage glossy; moderate, bushy growth; [Luc Varenne × Lafayette]

Punctata – See **Belle Herminie**, HGal

Punicea – See ***R. foetida bicolor*** ((Jacquin) Willmott)

Punkin Min, ob, 1983, Bennett, Dee; flowers orange with yellow eye, ages red, 5 petals, borne singly, no fragrance; foliage small, medium green, semi-glossy; upright growth; [Orange Honey × Orange Honey]; int. by Tiny Petals Nursery

Puppy Love Min, ob, 1978, Schwartz, Ernest W.; bud pointed; flowers pink, coral, orange blend, 1½ in., 23 petals, high-centered, borne mostly singly, slight fragrance; good repeat; foliage matte; prickles very few, soft. thin, pointed; upright, compact growth; PP4292; [Zorina × seedling]; int. by Nor'East Min. Roses; AOE, ARS, 1979

Pur Caprice S, w, Delbard; few prickles; int. by Georges Delbard SA, 1997

Pur Sang – See **Wiener Walzer**, F

Pure – See **Pure Hit**, MinFl

Pure Abundace – See **Great North Eastern Rose**, F

Pure and Simple S, w, 2002, Horner, Colin P.; flowers pure white, small, semi-dbl., borne in large clusters, slight fragrance; foliage small, medium green, glossy; prickles small, curved, moderate; growth spreading, low (45 cm.); garden decorative, groundcover; [Golden Future × Baby Love]; int. by Paul Chessum Roses, 2002

Pure Bliss HT, mp, 1999, Dickson, Alex; flowers pale pink, reverse mid-pink, 2¼-2½ in., full, borne mostly singly, moderate fragrance; foliage medium size, medium green, semi-glossy; prickles moderate; patio; upright, medium growth; [Elina × seedling]; int. by Dickson Nurseries Ltd., 1994; Gold Medal, Belfast, 1997

Pure Gold S, my; flowers amber to creamy yellow, large, dbl., borne in clusters of three, moderate fragrance; repeats quickly and freely; foliage dark green; growth upright, vigorous (4 × 3 ft.); int. by Harkness, 2002

Pure Hit MinFl, w, Poulsen; bud short; flowers ivory, 2-3 in., 30 petals, high-centered, borne singly and in clusters, moderate fragrance; good repeat; foliage dark green, glossy; prickles medium, short, straight; growth bushy, upright (40-60 cm.); PP9996; [Pink Delight × seedling]; int. by Poulsen Roser, 1996

Pure Love HT, w, 1988, Perry, Anthony; bud medium, pointed; flowers 4½ in., 35-40 petals, cupped, borne singly, slight fragrance; recurrent; foliage medium size, dark green, semi-glossy; prickles slight recurved, average, brown-green; upright, medium growth; hips globular, average, grey-red; PP6781; [Queen Elizabeth × World Peace]; int. by Co-Operative Rose Growers, 1987

Pure Magic Min, ob; [sport of Sweet Magic]; int. by Whartons, 1999

Pure Magic F, w, Matthews; int. by Matthews Nurseries, 2000

Pure Orange Typhoon Sport HT, ob; [sport of Typhoon]; int. by Vintage Gardens

Pure Perfume S, w, 2005, Zary, Keith W.; bud pointed, ovoid; flowers 3-4 in., very full, cupped, borne in small clusters, intense grapefruit fragrance; foliage large, dark green, glossy; prickles 6-8 mm., straight, greyed-orange, moderate; upright, branching, medium (5 ft.) growth; PP16864; [Fabulous! × Perfume Perfection (a.k.a. Cotillion)]; int. by Jackson & Perkins Wholesale, Inc., 2005

Pure Poetry F, yb, 1998, Zary, Dr. Keith W.; flowers yellow-orange with pink petal edges, 4 in., 30-35 petals, high-centered, then flat, borne in small clusters, slight fragrance; recurrent; foliage medium size, dark green, glossy; prickles numerous, straight; compact (2½ ft.) growth; PP10282; [seedling × Tournament of Roses]; int. by Bear Creek Gardens, Inc., 1997

Puregold HT, dy, 1961, Robichon; bud long, pointed; flowers rich yellow, 3-3½ in., 30 petals, high-centered, intense fragrance; foliage leathery, dark, glossy; vigorous, upright growth; PP1859; [Helen Fox × (Mrs Pierre S. duPont × Joanna Hill)]; int. as Fanion, Ilgenfritz Nursery, 1961

Purezza LCl, w, 1961, Mansuino, Q.; flowers dbl., pompon, borne in clusters of 39-50, moderate fragrance; may repeat; foliage small, glossy, leathery; thornless; growth very vigorous, climbing; [Tom Thumb × *R. banksiae lutescens*]; Gold Medal, Rome, 1960

Puritas HT, Borgatti, G.; int. in 1969

Purity B, w, 1899, Cooling; flowers pure white with light rosy center, medium; growth semi-climbing; [said to be Devoniensis × Madame Bravy]; Gold Medal, NRS

Purity LCl, w, 1917, Farrell; flowers pure unshaded white, 4 in., semi-dbl., globular, borne in small clusters; some autumn repeat; foliage bronze-green, glossy; prickles heavy; vigorous, climbing growth; [(*R. wichurana* × Marion Dingee) × Mme Caroline Testout]

Purple – See **Louis-Philippe**, Ch

Purple – See **Purple Parade**, Min

Purple 'n' Gold MinFl, m, 2004, Mander, George; flowers purple-red, reverse gold, 3-3½ in., full, high-centered, borne in small clusters, slight fragrance; foliage medium size, dark green, semi-glossy; prickles ¼ in., needlepoint; growth bushy, medium (2-2½ ft.); containers, garden, exhibition; [Hot Tamale × Florib. seedling]; int. by Select Roses, 2005

Purple Angel S, m; groundcover; spreading growth; int. by Willemse France, 2001

Purple Beauty HT, m, 1979, Gandy, Douglas L.; flowers red-purple, 5 in., 30 petals, high-centered, moderate damask fragrance; foliage leathery; growth vigorous, upright; [Eminence × Tyrius]

Purple Bengal Ch, dr, 1827, Vibert; flowers maroon shaded darker

Purple Buttons S, m, Rupert, Kim L.; flowers deep red-purple, 2 in., full, rosette, borne in clusters, moderate fragrance; recurrent; growth small (under 3 ft.); [Cardinal Hume × unknown]; int. in 1993

Purple Carpet S, m, Clements, John K.; int. in 1999

Purple Chateau HT, m, Teranishi; int. in 1996

Purple Cloud HT, m, Keisei Rose Nurseries, Inc.; flowers purple magenta, large, 40-50 petals, high-centered, intense fragrance; good repeat; short stems; growth to 4 ft.; int. in 1993

Purple Dawn MinFl, m, 1991, Bridges, Dennis A.; flowers velvety mauve, long-lasting, 1½ in., 25 petals, high-centered, borne usually singly or in sprays of 5-7, slight fragrance; foliage medium size, dark green, semi-glossy; upright, tall growth; [Party Girl × unknown]; int. by Bridges Roses, 1991

Purple East HMult, dp, 1900, Paul, W.; flowers light crimson, fading to deep pink to medium, 4 cm., semi-dbl., borne in tight clusters; early, non-recurrent; numerous prickles; [Turner's Crimson Rambler × Beauté Inconstante]

Purple Elf Min, m, 1964, Moore, Ralph S.; flowers fuchsia-purple, small, 43 petals; foliage glossy; dwarf, bushy (10 in.) growth; [Violette × Zee]; int. by Sequoia Nursery, 1963

Purple Fantasy Min, m, 1983, Dobbs, Annette E.; flowers deep purple, small, dbl., no fragrance; foliage small, medium green, matte; bushy growth; [Blue Mist × Snow Magic]; int. in 1982

Purple Floorshow S, m; flowers deep magenta purple with large, deep golden centers., 2-3 in., 10-12 petals, moderate fragrance; low (2 ft.), spreading (3 ft.) growth; int. by Harkness, 2002

Purple Fragrance – See **Shiko**, HT

Purple Gem – See **S.E.A. of Love**, F

Purple Haze Min, m, 1996, Justice, Jerry G.; flowers soft mauve with light tan shading at the throat, 2¾ in., full, borne mostly singly, intense fragrance; foliage medium size, medium green, semi-glossy; some prickles; bushy, medium growth; PPAF; [Twilight Trail × seedling]; int. by Justice Miniature Roses, 1996

Purple Haze – See **Leeds Castle**, S

Purple Heart HT, m, 1946, Moore, Ralph S.; bud long, pointed; flowers dahlia-purple to blackish red-purple, large, semi-dbl., cupped; upright, bushy growth; [Crimson Queen × Crimson Queen]; int. by Sequoia Nursery

Purple Heart F, m, 1999, Carruth, Tom; flowers magenta purple, 3½-4 in., 30-35 petals, cupped, borne in large clusters, intense clove and spice fragrance; foliage medium size, medium green, matte; prickles moderate; rounded, compact, bushy, medium (3½ ft.) growth; PP11513; [Stephen's Big Purple × International Herald Tribune]; int. by Weeks Roses, 1999

Purple Iceberg – See **Burgundy Iceberg**, F

Purple Imp Min, m, 1967, Wiliams, E.D.; bud ovoid; flowers magenta to purple, small, dbl.; foliage small, narrow, glossy; vigorous, very compact growth; [Baby Faurax × Red Imp]; int. by Mini-Roses

Purple Majesty Min, m, 1987, Williams, Ernest D.; bud short, pointed; flowers mauve, edged red, reverse reddish-mauve, 1½ in., 40 petals, high-centered, borne usually singly, slight fragrance; recurrent; foliage small, medium green, semi-glossy; prickles few, tan, needle-like, dilated at base; stems slender, wiry; growth bushy, medium; PP6894; [Tom Brown × Black Jack]; int. by Mini-Roses

Purple Mary F, m, Takatori; int. by Takatori Roses

Purple Meadow – See **Muraskino**, HT

Purple Mikado F, m, Tantau; florist rose; int. by Rosen Tantau

Purple Noisette – See **Purpurea**, N

Purple Parade Min, m, Poulsen; flowers mauve, medium, no fragrance; foliage dark; growth bushy, 20-40 cm.; int. by Poulsen Roser, 1996

Purple Passion HT, m, 1999, Zary, Dr. Keith W.; bud pointed, ovoid; flowers rich purple/lavender, reverse lavender, 4½-5 in., 30-35 petals, high-centered, borne singly and in clusters of 3-7, intense lemony fragrance; recurrent; foliage large, dark green, glossy; prickles moderate; upright, spreading, tall (5 ft.) growth; PP11801; [seedling × seedling]; int. by Bear Creek Gardens, Inc., 1999

Purple Pavement HRg, m, Baum; flowers purple-red with yellow stamens, large, semi-dbl., cupped, borne in small trusses, moderate fragrance; recurrent; foliage rugose, glossy; mounding (3 ft.) growth; hips plump, red

Purple Pleasure HT, m, 2001, Bryan Epstein; flowers mauve with darker edge, reverse lighter, 3-4 in., dbl., high-centered, borne mostly solitary, moderate fragrance; foliage medium size, medium green, semi-glossy; growth upright, medium (5 ft.); garden decorative, exhibition; [Fragrant Plum × Blue Bird]

Purple Popcorn S, m, 1991, Williams, J. Benjamin; flowers bluish purple, small, semi-dbl., borne in small, grape-like clusters, slight fragrance; foliage small, medium green, matte, disease-resistant; few prickles; low (12-18 in.), compact, bushy growth; [*R. chinensis minima* × (Sea Foam × The Fairy)]

Purple Prince F, m, 1993, Ilsink, G.P.; flowers dark mauve to light purple, medium, full, borne in large clusters; foliage medium size, dark green, semi-glossy; some prickles; medium (55 cm.), upright growth; int. by Interplant B.V., 1991

Purple Puff – See **Love Potion**, F

Purple Rain HT, m, 1995, Kawamoto, Hiromoto; bud medium, pointed; flowers mauve, 4-5 in., 24-30 petals, high-centered, borne mostly singly, intense fragrance; good repeat; foliage medium size, dark green, semi-glossy; few prickles; growth upright, medium; PP9987; [seedling × Blue Moon]; greenhouse rose; int. by Carlton Rose Nurseries, 1994

Purple Reign S, m, 1997, Carruth, Tom; flowers irregularly striped magenta and white, 1½-2½ in., 8-14 petals, borne in large clusters; foliage large, dark green, glossy; spreading, medium (60-70 cm.)growth; [Fragrant Plum × Roller Coaster]; int. by Michigan Bulb Co., 1997

Purple Simplicity S, m, 1998, Zary, Dr. Keith W.; bud long, pointed ovoid; flowers raspberry purple, 3 in., semi-dbl., high-centered, then flat, borne in clusters of 5-9, slight fragrance; free-flowering; foliage medium size, medium green, semi-glossy; prickles few, straight, thin; growth tall, bushy; hedging; PP11251; [seedling × Love Potion]; int. by Bear Creek Gardens, Inc., 1999

Purple Skyliner LCl, m, Cowlishaw; flowers purple, fading to mauve, small, borne in clusters, intense fragrance; growth large shrub or small climber; int. by C & K Jones, 2002

Purple Spires F, m, Hortico; int. in 1997

Purple Splendour F, m, 1976, LeGrice; flowers glowing purple, 4 in., 26 petals, slight fragrance; foliage dark; upright growth; [News × Overture]; int. by Roseland Nurs.

Purple Springs HRg, m, 2006, Olsen, Paul G; flowers semi-dbl., borne in small clusters, moderate fragrance; foliage medium size, medium green, semi-glossy; prickles small, straight, brown, moderate; growth bushy, medium (1½ m.); landscape, hedging; hardy to -40ºF; [Hansa × Rosa foliolosa]; int. by Brentwood Bay Nursery, 2006

Purple Sunset Min, m, 1992, Mander, George; flowers purple/cream bicolor, very attractive bicolor combination, medium, dbl., no fragrance; foliage small, dark green, glossy; few prickles; low (35-40 cm.), upright growth; [Rise 'n' Shine × MANpurple]

Purple Tiger F, m, 1991, Christensen, Jack E.; bud pointed, ovoid; flowers very deep purple with stripes and flecks of white and mauve-pink, 3½-4 in., full, borne in small clusters, moderate damask fragrance; foliage medium size, medium green, glossy; nearly thornless; stems very glabrous (shiny); medium (70-90 cm.), bushy growth; [Intrigue × Pinstripe]; int. by Bear Creek Gardens, 1992

Purple Times F, m, Tantau; flowers borne in large clusters; int. by Rosen Tantau, 1999

Purple Torch HT, m; flowers purple, large, dbl.; growth to 3 ft.; int. by Hortico, Inc., 2005

Purple Velvet S, m, Clements, John; flowers velvet purple. magenta-crimson in heat of summer, 4-5 in., 85 petals, old-fashioned, moderate wine fragrance; foliage serrated, matte green; growth vigorous, somewhat spreading (4 × 3 ft.); PPAF; int. by Heirloom, 2000

Purpurea – See **Purpurine de France**, HGal

Purpurea N, dr, 1822, Laffay, M.; flowers purple-crimson, poorly formed, semi-dbl.; possibly a Boursault × Noisette hybrid

Purpurea Ch, m, 1930, Chenault; growth small

Purpurea Misc OGR, m, Buist; no prickles on sepals or receptacle; flowers purple-crimson or purplish-rose; [*R. roxburghii* × unknown]

Purpurea di Bologna B, m, Ruston, D.; flowers purple, striped maroon, medium, dbl., cupped, borne in large clusters, intense fragrance; recurrent; growth to 6 ft.; [sport of Variegata di Bologna]; int. in 1980

Purpurea Plena – See **Pourpre Ancien**, Misc OGR

Purpurea Rubra M, m, before 1870; flowers violet-purple, well mossed, large, dbl., intense fragrance

Purpurea Velutina Parva – See **L'Obscurité**, HGal

Purpureo-Violaceo Magna – See **L'Évêque**, HGal

Purpuria – See **Purpurea**, Misc OGR

Purpurine F, m, Lens; bud long; flowers fuchsia-purple to rhodamine-purple, dbl.; foliage dark; vigorous, bushy growth; [(Peace × seedling) × Fashion]; int. by Galan

Purpurine de France HGal, m, before 1770; flowers brilliant purple-red, semi-dbl., moderate fragrance; foliage oval; nearly thornless; growth upright; possibly synonymous with *R. gallica officinalis*

Purpurtraum HWich, dr, 1923, Kayser & Seibert; flowers deep purple red with a white eye, 3 cm., semi-dbl., borne in medium to large clusters, no fragrance; foliage small, glossy; strong, bushy (12 ft.) growth; [Excelsa × unknown]

Purpurtraum 2000 S, m, Schultheis; flowers magenta-violet with golden stamens, semi-dbl., shallow cup, borne in clusters; low (2 ft.), bushy growth; int. by Rosen von Schultheis, 2000

Pusa Christina HT, mp, 1976, IARI; bud globular; flowers 3 in., 50 petals, high-centered; foliage soft; vigorous, upright growth

Pusa Pitambar F, yb, IARI; flowers golden yellow with shadings of pink, high-centered, borne in large clusters, intense fragrance; int. in 2000

Pusa Priya HT, lp, IARI; buds long; flowers pale pink, long lasting; stems sturdy; int. in 2000

Pusa Sonia HT, dy, 1968, IARI; bud long, pointed; flowers golden yellow, large, 24 petals; foliage leathery; vigorous, upright growth; [McGredy's Yellow × unknown]

Pusa Sonora HT, pb, 1984, Division of Floriculture and Landscaping; flowers rose pink, deeper reverse, medium, 5 petals; foliage medium green; bushy, upright growth; [Queen Elizabeth × First Prize]

Pushkala Min, w, Kasturi; flowers clear white, tiny, borne in large clusters; free-flowering; int. by KSG Son, 1973

Pushkarini F, w, Chiplunkar; int. in 1990

Pussta – See **New Daily Mail**, F

Pussta, Climbing – See **New Daily Mail, Climbing**, Cl F

Putidula – See **Le Rire Niais**, C

Puy du Fou – See **Exotica**, HT

Pye Colour F, mr, 1973, Dickson, A.; flowers turkey-red, ovate, 2 in., 30 petals; foliage leathery; free growth; [Marlena × Elizabeth of Glamis]; int. in 1972

Pygmae Min, or, 1978, Poulsen, Niels D.; bud globular; flowers bright orange-red, yellow center, 1 in., 13 petals, borne in clusters; foliage small, glossy, dark; low, compact, spreading, bushy growth; [Anytime × Minuette]; int. by D.T. Poulsen, 1977

Pygmee Min, yb, Delbard; flowers yellow shaded with apricot and flame; int. by Sauvageot, 1978

Pygmy – See **Pygmae**, Min

Pyramidale – See **Porcelaine**, HGal

Pyrenees – See **Kent**, S

Pyrenees Rose – See ***R. pendulina pyrenaica*** (Keller)

Pythagoras HSpn, pb, probably Vibert; flowers light pink, flecked deep pink, semi-dbl.; early bloom; foliage finely divided; dense, shrubby (3-4 ft.) growth; hips glossy, black

Pzazz – See **Pzazz Hit**, MinFl

Pzazz Hit MinFl, rb, Poulsen; flowers red blend, 5-8 cm., dbl., no fragrance; foliage dark; growth bushy, 40-60 cm.; int. by Poulsen Roser, 1996

QE2 HT, rb, Ruston, D.; [sport of Queen Elizabeth]

Quadra HKor, dr, Svejda, F.J. & Ogilvie, Ian S.; bud ovoid; flowers dark red, reverse slightly lighter, 60 petals, flat, somewhat quartered, borne singly or in clusters of up to 4, slight fragrance; recurrent; foliage dark green with red tinge, glossy; very low, trailing growth or may be trained as climber to 8 ft.; very hardy; PP9995; [seedling from B08 line × seedling from U11 line]; int. in 1994

Quadroon S, dr, Wright, Percy H.; flowers rich dark red, small, single; non-recurrent; growth rather poor; [supposedly Hansa × (Hansa × *R. nitida*)]

Quaker Beauty HT, ab, 1936, Brookins; bud long, pointed; flowers glowing apricot, large, high-centered; [sport of Joanna Hill]

Quaker Maid F, or, 1960, Byrum, Roy L.; bud ovoid; flowers nasturtium-red, 1½-2 in., 18-20 petals, flat, borne in clusters, moderate spicy fragrance; foliage leathery; vigorous, upright, bushy growth; PP1789; [Orange Sweetheart × Pinocchio]; originally registered as Pol; int. by Hill, Joseph H., Co., 1959

Quaker Star Gr, op, 1991, Dickson, Colin; flowers orange with silver reverse, aging to salmon with orange petal edges, large, very full, borne mostly singly, no fragrance; foliage medium size, dark green, glossy; prickles few, straight, small; upright, medium (4 ft.) growth; [Anisley Dickson × seedling]; int. by Roses by Fred Edmunds, 1991

Quantock Star HT, or, 1968, Heard; flowers vermilion shaded pink, small, dbl.; foliage variegated; free growth; [sport of Tropicana]

Quatre Saisons – See **Autumn Damask**, D

Quatre Saisons Blanc Mousseux M, w, 1835, Laffay, M.; bud very mossy; flowers medium, dbl., borne in large clusters; repeats sparingly in fall; growth medium (4 ft.); [sport of Autumn Damask]

Quatre Saisons Blanche – See **Quatre Saisons Blanc Mousseux**, M

Quatre Saisons Continue – See **Autumn Damask**, D

Quatre Saisons d'Italie P, dp, before 1815, Dupont, Andre; flowers vermilion, sometimes striped, medium, semi-dbl., borne in clusters of 3, moderate fragrance; foliage large, ovate, simply serrate; prickles very numerous, small, short, straight; brought from Florence to Luxembourg in 1795 by Dupont; re-introduced by Verdier in 1865; sometimes classed as D

Quatre Saisons Rose D, mp, 1580; flowers deep rose; possibly brought to France from Italy by Montaigne

Québec – See **Mme Marie Curie**, HT

Queen B, mp, 1900, Paul, W.; flowers pink, shaded darker, large, full

Queen – See **Queen Parade**, Min

Queen Adelaide – See **Yves Piaget**, HT

Queen Aishwarya – See **Aishwarya**, HT

Queen Alexandra HMult, mp, 1901, Veitch; flowers rosy white, medium, semi-dbl., borne in large corymbs

Queen Alexandra HMsk, ly, 1915, Pemberton; flowers light yellow, flushed with pink, stamens prominent, 2-3 cm., single, borne in large clusters, slight fragrance

Queen Alexandra – See **The Queen Alexandra Rose**, HT

Queen Ann HT, dr, 1949, Spandikow; bud long, pointed; flowers crimson, medium, dbl., high-centered; strong stems; vigorous growth; [sport of Better Times]

Queen Astrid – See **Koningin Astrid**, HT

Queen Beatrice HT, lp, 1909, Kramer; flowers bright silvery pink, large to medium, very dbl.; vigorous growth; [Mme Abel Chatenay × Liberty]

Queen Beatrix – See **Königin Beatrix**, HT

Queen Bee S, dr, 1985, Buck, Dr. Griffith J.; flowers 4-5 in., 35 petals, high-centered to cupped, borne 5-8 per cluster, moderate old rose fragrance; repeat bloom; foliage large, leathery, dark olive green; prickles awl-like, brown; erect, bushy, branching growth; hardy; [(Rosali × Music Maker) × (Square Dancer × Tatjana)]; int. by Iowa State University, 1984

Queen Bett's Min, w, 2001, Bell, Judy G.; flowers white blushed pink, gold and red stamens, red stigma, 1½ in., full, borne mostly solitary, slight fragrance; foliage medium size, dark green, semi-glossy; prickles small, straight, moderate; upright, medium growth; garden decorative, exhibition, containers; [Party Girl × Giggles]; int. by Michigan Mini Roses, 2002

Queen Charlotte HT, op, 1988, Harkness, R., & Co., Ltd.; flowers deep salmon-red, yellow base, reverse pink-red, aging paler, dbl., high-centered; foliage large, dark green, semi-glossy; prickles recurved, medium, reddish-green; upright, tall growth; hips ovoid, large, green; [Basildon Bond × Silver Jubilee]; int. by R. Harkness & Co., Ltd., 1989

Queen City Min, ob, 1987, Bridges, Dennis A.; flowers orange, yellow base, fading lighter, medium, 20 petals, high-centered, borne usually singly, slight fragrance; foliage medium size, medium green, semi-glossy; prickles long, straight, medium, light colored; bushy, medium growth; [Rise 'n' Shine × seedling]

Queen Dina Gr, dr, 1964, Soenderhousen; flowers deep scarlet, large, dbl.; foliage leathery; very vigorous, upright, bushy growth; [Cocorico × Geranium Red]; int. by Hoersholm Nursery

Queen Dorothy Bell HT, dr, 1940, Stell; flowers velvety scarlet, very dbl., globular; foliage light, leathery; vigorous growth; [sport of Oswald Sieper]; int. by Stell Rose Nursery

Queen Elizabeth Gr, mp, 1954, Lammerts, Dr. Walter; bud pointed; flowers 3½-4 in., 38 petals, high-centered to cupped, borne singly and in clusters, moderate fragrance; good repeat; foliage dark, glossy, leathery; very vigorous, upright, bushy growth; PP1259; [Charlotte Armstrong × Floradora]; int. by Germain's, 1954; President's International Trophy, NRS, 1955, Hall of Fame, WFRS, 1978, Gold Medal, Portland, 1954

Queen Elizabeth, Climbing Cl Gr, mp, 1957, Whisler; PP1615; [sport of Queen Elizabeth]; int. by Germain's, 1957

Queen Elizabeth Abricot – See **Apricot Queen Elizabeth**, Gr

Queen Elizabeth Blush – See **Blushing Queen**, Gr

Queen Elizabeth Jaune – See **Yellow Queen Elizabeth**, Gr

Queen Esther HT, w, 1985, Poole, Lionel; flowers cream, pale pink petal edges, spiraled, large, 35 petals; foliage medium size, medium green, matte; numerous prickles; [Golden Masterpiece × Peer Gynt]; int. in 1984

Queen Fabiola Gr, op, 1965, Hazenberg, G.; bud ovoid; flowers salmon-pink, medium, dbl., borne several together; foliage dark green; numerous prickles; [sport of Montezuma]; int. by S. C. Hazenberg, 1962

Queen Frances Connally HT, mr, 1939, Stell; flowers spectrum-red, base lemon-chrome, reverse yellow edged red; [sport of Katharine Pechtold]; int. by Stell Rose Nursery

Queen Gertrude Anne Windsor HT, dp, 1936, Dixie Rose Nursery; flowers darker; [sport of Francis Scott Key]

Queen Juliana – See **Orange Delight**, HT

Queen Louise Boren HT, op, 1935, Nicolas; flowers pink suffused salmon, large, dbl.; very vigorous growth; [(Emile Charles × La France) × Marechal Niel]; int. by Dixie Rose Nursery

Queen Lucia F, op, 1954, Maarse, G.; flowers salmon-pink, pompon form, dbl., borne in large trusses; vigorous growth; [Pinocchio × Tapis Rose]

Queen Lucia – See **Lichtkönigin Lucia**, S

Queen Mab Ch, ab, 1896, Paul, W.; flowers soft rosy apricot, center shaded orange, reverse tinted rose, dbl.; free-flowering; bushy, compact (2-3 ft.) growth

Queen Margaret Hunt HT, dr, 1936, Nicolas; bud long, pointed, spiral; flowers dark velvety crimson-maroon, stamens golden yellow, large, cupped; foliage leathery; very vigorous growth; [Templar × Ami Quinard]; int. by Dixie Rose Nursery

Queen Margrethe S, lp, 1994, Olesen; bud short, pointed to ovoid; flowers pastel pink, old-fashioned form, medium, very full, quartered, borne in small clusters, moderate apple fragrance; free-flowering; foliage small, medium green, glossy, clean; few prickles; stems strong, short to medium; low to medium (2 ft.), bushy, compact, rounded growth; PP9062; [seedling × Egeskov]; int. by Weeks Roses, 1995; Gold Star of the South Pacific, Palmerston North, NZ, 1992

Queen Marie HT, pb, 1925, Chervenka; flowers rose-pink, reverse deeper pink, base bronze yellow, dbl.; [Mme Butterfly × Lamia]

Queen Marie of Jugoslavia HT, my, 1935, Hicks; flowers bright yellow, slightly flushed pink; [sport of Mme Butterfly]

Queen Mary HT, yb, 1913, Dickson, A.; flowers bright canary yellow, shaded red, medium, semi-dbl., moderate fragrance; Gold Medal, NRS, 1913

Queen Mary HT, lp, 1911, Williams, A.; [Frau Karl Druschki × unknown]

Queen Mary 2 HT, w, 2004, Meilland International; flowers 8-10 cm., full, borne mostly solitary, intense fragrance; foliage dark green, glossy; growth upright, tall (5-6 ft.); garden decoration, cutting; PP16951; [Meiban × (Poulari × Lady Sylvia)]; int. by The Conard-Pyle Company, 2004

Queen Mother F, lp, Kordes; flowers small, semi-dbl., flat; low, spreading growth; int. in 1991

Queen Mum – See **Queen Mother**, F

Queen Nefertiti S, ab, Austin, David; flowers variable blends of apricot, soft yellow and pink, 4 in., very full, cupped, moderate fragrance; recurrent; foliage medium green; growth bushy, moderate (4 ft.); int. in 1988

Queen of Bath HT, dy, 1931, Bees; bud long, pointed; flowers deep buttercup-yellow, outer edged chrome-yellow, dbl., high-centered; foliage thick, glossy, bronze; vigorous growth; [Souv. de Claudius Pernet × Cleveland]

Queen of Beauty and Fragrance – See **Souv de la Malmaison**, B

Queen of Bedders B, dp, 1876, Noble; flowers deep carmine, well-shaped, medium to large, full; dwarf, compact growth; [Sir Joseph Paxton × unknown]

Queen of Bermuda Gr, or, 1961, Bowie; bud ovoid; flowers orange-vermilion, 4 in., 35 petals, high-centered, borne in small clusters, moderate fruity fragrance; foliage glossy, bronze; vigorous, bushy growth; [(Independence × Orange Triumph) × Bettina]; int. by Bermuda Rose Nursery, 1960

Queen of Bourbons B, pb, 1834, Mauget; flowers fawn and rose, small to medium, dbl., cupped, intense fragrance

Queen of Bourbons B, w, 1930, Burch; flowers pure white, moderate fragrance

Queen of Colors – See **Farbenkönigin**, HT

Queen of Denmark – See **Königin von Dänemark**, A

Queen of Denmark D, lp, 1846, Vibert; flowers light flesh pink

Queen of Diamonds – See **Scarlet Queen Elizabeth**, F

Queen of Diamonds Gr, mr, 1966, Dickson; bud ovoid; flowers light red, medium, dbl, borne several together; foliage dark green; [(Korona × unknown) × Queen Elizabeth]; int. by Spek, 1965

Queen of Edgely HP, mp, 1901, Florist's Exchange; flowers bright pink, large, deeply cupped; [sport of American Beauty]

Queen of England – See **Queen Elizabeth**, Gr

Queen of Fragrance HT, lp, 1915, Paul, W.; flowers shell-pink, tipped silver, well-shaped, large, dbl.; foliage soft; dwarf growth

Queen of Hearts Cl HT, mp, 1920, Clark, A.; bud globular; flowers rich pink, aging lighter, 4½ in., semi-dbl. to dbl., cupped, moderate fragrance; foliage dark green, glossy; numerous prickles; very vigorous, climbing growth; [Gustave Grunerwald × Rosy Morn]; int. by NRS Victoria

Queen of Hearts – See **Dame de Coeur**, HT

Queen of Hearts – See **Taser Bibi**, HT

Queen of Hearts S, mr, 2001, Harkness New Roses, Ltd.; flowers very full, borne in small clusters, intense fragrance; foliage medium size, dark green, glossy; prickles medium, hooked downwards, moderate; bushy, tall (100 cm.) growth; garden decoration; [KORphean × HARmusky]; int. in 2001

Queen of Hearts HT, rb, Kordes; flowers cherry red and apricot, large, full, cupped, borne mostly singly, slight fragrance; foliage glossy; strong (5 ft.) growth; int. by W. Kordes Söhne, 2005

Queen of Pearl HWich, lp, 1898, Van Fleet; non-remontant

Queen of Queens HP, pb, 1882, Paul, W.; flowers pink, with blush edges, large, full, globular; [Victor Verdier × (La Reine × Maiden's Blush)]

Queen of Queens, Climbing Cl HP, mp, 1892, Paul, W.; flowers very large; [sport of Queen of Queens]

Queen of Roses – See **Colour Wonder**, HT, 1964

Queen of Scarlet – See **Cramoisi Supérieur**, Ch

Queen of Spain HT, lp, 1907, Bide; flowers flesh pink, center darker, large, very full; [Antoine Rivoire × unknown]

Queen of Sweden S, lp, 2004; flowers very full, cupped, borne in small clusters, slight myrrh fragrance; foliage medium size, medium green, matte; prickles medium, hooked downward; growth upright, narrow, medium (3½ ft.); garden decorative; [seedling (medium pink English-type shrub) × Charlotte]; int. by David Austin Roses, Ltd., 2004

Queen of the Belgians – See **Reine des Belges**, Ayr

Queen of the Belgians HT, op, 1916, Hicks; bud long, pointed; flowers salmon-pink, semi-dbl.; Gold Medal, NRS, 1915

Queen of the Belgians Ayr, w; flowers small, very dbl.

Queen of the Dwarfs Min, dp, 1955, Kordes; flowers deep pink, dbl.; foliage rather coarse; growth to 10-12 in.

Queen o' the Lakes HT, dr, 1949, Brownell; bud ovoid, long, pointed; flowers large, dbl., high-centered, moderate fragrance; foliage glossy; vigorous, bushy growth; [Pink Princess × Crimson Glory]

Queen o' the Lakes, Climbing Cl HT, dr, 1965; int. by Stern's Nurseries, 1965

Queen of the Musks HMsk, pb, 1913, Paul, W.; bud coppery red; flowers deep blush and white, centers darker, small, semi-dbl., borne in large clusters, intense fragrance; recurrent bloom; foliage dark ivy-green; prickles numerous, small, bristly; bushy (3 ft.) growth

Queen of the Night HT, Sgaravatti, A.

Queen of the Prairies HSet, pb, 1843, Feast; flowers bright rose pink, frequently striped white, large, dbl., globular, borne in clusters of 10-15, moderate fragrance; foliage large, dark green; vigorous, climbing growth; hardy; [*R. setigera* × a Gallica]; Gold Medal, Mass. Hort. Society

Queen of the Violets – See **Reine des Violettes**, HP

Queen Olga of Greece – See **Reine Olga de Wurtemberg**, N

Queen Olga of Wurtemburg – See **Reine Olga de Wurtemberg**, N

Queen Parade Min, dp, Poulsen; flowers deep pink, medium, no fragrance; foliage dark; growth bushy, 20-40 cm.; int. by Poulsen Roser, 1996

Queen Thornless, Climbing Cl HT, dp, Kittle; bud pointed; flowers deep pink, 3-4 in., 20-40 petals, high-centered, moderate fragrance; intermittent bloom; foliage leathery, dull green; thornless; strong stems; vigorous, arching growth; PP2275; int. by Lincoln Nursery Co.

Queen Victoria – See **Brennus**, HCh

Queen Victoria – See **Souv d'un Ami**, T

Queen Victoria HP, lp, 1850, Fontaine; flowers blush-pink, large, dbl.; [La Reine × unknown]; int. by A. Paul

Queen Wilhelmina HT, ob, 1942, Deverman; flowers brilliant orange, base light orange-yellow; [sport of Hinrich Gaede]

Queen Wilhelmina – See **Golden Girls**, F

Queenie F, lp, 1962, Boerner; bud ovoid; flowers 4 in., 33 petals, cupped, borne in clusters, moderate fragrance; foliage leathery; vigorous, upright, bushy growth; PP2238; [(Pinocchio × unknown) × Spartan]; int. by J&P, 1962

Queenie Robinson HT, op, 1924, Easlea; bud long, pointed; flowers orange-cerise to flame-pink, semi-dbl.

Queenie's Love HT, dp, 1970, Verschuren, A.; bud globular; flowers begonia-rose, medium, dbl., moderate fragrance; foliage leathery; vigorous growth; [Libretto × Mme Butterfly]; int. by Stassen, 1968

Queen's – See **Queen's Palace**, S

Queen's Knight S, mp, 1980, Stoddard, Louis; bud short, conical; flowers 6-10 petals, cupped, borne 3 per cluster; profuse for 6 weeks; non-recurrent; foliage semi-glossy, deep green, 7 leaflets; prickles hooked; erect, arching, self-supporting growth; [Don Juan × *R. laxa*]

Queen's Palace S, mp, Poulsen; bud pointed to ovoid; flowers medium pink, 3 in., 20-25 petals, flattened, borne in large clusters; quick repeat; foliage medium size, dark green, semi-glossy; prickles moderate, ¼ in., straight, red; growth vigorous, compact (2 ft.),bushy; PP10821; [Sexy Rexy × seedling]; int. by Poulsen Roser, 1997

Queen's Scarlet Ch, mr, 1880, Hallock & Thorpe; flowers rich velvety scarlet, small, dbl.; foliage small; bushy, compact growth

Queen's Visit HT, dr, 1955, Viney; bud long, pointed; flowers dark velvety red veined darker, medium, dbl., high-centered; foliage leathery; vigorous growth; [Crimson Glory × Crimson Glory]; int. by Wynne, 1955

Queensday HT, ab, Tantau; flowers apricot-orange, large, full, high-centered, borne mostly singly; good repeat; greenhouse rose; int. by Rosen Tantau, 1997

Queensland Beauty HT, pb, 1934, Alderton & Williams; flowers coppery pink; [sport of Golden Dawn]

Queenstown HT, dr, 1991, Cattermole, R.F.; bud pointed; flowers deep crimson to ruby red, 5 in., 32 petals, cupped, borne up to 6 per cluster, slight fragrance; foliage leathery, mid-green, semi-glossy; upright, spreading growth; [Silent Night × Josephine Bruce]; int. by South Pacific Rose Nursery, 1991

Quercifolia – See **À Feuille de Chêne**, C

Querida HT, mp, 1994, Maltagliati, Mark G.; flowers 3-3½ in., full, borne mostly singly; foliage large, dark green, semi-glossy; few prickles; upright (5 ft.) growth; PP9769; [Silver Anniversary × unknown]; int. by Meilland-Star Roses, Inc., 1995

Quicksilver HT, m, 1986, Christensen, Jack E.; flowers pale lavender gray, large, 25 petals, high-centered, borne singly, moderate fragrance; foliage large, dark, matte; prickles medium, yellow-gray; tall, upright, bushy growth; [Blue Nile × Brandy]; int. by Michigan Bulb Co., 1985

Quickstep LCl, mp, Poulsen; flowers dusty rose, lightens with age, 8-10 cm., dbl., cupped, no fragrance; foliage dark green, glossy; bushy (10 ft.) growth; int. by Poulsen Roser, 2001

Quiet Reflections T, dy, Hay

Quiet Time MinFl, m, 1995, Bennett, Dee; flowers lavender-pink with inner petals of soft tan, small, full, borne mostly singly; foliage medium size, medium green, semi-glossy; bushy growth; [Lagerfeld × Ernie]; int. by Tiny Petals Nursery, 1995

Quietness S, lp, 2003, Buck, Dr. Griffith J.; flowers soft pink, 4 in., very full, borne in small clusters, intense spicy fragrance; foliage medium size, medium green, semi-glossy, disease-resistant; prickles medium, awl, light brown, moderate; growth spreading, tall (4-5 ft.); landscape, mixed plantings; [seedling × seedling]; tolerant of partial shade; int. by Roses Unlimited, 2003

Quinella HT, ob

Quintet – See **Victoria Park**, HT

Quiproquo HT, my, Richardier; int. by Pep. Jarrige, 1999

Quite Unforgettable Min, ob, 2005, Paul Chessum Roses; flowers semi-dbl., borne in small clusters, slight fragrance; foliage medium size, medium green, semi-glossy; prickles medium, sharp, pink, few; growth compact, medium (18 in.); bedding, containers; [seedling × seedling]; int. by World of Roses, 2005

Quito HT, yb; int. in 1999

Quo Vadis? HT, pb, 1961, Giacomasso; bud oval; flowers silvery pink becoming red, large, 50-60 petals; very vigorous growth; [Peace × (Baiser × unknown)]

R. B. Cater HP, dp, 1899, Cooling; flowers glossy carmine-magenta

R. B. Stewart HT, or, 2005, French, Bryan; flowers deep orange-red with small yellow center, yellow stamens, reverse lighter, 4 in., dbl., borne mostly solitary, intense spice fragrance; foliage medium size, semi-glossy; prickles moderate, 1/4 in., slight curve downward, yellow-green; growth upright, medium (28-32 in.); garden, cutting; not heat tolerant; [unnamed sport of Playboy × Vannie]; int. by Valley View Gardens, 2006

R. G. Casson HT, pb, 1923, Cant, B. R.; flowers rose and copper

R. K. Witherspoon HT, w, 2005, Pike, David V.B.; buds long, pointed; flowers white with pink-blushed petals, colors stronger in cool weather, 4-5 in., dbl., high-centered, borne mostly solitary, intense fragrance; foliage medium size, dark green, semi-glossy; prickles moderate; upright, medium growth; [sport of Tiffany]; int. by David V.B. Pike, 2006

R. M. S. Queen Mary HT, mp, 1937, Verschuren; flowers salmon-pink suffused orange, very large, dbl., cupped; foliage leathery; vigorous growth; [Briarcliff × Mrs Sam McGredy]; int. by Dreer

R. S. Hudson HT, yb, 1939, Wheatcroft Bros.; flowers yellow tinged red, large, well-formed; vigorous, upright growth

R. W. Proctor F, dp, 1947, Proctor; flowers deep rose-pink, 4 in., 10-12 petals, borne in trusses; foliage glossy; vigorous growth; [sport of Anne Poulsen]

Raalte's Golden Harvest S, dy, Interplant; int. in 1992

Raat-ki-Rani HT, mr, 1975, IARI; bud pointed; flowers velvety crimson-red, 4½ in., 30 petals; foliage glossy; vigorous, upright growth; [seedling × (Samourai × unknown)]; int. in 1975

Rabbie Burns HT, mr, 1960, Arnot; bud long, pointed; flowers bright light red, semi-dbl., intense fragrance; foliage dark; vigorous, upright growth; [Ena Harkness × Sutter's Gold]; int. by Croll, 1959

Rabble Rouser S, dy, 1998, Horner, Colin P.; flowers deep yellow, non-fading, paler reverse, 1½-2 in., semi-dbl., borne in large clusters; foliage small, medium green, very glossy; prickles moderate; bushy, tall growth; [(Anytime × Liverpool Echo) × (Flamenco × Rosa bella)]; int. as Celebration 2000, Paul Chessum Rose Specialist, 1999

Rabelais – See **Francois Rabelais**, F

Rachael Fox F, mr, 2006, Rawlins, Ronnie; flowers red, reverse red, 2½ in., dbl., borne in small clusters, moderate fragrance; foliage medium size, medium green, semi-glossy; prickles ½ in., triangle, few; growth compact (24 in.); garden decoration; [(Summer Wine × International Herald Tribune) × Ingrid Bergman]

Rachael's Smile LCl, or, 2007, Tolmasoff, Jan; flowers orange-red with yellow at very base, 3½ in., dbl., borne mostly solitary; very early blooming; foliage medium size, medium green, semi-glossy; prickles medium to large, tan, moderate; growth climbing, tall (12-14 ft.); trellises/fences; [unknown × unknown]; int. by Russian River Rose Company, 2001

Rachel HT, ob, 1929, Pemberton; flowers orange-buff, flushed carmine, large, dbl., high-centered; foliage dark; very vigorous growth; RULED EXTINCT 5/84

Rachel S, mp, 1984, Booth, Mrs. Rachel Y.; flowers medium, 35 petals, slight delicate fragrance; foliage medium size, medium green, matte; upright growth

Rachel – See **Augusta Luise**, S

Rachel MinFl, dp, 2005, Rickard, Vernon; flowers deep pink, reverse medium pink, 1½ in., full, borne mostly solitary, moderate fragrance; foliage medium size, dark green, semi-glossy; prickles small, 3mm., straight, red, few; growth upright, vigorous, tall, 30 in; exhibition, garden decoration; [Fairhope × Signature]; int. by Almost Heaven Roses, 2006

Rachel Bowes Lyon S, pb, 1980, Harkness, R., & Co., Ltd.; bud fat; flowers peach pink, reverse yellow, 12 petals, flat, borne in large clusters, moderate wild rose fragrance; good repeat; foliage small to medium size, medium green; prickles small, hooked; low, bushy growth; [Kim × ((Orange Sensation × Allgold) × *R. californica*)]; int. by Harkness, 1981

Rachel Buchanan Min, ly, 2000, Buchanan, Hedley; flowers cream-lemon, large, very full, borne mostly singly, slight fragrance; foliage medium size, dark green; few prickles; growth upright, tall; [sport of Pink Petticoat]

Rachel Crawshay HT, op, 1978, Harkness; flowers pink to orange-salmon, 5 in., 30 petals; foliage olive-green; [Fragrant Cloud × Mary Mine]; int. in 1977

Rachel Esta HT, w, 2002, Poole, Lionel; flowers white with pink edge, 5 in., full, high-centered, borne mostly solitary, intense fragrance; foliage medium size, medium green, semi-glossy; prickles medium, triangular, moderate; growth upright, bushy, vigorous, medium (3 ft.); exhibition, bedding; [(Hazel Rose × Cardiff Bay) × New Zealand]; int. by David Lister Roses, 2003

Rachel Farrant F, dy, 2001, Horner, Colin P.; flowers buttercup yellow, slightly paler reverse, medium, dbl., borne in small clusters, slight fragrance; foliage medium size, medium green, glossy; prickles medium, curved, moderate; growth compact, medium (110 cm.); garden decorative; [Simba × Prominent]; int. by Paul Chessum Roses, 2004

Rachel Jayne HT, op, 2001, Poole, Lionel; flowers coral/amber, 4 in., full, borne mostly solitary, intense fragrance; free-flowering; foliage medium size, dark green, glossy; prickles medium, long, angular; upright, bushy, medium growth; borders, beds; [Augustus Stone × Joanna Lumley]; int. by David Lister Roses, 2002

Rachel Kathleen F, mr; flowers bright red, dbl., cupped; int. by R. V. Rogers, 2006

Rachel Townsend HT, yb, 1963, Townsend; flowers golden yellow tipped carmine, 4-4½ in., 30 petals; foliage dark, glossy; free growth; [sport of Sultane]; int. by Townsend & Son

Rachelle F, mp, 1976, Warriner, William A.; bud long; flowers French rose, 2-3 in., 30 petals, nearly flat; upright growth; [Antigua × unnamed cultivar]; int. by J&P

Racy Lady HT, w, 1999, Dickson, Colin; flowers creamy white, reverse cream, 4½ in., full, borne mostly singly, moderate fragrance; foliage medium size, dark green, glossy; numerous prickles; upright, medium (3 ft.) growth; [Solitaire × Elina]; int. by Dickson Nurseries Ltd.

Rada HT, dr, 1985, Staikov, Prof. Dr. V.; flowers large, 75 petals; foliage medium green, glossy; [Baccará × seedling]; int. by Kalaydjiev and Chorbadjiiski, 1975

Radames HT, dr, 1984, Fumagalli, Niso; flowers large, 35 petals, intense fragrance; foliage large, medium green, glossy; upright growth; [seedling × seedling]; int. in 1983

Radar HT, or, 1953, Meilland, F.; bud long; flowers light geranium-red, well-formed, large, 45 petals; vigorous growth; [Charles Mallerin × Independence]; int. by URS

Radar, Climbing Cl HT, or, 1959, Meilland, Mrs. Marie-Louise; int. by URS

Radar Italiana HT, or, 1944, San Remo Exp. Sta.; bud pointed; flowers nasturtium-red edged rose, large, 32-34 petals; foliage bright green; vigorous, bushy growth; [Souv. de Denier van der Gon × Brazier]

Radcliffe Flame HT, mr, 1987, Thomson, Colin; flowers medium, full, no fragrance; foliage medium size, dark green, matte; upright growth; [Alec's Red × Grandpa Dickson]

Radhe S, pb, 2000, Horner, Colin P.; flowers deep and light pink with cream stripes, reverse pink and cream, 3½ in., dbl., borne in small clusters, moderate fragrance; foliage medium size, medium green, matte; prickles moderate; spreading, tall (4-5 ft.) growth; [(Wandering Minstrel × (Alexander × (Southampton × ((Little W Pet × New Penny) × Stars 'n' Stripes)))) × striped seedling]; int. by Warley Rose Gardens, 2002

Radiance HT, lp, 1904, Cook, J.W.; bud globular; flowers rose-pink, reverse lighter, large, 23 petals, cupped, intense damask fragrance; foliage leathery; vigorous growth; [Enchanter × Cardinal]; int. by P. Henderson, 1908

Radiance, Climbing Cl HT, lp, 1926, Griffing, W.D. (also Catt, 1928); flowers salmon pink with yellow, large, full; [sport of Radiance]

Radiant HT, or, 1962, Fletcher; bud spiral; flowers orange-flame, reverse shaded red, 4-5 in., 30 petals; foliage glossy; very free growth; RULED EXTINCT 9/87; [Mrs Sam McGredy × Fantasia]; int. by Tucker & Sons, 1962

Radiant Min, or, 1988, Benardella, Frank A.; bud medium, pointed, ovoid; flowers brilliant orange-red, 1¾ in., 23-27 petals, high-centered, then flat, borne singly, moderate spicy fragrance; foliage large, dark green, semi-glossy; prickles long, thin, straight, pointed slightly downward, gray-red; stems long, straight; upright, vigorous (18-30 in.) growth; no fruit; PP6569; [Sheri Anne × Sheri Anne]; int. by Nor'East Min. Roses, 1988

Radiant Beauty HT, mr, 1934, Cleveland Cut-Flower Co.; flowers deeper crimson than parent, not turning blue, dbl.; [sport of Francis Scott Key]

Radiant Glow F, or, 1953, Quinn; bud pointed; flowers bright orange-salmon tinted peach, medium, dbl., cupped, borne singly and in clusters; foliage leathery, light green; vigorous, upright growth; [Pinocchio × unknown]; int. by Roseglen Nursery

Radiant Gold HT, my, 1984, J&P; flowers large, 35 petals; foliage large, dark, glossy; upright growth; [Precilla × Sunshine]; int. by McConnell Nurs., Inc.

Radiant Perfume Gr, my, 2005, Zary, Keith W.; flowers 25-30 petals, borne mostly solitary, intense lemony fragrance; foliage large, dark green, glossy; prickles 12 mm., hooked downward, greyed-orange, moderate; upright (5-6 ft.), branching, very vigorous growth; PP14915; [Henry Fonda × seedling]; int. by J&P Retail, 2004

Radiant Superglaze HT, w, 1987, Greensitt, J.A.; flowers near white, large, very dbl., moderate fragrance; foliage large, dark green, glossy; [Gavotte × Erotika]; int. by Nostell Priory Rose Gardens, 1982

Radiation F, mr, 1960, deRuiter; flowers open, 3-3½ in., semi-dbl., borne in clusters; foliage glossy; vigorous growth; [Poulsen's Pink × Pompadour Red]

Radieuse HT, mr, 1955, Laperrière; bud long; flowers clear red, well-formed, large, 30-35 petals; vigorous, bushy growth; int. by EFR

Radiman F, ly, 1985, Staikov, Prof. Dr. V.; flowers 50 petals, cupped, borne in clusters of 5-35, moderate tea fragrance; foliage dark, glossy; vigorous growth; [Highlight × Masquerade]; int. by Kalaydjiev and Chorbadjiiski, 1975

Radio HT, yb, 1937, Dot, Pedro; flowers yellow slightly tinted pink, striped and marked rose, large, 50 petals, cupped, moderate spicy fragrance; foliage wrinkled, light green; vigorous growth; [sport of Condesa de Sástago]; int. by C-P

Radio Lancashire F, or, 1987, Bracegirdle, A.J.; flowers orange-red, reverse slightly lighter, rosette, medium, 38 petals, borne in sprays of 10-15, slight fruity fragrance; foliage medium size, dark green, glossy; prickles triangle-shaped, brown; upright, medium growth; hips round, orange; [Dusky Maiden × Matangi]; int. by Rosemary Roses, 1987

Radio Times S, mp, 1997, Austin, David; bud pointed ovoid, globular; flowers rich, clear pink, 2½-3 in., 95-110 petals, flat, borne in small clusters, intense fragrance; foliage medium size, medium green, semi-glossy; prickles numerous, straight or slighly hooked; bushy, speading, low (75 cm.) growth; PP9525; [seedling × seedling]; int. by David Austin Roses, Ltd., 1994

Radiosa HT, Aicardi; int. in 1956

Radium Pol, lp, 1913, Grandes Roseraies; flowers delicate pink, pearly gold at center, borne in clusters of 15-20

Radium HT, rb, 1922, Lippiatt; flowers carmine, shaded coppery red; [Beauté Lyonnaise × Capt. Hayward]

Radka HT, dy, Vecera, L.; flowers large, dbl.; int. in 1975

Radome F, lp, 1966, Nicol; flowers pale rose; [sport of Queen Elizabeth]; int. by Minier

Radox Bouquet F, mp, 1980, Harkness, R., & Co., Ltd.; flowers soft medium pink, 4 in., 30-50 petals, cupped, borne 1-3 per cluster, moderate rose/lilac fragrance; recurrent; foliage large, glossy, medium green; prickles large, dark; upright, rather open growth; [(Alec's Red × Piccadilly) × (Southampton × (Clare Grammerstorf × Fruhlingsmorgen))]

Radway Charm HT, dp, 1960; flowers deep pink, base deep yellow, 20 petals, moderate fragrance; vigorous growth; [Christopher Stone × McGredy's Wonder sport]; int. by Waterhouse Nurs., 1959

Radway Glow F, op, 1960; flowers coral-pink, 14 petals, borne in large, open clusters; foliage dull green; vigorous growth; int. by Waterhouse Nurs., 1960

Radway Jewel F, dr, 1960; flowers yellow, becoming orange and deep red, medium, 40 petals, borne in large clusters; foliage light green; int. by Waterhouse Nurs., 1960

Radway Pink F, mp, 1965; flowers rose-pink, large, 42 petals, borne in clusters; foliage dull green; very free growth; [Margaret × Korona]; int. by Waterhouse Nursery, 1965

Radway Scarlet F, mr, 1963, Waterhouse Nursery; low growth; [Karl Weinhausen × seedling]

Radway Sunrise S, ob, 1962; flowers yellow, shading through orange to red, 3½-4 in., 7 petals, borne in clusters, slight fragrance; free-flowering; foliage dark, glossy; very vigorous growth; [Masquerade × unknown]; int. by Waterhouse Nursery, 1962

Rae Dungan HT, yb, 1972, Dawson, George; bud long, pointed; flowers creamy yellow, edged deep pink, large, dbl., borne singly, moderate fragrance; moderate, intermittent repeat; foliage dark green; stems long; vigorous, upright growth; [Daily Sketch × Fred Streeter]

Raewyn Henry HT, mr, 2001, Poole, Lionel; flowers medium red, lighter reverse, 5½ in., full, high-centered, borne mostly solitary, slight fragrance; free-flowering; foliage medium size, dark green, matte; prickles medium, hooked down, moderate; growth upright, bushy, vigorous, medium (1 m.); exhibition, bedding; [Naomi Rebecca × Adrienne Berman]; int. by Style Gardens Centre, 2002

Raf – See **Rafaël Braeckman**, F

Rafaël Braeckman F, ob, RvS-Melle; [Mullard Jubilee × Satchmo]; int. in 1985

Rafaela G. de Peña Pol, ob, 1938, Dot, Pedro; flowers pure orange, dbl.; foliage bright green, leathery; vigorous, bushy growth

Raffel's Pride HT, mr, 1937, Raffel; bud small; flowers oriental red, reverse gold-splashed, open, dbl.; vigorous growth; [Talisman × unknown]; int. by Port Stockton Nursery

Raffel's Yellow HT, my, 1942, Raffel; flowers pure yellow, well-shaped, large, 25-35 petals; foliage bronze turning very dark; vigorous growth; [probably Mrs Beatty × Maid of Gold]; int. by Port Stockton Nursery

Raffles Bruce HT, ab, 1943, Bees; flowers apricot and gold, well-shaped, 3-4 in.; foliage dark; compact growth; [Mrs Sam McGredy × Aureate]; Gold Medal, NRS, 1943

Rafzerfeld HGal, mp

Ragamuffin Min, yb

Ragazzina F

Ragged Robin – See **Gloire des Rosomanes**, Ch

Raggedy Ann F, mr, 1956, Joseph H. Hill, Co.; bud short, pointed; flowers 13 petals, borne in clusters; foliage dark, leathery; vigorous, upright growth; PP1403; [Garnette × Sister Kenny]

Ragini F, mp, 1974, Pal, Dr. B. P.; buds medium, pointed; flowers large, semi-dbl., open, borne singly and several together; foliage medium size, dark green, glossy; growth very vigorous, upright (140 cm.); int. by K. S. G. Son, 1972

Ragtime F, r, 1986, Lens, Louis; flowers brownish red, medium, 25 petals, hybrid tea, borne in clusters of 7-18, slight fragrance; foliage brownish-green; low, bushy growth; [Little Angel × Goldtopas]; int. in 1980

Ragtime F, ab, 1980, Pearce, C.A.; flowers apricot-pink, 65 petals, borne 10-15 per cluster; foliage small, mid-green, glossy; prickles large, straight, red; bushy growth; [Vesper × Aloha]; int. by Limes Rose Nursery, 1981

Ragtime Min, pb, 1985, McGredy, Sam IV; flowers small, dbl.; foliage small, dark, matte; bushy growth; [Mary Sumner × seedling]; int. by McGredy Roses International, 1982

Ragtime LCl, dp, Poulsen; flowers deep pink, reverse lighter, 8-10 cm., dbl., no fragrance; recurrent bloom; foliage dark green, glossy; bushy (7-10 ft.) growth; int. by Poulsen Roser, 2000

Rahima Pol, mp, 2004, Valentic, Dzejna; flowers pink with golden center and white edged petals, reverse blush pink with white, semi-dbl., borne mostly solitary, no fragrance; foliage small, medium green, glossy; upright, medium (12-18 in.) growth; garden, decorative, containers; [seedling × seedling]

Rainbow T, pb, 1889, Sievers; flowers pink, striped carmine and blush, semi-dbl., moderate fragrance; recurrent; [sport of Papa Gontier]

Rainbow S, op, Mattock; flowers peachy-salmon, shaded orange and lemon, large, dbl.; recurrent; growth tall; can serve as small climber or shrub; int. in 1974

Rainbow 02 LCl, rb, Hiroshima; flowers striped; int. by Hiroshima Bara-en, 2002

Rainbow Bliss Min, rb, 1990, Marciel, Stanley G.; bud slender, tapering; flowers white with cream inside with red edges, reverse same, medium, 37-45 petals, cupped, borne mostly singly, slight damask fragrance; foliage small, dark green, glossy; prickles declining, brown-orange; upright, low growth; [seedling × Scarlet Sunblaze]; int. by DeVor Nurseries, Inc., 1989

Rainbow Cerise Min, dp, 1989, Marciel, Stanley G.; bud tapering, slender; flowers medium, 39-45 petals, cupped, borne singly, slight fruity fragrance; free-flowering; foliage medium size, dark green, glossy; bushy, medium growth; PP7560; [Scarlet Sunblaze × seedling]; int. by DeVor Nurseries, Inc.

Rainbow Crimson Min, dr, 1990, Marciel, Stanley G.; bud slender; flowers deep red, aging discolors slightly, small, 33 petals, cupped, borne singly, slight damask fragrance; foliage medium size, dark green, semi-glossy; prickles declining, slightly dark mauve; upright, low growth; [seedling × seedling]; int. by DeVor Nurseries, Inc., 1989

Rainbow Delight Min, mr; int. in 1998

Rainbow Eclipse Min, rb, 1989, Marciel, Stanley G.; bud pointed; flowers crimson-pink edges, center very light whitish-pink, fading to white, medium, 34-40 petals, cupped, borne singly, slight fragrance; foliage small, dark green, glossy; prickles declining, rusty-brown; bushy, medium growth; PP7637; [Scarlet Sunblaze × seedling]; int. by DeVor Nurseries, Inc.

Rainbow Gold Min, yb, 1991, Marciel, Stanley G.; bud ovoid; flowers yellow-orange blend, medium, dbl., cupped, then flat, borne in small clusters, slight musk fragrance; foliage small, dark green, semi-glossy; prickles moderate, pointed, thin, declining; upright, medium (54 cm.) growth; PP7914; [Amber Flash × Rhumba]; int. by DeVor Nurseries, Inc., 1991

Rainbow Hot Pink Min, dp, 1989, Marciel, Stanley G.; bud long, slightly urn-shaped; flowers deep pink, small, 26 petals, cupped, borne singly, very slight fragrance; free-flowering; foliage small, dark green, semi-glossy; prickles declining, mauve; stems strong, upright; bushy, upright, medium growth; PP7689; [Orange Sunblaze × seedling]; int. by DeVor Nurseries, Inc.

Rainbow Knock Out S, pb, Radler; bud slender; flowers light coral pink with yellow eye, 2 in., single, shallow cup to flat, borne in small clusters, slight spice fragrance; recurrent; foliage medium green, satiny finish; prickles 1-1½ cm., brown; vigorous, round, bushy (3 ft.) growth; hips greyed-orange; PP17346; [Radtee × Radral]; int. in 2007; AARS, All-American Rose Selections, 2007

Rainbow Magic Min, rb, 1999, Dickson, Colin; flowers cerise red, reverse yellow, 1¾ in., semi-dbl., borne in large clusters, slight fragrance; foliage small, medium green, glossy; prickles moderate; spreading, low (2 ft × 3 ft.) growth; patio; [Sunseeker × seedling]; int. by Dickson Nurseries, Ltd., 1999

Rainbow Nation – See **Camille Pissarro**, F

Rainbow Niagara – See **Tropical Sunset**, HT

Rainbow Pink Min, dp, 1989, Marciel, Stanley G.; bud ovoid, pointed; flowers deep pink, petals imbricated, small, 32 petals, high-centered, borne singly, slight spicy fragrance; free-flowering; foliage medium size, dark green, semi-glossy; prickles sparse, declining, purple; bushy, compact, medium growth; PP6875; [seedling × Orange Sunblaze]; int. by DeVor Nurseries, Inc.

Rainbow Red Min, mr, 1989, Marciel, Stanley G.; bud pointed; flowers small, 25-28 petals, flat, borne singly, slight spicy fragrance; foliage small, dark green, glossy; prickles declining, brown with orange; bushy, upright, compact, medium growth; PP6584; [Scarlet Sunblaze × Rumba]; int. by DeVor Nurseries, Inc.

Rainbow Robe HT, m, Kordes; flowers mauve, edges of outer petals turning red with exposure to sun, large, dbl., high-centered, intense fragrance; int. in 1991

Rainbow Shower LCl, pb, 1992, Little, Lee W.; flowers shrimp pink suffused with yellow and darker pink edge, aging, 3-3½ in., 5 petals; foliage medium size, medium green, glossy, disease-resistant; some prickles; tall (210 cm.), upright, spreading growth; [Altissimo × Playboy]; int. by Oregon Miniature Roses, 1992

Rainbow Sorbet F, yb, Lim, Ping; bud pointed; flowers bright yellow, red and orange petal edges, 3½ in., 15-18 petals, cupped, no fragrance; recurrent; foliage dark green, glossy; upright (to 5 ft.) growth

Rainbow Stanford Min, rb, 1989, Marciel, Stanley G.; bud pointed, slender; flowers bright red, aging discolors to a bright red-orange, medium, 12-15 petals, high-centered, borne singly, slight fruity fragrance; free-flowering; foliage medium size, dark green, glossy; prickles declining, reddish-brown; bushy, compact, medium growth; PP7559; [Candia × seedling]; int. by DeVor Nurseries, Inc.

Rainbow Sunblaze Min, yb, Meilland; flowers yellow with red petal edges, small, 30-40 petals, cupped, borne in clusters, no fragrance; recurrent; foliage medium green, semi-glossy; medium, bushy growth; PPAF; int. in 2005

Rainbow Sunrise Min, ob, 1989, Marciel, Stanley G.; bud pointed; flowers orange with tinge of red, reverse same, 1 in., 15-18 petals, cupped, borne singly, slight spicy fragrance; free-flowering; foliage small, medium green, glossy; prickles sparse, declining, brown; bushy, upright, medium growth; PP6583; [Amber Flash × Rumba]; int. by DeVor Nurseries, Inc.

Rainbow Surprise Min, ab, 1989, Marciel, Stanley G.; bud slender, tapering; flowers medium coral, reverse light coral, aging pink, 28 petals, cupped, borne singly, slight fruity fragrance; free-flowering; foliage small, dark green, glossy; prickles declining, mauve; bushy, upright, medium growth; PP7558; [Orange Sunblaze × seedling]; int. by DeVor Nurseries, Inc.

Rainbow Warrior – See **Modern Magic**, F

Rainbow Yellow Min, ob, 1989, Marciel, Stanley G.; bud pointed, urn-shaped; flowers tangerine orange with yellow base, aging lighter, 48 petals, cupped, borne singly, intense fruity fragrance; free-flowering; foliage medium size, medium green, matte; prickles declining, reddish-brown; bushy, upright, medium growth; PP7638; [seedling × Amber Flash]; int. by DeVor Nurseries, Inc.

Rainbow Yellow Parade Min, dy, 1990, Olesen, Pernille & Mogens N.; bud cupped, globular; flowers bright yellow, aging slightly, small, 28-30 petals, cupped, borne singly, slight damask fragrance; foliage small, dark green, semi-glossy; no prickles; upright, low, compact growth; [seedling × Texas]; int. by Poulsen Roser, 1985; Gold Medal, The Hague, 1988

Rainbow's End Min, yb, 1984, Saville, F. Harmon; bud long pointed; flowers deep yellow, red petal edges, aging red all over, 1¼-1¾ in., 30-35 petals, high-centered, borne singly and in small clusters, no fragrance; free-flowering; foliage small, dark green, glossy; prickles moderate, thin, pointed, angled slightly downward; upright (18 in.), bushy growth; hips globular, orange-red; PP5482; [Rise 'n' Shine × Watercolor]; int. by Nor'East Min. Roses; AOE, ARS, 1986

Rainbow's End, Climbing Min, yb, 1998, O'Brien, Susan; flowers yellow suffused with red at edges, 1½ in., 30-35 petals, high-centered, borne singly and in small clusters; foliage small, medium green, semi-glossy; prickles moderate, thin, angling downward; short, thick stems; climbing to 10 ft. growth; PP11257; [sport of Rainbow's End]; int. by Nor'East Miniature Roses

Raindrops Min, m, 1990, Saville, F. Harmon; bud ovoid; flowers light mauve-purple, light yellow at base, reverse lighter, 1½ in., 24 petals, high-centered, borne in sprays of 5-20, slight fragrance; foliage small, dark green, semi-glossy; prickles straight, slanted downward, small, gray-red; upright, medium growth; fruit not observed; PP7448; [Sachet × Rainbow's End]; int. by Nor'East Min. Roses, 1990

Raindrops S, pb, Williams, J. Benjamin; flowers medium pink, ivory reverse, semi-dbl.; compact growth; int. by Hortico Inc., 1997

Rainer Maria Rilke – See **Uwe Seeler**, F

Rainforest F, pb, 2004, Moore, Ralph S.; flowers pink, aging to light green with pink highlights, reverse white, 3 in., semi-dbl., borne in small clusters, slight fragrance; foliage medium size, medium green, semi-glossy; prickles small, straight, brown, few; upright, tall (3-4 ft. growth); pillar, specimen, cutting; [Sheri Ann × Scarlet Moss]; int. by Sequoia Nurs., 2004

Rainy F, mr, 2006, Scrivens, Len; flowers crimson, 4 in., very full, borne in large clusters; foliage medium size, dark green, matte; prickles straight, few; growth bushy, tall (4 ft.); garden decoration; [(seedling × Cuthbert Grant) × Big Purple]; int. in 2007

Rainy Day HT, mp, 1982, McGredy, Sam IV; flowers large, 20 petals; foliage large, dark, semi-glossy; bushy growth; [Trumpeter × Typhoon]; int. by McGredy Roses International

Raissa HT, mp, Cocker; int. in 1990

Raita HRg, Rieksta, Dr. Dz.

Raja of Nalagarh HT, or, 1979, Pal, Dr. B.P.; bud pointed; flowers bright orange-red with salmon tints, 4 in., 32 petals, high-centered, borne singly, slight fragrance; recurrent; foliage dark, leathery; vigorous, upright growth; [Samourai × Montezuma]; int. by Gopalsinamiengar, 1977

Raja Surendra Singh of Nalagarh – See **Raja of Nalagarh**, HT

Rajbala F, pb, 1976, Pal, Dr. B.P.; bud pointed; flowers open, 4 in., 10 petals; foliage large, glossy, light; very vigorous, upright, compact growth; [Delhi Princess × seedling]; int. by Indian Agric. Research Inst., 1975

Rajkumari HT, dp, 1976, IARI; bud pointed; flowers deep fuchsine-pink, 4 in., 70 petals; foliage glossy, light; vigorous, compact growth; [(Charles Mallerin × Delhi Princess) × seedling]; int. in 1975

Rajni – See **Orient Spice**, HT

Raketa HT, op, 1952, Shtanko, E.E.; flowers golden orange-pink, 5 in., 50 petals; foliage reddish bronze; vigorous, upright, compact growth; [Narzisse × Comtesse Vandal]

Rakete HT, mr, GPG Bad Langensalza; flowers large, dbl.; int. in 1972

Raktagandha HT, or, 1976, IARI; bud long, pointed; flowers vermilion, 3 in., 35 petals, high-centered; foliage glossy; vigorous, upright growth; [Christian Dior × Carrousel seedling]; int. in 1975

Rakthima HT, mr, IARI; flowers bright red, dbl., high-centered; recurrent; stems strong, straight; int. in 1991

Rakuen HT, ob, Keisei; int. by Keisei Rose Nurseries, 1996

Rakuhoku HT, pb, Keihan; int. by Keihan Gardening, 1990

Rakuyô HT, rb; int. in 1995

Rallye Pol, r, 1966, Delforge; bud ovoid; flowers cognac color with pink, large, dbl., borne in clusters; foliage dark, glossy; vigorous, upright growth; [Cognac × Fashion]

Ralph HT, ab, deVor; int. in 1993

Ralph Leighty F, w, 1972, Leighty; bud ovoid; flowers near white, medium, dbl., high-centered; foliage light, soft; moderate, upright growth; PP3545; [sport of Gene Boerner]; int. by McFadden, 1971

Ralph Moore Min, mr, 1999, Saville, F. Harmon; bud small, ovate; flowers dark cherry red, lighter reverse, medium, 20 -24 petals, high-centered, borne mostly singly, with some sprays, slight fragrance; free-flowering; foliage medium size, dark green, semi-glossy; prickles few, straight; upright, compact, well-branched, medium (16 in.) growth; hips near globular, deep orange; PP13056; [Sachet × seedling]; int. by Nor'East Miniature Roses, 2000; AOE, ARS, 2000

Ralph T Min, my, 2001, Moe, Mitchie; flowers single, borne mostly singly, slight fragrance; foliage small, medium green, semi-glossy; prickles few, very small, straight, white; growth upright, tall (24-30 in.); garden decoration, exhibition; [Klima × Blue Peter]; int. by Mitchie's Roses and More, 2001

Ralph Tizard F, op, 1979, Sanday, John; flowers pure salmon, pointed, 4 in., 28 petals, borne singly and several together, moderate fragrance; free-flowering; foliage medium size, dark green; prickles straight; growth average, vigorous; [Vera Dalton × Tropicana]

Ralph's Creeper S, rb, 1988, Moore, Ralph S.; bud small, long, pointed; flowers dark orange-red, bright yellow eye, reverse bright yellow to white, medium, 15-18 petals, loose, borne in sprays of 10-15, moderate apple-blossom fragrance; repeat bloom; foliage small, dark green, matte; prickles brownish, straight, inclined downward; spreading, low, groundcover growth; hips round, orange-red; PP6548; [Papoose × Playboy]; int. by Armstrong Nursery, 1988

Ramanas Rose – See ***R. rugosa*** (Thunberg)

Ramapo Min, mp, 1985, Zipper, Herbert; flowers small, 5 petals, borne singly; foliage small, medium green, matte; bushy growth; [Maytime × Libby]; int. by Magic Moment Miniature Roses

Ramat-Gan F, dy, 1975, Holtzman; bud urn-shaped; flowers deep lemon-yellow, 1 in., 25 petals, cupped to urn-shaped, moderate fragrance; foliage light; moderate growth; [Golden Masterpiece × Zorina]; int. by Holtzman Rose Nursery, 1974

Ramble and Tumble LCl, op, Kordes; flowers intense salmon pink, full, cupped, borne in clusters; late bloomer, rapid repeat; vigorous, spreading, tumbling growth; int. by Ludwig's Roses, 2004

Rambler-Königin HWich, mp, 1907, Kohler & Rudel; flowers small, full; somewhat remontant

Rambling Rector HMult, w, 1910, from England; flowers pink-white, 4 cm., semi-dbl., borne in large clusters, moderate fragrance; vigorous growth; hips small, oval; very probably an older rose, renamed

Ramblin' Red LCl, mr, 2001, Radler, William; bud slender, small to medium; flowers cardinal red, 3 in., 35 petals, borne in large clusters, slight spicy fragrance; recurrent; foliage deep green, satiny; prickles moderate; upright, vigorous (6-9 ft.) growth; PP14270; [Razzle × Henry Kelsey]

Rambling Rosie Cl Min, mr, Horner; flowers bright red with yellow eye, small, borne in large clusters; recurrent; foliage small, medium to dark green, glossy; vigorous (8-12 ft.) growth with flexible canes; [Super Excelsa × (Baby Love × Golden Future)]; int. in 2006

Ramira LCl, mp, W. Kordes' Sohne; flowers large, borne singly or in small clusters, slight fragrance; good repeat; foliage dark green, glossy; int. in 1988

Ramón Bach HT, ob, 1938, Dot, Pedro; flowers bright orange, edged lighter, reverse reddish-gold, stamens bright yellow, 80 petals, globular, intense fruity fragrance; foliage glossy, dark; vigorous growth; [Luis Brinas × Condesa de Sástago]; int. by C-P

Ramona S, mr, 1913, Dietrich & Turner; flowers carmine-crimson, fading to rose pink with age, large, single; some repeat; [sport of Anemone]; most characteristics like Anemone, but bloom deeper color

Ramona – See **Ramona Hit**, MinFl

Ramona Hit MinFl, dp, Poulsen; flowers deep pink, 5-8 cm., dbl., no fragrance; foliage dark; growth bushy, 40-60 cm.; int. by Poulsen Roser, 2000

Rampa Pal HT, pb, 1976, Pal, Dr. B.P.; bud ovoid; flowers fuchsia-pink, reverse lighter, 4½ in., 60 petals, high-centered; foliage glossy; moderate, upright, bushy growth; int. in 1975

Rampant HSem, w, 1830, Jacques; profuse bloom, sometimes in autumn

Ran S, mp, 1973, Lundstad; bud globular; flowers pink, open, small, semi-dbl.; foliage small, light, soft; vigorous, upright growth; [*R. cinnamomea* × *R. helenae* hybrid]; int. by Norges Landbruks-hogskole, 1972

Rancho Mirage F, mr, 2005, Rippetoe, Robert Neil; flowers small, single, borne in large clusters, no fragrance; foliage medium size, dark green, glossy; prickles moderate, medium, hooked, light tan; growth compact, short (2 ft.); bedding; [Dortmund × unknown]; int. in 2005

Randall HGal, mp; flowers dbl.; not as hardy as Alika; an old variety taken by early pioneers to western Canada

Randers F, yb, Poulsen; bud long, pointed ovoid; flowers yellow-apricot-orange blend, 2½-4 in., 28-33 petals, open cup, borne in large clusters, very slight fragrance; free-flowering; foliage dark green, glossy; prickles linear to slightly concave; bushy, upright (3 ft.) growth; PP15609; [seedling × Aspen]; int. by Poulsen Roser, 2002

Randfontein Gold Gr, my, Kordes; bud egg-shaped; flowers clear golden-yellow, dbl., cupped, borne in large clusters; vigorous, medium growth; int. by Ludwig's Roses, 1989

Randilla Geel – See **Randilla Jaune**, Min

Randilla Jaune Min, my

Randilla Rose Min, mp

Randilla Rouge Min, mr

Rangatarang HT, pb, Chiplunkar; int. in 1993

Range View Cream Tea – See **Devoniensis**, T

Ranger S, mr, Barni, V.; flowers red with vermilion highlights and yellow eye, single, borne in clusters, moderate fragrance; growth to 4-5 ft.; int. by Rose Barni, 1996; Gold Medal, Baden-Baden, 1996

Rangila HT, rb, Tejganga; int. in 1995

Rangitoto HT, m, 1992, Schuurman, Frank B.; flowers medium, very dbl.; foliage medium size, medium green, glossy; upright growth; [Champagne × Chantilly Lace]; int. by Riverland Nurseries, Ltd., 1990

Rangoli F, op, 1979, Thakur; bud tapered; flowers coral-pink, 3-3½ in., 25 petals, high-centered, slight fruity fragrance; foliage glossy; dwarf, bushy growth; [sport of Golden Slippers]; int. by Doon Valley Roses

Rangoli HT, w, Chakraborty, Dr. K.; flowers creamy white with strong pink flush, large, dbl.; int. in 1999

Rangshala HT, ab, 1971, IARI; bud pointed; flowers apricot, shaded peach and amber yellow, open, medium, dbl.; foliage glossy; moderate growth; [Margaret Spaull × unknown]; int. in 1969

Ranjana HT, or, 1976, Pal, Dr. B.P.; bud pointed; flowers rose-opal, 4½ in., 38 petals, intense fragrance; foliage dark, leathery; very vigorous, upright, bushy growth; [Samourai × unknown]; int. by Anand Roses, 1975

Rankende Johanna Tantau Cl Pol, 1942, Tantau, Math.

Rankende Miniature – See **Miniature, Climbing**, Cl Pol

Ranuncula HT, rb, Kordes; flowers red with soft yellow stripes and splashes, medium, dbl., cupped, borne mostly singly; recurrent; stems long; florist rose; int. by W. Kordes Söhne, 2005

Ranunculiflora HSet, lp, about 1846, Pierce; flowers pale flesh, darker center, small to medium, borne in clusters of 20-30, moderate fragrance; foliage rugose; prickles purplish

Ranunculus Musk Cluster HMsk, w; flowers pure white, very dbl.; very vigorous growth

Ranunkel Mikado F, dy, Tantau; greenhouse rose

Ranzan HT, dr, Keihan; int. by Keihan Gardening, 1990

Raoul Chauvry T, yb, 1896, Chauvry; flowers capucine yellow, shaded coppery, center apricot, large, dbl., moderate fragrance; [Mme Lombard × unknown]

Raoul Follereau HT, dp; flowers rose-magenta, large, very dbl., moderate fruit and spice fragrance; int. by Delbard, 2005

Raphael M, w, 1856, Robert; flowers well mossed, pinkish white, full, borne in clusters of 12-20; slightly recurrent bloom

Raphaela HT, ob, Tantau; bud long pointed, ovoid; flowers orange to orange-red, with thick petals, 5 in., 20 petals, high-centered, borne singly, slight fragrance; recurrent; foliage large, leathery, glossy; prickles moderate, hooked slightly downward, red; stems long (24-28 in.); vigorous, upright (6 ft. in greenhouse) growth; PP9064; [seedling × TANettelur]; originally a florist rose; int. by Rosen Tantau, 1994

Rapperswil HT, or, 1979, Huber; bud globular; flowers 4 in., 30 petals, cupped, intense fragrance; foliage dark, leathery; [Fragrant Cloud × Ena Harkness]; int. in 1975

Rapsodia F, ob

Rapture HT, pb, 1926, Traendly & Schenck; flowers deeper pink, flushed gold at base; [sport of Mme Butterfly]; growth much like parent

Rapture, Climbing Cl HT, pb, 1933, Dixie Rose Nursery

Raquel Meller HT, lp, 1958, Camprubi, C.; flowers soft pink, large, dbl., cupped, intense fragrance; foliage glossy; [Edith Krause × Fashion]; int. in 1957; Gold Medal, Geneva, 1956

Rare Edition F, rb, Kasturi; flowers scarlet, striped and splashed white; [sport of Kusum]; int. by KSG Son, 1982

Rashmi Pol, dr, Kasturi; flowers blackish crimson, globular; int. by KSG Son, 1977

Raspberry Beauty Min, mr, 1994, Williams, Ernest D.; flowers non-fading raspberry red, medium, full, high-centered, borne mostly singly; foliage small, medium green, semi-glossy; few prickles; medium (16-20 in.), bushy growth; [Angel Face × Anita Charles]; int. by Texas Mini Roses, 1994

Raspberry Bouquet S, rb, 2006, Brown, Ted; flowers red, reverse cream, 4 in., full, borne in large clusters, strong raspberry fragrance; foliage medium size, medium green, semi-glossy; prickles small, hooked, brown, moderate; growth upright, bushy, tall (4-6 ft.); exhibition, garden decorative; [Lydia (Kordes) × Cocktail (Meimick)]; int. in 2006

Raspberry Delight HT, rb, 1980, Taylor, Thomas E.; flowers medium red on outer petals shading to creamy coral on inner, 30 petals, high-centered, moderate raspberry fragrance; foliage medium green, semi-glossy; prickles hooked; upright, bushy growth; [Carrousel × First Prize]

Raspberry Ice – See **Hannah Gordon**, F

Raspberry Ice MinFl, rb, 1989, Zipper, Herbert; flowers white brushed with red, deeper red at petal edge, medium, 40 petals, no fragrance; foliage medium size, dark green, semi-glossy; mini-flora; upright growth; [High Spirits × Charmglo]; int. by Magic Moment Miniature Roses, 1989

Raspberry Meillandina Min, dp, Meilland

Raspberry Punch Min, dp, 1998, Zary, Dr. Keith W.; bud long, pointed ovoid; flowers full, 35 petals, high-centered, borne singly and in clusters of three to seven, slight fragrance; foliage medium size, dark green, semi-glossy; prickles moderate, straight; stems strong (6-8 in.); compact, upright, moderate (30 in.) growth; PP12050; [Tournament of Roses × seedling]; int. by Bear Creek Gardens, Inc., 1999

Raspberry Red F, mr; int. in 1995

Raspberry Ripple F, rb, Delbard; flowers red with white stripes, semi-dbl. to dbl., cupped to flat, borne in clusters; recurrent; vigorous (24-30 in.) growth; int. by Sanwell Nurseries, 1998

Raspberry Ripple HSet, pb

Raspberry Ripple Folies F, dp, J&P; int. in 2004

Raspberry Rose F, mr

Raspberry Royale S, dp; flowers raspberry red, dbl., cupped; foliage glossy; growth to 20 × 20 in.; int. by Burston Nurseries, 2003

Raspberry Ruffles F, dp, 1991, Taylor, Pete & Kay; bud pointed; flowers deep pink with white eye, deep pink reverse, aging lighter, medium, 18-20 petals, high-centered, opens flat, borne in sprays of 4-6, intense fragrance; foliage medium size, medium green, semi-glossy; upright, bushy, medium growth; [Garnette × seedling]; int. by Taylor's Roses, 1990

Raspberry Ruffles S, pb, Harkness Roses; flowers ruffled, raspberry with brushed white edges, 2½ in., 12 petals, slight fragrance; compact, upright (3½ ft.) growth with many canes; PPAF; int. by Heirloom Roses, 2005

Raspberry Rugostar HRg, dp, 2003, Meilland International; flowers mauve, reverse deep pink, 6-8 cm., 5 petals, flattened cup, borne in clusters, moderate spicy, sweet clove fragrance; recurrent; foliage large, light green, matte; prickles moderate; growth spreading, short (2-3 ft.); groundcover; hips sub-globose, 14 × 18 cm., orange-red; PP15937; [Schneekoppe × Frau Dagmar Hastrup]; int. by The Conard-Pyle Company, 2003

Raspberry Star Min, dp; int. by Regan Nursery, 2000

Raspberry Sunblaze Min, dp, 1998, Meilland; buds egg-shaped; flowers raspberry red with lighter reverse, 2 in., 50 petals, cupped, borne in small clusters and singly, no fragrance; free-flowering; foliage medium size, medium green, semi-glossy; prickles moderate, small; bushy, medium, compact (15 in.) growth; PP10666; [(Orange Sunblaze × Prince Meillandina) × Red Minimo]; int. by Conard-Pyle Co.

Raspberry Swirl S, rb, 1999, Walden, John K.; flowers red, white, pink stripe, reverse same, 2 in., dbl., borne in large clusters, slight apple scent fragrance; foliage small, dark green, glossy; prickles moderate; upright, arching, medium (3-4 ft.) growth; PP11996; [seedling × Plum Dandy]; int. by Bear Creek Gardens, Inc., 1999

Raspberry Swirls HT, pb, 2000, Edwards, Eddie; flowers raspberry, reverse white, 4-5 in., dbl., high-centered, borne mostly singly, slight fragrance; foliage large, medium green, semi-glossy; few prickles; growth upright, medium (4 ft.); [Crystalline × Suffolk]; int. by Johnny Becnel Show Roses

Raspberry Trail S, mr, Bell, Laurie; flowers rich raspberry red, very full; growth vigorous, low, spreading; groundcover; [seedling × Red Cascade]; int. by Bell Roses

Raspberry Wine – See **Malinovka**, F

Rassvet HT, pb, 1955, Klimenko, V. N.; flowers soft pink, base creamy yellow, medium, 48 petals; foliage dark; spreading growth; [Peace × unknown]

Rastede – See **Ledreborg**, F

Ratan HT, my, Bulsara, S.P.; flowers lemon yellow; int. in 1990

Ratgeber Rose HWich, mr, 1930, Verlag Praktischer Ratgeber; flowers light red, 4-5 cm., dbl., borne in small clusters

Rathernice HT, ob, 1957, Bishop; flowers coppery orange; foliage coppery; moderate growth; int. by Baker's Nursery

Ratnaar HT, mp, Pal, Dr. B.P.; flowers coral pink, large, dbl., high-centered; int. in 1985

Raubritter S, lp, 1936, Kordes; flowers medium, dbl., globular, borne in clusters, moderate fragrance; foliage leathery, wrinkled; vigorous, climbing growth; [Daisy Hill × Solarium]

Ravel HMsk, pb, 2000, Lens, Louis; flowers medium red, yellow stamens, 3 cm., single, borne in large clusters, moderate fragrance; recurrent; foliage medium size, medium green, semi-glossy; prickles moderate; growth bushy, medium (80-120 cm.); [*R. multiflora*

adenocheata × Ballerina]; int. by Louis Lens N.V., 1988

Ravel HT, dp; bud medium, ovate; sepals shorter than bud, generally simple to slightly foliated; flowers dark pink, reverse slightly lighter and veined, 5 in., 25 petals, high-centered, borne singly, very slight fragrance; free-flowering; foliage medium to large, dark green, semi-glossy; prickles moderate, hooked downward, 7 mm., tan to reddish-tan; narrow upright, vigorous (6 ft.) growth; hips funnel-shaped ; PP8632; [sport of Vivaldi]; int. by deRuiter, 1994

Ravellae HSpn, w, Christ; flowers creamy white

Raven S, dr, 1999, Fryer, Gareth; flowers deep velvety red, golden stamens, 1¼-1½ in., 20-25 petals, borne in very large clusters; foliage small, dark green, glossy; prickles moderate; upright, bushy, medium (3-4 ft.) growth; PP9211; [Lavaglut × ((Anytime × Liverpool Echo) × (New Penny × Unknown))]; int. as Daily Post, Fryer's Nurseries Ltd., 1992

Ravenna S, dp, Noack; flowers dark pink with lighter tones in center, 4 cm., single, shallow cup, borne in clusters, slight fragrance; free-flowering; upright (80 cm.), then spreading growth; crown frost hardy; int. by Noack Rosen, 2001

Ravensberg S, mr, Noack, Werner; flowers blood red with a darker overlay on the petal edges, small, dbl., borne in clusters, slight fragrance; recurrent; [Alpengruss × ((Ruth Leuwerik × Paprika (Tantau, 1958)) × (Lili Marlene × Molde))]; int. in 1986

Ravenswood Min, yb, 1992, Catt, Graeme Charles; flowers gold, outer petals flushed pink, ½ in., 18-20 petals, borne 3-4 per cluster; foliage healthy; upright, bushy growth; [Rise 'n' Shine × unknown]; int. by F.D. Catt Wholesale Nursery, 1989

Ravenswood Village HT, ly, 1996, Poole, Lionel; flowers light yellow, deeper in autumn, very large, full, high-centered, borne mostly singly; foliage medium size, medium green, glossy; some prickles; upright, medium growth; [Golden Splendour × Queen Esther]; int. by F. Haynes & Partners, 1997

Ravensworth Pol, my; flowers soft yellow; [sport of Perle d'Or]; identical to Perle d'Or in all respects except bloom color; int. by Ross Roses, 1998

Ravikanchan HT, lp, 2003, Bhate, N.B.; flowers large, full, borne mostly solitary, slight fragrance; foliage medium size, medium green, semi-glossy; prickles slightly pointed; bushy, medium growth; [sport of Garden Party]; int. in 2002

Raving Beauty HT, mp, 1948, Joseph H. Hill, Co.; bud ovoid, rose-red; flowers Tyrian rose, 3-4 in., 35-40 petals, globular; foliage leathery, dark; vigorous, upright growth

Ray Adeline HT, my, 1990, Bevard, Harry D.; bud pointed; flowers medium, 40 petals, high-centered, borne usually singly and in sprays of 2-4, moderate fragrance; foliage medium size, dark green, semi-glossy; prickles straight, hooked down, light green; upright growth; hips small, light green; [First Prize × King's Ransom]

Ray Bunge Cl HP, dp, 1959, Bunge; flowers dark rose, reverse lighter, 4-5 in., 30-40 petals, borne singly or clusters of 7-8; prolific early spring bloom, repeating later in season; foliage dark; very long stems; very vigorous (15½ ft.) growth; quite hardy; PP1637; [sport of Paul Neyron]; int. by Andrews Nursery Co., 1959

Ray of Hope F, mr, Cocker; flowers bright red, medium, semi-dbl., borne in clusters, slight fragrance; foliage large, dark green, glossy; bushy, upright (2½-3 ft.) growth; [seedling × Abbeyfield Rose]; int. in 1996

Ray of Sunshine S, my, 1990, Cocker, James & Sons; bud pointed; flowers clear, bright yellow, small, 15 petals, cupped, borne in sprays of 3-9, slight spicy fragrance; foliage small, dark green, glossy; prickles small, green; bushy, low growth; hips round, small, green; [Sunsprite × (Clare Grammerstorf × Fruhlingsmorgen)]; int. in 1988

Ray Still MinFl, mr, 2001, Hough, Robin; flowers velvety red petals, 1¾ in., dbl., exhibition, borne mostly solitary, slight fragrance; foliage large, dark green, semi-glossy; prickles medium, straight, moderate; growth bushy, tall (24-30 in.); [seedling × Halo Today]; int. in 2001

Ray Torey F, mr, 2003, Gill, Mathew; flowers medium, semi-dbl., borne in large clusters, slight fragrance; foliage medium size, medium green, semi-glossy; prickles small, hooked; compact, medium (50 cm.) growth; [unknown]; int. by Love 4 Plants, 2003

Raymond HT, pb, 1917, Pernet-Ducher; bud long, pointed; flowers peach-blossom-pink, center salmon-carmine, dbl.; [Rayon d'Or × unknown]

Raymond Blanc S, mp; flowers bright cerise pink, full, old fashioned, moderate almond fragrance; recurrent; bushy growth; int. by Pococks Roses, 2006

Raymond Carver S, ab, 2000, Horner, Colin P.; flowers apricot orange, reverse lighter, 11-12 cm., full, borne in small clusters; foliage large, medium green, glossy; prickles moderate; growth climbing, upright, tall (2 m.); hedges, pillars; [Summer Wine × Lichtkonigin Lucia]; int. by Peter Beales Roses, 1999

Raymond Chenault HKor, mr, 1963, Kordes, R.; flowers bright red, 4 in., 16 petals, borne in medium clusters, moderate fragrance; foliage dark, glossy; vigorous (9-12 ft.) growth; [*R.* × *kordesii* × Montezuma]; int. by W. Kordes Söhne, 1960

Raymond Chevalier-Appert, Climbing Cl HT, mr; flowers pale red, semi-dbl.

Raymond Kopa – See **Chris Evert**, HT

Raymond Nazereau F, dp, Adam; int. in 2000

Raymond Privat Pol, m, 1935, Privat; flowers violet, dbl., borne in clusters; vigorous growth

Raymond's Pearl F, yb, 1997, Rawlins, R.; flowers medium, 41 petals, borne in small clusters; foliage medium size, medium green, semi-glossy; some prickles; upright, medium (75 cm.) growth; [Amber Queen × Brown Velvet]

Rayon Butterflies S, pb, Rupert; flowers single; int. in during the 1980s

Rayon d'Or HT, my, 1910, Pernet-Ducher; flowers golden yellow, sometimes streaked crimson on the outer petals, large, dbl., globular; foliage large, glossy; [Mme Mélanie Soupert × (Soleil d'Or × unknown)]

Rayon d'Or HT, my, 1962, Combe; flowers well-formed

Ray's Joy F, ob, 2000, Jerabek, Paul E.; flowers orange-brownish, velvety, reverse orange, 3 in., full, borne singly or in small clusters, slight fragrance; foliage medium medium green, semi-glossy,new growth bronze; prickles moderate; growth upright, medium (3 ft.); int. by Freedom Gardens

Raywen Henry HT, mr, Poole; int. by David Lister Ltd., 2004

Razzle Dazzle F, rb, 1976, Warriner, William A.; flowers red, reverse white, 2½ in., 25 petals, slight fragrance; foliage dark, leathery; bushy growth; PP3995; int. by J&P, 1977; Gold Medal, Portland, 1978

Razzle Dazzle F, ob, Fryer, Gareth; flowers tangerine-orange, large, dbl., high-centered, borne in clusters, moderate fragrance; good repeat; foliage dark green, glossy; vigorous (2½ ft.), bushy growth; int. by Fryer's Roses, 1997

Razzmatazz Min, or, 1982, Warriner, William A.; bud pointed ovoid; flowers small, 27 -30 petals, flat, borne in clusters, no fragrance; free-flowering; foliage semi-glossy; prickles numerous, long, hooked slightly downward, brown; vigorous, upright (2 ft.) growth; PP5118; [Zorina × Fire Princess]; int. by J&P, 1981

Rea Silvia HT, or, 1959, Giacomasso; flowers fiery red; [Baiser × (Peace × seedling)]; int. in 1958

Reach for Recovery HT, mp, Delbard; bud globular; flowers large, full, borne mostly singly, intense fragrance; good repeat; tall growth; int. by Ludwig's Roses, 2001; Trial Ground Certificate, Durbanville, 2006

Ready MinFl, yb, 2006, Tucker, Robbie; flowers yellow with red edging, 1½ in., full, borne mostly solitary; foliage dark green, glossy; prickles ¼ to ½ in., straight with point slightly down, reddish brown; growth bushy, medium (to 30 in.); landscape, exhibition; [Cal Poly × Little Tommy Tucker]; int. by Rosemania, 2007

Reah Nicole MinFl, pb, 2004, Jalbert, Brad; flowers pink and cream, 1½-2 in., full, borne in small clusters, slight fragrance; foliage medium size, medium green, semi-glossy; prickles moderate, medium size, green; growth upright, 18 in. and up; cutting, garden decoration; [Loving Touch × Kristen]; int. in 2000

Real – See **Real Hit**, MinFl

Real Charmer Min, lp, 1992, Chaffin, Lauren M.; flowers 3-3½ in., full, borne in small clusters, moderate fragrance; foliage large, medium green, semi-glossy; tall (45 cm.), upright growth; [Gene Boerner × Crissy]; int. by Pixie Treasures Min. Roses

Real Hit MinFl, dr, Poulsen; flowers dark red, 5-8 cm., dbl., no fragrance; foliage dark; growth bushy, 20-40 cm.; PP13170; int. by Poulsen Roser, 2002

Reality LCl, mp, 2000, Brown, Ted; flowers medium pink, reverse lighter, 3½ in., full, borne in small clusters, moderate fragrance; foliage medium size, dark green, glossy, very thick, rubbery; prickles moderate; growth spreading, medium (6-8 ft.); [Esprit × seedling]

Rea's Rose HT, pb, Kordes; flowers coral pink with cream reverse, full, high-centered, borne mostly singly; recurrent; stems sturdy, medium long; medium to tall growth; int. by W. Kordes Söhne, 1997

Reba K. Rowland LCl, dr, 2003, Carruth, Tom; flowers deep velvet red, reverse slightly lighter red, 6½-8½ cm., full, borne in small clusters, slight fragrance; foliage large, dark green, glossy; prickles few, average, hooked slightly downward, greenish tan; growth spreading, climbing (250-380 cm.); garden decorative; PP15089; [(America × Marina) × (*R. soulieana* derivative × Dortmund)]; int. by Rowland Nursery, 2003

Reba McEntire Gr, or, 1998, McGredy, Sam IV; bud medium, ovoid; flowers 4-4½ in., 30-35 petals, cupped to high-centered, borne in small clusters, slight spicy fragrance; free-flowering; foliage large, dark green, glossy; prickles moderate, large, hooked slightly downward; bushy, medium (110cm.) growth; hips none observed ; PP11489; [(Howard Morrison × Red Perfection) × Maiden Voyage]; int. by McGredy, 1997; Gold Star of the South Pacific, Palmerston North, NZ, 1994

Rebecca HT, pb, 1930, Pemberton; bud large, long, pointed; flowers silvery pink, reverse salmon-pink, dbl.; foliage dark, leathery; vigorous growth; int. by Bentall

Rebecca HT, rb, 1974, Tantau, Math.; bud ovoid; flowers red, yellow reverse, well-formed, large, dbl.; vigorous, upright growth; [Konfetti × Piccadilly]; int. in 1970

Rebecca Min, dp, Style; flowers deep raspberry pink, dbl., cupped, borne in clusters; free-flowering; foliage medium green, glossy; growth to 2 ft.; [sport of Sweet Dream]; int. by Style Roses, 2004

Rebecca Anne Min, mp, 1993, Chaffin, Lauren M.; flowers large, very dbl., borne mostly singly; foliage medium size, medium green, semi-glossy; some prickles; medium (40-45 cm.), upright, bushy, vigorous growth; [Gene Boerner × Pink Petticoat]; int. by Pixie Treasures Min. Roses, 1993

Rebecca Claire HT, op, 1981, Law, M.J.; flowers coppery orange edged light coral, 28 petals, borne singly and in small clusters; foliage medium green, semi-glossy; prickles medium brown; vigorous, bushy growth; [Blessings × Redgold]; Gold Medal, RNRS, 1980, President's International Trophy, RNRS, 1980, Edland Fragrance Medal, ARS, 1980

Rebecca Gue B, mp, 1983, Gue, Derek J.; flowers distinction from parent not described; [sport of Mme Ernst Calvat]

Rebecca Kathleen F, mr; int. by Battersby Roses, 2002

Rebecca Louise S, mp, Clements, John; flowers soft candy pink, golden stamens., 3 in., 25 petals, borne consistently in clusters of 6; foliage bronzy early, turning dark green, glossy; upright (5 × 5 ft.) growth; PPAF; int. by Heirloom, 2000

Rebecca Paul HT, yb, 1997, Horner, Colin P.; flowers medium, dbl., borne in small clusters; foliage medium size, medium green, semi-glossy; bushy, medium (80 cm.) growth; [Silver Jubilee × Isobel Derby]; int. by Battersby Roses

Rebecca Susan HT, op, Athy, M.; flowers orange pink with shades of tan and brown, dbl., moderate fragrance; recurrent; int. by Hortico, Inc., 2006

Rebecca's Delight F, mp, 1975, Harkness; flowers soft salmon pink, shaded darker, large, 24 petals; foliage light green; vigorous, upright growth; [(Pink Parfait × Highlight) × Circus]; int. by Morse Roses, 1973

Rebekah HT, pb, 1988, McGredy, Sam IV; flowers large, full, high-centered, borne mostly singly, slight fragrance; recurrent; foliage large, dark green, glossy; upright growth; [Freude × Typhoo Tea]

Rebell HT, ob, 1973, Kordes; flowers dark orange, large, dbl., high-centered, intense fragrance; foliage leathery; vigorous, upright growth; [Brandenburg × seedling]; int. by Fey, 1971

Rebell HT, mr, 2006; flowers flower brilliant red, 11 cm., full, high-centered, borne singly and in small clusters, moderate fragrance; foliage medium size, dark green, very glossy; growth upright, medium, 80 cm; int. by W. Kordes' Söhne, 1996

Rebell 03 Kordana – See **Rebell Kordana**, Min full

Rebell Kordana Min, dr, Kordes; flowers full, cupped; int. as Rebell 03 Kordana, NewFlora

Rebellastar HT, Hetzel; int. in 1970

Recompense HT, dp, 1957, Ratcliffe; flowers deep pink, well-shaped, medium; moderate growth; [Charles P. Kilham × Polly]

Reconciliation HT, ab, Harkness, J.; flowers peach with hint of buff, 5-6 in., very full, high-centered, intense rose/clove fragrance; recurrent; foliage dark green, leathery; growth to 4 ft.; int. by Harkness, 1995

Record – See **Décor**, LCl

Recuerdo de Angel Peluffo HT, rb, 1928, Soupert & Notting; flowers cardinal-red, center garnet-red, large, dbl., moderate fragrance; [Mme Edouard Herriot × Duchess of Wellington]

Recuerdo de Antonio Peluffo T, yb, 1910, Soupert & Notting; flowers light yellow, edged pink, dbl.; [Mme Mélanie Soupert × Mme Constant Soupert]

Recuerdo de Blas Munné Cl HT, rb, 1948, Munné, M.; flowers carmine-red shaded cerise red; foliage dark; long, strong stems; very vigorous growth; [Maria Serrat × Recuerdo del Doctor Ferran]

Recuerdo de Felio Camprubi HT, rb, 1931, Camprubi, C.; flowers crimson suffused pink, reverse yellow suffused red, large, dbl.; vigorous growth; [Hugh Dickson × Souv. de Claudius Pernet]

Recuerdo del Doctor Ferrari HT, rb, 1935, Munné, B.; bud long, pointed; flowers scarlet-crimson, shaded fiery red, open, large, very dbl.; foliage dark; vigorous growth; [Sensation × Kitchener of Khartoum]

Red – See **Red Paillette**, Min

Red Abundance F, dr, Harkness; flowers blood red, 2½ in., full, cupped, borne in large clusters, slight fragrance; good repeat; foliage dark green, glossy; upright (2½ ft.), bushy growth; int. in 2005

Red Ace – See **Amanda**, Min

Red Ace Min, mr, 1981, Saville, F. Harmon; flowers 23 petals, high-centered, borne usually singly; prickles long, thin, straight; low, compact, bushy growth; PP4840; [Rise 'n' Shine × Sheri Anne]; int. by Nor'East Min. Roses, 1980

Red Admiral HT, mr, 1913, Paul, W.; flowers cerise, large, semi-dbl., borne in small clusters, slight fragrance

Red Admiral F, mr, 1940, Archer; flowers scarlet, borne in clusters

Red Alert Min, mr, 1991, Moore, Ralph S.; bud pointed, long; flowers medium red, slightly lighter reverse, aging similar, 4 cm., 35-40 petals, high-centered, borne usually singly or in sprays of 3-4, slight fragrance; foliage medium size, medium green, semi-glossy; prickles several, thin, straight; stems slender, wiry; upright, bushy, medium growth; hips none ; PP8193; [Orangeade × Rainbow's End]; int. by Sequoia Nursery, 1991

Red Alpha HT, dr, Meilland; flowers full, high-centered, borne mostly singly; recurrent; int. by Meilland Intl., 2006

Red American Beauty HT, mr, 1960, Morey, Dr. Dennison; bud ovoid; flowers scarlet overcast rose-red, 4½-5 in., 30-35 petals, high-centered, intense fragrance; foliage leathery, dark; long stems; vigorous, upright, bushy growth; PP1982; [Happiness × San Fernando]; int. by J&P, 1959

Red 'n' Fragrant – See **Firefighter**, HT

Red and White Delight – See **Peppermint Twist**, F

Red Arrow Min, mr, 1962, Moore, Ralph S.; flowers 1¼ in., 40 petals, high-centered, borne in clusters; foliage leathery; vigorous (12-18 in.) growth; [(*R. wichurana* × Floradora) × seedling]; int. by Sequoia Nursery, 1962

Red Azteca HT, mr, 1990, Select Roses, B.V.; bud pointed, tapering, slender; flowers bright red, no fading, large, 30-35 petals, cupped, borne singly; foliage large, dark green, glossy; prickles reddish, with yellow tip; upright, tall growth; [seedling × seedling]; int. by DeVor Nurseries, Inc.

Red Baby S, Embriaco, B.; int. in 1992

Red Baby Rambler – See **Mme Norbert Levavasseur**, Pol

Red Ballerina S, mr, 1976, Fryer, Gareth; flowers bright crimson, small, 10 petals; foliage glossy; [Ballerina × Evelyn Fison]; int. by Fryer's Nursery, Ltd.

Red Ballerina – See **Marjorie Fair**, S

Red Barrier – See **Ulmer Münster**, S

Red Beauty HT, mr, 1929, Dunlop; [sport of Matchless]; int. by Liggit

Red Beauty Min, dr, 1982, Williams, Ernest D.; flowers dark red, yellow hinge, small to medium, 35 petals, high-centered; foliage small, dark, glossy; bushy growth; [Starburst × Over the Rainbow]; int. by Mini-Roses, 1981

Red Belgic mr; flowers full; in England before 1759

Red Bells Min, mr, 1984, Poulsen Roser APS; flowers bright red, small, 35 petals, cupped, borne in clusters; foliage small, medium green, semi-glossy; groundcover; spreading (2 × 4 ft.) growth; [Mini-Poul × Temple Bells]; int. by John Mattock, Ltd., 1983

Red Berlin HT, mr, Olij; flowers dbl., high-centered, borne mostly singly; recurrent; florist rose; int. in 1999

Red Better Times HT, mr, 1937, Asmus; flowers bright clear red; [sport of Better Times]

Red Bird HT, mr, 1959, Manda, Jr., E.A.; flowers bright red; PP1687; [sport of Better Times]; int. by J&P, 1958

Red Bird LCl, mr, 1997, Giles, Diann; flowers medium, very dbl., borne mostly singly; foliage medium size, medium green, semi-glossy; spreading, medium (6-8 ft.) growth; [Crepe de Chine × Kardinal]; int. by Giles Rose Nursery

Red Blanket S, dp, 1979, Ilsink; flowers dull, deep pink, small, semi-dbl., borne in small clusters, slight fragrance; repeat bloom; foliage dark, glossy; prickles numerous, medium; vigorous (to 3-4 ft.) groundcover growth; [Yesterday × seedling]; int. by Dickson Nurseries, Ltd.

Red Blush A, mr, Sievers; flowers rose-red with darker edges, small, dbl., moderate fragrance; non-remontant; foliage soft green, glossy; arching growth; int. in 1988

Red Bonica S, mr; growth to 4 ft.; [sport of Bonica]; int. after 1986

Red Boy HT, or, 1939, Hansen, N.J.; bud long, pointed; flowers fiery orange-red, fading to dominant pink, open, single to semi-dbl.; foliage dark, glossy; vigorous, bushy growth; [Charles K. Douglas × Pres. Herbert Hoover]; int. by B&A

Red Brigand F, or, 1984, Sanday, John; flowers medium, 20 petals; foliage large, dark, semi-glossy; prickles short, slightly hooked; bushy growth; [Vera Dalton × Stephen Langdon]; int. by Sanday Roses, Ltd.

Red Built HT, dr; florist rose; int. by deRuiter, 2005

Red Button Min, dr, 1979, Moore, Ralph S.; bud short, pointed; flowers deep red, small, full; foliage very small, glossy; bushy, compact, spreading growth; [(*R. wichurana* × Floradora) × Magic Dragon]; int. by Sequoia Nursery, 1978

Red Calypso HT, dr; flowers large, full, high-centered, borne mostly singly; foliage glossy; stems very long

Red Camellia F, or, 1943, Krause; bud small; flowers orange-scarlet, 20-30 petals; foliage dark, leathery; vigorous, upright, bushy growth; [Baby Chateau × Folkestone]

Red Camellia HT, mr

Red Cameo Min, dr, 1993, Moore, Ralph S.; flowers dark red, do not burn, large, 6-14 petals, borne mostly singly; foliage medium size, medium green, semi-glossy; few prickles; medium (34-38 cm.), upright, bushy growth; [Anytime × Black Jade]; int. by Sequoia Nursery, 1994

Red Can Can Min, mr, 1977, Lyon; bud pointed; flowers cardinal-red, 2 in., 28 petals, moderate fruity fragrance; foliage dark; vigorous, upright growth; [seedling × unknown]

Red Candy F, mr, Wagner, S.; bud short; flowers simple light red with white eye, 8 petals, flat, borne in clusters, slight fragrance; foliage medium large, dark green, glossy; [sport of Candy Rose chance seedling]; int. by Res. Stn. f. Fruit Growing, Cluj, 1995

Red Carpet Cl F, dr, 1971, Williams, J. Benjamin; bud ovoid; flowers dark scarlet, overlaid darker, medium, dbl., globular; foliage large, dark, leathery; very vigorous, climbing growth; [Don Juan × Red Favorite]; originally registered as LCl

Red Carrousel Min, dp, 1984, Rumsey, R.H.; flowers small, full, slight fragrance; foliage glossy, leathery; bushy growth; [sport of Magic Carrousel]; int. by Roy H. Rumsey, Pty. Ltd.

Red Cascade Cl Min, dr, 1976, Moore, Ralph S.; bud pointed; flowers deep red, 1 in., 40 petals, cupped, borne singly or in small clusters, very slight fragrance; free-flowering; foliage small, leathery, semi-glossy; prickles moderate, straight; prostrate, bushy growth; hips none ; PP3962; [(*R. wichurana* × Floradora) × Magic Dragon]; int. by Sequoia Nursery; AOE, ARS, 1976

Red Cavalier S, mr, Courage; flowers rich red, ruffled, dbl., borne in small clusters; recurrent; int. by Ross Roses, 2002

Red Caviar F, dr, Olesen; bud pointed ovoid, broad base; flowers dark red, 8 cm., 30 petals, pompon, borne in large clusters, very slight fragrance; recurrent; foliage dark olive-green, glossy; prickles few, 5 mm., hooked downward, brown; upright to bushy (60-100 cm.) growth; PP16033; [Dalli Dalli × seedling]; int. by Poulsen Roser, 2003

Red Cécile Brünner – See **Pasadena Tournament**, F

Red Cécile Brünner, Climbing – See **Pasadena Tournament, Climbing**, Cl F

Red Cedar – See **Loving Memory**, HT

Red Centre LCl, or, Peden

Red Champ F, mr, Select; flowers bright red, 9 cm., 40-45 petals, high-centered, borne mostly singly; recurrent; stems 50-70 cm; florist rose; int. by Terra Nigra BV, 2001

Red Chateau HT, mr, 1999, Teranishi, K.; flowers crimson red, 35 petals, high-centered; growth to 3½ ft.; [(Samantha × seedling) × seedling]; int. by Itami Rose Nursery, 1997

Red Chatenay HT, mr, before 1910

Red Cheer Min, mr, 1978, Lyon; flowers cherry-red, 1 in., 45 petals; foliage very small, dark; compact, bushy growth; [seedling × seedling]; int. in 1975

Red Cheerful HT, dr, 1951, Blixen; bud pointed; flowers deep red, 4½ in., 30-40 petals, high-centered, moderate fragrance; foliage glossy, leathery, veined red; vigorous, upright growth; PP1556; [sport of Better Times]; int. by Woodlawn Gardens, 1951

Red Cherokee – See **Ramona**, S

Red Chief HT, mr, 1967, Armstrong, D.L.; bud large, ovoid; flowers 35-40 petals, high-centered, borne usually singly, but sometimes 2 or 3 per stem, intense fragrance; good repeat; foliage medium to large, leathery, semi-glossy; prickles several, medium, hooked slightly downward, brown; vigorous, upright, bushy growth; hips short, globular, smooth, chrysolite green; PP2927; [seedling × Chrysler Imperial]; int. by Armstrong Nursery

Red Coat – See **Redcoat**, F

Red Columbia HT, mr, 1920, Joseph H. Hill, Co.; flowers rich velvety scarlet, large, dbl.; foliage leathery; very vigorous growth; [sport of Columbia]

Red Corsair – See **Roter Korsar**, S

Red Corvette – See **Vital**, HT

Red Cottage S, rb, Dickson, Patrick; flowers single; int. in 1998

Red Cross HT, ob, 1916, Dickson, A.; flowers orange-crimson-scarlet, dbl., moderate fragrance; Ruled extinct 1969 ARA

Red Cross HT, mr, 1969, Gregory; flowers crimson scarlet, pointed, borne several together; foliage medium size, medium green; int. by C. Gregory & Son, 1967

Red Cross – See **Graf Lennart**, HT

Red Cupido Min, mr; bud ovoid, rounded; flowers 3-4 cm., 35-45 petals, rosette, borne in clusters of up to 9, no fragrance; recurrent; foliage smooth, leathery; compact (12 in.), rounded, dense growth; hips rarely observed ; PP9634; [seedling × seedling]; containers; int. by deRuiter

Red Curtain LCl, dr, Kordes; int. in 1994

Red Cushion F, dr, 1966, Armstrong, D.L.; bud pointed; flowers small, semi-dbl., borne in clusters; foliage dark, glossy, leathery; vigorous, bushy growth; PP2845; [Circus × Ruby Lips]; int. by Armstrong Nursery, 1966

Red Dagmar HRg, mr, Spek; int. in 1997

Red Damask – See ***R. gallica officinalis*** (Thory)

Red Damask D, mr, before 1789; flowers rose red, medium, dbl., intense fragrance

Red Dandy F, mr, 1960, Norman; flowers cherry-red, velvety, 3 in., 40 petals, high-centered, moderate fragrance; free-flowering; foliage dark green; vigorous, upright growth; [Ena Harkness × Karl Herbst]; int. by Harkness, 1959

Red Dawn S, mr, 1957, Simonet; flowers deep rose-red, well-formed; recurrent bloom; hardy; [New Dawn × unknown]; int. by Skinner

Red Deer – See **Waskasoo**, HRg dbl.

Red Delicious HT, mr, 1942, Joseph H. Hill, Co.; bud carmine, shaded oxblood-red; flowers brilliant rose-red, 4-6 in., 30-35 petals; foliage leathery, dark; stems weak necks; vigorous, upright growth; [Rome Glory × Chieftain]

Red Delicious S, mr, J&P; PP11221; int. in 1998

Red Delight HT, mr, Avansino; flowers bright red; RULED EXTINCT 11/86; [sport of Pink Delight]; int. by Mortensen, 1935

Red Delight Cl Min, mr, 1987, Williams, Ernest D.; bud pointed; flowers deep medium red, yellow at base, small, 33 petals, high-centered, borne singly and in sprays, intense spicy fragrance; foliage small, dark green, semi-glossy; prickles few, small, tan, slanted downwards; tall, bushy, upright growth; hips round, red; PP6547; [Golden Song × Magic Mist]; int. by Mini-Roses, 1986

Red Det Min, mr, 1986, Harkness; flowers dbl., flat, borne in clusters; foliage small, deep green, glossy; vigorous, bushy growth; [(Marlena × Kim) × Little Buckaroo]; int. by Rosen-Union, 1978

Red Det 80 Min, dr, Cocker; flowers dark scarlet-red, very dbl.; bushy, compact growth; int. as Red Ded, Cocker, 1980

Red Devil HT, mr, 1967, Dickson, A.; bud ovoid; flowers medium red, reverse lighter, large, 72 petals, high-centered, borne singly, moderate fragrance; foliage large, glossy; stems long; vigorous growth; PP3037; [Silver Lining × Prima Ballerina]; int. by J&P, 1970; Gold Medal, Portland, 1970, Gold Medal, Japan, 1967, Gold Medal, Belfast, 1969

Red Diadem F, dr, Tantau; int. in 1991

Red Dorothy Perkins – See **Excelsa**, HWich

Red Dot – See **Dart's Red Dot**, S

Red Dragon HP, dr, 1878, Paul, W.; flowers vivid crimson, large, very dbl., cupped; foliage grey-green; [Charles Lefèbvre × unknown]

Red Dragon F, mr, 1970, Cants of Colchester, Ltd.; flowers 3½-4 in., 5 petals; vigorous growth; [Anna Wheatcroft × seedling]

Red Dragon HT, mr, 2005, Poole, Lionel; flowers full, borne mostly solitary, slight fragrance; foliage medium size, dark green, semi-glossy; prickles moderate, medium size, slightly hooked, brown; upright, medium growth; garden decorative, exhibition; [Raewyn Henry × Unamed seedling (Hazel Rose × Cardiff Bay) × Red Planet]; int. in 2007

Red Druschki – See **Ruhm von Steinfurth**, HP

Red Duchess HT, mr, 1942, Brownell; bud long, pointed; flowers 3½-5 in., 35-45 petals, high-centered, moderate fragrance; foliage glossy, bronze; long, strong stems; vigorous, upright, bushy growth; [Pink Princess × Crimson Glory]

Red Duchess, Climbing Cl HT, mr, 1955, Brownell; PP1370

Red Echo Pol, or, 1932, Kluis & Koning; flowers vermilion tinted crimson, dbl., cupped; foliage dark, wrinkled; dwarf growth; [Echo × unnamed Hybrid Tea]; int. by J&P

Red Eden – See **Eric Tabarly**, LCl

Red Eden Rose – See **Eric Tabarly**, LCl

Red Elegance HT, dr, Twomey, Jerry

Red Elf Min, dr, 1949, deVink; bud ovoid; flowers dark crimson, ¾-1 in., 23 petals; foliage soft, tiny; vigorous, bushy, dwarf growth; [Eblouissant × Tom Thumb]; int. by C-P

Red Ellen Poulsen Pol, mr, 1918, Poulsen, S.; [sport of Ellen Poulsen]

Red Ember HT, or, 1953, Cant, F.; flowers flame, well-formed, 4-5 in., 30 petals; foliage glossy, dark; free growth

Red Emblem F, dr, 1959, Boerner; bud ovoid; flowers deep red, open, 2½ in., 30-35 petals, moderate fragrance; foliage leathery; upright, bushy growth; [(Garnette × unknown) × Pageant]; int. by J&P, 1959

Red Emperor F, dr, 1997, Brown, Ted; flowers large, dbl., borne in small clusters; foliage medium size, dark green, glossy; spreading, low (2ft.)growth; [Esprit × seedling]

Red Empress LCl, mr, 1957, Mallerin, C.; bud ovoid; flowers cardinal-red, 3½ in., 33 petals, high-centered to cupped, borne usually singly, sometimes in small clusters, intense tea fragrance; recurrent; foliage medium size, leathery; prickles several, medium, hooked downward, oval base; vigorous, climbing growth; PP1573; [(Holstein × Decor) × (Holstein × Decor)]; int. by EFR

Red Ensign HT, mr, 1947, Norman; flowers crimson, 4-5 in., 40-45 petals, high-centered, intense damask fragrance; foliage dark; very vigorous growth; [Crimson Glory × Southport]; int. by Harkness; Gold Medal, NRS, 1943

Red Euphoria S, mr, Interplant; flowers bright red, semi-dbl., borne in small clusters; int. by Jac. Verschuren-Pechtold, 1999

Red Explorer Cl Pol, dr, 1928, Penny; flowers deep brilliant crimson, small, dbl., borne in medium clusters; recurrent bloom; vigorous, climbing growth; [sport of Miss Edith Cavell]

Red Facade – See **Rotfassade**, LCl

Red Fairy – See **Burlington**, S

Red Fairy Pol, mr, 1995, Moore, Ralph S.; bud short, rounded; flowers cherry red, often with red line down center of petals, 1¼ in., 24-30 petals, rounded, borne in conical sprays, somewhat pendulous, slight fragrance; free-flowering; foliage long, bright medium green, semi-glossy; prickles some, hooked downward, brown; wiry, sturdy stems; bushy, medium, semi-cascading growth; hips small ; PP10150; [Simon Robinson × Simon Robinson]; int. by Sequoia Nurs., 1996

Red Fan HT, or, Keisei; int. by Keisei Rose Nurseries, 1991

Red Fantasy – See **Boksburg Fantasia**, HT

Red Fantasy S, mr; flowers 3 in., full, pompon, borne in clusters; free-flowering; foliage disease-resistant; low (2-3 ft.), spreading (5 ft.), groundcover growth

Red Favorite F, mr, 1954, Tantau, Math.; bud ovoid; flowers velvety oxblood-red, 2½ in., 13 petals, borne in trusses; good repeat; foliage dark, leathery, glossy; vigorous, bushy growth; [Karl Weinhausen × Cinnabar]; int. by C-P; ADR, 1950

Red Favorite, Climbing Cl F, mr, 1964, Münster; flowers medium, semi-dbl.; int. in 1958

Red Favourite – See **Red Favorite**, F

Red Fawn – See **Benikanoko**, HT

Red Festival – See **Festival Rouge**, F semi-dbl.

Red Figurine Min, dr, Saville; flowers bright crimson red, dbl., borne mostly singly; recurrent; slender, 8 in. stems; medium to tall growth; int. by Ludwig's Roses, 2001

Red Finch Pol, mp, 1937, Stielow, F.C.; flowers cerise, more cupped, more open, more dbl. than parent, borne in clusters; [sport of Mrs R.M. Finch]

Red Finesse – See **Rotilia**, F

Red Flame – See **Commandant Cousteau, Climbing**, Cl HT

Red Flare LCl, dr, 1954, Mansuino, Dr. Ada; bud globular; flowers carmine overcast spectrum-red, 4-4½ in.,

40 petals, cupped, borne singly and in small clusters, moderate fragrance; profuse bloom repeated sparingly; foliage dark, glossy; growth to 7-8 ft.; PP1366; [Reine Marie Henriette × Paul's Scarlet Climber]; int. by J&P, 1954

Red Fleurette S, mr

Red Flower Carpet S, mr, Noack, Werner; buds pointed; flowers pure velvet red with bright yellow stamens, 2 in., 25 petals, cupped to flat, borne in large trusses, no fragrance; recurrent; foliage dark green, glossy; prickles medium; growth spreading (2½ × 3 ft.); PP11308; [(Evelyn Fison × Paprika) × Flower Carpet]

Red Flush Min, mr, 1978, Schwartz, Ernest W.; bud ovoid; flowers rose red, satiny, 1½ in., 30-35 petals, cupped, borne usually in sprays of 3-7, no fragrance; fast repeat; foliage medium size, green, matte; prickles few, thin, pointed; very compact (15 in.) growth, breaks readily from soil; hips none observed ; PP4369; [Zorina × seedling]; int. by Nor'East Min. Roses; AOE, ARS, 1979

Red Fountain LCl, dr, 1974, Williams, J. Benjamin; bud ovoid, pointed; flowers scarlet, medium, 20-25 petals, cupped, borne in clusters, intense old rose fragrance; recurrent; foliage large, dark, leathery; prickles moderate, flat base, hooked downward, red; very vigorous, climbing growth; hips globular, smooth, persimmon orange; PP3615; [Don Juan × Blaze]; int. by C-P, 1975

Red France HT, mr; flowers bright red, full; PP11480; int. in 1999

Red Friendship S, mr, Verschuren; flowers bright red, small, dbl., borne in clusters; low (30 in.), sprawling growth; int. by Verschuren, 1986

Red Frost HT, rb, 1993, Lienau, David W.; flowers medium red, suffused white, shaded light yellow at base, 3-3½ in., full, high-centered; foliage medium size, dark green, glossy; some prickles; medium (90-120 cm.), bushy growth; [First Prize × seedling]; int. by Trophy Roses, Ltd., 1993

Red Garnette – See **Garnette**, F

Red Garter F, rb, 1997, Brown, Ted; flowers medium, single, borne in small clusters; foliage medium size, dark red turning dark green, glossy; upright, medium (4 ft.) growth; [Esprit × Stretch Johnson]

Red Germain Min, rb, 1976, Moore, Ralph S.; bud long, pointed; flowers red, reverse lighter, 1 in., 25 petals, flat; foliage small, leathery; vigorous, bushy growth; [(*R. wichurana* × Floradora) × (Oakington Ruby × Floradora)]; int. by Sequoia Nursery, 1975

Red Giant HT, mr, Kordes; flowers clear red, large, full, high-centered, borne mostly singly; good repeat; stems long, upright, firm; florist rose; int. by W. Kordes Söhne, 2002

Red Globe F, mr, 1971, Delforge; bud ovoid; flowers full,large, dbl.; foliage soft; moderate, bushy growth

Red Glory F, mr, 1963, Swim, H.C.; bud ovoid, pointed; flowers cherry to rose-red, 2½-3½ in., 11 petals, cupped to flat, borne in rounded clusters, slight fragrance; foliage leathery, semi-glossy; very vigorous, tall, bushy growth; good as fence or hedge; PP1885; [Gay Lady × (Pinocchio × Floradora)]; int. by Armstrong Nursery, 1958

Red Gold – See **Redgold**, F

Red Gruss an Coburg – See **Clotaria**, HT

Red Guard HT, rb, 1935, Verschuren; flowers dark blood-red, well-formed, very dbl.; very vigorous growth

Red Halo F, mr, 1968, Oliver, W.G.; flowers crimson, flat, borne in trusses; foliage glossy; vigorous, bushy growth; [Tabarin × Karl Herbst]

Red Haze – See **Beaulieu**, S

Red Head HT, mr, Dickson; int. in 1985

Red Hedge HRg, mr, 1958, Nyveldt; flowers single; hips small, red; [(*R. rugosa rubra* × *R. cinnamomea*) × *R. nitida*]

Red Hedges S, mr, Williams, J.B.; flowers bright red with yellow stamens, ruffled petals, semi-dbl., borne in masses of bloom; int. by Hortico, 2000

Red Hermosa – See **Queen's Scarlet**, Ch

Red Hill HT, mr, 1941, Clark, A.; flowers well-formed, large; [E.G. Hill × unknown]

Red Hiroshima HT, mr, Hiroshima; int. by Hiroshima Bara-en, 1990

Red Hit Min, dr, 1985, Olesen, Pernille & Mogens N.; flowers small, 20 petals, no fragrance; foliage small, dark, matte; low, bushy, compact growth; [Mini-Poul × seedling]; int. by Poulsen's Roses, 1984

Red Hoover HT, rb, 1937, Lens; flowers brilliant red, center salmon-red; [sport of President Herbert Hoover]

Red Hot S, mr, Carruth, Tom; flowers bright red, small, single, shallow cup to flat, borne in clusters; free-flowering; foliage small, medium green, glossy; vigorous, low (15-18 in.) growth; int. by C&K Jones, 2006; Best Miniature, Belfast, 2006

Red Hot Friendship F, rb, Fleming; int. by World of Roses, 2006

Red Immensee – See **Sommerabend**, S

Red Imp Min, dr, 1951, deVink; bud ovoid; flowers deep crimson, micro-mini, ¾-1 in., 54 petals, flat, slight fragrance; upright, bushy, dwarf (9 in.) growth; [Ellen Poulsen × Tom Thumb]; int. by C-P

Red Intuition HT, rb, Delbard; flowers mix of bright red and dark red in stripes and splotches, dbl., high-centered, borne mostly singly; stems long; vigorous, tall growth; originally a greenhouse rose; int. in 2004

Red Jacket HT, mr, 1950, Swim, H.C.; bud ovoid, pointed; flowers 3¾ in., 21 petals, urn-shaped, then flat, slight fragrance; foliage leathery; upright, bushy growth; [World's Fair × Mirandy]; int. by Stuart

Red Jewel HT, mr, Verbeek; bud medium, oval, violet-red; flowers currant red, reverse lighter, petals scalloped, 3-4 in., 44-62 petals, full, opening flat, borne several to a stem; foliage large, dark green, glossy; prickles moderate, 9 mm., reddish; growth bushy; hips pear-shaped, smooth, thin-walled; PP2546; [Poinsettia × (Baccara × seedling)]

Red Jewel Min, or, 1985, Interplant; flowers small, 20 petals, no fragrance; foliage small, medium green, semi-glossy; bushy growth; PP5769; [Amanda × seedling]; int. in 1984

Red Jewel HT, dr, deRuiter

Red Jonathan – See **Jonathan**, F

Red Joy HT, mr; int. in 1997

Red Kelly LCl, rb, Sutherland, P; int. in 1999

Red Knight LCl, dr, 1965, Booy, P.J.; flowers maroon, medium, very vigorous growth, semi-dbl., globular; recurrent bloom; [sport of Dr. Huey]; int. by Booy Rose Nursery

Red La France – See **Duchess of Albany**, HT

Red Lady HT, mr, Laperriére; flowers velvety red, dbl.; int. by Sauvageot, 1978

Red Leonardo da Vinci F, dr, Meilland; flowers rich, dark red, lightening in strong sun, dbl., rosette; free-flowering; robust, low growth; int. in 2004

Red-Letter Day HT, dp, 1914, Dickson, A.; flowers velvety rose-red, white streak in center of inner petals, stamens cinnamon, 3½ in., semi-dbl.; foliage glaucous sage-green; short stems; vigorous growth; Gold Medal, NRS, 1913

Red Lion HT, mr, 1964, McGredy, Sam IV; flowers red becoming rose-red, 5 in., 38 petals, high-centered; [Kordes' Perfecta × Detroiter]; int. by Spek

Red Love Min, mr, 1985, Williams, Ernest D.; flowers spiral form, small, 35 petals; foliage small, dark, semi-glossy to glossy; upright, bushy growth; [Tom Brown × Over the Rainbow]; int. by Mini Roses, 1984

Red Magic Min, mr, 1977, Lyon; bud pointed; flowers deep cherry-red, open, medium, 10-15 petals; vigorous, upright growth; [Red Can Can × unknown]; int. by L. Lyon Greenhouses

Red Magic – See **Randilla Rouge**, Min

Red Magic Carpet S, mr, 1999, McGredy, Sam IV; flowers cerise-red, yellow stamens, 3 in., semi-dbl., borne in small clusters, moderate fragrance; foliage medium size, semi-glossy; growth spreading, low (12 in.); groundcover; [Sexy Rexy × Eyeopener]; int. in 1994

Red Maid F, or, 1976, Sanday, John; flowers coral-red, 3 in., 18 petals; [Vera Dalton × Stephen Langdon]; int. in 1975

Red Malmaison – See **Malmaison Rouge**, B

Red Maman Cochet – See **Niles Cochet**, T

Red Maréchal Niel – See **Grossherzog Ernst Ludwig von Hesse**, Cl HT

Red Margo Koster Pol, mr

Red Martini HT, dr, 1967, Delforge; bud ovoid; flowers large, dbl.; foliage bronze; vigorous, bushy growth; [Chrysler Imperial × seedling]

Red Masquerade F, mr, 1965, Hill, A.; bud pointed; flowers red becoming darker, 2½-3 in., 10 petals, borne in clusters; vigorous growth; [Masquerade × Independence]

Red Masterpiece HT, dr, 1974, Warriner, William A.; bud ovoid to globular; flowers cardinal red, 4½-5 in., 45-50 petals, high-centered, borne usually singly, intense fragrance; foliage large, dark green, leathery; prickles moderate, long, hooked downward; vigorous, upright growth; PP3508; [(Siren × Chrysler Imperial) × (Carrousel × Chrysler Imperial)]; int. by J&P

Red Masterpiece, Climbing Cl HT, dr, Kasturi & Sriram; flowers very large; free-flowering; [sport of Red Masterpiece]; int. in 2004

Red Max Graf – See **Rote Max Graf**, HKor

Red Meidiland S, rb, 1989, Meilland, Alain A.; bud conical; flowers red with white eye, medium, 5 petals, cupped, borne in sprays of 7-15; repeat bloom; foliage medium size, dark green, glossy, disease-resistant; prickles gray-brown; spreading, medium, very winter hardy growth; hips globular, small, red; PP7116; [Sea Foam × (Picasso × Eyepaint)]; int. by The Conard-Pyle Co., 1989

Red Meillandina Min, mr, Meilland; int. in 1982

Red Meilove – See **Ondella**, F

Red Mercedes F, mr

Red Midinette Cl Min, mr, Orard; flowers bright red, yellow stamens, semi-dbl. to dbl., borne in clusters; recurrent; tall (8 ft.), vigorous growth; int. by Ludwig's Roses, 2004

Red Mikado F, mr, Tantau; florist rose; int. by Rosen Tantau

Red Mini-Wonder Min, dr, 1990, Selection Meilland; bud rounded; flowers currant red, cardinal red reverse, aging to dark red, small, 40-43 petals, cupped; foliage small, medium green, very dense, semi-glossy; prickles small, green to tan; bushy, low growth; PP7384; [(Anytime × Parador) × Mogral]; int. by Meilland, 1987

Red Minimo Min, dr, 1991, deRuiter, George; bud pointed ovoid; flowers Orient red, small, 22-25 petals, flat, borne in small clusters, no fragrance; free-flowering; foliage small, dark green, semi-glossy; prickles long, hooked slightly downward; stems short, strong; low, bushy growth; PP5770; [seedling × seedling]; int. by Bear Creek Gardens, 1986

Red Minimo, Climbing Cl Min, dr, Takefuji (Muto?); int. in 1998

Red Minuetto Min, mr; PPAF; int. by Greenheart Farms, 2004

Red Mirato – See **CentrO-Rose**, S

Red Monarch HT, dr, Meilland; flowers dbl., high-centered, borne mostly singly; good repeat; florist rose; int. by Meilland Intl., 2004

Red Moon Min, mr, 1995, Williams, Ernest D.; flowers 1-1½ in., full, borne in small clusters, no fragrance; foliage medium size, medium green, semi-glossy; some prickles; upright, bushy, climbing (5 ft.) growth; [Red Delight × Twilight Trail]; int. by Texas Mini Roses, 1995

Red Moon HT, m, Teranishi; int. by Itami Rose Garden, 2003

Red Moscow – See **Krasnaia Moskva**, HT

Red Moss – See **Henri Martin**, M

Red Moss, Climbing Cl M, mr, Foote; int. by B&A

Red Moss Rambler HWich, mr, Moore; bud mossy; flowers deep, bright crimson, semi-dbl., moderate fragrance; recurrent; numerous prickles; int. by Sequoia Nursery, 1988

Red Mountain Peak HT, mr, Taschner, Ludwig; flowers large, full, high-centered, borne usually singly; recurrent; tall growth; int. by Ludwig's Roses, 2004

Red Mozart – See **Rote Mozart**, S

Red-n-White Glory – See **Candystick**, HT

Red Nearly Wild F, mr, 1960, Brownell, H.C.; bud globular; flowers rose-red, small, single, cupped, borne in clusters; foliage soft; vigorous, bushy growth; [Nearly Wild × seedling]; int. by Brownell Roses, 1960

Red Nella HT, dp, Allender, Robert William; int. in 1991

Red Nelly HSpn, rb; flowers red, white at petal base, small, single; may by synonymous with *R. spinosissima* 'Single Red'

Red New Dawn – See **Étendard**, HWich

Red Niphetos – See **Lady Battersea**, HT

Red Nostalgie – See **Helmut Kohl Rose**, HT

Red One HT, dr; bud large, cylindrical; flowers, 11-12 cm., 22 petals, cupped, borne singly, no fragrance; recurrent; prickles numerous, strong, 1 cm., curved downward, green; upright (6 ft.), vigorous growth; hips pitcher shaped, 1 cm ; PP14468; [seedling × Tina]; int. by deRuiter, 2001

Red Opal F, mr, 1968, Northfield; bud pointed; flowers red, reverse cerise, flat, borne in small clusters; foliage small, dark; free growth; [Karl Herbst × Korona]

Red Orléans Rose – See **Maréchal Foch**, Pol

Red Pagode MinFl, mr, Poulsen; flowers medium red, 5-8 cm., dbl., no fragrance; foliage dark; cascading growth, hanging basket type; PP13592; int. by Poulsen Roser, 2000

Red Paillette Min, mr, Poulsen; flowers medium red, medium, no fragrance; foliage dark; growth narrow, bushy, 40-60 cm.; int. by Poulsen Roser, 1998

Red Parade F, mr, 1972, Patterson; bud ovoid; flowers carmine-red, medium, dbl., high-centered; foliage glossy, bronze; vigorous, bushy growth; [(Frolic × Peace) × Texan]; int. by Patterson Roses

Red Parfum Cl F, mr, Eve, A.; flowers soft red, 9 cm., dbl., borne in clusters, intense fragrance; foliage glossy; vigorous (10-13 ft.) growth; int. in 1972

Red Passion S, mr; int. by Kelly Nurseries, 2004

Red Pastel – See **Red Ribbon**, F

Red Pat S, mr; groundcover; spreading growth; int. by Melville Nurseries, 2003

Red Patio Wonder MinFl, mr, Jalbert; flowers crimson red, large, full, slight fragrance; recurrent; compact (14 in.), tidy growth; int. in 1999

Red Peace – See **Karl Herbst**, HT

Red Peace – See **Dame de Coeur**, HT

Red Pearl HT, mr, 1970, Watkins Roses; flowers bright red, pointed, 5 in., 40 petals; foliage large, dark; very vigorous growth; [Josephine Bruce × Kordes' Perfecta]

Red Pendant Min, dr, 1985, Williams, Ernest D.; flowers small, 35 petals, no fragrance; foliage small, medium green, very glossy; low, spreading growth; [Red Cascade × Red Cascade]; int. by Mini Roses, 1984

Red Perfection HT, dr, 1987, McGredy, Sam IV; flowers dark red, reverse slightly lighter, fading purple-red, medium, 50-60 petals, high-centered, moderate old rose fragrance; foliage large, dark green, semi-glossy; prickles slightly recurved, average, green; tall growth; hips globular, large, dark red; PP5426; [Karma × Arturo Toscanini]; int. by Co-Operative Rose Growers, 1986

Red Pet Ch, dr, 1888, Parker/G. Paul; flowers deep rich red, round, small, very dbl.; growth low, bushy; probably extinct

Red Petticoat F, mr, 1967, Watkins Roses; flowers blood-red, short petaled, dbl., flat, borne in trusses; foliage dark, glossy; very vigorous growth; [Buisman's Triumph × Lilli Marlene]

Red Pierre – See **Eric Tabarly**, LCl

Red Pinocchio F, dr, 1947, Boerner; flowers velvety carmine-red, 3 in., 28 petals, cupped, borne in clusters, moderate fragrance; vigorous, bushy growth; [(Pinocchio × unknown) × Donald Prior]; int. by J&P

Red Pistols Min, dy, 1982, Ballmer, Gordon W.; flowers deep golden yellow, small, 15-20 petals; foliage medium green, matte; prickles brown, needle-like; upright, bushy growth; [Rise 'n' Shine × seedling]; int. by Biotika International

Red Pixie – See **Heinzelmännchen**, F

Red Planet HT, dr, 1970, Dickson, Patrick; flowers crimson, 5½-6 in., 30-35 petals, high-centered, intense fragrance; foliage glossy; [Red Devil × seedling]; int. by A. Dickson; President's International Trophy, RNRS, 1969, Gold Medal, RNRS, 1969

Red Plume F, or, 1966, Sanday, John; flowers bright scarlet, 3 in., 35 petals, rosette, borne in clusters; foliage glossy; vigorous, bushy growth; [Masquerade × (Independence × unknown)]

Red Point F, mr, 1998, McGredy, Sam IV; flowers 9 cm., dbl., borne in small clusters, slight fragrance; foliage large, medium green, glossy; prickles moderate; bushy, medium (110 cm.) growth; [Maiden Voyage × Eyeopener]; int. by McGredy, 1993

Red Popcorn S, dp, Williams, J. Benjamin; flowers reddish-pink, small, dbl., pompon, borne in large sprays, slight fragrance; recurrent; foliage small, bluish-green; groundcover, small climber; spreading (2 ft.) growth; int. by Hortico, Inc., 2005

Red Poppy – See **Krasnyi Mak**, F

Red Premier HT, dp, 1924, Scott, R.; bud long, pointed; flowers bright carmine, large, dbl.; foliage leathery; vigorous growth; [sport of Premier]

Red Pride F, mr, 1968, Verbeek; bud ovoid; flowers small, dbl.

Red Prince – See **Fountain**, HT

Red Princess – See **Benihime**, Min

Red Prolific – See **Clos Vougeot**, F

Red Provence – See **Rubra**, C

Red Queen HT, mr, 1968, Kordes; bud ovoid; flowers large, dbl.; foliage dark; vigorous, upright growth; [Colour Wonder × Liberty Bell]; int. by McGredy & Son

Red Queen, Climbing Cl HT, mr; int. after 1968

Red Queen HT, mr, Kordes; flowers velvety red, large, dbl.; free-flowering; florist rose; int. as Marlena, W. Kordes Söhne, 1998

Red Radiance HT, dp, 1916, Gude Bros.; flowers brilliant cerise-red, large, 23 petals, cupped, intense damask fragrance; free-flowering; foliage leathery; vigorous growth; [sport of Radiance]

Red Radiance, Climbing Cl HT, dp, 1927, Pacific Rose Co. (also Catt, 1929); bud very large, long-pointed; flowers very large, dbl., moderate fragrance; foliage large, dark green, glossy; [sport of Red Radiance]

Red Rascal S, mr, 1986, Warriner, William A.; bud short, pointed ovoid; flowers bright red, 2 in., 30 petals, cupped, borne in sprays of 2-5, self cleaning, slight fragrance; recurrent; foliage small, medium green, semi-glossy; prickles medium, red to brown, hooked downward; stems strong, short; tall (3-4 ft.), vigorous, bushy growth; PP6693; [seedling × seedling]; int. by J&P

Red Recker HT, dr, Kasturi; flowers deep crimson, dbl., high-centered; int. by KSG Son, 1986

Red Reflection HT, mr, 1975, Warriner, William A.; bud ovoid, pointed; flowers velvet red with faint blue tint on reverse, 4-5 in., high-centered, slight fragrance; recurrent; foliage large, leathery; upright growth; [Tropicana × Living]; int. by J&P, 1964

Red Ribbon F, mr, McGredy, Sam IV; int. in 1973

Red Ribbon F, mr, 1997, Williams, J. Benjamin; flowers medium, dbl., borne in small clusters, moderate fragrance; foliage medium size, medium green, semi-glossy; upright, compact, medium (14-18 in.)growth; [Red Sunblaze × Pink Sweetheart]; int. by Paramount Roses

Red Ribbon HT, mr, Kordes; flowers brilliant red, large, dbl., high-centered, borne mostly singly; recurrent; stems moderately long; int. by W. Kordes Söhne, 2005

Red Ribbons S, dr, 1998, Kordes, W.; bud short, pointed ovoid; flowers bright red, 3 in., 20 petals, cupped, borne in large clusters, slight fragrance; recurrent; foliage medium size, dark green, glossy; prickles moderate, short, hooked downward, red; stems short, strong; growth low (2 × 5 ft.), spreading; PP9115; [Weisse Max Graf × Waltzertraum]; int. by Bear Creek Gardens, 1990; Gold Medal, Baden-Baden, 1991

Red Riddle – See **Red Ribbon**, F

Red Rider Cl F, rb, 1970, Guest; flowers red, base yellow, 2-3 in., 50 petals; foliage large, glossy; vigorous growth; [Circus × Danse de Feu]

Red Rider – See **Red Rover**, Min dbl.

Red Riding Hood – See **Rödhätte**, F

Red Riding Hood Min, dr, 1955, Robinson, T.; flowers brilliant dark red; [sport of Red Imp]

Red Ripples F, dr, 1942, Krause; bud globular; flowers deep red, petals wavy, small, semi-dbl., borne in large clusters; foliage leathery, glossy, wrinkled; upright, bushy growth; [Hamburg × Anne Poulsen]; int. by C-P

Red River F, Kordes

Red Robin – See **Gloire des Rosomanes**, Ch

Red Robin HT, rb, 1940, Brownell; flowers red, tending toward scarlet; vigorous growth

Red Robin S, rb, 2000, Lens, Louis; flowers deep pink to crimson, reverse lighter, small, semi-dbl., borne in large clusters, moderate fragrance; non-recurrent; foliage medium green, matte; prickles moderate; stems red; growth bushy, tall (200 cm.); [*R. helenae* × Robin Hood]; int. by Louis Lens N.V., 1992

Red Rock HT, mr, 1974, Meilland; flowers cherry-red, open, petals imbricated, 5 in., 35 petals; very vigorous growth; [(Royal Velvet × Chrysler Imperial) × Pharaoh]; int. by URS, 1973

Red Rocket S, mr, 1949, Longley, L.E.; bud ovoid; flowers crimson, large, semi-dbl., borne in clusters; non-recurrent; foliage large, dark, glossy, bronze; vigorous, upright growth; [Skyrocket × unknown]; int. by Univ. of Minn.

Red Rocky – See **Red Rock**, HT

Red Roma HT, mr; flowers large, dbl.

Red Romance S, dr; flowers deep red, small, semi-dbl. to dbl., cupped; growth to 20 × 20 in.; int. by Paul Chessum Roses, 2003

Red Rosamini Min, dr, 1988, deRuiter, George; flowers clear crimson, white at base, 1-1½ in., 30-40 petals, cupped, borne in small clusters; free-flowering; foliage medium size, medium green, matte; few prickles; bushy, medium (15 in.) growth; PP5976; [seedling × seedling]; int. by Conard-Pyle Co., 1988

Red Rose – See ***R. gallica*** (Linnaeus)

Red Rose Marie HT, rb, 1938, Mordigan Evergreen Nursery; bud ovoid; flowers cerise-red, large, dbl., high-centered; foliage dark, leathery; vigorous, bushy growth; [sport of Rose Marie]

Red Rose of Denman S, dr; int. in 1958

Red Rose of Lancaster – See ***R. gallica officinalis*** (Thory)

Red Roulette Min, mr

Red Rover HP, mr, 1864, Paul, W.; flowers fire-red, large, full

Red Rover Min, dr, 1991, Laver, Keith G.; bud pointed; flowers dbl., exhibition, loose, borne usually singly, no fragrance; foliage small to medium size, dark green, semi-glossy to glossy; bushy, low growth; [sport of Mountie]; int. by Springwood Roses, 1990

Red Ruffles F, dr, 1960, Von Abrams; bud pointed; flowers dull dark red, petals ruffled, 2½-3 in., 45 petals, cupped to flat, borne in large clusters, slight fragrance; foliage dark, glossy; vigorous, bushy, compact growth; PP2110; [Improved Lafayette × Carrousel]; int. by Peterson & Dering, 1960

Red Rugostar HRg, mr, Meilland; flowers carmine-red, medium-large, semi-dbl.; int. in 1995

Red Rum F, mr, 1976, Bees; flowers red, shaded scarlet, 2½ in., 24 petals; foliage dark; vigorous growth; [Handel × Arthur Bell]

Red Safrano – See **Safrano à Fleurs Rouges**, T

Red Sarong HT, dr, 1975, Golik; bud ovoid; flowers deep red, 5 in., 36 petals, high-centered, moderate fragrance; foliage dark, leathery; tall growth; [Baccará × Golden Showers]; int. by Dynarose, 1974

Red Satin HT, mr, 1994, Marciel, Stanley G. & Jeanne A.; flowers 3-3½ in., full, borne mostly singly; foliage large, medium green, matte; few prickles; low (55-60 cm.), upright growth; [Jacqueline × Prominent]; int. by DeVor Nurseries, Inc., 1993

Red Scentsation Min, mr, 2002, White, Wendy R.; bud ovate with an acuminate tip; flowers medium red, reverse streaked with burgundy, 2 in., 24 petals, high-centered, borne mostly solitary, with some small clusters, intense fragrance; recurrent; foliage medium size, dark green, matte; prickles thin, tapered, angled down; stems long; growth upright, bushy, medium (18-24 in.); cut flower, decorative, container; PP16040; [Taxi × ((Party Girl × Sparks) × New Zealand)]; int. by Nor' East Miniature Roses, 2003

Red Sea F, dr, Barni, V.; flowers deep red, semi-dbl., borne in large clusters, slight fragrance; recurrent; foliage dark green; compact (2 ft.) growth; int. by Rose Barni, 1990

Red Sea F, dr, 2006, Castillo, Angel; flowers single, borne in large clusters; foliage large, medium green, semi-glossy; prickles medium, slightly hooked, moderate; growth spreading, tall (48 in.); garden decorative; [pink Grandiflora seeding × orange-red Floribunda seedling]; int. by Angel Roses, 2007

Red Seafoam S, dp; flowers fuchsia pink, semi-dbl., borne in clusters, slight fragrance; low, spreading growth; int. by Martin & Kraus, 2000

Red Shadows Min, dr, 1984, Saville, F. Harmon; flowers show dark shadings on petal edges, small, dbl., high-centered, no fragrance; foliage small, medium green, semi-glossy; bushy, slightly spreading growth; [Tamango × Sheri Anne]; int. by Nor'East Min. Roses

Red Simplicity S, mr, 1991, Warriner, William A. & Zary, Keith W.; bud long, pointed ovoid; flowers bright red, a bit of blackening near petal edges, 3½-4 in., 20-25 petals, high-centered, then flat, borne singly and in small clusters, slight fragrance; foliage medium size, medium green, semi-glossy; prickles moderate, medium, hooked downward, red when young; medium, upright, spreading growth; PP8582; [seedling × Sun Flare]; int. by Bear Creek Gardens, 1992

Red Skelton HT, or, 1968, Whisler, D.; bud long, pointed; flowers vermilion, 5-6 in., 20-30 petals, high-centered to cupped, borne mostly singly, moderate fragrance; recurrent; foliage bronze-green when young, dark green when mature, leathery; prickles few, bronze; vigorous, upright growth; hips none observed; PP3020; [Rose Queen × Charlotte Armstrong]; int. by Germain's

Red Smith's Parish T, rb, 1997, Manners, Dr. Malcolm; flowers small, color variable, dbl., borne in small clusters, slight fragrance; recurrent; foliage medium size, light green, semi-glossy; bushy, medium (4-6 ft.) growth; [sport of Smith's Parish]

Red Soldier – See **Fusilier**, F

Red Soupert – See **Ma Petite Andrée**, Pol

Red Sparkler HT, rb, 1975, Buck, Dr. Griffith J.; flowers red, striped pink and white, 4-4½ in., 55 petals, cupped, intense damask fragrance; foliage dark, leathery; upright growth; [Scarlet Royal × Rouge Mallerin]; int. by Iowa State University, 1974

Red Spectacle S, dr, Poulsen; flowers crimson red, large, full, cupped; free-flowering; vigorous, tall (6-7 ft.) growth; int. in 1993

Red Spice F, dr, 1959, Boerner; bud short, flat topped; flowers 2-2½ in., 80-85 petals, cupped, moderate fragrance; foliage dark, leathery; vigorous, bushy growth; PP1784; [Spice × Garnette]; int. by J&P, 1958

Red Spire HT, or; flowers large, full, high-centered, borne mostly singly; stems strong; very tall, stiffly upright growth; int. by Ludwig's Roses, 2000

Red Spirit HT, mr, Zary; int. by Bear Creek Gardens, 2000

Red Spirit HT, mr, J&P; florist rose

Red Splendor HT, mr, 1954, Grillo; flowers bright red, 6 in., 55 petals; foliage leathery; vigorous, upright growth; [sport of Joyance]

Red Splendour F, dr, 1982, Davies, Gareth; flowers deeper red than Europeana, petals frilled, medium, dbl., borne in clusters, slight fragrance; foliage medium size, dark green, glossy; medium, bushy growth; [sport of Europeana]; int. in 1979

Red Sprite F, mr, 1976, LeGrice; flowers glowing red, 2-2½ in., 35 petals; foliage small, glossy, dark; low growth; int. in 1974

Red Star HT, mr, 1918, Verschuren; flowers scarlet-red, very large, semi-dbl., moderate fragrance

Red Star – See **Precious Platinum**, HT

Red Stone – See **Krasnokamenka**, F

Red Storm Min, dr

Red Success HT, rb, 1976, Paolino; bud oval; flowers blood-red, base cardinal-red, 4-4½ in., 40-45 petals, high-centered, borne mostly singly, slight fragrance; good repeat; foliage large, dark green, semi-glossy; prickles medium; stems long; vigorous, upright (5 ft.) growth; PP4037; [(Tropicana × Meialto) × ((((Meibrem × Zambra) × Tropicana) × ((Meibrem × Zambra) × Tropicana)) × Tropicana)]; greenhouse rose; int. by URS

Red Summer F, or, Noack, Werner; int. in 1996

Red Summerwind S, mr

Red Summit Min, dr, 1981, Lyon; bud ovoid, pointed; flowers 33 petals, borne usually singly; prickles long, thin, straight; low, compact, bushy growth; [seedling × seedling]; int. in 1980

Red Sunblaze – See **Prince Meillandina**, Min

Red Sweetheart Pol, rb, 1944, Krebs; bud pointed; flowers crimson-carmine, 1-1½ in., 25 petals, high-centered, moderate spicy fragrance; foliage small, glossy; strong stems; vigorous, bushy growth; [intercrossing of Cécile Brunner seedlings]; int. by Marsh's Nursery

Red Tag Min, rb, 1979, Williams, Ernest D.; bud ovoid, pointed; flowers medium red, white reverse, 1 in., 48 petals, high-centered, moderate fragrance; foliage small, glossy, dark; upright, spreading growth; [seedling × Over the Rainbow]; int. by Mini-Roses, 1978

Red Taifun – See **Red Typhoon**, F

Red Talisman HT, rb, 1931, Amling Bros.; flowers deep cerise, base yellow, intense fruity fragrance; recurrent; [sport of Talisman]

Red Talisman, Climbing Cl HT, rb

Red Tausendschön HMult, rb, 1931, Walter, L.; flowers vivid red with white eye, but varies considerably; [sport of Tausendschön]

Red Tornado HT, mr, 1999, McCall, Sharan; flowers medium red, reverse light red, 5-5½ in., full, borne mostly singly, slight fragrance; foliage medium size, dark green, glossy; prickles moderate; upright, medium (4 ft.) growth; [Dorothy Anne × Classic Touch]

Red Trail S, mr, Ilsink; flowers bright red with golden stamens, 3½ in., single; recurrent; low, spreading, groundcover growth; roots easily wherever it touches the ground; int. in 1991

Red Treasure HT, dr; int. by Inter-State Nurseries, 2001

Red Triumph Pol, or, 1956, Morse; [sport of Orange Triumph]

Red Trooper F, dr

Red Tropicana HT, or; int. by Certified Roses, 2006

Red Typhoon F, mr, Kordes; int. by NewFlora, 2006

Red Unique HT, mr; int. by deRuiter, 2000

Red Velvet F, mr, 1940, Kordes; bud ovoid; flowers vivid crimson, semi-dbl., cupped, slight fragrance; vigorous, compact growth; int. by Dreer

Red Velvet HT, dr, Tantau; flowers deep velvet red, large, full, high-centered, borne mostly singly, slight fragrance; good repeat; foliage glossy; stems very long; tall, upright growth; int. in 1994

Red Velvet F, dr, 1995, Pearce, C.A.; flowers deep red with a hint of brown, medium, full, borne in large clusters, slight fragrance; foliage medium size, dark green, semi-glossy; low (50 cm.), bushy, spreading growth; int. by Rearsby Roses, Ltd., 1996

Red Velvet – See **Velvet Flower Carpet**, S

Red Wagon Min, mr, 1981, Moore, Ralph S.; flowers 23 petals, borne 1-3 or more per cluster; foliage glossy; prickles brown; vigorous, bushy, rounded growth; [Little Darling × Little Chief]; int. by Moore Min. Roses, 1980

Red Wand Cl Min, mr, 1964, Moore, Ralph S.; bud small, ovoid-pointed; flowers light crimson-red, golden stamens, small, 18-25 petals, cupped, borne in clusters, slight green tea fragrance; recurrent; foliage small, semi-glossy, leathery; prickles moderate, slender, hooked slightly downward, brown; vigorous, climbing (3½-4 ft.) growth; PP2717; [((*R. wichurana* × Floradora) × Orange Triumph) × unknown miniature]; int. by Sequoia Nursery

Red Wand S, mr, Kordes; flowers bright blood-red, semi-dbl., borne in clusters; tall, strong growth; int. in 1994

Red Wave F, mr, 1964, Moore, Ralph S.; flowers tulip shaped, small; low growth; containers; [Carolyn Dean × unnamed Floribunda seedling]; int. by Sequoia Nursery

Red Wine HT, mr, 1970, Sanday, John; flowers large, 22 petals, high-centered, borne in clusters; foliage medium green, matte; upright growth; [Lilac Rose × seedling]

Red Wing S, ly, about 1950, possibly Doorenbos; flowers pale yellow, 3 cm., single, borne in clusters; prickles large, winged, translucent red; growth to 6 ft.; hardy; [probably *R. sericea pteracantha* × *R. hugonis*]

Red Wing – See **Napa Valley**, S

Red Wings F, dr, 1959, Boerner; bud ovoid; flowers rich dark red, large, 20 petals, cupped, moderate fragrance; foliage dark, leathery; vigorous, upright, bushy growth; PP1788; [(Improved Lafayette × Herrenhausen) × Lavender Pinocchio]; int. by J&P, 1959

Red Wonder F, dr, 1954, deRuiter; bud globular; flowers crimson-carmine, 3-3½ in., 24-28 petals, cupped, borne in large clusters, moderate fragrance; foliage medium size, leathery, semi-glossy; prickles several, straight, pointed downward; vigorous, bushy growth; hips none ; PP1341; [Better Times × polyantha seedling]; int. by C-P, 1954

Red Yesterday – See **Marjorie Fair**, S

Red Zinnia Min, dr; flowers frilly, long lasting; free-flowering; low growth

Red/White – See **Brandenburg Gate**, HT

Redcap F, mr, 1954, Swim, H.C.; bud ovoid; flowers semi-dbl., 18 petals, high-centered, borne in clusters; foliage leathery, semi-glossy; vigorous, upright, bushy growth; PP1292; [World's Fair × Pinocchio]; int. by Armstrong Nursery

Redcliffe F, mr, 1976, Sanday, John; flowers bright crimson, large, 15 petals; [seedling × Sarabande]; int. in 1975

Redcoat F, mr, 1981, Austin, David; bud pointed; flowers 10 petals, borne 1-5 per cluster, slight fragrance; free-flowering; foliage dark; prickles hooked, brown; bushy growth; [seedling × Golden Showers]; int. in 1973

Redcraze HT, ob, 1959, Doley; bud long, pointed; flowers orange-scarlet, medium, dbl., high-centered; foliage glossy, dark; vigorous, bushy growth; [Independence × Independence]

Reddy Teddy Min, ab, 1999, Schuurman, Frank B.; flowers 1½ in., dbl., borne mostly singly; foliage small, medium green, semi-glossy; prickles moderate; compact, low (8-12 in.) growth; [Sexy Rexy × Firefly]; int. by Franko Roses New Zealand, 1996

Redemption HT, dp, 2005, Edwards, Eddie & Phelps, Ethan; flowers deep pink, reverse deep pink, 5-6 in., full, borne mostly solitary; foliage large, dark green, glossy; few prickles; growth upright, tall (5-6 ft.); exhibition; [Veteran's Honor × Hot Princess]; int. in 2006

Redglo Min, mr, 1991, Williams, Ernest D.; flowers very color fast, velvety nap, outstanding substance, small, full, high-centered, borne mostly singly, slight fragrance; recurrent; foliage small, dark green, semi-glossy; some prickles; low (36 cm.), bushy growth; [Starburst × Over the Rainbow]; int. by Mini-Roses, 1992

Redgold F, yb, 1967, Dickson, A.; bud ovoid, pointed; flowers gold edged deep pink, 4½ in., 25 petals, high-centered, borne usually in clusters, slight fragrance; free-flowering; foliage medium size, dark green, leathery; prickles numerous, broad base, slightly hooked downward; vigorous, upright (2½ ft.) growth; PP3006; [((Karl Herbst × Masquerade) × Faust) × Piccadilly]; int. by J&P, 1971; Gold Medal, Portland, 1969

Redgold, Climbing Cl F, yb, 1972, Stratford (also Lynch, 1974); buds medium, ovoid; flowers gold with deep pink edging, medium, dbl, borne singly and several together; foliage medium size, medium green; [sport of Redgold]; int. by R. H. Rumsey, 1970

Redgold, Climbing Cl F, yb, 1980, Pekmez, Paul; bud cylindric; flowers borne 3-5 per cluster; foliage green, glossy; large growth; [sport of Redgold]; int. by Pekmez

Redhead Cl Min, dr, 1956, Moore, Ralph S.; flowers blood-red; growth to 2½ ft.; [((Soeur Thérèse × Skyrocket) × (seedling × Red Ripples)) × Zee]; int. by Sequoia Nursery

Redhot F, pb, 1988, McGredy, Sam IV; flowers hand-painted, medium, dbl.; foliage small, medium green, semi-glossy; bushy growth; [Eyepaint × Ko's Yellow]

Redhots Min, dr, 1983, Meredith, E.A. & Rovinski, M.E.; flowers 22 petals, high-centered, borne singly; foliage small, long, medium green, finely serrated; very small, tiny growth; [seedling × Darling Flame]; int. by Rosa de Casa Domingo

Rediffusion Gold F, dy, 1985, Harkness, R., & Co., Ltd.; flowers deep golden yellow, 70 petals, borne in clusters of 3-7; foliage small, light green, matte; prickles small; medium, bushy growth; [(Orange Sensation × Allgold) × Sunsprite]; int. by R. Harkness & Co., Ltd., 1984

Redipuglia HT, w, 1933, Ingegnoli; bud long, pointed; flowers pinkish white, reverse golden rose, base chrome-yellow, large, dbl.; vigorous growth

Redland Court F, ab, 1982, Sanday, John; flowers soft apricot, small, 20 petals, slight fragrance; foliage small, medium green, glossy; bushy growth; [Red Maid × Sarabande]; int. by Sanday Roses, Ltd.

Redlands Century HT, or, 1988, Perry, Anthony; flowers medium orange-red, aging slightly lighter, medium, semi-dbl., urn-shaped; foliage medium size, medium green, semi-glossy; prickles average, yellow-green; upright, medium growth; hips globular, small, orange; [World Peace × Command Performance]; int. by Co-Operative Rose Growers, 1988

Redneck Girl Min, op, 1995, Giles, Diann; flowers orange pink with white base, full; foliage small, dark green, semi-glossy; few prickles; spreading growth; int. by Giles Rose Nursery, 1995

Redonda HT, mr, 1968, Patterson; bud globular; flowers large, dbl.; foliage leathery, wrinkled; vigorous, upright growth; [Queen Elizabeth × Happiness]; int. by Patterson Roses

Redouté – See **De Marienbourg**, HSpn

Redouté S, lp, 1992, Austin, David; bud short, slightly pointed ovoid; flowers 3 in., 97 petals, cupped, quartered, borne in clusters of 1-6, moderate sweet, heavy fragrance; recurrent; vigorous (4 ft.) growth; PP8789; [sport of Mary Rose]

Redutea Glauca – See **De Marienbourg**, HSpn

Redway HT, mr, 1954, Waterhouse Nursery; flowers crimson-carmine, high-centered, moderate fragrance; foliage leathery; moderate, upright growth; [Ena Harkness × seedling]

Redwood F, rb, 1988, McGredy, Sam IV; flowers hand-painted, medium, 14 petals; foliage large, dark green, glossy; bushy growth; [Old Master × Wienerwald]

Redwood F, dr, Poulsen; flowers dark red, 8-10 cm., full, cupped, then rounded, no fragrance; bushy (60-100 cm.) growth; hips none; int. as Kronborg, Poulsen Roser, 1996

Redwood Empire Min, or, 1984, Moore, Ralph S.; flowers small, 20 petals; foliage small, medium green, semi-glossy; upright, bushy growth; [Rumba × Sheri Anne]; int. by Moore Min. Roses, 1983

Referenz F, mp, VEG; flowers dbl.; int. in 1983

Reflection HT, yb, 1952, Ratcliffe, R. & E.; bud long, pointed; flowers amber, reverse streaked scarlet, moderate fragrance; vigorous growth; [sport of Mme Henri Guillot]

Reflection HT, dr, Brady, M.; int. in 1995

Reflections F, mp, Simpson; flowers warm shell pink, dbl., borne in clusters; free-flowering; medium growth; int. by Matthews Nurseries, 2000

Reflets F, or, 1964, Croix, P.; flowers large, single; free-flowering; upright growth; [Gertrud Westphal × Sarabande]; Gold Medal, Orléans

Reflets de Saint Malo HT, pb, Adam; flowers pink with light yellow reverse, full, low-centered, intense fragrance; recurrent; foliage dark green, glossy; moderate growth; int. in 2003; Press Prize, Monza, Silver Medal, Paris, Fragrance Award, Madrid

Refresher HWich, w, 1929, Clark, A.; flowers pure white, 4 cm., single, borne in medium to large clusters; early; vigorous, climbing growth; int. by Hazlewood Bros.

Refulgence HEg, mr, 1909, Paul, W.; flowers scarlet, aging to crimson, large, semi-dbl.; foliage very fragrant; vigorous growth; very hardy

Reg Willis HT, dp, 1966, McGredy, Sam IV; flowers deep rose-pink, base yellow, well-formed, 4½ in.; [Golden Masterpiece × Karl Herbst]

Regal Cl Min, dp, 1999, Justice, Jerry G.; flowers old rose pink, reverse same, 1¾ in., very dbl., borne mostly singly, no fragrance; foliage medium size, medium green, glossy; prickles moderate; upright, climbing, medium to tall (6 ft.) growth; [Rosanna × unknown]; int. by Justice Miniature Roses, 1999

Regal Gold HT, dy, 1958, Dale; bud pointed; flowers clear golden yellow, open, 5 in., 40-45 petals; foliage glossy, leathery; vigorous, upright, bushy growth; [sport of Golden Rapture]; int. by Amling-DeVor Nursery, 1957

Regal Lady Min, pb, 1990, Jolly, Nelson F.; bud pointed; flowers white, edged pink, 27 petals, high-centered, borne usually singly or in sprays of 3-5, slight fragrance; foliage medium size, medium green, semi-glossy; no prickles; upright, spreading, tall growth; round fruit; [Sassy Lassie × First Prize]; int. by Rosehill Farm, 1990

Regal Pink HT, mp, 1980, Thomas, Dr. A.S.; [sport of Red Queen]

Regal Red S, mr, Cocker; int. in 1988

Regalia HT, rb, 1964, Robinson, H.; flowers cherry-red, reverse silver, well-formed, 5½ in., 60 petals; foliage bronze; [Rose Gaujard × seedling]

Regalis – See **Royale**, HGal

Regalis – See **Great Royal**, HGal

Regatta HT, w, 1986, Warriner, William A.; flowers large, 48 petals, high-centered, borne singly; foliage medium size, medium green, matte; prickles medium red to brown, hooked downward; medium, upright growth; no fruit; PP5896; [Bernadette × Coquette]; int. by J&P

Regatta HT, lp, 1994, Meilland, Alain A.; bud medium, ovoid; flowers soft dawn pink, large, 32-35 petals, high-centered, borne mostly singly, moderate spicy fragrance; free-flowering; foliage large, dark green, matte; prickles numerous, large, greenish tan; medium (3 ft.), bushy growth; PP8390; [Coppélia 76 × (Meinaregi × Laura 81)]; int. by SNC Meilland & Cie, 1992

Regeliana Flore Pleno – See **Kaiserin des Nordens**, HRg

Regeliana Rubra – See **Kaiserin des Nordens**, HRg

Régence HT, pb, 1970, Laperrière; bud globular; flowers flesh color edged bright pink, open, dbl.; foliage glossy; vigorous, bushy growth; int. by EFR, 1967

Regensberg F, pb, 1978, McGredy, Sam IV; flowers pink, edged white, white eye, yellow stamens, 4½ in., 21 petals, cupped, moderate fragrance; low, bushy growth; [Geoff Boycott × Old Master]; int. by McGredy Roses International, 1979; Gold Medal, Baden-Baden, 1980

Regensberg, Climbing Cl F, pb; int. by Greenhead Nursery, 2002

Regente Agricola HT, Moreira da Silva, A.

Reggae HT, ob, Tantau; flowers soft orange, reverse lighter, medium, dbl., high-centered, borne mostly singly; good repeat; stems 18 in. length; greenhouse rose; int. by Rosen Tantau, 1997

Regia – See **Beauté Tendre**, A

Regia Purpurea HGal, m, before 1835, Coquerel; flowers dark purple, center carmine, medium, full

Regierungsrat Rottenberger HMult, mp, 1926, Praskac;

flowers rich pink, lighter towards edges, reverse darker, 4-5 cm., dbl., flat, circular, borne in large clusters, strong musky fragrance; [Fragezeichen × Tausendschön]

Regierungsrat Stockert HP, lp, 1888, Soupert & Notting; flowers silky, silvery pink, reverse edged light carmine, large, full, moderate fragrance; [Dupuy-Jamain × Mme de Sévigné]

Regina C, mp, before 1885; flowers medium, very dbl., intense fragrance; prickles numerous, short, hooked, blackish green; stems strong; growth vigorous, tall

Regina HWich, w, 1916, Walsh; flowers creamy white tipped pink large panicles, single; foliage large, glossy; vigorous, climbing growth

Regina HT, or, Kordes; flowers orange-red, reverse yellow, dbl., high-centered, moderate fragrance; growth to 70-90 cm.; int. before 1976

Regina – See **Regina Palace**, MinFl

Regina HT, pb, Twomey

Régina Badet HRg, dp, 1908, Gravereaux & Müller; flowers deep violet pink, large, very dbl., flat, often quartered, intense fragrance; repeat bloom; foliage dark; bushy growth; [(Général Jacqueminot × Empereur du Maroc) × *R. rugosa*]

Regina Centifolia HRg, mp; recurrent; 3-5 ft. growth; int. by Rosen von Schultheis, 2001

Régina de Alvéar HT, w, 1922, Sauvageot, H.; flowers white, center slightly shaded pink, dbl.; [Mme Mélanie Soupert × Mme Segond Weber]

Regina della Neve – See **Magic Blanket**, S

Regina Dicta HGal, m, before 1791; flowers light violet, edged white, often mottled, medium, full; often shows proliferation

Regina Elena HT, mp, 1938, Grillo; bud long, pointed; flowers darker rose-pink than briarcliff, 5 in., 50 petals; foliage dark; [sport of Briarcliff]

Regina Lee MinFl, rb, 2005, Verlie W. Wells; flowers white edged red, reverse creamy white, 1¾-2 in., full, borne mostly solitary, slight fragrance; foliage medium size, dark green, semi-glossy; prickles ¾ in., hooked; growth spreading, medium (2½ ft.); garden, exhibition; [Soroptimist International × seedling]; int. by Wells Midsouth Roses, 2004

Regina Louise S, lp, 1999, Clements, John K.; flowers soft pink fading to white, fuchsia stamens tipped gold, 4 in., 25 petals, cupped, intense sweet fragrance; recurrent; medium (3½ ft.), bushy growth; int. by Heirloom Roses, 1999

Regina Pacis HT, w, 1945, Dot, Pedro; buds long; flowers 5 in., high-centered, intense fragrance; foliage soft; branching growth; [Nuria de Recolons × Ibiza]

Regina Palace MinFl, mp, Olesen; bud globular; flowers bright pink, fading slightly as they open, 5 cm., 65 petals, high-centered, borne usually singly, very slight fragrance; recurrent; foliage dark green, glossy; bushy (40-60 cm.) growth; PP15171; [Patricia Kordana Mini Brite × seedling]; int. by Poulsen Roser, 2002

Reginald Fernyhough HT, op, 1949, Bees; flowers pink lightly suffused orange, long, pointed, 5 in., 35 petals; foliage olive-green; very vigorous growth; [Southport × seedling]

Regine Min, pb, 1990, Hefner, John; flowers soft, light pink, silvery-pink reverse, small, 30 petals; foliage medium size, medium green, semi-glossy; bushy growth; [Little Darling × Party Girl]; int. by Kimbrew Walter Roses, 1990; AOE, ARS, 1990

Regine Crespin F, pb, Delbard; int. in 1990

Reginella – See **Sweet Home**, HT

Regulus T, pb, 1860, Robert & Moreau; flowers bright coppery pink, medium, dbl., flat, intense fragrance

Reichsgraf E. von Kesselstatt T, rb, 1898, Lambert; flowers brilliant carmine, aging to rose-pink, edged with crimson, very large, very dbl.; growth erect; [Princesse Alice de Monaco × Duchesse Marie Salviati]

Reichspräsident von Hindenberg HP, pb, 1933, Lambert, P.; flowers dark pink to carmine, veined lighter, reverse darker, button center, 6 in., very dbl., moderate fragrance; floriferous; foliage broad; very vigorous, bushy growth; [Frau Karl Druschki × Graf Silva Tarouca]

Reigen F, ob, GPG Bad Langensalza; flowers medium, dbl.; int. in 1984

Reiko HT, op, 1963, Teranishi, K.; bud long, pointed; flowers bright coral-peach, 3½-4 in., 25 petals, high-centered; foliage dark, leathery; vigorous, upright growth; [Spartan × Fred Streeter]; int. by Itami Rose Nursery

Reiko Min, lp, 1995, Jalbert, Brad; flowers medium pink, lighter pink reverse, 1 in., dbl., borne in small clusters, moderate fragrance; foliage medium size, medium green, glossy; some prickles; medium (12 in.), compact, bushy growth; [Winsome × Springwood Gold]; int. by Select Roses, 1995

Reims HT, yb, 1924, Barbier; bud long, pointed; flowers bright nankeen yellow shaded fiery red, orange-apricot and copper-pink, large

Reina Elisenda – See **Independence**, F

Reina Maria Christina – See **Maria Cristina**, T

Reinaerdiana F, Delforge; int. in 1974

Reine Amelia HGal, mp

Reine André HWich, 1900, Barbier; [L'Idéal × *R. wichurana*]

Reine Astrid HT, rb, 1937, Gaujard; bud long, pointed; flowers bright deep coppery red, reverse golden yellow, dbl., cupped; foliage glossy; vigorous growth

Reine Augusta Victoria – See **Kaiserin Auguste Viktoria**, HT

Reine Blanche – See **Hebe's Lip**, HEg

Reine-Blanche M, w, 1857, Moreau et Robert; flowers pure white, large, dbl., flat

Reine Blanche HP, w, 1868, Damaizin; flowers white, shaded light pink, large, full, globular; [La Reine × unknown]

Reine Carola de Saxe HT, pb, 1902, Gamon; flowers silvery pink on a deep salmony pink ground, large, full, moderate fragrance

Reine Chabeau HMsk, w, 2000, Lens, Louis; flowers creamy white, 2-3 cm., semi-dbl., borne in large, long, pyramid-shaped clusters, moderate fragrance; foliage light green, semi-glossy; prickles moderate; compact, upright, arching, medium (80-120 cm.) growth; [(Seagull × *R. multiflora nana*) × *R. multiflora nana*]; int. by Louis Lens N.V., 1994

Reine d'Angleterre T, dp; flowers carmine, shaded purple, medium, very full

Reine de Castille HP, dr, 1852, Lartay; flowers deep carmine red, large, full, globular

Reine de Castille B, mp, 1863, Pernet; bud rose-white; flowers bright rose, well-formed; vigorous growth

Reine de Danemark HP, lp, 1857, Granger; flowers flesh-lilac, large, full; foliage small, pointed, very serrate; nearly thornless

Reine de Fontenay HP, mp; flowers medium, full

Reine de la Lombardie Ch, dr, before 1835; flowers deep cerise passing to crimson purple, medium, dbl., globular

Reine de la Pape HP, m, 1863, Guillot; flowers violet pink, large, full

Reine de Perse HGal, lp, before 1825; flowers light cream-pink, small to medium, very dbl., intense fragrance

Reine de Portugal T, yb, Guillot et Fils; flowers coppery yellow shaded pink, large, very dbl.

Reine de Prusse HGal, mr, 1824, possibly Asselin; flowers bright red, aging to lilac pink, medium, full

Reine de Prusse – See **Duchesse d'Angoulême**, HGal, before 1860

Reine de Saxe C, mp, before 1820; flowers medium, dbl., moderate fragrance

Reine de Vibert HGal, m, about 1835, Vibert; flowers purple

Reine des Amateurs HGal, m, before 1829, Hébert, Mme.; flowers clear lilac, edged pale pink, well-shaped, very large

Reine des Ayrshire – See **Ayrshire Queen**, Ayr

Reine des Beautés HP, lp, 1870, Gonod; flowers light flesh pink with white, medium to large, full

Reine des Belges Ayr, w, 1832, Jacques; flowers creamy white, lightly touched with pink, 4-5 cm., very dbl., slight musk fragrance; non-recurrent; foliage evergreen; stems long, slender, reddish; mixed parentage of *R. sempervirens*, *R. arvensis*, and a China

Reine des Belges HCh, w, 1867, Cochet; sparse bloom; vigorous growth; [Globe Hip × *R. chinensis*]

Reine des Blanches HP, w, 1868, Avoux or Pernet; flowers white shaded pink, large, full; [La Reine × unknown]

Reine des Blanches HP, w, 1870, Crozy; flowers white, shaded light pink, large, full; [Victor Verdier × unknown]

Reine des Bordures – See **Border Queen**, F

Reine des Centfeuilles C, mp, 1824, from Belgium; flowers clear pink, reflexed, central rosette, very large, dbl., cupped/globular, moderate fragrance; foliage somber green; very vigorous growth

Reine des Couleurs – See **Farbenkönigin**, HT

Reine des Fées – See **Rosalie**, T

Reine des Fleurs HP, mr, 1846, Portemer; flowers crimson, edged with lilac-pink, large, full, globular

Reine des Francais – See **La Reine**, HP

Reine des Iles-Bourbons – See **Queen of Bourbons**, B, 1834

Reine des Mousseuses M, lp, about 1860, Moreau et Robert; flowers flesh pink, medium, full; possibly synonymous with Gloire des Mousseux

Reine des Nègres – See **Superbe en Brun**, HGal

Reine des Neiges – See **Frau Karl Druschki**, HP

Reine des Neiges, Climbing – See **Frau Karl Druschki, Climbing**, Cl HP

Reine des Pays-Bas HGal, dp, 1824, in Brussels; flowers velvety carmine, medium

Reine des Pays-Bas T, lp, 1858, Fontaine

Reine des Poêtes – See **Des Poêtes**, D

Reine des Pourpres – See **Pallas**, HGal

Reine des Reines – See **Queen of Queens**, HP

Reine des Roses – See **Colour Wonder**, HT, 1964

Reine des Vierges B, lp, 1844, Béluze; flowers pale pink, flesh towards center, medium, semi-dbl.

Reine des Violettes HP, m, 1860, Mille-Malet; flowers violet-red, large, 75 petals, intense fragrance; recurrent bloom; foliage sparse; [Pie IX × unknown]

Reine d'Espagne HP, mr, 1861, Fontaine; flowers brilliant red, medium, full; foliage light; bushy growth; sometimes classed as HGal

Reine d'Italie Ch, dr, 1886, Perny; flowers dark red with carmine

Reine du Congrès B, lp, 1842, Béluze; flowers flesh pink, shaded bright pink, medium, full

Reine du Dänemark – See **Königin von Dänemark**, A

Reine du Forez HT, rb, Croix; flowers red with silver reverse, nuanced with orange, 45 petals, globular; foliage dark green, resistant; upright growth; int. by Roseraie Paul Croix, 1969; Certificate of Merit, Monza, Certificate of Merit, Madrid

Reine du Matin HP, m, 1845, Béluze; flowers bluish lilac, medium, full

Reine du Midi HP, mp, 1867, Roland; flowers lilac pink,

very large, full, flat, moderate fragrance; [La Reine × unknown]

Reine Elisabeth HT, mr, 1955, Buyl Frères; flowers velvety blood-red; [Princesse Liliane × Ena Harkness]

Reine Elizabeth HT, rb, 1925, Opdebeeck; bud long, pointed; flowers coral-red, changing to prawn-red, tinted yellow, dbl.

Reine Elizabeth Pol, mr; flowers crimson, pompon, borne in clusters; compact, dwarf growth

Reine Emma des Pays-Bas T, my, 1879, Nabonnand, G.; flowers coppery yellow, reverse almost flame-colored, large, semi-dbl.

Reine France HT, op, Delbard-Chabert; flowers large, dbl.

Reine Lucia – See **Lichtkönigin Lucia**, S

Reine Marguerite – See **Tricolore**, HGal

Reine Marguerite d'Italie HT, mr, 1904, Soupert & Notting; flowers carmine red, vermilion toward center, very large, very full; foliage dark green; [Baron Nathaniel de Rothschild × Mme la Princesse de Bessaraba de Brancovan]

Reine Maria de Roumanie HT, w, 1927, Mühle; bud long, pointed; flowers marble-white, center yellow, dbl.; [Stadtrat Glaser × unknown]

Reine Maria Pia T, dp, 1880, Schwartz, J.; flowers deep pink, center crimson, lighter reverse, 9-10 cm., full, globular, borne singly or in small clusters, moderate fragrance; very vigorous growth; [Gloire de Dijon × unknown]

Reine Marie Henriette Cl T, mr, 1878, Levet, F.; bud large, plump, pointed; flowers pure cherry-red, fading to magenta, reverse lighter, 10-11 cm., dbl., moderate fragrance; foliage dark green; vigorous, climbing growth; [Mme Berard × Général Jacqueminot]; sometimes classed as a Cl HT or a N

Reine Mère d'Italie HT, dy, 1910, Bernaix; flowers apricot-ochre yellow, medium, dbl.

Reine Nathalie de Serbie T, lp, 1885, Soupert & Notting; flowers flesh pink and creme, shaded light yellow, large to very large, full, flat to globular; [Mme Lombard × Sulfureux]

Reine Olga de Wurtemberg N, mr, 1881, Nabonnand, G.; flowers bright red, 9 cm., dbl., moderate fragrance; reliable repeat; growth very vigorous; pillar

Reine Sammut S, pb, Guillot-Massad ?; int. by Roseraies Guillot, 1999

Reine Victoria B, mp, 1872, Labruyère/Schwartz; flowers rich pink, well-formed, large, dbl., cupped, intense damask fragrance; repeat bloom; foliage soft green; slender, upright (to 6 ft.) growth

Reiner Maria Rilke – See **Uwe Seeler**, F

Reinhard Bädecker HP, my, 1918, Kordes; flowers clear golden yellow, red shadings on edge and reverse, very large, dbl.; [Frau Karl Druschki × Rayon d'Or]

Reinhard Pusch HT, yb, Tagashira, Kazuso; flowers large, dbl.; int. by Hiroshima Bara-en, 1992

Rejoice Gr, pb, 1985, McMillan, Thomas G.; flowers salmon-pink blended with yellow, large, 40 petals, high-centered, borne in clusters of 1-6, moderate fragrance; foliage large, medium green, glossy; tall, upright, bushy growth; [Little Darling × Color Magic]; Gold Medal, ARC TG, 1985

Rejouissence HT, Croix; int. in 1977

Rekordblüher F, mp, 1965, Tantau, Math.; flowers rose-pink, 2-3 in., semi-dbl., borne in large trusses; foliage dark, glossy; bushy growth; int. by Wheatcroft Bros.

Rektor Foerster HT, pb, 1936, Weigand, C.; flowers solferino-pink, flushed yellow, large, dbl., high-centered; foliage leathery; vigorous growth; [Golden Ophelia × Mme Caroline Testout]; int. by Pfitzer

Relax S, or; flowers orange-red with yellow center, lighter reverse, yellow stamens, single, borne in small clusters; non-remontant; int. in 1979

Relax Meidiland – See **Relax Meillandecor**, S semi-dbl.

Relax Meillandecor S, pb, Meilland; flowers semi-dbl.; free-flowering; growth to 50 cm.; int. in 1993

Release – See **Nobilo's Chardonnay**, HT

Release HT, yb

Reliance HT, lp, 1909, Hill, E. G.; flowers light pink, edged creamy white, large, full; [Etoile de France × Chateau de Clos Vougeot]

Relief HT, w, 1919, Verschuren; flowers ivory-white, center yellowish-pink; [Kaiserin Auguste Viktoria × Sunburst]

Remarkable F, pb, 2004, Bridges, Dennis A.; flowers shades of pink with white and a little yellow, reverse lighter, 3½ in., full, borne in small clusters, slight fragrance; foliage medium size, dark green, semi-glossy; prickles to 7/16 in., slight curve pointing slightly; growth bushy, medium, vigorous (4 ft); garden, exhibition, cutting; [Tiki × Mixed pollen]; int. by Almost Heaven Roses, 2005

Rembrandt P, m, 1883, Moreau-Robert; flowers vermilion, sometimes striped with white, large, full; remontant; stems long, strong; growth vigorous

Rembrandt HT, ob, 1914, Van Rossem; flowers salmon, tinted orange-red, well-formed, large, 40 petals; foliage leathery; vigorous growth; [Frau Karl Druschki × Lyon Rose]; sometimes classed as HP

Rembrandt F, mr, 1964, McGredy, Sam IV; flowers bright scarlet, large, 15 petals, borne in clusters; foliage light green; [Tivoli × Independence]

Rembrandt van Ryn S, rb, Williams, J. Benjamin; flowers burgandy red with lighter striping and spotting, dbl., cupped, borne in clusters; upright growth; int. in 1997

Remember – See **Royal Copenhagen**, HT

Remember Me HT, ob, 1984, Cocker; flowers orange and yellow blend, large, 20 petals, high-centered; foliage small, dark, glossy; bushy, spreading growth; [Ann Letts × (Dainty Maid × Pink Favorite)]

Remembering Dee MinFl, w, 2007, Sparks, Richard & Carol; flowers pure white, 6 cm., 40-50 petals, borne singly and in small clusters; foliage medium size, medium green, semi-glossy; prickles moderate, 6-7 mm., slightly hooked; growth upright, well-branched, medium (40-60 cm.); garden, cutting, containers; [sport of Madeline Spezzano]; int. by Nor'East Miniature Roses/ Greenheart Farms, Inc., 2007

Remembering Michael HT, m, 2005, Halvorson, Donald A.; flowers mauve, reverse mauve, 4 in., full, borne mostly solitary, intense fragrance; foliage medium size, medium green, semi-glossy; prickles medium; growth bushy, medium (4-5 ft.); garden, exhibition; [Royal Highness × Charles de Gaulle]; int. by Halverson, Donald A., 2005

Remembrance HT, yb, 1953, Howard, A.P.; bud ovoid; flowers soft yellow edged dawn-pink, 4-5 in., 50 petals, high-centered; profuse bloom; foliage leathery, glossy, coppery green; vigorous, upright growth; RULED EXTINCT 4/92; [Fred Howard × seedling]; int. by H&S

Remembrance F, mr, 1992, Harkness, R., & Co., Ltd.; flowers scarlet, large, 32 petals, cupped, borne in sprays of 5-7, slight fragrance; foliage dark green, glossy; bushy growth; [Trumpeter × Southampton]; int. by R. Harkness & Co., Ltd.; Golden Prize, Glasgow, 1995

Reminiscence – See **Caramella**, S

Remuera F, w, 1998, McGredy, Sam IV; flowers white, 2¾ in., 26-41 petals, borne in large clusters; foliage small, medium green, semi-glossy; prickles moderate; bushy, low (40 cm.) growth; [Seaspray × Sexy Rexy]; int. by McGredy, 1991; Gold Star of the South Pacific, Palmerston North, NZ, 1989

Remy Martin – See **Magic Lantern**, Gr

Renae Cl F, mp, 1954, Moore, Ralph S.; bud pointed; flowers warm pink, 2½ in., 43 petals, cupped, borne in clusters, intense fragrance; recurrent bloom; foliage small, glossy; prickles few to none; vigorous, climbing growth; [Étoile Luisante × Sierra Snowstorm]; int. by Armstrong Nursery

Renaissance HT, rb, 1945, Gaujard; bud pointed; flowers red and gold, medium, dbl.; foliage glossy; low growth; RULED EXTINCT 10/86

Renaissance HT, ob, 1987, Gaujard, Jean; flowers brilliant orange, dbl., high-centered, moderate fragrance; foliage large; prickles small; rounded fruit; [seedling × Pampa]; int. in 1980

Renaissance HT, lp; flowers pale blush pink, dbl., high-centered, intense fruity, Damask fragrance; recurrent; bushy (2½ ft.) growth; int. by Harkness, 1994; Fragrance Award, Glasgow, 1996, Fragrance Award, Belfast, 1995

Renaissance HT, ab; greenhouse rose; int. by Grandiflora Nursery, 2002

Renaissance de Flecheres HT, my, Ducher; flowers yellow, petal edges turn white, full, cupped, moderate fragrance; free-flowering; growth to 3-4 ft.; int. by Roseraie Fabien Ducher, 2004

Renata HT, op, Williams, J. Benjamin; flowers orange and peach blend with hint of green, dbl., cupped, moderate fragrance; recurrent; growth to 4 ft.; int. by Hortico, Inc., 2005

Renata Tebaldi HT, ob, Delbard; flowers red-orange, large, dbl.; foliage large, brilliant green; int. by Sauvageot, 1987

Renate HT, w, 1925, Berger, V.; flowers cream-white, dbl.; [Kaiserin Auguste Viktoria × unknown]

Rendan F, rb, Keisei; int. by Keisei Rose Nurseries, 1987

Rendez-vous – See **Day of Triumph**, HT

Rendez-vous S, mp, 1986, Lucas, C.C.; flowers medium, semi-dbl., intense fragrance; foliage medium size, medium green, matte; bushy growth; [*R. wichurana* × Alain Blanchard]; int. in 1981

Rendez-vous HT, dp, 1987, Meilland; flowers rose-mauve, large, dbl., intense fragrance; Fragrance Award, Belfast, 1990

Rendez-vous HT, dr

Rendez Vous 81 HT, Meilland, L.; int. in 1981

Rendez-Vous HT, dp, J&P; cut flower rose; int. by Francis Aebi, 1993

Rene F, Byrum; PP4016

René André HWich, ab, 1901, Barbier; bud coppery; flowers saffron-yellow, becoming pale pink and carmine, 2-2½ in., semi-dbl., borne in clusters, moderate fragrance; very vigorous growth; [*R. wichurana* × L'Ideal]

René Boulanger B, lp, 1913, Boulanger; flowers flesh pink with salmon, large, full

René Buatois LCl, mp, 1936, Buatois; flowers ruddy pink; [sport of Leontine Gervais]

René Daniel HP, dp, 1868, Damaizin; flowers cherry-pink, aging to crimson, large, full

René d'Anjou M, dp, 1853, Robert; flowers deep pink, veined, small, dbl., globular; some repeat

René Denis N, ly, 1897, Denis; [sport of Mme Bérard]

René Goscinny HT, ob, Meilland; flowers warm orange suffused with vermillion, 80-90 petals, cupped, moderate fruity fragrance; vigorous (60-80 cm.) growth; int. by Meilland Richardier, 2005; Gold Rose, Geneva, 2001

René Javey HT, ab, 1934, Gillot, F.; flowers clear apricot, reverse salmon-pink shaded yellow, passing to, dbl.; foliage clear bronze green

Renée Brightman HT, rb, 1936, Hurran; flowers brilliant scarlet, shaded orange, reverse striped yellow, dbl.; vigorous growth; [Emma Wright × unknown]

Renee Columb HT, rb, Gaujard; int. in 1979

Renée Danielle HWich, my, 1913, Guillot, P.; flowers jonquil-yellow to golden yellow, passing to white, 5 cm., dbl., cupped, borne in small clusters; sometimes blooms again in autumn; foliage glossy, purplish; nearly thornless; vigorous, climbing growth

Renée Wilmart-Urban HT, pb, 1908, Pernet-Ducher; bud long, pointed; flowers salmon-flesh, edged carmine, large, dbl.

Renegade Min, mr, 1986, Lyon; flowers 52 petals, cupped, borne usually singly; foliage medium size, medium green, matte; prickles small, green; medium, upright growth; [seedling × seedling]; int. by M.B. Farm Min. Roses, Inc.

Renegade MinFl, lp, Spooner, Raymond A.; int. in 1995

Rene's Rose HT, pb, Dawson; int. in 1995

Renica – See **Rebecca**, HT

Rennie's Pink Min, pb, Rennie; flowers deep salmon pink inner petals blending to soft pink and white outer petals., hybrid tea, slight fragrance; recurrent; int. by Hortico, 2000

Renny Min, mp, 1989, Moore, Ralph S.; bud pointed; flowers medium rose pink, reverse lighter, old fashioned, medium, 25 petals, borne in sprays of 3-7, moderate fragrance; foliage medium size, medium green, matte; no prickles; upright, bushy, low growth; no fruit; [Anytime × Renae]; int. by Sequoia Nursery

Renny's Dream – See **Renny**, Min

Reno Gr, op, 1957, Silva; bud long, pointed, ovoid; flowers coral-salmon, wavy petals, 3-3½ in., 16-20 petals, globular, cupped, borne singly and in clusters; free-flowering; foliage bronze; prickles reddish-brown; vigorous (4 ft.), branching growth; hips round, yellow; PP1690; [Mrs Sam McGredy × Mme Henri Guillot]; int. by Booy Rose Nursery, 1957

Renoir Gr, pb, 1980, Hall, William W.; bud plump, pointed; flowers flesh pink with peach tones toward base, 18 petals, borne 1-4 per cluster, moderate tea fragrance; repeat bloom; foliage 7-9 leaflet,dark, smooth; prickles curved; vigorous, upright to arching growth; int. in 1982

Renoncule – See **Provins Renoncule**, HGal

Renoncule Pol, dp, 1913, Barbier; flowers deep pink tinted lighter, buttercup-like

Renoncule Noirâtre – See **Roi des Pourpres**, HGal

Renoncule Ponctuée HGal, mr, 1833, Vibert; flowers crimson, spotted and marbled with rose, medium, dbl.

Renouveau de Provins HT, or, 1970, Laperrière; bud ovoid; flowers geranium color, open, very large, 36 petals; foliage glossy; vigorous, bushy growth; [Magicienne × Numero Un]; int. by EFR, 1967

Renown HT, or, 1927, Burbage Nursery; flowers glowing orange-cerise, shaded cardinal, dbl.; [Red-Letter Day × Mrs Wemyss Quin]

Renown's Desert Glo – See **Della Balfour**, S

Renown's Rosario – See **Rosario**, S

Renown's Samaritan – See **English Sonnet**, F

Renown's Summer Lady – See **Summer Lady**, HT

Renzie Park Min, ob, Consigliero; int. in 2005

Repandia S, lp, 1983, Kordes, W.; flowers soft pink, small, semi-dbl., shallow cup, borne in clusters, moderate fragrance; foliage small, dark, glossy; low, spreading (to 5 ft.) growth; groundcover; [The Fairy × (*R. wichurana* × unknown)]; int. by Kordes Roses, 1982; ADR, 1986

Repartee HSpn, w

Repelsteeltje – See **Rumpelstilzchen**, S

Repens – See **Aimée Vibert**, N

Repens – See **Splendens**, Ayr

Repens Alba – See **Paulii**, HRg

Repens Meidiland S, w, 1987, Meilland, Mrs. Marie-Louise; bud conical; flowers single, 5 petals, flat to slightly cupped, borne in clusters of 5-10, no fragrance; moderate to low production; foliage medium size, light green, glossy; spreading, almost horizontal, strong growth; PP6598; [Swany × New Dawn]; int. in 1985

Repens Rosea – See **Paulii Rosea**, HRg

Rephidy HT, pb; flowers pink with darker pink edges, medium, full, high-centered; tall growth

Republic of Texas S, ly, 2005, Shoup, George Michael; buds bright yellow; flowers light yellow with pink tints, 1-1½ in., dbl., borne in small clusters, moderate fragrance; remontant; foliage small, dark green, semi-glossy; numerous prickles; spreading, medium (3-4 ft.) growth; container/border or in mass; [(The Fairy × *R. wichurana*) × Baby Love]; int. by Antique Rose Emporium, 2000

République de Genève HT, rb, Laperrière; flowers yellow heart and reverse, outer half of petals turning red, dbl., high-centered; free-flowering; int. in 1992

Resolut F, or, 1962, Tantau, Math.; bud oval; flowers 4-5 in., 30 petals, borne in large sprays; foliage glossy; upright, bushy growth

Resonanz F, mr, Noack; flowers bright red, bright yellow stamens, colorfast, 2½ in., semi-dbl., cupped, borne in clusters, slight fragrance; recurrent; foliage dark green, glossy; growth to 90-100 cm.; int. by Noack Rosen, 2006

Respect HT, mr, Spek; flowers bright red, full, high-centered, borne mostly singly; int. by Carlton Rose Nurseries, 2002

Resplenda HT, w, 1975, Golik; bud ovoid; flowers 4 in., 30 petals, moderate fruity fragrance; foliage glossy; moderate growth; [Queen of Bermuda × Golden Giant]; int. by Dynarose, 1974

Resplendent HP, lp, 1896, Williams, A.

Respond HT, pb, 1995, Sheldon, John & Robin; flowers dark pink blend, large, full, borne mostly singly, slight fragrance; foliage medium size, medium green, matte; upright, medium growth; [Sheer Elegance × seedling]

Responso F, yb, GPG Bad Langensalza; flowers medium, dbl.; int. in 1981

Ressins Etienne Gautier HT, pb, Dorieux; int. in 1996

Rest in Peace MinFl, w, Chessum, Paul; flowers creamy white, large, full; foliage medium green, glossy; growth to 3 ft.; int. in 1997

Restful HT, my, 1995, Sheldon, John & Robin; flowers large, full, borne mostly singly, slight fragrance; foliage medium size, medium green, matte; upright, tall growth; [Miyabi × Lanvin]

Restless HT, dr, 1938, Clark; flowers dark red, semi-dbl.; almost thornless

Restless Native S, or, 1973, Stoddard, Louis; bud ovoid; flowers orange-scarlet, base white, 2½ in., 8-12 petals, cupped; foliage large, dark, leathery; vigorous, compact, bushy growth; [Orangeade × *R. carolina*]

Results HT, pb, 1995, Sheldon, John & Robin; flowers red, white, pink, purple hues, depending on temperature, large, dbl., borne mostly singly; foliage medium size, dark green, matte; upright, tall growth; [Pristine × seedling]

Resurrection HT, dp, 1986, Kriloff, Michel; bud red; flowers bright pink, large, moderate sweet fragrance; foliage dark; [seedling × seedling]

Reta Elizabeth Lindsay – See **Lions International**, HT

Retina Min, mr, 1981, Williams, Ernest D.; flowers medium red, reverse lighter, base gold, 43 petals, borne singly, slight fruity fragrance; foliage green, matte; prickles straight, long, tan; bushy, spreading growth; [seedling × Over the Rainbow]; int. by Kimbrew-Walter Roses, 1980

Retour du Printemps HCh, dp, before 1835; flowers medium, semi-dbl.; Lawrenciana

Rétro S, mp, Meilland; flowers large, dbl.; int. in 1980

Rétro Blanc S, w

Reunion HT, pb; int. by Certified Roses, 2005

Reus HT, m, 1949, Dot, Pedro; bud long, pointed; flowers magenta, large, dbl., high-centered; [Cynthia × Manuelita]

Rêve de Capri HT, op, 1953, Buyl Frères; flowers salmon-orange and yellow; foliage bronze; compact, low growth; [Pres. Herbert Hoover × seedling]

Rêve de Deauville F, dy, Pineau; int. in 1982

Rêve de Môme HT, yb, Dorieux; flowers yellow with broad red edges, dbl., high-centered; foliage dark green, glossy; int. by Roseraies Dorieux, 2006; People's Choice, Monza, 2005

Rêve de Paris HT, op, Meilland; flowers rose-scarlet, large, dbl.; int. in 1985

Rêve de Valse F, mr, Tantau; flowers velvety blood red, dbl.

Rêve d'Hélène HT, mp, 1959, Orard, Joseph; flowers bright pink edged silvery, large; foliage clear green; free growth; [Michèle Meilland × seedling]

Rêve d'Or N, my, 1869, Ducher, Vve.; flowers buff-yellow tinted lighter at edges, fading to pale buff, medium to large, dbl., loose, borne in small clusters, moderate fragrance; foliage dark green, glossy, tinted red when young; vigorous, climbing growth; [Mme Schultz × unknown]

Rêve d'un Soir HT, m, Croix; flowers large, well-formed, intense fragrance; free-flowering; int. by Roseraie Paul Croix, 1997; Gold Medal, Baden-Baden, 1997

Rêve Rose F, mp, 1950, Mallerin, C.; flowers 60 petals, borne in large clusters; int. by Vilmorin-Andrieux

Réveil B, rb, 1854, Guillot père; flowers cherry red, tinted and shaded violet, large, full; growth to 80 cm.

Réveil HT, yb, 1924, Van Rossem; flowers golden yellow, reverse striped red, dbl.; [Mr Joh. M. Jolles × Mrs Wemyss Quinn]

Réveil de l'Empire HP, mp, 1852, Bernède; flowers silky pink, large, full

Réveil Dijonnais Cl HT, rb, 1931, Buatois; flowers cerise, golden yellow center, reverse yellow streaked carmine, 5 in., 13 petals, cupped, borne in small clusters, moderate fragrance; intermittent repeat; foliage thick, glossy, bronze; short stems; vigorous, climbing growth; [Eugene Furst × Constance]; Gold Medal, Portland, 1929

Réveil du Printemps HP, w, 1883, Oger; flowers delicate flesh white, large, very full

Reveille HT, pb, 1941, Nicolas; flowers light salmon-buff-pink, center deeper pink, open, large, 40-50 petals, cupped; foliage dark, leathery; vigorous, upright, bushy, compact growth; [Kidwai × Golden Main]; int. by J&P

Revelation HT, pb, 1938, Witter; bud long; flowers thulite-pink to rose-red, 4½-5 in., 35 petals, high-centered; foliage dark; very vigorous growth; [sport of Briarcliff]; int. by Evans City Cut Flower Co.

Revelry F, dp, 1959, Boerner, E. S.; bud large, blood-red, ovoid; flowers open rose-red, aging to rose-pink, very large, semi-dbl., open; continuous; foliage leathery, dark green, disease-resistant; growth vigorous, upright, bushy; PP1850; [Enchantment × seedling]; int. by J&P, 1959

Revelry HT, dr, 1998, Swisher, Stan; flowers dark red to purple, 4 in., full, borne mostly singly, moderate fragrance; foliage medium size, dark green, semi-glossy; upright, tall growth; [Pristine × National Velvet]; int. by Certified Roses, Inc., 1998

Revenante – See **La Revenante**, HGal

Révérence F, mr, 1962, Delforge; flowers geranium-red, 2 in., 26 petals, carnation-like, borne in large clusters; foliage dark, glossy; vigorous, upright growth; [Orange Triumph × seedling]

Reverend Alan Cheales HP, mr, 1897, Paul, G.; flowers pale pink, reverse darker, very large, dbl., peony-like

Rev. David R. Williamson HT, mr, 1921, Pernet-Ducher; bud long, pointed, deep coral-red; flowers coral-red, tinted orange, large, very full, globular, moderate fragrance

Rev F. Page-Roberts HT, yb, 1921, Cant, B. R.; bud long, pointed; flowers yellow shaded red, large, dbl., high-centered, intense fragrance; free-flowering; growth to 4 ft.; [Queen Mary × seedling]; Gold Medal, NRS, 1920

Rev. F. Page-Roberts, Climbing Cl HT, yb, 1931, Beverley; int. by W.B. Clarke

Rev. Floris Ferwerda – See **Ben Stad**, LCl

Rev. H. d'Ombrain B, mr, 1863, Margottin; flowers brilliant red, large, full, cupped; recurrent bloom; vigorous growth

Rev James Sprunt Cl HCh, mr, 1858, Sprunt; flowers crimson-red, larger than parent; [sport of Cramoisi Supérieur]; int. by P. Henderson, 1858

Rev. Peter Lewis F, rb, 2006, Pullen, Sarah Mary; flowers red striped, reverse red, 2-3 in., semi-dbl., borne in large clusters; foliage medium size, medium green, semi-glossy; prickles small, straight, light brown, moderate; growth upright, medium (30 in.); [Pirouette × seedling]; int. in 2006

Reverend Seidel HMsk, w, Robinson; flowers white with yellow stamens, small, single, flat, borne in large clusters, moderate fragrance; free-flowering; growth compact, Noisette-like; int. by Vintage Gardens, 2005

Rev T. C. Cole Cl T, dy, 1880, Cole, Rev T.C.; [Chromatella × Marechal Neil]

Rev. Williamson HT, or, 1921, Pernet-Ducher; bud long, pointed; flowers coral-red, shaded carmine, dbl.

Rev Williamson – See **Rev. David R. Williamson**, HT

Rêverie HT, ab, 1925, Ketten Bros.; flowers apricot, reverse shrimp-pink veined rose, dbl.; [Mme Mélanie Soupert × Jean C.N. Forestier]

Reverie – See **Träumerei**, F

Reversa Bslt, m, about 1810, Vilmorin; flowers violet purple, medium, semi-dbl., borne in small clusters; foliage lanceolate, glabrous, simply dentate at the tips; nearly thornless; stems glaucous, usually purple; hips ovoid, red

Reversa Pourpre – See **Maheca**, Bslt

Review HT, mp, 1951, Fletcher; flowers bright rose, reverse flesh, 6-7 in., 50 petals; foliage dull, green; medium, dwarf growth; [Mrs Henry Bowles × Trigo]; int. by Tucker

Revival HT, ab, 1981, Rose Barni-Pistoia; flowers honey amber, fading to creamy yellow, dbl., high-centered, slight fragrance; recurrent; stems strong; growth to 4 ft.; [sport of Folklore]; int. in 1979

Revolution Pol, or, GPG Bad Langensalza; flowers medium, semi-dbl., loose, borne in clusters; bushy (2 ft.) growth; int. in 1972

Révolution Française HT, mr, Meilland; int. in 1989

Revue HT, pb, Kordes; bud large; flowers white with pink edges, strong contrast, medium size, 40-45 petals, high-centered, borne usually singly, no fragrance; good repeat; foliage dark green, glossy; prickles few, bending downward; stems 60 cm.; vigorous, upright, bushy growth; PP14440; [seedling × seedling]; greenhouse rose; int. by W. Kordes Söhne, 2002

Revue de Dauville – See **Rêve de Deauville**, F

Reward HT, yb, 1934, Dickson, A.; bud long, pointed; flowers clear yellow shaded peach, medium; foliage dark, glossy; vigorous, bushy growth

Rex HT, mr, 1960, Spanbauer; bud long, pointed; flowers velvety cardinal-red, large, semi-dbl., cupped; foliage leathery, glossy; vigorous, upright growth; [Senior × Better Times]; int. in 1959

Rex Anderson HT, w, 1938, McGredy; flowers ivory-white, very well-formed, large, dbl., high-centered, moderate fruity fragrance; shy bloom; foliage gray-green; vigorous growth; [Florence L. Izzard × Mrs Charles Lamplough]; int. by J&P

Rexy's Baby F, lp, 1992, McGredy, Sam IV; flowers medium, full, borne in clusters, slight fragrance; foliage small, medium green, glossy; bushy (90 cm.) growth; [Sexy Rexy × (Freude × ((Anytime × Eyepaint) × Stars 'n' Stripes))]; int. by McGredy Roses International, 1992

Reynolda House HT, pb, 1992, Williams, J. Benjamin; flowers light pink with ivory and coral blend, medium, full, borne mostly singly, intense fragrance; foliage medium size, dark green, semi-glossy, disease-resistant; few prickles; upright, bushy, medium (3-4 ft.) growth; winter hardy; [Royal Highness × Command Performance]

Reynolds Hole B, mp, 1862, Standish & Noble; flowers medium, very dbl.

Reynolds Hole HP, rb, 1874, Paul, G.; flowers chestnut-brown-red, shaded scarlet-purple or amaranthe, large, full, globular; [Duke of Edinburgh × unknown]

Reynold's Rugosa HRg, mr, 2000, Reynolds, Ted; flowers 100 petals, borne mostly singly; foliage large, dark green, glossy; numerous prickles; bushy, medium growth; int. by Paul Chessum Roses, 2002

Rhapsody HT, ob, 1951, Houghton, D.; bud long, pointed; flowers orange, reverse terra-cotta, medium, 20 petals, high-centered; foliage leathery; vigorous, bushy growth; RULED EXTINCT 1/85; [Lulu × Cecil]; int. by Elmer Roses Co.

Rhapsody HT, mp, 1985, Warriner, William A.; flowers medium, 20 petals; foliage medium size, medium green, matte; [unnamed variety × unnamed variety]; int. by J&P

Rhapsody in Blue S, m, 1999, Cowlishaw, Frank; flowers dark purple/blue, reverse lighter, 2½ in., semi-dbl., borne in large clusters, intense fragrance; foliage medium size, light green, glossy; prickles moderate; upright, semi-climbing, tall (6-8 ft.) growth; [Summer Wine × seedling]; int. by Warner's Roses, 2000

Rhea Reid HT, mr, 1908, E.G. Hill, Co.; bud long, pointed; flowers crimson-red, large, dbl., high-centered, moderate fragrance; foliage soft; [American Beauty × red seedling]; Gold Medal, Bagatelle, 1908

Rhea Reid, Climbing Cl HT, mr, 1914, California Nursery Co.

Rheda-Wiedenbruck F, mp

Rheinaupark S, mr, 1983, Kordes; flowers large, 20 petals; foliage large, dark, glossy; upright, bushy growth; [(Gruss an Bayern × seedling) × (*R. rugosa* × unknown)]; int. by Kordes Roses

Rheingold T, my, 1889, Lambert

Rheingold HT, my, 1934, Leenders, M.; flowers golden yellow, large, very dbl.; foliage leathery, light; dwarf, bushy, compact growth; [Mrs T. Hillas × Mabel Morse]; int. by J&P

Rhode Island Red LCl, dr, 1958, Brownell; flowers 33 petals, cupped, moderate fragrance; remontant; foliage dark green, glossy; [Everblooming Pillar No. 73 × seedling]; int. in 1957

Rhodes Rose HMult, w

Rhodologue Jules Gravereaux T, yb, 1908, Fontes; flowers yellowish-pink, medium, very full, slight fragrance; [Marie Van Houtte × Mme Abel Chatenay]

Rhodophile Gravereaux HFt, yb, 1900, Pernet-Ducher; flowers dark yellow with pink, large, semi-dbl.; [Antoine Ducher × *R. foetida persiana*]

Rhona HT, mp, 1984, Gobbee, W.D.; flowers large, 20 petals; foliage medium size, medium green, semi-glossy; bushy growth; [Anne Letts × (Dainty Maid × Pink Favorite)]

Rhona Beck HT, lp, Kordes; bud long, slender; flowers porcelain-pink, dbl., high-centered, borne mostly singly, intense fragrance; free-flowering; vigorous, tall growth; int. by Ludwig's Roses, 2001

Rhona Catherine MinFl, dr, 2001, Bailey, John; flowers scarlet, crimson reverse, 3 in., dbl., borne in small clusters, moderate fragrance; foliage medium size, dark green, glossy; prickles small, slightly hooked, few; bushy, medium (42 in.) growth; garden decorative; [(Whisky Mac × Adrian Bailey) × (Adrian Bailey × Peer Gynt)]; int. in 2002

Rhonda LCl, mp, 1967, Lissemore; bud globular; flowers carmine-rose, 7-8 cm., dbl., borne in medium to large clusters; foliage dark, glossy; vigorous, climbing growth; PP2854; [New Dawn × Spartan]; int. by C-P, 1968

Rhosyn Margaret Williams HT, ob, Fryer; flowers two-tone brick and terracotta, dbl., spiral, moderate fragrance; recurrent; moderate growth; int. by Fryers Roses, 2005

Rhotare Pol, mr; flowers medium, semi-dbl.

Rhumba – See **Rumba**, F

Rhythm 'n' Blues LCl, dp, Poulsen; flowers warm pink with almost purple overtones, 10-15 cm., dbl., cupped, borne in clusters, no fragrance; free-flowering; foliage medium green, matte; bushy, strong (8-10 ft.) growth; int. by Poulsen Roser, 2000

Ria Wenning HT, dp, 1932, Leenders, M.; bud long, pointed; flowers carmine, semi-dbl.; vigorous growth; [Mme Maurice de Luze × Red Star]

Rialto – See **Rialto Palace**, MinFl

Rialto Palace MinFl, w, Poulsen; flowers white, 5-8 cm., semi-dbl., no fragrance; growth bushy, 20-40 cm.; PP15000; int. by Poulsen Roser, 2002

Ribambelle F, op, Croix; flowers luminous salmon-pink, borne in clusters of 25-30; free-flowering; foliage glossy; int. by Roseraie Paul Croix, 1972; 1st Certificate of Merit, Roseraie de la Haye, 1st Certificate of Merit, Madrid

Ribatejo F, w, 1962, Moreira da Silva; flowers white, center deep yellow; [Virgo × seedling]

Ribbon Parade Cl Min, rb; flowers apricot yellow and cherry red, well-formed, moderate fragrance; int. by Bell Roses

Ribbon Rose Min, lp; flowers shell pink, very full, cupped; recurrent; foliage light green, glossy; growth to 18-24 in.; sold to support Breast Cancer Care, a charity; int. in 2004

Riberhus – See **Grand Canyon**, F

Ric Rac F, rb, 1996, Chaffin, Lauren M.; flowers white edged red, non-fading color, long lasting, 2½-3 in., full; fast repeat; foliage small, medium green, semi-glossy; prickles moderate; upright, low (18-20 in.) growth; [Hannah Gordon × Pink Petticoat]; int. by Pixie Treasures Min. Roses, 1996

Ricarda F, op, Noack, Werner; int. in 1989

Riccordo di Fernando Scarlatti HP, dr, about 1925; flowers large, dbl., intense fragrance

Riccordo di Geo Chavez HT, dp, 1911, Bonfiglio, A.; flowers large, dbl.

Riccordo di Giosue Carducci HT, lp, 1909, Bonfiglio, A.; flowers very large, very dbl.

Riccordo di Giovanni Spotti HT, mr; flowers large, dbl.

Rich and Rare Min, rb, 1986, McCann, Sean; flowers scarlet, reverse white veined red, small, 35 petals, high-centered, borne singly; foliage small, dark, semi-glossy; bushy growth; [(Rise 'n' Shine × Siobhan) × Beauty Secret]; int. in 1987

Richard HT, dr, 1978, Ellick; bud long, pointed; flowers spinel-red, 4-5 in., 25-30 petals, intense fragrance; foliage light green; bushy, upright growth; [Gavotte × Memoriam]; int. by Excelsior Roses, 1979

Richard Buckley F, mp, 1994, Smith, Edward; flowers

pale salmon pink, medium, dbl., borne in small clusters; foliage medium size, medium green, matte; some prickles; low (45-55 cm.), bushy,compact growth; [Lady Taylor × Regensberg]; int. in 1992

Richard E. West HT, my, 1924, Dickson, A.; bud long, pointed; flowers large, dbl., moderate lemon fragrance; recurrent; foliage leathery; vigorous growth

Richard Hayes S, mp, 1974, Holmes, R.A.; flowers 4 in., moderate fragrance; foliage light; vigorous, tall, upright growth; [sport of Fred Loads]; int. by Wonnacott, 1965

Richard Smith – See **Général Jacqueminot**, HP

Richard Strauss S, pb, Noack, Werner; flowers rose-pink and white, 3 cm., single, shallow cup, borne in large clusters of up to 30; recurrent; upright (3-4 ft.) growth; int. by Noack Rosen, 1989

Richard Tauber HT, rb, Pouw; int. in 1986

Richardson Wright HT, pb, 1931, C-P; flowers pearl with carmine dashes and lemon reflexes, large, globular; foliage dark, leathery; vigorous growth; [Radiance × Ville de Paris]

Richelieu Ch, m, 1845, Verdier, V.; flowers violet-pink, large, very dbl., cupped; growth compact, branching

Richmond HT, mr, 1905, E.G. Hill, Co.; bud long, pointed; flowers bright scarlet, varying greatly at times, large, dbl., moderate damask fragrance; vigorous growth; [Lady Battersea × Liberty]

Richmond, Climbing Cl HT, mr, 1912, Dickson, A.; flowers red-scarlet, medium, full, moderate fragrance; [sport of Richmond]

Rick Stein – See **Rikita**, HT

Rickie-Tickie MinFl, or, 2003, Greenwood, Chris; flowers bright orange fading to pink, medium, single, borne mostly solitary, no fragrance; foliage medium size, dark green, semi-glossy; prickles medium, slightly curved upward, light greenish yellow; upright, medium (2-3 ft.) growth; [Sunset Celebration × First Prize]

Ricky Min, op, Hauser; int. in 1989

Ricky Hendrick MinFl, dr, 2006, Bridges, Dennis A.; flowers dark red, reverse slightly lighter, 2¼ in., full, high-centered, borne mostly solitary; recurrent; foliage medium size, dark green, semi-glossy, disease-resistant; prickles moderate, ¼ in., straight, slightly pointing down, light tan; growth spreading, medium (24-30 in.); garden, exhibition, containers; [Jennifer × Miss Flippins]; int. by Bridges Roses, 2006

Ricordo di Geo Chavez HT, mr, 1911, Gaetano, Bonfiglioli; flowers large, full

Ricordo di Giosue Carducci HT, lp, 1909, Gaetano, Bonfiglioli; flowers whitish pink, very large, very full

Ricordo di Leone Sgaravatti HT, Sgaravatti, A.

Ridgeway HT, pb, 1953, Ratcliffe; flowers salmon-pink shaded apricot, well-shaped, dbl.; foliage rather sparse; strong stems; very vigorous growth; [Princess Marina × Vanessa]

Rieder's Solin Cl HT, mr, 1930, Rieder; flowers large, dbl.

Riégo HCh, mp, 1831, Vibert; flowers bright carmine pink, large, full, globular, intense raspberry fragrance; foliage dark green, thick; growth branching, robust

Rifleman HT, or, 1980, Murray, Nola; bud ovoid; flowers light vermilion, large, 35-43 petals, high-centered; tall, very vigorous, bushy growth; [Tropicana × Orange Sensation]

Rigadoon – See **Dragon's Fire**, Min

Rigaudon F, dr, 1957, Combe; flowers dark red tinted geranium, dbl.; very dwarf, dense growth; [(Independence × seedling) × seedling]; int. by Japan Rose Society

Right Bright – See **Rite Brite**, F

Right Royal HT, mp, 1980, Hawken, Una; flowers silvery pink, 4 in., 30 petals; foliage dark; moderate growth; [Scented Air × Anne Letts]

Rigobec – See **Mon Pays**, Gr

Rigobec 2 – See **Neiges d'Été**, Min

Rigobec 3 – See **Danse Azteque**, Min

Rigoletto F, ab, 1954, Leenders, M.; flowers apricot-yellow tinted copper, well-formed, large, semi-dbl.; vigorous growth; [Floribunda seedling × Souv. de Claudius Pernet]

Rigoletto HT, pb, Kordes; flowers cream with pink edges, spreading down the petals, large, full, high-centered, borne usually singly; recurrent; stems long; int. by W. Kordes Söhne, 2005

Rijswijk F, ob, 1964, Buisman, G. A. H.; bud deep yellow; flowers orange-yellow, semi-dbl., borne in clusters; foliage dark, glossy; vigorous growth; [Goldmarie × Fata Morgana]

Rikita HT, ab, Tantau; flowers soft apricot with touch of pink, full, cupped, moderate sweet fragrance; recurrent; foliage glossy; int. in 2005

Riksbyggerosen F, or, 1978, Poulsen, Niels D.; flowers open, 3 in., 23 petals; foliage glossy, light green; low, compact growth; [Irish Wonder × seedling]; int. by Poulsen, 1969

Rilla – See **O'Rilla**, HT

Rim – See **Happiness**, HT

Rima HT, lp, 1964, Samuels; flowers light silvery pink; PP2570; [sport of Prima Ballerina]

Rimosa F, my, 1958, Meilland, F.; flowers Indian yellow to citron-yellow, well-formed, medium, 18-25 petals, borne in clusters; foliage leathery; upright, symmetrical, compact growth; [Goldilocks × Perla de Montserrat]; int. by URS

Rimosa, Climbing – See **Gold Badge, Climbing**, Cl F

Rimosa 79 – See **Gold Badge**, F

Rimrose F, my, 1959, Meilland, F.; buds small, pointed, dark yellow; flowers Indian-yellow, aging to lemon yellow, medium, semi-dbl., borne in small clusters; continuous; foliage leathery, disease-resistant; few prickles; growth vigorous, compact, bushy; [Goldilocks × Perla de Montserrat]; int. by URS, 1958

Rina HT, w, 1999, Yonzda, Kazuo; flowers cream white blended pink, 5 in., 32 petals, high-centered; foliage medium size, medium green, semi-glossy; tall (6 ft.) growth; [Royal Highness × Shizunomai]; int. in 1997

Rina Herholdt HT, pb, 1960, Herholdt, J.A.; bud long, pointed; flowers milky white, flushed deep pink at edges, darkening with age, 3½-4 in., 60 petals, semi-cupped, borne singly, moderate sharp, sweet fragrance; recurrent; foliage medium green, leathery, glossy; prickles moderate, broad base, slightly recurved; vigorous, upright, bushy growth; hips spherical ; PP1970; [Peace × seedling]; int. by Herholdt's Nursery, 1962

Rina Herholdt, Climbing Cl HT, pb, 1974, Arora, Bal Raj; bud large, long pointed; flowers ivory white, edged bright pink, large, full, high-centered, borne singly, slight fragrance; intermittent, moderate; foliage large, dark green, glossy; few prickles; stems medium; vigorous growth; [sport of Rina Herholdt]; int. by The Rosery, India, 1973

Rina Hugo HT, dp, Dorieux; flowers pinkish raspberry, large, 35-40 petals, high-centered, borne mostly singly, slight fragrance; recurrent; foliage dark green, glossy, resistant; vigorous, upright (5-7 ft.), slightly spreading growth; int. in 1993

Rinascimento S, pb, Barni, V.; flowers deep pink, striped white, dbl., cupped, intense fragrance; shrubby, open (4 ft.) growth; int. by Rose Barni, 1989

Ring-A-Ling HT, mp, Ringrose, Dr. V.P.; int. in 1995

Ring of Fire Min, yb, 1987, Moore, Ralph S.; bud ovoid to pointed; flowers yellow blended orange, reverse yellow, fading lighter, imbricated, 1½ in., 60 petals, high-centered, borne usually singly, but some small clusters, slight fragrance; foliage medium size, medium green, semi-glossy; prickles slender, sharp pointed, medium, green to brown; stems sturdy, wiry; upright, bushy, vigorous growth; no fruit; PP6618; [Pink Petticoat × Gold Badge]; int. in 1986; AOE, ARS, 1987

Ringfield HT, or, 1977, Plumpton, E.; flowers deep vermilion, 5 in., 30 petals; vigorous growth; [Ernest H. Morse × Fragrant Cloud]

Ringlet LCl, pb, 1922, Clark, A.; flowers white, tipped pink and lilac to medium, 2½ in., single, borne in clusters; good repeat; few prickles; vigorous, climbing growth; [Ernest Morel × Betty Berkeley]; int. by Brundrett

Rio Grande HT, dr, 1973, Tantau, Math.; bud ovoid; flowers velvety dark red, medium, dbl.; foliage soft; moderate, upright, bushy growth; [unknown × unknown]; int. by Ahrens & Sieberz

Rio Rita HT, w, 1931, Joseph H. Hill, Co.; bud long, pointed; flowers white tinged pink, large, dbl.; foliage glossy; vigorous growth; [Mme Butterfly × Premier]

Rio Rita, Climbing Cl HT, w, 1935, Elmer's Nursery; flowers velvety scarlet-crimson, very large, dbl., cupped, intense fragrance; foliage glossy; very vigorous growth; [sport of E.G. Hill]

Rio Rita MinFl, dy, 2005, Paul Chessum Roses; flowers dbl., borne in small clusters; foliage medium size, dark green, glossy; prickles large, long, yellow, few; growth bushy, medium (24 in.); bedding, containers; [seedling × seedling]; int. by World of Roses, 2005

Rio Samba HT, yb, 1991, Warriner, William A.; bud long, pointed, ovoid; flowers medium yellow fading to peach-pink, large, 25 petals, high-centered, borne singly and in small clusters, slight fragrance; foliage medium size, dark green, matte; prickles some, medium, hooked slightly downward; medium (110-120 cm.), upright, bushy growth; PP8361; [seedling × Sunbright]; int. by Bear Creek Gardens, 1993

Ripples F, m, 1971, LeGrice; flowers lilac-lavender, wavy petals, large, 18 petals, cupped, slight fragrance; foliage small, green, matte; [(Tantau's Surprise × Marjorie LeGrice) × (seedling × Africa Star)]

Rise 'n' Shine Min, my, 1977, Moore, Ralph S.; bud long, pointed; flowers rich medium yellow, 1½ in., 35 petals, high-centered, borne singly and in small clusters, moderate sweet tea rose fragrance; recurrent; foliage small, leathery, semi-glossy to matte; prickles moderate, slender, hooked downward, brown; bushy, upright growth; PP4231; [Little Darling × Yellow Magic]; int. by Sequoia Nursery; Miniature Rose Hall of Fame, ARS, 1999, AOE, ARS, 1978

Rise 'n' Shine, Climbing Cl Min, my, 1990, King, Gene; bud pointed; flowers medium yellow, aging lighter, small, 35 petals, high-centered, borne usually singly or in small clusters; foliage medium size, medium green, semi-glossy; prickles straight, inclined slightly downward, brown; upright, spreading, tall, climbing. growth; hips round, orange; [sport of Rise 'n' Shine]; int. by Sequoia Nursery, 1990

Rising Star F, mr, Harkness, R.; flowers velvety crimson-scarlet, dbl., high-centered, borne in clusters; recurrent; int. in 1995

Rising Star Min, pb, 1995, Jalbert, Brad; flowers cream with strong pink blend edges, 1-2 in., full, borne mostly singly, slight fragrance; foliage medium size, medium green, semi-glossy; some prickles; tall (18 in.) upright, bushy growth; [Sans Souci × Pink Petticoat]; int. by Select Roses, 1995

Rising Sun HT, rb, 1924, Hicks; bud long, pointed; flowers rich copper, base old-gold, cactus dahlia form, large

Risqué Gr, rb, 1985, Weeks, O.L.; bud short, pointed; flowers medium red, light yellow reverse, 4 in., 20-28 petals, high-centered, borne singly and several together, no fragrance; recurrent; foliage medium size, dark green, semi-glossy; prickles very few, flat, pointed down, reddish-brown; upright (4-4½ ft.), slightly spreading growth; PP5828; [Bob Hope × seedling]; int. by Weeks Wholesale Rose Growers

Rita F, mp, 1960, Fryers Nursery, Ltd.; flowers rich pink, dbl., borne in large clusters; foliage glossy; vigorous growth; [Karl Herbst × Pinocchio]

Rita F, rb, Vidal; int. by Rosales Vidal

Rita Applegate MinFl, ly, 1996, Bennett, Dee; flowers light yellow to softest gold with heart of deeper yellow/gold, 2 in., full, high-centered, borne mostly singly, moderate fragrance; foliage medium size, medium green, semi-glossy; prickles moderate; long-stemmed; growth upright, bushy, tall (80-90 cm.); [Pink Porcelain × unknown]; int. by Tiny Petals Nursery, 1997

Rita Barbera – See **Sophia Renaissance**, S

Rita Bugnet HRg, w, Bugnet; int. in 1958

Rita Jackson HT, rb, 1973, Jackson, F.; flowers striped carmine and yellow, large, dbl., high-centered, borne mostly singly, slight fragrance; stems long; upright, bushy growth; [sport of Tzigane]; int. in 1964

Rita Levi Montalcini F, ab, Barni, V.; flowers apricot-rose, dbl., borne in large clusters, moderate fragrance; recurrent; regular, compact (60-80 cm.) growth; int. by Rose Barni, 1991; Gold Medal, Geneva, 1991

Rita MacNeil – See **Big Daddy**, HT

Rita Perfumella HT, lp, Meilland; flowers light buff-colored pink, dbl., high-centered, borne usually singly; recurrent; florist rose; int. by Meilland Intl., 2005

Rita Sammons Pol, pb, 1925, Clarke, B.; flowers deep rose-pink, opening pink, edged lighter; [sport of Cécile Brunner]; int. by Clarke Bros.

Ritausma HRg, lp, Rieksta; bud slim; flowers soft blush and light pink, deeper in the center, medium, dbl., high-centered, moderate fragrance; foliage glossy; vigorous, arching (1 × 1 m.) growth; winter hardy; [*R. rugosa plena* × Abelzieds]; registered incorrectly as Polareis; int. in 1963

Rite Brite F, my, 1996, Giles, Diann; flowers 1½ in., full, slight fragrance; foliage small, medium green, matte; few prickles; low (3½ ft.), spreading, compact growth; [Sun Flare × Rise 'n' Shine]; int. by Giles Rose Nursery, 1995

Rittenhouse HT, ob, 1988, Williams, J. Benjamin; flowers fiery orange to copper blended, large, full, moderate fragrance; foliage large, dark green, glossy, disease-resistant; upright, vigorous, mass-blooming, winter hardy growth; [Queen Elizabeth × Zorina]; int. in 1989

Ritter Taler HT, rb

Ritter von Barmstede HKor, dp, 1959, Kordes; flowers very dark pink, lighter reverse white eye, 2 in., 20 petals, borne in clusters of 30-40; foliage light green, glossy; vigorous (10-15 ft.) growth; [*R. × kordesii* × a Polyantha]

Ritz LCl, mr, 1955, Horvath; flowers velvety red, 3 in., 11 petals, borne in clusters; recurrent bloom; vigorous (8-9 ft.) growth; [*R. setigera* × unknown]; int. by Wyant, 1955

Ritz F, mr, 1961, Gaujard; flowers bright scarlet, large, 16 petals; foliage dark, glossy; vigorous, well branched growth

Riva Ligure HT, dp, 1947, San Remo Exp. Sta.; bud pointed; flowers velvety carmine, 24-35 petals; foliage dark; vigorous, bushy growth; [seedling × Crimson Glory]

Rival HT, mr, 1954, Fletcher; flowers cherry-scarlet, loosely formed, 4-5 in., flat; foliage bronze; free growth; [Southport × The Rev. W.S. Crawford]; int. by Tucker, 1954

Rival de Paestum T, w, 1841, Béluze; bud tinged pink; flowers white, base blush and ivory, dbl.; foliage dark; moderate growth; often classed as a China

River City Jubilee Min, ob, 1996, Bell, Judy G.; flowers orange, tight, full, high-centered, borne in small clusters, no fragrance; foliage medium size, dark green, semi-glossy, very disease-resistant; some prickles; medium (16 in.), upright growth; [Jean Kenneally × Rainbow's End]; int. by Michigan Mini Roses, 1996

Riverbanks S, mp, 2005, Rippetoe, Robert Neil; flowers semi-dbl., borne in small clusters, moderate fragrance; foliage medium size, medium green, semi-glossy; prickles moderate, medium size, straight, tan; growth upright, medium (4 ft.); [Antoine Rivoire × Lila Banks]

Riverdance Min, dp, 1997, Kenny, David; flowers medium, dbl., borne in small clusters, moderate fragrance; foliage small, medium green, glossy; bushy, medium (28 in.) growth; [MEIdomonac × Freegold]

Riverdance Min, pb, Laver, Keith G.; bud pointed; flowers white with pink stripes, dbl., high-centered; foliage dark green, semi-glossy; growth to 12-15 in.; int. in 1998

Riverina Sunset T, mp, Hay

Rivers HP, mr, 1832, Laffay, M.; flowers bright crimson, large, dbl., borne in corymbs; recurrent bloom; vigorous growth

Rivers' George IV HCh, dr, 1830, Rivers; flowers vivid crimson, shaded with dark purple, dbl., loosely cupped; non-recurrent; stems branching shoots tinged with purple; vigorous growth; [thought to be Damask × *R. chinensis*]

Rivers' Musk Cluster HMsk, mp, before 1846, Rivers; flowers rosy buff, small, dbl., intense fragrance

Rivers' Single Crimson Moss M, dr, before 1838, Rivers; flowers brilliant crimson, changing to purplish crimson, large, single to semi-dbl.; foliage dark green

River's South Bank – See **Jujnoberejnaia**, F

Rivers' Super Tuscan – See **Tuscany Superb**, HGal

Riverview – See **Riverview Centennial**, HT

Riverview Centennial HT, dr; flowers very dark red, large, dbl.; strong, tall growth; int. in 1980

Riviera HT, or, 1939, Dot, Pedro; bud globular, yellow; flowers orange-scarlet, reverse lighter, base yellow, open, large, dbl., cupped; foliage glossy, wrinkled, dark; very vigorous, bushy growth; [Luis Brinas × Catalonia]; int. by J&P, 1940

Riviera HT, mr, J&P; int. in 1994

Riviera LCl, mr

Riviere de Diamant Min, w, Briant; int. in 1990

Rivierenhof F, pb, DVP Melle; flowers pink and red, large, borne in clusters; growth strong, branching; [Melglory × Guirlande d'Amour]; int. in 1998; Gold Medal, Dublin, 2000, Gold Medal, The Hague, 1998, Gold Medal, Rome, 2000, Gold Medal, Monza, 2002

Road to Freedom HT, m, 1995, Cowlishaw, Frank; flowers lilac, gold stamens, medium, dbl.; foliage medium size, medium green, glossy; low (15-20 in.), bushy, compact growth; [seedling × Lilac Charm]; int. by Rearsby Roses, Ltd., 1996

Roadman HT, w, 1977, Ota, Kaichiro; bud pointed; flowers near white, 6 in., 40-50 petals, high-centered; foliage leathery; upright growth; [Hawaii × Kordes' Perfecta]; int. in 1974

Roaming HT, dp, 1970, Sanday, John; flowers reddish-pink shades, pointed, large, 24 petals; foliage green, matte; [Vera Dalton × Tropicana]

Rob Roy F, dr, 1970, Cocker; flowers scarlet-crimson, 4½ in., 30 petals, hybrid tea, borne several together; free-flowering; foliage glossy; vigorous growth; [Evelyn Fison × Wendy Cussons]

Robbie Burns S, lp, 1987, Austin, David; flowers light pink, white center, small, 5 petals, moderate fragrance; foliage small, medium green, matte; bushy, strong (5 ft.) growth; hips large, mahogany; [Wife of Bath × *R. pimpinellifolia*]; int. in 1985

Robe de Neige S, w, 2000, Lens, Louis; flowers white with pink shades, reverse white, small, single, borne in large clusters; recurrent; foliage medium size, medium green, semi-glossy; prickles moderate; growth spreading, medium (60 cm.); [Serpent Vert × Ballerina]; int. by Louis Lens N.V., 1995

Robe de Soie S, lp, 2000, Lens, Louis; flowers pink, center white, reverse lighter, 3 cm., single, borne in large clusters, slight fragrance; recurrent; foliage medium size, dark green, glossy; prickles moderate; growth spreading, low (40 cm.); groundcover; [Serpent Vert × Ballerina]; int. by Louis Lens N.V., 1996

Robe d'Eté F, or, 1979, Lens; flowers salmon-orange, 3-3½ in., 22-24 petals, high-centered; foliage bronze; bushy, upright growth; [(Chatelaine × Mannequin) × (Montezuma × Floradora)]; int. in 1966

Robe Fleuri S, mp, 2000, Lens, Louis; flowers medium pink, white center, 2 cm., single, borne in large clusters, moderate fragrance; recurrent; foliage medium size, dark green, semi-glossy; prickles moderate; growth spreading, low (40-50 cm.); groundcover; [Serpent Vert × Ballerina]; int. by Louis Lens N.V., 1995

Robe Rose S, mp, 2000, Lens, Louis; flowers medium pink, white center, 2 cm., single, borne in large clusters, moderate fragrance; foliage medium size, medium green, semi-glossy; prickles moderate; growth spreading, low (40-50 cm.); [Serpent Vert × Ballerina]; int. by Louis Lens N.V., 1995

Robert P, pb, 1856, Robert; flowers carmine, marbled white

Robert Aliano HT, dr, 1998, Williams, J. Benjamin; flowers deep velvet red, dull reverse, 4½-5 in., dbl., high-centered, borne mostly singly; foliage large, dark green, semi-glossy; few prickles; strong, upright, tall (4-5 ft.) growth; [Chrysler Imperial × Mister Lincoln]; int. by J. Benjamin Williams & Associates, 1999

Robert Betten HT, mr, 1920, Schmidt, J.C.; flowers clear dark carmine-red, not turning blue, dbl.; [Frau Karl Druschki × Corallina]

Robert Bland S, dp, 1960, Wright, Percy H.; flowers open, small, dbl.; non-recurrent; foliage richgreen; thornless; vigorous, bushy growth; quite hardy; [((Hansa × *R. macounii*) × Betty Bland) × (*R. blanda* × Betty Bland)]

Robert Burns HT, mr; flowers scarlet, dbl., rounded, moderate fragrance; strong (3 ft.), healthy growth; int. in 2005

Robert Clements S, ob, Clements, John; bud long and pointed; flowers deep apricot-blush overlayed with orange-red, 4 in., 20 petals, high-centered, moderate sweet old rose fragrance; foliage bright green, glossy; well foliaged (3½ ft. × 3 ft.) growth; PPAF; int. by Heirloom, 2003

Robert Cotton HT, w, 1968, Golik; bud ovoid; flowers white, edges flushed pink, large, dbl.; foliage glossy, serrated, leathery; moderate growth; [Marcia Stanhope × Karl Herbst]; int. by Ellesmere Nursery

Robert Craig HWich, my, 1903, Hoopes & Thomas; bud yellow-apricot; flowers yellow, center darker; [*R. wichurana* × Beauté Inconstante]

Robert de Brie HP, m, 1860, Granger; flowers violet-pink with white stripes, large, dbl.

Robert Dubol HT, mr, 1946, Sauvageot, H.; flowers warm orient red, stamens golden, very dbl., high-centered; int. by Sauvageot

Robert Duncan HP, pb, 1897, Dickson, A.; flowers purplish pink, sometimes flamed brilliant red, well-formed, large, 70 petals, moderate Damask fragrance; repeat bloom; vigorous growth

Robert F. Kennedy HT, mr, 1968, Takatori, Yoshiho; flowers scarlet, high-centered, borne singly, intense fragrance; foliage dark green, semi-glossy; very vigorous, upright growth; [Chrysler Imperial × Ena Harkness]; int. by Parnass Rose Nursery

Robert Fortune M, m, 1853, Robert; flowers striped lilac and pale violet, 2½ in., dbl., globular

Robert Huey HT, dp, 1911, Dickson, A.; bud long, pointed; flowers carmine edged lighter, bluing slightly, dbl.; moderate growth

Robert le Diable HGal, m, before 1885; flowers scarlet-pink aging to deep purple, center often green, full, moderate fragrance; low (3 ft.), lax growth; sometimes classed as C; perhaps as early as 1831 (see Beales, and Prince)

Robert Léopold M, pb, 1941, Buatois; flowers salmon-flesh-pink edged light carmine, large, dbl., loose, moderate fragrance; remontant; upright (4 ft.) growth

Robert Perpétuel P, m, 1856, Robert; flowers violet-pink, medium, dbl., rosette when open; growth medium

Robert Pineau F, ob, Pineau; int. in 2000

Robert Scott HT, mp, 1901, Scott; flowers medium pink, edges flesh pink, very large, dbl.; [Merveille de Lyon × Belle Siebrecht]

Robert Stolz F, dr, deRuiter; flowers medium, semi-dbl.; int. in 1974

Roberta – See **Heritage**, S

Roberta HT, lp, 2005, Alberici, Marc; flowers light pink, reverse more light, 7-10 cm., single, borne mostly solitary; prickles normal, brown, numerous; growth to 100 cm.; garden decorative; [Nil Bleu × Abraham Darby]; int. by Alberici, Mark, 2007

Roberta Bondar LCl, my, 1993, Fleming, Joyce L.; flowers medium, full, borne 1-8 per truss, moderate fragrance; foliage large, dark green, semi-glossy; climbing (6-8 ft.) growth; [King's Ransom × Buff Beauty]; named for first Canadian woman in space; int. by Hortico Roses, 1993

Roberto Capucci HT, lp, Barni; flowers light pink deepening toward the center, 10-12 cm., full, old fashioned, cupped, moderate fragrance; foliage very large, glossy, light green; growth to 4 ft.; hips globular, orange, medium; [Antico Amore × Letizia]; int. by Rose Barni, 2001

Robertson Garden F, op, Kordes; flowers roses salmon-pink, dbl., borne in clusters, slight sweet fragrance; recurrent; foliage leathery, disease-resistant; low to medium growth; int. by Ludwig's Roses, 2005

Robespierre Pol, pb, 1976, Delforge, S.; bud full; flowers very dbl., 88 petals, cupped, moderate fragrance; foliage bronze; int. in 1975

Robi Min, or, 2000, Moore, Ralph S.; flowers orange-red, medium, very full, cupped, borne in small clusters, no fragrance; prolific; foliage medium size, medium green, semi-glossy; few prickles; growth bushy, spreading, medium (15-18 in.); [Pink Petticoat × Sincerely Yours]; int. by Sequoia Nurs.

Robin Min, mr, 1957, Dot, Pedro; bud urn-shaped; flowers rich red, 1¼ in., 65 petals, flat, borne in clusters of 15; foliage leathery, green, matte; vigorous, dwarf (12 in.), bushy growth; PP1663; [Perla de Montserrat × Perla de Alcanada]; int. by C-P, 1957

Robin HT, m

Robin Alonso MinFl, dr, 2005, Peter G. Alonso Jr.; flowers deep red, reverse medium red, over 3 in., full, borne mostly solitary; foliage large, dark green, semi-glossy; prickles ½ cm., curved, brown, moderate; growth compact, medium; exhibition; [sport of Caliente]; int. by Almost Heaven Roses, 2007

Robin Beard's Rugosa HRg, dp, Beard; flowers dark magenta pink with white flash at center, creamy yellow stamens, 5 in., semi-dbl., cupped to flat, intense fragrance; recurrent; growth to 4-5 ft.; [Roseraie de l'Hay × unknown]; int. by Mistydowns, 2003

Robin des Bois – See **Robin Hood**, HMsk

Robin Hood HP, mr, before 1850; flowers bright cherry red, large, full, globular

Robin Hood HT, mr, 1912, E.G. Hill, Co.; flowers soft bright rosy scarlet, changing to bright scarlet-crimson, dbl.

Robin Hood HMsk, mr, 1927, Pemberton; flowers cherry-red, single, borne in large clusters; recurrent bloom; vigorous (4-5 ft.), dense, compact growth; [seedling × Miss Edith Cavell]

Robin Red Breast MinFl, rb, 1983, Interplant; flowers dark red, white eye, reverse silver, small, single, borne in clusters, no fragrance; foliage small, medium green, glossy; prickles numerous, medium; bushy growth; [seedling × Eyepaint]

Robin Redbreast – See **Robin Red Breast**, MinFl

Robina HT, mr, Kordes; int. in 1988

Robinette HMult, rb, 1943, Moore, Ralph S.; flowers amaranth-red, white eye, open, small, single, borne in large clusters, intense fragrance; foliage glossy; growth to 10-12 ft.; [Hiawatha × Hiawatha]; int. by Hennessey

Robur – See **Red Empress**, LCl

Robusta B, mr, 1877, Soupert & Notting; flowers velvety red, aging to purple, large, full, borne in small clusters

Robusta S, mr, 1979, Kordes, W.; bud long, pointed; flowers single, 5-8 petals, shallow cup, borne in clusters, slight fragrance; foliage large, dark green, glossy, leathery; numerous prickles; very vigorous, upright (6-7 ft.), bushy growth; [seedling × *R. rugosa*]; ADR, 1980

Robusta Cl T, mp

Roby HMult, rb, 1912, Guillot, P.; bud deep pink; flowers rose red, yellow center, 6-7 cm., single, borne in medium to large clusters, moderate fragrance; [Léonie Lamesch × Leuchtstern]

Roccana Diane F, dp, 1985, Kirkham, Gordon Wilson; flowers deep pink, medium, 20 petals; foliage large, dark, glossy; upright growth; [Pink Favorite × Attraction]

Roche Centenary MinFl, mr, Dickson, Patrick; int. in 1993

Roche du Theil – See **Toprose**, F

Rochefort HT, ab, 1936, Mallerin, C.; flowers large, dbl., intense fruity fragrance; foliage leathery; vigorous growth; [Mrs Pierre S. duPont × Charles P. Kilham]; int. by C-P; Gold Medal, Portland, 1935

Rochelle Hudson HT, rb, 1937, Moore, Ralph S.; bud long, pointed; flowers carmine, base yellow, orange undertone deepening with age, semi-dbl., slight fruity fragrance; foliage dark; vigorous growth; [Isobel × Mme Edouard Herriot]; int. by Brooks & Son

Rochemenier Village – See **Britannia**, HT

Rochester F, ab, 1934, Nicolas; flowers buff, reverse orange-carmine, medium, dbl.; foliage leathery; vigorous, bushy growth; [Echo × Rev. F. Page-Roberts]; int. by J&P

Rochester Cathedral S, mp, 1985, Harkness, R., & Co., Ltd.; flowers medium to large, 58 petals, cupped, borne in clusters, moderate fragrance; repeat bloom; foliage medium size, dark, matte; medium, dense, spreading growth; [(seedling × ((Orange Sensation × Allgold) × *R. californica*)) × Frank Naylor]; int. in 1986

Rocio Elias HT, m, Viveros Fco. Ferrer, S L; flowers 32 petals, flat; [Carinella × Kardinal]

Rock 'n' Roll – See **Stretch Johnson**, S

Rock Creek S, rb, 2007, Garhart, Michael; flowers red with white eye, reverse red, small, 2½ in., single, borne in large clusters; foliage small, dark green, glossy; prickles small, hooked, light brown, few; growth bushy, short (24 in.); bedding, containers; hips numerous, bright orange; [Dortmund × Circus]

Rockabye Baby Min, dy, Dickson; flowers non-fading yellow, full, cupped, then pompon; free-flowering; foliage dark green, glossy; bushy, compact (20 in.) growth; int. by Dickson Nurseries, 2006

Rocket HT, mr, 1935, Nicolas; flowers brilliant scarlet, reverse crimson, large, dbl., high-centered; foliage leathery, dark, bronze; very vigorous growth; [Dame Edith Helen × Scorcher]; int. by J&P

Rocket – See **Raketa**, HT

Rocketeer – See **Rosalie Coral**, Cl Min

Rockin' Robin S, rb, 1999, Carruth, Tom; bud short, pointed to globular; flowers red, white and pink stripes and splashes, ruffled, 1½-2½ in., 40-45 petals, cupped, borne in large clusters, slight apple fragrance; foliage medium size, dark green, glossy; prickles moderate; fountainous, rounded, bushy (4 ft.) growth; PP10070; [Bonica × Roller Coaster]; int. by Weeks Roses, 1997

Rockwall Sesquicentennial S, lp, 2005, Shoup, George Michael; flowers very full, borne mostly solitary, moderate fragrance; remontant; foliage medium size, medium green, semi-glossy; numerous prickles; growth compact, medium (3-4 ft.); containers; [(Carefree Beauty × Granny Grimmetts) × City of York]; int. by Antique Rose Emporium, 1999

Rocky LCl, ob, 1979, McGredy, Sam IV; bud ovoid; flowers coral-orange, reverse whitish, 2-3 in., 18-25 petals, loosely cupped, borne mostly in clusters of 5 or more, slight fragrance; foliage medium size, leathery, semi-glossy, dark yellow-green; prickles few, long, straight, yellow-brown; stems strong, medium to long; vigorous, tall, bushy growth; PP4669; [Liverpool Echo × (Evelyn Fison × (Orange Sweetheart × Fruhlingsmorgen))]; int. by McGredy Roses International

Rocky Top MinFl, or, 2004, Verlie W. Wells; flowers orange, reverse lighter orange, 3 in., dbl., high-centered, borne mostly solitary, slight fragrance; foliage medium size, dark green, semi-glossy; prickles moderate, ¼ in., hooked; upright, medium growth; garden decoration, exhibition; [seedling × seedling]; int. by Wells MidSouth Roses, 2003

Rococo F, mr, 1964, McGredy, Sam IV; flowers scarlet, 3 in., 15 petals, borne in clusters; free growth; [Moulin Rouge × Fire Opal]; int. by Spek

Rod Stillman HT, lp, 1948, Hamilton; flowers light pink, base flushed orange, large, 35 petals, intense melons and peaches fragrance; foliage dark green; vigorous, tall growth; [Ophelia × Editor McFarland]

Röd Summerwind – See **Red Summerwind**, S

Roddy MacMillan HT, ab, 1982, Cocker, James; flowers large, 35 petals; foliage medium size, medium green, semi-glossy; bushy growth; [(Fragrant Cloud × Postillion) × Wisbech Gold]; int. by Cocker & Sons

Rodeo F, or, 1960, Kordes, R.; flowers bright scarlet, 3 in., dbl., borne in clusters of up to 10; foliage light green; bushy, low growth; [Obergärtner Wiebicke × Spartan]; int. by McGredy & Son, 1960

Rodeo Drive HT, mr, 1987, Christensen, Jack E.; flowers bright deep red, large, 32 petals, high-centered, borne usually singly; foliage medium to large, medium green, semi-glossy; prickles many attenuated, medium, reddish aging light brown; bushy, medium growth; fruit not observed; PP6813; [Merci × Pharaoh]; int. by Armstrong Nursery, 1986

Rodeo Kordana Min, or, Kordes; flowers dbl., high-centered, borne singly and in small clusters; int. by W. Kordes Söhne

Rödhätte F, mr, 1912, Poulsen, D.T.; flowers clear cherry-red, large, semi-dbl., borne in large clusters; foliage rich green; bushy, compact growth; [Mme Norbert

Levavasseur × Richmond or Liberty]; int. by Poulsen

Rödhätte, Climbing Cl F, mr, 1925, Grootendorst, F.J.

Rodheo HT, rb

Rodin – See **Anticipation**, HT

Rodin S, dp, Meilland; flowers clear pink, semi-dbl., shallow cup, borne in clusters; free-flowering; foliage very disease-resistant; growth to 60-70 cm.; descended in a direct line from Knock Out; int. by Meilland Richardier, 2005

Rödinghausen S, mr, Noack, Werner; flowers brilliant orange-red, lavender petal bases, slight fragrance; recurrent; hips brilliant orange; int. by Noack Rosen, 1987

Rodovrerosen – See **Poulsen's Fairy**, F

Rody S, mr, Tantau; flowers raspberry red, 2 in., dbl., borne in clusters, intense fragrance; free-flowering; foliage dark green, glossy; low (2 ft.), spreading growth; int. by Rosen Tantau, 1995

Roedean HT, pb, Benardella, Frank A.; flowers pink and white stripes, dbl., high-centered, moderate fragrance; recurrent; int. in 1993

Roelof Buisman HT, mr, 1966, Kordes, R.; bud ovoid; flowers bright pure red, well-formed, large; vigorous, upright, bushy growth; int. by Buisman, 1964

Roemer's Hip Happy S, mp, 2005, Shoup, George Michael; flowers small, single, shallow cup, borne in small clusters, moderate fragrance; foliage medium size, dark green, semi-glossy; few prickles; bushy, medium (4 ft.) growth; containers, landscape; hips very numerous; [(Carefree Beauty × Heritage) × Iceberg]; int. by Antique Rose Emporium, 2000

Roger Boudou Pol, mr, 1957, Privat; flowers very bright red; [Lafayette × unknown]

Roger Lambelin HP, rb, 1890, Schwartz, Vve.; flowers bright crimson fading maroon, petals margined white, very distinct, 30 petals, petals fringed; recurrent bloom; vigorous growth; [sport of Fisher Holmes]

Roger Lambelin Striped HP, rb, 1953, Hennessey; flowers deep maroon to pink stripes on white ground; recurrent bloom; [sport of Roger Lambelin]

Roger Secretrain LCl, Moreira da Silva, A.

Roi Albert HT, pb, 1925, Klettenberg-Londes; bud long, pointed; flowers bright carmine-rose, center tinted scarlet; [(Laurent Carle × unknown) × Mme Abel Chatenay]

Roi Alexandre HT, ob, 1937, Gaujard; flowers coppery orange, tinted salmon, over large, dbl.; foliage leathery, glossy, bronze; very vigorous growth

Roi d'Angleterre – See **Duc de Berry**, HGal

Roi de Nains Min, mr

Roi de Perse – See **Petite Junon de Hollande**, C

Roi de Rome – See **Enfant de France**, HGal

Roi de Siam Cl T, lp, 1825, Laffay, M.; flowers pale pink and cream, large, semi-dbl., moderate tea fragrance; cultiver now in commerce is probably not correct

Roi d'Écosse – See **King of Scots**, HSpn

Roi des Aunes S, dp, 1885, Geschwind, R.; flowers carmine tinted red, fading to medium pink, 5-6 cm., full, globular, borne in medium to large clusters; non-recurrent; very vigorous growth; [De la Grifferaie × unknown]

Roi des Bengales F, rb, 1958, Arles; flowers grenadine-red; vigorous, low growth; [(Hermosa × Gruss an Teplitz) × Independence]; int. by Roses-France

Roi des Bordures – See **Border King**, Pol

Roi des Cramoisis Ch, mr; flowers bright red, cupped

Roi des Pays-Bas D, dp, before 1826; flowers deep pink, large, dbl., cupped; foliage very large; from Holland

Roi des Pourpres – See **Mogador**, P

Roi des Pourpres HGal, dr, before 1817, Descemet; bud round, small; flowers dark crimson-purple, small, very dbl., pompon

Roi des Rois F, Delbard-Chabert; int. in 1955

Roi d'Italie T, w; flowers flesh white, medium, full

Roi Maximilian de Bavière HP, m, 1857, Touvais; flowers velvety purple, shaded darker, medium, full

Roi Soleil HT, my, 1962, Dorieux; bud long, pointed; flowers citron-yellow; very vigorous growth; [Peace × (Independence × unknown)]; int. by Le Blévenec; Gold Medal, Madrid, 1963

Róisín Ruddle S, ob, 2004, Kenny, David; flowers orange, reverse orange/yellow, 2½ cm., dbl., borne in large clusters, no fragrance; continuous; foliage light green, matte; prickles small, pointed; bushy, spreading, short growth; patio, groundcover; [Mr.J.C.B. × Pathfinder]

Roklea HT, ob, 1985, Tantau, Math.; flowers bright orange, large, 20 petals, high-centered, moderate fragrance; foliage large, dark, semi-glossy; upright growth; greenhouse rose; int. in 1975

Rokoko – See **Showy Pavement**, HRg

Rokoko S, ly, Tantau; flowers light yellow with rose tints, large, dbl., cupped; foliage large, dark green; wide, bushy, well-branched (4½ ft.) growth; int. by Rosen Tantau, 1987

Roland F, ob, 1961, Leenders, J.; flowers salmon-orange-red; low growth; [Karl Weinhausen × Independence]

Roland Garros HT, mr, Briant; int. in 1989

Roletta F, op, GPG Bad Langensalza; flowers salmon-orange/pink, large, dbl.; int. in 1983

Roller Coaster Min, rb, 1988, McGredy, Sam IV; bud short, pointed ovoid; flowers red and white striped, 2-2½ in., 10-15 petals, flat, borne in clusters, slight fragrance; scattered repeat; foliage small, medium green, glossy; prickles numerous, medium, straight to hooked downward, brown; vigorous, upright (5 ft.), arching growth; hips bright orange; PP7319; [(Anytime × Eyepaint) × Stars 'n' Stripes]; int. by McGredy Roses International, 1988

Roma HT, op, Spronk; [sport of Duet]; int. in 1970

Roma di Notte HT, Zandri, R.; int. in 1980

Romaine Desprez B, mr, before 1835, Desprez; flowers crimson, aging to light red, medium

Román HT, mp, 1961, Dot, Simon; flowers nilsson pink, becoming hermosa pink, large, 35 petals; [Asturias × Rosa de Friera]

Roman S, op, Poulsen; flowers orange pink and orange blend, 8-10 cm., full, high-centered, no fragrance; foliage dark green, glossy; bushy, low (40-60 cm.) growth; int. by Poulsen Roser, 2001

Roman Festival F, pb, 1968, Williams, J. Benjamin; bud ovoid; flowers coral, base yellow, medium, high-centered, borne in clusters; foliage dark, glossy; vigorous, low, compact growth; [Queen Elizabeth × Sumatra]

Roman Herzog F, or, Noack; flowers shiny red, non-fading, 8 cm., dbl., high-centered, borne in clusters, slight fragrance; recurrent; growth to 70-90 cm.; int. by Noack Rosen, 1999

Roman Holiday F, rb, 1966, Lindquist; bud ovoid; flowers orange turning blood-red, base yellow, medium, 28 petals, high-centered, borne in clusters, moderate fragrance; foliage dark, leathery; vigorous, bushy, low growth; PP2725; [(Pinkie × Independence) × Circus]; int. by Howard Rose Co.

Roman Palace – See **Roman**, S

Roman Triumph F, mr, 1978, Harkness; flowers large, 13 petals; foliage glossy; upright, bushy growth; [Jove × City of Leeds]; int. in 1977

Romana HT, rb, 1938, Ringdahl; bud long, pointed; flowers rose-red to light purple, open, large, dbl.; foliage leathery, glossy, dark; very vigorous growth; [sport of Better Times]

Romana HT, or, Roman, G., and Wagner, S.; flowers deep orange-red, 60-80 petals, high-centered; continuous bloom; foliage large, medium green, semi-glossy; [Rosabunda × Landora]; int. by Res. Stn. for Hort., 2003

Romana HT, rb, Vecera, L.

Romance HT, my, 1931, Towill; bud long, pointed; flowers golden yellow, shading toward lemon, open, large, dbl.; foliage thick; very vigorous growth; RULED EXTINCT 11/82; [Souv. de Claudius Pernet × Buttercup seedling]

Romance, Climbing Cl HT, lp, 1933, Beckwith; flowers shell-pink, fading to pale blush, large, semi-dbl to dbl, intense sweet fragrance; vigorous, climbing growth; [sport of Isa]

Romance HT, mp, 1983, Warriner, William A.; flowers medium salmon-pink, large, 35 petals; foliage large, medium green, semi-glossy; upright growth; PP5250; [Unnamed variety × Prominent]; int. by J&P

Romance – See **Romanze**, S

Romance Mikado F, pb, Tantau; flowers pink and cream blend, borne in clusters; florist rose; int. by Rosen Tantau

Romane Estenou S, op, Gilet; int. by Les Rosier du Berry, 2005

Romanina F, Zandri, R.; int. in 1974

Romantic S, mp, 1999, Poulsen; bud ovoid to globular; flowers medium pink, 3 in., 40-50 petals, borne 1-4 per stem, slight fragrance; free-flowering; foliage dark green, glossy; prickles moderate, straight to curved downward; bushy, upright (2-2½ ft.) growth; PP11540; [sport of Queen Margrethe]; int. by Poulsen Roser, 1998

Romantic Curiosa HT, yb; florist rose

Romantic Days – See **Honore de Balzac**, HT

Romantic Dreams – See **Marie Curie**, F

Romantic Fragrance – See **Guy de Maupassant**, F

Romantic Hedgerose F, mp, Kordes; int. in 1994

Romantic Moments – See **Jean Giono**, HT

Romantic Occasion – See **César**, S

Romantic Palace – See **Romantic**, S

Romantic Panarosa S, ab, Kordes; bud pointed; flowers creamy apricot with touch of pink, large, full, rosette; vigorous, tall growth; int. by Ludwig's Roses, 2004

Romantic Roadrunner HRg, dp, Uhl; flowers strong pink, large, dbl., rosette, intense fragrance; recurrent; foliage dark green, leathery; upright (70 cm.), but bushy, spreading growth; int. by W. Kordes Söhne, 2004

Romantic Ruffles F, mr; int. by Hole's Greenhouses & Gardens, 2002

Romantic Seranade – See **Abbaye de Cluny**, HT

Romantic Sunrise S, my, Meilland

Romantica HT, mp, 1962, Meilland, Mrs. Marie-Louise; bud oval; flowers phlox-pink, large, 40 petals, high-centered, slight fragrance; foliage leathery, glossy; very vigorous, upright growth; [Baccará × White Knight]; forcing variety; int. by URS

Romantica 76 HT, op

Romantique Meillandina – See **Candy Sunblaze**, Min

Romany F, op, 1965, McGredy, Sam IV; flowers salmon, well-formed, large, borne in clusters; free growth; [Orangeade × Mischief]; int. by Geest Industries

Romanze S, mp, 1985, Tantau, Math.; flowers medium, petals ruffled, 9 cm., 20 petals, borne in clusters, slight fragrance; recurrent; foliage medium size, dark green, semi-glossy; bushy, upright (5 ft.) growth; int. by Tantau Roses, 1984; Gold Medal, Baden-Baden, 1985, ADR, 1986

Rome Glory HT, mr, 1937, Aicardi, D.; bud ovoid; flowers scarlet, reverse cerise, 4-5 in., 55 petals, globular, moderate fragrance; recurrent; vigorous, bushy growth; [Dame Edith Helen × Sensation]; int. by J&P

Rome Glory, Climbing Cl HT, mr

Romeo HT, yb, 1918, Therkildsen; flowers Indian yellow,

suffused coppery pink; [(Edith Part × unknown) × Ophelia]

Romeo HWich, dr, 1919, Easlea; flowers deep red, small, dbl., high-centered, borne in small clusters; vigorous, climbing growth

Romeo Nieuwkoop, Jacob, Nieuwkoop, Jacob; PP4626

Romeo HT, dr, 1998, McGredy, Sam IV; flowers dark crimson-red, 4½ in., full, borne mostly singly, moderate fragrance; foliage large, dark green, semi-glossy; prickles moderate; bushy, tall (110 cm.) growth; [Howard Morrison × Harmonie]; int. by McGredy, 1995

Romeo F, or, Barni, Enrico; flowers bright geranium-red, 4-5 cm., 20-25 petals, high-centered, slight fragrance; foliage medium size, light green, matte; growth to 2-3 ft.; [Feeling × Mathias Meilland]; int. by Rose Barni, 2000

Romina HT, dp, Tantau; int. in 1994

Romstar HT, dr, Wagner, S.; bud long; flowers medium red, velvety, high centered, 34 petals, moderate fragrance; foliage medium size, medium-green, semi-glossy; [Baccara × Coronado]; int. by Res. Stn. f. Horticulture, Cluj, 1991

Romy HT, w, Select Roses, B.V.

Romy Schneider F, mr, Orard; int. in 1991

Ron West HT, pb, 1985, West, Ronald; flowers white with deep pink petal edges; [sport Admiral Rodney]

Ronald George Kent F, mp, 1992, Bracegirdle, A.J.; flowers 3-3½ in., dbl., borne in small clusters; foliage large, dark green, semi-glossy; few prickles; medium (86 cm.), bushy growth; [Pink Favorite × Piccasso]

Ronald Healy HT, pb, 1932, Dobbie; bud long, pointed; flowers old-rose, shaded salmon and yellow, dbl., high-centered; foliage glossy; bushy growth

Ronald McDonald – See **Philadelphia**, HT

Ronald Reagan HT, rb, 2005, Zary, Keith W.; bud long, pointed ovoid; flowers red, reverse white and red, 10-12 cm., 35 petals, high-centered, borne mostly solitary, slight fragrance; foliage medium size, dark green, glossy; prickles moderate, 6-10 mm., hooked downward, greyed orange; upright, branching, tall (150 cm.) growth; PP15061; [seedling × (seedling × Ingrid Bergman)]; int. by Jackson & Perkins Wholesale, Inc., 2004

Ronald Tooke HT, dr, 1927, Morse; flowers deep blackish crimson; [sport of Col. Oswald Fitzgerald]

Roncalli S, rb, Noack, Werner; int. in 1997

Ronce d'Autriche – See ***R. foetida*** (Herrmann)

Ronda – See **Ronda Palace**, MinFl

Ronda Palace MinFl, mr, Poulsen; flowers medium red, 5-8 cm., semi-dbl., no fragrance; foliage dark; growth bushy, 60-100 cm.; int. by Poulsen Roser, 2005

Ronde Endiablée F, or, 1963, Combe; flowers geranium-red, edged darker, large, semi-dbl.; foliage dark, glossy; moderate growth; Gold Medal, The Hague, 1964

Rondo HT, or, 1955, Tantau, Math.; bud ovoid; flowers 3½-4 in., 15-20 petals, high-centered, moderate fruity fragrance; foliage dark, leathery; vigorous, upright, compact growth; PP1454; [Danzig × (Crimson Glory × Floradora sister seedling)]; int. by J&P, 1955

Rongotai Rose S, dr, Ball; int. in 1995

Ronja – See **Mary Hayley Bell**, S semi-dbl.

Ronny Temmer F, mp, 1976, Delforge, S.; bud ovoid; flowers large, 44 petals, moderate fragrance; int. in 1974

Ronsard HFt, rb, 1932, Gaujard; bud long, pointed, yellowish edged red; flowers brilliant red, reverse yellow and cream, semi-dbl., cupped; sometimes recurrent; foliage leathery, dark; bushy, compact growth; [Conrad Ferdinand Meyer × *R. foetida bicolor*]; int. by J&P

Rooi Rose HT, mr, Kordes; bud pointed; flowers clear velvet red, dbl., high-centered, borne mostly singly, slight fragrance; recurrent; stems long, strong; medium growth; int. by Ludwig's Roses, 1993

Rookie Min, w, Fischer; [sport of Giggles]; similar to Giggles except for bloom color; int. in 2000

Roos Sonder Grense – See **RSG Roos**, F

Roosendaal F, mr, 1965, Buisman, G. A. H.; flowers medium, dbl.; foliage dark; [Gartendirektor Glocker × Alpine Glow]

Roquebrune HT, ob, 1959, Delforge; bud oval; flowers ochre-yellow edged orange, medium, dbl.; foliage dark, glossy; strong stems; moderate, bushy growth

Roro HT, 1954, San Remo Exp. Sta.

Rory Carlton HT, dp, 1996, Macredie, W.R.; flowers deep pink, full, borne mostly singly; foliage medium size, dark green, semi-glossy; few prickles; medium (100-120 cm.), upright growth; [Sylvia × Royal Highness]

Ros Gardner HT, pb, 2003, Poole, Lionel; flowers pink/cream, 4 in., full, borne mostly solitary; foliage medium size, medium green, glossy; prickles medium, triangular; growth upright, bushy, medium (30 in.); garden; [Silver Jubilee × New Zealand]; int. in 2004

R. abietorum (Greene) – See ***R. gymnocarpa*** (Nuttall)

R. abyssinica (R. Br.) Sp, w, 1814; flowers cream to white, borne in clusters, moderate clove fragrance; more prickly; tender growth; Eurosa, Synstylae, (14); from Ethiopia, Northern Somalia and Sudan

R. acicularis (Lindley) Sp, dp, 1805; flowers deep rose-pink, 1-1½ in., single, borne usually solitary, moderate fragrance; spring bloom, with some tendency to repeat; foliage large, thin, oblong, with 3-7 leaflets; prickles numerous, needle-like; erect, vigorous, dense, 3 ft. growth; hips usually pear-shaped, ½-1 in., bright red, bristly; extremely hardy; Eurosa, Cinnomomeae, (42); native to the colder areas of North America and Asia; intermediate between *R. blanda* and *R. cinnamomea*; introduced into England from Siberia in 1805

R. acicularis bourgeauiana (Crépin) – See ***R. acicularis sayi*** (Rehder)

R. acicularis carelica (Matsson) – See ***R. acicularis*** (Lindley)

R. acicularis engelmannii (Crépin) – See ***R. × engelmannii*** (Watson)

R. acicularis fennica (Lallemant) Sp, dp; tetraploid variant from Finland/Siberia

R. acicularis gmelinii (Bunge) – See ***R. acicularis fennica*** (Lallemant)

R. acicularis nipponensis (Koehne) Sp, dp, 1894; flowers 1½ in., single; European distribution made from the Botanic Garden in St. Petersburg; introduced into Britain and the U.S. in 1894; first discovered in 1864 on Fujiyama by Sugawa

R. acicularis rotundata (Rydberg) – See ***R. acicularis*** (Lindley)

R. acicularis sayi (Rehder) Sp, m, about 1834; flowers pale lavender, relatively large, 2½ in.; fruit subglobose; native to southwestern Canada and northwestern United States

R. acicularis sayi plena (Lewis) Sp, dp

R. acicularis taquetii (Léveillé) – See ***R. acicularis*** (Lindley)

R. acicularis × R. rugosa HRg, mr; flowers magenta-crimson, single; occasional autumn repeat; hips pear-shaped; natural hybrid from Japan

R. adenosepala (Wooton & Standley) Sp, dp, 1913; flowers deep pink, single; foliage large, gray-green; prickles deflexed or curved; hips round, glandular, large, bright scarlet; very hardy; Eurosa, Cinnamomeae, (14); native to North America and Europe; a form of *R. woodsii*

R. afzeliana (Fries) – See ***R. dumalis*** (Bechstein) single

R. agrestis (Savi) Sp, lp, about 1878; flowers pale pink or whitish, small; Eurosa, Caninae, (35, 42); often confused with *R. rubiginosa*; native to Europe and northern Africa

R. agrestis belgradensis Sp, lp; foliage glossy; prickles coral-red

R. agrestis gizellae ((Borbás) R.Keller) Sp, w; foliage dark green, heavily veined

R. agrestis inodora ((Fries) Keller)) – See ***R. inodora*** (Fries)

R. alabukensis Sp, my; flowers 2 in., single; non-recurrent; foliage fern-like; stems red

R. × alba (Linnaeus) – See **White Rose of York**

R. alba (Allioni) – See ***R. sempervirens*** (Linnaeus)

R. alba anglica minor – See **Alba Maxima**

R. alba cimbaefolia (Thory) – See **Cymbaefolia**

R. alba florepleno (hort. Ex Andrews) – See **Alba Maxima**

R. × alba incarnata (Weston) – See **Great Maiden's Blush**

R. × alba maxima – See **Alba Maxima**

R. × alba nivea – See **Alba Semi-plena**

R. × alba regalis (Thory) – See **Great Maiden's Blush**

R. alba rubicunda (Roessig) – See **Great Maiden's Blush**

R. alba rubicunda plena – See **Great Maiden's Blush**

R. × alba semi-plena (Seringe) – See **Alba Semi-plena**

R. × alba suaveolens (Dieck) – See **Alba Semi-plena**

R. albertii (Regel) Sp, w, 1877; flowers white to pale yellow, 1½ in., borne singly; once-blooming, in June; foliage small, with 5-9 leaflets; prickles long, sharp, red; growth erect, short (3 ft.); fruit oval, orange-red, crowned with persistent sepals; Eurosa, Cinnomomeae; native to the Tian-Shan Mountains of central Asia; allied to *R. willmottiae*

R. alpina (Linnaeus) – See ***R. pendulina*** (Linnaeus)

R. alpina speciosa (Lindl.) – See **Drummond's Thornless**

R. altaica (Willdenow) – See ***R. spinosissima altaica*** (Bean)

R. amblyotis (Meyer) Sp, mr, before 1917; flowers 2 in., single, borne mostly singly or in small clusters; hips subglobose or pyriform, ½-1 in., bright red; Eurosa, Cinnomomeae, (14); intermediate between *R. cinnamomea* and *R. rugosa*; native to Siberia and Alaska

R. amoyensis (Hance) – See ***R. cymosa*** (Trattinnick)

R. amygdalifolia (Seringe) – See ***R. laevigata*** (Michaux)

R. andegavensis (Bastard) – See ***R. canina andegavensis*** ((Bastard) Desportes)

R. × andersonii (hort.) – See **Andersonii**

R. andreae (Lange) Sp, 1874

R. anemoneflora (Fortune) Sp, w, 1844; flowers dull white, outer petals round, inner petals narrow and irregular, 1 in., very dbl., borne in corymbs; foliage having very narrow leaflets; stems long, thin, having a rusty appearance; climbing growth; Eurosa, Synstelae, (14); probably a natural hybrid between *R. moschata* and *R. banksiae*; found in eastern China

R. × anemonoides (Rehder) – See **Anemone**

R. angustiarum (Cockerell) – See ***R. arkansana*** (Porter)

R. apiifolia (Willdenow) – See ***R. centifolia bipinnata*** (Thory)

R. appennina (Borbás) – See ***R. serafinii*** (Viviani)

R. arizonica (Rydberg) Sp, mp, 1918; prickles deflexed or curved; hips round; a form of *R. woodsii*

R. arkansana (Porter) Sp, mp, 1880; flowers 1½ in., borne in corymbs; growth to 1½ ft.; Eurosa, Cinnamomeae, (28); native to the north-central U.S.; with somewhat larger blossoms and leaflets than *R. suffulta*

R. arkansana alba ((Rehder) Lewis) – See ***R. pratincola alba*** (Rehder)
R. arkansana plena (Lewis) Sp, lp
R. arkansanoides (Schneider) – See ***R. arkansana*** (Porter)
R. arkansanoides alba (Schneider) – See ***R. pratincola alba*** (Rehder)
R. × *arnoldiana* (Sargent) – See **Arnold Rose**
R. arvensis (Hudson) Sp, w, 1762; sepals long, smooth, pointed; flowers white, yellowish at base of petals, 1½-2 in., borne in custers of 3-7, slight musk-like fragrance; summer bloom; foliage dark green, widely-set, oval, simply dentate; prickles equal, sparse, hooked; stems long, very slender; creeping growth; hips dark red, almost round; Eurosa, Synstylae, (14); first mentioned by Caspar Bauhin in 1623; see also Lawrance, 1799; native to western, central and parts of southern Europe
R. arvensis ayreshirea (Seringe) – See **Ayrshire Rose**
R. arvensis capreolata ((Neill) Bean) – See **Ayrshire Rose**
R. arvensis splendens (Gentil) – See **Splendens**
R. × *aschersoniana* (Graebner) – See **Aschersoniana**
R. asperrima (Godet ex Boissier) Sp, mp, before 1885; flowers 1 in., single, borne singly; once-blooming; foliage small; prickles numerous, slender, straight; growth short (2 ft.); hips small, round, very prickly; not dependably hardy; Eurosa, Cinnamomeae; native to the Iranian mountains
R. atrovirens (Viviani) – See ***R. sempervirens*** (Linnaeus)
R. aurantiaca (hort. ex von Steudel) – See ***R. foetida bicolor*** ((Jacquin) Willmott)
R. austriaca (Crantz) – See ***R. gallica*** (Linnaeus)
R. austriaca pygmaea (Wallroth) – See ***R. gallica pumila*** (Seringe)
R. bakerii (Rydberg) – See ***R.* × *engelmannii*** (Watson)
R. balearica (Desfontaines) – See ***R. sempervirens*** (Linnaeus)
R. balsamea (Bess.) – See **Tackholmii**
R. baltica (Roth) – See ***R. spinosissima baltica*** (hort.) single
R. banksiae alba (hort.) – See ***R. banksiae banksiae*** (Aiton)
R. banksiae alba-plena (Rehder) – See ***R. banksiae banksiae*** (Aiton)
R. banksiae banksiae (Aiton) Sp, w, 1807; sepals united, reflexed after opening, not persistent; flowers small, dbl., borne in umbels; foliage small, with 3-5 leaflets, simply serrate, glabrous; prickles few, small, hooked; stems have scaling outer layer; growth large, climbing; hips small, round, smooth; discovered by William Kerr near Canton, China
R. banksiae grandiflora S, w; flowers white, tinged with violet at center, large than the species, single; probably a natural hybrid of *R. banksiae banksiae* and another rose
R. banksiae lutea (Rehder) Sp, ly; sepals united, reflexed after opening, not persistent; flowers straw yellow with a green eye, 1-1½ cm., dbl., borne in large clusters, no fragrance; foliage small, simply dentate, glabrous; nearly thornless; growth vigorous, climbing; brought to England by John Damper Parks about 1824
R. banksiae luteaplena (Rehder) – See ***R. banksiae lutea*** (Rehder)
R. banksiae lutescens (Voss) Sp, my, about 1816; sepals united, reflexed after flowering, not persistent; flowers single, borne in umbels; foliage simply serrate, small, glabrous; nearly thornless; hips small, round, smooth, yellow; discovered in Nanking by Dr. Clarke Abel, physician to Lord Amherst's embassy to China
R. banksiae normalis (Regel) Sp, w, about 1877; sepals united, reflexed after flowering, not persistent; flowers white, on slender pedicels, 1 in., single, borne in many-flowered umbels; early spring bloom; foliage evergreen, simply serrate, small, glabrous; virtually thornless; climbing (20 ft. or more) growth; hips small, round, smooth; Eurosa, Banksianae, (14); possibly discovered by Drummond and introduced in 1796
R. banksiana (Abel) – See ***R. banksiae banksiae*** (Aiton)
R. banksiopsis (Baker) Sp, dp, before 1914; flowers rose-pink, 1 in., single, borne in corymbs; once-blooming, in late June; hips coral-red to orange; not hardy; Eurosa, Cinnomomeae, (14); native to southern China; probably related to *R. caudata*; int. by E. H. Wilson, 1909
R. barbierana (Rehder) HWich, rb, before 1900, Barbier; flowers red lightly tinted orange, white center, 1½-2 in., single, borne in clusters of 20-50; foliage glabrous, oval; prickles short, upright, whitish-gray; [*R. wichurana* × Turner's Crimson Rambler]
R. batavica (Breiter) – See **Cabbage Rose**
R. beggeriana (Schrenk ex Fischer & Meyer) Sp, w, 1881; flowers 1½ in., borne in small clusters; late summer bloom; foliage pale green; dense, branched (5 ft.) growth; fruit small, round, dark red, without sepals; very hardy; Eurosa, Cinnomomeae, (14); considered to be an Asiatic relative of *R. eglanteria*; found in western China by Dr. J.E.T. Aitchison in 1881
R. beggeriana anserinifolia ((Boissier) Regel) Sp, w, before 1886; has more pubescent foliage than the type
R. belgica (Miller) – See **Summer Damask**
R. bella (Rehder & Wilson) Sp, mp, 1910; flowers pink, 1¾-2 in., single, borne mostly solitary, slight fragrance; foliage small, with 7-9 leaflets; prickles numerous, straight, slender; growth to 8 ft.; hips ovoid, scarlet, ¾ in.; Eurosa, Cinnomomeae, (28); from northern China
R. bella pallens (Rehder & Wilson) Sp, lp, 1910; lighter pink than the type
Rosa Belle Min, dp, 1988, King, Gene; flowers deep pink to yellow-cream at base, medium, 21 petals, high-centered, borne usually singly; foliage medium size, medium green, matte; prickles straight with hook, few, dark brown; bushy, medium growth; no fruit; [Vera Dalton × Party Girl]; int. by AGM Miniature Roses
R. bengalensis (Persoon) – See **Slater's Crimson China**
R. berberifolia (von Pallas) – See ***Hulthemia persica***
R. bicolor (Jacquin) – See ***R. foetida bicolor*** ((Jacquin) Willmott)
R. bifera (Persoon) – See **Autumn Damask**
R. bifera alba – See **White Four Seasons Rose**
R. billotiana (Crépin) – See ***R. tomentosa*** (Smith)
R. biserrata (Mérat) – See ***R. arvensis*** (Hudson)
R. blanda (Aiton) Sp, mp, 1773; sepals persistent; flowers pink, 2-2½ in., single, borne in clusters of 3-7 on smooth peduncles; spring bloom; foliage moderately large, thin, pale green, with 5-7 leaflets; stems brown; erect, branching, 6 ft. growth; hips small, round, red; hardy; Eurosa, Cinnamomeae, (14); found from Newfoundland to southeastern Saskatchewan, to northern Missouri and Pennsylvania; introduced to cultivation by James Gordon
R. blanda (Pursh) – See ***R. nitida*** (Willdenow)
R. blanda alba (Fernald) Sp, w, 1926
R. blanda carpohispida ((Schuette) Lewis) Sp, mp, 1898; prickles densely covered with fine bristles
R. blanda glandulosa (Schuette) Sp, mp, 1898; has small glands on the sepals
R. blanda hispida (Farwell) – See ***R. blanda carpohispida*** ((Schuette) Lewis)
R. blanda michiganensis (Erlanson) S, dp; possibly *R. blanda* × *R. palustris*, having deeper pink, broader petals than *R. blanda*
R. blanda schuetteana (Erlanson) Sp, dp; flowers deeper pink and with broader petals than the type
R. blanda willmottiana (Baker) Sp, mp, before 1910; flowers bright coral-pink; stems red
R. blinii (Léveillé) – See ***R. multiflora carnea*** (Thory)
R. blondaeana (Ripart ex Déséglise) – See ***R. canina blondaeana*** ((Ripart) Rouy)
Rosa Blossom F, lp; flowers blush pink, heavy bloom; low growth
Rosa Bonheur M, mp, Laffay, M.; flowers pink or bright rose, large, dbl.; moderate growth
R. × *borboniana* (Desportes) – See **Bourbon Rose**
R. bourgeauiana (Crépin) – See ***R. acicularis sayi*** (Rehder)
R. boursaulti (Sweet) – See **Boursault Rose**
R. boursaultiana (Desportes) – See **Boursault Rose**
R. boursaultii (Steudel) – See **Boursault Rose**
R. bracteata (Wendland) Sp, w, 1793; sepals reflex after flowering, deciduous; flowers milky white with golden stamens, with large ovate bracts, 2-2¾ in., single, borne singly on short stalks; spring-fall bloom; foliage half-evergreen, bright green, somewhat glossy above, sharply serrated; prickles stout, hooked, in pairs; stems procumbent or arching, extremely pubescent; climbing growth; hips large, globular, tomentose, orange-red; Eurosa, Bracteata, (14); native to southeastern China; naturalized in much of the southeastern U.S.
R. bracteata (Sieber ex Presl) – See ***R. wichurana*** (Crépin)
R. × *bracteata alba odorata* – See **Alba Odorata**
R. braunii (Keller) – See ***R.* × *involuta*** (Smith)
R. bridgesii Sp, mp, 1896; sepals persistent; flowers borne mostly solitary; foliage with distinct, blunt terminal leaflets; prickles paired at nodes; growth dwarf (4-30 in.), shrubby; hips globose; Eurosa, Cinnamomeae; native to central and northern Sierra Nevada and southern Cascades
R. britzensis (Koehne) Sp, lp, 1901; flowers pale pink changing to white, 3-4 in., borne singly or in pairs; early summer; foliage large, glossy; growth to 6 ft.; hips ovoid, large, brownish-red; Eurosa, Caninae, (35); native to mountains of southeastern Turkey
R. brownii (Trattinnick) – See ***R. brunonii*** (Lindley)
R. brunonii (Lindley) Sp, w, 1822; bud creamy white; sepals long; flowers pure white, 3-4 cm., single, borne in large clusters; foliage like *R. moschata* but dull green, downy; prickles hooked, stout, short; stems arching; growth very large (to 12 m.); hips red, round, shiny, small
R. burgundensis (Weston) – See **Burgundian Rose**
R. burgundiaca (Roessig) – See **Burgundian Rose**
R. calabrica (Huter ex Burnat. & Gremli) – See ***R. glutinosa*** (Sibthorp & Smith)
R. calendarum (Borkhausen) – See **Summer Damask**
R. californica (Chamisso & Schlechtendahl) Sp, mp, 1878; flowers medium to dark pink, 1½ in., single, borne singly and in clusters of up to 20; summer bloom; foliage medium size, with 5-7 broad, elliptic, 1 in. leaflets; prickles robust, straight and hooked; up to 8 ft. growth; thicket-forming; hips persistent, round, bright red, ½ in., with a distinct neck; Eurosa, Cinnamomeae, (28); extremely variable; native to the streambanks of the North American west coast from British Columbia to lower California and inland to Sierra Nevada foothills
R. californica nana (Rehder) Sp, mp, before 1949; growth very dwarf
R. californica plena (Rehder) S, mp, 1894; like the type, but with semi-double flowers
R. californica ultramontana (Watson) – See ***R. woodsii ultramontana*** ((S.Watson) Jeps.)
R. × *calocarpa* (Willmott) – See **Calocarpa**

R. calva ((Franch. & Sav.) Boulenger) – See ***R. multiflora calva*** (Franchet & Savatier)

R. camellia (Siebold) – See ***R. laevigata*** (Michaux)

R. campanulata (Ehrhart) – See ***R. × francofurtana*** (Muenchhausen)

R. candida (Davidov) – See ***R. micrantha*** (Borrer ex Sm.)

R. canina (Linnaeus) Sp, lp, before 1737; sepals reflexed, deciduous; bracts dilated; flowers white or pinkish, 2 in., single, borne singly or in few-flowered corymbs; summer bloom; foliage medium size, with 5-7 leaflets and adnate stipules; prickles numerous, scattered, hooked; stems long, upright, much-branched; growth to 10 ft.; hips ovoid, glabrous, scarlet; Eurosa, Caninae, (35, 42, 34)

R. canina andegavensis ((Bastard) Desportes) Sp, mp, 1809; variation with glabrous, eglandular foliage, but glandular hispid peduncles

R. canina andersonii (hort. ex Schneider) – See **Andersonii**

R. canina blondaeana ((Ripart) Rouy) Sp, 1861; glandular sepals; foliage leaflet teeth glandular, bi-serrate

R. canina burboniana (Redouté & Thory) – See **Bourbon Rose**

R. canina coriifolia ((Fries) Dumortier) – See ***R. coriifolia*** (Fries)

R. canina dumetorum (Desvaux) – See ***R. corymbifera*** (Borkhausen)

R. canina exilis (Keller) Sp, mp, before 1939; flowers 1 in., single; low (2 ft.) growth

R. canina froebelii (Christ) Sp, w, 1890; flowers small; originated at the Froebel Nurseries, Zurich, Switzerland; used as understock

R. canina inermis (hort.) Sp; prickles almost unarmed; growth vigorous; dog rose popular as an understock

R. canina insignis (Wolley-Dod) – See ***R. canina spuria*** ((Puget) Wolley-Dod)

R. canina lutetiana (Léman) Sp

R. canina spuria ((Puget) Wolley-Dod) Sp; foliage serrations almost entirely simple; large fruit

R. canina tomentella (Léman) – See ***R. obtusifolia*** (Desvaux)

R. cannabifolia – See **Cymbaefolia**

R. × cantabrigiensis (Weaver) – See **Cantabrigiensis**

R. capreolata (Neill) – See **Ayrshire Rose**

R. carelica (Fries) – See ***R. acicularis*** (Lindley)

R. carnea – See **Great Maiden's Blush**

R. carolina (Auth.) – See ***R. palustris*** (Marshall)

R. carolina (Linnaeus) Sp, mp, 1826; sepals widespreading, entire, falling soon after flowering; flowers bright pink, 2 in., borne singly or in small corymbs; summer bloom; foliage small, thin, lightly lustrous; prickles numerous, paired at the nodes, almost straight; growth to 3-6 ft.; hips round, red; Eurosa, Carolinae; native to North America, ranging from New Brunswick to Florida and west to Texas and Wisconsin

R. carolina alba (Rehder) Sp, w, 1880; flowers single

R. carolina flore pleno (Rehder) – See ***R. pennsylvanica plena*** (Marshall) dbl.

R. carolina florida (Donn) Sp, mp; native to Florida, Georgia, and Alabama; having smoother leaflets than type

R. carolina glandulosa (Farwell) Sp, mp, 1902; foliage leaflets glandular-serrate leaf-stalk glandular; leaflets and petioles are glandular; Massachusetts to Florida and southern Texas

R. carolina grandiflora (Rehder) Sp, mp, before 1949; blossoms and foliage slightly larger than the type; Maine to Michigan and south to Missouri

R. carolina inermis (Regel) – See ***R. palustris inermis*** (Schuette)

R. carolina lyonii (Pursh Palmer & Steyermark) – See ***R. carolina villosa*** (Rehder)

R. carolina nuttalliana (Rehder) – See ***R. palustris nuttalliana*** (Rehder)

R. carolina setigera (Crépin) – See ***R. nitida spinosa*** (Lewis)

R. carolina triloba (Rehder) Sp, mp, before 1949; flowers bright pink, petals 3-lobed; generally distributed throughout eastern North America; also known erroneously as *R. humilis triloba*

R. carolina villosa (Rehder) Sp, mp, 1887; foliage pubescent beneath; New England to Minnesota, south to Georgia and Kansas

R. carolinensis (Marshall) – See ***R. virginiana*** (Miller)

R. caroliniana (Michaux) – See ***R. palustris*** (Marshall)

R. caryophyllacea (Christ) – See ***R. agrestis gizellae*** ((Borbás) R.Keller)

R. cathayensis (Bailey) – See ***R. multiflora cathayensis*** (Rehder & Wilson)

R. cathayensis platyphylla ((Thory) Bailey) – See **Seven Sisters**

R. caudata (Baker) Sp, mr, about 1896; flowers bright red, 2 in., single, borne in small clusters; foliage slightly scented, with 7-9 leaflets; growth to 12 ft.; hips pear-shaped, orange-red, 1 in.; Eurosa, Cinnomomeae, (14, 28); from China; closely allied to *R. macrophylla*

R. × centifolia (Linnaeus) – See **Cabbage Rose**

R. × centifolia albomuscosa (Willmott) – See **Shailer's White Moss**

R. centifolia andrewsii (Rehder) – See **Muscosa Simplex**

R. centifolia anglica rubra (Redouté) – See **Rubra**

R. centifolia batavica (Clusius) C, dp, 1583; flowers deeper pink and larger than *R. × centifolia*

R. centifolia bipinnata (Thory) C, lp, before 1802; flowers medium, with distinctive waved petals, full, globular; foliage rounded, toothed as if crimped, resembling celery

R. × centifolia bullata (Thory) – See **Bullata**

R. centifolia cristata (Rehder) – See **Crested Moss**

R. × centifolia maxima – See **Rose des Peintres**

R. × centifolia minima – See **Rouletii**

R. × centifolia minor (Pródán) – See **Petite de Hollande**

R. × centifolia muscosa (Seringe) – See **Communis**

R. centifolia muscosa cristata (Hooker) – See **Crested Moss**

R. centifolia mutabilis (Thory) – See **White Provence**

R. centifolia nivea (Loisel.) – See **White Provence**

R. × centifolia parvifolia ((Ehrhart) Rehder) – See **Burgundian Rose**

R. × centifolia pomponia (Lindley) – See **Rose de Meaux**

R. centifolia prolifera foliacea (Redouté & Thory) – See **Prolifera de Redouté**

R. × centifolia provincialis (Bean) – See ***R. gallica officinalis*** (Thory)

R. centifolia sancta (Zabel) – See **St John's Rose**

R. centifolia simplex (Thory) – See **Ciudad de Oviedo** single

R. centifolia variegata – See **Variegata**

R. cerasocarpa (Rolfe) Sp, w, about 1914; flowers 1-1¼ in., borne in panicles; hips globose, about ½ in., intense red; Eurosa, Synstylae, (14); a form of *R. rubus*; native to central China

R. cerea (Roess. ex Red.) – See ***R. foetida*** (Herrmann)

R. charbonneaui (Léveillé) – See ***R. longicuspis*** (Bertoloni)

R. chavinii (Rapin ex Reuter) Sp, mp, 1905; flowers 2 in., single; ovoid, setose fruit; Eurosa, Caninae, (42); [perhaps a derivative of *R. canina × R. montana*]; native to mountainous areas of Europe; closely allied to *R. montana*

R. cherokeensis (Donn) – See ***R. laevigata*** (Michaux)

R. chinensis (Jacquin) Sp, mr, 1759; sepals reflex after flowering; flowers crimson or pink, rarely whitish, 2-2½ in., single to semi-dbl., loose, borne singly and in small clusters, no fragrance; recurrent bloom; foliage evergreen or partially so, typically with 3-5 ovate leaflets; few prickles; growth tall (4-6 ft.); hips ovate, smooth, about ¾ in., red; Eurosa, Chinensis, (14, 21, 28); brought to Holland possibly as early as 1704

R. chinensis fragrans (Thory) – See **Hume's Blush Tea-Scented China**

R. chinensis indica (Lindley) – See ***R. chinensis*** (Jacquin)

R. chinensis longifolia (Voss) Sp, dp, 1820; flowers single; foliage leaflets very long and narrow, like a willow; not now in cult.

R. chinensis manettii (Dippel) – See **Manettii**

R. chinensis minima (Voss) Sp, 1815; flowers white, pink or red, petals often pointed, 1½ in., semi-dbl.; growth variable; Eurosa, Chinensis

R. chinensis mutabilis (Rehder) – See **Mutabilis**

R. chinensis pseudindica ((Lindl.) Willmott) – See **Fortune's Double Yellow**

R. chinensis pumila – See ***R. chinensis minima*** (Voss)

R. chinensis semperflorens ((Curtis) Koehne) – See **Slater's Crimson China**

R. chinensis serratipetala – See **Serratipetala**

R. chinensis spontanea (Rehder & Wilson) Ch, dr, 1885; flowers deep red pink, or white, medium, single, borne mostly solitary; foliage oval to lanceolate, serrated; prickles scattered, small, hooked; growth medium shrub with climbing tendencies; hips medium (2 cm), yellow or orange; discovered near Ichang in central China by Dr. Augustine Henry

R. chinensis viridiflora (Dippel) – See **Green Rose**

R. chlorophylla (Ehrhart) – See ***R. foetida*** (Herrmann)

R. cinnamomea (Linnaeus) Sp, m, before 1600; sepals persistent; flowers purplish-red, 2 in., borne singly or few on short, naked pedicels, moderate fragrance; foliage medium size, with 5-7 leaflets and very large stipules; prickles few, short, curved; stems arching, slender, brown-tinged; growth to 6 ft.; hips round, scarlet, ½ in.; Eurosa, Cinnomomeae, (14, 28); native to a large area from western Europe to Japan; naturalized in parts of North America

R. cinnamomea (Linnaeus) – See ***R. pendulina*** (Linnaeus)

R. cinnamomea (Linnaeus) – See ***R. majalis*** (Herrmann) dbl.

R. cinnamomea plena (Rehder) – See ***R. majalis*** (Herrmann) dbl.

R. cinnamomea sewerzowii (Regel) – See ***R. beggeriana*** (Schrenk ex Fischer & Meyer)

R. clinophylla (Thory) Sp, w, before 1817; flowers white, slightly yellow at base, very large, 5 petals, flat, borne in small clusters; foliage elliptical, doubly dentate, gright green, glossy above; prickles scattered; hips numerous, large; tender; Eurosa, Bracteata, (14); very similar to *R. bracteata*

R. collina (Jacquin) Misc OGR, mp, before 1788; sepals short; flowers rose-colored; considered by Rehder to be a species; closely allied to *R. corymbifera*; found in many sections of Europe and western Asia

R. collina (De Candolle) – See ***R. corymbifera*** (Borkhausen)

R. collincola (Ehrhart) – See ***R. cinnamomea*** (Linnaeus)

R. × cooperi – See **Cooper's Burmese**

R. coreana (Keller) – See ***R. maximowicziana jackii*** (Rehder)

R. coriifolia (Fries) Sp, lp, 1878; flowers white to pale pink, short-pediceled, with large bracts, borne singly and in small corymbs; foliage leaflets gray-green, downy, very thick and hard; growth to 5 ft.; Eurosa, Caninae, (35); native to Europe and western Asia

R. coriifolia froebelii (Rehder) – See ***R. canina froebelii*** (Christ)

R. coronata (Crépin) – See ***R. × involuta*** (Smith)

R. coruscans (Waitz ex Link) – See ***R. rugosa chamissoniana*** (Meyer)

R. × coryana (Hurst) – See **Coryana**

R. corymbifera (Borkhausen) Sp, w, 1838; flowers light pink to white, 1¾-2 in., borne 1 to many per cluster; foliage leaflets downy; ovoid to subglobose, ¾ in. fruit; Eurosa, Caninae, (35, 42); very similar to *R. canina*; native to Europe, western Asia, and Africa

R. corymbosa (Ehrhart) – See ***R. palustris*** (Marshall)

R. corymbulosa (Rolfe) Sp, rb; flowers red with a white eye, ¾-1 in., borne in dense, umbel-like corymbs; almost thornless; growth to 6 ft.; hips almost round, coral-red, ½-1 in long; Eurosa, Cinnomomeae, (14); from central China; int. by E. H. Wilson in 1908

R. cretica sabina (Vibert) – See **Clémence Isaure**

R. crocantha (Boulenger) Sp, w, 1917; flowers ½ in., borne in many-flowered panicles; prickles curved, orange-yellow; hips globose, in., red; Eurosa, Synstylae, (14); native to western China

R. cucumerina (Trattinnick) – See ***R. laevigata*** (Michaux)

R. cursor (Rafinesque) – See ***R. setigera tomentosa*** (Torrey & Gray)

R. cuspidata (von Bieberstein) – See ***R. tomentosa*** (Smith)

R. cymbifolia (Léman) – See **Cymbaefolia**

R. cymosa (Trattinnick) Sp, w, 1904; flowers small, borne in many-flowered corymbs; hips small, globose, red; Eurosa, Banksianae, (14); closely related to *R. banksiae*; widely distributed in southern China; int. in 1904?

Rosa d'Abril HT, dp, 1948, Dot, Pedro; flowers carmine, large, very dbl., globular; very vigorous growth

R. daishanensis (Ku, T. C.) Sp, w, 1990; flowers borne in panicles of 8-12; foliage with 5-7 leaflets; growth small, climbing; Eurosa, Synstylae; native to eastern China

R. dalmatica (Kern.) – See ***R. glutinosa dalmatica*** (Kerner)

R. × damascena (Miller) – See **Summer Damask**

R. damascena aurora (Redouté) – See **Celestial**

R. × damascena bifera (Regel) – See **Autumn Damask**

R. damascena italica – See **Quatre Saisons d'Italie**

R. damascena rubra – See **Hebe's Lip**

R. damascena rubrotincta – See **Hebe's Lip**

R. × damascena semperflorens (Loiseleur-Deslongchamps & Michel) – See **Autumn Damask**

R. × damascena subalba (Redouté) D, w; bud darkish red; sepals elongate, pointed, pinnatifid; flowers white flushed with pink, single; foliage simply dentate; prickles unequal, some straight, some recurved, reddish

R. × damascena trigintipetala (Keller) – See **Trigintipetala**

R. damascena variegata (Thory) – See **York and Lancaster**

R. × damascena versicolor (Weston) – See **York and Lancaster**

R. davidii (Crépin) Sp, lp; sepals extremely long; flowers pink, 1½-2 in., single, borne in very large corymbs; foliage with deeply impressed veins; prickles sturdy, straight; erect, branching, 10 ft. growth; hips long-necked, bristly, orange-red; Eurosa, Cinnomomeae, (28); allied to *R. macropylla*; introduced from south-central China in 1908

R. davidii elongata (Rehder & Wilson) Sp, lp, 1908; flowers somewhat pendulous; with larger hips and leaflets, and more arching growth, than the type

R. davidii persetosa (Rolfe) – See ***R. persetosa*** (Rolfe)

R. davidii 'Syvdal' – See **Syvdal**, S

R. davurica (Pallas) Sp, m, 1910; flowers purple-pink, single; foliage small; prickles straight; ovate fruit; Eurosa, Cinnomomeae, (14); very similar to *R. cinnamomea*; from Manchuria

R. dawsoniana (Rehder) – See **Dawson**

Rosa de Ferra HT, pb, 1958, Dot, Pedro; flowers violet-pink with carmine reflections, large, 35 petals, intense fragrance; strong stems; vigorous growth; [Rosa Gallart × Paulette]; int. in 1956

Rosa de los Andes Gr, op, 1975, Gutierrez; bud ovoid; flowers pink-salmon-peach, 4-4½ in., 44-46 petals; vigorous growth; [sport of Duet]

R. deserta (Lunell) – See ***R. woodsii*** (Lindley)

R. dimorpha (Bess.) – See ***R. tomentosa*** (Smith)

R. diversifolia (Ventenat) – See **Slater's Crimson China**

R. doncasterii – See **Doncasterii**

R. doniana (Woods) – See ***R. × involuta*** (Smith)

R. × dulcissima (Lunell) Misc OGR; [*R. blanda × R. woodsii*]

R. dumalis (Bechstein) Sp, lp, 1872; sepals long; flowers single; foliage bluish green glaucous leaflets; heavily prickled; Eurosa, Caninae, (35); found in many parts of Europe and western Asia

R. dumetorum (Thuillier) – See ***R. corymbifera*** (Borkhausen)

R. dumetorum 'Laxa' – See ***R. canina froebelii*** (Christ)

R. × dupontii (Déséglise) – See **Dupontii**

R. durandii (Crépin) Sp, before 1904; differing slightly from *R. nutkana* in armament, foliage and/or stature

R. earldomensis – See **Earldomensis**

R. ecae (Aitchison) Sp, dy, 1880; flowers buttercup-yellow, short-stalked, 1-1¼ in., single, borne solitary; foliage very small, with 5-9 leaflets; numerous prickles; growth slender, arching (4 ft.); hips small, round; not dependably hardy; Eurosa, Pimpinellifoliae, (14); first collected in the hills of Afghanistan

R. eglanteria (Linnaeus) – See ***R. rubiginosa*** (Linnaeus)

R. eglanteria duplex (Weston) – See ***R. eglanteria duplex*** (Weston)

R. eglanteria eos – See **Eos**

R. eglanteria punicea (Thory) – See ***R. foetida bicolor*** ((Jacquin) Willmott)

R. ehrrhartiana (Trattinnick) – See **Burgundian Rose**

R. elasmacantha (Trautvetter) Sp, my, 1858; flowers light yellow, borne singly; prickles few, flattish; growth low, glabrous; Eurosa, Pimpinellifoliae, (28); native of the Caucasus

R. elegantula (Rolfe) Sp, mp, 1907; flowers pink or white, with golden anthers, small; free bloomer; summer; foliage dainty, fern-like, light green, with 7-11 leaflets; purple-crimson in autumn; prickles numerous, dense, fine; growth to 5-10 ft.; hips small, bright coral-red; Eurosa, Cinnomomeae, (14); from China

R. elegantula persetosa – See ***R. farreri persetosa*** (Stapf)

R. elliptica (Tausch ex Tratt.) – See ***R. inodora*** (Fries)

R. elongata (Roessig ex Stendel) – See ***R. palustris*** (Marshall)

R. elymaitica (Boissier & Haussknecht) Sp, mp, 1867; flowers pink or white, small, borne singly and in small clusters; foliage rigid, with 3-5 leaflets; prickles large, curved; branching, dwarf (3 ft.) growth; hips dark red, small; not hardy; Eurosa, Cinnomomeae, (14, 28); from northern Iran and Turkey

R. elymaitica albicans (Godet) Sp, w; flowers white or pink, small; foliage densely tomentose; similar to *R. elymaitica*, except for the foliage

R. engelmannii (Crépin) – See ***R. × engelmannii*** (Watson)

R. × engelmannii (Watson) Misc OGR, dp, 1891; [*R. nutkana × R. acicularis*]; slightly more bristly than the type; native to mountainous areas from British Columbia to Colorado

R. ernestii (Stapf ex Bean) – See ***R. rubus*** (Léveillé & Vaniot)

R. ernestii nudescens (Stapf) – See ***R. rubus nudescens*** ((Stapf) Rowley)

R. esquirolii (Léveillé & Vaniot) – See ***R. cymosa*** (Trattinnick)

R. exilis (ex Boutt.) – See ***R. canina exilis*** (Keller)

R. fargesii (Osborn) – See ***R. moyesii*** (Hemsley & Wilson)

R. fargesii (hort.) – See ***R. moyesii fargesii*** (Rolfe)

R. fargesii (Boulenger) Sp, w; flowers paniculate, 1¾ in.; Eurosa, Synstylae; closely related to *R. moschata*

R. farreri (Stapf) Sp, w; flowers pale pink to white, 1¼-1½ in.; hips ovoid to ellipsoid, red; Eurosa, Pimpinellifoliae

R. farreri persetosa (Stapf) Sp, mp, before 1900; flowers pink, smaller; prickles whole plant finely bristly; related to *R. sertata*

R. faureri (Léveillé) – See ***R. maximowicziana*** (Regel)

R. fauriei (Léveillé) – See ***R. acicularis*** (Lindley)

R. fedtschenkoana (Regel) Sp, w, 1876; flowers 1½-2 in., single, borne 1-4 together; some tendency to repeat; foliage small, thin, glaucous, with 7-9 leaflets; numerous prickles; growth branching, to 6 ft.; hips ovoid, bright-red, bristly; Eurosa, Cinnomomeae, (28); discovered in central Asia by Olga Fedtschenko in 1875; may be allied to *R. beggeriana*

R. fendleri (Crépin) – See ***R. woodsii fendleri*** (Rehder)

R. fenestrata (Donn) – See ***R. setigera*** (Michaux)

R. ferox (von Bieberstein) – See ***R. horrida*** (Fischer)

R. ferox (Regel) – See ***R. glutinosa*** (Sibthorp & Smith)

R. ferox (Lawrance) – See ***R. rugosa*** (Thunberg)

R. ferruginea (Villars) – See ***R. rubrifolia*** (Villars)

R. filipes (Rehder & Wilson) Sp, w, 1908; bud cream; flowers 1 in., single, borne in clusters of up to 100, moderate musk fragrance; foliage thin, coppery red when young, shallowly dentate; prickles few, small; stems arching; growth very tall (to 10 m.); hips globose, -½ in., scarlet; Eurosa, Synstylae, (14); native to western China; closely allied to *R. henryi*

R. fimbriata (Gremli) – See **Fimbriata**

R. fimbriatula (Greene) – See ***R. woodsii*** (Lindley)

R. floribunda (Steven) – See ***R. micrantha*** (Borrer ex Sm.)

R. floribunda (Baker) – See ***R. helenae*** (Rehder & Wilson)

R. florida (Poiret) – See ***R. multiflora carnea*** (Thory)

R. foecundissima (Münchhausen) – See ***R. majalis*** (Herrmann) dbl.

R. foetida (Herrmann) Sp, my, maybe before 1542; sepals upright, persistent; flowers bright yellow, 2-2½ in., single, borne in clusters of 1-3, moderate sickly sweet fragrance; summer bloom; foliage ovate, deeply bidentate, dark green, with 5-9 leaflets; numerous prickles; stems rich brown; upright, 10 ft. growth; hips almost round, dark red; Eurosa, Pimpinellifoliae, (28); native to Iran, Turkey, and neighboring countries

R. foetida bicolor ((Jacquin) Willmott) Sp, rb, about 1596; flowers orange-scarlet within, yellow reverse, 2-2½ in., single, cupped; foliage small, oval, deeply toothed; prickles long, brown at base, green at tip, straight; [sport of *R. foetida*]

R. foetida harisonii (hort. Ex Rehder) – See **Harison's Yellow**

R. foetida persiana (Rehder) Sp, my, 1837; flowers golden yellow, 3-4 in., dbl., globular; prickles numerous, brown; brought from Persia to England by Willock

R. foliolosa (Nuttall ex Torrey & Gray) Sp, mp, about 1880; flowers deep rose pink, 1½ in., borne singly or in few-flowered clusters; spring bloom; foliage very narrow, with 7-11 leaflets; almost thornless; growth to 1½ ft.; hips round, orange-red, ½ in.; Eurosa, Cinnamomeae, (14); first discovered in Arkansas; also found in various sections of Texas and Oklahoma

R. foliolosa alba (Rehder) Sp, w, 1919

R. foliolosa × R. rugosa HRg, mp; flowers rose-pink, single; growth compact (3 ft.)

R. forrestiana (Boulenger) Sp, dp; flowers rose, with large bracts, 1 in., borne singly or in small clusters; Eurosa, Cinnomomeae; a less-hardy relative of *R. multibracteata*; introduced from southwest China in 1922

R. fortuneana (Lindley) – See **Fortuniana**

R. fortuneana (Lem.) – See **Fortune's Double Yellow**

R. × *fortuniana* ((Lindley & Paxton)) – See **Fortuniana**

R. fortuniana (Lindl. & Paxton) – See **Fortune's Double Yellow**

R. fragariaeflora (von Steudel) – See ***R. cymosa*** (Trattinnick)

R. fragrans (Salisbury) – See ***R. palustris*** (Marshall)

R. franchetii (Koidzumi) – See ***R. luciae*** (Franchet & Rochebrune)

R. franchetii paniculigera (Makino) – See ***R. multiflora*** (Thunberg ex Murray)

R. × francofurtana (Muenchhausen) Misc OGR, m, maybe before 1629; bud protrusive, rounded; flowers purple, 2-3 in., semi-dbl.; summer bloom; foliage oval, villose beneath; prickles few, recurved; growth to 6 ft.; hips turbinate; [probably *R. cinnamomea* × *R. gallica*]

R. fraseri – See **Fraser's Pink Musk**

R. fraxinifolia (Borkhausen) – See ***R. pendulina*** (Linnaeus)

R. fraxinifolia (Lindley) – See ***R. blanda*** (Aiton)

R. freundiana (Graebner) – See **Dupontii**

R. froebelii (Christ) – See ***R. canina froebelii*** (Christ)

R. frutetorum (Besser) – See ***R. coriifolia*** (Fries)

R. fujisanensis (Makino) – See ***R. luciae*** (Franchet & Rochebrune)

Rosa Gallart HT, mp, 1935, Dot, Pedro; bud long, pointed; flowers rose-pink, large, dbl., cupped; foliage glossy; vigorous growth; [seedling × (Li Bures × Rose Marie)]

R. gallica (Linnaeus) Sp, dp, before 1500; bud bracts narrow or entirely lacking; sepals reflex and fall soon after flowering; flowers deep pink to crimson, 2-3 in., borne singly or in small clusters; summer bloom; intermixed, hooked prickles and bristles; stems stout pedicels; moderate (5 ft.), upright growth; hips subglobose or turbinate, brick-red; Eurosa, Gallicanae, (28); found growing naturally throughout Europe and western Asia

R. gallica agatha (Thory) – See **Francfort Agathé**

R. gallica agatha delphiniana – See **Enfant de France**

R. gallica agatha incarnate (Redouté) – See **Agathe Incarnata**

R. gallica centifolia (Regel) – See **Cabbage Rose**

R. gallica complicata – See **Complicata**

R. gallica conditorum (Dieck) – See **Conditorum**

R. gallica damascena (Voss) – See **Summer Damask**

R. gallica grandiflora – See **Alika**

R. gallica haplodonta ((Borbás) Braun) Sp, dp; foliage wild variety with simply serrate and woolly styles

R. gallica macrantha (hort.) – See **Gallica Macrantha**

R. gallica maxima (hort.) – See ***R. gallica officinalis*** (Thory)

R. gallica officinalis (Thory) Sp, dp, before 1600; flowers deep pink to rose red, with undertones of purple or magenta, prominent yellow stamens, semi-dbl., borne in clusters of 2-6, moderate fragrance; foliage dark, ovate, denticulate; prickles weak, sparse, unequal, almost straight; growth branching, compact (3 ft.); hips almost round, large, deep red; possibly as early as 1200; double-flowered form of *R. gallica*

R. gallica plena (Regel) – See ***R. gallica officinalis*** (Thory)

R. gallica pumila (Seringe) Sp, dp, before 1824; flowers red, single; growth dwarf (2 ft.); found in the wild in various parts of Europe, particularly Italy and Spain

R. gallica remensis (Wallroth) – See **Burgundian Rose**

R. gallica rosa mundi (Weston) – See ***R. gallica versicolor*** (Linnaeus)

R. gallica semi-duplex (Linnaeus) – See ***R. gallica officinalis*** (Thory)

R. gallica splendens – See ***R. × francofurtana*** (Muenchhausen)

R. gallica variegata (Thory) – See ***R. gallica versicolor*** (Linnaeus)

R. gallica velutinaeflora ((Déséglise & Ozanon) Rouy) – See ***R. velutinaeflora*** (Déséglise)

R. gallica versicolor (Linnaeus) Sp, pb, before 1581; flowers striped white, pink and red, with yellow stamens, semi-dbl., borne in cluster of 3-4, moderate fragrance; foliage medium green, elliptical; [assumed to be a sport of *R. gallica officinalis*]; described by L'Obel in 1581 and Charles de l'Ecluse in 1583

R. gebleriana (Schrenk) – See ***R. laxa*** (Retzius)

R. gentiliana (Rehder & Wilson) – See ***R. henryi*** (Boulenger)

R. gentiliana (Léveillé & Vaniot) Sp, w, 1907; flowers creamy white, semi-dbl., borne in dense clusters; stems red glandular branches; vigorous shrub growth; hips red; Eurosa, Synstylae, (14)

R. gentilis (Sternb.) – See ***R. pendulina gentilis*** (Keller)

R. germanica (Gordon) – See ***R. × francofurtana*** (Muenchhausen)

R. gigantea (Collett ex Crépin) Sp, w, 1889; bud slim, pointed, pale yellow; sepals entire, narrowly triangular; flowers creamy white, with deep orange anthers, 4-5 in., single, borne in arching sprays, moderate fragrance; produced over a period of several months; foliage large, dark green, glossy, evergreen, with 5-7 leaflets; prickles stout, hooked; vigorous growth; climbing to 50 ft.; hips globose or depressed-globose, red, thick, large; Eurosa, Chinensis, (14)

R. gigantea erubescens (Focke) – See ***R. × odorata erubescens*** (Rehder & Wilson) single

R. giraldii (Hesse) – See ***R. rubrifolia*** (Villars)

R. giraldii (Crépin) Sp, pb, 1897; flowers pink with white center, 1 in., single, borne singly or in small clusters; foliage gray-green; almost thornless; stems reddish; growth to 6 ft.; hips small, red; Eurosa, Cinnomomeae, (14); from central China; closely related to *R. sertata*

R. giraldii venulosa (Rehder & Wilson) Sp, pb, 1907; more dwarf and compact than the type

R. glabrata (Déséglise) – See ***R. × spinulifolia*** (Dematra)

R. glandulosa (Bellardi) – See ***R. pendulina*** (Linnaeus)

R. glauca (Pourret) – See ***R. rubrifolia*** (Villars)

R. glauca (Villars, not Poirret) – See ***R. dumalis*** (Bechstein) single

Rosa glauca Nova – See **Glauca Nova**, S

R. glaucodermis (Greene) – See ***R. gymnocarpa*** (Nuttall)

R. glaucophylla (Ehrhart) – See ***R. hemisphaerica*** (Herrmann)

R. glomerata (Rehder & Wilson) Sp, w, 1908; flowers 1 in., borne in dense corymbs, moderate fragrance; growth to 20 ft.; hips subglobose, about in., orange-red; Eurosa, Synstylae; closely related to *R. longicuspis*

R. glutinosa (Sibthorp & Smith) Sp, w, 1821; flowers white tinged pink, small, moderate pine-scented fragrance; foliage pine-scented; numerous prickles; dwarf growth; hips globose, small; Eurosa, Caninae, (35, 42); ranging from Spain eastward to Iran; first described by Tournefort in 1703; considered to be a Mediterranean representative of *R. rubiginosa*

R. glutinosa dalmatica (Kerner) Sp, mp, 1882; ellipsoid fruit

R. gmelinii (Bunge) – See ***R. acicularis fennica*** (Lallemant)

R. godeti (Grenier) – See ***R. marginata godetii*** ((Grenier) Rehder)

R. gorenkensis (Fisch. ex Sprengel) – See ***R. majalis*** (Herrmann) dbl.

R. graciflora (Rehder & Wilson) Sp, lp, 1932; flowers pale pink, 1½ in., single; almost thornless; native to western China

R. graciliflora (Rehder & Wilson) Sp, mp, 1908; flowers pale rose, 1½ in., borne solitary, but numerous along the stem; Eurosa, Pimpinellifoliae

R. grandiflora (Lindley) – See ***R. spinosissima altaica*** (Bean)

R. grandiflora (Salisbury) – See ***R. gallica*** (Linnaeus)

R. granulifera (Rydberg) Sp, mp; prickles deflexed or curved; hips round; a form of *R. woodsii*

R. granulosa (Keller) – See ***R. maximowicziana*** (Regel)

R. gratiosa (Lunell) – See ***R. blanda*** (Aiton)

R. gratiosa (Lunell) – See ***R. × dulcissima*** (Lunell)

R. gratissima (Greene) Sp, mp; foliage bright green, thin, scented; growth branching, compact, to 6 ft.; allied to *R. californica*

R. graveolens (Gren. & Godr.) – See ***R. inodora*** (Fries)

R. grosse-serrata (Nelson) – See ***R. macounii*** (Greene)

Rosa Gruss an Aachen F, pb, 1930, Spek; flowers satiny yellowish-pink, large, full; [sport of Gruss an Aachen]

R. gymnocarpa (Nuttall) Sp, lp, 1893; flowers pale pink, 1 in., single, borne singly; early summer; foliage rather broad, with 5-9 leaflets; prickles paired, very slender; stems short lateral branchlets; variable, 4-10 ft. growth; hips small, subglobose, orange-red; Eurosa, Cinnomomeae, (14); a forest-edge plant, from central British Columbia to central California and east to Idaho; first described in 1840

R. gypsicola (Blocki) – See ***R. dumalis*** (Bechstein) single

R. × *hardii* (Paxton) – See ***Hulthemia hardii***

R. × *harisonii* (Rivers) – See **Harison's Yellow**

R. × *harisonii vobergii* ((Graebn. ex Späth) Rehder) – See **Vobergii**

R. hawrana (Kmet) Sp, lp, 1914; flowers 2 in.; globose, densely bristly fruit; Eurosa, Caninae, (28); similar to *R. pomifera*, except in leaf formation; from Hungary

R. headleyensis – See **Headleyensis**

R. heckeliana (Trattinnick) Sp, lp; flowers pink, small, borne singly or in pairs; foliage small, with 5-7 almost-round, in. leaflets; dwarf (3 ft.) growth; Eurosa, Caninae; found by Heckel in Sicily; originally described by Cupani in 1713; ranging from Sicily to Syria

R. helenae (Rehder & Wilson) Sp, w, 1907; sepals long, laterally lobed; flowers aging to light pink, with reflexed petals and conspicuous yellow stamens, 1½ in., single, borne in corymbs of 30-50, moderate fragrance; late spring; stems long, slender, arching; growth to 15 ft.; hips ovoid or oblong-obovoid, about ½ in., scarlet; Eurosa, Synstylae, (14); native to west and central China, Vietnam, Laos, and Cambodia

R. heliophila (Greene) – See ***R. suffulta*** (Greene)

R. heliophila alba (Rehder) – See ***R. pratincola alba*** (Rehder)

R. hemisphaerica (Herrmann) Sp, my; bud yellowish-green; flowers sulfur-yellow, nodding, 1½ in., single, cupped, borne mostly solitary, no fragrance; late spring; foliage bluish-green, oval, simply dentate, small; prickles numerous, curved; growth to 8 ft.; Eurosa, Pimpinellifoliae, (28); first mentioned by Ludovico Berthema in 1503; rarely opens properly except in a hot, dry climate

R. hemisphaerica plena (Rehder) – See ***R. foetida persiana*** (Rehder)

R. hemisphaerica rapini ((Boissier) Rowley) Sp, my, 1933

R. hemsleyana (Täckholm) Sp, lp; flowers 2 in., single, borne in small clusters; late spring; foliage oval, with 7-9 leaflets; stems long; growth 5 × 4 ft.; hips ovoid, with a distinct neck, bristly, about 1 in.; Eurosa, Cinnomomeae, (42); introduced from central China in 1904

R. henryi (Boulenger) Sp, w, 1907; flowers 1½ in., moderate fragrance; summer bloom; stems occasionally purple-tinged; globose, about in. fruit; Eurosa, Synstylae, (14); closely related to *R. helenae*

R. heterophylla (Woods) – See ***R. mollis*** (Smith)

R. × *heterophylla* (Cochet-Cochet) – See **Proteiformis** semi-dbl.

R. × *hibernica* (Smith) – See **Hibernica**

R. × *hibernica* (Hooker) – See **Tackholmii**

R. × hibernica cordifolia (Baker) S, mp

R. × hibernica glabra (Baker) S, mp

R. × *hibernica wilsonii* (Baker) – See ***R. × hibernica cordifolia*** (Baker)

R. × *highdownensis* (Hillier) – See **Highdownensis**

R. × *hillieri* (Hillier) – See **Hillier Rose**

R. hirtula (Nakai) – See ***R. roxburghii hirtula*** (Rehder & Wilson)

R. hispanica (Boissier & Reuter) – See ***R. pouzinii*** (Trattinnick)

R. hispida (Poiret) – See ***R. villosa*** (Linnaeus)

R. hispida (Sims) – See ***R. spinosissima hispida*** (Koehne)

R. hoffmeisteri (Klotzsch) – See ***R. macrophylla*** (Lindley)

R. holodonta (Stapf) – See ***R. moyesii rosea*** (Rehder & Wilson)

R. hookeriana (Wallich) – See ***R. macrophylla*** (Lindley)

R. horrida (Fischer) Sp, w, 1796; flowers 1½ in., borne in small corymbs; foliage very small, roundish leaflets; prickly; low shrub growth; hips subglobose, -½ in. across, dark red; Eurosa, Caninae, (35); common in southeastern Europe and Asia Minor

R. hudsoniana (Thory) – See ***R. palustris*** (Marshall)

R. hudsoniana scandens (Thory) – See ***R. palustris scandens*** dbl.

R. hugonis (Hemsley) Sp, my, 1905; flowers 2½ in., single, borne solitary on slender glabrous pedicels; early spring; growth to 6 ft., branches drooping; hips depressed-globose, deep scarlet; Eurosa, Pimpinellifoliae, (14); seeds brought from north-central China to Kew Gardens in 1899

R. hugonis flora pleno – See **Double Hugonis** dbl.

R. humilis (Tausch, not Marshall) – See ***R. gallica pumila*** (Seringe)

R. humilis (Marshall) – See ***R. carolina*** (Linnaeus)

R. humilis (Besser) – See ***R. marginata*** (Wallroth)

R. humilis lucida (Best) – See ***R. virginiana*** (Miller)

R. humilis villosa (Best) – See ***R. carolina villosa*** (Rehder)

R. humilis × R. rugosa HRg, mr; flowers almost crimson, single; flowering throughout summer

R. hypoleuca (Wooton & Standl.) Sp, mp; prickles straight; hips round; a form of *R. woodsii*

R. hystrix (Lindley) – See ***R. laevigata*** (Michaux)

R. illinoiensis (Baker) – See ***R. spinosissima*** (Linnaeus)

R. ilseana (Crépin) – See ***R. rubrifolia*** (Villars)

R. incarnata (Miller) – See **Great Maiden's Blush**

R. inconsiderata (Déséglise) – See ***R. pouzinii*** (Trattinnick)

R. indica (Lindley) – See ***R. chinensis*** (Jacquin)

R. indica (Linnaeus) – See ***R. cymosa*** (Trattinnick)

R. indica creunta (Redouté & Thory) – See **Sanguinea**

R. indica humilis (De Candolle) – See ***R. chinensis minima*** (Voss)

R. indica longifolia (Willdenow) – See ***R. chinensis longifolia*** (Voss) single

R. indica ochroleuca (Lindley) – See **Parks' Yellow Tea-Scented China**

R. indica odoratissima (Lindley) – See **Hume's Blush Tea-Scented China**

R. indica pumila (Thory) – See ***R. chinensis minima*** (Voss)

R. indica semperflorens ((Curtis) Seringe) – See **Slater's Crimson China**

R. indica sertulata (Redouté) – See **Slater's Crimson China**

R. indica vulgaris (Lindley) – See ***R. chinensis*** (Jacquin)

R. inermis (Thory) – See ***R. × francofurtana*** (Muenchhausen)

R. inermis morletii – See **Morletii**

R. inodora (Fries) Sp, w, 1875; flowers white or pink, 1-1½ in., no fragrance; hips ovoid, bright red; Eurosa, Caninae, (35, 42); native to the British Isles; very similar to *R. agrestis*, with leaves that are broader and more hairy

R. inodora (Hooker) – See ***R. obtusifolia*** (Desvaux)

R. intermedia (Carriere) – See ***R. multiflora*** (Thunberg ex Murray)

R. involucrata (Roxburgh) – See ***R. clinophylla*** (Thory)

R. × involuta (Smith) Misc OGR, lp, before 1800; flowers pale pink, single; growth moderate; [*R. spinosissima* × *R. tomentosa*]; from Scotland

R. × involuta wilsonii ((Borrer) Baker) Misc OGR, before 1862; vigorous, shrubby growth

R. irridens (Focke) – See ***R. longicuspis*** (Bertoloni)

R. × *iwara* (Regel) – See **Iwara**

R. jackii (Rehder) – See ***R. maximowicziana jackii*** (Rehder)

R. jackii pilosa (Nakai) – See ***R. maximowicziana pilosa*** (Nakai)

R. × jacksonii (Willmott) S, mr, before 1910; flowers bright crimson; very free bloomer; [*R. rugosa* × *R. wichurana*]

R. jasminoides (Koidzumi) – See ***R. luciae*** (Franchet & Rochebrune)

R. jundzilli (Besser) – See ***R. marginata*** (Wallroth)

R. jundzilli godetii (Keller) – See ***R. marginata godetii*** ((Grenier) Rehder)

Rosa Kaiserin HT, mp; flowers large, dbl.

R. hakonensis (Koidzumi) – See ***R. luciae*** (Franchet & Rochebrune)

R. kamtchatica (Ventenat) – See **Kamtchatica**

R. kelleri (Baker) – See ***R. maximowicziana jackii*** (Rehder)

R. kentuckensis (Rafinesque) – See ***R. setigera tomentosa*** (Torrey & Gray)

R. klukii (Bess.) – See ***R. inodora*** (Fries)

R. × kochiana (Koehne) S, dp, before 1869; flowers deep rose, 1½ in., borne solitary in clusters of 3; foliage small, with 9-11 leaflets; numerous prickles; probably *R. spinosissima* × *R. carolina*

R. × koehneana (Rehder) S, m, before 1893; flowers purplish red, large; [*R. carolina* × *R. rugosa*]

R. kokanica (Regel) Sp, w; flowers white to pale yellow, borne singly; foliage with 5-7 leaflets; growth small; hips very small, dark purple; Eurosa, Pimpinellifoliae; native to SW Asia

R. × kordesii (Wulff) HKor, dp, 1941, Kordes, W.; flowers bright red-pink, 2 in., semi-dbl., cupped; non-recurrent; foliage dark green, glossy; growth open, lax; hips elliptic-ovoid, vermilion; very hardy; [Max Graf × unknown]

R. koreana (Komarov) Sp, lp, 1917; flowers white, flushed pink, 1 in.; foliage elliptic, with 7-11 leaflets; stems dark red; growth very dense, to 3 ft.; hips ovoid, ½ in. long, orange-red; Eurosa, Pimpinellifoliae, (14); from Korea; a form of *R. spinosissima*

R. korsakoviensis (Léveillé) – See ***R. acicularis*** (Lindley)

R. kotschyana (Boissier) Sp, before 1885; a natural hybrid of *R. orientalis*

R. kunmingensis (Ku, T. C.) Sp, w; flowers dbl., about 1 in., borne in corymbs of 5-7; foliage with 7-9 leaflets; growth tall (9 ft.); Eurosa, Synstylae; native to Yunan province of China

R. kweichowensis (Yu, T. T., and Ku, T. C.) Sp, w, 1981; flowers borne in corymbs of 7-17; foliage semi-evergreen; Eurosa, Microphyllae; native to Guizhou province in southwest China

R. laevigata (Michaux) Sp, w, 1803; sepals erect, persistent; flowers pure white, rarely rose, with golden stamens, 2½-3½ in., single, borne mostly singly, moderate fragrance; early spring; foliage moderately large, dark green, glossy, leathery, 3-leaflets; prickles small, scattered, reddish brown, hooked; tall, climbing growth; hips large, oblong, red, bristly; Eurosa, Laevigatae, (14); native to Southern China and Indo-China; first mentioned botanically by Plukenet in 1696

R. latibracteata (Boulenger) Sp, mp, 1936; flowers borne in two's or corymbose; foliage bracts broad, leaflets 7, up to 1 in long; a form of *R. multibracteata*

R. laurentiae (Andrews) – See ***R. chinensis minima*** (Voss)

R. lawranceana (Sweet) – See ***R. chinensis minima*** (Voss)

R. laxa (Retzius) Sp, w, 1803; flowers white, occasionally light pink, small, single; early summer; foliage small, light green, oblong; prickles large, robust, hooked; growth vigorous; hips oblong-ovoid, small, bright red; very hardy; Eurosa, Cinnomomeae, (28); closely related to *R. cinnamomea*; useful as an understock

R. laxa (Froebel, not Retzius) – See ***R. canina froebelii*** (Christ)

R. lebrunei (Léveillé) – See ***R. multiflora carnea*** (Thory)

R. lehmanniana (Bunge) – See ***R. beggeriana*** (Schrenk ex Fischer & Meyer)

R. × *leonida* (Moldenke) – See **Maria Leonida**

R. leschenaultii (Wight & Arnott) Sp, w, 1830; flowers larger than those of *R. moschata*, borne in few-flowered corymbs; hips round, red; Eurosa, Synstylae, (14); similar to *R. brunonii*, but also resembling *R. sempervirens*; generally assumed to be a close relative of *R. moschata*

R. leucantha (Loisel.) – See ***R. canina*** (Linnaeus)

R. × *lheritierana* (Thory) – See **Boursault Rose**

R. libanotica (Boissier) – See ***R. glutinosa*** (Sibthorp & Smith)

R. lindleyana (Trattinnick) – See ***R. clinophylla*** (Thory)

R. linkii (Dehnh.) – See ***R. multiflora*** (Thunberg ex Murray)

R. longicuspis (Bertoloni) Sp, w, 1904; bud narrow; sepals long, reflexing after flowering; flowers reverse of petals silky, 1½ in., single, borne in clusters of 5-15, moderate fruity fragrance; foliage evergreen or semi-evergreen, long, dark, glossy, leathery; prickles short, flat, straight, numerous; stems reddish mahogany when young; growth to 20 ft.; hips ovoid, scarlet or orange-red; tender; Eurosa, Synstylae, (14); native to northeastern India, western China, and Mianmar

R. longicuspis lucens Sp, w; a form of *R. longicuspis*, having shorter leaflets and petal-backs which are not silky

R. longifolia (Willdenow) – See ***R. chinensis longifolia*** (Voss) single

R. lucens (Rolfe) – See ***R. longicuspis*** (Bertoloni)

R. luciae (Franchet & Rochebrune) – See ***R. wichurana*** (Crépin)

R. luciae (Franchet & Rochebrune) Sp, w, 1880; related to *R. wichurana*; flowers smaller, and habit more upright

R. luciae fujisanensis (Makino) – See ***R. luciae*** (Franchet & Rochebrune)

R. luciae taquetiana (Boulenger) – See ***R. wichurana*** (Crépin)

R. luciae wichuraiana (Crépin) – See ***R. wichurana*** (Crépin)

R. lucida (lawrance) – See ***R. bracteata*** (Wendland)

R. lucida (Ehrhart) – See ***R. virginiana*** (Miller)

R. lucida alba (hort.) – See ***R. virginiana*** (Miller)

R. lurida (Andrews) – See ***R. rubrifolia*** (Villars)

R. lutea (Miller) – See ***R. foetida*** (Herrmann)

R. lutea bicolor (Sims) – See ***R. foetida bicolor*** ((Jacquin) Willmott)

R. lutea hoggii (D.Don) – See **Harison's Yellow**

R. lutea persiana (Lemaire) – See ***R. foetida persiana*** (Rehder)

R. lutea plena (hort.) – See ***R. foetida persiana*** (Rehder)

R. lutea punicea (Miller) – See ***R. foetida bicolor*** ((Jacquin) Willmott)

R. lutescens (Pursh) – See ***R. spinosissima hispida*** (Koehne)

R. lutetiana ((Léman) Baker) – See ***R. canina lutetiana*** (Léman)

R. lyellii (Lindley) – See ***R. clinophylla*** (Thory)

R. lyonii (Pursh) – See ***R. carolina villosa*** (Rehder)

R. lyonii alba (Rehder) – See ***R. carolina alba*** (Rehder) single

R. macartnea (Dumont de Courset) – See ***R. bracteata*** (Wendland)

R. macdougalii (Holzinger) – See ***R. nutkana hispida*** (Fernald)

R. macounii (Rydberg) – See ***R. woodsii*** (Lindley)

R. macounii (Greene) Sp, lp, before 1826; flowers pale pink, small, single; foliage large, pale green; stems light brown, straight; low, bushy growth; hips round, orange-red; extremely hardy; Eurosa, Cinnomomeae, (14, 21); a form of *R. woodsii*

R. macrantha (Desportes) – See **Gallica Macrantha**

R. macrocarpa Sp, ly, 1882; discovered in Manipur by George Watt; probably synonymous with *R. odorata gigantea*

R. macrophylla (Lindley) Sp, dp, 1818; flowers light red, 2 in., single, borne in groups of 1-3; leaves composed of 9-11 elliptic, 1-2 in. leaflets; prickles few, straight, intermixed with bristles; stems reddish-brown; growth erect, vigorous (8-10 ft.); hips oblong-ovoid, 1-1½ in. long, bristly, red, with persistent sepals; Eurosa, Cinnomomeae, (14, 28); native to the Himalayas

R. macrophylla (Crépin) – See ***R. hemsleyana*** (Täckholm)

R. macrophylla acicularis (Vilmorin) – See ***R. persetosa*** (Rolfe)

R. macrophylla coryana – See **Coryana**

R. macrophylla crasseaculeata (Vilmorin) – See ***R. setipoda*** (Hemsley & Wilson)

R. macrophylla doncasterii – See **Doncasterii**

R. macrophylla glaucescens (Hillier) Sp, mp; flowers clear pink, large, single; foliage and stems glaucous; brought to England by Forrest

R. macrophylla gracilis (Vilmorin & Bois) – See ***R. persetosa*** (Rolfe)

R. macrophylla rubricaulis (Hillier) Sp, mp; flowers pink with lilac-blue tints; foliage reddish-green; stems tinged purple; less hardy than the type

R. macrophylla rubrostaminea (Vilmorin) – See ***R. moyesii*** (Hemsley & Wilson)

R. majalis (Herrmann) Sp, m, 1596; flowers dbl., moderate over-ripe raspberry fragrance; completely sterile

R. majalis flore simplici Sp, mp; flowers single

R. × malyi (Kerner) S, dr, 1902; flowers deep, bright red, 1½ in., borne singly; foliage similar to spinosissima; growth to 6 ft.; hips scarlet, ovoid, ¾ in.; probably *R. pendulina* × *R. spinosissima*; first recorded in 1902 by Keller; from Austria

Rosa Mamie HT, mr, 1956, Asseretto, V.; bud ovoid; flowers bright rose, large, 35 petals, moderate fragrance; long stems; vigorous growth; PP1356; [sport of Rome Glory]

R. manca (Greene) Sp, mp; flowers 2 in., borne singly; growth low (2 ft.); native to the southern Rocky Mountains

R. manettii (hort.) – See **Manettii**

R. maracandica (Bunge) Sp, lp; a dwarf (3 ft.) form of *R. webbiana*

R. × marcyana (Boullu) S, m; flowers pink to light purple, with notched petals, 2½-3 in., single; some repeat; stems long-stalked; low (2 ft., rarely 4 ft.) growth; hips almost round; first found near Marcy l'Étoile, France; presumed to be a natural hybrid between *R. gallica* and *R. tomentosa*

R. × mareyana (Boullu ex Déséglise) – See ***R. × marcyana*** (Boullu)

R. marginata (Wallroth) Sp, lp, 1870; sepals deciduous; flowers pink, 2-2½ in., borne singly or in small corymbs; prickles uniform; growth vigorous, 5-6 ft.; hips round, red; Eurosa, Caninae, (42); from Europe and western Asia; shows some relationship to *R. gallica*

R. marginata godetii ((Grenier) Rehder) Sp, lp; flowers small; low shrub growth

R. × mariae-graebneriae (Ascherson & Graebner) – See **Maria Graebner**

R. marrettii (Léveillé) Sp, mp, 1908; flowers rose-pink, 1½-2 in., borne usually in clusters of 3-6; foliage oblong; stems dark purple; hips subglobose, red, -½ in.; very hardy; Eurosa, Cinnomomeae, (14); from the island of Sakhalin; closely related to *R. cinnamomea*

R. maximilianii (Nees) – See ***R. woodsii*** (Lindley)

R. maximowicziana (Regel) Sp, w, before 1880; flowers 1½ in., borne in many-flowered corymbs; partially climbing. growth; Eurosa, Synstylae, (14); native to Korea and Manchuria

R. maximowicziana jackii (Rehder) Sp, w, 1905; prickles without bristles

R. maximowicziana pilosa (Nakai) Sp, w, 1916; flowers leaf and stalks pubescent

R. melina (Greene) Sp, mp; flowers rose pink, 2 in., borne singly; growth well-branched, 3 ft.; native to Colorado and Utah

R. mexicana (Watson, not Willdenow) – See ***R. carolina glandulosa*** (Farwell)

R. michiganensis (Erlanson) Sp, mp; intermediate between *R. blanda* and *R. palustris*

R. micrantha (Borrer ex Sm.) Sp, lp, before 1800; flowers pale pink, small; very vigorous (6 ft.) growth; Eurosa, Caninae, (35, 42); closely resembling *R. eglanteria*; common throughout Europe and Asia Minor, and has naturalized in parts of the U.S.

R. microcarpa (hort.) – See ***R. multiflora*** (Thunberg ex Murray)

R. microcarpa (Lindley) – See ***R. cymosa*** (Trattinnick)

R. microphylla (Roxburgh) – See ***R. roxburghii*** (Trattinnick)

R. × microphylla alba odorata – See **Alba Odorata**

R. microphylla hirtula (Regel) – See ***R. roxburghii hirtula*** (Rehder & Wilson)

R. × micrugosa (Henkel) S, lp, before 1905; flowers 3 in., single to semi-dbl.; some repeat; hips orange-red, depressed-globose, about 1 3/4 in. diameter; [*R. roxburghii* × *R. rugosa*]; spontaneous hybrid, originating in the Botanical Garden at Strasbourg

R. × micrugosa alba – See **Micrugosa Alba**

R. minutifolia (Engelmann) Sp, 1882; flowers pink or white, short-pediceled, 1 in., borne singly or in small clusters; early spring; foliage very small, gray-green, deeply laciniated, ovate, 5-7 ½ in. leaflets; prickles slender, brown, extending beyond the leaves; growth to 4 ft., in thickets; hips bristly, round, red, about in. in diameter; Minutifoliae (Hesperhodos), (14); first discovered by C. C. Parry in 1882; native to west coast of Baja California and southern California

R. mirifica (Greene) – See ***R. stellata mirifica*** (Greene)

R. × mitcheltonii – See **Mitcheltonii**, S

R. mitissima (Gmelin) – See ***R. spinosissima inermis*** (Rehder)

R. mohavensis (Parish) – See ***R. woodsii*** (Lindley)

R. mohavensis (Parish) Sp, dp; flowers small; prickles numerous, straight; growth much-branched, to 3 ft.; hips round; confined to a very small area in southern California; a form of *R. woodsii*

R. mokanensis (Léveillé) – See ***R. wichurana*** (Crépin)

R. mollis (Smith) Sp, dp, 1818; flowers deep pink, rarely white, 1½-2 in., single, borne 1-3 together; summer bloom; foliage dark gray-green; few prickles; stems tinged purple; compact (4 ft.) growth; hips small, round or pear-shaped, somewhat pendulous; Eurosa, Caninae, (28); possibly related to *R. rubrifolia* and *R. pendulina*

R. mollissima (Willdenow) – See ***R. mollis*** (Smith)

Rosa Monnet – See **Mme Rosa Monnet**, HP

R. monophylla (hort. ex von Steudel) – See ***Hulthemia persica***

R. monstrosa (Breiter) – See **Green Rose**

R. montana (Chaix) Sp, lp, 1872; flowers pink, 1½ in., borne singly or in small clusters; foliage tinged red; vigorous growth (5-10 ft.); oblong-ovoid, ¾ in. fruit; Eurosa, Caninae, (42); native to the mountains of Central Europe; very similar to *R. canina*

R. montana chavinii ((Rapin ex Reuter) Christ) – See ***R. chavinii*** (Rapin ex Reuter)

R. montezumae (Humboldt & Bonpland) Sp, dp, 1825; flowers pale red, 1½ in.; June-blooming; growth to 3 ft.; Eurosa, Caninae, (35); discovered in Mexico; very similar to *R. eglanteria*

R. monticola (Aiton) Sp, dp, before 1794; prickles moderate; stems reddish-brown; hips bright red; extremely hardy; resembles both *R. montana* and *R. cinnamomea*

R. morrisonensis (Hayata) Sp, lp; a form of *R. webbiana*, with shorter, more uniform prickles and smaller leaflets

R. moschata (Herrmann) Sp, w, 1540; sepals lanceolate, 2 entire, 3 pinnatifid; flowers white, on slender pedicels, 1½-2 in., single to semi-dbl., borne usually in 7-flowered corymbs, moderate musk fragrance; summer-fall bloom; remontant in warm, humid climates; foliage oblong, acute, serrate, dark green, glossy; prickles small, uniformly hooked; hips round, small, red; Eurosa, Synstylae, (14)

R. moschata abyssinica (Rehder) – See ***R. abyssinica*** (R. Br.)

R. moschata adenochaeta – See ***R. multiflora adenochaeta*** ((Koidz.) Ohwi ex H.Ohba)

R. moschata autumnalis – See ***R. moschata*** (Herrmann)

R. moschata flore semipleno (Thory) – See ***R. moschata plena*** (Weston) dbl.

R. moschata grandiflora – See **Moschata Grandiflora**

R. moschata helenae (Rehder & Wilson) – See ***R. helenae*** (Rehder & Wilson)

R. moschata leschenaultii (Crépin) – See ***R. leschenaultii*** (Wight & Arnott)

R. moschata micrantha (Crépin) – See ***R. helenae*** (Rehder & Wilson)

R. moschata nastarana (Christ) – See **Nastarana**

R. moschata nepalensis (Lindley) – See ***R. brunonii*** (Lindley)

R. moschata nivea (Lindley) – See **Dupontii**

R. moschata pissardii (Bean) – See **Nastarana**

R. moschata plena (Weston) Sp, w, before 1596; flowers dbl.

R. moschata sempervirens – See ***R. sempervirens*** (Linnaeus)

R. moyesii (Hemsley & Wilson) Sp, mr, 1906; flowers deep blood-red through deep rose to light pink, 1¾-2½ in., single, borne singly or in pairs; summer bloom; foliage large, light green; nearly thornless; growth to 10 ft.; hips pitcher-shaped, orange-red; Eurosa, Cinnomomeae, (42); from south-central China; first collected by E. A. Pratt in 1894

R. moyesii fargesii (Rolfe) Sp, mr, 1916; flowers rich rose-red, 1½ in., single; foliage leaflets smaller than the type, broad-oval to suborbicular; growth to 8 ft.

R. × moyesii hillieri – See **Hillier Rose**

R. moyesii rosea (Rehder & Wilson) Sp, lp, 1908; flowers with dark purple calyces, single; leaves coarsely serrate; growth to 8-10 ft.; Eurosa, Cinnomomeae, (28); from China

R. mulliganii (Boulenger) Sp, w, 1917-1919; flowers 2 in.; ovoid, ½ in. long fruit; Eurosa, Synstylae, (14); raised at Wisley (RHS) from seed collected in China by Forrest in 1917

R. multibracteata (Hemsley & Wilson) Sp, lp, 1910; flowers pink, with numerous crowded bracts, 1¼ in., single, borne in large panicles, but occasionally produced individually along the stems; intermittent bloom from June to Sept.; foliage small, with 7-9 leaflets; stems slender; much-branched, 6 ft. growth; hips ovoid, orange-red, -½ in. long; not dependably hardy; Eurosa, Cinnomomeae, (28); resembling *R. willmottiae*; first collected by E. H. Wilson in the Min River valley in China in 1904

R. multiflora (Thunberg ex Murray) Sp, w, 1784; flowers usually white, with prominent golden stamens, 2½-3 cm., borne in many-flowered pyramidal corymbs; summer bloom; foliage having deeply toothed or fringed stipules, 7-11 leaflets; prickles moderate, stout, recurved; growth with recurving or climbing branches; hips small, globular, bright red; Eurosa, Synstylae, (14, 28); not introduced into Europe until 1862; date of 1804 sometimes quoted refers to *R. multiflora carnea*

R. multiflora adenochaeta ((Koidz.) Ohwi ex H.Ohba) Sp, dp; flowers deep bright pink, fading lighter, single, borne in clusters, slight fragrance

R. multiflora alba Sp, w; flowers flesh, aging to white, medium, very dbl.; introduced to Europe in 1844 from Japan

R. multiflora calva (Franchet & Savatier) Sp, w, before 1900

R. multiflora carnea (Thory) Sp, lp, 1804; flowers pearly pink, fading to white, 4 cm., dbl., borne in small clusters; foliage 5-7 leaflets; few prickles; possibly a natural hybrid of *R. chinensis* and *R. multiflora cathayensis*; sent by Thomas Evans to the English East India Company

R. multiflora cathayensis (Rehder & Wilson) Sp, lp, 1907; flowers rosy pink, fading to pale pink, having prominent yellow stamens, 4 cm., single, flat, borne in rather flat corymbs; presumed to be a variant of *R. multiflora calva*

R. multiflora dawsoniana (hort.) – See ***R. multiflora roseiflora*** ((Focke) Rehder)

R. multiflora grandiflora – See **Moschata Grandiflora**

R. multiflora nana (hort.) Pol, w, after 1875; flowers white to pink, very small, single to semi-dbl., borne in clusters; recurrent bloom; bushy, dwarf (1-2 ft.) growth

R. multiflora platyphylla (Rehder & Wilson) – See **Seven Sisters**

R. multiflora plena (Regel) – See ***R. multiflora carnea*** (Thory)

R. multiflora roseiflora ((Focke) Rehder) Sp, lp; flowers 1 in., semi-dbl.

R. multiflora thunbergiana (Thory) – See ***R. multiflora*** (Thunberg ex Murray)

R. multiflora watsoniana (Matsumura) – See ***R. watsoniana*** (Crépin)

Rosa Mundi – See ***R. gallica versicolor*** (Linnaeus)

R. mundi – See ***R. gallica versicolor*** (Linnaeus)

Rosa Mundi T, dr, 1898, Conard & Jones; flowers deep crimson, large, cupped

Rosa Munné HT, rb, 1952, Munné, M.; flowers red to saffron-pink, large, dbl.; foliage clear green; very vigorous growth; [Maria Serrat × Paz Vila]

R. muriculata (Greene) – See ***R. gymnocarpa*** (Nuttall)

R. murielae (Rehder & Wilson) Sp, w, 1904; flowers pale pink to white, 1 in., single, borne in clusters of 3-7; foliage small, pointed; prickles numerous, reddish-pink; growth well-branched, to 8 ft.; hips ellipsoid, orange-red, ½-¾ in.; Eurosa, Cinnomomeae, (28); from southwestern China

R. muscosa (Aiton) – See **Communis**

R. muscosa alba (Thory) – See **Shailer's White Moss**

R. muscosa anemonflora (Redouté & Thory) – See **De La Flèche**

R. muscosa multiplex (Redouté) – See **Communis**

R. muscosa simplex (hort. Ex Andrews) – See **Muscosa Simplex** single

R. mutabilis (Correvon) – See **Mutabilis**

R. myriacantha (De Candolle) – See ***R. spinosissima myriacantha*** (Koehne)

R. myriadena (Greene) – See ***R. yainacensis*** (Greene)

R. naiadum (Lunell) – See ***R. macounii*** (Greene)

R. nankinensis (Lour.) – See ***R. chinensis*** (Jacquin)

R. nanothamnus (Boulenger) Sp, mp, 1935; Eurosa, Cinnomomeae, (14)

R. nemorosa (Libert ex Lejeune) – See ***R. micrantha*** (Borrer ex Sm.)

R. neomexicana (Cockerell) Sp, mp; a form of *R. woodsii* with pyriform fruits

R. nipponensis (Crépin) – See ***R. acicularis nipponensis*** (Koehne)

R. nitida (Willdenow) Sp, mp, 1807; flowers bright pink, 1-2 in., single, borne solitary, or in few-flowered corymbs on slender stems; summer bloom; foliage small, glossy, bright green, with 7-9 leaflets; prickles small, straight; stems red-tinged; dwarf (1½ ft.) growth; hips 1/2 in., round, red; very hardy; Eurosa, Cinnamomeae, (14)

R. nitida spinosa (Lewis) Sp, mp; stems with enlarged prickles; native to New England and eastern Canada

R. nivea (De Candolle) – See ***R. laevigata*** (Michaux)

R. × noisettiana (Thory) N, w, 1814, Noisette; flowers blush white

R. noisettiana manettii (Rehder) – See **Manettii**

R. nutkana (Presl) Sp, mp, 1876; flowers pink, 2-2½ in., single, borne usually singly; summer bloom; prickles moderate; stems dark brown-tinged; growth to 5 ft.; hips round, red, ¾ in.; Eurosa, Cinnamomeae, (42); found on the Pacific coast of North America, from southern Alaska to northern California, eastward to southwestern Wyoming

R. nutkana hispida (Fernald) Sp, mp; differs from the type in having hips covered with bristly protuberances

R. nuttalliana (Rehder) – See ***R. palustris nuttalliana*** (Rehder)

R. obtusifolia (Desvaux) Sp, 1905; flowers white or rose, 1¼ in., single, borne singly or in small clusters; foliage with 5-7 leaflets, 1½ in. long, evenly serrated; growth to 12 ft.; ovoid, ½-¾ in. fruit; Eurosa, Caninae, (35); from Europe

R. ochroleuca (Swartz) – See ***R. spinosissima luteola*** (Rehder)

R. odorata (Sweet) – See **Hume's Blush Tea-Scented China**

R. × odorata erubescens (Rehder & Wilson) Misc OGR, lp, before 1949; flowers single; recurrent; possibly the ancestral form of both Park's Yellow and Hume's Blush; found in many parts of southern and western China

R. odorata gigantea ((Crépin) Rehder & Wilson) – See ***R. gigantea*** (Collett ex Crépin)

R. odorata macrocarpa (Watt) – See ***R. macrocarpa***

R. odorata ochroleuca (Lindley) – See **Parks' Yellow Tea-Scented China**

R. odorata pseudindica (Rehder) – See **Fortune's Double Yellow**

R. officinalis (Thory) – See ***R. gallica officinalis*** (Thory)

R. olympica (Donn) – See ***R. gallica*** (Linnaeus)

R. olympica (Déséglise) Sp; a natural hybrid of *R. orientalis*

R. omeiensis (Rolfe) Sp, w; flowers small, with 4 petals, single; leaves composed of 9-17 finely-divided, fernlike leaflets; prickles flattened, wide-based; growth vigorous, to 10 ft.; hips bright crimson, 1/2 in., pear-shaped, borne on bright yellow stalks; first discovered on Mt. Omei by Faber in 1886, but introduced into England by E.H. Wilson in 1901

R. omeiensis atro-sanguinea Sp, w; hips entirely crimson

R. omeiensis chrysocarpa ((Rehder) Rowley) – See ***R. sericea chrysocarpa*** ((Rehder) S.G.Haw)

R. omeiensis polyphylla (Geier) – See ***R. sericea polyphylla*** (Geier)

R. omeiensis pteracantha (Rehder & Wilson) – See ***R. sericea pteracantha*** (Franchet)

R. omeiensis pteracantha lutea Sp, ly

R. omeiensis pteragonis – See **Pteragonis**

R. omissa (Déséglise) – See ***R. sherardii*** (Davies)

Rosa Orange Triumph Pol, mp, 1943, Verschuren; flowers small, semi-dbl.

R. orbicularis (Baker) Sp, 1908; differs from *R. webbiana* in having almost round, 1/2 in. leaflets; from southwest China

R. oreophila (Rydberg) Sp; differing slightly from *R. nutkana* in armament, foliage and/or stature

R. orientalis (Dupont) Sp, lp, 1905; flowers pink, medium, short-pediceled, borne singly; dwarf growth; Eurosa, Caninae, (35); closely allied to *R. rubiginosa*; native to the mountains of Asia Minor

R. oxyacanthos (Koch) – See ***R. × kochiana*** (Koehne)

R. oxyodon (Boissier) – See ***R. pendulina oxyodon*** (Rehder)

R. paestana – See **Rose du Roi**

R. palustris (Marshall) Sp, mp, 1726; flowers pink or white, 2 in., borne in small corymbs; intermittent from June to August; growth to 8 ft.; Eurosa, Cinnamomeae, (14); inhabiting swampy areas from lower Quebec to Florida and west to Iowa

R. palustris inermis (Schuette) Sp, mp; thornless

R. palustris nuttalliana (Rehder) Sp, mp, before 1949; has somewhat larger blossoms and blooms later (July-Sept.) than the type

R. palustris scandens Sp, mp, before 1824; flowers dbl.; spring bloom

R. parmentieri (Léveillé) – See ***R. davidii elongata*** (Rehder & Wilson)

R. parviflora (Ehrhart) – See ***R. carolina*** (Linnaeus)

R. parviflora glandulosa (Crépin) – See ***R. carolina glandulosa*** (Farwell)

R. parviflora provincialis – See **Blandford Rose**

R. parvifolia (Ehrhart) – See **Burgundian Rose**

R. parvula (Gren. ex Déséglise) – See **Très-Petite Fleur**

R. × paulii (Rehder) – See **Paulii Rosea**

R. × paulii rosea ((Darl.) Rehder) – See **Paulii Rosea**

R. pendulina (Linnaeus) Sp, dp, 1753; flowers purple-crimson, 1½ in., single, borne singly or in clusters of 2-5; very early spring; foliage oblong, with 5-13 leaflets; nearly thornless; stems bright red-brown where exposed to the sun; growth scrubby, medium (3-5 ft.); hips orange-red, urn-shaped, pendulous, 1 in. long; extremely hardy; Eurosa, Cinnomomeae, (28); native to the Alps of central and southern Europe; supposedly introduced into England in the early 17th century

R. pendulina gentilis (Keller) Sp, dp, 1910; flowers deep pink; stems bristly; growth low

R. pendulina haematodes Sp, dp; from Corsica; a form of *R. pendulina* blooming in small clusters and having bright red mid-ribs of the stipules

R. pendulina laevis (Thory) Sp, rb, about 1820; flowers bright red, whitening towards the base, 5 petals; foliage ovate, glabrous, almost always bidentate; nearly thornless; stems reddish; native to the Alps and southern France

R. pendulina malyi (Keller) – See ***R. × malyi*** (Kerner)

R. pendulina oxyodon (Rehder) Sp, mp, 1896; flowers deep rose-pink, 2½ in., single; foliage soft green, with 9 leaflets; growth compact (3-4 ft.); hips semi-pendent, dark red, almost globose; a variant of *R. pendulina*, native to the Caucasus Mountains

R. pendulina plena Sp, dp; flowers deep pink with darker veining; a form of *R. pendulina*

R. pendulina pyrenaica (Keller) Sp, mp, 1815; leaves glandular; stems less red-tinted than the type; dwarf growth

R. pennsylvanica (Andrews) – See ***R. virginiana*** (Miller)

R. pennsylvanica plena (Marshall) Sp, mp, 1803; flowers dbl.

R. pennsylvanica (Wangenheim) – See ***R. carolina*** (Linnaeus)

R. pennsylvanica flore pleno (Andrews) – See ***R. pennsylvanica plena*** (Marshall) dbl.

R. pensylvanica (Michaux) – See ***R. palustris*** (Marshall)

R. × penzanceana (Rehder) – See **Lady Penzance**

R. persetosa (Rolfe) Sp, dp, 1895; flowers deep pink, 1 in., single, borne in large panicles; numerous prickles; growth vigorous; Eurosa, Cinnomomeae, (14); appears to be a natural hybrid of *R. macrophylla* and *R. acicularis*; from western China

R. persica (Michaux) – See ***Hulthemia persica***

R. phalloidea – See ***R. sempervirens latifolia*** (Thory)

R. phoenicia (Boissier) Sp, w, about 1885; flowers snow white, 2 in., single, borne in many-flowered panicles; not hardy; Eurosa, Synstylae, (14); from Aisa Minor; closely allied to *R. moschata*

R. pimpinellifolia (Linnaeus) – See ***R. spinosissima*** (Linnaeus)

R. pimpinellifolia elasmacantha (Trautvetter) – See ***R. elasmacantha*** (Trautvetter)

R. pimpinellifolia hispida (Godet) – See ***R. spinosissima hispida*** (Koehne)

R. pimpinellifolia inermis (De Candolle) – See ***R. spinosissima inermis*** (Rehder)

R. pimpinellifolia (Christ) – See ***R. tuschetica*** (Boissier)

R. pineliensis (Almq.) – See ***R. coriifolia*** (Fries)

R. pinetorum (Heller) Sp, dp; flowers deep rose, floral tube usually not glandular, 1½ in., borne singly; foliage leaflets doubly serrate, with gland-tipped teeth; growth to 3 ft.; Eurosa, Cinnomomeae; thought to be a natural hybrid of *R. nutkana* and *R. californica*

R. pisocarpa (Grav) Sp, mp, 1877; flowers pink, lilac-tinged on short pedicels, 1 in., single, borne in corymbose clusters; intermittent from June to August; prickles few, weak; growth slender, to 6 ft.; hips globose, with a very short neck, numerous, small; Eurosa, Cinnomomeae, (14); ranging from central Alaska to Utah and California

R. pisocarpa ultramontana ((S. Watson) M. Peck) – See ***R. woodsii ultramontana*** ((S.Watson) Jeps.)

R. pissardii (Carrière) – See **Nastarana**

R. platyacantha kokanica – See ***R. kokanica*** (Regel)

R. platyacantha variabilis – See ***R. kokanica*** (Regel)

R. platyphylla ((Thory) Takasima, not Rau) – See **Seven Sisters**

R. poetica (Lunell) – See ***R. woodsii fendleri*** (Rehder)

R. pokornyana (Kmet) Misc OGR, dp, 1916; flowers 1½ in.; foliage purplish; prickles purplish; a *R. rubrifolia* × *R. canina hybrid*

R. × pokornyana (Kmet) – See **Pokornyana**

R. × polliniana (Sprengel) – See **Polliniana**

R. polyantha (Roessig) – See **Summer Damask**

R. polyantha (Siebold & Zuccarini, not Roessig) – See ***R. multiflora*** (Thunberg ex Murray)

R. polyantha grandiflora – See **Moschata Grandiflora**

R. pomifera – See ***R. spinosissima*** (Linnaeus)

R. pomifera (Herrmann) – See ***R. villosa*** (Linnaeus)

R. pomifera duplex (Weston) – See **Duplex**

R. pomponia (Thory ex Redouté) – See **Burgundian Rose**

R. pomponia (Roessig or Thory) – See ***R. × centifolia pomponia*** (Lindley)

Rosa Poncheaux – See **Poncheau-Capiaumont**, HCh

R. portlandica (Roessig) – See **Duchess of Portland**

R. pouzinii (Trattinnick) Sp, mp, 1905; flowers pink, small, borne singly or in small clusters; ellipsoid, small fruit; not dependably hardy; Eurosa, Caninae, (42); found in parts of southern Europe and northern Afica; similar to *R. micrantha* (Smith)

R. praelucens (Byhouwer) Sp, lp; hips near to *R. roxburghii*, but less bristly, leaflets larger; Microphyllae (Platyrhodon)

R. pratensis (Rafinesque) – See ***R. carolina*** (Linnaeus)

R. pratincola (Greene) – See ***R. suffulta*** (Greene)

R. pratincola alba (Rehder) Sp, w, 1901

Rosa Prattigora S, mr, 1956, Kordes, W.; bud long, pointed; flowers light red, very large, open, borne in small clusters, slight fragrance; continuous; foliage light green, leathery; stems light brown; growth vigorous, upright, bushy (to 6 ft.); [*R. prattii* × *R. rugosa alba*]

R. prattii (Hemsley) Sp, mp, 1903; flowers deep pink, ¾ in., borne in small clusters; foliage dainty; growth slender, to 6 ft.; hips tiny, ovoid, scarlet; Eurosa, Cinnomomeae, (14); from southwestern China; related to *R. sertata*

R. primula (Boulenger) Sp, ly, 1936; flowers yellowish-white, short-stemmed, single, intense incense fragrance; very early spring; foliage small, stiff, incense-scented; numerous prickles; thin, flexible stems; growth to 6-7 ft.; hips bright red; Eurosa, Pimpinellifoliae, (14); discovered by Meyer, near Samarcande, about 1890, but not introduced until 1910; historically confused with *R. ecae*

R. procera (Salisbury) – See **White Rose of York**

Rosa Prominent Gr, mp, Sieber; flowers large, dbl; [sport of Prominent]; int. by Kordes, 1982

R. prostrata (De Candolle) – See ***R. sempervirens prostrata*** (Desvaux)

R. × proteiformis (G.D. Rowley) – See **Proteiformis** semi-dbl.

R. provincialis (Miller) – See ***R. gallica officinalis*** (Thory)

R. provincialis (Miller) – See **Cabbage Rose**

R. provincialis alba (Andrews) – See **White Provence**

R. provincialis minor – See **Burgundian Rose**

R. × pruhoniciana (Kriechbaum) – See **Hillier Rose**

R. pseudindica (Lindley) – See **Fortune's Double Yellow**

R. pseudo-scabrata (Blocki ex R.Keller) – See ***R. canina*** (Linnaeus)

R. puberulenta (Rydberg) Sp, mp; prickles deflexed or curved; hips round; a form of *R. woodsii*

R. pubescens (Baker) – See ***R. rugosa plena*** (Byhouwer)

R. pulchella (Salisbury) – See ***R. spinosissima*** (Linnaeus)

R. pulverulenta (von Bieberstein) – See ***R. glutinosa*** (Sibthorp & Smith)

R. pumila (Scop.) – See ***R. gallica pumila*** (Seringe)

R. punicea (Miller) – See ***R. foetida bicolor*** ((Jacquin) Willmott)

R. pusilla (Rafinesque) – See ***R. carolina villosa*** (Rehder)

R. pustulosa (Bertol.) – See ***R. glutinosa*** (Sibthorp & Smith)

R. pyrenaica (Gouan) – See ***R. pendulina pyrenaica*** (Keller)

R. pyrifera (Rydberg) – See ***R. woodsii*** (Lindley)

R. pyrifera (Rydberg) Sp, w; flowers 1½ in., single, borne in small clusters; hips ellipsoid or pear-shaped, with a distinct neck; native to the Rocky Mountains; a form of *R. woodsii*

R. rapa (Bosc) – See **Rose d'Amour**

R. rapini (Boissier & Balansa) – See ***R. hemisphaerica*** (Herrmann)

R. rapini (Boissier) – See ***R. hemisphaerica rapini*** ((Boissier) Rowley)

R. reclinata (Thory) – See **Boursault Rose**

R. reducta (Baker) – See ***R. multibracteata*** (Hemsley & Wilson)

R. redutea rubescens (Thory) – See ***R. nitida*** (Willdenow)

R. regeliana ((Linden & André)) – See ***R. rugosa*** (Thunberg)

R. regelii (Reut.) – See ***R. beggeriana*** (Schrenk ex Fischer & Meyer)

R. remensis (De Candolle) – See **Burgundian Rose**

R. repens (Scopoli) – See ***R. arvensis*** (Hudson)

R. reuteri (Godet) – See ***R. dumalis*** (Bechstein)

R. × reversa (Waldstein & Kitaibel) Misc OGR, mr, 1820; foliage very dark green; growth upright, to 5 ft.; hips scarlet, 3/4 in., obovoid, pendulous; assumed to be *R. pendulina* × *R. spinosissima*; found in the Alps and southern Europe

R. richardii (Rehder) – See **St John's Rose**

R. rouletii (Correvon) – See **Rouletii**

R. roxburghii (Trattinnick) Sp, mp, before 1814; bud prickly, like a chestnut burr; sepals alternating prickly and smooth; flowers lilac pink on short pedicels, 2-2½ in., dbl., borne often singly; spring-summer bloom; foliage small, deep green, with 9-15 leaflets; prickles dark red, upturned, paired at the base of each leaf stem; stems angularly jointed, gray-brown, peeling; growth to 6 ft.; depressed-globose, 1-1½ in. fruit; Microphyllae (Platyrhodon), (14)

R. roxburghii hirtula (Rehder & Wilson) Sp, mp, before 1862; flowers lilac pink; foliage pubescent beneath; Microphyllae (Platyrhodon), (14); collected by Maximowicz in central Japan

R. roxburghii normalis (Rehder & Wilson) Sp, lp, 1864; flowers white to light pink, single, borne singly and in small clusters; Microphyllae (Platyrhodon), (14); found in Szechuan, China; color varies naturally from blush pink to deep purple-pink

R. roxburghii plena (Rehder) Sp, dp, 1820; flowers dbl.; recurrent; found in Canton, China, by Roxburgh

R. roxosa (Henkel) – See ***R. × micrugosa*** (Henkel)

R. rubella (Smith) – See ***R. × reversa*** (Waldstein & Kitaibel)

R. rubeoides (Andrews) – See ***R. multiflora carnea*** (Thory)

R. rubicans (Roessig) – See **Great Maiden's Blush**

R. rubifolia (Robert Brown) – See ***R. setigera tomentosa*** (Torrey & Gray)

R. rubiginosa (Linnaeus) Sp, lp, before 1551; flowers very light pink or white, with darker edges, 2 in., single, borne singly or in few-flowered corymbs; foliage glandular and fragrant (apple), with 5-7 oval, small leaflets; vigorous, to 8 ft. growth; hips small, round or ovoid, orange to scarlet, numerous; Eurosa, Caninae, (35, 42); common in the British Isles and other parts of Europe; naturalized in western Asia, northern Africa, and North America

R. rubiginosa (Britton & Brown) – See ***R. micrantha*** (Borrer ex Sm.)

R. rubiginosa dimorphacantha (Martinis) – See ***R. eglanteria duplex*** (Weston)

R. rubiginosa duplex Sp, m; flowers reddish-purple, 10 petals; first described by Parkinson in 1629; flowers more fragrant than type, but foliage less so.

R. rubiginosa magnifica – See **Magnifica**

R. rubiginosa nemoralis (Thory) – See ***R. micrantha*** (Borrer ex Sm.)

R. rubiginosa parvifolia (Willdenow) – See ***R. pouzinii*** (Trattinnick)

R. rubra (Blackwell) – See ***R. gallica*** (Linnaeus)

R. rubra plena spinosissima pedunculo muscosa (Boerhaave) – See **Communis**

R. rubrifolia (Villars) Sp, mp, 1789; flowers vivid pink, 1½ in., star-like, borne 1-3 together; spring bloom; foliage reddish tinged, bluish green, with 5-7 small leaflets; almost thornless; growth to 5-8 ft.; hips subglobose, bright red; very hardy; Eurosa, Caninae, (28); native to the mountains of central and southern Europe

R. rubrifolia livida (Host) Sp, mp; foliage somewhat darker than type

R. rubrifolia pubescens (Koch) Sp, mp; foliage slightly pubescent

R. rubrispina (Bosc ex Poir.) – See ***R. nitida*** (Willdenow)

R. rubrosa (Preston) – See **Carmenetta**

R. rubro-stipullata (Nakai) – See ***R. marrettii*** (Léveillé)

R. × rubrosa (Preston) S, mp, before 1903; flowers large; [*R. glauca* × *R. rugosa*]

R. rubus (Léveillé & Vaniot) Sp, w, 1907; sepals downy; flowers single, borne in dense corymbs, moderate fragrance; foliage greyish-green, simple dentate; prickles short, hooked; stems purplish; climbing, 20 ft. growth; hips subglobose, about in., dark scarlet; Eurosa, Synstylae, (14); native to western and central China; closely related to *R. helenae*

R. rubus nudescens ((Stapf) Rowley) Sp, w

R. rudiuscula (Greene) Sp, mp, 1917; flowers pink, 2 in., borne in small corymbs; foliage with 5-9 leaflets; prickles very bristly; hips globose, 1/2 in., red; Eurosa, Carolinae, (28); occurring from northern Oklahoma to Wisconsin

R. × ruga (Lindley) – See **Ruga**

R. rugosa (Thunberg) Sp, m, before 1846; flowers purple or white, 2½-3½ in., borne singly or in small clusters; spring-fall bloom; foliage rugose, shining, darkgreen; growth to 6 ft.; hips depressed-globose, to 1 in., brick-red; Eurosa, Cinnomomeae, (14); botanists now agree that forms 'rubra' and 'regeliana' are indistinguishable from the type

R. rugosa alba (Rehder) Sp, w, 1784; bud delicately tinted pink; flowers large, single, borne singly or in small clusters; from Russia

R. rugosa albiflora (Koidzumi) – See ***R. rugosa alba*** (Rehder)

R. rugosa albo-plena (Rehder) Sp, w, before 1949; flowers dbl.; probably a sport of *R. rugosa alba*

R. × rugosa atropurpurea (hort.) – See **Atropurpurea**

R. × rugosa calocarpa (hort.) – See **Calocarpa**

R. rugosa chamissoniana (Meyer) Sp; almost thornless

R. × rugosa kamtchatica ((Ventenat) Regel)) – See **Kamtchatica**

R. rugosa plena (Byhouwer) Sp, m, about 1880; flowers magenta-purple, dbl.; very hardy shrub on the prairies, where it is called Empress of the North; from Russia

R. rugosa rebro-plena (Rehder) – See ***R. rugosa plena*** (Byhouwer)

R. rugosa regeliana (Wittmack) – See ***R. rugosa*** (Thunberg)

R. × rugosa repens alba – See **Paulii**

R. × rugosa repens rosea (Paul) – See **Paulii Rosea**

R. rugosa rosea (Rehder) Sp, mp, before 1949; flowers single

R. rugosa rubra (Rehder) – See ***R. rugosa*** (Thunberg)

R. rugosa scabrosa (hort.) – See **Scabrosa**

R. rugosa thunbergiana (Meyer) – See ***R. rugosa rugosa***

R. rugosa typica (Regel) – See ***R. rugosa*** (Thunberg)

R. × rugotida – See **Rugotida**

R. ruscinonensis (Grenier & Déséglise) – See ***R. moschata*** (Herrmann)

R. russeliana (Loudon) HSem; [*R. sempervirens* × *R. chinensis*]

R. rydbergii (Greene) – See ***R. arkansana*** (Porter)

R. sabini (Woods) – See ***R. × involuta*** (Smith)

R. × salaevensis perrieri ((Songeon ex Déséglise) Rouy) S; flowers rose-purple, borne 1-3 together; [*R. dumalis* × *R. pendulina*]

R. salicifolia (Thory) – See ***R. palustris*** (Marshall)

R. salictorum (Rydberg) Sp, mp; flowers pink, 1½ in., borne in corymbs; foliage leaflets ovate oblong, mostly 2 in long, 5-7; prickles nearly spineless; growth to about 12 ft.; hips globose, about 1/2 in.; Eurosa, Cinnomomeae, (14); a form of *R. woodsii*

R. sancta (Richard) – See **St John's Rose**

R. sandbergii (Greene) – See ***R. woodsii*** (Lindley)

R. sarrulata (Rafinesque) – See ***R. carolina glandulosa*** (Farwell)

R. saturata (Baker) Sp, dp, 1914; flowers bright pink, anthers purple, 2 in., borne usually solitary; foliage large; nearly thornless; stems brownish-green; growth erect, branching, to 8 ft.; hips numerous, globose-ovoid, ¾ in. long, coral-red; Eurosa, Cinnomomeae, (28); from central and southwest China; introduced in 1906; related to *R. moyesii*

R. saxatilis (Steven) – See ***R. corymbifera*** (Borkhausen)

R. sayi (Schweinitz) – See ***R. acicularis*** (Lindley)

R. sayi (Watson, not Schweinitz) – See ***R. acicularis sayi*** (Rehder)

R. scandens (Miller) – See ***R. sempervirens scandens*** (De Candolle)

R. × scharnkeana (Graebner) – See **Scharnkeana**

R. scopulosa (Briquet) – See **Pokornyana**

R. semperflorens (Curtis) – See **Slater's Crimson China**

R. semperflorens minima (Sims) – See ***R. chinensis minima*** (Voss)

R. sempervirens (Linnaeus) Sp, w, 1629; bud small, ovoid; flowers single, borne in few-flowered corymbs, moderate musky fragrance; summer bloom; foliage evergreen, small, dark green, glossy, persistent; prickles few, small, hooked, red; stems thin, flexible, bright green; growth climbing or trailing, vigorous; hips small, round or ovoid, orange-red, 1-2 cm; Eurosa, Synstylae, (14, 21, 28); native to the Mediterranean region; possibly intermediate between *R. moschata* and *R. arvensis*

R. sempervirens anemoniflora (Regel) – See ***R. anemoneflora*** (Fortune)

R. sempervirens latifolia (Thory) Sp, w, before 1824; differing from the type in leaf formation

R. sempervirens leschenaultiana (Redouté & Thory) – See ***R. leschenaultii*** (Wight & Arnott)

R. sempervirens major – See **Plena**

R. sempervirens micrantha (Rouy) Sp, w; differing from the type in leaf formation

R. sempervirens microphylla (De Candolle) Sp, w; differing from the type in leaf formation

R. sempervirens odorata – See **Triomphe de Bolwyller**

R. sempervirens prostrata (Desvaux) Sp, w; flowers borne mostly solitary; foliage small; stems weak, trailing; ovoid fruit

R. sempervirens scandens (De Candolle) Sp, w, before 1750; subglobose fruit; canes more rigid than the type; flowers borne more freely, and with stronger fragrance

R. sepium (Thuillier) – See ***R. agrestis*** (Savi)

R. serafinii (Viviani) Sp, lp, 1914; flowers pink, very short-stalked, 1 in., borne singly; globose-ovoid fruit; Eurosa, Caninae, (35); closely allied to *R. rubiginosa*; native to the Mediterranean region; first described in 1824

R. seraphini (Viviani) – See ***R. serafinii*** (Viviani)

R. seraphinii – See ***R. sicula*** (Trattinnick)

R. sericea (Lindley) Sp, w, 1822; flowers creamy white, 1-2 in., 4-5 petals; early spring; foliage with 7-11 leaflets; prickles prominent; growth to 12 ft.; hips globose or turbinate; Eurosa, Pimpinellifoliae, (14); from the Himalayas

R. sericea chrysocarpa ((Rehder) S.G.Haw) Sp, w, before 1949; hips bright yellow

R. sericea denudata (Franchet) Sp, w; prickles branches unarmed

R. sericea hookeri (Regel) Sp, w; prickles branches glandular

R. sericea nigra Sp, w; differs from the type in having almost-black canes and ruby-red prickles

R. sericea omeiensis ((Rolfe) A.V.Roberts) – See ***R. omeiensis*** (Rolfe)

R. sericea omeiensis pteracantha – See ***R. sericea pteracantha*** (Franchet)

R. sericea polyphylla (Geier) Sp, w, 1934; foliage leaflets numerous

R. sericea pteracantha (Franchet) Sp, w, 1890; flowers 4 petals, shallow cup, borne all along stems, moderate fragrance; non-remontant; foliage fern-like; prickles large, wing-like, deep red, semi-transparent when young; vigorous (5 ft.), vase shaped growth

R. serpens (Wibel) – See ***R. arvensis*** (Hudson)

R. sertata (Rolfe) Sp, mp, 1904; flowers rose or rose-purple, on short branchlets, 2-2½ in., single; foliage deep green, with 7-15 leaflets; prickles moderate; stems maturing to reddish-brown; slender, graceful, 7 ft. growth; hips ovoid, deep red, 3/4 in.; Eurosa, Cinnomomeae, (14); from central and western China; possibly related to *R. moyesii*

R. setigera (Michaux) Sp, dp, 1810; sepals short, ovate, pointed; flowers deep rose, fading to whitish, 2 in., 5 petals, borne in loose clusters of 5-15 at branch tips; summer bloom; foliage soft, seemingly puckered, unequally dentate; prickles small, reddish, hooked, sparse; growth to 6 ft., branches recurving or climbing; hips globular, in., red; Eurosa, Synstylae, (14); native to eastern North America; functionally dioecious

R. setigera inermis (Palmer & Steyermark) Sp, dp, 1924; leaves glabrous; a spineless form of *R. setigera*

R. setigera serena (Palmer & Steyermark) Sp, dp, 1924; leaves pubescent; no prickles; a thornless version of *R. setigera*

R. setigera tomentosa (Torrey & Gray) Sp, dp, 1811; flowers somewhat small and more numerous than the type; leaves tomentose beneath, dull above; first recorded by Robert Brown

R. setigera variegata Sp, pb

R. setipoda (Hemsley & Wilson) Sp, lp, 1895; flowers rose-pink, 2 in., single, borne in large, loose corymbs; summer bloom; foliage sweetbriar-scented, with 7-9 leaflets; prickles numerous, straight, wide-based; growth to 10 ft.; hips large, pear-shaped, crimson; Eurosa, Cinnomomeae, (28, 42); native to central China

R. setipoda (Rolfe) – See ***R. hemsleyana*** (Täckholm)

R. sherardii (Davies) Sp, dp, 1933; flowers deep pink, 1½-2 in.; foliage bluish green; growth densely branched, 6 ft.; hips ovoid or pear-shaped, ½-¾ in.; Eurosa, Caninae, (28); northern and central Europe

R. sherardii perthensis (Harrison) Sp, dp, 1900; remarkable variety with densely glandular hispid fruit

R. sibirica (Stephan ex Ledeb.) – See ***R. spinosissima altaica*** (Bean)

R. sicula (Trattinnick) Sp, before 1894; flowers deep red to whitish, short-stalked, 1-1¼ in., borne mostly singly, rarely in clusters of up to 4; small, globose fruit; Eurosa, Caninae, (35); first discovered in Sicily, but native to large areas of southern Europe and northern Africa

R. silverhielmii (Schrenk) – See ***R. beggeriana*** (Schrenk ex Fischer & Meyer)

R. silvestris (Herrmann) – See ***R. arvensis*** (Hudson)

R. simplicifolia (Salisbury) – See ***Hulthemia persica***

Rosa Sinfonie F, mp, VEG; flowers medium, semi-dbl.

R. sinica (Linnaeus) – See ***R. chinensis*** (Jacquin)

R. sinica (Aiton) – See ***R. laevigata*** (Michaux)

R. sinowilsonii (Hemsley & Wilson) Sp, w, 1904; flowers 1½ in., borne in large, loose corymbs; hips subglobose, small, red; half hardy; Eurosa, Synstylae, (14); a form of *R. longicuspis*, having buds more rounded, larger foliage, and bearing blooms in larger clusters

R. solandri (Trattinnick) – See ***R. blanda*** (Aiton)

R. sonomensis (Greene) Sp, mp; flowers bright pink, 1-1½ in., borne in in dense few-flowered corymbs; growth to 1 ft.; Eurosa, Cinnomomeae

R. soongarica (Bunge) – See ***R. laxa*** (Retzius)

R. sorbiflora (Focke) – See ***R. cymosa*** (Trattinnick)

R. soulieana (Crépin) Sp, w, 1896; bud pale yellow; flowers sulphur yellow at opening, changing quickly to creamy white, 1½ in., single, borne in compact corymbs, moderate fragrance; June bloom; foliage grey-green, simply dentate; prickles numerous, large, curved; growth to 12 ft.; hips ovoid or subglobose, -½ in. long, orange-red; Eurosa, Synstylae, (14); indigenous to the semi-arid regions of China and Tibet; first discovered by Father Jean André Soulié

R. × spaethiana (Graebner) – See **Spaethiana**

R. spaldingii (Crépin) Sp, before 1904; differing slightly from *R. nutkana* in armament, foliage and/or stature

R. sphaerica (Gren.) – See ***R. canina*** (Linnaeus)

R. spinosissima (Rydberg) – See ***R. cinnamomea*** (Linnaeus)

R. spinosissima (Linnaeus) Sp, w, before 1600; sepals persistent; flowers usually white with a tinge of blush, but sometimes pink or yellow, 1¼-2 in., single, cupped, opening flat, borne on short branches along the stems; spring bloom; foliage small, nearly round to oblong-ovate, with 7-9 leaflets; erect, 3-4 ft. growth; hips globular, black, ½ in.; hardy; Eurosa, Pimpinellifoliae, (28); ranging over Europe and temperate Asia

R. spinosissima altaica (Bean) Sp, w, about 1820; flowers white, tinged sulphur, 3 in., single; few prickles; growth rounded, to 6 ft.; hips purple-black, small, round; found originally in the Altai Mountains of Siberia

R. spinosissima andrewsii (Rehder) Sp, mr, before 1949; flowers light red, large, dbl.

R. spinosissima baltica (hort.) Sp, ly; flowers single; unrecorded botanically

R. spinosissima bicolor (Andrews) Sp, pb, before 1832; flowers pale pink becoming cream flushed with pink, semi-dbl., cupped

R. spinosissima ciphiana (Siebold) Sp, pb, 1684; flowers variegated pink and white; reported as growing wild in Perthshire, England

R. spinosissima fulgens (Bean) Sp, mp; flowers bright rose

R. spinosissima hispida (Koehne) Sp, my, before 1781; flowers sulfur-yellow, 2½-3 in.; growth vigorous, 6 ft.; thought to have been introduced from Iceland;

R. spinosissima inermis (Rehder) Sp, lp, before 1949; nearly thornless; growth moderate

R. spinosissima lutea (Bean) Sp, my; flowers bright yellow

R. spinosissima lutea plena – See **Williams' Double Yellow**

R. spinosissima luteola (Rehder) Sp, ly, before 1949; flowers pale yellow, 2 in.; similar to *R. spinosissima hispida*; from northern China

R. spinosissima mitissima (Koehne) – See ***R. spinosissima inermis*** (Rehder)

R. spinosissima myriacantha (Koehne) Sp, w, before 1820; flowers white, blushed, small; foliage very small; numerous prickles; common in Spain and southern France

R. spinosissima nana (Rehder) Sp, w, before 1949; flowers semi-dbl.; hips oval; from Austria

R. spinosissima pimpinellifolia (Seymour) – See ***R. spinosissima*** (Linnaeus)

R. spinosissima rosea (hort.) – See ***R. spinosissima*** (Linnaeus)

R. × spinulifolia (Dematra) S, mp; sepals persistent; flowers 2-2½ in., single, borne in clusters of 1-3; summer bloom; foliage medium size, with numerous bristles on the midrib; prickles large, straight, slender; growth to 5 ft.; hips ovoid, bright red; [a natural hybrid of *R. pendulina* × *R. tomentosa*]; discovered in 1802; native to parts of Switzerland

R. spinulifolia dematriana – See ***R. × spinulifolia*** (Dematra)

R. spithamea (Watson) Sp, mp; flowers small, single, borne mostly solitary; prickles straight; growth very low (20 in. or less), rhizomatous; Eurosa, Cinnomomeae, (28); stalked glands on sepals, hips and pedicel; allied to *R. californica*; native to Coast Range of northern California

R. spithamea sonomensis ((Greene) Jeps.)) Sp, mp; flowers deep lavender-pink, straw-colored stamens, slight fragrance; non-remontant; foliage often double serrate, with gland-tipped teeth; very low (12 in.), spreading growth

R. stellata (Wooton) Sp, m, 1897; flowers deep rose-purple, 1¾-2¼ in., borne singly; foliage broadly cuneate, obovate, with 3 small (½ in.) leaflets; prickles numerous, slender, pale yellow; growth compact, bushy, freely suckering, to 2 ft.; hips turbinate, galbrous or puberulent with scattered short bristles; Minutifoliae (Hesperhodos), (14); native to the lower elevations of the San Andres Mountains of New Mexico

R. stellata erlansoniae (Lewis) Sp, m; Minutifoliae (Hesperhodos)

R. stellata mirifica (Greene) Sp, m, 1910; flowers bright purplish-pink, large, single; free-flowering; foliage usually with 5 leaflets; prickles floral branches gladrous with many internodal glands; compact (4 ft.) growth; Minutifoliae (Hesperhodos), (14); native to the mountains of northern New Mexico

R. stellata mirifica mirifica (Lewis) Sp, m; Minutifoliae (Hesperhodos)

R. stellata stellata (Lewis) Sp, m; prickles few internodal; Minutifoliae (Hesperhodos)

Rosa Stern – See **Bel Ange**, HT

Rosa Sternenflor S, mp, Schultheis; flowers bright pink, fading to white, yellow stamens, small, single, flat, borne in large clusters, moderate fragrance; recurrent; low (2 ft.), spreading growth; [Sternenflor × unknown]; int. by Rosen von Schultheis, 1995

R. stricta (Macoun) – See ***R. acicularis*** (Lindley)

R. stylosa (Desvaux) Sp, w, 1838; flowers white or light pink, 1½-2 in., borne in small corymbs; prickles sturdy, hooked; growth tall, arching; hips numerous, ovoid, red; native to Europe

R. suavifolia (Lightfoot) – See ***R. rubiginosa*** (Linnaeus)

R. subblanda (Rydberg) – See ***R. blanda*** (Aiton)

R. subglobsa (Sm.) – See ***R. sherardii*** (Davies)

R. subglosa – See ***R. tomentosa subglobosa*** (Smith)

R. × sublaevis (Boullu) – See **Sublaevis**

R. subnuda (Lunell) – See ***R. macounii*** (Greene)

R. subserrulata (Rydberg) Sp, mp, 1930; flowers rose solitary, 2 in.; growth to 2½ ft.; Eurosa, Carolinae, (14, 28); native to Missouri, Arkansas, Oklahoma and Texas; differing only in foliage from *R. carolina*

R. suffulta (Greene) Sp, lp; flowers 1½ in., single, borne in corymbs; first flush on old wood, 2nd flush on new laterals; foliage large, with 7-11 leaflets; numerous prickles; growth dense, low (18 in.); hips globose, large; very hardy; native to the Great Plains, from central Alberta ot northern Texas; exceptionally drought-resistant

R. suffulta alba (Rehder) – See ***R. pratincola alba*** (Rehder)

R. sulphurea (Aiton) – See ***R. hemisphaerica*** (Herrmann)

R. sulphurea nana – See **Pompone Jaune**

R. surculosa (Woods) – See ***R. canina*** (Linnaeus)

R. sweginzowii (Koehne) Sp, mp, 1909; flowers bright pink, 1¾ in., single, borne usually singly, but occasionally in groups of 3; foliage with 7-11 elliptic leaflets; prickles large, brown-red, flat, interspersed with smaller ones; growth vigorous, to 15 ft.; hips oblong, 1 in., bright red; Eurosa, Cinnomomeae, (42); often regarded as synonymous with *R. moyesii rosea*, but it is not; introduced from northwest China by E. H. Wilson in 1910

R. sweginzowii inermis (C.Marquand & Airy Shaw) – See ***R. wardii*** (Mulligan)

R. sweginzowii macrocarpa (hort.) Sp, dp; flowers cerise, large, orange stamens, single, slight fragrance; non-remontant; prickles large, flattened; vigorous (10 ft.) growth; hips bottle shaped, large, orange

R. sylvatica (Gaterau) – See ***R. gallica*** (Linnaeus)

R. sylvestris pomifera – See ***R. spinosissima*** (Linnaeus)

R. systyla (Bast.) – See ***R. stylosa*** (Desvaux)

R. × tackholmii (Hurst) – See **Tackholmii**

R. taiwanensis (Nakai) Sp, w, 1916; flowers borne in large corymbs; prickles hooked; climbing growth; hips red, globose; native to the mountains of Taiwan

R. taqueti (Léveillé) – See ***R. wichurana*** (Crépin)

R. taurica (M.Bieb.) – See ***R. corymbifera*** (Borkhausen)

R. terebinthinacea – See ***R. × marcyana*** (Boullu)

R. ternata (Poiret) – See ***R. laevigata*** (Michaux)

R. tetrapetala (Royle) – See ***R. sericea*** (Lindley)

R. thea (Savi) – See **Hume's Blush Tea-Scented China**

R. thoryi (Trattinnick) – See **Seven Sisters**

R. thunbergii (Trattinnick) – See ***R. multiflora*** (Thunberg ex Murray)

R. thyrsiflora (Leroy ex Déséglise) – See ***R. multiflora*** (Thunberg ex Murray)

R. tomentella (Léman) Sp, lp; very similar to *R. canina*

R. tomentosa (Smith) Sp, lp, 1820; flowers pale pink, on longer pedicels, 1½ in.; foliage grayish green, downy; growth to 8 ft.; smaller fruit; Eurosa, Caninae, (35); intermediate between *R. mollis* and *R. canina* and closely allied to *R. pomifera*; distributed throughout Europe

R. tomentosa subglobosa (Smith) Sp, lp, 1824; prickles hooked; subglobose fruit; hips and prickles slightly different from the type

R. trachyphylla (Rau) – See ***R. marginata*** (Wallroth)

Rosa Traum F, mp, 1976, Kordes; bud pointed; flowers 2½ in., 32 petals, high-centered; foliage glossy; vigorous, upright, bushy growth; [Duftwolke × seedling]; int. by Dehner & Co., 1974

R. trifoliata (Bosc) – See ***R. laevigata*** (Michaux)

R. trifoliata (Rafinesque) – See ***R. setigera*** (Michaux)

R. trigintipetala (Dieck. Ex Koehne) – See **Trigintipetala**

R. triphylla (Roxburgh) – See ***R. anemoneflora*** (Fortune)

R. tsinlingensis (Pax & Hoffman, K.) Sp, w, 1922; flowers borne singly, late in season; foliage with 7-13 leaflets; prickles slightly ascending; hips red-brown, ovoid; Eurosa, Pimpinellifoliae; native to the mountains of northern China

R. turbinata (Aiton) – See ***R. × francofurtana*** (Muenchhausen)

R. turkestanica (Regel) Sp, ly, 1900; flowers pale yellow, single, borne in clusters of 1-3; subglobose fruit; Eurosa, Pimpinellifoliae; from Turkestan, closely related to *R. spinosissima*

R. tuschetica (Boissier) Sp, mp, about 1945; foliage differs from *R. glutinosa* in the leaflets; ovate (not obovate) fruit; Eurosa, Caninae; native to the Daghestan Mountains of Russia

R. uchiyamana ((Makino) Makino) – See ***R. multiflora cathayensis*** (Rehder & Wilson)

R. ultramontana (Heller) Sp, mp; prickles straight; hips round; a form of *R. woodsii*

R. unguicularis (Bertol.) – See ***R. webbiana*** (Royle)

R. uniflorella (Buzunova) Sp, w; flowers borne singly; native to seashores of eastern China

Rosa Union HT, Dot

R. usitatissima (Gater.) – See **White Rose of York**

R. velutinaeflora (Déséglise) Sp, pb, before 1872; flowers described by Déséglise as deep velvety red; late spring; hips pyriform, reddish-orange; rose now in commerce is mauve-pink, large

R. vernonii (Greene) – See ***R. stellata*** (Wooton)

Rosa Verschuren HT, lp, 1904, Verschuren; flowers large, full, loose

R. villosa (Linnaeus) Sp, mp, 1771; bud round; flowers bright blush to pink, 1½-2 in., single, borne in small clusters; summer bloom; foliage large, grayish green, with 5-9 long, deeply dentate leaflets; prickles numerous, green, straight, very pointed; densely branched, 6 ft. growth; hips ovoid or subglobose, bristly, large (to 1 in.), scarlet; Eurosa, Caninae, (28); native to Europe and western Asia

R. villosa (Smith) – See ***R. × involuta*** (Smith)

R. villosa (Linnaeus) – See ***R. mollis*** (Smith)

R. villosa mollissima (Rau) – See ***R. mollis*** (Smith)

R. villosa pomifera (Redouté) – See ***R. villosa*** (Linnaeus)

R. vilmorinii (Bean) – See ***R. × micrugosa*** (Henkel)

R. viminea (Linnaeus) – See ***R. spinosissima*** (Linnaeus)

R. virginiana (Miller) Sp, mp, before 1724; flowers bright pink, 2 in., single, borne mostly singly or in small clusters; summer bloom; foliage extremely glossy; prickles moderate; stems reddish-brown; erect, 6 ft. growth; fruit bright red, round, persistent, remaining plump until next spring; Eurosa, Carolinae, (28); widely distributed in eastern North America; probably the first North American species to be cultivated in Europe

R. virginiana (Du Roi) – See ***R. palustris*** (Marshall)

R. virginiana alba (Willmott) – See ***R. carolina alba*** (Rehder) single

R. virginiana blanda (Koehne) – See ***R. blanda*** (Aiton)

R. virginiana humilis (Schneider) – See ***R. carolina*** (Linnaeus)

R. virginiana lamprophylla (Rehder) Sp, mp, 1881; foliage extremely lustrous; growth compact; native to the New England states

R. virginiana plena (Rehder) – See **Rose d'Amour**

R. viridiflora (hort.) – See **Green Rose**

Rosa Vollendung F, pb, 1943, Kordes; bud long, pointed; flowers salmon-pink, reverse capucine-red, large, dbl., borne in clusters; foliage leathery, wrinkled; vigorous, bushy growth; [Crimson Glory × Else Poulsen]

R. vobergii (Graebner ex Späth) – See **Vobergii**

R. × wadeii (Hurran) HRg, op; flowers salmon-pink, 3 in., single; June; foliage rough, yellowish; growth low, sprawling; [*R. rugosa* × *R. moyesii*]; introduced in 1919

R. × waitziana (Trattinnick) – See **Waitziana**

R. × waitziana macrantha (Rehder) – See **Gallica Macrantha**

R. wallichii (Trattinnick) – See ***R. sericea*** (Lindley)

R. walpoleana (Greene) – See ***R. rubiginosa*** (Linnaeus)

R. wardii (Mulligan) Sp, w; flowers borne up to 3 together; prickles almost unarmed

R. wardii culta (Mulligan) Sp, w, 1924; flowers smaller than *R. wardii*, pedicels often glandular, 1¼ in.

R. × warleyensis (Willmott) – See **Warleyensis**

R. watsoniana (Crépin) Sp, lp, about 1870; flowers white to light pink, very small, semi-dbl., borne in large pyramidal corymbs; foliage long, very narrow, waved, pale blue-green, often mottled white; prickles few, very sharp; stems thin, red-green; growth slender (4 ft.); int. as *R. multiflora watsoniana*, from a Japanese garden

R. watsonii (Baker) – See ***R. coriifolia*** (Fries)

R. webbiana (Royle) Sp, lp, 1879; flowers large, single, borne mostly singly; foliage small, with 5-9 leaflets; prickles yellow, straight, ½ in.; stems blue-tinged; growth slender, to 6 ft.; hips ovoid, bright red, 3/4 in.; not dependably hardy; Eurosa, Cinnomomeae, (14); from the lower Himalayas

R. webbiana (Wall.) – See ***R. sertata*** (Rolfe)

R. wichurae (K.Koch) – See ***R. multiflora*** (Thunberg ex Murray)

R. wichurana (Crépin) Sp, w, 1886; flowers 1½-2 in., single, borne in clusters of 6-10, moderate clover fragrance; late summer, with some intermittent repeat; foliage half evergreen, glossy, simply dentate; prickles strong, curved; growth prostrate with creeping branches; hips ovoid, to ½ in., bright red; Eurosa, Synstylae, (14); introduced into Europe around 1860; first described in 1886; native to eastern China, Korea, and southern Japan

R. wichurana grandiflora S, w; flowers 2-2½ in.; assumed to be a tetraploid form; discovered in the fields of an English nursery

R. wichurana rubra (André) – See ***R. barbierana*** (Rehder)

R. wichurana variegata (Uyeki) Sp, w, 1956; flowers single, slight fragrance; non-recurrent; foliage green, heavily spashed with cream and pink (changing to white).; groundcover; spreading growth; hips red; may be several versions under this name; int. by Lens, 1982

R. wichurana yakachinensis Sp, w; flowers very small; foliage leaflets formed like a reversed spoon

R. willdenowii (Sprengel) – See ***R. davurica*** (Pallas)

R. willmottiae (Hemsley) Sp, m, 1907; flowers rose-purple, short-stalked, on short lateral branchlets, 1-1¼ in., borne mostly singly; spring bloom; foliage small, fragrant, with 7-9 leaflets; prickles paired, long, pointed, pale-brown; dense, 5-10 ft. growth; hips orange-red, ½ in.; Eurosa, Cinnomomeae, (14); from China; introduced by Wilson in 1904

R. willmottiana (Léveillé) – See ***R. longicuspis*** (Bertoloni)

R. wilsonii (Borrer) – See ***R. × involuta wilsonii*** ((Borrer) Baker)

R. wilsonii – See ***R. × micrugosa*** (Henkel)

R. wilsonii (hort.) – See ***R. gentiliana*** (Léveillé & Vaniot)

R. × wintoniensis (Hillier) – See **Wintoniensis**

R. woodsii (Lindley) Sp, mp, 1820; flowers pink, rarely white, on very short, smooth pedicels, 1½-2 in., single, borne singly or in clusters of 3; summer bloom; foliage small, obovate, with 5-7 leaflets; prickles numerous, straight or slightly curved; growth to 6 ft.; hips globose, with a distinct, short neck; Eurosa, Cinnomomeae, (14); found in central North America, from Alberta south to Texas, Iowa west to Oregon

R. woodsii adenosepala (Wooton & Standley) – See ***R. adenosepala*** (Wooton & Standley)

R. woodsii fendleri (Rehder) Sp, mp, 1888; a form of *R. woodsii* which is taller and more slender, and has smaller flowers and hips and fewer prickles

R. woodsii mohavensis ((Parish) Jepson) – See ***R. woodsii*** (Lindley)

R. woodsii ultramontana ((S.Watson) Jeps.) Sp, mp, 1888; flowers 2 in., borne in clusters of 3-10; subglobose, small fruit; Eurosa, Cinnomomeae, (14); native to high Sierra Nevada north to British Columbia

R. xanthina ((Auth., not Lindley)) – See ***R. ecae*** (Aitchison)

R. xanthina (Lindley) Sp, my, 1820; sepals persistent; flowers short-stalked, 1¾ in., dbl., borne mostly singly; foliage small, oval, in units of 7-13; prickles numerous, straight; stems brown-tinged; branching, 8 ft. growth; hips globose, red, in.; Eurosa, Pimpinellifoliae, (14); cultivated in Asia for centuries, but not introduced into Europe and America until 1906

R. xanthina ecae ((Aitchinson) Boulenger) – See ***R. ecae*** (Aitchison)

R. xanthina kokanica – See ***R. kokanica*** (Regel)
R. xanthina slingerii – See **Allard**
R. xanthina spontanea (Rehder) – See **Canary Bird**
R. xanthinoides (Nakai) – See ***R. xanthina*** (Lindley)
R. xanthocarpa (Watt) – See ***R. macrocarpa***
R. yainacensis (Greene) Sp, 1912; flowers more numerous; smaller fruit
R. yesoensis (Makino) – See **Iwara**
R. zagrabiensis (Vukotinovics & Braun) Sp, lp; flowers single, borne in clusters of 1-3; prickles moderate; growth to 10 ft.; Eurosa, Caninae; from Hungary
Rosa Zwerg HRg, mp, Baum; flowers medium, semi-dbl., flat, moderate fragrance; recurrent; spreading, low (2 ft.) growth; hips orange-red; very winter hardy; int. in 1984
Rosabel Walker HT, mr, 1922, Cant, F.; bud long, pointed; flowers brilliant velvety crimson, large, dbl.; very vigorous, bushy, spreading growth
Rosabell MinFl, mp, 1988, Cocker, James & Sons; flowers medium, incurving petals, dbl., cupped, borne in clusters, slight fragrance; foliage medium size, medium green, semi-glossy; bushy (15 in.) growth; patio; [(National Trust × Wee Man) × Darling Flame]; int. in 1986; Gold Award, Auckland, NZ, 1994
Rosabella HT, mr, 1941, Giacomasso; flowers red with cerise reflections, very large; foliage abundant; long stems; [Mrs J.D. Russell × Julien Potin]
Rosabella F, op, 1955, Maarse, G.; flowers salmon-pink shaded orange, well-shaped, very dbl., borne in very large clusters; vigorous growth; [Pinocchio × unknown]
Rosabelle Cl T, op, 1900, Bruant; bud long; flowers light pink with salmon reflections, pink reverse, large, borne in small clusters; remontant; foliage glossy, bronze, purplish when young; numerous prickles; [Fortune's Double Yellow × Mme de Tartas]
Rosabelle Barnett F, op, 1970, Gregory; flowers coral, 2½ in., 32 petals, globular; foliage dark; very free growth; [Tropicana × unknown]
Rosabunda F, dp, Wagner, S.; bud cylindrical and short; 30 petals, cupped, borne in flowers in clusters of 3-9 florets, moderate fragrance; foliage dark green, medium large, glossy; [Frankfurt am Main × Maria Callas]; int. by Res. Stn. f. Hortiuclture, Cluj, 1978
Rosada Min, op, 1950, Dot, Pedro; flowers peach edged pink, 25 petals, cupped; foliage small, glossy; compact (7-8 in.) growth; [Perla de Alcanada × Rouletii]; int. by URS
Rosadoll F, pb, Roman, G., and Wagner, S.; flowers intense mauvish-pink, small to medium, semi-dbl., flat, borne in clusters, slight fragrance; foliage medium size, dark green, glossy, healthy; [Rusticana × Lavender Dream]; int. by Res. Stn. for Hort., 2005
Rosadora F, lp, Wagner, S.; flowers 25 petals, rosette, slight fragrance; leaves small, medium green, glossy; growth spreading; [Candy Rose × Yesterday]; int. by Res. Stn. f. Fruit Growing, Cluj, 1996
Rosagold F, dy, Wagner, S.; bud medium long; flowers yellow-apricot, 35 petals, cupped, borne in clusters, intense very fragrance; foliage medium large, light green, glossy; vigorous upright tall growth; [Vigorosa × Allgold]; int. by Res. Stn. f. Fruit Growing, Cluj, 1996
Rosalba HT, pb, 1934, Borgatti, G.; bud long, pointed, streaked carmine; flowers lilac-pink, center shaded salmon-pink, large, dbl.; vigorous growth; [Souv. de Claudius Pernet × Willowmere]
Rosaleda HT, yb, 1958, Moreira da Silva; flowers yellow and white, well-formed, large, dbl.; foliage dark; strong stems; upright, bushy growth; [Monte Carlo × Michele Meilland]
Rosaleen HMsk, dr, 1932, Bentall; flowers crimson, small, dbl., borne in large clusters, slight fragrance; recurrent bloom
Rosaleen Dunn HT, mr, 1942, McGredy; flowers crimson-red, 5½ in., 22 petals, cupped; foliage dark; vigorous growth; int. by J&P
Rosaletta Min, pb, Fryer, Gareth; int. in 1988
Rosali F, mp, 1973, Tantau, Math.; bud long, pointed; flowers large, dbl., moderate fragrance; vigorous, upright growth; RULED EXTINCT 4/85; [seedling × Junior Miss]; int. in 1971
Rosali F, mp, 1985, Tantau, Math.; flowers apple blossom pink, medium, 20 petals, borne in clusters, no fragrance; free-flowering; foliage medium size, medium green, glossy; compact, bushy, low growth; winter hardy; int. in 1983
Rosali 83 – See **Rosali**, F, 1985
Rosalia HT, dp, 1954; bud long, pointed, light cerise; long stems; int. by Cant, F.
Rosalie – See **Unique Carnée**, C
Rosalie T, mp, 1884, Ellwanger & Barry; flowers clear pink, medium, very full, moderate fragrance; [Marie Van Houtte × unknown]
Rosalie – See **Rosella Sweet**, HT
Rosalie Coral Cl Min, ob, 1992, Warner, Chris; bud short, pointed ovoid; flowers bright coral-orange, reverse yellow, 1-1½ in., 20 petals, flat, quilled, borne in large clusters, slight fragrance; recurrent; foliage small, medium green, glossy; prickles few, hooked downward; medium (175-190 cm.), bushy growth; PP9013; [(Elizabeth of Glamis × (Galway Bay × Sutter's Gold)) × Anna Ford]; int. in 1991
Rosalie Richardson HT, lp, 1932, Evans; flowers soft pink
Rosalina S, dp, 1998, Kordes, W.; bud short, slender, pointed; flowers dark pink with traces of lavendar, dark pink reverse, 3 in., 5 petals, cupped to flat, borne in small clusters, slight fragrance; foliage medium size, medium green, dull, Rugosa-like; prickles numerous, narrow, sharp, hooked downward; stems short, strong; bushy, medium (3-4 ft.), sprawling growth; hedges; PP9011; [The Fairy × seedling]; int. by Bear Creek Gardens, 1992
Rosalind HT, op, 1918, Pierson, F.R.; bud bright coral; flowers apricot-pink becoming shell-pink, dbl.; [sport of Ophelia]
Rosalind HT, pb, Bell; int. in 1993
Rosalind Orr English HT, op, 1905, E.G. Hill, Co.; flowers salmon-pink, large, dbl.; [Mme Abel Chatenay × Papa Gontier]
Rosalind Russell HT, mp, 1950, Grillo; bud long, well formed; flowers bright pink, 5 in., 45-50 petals, high-centered; foliage dark, leathery; very vigorous, upright growth; [Briarcliff × Regina Elena]
Rosalinda HT, dp, 1945, Camprubi, C.; flowers carmine, well-formed, large, very dbl.; very vigorous growth; [Editor McFarland × Comtesse Vandal]
Rosalinda F, mp, Wagner, S.; flowers medium pink, 39 petals, cupped, borne in clusters, slight fragrance; foliage medium green, semi-glossy; growth vigorous; [(Frankfurt am Main × Maria Callas) × Foc de Tabara]; int. by Res. Stn. f. Horticulture, Cluj, 1994
Rosalinde F, mp, 1944, Krause; bud round, fat; flowers clear, soft pink, dbl., cupped, borne in large clusters, moderate apples fragrance; recurrent; foliage dark; stout, upright growth
Rosalita HMsk, w, 2000, Lens, Louis; flowers white with yellow button center, 5-6 cm., single, borne in large clusters; foliage large, brown-green and dark green, glossy; few prickles; bushy, medium (120-150 cm.) growth; [(Trier × Surf Rider) × *R. helenae*]; int. by Louis Lens N.V., 1997
Rosalpina HT, pb, 1958, Giacomasso; flowers coppery pink, very large, 50 petals; foliage glossy; strong stems; very vigorous growth; [Signora × unnamed variety]; int. in 1953
Rosalynn Carter Gr, or, 1973, deRuiter; flowers coral-red with orange tones, 3½-4 in., 30 petals, high-centered, moderate spicy fragrance; tall, vigorous, bushy, upright growth; [Mischief × (Queen Elizabeth × Scania)]; originally registered as HT; re-registered as Rosalynn Carter, ARA 1979; int. by C-P, 1978
Rosamaria S, Mansuino; int. in 1974
Rosamond HT, op, 1927, Burbage Nursery; flowers orange-salmon, stamens golden, single; [Red-Letter Day × *R. foetida bicolor*]
Rosamunde F, pb, 1941, Leenders, M.; flowers salmon-carmine, reverse hydrangea-pink, large, dbl.; [seedling × Permanent Wave]
Rosamunde F, mp, Kordes; int. in 1975
Rosanna HT, mp, 1959, Biga, Valentino; bud urn shaped; flowers spinel-rose, open, medium to large; foliage leathery; vigorous, upright, compact growth; RULED EXTINCT 4/77; [Baccará × Gruss an Coburg]
Rosanna LCl, op, 1985, Kordes, W.; flowers salmon pink, large, 35 petals, camellia, moderate fragrance; foliage medium size, medium green, glossy; upright, tall growth; [Coral Dawn × seedling]; int. in 1982; Gold Certificate, The Hague, 2006
Rosanna LCl, op, 2006, W. Kordes' Söhne; flowers salmon pink, 11 cm., full, borne in small clusters, slight fragrance; recurrent; foliage large, glossy; spreading, tall (200 cm.) growth; int. by W. Kordes' Söhne, 2002; Honorable Mention, Hradec Králové, 2006
Rosaperle S, mp; groundcover; int. in 2002
Rosarama HT, op, Martin; int. in 1988
Rosario S, mp, Tantau; flowers bright pink, dbl., cupped, borne in loose clusters, moderate fragrance; foliage dark green, glossy; vigorous, arching growth; int. by Rosen Tantau, 1993
Rosario Algorta HT, ly, 2006, McCann, Sean; flowers cream, reverse cream, 3 in., dbl., borne mostly solitary; foliage medium size, dark green, semi-glossy; prickles medium, straight, light brown, moderate; growth upright, 36 in.; [seedling × seedling]; int. in 2006
Rosarito HT, Moreira da Silva, A.
Rosarium den Blakken F, lp, RvS-Melle; int. in 1998
Rosarium Dortmund LCl, pb, Noack, Werner; flowers bright pink, 4 cm., dbl., rosette, borne in large clusters; recurrent; growth to over 8 ft.; int. as Deutsches Rosarium Dortmund, Noack Rosen, 1995
Rosarium Glücksburg – See **Glücksburg**, S
Rosarium Uetersen LCl, dp, 1977, Kordes, W.; bud ovoid, pointed; flowers deep pink, silvery reverse, ruffled petals, 10-12 cm., very dbl., borne in large clusters, moderate fragrance; recurrent; foliage large, medium green, glossy; vigorous, climbing (10 ft.) growth; [Karlsruhe × seedling]
Rosary – See **Roserie**, HMult
Rosata – See **Rosada**, Min
Rosatherapy HT, dp, 2000, Chiplunkar, C.R.; flowers dark pink, reverse light pink, medium, very full, high-centered, borne mostly singly, slight fragrance; foliage medium size, medium green, semi-glossy; prickles moderate; compact, medium (2½-3 ft.) growth; [sport of Ace of Hearts]; int. by K.S.G. Sons Roses, 1996
Rosatop F, mr, Roman, G., and Wagner, S.; flowers carmine-red with a white eye, small to medium, semi-dbl., flat, slight fragrance; foliage small to medium, dark green, semi-glossy; int. by Res. Stn. for Hort., 2004
Rosazwerg – See **Rosa Zwerg**, HRg
Röschen Albrecht F, or, Tantau; flowers medium, semi-dbl.; int. in 1981
Rose 2,000 F, op, 1998, Cocker, Ann G.; flowers coral vermilion, lighter reverse, ½-1½ in., 8-14 petals, borne

in large clusters; foliage medium size, dark green, glossy; prickles moderate amount, small, slightly hooked; bushy, low, rounded growth; [Trumpeter × Clydebank Centenary]; int. by James Cocker & Sons, 1998

Rose à Bois Jaspé S, mr, 1876, Brassac; flowers bright carminy cherry red, large, full; hybrid canina

Rose à Cent Feuilles – See **Cabbage Rose**, C

Rose à Feuilles de Laitue – See **Bullata**, C

Rose à Feuilles Luisantes M, lp, 1843, Vibert; flowers soft pink edged blush, medium, dbl., globular, borne in clusters; foliage glossy; branching growth

Rose à Parfum de Bulgarie D, mp; flowers medium, dbl., intense fragrance; possibly the same as Kazanlik

Rose à Parfum de Grasse D, mp, before 1867; flowers medium, dbl., intense fragrance

Rose à Parfum de l'Hay HRg, mr, 1901, Gravereaux; flowers cherry-carmine-red, turning blue in heat, large, dbl., globular, intense fragrance; recurrent bloom; foliage not typically rugose; vigorous (5 ft.) growth; [(Summer Damask × Général Jacqueminot) × *R. rugosa*]

Rose Aimée HT, m, 1955, Gaujard; flowers gold, flushed and splashed crimson, well-formed, dbl.; very vigorous, bushy growth; [Peace × seedling]

Rose Angle Ayr, mp, before 1838, Martin; flowers bright lilac rose, semi-dbl., cupped; foliage very fragrant; very vigorous growth

Rose Angle Blush – See **Rose Angle**, Ayr

Rose Anil Gr, m, Viraraghavan, M.S.; int. in 1998

Rose Anil – See **Twilight Secret**, Gr

Rose Anne Cl HT, ob, 1938, Thomas; flowers orange-apricot, base deeper yellow, semi-dbl., cupped; recurrent bloom; foliage large, glossy; very vigorous, climbing (15 ft.) growth; RULED EXTINCT 4/77; [Francesca × Margaret McGredy]; int. by Armstrong Nursery

Rose Apples HRg, dp, 1895, Paul; flowers carmine-rose, large, semi-dbl., moderate fragrance; vigorous growth

Rose Ayez – See **Spectabilis**, HSem

Rose Baby – See **Royal Salute**, Min

Rose Ball S, lp, Beales; flowers soft powder pink, full, globular, borne in dense clusters, slight fragrance; recurrent; foliage green tinted maroon; bushy (3-4 ft.) growth; int. by Peter Beales Roses, 2002

Rose Bampton HT, dp, 1940, Van Rossem; bud carmine; flowers bright China-red, 5½ in., 50 petals, camellia-like; foliage dark; vigorous growth; [Charles P. Kilham × Margaret McGredy]; int. by J&P

Rose Bansal HT, yb, 1972, Friends Rosery; flowers yellow, petal edges sometimes crimson; [sport of Ambossfunken]

Rose Bayard – See **Pearl Essence**, HT

Rose Benary HT, mp, 1908, Lambert, P.; flowers pink, yellow center, large, dbl., moderate fragrance; [Ferdinand Batel × Liberty]

Rose Bengal HT, rb, Ghosh, Mr & Mrs S.; flowers dark, velvety crimson, creamy white reverse, dbl., high-centered, moderate sweet fragrance; int. in 2001

Rose Berkley HT, op, 1928, McGredy; bud long, pointed; flowers deep rosy salmon-pink suffused orange, base orange, large, high-centered; foliage rich green, glossy; very vigorous growth

Rose Bicolore HT, ob, Croix

Rose Blanche HT, w, Croix

Rose Bleu HGal, m, about 1810, Descemet; flowers purple with bluish marbling

Rose Bleu – See **Charles de Mills**, HGal

Rose Bleue HT, m

Rose Bordée de Blanc – See **Comtesse de Chamoïs**, C

Rose Bowl HT, mr, 1961, Morey, Dr. Dennison; bud urn shaped; flowers bright red, large, 35 petals, high-centered, intense fragrance; foliage leathery; long, strong stems; vigorous, upright, bushy growth; PP2188; [Mardi Gras × Chrysler Imperial]; int. by J&P, 1961

Rose Bradwardine HEg, mp, 1894, Penzance; flowers clear rose-pink, center white, single, borne in graceful clusters; seasonal bloom; foliage very fragrant; vigorous growth

Rose Bretagne S, mp

Rose Brillante – See **Brillante**, HGal

Rose Bruford HT, ab, 1961, Wheatcroft Bros.; flowers creamy peach, shaded rosy bronze; [sport of Soraya]

Rose Buffon – See **Buffon**, P

Rose Capucine – See ***R. foetida bicolor*** ((Jacquin) Willmott)

Rose Cascade LCl, lp, Delbard; int. in 1995

Rose Céleste Cl HT, lp, 1986, Delbard; flowers light pink, darker at center, large, 33 petals, cupped, borne in small clusters, moderate fragrance; vigorous, climbing (to 9 ft.) growth; [(Queen Elizabeth × Provence) × (Sultane × Mme Joseph Perraud)]; int. in 1979

Rose Charm HT, mp, 1934, Scittine; flowers sanguineous pink; [sport of Talisman]; int. by Lainson

Rose Châtaigne – See ***R. roxburghii*** (Trattinnick)

Rose Cheal HT, mp, 1970, Herincx; flowers rose-pink, spiral form, 4-5 in., 42 petals; foliage glossy, dark; free growth; [New Style × Scarlet Queen Elizabeth]

Rose Cherry Pastel Min, mr

Rose Chou de Hollande – See **Cabbage Rose**, C

Rose City of Nashik HT, dp, Bulsara; [sport of Christian Dior]; int. in 1990

Rose Cornet – See **Cornet**, HP

Rose Country Min, lp, 2001, Sproul, James; bud pointed; flowers medium, 25-35 petals, borne singly and in small clusters, slight fragrance; foliage medium size, dark green, semi-glossy; prickles medium, few; growth upright, bushy (30-36 in.); garden decorative; disease-resistant; [Sexy Rexy × Michel Cholet]; int. by Sproul Roses By Design, 2001

Rose Csárdás F, mr, Berger, W.; flowers medium, dbl.; int. in 1965

Rose d'Amour Misc OGR, dp; bud deep pink with long sepals; flowers rose pink, outer petals fading to pale pink receptacle wide, semi-dbl., moderate fragrance; summer bloom; foliage leaflets 5-7, rich green, marked with red on leaf stalks & stipules; prickles mixed sizes, scattered; lax growth to 10 ft.; cultivated in Europe since 1768

Rose d'Amour HT, rb, 1936, Gaujard; flowers brown-red, reverse yellow, open, large, dbl.; foliage glossy, dark; vigorous growth

Rose d'Amour – See **Remember Me**, HT

Rose d'Anjou T, dp, before 1836, Vibert; flowers dark pink, center lighter, large, dbl, slight fragrance

Rose d'Annecy S, mp, Adam; flowers clear, bright pink, medium, dbl., borne in clusters, slight fragrance; recurrent; bushy (80 × 60 cm.) growth; int. in 1995; Golden Rose, Geneva, 1995

Rose Dawn HT, pb, 1924, Towill; bud long, pointed; flowers soft shell-pink, base yellow, large, dbl., high-centered; foliage light; vigorous growth; [(Joseph Hill × (Mrs George Shawyer × Unknown)) × Ophelia]

Rose de Batavie – See **Cabbage Rose**, C

Rose de Bengale – See **Sanguinea**, Ch

Rose de Cahors F, rb, Reuter; flowers dark red with silver reverse, dbl., borne in clusters, slight fragrance; recurrent; vigorous (70-80 cm.) growth; int. in 2006

Rose de Cornouaille F, mp, Harkness; flowers pastel pink, large, full, shallow cup, abundant, moderate fragrance; recurrent; foliage dark green; growth to 3 ft.; int. in 2003

Rose de Dijon – See ***R. × centifolia pomponia*** (Lindley), C

Rose de France – See ***R. gallica*** (Linnaeus)

Rose de France HP, mp, 1893, Verdier, E.; flowers carmine pink, reverse silvery, medium to large, full

Rose de France HT, op, 1942, Gaujard; bud ovoid; flowers brilliant salmon tinted orange, very large, dbl.; foliage glossy; dwarf growth

Rose de la Floride – See **Blush Boursault**, Bslt

Rose de La Maître-Ecole HGal, m, 1831, Coquereau; flowers soft pink to lilac, center petals not opening, very large, dbl., cupped, borne in clusters of 2-3, intense fragrance; foliage dark green, oval, medium to large; some prickles, intermixed with fine bristles

Rose de la Petite Chabote F, pb, Lens; flowers pink changing to white, small, dbl., cupped, borne in large clusters, slight fragrance; recurrent; foliage dark green; growth to 80 cm.; int. by Louis Lens SA, 2005

Rose de la Reine – See **La Reine**, HP

Rose de l'Hymen – See **Plena**, A

Rose de Limoux HT, my, Tantau; flowers yellow ocher, dbl., cupped, borne singly and in clusters, slight fragrance; recurrent; robust, medium growth; int. in 2005

Rose de l'Inde Ch, dp

Rose de Lyon HT, ob, 1945, Gaujard; bud pointed; flowers orange-yellow, medium, dbl.; foliage glossy

Rose de Mai – See ***R. majalis*** (Herrmann) dbl.

Rose de Meaux C, dp, before 1814; flowers deep rose, small, very dbl., flat, rosette, borne singly or in clusters of 2-3, moderate fragrance; nonrecurrent; foliage small, clear green; prickles numerous, narrow, straight; growth dwarf, bushy (80 cm.); possibly from Dominique Séguier, Bishop of Meaux, 1637

Rose de Meaux White C, w, before 1824; flowers white with pink centers; white form of *R. centifolia pomponia*

Rose de Montfort F, dp, Adam; int. in 1993

Rose de Pâques – See ***R. majalis*** (Herrmann) dbl.

Rose de Puebla – See **François Fontaine**, HP

Rose de Rennes HT, lp, Adam, M.; int. in 1995; Gold Medal, Baden-Baden, 1995

Rose de Rescht P, dp, about 1880, from Iran; flowers bright fuchsia-red, fading with lilac tints, very dbl., rosette, borne mostly singly, intense damask fragrance; recurrent; foliage dense; vigorous, compact growth; originally introduced into England about 1880, but was then forgotten about and re-introduced in the 1940's.

Rose de Schelfhout HGal, lp, 1840, Parmentier; flowers delicate pink, full, quartered, moderate fragrance; non-remontant

Rose de Tavel F, dp, Reuter; flowers intense deep pink, dbl., high-centered, borne in clusters, slight fruity fragrance; recurrent; growth to 70-80 cm.; int. in 2003

Rose de Trianon P, mp, about 1830, Vibert; flowers medium, dbl., cupped, borne in large clusters; growth small, vigorous; probably extinct

Rose de Trianon Double – See **Adèle Mauzé**, P

Rose de Van Huysum – See **Celsiana**, D

Rose des Alpes – See ***R. pendulina*** (Linnaeus)

Rose des Blés LCl, rb, Eve; flowers bright shades of red, dbl., cupped, slight fragrance; recurrent; vigorous (180-250 cm.) growth; int. by Les Roses Anciennes de Andre Eve, 2006

Rose des Cisterciens S, pb, Delbard; flowers clear yellow and dusty pink stripes, petals waved and imbricated, large, very dbl., moderate citron and fruit fragrance; growth to 1 m.; int. by George Delbard SA, 1998

Rose des Maures HGal, dr; flowers deep plum-crimson, yellow stamens, 2½ in., semi-dbl. to dbl., rosette, borne singly or in clusters of 2-7, slight fragrance; non-remontant; foliage medium green, oval, with 3 leaflets; prickles numerous, hooked; vigorous, upright (4 ft.) growth; a very old variety, believed lost, but rediscovered by Sackville-West in 1947 at Sissinghurst

Rose des Parfumeurs – See **Rose du Puteaux**, D

Rose des Peintres C, mp, before 1806; flowers pink, tending toward scarlet, darker at center, sometimes with faint white stripes, very large, full, cupped, borne in small clusters; foliage very large, dull green, deeply toothed; prickles nearly straight, unequal

Rose d'Espérance HT, dr, 1918, Verschuren; flowers dark red to deep black, medium, dbl.

Rose d'Evian T, pb, 1895, Bernaix, A.; bud long, magenta; flowers pink, center carmine, very large, very dbl., cupped; foliage glossy

Rose d'Herbeys – See **Souv de J. B. Guillot**, T

Rose d'Hivers D, w; flowers whitish, center shell-pink, well-shaped

Rose d'Or HT, dy, 1941, Gaujard; bud long, pointed; flowers intense yellow, 4½-5 in., 35 petals; foliage dark, bronze, glossy; very vigorous growth; [Julien Potin × seedling]; int. by J&P

Rose d'Or de Montreux F, dy, Adam, M.

Rose d'Orsay – See **D'Orsay Rose**, Misc OGR

Rose Dot HT, rb, 1962, Dot, Simon; flowers red, reverse white, large, 35 petals, intense fragrance; foliage dark; vigorous, upright growth; [Baccará × Peace]

Rose du Barri HT, pb, 1940, Archer; flowers salmon-pink, reverse carmine, large, single; vigorous growth

Rose du Ciel HT, pb, 1970, Delbard-Chabert; flowers cream-white broadly edged carmine-pink, large, dbl., globular; foliage dark, glossy; vigorous, bushy growth; [Chic Parisien × (Michele Meilland × Bayadere)]; int. in 1966

Rose du Maître d'École – See **Rose de La Maître-Ecole**, HGal

Rose du Prince HT, mr, 1962, Dorieux; bud long, pointed; flowers strawberry-rose, large, dbl.; foliage leathery, light green; vigorous, upright growth; [Blanche Mallerin × Profusion]; int. by Pin, 1959

Rose du Puteaux D, mp, before 1826; flowers rose pink to rose red, moderate fragrance; recurrent; a form of Quatre Saisons, cultivated at Puteaux, near Paris, for the perfume industry; sometimes credited to Cochet

Rose du Roi P, mr, about 1819, Souchet or Ecoffé; flowers bright red shaded violet, large, semi-dbl., intense fragrance; remontant bloom; foliage clear green, slightly fluted; vigorous growth; cultivar widely sold under this name may be misidentified; int. by Souchet

Rose du Roi à Fleurs Blanches – See **Célina Dubos**, D

Rose du Roi à Fleurs Pourpres P, dr, 1844, Varangot; flowers crimson, shaded with purple, large, medium, full, cupped; repeats sparingly; growth branching, moderate (4 ft.); breeder and date based on Revue Horticole, 1846; usually considered to be a sport of Rose du Roi, but is not, according to Joyaux

Rose du Roi Panachée – See **Panachée de Lyon**, P

Rose du Roi Strié – See **Capitaine Rénard**, P

Rose du Saint Sacrament – See ***R. majalis*** (Herrmann) dbl.

Rose du Sérail – See **La Belle Sultane**, HGal

Rose Dubreuil – See **Rose Edouard**, B

Rose d'York – See **Duc d'York**, A

Rose Edouard B, mp, 1818, Perichon/Neumann; bud pointed; flowers bright pink, small, dbl., cupped, often muddled, moderate sweet with hint of pepper fragrance; recurrent; foliage gray-green, waxy; broad, tall (5-6 ft.) growth; [Tous-les-Mois (DP) × Parsons' Pink]

Rose Edward – See **Bourbon Rose**, B

Rose Elf – See **Rosenelfe**, F

Rose Ellen S, lp, Lykke; int. in 1995

Rose Eutin F, mp, 1958, Hennessey; flowers rose-pink; [sport of Eutin]

Rose Festival S, mr, Sutherland, P; [Black Beauty × Candy Cane]; int. by Golden Vale Nursery, 1996

Rose Foncé – See **Rubra**, M

Rose For Elaine HT, ob, 2003, Rawlins, R.; flowers orange brown, medium, dbl., borne in small clusters, moderate fragrance; foliage medium size, medium green, semi-glossy; prickles 2 cm., scimitar-shaped, moderate; upright, medium (36 in.) growth; garden; [Edith Holden × (Baby Love × Amber Queen)]; int. in 2003

Rose Foucheaux – See **Foucheaux**, HGal

Rose Fukuoka HT, pb, 1985, Ota, Kaichiro; flowers blend of light, medium and deep pink, (deeper at petal edges, 27 petals, high-centered; foliage small, dark, glossy; compact growth; [(Utage × Kordes' Perfecta) × Miss Ireland]; int. in 1983

Rose Fukuyama HT, dp, Hiroshima; int. by Hiroshima Bara-En, 1985

Rose Garnette Pol, mp

Rose Gaujard HT, rb, 1958, Gaujard; bud small to medium, ovoid to globular; flowers cherry-red, reverse pale pink and silvery white, 3-4 in., 80 petals, high-centered to cupped, borne usually singly, slight fragrance; free-flowering; foliage leathery, glossy; prickles several, medium, hooked downward, brown; stems medium; vigorous, bushy growth; PP1829; [Peace × (Capucine Bicolore × Opera)]; int. by Armstrong Nursery, 1964; Gold Medal, NRS, 1958

Rose Gaujard, Climbing Cl HT, rb, 1964, Nakashima, Tosh; [sport of Rose Gaujard]

Rose Gaujard × Leverkusen S, rb, Scholle, E.; flowers white with red edges, large, single to semi-dbl.; recurrent; tall (200 cm.), arching growth

Rose Gilardi Min, rb, 1987, Moore, Ralph S.; bud slender, mossy; flowers red and pink striped, aging well, small, 12-15 petals, informal, borne in small clusters, slight fragrance; recurrent; foliage small, medium green, semi-glossy; prickles slender, straight, small to medium, brownish; bushy, spreading, medium growth; hips oblong, covered with prickles, orange; [Dortmund × ((Fairy Moss × (Little Darling × Ferdinand Pichard)) × seedling)]; int. in 1986

Rose Hannes HT, w, 1982, Wheatcroft, Christopher; flowers large, dbl.; foliage medium size, medium green, glossy; upright growth; [Pascali × seedling]; int. by Timmerman's Roses

Rose Hill HT, dp, 1928, Joseph H. Hill, Co.; bud long, pointed; flowers darker than briarcliff, very large, dbl., high-centered; [sport of Columbia]

Rose Hills Red Min, dr, 1977, Moore, Ralph S.; bud pointed; flowers deep red, 1½ in., 30 petals; foliage glossy, leathery; vigorous, upright growth; [(*R. wichurana* × Floradora) × Westmont]; int. by Sequoia Nursery, 1978

Rose Iga F, mr, 1985, Meilland, Mrs. Marie-Louise; bud oblong; flowers carmine-pink suffused with a scarlet blush on the edges, 3-3½ in., 17-20 petals, borne in clusters, no fragrance; recurrent; foliage medium size, dark green, semi-glossy; bushy (1 m.) growth; hips orange; PP6281; [Coppélia 76 × (Curiosa × City of Leeds)]; int. by Meilland & Son, 1981

Rose Impériale HT, ob, 1942, Gaujard; flowers flame and gold, over large, very dbl., globular; foliage dark, glossy; vigorous growth; Gold Medal, Bagatelle, 1941

Rose Jacques – See **Rosier de Bourgon**, B

Rose Jay – See **Clémentine**, HEg

Rose Lée – See **Léa**, HGal

Rose Lelieur – See **Rose du Roi**, P

Rose Love HT, or, Delbard; flowers tender orange, dbl.; int. by Sauvageot, 1978

Rose MacKenzie MinFl, dr, 2005, Jalbert, Brad; flowers very dark, velvety red, 2 in., full, borne in large clusters, slight fragrance; foliage medium size, dark green, glossy; prickles medium, pointed, dark, numerous; growth bushy, medium (2 ft.); [Thelma's Glory × Glad Tidings]; int. in 2005

Rose Magic Min, rb, 1999, Giles, Diann; flowers white and red edge, white reverse, medium, full, borne in small clusters; foliage medium size, dark green, semi-glossy; few prickles; upright, medium growth; [Little Darling × Kristen]; int. by Giles Rose Nursery, 1999

Rose Marguerite – See **Tricolore**, HGal

Rose Marie HT, mp, 1918, Dorner; flowers clear rose-pink, very large, dbl., cupped, moderate fragrance; recurrent; foliage glossy, dark; vigorous growth; [Hoosier Beauty × Sunburst]

Rose Marie, Climbing Cl HT, mp, 1927, Pacific Rose Co.; bud very large, long-pointed; flowers very large, dbl.; [sport of Rose Marie]

Rose-Marie S, w, 2003, Austin, David; flowers very full, borne in small clusters, intense fragrance; foliage medium size, dark green, semi-glossy; prickles few, 9 mm., concave, curved inwards; upright growth; garden decorative; [sport of Heritage]; int. by David Austin Roses, Limited, 2003

Rose Marie F, m

Rose Marie Reid HT, mp, 1956, Whisler; bud globular; flowers Neyron rose, 5-6 in., 48 petals, cupped, moderate fragrance; foliage dark, leathery; vigorous growth; PP1487; [Charlotte Armstrong × Katherine T. Marshall]; int. by Germain's, 1956

Rose-Marie Viaud HMult, m, 1924, Igoult; flowers same as parent except bluer and more double, 3 cm., dbl., rosette, borne in large clusters, no fragrance; thornless; [Veilchenblau × unknown]; int. by Viaud-Bruant

Rose Mary HT, mp

Rose Mauve – See **Bourbon**, HGal

Rose Meillandécor – See **Pink Meidiland**, S

Rose Merk HT, or, 1931, Cant, F.; flowers bright geranium-red; vigorous growth

Rose Mille A, w, 1826, Cartier; flowers pure white, medium, full

Rose Minarett F, mp, Noack, Werner; int. in 1997

Rose mit Herz S, dr, Huber; int. in 2003

Rose Moet HT, my, 1962, Dorieux; flowers golden yellow, large, dbl.; foliage leathery; long, strong stems; int. by Pin

Rose Mousseuse Ordinaire – See **Communis**, M

Rose Music F, dp, Kakujitsu-en; int. in 1988

Rose Myra Grimbley HT, mp, 2002, Webster, Robert; flowers large, full, borne in small clusters, moderate fragrance; foliage medium size, medium green, semi-glossy; prickles moderate, 8 mm., triangular; bushy, medium (36 in.) growth; bedding; [Dave Hessayon × ((Matangi × Memorium) × Gold Bunny)]

Rose Nabonnand T, pb, 1883, Nabonnand, G.; flowers salmon-pink tinted yellow, large, full, intense fragrance; few prickles

Rose Neumann – See **Rose Edouard**, B

Rose Noble HT, lp, 1927, Mühle; bud long, pointed; flowers silvery pink, semi-dbl.; [Mme Caroline Testout × unknown]

Rose Nuggets Min, lp, 1991, Michelis, Dorothy; bud pointed; flowers light pink, aging lighter, self-cleaning, many petaloids, small, 30 petals, high-centered, borne singly, no fragrance; foliage small, dark green, glossy, frequently 7 leaflets; very full, bushy, low growth; [sport of Red Ace]; int. by Justice Miniature Roses, 1992

Rose O'Bree F, O'Bree, Nancy

Rose Odyssey 2000 HT, w, 1999, Ballin, Don & Paula; flowers cream with pink edge, 4-5 in., full, high-centered, borne mostly singly, moderate fragrance; foliage medium to large, medium to dark green, semi-glossy; prickles moderate; upright, bushy, medium (3½-4½ ft.) growth; PP11091; [sport of Garden Party]; int. by Arena Rose Co., 1999

Rose Œillet de Saint-Arquey (Vilfroy) – See **Serratipetala**, Ch

Rose of Castile – See **Summer Damask**, D

Rose of Clifton F, yb, 1978, Sanday, John; bud pointed; flowers gold edged peach-pink, large, 27 petals; foliage dark, matte; vigorous, upright growth; [Vera Dalton × Parasol]

Rose of Freedom HT, mr, 1948, Swim, H.C.; bud ovoid; flowers clear rose red, 3½-4½ in., 50 petals, intense tea and spice fragrance; foliage leathery, dark; vigorous, upright, bushy growth; [Charlotte Armstrong × Night]; int. by Mt. Arbor Nursery

Rose of Hope HT, my, 2004, Astor Perry; flowers medium, full, borne mostly solitary, slight fragrance; foliage medium size, medium green, semi-glossy; prickles few, average, curved; bushy, medium (50 in.) growth; garden decoration; [Grandpa Dickson × seedling]; int. by Certified Roses, Inc., 2004

Rose of Lidice HT, yb, 1961, Wheatcroft Bros.; flowers lemon-yellow shaded poppy red; [sport of Tzigane]

Rose of Love – See ***R. gallica pumila*** (Seringe)

Rose of Miletus – See ***R. gallica*** (Linnaeus)

Rose of Narromine – See **Heart O' Gold**, Gr

Rose of Paestum – See **Summer Damask**, D

Rose of Picardy S, mr, 2004; flowers single, borne in small clusters, slight fragrance; foliage medium size, medium green, matte; prickles medium, concave curved inward; growth compact, narrow bushy, vigorous, medium (100 cm.); garden decorative; [seedling (deep pink English-type shrub) × seedling (deep pink English-type shrub)]; int. by David Austin Roses, Ltd., 2004

Rose of Provence – See **Cabbage Rose**, C

Rose of Provins – See ***R. gallica*** (Linnaeus)

Rose of Provins – See ***R. gallica officinalis*** (Thory)

Rose of Rhone – See **Cabbage Rose**, C

Rose of Rove – See **Cabbage Rose**, C

Rose of the Tombs – See **St John's Rose**, S

Rose of Torridge HT, dp, 1961, Allen, E.M.; flowers deep pink, 6 in., 36 petals; foliage glossy; vigorous growth; [Karl Herbst × Pink Charming]

Rose of Tralee S, op, 1964, McGredy, Sam IV; flowers deep pink shaded salmon, 4 in., 35 petals, borne in small clusters, slight fragrance; foliage dark; very vigorous, bushy growth; [Leverkusen × Korona]

Rose of Wagga Wagga – See **Sun Goddess**, HT

Rose 1 F, w, Teranishi; int. in 1999

Rose Opal HT, dp, 1961, LeGrice; flowers pink-opal, well-formed, 4-5 in., 25-30 petals, moderate fragrance; foliage dark (reddish when young); vigorous, upright, bushy growth; PP2190; [Wellworth × Independence]; int. by Wayside Gardens Co.

Rose Osaka HT, dr, 2003, Teranishi, Kikuo; flowers 15 cm., very full, borne mostly solitary, slight fragrance; foliage large, medium green, semi-glossy; prickles large; growth upright, tall (150 cm.); garden, exhibition; [(Helene Schoen × seedling) × seedling]; int. by Itami Rose Garden, 2003

Rose Parade F, pb, 1974, Williams, J. Benjamin; bud ovoid; flowers coral-peach to pink, large, dbl., cupped; foliage large, glossy; vigorous, bushy, compact growth; [Sumatra × Queen Elizabeth]; int. by Howard Rose Co.

Rose Pavot – See **Grosse Mohnkopfs Rose**, S

Rose Pearl – See **Bremer Stadtmusikanten**, S

Rose-Pink Ophelia – See **Pink Ophelia**, HT

Rose Pluton – See **Pluton**, HGal

Rose Ponceau – See **Poncheau-Capiaumont**, HCh

Rose Poncheaux – See **Poncheau-Capiaumont**, HCh

Rose Prolifère – See **Prolifera de Redouté**, C

Rose Queen HT, mp, 1911, Hill, E. G.; bud long, pointed

Rose Queen HT, or, 1964, Whisler; bud globular; flowers 4-5 in., 38 petals, high-centered, moderate fragrance; foliage leathery, dark; vigorous, upright, bushy growth; PP2203; [Chrysler Imperial × seedling]; int. by Germain's, 1962

Rose Rhapsody HT, dp, 1999, Zary, Dr. Keith W.; bud long, pointed ovoid; flowers deep, dusty pink, 5-6½ in., 41-50+ petals, high-centered, borne mostly singly, intense citrus fragrance; recurrent; foliage large, dark green, glossy; prickles moderate, medium size, hooked downward; stems medium, strong; upright, spreading, tall (4½-5 ft.) growth; PP11046; [Fragrant Cloud × Ingrid Bergman]; int. by Bear Creek Gardens, Inc., 1999

Rose Sachet HT, dp, J&P; int. in 1998

Rose Sachet – See **Rose Rhapsody**, HT

Rose Schelfhout – See **De Schelfhout**, HGal

Rose Sherbet F, dp, 1970, Pal, Dr. B.P.; bud globular; flowers deep rose-pink, medium, dbl., intense fragrance; foliage glossy; vigorous, upright, open growth; [Gruss an Teplitz × unknown]; int. by Indian Agric. Research Inst., 1962

Rose Tulipe HFt, yb, before 1817, Dupont/Noisette; flowers yellow with poppy bands

Rose Two Thousand – See **Rose 2,000**, F

Rose Unique – See **White Provence**, C

Rose Valmae S, mr, 1981, Watts, Mrs. M.A.; flowers decorative, 40 petals, borne in clusters of 3; foliage light green, 7 leaflet; upright, medium growth

Rose van Sian – See **Cardinal de Richelieu**, HGal

Rose Verreux D, dp, before 1848; flowers red, tinged lilac, paler at edges, medium, full, globular

Rose Verte HT, w, Croix; flowers creamy white with green tinges and touch of apricot in center; int. by Roseraie Paul Croix, 1989

Rose Window Min, ob, 1979, Williams, Ernest D.; bud ovoid, pointed; flowers orange, yellow, and red blend, 1 in., 15-20 petals, hybrid tea, borne singly, slight fragrance; recurrent; foliage small, dark green, rounded leaflets; prickles small, thin; spreading, bushy growth; [seedling × Over the Rainbow]; int. by Mini-Roses, 1978

Rose Yokohama HT, dy, 2000, Hirabayashi, Hiroshi; flowers large, very full, borne mostly singly, moderate tea fragrance; foliage large, dark green, semi-glossy, leathery; numerous prickles; growth upright, medium; [seedling × seedling]; int. by Keisei Rose Nursery; Bronze Medal, JRC, 1998

Rosea – See **Gallica Alba**, HGal

Rosea Bslt, lp, 1824, Boursault; [*R. banksiae alba-plena* × unknown garden variety]

Rosea F, Delforge; int. in 1974

Rosea Centfeuilles HP, dp, Touvais

Roseanna Cl Min, dp, 1977, Williams, Ernest D.; bud long, pointed; flowers deep pink with slightly darker reverse, 1-1½ in., 50+ petals, high-centered, borne singly and in clusters; recurrent in cycles; foliage glossy, firm, medium green; tall, semi-climbing growth; [Little Darling × seedling]; int. by Mini-Roses, 1976

Roseanne HT, dr; int. by Springhill, 2000

Roseate Cl HT, mr, 1931, Clark, A.; flowers large, semi-dbl., cupped; foliage wrinkled; vigorous, climbing growth; good as a pillar; int. by Ivanhoe Hort. Soc.

Roseball S, lp, 2006, Beales, Amanda; flowers light pink, reverse light pink, 15 cm., dbl., borne in large clusters; foliage medium size, dark green, semi-glossy; prickles moderate; growth bushy, medium (1 m.); hedging; [Bonica × English Miss]; int. by Peter Beales Roses, 2002

Roseberry Blanket S, dp, Kordes; flowers fuchsia-toned, 2½ in., 15-20 petals, borne in clusters, slight spicy fragrance; groundcover; spreading growth; PPAF; int. by J&P, 2004

Rosebud S, pb, Demits; flowers single; hybrid filipes; int. in 1997

Rosecarpe HT, yb, 1993, Poole, Lionel; flowers cream shaded pink, 3-3½ in., full, borne mostly singly; foliage large, dark green, semi-glossy; some prickles; medium (100 cm.), upright growth; [Selfridges × Mischief]; int. by Battersby Roses, 1994

Rosée du Matin – See **Elisa**, A

Rosee O'Bree F, mp, 1998, O'Bree, Nancy; flowers medium pink, lighter reverse, multi-clored, ¾-2½ in., dbl., borne in large clusters; foliage medium green, semi-glossy; prickles moderate; spreading, rambling, medium growth; [seedling]

Roseford LCl, lp, 1982, Jerabek, Paul E.; bud ovoid; flowers light pink, slightly darker reverse, 28 petals, cupped, borne 6 per cluster, slight fragrance; repeats well; foliage dark, semi-glossy; prickles straight, red; bushy growth; [seedling × seedling]; Bronze Medal, ARC TG, 1986

Roseglen Bouquet F, pb, 1953, Quinn; flowers ivory-white edged deep pink, small, very dbl., high-centered; foliage dark, glossy, leathery; vigorous, upright growth; [Pinocchio × unknown]; int. by Roseglen Nursery

Rosehill – See **Egeskov**, F

Roseketeer Min, ob, 2001, Bennett, Dee; flowers soft orange with a bright white eye, 1-1½ in., single, borne mostly solitary, no fragrance; foliage medium size, medium green, semi-glossy; few prickles; growth compact, low (1-2 ft.); garden decorative, containers, exhibition; [Angel Face × seedling]; int. by Tiny Petals Nursery, 2001

Rösel Dach Pol, mr, 1906, Walter; flowers cherry red, edges lighter, very full

Rosel Vogel S, m, 1938, Vogel, M.; flowers small, dbl.

Roseland Rosette F, dp, 1952, Houghton, T.B.; bud globular; flowers deep rose-pink, small, dbl.; vigorous, bushy growth; [sport of Crimson Rosette]

Roselandia HT, my, 1924, Stevens, W.; flowers darker and larger; [sport of Golden Ophelia]; int. by Low

Roselandia, Climbing Cl HT, my, 1933, Lens

Roselette F, mp, 1957, Lens; flowers soft salmon-pink; foliage bright green; very vigorous growth; [Orange Triumph × Alain]

Roselina – See **Rosalina**, S

Roseline de Kersa HT, dp; int. in 1997

Rosella F, pb, 1930, Prior; flowers salmon-rose-pink, ruffled, semi-dbl., borne in large trusses; vigorous growth; [sport of Else Poulsen]

Rosella Cl HT, pb, 1931, Dot, Pedro; bud long, pointed; flowers velvety carmine, base yellow, orange undertone, 2¾ in., single, borne in clusters; foliage large, glossy; vigorous (8 ft.) growth; [(Mme Edouard Herriot × Roger Lambelin) × unknown]; int. by C-P

Rosella – See **Bobby Dazzler**, F

Rosella S, dp, 2001, Ferrer, Fco.; flowers single, borne in small clusters, slight fragrance; foliage medium green; growth medium (1 m.); [Heideschnee × Purple Rain]; int. by Roses Noves Ferrer S.L., 2000

Rosella Grace Cremer F, dp, 1957, Cremer; bud conical to ovoid; flowers dark Tyrian rose, reverse lighter, rosette center, medium, 35-40 petals, moderate fragrance; very vigorous, bushy growth; PP1607; [sport of Garnette]

Rosella Sweet HT, op, 1930, Pernet-Ducher; flowers nasturtium-yellow suffused salmon-pink, large; int. by Dreer

Rosellana F, mp, Barni, V.

Rosemarie Hinner HT, mp, 1949, Hinner, P.; bud long, pointed; flowers large, high-centered; foliage leathery, light green; very vigorous, upright, bushy growth; [Frau

Karl Druschki × (Ellen × Una Wallace)]; int. by Bauské Bros. & Hinner

Rosemarin Min, pb, 1965, Kordes, R.; flowers light pink, reverse light red, small, globular, borne several together, slight fragrance; recurrent; foliage glossy, light green; dwarf, bushy growth; [Tom Thumb × Dacapo]

Rosemary HGal, m, 1842, Vibert; flowers lilac-pink, spotted white, large, full, rosette; foliage large, marbled with yellowish splotches; [Boule de Neige × unknown]

Rosemary HT, lp, 1907, Hill, E. G.; flowers deep carmine, reverse permeated old gold, medium, full

Rosemary, Climbing Cl HT, lp, 1920, Dingee & Conard; flowers very large, dbl.; [sport of Rosemary]

Rosemary Cl HT, lp, 1925, Cant, F.; bud long, pointed; flowers pink shaded old-gold, very dbl., high-centered; free, recurrent boom; foliage leathery; pillar growth

Rosemary F, dp, Schenkel; bud ovoid; flowers rose-pink, 2½ in., 55-60 petals, flat, borne in clusters, moderate fragrance; foliage leathery; vigorous, bushy growth; PP1398; [sport of Garnette]; int. by Amling-DeVor Nursery, 1955

Rosemary Min, mp; flowers apple-blossom-pink

Rosemary Clooney F, ab, 1985, French, Richard; flowers creamy apricot, 20 petals, borne in clusters of 3-6; foliage small, medium green, matte; prickles small, red; upright, bushy growth; [Vera Dalton × Elizabeth of Glamis]

Rosemary Duncan F, my, 1964, Duncan; flowers yellow, edged lighter, medium, 40 petals; foliage glossy; vigorous, bushy growth; [sport of Pinocchio]

Rosemary Eddie F, mp, 1956, Eddie; flowers bright pink, well-formed; [New Dawn × Fashion]

Rosemary Foster LCl, lp, 2000, Foster, Maurice; flowers medium pink, fading to white, slightly darker at edges, orange stamens, 3 cm., single, borne in very large clusters, slight fragrance; foliage large, medium green, semi-glossy; prickles moderate; growth climbing, vigorous, tall (35 ft.); [Kiftsgate × unknown]; int. by White House Farm, 1996

Rosemary Gandy F, yb, 1959, Gaujard; flowers yellow and coppery, medium, semi-dbl., cupped, moderate fragrance; foliage glossy, bronze; bushy, strong, upright growth; [(Tabarin × unknown) × Jolie Princesse seedling]; int. by Gandy's Roses, 1958

Rosemary Harkness HT, op, 1985, Harkness, R., & Co., Ltd.; flowers orange-salmon, orange-yellow reverse, medium-large, 35 petals, intense fragrance; foliage large, dark, semi-glossy; bushy growth; [Compassion × (Basildon Bond × Irish Gold)]; Gold Medal, Belfast, 1987, Fragrance Award, Belfast, 1987

Rosemary Ladlau S, m, Delbard; int. by Ludwig's Roses, 2002; Fragrance Award, Durbanville, 2006, Trial Ground Certificate, Durbanville, 2006

Rosemary McCoy HT, pb, 2004, Larry Burks; flowers pink blend, reverse pink, medium, full, borne mostly solitary, slight fragrance; foliage medium size, dark green, semi-glossy; prickles average, curve, few; upright, medium (60 in.) growth; garden; [seedling × seedling]; int. by Certified Roses, Inc., 2004

Rosemary Murray F, my, Harkness; flowers yellow, fading toward white on outer petals, full, rosette, moderate fragrance; recurrent; growth to 80 cm.; int. by R. Harkness & Co., 2005

Rosemary Roache's Burnett HSpn, pb, Roache, Rosemary; flowers lilac-pink centers with cream edges, medium, semi-dbl., shallow cup, borne in small clusters, intense fragrance; recurrent; foliage fine, ferny; growth to 3 × 3 ft.; hips elongated, black; [Irish Rich Marble × unknown]; this may be Irish Rich Marble and not a seedling of it

Rosemary Rose F, dp, 1957, deRuiter; flowers medium, dbl., camellia-shaped, borne in large trusses, moderate fragrance; foliage coppery; vigorous, bushy growth; [Gruss an Teplitz × Floribunda seedling]; int. by Gregory, 1954; Gold Medal, Rome, 1954, Gold Medal, NRS, 1954

Rosemary Stone HT, mp, 1970, Stone; flowers pink, very dbl., high-centered; foliage leathery; moderate, upright growth; [sport of Waltzing Matilda]

Rosemary Viaud – See **Rose-Marie Viaud**, HMult

Rosemary's Dream Min, lp, 2000, Sawyer, Rosemary; bud ovoid; flowers light pink, aging to almost white, reverse white, medium, full, high-centered, borne mostly singly, slight fragrance; foliage medium size, medium green, semi-glossy; prickles moderate; upright, bushy, medium (24 in.) growth; [sport of Chelsea Belle]

Rosemeade HT, or, 2003, Rawlins, R.; flowers vermilion, medium, full, borne in small clusters, slight fragrance; foliage medium size, medium green, semi-glossy; prickles moderate, 1 cm., triangular; upright, medium (33 in.) growth; garden; [Sexy Rexy × Kanagem]

Rosemere Cancer Foundation HT, mr, 2004, Poole, Lionel; flowers 5 in., full, spiral-shaped, borne mostly solitary, slight fragrance; free-flowering; foliage medium size, dark green, semi-glossy; prickles medium, triangular; growth upright, bushy, medium (3 ft.); garden, bedding, exhibition; [Raewyn Henry × Red Planet]; int. in 2005

Rosemonde – See ***R. gallica versicolor*** (Linnaeus)

Rosemonde D, pb, 1825, Toutain; flowers pink, plumed white; probably the same as *R. gallica versicolor*

Rosemoor S, lp, 2004; flowers very full, borne in small clusters, intense fragrance; foliage medium size, dark green, semi-glossy; prickles medium, linear; growth bushy, narrow, vigorous, medium (100 cm.); garden decorative; [Sharifa Asma × unnamed seedling (light pink modern type shrub)]; int. by David Austin Roses, Ltd., 2004

Rosen-Lambert LCl, dr, 1937, Vogel, M.; flowers oxblood-red, very large, dbl.; foliage large, bronze, leathery; vigorous, climbing (9 ft.) growth; [Fragezeichen × American Pillar]; int. by P. Lambert

Rosen-Müller S, mr, 1940, Vogel, M.; flowers medium, single

Rosenau F, dr, Eggert; flowers glowing dark red, large, dbl., borne in clusters, slight fragrance; recurrent; even, low (50 cm.) growth; winter hardy; int. in 1961

Rosenborg F, lp, Poulsen; flowers light pink, deeper in center, 10-15 cm., full, cupped, borne in clusters, no fragrance; recurrent; foliage dark green, glossy; bushy, medium (60-100 cm.) growth; int. by Poulsen Roser, 2000

Rosenburg Riederburg – See **Countess Celeste**, S

Rosendal F, pb, Poulsen; flowers pink blend, 8-10 cm., dbl., cupped, borne in clusters, no fragrance; recurrent; foliage dark green, glossy; bushy, tall (100-150 cm.) growth; PP13451; int. by Poulsen Roser, 2001

Rosendel F, m

Rosendorf Schmitshausen LCl, dr, Cocker; flowers dark scarlet-crimson, large, dbl., borne usually singly, slight fragrance; good repeat; foliage dark green; int. in 1977

Rosendorf Sparrieshoop S, lp, Kordes; flowers pale pink with bright pink highlights, large, 15 petals, cupped, borne in clusters, moderate apple fragrance; recurrent; foliage medium green, glossy; bushy (4½ ft.) growth; int. in 1988

Rosendorf Steinfurth S, mp, Schultheis; flowers medium pink, fading to white, small, semi-dbl., cupped, borne in clusters, slight fragrance; fast repeat; foliage medium green; growth to 8-10 ft.; int. by Rosen von Schultheis, 1993

Rosendorf Ufhoven HEg, dr, 1949, W. Kordes Söhne; flowers magenta-crimson, very large, very dbl., globular, borne in small clusters; non-recurrent; foliage leathery, glossy, dark; weak stems; vigorous, upright, bushy growth; [Gen. MacArthur × Magnifica]

Rosenelfe F, mp, 1939, Kordes; bud long, pointed; flowers 2½ in., dbl., high-centered, borne in clusters, moderate fragrance; foliage leathery, glossy, light; vigorous, bushy growth; [Else Poulsen × Sir Basil McFarland]; int. by Dreer

Rosenella HT, mp, 1964, Mondial Roses; flowers clear pink, reverse brighter

Rosenfee F, lp, Boerner; int. in 1967

Rosenfest LCL, op, GPG Roter Oktober; flowers pale crimson/cherry, large, semi-dbl., borne in clusters, moderate fragrance; foliage large, glossy, rounded; strong (8-12 ft.) growth; [(Dortmund × unknown) × seedling]; int. in 1981

Rosenholm LCl, lp, Poulsen; flowers small to medium, dbl., borne in clusters, no fragrance; good repeat; foliage dark green, glossy; bushy, tall (200-300 cm.) growth; int. by Poulsen Roser, 1994

Rosenkavalier F, dp, 1965, Verschuren, A.; flowers deep rose, 45 petals, borne in clusters, intense fragrance; foliage dark; vigorous, upright, bushy growth; int. by Stassen, 1963

Rosenkavalier F, or, Huber; int. in 1995

Rosenkreis Neunkirchen F, mr, Michler, K. H.; flowers luminous red, semi-dbl.; int. in 1995

Rosenmärchen – See **Pinocchio**, F

Rosenmärchen, Climbing – See **Pinocchio, Climbing**, Cl F

Rosenmärchen F, mp, Kordes; flowers strong pink; int. in 1992

Rosenpfarrer Meyer HT, or, 1930, Soupert & Notting; flowers coral-red passing to prawn-red, semi-dbl.; very vigorous growth; [Mme Edouard Herriot × Louise Catherine Breslau]

Rosenprinz S, dp, Wänninger, Franz; flowers small, dbl.; very low, almost dwarf growth; int. in 1990

Rosenprinzessin HT, mp, 1976, Hetzel; bud ovoid; flowers 3½-5 in., dbl., moderate fragrance; foliage glossy; upright growth; [Nordia × Sans Souci]; int. in 1975

Rosenprinzessin Pol, dp, Hetzel; flowers rich pink, slight fragrance; free-flowering; low growth; int. in 1993

Rosenprinzessin Andrea HT, mr, Hetzel; int. in 1993

Rosenprinzessin Evi – See **Rosenprinzessin**, HT

Rosenprofessor Sieber F, mp, 2006; flowers pure pink, aging to porcelain pink, 5 cm., dbl., borne in small clusters; foliage medium size, dark green, glossy; compact, medium (70 cm.) growth; int. by W. Kordes' Söhne, 1997

Rosenreigen – See **Cape Cod**, S

Rosenresli S, dp, 1987, Kordes, W.; flowers blend of orange pink to carmine red, 4 in., full, high-centereed, borne singly or in small clusters, intense tea rose fragrance; recurrent; foliage medium size, dark green, glossy; vigorous (5 ft.), bushy, arching, possibly climbing growth; [(New Dawn × Prima Ballerina) × seedling]; int. in 1986; ADR, 1984

Rosenrot HT, mr, Tantau; flowers velvety deep crimson, moderate fragrance; int. in 1978

Rosenstadt Freising S, w, Kordes; bud pointed, reddish; flowers white with red edges, aging to white with red splashes and pink tones, 7 cm., dbl., cupped, borne in clusters, slight fragrance; recurrent; foliage dark green, glossy; upright (4 ft.), bushy growth; int. by W. Kordes Söhne, 2004; Silver Medal, Rome, 2002, Silver Medal, Monza, 2002, Silver Medal, Kortrijk, 2002

Rosenstadt Zweibrücken S, pb, 2006; flowers pink-red, center golden yellow, yellow stamens, 7 cm., semi-dbl., cupped, borne in large clusters; recurrent; foliage medium size, deep green, glossy; bushy, medium (3 ft.) growth; int. by W. Kordes' Söhne, 1989

Rosentanz – See **Biddulph Grange**, S

Rosenthal – See **Tatjana**, HT

Rosenwalzer S, pb, Dickson, Patrick; int. in 1993

Rosenwunder HEg, dp, 1934, Kordes; bud long, pointed; flowers rose pink to rose red, 3 in., semi-dbl., globular to cupped, borne in small clusters; non-recurrent; foliage large, leathery, glossy, wrinkled; very vigorous, bushy growth; hips squat, turban-shaped, fleshy, bright orange; [W.E. Chaplin × *R. rubiginosa*]

Rosenzauber – See **White Fleurette**, S

Rosenzauber F, lp, Wänninger, Franz; flowers medium, semi-dbl.; int. in 1991

Roseraie de Blois HT, mr, Dorieux; int. in 1991; Gold Medal, Rome, Gold Medal, Cannes

Roseraie de l'Hay HRg, dr, 1901, Cochet-Cochet; flowers crimson-red changing to rosy magenta, 4 in., dbl., intense fragrance; recurrent bloom; foliage medium green, rugose; vigorous (4-5 ft.) growth; [*R. rugosa rubra* × unknown]

Roseraie du Châtelet F, pb, Sauvageot; flowers rose-carmine and bengal-rose, dbl., rosette; int. in 1999

Roserie HMult, mp, 1917, Witterstaetter; flowers Tyrian pink, base white, darkening with age, 3¾ in., semi-dbl., open, borne in clusters; foliage large, rich green, leathery, glossy; thornless; very vigorous, climbing growth; [sport of Tausendschön]

Roseromantic F, w, 1984, Kordes, W.; bud light pink; flowers light pink to white, medium, 5 petals, shallow cup, borne in large clusters, slight fragrance; foliage small, dark green, glossy; bushy, spreading (2 ft.) growth; [seedling × Tornado]; Gold Medal, Baden-Baden, 1982

Roses Are Red S, rb, 2005, Moore, Ralph; flowers red with darker red eye, 2½ in., semi-dbl., cupped, borne in clusters of 3-5; scattered repeat; foliage large, dark green; numerous prickles; arching (6 ft.) growth; [Tigris × Playboy]; hybrid Hulthemia; int. by Sequoia Nursery, 2005

Rosetime Min, dr, 1990, Benardella, Frank A.; flowers medium red, brushed with dark red, upright, medium, full, slight fragrance; foliage medium size, medium green, matte; upright growth; [Rise 'n' Shine × Black Jade]; int. by Kimbrew Walter Roses, 1989

Rosetone Min, mp, 1977, Moore, Ralph S.; bud ovoid, pointed; flowers 1 in., 60 petals, high-centered; foliage small, dark, leathery; very bushy growth; [Dream Dust × Little Chief]; int. by Sequoia Nursery

Rosetta Min, rb, 1991, Spooner, Raymond A.; flowers white center, red on outer half of petals, medium, full, borne singly and in sprays, no fragrance; foliage small, medium green, semi-glossy, disease-resistant; bushy (34 cm.) growth; [Scamp × seedling]; int. by Oregon Miniature Roses, 1992

Rosette Pol, mr, 1926, Grandes Roseraies; flowers fuchsia-red, medium, dbl.; semi-dwarf growth

Rosette HT, or, 1934, Dickson, A.; flowers rose red, shaded orange, base yellow, well-formed, large, dbl.; vigorous, bushy growth

Rosette F, op, Archer; flowers peach-pink, dbl., borne in clusters; vigorous growth

Rosette de la Légion d'Honneur HT, op, 1896, Bonnaire; flowers salmon-pink, medium, semi-dbl.

Rosette Delizy T, yb, 1922, Nabonnand, P.; flowers yellow, apricot reflexes, outer petals dark carmine, well-formed, dbl., slight fragrance; free-flowering; vigorous (3-5 ft.) growth; [Général Galliéni × Comtesse Bardi]

Rosetti Stone – See **Rossetti Rose**, F

Roseville College – See **The Roseville College Rose**, HT

Rosewood HT, dp, 1998, Prescott, Cheryl; flowers neon pink, dbl., 4-4½ in., dbl., borne in small clusters; foliage medium size, medium green, semi-glossy; prickles moderate; compact, medium growth; [sport of Kardinal]

Roseworld HT, mr, 1994, Simpson, Nola; flowers 3-3½ in., full, borne mostly singly; foliage medium size, medium green, semi-glossy; few prickles; medium, upright growth; [Melina × Mme G. Delbard]; int. by Simpson, 1994

Rosey Garland HMult, mp, Robinson; flowers rose pink, borne in clusters, moderate fragrance; non-remontant; vigorous growth; [sport of The Garland]; int. by Vintage Gardens, 2002

Rosey Gem Min, mp, 1972, Meilland; flowers Neyron rose, small, 50-60 petals, cupped, then flat, borne in compact trusses; recurrent; foliage small, semi-glossy, dark green; medium, bushy, vigorous growth; [sport of Scarlet Gem]; int. by L. Dol

Rosey Lou Min, pb, McCann, Sean; flowers medium, dbl., slight fragrance; foliage medium; int. by Ashdown Roses, 2005

Rosi Mittermeier – See **Luminion**, F

Rosie Min, pb, 1987, Benardella, Frank A.; bud medium, pointed; flowers cream with pink edges, 1¼ in., 30-33 petals, high-centered, borne singly and in sprays, slight fragrance; recurrent; foliage medium size, medium green, semi-glossy; prickles long, thin, straight, angled slightly downward; upright, bushy, medium (14-16 in.) growth; fruit not observed; PP6508; [Rise 'n' Shine × (Sheri Anne × Laguna)]; int. by Nor'East Min. Roses, 1987

Rosie Jane F, mp, 2005, Paul Chessum Roses; flowers single, borne mostly solitary, no fragrance; foliage medium size, medium green, semi-glossy; prickles small, short, red, few; growth bushy, medium (24 in.); bedding, containers; [seedling × seedling]; int. by World of Roses, 2005

Rosie Larkin S, m, Fryer, Gareth; flowers lavender, dainty, small, dbl., cupped, borne in clusters; recurrent; neat, compact growth; int. in 1993

Rosie O'Donnell HT, rb, 1999, Winchel, Joseph F.; bud pointed to ovoid, long; flowers velvety scarlet red with creamy yellow reverse, 5-5½ in., 30-35 petals, high-centered, borne mostly singly, slight tea fragrance; recurrent; foliage large, dark green, matte to semi-glossy; prickles several, long, almost straight, angled downward; strong, long stems; medium, upright, slightly spreading growth; PP11382; [unknown × unknown]; int. by Weeks Roses, 1998

Rosier à Feuilles de Pimprenelle – See ***R. spinosissima*** (Linnaeus)

Rosier à Fruit – See ***R. villosa*** (Linnaeus)

Rosier Cannelle – See ***R. majalis flore simplici*** single

Rosier-Corail sans Épines – See ***R. virginiana*** (Miller)

Rosier d'Amérique – See ***R. setigera*** (Michaux)

Rosier d'Amérique à Feuilles de Grande Pimprenelle – See ***R. virginiana*** (Miller)

Rosier d'Amour HGal, m, before 1806, possibly Crantz; sepals lanceolate; flowers whitish outside light purple within, large, 5 petals, borne in small clusters, moderate fragrance; foliage ovate, doubly dentate; prickles straight or slightly curved; growth branching; hips somewhat bristly, reddish or orange, persistent

Rosier d'Autriche – See **Rosier d'Amour**, HGal

Rosier de Bourgogne à Grandes Fleurs – See **Petite de Hollande**, C

Rosier de Bourgon B, dp, 1821, Breon/Jacques; flowers deep pink with lilac, medium, semi-dbl., cupped; somewhat remontant; [Rose Edouard × unknown]

Rosier de Damas D, mp, about 1840, from France; flowers medium, dbl., moderate fragrance

Rosier de Grèce – See ***R. rubiginosa*** (Linnaeus)

Rosier de la Chine – See ***R. laevigata*** (Michaux)

Rosier de la Malmaison – See **Quatre Saisons d'Italie**, P

Rosier de Normandie – See **Vivid**, B

Rosier de Philippe Noisette – See ***R. × noisettiana*** (Thory), N

Rosier de Portland – See **Duchess of Portland**, P

Rosier de Thionville – See **Quatre Saisons Blanc Mousseux**, M

Rosier des Dames – See **Petite de Hollande**, C

Rosier des Marais – See ***R. palustris*** (Marshall)

Rosier des Quatre Saisons – See **Autumn Damask**, D

Rosier d'Or Pol, ob, 1969, Delbard; flowers orange-yellow, shaded apricot-yellow, 2½-3½ in., 20-28 petals; [Zambra × (Orléans Rose × Goldilocks)]; int. by Trioreau

Rosier du Bengale – See **Slater's Crimson China**, Ch

Rosier Évêque – See **The Bishop**, C

Rosier Gloriette Min, op; flowers orange-salmon, rosette form

Rosier Jaune – See ***R. foetida*** (Herrmann)

Rosier Lisse – See ***R. laevigata*** (Michaux)

Rosier Mousseux – See **Communis**, M

Rosier Muscade d'Alexandrie – See ***R. moschata*** (Herrmann)

Rosier Panaché d'Angleterre – See **York and Lancaster**, D

Rosier Petit à Cent Feuilles – See **Petite de Hollande**, C

Rosier Ponceau – See ***R. foetida bicolor*** ((Jacquin) Willmott)

Rosier sans Épines des Alpes – See ***R. pendulina*** (Linnaeus)

Rosier Tenuifolia HRg, w, 1904, Bénard; foliage finely lacinate and curled; [*R. rugosa alba* × *R. pimpinellifolia*]

Rosière d'Enghien B, lp, 1875, Dallemagne; flowers whitish pink, small

Rosiériste Chauvry HP, mr, 1885, Gonod; flowers shining fiery red, large, full, globular; [Victor Verdier × unknown]

Rosiériste Gaston Lévêque HT, dp, 1932, Dot, Pedro; bud long, pointed; flowers brilliant carmine, large, dbl., cupped; foliage dark; very vigorous growth; [Mme Butterfly × Jean C.N. Forestier]

Rosiériste Harms HP, mr, 1879, Verdier, E.; flowers velvety scarlet, large, full; foliage delicate green, deeply serrated; prickles numerous, very fine and pointed; growth upright

Rosiériste Jacobs HP, mr, 1880, Ducher; flowers velvety bright red, shaded darker, large, full, globular; repeats well

Rosiériste Max Singer HMult, dr, 1885, Lacharme, F.; flowers ruby-red, aging lighter, 7-8 cm., dbl., cupped, borne singly or in small clsuters, moderate tea fragrance; good repeat; foliage large; few prickles; growth vigorous (2½ m.); [Polyantha Alba Plena Sarmentosa × Général Jacqueminot]

Rosiériste Pajotin-Chédane Pol, dr, 1934, Délépine; flowers deep red, with white, thread-like markings, semi-dbl., cupped, borne in clusters on strong stems; foliage leathery; strong stems; vigorous, bushy growth; int. by Pajotin-Chédane

Rosiériste Philbert Boutigny HT, mp, 1904, Boutigny, P.; flowers carmine, globular; [Reine Marie Henriette × Victor Hugo]

Rosika – See **Radox Bouquet**, F

Rosilia – See **Rosalie Coral**, Cl Min

Rosina Min, my, 1951, Dot, Pedro; flowers sunflower-yellow, small, 16 petals, borne in clusters, slight fragrance; foliage glossy, light; dwarf, compact growth; [Eduardo Toda × Rouletii]; int. by URS, 1935

Rosine HT, pb, 1935, Lens; bud citron-yellow with red; flowers flesh-pink, base clear salmon, very dbl.; foliage bronze

Rosine Dupont HCh, w, Jacques; flowers flesh white, center violet, medium, very full

Rosine Margottin HP, lp, 1849, Margottin; flowers very pale flesh pink, medium, full

Rosita HT, lp, 1956, Delforge; bud long; flowers soft pink, large, dbl.; foliage glossy; vigorous growth; [The Doctor × seedling]

Rosita – See **Rosita Parade**, MinFl

Rosita Mauri HT, dp, 1914, Ketten Bros.; flowers deep rose-pink, large, full, borne mostly solitary; [Mme Abel Chatenay × Étoile de France]

Rosita Missoni HT, yb, Barni, V.; flowers yellow and red striped, medium, dbl., cupped, moderate fragrance; free-flowering; vigorous, tall growth; int. by Rose Barni, 1999

Rosita Parade MinFl, yb, Poulsen; flowers yellow with red edges, 5-8 cm., semi-dbl., slight wild rose fragrance; foliage dark; growth bushy, 20-40 cm.; PP13111; int. by Poulsen Roser, 2000

Rosita Vendela HT, dp, Tantau; greenhouse rose; int. by Australian Roses, 2004

Roslyn HT, dy, 1929, Towill; bud long, pointed, deep orange; flowers golden yellow, reverse darker orange, large, semi-dbl.; vigorous, compact growth; [Souv. de Claudius Pernet × Buttercup]

Roslyn, Climbing Cl HT, dy, 1937, Vestal

Roslyne – See **Strawberry Ice**, F

Rosmari HT, pb, 1962, Dot, Simon; bud pointed; flowers pink, reverse purplish, 30 petals; strong stems; vigorous, upright growth; [Vigoro × First Love]

Rosmarin – See **Rosemarin**, Min

Rosmarin Min, dp, 2006; flowers full, borne in small clusters; foliage tiny, dark green, dense; compact, short (20 cm.) growth; int. by W. Kordes' Söhne, 1989

Rosmarin 89 – See **Rosmarin**, Min

Rosnella Gr, Moro, L.; int. in 1958

Rosomane Alix Huguier HT, w, 1895, Bonnaire; flowers white with flesh pink reflections, center tinted salmon, very large, full

Rosomane E. P. Roussel HT, mr, 1907, Guillot; flowers glossy light crimson, reverse bright carmine, very large, full, moderate fragrance

Rosomane Gravereaux HT, w, 1899, Soupert & Notting; bud large, long; flowers silvery white, exterior tinted very lightly with flesh pink, very large, very full

Rosomane Hubert T, dy, 1883, Bernède; [Gloiire de Dijon × unknown]

Rosomane Narcisse Thomas T, rb, 1908, Bernaix fils; flowers crimson suffused apricot-yellow, small

Rosorum F, or, 1959, Buisman, G. A. H.; flowers orange-scarlet, semi-dbl., borne in large clusters; foliage dark, glossy; vigorous, upright growth; [Buisman's Triumph × Alpine Glow]

Ross Gowie HT, dr, 1968, Gowie; flowers conical, large; vigorous, tall growth; int. by Gandy Roses, Ltd.

Ross Rambler LCl, w, 1938; flowers small, single; blooms all summer; growth to 9 ft.; very hardy; discovered at the Dominion Forestry Station, Indian Head, Saskatchewan; probably a hybrid of *R. beggeriana*; int. by P.H. Wright

Rossana HT, dr, 1958, Buyl Frères; flowers blood-red, well-shaped, large, dbl.; vigorous, spreading growth; [Orange Delight × Tudor]

Rossetti Rose F, mp, Harkness; flowers large, delicate mid pink, very dbl., borne in large clusters, slight herbal fragrance; repeats freely; foliage dark green; bushy (3 × 3 ft.) growth; int. by R. Harkness & Co., 2004

Rossi HT, my, Select; flowers 5 in., 25-35 petals, high-centered, borne mostly singly; recurrent; stems 70-90 cm; florist rose; int. by Terra Nigra BV, 2003

Rossini HT, pb, deRuiter; florist rose; int. by deRuiter's New Roses Intl. BV

Rosslyn HP, mp, 1900, Dickson, A.; flowers rosy flesh, large, full

Rosso Giacomasso HT, Giacomasso; int. in 1967

Rostock HMsk, lp, 1937, Kordes; bud long, pointed; flowers very large, dbl., cupped, borne in clusters, slight fragrance; recurrent; foliage leathery, glossy, dark; very vigorous, bushy (4 ft.) growth; [Eva × Louise Catherine Breslau]

Roswytha F, mp, 1968, van der Meyden; bud ovoid; flowers pink, small, very dbl., borne in clusters; foliage dark; [sport of Carol]

Rosy Min, mp, Chandrakant; flowers non-fading pink, very full, rosette; free-flowering; [sport of Don Don]; int. in 1993

Rosy Ann MinFl, op, 2000, Lens, Louis; flowers orange pink, 2-3 cm., full, borne in small clusters, slight fragrance; recurrent; foliage medium size, medium green, glossy; prickles moderate; growth bushy, low (25 cm.); [Little Angel × Papillon Rose]; int. by Louis Lens N.V., 1993

Rosy Border – See **Santa Barbara**, S

Rosy Carpet S, dp, 1983, Interplant; flowers deep pink to red, 5 petals, shallow cup, borne in clusters, moderate fragrance; repeat blooming; foliage medium size, dark, glossy; prickles numerous, medium; spreading (to 4 ft.) growth; [Yesterday × seedling]

Rosy Cheeks HT, rb, 1976, Anderson's Rose Nurseries; flowers red, reverse yellow, 7 in., 35 petals, intense fragrance; foliage dark, glossy; [unknown × Irish Gold]; int. in 1975

Rosy Cheeks S, op, Moore; flowers coral pink, small, semi-dbl., borne in clusters; recurrent; foliage small, glossy; vigorous, spreading (3 × 6 ft.) growth; int. by Ludwig's Roses, 1984

Rosy Cheeks, Climbing Cl HT, rb, 1984, Anderson's Rose Nurseries; int. in 1985

Rosy Creeper – See **Suma**, S

Rosy Cushion S, pb, 1979, Ilsink; bud ovate; flowers pink with white toward center, small, 6 petals, flat, borne in large clusters, very slight fragrance; free-flowering; foliage dark green, glossy; prickles numerous, medium, straight; vigorous, sprawling (3 × 4 ft.) growth; [Yesterday × seedling]; int. by Dickson Nursery, Ltd.

Rosy Dawn Min, yb, 1982, Bennett, Dee; bud ovoid; flowers yellow, edged deep pink, medium, 25-30 petals, cupped, borne singly, slight tea fragrance; recurrent; foliage small, medium green, glossy; prickles small, slender, reddish; vigorous, erect (24 in.) growth; PP5274; [Magic Carrousel × Magic Carrousel]; int. by Tiny Petals Nursery

Rosy Floorshow S, pb; flowers rosy pink with white eye, 3½ in., 75 petals, cupped; foliage mid-green; growth compact, bushy plant (3 × 2 ft.); int. by Harkness, 1999

Rosy Forecast Min, dp, 1993, Laver, Keith G.; flowers deep pink, medium, dbl., borne in small clusters, moderate fragrance; foliage small, dark green, matte; few prickles; low (15-18 cm.), compact growth; [(June Laver × Ontario Celebration) × Potluck Purple]; int. by Springwood Roses, 1994

Rosy Future F, dp, 1992, Harkness, R., & Co., Ltd.; flowers carmine, small, dbl., borne in large clusters, moderate fragrance; foliage small, dark green, semi-glossy; few prickles; medium (60 cm.), upright growth; patio; [Radox Bouquet × Anna Ford]; int. by Harkness New Roses, Ltd., 1991

Rosy Glow HT, mp, 1947, Joseph H. Hill, Co.; bud long, pointed; flowers hermosa pink, 4-5 in., 25-35 petals, high-centered; foliage leathery; vigorous, bushy growth; [sport of Better Times]

Rosy Glow F, mp, Hensen

Rosy Hedge – See **Rosy Cushion**, S

Rosy Hit Min, op, Poulsen; flowers warm orange-pink, yellow on reverse, dbl., cupped, borne singly and in clusters; recurrent; vigorous, tall growth; int. in 1994

Rosy Jewel Min, pb, 1959, Morey, Dr. Dennison; bud ovoid; flowers rose-red, reverse lighter, center white, 1 in., 25 petals, moderate fragrance; low (6-8 in.), compact growth; PP1899; [Dick Koster × Tom Thumb]; int. by J&P, 1959

Rosy Koster Pol, mp

Rosy La Sevillana – See **Pink La Sevillana**, F

Rosy La Sevillana, Climbing Cl F, mp, Meilland; [sport of Rosy La Sevillana]; int. in 1993

Rosy Life HT, mp, 1971, Delbard; flowers sparkling pink, 3-4 in., 25 petals; foliage glossy; vigorous growth; [Walko × Souv. de J. Chabert]; int. by Laxton & Bunyard Nursery

Rosy Mantle LCl, mp, 1968, Cocker; flowers pale coral pink, 12-14 cm., dbl., borne in small clusters, moderate fragrance; recurrent; foliage dark, glossy; growth to 8-10 ft.; [New Dawn × Prima Ballerina]

Rosy Meillandina – See **Air France**, Min

Rosy Minimo Min, mp

Rosy Minuetto Min, lp, 2000, Meilland International; flowers 2-3 cm., very full, borne in small clusters, no fragrance; foliage medium size, medium green, semi-glossy; prickles moderate; compact, medium (8-12 in.) growth; PP17561; [sport of Fuchsia Minuetto]; int. by Conard-Pyle Co., 1999

Rosy Morn HP, op, 1878, Paul, W.; flowers soft peach shaded salmon-pink, well-formed, very large; very vigorous growth; [Victor Verdier × unknown]

Rosy Morn LCl, mp, 1914, Clark, A.; flowers large; [Frau Karl Druschki × unknown]

Rosy Morn Pol, mp, 1930, Burbage Nursery; flowers rose-pink, large, borne in large clusters; vigorous growth

Rosy Morn – See **Improved Cécile Brünner**, HG

Rosy Outlook LCl, pb, 1999, Carruth, Tom; flowers deep pink striped white, large, dbl., borne in large clusters, slight fragrance; foliage large, dark, green, glossy; prickles moderate; spreading, climbing, tall (10-12 ft.) growth; hardy; [Tournament of Roses × Roller Coaster]; int. by Weeks Roses, 1999

Rosy Pagode MinFl, mp, Poulsen; flowers medium pink, 5-8 cm., dbl., slight wild rose fragrance; foliage dark; growth broad, bushy, 40-60 cm.; PP14942; int. by Poulsen Roser, 2002

Rosy Paillette – See **Pink Parade**, Min

Rosy Pillow S, dp, Kontor; int. in 1998

Rosy Potluck Min, mp, 1995, Laver, Keith G.; flowers medium, full, borne in small clusters, moderate fragrance; foliage small, dark green, semi-glossy; few prickles; low (20-30 cm.), compact growth; int. by Springwood Roses, 1995

Rosy Purple HMsk, m, Lens, Louis; flowers reddish-purple, yellow stamens, small, single, flat, borne in clusters, slight fragrance; recurrent; foliage disease-resistant; tall (5+ ft.) growth; int. in 1995

Rosy Star HT, dp; flowers bright, strong pink, dbl., high-centered

Rosy Vision S, mp, 2005, Arnold, Dr. Neville, and Arnold, Catherine; flowers pink, reverse pink with yellow base, large, full, borne in large clusters, no fragrance; foliage medium size, medium green, semi-glossy, disease-resistant; prickles ½ in., hooked slightly downward, reddish brown, numerous; growth bushy, medium (5 ft.); [L 83 × Dornroshen]; int. by Canadian Rose Society, 2006

Rosy Wings HT, dp, 1962, Delforge; flowers pink shaded light red, 2-2½ in., 35 petals, globular; foliage dark, glossy; vigorous growth; [Pink Spiral × seedling]

Rosy Wings S, rb, 1997, Mekdeci, John; flowers large, 8-15 petals, borne in large clusters; foliage large, medium green, glossy; spreading, tall (6 ft.) growth; [Dornroschen × Golden Wings]; int. by Hortico

Rosycola Panarosa F, r, Delbard; flowers deep scarlet orange, maturing to orange brown, petals curly, semi-dbl., open, borne in clusters; recurrent; vigorous growth; int. by Ludwig's Roses, 2001

Rotaria Min, or

Rotarian HT, mr, 1921, Lemon; bud long, pointed; flowers bright cherry-crimson, 35-40 petals; [Ophelia × unknown]

Rotary Centennial Rose S, dy, Taschner, Ludwig; int. by Ludwig's Roses, 2003

Rotary Jubilee HT, yb, 1973, Lindquist; bud ovoid; flowers yellow blend, creamy yellow, large, dbl., high-centered, moderate fragrance; foliage large, glossy, dark, leathery; vigorous, bushy growth; [Queen Elizabeth × Peace]; int. by Bell Roses, Ltd., 1971

Rotary-Lyon HT, yb, 1936, Chambard, C.; bud long, pointed, well formed, golden pink; flowers old-gold shaded carmine, reverse yellow, stamens deep yellow, dbl., cupped; foliage dark; very vigorous growth

Rotary President F, or, 1976, Wood; flowers deep vermilion, 4 in., dbl., intense fragrance; foliage small, plum color, turning dark green; dwarf, bushy growth; [Fairlight × Summer Holiday]

Rotary Rose HT, dr, 1990, Meilland, Alain A.; bud pointed; flowers 27 petals, high-centered, borne usually singly; foliage medium green; prickles large, red; vigorous, upright growth; PP7408; [(Mister Lincoln × Pres. Leopold Senghor) × Karl Herbst]; int. by Rotary Rose Co., 1989

Rotary Sunrise HT, yb, Fryer; flowers golden orange, bright orange at petal edges, dbl., high-centered, borne mostly singly, moderate fragrance; recurrent; medium growth; int. by Fryer's Roses, 2004

Rote Apart – See **Scarlet Pavement**, S

Rote Apart S, mr, Uhl, J.; int. in 1991

Rote Better Times HT, mr, 1940, Noack, Werner; flowers large, dbl.

Röte Centifolie C, dr, 1938, Krause; flowers deep red, medium, very dbl., intense fragrance

Rote Else Poulsen F, dp, 1934, Koopmann; [sport of Else Poulsen]; int. by Tantau Roses

Rote Flamme HKor, dr, Kordes; flowers dark blood-red, 8-9 cm., dbl., borne in small clusters, no fragrance; some repeat; foliage large, dark green, glossy; bushy, upright (13 ft.) growth; int. in 1967

Rote Fox – See **Scarlet Pavement**, S

Rote Gabrielle Privat Pol, mr, 1940, Koopmann; [sport of Gabrielle Privat]

Rote Hannover S, mr; int. in 1998

Rote Hermosa – See **Queen's Scarlet**, Ch

Rote Hermosa Ch, mr, 1899, Geissler; flowers carmine-red, medium, dbl., moderate fragrance

Rote Hiroshima HT, mr, Tagashira, Kazuso; flowers carmine-red, large, dbl.; int. in 1990

Rote Krimrose HGal, dp; flowers bright pink to purple-pink, yellow stamens, large, full, intense fragrance; bushy, upright (5 ft.) growth; the Oilrose of Crimea

Rote Max Graf HKor, mr, 1980, Kordes, W.; bud medium, ovoid; flowers deep red with white at petal base, 7 cm., 6 petals, borne in large clusters, moderate fragrance; recurrent; foliage small, leathery, matte; prickles dark brown; vigorous, trailing groundcover growth; [*R. × kordesii* × seedling]; Gold Medal, Baden-Baden, 1981

Rote Mevrouw G. A. van Rossem HT, or, 1934, Kordes; flowers nasturtium-red, reverse lightly tinted yellow, large, dbl., open, intense fragrance; foliage glossy, dark; vigorous growth; [sport of Mev. G.A. van Rossem]

Rote Mozart S, or, Kordes; int. in 1989

Rote Perle F, dr, 1962, Tantau, Math.; flowers deep red, 1½ in., 25 petals; foliage dark; vigorous, bushy growth

Rote Pharisäer HT, mr, 1927, Hinner, W.; bud very long, pointed; flowers well-shaped, large, dbl.; foliage reddish green,leathery; very vigorous growth; [Pharisaer × George C. Waud]

Rote Rapture HT, mr, 1934, Weber, J.; flowers bright cherry-red; [sport of Rapture]

Rote Tausendschön HMult, mr, 1918, Isenhut, Frau; flowers ruby red; [Tausendschön × Bordeaux]

Rote Teschendorffs Jubiläumsrose Pol, dp, 1930, Grunewald; flowers dark crimson-pink to light red, large, dbl., borne in large clusters; vigorous growth; int. by Teschendorff

Rote Woge S, mr, Meilland; flowers dbl., cupped, borne in clusters; spreading (80-100 cm.) growth; int. in 1992

Rotelfe HT, dr, 1922, Tantau; flowers very dark red, medium, semi-dbl.; RULED EXTINCT 4/85; [Château de Clos Vougeot × Ulrich Brunner Fils]

Rotelfe F, mr, 1985, Tantau, Math.; flowers medium, semi-dbl.; foliage small, medium green, semi-glossy; groundcover; spreading growth

Roter Champagner HT, dp, 1963, Tantau, Math.; bud pointed; flowers red champagne color, large, dbl.; foliage bright green; long, strong stems; vigorous, upright growth

Roter Kobold F, dr, Interplant; int. in 1994

Roter Korsar S, dr, 2006, W. Kordes' Söhne; flowers brilliant dark red, not bluing, 9 cm., semi-dbl., shallow cup, borne in clusters of 10-12, very slight fragrance; foliage medium size, dark green, slightly glossy; bushy, tall (4-5 ft.) growth; int. as Red Corsair, Palatine Roses; Winner-Shrub, Dublin, 2006, Silver Medal, Kortrijk, 2006

Roter Schmetterling HFt, mr, 1935, Vogel, M.; flowers medium, semi-dbl.

Roter Stern HT, mr, Meilland; flowers geranium red, dbl., cupped, borne mostly singly, very slight fragrance; recurrent; medium growth; int. in 1958

Rotes Meer Pol, or, 1960, Verschuren, A.; flowers dbl., borne in large clusters; foliage glossy, dark; upright, bushy, symmetrical growth; [Orange Triumph × seedling]; int. by van Engelen

Rotes Meer – See **Purple Pavement**, HRg

Rotes Phænomen HRg, m, Baum; flowers dark magenta purple, intense fragrance; foliage rough; numerous prickles; dense growth; hips round; int. in 2002

Rotesmeer – See **Purple Pavement**, HRg

Rotfassade LCl, mr, Noack, Werner; flowers red with white base and yellow stamens, 6 cm., semi-dbl., cupped to flat, borne in clusters; recurrent; foliage medium to dark green, glossy; growth to 10 ft.; int. by Noack Rosen, 1997

Rothsay F, or, 2000, Brown, Ted; flowers bright orange-red, 3½ in., dbl., borne in small clusters, slight fragrance; foliage medium size, dark green, semi-glossy; few prickles; bushy, medium (3 ft.) growth; [Royal Occasion × seedling]

Rotilia F, mr, 2006, W. Kordes' Söhne; bud small, pointed, dark red; flowers brilliant crimson, 5 cm., semi-dbl., cupped, borne in large clusters, moderate fragrance; recurrent; foliage medium size, deep dark green, very glossy; bushy, compact, medium (60 cm.) growth; int. by W. Kordes' Söhne, 2000; Golden Rose, Hague, 2003, Gold Medal, Glasgow, 2006, Gold Medal, Dublin, 2001

Rotkäppchen Pol, mr, 1887, Geschwind, R.; flowers magenta-red, 6 cm., 30 petals, rosette, borne in small clusters; good repeat; bushy (50 cm.) growth; winter hardy

Rotorua F, or, 1963, McGredy, Sam IV; bud ovoid; flowers orange-scarlet, large, 27 petals, high-centered, borne in clusters; foliage leathery, dark; short, strong stems; very vigorous, bushy growth; [Independence × Spartan]; int. by Avenue Nursery, 1962

Rotraut Pol, dr, 1931, Grunewald; flowers dbl., borne in clusters; vigorous growth; [sport of Miss Edith Cavell]

Rotrou M, m, 1849, Vibert; flowers reddish-violet, medium, dbl.

Rouge – See **Rubra**, C

Rouge – See **Rubra**, M

Rouge – See **Red Damask**, D

Rouge HSpn, mp, about 1808, Descemet; bud nearly round; flowers delicate flesh pink, medium, dbl., borne mostly singly on the secondary branches; foliage round or elliptical, simply dentate; prickles unequal, short, almost straight; hips cherry-sized, red at first, blackening at maturity

Rouge Pol, mr, 1934, Verschuren; flowers brilliant scarlet-crimson, open, semi-dbl.; foliage leathery; strong stems; dwarf growth; int. by J&P

Rouge Adam HT, dr, Adam, M.; flowers velvety dark red, full to very full, high-centered, borne singly, slight fragrance; recurrent; foliage medium size, dark green, glossy; bushy, medium growth; int. in 1996

Rouge Admirable – See **Pourpre Charmant**, HGal

Rouge Admirable – See **Orphise**, HGal

Rouge Admirable Strié HGal, m, before 1836, Vibert; flowers striped purple

Rouge Agréable – See **Junon**, HGal

Rouge Angevine HP, mr, 1907, Chedane-Pajotin; flowers large, dbl.

Rouge Baiser HT, mr, Delbard; flowers red to reddish-orange, high-centered; greenhouse variety

Rouge Captain Christy HT, dp, 1898, Perrier; [sport of Captain Christy]

Rouge Champion HT, mr, 1956, Buyl Frères; flowers bright red, 40-50 petals; very vigorous growth; [Happiness × Princesse Liliane]

Rouge de Belgique HGal, mr, before 1791; flowers large, dbl.; foliage dark green, often marbled yellow, wavy edges; Agathe group

Rouge de Paris F, mr, 1958, Delbard-Chabert; flowers light red, 3 in., 35-45 petals; foliage purplish; vigorous, bushy growth; [(Floradora × unknown) × (Orange Triumph × unknown)]; int. by Stark Bros., 1964

Rouge de Parme HT, pb, 1963, Dorieux; flowers mauve-pink, large, dbl., high-centered; foliage dark, dull; [(Peace × Fred Edmunds) × Buccaneer]; int. by Le Blévenec

Rouge Dorieux HT, mr, 1970, Dorieux; bud pointed; flowers cherry-red, open, over large, dbl.; foliage dark, glossy, leathery; vigorous, upright growth; [seedling × Ena Harkness]; int. by Vilmorin, 1967

Rouge Dot HT, mr, 1962, Dot, Simon; flowers currant-red, 40 petals; vigorous growth; [Baccará × Lydia]

Rouge Éblouissant – See **Assemblage de Beauté(s)**, HGal

Rouge et Or – See **Redgold**, F

Rouge et Or, Climbing – See **Redgold, Climbing**, Cl F, 1980

Rouge Formidable HGal, mr, before 1811; flowers crimson-violet-purple, medium, very dbl.

Rouge Koster Pol, mr

Rouge Mallerin HT, mr, 1934, Mallerin, C.; bud long, pointed; flowers brilliant red, large, dbl., high-centered, intense damask fragrance; compact growth; [Mme Van de Voorde × Lady Maureen Stewart]; int. by C-P

Rouge Marbrée B, rb; flowers red and violet

Rouge Meidiland – See **Red Meidiland**, S
Rouge Meilland – See **Happiness**, HT
Rouge Meilland, Climbing – See **Happiness, Climbing**, Cl HT

Rouge Meilland HT, mr, 1985, Meilland, Mrs. Marie-Louise; flowers large, very full, no fragrance; foliage large, dark green, semi-glossy; upright growth; [((Queen Elizabeth × Karl Herbst) × Pharoah) × Antonia Ridge]; int. by Meilland Et Cie, 1982

Rouge Meillandécor – See **Red Meidiland**, S

Rouge Pineau F, Pineau; int. in 1980

Rouge Prolific – See **Clos Vougeot**, F
Rouge Rayé – See **Beauté Tendre**, HGal

Rouge Royale HT, rb, 2001, Meilland International; bud ovoid; flowers velvety red, reverse geranium red, 6-7 in., very full, cupped, borne mostly solitary, intense fragrance; recurrent; foliage large, medium green, glossy; prickles moderate, large, slightly concave undersurface; growth upright, medium (5-6 ft.); garden decorative, cutting; hips none ; PP14039; [Charlotte Rampling × (Ambassador × Meicapula)]; int. by The Conard-Pyle Company, 2001; Perfume Prize, Orléans, 2006

Rouge Striée – See **Striata**, S

Rouge Superbe Actif HGal, dr, before 1811; bud round; flowers velvety crimson, small, very dbl., moderate fragrance

Rouge Vif – See **Capricornus**, C
Rougeau Virginale – See **Héloïse**, C

Rougemoss F, or, 1973, Moore, Ralph S.; bud ovoid, pointed; sepals covered densely with bristles mimicking moss; flowers scarlet, 2½ in., 30-40 petals, cupped, borne singly and in small clusters, moderate fragrance; recurrent; foliage medium to dark green, leathery, glossy; prickles numerous, medium, slender, straight, sharp, brown; vigorous, bushy (2½-3 ft.) growth; hips none ; PP3563; [Rumba × Moss hybrid]; int. by Sequoia Nursery, 1972

Rouletii Ch, mp, 1815, rediscovered in 1922 by Major Roulet; flowers rose-pink, ½ in., dbl.; recurrent bloom; dwarf growth; sometimes considered (Jäger) to be a dwarf form of *R. semperflorens* or R. *bengalensis*; possibly synonymous with *R. semperflorens minima* (Lawrence)

Rouletii, Climbing Cl Ch, mp; possibly synonymous with Pompon de Paris, Cl.

Rouletti, Climbing – See **Pompon de Paris, Climbing**, Cl Ch

Round Robin Min, mr, Hannemann, F.; [Avandel × Oz Gold]; int. by The Rose Paradise, 1990

Roundabout Min, mr, 1985, Zipper, Herbert; flowers small, 20 petals, borne mostly singly; foliage medium size, medium green, matte; bushy growth; [Double Joy × Libby]; int. by Magic Moment Miniature Roses

Roundelay Gr, dr, 1954, Swim, H.C.; bud ovoid; flowers medium-large, 3-4 in., 35-40 petals, high-centered, then flat, borne mostly in clusters of 3-4, some singly, moderate tea fragrance; free-flowering; foliage dark green, glossy, leathery; prickles numerous, medium, hooked slightly downward, tawny; stems strong, long; very vigorous growth; hips globular, smooth, green; PP1280; [Charlotte Armstrong × Floradora]; int. by Armstrong Nursery; Gold Medal, Geneva, 1954

Roundelay, Climbing Cl Gr, dr; flowers deep crimson red; recurrent; vigorous (10 ft.) growth; [sport of Roundelay]; discovered in Australia; int. in 1970

Rountuit HRg, pb, Moore, Ralph; flowers rose pink, 2½ in., very dbl.; borne all season; growth somewhat spreading, to 5 ft.; int. by Sequoia Nursery, 2000

Roussillon F, mr

Route 66 S, m, 2001, Carruth, Tom; flowers velvet black/purple with white eye, 5-7 cm., single, borne in large clusters, Intense clove fragrance; foliage medium size, dark green, semi-glossy; prickles few, average, almost straight, light brown; growth bushy, medium (90-110 cm.); garden decorative; PP15374; [((Sweet Chariot × Blue Nile) × Purple Splendor) × ((International Herald Tribune × *R. soulieana derivative*) × (Sweet Chariot × Blue Nile))]; int. by Armstrong Garden Centers, 2001

Routrou – See **Rotrou**, M

Roville LCl, mp, 2002, Eve, André; flowers carmine pink, silvery reverse, 8 cm., single, borne in large clusters, slight fragrance; recurrent; foliage medium size, medium green, matte; prickles moderate; growth tall (4-5 m.), climbing; [Red Parfum × Phyllis Bide]

Rowdy Roy MinFl, rb, 2005, Bennett, Dee; flowers variable in color, from scarlet to deep burgundy with pink to white striping, 2½-3 in., full, borne mostly solitary, slight fragrance; foliage medium size, medium green, matte; prickles small, straight; growth compact, short (2-2½ ft.); garden, cut flower, exhibition; [October × Fool's Gold]; int. by Tiny Petals Nursery, 2005

Rowena HWich, dp, 1912, Paul, W.; flowers carmine, changing to mauve-pink, small, dbl., borne in clusters; vigorous, climbing growth

Roxana HT, yb, 1933, Dickson, A.; bud large, long, pointed; flowers orange-yellow and copper, open, semi-dbl.; foliage glossy, light; vigorous, bushy growth

Roxana HT, or, Urban, J.

Roxane HT, yb, Laperrière; flowers Indian-yellow with red-carmine edges, dbl., slight fruity fragrance; foliage glossy; moderate growth; int. by Roseraie Laperrière, 1990; Golden Rose, Geneva, 1990

Roxane, Climbing Cl HT, yb, Laperrière; flowers yellow with carmine red edges, slight fruity fragrance; growth to 3-5 m.; [sport of Roxane]; int. by Roseraie Laperrière, 2000

Roxanne F, Laperrière; int. in 1990

Roxburghe Rose HT, or, Cocker; flowers dbl.; int. in 1991

Roxburghiana – See **Grevilii**, HMult single
Roxelana – See **Roxelane**, HCh

Roxelane HGal, dp, 1811; flowers semi-dbl.

Roxelane HCh, mp, about 1825, Prévost; flowers medium pink, inner petals often marked with white, small, dbl., cupped; sometimes classed as HGal

Roxette F, op, Select; flowers salmon pink, 9 cm., 30-40 petals, high-centered, borne mostly singly; recurrent; florist rose; int. by Terra Nigra BV, 2003

Roxie HT, mr, 1995, Sheldon, John & Robin; flowers medium, full, borne mostly singly, slight fragrance; foliage medium size, medium green, matte; upright, medium growth; [Sheer Bliss × Headliner]

Roxie MinFl, op, 2001, Tucker, Robbie; flowers light orange, 2 in., dbl., high-centered, borne in small clusters, no fragrance; foliage dark green, glossy; prickles 1 cm., straight to slightly downward, red on new growth; growth bushy, medium (to 30 in.); exhibition, cutting, garden decorative; [Elsie Melton × Kristin]; int. by Rosemania, 2001

Roxie Baby HT, op, 1998, Tucker, Robbie; flowers orange to pink, reverse lighter, 3-4 in., 65 petals, high-centered, borne mostly singly; foliage dark green, glossy; upright, medium (5 ft.) growth; [Elizabeth Taylor × Hoagy Carmichael]; int. by Rosehill Nursery, 1999

Roxy – See **Roxy 2001**, HT

Roxy 2001 HT, mr, Kordes; flowers large, dbl., high-centered, borne mostly singly; good repeat; stems long (80 cm) in greenhouse; florist rose; int. by W. Kordes Söhne, 2001

Roxy Kordana Mini Brite Min, mr, Kordes; bud long, blunt topped; flowers medium red, reverse slightly darker, occasional white streak, 2-2¼ in., 35-40 petals, high-centered, then flat, borne singly and in small clusters, no fragrance; free-flowering; foliage leathery, glossy; prickles moderate, short, straight; stems 8-10 in.; vigorous, upright (3 ft.) growth; PP11148; [seedling × seedling]; int. in 1998

Roy Black – See **Karen Blixen**, HT
Roy Castle Rose – See **Courage**, HT
Royal – See **Royal Parade**, Min

Royal Min, mp, Poulsen; int. in 2000

Royal Air Force HT, m, 1969, Laperrière; flowers light lavender-blue, 6 in., 35 petals, high-centered, slight tea and lavender fragrance; foliage dark, matte; int. by Wheatcroft Bros.

Royal Albert Hall HT, rb, 1972, Cocker; flowers wine-red, reverse gold, 5 in., 32 petals, intense tea fragrance; foliage dark; compact growth; [Fragrant Cloud × Postillon]

Royal Amber S, ab, Clements, John; flowers rich apricot-amber, very ruffled, 4 in., 33 petals, pompon, moderate old rose fragrance; recurrent; bronzy red leaves become medium green, matte; compact (4 × 3½ ft.) growth; PPAF; int. by Heirloom, 2000

Royal America LCl, w, 1994, Cooper, Curt; flowers ivory, medium, semi-dbl., borne in small clusters, slight fragrance; foliage medium size, light green, matte; tall, bushy, spreading growth; [sport of America]; int. by Certified Roses, Inc., 1995

Royal Amethyst HT, m, 1989, deVor, Paul F.; bud pointed; flowers lavender, large, 32 petals, borne singly, intense fruity fragrance; foliage medium size, medium green, glossy; prickles declining, henna; upright, tall growth; hips globular, tangerine-orange; [Angel Face × Blue Moon]; int. by DeVor Nurseries, Inc.; Gold Medal & FA, Portland, 1996

Royal Anniversary F, mr, 1993, Harkness; flowers crimson, yellow base, reverse mid-pink, aging dark red, 2½ in., 24 petals, slight fruity fragrance; foliage small, dark green, glossy; bushy, low growth; [Intrigue × Anna Ford]; int. as Ruby Anniversary, Harkness New Roses, Ltd., 1992; Gold Medal, Belfast, 1995

Royal Ascot HT, pb, 1970, Delbard-Chabert; flowers pink, reverse shaded crimson, large, semi-dbl., high-centered; foliage glossy, leathery; vigorous, bushy growth; [Chic Parisien × (Grande Premiere × (Sultane × Mme Joseph Perraud))]; int. in 1968

Royal Baby F, mr, 1982, Bracegirdle, Derek T.; flowers medium, 20 petals; foliage small, medium green, semi-glossy; upright growth; [Generosa × Baby Darling]; int. by Arthur Higgs Roses

Royal Baccara HT, mr, Meilland; flowers velvety red, dbl., high-centered, bonre mostly singly; good repeat; florist rose; int. by Meilland Intl., 2002

Royal Ballgown – See **The Fisherman's Cot**, F

Royal Bassino S, mr, Kordes; flowers bright red to scarlet with yellow stamens, medium, semi-dbl., shallow cup to flat, borne in clusters, slight fragrance; continuous blooms; medium (2-3 ft.), spreading, groundcover growth

Royal Bath & West Gr, lp, 1977, Sanday, John; flowers pastel pink, 4 in., 20 petals; foliage green, matte; [seedling × Prima Ballerina]

Royal Beauty HT, dr, 1940, Coddington; flowers dark velvety red, 5 in., 25 petals, high-centered, moderate spicy fragrance; foliage bronze; [sport of Better Times]

Royal Blush A, lp, Sievers; flowers pale flesh pink, 4-5 in., very full, cupped, intense fragrance; arching (5 ft.) growth; int. in 1988

Royal Bonica S, mp, 1994, Meilland, Alain A.; bud oval; flowers cardinal red, suffused with Neyron rose, medium, 53 petals, globular, then cupped, borne usually in small clusters, slight fragrance; recurrent;

foliage medium size, medium green, semi-glossy; some prickles; bushy, medium (3 ft.), upright growth; PP8840; [sport of Bonica]; int. by The Conard-Pyle Co., 1993

Royal Bouquet – See **Diadem**, F dbl.

Royal Bright HT, my, 1977, Kono, Yoshito; bud ovoid; flowers 6 in., very dbl., high-centered; vigorous, upright growth; [Garden Party × (Bronze Masterpiece × Memoriam)]; int. in 1976

Royal Canadian HT, mr, 1967, Boerner, E. S.; bud ovoid; flowers deep, clear red, very large, dbl., open, borne singly and several together; foliage large, leathery; vigorous, upright growth; [seedling × seedling]; int. by J&P

Royal Canadian HT, mr, 1968, Morey, Dennison H., Jr.; buds large, ovoid to urn-shaped; flowers scarlet, 5-5½ in., 25-30 petals, cupped, borne mostly singly; free-flowering; foliage leathery, glossy; prickles moderate, medium, hooked downward; stems medium, strong; growth upright, vigorous; no hips; PP2736

Royal Carpet Min, mr, 1985, Williams, Ernest D.; flowers small, dbl., borne in clusters, no fragrance; foliage small, dark, semi-glossy; groundcover; spreading growth; PP5909; [Red Cascade × Red Cascade]; int. by Mini-Roses, 1984

Royal Celebration F, m, Carruth, Tom; flowers velvet purple, dbl., cupped, borne in clusters, intense clove fragrance; recurrent; foliage semi-glossy; slender, fairly short growth; int. by C&K Jones, 2004

Royal Chinook HT, mr, 1939, Chase; flowers brilliant rose-red; [sport of Rapture]

Royal Circus HT, rb, Kordes; flowers bright red, reverse yellow suffused with red from the outer edge, medium, full, high-centered, borne mostly singly; recurrent; stems medium; [sport of Circus (Korlumara)]; florist rose; int. by W. Kordes Söhne, 2005

Royal City Min, dr, 1989, Rennie, Bruce F.; bud ovoid; flowers medium, 23 petals, high-centered, urn-shaped, borne singly; foliage medium size, medium green, semi-glossy; prickles hooked, medium, yellow; upright, tall growth; hips globular, medium, ornage-red; [Goldmarie × Pink Sheri]; int. by Rennie Roses International, 1990

Royal Class HT, dr; flowers deep classic red; int. by Carlton Rose Nurseries, 2004

Royal Cluster HMult, lp, 1899, Dawson; flowers blush white, 4 cm., single, borne in clusters of up to 100; [Hermosa × Dawson]; int. by Conard & Jones, 1899

Royal Copenhagen HT, lp, Olesen; bud pointed ovoid; flowers light blush pink, 3½-4 in., 25-30 petals, hybrid tea, borne one to a stem, moderate old rose with lemon and grapefruit fragrance; recurrent; foliage very glossy; prickles medium, deeply concave; upright, bushy (100-150 cm.) growth; PP15195; [seedling × Tivoli Gardens]

Royal Dane HT, ob, 1973, Poulsen, D. T.; flowers orange, outer petals red, 4-6 in., full, high-centered, borne mostly singly, intense sweet fragrance; recurrent; foliage large, dark, glossy, leathery; vigorous, upright, bushy growth; [(Tropicana × (Baccará × Princesse Astrid)) × Hanne]; int. by Kordes, 1971; Gold Medal, James Mason, 1992

Royal Dawn LCl, mp, 1964, Morey, Dr. Dennison; flowers coral-pink, large, 35 petals, moderate fragrance; foliage dark, glossy; vigorous, climbing growth; [Royal Sunset × Aloha]; int. by J&P, 1962

Royal Delight – See **Royal Success**, HT

Royal Dot HT, pb, Dot, P.; flowers well-formed; int. in 1980

Royal Dream HT, dp, Kordes; bud long, pointed ovoid, blunt tip; flowers 3½-4 in., 25 -30 petals, high-centered, borne mostly singly, slight fragrance; recurrent; foliage large, leathery, matte; prickles few, short, hooked slightly downward; stems strong, 18-22 in.; vigorous, upright (5½ ft.) growth; PP11353; [sport of Dream]; greenhouse rose; int. by W. Kordes Söhne, 1997

Royal Edward S, mp, 1994, Ogilvie, Ian S.; bud ovoid; flowers medium pink, fading to pale pink, 2 in., 18 petals, flat, borne mostly in large clusters, slight fragrance; heavy spring bloom, lesser repeat; foliage small, medium green, glossy; few prickles; low (45 cm.), bushy, spreading growth; winter hardy ; PP9972; [*R.* × *kordesii* × ((*R.* × *kordesii* × (Red Dawn × Suzanne)) × Zeus)]; int. by Agriculture Canada, 1994

Royal Emblem HT, w, 2003, Ishii, Tsuyoshi; flowers semi-dbl., borne in small clusters, slight fragrance; foliage small, dark green, glossy; prickles medium, sharp, moderate; growth spreading, medium (5 ft.); ground cover, weeping standard; [*R. yakushimensis* × unknown]

Royal Époux HP, mp, 1859, Damaizin; flowers bright glossy pink, large, full

Royal Flare HT, rb, 1988, Wambach, Alex A.; flowers red and white blend, large, high-centered, borne singly; foliage medium size, dark green, disease-resistant; prickles down-turned, dark green; upright, medium growth; [Pristine × Standout]

Royal Flush LCl, pb, 1970, Fuller; bud ovoid; flowers cream, edges blending pink, medium, semi-dbl., cupped; repeat bloom; foliage dark, leathery; vigorous, upright, climbing growth; [Little Darling × Suspense]; int. by Wyant

Royal Flush MinFl, pb, Pearce; int. in 1992

Royal Garnet Min, mr; flowers rich, moderate fragrance; moderate growth

Royal Gem F, lp, Brooks, M.L.; int. in 1959

Royal Gold LCl, my, 1958, Morey, Dr. Dennison; bud medium, ovoid; flowers golden yellow, 4-5 in., 35-45 petals, cupped, borne singly and in clusters of 3-7, moderate fruity fragrance; recurrent; foliage large, dark green, glossy; prickles numerous, medium, straight; stems medium, strong; vigorous, pillar (5-7 ft.) growth; hips none ; PP1849; [Goldilocks, Climbing × Lydia]; int. by J&P, 1957

Royal Highness HT, lp, 1962, Swim & Weeks; bud long, pointed; flowers soft light pink, 5-5½ in., 40-45 petals, high-centered, borne mostly singly, intense tea fragrance; recurrent; foliage large, dark, glossy, leathery; prickles several, long, straight, brown; stems long, strong; tender, upright, bushy growth; hips globular, smooth ; PP2032; [Virgo × Peace]; int. by C-P, 1962; Gold Medal, Portland, 1960, Gold Medal, Madrid, 1962, David Fuerstenberg Prize, ARS, 1964

Royal Lady Min, m, 1993, Williams, Ernest D.; flowers lavender pink, petals ruffled, medium, full, borne mostly singly, intense fragrance; foliage small, medium green, semi-glossy; few prickles; medium (40 cm.), bushy growth; [Angel Face × Twilight Beauty]; int. by Mini Roses of Texas, 1993

Royal Lavender LCl, m, 1961, Morey, Dr. Dennison; bud medium, ovoid; flowers lavender tinted gray and pink, 3 in., 35-40 petals, cupped, borne in clusters, intense old rose (centifolia) fragrance; intermittent; foliage large, dark green, leathery; prickles moderate, medium, hooked downward; stems medium, strong; vigorous (6-9 ft.) growth; hips none ; PP2194; [Lavender Queen × Amy Vanderbilt]; int. by J&P, 1961

Royal Lustre HT, op, McGredy; flowers orange-buff overlaid salmon, 6-7 in., 45 petals; foliage coppery; very free growth; [Mrs Sam McGredy × Crimson Glory]

Royal Mail F, rb, 1985, Anderson's Rose Nurseries; flowers red with yellow petal edges, small, 20 petals, no fragrance; foliage small, medium green, glossy; upright, bushy growth; [seedling × Manx Queen]; int. in 1986

Royal Marbré HGal, m, before 1837, Moreau & Robert; flowers lilac and purple, marbled (striped) pink, medium, very dbl.; upright, bushy (5 ft.) growth

Royal Meillandina – See **Royal Sunblaze**, Min

Royal Midinette S, rb, Moore; flowers gold-cream and deep royal red, borne in clusters; foliage dark green; medium, vigorous, arching growth; int. in 1997

Royal Occasion F, or, 1976, Tantau, Math.; bud long, pointed; flowers luminous orange-scarlet, 3 in., 20 petals, cupped, borne in small clusters, slight fragrance; recurrent; foliage glossy, large, leathery; prickles numerous, narrow base, brown; stems long; upright, compact, strong (3 ft.) growth; hips round, smooth, orange-scarlet; PP3824; [Walzertraum × Europeana]; int. by H. Wheatcroft, 1974; ADR, 1974

Royal Pageant – See **Della Balfour**, S

Royal Palace MinFl, yb, Poulsen; bud short, globular; flowers yellow-orange, 2 in., 20-28 petals, flat, borne singly, slight fruity fragrance; recurrent; foliage medium size, dark, glossy; prickles few, 3-4 mm., concave; bushy (40-60 cm.) growth; PP13277; [Flora Danica × Easter]; int. by Poulsen Roser, 2000

Royal Parade Min, mp, Poulsen; flowers medium pink, medium, dbl., no fragrance; growth bushy, 20-40 cm.; int. by Poulsen Roser, 1996

Royal Parks HT, ab, Harkness; flowers copper shading blending with apricot and caramel, 4½ in., 35 petals, high-centered, borne mostly singly, moderate sweet & spicy fragrance; recurrent; foliage leathery; strong (4 ft.) growth; int. by R. Harkness & Co, 2005

Royal Pashmina HT, dp, Kordes; flowers rich pink, medium, dbl., cupped, borne mostly singly; recurrent; stems medium; [sport of Pascha]; florist rose; int. by W. Kordes Söhne, 2005

Royal Perfection HT, or, 1964, Delbard; flowers orange-coral, 4½ in., 20 petals; vigorous growth; [Rome Glory × Bayadere]; int. by Laxton & Bunyard Nursery, 1964

Royal Philharmonic HT, w, Harkness; flowers white with a hint of pink, full, high-centered, borne mostly singly, slight fragrance; recurrent; medium to tall growth; int. by R. Harkness & Co., 1997

Royal Porcelain Cl HT, mp, 1992, Little, Lee W.; flowers 3-3½ in., full, high-centered, borne in small clusters on strong upright laterals; foliage large, disease-resistant; some prickles; tall (260 cm.), upright, spreading growth; [Pele × Altissimo]; int. by Heirloom Old Garden Roses, 1992

Royal Princess Min, pb, 1982, Lyon; bud ovoid; flowers pink and yellow blend, 65 petals, borne singly and in small clusters, moderate fruity fragrance; foliage dark, leathery; prickles hooked, bronze; upright, bushy growth; [seedling × seedling]; int. in 1981

Royal Princess S, Meilland; int. by Keisei Rose Nurseries, 1997

Royal Prophyta HT, mp, deRuiter; flowers cerise, full, cupped, borne mostly singly; recurrent; [sport of Prophyta]; florist rose; int. by deRuiter's New Roses Intl., 2001

Royal Queen Gr, w, 1965, Verschuren; bud ovoid; flowers greenish white, medium, dbl., borne several together; foliage dark green; [sport of Queen Elizabeth]

Royal Queen, Cl. Cl Gr, w, after 1965

Royal Queen Elizabeth – See **Royal Queen**, Gr

Royal Queen Elizabeth, Cl. – See **Royal Queen, Cl.**, Cl Gr

Royal Red HT, mr, 1924, E.G. Hill, Co.; bud pointed; flowers intense crimson-scarlet, very large, dbl.; foliage leathery; vigorous growth

Royal Red HT, dr, 1956, Lowe; flowers deep scarlet, well-formed; moderate growth; [sport of Happiness]

Royal Red HT, mr, 1985, Kordes, W.; flowers 20 petals; foliage dark, glossy; upright growth; [seedling × seedling]; int. by Paul Pekmez

Royal Red – See **Rouge Royale**, HT

Royal Robe S, mr, 1946, Wright, Percy H.; flowers crimson, almost purple, rather large, semi-dbl.; non-recurrent; vigorous growth; [(*R. rugosa* × Hybrid Perpetual) × (*R. multiflora* × *R. blanda*)]

Royal Romance HT, my, 1975, Fryer, Gareth; flowers bright lemon-yellow, 5 in., 30 petals, moderate fragrance; foliage leathery; very free growth; [Pink Parfait × seedling]; int. by Fryer's Nursery, Ltd., 1974

Royal Romance – See **Liselle**, HT

Royal Rose HT, mp, 1999, Teranishi, K.; flowers rose pink, 80 petals, high-centered; growth to 4½ ft.; [Happiness × Peter Frankenfeld]; int. by Itami Rose Nursery, 1987

Royal Ruby Min, mr, 1974, Morey, Dr. Dennison; bud small, globular; flowers red, base white, small, full, globular, borne singly and in small clusters, slight sweet fragrance; free-flowering; foliage small, dark green, leathery. glossy; stems long; vigorous, upright (12-18 in.) growth; [Garnette × (Tom Thumb × Ruby Jewel)]; int. by Pixie Treasures Min. Roses, 1972

Royal Salute Min, mr, 1977, McGredy, Sam IV; flowers rose-red, 1½ in., 30 petals, rosette, borne in trusses; free-flowering; foliage small, dark green, matte; compact (2 ft.) growth; [New Penny × Marlena]; int. by Mattock, 1976

Royal Scarlet HP, mr, 1899, Paul, G.; flowers bright scarlet-red; recurrent; [Mme Rady × Cheshunt Scarlet]

Royal Scarlet HT, mr, 1969, Kraus; bud ovoid; flowers scarlet-red, large, dbl., high-centered, moderate fragrance; foliage glossy; vigorous, bushy growth; [McGredy's Scarlet × Christian Dior]; int. by Wyant, 1966

Royal Scarlet Hybrid HWich, mr, 1926, Chaplin Bros.; flowers bright crimson red, 6-7 cm., semi-dbl., borne in small clusters, slight fragrance; foliage small, glossy

Royal Scot HT, yb, 1928, Dobbie; flowers golden yellow, edged crimson, open, semi-dbl.; foliage dark; vigorous growth

Royal Show HT, mr, 1973, Gregory; flowers light red to deeper red, pointed, 4 in., 27 petals, borne singly, slight fragrance; recurrent; foliage medium green, glossy; vigorous (3 ft.) growth; [Queen Elizabeth × unknown]

Royal Show S, mr, Meilland; bud tinted crimson; flowers vermilion, 3 in., dbl., borne in large clusters, no fragrance; foliage dark green; int. in 1983; Gold Medal, Durbanville, 1984

Royal Smile HT, w, Beales, Peter; flowers creamy white with soft pink shadings, dbl., cupped, intense fragrance; free-flowering; short to medium growth; int. by Peter Beales Roses, 1980

Royal Star & Garter LCl, mp, Fryer; flowers candy pink, large, dbl., cupped, borne in clusters of several together., moderate fragrance; constant bloom.; stems long, supple; growth to 8-9 ft.; int. by Fryer's, 2001

Royal Success HT, mr, 1987, Christensen, Jack & Carruth, Tom; flowers large, 30 petals, high-centered, borne usually singly; foliage medium size, medium green, semi-glossy; prickles normal, light green to tan; upright, bushy, tall growth; fruit not observed; PP6910; [Red Success × Royalty]; int. by Armstrong Nursery, 1986

Royal Sunblaze Min, my, 1987, Schwartz, Ernest W.; bud ovoid; flowers lemon yellow, quilled petals, 4-5 cm., very dbl., rosette, borne in small clusters, slight fragrance; free-flowering; foliage medium size, medium green, semi-glossy; prickles red; compact, bushy (15 in.) growth; PP5690; [seedling × seedling]; int. by SNC Meilland & Cie, 1984

Royal Sunset LCl, ab, 1960, Morey, Dr. Dennison; bud large, ovoid; flowers 4½-5 in., 20 petals, cupped, borne singly and several together, moderate fruity fragrance; recurrent; foliage large, leathery; prickles numerous, medium, straight; stems medium, strong; vigorous, upright (6 ft.) growth; hips none ; PP2072; [Sungold × Sutter's Gold]; int. by J&P, 1960; Gold Medal, Portland, 1960

Royal Tan HT, m, 1956, McGredy, Sam IV; flowers pale purple feathered violet and chocolate, high-pointed, 5 in.; foliage dark; vigorous growth; [Charles P. Kilham × Mrs Sam McGredy]

Royal Touch F, rb, 1983, Anderson's Rose Nurseries; flowers red, reverse silver, medium, 20 petals; foliage medium size, medium green, semi-glossy; upright growth; [Orange Sensation × Elizabeth of Glamis]

Royal Velvet HT, dr, 1960, Meilland, F.; flowers rich, velvety cardinal-red, 4-5 in., 55-65 petals; vigorous, tall growth; PP1911; RULED EXTINCT 3/86 ARM.; [(Happiness × Independence) × (Happiness × Floradora)]; int. by C-P, 1959

Royal Velvet HT, dr, 1986, Meilland, Mrs. Marie-Louise; flowers large, 28 petals, high-centered, borne mostly singly; prickles large, straw-colored; medium, bushy growth; hips globular, small, medium green; [(Exciting × Suspense) × Duke of Windsor]; int. by Wayside Gardens Co.

Royal Victoria Min, op, 1991, Laver, Keith G.; flowers coral pink, white reverse, small, very full, cupped, borne mostly singly, moderate fragrance; recurrent; foliage small, medium green, semi-glossy; tall, upright, bushy growth; [(Painted Doll × June Laver) × Mountie]; int. by Springwood Roses, 1991

Royal Victoria Hospital F, pb; int. by White Rose, 2002

Royal Virgin Rose – See **Aimable Rouge**, HGal, 1819-1820

Royal Visit HT, op, 1939, Eddie; flowers deep tangerine-orange, reverse coral passing to apricot, dbl.; foliage leathery, glossy, dark; bushy growth; [Picture × Mrs Pierre S. duPont]

Royal Volunteer HT, ob, 1988, Cocker, James & Sons; flowers orange-red and yellow blended, medium, full; foliage medium size, light green, semi-glossy; upright growth; [Yellow Pages × Alexander]

Royal Wedding F, ab, 1998, Zary, Dr. Keith W.; bud globular; flowers pink-amber, 3½-4 in., 40-45 petals, cupped, borne mostly singly, with some small clusters, moderate fragrance; recurrent; foliage medium size, dark green, semi-glossy; prickles moderate, straight to hooked slightly downward; stems short; compact (3½ ft.), vigorous, old-fashioned growth; PP11170; [Impatient × Amber Queen]; int. by Bear Creek Gardens, Inc., 1998

Royal Welcome HT, rb, 1955, Homan; flowers velvety dark red, reverse deep rosy pink, well-formed; foliage glossy; vigorous growth; [Crimson Glory × Peace]; int. by G.A. Williams, 1955

Royal Welsh Show HT, w, 2000, Poole, Lionel; flowers full, high-centered, borne in small clusters, slight fragrance; foliage medium size, medium green, semi-glossy; few prickles; bushy, vigorous, medium (36 in.) growth; [Solitaire × Hazel Rose]; int. in 2004

Royal William HT, dr, 1984, Kordes, W.; flowers deep crimson red, large, 35 petals, high-centered, moderate spicy fragrance; free-flowering; foliage large, dark, semi-glossy; upright, bushy (3½ ft.) growth; [Feuerzauber × seedling]; Rose of the Year, 1987, Fragrance Award, The Hague, 1989

Royal William, Climbing Cl HT, dr, 1995, Newman, F. S.; flowers other growth similar to parent; [sport of Royal William]; int. by Abbey Rose Gardens

Royal Worcester S, w, 1992, Robinson, Thomas, Ltd.; flowers peachy cream, large, semi-dbl., borne in large clusters, moderate fragrance; foliage medium size, dark green, very glossy; some prickles; low to medium (60 cm.), bushy, compact growth; [Simon Robinson × Gina Louise]; int. by Thomas Robinson, Ltd., 1991

Royale HGal, lp, before 1811, Godefroy; flowers light pink or cerise, edges lighter, mottled with red, medium, dbl., borne in small clusters; foliage stiff, bidentate; prickles numerous, slender, unequal; Agathe group

Royale – See **Belle Époque**, HT

Royale Aurore – See **Celestial**, A

Royale de Mulhouse F, w, Sauvegeot; int. by Roseraies Barth, 2005

Royale Perfection HT, or, Delbard-Chabert; flowers large, dbl.; int. in 1964

Royale Perfection – See **Royal Perfection**, HT

Royale Veloutée – See **Holoserica Regalis**, HGal

Royalet HT, mr, 1977, Herholdt, J.A.; flowers crimson-red, 4½-5½ in., 35-40 petals; foliage dark; upright, bushy growth; [seedling × Chrysler Imperial]; int. in 1968

Royalglo Min, m, 1987, Williams, Ernest D.; flowers non-fading, small, 40 petals, high-centered, borne usually singly, intense damask, sweet fragrance; foliage small, dark green, semi-glossy; prickles few, long, light tan; bushy, medium growth; no fruit; PP6673; [Angel Face × Anita Charles]; int. by Mini-Roses

Royalist HT, mp, 1954, McGredy, Sam IV; flowers deep rose-pink, large, 28 petals, high-centered; foliage dull green; very free growth; [(Billy Boy × Blossom) × Mrs Redford]

Royalty HT, dr, 1976, Jelly; bud globular, pointed; flowers deep cardinal red, 4-4½ in., 20-22 petals, high-centered to cupped, borne mostly in small clusters; free-flowering; foliage leathery; prickles few, medium, hooked downward; stems long, strong; vigorous growth; hips medium, globular body with conspicuous neck, smooth ; PP4057; [Forever Yours × Love Affair]; originally a greenhouse rose; int. by E.G. Hill Co., 1976

Royalty Bailey, Dorothy J., Bailey, Dorothy J.; PP4397

Royat Mondain HP, mr, 1901, Veysset; flowers crimson red, large, petals pointed, some edges thinly bordered white, full

Royden F, my, 1989, Cattermole, R.F.; flowers bright gold, fading quickly to white, 40 petals, cupped, borne in sprays; foliage light green, glossy; tall, upright growth; [Liverpool Echo × Arthur Bell]; int. by South Pacific Rose Nursery

Roydon Hall F, mr, 1985, Scrivens, Len; flowers large, 35 petals, no fragrance; foliage medium size, medium green, semi-glossy; bushy growth; [City of Leeds × (Paprika × Rose Gaujard)]; int. in 1983

Roze Koningin HT, mr, 1938, Lens; bud long, pointed; flowers medium red, passing to pink, well-formed large, dbl.; vigorous growth; [(Lady Sylvia × unknown) × Étoile de Hollande]

Rozenamateur A. Bok F, mr, 1961, Buisman, G. A. H.; flowers bright red, single, borne in large clusters; foliage dark; vigorous, upright growth; [Prinses Christina × Kathe Duvigneau]

Rozenmini Min, pb; flowers medium pink with white streaks, small, single, shallow cup to flat, borne in clusters; recurrent; growth to 12 in.

Rozorina – See **Zorina**, F

Roztomila F, w, Urban, J.

RSG Roos F, or, Taschner, Ludwig; flowers bright vermilion orange, intensifying to red, yellow base, medium, dbl., high-centered, borne in small clusters; free-flowering; foliage large, medium green; stems straight; tall, upright growth; int. by Ludwig's Roses, 2004

Ruatara LCl, dp, Nobbs; int. in 1995

Rubaiyat HT, dp, 1946, McGredy; bud long, pointed; flowers rose-red, reverse lighter, 4½-5 in., 25 petals, high-centered, intense Damask & spice fragrance; foliage dark, leathery; vigorous, upright growth; [(McGredy's Scarlet × Mrs Sam McGredy) × (seedling × Sir Basil McFarland)]; int. by J&P; Gold Medal, Portland, 1945

Ruban Doré – See **Tricolore**, HGal

Ruban Rouge F, dr, 1957, Lens; bud globular; flowers deep velvety red, borne in clusters; foliage dark, leathery; vigorous growth; [Alain × Cinnabar]

Rubella F, dr, 1973, deRuiter; flowers deep red, 2½-3 in., 24 petals, open, borne in trusses; free-flowering; bushy growth; hardy; [Kimono × Lilli Marleen]; int. by De Ruiter New Roses, 1972

Rubens HP, mr, 1852, Laffay; flowers amaranth-red, loose

Rubens T, w, 1859, Robert; flowers white, shaded with rose, center bronzy yellow, large, wavy petals, dbl., cupped, moderate fragrance; free-flowering; dense (3-5 ft.), spreading growth

Rubens HP, yb, 1864, Verdier

Rubens HT, mr, 1978, Gaujard; bud pointed; flowers vermilion red, large, dbl.; vigorous growth; [Rose Gaujard × Miss France]; int. in 1972

Rübezahl HT, mr, 1917, Krüger; flowers large, dbl.; [Julius Fabianics de Misefa × Mrs W. J. Grant]

Rubiela F, w, NIRP; int. by Roseraies Barth, 2005

Rubies 'n' Pearls Min, m, 1992, Mander, George; flowers purple/cream bicolor, 2 in., dbl., cupped, slight fragrance; recurrent; foliage small, medium green, semi-glossy; few prickles; stems long; low (40-50 cm.), upright, bushy growth; [Rise 'n' Shine × MANpurple]

Rubiginosa – See **Rubra**, C

Rubiginosa – See **Hebe's Lip**, HEg

Rubin HMult, mr, 1899, Kiese; flowers crimson to spinel-red, 4-5 cm., semi-dbl., borne in clusters of 10-30, moderate fragrance; growth to 10-12 ft.; [Daniel Lacombe × Fellemberg]; int. by Schmidt, 1899

Rubin HT, or, 1956, Lens; flowers orange-red, base yellow, large, semi-dbl.; vigorous growth; [Mme Henri Guillot × Grande Duchesse Charlotte]

Rubin F, dr, 1962, Kordes; bud long, pointed; flowers deep red, dbl., borne in broad clusters; foliage dark; bushy, compact, low growth; int. by Dehner & Co.

Rubina F, dr, Dickson, Patrick; int. in 1989

Rubinette F, dr, 1971, deRuiter; flowers deep red, large, 28 petals; foliage dark; vigorous, upright growth; [(Mandrina × Baccará) × (Mandrina × Baccara)]; int. by Carlton Rose Nurseries

Rubino S, Mansuino; int. in 1966

Rubis Pol, rb, 1926, Nonin; flowers bright ruby-red, center white, medium, borne in clusters; dwarf growth; [Merveille des Rouges × Jessie]

Rubis Cl HT, mr, 1948, Mallerin, C.; flowers blood-red, 4 in., dbl., intense fragrance; foliage bronze; vigorous growth; [Mme G. Forest-Colcombet × unknown]; int. by URS

Rubor HT, mp, 1947, Dot, Pedro; flowers Neyron pink, dbl.; foliage dark; very vigorous growth; [Cynthia × Director Rubió]

Rubra C, mr, before 1629; flowers crimson red, 3 in., dbl., slight fragrance; foliage large

Rubra M, mr, before 1777, from England; flowers deep pink to medium red, medium, dbl.

Rubra – See **Jenny**, HCh

Rubra – See ***R. barbierana*** (Rehder), HWich

Rubra Plena – See **Rouge**, HSpn

Rubra Variegata – See **Striata**, S

Rubro-Purpurea – See **Red Damask**, D

Rubrosa – See **Carmenetta**, S

Rubrotincta – See **Hebe's Lip**, HEg

Ruby Pol, mr, 1932, deRuiter; flowers glowing scarlet; int. by Sliedrecht & Co.

Ruby Min, dr, 2002, Benardella, Frank; flowers dark red, medium red reverse, 1½-2 in., dbl., borne mostly solitary, slight fragrance; foliage medium size, dark green, semi-glossy; prickles 5/16 in., slightly angled down, moderate; growth upright, medium (24-30 in.); containers, cutting, exhibition; [Jennifer × Kristin]; int. by Nor'East Miniature Roses, 2002; AOE, ARS, 2001

Ruby Anniversary – See **Royal Anniversary**, F

Ruby Baby Min, rb, 2000, Christopher, Lonnie H.; flowers red-orange, reverse yellow, 1½ in., dbl., high-centered, borne mostly singly, slight fragrance; foliage medium size, medium green, semi-glossy; prickles moderate; upright, medium (12-18 in.) growth; [sport of Hot Tamale]

Ruby Bay HMsk, mr; flowers ruby red, small, semi-dbl., borne in clusters; shrubby (5 ft.), semi-climbing growth; [Ballerina × unknown]; int. by Tasman Bay Roses, 1994

Ruby Belle Min, dr, Bell, Laurie; flowers deep velvety red, moderate fragrance; free-flowering; medium growth; int. by Bell Roses

Ruby Border – See **Sausalito**, S

Ruby Celebration F, dr, Pearce; bud near black; flowers very dark red, small, semi-dbl. to dbl., cupped to flat, borne in clusters; recurrent; foliage matte, disease-resistant; medium (2-3 ft.) growth; int. in 1995

Ruby Dee Gr, mr, 1968, Patterson; bud ovoid; flowers large, dbl., high-centered, borne in clusters, moderate fragrance; foliage dark, glossy; vigorous, upright growth; PP3074; [Queen Elizabeth × Happiness]; int. by Patterson Roses

Ruby Garland LCl, mr, Pearce; flowers ruby red, medium, dbl., high-centered; recurrent; supple canes, tall growth; int. by Ludwig's Roses, 2005

Ruby Gem HT, mr, 1962, Leenders, J.; flowers bright red, large, 28 petals; [seedling × Red Favorite]

Ruby Glow LCl, mr, 1955, Jacobus, Martin; bud short, oval; flowers spectrum-red, open, 3 in., 13-15 petals, borne in clusters, moderate fragrance; foliage glossy; moderate pillar (7 ft.) growth; [Dream Girl × New World]; int. by B&A, 1955

Ruby Gold – See **Jean Ducher**, T

Ruby Jewel Min, mr, 1959, Morey, Dr. Dennison; bud ovoid; flowers ruby-red, reverse lighter, open, ½ in., 35-40 petals, moderate fragrance; foliage glossy; low (6-8 in.), compact growth; PP1907; [Dick Koster × Tom Thumb]; int. by J&P, 1959

Ruby Lips F, mr, 1959, Swim, H.C.; bud short, ovoid, pointed; flowers bright cardinal-red, 3 in., 18-20 petals, loose, borne in clusters, slight fragrance; recurrent; foliage medium size, leathery, semi-glossy; prickles several, medium, almost straight, brown; stems short to medium; vigorous, semi-spreading, bushy growth; hips globular, smooth, orange; PP1775; [World's Fair × Pinocchio]; int. by Armstrong Nursery, 1958

Ruby Magic Min, mr, 1986, Moore, Ralph S.; flowers cherry red, small to medium, 20 petals, borne singly and in sprays of 3-5, slight fragrance; foliage small to medium size, medium green, semi-glossy; prickles brown; medium, upright, bushy growth; usually no fruit; [Orangeade × Pinstripe]; int. by Moore Min. Roses

Ruby Manwaring HT, dp, 1932, Longley; flowers rich rosy cerise; [sport of Betty Uprichard]

Ruby Meidiland S, mr, 2001, Meilland International; bud globose, small to medium; flowers show shades of red, 1½ in., 15 petals, cupped, borne in large clusters, no fragrance; free-flowering; foliage small, dark green, glossy; prickles moderate; growth bushy, low (3 ft.); landscape; PP13500; [(Red Meidiland × Scarlet Meidiland) × The Fairy]; int. by The Conard-Pyle Company, 2000

Ruby Pendant Min, m, 1980, Strawn, Leslie E.; bud pointed; flowers red-purple, 25-30 petals, high-centered, borne singly, slight fragrance; recurrent; foliage reddish-green; prickles needle-shaped; vigorous growth; [(Lotte Gunthart × Salvo) × Baby Betsy McCall]; int. by Pixie Treasures Min. Roses, 1979

Ruby Princess HT, mr, 1949, Grillo; flowers velvety red, 5 in., 50 petals; [sport of Jewel]

Ruby Princess Min, rb, 2002, Moore, Ralph S.; flowers ruby red, reverse red, 1 in., dbl., borne mostly solitary; foliage small, medium green, semi-glossy; prickles small, pointed, green, few; growth compact, short (12 in.); potted plant, specimen; [Joycie × Cherry Magic]; int. by Sequoia Nurs., 2002

Ruby Queen HWich, dp, 1899, Van Fleet; flowers deep rose-pink, reverse lighter, 4-5 cm., dbl., loose, borne in clusters of 5-7; non-recurrent; foliage small, medium green, glossy; numerous prickles; stems stiff; growth to 10 ft.; [*R. wichurana* × Cramoisi Supérieur]; int. by Conard & Jones

Ruby Rain Cl Min, mr

Ruby Ring HWich, w, 1926, Clark, A.; flowers white with ruby edge, 4-5 cm., dbl., borne in clusters of 5-15; foliage glossy

Ruby Ruby Min, mr, 2003, Carruth, Tom; buds shapely; flowers stable cherry red, 3-4 cm., full, high-centered, borne in large clusters, slight fragrance; recurrent; foliage small, dark green, glossy; prickles average, almost straight; growth bushy, slightly spreading, medium (45-60 cm.); garden decoration; PP15066; [Santa Claus × (Trumpeter × Red Minimo)]; int. by Weeks Roses, 2004

Ruby Star Min, dr, 1991, Umsawasdi, Dr. Theera; flowers small, 5 petals, borne mostly singly, no fragrance; foliage medium size, dark green, semi-glossy; upright, bushy, tall (24 cm.) growth; [High Spirits × seedling]

Ruby Superior Pol, mr, deRuiter; flowers have more lasting color; [sport of Ruby]

Ruby Talisman HT, mr, 1935, Eddie; flowers rich ruby-red, more shapely than parent, with reflexed petals; [sport of Talisman]

Ruby Treasure Min, dr, Hannemann, F.; [Oz Gold × Lemon Delight]; int. by The Rose Paradise

Ruby Tuesday Min, dr, 1988, Rennie, Bruce F.; flowers dark, velvety red, reverse lighter, aging darker, small, 25-30 petals, cupped pompom, no fragrance; foliage small, dark green, semi-glossy; prickles slightly hooked, small, brownish; bushy, low growth; hips round, small, red-orange; [Pink Sheri × Black Jack]; int. by Rennie Roses International, 1989

Ruby Ulrick F, dp, 1953, Ulrick, L.W.; flowers deep pink, base white, dbl., borne in clusters; foliage leathery; very vigorous growth; [Mrs Tom Henderson × Gloria Mundi]

Ruby Velvet F, dr, 1999, Hintlian, Nancy Sears; flowers dark red, turning purple with age, lasts well, 5 in., 41 petals, borne in small clusters; foliage medium size, medium green, semi-glossy; prickles numerous, very large; spreading, medium (4 ft.) growth; [The Dark Lady × Oklahoma]

Ruby Vigorosa – See **Rotilia**, F

Ruby Voodoo S, dr, 2004, Starnes, John A. Jr.; flowers deep red, 3 in., very full, borne mostly solitary, intense rich, sweet fragrance; early summer; foliage medium size, medium green, matte; prickles small, cats claw; upright, short growth; short shrub or medium pillar; [General Jacqueminot × Stephen's Big Purple]; int. by John A. Starnes Jr., 2004

Ruby Wedding HT, dr, 1980, Gregory; bud flat, pointed; flowers deep, velvety red, medium, 44 petals, borne 3-4 per cluster, moderate fragrance; good repeat; foliage medium green; prickles slightly hooked; vigorous (3 ft.), somewhat spreading growth; [Mayflower × seedling]; int. in 1979

Ruby Wedding, Climbing Cl HT, dr; vigorous (12 ft.) growth; [sport of Ruby Wedding]; int. after 1979

Ruby Wedding Anniversary F, mr; flowers brilliant red, slight fragrance; medium growth; int. in 2005

Ruby Wedding Celebration F, w; int. by Love4Plants, 2005

Ruby Wishes – See **Scarlet Hit**, MinFl

Rudelsburg HMult, dp, 1919, Kiese; flowers shining carmine-rose, fading to slatey pink, 3-4 cm., semi-dbl., flat, borne in large clusters; non-recurrent; no prickles; vigorous, climbing growth

Rudi Korte Pol, or, 1929, Kersbergen; flowers medium, semi-dbl.

Rudi Neitz HT, yb, Dorieux; bud long, pointed; flowers golden-yellow with touch of pink on petal edges, cupped; foliage deep green, glossy; prickles very few; stems long, straight; vigorous, medium growth; int. by Ludwig's Roses, 2004

Rudola F, mr, 1974, deRuiter; bud ovoid; flowers light geranium-red, open, large, semi-dbl.; foliage leathery; very vigorous, bushy growth; [Dacapo × Kimono]; int. in 1972

Rudolf Alexander Schröder HT, w, 1930, Kordes; bud long, pointed; flowers white, center tinted lemon, large, dbl., high-centered; foliage leathery, light; vigorous growth; [Mrs Herbert Stevens × Pius XI]

Rudolf Schmidt's Jubiläumsrose F, my, 1958, Kordes; flowers golden yellow, large, semi-dbl., high-centered, borne in clusters, moderate fragrance; foliage light green, glossy; very vigorous, upright, bushy growth; int. by R. Schmidt, 1955

Rudolf Schock HT, mr, 1970, Verschuren, A.; flowers bright currant-red, large, dbl., moderate fragrance; foliage dark, leathery; vigorous growth; [Josephine Bruce × seedling]; int. by Stassen, 1968

Rudolf von Bennigsen LCl, mp, 1932, Lambert, P.; bud pointed; flowers rosy-pink, edges fading, large, semi-dbl., borne in clusters of 5-20, slight fragrance; recurrent bloom; foliage broad, dark, glossy; vigorous, bushy, semi-climbing growth; [(Geheimrat Dr. Mittweg × Souv. de Paul Neyron) × Joanna Hill]

Rudolph Kluis Pol, mr, 1922, Kluis & Koning; bud globular; flowers pure vermilion-red, dbl.; foliage rich green, glossy; bushy growth; [sport of Ellen Poulsen]

Rudolph Kluis Superior Pol, mr, 1928, Kluis; flowers glowing scarlet; more compact growth than Rudolph Kluis; [sport of Ellen Poulsen]

Rudolph Timm F, rb, 1951, Kordes; flowers white, reverse red, open, 2 in., 15-20 petals, borne in trusses to 40; foliage glossy, light green; very free growth; [(Johannes Boettner × Magnifica) × (Baby Chateau × Else Poulsen)]; int. by Wheatcroft Bros.

Rudolph Valentino HT, op, 1929, Pernet-Ducher; flowers lively shrimp-pink or coral-red, suffused golden coppery, dbl.; vigorous growth; int. by Dreer

Rudy Rambler ClMin, mr; int. by Harvest Moon Farms, 2005

Ruffian MinFl, op, 2000, Clemons, David E.; flowers orange pink, reverse light pink, 1½ in., dbl., high-centered, borne mostly singly, slight fragrance; foliage medium size, dark green, semi-glossy; prickles moderate; growth upright, medium (24-36 in.); [Corina × Child's Play]; int. by Suncrest Roses, 2003

Ruffled Cloud S, dp, 2007, Zary, Keith W.; flowers deep pink, reverse medium pink, 4 in., dbl., blooms borne in small clusters; foliage medium size, medium green, glossy; prickles 6-8 mm., straight, greyed-orange, few; growth bushy, medium (3½ ft.); landscape, bedding; [Morden Blush × seedling]; int. by Jackson & Perkins Wholesale, Inc., 2007

Ruffles HT, mp, 1994, Perry, Astor; flowers magenta pink, ruffled petals, medium, full, high-centered, borne mostly singly, slight fragrance; recurrent; foliage large, medium green; some prickles; tall, upright growth; [seedling × Alec's Red]; int. by Certified Roses, Inc., 1997

Ruffle's Dream S, yb

Ruffles 'n' Flourishes S, rb, 1994, Clements, John K.; flowers violet red and gold, medium, dbl., borne in small clusters; foliage medium size, reddish green, glossy; few prickles; low (18 in.), upright, bushy growth; [Sexy Rexy × Whistle Stop]; int. by Heirloom Old Garden Roses, 1994

Ruffle's Passion S, m

Rufus Pol, mr, 1925, Allen; flowers intense scarlet, dbl., borne in clusters; compact growth; [sport of Orléans Rose]

Ruga Ayr, w, before 1820; flowers creamy flesh pink, fading lighter, 5-6 cm., semi-dbl., cupped, borne in small clusters, moderate tea fragrance; non-recurrent; numerous prickles; stems long, slender; trailing (up to 30 ft.) growth; [thought to be *R. arvensis* × *R. odorata*]; brought to England from Italy by John Lindley

Rugelda HRg, yb, 2006; flowers citron yellow edged reddish, 9 cm., dbl., cupped, borne in large clusters, moderate fragrance; recurrent; foliage dark green, glossy; numerous prickles; bushy, tall (200 cm.) growth; int. by W. Kordes' Söhne, 1989

Rugosa Copper S, ob, 1958, Gaujard; flowers coppery orange, large; recurrent bloom; vigorous growth; [Conrad Ferdinand Meyer × seedling]; int. in 1955

Rugosa Magnifica – See **Magnifica**, HRg

Rugosa Ottawa HRg, m, L'Assomption; flowers 5 petals, flat

Rugosa Rose – See ***R. rugosa*** (Thunberg)

Rugosa Superba – See **Scabrosa**, HRg

Rugotida HRg, 1950, Darthuis

Rugspin HRg, dr, Petersen; flowers deep scarlet crimson, large, single, flat, moderate fragrance; recurrent; foliage dark green, glossy; healthy (4 ft.) growth; hips rounded; int. in 1966

Ruhm der Gartenwelt HP, dr, 1904, Jacobs; flowers fiery red, large, dbl.; [American Beauty × Francis Dubreuil]

Ruhm von Steinfurth HP, mr, 1920, Weigand, C.; bud long, pointed; flowers bright carmin, large, 34 petals, cupped, intense fragrance; recurrent; foliage dark, leathery; vigorous growth; [Frau Karl Druschki × Ulrich Brunner Fils]; int. by H. Schultheis

Ruhm von Thalwitz HP, mr, 1866, Peters; flowers poppy red with salmon pink reflections, medium to large, full

Ruimz15 HT, w, de Groot; Henk; PP16139; [sport of Ruiliro]

Ruiy5451 HT, or, de Groot; H. C. A.; PP15993

Rukhsaar HT, w, 1971, Singh; flowers cream, center shell-pink, medium, dbl., high-centered; foliage glossy; moderate growth; [Virgo × Open pollination]; int. by Gopalsinamiengar, 1969

Rum Butter Min, ab, 1991, Taylor, Pete & Kay; bud pointed; flowers apricot with yellow base, with a lavender cast blended with apricot, small, semi-dbl., high-centered, borne singly and in sprays of 4-5, no fragrance; foliage medium size, medium green, semi-glossy; upright, bushy, medium growth; [Azure Sea × seedling]; int. by Taylor's Roses, 1990

Rum Candy Min, r, 1990, Umsawasdi, Dr. Theera; flowers brownish apricot, light apricot shaded light pink when fully open, small, semi-dbl., borne mostly singly, slight fragrance; foliage small, light green, matte; upright, bushy, low (18 cm.) growth; [Twilight Trail × seedling]

Rumba HT, op, 1956; bud long, pointed; flowers salmon-orange, intense fragrance; long stems; [Talisman × unknown]; int. by Faassen-Houba

Rumba F, rb, 1961, Poulsen, S.; bud ovoid; flowers poppy-red, center yellow, 2-2½ in., 30-35 petals, cupped, borne in clusters, slight spicy fragrance; recurrent; foliage dark, glossy, leathery; vigorous, bushy growth; PP1919; [Masquerade × (Poulsen's Bedder × Floradora)]; int. by McGredy & Son, 1960

Rumba, Climbing Cl F, rb, 1972, Bansal, O.P.; flowers medium, dbl, cupped; [sport of Rumba]; int. by Bansal Roses

Rumpelstilzchen S, dr, 1956, deRuiter; flowers deep red, small, single; dwarf growth; int. by Willicher Baumschulen

Running Maid S, m, 1986, Lens, Louis; flowers lilac-red, white eye, 2 in., 5 petals, borne in clusters of 3-32, intense fragrance; recurrent bloom; foliage deep reddish-green, glossy; prickles hooked, brown; spreading growth; groundcover; [*R. multiflora* × (*R. wichurana* × Violet Hood)]; int. in 1985; Rose of the Century, Lyon, 1983, Silver Medal, Munich, 1983, Gold Medal, Dusseldorf, 1987

Rupali F, dp, 1973, IARI; buds medium, pointed; flowers deep rose-pink, medium, dbl, open, borne singly and several together; foliage medium size, green; growth very vigorous, upright; [Sweet Afton × Delhi Princess]; int. in 1971

Rupert Brooke HT, pb, 1928, Easlea; flowers fawn-pink to cream, dbl.; [Miss Cynthia Forde × Mrs Wemyss Quin]

Rural Rhythm S, lp, 1985, Buck, Dr. Griffith J.; flowers 4 in., 30 petals, shallow cupped, borne 1-5 per cluster, moderate myrrh fragrance; repeat bloom; foliage dark, leathery; prickles awl-like, tan; erect, bushy, spreading growth; hardy; [Carefree Beauty × The Yeoman]; int. by Iowa State University, 1984

Ruritania HT, or, 1971, Curtis, E.C.; bud ovoid; flowers medium, very dbl., intense fragrance; foliage dark, leathery; vigorous, upright growth; [Miss Hillcrest × Hawaii]; int. by Kimbrew, 1972

Rusalka LCl, dp, 1934, Brada, Dr.; flowers carmine to sunset-rose, base yellow, very large, semi-dbl., high-centered; profuse, repeated bloom; foliage glossy, light; climbing growth; [Tausendschön × Farbenkonigin]; int. by Böhm

Rush S, pb, 1986, Lens, Louis; flowers pink, white eye, 2 in., 5 petals, borne in clusters of 3-32, moderate fruity fragrance; recurrent; foliage light green; prickles hooked, brownish-green; upright, bushy growth; [(Ballerina × Britannia) × *R. multiflora*]; int. in 1983; Gold Medal, Rome, 1982, Silver Medal, Le Roeulx, 1981, Silver Medal, Kortrijk, 1984, Silver Medal, Baden Baden, 1982

Rushing Stream S, w, 1997, Austin, David; flowers single, borne in large clusters, slight clove fragrance; foliage large, light green, glossy; few prickles; broad, bushy, medium (1½ ft.) growth; int. by David Austin Roses, Ltd., 1986

Rushton-Radclyffe HP, mr, 1864, Verdier, E.; flowers bright cherry red, large, full

Ruskin HRg, dr, 1928, Van Fleet; bud ovoid; flowers deep crimson, large, petals twisted, 50 petals, cupped, intense fragrance; sparingly recurrent; foliage large, rich green, leathery; vigorous, bushy (4-5 ft.) growth; hips rare; [Souv. de Pierre Leperdrieux × Victor Hugo]; int. by American Rose Society

Russell Supreme HT, lp, 1927, Pacific Rose Co.; [sport of Mrs Charles E. Russell]

Russelliana HMult, m, before 1826, Cormack & Sinclair; flowers magenta-crimson fading to mauve, 5-7 cm., dbl., flat, borne in clusters, moderate fragrance; foliage coarse; growth to 20 ft.

Russell's Cottage – See **Russelliana**, HMult

Russet Beauty Min, or, 1985, Olesen, Pernille & Mogens N.; flowers small, 46 petals, borne in clusters of 3-15; foliage matte; prickles straight, brown; compact, bushy growth; [Mini-Poul × seedling]; int. by Ludwigs Roses Pty. Ltd., 1983

Rust Spot Min, or, 2003, Barnes, Karen W.; flowers full, borne mostly solitary, no fragrance; foliage medium size, medium green, semi-glossy; prickles small, curved, red/brown, few; compact, short (18 in.) growth; containers; [seedling × seedling]; int. by Karen W. Barnes, 2003

Rustica HSpn, yb, 1929, Barbier; flowers straw-yellow and gold, center apricot, reverse citron-yellow, semi-dbl., moderate fragrance; non-recurrent bloom; growth to 6 ft.; [Mme Edouard Herriot × Harison's Yellow]

Rustica F, yb, 1981, Meilland, Mrs. Marie-Louise; bud very long; flowers yellow-peach blend, reverse buff yellow-orange, 35 petals, cupped, borne in clusters, slight fragrance; good repeat; foliage dark green, semi-matte, dense; half-upright growth; [(Queen Elizabeth × seedling) × Sweet Promise]; int. by Meilland Et Cie, 1979

Rustica 91 – See **Topaz Jewel**, HRg

Rusticana – See **Poppy Flash**, F

Rusticana, Climbing – See **Poppy Flash, Climbing**, Cl F

Rusticana F, lp, Wagner, S.; bud short; flowers pale pink, 15 petals, flat, borne in clusters, slight fragrance; foliage medium large, dark green, glossy; groundcover; spreading growth; [Candy Rose × Yesterday]; int. by Res. Stn. f. Fruit Growing, Cluj, 1995

Rustler's Dream S, lp, 2006, Ponton, Ray; flowers very full, borne in small clusters; recurrent; foliage medium green, semi-glossy, disease-resistant; prickles medium, straight, moderate; growth compact, medium (4 ft.); [(Paloma Blanca × Hippolyte) × Baby Love]; int. in 2006

Ruston's Blush HG, w, Morley, Dr B.; [sport of *R. gigantea* hybrid]

Rusty F, r; flowers burnt orange to russet, striped, semi-dbl., borne in trusses, slight fragrance; recurrent; strong growth; int. by Certified Roses, 2004

Ruth HT, ob, 1921, Pemberton; flowers orange flushed carmine, large, dbl., high-centered; vigorous, bushy growth

Ruth HGal, mr, 1947, Wright, Percy H.; flowers less bright than Alika, more double than Alika, dbl.; non-recurrent; upright growth (to 7 ft.); [Mary L. Evans × Alika]

Ruth, Climbing Cl HT, ob; flowers light orange shaded to red at edges, very large, very dbl.; recurrent bloom; foliage very large, glossy, olive-green; vigorous, climbing growth; not hardy

Ruth Alexander LCl, ob, 1937, Wilber; bud long, pointed; flowers orange, base yellow, large, semi-dbl., high-centered; foliage leathery, glossy, bronze; vigorous, climbing growth; [Myra × Constance Casson]; int. by Bertsch

Ruth Christine Cl F, pb, 2004, Horner, Colin P.; flowers pink/cream stripes, reverse cream, 3 in., full, borne in large clusters, intense fragrance; foliage medium size, medium green, semi-glossy; prickles medium, curved; growth upright, tall (6-8 ft.); garden decoration; [seedling × Summer Wine]; int. by Warley Rose Gardens Ltd. (Warley Roses), 2007

Ruth Clements S, op, Clements, John; flowers blend of coral-pink and soft pink, 4 in., 69 petals, moderate green apple fragrance; free-flowering; foliage matte green.; very bushy (4½ × 3½ ft.) growth; PPAF; int. by Heirloom Roses, 2000

Ruth Harker HT, mp, 1981, Harkness, R., & Co., Ltd.; flowers large, 46 petals, borne singly and in small clusters, intense fragrance; foliage large, medium green, matte to semi-glossy; prickles slightly curved, reddish; upright, bushy growth; [Fragrant Cloud × Compassion]

Ruth Hewitt F, w, 1963, Norman; flowers 4 in., 36 petals, cupped, borne in open clusters; foliage dark; vigorous, compact growth; [seedling × Queen Elizabeth]; int. by Harkness, 1962

Ruth Knopf LCl, mp

Ruth Leuwerik F, mr, 1961, deRuiter; flowers bright red, 3 in., 30 petals, borne in clusters, moderate fragrance; foliage bronze; vigorous, bushy growth; [Kathe Duvigneau × Rosemary Rose]; int. by Gandy Roses, Ltd.

Ruth Leuwerik, Climbing Cl F, mr

Ruth Pennington F, my, Kordes; int. in 1993

Ruth Shamburger F, lp, 1934, Shamburger, C.S.; [sport of Kirsten Poulsen]

Ruth Staley Min, mp, 1990, Bennett, Dee; bud ovoid; flowers medium shell pink, reverse lighter, medium, 25 petals, high-centered, borne singly and occaisionally in clusters of 3-5, moderate fruity fragrance; foliage medium size, dark green, semi-glossy, disease-resistant; prickles slender, straight, red; upright, tall growth; hips globular, green-brown; [Electron × Peachy Keen]; int. by Tiny Petals Nursery, 1989

Ruth Turner Pol, dp, 1941, Moore, Ralph S.; flowers rose-pink, small, dbl., high-centered, borne in clusters of 5-10; foliage glossy, pointed; vigorous, bushy growth; [Étoile Luisante × Sierra Snowstorm]; int. by California Roses

Ruth Vestal Cl T, w, 1908, Vestal; flowers snow-white, well-formed, very large; recurrent bloom; vigorous growth; [sport of The Bride climbing]

Ruth Warner F, m, 1984, Warner, A.J.; flowers deep lavender, medium, 48 petals, high-centered, borne singly and in clusters up to 5, intense fragrance; foliage dark, smooth; prickles very few; upright growth; [Little Darling × Angel Face]; int. in 1978; Bronze Medal, ARC TG, 1983

Ruth Woodward F, or, 1992, Dickson Nurseries; flowers 3-3½ in., full, borne in small clusters; foliage medium size, medium green, semi-glossy; some prickles; medium, bushy growth; [Wishing × seedling]

Ruthchen Pol, mr, 1937, Vogel, M.; flowers carmine-red, medium, dbl.

Ruthe HT, yb

Ruthie Min, w, 1988, Bennett, Dee; flowers cream-white with pink blush on outer petals, aging paler with deeper blush, 2 in., 25-30 petals, cupped, borne usually singly, moderate damask fragrance; recurrent; foliage medium size, medium green, semi-glossy, aging darker; prickles hooked slightly downward, yellow to reddish; upright, tall growth; hips globular, green-brown; PP7189; [Sonia × Little Melody]; int. by Tiny Petals Nursery

Rutilant HT, mr, 1962, Arles, F.; bud ovoid; flowers carthamus-red, open, medium, semi-dbl.; foliage glossy; vigorous, bushy growth; [Gloire de Cibeins × Independence]; int. by Roses-France, 1960

Rutland Cover – See **Aberdeen**, S

Ruyton HT, mp, Bell, Ronald J.; flowers strong pink in center, petals fading quickly to blush pink as they open, dbl., high-centered, very slight fragrance; recurrent; medium growth; int. by Bell, 1989

Ruyton Girl's School – See **Ruyton**, HT

Ruzova Lavina F, dp, Strnad

Ruzyne HT, rb, 1936, Mikes Böhm, J.; flowers carmine-red marked rose, large

Ryokkoh F, ly, 1999, Suzuki, Seizo; flowers light yellow green turning to green, 1-2 in., 15-20 petals, no fragrance; foliage dark green, leathery; growth to 3-4 ft.; [Bridal Pink × (seedling × Tasogare)]; int. by Keisei Rose Nurseries, 1991; Gold Medal, Baden-Baden, 1989

Ryokukou F, ly

Rythm 'n Blues LCl, mp, Poulsen; flowers medium pink, 10-15 cm., semi-dbl., no fragrance; foliage matte; growth bushy, 200-300 cm.; int. by Poulsen Roser, 2000

S. A. Prince Youssof Kamal HP, rb, 1922, Nabonnand, P.; bud long, pointed; flowers crimson, streaked brilliant scarlet, large, semi-dbl.; [Souv. de Mme Chedane-Guinoisseau × Ulrich Brunner Fils]

S. A. R. Ferdinand Ier HRg, mp, 1901, Gravereaux

S. & M. Perrier HT, pb, 1936, Mallerin, C.; flowers very pale rose-pink, with orange glow, large, 60 petals, high-centered; foliage glossy; vigorous growth; [Magdalena de Nubiola × Pres. Cherioux]; int. by C-P

S. Antonio di Padova HT, Sgaravatti, A.; int. in 1960

S. M. Alexander I – See **Roi Alexandre**, HT

S. M. Gustave V – See **Sa Majesté Gustave V**, HP

S. M. I. Abdul-Hamid HRg, mr, 1901, Gravereaux; flowers purple red

S. S. Pennock HT, pb, 1922, Kordes; flowers light rose-pink, with sulfur-yellow sheen, dbl., moderate fragrance; [Lieutenant Chaure × Mrs George Shawyer]

S. S. Pennock, Climbing Cl HT, pb, 1932, Lens; [sport of S. S. Pennock]; int. by J&P

S. W. A. L. K. Cl Min, mr, 1999, McCann, Sean; flowers barn red, 2¼ in., full, high-centered, borne mostly singly, slight fragrance; recurrent; foliage medium size, dark green, glossy; prickles moderate; climbing (6-7 ft.) growth; trellis or fence for support; [seedling × seedling]; int. by Justice Miniature Roses, 1998

S.E.A. of Love F, m, 1992, Mander, George; flowers purple/cream bicolor, mauve color intensifies with sun and aging, 3-3½ in., full, high-centered; recurrent; foliage medium size, dark green, semi-glossy; prickles very few; medium (3-4 ft.), bushy growth; [Rise 'n' Shine × MANpurple]

Sa Majesté Gustave V HP, dr, 1922, Nabonnand, P.; bud long, pointed, brilliant crimson; flowers carmine, reverse crimson, well-formed, very large, 30 petals, cupped, moderate fragrance; vigorous growth; [Frau Karl Druschki × Avoca]

Saarbrücken S, mr, 1959, Kordes; flowers scarlet-red, 3 in., semi-dbl., borne in clusters of up to 20; foliage dark; vigorous, bushy (5 ft.) growth

Saarlandwelle HT, or, Hetzel; int. in 1976

Sabaudia HT, pb, 1934, Cazzaniga, F. G.; flowers pink with gold reflections, base light chrome-yellow, large, dbl., cupped; foliage leathery, glossy, dark; vigorous, bushy growth; [*R. foetida hybrid* × Harison's Yellow]

Sabine HT, ob, 1958, Buyl Frères; flowers salmon, well-formed, 40 petals; vigorous growth; [Dame Edith Helen × seedling]

Sabine HT, dp, 1965, Tantau, Math.; bud pointed; flowers cherry-red, medium, 30 petals, urn-shaped, intense fragrance; foliage dark, glossy; upright, bushy growth; int. by Wheatcroft Bros., 1963

Sabine HT, pb, RvS-Melle; flowers fresh pink with yellow heart, dbl., high-centered; moderate growth

Sabine Plattner F, op, Taschner, Ludwig; bud pointed; flowers deep salmon, dbl., cupped, borne singly and in clusters; recurrent; vigorous (6 ft.) growth; int. by Ludwig's Roses, 2004

Sabine Rancy HT, Croix; int. in 1972

Sabine Ruf F, mp, Hetzel; int. in 1988

Sabine Sinjen – See **Sabine**, HT, 1965

Sabinia HT, pb, 1940, Aicardi, D.; bud ovoid; flowers dark eglantine-pink passing to reddish-yellow, large, dbl., high-centered; foliage dark, leathery; very vigorous, upright growth; [Julien Potin × Sensation]; int. by Giacomasso; Gold Medal, Rome, 1939

Sable Chaud – See **Puerto Rico**, F

Sabra Min, mp, 1999, Justice, Jerry G.; flowers medium pink, reverse light pink, 1¾ in., single, borne mostly singly; foliage large, light green, dull; upright, medium (18-21 in.) growth; [(Fairy Moss × unknown) × unknown]; int. by Justice Miniature Roses, 1999

Sabre Dance F, rb, 1976, Bees; flowers scarlet, reverse gold, 4 in., 40 petals, high-centered, slight fragrance; foliage dark; vigorous growth; [Mildred Reynolds × Arthur Bell]; int. in 1975

Sabrina HT, rb, 1960, Meilland, Mrs. Marie-Louise; flowers crimson, reverse amber-yellow marked crimson, 5 in., 35 petals, high-centered, intense fragrance; foliage dark, leathery; vigorous, bushy growth; ruled extinct ARA 1985; [Grand Gala × Premier Bal]; int. by Wheatcroft Bros., 1960

Sabrina HT, ab, 1985, Meilland, Mrs. Marie-Louise; flowers apricot-orange, large, 35 petals; upright growth; PP4520; [(Sweet Promise × Golden Garnette) × ((Zambra × Suspense) × (King's Ransom × Whisky Mac))]; int. by Meilland Et Cie, 1977

Sacajawea F, mr, 1983, Elliott, Charles P.; bud small, short, flat top; flowers have ruffled petals, 1¾ in., 20 petals, cupped, borne singly and in flat clusters, very slight fragrance; recurrent; foliage medium size, medium green, smooth; prickles medium, hooked downward; stems short; vigorous, upright (3 ft.) growth; PP4892; [(Baccará × Garnet) × unknown]; int. in 1982

Sacha HT, mr, Spek; bud long, pointed ovoid; flowers bright red, occasional white streak on guard petals, medium, 25-30 petals, high-centered, borne singly, slight fragrance; good repeat; foliage medium size, leathery; prickles medium to few, short, hooked slightly downward; stems medium, strong; growth vigorous, upright (5 ft.); PP9540; [sport of Calibra]; greenhouse rose; int. by Bear Creek Gardens, 1996

Sachalin HRg, pb; flowers medium pink in center, blending to blush pink on outer petals, dbl., cupped, moderate spicy, clove fragrance; recurrent; foliage wrinkled; vigorous, medium growth; int. in 1988

Sachet Min, m, 1986, Saville, F. Harmon; bud small, ovate, pointed; flowers lavender, yellow stamens, 1½-2 in., 30 petals, urn-shaped, then flat, borne singly and in small sprays, intense damask fragrance; foliage small, dark, semi-glossy; prickles few, medium, thin, angled slightly downward; medium upright, bushy growth; PP5967; [Unnamed yellow Miniature × Shocking Blue]; int. by Nor'East Min. Roses

Sachiko HT, rb, Takatori; int. by Takatori Roses

Sächs. Lichtenstein S, lp, Noack, Werner; flowers medium-large, semi-dbl.; int. in 1996

Sachsengruss HP, lp, 1912, Neubert; flowers soft flesh, well-formed, very large, full, moderate sweet fragrance; recurrent; thornless; stems short; vigorous, tall growth; [Frau Karl Druschki × Mme Jules Gravereaux]; int. by Hoyer & Klemm

Sachsenrose Pol, dp; flowers carmine-pink, small, semi-dbl.

Saclay F, pb, 1970, Inst. National Agronomique; flowers opal, 2-3 in., 20-22 petals, cupped; foliage dull, sage-green; bushy growth; [sport of Miss France]; int. by Commissariat a l'Energie Atomique

Sacramento HT, dr, GPG Bad Langensalza; flowers dark velvety red, medium, dbl.; int. in 1981

Sacred Fire – See **Olympic Torch**, HT

Sacred Heart – See **Caroline de Monaco**, HT

Sacred Heart HT, dr, 2002, Weeks, O.L.; flowers 4 in., full, high-centered, borne mostly solitary, moderate fragrance; foliage medium size, medium green, semi-glossy; prickles average, recurved, moderate; upright, medium (5 ft.) growth; garden decorative; [Chrysler Imperial × Happiness]; int. by Certified Roses, Inc., 2002

Sadabahar F, mp, 1970, IARI; bud pointed; flowers pink, open, medium, semi-dbl.; foliage glossy, dark; very vigorous, bushy growth; [Frolic × unknown]

Sadabahar, Climbing Cl F, mp, IARI; flowers borne in large clusters; [sport of Sadabahar]; int. in 1991

Sadaranga HT, mp, 1978, Hardikar, Dr. M.N.; bud ovoid; flowers 4½ in., 60 petals, globular; foliage glossy; vigorous, upright, compact growth; [Kronenbourg × Peace]; int. in 1977

Saddler's Gold F, ab, 1995, Horner, Heather M.; flowers amber gold, 2½ in., dbl., borne in small clusters; foliage medium size, medium green, semi-glossy; medium (50 cm.), bushy growth; [Gingernut × Gold Bunny]; int. by Warley Rose Gardens, 1997

Saddleworth HT, w, 2000, Rawlins, R.; flowers semi-dbl., slight fragrance; foliage medium size, medium green, semi-glossy; prickles moderate; growth upright, medium; [Golden Future × (Sheri Ann × (Queen Elizabeth × *R. laxa* (Retzius)))]

Saddleworth Male Voice Choir F, rb, 2003, Rawlins, R.; flowers crimson with white stripe, reverse magenta, large, single, borne in small clusters, no fragrance; foliage medium size, medium green, semi-glossy; prickles ½ in., hooked; growth bushy, medium (42 in.); garden; [Golden Future × Crazy For You]

Sadie Min, w, Desamero, Luis; flowers very dbl., high-centered; [sport of Irresistible]

Sadie Hawkins Min, pb, 1990, Spooner, Raymond A.; bud globular; flowers medium pink with white stripes, reverse white, aging lighter, 16 petals, moderate fruity fragrance; foliage medium size, medium green, matte; no prickles; bushy, medium growth; hips globular, medium green; [Roller Coaster × seedling]; int. by Oregon Miniature Roses, 1990

Sadler Min, op, 1983, Bischoff, Francis J.; flowers orange pink, small, 43 petals, high-centered; foliage medium green, matte; upright growth; [Faberge × Darling Flame]; int. by Kimbrew-Walter Roses

Sadler's Wells S, pb, Beales, Peter; flowers silvery-pink, laced with cherry red at the edges, semi-dbl., shallow cup, borne in large clusters, slight fragrance; free-flowering; foliage dark green, glossy; vigorous (4 ft.) growth; int. by Peter Beales Roses, 1983

Safari F, my, 1970, Tantau, Math.; flowers large, 22 petals, cupped, borne in trusses; vigorous, compact growth; int. in 1966

Safari F, ab, Kordes; int. by W. Kordes Söhne, 1998

Safari S, op, Clements, John; flowers soft coppery-bronze shading to rich coral toward the outer edge of the petals, 3-4 in., 35 petals, deeply cupped., moderate sweet fragrance; free-flowering; growth compact, bushy plant (3½ × 3 ft.); PPAF; int. by Heirloom Roses, 2004

Safe Haven F, mr, J&P; flowers medium, dbl., cupped, borne in large clusters, slight fragrance; free-flowering; foliage medium green, glossy; bushy, strong (3 ft.) growth; int. in 2006

Saffex Rose F, m, Kordes; int. in 1993

Saffo HT, 1934, Aicardi, D.

Saffron Minuetto Min, dy, 2000, Meilland International; flowers deep yellow, reverse medium yellow, 2-3 cm., very full, no fragrance; foliage medium size, dark green, glossy; prickles moderate; compact, medium (8-12 in.) growth; containers, forcing; PPAF;

[unknown]; int. by Conard-Pyle Co., 1999

Safrano T, ab, 1839, Beauregard; bud pointed; flowers saffron and apricot-yellow, large, semi-dbl., moderate fragrance; good repeat; vigorous growth

Safrano à Fleurs Rouges T, yb, 1867, Oger; flowers saffron yellow, shaded with coppery red, medium, semi-dbl.; [sport of Safrano]

Saga S, w, 1974, Harkness; flowers cream-white, 2½ in., 12 petals, borne in clusters; free-flowering; foliage medium green; [Rudolph Timm × (Chanelle × Piccadilly)]

Saga Holiday F, ob, 1993, Harkness; flowers orange, orange-pink reverse, 4 in., 28 petals, high-centered, loose, borne in clusters of 3-5, slight spicy fragrance; foliage medium size, purplish, glossy; bushy, medium growth; [seedling × Amber Queen]; int. by Harkness New Roses, Ltd., 1993

Sagano HT, op, Keihan; int. by Keihan Gardening, 1982

S'Agaró HT, mr, 1959, Dot, Simon; bud long, pointed; flowers geranium-red, large, 30 petals, high-centered; foliage dark, glossy; compact growth; [Angels Mateu × (Radar × Grand'mere Jenny)]

Sagittarius F, mp, Chessum, Paul; flowers strong pink, dbl., borne in clusters; foliage glossy; bushy (75 cm.) growth; int. by Burston Nurseries, 2004

Sahara HT, w, 1956, Stevenson; bud golden yellow; flowers creamy buff, well-shaped; rather late bloom; very vigorous, upright growth; [Mrs Wemyss Quinn × Mev. G.A. van Rossem]; int. by Waterer

Sahara S, yb, Tantau; flowers golden yellow with bronze red shades, dbl.; free-flowering; foliage medium green, glossy; int. by Tantau Rosen, 1996

Sahara F, w, Olij; bud conical, elongated; flowers cream with light yellow and orange tints, 3½-4 in., 35 petals, high-centered, borne 1-3 per stem; good repeat; foliage medium green; prickles numerous, medium, greenish to yellow-brown; erect (4-5 ft.) growth; PP10281; [Prophyta × Olytel]; greenhouse rose; int. in 1997

Sahasradhara HT, pb, Thakur, Arpi; flowers deep pink with white streaks; [sport of Century Two]; int. in 1981

Sai-Un HT, ob, 1986, Suzuki, Seizo; flowers yellow-orange shaded deep orange-red, large, 50 petals, high-centered, moderate fragrance; foliage dark, glossy; prickles slanted downward; upright growth; [(Miss All-American Beauty × Kagayaki) × seedling]; int. by Keisei Rose Nursery, 1980

Sai Zan Tsuin HCh, ab

Sai Zhao Jun HCh, ab; flowers blush pink, sometimes with honey tints, 2-2½ in., dbl., flat, moderate old rose fragrance; recurrent; growth to 5 ft.

Saïd F, rb, 1964, Arles; bud ovoid; flowers cinnabar-red, reverse dark red, medium, 28 petals, cupped, borne in clusters; short stems; [Aloha × Pioupiou]; int. by Roses-France

Saigon HT, yb, 1943, Gaujard; flowers dark yellow with coppery pink tints, large, dbl.

Saiki HT, ly, Hiroshima; int. by Hiroshima Bara-en, 1999

Sailoz Mookherjea F, or, 1974, Pal, Dr. B.P.; flowers cadmium-orange to orange-vermilion, 3 in., 20 petals, high-centered; very vigorous growth; [unknown × unknown]

Saint Alban F, mr, 1977, Harkness; flowers 3 in., 15 petals; foliage glossy; dwarf growth; [Marlena × unknown]

St Alban S, my, 2004; flowers medium yellow, reverse light yellow, 6½ cm., very full, borne in small clusters, slight fragrance; foliage medium size, dark green, semi-glossy; prickles medium, hooked downward; growth bushy, narrow / branching, medium (4 ft.); garden decorative; [Ausgold × seedling (medium pink English-type shrub)]; int. by David Austin Roses, Ltd., 2003

St Alban's Gem S, m

St. Andrews – See **Valentine Heart**, F

St Boniface F, or, 1982, Kordes, W.; flowers bright vermilion red, medium, 35 petals, hybrid tea form, slight fragrance; foliage medium size, dark, semi-glossy; upright (2 ft.), bushy growth; [Diablotin × Traumerei]

St. Brennus – See **Brennus**, HCh

St. Brigid's Rose HT, pb; int. by Nieuwesteeg Rose Nursery, 1999

St Bruno F, dy, 1986, Sealand Nurseries, Ltd.; flowers large, 35 petals, intense fragrance; foliage medium size, medium green, semi-glossy; bushy growth; [Arthur Bell × Zambra]; int. in 1985; Edland Fragrance Medal, ARS, 1986

St Catherine LCl, pb

St Cecilia S, lp, 1987, Austin, David; flowers pale buff yellow, fading cream, medium, 40 petals, cupped, borne usually singly, moderate myrrh fragrance; repeat bloom; foliage small, medium green, matte; bushy, low, medium growth; no fruit; PP8157; [seedling × seedling]

St Christopher HT, dy, Harkness, R.; flowers intense deep yellow, 4 in., 20 petals, high-centered, moderate fruity/tea fragrance; vigorous (3½ ft.) growth; int. by R. Harkness & Co., 1996; Gold Medal, Belfast, 1998

St Clair's Rose HT, w

St Clare S, ab, 2005, Horner, Colin P.; flowers buff/apricot, reverse pale yellow, large, full, borne in small clusters, intense fragrance; foliage medium size, medium green, glossy; prickles medium, curved, numerous; growth upright, tall (4-5 ft.); garden decoration; [Arthur Bell × Perdita]; int. by Peter Beales Roses, 2006

St Dunstan's Rose S, w, Kirkham, Gordon Wilson; buds lemon yellow; flowers white, sometimes yellow streaked, full, rosette, intense fragrance; foliage pale green, glossy; growth to 3-4 ft.; commemorating the War Blind Association; int. by C&K Jones, 1991

Saint-Émilion HT, mr, Briant; int. by Jacques Briant, 2001

St Ethelburga S, lp, 2006, Beales, Amanda; flowers soft pink, 15 cm., very full, cupped, borne in large clusters, intense clove fragrance; free-flowering; foliage medium green, semi-glossy; prickles average, hooked, moderate; growth bushy, medium (4 ft.); containers, hedging; int. by Peter Beales Roses, 2003

Saint-Exupéry HT, m, 1960, Delbard-Chabert; flowers mauve tinted silvery, fading quickly, 5 in., dbl., high-centered, borne mostly solitary, slight fragrance; vigorous, bushy growth; [(Christopher Stone × Marcelle Gret) × (Holstein × Bayadere)]

Saint-Exupéry S, mp; flowers Indian-rose, large, dbl., cupped, intense rose fragrance; growth to 80 cm.; int. by Delbard, 2003

Saint Fiacre Pol, or, 1965, Delforge; bud ovoid; flowers geranium-red, single, cupped, borne in clusters; vigorous, upright growth; [Reverence × Sumatra]

Saint Fiacre d'Orléans Pol, op, Eve, A.; flowers salmon-pink, 6 cm., full, turbinate, borne in large clusters; recurrent; compact (2 ft.) growth; int. as Saint-Fiacre d'Orléans, Les Roses Anciennes de André Eve, 1997

St Francis Xavier T, dr, 2004, Thomson, George L.; flowers deep crimson, 4 in., very full, borne in small clusters, intense fragrance; foliage medium size, dark green, glossy; prickles medium, hooked; growth bushy, medium (3-4½ ft.); garden decorative; [Francis Dubrieul × Papa Gontier]; int. by Ross Roses, 2004

Saint Galmier S, w, Eve, André; flowers 3 cm.; foliage glossy; lax, groundcover or climbing growth; hips small, red; int. by Les Roses Anciennes de André Eve, 2005

St Helena HT, ly, 1912, Cant, B. R.; flowers creamy yellow, center pinkish, large, full; RULED EXTINCT 6/83; Gold Medal, RNRS, 1912

St Helena F, mp, 1983, Cants of Colchester, Ltd.; flowers medium lilac pink, medium, 20 petals, cupped, slight fragrance; free-flowering; foliage medium size, medium green, semi-glossy; upright, compact growth; [Jubilant × Prima Ballerina]

St Hilaire (*R. blanda* form), mp; no prickles

St Hildas HT, ab; flowers bright bronze-yellow, borne in clusters, moderate fragrance; stems moderately long; medium growth; int. in 1996

St Hughs HT, my, 1987, Kordes, W.; flowers creamy yellow, large, full, moderate fragrance; foliage medium size, medium green, semi-glossy; upright, bushy growth; [seedling × seedling]; int. by The Rose Nursery, 1986

St Ignatius HT, dy, Courage; flowers clear yellow, semi-dbl. to dbl., star-like, intense fragrance; recurrent; int. by Ross Roses, 2001

St Ingebert HP, w, 1926, Lambert, P.; bud long, pointed; flowers white, center yellowish and reddish, large, 62 petals; vigorous growth; [Frau Karl Druschki × Mme Mélanie Soupert]

St John F, w, 1994, Harkness; flowers medium, dbl., borne in small clusters, slight fragrance; foliage medium size, medium green, glossy; few prickles; low (60 cm.), bushy, spreading growth; [Prima × Grace Abounding]; int. by Harkness New Roses, Ltd., 1994

St. John Nonacentenary F, w, Poulsen; flowers white with soft apricot-cream in the center, dbl., low-centered, borne in dense clusters; recurrent; growth medium; int. by Ludwig's Roses, 2000

St John Ogilvie – See **Festival Fanfare**, S

St John's Rose S, lp, before 1867; flowers rose to salmon-pink, 2-2½ in., single, borne in small corymbs; foliage somewhat rugose; prickles robust, hooked; growth low, trailing; [*R. gallica* × *R. phoenicia*]; introduced in Europe by Dammann around 1895; described by Rehder in 1902; known from Ethiopian & Egyptian tombs between 100-400 AD

St Katherine's S, m, Pearce

Saint Louis Gr, w, 1989, Maltagliati, Mark G.; flowers white to ivory; PP6908; [sport of Lifirane]; int. by Conard-Pyle Co., 1989

St Lucia HT, mp, 1975, Tantau, Math.; bud ovoid; flowers pink, medium, dbl., moderate fragrance; foliage glossy; moderate, upright, bushy growth; [unknown × unknown]; int. by Ahrens & Sieberz

St Margaret's HT, ob, Bell, Ronald J.; int. in 1998

St Mark's Rose – See **Rose d'Amour**, Misc OGR

Saint Mary Min, m, 1986, Moore, Ralph S.; flowers deep red-purple, small, dbl., cupped, slight fragrance; foliage small, medium green, semi-glossy; prickles small, brown; medium, upright, bushy growth; no fruit; [Little Chief × Angel Face]; int. by Moore Min. Roses

St Nicholas D, dp, Hilling; flowers rich pink, yellow stamens, medium, semi-dbl., moderate apple fragrance; vigorous, erect (3 ft.) growth; [sport of Hebe's Lip]; probably a very old variety; found in England and re-introduced in 1950; int. by Hilling, 1950

Saint Patrick – See **St Patrick**, HT

St Patrick HT, yb, 1999, Strickland, Frank A.; flowers yellow gold, shaded green in heat, 5 in., 30-35 petals, high-centered, borne mostly singly, slight fragrance; foliage large, medium green, matte; prickles moderate; upright, bushy, medium (3-4 ft.) growth; PP9591; [Brandy × Gold Medal]; int. by Weeks Roses, 1996

St Paul F, yb, 1959, Kordes, R.; bud long, pointed; flowers golden yellow edged red to pink, becoming fused, open, 3 in., 15 petals, borne in clusters, moderate fragrance; foliage large, dark green, glossy; very vigorous, upright, bushy growth; [Masquerade × Spek's Yellow]; int. in 1958

St. Pauli – See **St Paul**, F

St Piers F, mp; flowers rose pink, medium, full, cupped, borne in clusters, slight to moderate fragrance; good repeat; foliage dark green, glossy; modest (2-3 ft.) growth; int. by Harkness, 1998

St Priest de Breuze Ch, rb, 1838, Desprez; flowers rich deep crimson with rose center, medium, dbl., globular; upright (3-4 ft.) growth

St Prist de Breuze – See **St Priest de Breuze**, Ch

St Quentin HT, rb, 1986, Kriloff, Michel; flowers red, silver petal edges; foliage dark, glossy; [seedling × Tropicana]

St Richard of Chichester – See **Sherlock Holmes**, S

St Swithun S, lp, 1994, Austin, David; flowers pale pink, large, very dbl., borne in small clusters, moderate fragrance; foliage medium size, medium green, semi-glossy; some prickles; medium (4-5 ft.), bushy growth; PP9010; [Mary Rose × seedling]; int. by David Austin Roses, Ltd., 1993

St Theresa HT, op, Williams, J.B.; flowers warm coral pink, dbl., cupped, borne in clusters; recurrent; int. by Hortico, 2002

St Tiggywinkles – See **Pink Bassino**, F

Saint-Victor HT, mr, Croix; flowers large; free-flowering; foliage resistant; int. by Roseraie Paul Croix, 1979; Gold Medal, Genoa, Certificate of Merit, Roeulx

Saint-Vincent F, mr, Delbard, Georges; flowers dbl., open, borne in clusters; good repeat; foliage disease-resistant; medium, stocky growth; int. by George Delbard SA, 1994

St Wilfrid's Hospice F, mr, 1994, Sawday, Mrs. D.R.; flowers medium, semi-dbl., borne in small clusters, slight fragrance; foliage small, medium green, semi-glossy; some prickles; medium, bushy growth; [sport of Len Turner]; int. by Apuldram Roses, 1995

Sainte-Genevieve S, w, Guimont, G.; non-remontant; int. in 1987

Saison Bluete HT, dy

Sakaura-Hime Min, lp; flowers light to medium pink, large, dbl., pompon, borne in clusters; recurrent; int. before 1979

Sakura-Gasumi F, lp, 1999, Suzuki, Seizo; flowers pale pink, turning deeper, 1½-2 in., 20-25 petals; foliage dark green, semi-glossy; dwarf, compact (1 ft.) growth; [seedling × seedling]; int. by Keisei Rose Nursery, 1990; Gold Medal, Japan Rose Concours, 1990

Sakura-Gasumi, Climbing Cl F, lp, Washimi; [sport of Sakura-Gasumi]; int. by Keisei Rose Nurseries, 2001

Sakuragai F, lp, Keisei; int. by Keisei Rose Nurseries, 1996

Sakuragasumi – See **Sakura-Gasumi**, F

Salam Aleik HT, mr; flowers pure red, very large, dbl.

Salamanca S, ab, Poulsen; flowers apricot blend, 5-8 cm., 25 petals, no fragrance; foliage dark; growth bushy, 60-100 cm.; int. by Poulsen Roser, 2005

Salamander HP, mr, 1891, Paul, W.; flowers bright scarlet-crimson, large, dbl., cupped; non-recurrent; upright growth

Salambo HT, mr, 1959, Kordes, R.; flowers carthamus-red; int. by Vilmorin-Andrieux

Salammbô LCl, dr, Delbard; flowers dark, velvety crimson, medium, very full, borne in small clusters, slight fragrance; growth to 7-8 ft.; [Grimpant Delbard × Perle Noire]; int. by George Delbard SA, 1994

Salazar HT, rb, Moreira da Silva; flowers bright velvety red with salmon reflections, petals waved

Salden Monarch HT, mp, 1970; flowers large, dbl.; foliage glossy; vigorous growth; [Ballet × unknown]; int. by Carrigg, 1968

Salet M, mp, 1854, Lacharme, F.; bud well mossed; flowers rosy pink, lighter at edges, very large, full, cupped to flat, moderate fragrance; some recurrence; vigorous growth; apparently part Damask

Salita LCl, or, 2006; bud large, ovoid; flowers orange scarlet, 9 cm., full, high-centered, borne in small clusters, no fragrance; foliage reddish when young, later dark green, glossy; upright, tall (250 cm.) growth; int. by W. Kordes' Söhne, 1987

Salita Kordana Min, or, Kordes; compact growth; int. by NewFlora, 2006

Sallie HT, w, 1915, Cant, B. R.; flowers cream white, center darker with yellow reflections, large, full

Sallie Lewis HT, ab, 1924, Morse; bud long, pointed; flowers creamy apricot, center deeper, dbl., intense fragrance; [Mme Charles Lutaud × Gladys Holland]; similar to Souv. de Mme. Boullet

Sallijane HT, pb, 2001, Adlong, Paula; flowers medium, full, borne mostly singly, slight fragrance; [Crystalline × Elizabeth Taylor]; int. in 2001

Sally HT, mp, 1938, Spandikow; bud long, pointed; flowers pink, dbl., high-centered; foliage leathery; long stems; vigorous growth; RULED EXTINCT 3/81; [Mrs Charles Russell × Mme Butterfly]; int. by Eddie

Sally F, ab, 1981, Walker, B.; flowers pale apricot, fading to ivory, with pink veins; [sport of Elizabeth of Glamis]; int. by Homeric Rose Nurseries

Sally Alder HT, mp, 1944, Moss; bud long, pointed; flowers pink, medium, semi-dbl., high-centered; foliage dark; moderate, bushy growth; [Portadown × seedling]; int. by F. Mason

Sally Forth S, yb, Peden, R.

Sally Holmes S, w, 1976, Holmes, R.; bud pointed, apricot; flowers creamy white, 3½-4 in., single, borne in large clusters; recurrent; foliage dark, glossy; few prickles; straight, long stems; vigorous, bushy growth; [Ivory Fashion × Ballerina]; int. by Fryer's Nursery, Ltd., 1976; Gold Medal, Portland, 1993, Gold Medal, Baden-Baden, 1980, Fragrance Award, Glasgow, 1993

Sally Jane – See **Sallijane**, HT

Sally Jean HT, ab, 2001, Thomson, George L.; flowers golden apricot, lighter reverse, 6 in., full, borne mostly solitary, intense fragrance; foliage large, medium green, semi-glossy; prickles large, hooked, few, brown; stems long; growth upright, tall (6-7 ft.); garden decorative; [King's Ransom × Papa Meilland]; int. by Ross Roses, 2001

Sally Kane HT, w, Fryer; flowers creamy white with green tints on outer petals and champagne in the center, large, full, high-centered, borne usually singly, moderate fragrance; recurrent; foliage dark green, dense; medium growth; int. by Fryers Roses, 2006

Sally Krisman HT, w, 2002, Poole, Lionel; flowers cream to pale pink, 4½ in., full, borne mostly solitary, slight fragrance; foliage medium size, medium green, glossy; prickles medium, hooked down, moderate; growth upright, bushy, medium (3 ft.); garden decorative, exhibition; [Joanna Lumley × New Zealand]

Sally Mac F, ab, 1981, McCann, Sean; flowers apricot-pink blend, yellow at base, 40 petals, borne in clusters of 4; foliage medium size, dark, glossy; prickles hooked, red-brown; vigorous, upright growth; [(Joyfulness × Paddy McGredy) × (Circus × Joyfulness)]; int. by Hughes Roses

Sally Pigtail HT, pb, 1959, Mee; flowers cream flushed rose-pink, high pointed, large, 32 petals; free growth; [Wilfred Pickles × Karl Herbst]

Sally Tite HT, dr, 1930, Dickson, S.; flowers glowing crimson, over large, dbl., high-centered; int. by Armstrong Nursery

Sally's Rose HT, pb, 1994, Cants of Colchester, Ltd.; flowers pale pink and cream, shaded apricot, medium, dbl., high-centered, slight fragrance; foliage reddish when young, maturing to dark green, glossy; numerous prickles; short (60 cm.), bushy growth; [Amber Queen × Remember Me]; int. by Cants of Colchester Ltd., 1994; Fragrance Award, Glasgow, 1997

Salmo S, op, Olesen; flowers salmon-pink to orange, 5-8 cm., dbl., high-centered, borne in clusters, slight fragrance; free-flowering; foliage dark green, glossy; bushy, low (40-60 cm.) growth; int. as Coral Midinette, Ludwig's Roses

Salmon Cl Min, op; int. in 1994

Salmon Abundance – See **St Piers**, F

Salmon Ange HT, op

Salmon Arctic LCl, lp, 1954, Brownell; flowers dawn-pink, 3½-4½ in., 90-100 petals; growth like a hybrid tea, followed by 4-5 ft. canes; PP1297; [seedling × Break o' Day, Climbing]

Salmon Beauty Pol, op, 1929, Wezelenburg; flowers peach-pink, passing to soft salmon, medium, very dbl., borne in clusters; dwarf growth; [sport of Orange King]

Salmon Button Min, ob

Salmon Charm – See **Ginger Rogers**, HT

Salmon Cupido Min, op, Pouw; bud ovoid; flowers salmon, 1½ in., 78 petals, rosette, borne singly and in large sprays, very slight fragrance; free-flowering; foliage dark green, glossy; prickles moderate, 4 mm., straight, brown; upright (15 in.), spreading growth; PP12642; [seedling × seedling]; containers; int. by Greenheart Farms, 2004

Salmon Dream MinFl, op; int. in 1999

Salmon Drops Gr, op, Williams, J. Benjamin; flowers salmon-pink, dbl., high-centered, intense fragrance; foliage glossy; int. by Hortico, 1999

Salmon Gaujard HT, op, Gaujard; flowers salmon-pink, large, full, high-centered; vigorous, sturdy growth; int. in 1985

Salmon Glory Pol, op, 1937, deRuiter; flowers pinkish salmon; [sport of Gloria Mundi]

Salmon Glow F, op, 1970, Sanday, John; flowers salmon, 3 in., 25 petals; foliage matte green; compact, bushy growth; [Vera Dalton × seedling]

Salmon Impressionist S, op, Lim, P, & Twomey, J.; bud medium, rounded; flowers coral, maturing to mauve-pink, 3½ in., 30 petals, tea rose form, borne in cluster of about 8, moderate fragrance; recurrent; foliage medium to dark green, satiny, disease-resistant; compact, upright (3 ft.), bushy growth; PP15739; [Unnamed seedling 4-43A × Lillian Gibson]; int. by Bailey Nurseries, 2004

Salmon-King F, rb, 1972, Ellick; flowers red, inside orange-red, high pointed, 5 in., 28-30 petals, intense fragrance; foliage glossy; vigorous, bushy growth; [Show Girl × Orange Sensation]; int. by Excelsior Roses

Salmon LD S, op, Rogue Valley Roses; flowers salmon; [sport of Leonard Dudley Braithwaite]; like its parent except in flower color; int. by Rogue Valley Roses, 2007

Salmon Marvel F, op, 1959, deRuiter; flowers orange-salmon, 2½-3 in., 44 petals, rosette, borne in trusses;

foliage dark, glossy, crinkled; bushy, upright growth; [Red Pinocchio × Signal Red]; int. by Blaby Rose Gardens, 1958

Salmon Midinette Cl Min, op, Moore; flowers deep salmon-pink, borne singly and in clusters; recurrent; vigorous, tall (4 m.), willowy growth; int. in 1996

Salmon Panarosa S, op, Kordes; flowers deep salmon, medium, dbl., high-centered; upright, tall growth; int. by Ludwig's Roses, 2004

Salmon Perfection F, rb, 1952, deRuiter; flowers scarlet-red shaded orange, medium, 25 petals, cupped, borne in trusses; foliage dark, leathery; vigorous growth; int. by A. Dickson

Salmon Pink Garnette Pol, op

Salmon Queen Pol, op, 1923, Den Ouden; flowers deep salmon; [sport of Juliana Rose]

Salmon Radiance – See **Mrs Charles J. Bell**, HT

Salmon Rosamini Min, op, deRuiter; flowers orange salmon, pompon; free-flowering; vigorous, tall, densely branched growth; int. by Ludwig's Roses, 1984

Salmon Sensation – See **Marion**, F

Salmon Sorbet F, pb

Salmon Spire HT, op, Kordes; bud long; flowers clear salmon-pink, dbl., high-centered, borne mostly singly, intense fragrance; recurrent; vigorous, tall (8 ft.) growth; int. in 1993

Salmon Splash F, ob, K&S; flowers salmon with white stripes and splashes, borne in large sprays; free-flowering; compact growth; [sport of Orange Splash]; int. by KSG Son, 1997

Salmon Spray F, pb, 1923, Grant; flowers light salmon-pink, reverse shaded carmine, semi-dbl., cupped, borne in clusters, moderate fragrance; recurrent; foliage rich green, leathery; very vigorous, bushy growth; [Orléans Rose, Climbing × Midnight Sun]; int. by Kershaw

Salmon Sprite F, op, 1964, LeGrice; flowers salmon suffused strawberry, 3 in., 40 petals, borne in clusters of up to 15; upright growth; [seedling × Jiminy Cricket]

Salmon Sunblaze Min, op, 1996, Meilland International SA; bud egg-shaped, medium; flowers salmon pink, 1½-2 in., 35-40 petals, cupped, borne in small clusters; free-flowering; foliage small, dark green, semi-glossy; prickles numerous, small, pinkish; compact, upright, low (12-16 in.) growth; PP10015; [Parador × (Lady Sunblaze × Dwarf Queen '82)]; int. by The Conard-Pyle Co., 1997

Salmon Sunsation S, op, Kordes; flowers deep salmon, dbl., cupped, borne in clusters; low, groundcover growth; int. by Ludwig's Roses, 1989

Salmon Symphony HT, op

Salmon Vigorosa – See **Electric Blanket**, F

Salmona HT, op, Ghosh, Mr. & Mrs. S.; bud long; flowers salmon, veined deeper salmon, dbl., high-centered; int. in 2001

Salmone Gr, lp, 1968, Faassen-Gouba; bud ovoid; flowers medium, borne in clusters; foliage dark; [sport of Queen Elizabeth]

Salmonea Pol, op, 1927, Cutbush; flowers salmon-pink

Salomé HT, op, 1945, Gaujard; bud ovoid; flowers salmon-flesh-pink, medium, dbl.; foliage glossy; very vigorous, upright growth

Salomé F, pb, 1958, Buyl Frères; flowers rose-orange, dbl.; vigorous growth

Salome HT, yb; florist rose; int. by Terra Nigra BV, 2002

Salomon HGal, pb, about 1825, Cartier; flowers dark pink, striped white, large, full

Salou F, pb, 1971, Delforge; bud long, pointed; flowers deep pink to flesh-pink, open, large, dbl.; foliage dark, leathery; very vigorous, upright growth; [Astoria × Tiffany]

Salsa HT, dr, 1990, Warriner, William A.; bud ovoid, pointed; flowers large, 30-35 petals, high-centered, urn-shaped, borne singly, moderate damask fragrance; foliage medium size, dark green, semi-glossy; few prickles; upright, tall growth; PP6971; [Showstopper × seedling]; int. by Bear Creek Gardens

Salsa F, dr, 2001, Zary, Keith; bud pointed, ovoid; flowers bright, velvety red, 3½-4 in., 20 petals, shallow cupped, borne in small clusters, slight light, fresh fragrance; repeats well; foliage medium size, dark green, glossy; prickles moderate; growth upright, medium (3 ft.); garden decorative; PP14245; [Showbiz × unnamed red floribunda seedling]; int. by J&P, 2002

Salsa – See **Cheek to Cheek**, LCl

Salt Lake S, my, Poulsen; flowers medium yellow, 5-8 cm., semi-dbl., cupped to flat, borne in clusters, very slight fragrance; recurrent; foliage dark green, glossy; broad, bushy (60-100 cm.) growth; int. as Silk Border, Poulsen Roser, 2005; Silver Medal, Geneva, 2006, Gold Medal, Buenos Aires, 2006

Saltaire HT, dr, 1925, Dickson, A.; bud long, pointed; flowers deep velvety crimson, dbl.

Saltatina F, or, 1979, Lens, Louis; bud ovoid; flowers orange-copper to red, open, 2½-3 in., 18-22 petals, moderate spicy fragrance; foliage dark; bushy, spreading growth; [Zorina × Fillette]; int. in 1974

Saltwell Park F, mr, 1976, Wood; flowers very deep scarlet, 3 in., 20 petals; foliage dark; moderate, upright growth; [Paddy McGredy × Arabian Nights]

Saluda Min, ob, 2006, Williams, Michael C.; flowers light, creamy orange, small, dbl., high-centered, borne in small clusters; recurrent; foliage small, dark green, matte; prickles few, less than ¼ in., straight, dark reddish brown; growth upright, medium (18-22 in.); garden decoration, borders, containers; [Finest Hour × Party Girl]; int. by Bridges Roses, 2007; Award of Excellence, ARS, 2007

Salut HT, op, VEG; flowers salmon-orange, large, dbl.; int. in 1987

Salut à la Suisse – See **Red Favorite**, F

Salut d'Aix la Chapelle – See **Gruss an Aachen**, F

Salutation LCl, op, 1972, Oliver, W.G.; flowers salmon, 2½ in., 38 petals; foliage glossy, dark; very vigorous growth; [Salute × Mme Isaac Pereire]

Salute F, rb, 1959, McGredy, Sam IV; flowers cherry and ochre bicolor, 1½ in., 20 petals, borne in trusses; foliage dark, leathery; free growth; [Masquerade × Lady Sylvia]; int. by McGredy & Son, 1958

Salute Min, dr, 2003, White, Wendy R.; flowers 1½-1¾ in., dbl., borne mostly solitary; foliage medium size, dark green, matte, good disease resistance; prickles ¼ in., angled slightly downward; upright (15-22 in.), compact, bushy growth; cut flower, exhibition; PP15899; [(Vista × Party Girl) × (Party Girl × Teddy Bear)]; int. by Nor East Miniature Roses, Inc., 2004; Certificate of Merit, Rose Hills, 2006, Award of Excellence, ARS, 2004

Salvation F, mr, 2001, Thomson, George L.; flowers velvet red, 2-2½ in., semi-dbl., borne in large clusters, slight fragrance; free-flowering; foliage medium size, dark green, glossy; prickles medium, hooked, brown, numerous; growth bushy, low (3-3½ ft.); garden decorative; [Trumpeter × Showbiz]; int. by Ross Roses, 2001

Salvation F, ab, Harkness; flowers amber infused with apricot, full, pompon, borne in clusters of 3-7, moderate fruity fragrance; recurrent; compact, sturdy, bushy growth; int. by R. Harkness & Co., 2005

Salvo HT, mr, 1959, Herholdt, J.A.; flowers velvety crimson, 5 in., 45 petals; vigorous, bushy growth; [Happiness × Grand Gala]; int. by Herholdt's Nursery

Salza S, dp, Berger, W.; flowers carmine-pink, medium, dbl.; int. in 1956

Salzagold HT, dy

Salzajubiläum F, or, GPG Bad Langensalza; flowers salmon-red, large, semi-dbl.; int. in 1982

Salzaperle HT, mp, GPG Bad Langensalza; flowers large, dbl.; int. in 1977

Salzaquelle HT, m, GPG Bad Langensalza; flowers light lilac, large, dbl.; int. in 1977

Salzburg S, op, W. Kordes Söhne; flowers medium, dbl.; int. in 1967

Sam F, r, 1984, Stephens, Paddy; flowers russet, reverse cream, 20 petals; foliage medium size, dark, glossy; bushy growth; [Brown Eye × seedling]; int. in 1981

Sam Buff – See **Afterglow**, HT

Sam Ferris F, ob, 1967, Ellick; flowers orange-scarlet, dbl., borne in trusses; vigorous growth; [sport of Heidleberg]

Sam Houston – See **Sam Houston Rose**, S

Sam Houston Rose S, pb, Antique Rose Emporium; bud long, pointed; flowers medium pink fading into yellow eye, outer petals fade to pale pink, 3 in., semi-dbl., loose, flat, borne in small clusters, no fragrance; recurrent; growth to 3-4 ft.; [Carefree Beauty (Katy Road Pink) × Mrs. Oakley Fisher]; int. in 1996

Sam McGredy HT, yb, 1937, McGredy; flowers dark cream, base sunflower-yellow, large, high-centered, slight fragrance; foliage dark, leathery; vigorous growth; [Delightful × Mrs Charles Lamplough]; Gold Medal, NRS, 1935

Sam Trivitt Min, ab, 2000, Sproul, James; bud pointed; flowers light golden apricot, 1½ in., full, high-centered, borne singly or in small clusters, slight fragrance; foliage medium size, dark green, semi-glossy; few prickles; growth upright, bushy, medium (3 ft.); [Chipmunk × (San Jose Sunshine × Prima Donna)]; int. by Roses By Design

Samandi F, w, 1997, Rawlins, R.; flowers dbl., borne in small clusters; foliage medium; medium (1 m.) growth; [Sexy Rexy × Brownie]

Samantha HT, mr, 1974, Warriner, William A.; bud ovoid, pointed; flowers currant red, 4 in., 45-50 petals, high-centered, borne singly and several together, slight fragrance; recurrent; foliage medium size, leathery; prickles moderate, long, straight; stems long, strong; vigorous, upright growth; PP3727; [Bridal Pink × seedling]; flora-tea; int. by J&P

Samantha, Climbing Cl HT, mr; [sport of Samantha]

Samantha HT, dr, Noack, Werner; int. in 1984

Samantha Barker HT, ly, 2001, Webster, Robert; flowers lemon yellow, changing to cream/lemon blend late in season, medium, full, borne in small clusters, intense fragrance; foliage medium size, medium green, glossy; prickles 8-10 mm., triangular, moderate; growth compact, low (30 in.); bedding; [The Marquess of Bristol × Indian Summer]; int. by Handley Rose Nurseries, 2003

Samantha Ruth Min, yb, 1994, Wells, Verlie W.; flowers blend of cream, orange and pink, large, very full, high-centered, borne mostly singly, slight fragrance; foliage medium size, dark green, semi-glossy; some prickles; medium, upright growth; [(Party Girl × Magic Carrousel) × seedling]; int. by Wells Mid-South Roses, 1994

Samara HT, dy, Noack, Werner; flowers golden yellow,

4 in., dbl., high-centered; free-flowering; moderate growth; int. by Noack Rosen, 1989

Samaritan – See **English Sonnet**, F

Samatigui – See ***R. leschenaultii*** (Wight & Arnott)

Samba F, yb, 1963, Poulsen, N.; flowers cream yellow rimmed vermilion, 2½ in., 15 petals, high-centered, borne in clusters; foliage dark green; int. by McGredy & Son, 1962

Samba F, yb, 1964, Kordes, R.; bud globular; flowers golden yellow touched red, becoming fiery red, 6 cm., dbl., borne in clusters, no fragrance; recurrent; foliage dark green, glossy; upright (2 ft.), bushy growth; int. by W. Kordes Söhne, 1964

Samba F, ob, Kordes; flowers copper-orange, sweetheart size, full, high-centered, borne mostly singly; recurrent; stems moderate; florist rose; int. by W. Kordes Söhne, 2005

Samba Kordana Min, yb, Kordes; flowers deep yellow, edged red, full, cupped; int. by W. Kordes Söhne

Sambina HT, pb; florist rose; int. by Terra Nigra BV, 2002

Sammetglut F, dr, 1943, Kordes; bud long, pointed; flowers crimson, open, very large, semi-dbl., borne in clusters; foliage dark, leathery; very vigorous, upright, bushy growth; [Holstein × Kardinal]

Sammi Minijet Min, op, Meilland; flowers salmon, dbl., rosette, borne in clusters; containers

Sammy HMsk, dr, 1921, Pemberton; bud small; flowers carmine, single, borne in erect clusters; recurrent bloom; foliage glossy, bronze; very vigorous, bushy growth; [(Trier × Gruss an Teplitz) × unknown]

Sammy F, ab, Athy, Mike; bud pinky red; flowers apricot, ruffled, full, rosette, intense musk fragrance; recurrent; low to medium growth; int. by DeBoer Roses, 2004

Samoa – See **Fred Cramphorn**, HT

Samoa Sunset HT, ob, 1965, Lone Star Rose Nursery; flowers chrome-yellow and copper-orange, open, large, dbl.; foliage glossy, bronze; vigorous, bushy, compact growth; [sport of McGredy's Sunset]

Samouraï – See **Scarlet Knight**, Gr

Samourai, Climbing – See **Scarlet Knight, Climbing**, Cl Gr

Samptosa F, dr, Institut für Obstbau Dresden Pillnitz; flowers large, dbl.; int. in 1969

Samsø – See **Megenaris**, F

Samson Min, mr, 1986, Saville, F. Harmon; flowers brilliant scarlet red, 28 petals, urn-shaped, borne in sprays of 20-60; foliage large, dark, semi-glossy; prickles long, thin; tall, upright growth; [Sheri Anne × (Yellow Jewel × Tamango)]; int. by Nor'East Min. Roses

Samuel Holland – See **Captain Samuel Holland**, S

Samuel Marsden Ch, mp, 1989, Nobbs, Kenneth J.; [sport of Slater's Crimson China]; int. in 1987

Samuel Pepys HT, w, 1934, Cant, B. R.; flowers white, center slightly shaded cream, very large, dbl., globular; foliage leathery; bushy growth

San Antonio Gr, or, 1967, Armstrong, D.L.; bud ovoid, medium; flowers cardinal red, 3½-5 in., 35-45 petals, high-centered to cupped, borne singly and in small clusters, slight fragrance; free-flowering; foliage dark, glossy, leathery; prickles several, short, almost straight; stems strong, medium to long; very vigorous, upright, bushy growth; hips globular, rough, apricot-orange to hazel; PP2844; [Roundelay × El Capitan]; int. by Armstrong Nursery

San Diego HT, ob, 1937, Hieatt, Forrest L.; bud medium to large, ovoid; flowers deep orange-yellow, shading to apricot, fading to soft buff, large, dbl., strong fruity fragrance; good repeat bloom; foliage glossy; growth vigorous upright, bushy (3 ft.)

San Diego HT, my, 1968, Armstrong, D.L.; bud ovoid; flowers light yellow, large, 50 petals, high-centered, moderate fragrance; foliage leathery; vigorous, upright, bushy, compact growth; PP2900; [Helen Traubel × Tiffany]; int. by Armstrong Nursery

San Diego HT, pb, deVor; int. in 1993

San Fernando HT, mr, 1948, Morris; bud fat; flowers scarlet, large, 30 petals, high-centered, intense fruit/tea fragrance; recurrent; vigorous, upright growth; [Heart's Desire × (Crimson Glory × Poinsettia)]; int. by Western Rose Co.

San Fernando, Climbing Cl HT, mr, 1951, Whisler; [sport of San Fernando]; int. by Germain's

San Francisco HT, mr, 1962, Lammerts, Dr. Walter; bud ovoid; flowers signal-red, 4-5 in., 40 petals, high-centered; foliage dark, glossy, leathery; vigorous, compact, branching growth; [Dean Collins × Independence]; int. by Germain's, 1962

San Francisco Sunset MinFl, or, 2004, McCann, Sean; flowers dbl., borne in small clusters, slight fragrance; foliage medium size, medium green, semi-glossy; prickles medium, straight; growth upright, medium (24 in.); garden decoration; [Kiss'n'tell × (Orangeade × Alexander)]; int. in 1997

San Gabriel HT, op, 1947, Morris; bud long, pointed; flowers deep salmon-pink, 5½ in., 45 petals, high-centered; foliage dark, leathery; vigorous, bushy growth; [Poinsettia × unnamed variety]; int. by Germain's

San Gabriel S, yb, 2002, Ponton, Ray; flowers yellow-red, 2-3 cm., single, borne in small clusters, moderate fragrance; foliage medium green, semi-glossy; prickles medium, hooked, moderate; growth upright, medium (3-4 ft.); landscape; [Katy Road Pink × Reveil Dijonnaise]; int. by Chamlee's Rose Nursery, 2002

San Joaquin HT, ob, 1939, Moore, Ralph S.; flowers glowing orange; [sport of Talisman]

San Jordi HT, Camprubi, C.

San José HT, ob, 1933, Denoyel, Vve.; bud ovoid; flowers orange-salmon suffused gold, very large, dbl.; foliage glossy; very vigorous growth; int. by J&P

San Jose Sunshine Min, dy, 1991, Jacobs, Betty A.; bud pointed; flowers deep golden yellow, aging light yellow with orange highlights, medium, 25-30 petals, high-centered, borne usually singly or in sprays of up to 10, slight fruity to tea fragrance; foliage medium size, medium green, matte; bushy, spreading, medium to tall growth; [(Rise 'n' Shine × Redgold) × Summer Madness]; int. by Sequoia Nursery, 1991

San Luis Rey HT, dy, 1947, Morris; bud ovoid; flowers deep saffron-yellow, 4½ in., 40 petals, cupped, intense orange-clove tea fragrance; foliage dark, glossy; bushy growth; [Lady Forteviot × Pedralbes]; int. by Germain's

San Rafael Rose – See **Fortune's Double Yellow**, Misc OGR

San Valentin Pol, Dot, Simon; int. in 1971

Sanbi HT, pb, Suzuki; int. by Keisei Rose Nurseries, 1991

Sanchette HGal, dp, 1837, Vibert; flowers crimson pink to rose, medium to large, full, cupped; growth erect

Sancta – See **St John's Rose**, S

Sanctus HKor, w, 1982, James, John; flowers pure white, large, 36 petals, high-centered, borne singly, moderate fragrance; repeat bloom; foliage large, dark, leathery; prickles large, straight, rust-brown; vigorous, upright, tall growth; [Borealis × Borealis]; int. in 1978

Sandalwood Min, r, 1995, Jalbert, Brad; flowers russet with lighter edges, 1 in., dbl., borne in small clusters, no fragrance; foliage medium size, medium green, glossy; some prickles; medium (12 in.), compact, bushy growth; [Blushing Blue × Springwood Gold]; int. by Select Roses

Sandar HT, rb, 1946, Laperrière; flowers carmine, center yellow, large, 25 petals; foliage dark; very vigorous growth; [Charles P. Kilham × Lleida]

Sandberg HT, pb

Sandefjord – See **Hertfordshire**, S

Sander's White Rambler HWich, w, Sander; flowers golden stamens, 3 cm., dbl., rosette, borne in large clusters, moderate fragrance; some autumn repeat; foliage bright green, glossy; vigorous growth; int. by Sander & Son, 1912

Sandhya Bela F, ob, 1974, Pal, Dr. B. P.; buds small, ovoid; flowers orange with lighter reverse, medium, semi-dbl., open, borne singly and several together; foliage medium size, glossy; growth vigorous, bushy, open (60 cm.); [Zambra × unknown]; int. by K. S. G. Son, 1971

Sandolina de Major HT, dp, 1978, W. Kordes Söhne; bud ovoid; flowers deep pink, 4 in., 57 petals, cupped, moderate fragrance; vigorous, upright growth; [Dr. A.J. Verhage × Königin der Rosen]; int. by Willemse, 1977

Sandra HT, op, 1982, Kordes, W.; bud long; flowers salmon, large, 35 petals, high-centered, slight fragrance; foliage medium size, medium green, matte; upright, medium growth; [Mercedes × seedling]; int. in 1981

Sandra – See **Flamingo Meidiland**, S

Sandra – See **Sandra Renaissance**, S

Sandra HT, op, Kordes; flowers ivory with coral-pink edges spreading down the petals, dbl., high-centered, borne mostly singly; recurrent; stems long, strong; vigorous, upright growth; int. in 2002

Sandra Kim – See **Flamingo Meidiland**, S

Sandra Kordana Min, op, Kordes

Sandra May Williamson HT, mp, Williamson; flowers single; int. in 1988

Sandra Renaissance S, m, Poulsen; bud pointed ovoid; flowers lavender and purple, 4-6 in., 30 petals, deep cup, borne singly and in small clusters, moderate floral fragrance; recurrent; foliage dark, glossy; prickles some, deeply concave; upright (3-5 ft.), bushy growth; PP15730; [seedling × Evening Star]; int. by Poulsen Roser, 2002

Sandrina S, Embriaco, B.; int. in 1996

Sandrina HT, yb, Kordes; int. in 1997

Sandrine F, lp, Eve, A.; flowers pale pink, 4 in., dbl., high-centered; recurrent; growth to 3-4 ft.; int. by Les Roses Anciennes de Andre Eve, 1975

Sandringham F, my, 1955, Kordes; flowers 2½ in., 30 petals, borne in large clusters; foliage light green, glossy; vigorous, tall growth; int. by Morse

Sandringham Centenary HT, op, 1980, Wisbech Plant Co.; bud pointed; flowers deep salmon-pink, 22 petals, borne singly; foliage dark, glossy; vigorous, upright growth; [Queen Elizabeth × Baccará]

Sandringham Century – See **Sandringham Centenary**, HT

Sands of Time Min, r, 1990, Williams, Ernest D.; bud short. pointed; flowers soft russet, 1½ in., 32 petals, high-centered, borne usually singly, moderate fragrance; recurrent; foliage small, medium green, semi-glossy; prickles few, slender, long, almost straight, tan; stems slender, wiry; upright, bushy growth; hips few ; PP7607; [Tom Brown × Twilight Trail]; int. by Mini-Roses, 1989

Sandton City – See **Coral Meidiland**, S

Sandton Smile – See **Anna Livia**, F

Sandy HT, op, Wisbech Plant Co.; flowers coppery-pink, large, dbl.; int. in 1981

Sandy F, ly, Spek; flowers pale yellow to apricot, 9

cm., 30-35 petals, high-centered, borne mostly singly; recurrent; prickles moderate; stems medium length; florist rose; int. by Jan Spek Rozen, 2002

Sandy Lundberg Min, w, 2000, Giles, Diann; flowers medium, full, high-centered, borne singly and in small clusters, no fragrance; foliage medium size, medium green, matte; few prickles; upright, medium (2½ ft.) growth; [Party Girl × seedling]; int. by Giles Rose Nursery

Sang – See **Hector**, HGal

Sang de Boeuf – See **Sanguineo-Purpurea Simplex**, HGal

Sang de Venus P, mr, 1823, Bizard

Sangerhausen HMsk, dp, 1938, Kordes; bud long, pointed; flowers large, semi-dbl., cupped, borne in large clusters, slight fragrance; recurrent; foliage large, leathery, wrinkled; vigorous (4-5 ft.), bushy growth; [Ingar Olsson × Eva]

Sangerhäusen Jubiläumsrose – See **Floral Fairy Tale**, F

Sanglant Ch, mp, 1873, Cherpin/Liabaud; flowers varying from light to dark pink

Sangria F, or, 1966, Meilland, Mrs. Marie-Louise; flowers semi-dbl., borne in large trusses; vigorous growth; [Fire King × (Happiness × Independence)]; int. by URS; Gold Medal, The Hague, 1966, Gold Medal, Geneva, 1966

Sangria F, dp, Meilland; flowers fuchsia pink tinted carmine, 60-80 petals, rosette, borne in small clusters; growth compact (80-90 cm.); int. in 1992

Sanguinaire HRg, or, 1933, Gillot; bud long, pointed; flowers brilliant oxblood-red with orange, stamens yellow, open, 4 in., 18 petals; repeats sparingly; foliage glossy; short stems; growth shrub or pillar (6½ ft.); [Bergers Erfolg × Capt. Ronald Clerk]

Sanguine d'Angleterre – See **Hector**, HGal

Sanguinea – See **De La Flèche**, M

Sanguinea Ch, dr, before 1818; flowers velvety, vivid purple crimson, petals concave with white base, very dbl., globular; branches, leaves, and flowered stalks very purple; weak, spreading growth

Sanguineo-Purpurea Atra – See **Ombre Superbe**, HGal

Sanguineo-Purpurea Simplex HGal, dr, before 1820; flowers oxblood red, medium, single; foliage oval, singly dentate, light green upper, dull green reverse; prickles moderate

Sanjith F, pb, K&S; flowers bright pink with broad white eye, single, shallow cup, borne in clusters; recurrent; compact growth; int. by KSG Son, 2001

Sanka HT, ob, Keisei Rose Nurseries, Inc.; flowers dbl., high-centered; int. by Keisei Rose Nurseries, 1986

Sankt Anton Pol, mr, 1971, Delforge; bud long, pointed; flowers brilliant red, open, small, single; profuse, continuous bloom; foliage leathery; vigorous, upright growth; [Alain × seedling]

Sanktflorian F, mr, Meilland; flowers medium to large, dbl.; int. in 1971

Sanlam-Roos – See **Jacqueline Nebout**, F

Sanmez F, rb, 1979, Sande; flowers 27-32 petals; int. by Pekmez

Sanremo HT, mr, 1962, Mansuino, Q.; bud ovoid, pointed; flowers cardinal-red, 5½-6 in., 20-30 petals, high-centered, moderate fragrance; foliage glossy; strong stems; vigorous, upright, bushy growth; PP2134; [(Pink Delight × Rome Glory) × Baccará]; int. by Carlton Rose Nurseries

Sans Pareille Pourpre HGal, dr, before 1811; bud oval; flowers velvety crimson-violet, full, moderate fragrance; foliage long, pointed, regularly dentate; prickles stright, red, pointed, unequal

Sans Pareille Rose HGal, dp, before 1811; bud oval; flowers delicate rose pink, lighter at edges, large, very dbl., moderate fragrance; foliage long, pointed, regularly dentate; prickles straight, red, pointed, few

Sans Sépales M, lp, 1839; flowers silvery flesh-pink, medium, dbl.

Sans souci – See **Moulin Rouge**, F

Sans Souci Pol, or, Schmid, P.; flowers small, dbl.; int. in 1960

Sans Souci Min, dp, 1986, Laver, Keith G.; flowers deep fuchsia pink, fading slightly, medium, 40 petals, high-centered, borne usually singly, slight fragrance; foliage medium size, light green, matte; prickles numerous, very fine, light brown; bushy, medium growth; hips oblong, narrow, red; [Rise 'n' Shine × Ontario Celebration]; int. by Springwood Roses, 1986

Sans Souci F, w, Barni, V.; flowers creamy blush white with apricot tones in center, large, dbl., borne in large clusters, moderate fragrance; vigorous (3 ft.) growth; int. by Rose Barni, 1996; Gold Medal, Baden-Baden, 1996, Best Italian Rose and Silver Medal, Monza, 1995

Santa Anita HT, mp, 1932, Howard, F.H.; bud long, pointed; flowers warm, clear pink, 3½-4 in., 22 petals, high-centered, moderate fragrance; foliage light; vigorous, bushy growth; [(Mrs J.D. Eisele × seedling) × E.G. Hill]; int. by H&S

Santa Anita, Climbing Cl HT, mp, 1946, Howard, F.H.; [sport of Santa Anita]; int. by H&S

Santa Barbara S, mp, Olesen, P & M; bud long, pointed ovoid; flowers medium pink, 3 in., 17-22 petals, flat, borne in large clusters, moderate fragrance; recurrent; foliage dark, glossy; prickles moderate, medium, yellow-green, linear to deeply concave; bushy (3-4 ft.) growth; PP14422; [seedling × La Sevillana]; int. as Rosy Border, Poulsen Roser, 2000

Santa Catalina Cl F, lp, 1970, McGredy, Sam IV; bud dark pink; flowers pale pink, reverse darker, 3½ in., 18 petals, borne in small clusters; foliage dark green, glossy; vigorous, tall (15 ft.) growth; [Paddy McGredy × Gruss an Heidelberg]; originally registered as LCl; int. by McGredy

Santa Claus Min, dr, 1991, Olesen, Pernille & Mogens N.; bud long, well-formed; sepals sepal insides tinted red; flowers velvety dark red, medium, dbl., high-centered, borne mostly singly, slight fragrance; foliage medium size, dark green, glossy; few prickles; medium (50-60 cm.), upright, bushy growth; PP9063; [Floribunda seedling × Miniature seedling]; int. by Weeks Roses, 1995

Santa Claus HT, rb, Ghosh, Mr. & Mrs. S.; flowers carmine red with white reverse, large, full, high-centered; free-flowering; int. in 1998

Santa Fe HT, op, 1967, McGredy, Sam IV; flowers deep salmon-pink, reverse lighter, large, dbl.; [Mischief × Tropicana]; int. as Santa Fé, McGredy

Santa Fe HT, my, 1993, Zary, Dr. Keith W.; bud long, pointed ovoid; flowers rich, medium yellow, 5-5½ in., 35-40 petals, high-centered, borne singly, moderate musk fragrance; good repeat; foliage large, dark green, matte; prickles few, medium to short, hooked downward; stems long, strong, straight; vigorous, upright (6-7 ft.) growth; PP9329; [Emblem × seedling]; greenhouse rose; int. by Bear Creek Gardens, 1993

Santa Maria F, mr, 1969, McGredy, Sam IV; flowers scarlet, borne in trusses; foliage small; [Evelyn Fison × (Ma Perkins × Moulin Rouge)]; int. by McGredy

Santa Rita HT, op, 1961, Lens; flowers salmon-pink, well-formed, large; vigorous growth; [Independence × Papillon Rose]

Santa Rosa Ch, mp, 1899, Burbank; flowers bright rose-pink shading lighter, large, dbl., moderate fragrance; recurrent; moderate growth; [Hermosa × Bon Silene (or a seedling thereof)]; int. as Burbank, Burpee

Santa Rosa F, op, 1959, Silva; bud ovoid; flowers salmon-pink tipped brick, small, dbl., globular, intense fragrance; foliage glossy, soft, bronze; vigorous, bushy growth; [Golden Salmon × Pinocchio]; int. in 1954

Santa Rosa S, mr, Poulsen; flowers medium red, 5-8 cm., slight wild rose fragrance; foliage dark; growth broad, bushy, 100-150 cm.; PP15230; int. as Special Border, Poulsen Roser, 2002

Santa Tereza d'Avila HT, op, 1959, Moreira da Silva; flowers salmon-pink and orange, reverse gold, well-formed; foliage glossy; vigorous growth; [Monte Carlo × Michele Meilland]; Gold Medal, Madrid, 1959

Santana LCl, mr, 1985, Tantau, Math.; flowers vermilion-red, 4 in., 20 petals, borne in small clusters, no fragrance; foliage large, medium green, glossy; upright growth

Santiago F, mr, Adam

Saohime HT, lp, 1999, Hayashi, Shunzo; flowers clean, light pink, 38 petals, high-centered; foliage medium green, half-leathery; growth to 3½ ft.; [Gavotte × Bridal Robe]; int. in 1990; Bronze Medal, Japan Rose Concours, 1992

Saonara HT, mr, 1962, Borgatti, G.; flowers geranium-red, dbl.; foliage dark; strong stems; vigorous growth; [Baccará × Peace]; int. by Sgaravatti

Saphir – See **Song of Paris**, HT

Saphir HT, m, Tantau; flowers lavender-pink, 4 in., 30 petals, moderate spicy fragrance; recurrent; int. in 1989

Sapho HGal, pb, 1818, Vibert; flowers purple center, edges a mixture of deep pink and delicate pink, medium, very dbl., flat; Agathe group

Sapho P, w, 1847, Vibert; flowers white, shaded flesh pink, small, full, borne in large clusters

Sapho HT, ob, 1933, Gaujard; flowers salmon, tinted coppery, very large, dbl.; foliage leathery, glossy, dark; very vigorous growth

Sappho T, pb, 1889, Paul & Son; flowers fawn shaded pink, center yellow, large, full, moderate like Gloire de Dijon fragrance; vigorous growth

Sappho A, w; may not really exist

Sara – See **Pompon Varin**, C

Sara HT, mp, 1997, J&P

Sara F, dr; int. by Jan Spek Rozen, 2000

Sara HT, pb, 2005, Alberici, Marc; flowers pink blend, reverse light pink, 10-12 cm., very full, borne in large clusters, intense fragrance; foliage large, light green, glossy, blackspot-resistant; prickles normal, straight; growth upright, bushy, tall (more than 1 m.); garden decoration; [Allgold (my) × Yves Piaget (dp)]; int. in 2006

Sara May Price LCl, mp, 2005, Cunningham, Sam; flowers medium pink, reverse light pink, 4+ in., very full, borne mostly solitary, intense fragrance; foliage large, dark green, semi-glossy; prickles few, ¼ in., triangular, brown; growth upright, open, tall (11 ft.); lattice, fence; [Maman Cochet, Cl. × New Dawn (?)]; int. in 1988

Sarabande F, or, 1958, Meilland, F.; flowers light orange-red, stamens yellow, 2½ in., 13 petals, cupped to flat, borne in large trusses, slight fragrance; recurrent; foliage semi-glossy; low, bushy growth; PP1761; [Cocorico × Moulin Rouge]; int. by URS, 1957; Gold Medal, Rome, 1957, Gold Medal, Portland, 1958, Gold Medal, Geneva, 1957, Gold Medal, Bagatelle, 1957

Sarabande, Climbing Cl F, or, 1970, Meilland; [sport of Sarabande]; int. by URS; Gold Medal, Japan, 1968

Saragat HT, rb, 1968, Malandrone; flowers deep strawberry to cream, large, dbl., globular; foliage leathery;

very vigorous growth; [seedling × seedling]

Sarah C, mp, 1822, Calvert; flowers medium pink, center brighter

Sarah – See **Jardins de Bagatelle**, HT

Sarah S, op, Clements, John; flowers soft pink, peach and coral., 3½ in., 30 petals, intense fruity fragrance; foliage rich green; vigorous, bushy (3-4 ft.) growth; PPAF; int. by Heirloom, 2001

Sarah Min, ab, Hannemann, F.; [Poker Chip × Holy Toledo]; int. by The Rose Paradise

Sarah Ann Morgan Min, w, 2003, Hover, Flora C.; flowers full, borne in small clusters, slight fragrance; foliage medium size, medium green, semi-glossy; prickles in., straight, moderate; growth bushy, tall (4 ft.); garden decorative, exhibition; [sport of Giggles]; int. in 2002

Sarah Anne MinFl, mp, 2002, Read, Allan; flowers medium, colour varying from white with pink splashes to solid pink, 2½ in., full, borne in large clusters, no fragrance; foliage medium size, medium green, semi-glossy; prickles 3/16 in. pointed, few; growth compact, medium (3 ft.); garden decorative, exhibition; [Bluesette × unknown]; int. by Villa Rosa, 2003

Sarah Arnot HT, mp, 1958, Arnot, David; flowers warm rose-pink, 4½ in., 25 petals, moderate fragrance; foliage leathery; vigorous, upright growth; [Ena Harkness × Peace]; int. by D. W. Croll Ltd., 1957; Gold Medal, NRS, 1958

Sarah Bacherach F, mp, 1965, Buisman, G. A. H.; flowers pink, medium, dbl.; foliage dark; [Harmonie × Buisman's Triumph]

Sarah Bernhardt Cl HT, dr, 1906, Dubreuil; flowers scarlet-crimson, very large, semi-dbl.

Sarah Coventry F, dr, 1959, Boerner; bud ovoid; flowers cardinal-red, open, medium, 40-45 petals, cupped, borne in irregular clusters, moderate fragrance; foliage bright green; vigorous, compact, bushy growth; PP1611; [Red Pinocchio × Garnette]; int. by Stuart, 1956

Sarah Darley HT, dy, 1938, Wheatcroft Bros.; flowers clear deep golden yellow, well-shaped; foliage dark; vigorous growth

Sarah, Duchess of York – See **Duchess of York**, F

Sarah Elizabeth F, ab, 1998, Chaffin, Lauren M.; flowers apricot blend, 2½-3 in., 41 petals, old-fashioned, rosette, borne in small clusters, slight fragrance; foliage medium size, dark green, glossy; prickles few, medium, straight; upright, medium growth; [City of Auckland × seedling]; int. by Pixie Treasure Roses, 1998

Sarah Eluned F, pb, 2004, Paul Chessum Roses; flowers small, semi-dbl., borne in small clusters, slight fragrance; foliage medium size, medium green, matte; growth compact, short (50 cm.); bedding, borders, containers; [seedling × seedling]; int. by Love4Plants Ltd, 2004

Sarah Hill F, mp, 1956, Joseph H. Hill, Co.; bud short, pointed; flowers phlox-pink, open, 2½-3 in., 25-30 petals, slight spicy fragrance; foliage dark, leathery; vigorous, upright, bushy growth; PP1397; [Garnette × Pink Bountiful]

Sarah Jane HT, pb, 1970, Heath, W.L.; flowers rose-pink, edged deeper, reverse white, 4½-5 in., 35 petals; foliage glossy; very vigorous, tall growth; [sport of Rose Gaujard]

Sarah Jayne Min, ob, 2003, Eagle, B & D; flowers orange with yellow base, reverse orange, 3-3½ cm., dbl., borne mostly solitary, slight fragrance; foliage medium size, dark green, matte; prickles small, straight; growth upright, tall (50-60 cm.); garden, cutting; [Patio Flame × Golden Angel]; int. by Southern Cross Nurseries, 1996

Sarah Jo F, rb, 1993, Mehring, Bernhard F.; flowers red with white eye, salmon reverse, medium, dbl., borne in small clusters; foliage large, dark green, glossy; some prickles; medium (60 cm.), upright, bushy growth; [Sheri Ann × Dortmund]; int. by Mehring, 1994

Sarah Juanita S, my, 2003, Ponton, Ray; flowers 3-4 in., dbl., borne in small clusters, moderate fragrance; recurrent; foliage medium size, dark green, glossy, disease-resistant; prickles medium, curved, few; growth compact, short (1-2 ft.); bedding, hedge, container; decorative hips; [Lillian Austin × Baby Love]; int. by Peaceful Habitations, 2003

Sarah Lynn HT, mp, 1991, Ohlson, John; flowers medium, full, borne mostly singly, slight fragrance; foliage large, dark green, semi-glossy; strong stems; vigorous, medium, compact growth; [seedling × Prima Ballerina]; Bronze Medal, ARC TG, 1991

Sarah Maud HT, dy, 1934, Mallerin, C.; bud long; flowers golden yellow, large; foliage bright, dark; very vigorous growth

Sarah Nesbitt T, yb, 1910, Dorrance; flowers light carnation-yellow, center darker; [sport of Mme Cusin]

Sarah Penrose HT, yb, 2005, Webster, Robert; flowers yellow, outer petals lemon, 5 in., very full, borne mostly solitary, slight fragrance; foliage medium size, light green, matte; prickles moderate, 8 mm., slightly hooked; growth compact, medium (30 in.); bedding; [Golden Wedding × Golden Giant]

Sarah Philp Min, ab

Sarah Robinson Min, ab, 1982; flowers soft apricot, small, 20 petals, intense fragrance; foliage small, dark, glossy; compact, bushy growth; [Rumba × Darling Flame]; int. by Thomas Robinson, Ltd.

Sarah Van Fleet HRg, mp, 1926, Van Fleet; flowers wild-rose-pink, large, semi-dbl., cupped, intense fragrance; recurrent bloom; foliage leathery, rugose; compact (6-8 ft.) growth; [*R. rugosa* × My Maryland]; int. by American Rose Society

Sarah Wright HT, dp, 1927, Morse; bud long, pointed; flowers rose-pink, dbl.; [Ophelia × Emma Wright]

Sarah's Rose HT, op; int. by Rearsby Roses, 2003

Sarajean Min, pb, 1980, Williams, Ernest D.; bud pointed; flowers peach-pink, 1 in., 50 petals, globular, moderate fragrance; foliage small, bronze-green, glossy; upright, bushy growth; PP4755; [seedling × Over the Rainbow]; int. by Mini-Roses, 1979

Saramouche Min, rb, Delbard; flowers striped; int. by Georges Delbard SA, 2002

Sarasota Spice N, w, 2006, Starnes, John A., Jr.; flowers dbl., borne in large clusters, intense cinnamon-clove fragrance; foliage medium size, medium green, matte; prickles small, cats claw, tan, moderate; growth upright, climbing, medium (6 ft.); pillar/climber; [The Gift × Blush Noisette]; at times produces massive panicles of dozens of blooms; int. in 2005

Saratoga F, w, 1963, Boerner; bud ovoid; flowers 33 petals, gardenia-like, borne in irregular clusters, intense fragrance; foliage glossy, leathery; vigorous, upright, bushy growth; PP2299; [White Bouquet × Princess White]; int. by J&P

Sardane F, rb, 1962, Laperrière; bud long; flowers coral-red tinted silvery, 3 in., 35-40 petals; foliage bright green; very bushy, compact growth; int. by EFR

Saremo S, mp, Noack; flowers soft, medium pink, 3-4 in., full, borne in clusters, slight fragrance; recurrent; spreading (4 × 4 ft.) growth; hips decorative; int. by Noack Rosen, 2001

Sargent HWich, pb, 1912, Dawson; flowers apple-blossom-rose to pale pink, base amber-yellow, 3 in., semi-dbl., borne in large clusters, moderate fragrance; growth to 10-12 ft.; [(*R. wichurana* × Turner's Crimson Rambler) × Baronne Adolphe de Rothschild]; int. by Eastern Nursery

Sari Hou S, lp, 2003, Law, Stephen; flowers 2-3 in., dbl., borne in small clusters, slight fragrance; foliage small, medium green, matte; prickles small; growth to 2-3 ft.; decorative; [Morden Centennial × unknown (open pollinated)]

Sarie HT, mp, 1976, Herholdt, J.A.; flowers 4½-5 in., 35 petals; foliage glossy, bright green; vigorous growth; [Pink Favorite × Nightingale]; int. by Roselandia, 1977

Sarie Marais HT, pb, Kordes

Sarie Mareis F, mr, 1950, Leenders, M.; flowers glowing scarlet; [Irene × Donald Prior]

Saris Sepals M, mp, 1839

Saroda – See **Sharada**, Gr

Saroja F, pb, Pal, Dr. B.P.; int. in 1984

Sarong – See **Lincoln Cathedral**, HT

Saroor F, or, 1971, Singh; bud ovoid; flowers orange-scarlet, open, large, dbl.; foliage large, leathery; upright growth; [Gertrud Westphal × Open pollination]; int. by Gopalsinamiengar, 1969

Sarvesh HT, or, K&S; bud pointed, long; flowers intense, deep orange-red, large, dbl., high-centered; free-flowering; sturdy growth; int. by KSG Son, 2004

Sasa F, rb, Delbard; int. in 1995

Saskabec – See **Tant Mieux**, S

Saskia F, mp, 1961, Buisman, G. A. H.; flowers single, borne in large clusters; foliage dark; bushy growth; [Pinocchio × Gartenstolz]

Sassy F, dr, 1986, Jelly, Robert G.; flowers sweetheart, small, 20 petals, high-centered, borne usually singly; foliage small, medium green, matte; prickles only on peduncle; upright growth; hips small, globular, greyed-red; PP4559; [Little Leaguer × Mary DeVor]; int. by E.G. Hill Co., 1985

Sassy Cindy MinFl, rb, 2006, Bridges, Dennis; flowers bright red, reverse light yellow to white, 2 in., full, high-centered, borne mostly solitary, slight fragrance; recurrent; foliage medium size, dark green, semi-glossy; prickles moderate, ¼ in., sharp, pointed slightly downward, tan; upright, tall (28-36 in.) growth; exhibition, containers, garden decorative; [Purple Dawn × Trickster]; int. by Bridges Roses, 2005

Sassy Girl Min, op, 2000, Moe, Mitchie; flowers orange-pink, 2½ in., full, high-centered, borne mostly singly, slight fragrance; foliage medium size, medium green, semi-glossy, disease-resistant; few prickles; growth upright, vigorous, medium (15-18 in.); [Violet Mist × unknown]; int. by Mitchie's Roses and More

Sassy Lassy Min, yb, 1976, Williams, Ernest D.; bud pointed; flowers yellow and pink blend, 1 in., 28 petals, cupped to high-centered, borne singly or several together, slight fragrance; foliage small, bronze, glossy, leathery; upright, spreading growth; PP4036; [seedling × Over the Rainbow]; int. by Mini-Roses, 1975

Satan HT, dr, 1939, Pahissa; flowers very dark red, reverse lighter, large, semi-dbl. to dbl., high-centered, moderate fragrance; foliage leathery; bushy growth; [(Mme Edouard Herriot × Angèle Pernet) × Mari Dot]; int. by J&P

Satanas – See **Satan**, HT

Satchmo F, or, 1970, McGredy, Sam IV; flowers bright scarlet, 3 in., 25 petals, hybrid tea, borne in large clusters, slight fragrance; foliage reddish early, then dark green; bushy, compact growth; [Evelyn Fison × Diamant]; int. by McGredy; Gold Medal, The Hague, 1970

Satellite HT, dr, 1959, Priestly; bud pointed; flowers deep crimson, 4½ in., 30 petals, high-centered, intense fragrance; foliage dark, glossy; vigorous, upright, compact growth; [Editor McFarland × William Harvey]; int. in 1958

Satellite HT, or, 1985, Delbard, Georges; flowers vermilion, medium, 28 petals, high-centered, borne mostly singly, moderate fragrance; good repeat; foliage medium size, medium green, semi-glossy; moderate, bushy growth; [((Tropicana × Samourai) × (Tropicana × (Rome Glory × Impeccable))) × Granada]; int. in 1982

Satin HT, dp; flowers deep satiny pink, dbl., high-centered, borne mostly singly; recurrent; growth to 3½ ft.; int. by Hortico Inc., 1996

Satin HT, ab, Tantau; thornless; greenhouse rose; int. by Sovereign Nursery Pty Limited, 2002

Satin Beauty HT, op, Kordes; flowers clear salmon, softening to cream salmon in the sun, dbl., high-centered, borne mostly singly; recurrent; few prickles; stems long, strong, upright; medium growth; int. by Ludwig's Roses, 2002

Satin Doll F, ly, 1986, Warriner, William A.; flowers cream to pale apricot; [sport of Pacifica]; int. by J&P

Satin Ribbon HT, yb, Delbard; bud creamy yellow; flowers deep yellow with light apricot tones; moderate growth; int. in 2001

Satin Tears F, mp, Williams, J.B.; flowers pink with yellow stamens, semi-dbl.; recurrent; int. by Hortico, 2004

Satin Touch – See **First Gold**, HT

Satina S, mp, Tantau; flowers medium, semi-dbl., rosette, borne in large clusters, slight fragrance; free-flowering; foliage deep green, glossy; compact, bushy growth; int. by Rosen Tantau, 1992

Satinette Pol, w, 1971, Delforge; bud ovoid; flowers large, dbl., cupped; foliage large, light, leathery; vigorous, upright growth; [Maria Delforge × Irene of Denmark]

Satinglo F, mp, 1954, Boerner; bud globular; flowers glowing coral, 2½ in., 45-50 petals, cupped, borne in clusters, moderate fragrance; foliage leathery, glossy; vigorous growth; PP1285; [(Pinocchio × unknown) × Vogue]

Satisfaction HT, dp, 1960, Verbeek; flowers carmine-pink, large, dbl., intense fragrance; [Parfum × seedling]; int. in 1958

Satmir HT, dr, 1956, Dot, Pedro; flowers carmine-red, dbl.; long, strong stems; very vigorous growth; [Satan × Mirandy]

Saturday HT, pb, McGredy, Sam IV; flowers rose pink with yellow tones in center, large, dbl., borne singly and several together, slight fragrance; recurrent; foliage dark green; stems strong; strong, upright (100 cm.) growth; int. in 1990

Saturday Star HT, ab, Kordes; int. in 1994

Saturn HT, ob, J&P; PP9326; int. in 1997

Saturnia HT, rb, 1936, Aicardi, D.; bud long, pointed; flowers bright scarlet with gold, large, 20 petals, cupped, moderate fruity fragrance; foliage dark, glossy; vigorous growth; [Julien Potin × Sensation]; int. by J&P; Gold Medal, Portland, 1938, Gold Medal, Rome, 1933

Satvika HT, rb, K&S; flowers hand-painted scarlet-crimson with prominent white base, silvery white reverse, dbl.; free-flowering; int. by KSG Son, 2001

Saucy Sue F, mp, 1975, Lowe; flowers large, 20-25 petals, moderate fragrance; free growth; [Pink Parfait × Europeana]; int. in 1973

Saudade d'Anibal de Morais HT, dr, 1935, Moreira da Silva; bud velvety crimson; flowers salmony crimson-red, dbl.; vigorous growth; [Sir David Davis × Pres. Jac. Smits]

Saul HT, dp, 1970, Gandy, Douglas L.; flowers light rose-madder, 4 in., 28 petals; foliage large, dark; upright growth; [Tropicana × Sterling Silver]

Saumonia HT, op; int. in 1998

Sausalito S, mr, Olesen; bud urceolate; flowers medium red, reverse lighter, 5 cm., 30-35 petals, open cup, flowers borne in large panicles, slight floral fragrance; recurrent; foliage dark green, glossy; prickles numerous, 7 mm., concave, brown; broad, bushy (60-100 cm.) growth; PP16583; [Charming Cover × seedling]

Savanin Min, rb, 1987, Saville, F. Harmon; flowers medium red with yellow center, small, dbl.; foliage small, medium green, semi-glossy; bushy growth; [Rise 'n' Shine × Zinger]; int. by SNC Meilland & Cie, 1986

Savannah HT, ab, 1980, Weeks, O.L.; bud ovoid, pointed; flowers soft apricot, 4-4½ in., 32 petals, cupped, borne singly or 2-3 per cluster, slight spicy fragrance; recurrent; foliage moderately leathery; prickles long, hooked down; vigorous, upright growth; PP4735; [seedling × Arizona]

Savannah Miss Min, ab, 1990, Chaffin, Lauren M.; bud pointed; flowers dark apricot, edges lighter, medium apricot reverse, fading to soft pink, medium, 40-50 petals, high-centered, borne singly, moderate fragrance; foliage medium size, medium green, semi-glossy; prickles needle-shaped, light tan; bushy, tall growth; hips globular, medium green; [Pounder Star × Ann Moore]; int. by Pixie Treasures Min. Roses

Savanne HT, dy, Noack, Werner; int. in 1985

Savaria Pol, Mark; int. in 1972

Save the Children F, mr, 1986, Harkness; flowers bright red, patio, dbl., cupped, borne in clusters; foliage dark, semi-glossy; prickles narrow, straight; low, bushy, compact growth; [Amy Brown × Red Sprite]

Saverne HT, rb, 1937, Heizmann, E.; flowers nasturtium tinted brownish red, reverse tinted yellow, large, dbl.; foliage bright, bronze; int. by A. Meilland

Savkar HT, mr, Patil, B.K.; int. in 1988

Savoia HT, m, 1937, Aicardi, D.; bud pointed, rosy lilac; foliage glossy; vigorous growth; [Julien Potin × Sensation]; int. by Giacomasso

Savoy Hotel HT, lp, 1987, R. Harkness & Co., Ltd.; flowers light phlox pink, reverse shaded deeper, large, 40 petals, high-centered, borne usually singly, slight fragrance; foliage medium size, dark green, semi-glossy; prickles small, reddish-green, fairly straight, narrow; bushy, medium growth; hips rounded, average, green; [Silver Jubilee × Amber Queen]; int. in 1989; Gold Medal, Dublin, 1988

Savrojet Min, dp, 1987, Saville, F. Harmon; flowers deep pink, moderately small, dbl., no fragrance; foliage small, medium green, semi-glossy; bushy growth; [(Tamango × Yellow Jewel) × Watercolor]; int. by SNC Meilland & Cie, 1985

Saxo – See **Paul Shirville**, HT

Saya Min, ob

Sayokyoku Min, lp, 1999, Hirabayashi, Hiroshi; flowers soft pink, 2-2½ in., 45-50 petals, hybrid tea, slight fragrance; foliage dark green, leathery; growth to 1½-2 ft.; [Sonia × Petite Folie]; int. by Keisei Rose Nurseries, 1996; Gold Medal, Japan Rose Concours, 1994

Sayonara HT, yb, 1959, Grillo; bud long, pointed; flowers yellow blend tinted pink, 5 in., 50 petals; foliage leathery; vigorous, upright growth; [sport of Sunnymount]

Sazanami Min, lp, 1986, Suzuki, Seizo; flowers soft pink, small, 60 petals, flat, borne 2-5 per cluster, moderate fragrance; foliage dark green, semi-glossy; prickles slanted downward; bushy growth; [(Yorokobi × unknown) × Yellow Doll]; int. by Keisei Rose Nursery, 1984; Gold Medal, Japan, 1980

Sázava S, mr, Pajer, J.; flowers medium, semi-dbl.; int. in 1964

Scabrata S, m; flowers rich pinkish purple, large, single; foliage downy; [*R. corymbifera* × *R. gallica*]

Scabriusculus HBc, w, before 1822, Noisette; flowers single; foliage small; prickles needle-like, straight, intermixed with numerous bristles; stems thin

Scabrosa HRg, m, 1950; flowers mauve-pink, stamens light sulfur, 5 in., 5 petals, borne in clusters of 5 or more, moderate carnation fragrance; recurrent bloom; foliage light, glossy, soft; very bushy (5 ft.) growth; hips large, bright red; int. by Harkness

Scala – See **Clubrose Scala**, F

Scala HT, dp, Gaujard

Scaldia HT, Delforge; int. in 1987

Scamp Min, mr, 1985, Saville, F. Harmon; flowers micro-mini, small, 35 petals, high-centered, slight fragrance; foliage small, medium green, semi-glossy; compact, bushy growth; [Baby Katie × (Yellow Jewel × Tamango)]; int. by Nor'East Min. Roses, 1984

Scandale HT, pb, 1959, Gaujard; bud pink; flowers crimson shaded coppery, 4 in., 25 petals, moderate fragrance; foliage glossy, dark; long stems; vigorous, upright growth; [Peace × Opera]

Scandens Ayr, w, before 1804, from Italy; flowers salmony cream white, darker edges, darker reverse, 5 cm., semi-dbl., borne in clusters of up to 15, strong musky fragrance; moderately vigorous growth; possibly *R. arvensis* × *R. gallica*

Scandia Pol, op, 1951, van de Water; flowers salmon-orange; [sport of Margo Koster]; int. by van Nes

Scandia HT, m, Cooper; flowers pale mauve blend, dbl., slight fragrance; [sport of Paradise]; int. in 1996

Scandica – See **Scania**, F

Scania F, dr, 1965, deRuiter; flowers deep red, well-formed, 3½ in., borne in clusters, slight fragrance; foliage matte; vigorous (80-100 cm.) growth; [Cocorico × seedling]

Scar P97 Misc OGR, lp, Scarman; int. in 1997

Scaramouche F, mr, 1969, Fankhauser; bud long, pointed; flowers coral-red, large, 30-35 petals, high-centered; foliage leathery; vigorous, compact, tall growth; [Ma Perkins × Duet]

Scarborough Fair S, lp, 2004; flowers soft pink, golden stamens, 5½ cm., semi-dbl. to dbl., globular to cupped, borne in small clusters, moderate old rose to musk fragrance; recurrent; foliage medium size, dark green, matte; prickles medium, concave, curved inward; growth bushy, narrow, branching, short (75 cm.); garden decorative; [seedling (medium yellow English type shrub) × seedling (light pink English type shrub)]; int. by David Austin Roses, Ltd., 2003

Scarlano HSet, mr, 1938, Horvath; flowers cerise-red, open, semi-dbl., borne in clusters; sometimes recurrent bloom; foliage leathery, dark; short, strong stems; bushy (2½ ft.) growth; [(*R. setigera* × Papoose) × Paul's Scarlet Climber]; int. by Wayside Gardens Co.

Scarlet – See **Scarlet Hit**, MinFl

Scarlet – See **Scarlet Parade**, Min

Scarlet Abundance – See **Remembrance**, F

Scarlet Adventurer HT, dr, 1958, Lowe; flowers scarlet, medium, dbl.; foliage dark; int. by Wm. Lowe & Son, 1957

Scarlet Beauty HT, dr, 1934, Vestal; flowers crimson-scarlet, very large, dbl.; vigorous growth; [Mme Butterfly × Premier Supreme]

Scarlet Bedder HT, ob, 1927, Henderson, W.H.; flowers rich orange-scarlet; dwarf growth; [Mme Edouard Herriot × Gen. MacArthur]

Scarlet Betty Uprichard HT, dr, 1930, Allen; bud long, pointed, shaded black; flowers intense scarlet, semi-dbl., cupped; foliage thick, light; vigorous growth; [Betty Uprichard × unknown]

Scarlet Button Pol, dr, 1932, Dreer; flowers brilliant scarlet; [sport of Locarno]

Scarlet Crampel Pol, dr; flowers scarlet; [sport of Paul Crampel]

Scarlet Else F, dr, Kordes; flowers scarlet, 3-4 in., 10-12 petals, borne in trusses; foliage leathery; very free growth; [Else Poulsen × Hybrid Tea seedling (red)]

Scarlet Emperor HT, mr, 1961, LeGrice; flowers scarlet-red, large, dbl., high-centered; vigorous, upright growth; [Karl Herbst × Fandango]; int. by Wayside Gardens Co.

Scarlet Fire – See **Scharlachglut**, HGal

Scarlet Flame HT, mr, 1934, Burbank; flowers brilliant red, petals recurved and fringed, large, dbl.; very vigorous growth; int. by Stark Bros.

Scarlet Garnette F, mr, 1971, Newberry; flowers scarlet, small, 45 petals, globular; foliage dark; vigorous growth; [sport of Garnette]

Scarlet Gem Min, or, 1961, Meilland, Alain A.; bud ovoid; flowers orange-scarlet, 1 in., 58 petals, cupped, borne singly and in irregular clusters, slight fragrance; recurrent; foliage dark, glossy, leathery; prickles several, brown; stems short; bushy, dwarf (12-15 in.) growth; PP2155; [(Moulin Rouge × Fashion) × (Perla de Montserrat × Perla de Alcanada)]; int. by C-P, 1961

Scarlet Glory HT, ob, 1925, Dickson, A.; bud long, pointed; flowers orange-scarlet, dbl., high-centered; foliage leathery, rich green

Scarlet Glow HT, dr, 1945, Sodano, A.; flowers brilliant velvety scarlet; [sport of Briarcliff]; int. by St. Leonards Farms

Scarlet Glow – See **Scharlachglut**, HGal

Scarlet Grevillea – See **Russelliana**, HMult

Scarlet Hit MinFl, dr, Olesen, L & M; bud pointed ovoid to globular; flowers open quickly, 2 in., 18-22 petals, flat, borne in sprays of 8-10, very slight fragrance; free-flowering; foliage dark green, semi-glossy; prickles numerous, slight downward curve; growth vigorous, compact (50 cm.), upright to bushy; PP12490; [H. C. Andersen × Red Minimo]; int. by Poulsen Roser, 1996

Scarlet Kardinal HT, or, Tapanchev; [sport of Kardinal]; int. by Erica Intl., 2001

Scarlet Knight Gr, mr, 1966, Meilland, Mrs. Marie-Louise; bud medium, ovoid with a conspicuous neck; flowers crimson-scarlet, 4-5 in., 25-30 petals, cupped, borne singly and in small clusters, slight tea fragrance; recurrent; foliage large, leathery; prickles several, brownish; vigorous, upright, bushy growth; hips medium, globular, smooth, green, shaded red; PP2692; [(Happiness × Independence) × Sutter's Gold]; int. as Samourai, URS, 1966; Gold Medal, Madrid, 1966

Scarlet Knight, Climbing Cl Gr, mr, 1974, Jack; [sport of Scarlet Knight]; int. by A. Ross & Son, 1972

Scarlet Lady Min, mr, 1991, Jolly, Nelson F.; bud ovoid; flowers medium red, aging light pink, large, 30 petals, cupped, borne singly, no fragrance; foliage medium size, dark green, semi-glossy; upright, medium growth; [Anita Charles × Chris Jolly]; int. by Rosehill Farm, 1991

Scarlet Leader Pol, ob, 1927, Wezelenburg; flowers brilliant orange-scarlet, large, dbl., borne in clusters

Scarlet Maria Leonida HBc, mr, before 1846, Rivers; flowers crimson red, large, full, cupped

Scarlet Mariner F, mr, 1972, Patterson; flowers bright scarlet-red, medium, dbl., high-centered; foliage leathery; vigorous, bushy growth; [seedling × Showboat]; int. by Patterson Roses

Scarlet Marvel F, mr, 1960, deRuiter; flowers orange-scarlet, 2½ in., 45-50 petals, flat, borne in clusters; foliage leathery; vigorous, compact growth; PP1771; [Alain × Floribunda seedling]; int. by C-P, 1959

Scarlet Meidiland S, mr, 1987, Meilland, Mrs. Marie-Louise; bud oval; flowers light cherry red, reverse dark carmine pink, 1½ in., 15-20 petals, borne in clusters of 10-15, no fragrance; recurrent; foliage medium size, dark green, glossy; spreading growth; PP6087; [MEItiraca × Clair Matin]; int. by SNC Meilland & Cie, 1985; Gold Medal, Frankfurt, 1989

Scarlet Meillandécor – See **Scarlet Meidiland**, S

Scarlet Meillandina – See **Scarlet Sunblaze**, Min

Scarlet Midinette Min, mr, Horner; flowers scarlet-red, small, dbl., high-centered; free-flowering; vigorous (5-7 ft.) growth; int. by Ludwig's Roses, 2003

Scarlet Mimi F, dr, Suzuki, Seizo; bud medium, conical; flowers bright red, 2½ in., 21 petals, cupped, borne singly and in clusters of up to 9, no fragrance; good repeat; foliage dark green, semi-glossy; prickles very few, small, greenish; vigorous, upright (3-4 ft.) growth; PP8484; [seedling × Sassy]; greenhouse rose; int. in 1992

Scarlet Moss – See **De La Flèche**, M

Scarlet Moss Min, mr, 1988, Moore, Ralph S.; bud long, pointed, mossy; very mossy sepals; flowers intense scarlet-red, 2 in., 12-15 petals, high-centered, then flat, borne singly and in loose sprays of 3-10, no fragrance; free-flowering; foliage medium size, medium green, glossy, leathery; prickles slender, various, green to brown; stems slender, wiry; upright, bushy, tall growth; hips round, elongated, orange; PP7128; [(Dortmund × Miniature seedling) × (Dortmund × Miniature striped seedling)]; int. by Sequoia Nursery

Scarlet Ovation Min, mr, deRuiter; int. in 2000

Scarlet Panarosa HRg, mr, Moore; flowers scarlet, large, semi-dbl., loose, borne in clusters; recurrent; foliage dark green, rugose; robust growth; int. by Ludwig's Roses, 2004

Scarlet Parade Min, dr, Poulsen; flowers dark red, medium, dbl., slight wild rose fragrance; foliage dark; growth bushy, 20-40 cm.; PP11543; int. by Poulsen Rosen, 2000

Scarlet Patio MinFl, mr, Kordes; flowers bright scarlet, semi-dbl. to dbl., cuppped, borne in clusters, slight fragrance; recurrent; foliage bright green; dainty (18-24 in.) growth; int. in 1993

Scarlet Pavement S, mr, Uhl, J.; bud pink; flowers light fuchsia red, semi-dbl., borne in clusters, moderate fragrance; recurrent; spreading (2½ × 3 ft.) growth; hips numerous, dark red; int. in 1991

Scarlet Pearl F, rb, 1993, Mander, George; flowers scarlet red with white eye and white reverse, medium, 5 petals, borne in large clusters, slight fragrance; foliage medium size, dark green, glossy; prickles numerous on basals, few on laterals; medium (90-100 cm.), bushy, spreading, very vigorous growth; [Pink Meidiland × seedling]; int. by Christie Nursery, Ltd., 1993

Scarlet Pimpernel – See **Scarlet Gem**, Min

Scarlet Provence C, mr, before 1867; flowers faint carmine

Scarlet Queen F, dr, 1939, Kordes; bud long, pointed; flowers pure scarlet, open, large, dbl., borne in clusters; foliage glossy, leathery, bronze; long stems; vigorous, bushy growth; [Dance of Joy × Crimson Glory]; int. by Morse

Scarlet Queen Elizabeth F, or, 1965, Dickson, Patrick; flowers flame-scarlet, medium, dbl., globular, borne in clusters, slight fragrance; foliage dark; vigorous, tall growth; [(Korona × seedling) × Queen Elizabeth]; int. by A. Dickson & Sons, 1962; Golden Rose, The Hague, 1973, Gold Medal, The Hague, 1973

Scarlet Ribbon Cl Min, dr, 1961, Moore, Ralph S.; bud ovoid; flowers red, sometimes almost maroon, 1¼ in., 50 petals, high-centered; vigorous (3 ft.) growth; [((Soeur Thérèse × Wilhelm) × (seedling × Red Ripples)) × Zee]; int. by Sequoia Nursery, 1961

Scarlet Ripple S, rb, Williams, J.B.; flowers ruffled petals of pink, dark red and white stripes, yellow stamens, cupped, borne in clusters; recurrent; foliage medium green; bushy growth; int. by Hortico, 2004

Scarlet Rosamini Min, mr, deRuiter; flowers bright scarlet red, cupped; free-flowering; foliage glossy; vigorous, neat growth; int. in 1989

Scarlet Royal HT, mr, 1963, Park; flowers scarlet, base yellow, well-formed; vigorous growth; [Karl Herbst × Independence]; int. by Tantau Roses

Scarlet Ruffles Min, or, 1990, Gruenbauer, Richard; bud pointed; flowers orange-red with yellow eye, aging to light red, loose, large, 8 petals, intense spicy fragrance; foliage medium size, dark green, glossy; prickles straight, slightly hooked downwards, tan; spreading, medium growth; hips oblong, gold and orange; [Poker Chip × Zinger]; int. by Richard Gruenbauer, 1984

Scarlet Sensation LCl, dr, 1954, Brownell; bud high pointed, crimson; flowers rose-madder, 3½-4½ in., 35 petals, borne in clusters, moderate fragrance; free bloom; growth like a hybrid tea, followed by 4-5 foot canes; PP1261; [seedling × Queen o' the Lakes]

Scarlet Showers LCl, mr; flowers bright red; recurrent; [Golden Showers × Chrysler Imperial]; int. by Gandy's Roses

Scarlet Spreader S, dr, 1995, Williams, J. Benjamin; flowers dark scarlet red, 1-1½ in., 6-14 petals, borne in small clusters; foliage small, dark green, glossy; some prickles; dwarf, spreading, low (10-12 in.) growth; [seedling × Red Fountain]; int. by J. Benjamin Williams & Associates, 1996

Scarlet Star LCl, mr, 1999, Williams, J. Benjamin; bud pointed, small to medium; flowers smoky red, 2½-3 in., 20 -25 petals, informal, borne in large clusters, slight spicy fragrance; foliage large, medium green, semi-glossy; prickles numerous, curved and hooked; climbing, upright, bushy, tall (12-15 ft.) growth; PP11834; [Red Fountain × Mister Lincoln]; int. by Conard-Pyle, 1999

Scarlet Sunblaze Min, dr, 1982, Meilland, Mrs. Marie-Louise; bud medium, conical; flowers currant red, 5½ cm., 20-30 petals, cupped, borne in clusters of 3-21, no fragrance; free-flowering; foliage medium size, dark green, matte; prickles average, small, slender, curved downward; bushy (20 in.) growth; PP4681; [Tamango × (Baby Bettina × Duchess of Windsor)]; int. by C-P, 1980

Scarlet Sunset F, or, 1970, deRuiter; flowers small, 12 petals, borne on trusses; foliage dark, leathery; moderate bushy growth; [Orange Sensation × seedling]; int. by Geo. deRuiter

Scarlet Sweet Brier – See **La Belle Distinguée**, HEg

Scarlet Swimmer Min, rb; flowers red with yellow center; [sport of Tracey Wickham]; int. by Australian Roses, 2001

Scarlet Triumph F, rb, 1951, Poulter; bud ovoid; flowers deep scarlet, base yellow, small, semi-dbl., cupped, borne in clusters; foliage glossy, light green; vigorous, bushy growth; [sport of Orange Triumph]

Scarlet Velvet S, mr, Clements, John; flowers velvety scarlet, 4 in., very full, cupped, quartered, borne singly and in clusters, slight to moderate fruity tea fragrance; recurrent; compact (3 ft.) growth; int. by Heirloom Roses, 2006

Scarlet Waves F, mr, 1961, Bennett, H.; flowers bright scarlet, ruffled petals; tall growth; [(Florence Mary Morse × Border Queen) × Mrs Inge Poulsen]; int. by Pedigree Nursery

Scarlet Wonder F, or, 1959, deRuiter; flowers bright orange-scarlet, 3 in., semi-dbl., flat, borne in clusters; foliage dark, glossy; vigorous growth; [Signal Red × Fashion]; int. by Blaby Rose Gardens, 1958

Scarletina Min, or, 1985, Hardgrove, Donald L.; flowers spiraled, dbl., borne mostly singly; foliage small, medium green, semi-glossy; upright, bushy growth; [Futura × Poker Chip]; int. by Rose World Originals

Scarlett O'Hara Pol, rb, 1947, Klyn; bud ovoid; flowers brilliant red, overcast orange, open, large, dbl., borne in clusters; foliage leathery; vigorous, bushy growth; RULED EXTINCT 2/88; [sport of Gloria Mundi]

Scarlett O'Hara Gr, mr, 1987, Christensen, Jack & Carruth, Tom; flowers medium, 35 petals, high-centered, borne usually singly; foliage medium size, medium green, semi-glossy; nearly thornless; upright, tall growth; PP9++; [Red Success × Mary DeVor]; int. by Armstrong Nursery, 1986

Scarletta Min, mr, deRuiter; flowers scarlet red, small, dbl.; recurrent; growth to 2 ft.; int. in 1972

Scarletta, Climbing Cl Min, mr; [sport of Scarletta]; int. after 1972

Scarman's Crimson China Ch, mr, Scarman; flowers medium red, fading quickly, dbl., borne in clusters; growth to 80 cm.; int. in 1995

Scent From Above LCl, my, 2005, Warner, Christopher H. ; bud long, pointed ovoid; flowers golden yellow, 10 cm., 25-30 petals, high-centered, borne in small clusters of 3-5, moderate spicy fragrance; recurrent; foliage medium size, dark green, glossy; prickles 6-8 mm., hooked slightly downward, greyed-yellow, moderate; growth upright, branching and vigorous, tall (3-4 m.); climber; PP17126; [Laura Ford × Amanda]; int. by Jackson & Perkins Wholesale, Inc., 2005

Scent-Sation HT, ob, Fryer, Gareth; flowers blend of creamy gold and peach pink, medium to large, dbl., high-centered, intense fragrance; recurrent; foliage dark green; vigorous, bushy, upright growth; int. by Fryer's Roses, 1998

Scent to Remember F, ab, 2005, Somerfield, Rob; flowers peach/apricot, reverse dark apricot, 10 cm., full, borne in small clusters, moderate fragrance; foliage small, dark green, glossy; prickles medium, moderate; growth bushy, medium (1¼ m.); [Enchantment × Warm Wishes]; int. in 2006

Scentasia Min, ly, 1999, Schuurman, Frank B.; flowers creamy yellow, 1½-2 in., full, borne in large clusters, moderate fragrance; foliage large, medium green, semi-glossy; few prickles; spreading, tall (20-28 in.) growth; [Tinkerbell × Little Nugget]; int. by Franko Roses New Zealand, Ltd., 1997

Scented Abundance – See **Victorian Spice**, F

Scented Air F, op, 1965, Dickson, Patrick; flowers salmon-pink, well-formed, 5 in., dbl., borne in clusters; foliage very large; vigorous growth; [(Spartan × unknown) × Queen Elizabeth]; int. by A. Dickson; Gold Medal, The Hague, 1965, Gold Medal, Belfast, 1967

Scented Bouquet ; [My Choice × Great Venture]

Scented Bowl HT, dr, 1970, Pal, Dr. B.P.; bud ovoid; flowers bright red, medium, dbl., intense fragrance; foliage glossy; open, upright growth; [Gen. MacArthur × unknown]; int. by Indian Agric. Research Inst., 1965

Scented Carpet S, m, Warner, Chris; bud lanceolate; flowers red-purple, 2 in., single, borne is small terminal clusters, moderate sweet fragrance; foliage dark green, glossy; prickles dense, triangular, sharp; vigorous, low (16 in.), spreading (5 ft.), freely branching growth; hips ovoid, fleshy, smooth ; PP15981; [Grouse × Yesterday]; int. in 2002

Scented Dawn – See **Polka**, LCl

Scented Memory HT, ab, Poulsen; flowers apricot blend with pink flush, 10-15 cm., full, cupped, borne one to a stem, moderate fragrance; foliage large, dark green, glossy; narrow, upright (3-5 ft.), bushy growth; int. by Poulsen Roser, 2003; Honorable Mention, Hradec Králové, 2006, Gold Medal, The Hague, 2006, Certificate of Merit, Orléans, 2006

Scented Star HT, lp, 1974, Lowe; flowers coral-pink, 5-5½ in., 30-35 petals, high-centered, intense fragrance; foliage dark; moderate growth; [Fragrant Cloud × Spek's Yellow]; int. in 1973

Scented Whisper – See **Martin des Senteurs**, F

Scentillating Blues MinFl, m, 2003, Eagle, B & D; flowers dbl., borne mostly solitary, intense fragrance; foliage medium size, medium green, matte; prickles small, straight; growth upright, tall (65-70 cm.); garden, cutting, exhibition; [Winter Magic × Sachet]; int. by Southern Cross Nurseries, 2000

Scentimental F, rb, 1999, Carruth, Tom; bud pointed to globular; flowers striped burgundy and white, or cream, or red, opening quickly, 4-4½ in., 25-30 petals, cupped, borne in small clusters, intense spicy & Damask fragrance; foliage large, quilted, medium green, semi-glossy; prickles moderate; compact, rounded, medium (3-4 ft.) growth; hips short, globular ; PP10126; [Playboy × Peppermint Twist]; int. by Weeks Roses, 1997

Scentsational Min, m, 1995, Saville, F. Harmon; bud ovoid; flowers light mauve with pink tones, 2 in., 24 -30 petals, high-centered, borne mostly singly, but some clusters of up to 7, intense lilac fragrance; recurrent; foliage medium green, semi-glossy; prickles on main canes few, on laterals numerous, angled downward; stems long; vigorous, upright (24-30 in.), branching growth; hips globular ; PP9798; [Lavender Jade × Silverado]; int. by Nor'East Miniature Roses, 1996

Scepter'd Isle S, lp, 1997, Austin, David; bud short, pointed ovoid; flowers soft pink, 4 in., 45 petals, cupped, borne in small clusters, intense myrrh fragrance; good repeat; foliage medium size, dark green, semi-glossy; prickles some, medium, hooked downward; narrow, bushy (4 ft.) growth; PP10969; [seedling × Heritage]; int. by David Austin Roses, Ltd., 1996; Henry Edland Fragrance Award, RNRS

Sceptre HT, ob, 1923, McGredy; flowers bright flame, base shaded orange, reverse dull yellow; low growth

Schackenborg – See **Countess Celeste**, S

Schaffners Erfolg F, mr, 1958, Tantau; flowers bright scarlet, 2 in., 30 petals, borne in well-spaced clusters; foliage medium green; vigorous, bushy growth; [Red Favorite × Fanal]; int. in 1955

Scharlachglut HGal, dr, 1952, Kordes; flowers scarlet-crimson, golden stamens, 5 in., single, borne in clusters; foliage dull green; vigorous (8-10 ft.), dense, arching, spreading growth; hips large, urn-shaped, sealing-wax red; [Alika × Poinsettia]; originally registered as S

Scharnkeana S, m, before 1900; flowers rose-purple, borne in small clusters; growth to 3 ft.; a natural hybrid of *R. californica* × *R. nitida*

Schéhérazade HT, mr, 1942, Mallerin, C.; bud large, oval; flowers fiery red, dbl., cupped, slight fragrance; foliage dark, glossy; vigorous, bushy growth; int. by A. Meilland; Gold Medal, Rome, 1940

Scherzo F, rb, 1976, Paolino; bud pointed; flowers bright scarlet, reverse white and crimson, large, 40 petals, spiraled, borne in clusters, moderate fragrance; foliage dark; vigorous, bushy growth; [Tamango × Frenzy]; int. by URS; Gold Medal, Belfast, 1975

Schiehallion HT, mr, 1982, MacLeod, Major C.A.; flowers 4½ in., 50 petals; foliage medium size, medium green, glossy; upright growth; [Red Planet × Bonnie Anne]

Schiller HMult, mp, 1913, Lambert, P.; flowers clear pink, medium, borne in clusters; [Trier × Lady Mary Fitzwilliam]

Schirus HT, w, Schreurs; Petrus Nicolaas Johannes; PP15725

Schleswig – See **Maid of Honour**, F

Schleswig 87 F, dp, Kordes; int. in 1987

Schleswig-Holstein HT, rb, 1921, Engelbrecht; flowers reddish-yellow, large, semi-dbl., cupped, borne singly or in small clusters; foliage glossy; [sport of Mme Edouard Herriot]

Schloss Balthasar F, op, Kordes; int. by W. Kordes Söhne, 1997

Schloss Dryburg Cl HT, dy, GPG Bad Langensalza; flowers luminous golden yellow, 4 in., dbl., borne in small clusters; foliage small; prickles numerous, large; [Lydia × Le Rêve]; int. in 1969

Schloss Eutin S, ab, Kordes; bud rounded, cream-apricot; flowers soft apricot with darker center, 8 cm., full, imbricated, camellia-like, borne mostly in large clusters, slight sweet fragrance; recurrent; foliage medium size, dark green, glossy; vigorous, upright (4 ft.), arching growth; [sport of Bremer Stadtmusikanten]; int. by W. Kordes Söhne, 2006

Schloss Friedenstein HMult, m, 1915, Schmidt, J. C.; flowers reddish-violet, 3-4 cm., dbl., moderate fragrance; [Veilchenblau × Mme Norbert Levavasseur]

Schloss Glücksburg – See **English Garden**, S

Schloss Heidegg – See **Pink Meidiland**, S

Schloss Herrenchiemsee – See **Canyonlands**, F

Schloss Linderhof – See **Redwood**, F

Schloss Luegg HMult, mp, 1886, Geschwind; flowers shining carmine pink, full; [de la Grifferaie × unknown]

Schloss Mannheim F, or, 1975, Kordes; flowers red-orange, medium, dbl., globular, borne in clusters, slight fragrance; free-flowering; foliage dark green, medium size, leathery; vigorous, upright, bushy growth; [Marlena × Europeana]; ADR, 1972

Schloss Moritzburg F, dr, 1967, Haenchen, E.; flowers medium, semi-dbl., cupped; foliage dark, leathery; vigorous growth; [Donald Prior × unknown]; int. by Teschendorff

Schloss Neuschwanstein – See **Yellowstone**, F

Schloss Seusslitz HSpn, ly, 1933, Dechant; flowers creamy yellow, fading to white, 2½-3 in., semi-dbl., flat, borne in small clusters; once-blooming, very early; moderate growth; [Frau Karl Druschki × Harison's Yellow]

Schlosser's Brilliant – See **Detroiter**, HT

Schlössers Brilliant, Climbing – See **Detroiter, Climbing**, Cl HT

Schlossgarten S, mp, GPG Bad Langensalza; flowers large, dbl., high-centered, borne singly and in clusters; upright growth; int. in 1989

Schmetterling HFt, yb, 1905, Müller, Dr. F.; flowers yellow and red, medium, semi-dbl.

Schmid's Ideal (strain of *R. canina*), lp; prickles thorny; growth used as an understock; int. by R. Schmid

Schmid's Rekord S, lp, 1930, Schmid, R.; flowers soft pink, golden stamens, 5 petals, moderate fragrance;

spring-flowering; moderate (3-5 ft.) growth; hybrid canina

Schnee-Eule – See **White Pavement**, HRg

Schneeball HWich, w, 1905, Weigand, C.; flowers semi-dbl., borne in clusters, moderate fragrance

Schneeberg – See **Pristine Pavement**, HRg

Schneeflocke – See **Parsla**, HRg

Schneeflocke – See **White Flower Carpet**, F

Schneekönigen – See **Frau Karl Druschki**, HP

Schneekönigin – See **Magic Blanket**, S

Schneekopf Pol, w, 1903, Lambert, P.; flowers snow-white or light pink, regular form; recurrent bloom; vigorous growth; [Mignonette × Souv. de Mme Sablayrolles]; sometimes classified as HP

Schneekoppe – See **Snow Pavement**, HRg

Schneeküsschen Min, w, 2006; flowers white, suffused pink, 3 cm., dbl., borne in small clusters; foliage tiny, fresh green; growth compact, short (30 cm.); int. by W. Kordes' Söhne, 1993

Schneelicht HRg, w, 1894, Geschwind, R.; flowers pure white, large, single, borne in clusters; very vigorous, climbing growth; makes an impenetrable, prickly hedge; very hardy; [*R. rugosa* × *R. phoenicia*]

Schneeprinzessin HT, w, 1946, Meilland, F.; bud long; flowers large; vigorous growth; int. by Pfitzer

Schneeschirm F, w, 1946, Tantau; flowers white, center tinted rose-yellow, large, single, shallow cup, borne in clusters; foliage dark; low, bushy, spreading growth; [Johanna Tantau × (Karen Poulsen × Stammler)]

Schneesturm S, w, Tantau; President's International Trophy, RNRS, 1992, ADR, 1993

Schneeteppich – See **Snow Carpet**, Min

Schneewalzer F, w, 1973, Tantau, Math.; bud ovoid; flowers large, dbl.; moderate, upright growth

Schneewalzer 87 LCl, w, Tantau; flowers very pale lemon-white, 5-6 in., dbl., high-centered, borne singly or in small clusters; foliage large, dark green, glossy; tall, bushy growth; int. by Rosen Tantau, 1987

Schneeweisschen Min, w, Tantau; flowers clean white, full, rosette, no fragrance; growth to 12-16 in.; containers; int. by Rosen Tantau, 1992

Schneewittchen Pol, ly, 1901, Lambert, P.; flowers yellow fading to white, dbl., rosette, borne in clusters; foliage glossy; low (16 in.) growth; [Aglaia × (Paquerette × Souv. de Mme Levet)]

Schneewittchen – See **Iceberg**, F

Schneewittchen, Climbing – See **Iceberg, Climbing**, Cl F

Schneewolke S, w, Noack, Werner; int. in 1996

Schneezwerg HRg, w, 1912, Lambert, P.; flowers snow-white, stamens golden yellow, small, semi-dbl., flat, borne in clusters of 3-10; recurrent bloom; foliage dark, glossy, rugose; prickles spiny; vigorous (3-4 ft.) growth; hips abundant, small, red; [possibly *R. rugosa* × Polyantha hybrid]

Schoener's Musk HMsk, w, Schoener; flowers milk-white, medium enormous trusses; vigorous, pillar growth

Schoener's Nutkana S, mp, 1930, Schoener; flowers clear rose-pink, 4 in., single, blooms on arching canes, moderate fragrance; non-recurrent; foliage grey-green; few prickles; stems red-brown; vigorous, shrub (4-6 ft.) growth; [*R. nutkana* × Paul Neyron]; int. by C-P

Scholle's Golden Moss M, dy, Scholle, E.; flowers amber-yellow, medium, dbl.; int. in 1985

Schön Ingeborg HP, lp, 1921, Kiese; flowers light pink with darker center, large, dbl., shallow cup; recurrent; upright (5 ft.) growth; [Frau Karl Druschki × Natalie Böttner]

Schöne aus Kaiserslautern F, op, 1958, Kordes; bud long, pointed; flowers orange tinted salmon-red, 4 in., 30 petals, high-centered, intense fragrance; free, intermittent bloom; foliage dark, leathery; strong stems; very vigorous, upright, bushy growth; [R.M.S. Queen Mary × Obergärtner Wiebicke]; int. in 1957

Schöne Berlinerin HT, mp, Tantau; flowers warm, bright rose pink, 8-10 cm., dbl., high-centered, slight fragrance; recurrent; strong (80-100 cm.) growth; int. by Rosen Tantau, 1986

Schöne Dortmunderin F, mp, Noack, Werner; flowers intense pure pink, 2 in., dbl., cupped, borne in clusters; recurrent; upright (60-70 cm.) growth; int. by Noack Rosen, 1991

Schöne Münchnerin F, mr, 1985, Kordes, W.; flowers 22 petals, cupped, borne 2-3 per cluster; foliage medium size, medium green, semi-glossy; prickles medium, green; bushy growth; [Sympathie × Tornado]; int. by Kordes

Schöne von Holstein Pol, mp, 1919, Tantau; flowers pure hermosa pink, yellow stamens, dbl., cupped, borne in large clusters, no fragrance; recurrent; foliage apple green; [Orléans Rose × unknown]

Schöne von Kaiserslautern – See **Schöne aus Kaiserslautern**, F

Schöne von Marquardt HWich, rb, 1928, Clauberg; flowers bright dark red, variegated with white; vigorous, climbing growth; [sport of Sodenia]

Schonerts Meisterklasse HT, or, 1952, Leenders, M.; flowers salmon and coral-red, well-formed, very large, dbl.; vigorous growth

School Days Min, dy, 1993, Saville, F. Harmon; flowers medium, full, borne mostly singly, no fragrance; foliage medium size, medium green, semi-glossy; few prickles; medium (14-18 in.), bushy, compact growth; [Klima × Sonnenkind]; int. by Nor'East Min. Roses, 1994

School Girl LCl, ab, 1964, McGredy, Sam IV; flowers orange-apricot, 4 in., dbl., loose, flat, borne mostly solitary, moderate fragrance; recurrent bloom; foliage dark green, glossy, sparse; prickles numerous, large; fairly vigorous (10 ft.) growth; [Coral Dawn × Belle Blonde]; int. by McGredy

Schoolgirl – See **School Girl**, LCl

Schoone Gezelle Blomme HMsk, w, 2000, Lens, Louis; flowers semi-dbl., open, borne in large clusters; foliage medium size, dark green, semi-glossy; prickles moderate; growth bushy, spreading, medium (80-120 cm.); [Fil d'Ariane × Tapis Volant]; int. by Louis Lens N.V., 1999; Landscape Rose Certificate, Paris, 2003

Schrenat HT, dp, Schreurs, Petrus Nicolaas Johannes; PP16075

Schubert S, pb, 1986, Lens, Louis; flowers pink, white-eye, 1 in., 5 petals, borne in clusters of 7-60, slight fragrance; recurrent; foliage small; prickles very hooked, greenish-brown; bushy, spreading growth; [Ballerina × *R. multiflora*]; int. in 1984

Schulenfest S, ly, 2006, Ponton, Ray; flowers full, borne mostly solitary; foliage dark green, semi-glossy; prickles medium, straight, moderate; growth compact, short (2 ft.); [Lilian Austin × Schulenberg Apricot]; int. in 2006

Schuss S, lp, Meilland; flowers carmine pink, small, dbl., cupped, borne in clusters; spreading, trailing growth; int. in 1989

Schwabenland HRg, mp, 1928, Berger, V.; flowers amaranth-pink, open, large, dbl.; profuse, repeated bloom; foliage large, rich green, leathery; vigorous (3 ft.) growth; [(*R. rugosa* × unknown) × Elizabeth Cullen]; int. by Pfitzer

Schwabenmädel F, dr; flowers velvety dark red, dbl., cupped, borne in clusters; bushy, well-branched growth

Schwäbische Heimat HT, dr, 1934, Pfitzer; flowers deep amaranth-red, dbl.; [sport of Jonkheer J.L. Mock]

Schwanensee – See **Swan Lake**, LCl

Schwarzaldmädel F, Hetzel, K.; int. in 1977

Schwarze Madonna HT, dr, 2006; bud velvety black; flowers velvety black-red, 11 cm., full, high-centered, borne mostly solitary, slight fragrance; recurrent; foliage reddish at first, then deep dark green, glossy; vigorous, upright (80 cm.) growth; int. by W. Kordes' Söhne, 1992

Schwarze Rose – See **Norita**, HT

Schwarzer Samt HKor, dr, Hänchen; buds medium, long pointed; flowers dark velvety blackish red, 7-9 cm., semi-dbl., open, borne several together and in clusters, slight fragrance; continuous; foliage medium size, dark green, glossy, leathery; [Alain × Oskar Scheerer]; int. by Teschendorff, 1969

Schwarzwaldfeuer – See **Charming Cover**, S

Schwarzwaldmädel F, ob, Hetzel; flowers orange with red tones, moderate fragrance; recurrent; int. in 1977

Schweizer Garten F, ly, Huber; flowers white with yellow centers, 9 cm., 25-30 petals, cupped, borne in clusters of 10-12, slight fragrance; recurrent; foliage copper-colored when new, then dark green, glossy; bushy (80-120 cm.) growth; int. by Richard Huber AG, 2001

Schweizer Gold HT, ly, 1975, Kordes; bud ovoid; flowers dbl., high-centered; foliage large, light; vigorous growth; [Peer Gynt × King's Ransom]; int. by Horstmann; Gold Medal, Baden-Baden, 1972

Schweizer Gold HT, dy, Urban, J.

Schweizer Gruss – See **Red Favorite**, F

Schweizer Gruss, Climbing – See **Red Favorite, Climbing**, Cl F

Schweizer Woche HT, w, Huber; bud roundish; flowers creamy white, some with yellow or apricot tints, dbl., borne mostly singly, intense tea rose fragrance; foliage dark green, leathery; stems strong; upright, medium growth; int. by Richard Huber AG, 1989

Schwerin HMsk, dp, 1937, Kordes; bud long, pointed; flowers light crimson, open, cupped, borne in large clusters, moderate musk fragrance; profuse, intermittent bloom; foliage large, leathery, glossy, bronze; long, strong stems; very vigorous, bushy growth; [Eva × D.T. Poulsen]

Scintillation S, lp, 1967, Austin, David; flowers blush pink, small, semi-dbl., shallow cup to flat, borne in large clusters, intense fragrance; non-remontant; foliage dark, matte; vigorous, wide growth; [*R. macrantha* × Vanity]; int. by Sunningdale Nursery, 1968

Scipion HP, pb, 1852, Avoux & Crozy; flowers shining carmine pink with white, large, full

Scipion Cochet B, dp, 1850, Cochet, S.; flowers bright pink to grenadine, medium, dbl.

Scipion Cochet HP, dr, 1887, Verdier, E.; flowers glowing velvety chestnut purple, shaded fiery carmine-scarlet, large, full

Scoop F, or, Richardier; flowers vivid orange, dbl.; growth to 80-90 cm.; int. by Meilland-Richardier, 1998

Scoop Jackson Gr, dr, 1980, McGredy, Sam IV; flowers large, 20 petals; foliage glossy; upright growth; [Kalahari × John Waterer]; int. by Roses by Fred Edmunds, 1981

Scorcher HWich, dr, 1922, Clark, A.; flowers brilliant scarlet-crimson, 8-9 cm., semi-dbl., flat, borne singly or in small clusters; some repeat; foliage small, dark green, glossy; vigorous, climbing or pillar (to 10 ft.)

growth; [Mme Abel Chatenay × seedling]; int. by Hackett

Scorpio HT, mr; flowers bright crimson, dbl., high-centered; recurrent; foliage glossy; stems stiff, upright; moderate growth; int. by Burston Nurseries, 2004

Scotch Blend HT, pb, 1976, J&B Roses; bud long, pointed; flowers 5-6 in., 35 petals, high-centered; foliage dark, leathery; upright growth; [Queen Elizabeth × Peace]; int. by Eastern Roses, 1975

Scotch Briar – See ***R. spinosissima*** (Linnaeus)

Scotch Double White – See **Double White Burnet**, HSpn

Scotch Heather HSpn, yb, Sutherland; flowers single; int. in 1996

Scotch Perpetual – See **Perpetual Scotch**, HSpn

Scotch Rose – See ***R. spinosissima*** (Linnaeus)

Scotch Yellow HT, my, Mercer; int. in 1991

Scotland Wink F, dp, Adam; int. by Pep. de la Guerinais, 2001

Scotland Yard HT, ab

Scotland's Trust HT, lp, 1992, Cocker, James & Sons; flowers light pink, silver reverse, moderately well-shaped, medium, dbl.; foliage medium size, medium green, matte; some prickles; medium (16-20 cm.), upright growth; [Sunblest × Prima Ballerina]

Scott Cl Min, mr, 2000, Moe, Mitchie; flowers bright red, 1-1½ in., dbl., borne in small clusters, slight fragrance; foliage medium size, dark green, semi-glossy; few prickles; growth vigorous, climbing, upright (30-36 in.); [Klima × select pollen]; int. by Mitchie's Roses and More, 2000

Scott Chait MinFl, ob, 2003, Zipper, Herbert; flowers orange, reverse cream, 1-1½ in., full, borne mostly solitary, slight fragrance; foliage medium size, medium green, matte; prickles few, 4 mm., hooked; growth bushy, medium (24-36 in.), very vigorous; exhibition, garden, cutting; [Tiki × Percussion]; int. by Island Roses, 2003

Scott Williams F, yb, Hannemann, F.; [Oz Gold × Gold Bunny]; int. by The Rose Paradise, 1992

Scottish Celebration F, pb; int. by Greenhead Nursery, 2004

Scottish Highlands S, ob, Cocker; flowers bronzy-copper, 7 in., very full, moderate fragrance; recurrent; strong (4-5 ft.) growth; int. in 1991

Scottish Soldier S, yb, Williams, J. Benjamin; flowers yellow with red tints on some petal edges, semi-dbl., cupped to flat; int. in 1996

Scottish Special Min, lp, 1985, Cocker, Ann G.; flowers patio, large, semi-dbl.; foliage small, medium green, semi-glossy; bushy growth; [Wee Man × Darling Flame]

Scottish Tartans F, yb; flowers begin yellow, red starts on petal edges as it opens, spreading down the petals, semi-dbl. to dbl., borne in clusters; recurrent

Scott's Columbia HT, dp, 1928, Scott, R.; flowers clear bright pink; [sport of Columbia]

Scout – See **Boy Scout**, HT

Scouts Honor F, w; int. in 2006

Scrabo F, op, 1970, Dickson, A.; flowers light salmon-pink, large, dbl., high-centered, moderate fragrance; free growth; [Celebration × Elizabeth of Glamis]

Scudbuster Min, or, 1991, Clements, John K.; flowers intense rocket flame orange, medium, very full, high-centered, borne mostly singly, slight fragrance; foliage small, dark green, semi-glossy; some prickles; medium (35 cm.), upright growth; [seedling × seedling]; int. by Heirloom Old Garden Roses, 1992

Sea Foam HBc, w, 1919, Paul, W.; flowers white, shaded slightly with cream, small, dbl.; foliage dark green, glossy; [Mermaid × a Polyantha]

Sea Foam S, w, 1964, Schwartz, Ernest W.; bud short, pointed, globular with conspicuous neck; flowers white to cream, 2-2½ in., 60-70 petals, high-centered to cupped, borne in clusters, slight spicy fragrance; recurrent; foliage small, glossy, leathery; prickles numerous, pointed downward, brown; vigorous, climbing trailer, semi-prostrate growth; hips globular, smooth, green; PP2463; [((White Dawn × Pinocchio) × (White Dawn × Pinocchio)) × (WhiteDawn × Pinocchio)]; int. by C-P; Gold Medal, Rome, 1963, David Fuerstenberg Prize, ARS, 1968

Sea Foam Rosa S, Zandri, R.; int. in 1971

Sea Jack HT, lp; flowers baby pink; vigorous growth; [sport of Confidence]

Sea Mist HT, w, 1962, Armbrust, F. J.; bud long, pointed; flowers cream, center golden, large, semi-dbl., high-centered, slight fragrance; foliage leathery; vigorous growth; [Helen Traubel × Golden Harvest]; int. by Langbecker, 1960

Sea Nymph Min, pb, 1986, McDaniel, Earl; flowers petals blush pink, edged coral, large, 48 petals, high-centered, borne singly; foliage medium size, medium green, semi-glossy; prickles medium, curved; upright, bushy growth; [seedling × seedling]; int. by McDaniel's Min. Roses

Sea of Fire F, or, 1954, Kordes; flowers orange-scarlet, 3 in., semi-dbl., open wide, borne in small clusters, slight fragrance; recurrent; foliage dark, leathery; vigorous, upright, bushy growth; [(Baby Chateau × Else Poulsen) × Independence]; int. by Wheatcroft Bros., 1954

Sea of Tranquility HT, ab, 1991, Keene's Rose Nursery; bud classical, delicate light pink; flowers opening to apricot-pink blush, lighter reverse, holds color, 4¾ in., 40-45 petals, high-centered, borne singly, slight sweet fragrance; foliage light green, small, disease-resistant; upright (up to 5 ft.), non-spreading growth; [sport of Sylvia]

Sea Pearl F, pb, 1964, Dickson, Patrick; bud long, pointed; flowers soft pink, reverse flushed peach and yellow, well-formed, 4½ in., 24 petals, borne in clusters; foliage dark; stems strong, straight; upright, bushy (4 ft.) growth; [Kordes' Perfecta × Montezuma]; int. by A. Dickson

Sea Rodney Min, m, McCann, Sean; flowers mauve and white, intense fragrance; int. by Australian Roses, 2001

Sea Spray HMsk, w, 1923, Pemberton; flowers stone-white, flushed pink, semi-dbl., borne in small clusters; non-recurrent; growth to 3-5 ft.

Sea Spray – See **Seaspray**, Min

Seabird HT, my, 1913, Dickson, H.; flowers primrose-yellow, paling to creamy yellow, medium, dbl.; vigorous growth

Seabreeze Min, mp, 1976, Lemrow, Dr. Maynard W.; bud short, pointed; flowers from dusty rose to lavender pink, cream shadings on reverse, 1 in., 25-35 petals, cupped, ruffled, borne in clusters of 7-12, slight fragrance; recurrent; foliage light to medium green; prickles very few, slight downward curve; very vigorous, upright (15-18 in.), bushy growth; hips globular, orange-red; PP4025; [White Fairy × seedling]; int. by Nor'East Min. Roses

Seacombe w, Bates, Michael; int. by Vintage Gardens, 2001

Seafair HT, ab, 1960, Von Abrams; bud long, pointed; flowers deep apricot, large, 45 petals, high-centered; foliage glossy; vigorous, upright, symmetrical growth; RULED EXTINCT 4/86; [Charlotte Armstrong × Signora]; int. by Peterson & Dering, 1959

Seafarer F, or, 1986, Harkness; flowers large, 30 petals, cupped, borne in clusters of 3-5; foliage medium size, dark, glossy; prickles medium, red; medium, bushy growth; hips medium, green; [Amy Brown × Judy Garland]

Seager Wheeler HSpn, lp, 1947, Wheeler; flowers semi-dbl.; non-recurrent; growth to 6 ft.; hardy; [*R. spinosissima altaica* × unknown]; int. by P.H. Wright

Seagull HMult, w, 1907, Pritchard; bud tinged pink; flowers pure white, stamens golden, 3 cm., single, borne in large clusters, moderate fragrance; non-remontant; foliage grey-green; prickles large; very vigorous growth; [*R. multiflora* × Général Jacqueminot]

Seale Peach Min, ab, Seale; int. by Seale Nurseries

Sealily Min, pb, 1984, Lemrow, Dr. Maynard W.; flowers white, petals edged pink, small, 35 petals; foliage medium size, dark, semi-glossy; [Max Colwell × unknown]

Sealing Wax HMoy, mp, 1938, Royal Hort. Soc.; flowers large; hips abundant, brilliant red; [*R. moyesii* × unknown]

Sean S, w, Sutherland, P; [sport of Mme Segond Weber]; int. by Golden Vale Nursery, 2000

Sean and Joan F, ob, 2000, Bossom, Bill; flowers orange, reverse lighter, large, dbl., borne in small clusters, slight fragrance; foliage medium size, dark green, glossy; prickles moderate; upright (4½ ft.) growth; [Sexy Rexy × Edith Holden]

Search for Life HT, mr, 1988, Williams, J. Benjamin; flowers large, full, high-centered; foliage large, dark green, semi-glossy; vigorous, hardy, abundant growth; [Miss All-American Beauty × Mister Lincoln]

Seashell HWich, mp, 1916, Dawson; flowers large, semi-dbl., borne in large clusters; foliage glossy

Seashell HT, op, 1975, Kordes, R.; bud short, pointed; flowers burnt-orange, imbricated, 3-4 in., 48 petals, slight fragrance; free-flowering; upright growth; PP3685; [seedling × Colour Wonder]; int. by J&P, 1976

Seashore HT, op, Williams, J. B.; int. by Hortico, 1996

Seasons S, ob; flowers single; int. by Rozenwerkerij De Wilde Bussum, 2003

Seaspray Min, pb, 1983, McGredy, Sam IV; flowers pale pink flushed red, medium, semi-dbl., moderate fragrance; foliage medium size, medium green, matte; bushy growth; [Anytime × Moana]; int. by John Mattock, Ltd, 1982

Seattle Scentsation Min, pb, 1996, Saville, F. Harmon; bud small, ovate, pointed; flowers yellow, apricot base and mauve-pink, large, 18-20 petals, flat, borne singly and in small clusters, intense classic rose fragrance; recurrent; foliage small, dark green, semi-glossy; prickles very few, short, thin, straight; stems variable; medium (26-30 in.), upright, bushy, vigorous growth; hips pear-shaped ; PP9821; [Lavender Jade × New Zealand]; int. by Nor'East Min. Roses, 1996; Named in honor of ARS Spring Convention, Seattle, WA, ARS, 1996

Seattle Sunrise MinFl, ab, 2005, Moe, Mitchie; flowers dbl., high-centered, borne mostly solitary, slight fragrance; foliage medium size, dark green, semi-glossy; prickles few, medium, hooked down, light tan; growth upright, medium (18-24 in.); exhibition, garden; [(Pristine × Selfridges) × Finest Hour]; int. by Nor'East Miniature Roses, 2006

Sebago – See **Tyler**, HT

Sebastian Kneipp HT, w, 2006; bud rounded, medium, green-white; flowers cream with a yellow-pink center, 11 cm., full, quartered, borne mostly solitary, strong, sweetish fragrance; foliage medium size, dark green, glossy; growth bushy, medium (120 cm.); int. by W. Kordes' Söhne, 1997

Sebastian Schultheis Gr, dp, Schultheis; flowers bright carmine pink, dbl., cupped, borne mostly in clusters, slight fragrance; free-flowering; stems long; upright, tall, bushy growth; [Queen Elizabeth × unknown]; int. by Rosen von Schultheis, 1979

Sebastopol Queen HMult, w; flowers white with blushed edges, single, borne in large clusters, slight fragrance; non-remontant; hips abundant, soft salmon-orange; chance seedling; may be from *R. soulieana* crossed with a multiflora rambler; int. by Vintage Gardens, 2003

Secco HT, yb, Sasaki; int. in 1997

Second Chance HT, pb, 1989, Stoddard, Louis; bud ovoid; flowers coral-orange, tips orange-red, reverse deep pink, aging medium pink with red edges, 35 petals, high-centered, moderate damask fragrance; foliage medium size, medium green to maroon, semi-glossy, a bit rugose; bushy, slightly spreading growth; [Carefree Beauty × Sonia]; int. in 1991

Secret HT, pb, 1992, Tracy, Daniel; bud ovoid; flowers light creamy pink edged with deep pink, 4-4½ in., 30-40 petals, cupped, borne mostly singly, intense sweet and spicy fragrance; recurrent; foliage large, medium green, semi-glossy; prickles some, medium, reddish green; strong stems; tall (120-130 cm.), bushy growth; PP8494; [Pristine × Friendship]; int. by The Conard-Pyle Co., 1994

Secret Love HT, dr, 1973, Armstrong, D.L.; bud ovoid; flowers deep red, large, dbl., high-centered, moderate fragrance; foliage leathery; moderate, upright, bushy growth; PP3584; [seedling × seedling]; int. by Armstrong Nursery

Secret Obsession Min, lp, 1995, Rennie, Bruce F.; flowers 3 in., full, borne mostly singly; foliage large, medium green, semi-glossy; few prickles; tall (24-30 in.), upright growth; [seedling × Innocent Blush]; int. by Rennie Roses International, 1994

Secret Recipe Min, rb, 1994, Moore, Ralph S.; bud pointed, mossy; flowers combination of burgundy, red and white stripes, yellow stamens, 1¾ in., semi-dbl., flat, borne mostly singly, slight fragrance; foliage medium size, medium green, semi-glossy; some prickles; upright, bushy (12-18 in.) growth; [Little Darling × seedling]; int. by Sequoia Nursery, 1995

Secrétaire Allard HP, mr, 1869, David; flowers velvety scarlet-vermilion, large, full

Secrétaire Belpaire HT, op, 1934, Lens; flowers brilliant salmon-pink, large, dbl.; foliage bright bronze; vigorous growth; [Angèle Pernet × Mme Edouard Herriot]

Secrétaire Général Delaire HP, dr, 1899, Corboeuf; flowers very large, very full; [Baronne Adolphe de Rothschild × Alphonse Soupert]

Secrétaire J. Nicolas HP, m, 1883, Schwartz; flowers dark red and velvety purple, reverse lighter, large, full, cupped, globular, borne mostly solitary; foliage light green, finely dentate; prickles thin, pointed, numerous; growth upright

Secrétaire Jean Nicolas – See **Secrétaire J. Nicolas**, HP

Secretaris Zwart HT, dp, 1918, Van Rossem; flowers bright rose, reverse silvery rose, large, full, globular, moderate fragrance; recurrent; [Gen. MacArthur × Lyon Rose]

Sedana S, ob, Noack; flowers cream-orange to apricot, some soft pink tones, 2 in., semi-dbl., shallow cup, borne in clusters; recurrent; foliage medium green, glossy, leathery; low (2 ft.), bushy growth; int. by Noack Rosen, 2006

Sedana Flower Carpet – See **Sedana**, S

Sedgebrook HT, lp, 1987, Murray, Nola; flowers very pale pink, almost white, 47 petals, high-centered; foliage large, medium green, flat; prickles pointed, brown; low growth; [(Chanelle × Prima Ballerina) × Deep Secret]; int. in 1986

Séduction Pol, mp, 1927, Turbat; flowers peach-blossom-pink, large, dbl., borne in clusters of 50-60; few prickles; dwarf growth

Seduction – See **Matilda**, F

Seduction HT, op, Meilland; flowers intense salmon-pink, dbl., high-centered, borne mostly singly; recurrent; cut flower rose; int. by Meilland Intl., 1999

Seduction, Climbing Cl F, pb, 2001, Nieuwesteeg, John; flowers white, edged pink, large, semi-dbl. to dbl., borne in small clusters, slight fragrance; foliage medium to large, dark green, semi-glossy; prickles large, hooked, moderate; growth climbing; [sport of Matilda]

Seefeld F, rb, 1958, Delforge; bud oval; flowers red tinted lighter, open, medium, dbl., borne in large clusters; foliage glossy; very vigorous, bushy growth; [Fashion × Orange Triumph]

Seftopolis Gr, dp, 1985, Staikov, Prof. Dr. V.; flowers deep pink, large, 36 petals; foliage glossy, leathery; vigorous growth; [Queen Elizabeth × seedling]; int. by Kalaydjiev and Chorbadjiiski, 1977

Segovia HT, Combe, M.; int. in 1964

Segovia S, pb, Olesen; bud urceolate with pointed apex; flowers varying shades of light to medium pink, 5 cm., very full, globular, to rosette, borne singly and in small clusters, slight fragrance; recurrent; foliage dark green, glossy; prickles numerous, 4-5 mm., hooked downward; upright to bushy (60-100 cm.) growth; PP16961; [seedling × Bernstorff]; int. by Poulsen Roser, 2005; Silver Medal, Baden-Baden, 2006, City of Zweibrücken Prize, Baden-Baden, 2006, Bronze Medal, Rome, 2006

Séguier HGal, m, 1853, Robert; flowers purple/violet with white stripes, medium, dbl.

Sehnsucht F, dr

Sei-Ka – See **Olympic Torch**, HT

Sei-Ka, Climbing – See **Seika, Climbing**, Cl HT

Seigneur d'Harzelhaard HGal, m, about 1845, Calvert; flowers dark violet-purple, center red, medium, full

Seika HT, ob, Teranishi; flowers single; int. in 1966

Seika – See **Olympic Torch**, HT

Seika, Climbing Cl HT, rb, Keisei; [sport of Olympic Torch]; int. in 1985

Seiko HT, dy, 1977, Keisei Rose Nurseries; buds ovoid; flowers non-fading, deep lemon yellow, dbl, high-centered, borne in clusters; foliage large, semi-glossy; growth very vigorous; int. by Keisei Rose Nursery, 1975

Seion HT, my, 1988, Yokota, Kiyoshi; flowers large, 35-40 petals, high-centered, moderate fragrance; foliage light green; few prickles; upright, medium growth; hips medium, pale orange; [Grandpa Dickson × Sunblest]

Seiryoden HT, pb, Kuroda; int. in 1961

Seiryu HT, m, 2005, Kobayashi, Moriji; flowers 12 cm., dbl., borne mostly solitary, slight fragrance; foliage medium size, light green, matte; prickles medium; growth upright, 160 cm; cutting, garden; [Ondina × (Madame Violet × seedling)]

Seisho HT, pb, 1999, Ohkawara, Kiyoshi; flowers soft pink, deep pink petal edge, 5½ in., 30-35 petals, high-centered; foliage dark green; growth to 5 ft.; [Michele Meilland × Maria Teresa Bordas]; int. by Komaba Rose Nursery, 1992

Seishun HT, dp, Hiroshima; int. by Hiroshima Bara-en, 1996

Sekel S, yb, 1985, Lundstad, Arne; flowers light yellow with red spreading down from the petal edges, large, 11 petals, shallow cup, borne in large clusters of up to 21, slight fragrance; foliage dark, leathery, glossy; vigorous, upright growth; [Lichterloh × Zitronenfalter]; int. by Agricultural University of Norway, 1984

Seki-Yoh HT, or, 1986, Suzuki, Seizo; flowers large, 52 petals, high-centered; foliage dark, leathery, semi-glossy; upright, compact growth; [Miss France × Christian Dior]; int. by Keisei Rose Nursery, 1975

Selandia LCl, mp, 1913, Poulsen, D.T.; flowers medium pink, fading to light rose pink, reverse lighter, 4 cm., dbl., borne in medium to large clusters; foliage glossy; vigorous growth; [Mme Norbert Levavasseur × Dorothy Perkins]

Selena HT, dr, deVor; int. in 1996

Selenia F, w, J&P; flowers white with cream centers, large, dbl., high-centered; free-flowering; compact, low, well-branched growth; int. by Rose Barni, 2002

Selfridges – See **Berolina**, F

Selfridges HT, dy, 1984, Kordes, W.; bud large; flowers amber yellow, large, 35 petals, high-centered, borne mostly singly, moderate fragrance; foliage medium size, medium green, semi-glossy; upright growth; int. by John Mattock, Ltd, 1984; ADR, 1986

Sélima Dubos – See **Célina Dubos**, D

Selina HMsk, dp, 1992, Reynolds, Ted; flowers deep pink, medium, single, borne in small clusters; foliage small, medium green, semi-glossy; few prickles; medium, spreading growth; [Cornelia × Trier]; int. by Reynolds Roses, 1992

Selvetta HT, pb, 1983, Cazzaniga-Como; flowers light pink, petals edged salmon, large, 40 petals, high-centered, no fragrance; foliage medium size, dark, matte; upright growth; int. by Rose Barni-Pistoia, 1982

Selwyn Bird HT, or, 1970, Cocker; flowers salmon-cerise, 35 petals, high-centered, moderate fragrance; foliage dark, glossy; vigorous growth; [Fragrant Cloud × Stella]; int. by David Austin, Ltd., 1969

Selwyn Toogood Min, mp, 1984, Eagle, Barry & Dawn; flowers small, 33 petals, high-centered; foliage small, light green; prickles light moss on stems; bushy, upright growth; [Heidi × unknown]; int. by Southern Cross Nursery, 1983

Sémèlé T, w, about 1844, Guérin or Boyau; flowers flesh white, aging darker, medium, dbl.

Semi (*R. laxa* form), w, 1913; flowers small; blooms all summer; tall (8 ft.) growth; hips bright red; very hardy

Semi-Double M, dp, before 1826, Vibert; flowers large, semi-dbl.

Semi-Double Marbled Rose – See **Marmorea**, HGal

Semi-Double Striped Moss – See **Panachée**, M

Semi-Plena – See **Alba Semi-plena**, A

Semillante HT, Combe, M.; int. in 1976

Sémiramis D, pb, 1841, Vibert; flowers salmon-rose, center fawn, large, dbl.

Semiramis HT, yb, 1957, Motose; bud pointed; flowers rose, center buff or amber, 5 in., 35-45 petals, high-centered, intense raspberry fragrance; foliage dark, glossy; vigorous growth; PP1552; [Capistrano × (Peace × Crimson Glory)]

Sémonville A, w, before 1815, Charpentier; flowers white with coppery yellow-pink, medium, semi-dbl.; foliage veined; prickles long, intermixed with glandular bristles; [Evratina × unknown]

Sémonville à Fleurs Doubles A, pb, 1823, Hardy; flowers pink tinted yellow-copper, large, dbl.

Semperflorens – See **Slater's Crimson China**, Ch

Sempervirens Major – See **Plena**, HSem

Sempervirens Pleno – See **Plena**, HSem

Sénat Romain – See **Duc de Guiche**, HGal

Sénateur Amic Cl T, mr, 1924, Nabonnand, P.; bud long, pointed; flowers brilliant carmine, large, semi-dbl., cupped; very vigorous growth; [*R. gigantea* × General MacArthur]

Sénateur Belle HT, op, 1900, Pernet-Ducher; flowers salmon pink, center dark golden, edges shaded carmine, medium, full, globular

Sénateur Favre – See **François Fontaine**, HP

Sénateur La Follette – See **La Follette**, Cl T

Sénateur Laubet – See **Sénateur Loubet**, T

Sénateur Loubet T, yb, 1891, Reboul; flowers delicate pink on a ground of metallic yellow, changing to poppy, large, very full; growth dwarf but vigorous

Sénateur Mascuraud HT, ly, 1909, Pernet-Ducher; flowers light yellow, center darker, dbl.

Sénateur Potié HT, ob, 1937, Dot, Pedro; flowers orange-yellow, large, semi-dbl., cupped; foliage glossy, bronze; vigorous growth; [Mme Butterfly × Carito MacMahon]

Sénateur Réveil HP, rb, 1863, Damaizin; flowers shining crimson, shaded dark purple, large, full

Sénateur Saint-Romme HT, op, 1904, Schwartz; bud light red; flowers salmon on a pink ground, large, full

Sénateur Vaïsse HP, rb, 1859, Guillot Père; flowers red, shaded darker, large, 32 petals; occasionally recurrent bloom; upright growth; [Général Jacqueminot × unknown]

Senator HT, mr, 1926, Florex Gardens; bud long, pointed; flowers brilliant scarlet, dbl.; [Red Columbia × Premier]

Senator Burda HT, dr, 1988, Meilland, Mrs. Marie-Louise; flowers brilliant currant-red, large, full, high-centered, intense fragrance; recurrent; foliage large, medium green, semi-glossy; upright, strong, floriferous growth; [(Karl Herbst × (Royal Velvet × Suspense)) × Erotika]; int. by SNC Meilland & Cie; Fragrance Award, l'Hay, 1985

Senator Joe T. Robinson HT, dr, 1938, Vestal; bud long, pointed; flowers dark crimson, semi-dbl., cupped; foliage leathery; vigorous growth; [Harvard × David O. Dodd]

Senator McNaughton T, w, 1895 or before, California Nursery Co.; flowers creamy white, large, full; foliage glossy; [sport of Perle des Jardins]

Senbatsuru HT, w, Hiroshima; int. by Hiroshima Bara-en, 1994

Send in the Clowns HWich, mp, Clements, John; flowers candy pink, small to medium, dbl., borne in clusters; foliage dark green, glossy; vigorous (12 ft.) growth; int. in 1997

Seneca Queen HT, pb, 1965, Boerner; flowers apricot-pink, reverse darker, 6 in., 50 petals, high-centered, moderate fragrance; foliage leathery; vigorous growth; PP2629; [((Serenade × unknown) × Fashion) × Golden Masterpiece]; int. by J&P

Sénégal Cl HT, dr, 1944, Mallerin, C.; flowers very dark crimson, aging to brown/black, 3 in., dbl., intense fragrance; recurrent; very vigorous growth; [Guinée × unknown]; int. by A. Meilland

Senff (strain of *R. canina*), lp; almost thornless; growth sometimes used as understock; similar to Kukolinsky, but somewhat more disease-resistant; int. by Senff

Sengodea HT, pb; flowers white with lavender pink edges, dbl., high-centered; int. in 1995

Senhora da Graça HT, rb, Moreira da Silva; flowers red with carmine reflections

Senior HT, rb, 1932, Spanbauer; bud pointed; flowers scarlet-crimson, open, dbl.; foliage thick; long stems; very vigorous growth; [Richmond × Général Jacqueminot]; int. by Hill Floral Products Co.

Senior Prom HT, dp, 1964, Brownell, H.C.; bud long, pointed; flowers China rose pink, 4½ in., 35-40 petals, high-centered, borne singly and several together, slight fragrance; recurrent; foliage abundant, dark green, glossy; prickles several, short, hooked slightly downward, red to brown; stems long, strong; vigorous, upright growth; hips short, globular, smooth, green; PP2521; [Pink Princess × Queen Elizabeth]; int. by Brownell Sub-Zero Roses, 1964

Señor Philippe LCl, m; flowers lilac-pink, center paler, dbl.; vigorous growth

Señora de Bornas HT, mr, 1958, Camprubi, C.; flowers vermilion-red, medium, very dbl., cupped, intense fragrance; foliage glossy; vigorous, upright growth; [J.M. Lopez Pico × Concerto]; int. in 1955

Señora de Carulla F, mr, 1961, Torre Blanca; flowers cerise-red; Gold Medal, Madrid, 1961

Señora Gari HT, yb, 1935, Dot, Pedro; bud long, pointed; flowers deep orange-yellow, very large, dbl., high-centered; sprawling growth; [Mari Dot × Constance]; int. by C-P

Señora Leon de Aujuria HT, ob, 1935, La Florida; flowers orange; foliage glossy; vigorous growth

Señorita F, rb, 1991, Warriner, William A.; flowers orange-red to red on top of petal with a yellow petal base and yellow-tan reverse, medium, full, borne in large clusters, slight fragrance; foliage medium size, dark green, semi-glossy; numerous prickles; upright (75 cm.), bushy growth; [seedling × Matador]; int. by Bear Creek Gardens, 1992

Señorita Carmen Sert HT, yb, 1917, Pernet-Ducher; flowers Indian yellow, shaded pale pink, edged bright carmine, dbl.; [Marquise de Sinéty × unknown]

Señorita de Alvarez HT, mp, 1931, Cant, B. R.; bud long, pointed; flowers glowing salmon, very large, single, cupped; foliage leathery, dark; vigorous growth; Gold Medal, NRS, 1930

Sensass Delbard Cl HT, mr, 1986, Delbard; flowers bright velvety red, 3 in., 28 petals, cupped, borne in small clusters, no fragrance; foliage dark green, glossy; vigorous, climbing (to 10 ft.) growth; [(Danse du Feu × (Orange Triumph × Floradora)) × (Tenor × unknown)]; int. in 1973

Sensation HT, ob, Tracy, Sr.; Daniel L.; bud medium, ovoid; flowers orange blend with peach tones, 5½-6 in., 26-30 petals, high-centered, borne mostly singly, moderate fragrance; foliage large, medium green, leathery; prickles medium to large, thin, downward angle; growth vigorous, bushy, upright (24 in.); PP8355; [Capella × Golden Fantasie]; int. by E.G. Hill, 1992

Sensation HT, mr, 1922, Joseph H. Hill Co.; bud long, pointed; flowers scarlet-crimson, 5 in., 36 petals, open, moderate fragrance; foliage dark green; free, branching growth; [Hoosier Beauty × Premier]

Sensucht F, Noack, Werner; int. in 1978

Sensuous – See **Sensuous Parade**, Min

Sensuous Parade Min, mr, Poulsen; flowers medium red, medium, dbl., no fragrance; growth bushy, 20-40 cm.; int. by Poulsen Roser, 2000

Senta Schmidt Pol, ob, 1930, Schmidt, R.; flowers coppery orange, semi-dbl.; foliage small, soft, light; dwarf growth; [sport of Suzanne Turbat]

Senteur des Iles – See **Fulton MacKay**, HT

Senteur Royale – See **Duftrausch**, HT

Senteur Royale HT, m, Tantau; flowers violet-magenta, 12 cm., very full, cupped, intense fragrance; recurrent; foliage glossy, disease-resistant; compact, upright (60-80 cm.) growth; int. by Rosen Tantau, 2005

Sentimental – See **Eva Gabor**, HT

Sentinel HT, pb, 1934, Clark, A.; flowers velvety cerise, reverse silvery cerise, large, dbl., cupped; foliage glossy; vigorous growth; int. by Wyant

Sentir HT, rb, Christensen; int. in 1998

Sentry HT, dr, 1948, Fletcher; bud long, pointed; flowers clear crimson, 4-5 in., 25 petals; dwarf, compact growth; int. by Tucker

Sentyana Min, m; flowers purple, well-formed, full, high-centered; int. in 1994

Sentyna F, op, 1993, Ilsink, G.P.; flowers light salmon pink, medium, dbl., borne in sprays; foliage medium size, medium green, glossy; few prickles; tall (80 cm.), upright growth; int. by Interplant B.V., 1990

Seppenrade S, ob, Scholle, E.; flowers salmon-orange, large, dbl.; int. in 1970

Seppenrade Elfe HKor, mr, Scholle, E.; flowers crimson, medium, dbl., borne in medium clusters; int. in 1975

September Dawn HT, dy, 2007, Burks, Larry; flowers golden yellow, reverse deep yellow, medium, 4½ in., full, borne mostly solitary; foliage medium size, dark green, semi-glossy; prickles average, slightly recurved, brownish green, moderate; growth upright, medium (50 in.); garden decoration; [unknown × unknown]; int. in 2007

September Days Min, dy, 1978, Saville, F. Harmon; bud pointed; flowers reflexed, micro-mini, 1½ in., 40 petals, high-centered, moderate fragrance; foliage glossy; upright, compact growth; [Rise 'n' Shine × Yellow Jewel]; int. by Days Inn, 1976

September Eighteenth HT, pb, 1991, Williams, J. Benjamin; bud ovoid; flowers shell pink, reverse deep coral pink, aging light pink, medium, dbl., high-centered, borne usually singly or in sprays of 3-4, intense damask fragrance; foliage large, light green, semi-glossy; medium, bushy growth; [Carla × Queen Elizabeth]

September Morn HT, pb, 1913, Dietrich & Turner; flowers flesh-pink, center deeper, large, full, flat, moderate fragrance; recurrent; vigorous growth; [sport of Mme Pierre Euler]

September Mourn F, w, 2003, Meilland International; bud narrow, ovoid; flowers large, very similar to Iceberg, but with better form, 3½ in., 36 petals, cupped, borne in small clusters; recurrent; foliage large, medium green, semi-glossy; few prickles; bushy, medium (3-4 ft.) growth; specimen, hedge, landscape; [(Iceberg × Sunsprite) × Sun Flare]; int. by The Conard-Pyle Co., 2003

September Song Gr, ab, 1981, Buck, Dr. Griffith J.; bud ovoid; flowers apricot-pink, outer petals fading to blush, 28 petals, cupped, borne singly and in clusters of 5-8, moderate fruity fragrance; foliage dark, tinted with copper, semi-glossy, leathery; prickles thin, awl-like; erect, bushy growth; [(Vera Dalton × Prairie Princess) × (Apricot Nectar × Prairie Princess)]; int. by Iowa State University

September Wedding HT, mp, 1964, Schloen, J.; bud ovoid; flowers deep pink, reverse darker, large, dbl., high-centered; foliage dark, glossy; vigorous, tall, compact growth; [sport of Montezuma]; int. by Ellesmere Nursery

Septime HGal, m, about 1845, Calvert; flowers light purple, center petals often white, medium, full

Sequoia HT, ob, 1939, Verschuren-Pechtold; flowers ripe pumpkin-flesh shaded apricot, dbl., globular; foliage leathery, bronze; vigorous growth; int. by Dreer

Sequoia, Climbing Cl HT, ob, 1940, Swim, H.C.; [sport of Sequoia]; int. by Armstrong Nursery

Sequoia Gold Min, my, 1987, Moore, Ralph S.; flowers medium yellow, fading lighter, medium, 30 petals, high-centered, borne usually singly, moderate fruity fragrance; foliage medium size, medium green, glossy; prickles slender, medium, pale green-brown; bushy, spreading growth; hips round, orange; PP6617; [(Little Darling × Lemon Delight) × Gold Badge]; int. in 1986; Rose of the Year, Auckland, NZ, 1995, AOE, ARS, 1987

Sequoia Jewel Min, mr, 1990, Moore, Ralph S.; bud rounded; flowers medium, 33 petals, cupped, borne in sprays of 3-7; foliage medium size, medium green, matte; prickles straight, short, brown; upright, bushy, medium growth; hips round, medium, orange-red; [Sheri Anne × Paul Neyron]; int. by Sequoia Nursery, 1990

Sequoia Ruby Cl Min, mr, 1995, Moore, Ralph S.; flowers cherry red, yellow stamens, 2 in., dbl., cupped, borne in small clusters, no fragrance; recurrent; foliage medium size, dark green, matte; some prickles; tall (5 ft.), arching shrub, upright, bushy spreading growth; [(Little Darling × Yellow Magic) × Floradora]; int. by Sequoia Nursery, 1996

Sequoia Twist Min, yb, 2004, Moore, Ralph S.; flowers yellow/orange, varying in pattern, reverse yellow, 1½-2 in., semi-dbl., borne in small clusters, moderate fragrance; foliage medium size, medium green, semi-glossy; prickles small, straight; growth spreading, medium (15-18 in.); containers, specimen, borders; [sport of Sequoia Gold]; int. by Sequoia Nurs., 2005

Serafina Longa HT, dp, 1933, La Florida; flowers old-rose, heavily veined, well-formed, large; vigorous growth; [Mme Butterfly × Mme Abel Chatenay]

Seraphim – See **Seraphine**, HSet

Seraphine HSet, pb, 1840, Prince Nursery; flowers soft pink, center darker, very dbl.

Serena HT, Lens; int. in 1955

Serena S, mr, Mekdeci; flowers rose red, very full, intense fragrance; free-flowering; foliage glossy; few prickles; tolerates partial shade.; int. in 1996

Serenade HT, ob, 1949, Boerner; bud ovoid; flowers coral-orange, 4-4½ in., 28 petals, cupped, loose, slight fragrance; free-flowering; foliage glossy, leathery; vigorous, upright growth; [Sonata × R.M.S. Queen Mary]; int. by J&P

Serenade LCl, lp, Poulsen; flowers light mauve-pink, 5-8 cm., 15-20 petals, cupped, borne in clusters, no fragrance; recurrent; foliage matte; growth bushy, 150-200 cm.; int. by Poulsen Roser, 2004

Serenata HT, op, Barni, V.; int. in 1998

Serendipity S, ob, 1978, Buck, Dr. Griffith J.; bud ovoid, pointed; flowers orange to buttercup-yellow, 4-5 in., 20-25 petals, cupped, borne in clusters, moderate fragrance; foliage dark green, glossy, leathery; vigorous, upright, spreading, bushy growth; winter hardy; [(Western Sun × Carefree Beauty) × (Apricot Nectar × Prairie Princess)]; int. by Iowa State University

Serendipity F, my, Harkness; flowers canary yellow, large, cupped, borne in clusters, moderate fragrance; recurrent; medium growth; int. by De Boer Roses, 2000

Serene HT, w, 1940, Mallerin, C.; bud long, pointed, light buff; flowers shining silvery white, open, very large, 30-40 petals; foliage sparse, soft; vigorous, upright growth; int. by C-P

Serene Bouquet Min, pb, 1998, Laver, Keith G.; flowers pink with white reverse, 1½-2 in., very dbl., borne in sprays of 5; foliage medium size, medium green, matte; some prickles; upright, vigorous growth; [seedling × Antique Gold]; int. by Springwood Roses, 1998

Serenella HT, 1954, Cazzaniga, F. G.

Serenella '99 Min, dy, Barni; flowers deep lemon yellow, 2 in., 35 petals, borne in clusters of 3-5, no fragrance; recurrent; foliage small; growth to 12-16 in.; int. by Rose Barni, 2000

Serenissima LCl, m, 1981, Takatori, Yoshiho; bud pointed; flowers light lilac, 38 petals, intense fragrance; recurrent bloom; foliage large, light green, matte; prickles straight, reddish-green; upright growth; int. by Rose Barni-Pistoia, 1980

Serenissima – See **Cotillion**, F, 1999

Sérénité HT, my, 1946, Gaujard; bud pointed; flowers chrome-yellow, large; foliage reddish; stiff stems; very vigorous growth; RULED EXTINCT 7/86

Sérénité HT, my, 1987, Gaujard, Jean; flowers coppery-yellow, dbl., high-centered, borne singly, intense fragrance; foliage large, medium green; prickles large; tall growth; rounded fruit; [John Armstrong × Tanagra]; int. in 1980

Sérénité St. Michel F, my, Adam; int. by Pep. de la Guerinais, 2000

Serenity S, lp, 2000, Brown, Ted; flowers semi-dbl., borne in large clusters, moderate fragrance; foliage large, dark green, dull; prickles moderate; growth upright, tall (6-7 ft.); [Esprit × seedling]

Serenity F, lp, Snetsinger; [sport of Playgirl]

Serezo F, lp, Kakujitsu; int. in 1997

Serge Basset HT, dr, 1918, Pernet-Ducher; flowers brilliant garnet-red, dbl.

Sergeant Pepper Min, or, 1992, W. Kordes Söhne; flowers large, semi-dbl., borne in small clusters, no fragrance; free-flowering; foliage small, dark green, glossy; some prickles; low (45-60 cm.), upright, bushy, spreading growth; [seedling × LAVglut]; int. by Bear Creek Gardens, 1992

Sergent Ulmann HT, dr, 1930, Mallerin, C.; bud long, pointed; flowers deep garnet, lightened with scarlet, open, very large, semi-dbl.; foliage leathery, bronze; vigorous growth; [Grenoble × Mme Van de Voorde]

Serin – See **Luteola**, HFt

Serpent Rose S, mp, 2000, Lens, Louis; flowers single, borne in small clusters, moderate fragrance; non-recurrent; foliage small, light green, glossy; prickles moderate; growth spreading, low; groundcover; [Serpent Vert × Ballerina]; int. by Louis Lens N.V., 1994

Serpent Vert – See **Green Snake**, S

Serratipetala Ch, pb, 1831, Jacques; flowers medium, petals fringed, outer crimson, inner pink, full, flat, slight fragrance; recurrent; stems red-green, smooth; probably introduced by Jacques in 1831, but lost for many years and reintroduced by Vilfroy, 1912

Seseragi HT, m, Hiroshima; int. by Hiroshima Bara-en, 1996

Set of Gold HT, yb, Delbard; int. in 1994

Setina Cl HCh, lp, 1879, Henderson; flowers silvery-rose, medium, full, globular, moderate fragrance; varies considerably; [sport of Hermosa]; int. by P. Henderson

Setsuko HT, w, 1999, Sasaki, Keiji; flowers cream white, blended red in petal edge, 5 in., 37 petals; foliage dark green, half leathery; growth to 4½ ft.; [Marchenkonigin × Hakuchoh]; int. in 1996

Seven Seas F, m, 1972, Harkness; flowers lilac, wavy, stamens powder yellow, 4 in., 26 petals, shallow cup, moderate Tea-Damask fragrance; recurrent; foliage large, glossy; [Lilac Charm × Sterling Silver]; int. in 1971

Seven Sisters HMult, pb, 1815; flowers pale rose to mauve-purple, varying considerably in size and petalage, borne in clusters of 8-30, moderate fragrance; non-remontant; foliage somewhat rugose; vigorous, tall growth; possibly a natural cross of *R. multiflora carnea* and *R. rugosa*; sent from China to Charles Greville of London in 1815

Seven Sisters Rose – See **Seven Sisters**, HMult

Seventeen F, pb, 1960, Boerner; bud ovoid; flowers pink-coral, large, 20-25 petals, cupped, borne in pyramidal clusters, intense fragrance; foliage dark, leathery; vigorous, upright growth; PP1765; [(Pinocchio × unknown) × Fashion seedling]; int. by J&P, 1959

Seventh Heaven HT, dr, 1966, Armstrong, D.L. & Swim, H. C.; flowers large, dbl., high-centered; foliage glossy; upright, bushy growth; PP2832; [seedling × Chrysler Imperial]; int. by Armstrong Nursery

Seventh Heaven HT, ob, Fryer; flowers apricot orange, mid-sized, dbl., moderate fragrance; repeats well; foliage glossy, dark green; vigorous, bushy (3 ft. × 2 ft.) growth; int. by Fryer's Roses, 2004

Séverine HT, rb, 1918, Pernet-Ducher; flowers coral-red, passing to shrimp-red, semi-dbl.; foliage bronze; vigorous growth

Severn Vale HT, ob, 1967, Sanday, John; flowers salmon, 4½ in., high-centered; free growth; [sport of Beauté]

Sevillana – See **La Sevillana**, F

Sevilliana S, pb, 1976, Buck, Dr. Griffith J.; bud ovoid, pointed; flowers light claret-rose, stippled red, yellow from base, 3½-4 in., 15 petals, cupped, moderate spicy fragrance; recurrent; foliage tinted copper, leathery; upright, bushy growth; [(Vera Dalton × Dornroschen) × ((World's Fair × Floradora) × Applejack)]; int. by Iowa State University

Sexy Rexy F, mp, 1985, McGredy, Sam IV; bud pointed, ovoid to ovoid globular with conspicuous neck; flowers creamy medium to light pink, medium, 39 -51 petals, cupped, borne in large clusters, slight fragrance; good repeat; foliage small, light green, glossy; prickles several, medium, hooked slightly downward, yellow-green; stems medium; compact, upright, bushy growth; hips globular, smooth, bright orange; PP6713; [Seaspray × Dreaming]; int. by McGredy Roses International, 1984; Golden Prize, Glasgow, 1989, Rose of the Year, Auckland, NZ, 1991, Gold Star of the South Pacific, Palmerston North, NZ, 1984, Gold Medal, Portland, 1990

Sfinge HT, rb, 1954, Aicardi, D.; flowers deep red edged rose; long stems; vigorous, upright growth; [Julien Potin × Sensation]; int. by Giacomasso

Shabnam F, w, 1976, IARI; bud ovoid; flowers white, center pinkish, open, 2 in., 85 petals; foliage soft; upright, open growth; [Baby Sylvia × unknown]; int. in 1975

Shades of Autumn HT, rb, 1943, Brownell; flowers red to pink with some yellow, center yellow, large, dbl., intense fragrance; free-flowering; foliage glossy, leathery; vigorous, compact, upright, bushy growth; [Golden Glow × Condesa de Sástago]

Shades of Pink F, pb, 1985, Mander, George; flowers pink with white eye, imbricated, large, 33 petals, borne in large clusters, no fragrance; foliage medium green, glossy; prickles curved, hooked; bushy, upright growth; [Robin Hood × Pascali]

Shadow HT, dr, Dawson; flowers black red, medium, dbl.; stems long; medium growth; int. in 1966

Shadow Dance F, rb, 1969, Fankhauser; bud ovoid; flowers silver-pink edged red, small, 30-35 petals; foliage glossy, leathery; vigorous, low, compact growth; [Pink Parfait × Crimson Glory]

Shadow Dancer LCl, pb, 1999, Moore, Ralph S.; bud very pointed to somewhat ovoid; flowers striped, swirled two-tone pink, 3½-4 in., 14-18 petals, cupped, borne usually in large clusters, sometimes singly, slight fruity fragrance; recurrent; foliage medium size, dark green, holly-like; prickles moderate, straight, angled downward; stems medium to long; climbing, tall (8-10 ft.) growth; hips globular ; PP11089; [(Dortmund × unknown) × Dortmund]; int. by Weeks Roses, 1998

Shady Charmer Min, yb, 1990, Williams, Michael C.; bud ovoid; flowers light yellow base with light pink edges, aging cream, medium, 43 petals, high-centered, slight spicy fragrance; foliage medium size, dark green, semi-glossy; prickles straight, very few, small,lightgreen; bushy, medium growth; no fruit; [Party Girl × Anita Charles]; int. by The Rose Garden & Mini Rose Nursery, 1990

Shady Flame Min, or, 1981, Jolly, Betty J.; flowers 35 petals, high-centered, borne usually singly; foliage small, light green; prickles straight; compact, bushy growth; [Prominent × Zinger]; int. by Rosehill Farm

Shady Lady Min, dy, 1981, Jolly, Betty J.; flowers yellow-orange, 35 petals, high-centered, borne mostly singly; foliage tiny, green; no prickles; upright, bushy growth; [(Prominent × Zinger) × Puppy Love]; int. by Rosehill Farm

Shady Lady – See **Lutin**, S

Shady Lane HT, pb, 1990, Bridges, Dennis A.; bud ovoid; flowers deep pink to white base, aging deeper pink, large, 35 petals, high-centered, borne usually singly, intense damask fragrance; foliage medium size, dark green, semi-glossy; prickles medium, pointed downwards, light green; upright, medium growth; [Thriller × Just Lucky]; int. by Bridges Roses

Shafter – See **Dr Huey**, HWich

Shaida HT, or, 1979, Lens, Louis; bud long, pointed; flowers red-orange-salmon, 3½-4½ in., 28-32 petals, high-centered, borne 3-7 per cluster, slight fragrance; recurrent; foliage dark green, leathery; prickles triangular; vigorous, upright growth; [(Fandango × Fillette) × Coloranja]; int. by Louis Lens, 1976

Shailer's Provence C, lp, before 1799, Shailer; flowers lilac-pink, base white, inner petals rolled and wrinkled, dbl., cupped, often borne in clusters of 2 or 3, moderate fragrance; foliage small; vigorous (4-5 ft.), branching growth; [*R. centifolia* × R. *lheritieranea*]

Shailer's White Moss M, w, 1788, Shailer; flowers flesh white, center darker, large, dbl., cupped; [sport of Common Moss]; very often confused with White Bath, and probably mixed in commerce

Shakespeare – See **Kean**, HGal

Shakespeare Festival Min, my, 1979, Moore, Ralph S.; bud long, pointed; flowers clear yellow, 1½ in., 35-45 petals, high-centered, borne singly and several together, moderate tea fragrance; recurrent; foliage medium green, matte; prickles average, slender, hooked downward, brown; stems slender, wiry; bushy, compact (12-14 in.) growth; hips apple-shaped ; PP4656; [Golden Angel × Golden Angel]; int. by Sequoia Nursery

Shakespeare Garden Eglantine HEg, w; flowers white with yellow stamens, single, moderate fragrance; non-remontant; chance seedling found in the old Shakespeare Garden at the Huntington

Shakira HT, dp, Meilland; flowers fuchsia-pink, full, high-centered, borne mostly singly; recurrent; cut flower rose.; int. by Meilland Intl., 2004

Shaleen Surtie-Richards HT, op, Taschner, Ludwig; flowers coral-pink, large, dbl., borne mostly singly, intense fragrance; recurrent; medium growth; [sport of Electron]; int. by Ludwig's Roses, 1996

Shalimar HWich, yb, 1914, Burrell; flowers creamy blush, picotee edge of bright rose-pink, medium, dbl., borne in very large clusters; occasional autumn repeat; vigorous, climbing growth; [sport of Minnehaha]

Shalimar HT, pb, Ghosh, Mr. & Mrs. S.; flowers large, dbl., high-centered; int. in 1998

Shalom F, or, 1978, Poulsen, Niels D.; bud globular; flowers 3½-4 in., 23 petals, no fragrance; foliage dark green, glossy; vigorous, bushy, upright (150-200 cm.) growth; [(Korona × unknown) × (Korona × unknown)]; int. by Poulsen, 1973

Shandon HT, dr, 1899, Dickson, A.; flowers deep carmine, center lighter, large, dbl., intense fragrance

Shanghai Autumn HT, yb; flowers medium yellow, edges shaded pink; free-flowering

Shanghai Princess HCh, lp, Clements, John; flowers soft pink, small; recurrent; foliage dark green; rounded, bushy (2½ ft.) growth; int. in 1993

Shangri-La HT, mp, 1945, Howard, F.H.; bud long, pointed; flowers silvery pink, open, 3½-4½ in., 35 petals; foliage leathery; long stems; very vigorous, upright, bushy growth; [Mrs J.D. Eisele × Pres. Herbert Hoover]; int. by H&S

Shania HT, dp, Delbard; flowers bright cerise pink, large, full, high-centered, borne mostly singly; recurrent; stems long; tall, strong growth; int. by Ludwig's Roses, 2005

Shankar Jaikishan HT, rb, 2005, Shastri, N.V.; flowers red, reverse light red turning silvery, 4½ in., very full, borne mostly solitary, no fragrance; foliage medium size, dark green, matte; prickles medium, crooked; upright, medium (40 in.) growth; garden decoration, exhibition; [Captain Harry Stebbings × Christian Dior]; int. by N.V.Shastri, 1997

Shannie Min, pb, 1997, Giles, Diann; flowers medium, very dbl., borne mostly singly; foliage medium size, medium green, semi-glossy; upright, medium (2½ ft.) growth; [Little Darling × Magic Carrousel]; int. by Giles Rose Nursery

Shannon HT, mp, 1965, McGredy, Sam IV; bud ovoid, pointed; flowers rosy-pink, reverse slightly darker, 5 in., 58 petals, high-centered, borne singly; recurrent; foliage large, dark green, semi-glossy, rounded; prickles large, slightly hooked, red to tan; stems stout, erect; vigorous, upright (4-5 ft.), spreading growth; PP2919; [Queen Elizabeth × McGredy's Yellow]; int. by McGredy

Shantaraj HT, dr, K&S; flowers large, full, high-centered, intense tea fragrance; int. in 1998

Shanthi Pal HT, op, Pal, Dr. B.P.; flowers salmon, touched coral, large, dbl., high-centered; int. in 1989

Shanti HT, rb, Tantau; flowers bright red, white reverse, medium, dbl., high-centered, borne mostly singly; good repeat; stems medium to long; florist rose; int. by Rosen Tantau, 2002

Shantung F, pb, 1989, Delbard & Chabert; flowers mottled pink, cream and red, large, 22 petals, flat; foliage matte; vigorous growth; [(Orléans Rose × Goldilocks) × (Bordure Rose × unknown)]; int. in 1988

Shantung Yellow Ch, my, before 1867; virtually identical to Marechal Niel

Shanty – See **Shanti**, HT

Sharada Gr, lp, 1985, Gupta, Dr. M.N., Datta, Dr. S.K. & Nath, P.; [sport of Queen Elizabeth]; int. by National Botanical Research Institute, 1983

Shari HT, pb, 1992, Perry, Astor; flowers lighter than Swarthmore, petals do not burn, large, full, slight fragrance; foliage medium size, medium green, matte; upright (185 cm.) growth; [sport of Sweetie Pie]; flowers, growth and foliage same as Swarthmore, flower color lighter; int. by Hortico Roses, 1993

Sharifa – See **Sharifa Asma**, S

Sharifa Asma S, lp, 1995, Austin, David; bud rounded; flowers blush pink, fading to almost white on outer petals, 3-4 in., 90 petals, cupped, then rosette, borne singly and in small clusters, moderate fruity (white grapes and mulberry) fragrance; recurrent; foliage dark green, semi-glossy; numerous prickles; bushy, upright (3 ft.) growth; hips none ; PP8143; [Mary Rose × Admired Miranda]; int. by David Austin Roses, Ltd., 1989

Sharon HT, lp, 1962, Spandikow; bud long, pointed; flowers soft pink edged lighter, base light yellow, reverse darker pink, 5½ in., 35-40 petals, high-centered; foliage leathery, dull; vigorous, upright growth; PP2232; [Golden Rapture × Happiness]

Sharon Anne F, ob, 1993, Bossom, W.E.; flowers orange salmon, medium, dbl., borne in large clusters; foliage large, medium green, semi-glossy; few prickles; tall to medium (120 cm.), upright growth; [Sharon Lorraine × Brown Velvet]; int. by Bossom, 1993

Sharon Frances HT, pb, 1999, Poole, Lionel; flowers light pink blending to peach center, 5½-6 in., full, borne mostly singly, slight fragrance; foliage large, dark green, glossy; some prickles; upright, tall (3 ft.) growth; [Tom Foster × Ravenswood Village]

Sharon Lorraine F, rb, 1981, Bossom, W.E.; bud pointed; flowers ivory yellow, aging red, reverse red, full, borne 30-36 per cluster; foliage dark, semi-glossy; prickles long, red; medium, upright (2-2½ ft.) growth; [seedling × seedling]; int. in 1978

Sharon Louise HT, w, 1968, Parkes, Mrs M.H.; bud ovoid; flowers near white, center pale pink, medium, dbl., slight fragrance; foliage dark, leathery; vigorous, tall, bushy growth; [Queen Elizabeth × Virgo]

Sharon Marie HT, rb, 2006, Saffell, Jack C.; flowers white edged magenta, reverse white, 5 in., full, borne mostly solitary; foliage large, dark green, semi-glossy; prickles , facing downward, copper-bronze, moderate; growth upright, medium (5 ft.); exhibition, garden decorative; [Lynn Anderson × Sheer Elegance]; int. in 2006

Sharon Muxlow Min, op, 1980, Dobbs; bud globular; flowers bright coppery orange, 1 in., 25 petals, flat; foliage leathery; upright growth; [Anytime × Persian Princess]; int. by Min. Plant Kingdom

Sharon's Delight S, w, 1996, Moore, Ralph S.; flowers pure white, yellow stamens, 3½ in., single, shallow cup, borne in small clusters; free-flowering; foliage medium size, medium green, semi-glossy; few prickles; bushy, medium (2-3 ft.) growth; [Golden Angel × Safrano]; int. by Sequoia Nursery, 1996

Sharon's Love S, lp, 2000, Lens, Louis; flowers pale pink, reverse lighter, red stamens, petals wavy, 4 in., single, flat, borne in small clusters, slight fragrance; recurrent; foliage medium size, medium green, semi-glossy; prickles moderate; growth upright, medium (120-150 cm.); [Rudolf Timm × Maria-Mathilda]; int. by Louis Lens N.V., 1998

Shasta F, w, 1962, Schwartz, Ernest W.; bud pointed; flowers 4 in., 20-25 petals, open, borne in clusters, moderate fragrance; free-flowering; foliage leathery; vigorous, bushy growth; [Paul's Lemon Pillar × Fashion]; int. by Wyant, 1962

Shatadhara F, mp, Chiplunkar; flowers rose pink, yellow stamens, flat, borne in large clusters; int. in 1991

She F, or, 1962, Dickson, Patrick; flowers salmon-opal, base lemon, 2½ in., 19 petals, borne in clusters; moderate, bushy growth; [(Independence × Fashion) × Brownie]; int. by A. Dickson & Sons, 1962

Shearer's Delight HRg, m, Sutherland; int. by Golden Vale Nursery, 2002

Sheelagh Baird Pol, pb, 1934, Cant, F.; flowers shell-pink, overlaid rich rose pink, base yellow, large, dbl., borne in large trusses; vigorous growth

Sheena F. Gordon HT, dy, 2000, Rawlins, R.; flowers 3 in., full, borne in small clusters, slight fragrance;

foliage medium size, medium green, glossy; prickles 1 cm., triangular, moderate; growth upright, medium (3 ft.); garden decorative; [Golden Quill × Lichtkonigin Lucia]

Sheer Bliss HT, w, 1985, Warriner, William A.; flowers white with pink center, large, 35 petals, high-centered, borne singly, moderate spicy fragrance; foliage medium size, medium green, matte; prickles medium brown; medium, upright, bushy growth; PP6282; [White Masterpiece × Grand Masterpiece]; int. by J&P, 1987; Gold Medal, Japan, 1984

Sheer Delight F, or, 1992, Harkness, R., & Co., Ltd.; flowers vermilion, small, dbl., borne in large clusters, no fragrance; free-flowering; foliage small, light green, semi-glossy; few prickles; low (40 cm.), bushy growth; patio; [Bobby Dazzler × Little Prince]; int. by Harkness New Roses, Ltd., 1991

Sheer Elegance HT, op, 1990, Twomey, Jerry; bud pointed; flowers soft creamy pink with dark pink edges, 4½ in., 30-35 petals, high-centered, borne singly, moderate musk fragrance; good repeat; foliage large, dark green, glossy; prickles slightly curved, red with green; stems long; upright, tall (5 ft.) growth; hips pear-shaped, yellow-orange; PP7901; [Pristine × Fortuna]; int. by DeVor Nurseries, Inc., 1990; Gold Medal, Portland, 1994

Sheer Elegance, Climbing Cl HT, op, 1995, deVor, Bill; flowers pink blend, 3-3½ in., full, slight fragrance; foliage large, dark green, semi-glossy; few prickles; tall (315-345cm.), upright, branching growth; [sport of Sheer Elegance]; int. by DeVor Nursery, 1994

Sheer Grace HT, pb, Patil, B.K.; flowers pink with white stripes and streaks; [sport of Sheer Bliss]; int. by Icospin, 1995

Sheer Magic HT, ob, 2007, Zary, Keith W.; flowers coral-red and cream blend, reverse coral-orange and cream blend, 4-4½ in., full, blooms borne mostly solitary; foliage medium size, dark green, glossy; prickles 8-10 mm., hooked downward, greyed-orange, moderate; growth upright, medium (5 ft.); [Sheer Elegance × Color Magic]; int. by Jackson & Perkins Wholesale, Inc., 2007

Sheer Stripes S, pb, 1999, Lowe, Malcolm; flowers dark pink and white stripes, 3 in., single, shallow cup to flat, borne in small clusters, slight fragrance; recurrent; foliage medium size, medium green, semi-glossy; few prickles; upright, tall (6 ft.) growth; [Hurdy Gurdy × Heritage]

Sheerwater HT, ly, 1977, Plumpton, E.; flowers beige to cream, veined carmine, 5 in., 35 petals; foliage dark, matte green; free growth; [My Choice × Premier Bal]

Sheffield Pride Min, mp, 1994, Webster, Robert; flowers medium, very dbl., borne in small clusters; foliage small, dark green, semi-glossy; some prickles; low, compact growth; [Robin Red Breast × Matangi]; int. by Handley Rose Nurseries, 1995

Sheila HT, mp, 1895, Dickson, A.

Sheila Pol, op, 1930, Walsh, J.; flowers orange-salmon flowers; int. by Beckwith

Sheila Bellair HT, op, 1937, Clark, A.; bud long, pointed; flowers salmon-pink, large, semi-dbl., cupped, moderate fragrance; recurrent; foliage rich green, leathery; bushy (4 ft.) growth; [Miss Mocatta × unknown]; int. by NRS Victoria

Sheila Fleming Gr, mp, 1995, Fleming, Joyce L.; flowers medium pink with darker edges, prominent stamens, medium, 5 petals, flat, borne 15-20 per cluster, moderate fragrance; recurrent; foliage medium size, medium green, matte; upright (120 cm.), bushy growth; [Märchenland × Montezuma]; int. by Hortico Roses, 1994; 1st prize, Unnamed Seedling, Toronto Show, 1992

Sheila MacQueen F, w, 1988, R. Harkness & Co., Ltd.; flowers chartreuse green with apricot tint at certain seasons, medium, 24 petals, cupped, borne in sprays of 3-9, slight peppery fragrance; foliage medium size, medium green, semi-glossy; prickles broad, straight, green; upright, medium growth; hips rounded, medium, green; [Greensleeves × Letchworth Garden City]; int. by R. Harkness & Co, 1988

Sheila MacQueen F, lp, Harkness; flowers shell pink, fading to blush as petals open, dbl., cupped, borne in clusters, moderate fragrance; recurrent; moderate (2½-3 ft.) growth; often confused with Harwotnext, also named Sheila MacQueen; int. by R. Harkness & Co., 1994

Sheila Mitchell HT, yb, 1998, Mitchell, Harold V.; flowers yellow shading to pink, reverse lemon yellow, 5 in., 41 petals, high-centered, borne mostly singly; foliage large, medium green, semi-glossy; prickles moderate; compact, medium (3 ft.) growth; [Trumpeter × Grandpa Dickson]; int. by Nicholas Maple, 2000

Sheila Sorensen HT, mp, 2005, Paul Chessum Roses; flowers 7 cm., full, borne mostly solitary, moderate fragrance; recurrent; foliage medium size, medium green, semi-glossy; prickles moderate, medium size; growth upright, medium (80 cm.); bedding, garden decorative; [seedling × seedling]; int. by Love4Plants Ltd, 2004

Sheila Wilson HT, mr, 1910, Hall; flowers light scarlet; vigorous growth; int. by A. Dickson

Sheila's Perfume F, yb, 1982, Sheridan, John; flowers yellow, petals edged red, 4-5 in., 20-25 petals, high-centered, borne mostly singly, intense sweet fragrance; recurrent; foliage medium size, dark green, semi-glossy; medium, bushy growth; [Peer Gynt × (Daily Sketch × (Paddy McGredy × Prima Ballerina))]; int. by Harkness New Roses, Ltd., 1985; Gold Star of the South Pacific, Palmerston North, NZ, 1993, Gamble Fragrance Medal, ARS, 2005, Edland Fragrance Medal, ARS, 1991

Shelby Wallace Cl Pol, op, 1929, Moore, Ralph S.; flowers light salmon-pink, small, semi-dbl.; [Cécile Brunner, Climbing × unknown]

Sheldon's Honor HT, w, 1995, Sheldon, John & Robin; flowers full, borne in small clusters, slight fragrance; foliage medium size, medium green, matte; upright, medium growth; [Sheer Bliss × Anastasia]

Shell Beach Min, w, 1983, Thomas Robinson, Ltd.; bud soft pink; flowers creamy white, 28 petals, borne in clusters; foliage small, medium green, semi-glossy; bushy growth; [Simon Robinson × Simon Robinson]

Shell-Pink Radiance – See **Mrs Charles J. Bell**, HT

Shell Queen Gr, lp, 1961, Allen, L.C.; flowers shell pink, fading white; [sport of Queen Elizabeth]

Shellbrook Pink HRg, mp; int. by Russian Roses for the North, 2003

Shellbrook Rose (form of *R. acicularis*), dr; long, bottle-shaped fruit

Shelley Higgins HT, ab, 1998, Reynolds, Ted; flowers apricot-peach blend, dbl., high-centered, borne mostly singly, intense spicy fragrance; foliage medium size, medium green, semi-glossy; some prickles; upright, medium growth; [Westerland × seedling]; int. by Ted Reynolds Roses International, 1998

Shelly HT, pb, 1988, Melville Nurseries Pty., Ltd.; flowers pale pink with cyclamen-pink shading, reverse flecked and striped with pink-silver, large, 20-25 petals, decorative, borne in sprays of 5-6, slight sweet fragrance; foliage dark green, glossy, disease-resistant; prickles slightly hooked, beige-cream; medium growth; [sport of Francine]

Shelly Renee Min, pb, 1989, Saville, F. Harmon; bud medium, ovate; flowers shrimp pink, reverse peach, aging light pink to white, 1 in., 35 -38 petals, cupped, to flat, borne in clusters, slight fragrance; recurrent; foliage small, dark green, semi-glossy; prickles average, long, thin, slanted slightly downwards, olive green; vigorous, compact (12-14 in.) growth; PP6952; [sport of Spice Drop]; int. by Nor'East Min. Roses, 1989

Shenandoah LCl, dr, 1935, Nicolas; bud long, pointed; flowers crimson, large, semi-dbl., high-centered, intense fragrance; foliage large, glossy; vigorous, climbing (10 ft.) growth; [Étoile de Hollande × Schoener's Nutkana]; int. by C-P

Shenandoah – See **Everglades**, F

Shenandoah MinFl, dr, 2006, Bridges, Dennis A.; flowers dark red, reverse lighter, 2¼ in., dbl, high-centered, borne mostly solitary, moderate slightly sweet fragrance; recurrent; foliage medium size, dark green, semi-glossy, disease-resistant; prickles moderate, ¼ in., curved slightly downward, tan; growth upright, medium (24-28 in.); garden, exhibition, containers, cutting; [Dr. John Dickman × Miss Flippins]; int. by Bridges Roses, 2006

Shepherdess F, yb, 1967, Mattock; flowers yellow flushed salmon, 3½-4 in., dbl., borne in clusters; foliage dark, glossy, leathery; vigorous growth; [Allgold × Peace]

Shepherd's Delight F, rb, 1958, Dickson, A.; flowers flame and yellow, 3 in., 15 petals, borne in trusses, slight fragrance; foliage dark green; vigorous growth; [(Masquerade × unknown) × Joanna Hill]; int. by A. Dickson & Sons, 1957; Gold Medal, NRS, 1958

Shepherd's Oriole – See **Golden Oriole**, T

Sherbert Fizz S, lp; flowers dbl., borne in clusters; foliage glossy; compact (2 ft.) growth; int. by Paul Chessum Roses, 2003

Sherbet Fizz – See **Sherbert Fizz**, S dbl.

Sheri Anne Min, or, 1975, Moore, Ralph S.; bud long, pointed; flowers orange-red, base yellow, 1-1½ in., 17-20 petals, cupped, flowers borne singly or several together, moderate sweet fragrance; recurrent; foliage glossy, leathery; prickles few, medium, hooked slightly downward, brown; upright, bushy growth; hips numerous, fairly large ; PP3826; [Little Darling × New Penny]; int. by Sequoia Nursery, 1973; AOE, ARS, 1975

Sheridan Pink F, dp; int. in 1998

Sheriskep – See **Mary May**, F

Sherlock Holmes S, lp, Hortico; flowers soft lavender-pink, fading to white, semi-dbl. to dbl., open cup, slight fragrance; recurrent; moderate (3 ft.) growth; int. by Hortico, Inc., 2006

Sheroo HT, mr, Shastri, Dr. N.V.; flowers flower bright, medium red, large, dbl., high-centered; [Pristine × Swarthmore]; int. in 2002

Sherrill Anne S, pb, 1999, Byrnes, Robert; flowers blush pink, reverse medium pink, 4 in., 41 petals; foliage medium size, medium green, semi-glossy; few prickles; upright, medium (4-5 ft.) growth; [Country Dancer × Country Dancer]; int. by Overbrooke Gardens, 1999

Sherry F, r, 1960, McGredy, Sam IV; flowers dark sherry color, coppery-orange to terracotta, 2½ in., 14 petals, borne in clusters, slight fragrance; foliage dark green; vigorous growth; [Independence × Orange Sweetheart]; int. by McGredy & Son, 1960

Sherry Parks Sunrise MinFl, ab, 2005, Jalbert, Brad; flowers apricot, sometimes with slight salmon veining, 2½-3 in., very full, old-fashioned, borne in small clusters, slight fragrance; foliage medium green, glossy; prickles medium, pointed, green, moderate; growth bushy, medium (20 in. or more); [Graduation Day × Fellowship]; int. by Select Roses, 2005

Sherwood F, my, Harkness; flowers citron yellow, very dbl., moderate spicy fragrance; int. in 1999

Shi Tz-mei – See **Crimson Rambler**, HMult

Shi-un HT, m, 1985, Suzuki, Seizo; flowers deep lilac purple, reverse deeper, 30-35 petals, high-centered, borne usually singly, moderate sweet fragrance; foliage dark, leathery, semi-glossy; prickles slanted downward; vigorous, upright, bushy growth; [(Blue Moon × Twilight) × (Red American Beauty × Happiness)]; int. by Keisei Rose Nursery, 1984

Shigyoku HGal, m; int. before 1883

Shii Yan Fueh HCh, mp

Shikibu HT, m, Hiroshima; int. by Hiroshima Bara-en, 1999

Shiko HT, m, Keisei; int. by Keisei Rose Nurseries, 1993

Shiloh Hill Rose F, rb, 2005, Jalbert, Brad; flowers red, reverse silver-white, 2-3 in., full, borne in large clusters, no fragrance; foliage medium size, dark green, glossy; prickles medium, pointed, reddish, moderate; growth bushy, medium (2½-3 ft.); [Thelma's Glory × Glad Tiding's]; int. by Select Roses, 2006

Shimmering Dawn F, mp, 1965, Verschuren; bud rose-pink; flowers blush-pink, 3 in., borne in clusters; foliage dark, glossy; very vigorous growth

Shimmering Silk HT, rb, 1968, Barter; flowers cerise tinted silvery pink, large, dbl.; foliage dark; vigorous, upright growth; [Ena Harkness × Molly Doyle]

Shimsha HT, pb, Kasturi; int. in 1976

Shin-sei HT, dy, 1978, Suzuki, Seizo; bud pointed; flowers well-formed, large, 35-45 petals, high-centered, borne singly, moderate fragrance; recurrent; foliage medium large, medium green, glossy; prickles slanted downward; upright, bushy growth; [(Ethel Sanday × Lydia) × Koto]; int. by Keisei Rose Nursery, 1979

Shin-Setsu LCl, w, 1974, Suzuki, Seizo; bud ovoid; flowers white, center soft cream, large, very dbl., high-centered, moderate fragrance; foliage glossy, dark; very vigorous, climbing growth; [(Blanche Mallerin × Neige Parfum) × (New Dawn × unknown)]; int. by Keisei Rose Nursery, 1969

Shine On Min, op, 1999, Dickson, Colin; flowers nasturtium red, reverse azalea pink, 2½ in., dbl., cupped, borne in small clusters; free-flowering; foliage small, medium green, semi-glossy; prickles moderate; compact, low (22 in.) growth; [Sweet Magic × seedling]; int. by Dickson Nurseries, Ltd., 1994

Shiner – See **Aberdeen**, S

Shining Coral HT, pb, 1992, Davidson, Harvey D.; flowers coral pink, 4 in., 22-24 petals, cupped, borne singly and in small clusters, moderate fruity fragrance; foliage large, dark green, very glossy; medium, bushy growth; [Shining Ruby × (Honey Favorite × (Little Darling × Traviata))]; int. by C & L Valley Rose Co., 1992

Shining Flare HT, or, 1992, Davidson, Harvey D.; bud ovoid; flowers 4½ in., 22-26 petals, cupped, borne in sprays, slight fruity fragrance; foliage medium size, dark green, very glossy; prickles sharp pointed, slight downward curvature; bushy, upright, medium growth; PP8911; [Shining Ruby × (Smooth Sailing × Futura)]; int. by C & L Valley Rose Co., 1992

Shining Hope – See **Our Lady of Guadalupe**, F

Shining Hour Gr, dy, 1990, Warriner, William A.; bud short, pointed ovoid; flowers deep, bright yellow, 4 in., 30-35 petals, high-centered, borne singly and in sprays, moderate fruity fragrance; recurrent; foliage large, dark green, semi-glossy; prickles fairly long, hooked downward, red to yellow; stems medium, strong; upright, bushy, medium growth; PP7949; [Sunbright × Sun Flare]; int. by Bear Creek Gardens, 1991

Shining Light F, ab, 2000, Cocker, A.G.; flowers apricot, reverse golden, 1 in., dbl., cupped, borne in large clusters, slight fragrance; free-flowering; foliage small, medium green, glossy; prickles moderate; growth bushy, medium (2 ft.); patio; [Prima Ballerina × Ohshima Rose]; int. by James Cocker & Sons, 2000

Shining Rose – See ***R. nitida*** (Willdenow)

Shining Ruby HT, mr, 1992, Davidson, Harvey D.; flowers medium red, fading to blue, 5½ in., 24-26 petals, cupped, borne in sprays, moderate spicy fragrance; foliage large, dark green, very glossy; bushy, medium growth; [Pink Favorite × Simon Bolivar]; int. by C & L Valley Rose Co., 1992

Shining Star HT, my, 1945, Mallerin, C.; bud long, pointed; flowers vivid chrome-yellow, large, dbl., moderate fruity fragrance; foliage dark, leathery; [Soeur Thérèse × Feu Pernet-Ducher]; int. by C-P

Shining Star – See **Tulsa**, HT

Shining Sun – See **Mrs Paul Goudie**, HT

Shining Sun HT, yb, 1932, Van Rossem; bud long, pointed, golden yellow splashed scarlet; flowers yellow deepening to reddish center, dbl.; foliage thick, bronze; vigorous growth; [Charles P. Kilham × Julien Potin]

Shinju HT, lp, 1986, Harada, Toshiyuki; bud large, ovoid; flowers light pink, paler at petal edges, large, 28 petals, high-centered, borne singly or in small clusters, moderate fragrance; foliage medium green, leathery; prickles numerous, medium, slanted downward; vigorous, upright growth; [Royal Highness × Garden Party]; int. in 1976

Shinjugai F, w; int. by Keisei Rose Nurseries, 2004

Shinsei – See **Shin-sei**, HT

Shirakawa HT, w; int. by Keihan Gardening, 1995

Shiralee HT, yb, 1965, Dickson, Patrick; flowers yellow flushed orange, 5½ in., 36 petals, high-centered, moderate fragrance; vigorous, tall growth; [seedling × Kordes' Perfecta]; int. by A. Dickson; Gold Medal, Japan, 1964

Shire County HT, op, 1990, R. Harkness & Co., Ltd.; bud ovoid; flowers peach on primrose yellow base, reverse salmon rose on primrose, medium, 33 petals, cupped, borne usually singly, moderate fragrance; foliage medium size, medium green, semi-glossy; prickles recurved, medium, reddish; bushy, medium growth; [Amy Brown × Bonfire Night]; int. in 1989

Shirley HT, rb, 1933, Dickson, A.; bud shaded russet; flowers light prawn-red, base yellow; vigorous growth

Shirley HT, rb; flowers bright red with white reverse, dbl., high-centered, star-shaped; stems long; narrow, upright, medium to tall growth; int. by Ludwig's Roses, 2003

Shirley A. Ryals F, pb, 2000, Giles, Diann; flowers medium, dbl., high-centered, borne in small clusters, no fragrance; foliage medium size, medium green, semi-glossy; few prickles; compact, medium (4 ft.) growth; [Sun Flare × Simplicity]; int. by Giles Rose Nursery, 2000

Shirley Hibberd T, my, 1874, Levet, F.; flowers small; [Mme Falcot × unknown]

Shirley Holmes HT, ob, 1960, Mee; bud long, pointed; flowers golden orange, 4 in., 30 petals, intense fragrance; vigorous, bushy growth; [McGredy's Yellow × Ethel Sanday]; int. by Edenvale Nursery, 1958

Shirley Laugharn HT, yb, 1976, Swim, H.C.; bud ovoid; flowers creamy yellow, edged pink, 5 in., 35 petals, moderate fruity fragrance; foliage dark; very vigorous, upright, slightly spreading growth; [Granada × Garden Party]; int. by Laugharn, 1974

Shirley Marie Min, mp, 2000, Schramm, Dwayne; flowers light pink, reverse medium pink, 1½ in., dbl., borne mostly singly, slight fragrance; foliage medium size, light green, semi-glossy; few prickles; upright, medium (1½-2 ft.) growth; [Why Not × Why Not]

Shirley Rose HT, pb, 1966, Lawrence; flowers cream and carmine, loose, 5 in.; foliage dark; upright growth; [sport of Eden Rose]

Shirley Spain F, mr, 1993, Cocker; flowers glowing russet red, medium, dbl., borne in small clusters; foliage medium size, dark green, glossy; some prickles; medium, compact growth; [seedling × Roddy McMillan]; int. by James Cocker & Sons, 1992

Shirley Temple HT, ly, 1936, Engle; flowers light yellow, edged lemon-yellow; [sport of Joanna Hill]; int. by Wyant

Shirpa LCl, op, Eve, A.; flowers dark coral pink, 3 in., loose; free-flowering; vigorous (10-13 ft.) growth; int. by Les Roses Anciennes de Andre Eve, 1976

Shiun – See **Shi-un**, HT

Shizu no Mai HT, lp, 1991, Ohtsuki, Hironaka; flowers light pastel pink, large, 32-35 petals, high-centered, borne usually singly, slight fragrance; foliage medium size, dark green, semi-glossy; sturdy, upright growth; [Jana × Madame Violet]

Shleby Belogorsky HMsk, w; int. in 1996

Shobha HT, ob, Friends Rosery; flowers orange with broad white stripes, large, dbl.; [sport of Otohime]; int. in 1988

Shocking Pol, rb, 1967, Hémeray-Aubert; flowers dark red, reverse lighter, 3 in., high-centered, borne in clusters; foliage dark, glossy; very low, erect growth; [Red Favorite × Alain]; int. by McGredy & Son

Shocking Min, m, Poulsen; int. in 2000

Shocking Blue F, m, 1975, Kordes; bud very large, pointed; flowers lilac-mauve, 2½-3½ in., 28 petals, high-centered to cupped, borne in clusters, intense fragrance; recurrent; foliage large, dark green, glossy, leathery; prickles few, medium, hooked downward, brown; vigorous, upright, bushy growth; PP3846; [(Zorina × seedling) × Silver Star]; int. in 1974

Shocking Blue, Climbing Cl F, m; [sport of Shocking Blue]; int. after 1974

Shocking Pink HT, mp, 1970, McCannon; flowers large, dbl., cupped, intense fragrance; foliage leathery; vigorous, upright growth; PP3072; [sport of Pink Sensation]; int. by DeVor Nurseries, Inc., 1968

Shocking Sky F, m, Kordes; bud pointed; flowers lavender-mauve with red edges, medium, dbl., high-centered, borne singly, in clusters and in candelabras, moderate fragrance; recurrent; vigorous, medium growth; flora-tea; int. in 1994

Shogun LCl, pb, Tantau; flowers deep pink, lighter reverse, 3-4 in., dbl., high-centered, borne usually in clusters, slight fragrance; recurrent; strong (10-13 ft.) growth; int. by Rosen Tantau, 2000

Shola F, mr, 1971, IARI; bud pointed; flowers sparkling orient red, medium, dbl.; foliage leathery; vigorous, dwarf growth; [Anna Wheatcroft × unknown]; int. in 1969

Shona F, op, 1982, Dickson, Patrick; flowers medium coral pink, 23 petals, borne in clusters, slight fragrance; foliage medium size, medium green, semi-glossy; bushy growth; [Bangor × Anabell]; int. by Dickson Roses, 1982

Shooting Star Min, yb, 1972, Meilland; bud ovoid; flowers yellow, tipped red, small, dbl., cupped, slight fragrance; foliage small, light, soft; vigorous, dwarf growth; [Rumba × (Dany Robin × Perla de Montserrat)]; int. by C-P

Shooting Star F, yb, Diby's; flowers yellow, turning to

pink, aging to crimson, borne in well-formed trusses; int. in 2005

Shootout Min, ab, 1981, Borst, Jim; bud ovoid; flowers apricot-orange, 28 petals, borne singly; foliage medium green; prickles long, triangular, light green; vigorous, bushy growth; [Tiki × Darling Flame]; int. by Kimbrew-Walter Roses

Short 'n' Sweet Min, dp, 1984, Bennett, Dee; flowers deep pink, very small, 35 petals; foliage medium size, medium green, semi-glossy; bushy, spreading growth; [Sheri Anne × seedling]; int. by Tiny Petals Nursery

Shortcake Min, rb, 1991, Keisei Rose Nurseries, Inc.; bud ovoid, pointed, short; flowers red, white reverse, red color pales with age, blues slightly, 2 in., 30-35 petals, cupped, borne in flat clusters of 5-10, slight fragrance; recurrent; foliage large, dark green, glossy; prickles normal, medium, straight, red to brown; stems short (6 in.), strong; upright, bushy, tall (30 in.) growth; PP8602; [seedling × seedling]; int. by Bear Creek Gardens/Jackson & Perkins, 1991

Shot Silk HT, pb, 1924, Dickson, A.; flowers cherry-cerise, shading to golden yellow at base, medium, 27 petals, loose, intense tea fragrance; recurrent; foliage glossy, slightly curled; vigorous, compact (3 ft.) growth; [(Hugh Dickson × unknown) × Sunstar]; Gold Medal, NRS, 1923

Shot Silk, Climbing Cl HT, pb, 1931, Knight, G. (also Low, 1935); flowers pale-cerise with a golden glow and orange center, large, dbl., high-centered to loose; foliage large, dark green, glossy; growth to 10 ft.; [sport of Shot Silk]

Show HT, lp, RvS-Melle; [Frederik Chopin × Mme Butterfly]; int. in 1993

Show 'n' Tell Min, ob, 1988, Jacobs, Betty A.; bud long, pointed; flowers bright, velvety orange-red, white border, reverse white, 1¾ in., 25-30 petals, high-centered, borne singly and in loose sprays, slight spicy fragrance; free-flowering; foliage medium size, medium green, semi-glossy, disease-resistant; prickles moderate, light brown; stems slender, wiry; spreading, tall growth; hips ball-shaped, orange to russet; PP7375; [Rocky × (Matangi × Honey Hill)]; int. by Four Seasons Rose Nursery

Show Carpet Min, lp, 1995, Laver, Keith G.; flowers pale pink with deeper tones, small, micro-mini, dbl., borne in large clusters, slight fragrance; foliage small, dark green, glossy; upright growth; [seedling × seedling]; int. by Springwood Roses, 1996

Show Garden LCl, mp, 1954, Brownell; bud medium, pointed; flowers crimson to rose-bengal, then magenta, 4-5 in., 40-45 petals, rounded, borne singly and in small clusters, slight tea fragrance; remontant; prickles several, in., red to clear; stems long, stiff; growth like a hybrid tea, with additional canes going to 10 ft.; PP1295; [seedling × Queen o' the Lakes]

Show Girl HT, mp, 1946, Lammerts, Dr. Walter; bud long, pointed; flowers rose-pink, deepening to claret pink, 3½-4½ in., 15-20 petals, high-centered, moderate fragrance; foliage leathery; vigorous, upright, bushy growth; [Joanna Hill × Crimson Glory]; int. by Armstrong Nursery; Gold Medal, NRS, 1950

Show Girl, Climbing Cl HT, mp, 1949, Chaffin; [sport of Show Girl]; int. by Armstrong Nursery

Showbiz F, mr, 1983, Tantau, Math.; bud short, globular, blunt top; flowers bright medium red, 2½-3½ in., 20-30 petals, flat, borne in clusters, slight sweet fragrance; recurrent; foliage medium size, dark, semi-glossy; prickles normal, long, hooked downward; stems short; bushy, low (2-2½ ft.) growth; PP4844; [Dream Waltz × Marlena]

Showbiz, Climbing Cl F, mr, Tejganga; flowers scarlet-red, borne in large clusters; [sport of Showbiz]; int. in 1995

Showboat F, yb, 1964, Patterson; bud ovoid; flowers deep yellow on pink to cream ground, 2½ in., 30 petals, moderate fragrance; foliage leathery; moderate, bushy growth; PP2661; [Carrousel × seedling]; int. by Patterson Roses, 1963

Showbound Min, op

Showcase Min, ab, 1984, Stoddard, Louis; flowers small, 35 petals; foliage small, light green, semi-glossy; bushy growth; [Rise 'n' Shine × Over the Rainbow]; int. in 1986

Showdown Min, dr, 1996, Williams, Ernest D.; flowers 1¼ in., full, borne mostly singly, no fragrance; foliage dark green, semi-glossy; some prickles; medium (16-18 in.), upright, bushy growth; [Rise 'n' Shine × Twilight Trail]; int. by Texas Mini Roses, 1996

Shower of Gold HWich, my, 1910, Paul, G.; flowers golden yellow, rapidly fading to pale yellow, 7-8 cm., dbl., rosette, borne in clusters of 5-15, no fragrance; non-recurrent; foliage coppery green, glossy, fern-like; very vigorous, climbing growth; [Jersey Beauty × Instituteur Sirdey]

ShowMotion S, yb; flowers light yellow with apricot-tan tones, full, cupped; int. by Richard Huber AG, 2006

Showoff LCl, mr, 1952, Moffet; flowers scarlet, medium to large, very dbl., cupped, borne in large clusters; profuse, repeated bloom; vigorous growth; [sport of Blaze]; int. by Earl May Seed Co.

Showoff HT, rb, 1986, Christensen, Jack E.; flowers velvety brilliant red, reverse silvery blend, large, 35 petals; foliage large, dark, semi-glossy; upright, bushy growth; [Typhoo Tea × Snowfire]; int. by Armstrong Nursery

Showpiece HT, mr, 1958, Ratcliffe; flowers bright scarlet

Showqueen HT, mp, Williams, J. Benjamin; flowers pink with lavender shading, dbl., high-centered, borne mostly singly; recurrent; stems long; int. by Hortico Inc., 1997

Showstopper HT, dr, 1981, Warriner, William A.; bud pointed; flowers deep red, spiral, 33 petals, borne singly or 3-4 per cluster, intense fragrance; foliage large; prickles long; strong, upright, bushy growth; PP4851; [seedling × Samantha]; int. by J&P

Showtime HT, mp, 1970, Lindquist; flowers large, dbl., high-centered, blooms in flushes, moderate fruity fragrance; foliage glossy, leathery; vigorous, bushy growth; PP3044; [Kordes' Perfecta × Granada]; int. by Howard Rose Co., 1969

Showy Gold F, dy

Showy Miss HT, dp; flowers warm, unfading pink; free-flowering; short growth; flora-tea

Showy Pavement HRg, mp, Baum; flowers large, dbl., intense fragrance; low, arching, spreading (2 ft.) growth

Showy Pinocchio Min, yb, Delbard; flowers golden yellow striped and splashed with deep tangerine, fading lighter, dbl., cupped, borne in small clusters; medium growth; int. in 2001

Shree Dayananda HT, dp, 1980, Hardikar, Dr. M.N.; bud ovoid; flowers deep pink, 90 petals, moderate fragrance; foliage small, green; prickles beak-shaped; bushy, dwarf growth; [Scarlet Knight × Festival Beauty]; int. in 1979

Shreveport Gr, ob, 1981, Kordes, R.; bud ovoid, pointed; flowers orange, 3½-4½ in., 50 petals, globular to cupped, borne 1-3 per cluster, slight tea fragrance; recurrent; foliage large; prickles small, hooked downward; stems medium, strong; tall, upright, vigorous growth; hips short, ovoid, smooth, yellow-green; PP5157; [Zorina × Uwe Seeler]; int. by Armstrong Nursery

Shrewsbury Show HT, dr, Fryer, Gareth; flowers crimson, unfading, spiral; int. by Fryers Roses, 1988

Shreyasi HT, m, IARI; flowers plum red with silvery grey reverse, petal base yellow, moderate fragrance; free-flowering; int. in 1992

Shri Swamy Samarth LCl, dp, Patil, B.K.; int. in 1992

Shrimp – See **Shrimp Hit**, MinFl

Shrimp Hit MinFl, or, Poulsen; bud broad ovate; flowers bright orange-red, 1½-2 in., 20-30 petals, flat, borne in small clusters, no fragrance; free-flowering; foliage dark; prickles few, concave to flat, yellow-green; bushy, compact (16-20 in.) growth; PP12987; [Everglades × Victory Parade]; int. by Poulsen Roser, 2001

Shrimp Pink Castle – See **Canyonlands**, F

Shringar F, dp, 1974, IARI; buds small, pointed; flowers deep camellia-rose with lighter reverse and base, medium, semi-dbl., open, borne singly and in small clusters; foliage medium size, glossy; growth vigorous, upright (90 cm.); [Eiffel Tower × Suryodaya]; int. in 1972

Shropshire Lass S, lp, 1970, Austin, David; flowers blush-pink, fading to white, golden stamens, 5 in., single to semi-dbl., flat, borne singly and in small clusters, moderate myrrh fragrance; summer bloom; robust, large (8 ft.) growth; [Mme Butterfly × Mme Legras de St. Germain]; int. by David Austin Roses, 1969

Shrubby Pink – See **Sunday Times**, F

Shu-getsu HT, dy, 1985, Suzuki, Seizo; flowers large, 38 petals, high-centered, moderate fragrance; foliage large, dark, glossy; prickles large, straight; upright, bushy growth; [Seiko × King's Ransom]; int. by Keisei Rose Nursery, 1984

Shu-oh HT, or, 1986, Suzuki, Seizo; flowers medium, cupped, moderate fragrance; foliage dark, semi-glossy; prickles slanted downward; upright growth; [San Francisco × Pharaoh]; int. by Keisei Rose Nursery, 1982

Shugetsu – See **Shu-getsu**, HT

Shunpo HT, lp, Suzuki, Seizo; int. in 1987

Shunyo HT, ob, 1985, Kono, Yoshito; flowers light yellow orange, large, 33 petals, high-centered; foliage glossy; prickles sickle-shaped; vigorous, upright growth; [(Golden Sun × Summer Holiday) × (Garden Party × Narzisse)]; int. in 1984

Shurpee HT, mr

Shuzao Red S, mr; from China

Shy Beauty Min, mp, 1985, Lyon; flowers small, 55 petals, borne singly; foliage medium size, medium green, semi-glossy; bushy growth; [seedling × unknown]; int. by M.B. Farm Min. Roses, Inc.

Shy Girl Min, w, 1989, Warriner, William A.; bud ovoid, pointed; flowers medium, 80 petals, high-centered, borne usually singly and in sprays of 2-4; foliage medium size, dark green, semi-glossy; prickles straight, short; upright, spreading, low growth; no fruit; PP6514; [Petticoat × Red Minimo]; int. by Bear Creek Gardens, 1988

Shy Maiden F, rb, 1984, Anderson's Rose Nurseries; flowers white with red petal edges, large, 35 petals; foliage medium size, light green, glossy; bushy growth; [Iceberg × Iceberg]

Si Min, w, Dot, Pedro; flowers rosy white, micro-mini, ¾-1 in., semi-dbl.; foliage dark green; dwarf growth; [Perla de Montserrat × (Anny × Tom Thumb)]; int. in 1957

Si Bemol Min, m, 1986, Lens, Louis; flowers lilac blue and white, small, 30 petals, borne in clusters of 3-24;

foliage dark; prickles few, green; bushy growth; [(Little Angel × Le Vesuve) × Mr Bluebird]; int. in 1980

Sibelius HT, mr, 1959, Verschuren; flowers velvety crimson, dbl., high-centered; vigorous growth; [New Yorker × Étoile de Hollande]; int. by Blaby Rose Gardens, 1958

Sibelius HMsk, m, 2000, Lens, Louis; flowers dark mauve, 1 in., semi-dbl., cupped, borne in large clusters; recurrent; foliage small, dark green, glossy; prickles moderate; upright, medium (80-120 cm.) growth; hedge; [Mister Bluebird × Violet Hood]; int. by Louis Lens N.V., 1984

Sibilla HT, dr, Barni, V.; int. in 1987

Sibylle F, op

Sicilian Rose – See ***R. sicula*** (Trattinnick)

Siddartha HT, rb, Kasturi; flowers red with stripes and splashes of white and green; [sport of Christian Dior]; int. by KSG Son, 1973

Side Kick Min, or, 1995, Chaffin, Lauren M.; flowers orange-red, medium, 40-60 petals, borne mostly singly; foliage medium size, medium green, semi-glossy; few prickles; medium (30 cm.), bushy growth; [Dandenong × Ann Moore]; int. by Pixie Treasures Miniature Rose Nursery, 1996

Sidi-Brahim HT, dy, 1953, Robichon; flowers jonquil-yellow, dbl.; strong stems; [Feu Pernet-Ducher × Mme Rene Lefevre]

Sidney Peabody F, dp, 1956, deRuiter; flowers reddish-pink, well-formed, large, 36 petals, borne in clusters; foliage dark, leathery; very vigorous growth; [Rome Glory × Floribunda seedling]; int. by Gandy Roses, Ltd., 1955

Sidonie HP, mp, 1847, Vibert; flowers rosy blush to salmon or flesh, medium, full, quartered, borne in small clusters, moderate damask fragrance; recurrent; [Belle de Trianon × unknown]; sometimes classed as either Damask Perpetual or Portland; int. by Vibert

Siegeslied – See **Bouquet**, F

Siegesperle Pol, ly, 1915, Kiese; flowers small, semi-dbl.; [Tausendschön × unknown]

Siegfried T, op, 1893, Drögemüller; flowers dark salmon pink, large, full, semi-globular; [Gloire de Dijon × unknown]

Siegfried Sassoon – See **Spiced Coffee**, HT

Sieguier HGal, m, 1853, Robert

Siena Vigorosa – See **Maxi Vita**, F

Sierra Dawn HT, pb, 1967, Armstrong, D.L.; bud long, pointed; flowers bright pink blend, large, dbl., high-centered, moderate fragrance; foliage dark, bronze, leathery; vigorous, upright, bushy growth; PP2914; [Helen Traubel × Manitou]; int. by Armstrong Nursery

Sierra Glow HT, pb, 1942, Lammerts, Dr. Walter; bud ovoid; flowers shrimp-pink, reverse strawberry-pink, 3½-4½ in., 33 petals, high-centered, moderate fragrance; recurrent; foliage leathery; vigorous, bushy, spreading growth; [Crimson Glory × Soeur Thérèse]; int. by Armstrong Nursery

Sierra Gold HT, my, 1960, Lammerts, Dr. Walter; bud urn shaped; flowers Indian yellow, 4-4½ in., 45-55 petals, high-centered; foliage leathery, semi-glossy; upright, compact growth; PP2036; [Queen Elizabeth × Tawny Gold]; int. by Amling-DeVor Nursery, 1960

Sierra Lynn HT, rb, 1999, Giles, Diann; flowers medium, full, borne mostly singly; foliage medium size, dark green, semi-glossy; few prickles; upright, medium (4-5 ft.) growth; [Vera Dalton × Paradise]; int. by Giles Rose Nursery, 1999

Sierra Skye HT, mr, Ping Lim; bud round to oval; flowers deep red with orange tones on petal edge, 2½-3 in., 30 petals, pompon, borne in clusters; recurrent; foliage medium green, satiny; growth shrub or climber, depending upon climate; hips 0.5; PP16661; [Orange Fire × seedling 5-180A]; int. by Bailey Nurseries, 2004

Sierra Snowstorm S, ly, 1936, Moore, Ralph S.; bud long, pointed, cream and yellow; flowers open, 2 in., single, borne in clusters; abundant, recurrent bloom; foliage large, leathery, glossy, light; vigorous (5-6 ft.), bushy, arching growth; [Gloire des Rosomanes × Dorothy Perkins]; int. by Henderson's Exp. Gardens and Brooks & Son

Sierra Sun HT, rb

Sierra Sunrise Min, yb, 1980, Moore, Ralph S.; bud medium, pointed; flowers soft yellow, petals tipped pink, 1½ in., 35-45 petals, cupped, open, borne singly or 3-5 per cluster, slight fragrance; foliage medium size, medium green; prickles long, straight; vigorous, bushy, upright growth; PP4662; [Little Darling × Yellow Magic]; int. by Sequoia Nursery; Gold Star of the South Pacific, Palmerston North, NZ, 1984

Sierra Sunset LCl, yb, 1961, Morey, Dr. Dennison; bud pointed; flowers blend of yellow, peach, orange and red, 6 in., full, high-centered, borne in clusters, intense fruity fragrance; foliage glossy; vigorous (6-8 ft.) growth; PP2322; [(Capt. Thomas × Joanna Hill) × Mme Kriloff]; int. by J&P, 1961

Sierra's Smile Min, ob, 2004, Wells, Verlie W.; flowers gray orange, 2 in., very full, borne mostly solitary, no fragrance; foliage medium size, dark green, semi-glossy; prickles ¼ in., straight; spreading, medium (2 ft.) growth; exhibition, garden decoration; [seedling × seedling]; int. by Wells MidSouth Roses, 2004

Sieska Fervid F, Klimenko, V. N.

Siesta F, or, 1966, Meilland; flowers light vermilion on cream base, large, semi-dbl.; free-flowering; foliage glossy, leathery; very free growth; [Sarabande × Dany Robin]; int. by URS

Siesta S, pb, Meilland; flowers magenta pink with white eye, small, single, borne in large clusters; bushy (3-4 ft.) growth; int. by Meilland Richardier, 2001

Sif LCl, ob, 1969, Lundstad; flowers tangerine-orange, large, 25 petals, cupped; foliage dark, glossy; vigorous, climbing growth; [Traumland × Royal Gold]

Sight Saver HT, lp, Fryer, Gareth; flowers soft pink, 4 in., 30-35 petals, high-centered, borne singly and in small clusters, intense tea fragrance; recurrent; rounded, medium (3 ft.) growth; int. by Fryer Roses, 1997

Sightsaver – See **Sight Saver**, HT

Siglinde F, Noack, Werner; int. in 1972

Signal Red Pol, mr, 1949, deRuiter; flowers scarlet, 2 in., rosette, borne in large trusses; foliage glossy, bronze; vigorous, bushy growth; [DeRuiter's Herald × Polyantha seedling]; int. by Gandy Roses, Ltd.

Signal Rot F, VEG; int. in 1982

Signalfeuer F, or, 1959, Tantau, Math.; flowers cinnabar to orange, dbl., borne in clusters; bushy growth; [Lumina × Cinnabar seedling]

Signature HT, pb, 1998, Warriner, William A.; bud long, pointed, ovoid, deep pink; flowers deep pink and cream blend, light pink and cream reverse, 5-6 in., 30-35 petals, high-centered, borne singly, moderate fragrance; foliage large, dark green, semi glossy; numerous prickles; upright, bushy, tall (4-5 ft.) growth; PP9539; [Honor × First Federal Renaissance]; int. by Bear Creek Gardens, Inc., 1996

Signe Relander HRg, dr, 1928, Poulsen, D.; flowers bright dark red, small, fringed petals, dbl., borne in clusters, moderate fragrance; recurrent bloom; vigorous (6½ ft.) growth; [*R. rugosa* hybrid × Orléans Rose]; int. by Poulsen, 1928

Signet HT, dp, 1938, Montgomery Co.; bud long, pointed; flowers deep pure pink, large, dbl., high-centered; foliage leathery; very vigorous growth; [Premier × Talisman]

Signora HT, ob, 1936, Aicardi, D.; bud long, pointed; flowers orange-apricot, suffused gold, outer petals magenta-pink, large, 27 petals, cupped, moderate fragrance; foliage glossy; vigorous growth; [Julien Potin × Sensation]; int. by J&P; Gold Medal, Portland, 1937

Signora, Climbing Cl HT, ob; flowers deep salmon, pink at center, darker edges, 6 in.; [sport of Signora]

Signora Maria Sgaravatti HT, Sgaravatti, A.

Signora Piero Puricelli – See **Signora**, HT

Sika HT, op, Dorieux; flowers bright, dbl., high-centered; free-flowering; int. in 1974

Sila HT, op, Cocker; int. in 1983

Silberlachs F, op, 1944, Tantau; flowers pale salmon, 6-8 petals, borne in clusters of 3-10; foliage light green; upright, bushy growth; [Rosenelfe × Hamburg]

Silberzauber F, mp, GPG Bad Langensalza; flowers large, dbl.; int. in 1985

Silchester Sunset HT, rb, 2004, Paul Chessum Roses; flowers small, dbl., borne in small clusters, slight fragrance; foliage medium size, medium green, semi-glossy; growth upright, medium (80 cm.); beds, borders; [seedling × seedling]; int. by Love4Plants, Ltd., 2004

Silène T, op, before 1866; flowers flesh pink, large, full, moderate fragrance

Silent Night HT, yb, 1969, McGredy, Sam IV; flowers creamy yellow suffused pink, well-formed; [Daily Sketch × Hassan]; Gold Medal, Geneva, 1969

Silhouette – See **Oregold**, HT

Silhouette – See **Honor**, HT

Silhouette HT, w, 1981, Warriner, William A.; bud broad, oval, pointed; flowers creamy white, 5 in., 45-50 petals, high-centered, borne singly; free-flowering; foliage large, light green; prickles brown, hooked down; slightly angular growth; PP4813; [Tonight × Coral Satin]; int. by J&P, 1984

Silhouette HT, dp, Richardier; int. in 1999

Silk HT, w; florist rose; int. by deRuiter, 2001

Silk Border – See **Salt Lake**, S

Silk Butterflies – See **Mateo's Silk Butterflies**, Ch

Silk Button Min, w, Kordes; bud pointed; flowers cream, dbl., star-shaped; free-flowering; few prickles; stems long, slender; vigorous, tall growth; int. in 1991

Silk Hat HT, m, 1986, Christensen, Jack E.; flowers red purple, cream reverse, large, 45 petals, high-centered, borne usually singly, moderate damask fragrance; foliage large, medium green, matte; medium, upright, bushy growth; no fruit; [Ivory Tower × (Night 'n' Day × Plain Talk)]; int. by Armstrong Nursery, 1985

Silk 'n' Satin Min, ab, 1996, Bell, Judy G.; flowers apricot, with bright yellow stamens, 1½ in., 8-9 wide petals, borne in small clusters, no fragrance; foliage small, light green, matte; no prickles; low (10 in.), bushy, spreading growth; winter hardy; [seedling × unknown]; int. by Michigan Mini Roses, 1997

Silk Parasol – See **Kinugasa**, HT

Silk Road Cl Min, w, 2003, Ishii, Tsuyashi; flowers single, borne in small clusters, slight fragrance; foliage small, medium green, glossy; prickles small, numerous; growth spreading, tall (200 cm.); ground cover, weeping standard; [*R. yakushimensis* × Snowball]

Silk Sash HT, pb, 1971, Fankhauser; flowers pastel pink, reverse silvery pink, very large, 85 petals, high-centered; foliage dark, leathery; vigorous, upright growth; [Memoriam × Elizabeth Fankhauser]

Silken Laumann Min, ob, 1993, Laver, Keith G.; flowers luminous orange, yellow reverse, large, full, high-centered, borne in large clusters, slight fragrance; foliage medium size, medium green, matte; few prickles; medium (18 in.), bushy growth; [June Laver × Potluck Red]; int. by Springwood Roses, 1994

Silky Mist HT, lp, Simpson; bud long; flowers soft pink, high-centered; medium growth; int. in 1989

Silky Petals HT, dp, Ghosh, Mr. & Mrs. S.; flowers bright, clear, deep pink, dbl., high-centered; int. in 1998

Silva HT, pb, 1964, Meilland, Alain A.; bud long, pointed; flowers yellowish-salmon shaded bright rose, 5½ in., 38 petals, high-centered, borne mostly singly, slight fragrance; foliage dark, glossy, leathery; vigorous, upright growth; [Peace × Confidence]; int. by URS, 1964; Gold Medal, The Hague, 1964

Silva HT, op, Keisei

Silva Graça HT, ob, 1956, Moreira da Silva; flowers salmon and yellow shaded pink, well-shaped; [Michèle Meilland × Comtesse Vandal]

Silvabella HT, pb, 1967, Guiseppe, M.; flowers deep pink, reverse carmine-pink, large, dbl., cupped; foliage leathery; upright, bushy growth; [Dr. Debat × Eden Rose]

Silver Angel F, m, 1998, Giles, Diann; flowers light silver mauve, dbl., borne in small clusters; foliage medium green, semi-glossy; bushy, medium (3 ft.) growth; [sport of Angel Face]; int. by Giles Rose Nursery, 1996

Silver Anniversary HT, m, 1991, Christensen, Jack E.; bud long, pointed ovoid; flowers medium lavender, spot of yellow at base, aging paler, 4½-5 in., 25-30 petals, high-centered, borne singly, intense damask fragrance; recurrent; foliage large, very dark green, semi-glossy to glossy; prickles ordinary, ¼ in. straight, red to brown; long, straight, sturdy stems; tall, upright, bushy growth; PP7658; [Crystalline × Shocking Blue]; int. by Bear Creek Gardens, 1990

Silver Anniversary – See **Karen Blixen**, HT

Silver Anniversary HT, m, Meilland

Silver Beauty F, m, 1956, Verschuren; flowers silvery rose-madder; vigorous, bushy growth; [La France × unknown]; int. by Gandy Roses, Ltd.

Silver Bell F, lp, 1976, Takatori, Yoshiho; bud ovoid; flowers soft light pink, 2 in., 35 petals, high-centered; foliage glossy; vigorous, upright growth; [Gene Boerner × seedling]; int. by Japan Rose Nursery

Silver Celebration Gr, w; flowers pure white, dbl., cupped, borne in clusters, moderate fragrance; good repeat; foliage semi-glossy; tall growth; int. in 1980

Silver Chalice F, lp, Williams, J.B.; flowers silvery pink., single, slight fragrance; foliage reddish; growth to 5 ft.; int. by Hortico, 2004

Silver Charm F, m, 1968, LeGrice; flowers lavender-blue, large, semi-dbl., borne in large trusses; foliage dark; vigorous, low growth; [Lilac Charm × Sterling Silver]; int. by Roseland Nurseries, 1968

Silver Cloud F, r, Moore; flowers silver and coffee with cream, dbl., flat, borne in clusters, slight fragrance; free-flowering; sturdy, vigorous, medium growth; int. by Sequoia Nursery, 1990

Silver Cloud LCl, pb, Benny, David; flowers rich rose magenta, paling to silver tips at the petal margins, dbl, moderate rose/apple fragrance; int. by Camp Hill Roses, 2004

Silver Columbia HT, pb, 1924, Leonard; flowers clear silver-pink; [sport of Columbia]

Silver Dawn LCl, w, 1942, Zombory; flowers creamy white, center deeper, stamens golden yellow, open, large, 90-100 petals; foliage large, leathery, glossy, dark; vigorous (10-12 ft.), compact, climbing growth; [Silver Moon × Silver Moon]

Silver Dawn S, w, 2005, Viraraghavan, M.S. Viru; flowers single, borne in small clusters; foliage large, medium green, glossy; prickles medium, pointed; growth bushy, tall (5 ft.); garden decorative; [(Bonica × *R. clinophylla*) × Silver Moon]; int. by Roses Unlimited, 2004

Silver Dream F, lp, 1993, Ilsink, G.P.; flowers silver pink, medium, dbl., borne in sprays; foliage medium size, medium green, semi-glossy; few prickles; medium (60 cm.), upright growth; int. by Interplant B.V., 1992

Silver Enchantment HT, rb, 1971, Gregory; flowers rich red, reverse silver, conical, large, 36 petals; foliage dark; very free growth; [Tropicana × unknown]

Silver Fox HT, w, 1992, Marciel, Stanley G. & Jeanne A.; bud medium, pointed, slender; flowers clear white, 3-4 in., 26-30 petals, imbricated, then flat, borne mostly singly, slight fragrance; recurrent; foliage large, dark green, semi-glossy; prickles some, thin, straight, slightly wing-shaped; stems long; tall (210 cm.), upright growth; hips globose ; PP8931; [seedling × seedling]; florist rose; int. by DeVor Nurseries, Inc., 1994

Silver Gem F, m, 1969, deRuiter; flowers silver-mauve, large, semi-dbl., borne in trusses; foliage dark, leathery; bushy growth

Silver Ghost S, w, Kordes; flowers pure white, yellow stamens, 1½-2 in., single, shallow cup, borne in clusters, no fragrance; recurrent; foliage disease-resistant; upright (2 ft.), bushy growth; int. by Notcutts Nurseries, 2004; President's Intl. Trophy, RNRS, 2001, Certificate of Merit, Glasgow, 2006

Silver Jubilee HT, yb, 1937, Dickson, A.; flowers light golden yellow, base chrome, edged canary, very large, dbl.; foliage very large, glossy; vigorous growth; RULED EXTINCT 4/77

Silver Jubilee HT, pb, 1977, Cocker; bud long, pointed; flowers silvery pink, reverse darker, 5 in., 30-35 petals, high-centered, borne mostly singly, moderate fragrance; recurrent; foliage dark green, glossy; vigorous (5 ft.) growth; [((Highlight × Colour Wonder) × (Parkdirektor Riggers × Piccadilly)) × Mischief]; int. by James Cocker & Sons, 1978; Gold Medal, Belfast, 1980, President's International Trophy, RNRS, 1977, Gold Medal, RNRS, 1977, Gold Medal, Portland, 1981

Silver Jubilee, Climbing Cl HT, pb, 1983, Cocker; int. in 1985

Silver Lady F, m, 1991, Taylor, Pete & Kay; flowers pale lavender, with a hint of darker lavender on edges of petals, large, dbl., borne singly and in small clusters, no fragrance; foliage medium size, medium green, semi-glossy; some prickles; medium (90 cm.), upright, bushy growth; [Azure Sea × seedling]; int. by Taylor's Roses, 1993

Silver Lining HT, pb, 1960, Dickson, A.; flowers silvery rose, edges deeper, 5 in., 30 petals, high-centered, borne mostly singly, intense fragrance; recurrent; vigorous (4 ft.) growth; [Karl Herbst × Eden Rose seedling]; int. by Dickson & Sons, 1959; Gold Medal, Portland, 1964, Gold Medal, NRS, 1958

Silver Lining, Climbing Cl HT, pb, 1997, Dickson, Alex; flowers large, very dbl.; foliage medium size, medium green, glossy; numerous prickles; tall, spreading growth, with 10-12 canes ranging in size to 10-20 ft.; [sport of Silver Lining]

Silver Moon HWich, w, 1910, Van Fleet; bud long, pointed; flowers creamy white, base amber, stamens darker, 8-11 cm., single to semi-dbl., borne mostly solitary; may show some repeat; foliage large, dark, leathery, glossy; very vigorous (to 20 ft or more) growth; [*R. wichurana* × Devoniensis]; DNA studies have proved that this is not a HLaev; int. by P. Henderson

Silver Peach Min, ab, Hannemann, F.; [Silver Jubilee × Oz Gold]; int. by The Rose Paradise, 1989

Silver Peak – See **Ginrei**, F

Silver Phantom Min, m, 1988, Rennie, Bruce F.; bud pointed; flowers silver-lavender, large, 33 petals, high-centered, borne usually singly, slight licorice fragrance; foliage medium size, dark green, semi-glossy; prickles hooked, medium, light tan-red to dark; upright, bushy, tall growth; hips globular, medium, yellow-orange; [Shocking Blue × Angelglo]; int. by Rennie Roses International, 1989

Silver Pink F, lp, 2000, Lens, Louis; flowers medium, full, cupped, borne in large clusters; recurrent; foliage medium size, dark green, glossy; prickles moderate; growth bushy, medium (60-80 cm.); [(*R. multiflora adenocheata* × Ballerina) × Running Maid]; int. by Louis Lens N.V., 1990

Silver Princess HT, ob, 1934, Burbank; bud salmon-yellow to delicate pink; flowers almost ivory-white, tinged pink, very large, semi-dbl.; vigorous growth; int. by Stark Bros.

Silver Queen HP, pb, 1887, Paul, W.; flowers silvery pink and red, shaded rose pink in center, large, full, cupped; [sport of Queen of Queens]

Silver Queen HT, w

Silver River S, w, 2000, Lens, Louis; flowers white, shaded pink, reverse white, 3 cm., single, borne in large clusters; recurrent; foliage medium size, medium green, semi-glossy; prickles moderate; growth spreading, medium (40 cm.); groundcover; [(*R. multiflora adenocheata* × Ballerina) × Running Maid]; int. by Louis Lens, 1989

Silver Salmon – See **Silberlachs**, F

Silver Shadows HT, m, 1985, Buck, Dr. Griffith J.; flowers light blue-lavender, large, 33 petals, cupped, borne 3-5 per cluster, intense fragrance; repeat bloom; foliage large, dark, leathery; prickles awl-like, tan; upright, bushy growth; hardy; [(((Soir d'Automne × Music Maker) × Solitude) × (Blue Moon × Tom Brown)) × Autumn Dusk]; int. by Iowa State University, 1984

Silver Slippers Min, m, 1991, Chaffin, Lauren M.; bud slender; flowers unique silvery lavender, medium, full, borne mostly singly, moderate fragrance; foliage medium size, medium green, semi-glossy; medium (30 cm.), bushy growth; [Deep Purple × Jennifer]; int. by Pixie Treasures Min. Roses, 1992

Silver Spoon HT, m, 1985, Weeks, O.L.; bud large, long pointed; flowers silvery lavender, center and reverse appearing slightly darker, 4½-5 in., 25-35 petals, high-centered, borne singly, no fragrance; recurrent; foliage large, medium green, semi-glossy; prickles few, narrow, pointing downward, brownish; upright (4-5 ft.), bushy, spreading growth; PP5858; [Louisiana × seedling]; int. by Weeks Wholesale Rose Growers

Silver Star HWich, w, 1918, Undritz, Frederick R. M.; flowers white with cream tints, large, dbl., moderate fragrance

Silver Star HT, m, 1966, Kordes, R.; flowers lavender, well-formed, 5 in., dbl., classic hybrid tea, borne singly, intense fragrance; free-flowering; foliage dark green; vigorous growth; [Sterling Silver × (Magenta (F) × seedling)]; int. by McGredy & Son, 1966

Silver Star Gr, m, Weeks, O.L.; bud large, ovoid; flowers light to medium lavender, 4 in., 24-30 petals, cupped, borne in small clusters, slight fragrance; recurrent; foliage medium green, semi-glossy; prickles numerous, straight to slightly hooked downward; bushy (4-5 ft.) growth; PP14434; [Sterling Silver × Silver Spoon]; int. by Weeks, 2001

Silver Tips Min, pb, 1961, Moore, Ralph S.; bud pointed; flowers pink, reverse and tips silvery, becoming soft lavender, 1 in., 50 petals, slight fragrance; foliage leathery; vigorous, bushy (10-12 in.) growth; [(*R. wichurana* × Floradora) × Lilac Time]; int. by Sequoia Nursery, 1961

Silver Wedding HT, w, 1921, Amling Co.; flowers almost identical to parent; [sport of Ophelia]

Silver Wedding HT, w, Gregory; flowers white to cream, dbl., high-centered, borne mostly singly, slight fragrance; free-flowering; foliage dark green; bushy (2½ ft.) growth; int. in 1976

Silver Wedding Celebration F, w; flowers pure white, medium, full, cupped, borne in clusters; recurrent; foliage medium green; bushy (3 ft.), spreading growth

Silver Wings HT, w, 1943, McGredy; bud long, pointed; flowers ivory-white, large, dbl., high-centered; foliage glossy; vigorous, upright, bushy growth

Silver Wishes – See **Pink Hit**, Min

Silver World – See **Ginseikei**, F

Silverado HT, m, 1986, Christensen, Jack E.; bud long, pointed ovoid; flowers soft silvery lavender blushed ruby, reverse creamy white, 4½-5 in., 28-34 petals, high-centered, borne singly or in clusters of 2 or 3, slight fruity fragrance; foliage medium size, dark green, matte; prickles large, hooked slightly downward; stems average, strong; medium, bushy growth; hips globular to pear-shaped, orange; PP6861; [(Ivory Tower × Angel Face) × Paradise]; int. by Armstrong Garden Ctrs, 1987

Silverelda HT, pb, Riethmuller; flowers veined silvery buff-pink, edged lighter, base yellow, 35 petals; foliage glossy; vigorous, compact growth; [Heinrich Wendland × Nancy Wilson]

Silverhill Min, pb, 1996, Taylor, Franklin; flowers pink with mauve tint, blending to cream center and cream reverse, large, full, high-centered; foliage medium size, medium green, semi-glossy; some prickles; medium (36 in.), upright, bushy growth; [Azure Sea × seedling]; int. by Taylor's Roses, 1997

Silvery Moon HT, m, 1982, Leon, Charles F., Sr.; flowers lilac, large, 35 petals; foliage medium size, medium green, leathery, matte; upright growth; [Silver Star × Blue Moon]; int. in 1981

Silvia D, m, 1819, Vibert; flowers light rose-purple, large, dbl.; foliage oval, large

Silvia HT, yb, 1920, Pierson, F.R.; flowers sulfur-yellow shading to white; [sport of Ophelia]

Silvia S, dy, Poulsen; flowers deep yellow, 8-10 cm., dbl., no fragrance; foliage dark; growth bushy, 40-60 cm.; PP13104; int. by Poulsen Roser, 2000

Silvia Hit – See **Silvia**, S

Silvia Leyva HT, mr, 1933, Dot, Pedro; flowers cardinal-red, large, dbl., cupped; foliage glossy; vigorous growth; [Mrs C.W. Edwards × Mari Dot]; int. by C-P

Silvina Donvito F, dy, Barni; flowers ochre-apricot, 6-7 cm., 30-35 petals, cupped, borne in clusters, moderate fragrance; free-flowering; foliage medium size, light green; compact (40-60 cm.), uniform growth; [seedling × Rita Levi Montalcini]; int. by Rose Barni, 2003

Simba – See **Helmut Schmidt**, HT

Simerose HT, rb, 1939, Meilland, F.; bud long; flowers nasturtium-red, reverse golden yellow; vigorous growth; [Charles P. Kilham × (Charles P. Kilham × Margaret McGredy)]

Simfonia HT, w, Wagner, S.; flowers 29 petals, high-centered, borne mostly singly or in clusters; foliage dark green, semi-glossy; growth vigorous upright; [Mount Shasta × Pascali]; int. by Res. Stn. f. Horticulture, Cluj, 1977

Similor N, pb, 1840, Boyau; flowers yellowish-carmine, center pink, fading white shaded red, small, very full

Simina F, mp, Wagner, S.; flowers clear pink, 40 petals, cupped, borne in clusters, moderate fragrance; foliage large, dark green, glossy; growth vigorous tall upright; [Vigorosa × Allgold]; int. by Res. Stn. f. Fruit Growing, Cluj, 1997

Simon Bolivar HT, or, 1966, Armstrong, D.L.; bud ovoid; flowers bright orange-red, 4-5 in., 30-40 petals, high-centered, borne singly and in small clusters, slight fragrance; good repeat; foliage dark, glossy, leathery; prickles numerous, medium, straight to hooked downward, reddish brown; stems medium, strong; vigorous, upright, bushy growth; PP2705; [Roundelay × El Capitan]; int. by Armstrong Nursery

Simon de St Jean HP, m, 1861, Liabaud; flowers velvety purple, dbl.

Simon Dot HT, or, 1979, Dot, Simon; flowers orange-red, lighter reverse, 5 in., 35 petals, cupped, intense fragrance; foliage dark, upright growth; [Pharaoh × Rose Dot]; int. in 1978

Simon Estes S, mp, 2006, Buck, Dr. Griffith J.; flowers full, borne mostly solitary; foliage medium size, medium green, semi-glossy; prickles ½ in., awl, brownish-tan, moderate; growth upright, medium (3-4 ft.); garden decorative; [Carefree Beauty × (The Yeoman × Country Dancer)]; int. by Roses Unlimited, 2006

Simon Fraser S, mp, 1992, Svejda, Felicitas, & Ogilvie, Ian S.; bud ovoid; flowers have 5 petals during intial bloom flush, subsequent cycles have 20+ petals, 2 in., single, then double, cupped, then flat, borne singly and in small clusters, slight fragrance; foliage dark green, semi-glossy; prickles some, slightly concave, brown; low (60 cm.), upright growth; extremely winter hardy; PP9178; [((Bonanza × Arthur Bell) × (Red Dawn × Suzanne)) × ((*R.* × *kordesii* × unknown) × Champlain)]; int. by Agriculture Canada, 1992

Simon Robinson Min, mp, 1982, Thomas Robinson, Ltd.; flowers small, single, borne in large clusters, moderate fragrance; foliage small, dark green, glossy; compact, low, bushy growth; [*R. wichurana* × New Penny]

Simona HT, ab, 1982, Tantau, Math.; flowers large, 20 petals, moderate fragrance; foliage large, medium green, matte; upright growth; int. in 1979

Simone HT, w, 1924, Buatois; flowers flesh-white, center deeper pink, passing to creamy white, dbl.; [Mme Caroline Testout × Paul Monnier]

Simone HT, m, 1958, Mallerin, C.; bud ovoid; flowers pastel lilac, 6 in., 50 petals, high-centered, moderate fragrance; foliage leathery, dark, glossy; vigorous growth; PP1847; [(Peace × Independence) × Grey Pearl]; int. by Hémeray-Aubert, 1957

Simone Damaury HT, dr, 1925, Soupert & Notting; bud long, pointed; flowers brilliant crimson, semi-dbl.; [Liberty × Gen. MacArthur]

Simone de Chevigné HT, pb, 1924, Pernet-Ducher; flowers flesh-pink, shaded yellow, dbl.

Simone de Nanteuil HT, pb, 1925, Schwartz, A.; bud long, pointed; flowers rosy white, tinted carmine-pink, reverse flesh, dbl.; [Ophelia × Mme Vittoria Gagniere]

Simone Guérin HT, my, 1929, Mallerin, C.; flowers coral-yellow, large, semi-dbl., high-centered, slight fragrance; foliage glossy, dark green; vigorous growth; [Constance × unnamed Hybrid Tea seedling]

Simone Labbé HT, ab, 1922, Ketten Bros.; bud long, pointed; flowers apricot-yellow, passing to clear saffron-yellow, dbl.; [Le Progres × Lady Greenall]

Simone Mayery HT, yb, 1937, Chambard, C.; bud long, pointed, cream-yellow, shaded carmine-pink; flowers cream, center dark yellow, very large, cupped; foliage bronze; vigorous growth

Simone Merieux HT, rb, 1982, Gaujard; flowers large, full; foliage large, dark green, semi-glossy; int. as Meduse, Roseraies Gaujard, 1981

Simone Thomas T, rb, before 1927; flowers carmine to coppery-red

Simonet – See **Metis**, S

Simonet's Double Pink Rugosa HRg, mp, Simonet; flowers pink, smaller than Hansa, very dbl.; non-recurrent; hardy; [*R. macounii* × Mme Georges Bruant]; int. by P.H. Wright

Simple – See **Single**, M

Simple Gifts – See **Pink Bassino**, F

Simple Pleasures Min, rb, 1999, Taylor, Franklin "Pete" & Kay; flowers red petals, white eye, yellow stamens, 1¾ in., single, borne mostly singly; foliage medium size, medium green, semi-glossy; few prickles; upright, spreading, medium (18 in.) growth; int. by Taylor's Roses, 1998

Simple Simon Min, mp, 1955, deVink; flowers carmine-rose, base yellow, dbl.; [(*R. multiflora nana* × Mrs Pierre S. duPont) × F2Tom Thumb]; int. by T. Robinson, Ltd.

Simple Splendor Min, yb, 2003, Carle, Mary C.; flowers med. yellow with crimson edges, fading to pink, yellow stamens, 2 in., single, flat, wavy petals, borne solitary and in small clusters, slight fragrance; recurrent; foliage medium size, medium green, semi-glossy; prickles medium, hooked, green, few; growth upright, medium (18 in.); garden, exhibition; [sport of Autumn Splendor]; int. by Mary C. Carle, 2003

Simplex Min, w, 1961, Moore, Ralph S.; bud long, pointed, apricot; flowers 1½ in., single, flat, borne in small clusters, slight fragrance; recurrent; foliage leathery; vigorous, bushy (12-14 in.) growth; [(*R. wichurana* × Floradora) × seedling]; int. by Sequoia Nursery, 1961

Simplex A, w

Simplex Multiflora HMult, pb, 1905

Simplicity HT, w, 1909, Dickson, H.; bud cup-shaped; flowers pure white, large, single, open; foliage glossy, rich green; declared extinct, ARA 1979

Simplicity F, mp, 1979, Warriner, William A.; bud long, pointed; flowers phlox pink, 3-4 in., 14-20 petals, flat, borne several together, very slight fragrance; free-flowering; foliage large, leathery; prickles normal, hooked slightly downward; stems long, strong; bushy, upright growth; PP4089; [Iceberg × seedling]; int. by J&P, 1979; Gold Medal, NZ, 1976

Simplicity F, op, 2000, Lens, Louis; flowers light salmon-pink, 6 cm., semi-dbl. to dbl., cupped to flat, borne in large clusters, moderate fragrance; foliage medium size, medium green, glossy; few prickles; growth bushy, medium (60-70 cm.); [Little Angel × Pascali]; int. by Louis Lens N.V., 1990

Simply S, mp, Noack; flowers soft pink, 1½ in., dbl., cupped, borne in clusters; recurrent; upright (3 ft.), arching growth; int. by Noack Rosen, 2003

Simply Beautiful MinFl, m, 2003, Wells, Verlie W.; flowers lavender blend, 2 in., dbl., borne mostly solitary, intense fragrance; foliage medium size, medium green, semi-glossy; prickles moderate, 3/16 in., straight; growth upright, medium (24 in.); garden, exhibition; [Tom Brown × seedling]; int. by Wells Mid-South Roses, 2002

Simply Charming F, op, Delbard; flowers soft pink with cream eye, intensifying to coral, prominent stamens, single, shallow cup to flat, borne in clusters, slight fragrance; recurrent; medium (5 ft.) growth; int. by Ludwig's Roses, 2005

Simply Divine F, rb, 1978, Anderson's Rose Nurseries; flowers large, 18 petals; foliage dark; [Elizabeth of Glamis × Evelyn Fison]

Simply Elegant Min, m, 1993, Buster, Larry S.; flowers light lavender inside with darker reverse, large, full, borne mostly singly; foliage medium size, medium green, matte; some prickles; upright, compact (50 cm.) growth; [Lady X × Winsome]; int. by Kimbrew Walter Roses, 1993

Simply Elegant Gr, dy, Delbard; flowers full, cupped, moderate fragrance; medium growth; int. in 2001

Simply Heaven HT, ly, Dickson; flowers light lemon, tinted bronze, large, dbl., high-centered, borne mostly singly; foliage dark green, glossy; stems long; tall, healthy growth; int. by Dickson Nurseries, 2002; Gold Medal, RNRS, 1999

Simply Irresistible HT, w, 1996, Datt, Braham; flowers white with pink tones, reverse cream with pink tones, medium, dbl., borne in small clusters, moderate fragrance; foliage medium size, medium green, semi-glossy; few prickles; upright, medium (4½ ft.) growth; [First Prize × Garden Party]; int. by Certified Roses, Inc.

Simply Magic – See **Les Amoureux de Peynet**, F

Simply Marvelous! F, m, 2001, Zary, Keith; bud pointed, ovoid; flowers lavender with soft pink edges, 3-4 in., 30 petals, high-centered, borne in large clusters, moderate antique rose fragrance; good repeat; foliage medium size, dark green, glossy; prickles moderate; growth upright, medium (3½ ft.); garden decorative; PP13183; [Pink Pollyanna × Arosedi]; int. by J&P, 2002

Simply Sunblaze – See **Spot Meillandina**, Min

Simply the Best – See **Top Notch**, HT

Simpson's Red HT, dr, 1977, Simpson, J.W.; flowers large, full; [Red Lion × Grande Amore]; int. by Lower Rangitikei Rose Soc.

Simpson's Ruby F, mr, Horner; int. by Warley Rose Gardens, 2006

Simsalabim HT, yb, Kordes; flowers striped; int. in 2002

Sinbad HT, op, 1964, Leenders, J.; flowers salmon-pink; [Pink Lustre × Circus]

Sincera – See **Amistad Sincera**, HT

Sincerely Mine Min

Sincerely Yours Min, mr, 1991, Moore, Ralph S.; flowers rich red, yellow stamens, medium, semi-dbl., borne in small clusters, no fragrance; foliage medium size, medium green, semi-glossy; some prickles; medium (20-24 cm.), bushy growth; [Sheri Anne × Dortmund]; int. by Sequoia Nursery, 1992; AOE, ARS, 1992

Sincerity HT, ob, 1940, LeGrice; bud long, pointed; flowers flesh, shaded amber and orange, large, dbl.; foliage dark, leathery; vigorous, compact growth; [(Comtesse Vandal × unknown) × Mrs Sam McGredy]

Sindoor F, or, 1981, Division of Vegetable Crops and Floriculture; bud long, pointed; flowers 23 petals, borne singly or 15 per cluster, no fragrance; foliage large, glossy, coppery when young; prickles straight, bending downward; upright, tall growth; [Sea Pearl × Suryodaya]; int. in 1980

Singalong Min, op, 1988, McGredy, Sam IV; flowers salmon-orange and yellow, medium, full; foliage small, medium green, glossy; patio; bushy growth; [(Anytime × Eyepaint) × New Year]

Singin' in the Rain F, ab, 1994, McGredy, Sam IV; flowers apricot/copper, medium, 25-30 petals, ruffled, borne in large clusters, moderate sweet musk fragrance; foliage medium size, dark green, glossy; some prickles; medium (3-4 ft.), upright, free-branching growth; PP8362; [Sexy Rexy × Pot O'Gold]; int. by Edmunds Roses, 1994; Gold Medal, RNRS, 1991

Single M, lp, 1807, Wandes; flowers rose pink, medium, single; foliage unequally dentate; prickles numerous, straight, sharp

Single Bliss Min, pb, 1980, Saville, F. Harmon; bud short, pointed; flowers deep pink and white, 5 petals, flat, borne in clusters of 5-30; foliage very small, very glossy; prickles straight; very compact, bushy growth; [Seabreeze × Baby Betsy McCall]; int. by Nor'East Min. Roses

Single Charm Min, pb, 1991, Umsawasdi, Dr. Theera; flowers hand-painted white with pink edge, small, 5 petals, borne mostly singly, no fragrance; foliage small, medium green, matte; tall, upright, bushy growth; [Jennifer × seedling]

Single Cherry HSpn, pb; flowers cerise red, medium, single

Single Chestnut Rose – See ***R. roxburghii normalis*** (Rehder & Wilson)

Single Crimson Moss Rose – See **Rivers' Single Crimson Moss**, M

Single Moss – See **Communis**, M

Single Red – See **Red Nelly**, HSpn

Single's Better Min, mr, 1985, Saville, F. Harmon; bud mossy; flowers medium red, yellow hinge, mini-moss, small, 5 petals; foliage medium size, medium green, semi-glossy; bushy growth; [(Yellow Jewel × Tamango) × ((Little Chief × Sarabande) × (Lemon Delight × LemonDelight))]; int. by Nor'East Min. Roses

Sinica Anemone – See **Anemone**, S

Sinjun HT, w, Harada; flowers white with touch of pink in center, dbl., high-centered; free-flowering

Sinoia Pol, ob

Sinsetu – See **Shin-Setsu**, LCl

Siobhan F, rb, 1985, McCann, Sean; flowers red, reverse yellow, medium, 20 petals, hybrid tea form, borne in small clusters, slight fragrance; recurrent; foliage medium size, dark bronze, semi-glossy; upright (3-5 ft.) growth; [Maxi × Copper Pot]; int. in 1984

Sioux HT, op, Kordes ; bud slender, salmon-orange; flowers salmon pink, medium, dbl., high-centered, borne usually singly; good repeat; few prickles; stems long; florist rose; int. by W. Kordes Söhne, 2001

Sioux Beauty S, rb, 1927, Hansen, N.E.; flowers bright rose, center dark crimson, 100 petals; non-recurrent bloom; hardy; [Tetonkaha × American Beauty]

Sir Min, ab, 1992, Jolly, Marie; flowers medium, semi-dbl., moderate fragrance; foliage medium size, dark green, semi-glossy; few prickles; medium growth; [Olympic Gold × Rise 'n' Shine]; int. by Rosehill Farm, 1993

Sir Alexander N. Rochfort HT, ob, 1917, Le Cornu; flowers flesh, center darker; [Lady Alice Stanley × Marquise de Sinéty]

Sir Arthur Streeton HT, mp, 1940, Clark, A.; flowers pink, well-formed

Sir Basil McFarland HT, ob, 1931, McGredy; bud long, pointed; flowers orange-salmon-pink, flushed yellow, dbl., high-centered; foliage thick; vigorous growth

Sir Billy Butlin HT, or, 1969, Gandy, Douglas L.; flowers red-orange, large, 30 petals, cupped, slight fragrance; foliage bronze; vigorous, upright growth; [Bettina × Majorca]

Sir C. V. Raman HT, or, Pal, Dr. B.P.; flowers scarlet, large, dbl.; free-flowering; int. in 1989

Sir Cedric Morris LCl, w, 1980; bud small, globular; flowers small, 5 petals, borne 20-40 per cluster, slight fragrance; summer bloom only in large quantity; foliage elongated, large; prickles large; very vigorous growth; [*R. rubrifolia* × *R. mulligani*]; from the garden of Sir Cedric Morris, at Benton End, Hadleigh; int. by Peter Beales, 1979

Sir Cliff Richard – See **Cliff Richard**, F

Sir Clough S, dp, Austin, David; flowers deep, brilliant pink, large, semi-dbl., shallow cup, moderate fragrance; good repeat; tall (5 ft.), strong, arching growth; int. by David Austin Roses, 1983

Sir Dallas Brooks HT, mr, 1963, Smith, R.W.; bud long, pointed; flowers large, dbl., high-centered, moderate fragrance; foliage leathery; vigorous, upright, open growth; [Ena Harkness × Charles Mallerin]; int. by T.G. Stewart, 1962

Sir David Davis HT, rb, 1926, McGredy; bud long, pointed; flowers deep glowing crimson, base light yellow, dbl., high-centered; foliage dark, leathery; vigorous growth

Sir David Reid HT, mr, 1941, Dickson, A.; flowers crimson-red, large, 25 petals, flat

Sir Donald Bradman – See **Botero**, HT very dbl.

Sir Edward Elgar S, mr, 1995, Austin, David; flowers cerise-crimson, medium, very dbl., cupped, borne mostly singly; foliage medium size, medium green, semi-glossy; numerous prickles; medium (75 cm.), upright, bushy, compact growth; [Mary Rose × The Squire]; int. by David Austin Roses, Ltd., 1992

Sir Edward's Rose HT, mp, Dawson; int. in 1998

Sir Frederick Ashton HT, w, Beales, Peter; flowers white to cream, large, dbl., intense sweet fragrance; foliage dark green, leathery; stems strong; upright, vigorous growth; [sport of Anna Pavlova]; int. by Peter Beales Roses, 1987

Sir Galahad F, dp, 1967, Harkness; flowers deep pink, medium, dbl.; foliage glossy; [Pink Parfait × Highlight]

Sir Galahad – See **Great North Eastern Rose**, F

Sir Garnet Wolseley HP, mr, 1875, Cranston; flowers rich vermilion shaded bright carmine, very large, full, borne mostly solitary; prickles coppery brown; [Prince Camille de Rohan × unknown]

Sir Harry HT, my, 1990, Bracegirdle, A.J.; bud ovoid; flowers medium, 30 petals, high-centered, borne usually singly, slight fruity fragrance; foliage medium size, dark green, glossy; prickles triangular, brown; bushy, medium growth; hips round, orange; [Irish Gold × (Pink Favorite × Golden Autumn)]; int. by Gregory's Roses, 1989

Sir Harry Pilkington HT, mr, 1973, Tantau; flowers well-formed, 4-5 in., 30 petals, high-centered, borne mostly singly; foliage dark; [Inge Horstmann × Sophia Loren]

Sir Henry HRg, m, Kordes; flowers dark magenta, dbl., cupped, moderate fragrance; recurrent; foliage dark green, semi-glossy; bushy (3 ft.), strong growth; int. by W. Kordes Söhne, 1988

Sir Henry Seagrave HT, ly, 1932, Dickson, A.; bud long, pointed; flowers light primrose-yellow, large, dbl., high-centered, intense fragrance; good repeat; foliage leathery; Gold Medal, NRS, 1932

Sir J. C. Bose HT, dp, Ghosh, Mr. & Mrs. S.; flowers deep pink, reverse darker, dbl., high-centered; vigorous growth; int. in 2004

Sir John A. Macdonald – See **John A. Macdonald**, Gr

Sir John Mills LCl, mp, 2006, Beales, Amanda; flowers glowing pink, outer edges fading lighter, 10 cm., full, hybrid tea, borne mostly solitary, moderate fragrance; recurrent; foliage medium size, dark green, glossy; prickles average, hooked, moderate; growth upright, medium (2½ m.); small climber for walls, fences, obelisks; [Armada × Westerland]; int. by Peter Beales Roses, 2005

Sir John Sebright Ayr, mp, before 1866; flowers bright carmine, small, dbl.

Sir Joseph Min, pb, 2004, Smith, Joe and Landers, Brenda; flowers striped with deep pink, medium pink, and light pink, 1½ in., dbl., borne mostly solitary, no fragrance; foliage medium green, semi-glossy; upright, short growth; [sport of Aristocrat]; int. in 2005

Sir Joseph Paxton B, dr, 1852, Laffay, M.; flowers deep red tinted violet, well-formed, medium, full, borne in small clusters, moderate fragrance; recurrent; foliage grey green; upright (6 ft.), narrow growth

Sir Lancelot F, ab, 1967, Harkness; flowers apricot-yellow, 3-4 in., semi-dbl., cupped, slight fragrance; recurrent; foliage light green, glossy; upright growth; [Vera Dalton × Woburn Abbey]

Sir Lancelot F, dp, Harkness; flowers dark rose pink, moderate fruity fragrance; large growth; original denomination of Harglisser was withdrawn at request of French authorities; int. by R. Harkness, 1999

Sir Matthew Nathan HT, dp, 1927, Harrison, A.; [Rhea Reid × Laurent Carle]

Sir Neville Marriner F, pb, 1997, Langdale, G.W.T.; flowers camelia pink, medium, very full, high-centered, borne mostly singly or in small clusters; foliage medium size, medium green, semi-glossy; few prickles; upright, medium (3 × 2 ft.) growth; [seedling × Painted Doll]; int. by Battersby Roses

Sir Paul Smith LCl, ab, 2006, Beales, Amanda; flowers full, borne in large clusters; foliage medium size, medium green, semi-glossy; prickles large, hooked, moderate; growth spreading, medium (2-3 m.); [Louise Odier × Aloha]; int. by Peter Beales Roses, 2006

Sir Robert Duff Cl T, lp, 1893, Johnson; [Gloire de Dijon × unknown]

Sir Rowland Hill HP, m, 1888, Mack; flowers dark purple/red, large, very dbl.; [sport of Charles Lefebvre]

Sir Thomas Lipton HRg, w, 1900, Van Fleet; bud ovoid; flowers very white, medium, dbl., round and cupped, intense fragrance; recurrent; foliage dark, leathery; vigorous (6-8 ft.), bushy growth; [*R. rugosa* (alba?) × Clotilde Soupert]; int. by Conard & Jones

Sir Tristram F, mr, Attfield; flowers velvety red; medium growth; int. in 2003

Sir Walter Raleigh HT, ob, 1919, Le Cornu; bud long, pointed; flowers coppery reddish-salmon, reverse deep crimson, dbl.; [Lady Pirrie × seedling]

Sir Walter Raleigh S, mp, 1994, Austin, David; bud medium, ovate pointed; flowers warm medium pink, 4 in., very dbl., flat cup, borne mostly singly or in small clusters, intense fragrance; recurrent; foliage medium size, medium green, semi-glossy; prickles few, slightly recurved, brown; medium (4 ft.), upright, bushy growth; PP7213; [Lilian Austin × Chaucer]; int. by David Austin Roses, Ltd., 1985

Sir Walter Raleigh Mutant S, ob; flowers orange, moderate fragrance; growth to 1 m.; [sport of Sir Walter Raleigh]

Sir Wilfrid Laurier LCl, lp; flowers clear rosy pink, dbl., hybrid tea, moderate fragrance; pillar rose growth, remains upright with little support

Sir William Butlin – See **Sir Billy Butlin**, HT

Sir William Leech – See **William Leech**, HT

Sir Winston Churchill HT, op, 1956, Dickson, A.; flowers salmon-pink shaded orange, 5 in., 48 petals, high-centered, moderate fragrance; foliage dark green, glossy; very vigorous growth; [seedling × Souv. de Denier van der Gon]; int. by A. Dickson & Sons, 1955; Gold Medal, NRS, 1955

Siren F, or, 1953, Kordes; bud ovoid; flowers bright scarlet-red, 3-3½ in., 18 petals, cupped, borne in clusters; foliage leathery; vigorous, compact growth; [(Baby Chateau × Else Poulsen) × Independence]; int. by J&P; Gold Medal, NRS, 1952

Sirena – See **Charlotte Klemm**, Ch

Sirena HT, rb, 1941, Aicardi, D.; bud ovoid; flowers cardinal-red, center shaded yellow, very large, dbl., cupped; foliage leathery; very vigorous growth; [Saturnia × Anemone]; int. by Giacomasso

Sirene – See **Charlotte Klemm**, Ch

Sirenella HT

Sirenetta Min, ab

Sirius Cl HT, mr, 1939, Fitzhardinge; bud long, pointed; flowers cherry-red, center lighter, large, dbl.; intermittent bloom; vigorous, climbing (15 ft.), open habit growth; [seedling × Lubra]; int. by Hazlewood Bros.

Sirocco F, or, 1971, Delforge; bud globular; flowers vermilion-red, large, very dbl., cupped; foliage dark, leathery; vigorous, bushy growth; [Independence × Orangeade]

Sirohi Sunrise HG, ob, 2005, Viraraghavan, M.S. Viru; flowers full, borne mostly solitary; foliage large, medium green, glossy; prickles large, triangular; growth pillar-like, tall (8 ft.); garden decorative; [Brown Velvet × (Carmousine × *R. gigantea*)]; int. by Roses Unlimited, 2004

Sis Min, w, 1998, Bridges, Dennis A.; flowers delicate white with a hint of pink, firm substance, 1½ in., dbl., high-centered, borne mostly singly, slight fragrance; recurrent; foliage small, medium green, semi-glossy; few prickles; stems long; strong, bushy, slightly spreading growth; disease resistant; [Party Girl × Cape Hatteras]; int. by Bridges Roses, 1998

Sisena – See **Charlotte Klemm**, Ch

Sisi Ketten Pol, dp, 1900, Gebrüder Ketten; flowers peach pink veined carmine, large, dbl.; [Mignonette × Safrano]

Sisley HP, mr, 1835, Sisley; flowers rosy crimson, medium, full, flat

Sissel – See **Sissel Renaissance**, S

Sissel Renaissance S, lp, Olesen; bud pointed ovoid; flowers blush pink to creamy white, 4 in., 45-50 petals, deep cup, borne in clusters (usually of 3), moderate fragrance; recurrent; foliage dark green; prickles few, 7 mm., concave, dark brown; narrow, bushy (75 cm.) growth; PP15388; [Clair Renaissance × seedling]; int. by Poulsen Roser, 2003

Sissi – See **Blue Moon**, HT

Sissi, Climbing – See **Blue Moon, Climbing**, Cl HT

Sissinghurst Castle – See **Rose des Maures**, HGal

Sister Elizabeth S, mp, 2006; flowers very full, borne in small clusters; foliage medium size, medium green, matte; prickles medium, concave, curved inward, red, numerous; growth compact, bushy, short (80 cm.); garden decorative; [seedling × seedling]; int. by David Austin Roses, Ltd., 2006

Sister Hellie F, w, 2003, Jellyman, J.S.; flowers pearl pink to white, reverse white and pink, 2 in., single, borne in small clusters, moderate fragrance; foliage medium size, dark green, semi-glossy; prickles 8 mm., slightly curved, few; growth compact, medium (3 ft.); garden, bedding; [Marylin Ross × (Jean Kenneally × (Sue Lawley × Sue Lawley))]

Sister Joan F, op, 1997, Kenny, David; flowers large, dbl., borne in small clusters; foliage large, dark green, semi-glossy; some prickles; upright, bushy, tall (3½ × 2½ ft.)growth; [(Mary Sumner × Kiskadee) × Maestro]

Sister Kenny F, mr, 1954, Joseph H. Hill, Co.; bud ovoid; flowers scarlet, medium, 10-12 petals, flat, borne in clusters; foliage leathery; very vigorous, upright growth; [Baby Chateau × Red Delicious]; int. by H&S

Sister Susan HT, rb, Oliver, F.; bud ovoid, yellow stained crimson; flowers cream tinted flesh, center copper-orange, base yellow, medium, 48 petals, high-centered; foliage leathery, glossy, dark; vigorous, spreading growth; [Mrs Sam McGredy × Soeur Thérèse]

Sister Thérèse – See **Soeur Thérèse**, HT

Sisters at Heart F, ab, Zary, Keith; bud pointed ovoid; flowers light apricot, 4 in., 35-40 petals, hybrid tea, borne in clusters, moderate spicy fragrance; recurrent; foliage dark green, glossy; stems 14-16 in.; medium (3 ft.) growth; PPAF; int. by Jackson & Perkins, 2006

Sister's Fairy Tale – See **Home & Garden**, F

Sitting Bull HSet, dp, Horvath; flowers deep pink, semi-dbl.; non-recurrent; growth to 6-8 ft.; not hardy

Sitting Pretty Min, pb, 1986, Bennett, Dee; bud ovoid; lacy sepals; flowers apricot-pink, yellow base, 35-40 petals, high-centered, borne usually singly, occasionally in small clusters, moderate damask fragrance; foliage medium size, medium green, semi-glossy; prickles small, straight, red; stems long, with long peduncle; medium (2-3 ft.), upright, bushy growth; hips globular, 1/2 in., yellowish-green; PP6454; [Sonoma × Mabel Dot]; int. by Tiny Petals Nursery

Siwa S, mp, 1910, Geschwind; flowers medium, full, flat, no fragrance; once-blooming; upright (5 ft.) growth; hybrid canina

Six Flags Gr, mr, 1962, Swim, H.C.; flowers cherry-red, 3½-4 in., 25-30 petals, high-centered; foliage slender, leathery, semi-glossy; vigorous, upright, spreading growth; [First Love × Roundelay]; int. by Poulsen

Six Fours Auri Misc OGR, w

Sixteen Candles F, pb, Harkness; bud pointed ovoid; flowers blend of peach and pink, 4 in., 25 petals, cupped, borne in clusters, slight sweet fragrance; recurrent; foliage dark green, glossy; stems 10-16 in.; compact, upright (3-4 ft.) growth; PPAF; int. in 2006

Sixth Sense F, pb, J&P; flowers cerise pink with silver-pink stripes and white eye, semi-dbl., flat, borne in clusters; free-flowering; foliage dark green; bushy, compact, short growth; int. in 1996

65 Roses S, w, Thomson; flowers clear white with yellow stamens, single, flat, borne in clusters, intense sweet clove fragrance; stems long; medium to tall growth; named for Cystic Fibrosis research; int. by Ross Roses, 2001

Sizzle Pink HT, dp, 1989, Marciel, Stanley G.; bud slender, tapering; flowers deep pink, sweetheart, large, 25 petals, cupped, borne singly; foliage large, dark green, matte; prickles declining, olive green; upright, tall growth; PP7562; [seedling × seedling]; int. by DeVor Nurseries, Inc.

Sizzler Min, or, 1978, Saville, F. Harmon; flowers 1-1½ in., 28 petals, high-centered, moderate spicy fragrance; vigorous, upright, spreading growth; [Sheri Anne × Prominent]; int. by Nor'East Min. Roses, 1975

Sjoukji Dijkstra Pol, mr, 1966, Buisman, G. A. H.; bud ovoid; flowers scarlet, medium, semi-dbl., borne in large clusters; compact growth; [Chatter × Paprika]

Skaggarak F, mr, 1970, Poulsen; flowers clear red, 3½-5 in., 18-20 petals, open, borne several together, slight fragrance; free-flowering; vigorous growth; hardy; [Irish Wonder × seedling]

Skaidra HRg, Rieksta, Dr. Dz.

Skarlagen General MacArthur HT, dr, 1985, Poulsen, S.; flowers scarlet, large, dbl.; foliage medium size, dark, semi-glossy; upright growth; [General MacArthur × seedling]; int. by Poulsen's Roses, 1930

Skinner's Rambler LCl, lp, 1956, Skinner; bud small, long, pointed; flowers pale pink, open, small, 5 petals, borne in clusters of 10-40; foliage soft green; very vigorous, climbing (20 ft. annually) growth; [*R.*

maximowicziana × unknown]; int. by Univ. of NH, 1955

Skinner's Red S, mr, Skinner

Skogul F, dp, 1969, Lundstad; flowers rose-madder, open, 18 petals, borne in clusters; foliage dark, glossy; vigorous growth; [Lichterloh × Lumina]

Skvost HT

Sky High LCl, mp, 2001, Cowlishaw, Frank; flowers medium, dbl., borne in large clusters, moderate fragrance; foliage medium size, medium green, semi-glossy; prickles medium, sharp, moderate; growth upright, tall (2½ m.); garden decorative; int. by Rearsby Roses Ltd., 2001

Sky Tower LCl, mp, 2004, Somerfield, Rob; flowers lighter pink, reverse bright pink, medium, dbl., borne in large clusters, no fragrance; foliage large, dark green, glossy; prickles medium, downward facing, numerous; stems long; growth bushy, tall (10 ft.), climbing; [Strawberry Ice × Hot Chocolate]; int. in 2004; Best Climber, Hamilton, NZ, 2006

Skylark F, mp, 1959, deVor, Paul F.; bud urn shaped; flowers pink, reverse darker, 2½ in., 55-65 petals, high-centered, borne in clusters of 3-15; foliage glossy; very vigorous, upright growth; PP1678; [sport of Carol Amling]; int. by Amling Bros., 1958

Skyline HT, my, Tantau; bud long, pointed ovoid; flowers clear yellow, outer petals fade, 4 in., 30 petals, high-centered, borne singly, moderate fragrance; recurrent; foliage large; prickles medium, hooked slightly downward; stems long, strong; vigorous, upright (5-6 ft.) growth; PP9065; [seedling × seedling]; int. in 1991

Skyliner LCl, Delforge; int. in 1980

Skylon HT, rb, 1952, Lowe; bud very long, pointed; flowers orange shaded peach, veined red, 5½-6 in., 26 petals; foliage glossy; very free growth; [sport of Mme Henri Guillot]

Skyrocket HMsk, dr, 1934, Kordes; bud long, pointed, black-red; flowers bright blood red, 2 in., semi-dbl., cupped to flat, borne in very large clusters, moderate fragrance; recurrent bloom; foliage large, glossy, leathery; vigorous, bushy (6-8 ft.) growth; [Robin Hood × J.C. Thornton]

Sky's the Limit LCl, my, 2005, Carruth, Tom; flowers clear, pure yellow, ruffled, 8-10 cm., 20-25 petals, borne in large clusters, moderate fruity fragrance; free-flowering; foliage medium size, medium green, glossy; prickles moderate, average, almost straight, beige; climbing, tall (10-12 ft.) growth; garden decoration; [Princess Marianna × *R. soulieana* derivative]; int. by Weeks Roses, 2007

Slater's Crimson China Ch, mr, 1790; flowers velvety red-crimson, 2½ in., dbl., borne usually solitary; foliage shows a tint of purple when young; slender stems; growth medium (3-4 ft.); hips round, scarlet; introduced by Slater

Slats HT, mp, 1999, Edwards, Eddie; flowers 6 in., full, borne mostly singly, moderate fragrance; foliage large, medium green, semi-glossy; prickles moderate; upright, tall (5-6 ft.) growth; [Louise Estes × Great Scott]; int. by Johnny Becnel Show Roses, 1999

Slava HT, rb, 1987, Williams, J. Benjamin; flowers scarlet red, reverse ivory white, large, 34 petals, high-centered, borne singly, moderate damask fragrance; foliage large, dark green, glossy, disease-resistant; prickles medium, few, yellow-green, hooked downwards; upright, bushy, tall growth; hips rounded, medium, pumpkin-orange; [Garden Party × Love]; int. in 1988

Sláva Böhmova HT, rb, 1930, Böhm, J.; bud long; flowers salmon-red, base golden yellow, large, dbl.; foliage blood-red, mahonia-like; [Covent Garden × Golden Emblem]

Slavia Cl Pol, w, 1934, Brada, Dr.; bud pink; flowers rosy white, 4 cm., dbl., borne in small clusters, intense fragrance; recurrent bloom; vigorous growth; [Tausendschön × unknown]; int. by Böhm

Slávuse HT, w, 1936, Brada, Dr.; flowers formed like a cactus dahlia

Sleeping Beauty – See **Dornröschen**, S

Sleeping Beauty HT, w, 1968, Morey, Dr. Dennison; bud long, pointed; flowers large, dbl., high-centered, moderate fragrance; foliage leathery; vigorous, upright growth; [(Frau Karl Druschki × Rex Anderson) × Virgo]; int. by General Bionomics

Sleeping Beauty HT, pb, Hiroshima; int. by Hiroshima Bara-en, 2004

Sleeping Beauty MinFl, pb, 2005, White, Wendy R.; flowers salmon, reverse light pearl salmon, 1?-2? in., very full, borne in large clusters, intense fragrance; foliage medium size, medium green, semi-glossy, disease-resistant; prickles 5/16, tapered, hooked, slight angle, dark, mahogany brown; growth compact, bushy, medium (18-22 in.); garden perennial, borders; [seedling × New Zealand]; int. by Nor'East Miniature Roses, 2005

Sleepy Pol, mp, 1958, deRuiter; flowers very small, dbl., borne in trusses; [(Orange Triumph × Golden Rapture) × Polyantha seedling]; int. by Gregory & Son, 1955

Sleepy Time Min, op, 1974, Moore, Ralph S.; bud long, pointed; flowers soft peach to soft salmon-pink, small, dbl.; foliage small, light, leathery; vigorous, dwarf, upright, bushy growth; [Ellen Poulsen × Fairy Princess]; int. by Sequoia Nursery, 1973

Sleigh Bells HT, w, 1950, Howard, P.J.; bud ovoid, cream; flowers white, center creamy, open, large, 40 petals, cupped, intense fragrance; recurrent; foliage leathery, glossy; very vigorous, upright growth; [Capt. Thomas × Eternal Youth]; int. by H&S

Sleigh Bells, Climbing Cl HT, w, Wilkins; [sport of Sleigh Bells]; int. in 1995

Slot van Laarne S, lp, RvS-Melle; [*R. fedtschenkoana* × Pernille Poulsen]; int. in 1992

Sly Fox S, mr, Kordes; flowers bright red, yellow stamens, dbl., cupped, borne in clusters; recurrent; foliage glossy; moderate (3-4 ft.), spreading growth; int. by Ludwig's Roses, 2003

Small Fantasy Min, lp, 1983, Dobbs, Annette E.; flowers small, dbl.; foliage small, light green, semi-glossy; bushy growth; [Snow Magic × Blue Mist]; int. in 1982

Small-flowered Rose – See ***R. micrantha*** (Borrer ex Sm.)

Small Miracle Min, w, 1993, Warriner, William A.; bud plump, short, pointed ovoid; flowers clean white, 1½-2 in., 20-24 petals, classic hybrid tea, borne in clusters, slight fragrance; recurrent; foliage small, dark green, glossy, resistant to powdery mildew; prickles few, short, hooked downward; upright (20-24 in.), bushy growth; PP8850; [Libby × Sun Flare]; int. by Bear Creek Gardens, 1993

Small Slam Min, dr, 1984, Laver, Keith G.; flowers small, dbl.; foliage small, dark, semi-glossy; bushy growth; [Nic Noc × Party Girl]

Small Talk F, my, 1963, Swim & Weeks; flowers 2½ in., 33 petals, high-centered, borne in large clusters; foliage leathery, glossy, dark; compact, low growth; PP2226; [Yellow Pinocchio × Circus]; int. by Weeks Roses, 1963

Small Victories F, mr, Drummond; int. by Greenbelt Farm, 1996

Small Virtue Min, w, 1986, Jolly, Marie; flowers small, 48 petals, high-centered, borne singly and in sprays of 2-7; foliage small, medium green, semi-glossy; prickles medium pink; low, bushy growth; fruit not observed; [Party Girl × Snow Bride]; int. by Rosehill Farm, 1983

Small Wonder Min, pb, 1984, Hardgrove, Donald L.; flowers light pink, darker reverse, small, dbl., high-centered, borne singly, no fragrance; foliage small, medium green, semi-glossy; upright, bushy growth; [Futura × Orange Honey]; int. by Rose World Originals, 1983

Small World Min, or, 1975, Moore, Ralph S.; bud pointed; flowers rich orange-red, 2½ in., 21 petals, flat; foliage small, glossy, leathery; dwarf, compact growth; PP4027; [Little Chief × Fire Princess]; int. by Sequoia Nursery

Smart F, op, Kordes; flowers salmon orange, medium, dbl., urn-shaped, borne mostly singly; recurrent; stems medium (16 in.); florist rose; int. by W. Kordes Söhne, 1999

Smart Kordana Min, mp, Kordes; flowers dusky pink, full, high-centered to cupped, borne mostly singly; container plant; int. by W. Kordes Söhne

Smart Roadrunner HRg, dp, Uhl; flowers deep magenta pink, yellow stamens, 2 in., semi-dbl. to dbl., cupped, borne in trusses, moderate fragrance; recurrent; foliage dense, semi-glossy; bushy, upright (2 ft.) growth; groundcover; int. by W. Kordes Söhne, 2004; ADR, 2003

Smarty S, lp, 1979, Ilsink; flowers pale pink with large white eye, 2 in., single, flat, borne in clusters, no fragrance; recurrent; foliage bright green, matte; prickles numerous, small; vigorous, bushy (3 ft. × 4 ft.) growth; groundcover; [Yesterday × seedling]; int. by Dickson Nurseries, Ltd.

Smell Me HT, dp, Pearce; flowers deep magenta pink, large, dbl., high-centered, intense fragrance; recurrent; vigorous, tall growth; int. by Ludwig's Roses, 2005

Smerisal HT, op

Smile S, pb, Clements, John; flowers pink, edges tinged copper, white eye, golden stamens, 3½-4 in., 12 petals, flat, borne in clusters of 12-24, moderate fruity fragrance; free-flowering; upright (4½ ft.), arching growth; PPAF; int. by Heirloom, 2002

Smile – See **Emi**, F

Smile Kordana Min, my, Kordes; flowers dbl.; int. by W. Kordes Söhne

Smiles F, lp, 1937, Nicolas; flowers light salmon-pink, semi-dbl., borne in clusters, slight fragrance; recurrent; foliage leathery; compact, bushy growth; [Echo × Rev. F. Page-Roberts]; int. by J&P

Smiles Min, my, 1982, Warriner, William A.; flowers medium, 35 petals; foliage small, light green, semi-glossy; upright, bushy growth; PP5577; [Spanish Sun × Calgold]; int. by J&P, 1984

Smiley F, ob, 1980, Murray, Nola; bud pointed; flowers orange, apricot, yellow, shapely, 2½ in., 21 petals; foliage matte green; tall, vigorous, upright growth; [Arthur Bell × Little Darling]

Smiling Susan S, op, Delbard; flowers blend of light peach to burnt orange, semi-dbl., cupped, open, borne in large clusters; vigorous, large, arching growth; large shrub or small climber; int. by Ludwig's Roses, 2001

Smiling Through F, or, 1976, Anderson's Rose Nurseries; flowers orange to red, 3 in., 27 petals; foliage glossy, light; [Orange Sensation × Mme Louis Laperriere]

Smiling Wings F, dp

Smithfield Rose S, ob, Taschner, Ludwig; flowers blend of bright orange, apricot, peach and yellow, large, dbl., loose, borne in clusters; free-flowering;

medium, broad growth; int. by Ludwig's Rose, 1999

Smithii – See **Smith's Yellow China**, T

Smith's Parish – See **Fortune's Five-colored Rose**, T

Smith's Yellow China T, dy, 1834, Smith; flowers sulphur yellow, large, full, cupped; [Blush Noisette × Parks' Yellow Tea-Scented China]

Smits' Briar HRg; [*R. rugosa* × *R. canina*]; used for understock; int. by Smits

Smoke Screen HT, or, Benardella, Frank; int. by Bell Roses, 1997

Smoke Signals Min, m, 1990, Williams, Ernest D.; bud short, pointed; flowers smoky, lavender-gray, adding pinkish tone with aging, 1½ in., 30-40 petals, high-centered, borne usually singly, intense fragrance; recurrent; foliage small, medium green, glossy; prickles few, slender, hooked slightly downward, tan; stems slender, wiry; upright (12-14 in.), bushy growth; PP7604; [(Tom Brown × (Rise 'n' Shine × Watercolor)) × Twilight Trail]; int. by Mini-Roses, 1989

Smoked Salmon Min, pb, 2007, Chapman, Bruce; flowers 4-5 cm., dbl., blooms borne in small clusters; foliage small, dark green, glossy; prickles small, hooked, brown, few; growth upright, short; garden decoration; [Rise 'n' Shine × First Prize]; int. by Ross Roses, 2007

Smokey Joe HT, ob, Williams, J. Benjamin; flowers orange, yellow base, smokey overlay, full, high-centered, slight fragrance; int. by Hortico Inc., 1998

Smokey Joe HT, or, Cocker; bud deep copper-orange; flowers burne orange-scarlet with a smokey edge, dbl., high-centered, slight fragrance; medium to tall growth; int. by De Boer Roses, 2003

Smokey Joe's Cafe HT, dp, 1999, Sheridan, John; flowers 3½-4 in., dbl., borne in small clusters; foliage medium size, medium green, semi-glossy; few prickles; upright, medium (2½ ft.) growth; [Red Planet × Pretty Lady]

Smoking Gun Min, m, 2003, Moe, Mitchie; flowers light mauve, 1½ in., dbl., high-centered, borne mostly solitary, slight fragrance; foliage small, light green, semi-glossy; prickles small, straight, light tan, few; growth upright, medium (18-20 in.); exhibition, garden decorative; [Vista × Anne Hering]; int. by Mitchie's Roses and More, 2003

Smoky HT, rb, 1970, Combe; bud medium, ovoid; flowers smoky oxblood-red shaded burgundy, medium, dbl., open, borne mostly singly, slight fragrance; free-flowering; foliage medium size, medium green; stems medium; vigorous, upright growth; int. by J&P, 1968

Smoky Mountain Min, m, 1988, Bridges, Dennis A.; bud pointed; flowers deep mauve, medium, 24 petals, high-centered, borne usually singly; foliage medium size, dark green, semi-glossy; prickles straight, pointed, small, tan; upright, medium growth; [Black Jade × seedling]; int. by Bridges Roses, 1989

Smooth Angel HT, ab, 1986, Davidson, Harvey D.; bud medium, globular; flowers apricot blending to cream at edges, 5 in., 36-48 petals, cupped, borne mostly singly, intense fruity fragrance; recurrent; foliage medium size, medium green, matte; no prickles; medium (1 m.), bushy, spreading growth; no fruit; PP6146; [Smooth Sailing × Royal Flush]; int. by Gurney Seed

Smooth Ballerina F, lp, 2006, Davidson, Harvey; bud ovoid; flowers light pink with slight white stripe, reverse light pink, 8-9 cm., 48-52 petals, globular, borne in small clusters, moderate fragrance; rapid repeat; foliage medium size, medium green, matte; growth upright, medium (1¼ m.); garden; hips round, olive green with orange tints; PP15662; [Pink Empress × (Blue Moon × Roller Coaster)]; int. by Mea Nursery, 2006

Smooth Buttercup F, dy, 2003, Davidson, Harvey; bud ovoid; flowers deep butter yellow, ruffled petals, 2½-3½ in., 24-26 petals, globular, borne in clusters of 3-14, moderate fragrance; fast repeat; foliage medium size, medium green, matte; upright (2½ ft.), medium growth; garden; hips few, round, orange; PP16014; [Kika × (Basildon Bond × Arthur Bell) × Midas Touch]; int. by Monrovia Nursery, 2003

Smooth Delight HT, op, 2006, Davidson, Harvey; bud ovoid; flowers peach, 11-12 cm., 34-36 petals, globular, borne mostly solitary, moderate fragrance; recurrent; foliage medium green, glossy; growth upright, medium (1¼ m.); garden; hips none ; PP15907; [yellow HT (6830CP) seedling × Smooth Sailing]; int. by Mea Nursery, 2006

Smooth Lady HT, mp, 1986, Davidson, Harvey D.; bud slender, tapering; flowers open fast, 4-4½ in., 21-26 petals, high-centered, to loose, borne in clusters of 1-3, moderate spicy fragrance; foliage large, medium green, very glossy; no prickles; tall (5 ft.), upright, bushy growth; hips medium, globular, orange; PP6147; [Smooth Sailing × ((Polly × Peace) × Circus)]; int. by Gurney Seed

Smooth Melody F, rb, 1990, Davidson, Harvey D.; bud ovoid, pointed; flowers red with white center, white reverse with red on outer edge, aging darker, 3½ in., 26 petals, cupped to flat, borne in small clusters, intense fruity fragrance; fast repeat; foliage medium size, dark green, semi-glossy; thornless; growth vigorous, upright (3-4 ft.); hips round, rarely sets seed; PP7729; [Royal Flush × Smooth Lady]; int. by Harvey Davidson, 1979

Smooth Moonlight HT, m, 2006, Davidson, Harvey; bud ovoid; flowers lavender-pink, aging lavender, 10-12 cm., 36-40 petals, globular, borne mostly solitary, intense Damask fragrance; rapid repeat; foliage medium size, dark green, glossy; growth compact, medium (1 m.); garden decoration; hips round, 1 in., olive green with orange tones; PP15667; [Smooth Perfume × Blue Boy]; int. by Mea Nursery, 2006

Smooth Perfume HT, lp, 1990, Davidson, Harvey D.; bud pointed, ovoid, large; flowers cream to light pink, very light mauve on edge, 5 in., 28-30 petals, cupped, open fast, borne singly and in small clusters, intense damask fragrance; recurrent; foliage medium size, medium green, semi-glossy; thornless; upright, bushy, medium (3-4 ft.) growth; hips rounded, flat base; PP7728; [(Smooth Sailing × Medallion) × Blue Moon]; int. by Harvey Davidson, 1979

Smooth Prince HT, mr, 1990, Davidson, Harvey D.; bud ovoid to globular, large; flowers 26-28 petals, cupped, flat center, urn-shaped, usually borne singly, slight fruity fragrance; good repeat; foliage medium size, medium green, semi-glossy; thornless; vigorous, upright (4 ft.) growth; hips oblong, rarely sets seed; PP7706; [Smooth Sailing × Old Smoothie]; int. by Harvey Davidson, 1979

Smooth Princess HT, w, 2000, Davidson, Harvey; flowers full, borne mostly singly, moderate fragrance; foliage medium size, medium green, semi-glossy; thornless; growth upright, medium to tall (1½ m.); [(Smooth Sailing × (Blue Moon × Roller Coaster)) × Kika]; int. by Monrovia Nursery, 2002

Smooth Queen HT, yb, 2006, Davidson, Harvey; bud ovoid; flowers yellow, shaded pink, 12 cm., 34-36 petals, globular, borne mostly solitary, intense fragrance; recurrent; foliage medium size, dark green, semi-glossy; growth upright, medium (1¼ m.); garden; hips none ; PP17482; [Kika × Remember Me]; int. by Mea Nursery, 2006

Smooth Romance HT, w, 1992, Davidson, Harvey D.; flowers cream with tinge of pink in center, 4¾ in., 42-45 petals, urn-shaped, borne usually singly, moderate fragrance; fast repeat; foliage medium size, medium green, glossy; thornless; stems straight, upright; upright, bushy, tall growth; hips will not set seed; [Smooth Sailing × Portrait]; int. by Hortico Roses, 1991

Smooth Sailing Gr, w, 1977, Davidson, Harvey D.; flowers cream color, 4 in., 30 petals, slight fragrance; foliage dark, glossy; tall growth; [Little Darling × Pink Favorite]; int. by Burgess Seed & Plant Co.

Smooth Satin HT, mp, 1993, Davidson, Harvey D.; bud ovoid; flowers light to medium pink, reverse slightly darker, 4½ in., 35-40 petals, globular, borne mostly singly, moderate fragrance; recurrent; foliage large, medium green, glossy; nearly thornless; medium (4 ft.), upright, bushy growth; hips does not set seed ; PP8910; [Smooth Lady × Smooth Sailing]; int. by C & L Valley Rose Co.

Smooth Snowflake HT, w, 2006, Davidson, Harvey; flowers 9-10 cm., full, borne mostly solitary, moderate fragrance; foliage medium size, medium green, matte; growth compact, medium (1 m.); garden decoration; [Kika × (Singing in the Rain × Joro)]; int. by Mea Nursery, 2006

Smooth Talk F, w, 1988, Weeks, O.L.; bud long, pointed ovoid; flowers ivory-white, aging bright white, abundant, 3 in., 25-35 petals, high-centered, borne in clusters of 3-7, slight anise fragrance; recurrent; foliage medium size, medium green, semi-glossy; prickles few, pointed, small, yellow-brown; upright, bushy, compact (3-3½ ft.) growth; exhibition; PP7156; [seedling × seedling]; int. by Weeks Wholesale Rose Growers, 1988

Smooth Touch – See **Smooth Buttercup**, F

Smooth Velvet HT, dr, 1986, Davidson, Harvey D.; bud pointed ovoid; flowers velvety dark red, 5 in., 38-42 petals, cupped, borne usually singly, slight damask fragrance; recurrent; foliage large, light green, matte; tall (7-8 ft.), upright growth; hips medium, globular, orange; PP6152; [Smooth Lady × Red Devil]; int. by Gurney Seed

Smuts Memory HT, dr, 1950, Leenders, M.; flowers brilliant deep crimson-red; [Sensation × World's Fair]

Snappie HT, rb, 1990, Bridges, Dennis A.; bud pointed; flowers medium red with yellow at base, reverse creamy-yellow, aging, 52 petals, high-centered; foliage medium size, dark green, semi-glossy; prickles curved slightly downward, medium, deep pink; upright, medium growth; [Lady X × Wini Edmunds]; int. by Bridges Roses, 1990

Snedronningen – See **Frau Karl Druschki**, HP

Sneeuwwitje – See **Iceberg**, F

Sneezy Pol, dp, 1958, deRuiter; flowers Neyron rose, small, single, slight fragrance; free-flowering; foliage dark green, glossy; vigorous growth; int. by Gregory & Son, 1955

Snehurka Pol, w, 1937, Böhm, J.; flowers small, dbl.

Snehurka Min, Vik

Snehurka Min, w, Urban, J.

Sneprincess Pol, w, 1958, Bang; bud ovoid; flowers pure white, small, dbl., cupped, borne in clusters; foliage light green, glossy; moderate, upright, bushy growth; [sport of Mothersday]; int. in 1953

Sneprinsesse Pol, w, 1946, Grootendorst, F.J.; flowers small, globular, borne in clusters; bushy growth; [sport of Dick Koster]

Sniedze HRg, Rieksta, Dr. Dz.

Sniffer HRg, m, 2004, Bock, Chuck; flowers beet purple with white eye and white streaks, 4 in., semi-dbl., borne in small clusters, intense clove fragrance; remontant; foliage medium size, dark green, glossy, disease-resistant; prickles straight; growth bushy, wide, dense, short (33 in.); landscape, borders; hips red; hardy; [hybrid rugosa seedling × Miniature seedling]; int. in 2006

Sno Min, w, 1983, Meredith, E.A. & Rovinski, M.E.; flowers 48 petals, high-centered, borne in clusters of 1-3, intense fragrance; foliage narrow, light green, matte; sprawling growth; [seedling × Gold Pin]; int. by Casa de Rosa Domingo

Sno Cone F, rb, 1996, Chaffin, Lauren M.; flowers white edged red, 2½-3 in., dbl., borne in small clusters; foliage small, medium green, semi-glossy, disease-resistant; prickles moderate; bushy, low (18 in.) growth; [Hannah Gordon × Pink Petticoat]; int. by Pixie Treasures Min. Roses, 1996

Snodoll Min, w, 1987, Travis, Louis R.; flowers 30-40 crinkled, translucent petals, borne singly, slight fruity fragrance; foliage small, medium green, semi-glossy; prickles bowed, white; upright growth; no fruit; [Yellow Doll × Yellow Doll]; int. in 1986

Snookie Min, ob, 1984, Bennett, Dee; flowers deep orange, blushing red with age, very small, 33 petals; foliage medium green, semi-glossy; bushy, tiny growth; [Torchy × Orange Honey]; int. by Tiny Petals Nursery

Snoopy HT, rb, 1973, Cadle's Roses; flowers carmine, reverse silver, very large, 28 petals, urn-shaped, moderate spicy fragrance; foliage large, glossy; [Paddy McGredy × Rose Gaujard]

Snövit – See **Blanche Neige**, Pol

Snövit Pol, w, 1946, Grootendorst, F.J.; flowers pure white; [sport of Dick Koster]

Snow Min, w, Poulsen; flowers white, medium, semi-dbl., slight wild rose fragrance; foliage dark; growth bushy, 20-40 cm.; PP10649; int. by Poulsen Roser, 1998

Snow – See **Snow Hit**, MinFl

Snow Angel S, w, 1993; flowers white with a light pink tone and a hint of yellow near petal base, medium, very dbl.; foliage small, dark green, semi-glossy; some prickles; medium (5 ft.), upright, bushy growth; [sport of Pink Pollyanna]; int. by Bear Creek Gardens, 1993

Snow Ballet S, w, 1977, Clayworth; flowers pure white, 4-5 cm., 45 petals, cupped, slight fragrance; foliage small, dark green, glossy; growth to 16-20 in.; [Sea Foam × Iceberg]; int. by Harkness New Roses, Ltd., 1977; Gold Medal, Baden-Baden, 1980

Snow Bear S, w, 1993, Adams, Dr. Neil D.; flowers 3-3¼ in., dbl., borne in clusters of 3-5; foliage medium size, dark green, semi-glossy; some prickles; upright (4 ft.) growth; [Dornroschen × Rosanna]; int. by Rosehaven Nursery, 1993

Snow Bride Min, w, 1982, Jolly, Betty J.; flowers medium, 20 petals, high-centered, borne mostly singly, slight fragrance; recurrent; foliage medium size, medium green, semi-glossy; bushy growth; PP5579; [Avandel × Zinger]; int. by Rosehill Farm; AOE, ARS, 1983

Snow Bunny Min, w, 2000, Moe, Mitchie; flowers dbl., high-centered, borne mostly singly, slight fragrance; foliage small, medium green, semi-glossy; few prickles; growth upright, medium (10-12 in.); micro-mini; [Grace Seward × Blue Peter]; int. by Mitchie's Roses and More

Snow Bunting S, w, 2000, Brown, Ted; flowers white with pale pink center, 2½ in., full, borne in large clusters, slight fragrance; foliage medium size, dark green, glossy; few prickles; bushy, low (4 ft.) growth; [Meidomonac × seedling]

Snow-Bush Rose – See **Dupontii**, Misc OGR

Snow Cap – See **Snowcap**, Min

Snow Carol HT, w, Teranishi; int. in 1998

Snow Carpet Min, w, 1979, McGredy, Sam IV; bud pointed, tapered; flowers pure white, open quickly, 1 in., 55 petals, high-centered, to loose, borne singly and in sprays, slight tea fragrance; foliage tiny, glossy, leathery; prickles few, long, recurved, red; low (8-10 in.), spreading (5 ft.) growth; hips oval, orange-red; PP4612; [New Penny × Temple Bells]; int. in 1980; Gold Medal, Baden-Baden, 1982

Snow Cloud S, w, Tantau; int. in 1993

Snow Cover – See **Niagara**, S

Snow Cream HT, w, 1986, Bridges, Dennis A.; flowers cream, yellow stamens, medium, single to semi-dbl., flat, borne singly and in clusters of 4-8; recurrent; foliage medium size, dark, glossy; prickles medium, red, hooked; medium, upright, vigorous growth; [Garden Party × Portrait]; int. by Bridges Roses

Snow Crystal HT, w, 1982, Verschuren, Ted; flowers large, 20 petals; foliage large, light green, semi-glossy; [Sonia × Pascali]; int. by H.A. Verschuren, 1978

Snow Crystal HT, w, 2003, Rawlins, R.; flowers medium, full, borne mostly solitary; foliage medium size, dark green, glossy; prickles 2 cm., triangular; growth upright, tall (45 in.); garden, exhibition; [Solitaire × Silver Anniversary]; int. in 2003

Snow Dolphin HT, w, Asami; int. in 1987

Snow Drop Min, w; int. in 1975

Snow Drop Min, w, Welsh; int. by Oregon Miniatures, 1996

Snow Dwarf – See **Schneezwerg**, HRg

Snow Fairy F, w, 1964, Camprubi, C.; bud pointed; flowers 18 petals, cupped, borne in clusters, moderate fragrance; foliage dark, glossy, leathery; vigorous, bushy growth; PP2376; [Virgo × Katharina Zeimet]; int. by C-P, 1963

Snow Flurry F, w, 1952, Moore, Ralph S.; bud small, long, pointed, tinted pink in cool weather; flowers open, semi-dbl., borne in clusters; foliage leathery, glossy, dark; vigorous, bushy growth; [seedling × Red Ripples]; int. by Marsh's Nursery

Snow Goose S, w, 1997, Austin, David; bud creamy, pink-tipped, pointed; flowers white with very narrow petals, 1-2 in., full, pompon, borne in small clusters, slight sweet, musk fragrance; good repeat; foliage small, dark green, smooth; few prickles; bushy (8-10 ft.) growth; tall shrub or short climber; int. by David Austin Roses, Ltd., 1997

Snow Gosling F, w, Poulsen; flowers 3 in., dbl., cupped, borne in clusters, moderate fragrance; free-flowering; upright (3 ft.) growth; int. by Poulsen Roser, 1982

Snow Hedge HRg, w, 1963, Nyveldt; flowers pure white, medium, single; hips red; [(*R. rugosa rubra* × *R. cinnamomea*) × *R. nitida*]

Snow Hit MinFl, w, Poulsen; flowers creamy white, 5-8 cm., full, cupped, borne in clusters, moderate fragrance; recurrent; foliage dark green, glossy; bushy (40-60 cm.) growth; int. by Poulsen Roser, 2000

Snow Infant Min, w, 1990, Yamasaki, Kazuko; bud ovoid; flowers light green, reverse white, aging white, small, full, borne in sprays, no fragrance; foliage small, light green, semi-glossy; prickles small, light green; upright, medium growth; hips ovoid, small, red; [Katharina Zeimet × seedling]

Snow Kiss Min, w, Kordes; int. in 1997

Snow Magic Min, w, 1976, Moore, Ralph S.; bud short pointed, light pink; flowers medium, 40 petals, cupped, borne in clusters, slight fragrance; free-flowering; foliage small, soft, light to medium green; bushy, spreading growth; [from unnamed polyantha seedling × unknown]; int. by Sequoia Nursery

Snow Maiden Min, w, 1995, Justice, Jerry G.; flowers pure white with ivory to bone white throat, reverse pure white, pink in cool temp, full, borne mostly singly, slight fragrance; foliage medium size, dark green, glossy; few prickles; upright, medium growth; [Snow Twinkle × seedling]; int. by Justice Miniature Roses, 1996

Snow Meillandina Min, w, Meilland; bud large, ovoid; flowers white with yellow tones in center, 2½ in., 85 -95 petals, cupped, borne singly and in small clusters, slight fragrance; free-flowering; foliage dark green, glossy; prickles normal, medium to large, greenish-pink to tan; bushy (12 in.) growth; PP8063; [sport of Lady Sunblaze]; int. in 1991

Snow on the Heather – See **Moon River**, S

Snow Owl – See **White Pavement**, HRg

Snow Parade – See **Snow**, Min

Snow Pavement HRg, w, Baum; bud light lavender-pink; flowers white with lavender tint, semi-dbl., cupped, borne in clusters, moderate fragrance; foliage light green; groundcover; spreading (2½ ft.) growth; hips red; very hardy

Snow Princess F, w, 1991, Laver, Keith G.; flowers medium, full, borne in large clusters, no fragrance; foliage large, dark green, glossy; some prickles; bushy, low (45 cm.), compact growth; [Regensberg × June Laver]; int. by Springwood Roses, 1992

Snow Princess – See **Yukihime**, Min

Snow Queen – See **Frau Karl Druschki**, HP

Snow Queen, Climbing – See **Frau Karl Druschki, Climbing**, Cl HP

Snow Queen HT, w, Taschner, Ludwig; flowers pure white, dbl., high-centered, borne mostly singly, moderate damask fragrance; recurrent; stems long; medium to tall growth; [sport of Bewitched]; int. by Ludwig's Roses, 2001

Snow Rambler HMult, w, Nieuwesteeg, J.; int. by Golden Vale Nursery, 1995

Snow Ruby MinFl, rb, Clements, John; flowers velvety red, white reverse, dbl., cupped, spiral, borne mostly singly, slight fresh fragrance; medium growth; int. by Heirloom Roses, 1996

Snow Shower Min, w, 1992, Warriner, William A. & Zary, Keith W.; bud short, pointed ovoid; flowers snow white, 1-1½ in., 45-50 petals, high-centered to flat, borne singly and in small clusters, no fragrance; recurrent; foliage small, medium to dark green, glossy; prickles some, short, hooked downward; stems 5-6 in.; growth low (25-40 cm.), spreading (60-75 cm.) across; groundcover; PP9374; [Immensee × Roller Coaster]; int. by Bear Creek Gardens, 1993

Snow Showers Polyantha, w, 2004, Wilke, William; flowers pure white, reverse white, 1 in., dbl., borne in very large sprays on long stems, no fragrance; foliage medium size, medium green, semi-glossy; prickles in., straight out; stems long; growth upright, medium (2½-3 ft.); garden, hedge; [Sweet Afton × unknown]

Snow Spray F, w, 1957, Riethmuller; flowers pure white, stamens yellow, dbl.; dwarf growth; [Gartendirektor Otto Linne × Gartendirektor Otto Linne]

Snow Sunblaze – See **Snow Meillandina**, Min

Snow Twinkle Min, w, 1987, Moore, Ralph S.; bud long, pointed; flowers ivory to white, opening to a star shape, 1½ in., 35 -45 petals, high-centered, borne singly and in small, loose sprays, slight fragrance; free-flowering; foliage small, medium green, semi-glossy to matte; prickles small, slender, slightly curved downward, brown; stems slender, wiry; bushy, medium growth; hips round, orange; PP6822; [(Little Darling × Yellow Magic) × Magic Carrousel]

Snow Waltz – See **Schneewalzer 87**, LCl

Snow Waltz HT, w

Snow White HT, w, 1938, Dot, Pedro; flowers well-formed, large; [White Ophelia × Nuria de Recolons]

Snow White HT, w, 1941, Joseph H. Hill Co.; bud long, pointed; flowers large, dbl., high-centered, moderate fragrance; foliage leathery, dark; vigorous, bushy, compact growth; [Joanna Hill × White Briarcliff]

Snow White – See **Sneprinsesse**, Pol

Snow White Min, w, 1955, Robinson, T.; flowers white tinted blush, 1 in., dbl., borne in clusters; low (3-6 in.), spreading growth; [Little Princess × Baby Bunting]; micro-mini

Snow White HT, w, Sealand Nurseries, Ltd.; flowers oystershell white with pink blush on guard petals, dbl., high-centered, slight fragrance; recurrent; tall, spreading growth; int. in 1987

Snow White, Climbing Cl HT, w, Cant, F.

Snow Wonder Min, w, 1980, Lyon; bud ovoid, pointed; flowers 48 petals, borne 3-5 per cluster; foliage tiny, medium green; prickles tiny, curved; vigorous, bushy growth; [Red Can Can × Baby Betsy McCall]; int. in 1978

Snowball – See **Boule de Neige**, B

Snowball Pol, w, 1901, Walsh; flowers dbl.; ruled extinct ARA 1985

Snowball – See **Angelita**, Min

Snowballet – See **Snow Ballet**, S

Snowbank F, w, 1937, Nicolas; flowers white tinted blush, changing to white, large, 30 petals, cupped; foliage leathery, dark; dwarf growth; [Mrs E.P. Thom × Gloria Mundi]; int. by J&P

Snowbelt Pol, w, 1997, Jerabek, Paul E.; flowers medium, dbl., borne in large clusters; foliage medium size, light green turning medium green, semi-gloss; some prickles; medium, bushy growth; [seedling × seedling]

Snowbird HT, w, 1936, Hatton; bud long, pointed; flowers white, center creamy, very dbl., old-fashioned, intense sweet fragrance; recurrent; foliage leathery; vigorous, compact, bushy growth; [Chastity × Louise Crette]; int. by C-P

Snowbird, Climbing Cl HT, w, 1949, Weeks; flowers white, tinged lemon-yellow, 4 in., very dbl.; recurrent; vigorous, tall (15 ft.) growth; [sport of Snowbird]

Snowblush Min, rb, 1991, Clements, John K.; flowers purest white, edges red, medium, very full, high-centered, borne mostly singly, no fragrance; foliage medium green, matte; some prickles; tall (50 cm.),upright growth; [Minuette × seedling]; int. by Heirloom Old Garden Roses, 1992

Snowbound Min, w, 1989, Laver, Keith G.; bud ovoid; flowers ivory, reverse white, aging white, small, 55 petals, urn-shaped, borne usually singly; foliage small, dark green, matte, disease-resistant; prickles straight, narrow, greenish-brown; bushy, low, compact growth; hips round, yellow-orange; [Tabris × June Laver]; int. by Springwood Roses, 1989

Snowcap Min, w; flowers antique white, creamy center, very dbl., rosette, borne in dense clusters, slight fragrance; free-flowering; mounded (12-18 in.) growth; int. by Harkness, 1999

Snowcone S, w, 2007, Zary, Keith W.; flowers pure white, yellow stamens, 1 in., single, shallow cup, blooms borne in large clusters, slight fragrance; foliage small, dark green, glossy; prickles few, 4-6 mm., hooked downward, greyed-orange; growth upright, short (2 ft.); mini shrub, mixed perennial beds; PPAF; [seedling × seedling]; int. by Jackson & Perkins Wholesale, Inc., 2006

Snowdance F, w, 1971, deRuiter; flowers 3 in., 36 petals, slight fragrance; moderate, bushy growth; [Orange Sensation × Iceberg]

Snowdon HRg, w, Austin, David; flowers pure white, medium, dbl., flat, borne in clusters, slight fragrance; recurrent; large (7 × 7 ft.) growth; int. in 1989

Snowdrift HWich, w, 1913, Walsh; flowers pure white, small, dbl., borne in clusters of 20-30; foliage very large, light; vigorous (8-12 ft.) growth; ruled extinct ARA 1985

Snowdrift HWich, w, 1914, Smith, W. R.; flowers pure white, small, dbl., borne in clusters of 20-30; non-recurrent; foliage large

Snowdrift S, w, 1985, Williams, J. Benjamin; flowers small, 35 petals, borne in large sprays, slight fragrance; repeat bloom; foliage medium size, dark, semi-glossy; low, spreading growth; [Sea Foam × The Fairy]; int. in 1986

Snowdrop – See **Amorette**, Min

Snowdwarf – See **Schneezwerg**, HRg

Snowfall Cl Min, w, 1988, Lemrow, Dr. Maynard W.; bud medium, ovoid, recessed center; flowers white, reverse greenish-white, 1½ in., 40-50 petals, flat, then pompon, borne usually singly or in sprays of 2-5, no fragrance; recurrent; foliage medium size, medium green, semi-glossy; prickles short, pointed, small, straight; spreading, tall, profuse, hardy growth; no fruit; PP6706; [Jeanne Lajoie × seedling]; int. by Nor'East Min. Roses, 1988

Snowfire HT, rb, 1973, Kordes, R.; bud large, pointed ovoid; flowers bright red, reverse white, 4-6 in., 25-35 petals, cupped, flat top, borne singly, slight fruity fragrance; recurrent; foliage large, dark, leathery; prickles numerous, long, hooked downward, brown; stems medium, strong; vigorous, medium growth; PP3014; [Detroiter × Liberty Bell]; int. by J&P, 1970

Snowflake – See **Marie Lambert**, T

Snowflake T, w, 1890, Strauss & Co.

Snowflake HWich, w, 1922, Cant, F.; flowers pure white, 4 cm., dbl., globular, borne in small to medium clusters, intense fresh fragrance; non-recurrent; foliage dark green, glossy; vigorous, climbing growth; Gold Medal, NRS, 1921

Snowflake Min, w, 1978, Ludwig Roses; flowers white with faint pink center, dbl.; free-flowering; vigorous growth; [sport of Chipper]; int. by Ludwig's Roses, 1977

Snowflake – See **White Flower Carpet**, F

Snowflake Min, w, 1999, Schuurman, Frank B.; flowers 1 in., full, borne in small clusters, no fragrance; foliage small, light green, semi-glossy; prickles moderate; compact, low growth; int. by Franko Roses New Zealand, Ltd., 1996

Snowflakes Min, w, 1954, Moore, Ralph S.; flowers small, dbl.; dwarf (6 in.) growth; [(*R. wichurana* × Floradora) × Zee]; int. by Sequoia Nursery

Snowgoose F, w, 1986, Barrett, F.H.; flowers small, 20 petals, borne in clusters; foliage medium size, medium green, semi-glossy; upright growth; [Seaspray × Iceberg]

Snowhite Climber LCl, w, 1938, Burbank; flowers large, dbl.; long, strong stems; vigorous climbing growth; int. by Stark Bros.

Snowline F, w, 1971, Poulsen, Niels D.; flowers white with creamy center, 3-4 in., 31 petals, cupped, borne in clusters, slight wild rose fragrance; recurrent; foliage dark green, glossy; bushy (3-5 ft.) growth; int. by McGredy, 1970; ADR, 1970

Snowman HT, w, 1984, John Mattock, Ltd.; flowers large, dbl., moderate fragrance; foliage large, dark, semi-glossy; upright, bushy growth; [(Peer Gynt × Isis) × Lady Seton]; int. in 1983

Snowsong HT, w, 1961, Jelly; bud long, pointed; flowers white, base yellow, 4½ in., 20 petals, slight sweetbriar fragrance; foliage dark, glossy; moderately vigorous, upright growth; PP2165; [Snow White × (Snow White × unknown)]; int. by E.G. Hill Co., 1961

Snowsong Supreme HT, w, 1969, Jelly; bud long, pointed; flowers white, base greenish, medium, high-centered, moderate fragrance; moderate growth; PP2624; [Snowsong × White Butterfly]; int. by E.G. Hill Co., 1965

Snowstorm HMsk, w, 1907, Paul; flowers pure white, small, semi-dbl., borne in clusters of 6-20; recurrent bloom; vigorous growth; [*R. moschata* × a climber]

Snowy Jewel F, w; int. by de Ruiter, 2001

Snowy Summit – See **Clos Fleuri Blanc**, F

Snuffy HT, op, 2005, Smith, John T; flowers orange, reverse coral pink, 5-6 in, dbl., high-centered, borne mostly solitary; foliage large, dark green, semi-glossy; prickles large, straight, white, moderate; growth vigorous, branching, spreading, tall (48 in.); exhibition; [Gemini × Veterans' Honor]; int. by same, 2007

Snuggles Min, mp, 1995, Rennie, Bruce F.; flowers 1½ in., dbl., borne in small clusters; foliage medium size, medium green, semi-glossy; some prickles; medium (15-18 in.), bushy growth; int. by Rennie Roses International, 1993

So In Love F, w, Umsawasdi, Dr. Theera; flowers near white, medium, full, borne mostly singly, moderate fragrance; foliage medium size, medium green, semi-glossy; few prickles; medium, bushy, spreading growth; [Golden Wings × unknown]; int. in 1996

So Pretty HT, mp, Meilland; flowers light, creamy pink, full, high-centered, borne mostly singly; good rebloom; florist rose; int. by Meilland Intl., 2004

Soaring Flight HWich, pb, Clements, John K.; flowers salmon pink with gold and apricot centers, 3 in., 8-12 petals, cupped, borne in clusters, moderate sweet/honey fragrance; recurrent; foliage dark green; vigorous, tall (14 ft.) growth; int. by Heirloom Roses, 1996

Soaring Spirits LCl, pb, 2004, Carruth, Tom; flowers pastel pink, yellow & cream stripes, 10-13 cm., single, borne in large clusters, moderate apple fragrance; foliage large, light green, glossy; prickles mixed, almost straight; growth spreading, climbing, tall (210-250 cm.); garden decoration; [Berries 'n' Cream × Fourth of July]; int. by Weeks Roses, 2005

Soaring Wings HT, ob, 1979, W. Kordes Söhne; bud ovoid; flowers deep dusky orange, golden base, large, 64 petals, high-centered, borne mostly singly, moderate fragrance; recurrent; foliage medium green, matte; numerous prickles; vigorous, upright, bushy growth; [Colour Wonder × unknown]; int. by Ludwigs Roses Pty. Ltd.

Sobhag F, ob, 1973, Bansal, O.P.; bud urn shaped; flowers orange, open, medium, semi-dbl., moderate fragrance; foliage glossy, dark, leathery; vigorous, bushy growth; [Orangeade × unknown]; int. by Bansal Roses, 1972

Social Climber LCl, mp; bud pointed, ovoid; flowers 4 in., very full, cupped, moderate spicy fragrance; good repeat.; foliage glossy, dark green.; branching (6 ft.) growth; PPAF; int. by J&P, 2004

Société d'Horticulture de Melun et Fontainebleau HP, w, 1852, Cochet; flowers white, center creamy yellow, medium, full

Society Special Min, ob, 1996, Warner, Chris; flowers yellow with red reverse, small, full, borne in small clusters; foliage small, medium green, semi-glossy; few prickles; upright, bushy, tall growth; [Laura Ford × Anne Harkness]; int. by Warner's Roses, 1997

Sococ HT, ab; flowers dbl., moderate fragrance

Socrate T, pb, 1858, Moreau et Robert; flowers deep rose tinged fawn, large, dbl.

Sodenia HWich, rb, 1911, Weigand, C.; flowers bright carmine changing to deep pink, streaked with white to medium pink, 5 cm., dbl., borne in large clusters, no fragrance; good repeat; foliage small, glossy; vigorous, climbing growth

Sodori-Himé HT, w, 1979, Onodera, Toru F.; flowers 4½ in., 30 petals, high-centered, slight fragrance; foliage dark; bushy growth; [White Knight × White Prince]; int. by S. Onodera, 1975

Soestdijk F, ob, 1949, Leenders, M.; flowers deep orange, base buttercup-yellow, medium, semi-dbl.; vigorous, compact growth; [Vanessa × seedling]

Soeur Bernède de St Vincent de Paul HP, dp, 1879, Bernède; flowers large, very full; [Jules Margottin × unknown]

Soeur Emmanuelle HT, m, Delbard; bud deep rosy mauve; flowers rose-lilac, very full, cupped, intense herbal fragrance; vigorous (1 m.) growth; int. in 2005

Soeur Kristin HKor, my, 1984, James, John; flowers large, 20 petals, borne singly; repeat bloom; foliage medium size, medium green, glossy; semi-spreading growth; [Blanche Mallerin × (*R.* × *kordesii* × (Van Bergen × Soeur Thérèse))]; int. in 1978

Soeur Marie-Ange F, w, 1957, Privat; flowers snow-white, very dbl.; bushy, dwarf growth

Soeur Marthe M, dp, 1848, Vibert; bud mossed; flowers light pink, darker at center, 7-8 cm., full, cupped, moderate fragrance; once-bloomer; stems mossed; upright (3-5 ft.) growth

Soeur Thérèse HT, yb, 1931, Gillot, F.; bud long, pointed; flowers golden yellow flushed and edged carmine, large, 25 petals, cupped, slight fragrance; free-flowering; foliage leathery, bronze; vigorous, bushy growth; [(Général Jacqueminot × Juliet) × Souv. de Claudius Pernet]; int. by C-P

Soeur Thérèse, Climbing Cl HT, yb, 1953, Shira; [sport of Soeur Thérèse]

Sofiero F, mp, Poulsen; flowers medium pink, lightening as they open, 10-15 cm., full, cupped, borne in clusters, no fragrance; recurrent; foliage dark green, glossy; bushy, medium (60-100 cm.) growth; int. by Poulsen Roser, 2000

Soft Blush F, lp; flowers soft pearly pink, dbl., rosette; foliage glossy; stems long; growth medium

Soft Cover – See **Annapolis**, S

Soft Meidiland S, pb, Meilland; flowers soft pink with showy white base, single, borne in large sprays, slight fragrance; recurrent; low (2 ft.), spreading growth; int. by Hortico, Inc., 2005

Soft Morning F, ab, 2006; flowers medium, full, borne mostly solitary, no fragrance; foliage medium size, medium green; spreading, medium growth; [sport of Rose Parade]; int. by Roses Unlimited, 2006

Soft Scent F, pb, 1988, Rennie, Bruce F.; bud ovoid; flowers pink blend, reverse light pink, sweetheart, medium, 48 petals, high-centered, urn-shaped, borne usually singly, intense spicy fragrance; foliage medium size, dark green, semi-glossy; prickles straight, medium, red; bushy, medium growth; hips elongated, medium, orange; [Paul Shirville × California Girl]; int. by Rennie Roses International, 1990

Soft Steps Min, pb, 1986, Florac, Marilyn; flowers creamy, petal edges pink, medium, 33 petals, cupped, borne singly; foliage medium size, medium green, semi-glossy; prickles small, reddish; tall, upright growth; [Avandel × unknown]; int. by M.B. Farm Min. Roses, Inc.

Soft Touch Min, ab, 1982, Warriner, William A.; flowers medium, semi-dbl.; foliage medium size, medium green, semi-glossy; PP5578; [Bridal Pink × Fire Princess]; int. by J&P, 1984

Softee Min, w, 1983, Moore, Ralph S.; flowers creamy white, small, 35 petals, slight fragrance; foliage small to medium size, medium green, matte; no prickles; bushy (2 ft.), spreading growth; [seedling × seedling]; int. by Moore Min. Roses, 1982

Softee, Climbing Cl Min, w, Hannemann, F.; [sport of Softee]; int. by The Rose Paradise, 1992

Softly Softly F, pb, 1977, Harkness; flowers pink and creamy pink, 5 in., 35 petals, hybrid tea, borne several together, slight fragrance; free-flowering; foliage leathery, medium green, large; free and hardy growth; [White Cockade × ((Highlight × Colour Wonder) × (Parkdirektor Riggers × Piccadilly))]

Softy HT, lp, Tantau; flowers small, dbl.; int. in 1990

Softy Pol, lp, Tantau; flowers small, dbl.; int. in 1992

Sogno HT, mr, 1974, Calvino; bud ovoid, globular; flowers orient red to geranium-like, open, medium, dbl., cupped; foliage large, dark, leathery; vigorous, upright, bushy growth; PP2933

Sogno Rosa – See **Pink Traumland**, F

Soir d'Automne HT, m, 1966, Dot; bud long, pointed; flowers violet, medium, dbl., cupped; foliage light green, leathery; vigorous growth; [(Sterling Silver × Intermezzo) × (Sterling Silver × Simone)]; int. by Minier

Soir de Fete HT, my, Croix; int. by Roseraie Paul Croix

Soir d'Eté F, mr, Croix; flowers rose red, slight fragrance; free-flowering; growth medium; int. as Soir d'Été, Roseraie Paul Croix, 1977; Certificate of Merit, Roeulx

Soiree – See **Soiree de Bonheur**, S

Soirèe Min, ob, Teranishi; int. by Itami Rose Garden, 1997

Soiree de Bonheur S, op, Croix; flowers salmon pink, semi-dbl., borne in clusters, slight fragrance; free-flowering; vigorous (8 ft.) growth; int. in 1993; Gold Medal, Saverne, 1996, Silver Medal, Bagatelle, 1996, Gold Medal, Geneva, 1996, Gold Medal, Baden-Baden, 1996

Solar Flair Min, rb, 1996, Tucker, Robbie; flowers bright crimson with yellow reverse, small, 6-14 petals, borne mostly singly or in small clusters, no fragrance; foliage small, dark green, glossy; some prickles; compact, low growth; [Rise 'n' Shine × Captivation]

Solar Flair MinFl, yb, 2004, Benardella, Frank; flowers yellow with red edges, 2-2½ in., full, high-centered, borne mostly solitary, slight fragrance; foliage medium size, dark green, glossy; prickles ¼ in. long, pointed down; growth upright, medium (2-2½ ft.); exhibition;cut flowers;decorative; [Antique Gold × Brett's Rose]; int. by NorEast Miniature Roses, 2005

Solar Flare – See **Solarflash**, HT

Solar Flare F, ob, Tolmasoff, Jan; flowers burnt orange with some gold on the reverse, 1½ in., no fragrance; blooms continuously; growth to 2½ ft.; [sport of Charisma]; int. by Rusian River Rose Co., 2001

Solar Flash – See **Solarflash**, HT

Solar Sensation HT, ob, 2000, Giles, Diann; flowers large, full, borne mostly singly, no fragrance; foliage dark green, semi-glossy; numerous prickles; upright, medium (4 ft.) growth; [Vera Dalton × unknown]; int. by Giles Rose Nursery

Solarflare – See **Solarflash**, HT

Solarflash HT, or, 1996, Pallek, Otto; flowers bright vermilion, vibrant dark orange, with dark petal edge, medium to large, full, borne mostly singly; foliage medium size, dark green, semi-glossy; prickles some to numerous; medium to low (2½-3 ft.), compact growth; [seedling × Hot Pewter]; int. by Pallek, 1995

Solaria HT, or, 1979, W. Kordes Söhne; bud long, pointed; flowers dbl., cupped; foliage dark; upright growth; [(Anabell × Zorina) × seedling]; int. by Barni, 1976

Solarium HWich, w, 1925, Turbat; flowers velvety vermilion-red, stamens yellow, 6 cm., single, borne in clusters of 15-20; foliage rich glossy green; very vigorous, climbing growth

Soldier Boy LCl, mr, 1953, LeGrice; flowers scarlet, 4 in., single, borne in small clusters, slight fragrance; recurrent; vigorous, pillar growth; hips red; [seedling × Guinee]

Soldier's Pride HT, dr, 1987, MacLeod, Major C.A.; flowers medium, full; foliage medium size, dark green, semi-glossy; upright growth; [Red Planet × Clare]

Sole di San Remo S, Mansuino; int. in 1975

Soleil Brillant HGal, dp, before 1790; bud yellow-green; flowers medium, moderate fragrance; from Holland; Agathe group

Soleil d'Angers HFt, yb, 1910, Détriché; flowers orange-yellow, medium, very dbl., cupped to flat; [sport of Soleil d'Or]

Soleil de France HT, yb, 1931, Mermet; flowers sun-yellow, center reddish, large, dbl.; foliage thick; vigorous growth; [Souv. de Claudius Pernet × seedling]; int. by J&P

Soleil de Lyon F, op, 1955, Robichon; flowers salmon-pink; vigorous growth; int. by Pin

Soleil de Minuit HT, Delbard-Chabert

Soleil de Rustica LCl, dy, Cognet; flowers golden yellow, large

Soleil d'Été HT, my, Orard; int. by Vilmorin, 2000

Soleil d'Été – See **Summer Sunshine**, HT

Soleil d'Or HFt, yb, 1900, Pernet-Ducher; bud long, pointed; flowers orange-yellow to ruddy gold, shaded nasturtium-red, large, full, globular to flat, moderate citrus, orange fragrance; recurrent; foliage rich green, smooth; prickles thin, straight; vigorous, upright growth; [Antoine Ducher × *R. foetida persiana*]

Soleil d'Orient Cl HT, rb, 1935, Croibier; bud long, pointed; flowers Indian red, shaded yellow, 4 in., dbl.; occasional repeat; foliage glossy; long stems; vigorous, climbing (6 ft.) growth; [Frau Karl Druschki × Mme Edouard Herriot]

Soleil Levant LCl, ob, 1956, Mondial Roses; flowers scarlet/orange, single; [Spectacular × unknown]

Soleil Rouge HT, rb, Dorieux; int. by Roseraies Dorieux, 2002

Soleillade F, dy, Dorieux; int. by Roseraies Dorieux, 1997

Solero HT, dy, Kordes; flowers brass yellow, full, high-centered, borne mostly singly; recurrent; stems medium; int. by W. Kordes Söhne, 2005

Solette HT, ab, Kordes; int. by W. Kordes Söhne, 1999

Solfatare – See **Solfaterre**, N

Solfaterre N, my, 1843, Boyau; flowers sulphur yellow, 9 cm., dbl., cupped, borne in clusters of 3-5; remontant; numerous prickles; vigorous growth; [Lamarque × unknown]

Solid Gold HT, my, 1982, Leon, Charles F., Sr.; flowers golden yellow, large, 36 petals, borne 3-6 per cluster; foliage dark, glossy; vigorous growth; [((Royal Gold × unknown) × Golden Giant) × (Bright Gold × PhyllisGold seedling)]

Solidor HT, my, Meilland; flowers intense yellow, large, dbl.; int. in 1986

Solidor HT, dy, Meilland; flowers dbl., high-centered, borne mostly singly; PPAF; florist rose; int. by Meilland Intl., 1999

Soliman F, VEG; int. in 1975

Solistka Baleta HT, yb, 1955, Klimenko, V. N.; flowers soft lemon-yellow edged pink, large; [(Peace × Crimson Glory) × Poinsettia]

Solitaire F, mp, 1970, Cants of Colchester, Ltd.; flowers coral-pink, reverse silvery, 3 in., 25 petals; foliage glossy, dark; vigorous growth; [Queen Elizabeth × Elysium]

Solitaire HT, yb, 1987, McGredy, Sam IV; flowers yellow tinted pink, reverse yellow, fading without blanching, large, 25 petals, cupped, borne in clusters of 2 or 3, slight fragrance; foliage medium size, dark green, semi-glossy; prickles slightly hooked, large, reddish-brown; bushy, strong growth; no fruit; [Freude × Benson & Hedges Gold]; int. by Sealand Nursery, 1987; President's International Trophy, RNRS, 1985

Solitaire, Climbing Cl F, yb, 1997, Earnshaw, Ronald; flowers medium, dbl., moderate fragrance; foliage medium size, medium green, semi-glossy; numerous prickles; upright (7ft.) growth; [sport of Solitaire]

Solitude Gr, ob, 1991, Olesen, Pernille & Mogens N.; bud large, elongated; flowers orange-yellow with red on petal edges, 4½-5 in., 20-23 petals, cupped, borne singly and in clusters of 3-10, slight spicy fragrance; recurrent; foliage medium size, medium green, semi-glossy; prickles few to moderate, medium size, tan; medium (4 ft.), bushy growth; PP8230; [Selfridges × seedling]; int. by Conard-Pyle Co., 1992

Solitude Min, pb, McCann, Sean

Soller HT, my, 1949, Dot, Pedro; bud long, pointed; flowers overlarge, very dbl.; foliage glossy, bronze; bushy growth; [Eduardo Toda × Senateur Potie]

Solliden HT, rb, 1924, Leenders, M.; bud long, pointed; flowers carmine, reverse shaded ochre, open, large, semi-dbl.; foliage dark; vigorous growth; [(Mme Mélanie Soupert × George C. Waud) × Mme Edouard Herriot]

Solliden – See **Canyonlands**, F

Solo LCl, mr, 1959, Tantau, Math.; flowers fiery crimson, large, dbl., borne in small clusters, slight fragrance; recurrent; foliage dark, leathery; vigorous growth; [Crimson Glory × unknown]; int. in 1956

Solo HT, rb, Tantau; int. by Australian Roses, 2004

Solo Mio – See **Sophia Renaissance**, S

Solstice Gr, ly, 2007, Zary, Keith W.; flowers full, blooms borne in small clusters; foliage medium size, dark green, semi-glossy; prickles 8-10 mm., hooked downward, greyed-orange, moderate; growth upright, tall, 5-6 ft.; [seedling × seedling]; int. by Jackson & Perkins Wholesale, Inc., 2005

Solus S, or, 1967, Watkins Roses; flowers bright orange-scarlet, 2½ in., 19 petals, borne in clusters; foliage dark, glossy, leathery; very vigorous growth; [Kathleen Ferrier × Dickson's Flame]

Solvang HT, dr, 1988, Olesen, Pernille & Mogens N.; flowers large, 6-14 petals; foliage large, dark green, glossy; prickles average; bushy, vigorous growth; [Vision × seedling]; int. by Poulsen Roser ApS, 1987

Soma HT, m, 1981, Division of Vegetable Crops and Floriculture; bud long, pointed; flowers mauve blend, 40 petals, borne 8 per cluster, no fragrance; foliage dark, leathery; prickles straight; bushy growth; [Chandrama × Surekha]; int. in 1980

Somasila – See **Spice Trail**, HT

Sombrero F, pb, 1962, McGredy, Sam IV; flowers cream flushed pink, well-formed, 4 in., 25 petals; foliage light green; vigorous growth; [Masquerade × Rubaiyat]; int. by McGredy & Son, 1962

Sombreuil LCl, w, about 1880; flowers creamy white, 3 in., very dbl., flat, borne singly and in small clusters, slight fragrance; foliage large, medium green, semi-glossy; growth climbing, tall (8-12 ft.); not synonymous with Mlle de Sombreuil

Someday Soon Min, ly, 1992, McCann, Sean; flowers light yellow framed in creamy white outer petals, reverse cream, 1½ in., 52 petals, high-centered, borne singly, slight spicy fragrance; foliage medium size, light green, matte, highly serrated; upright, medium growth; [Miniature seedling × Antique Silk]; int. by Justice Miniature Roses, 1993

Somersault HT, yb, 1993, Zary, Dr. Keith W.; flowers yellow and rose red/orange blend, medium, full, borne in clusters; foliage small, dark green, glossy; some prickles; low (45-50cm.), upright, bushy growth; int. by Bear Creek Gardens

Something Else Min, rb, 1991, Saville, F. Harmon; flowers white with very contrasting red edge, medium, dbl., cupped, borne usually singly, slight fragrance; foliage small, medium green, semi-glossy; upright, bushy, medium growth; PP7769; [(Yellow Jewel × Tamango) × Party Girl]; int. by Nor'East Min. Roses, 1985

Something for Judy MinFl, pb, 1995, Bennett, Dee; flowers cream with deep pink blush, medium, dbl., borne mostly singly; foliage medium size, medium green, semi-glossy; tall (2-3 ft.), bushy growth; [Angel Face × Big John]; int. by Tiny Petals Nursery, 1995

Something Special HT, ly, McGredy; flowers pale yellow with hints of apricot and peach, dbl., high-centered, intense fragrance; recurrent; foliage dark green, glossy; upright (3-3½ ft.) growth; int. in 1999

Something Special F, pb, 2001, Hill, Ernest H.; flowers salmon peach, lighter reverse, 2½ in., dbl., high-centered, borne in large clusters, slight fragrance; foliage medium size, dark green (dark copper when young), glossy; numerous prickles; growth upright, medium (2-3 ft.)

Sommerabend S, dr, Kordes; flowers vivid dark red, 1½ in., single, cupped, borne in clusters, no fragrance; recurrent; foliage medium size, glossy; low (12 in.), bushy, spreading growth; groundcover; int. by W. Kordes Söhne, 1995; ADR, 1996

Sommerduft HT, dr, 1985, Tantau, Math.; flowers very dark red, medium-large, 20 petals, high-centered, borne mostly singly, moderate spicy fragrance; recurrent; foliage medium size, dark, semi-glossy; stems long, strong; upright growth; int. by Rosen Tantau, 1986

Sommerfreude F, lp, Noack; flowers scrolled, scrolled, slight fragrance; recurrent; foliage olive green, glossy; int. by Noack Rosen, 1988

Sommerlachen F, ob, GPG Bad Langensalza; flowers coppery orange and dark golden yellow, large, dbl.; int. in 1972

Sommerliebe HT, or, Pörschmann; flowers large, dbl.; int. in 1975

Sommerliebe F, ob, GPG Bad Langensalza; flowers coppery-pink, large, dbl.; int. in 1986

Sommermärchen F, dp, 1945, Tantau; flowers dark rose, petals shell-shaped, large, single, borne in clusters of 12-18; foliage light green, leathery; upright, vigorous, bushy growth; [Prof. Gnau × Baby Chateau]

Sommermärchen F, dp, 2006; flowers non-fading, petals ruffled, 4 cm., semi-dbl., cupped, borne in large clusters, slight fragrance; recurrent; foliage dark green, glossy, robust; bushy, medium (50 cm.), wide growth; int. by W. Kordes' Söhne, 1992; Silver Medal, Monza, Gold Medal, Geneva, Gold Medal, Baden-Baden

Sommermelodie – See **Appleblossom**, S

Sommermond F, my, Kordes; flowers canary yellow, fading to cream; continuous bloom; growth medium and spreading; int. in 1991

Sommermorgen – See **Baby Blanket**, S

Sommernachtstraum Pol, rb, 1944, Krause; flowers carmine-red with white, medium, single

Sommerschirm F, Tantau; int. in 1993

Sommerschnee Min, w, Hetzel, Karl; int. by Treffing-Hofmann, 1999

Sommerschnee F, w, VEG; flowers large, dbl.

Sommerspiel S, dp; int. by Richard Huber AG, 2005

Sommertag – See **Summer Holiday**, HT

Sommertraum F, pb, 1965, van Engelen, A. J.; flowers pink, red and yellow, semi-dbl., borne in clusters; foliage dark; [Masquerade × seedling]; int. by van Engelen, 1962

Sommerwind – See **Surrey**, S

Sommerwind Fuchsia S, dp, Vidal; int. by Rosales Vidal, after 1988

Sommesson HGal, mp, before 1820, Pelletier; flowers lilac pink, small, full; prickles numerous, strong, crooked; Agathe group

Sommet LCl, or, 1960, Mallerin, C.; flowers well-formed, dbl.; foliage bright green; vigorous growth; int. by Hémeray-Aubert

Somskywer – See **Sky Tower**, LCl

S. A. R. Mme La Princesse de Hohenzollern, Infante de Portugal – See **Princesse Hohenzollern**, T

Sonata HT, pb, 1942, Van Rossem; bud long, pointed; flowers red becoming lively pink, reverse darker, 4 in., 30 petals, high-centered, moderate fruity fragrance; foliage glossy; vigorous, bushy growth; int. by J&P

Sonata – See **Songfest**, Min

Sonata in Pink Min, pb, 1991, Jolly, Marie; flowers medium pink fading to light pink, 1¼ in., 24 petals, borne mostly singly; foliage medium size, medium green, semi-glossy; few prickles; medium (44 cm.), upright growth; [Chris Jolly × Chattem Centennial]; int. by Rosehill Farm, 1992

Sonatina F, lp, 1982, Sanday, John; flowers small, 35 petals; foliage medium size, dark, semi-glossy; [Red Maid × Sarabande]; int. by Sanday Roses, Ltd.

Sondermeldung – See **Independence**, F

Song and Dance HT, ob, Fryers; flowers bright coral-orange, dbl., urn-shaped, moderate fragrance; recurrent; foliage dark green, dense; vigorous (85 cm.) growth; int. by Fryers Roses, 2006

Song Bird Gr, w, 1979, Ryan, C.; PP4419; [sport of Tammy]; int. by J. Hill Co., 1978

Song of Paris HT, m, 1967, Delbard-Chabert; bud short, ovoid to globular; flowers silvery lavender, 4 in., 35-45 petals, high-centered, borne singly or in small clusters, moderate fragrance; recurrent; foliage leathery, glossy; prickles several, medium, almost straight, brown; stems medium, strong; upright growth; PP2669; [(Holstein × Bayadere) × Prelude]; int. by Armstrong Nursery, 1964

Song of Songs HT, dr, 1998, Poole, Lionel; flowers dark red, 5½ in., very dbl., high-centered, borne mostly singly; foliage medium size, dark green, semi-glossy; some prickles; upright, bushy, medium (3½ ft.) growth; [Adrienne Berman × (Royal William × Gabi)]

Song of the Stars HGal, m, 2004, Barden, Paul; flowers dark purple with paler spots, reverse light mauve, 3 in., 30 petals, shallow cup, borne in small clusters, moderate fragrance; spring-blooming, non-recurrent; foliage small, dark green, matte; prickles ¼ in., straight; growth bushy, some suckering, medium (4-5 ft.); specimen, border shrub; [Alain Blanchard × Alain Blanchard]; int. in 2005

Songfest Min, mp, 1987, Zipper, Herbert; flowers small, very dbl., high-centered, borne singly; foliage small, medium green, matte; bushy, compact growth; [Queen Elizabeth × Baby Katie]; int. by Magic Moment Miniature Roses

Songs of Praise – See **Red Abundance**, F

Sonia HT, rb, 1938, Horvath; flowers cherry-red, center orange, semi-dbl., camellia-like; occasional repeat; foliage glossy, dark; short stems; vigorous, bushy growth; hardy; [(*R. multiflora* × *R. canina*) × Hortulanus Budde]; int. by Wayside Gardens Co.

Sonia Gr, pb, 1971, Meilland; bud long, somewhat cylindrical; flowers pink suffused coral to yellow, 4-4½ in., 30 petals, high-centered, borne mostly singly, intense fruity fragrance; recurrent; foliage glossy, dark, leathery; prickles moderate, medium, straight to slightly hooked; upright growth; hips rounded, orange-yellow; PP3095; [Zambra × (Baccará × White Knight)]; originally registered as F; patent issued as Gr; int. by C-P

Sonia, Climbing Cl Gr, pb, 1979, Meilland, Mrs. Marie-Louise; bud coral pink; flowers dusky pink, quartered, flat, strong fruity fragrance; [sport of Sonia]; int. as Sweet Promise, Climbing, Meilland & Co SNC, 1976

Sonia Meilland – See **Sonia**, Gr

Sonia Meilland, Climbing – See **Sonia, Climbing**, Cl Gr

Sonia Rykiel S, op, Guillot-Massad; flowers soft pink, tinted amber, large, full, cupped, quartered, borne singly and in small clusters, strong fruity fragrance; growth spreading, bushy (5 ft.); int. in 1995; Prix de la Rose, Association des Journalistes du Jardin, 2002

Sonia Sunblaze Min, mp, 2003, Meilland International; bud conical, pointed; flowers full, cupped, borne in small clusters, no fragrance; recurrent; foliage medium size, medium green, matte; prickles moderate, hooked downward, pink to brown; growth upright, tall 2 ft.); garden, container; hips none ; PP14069; [Apricot Sunblaze × (Cumba Meillandina × Meisancho)]; int. by The Conard-Pyle Company, 2003

Sonia Supreme Gr, ab, Williams, J. B.; flowers salmon-peach with yellow base, dbl., high-centered; spreading, upright growth; [Sonia × unknown]; int. by Hortico, 1996

Sonja – See **Sonja Parade**, MinFl

Sonja 92 Gr, mp

Sonja Henie HT, pb, 1949, Hinner, P.; bud long, pointed to ovoid; flowers pink, reverse darker, very large, very dbl., high-centered; foliage leathery, dark; vigorous, upright growth; [Briarcliff Supreme × Rosemarie Hinner]; int. by Bauské Bros. & Hinner

Sonja Horstmann HT, mr

Sonja Parade MinFl, yb, Poulsen; bud pointed ovoid to globular; flowers yellow with red to pink edges, 2 in., 80-85 petals, high-centered, borne mostly singly, slight fragrance; recurrent; foliage dark; bushy, compact (20-40 cm.) growth; PP15120; [sport of Mistral Parade]; container rose; int. by Poulsen Roser, 2003

Sonne der Freundschaft F, dy, GPG Bad Langensalza; flowers golden yellow, medium, semi-dbl. to dbl., cupped, borne singly or several together, slight fragrance; foliage dark green, glossy; bushy, low growth; int. in 1978

Sonne des Allgäus – See **Amber Sun**, S

Sonnengold HT, dy, 1936, Kordes; bud long, pointed; flowers golden yellow, large, dbl., high-centered; foliage leathery, glossy, light; bushy growth; [Lilian × Sir Basil McFarland]

Sonnenkind Min, dy, 1987, Kordes, W.; flowers deep golden yellow, medium, dbl., high-centered, slight fragrance; recurrent; foliage small, dark green, semi-glossy; bushy, upright (14 in.) growth; [seedling × Goldmarie]; int. in 1986

Sonnenlicht HSpn, my, 1910, Krüger; flowers canary-yellow, semi-dbl., moderate fragrance; non-recurrent; vigorous growth; [Lady Mary Fitzwilliam × Harison's Yellow]; int. by Kriese

Sonnenröschen F, dy, 1977, W. Kordes Söhne; bud ovoid; flowers deep yellow, 4 in., full, cupped; foliage glossy; vigorous, bushy growth; [Arthur Bell × Yellow seedling]; int. by Dehner & Co.

Sonnenröschen Min, w, Kordes; flowers ivory, conspicuous yellow stamens, 3 cm., single, shallow cup, borne in clusters of 3-6, moderate fragrance; recurrent; foliage small, dense, dark green, very glossy; upright, compact (12 in.), wide growth; int. by W. Kordes Söhne, 2005

Sonnenschirm S, my, Tantau; flowers lemon yellow, 6-8 cm., 33 petals, cupped, borne in clusters; foliage dark green, glossy; low (2 ft.), spreading growth; int. by Rosen Tantau, 1993; President's Intl. Trophy, RNRS, 1995

Sonnenuntergang F, deRuiter; int. in 1970

Sonnet HT, lp, 1961, Boerner; bud ovoid; flowers light salmon-pink, 5 in., 58 petals, cupped, moderate fragrance; foliage leathery; vigorous, upright growth; PP2167; [Golden Masterpiece × Spartan]; int. by J&P, 1962

Sonningdean HWich, 1916, Hicks, Elisha

Sonny S, ab, Peden, G.H.; int. in 1995

Sonnychild HT, yb, 1949, Lowe; flowers yellow, reverse edged scarlet, 6 in., 20 petals; foliage glossy; vigorous growth

Sonoma F, mp, 1971, Armstrong, D.L.; flowers medium salmon-pink, medium, dbl., high-centered, moderate fragrance; foliage leathery; vigorous, upright, bushy growth; PP3302; [Sumatra × Circus]; int. by Armstrong Nursery, 1973

Sonora F, yb, 1962, Boerner; bud ovoid; flowers buff-yellow flushed to pink, 3½-4 in., 30 petals, cupped, borne several together, moderate tea fragrance; recurrent; foliage large, leathery, dark green; prickles numerous, medium, hooked downward; stems medium, strong; vigorous, upright growth; hips none ; PP2223; [Orange Mist × Mayday]; int. by J&P, 1962

Sonora Sunset HT, m, deVor; int. in 1995

Sonrisa HT, dr, 1969, Swim & Weeks; flowers deep crimson-red, medium-large, 48 petals, high-centered, intense damask fragrance; foliage dark, leathery; vigorous, upright growth; PP3007; [Mister Lincoln × Night 'n' Day]; int. by Weeks Wholesale Rose Growers

Sophia HT, pb, 1988, Weddle, Von C.; flowers medium pink with persimmon-orange, large, 27 petals, high-centered, borne usually singly, moderate fruity fragrance; foliage large, dark green, glossy; no prickles; upright, tall growth; no fruit; [First Prize × Dolce Vita]; int. by Hortico Roses, 1988

Sophia – See **Sophia Renaissance**, S

Sophia HT, mp, Pekmez; int. by Pep. Maillard, 2002

Sophia Fleur F, ly, 1977, Timmerman's Roses; flowers creamy yellow; [sport of Elizabeth of Glamis]; int. in 1978

Sophia Loren HT, mr, 1967, Tantau, Math.; flowers bright, velvety red, well-formed, large, 33 petals; foliage glossy; vigorous, upright growth

Sophia Neate T, op, 1910, Bide; flowers bright salmon pink, reverse darker, large, full

Sophia Renaissance S, dy, Olesen; bud long, pointed; flowers deep amber yellow, 4-5 in., 70-90 petals, cupped, borne 1-3 per stem, moderate fruity, herbaceous fragrance; foliage large, matte; prickles many on older wood, few on newer, deeply concave; vigorous, upright to bushy (3-4 ft.) growth; PP12268; [seedling × seedling]; int. by Poulsen, 1999

Sophia Smith HT, m, 1996, Linck, Robert G.; flowers pinkish-mauve with salmon center, reverse pinkish-mauve suffused on buff, to yellow at petal base, 8-10 cm., very dbl., borne mostly singly; foliage medium size, dark green; prickles moderate; upright, medium (5 ft.) growth; [Lady X × (Blue Moon × Great News)]; int. by Linck, 1996

Sophia's Song HT, op, 1989, Marciel, Stanley G.; bud slender, tapering; flowers coral, large, 32 petals, high-centered, borne singly, slight fruity fragrance; foliage medium size, dark green, semi-glossy; prickles declining, copper brown with pea green tinges; upright, tall growth; PP7455; [Emily Post × Prominent]; int. by DeVor Nurseries, Inc.

Sophie F, lp, Eve, A.; bud long; flowers pale pink, 8 cm., semi-dbl., cupped, borne in clusters, intense fragrance; upright (3-4 ft.) growth; int. by Les Roses Anciennes de Andre Eve, 1972

Sophie HT, lp, Tantau; int. by Rosen Tantau, 2000

Sophie Coquerel HP, mp, 1842, Coquerel; flowers very large, full

Sophie de Bavière A, mp, before 1826, Cottin/Vibert; flowers clear pink, very regular, medium, dbl.

Sophie de Marsilly M, pb, 1863, Moreau et Robert; flowers pink with light white stripes, dbl., globular; some repeat; vigorous, upright growth

Sophie Deborah HT, ob, 1999, Kirkham, Gordon Wilson; flowers 3 in., dbl., borne in small clusters; foliage medium size, dark green, semi-glossy; prickles moderate; upright, medium (2½ ft.) growth; [Prunella × Mary Sumner]

Sophie Ella Sloane Hicks F, pb, 2005, Paul Chessum Roses; flowers 6 cm., dbl., borne in small clusters; foliage small, light green, semi-glossy; growth compact, medium (60 cm.); containers, garden decorative; [seedling × seedling]; int. by Love4Plants Ltd, 2004

Sophie MacKinnon HT, dr, 1937, Clark, A.; flowers deep red, large, dbl.; vigorous growth; [John Cromin × unknown]; int. by NRS Victoria

Sophie Ortlieb HP, mp, 1933, Walter, L.; bud long, pointed; flowers silvery pink, very large, dbl.; foliage wrinkled; very vigorous, open growth; [Georg Arends × seedling]

Sophie Thomas Cl HT, my, 1931, Thomas; flowers deep yellow, passing to lighter yellow but not cream, large, dbl.; foliage good; long, strong stems; vigorous growth; [climbing seedling × Los Angeles]; int. by H&S

Sophie's Perpetual Ch, pb, before 1905, Paul, W.; flowers pale pink, overlaid with deep pink and cerise red, globular; foliage dark green; growth to 8 ft.; sometimes classed as B; re-introduced by Humphrey Brooke, 1960

Sophileo HT, or, 1993, McGredy, Sam IV; flowers medium, dbl.; foliage medium size, medium green, semi-glossy; medium, bushy growth; int. by Golden Fields Nursery

Sophisticate HT, pb, 2003, McCann, Sean; flowers pink, reverse silver, large, dbl., borne mostly solitary, moderate fragrance; foliage medium size, medium green, semi-glossy; bushy, medium growth: garden decorative; [Sally Mac × seedling]

Sophisticated Lady Gr, lp, 1986, Epperson, Richard G.; flowers 25 petals, high-centered, borne usually singly, slight fruity fragrance; foliage medium size, medium green, semi-glossy; prickles medium, hooked, dull red; upright, tall growth; [Queen Elizabeth × Arlene Francis]; int. in 1985

Sophisticated Lady HT, ab, 2006, Rippetoe, Robert, Neil; flowers single, borne mostly solitary, strong fruity fragrance; foliage large, dark green, semi-glossy; prickles medium, straight, tan, moderate; growth bushy, 2½ ft.; garden decorative, cutting, exhibit; [Just Joey × unknown]; int. by Robert Neil Rippetoe, 2006

Sophocle HT, m, 1978, Gaujard; flowers velvety purple-red, large; [Rose Gaujard × Credo]; int. in 1974

Sophy's Rose S, rb, 1999, Austin, David; bud short, pointed ovoid; flowers red-purple, 3½ in., 82 petals, cupped, domed, borne singly and in small clusters, moderate light tea fragrance; recurrent; foliage medium size, medium green, semi-glossy; prickles moderate, medium to short, hooked downward; strong, bushy, vigorous, medium (3½ ft.) growth; PP11422; [Prospero × seedling]; int. by David Austin Roses, Ltd., 1997

Soprano F, or, 1961, Lens; flowers large, dbl.; vigorous growth; [Mannequin × Aztec]

Soraya HT, or, 1958, Meilland, F.; bud pointed; flowers orange-red, reverse crimson-red, large, 30 petals, cupped, slight fragrance; foliage glossy; vigorous, bushy growth; [(Peace × Floradora) × Grand'mere Jenny]; int. by URS, 1955

Soraya, Climbing Cl HT, or, 1960, Meilland; flowers orange vermilion, reverse darker, 5-6 in.; [sport of Soraya]; int. by Barni, 1960

Soraya – See **Soraya Hit**, MinFl

Soraya Hit MinFl, mp, Poulsen; flowers medium pink, 5-8 cm., dbl., no fragrance; foliage dark; growth bushy, 40-60 cm.; int. by Poulsen Roser, 2000

Sorbet LCl, lp, Meilland; flowers light pink, reverse lighter, medium, semi-dbl. to dbl., borne singly or in small clusters; recurrent; foliage dark green; bushy (8 ft.) growth; int. in 1993

Sorbet – See **Golden Nugget**, HT

Sorbet Bouquet F, pb, 1999, Zary, Dr. Keith W.; bud long, pointed ovoid; flowers rose pink, reverse light yellow, 4 in., 30 petals, high-centered, borne singly and several together, slight fragrance; recurrent; foliage medium size, dark green, glossy; prickles moderate, medium, hooked downward; stems strong; bushy, upright, medium (3½ ft.) growth; PP12128; [Tournament of Roses × floribunda seedling]; int. by Bear Creek Gardens, Inc., 2000

Sorbet Framboise S, pb, Delbard; flowers white with red and pink stripes, medium, semi-dbl., cupped, borne in clusters, slight fragrance; free-flowering; growth to 100 cm.; int. in 1994

Sorbet Fruite, Cl. Cl F, yb, Meilland; flowers red and yellow blend, dbl.; growth to 2 m. plus; int. by Meilland Richardier, 2002

Sorbet Pêche-Abricot S, yb, Delbard; int. by Georges Delbard SA, 2003

Sorcerer Min, mr, 1994, Saville, F. Harmon; bud small, pointed, ovate; flowers bright, medium red, 1¾ in., 22-26 petals, high-centered, borne mostly singly, no fragrance; free-flowering; foliage small, medium green, semi-glossy; prickles some, thin, straight, angled downward; medium (16-20 in.), upright, bushy growth; PP9507; [Ginger Snap × Rainbow's End]; int. by Nor'East Min. Roses, 1995

Sorcier LCl, ob, 1958, Hémeray-Aubert; flowers bright orange; recurrent bloom; foliage bronze; vigorous growth; [seedling × Spectacular]

Søren Kanne – See **Everglades**, F

Soroptimist International Min, pb, 1995, Benardella, Frank A.; flowers shrimp pink and ivory, opening to star shape, large, very dbl., high-centered, borne singly and in clusters, slight fragrance; recurrent; foliage large, dark green, glossy; no prickles; tall (24in.), upright, bushy growth; [Party Girl × Rosie]; int. as The Soroptimist Rose, C. & K. Jones

Soroptomist HT, dy, 1960, Verbeek; flowers orange-yellow, well-formed, 4 in., full; foliage glossy; vigorous growth; [Golden Scepter × seedling]; int. in 1958

Sorraya HT, dy, Meilland; flowers dbl., high-centered, borne mostly singly; florist rose; int. as Golden Starlite, Meilland Intl, 2002

Sorrento S, mr, Noack; flowers bright red, 2 in., dbl., open cup, borne in clusters; recurrent; foliage dark green, glossy; bushy (70-80 cm.) growth; int. by Noack Rosen, 2006

SOS Children's Rose F, ob, Delbard; bud long, pointed, apricot orange; flowers reddish-gold with irregular yellow stripes, aging to blend of pinks, dbl., cupped, borne singly and in clusters; recurrent; stems medium long, strong; vigorous, medium growth; int. by Ludwig's Roses, 2001

Soshun F, lp, Keisei; int. by Keisei Rose Nurseries, 1991

Souchet – See **Rose des Peintres**, C

Souchet B, m, 1842, Souchet; flowers purple/pink, large, dbl., intense fragrance; foliage glossy; prickles large, hooked, red

Soufflé de Zéphire A, w, about 1815, Descemet

Soukara-Ibara – See **Crimson Rambler**, HMult

Soul Mate HT, pb, 2005, Smith, John T.; flowers dark pink, reverse lighter, 4½-5 in., full, borne mostly solitary; foliage large, dark green, semi-glossy; prickles large, slightly downward, red, moderate; growth bushy, medium (3½-4½ ft.); hedging, exhibition; [Gemini × Donna Darling]; int. by same, 2007

Soulmate Min, w, 2007, Paul Chessum Roses; flowers dbl., borne in small clusters; foliage large, medium green, semi-glossy; prickles medium, sharp, yellow, few; growth bushy, medium (24 in.); beds, borders, containers; [seedling × seedling]; int. by World of Roses, 2005

Souma HT, mp, 1977, Souma Rose Soc.; flowers 6 in., 45 petals, high-centered; foliage glossy, dark; vigorous, upright growth

Soupert & Notting, Frères T, yb, 1871, Levet; flowers yellow-white, with pink and lilac reflections, edges crimson, medium, full

Soupert et Notting M, dp, 1874, Pernet père; bud moderately mossy; flowers deep pink, very large, full, globular, then flat, borne in small clusters, intense fragrance; recurrent bloom; foliage 5 leaflets per leaf, small, greyish-green; dwarf (3 ft.) growth

Source d'Or LCl, yb, 1913, Turbat; flowers amber-yellow, edged creamy yellow, 5-6 cm., very dbl., borne in small clusters, intense fragrance; abundant, non-recurrent bloom; foliage glossy, dark; short stems; growth to 6-8 ft.

Sourire d'Antan HMsk, dp, 2000, Lens, Louis; flowers rose fuchsia, small, dbl., cupped, borne in large clusters, moderate fragrance; recurrent; foliage medium size, medium green, semi-glossy; few prickles; bushy, medium (100 cm.) growth; [(*R. multiflora* × *R. multiflora*) × Violet Hood]; int. by Louis Lens N.V., 1988

Sourire de France HT, ob, 1940, Meilland, F.; bud oval; flowers orange, base ochre-yellow, open, medium, dbl.; foliage leathery, glossy; vigorous, bushy growth; [Ampere × (Charles P. Kilham × Capucine Chambard)]; int. by A. Meilland

Sourire d'Enfant HT, ly, Orard; flowers pale yellow, dbl., moderate fragrance; int. in 1990

Sourire d'Orchidée S, lp, Croix; bud pink; flowers light mauve-pink, reverse darker, with yellow stamens, 1½-2 in., single, flat, borne in large clusters, slight fragrance; reliable repeat; foliage small, light green, matte; growth climbing, tall (to 15 ft.), as arching shrub (6-8 ft.); int. by Paul Croix, 1983; Golden Rose, Geneva, 1985, Bronze Medal, Rome, Bronze Medal, La Haye, Bronze Medal, Baden-Baden

Sourire Rose HMsk, lp, 2000, Lens, Louis; flowers pale pink, reverse lighter, 6-7 cm., semi-dbl., shallow cup, borne in large clusters, slight fragrance; recurrent; foliage light green, glossy, disease-resistant; few prickles; upright, tall (6 ft.) growth; [Trier × Maria Teresa]; int. by Louis Lens N.V., 1996

Sousse HT, lp, 1942, Meilland, F.; flowers large, dbl.

Sousyun F, w

South Africa Gr, dy, Kordes; flowers golden yellow, large, dbl., high-centered, borne in large clusters, moderate fragrance; free-flowering; foliage very disease-resistant; vigorous (5 ft.) growth; int. by Ludwig's Roses, 2001; Golden Prize, Glasgow, 2006

South Moon S, w, 1998, Giles, Diann; flowers pure white, yellow stamens, full, borne in large clusters, intense fragrance; foliage medium size, medium green, semi-glossy; upright, medium (4 ft.) growth; [sport of Belle Story]; int. by Giles Rose Nursery, 1997

South Orange Perfection HWich, pb, 1899, Horvath; flowers blush-pink, turning white, 3 cm., dbl., rosette, borne in clusters of about 20, moderate fragrance; very hardy; [*R. wichurana* × Cramoisi Supérieur]; int. by W.A. Manda

South Pacific F, dy, 1988, Christensen, Jack E.; flowers medium, hold color well, 26 petals, cupped, borne in sprays of 4-6; foliage medium size, medium green, glossy; prickles hooked slightly downward, medium, few,green to tan; bushy, medium growth; no fruit; [Sunsprite × seedling]; int. by Bear Creek Gardens, 1988

South Seas HT, op, 1962, Morey, Dr. Dennison; bud large, ovoid; flowers coral-pink, 6-7 in., 45-50 petals, cupped to flat, borne singly and several together, moderate fragrance; recurrent; foliage large, dark green, leathery; prickles normal, medium, hooked downward; stems long, strong; vigorous, upright growth; hips none ; PP2184; [Rapture × HT, Climbing seedling]; int. by J&P, 1962

Southampton F, ab, 1971, Harkness; bud pointed; flowers apricot-orange, flushed red on guard petals, 3 in., 28 petals, cupped, borne in clusters, moderate fragrance; free-flowering; foliage glossy; vigorous (3½ ft.) growth; [(Ann Elizabeth × Allgold) × Yellow Cushion]; Gold Medal, Belfast, 1974

Southend Jubilee F, dp, 1965, McCreadie; flowers deep pink, 2½ in., semi-dbl., flat, borne in clusters; very vigorous, bushy growth; int. by Southend-on-Sea Parks Dept.

Southern Alps Min, w, 2003, Eagle, B & D; flowers have slightly pale pink center before flower opens fully, 3½ cm., very full, borne in small clusters, no fragrance; foliage small, dark green, matte; growth upright, tall (120 cm.); shrub or short climber, garden decoration; [Jeanne Lajoie × seedling]; int. by Southern Cross Nurseries, 1996

Southern Aurora F, rb, 1999, Le Fevre, Ian; flowers red, reverse orange, 3 in., dbl.; foliage medium size, medium green, semi-glossy; few prickles; upright, medium (4½ ft.) growth; [sport of Redgold]

Southern Beauty HP, mp, 1888, Nanz & Neuner

Southern Beauty HT, 1897, Dingee & Conard

Southern Beauty HT, pb, 1926, Rowe; flowers deep rose-pink, edged light pink; [sport of Columbia]

Southern Belle HT, Perry, Anthony; PP2831

Southern Belle HT, pb, 1981, Swim, H.C. & Ellis, A.E.; bud ovoid, long, pointed; flowers deep pink, white reverse, spiraled, 28 petals, borne singly; foliage large, semi-glossy; prickles long, narrow; medium, upright, spreading growth; PP5077; [Pink Parfait × Phoenix]; int. by Armstrong Nursery

Southern Breeze HT, m, 2004, Adlong, Paula; flowers full, borne in large clusters, slight fragrance; foliage medium size, medium green, matte; prickles average; upright, tall growth; [Crystalline × Louise Estes]; int. in 2004

Southern Charm Min, yb, 1992, Bridges, Dennis A.; flowers shades of light yellow and pink, pink intensifying with sun, large, 25-40 petals; foliage large, medium green, semi-glossy; no prickles; medium (40-45 cm.), upright, bushy, slightly spreading growth; [Baby Katie × unknown]; int. by Bridges Roses

Southern Cross HT, mp, 1931, Clark, A.; flowers pink, dbl., globular; bushy growth; [Joseph Hill × Gen. MacArthur]; int. by Ballarat Hort. Soc.

Southern Cross F, dy, Jack; [sport of Redgold]; int. in 1977

Southern Dawn Min, lp, 2003, Eagle, B & D; flowers light pink, reverse deeper pink, with unusual fluting when open, 3½ cm., semi-dbl., borne in small clusters, no fragrance; very quick repeat; foliage small, dark green, semi-glossy, disease-resistant; prickles small, straight; growth bushy, medium (40-45 cm.); garden, containers, exhibition; [Kapiti × seedling]; int. by Southern Cross Nurseries, 2000

Southern Delight Min, yb, 1991, Moore, Ralph S.; bud pointed; flowers yellow edged with red, aging to pink and yellow, 1¾ in., 40 petals, high-centered to rounded, borne singly and in small clusters, slight fragrance; recurrent; foliage medium size, medium green, semi-glossy; prickles few, slightly inclining downwards; medium (14-16 in.), upright, bushy growth; PP8815; [Little Darling × Rise 'n' Shine]; int. by Sequoia Nursery, 1992

Southern Honey Min, my, 2003, Eagle, B & D; flowers blushed pink on petal edges as flower ages, large, full, borne in small clusters, slight fragrance; foliage medium size, dark green, semi-glossy; prickles small, straight; growth bushy, medium (40 cm.); garden, cutting; [Golden Angel × San Jose Sunshine]; int. by Southern Cross Nurseries, 1998

Southern Lady HT, pb, 1989, Bridges, Dennis A.; bud pointed; flowers light pink, center flesh tones, reverse slightly darker pink, full, high-centered, moderate fragrance; foliage medium size, dark green, semi-glossy; prickles downward pointed, medium, tan; upright, medium growth; [Lady X × Flaming Beauty]; int. by Bridges Roses, 1989

Southern Spring Min, m, 1989, Bridges, Dennis A.; bud ovoid; flowers light mauve shaded pink, reverse lighter mauve edges, darker, 65 petals, moderate fragrance; foliage medium size, dark green, matte; prickles slightly downward pointed, medium, tan; bushy, low growth; [Twilight Trail × seedling]; int. by Bridges Roses, 1989

Southern Sun HT, ob, Herholdt; flowers blend of gold, orange and red, large, dbl., high-centered, borne singly and in clusters, moderate fragrance; recurrent; vigorous, medium growth; int. in 1986

Southern Sunrise MinFl, ob, Eagle, Dawn; flowers bright orange with yellow reverse, 40 petals; low growth; [Orange Honey × unknown]; int. by Southern Cross Nurseries, 1999

Southern Sunset HT, ob, 1997, Viraraghavan, M.S. Viru; flowers silky orange with yellow reverse and copper overtones, 4 in., full, borne mostly singly, slight fragrance; foliage large, dark green, glossy; numerous prickles; upright, compact, medium (2½ ft.) growth; int. as Tamrabarani, KSG Son, 1988

Southport HT, mr, 1933, McGredy; bud long, pointed; flowers bright scarlet, 18 petals, cupped; vigorous growth; [(George Dickson × Crimson Queen) × Souv. de George Beckwith]; Gold Medal, NRS, 1931

Southport, Climbing Cl HT, mr, 1946, Howard Rose Co.; [sport of Southport]

Soutine HT, rb; flowers white with crimson stripes that widen with age, dbl., globular, slight fragrance; recurrent; int. in 2000

Souvenance HT, m, 1979, Lens; bud very long, pointed; flowers deep lavender-lilac, 3½-4½ in., 25-30 petals, high-centered, intense fragrance; foliage dark; moderately vigorous growth; [seedling × Sterling Silver]; int. in 1965

Souvenir HT, dy, 1930, Pierson, A.N.; bud pointed; flowers golden yellow, 36-42 petals; foliage glossy; vigorous growth; [sport of Talisman]

Souvenir F, ob, Kordes/Grootendorst; bud pointed; flowers orange, medium, dbl., rosette, borne in large clusters; foliage fresh green, glossy; low, bushy, compact growth; int. in 1991

Souv d'Adèle Launay B, mr, 1872, Moreau et Robert; flowers bright rose pink, large, full, globular

Souv d'Adolphe de Charvoik HWich, lp, 1911; flowers bright pink, 4 cm., semi-dbl., borne in clusters of 5-15, slight fragrance; once-blooming; foliage light green, glossy; thornless; vigorous (5 m.) growth

Souv d'Adolphe Thiers HP, mr, 1877, Moreau et Robert; flowers red, tinged with vermilion, very large, dbl., moderate fragrance

Souv d'Adolphe Turc Pol, op, 1924, Turc; flowers clear salmon-pink, 3 cm., semi-dbl. to dbl., cupped, borne in large clusters, slight fragrance; good repeat; low (2 ft.) growth

Souv d'Adrien Bahivet HP, dp, 1867, Cochet; flowers carmine, shaded violet-purple, large, full

Souv d'Aimée Terrel des Chenes Ch, op, 1897, Widow Schwartz; flowers coppery-pink, small, dbl.

Souv d'Alexandre Bacot HT, mr, 1958, Arles; flowers geranium-red, large, 50 petals; very vigorous growth; [Crimson Glory × Independence]; int. by Roses-France

Souv d'Alexandre Bernaix HT, dr, 1926, Bernaix, P.; flowers crimson-scarlet, shaded darker, very large, dbl., cupped; foliage purplish green; vigorous growth; [Étoile de Hollande × Gen. MacArthur]

Souv d'Alexandre Hardy HP, mr, 1898, Lévêque; flowers maroon, tinted carmine and vermilion, large, dbl.

Souv d'Aline Fontaine HP, lp, 1879, Fontaine; flowers flesh pink, aging lighter, very dbl.

Souv d'Alma de l'Aigle – See **Andenken an Alma de l'Aigle**, HMsk

Souv d'Alphonse Lavallée HP, dr, 1884, Verdier, C.; flowers dark velvety crimson to maroon, 8 cm., full, cupped, moderate fragrance; recurrent; few prickles; growth to 6 ft.; int. by C. Verdier

Souv d'André Raffy HP, dr, 1899, Vigneron; flowers vermilion red, with velvety touches, large, dbl., globular, intense fragrance

Souv d'Angèle Opdebeeck HT, my, 1926, Verschuren; bud golden yellow, long, pointed; flowers canary-yellow, large, dbl., moderate fragrance; [Golden Ophelia × Golden Emblem]

Souv d'Angelique N, lp

Souv d'Anne Frank F, ob, 1960, Delforge; flowers orange tinted yellow and salmon, medium, 17 petals, cupped, borne in clusters; foliage glossy, dark; moderate, bushy growth; [Reve de Capri × Chanteclerc]

Souv d'Anne-Marie HT, op, 1902, Gebrüder Ketten; flowers yellowish salmon-pink, large, dbl.; [Safrano × Mme Caroline Testout]

Souv d'Anselme B, dp; flowers bright cherry red, large, dbl., cupped

Souv d'Antonin Poncet HT, dr, 1921, Schwartz, A.; bud long, pointed; flowers carmine, flecked paler, dbl.; [Mme Maurice de Luze × Lady Ashtown]

Souv d'Arthur de Sansal HP, mp, 1876, Guénoux; flowers clear rose, large, dbl., intense fragrance; [Jules Margottin × unknown]

Souv d'Auguste Legros T, mr, 1890, Bonnaire; flowers red-crimson, large

Souv d'Auguste Métral HT, dr, 1895, Guillot, P.; flowers varying from purple red to crimson, large, full, moderate fragrance

Souv d'Auguste Rivière HP, rb, 1877, Verdier; flowers rich crimson red, purple and scarlet, large, full; foliage delicate green, irregularly toothed; prickles numerous, unequal, very sharp, reddish; growth upright

Souvenir de Adolphe Turc – See **Souv d'Adolphe Turc**, Pol

Souv de Amand Opdebeeck HT, yb, 1936, Belge; bud long, pointed; flowers yellowish apricot-pink, edged pink, very large, dbl., high-centered; foliage leathery, bronze; very vigorous growth; int. by Opdebeeck

Souv de Bélicant-Gibey T, pb, 1902, Bonnaire; flowers fresh pink, center coppery, large, full

Souv de Ben-Hur HT, mr, 1960, Verschuren; bud pointed; flowers crimson-scarlet, 5 in., dbl.; very vigorous growth; [Ena Harkness × Charles Mallerin]; int. by Blaby Rose Gardens, 1960

Souv de Béranger HP, mp, 1857, Bruant; flowers rose, large, dbl.; moderate growth

Souv de Bernardin de St. Pierre HP, dr, 1864, Guillot; flowers velvety dark crimson with slatey violet-red, large, full

Souv de Bertrand Guinoisseau HP, m, 1895, Chédane-Guinoisseau; flowers purple red nuanced crimson, large, very dbl., moderate fragrance

Souv de Brod – See **Erinnerung an Brod**, HSet

Souv de Caillat HP, rb, 1867, Verdier, E.; flowers purple and flame, large, full, borne in small clusters

Souv de Catherine Fontaine HT, yb, 1934, Soupert, C.; bud long, pointed; flowers brownish yellow, center brick-red, reverse coral-red, very large; [Souv. de Jean Soupert × Mme Edouard Herriot]

Souv de Catherine Guillot T, rb, 1895, Guillot, P.; bud long, nasturtium red; flowers coppery carmine, center shaded orange, large, dbl., intense fragrance; weak growth

Souv de Charles Gouverneur HT, pb, 1927, Chambard, C.; bud long, pointed; flowers flesh-pink, center salmon-orange, very large

Souv de Charles Laemmel HT, yb, 1919, Gillot, F.; bud very large, ovoid; flowers golden yellow, streaked orange and shaded pink, large, full, intense fragrance; foliage dark green, glossy; growth upright, vigorous; [Frau Karl Druschki × Soleil d'Or]

Souv de Charles Montault HP, dr, 1862, Robert & Moreau; flowers velvety purple suffused with crimson, large, full, cupped

Souv de Charles Verdier HP, m, 1894, Verdier, E.; flowers purple-violet, shaded crimson and slate-purple, medium to large, full

Souv de Charles Verdier HP, dp, 1900, Lévêque; flowers dark carmine, shaded purple, large, full

Souv de Christophe Cochet HRg, mp, 1894, Cochet-Cochet; flowers bright flesh pink, flushed carmine, 6 cm., semi-dbl. to dbl., cupped, open, moderate fragrance; non-recurrent; foliage dark green, leathery; upright (5 ft.), bushy growth; hips large, bright red; [*R. × kamtchatika* 'Alba Simplex' × Comte d'Epremesnil]

Souv de Clairvaux T, pb, 1890, Verdier, E.; flowers China pink, with apricot yellow at base, tinted carmine, medium to large, full, moderate fragrance; foliage glossy

Souv de Claude Vially HT, rb, 1931, Reymond; bud long, pointed; flowers light red, tinted pink and aurora

Souv de Claudius Denoyel Cl HT, dr, 1920, Chambard, C.; bud long, pointed; flowers rich crimson-red, tinted scarlet, large, dbl., cupped, moderate fragrance; sparse, recurrent bloom; vigorous, climbing growth; [Château de Clos Vougeot × Commandeur Jules Gravereaux]

Souv de Claudius Pernet HT, my, 1920, Pernet-Ducher; bud long, pointed; flowers pure sunflower-yellow, center deeper, large, 28 petals, moderate fragrance; foliage large, glossy, rich green; long, strong stems; growth vigorous, branching; [Constance × unnamed variety]; very susceptible to foliage diseases; Gold Medal, Bagatelle, 1920

Souv de Claudius Pernet, Climbing Cl HT, my, 1925, Western Rose Co.; flowers sunflower yellow, 6 in., full, globular, moderate fragrance; [sport of Souv de Claudius Pernet]; (also Schmidt, 1932, Gaujard, 1933, Square, 1937)

Souv de Clermonde HT, pb, 1925, Pernet-Ducher; flowers salmon-rose, center darker, shaded yellow, semi-dbl.

Souv de Coulommiers HP, dr, 1868, Desmazures; flowers dark scarlet with violet reflections, large, full

Souv de David d'Angers T, dr, 1856, Moreau-Robert; flowers dark red, shaded maroon, very large, dbl.

Souv de Denier van der Gon HT, yb, 1935, Verschuren-Pechtold; bud long, pointed; flowers reddish-yellow to golden yellow, large, dbl., moderate fragrance; very vigorous growth; [Roselandia × Souv. de Claudius Pernet]

Souv de Ducher HP, m, 1874, Verdier, E.; flowers purple, center velvety dark violet, medium, full

Souv de Ernest H. Morse – See **Ernest H. Morse**, HT

Souv de F. Bohé HT, op, 1922, Chambard, C.; bud long, pointed; flowers orange-salmon, 35 petals; [Willowmere × seedling]

Souv de Fernand Leroy HSpn, pb, Brochet-Lanvin; flowers striped, small, pompon; non-remontant

Souv de Francis Borges HT, ob, 1932, Chambard, C.; flowers flesh, center orange, very large; vigorous growth; [Mme Leon Pain × seedling]

Souv de François Gaulain T, rb, 1889, Guillot; flowers crimson and violet, moderate fragrance

Souv de François Graindorge HT, yb, 1928, Grandes Roseraies; bud long, pointed; flowers ochre-yellow, base Indian yellow, dbl.; [Benedicte Sequin × Lady Hillingdon]

Souv de François Mercier HT, ob, 1923, Laperrière; bud long, pointed; flowers light coppery rose, edged deeper, dbl.; [sport of Antoine Rivoire]

Souv de François Richardier HT, rb, 1923, Richardier; flowers bright carmine-pink, tinted cherry

Souv de Gabriel Luizet HT, yb, 1922, Croibier; flowers sulfur-yellow tinted salmon, passing to deep rich yellow and later straw yellow, dbl.; [(Mme Mélanie Soupert × unknown) × Lyon Rose]

Souv de Gabrielle Drevet T, op, 1884, Guillot et Fils; flowers salmon-pink, base coppery, large, well-formed, intense fragrance

Souv de Gaston Commagères HT, ob, 1954, Privat; flowers orange-ivory veined yellow, edge veined pink, very dbl.; vigorous, bushy growth

Souv de Général Gange B, dp, 1855, de Fauw; flowers lilac pink, aging to red, medium, full

Souv de Geneviève Godard T, mp, 1893, Godard

Souv de George Beckwith HT, pb, 1919, Pernet-Ducher; bud long, pointed; flowers shrimp-pink, tinted chrome-yellow, base deeper, very large, 55 petals, globular; foliage glossy; very vigorous growth; [seedling × Lyon Rose]

Souv de George Knight HT, my, 1926, Knight, J.; flowers nankeen yellow; [sport of Rayon d'Or]

Souv de George Sand T, yb, 1876, Widow Ducher; bud carmine; flowers salmony yellow, reverse ribboned lilac, very large, full

Souv de Georges Pernet HT, op, 1921, Pernet-Ducher; bud globular; flowers medium salmon-pink, large, 31 petals, rosette, borne in clusters, intense fragrance; foliage dark, bronze; vigorous growth; [seedling × Mme Edouard Herriot]; Gold Medal, Bagatelle, 1921

Souv de Georges Pernet, Climbing Cl HT, op, 1927, Pernet-Ducher; flowers red exterior, carmine interior, large, full; [sport of Souv de Georges Pernet]

Souv de Germain de Saint-Pierre T, dr, 1882, Nabonnand; flowers purple-red, large, full, borne in small clusters

Souv de Gilbert Nabonnand T, pb, 1920, Nabonnand, P.; flowers yellow base edged carmine-pink, dbl., intense fragrance; vigorous growth

Souv de Giosue Carducci – See **Ricordo di Giosue Carducci**, HT

Souv de Gonod HP, mr, 1890, Gonod; flowers cherry red, very large, full; [Baronne Adolphe de Rothschild × unknown]

Souv de Grégoire Bordillon HP, mr, 1889, Moreau et Robert; flowers bright red nuanced vermilion, very large, full, globular; foliage dark green; prickles sharp, dense

Souv de Greuville S, m, Schultheis; flowers soft lilac-pink, fading to white, small, dbl., pompon, borne in clusters, slight fragrance; recurrent; foliage medium green; low (60-80 cm.), bushy growth; int. by Rosen von Schultheis, 2004

Souv de Gustave Prat HT, ly, 1909, Pernet-Ducher; flowers pure light sulfur-yellow, large, dbl.

Souv de Gustave Schickelé HT, yb, 1927, Ketten Bros.; bud long, pointed; flowers chrome-yellow, reverse bright rosy scarlet, shaded apricot, dbl.; [Mme Edouard Herriot × Duchess of Wellington]

Souv de H. A. Verschuren HT, yb, 1922, Verschuren; bud long, pointed; flowers yellow to orange-yellow, pink tones on edges, large, 38 petals, high-centered, moderate fragrance; vigorous growth; [seedling × Golden Ophelia]

Souv de H. A. Verschuren, Climbing Cl HT, yb, 1927, H&S; [sport of Souv de H. A. Verschuren]

Souv de Henri Faassen HT, pb, 1929, Faassen-Hekkens; bud long, pointed; flowers deep pink, base orange-yellow, open, large, semi-dbl.; foliage bronze; very vigorous growth; [Betty Uprichard × (Mrs George Shawyer × Los Angeles)]

Souv de Henri Lévêque de Vilmorin HP, dr, 1899, Lévêque; flowers deep velvety crimson, large, full; foliage dark green

Souv de Henri Venot HT, mr, 1931, Lens; flowers brilliant red, very dbl.; foliage dark; vigorous growth; [Lord Charlemont × Red Star]

Souv de Henry Clay HSpn, lp, 1854, Boll; flowers light lilac pink, medium; some repeat in autumn

Souv de Henry Graham HT, yb, 1915, Dickson; flowers creamy yellow with carmine reflections, large, full, moderate fragrance

Souv de J. B. Guillot T, or, 1897, Guillot; flowers bright coppery-red, shaded crimson, large, full; growth to 1 m.

Souv de J. B. Weibel HT, dr, 1930, Sauvageot, H.; flowers carmine, very large, dbl., cupped; foliage dark; very vigorous, bushy growth; [(Mrs Bullen × unknown) × Edouard Mignot]; int. by F. Gillot, 1930

Souv de J. Chabert F, mr, 1956, Delbard-Chabert; flowers well-formed, large, dbl., borne in clusters of 3-6; foliage dark, bronze; vigorous, low growth; [Francais × seedling]

Souv de J. Mermet HWich, dr, 1934, Mermet; flowers silvery carmine, reverse lighter to medium, 4-5 cm., full, rosette, borne in small to medium clusters, slight fragrance; repeats in autumn; foliage bronze-green, glossy; very vigorous, tall growth

Souv de J. Passinge HT, op, 1912, Chambard; flowers coppery dawn pink, shaded carmine and dark yellow, large, full, moderate fragrance

Souv de Jacques Verschuren HT, op, 1950, Verschuren-Pechtold; bud long, pointed; flowers apricot-salmon, large, dbl.; foliage leathery, dark; vigorous, bushy growth; [Katharine Pechtold × Orange Delight]

Souv de Jean Croibier HT, pb, 1921, Croibier; flowers bright salmon-pink shaded chamois, center coral-red shaded yellow, dbl.; [Mme Mélanie Soupert × Lyon Rose]

Souv de Jean Ginet HT, mr, 1935, Brenier, E.C.; flowers scarlet-red, base coppery, reverse golden yellow; int. by Buatois

Souv de Jean Sisley HP, m, 1891, Dubreuil; flowers dark carmine-purple, shaded magenta and amaranth, large, full

Souv de Jean Soupert HT, my, 1929, Soupert & Notting; bud long, pointed; flowers golden yellow, very large, semi-dbl., cupped; foliage bronze; vigorous growth; [Ophelia × Feu Joseph Looymans]

Souv de Jeanne Balandreau – See **Souv de Mme Jeanne Balandreau**, HP

Souv de Jeanne Cabaud T, yb, 1896, Guillot, P.; flowers coppery yellow, tinted with apricot and carmine, very large, full, moderate fragrance

Souv de John E. Knight HT, ob, 1928, Knight, J.; flowers terra-cotta, salmon-pink and flesh streaked yellow; foliage dark; vigorous growth

Souv de John Gould Veitch HP, dr, 1872, Verdier, E.; flowers deep crimson, shaded violet-purple, large, full

Souv de Josefina Plà HT, mr, 1929, Munné, B.; flowers bright red, large, semi-dbl.; vigorous growth; [Étoile de Hollande × Mme Butterfly]

Souv de Joseph Besson HT, rb, 1931, Brenier, E.C.; flowers reddish-orange, base yellow

Souv de Jules Godard T, w, 1894, Godard; flowers flesh white, medium, full, moderate fragrance

Souv de Jules Nicolas Mathieu Lamarche Pol, rb, 1934, Soupert, C.; flowers cardinal-red, base yellow, very small, single, borne in large panicles; [Eblouissant × Petit Constant]

Souv de Julie Gonod HP, mp, 1871, Gonod; flowers glowing silky pink, large, full

Souv de la Bataille de Marengo – See **Russelliana**, HMult

Souv de la Comtesse de Roquette-Buisson HT, lp, 1908, Ketten; flowers flesh pink, aging to flesh-white, tinted salmon, very large, very full, moderate fragrance; [Laure Wattine × William Askew]

Souv de la Malmaison B, lp, 1843, Béluze; flowers creamy flesh, center rosy shaded, 4 in., dbl., quartered, flat, intense spicy fragrance; repeat bloom; dwarf, bushy (2 ft.) growth; [Mme Desprez (B) × a Tea rose (possibly Devoniensis)]; Old Rose Hall of Fame, WFRS

Souv de la Malmaison, Climbing Cl B, lp, 1893, Bennett; flowers blush white, slightly darker at center, 10-12 cm., very full, flat, quartered, moderate fragrance; [sport of Souv de la Malmaison]

Souv de la Malmaison Rose – See **Leweson-Gower**, B

Souv de la Malmaison Rouge – See **Malmaison Rouge**, B

Souv de la Princesse Amélie des Pays-Bas HP, m,

1873, Liabaud; flowers grenadine red shaded purple, large, dbl., globular

Souv de la Princesse de Lamballe – See **Queen of Bourbons**, B, 1834

Souv de la Reine d'Angleterre HP, mp, 1855, Cochet Freres; flowers bright pink, large, dbl.; recurrent bloom; very vigorous growth; [La Reine × unknown]

Souv de la Reine des Belges HP, pb, 1850, de Fauw; flowers fiery light carmine, edges bright carmine, medium

Souv de la Reine des Pay-Bas HP, m, 1876, Schwartz; flowers purple with darker reflections

Souv de la Russie HT, pb, 1905; flowers dark pink, marbled white

Souv de Lady Ashburton T, rb, 1890, Verdier, C.; flowers rich coppery red, suffused with pale orange yellow

Souv de Laffay HP, mr, 1878, Verdier, E.; flowers crimson-red, large, very full, borne in small clusters; foliage oblong, dark green, regularly toothed; prickles large, short, upright; growth upright, short

Souv de l'Ami Labruyère HP, mp, 1884, Gonod; flowers outer petals China pink, center darker; growth upright

Souv de l'Amiral Courbet T, mr, 1885, Pernet père; flowers bright fiery red, medium, dbl., globular, borne in large clusters; growth upright

Souv de Laurent Guillot T, pb, 1894, Bonnaire; flowers China pink with peach yellow center, edges carmine, large, full; foliage bronze-green

Souv de l'Aviateur Métivier HWich, ly, 1913, Tanne; flowers clear yellow, passing to white, dbl.; vigorous, climbing growth; [*R. wichurana* × Mme Ravary]

Souv de l'Aviateur Olivier de Montalent HWich, rb, 1913, Tanne; flowers dull rose, base salmon, dbl., borne in clusters; profuse bloom, rarely recurrent; foliage very glossy, dark; vigorous, climbing growth; [*R. wichurana* × Anna Olivier]

Souv de Léon Gambetta HP, pb, 1908, Vigneron; flowers flesh pink, nuanced carmine red, 5 in.; foliage bright green; prickles large recurved; [Victor Verdier × unknown]

Souv de Léon Roudillon HP, dr, 1908, Vigneron; flowers deep velvety red, fiery red center, large, full; foliage dark green; [Général Appert × Louis Van Houtte]

Souv de Leveson Gower HP, mr, 1852, Guillot père; flowers dark red, changing to ruby, very large, full

Souv de l'Exposition de Bordeaux HMult, lp, 1905, Puyravaud; flowers pale pink, lighter at center, 5-6 cm., dbl., globular, borne in clusters of more than 40; none-recurrent; prickles close-set, straight, reddish; [Turner's Crimson Rambler × Simon de St Jean]

Souv de l'Exposition de Brie – See **Maurice Bernardin**, HP

Souv de l'Exposition de Londres B, mr, 1851, Guillot père; flowers velvety poppy red, medium to large, full

Souv de Lilette HT, w, 1937, Chambard, C.; bud very long; flowers snow-white, large; foliage slightly bronze; compact, bushy growth

Souv de Louis Amade S, mp, Delbard; flowers lilac pink, dbl., globular to cupped, moderate licorice fragrance; free-flowering; moderate (2-3 ft.) growth; int. in 1998

Souv de Louis Bertrand HWich, 1910, Béluze

Souv de Louis Eugene Rantz HT, Rantz, Louis M.; PP2828

Souv de Louis Gaudin B, dr, 1864, Trouillard; flowers reddish-purple, almost black, medium, full

Souv de Louis Moreau HP, mr, 1891, Moreau & Robert; flowers flame red, aging to dark crimson, large, full, globular

Souv de Louis Simon – See **Mrs Miniver**, HT

Souv de Louis Van Houtte – See **Crimson Bedder**, HP

Souv de Lucie N, dp, 1893, Schwartz; bud small, crimson; flowers cerise pink, lighter reverse to medium, 5 cm., dbl., flat, borne in small clusters; foliage small, glossy; [Fellemberg × Ernestine de Barante]

Souv de Lucienne Valayer HT, pb, 1938, Chambard, C.; bud long; flowers soft pink, shaded light salmon, very large, cupped; vigorous, bushy growth

Souv de Ma Petite Andrée T, w, 1901, Chauvry; flowers cream-white, edged pearly pink, large, very full, moderate fragrance; [Mme Clément Massier × unknown]

Souv de Mme A. Henneveu T, pb, 1892, Bernaix; flowers silky China pink, sometimes with coppery amaranthe, dbl.

Souv de Mme A. Hess HT, pb, 1936, Chambard, C.; bud long, pointed; flowers shrimp-pink, center deep coral, very large, cupped; foliage bronze; very vigorous, bushy growth; [seedling × Ami F. Mayery]

Souv de Mme Achille van Herreweghe HT, dr, 1936, Van Herreweghe-Coppitters; flowers carmine-red; vigorous growth

Souv de Mme Alexandre Mathian T, w, 1903, Bonnaire; flowers ivory white, base apricot-yellow, large, full, globular

Souv de Mme Alfred Vy HP, dr, 1880, Jamain; flowers deep currant red, large, full

Souv de Mme Auguste Charles B, mp, 1866, Moreau et Robert; flowers light pink tinged salmon, medium, full, rounded, pompon, slight fruity fragrance; recurrent; angular (3-5 ft.) growth

Souv de Mme Augustine Gillot HT, op, 1920, Gillot, F.; bud long, pointed; flowers salmony flesh-pink, base salmon-yellow, reverse silvery flesh; [Frau Karl Druschki × Lyon Rose]

Souv de Mme Berthier HP, dr, 1881, Berthier/Liabaud; flowers velvety red, sometimes streaked white, large, very full; very remontant; growth to 5 ft.; [Victor Verdier × Jules Margottin]

Souv de Mme Boll HP, rb, Boyau; flowers rich red blend, full, cupped, moderate fragrance; recurrent; large (5 ft.) growth; int. by Souvenir de Madame Boll, 1866

Souv de Mme Boullet HT, dy, 1921, Pernet-Ducher; bud long, pointed; flowers golden yellow with apricot tones, large, dbl., cupped, borne mostly singly, moderate tea fragrance; recurrent; foliage bronzy-purple; stems wiry; vigorous, spreading (4 ft.) growth; [Sunburst × unnamed variety]

Souv de Mme Boullet, Climbing Cl HT, dy, 1930, H&S; [sport of Souv de Mme Boullet]

Souv de Mme Breuil B, dp; flowers deep cerise magenta, large, full, pompon, intense fragrance; recurrent; arching (2 m.) growth

Souv de Mme Breul B, mr, 1889, Levet; flowers light red, large, full; foliage dark green; prickles large

Souv de Mme C. Chambard HT, op, 1931, Chambard, C.; flowers coral-rose-pink, center flushed gold, large, semi-dbl., cupped; vigorous growth; int. by C-P

Souv de Mme C. Chambard, Climbing Cl HT, op, 1935, Armstrong, J.A.; [sport of Mme C. Chambard]

Souv de Mme Camusat HT, lp, 1897, Bonnaire; flowers flesh pink, carmine at center, large, full

Souv de Mme Canel HT, rb, 1932, Gillot, F.; flowers carmine-orange, large, very dbl.; foliage pointed, bronze; robust, bushy growth

Souv de Mme Chédane-Guinoisseau HP, mr, 1900, Chédane-Guinoisseau; flowers bright geranium red, very large, dbl.

Souv de Mme de Corval HP, dp, 1867, Gonod; flowers dawn pink, medium, dbl.; recurrent

Souv de Mme Durand HT, yb, 1954, Privat; flowers naples yellow, base bright yellow, edges veined pink, dbl., globular; foliage glossy; strong stems

Souv de Mme Dussordet HP, mp, 1860, Clément/Guillot

Souv de Mme Ernest Cauvin HT, pb, 1898, Pernet-Ducher; flowers flesh pink, bordered brighter pink, center light yellow to orange-yellow, large, very full; few prickles; growth upright

Souv de Mme Ernest Oudin HT, w, 1906, Bonnaire; flowers white, shaded bluish, large, full

Souv de Mme Eugène Verdier HT, w, 1894, Pernet-Ducher; flowers white, base saffron-yellow, large, very full; foliage finely serrated; growth upright; [Lady Mary Fitzwilliam × Mme Chedane-Guinoisseau]

Souv de Mme Eugène Verdier HP, pb, 1894, Jobert; flowers bright pink, reverse silver, full, globular

Souv de Mme F. Zurich HT, mp, 1910, Puyravaud; flowers silvery pink, large, dbl.; [Laure Wattinne × Mme Bérard]

Souv de Mme Faure HP, dr, 1888, Bernaix; flowers dark, velvety carmine, shaded purple, very large, very full, globular

Souv de Mme Fontaine – See **Toujours Fleuri**, B

Souv de Mme Frogère HP, w, 1900, Chédane-Guinoisseau; flowers white, shaded pink, very large, full

Souv de Mme Gauthier-Dumont HT, mr, 1921, Guillot, P.; bud long, pointed; flowers scarlet

Souv de Mme H. Thuret HP, pb, 1922, Texier; flowers salmon-pink, center shrimp-red, edged chrome, well-formed, cupped; foliage rich green; very vigorous growth; [Frau Karl Druschki × Lyon Rose]; int. by P. Nabonnand

Souv de Mme Hélène Lambert T, pb, 1885, Gonod; flowers pink-yellow, reverse dark flesh pink, medium to large; [Beauté de l'Europe × unknown]

Souv de Mme Hennecart HP, mp, 1869, Carré/Cochet; flowers glossy pink fading to icy pink, large, dbl.

Souv de Mme Jeanne Balandreau HP, mr, 1899, Vilin; flowers red, shaded vermilion, medium, full, globular to cupped; recurrent; foliage dark grey-green; upright (3-5 ft.) growth; [sport of Ulrich Brunner Fils]; int. by Robichon, 1899

Souv de Mme Joseph Métral Cl HT, mr, 1887, Bermaix; flowers bright cerise, illuminated with crimson and vermilion, 9-10 cm., very dbl.; [Mme Bérard × Eugene Fürst]

Souv de Mme Jules Pages HMult, pb, 1937, Reiter; flowers deep pink shaded orange and red, open, small, dbl.; free, intermittent bloom; vigorous, climbing or pillar growth; [Phyllis Bide × Eblouissant]; int. by Stocking

Souv de Mme Krenger HT, op, 1919, Chambard, C.; flowers pure salmon-orange, passing to coppery pink, dbl.; [Mme Mélanie Soupert × Willowmere]

Souv de Mme l'Advocat N, op, 1899, Veysset; flowers coppery pink, medium, dbl.; [sport of Duarte de Oliveira]

Souv de Mme Lambard T, yb, 1890, California Nursery Co.; flowers canary yellow, shaded and tinted with salmon rose, large

Souv de Mme Lefèbvre HT, rb, 1929, Richardier; flowers oriental red, passing to pink, golden yellow and red; vigorous growth

Souv de Mme Léonie Viennot Cl T, yb, 1898, Bernaix, A.; flowers deep peachy yellow-pink, aging to paler pink, reverse silvery, 10 cm., very dbl., intense tea fragrance; foliage dark green; vigorous (10-15 ft.) growth; [Gloire de Dijon × unknown]

Souv de Mme Levet T, ob, 1891, Levet, F.; flowers orange-yellow, large, full; foliage dark green; few prickles; growth vigorous; [Mme Carot × Mme Eugène Verdier]

Souv de Mme Louise Cretté HT, yb, 1924, Cretté; flowers golden yellow, shaded coral and red, dbl.; [Mme Edouard Herriot × unknown]; int. by C. Chambard

Souv de Mme Morin-Latune HT, dp, 1920, Bernaix, P.; bud long, pointed; flowers cream-rose, dbl.

Souv de Mme Pidoux HT, yb, 1926, Chambard, C.; bud long, pointed; flowers chrome-yellow, reverse pink, cupped; [seedling × Mrs Aaron Ward]

Souv de Mme Robert HP, lp, 1879, Moreau et Robert; flowers icy salmon-pink, center brighter, large, dbl.; [Jules Margottin × unknown]

Souv de Mme Rousseau – See **Souv de Monsieur Rousseau**, HP

Souv de Mme Sablayrolles T, ab, 1891, Bonnaire; flowers apricot-pink edged with carmine, large, full, globular, borne mostly solitary; [Devoniensis × Souv d'Elise Vardon]

Souv de Mme Sadi Carnot HP, dr, 1898, Lévêque; flowers deep carmine red nuanced purple, very large; foliage glaucous green; [Mme Victor Verdier × unknown]

Souv de Mme Salati-Mongellaz HP, dp, 1937, Croibier; bud long, pointed; flowers satiny rose-pink, very large, dbl.; foliage dark; very vigorous growth; [Frau Karl Druschki × seedling]

Souv de Mme Victor Verdier HP, dp, 1883, Verdier, E.; flowers shining dark pink, reverse lighter, large, full

Souv de Mme William Wood HP, m, 1865, Verdier, E.; flowers purple; vigorous growth; [Général Jacqueminot × unknown]

Souv de Madeleine Rouillon HT, ob, 1929, Bernaix, P.; bud long, pointed; flowers orange, base yellow, dbl.; [Manon × Elvira Aramayo]

Souv de Mlle Élise Châtelard Pol, mr, 1891, Bernaix; flowers carmine red

Souv de Mlle Juliet de Bricard Pol, lp, 1934, Délépine; flowers pale rosy pink, 2 in., very dbl., globular, borne in clusters; recurrent; foliage glossy, dark; vigorous (2 ft.), bushy growth; [Cécile Brunner × Yvonne Rabier]; int. by Pajotin-Chédane

Souv de Mlle Victor Caillet T, w, 1892, Bernaix; flowers pure white, medium, full

Souv de Malmedy HGal, mp, Scarman; flowers clear pink, full, shallow cup; growth to 4 ft.; int. in 1996

Souv de Maman Corboeuf HP, mp, 1900, Corboeuf; flowers medium, dbl.

Souv de Marcel Proust HT, my, Delbard; flowers intense yellow, large, full, cupped, quartered, intense citronelle fragrance; free-flowering; foliage medium green; moderate, branching growth; int. by Georges Delbard SA, 1992; Gold Medal, Baden-Baden, 1992, Fragrance Award, Nantes, 1995, Fragrance Award, Monza, 1992

Souv de Marcelle Balage HT, pb, 1930, Bernaix, P.; bud long, pointed; flowers satiny flesh-pink, center slightly tinted salmon, very large, dbl., cupped, intense fragrance; foliage dark; [Willowmere × Mme Pizay]

Souv de Maria Clotilde HT, ly, 1934, Carneiro; bud long; flowers amber-white, often passing to light yellow, center sometimes flesh-pink, large, dbl., moderate fragrance; vigorous growth; [sport of Mme Abel Chatenay]; int. by Ketten Bros.

Souv de Maria de Zayas HT, mr, 1906, Soupert & Notting; bud long, pointed; flowers carmine red veined deep red, very large, dbl., moderate fragrance; [seedling × Papa Gontier]

Souv de Maria Zozaya HT, or, 1903, Soupert & Notting; bud long; flowers coral-red, silvery center, very large, full; [Souv de Wootton × Mrs W. J. Grant]

Souv de Marie Finon HT, ab, 1924, Croibier; flowers apricot-yellow passing to clear yellow shaded salmon, dbl.

Souv de Marie-Thérèse HT, w, Chabanat; flowers ivory-white; low growth; int. by Roses-France

Souv de Marie Thérèse Privat Pol, mr, 1935, Privat; flowers bright vermilion, well-formed, very dbl., borne in clusters of 40-50; foliage bright green; dwarf, good habit growth

Souv de Marques Loureiro HT, rb, 1912, Ketten Bros.; flowers light red shading to rose, tinted yellow and purple, dbl.; [Mons. Paul Lédé × Mme Hoste]

Souv de Maurice Chevalier Gr, dr, 1982, Delbard, Georges; flowers semi-dbl., borne in clusters; [(Walko × Impeccable) × (Papa Meilland × (Baccará × Michele Meilland))]

Souv de McKinley HT, lp, 1902, Godard; flowers delicate pink, full, moderate fragrance; recurrent; [Magna Charta × Captain Christy]; sometimes classed as HP or P

Souv de Mère Fontaine HCh, mr, 1874, Fontaine; flowers bright red, nuanced carmine, very large, full

Souv de Mon Ecole S, dr

Souv de Monsieur Boll HP, mr, 1866, Boyau; flowers bright cherry red, very large, full

Souv de Monsieur Bruel – See **Souv de Mme Breul**, B

Souv de Monsieur Claude Dupont T, dp, 1893, Godard; flowers dark pink, shaded red, large, full; [Souv de Victor Hugo × unknown]

Souv de Monsieur Droche HP, mp, 1881, Pernet père; flowers carmine-rose, large, dbl., globular

Souv de Monsieur Dussordet – See **Souv de Mme Dussordet**, HP

Souv de Monsieur Faivre HP, mr, 1879, Levet; flowers poppy red with slate reflections, very large, full

Souv de Monsieur Frédéric Vercellone HT, pb, 1906, Schwartz; flowers carmine pink, lightly coppery, nuanced blush white tinted bright carmine, large, full; [Antoine Rivoire × André Schwartz]

Souv de Monsieur Poncet P, lp, 1892, Pernet; flowers light pink, large, dbl

Souv de Monsieur Rousseau HP, mr, 1861, Fargeton; flowers scarlet, changing to crimson, shaded maroon, velvety, large, dbl.

Souv de Némours B, mp, 1859, Hervé; flowers fresh rose, reverse darker, large, full, moderate fragrance; recurrent; medium growth

Souv de Norah Lindsay LCl, mp; flowers bright pink, stamens golden, very large, single; vigorous, pillar growth

Souv de Nungesser HT, dr, 1927, Croibier; flowers brilliant deep carmine-red, dbl.; [Mme Maurice de Luze × Laurent Carle]

Souv de Papa Calame HT, dp, 1922, Guillot; flowers large, dbl.

Souv de Paul Grandclaude HT, yb, 1923, Sauvageot, H.; bud large, long, pointed; flowers yellow, shaded pink and in autumn light brown, semi-dbl.; [Mme Mélanie Soupert × Beauté de Lyon]

Souv de Paul Neyron T, yb, 1871, Levet, A.; flowers salmon-yellow edged pink, semi-globular, large; very vigorous growth; [Ophirie × unknown, or Devoniensis × Souv de la Malmaison]

Souv de Paul Raudnitz HWich, lp, 1910, Cochet-Cochet; flowers white tinged with salmon, 3-4 cm., very dbl., borne in clusters of 25-35; some autumn repeat; foliage elliptical, bright green, glossy; prickles strong, slightly hooked, sparse, gray; [*R. wichurana* × Turner's Crimson Rambler]

Souv de Périgueux HT, mr, 1913, Croibier; flowers bright, glossy carmine-red, large, full; [Mme M. de Luze × Liberty]

Souv de Philémon Cochet HRg, w, 1899, Cochet-Cochet; flowers white, center rose tinged salmon, 10-12 cm., very full, moderate fragrance; recurrent; medium growth; [sport of Blanc Double de Coubert]; same as Blanc Double de Coubert except for slight color difference

Souv de Pierre Dupuy B, dr, 1876, Levet; flowers deep velvety red, 3 in., full, globular, borne singly and in small clusters, moderate fragrance; some repeat; [Général Jacqueminot × unknown]

Souv de Pierre Guillot HT, ob, 1928, Guillot, M.; bud long, pointed; flowers coral-orange-yellow blend, dbl.; [Marie Adélaide × seedling]

Souv de Pierre Ketten HT, pb, 1928, Ketten Bros.; bud long, pointed; flowers bright rose, inside pink, base chrome-yellow, 30-35 petals, intense fragrance; [Mme Mélanie Soupert × Pilgrim]

Souv de Pierre Leperdrieux HRg, mr, 1895, Cochet-Cochet; flowers bright wine red, 9-10 cm., semi-dbl., borne in large clusters; large fruit

Souv de Pierre Notting T, yb, 1902, Soupert & Notting; bud long, pointed; flowers sunflower-yellow tinted apricot and coppery yellow, edged rose, very dbl., cupped, slight fragrance; free-flowering; foliage rich green, soft; [Maréchal Niel × Maman Cochet]

Souv de Pierre Notting, Climbing Cl T, ab, 1913, Cant, F.; flowers apricot yellow with hints of gold, fading to pink, edged carmine, 10 cm., very full, borne in small clusters; [sport of Souv de Pierre Notting]

Souv de Pierre Sionville HP, mr, 1906, Boutigny; flowers bright red, large, very full, cupped; sometimes classed as HT

Souv de Pierre Vibert M, rb, 1867, Moreau et Robert; flowers dark red, shaded carmine and violet, large, dbl., slight fragrance; sometimes recurrent bloom; moderate growth

Souv de Poiteau HP, op, 1868, Margottin; flowers bright salmon pink, large, full, cupped

Souv de Prosper Fraissenon HT, m, 1927, Richardier; bud long, pointed; flowers geranium-red tinted violet

Souv de R. B. Ferguson HT, pb, 1922, Ferguson, W.; flowers shell-pink and apricot, sometimes shaded rose-pink and cerise; [seedling × Constance]

Souv de Raymond Gaujard HT, yb, 1943, Gaujard; bud ovoid; flowers golden yellow, reverse often veined red, open, medium, dbl.; foliage dark, glossy; vigorous, upright growth

Souv de René Bahaud T, op, 1897, Bahaud; flowers salmon pink, opening golden yellow, aging to China pink, large, full

Souv de René Grognet HT, ob, 1921, Chambard, C.; bud long, pointed; flowers coppery orange-yellow, shaded carmine

Souv de Robert Schuman S, ab, Guillot-Massad; flowers amber yellow, fading to white, semi-dbl., cupped to flat, borne in clusters; recurrent; foliage dark green, glossy; int. by Roseraies Guillot, 2006

Souv de Romain Desprez HP, lp, 1871, de Sansal; flowers flesh pink, shaded slate, center brighter, very large, full

Souv de Rose Berkley – See **Rose Berkley**, HT

Souv de Rose-Marie HMsk, ly, 2000, Lens, Louis; flowers ochre, changing to light yellow, reverse light yellow, 5-6 cm., single, shallow cupped, borne in large clusters, moderate fragrance; recurrent; foliage medium size, medium green, semi-glossy; prickles moderate; growth upright, medium (80-100 cm.); hedges; [Trier × Mutabilis]; int. by Lens Roses, 1998

Souv de S. A. Prince T, w, 1889, Dingee & Conard; flowers pure white, large, full, globular; [sport of Souv. d'un Ami]

Souv de St Anne's B, lp, before 1916; flowers blush-pink, medium, semi-dbl., moderate fragrance; recurrent bloom; medium to tall growth; [sport of Souv. de la Malmaison]; from the garden of Lady Ardilaun, at Saint-Anne, near Dublin; int. by Hilling, 1950

Souv de Saintonge N, w, 1904, Chauvry; flowers white, base canary yellow

Souv de Shelby Wallace – See **Shelby Wallace**, Cl Pol

Souv de Simon de St Jean HP, mr

Souv de Solférino HP, dp, 1861, Margottin; flowers velvety carmine, shaded brown, large, full

Souv de Spa HP, dr, 1873, Gautreau; flowers deep red with scarlet reflex, large, full, globular; [Mme Victor Verdier × unknown]

Souv de Thérèse Levet T, dr, 1886, Levet, A.; flowers crimson, shaded pink at the center, large, full, globular to cupped, moderate sweet fragrance; foliage dark green; prickles large, hooked; compact (4 ft.), spreading growth; [Adam × unknown]

Souv de Victor Hugo HP, lp, 1885, Pernet père; flowers bright satiny pink, very large, very dbl., globular; foliage thick, light green; growth upright; [Ambrogio Maggi × unknown]

Souv de Victor Hugo T, pb, 1886, Bonnaire; flowers China-pink, center salmon-pink, large, dbl., intense fragrance; recurrent; stems purple-red; upright growth; [Duchesse de Brabant × Regulus]

Souv de Victor Landeau B, mr, 1890, Moreau et Robert; bud rose; flowers vivid red, large, moderate fragrance; recurrent

Souv de Victor Landeau HP, pb, Moreau et Robert; flowers pale pink to mauve rose, large, dbl., globular

Souv de Victor Verdier HP, rb, 1878, Verdier, E.; flowers scarlet poppy-red nuanced purple crimson, flame, and violet, large, full; very remontant; foliage oval, delicate green, regularly toothed; prickles numerous, recurved, sharp; growth upright

Souv de William Robinson T, op, 1899, Bernaix fils; bud ovoid; flowers peony-pink, with salmon, partly cream white and apricot yellow with violet veins

Souv de William Wood HP, dr, 1864, Verdier, E.; flowers dark blackish purple, centers flame red, large, full, semi-globular, moderate fragrance; [General Jacqueminot × unknown]

Souv de Yeddo HRg, mp, 1874, Morlet; flowers silky China pink, shaded white, large, dbl.; [*R. rugosa* × a Tea]

Souv d'E. Guillard HT, rb, 1912, Chambard, C.; flowers reddish-yellow shaded coppery carmine, large, dbl.; very vigorous, branching growth; [Beauté Inconstante × Le Progres]; Gold Medal, Bagatelle, 1914

Souv d'Elise Vardon T, w, 1855, Marest; flowers creamy white, center yellowish, very large, dbl., globular, moderate fragrance; recurrent; foliage leathery, glossy; moderate (3-4 ft.) growth

Souv d'Emile Mayrisch HT, dr, 1932, Ketten Bros.; flowers dark crimson-garnet, well-formed, large, 35-40 petals; stiff stems; vigorous growth

Souv d'Émile Peyrard T, w, 1900, Bonnaire; flowers pearly white, edges tinted pink

Souv d'Emile Zola Cl HT, lp, 1907, Begault-Pigné; bud bright pink; flowers light silvery pink, very large, full; [La France de '89 × unknown]

Souv d'Emmanuel Buatois HT, rb, 1932, Buatois; bud long, pointed; flowers coral-red shaded shrimp-red, reverse clear rose, base golden, dbl.; foliage leathery, bronze; vigorous growth; [Mme Edouard Herriot × Souv. de Claudius Pernet]

Souv d'Enghien M, mp, about 1830, Parmentier; flowers bright pink, medium, full

Souv d'Ernest Thébault HWich, dr, 1921, Thébault; flowers small, dbl., borne in clusters of 10-20; vigorous, climbing growth

Souv d'Espagne T, yb, 1888, Pries/Ketten Bros.; flowers coppery yellow and rose, edged with pinkish carmine, medium, dbl., cupped

Souv d'Henri Puyravaud HT, w, 1901, Puyravaud; flowers white, center tinted chrome yellow, large, full; [Lady Mary Fitzwilliam × Lady Emily Peel]

Souv di Castagneto HP, lp, Scarman; int. by re-introduced by Scarman, 1988

Souv du Baron de Rochetaillée HP, m, 1888, Liabaud; flowers purple, large, full

Souv du Baron de Rothschild B, mp, 1868, Avoux / Crozy; flowers carmine pink, large, full

Souv du Baron de Sémur HP, m, 1874, Lacharme, F.; flowers deep purple-red shaded fiery red and black, large, dbl.; vigorous growth; [Charles Lefebvre × unknown]

Souv du Capitaine Crémona HT, rb, 1928, Bernaix, P.; flowers salmon-carmine over yellow ground, dbl.; [Admiration × Gorgeous]

Souv du Capitaine Fernand Japy HT, mr, 1922, Sauvageot, H.; flowers purple pink, large, dbl.; [Le Progres × Les Rosati]

Souv du Capitaine Ferrand HT, rb, 1939, Gaujard; bud long, well formed; flowers nasturtium-red, reverse golden yellow; erect, vigorous growth

Souv du Comte Cavour HP, mr, 1861, Margottin; flowers velvety crimson shaded darker crimson, large, full

Souv du Comte Cavour HP, dr, 1861, Robert & Moreau; flowers dark bluish-red

Souv du Docteur Albert Reverdin HT, rb, 1930, Bernaix, P.; bud long, pointed; flowers brilliant carmine, shaded vermilion, large, very dbl.; foliage dark; strong stems; vigorous growth; [George C. Waud × Mrs Edward Powell]

Souv du Docteur Jamain HP, dr, 1865, Lacharme, F.; flowers plum shaded deep crimson, yellow stamens, small to medium, dbl., cupped, moderate old rose fragrance; recurrent; few prickles; growth arching, tall (5-9 ft.); [Charles Lefebvre × unknown]

Souv du Dr Passot T, mr, 1889, Godard; flowers velvety crimson red, fading lighter, large, full

Souv du Dr Abel de Bouchard T, w, 1900, Chauvry; flowers white, center greenish-yellow, coppery reflections, very large, moderate fragrance; [Mme Eugene Verdier × unknown]

Souv du Lieutenant Bujon B, mr, 1891, Moreau et Robert; flowers light red, aging to carmine, very large, dbl., moderate fragrance; foliage dark green

Souv du Papa Calame HT, pb, 1921, Gillot, F.; bud long, pointed; flowers carmine-pink, reverse silvery pink, stamens salmon, dbl.; [sport of Jonkheer J.L. Mock]

Souv du Petit Roi de Rome HP, lp, 1850, Béluze; flowers flesh pink, center darker

Souv du Président Carnot HT, lp, 1894, Pernet-Ducher; bud long, pointed; flowers flesh-pink, center shell-pink, full, moderate fragrance; recurrent; foliage medium green, matte; moderate growth; [Lady Mary Fitzwilliam × unknown]

Souv du Président Carnot, Climbing Cl HT, lp, 1926, Grandes Roseraies; [sport of Souv du Président Carnot]

Souv du Président Daurel HT, dp, 1906, Chauvry; flowers large, dbl.; [sport of Mme Caroline Testout]

Souv du Président Lincoln B, mr, 1865, Moreau et Robert; flowers crimson red, shaded black, medium, full, slight fragrance; some repeat; bushy (5 ft.) growth

Souv du Président Plumecocq HT, rb, 1958, Laperrière; flowers bright red, reverse marked silvery, large, dbl.; foliage bronze; very vigorous, well branched growth; [seedling × Peace]; int. by EFR

Souv du Président Porcher HP, dp, 1880, Granger, T.; flowers dark pink, reverse lighter, large, full; foliage light green; few prickles; growth upright

Souv du Prince Charles d'Arenberg N, my, 1897, Soupert & Notting; flowers canary yellow, center darker, large, full, moderate fragrance; [Rêve d'Or × Duchesse d'Auerstädt]

Souv du Reverend Père Planque HT, ob, 1932, Bel; flowers orange-chrome-yellow, fading lighter, large, full; foliage very glossy; very vigorous growth; [seedling × Souv. de Georges Pernet]

Souv du Rosiériste Gonod HP, mr, 1889, Ducher fils; flowers cerise red, veined bright pink, very large, dbl., intense fragrance

Souv du Rosiériste Rambaux T, pb, 1883, Rambaux; bud ovoid; flowers straw yellow, heavily bordered with bright rose, cupped, intense tea fragrance; foliage medium size, glossy; [Bon Silène × unknown]

Souv du Sénateur Bazire HMult, m, 1918, Lottin; flowers violet, center violet-rose, semi-dbl., borne in clusters of 25-50; [Veilchenblau × Bordeaux]

Souv du Sergent Cretté HT, yb, 1921, Chambard, C.; bud long, pointed; flowers coppery golden yellow, shaded carmine, very large, cupped; foliage bronze; very vigorous growth; [Mme Mélanie Soupert × seedling]

Souv d'un Ami T, lp, 1846, Bélot-Défougère; flowers pale rose tinged salmon, very large, dbl., cupped, intense fragrance; recurrent; vigorous growth

Souv d'un Frère B, dr, 1850, Oger; flowers purple-red and carmine, medium, dbl.

Souv of Miami HT, dr, 1925, Cook, J.W.

Souv of Portland HT, m, 1910, Dickson, H.; flowers dark purple, large, full

Souv of Stella Gray T, ob, 1907, Dickson, A.; flowers deep orange splashed apricot, salmon and crimson, small to medium, semi-dbl.

Souv of the Old Rose Garden HT, pb, 1929, Cant, B. R.; flowers silvery pink, brighter inside, very large, dbl., globular; foliage glossy, light; strong stems; vigorous growth; Gold Medal, NRS, 1928

Souv of Wootton HT, mr, 1888, Cook, J.W.; flowers rich velvety red, very large, dbl.; foliage dark, leathery; vigorous growth; [Bon Silène × Louis van Houtte]

Souv of Wootton, Climbing Cl HT, mr, 1899, Butler; flowers bright magenta red, large, full, cupped, borne singly and in small clusters; [sport of Souv of Wooton]

Souviens-Toi F, yb, 1986, Kriloff, Michel; flowers medium yellow, petals edged and washed carmine, large, 38 petals, moderate fragrance; foliage matte

Sovereign HT, dy, 1922, Cant, B. R.; flowers deep yellow and old-gold, open, cupped, intense fruity fragrance; foliage glossy, dark, bronze; vigorous growth; [Queen Mary × seedling]

Sovrana HT, ob, 1930, Aicardi, D.; flowers orange streaked yellow, well-formed, large; very vigorous, upright growth; [Julien Potin × (Signora × unknown)]; int. by Giacomasso

Sowetan Peace HT, dp; int. by J&P, 1994

Sox Min, rb, 1986, Williams, Michael C.; flowers medium red with a white eye, 1 in., 7 petals, borne singly; foliage medium size, dark; prickles small, straight; medium, upright growth; hips small, globular, orange; [Baby Katie × Angel Darling]; int. by The Rose Garden & Mini Rose Nursery

Soyécourt HT, rb, 1921, Jersey Nursery; flowers blood-red, overlaid orange; [Gen. MacArthur × George C. Waud]

Space Girl LCl, dr, 1966, Barter; flowers dark crimson, very large, dbl.; foliage dark; vigorous, climbing growth; [Queen Elizabeth × Étoile de Hollande]

Space Invader S, lp, 1990, Dickson, Patrick; flowers large, full, moderate fragrance; foliage medium size, medium green, semi-glossy; spreading growth; [seedling × Temple Bells]; int. by Dickson Nurseries, Ltd.

Space Odyssey Min, rb, 1999, Carruth, Tom; flowers red with white eye, reverse white, 1-1½ in., semi-dbl., shallow cup, borne in small clusters, slight fragrance; recurrent; foliage small, dark green, glossy; few prickles; compact, spreading, low (16-20 in.) growth; PP13514; [Santa Claus × Times Square]; int. by Weeks Roses, 2000

Space Probe Min, rb, 1995, Williams, Ernest D.; flowers red edges on white petals, medium, dbl., moderate fragrance; foliage small, medium green, semi-glossy; some prickles; medium, upright, bushy growth; [Little Darling × Over the Rainbow]; int. by K&C Roses, 1995

Space Walk Min, m, 1991, Williams, Ernest D.; flowers mauve-tan/yellow, russet reverse, small, full, borne mostly singly, intense fragrance; foliage small, dark green, semi-glossy; few prickles; low (30 cm.), bushy growth; [seedling × Twilight Trail]; int. by Mini-Roses, 1992

Spaethiana S, m; flowers purple, large, single, borne in clusters; may possibly repeat; [*R. palustris* × *R. rugosa*]; possibly 1902 or earlier

Spangles F, lp, 1994, Gandy, Douglas L.; flowers pale pink, speckled, medium, dbl., borne in large clusters, moderate musk fragrance; foliage medium size, light green, semi-glossy; numerous prickles; medium, upright, compact growth; [Florence Nightingale × Silver Jubilee]; int. by Gandy Roses, Ltd., 1995; TGC, RNRS, Certificate of Merit, Belgium

Spanish Beauty – See **Mme Grégoire Staechelin**, LCl

Spanish Dancer Min, or, 1986, Moore, Ralph S.; flowers small, 18 petals, open, borne in sprays of 5-7; foliage medium size, medium green, semi-glossy; prickles small, brown; medium, bushy, spreading growth; no fruit; [Sarabande × Little Chief]; int. by Moore Min. Roses, 1980

Spanish Dancer HT, pb, Meilland; flowers cream, edged strong pink, full, pompon; int. by Meilland Intl., 2002

Spanish Enchantress S, pb; int. in 1999

Spanish Eyes F, op, 1978, Takatori, Yoshiho; flowers orange-salmon, reverse yellow; [sport of Prominent]; int. by Japan Rose Nursery, 1981

Spanish Fort Min, pb, 2003, Taylor, Franklin & Kay; flowers medium pink, yellow base, reverse lighter, 2 in., dbl., borne mostly solitary, slight fragrance; foliage medium size, medium green, semi-glossy; prickles medium, slight hook, brown, few; growth upright, medium (2 ft.); garden/decorative; [unknown × unknown]; int. by Taylor, Franklin & Kay Taylor, 2003

Spanish Gold HT, dy, 1960, Fletcher; flowers straw-yellow; tall, bushy growth; int. by Tucker

Spanish Lady HT, rb; flowers striped

Spanish Main – See **Marquesa del Vadillo**, HT

Spanish Musk Rose HMsk, w, before 1629; flowers white, sometimes shade pink at center, medium, single

Spanish Orange F, ob, 1966, deRuiter; flowers orange, 1½ in., very dbl., borne in clusters; foliage dark, glossy; very free growth; int. by Gregory & Sons

Spanish Rhapsody S, pb, 1985, Buck, Dr. Griffith J.; flowers deep pink, tinted orange and freckled red, large, 30 petals, shallow cup, borne 1-8 per cluster, moderate raspberry fragrance; recurrent; foliage medium-large, leathery, dark olive green; prickles awl-like; upright, bushy, branching growth; hardy; [Gingersnap × Sevilliana]; int. by Iowa State University, 1984

Spanish Sun F, dy, 1966, Boerner; bud large, ovoid; flowers imbricated, 3½-4½ in., 35-40 petals, borne singly and several together, intense russet apple fragrance; recurrent; foliage glossy, leathery; prickles normal, medium, some hooked downward and some upward; stems long, strong; vigorous, bushy growth; hips none ; PP2809; [Golden Garnette × Yellow Pinocchio climbing seedling]; int. by J&P, 1966

Spanky Min, yb, 1986, Bridges, Dennis A.; flowers bright yellow, shaded pink to red, reverse yellow, aging pink, dbl., high-centered; foliage large, medium green, semi-glossy; prickles few, pink, small; medium, upright growth; [Rise 'n' Shine × unknown]; int. by Bridges Roses

Sparkels HT, rb, 1956, Webber; bud urn shaped; flowers red striped white, medium, 35-50 petals, high-centered; foliage leathery; [sport of Briarcliff]

Sparkie Min, mr, 1957, Moore, Ralph S.; flowers bright red, becoming darker, 6 petals, borne in clusters; foliage glossy; vigorous (12-16 in.) growth; [(*R. wichurana* × Floradora) × Little Buckaroo]; int. by Sequoia Nursery

Sparkle HT, pb, 1949, Brownell; bud pointed, ovoid; flowers white turning cream, rose-pink and yellow toward center, large, dbl., high-centered, moderate fragrance; foliage glossy, light green; vigorous, upright, bushy growth; [Pink Princess × Shades of Autumn]

Sparkle Berry – See **Merlot**, Min

Sparkle On F, mr

Sparkle Plenty F, ob, 1976, Patterson; bud ovoid; flowers bright orange, to open, 3 in., 25 petals, high-centered; foliage dark, leathery, wrinkled; vigorous growth; [Ma Perkins × Engagement]; int. by Patterson Roses

Sparkler Pol, mr, 1929, deRuiter; flowers clear red touched with scarlet, slight fragrance; recurrent; [sport of Golden Salmon]; int. by Sliedrecht & Co., 1929

Sparkler – See **Clos Fleuri Rouge**, F

Sparkler – See **Kent**, S

Sparkling Burgundy F, dr, 1965, Williams, J. Benjamin; flowers burgundy-red, open, medium, dbl., borne in clusters; foliage dark, leathery, glossy; vigorous, upright growth; [Queen Elizabeth × Carrousel]

Sparkling Burgundy II Gr, dr, Williams, J. Benjamin; flowers dark scarlet, prominent golden stamens, single; int. by Hortico, Inc., 1996

Sparkling Cupido Min, dp, deRuiter; int. by Greenheart Farms, 2004

Sparkling Fire F, mr, 2000, Brown, Ted; flowers very bright red, 4 in., semi-dbl., borne in large clusters, slight fragrance; foliage medium size, medium green, semi-glossy; numerous prickles; upright, medium (4 ft.) growth; [Esprit × Stretch Johnson]

Sparkling Orange HT, rb, 1989, Marciel, Stanley G.; bud tapering; flowers vermilion, reverse scarlet, aging to rose, sweetheart, large, dbl., borne singly, intense musk fragrance; foliage large, dark green, glossy; prickles variation, reddish-brown; upright, tall growth; [Sonia × Prominent]; int. by DeVor Nurseries, Inc.

Sparkling Pink – See **Pebble Beach**, S

Sparkling Rouge Min, rb, Delbard; flowers deep red, heavily brushed with creamy white, full, cupped to flat; tall growth

Sparkling Ruffle S, rb

Sparkling Scarlet Cl F, mr, 1971, Meilland; flowers scarlet-red, 2½ in., 13 petals, borne in clusters, moderate fruity fragrance; recurrent; foliage large, semi-glossy; to 7-10 ft. growth; [Danse des Sylphes × Zambra]; int. by URS, 1970; Gold Medal, Paris, 1969

Sparkling White – See **Kent**, S

Sparkling Yellow – See **Lexington**, S

Sparks Min, mr, 1995, Saville, F. Harmon; bud oval, pointed; flowers bright scarlet, 1½ in., 18-24 petals, high-centered, borne mostly in clusters, no fragrance; recurrent; foliage small, medium green, semi-glossy; few prickles; compact, upright (14-16 in.) growth; hips globular to bowl-shaped ; PP9799; [(Zorina × Baby Katie) × Red Minimo]; int. by Nor'East Miniature Roses, 1996

Sparrieshoop S, lp, 1953, Kordes; bud long, pointed; flowers light salmon-pink, gold stamens, 4 in., single, borne in large sprays, intense fragrance; repeat bloom; foliage leathery; very vigorous (5 ft.), upright, bushy growth; [(Poulsen's Pink × Siren) × (Johannes Böttner × *R. rubiginosa magnifica*)]; Gold Medal, Portland, 1971

Spartan F, or, 1956, Boerner; bud large, pointed ovoid; flowers orange-red to reddish-coral, 3-3½ in., 25-30 petals, high-centered, borne singly and in clusters, intense sweet briar/geranium fragrance; quick repeat; foliage dark, leathery, glossy; prickles normal, medium, straight or hooked downward; stems medium, strong; vigorous, bushy growth; hips none ; PP1357; [Geranium Red × Fashion]; int. by J&P, 1955; President's International Trophy, NRS, 1954, Gold Medal, Portland, 1955, Gold Medal, NRS, 1954, Gold Medal, ARS, 1961

Spartan, Climbing Cl F, or, 1958, Martinez (also Kordes, 1960; Boerner, 1965); PP1616; [sport of Spartan]; same as bush form except for climbing habit; int. by J&P, 1964

Spartan Blaze Min, rb, 1991, Gruenbauer, Richard; bud ovoid; flowers red with yellow reverse, medium, dbl., high-centered, borne usually singly, slight fragrance; foliage medium size, medium green, semi-glossy; upright growth; [Poker Chip × Rise 'n' Shine]; int. by Flowers 'n' Friends Miniature Roses, 1991

Spartan Dawn Min, yb, 1990, Gruenbauer, Richard; bud rounded; flowers yellow with orange edges, reverse yellow to cream to orange, 30 petals, no fragrance; foliage medium size, medium green, matte; few or no prickles; bushy, medium growth; hips round, flat on top, orange-red; [Rise 'n' Shine × Hokey Pokey]; int. by Richard Gruenbauer

Spartan II F, Moreira da Silva, A.

Späth 250 – See **Späth's Jubiläum**, F

Späth's Jubiläum F, or, 1976, Kordes; bud ovoid; flowers 2½ in., 22 petals, high-centered; foliage dark, soft; vigorous, upright, bushy growth; [Castanet × seedling]; int. in 1970

Speaker Sam HT, yb, 1962, Dean; flowers light yellow edged red; PP2053; [sport of Peace]; int. by Arp Nursery Co., 1962

Spearmint Min, w; bud pointed; flowers creamy white, dbl., cupped; recurrent; medium growth; [sport of Angela Rippon]; int. after 1977

Special Angel Min, m, 1992, Stoddard, Louis; flowers mauve, tipped in pink, 1½ in., dbl., high-centered, borne mostly singly; foliage medium size, dark green, semi-glossy; few prickles; tall (60-70 cm.), upright, bushy growth; [Jean Kenneally × (Rise 'n' Shine × Acey Deucy)]; int. by Bridges Roses, 1992

Special Anniversary HT, mp, Smith, Edward; flowers rose pink, dbl., globular, intense fragrance; foliage dark green, glossy; short (3 ft.), bushy growth; int. by Whartons Nurseries Ltd., 2003

Special Bond S, mp, Bond; flowers medium pink in center, petals fade as they open, large, full, intense fragrance; prickles very few; medium growth; int. by Ross Roses, 2002

Special Border – See **Santa Rosa**, S

Special Child F, w, 2001, Rosen Tantau; flowers white, shadings of pink, 6 cm., dbl., cupped, borne in large clusters, slight fragrance; recurrent; foliage large, medium green, glossy; prickles medium, curved, moderate; compact, bushy, medium growth; garden, containers; [seedling × seedling]

Special Effects F, ob, 2006, Desamero, Luis; flowers orange & white striped, 4½ in., full, borne in small clusters; foliage medium size, dark green, matte; prickles small, straight, reddish, moderate; growth upright, tall (4 ft.); [sport of Scentimental]; int. in 2006

Special Event HT, m; int. by Burston Nurseries, 2005

Special Friend Min, lp, Kirkham; flowers blush pink with salmon heart, full, cupped, borne usually in clusters of 5-8, slight fragrance; recurrent; foliage pale green, glossy; dense (18 in.) growth; int. in 1999

Special Guest HT, mr, 1992, Guest, M.M.; flowers crimson, 3-3½ in., very dbl., borne singly; foliage medium size, medium green, semi-glossy; numerous prickles; medium (70 cm.), bushy growth; [sport of Jan Guest]; int. in 1990

Special Merit HT, mr, 1991, Wambach, Alex A.; bud medium, ovoid, pointed; flowers large, 30 petals, high-centered, borne singly, slight spicy fragrance; recurrent; foliage medium size, dark green, semi-glossy; prickles average, medium, curved downward; stems long (24 in.); medium (5 ft.), upright, bushy growth; hips globular ; PP9862; [seedling 83-1 × First Prize]; int. in 1993

Special Moment F, ab; int. by Burston Nurseries, 2005

Special Occasion HT, ab, Fryer, Gareth; flowers coppery-apricot, 4-5 in., 25-30 petals, high-centered, borne mostly singly, moderate fruity/myrrh fragrance; quick repeat; foliage dark green, glossy; neat, bushy (4 ft.) growth; int. by Fryers Nursery, 1995; Gold Medal, Genoa, 1995

Special Reserve Pol, dp, diCillo; int. by Freedom Gardens, 2002

Special Son Min, mr; int. by Burston Nurseries, 2005

Special Wishes – See **Carrot Top**, Min

Speckled Delight HT, rb, Patel

Spectabile – See **Spectabilis**, HSem

Spectabilis HSem, m, before 1832; bud dark crimson; flowers bright rosy lilac, fading to white, medium, dbl., cupped, borne in small, loose clusters, intense musky fragrance; occasionally repeats in autumn; vigorous, climbing growth; [possibly *R. sempervirens* × Noisette hybrid]; possibly by Jacques; int. by Vibert, 1832

Spectacular LCl, or, 1953, Mallerin, C.; bud ovoid; flowers scarlet-red, medium, 33 petals, cupped, borne singly or in small clusters, moderate old rose fragrance; recurrent bloom; foliage glossy, bronze; prickles average, short, straight to hooked downward; vigorous, climbing (8-10 ft.) growth; PP1416; [Paul's Scarlet Climber × *R. multiflora* seedling]; int. by EFR, 1953

Spectacular – See **Spectacular Palace**, MinFl

Spectacular Palace MinFl, ab, Poulsen; flowers apricot blend, 5-8 cm., dbl., no fragrance; foliage dark; growth bushy, 40-60 cm.; PP15569; int. by Poulsen Roser, 2003

Spectra LCl, yb, Meilland; flowers yellow suffused with red on upper surface, numerous short, irregular petals in center, 3-4 in., very full, borne singly or in small clusters of 2 or 3, slight fragrance; abundant in spring, sporadic thereafter; foliage large, deep green, glossy; few prickles; growth vigorous, well branched, long arching canes; PP5396; [(Kabuki × Peer Gynt) × ((Zambra × Suspense) × King's Ransom)]; int. in 1983

Spectrum LCl, mr, Thomas; int. by Thomas for Roses

Spedeni – See **Denice**, HT

Speechless Min, ob, 1987, King, Gene; flowers dark to light orange, fading darker, medium, 30 petals, high-centered, borne usually singly, no fragrance; foliage dark green, semi-glossy; prickles medium, hooked, red, with brown tips; upright, bushy growth; hips oval, medium, green; [seedling × Watercolor]; int. by AGM Miniature Roses, 1987

Speelwark HT, yb, 2006; bud large, pointed, red with yellow stripes; flowers flower cream and golden yellow flushed with vermilion and pink, fading to reddish, 12 cm., full, high-centered, borne mostly solitary, intense fragrance; foliage medium size, reddish, then dark green, glossy; upright, medium (80 cm.) growth; int. by W. Kordes' Söhne, 1999

Spek's Centennial – See **Singin' in the Rain**, F

Spek's Improved HRg

Spek's Yellow – See **Golden Scepter**, HT

Spek's Yellow, Climbing – See **Golden Scepter, Climbing**, Cl HT

Spellbinder HT, pb, 1974, Warriner, William A.; bud ovoid; flowers ivory to crimson, large, dbl., high-centered; foliage large, dark, leathery; vigorous growth; PP3571; [South Seas × seedling]; int. by J&P, 1975

Spellbound HT, dr, 1949, Sodano, J.; flowers deep velvety red, becoming darker, 5½-6 in., 25-30 petals, moderate fragrance; foliage dark; thornless; very vigorous, upright growth; [sport of Better Times]; int. by Amling-DeVor Nursery

Spellbound – See **Flora Danica**, HT

Spellbound HT, op, 2007, Zary, Keith W.; flowers coral pink, 4½ in., full, high-centered, blooms borne mostly solitary; foliage medium size, dark green, semi-glossy; prickles few, 8-10 mm., hooked downward, greyed-orange; growth upright, medium (5 ft.); [Ingrid Bergman × Pristine]; int. by Jackson & Perkins Wholesale, Inc., 2006

Spellcaster Gr, m, 1991, Warriner, William A.; bud short, pointed ovoid; flowers lavender and deep mauve, heavy substance, 4 in., 25-30 petals, high-centered, borne mostly singly or in small clusters, moderate lemon fragrance; recurrent; foliage large, dark green, glossy; prickles some, medium, hooked downward; stems strong, 12-14 in.; tall (145-160 cm.), upright, spreading, very full, uniform growth; PP8568; [seedling × Angel Face]; int. by Bear Creek Gardens, 1992

Spencer – See **Spenser**, HP

Spencer's Delight HT, ab, 1998, Spencer, Keith V.; flowers coral pink, reverse soft amber, 3½-4½ in., full, high-centered, borne mostly singly, moderate fragrance; foliage medium size, dark green, semi-glossy; prickles moderate; long, straight stems; vigorous, upright, tall (48-62 in.) growth; [sport of Maid of Honor]

Spenser HP, lp, 1892, Paul, W.; flowers soft pink, moderate fragrance; [sport of Merveille de Lyon]

Speragina T, dp, Hay

Spes HT, mp, Urban, J.; flowers large, very dbl.; int. in 1970

Sphinx HT, lp, 1970, Gaujard; flowers bright pink tinted lighter, very large, dbl., moderate fragrance; foliage leathery; vigorous, bushy growth; [Rose Gaujard × Gail Borden]; int. in 1967

Spice F, or, 1954, Boerner; bud globular; flowers scarlet-red, 3 in., 53 petals, cupped, borne in clusters; foliage glossy; vigorous, compact, upright growth; [(Goldilocks × Floradora) × unnamed Floribunda seedling]; int. by J&P, 1954

Spice 'n' Nice HT, lp, Twomey, Jerry

Spice Drop Min, op, 1982, Saville, F. Harmon; bud small, ovoid; flowers light salmon-pink, 1 in., 25-35 petals, hybrid tea, borne singly and in sprays, slight fragrance; recurrent; foliage small, medium green, glossy; prickles few, short, straight, thin, slanting slightly downward; compact (8 in.), bushy, micro-mini growth; PP5089; [(Sheri Anne × Glenfiddich) × (unnamed moss seedling × (Sarabande × Little Chief))]; int. by Nor'East Min. Roses

Spice of Life F, ob, Dickson; bud reddish pink; flowers orange blend with scarlet edges, reverse suffused with lemon yellow, dbl., cupped, borne in large clusters, slight fragrance; recurrent; foliage dense, red when young; upright (3-4 ft.), bushy growth; int. by Dickson Roses, 2004; Winner-Floribunda, Dublin, 2006, Dept. of Ag. Award, Belfast, 2006

Spice So Nice LCl, ab, 2000, Carruth, Tom; bud mossed, pointed to somewhat ovoid; flowers ruffled petals of apricot orange with yellow reverse and eye, 3-4 in., 30 petals, cupped, borne in clusters on old and new wood., moderate fragrance of spice, while rubbed buds smell of juniper; recurrent; foliage large, dark green (dark red new growth), glossy, quilted; prickles moderate, medium-large, straight; stems strong, short to medium; growth spreading, tall (180-250 cm.); garden decorative, climber; hips rounded to globular ; PP16154; [Westerland × Flutterbye]; int. by Weeks Roses, 2002

Spice Trail HT, pb, 2006, Viraraghavan, M.S. Viru; bud pointed; flowers soft pink edged darker, up to 5 in., dbl., borne mostly solitary, intense fragrance; foliage medium size, medium green, semi-glossy; prickles medium, pointed, grey, moderate; growth bushy, medium (3-4 ft.); garden decorative; [Pristine × Orient Spice]; int. by Roses Unlimited in USA / KSG SONS in India, 1984

Spice Twice HT, ob, 1998, Zary, Dr. Keith W.; bud long, pointed ovoid; flowers orange, 5-6 in., 30-35 petals, high-centered, borne mostly singly, moderate ginger fragrance; recurrent; foliage medium size, dark green, semi-glossy; prickles moderate, hooked downward; stems strong, medium; upright, tall (5 ft.) growth; PP8628; [Spirit of Glasnost × Kardinal]; int. by Bear Creek Gardens, Inc., 1997

Spiced Coffee HT, r, 1991, McGredy, Sam IV; flowers pale lavender with brown overtones, large, dbl., cupped, borne mostly singly, intense fragrance; recurrent; foliage medium size, medium green, matte; upright, medium growth; [Harmonie × Big Purple]; int. by McGredy Roses International, 1991

Spicy Min, yb, Delbard; flowers blend of ochre and tan with splashes of cinnamon; medium growth

Spicy HT, ob, Kordes; bud large, triangular; flowers bronze gold, reverse copper red, fading to rose pink, full, high-centered, star shape, borne singly and several together, moderate fragrance; recurrent; stems long, sturdy; vigorous, upright growth; florist rose; needs disbudding and spraying; int. in 1999

Spicy Minijet – See **Potluck Yellow**, Min

Spielplatz DRS HT, yb, Huber

Spin Out F, ob

Spinning Wheel S, rb, 1991, Williams, J. Benjamin; flowers cherry red with ivory striping, large, full, borne in large clusters, slight fragrance; recurrent; foliage large, dark green, semi-glossy; tall, upright, spreading growth; [Handel × Love]

Spion-Kop F, mr, 1968, Ellick; flowers signal-red, 3-5 in., 30-35 petals; foliage light, bronze, matte green; vigorous growth; [Evelyn Fison × Orange Sensation]

Spirit HT, mr

Spirit Abundance – See **Spirit of Tollcross**, F

Spirit of '76 Gr, or, 1971, Whisler, D.; bud ovoid; flowers medium, dbl., moderate fragrance; foliage large, glossy, dark; vigorous, upright growth; PP3820; [Queen Elizabeth × San Francisco]; int. by Gro-Plant Industries

Spirit of Canada F, dr, 1995, Fleming Joyce; flowers dark red enriched with flashes of scarlet, prominent stamens, medium, 10 petals, flat, borne in small and large clusters, moderate fragrance; recurrent; foliage medium size, medium green, semi-glossy; numerous prickles; upright, bushy, tall growth; [Bambula × Red Max Graf]; int. by Hortico Roses, 1995

Spirit of Freedom S, lp, 2005; bud globular; flowers very full, cupped, borne in clusters of up to 15, intense myrrh fragrance; recurrent; foliage medium size, dark green, semi-glossy; prickles medium, concave; stems strong; growth bushy, branching, tall (5-6 ft.); garden decorative; hips cupped, green; PP14973; [seedling (pink English type shrub) × Abraham Darby]; int. by David Austin Roses, Ltd., 2002

Spirit of Glasnost HT, pb, 1991, Warriner, William A.; flowers coral pink and ivory blend, large, full, borne mostly singly, moderate fragrance; foliage medium size, dark green, semi-glossy; upright, spreading growth; [seedling × seedling]; int. by Bear Creek Gardens, 1991

Spirit of Hope – See **Reba McEntire**, Gr

Spirit of Ocean City HT, rb, Williams, J. B.; flowers red with yellow reverse, large, dbl., borne mostly singly, moderate fragrance; foliage large, mahogany to dark green, glossy, disease-resistant; vigorous, tall (6 ft.), bushy growth; [Oregold × Tropicana]; int. in 1996

Spirit of Peace – See **Paul Ricard**, HT

Spirit of Peace HT, yb, 1992, Warriner, William A.; flowers apricot yellow, opening with pink tinge where sun strikes the blooms, large, full, classic hybrid tea, borne mostly singly, slight spiced honey fragrance; recurrent; foliage medium size, dark green, semi-glossy; some prickles; tall (170-180 cm.), upright,spreading growth; [Pristine × seedling]; int. by Bear Creek Gardens

Spirit of Pentax F, or, 1990, Harkness, R., & Co., Ltd.; bud pointed; flowers bright red, bright orange-red reverse, aging deeper, to roan, medium, 21 petals, high-centered to rounded, borne in clusters of 3-7, slight fragrance; recurrent; foliage small to medium size, dark green, glossy; prickles straight, narrow, small to medium, medium green; upright, medium growth; [Alexander × Remember Me]; int. by R. Harkness & Co., Ltd.

Spirit of SACS – See **Pure Magic**, F

Spirit of Southland F, ob, Attfield; flowers blend of orange, red and yellow, dbl., high-centered; tall growth; int. in 1999

Spirit of the Heath HT, mp, 2001, Poole, Lionel; flowers full, borne in small clusters, slight fragrance; foliage large, dark green, very glossy; prickles medium, triangular, few; growth upright, bushy, medium (1 m.), very vigorous & strong; garden, exhibit; [Hazel Rose × Silver Jubilee]; int. in 2002

Spirit of Tollcross F, or, Harkness; flowers vermilion, often with white stripe in center of petals, dbl., cupped to flat, borne in clusters; recurrent; medium growth; int. in 1998

Spirit of Youth – See **Senator Burda**, HT

Spitfire HT, mr, 1943, Joseph H. Hill, Co.; bud oxblood-red; flowers carmine, open, 2-3 in., 25-30 petals; foliage dark, leathery; short stems; vigorous, upright, much branched growth; RULED EXTINCT 6/86; [Better Times × Colleen Moore]

Spitfire Min, mr, 1986, McDaniel, Earl; flowers large, 38 petals, high-centered, borne singly; foliage medium size, medium green, matte; prickles thin, light green; upright, bushy growth; [seedling × seedling]; int. by McDaniel's Min. Roses

Spitfire Improved HT, dr, 1949, Joseph H. Hill, Co.; bud medium, short-pointed, ovoid; flowers velvety dark carmine, 4-5 in., semi-dbl., globular; foliage leathery, dark; vigorous, upright, bushy growth; RULED EXTINCT 6/86; [sport of Spitfire]

Spitfire Paddy HT, ob, 2004, McCann, Sean; flowers orange-yellow, 4 in., full, borne mostly solitary, slight fragrance; foliage medium size, dark green, semi-glossy; prickles large, straight; growth upright, medium (36 in.); garden decoration; [Piccadilly × seedling.]; int. in 2004

Spitzenschleier S, lp, VEG; flowers small, single

Splash HT, w, Becnel, Johnny; flowers white with splashes of pink; [sport of Moonstone]

Splendens – See ***R. × francofurtana*** (Muenchhausen), Misc OGR

Splendens Ayr, w, about 1835, from England; bud crimson; flowers pale flesh to creamy blush, fading to white, 6-7 cm., semi-dbl. to dbl., globular, strong myrrh fragrance; pendulous growth

Splendid F, w, Roman, G., and Wagner, S.; flowers cream-white, flushed pink, large, 30 petals, borne in clusters, slight fragrance; foliage large, dark green, glossy; [Centennaire de Lourdes × Clare Grammerstorf]; int. by Res. Stn. for Hort., 1997

Splendid Garland – See **The Garland**, HMult

Splendid Garland HSem, lp, 1835, Wells; flowers medium, dbl.

Splendid Lady HT, w, 2001, Clemons, David; flowers white with pink edges, reverse white, 4 in., very full, exhibition, borne mostly solitary, slight fragrance; foliage medium size, dark green, semi-glossy; prickles moderate; growth upright, medium; garden decorative; [Lynn Anderson × select pollen]; int. by Suncrest Roses, 2001

Splendid Sweet-Brier – See **Splendens**, Ayr

Splendor HT, or, 1933, Sauvageot, H.; bud long, pointed; flowers orange-carmine, dbl., cupped, moderate fragrance; foliage leathery, glossy; vigorous growth; [La Marechale Petain × Souv. de Claudius Pernet]; int. by C-P

Splendor HT, mr, 1940, Abrams, Von; bud long; flowers rose-red, reverse slightly lighter, pointed, 4-5 in., dbl.; foliage dark; [sport of Better Times]

Splendora S, dp, 2004, Ponton, Ray; flowers uniform deep pink, medium, full, borne mostly solitary, slight fragrance; foliage medium size, light green, semi-glossy; prickles large and small, hooked; spreading, medium (4-5 ft.) growth; [Lillian Austin × San Gabriel]

Splish Splash Min, pb, 1993, Moore, Ralph S.; flowers deep pink, yellow heart and reverse, large, full, cupped to rosette, borne in small clusters, slight fragrance; recurrent; foliage medium size, medium green, semi-glossy; few prickles; medium (30 cm.), bushy, spreading growth; [Sequoia Gold × Little Artist]; int. by Sequoia Nursery, 1994

Splish Splash S, w, Kordes

Spode HT, ob, 1973, Fryers Nursery, Ltd.; flowers orange-scarlet, flushed cream, long, pointed, 6 in., 35 petals, intense fragrance; foliage glossy, dark; [Diorama × Fragrant Cloud]

Spong C, mp, 1805, Spong; flowers rose-pink, richer in center, small, very dbl., cupped, borne in small clusters, slight to moderate fragrance; early bloom; foliage ovate-pointed, serrate, gray-green; branching, dwarf, compact (to 4 ft.) growth; int. in 1805

Sporting Duo F, ob, Harkness, R.; flowers orange with tones of red and pink, large, dbl., cupped, borne in clusters; medium growth; int. in 1995

Spot Meillandina Min, dp, 1994, Meilland, Alain A.; flowers rose bengal, small, 74 petals, borne in small clusters, no fragrance; foliage medium size, dark green, semi-glossy; few prickles; low (20-25 cm.), bushy growth; [(Orange Sunblaze × Pink Symphony) × Red Minimo]; int. by SNC Meilland & Cie, 1992

Spot Minijet – See **White Mini-Wonder**, Min

Spot o' Gold Min, my, 1992, Weeks, Michael W.J.; flowers yellow stamens, medium, single, borne in small clusters; foliage medium size, medium green, semi-glossy; some prickles; bushy (20 cm.) growth; [Rise 'n' Shine × unknown]

Spotlight HT, my, 1969, Dickson, A.; flowers peach and gold, globular; foliage dark; free growth; [seedling × Piccadilly]

Spotlight Min, ob, 1999, Moore, Ralph S.; flowers bright orange, blended rose, with white star-shaped eye, reverse white, 1½ in., 5 petals, borne mostly singly, no fragrance; recurrent; foliage medium size, medium green, semi-glossy; bushy, compact (12-18 in.) growth; [Orangeade × Little Artist]; int. by Sequoia Nursery, 1999

Spotted Gold F, yb; flowers clear yellow, reverse red gold over yellow, dbl., cupped, borne singly and in clusters; recurrent; stems sturdy; medium growth; int. by Kordes, 1994

Spowest – See **Dr Mark Weston**, Min

Spray Cécile Brünner Pol, pb, 1941, Howard Rose Co.; bud long, pointed; flowers bright pink on yellow, edged clear pink, center yellowish, dbl., borne in large sprays, moderate fragrance; foliage sparse, soft, dark; compact, bushy growth; [sport of Mlle Cécile Brunner]

Spray Wit S, w, Yanagisawa

Spreeathen HT, mr, Rupprecht-Radke; flowers large, dbl.; int. in 1968

Spreeglut S, dr, Kopenick; flowers small to medium, semi-dbl., shallow cup, borne singly or several together; free-flowering; upright (4 ft.), branching growth; int. by Institut für Zierpflanzenbau Berlin, 1985

Spring – See **Wesnianka**, HT

Spring Min, dy, Poulsen; flowers deep yellow, medium, dbl., slight wild rose fragrance; foliage dark; growth bushy, 20-40 cm.; PP10738; int. by Poulsen Roser, 2000

Spring – See **Spring Palace**, MinFl

Spring Beauty Min, pb, 1983, Williams, Ernest D.; flowers pastel pink and yellow blend, small, 35 petals; foliage small, medium green, glossy; upright growth; [Little Darling × Over the Rainbow]; int. by Mini-Roses, 1982

Spring Beginning – See **Frühlingsanfang**, HSpn

Spring Belle Min, dp; flowers deep rose pink, large, hybrid tea; tall growth

Spring Bouquet Min, pb, 1985, Bennett, Dee; flowers crimson pink, blended with yellow, medium, high-centered; foliage medium size, medium green, semi-glossy; upright, bushy growth; [Portrait × Party Girl]; int. by Tiny Petals Nursery

Spring Break HT, dp, 1993, Strickland, Frank A.; flowers deep florescent pink, medium, dbl., high-centered, borne mostly singly, no fragrance; foliage medium size, medium green, matte; some prickles; medium, upright growth; [Secret Love × Kardinal]; int. by Strickland, 1994; Silver Medal, ARC TG, 1995

Spring Bride LCl, w; flowers blush white, slight fragrance; tall (12-15 ft.) growth; int. by Paul Chessum Roses, 2003

Spring Carnival Min, r, Benardella, Frank; flowers deep tan and orange apricot tonings, well-formed; free-flowering; strong, tall growth

Spring Charm – See **Frühlingszauber**, HSpn

Spring Fever HT, ob, 1985, Christensen, Jack E.; flowers apricot, pink and orange blend, large, 35 petals; foliage large, dark, semi-glossy; [Gingersnap × Brandy]; int. by Armstrong Nursery

Spring Fling Min, mr, 2006, Meyer, Lawrence; flowers bright clear red, 3-5 cm., single, borne mostly solitary; foliage small, dark green, glossy; prickles average, slightly hooked, beige, few; growth compact, short (30-45 cm.); garden decoration; [sport of Gizmo]; int. by Nor'East Miniature Roses, Inc., 2006

Spring Fragrance – See **Frühlingsduft**, HSpn

Spring Fragrance – See **Vesenii Aromat**, HT

Spring Fragrance – See **Shunpo**, HT

Spring Frolic Min, my, 1979, Williams, Ernest D.; bud ovoid; flowers dbl., 70 petals, pompon, intense fragrance; low, compact, spreading growth; [(Little Darling × Gold Coin) × Golden Angel]; int. by Mini-Roses, 1978

Spring Frost Min, w, 1979, Schwartz, Ernest W.; flowers pure white, ruffled, 1 in., 17 petals; foliage small; low, very compact growth; int. by Bountiful Ridge Nursery, 1978

Spring Gold – See **Frühlingsgold**, HSpn

Spring Gold Min, dy

Spring Hill's Freedom S, mr, 1990, Twomey, Jerry; bud ovoid, pointed; flowers scarlet red, 7 cm., 30-35 petals, cupped, borne singly, slight musk fragrance; free-flowering; foliage medium size, medium green, semi-glossy; prickles slightly curved, red-purple; stems strong, upright; vigorous, upright, medium growth; PP7868; [Samantha × seedling]; int. by DeVor Nurseries, Inc., 1990

Spring Hill's Pink Freedom S, mp; flowers salmon pink to rose pink, 3½ in., dbl., cupped, borne in clusters, slight fragrance; free-flowering; bushy (4-6 ft.) growth; int. by Spring Hill, 1997

Spring Melody Min, ob, 1983, Williams, Ernest D.; flowers orange, small, 35 petals, slight fragrance; foliage small, bronze green, semi-glossy; bushy (12 in.) growth; [Little Darling × Over the Rainbow]; int. by Mini-Roses

Spring Morning – See **Frühlingsmorgen**, HSpn

Spring Palace MinFl, mp, Olesen; bud pointed ovoid; flowers medium pink, aging lighter, 5 cm., 40-45 petals, rosette, borne in clusters, very slight fragrance; recurrent; foliage dark green, glossy; prickles numerous, 6 mm., concave, olive green; bushy, 40-60 cm. growth; PP15831; [Fredensborg × seedling]; int. by Poulsen Roser, 2003

Spring Parade – See **Spring**, Min

Spring Snow – See **Frühlingsschnee**, HSpn

Spring Song S, dp, 1954, Riethmuller; flowers rich carmine-pink, semi-dbl., moderate fragrance; vigorous, tall growth; [Gartendirektor Otto Linne × unknown]

Spring Song Min, pb, 1957, Moore, Ralph S.; flowers pink tinted salmon, small, full, rosette, borne in clusters, no fragrance; recurrent; foliage medium green, glossy; bushy (18-24 in.), spreading growth; [(*R. wichurana* × Floradora) × Thumbelina]; int. by Sequoia Nursery

Spring Time Min, w, 1991, Williams, J. Benjamin; bud pointed; flowers ivory with light red edge, reverse ivory with light yellow base, small, 26 petals, high-centered, borne usually singly, intense damask fragrance; foliage small, dark green, semi-glossy; bushy, low growth; [Easter Morning (F2) × Toy Clown]; int. by White Rose Nurseries, Ltd., 1990

Spring Time HT, pb, Ghosh, Mr. & Mrs. S.; flowers blend of pink, orange and apricot, large, high-centered; free-flowering; int. in 2003

Springfields F, ob, 1977, Dickson, A.; flowers orange, red, gold, 3 in., 48 petals, cupped; [Eurorose × Anabell]; int. in 1978

Springhill Freedom – See **Spring Hill's Freedom**, S

Springs 75 – See **Dolly**, F

Spring's A Comin' MinFl, pb, 2001, Wells, Verlie; flowers white with pink edge, 2 in., dbl., high-centered, borne mostly solitary; foliage medium size, dark green, semi-glossy; prickles medium, hooked, few; growth upright, tall (3-4 ft.); garden decorative, exhibition; [seedling × seedling]; int. by Well's Mid-South Roses, 2002

Springtime F, lp, 1935, Howard, F.H.; flowers wild-rose-pink, center white, semi-dbl., cupped, borne in clusters; foliage leathery; bushy growth; RULED EXTINCT 7/90; [Miss Rowena Thom × seedling]; int. by Dreer

Springtime S, ly, Lens; flowers soft yellow, 4 cm., single, shallow cup; once-blooming; foliage light green; compact (4½-6 ft.) growth; int. in 1984

Springtime S, mp; int. by Heirloom, 2004

Springvale HT, w, 1976, Miller, J.; flowers white to pink, 4 in., 50 petals, high-centered; foliage dark; [sport of Mme A. Meilland]

Springwood Beauty Min, op, 1995, Laver, Keith G.; flowers orange pink, reverse lighter, medium, full, borne mostly singly, no fragrance; foliage small, medium green, semi-glossy; few prickles; bushy, low growth; [seedling × Apricot Doll]; int. by Springwood Roses, 1995

Springwood Classic Min, mp, 1999, Laver, Keith G.; flowers 2 in., full, borne in small clusters, no fragrance; foliage medium size, medium green, semi-glossy; few prickles; bushy, medium (10-12 in.) growth; [seedling × seedling]; int. by Springwood Roses, 1999

Springwood Coral Min, or, 1988, Laver, Keith G.; flowers coral-pink, turning slightly white at stem, loose, large, 23 petals, borne in sprays of 3-4, intense fragrance; foliage large, light green, matte; prickles curved, red; bushy, medium growth; hips round, light orange; [Helmut Schimdt × Potluck]; int. by Springwood Roses, 1986

Springwood Gold Min, my, 1989, Laver, Keith G.; bud pointed; flowers deep, buttery yellow, reverse lighter, medium, 20 petals, high-centered, borne usually singly; foliage small, medium green, semi-glossy; prickles very narrow, straight, green; upright, bushy, medium growth; hips globular, light orange; [Rise 'n' Shine × June Laver]; int. by Springwood Roses

Springwood Mauvette Min, m, 1995, Laver, Keith G.; flowers deep mauve, medium, full, borne mostly singly, slight fragrance; foliage medium size, dark green, glossy; numerous prickles; spreading, bushy growth; [Blue Ice × seedling]; int. by Springwood Roses, 1996

Springwood Pink Min, dp, 1992, Laver, Keith G.; flowers deep pink, 1½ in., dbl., borne in small clusters; foliage medium size, medium green, matte; some prickles; low (30-40 cm.), spreading growth; containers; [Maurine Neuberger × (June Laver × Ontario Celebration)]; int. by Springwood Roses

Springwood Pink Satin Min, mp, 1997, Laver, Keith G.; flowers small, very dbl., borne in small clusters; foliage medium size, medium green, semi-glossy; few prickles; compact, bushy, low growth; [Pleasantly Pink × Springwood Ruby]; int. by Springwood Roses

Springwood Purple Min, dp, 1990, Laver, Keith G.; flowers fuchsia, medium to large, 25-30 petals, loose, borne in sprays of 3, no fragrance; foliage large, medium green, semi-glossy; bushy, spreading, medium, very compact growth; [June Laver × (Small Slam × Mountie)]; int. by Springwood Roses, 1990

Springwood Red Min, dr, 1988, Laver, Keith G.; flowers deep red, aging slightly lighter, small, full, urn-shaped, borne usually singly; foliage small, medium green, matte; prickles slightly recurved, light yellow-green; bushy, low growth; hips ovoid, orange; [Small Slam × Mountie]; int. by Springwood Roses

Springwood Red Victor Min, dr, 1995, Laver, Keith G.; flowers dark red, small, 40-60 petals, borne 3-10 per clusters; foliage medium size, medium green, semi-glossy; some prickles; medium (30-33 cm.), upright, compact growth; [seedling × seedling]; int. by Springwood Roses, 1995

Springwood Ruby Min, dr, 1993, Laver, Keith G.; flowers 1½ in., full, borne in small clusters, no fragrance; foliage medium size, medium green, matte; some prickles; low (20-25 cm.), compact growth; [(Breezy × June Laver) × (June Laver × Ontario Celebration)]; int. by Springwood Consultants, Ltd.

Springwood White Min, w, 1991, Laver, Keith G.; flowers medium, very full, borne mostly singly, no fragrance; foliage small, medium green, matte; few prickles; low (22 cm.), bushy growth; [Loving Touch × June Laver]; int. by Springwood Roses, 1991

Sprint F, mr, 1961, Gaujard; bud oval; flowers bright red, open, 2½ in., 12 petals, borne in clusters; foliage glossy, dark; vigorous growth; [Jolie Princesse × Chanteclerc]

Sprinter HT, dy, Ilsink; flowers bright yellow, dbl., high-centered; free-flowering; short to medium growth; int. in 1989

Spruce Up Min, dp

Spun Gold HT, my, 1941, McGredy; flowers gold, 4½ in., 27 petals, high-centered; foliage glossy, leathery; vigorous, bushy, fairly compact growth; [seedling × Portadown Glory]; int. by J&P

Spunglass HT, w, 1989, Marciel, Stanley G.; bud pointed; flowers very large, 50 petals, cupped, borne singly, slight spicy fragrance; foliage large, dark green, glossy; prickles declining, pea green; upright, tall growth; PP7613; [seedling × Angel]; int. by DeVor Nurseries, Inc.

Spunky Min, mr, 1993, Bell, Judy G.; flowers medium, dbl., borne in small clusters, no fragrance; foliage small, dark green, glossy; numerous prickles; medium (16 in.), bushy, upright growth; [Dale's Sunrise × J. Michael]; int. by Michigan Mini Roses, 1994

Sputnik F, or, 1958, Maarse, G.; flowers semi-dbl., borne in large trusses of 25-30; low, bushy growth; [Jiminy Cricket × Gloria Mundi]

Square Dancer S, dp, 1972, Buck, Dr. Griffith J.; bud ovoid; flowers deep pink, large, dbl., cupped, moderate fragrance; repeat bloom; foliage large, dark, leathery; vigorous, upright, bushy growth; [Meisterstuck × ((World's Fair × Floradora) × Applejack)]; int. by Iowa State University, 1973

Squatter's Dream S, my, 1923, Clark, A.; flowers medium yellow, becoming lighter, golden stamens, medium to large, single to semi-dbl., shallow cup, moderate fragrance; recurrent; foliage dark bronze-green; no prickles; dwarf (4 ft.), bushy growth; [seedling from *R. gigantea*]; int. by Hackett

Srdce Evropy HWich, dp, 1937, Böhm, J.; flowers deep pink, white center, 4½-5 cm., single, borne in very large clusters, slight fragrance; numerous prickles

Srebra F, pb, 1985, Staikov, Prof. Dr. V.; flowers pink, shaded mauve, dbl., borne in clusters of 5-20, moderate tea fragrance; foliage dark, glossy; bushy growth; [Highlight × Masquerade]; int. by Kalaydjiev and Chorbadjiiski, 1975

Sri Chinmoy F, my, 2005, Paul Chessum Roses; flowers medium yellow, 6 cm., dbl, borne in small clusters, moderate fragrance; foliage medium size, medium green, matte; growth compact, medium (75 cm.); beds, borders, containers; int. by Love4Plants, Ltd., 2004

Sri Sri Paramananda Yogananda HT, ab, Ghosh, Mr. & Mrs. S.; flowers apricot and pink blend, reverse medium yellow, high-centered; int. by KSG Son, 2006

Srinivasa HT, rb, Kasturi; flowers red with white reverse, full, high-centered; int. by KSG Son, 1969

St. Francis – See **Pompon de Saint-François**, C

St. Katherine's Min, m, Pearce; bud slender; flowers deep mauve, semi-dbl., intense fragrance; recurrent; low, arching growth; containers; int. in 1995

Staatspräsident Päts HT, my, 1937, Weigand, C.; bud long, pointed; flowers amber-yellow, very varying, very large, dbl.; foliage leathery, dark; vigorous growth; [Ophelia × Souv. de Claudius Pernet]; int. by Spath

Staccato F, mr, 1965, van de Water; bud ovoid; flowers vermilion-red, open, medium, 14-20 petals; moderately vigorous, bushy growth; [sport of Cantate]; originally registered as Pol; int. by Klyn, 1959

Stacey F, yb, 1965, Verschuren, A.; flowers maize-yellow tinted blush, 4-5 in., 25-30 petals, borne in clusters; foliage dark, glossy, leathery; vigorous growth; int. by Blaby Rose Gardens

Stacey Sue Min, lp, 1976, Moore, Ralph S.; bud short, pointed; flowers soft pink, 1 in., 50-70 petals, rounded, borne usually in small clusters, slight sweet fragrance; recurrent; foliage small, medium green, glossy; prickles several, slender, slightly curved, inclined downward, brown; stems sturdy, wiry, short to medium; short (10-12 in.), bushy, rounded growth; hips few to none ; PP4158; [Ellen Poulsen × Fairy Princess]; int. by Sequoia Nursery

Stacey's Star F, pb, 1996, Horner, Colin P.; flowers blends of pink, short center petals much darker pink, 2½ in., full, flat, borne in clusters, moderate fragrance; foliage small, medium green, semi-glossy; some prickles; low (50 cm.), bushy growth; int. by Battersby Roses, 1998

Stad den Haag F, mr, 1969, McGredy, Sam IV; flowers scarlet, open, large, 20 petals; foliage glossy; free growth; [Evelyn Fison × (Spartan × Red Favorite)]

Stad Kortrijk S, rb, Kordes; flowers creamy white with splotches of red and pink, dbl., cupped, borne in small clusters, slight fragrance; recurrent; foliage dark green, resistant; vigorous (4 ft.) growth; int. in 2003

Stadt Basel – See **Rustica**, F

Stadt Darmstadt Pol, mr, 1966, deRuiter; bud ovoid; flowers bright red, small, semi-dbl., borne in clusters; foliage dark; [Red Favorite × The Doctor]

Stadt den Helder F, mr, 1982, Interplant; flowers bright red, medium, 20 petals, cupped, borne in sprays, slight fragrance; recurrent; foliage large, dark green, matte; upright (3-5 ft.) growth; [Amsterdam × (Olala × Diablotin)]; int. in 1979

Stadt Eltville F, mr, Tantau; flowers bright red, 3-4 in., dbl., high-centered, borne in clusters, no fragrance; recurrent; foliage reddish when young, then dark green; medium growth; int. by Rosen Tantau, 1990; Gold Medal, Durbanville, 1989

Stadt Essen Pol, mr, 1937, Tantau, Math.; flowers medium, dbl.

Stadt Ettelbrück S, mr, Lens, Louis; flowers medium-large, semi-dbl.; int. in 1981

Stadt Hildesheim – See **Coral Meidiland**, S

Stadt Hockenheim HMsk, ob, Weihrauch

Stadt Kiel S, mr, 1964, Kordes, R.; flowers cinnabar-red, medium, 30 petals, borne in large clusters, slight fragrance; foliage dark green; very vigorous, bushy growth; int. by Morse, 1963

Stadt Luzern F, op, Huber; flowers bright salmon, borne singly and in clusters, slight fragrance; recurrent; foliage dark green; stems long, strong; strong, upright (80-100 cm.) growth; best in partial shade; int. by Richard Huber AG, 1967

Stadt Pilsen – See **Plzen**, HT

Stadt Potsdam S, mr, Tantau; flowers blood-red; int. by Rosen Tantau, 2003

Stadt Pottrop F, deRuiter; int. in 1961

Stadt Rosenheim S, or, 1961, Kordes, R.; flowers dbl., borne in clusters (up to 10); foliage glossy, light green; vigorous, upright growth; ADR, 1960

Stadt Wurzburg HT, Kordes, R.; int. in 1987

Stadt Wurzburg – See **Veldfire**, HT

Stadtholder – See **Hybride Stadtholder**, HCh

Stadtrat F. Köhler HT, mr, 1906, Geduldig; bud pointed; flowers very large, very full, borne mostly solitary

Stadtrat Glaser HT, yb, 1910, Kiese; bud long; flowers sulfur-yellow edged soft red, large, full

Stadtrat Meyn Pol, mr, 1919, Tantau; flowers luminous brick-red, large, full, cupped, borne in pyramidal clusters, slight fragrance; recurrent; [Orléans Rose × unknown]

Staffa HSpn, w; flowers milk white shading to yellow at center, occasionally mottled pink, large, 20-40 petals, strong fragrance; growth moderate (90-120 cm.); very hardy; from Scotland, about 1832

Stagecoach Min, op, 1987, King, Gene; flowers medium salmon pink, medium, 18 petals, high-centered, borne usually singly or in sprays of 3-5; foliage medium size, light green, matte; prickles straight, white; upright, spreading growth; hips oval, green; [Vera Dalton × Orange Honey]; int. by AGM Miniature Roses, 1987

Stained Glass Min, pb, 2003, Barnes, Karen W.; flowers 1½ in., full, borne mostly solitary, no fragrance; foliage medium size, medium green, semi-glossy; prickles ¼, slightly curved, brown, few; bushy (12 in.) growth; containers; [unknown × unknown]; int. by Karen W. Barnes, 2003

Stainless Steel HT, m, 1991, Carruth, Tom; bud pointed to ovoid; flowers clean, silvery gray lavender, 5-6 in., 22-28 petals, high-centered, borne mostly singly, with some clusters, intense sweet fragrance; recurrent; foliage large, medium green, semi-glossy; some prickles; stems long, strong; tall to medium (130-150 cm.), vigorous growth; PP10188; [Blue Nile × Silverado]; int. by Weeks Roses, 1995

Stairway to Heaven Cl F, mr, 2002, Zary, Keith; bud pointed, ovoid; flowers ruffled, 3½-4 in., 25-35 petals, high-centered, borne in small clusters, slight light, sweet fragrance; recurrent; foliage medium size, dark green, glossy; prickles moderate; stems strong, medium; growth upright, spreading, tall (10-12 ft.); hips pear-shaped, yellow-green; PP14333; [Dynamite × Dream Weaver]; int. by Jackson & Perkins, 2002

Stamela F, (Holland)

Stämmler HP, mp, 1933, Tantau; flowers rose-pink, large, very dbl., cupped, intense fragrance; foliage glossy; vigorous (120-140 cm.) growth; [Victor Verdier × Arabella]; int. by C-P

Standard of Marengo – See **Étendard de Marengo**, HP

Standing Pol, dr, 1969, Delforge; flowers open, medium, dbl.; foliage dark, glossy; vigorous growth; [Atlantic × seedling]

Standing Ovation HT, rb, 1998, Tucker, Robbie; flowers white with red edge, 4½ in., very dbl., high-centered, borne singly or in small clusters, slight fragrance; recurrent; foliage medium size, dark green, semi-glossy; prickles moderate; upright, medium (4-5 ft.) growth; [Elizabeth Taylor × White Masterpiece]; int. by Edmunds Roses, 1999

Standout HT, rb, 1978, Weeks; bud ovoid, pointed; flowers red, white reverse, 3-4 in., full, high-centered, slight tea fragrance; vigorous, upright growth; PP4583; [Tiffany × Suspense]; int. by Weeks Wholesale Rose Growers, 1977

Stanislas Dubourg B, dp, about 1850, Pradel; flowers medium, full

Stanley Duncan Min, ab

Stanley Gibbons HT, op, 1976, Gregory; flowers salmon-orange, pointed, 4 in., 28 petals; foliage glossy, dark; [Fragrant Cloud × Papa Meilland]

Stanley Matthews HT, dr, 1964, Latham; flowers crimson-scarlet, 4½-5 in., 26 petals; foliage glossy, light green; vigorous growth; [(Independence × Crimson Glory) × Happiness]

Stanwell Perpetual HSpn, w, before 1836, Lee; flowers blush, medium, dbl., cupped, very early first bloom, moderate fragrance; recurrent; foliage very small; numerous prickles; moderate, spreading growth; [Duchess of Portland × *R. spinosissima*]; found in a garden at Stanwell

Stanza F, lp, 1971, Pal, Dr. B.P.; bud ovoid; flowers light pink, center darker, open, medium, semi-dbl.; foliage glossy, dark; very vigorous, bushy growth; int. by K. S. G. & Son, 1969

Star Burst S, Ilsink, Peter; int. in 1994

Star Child F, rb, 1987, Dickson, Patrick; flowers small, 6-14 petals; foliage small, medium green, glossy; strong, straight stems; bushy, prolific growth; PP7312; [Eyepaint × (Liverpool Echo × Woman's Own)]; int. in 1988

Star Dance F, w; int. by Sheridan Nurseries Ltd., 2002

Star Delight HRg, mp, 1990, Moore, Ralph S.; bud pointed; flowers rose pink, white base, silvery pink reverse, medium, 5 petals, flat, borne usually singly and in sprays of 3-5; repeat bloom; foliage medium size, olive to bluish-green, semi-glossy; upright, bushy, tall growth; [Yellow Jewel × Rugosa Magnifica]; int. by Sequoia Nursery, 1990

Star Dust – See **Hoshikage**, HT

Star Dust HBc, w, 2002, Moore, Ralph S.; flowers white/yellow, reverse white, 1-1½ in., dbl., borne in small clusters; foliage medium size, medium green, semi-glossy; prickles small, pointed, green, few; growth bushy, medium (18-24 in.); containers, specimen; [un-named seedling × Out of Yesteryear]; int. by Sequoia Nurs., 2002

Star Gazer HT, pb

Star Magic S, pb, 1995, Moore, Ralph S.; flowers pink blend, small, 5 petals, borne in small clusters; foliage small, dark green, glossy; some prickles; groundcover; medium (3 × 8 ft.), spreading, compact growth; [Sequoia Gold × MORmuri]; int. by Sequoia Nursery, 1996

Star of Bethlehem HWich, w, 1947, Fisher, R.C.; flowers with red stamens, 3-3½ in., 5 petals; moderate bloom; foliage glossy; [Innocence × Silver Moon]

Star of Hurst HWich, 1916, Hicks, Elisha

Star of Persia HFt, my, 1919, Pemberton; flowers bright yellow, stamens golden, 3-5 cm., semi-dbl., borne singly or in small clusters, slight fragrance; vigorous (8-10 ft.) growth; [*R. foetida* × Trier]

Star of Queensland HT, w, 1909, Williams, A.; flowers creamy white, medium, full, high-centered; foliage grayish green; vigorous, bushy growth; [Étoile de France × Earl of Dufferin]

Star of Thailand HT, w, 1978, Chinprayoon; flowers creamy white, medium, full, high-centered; foliage grayish green; vigorous, bushy growth; [Mount Shasta × Pascali]; int. by Chavalit Nursery, 1977

Star of the Nile S, dp, Clements, John; flowers intense pink, 4 in., 80 petals, moderate fruity/sweet myrrh fragrance; free-flowering; foliage bronzy red turning to dark green, matte; upright (4 ft.) growth; PPAF; int. by Heirloom Roses, 2000

Star of the Republic S, ob, 2005, Shoup, George Michael; flowers peachy-apricot, center deeper, 3½ in., very full, cupped, quartered, borne mostly solitary, moderate fragrance; strong fall repeat; foliage large, dark green, semi-glossy; few prickles; growth spreading, tall (8 ft.); hedging; [Graham Thomas × *R. wichuriana*]; int. by Antique Rose Emporium, 1998

Star of Tokio Min, Dot, Simon; int. in 1984

Star of Waltham HP, mr, 1875, Paul, W.; flowers carmine-crimson, mottled pink reverse, medium, dbl., semi-globular, moderate fragrance; recurrent; foliage very large; occasional red prickles; stems smooth, green; growth medium to tall

Star Performer Cl Min, mp, 1999, Warner, Chris; bud obovate; flowers satin pink, reverse medium pink, 4 cm., 20-25 petals, borne in small clusters, slight sweet fragrance; recurrent; foliage small, medium green, glossy; prickles few, curved; upright, tall (7 ft.) growth; for walls, fences, pillars; hips globular ; PP13877; [Laura Ford × Congratulations]; int. by Warner's Roses, 1999

Star Quality F, mp, 2005, Somerfield, Rob; flowers smokey pink, 8 cm., semi-dbl., borne in large clusters, no fragrance; foliage medium size, light green, matte; prickles medium, moderate; bushy, medium (1 m.) growth; [Hans Christian Andersen × Class Act]; int. in 2006

Star Trail – See **Colibre 79**, Min

Star Twinkle Min, pb, 1978, Moore, Ralph S.; bud pointed; flowers pink, coral and orange, 1 in., 5 petals, star shaped; recurrent; foliage glossy; bushy, compact, low growth; [Fairy Moss × Fire Princess]; int. by Sequoia Nursery

Star 2000 HT, or, Pekmez, Paul; flowers intense vermilion, large, 32-34 petals, high-centered, borne mostly singly, slight fragrance; good repeat; foliage medium size, medium green, semi-glossy; upright (60-80 cm.) growth; int. by NIRP Intl., 1992

Star Wheel F, rb, Zary, Keith; bud long, pointed ovoid; flowers white edged in red, 3½ in., 40-45 petals, high-centered, borne in flat clusters of 5-7, slight fragrance; good repeat; foliage large, leathery, glossy; prickles few, long, hooked slightly downward; stems strong, long (20-24 in.); vigorous, upright (6 ft.) growth; PP11738; [Princess × Purple Tiger]; florist rose; int. by Bear Creek, 1999

Starbright – See **Lily White**, HT

Starbright HT, w, 1962, Boerner; bud ovoid; flowers 4 in., 43 petals, high-centered, moderate fragrance; foliage glossy, dark; vigorous, upright growth; PP2128; [Princess White × Hybrid Tea seedling]; int. by J&P, 1962

Starburst Gr, rb, 1969, Meilland, Mrs. Marie-Louise; bud ovoid; flowers red and yellow, medium, dbl., high-centered; foliage glossy; vigorous, bushy growth; PP2974; [Zambra × Suspense]; int. by C-P

Starburst F, ly; PP10577; int. by J&P, 1997

Starburst S, my, Williams, J.B.; flowers bright yellow, dbl., high-centered, slight fragrance; foliage glossy, green; prickles quite thorny; growth to 4 ft.; int. by Hortico Inc., 2004

Stardance MinFl, w, 1982, Williams, J. Benjamin; bud broadly ovoid; flowers white, deep yellow stamens, 5-6 cm., 35 petals, cupped to flat, borne in small clusters, slight fragrance; good repeat; foliage small, medium green, semi-glossy; prickles few, medium, straight, straw; bushy, semi-erect (60-80 cm.) growth; PP5222; [Ma Perkins × (Charlie McCarthy × Easter Morning)]; int. by C-P

Stardust HT, w, 1939, Florex Gardens; flowers rose-red; RULED EXTINCT 5/92; [sport of Better Times]

Stardust – See **Sun Runner**, S

Stardust HT, w, 1992, Marciel, Stanley G. & Jeanne A.; flowers 3-3½ in., full, borne mostly singly, no fragrance; foliage large, medium green, semi-glossy; some prickles; tall (230 cm.), upright growth; [Coquette × unnamed seedling 64022-39]; int. by DeVor Nurseries, Inc.

Stardust F, m, Pearce; flowers lilac magenta, golden stamens, semi-dbl., shallow cup, borne in clusters, intense fragrance; recurrent; very few prickles; dwarf (18-24 in.) growth; int. in 1995

Stardust Memory F, ab, 2001, Kenny, David; flowers apricot with apricot/pink reverse, old-fashioned, 3 in., full, flat, borne in small clusters, moderate fragrance; foliage medium size, medium green, glossy; prickles moderate, medium, straight; growth bushy, medium; garden decorative; [Sexy Rexy × (Mary Sumner × Kiskadee)]

Starfire Gr, mr, 1959, Lammerts, Dr. Walter; bud short, pointed; flowers bright rose red, 4-5 in., 25-34 petals, high-centered to cupped, borne in clusters, moderate spicy fragrance; recurrent; foliage large, glossy; prickles numerous, long, straight; vigorous, tall, bushy growth; PP1742; [Charlotte Armstrong × (Charlotte Armstrong × Floradora)]; int. by Germain's, 1959

Starfire, Climbing Cl F, mr, Jack, V.; [sport of Starfire]; int. in 1972

Stargazer F, ob, 1976, Harkness; flowers orange-red, yellow eye, small to medium, single, borne in large clusters, slight fragrance; free-flowering; foliage medium size, medium green, matte; medium, bushy growth; [Marlena × Kim]; int. in 1977; Trial Ground Certificate, RNRS, 1975

Starglo Min, w, 1974, Williams, Ernest D.; bud long, pointed; flowers creamy white with hint of pink, small, dbl., high-centered, slight fragrance; free-flowering; foliage small, leathery; vigorous, bushy growth; [Little Darling × Jet Trail]; int. by Mini-Roses, 1973; AOE, ARS, 1975

Stargold HT, my, 1936, Brownell; bud long, pointed; flowers yellow, often splashed red, 32 petals, high-centered, intense fragrance; foliage dark, glossy; long, strong stems; branching, upright growth; [(Mary Wallace × Mary Wallace) × (seedling × seedling)]; int. by Inter-State Nursery

Starina Min, or, 1965, Meilland, Mrs. Marie-Louise; bud short, ovoid; flowers orange-scarlet, 1½ in., 23-28 petals, high-centered, borne singly and in small clusters, very slight fragrance; recurrent; foliage small, leathery, glossy; prickles several, brown; vigorous, dwarf growth; PP2646; [(Dany Robin × Fire King) × Perla de Montserrat]; int. by C-P; Miniature Rose Hall of Fame, ARS, 1999, Gold Medal, Japan, 1968, ADR, Germany, 1971

Starina, Climbing Cl Min, or, 1982, Asami, Hitoshi; [sport of Starina]; int. in 1979

Starion HT, pb, Dorieux; flowers pale yellow and white, pink petal edges, dbl., high-centered, moderate fragrance; int. in 1987; Plus Belle Rose de France, 1986

Starion HT, rb, NIRP; flowers shades of light red and medium to deep pink, 4 in., 40 petals, cupped, borne mostly singly, slight fragrance; recurrent; few prickles; stems long (50-70 cm); growth upright; florist rose; int. by NIRP Intl., 2007

Stark Whitecap F, w, 1959, Boerner; flowers pure white, 3 in., 30-35 petals, cupped, borne in clusters; foliage glossy; vigorous, upright growth; [Glacier × Garnette]; int. by Stark Bros.

Starkrimson HT, dr, 1963, Morey, Dr. Dennison; flowers scarlet-red, 4½ in., 48 petals, cupped, intense fragrance; foliage leathery; vigorous, upright growth; PP1964; [Happiness × San Fernando]; int. by Stark Bros., 1961

Starla Min, w, 1990, Chaffin, Lauren M.; bud pointed; flowers medium, 20-25 petals, high-centered, borne singly, slight fruity fragrance; recurrent; foliage medium size, medium green, semi-glossy; prickles needle-shaped, tan; bushy, medium (18-24 in.) growth; [Honor × Rainbow's End]; int. by Pixie Treasures Min. Roses, 1991

Starlet F, my, 1957, Swim, H.C.; bud pointed; flowers 2½ in., 60 petals, high-centered, borne in clusters; foliage dark, leathery, glossy; vigorous, compact, upright growth; PP1694; [Goldilocks × seedling]; int. by Armstrong Nursery

Starlet MinFl, w, Poulsen; flowers white, 5-8 cm., dbl., no fragrance; growth bushy, 20-40 cm.; int. by Poulsen Roser, 2005

Starlight HT, ob, 1934, Wood & Ingram; flowers orange and buff, moderate fragrance; vigorous growth; RULED EXTINCT 3/87

Starlight – See **Lagerfeld**, Gr

Starlight HT, my, 1987, Guest, M.M.; flowers medium, full; foliage large, light green, matte; bushy growth; [Devotion × Benson & Hedges Gold]

Starlight – See **Starlight Parade**, Min

Starlight Min, ab, Coyier, Duane L.; flowers ¾ in., dbl., high-centered, pointed, borne in small clusters, no fragrance; good repeat; foliage small, medium green, matte; compact, low (12 in.) growth; containers, decorative; [sport of Rainbow Surprise]; int. by Coyiers Roses, 2003

Starlight Express LCl, dp, Robinson, T.; moderate (8 ft.) growth; int. in 1997

Starlight Fantasy F, w, Zary; bud long, pointed ovoid; flowers white with yellow tones in center, 3½ in., 25-30 petals, high-centered, flattens, borne in clusters of 4-7, no fragrance; good repeat; foliage large, leathery; prickles normal, medium size, hooked slightly downward; stems strong, 18-22 in. long; vigorous, upright (5½ ft.) growth; PP11841; [Princess × seedling]; florist rose; int. by Bear Creek Gardens, 1999

Starlight Parade Min, w; bud short, pointed ovoid; flowers white, 1 in., 25 petals, high-centered, then flat, borne singly and several together, no fragrance; recurrent; foliage dark green, glossy; prickles few, short, straight; stems short, strong; bushy, upright (16-18 in.) growth; PP9016; [Evita × seedling]; int. by Poulsen, 1991

Starlina Min, mp

Starlite HT, w, 1942, Nicolas; bud long, pointed; flowers clear white, center tinted cream, large, full, high-centered; foliage dark, soft; vigorous, upright, bushy growth; RULED EXTINCT 3/87; [seedling × White Briarcliff]; int. by J&P

Starlite HT, my, Meilland; bud spherical; flowers sunny yellow, full, pompon, moderate fragrance; free-flowering; bushy, moderate (80 cm.) growth; int. in 1989

Starlite F, ly, Meilland; bud conical; flowers lemon yellow, outer petals whiten, 4 in., 33 petals, cupped, borne mostly singly, slight anise fragrance; good repeat; foliage dark green, glossy; prickles numerous, small, light brown; erect (4 ft.) growth; PP9581; [Golden Times × (Meitaranja × Golden Garnette)]; florist rose; int. by Meilland Intl., 1995

Starry Bouquet S, rb, Clements, John K.

Starry Eyed – See **Star Delight**, HRg

Starry Eyed S, yb, 1997, Horner, Colin P.; flowers yellow to ivory with deep pink to red edges, reverse yellow, small, single, borne in large clusters, slight fragrance; free-flowering; foliage small, light green, dull; few prickles; spreading, bushy, low (90cm.) growth, can be trained as climber; [(Anna Ford × Little Darling) × ((Sea Foam × Little Darling) × (Hamburger Phoenix × Prelude))]; int. by Paul Chessum Roses

Starry Night S, w, Orard; bud pointed, conspicuous neck; flowers white with bright yellow stamens, 2½ in., 5 petals, borne in clusters of 5-25, no fragrance; free-flowering; foliage small, dark green, glossy; prickles few, straight or hooked slightly downward; stems long, strong; low (18-24 in.), spreading (3-5 ft.) growth; hips none; PP14785; [Anisley Dickson × *R. wichurana*]; int. by Edmunds' Roses, 2002; AARS, 2002

Stars 'n' Stripes Min, rb, 1976, Moore, Ralph S.; bud long, pointed; flowers striped red and white, 1½ in., 18-23 petals, high-centered, soon flat, borne singly and in small clusters, moderate sweet fragrance; recurrent; foliage small, light to medium green, semi-glossy; prickles few, small, hooked slightly downward, brown; bushy, upright (16-20 in.) growth; hips few ; PP4029; [Little Chief × (Little Darling × Ferdinand Pichard)]; int. by Sequoia Nursery, 1976

Stars and Stripes S, pb, Williams, J.B.; flowers pink and white striped., semi-dbl., slight fragrance; recurrent; int. by Hortico, 2004

Stars 'n' Stripes Forever S, rb, Clements, John; flowers pink with stripes of white and dark pink, 2½ in., 10-16 petals, cupped, moderate fragrance; recurrent; foliage glossy; tidy, even, bushy growth; int. by Heirloom Roses, 2003

Starscent HT, pb, 1976, Parkes, Mrs M.H.; flowers rich pink, base yellow, 4½ in., 20 petals; foliage dull, blue-green; upright growth; [Silver Star × Peter Frankenfeld]; int. by Rumsey

Starshine HT, yb, 1972, Hamm; flowers pink and yellow blend, very large, dbl., globular; foliage glossy; vigorous, bushy growth; [Peace × Condesa de Sástago]; int. by Five M Nursery, 1971

Starshine – See **Tulsa**, HT

Starship MinFl, yb, 2002, Bridges, Dennis; flowers yellow blushed with coral, reverse yellow, 2½ in., full, high-centered, borne mostly solitary, no fragrance; recurrent; foliage medium size, medium green, semi-glossy; prickles ¼ in., pointed, slight downward curve, moderate; growth upright, tall (2½-3 ft.); garden, exhibition, containers, cutting; [Summer Sunset × select pollen]; int. by Bridges' Roses, 2003

Starstruck Min, ob, 1986, Bennett, Dee; flowers deep golden orange with petals edged red, reverse medium red, 32 petals; foliage medium size, medium green, semi-glossy; prickles small, thin, reddish; low, spreading growth; hips globular, in., brownish; [October × Orange Honey]; int. by Tiny Petals Nursery

Starstruck – See **Concerto**, S

Start F, or, VEG; flowers medium, semi-dbl.

Starting Over Gr, pb, 2001, Byrnes, Robert L.; flowers silvery pink, mauve/pink reverse, some striping, large, dbl., borne mostly solitary, moderate fragrance; foliage medium green, semi-glossy; few prickles; growth upright, medium; specimen; very disease resistant and hardy.; [Country Dancer × Fragrant Plum]; int. by Overbrooke Gardens, 2001

Startler HT, or, 1955, Robinson, H.; flowers orange-scarlet, base rich yellow, well-formed; vigorous growth; [Hector Deane × Mary Wheatcroft]

State of Maine HT, w, 1930, de Bree; flowers white, center slightly tinged greenish, large, very dbl., high-centered; [sport of Lady Ursula]

Stately HT, lp, 1930, Clark, A.; bud long, pointed; flowers pale flesh, center deeper, well-shaped, large, dbl., high-centered; vigorous growth; [Souv. de Gustave Prat × seedling]; int. by Hackett

Statesman HT, dr, 1991, Burks, Larry; flowers large, full, borne mostly singly, slight fragrance; foliage medium size, medium green, matte; medium, bushy growth; [seedling × seedling]; int. by Co-Operative Rose Growers, 1991

Steadfast HT, ob, 1939, Clark, A.; flowers amber, flushed yellow and pink, semi-dbl.; vigorous growth; [Mme Auguste Choutet × unknown]; int. by T.G. Stewart

Steeple Rose – See **Prolifera de Redouté**, C

Steeple Rose C, dp; bud full, globular, large; flowers rich rosy crimson with large green foliage; [perhaps a sport of Prolifera de Redoute]

Stefanie Gachot – See **Benikanoko**, HT

Stefanovitch, Climbing Cl HT, dr, 1943, Meilland, F.; flowers large, dbl.; recurrent bloom; vigorous growth; [sport of Lemania]

Steffi Graf HT, mp, Hetzel; flowers medium pink, reverse with brownish tones, large, full, high-centered, borne singly or in small clusters, intense fragrance; recurrent; bushy, moderate growth; int. in 1993

Steiler Rambler – See **Steyl Rambler**, HMult

Steino HT, my, 1965, Stein; bud ovoid; flowers dbl.; foliage dark; [sport of Golden Rapture]

Steliana HT, mr, Roman, G., and Wagner, S.; flowers carmine-red, large, 50 petals, spiral-shaped, slight fragrance; foliage large, dark green, leathery, glossy; [Romstar × Peace]; int. by Res. Stn. for Hort., 2005

Stella HMult, rb, 1905, Soupert & Notting; flowers bright red, white center, 3-4 cm., single, borne in small clusters; [Turner's Crimson Rambler × seedling]

Stella Gr, pb, 1959, Tantau, Math.; bud ovoid; flowers blush, edged deep pink on outer petals, 4-5 in., 36 petals, high-centered, borne in clusters; recurrent; foliage dark green, leathery; few prickles; vigorous, upright growth; [Horstmann's Jubilaumsrose × Peace]; int. in 1958; Gold Medal, NRS, 1960

Stella di Bologna HT, m, 1909, Bonfiglio, A.; flowers violet pink, lighter at base, large, dbl., moderate fragrance; [L'Innocence × unknown]

Stella Dorata – See **Goldstern**, HKor

Stella Duce F, dr, 1956, Leenders, M.; flowers dark crimson-red, stamens deep gold; vigorous growth

Stella Elisabeth Min, w, 1983, Moore, Ralph S.; flowers creamy white, petals edged light pink, small, 35 petals; foliage small, medium green, semi-glossy; bushy growth; [seedling × seedling]; int. by Roy H. Rumsey, Pty. Ltd.

Stella Giles F, ab; int. by Melville Nurseries, 1999

Stella Mattutina HT, lp, 1958, Giacomasso; flowers flesh-pink, well-formed, large, 35 petals; foliage glossy; vigorous growth; [Numa Fay × Asso Francesco Baracca]; int. in 1951

Stella Pacis HT, ob, 1946, Giacomasso; flowers combination of orange, salmon, red and yellow, large; vigorous growth; [Julien Potin × Mme G. Forest-Colcombet]

Stella Polaris HRg, w, 1890, Jensen; flowers silvery white, large, single; recurrent bloom; foliage dark; vigorous (4 ft.) growth

Stellmacher S, mr, 1937, Tantau; flowers bright red, full, borne in small clusters, moderate fragrance; abundant, recurrent; growth to 5 ft.; hardy; [D.T. Poulsen × Stammler]

Stelvio Coggiatti F, dy, Barni, V.; flowers deep, intense yellow, full, cupped, borne in clusters, moderate fragrance; free-flowering; foliage dark green, glossy; regular, compact (40-60 cm.) growth; int. by Rose Barni, 1999

Stephan Pol, mp, 1967, Delforge; bud ovoid; flowers cyclamen-pink, large, dbl., borne in clusters; foliage glossy; vigorous, upright growth; [Maria Delforge × Arc-en-Ciel]

Stéphanie – See **Aspasie**, HGal

Stephanie Cl HT, lp, 1973, Gatty, Joseph; flowers open, large, semi-dbl.; profuse, repeated bloom; foliage glossy; vigorous, climbing growth; [Coral Dawn × Titian]

Stephanie Ann Min, mp, 1979, Lyon; bud long, pointed; flowers Neyron rose, 1 in., 16 petals; foliage tiny; upright, bushy growth; int. in 1978

Stephanie Ann HT, rb, Edwards, Eddie, & Phelps, Ethan; flowers red and white, 4-5 in., full, borne mostly solitary, slight fragrance; foliage large, dark green, semi-glossy; prickles hooked; upright, medium growth; exhibition, garden decoration; [Veteran's Honor × White Success]; int. by K&M Nursery, 2005

Stéphanie de Monaco – See **Portrait**, HT

Stephanie Diane HT, mr, 1980, Bees; flowers scarlet-red, paler center, 5 in., 50 petals, imbricated, borne singly and in clusters of 3, slight sweet fragrance; recurrent; foliage large, medium green, semi-glossy; prickles slightly hooked; moderately vigorous, upright growth; [Fragrant Cloud × Cassandra]; int. in 1971

Stéphanie et Rodolphe – See **Fiançailles de la Princesse Stéphanie et de l'Archiduc Rodolphe**, N

Stephanie Jo HT, w, Allender, Robert William; [sport of Sylvia]; int. in 1995

Stephen F. Austin S, yb, 2006, Shoup, George Micheal; flowers light yellow to cream, orange stamens, 3 in., semi-dbl., cupped, borne mostly solitary, moderate fragrance; recurrent; foliage large, dark green, semi-glossy; numerous prickles; upright, tall (6 ft.) growth; hedging; [Carefree Beauty × Graham Thomas]; int. by Antique Rose Emporium, 2000

Stephen Foster LCl, mp, 1950, Rosen, H.R.; bud ovoid; flowers pink, recurved, 3½-4 in., 20 petals; vigorous, upright growth, spreading to 15 ft. or more; [seedling × Black Knight]

Stephen Langdon F, dr, 1969, Sanday, John; flowers deep scarlet, large, semi-dbl., slight fragrance; foliage dark green; vigorous, compact growth; [Karl Herbst × Sarabande]

Stephens' Big Purple HT, m, 1986, Stephens, Pat; bud large; flowers reddish-purple, 5 in., 35 petals, high-centered, borne mostly singly, intense fragrance; recurrent; foliage large, medium green, matte; prickles few, medium, recurved; stems long; upright (4-5 ft.) growth; PP6262; [seedling × Purple Splendour]; int. by McGredy Roses International, 1986

Stephens' Rose Big Purple – See **Stephens' Big Purple**, HT

Steppin' Out HT, mp, 1995, Bridges, Dennis A.; flowers

clear pink, large, 30-35 petals, high-centered, borne mostly singly, moderate fragrance; recurrent; foliage medium size, dark green, semi-glossy; few prickles; medium (4½ ft.), bushy growth; [Kardinal × Thriller]; int. by Bridges Roses, 1995

Sterckmanns – See **Triomphe de Sterckmanns**, HGal

Stereo F, or, 1979, Lens, Louis; bud long, pointed; flowers pure orange, open, 3-3½ in., 18-24 petals; foliage brownish, leathery; bushy growth; [Baccará × (Ole × Independence)]; int. by Spek, 1972

Sterkmanns HGal, mr, 1847, Vibert; flowers large, dbl.

Sterling HT, mp, 1933, E.G. Hill, Co.; bud long, pointed; flowers brilliant pink, base yellow, large, 35 petals; foliage glossy; vigorous growth; [Mme Butterfly × seedling]; Gold Medal, Portland, 1938, Gertrude M. Hubbard, ARS, 1939

Sterling – See **Sterling Parade**, MinFl

Sterling '95 HT, m; int. by J&P, 1995

Sterling Parade MinFl, mr, Poulsen; flowers medium red, 5-8 cm., dbl., no fragrance; foliage dark; growth bushy, 20-40 cm.; PP16077; int. by Poulsen Roser, 2001

Sterling Silver HT, m, 1956, Fisher, E. G.; bud long, pointed; flowers lilac, becoming lighter, large, 30-35 petals, high-centered to cupped, borne singly, intense fragrance; recurrent; foliage large, dark green, glossy; very few prickles; stems strong, but not heavy; vigorous, upright (4 ft.) growth; PP1433; [seedling × Peace]; int. by J&P, 1956

Sterling Silver, Climbing Cl HT, m, 1963, Miyawaki; seldom blooms on new wood; tall (8-10 ft.) growth; PP2473; [sport of Sterling Silver]

Sterling Star HT, m, 1997, Ortega, Carlos; flowers large, 41 petals, borne mostly singly; foliage medium size, medium green, dull; upright, tall (8-10ft.) growth; [Lauren Elizabeth × Sterling Silver]; int. by Aebi Nursery

Stern von Prag HRg, dr, 1924, Berger, V.; flowers dark blood-red, large, dbl.; foliage large, dark; very vigorous, bushy growth; [(*R. rugosa* × Edward Mawley) × unknown]; int. by Faist

Sternenflor S, w, Schultheis; flowers small, single, flat, borne in large clusters, moderate fragrance; free-flowering; foliage dark green, glossy; low (30-40 cm.), spreading growth; hips round, small, red; int. in 1989

Sterntaler – See **Golden Fairy Tale**, HT

Steve Chase F, ob, 2006, Rippetoe, Robert Neil; flowers creamy, blushing orange, aging to mostly orange, 3-4 in., full, borne mostly solitary; good repeat; foliage medium size, dark green, glossy; prickles large, slightly curved, tan, moderate; growth bushy, medium (2½ ft.); bedding, exhibition, hedging; hips few; [Little Darling × unknown]; int. by Robert Neil Rippetoe, 2006

Steve Clark HT, ly, 2002, Poole, Lionel; flowers cream flushed pink, 4½-5 in., dbl., borne in small clusters; recurrent; foliage large, medium green, glossy; prickles medium, long, pointed, moderate; growth upright, medium (3 ft.); garden, beds, borders; [Silver Jubilee × Pedrus Aquarius]; int. in 2003

Steve Redgrave – See **Pure Gold**, S

Steve Silverthorne HT, pb, 1991, Fulgham, Mary; flowers white with pink blushing, large, full, borne mostly singly, slight fragrance; foliage large, medium green, semi-glossy; medium, upright growth; [Dorothy Anne × Headliner]

Stevens Rose – See ***R. majalis*** (Herrmann) dbl.

Stevens,Climbing – See **Mrs Herbert Stevens, Climbing**, Cl HT

Stevie Min, w, 1992, Buster, Larry S.; flowers 3 cm., 53 petals, borne mostly singly; foliage small, medium green, matte; some prickles; low (42 cm.), upright, compact growth; [Frau Karl Druschki × Miniature seedling]

Steyl Rambler HMult, mr, 1915, Leenders, M.; flowers light geranium-red to medium, 3-4 cm., dbl., borne in large clusters; non-recurrent

Stifontein Rose HT, ob, Tantau

Stile '800 HT, ab, Barni, Enrico; flowers warm apricot and salmon, 9-11 cm., 40 petals, cupped, strong fragrance; recurrent; foliage large, deep green; vigorous (90-110 cm.) growth; [Antico Amore × Louis de Funes]; int. by Rose Barni, 2000; Grand Prize & Gold Fragrance Medal, Nantes, 1999

Sting – See **Patte de Velours**, S

Stint S, or, Williams, J. Benjamin; flowers more orange than red, single, flat, borne in clusters, slight fragrance; recurrent; growth to 3 ft.; int. by Hortico, Inc., 2006

Stirling Castle F, mr, 1978, Cocker; flowers bright scarlet, 3 in., 18-20 petals; foliage matte; low, compact growth; [(Anne Cocker × Elizabeth of Glamis) × (Orange Sensation × The Optimist)]

Stockton Beauty HT, pb, 1948, Raffel; bud long, pointed; flowers deep salmon-pink, base yellow, large, dbl., open, moderate fragrance; foliage soft; very vigorous, bushy growth; [sport of Banner]; much like Charlotte Armstrong except for color; int. by Port Stockton Nursery

Stockton Red Cl HT, mr, 1962, Raffel; flowers clear red, well-formed; very long stems, vigorous growth; int. by Port Stockton Nursery

Stokes HT, op, 1982, Perry, Astor; flowers peach, reverse salmon, large, 35 petals, high-centered, slight fruity fragrance; foliage medium green, matte; prickles very few; medium-tall growth; [Susan Massu × yellow seedling]; int. by Perry Roses

Stolen Dream Min, mp, 1995, Williams, Michael C.; flowers medium pink, touch of yellow at base of petals, large, dbl., no fragrance; foliage small, dark green, semi-glossy; upright (55 cm.) growth; int. by The Mini Rose Garden, 1995

Stolen Moment Min, m, 1990, McCann, Sean; flowers mauve blend, small, 6-14 petals; foliage small, medium green, semi-glossy; bushy growth; [Kiss 'n' Tell × (Aunty Dora × Charles de Gaulle)]

Stonelea Rambler HMsk, lp, Nieuwesteeg, J.; int. in 1994

Stop Street S, mr, Kordes; flowers bright red, semi-dbl., cupped, borne in large clusters; recurrent; vigorous, tall growth; int. by Ludwig's Roses, 2000

Stoplite Pol, mr, 1955, Jelly; flowers rose-red, medium, 45-55 petals, moderate fragrance; vigorous, upright growth; PP1315; [Garnette × seedling]; int. by E.G. Hill Co., 1955

Stormly HT, op, 1966, Caranta, M. & H.; flowers coral, reverse red-pink, oval, cupped; foliage dull; tall growth; [(Eclipse × Michele Meilland) × Baccará]

Stormy Mountain – See **Ranzan**, HT

Stormy Weather Min, m, 1994, Williams, Ernest D.; flowers medium lavender, medium, full, high-centered, borne mostly singly, moderate fragrance; foliage small, medium green, semi-glossy; few prickles; tall (24-30 in.), upright growth; [seedling × Twilight Trail]; int. by Texas Mini Roses, 1994

Straight Arrow HT, pb, 2003, Streeper, Richard; flowers medium pink to medium red, 4½ in., dbl., borne mostly solitary, slight fragrance; recurrent; foliage large, dark green, glossy, mildew-free; prickles hooked; very long, straight stems; growth upright, tall (5-7 ft.); garden, exhibition; [seedling × First Prize]; int. by Blue Ribbon Roses, 2004

Strange Music Min, rb, 1986, Moore, Ralph S.; bud mossy; flowers red, striped white, reverse near white, medium, 50 petals, high-centered, borne in clusters of 5-7, no fragrance; recurrent; foliage medium size, medium green, matte; prickles small to medium, straight, brown; bushy, spreading growth; [Little Darling × (Fairy Moss × (Little Darling × Ferdinand Pichard))]; int. by Moore Min. Roses, 1982

Stratford HT, op, 1936, Nicolas; bud long-pointed, ovoid; flowers luminous pink tinted salmon, very dbl.; foliage leathery; long stems; very vigorous, bushy growth; [(Emile Charles × La France) × Marechal Niel]; int. by Dixie Rose Nursery

Stratosféra HSet, dp, 1934, Böhm, J.; flowers purple-red, 4-6 cm., semi-dbl., cupped, borne in small clusters, moderate fragrance; once-bloomer; upright, tall (2 m.) growth; [Geschwind's Nordlandrose × *R. centifolia*]

Strauchmaskerade S, yb

Strawberries and Cream Min, yb, 1996, Bees of Chester; flowers light yellow, pink and red striped, small, full, borne in small clusters, slight fragrance; foliage small, medium green, semi-glossy; some prickles; compact, medium (50-70 cm.) growth; [seedling × seedling]; int. by L W Van Geest Farms, Ltd., 1995

Strawberry HT, mr, 1950, Fletcher; flowers strawberry, reverse deep flesh, 5½-6 in., 35-40 petals; foliage light green; vigorous, compact growth; [McGredy's Pink × Phyllis Gold]; int. by Tucker

Strawberry Blonde Gr, or, 1966, Armstrong, D.L.; bud urn-shaped; flowers light orange-red, medium, 25 petals, high-centered, moderate spicy fragrance; recurrent; foliage dark green, leathery; very vigorous, upright, bushy growth; PP2707; [Ma Perkins × Spartan]; int. by Armstrong Nursery

Strawberry Cream F, pb, 1972, Ellick; flowers strawberry-pink, streaked cream, 3 in., 45 petals; foliage light; vigorous, low growth; int. by Excelsior Roses

Strawberry Crush F, mr, 1976, Dickson, A.; flowers unfading scarlet, 3 in., full, slight fragrance; foliage red when young, then rich green, glossy; [Bridal Pink × Franklin Engelmann]; int. in 1974

Strawberry Delight Min, pb, 1989, Rennie, Bruce F.; bud pointed; flowers white with medium pink freckles, reverse white with pink edg, 28 petals, high-centered; foliage medium size, dark green, semi-glossy; prickles straight, medium, brown; spreading, medium growth; fruit not observed; [Little Darling × California Dreaming]; int. by Rennie Roses International, 1990

Strawberry Fair F, mr, 1966, Gregory; flowers scarlet, 2 in., dbl., borne in clusters; foliage dark; vigorous, bushy growth; [Orangeade × unknown]

Strawberry Fayre MinFl, rb; flowers striped white, pink and red, full; foliage dark green, glossy; medium (20-30 in.) growth; int. by Bear Creek Gardens, 1991

Strawberry Fields S, m, 2001, Rawlins, R.; flowers purple with pink flecks, reverse purple, 1 in., dbl., borne in small clusters, slight fragrance; foliage small, medium green, semi-glossy; prickles small, few; growth spreading, low (18 in.); garden decorative; [Intrigue × Christopher Columbus]; int. by Pocock's Roses, 2001

Strawberry Hill S, lp, 2006; flowers very full, borne in small clusters; foliage medium size, dark green, glossy; prickles medium, concave, curved inward, dark red, moderate; growth bushy, vigorous, medium (120 cm.); garden decorative; [seedling × seedling]; int. by David Austin Roses, Ltd., 2006

Strawberry Ice F, w, 1976, Delbard, G.; flowers

bordered cyclamen pink, center cream white, 3-3½ in., 22-25 petals, borne several together; foliage dark, slightly glossy; compact, bushy, low growth; [((Goldilocks × Virgo) × (Orange Triumph × Yvonne Rabier)) × Fashion]; originally registered as Pol; re-registered as Bordure Rose, F, 1986; int. by Bees Ltd, 1975; Silver Medal, Courtrai, 1974, Silver Medal, Monza, 1974, Silver Medal, Geneva, 1974, Gold Medal, Roeulx, 1974

Strawberry Kiss Min, rb, 1991, Clements, John K.; flowers white edged red, medium, dbl., high-centered, borne mostly singly, no fragrance; foliage small, light green, semi-glossy; some prickles; medium (35 cm.), upright, bushy growth; [seedling × seedling]; int. by Heirloom Old Garden Roses, 1989

Strawberry Parfait – See **Imperatrice Farah**, HT

Strawberry Romance HT, pb, 2003, Sheldon, John; flowers red, pink & cream, aging to almost white, 5-6 in., full, high-centered, borne mostly solitary; recurrent; foliage medium size, medium green, matte; prickles medium, pointed; bushy, medium growth; PPAF; [Pristine × Gold Medal]; int. by Certified Roses, Inc., 2004

Strawberry Shake Min, rb, 2001, Siddiqui, Tariq; flowers white with red edges, large, dbl., high-centered, borne mostly solitary, slight fragrance; foliage medium size, medium green, matte; prickles moderate; growth upright, tall (40 in.); garden decorative, exhibition; [Irresistible × select pollen]

Strawberry Social F, mr, 1980, Taylor, Thomas E.; bud ovoid; flowers 23 petals, high-centered, borne 3-7 per cluster; foliage medium green, semi-glossy; prickles hooked; upright to spreading, bushy growth; [Pink Parfait × Chrysler Imperial]

Strawberry Sundae Min, w, 1985, Leon, Charles F., Sr.; flowers ivory flushed pink, medium, 35 petals; foliage medium size, light to medium green, semi-glossy; bushy, spreading growth; [(Kathy Robinson × seedling) × (Kathy Robinson × seedling)]

Strawberry Swirl Min, rb, 1978, Moore, Ralph S.; bud ovoid, pointed, lightly mossed; flowers red mixed with white, 1 in., 48 petals, high-centered, borne in clusters; recurrent; bushy, spreading growth; PP4495; [Little Darling × unnamed Miniature seedling]; int. by Sequoia Nursery

Strawrose Pol, mr, Schneider, S.; int. by Freedom Gardens, 1998

Streaker HRg, m, 2004, Bock, Chuck; flowers frosted orchid, reverse orchid, streaked, white eye, 4½ in., dbl., borne in small clusters, intense clove fragrance; recurrent; foliage large, dark green, semi-glossy; prickles straight; bushy, wide, dense growth; landscape, borders; hips orange-red; winter hardy; [un-named Hybrid Rugosa Seedling × un-named Miniature Rose Seedling]; int. by Chuck Bock

Stream HT, lp, 2003, Yasuda, Yuji; flowers dbl., borne mostly solitary, slight fragrance; foliage medium size, dark green, matte; prickles medium, hooked; growth upright, medium (4 ft.); cutting, garden; [Marchenkonigin × Seisho]; int. by Ogura Bara-en, 2003

Street Party Min, ob; int. in 2001

Street Wise Min, op, 1996, McCann, Sean; flowers orange and pink, reverse yellow at throat, 60 petals, borne mostly singly; foliage medium size, medium green, semi-glossy; numerous prickles; upright, medium growth; PPAF; [Rise 'n' Shine × Siobhan]; int. by Justice Miniature Roses, 1996

Stretch Johnson S, rb, 1988, McGredy, Sam IV; bud small; flowers red with yellow eye, reverse pink with yellow tones, 4 in., semi-dbl., flat, borne in sprays of 5-25, slight sweet fragrance; recurrent; foliage large, medium green, semi-glossy; prickles few. thin, slightly curved downward; bushy, vigorous (2 m.) growth; hips globular, ½ in.; PP7472; [Sexy Rexy × Maestro]; int. by McGredy Roses International, 1988; Gold Medal, RNRS, 1988, Golden Rose, The Hague, 1993

Striata S, rb, before 1817, from England; flowers crimson, striped with white, large, full; foliage oval, finely toothed, pale green; prickles reddish, sparse

Strike It Rich Gr, yb, 2005, Carruth, Tom; buds long; flowers yellow gold blended with orange-red, 9-11 cm., full, borne in large clusters, intense spice and fruit fragrance; recurrent; foliage medium size, medium green, semi-glossy; prickles moderate, average, pointed, brown; stems dark red; upright, vigorous, tall (175 to 200 cm.) growth; [CHRiscinn × Mellow Yellow]; int. by Weeks Roses, 2007; AARS, All-American Rose Selections, 2007

Strilli F, my, Kordes; flowers clear, unfading yellow, medium, dbl., high-centered, borne singly and in clusters, slight fragrance; free flowering, prolific; medium growth; int. in 1993

String of Pearls S, w, Williams, J. Benjamin; flowers white, shaded pearl pink; vigorous, compact (3 ft.) growth; int. in 1981

String of Pearls F, w, 1985, Gandy's Roses, Ltd.; flowers near white, medium, semi-dbl.; foliage medium size, dark, semi-glossy; dwarf, bushy growth; [Meg, Climbing × Sunsprite]; int. by Rearsby Roses, Ltd.

String of Pearls Min, op, deRuiter; flowers coral pink, fading to pearl pink, narrow petals, small, dbl., pompon, moderate fragrance; recurrent; moderate growth; containers, borders; int. in 1991

String of Rubies Min, dp, Taschner, Ludwig; bud oval; flowers pleasing medium to deep pink, pompon, moderate fragrance; medium growth; containers, borders; [sport of String of Pearls]; int. by Ludwig's Roses, 2001

Striped Crimson Perpetual – See **Panachée de Lyon**, P

Striped Fairy Rose Min, rb

Striped Festival Min, rb, 1999, Laver, Keith G.; flowers velvety red with salmon stripes, 2½ in., dbl., high-centered, borne mostly singly, slight fragrance; foliage medium size, medium green, semi-glossy; prickles moderate; easy-growing, upright, medium (12-15 in.) growth; int. by Springwood Roses, 1999

Striped La France – See **Mme Angélique Veysset**, HT

Striped Meillandina – See **Strange Music**, Min

Striped Moss – See **Panachée**, M

Striped Moss – See **Panachée Pleine**, M

Striped Moss – See **Œillet Panachée**, M

Striped Pet Min, pb, 1993, Laver, Keith G.; flowers variable pink stripes on white, large, dbl., borne singly; foliage medium size, dark green, matte; few prickles; low (25-30 cm.), upright,compact growth; [June Laver × (June Laver × Ontario Celebration)]; int. by Springwood Roses, 1993

Striped Radiance HT, rb, 1919, Vestal; flowers red, distinctly striped white; [sport of Red Radiance]

Striped Texas Centennial HT, ob, 1950, Heckmann; flowers orange-red with dark yellow striping, large, dbl.

Striped Unique – See **Unique Panachée**, C

Stripey Fred Min, rb; flowers striped; int. by Burston Nurseries, 2005

Stripez HT, pb, 1942, Janssen; flowers striped and variegated; [sport of Better Times]; int. by Premier Rose Gardens

Stroke-o-Luck F, yb

Stroller F, rb, 1970, Dickson, A.; bud loose; flowers cerise, reverse gold, dbl., borne in trusses; foliage matte; [Manx Queen × Happy Event]

Strombergzauber – See **Super Elfin**, LCl

Stromboli S, rb, Poulsen; flowers red with orange and yellow tones, 8-10 cm., full, slight wild rose fragrance; bushy, low (20-40 cm.) growth; hips none; int. by Poulsen Roser, 2004

Stromboli Palace – See **Stromboli**, S

Stryke Me Pink S, mp, Tantau; flowers medium to porcelain pink; quick repeat; int. in 1998

Stryker HT, pb, 1994, Edwards, Eddie; flowers pink and white, veining in outer petals, 3 in., full, borne mostly singly, slight fragrance; foliage medium size, dark green, glossy; tall, bushy, upright growth; [Pristine × Suffolk]

Stuart's Quarry HT, pb, 1977, Bailey; bud high centered; flowers pale bluish pink, reverse silver, 4 in., 30 petals; bloom repeats quickly; foliage small, glossy, dark; [Silver Lining × Anne Letts]

Studienrat Schlenz Cl HT, mp, 1926, Lambert, P.; flowers rose-pink, reverse darker, large, dbl., moderate fragrance; non-recurrent; growth to 6½-8 ft.; [Mrs Aaron Ward × Frau Karl Druschki]

Stunning HT, m, Olesen; bud globular; flowers light lavender, 8 cm., very full, globular, borne in large clusters, slight wild rose fragrance; recurrent; foliage dark green, glossy; prickles normal, deeply concave; narrow, bushy (60-100 cm.) growth; PP15406; [seedling × seedling]; int. by Poulsen Roser, 2003

Sturdy Gertie HT, op, 1949, Taylor, C.A.; flowers coral-pink, medium, 30 petals, moderate raspberry fragrance; foliage small, dark, glossy, somewhat ribbed; [Pink Princess × Peace]

Stuttgart HT, my, 1928, Berger, V.; bud long, pointed; flowers pure yellow, medium; [Edith Cavell × Mrs Franklin Dennison]; int. by Pfitzer

STW-1 S, mr, Moore, Ralph; flowers light red, fading to pinkish-red, 8-12 petals, flat, borne in clusters, slight fragrance; blooms in large flushes; tall, V-shaped growth; [Soeur Therese × Wilhelm]; used primarily as breeding stock; never formally introduced.; int. by Sequoia Roses, before 1951

Stylish HT, pb, 1953, Robinson, H.; flowers rose-pink, base yellow, 5-6 in., high-centered; foliage dark, glossy; vigorous growth

Su Excelencia Señora de Franco F, mr, 1958, Camprubi, C.; bud long, pointed; flowers medium, dbl., cupped; foliage dark, glossy; vigorous, upright growth; [Cocorico × Independence]; int. in 1956

Su-Spantu F, m, 1962, Borgatti, G.; flowers purplish pink, 25 petals, borne in clusters of 7-8; upright growth; [Alain × Independence]; int. by Sgaravatti

Subaru F, mr, 1977, Kikuchi, Rikichi; bud pointed; flowers single, 5 petals; foliage dark; low growth; [Masquerade × Permanent Wave]

Sublaevis Ayr, op; flowers salmon pink, fading to rose pink, small, single, borne in small clusters; possibly *R. arvensis* × a gallica

Sublime HT, op, 1931, Amling Co.; bud long, pointed; flowers orange-salmon, suffused scarlet, semi-dbl.; long stems; very vigorous growth; [sport of Talisman]

Sublime S, dp, Tantau; groundcover; int. by Rosen Tantau, 2002

Sublime Min, rb, 2003, Tucker, Robbie; flowers white with red edging, reverse white, 2 in., dbl., borne mostly solitary, no fragrance; foliage medium size, light green, matte; prickles numerous, small, straight, light green; compact, short (to 18 in.) growth; [seedling × Dancing Flame]; int. in 2004

Sublimely Single – See **Altissimo**, LCl

Subnigra HGal, m, before 1811; bud round, slightly pointed; flowers violet purple tending towards black, medium, semi-dbl.; possibly synonymous with either Cramoisie Éblouissante or Superbe en Brun

Subnigra Marron – See **Subnigra**, HGal

Substitut Jacques Chapel HT, pb, 1922, Bernaix, P.; flowers peach-blossom-pink, edged rose-pink, base shaded citron-yellow; [Mme Mélanie Soupert × Lyon Rose]

Subviolacea – See **Ternaux**, Ch

Succes S, lp, 1954, deRuiter; flowers pinkish white, single, borne in trusses; foliage dark, glossy; [*R. canina* × unknown]

Succès Fou HT, mr, 1963, Delbard-Chabert; bud long; flowers deep cherry-red, well-formed; vigorous growth; [Walko × Souv. de J. Chabert]

Success Story – See **Weight Watcher Success**, HT

Suchitra F, pb, 1974, IARI; buds large, long pointed; flowers Rhodamine-pink with mimosa-yellow reverse and base, large, dbl, high-centered, borne in clusters; foliage large, dark green, soft; growth very vigorous, compact, bushy (90 cm.); [Lady Frost × Swati]; int. in 1972

Sudha HT, yb, Datta, Sekhar; flowers bright yellow with pink, dbl., moderate fragrance; [sport of Lido di Roma]; int. in 2005

Sudhanshu HT, lp, 2006, Jagtap, Ramrao S.; flowers light pink deepening at center, reverse light pink, 10-12 cm., high-centered, borne mostly solitary, strong fragrance; prickles 5 mm., cream, few; growth to 1-1½ m.; bedding; [Lilac Airs × Paradise]; int. by Jagtap Nursery Garden Center, 2005

Sue Belle Min, ob, 1992, Taylor, Franklin "Pete" & Kay; flowers orange with yellow eye, yellow stamens, aging to pink, large, 6-14 petals; foliage small, medium green, semi-glossy; some prickles; medium (40 cm.), upright, bushy growth; [Party Girl × Poker Chip]; int. by Taylor's Roses, 1993

Sue Betts F, or, 1988, Betts, John; flowers long lasting color, large, dbl., cupped, borne in sprays of 65-120, moderate fragrance; foliage medium size, medium green, semi-glossy; prickles sharp, thin, brown; bushy, low growth; hips round, red; [sport of Europeana]; int. by Wisbech Plant Co., 1987

Sue Earley F, w, 2005, Paul Chessum Roses; flowers white blend, 4 cm., semi-dbl., borne in large clusters, slight fragrance; foliage small, medium green, semi-glossy; growth compact, short; [seedling × seedling]; int. by Love4Plants Ltd, 2005

Sue Hipkin HT, ab, Harkness; flowers apricot, blushed pink, medium, dbl., imbricated, intense fragrance; recurrent; foliage dark green; vigorous, bushy (4 ft.) growth; int. in 1997

Sue Jo Min, r, 1990, Williams, Ernest D.; flowers russet, outside petals tan-lavender, inside petals golden-amber, 1½ in., 33 petals, high-centered, borne mostly singly, intense fragrance; recurrent; foliage small, medium green, glossy; prickles few, slender, inclined downward, tan; stems slender, wiry; upright, bushy growth; PP7606; [Tom Brown × Twilight Trail]; int. by Mini-Roses, 1989

Sue Lawley F, rb, 1980, McGredy, Sam IV; bud small, pointed; flowers medium red, petals edged light pink all around, ruffled, 4½ in., 19 petals, high-centered, then flat, borne in large sprays, slight fruity fragrance; free-flowering; foliage medium size, leathery, matte, red when young; prickles small, straight, pointed; bushy, compact (25-30 in.) growth; hips globular, small ; PP4993; [(((Little Darling × Goldilocks) × (Evelyn Fison × (Coryana × Tantau's Triumph))) × (John Church × Elizabeth of Glamis)) × (Evelyn Fison × (Orange Sweetheart × Fruhlingsmorgen))]; Gold Star of the South Pacific, Palmerston North, NZ, 1981

Sue Leat HT, pb, 1984, Summerell, B.L.; flowers medium pink on outer half of petals, golden yellow on lower, 20 petals, moderate fragrance; prickles brown; upright growth; [Golden Slippers × Anne Letts]; int. in 1983

Sue Ryder F, op, 1980, Harkness; bud slim; flowers salmon orange, reverse shaded yellow, 20 petals, cupped, borne in large clusters; free-flowering; foliage medium size, mid-green, semi-glossy; prickles small; vigorous, medium, bushy growth; [Southampton × ((Highlight × Colour Wonder) × (Parkdirektor Riggers × Piccadilly))]; int. in 1983

Sue Watkins F, mp, 2002, Bossom; flowers medium pink, reverse lighter, 2½ in., semi-dbl., borne in small clusters, slight fragrance; foliage small, medium green, semi-glossy; prickles moderate, ¼ in., slender, pointed, triangular; growth bushy, medium (2½ ft.); garden decorative, containers; [City of London × Anna Ford]

Suela HT, dy; flowers deep yellow, petal edges fading white, medium to large, dbl., blooms in flushes, no fragrance; recurrent; int. by Tantau, 2002

Suffolk HT, w, 1984, Perry, Astor; flowers white with pink petal tips, large, very full, high-centered, borne mostly singly, slight fragrance; recurrent; foliage large, medium green, matte; upright growth; [Garden Party × unnamed yellow seedling]; int. by Perry Roses, 1984

Suffolk – See **Lexington**, S

Suffolk – See **Bassino**, S

Sugandha HT, dr, P. Bhattacharjee & Sons; flowers crimson, large, slight fragrance; int. in 1963

Sugandha Raj HT, dr, Datt, Brahm; flowers non-fading crimson red, full, moderate fragrance; int. in 1992

Sugandhini HT, lp, 1971, IARI; bud pointed; flowers medium, dbl., intense fragrance; foliage glossy, light; bushy growth; [Margaret Spaull × unknown]; int. in 1969

Sugar & Spice Min, lp, Pearce; flowers soft pink, dbl., pompon, slight fragrance; free-flowering; foliage light green, disease-resistant; low (12 in.) growth; int. in 2000; Gold Medal, Glasgow, 2003

Sugar Babe Min, lp, 1979, Lyon; bud long, pointed; flowers 1 in., 16 petals; foliage bronze; compact growth; int. in 1978

Sugar Baby Min, dp, Tantau; flowers rich pink, small, dbl., cupped, borne in clusters, moderate fragrance; free-flowering; low (12 in.) growth; int. in 1997

Sugar Bear Min, w, 1987, Bridges, Dennis A.; flowers medium, 18 petals, high-centered, borne singly; foliage medium size, medium green, semi-glossy; prickles straight, pointed, medium, light green; upright, medium growth; [Heartland × seedling]

Sugar Bells HT, w; bud globular; flowers creamy white; medium growth; [sport of Joybells]; int. by Ludwig's Roses, 2003

Sugar Candy Pol, mp, 1951, Proctor; flowers pink, very small, dbl.; profuse, repeated bloom; compact growth

Sugar Cookie Min, mp, 2003, Chaffin, Lauren; flowers medium pink, white at base, reverse white, 2 in., dbl., borne mostly solitary, slight fragrance; foliage medium size, medium green, semi-glossy; prickles medium, straight, moderate; growth bushy, medium (14-16 in.); garden, containers; [Matangi × Little Artist]; int. by Pixie Treasures Roses, 2003

Sugar Daddy HT, dp; int. by J&P, 1992

Sugar Elf Min, pb, 1975, Moore, Ralph S.; bud long, pointed; flowers pink and gold blend, 1 in., 15 petals; foliage glossy, leathery; bushy, spreading growth; int. by Sequoia Nursery, 1974

Sugar Magnolia F, w, 1999, Taylor, Franklin "Pete" & Kay; flowers white, burgundy pistil and stamens, set against fleshtone petals, 2¾ in., dbl., borne in small clusters; foliage medium size, dark green, semi-glossy; few prickles; upright, bushy (3 ft.) growth; int. by Taylor's Roses, 1998

Sugar 'n' Spice Min, lp, 1985, Bennett, Dee; flowers light peach-pink, medium, 28 petals, high-centered; foliage medium size, medium green, semi-glossy; upright, bushy growth; PP6139; [Futura × Avandel]; int. by Tiny Petals Nursery

Sugar Plum HT, mp, 1954, Swim, H.C.; bud ovoid; flowers Tyrian rose, 4-5 in., 55 petals, high-centered, moderate spicy fragrance; foliage dark, glossy, leathery; vigorous, upright, bushy growth; [Crimson Glory × Girona]; int. by Breedlove Nursery, 1954

Sugar Plum Min, m, 1994, Moore, Ralph S.; flowers lavender purple, opening to expose a silver shading on inside of petals, 1½-2½ in., semi-dbl., borne mostly singly or in small clusters, no fragrance; foliage medium size, medium green, semi-glossy; medium (12-16 in.), bushy, spreading growth; [Anytime × Angel Face]; int. by Sequoia Nursery, 1995

Sugar Plum – See **Gloriana 97**, Cl Min

Sugar Plum Fairy Min, m, Hannemann, F.; [Sweet Chariot × seedling]; int. by The Rose Paradise

Sugar Sweet F, pb, 1973, Sanday, John; flowers soft pink, reverse yellow and pink, 3-4 in., 13 petals, high-centered; foliage green, matte; [Wendy Cussons × Prima Ballerina]; Edland Fragrance Medal, ARS, 1974

Sugarland Run S, my; flowers bright yellow, 5 cm., semi-dbl. to dbl., open cup, borne in clusters, very slight fragrance; recurrent; foliage dark green, glossy; growth bushy, 40-60 cm.; int. by Poulsen Roser, 2005

Suhasini F, lp, 1974, Pal, Dr. B. P.; buds medium, pointed; flowers soft pink, medium, dbl, borne singly and several together; foliage medium size, glossy; growth vigorous, upright (105 cm.); [Queen Elizabeth × unknown]; int. by K. S. G. Son, 1972

Suitor Pol, lp, 1942, Clark, A.; flowers light pink; growth low; int. in 1942

Sujata HT, dr, 1973, IARI; buds very large, long pointed; flowers deep crimson red, large, dbl, high-centered, borne singly; foliage medium size, dark green, leathery; growth vigorous, bushy, compact; int. in 1971

Sukumari F, w, 1985, Gupta, Dr. M.N. & Datta, Dr. S.K.; flowers rosy white; [sport of America's Junior Miss]; int. by National Botanical Research Institute, 1983

Sulcova Kladenska Pol, lp, 1936, Sulc; flowers bright pink; vigorous growth

Sullivan – See **Sullivan Hit**, MinFl

Sullivan Hit MinFl, my, Poulsen; flowers medium yellow, 5-8 cm., dbl., no fragrance; growth bushy, 20-40 cm.; int. by Poulsen Roser, 2005

Sulphur Rose – See ***R. hemisphaerica*** (Herrmann)

Sulphurea – See **Multiplex**, Misc OGR

Sulphurea HSpn, ly, before 1838, Hardy; flowers pale straw yellow, large, semi-dbl., cupped; foliage small, almost round, finely toothed, yellowish-green; prickles very fine, uneven, rather crooked

Sulphurea T, ly, 1900, Paul, W.; flowers sulfur-yellow, large, full

Sulphurea Nana – See **Pompone Jaune**, Misc OGR

Sulphureux T, dy, Ducher; flowers sulphur-yellow

Sultan of Zanzibar HP, m, 1876, Paul & Son; flowers purplish maroon, medium, globular; [Duke of Edinburgh × unknown]

Sultana – See **Regina**, C

Sultane HT, rb, 1946, Meilland, F.; bud long, pointed; flowers vermilion, reverse gold, petals quilled, 5 in., 40 petals, slight fragrance; recurrent; foliage leathery, bronze; [J.B. Meilland × Orange Nassau]

Sultane, Climbing Cl HT, rb, after 1946; [sport of Sultane]

Sultane Favorite – See **Félicie**, HGal

Sultry HT, ab, 2000, Zary, Keith; flowers apricot yellow, 5½ in., full, high-centered, borne mostly singly, moderate fragrance; recurrent; foliage large, dark green, glossy; prickles moderate; upright, tall (6 ft.) growth; PP12126; [(Legend × unknown) × (Tansenfrie × unknown)]; int. by Bear Creek Gardens, 2001

Suma S, dp, Onodera, Toru F.; flowers rose-pink, 1 in., 12-18 petals, cupped, borne in clusters, slight fragrance; foliage small, dense; low (1-2 ft.), spreading (5-6 ft.) groundcover growth; int. as Rosy Creeper, Heirloom Roses

Suma no Ura HT, mr, 1986, Teranishi, K.; flowers crimson, full, high-centered, borne singly, no fragrance; foliage small, medium green, semi-glossy; prickles large, reddish-brown; medium, bushy growth; [(Rob Roy × Himatsuri) × unnamed seedling.]; int. by Itami Rose Nursery, 1980

Suman HT, lp, Ghosh, Mr. & Mrs. S.; flowers soft pink, broad petals, large, high-centered, moderate fragrance; int. in 1998

Sumatra F, or, 1957, Mallerin, C.; bud ovoid; flowers signal-red, 3 in., 26 petals, globular, borne in pyramidal clusters, moderate fragrance; foliage leathery; moderate, upright growth; PP1572; [Olga × Fashion]; int. by C-P, 1957

Sumire-no-Oka LCl, m, 2005, Kobayashi, Moriji; flowers dbl., borne in small clusters, intense fragrance; foliage medium size, medium green, matte; prickles medium; spreading (200 cm.) growth; containers; [seedling × seedling]; int. by Kairyo-Een, 2005

Summer – See **Summer Palace**, S

Summer Beauty Min, dy, 1987, Williams, Ernest D.; flowers small, dbl., high-centered, borne usually singly or in sprays of 3-5, moderate fragrance; foliage small, dark green, semi-glossy; prickles very few, thin, short, light; upright, bushy, medium growth; no fruit; [seedling × seedling]; int. by Mini-Roses, 1986

Summer Beauty – See **Aprikola**, F

Summer Blossom F, mp, 1971, deRuiter; flowers soft geranium-pink, open, 2-3 in.; upright, bushy growth; [Orange Sensation × Kimono]

Summer Blush A, dp, Sievers, Rolf; flowers deep pink to medium red, full, cupped, moderate fragrance; spring flowering; medium growth; int. in 1988

Summer Breeze – See **Surrey**, S

Summer Breeze Min, op, 1991, Taylor, Pete & Kay; flowers light orange-pink, ages lighter, yellow base, reverse slightly darker, medium, full, borne mostly singly or in small clusters, slight fragrance; foliage medium size, medium green, semi-glossy; some prickles; low (40 cm.), spreading growth; [Baby Katie × Poker Chip]; int. by Taylor's Roses, 1992

Summer Breeze – See **Linderhof**, S

Summer Breeze F, mp, Meilland

Summer Butter Min, dy, 1979, Saville, F. Harmon; bud ovoid, pointed; flowers deep yellow, slightly fading as it ages, 1-1½ in., 20-25 petals, cupped, borne mostly singly, intense spicy-sweet fragrance; recurrent; foliage medium size, glossy; prickles moderate, straight, pointed; vigorous, compact growth; hips round ; PP4457; [Arthur Bell × Yellow Jewel]; int. by Nor'East Min. Roses

Summer Charm S, pb, Williams, J.B.; flowers pink fading to white, borne in masses of blooms; recurrent; upright growth; int. by Hortico Inc., 2003

Summer Cloud Min, w, 1990, Zipper, Herbert; bud ovoid; flowers white with hint of pink, large, 65 petals, high-centered, urn-shaped, borne singly and in sprays of 3-4; foliage medium size, medium green, semi-glossy; prickles straight, small, few, light brown; bushy, medium growth; hips globular, medium, brown-orange; [Roundabout × Erfurt]; int. by Magic Moment Miniature Roses, 1990

Summer Crest HT, dp, 1982, Herholdt, J.A.; flowers deep pink, large, dbl.; foliage medium size, medium green, semi-glossy; [Miss All-American Beauty × seedling]

Summer Damask D, lp, before 1600; sepals not persistent; flowers highly variable in color from almost white to dark pink, medium, semi-dbl. to dbl., loose, borne in small to medium clusters, intense fragrance; early summer; foliage oval acute, gray-green, reverse lighter, downy, usually with 5-7 leaflets; prickles moderate, short, hooked; stems long, arching, pale green; growth to 5-7 ft.; hips obovoid, bristly, about 1 in., bright red, (28, 35); referenced by Virgil about 50 B.C., and later by Pliny; probably introduced into Europe by the Romans, but lost and reintroduced during the Crusades

Summer Dawn Pol, mp, 1950, Proctor; flowers soft rose-pink, globular, moderate fragrance; recurrent; foliage small, dainty; [sport of Margo Koster]

Summer Dawn Min, op, Benardella, Frank; flowers deep coral pink with copper tonings, borne mostly singly, moderate fragrance; recurrent; medium growth; int. by Bell Roses

Summer Days HT, ly, 1976, Bees; flowers pale yellow, large, 36 petals, high-centered; vigorous growth; [Fragrant Cloud × Dr. A.J. Verhage]

Summer Dream HT, ab, 1986, Warriner, William A.; bud pointed ovoid; flowers apricot-pink, 5½ in., 30-35 petals, high-centered, borne singly, slight fruity fragrance; recurrent; foliage medium size, medium green, matte; prickles numerous, long, straight, brown; stems long, strong; upright, tall (5 ft.) growth; PP5640; [Sunshine × seedling]; int. by J&P, 1987

Summer Dream F, ab, Fryer, Gareth; bud globular; flowers peachy-apricot, large, dbl., cupped, borne in clusters, moderate fragrance; free-flowering; foliage light green; vigorous, medium growth; [sport of Sweet Dream]; int. in 1990

Summer Evening – See **Sommerabend**, S

Summer Evening Min, ob, 1999, Jolly, Betty J.; flowers orange and white, reverse white, 1¾ in., full, high-centered, borne mostly singly, no fragrance; foliage medium size, dark green, semi-glossy; few prickles; upright, medium (14 in.) growth; [Tennessee × Kristin]; int. by Langenbach, 1998

Summer Fantasy – See **Julie Lynne Zipper**, S

Summer Fashion F, yb, 1986, Warriner, William A.; bud pointed ovoid; flowers light yellow edged pink, pink spreading with age, 5 in., 20-30 petals, high-centered, borne singly and in flat clusters, moderate fragrance; recurrent; foliage large, medium green, semi-glossy; prickles numerous, long, hooked downward; stems short, strong; vigorous, upright (under 3 ft.) growth; PP5860; [Precilla × Bridal Pink]; int. by J&P, 1985

Summer Festival Min, rb, 1997, Laver, Keith G.; flowers medium, 41 petals, borne singly and in small clusters; foliage medium size, dark green, semi-glossy; some prickles; upright, compact, bushy, medium growth; [seedling × Painted Doll]; int. by Springwood Roses

Summer Fever F, or, Mehring; flowers scarlet, medium, dbl., open cup; free-flowering; foliage large, glossy; neat, bushy (2 ft.) growth; int. in 2006

Summer Fever HT, my

Summer Fields F, dp, 1971, Mattock; flowers light scarlet, yellow eye, 5 in., 17 petals, moderate fragrance; recurrent; foliage red when young, then green, matte; hips large, orange; [Tropicana × Goldmarie]

Summer Fragrance – See **Sommerduft**, HT

Summer Frost F, w, 1962, Boerner; bud ovoid; flowers white with slight yellow tones in center early, 4½ in., 30-35 petals, cupped, borne singly and several together, moderate tea fragrance; recurrent; foliage medium size, leathery, dark green; prickles normal, medium length, straight; stems medium, strong; vigorous, bushy, compact growth; PP2115; [Princess White × Golden Masterpiece]; int. by Home Nursery Products Corp., 1962

Summer Glory HT, my, 1961, Leenders, J.; flowers lemon, well-formed, large; upright growth; [Dr. van Rijn × seedling]

Summer Glow HT, yb, Courage; flowers soft yellow, pink blush spreading with age, dbl., cupped, moderate sweet fragrance; recurrent; foliage dark green; medium (4-5 ft.) growth; int. by Mistydowns, 2001

Summer Gold – See **Fragrant Gold**, HT

Summer Gold – See **Yellowstone**, F

Summer Harvest Min, ob, 1998, Chaffin, Lauren M.; flowers very bright orange blend, gold stamens, 2 in., 5 petals, borne in small clusters; foliage large, dark green, glossy; prickles moderate, medium, straight; bushy, tall (24 in.) growth; [Ann Moore × Sequoia Gold]; int. by Pixie Treasures Roses, 1998

Summer Holiday HT, or, 1967, Gregory; flowers vermilion, 48 petals, high-centered, moderate fragrance; recurrent; foliage semi-glossy; very vigorous growth; [Tropicana × unknown]; int. in 1967

Summer Joy HWich, dp, 1911, Walsh; bud pure white; flowers dark rose-pink, dbl., cupped, borne in clusters, moderate fragrance; foliage large, glossy; vigorous, climbing (18-20 ft.) growth

Summer Jubilee S, rb, Williams, J.B.; flowers light red and ivory, borne in clusters; recurrent; foliage dark green, glossy; low, compact growth; int. by Hortico Inc., 2003

Summer Lady HT, pb, Tantau; bud long; flowers creamy pink overlaid with deeper salmon tones, dbl., high-centered, borne mostly singly, moderate fragrance; recurrent; foliage large, leathery; upright, medium growth; int. by Rosen Tantau, 1991

Summer Love F, ab, 1985, Cowlishaw, Frank; flowers light apricot, large, 27 petals, hybrid tea, borne in clusters of 5-10, moderate spicy fragrance; foliage large, dark, semi-glossy; upright growth; [Pink Parfait × Cynthia Brooke]; int. in 1986

Summer Madness Min, my, 1987, Jacobs, Betty A.; flowers medium golden yellow, gold stamens, fading white, deeper in cool weather, petals reflexed, 20-25 petals, high-centered, slight fruity tea fragrance; foliage medium medium green matte; prickles long, red to light brown; bushy, medium growth; hips round, small, orange-red; [Party Girl × Sun Flare]; int. by Four Seasons Rose Nursery

Summer Magic Min, op, 1990, Jolly, Marie; bud ovoid; flowers light pink blended apricot, reverse cream center, pink edging, 150 petals, high-centered, slight fruity fragrance; foliage small, medium green, matte; no prickles; bushy, spreading, medium growth; [Fashion Flame × Anita Charles]; int. by Rosehill Farm, 1991

Summer Meeting F, my, 1968, Harkness, R.; flowers large, 45 petals, borne in trusses; foliage glossy; compact, bushy growth; [Selgold × Circus]; int. by J. L. Harkness, 1968

Summer Memories F, w, Kordes; flowers creamy white, large, full, cupped, slight fragrance; recurrent; foliage medium green; bushy, upright growth; int. by Mattock's Roses, 2005

Summer Morning – See **Baby Blanket**, S

Summer Night MinFl, yb, 2005, Wells, Verlie W.; flowers yellow-orange, 2¼ in., dbl., borne mostly solitary, slight fragrance; foliage medium size, dark green, semi-glossy; prickles ¼ in., hooked; upright, spreading, medium growth; garden decorative, exhibition; [seedling × seedling]; int. in 2004

Summer Pageant F, yb

Summer Palace S, w, Olesen; bud pointed; flowers white with yellow tones in center, 3 in., 50-60 petals, cupped, borne in clusters, slight wild rose fragrance; recurrent; foliage medium size, dark green, glossy; prickles few, concave to linear; bushy, compact (40-60 cm.) growth; PP10730; [Sexy Rexy × seedling]; int. by Poulsen Roser, 1998

Summer Perfume LCl, mr, 1962, Leenders, J.; flowers vermilion-red, 19 petals; [Coral Dawn × Cocorico]

Summer Promise HT, ly, 1971, Von Abrams; flowers very large, dbl., high-centered; foliage glossy; vigorous growth; int. by United Rose Growers, 1969

Summer Queen HT, w, 1966, Delforge; flowers ivory-white, center tinted pink; [sport of Queen Elizabeth]

Summer Rainbow HT, pb, 1966, Jelly; bud medium, pointed ovoid; flowers pink, reverse yellow, 6 in., 45-50 petals, high-centered, borne singly, slight tea fragrance; free-flowering; foliage medium size, glossy, leathery; prickles several, reddish brown; stems medium to long; vigorous, bushy growth; PP2746; [Peace × Dawn]; int. by C-P; Gold Medal, Portland, 1966

Summer Samba F, op, 2000, Zary, Keith; bud long, pointed ovoid; flowers apricot orange, reverse apricot yellow, 4 in., 25-30 petals, high-centered, borne singly and in small clusters, moderate sweet damask fragrance; recurrent; foliage large, dark green, glossy; prickles moderate, medium, straight to hooked slighty downward; stems strong (14-18 in.); growth upright, medium (3½ ft.); landscape, containers; PP12114; [Sexy Rexy × Summer Fashion]; int. by Bear Creek Gardens, 2001

Summer Scent Min, lp, 1990, Rennie, Bruce F.; bud ovoid; flowers medium pink with white center, reverse lighter, medium, 30 petals, high-centered, borne singly, moderate spicy fragrance; foliage medium size, dark green, glossy; prickles straight, small, few, brown; bushy, low growth; fruit not observed; [Paul Shirville × seedling]; int. by Rennie Roses International, 1990

Summer Serenade F, ab, 1987, Smith, Edward; flowers apricot to gold, fading to cream, medium, 25 petals, urn-shaped; foliage medium size, dark green, glossy; prickles medium, pointed, brown; upright, medium growth; hips round, small, orange; [(seedling × Zambra) × Baby Bio]; int. as Summer Sérénade, Wheatcroft Roses, 1987; Gold Medal, Geneva, 1986, Gold Medal, Bagatelle, 1986

Summer Snow, Climbing Cl F, w, 1936, Couteau; flowers semi-dbl., cupped, borne in large clusters; sparse recurrent bloom; foliage leathery; vigorous, pillar (8-10 ft.) growth; [Tausendschön × unknown]; int. by J&P

Summer Snow F, w, 1938, Perkins, C.H.; flowers large, cupped, borne in large clusters, slight fragrance; heavy, recurrent; foliage light green; bushy growth; [sport of Summer Snow, Climbing]; int. by J&P

Summer Snow – See **Gourmet Popcorn**, Min

Summer Snowflake – See **Katharina Zeimet**, Pol

Summer Snows – See **Neiges d'Été**, Min

Summer Song F, ob, 1962, Dickson, Patrick; flowers orange and yellow, large, 12 petals, borne in clusters; foliage glossy; low, bushy growth; [seedling × Masquerade]; int. by A. Dickson

Summer Song S, ob, 2006; bud rounded; flowers burnt orange, 9½ cm., very full, globular, then cupped, borne in small clusters, intense fragrance; foliage medium size, dark green, semi-glossy; prickles moderate, medium, concave, curved inward, red; growth upright, bushy, medium (120 cm.); garden decorative; [seedling × seedling]; int. by David Austin Roses, Ltd., 2005

Summer Spice Min, ab, 1983, Bridges, Dennis A.; flowers light apricot, medium, 35 petals; foliage medium size, medium green, semi-glossy; spreading growth; [Sheri Anne × seedling]

Summer Splash MinFl, my, 2003, Chaffin, Lauren; flowers dbl., borne mostly solitary, slight fragrance; foliage medium size, medium green, semi-glossy; prickles straight, moderate; growth upright, medium (18-24 in.); garden, containers; [Rise 'n' Shine × Dorola]; int. by Pixie Treasures Roses, 2003

Summer Sun LCl, my, 1993, Adams, Dr. Neil D.; flowers medium, dbl., borne in large clusters; repeat bloom; foliage medium size, dark green, semi-glossy; some prickles; tall (6 ft.), spreading growth; hardy; [Prairie Princess × Lichtkonigin Lucia]; int. by Rosehaven Nursery, 1993

Summer Sunrise S, lp, 2006, Beales, Amanda; flowers dbl., borne in small clusters, slight fragrance; foliage small, medium green, glossy; prickles moderate, 6-8 mm., deeply concave; growth spreading, bushy, short (40-60 cm.); groundcover, containers; [Bonica × New Dawn]; int. by Peter Beales Roses, 1994

Summer Sunset Min, yb, 1993, Bridges, Dennis A.; flowers bright yellow with salmon pink shading, medium, dbl., high-centered, borne mostly solitary; foliage small, medium green, semi-glossy; some prickles; medium (45 cm.), bushy, compact growth; [Fancy Pants × seedling]; int. by Bridges Roses, 1993

Summer Sunset S, dp, 2006, Beales, Amanda; flowers deep pink, reverse deep pink, 4-6 cm., semi-dbl., borne in small clusters; foliage small, dark green, glossy; prickles 6-8 mm., concave, moderate; growth spreading, bushy, short (60 cm.); groundcover, containers; [New Dawn × Robin Redbreast]; int. by Peter Beales Roses, 1994

Summer Sunset HT, ob; flowers orange and yellow blend, dbl., high-centered; foliage dark green

Summer Sunshine HT, dy, 1962, Swim, H.C.; bud ovoid; flowers canary yellow, 3½-5 in., 22-28 petals, high-centered to cupped, borne usually singly, slight fragrance; recurrent; foliage leathery, dark green, semi-glossy; prickles few to several, medium, straight to hooked downward, brown; vigorous, upright, well-branched growth; PP2078; [Buccaneer × Lemon Chiffon]; int. by Armstrong Nursery, 1962

Summer Sunshine, Climbing Cl HT, dy

Summer Surprise Min, mp, 1991, Gruenbauer, Richard; bud rounded; flowers pink with yellow stamens, slightly darker reverse, aging light pink, medium, 60 petals, rosette, no fragrance; foliage small, medium green, matte; bushy, low growth; [Libby × seedling]; int. by Flowers 'n' Friends Miniature Roses, 1990

Summer Sweet S, pb

Summer Sweet HT, ly, Bell, Laurie; flowers creamy pale primrose yellow, well-formed, moderate fragrance; free-flowering; medium growth; int. by Bell Roses

Summer Symphony Min, yb, 1985, Hardgrove, Donald & Mary; flowers large, dbl., high-centered, intense fragrance; foliage medium size, medium green, semi-glossy; bushy, spreading growth; [Lady Eve × Little Darling]; int. by Rose World Originals, 1984

Summer Tan F, lp, 1979, Sheridan, John; flowers flesh-pink; foliage medium green, semi-glossy; vigorous, compact growth; [Golden Slippers × Picasso]

Summer Time – See **Summertime**, Cl Min

Summer Wedding Min, mp, 1995, Jalbert, Brad; flowers medium, full, borne in small clusters, slight fragrance; foliage medium size, medium green, semi-glossy; few prickles; compact, bushy, medium growth; [Maurine Neuberger × Sexy Rexy]; int. by Select Roses, 1996

Summer Wind S, op, 1975, Buck, Dr. Griffith J.; bud ovoid, pointed; flowers orange-pink, aging to rose pink, 3½-4 in., single to semi-dbl., flat, borne singly and in clusters, moderate spicy clove fragrance; foliage dark green, leathery; prickles large; moderately vigorous, erect, bushy growth; [(Fandango × Florence Mary Morse) × Applejack]; int. by Iowa State University

Summer Wine LCl, op, 1985, Kordes, W.; bud conical; flowers salmon pink, red stamens, 3 in., single, flat, borne mostly in clusters, moderate fruity fragrance; recurrent; foliage large, medium green, semi-glossy; prickles large; upright (8 ft.), bushy growth; int. by John Mattock, Ltd

Summerdale Min, dy, 1991, Taylor, Pete & Kay; bud pointed; flowers deep yellow, aging lighter, medium, 30-35 petals, cupped, loose, borne usually singly and in sprays of 3-4, no fragrance; foliage small, medium green, matte; bushy, low growth; [Rise 'n' Shine × seedling]; int. by Taylor's Roses, 1990

Summerrose S, lp, 1982, Interplant; flowers 2 in., 6-8 petals, borne in large clusters, moderate fragrance; foliage medium size, medium green, matte; prickles numerous, long; groundcover; spreading growth; [Yesterday × seedling]; int. in 1981

Summer's Kiss – See **Paul Ricard**, HT

Summertime HT, mp, 1957, Boerner; bud medium, ovoid; flowers cameo-pink overcast rose-pink, 4-4½ in., 65-70 petals, high-centered, borne in irregular clusters, intense Old Rose (centifolia) fragrance; free-flowering; foliage medium size, glossy, olive-green; prickles normal, medium, hooked downward; stems medium; vigorous, upright, bushy growth; PP1541; [Diamond Jubilee × Fashion]; int. by J&P, 1957

Summertime Cl Min, ly, 2003, Warner, Chris; flowers lemon with cream rim, reverse pale yellow, medium, dbl., borne singly and in clusters, no fragrance; free-flowering; foliage small, medium green, semi-glossy, very disease-resistant; prickles moderate; growth upright, tall (7-8 ft.); garden decorative; [Laura Ford × Golden Future]; int. by Warner Roses, 2005

Summertime HT, ly, Meilland; flowers light yellow, out petals fading, dbl., high-centered, borne mostly singly; recurrent; florist rose; int. by Meilland intl., 2004

Summerwind – See **Surrey**, S

Summerwine HT, mp, 1975, Warriner, William A.; bud ovoid, pointed; flowers 4-6 in., 45 petals; foliage leathery; [Tiffany × South Seas]; int. by J&P, 1974

Summit LCl, mr, Williams, J. B.; flowers candy-apple red, dbl., moderate fragrance; foliage dark green; growth to 6 ft.; int. by Hortico, Inc., 2005

Sun – See **Sun Hit**, MinFl

Sun Blush HT, yb, 1981, Anderson's Rose Nurseries; flowers 37 petals, high-centered, borne singly or 4 per cluster; foliage mid-green; prickles broad based, dark red; upright growth; [Circus × Summer Sunshine]

Sun Chariot Min, my, 1995, Jalbert, Brad; flowers medium yellow with blush of salmon on edges, bright gold stamens, medium, dbl., borne in small clusters, moderate fragrance; foliage medium size, dark green, matte; numerous prickles; medium, upright, tall growth; [Pink Petticoat × Bright Smile]; int. by Select Roses, 1996

Sun City HT, yb, 1985, Kordes, R.; flowers deep yellow with red petal edges, red spreading, 32 petals, high-centered, star-shaped, borne singly and in clusters of 2 or 3, slight fragrance; foliage deep green, red when young, leathery; prickles dark brown; upright, tall growth; [((New Day × Minigold) × seedling) × MEItakilor]; int. by Ludwigs Roses Pty. Ltd.

Sun City 2 HT, yb, Kordes; flowers deep yellow with orange-red spreading down from petal edges, dbl., high-centered, moderate fragrance; stems strong; medium to tall growth; int. by Ludwig's Roses

Sun Cover – See **Aspen**, S

Sun Drops Min, my, 1986, Lyon; flowers 35 petals, cupped, borne usually singly; foliage medium size, medium green, matte; prickles very small, reddish; low, bushy growth; [seedling × Redgold]; int. by M.B. Farm Min. Roses, Inc.

Sun Dust – See **Sundust**, Min

Sun Flare F, my, 1982, Warriner, William A.; bud pointed ovoid; flowers 4 in., 20-30 petals, flat, borne singly and 3-12 per cluster, very slight fragrance; recurrent; foliage small, glossy, disease-resistant; prickles numerous, long, pointing downwards, reddish; low, compact (3 ft.) growth; PP5001; [Sunsprite × seedling]; int. by J&P, 1983; Gold Medal, Portland, 1985, Gold Medal, Japan, 1981

Sun Flare, Climbing Cl F, my, 1983, Warriner, William A.; [sport of Sun Flare]; int. by J&P, 1987

Sun Flare, Climbing Cl F, my, 1987, Burks, Joe J.; flowers medium yellow, fading lighter, large, 20 petals, cupped, borne in sprays of 3-5, slight licorice fragrance; recurrent; foliage medium size, medium green, semi-glossy; prickles short, yellow-green, slightly curved; spreading, tall (14 ft.) growth; hips globular, medium, orange-red; PP6509; [sport of Sun Flare]; int. by Co-Operative Rose Growers, 1987

Sun Glory HT, dy, 1987, Warriner, William A.; flowers medium, 30 petals, high-centered, borne singly, slight fruity fragrance; foliage medium size, medium green, matte; prickles long, red, pointed slightly downwards; upright growth; no fruit; PP6612; [Golden Emblem × seedling]; int. by J&P

Sun Glow HT, op, 1934, Florex Gardens; bud long, pointed; flowers dark coral-pink, large, dbl., high-centered; foliage glossy; long, strong stems; very vigorous growth; [sport of Talisman]

Sun God HT, pb, 1930, Klyn; flowers shrimp-pink, yellow, and orange-copper, very dbl.; foliage leathery, bronze; short stems; dwarf growth; [seedling × Mme Edouard Herriot]; int. by Wayside Gardens Co.

Sun Goddess HT, dy, 1993, Warriner, William A.; bud long, pointed ovoid; three moderately bearded sepals; flowers bright yellow, 3 in., 20-25 petals, high-centered, flattens, borne mostly singly, moderate fragrance; recurrent; foliage medium size, dark green, matte; prickles some, medium, straight to hooked slightly downward; stems long; tall, upright, spreading growth; PP7659; [Sunbright × seedling]; int. by Bear Creek Gardens, 1993

Sun Gold HT, my, 1935, Elmer's Nursery; flowers pure yellow, large, dbl.; foliage glossy, dark; very vigorous growth; RULED EXTINCT 3/83

Sun Hit MinFl, my, Olesen; bud long, pointed ovoid; flowers medium to deep, bright yellow, 2½ in., 30-35 petals, cupped, borne singly and several together, slight fragrance; recurrent; foliage dark green, glossy; prickles normal, short, hooked downward; stems strong, short; upright, bushy (40-60 cm.) growth; PP9716; [seedling × Goldmarie 82]; int. by Poulsen Roser, 1996

Sun Honey Min, my, 1984, Moore, Ralph S.; [sport of Orange Honey]; int. by Moore Min. Roses, 1983

Sun King HT, my, 1954, Meilland, F.; bud long, pointed ovoid with conspicuous neck; flowers bright lemon-yellow, large, 45 petals, high-centered, borne mostly singly, moderate fragrance; recurrent; foliage dark green, glossy, leathery; prickles several, medium, slighty hooked downward; stems medium; vigorous, upright, bushy growth; hips none ; PP1342; [Peace × Duchesse de Talleyrand]; int. by C-P, 1954

Sun King HT, my, 1976, Paolino; flowers yellow-ocher, large, 30 petals, high-centered, slight fragrance; free-flowering; foliage small, matte; vigorous, upright growth; [(Soroya × Signora) × King's Ransom]; int. by URS, 1972

Sun King HT, dy, Meilland; flowers bright, sunny, lemon yellow, dbl., high-centered, borne mostly singly; good repeat; florist rose; int. by Meilland Intl., 2004

Sun King '74 – See **Sun King**, HT, 1976

Sun Kissed MinFl, yb, 2003, Chaffin, Lauren M.; flowers yellow w/ blush pink edges, reverse medium yellow, 2½ in., full, borne mostly solitary, slight fragrance; foliage medium size, medium green, semi-glossy; prickles straight; growth upright, bushy, medium (2-3 ft.); garden, containers; [Honor × Rise 'n' Shine]; int. by Pixie Treasures Miniature Roses, 2004

Sun Princess Min, lp, Laver, Keith G.; flowers light salmon-pink, small, 35 petals, slight fragrance; foliage small, medium green, semi-glossy; bushy, spreading growth; [(Dwarfking '78 × Starina) × Lemon Delight]; int. in 1984

Sun-Ray HT, my, 1932, Bentall; flowers golden yellow, semi-dbl.; vigorous growth

Sun Runner S, ly, 1998, Ilsink/Interplant; bud short, pointed ovoid; flowers light, bright yellow, 1½ in., 5-10 petals, shallow cup, borne in large clusters, self cleaning, slight fragrance; recurrent; foliage small, dark green, glossy; prickles moderate, short, red; spreading (3 ft.), mounding (18 in.), low, growth; PP10240; [seedling × seedling]; int. by Bear Creek Gardens, 1992

Sun Sparkle Min, yb, 1984, Lyon; flowers yellow blended red, small, 20 petals; foliage small, medium green, semi-glossy; upright, bushy growth; [Dandy Lyon × seedling]

Sun Sprinkles Min, dy, 1999, Walden, John K.; bud pointed ovoid; flowers stable deep yellow, 2 in., 25-30 petals, high-centered, flattens, borne mostly singly and in small clusters, slight sweet, myrrh fragrance; recurrent; foliage medium size, dark green, glossy; prickles moderate; stems normal, short, hooked downward; compact, low (18-20 in.) growth; PP11883; [Yellow Jacket × (Ferris Wheel × seedling)]; int. by Bear Creek Gardens, 2001; AOE, ARS, 2001

Sun Up HT, lp, 1951, Brownell; flowers China-pink, large, dbl., moderate fragrance; vigorous growth; [sport of Break o' Day]

Sun Valley HT, dy, 1952, Whisler; bud ovoid; flowers golden yellow, open, 4-5 in., 30-35 petals, intense spicy fragrance; foliage dark, leathery; vigorous, upright growth; PP1135; [Soeur Thérèse × Mark Sullivan]; int. by Germain's

Sun Valley, Climbing Cl HT, dy, Whisler; [sport of Sun Valley]

Sun Valley S, dy, Poulsen; flowers deep yellow, 8-10 cm., semi-dbl., open cup, borne in clusters, slight wild rose fragrance; recurrent; foliage dark green, glossy; bushy (100-150 cm.) growth; int. as Sunburst Border, Poulsen Roser, 2000

Sunabro – See **Ambrosia**, Gr

Sunanda HT, pb, Ghosh, Mr. & Mrs. P.; flowers deep pink with purple shadings, lighter reverse, large, dbl., high-centered, moderate tea fragrance; int. in 1998

Sunbeam T, 1908, California Rose Co.; [sport of Golden Gate]

Sunbeam HT, yb, 1912, Cant; flowers dark golden yellow, shaded peach, aging to fawn, large, full

Sunbeam – See **Margo Koster**, Pol

Sunbeam Min, my, 1957, Robinson, T.; flowers rich yellow, intense fragrance; free-flowering; dwarf (14-18 in.) growth; [(Tom Thumb × Polly Flinders) × Golden Scepter]

Sunbeam, Climbing – See **Margo Koster, Climbing**, Cl Pol

Sunbeam HT, ab, 1987, Kordes, W.; flowers large, full; foliage large, dark green, semi-glossy; bushy growth; int. in 1986

Sunbeam HT, ab, Kordes; flowers copper-yellow, medium, full, high-centered, borne mostly singly; recurrent; stems long; int. by W. Kordes Söhne, 1999

Sunbeam Kordana Min, my, Kordes; flowers golden-yellow, full; int. by W. Kordes Söhne, 2005

Sunbeam 2000 – See **Sunbeam**, HT

Sunbird Min, my, 1988, Poulsen Roser APS; flowers medium yellow opening to light yellow, fading to light pastel, 25-30 petals, high-centered; foliage medium size, dark green, matte, convex; bushy, medium growth; hips ovoid, few, pale orange-red; [Mini-Poul × seedling]; int. by Conard-Pyle Co., 1988

Sunbird – See **Hot Tamale**, Min

Sunblaze – See **Orange Sunblaze**, Min

Sunblaze – See **Sunny Meillandina**, Min

Sunblest HT, dy, 1971, Tantau, Math.; flowers 5 in., 38 petals; foliage glossy; [seedling × King's Ransom]; int. by Wheatcroft Bros., 1970; Gold Star of the South Pacific, Palmerston North, NZ, 1971, Gold Medal, Japan, 1971

Sunblest, Climbing – See **Clinora**, Cl HT

Sunbonnet F, dy, 1969, Swim & Weeks; bud pointed; flowers bright greenish yellow, medium, 30-38 petals, high-centered, borne usually in clusters, moderate fragrance; recurrent; foliage dark green, leathery; prickles numerous, medium, straight to slightly hooked downward; vigorous, low, bushy growth; hips short, globular, yellow-russet; PP2815; [Arlene Francis × (Circus × Sweet Talk)]; int. by Weeks Wholesale Rose Growers, 1967

Sunbonnet Min, dy, Delbard; flowers golden-yellow; free-flowering; bushy, short growth

Sunbonnet Sue S, yb, 1985, Buck, Dr. Griffith J.; flowers yellow stippled with scarlet, large, 25 petals, high-centered, borne singly or in cluster up to 10, moderate sweet fragrance; repeat bloom; foliage large, leathery, semi-glossy, medium green; prickles small, awl-like, brown; upright, bushy growth; hardy; [Gold Dot × Malaguena]; int. by Iowa State University, 1984

Sunbright HT, my, 1978, Warriner, William A.; bud long, pointed ovoid; flowers chrome yellow, 4-5 in., 25-35 petals, high-centered, flattens, borne singly and several together, very slight fragrance; recurrent; foliage medium size, leathery; prickles numerous, long, straight; stems medium; vigorous, upright growth; PP4438; [seedling × New Day]; int. by J&P, 1984

Sunburn S, yb, Rupert, Kim; flowers open yellow and turn pink in the sun, single, borne singly and in clusters; bushy growth

Sunburnt F, ob, 1997, Giles, Diann; flowers small, dbl., borne in small clusters; foliage medium size, medium green, semi-glossy; spreading, medium

(3½ ft.) growth; [Dalton × unknown]; int. by Giles Rose Nursery

Sunburnt Country – See **Ave Maria**, HT

Sunburst HT, yb, 1912, Pernet-Ducher; bud long, pointed; flowers variable yellow, toward orange, dbl., cupped; Gold Medal, NRS, 1912

Sunburst, Climbing Cl HT, dy, 1914, Howard Rose Co. (also Low, 1915); [sport of Sunburst]

Sunburst – See **Mme Joseph Perraud**, HT

Sunburst S, or, John Clements; flowers bright orange-red, 3½ in., 18 petals, shallow cup, moderate fragrance; free-flowering; foliage disease-resistant; bushy (4½-5 ft.) growth; int. by Heirloom Roses, 2003

Sunburst HT, ob; int. by Love4Plants Ltd., 2005

Sunburst Border – See **Sun Valley**, S

Sunburst Jewel HT, rb, 1979, Herholdt, J.A.; bud pointed; flowers red, reverse pale gold, 35 petals; bushy growth; [Muchacha × seedling]

Suncharm MinFl, dy, Harkness; flowers golden amber, dbl., cupped; foliage dark green, glossy; compact, bushy growth; int. by R. Harkness, 1998

Suncluster F, my, Kordes

Sundance F, yb, 1957, Poulsen, S.; flowers orange-yellow changing to bright rose-pink, 2½ in., 22 petals, borne in trusses; foliage light green, matte, thin; vigorous, tall (4 ft.), upright, uneven growth; [Poulsen's Supreme × Eugene Furst]; int. by Poulsen; Gold Medal, NRS, 1954

Sundance HT, dy, 1992, Warriner, William A.; flowers 3-3½ in., very dbl., borne mostly singly; foliage large, dark green, semi-glossy; some prickles; tall (180-120 cm.), upright growth; [seedling × Emblem]; int. by Bear Creek Gardens, 1991

Sundance – See **Sundance Palace**, MinFl

Sundance HT, yb, 2005, Zary, Keith W.; bud long, pointed ovoid; flowers bright yellow, tipped orange, 9-11 cm., 25 petals, high-centered, borne singly and in small clusters of 3-5, moderate spicy fragrance; foliage large, dark green, glossy; prickles few, 8-10 mm., straight, greyed-yellow; stems medium, strong; upright, branching, medium (140-160 cm.) growth; PP16388; [seedling × AROgoru]; int. by Jackson & Perkins Wholesale, Inc., 2004

Sundance Palace MinFl, dy, Olesen ; bud blunt to ovoid; flowers 6 cm., 15 -20 petals, borne singly and in small clusters, slight citrus fragrance; recurrent; foliage glossy; prickles moderate, straight; vigorous, compact (2 ft.), bushy growth; PP11611; [Fragrant Delight × seedling]; int. by Poulsen, 1999

Sundancer HT, yb, deVor; flowers large, moderate fragrance; blooms in flushes; int. in 1995

Sunday Best Cl HP, rb, 1924, Clark, A.; bud long, pointed; flowers brilliant red, center white, single, borne in clusters; long seasonal bloom; foliage wrinkled; vigorous, climbing growth; [Frau Karl Druschki × unknown]; int. by NRS Victoria

Sunday Brunch Min, yb, 1984, Moore, Ralph S.; flowers soft creamy yellow, petal tips becoming red, which spreads, 20 petals, variable, moderate fragrance; foliage small to medium size, medium green, semi-glossy; vigorous, upright, bushy growth; [Rumba × Peachy White]; int. by Moore Min. Roses, 1983

Sunday China S, mp, 1997, Giles, Kevin; flowers borne in large clusters; foliage small, medium green, dull; compact, low (2½ ft.)growth; [Champney's Pink Cluster × seedling]; int. by Giles Rose Nursery

Sunday Lemonade HT, lp, 1986, Molder, W.A.; flowers pale pink, 30 petals, high-centered to cupped, borne usually singly, intense fruity fragrance; recurrent; foliage medium size, dark, matte; prickles medium, amber, hooked downward; upright, medium-tall growth; [sport of Lemon Spice]; int. by Rose Acres

Sunday Press HT, mr, 1971, Kordes; flowers 4½ in., 53 petals, high-centered; int. by McGredy & Son, 1970

Sunday Times F, dp, 1972, McGredy, Sam IV; flowers deep rosy pink, medium, dbl., globular; foliage light; moderate, dwarf growth; int. by Kordes

Sunderland Supreme HT, lp, 1987, Greensitt, J.A.; flowers medium, full; foliage medium size, medium green, semi-glossy; upright growth; [Paul Neyron × Royal Highness]; int. by Nostell Priory Rose Gardens, 1980

Sundial HT, my, 1987, Christensen, Jack E.; flowers medium, bright yellow, medium, 30 petals, high-centered, borne usually singly, slight spicy fragrance; foliage medium size, medium green, glossy; prickles numerous, normal, small and large, light green-tan; upright, bushy, medium growth; no fruit; [(Golden Wave × (American Heritage × First Prize)) × ((Camelot × First Prize) × Yankee Doodle)]; int. by Armstrong Nursery, 1986

Sundown HT, mp, 1934, Scittine; bud globular; flowers pink, large, 35-40 petals; foliage glossy; very vigorous growth; [sport of Talisman]; int. by Lainson

Sundown LCl, ob; flowers two-toned yellow and orange, moderate fragrance

Sundowner Gr, ab, 1978, McGredy, Sam IV; flowers golden orange, fading to salmon orange, 4 in., 35-40 petals, classic, borne mostly singly, intense fruity fragrance; recurrent; foliage large, leathery; prickles medium, pointed; tall (5½ ft.), upright, vigorous growth; hips globular ; PP4309; [Bond Street × Peer Gynt]; int. by Edmunds Roses

Sundra F, dr, 1968, Gaujard; bud pointed; flowers large, semi-dbl., cupped; foliage glossy; vigorous, bushy growth; [Club × Lilli Marlene]

Sundream F, Leenders; int. in 1971

Sundry S, rb, Williams, J. Benjamin; flowers red with a few pink and white stripes, semi-dbl., flat, moderate fragrance; recurrent; growth to 4 ft.; int. by Hortico, Inc., 2006

Sundust Min, yb, 1977, Moore, Ralph S.; bud pointed; flowers yellow with apricot tones, more yellow in warm weather, 1½ in., 23 petals, borne singly and in clusters, moderate fruity fragrance; free-flowering; foliage small, light green; low, bushy, compact growth; [Golden Glow × Magic Wand]; int. by Sequoia Nursery, 1977

Suneva – See **Flower Carpet Yellow**, S

Sunfire F, or, 1974, Warriner, William A.; bud ovoid, blunt; flowers mandarin-red, 3½ in., 30 petals, high-centered, borne singly and in rounded clusters, slight fragrance; recurrent; foliage large, leathery; prickles ordinary, broad base, hooked downward; stems long, strong; vigorous, upright, bushy growth; PP3510; [Tropicana × Zorina]; int. by J&P, 1974

Sunflare – See **Sun Flare**, F

Sungirl F, yb, 1981, Rose Barni-Pistoia; flowers deep yellow, light red on petal tips, 25 petals; foliage medium size, deep green, glossy; prickles reddish-green; upright growth; [Charleston × seedling]

Sunglo F, or, 1976, Kuramoto, H.; bud ovoid; flowers open, 3 in., 25 petals, flat, slight fruity fragrance; PP3725; [sport of Woburn Abbey]; int. by J&P

Sunglow – See **McGredy's Orange**, HT

Sunglow Min, my, Olesen; flowers dbl., 25-30 petals, moderate wild rose fragrance; foliage dark green, glossy; growth bushy, low (40-60 cm.); PP13493; int. by Poulsen Roser, 2000

Sunglow – See **Sunglow Palace**, MinFl

Sunglow Palace MinFl, my, Poulsen; flowers medium yellow, 5-8 cm., dbl., no fragrance; foliage dark; growth bushy, 40-60 cm.; int. by Poulsen Roser, 2005

Sungold Cl HT, my, 1939, Thomas; bud long, pointed; flowers bright golden yellow, large, dbl., slight fragrance; foliage glossy, dark; vigorous (15-18 ft.) growth; [Margaret Anderson × Souv. de Claudius Pernet, Climbing]; int. by Armstrong Nursery

Sungold Min, ob, 1983, Moore, Ralph S.; flowers yellow overlaid with orange on outer half of petals, reverse light yellow, 20 petals, cupped, then flat, no fragrance; foliage small, medium green, matte to semi-glossy; upright, bushy growth; [Rumba × Lemon Delight]; int. by Moore Min. Roses, 1982

Suni F, pb, Barni, V.; flowers creamy white with carmine edges spreading down the petals, large, dbl., high-centered, moderate fragrance; recurrent; strong, robust (40-60 cm.) growth; int. by Rose Barni, 1993; Special Prize for Rebloom, Genoa, 1994, Golden Rose, Geneva, 1993

Sunil Gavaskar F, m, 1986, Hardikar, Dr. M.N.; flowers 3 in., 60 petals, cupped, borne in clusters of 7 or more, no fragrance; foliage large, dark, leathery; prickles light green, needle-like; dwarf, bushy growth; [(First Rose Convention × Scarlet Knight) × Ena Harkness]; int. in 1985

Sunita S, ob, Clements, John; flowers soft golden orange, deep orange shaded light crimson on petal edges, 3 in., dbl., hybrid tea, moderate honey/ spice fragrance; recurrent; growth to 3½ ft.; int. by Heirloom Roses, 2006

Sunking F, dy

Sunkissed HT, yb, 1981, Tantau, Math.; bud ovoid, pointed; flowers yellow-orange, borne singly, no fragrance; foliage leathery; prickles long, light green, hooked down; upright growth; PP4799; [Minigold × Precilla]; int. by J&P, 1980

Sunkist HT, ob, 1932, E.G. Hill, Co.; flowers orange-copper; [sport of Joanna Hill]

Sunkist Min, my, Moore, Ralph; flowers bright yellow; medium growth; int. by Bell Roses, 2001

Sunlight HT, my, 1958, Meilland, F.; bud ovoid with conspicuous neck; flowers canary yellow, fading to light yellow, 4 in., 43-48 petals, high-centered to cupped, borne usually singly, moderate tea fragrance; recurrent; foliage medium size, leathery; prickles numerous, medium, straight; stems medium; vigorous, upright, bushy growth; hips ovoid, smooth, green; PP1576; [(Eclipse × Ophelia) × Monte Carlo]; int. by URS, 1956

Sunlight, Climbing Cl HT, my, 1963, Meilland, Mrs. Marie-Louise; [sport of Sunlight]; int. by URS

Sunlight HT, dy, Meilland; flowers golden yellow, tinged with orange on reverse, full, high-centered, borne mostly singly; recurrent; florist rose; int. by Meilland Intl., 2004

Sunlight Romantica S, my, Meilland; flowers bright golden-yellow, very full, cupped, moderate fragrance; recurrent; low to medium growth; int. in 2002

Sunlit HT, ab, 1937, Clark, A.; flowers rich apricot, medium, dbl., globular to cupped, intense fragrance; free-flowering; foliage dark green; compact growth; int. by NRS Victoria

Sunmaid Min, ob, Spek; flowers golden yellow with orange edges spreading down the petals, turning red with age, 40 petals, rosette, no fragrance; recurrent; foliage medium green; upright (18-24 in.) growth; int. in 1972

Sunmist F, ly, 1940, Kordes; bud pointed; flowers

clear light sulfur-yellow, open, semi-dbl.; foliage leathery; vigorous growth; [(Eva × Golden Rapture) × Hede]; int. by Dreer

Sunningdale HT, mp, 1929, Hicks; bud long, pointed; flowers reddish-carmine passing to cherry-pink, dbl., high-centered

Sunny F, my, 1952, Moore, Ralph S.; bud pointed, yellow overlaid red; flowers lighter yellow, open, small, semi-dbl.; foliage leathery, glossy; vigorous, upright, bushy growth; [seedling × Goldilocks]; int. by Marsh's Nursery

Sunny Min, my, Poulsen; int. in 2000

Sunny Abundance F, yb; flowers yellow with pink blush on petal edges, medium, 30 petals, imbricated, borne in clusters, slight fruity fragrance; free-flowering; foliage dark green, glossy; upright (3 ft.) growth; int. by Harkness, 1999

Sunny Afternoon Min, yb, 1995, Taylor, Franklin; flowers light yellow, outer edges pinkish/apricot tinge, 1½ in., dbl., borne mostly singly; foliage medium size, medium green, semi-glossy; some prickles; medium, upright, bushy growth; [Party Girl × Elina]; int. by Taylor's Roses, 1995

Sunny Boy HT, pb, 1961, Delforge; flowers buff-pink, tinted gold and lilac, center darker, well-formed; foliage bronze; [Mme Butterfly × The Queen]

Sunny California HT, my, 1936, Hanshaw, E.; bud long, pointed; flowers yellow like Ville de Paris, very large, dbl., cupped; [sport of Feu Joseph Looymans]

Sunny Child Min, dy, 1985, Verschuren, Ted; flowers small, 8 petals; foliage medium size, light green; no prickles; spreading, low growth; [Gold Bunny × seedling]; int. by H.A. Verschuren

Sunny Day Min, dy, 1987, Saville, F. Harmon; bud long, pointed; flowers bright yellow, fading lighter, slight red blush on edges, 1½ in., 30 petals, high-centered, then flat, borne singly and in small clusters, slight spicy fragrance; recurrent; foliage small, dark green, semi-glossy; prickles long, thin, angled slightly downwards; upright, bushy, low (14-16 in.) growth; no fruit; PP6213; [Golden Slippers × Rise 'n' Shine]; int. by Nor'East Min. Roses, 1987

Sunny Days HT, my, 1939, Verschuren; bud long, pointed; flowers chrome-yellow at edges, large, dbl., high-centered; foliage leathery, dark; vigorous growth; RULED EXTINCT 11/86; int. by Dreer

Sunny Daze HT, my; flowers clear yellow, slight darkening on edges, dbl., high-centered, intense lemon fragrance; recurrent; foliage dark green, glossy, leathery; growth to 5 ft.

Sunny Delight HT, my; flowers bright yellow, dbl., high-centered, moderate fragrance; recurrent; foliage dark green, glossy; vigorous (4 ft.) growth

Sunny Dew – See **Sunnydew**, Min

Sunny Honey F, yb, 1973, Dickson, Patrick; flowers yellow-pink blend, reverse red, 4 in., 20-25 petals, high-centered, moderate fragrance; recurrent; foliage large, dark; [Happy Event × Elizabeth of Glamis]; int. by Dickson's of Hawlmark, 1972

Sunny Jean HT, my, Zary, Keith; int. by Bear Creek Gardens, 2000

Sunny Jersey HT, ab, 1928, Le Cornu; flowers bronze, apricot, salmon and orange; [sport of Mme Edouard Herriot]

Sunny June S, dy, 1952, Lammerts, Dr. Walter; bud long, pointed; flowers deep canary-yellow, 3-3½ in., 5 petals, cupped to flat, borne in large clusters, slight spicy fragrance; foliage large, dark green, glossy; prickles few, medium, hooked downward; stems strong, short; upright, compact, pillar or shrub (8 ft.) growth; hips none, cultivar sterile ; PP1239; [Crimson Glory × Capt. Thomas]; int. by Descanso Distributors

Sunny Kordana – See **Sunny Kordana Mini Brite**, Min

Sunny Kordana Mini Brite Min, my, Kordes; int. by Jackson & Perkins, 1998

Sunny Leonidas HT, ob, Meilland; flowers orange with yellow reverse, dbl., high-centered, borne mostly singly; recurrent; int. by Meilland Intl., 2002

Sunny Maid F, my, 1949, Fletcher; flowers bright yellow, 4 in., 6-8 petals, borne in clusters; foliage glossy, light green; very vigorous, upright growth; [(Golden Rapture × Fred Walker) × seedling]; int. by Tucker

Sunny Meillandina Min, ob, 1986, Meilland, Mrs. Marie-Louise; bud slightly globular; flowers light orange-yellow, pale yellow reverse, 2 in., 35 petals, cupped, borne 1-5 per stem, no fragrance; free-flowering; foliage small, dark green, matte; bushy (12 in.) growth; PP6810; [(Sarabande × Moulin Rouge) × (Zambra × Meikim)]; int. by Meilland, 1985

Sunny Milva HT, yb, Tantau; int. by Australian Roses, 2004

Sunny Morning Min, my, 1977, Moore, Ralph S.; bud medium long, pointed; flowers medium to creamy yellow, 1-1½ in., 30-35 petals, flat, borne singly or several together, moderate sweet fragrance; recurrent; foliage small, medium green, leathery; prickles normal, medium length, straight, inclined downward; stems strong, medium; bushy, upright (12-16 in.) growth; hips none ; PP3800; [Golden Glow × Peachy White]; int. by Sequoia Nursery, 1974

Sunny Prophyta HT, dy, van der Hoorn; bud medium, ovate; flowers clear yellow, 3 in., 26 petals, high-centered, borne mostly singly, very slight fragrance; good repeat; foliage medium size, leathery, semi-glossy; prickles normal, hooked downward; stems 20 in.; narrow, vigorous, bushy growth; hips pitcher-shaped, large seed vessel at petal fall ; PP9391; [sport of Ruirovingt]; cut flower variety; int. by deRuiter

Sunny Rose S, ly, 2006; bud small, rounded; flowers pale yellow, 3 cm., dbl., cupped to flat, borne in small clusters, no fragrance; recurrent; foliage small, dark green, very glossy; bushy, short (40 cm.,) growth; int. by W. Kordes' Söhne, 2001

Sunny Royal 21st Century Cl Min, dp, 2003, Ishii, Tsuyashi; flowers dbl., borne in small clusters, slight fragrance; foliage small, medium green, semi-glossy; prickles moderate; spreading, tall (10 ft.) growth; [*R. wichurana* × miniature]

Sunny Sam F, my, 1997, Nolan, Gordon D.; flowers medium, 41 petals, borne in small clusters; foliage medium size, medium green, semi-glossy; upright, compact, low (2½-3ft.) growth; [(Gold Bunny × Gold Bunny) × seedling]

Sunny San Joaquin F, rb, 1962, Raffel; flowers cerise-red, reverse tinted ivory, well-shaped, borne in large clusters; tall growth; [Little Darling × Gertrude Raffel]; int. by Port Stockton Nursery

Sunny Side Up F, ob, 1994, Chaffin, Lauren M.; flowers blended soft yellow to tangerine, 3-3½ in., 6-14 petals, borne in small clusters; foliage medium size, dark green, glossy; some prickles; medium (2-3 ft.), bushy growth; [City of Auckland × Rainbow's End]; int. by Pixie Treasures Min. Roses, 1994

Sunny Sky – See **Souvenir**, F

Sunny Sky HT, yb, Kordes; flowers copper-yellow, large, full, high-centered, borne mostly singly; good repeat; stems medium to long; florist rose; int. by W. Kordes Söhne, 2000

Sunny South HT, pb, 1918, Clark, A.; flowers soft pink flushed carmine, base yellow, large, semi-dbl., cupped, moderate fragrance; free-flowering; foliage rich green; stems long; very vigorous (5 ft.) growth; [Gustav Grunerwald × Betty Berkeley]; int. by NRS Victoria

Sunny Sunblaze – See **Sunny Meillandina**, Min

Sunny Today F, dy, 1971, Whisler, D.; flowers clear deep yellow, petals quilled, medium, dbl., high-centered, moderate fruity fragrance; recurrent; foliage glossy, dark green; moderate, bushy growth; [(Summer Sunshine × Gold Cup) × Isobel Harkness]; int. by Gro-Plant Industries, 1970

Sunny Waterfall Min, my, 2000, Meilland International; bud ovoid; flowers aureolin yellow, reverse straw yellow, 2½-3½ cm., 100 petals, flattened, borne in clusters of 6-15, slight fragrance; free-flowering; foliage medium size, dark green, semi-glossy; prickles moderate, small, pinkish; spreading, low (20-30 cm.) growth; hanging basket; PP10543; [(Meiplarzon × Yellow Meillandina) × Katharina Zeimet]; int. by Conard-Pyle Co.

Sunny Yellow HT, dy; int. by Pep. Jacques Briant, 2004

Sunnybrook HT, my; flowers creamy primrose yellow, dbl., high-centered

Sunnydew Min, dy, 1979, Schwartz, Ernest W.; bud ovoid; flowers clear yellow, 1 in., 18 petals, high-centered, slight fragrance; free-flowering; foliage small; bushy, well-branched, spreading growth; [Yellow Doll × seedling]; int. by Bountiful Ridge Nursery, 1978

Sunnymount HT, my, 1936, Grillo; bud sharp pointed but short; flowers buttercup-yellow, large, 50 petals; foliage leathery; vigorous growth; [sport of Joanna Hill]

Sunnyside HT, op, 1949, Andre; bud pointed, orange; flowers pink shaded orange, 4½-5 in., 24-30 petals, high-centered; very vigorous growth; [sport of Yellow Gloria]; int. by Andre Greenhouses

Sunnyside Min, yb, 1963, Lens; flowers yellow, becoming pink and then red; vigorous growth; [(Purpurine × Miniature seedling) × Rosina]

Sunnyside – See **Niagara**, S

Sunnyside '83 Min, yb, 1986, Lens, Louis; flowers yellow, spotted red, small, 20 petals, borne in clusters of 3-22, moderate fruity fragrance; foliage small; prickles small, hooked, green; bushy growth; [Little Angel × (Rosina × seedling)]; int. in 1983

SunQueen F, yb, 2005, Singer, Judith A.; flowers glowing yellow, fading to white, reverse white, 3½ in., very full, borne in small clusters, moderate fragrance; foliage small, dark green, glossy; prickles small, straight, beige to light brown, moderate; growth upright, medium; [Loving Touch × seedling]; int. in 2006

Sunrise T, op, 1899, Piper; bud long, pointed, scarlet and yellow; flowers salmon-rose, center yellow, salmon and orange, medium, dbl.; foliage glossy; [sport of Sunset (T)]

Sunrise HT, mp, 1939, Dot, Pedro; bud long, pointed; flowers salmon, open, large, dbl.; foliage glossy, bronze; vigorous, bushy growth; [Pilarin Vilella × Rosa Gallart]

Sunrise – See **Freisinger Morgenröte**, S

Sunrise HT, yb; flowers light golden yellow with pink edges on opened petals, medium, dbl., high-centered, slight fragrance; foliage glossy; bushy, medium growth; int. by Karl Zundel, 2003

Sunrise at Heirloom S, ob, Clements, John; flowers firey orange, ruffled, 3 in., 15-20 petals, cupped to flat, no fragrance; profuse; foliage shiny green; bushy (3 ft.) growth; PPAF; int. by Heirloom Roses, 2003

Sunrise Cupido Min, ob, Pouw; bud pear-shaped; flowers orange, salmon pink and yellow, 4 cm., 25 petals, rosette, cupped, borne singly and in small clusters, no fragrance; recurrent; foliage dark green, leathery; prickles very few, short; compact, uniform growth; PP10685; [seedling × seedling]; container rose; int. by Greenheart Farms, 2001

Sunrise-Sunset HT, pb, 1971, Swim & Weeks; bud pointed, with conspicuous neck; flowers blended pink, cream and lavender, 5 in., 46-52 petals, high-centered, borne mostly singly, slight fragrance; recurrent; foliage glossy, light to dark green, leathery; prickles numerous, medium, almost straight, brown to dull green; stems long, strong; vigorous, upright growth; PP3244; [Tiffany × (seedling × Happiness)]; int. by Weeks Wholesale Rose Growers, 1971

Sunrise Sunset S, pb, Ping Lim; bud medium, pointed; flowers bright fuchsia-pink with apricot yellow centers, 2-2½ in., 13-19 petals, cupped, borne in clusters of about 5, slight fragrance; blooms constantly; foliage slightly blue-green, semi-glossy; dense, spreading (2-3 ft.) growth; PP16770; [seedling × seedling]; int. by Sunrise Sunset, 2004

Sunsation – See **Veldfire**, HT

Sunsation HT, pb, 1996, Carruth, Tom; flowers yellow striped pink, 5 in., full, borne mostly singly, intense fragrance; foliage large, light green, dull; some prickles; upright, bushy, medium growth; PPAF; [Celebrity × Peppermint Twist]; int. by Michigan Bulb Co., 1996

Sunsational HT, yb, 2001, Epstein, Bryan; flowers yellow with white edges, reverse lighter, 4-4½ in., full, high-centered, borne mostly solitary, moderate fragrance; foliage dark green, semi-glossy; growth upright, medium (5 ft.); garden decorative, exhibition; [sport of Veldfire]

Sunseeker – See **Duchess of York**, F

Sunset T, dy, 1883, Henderson, P.; flowers orange-yellow, medium, full, moderate tea-rose fragrance; recurrent; tall growth; [sport of Perle des Jardins]

Sunset Cl HT, yb, 1947, Marsh; flowers peach and apricot, reverse yellow, 5 in., 45-60 petals, cupped; vigorous growth; [sport of Faience]; int. by Marsh's Nursery

Sunset – See **Sunset Parade**, Min

Sunset Min, yb, Benardella, Frank; flowers yellow, edged red, dbl., imbricated; free-flowering; int. by Treloar Roses, 1999

Sunset Beauty LCl, op, 2006, Webster, Robert; flowers peach pink and gold, 2½ in., semi-dbl., borne in large clusters; foliage medium size, medium green, glossy; prickles 8 mm., triangular, numerous; growth upright, climbing, medium (12 ft.); [Western Sun × Sue Lawley]; int. by Handley Rose Nurseries, 2006

Sunset Boulevard F, op; flowers salmon-pink, medium, dbl., high-centered, borne in clusters, slight fragrance; recurrent; foliage dark green, glossy, disease-resistant; upright (3 ft.) growth; int. by Harkness, 1997; Rose of the Year, Roses UK, 1997, Golden Prize, City of Glasgow, 1998

Sunset Celebration HT, ab, 1999, Fryer, Gareth; bud pointed to ovoid; flowers creamy apricot/amber blend, 4½-5 in., 35-40 petals, high-centered, borne mostly singly, moderate fruity fragrance; recurrent; foliage large, medium green, semi-glossy; prickles moderate, long, straight; stems strong, medium; upright, bushy, medium (3½-4 ft.) growth; hips very round to globular, smooth ; PP9718; [Pot O'Gold × seedling]; int. as Warm Wishes, Fryer's Nurseries Ltd., 1994; Golden Rose, The Hague, 1997, Gold Medal, Belfast, 1996

Sunset Folies F, rb, Meilland; florist rose; int. by Australian Roses, 2004

Sunset Glory HT, ab, 1947, Boerner; bud ovoid; flowers golden yellow overlaid dusty rose-pink, 4-4½ in., 35-40 petals, cupped, moderate fruity fragrance; vigorous, upright, compact growth; [sport of McGredy's Sunset]; int. by J&P

Sunset Glow – See **Canarienvogel**, Pol

Sunset Jubilee HT, pb, 1973, Boerner; bud ovoid; flowers medium pink, tinted lighter, large, dbl., high-centered; foliage large, light, leathery; vigorous, upright, bushy growth; [Kordes' Perfecta × (Pink Duchess × unknown)]; int. by J&P

Sunset Memory LCl, ab, Itami; int. by Itami Rose Garden, 2003

Sunset Parade Min, dy, Poulsen; flowers deep yellow, medium, dbl., slight wild rose fragrance; bushy (20-40 cm.) growth; int. by Poulsen Roser, 1996

Sunset Party Min, yb, Benardella, Frank; flowers two-tone yellow and red, intense fragrance; medium growth

Sunset Song HT, ab, 1980, Cocker, James; bud pointed; flowers golden amber, medium, 46 petals, hybrid tea, borne 1-5 per cluster, slight fragrance; free-flowering; foliage large, glossy, light olive green; prickles beak-shaped, red-brown; upright growth; [(Sabine × Circus) × Sunblest]; int. in 1981

Sunset Strip – See **Rodeo Drive**, HT

Sunshine HT, yb, 1918, Chaplin Bros.; bud long, pointed; flowers golden yellow, shaded apricot, dbl.

Sunshine Pol, ob, 1927, Robichon; bud ovoid; flowers golden orange, small, dbl., borne in clusters, moderate sweet fragrance; free-flowering; foliage glossy; dwarf growth; [George Elger × William Allen Richardson]; int. by Cutbush

Sunshine HT, my, Kordes; flowers pleasant yellow; free-flowering; [sport of Sunbeam 2000]; int. by W. Kordes Söhne, 2002

Sunshine LCl, my

Sunshine Abundance – See **Sunny Abundance**, F

Sunshine Flower Carpet – See **Celina**, S

Sunshine Girl – See **Living Fire**, F

Sunshine Girl Min, my, 1985, Woolcock, Edward P.; flowers small, 35 petals, multi-star shaped, slight fragrance; foliage small, medium green, semi-glossy; upright growth; [Sunsilk × Rise 'n' Shine]; int. by Pixie Treasures Min. Roses

Sunshine Princess F, yb, 1983, Anderson's Rose Nurseries; flowers medium, 20 petals; foliage medium size, medium green, semi-glossy; bushy growth

Sunshine Sally S, my, Moore, Ralph; bud clear yellow; flowers soft yellow, 1½-2 in., dbl., borne in clusters and sprays; foliage glossy; growth shrub (5 × 5 ft.) or can be trained as a climber; int. by Sequoia Nursery, 2000

Sunshower F, my, 1975, Golik; bud ovoid; flowers bright yellow, ruffled, 2½ in., 16 petals; foliage glossy, light; moderate growth; [Golden Showers × Prairie Fire]; int. by Dynarose, 1974

Sunsilk F, my, 1976, Fryer, Gareth; flowers lemon-yellow, 5 in., 30 petals, cupped, slight fragrance; foliage dark; [Pink Parfait × Redgold seedling]; int. by Fryer's Nursery, Ltd., 1974; Gold Medal, Belfast, 1976

Sunsmile Min, my, 1989, Warriner, William A.; bud ovoid; flowers medium, 48 petals, high-centered, borne singly and in sprays of 2-3; foliage medium size, medium green, semi-glossy; prickles straight to slightly hooked downward, brown; bushy, spreading, compact, vigorous growth; [Spanish Sun × Calgold]; int. by Bear Creek Gardens, 1989

Sunsong Gr, ob, 1975, Poulsen; bud globular to urn-shaped; flowers opening pure strong orange, aging to coral blend, 3 in., 55-70 petals, informal, borne in clusters, slight tea/musk fragrance; foliage medium size, glossy, leathery; upright, bushy growth; PP3794; [Folie d'Espagne × (Zambra × Danish Pink)]; patent issued to Olaf Soenderhousen; int. by Armstrong Nursery, 1976

Sunsplash Min, dy, 1989, Warriner, William A.; bud short, ovoid, pointed; flowers deep yellow, aging pale yellow on petal edges, 1½ in., 40-45 petals, flat, borne in sprays of 18-21, very slight fragrance; free-flowering; foliage medium size, medium green, very glossy, attractive; prickles few, long, slightly hooked downward, red to green-tan; stems medium; bushy, upright (2 ft.), spreading growth; PP7127; [Rise 'n' Shine × Sun Flare]; int. by Bear Creek Gardens

Sunsplash F, ab, 2001, Cocker, A.G.; flowers light apricot, reverse cream, medium, full, quartered, borne in small clusters, moderate sweet fragrance; foliage medium size, dark green, glossy, deeply veined; prickles moderate, 6 mm., straight; growth compact, bushy, medium (2-2½ ft.); garden, decorative; [Indian Summer × seedling]; deeply veined leaves; int. by James Cocker & Sons, 2003

Sunspot F, my, 1965, Fisher, G.; flowers mimosa-yellow, large, dbl., cupped, borne in clusters; foliage leathery; vigorous, bushy growth; PP2576; [Golden Anniversary × Masquerade]; int. by C-P

Sunspray Min, dy, 1980, Christensen, Jack E.; bud ovoid, long, pointed; flowers bright deep yellow, 1½ in., 12-18 petals, cupped, borne singly or several per cluster, slight tea fragrance; recurrent; foliage semi-glossy, dark green; prickles few, medium to long, almost straight; stems long, strong; vigorous, upright growth; hips globular, smooth, orange; PP5035; [Gingersnap × Magic Carrousel]; int. by Armstrong Nursery, 1981

Sunsprite F, dy, 1973, Kordes, R.; bud ovoid, blunt top; flowers bright yellow, 3-3½ in., 25-30 petals, high-centered, borne singly and in flat clusters, intense fragrance; recurrent; foliage medium size, light green, semi-glossy; prickles moderate, long, hooked downward; stems medium; upright growth; PP3509; [seedling × Spanish Sun]; int. as Friesia, Kordes; James Mason Gold Medal, 1988, Gold Star of the South Pacific, Palmerston North, NZ, 1975, Gold Medal, Baden-Baden, 1972, Gamble Fragrance Award, ARS, 1979

Sunsprite, Climbing Cl F, dy, 1989, Kroeger, Henry; [sport of Sunsprite]

Sunstar HT, or, 1921, Dickson, A.; bud long, pointed; flowers orange and red, medium, semi-dbl., intense fragrance; foliage light green; vigorous, bushy growth; [Mrs C.V. Haworth × Hugh Dickson]; Gold Medal, NRS, 1917, Gold Medal, Bagatelle, 1923

Sunstar, Climbing Cl HT, or, 1925, Dickson, A.; [sport of Sunstar]

Sunstone HT, yb, 1959, Fletcher; bud long; flowers bright yellow splashed red, 6 in.; foliage glossy, bronze; strong stems; vigorous, tall growth; [Bridget × Marcelle Gret]; int. by Tucker & Sons, 1957

Sunstrike F, dy, 1974, Warriner, William A.; bud small, pointed, ovoid; flowers medium, dbl., high-centered; foliage large, light, leathery; very vigorous, bushy growth; [Spanish Sun × (Buccaneer × Zorina)]; int. by J&P

Sunstruck Min, yb, 1979, Lyon; bud long, pointed; flowers aureolin-yellow and signal-red, 2 in., 20

petals, intense fragrance; foliage dark; upright growth; [Redgold × unknown]; int. in 1978

Sunstruck HT, ab, 2004, Carruth, Tom; flowers apricot gold edged darker, reverse apricot gold with a yellow fan veination, 11-14 cm., full, high-centered, borne mostly solitary, slight fruity fragrance; recurrent; foliage large, dark green, semi-glossy; prickles medium, straight; stems long; growth upright, medium (140-160 cm.); garden decoration; [Sunset Celebration × (Voodoo × seedling)]; int. by Weeks Roses, 2005

Suntan HT, dy, 1939, Hansen, N.J.; flowers deep orange-yellow, fading slowly, large, 35 petals; foliage leathery, dark, bronze; strong stems; RULED EXTINCT 4/92; [Nanjemoy × Mrs Pierre S. duPont]; int. by B&A

Suntan HT, op, 1940, Yoder; bud long, pointed; flowers buff-salmon, base yellow, reverse light coral-red, large, 25 petals, cupped, moderate fragrance; vigorous, upright growth; RULED EXTINCT 4/92; [sport of Mrs Franklin D. Roosevelt]

Suntan Min, r, 1992, Ilsink, G.P.; flowers bronze, little fading, 1½ in., 30 petals, urn-shaped, borne in sprays, slight fragrance; foliage small, dark green, glossy; upright, bushy, low (30 cm.) growth; [seedling × The Fairy]; int. by Interplant B.V., 1989; Golden Rose, The Hague, 1996

Suntan Beauty Min, r, 1990, Williams, Ernest D.; bud short, pointed; flowers tan to russet with rosy highlights, 1½ in., 33-45 petals, high-centered, borne usually singly, moderate fragrance; recurrent; foliage small, dark green, glossy, disease-resistant; prickles few, slender, short, hooked downward, light tan; stems slender, wiry; bushy, upright growth; hips few ; PP7596; [(Angel Face × Golden Angel) × Yellow Jewel]; int. by Mini-Roses, 1989

Super Aribau HT, dr, 1960, Dot, Pedro; flowers crimson-carmine, reverse silvery crimson, large, 24 petals; strong stems; upright, vigorous growth; [Aribau × Director Rubió]

Super Bianca – See **Heinrich Blanc**, LCl

Super Bowl – See **Cologne**, Gr

Super Cascade Coral Min, op, 1996, Jalbert, Brad; flowers coral, petals very frilly, 1½ in., very dbl., borne in large clusters, slight fragrance; foliage medium size, dark green, glossy; few prickles; spreading, medium (12 in.), cascading growth; [Orange Honey × Sexy Rexy]; int. by Select Roses, 1997

Super Celeste F, op; int. in 1999

Super Chief HT, mr, 1976, Patterson; bud globular; flowers bright red, aging darker, 5 in., 60-65 petals, high-centered; foliage dark; vigorous growth; [Queen Elizabeth × Happiness]; int. by Patterson Roses

Super Congo HT, dr, 1950, Meilland, F.; bud ovoid; flowers velvety dark blood-red, medium, 30 petals, slight fragrance; foliage dull green; upright growth; [Congo × Léonce Colombier]

Super Delilah HT, m, Scherman; flowers lavender, very large, dbl., high-centered; PPAF; int. by Carlton Rose Nurseries, 2002

Super Derby – See **Easter Bonnet**, HT

Super Disco F, pb, Olij, Huibert W. ; bud small, conical; flowers light cardinal pink suffused red, reverse cream yellow suffused pink, 8 cm., 27 -30 petals, cupped, borne mostly singly, slight fragrance; recurrent; foliage dark green, semi-glossy; prickles few, small, greenish-pink; upright, bushy growth; PP8862; [Fantasia × Vivaldi]; florist rose; int. by Conard Pyle, 1994

Super Dorothy HWich, mp, Hetzel; flowers medium to deep pink, fading to white, reverse lighter, 4-5 cm., semi-dbl., borne in large clusters, slight green apple fragrance; recurrent; foliage small, glossy; prickles moderate; vigorous (12 ft.) growth; int. in 1986

Super-Dupont – See **Dolly Madison**, HT

Super Elfin LCl, or, 1996, Hetzel, Karl; flowers orange-scarlet, 2 in., dbl., high-centered, loose, borne in large clusters, slight fragrance; recurrent; foliage medium size, dark green, glossy; rambling, medium (300 cm.) growth; int. by Eurosa, 1997

Super Excelsa LCl, mr, Hetzel; flowers carmine-crimson, occasional white stripe, reverse lighter, 3½ cm., dbl., cupped, borne in very large clusters, slight fragrance; good repeat; vigorous (12 ft.) growth; [unknown × unknown]; int. in 1986

Super Fairy LCl, lp, 1996, Helzel, Karl; flowers delicate pink, 1¼ in., dbl., cupped, borne in large clusters, moderate green apple fragrance; repeat bloom; foliage medium size, medium green, glossy; rambling (300-500 cm.) growth; int. by Eurosa, 1997

Super Gamusin HT, m, 1962, Dot, Pedro; flowers chamois to mauve; [Grey Pearl × Tristesse]

Super Gold HT, ly, 1999, Winchel, Joseph F.; flowers 2½ in., dbl., borne mostly singly, slight fragrance; foliage large, dark green, glossy; few prickles; upright, tall (36 in.) growth; PP12739; [Gold Medal × seedling]; int. by Coiner Nursery, 2000

Super Green HT, w; flowers greenish white, ruffled edges; foliage dark; int. by Carlton Roses, 2004

Super Harrington HT, dr, 1938, Brown, John; bud oval; flowers dark crimson, mottled scarlet, medium, dbl., loose, moderate fragrance; foliage leathery; vigorous, upright growth; [Tassin × Victoria Harrington]; int. by A. Meilland

Super Lass LCl, pb, Hetzel; flowers lilac-pink with cream-white eye, flat, borne in large trusses, moderate fragrance; recurrent; vigorous (8-10 ft.) growth; int. in 1999

Super Nova F, dp; PP11153; int. by J&P, 1997

Super Pink LCl, mp, 2000, Lens, Louis; flowers pure, clear pink, 8-12 cm., full, cupped, borne in small clusters; recurrent; foliage large, dark green, glossy; prickles moderate; growth upright, tall (2-2½ m.); [Jour de Fete × Maria Teresa]; int. by Louis Lens N.V., 1992

Super Prince Tango F, Delbard; int. in 1971

Super Rugostar HRg, mr; flowers bright red, small, dbl., cupped to flat, borne in clusters; recurrent; int. by Belle Epoque, 1998

Super Sparkle LCl, dr, 1996, Hetzel, Karl; flowers crimson scarlet, 2 in., dbl., borne in large clusters, slight fragrance; reliable repeat; foliage medium size, dark green, glossy; rambling, climbing (300 cm.) growth; int. by Eurosa, 1997

Super Star – See **Tropicana**, HT

Super Star, Climbing – See **Tropicana, Climbing**, Cl HT

Super Star Supreme HT, or, 1982, U.S. Patent Sales, Inc.; flowers deeper color; [sport of Tropicana]

Super Sun HT, my, 1967, Bentley; flowers maize-yellow; [sport of Piccadilly]

Super Swany – See **White Meidiland**, S

Super Tabarin F, ob, 1965, Gaujard; flowers coppery, reverse orange, semi-dbl.; vigorous growth; [Faust × Tabarin]

Super Tan Min, op, Interplant; flowers coppery orange, small to medium, semi-dbl.; int. in 1995

Superb HT, lp, 1924, Evans; flowers pale pink, tinted blush; [Mme Caroline Testout × Willowmere]

Superb Pol, dr, 1927, deRuiter; flowers crimson, dbl.

Superb, Climbing Cl Pol, dr, 1933, Guillot, P.; [sport of Superb]

Superb Striped Unique – See **Unique Panachée**, C

Superb Tuscan – See **Tuscany Superb**, HGal

Superb Tuscany – See **Tuscany Superb**, HGal

Superba HSet, lp, 1843, Feast; flowers pale pink, varying to flesh and white, very dbl., borne in large clusters

Superba Pol, dr, 1927, de Ruiter; either a sport or seedling of Orléans Rose

Superba, Climbing Cl Pol, mr, 1932, Guillot; flowers scarlet-crimson, large; [sport of Superba]

Superba HT, dp, 1940, Aicardi, L.; flowers intense rose with yellow reflections, overlarge; long stems; [Julien Potin × seedling]; int. by Giacomasso

Superba HMoy, dr; flowers dark crimson, large, dbl.; no fruit; [Charles P. Kilham × *R. moyesii*]; int. by Van Rossem

Superbe – See **Cramoisie Triomphante**, HGal

Superbe A, w, before 1846; flowers full

Superbe Brune – See **Achille**, HGal

Superbe Cramoisie C, mr, about 1850, Robert; flowers crimson, very large, full

Superbe du Bengale – See **Louis-Philippe**, Ch

Superbe en Brun HGal, m, before 1810, Dupont; flowers deep velvety purple, 2 in., dbl., flat; prickles hooked, paired

Superbissima – See **Admirable**, HGal

Supercandy Gr, Mansuino; int. in 1967

Superga HT, lp, 1958, Giacomasso; flowers rose-pearl, high pointed; foliage dark, glossy; long stems; very vigorous growth; [sport of Savoia]; int. in 1956

Superglo Min, or, 1985, Spooner, Raymond A.; flowers small, semi-dbl.; foliage small, medium green, semi-glossy; bushy growth; [((Prominent × Rise 'n' Shine) × Trumpeter) × Chattem Centennial]

Superior F, ab, 1968, LeGrice; flowers apricot-yellow, semi-dbl., borne in trusses; foliage dark, glossy; vigorous, low growth; [Masquerade × Amberlight]; int. by Roseland Nurs.

Supernova S, w, Barni; flowers pure white, dbl., pompon, borne in clusters, moderate fragrance; recurrent; low (2 ft.), arching, sprawling growth; groundcover; int. by Rose Barni, 2003

Superstition HT, m; flowers deep lavender, some with reddish edges, dbl., high-centered, blooms in flushes; recurrent; foliage dark green, glossy.; int. by Carlton Rose Nurseries, 2002

Suplesse HT, w, Tantau; florist rose; int. by Rosen Tantau

Supra HT, dy, 1984, Meilland, Mrs. Marie-Louise; flowers flora-tea, large, 20 petals, no fragrance; foliage medium size, dark, semi-glossy; upright growth; PP5042; [((Zambra × (Baccará × White Knight)) × Golden Garnette) × seedling]; int. by Meilland Et Cie, 1980

Supravat HT, mp, Ghosh, Mr. & Mrs. S.; flowers large, dbl., high-centered; int. in 1996

Supreme HT, my, 1963, LeGrice; flowers lemon-yellow, well-formed, 4½-5 in., 40-45 petals; foliage dark, leathery, glossy; vigorous, tall growth; [Golden Masterpiece × Ethel Sanday]

Supreme Cover – See **Mystic**, S

Supreme Rendezvous HT, pb, 1961, Langbecker; flowers cream to pale pink, edged carmine; [sport of Day of Triumph]

Supreme's Sister F, mp, 1965, Jones; bud red; flowers coppery salmon to salmon-pink, medium, 42 petals; foliage leathery, bronze; low, bushy growth; int. by Hennessey, 1960

Supriya HT, pb, Sen, Dr. N.C.; flowers pure pink with cream and white stripes and splashes, dbl., high-centered; [sport of Princess Margaret of England]; int. in 1982

Surabhi HT, mp, 1976, IARI; bud long, pointed; flowers phlox-pink, 80 petals, high-centered, intense fragrance; foliage glossy, dark; upright, compact growth; [Oklahoma × Delhi Princess]; int. in 1975

Surain HT, mp, 1985, Elliott, Charles P.; flowers large, 35 petals, high-centered; upright growth; [seedling × Forever Yours]

Surbrunnsgatan HP, mp; flowers strong pink, edges lighter, large, full, cupped, borne mostly singly, moderate fragrance; recurrent; upright (4 ft.) growth; from Sweden

Surekha HT, or, 1971, IARI; bud pointed; flowers coral-red, large, dbl.; foliage dark, leathery; very vigorous, upright growth; [Queen Elizabeth × unknown]

Surf F, op, Laperrière; int. by Roseraie Laperrière, 2000

Surf Rider S, w, 1970, Holmes, R.A.; flowers creamy white, medium, 25 petals, loose, borne in large trusses, moderate musk fragrance; recurrent; foliage bright, glossy; very vigorous, erect (6 ft.) growth; [Ivory Fashion × Ballerina]; int. by Fryer's Nursery, Ltd., 1968

Surfer Girl Min, or, 1988, Rennie, Bruce F.; flowers light orange-red, salmon, reverse lighter, medium, 25-30 petals, high-centered, borne usually singly, moderate spicy fragrance; foliage medium size, medium green, matte; prickles hooked, medium, transparent yellow-brown; bushy, medium growth; hips round, small, yellow-orange; [Pink Sheri × Paul Shirville]; int. by Rennie Roses International

Surf's Up Min, ob, 1984, Lemrow, Dr. Maynard W.; flowers orange, yellow reverse, small, 35 petals, high-centered, borne singly; foliage small, medium green, semi-glossy; upright growth; [Avandel × seedling]

Surfside Min, pb, 1988, Williams, Michael C.; flowers medium pink to creamy yellow to creamy white, 24 petals, high-centered, borne usually singly; foliage large, light green, semi-glossy; prickles curved down, very few, red-green; upright, medium growth; hips round, medium, green orange-yellow; [Tiki × Party Girl]; int. by The Rose Garden & Mini Rose Nursery

Surkhab HT, m, 1976, Pal, Dr. B.P.; bud globular; flowers Tyrian purple, reverse silvery amaranth, 4 in., 76 petals, cupped, intense fragrance; foliage leathery; very vigorous, upright, compact growth; int. by Anand Roses, 1975

Surpasse Singleton – See **Illustre**, HGal

Surpasse Tout HGal, mr, before 1811; flowers rosy crimson, fading cerise-pink, medium, full, cupped to flat, moderate fragrance; once blooming; foliage large; upright (3 ft.) growth; probably from Holland; int. by Hardy

Surprise HT, mp, 1925, Van Rossem; flowers salmon-pink, dbl., cupped; [Frau Karl Druschki × Mme Edouard Herriot]

Surprise – See **Golden Holstein**, F

Surprise! S, w; flowers white with pink blush in center, dbl., globular, intense fragrance; medium growth; int. by Pococks Roses, 2004

Surprise Party – See **Charisma**, F

Surprise Surprise Min, m, 1994, Moore, Ralph S.; flowers mauve-lavender with occasional petals being striped red, medium, semi-dbl., shallow cup to flat, borne in clusters, no fragrance; recurrent; foliage small, dark green, semi-glossy; few prickles; low (12-16 in.), bushy, compact growth; [sport of Cherry Magic]; int. by Sequoia Nursery, 1994

Surprise Treat F, dr, Delbard; flowers deep red with prominent yellow stamens; int. by Bell Roses, 2001

Surrey S, lp, 1985, Kordes, W.; flowers soft pink, medium, semi-dbl., cupped, borne in clusters; recurrent; foliage small, medium green, semi-glossy; bushy (2-3 ft.), spreading growth; [The Fairy × seedling]; Gold Medal, RNRS, 1987, Gold Medal, Genoa, 1989, Gold Medal, Baden-Baden, 1987

Surrey – See **Patio Princess**, S

Surville HT, mr, 1924, Croibier; bud fat, deep rose red; flowers Indian red, shaded cerise, golden stamens, dbl., globular, moderate fragrance; recurrent; [Mme Edouard Herriot × unknown]

Survivor HKor, dr, Svejda, Dr. Felicitas; flowers dark scarlet, large; bushy (5 ft.), arching growth; int. by Agriculture Canada, 1975

Surya Kiran F, or, 1980, Pal, Dr. B.P.; bud pointed; flowers 19 petals, borne 2-14 per cluster; foliage large, glossy; prickles hooked; tall, upright, vigorous, open growth; [Flamenco × Orangeade]; int. by Friends Rosery, 1979

Surya Shikha HT, pb, Diby; flowers striped and splashed pink and yellow, large, dbl.; free-flowering; [sport of Grand Opera]; int. in 1992

Suryodaya F, ob, 1968, IARI; bud ovoid; flowers bright orange, medium, semi-dbl.; foliage dark, leathery; very vigorous, upright growth; [Orangeade × unknown]

Susan F, mr, 1955, Robinson, H.; flowers crimson, well-formed, semi-dbl., borne in large clusters; foliage dark; bushy, compact growth; [Donald Prior × Our Princess]

Susan HT, lp, Kordes; flowers pale pink, sometimes deeper in center, dbl., high-centered, borne mostly singly, intense fragrance; recurrent; foliage leathery; robust growth; int. by Treloar Roses, 1996

Susan S, w, Poulsen; flowers white with ivory tones in center, 10-15 cm., full, moderate fragrance; foliage dark green, glossy; bushy, tall (100-150 cm.) growth; int. by Poulsen Roser, 2000

Susan Ann – See **Southampton**, F

Susan Beckwith HT, mp, 1998, Beckwith, R.; bud short, squat; flowers medium pink, apricot base, opens flat, 4-4½ in., very dbl., flat, borne in clusters; foliage medium size, medium green, semi-glossy; prickles moderate; bushy, medium (2½ ft.) growth; [Dr. Sybil Johnston × seedling]; int. by Battersby Roses, 1998

Susan Blixen – See **Karen Blixen**, HT

Susan Daniel – See **The English Lady**, F

Susan Devoy – See **Cardinal's Robe**, HT

Susan Elizabeth HT, pb, 1990, Schlueter, Barry; bud ovoid; flowers cream tipped with very deep purple-pink, reverse cream to pale yellow at base, edging broadening with age, full, high-centered, slight fruity fragrance; foliage medium size, medium green, semi-glossy; prickles slightly recurved, sparse, red; upright, medium growth; fruit not observed; [Pristine × Akebono]; int. by Schlueter Rose Culture, 1989

Susan Hampshire HT, lp, 1976, Paolino; flowers light fuchsia-pink, 5½ in., 40 petals, globular, intense fragrance; free-flowering; foliage medium green, matte; vigorous, upright growth; [(Monique × Symphonie) × Miss All-American Beauty]; int. by URS, 1972

Susan Hayward Cl HT, lp, 1967, Hayward; flowers light pink, center and reverse darker, large, dbl., high-centered; foliage dark, glossy; vigorous, climbing, open habit growth; [Fontanelle × Gen. MacArthur]

Susan Irvine HG, pb, 1997, Thomson, George L.; flowers rose pink, cream center, prominent gold stamens, 2½-3½ in., 8-14 petals, borne in large clusters, moderate fragrance; foliage medium size, medium green, semi glossy; bushy, medium (5 ft.) growth; [Mrs. Mary Thomson × *R. gigantea* seedling]

Susan Jellicoe F, w, 1994, Horner, Calvin; flowers cream/pink blend, 3 in., full, borne singly and in small clusters, intense fragrance; foliage medium size, medium green, semi-glossy; some prickles; medium (100 cm.), upright, bushy growth; [Keepsake × Pot O'Gold]; int. by Horner, 1993

Susan Louise T, lp, 1929, Adams, Charles E.; bud very long, pointed, deep pink; flowers flesh-pink, reverse deeper, semi-dbl., loose, slight fragrance; recurrent; vigorous (4-5 ft.), bushy growth; [Belle Portugaise × unknown]; int. by Stocking, 1929

Susan Massu HT, yb, 1973, Kordes, R.; bud ovoid; flowers light yellow and salmon blend, large, dbl., cupped, moderate fragrance; foliage glossy, dark, leathery; vigorous, upright growth; [Colour Wonder × Liberty Bell]; int. by Kordes, 1970; Gold Medal, Baden-Baden, 1968

Susan Munro HT, mp, 2001, Jellyman, J.S.; flowers medium pink with light pink reverse, 4½ in., dbl., borne mostly solitary; foliage medium size, dark green, semi-glossy; prickles few, small, curved; growth compact, bushy, medium (2½ ft.); bedding; [Jean Kenneally × (Starina × Peachy White)]

Susan Noel Min, ab, 1986, Jolly, Nelson F.; flowers light apricot, small, 80 petals, urn-shaped, borne usually singly; foliage small, medium green, semi-glossy; prickles small, slightly hooked, gray-orange; medium, upright growth; small, globular fruit; [Rise 'n' Shine × Orange Honey]; int. by Rosehill Farm

Susan Renaissance – See **Susan**, S

Susan Schneider S, yb, 1999, Jerabek, Paul E.; flowers med. yellow, turning orange pink, then red, reverse med. yellow, 3 in., 8-14 petals, borne in small clusters, slight fragrance; foliage medium size, medium green, glossy; prickles moderate, tan; spreading, medium (5 ft.) growth; int. by Freedom Gardens, 1998

Susan Wilce HT, w, 2006, Poole, Lionel; flowers full, high-centered, borne mostly solitary; foliage medium size, medium green, glossy; prickles medium, hooked, brown, moderate; growth upright, medium (3 ft.); exhibition; [Silver Anniversary × New Zealand]; int. by David Lister, 2007

Susana Marchal HT, or, 1958, Dot, Pedro; bud pointed; flowers coral-red, large, 18 petals, high-centered; foliage clear green; strong stems; upright growth; [Cynthia × Vive la France]; int. in 1953

Susane Dot Cl HT, dr, 1963, Dot, Simon; flowers crimson, large, 32 petals; vigorous growth; [Queen Elizabeth × Peace, Climbing]

Susanna Pol, lp, 1914, Weigand, C.; flowers small, dbl.; [sport of Tausendschön]

Susanna Tamaro HT, op, Barni; flowers salmon-pink, full, borne mostly singly, intense fragrance; free-flowering; foliage deep green; vigorous (3-4 ft.), bushy growth; int. by Rose Barni, 2004

Susanne S, yb, Huber; flowers golden yellow in center, whitish on outer petals, full, slight fragrance; growth to 4-5 ft.; int. by Richard Huber AG, 2006

Susanne Marie F, pb, 2000, Schramm, Dwayne; bud deep pink; flowers medium pink, edged deep pink, reverse deep pink, 2-3 in., full, borne mostly singly, no fragrance; foliage medium size, medium green, semi-glossy; few prickles; upright, medium (2-3 ft.) growth; [Gene Boerner × Gingersnap]

Sushma F, m, Kasturi; int. in 1975

Susie HT, mp, 1955, Spandikow; flowers pink, base yellow, 4-6 in., 45-50 petals, high-centered; foliage leathery; vigorous, bushy growth; PP1423; RULED

EXTINCT 11/90; [Mme Butterfly × Sally]

Suspense HT, rb, 1960, Meilland, F.; bud ovoid; flowers turkey-red, reverse yellow-ochre, 4½-5 in., 58 petals, high-centered; foliage leathery, dark, glossy; vigorous, upright, bushy growth; PP1944; [Henri Mallerin × (Happiness × Floradora)]; int. by C-P, 1960

Suspense, Climbing Cl HT, rb; [sport of Suspense]

Suspense F, w, Asaoka, Keisuke; bud yellow; flowers greenish-white to white, petal tips very light pink; PP4660; [sport of Faberge]; same as Fabergé except for bud and bloom color

Sussex S, ab, Poulsen; flowers peachy-apricot, scalloped petals and amber stamens, 3 in., dbl., cupped, borne in large clusters, slight fragrance; free-flowering; foliage medium to dark green, glossy; compact (2-3 ft.), bushy growth; int. in 1991

Sutter's Gold HT, ob, 1950, Swim, H.C.; bud orange overlaid indian red; flowers golden orange, often with red on outer petals, 4-5 in., 33 petals, high-centered, borne usually singly, intense fragrance; recurrent; foliage dark, leathery; very vigorous, upright growth; [Charlotte Armstrong × Signora]; int. by Armstrong Nursery; Gold Medal, Geneva, 1949, James Alexander Gamble Fragrance Medal, ARS, 1966, Gold Medal, Portland, 1946, Gold Medal, Bagatelle, 1948

Sutter's Gold, Climbing Cl HT, ob, 1950, Weeks; bud vermilion; flowers golden yellow with ruddy guard petals, 5 in., borne mostly solitary, moderate fragrance; scattered repeat bloom; vigorous (10-14 ft.) growth; [sport of Sutter's Gold]; int. by Armstrong Nursery

Sutton Place Gr, pb, 1991, Williams, J. Benjamin; flowers white with dark salmon-pink edge, aging to pink, single, borne singly and in clusters of 5-6, intense fragrance; foliage large, dark green, semi-glossy; tall, upright, bushy growth; [Queen Elizabeth × (Carla × Command Performance)]; int. in 1996

Suzaku HT, ob, Keihan; int. in 1977

Suzan Ball F, ab, 1958, Warriner, William A.; bud conical; flowers salmon-coral, to loosely open, 2½-3½ in., 25 petals, high-centered, borne in clusters, moderate spicy fragrance; foliage dark; vigorous, upright growth; PP1588; [Tom Breneman × Fashion]; int. by H&S, 1956

Suzanne HSpn, op, 1950, Skinner, Dr. F. L.; flowers pale coral-pink, medium, dbl., cupped, moderate fragrance; occasional repeat; foliage small, dark, turning bronze purple and red in autumn; tall (4-5 ft.), arching growth; hips bright red, turning purple; cold hardy; [second generation *R. laxa* × *R. spinosissima*]; int. in 1949

Suzanne Albrand Pol, mr, 1930, Turbat; flowers bright red, large, borne in large clusters; foliage glossy; vigorous growth

Suzanne Balitrand HT, or, 1942, Mallerin, C.; flowers coral edged fiery red, stamens yellow; int. by A. Meilland

Suzanne Bidard Pol, mp, 1914, Vigneron; flowers small, dbl.

Suzanne Blanchet T, lp, 1885, Nabonnand, G.; flowers flesh-pink, large

Suzanne Carrol of Carrolton HP, mp, 1924, Nabonnand, P.; flowers light satiny rose and salmon, large, semi-dbl.; vigorous growth; [Frau Karl Druschki × Mme Gabriel Luizet]

Suzanne Dolard Pol, dr, Gaujard; flowers medium, semi-dbl.; int. in 1966

Suzanne Étienne HMult, w, 1909, Cochet

Suzanne Finger HT, 1908, Walter

Suzanne Hester Cl HT, w, 1950, Hester; bud ovoid; flowers white, base tinted yellow, 30 petals, high-centered; foliage glossy; vigorous growth; [sport of Marie Maass]

Suzanne-Marie Rodocanachi HP, mp, 1883, Lévêque; flowers dark rosy cerise, shaded and bordered lighter, well-formed, 45 petals, globular; profuse bloom, somewhat recurrent; [Victor Verdier × unknown]

Suzanne Meyer Pol, w, 1926, Walter, L.; flowers white shaded soft pink, center bright rose-pink, medium; medium growth; [Tausendschön × Rosel Dach]

Suzanne Michela HT, my, 1932, Chambard, C.; bud long, pointed; flowers pure chrome-yellow, very large, dbl., cupped; very vigorous growth; [Mme la Generale Ardouin × seedling]

Suzanne Miller Pol, mr, 1927, Wezelenburg; flowers clear bright cherry-red, medium, dbl., borne in clusters; low, bushy growth

Suzanne Turbat Pol, ob, 1919, Turbat; flowers coral-red, shaded shrimp-pink, medium, dbl., cupped, borne in clusters of 10-20; dwarf growth; [(Petit Constant × unknown) × seedling]

Suzanne Villain HT, pb, 1935, Ketten Bros.; flowers peach-blossom-pink suffused cherry-red, reverse salmon-pink, 60-65 petals; foliage rich green; vigorous, bushy growth; [(Rev. Williamson × Gorgeous) × Mrs John Bell]

Suzanne Wood HP, mp, 1869, Verdier, E.; flowers large, dbl.

Suzette van der Merwe HT, w; int. by J&P, 1994

Suzon LCl, pb, Eve; flowers blend of pink, apricot and yellow, 8 cm., semi-dbl., cupped, borne in large clusters, moderate sweet, musky fragrance; vigorous, very tall (to 8 m.), fast growth; [Kiftsgate × Joseph's Coat]; int. by Les Roses Anciennes de Andre Eve, 1994

Suzon Lotthé HT, pb, 1951, Meilland, F.; bud peach; flowers pearl-pink, flushed deeper toward edge, 4-5 in., 60 petals, high-centered, borne mostly singly, intense damask fragrance; recurrent; foliage dark; few prickles; very vigorous growth; [Peace × (Signora × Mrs John Laing)]; int. by C-P

Suzon Lotthé, Climbing Cl HT, pb, 1964, Trimper, K.; vigorous (10 ft.) growth; [sport of Suzon Lotthé]; int. by Ruston, 1964

Suzy Min, mp, 1991, Bridges, Dennis A.; bud pointed; flowers medium pink, near white at base blending to light pink, lightens slightly with age, medium, 38-40 petals, high-centered, borne singly or in sprays of 3-5, slight fragrance; foliage medium size, dark green, semi-glossy; bushy, medium growth; PP7738; [Party Girl × seedling]; int. by Bridges Roses, 1991; AOE, ARS, 1991

Suzy LCl, yb, Eve; flowers yellow to pale peach, 10 cm., dbl., cupped, quartered, borne in large clusters, moderate fruity fragrance; growth very tall (to 10 m.); int. by Les Roses Anciennes de Andre Eve, 1994

Suzy Q Min, mp, 1991, Warriner, William A. & Zary, Keith W.; bud ovoid; flowers medium shell pink, deeper color at petal margins, medium, 40-45 petals, cupped, no fragrance; foliage medium size, dark green, glossy; upright, bushy, medium growth; [Rose Hills Red × Baby Ophelia]; int. by Bear Creek Gardens/Jackson & Perkins, 1991

Svatopluk Cech LCl, dy, 1936, Brada, Dr.; bud buff; flowers orange-yellow, medium, full, intense fragrance; recurrent bloom; vigorous growth; int. by Böhm

Svaty Václav HT, w, 1936, Berger, A.; flowers white, center yellowish, large

Svensk Pimpinelle HSpn, w

Svetla Albena F, yb, 1986, Staikov, Prof. Dr. V.; flowers opening yellow orange, aging red, 85 petals, borne in large clusters; foliage dark; vigorous, upright growth; [Highlight × Masquerade]; int. by Kalaydjiev and Chorbadjiiski, 1974

Svetlana F, dy, Urban, J.

Svitani HT, my, Kavka

Svornost Pol, dr, 1935, Böhm, J.; flowers pure dark red, with fiery streaks, borne in large clusters; [sport of Orléans Rose]

Swagatam HT, ab, 1989, Patil, B.K.; flowers light pink, reverse apricot; [sport of Surkhab]; int. by K.S.G. Son's Roses, 1987

Swami HT, lp, 1979, Hardikar, Dr. M.N.; bud long, pointed; flowers 5 in., 100 petals, high-centered, moderate fragrance; very vigorous, upright growth; [Scarlet Knight × Festival Beauty]; int. in 1973

Swamp Rose – See ***R. palustris*** (Marshall)

Swamp Rose – See ***R. palustris scandens*** dbl.

Swan S, w, 1987, Austin, David; flowers white, tinged buff, reverse white, large, very dbl., rosette, borne usually singly or in small clusters, moderate fruity fragrance; repeat bloom; foliage large, light green, semi-glossy; prickles few, hooked, medium, brownish-red; upright, tall growth; no fruit; PP7564; [Charles Austin × (seedling × Iceberg)]; int. by David Austin Roses, 1987

Swan – See **Hakucho**, HT

Swan Lake LCl, w, 1968, McGredy, Sam IV; flowers white, center tinged pinkish, large, 50 petals, inbricated, borne in small clusters, slight fragrance; free-flowering; foliage dark green; vigorous (8 ft.) growth; [Memoriam × Gruss an Heidelberg]

Swansdown HT, w, 1928, Dickson, A.; bud large, long, pointed; flowers creamy white, center deeper cream, dbl., spiral; foliage olive-green; fairly vigorous growth

Swansong Min, w, 1988, McCann, Sean; flowers small, dbl., intense fragrance; foliage small, medium green, semi-glossy; bushy growth; [(Rise 'n' Shine × Party Girl) × Margaret Merril]

Swantje F, w, 1936, Tantau; flowers snow-white, 3 in., dbl., borne in clusters, slight fragrance; recurrent; foliage glossy, deep green; very vigorous, bushy growth; [Johanna Tantau × (Prof. Gnau × Joanna Hill)]

Swany S, w, 1977, Meilland, Mrs. Marie-Louise; bud ovoid; flowers pure white, large, 95 petals, cupped, slight fragrance; free-flowering; foliage glossy, bronze; very vigorous, spreading (2 × 6 ft.) growth; groundcover; [*R. sempervirens* × Mlle Marthe Carron]; int. by URS, 1977

Swany Folies F, w, Meilland; int. by Australian Roses, 2004

Swany Mimi HT, w, Meilland; flowers white with yellow tint in heart, dbl., high-centered, borne mostly singly; recurrent; int. by Meilland Intl., 2004

Swany River HT, w, 1982, Herholdt, J.A.; flowers large, dbl., moderate fragrance; foliage medium size, dark, semi-glossy; upright growth; [Pascali × seedling]

Swarthmore HT, pb, 1964, Meilland, Alain A.; bud pointed ovoid, with conspicuous neck; flowers blended shades of pink, petal edges will blacken in heat, 4 in., 45-55 petals, high-centered, borne mostly singly, slight tea fragrance; recurrent; foliage dark green, leathery; prickles several, reddish-brown; stems long, strong; vigorous, tall, bushy growth; PP2444; [(Independence × Happiness) × Peace]; int. by C-P, 1964

Swarthmore, Climbing Cl HT, pb, 1976, Thomas,

Dr. A.S.; [sport of Swarthmore]; int. by A. Ross & Son, 1973

Swashbuckle HT, or, Dawson; int. in 1990

Swati Pol, w, 1968, IARI; bud pointed; flowers white, edged deep pink, open, small, semi-dbl.; foliage dark, leathery; moderate, bushy growth; [Winifred Coulter × unknown]

Swedish Doll Min, op, 1976, Moore, Ralph S.; bud long, pointed; flowers bright coral pink, 1½ in., 22-28 petals, high-centered, then open, borne singly or several together in loose cluster, very slight fragrance; recurrent; foliage small, medium green, glossy, leathery; prickles normal, large, straight, angled slightly downward, brown; stems medium, sturdy, wiry; vigorous, upright, branched growth; PP4160; [Fire King × Little Buckaroo]; int. by Sequoia Nursery

Sweepstakes HT, op, 1977, McGredy, Sam IV; bud long, pointed; flowers coral-orange to salmon-pink, imbricated, 3½-5 in., 35 petals, high-centered, moderate fragrance; upright, spreading, bushy growth; PP4503; [Prima Ballerina × Ginger Rogers]; int. by Armstrong Nursery, 1978

Sweet Min, my, 1980, Lyon; bud long, pointed; flowers 50 petals, borne 1-3 per cluster; foliage tiny, glossy, deep green; prickles tiny, curved; compact, bushy growth; [seedling × seedling]; int. in 1979

Sweet HT, ob, Poulsen; int. in 1997

Sweet Min, mp, Poulsen; flowers medium pink, medium, dbl., no fragrance; foliage dark; growth bushy, 20-40 cm.; int. by Poulsen Roser, 1999

Sweet Adeline HT, mp, 1929, Joseph H. Hill, Co.; bud long, pointed; flowers rose-pink, large, semi-dbl.; [Rapture × Souv. de Claudius Pernet]

Sweet Adeline S, mp, Erskine, Robert; flowers soft pink, 20-40 petals, cupped, borne in clusters, moderate fragrance; non-remontant; durable (4-5 ft.) growth; winter hardy; [Will Alderman × Victory Year]

Sweet Afton HT, w, 1964, Armstrong, D.L. & Swim, H. C.; flowers near white, reverse pale pink, 4½-5 in., dbl., high-centered, intense sweet fragrance; recurrent; foliage dark green, leathery; tall (5 ft.), spreading, bushy growth; PP2654; [(Charlotte Armstrong × Signora) × (Alice Stern × Ondine)]; int. by Armstrong Nursery

Sweet Akito HT, mp, Tantau; flowers clean pink, slow opening, dbl., high-centered; [sport of Akito]; int. by Carlton Roses, 2004

Sweet Allison MinFl, rb, 1985, Jolly, Nelson F.; flowers orange-red shading to yellow or white, reverse cream, deeper, 35 petals; foliage medium size, medium green, semi-glossy; upright, bushy growth; [Bonny × (Tiki × seedling)]; int. by Rosehill Farm

Sweet Amazone HT, op

Sweet Amy HT, mp, 1999, Edwards, Eddie; flowers medium pink, reverse lighter, 4-5 in., full, borne mostly singly, intense fragrance; recurrent; foliage medium size, dark green, glossy; prickles moderate; upright, medium (5 ft.) growth; [Crystalline × Stainless Steel]; int. by Johnny Becnel Show Roses, 1999

Sweet and Low F, pb, 1962, Schwartz, Ernest W.; bud globular; flowers salmon-pink, center lighter, small, 36 petals, borne in large clusters; foliage glossy, bronze; compact, low growth; [Pinocchio × Sweet Fairy]; int. by Wyant, 1962

Sweet 'n' Pink HT, dp, 1976, Weeks; bud ovoid, pointed; flowers soft pink in heart, blending to deeper pink toward outer edges, 4-4½ in., 48 petals, high-centered, borne singly and in small clusters of 2-3, intense fragrance; free-flowering; foliage large, dark green, waxy; prickles numerous, medium, straight, brown; stems medium; upright, branching growth; PP4003; [(Prima Ballerina × seedling) × seedling]; int. by Weeks Wholesale Rose Growers

Sweet Anise Rose – See **Narcisse**, T

Sweet Arlene MinFl, m, 2001, Bennett, Dee; flowers very pale lavender, 2½-3 in., full, high-centered, borne in small clusters, intense fragrance; foliage medium size, medium green, semi-glossy; prickles moderate; growth upright, vigorous, medium (2½-3 ft.); garden, cutting, exhibition; [Lagerfeld × Ernie]; int. by Tiny Petals Nursery, 2002

Sweet Ballymaloe S, mp; int. by Hosford's Geraniums & Garden Center, 2001

Sweet Bouquet – See **Focus**, HMsk

Sweet Bouquet HT, lp, Burrows, Steven; int. by Burrows, 1996

Sweet Briar Queen F, mp, 1960, Schenkel; flowers rose-pink, 2 in., 45-50 petals, flat, borne in clusters, moderate fragrance; foliage maroon when young, leathery; vigorous, branching growth; PP2046; [sport of Rosemary]; int. by H.R. Schenkel, Inc.

Sweet Brier Rose – See ***R. rubiginosa*** (Linnaeus)

Sweet Butterfly Min, m, 1989, Laver, Keith G.; bud rounded; flowers mauve pink, pointed, open, loose, medium, 12-15 petals, flat, star-like, borne singly, intense fragrance; foliage medium size, medium green, matte; prickles short, pointed, beige; bushy, low growth; hips globular, yellow; [(Dwarfking × Baby Katie) × (Small Slam × Mountie)]; int. by Springwood Roses

Sweet Candia HT, pb, Meilland; flowers orchid pink, edged Neyron pink, dbl., cupped, borne mostly singly; recurrent; florist rose; int. by Meilland Intl., 1998

Sweet Caress F, mp, 1959, Boerner; bud ovoid; flowers rose-pink, large, 55-60 petals, moderate fragrance; foliage leathery, glossy; vigorous, upright growth; [Pigmy Red × Demure]; int. by J&P, 1959

Sweet Caroline Min, rb, 1998, Williams, Michael C.; flowers white with light to medium red on outer petals, 1½ in., dbl., high-centered, borne mostly singly, no fragrance; recurrent; foliage medium size, dark green, semi-glossy; prickles moderate, small; tall (28-36 in.), slightly spreading growth; [seedling × unknown]; int. by The Mini Rose Garden, 1999; AoE, ARS, 1999

Sweet Chariot Min, m, 1985, Moore, Ralph S.; bud small, ovoid to pointed; flowers lavender to purple blend, 1½ in., 55-60 petals, cupped, then rounded, borne in clusters of 5-20, intense fragrance; recurrent; foliage small, medium green, matte; prickles several, short, curved to straight, brown; stems slender, wiry; low (12 in.), spreading growth; hips few to none ; PP5975; [Little Chief × Violette]; int. by Moore Min. Roses, 1984

Sweet Chariot – See **Anjou Palace**, S

Sweet Charity HT, w, 1969, Park, F.; flowers waxy white, sometimes marked pink, medium, semi-dbl., moderate fragrance; recurrent; foliage dark, glossy; vigorous, upright growth; int. by Moulton-Jones, 1967

Sweet Chateau HT, lp, Teranishi; int. by Itami Rose Garden, 2002

Sweet Cheeks MinFl, yb, 2003, Strickland, Frank A.; flowers yellow blend, reverse yellow, 4 in., semi-dbl., high-centered, borne in small clusters, intense fragrance; foliage medium green, semi-glossy; prickles ¼ in., slight hook down, reddish brown; upright, medium (18 in.) growth; exhibition; [Little Darling × (Funkuhr × Funkuhr)]; int. by Rosemania, 2004

Sweet Cherry HT, mr, 1960, Dickson, A.; flowers cherry-red and yellow, large, high-centered; [Margaret × Karl Herbst]

Sweet Cover – See **Monticello**, S

Sweet Diana HT, lp; int. by Hortico, 1999

Sweet Diana Min, dy, 2001, Saville, F. Harmon; bud ovate; flowers deep yellow, medium yellow reverse, 1 in., 20 petals, high-centered, then flat, borne in small clusters, very slight fragrance; recurrent; foliage medium size, dark green, matte, disease-resistant; prickles few, 5/16 in., angled slightly down; growth bushy, medium (14-18 in.); borders, containers, exhibition, cutting; hips apple-shaped ; PP16797; [Cal Poly × June Laver]; int. by Nor'East Miniature Roses, 2002; Award of Excellence, ARS, 2002

Sweet Dream F, ab, 1988, Fryers Nursery, Ltd.; flowers peach-apricot, medium, dbl., globular, borne in clusters, moderate fragrance; free-flowering; foliage medium size, medium green, semi-glossy; low (18-24 in.), bushy growth; [seedling × seedling]; Rose of the Year, Roses UK, 1988, James Mason Gold Medal, RNRS & BRGA, 1998

Sweet Dreams HT, pb, 1976, Takatori, Yoshiho; bud long, pointed; flowers light pink, reverse deep pink, 6 in., 45-50 petals, high-centered, slight tea fragrance; foliage dark; vigorous, very upright growth; [JRN. No. 8 seedling × Royal Highness]; int. by Japan Rose Nursery, 1977

Sweet Dreams MinFl, lp; int. by J&P, 1995

Sweet Ecstasy S, m, 1999, Hintlian, Nancy Sears; flowers purple-crimson, turning more purple with age, 5 in., 41 petals, borne mostly singly, intense lasting fragrance; foliage large, dark green, semi-glossy; prickles moderate; upright, vigorous, medium (5 ft.) growth; [The Dark Lady × Oklahoma]

Sweet Fairy Min, lp, 1946, deVink; flowers soft pink, 1 in., 57 petals, cupped to rosette, moderate sweet fragrance; foliage small, dark; vigorous, dwarf (6-8 in.) growth; [Tom Thumb × seedling]; int. by C-P

Sweet Fragrance F, pb; int. by Treloar Roses, 1999

Sweet Frédérique S, pb, Interplant; int. by Rozenkwerkerij De Wilde Bussum, 1997

Sweet Freedom HT, w, Zary, Keith; bud long, pointed; flowers ivory, hint of green on outer petals, 4 in., 25-30 petals, cupped, borne mostly singly, moderate honeysuckle fragrance; recurrent; foliage dark green, glossy; stems 16-20 in.; growth to 5 ft.; PPAF; int. by Jackson & Perkins, 2006

Sweet Gesture F, mp, 1991, McGredy, Sam IV; bud small, pointed; flowers clear pink, 3-3½ in., 55-60 petals, high-centered, then flat, borne in clusters of 6-12, slight sweet fragrance; recurrent; foliage large, medium green, semi-glossy; prickles numerous, short, slightly hooked; upright, bushy (100 cm.) growth; PP9275; [(Sexy Rexy × New Year) × West Coast]; int. by McGredy Roses International, 1992

Sweet Hannah Min, my, Moore; flowers light yellow, changing to deeper yellow as it ages, 1½ in., full, cupped to rosette, borne singly and in small clusters, moderate fragrance; recurrent; foliage dark green, glossy; growth to 12-18 in.; int. in 1998

Sweet Harmony F, pb, 1962, Gaujard; flowers canary-yellow edged crimson-pink, large, 36 petals, borne in clusters, moderate spicy fragrance; free-flowering; foliage glossy, light green; vigorous (3 ft.) growth; [Peace × Masquerade]; int. by Gandy's Roses, Ltd., 1962

Sweet Haze S, lp, Tantau; flowers pale pink with

red stamens, single, flat, borne in clusters; heavy spring bloom; foliage disease-resistant; int. by Rosen Tantau, 2004

Sweet Heart Shelley HT, mr, 2005, Poole, Lionel; flowers 4½ in., full, borne mostly solitary, moderate fragrance; foliage medium size, medium green, semi-glossy; prickles medium, slightly hooked, brown, moderate; growth upright, medium (3 ft.); garden decoration, exhibition; [Red Planet × Raewyn Henry]; int. by David Lister (Roses), 2006

Sweet Home HT, dp, 1970, Meilland, Mrs. Marie-Louise; flowers carmine-lake with vermilion red reverse, large, 35 petals, high-centered to cupped, slight fruity fragrance; foliage large, leathery; vigorous growth; [(Jolie Madame × Baccará) × (Baccará × Jolie Madame)]; int. by URS

Sweet Home Alabama Min, pb, 1995, Taylor, Franklin; flowers magenta pink with white reverse, white eye, 1½ in., full, borne mostly singly; foliage medium size, medium green, semi-glossy; some prickles; upright, bushy, medium growth; [Party Girl × Azure Sea]; int. by Taylor's Roses, 1996

Sweet Honesty Min, w

Sweet Honey HT, ly, Kordes; bud slender; flowers honey-cream, dbl., high-centered, moderate sweet fragrance; recurrent; prickles very few; medium to tall growth; int. by W. Kordes Söhne, 1999

Sweet India HT, w, Tejganga; flowers creamy white, large, full, intense fragrance; free-flowering; [sport of Sweet Surrender]; int. by Tejganga Roses, 1996

Sweet Inspiration F, mp, 1991, Warriner, William A.; bud short, pointed ovoid; flowers medium pink with some cream coloration at petal base, 4 in., full, high-centered, then flat, borne in large clusters, slight fragrance; fast repeat; foliage medium size, medium green, matte; prickles few, hooked slightly downward; stems short; upright (85-100 cm.), bushy growth; PP8581; [Sun Flare × Simplicity]; int. by Bear Creek Gardens, 1993

Sweet Interlude HT, pb, 1990, Wambach, Alex A.; bud pointed; flowers white center with pink edging, large, slow opening, 32 petals, high-centered, borne singly, intense fragrance; foliage medium green, disease-resistant; prickles moderate, brown; upright, bushy, medium growth; [Pristine × Olympiad]; int. in 1989

Sweet Juliet S, ab, 1994, Austin, David; bud rounded with long cuspidate apex; flowers apricot-yellow, fading lighter, medium, 90 petals, cupped, borne singly and in small clusters, moderate sweet, fruity fragrance; recurrent; foliage medium size, medium green, semi-glossy; prickles some, 9 mm., reddish; upright, bushy (39 in.) growth; PP8153; [Graham Thomas × Admired Miranda]; int. by David Austin Roses, Ltd., 1989; Gold Medal Fragrance Award, Belfast, 1992

Sweet Keri HT, lp, 1988, Wilson, George D.; flowers light pale pink, large, 44 petals, high-centered, borne singly; foliage medium green, large; prickles triangular, red; medium, upright growth; [Judith Marten × Folklore]

Sweet Lady – See **The McCartney Rose**, HT

Sweet Lady – See **Sue Hipkin**, HT

Sweet Lara HT, m, 2004, Edwards, Eddie; flowers white to very pale lavender, deeper lavender highlights on petal edges, 5½ in., full, high-centered, borne mostly solitary, intense fragrance; recurrent; foliage medium size, dark green, semi-glossy; growth upright, medium (5 ft.); exhibition; [Crystalline × Barbra Streisand]; int. by K&M Nursery

Sweet Lavender HMult, pb, 1912, Paul; flowers blush, edged mauve, single, borne in large clusters

Sweet Lavinia HT, my, 1967, McTeer, F.; flowers high-centered, high-centered; foliage glossy; [Golden Scepter × Peace]; int. by G. McTeer

Sweet Lelanie HT, lp, 1967, Duehrsen; flowers light pink, base yellow, large, dbl., globular; foliage wrinkled, bronze; vigorous, upright growth; [Charlotte Armstrong × seedling]; int. by Elmer Roses Co.

Sweet Lemon Dream Min, ly; int. by Wharton's Nurseries, 2003

Sweet Little Queen – See **The Sweet Little Queen of Holland**, T

Sweet Love HT, mp, 1985, Rijksstation Voor Sierplantenteelt; flowers medium-large, 90 petals, flat, borne singly and in clusters of up to 7, no fragrance; foliage matte, dark; prickles red; upright growth; [Queen Elizabeth × Duke of Windsor]; int. in 1980

Sweet Magic Min, ob, 1987, Dickson, Patrick; flowers orange-gold, small, dbl., cupped, borne in clusters, slight sweet fragrance; recurrent; foliage small, medium green, glossy; bushy (15-18 in.) growth; [Peek A Boo × Bright Smile]; Rose of the Year, Roses UK, 1987

Sweet Maid HT, lp, 1950, Moss; bud pointed; flowers porcelain-pink, semi-dbl.

Sweet Mandarin Min, ob, 1979, Schwartz, Ernest W.; bud pointed; flowers light orange, small, 16 petals, flat, moderate fragrance; foliage small, soft; compact growth; [Sweet and Low × Gypsy Moth seedling]; int. by Bountiful Ridge Nursery, 1978

Sweet Marie Min, ob; flowers orange-yellow blend, semi-dbl.; free-flowering; foliage very glossy; low (10-14 in.) growth

Sweet Marvel Min, w, deRuiter

Sweet Meidiland S, lp, Meilland; flowers soft pink, small, semi-dbl., globular, borne in clusters; free-flowering; compact (3 ft.) growth; int. in 2003

Sweet Melina HT, Tantau; int. in 2002

Sweet Melody Min, ab, Fischer; flowers almost white with touch of apricot; medium to tall growth; [sport of Pierrine]; int. in 1998

Sweet Melody F, Leenders

Sweet Memorie HT, mp, 1937, Hieatt; flowers pink, base yellow, reverse purplish, large, semi-dbl., cupped; foliage leathery; vigorous growth; [Mrs C.W. Edwards × Rose Marie]

Sweet Memories – See **Summer Dream**, F

Sweet Memories MinFl, my, Whartons Roses; flowers lemon yellow, medium, full, cupped, borne in clusters, slight fragrance; recurrent; foliage light green; bushy growth; [sport of Sweet Dream]; int. by Whartons Nurseries Ltd., 1995

Sweet Memory F, lp, 1991, Yasuda, Yuji; bud pointed; flowers 4 in., 30 petals, high-centered, moderate fragrance; foliage medium size, medium green, matte; bushy, medium growth; [Hana-Gasumi × (Lady X × Paradise)]

Sweet Mimi HT, mp, 1982, Hauser, Victor; flowers large, 20 petals, moderate fragrance; foliage medium size, reddish green, semi-glossy; bushy growth; [Tropicana × Elizabeth Harkness]; int. by Roseraies Hauser, 1981

Sweet Moments HT, lp, Schreurs; int. by Australian Roses, 2004

Sweet Moon F, m, Teranishi; int. by Itami Rose Garden, 2002

Sweet Mystery Min, ob, 1987, Florac, Marilyn; flowers deep orange fading to pink, medium, 90 petals, cupped, borne usually singly, moderate damask fragrance; foliage medium size, dark green, semi-glossy; prickles few, green; bushy, medium growth; [Care Deeply × Red Can Can]

Sweet Nell F, ob, 1984, Cocker, Alexander M.; flowers orange, large, 35 petals; foliage medium size, medium green, semi-glossy; upright growth; [Anne Cocker × (Mischief × ((Sabine × Circus) × (Tropicana × Circus)))]; int. by Cocker & Sons, 1984

Sweet Nothings Min, m, 2001, Zary, Keith; bud short, pointed, ovoid; flowers deep lavender, 1½-2 in., 20-25 petals, cupped, borne in large clusters, moderate antique rose fragrance; free-flowering; foliage small, light green, glossy; prickles moderate, medium size, hooked downward; stems strong; vigorous, compact (2½ ft.) growth; garden decorative; hips very few; PP12995; [La Marne × lavender miniature seedling]; int. by J&P, 2002

Sweet Paillette – See **Sweet**, HT

Sweet Party – See **Sweet**, Min

Sweet Passion Tea, dp, 2003, Starnes, John A. Jr.; flowers magenta pink, reverse silvery pink, 4 in., very full, borne mostly solitary, intense citrus peel and old rose fragrance; very remontant; foliage medium size, medium green, semi-glossy; prickles few, tiny, straight bristles, beige; bushy, short (3 ft.) growth; specimen; [Duchesse de Brabant × Francis Dubreuil]; int. by John A. Starnes Jr., 1999

Sweet Pea Pol, m, 2006, Shoup, George Michael; flowers lavender and mauve, bright yellow stamens, 1-1½ in., full, borne in large clusters, moderate fragrance; remontant; foliage small, medium green, semi-glossy; prickles moderate; compact, short (2-3 ft.) growth; [Lavender Pink Parfait × Lavender Pink Parfait]; int. by Antique Rose Emporium, 1996

Sweet Perfume – See **Indian Summer**, HT

Sweet Perfumella HT, op, Meilland; int. by Australian Roses, 2004

Sweet Petite Min, mp, Fryer, Gareth; flowers salmon-pink; free-flowering; int. by Fryer's Roses, 1994

Sweet Pickins Min, lp, 1987, Bennett, Dee; flowers pale pink, medium, 35-40 petals, urn-shaped, borne usually singly, moderate fruity fragrance; foliage medium size, medium green, semi-glossy; prickles slender, straight, small, reddish; micro-mini upright, bushy, medium growth; hips globular, medium, brown; PP6788; [Futura × Party Girl]; int. by Tiny Petals Nursery

Sweet Prince HT, pb, 1984, Stoddard, Louis; flowers deep pink, petals edged medium red, 3½ in., 20 petals, borne singly, intense fragrance; foliage large, dark, matte; heavily prickled; bushy growth; [Honey Favorite × Granada]; int. in 1987

Sweet Promise – See **Sonia**, Gr

Sweet Promise, Climbing – See **Sonia, Climbing**, Cl Gr

Sweet Raspberry Min, dp, 1984, Jolly, Nelson F.; flowers deep purplish pink, small, 28 petals, urn-shaped to flat, slight fragrance; free-flowering; foliage small, medium green, matte; bushy growth; [Little Rascal × Cinderella]; int. by Rosehill Farm

Sweet Remembrance HT, my, Kirkham; flowers bright yellow, fading to cream primrose, golden stamens, semi-dbl. to dbl., flat, opens quickly; foliage glossy; strong, upright, medium growth; int. by Henry Street Nursery, 2003

Sweet Repose F, yb, 1956, deRuiter; bud medium, ovoid, with conspicuous neck; flowers maize-yellow tinged carmine, becoming carmine, 3-4 in., 23-28 petals, high-centered, to cupped, borne in large clusters, moderate sweet fragrance; recurrent; foliage dense, leathery, parsley-green; prickles numerous, medium, hooked downward; vigorous, upright, bushy growth; hips short, globular, smooth, fern green; PP1533; [Golden Rapture × unnamed Floribunda seedling]; int. by Gandy, 1955; Gold Medal, NRS, 1955

Sweet Repose, Climbing Cl F, yb

Sweet Revelation – See **Sue Hipkin**, HT

Sweet Revenge Min, ob, 1995, Bennett, Dee; flowers soft orange with blush of deep orange on outer petals, 2 in., 25 -35 petals, urn-shaped to cupped, borne mostly singly; recurrent; foliage medium size, dark green, semi-glossy; prickles moderate, slender, hooked slightly downward; tall (2-3 ft.), bushy growth; PP9776; [Tony Jacklin × Pucker Up]; int. by Tiny Petals Nursery, 1995

Sweet Rosamini Min, lp, deRuiter; int. in 1987

Sweet Saffron Min, my, 2003, Denton, James A.; flowers quilling to star shape, 1¾ in., full, borne mostly solitary, no fragrance; foliage large, dark green, glossy; prickles moderate, small, straight, red brown; upright, medium (20 in.) growth; garden/patio/exhibition; [Amber Sunset × Louis Desamero]; int. by James A Denton, 2003

Sweet Salmon F, Leenders

Sweet San Carlos F, m, 2006, Coiner, Jim; flowers medium, semi-dbl., borne in small clusters; foliage small, dark green, glossy; prickles ¼ in., triangle, red, moderate; growth compact, medium (3½ ft.); garden decorative; [seedling × seedling]; int. by Coiner Nursery, 2006

Sweet Scent Min, mp, 1993, Rennie, Bruce F.; flowers medium, full, moderate fragrance; foliage small, medium green, semi-glossy; few prickles; medium, upright growth; [Party Girl × Silver Phantom]; int. by Rennie Roses International, 1994

Sweet Sensation – See **Liebeslied**, F

Sweet Seventeen HT, lp, 1923, Clark, A.; flowers semi-dbl.; foliage light, wrinkled; bushy, dwarf growth; [Frau Karl Druschki × Bardou Job]; int. by NRS Victoria

Sweet Seventeen Gr, mp, 1960, Leenders, J.; flowers pink, small; vigorous growth; [Fred Howard × Cocorico]

Sweet Shaddow HT, mr, 1963, Barter; flowers scarlet, edged darker, 4½ in., 22 petals; foliage dark; vigorous growth; [Queen Elizabeth × Étoile de Hollande]

Sweet Shadow HT, dr, 1965, Barter; flowers vivid scarlet, almost black edged, petals reflexed, borne mostly singly, moderate sweet fragrance; foliage large, dark green

Sweet Shirley Min, mp, 1991, Clements, John K.; flowers medium pink, lighter reverse, medium, dbl., high-centered, borne mostly singly, slight fragrance; foliage small, medium green, semi-glossy; some prickles; bushy (40 cm.), spreading growth; [Tweedle Dee × seedling]; int. by Heirloom Old Garden Roses, 1991

Sweet Shot HT, mp, deRuiter; int. by deRuiters New Roses Intl., 2001

Sweet Sixteen F; PP3585

Sweet Sixteen HT, pb, 1943, Lammerts, Dr. Walter; bud long, pointed; flowers salmon-pink, base yellow, 4-5 in., 16-20 petals, intense fragrance; vigorous, upright, bushy growth; [Mrs Sam McGredy × Pres. Herbert Hoover]; int. by Armstrong Nursery

Sweet Sixteen S, ab, Clements, John; flowers soft pink blended with soft peach, golden stamens, 4 in., 70 petals, borne in clusters, moderate peach fragrance; foliage crimson red when new, maturing to rich, leathery green; upright (4 × 3 ft.) growth; PPAF; int. by Heirloom Roses, 2002

Sweet Sonata – See **Johann Strauss**, F

Sweet Song F, mp, 1971, Meilland; flowers 4½ in., 35 petals, moderate fruity fragrance; bushy growth; [Fidélio × Bettina]

Sweet Success Gr, lp, Pottschmidt

Sweet Sue HT, op, 1940, Lammerts, Dr. Walter; bud long, pointed, flame to blood-red; flowers coral-pink, stamens maroon, single, cupped, moderate spicy fragrance; vigorous growth; [Joanna Hill × Night]; int. by Armstrong Nursery

Sweet Sue Min, lp, 1979, Bennett, Dee; bud ovoid; flowers very small, 13 petals, high-centered, borne in clusters of 10-25; foliage small, dark; bushy growth; [Pink Ribbon × Pink Ribbon]; int. by Tiny Petals Nursery

Sweet Sultan Cl HT, dr, 1959, Eacott; flowers crimson shaded maroon, 4 in., 5 petals, borne in trusses, intense fragrance; recurrent; vigorous, pillar growth; [Independence × Honour Bright]; int. by LeGrice Roses, 1958

Sweet Sunblaze – See **Pink Symphony**, Min

Sweet Sunsation S, lp, Kordes; flowers soft pink, fading with age, large, semi-dbl.; spreading, bushy growth

Sweet Sunshine Min, my, 1982, Moore, Ralph S.; flowers small, 20 petals, intense fragrance; foliage small, medium green, semi-glossy; upright, bushy growth; [Rumba × Yellow Jewel]; int. by Moore Min. Roses, 1981

Sweet Surrender HT, mp, 1982, Weeks, O.L.; bud pointed; flowers medium silvery pink, large, 40 petals, cupped, borne usually singly, intense tea fragrance; recurrent; foliage dark green, leathery; stems long, strong; medium to tall growth; [seedling × Tiffany]; int. by Weeks Wholesale Rose Growers, 1983

Sweet Symphony – See **Debut**, Min

Sweet Talk F, ly, 1964, Swim & Weeks; flowers lemon to white, dbl., borne in clusters, moderate fragrance; foliage light green, leathery; low, uniform., bushy growth; PP2542; [Frolic × Lavender Pinocchio]; int. by Weeks Wholesale Rose Growers

Sweet Tangela MinFl, yb, 2002, Giles, Diann; flowers yellow/pink, medium, full, borne in large clusters, slight fragrance; foliage medium size, medium green, matte; growth upright, low, garden, exhibition; [seedling × seedling]; int. by Giles Rose Nursery, 2001

Sweet Thoughts HT, lp, 1965, Cant, F.; flowers 5 in.; vigorous growth; [Kordes' Perfecta × Show Girl]

Sweet Twilight Cl HT, ly, 1954, Motose; flowers buff-yellow, center darker, 4-5½ in., 25 petals, high-centered, moderate fruity fragrance; abundant, recurrent bloom; vigorous (15-30 ft.) growth; PP1343; [sport of Tawny Gold]

Sweet Unique HT, pb, deRuiter; bud large, soft pink; flowers medium pink, edges darker, reverse lighter, dbl., high-centered, borne mustly singly; good repeat; stems long; florist rose; int. by deRuiter New Roses Intl.

Sweet Valentine Gr, mp, 2000, Zary, Keith; bud long, pointed ovoid; flowers warm pink, 5 in., 30-35 petals, high-cent., then flattens, borne singly and in large, open clusters, moderate spicy peach fragrance; recurrent; foliage large, dark green, glossy; prickles moderate, medium size, hooked slightly downward; stems strong, 12-16 in.; upright, medium (5 ft.) growth; PP12121; [Brandy × Tournament of Roses]; int. by Bear Creek Gardens, 2001; Gold Medal, Baden-Baden, 2000

Sweet Valentine Min, dr, Benardella, Frank; flowers deep, velvety red, classic hybrid tea form; free-flowering; medium, bushy growth

Sweet Velvet F, mr, 1969, Martin, J.; flowers velvety scarlet, large, dbl., hybrid tea, moderate sweet fragrance; foliage small, leathery, glossy; moderate growth; [Leverkusen × S'Agaro]; int. by Gandy Roses, Ltd.

Sweet Vibes F, lp, 1999, Giles, Diann; flowers medium, dbl., borne in small clusters; foliage medium size, medium green, glossy; few prickles; compact, medium growth; [Sun Flare × Simplicity]; int. by Giles Rose Nursery, 1999

Sweet Vigorosa – See **Neon**, F, 2006

Sweet Vivid Min, pb; flowers pink, yellow center, well-formed, dbl.; vigorous growth

Sweet Vivien F, pb, 1963, Raffel; bud ovoid; flowers pink, center white and light yellow, 3 in., 17 petals, shallow cup to flat, borne in clusters, slight honey/spice fragrance; recurrent; foliage small, dark, glossy; stems short; very compact, bushy growth; large, pear-shaped fruit; [Little Darling × Odorata]; int. by Port Stockton Nursery, 1963

Sweet Wonder MinFl, ab; flowers apricot-orange-peachy-pink, full, pompon, borne in clusters, slight fragrance; good repeat; foliage glossy; upright (2 ft.) growth; int. in 1999

Sweetbriar – See ***R. rubiginosa*** (Linnaeus)

Sweetcorn Min, yb, Hannemann, F.; int. by The Rose Paradise, 1991

Sweetheart HWich, w, 1901, Walsh; bud rose-pink; flowers white with faint blush to medium, 2½ in., very dbl., borne in clusters of 10-15, moderate fragrance; foliage small, glossy, dark; vigorous, climbing growth; RULED EXTINCT 4/80; [*R. wichurana* × Bridesmaid]

Sweetheart HT, mp, 1980, Cocker, James; bud ovoid; flowers rose pink, yellow base, 52 petals, imbricated, borne singly, moderate fragrance; recurrent; foliage large, medium green, semi-glossy; vigorous, upright (2½-3 ft.) growth; [Peer Gynt × (Fragrant Cloud × Gay Gordons)]; Fragrance Award, Belfast, 1982

Sweetheart Rose – See **Mlle Cécile Brünner**, Pol

Sweetheart Rose,Climbing – See **Mlle Cécile Brünner, Climbing**, Cl Pol

Sweetie – See **Peach Clementine**, Min

Sweetie Pie HT, lp, 1970, Hyde; flowers light pink, outer edges darker; [sport of Swarthmore]; int. by House of Roses, 1971

Sweetie Pie Min, dp, Bell; flowers carmine pink with salmon tonings, full, flat; medium growth; int. by Bell Roses

Sweetlips Minijet Min, mp, Meilland

Sweetness HT, mp, 1919, McGredy; flowers intense rose-pink, shaded scarlet, well-formed

Sweetness HT, ab, 1937, Dickson, A.; bud long, pointed; flowers apricot-yellow shaded pink, spiral, reflexed petals, large, dbl.; foliage glossy; very vigorous growth; Gold Medal, NRS, 1935

Sweetnesse HT, mp, Tantau; int. by Rosen Tantau, 1995

Sweetwaters HT, op, 1988, McGredy, Sam IV; flowers medium salmon-pink, large, full, slight fragrance; foliage large, dark green, glossy; upright, tall, very big growth; [((Sympathie × Red Lion) × Pharaoh) × (Tombola × (Elizabeth of Glamis × ((Circus × Golden Fleece) × Ferry Porsche)))]; int. by McGredy Roses International, 1986

Swet Sultain – See **Sweet Sultan**, Cl HT

Swift S, w, Poulsen; flowers white, 5-8 cm., full, slight wild rose fragrance; foliage dark, glossy; groundcover; low (1-1½ ft.) growth; int. in 1992

Swing F, lp, 1993, Ilsink, G.P.; flowers cream pink, medium, dbl., borne in sprays; foliage medium size, dark green, glossy; few prickles; medium (60 cm.), upright growth; int. by Interplant B.V., 1990

Swinger Min, my, 1984, Jolly, Nelson F.; flowers 35 petals, high-centered, borne usually singly, slight fragrance; recurrent; foliage medium size, medium green, semi-glossy; prickles moderate, slightly hooked; spreading growth; hips globular ; PP6560; [Rise 'n' Shine × Puppy Love]; int. by Rosehill Farm

Swinging Sixties F, yb; int. in 1995

Swingtime F, rb, 1965, Morgan; bud pointed; flowers crimson, reverse buff-white, medium, full, cupped, moderate sweetbriar fragrance; vigorous, upright growth; PP2331; [Little Darling × (Red Pinocchio × Masquerade)]; int. by Carlton Rose Nurseries, 1963

Swisa – See **White Satin**, HT

Swiss Bliss Min, my, 1988, Lemrow, Dr. Maynard W.; flowers aging lighter, decorative, small, 45-50 petals, borne singly or in sprays of 3-5; foliage small, medium green, matte, serrated; prickles reddish-brown; upright, bushy, medium growth; [Anytime × seedling]

Swiss Fire HT, or, 1979, Huber; bud globular, flowers orange-red; flowers 4-4½ in., 50 petals; foliage dark; upright growth; [Fragrant Cloud × Ena Harkness]; int. in 1975

Swiss Gold – See **Schweizer Gold**, HT, 1975 dbl.

Swiss Lass Min, rb, 1987, Lemrow, Dr. Maynard W.; flowers red, reverse almost all white, medium, very dbl.; foliage small, medium green, semi-glossy; upright growth; [seedling × seedling]

'Swonderful F, yb, 1999, Schakelford, Grace; flowers yellow-orange, reverse lighter, similar to Little Darling, 1½ in., full, high-centered, borne in small clusters, moderate fragrance; foliage small, dark green, glossy; prickles moderate; upright, medium (4 ft.); patio growth; [Pink Petticoat × Redgold]; int. in 1998

Sword of Hope HT, mr, 1964, Von Abrams; bud long, pointed; flowers 5-6 in., 45 petals, high-centered; foliage glossy; vigorous, upright growth; int. by Peterson & Dering

Sybil HT, op, 1921, Bees; bud long, pointed; flowers silvery salmon-rose, center orange-salmon, very dbl., moderate fragrance; [Sunburst × Mary, Countess of Ilchester]

Sybil Hipkin HT, dy, Dawson; flowers deep bright yellow, dbl., cupped, borne singly and in small clusters, moderate fragrance; recurrent; stems long; upright growth; int. in 1978

Sybil Thorndike HT, mr, 1976, Kordes; flowers full, 5 in., 25 petals; foliage dark; [Liebeszauber × seedling]; int. by Harry Wheatcroft Gardening

Sydney HP, mp, 1908, Moore, A.K.; [sport of Prince Camille de Rohan]

Sydney HCh, mp, 1978, Svedja, Felicitas; bud ovoid; flowers phlox-pink, 3-3½ in., 20 petals, cupped, intense fragrance; foliage rugose, yellow-green; bushy, spreading growth; [Old Blush × Dagmar Hastrup]; int. by Canada Dept. of Agric., 1977

Sydonie – See **Sidonie**, HP

Sydonie Dorizy B, op, 1846, Dorizy; flowers peach pink, aging to red, shaded lilac, medium

Sylph T, w, 1895, Paul, W.; flowers white tinted with peach, large, high-centered

Sylphide F, dp

Sylphide HGal, w; flowers white with pink edges; probably extinct

Sylt HKor, dr, 1982, Kordes, W.; flowers bright crimson, medium, semi-dbl., slight fragrance; recurrent; foliage medium size, dark, glossy; spreading growth; hips long, orange-red; [*R.* × *kordesii* × seedling]; int. in 1981

Sylvaine HT, lp

Sylvan Sunset HT, pb, 1980, Taylor, Thomas E.; bud pointed; flowers 28 petals, high-centered; foliage medium green, semi-glossy; prickles hooked; vigorous, upright, tall, bushy growth; [Swarthmore × First Prize]

Sylvana HT, w, Huber

Sylvander S, my, Preston, Isabella; flowers clear yellow, large, single; dwarf (2-3 ft.) growth; [*R.* × *harisonii* × unknown]; int. by Agriculture Canada

Sylvanus Thompson HT, mr, 2002, Poole, Lionel; flowers brilliant red, 5½ in., very full, high-centered, borne mostly solitary, slight fragrance; foliage large, dark green, semi-glossy; prickles large, slightly hooked down, moderate; growth upright, bushy, medium (3 ft.); garden decorative, exhibition, bedding; [(Gavotte × Spirit of the Heath) × Mike Thompson)]; int. by David Lister Roses, 2003

Sylvia – See **Silvia**, D

Sylvia HWich, ly, 1911, Paul, W.; flowers pale lemon-yellow, passing to white, dbl.; moderate growth

Sylvia HT, my, 1949, Foster; flowers buttercup-yellow, 25 petals, moderate fruity fragrance; RULED EXTINCT 1/79; [sport of Golden Gleam]

Sylvia – See **Congratulations**, HT

Sylvia Dot F, lp, 1970, Dot, Simon; bud pointed; flowers salmon, medium, 30 petals, high-centered; foliage glossy, bronze; upright, dense growth; [Queen Elizabeth × Orient]; int. by Minier, 1965

Sylvia Groen HT, pb, 1935, Groen; flowers coral-rose, shaded crimson; vigorous, upright growth; [sport of Pres. Herbert Hoover]

Sylvia Louise HT, op, 1980, Shaw, H.C.W.; flowers pink and orange blend; foliage glossy; [Ena Harkness, Climbing × unknown]; int. in 1973

Sylvie Briant HT, op

Sylvie Leblanc F, w

Sylvie Vartan Pol, mp, Eve; flowers bright pink, 8 cm., dbl., borne in clusters, slight fragrance; recurrent; foliage dark green, healthy; bushy (70-100 cm.) growth; int. by Les Roses Anciennes de Andre Eve, 1968

Sylvor HT, Croix; int. in 1971

Symbol F, mr

Symbol Miru HWich, w, 1937, Böhm, J.; flowers lemon yellow, fading to white, 6-8 cm., dbl., borne singly or in small clusters, moderate fragrance

Symbole S, mr, 1945, Robichon; bud thick, pointed; flowers carmine, well-shaped, very large; long, strong stems; vigorous growth; [Mev. G.A. van Rossem × Roseraie de l'Hay]; int. by Vilmorin-Andrieux

Symmetry HP, mr, 1910, Paul, G.; [Mrs John Laing × unknown]

Sympathie HKor, mr, 1964, Kordes, R.; flowers velvety dark red, opens quickly, 9 cm., dbl., high-centered, borne in small clusters, intense fragrance; some repeat; foliage glossy, dark; very vigorous (9-12 ft.) growth; [Wilhelm Hansmann × Don Juan]; int. by Kordes, 1964; ADR, 1966

Symphonette Min, pb, 1974, Morey, Dennison; bud ovoid; flowers light pink, reverse deep pink, small, dbl., moderate fragrance; foliage small, glossy, leathery; vigorous, dwarf, bushy growth; [Cécile Brunner × Cinderella]; int. by Pixie Treasures Min. Roses, 1973

Symphonie HT, pb, 1951, Meilland, F.; bud pointed, ovoid to globular; flowers shades of pink, broad petals, veined carmine-pink, 4½-5 in., 25 petals, high-centered, moderate fragrance; recurrent; foliage glossy, leathery; vigorous, upright, bushy growth; [Peace × (Signora × Mrs John Laing)]; int. by C-P; Gold Medal, NRS, 1949

Symphonie, Climbing Cl HT, pb, Elmer's Nursery; [sport of Symphonie]

Symphonie Lumiere Min, yb, Meilland

Symphonie No. 1 Min, mp, Meilland; int. by Rosas Hisaki

Symphonie No. 3 Min, ob, Meilland; int. by Rosas Hisaki

Symphony HP, lp, 1935, Weigand, C.; bud long, pointed; flowers large, dbl., cabbagy, moderate fragrance; recurrent; foliage leathery, dark; [Frau Karl Druschki × Souv. de Claudius Pernet]; int. by P.J. Howard

Symphony S, ly, 1994, Austin, David; flowers soft yellow, deeper in center, 3-4 in., very dbl., rosette, borne in small clusters, slight spicy fragrance; recurrent; foliage medium size, light green, glossy; medium (120 cm.), upright, bushy growth; [The Friar × Yellow Cushion]; int. by David Austin Roses, Ltd., 1986

Syr S, dr, 1978, Lundstad; bud pointed, ovoid; flowers 4 in., 23 petals, high-centered, borne in small clusters, slight fragrance; recurrent; foliage glossy, dark; very vigorous, upright (5-7 ft.) growth; [Stadt Rosenheim × Sangerhausen]; int. by Agricultural University of Norway, 1977

Syracuse HT, mr, 1930, Mallerin, C.; bud crimson; flowers scarlet-crimson, large, dbl.; foliage dark, leathery; vigorous growth; [Mme G. Forest-Colcombet × Aspirant Maumejean]; int. by C-P

Syrikit HT, Mondial Roses; int. in 1969

Syringa HWich, w, 1931, Browning; flowers medium to large, 4-5 cm., single, borne in clusters of 5-20

Syrius HGal, mp, before 1836, Coquerel; flowers glossy carmine, large, full

Syvdal S, dp, Olsen, Aksel; hips large, bottle-shaped, orange-red; hybrid of *R. davidii*; int. in 1960

T. B. McQuesten F, ab

T. F. Crozier HT, dy, 1918, Dickson, H.; flowers deep canary-yellow, fading to white, dbl., high-centered

T. V. Times HT, dr, 1970, Dickson, A.; flowers crimson, ovate, 5½ in., 35 petals; foliage very large, dull; very free growth; [Gallant × (Brilliant × seedling)]

T. W. Girdlestone HP, mr, 1891, Dickson, A.; flowers glossy vermilion-red, shaded salmon red, very large, full

Ta Nase Pisnicka Ceska Pol, mp, 1938, Böhm, J.; flowers small, dbl.

Ta Ta Min, mp, 1989, Williams, Ernest D.; flowers small, 33 petals, no fragrance; foliage small, medium green, semi-glossy, dense; bushy growth; [Tom Brown × Over the Rainbow]; int. in 1988

Tabarin F, mp, 1956, Gaujard; bud oval; flowers salmon-pink flushed yellow and copper-orange to red, 3-4 in., semi-dbl.; foliage light green; vigorous, bushy growth; [Opera × Masquerade]

Tabatha HT, pb, 2005, Edwards, Eddie & Phelps, Ethan; flowers blush pink with deeper pink edges, 5 in., very full, high-centered, borne mostly solitary; foliage medium size, dark green, glossy; prickles medium, hooked; growth upright, tall (5 ft.); exhibition; [Gemini × White Success]; int. by Johnny Becnel Show Roses, 2005

Table Mountain HT, pb; flowers white center, pink petal edges, and green on reverse, dbl., high-centered; recurrent; growth 5 × 4 ft.; int. by Kordes, 1990

Table Queen HT, ob, Williams, J.B.; flowers deep orange, very dbl., high-centered; int. by Hortico, 2003

Tablers' Choice F, rb, 1974, Harkness; flowers deep red, yellow reverse, 4 in., 38 petals; foliage glossy; [(Ann Elizabeth × Allgold) × (Tropicana × Piccadilly)]

Taboo HT, dr, 1993, Evers, Hans & Rosen Tantau; bud pointed, ovoid, almost black; flowers deepest red, velvety, 4-5 in., 25-30 petals, high-centered, borne mostly singly, moderate sweet citrus fragrance; recurrent; foliage large, dark green, semi-glossy; prickles some, large, hooked downward; stems long, strong; tall (170 cm.), upright, bushy growth; PP7665; [seedling × seedling]; int. by Bear Creek Gardens, 1994

Tabris – See **Hannah Gordon**, F

Tabriz HT, lp, 1986, Kriloff, Michel; flowers soft pink, petals quill, large, dbl., high-centered; recurrent; few prickles; [Belle Epoque × seedling]

Tache de Beauté F, op, 1986, Lens, Louis; flowers 2 in., 22 petals, high-centered, borne in clusters of 3-24; foliage dark; prickles hooked, brown; upright, bushy growth; [Little Angel × Picasso]; int. in 1982

Tackholmii S, mp, before 1922; flowers pink, solitary or few; early flowering; vigorous, erect, shrub growth

Tacoma HT, ab, 1921, Chervenka; bud long, pointed; flowers flaming apricot, dbl.; [Mme Butterfly × Honeymoon]

Taconis F, or, 1968, deRuiter; flowers orange-scarlet, borne in trusses; foliage glossy; vigorous growth; [Ruth Leuwerik × City of Nottingham]; Gold Medal, Baden-Baden, 1968

Taffeta HT, pb, 1947, Lammerts, Dr. Walter; bud urn-shaped; flowers pink-yellow blend, 3-3½ in., 20 petals, moderate fragrance; foliage leathery, glossy, bronze-green; vigorous, upright growth; [Mrs Sam McGredy × Pres. Herbert Hoover]; int. by Armstrong Nursery

Taffeta, Climbing Cl HT, pb, 1954, Armstrong, J.A.; int. by Weeks Roses

Taffeta Cl Min, w, Warner, Chris; flowers pure white, quartered, moderate fragrance; recurrent; int. in 1997; Gold Star of the South Pacific, Palmerston North, NZ, 1997

Taffy Min, yb, 1988, Baker, Larry; flowers soft, pastel butter yellow, tipped light pink, reverse pure pink, 33 petals, high-centered; foliage small, medium green, matte; prickles nearly straight, small, light brown; growth bushy, low, compact, full; [seedling × seedling]

Taft Rose HT, op, before 1911; flowers salmon-pink, shaded with chrome-yellow; [Kaiserin Auguste Viktoria × Mme Cusin]

Tag-a-long Min, rb, 1992, Moore, Ralph S.; flowers contrast of reddish-lavender against white, large, semi-dbl., borne in small clusters, no fragrance; recurrent; foliage medium size, medium green, new bronze, matte; few prickles; medium (30-40 cm.), upright, bushy growth; [(Little Darling × Yellow Magic) × Make Believe]; int. by Sequoia Nursery, 1993

Tagore F, my, 1955, Maarse, G.; flowers yellow-ochre, reverse shaded orange, borne in clusters; compact growth; [Pinocchio × unknown]

Tahiti HT, yb, 1947, Meilland, F.; flowers amber-yellow suffused carmine, 6 in.; foliage glossy, dark; [Peace × Signora]

Tahitian Moon S, ly, Ping Lim; flowers soft, pale yellow, center darker, 2 in., very full, cupped, quartered, borne in clusters; foliage glossy, dark green; growth low in cool climates, 6 ft. and more in warm zones; PP16994; int. by Bailey Nurseries, 2004

Tahitian Sunset HT, ab, 2007, Zary, Keith W.; bud pointed ovoid; flowers apricot yellow with pink blend, 5 in., 25-30 petals, blooms borne mostly solitary, intense licorice fragrance; recurrent; foliage medium size, dark green, semi-glossy; prickles few, 8-10 mm., hooked downward, greyed-orange; upright, tall (5 ft.) growth; [seedling × Sun Goddess]; int. by Jackson & Perkins Wholesale, Inc., 2006

Tahore HT, mp, 1958, Buyl Frères; flowers rose, large, 45-50 petals, high-centered; foliage glossy; strong stems; vigorous, upright growth; [Peace × seedling]

Tai-Gong F, or, 1976, Kordes; bud long, pointed; flowers orange to red, large, 28 petals, high-centered; foliage glossy, dark; vigorous, upright growth; [Klaus Stortebeker × seedling]; int. in 1974

Taïcoun HRg, mp, before 1872

Taifun – See **Typhoon**, HT

Taifun – See **Typhoon**, F

Taiga F, mp, 1972, Tantau, Math.; bud globular; flowers pink, medium, dbl.; vigorous, upright growth; [Geisha × Junior Miss]

Taiga HT, rb, Tantau; int. in 2003

Taihape Sunset HT, ob, Kordes; flowers orange, backed with yellow, dbl.; recurrent; medium to tall growth; int. in 1987

T'Aime HT, Shinoda, D. S. & Umeda, G. Y.; PP3960

Taischa HT, m, Robinson; flowers blend of various mauve shades, quilled, full, flat, moderate fragrance; recurrent; [Rêve d'Or × Lavender Pinocchio]; int. by Vintage Gardens, 1989

Taj Mahal HT, dp, 1972, Armstrong, D.L.; bud medium, ovoid; flowers deep pink, 5-6 in., 45-50 petals, high-centered, cupped, borne mostly singly, moderate fragrance; recurrent; foliage large, leathery, olive green; prickles several, hooked slighty downward, reddish brown; vigorous, upright, bushy growth; hips globular, strong yellow; PP3314; [Manitou × Grand Slam]; int. by Armstrong Nursery

Takao HT, yb, 1986, Okamoto, K.; flowers deep yellow, aging scarlet, medium, 33 petals, high-centered, borne usually singly, moderate damask fragrance; recurrent; foliage medium size, medium green; prickles deep brown; medium, bushy growth; [(Masquerade × Lydia) × (Montezuma × Miss Ireland)]; int. by K. Hirakata Nursery, 1975

Takapuna Min, op, 1978, McGredy, Sam IV; flowers light peach-pink, medium, 37 petals; tall, spreading growth; [New Penny × ((Clare Grammerstorf × Cavalcade) × Elizabeth of Glamis)]; int. by McGredy Roses International

Takatori Prominent F, op, 1981, Takatori, Yoshiho; flowers orange-salmon; [sport of Prominent]; int. by Japan Rose Nursery

Talia S, Barni, V.; int. in 1990

Talisman HT, yb, 1929, Montgomery Co.; bud pointed; flowers golden yellow and copper, medium, 25 petals, cupped to flat, moderate fruity, clove fragrance; recurrent; foliage light green, leathery, glossy; vigorous growth; [Ophelia × Souv. de Claudius Pernet]; John Cook Medal, ARS, 1932, Gertrude M. Hubbard, ARS, 1929

Talisman, Climbing Cl HT, yb, 1930, Western Rose Co. (also Dixie, 1932); flowers scarlet red and golden yellow, medium, semi-dbl., very fragrance; [sport of Talisman]

Talisman No. 5 HT, yb; flowers deeper color; free bloom

Tall Poppy – See **Linda Campbell**, HRg

Tall Story F, my, 1984, Dickson, Patrick; flowers soft primrose yellow, medium, semi-dbl., shallow cup to flat, borne in clusters; free-flowering; foliage medium size, light green, glossy; low, spreading growth; [Sunsprite × Yesterday]; int. by Dickson Nurseries, Ltd.

Tallulah HT, yb, 1983, Bees; flowers gold with deep pink petal edges, large, 20 petals, cupped; foliage medium size, dark, semi-glossy; bushy growth; [Astral × Piccadilly]

Tallyho HT, dp, 1948, Swim, H.C.; bud urn-shaped; flowers deep pink, 3½-4 in., 35 petals, high-centered, intense spicy fragrance; recurrent; foliage leathery; vigorous, upright, bushy growth; [Charlotte Armstrong × seedling]; int. by Armstrong Nursery; David Fuerstenberg Prize, ARS, 1951

Tallyho, Climbing Cl HT, dp, 1952, Armstrong, J.A.; int. by Armstrong Nursery

Tam o'Shanter F, yb, 1969, Cocker; flowers yellow and red, dbl., borne in clusters; low, compact growth; [Orange Sensation × Circus]

Tam Tam F, my, 1961, Boerner; bud ovoid; flowers yellow flushed pink, 3 in., 35-40 petals, cupped, moderate fragrance; foliage glossy; vigorous, upright growth; PP2181; RULED EXTINCT 1/88; [(Goldilocks × unknown) × Demure seedling]; int. by J&P, 1961

Tam-Tam Min, lp, 1988, Onodera, Toru F.; flowers inner petals upright, 18-20 petals, flat, borne in large clusters; foliage small, light green; hips elongated, orange; [(Nozomi × Nozomi) × Bo-Peep]

Tama HT, op, 1989, Sato, Kohi; bud pointed; flowers salmon-pink, fringed with pink, reverse creamy yellow, large, 35 petals, high-centered, urn-shaped, borne in sprays of 2 or 3, slight fragrance; foliage dark green; prickles small, lower part hollow; upright, tall growth; [Red Lion × Garden Party]

Tamango F, dr, 1967, Meilland, Mrs. Marie-Louise; flowers rose red with crimson shading, large, 35 petals, cupped, borne in large clusters, slight fragrance; free-flowering; foliage clear green; vigorous, free growth;

PP2857; [(Alain × Mutabilis) × (Radar × Caprice)]; int. by Wheatcroft Bros.

Tamango F, dr, Olij; flowers full, cupped, borne in clusters; recurrent; int. in 1998

Tamango Folies – See **Tamango**, F full

Tamara HT, mr, 1969, Mondial Roses; flowers geranium-red, dbl., high-centered; foliage dark; very vigorous growth; [Parel van Aalsmeer × Independence]; int. by Station Experimentale de Roses de Coninck Dervaes, 1966

Tamara F, ab, Kordes; flora-tea; int. in 1988

Tamarisk HT, mp, 1954, Ratcliffe, R. & E.; flowers clear rose-pink, camellia-like, intense fragrance; foliage leathery, dull green; very vigorous growth; [Mme Butterfly × Signora]

Tamayuru HT, ob, Hiroshima; int. by Hiroshima Bara-en, 2002

Tambourine F, rb, 1959, Dickson, A.; flowers cherry-red, base yellow, reverse light burnt-orange, large, 25 petals, borne in clusters, slight fragrance; foliage dark, veined; vigorous, tall, bushy growth; [(Independence × unknown) × Karl Herbst]; int. by Dickson & Sons, 1958

Tambourine F, ob; flowers golden orange, outer petals turning reddish-orange, medium, dbl., cupped, borne in clusters, slight fragrance; recurrent; vigorous, rounded (3 ft.) growth; int. by Harkness, 1998

Tammy Pol, lp, 1974, Byrum (possibly Sweet, Jack); flowers medium, dbl., high-centered, moderate fragrance; foliage large, leathery; vigorous, upright, bushy growth; PP3094; [Seventeen × Jack Frost]; int. by Joseph H. Hill Co., 1972

Tammy Darlene Min, pb, 2004, Rickard, Vernon; flowers light pink, reverse white, 2 in., dbl., borne singly and in small clusters, no fragrance; foliage medium size, medium green, semi-glossy; prickles moderate, angled down, red; growth bushy, tall (36 in.); exhibition, garden decoration; [Fairhope × Sweet Caroline]; int. by Almost Heaven Roses, 2004

Tamora S, ab, 1992, Austin, David; flowers apricot yellow, 3-4 in., very dbl., cupped, borne in small clusters, intense unusual myrrh fragrance; recurrent; foliage small, dark green, semi-glossy; some prickles; medium (90 cm.), bushy growth; [Chaucer × Conrad Ferdinand Meyer]; int. by David Austin Roses, Ltd., 1983

Tamouree F, Combe

Tampa Bay Min, ob, 1989, King, Gene; bud pointed; flowers orange, edges aging darker, medium, 18 petals, high-centered, borne singly, slight fruity fragrance; foliage medium size, medium green, matte; prickles straight, red; growth upright, medium; hips ovoid, orange; [(Arthur Bell × Orange Honey) × Baby Diana]; int. by BDK Nursery, 1988

Tampico HT, or, 1974, Warriner, William A.; bud ovoid, long, pointed; flowers coral-pink, 4-5 in., 30-35 petals, high-centered, borne mostly singly, slight fragrance; recurrent; foliage large, leathery; prickles normal, long, hooked downward; stems long, strong; vigorous, upright growth; PP3677; [South Seas × Hawaii]; int. by J&P, 1976

Tamrabarani – See **Southern Sunset**, HT

Tan Cho HT, rb; int. by Keisei, 1986

Tanagra HT, or, 1969, Gaujard; bud long, pointed; flowers large, dbl.; foliage soft; vigorous, upright growth; [Queen Elizabeth × Tropicana]

Tanche – See **Tan Cho**, HT

Tancrède HP, mr, 1876, Oger; flowers medium, full, globular

Tane F, r, 1980, Simpson, J.W.; bud pointed; flowers 38 petals, high-centered, borne 4-10 per cluster, no fragrance; foliage small, dark, very glossy; prickles short, straight, dark brown; vigorous, upright growth; [(Orangeade × Megiddo) × (seedling × Jocelyn)]

Tanecnice F, mr, Strnad

Tangeglow – See **Star Child**, F

Tanger HT, rb, 1949, Dot, Pedro; bud ovoid; flowers crimson, reverse yellow, large, 60 petals; moderate, compact growth; [Condesa de Sástago × Peace]

Tanger Folies F, ob, Keisei; flowers orange, yellow reverse, dbl., cupped, borne in clusters; recurrent; int. by Meilland Intl., 2004

Tangerina HT, ob, Dickson; int. in 2004

Tangerine HT, op, 1942, Joseph H. Hill, Co.; bud globular, coral-red; flowers light salmon-orange, 3½-4 in., 30-35 petals; foliage dark, leathery; strong stems; vigorous, very upright, well branched growth; [Capt. Glisson × R.M.S. Queen Mary]

Tangerine Contempo F, ob, 1985, Gupta, Dr. M.N. & Datta, Dr. S.K.; flowers tangerine orange; [sport of Contempo]; int. by National Botanical Research Institute, 1983

Tangerine Dream – See **Marmalade Skies**, F

Tangerine Jewel HBc, ob, 2002, Moore, Ralph S.; flowers orange, reverse orange/pink, 2-2½ in., single, borne in small clusters, moderate fragrance; foliage medium size, medium green, semi-glossy; prickles few, small, pointed, light green; growth bushy, medium (24-36 in.); garden shrub, containers, specimen; [Joycie × Out of Yesteryear]; int. by Sequoia Nurs., 2002

Tangerine Mist Min, ob, 1988, Rennie, Bruce F.; flowers orange, medium, 15 petals, high-centered, borne singly, moderate fruity fragrance; foliage medium size, light green, glossy; prickles straight, medium, red-brown; upright growth; hips round, small, orange; [(Avandel × seedling) × Gold Mine]; int. by Rennie Roses International, 1988

Tangerine Twist Min, ob, 1996, Williams, Michael C.; flowers medium orange with yellow, light yellow reverse edged orange, medium, dbl., high-centered, borne singly and in small clusters, no fragrance; recurrent; foliage medium size, medium green, semi-glossy; few prickles; upright, medium growth; [Pierrine × unknown]; int. by The Mini Rose Garden, 1996

Tangier HT, rb, 1955, Parmentier, J.; bud long, pointed; flowers peach-red to scarlet-copper, medium, 60 petals, high-centered; vigorous, bushy growth; PP1400; [Katharine Pechtold × R.M.S. Queen Mary]

Tango HT, mr, 1937, H&S; flowers scarlet, reverse bronze, base shaded old-gold; vigorous growth; [seedling × Talisman]

Tango HT, mr, 1955, Delforge; bud long; flowers tango-red, open, large, dbl.; foliage dark, glossy; vigorous, bushy growth; [The Doctor × Karl Herbst]

Tango – See **Stretch Johnson**, S

Tango HT, ob; int. by J&P, 1992

Tango LCl, lp, Poulsen; flowers light pink, 5-8 cm., dbl., no fragrance; foliage dark; growth bushy, 100-150 cm.; PP15956; int. by Poulsen Roser, 2002

Tango Rose HT, ob, 1979, Delbard; bud pointed; flowers salmon-orange, large, 35-40 petals; foliage matte green; bushy growth; [(Belle Rouge × (Gloire de Rome × Gratitude)) × ((Dr. Schweitzer × Tropicana) × (Ena Harkness × Quebec))]; int. in 1978

Tania Verstak HT, mr, 1964, Armbrust; flowers rich red, large, dbl.; foliage light green, soft; vigorous, upright growth; [Charlotte Armstrong × Happiness]; int. by Langbecker, 1962

Tanned Beauty – See **Triolet**, HT

Tanned Toddler F, ab; flowers buff apricot, medium, hybrid tea, moderate fragrance; free-flowering; stems short, firm; short, compact growth; int. by Ludwig's Roses, 2000

Tant Mieux S, ob, 1983, Wright, Percy H.; flowers tangerine, yellow center, 5 petals, borne in clusters, no fragrance; foliage medium size, medium green, glossy; bushy growth; [*R. gallica* × Maria Stern]; int. by Gilles Gailloux, 1984

Tantaliser F, ab

Tantalizing Mary MinFl, yb, 2000, McCann, Sean; flowers yellow, aging to apricot centers, medium, full, borne mostly solitary, intense fragrance; foliage medium size, medium green, glossy; some prickles; growth upright, medium; garden decorative; [Ladies View × (Someday Soon × New Dawn)]

Tantalizing Red HT, m, 2001, Coiner, Jim; flowers large, 38 petals, high-centered, then flat, borne in small clusters, slight fragrance; recurrent; foliage large, dark green, matte; prickles average, in.; stems long; growth upright, vigorous, tall (5 ft.); hips round, 1/2 in., olive green; PP16200; [seedling × seedling]

Tantallon HT, mp, 1934, Dobbie; flowers salmon-pink, base yellow, reverse cerise-red touched orange, dbl.; foliage glossy, dark; dwarf, stocky growth

Tantarra HT, r, Gardner; flowers soft tan, toned pink and apricot, moderate fragrance; recurrent; bushy growth; int. in 1996

Tantau's Delight F, or, 1951, Tantau; bud long, pointed; flowers open, large, semi-dbl., borne in clusters; foliage dark, glossy; vigorous, bushy growth; [Cinnabar × Kathe Duvigneau]

Tantau's Konfetti HT, ob, Tantau; flowers orange blend, reverse yellow with orange edges, dbl., high-centered, borne mostly singly; recurrent; stems long; cut flower rose; int. by Rosen Tantau, 1991

Tantau's Surprise F, mr, 1951, Tantau; flowers blood-red, large, full, borne in clusters of 5-8; foliage dark, glossy; upright growth; [Bouquet × Hamburg]

Tantau's Triumph – See **Cinnabar**, F

Tantau's Triumph, Climbing Cl Pol, mr, Rosarium Sangerhausen; flowers medium, semi-dbl.; int. in 1957

Tantau's Ueberraschung – See **Tantau's Surprise**, F

Tante Frieda HT, mr, Michler, K. H.; flowers large, dbl.; int. in 1995

Tantivvy Pol, mr, 1954, Ratcliffe; flowers crimson-scarlet, semi-dbl., rosette; compact, bushy growth; [sport of Gloire du Midi]

Tanya HT, ob, 1960, Combe; bud pointed; flowers deep orange to apricot-orange, 5 in., 48 petals, high-centered, moderate fragrance; foliage leathery, glossy; vigorous, upright growth; PP1712; [Peace × (Peace × Orange Nassau)]; int. by Vilmorin-Andrieux

Tanya Kim HT, my, 1976, Marks; flowers clear yellow, 4½ in., 24 petals, intense fragrance; foliage glossy; [sport of Whisky Mac]; int. in 1975

Tanya Marie Min, rb, 2002, Fletcher, Ira R.; flowers red with white center, 3½ cm., single, borne mostly solitary, no fragrance; foliage small, medium green, matte; prickles moderate, 6 mm., very fine, slightly curved; bushy, medium (60 cm.) growth; [Grace Seward × Hanini]

Taora F, or, Tantau, Math.; bud long, pointed; flowers large, dbl.; foliage glossy; very vigorous, bushy growth; [Fragrant Cloud × Schweizer Gruss]; int. in 1968; ADR, 1969

Taos – See **Amber Cover**, S

Tapestry HT, rb, 1959, Fisher, G.; bud pointed; flowers red, yellow and pink, 4½-6 in., 38 petals, high-centered, moderate spicy fragrance; foliage glossy; upright, bushy growth; PP1812; [Peace × Mission Bells]; int. by C-P, 1959

Tapestry S, ab, 2001, Thomson, George L.; flowers apricot to coppery-pink, lighter reverse, medium, very full, borne in small clusters, moderate fragrance; foliage medium size, dark green, glossy; prickles medium, hooked; growth spreading, medium (4½-5½ ft.); garden decorative; [(Rugelda × unknown) × Howard Florey]; int. by Ross Roses, 2001

Tapis – See **Tapis Rose**, F

Tapis Afghan Pol, dr, 1979, Pekmez, Paul; bud round; flowers 1-2 in., 15 petals, cupped; dwarf growth; [Marlena × Lampion]; int. in 1975

Tapis Blanc Pol, w, 1927, Turbat; flowers pure white, center tinted cream, large, dbl., borne in clusters; bushy, dwarf growth

Tapis de Soie – See **Wee Man**, Min

Tapis d'Orient – See **Yesterday**, Pol

Tapis Jaune Min, my, 1976, deRuiter; flowers dbl., 20 petals; foliage small, glossy, dark; low, compact growth; [Rosy Jewel × Allgold]; int. by Kwekerij Rosa, 1973

Tapis Magique – See **Magic Carpet**, S

Tapis Persan – See **Eye Paint**, F

Tapis Rose F, mp, 1950, Meilland, F.; bud ovoid; flowers rose-pink, 2-2½ in., full, high-centered, borne in clusters; foliage leathery, dark; vigorous, upright, bushy growth; [Pinocchio × Mme Jules Gouchault]; int. by C-P

Tapis Rouge – See **Eyeopener**, S

Tapis Rustic S, mr

Tapis Volant S, pb, 1986, Lens, Louis; flowers white-pink blend, 2 in., semi-dbl., borne in clusters of 7-35, moderate fruity fragrance; recurrent bloom; foliage reddish green; prickles hooked, reddish-brown; groundcover; spreading growth; [(*R. luciae* × unknown) × (*R. multiflora* × Ballerina)]; int. in 1982; Gold Medal, Kortrijk, 1987

Tapti Gr, lp, Kasturi, G.; flowers delicate pink, large, moderate spicy fragrance; [sport of Camelot]; int. by KSG Son, 1978

Tara – See **Tara Allison**, Min

Tara Allison Min, or, 1987, McGredy, Sam IV; flowers small, semi-dbl.; foliage small, medium green, semi-glossy; bushy growth; [Wanaka × Eyepaint]; int. by Justice Miniature Roses, 1986

Tara Red HT, dr, 1975, Golik; bud ovoid; flowers carmine-red, becoming very dark, 6 in., 38 petals, high-centered, moderate fragrance; foliage leathery; tall growth; [Peace × Charles Mallerin]; int. by Dynarose, 1974

Taranaki Dawn F, ab, 2001, Sherwood, George; flowers apricot/cream, apricot/pink reverse, 8 cm., dbl., borne in large clusters, slight fragrance; foliage medium size, medium green, semi-glossy; prickles moderate, 8 mm., slightly curved; growth upright, tall (1½ m.); garden decorative; [Kate Sheppard × Kate Sheppard]; int. by Egmont Roses, 2001

Taranga F, mr, 1983, Tantau, Math.; flowers medium, semi-dbl. to dbl., cupped, borne in large clusters, slight fragrance; free-flowering; foliage medium size, medium green, semi-glossy; bushy, upright (3 ft.) growth; int. in 1981

Tarantella HT, dy, 1936, Tantau; flowers deep golden yellow, large, dbl., cupped; foliage light, wrinkled; vigorous, bushy growth; [Charles P. Kilham × Pres. Herbert Hoover]

Tarantella HT, yb, 1986, Kordes, W.; flowers creamy yellow, petals edged and marked with pink, large, 54 petals, high-centered, borne singly; recurrent; foliage medium size, medium green, glossy; prickles light brown; upright growth; [Colour Wonder × Wiener Charme]; int. by Horstmann, 1979

Tarantella HT, w, Spek; flowers white to blush pink; florist rose; int. by Terra Nigra BV, 2003

Tarantelle – See **Tarentelle**, HT

Tarde Gris HT, m, 1970, Dot, Simon; flowers soft lilac, large, 25 petals, moderate fragrance; foliage dark; upright growth; [(Sterling Silver × Intermezzo) × (Sterling Silver × Simone)]; int. by Roses Dot, 1966

Tarentelle HT, op, 1965, Laperrière; flowers Orient red with reflections of rose salmon, full; foliage bronze; vigorous, bushy growth; [(Beauté × Ma Fille) × Magicienne]; int. by EFR

Target F, rb, 1986, Warriner, William A.; flowers white with red petal edges, 25 petals, high-centered, borne usually singly; foliage medium size, medium green, semi-glossy; prickles straight, large and small; upright, bushy, medium growth; PP6255; [Prominent × seedling]; int. by J&P

Taro HT, my, 1977, Ota, Kaichiro; bud oval; flowers high pointed, 5½ in., 35 petals; foliage dark, leathery; vigorous, upright growth; [Edith Krause × Narzisse]

Tarragona HT, ab, 1945, Dot, Pedro; flowers apricot-yellow, open, 25-35 petals, high-centered; foliage glossy; upright growth; [Duquesa de Peñaranda × Federico Casas]

Tarragona – See **Diputacion de Tarragona**, HT

Tarrawarra Pol, pb, Nieuwesteeg, J.; int. in 1992

Tartarus HP, m, 1887, Geschwind; flowers violet purple; [Erinnerung an Brod × Souv du Dr Jamain]

Tartufe F, mr, 1956, Buyl Frères; flowers dark geranium-red, 28 petals; moderate growth; [Pompadour Red × Independence]

Taryn Min, op

Tarzan LCl, mr, 1955, Delbard-Chabert; flowers coppery carmine, darker reverse, medium, dbl., moderate fragrance; free, recurrent bloom; foliage dark bronze-green, glossy; very vigorous growth

Tascaria S, mr, Noack; flowers bright red, 2 in., semi-dbl., open cup, borne in clusters; recurrent; foliage medium to dark green, glossy; vigorous, broad (4 × 4 ft.) growth; int. by Noack Rosen, 2005; ADR, 2004

Taser Bibi HT, mr, Ghosh, Mr. & Mrs. S.; flowers bright, velvet scarlet red, large, dbl., high-centered; int. in 2000

Tasja HT, w, RvS-Melle

Tasman Min, dp, 1983, Murray, Nola; flowers deep pink, small, 17 petals, flat; foliage medium size, dark, leathery; compact growth; [Smiley × ((((Pink Parfait × Una Hawken) × Anytime) × ((Pink Parfait × Una Hawken) × Anytime)) × Anytime)]

Tasman Bay LCl, w, Pratt, Florence; flowers single, borne in large sprays; early flowering; vigorous (4 m.) growth; int. in 1994

Tasman Venture S, dr, 2004, Marriner, Max; flowers dark red, reverse darker, medium, single, borne in small clusters, slight fragrance; foliage medium size, medium green, matte; prickles 2 cm., average; growth spreading, tall (2 m.); garden decorative; [Altissimo × Penelope]; int. in 2004

Tasogare F, m, 1977, Kobayashi, Moriji; bud cupped; flowers 2½-4 in., 18 petals, flat; foliage glossy; vigorous, spreading growth; [Gletscher × (Sterling Silver × Gletscher)]; int. in 1977

Tassie Corraline HT, mr, 2007, Eiszele, L. H.; flowers 11 cm., dbl., borne mostly solitary; foliage medium size, medium green, matte; prickles small, hooked, red, moderate; growth upright, short (30 in.); [unknown × unknown]

Tassie Laua-Maree F, dp, 2007, Eiszele, L. H.; flowers deep pink, reverse pink blend, 9 cm., very full, borne in small clusters; foliage medium size, dark green, semi-glossy; prickles medium, regular, red, moderate; growth upright, medium (1½ m.); [Pink Perpetue × unknown]

Tassie Mme Mariah F, w, 2007, Eiszele, L. H.; flowers white blend, 9 cm., very full, borne in small clusters; foliage medium size, medium green, semi-glossy; few prickles; growth upright, medium (20 in.); borders; [Iceberg × unknown]

Tassie Melanie HT, lp, 2007, Eiszele, L. H.; flowers 10 cm., dbl., borne mostly solitary; foliage medium size, medium green, matte; prickles medium, regular, red, moderate; growth upright, medium (1½ m.); [Proud Titania × unknown]

Tassie Princess F, dp, 1999, Elszele, L. H.; flowers 2-2½ in., dbl., borne in small clusters; foliage small, medium green, semi-glossy; few prickles; bushy, low (36 in.) growth

Tassili HT, ly, Orard; flowers sable yellow, dbl.; int. in 1993

Tassin HT, mr, 1942, Meilland, F.; bud ovoid; flowers large, dbl., urn-shaped, moderate fragrance; recurrent; foliage leathery; vigorous, upright (4 ft.) growth; [National Flower Guild × Lemania]; int. by A. Meilland

Tassin, Climbing Cl HT, mr, Moreira da Silva; [sport of Tassin]; int. in about 1950

Taste of Honey F, ob, 1977, Young, S.A.; bud ovoid; flowers honey color, aging pink, open, large, dbl.; foliage leathery; vigorous, upright growth; [sport of Elizabeth of Glamis]

Tata Centenary HT, rb, 1978, Pradhan, Rauf, Murmu, Ghosh; flowers deep carmine, striped pale yellow, reverse buff, large, dbl., high-centered, slight fragrance; recurrent; [sport of Pigalle]; int. by Telco Nursery, 1974

Tata Centenary, Climbing Cl HT, rb, K&S; [sport of Tata Centenary]; int. by KSG Son, 1995

Tate's Multiflora ; clone of *R. multiflora*; used for understock

Tathgata HT, w, Ghosh, Mr. & Mrs. S.; flowers white with slight pink blush, large, full, high-centered; int. in 1999

Tatiana S, op, Monteith, Joan; flowers apricot-orange, large, semi-dbl., shallow cup to flat, intense fragrance; recurrent; medium growth; [Heritage × Westerland]

Tatik Brada HP, op, 1933, Brada; flowers large, full

Tatjana HT, dr, 1973, Kordes, R.; bud long, pointed; flowers large, dbl., cupped, intense fragrance; foliage leathery, soft; vigorous, upright growth; [Liebeszauber × President Dr. H.C. Schroder]; int. by Kordes, 1970

Tatoo LCl, dr, Poulsen; flowers 2-3 in., dbl., cupped, borne in clusters, very slight fragrance; recurrent; foliage small, dark green, glossy; vigorous (5-7 ft.) growth; int. by Poulsen Roser, 2002

Tattletale Min, mp, 1989, Zipper, Herbert; flowers deep pink, small, 33 petals, borne singly and in sprays, no fragrance; foliage small, dark green, semi-glossy; bushy, compact growth; [High Spirits × Charmglo]; int. by Magic Moment Miniature Roses, 1989

Tatton F, ob, Fryer; flowers burnt orange, large, full, cupped, borne in clusters, moderate fruity fragrance; recurrent; foliage large, disease-resistant; vigorous, medium growth; int. by Fryers Roses, 2001

Tattooed Lady Min, rb, 1993, McCann, Sean; flowers red, yellow reverse, yellow stripes and veins, large, dbl., borne mostly singly, slight fragrance; foliage medium size, dark green, bronze, glossy; numerous prickles; medium (12-14 in.), upright growth; [Siobhan × (Picasso × Near You)]; int. by Justice Miniature Roses, 1994

Taubie Kushlik HT, pb, Kordes; flowers silvery pink, deeper reverse, dbl., high-centered, borne mostly singly, slight fragrance; recurrent; vigorous, medium growth; int. in 1991

Taunusblümchen HMult, m, 1902, Weigand, C.; flowers violet-pink, 4-5 cm., semi-dbl., borne in clusters of 10-20; [Turner's Crimson Rambler × Mlle Blanche Rebatel]

Taupo F, op, 1978, McGredy, Sam IV; flowers light rose-salmon, flora-tea, 5 in., full; tall growth; [Liverpool Echo × Irish Mist]; int. by McGredy

Tauranga Centennial F, or, 1983, Wareham, Phyllis E.; flowers orange-red, center yellow, large, 22 petals, borne in clusters of 3; prickles light brown; upright growth; [Arthur Bell × (Alexander × Sympathy)]

Taurinia HT, mp, 1942, Aicardi; bud ovoid; flowers bright salmon-pink, large, very dbl., cupped; foliage leathery; very vigorous growth; [Julien Potin × Sensation]; int. by Giacomasso

Tauro F, dr, 1959, Bofill; bud globular; flowers oxblood-red, large, dbl., borne in clusters; foliage glossy; upright growth; [Poinsettia × Alain]; int. by Torre Blanca, 1958

Taurus Min, or, 1978, Ellick; bud pointed, ovoid; flowers vermilion, 2-3 in., 35-40 petals; foliage dark; compact, upright growth; [Baby Masquerade × (Spion-Kop × Evelyn Fison)]; int. by Excelsior Roses

Taurus F, ab; flowers salmon-pink, outer petals fading lighter, dbl., borne in clusters, slight fragrance; foliage medium green; to 75 cm. growth; int. by Burston Nurseries, 2004

Tausendschön HMult, pb, 1906, Kiese; flowers deep rose-pink, center white, fading lighter, 6 cm., dbl., cupped, borne in clusters of 20-40; foliage soft green; climbing (8-10 ft.) growth; [Daniel Lacombe × Weisser Herumstreicher]; int. by Schmidt

Tawny Gold HT, dy, 1951, Leenders, M.; bud pointed; flowers tawny gold, well-shaped, 5 in., 25 petals, high-centered, intense fragrance; foliage leathery; bushy, compact growth; [Vanessa × Burgemeester van Oppen]; int. by J&P

Tawny Superior HT, my, 1958, Leenders, M.; flowers golden yellow

Tawny Tiger F, r, Fryer; flowers dark orange striped and rippled with terracotta and brown, semi-dbl., cupped, loose, borne in good-sized clusters, moderate fragrance; repeats well; foliage glossy; bushy (70 cm.) growth; int. by Fryer's Roses, 2003

Taxi F, rb, 1969, Trew, C.; flowers mandarin red, reverse soft rose, pointed, large, dbl.; foliage dark, matte; RULED EXTINCT 12/85; [Isabelle de France × Basildon Belle]; int. by Basildon Rose Gardens

Taxi HT, dr, 1986, Poulsen, Niels D.; flowers large, 35 petals, exhibition, borne usually singly, intense fragrance; foliage large, dark, matte; vigorous, upright growth; [Fragrant Cloud × Gisselfeld]; int. by Poulsen's Roses, 1977

Tay Caitlin Min, ab, 1997, Garrett, Troy O.; flowers dbl., borne mostly singly; foliage medium size, medium green, semi-glossy; some prickles; upright, medium (16-22in.) growth; [sport of Queen City]

Taylors Gold HT, my, 1990, Horner, Heather M.; bud ovoid; flowers do not fade, medium, 48 petals, cupped, borne singly and in sprays of 5; foliage medium size, medium green, semi-glossy; prickles narrow, small, brown; bushy, medium growth; fruit not known; [Prominent × Helmut Schmidt]; int. in 1989

Tchaikovski Gr, w, 2003, Meilland International; flowers white with apricot blush in center, 6-9 cm., very full, borne in small clusters; foliage medium size, dark green, semi-glossy; prickles moderate; growth bushy, tall (5-6 ft.); garden; [(Anthony Meilland × Landora) × Centenaire de Lourdes]

Tchin-Tchin – See **Parador**, HT

Tchin-Tchin F, or, 1978, Paolino; flowers large, 20 petals, cupped, borne in clusters of 3-17, slight fragrance; foliage matte; very vigorous growth; [((Sarabande × MEIkim) × (Alain × Orange Triumph)) × Diablotin]; int. as Parador, URS; Gold Medal, Tokyo, 1978

Tchin-Tchin, Climbing Cl F, ob, Meilland; [sport of Tchin-Tchin]; int. in 1995

Te Awamutu Centennial HT, rb, 1985, Stephens, Pat; flowers white, edged medium red, 35 petals, slight fragrance; foliage dark, glossy; bushy growth; [Strawberry Ice × seedling]; int. in 1985

Te Kawanata Hou S, w, Nobbs

Te Kowhai F, dr, 1960, Bennett, H.; flowers dark velvety red, reverse white overlaid red; [(Florence Mary Morse × Border Queen) × Confidence]; int. by Pedigree Nursery

Te Moana HT, pb, 1980, Simpson, J.W.; bud pointed; flowers 38 petals, high-centered, borne mostly singly, intense fragrance; foliage dark, semi-glossy; prickles brown; medium, bushy, upright growth; [(Gypsy Moth × Percy Thrower) × First Prize]; Gold Star of the South Pacific, Palmerston North, NZ, 1981

Tea Clipper S, ab, 2006; flowers very full, borne in small clusters; foliage medium size, dark green, matte; prickles medium, concave, curved inward, yellow blend, few; growth bushy, vigorous, medium (120 cm.); garden decorative; [seedling × seedling]; int. by David Austin Roses, Ltd., 2006

Tea Party Min, ab, 1973, Moore, Ralph S.; flowers orange-apricot to pink, small, dbl.; foliage small, light; vigorous, dwarf, bushy growth; [(*R. wichurana* × Floradora) × Eleanor]; int. by Sequoia Nursery, 1972

Tea Rambler HMult, op, 1904, Paul, W.; bud pointed; flowers soft salmon-pink, 4-5 cm., dbl., flat, borne in clusters of 3-15, moderate fragrance; early; foliage dark green, edged red; vigorous, climbing growth; [Turner's Crimson Rambler × a climbing Tea (possibly Gloire de Dijon)]

Tea Rose – See **Hume's Blush Tea-Scented China**, T

Tea-Scented Ayrshire – See **Ruga**, Ayr

Tea-Scented Rose – See **Hume's Blush Tea-Scented China**, T

Tea Time F, mp, 1960, Boerner; bud ovoid; flowers clear pink, medium, 60-65 petals, high-centered, borne in clusters; foliage leathery; vigorous, bushy growth; [Floribunda seedling × Demure]; int. by J&P, 1960

Tea Time HT, ob, Tantau; flowers smoky orange with brown shades, petals ruffled, medium, dbl., rosette, borne singly and in clusters, slight fragrance; recurrent; upright (3 ft.) growth; int. in 1994

Teacher's Pet HT, ab, 1980, Taylor, Thomas E.; bud ovoid, pointed; flowers apricot, 30 petals, high-centered; foliage dark green with red mid-rib and edges; prickles straight; upright, bushy growth; [First Prize × Bonsoir]

Tear Drop Min, w, 1989, Dickson, Patrick; flowers pure white with yellow stamens, small, semi-dbl., flat, borne in clusters, slight fragrance; recurrent; foliage small, medium green, glossy; bushy, compact growth; [Pink Spray × Bright Smile]; int. by Dickson Nurseries, Ltd., 1989

Tease F, ob, 1967, Boerner; bud ovoid, coppery; flowers golden yellow, dbl., cupped; foliage leathery; vigorous, upright growth; [Yellow Pinocchio × Fashion seedling]; int. by J&P

Teasing Georgia S, yb, 1998, Austin, David; flowers deep yellow in center, paler yellow on outer petals, large, very dbl., cupped, borne mostly singly, moderate tea rose fragrance; good repeat; foliage medium size, semi-glossy, disease-resistant; few prickles; branching, strong, graceful, medium (3½ ft.) growth; [Charles Austin × seedling]; int. by David Austin Roses, Ltd., 1998; Henry Edland Medal for fragrance, RNRS, 2000

Teatime F, pb; flowers creamy white with heavy blush of soft pearly pink, slight fragrance; foliage disease-resistant; short growth

Technikon Pretoria HT, yb, Kordes; bud triangular, deep yellow; flowers deep yellow with bright orange-red edges growing as it opens, dbl., high-centered; recurrent; short growth; int. in 1993

Ted Allen HT, ly, 1997, Guest, M.M.; flowers medium, dbl., borne mostly singly; foliage medium size, medium green, dull; some prickles; upright, medium (28 in.) growth; [Manx Queen × (Manx Queen × Rosa Bella)]

Ted Carnac LCl, 1968, Gowie; vigorous growth; int. by Gandy's Roses

Ted Gore F, dp, 1992, Horner, Colin P.; flowers deep pink, medium, full, borne in large clusters; foliage medium size, medium green, semi-glossy; some prickles; medium (80 cm.), bushy growth; [Miss Ireland × Lilac Charm]; int. in 1993

Ted Goves HT, mr, 1985, Kirkham, Gordon Wilson; flowers medium, 20 petals, intense fragrance; foliage medium size, dark, matte; [Prima Ballerina × Teenager]; int. in 1983

Tedcastle HP, m, 1940, Tedcastle; flowers purple, open, very dbl., cupped; foliage glossy; upright, bushy growth; [Ulrich Brunner Fils × Paul Neyron]

Teddy HT, lp, Pratt, Florence; bud pink; flowers pale peach-pink, dbl.; medium growth; [Margaret Merril × unknown]; int. in 1994

Teddy Bear Min, r, 1990, Saville, F. Harmon; bud small, ovate; flowers terra-cotta, reverse lighter, aging to mauve-pink, ¾ in., 28 petals, high-centered, then flat, borne singly or in clusters of 5-20, slight fragrance; recurrent; foliage medium size, dark green, semi-glossy; prickles slight downward curve, medium, purple; upright, bushy, medium, vigorous growth; hips ovoid to globular, brownish-orange; PP7424; [Sachet × Rainbow's End]; int. by Nor'East Min. Roses, 1990

Teddy Bear, Climbing Cl Min, r, Saito; int. in 1997

Teddy's Coat F, dy

Ted's Red HT, mr, 1992, Reynolds, Ted; flowers 3-3½ in., full, borne mostly singly; foliage medium size, medium size, semi-glossy; few prickles; medium, upright growth; [Alec's Red × seedling]; int. by Reynolds Roses

Teenager F, pb, 1958, Boerner; bud ovoid; flowers La France pink, lightly overcast shrimp-pink, 3½ in., 55-60 petals, high-centered to cupped, intense fragrance; foliage leathery; strong stems; vigorous, upright growth; [Demure × Demure]; a greenhouse variety; int. by J&P

Teenager HT, yb, 1960, Arnot; flowers yellow shaded pink and carmine, loosely formed, 4-5 in., 25 petals, intense fragrance; foliage dark, leathery; vigorous, upright growth; [Ena Harkness × Sutter's Gold]; int. by Croll, 1958

Teeny Bopper Min, rb, 1989, Bennett, Dee; bud ovoid; flowers white with red blush on outer petals, aging red with white, semi-dbl., cupped, slight damask fragrance; foliage small, medium green, semi-glossy; no prickles; micro-mini, bushy growth; hips globular, yellow-green-orange; PP7449; [Little Squirt × seedling]; int. by Tiny Petals Nursery, 1988

Teeny Weeny – See **Buttons 'n' Bows**, Min

Tegala S, dp, 1927, Hansen, N.E.; flowers deep pink, semi-dbl.; non-recurrent; growth to 5 ft.; very hardy; [Tetonkaha × Alika]

Teide LCl, mr, 1948, Dot, M.; flowers carmine, 3 in., full; foliage reddish; [Texas Centennial × Guinee]

Tejas LCl, pb, 2002, Ponton, Ray; flowers white to pink, 2 in., single, borne in small clusters; recurrent bloom; foliage medium size, medium green, semi-glossy; prickles medium, straight, moderate; growth upright, tall (10-12 ft.); pillar, fence; hips numerous; [Katy Road Pink (Carefree Beauty) × Reveil Dijonnais]; int. by Peaceful Habitations Rose Garden, 2003

Téléthon HT, ab, Delbard; flowers cream edges, apricot center, full, pointed to rosette, intense lilac and fruit fragrance; recurrent; foliage glossy; growth to 80 cm.; int. by George Delbard SA, 2005; Certificate of Merit, Belfast, 2006

Telford's Promise S, ob, 1992, Warner, Chris; flowers coppery salmon, small, semi-dbl., borne in large clusters; foliage small, medium green, glossy; few prickles; spreading (60 cm.) growth; [Mary Sumner × Nozomi]; int. in 1990

Tell Belle S, or, 2001, Hiltner, Martin J.; flowers small, full, borne in small clusters, intense fragrance; foliage medium size, medium green, semi-glossy; prickles moderate, 1/4- in., straight; spreading, medium (2-2½ ft.) growth; [Show 'n' Tell × Hawkeye Belle]

Telluride S, pb, Poulsen; flowers pale pink and white, small, single, slight wild rose fragrance; foliage dark; growth broad, bushy, 60-100 cm.; PP12575; int. as Butterflies Cover, Poulsen Roser, 1998

Telstar F, ob, 1963, Gandy, Douglas L.; flowers orange to orange-buff, flushed scarlet, large, 14 petals, borne in clusters of up to 5, moderate fragrance; foliage dark; vigorous, upright growth; [Flash × Masquerade]

Temno HT, m, 1936, Böhm, J.; flowers dark maroon, fairly large, dbl.; vigorous growth; int. by J&P

Temper Tantrum Min, dr, 1987, Jolly, Marie; flowers white center, medium, 30 petals, high-centered, borne usually singly or in sprays of 2; foliage small, medium green, semi-glossy; no prickles; upright, medium growth; no fruit; [Red Beauty × Libby]; int. by Rosehill Farm, 1988

Temperament F, mr, 1959, Tantau, Math.; flowers light scarlet, open, 2½ in., 24 petals, borne in clusters; foliage glossy, leathery; vigorous, upright growth; [Fanal × Karl Weinhausen]; int. in 1957

Tempest, Climbing LCl, rb, 1962, Verschuren; bud pointed; flowers yellow, pink and orange-red, 2½-3 in., 26 petals, borne in clusters; foliage dark, glossy; vigorous growth; [Masquerade × seedling]; int. by Blaby Rose Gardens, 1962

Tempi Moderni F, ob, Barni, V.; bud golden yellow; flowers golden yellow, flushed with vermilion orange which spreads with age, dbl., cupped, borne in clusters, slight fragrance; recurrent; vigorous (60-80 cm.) growth; int. by Rose Barni, 1996; Best Italian Rose, Monza, 1996

Tempie Lee HT, pb, 1991, Whittington, Sr., J.O.; flowers medium, full, high-centered, borne mostly singly, slight fragrance; foliage medium size, medium green, semi-glossy; some prickles; stems long; vigorous, medium, spreading growth; [sport of Elizabeth Taylor]; int. by Edmunds' Roses, 1998

Templar HT, mr, 1924, Montgomery Co.; flowers bright red, dbl., globular; foliage dark, leathery; vigorous growth; [Premier × seedling]; int. by A.N. Pierson; Gold Medal, NRS, 1925

Temple Bells Cl Min, w, 1972, Morey, Dennison; flowers single, 7 petals, slight fragrance; foliage small, glossy; growth tall; climber (if supported) or groundcover; [*R. wichurana* × Blushing Jewel]; int. by McGredy, 1971

Temple d'Apollon HGal, dr, 1816, possibly Prévost; bud long, pointed; sepals short; flowers velvety violet-crimson, large, semi-dbl.

Temple Flame F, or, 1970, Pal, Dr. B.P.; flowers orange flushed red, open, medium, semi-dbl.; foliage leathery; very vigorous, upright, compact growth; [Orangeade × unknown]; int. by Indian Agric. Research Inst., 1965

Tempo LCl, dr, 1974, Warriner, William A.; bud ovoid; flowers deep red, large, very dbl., slight fragrance; recurrent; foliage large, glossy, dark; climbing growth; [Ena Harkness, Climbing × unknown]; int. by J&P, 1975

Tempo F, mr, Meilland; flowers brilliant cardinal red; growth to 50-60 cm; mass plantings; int. by Sauvageot, 1977

Temptation LCl, mr, 1950, Jacobus; bud ovoid, carmine-red; flowers rose-red, open, large, 40 petals; free, recurrent boom; foliage large, glossy; vigorous, climbing growth; good pillar; very hardy; [(New Dawn × Crimson Glory) × Dream Girl]; int. by B&A

Temptation F, or, 1992, Robinson, Thomas, Ltd.; flowers 3-3½ in., 5 petals, borne in small clusters; foliage medium size, medium green, semi-glossy; some prickles; low (70 cm.), dense, bushy, compact growth; [Orange Sensation × seedling]; int. by Thomas Robinson, Ltd.

Temptation HT, mr; int. by Interplant, 1995

Temptress HT, mr, 1948, Joseph H. Hill, Co.; bud long, pointed, crimson; flowers carmine, medium, 35-40 petals, cupped; foliage leathery, dark; vigorous, upright, bushy growth; [(Lucile Hill × Chieftain) × seedling]

Temptress HT, w, 1998, Wambach, Catherine; flowers white, 4½-5 in., full, high-centered, borne singly, moderate fragrance; foliage medium size, medium green, semi-glossy; few prickles; upright, tall (5½ ft.) growth; [Elsie Melton × Elina]; int. by Certified Roses, Inc., 1999

Temptress – See **Roter Korsar**, S

Tempus-Fugit HT, mr, 1976, Ellick; flowers cardinal-red, 3-4 in., 40-45 petals, moderate fragrance; foliage glossy, dark; very free growth; [Chopin × Heidelberg]; int. in 1977

Ten Sisters – See **Crimson Rambler**, HMult

Ten Ten – See **Ten Ten CFRB**, HT

Ten Ten CFRB HT, mr, McGredy; flowers striking, velvet red, dbl., cupped; recurrent; stems long; int. in 1987

Ten Thousand Leaves – See **Manyo**, F

Tenacious F, yb, McGredy; flowers striped cherry red, lemon, and yellow maturing to blush pink, loose, slight fragrance; foliage bright green, glossy; short to medium growth; int. in 2004; Certificate of Merit, Glasgow, 2006

Tenacity S, mr, Williams, J. Benjamin; flowers semi-dbl., flat, borne in clusters, slight fragrance; recurrent; foliage reddish; stems reddish; growth to 2 ft.; int. by Hortico, Inc., 2006

Tendence F, dy, Noack; int. by Noack Rosen, 2002

Tender Min, mp, Olesen; PP11499; int. in 1998

Tender Blush A, lp, Sievers; flowers blush pink, 4½ in., very full, cupped; once blooming; tall (5-6 ft.), arching growth; [bred from Maiden's Blush]; int. in 1988

Tender Love Min, lp, 1980, Strawn, Leslie E.; bud slender, tapering; flowers 23 petals, borne mostly singly, sometimes 3-5 per cluster; foliage glossy, medium green; prickles dilated at base; tall, upright growth; [Doris Ashwell × Sheri Anne]; int. by Pixie Treasures Min. Roses

Tender Love F, lp, 1997, Bossom, W.E.; flowers very dbl., 41 petals, high-centered, borne in large clusters, no fragrance; foliage medium size, light green, glossy; some prickles; growth upright, medium (90 cm.); [Sexy Rexy × seedling]

Tender Love HT, mp, Ghosh, Mr. & Mrs. S.; bud long, tapering; flowers rosy pink, broad petals; free-flowering; vigorous growth; int. in 2000

Tender Loving Care F, mp, 1993, Bossom, W.E.; flowers medium pink, 4 in., 20 petals, borne in large clusters; foliage medium size, dark green, semi-glossy; some prickles; medium to tall (90 cm.), upright growth; [Pearl Drift × (Dublin Bay × seedling)]; int. by F. Haynes & Partners, 1995

Tender Mercy Min, mr, 1995, Rennie, Bruce F.; flowers 1-1½ in., dbl., borne mostly singly; foliage small, medium green, glossy; few prickles; low (12-15 in.), compact growth; [California Dreaming × seedling]; int. by Rennie Roses International, 1992

Tender Night F, mr, 1971, Meilland; flowers 4 in., 25 petals, slight fruity fragrance; foliage matte, dark; upright growth; [Tamango × (Fire King × Banzai)]; Gold Medal, Rome, 1971

Tender Night, Climbing Cl F, mr, 1979, Meilland, Mrs. Marie-Louise; int. by Meilland & Co SNC, 1976

Tender One – See **Nejenka**, F

Tender Spirit S, op, Williams, J. Benjamin; flowers single; int. by Hortico, Inc., 2005

Tenderly HT, Delforge; int. in 1984

Tenderly Yours Min, w, 1993, Rennie, Bruce F.; flowers small, white, full; foliage small, medium green, semi-glossy; some prickles; low, spreading growth; [Party Girl × Tooth of Time]; int. by Rennie Roses International, 1993

Tenderness HT, lp, Delbard; flowers pale pink, large, dbl., high-centered, borne mostly singly; recurrent; foliage light green; stems straight, rigid, medium to long; florist rose; int. in 2003

Tendresse – See **Sachsengruss**, HP

Tendresse HT, pb, 1985, Delbard, Georges; flowers light pink, reverse apricot-pink, large, dbl., high-centered, moderate fragrance; free-flowering; foliage dense; growth to 50-100 cm.; [(Michèle Meilland × Bayadère) × (Grace de Monaco × Present Filial)]; int. by Delbard Roses, 1980

Tendresse – See **Comtesse de Ségur**, S

Tendresse Admirable – See **Marie-Louise**, D

Tendresse d'Apollon HGal, m, before 1836, Prévost; flowers lilac pink, edges fading to white, medium, full

Tenerezza HT, rb, 1974, Calvino; bud ovoid, long, pointed; flowers spinel-rose to cherry-red, medium, dbl., cupped, moderate fragrance; foliage large, dark, leathery; vigorous, upright, bushy growth; PP2932; [seedling × Ninfa Rossa]

Teneriffe HT, op, 1973, Timmerman's Roses; flowers deep orange, yellowish reverse, pointed, 5 in., 45 petals, intense fragrance; foliage glossy; [Fragrant Cloud × Piccadilly]; int. in 1972

Tennessee Min, op, 1988, King, Gene; flowers coral to white, reverse light coral to white, aging darker coral, medium, 18 petals, high-centered, borne singly or in small clusters; recurrent; foliage medium size, light green, matte; prickles straight, light green; upright, tall growth; hips oval, large, orange; [Kiskadee × Orange Honey]; int. by AGM Miniature Roses

Tennessee HT, ob, Van de Meer, Peter; bud long, pointed; flowers orange with darker edges and yellow base, 9 cm., 30-40 petals, cupped, then flat, borne usually singly, very slight fragrance; recurrent; foliage dark green; upright (80 cm.) growth; hips round, orange; PP9170; [Eliora × Cocktail]; int. by Terra Nigra, 1988

Tennessee Belle HSet, mp, before 1898, from U.S.A.; flowers bright rosy blush, large, dbl., borne in clusters, moderate fragrance; vigorous, climbing growth

Tennessee Sunrise MinFl, ob, 2001, Wells, Verlie; flowers 2½ in., full, borne mostly solitary, moderate fragrance; foliage medium size, dark green, semi-glossy; prickles moderate, short, straight; growth upright, medium (24-36 in.); garden decorative, exhibition; [seedling × seedling]; int. by Mid-South Roses, 2002

Tennessee Sunset MinFl, yb, 2002, Wells, Verlie W.; flowers pink with yellow base, medium, full, borne in small clusters, slight fragrance; foliage medium size, medium green, semi-glossy; prickles few, 1/4 in., hooked; growth compact, medium; [seedling ×

seedling]; int. by Wells MidSouth Roses, 2002

Tennessee Waltz Min, pb, 2005, Wells, Verlie W.; flowers white at base, pink edges, reverse white, 1½ in., semi-dbl., borne mostly solitary; foliage medium size, medium green, semi-glossy; prickles few, ¼ in., straight; growth upright, medium (2-3 ft.); garden decorative, exhibition; [Figurine × mixed pollen]; int. by Wells Midsouth Roses, 2005

Ténor LCl, mr, 1963, Delbard-Chabert; flowers velvety red, medium, semi-dbl., borne in small to medium clusters, no fragrance; early; very vigorous growth

Tentation HT, op, 1970, Dorieux; bud pointed; flowers carmine-pink to orange, large, dbl.; foliage glossy; vigorous, upright growth; [Touggout × Flaminaire]; int. by Vilmorin

Tenth Rose Convention HT, dy, Patil, B.K.; flowers dbl., high-centered; int. in 1990

Teodora HT, mr, 1983, Stoddard, Louis; flowers large, 30 petals, cupped; foliage large, brownish-green, matte; prickles reddish-green; upright growth; [Honey Favorite × Command Performance]; int. by Rose Barni-Pistoia

Teodora HT, mr, Barni; bud globular; flowers brilliant red, large, dbl., slight fragrance; medium (4 ft.) growth; int. by Rose Barni, 2003

Tequila F, ob, 1983, Meilland, Mrs. Marie-Louise; flowers light yellow, overlaid with orange, stained carmine on outer edges, 20 petals; foliage medium size, dark, matte; bushy growth; [Poppy Flash × (Rumba × (MEIkim × Fire King))]; int. by Meilland Et Cie

Tequila F, ob, Meilland; flowers orange with yellow tones, dbl., high-centered, borne mostly singly; recurrent; florist rose; int. by Meilland Intl., 1998

Tequila F, ob, Meilland; flowers bright orange, semi-dbl., cupped to flat, borne in clusters; growth to 70 cm.; int. by Rosen von Schultheis, 2003

Téquila F, ab; bud conical; flowers 3-3½ in., 29 petals, cupped, borne in clusters of 2-5, no fragrance; free-flowering; foliage dark green, semi-glossy; growth bushy, 80-90 cm.; PP16342; [Golden Holstein × Bonica]; int. by Meilland, 2004

Tequila Sunrise HT, rb, 1989, Dickson, Patrick; flowers deep yellow heavily edged in scarlet red, 4 in., 40 petals, spiral, slight tea fragrance; recurrent; foliage medium size, medium green, glossy; bushy growth; [Bonfire Night × Freedom]; int. by Dickson Nurseries, Ltd., 1989; Gold Medal, RNRS, 1988, Gold Medal, Belfast, 1991

Tequila Sunset F, ob, 1991, Williams, J. Benjamin; bud ovoid; flowers brilliant orange and yellow blend, petals quilled, medium, 32 petals, urn-shaped, borne in sprays of 3-7, moderate fruity fragrance; foliage medium size, medium green, semi-glossy; growth upright, bushy, medium; [Redgold × Tropicana]; int. by Paramount Nursery, 1992

Teresa Finotti-Masieri HT, m, 1929, Ketten Bros.; bud long, pointed; flowers brilliant purple-rose, rosy scarlet reflexes, bordered yellow; [George C. Waud × Souv. de Gabriel Luizet]

Teresa Ozores Cl HT, lp, 1958, Camprubi, C.; bud ovoid; flowers soft pearly pink, large, dbl., cupped, intense fragrance; vigorous growth; [Frau Karl Druschki × Lady Sylvia]; int. in 1957

Ternata – See ***R. laevigata*** (Michaux)

Ternaux Ch, m, about 1830, Ternaux; flowers violet'purple, medium, full

Terra Cotta – See **Terracotta**, HT

Terra Jubilee F, ab, Zary, Dr. Keith W.; flowers soft apricot, fading to almost white, large, semi-dbl., flat, moderate fragrance; recurrent; int. in 1996; Golden Rose, The Hague, 1997

Terracotta HT, r; bud conical; flowers brick red, 12-14 cm., dbl., cupped, high-centered, borne mostly singly, no fragrance; recurrent; foliage medium green, semi-glossy; prickles numerous, medium, tan; upright (4-5 ft.) growth; PP10622; [sport of Leonidas]; florist rose; int. by Meilland, 1999

Terracotta, Climbing Cl HT, r, Meilland; int. in 2001

Terracotta HT, r, Simpson; flowers reddish-brown, dbl., high-centered, slight fragrance; growth medium to tall; many sources show code-form name as Simchoca, but NZ authority says it is Simchoka; int. as Chocolate Prince, De Boer Roses, 2003; Gold Medal, Durbanville, 2006

Terrazza Amore F, dr, de Ruiter; flowers dbl, borne in clusters; PPAF; int. by Nor'East Min. Roses, 2007

Terrazza Bella F, pb, de Ruiter; flowers dbl; int. by Nor'East Min. Roses, 2007

Terrazza Corazon F, mr, de Ruiter; flowers dbl.; int. by Nor'East Min. Roses, 2007

Terrazza Del Sol F, my, de Ruiter; flowers dbl; int. by Nor'East Min. Roses, 2007

Terrazza Rosa F, dp, de Ruiter; flowers hot pink, dbl.; int. by Nor'East Min. Roses, 2007

Terrazza Sunset F, ob, de Ruiter; flowers orange and apricot, dbl.; int. by Nor'East Min. Roses, 2007

Terrazza Voila F, op, de Ruiter; flowers peachy pink, dbl.; int. by Nor'East Min. Roses, 2007

Terrell Anne F, lp, 1991, Greenwood, Chris; bud ovoid; flowers medium, full, high-centered, borne in small clusters, slight fragrance; foliage medium size, medium green, glossy; some prickles; medium (90 cm.), upright growth; [sport of Gene Boerner]

Terri King HT, yb, 2001, Moe, Mitchie; flowers 3-4 in., dbl., high-centered, borne mostly solitary, moderate fragrance; foliage medium size, medium green, semi-glossy; prickles few, medium, hooked, light brown; growth upright, tall (3-4 ft.); garden decorative, exhibition, greenhouse; [Pristine × Selfridges]; int. by Mitchie's Roses and More, 2001

Terry Ann F, yb, 2003, Rawlins, R.; flowers primrose with pink edge, reverse primrose, medium, dbl., borne in small clusters, intense fragrance; foliage medium size, dark green, glossy; prickles moderate, 1½ cm., hooked; growth upright, tall (48 in.); garden; [Golden Future × Baby Face]; int. in 2003

Terry Edwards F, my, 2001, Webster, Robert; flowers 3½-4 in., very full, borne in small clusters; foliage medium size, medium green, semi-glossy; prickles moderate, 15 mm., triangular; growth bushy, medium (36 in.); bedding; [Arizona Sunset × The Lady]; int. by Handley Rose Nurseries, 2003

Terry O' F, rb, 1977, Hughes; flowers dark red, reverse copper yellow; [sport of Redgold]; int. by Hughes Roses, 1976

Terry Wogan F, dy

Tersicore S, Barni, V.; int. in 1985

Teschendorffs Jubiläumsrose Pol, dr, 1928, Teschendorff; flowers vivid rosy crimson, darker than Orleans Rose and more brilliant; [sport of Orléans Rose]

Teschendorffs Jubiläumsrose, Rankende Cl F, dp, 1930, Teschendorff; flowers deep pink, fading to medium pink, small, dbl., borne in medium clusters

Teschendorff's Unterlage HMult, dp, about 1911

Tesco Bernstein F, dy, 1973, Haenchen, E.; bud ovoid; flowers brownish yellow, open, medium, semi-dbl., globular; foliage glossy, dark, leathery; vigorous, bushy growth; [Cognac × Allgold]; int. by Teschendorff, 1972

Tesco Bernstein – See **Bernstein**, Pol

Tesco Blickfang F, or, 1973, Haenchen, E.; bud ovoid; flowers dark vermilion-red, large, dbl.; foliage dark, soft; vigorous, upright, bushy growth; [Dicksons Flame × Circus]; int. by Teschendorff, 1972

Tesco Brennpunkt F, or, 1973, Haenchen, E.; bud ovoid; flowers bright vermilion-red, open, medium, semi-dbl.; foliage dark, soft; vigorous, upright growth; [Highlight × Dicksons Flame]; int. by Teschendorff, 1972

Tesco Goldteppich F, my, 1973, Haenchen, E.; bud ovoid; flowers medium, semi-dbl., cupped; foliage glossy, dark, leathery; vigorous, bushy growth; [Cognac × Allgold]; int. by Teschendorff, 1972

Tesco Lichtblick S, ob, 1973, Haenchen, E.; flowers pink and orange-pink on yellow ground, large, dbl., high-centered; abundant, continuous bloom; foliage glossy, leathery; vigorous, upright growth; [Yellow Holstein × Heidelberg]; int. by Teschendorff, 1972

Tesco Romanze F, pb, 1973, Haenchen, E.; bud globular; flowers pink, center white, open, small, semi-dbl.; foliage small, glossy, dark, leathery; vigorous, dwarf, bushy growth; [Marchenland × unknown]; int. by Teschendorff, 1972

Tesorino Min, lp, 1983, Rose Barni-Pistoia; flowers fresh light pink, small, 20 petals, borne in clusters, no fragrance; free-flowering; foliage small, light green, matte; prickles light green; low (30-50 cm.), spreading growth; groundcover; [seedling × seedling]; int. in 1982

Tess HMult, mp, 1939, Beckwith; flowers Neyron pink, passing to deeper pink, center brighter, large, dbl.; foliage large, rich green; strong stems; very vigorous growth; RULED EXTINCT 11/91

Tess Min, lp, 1991, Clements, John K.; flowers flesh pink, medium, semi-dbl., high-centered, borne mostly singly, no fragrance; foliage small, medium green, semi-glossy; few prickles; medium (30 cm.), bushy growth; [Cupcake × seedling]; int. by Heirloom Old Garden Roses, 1992

Tess HT, lp, 1998, McGredy, Sam IV; flowers large, light pink to creamy apricot, 4½ in., very full, cupped, borne mostly singly, slight fragrance; recurrent; foliage large, medium green, semi-glossy; prickles moderate; growth bushy, tall (120 cm.); [((Sexy Rexy × New Year) × (Freude × Courvoisier × Arthur Bell)) × Dreaming]; int. by McGredy, 1997

Tess of the d'Urbervilles S, dr, 1999, Austin, David; flowers dark, crimson red, large, very dbl., cupped, borne in small clusters, moderate fragrance; foliage large, dark green, semi-glossy; numerous prickles; branching, medium (3 ft.) growth; [The Squire × seedling]; int. by David Austin Roses, Ltd., 1998

Tessa F, mp, Gandy; flowers lilac-pink to rosey pink, slight fragrance; recurrent; foliage matte; compact, upright, medium growth; int. by Gandy's Roses, 2003

Tessa O'Keeffe F, dy, 1999, Kenny, David; flowers 3 in., dbl., borne in small clusters; foliage medium size, dark green, glossy; few prickles; bushy, medium (30 in.) growth; [Friesia × Kiskadee]

Testa Rossa – See **Holsteinperle**, HT

Tête de Pavot – See **Grosse Mohnkopfs Rose**, S

Tête d'Or F, my; flowers medium yellow, outer petals lighter, very dbl., shallow cup, borne usually in clusters, slight fragrance; big spring flush, recurrent; low (50-60 cm.), compact growth; int. by Meilland, 2005

Teton Beauty HRg, dp, 1927, Hansen, N.E.; flowers rich pink to crimson, dbl., cupped; recurrent bloom; foliage rugosa-like; very hardy; [Tetonkaha × American Beauty]

Tetonkaha HRg, dp, 1912, Hansen, N.E.; flowers deep rich pink, medium, semi-dbl.; profuse, non-recurrent bloom; vigorous (6 × 6 ft.) growth; hardy; [*R. macounii* × *R. rugosa* hybrid]

Teutonia HT, dp, Noack, Werner

Tewantin Cl HT, dp, 1953, Ulrick, L.W.; bud globular; flowers deep pink, large, dbl.; long stems; vigorous (12 ft.) growth; [Editor McFarland × Editor McFarland]

Texan Gr, mr, 1956, Lindquist; bud ovoid; flowers rose-red, 3½-4 in., 23 petals, high-centered, borne singly and in clusters, moderate fragrance; foliage dark, leathery; vigorous, upright growth; PP1471; [Improved Lafayette × Peace]; int. by Howard Rose Co.

Texas Min, my, 1985, Olesen; bud long, pointed ovoid; flowers buttercup yellow, 2 in., 20 petals, high-centered, borne singly and several together, slight apple-rose fragrance; recurrent; foliage small, medium green, semi-matte; prickles some, short, slightly curved, green; upright (40-50 cm.), bushy growth; hips globular, 15 mm., yellow-orange; PP6261; [Mini-Poul × seedling]; int. by John Mattock, Ltd, 1984

Texas HT, my, Kordes; bud long, pointed ovoid; flowers bright yellow, 4½-5 in., 35 -40 petals, high-centered, borne singly, intense fruity fragrance; recurrent; foliage large, dark green, leathery, glossy; prickles average, short, hooked downward; stems long; vigorous, upright growth; PP8617; [seedling × Cocktail 80]; int. in 1993

Texas Centennial HT, rb, 1935, Watkins, A.F.; flowers vermilion-red with some gold, center lighter, dbl., intense fragrance; recurrent; tall growth; [sport of Pres. Herbert Hoover]; int. by Dixie Rose Nursery; Gold Medal, Portland, 1935

Texas Centennial, Climbing Cl HT, rb, 1936, Dixie Rose Nursery (also Armstrong Roses, 1942); [sport of Texas Centennial]

Texas Centennial Panachée HT, ob, 1939, Tantau, Math.; flowers light orange with white stripes, large, dbl.

Texas Girl HT, yb, 1991, Meilland, Alain A.; flowers creamy yellow, large, full, slight fragrance; foliage large, medium green; tall, upright growth; PP7784; [sport of Lovely Girl]; int. by The Conard-Pyle Co., 1991

Texas Gold HT, my, 1935, Wolfe; flowers golden yellow occasionally tinged pink, large, dbl.; [sport of Pres. Herbert Hoover]

Texas Queen HT, mp, 1965, Leidy; flowers base cream, shading to light and darker pink, large, 100 petals, intense fragrance; foliage light green, soft; almost thornless; vigorous growth; PP2565; [sport of Tip Toes]; int. by Wilson Nursery

Texas Sunrise Min, yb, 1991, Umsawasdi, Dr. Theera; flowers yellow at times with pinkish edge, small, dbl., borne mostly singly, no fragrance; foliage medium size, medium green, semi-glossy; upright, bushy growth; [sport of Arizona Sunset]

Texas Wax HMult, lp, before 1935; [probably *R. multiflora* × *R. odorata*]

Thaïs – See **Lady Elgin**, HT

Thalassa HT, m, Dorieux; int. in 1978

Thalia – See **Thalie La Gentille**, HGal

Thalia HMult, w, 1895, Schmitt; bud pinkish; flowers very pure white, 3 cm., dbl., borne in large clusters, moderate fragrance; early, non-recurrent; few prickles; [*R. multiflora* × Paquerette]; int. by P. Lambert

Thalia Remontant HMult, w, 1903, Lambert, P.; flowers pure white, 2½-3 cm., semi-dbl. to dbl., borne in large clusters, strong musky fragrance; freely remontant; upright (8 ft.), branching growth; [(Thalia × unknown) × Mme Laurette Messimy]

Thalie La Gentille HGal, dp, before 1811, possibly Descemet; flowers deep rose, small, very full, cupped, moderate fragrance; sometimes classed as C

Thandi HT, dp; flowers deep petunia pink, dbl., high-centered; stems long; vigorous, tall growth; [sport of Mother's Value]; int. in 2000

Thanet Ballerina HT, w, 1974, Court; flowers pearl-white, blushed pink, moderate fragrance; foliage rich green; vigorous growth; [sport of Prima Ballerina]; int. by Thanet Roses, 1973

Thank You MinFl, pb, Chessum, Paul; flowers deep pink with shades of pink, yellow centers, semi-dbl., cupped, borne in clusters; foliage glossy; growth to 2 ft.; int. in 1996

Thank You HT, pb, 2004, Thomson, George L.; flowers dark pink, reverse lighter, 15 cm., full, borne mostly solitary, intense fragrance; foliage medium size, medium green, semi-glossy; prickles small, hooked; growth upright, medium (4-5 ft.); garden decorative; [Baronne E. de Rothschild × Kordes Perfecta]; int. by Ross Roses, 2001

Thanks To Sue MinFl, ab, 2004, Moore, Ralph S.; bud peach-apricot; flowers peachy-pink, 2 in., semi-dbl., borne mostly solitary, moderate fragrance; fast repeat; foliage medium size, medium green, semi-glossy; prickles small, straight; growth upright, spreading, tall (30 in.); specimen, containers, exhibition; [Joycie × Playboy]; int. by Sequoia Nurs., 2005

Thanksgiving HT, ob, 1963, Warriner, William A.; bud ovoid; flowers bronze shades, reverse orange-red, 3½ in., 38 petals, high-centered; foliage dark, leathery; vigorous growth; [Fred Howard × seedling]; int. by Howard's California Flowerland, 1962

Thanksgiving HT, pb, Howard, A. P.; buds medium, conical; flowers porcelain-rose with coppery tones, base of petals barium yellow, 4-4½ in., 35-45 petals, high-centered, borne mostly singly; foliage medium size, medium green; growth upright, branching, tall (5-7 ft.); hips ovoid, dark green; PP2524; [Louis Philippe × The Doctor]

Thanx Mom HT, dp, 1998, Muha, Julius; flowers hot fuschia pink, 4-4½ in., full, decorative, borne in small clusters, intense raspberry fragrance; recurrent; foliage medium size, medium green, semi-glossy; prickles moderate; growth bushy, medium (3 ft.); [Lancome × Stephens' Big Purple]; int. by Hortico, Inc., 1998

Thanx Mum – See **Thanx Mom**, HT

Thari S, dr

That's Incredible – See **Incredible**, S

That's Jazz LCl, dr, Olesen; bud pointed ovoid; flowers intense dark red, 10 cm., 45-50 petals, flat, borne in small to medium clusters, moderate spicy, floral fragrance; recurrent; foliage large, dark green, glossy; prickles few, 6 mm., curved downward, light green; growth bushy, 200-300 cm.; PP12552; [seedling × Norita]; int. by Poulsen, 1997

Thé a Fleur Gigantesque – See **Gigantesque**, T

The Abbottsford Rose S, m, 2002, Williams, J. Ben; flowers lavender pink, reverse purplish pink, ½-1 in., single, borne in large clusters, slight fragrance; foliage small, medium green, matte; prickles small, curved down; stems arching, with numerous branches; growth bushy, medium (3-4 ft.); landscape, hedging; [*R. chinensis* × *R. multiflora nana*]; similar to *R. multiflora*; int. by Certified Roses, Inc., 2003

The Abyssinian Rose – See ***R. abyssinica*** (R. Br.)

The Adjutant HT, mr, 1922, Pemberton; bud long, pointed; flowers bright red, dbl.

The Adjutant, Climbing Cl HT, mr; flowers large, dbl.

The Alamo HT, mr, 1958, Meilland, F.; bud ovoid; flowers cardinal red, 3½-4½ in., 110 petals; foliage leathery; vigorous, upright, bushy growth; PP1689; [Happiness × Independence]; int. by Co-operative Rose Growers, 1957

The Alexandra T, op, 1900, Paul, W.; flowers light salmon-pink, large, dbl.

The Alexandra Rose S, pb, 1994, Austin, David; flowers coppery pink, medium, 5 petals, borne in large clusters; foliage medium size, medium green, semi-glossy; few prickles; bushy, compact (51 in.) growth; [Shropshire Lass × Heritage]; int. by David Austin Roses, Ltd., 1992

The Allies Pol, w, 1930, Heers; flowers white suffused pale pink, small, dbl., open, borne in clusters, slight fragrance; foliage small, glossy; dwarf, bushy growth

The Alnwick Rose – See **Alnwick Castle**, S

(The) Apothecary's Rose of Provins – See ***R. gallica officinalis*** (Thory)

The Archbishop HT, pb, 2004, Thomson, George L.; flowers smoky pink, reverse silver, medium, full, borne mostly solitary, moderate fragrance; foliage medium size, dark green, glossy; prickles medium, hooked; growth upright, medium to tall, (4½-5½ ft.); garden decorative; [Baronne E. de Rothschild × Granada]; int. by Ross Roses, 2002

The Attenborough Rose F, lp, Dickson; flowers delicate pink with green tinge on petal edges, large, dbl., cupped, borne in clusters of 4-17; recurrent; foliage medium green, glossy; few prickles; vigorous, upright to bushy growth; int. by Dickson Roses, 2005

The Audrey Hepburn Rose – See **UNICEF**, F

The Auld Mug HT, pb, Matthews; flowers antique pink, paling to beige, dbl., cupped; foliage medium green; upright, medium growth; int. by Matthews Nurseries, 2000

The Australian Bicentennial HT, mr, 1987, Bell, Ronald J.; flowers medium to deep red, well-formed, 30 petals, borne usually singly, intense fragrance; foliage medium size, medium green, glossy, disease-resistant; prickles curved, green; tall, branching, average growth; [(Daily Sketch × unknown) × Red Planet]; named in commemoration of the Australian Bicentennial and the World Federation Rose Convention, 1988; int. by Roy H. Rumsey, Pty. Ltd., 1988

The Backpackers Rose – See **Caroline Clarke**, HT

The Bairn HT, dy, 1977, Wood; flowers golden yellow, large, 40-50 petals; foliage dark, leathery; dwarf growth; [Arthur Bell × seedling]

The Beacon HWich, rb, 1922, Paul, W.; flowers bright fiery-red with white-eye (as in American Pillar), 5 cm., semi-dbl., cupped, borne in large clusters, no fragrance; foliage apple-green, glossy; numerous prickles; vigorous, climbing (to 8 ft.) growth

The Belle Canadese HT, lp, 2006, Gareffa, N.; flowers delicate, creamy, light pink with a bit of yellow at the base, 3-4 in., full, borne mostly solitary, intense fragrance; continuous bloom; foliage medium size, medium green, semi-glossy; prickles small, slightly hooked, moderate; growth upright, short (about 2 ft.); [Savoy Hotel × seedling]

The Bells of Hiroshima – See **Hiroshima no Kane**, HT

The Beloved – See **Priyatama**, HT

The Bishop HT, dr, 1937, Dickson, A.; flowers bright crimson, large, dbl.; foliage dark; vigorous growth; Gold Medal, NRS, 1937

The Bishop C, m; flowers unusual shade of cerise-magenta, fading bluish purple, rosette, flat; early bloom; slender, upright (4-5 ft.) growth

The Bishop of Bradford S, dy, Pearce, J.; flowers deep old gold, moderate fragrance; foliage dark green, matte; numerous prickles; growth to 12-15 in.; [sport of Maigold]; int. by Cants of Colchester, 2006

The Bourbon Jacques – See **Bourbon Rose**, B

The Braintree Rose – See **The John Ray Trust Rose**, F

The Bride T, w, 1885, May; flowers white tinged pink; [sport of Catherine Mermet]

The Bride HT, w, 1963, Herholdt, J.A.; bud pointed, ivory-white; flowers well-formed, 30 petals; foliage glossy; [White Swan × seedling]; int. by Herholdt's Nursery

The Brownie Rose F, my, Harkness; flowers clear yellow, dbl., cupped, borne in clusters, moderate fragrance; recurrent; medium (1 m.) growth; int. by R. Harkness & Co., 2005

The Bull – See **Taurus**, F

The Cambridge Rose – See **Cantabrigiensis**, S

The Care Rose S, dy, 1999, Horner, Heather M.; flowers buttercup yellow, reverse medium yellow, small, semi-dbl., borne in small clusters; foliage small, medium green, glossy; few prickles; compact, low (2 ft.); patio growth; [Apricot Sunrise × (Golden Future × Baby Love)]

The Carer's Rose HT, w, 2000, Thomson, George L.; flowers white with rose on outer petals, 5 in., dbl., borne mostly singly, moderate fragrance; foliage medium size, dark green, glossy; few prickles; growth upright, medium (4-5 ft.); [Francis Phoebe × Ophelia]

The Caron Keating Rose F, ab, Harkness; flowers apricot in center, outer petals fading lighter, 4 in., dbl., high-centered, borne in trusses, slight fragrance; free-flowering; vigorous, bushy (80 cm.) growth; int. by R. Harkness & Co., 2006

The Charlestonian N, w, 2000, Patterson, William M.; flowers light pink, reverse white, 1 in., very full, borne in small clusters, slight fragrance; foliage medium size, medium green, semi-glossy; prickles moderate; growth spreading, medium (6 ft.); [Champneys' Pink Cluster × unknown]; int. by Roses Unlimited, 2001

The Cheshire Regiment HT, ab, Fryer, Gareth; flowers apricot-salmon, high-centered; free-flowering; disease-resistant foliage; sturdy (3 ft.) growth; int. by Fryer's Roses, 1995

The Chief HT, ob, 1940, Lammerts, Dr. Walter; bud long, pointed; flowers flame, coral and copper, 4-6 in., 35 petals; vigorous, bushy, spreading growth; [Charles P. Kilham × Pres. Herbert Hoover]; int. by Armstrong Nursery

The Children's Rose HT, my; int. by Meilland, 1989

The Children's Rose – See **Frederic Mistral**, HT

The Children's Rose – See **Gina Lollobrigida**, HT

The Clerk S, dr, Jerabek, Paul E.; int. in 1997

The Cluster Rose – See ***R. glomerata*** (Rehder & Wilson)

The Colour Purple Min, m, 2004, Jalbert, Brad; flowers deep purple, 1¼ in., dbl., borne mostly solitary, moderate lemon fragrance; foliage medium size, dark green, very glossy, dark when new; prickles small, dark, moderate; growth upright, medium (14 in.); containers, garden decoration; [Loving Touch × Rubies]; int. in 2004

The Colwyn Rose F, m, Cowlishaw, Frank; flowers lavender to mauve, dbl., cupped to pompon, borne in clusters, slight fragrance; recurrent; int. by Fryer, 1992

The Commodore – See **Kommodore**, F

The Compass Rose S, w, Kordes; flowers pure white with red stamens, semi-dbl., cupped, borne in clusters, intense fragrance; recurrent; foliage dark green, glossy; medium (3 ft.) growth; int. in 1997; Edland Fragrance Award, RNRS, 1995

The Compassionate Friends – See **Compassionate Friend**, F

The Conductor – See **Dirigent**, HMsk

The Constance Pink F, yb, 2003, Rawlins, R.; flowers yellow with pink edge, small, dbl., borne in small clusters; foliage medium size, dark green, glossy; prickles 1 cm., triangular, moderate; growth upright, medium (1 m.); garden; [Golden Future × (Silver Jubilee × Pretty Lady)]

The Cottage Rose – See **Cottage Rose**, S, 1994

The Countryman S, mp, 1987, Austin, David; bud oval; flowers greyish-rose, 6-8 cm., 40 petals, rosette, borne singly and in sprays of 3-5, intense damask fragrance; repeat bloom; foliage medium size, medium green, matte; prickles hooked, small, downward pointing, pale; spreading, bushy, medium growth; hips ovoid, medium, red; PP7556; [Lilian Austin × Comte de Chambord]

The Coxswain HT, pb, 1984, Cocker, Alexander M.; flowers cream and pink blend, large, 35 petals, intense fragrance; foliage medium size, medium green, semi-glossy; bushy growth; [(Tropicana × Ballet) × Silver Jubilee]; int. by Cocker & Sons, 1985

The Creakes Rose MinFl, ab, 2006, Paul Chessum Roses; flowers 4 cm., dbl., borne in small clusters; foliage medium size, dark green, semi-glossy; prickles large, sharp, tan/pink, numerous; growth bushy, medium (30 in.); garden decoration, beds, borders; int. by World of Roses, 2005

The Crepe Rose – See **Paul Perras**, HP

The Dahlia Rose F, pb, 2004, Moore, Ralph S.; flowers medium pink to white, hand-painted, reverse white, 3 in., very full, borne in small clusters, slight fragrance; foliage medium size, medium green, semi-glossy; prickles small, straight, light green, few; growth spreading, medium (28-36 in.); containers, landscape, cutting; [Fairy Moss × Old Master]; int. by Sequoia Nurs., 2004

The Daldry Rose F, rb, 2006, Horner; flowers red/deep pink with yellow eye, reverse lighter with white veining, 1½ in., semi-dbl., borne in small clusters; foliage medium size, dark green, semi-glossy; prickles large, hooked, deep red, few; growth bushy, medium (3½ ft.); garden decorative; [seedling × (Robin Hood × seedling) × Nice 'n' easy]; int. by Warley Roses, 2007

The Dandy HT, dr, 1905, Paul, G.; flowers fiery maroon crimson, small; [Bardou Job × unknown]

The Daniel HT, dr, 1990, Williams, J. Benjamin; bud ovoid; flowers dark velvety red, reverse burgundy, medium, 36 petals, high-centered, borne usually singly, no fragrance; foliage large, dark green, semi-glossy; few prickles; upright, medium growth; fruit not observed; [Chrysler Imperial × Queen Elizabeth]; int. by The Peninsula Nursery, 1990

The Dark Lady S, dr, 1994, Austin, David; bud long, pointed, globular; flowers dark ruby red, 3-3½ in., very full, cupped, flattens, borne singly and in small clusters, moderate fragrance; recurrent; foliage medium size, dark green, semi-glossy; prickles some, medium, hooked downward; stems 12-18 in.; medium (3 ft.), upright, bushy growth; PP8677; [Mary Rose × Prospero]; int. by David Austin Roses, Ltd., 1991

The Dawson Rose – See **Dawson**, HMult

The Dazzler Cl HT, mr, 1955, Marsh's Nursery; flowers bright red, petals ruffled, single; profuse, repeated bloom; [Dainty Bess, Climbing × unknown]

The Didgemere Rose S, my, 1998, Ferguson, B.; flowers medium yellow, 2½-3 in., full, borne mostly singly, moderate fragrance; recurrent; foliage medium size, medium green, dull; prickles small, slightly hooked; upright, low (3-4ft.) growth; [Sunsprite × Trier]; int. by Burston Nurseries, Inc., 1998

The Dixon Rose S, mp, Clements, John; flowers single; upright (4 ft.) growth; int. by Heirloom Roses, 2004

The Doctor HT, mp, 1936, Howard, F.H.; flowers satiny pink, well-formed, 6 in., 25 petals; foliage soft, light; dwarf, bushy growth; [Mrs J.D. Eisele × Los Angeles]; int. by Dreer; Gold Medal, NRS, 1938

The Doctor, Climbing Cl HT, mp, 1950, Dyess; flowers silky pink, 6 in., intense fragrance; [sport of The Doctor]; int. by Reliance Rose Nursery

The Doll's Festival – See **Hinamatsuri**, F

The Dove – See **Dove**, S

The Dove F, w, 1985, Tantau, Math.; flowers medium, 20 petals, no fragrance; foliage medium size, light green, glossy; upright growth

The Dowager Countess of Roden HT, lp, 1919, Paul, W.; flowers bright silvery pink, dbl.; [Viscountess Enfield × George C. Waud]

The Duke HT, rb, 1956, Von Abrams; bud globular; flowers carmine-red, reverse gold, 5-6 in., 55 petals, high-centered, borne in clusters of 3-15, slight fragrance; foliage semi-glossy; vigorous, open growth; PP1522; [Applause × Peace]; int. by Peterson & Dering, 1956

The Ednaston Rose LCl, w

The Edwardian Lady – See **Edith Holden**, F

The Endeavour S, op, Austin, David; flowers salmon pink with yellow background, full, shallow cup, moderate spicy fragrance; free-flowering; foliage dark; growth to 4 ft.; favors hot weather

The English Lady F, ab, Harkness; flowers apricot-pink, fading lighter, 4 in., dbl., cupped, borne in clusters, moderate fruity fragrance; recurrent; medium (100 cm.), rounded growth; int. as Susan Daniel, R. Harkness & Co., 2005

The Fairy Pol, lp, 1932, Bentall, Ann; flowers pink, small, dbl., rosette, borne in clusters, no fragrance; recurrent bloom; foliage glossy, small; compact, arching, spreading growth; hardy; [Paul Crampel × Lady Gay]; int. by J.A. Bentall

The Fairy Queen – See **Fairy Queen**, Pol

The Farmer's Wife F, lp, 1962, Boerner; bud ovoid; flowers 4½ in., 38 petals, cupped, borne in clusters, intense fragrance; foliage leathery, glossy; upright, moderate growth; PP2196; [Queen Elizabeth × Spartan]; int. by J&P, 1962

The Farquhar Rose – See **Farquhar**, HWich

The Faun – See **Bossa Nova**, F

The Fisherman's Cot F, op, 1991, Harkness, R., & Co., Ltd.; bud pointed; flowers light salmon pink, aging to deeper pink, 3-4 in., 28 petals, cupped, borne in sprays of 3-9, moderate sweet, slightly pungent fragrance; recurrent; foliage small to medium size, dark green, semi-glossy; upright (3 ft.), spreading growth; [Radox Bouquet × Anna Ford]; int. as Royal Ballgown, Heirloom Roses

The Flower Arranger F, ab, 1984, Fryers Nursery, Ltd.; bud large; flowers peach, well-formed, semi-dbl., borne in trusses; foliage large, dark, glossy; upright growth; [seedling × seedling]

The Fordham Rose HT, rb, Williams, J. Benjamin; flowers medium red with plum edges, dbl., high-centered, moderate fragrance; foliage large, dark green, disease-resistant; int. in 1995

The French Strumpet HGal, dp, 2006, Hulse, Merrill; flowers a mix of OGR and modern form, 1½ in., dbl., borne in small clusters, slight fragrance; once-blooming, in Spring; foliage medium green, typical Gallica; prickles moderate, 1/16 in., setaceous, brown; growth spreading, tall (6 ft.); specimen; [unknown × unknown]

The Friar S, lp, 1969, Austin, David; flowers blush, edged white, medium, 10 petals; repeat bloom; foliage dark; [Ivory Fashion × seedling]

The Garden Editor Min, dy, 1989, Williams, Ernest D.; flowers small, 33 petals, moderate fragrance; foliage small, medium green, glossy; upright, bushy growth; [Gold Badge × Yellow Jewel]; int. in 1988

The Garland HMult, w, 1835, Wood or Wells; flowers faint yellow, pink, and white, semi-dbl., borne in corymbose clusters, moderate musk fragrance; late-season, not recurrent; prickles numerous, large; moderate climbing (8 ft.) growth; [probably *R. moschata* × *R. multiflora*]; sometimes classed as HMsk or Hsemp

The Gathering – See **Daniel Boon**, S

The Gem – See **Marie van Houtte**, T

The General HT, mr, 1920, Pemberton; flowers blood-red, flushed lighter, large, dbl., globular, moderate damask fragrance; foliage dark, bronze, leathery; vigorous, low growth

The Generous Gardener S, lp, 2004; flowers soft pink in center, very pale on outer petals, 6 cm., very full, cupped, borne in small clusters, intense fragrance; recurrent; foliage large, dark green, glossy; prickles medium, concave; growth bushy, arching, tall (150 cm.); garden, decorative; [Sharifa Asma × seedling (unnamed pink English-type shrub)]; int. by David Austin Roses, Ltd., 2002; Fragrance Award, The Hague, 2006, Silver Certificate, The Hague, 2006

The Gentleman HT, yb, 1958, Hay; bud long; flowers creamy yellow flushed pink, semi-dbl.; [seedling × Irish Fireflame]; int. by Marsh's Nursery

The Gift Pol, w, Demits; flowers pure white with yellow stamens, very small, single, flat, borne in long clusters, slight sweet fragrance; recurrent; foliage disease-resistant; vigorous, low growth; hips tiny, prolific, currant red; int. in 1981

The Gold Award Rose F, dy, Olesen; flowers deep yellow, reverse lighter, 2½-3 in., very full, open cup, borne in large clusters, very slight fragrance; recurrent; foliage dark green, glossy; prickles some, 6 mm., linear to concave; bushy (40-60 cm.) growth; PP15499; [Unnamed plant × Joey's Palace]; int. by Cants of Colchester, 2003

The Governator MinFl, or, 2003, Greenwood, Chris; flowers brilliant orange-red, long-lasting, 2-3 in., full, high-centered, borne mostly solitary, no fragrance; recurrent; foliage medium green, matte; prickles medium, slighly hooked downward, pale amber; growth compact, medium (1-2 ft.); garden decoration, exhibition; [Silverado × Ingrid Bergman]; int. in 2004

The Grace Land Rose S, mp, 2000, Horner, Colin P.; flowers medium pink, reverse lighter, 5 cm., dbl., borne in large clusters, slight fragrance; foliage small, medium green, semi-glossy; numerous prickles; growth spreading, medium (60 cm.); patio, containers; [(Robin Red Breast × Lichtkonigin Lucia) × Pretty Lady]

The Great Showman HT, dp, Shastri, Dr. N.V.; flowers deep, clear pink, large, dbl.; prickles very few; vigorous growth; int. in 2004

The Green Rose – See **Green Rose**, Ch

The Guthrie Rose MinFl, rb, 2006, Wells, Verlie W.; flowers red and yellow, reverse light red with white base, 1½ in, dbl., borne in small clusters; foliage medium size, dark green, semi-glossy; prickles 3/16 in., hooked, few; growth upright, bushy, medium (36-45 in.); garden decorative, exhibition; [seedling × Memphis King]; int. by Wells MidSouth Roses, 2006

The Halcyon Days Rose – See **Rosarium Uetersen**, LCl

The Herbalist S, dp, 1994, Austin, David; flowers deep pink, medium, 6-14 petals, borne in small clusters; foliage medium size, medium green, semi-glossy; some prickles; medium (90 cm.), bushy, spreading growth; [seedling × Louise Odier]; int. by David Austin Roses, Ltd., 1991

The Holt S, dp, Mehring, Bernhard F.; Gold Medal, Glasgow, 1997

The Hon Mrs Cat D, mp, Scarman; non-remontant; growth to 4 ft.; int. in 1995

The Hughes – See **Bridesmaid**, T

The Hunter – See **Hunter**, HRg

The Impressionist LCl, yb, Clements, John; flowers color varies from yellow to pumpkin orange, 4 in., 100 petals, moderate honey/peachy myrrh fragrance; recurrent; foliage dark green with slight blue cast; growth to 9-12 ft. high, 6-8 ft. wide; PPAF; int. by Heirloom Roses, 2000

The Indian HT, dr, 1939, Clark, A.; flowers very dark red, large, semi-dbl.; vigorous growth; [Sensation × seedling]; int. by Brundrett

The Ingenious Mr Fairchild S, pb, 2004; flowers lavender pink, reverse lighter mauve, 7 cm., very full, borne in small clusters, moderate fragrance; foliage medium size, dark green, semi-glossy; prickles medium, deeply concave; growth bushy, broad, branching, medium (120 cm.); garden decorative; [seedling (medium pink English-type shrub) × seedling (medium pink English-type shrub)]; int. by David Austin Roses, Ltd., 2003

The Ionian Rose – See **Phyllis McDonald**, HT

The J. S. E. Rose F, dy, Kordes

The Jacobite Rose – See **Alba Maxima**, A

The Jester Gr, yb, 1960, Leenders, J.; flowers yellow changing to red, compact, dbl., borne in clusters, slight fragrance; foliage dark; [Masquerade × High Noon]; int. by British Hort. Co., 1959

The John Ray Trust Rose F, dy, 2001, Horner, Heather M.; flowers deep yellow, medium yellow reverse, 8 cm., semi-dbl., borne in small clusters, moderate fragrance; foliage medium size, medium green, glossy; prickles medium brown, curved, moderate; growth upright, tall (110 cm.); garden decorative; [(Buttons × (Korp × Southampton)) × Pretty Lady]; int. by Warley Rose Gardens, 2002

The Jubilee Rose – See **P. G. Wodehouse**, HT

The Karnival – See **Cocorico**, F

The King's Rubies HMult, mr, Clements, John; flowers deep ruby red, 2 in., very full, cupped, borne in large clusters; once-blooming, long season; vigorous (15 ft.) growth; int. by Heirloom Roses, 2000

The Knight S, dr, 1969, Austin, David; flowers crimson turning purple and mauve, petals soft, medium, 80 petals, flat, moderate Damask fragrance; recurrent; foliage dark green; [Chianti × seedling]

The Ladakh Rose – See **Ladakh Rose**, Ch

The Lady HT, yb, 1986, Fryer, Gareth; flowers honey yellow, petals edged salmon, well-formed, large, 35 petals, high-centered, borne singly and in clusters, slight fragrance; recurrent; foliage medium size, medium green, semi-glossy; upright growth; [Pink Parfait × Redgold]; int. by Fryer's Nursery, Ltd., 1985; Gold Medal, Baden-Baden, 1987

The Lady Scarman HMsk, w, Scarman; flowers white; recurrent; growth to 5 ft.; there are reports of a version growing 12 ft. tall; int. in 1985

The Lifeline Rose F, rb, 2000, Walsh, Richard; flowers red, reverse white, large, full, borne in small clusters, slight fragrance; free-flowering; foliage medium size, dark green, semi-glossy; numerous prickles; compact, medium growth

The Lion HMult, dp, 1901, Paul, G.; flowers bright crimson, white center, 7-10 cm., single, flat, borne in small clusters, no fragrance; [Turner's Crimson Rambler × Beauté Inconstante]

The Lion – See **Leo**, F

Thé Maréchal – See **Lamarque**, N

The Marquess of Bristol HT, yb, 1998, Webster, Robert; flowers yellow, pink edge, yellow reverse, 4-5 in., dbl., borne mostly singly, slight fragrance; foliage medium size, medium green, glossy; prickles moderate, medium, hooked; upright, medium growth; [Pristine × Remember Me]; int. by Handley Rose Nurseries, 1999

The Master HT, lp, Datta, Sekhar; bud pointed; flowers baby pink, well-formed; free-flowering; strong growth; int. in 2005

The Master Cutler HT, mr, 1954, Liberty Hill Nurs.; flowers cherry-red shaded rose, well-formed, very large, dbl.; vigorous growth; [sport of The Doctor]

The Matsukawa Rose – See **Forever Friends**, S

The Matthew HT, pb, 1997, Jellyman, J.S.; flowers medium, very dbl.; few prickles; [Silver Jubilee × Pres. Petts]; int. by Bristol Workways Ltd.

The Mayflower S, pb, 2002, Austin, David; flowers very dbl., borne in small clusters, moderate fragrance; foliage medium size, dark green, matte, leathery; prickles few, medium, concave; growth bushy, upright, medium (120 cm.); garden decorative; [peachy-pink English-type shrub × yellow English-type shrub]; int. by David Austin Roses, Ltd., 2001

The McCartney Rose HT, mp, 1995, Meilland, Alain; bud oval, medium; flowers medium pink, reverse lighter, 4½-5 in., 20-22 petals, cupped, borne mostly singly and in small clusters, intense fragrance; good repeat; foliage large, medium green, semi-glossy; prickles numerous, medium, brownish; bushy, medium growth; PP8391; [(Nirvana × Papa Meilland) × First Prize]; int. by The Conard-Pyle Co.; Gold Medal, LeRoelx, 1988, Gold Medal, Paris, 1988, Gold Medal, Monza, 1988, Gold Medal, Geneva, 1988

The McClaren Rose Min, dy, Jalbert; int. in 2000

The Mencap Rose – See **Brian Rix**, S

The Merrion Rose MinFl, rb, 2003, Kenny, David; flowers pink/red with yellow eye, reverse yellow, 2 in., single, borne in large clusters, slight fragrance; continuous; foliage small, medium green, semi-glossy; prickles small, hooked downward, light brown; growth spreading, medium (2 ft. × 2 ft.); patio, containers; [New Year × Eyeopener]; int. in 2004

The Meteor HT, dr, 1887, Evans; bud large; flowers velvety crimson, large, semi-dbl., moderate fragrance

The Miller S, mp, 1981, Austin, David; bud globular; flowers 40 petals, rosette, borne 1-4 per cluster, moderate fragrance; recurrent; foliage medium green; prickles hooked, red; upright, bushy growth; [Baroness Rothschild × Chaucer]; int. in 1970

The Moth – See **Moth**, S

The Mountie F, mr, 1949, Eddie; flowers cherry-red, medium, 12-15 petals, borne in huge trusses; foliage leathery, glossy, light green; bushy growth; [Springtime × World's Fair]

The Mouse – See **Grey Pearl**, HT

The Nanango Rose – See **Kathleen Kellehan**, S

The New Century – See **New Century**, HRg

The New Dawn – See **New Dawn**, LCl

The New Riviera Rose – See **Fortuna**, T

The Nightwatch S, rb, Williams, J.B.; flowers wine red and pink stripes, aging to purple-pink, borne in large clusters; foliage dark green; growth spreading; int. by Hortico, 2003

The Nun S, w, Austin, David; flowers creamy white, semi-dbl., deeply cupped, borne in sprays, slight fragrance; free-flowering; stems slim, plentiful; upright (4 ft.) growth; int. by David Austin Roses, 1987

The Nurse S, w; int. by Heirloom, 2004

The Observer HT, ab, Fryer, Gareth; flowers deep, non-fading apricot yellow, shapely; free-flowering; int. in 1992

The Old Fashioned Rose HT, 1930, Archer; flowers deep crimson, dbl.; very vigorous growth

The Optimist – See **Sweet Repose**, F

The Painter – See **Michelangelo**, F

The Papworth Hospital Rose HT, dr, 2004, Paul Chessum Roses; flowers 7 cm., dbl., borne mostly solitary, slight fragrance; foliage medium size, medium green, semi-glossy; prickles moderate, medium, green; growth upright, medium (90cm.); bedding, borders, containers; int. by Love4Plants Ltd, 2004

The Pearl – See **Purezza**, LCl

The People – See **People**, F

The People's Princess F, mp, 1997, Bees; flowers very dbl., borne in small clusters; foliage medium size, medium green, semi-glossy; upright, medium growth; [seedling × seedling]; int. by L.W. Van Geest Farms Ltd., 1997

The Physician LCl, lp, 2007, Mattock, Robert; flowers very full, usually quartered, borne in small clusters; foliage medium size, dark green, glossy; prickles medium, slightly hooked concave lower, moderate; growth climbing, tall (2½-3 m.); [sport of Penny Lane]; int. by Robert Mattock Roses, 2007

The Pilgrim S, my, 1993, Austin, David; bud globular, pointed ovoid; flowers yellow in center, fading to creamy white on outer petals, 2½-3¼ in., 170 petals, cupped, borne singly and in small clusters, intense tea and myrrh fragrance; recurrent; foliage bright green, leathery; prickles few, medium, hooked downward; stems medium to long; strong, upright (3-3½ ft.) growth; PP8678; [Graham Thomas × Yellow Button]

The Pink Professor – See **Debonnaire**, S

The Poet S, dy, Clements, John; flowers deep primrose yellow, 3½ in., very full, cupped, intense fresh fragrance; recurrent; foliage deep green, glossy, holly-like; compact (3 ft.) growth; PPAF; int. by Heirloom Roses, 2003

The Polar Star – See **Polstjärnan**, LCl

The Pompeii Rose – See **Summer Damask**, D

The Portland from Glendora – See **Joasine Hanet**, P

The Portland Rose – See **Duchess of Portland**, P

The Prince S, dr, Austin, David; bud long, globular, cuspidate apex; flowers dark magenta, 2¾ in., 125 petals, deeply cupped, flattens, borne singly and in clusters of up to 12, intense old rose fragrance; recurrent; foliage dark green, leathery; prickles numerous, straight, slanted downward; short (30-36 in.), upright, bushy growth; PP8813; [Lilian Austin × The Squire]; int. by David Austin Roses, 1990

The Prince Imperial F, dp, Delbard; bud globular; flowers deep pink with touch of orange, large, dbl., cupped, borne in clusters, slight fragrance; recurrent; medium growth; int. in 1995

The Prince's Trust LCl, mr; flowers cherry red, 3½ in., dbl., borne in large clusters, from top to bottom, moderate sweet, spice fragrance; recurrent; foliage dark green; vigorous (10-12 ft.) growth; int. by Harkness, 2002

The Princess Elizabeth HT, ob, 1927, Wheatcroft Bros.; flowers orange-yellow, edged deep cerise, large, dbl.; [sport of The Queen Alexandra Rose]

The Princess of Wales – See **Princess of Wales**, F

The Prioress S, lp, 1969, Austin, David; flowers blush to white, yellow stamens, medium, dbl., cupped, moderate fragrance; recurrent; vigorous, upright (4 ft.) growth; [La Reine Victoria × seedling]

The PTA News Centenary HT, ab, McGredy; flowers apricot cream, deeper in center, large, dbl., high-centered, borne singly; recurrent; foliage glossy; vigorous, tall growth; [Solitaire × New Zealand]; int. by Ludwig's Roses, 1999

The Puritan HT, w, 1886, Bennett; flowers white, tinged light yellow at base, large, moderate fragrance; [Mabel Morrison × Devoniensis]

The Queen – See **Souv de S. A. Prince**, T

The Queen HT, ob, 1954, Lowe; bud pointed; flowers orange suffused salmon, medium, 26-30 petals; very free growth

The Queen HMsk, dr, before 1960; flowers dark purple-crimson, large, semi-dbl.

The Queen Alexandra Rose HT, rb, 1918, McGredy; bud old gold; flowers bright red, reverse shaded old-gold, base orange, 5 in., dbl., cupped, moderate fragrance; foliage glossy, dark; bushy growth; Gold Medal, NRS, 1917

The Queen Alexandra Rose, Climbing Cl HT, rb, 1929, Lindecke; flowers light red, orange center, large, full, moderate fragrance; [sport of The Queen Alexandra Rose]; int. by Kordes

The Queen Alexandra Rose, Climbing Cl HT, rb, 1931, Harkness

The Queen Elizabeth Rose – See **Queen Elizabeth**, Gr

The Queen Elizabeth Rose, Climbing – See **Queen Elizabeth, Climbing**, Cl Gr

The Queen Mother – See **August Seebauer**, F

The Queen Mother F, mp, 1959, Stedman; flowers soft rosy pink, large, 45-50 petals, borne on large trusses; foliage glossy, light green; vigorous growth; [sport of Nymph]

The Queen of Persia HT, ob, 1940; flowers light orange-yellow, large, dbl.

The Quest – See **Wandering Minstrel**, F

The Rajah HT, dr, 1937, Clark, A.; flowers deep red, dbl.; bushy growth; [Red-Letter Day × unknown]; int. by NRS Victoria

The Reeve S, dp, 1981, Austin, David; bud globular; flowers 58 petals, cupped, borne 1-5 per cluster, intense fragrance; repeat bloom; foliage red, turning to green; prickles hooked, red; spreading, shrubby growth; [Lilian Austin × Chaucer]; int. in 1973

The Rhenish Rose HT, lp, Kordes; flowers creamy pale pink, dbl., high-centered, borne mostly singly; recurrent; stems sturdy; medium growth; int. in 2000

The Ribbon Rose – See **Ribbon Rose**, Min

The Ridge School – See **Princess Alexandra**, S

The Robe HT, dr, Tantau

The Rose Tatoo HT, m, 1958, Gaujard; flowers salmon-pink tipped and spotted lavender, large, semi-dbl.; foliage leathery; very vigorous, upright growth; [(Opera × unknown) × (Opera × seedling)]

The Roseville College – See **The Roseville College Rose**, HT

The Roseville College Rose HT, yb; int. in 1990

The Rotarian – See **Rotary Sunrise**, HT

The Royal Brompton Rose – See **Yves Piaget**, HT

The Royal Society of Organists Rose F, lp, Tantau; int. by Pocock's Roses, 2004

The Rugby Rose HT, ob, Gandy, Douglas; flowers apricot-orange, well-shaped, long-lasting, large, slight fragrance; foliage olive green, disease-resistant; commissioned by the Rugby Burough Council; int. by Gandy's Roses, 2001

The St. Edmund's Rose – See **Bonita Renaissance**, S

Thé Sapho – See **Mistress Bosanquet**, B

The Scorpion – See **Scorpio**, HT

The Scotsman HT, m, Olesen; bud pointed ovoid; flowers lavender, 10-15 cm., 25-30 petals, high-centered, flattens, borne singly, slight spicy fragrance; recurrent; foliage dark green, glossy; prickles few, 5-8 mm., deeply concave; bushy, medium (2-3 ft.) growth; PP13293; [Karen Blixen × Mainzer Fastnacht]; int. by Poulsen Roser, 2001

The Seckford Rose – See **Pink Robusta**, S

The Senator HT, mr, 1981, Weeks, O.L.; bud ovoid, long; flowers bright medium red, petals loosely rolled outward, 46 petals, borne mostly singly, slight musk fragrance; foliage large, leathery, wrinkled, dark; prickles long, narrow-based, brown, curved down; tall, upright growth; PP4709; [seedling × Suspense]; int. in 1980

The Service Rose – See **Women in Military**, S

The Shepherdess S, ab, 2006; flowers rich apricot-pink, fading to pale apricot on outer petals, 7 cm., very full, deeply cupped, borne in small clusters, moderate fruity fragrance; recurrent; foliage medium size, dark green, semi-glossy; prickles few, medium, deeply concave, light green; growth upright, medium (100 cm.); garden decorative; [seedling × seedling]; int. by David Austin Roses, Ltd., 2005

The Sir Steven Redgrave Rose – See **Pure Gold**, S

The Sobell Rose F, dp, 2004, Paul Chessum Roses; flowers strong deep pink, 5 cm., full, borne in small clusters, slight fragrance; foliage medium size, medium green, semi-glossy; growth compact, medium (60 cm.); beds, borders, containers; int. by Love4Plants, 2004

The Soham Rose F, lp, Harkness; flowers pearl blush, dbl., high-centered, slight fragrance; recurrent; growth to 3 ft.; int. by R. Harkness and Co., 2004

The Songbird Rose – See **Pleine de Grâce**, S

The Soroptimist Rose – See **Soroptimist International**, Min

The Soroptimist Rose – See **Stella Giles**, F

The Spiedel Rose F, or, 2000, Jellyman, J.S.; flowers orange-red, reverse lighter, 3 in., semi-dbl., borne mostly singly, slight fragrance; recurrent; foliage large, medium green, glossy; few prickles; growth compact, tall (3 ft.); [Wembley Stadium × Alexander]

The Squire S, dr, 1981, Austin, David; bud globular; flowers very dark red, large, heavy, 120 petals, cupped, borne 1-3 per cluster, intense old rose fragrance; recurrent; foliage dark; prickles straight; open, bushy (3 ft.) growth; [The Knight × Château de Clos Vougeot]; int. in 1976

The St Mark's Rose – See **Rose d'Amour**, Misc OGR

The Stork HT, mp, 1952, Whisler; bud long, pointed; flowers carmine-rose, 5-5½ in., 28 petals, high-centered; foliage leathery; bushy growth; [seedling × The Doctor]; int. by Germain's

The Sulgrave Rose F, ob, 2000, Horner, Colin P.; flowers orange yellow, reverse creamy yellow, 5 cm., single, borne in large clusters, moderate fragrance; foliage medium size, light green, semi-glossy; prickles moderate; bushy, medium (100 cm.) growth; [(Robin Red Breast × Lichtkonigin Lucia) × (seedling × *R. longicuspis*)]

The Sun F, op, 1974, McGredy, Sam IV; flowers salmon-orange, large, 15 petals; [(Little Darling × Goldilocks) × Irish Mist]; int. by McGredy Ltd., 1973; Gold Medal, Madrid, 1973

The Sunflower – See **La Soleil**, F

The Surgeon HT, mp, 1956, Verschuren; flowers darker rose-pink, more vigorous than the doctor, dbl.; [The Doctor × unknown]; int. by Blaby Rose Gardens

The Sweet Little Queen of Holland T, yb, 1897, Soupert & Notting; bud long; flowers rich golden yellow, center shaded with orange and blush, large, dbl.; [Céline Forestier × Mme Hoste]

The Temptations HT, pb, 1990, Winchel, Joseph F.; bud pointed; flowers pink blend, medium pink reverse, aging slightly lighter, 4 in., 25-30 petals, high-centered, borne singly and in small clusters, moderate fruity fragrance; recurrent; foliage medium size, dark green, semi-glossy, disease-resistant; prickles slightly hooked, medium, green; upright, tall growth; hips oval, medium, orange; PP8516; [Paradise × Admiral Rodney]; int. by Joseph F. Winchel, 1984; Gold Medal, ARC TG, 1989

The Texan – See **Texan**, Gr

The Times Rose – See **Mariandel**, F

The Twins – See **Gemini**, HT

The Twins Rose S, ob, Delbard; flowers bright orange,

dbl., deep cup; recurrent; stems firm, medium-long; vigorous, medium growth; int. by Ludwig's Roses, 2001

The Valois Rose Min, yb, Kordes

The Venerable Bede F, yb, 1973, Wood; flowers yellow to cherry, 3-3½ in., 20-30 petals; foliage small, glossy; moderate, free growth; [John Church × Bobby Shafto]; int. by Homedale Nursery

The Wallflower HMult, mr, 1901, Paul, G.; flowers bright red, 4-5 cm., semi-dbl., borne in medium clusters, moderate fragrance; late; prickles few, large; vigorous growth; [Crimson Rambler × Beauté Inconstante]

The Wasa Star – See **Polstjärnan**, LCl

The Wedding Rose S, w, 1999, Gear, Ian Robert; flowers medium, inner petals tinged lemon to white, outer petals white, very dbl., somewhat quartered, borne in small clusters, slight fragrance; free-flowering; foliage dark blue/green, semi-glossy; prickles moderate; upright, compact, bushy, medium (3 ft.) growth; [Enchantment × English Miss]; int. by De Boer Roses, 1999

The Whitgift Rose HT, pb, 2000, Carlile, Adrian; flowers pink, reverse yellow, 4 in., full, borne mostly singly, moderate fragrance; foliage medium size, medium green, semi-glossy; few prickles; growth upright, medium; [(Lovely Lady × unknown) × unknown]; int. by LeGrice Future Plants, 2000

The Wife of Bath – See **Wife of Bath**, S

The Wild One S, w, 1998, Thomson, George L.; flowers cream with touch of rose, reverse lighter, stamens gold, 4½-5½ in., single, borne in small clusters; foliage large, light green, semi-glossy; numerous prickles; upright, medium (4 -5 ft.) growth; [Wild Flower × Ophelia]

The Wilson Rose – See ***R. sinowilsonii*** (Hemsley & Wilson)

The World – See **Die Welt**, HT

The Wright Brothers HT, pb, 2005, Eddie Edwards & Ethan Phelps; flowers light to medium pink with shading on the petal edges, 4½ in., full, high-centered, borne mostly solitary, intense fragrance; recurrent; foliage medium size, dark green, glossy; prickles hooked, moderate; growth upright (5-6 ft.); exhibition; [Hot Princess × Signature]; int. in 2005

The Wyevale rose – See **Rose Iga**, F

The Yank HT, mr, 1942, Joseph H. Hill, Co.; flowers rose-red, very large, 55-60 petals; foliage leathery, dark; long, strong stems; very vigorous, upright, much branched growth; [Chieftain × Lucile Hill]

The Yeoman S, op, 1969, Austin, David; flowers salmon-pink, medium, 50 petals, cupped to flat, intense fragrance; recurrent bloom; moderate (100 cm.) growth; [Ivory Fashion × (Constance Spry × Monique)]

The Yvonne Arnaud Theatre Rose F, mr, 2005, Paul Chessum Roses; flowers dbl., borne in small clusters, slight fragrance; foliage medium size, dark green, glossy; prickles large, sharp, red/pink, moderate; growth upright, medium (36 in.); bedding, containers; [seedling × seedling]; int. by World of Roses, 2005

Thea Harrison HT, lp, 1927, Harrison, A.

Thea Russel F, mr, 1954, Leenders, M.; flowers bright red; vigorous growth; [Ambassadeur Nemry × Cinnabar]

Théagène – See **Pucelle de Lille**, HGal

Théano HWich, lp, 1894, Geschwind, R.; flowers small, semi-dbl., cupped, borne in small clusters, no fragrance

Theda Mansholt Gr, my, 1966, Buisman, G. A. H.; bud ovoid; flowers medium, dbl.; foliage dark; upright growth; [Peace × Garden Party]

Thelma HWich, op, 1927, Easlea; flowers coral-pink, suffused carmine-red, center lighter, 3 in., semi-dbl., borne in clusters of 3-10; foliage light green, glossy; few prickles; vigorous, climbing growth; [*R. wichurana* × Paul's Scarlet Climber]

Thelma Amling Pol, w, 1942, Amling Bros.; bud globular; flowers small, semi-dbl.; foliage small, leathery; short stems; vigorous, bushy growth; [sport of Mrs R.M. Finch]; int. by J.H. Hill Co.

Thelma Bader HT, ob, 1958, Lathan; flowers orange-scarlet to salmon-pink, 3 in., 20 petals; foliage dark, glossy; moderately vigorous growth; [seedling × (Independence × Fashion)]; int. in 1957

Thelma Barlow HT, mp, Fryer; flowers porcelain pink, large, dbl., high-centered, moderate fragrance; good repeat; foliage dark green; upright (4 ft.) growth; int. by Fryer's Roses, 2002

Thelma Walton HT, pb, 1974, Walton; flowers deep pink, lightly edged silver, very large, very dbl., high-centered; foliage glossy, dark; vigorous, upright growth; [sport of Red Devil]; int. by Cooke, 1970

Thelma's Glory MinFl, dp, 2004, Jalbert, Brad; flowers self-cleaning, 2 in., semi-dbl., borne in large clusters, slight fragrance; foliage medium size, dark green, very glossy; prickles moderate, medium, hooked, green; growth bushy, medium (16-20 in.), very round; low hedge, containers, garden; very hardy; [Anytime × Flower Carpet]; int. in 1999

Thémis B, lp, about 1836, Bertin; flowers flesh pink, medium, semi-dbl.

Themis F, Gaujard; int. in 1984

Theodor Körner S, mp, Lützow; flowers large, very full, shallow cup, moderate fruity fragrance; foliage red when young, matures to full green, large; upright (200 cm.), strong growth; int. by Gartenbau Lützow, 1999

Theodora HT, dr, 1985, Staikov, Prof. Dr. V.; flowers large, 16 petals; [Apricot Nectar × Dame de Coeur]; int. by Kalaydjiev and Chorbadjiiski, 1984

Theodora Milch HWich, mp, 1906, Weigand, C.; flowers very dbl., flat, borne in small to medium clusters, moderate fragrance; foliage small, glossy

Théodore Liberton HP, mr, 1887, Soupert & Notting; flowers carmine red nuanced madder pink, fading to deep pink, reverse light purple, large, dbl., moderate fragrance

Theodore Roosevelt HT, dr, 1987, Burks, Larry; flowers deep red, fading slightly lighter, medium, 6-14 petals, high-centered, borne singly; foliage large, medium green, semi-glossy; prickles average, light yellow-green; upright, tall growth; hips globular, large, dark red; [sport of Alamo]; int. by Co-Operative Rose Growers, 1986

Theone C, mp, before 1820, Noisette; flowers medium, very full; foliage oval, lightly dentate; prickles large and small, flattened and hooked

Theresa HT, ab, 1909, Dickson, A.; flowers dark orange-apricot, aging to pink, shaded carmine, dbl.

Theresa Morley HT, dp, 1928, H&S; flowers brilliant carmine-cerise, dbl.; [Mme Segond Weber × Lady Battersea]

Theresa Scarman HGal, lp, Scarman; flowers soft pink, full, cupped, non-remontant, intense fragrance; growth to 4 ft.; hardy; int. in 1996

Therese Bauer HSet, mp, 1963, Ludwig; flowers open, large, semi-dbl., borne in clusters; profuse, repeated bloom; very vigorous, upright growth; [(Hansa × *R. setigera*) × *R. setigera*]; int. by Kern Rose Nursery

Thérèse Bonnaviat HT, lp, 1934, Chambard, C.; bud long, pointed; flowers clear pink, center coppery pink, very large; foliage purplish green; very vigorous growth; [Mrs Arthur Robert Waddell × seedling]

Thérèse Bugnet HRg, mp, 1950, Bugnet; bud conical but square-tipped; flowers rose aging pale pink, white center line on top of petals, 4 in., 35 petals, borne in small clusters, moderate spicy fragrance; repeat bloom; foliage quilted, grey-green; vigorous, 5-6 ft. growth; [((*R. acicularis* × *R. rugosa kamtchatica*) × (*R. amblyotis* × *R. rugosa plena*)) × Betty Bland]; int. by P.H. Wright

Therese de Lisieux HT, w, Orard; flowers pure white, dbl., high-centered, slight fragrance; foliage dark green, matte; growth to 80-100 cm.; int. in 1992

Thérèse Lambert T, pb, 1887, Soupert & Notting; flowers delicate rose, base of petals tinged with gold, center pale silvery salmon, very, full; [Mme Lambard × Socrate]

Thérèse Margat B, mp

Thérèse Schopper HT, mr, 1933, Kordes; bud long, pointed, blood-red; flowers nasturtium-red, reverse yellow, open, large, semi-dbl., high-centered; foliage leathery, dark; vigorous growth; [(Charles P. Kilham × Mev. G.A. van Rossem) × Lady Forteviot]

Therese Welter – See **Baronne Henriette de Loew**, T

Therese Zeimet-Lambert HT, dp, 1922, Lambert, P.; bud long, pointed; flowers deep rose, yellow ground, base orange, large, dbl., high-centered; foliage glossy, bronze; vigorous growth; [Richmond × Mrs Aaron Ward]

Theresette S, mp, 1987, James, John; flowers deep soft pink edged white, carnation-like, medium, dbl., frilly, borne in clusters, moderate fragrance; foliage small, medium green, semi-glossy, disease-resistant; bushy, hardy, compact, dwarf growth; [Arctic Glow × Therese Bugnet]; int. in 1986

Theresia S, lp, 1925, Alfons; flowers small, single; hybrid canina

Theresie F, ab, Noack; flowers salmon to apricot-pink, 4-5 cm., semi-dbl., shallow cup to flat, borne in clusters; recurrent if deadheaded; foliage dark green, glossy; low (50-70 cm.) growth; hips decorative; int. by Noack Rosen, 2004

Thermidor S, ly, 1909, Corboeuf-Marsault; flowers medium, dbl., moderate fragrance; [Turner's Crimson Rambler × Perle des Jardins]

Thicket Rose – See ***R. corymbifera*** (Borkhausen)

Thin Ink – See **Usuzumi**, HT

Think Pink Min, mp, 1983, Bennett, Dee; flowers golden stamens, small, 28 petals, intense apple fragrance; foliage small, medium green, semi-glossy; bushy growth; [Electron × Little Chief]

Thinking of You HT, mr, Fryer; bud long, dark; flowers velvety, shaded blood red and deep crimson, dbl., high-centered, borne mostly singly, slight fruity fragrance; recurrent; foliage bright red when young, turning green with maturity; medium (85 cm.) growth

Thirza HT, or, 1932, Bentall; flowers orange-scarlet

This Is The Day Min, r, 2003, Sproul, James A.; flowers red/orange, 1½ in., dbl., hybrid tea, borne mostly solitary, no fragrance; recurrent; foliage medium size, dark green, semi-glossy; prickles few, average, slightly hooked; growth bushy, medium (24 in.); garden, exhibition; PPAF; [Chipmunk × Michel Cholet]; int. by Sproul Roses By Design, 2003; AOE, ARS, 2003

This Little Piggy Min, mp, 2005, Moe, Mitchie; flowers dbl., high-centered, borne mostly solitary, slight fragrance; foliage small, dark green, matte; prickles few, small, straight, light brown; growth compact, short (12-14 in.); exhibition, garden decoration; [Miss Flippins × Anne Hering]; int. by Mitchie's Roses and More, 2005

Thisbé HCh, lp, about 1825, Noisette; flowers light flesh pink, medium, full, moderate hyacinth fragrance

Thisbé B, m, 1850, Robert

Thisbe HMsk, ly, 1918, Pemberton; flowers chamois-yellow, medium, dbl., rosette, borne in large clusters, intense musky fragrance; recurrent; vigorous, bushy (5 ft.) growth; [sport of Daphne]

Thomas A. Edison HT, pb, 1931, Bernaix, P.; bud long, pointed; flowers two-toned pink, very large, dbl., cupped, moderate fragrance; recurrent; very vigorous growth; int. by C-P

Thomas Affleck S, dp, 2005, Shoup, George Michael; flowers deep cerise pink, large, dbl., deeply cupped, borne mostly solitary, moderate fragrance; recurrent; foliage large, dark green, semi-glossy; few prickles; bushy, tall (6 ft.) growth; hedging; hips large; [Carefree Beauty × Basye's Blueberry]; int. by Antique Rose Emporium, 1996

Thomas Andrew Elliott HT, yb, 1995, Thomas, D.; flowers golden yellow with yellow and pink reverse, 4 in., 41 petals, borne mostly singly; foliage medium size, medium green, semi-glossy; some prickles; medium (50-60 cm.), upright growth; [Grandpa Dickson × ((City of Gloucester × seedling) × Polarstar)]

Thomas Barton – See **Charlotte Rampling**, HT

Thomas Garces HT, Dot, Simon; int. in 1986

Thomas H. Elliott HT, w; int. by Handley Rose Nurseries, 2002

Thomas Methven HP, dp, 1869, Verdier, E.; flowers bright carmine, large, full

Thomas Mills HP, dp, 1873, Verdier, E.; flowers rosy crimson, large, dbl., cupped; non-recurrent; vigorous growth

Thomas Rivers HP, m, 1857, Margottin; flowers lilac, large, full

Thor HSet, dr, 1940, Horvath; bud ovoid; flowers crimson-red, 4-5 in., 58 petals, slight damask fragrance; foliage large, leathery, dark; numerous prickles; vigorous, climbing (8-10 ft.) growth; [(Alpha × *R. xanthina*) × Pres. Coolidge]; int. by Wayside Gardens Co.

Thor Supreme LCl, dr, 1951, Horvath; flowers dark crimson edged deeper, 4 in., intense damask fragrance; foliage large, leathery, dark; vigorous, climbing growth; int. by Wyant

Thora Hird F, w, 1988, Bracegirdle, A.J.; flowers white deepen to cream in center with pink veins, loose, medium, 40 petals, moderate sweet fragrance; foliage medium size, dark green, semi-glossy; prickles straight, brown; bushy, medium growth; hips round, amber; [Chinatown × Picasso]; int. by Rosemary Roses, 1987

Thora McCrea HT, mr, 1987, Summerell, B.L.; flowers 20-25 petals, high-centered; foliage dark green; prickles red-brown; well-shaped, upright, medium growth; [Pink Parfait × Crimson Glory]

Thoresbyana – See **Bennett's Seedling**, Ayr

Thorin HP, mp, 1866, Lacharme; flowers brilliant carmine pink, large, dbl., widely cupped

Thornbury Castle – See **Radox Bouquet**, F

Thornfree Wonder HMult, w, 1986, Nobbs, Kenneth J.; flowers peach pink, fading to white, 14 petals, cupped, blooms in clusters of up to 14; summer bloom; no prickles; long canes; spreading growth; int. in 1985

Thornhem – See **Milky Way**, HT

Thornless Beauty HT, dr, 1938, Grillo; bud long, pointed, dark crimson-red; flowers light crimson-red, 4 in., 50 petals; foliage leathery; thornless; long, strong stems; vigorous growth; [sport of Better Times]

Thornless Beauty F, op, Patil, B.K.; flowers salmon-pink, large, semi-dbl.; medium growth; [sport of City of Lucknow]; int. by Icospin, 1990

Thornless Blush HT, lp, 1954, Grillo; bud globular; flowers blush-pink, 4½ in., 70 petals, high-centered; foliage leathery; thornless; very vigorous, upright growth; [sport of Rosalind Russell]

Thornless Fringedale HT, lp, 1955, Grillo; flowers 4 in., 25 petals; thornless; [sport of Thornless Beauty]

Thornless Glory LCl, lp, 1935, Izzo; flowers clear pink, 3 in., 20 petals; early summer bloom; thornless; long stems; vigorous, climbing growth

Thornless Mirage HT, mr, 1955, Grillo; flowers red suffused blush-pink, 5 in., 25 petals; thornless; [sport of Jewel]

Thornless Premier HT, mp, 1955, Grillo; bud globular, pointed; flowers rich pink, 4½ in., 75 petals; thornless; [Victory Stripe × Jewel]

Thornless Victory Stripe HT, rb, 1955, Grillo; bud long, pointed; flowers dark red and blush-pink, striped, 5 in., 50 petals; thornless; [Victory Stripe × Jewel]

Thoughtful HT, pb, 1995, Sheldon, John & Robin; flowers dark pink blend, large, full, borne mostly singly; foliage medium size, dark green, matte; upright, medium growth; [Pristine × Nightingale]

Thoughts Of Eileen Min, ab, 2005, Paul Chessum Roses Ltd; flowers 3 cm., single, borne in small clusters, slight fragrance; foliage small, medium green, semi-glossy; prickles few, small, short, red; growth bushy, tall (24 in.); bedding, borders, containers; [seedling × seedling]; int. by Love4Plants Ltd T/as World of Roses, 2005

Thoughts of Yesteryear S, lp, 2001, Byrnes, Robert L.; flowers blush pink, light pink and peach reverse, 3 in., full, borne in small clusters, moderate fragrance; foliage medium green, semi-glossy; few prickles; bushy, medium growth; [sport of Goldbusch]; int. by Overbrooke Gardens, 2001

Thoughts of You Min, dp; flowers pinky-red, cupped, borne in clusters, slight fragrance; free-flowering; foliage medium green; compact (18-24 in.) growth; int. in 1999

Thousand Beauties – See **Tausendschön**, HMult

Three Cheers F, dp, Dickson; flowers cerise pink, fading with age, dbl., shallow cup, borne in clusters; free-flowering; foliage dense, medium green, glossy; rounded (85 cm.) growth; int. by Dickson Roses, 2005

Three-Leaf Rose – See ***R. anemoneflora*** (Fortune)

Three Weddings ClMin, pb, Pallek; int. by Palatine Roses, 2004

Threepenny Bit Rose – See ***R. farreri persetosa*** (Stapf)

Thriller HT, pb, 1987, Bridges, Dennis A.; flowers white center, pink edges, reverse slight pink edging, pink highlights with sun, large, 28-30 petals, high-centered, borne singly, moderate fruity fragrance; recurrent; foliage medium size, dark green, glossy; prickles medium, long, light green, pointed downwards; upright, medium, strong growth; [Lady X × Flaming Beauty]; int. by Bridges Roses, 1986

Thumbelina Min, rb, 1954, Moore, Ralph S.; flowers cherry-red, white eye, small, semi-dbl.; foliage dark, glossy; dwarf (6-8 in.), bushy growth; [Eblouissant × Zee]; int. by Sequoia Nursery

Thumbelina Min, ly, 1999, Schuurman, Frank B.; flowers 1¾ in., dbl., borne in small clusters; foliage medium size, medium green, glossy; prickles moderate; patio; compact, medium growth; [Champagner × Tinkerbell]; int. by Franko Roses New Zealand, Ltd., 1998

Thumbs Up S, yb, 2005, Horner, Colin P.; flowers light yellow, striped pink, reverse paler, 10-12 cm., full, cupped, borne in small clusters, intense fragrance; free-flowering; foliage medium size, medium green, matte; prickles medium, curved, few; growth upright, tall (4-6 ft.); garden decoration; [(Southampton × ((New Penny × Little White Pet) × Stars 'n' Stripes)) × Graham Thomas]; int. by Peter Beales Roses, 2006

Thunder Bolt HT, dr, Shastri, Dr. N.V.; bud long, tapered; flowers deep, sparkling red, large, broad; int. in 2002

Thunder Cloud Min, or, 1979, Moore, Ralph S.; bud ovoid; flowers currant red, showing more orange in bright sunlight, 1-1½ in., 70-80 petals, rounded, carnation-like, borne in tight clusters of 3-7, very slight fragrance; recurrent; foliage small, glossy, leathery, pointed; prickles average, slender, inclined downward, brown; stems slender, wiry; growth vigorous, bushy, upright (12-14 in.); hips none ; PP4624; [Little Chief × Fire Princess]; int. by Sequoia Nursery

Thunderbird F, mr, 1959, deVor, Paul F.; bud urn-shaped; flowers rose-red, 2½ in., 48 petals, high-centered, borne in clusters of 3-8; vigorous, spreading growth; PP1677; [sport of Skylark]; int. by Amling Bros., 1958

Thunderbolt HT, pb, 1991, Bridges, Dennis A.; bud ovoid; flowers pink blend, white reverse, color intensifies with age, medium, 45 petals, urn-shaped, borne singly, slight fragrance; foliage medium size, dark green, matte; bushy, medium growth; [Lady X × Flaming Beauty]; int. by Bridges Roses, 1990

Thungabhadra HT, ob, Kasturi; flowers coppery orange with carmine; int. by KSG Son, 1985

Thusnelda HRg, mp, 1886, Müller, Dr. F.; flowers soft rose pink, fading lighter, large, semi-dbl., cupped, moderate fragrance; non-recurrent; foliage rugose; vigorous, upright (100-150 cm.) growth; [*R. rugosa alba* × Gloire de Dijon]

Thyra Hammerich HP, lp, 1868, Hugues Vilin; flowers white slightly tinted flesh pink, more intense at base, large, very dbl., cupped, moderate sweet fragrance; repeats in late summer; foliage light violet; prickles few, small, hooked; growth to 5 ft.; [Duchesse de Sutherland × unknown]

Thyrion HT, McGredy, Sam IV; int. in 1969

Tiamo HT, dr, Spek; flowers brilliant dark red, medium, dbl.; strong, medium to tall growth; florist rose; int. in 1996

Tiara F, w, 1960, Boerner; bud ovoid, medium; flowers 3 in., 45-50 petals, cupped, borne in clusters, moderate tea fragrance; recurrent; foliage leathery; prickles average, medium, straight; stems long, strong; vigorous, bushy growth; hips none ; PP1981; [Chic × Demure seedling (white)]; florist rose; int. by J&P, 1960

Tibeert S, Delforge; int. in 1991

Ticino F, mr, Huber; flowers vermilion red, large, dbl.; int. in 1979

Tick-Tock – See **Anytime**, Min

Ticker Tape ClMin, op; int. by Burston Nurseries, 2005

Tickle Me Pink Min, mp, 1989, Chaffin, Lauren M.; bud pointed; flowers medium pink to soft cream at base, reverse cream blush, aging, dbl., moderate spicy fragrance; foliage small, medium green, semi-glossy; prickles needle-like, light tan; bushy, low growth; hips globular, rare, medium green; [Osiria × Magic Carrousel]; int. by Pixie Treasures Min. Roses

Tickled Pink HT, mp, 1963, Lammerts, Dr. Walter; bud long, pointed; flowers medium, dbl., high-centered, moderate spicy fragrance; upright, bushy growth; PP2369; [Queen Elizabeth × Fashion]; int. by Amling-DeVor Nursery

Tickled Pink HT, pb, 1999, Schuurman, Frank B.; bud large, pointed; flowers 5 in., 36-42 petals, imbricated, borne mostly singly, moderate old rose fragrance; recurrent; foliage large, medium green, glossy; prickles very few; upright, tall (4 ft.) growth; PP11400; [Jacaranda × Gold Medal]; int. by Franko Roses New Zealand, Ltd., 1997

Tickled Pink F, mp, Fryer; flowers large, full, hybrid tea, borne in clusters, slight fragrance; free-flowering; foliage very disease-resistant; vigorous, medium growth; int. by Fryers Roses, 2007; Rose of the Year, Roses UK, 2007

Tickles F, pb, 1999, Dykstra, Dr. A. Michael; flowers pink and cream stripes, reverse same, 2½ in., semi-dbl., borne in small clusters, slight fragrance; few prickles; [(Pristine × Typhoo Tea) × Hurdy Gurdy]; int. by Certified Roses, 2000

Tidal Wave S, pb, 2004, Brown, Ted; flowers pink, yellow, cream, and orange, reverse cream with pink edges, 4 in., dbl., borne in large clusters, slight fragrance; foliage medium size, medium green, semi-glossy; prickles medium, slightly hooked; growth upright, medium (6½ ft.); garden decorative; [Nymphenberg × seedling]; int. in 2005

Tidbit Rose – See **Conditorum**, HGal

Tiddly Winks Min, yb, 2006, Carruth, Tom; flowers yellow with a broad cerise edging, reverse yellow, retaining color well, 3-5 cm., dbl., borne in small clusters; foliage small, medium green, semi-glossy; prickles small, straight, beige, moderate; growth compact, rounded, bushy, short (30-45 cm.); garden decoration; [(Golden Holstein × Easy Going) × Neon Cowboy]; int. by Weeks Roses, 2008

Tidewater MinFl, w, 1991, Bridges, Dennis A.; bud pointed; flowers ivory white with slight pink tints, 2½ in., 30-36 petals, high-centered, borne usually singly, moderate fruity fragrance; recurrent; foliage medium size, medium green, matte; prickles few, flat, 5 mm.; stems long; bushy, spreading, medium growth; hips globular, 1.5-2 cm., green with medium orange shades; PP8531; [Jennifer × unknown]; int. by Bridges Roses, 1991

Tiecelijn HT, Delforge; int. in 1990

Tien Shan Rose – See ***R. primula*** (Boulenger)

Tiergarten HMult, dy, 1904, Lambert; flowers ochre-yellow, aging to white, small, full; [Euphrosyne × Safrano]

Tiergartendirektor Timm F, dp, 1944, Kordes; bud long, pointed; flowers carmine-pink, open, very large, semi-dbl., borne in clusters; foliage dark, glossy; very vigorous, upright growth; [Sweetness × Hamburg]

Tiernan's Gold Min, my, 2001, McCann, Sean; flowers yellow fading to white, small, semi-dbl., borne in small clusters; foliage medium size, light green, semi-glossy; few prickles; compact, low growth; [Rise 'n' Shine × Amy Rebecca]

Tiffany HT, pb, 1954, Lindquist, R. V.; bud long, pointed ovoid; flowers pink-yellow blend, 4-5 in., 25-30 petals, high-centered, borne usually singly, intense tea fragrance; recurrent; foliage dark green, leathery, semi-glossy; prickles several, medium to long, almost straight, cinnamon; stems long, straight; vigorous, upright growth; hips turbinate, green; PP1304; [Charlotte Armstrong × Girona]; int. by Howard Rose Co., 1954; James Alexander Gamble Fragrance Medal, ARS, 1962, Gold Medal, Portland, 1954, David Fuerstenberg Prize, ARS, 1957

Tiffany, Climbing Cl HT, pb, 1958, Lindquist, R. V.; bud medium, pointed ovoid; flowers pink/yellow blend, 4-5 in., 25-30 petals, high-centered, borne usually singly, intense tea fragrance; recurrent; foliage dark green, leathery, semi-glossy; prickles several, medium to long, almost straight, cinnamon; stems medium; vigorous, upright, climbing growth; hips turbinate, green; PP1836; [sport of Tiffany]; like parent except for taller growth and shorter stems; int. by Howard Rose Co., 1958

Tiffany S, mp, Poulsen; flowers medium pink, 8-10 cm., dbl., moderate fragrance; foliage dark; growth bushy, 20-40 cm.; PP15722; int. by Poulsen Roser, 2001

Tiffany Hit – See **Tiffany**, S

Tiffany Lite MinFl, w, 1998, Giles, Diann; flowers large, white, dbl., borne in small clusters, slight fragrance; foliage medium size, medium green, semi-glossy; growth upright, bushy (3-4 ft.); [sport of Tiffany Lynn]; int. by Giles Rose Nursery, 1997

Tiffany Lynn MinFl, pb, 1985, Jolly, Nelson F.; flowers light to medium pink at edges, blending to white in center, large, 21 petals, high-centered, borne singly and in small clusters, slight fragrance; recurrent; foliage medium size, medium green with red edges, semi-glossy; prickles slanted downward; stems long; upright, bushy growth; [(Tiki × seedling) × Party Girl]; int. by Rosehill Farm

Tiffie Min, lp, 1980, Bennett, Dee; bud long, pointed; flowers soft pink, sometimes apricot, 15-20 petals, high-centered, borne singly, moderate lilac fragrance; foliage medium green; prickles large, red; upright growth; [Little Darling × Over the Rainbow]; int. by Tiny Petals Nursery, 1979

Tifton HT, yb, 1983, Perry, Astor; flowers brilliant yellow, petal tips red, red spreading with age, large, very full, high-centered, borne usually singly, moderate fragrance; recurrent; foliage large, medium size, semi-glossy; tall, bushy growth; [Fire Magic × Oregold]; int. by Perry Roses

Tiger HT, rb, McGredy, Sam IV; bud medium, ovoid; flowers orange-red, reverse yellow, 5-5½ in., 38-43 petals, high-centered, borne singly, slight sweet fragrance; foliage large, medium green, glossy, deeply dentate; prickles few, on main stalks and laterals; growth upright, vigorous, tall (5 ft.); [Penthouse × Macputar]; int. in 1990

Tiger Belle F, ob, 1962, Jelly; bud ovoid; flowers light signal-red, 2-2½ in., 25-35 petals, cupped; moderate growth; [Orange Sweetheart × Lovelight]; int. by E.G. Hill Co., 1962

Tiger Butter Min, dy, 1982, Strawn, Leslie E.; flowers small, 20 petals; foliage small, dark, semi-glossy; upright, bushy growth; [Sunblest × Over the Rainbow]; int. by Pixie Treasures Min. Roses

Tiger Cub Min, yb, Olesen; flowers yellow with red stripes, aging more toward red, 5-8 cm., dbl., cupped, borne in small clusters, no fragrance; recurrent; foliage dark green, glossy; bushy, low (40-60 cm.) growth; int. by Poulsen, 1998

Tiger Eyes S, yb, Warner; flowers yellow with red eye, single; recurrent; growth to 3-4 ft. high and twice as wide; bred from *Hulthemia persica*; int. by Ludwig's Roses, 2005

Tiger Paws Min, ob, 1994, Laver, Keith G.; flowers orange with yellow reverse, large, full, borne mostly singly, no fragrance; foliage medium size, medium green, matte; medium (20 cm.), compact growth; [Painted Doll × seedling]; int. by Springwood Roses, 1994

Tiger Stripes Min, yb, 1992, Clements, John K.; flowers unusual striped color combination, yellow, striped orange, medium, full, no fragrance; foliage small, medium green, semi-glossy; few prickles; low (25 cm.), bushy, compact growth; [seedling × seedling]; int. by Heirloom Old Garden Roses, 1991

Tiger Tail F, ob, 1991, Christensen, Jack E.; flowers deep orange, white or cream colored stripes, cream colored reverse, medium, full, borne in small clusters, no fragrance; foliage medium size, medium green, glossy; medium, bushy growth; [Matangi × Pinstripe]; int. by Bear Creek Gardens, 1992

Tiglia S, yb, 1962, Leenders, J.; flowers creamy yellow tinged pink, dbl.; recurrent bloom; [Ma Perkins × High Noon]

Tigress F, yb; int. by Terra Nigra BV, 2002

Tigress Gr, m, 2005, Zary, Keith; bud long; flowers striped with 2 slightly differing red-purples and white, reverse striping of red-purple and white, 9-11 cm., 25 petals, high-centered, borne singly and in small clusters, intense sweet gardenia fragrance; recurrent; foliage large, dark green, glossy; prickles few, 10mm., hooked downward, brown; stems strong, 18 in.; growth upright, branching, medium (1¼-1½ m.); PP13777; [Purple Tiger × seedling]; int. by Jackson & Perkins Wholesale, Inc., 2003

Tigris S, yb, 1986, Harkness; flowers yellow, dark red eye, 1 in., dbl., slight fragrance; recurrent; foliage small, light green, variable in shape; prickles gooseberry-like; stems slim; compact, rounded, wiry growth; [*Hulthemia persica* × Trier]; int. in 1985

Tiki F, pb, 1964, McGredy, Sam IV; flowers light pink and white blend, well-formed, flora-tea, large, 30 petals; foliage dark; vigorous growth; [Mme Léon Cuny × Spartan]; int. by McGredy

Tiki, Climbing Cl F, pb

Till Uhlenspiegel HEg, rb, 1950, W. Kordes Söhne; bud pointed; flowers bright red, white eye, 5 petals, borne in clusters; non-recurrent; foliage large, glossy, dark reddish-green; tall (to 10 ft.), arching growth; [Holstein × Magnifica]

Tillicum HT, 1924, Wilber; flowers deep rose-pink shaded orange, dbl.; [Général Jacqueminot × Old Gold]

Tilly Ashton Gr, lp, Nieuwesteeg, J.; [sport of Queen Elizabeth]; int. in 1996

Tilt Symphonie Min, dr, Meilland; flowers bright red, dbl., borne in clusters; free-flowering; bushy (12-16 in.) growth; int. in 1994

Tim Page HT, 1920, Page; flowers rich daffodil yellow; int. by Easlea

Timeless HT, w, Pouw; bud ovate; flowers cream, fades quickly to white., 11 cm., 30 petals, high-centered, borne singly, very slight fragrance; recurrent; foliage dark green, leathery, semi-glossy; prickles normal, average size, concave, reddish-brown; vigorous, narrow, bushy growth; hips pitcher-shaped, large ; PP9421; [seedling × seedling]; int. by De Ruiter, 1995

Timeless HT, dp, 1998, Zary, Dr. Keith W.; bud long, pointed ovoid; flowers red to deep pink, deep pink reverse, 4½ in., 25-30 petals, high-centered, borne singly and in small clusters, slight fragrance; recurrent; foliage medium size, dark green, semi-glossy, leathery; prickles numerous, medium length, hooked downward; stems medium; upright, bushy growth; PP11369; [Spirit of Glasnost × Kardinal]; int. by Bear Creek Gardens, Inc., 1997

Timeless Beauty – See **Mariandel**, F

Timeless Delight Min, m, 1995, Rennie, Bruce F.; flowers 2¼ in., dbl., borne mostly singly; foliage large, medium green, dull; some prickles; tall (24-36 in.), upright growth; [Silver Phantom × Innocent Blush]; int. by Rennie Roses International, 1996

Times Past LCl, mp; flowers shell pink, very dbl., cupped, moderate fruity fragrance; free-flowering; foliage matte, mid-green; growth climber to 8 ft.; int. by Harkness, 2002

Times Square HT, ob, 1943, Lammerts, Dr. Walter; bud peach; flowers orange, center golden yellow, large; foliage leathery, glossy; vigorous growth; [Mrs Sam McGredy × Pres. Herbert Hoover]; int. by Armstrong Nursery

Timmie Arkles F, lp, 1954, Boerner; flowers 3 in., dbl., flat, borne in clusters of 30-40, moderate fruity fragrance; vigorous growth; PP1320; [Mrs R.M. Finch × (Improved Lafayette seedling × Rochester seedling)]; int. by J&P

Timm's Jubilaümsrose F, or, 1976, Kordes; bud globular; flowers 2 in., 27 petals, globular; foliage soft; vigorous, upright, bushy growth; [Marlena × Europeana]; int. by Timm & Co., 1975

Timmy Williams F, or, 2001, Kenny, David; flowers orange/salmon, orange reverse, 3 in., dbl., borne in small clusters; foliage medium size, medium green (red when young), semi-glossy; prickles medium, hooked, moderate; growth upright, bushy, medium (3 ft.); garden decorative; [(Mary Sumner × Kiskadee) × Spek's Centennial]

Timothy Berlen Min, ob, 1987, Jolly, Marie; flowers orange, yellow center, reverse yellow fading dark pink, medium, 20 petals, high-centered; foliage small, medium green, semi-glossy; prickles bayonet-shaped, light pink; upright, spreading, low growth; hips round, green-yellow-orange; [Anita Charles × Poker Chip]; int. by Rosehill Farm, 1988

Timothy Eaton HT, op, 1968, McGredy, Sam IV; flowers salmon-pink, well-formed, dbl., slight fragrance; recurrent; [Radar × Mischief]

Tina F, ob, Tantau; florist rose; int. by Rosen Tantau

Tina Marie HP, w; flowers white touched with pink, moderate fragrance; recurrent; foliage large, drooping, grey-green; tall growth; [sport of Grandmother's Hat]

Tina Turner HT, ob, 1992, Thompson, Robert; flowers medium, full, borne mostly singly, moderate fragrance; foliage large, dark green, glossy; some prickles; bushy (60 cm.) growth; [Silver Jubilee × Doris Tysterman]; int. by Battersby Roses, 1990

Tineke HT, w, 1990, Select Roses, B.V.; bud pointed, ovoid; flowers creamy white, 4 in., 50-55 petals, cupped with high center, borne singly, very slight fragrance; recurrent; foliage large, dark green, semi-glossy; prickles yellow-green with reddish tip; stems strong, upright; upright, tall growth; hips pear-shaped ; PP8055; [seedling × seedling]; int. by DeVor Nurseries, Inc., 1990

Tineke van Heule F, lp, 1986, Lens, Louis; flowers 7-12 petals, borne in clusters of 3-12; foliage large, leathery, greenish-brown; prickles few, reddish-brown; upright, bushy growth; [seedling × City of Belfast]; int. in 1985

Tinker Bell Min, mp, 1954, deVink; bud ovoid; flowers bright rose-pink, 1½ in., 60 petals, cupped, borne in irregular clusters, very slight fragrance; free-flowering; foliage small, leathery; prickles few, medium, straight; stems medium; dwarf (8 in.), bushy growth; no hips; PP1293; [Ellen Poulsen × Tom Thumb]; int. by C-P

Tinkerbell F, lp, 1999, Schuurman, Frank B.; bud small, pointed; flowers soft, light pink, 1½-2½ in., 26-30 petals, slightly cupped, borne in large clusters and sprays, moderate fruity fragrance; recurrent; foliage medium size, dark green, glossy; prickles moderate, 1 cm., thin, straight, brown with green tips; stems 16-20 in.; upright, medium (2 ft.) growth; PP10940; [White Dream × Evelien]; int. by Franko Roses New Zealand, Ltd., 1993

Tino Rossi HT, mp, Meilland; flowers soft rose pink, large, dbl., high-centered, borne mostly singly, intense fragrance; free-flowering; vigorous (90-100 cm) growth; int. in 1990; Fragrance Cup, Bagatelle, 1989

Tinseltown HT, pb, Edwards, Eddie; int. in 1996

Tintagel LCl, w, McLeod, J.; [possibly a *R. brunonii* seedling]

Tintin F, or, 1964, Mondial Roses; flowers cinnabar-red, large, semi-dbl., cupped, borne in large clusters; moderate growth

Tintinara HT, or, 1999, Dickson, Colin; flowers poppy red, reverse geranium-lake, 5 in., full, high-centered, borne in small clusters, slight fragrance; recurrent; foliage large, medium green, glossy; prickles moderate; upright, tall (40 in.) growth; [Melody Maker × seedling]; int. by Dickson Nurseries, Ltd., 1996

Tinwell Moss M, dp, before 1827, Tinwell/Lee; bud large, well mossed; flowers very dark rose pink, large, dbl.; foliage large

Tiny Bubbles Min, w, 1990, Warriner, William A.; bud ovoid; flowers ivory, near white, fading to white, medium, dbl., cupped, borne usually singly, no fragrance; foliage medium size, medium green, semi-glossy; prickles straight, slightly angled downward, green-yellow; upright, spreading, medium growth; [Zorina × Funny Girl]; int. by Bear Creek Gardens, 1990

Tiny Dancer Min, lp, 1990, Williams, J. Benjamin; flowers bright, light coral pink, 34 petals, high-centered, borne usually singly, slight spicy fragrance; foliage small, dark green, dwarf; prickles very few; upright, low growth; [(Carla × Sonia) × (Circus × Ma Perkins)]; int. by Young's American Rose Nursery, 1990

Tiny Flame Min, or, 1969, Moore, Ralph S.; flowers coral-orange-red, micro-mini, very small, dbl., rosette, borne in clusters; free-flowering; foliage very small; dwarf (6 in.), bushy growth; [(*R. wichurana* × Floradora) × New Penny]; int. by Sequoia Nursery

Tiny Grace HT, pb, Teranishi; int. by Itami Rose Garden, 2005

Tiny Jack Min, mr, 1962, Moore, Ralph S.; bud pointed; flowers 1-1½ in., 28 petals, cupped; foliage leathery, dark; vigorous, bushy (12-14 in.)growth; PP2484; [(*R. wichurana* × Floradora) × (Oakington Ruby × Floradora)]; int. by Blue Ribbon Plant Co., 1962

Tiny Jewel S, lp, Williams, J.B.; flowers blush pink, golden stamens, single, borne in clusters; growth low; groundcover; int. by Hortico, 2003

Tiny Jill Min, mp, 1962, Moore, Ralph S.; bud pointed; flowers dbl., 45 petals, high-centered, moderate fragrance; foliage glossy; vigorous, bushy (12-14 in.) growth; PP2483; [(*R. wichurana* × Floradora) × Little Buckaroo]; int. by Blue Ribbon Plant Co., 1962

Tiny Love Min, dr, 1981, Lyon; bud ovoid; flowers 11 petals, cupped, borne 1-3 per cluster, intense fragrance; foliage dark; prickles straight; open, bushy growth; [seedling × seedling]; int. in 1980

Tiny Petals Min, rb, 1992, Bennett, Dee; flowers geranium lake with cream reverse, 1½-2 in., 25-35 petals, high-centered, borne mostly singly, very slight fragrance; recurrent; foliage small, dark green, semi-glossy, disease-resistant; prickles some, average, slender, hooked slightly downward; stems long; medium (60-80 cm.), bushy growth; PP9319; [San Antonio × Jean Kenneally]; int. by Tiny Petals Nursery, 1993

Tiny Stars Min, rb, 1987, Travis, Louis R.; flowers white with red narrow edges, small, 12 petals, cupped, borne usually singly and in clusters of 3-4, no fragrance; foliage small, medium green, matte; almost thornless; micro-mini; bushy, low growth; no fruit; [Magic Carrousel × Magic Carrousel]; int. in 1986

Tiny Tears Min, mp, 1979, Bennett, Dee; bud ovoid; flowers soft pink, yellow stamens, very small, 5 petals, borne in clusters of 10-25; foliage glossy, dark, small; trailing (12 in.) growth; [Pink Ribbon × Pink Ribbon]; int. by Tiny Petals Nursery

Tiny Tim F, my, 1943, Brownell; bud long, pointed; flowers clear yellow, open, small, 23 petals, high-centered; foliage glossy; moderately vigorous, compact to open growth; [Golden Glow × Shades of Autumn]

Tiny Tot Min, mp, 1955, Robinson, T.; flowers deep cerise-pink; very dwarf growth

Tiny Tot Min, ab, Benardella, Frank A.; flowers pastel shades of apricot, yellow and pink, dbl., high-centered, borne usually one to a stem; recurrent; long stems; tall, vigorous growth; int. in 1990

Tiny Visions Min, rb, 1981, Lyon; bud long; flowers crimson with white center, 5 petals, cupped, borne mostly singly; foliage dark, apple-scented; prickles very tiny, hooked, brown; very tiny, bushy growth; [seedling × seedling]; int. in 1980

Tiny Warrior Min, rb, 1976, Williams, Ernest D.; bud ovoid; flowers 1 in., 34 petals, flat; foliage small, glossy, very dark, embossed; upright, bushy growth; [Starburst × Little Chief]; int. by Mini-Roses, 1975

Tione Pietro – See **Pietro Tione**, HT

Tip Toes HT, op, 1948, Brownell; bud pointed; flowers salmon-pink, shading to yellow at base, large, semi-dbl., high-centered, moderate fragrance; foliage glossy; vigorous, upright growth; [(Général Jacqueminot × Dr. W. Van Fleet) × Anne Vanderbilt]

Tip-Top Pol, w, 1909, Lambert, P.; flowers white, tipped Tyrian rose, aging white and pale yellow, reverse white, dbl.; bushy, dwarf growth; [Trier × *R. foetida bicolor* seedling]

Tip Top F, op, Tantau, Math.; flowers salmon-pink, fading lighter, large, semi-dbl. to dbl., cupped, borne in clusters, moderate fragrance; free-flowering; foliage disease-resistant; short (2 ft.), vigorous growth; int. by Wheatcroft Bros., 1964

Tip Top, Climbing Cl F, op

Tipo Ideale – See **Mutabilis**, Ch

Tipper Min, mp, 1988, Jolly, Marie; flowers medium pink, touch of coral early, aging lighter, 1½ in., 32-36 petals, high-centered, borne singly, slight fragrance; recurrent; foliage medium size, medium green, semi-glossy; prickles very few, medium, bayonet, light brown; stems long, straight; upright, medium growth; hips round, 1.4 cm., orange; PP7340; [Chris Jolly × Chattem Centennial]; int. by Rosehill Farm, 1988; AOE, ARS, 1989

Tipperary HT, my, 1917, McGredy; bud long, pointed; flowers golden yellow, semi-dbl.; [Mrs Aaron Ward × unknown]

Tipsy HT, dp, 1969, Trew, C.; flowers soft rose, reverse geranium-red, pointed, large, dbl.; foliage dark, dull; free growth; [Basildon Belle × seedling]; int. by Basildon Rose Gardens

Tipsy Imperial Concubine T, pb; flowers soft pink with tones of lemon and red, large, full, globular, moderate fragrance; recurrent; moderate (2-3 ft.) growth; int. by re-introduced by Le Rougetel, 1989

Tipu's Flame S, rb, 2005, Viraraghavan, M.S. Viru; flowers bright red, reverse white, 4 in., full, borne in small clusters, slight fragrance; foliage medium size, dark green, semi-glossy, dense; prickles numerous, large, triangular pointing down, grey; growth bushy, shrubby, medium (3½ ft.); garden decoration; [Alliance × Priyatama]; int. by K.S.G. Sons Roses, 1990

Tira-Mi-Su HT, ab, 1999, Teranishi, K.; flowers pale copper and orange blend, 5 in., 28 petals, slight fragrance; growth to 4½ ft.; [(Julia × seedling) × seedling]; int. by Itami Rose Nursery, 1994

Tirza HT, mr, 2002, Poole, Lionel; flowers full, high-centered, borne mostly solitary, slight fragrance; foliage medium size, medium green, semi-glossy; prickles moderate, medium, slightly hooked; growth upright, bushy, medium (1 m.); garden decorative, exhibition; [Adrienne Berman × (Royal William × Gabi)]

Titania Ch, rb, 1915, Paul, W.; flowers deep salmon-red, shaded clear yellow at base, small, dbl.; dwarf, bushy growth

Titania Pol, lp, 1938, Leenders, M.; flowers salmon-flesh to rosy white, large, very dbl.; foliage leathery, dark; vigorous, bushy growth; [Mev. Nathalie Nypels × seedling]

Titanic F, w, McGredy; flowers creamy white edged with blush pink, 4 in., 20 petals, high-centered, moderate tea fragrance; recurrent; foliage shiny, dark green; sturdy (3½ × 3 ft.) growth; int. in 1999

Titi Parisien F, dr, 1959, Delbard-Chabert; flowers crimson, center lighter, stamens ivory, 3 in., 5 petals; bushy, low growth; [(Francais × unknown) × ((Orange Triumph × unknown) × Floradora)]

Titian F, dp, 1950, Riethmuller; flowers dusky cerise pink, large, dbl., rounded, then flat, borne in clusters, slight fragrance; recurrent; vigorous, tall growth

Titian, Climbing Cl F, dp, 1964, Kordes

Tivoli F, mp, 1955, Poulsen, S.; flowers warm rose-pink, center yellow, well-formed, 3 in., 24 petals, borne in clusters; foliage dark, glossy; very vigorous growth; [Poulsen's Supreme × (Souv. de Claudius Denoyel × Hvissinge-Rose)]; int. by McGredy, 1954

Tivoli – See **Tivoli Gardens**, HT

Tivoli 150 – See **Tivoli Gardens**, HT

Tivoli Gardens HT, my, 1994, Olesen, Pernille & Mogens N.; flowers soft yellow, 4-5 in., 50-65 petals, cupped, borne in small clusters, slight fragrance; recurrent; foliage large, dark green, semi-glossy; some prickles; tall (100-150 cm.), spreading growth; int. by Cants of Colchester Ltd., 1995

Tiz – See **Tzigane**, HT

Tiziana F, op, 1969, Cazzaniga, F. G.; bud pointed; flowers copper-pink, large, semi-dbl.; foliage light green; vigorous, compact growth; [Papillon Rose × Gay Paris]

To Mummy – See **Blossom Blanket**, S

Tobago F, ab, 1982, Delbard, Georges; flowers yellow apricot, outer petals aging pink, large, 35 petals, cupped, borne in clusters, moderate citrus fragrance; recurrent; foliage medium size, dark green, semi-glossy; vigorous, upright growth; [Avalanche × (Zambra × Orange Sensation)]; int. by George Delbard SA, 1981; Golden Rose, Geneva, 1981

Tobo Min, dy, 1989, King, Gene; bud pointed; flowers medium, 32 petals, high-centered, borne singly and in small clusters, slight fruity fragrance; recurrent; foliage medium size, light green, matte; prickles straight, slightly crooked, red to brown; upright, bushy, medium growth; hips ovoid, green; [Arthur Bell × Rise 'n' Shine]; int. by AGM Miniature Roses

Toboné – See **Prima Donna**, Gr

Toby Jo Min, yb, 1997, Garrett, Troy O.; flowers yellow and orange, lighter reverse, pink tips, 1 in., dbl., borne singly, no fragrance; foliage medium size, medium green, semi glossy; few prickles; upright, medium (16-20 in.) growth; [sport of Old Glory]

Toby Tristram HMult, w; bud pink; flowers cream, fading to white, 3 cm., single, moderate musk fragrance; some repeat; foliage medium green, soft; vigorous, very tall growth; rediscovered by Mrs. Targett; int. in about 1970

Tocade – See **Arizona**, Gr

Tocade F, yb; flowers yellow, striped rose pink, dbl., cupped, borne in clusters; recurrent; foliage semi-glossy; vigorous (90-110 cm) growth; int. by Meilland, 2000

Toccata F, or, 1959, Lens; flowers well-formed, borne in large clusters; low growth; [Independence × Cinnabar]

Toccata HT, mp, 1963, Sanday, John; flowers light rose edged darker, reverse silvery, becoming redder, 5 in., 27 petals; vigorous growth; [Karl Herbst × seedling]

Today Gr, ob, 1989, McGredy, Sam IV; bud ovoid; flowers light orange blending to yellow, medium, 33 petals, cupped, borne usually singly, slight fragrance; recurrent; foliage medium size, dark green, glossy; prickles recurved, medium, brown; bushy, medium growth; hips globular, medium, orange-red; PP7202; [(Typhoo Tea × (Yellow Pages × Kabuki)) × ((Yellow Pages × Kabuki) × (MACjose × Typhoon))]; int. by Co-Operative Rose Growers, 1988

Toddler F, pb, 1976, LeGrice; flowers pink, reverse deeper, 2 in., 19 petals; foliage small, dark; very low, bushy growth; [seedling × seedling]; int. in 1977

Todoroki HT, dr, 1977, Keisei Rose Nurseries, Inc.; bud pointed; flowers 6½ in., 33 petals, high-centered; foliage dark; vigorous growth; [(Pharaon × Kagayaki) × Yu-Ai]

Toffee Min, ob, 1992, McCann, Sean; flowers bright orange, yellow eye, dark orange stamens, 1 in., 18 petals, urn-shaped, loose, borne singly, slight fruity fragrance; recurrent; foliage medium size, medium green, semi-glossy, disease-resistant; bushy, medium growth; [Bloomsday × unnamed Min seedling]; int. by Justice Miniature Roses, 1993

Together For Ever – See **Caring For You**, Cl F

Together Forever F, op, Dickson; flowers orange with yellow center, turning to pale peach-pink, 4 in., 23 petals, cupped, borne in clusters of 5-25; recurrent; foliage dense, light to medium green, semi-glossy; upright to bushy (95 cm.) growth; int. by Dickson Roses, 2006

Togo HT, Cazzaniga, F. G.; int. in 1959

Toison d'Or HT, ab, 1921, Pernet-Ducher; flowers apricot-yellow, shaded orange-red, dbl.; Gold Medal, Bagatelle, 1922

Toison d'Or – See **Golden Fleece**, F

Tojo F, mr, McGredy, Sam IV; flowers dbl., cupped, borne in clusters; recurrent; int. in 1978

Tokay F, ab, 1999, Zipper, Herbert; flowers apricot suffused with pink, reverse soft pink to apricot, 3 in., full, borne mostly singly, slight fragrance; foliage medium size, dark green, semi-glossy; prickles moderate; upright, tall (4-5 ft.) growth; [Olympic Gold × Spanish Sun]; int. by Island Roses, 1999

Token HT, yb, 1933, Montgomery Co.; bud ovoid; flowers glowing orange, open, large, dbl.; foliage glossy; strong stems; vigorous growth; [Mme Butterfly × Premier Supreme]

Token Glory HT, or, 1959, Grillo; bud pointed; flowers orange, 4 in., 40 petals, moderate fragrance; foliage dark, leathery; long stems; very vigorous, upright, bushy growth; [sport of Token Supreme]; int. in 1957

Token Supreme HT, ob, 1940, Grillo; flowers deep orange, 5 in., 35 petals; [sport of Token]

Tokimeki F, dp, Ichibashi; int. in 1995

Tokonatsu HT, ob, Keisei; int. by Keisei Rose Nurseries, 2005

Tokyo Cl F, my, 1972, Oliver, W.G.; flowers 3 in., 5 petals; profuse May-June bloom; foliage light; vigorous growth; [Salute × Canary Bird]

Toledo S, yb, Poulsen; flowers yellow blend, 8-10 cm., dbl., no fragrance; foliage matte; growth bushy, 20-40 cm.; PP15041; int. by Poulsen Roser, 2003

Toledo Gold HT, my

Toledo Hit – See **Toledo**, S

Toliman Min, m; int. in about 1992

Tolstoï HSet, mp, 1938, Böhm, J.; flowers pale pink, reverse slightly darker, 8-10 cm., dbl., globular, intense fragrance; non-remontant; tall (2 m.) growth

Tom Barr HT, op, 1932, McGredy; bud long, pointed; flowers salmon and scarlet, suffused yellow and orange, large, dbl., high-centered; vigorous growth

Tom Breneman HT, dp, 1950, Howard, F.H.; bud ovoid; flowers rose-pink, red stamens, 4-4½ in., 30-40 petals, globular, intense fragrance; recurrent; foliage leathery, dark; very vigorous, upright growth; [Mauna Loa × R.M.S. Queen Mary]; int. by H&S

Tom Breneman, Climbing Cl HT, dp, 1954, H&S

Tom Brown F, r, 1964, LeGrice; flowers orangy-brown, reverse brownish-red, well-shaped, 3 in., 32 petals, borne singly and in clusters, intense fragrance; recurrent; foliage leathery, dark; vigorous, bushy growth; [seedling × Amberlight]

Tom Foster HT, my, Poole, Lionel; flowers medium yellow, large, very dbl., borne mostly singly, moderate fragrance; foliage medium size, dark green, semi-glossy; some prickles; bushy, medium growth; [Gertrude Shilling × Helmut Schmidt]; int. by Battersby Roses, 1996

Tom Maney LCl, mp, 1953, Maney; bud ovoid; flowers rose-pink, 4-5 in., 35-40 petals, cupped, borne in clusters of 3-4; non-recurrent; foliage leathery, dark; vigorous, climbing (15-20 ft.) growth; quite hardy; [*R. maximowicziana pilosa* × Kitchener of Khartoum]; int. by Iowa State College

Tom Pilliby F, or, 1963, Combe; flowers semi-dbl., borne in large clusters; vigorous growth

Tom Thumb Min, rb, 1936, deVink; flowers deep crimson, center white, ½-1 in., semi-dbl., shallow cup to flat, borne singly and in clusters; recurrent; foliage leathery, light green; very dwarf (8-12 in.) growth; [Rouletii × Gloria Mundi]; int. by C-P

Tom Tom F, dp, 1958, Lindquist; bud ovoid; flowers Neyron rose, 3-3½ in., 25 petals, high-centered to flat, borne in clusters, slight spicy fragrance; recurrent bloom; foliage dark green, semi-glossy; prickles several, medium, hooked slightly downward, russet; vigorous, upright, bushy growth; hips none ; PP1671; [Improved Lafayette × Floradora]; int. by Howard Rose Co., 1957

Tom Tom, Climbing Cl F, dp, 1962, Lindquist; PP2173; int. by Howard Rose Co.

Tom Wood HP, mr, 1896, Dickson, A.; flowers cherry-red, 8 cm., dbl., cupped, borne in clusters, moderate fragrance; recurrent; compact (3-4 ft.) growth

Tomás Batâ HP, dr, 1932, Böhm, J.; flowers shaded crimson, passing to maroon, large, dbl.; foliage leathery, glossy, dark; very vigorous growth; [Fisher Holmes × Prince Camille de Rohan]

Tomato Rose – See ***R. rugosa*** (Thunberg)

Tombola F, dp, 1967, deRuiter; flowers deep pink, 4 in.; foliage dark, glossy; vigorous, upright, bushy growth; [Amor × (Ena Harkness × Peace)]

Tombola HT, op, Spek; flowers pale salmon pink, 4½ in., 30-35 petals, high-centered, borne mostly singly; recurrent; foliage dark green; few prickles; stems long; florist rose; int. by Jan Spek Rozen, 2002

Tomboy Min, mp, 1989, Zipper, Herbert; flowers small, 5 petals, no fragrance; foliage small, dark green, semi-glossy; upright, spreading growth; [Maytime × Poker Chip]; int. by Magic Moment Miniature Roses, 1989

Tomkins Red F, dr, 1943, Brownell; bud long, pointed; flowers deep velvety crimson turning maroon, open, 18 petals, borne in clusters, moderate fragrance; foliage dark, glossy; long stems; vigorous, compact, upright growth; [(Dr. W. Van Fleet × Général Jacqueminot) × Nigrette]

Tommelise – See **Hertfordshire**, S

Tommy HT, pb, Schreurs; flowers pink with green tips, borne mostly singly; recurrent

Tommy Bright F, mr, 1961, Boerner; bud ovoid; flowers scarlet-red, large, 35-40 petals, cupped, moderate fragrance; foliage leathery; strong stems; very vigorous, upright growth; PP2129; [(Chatter × unknown) × Garnette Supreme]; int. by J&P, 1961

Tommy Thompson HT, or, 1976, Golik; bud ovoid; flowers 5 in., 50 petals, high-centered, moderate spicy fragrance; foliage glossy, very dark; moderate growth; [Queen o' the Lakes × Tropicana]; int. by Dynarose, 1974

Tommy Tucker Min, lp, 1955, Robinson, T.; flowers silvery pink, 1 in., dbl., borne in clusters; [Rouletti × Tom Thumb]

Tomorrow F, dy, Christensen; int. in 1989

Tom's Pink Pol, mp, Horsfield; flowers 4 cm., moderate fragrance; compact (40 cm.) growth; int. in 1986

Tonehime HT, w, 1985, Kikuchi, Rikichi; flowers white, creamy center, large, 30 petals, high-centered, borne mostly singly; foliage small, dark, glossy; few prickles; vigorous, slender, tall growth; [Mizuho × Sodori-Hime]; int. in 1984

Tonga HT, ob, 1955, Lowe; flowers deep golden orange, outer petals veined bronze and scarlet, dbl.; foliage dark, leathery; vigorous, upright growth

Toni Corsari F, dr, 1961, Delforge; flowers velvety deep red, medium, semi-dbl., borne in large clusters; bushy, low growth; [Red Favorite × seedling]

Toni Lander F, ob, 1961, Poulsen, D. T.; flowers salmon-orange, 3 in., 22 petals, borne in large clusters; foliage dark; bushy growth; [Independence × Circus]; Gold Medal, Madrid, 1960

Toni Thompson's Musk HMsk, w, Thompson, T.; [*R. brunonii* × unknown]

Tonia HT, m, 1992, Franklin-Smith, Roger; flowers light lavender/mauve with deeper tones (silvery lavender) at edges, 3-3½ in., full, intense fragrance; foliage medium size, medium green, matte; some prickles; upright (175-180 cm.), vigorous growth; [Lagerfeld × Remember Me]; int. in 1995

Tonia's Friendship HT, pb, 2004, Poole, Lionel; flowers ivory, edged pink, reverse ivory/pink, 5 in., full, borne in large clusters, intense fragrance; foliage medium size, medium green, semi-glossy; prickles moderate, medium size, slightly hooked; growth upright, bushy, medium (1 m.); garden decorative; [(Hazel Rose × Cardiff Bay) × New Zealand]; int. in 2005

Tonic Meillandina Min, mr, Meilland

Tonight HT, mr, 1973, Warriner, William A.; bud ovoid; flowers bright red, large, dbl., high-centered; foliage leathery; vigorous growth; PP3522; [seedling × Forever Yours]; int. by J&P

Tonimbuk HT, pb, Dawson; flowers flower blush pink with tints of strong pink, dbl., high-centered, very slight fragrance; recurrent; foliage dark green; medium growth; int. before 1990

Toniro HT, yb, Hiroshima; int. by Hiroshima Bara-en, 1998

Tonnere F, dr, 1956, Mallerin, C.; flowers deep velvety red, 3 in., 24 petals, borne in large clusters; foliage dark; vigorous, bushy growth; [Holstein × Francais]; int. by Wheatcroft Bros., 1954

Tonner's Fancy HG, w, 1928, Clark, A.; flowers white, tinted pink, fading to cream, large, semi-dbl., globular, moderate fragrance; non-remontant; vigorous, climbing (15 ft.) growth; [(*R. gigantea* × unknown) × seedling]; int. by Gill & Searle

Tonsina HT, ob

Tony Jacklin F, op, 1974, McGredy, Sam IV; flowers orange-salmon, flora-tea, 4 in., 30 petals, hybrid tea, slight fragrance; foliage dark green, glossy; tall growth; int. by McGredy & Son, 1972; Gold Medal, Portland, 1986, Gold Medal, Madrid, 1972

Tony Peace HT, ab, 1967, Brundrett; flowers buff-yellow to apricot; [sport of Peace]; int. in 1964

Tony Spalding HT, dr, 1933, McGredy; flowers brilliant crimson, semi-dbl., high-centered; foliage glossy; very vigorous growth

Tony's Two Tone F, pb, 2002, Hiltner, Martin; flowers deep pink, reverse light yellow, 2-3 in., dbl., borne in small clusters; foliage medium size, light green, semi-glossy; prickles moderate, hooked down; growth spreading, low, short (2½ ft.); decorative, garden; [Lynn Anderson × ((Carefree Beauty × Picasso) × Unknown)]; int. in 2003

Too Cute Pol, lp, Rupert; flowers light pink fading to white, 1½-2 in., very full, rosette, borne in large clusters, slight fragrance; recurrent; growth low, compact, bushy; int. in 2001

Too Hot To Handle LCl, or, 1998, McGredy, Sam IV; flowers orange-red, 2¾ in., dbl., borne in small clusters, slight fragrance; foliage large, dark green, glossy; prickles moderate; upright, tall (150 cm.) growth; [Waiheke × Eyeopener]; int. by McGredy, 1995

Toorenburg F, ab, Kordes

Tooth of Time Min, w, 1990, Rennie, Bruce F.; bud pointed; flowers white with cream, small, 25 petals, urn-shaped, borne usually singly and in sprays of 3-5, slight spicy fragrance; foliage small, dark green, semi-glossy; prickles hooked downward, medium, light yellow; growth bushy, medium; [Party Girl × Paul Shirville]; int. by Rennie Roses International, 1990

Tootie Min, mp; flowers 30-35 petals, slight fragrance; free-flowering; foliage small; compact (12-18 in.), rounded growth; int. by PanAm Nursery, 2003

Tootsie F, pb, 1991, Greenwood, Chris; flowers deep pink painted white, reverse mostly white, aging with a slight fading of pink, medium, 20 petals, loose, borne in sprays of 5-7, slight fragrance; foliage medium size, dark green, glossy, disease-resistant; upright, bushy, rounded, medium growth; [Angel Face × Old Master]; int. by Armstrong Garden Centers, 1991

Top Billing HT, dr, Ludwig; flowers crimson red, large, dbl., pointed, urn-shaped, borne mostly singly; recurrent; foliage dark green, glossy; stems sturdy, long; growth medium, rounded plant

Top Brass – See **Brass Monkey**, LCl

Top Choice Min, op, 1985, Hardgrove, Donald L.; flowers medium salmon-pink, medium, 36 petals; foliage small, medium green, semi-glossy; dense, spreading, bushy growth; [Gingersnap × Baby Katie]; int. by Rose World Originals

Top Contender MinFl, dy, 2006, Wells, Verlie W.; flowers dbl., borne mostly solitary; foliage medium size, medium green, semi-glossy; prickles ¼ in., straight, few; growth upright, medium (36-40 in.); garden decorative, exhibition; [sport of Memphis Music]; int. by Wells MidSouth Roses, 2006

Top Gear – See **Little Artist**, Min

Top Gun Min, pb, 1990, King, Gene; bud pointed; flowers peony pink, yellow base, apricot yellow reverse, medium, 28 petals, high-centered, borne usually singly, no fragrance; foliage medium size, medium green, semi-glossy; tall, upright growth; [(Rainbow's End × Vera Dalton) × Vera Dalton]; int. by AGM Miniature Roses, 1990

Top Hat F, ab, 1968, Fankhauser; bud ovoid; flowers apricot-blush, medium, dbl., high-centered; foliage small, dark, glossy; compact, low growth; [Ma Perkins × Garden Party]; int. by A. Ross & Son

Top Hit – See **Carrot Top**, Min

Top Marks Min, or, Fryer, Gareth; flowers bright vermilion, dbl., cupped, borne in clusters, slight fragrance; recurrent; foliage disease-resistant; compact (18 in.), bushy growth; Rose of the Year, RosesUK, 1992, Gold Medal, The Hague, Gold Medal, RNRS, 1990, Bronze Medal, Baden-Baden

Top Meillandina – See **Autumn Sunblaze**, Min

Top Mode HT, w, Hiroshima; int. by Hiroshima Bara-en, 1996

Top Notch HT, ab, 1998, McGredy, Sam IV; flowers golden-apricot, 4 in., 30-40 petals, high-centered, borne mostly singly, intense fruit & anise fragrance; recurrent; foliage large, medium green, glossy; prickles moderate; bushy (120 cm.) growth; PPAF; [Spek's Centennial × New Year]; Rose of the Year, Roses UK, 2002

Top of the Bill Min, dp, Genesis; flowers fuchsia-pink, semi-dbl. to dbl., cupped, moderate fragrance; recurrent; foliage dark green, glossy; moderate (12-24 in.) growth; int. in 1996; Silver Medal, The Hague, 2006

Top Rose – See **Toprose**, F

Top Secret Min, mr, 1971, Moore, Ralph S.; [sport of Beauty Secret]; int. by Sequoia Nursery

Top Secret HT, dr, Meilland

Top Star – See **Legend**, HT

Top Star HT, ob, Noack, Werner

Top Symphonie Min, ob, Meilland; int. by René Dessevre, 2002

Topaz Pol, yb, 1937, Tantau; flowers lemon-yellow, petals edged cream, reverse lemon and cream, small, very dbl., high-centered, slight fragrance; foliage small, leathery; dwarf, spreading growth; [Joanna Tantau × (Prof. Gnau × Julien Potin)]; int. by C-P

Topaz F, r, 1985, Warriner, William A.; flowers tan, medium, 35 petals; foliage medium size, medium green, semi-glossy; upright growth; [seedling × Intrigue]; int. by J&P, 1986

Topaz Jewel HRg, my, 1987, Moore, Ralph S.; bud large, pointed; flowers medium yellow fading to cream, 3-3½ in., 20-30 petals, cupped, borne usually in sprays of 5-8, moderate fruity fragrance; repeat bloom; foliage large, medium green, rugose, matte; prickles numerous, hooked downward, brown, in variable sizes; upright, bushy, spreading, vigorous growth; no fruit; PP6793; [Golden Angel × Belle Poitevine]; int. by Wayside Gardens, 1987

Topaze F, ab, Guillot-Massad; flowers apricot-pink, dbl., rosette, borne in clusters, moderate apple fragrance; recurrent; foliage bright, glossy; low (50 cm.) growth; int. by Roseraies Guillot, 1995

Topaze Orientale HT, yb, 1967, Delbard-Chabert; flowers maize-yellow to light pink, 5-6 in., dbl., high-centered, moderate fragrance; tall growth; [Sultane × Queen Elizabeth]; int. by Cuthbert, 1965

Topeka F, mr, 1978, Wisbech Plant Co.; bud long, pointed; flowers 3 in., 21 petals, flat; foliage glossy; vigorous, upright growth; [Vera Dalton × seedling]

Topkapi – See **Topkapi Palace**, S

Topkapi Palace S, dp, Olesen; bud ovoid; flowers deep pink to light red, 2-3 in., 55-60 petals, rounded, then flat, borne singly and in small clusters, slight wild rose fragrance; recurrent; foliage dark; prickles few, 5-7 mm, linear to concave, light pink; stems 14-18 in.; bushy (2-2½ ft.) growth; PP10883; [sport of Queen Margrethe]; int. by Poulsen, 1996

Topper HT, mr, 1959, Joseph H. Hill, Co.; bud short, pointed; flowers signal-red to crimson, 3-3½ in., 25-30 petals, high-centered to open; foliage dark, leathery; long, strong stems; vigorous, upright growth; PP1566; [Pink Bountiful × Sister Kenny]; for greenhouse use

Toprose F, dy, 1992, Cocker, James; flowers bright yellow, 3-3½ in., full, cupped to flat, borne in clusters, slight fragrance; recurrent; foliage large, medium green, glossy; some prickles; medium (75 cm.), upright growth; [((Chinatown × Golden Masterpiece) × Adolf Horstmann) × Yellow Pages]; int. by James Cocker & Sons, 1991; Gold Medal, Baden-Baden, 1987

Topsi F, or, 1973, Tantau, Math.; bud ovoid; flowers orange-scarlet, medium, semi-dbl., spiral to open, slight fragrance; recurrent; moderate, dwarf growth; [Fragrant Cloud × Signalfeuer]; int. in 1971; President's International Trophy, RNRS, 1972, Gold Medal, RNRS, 1972

Topsi's Friend F, lp, 1981, Anderson's Rose Nurseries; flowers 15 petals, rosette, borne 5 per cluster; foliage light green, glossy; prickles green; upright growth; [Dreamland × Topsi]

Topsy – See **Perfectly Red**, HT

Topsy Turvy F, rb, 2005, Carruth, Tom; flowers scarlet red, reverse white, 8-10 cm., 10-15 petals, open pinwheel, borne in large clusters, slight apple fragrance; recurrent; foliage medium size, dark green, glossy, new shoots dark red; prickles numerous, average, almost straight, taupe; growth bushy, very rounded, medium (60 to 70 cm.); garden decoration; PPAF; [Countess Celeste × Betty Boop]; int. by Weeks Roses, 2006

Toque Rouge – See **Asso di Cuori**, HT

Torch, Climbing Cl Pol, or, 1942, deRuiter; flowers scarlet-orange, white eye, 1½ in., 15 petals, borne in clusters; foliage glossy, dark; vigorous, climbing (6-8 ft.) growth; [sport of Unnamed orange Polyantha seedling, climbing]

Torch of Liberty Min, or, 1986, Moore, Ralph S.; bud long, pointed; flowers orange-red, silver reverse, 1½ in., 20-30 petals, high-centered, borne singly and several together, slight fragrance; recurrent; foliage small, medium green, semi-glossy; few prickles; upright, bushy growth; hips ball-shaped, orange; PP6254; [Orangeade × Golden Angel]; int. by Moore Min. Roses, 1985

Torch Song HT, or, 1959, Meilland, F.; bud ovoid; flowers vermilion, 5 in., 30-35 petals, high-centered; foliage dark, leathery; vigorous, upright, bushy growth; PP1760; [(Peace × Floradora) × Grand'mere Jenny]; int. by C-P, 1959

Torche Rose – See **Pink Torch**, S

Torchlight F, or, 1951, LeGrice; flowers brilliant orange-scarlet shaded deeper, large, 5-8 petals, borne in clusters of up to 30, moderate fragrance; foliage dark; vigorous growth; [Dusky Maiden × Holstein]

Torchy F, or, 1969, Armstrong, D.L.; bud pointed to urn-shaped; flowers brick-orange, medium, dbl., high-centered, moderate fragrance; foliage leathery; moderate, bushy growth; PP3016; [Heat Wave × Spartan]; int. by Armstrong Nursery

Toreador HT, pb, 1919, Paul, W.; flowers rosy red, reverse golden yellow, medium, semi-dbl.

Toresky F, lp, 1931, Padrosa; flowers light pink with white eye, dbl., cupped, borne in large clusters; foliage wrinkled, light; dwarf growth; [Perle d'Or × Antoine Rivoire]

Toresky, Climbing Cl F, lp, 1958, Bofill, F.; int. by Rosas Torre Blanca, 1956

Torino F, mp, 1960, Mansuino, Q.; flowers spinel-rose, small to medium; vigorous growth; [seedling × Cocorico]

Tornado F, or, 1973, Kordes, R.; flowers bright scarlet, 6 cm., semi-dbl., cupped, borne in clusters; recurrent; foliage large, dark green, glossy, leathery; vigorous, bushy (2 ft.), open growth; [Europeana × Marlena]; int. by Kordes, 1973; ADR, 1972

Tornado Kordana Min, mr, Kordes; flowers dbl., high-centered; int. by W. Kordes Söhne

Tornella S, dr, Noack; flowers velvety dark red, 8 cm., dbl., cupped, borne in clusters; recurrent; foliage dark green, glossy, leathery; upright (5 ft.), bushy growth; int. by Noack Rosen, 2006

Tornerose F, mr, Roldskov; flowers small, 20-40 petals, cupped to flat, borne in clusters, no fragrance; recurrent; int. in 1995

Toro – See **Uncle Joe**, HT

Toro de Fuego S, Delbard-Chabert; int. in 1970

Torrero F, ob, 1961, Leenders, J.; flowers pink-orange-red, 3 in., 18 petals, flat; [Ma Perkins × Cocorico]

Torrida HP, pb, 1839, Boyau; flowers velvety dark carmine-purple, streaked white, medium, dbl.

Torvill & Dean HT, pb, 1985, Sealand Nurseries, Ltd.; flowers pink, yellow reverse, medium, 35 petals, high-centered, slight fragrance; recurrent; foliage medium size, dark, semi-glossy; upright growth; [Irish Gold × Alexander]; int. in 1984

Tosca F, or, 1972, Warriner, William A.; bud long, pointed; flowers open, medium, dbl.; foliage large, leathery; very vigorous, upright growth; PP3347; [seedling × Ginger]; int. by J&P

Toscana HT, dp, 1954, Cazzaniga, F. G.; flowers deep pink, dbl.; vigorous growth; int. by Fedi

Toscana – See **Tosca**, F

Toscana F, mr, Kordes; flora-tea; int. in 1991

Toscana – See **Gärtnerfreude**, S

Toscanini HT, lp, Olij ; bud large, ovoid; flowers light pink to cream, reverse darker, 12 cm., very full, high-centered, borne usually singly, slight woodsy fragrance; recurrent; foliage dark green, semi-glossy; prickles numerous, medium, tan; erect (5-6 ft.) growth; PP11494; [Prophyta × (Meibrimel × Super Disco)]; int. in 1999

Rosier des Turcs – See ***R. hemisphaerica*** (Herrmann)

Total Recall Min, or, 1985, Saville, F. Harmon; flowers medium, dbl., no fragrance; foliage small, medium green, semi-glossy; bushy growth; [Zorina × Baby Katie]; int. by Nor'East Min. Roses, 1984

Totenviksrosen HSpn

Totote Gélos HT, w, 1915, Pernet-Ducher; bud long, pointed; flowers flesh-white, center shaded chrome-yellow, dbl.

Tottie F, mr, 1961, Borgatti, G.; flowers purplish red, 3 in., 35-40 petals, borne in clusters of 6; vigorous, bushy growth; [Alain × Fashion]; int. by Sgaravatti

Totty's Red HT, dr, 1926, Totty; flowers crimson-scarlet; [sport of Premier]

Touch of Class HT, op, 1985, Kriloff, Michel; bud pointed ovoid; flowers medium pink, shaded coral and cream, 4½-5½ in., 25-35 petals, high-centered, borne mostly singly, slight fragrance; recurrent; foliage large, dark green, semi-glossy; prickles several, medium, slightly hooked downward; stems strong, medium to long; upright, bushy growth; hips long, ovoid, conspicuous neck, very smooth ; PP5165; [Micaela × (Queen Elizabeth × Romantica)]; int. by Armstrong Nursery, 1984; Gold Medal, Portland, 1988

Touch o' Cloves Min, r, 1995, Williams, Ernest; flowers 1-1¼ in., dbl., borne mostly singly; foliage medium size, dark green, semi-glossy; few prickles; upright (18 in.), bushy growth; [seedling × Twilight Trail]; int. by Texas Mini Roses, 1995

Touch of Elegance Min, w, 1989, Leon, Charles F., Sr.; bud pointed; flowers white with creamy yellow center, large, dbl., high-centered, borne singly and in small clusters; foliage medium size, medium green, semi-glossy; upright, tall growth; [(Gavotte × Buccaneer) × unnamed Miniature seedling]; int. by John Carrigg, 1987

Touch of Fire Min, ob, 1989, Rennie, Bruce F.; bud ovoid; flowers orange-yellow, reverse light orange, aging apricot-orange, 25 petals, urn-shaped, moderate spicy fragrance; foliage small, medium green, semi-glossy; prickles straight, small, orange-red; bushy growth; no fruit; [Tangerine Mist × California Girl]; int. by Rennie Roses International, 1989

Touch of Glamour Min, w; flowers delicate pink, full, shallow cup, rosette; recurrent; compact (20 in.) growth; int. by Love4Plants, 2005

Touch of Kiwi HT, yb, 1989, Cattermole, R.F.; bud tapering; flowers creamy yellow, 1/4" wide orange margin on petals, dbl.; foliage medium green; prickles pointed, light brown, varying size; upright growth; [Kiwi Queen × Command Performance]; int. by South Pacific Rose Nursery

Touch of Magic HT, or, 1979, Patterson; bud globular; flowers 5 in., 40-45 petals, high-centered, intense fragrance; very vigorous growth; [San Francisco × Peace]; int. by Patterson Roses, 1977

Touch o' Midas Cl Min, yb, 1985, Williams, Ernest D.; flowers deep yellow, petals edged deep pink, small, 35 petals, borne singly; foliage small, dark, semi-glossy; upright (to 5 ft.) growth; [Little Darling × Over the Rainbow]; int. by Mini-Roses

Touch of Raspberry HT, dp, 1989, Marciel, Stanley G.; bud slender, tapering; flowers deep pink, large, 30 petals, cupped, borne singly, slight fruity fragrance; foliage large, dark green, semi-glossy; prickles declining, light lime green with mauve tinges; upright, tall growth; PP7548; [Love Affair × Paul's Pink]; int. by DeVor Nurseries, Inc.

Touch of Velvet HT, rb, 1989, Leon, Charles F., Sr.; bud pointed, long; flowers magenta red with lighter tones, 31 petals, high-centered, borne usually singly and in small clusters, moderate fragrance; foliage medium size, dark green, semi-glossy; upright, tall growth; [(First Prize × Gypsy) × seedling]; int. by John Carrigg, 1987

Touch of Venus HT, w, 1970, Armstrong, D.L.; flowers near white, center shaded pink, large, dbl., high-centered, intense fragrance; foliage large, leathery; vigorous, upright growth; [Garden Party × Sweet Afton]; int. by Armstrong Nursery, 1971

Touch-Up Min, pb, 1990, Jacobs, Betty A.; bud pointed; flowers medium pink with cream border, reverse cream, hand-painted, 30 petals, high-centered, moderate tea fragrance; foliage medium size, medium green, matte; prickles straight, large, red to tan; growth upright, bushy, tall; hips round, medium, russet-orange; [Scarlet Knight × (Matangi × Honey Hill)]; int. by Four Seasons Rose Nursery, 1989

Touchdown Min, mr, 1989, Jolly, Nelson F.; bud ovoid; flowers reverse red with white center, aging bluish, small, 40 petals, urn-shaped, no fragrance; foliage small, medium green, matte; no prickles; low, upright growth; no fruit; [Sheri Anne × Anita Charles]; int. by Rosehill Farm, 1989

Touché Min, op, 1995, Laver, Keith G.; flowers orange-pink, medium, 40-60 petals, borne in small clusters; foliage medium size, medium green, semi-glossy; prickles mossed; bushy, medium growth; [seedling × seedling]; int. by Springwood Roses, 1996

Touche HT, rb; int. by K&M Nursery, 2003

Touching Lives F, dy, 2004, Paul Chessum Roses; flowers full, borne in small clusters, moderate fragrance; recurrent; foliage large, medium green, semi-glossy; prickles moderate, medium, green; growth compact, bushy, medium (85 cm.); bedding, containers; [n/a × seedling]; int. by Love4Plants Ltd, 2004

Touggourt F, or, 1963, Arles; bud globular; flowers orange-shrimp-pink, open, large, dbl.; foliage dark, leathery; vigorous, bushy growth; [(Gruss an Teplitz × Independence) × (Floradora × Independence)]; int. by Roses-France, 1959

Toujours Fleuri B, m, 1856, Cherpin; flowers dark violet, large

Toulouse Lautrec HT, my, 1994, Meilland, Alain A.; bud globular; flowers clear lemon yellow, 3-4 in., 87-90 petals, cupped, borne mostly singly, very slight fragrance; good repeat; foliage medium size, medium green, glossy; prickles numerous, medium, greenish; medium (70-80 cm.), bushy growth; PP9582; [Ambassador × (King's Ransom × Sunblest)]; int. by SNC Meilland & Cie, 1992

Tour de France F, or, 1963, Mondial Roses; flowers deep orange-scarlet shaded blood-red, large to medium, semi-dbl.; vigorous, bushy growth; [(Alain × Orange Triumph) × seedling]

Tour de Malakoff C, m, 1856, Pastoret; flowers mauve-pink shaded purple, heavily veined, center green, large, dbl., deeply cupped, borne singly and in clusters of 2-3, moderate fragrance; non-remontant; foliage oblong, pointed, with 3-5 leaflets; prickles few, only on old wood; sprawling (7 ft.) growth; int. by Soupert & Notting

Tour Eiffel – See **Eiffel Tower**, HT

Tour Eiffel 2000 LCl, mr, Delbard; flowers semi-dbl., cupped, borne in clusters, slight fresh fragrance; recurrent; foliage disease-resistant; vigorous (8-10 ft.) growth; a rugosa included in parentage somewhere; int. by Georges Delbard SA, 1998

Tour Malakoff HGal, m, 1856, Robert; flowers lilac/flesh pink, 10-12 cm., full, globular

Touraine – See **H. C. Andersen**, F

Tourbillon F, rb, 1959, Delbard-Chabert; flowers red, reverse silvery pink, well-formed, 3-4 in., 30-35 petals, borne in clusters of 6-8; very vigorous, bushy growth; RULED EXTINCT 4/85; [Michèle Meilland × (Incendie × (Floradora × Orange Triumph))]

Tourbillon F, pb, 1985, Delbard, Georges; flowers deep pink, yellow reverse, large, 20 petals, moderate fragrance; foliage small, medium green, semi-glossy; upright growth; [Zambra × ((Orléans Rose × Goldilocks) × (Spartan × Fashion))]; int. in 1981

Tourmaline HT, pb, 1970, Delbard-Chabert; flowers creamy white, widely edged carmine, large, 28 petals, high-centered, cupped, very slight fragrance; recurrent; foliage light green; moderate growth; [Michèle Meilland × Chic Parisien]; int. by Cuthbert, 1965; Gold Medal, Madrid, 1965

Tournament of Roses Gr, pb, 1988, Warriner, William A.; bud pointed ovoid; flowers light coral pink, reverse deep pink, aging coral pink, 3-4 in., 25-30 petals, high-centered, borne singly and several together, very slight fragrance; recurrent; foliage large, dark green, semi-glossy, disease-resistant; prickles large; stems strong, medium length; upright, bushy, medium growth; PP6725; [Impatient × seedling]; int. by J&P, 1989

Tournee F, dy, VEG; flowers luminous golden yellow, medium, semi-dbl.

Toussaint L'Ouverture B, m, 1849, Miellez; flowers deep violet red, medium, full; sometimes classed as Ch

Tove Pedersen F, dr

Tower Bridge HT, mr, Harkness; flowers light crimson, 4½ in., 80 petals, intense spice/berry fragrance; recurrent; growth to 4½ ft.; int. in 1995

Town Crier HT, ly, 1960, Joseph H. Hill, Co.; bud pointed ovoid; flowers straw-yellow, 5-6 in., 30-35 petals, high-centered, borne singly, moderate tea fragrance; recurrent; foliage large, dark green, glossy; prickles several, medium, hooked downward; stems long, strong; vigorous, upright, well-branched growth; PP1807; [Peace × Yellow Perfection]; int. in 1961

Town Talk F, or, 1969, Swim & Weeks; bud ovoid; flowers small, dbl., cupped; foliage dark, leathery; moderate growth; PP2709; [(Circus × Garnette) × Spartan]; originally registered as Pol; patent issued as Pol; int. by Weeks Wholesale Rose Growers, 1966

Town Talk, Climbing Cl F, or, 1976, Weeks, O. L.; PP3909; int. by Weeks Wholesale Rose Growers, 1975

Townsend HSpn, mp, before 1885, from Scotland; flowers carmine striped with crimson, small, dbl.; non-recurrent; int. before 1885

Townswoman HT, rb, 1973, Anderson's Rose Nurseries; flowers red-purple, reverse silver, 5 in., 35 petals, globular; foliage light; free growth; [seedling × Piccadilly]

Toy Balloon Min, dr, 1979, Moore, Ralph S.; bud ovoid, pointed; flowers deep scarlet crimson, 1½ in., 45-50 petals, high-centered, slight fragrance; recurrent; foliage dark; bushy, spreading growth; PP4512; [Fairy Moss × Fire Princess]; int. by Sequoia Nursery

Toy Clown Min, rb, 1966, Moore, Ralph S.; flowers white edged red, small, semi-dbl., borne mostly singly; recurrent; foliage small, leathery; bushy, dwarf growth; PP2909; [Little Darling × Magic Wand]; int. by Sequoia Nursery; AOE, ARS, 1975

Toy Soldier Min, rb, 1985, Curtis, Thad; flowers red-white blend, medium, 20 petals; foliage medium size, medium green, semi-glossy; bushy growth; [Pink Parfait × Over the Rainbow]; int. by Hortico Roses

Toyland Min, mr, 1978, Lyon; bud ovoid; flowers Indian red, 1 in., 10 petals; foliage tiny; compact, bushy growth; int. in 1977

Toynbee Hall – See **Bella Rosa**, F

Tracey Wickham Min, yb, 1984, Welsh, Eric; flowers bright yellow, petals edged bright red, small, 30 petals, hybrid tea, borne singly and in clusters, moderate fragrance; foliage medium size, medium green, semi-glossy; upright growth; [Avandel × Redgold]; int. by Rose Hill Roses

Traci Min, w, 2001, Giles, Diann; flowers white with pink edge, medium, full, borne in large clusters, slight fragrance; foliage medium size, dark green, glossy; prickles few, medium, curved; growth spreading, medium; garden decorative; [seedling × seedling]; int. by Giles Rose Nursery, 2001

Trade Wind HT, rb, 1964, Von Abrams; bud long, pointed; flowers dark red, reverse silver, 5 in., 55 petals, high-centered, intense fragrance; foliage glossy; vigorous, tall growth; PP2664; [(Multnomah × seedling) × (Carrousel × seedling)]; int. by Peterson & Dering, 1964

Trade Winds – See **Trade Wind**, HT

Tradescant S, dr, 1994, Austin, David; bud short, pointed ovoid; flowers very dark purplish-red, 2½ in., very full, cupped, then rosette, borne in small clusters, moderate sweet fragrance; recurrent; foliage medium size, dark green, semi-glossy; prickles some, medium, straight to hooked downward; stems long; bushy, spreading growth; PP9009; [Prospero × seedling]; int. by David Austin Roses, Ltd., 1993

Tradition HT, mr, 1965, Kordes, R.; flowers scarlet-crimson, 4½ in., 35 petals; [Detroiter × Don Juan]; int. by McGredy

Tradition LCl, mr, 2006; flowers luminous deep red, conspicuous yellow stamens, 8 cm., semi-dbl., cupped to flat, borne in large clusters, slight fragrance; recurrent; foliage medium size, dark green, very glossy; bushy, upright (10 ft.) growth; int. by W. Kordes' Söhne, 1995

Tradition 95 – See **Tradition**, LCl

Traditional Home HT, m, 1998, Winchel, Joseph F.; flowers pinkish, high-centered, 4 in., dbl., high-centered, borne mostly singly; foliage medium size, dark green, semi-glossy; prickles moderate; growth upright, medium (5 ft.); [unknown × unknown]; int. by Certified Roses Inc., 1998

Traditional Home Rose 2001 – See **Mary Adrienne**, S

Trafalgar Cl HT, Fell, J.B.; [Mons Desir × Gruss an Teplitz]

Trafalgar Square F, mp, 1965, Van den Akker Bros.; flowers large, dbl.; vigorous growth

Trailblazer F, or, 1976, Harvey, R.E.; bud long, pointed; flowers 2½ in., 22 petals, high-centered, slight fragrance; foliage glossy; [Albert × Orange Sensation]; int. by Kimbrew-Walter Roses, 1975

Trailblazer – See **Michel Lis le Jardinier**, HT

Trakiika HT, dr, 1985, Staikov, Prof. Dr. V.; flowers large, 25 petals, cupped, moderate fragrance; foliage dark; vigorous, upright, bushy growth; [Tallyho × Spartan]; int. by Kalaydjiev and Chorbadjiiski, 1974

Tramonto HT, yb, 1943, Giacomasso; flowers yellow and orange, darker at edges, large, dbl., high-centered, borne mostly singly

Tramonto Estivo F, yb, Barni; flowers yellow shading to orange, turning bright red and carmine, single, shallow cup, borne in clusters, moderate fragrance; recurrent; foliage dark green; vigorous, bushy (2-3 ft.) growth; int. by Rose Barni, 2004

Tranquil HT, dp, Dawson; int. in 1977

Tranquility Cl Pol, op, before 1952, Radmore; flowers coral-salmon, rosette form, small, borne in trusses; foliage light green; vigorous growth; RULED EXTINCT 11/82; [sport of Princess van Orange]

Tranquility HT, ab, 1983, Barrett, F.H.; flowers pale apricot, peach and yellow blend, 35 petals, borne mostly singly; foliage medium size, dark, glossy; upright growth; [Whisky Mac × Pink Favorite]; int. by John Mattock, Ltd., 1982

Tranquility S, lp, Clements, John; flowers delicate light pink shading to near white, 4 in., 60 petals, borne individually and in small clusters, intense myrrh fragrance; foliage bronzy red maturing to dark green; bushy, compact (3 × 3 ft.) growth; PPAF; int. by Heirloom Roses, 2004

Transit F, VEG; int. in 1984

Transon-Goubault HGal; flowers bright red, edges darker, large, full

Transparente – See **Vilmorin**, M

Träumerei F, ob, 1974, Kordes; bud long, pointed; flowers salmon orange, 7 cm., dbl., cupped, borne singly or in clusters, intense fragrance; recurrent; foliage large, dark green, leathery; vigorous, upright, bushy growth; [Colour Wonder × seedling]; int. in 1974

Traumland F, lp, 1959, Tantau, Math.; flowers light peach-pink, well-formed, 20 petals, borne in clusters, slight fragrance; recurrent; foliage dark, leathery; upright, bushy growth; [Cinnabar Improved × Fashion]; int. in 1958

Travemünde F, mr, 1970, Kordes; bud ovoid; flowers dbl., borne in large clusters, no fragrance; recurrent; foliage dark green, matte; bushy, compact (50 cm.), vigorous growth; [Lilli Marleen × Ama]; originally registered as Pol; int. by Buisman, 1968; ADR, 1966

Traverser HG, yb, 1928, Clark, A.; flowers yellow and cream, 11 cm., semi-dbl. to dbl., borne in clusters; vigorous, climbing growth

Travesti F, yb, 1965, deRuiter; flowers yellow to carmine-red, medium, 38 petals, cupped, borne in clusters, moderate fragrance; recurrent; foliage dark; vigorous, bushy growth; [Orange Sensation × Circus]

Traveston Cl HT, dr, 1953, Ulrick, L.W.; bud long, pointed; flowers crimson, medium, semi-dbl.; vigorous growth; [Black Boy × Editor McFarland]

Travesty F, deRuiter; int. in 1965

Traviata HT, rb, 1964, Meilland, Alain A.; bud ovoid, pointed; flowers bright red blending to white base, 4½ in., 30-35 petals, high-centered, cupped, borne in clusters, moderate tea fragrance; free-flowering; foliage leathery; vigorous, bushy growth; PP2283; [Baccará × (Independence × Grand'mere Jenny)]; int. by URS, 1962

Traviata HT, dr, 1998, Selection Meilland; bud large, globular; flowers dark currant red, 6.5-7 cm., very full, hollow cup, borne singly and in small clusters, very slight fragrance; recurrent; foliage large, dark green, glossy; prickles numerous, large, brown; stems 18-24 in.; upright, medium growth; PP10845; [(Porta Nigra × Paolo) × William Shakespeare]; int. by Conard-Pyle Co., 1997

Treasure HT, ab, 1929, Fletcher; bud pointed; flowers apricot-pink, 6 in., dbl.; foliage glossy, dark; very vigorous growth; [Golden Rapture × Fred Walker]; int. by Tucker

Treasure Box F, pb; flowers bright pink with silvery white reverse, borne in clusters, moderate sweet fragrance; free-flowering; strong, medium growth

Treasure Chest HT, my, 1968, Whisler, D.; bud ovoid; flowers large, dbl., high-centered; foliage glossy; vigorous, upright growth; PP2992; [Charlotte Armstrong × Fred Howard]; int. by Germain's

Treasure Gold HT, my, 1950, Brownell; bud ovoid, pointed; flowers yellow, some petals splashed red, 4 in., 38 petals, moderate fragrance; upright, branching growth; [Pink Princess × Free Gold]

Treasure Island HT, op, 1938, Raffel; bud long, pointed; flowers light salmon, reverse flaming coppery pink, base orange, large, dbl., high-centered; foliage leathery, bronze; vigorous growth; [Comtesse Vandal × Mme Nicolas Aussel]; int. by Port Stockton Nursery

Treasure Island, Climbing Cl HT, op, 1941, Hennessey

Treasure Isle F, op, 1967, Raffel; bud slender, pointed; flowers salmon-pink, reverse coppery, small, dbl., moderate fragrance; recurrent; foliage glossy; vigorous, bushy growth; [seedling × Treasure Island]; int. by Port Stockton Nursery

Treasure Trove LCl, ab, 1977, Treasure; flowers apricot, mauve-pink and cream, 1½-2 in., 23 petals, cupped, borne in large clusters, intense fragrance; non-remontant; vigorous growth; hips numerous, red; [Kiftsgate × unknown]

Treasure Trove HT, my, Warriner, William A.; int. in 1991

Treasure Trow – See **Treasure Trove**, LCl

Treasured Memories F, yb, 2001, Kenny, David; flowers red, petals edged with yellow, 3 in., dbl., borne in large clusters, moderate fragrance; foliage medium size, dark green, glossy; growth bushy, medium (3 ft.); garden decorative; [Golden Wedding × Bright Smile]

Treasured Memories F, dr, Dickson; flowers dark red, bright yellow stamens, small, semi-dbl., shallow cup, borne in clusters; recurrent; foliage dense, small, glossy; bushy, spreading growth; int. by Dickson Roses, 2006; Certificate of Merit, Belfast, 2006

Treasured Moments – See **Stardust Memory**, F

Treasured Moments F, ab, 2000, Kenny, David

Trelleborg F, ab, Olesen; bud long; flowers orangy-apricot, 7-8 cm., full, cupped, borne in small clusters of 3-8, slight wild rose fragrance; recurrent; foliage dark green, glossy; prickles few, 8-10 mm, greyed-yellow; bushy, compact (60-100 cm) growth; [seedling × Avon]; int. by Poulsen Roser, 2001

Tremblevif S, mr, Gilet; int. by Les Rosiers du Berry, 2005

Trend HT, op, VEG; flowers large, dbl.

Très-Petite Fleur HMult, lp, 1866, Cochet; flowers pale pink, fading to pinky-white, ½ in., dbl., borne in large clusters; spring; foliage ovate, sharply pointed, finely toothed; prickles small, few, nearly straight

Trésarin HGal, m, about 1845, Calvert; flowers purple, medium, very full

Tresor HT, ab, Kriloff

Tresor de Thorigny S, w; flowers white with some blush pink tints, yellow stamens, 1½ in., dbl., cupped to flat, loose, borne in clusters, slight fragrance; recurrent; vigorous, arching growth; landscape shrub, climber

Tressor HT, ob; int. by Carlton Rose Nursery, 2002

Trevi Fountain LCl, ob

Trevor Griffiths S, dp, 1997, Austin, David; flowers dusky pink, large, very full, loose to flat, borne in small clusters, intense oaky claret fragrance; recurrent; foliage medium size, dark green, dull, rough texture; some prickles; upright, spreading, medium (105 cm.) growth; [Wife of Bath × Hero]; int. by David Austin Roses, Ltd., 1994

Triade S, mr, Noack; flowers bright red, yellow stamens, 4 cm., semi-dbl. to dbl., shallow cup, borne in clusters; recurrent; foliage medium green, glossy; compact, bushy, upright (4 ft.) growth; int. by Noack Rosen, 2004

Trianon F, pb, 2000, Lens, Louis; flowers pink with apricot, 5 cm., semi-dbl., borne in small clusters, moderate fragrance; recurrent; foliage medium size, medium green, semi-glossy; prickles moderate; bushy, medium (80 cm.) growth; [(*R. multiflora adenocheata* × Ballerina) × Buff Beauty]; int. by Louis Lens N.V., 1990

Triathlon S, pb; flowers shades of pink, yellow stamens, small, dbl., cupped, borne in clusters; recurrent; low, bushy growth; int. in 1998

Tribute HT, dp, 1982, Warriner, William A.; bud long, pointed ovoid; flowers deep pink, loose form, 4½ in., 30 petals, high-centered, borne singly and several together, slight fragrance; recurrent; foliage large, dark green, leathery; prickles numerous, reddish, hooked downward; stems long, strong; upright growth; PP4850; [seedling × seedling]; int. by J&P, 1983

Tribute HT, w, Chakraborty, Dr. K.; flowers cream white, gain red flush as they age, large, full, intense fragrance; free-flowering; upright growth; int. in 2000

Tricentenaire HT, mp, 1949, Lens; bud long, pointed; flowers pink, center deeper, medium, 25 petals, high-centered; foliage leathery, small; vigorous growth; [Charles P. Kilham × Neville Chamberlain]

Tricia LCl, lp, 1942, O'Neal; bud long, pointed; flowers flesh-pink to ivory-pink, dbl., high-centered, intense fragrance; foliage dark, glossy; growth vigorous (about 8 ft.); hardy; [New Dawn × unknown]

Tricia F, w, 1972, Warriner, W. A.; buds medium, long pointed; flowers white with ivory overcast, medium, dbl, high-centered, borne singly and several together, slight fragrance; PP3235; [sport of Bridal Pink]; int. by J&P, 1972

Tricia's Joy LCl, op, 1986, McKirdy, J.M.; flowers deep coral pink, large, 35 petals, moderate fragrance; foliage medium size, dark, semi-glossy; vigorous growth (to 18 ft.); [Mme Caroline Testout, Climbing × Blessings]; int. by John Sanday Roses, Ltd., 1973

Trick Or Treat Min, ob, 1996, Taylor, Franklin "Pete" & Kay; flowers orange blending to yellow base, 1½ in., 41 petals, flat, borne mostly singly; foliage small, medium green, semi-glossy; few prickles; medium (24 in.), upright, bushy growth; [seedling × seedling]; int. by Taylor's Roses, 1997

Trickster Min, rb, 1995, Bridges, Dennis A.; bud medium; flowers red with pale pink to white reverse, medium, 28-32 petals, high-centered, borne mostly singly, moderate fruity fragrance; recurrent; foliage small, medium green, semi-glossy; prickles moderate, medium length; medium (18 in.), slightly spreading growth; hips globular, medium green; PP9931; [Jennifer × Red Beauty]; int. by Bridges Roses, 1995

Tricolore HGal, rb, before 1821, Stegerhoek; flowers velvety crimson purple striped with yellowish-white, small, full; growth erect

Tricolore HGal, pb, 1827, Lahaye père; flowers lilac-pink, fringed at edges, dotted and mottled white, small, dbl., moderate fragrance; non-remontant; thornless; sturdy, upright (4 ft.) growth

Tricolore HMult, pb, 1863, Robert et Moreau; flowers lilac-pink, toothed and deckled white, 7 cm., full, globular, borne in corymbs of 20-50; non-recurrent; growth more vigorous than Gallica of the same name; [*R. multiflora* × unknown]

Tricolore HWich, rb, 1906, Weigand, C.; flowers variegated red, white, and pink, 5-6 cm., dbl., flat, borne in medium clusters, slight fragrance; foliage small, dark green

Tricolore de Flandre HGal, pb, 1846; flowers pale blush, striped bright pink, fading to mauve, with a small green eye, small, full, rosette, moderate fragrance; non-remontant; foliage dark green, oval; prickles very few; moderate (3 ft.) growth; possibly from Parmentier; int. by Van Houtte

Tricolore d'Enghien P, pb, about 1830, Parmentier; flowers carmine, shaded dark purple, striped white, small, full

Tricolore d'Orléans HGal, rb; flowers red, striped white, medium, full

Trier HMult, w, 1904, Lambert, P.; bud salmony pink; flowers rosy white, base straw-yellow, small, semi-dbl., borne in clusters of 30-50, moderate fragrance; moderate repeat; foliage dark green, glossy; prickles few, red; growth to 6-8 ft.; probably an Aglaia self-seedling, but Aglaia × Mrs. R. G. Sharman-Crawford has been noted

Trier 2000 – See **Anna Livia**, F

Trieste F, Mansuino; int. in 1960

Trifling MinFl, rb, Williams, J. Benjamin; flowers soft red with white tones and eye, single, shallow cup to flat, borne in large clusters, slight fragrance; recurrent; foliage medium green, matte; growth to 2 ft.; int. by Hortico, Inc., 2006

Trigintipetala D, mp, 1899; flowers bright pink, aging to white, medium, semi-dbl. to dbl.; non-recurrent; foliage clear green, oval, with 5-7 leaflets; prickles large, numerous; [*R. gallica* × *R. damascena*]; first described in 1689; often thought to be the same as Kazanlik, and possibly Prof. Émile Perrot

Trigo HT, ab, 1931, Dickson, A.; bud long, pointed; flowers Indian yellow, reverse apricot, tinted cerise, large, dbl., high-centered; foliage thick, bronze, glossy; vigorous growth; Gold Medal, NRS, 1931

Trilby HT, op, 1927, Dobbie; flowers rich salmon, dbl.

Trinity T, w; flowers pale pink to white, gold stamens, nodding, 4 in., semi-dbl., borne usually singly, moderate fragrance; free-flowering; foliage dark; vigorous, bushy, spreading growth; discovered in Bermuda

Trinity HT, pb, 1977, de Freitas; flowers variegated pink and yellow, medium, dbl., globular, intense fragrance; vigorous, upright, compact growth; [Korovo × unknown]; int. in 1976

Trinity S, dr, 1994, McGredy, Sam IV; flowers deep scarlet, small, dbl., slight fragrance; recurrent; foliage small, dark green, semi-glossy; spreading (90 cm.) growth; [Sexy Rexy × Eyeopener]; int. by McGredy Roses International, 1994

Trinity Rambler LCl, dp

Trinket Min, mp, 1965, Moore, Ralph S.; flowers phlox-pink, micro-mini, small, dbl., cupped to rosette, borne in clusters; free-flowering; foliage glossy; vigorous, bushy, dwarf (10 in.) growth; [(*R. wichurana* × Floradora) × Magic Wand]; int. by Sequoia Nursery

Trintago HT, mr, 1962, Leenders, J.; flowers cardinal-red, well-formed, dbl.; [Souv. de Jacques Verschuren × Charles Mallerin]

Trio F, pb, 1966, Dickson, A.; flowers gold and pink, well-formed, large; [Kordes' Perfecta × Shot Silk]

Triodene F, op, Kordes

Triolet HT, ab, Orard; flowers creamy apricot-salmon, darker reverse, dbl., borne mostly singly, moderate fragrance; recurrent; stems long; vigorous, medium growth; int. as Tanned Beauty, Ludwig's Roses

Triomphe Angevin Pol, mr, 1934, Délépine; flowers cerise-red, semi-dbl., cupped, borne in clusters, slight fragrance; recurrent; foliage glossy; very vigorous, bushy growth; int. by Pajotin-Chédane

Triomphe Briard F, op, 1958, Robichon; flowers coral, dbl., borne in clusters; foliage glossy; moderate growth; [seedling × Fashion]

Triomphe d'Alencon HP, dp, 1858, Touvais; flowers intense red, very large, dbl.

Triomphe d'Amiens – See **Général Jacqueminot**, HP

Triomphe d'Avranches HP, mr, 1855, Baudry; flowers scarlet-amaranth, shaded velvety carmine, edged white, large, full

Triomphe de Bollvillers – See **Triomphe de Bolwyller**, HSem

Triomphe de Bolwyller HSem, w, about 1860, Baumann; flowers white, center tinted yellow, large, globular, moderate fragrance; non-remontant; apparently a hybrid between *R. sempervirens* and a Tea

Triomphe de Brabant – See **Duchesse d'Angoulême**, HGal, before 1860

Triomphe de Caen HP, dr, 1861, Oger; flowers deep velvety grenadine, shaded with purple, large, full

Triomphe de Caen – See **Prince Arthur**, HP

Triomphe de Coulommiers – See **Souv de Coulommiers**, HP

Triomphe de Flore HGal, lp, before 1821; flowers delicate blush pink, medium, very dbl.; from Rouen

Triomphe de France HP, mp, 1875, Garçon; flowers bright carmine rose, very large, very dbl., moderate fragrance

Triomphe de Guillot Fils T, pb, 1861, Guillot fils; flowers apricot-pink at center, lighter edges, 9 cm., dbl.

Triomphe de Guillotière T, w, 1861, Guillot; flowers white, shaded cream, medium, dbl.

Triomphe de Guillotière S, w, 1863, Guillot et Fils; flowers white tinged pink; [probably *R. roxburghii* × *R. odorata*]

Triomphe de Jaussens HGal, dp, before 1850; flowers bright carmine, shaded purple

Triomphe de la Duchèr B, lp, 1846, Béluze; flowers pale rose, medium, full, borne in large clusters

Triomphe de la Malmaison HT, dp, 1946, Gaujard; flowers dark satiny pink, very large, petals reflexed; foliage dark; vigorous growth

Triomphe de la Terre des Roses HP, mp, 1864, Guillot père; flowers violaceous pink, large, dbl.; freely remontant; moderately vigorous growth

Triomphe de Laffay HCh, w, about 1830, Laffay; flowers delicate flesh, changing to white, expanded, large, very dbl.; recurrent; pendulous growth

Triomphe de l'Exposition HP, mr, 1855, Margottin; flowers cherry-red, 4-5 in., 55 petals, borne singly or in small clusters; recurrent bloom; foliage elongated oval, deeply serrate, dark green, glossy; prickles few, strong, very sharp, slightly curved; vigorous, bushy growth

Triomphe de Lille D, lp, before 1826, Vibert; flowers white, with a pink center, medium, full; foliage deeply serrate; prickles rare, slender, mixed wtih numerous glandular bristles

Triomphe de Luxembourg – See **Triomphe du Luxembourg**, T

Triomphe de Lyon HP, mr, 1859, Cordier; flowers velvety crimson, medium, semi-dbl.

Triomphe de Milan T, w, 1877, Widow Ducher; flowers white, with a deep yellow center, large, full, no fragrance; growth vigorous, upright

Triomphe de Nancy HP, dr, 1862, Crousse; flowers velvety dark crimson, large, full

Triomphe de Paris HP, dp, 1852, Margottin; flowers carmine, shaded velvety blackish-red, very large, very full

Triomphe de Pernet Père HT, m, 1890, Pernet; flowers reddish-violet, large, very dbl.; [Monsieur Désir × Général Jacqueminot]

Triomphe de Plantier B, pb, 1837, Plantier; flowers lilac pink, center carmine, large, very full

Triomphe de Rennes N, my, 1857, Panaget or Lancezeur; flowers canary yellow, center gold, very large, full; [Lamarque × unknown]

Triomphe de Rennes HGal, dr; flowers purple-red, shaded slate, very large, very full

Triomphe de Rouen D, mp, 1826, Lecomte; flowers soft pink, touched lilac, large, full

Triomphe de Saintes – See **Le Triomphe de Saintes**, HP

Triomphe de Sterckmanns HGal, dp, 1847, Vibert; flowers large, full

Triomphe de Toulouse HP, rb, 1873, Brassac; flowers red, shaded with violet-crimson, large, full

Triomphe de Valenciennes HP, lp, 1847, Schneider; flowers flesh pink shaded carmine, striped purple-violet, large, full; may have been re-introduced by Baudry in 1859

Triomphe de Vibert HGal, mr, about 1835, Vibert; flowers carmine-red, medium, full

Triomphe des Beaux-Arts HP, m, 1857, Fontaine; flowers velvety dark purple, large, full; [Général Jacqueminot × unknown]

Triomphe des Noisettes N, dp, 1887, Pernet père; flowers bright rose, fading lighter, 9-10 cm., full, often quartered, borne in small clusters; foliage very dark green; prickles numerous, protrusive; [Général Jacqueminot × Ophirie]

Triomphe d'Orléans HP, dr, 1902, Corboeuf; flowers red and deep violet; [Général Jacqueminot × Général de la Martinière]

Triomphe du Luxembourg T, pb, 1835, Hardy; flowers salmon-buff shaded rose, full; recurrent; growth to 3 ft.

Triomphe Orléanais Pol, mr, 1912, Peauger; flowers cherry-red, 1½-2 in., semi-dbl., borne in large clusters; foliage leathery, glossy, bright; vigorous growth

Triomphe Orléanais, Climbing Cl Pol, mr, 1922, Turbat; flowers small, semi-dbl., borne in medium to large clusters; non-recurrent

Triple Treat – See **Rosenstadt Freising**, S

Tristesse HT, m, 1953, Camprubi, C.; flowers gray-mauve, medium, 30-40 petals, flat; foliage glossy; vigorous growth; [Charles P. Kilham × Betty Uprichard]

Tristeza – See **Tristesse**, HT

Triton HT, yb, 1978, Dickson, Patrick; flowers white to light yellow, petals edged pink, large, 47 petals; upright growth; [Colour Wonder × Tzigane]

Triumphant HSet, mp, 1850, Pierce; flowers deep rose pink, aging to pale violet, medium, very dbl., borne in clusters of 20-30; foliage very large, undulated, deeply and sharply serrated; [*R. setigera* × unknown]

Trix Pol, or, VEG; flowers medium, dbl.

Trixx! HT, ob, Schreurs; greenhouse rose; int. by Yates Botanicals, 2002

Trocadero HT, mr, 1964, Delforge; bud pointed, bright red; foliage bronze; vigorous growth; [Karl Herbst × seedling]

Trocadero 'D' HT, Delforge; int. in 1989

Troika, Climbing Cl HT, 1964, Thomas, Dr. A.S.; int. by Rumsey

Troika – See **Royal Dane**, HT

Troilus S, ab, 1992, Austin, David; flowers creamy apricot to honey-buff, 3-3½ in., very full, cupped, borne in large clusters, intense sweet fragrance; recurrent; foliage large, dark green, semi-glossy; some prickles; medium (110 cm.), upright growth; [(Duchesse de Montebello × Chaucer) × Charles Austin]; int. by David Austin Roses, Ltd., 1983

Troja HT, w, 1927, Mikes; bud long, pointed, cream-yellow; flowers creamy white, full, moderate fragrance; vigorous, bushy growth; [sport of Mrs Herbert Stevens]; int. by Böhm, 1928

Trojan Gr, yb, 1961, Von Abrams; bud long, pointed; flowers pastel pink, reverse yellow, 5 in., 40 petals, high-centered; foliage leathery; upright growth; [Sutter's Gold × (Mme Henri Guillot × seedling)]; int. by Peterson & Dering, 1961

Trojan Victory HT, dr, 1986, Kordes, R.; bud ovoid; flowers deep red, reverse lighter, 4½ in., 50-55 petals, high-centered, borne singly, slight damask fragrance; recurrent; foliage medium size, medium green, semi-glossy; prickles medium, hooked downward; stems long, strong; medium, spreading growth; PP5678; [seedling × Uwe Seeler]; int. by J&P

Trollhattan HRg, dp, Essunga Planteskole; flowers rosy lilac that blush irregularly to pale lavender pink, petals twisted, large, dbl.

Trompeter von Säckingen HMult, m, about 1890, Geschwind, R.; flowers purple red, aging to cerise and medium pink, lighter reverse, 5-6 cm., full, flat, borne in small clusters, moderate fragrance; non-remontant; strong, upright (5 ft.) growth

Trophée LCl, mr, 1970, Robichon; flowers medium to large, 4 in., dbl., borne in clusters, no fragrance; recurrent; foliage glossy; vigorous, climbing growth; [Valenciennes × Etendard]; int. by Ilgenfritz Nursery, 1968

Trophy – See **Trophée**, LCl

Tropical F, Cazzaniga, F. G.; int. in 1966

Tropical Amazone HT, ob, deRuiter; flowers soft orange, dbl., high-centered, borne mostly singly; recurrent

Tropical Fragrance S, mr, Clements, John; flowers crimson red, yellow stamens, 4 in., 18-24 petals, shallow cup to flat, borne in clusters of 5 to 10, moderate citrus/honey/spice fragrance; recurrent; foliage leathery, dark green; compact (3 × 2½ ft.) growth; PPAF; int. by Heirloom Roses, 2002

Tropical Oasis F, r, 2004, Mueller, Joanna; flowers russet, reverse russet/orange, medium, full, borne mostly solitary, no fragrance; foliage semi-glossy, dense; growth upright, short; garden decoration; [Tropicana × Hot Cocoa]; int. by Joanna Mueller

Tropical Paradise HT, ob, 1996, Rodgers, Shafter R.; flowers orange blend, reverse orange blend with yellow gold, 4½ in., dbl., high-centered, borne mostly singly, moderate fragrance; recurrent; foliage large, dark green, glossy; few prickles; upright, tall (5 ft.) growth; [South Seas × First Prize]; int. by Certified Roses, Inc.

Tropical Passion HT, or, Strahle, B. Glen; int. in 1999

Tropical Sherbet F, yb, Keihan; int. by Keihan Gardening, 2003

Tropical Skies HT, yb, Ilsink; flowers yellow with pink and red edges, dbl., high-centered, moderate fragrance; recurrent; foliage dark green; medium to tall growth; int. by Interplant, 1997

Tropical Sunrise Gr, dy, 1992, Hoy, Lowel L.; flowers deep yellow aging to medium yellow, 4 in., 21 petals, high-centered, borne singly and in small clusters; foliage medium size, medium green, semi-glossy; upright, medium growth; [Golden Fantasie × seedling]; int. by DeVor Nurseries, Inc.

Tropical Sunset HT, yb, 1998, McGredy, Sam IV; bud big, pointed, yellow with orange-red; flowers yellow, striped pink and orange, aging lighter, 4-4½ in., dbl., cupped, borne mostly singly, slight spice fragrance; recurrent; foliage large, light green, matte; prickles moderate; bushy, tall (4 ft.) growth; PP11484; [Louise Gardner × (Auckland Metro × Stars 'n' Stripes seedling)]; int. by McGredy, 1995; Trial Ground Certificate, Durbanville, 2006

Tropical Twist Min, op, 1998, Walden, John K.; bud pointed ovoid; flowers coral-orange and apricot with yellow-cream reverse, 1½-1¾ in., 30-35 petals, high-centered, borne mostly singly, floriferous, very slight fragrance; recurrent; foliage medium size, dark green, glossy; prickles moderate, short, angled downward; compact, upright (22-24 in.) growth; hedging or border; PP10882; [(Funny Girl × Galaxy) × Pink Polyanna]; int. by Bear Creek Gardens, Inc., 1997; AOE, ARS, 1997

Tropicana HT, or, 1960, Tantau, Math.; bud pointed; flowers coral-orange, well-formed, 5 in., 30-35 petals, high-centered, cupped, borne singly and in clusters, intense fruity fragrance; recurrent; foliage dark, glossy, leathery; prickles normal, medium, straight or hooked upward; stems long, strong; vigorous, upright growth; PP1969; [(seedling × Peace) × (seedling × Alpine Glow)]; original registration (1961 ARS Annual) is for Super Star; int. as Super Star, Wheatcroft Bros., 1960; Gold Medal, NRS, 1960, President's International Trophy, NRS, 1960, Gold Medal, Portland, 1961, Gold Medal, ARS, 1967

Tropicana, Climbing Cl HT, or, 1966, Blaby; bud pointed; PP2701; [sport of Tropicana]; patent issued to Boerner; separate registration published in 1970; int. by J&P

Tropico Sunblaze Min, my, Meilland; int. in 1995

Tropique LCl, or, 1956, Delbard-Chabert; flowers velvety crimson, 3 in., dbl., borne singly or in small clusters; recurrent; foliage small, dark green, glossy, some bronze tones

Troubadour HWich, mr, 1911, Walsh; flowers bright red, shaded maroon, sometimes streaked with white to medium pink, 5-6 cm., dbl., borne in clusters of 10-25; free seasonal bloom; foliage large, glossy, dark; vigorous, climbing growth

Troubadour HT, Buyl Frères; flowers rose-copper, large, dbl.; free bloom; strong stems; moderate growth; RULED EXTINCT; int. in 1956

Troubadour of Love HT, dr

Trpaslik Min, Strnad

Truby King F, dp, 1965, Harris, L.M.; flowers carmine, open, large, semi-dbl., borne in large clusters; foliage leathery, glossy, bronze; vigorous, tall growth; [Border Queen × Helen Traubel]; int. by Cutler, 1957

Trudor – See **Micaëla**, HT

Trudy Mimi F, dp, Meilland

True Min, ob, Olesen; flowers dbl., 25-30 petals, borne mostly solitary, slight fragrance; foliage dark green, glossy; growth bushy, low (40-60 cm.); int. by Poulsen Roser, 2000

True Friend T, ly, 1905, California Nursery Co.

True Gold Min, dy, 1997, Laver, Keith G.; bud egg-shaped, golden; flowers medium, very full, cupped, borne mostly singly, no fragrance; foliage medium size, medium green, dull; few prickles; upright, bushy, medium growth; [Antique Gold × Yellow Bouquet]; int. by Springwood Roses

True Love HT, dr, 1971, Delbard; flowers deep red, 3½-4 in., 30 petals; foliage glossy; moderately vigorous growth; int. by Laxton & Bunyard Nursery, 1970

True Love – See **Yorkshire Bank**, HT

True Love – See **P. G. Wodehouse**, HT

True Vintage Min, mr, 1999, McCann, Sean; flowers medium red to fuchsia, reverse silver/light red, medium, semi-dbl., borne mostly singly, slight fragrance; recurrent; foliage medium size, medium green, semi-glossy; numerous prickles; compact, medium (16-18 in.) growth; [Rose Gilardi × Stolen Moment]; int. by Justice Miniature Roses, 1999

Truly Amazing HT, ab, Athy; bud reddish apricot; flowers apricot-pink, red stamens, moderate fragrance; medium growth; int. by Tasman Bay Roses, 2004

Truly Fair F, w, 1953, Ratcliffe; flowers cream, center apricot, small, semi-dbl., borne in sprays of 4-5; bushy growth

Truly Yours HT, ob, 1973, Robinson, H.; flowers coral-salmon to orange, 5 in., 44 petals, globular, intense fragrance; foliage large; vigorous, upright growth; [Miss Ireland × Stella]; Edland Fragrance Medal, ARS, 1971

Truly Yours HT, lp, 2004, Carruth, Tom; flowers light salmon pink, 10-13 cm., full, borne mostly solitary, slight fragrance; recurrent; foliage large, medium green, matte; prickles moderate, medium, almost straight; growth very compact, medium (60-90 cm.); garden decoration; [((O Sole Mio × seedling) × unknown) × Koronam]; int. by Weeks Roses, 2006

Trump – See **Honey**, HT

Trump Card HT, pb, 2007, Orent, Cliff; flowers pink, reverse yellow, 8½-11 cm., dbl., borne mostly solitary; prickles ¾-1 cm., almost straight, moderate, greyed orange; growth tall (120-140 cm.); garden decoration, cutting; [sport of Rosie O'Donnell]; int. by Ashdown West, 2007

Trumpet F, my, 1963, Von Abrams; bud small, long-pointed; flowers medium yellow, 4 in., 15-22 petals, cupped, borne in clusters; foliage glossy; growth vigorous, upright (4 ft.); [Goldilocks × Captain Thomas]; int. by Peterson & Dering, 1962

Trumpeter F, or, 1976, McGredy, Sam IV; bud ovoid; flowers bright orange-scarlet, 6-8 cm., 35-45 petals, cupped, borne usually in small clusters, slight fragrance; free-flowering; foliage medium green, glossy; prickles several, medium, slightly hooked downward, brown; bushy, compact growth; hips short, globular, reddish-orange; PP4297; [Satchmo × seedling]; int. by McGredy Roses International, 1977; James Mason Medal, RNRS, 1991, Gold Medal, Portland, 1977, Gold Medal, NZ, 1977

Trumpeter, Climbing Cl F, op; [sport of Trumpeter]; int. in about 1997

Truper – See **Persepolis**, HT

Tryfosa – See **Redwood**, F

Trylon – See **Shining Star**, HT

Tschaika HT, lp, Klimenko, V. N.; flowers large, dbl.; int. in 1959

Tschernowa Ukraijna HT, mr, 1940, Kosteckij; flowers large, semi-dbl.

Tschin-Tschin F, mr, Meilland; flowers luminous red, medium, dbl.; int. in 1973

T-620038 Sp; clone of *R. multiflora*; used for understock

Tsukiakari HT, w, 1985, Ota, Kaichiro; flowers creamy white, large, 35 petals, high-centered, globular, borne singly or in small clusters, no fragrance; foliage medium green, semi-glossy; prickles medium; bushy growth; [Utage × Anne Letts]; int. in 1984

Tsurumi 90 HT, ob, Keihan; int. by Keihan Gardening, 1990

Tsuzuki F, pb; flowers soft pink with white tones and white eye, stamens yellow, semi-dbl., shallow cup; foliage bright green, disease-resistant; small, compact growth

Tubantia HT, op, Verbeek; flowers reddish-orange and pink, large, dbl.; int. in 1975

Tucan HT, yb, Tantau; flowers yellow with red-orange edges, suffused down petals as it opens, medium, dbl., high-centered, borne mostly singly; recurrent; stems medium to long; florist rose; int. by Rosen Tantau, 2003

Tucker's Folly HT, pb, 1951, Fletcher; flowers glowing cerise overlaid orange, 6-7 in., 35-40 petals; foliage bronze; very vigorous growth; int. by Tucker

Tucker's Yellow HT, dy, Tucker; flowers deep golden yellow; [sport of Max Krause]

Tudelum Min, dp, 1987, King, Gene; flowers deep pink to lighter shades, petal edges darken on opening, 30 petals, high-centered, no fragrance; foliage medium size, medium green, matte; prickles straight, medium, light pink; upright, bushy, medium, vigorous growth; no fruit; [Baby Katie × Watercolor]; int. by AGM Miniature Roses, 1987

Tudor HT, mr, 1953, Verschuren-Pechtold; flowers spectrum-red overcast scarlet-red, 5 in., 20-25 petals, high-centered; long stems; vigorous growth; [Katharine Pechtold × Crimson Glory]; int. by J&P

Tudor Prince Gr, mr, 1960, Leenders, J.; bud long, pointed, chestnut; flowers bright red shaded geranium-red, large, 30-40 petals; foliage glossy, dark; vigorous, upright growth; [Independence × Buccaneer]; int. by Brit. Hort. Co., 1959

Tudor Rose S, Porter, L.; [*R. brunonii* × unknown]; int. in 1989

Tudor Sunsation S, lp, Kordes; flowers lightly brushed pink, deep cup, borne in fan-like clusters; recurrent; compact, prostrate, groundcover growth; int. by Ludwig's Roses, 1997

Tudor Victory HT, dr, 1988, Bracegirdle, Derek T.; flowers dusky, dark red, reverse medium red, aging purple, medium, 27 petals, high-centered, born in sprays of 2-3, slight damask fragrance; foliage large, medium green, semi-glossy; prickles straight, large, red; upright, tall growth; [Queen Elizabeth × John Waterer]

Tuhua HMult, ab, 1980, Murray, Nola; bud small, pointed; flowers 11 petals, borne 3-5 per cluster, no fragrance; early bloomer with some repeat; foliage small, glossy; prickles small, red-brown; vigorous, lax, tall growth; [Iceberg × Tausendschon]

Tulipe Paltot – See **Unique Panachée**, C

Tullamore S, op

Tulsa HT, yb, Perry, Astor; flowers yellow with red tones on petal edges, dbl., high-centered; recurrent; tall growth; int. in 1995

Tulsa Town Min, ob, 2003, Wells, Verlie W.; flowers semi-dbl., borne mostly solitary, intense fragrance; foliage medium size, dark green, semi-glossy; prickles ¼ in., straight; upright, medium growth; garden, exhibition; [seedling × seedling]; int. by Wells MidSouth Roses, 2003

Tumbarumba Schoolhouse HMult, dp

Tumbling Waters S, w, Olesen; bud short, pointed ovoid; flowers creamy white, small, semi-dbl. to dbl., shallow cup, borne usually 6-10 per stem, slight fragrance; recurrent; foliage dark green, glossy; prickles few, 5 mm, curving downward; growth broad, bushy, 60-100 cm.; PP12556; [seedling × *R. multiflora nana*]; int. by Poulsen Roser, 1998

Tumulte HT, Kordes, R.

Tunusblumchen LCl, m

Tupa HT, mr, Ghosh, Mr. & Mrs. S.; flowers non-fading; free-flowering; int. in 2003

Tupperware HT, pb, 1982, Williams, J. Benjamin; bud ovoid, pointed; flowers carmine pink, reverse silver, 65 petals, high-centered, borne singly or in cluster of up to 5, moderate fragrance; foliage large, dark, glossy; prickles medium; vigorous, upright growth; [(Pink Peace × Queen Elizabeth) × (Kordes' Perfecta × Peace)]; int. by Tupperware Home Parties

Turbinata – See **Venusta**, A

Turbo HRg, mp, 1994, Meilland, Alain A.; bud oblong, medium; flowers fuchsia pink, 3½-5 in., 21-23 petals, flat cup, borne singly and in small clusters, no fragrance; good repeat; foliage medium size, light green, semi-glossy; prickles numerous, medium to large, greenish; tall (130-140 cm.), bushy growth; PP9468; [(Frau Dagmar Hastrup × Manou Meilland) × Pink Grootendorst]; int. by SNC Meilland & Cie, 1993

Turbo Meidiland – See **Turbo**, HRg

Turbo Rugostar – See **Turbo**, HRg

Turbulance F, rb, 1999, Giles, Diann; flowers large, single, borne in small clusters; foliage medium size, light green, glossy; prickles moderate; bushy, medium growth; [Pink Favorite × Scentimental]; int. by Giles Rose Nursery, 1999

Turenne HGal, dp, 1846, Vibert (?); flowers rose-red, large, full, cupped to flat; growth to 4 ft.

Turenne HP, dr, 1861, Verdier, V.; flowers maroon, medium, full; vigorous growth; [sport of Général Jacqueminot]

Turenne Ch, m, Laffay; flowers violet

Turgida – See **Turneps**, S

Türke's Rugosa-Sämling HRg, pb, 1923, Türke; bud long, pointed; flowers peach-pink on yellow ground, large, semi-dbl., intense fragrance; foliage dark, leathery; strong stems; vigorous (2½-3 ft.) growth; [Conrad Ferdinand Meyer × Mrs Aaron Ward]; int. by Teschendorff

Turlock High Min, my, 1991, Clements, John K.; flowers bright yellow, small, full, borne mostly singly, intense fragrance; recurrent; foliage small, dark green, semi-glossy; some prickles; medium (40 cm.), upright, bushy growth; [Rise 'n' Shine × seedling]; int. by Heirloom Old Garden Roses, 1992

Turn of the Century F, lp, 1997, Sealand Nurseries, Ltd.; flowers medium, dbl., borne in small clusters; foliage medium size, semi-glossy; some prickles; upright, medium (2-2½ ft.) growth; [Elizabeth of Glamis × seedling]; int. by Gregory Roses

Turneps S, dp, before 1770; sepals very long, incised; flowers deep rose, medium to large, dbl., borne in small clusters; foliage ovoid-oblong, smooth, tinted purple beneath; prickles sparse, unequal, intermixed with crimson bristles; stems tinted red

Turner's Crimson Damask – See **Crimson Damask**, D

Turner's Crimson Rambler – See **Crimson Rambler**, HMult

Turnip Rose – See **Turneps**, S

Turnvater Jahn HP, pb, 1927, Müller, Dr. F.; flowers white with pink, very large, dbl.; [Frau Karl Druschki × (Mme Abel Chatenay × General MacArthur)]

Tuscan Beauty HGal, m, 1999, Hintlian, Nancy Sears; flowers red-lavender, aging to near purple, 4-4½ in., 41 petals, borne mostly singly; foliage medium size, medium green, semi-glossy; prickles moderate; spreading, tall (6 ft.) growth; [Superb Tuscan × Big Purple]

Tuscan Charm F, dy, Benny, David; flowers dusky yellow, edges bronze, medium, dbl, borne in trusses; free-flowering; foliage medium green, glossy; medium growth; int. by Camp Hill Roses

Tuscan Sun F, ab, 2005, Zary, Keith; bud pointed ovoid; flowers apricot-orange, 8-10 cm., 25 petals, high-centered, borne in small clusters of 3-7, slight spicy fragrance; recurrent; foliage large, dark green, glossy; prickles 8-10 mm., hooked slightly downward, greyed-orange, moderate; stems 10-12 in.; growth upright, branching, medium (100-120 cm.); PP17083; [Singin' in the Rain × (Pink Pollyanna × Impatient)]; int. by Jackson & Perkins Wholesale, Inc., 2005

Tuscany HGal, m, before 1598; flowers velvety blackish-crimson to deep purple, sometimes touched with white lines, yellow stamens, large, semi-dbl., flat, borne singly or in clusters of 2-5; foliage medium green, small, rounded; numerous prickles; vigorous, upright growth

Tuscany Superb HGal, m, before 1837, Rivers; flowers dark, velvety blackish-red, yellow stamens, large, semi-dbl. to dbl., borne singly or in clusters of 2-3; foliage light green, large, oval; [Tuscany × unknown]

Tuscia HT, mr, Barni, V.; flowers cherry red, full, high-centered, no fragrance; growth to 80 cm.; int. in 1993

Tut's Treasure Min, dy

Tutti-Frutti Min, yb, 1991, Christensen, Jack E.; bud ovoid, pointed; flowers yellow with red-orange stripes, medium, 25-30 petals, cupped, slight fragrance; foliage medium size, dark green, semi-glossy; bushy, spreading, medium growth; [Fool's Gold × Pinstripe]; int. by Bear Creek Gardens/Jackson & Perkins, 1991

Tutti Frutti – See **Pearl Sevillana**, S

Tutu Min, pb, 1979, Rovinski & Meredith; bud ovoid; flowers pink and rose, 1 in., 40 petals, high-centered, slight fragrance; upright, bushy growth; [Over the Rainbow × seedling]; int. by Kingsdown Nursery, 1978

Tutu Mauve F, m, 1963, Delbard-Chabert; flowers magenta shaded mauve and rose, well-formed, 4 in., 30 petals; bushy, low growth; Gold Medal, Madrid, 1962

Tutu Petite F, pb, 1967, Samuels; flowers pink, reverse darker, semi-dbl., borne in clusters; foliage glossy, light; compact, bushy growth; [Rudolph Timm × unknown]

Tuxedo HT, dr, 1989, Christensen, Jack E.; bud ovoid; flowers large, 45 petals, urn-shaped, borne singly; foliage medium size, medium green, semi-glossy; prickles broad, hooked downward, red-brown; upright growth; [Portland Trailblazer × Olympiad]; int. by Bear Creek Gardens, 1988

Tweedle Dee Min, op, 1987, Bennett, Dee; flowers coral pink, reverse lighter, small, 35-40 petals, urn-shaped, borne usually singly, slight fragrance; recurrent; foliage small, medium size, semi-glossy; no prickles; micro-mini; upright, bushy, low growth; hips globular, small, brown; [Deep Purple × Cupcake]; int. by Tiny Petals Nursery, 1986

Tweetie Min, lp, 1974, Moore, Ralph S.; bud ovoid, long, pointed; flowers soft pink, small, dbl.; foliage small, light, leathery; moderate, dwarf, bushy growth; [Perle d'Or × Fairy Princess]; int. by Sequoia Nursery, 1973

Tweety S, my, 2003, Umsawasdi, Dr. Theera & Chantana; flowers medium, dbl., borne in large clusters, slight fragrance; foliage medium size, medium green, semi-glossy; prickles small, curved; growth spreading, bushy, medium (4 ft.); [(Loving Touch × Rainbow's End) × Summer Madness]; int. by Certified Roses, 2003

Twenty-Fifth F, dr, 1997, Beales, Peter; flowers deep red, golden yellow stamens, 2½ in., semi-dbl., shallow cup to flat, borne in large clusters, slight fragrance; foliage medium size, dark green, semi-glossy; some prickles; growth compact, low (2ft.); [Redbreast × Pearl Drift]; int. by Peter Beales Roses, 1996

21st Century – See **Twenty First Century**, HT

Twenty First Century HT, dy, 1999, Perry, Astor; flowers large, full, borne mostly singly, slight fragrance; foliage medium size, dark green, semi-glossy; few prickles; upright, tall (5 ft.) growth; [Butterscotch × Mandelon]; int. by Certified Roses, Inc., 2000

Twenty-First Century HT, pb; flowers blend of pink and peach with yellow reverse, dbl., cupped, slight fragrance; low to medium growth; int. in 1999

21 Again! – See **Regatta**, HT, 1994

Twice as Nice HT, rb, 1985, Patterson, Randell E.; flowers white blending to red at edges, large, 40 petals, intense fragrance; foliage large, dark, semi-glossy; [Peace × Mirandy]; int. in 1984

Twice in a Blue Moon HT, m, Tantau; flowers silvery lilac, full, cupped, borne mostly singly, moderate to intense fragrance; recurrent; foliage medium green, glossy; upright growth; int. in 2004; Tollcross Fragrance Prize, Glasgow, 2006, Peoples' Choice, Glasgow, 2006

Twilight HT, m, 1955, Boerner; bud pointed; flowers lavender-lilac, reverse silvery, 4½ in., 30-35 petals, high-centered, moderate fragrance; foliage dull green; bushy, upright growth; PP1434; [Grey Pearl × Lavender Pinocchio]; int. by J&P, 1955

Twilight – See **Tasogare**, F

Twilight S, dp, Noack, Werner; part of Flower Carpet series; int. by Noack Rosen, 1997; PIT, RNRS, 1994

Twilight Min, rb, Bell; flowers red and yellow blend; free-flowering; bushy, medium growth; int. by Bell Roses

Twilight Beauty Min, m, 1978, Williams, Ernest D.; bud long, pointed; flowers red-purple, 1-1½ in., 40 petals, high-centered, moderate fragrance; bushy, spreading growth; [Angel Face × Over the Rainbow]; int. by Mini-Roses, 1977

Twilight Dream Min, m, 1992, Williams, Ernest D.; flowers medium, have good color stability, heavy substance, very dbl., high-centered, borne mostly singly, intense fragrance; good repeat; foliage small, dark green, glossy; few prickles; low (30 cm.), bushy growth; hardy; [Tom Brown × Twilight Beauty]

Twilight Glow – See **Polka**, LCl

Twilight Mist – See **Yugiri**, HT

Twilight Mist LCl, m, Robinson, P.; flowers soft lavender, large, semi-dbl., shallow cup, blooms in profusion, moderate fragrance; non-remontant; large growth; [Montecito × unknown]; int. in 1995

Twilight Secret Gr, m, 2005, Viraraghavan, M.S. Viru; flowers magenta pink, large, full, cupped, borne in small clusters; foliage medium size, dark green, semi-glossy; prickles ¼ in., pointed; bushy, medium growth; garden decorative; [(Vanamali × seedling) × Deep Purple]; int. by KSG Son, 2000

Twilight Skies Min, m, 2003, Moore, Ralph S.; flowers semi-dbl., borne in small clusters, slight fragrance; foliage medium size, medium green, semi-glossy; prickles small, straight, light green; growth bushy, medium (15 in.); containers, borders; [Vi's Violet × Anytime]; int. by Sequoia Nurs., 2003

Twilight Time Min, m

Twilight Trail Min, m, 1985, Williams, Ernest D.; bud long, pointed; flowers lavender-tan, 3 cm., 30-35 petals, high-centered, borne singly and several together, intense fragrance; recurrent; foliage small, dark green, semi-glossy; prickles average, slender; stems slender, wiry; upright, bushy growth; PP6198; [Angel Face × Anita Charles]; int. by Mini-Roses

Twilight Tryst HT, m, 2006, Viraraghavan, M.S. Viru;

flowers rich, deep purple, up to 5 in, single, borne mostly solitary, intense fragrance; foliage large, medium green, semi-glossy; prickles small, downward pointing, grey, few; growth bushy, medium (to 4 ft.); garden decorative; [(Vanamali × Seedling) × Deep Purple]; int. by Roses Unlimited, 2007

Twilight Zone Min, mr, 1985, Hardgrove, Donald L.; flowers well-formed, medium, 60 petals; foliage small, dark, semi-glossy; bushy, dense growth; [Scarlet Knight × Big John]; int. by Rose World Originals

Twilight Zone Gr, m, Williams, J. Benjamin; flowers lavender with yellow reverse, dbl., high-centered, slight fragrance; recurrent; low growth; int. in 1996

Twin HT, w, Kordes; flowers wihte with green tint on outer petals and slight pink tone in center, medium, full, high-centered, borne mostly singly; recurrent; stems medium; [Duett × Not stated]; florist rose; int. by W. Kordes Söhne, 2002

Twin Kordana Min, pb, Kordes; flowers deep pink with cream stripes and splotches, lighter reverse, full, high-centered; int. by W. Kordes Söhne

Twin Peaks – See **Ain't She Sweet**, HT

Twin Pinks Min, pb, 1991, Clements, John K.; flowers two-tone pink, medium, dbl., high-centered, borne in small clusters, slight fragrance; foliage small, medium green, semi-glossy; some prickles; low (30 cm.), bushy, compact growth; [seedling × seedling]; int. by Heirloom Old Garden Roses, 1991

Twin Sisters S, mr, Williams, J.B.; flowers bright red, borne in masses of blooms; recurrent; spreading, groundcover growth; int. by Hortico, 2003

Twinkie Min, lp, 1975, Moore, Ralph S.; bud pointed; flowers light clear pink, 1 in., 40 petals; foliage small, glossy; upright, very bushy growth; [(*R. wichurana* × Floradora) × Eleanor]; int. by Sequoia Nursery, 1974

Twinkle Min, ly, 1992, Ilsink, Peter; flowers light yellow, do not fade, 2 in., 10 petals, urn-shaped, borne singly, slight fragrance; recurrent; foliage medium size, medium green, matte; upright, low (40 cm.) growth; [McShane × seedling]; int. by Interplant B.V., 1989

Twinkle – See **Kirari**, F

Twinkle Bright Min, yb; free-flowering; growth to 20-24 in.; int. by Russian River Roses, 1998

Twinkle Charm Min, mr; free-flowering; growth to 20-24 in.; int. by Russian River Roses, 1998

Twinkle Eyes Min, rb; free-flowering; growth to 20-24 in.; int. by Russian River Roses, 1998

Twinkle Pink Min, mp; free-flowering; growth to 20-24 in.; int. by Russian River Roses, 1998

Twinkle Star Min, w; free-flowering; growth to 20-24 in.; int. by Russian River Roses, 1998

Twinkle Toes Min, mr, 1982, Lyon; flowers small, semi-dbl.; foliage small, medium green, semi-glossy; very compact growth; [Merry Christmas × seedling]

Twinkle Twinkle Min, ab, 1981, Bennett, Dee; bud pointed; flowers white with apricot petal edges, aging dark pink, 23 petals, blooms borne singly, slight tea fragrance; foliage medium green, semi-glossy; prickles very fine, curved; slender, straight, upright growth; [Contempo × Sheri Anne]; int. by Tiny Petals Nursery

Twinkler Min, pb, Datt, Braham

Twinkles Min, w, 1954, Spek; bud flesh; flowers small, 43 petals, moderate fragrance; compact, dwarf (8 in.) growth; PP1407; [Perla de Montserrat × polyantha seedling]; introduced as a miniature Hybrid China; int. by J&P, 1954

Twins HMsk, m, 2000, Lens, Louis; flowers lilac pink, fading toward cream, reverse lighter, 3-4 cm., single, borne in very long, large clusters, intense fragrance; recurrent; foliage large, brown to dark green, semi-glossy; prickles moderate; growth bushy, tall (125-150 cm.); [Trier × Felicia]; int. by Louis Lens N.V., 1994

Twirly Whirly S, dr, Peden, R.

Twist LCl, pb, Poulsen; flowers striped pink, red and cream, 10-15 cm., dbl., borne usually in clusters, no fragrance; recurrent; foliage dark green, glossy; bushy (150-200 cm.) growth; int. by Poulsen Roser, 2000

Twist 'n' Twirl Gr, or, Delbard; flowers orange-red, overlaid with stripes and splashes of silvery white, dbl., cupped, borne in clusters; recurrent; medium growth; int. in 2001; Children's Choice, Hamilton, NZ, 2006

Twister Cl Min, rb, 1997, Moore, Ralph S.; flowers striped red and white, 1½ in., full, rosette, borne in small clusters, slight fragrance; recurrent; foliage medium size, medium green, dull; few prickles; upright, climbing, tall (5-6 ft.) growth; [Little Darling × Little Magic]; int. by Sequoia Nurs.

Two Sisters S, w, 1993, Williams, J. Benjamin; flowers light pink to white, color variable, medium, full, borne in large clusters, slight fragrance; recurrent; foliage medium size, dark green, semi-glossy; some prickles; medium (3½-4 ft.), bushy, spreading growth; [Sea Foam × The Fairy]; int. by J.B. Williams & Associates, 1993

2004 Better Homes & Gardens Rose – See **Sunstruck**, HT

Two Thumbs Up HT, ab, 1999, Giles, Diann; flowers 5 in., full, borne mostly singly; foliage medium size, medium green, dull; few prickles; upright, medium (5 ft.) growth; [South Seas × St Patrick]; int. by Giles Rose Nursery

Two-Timer Min, ob, 1991, Moore, Ralph S.; bud ovoid; flowers orange-red with lighter shades of orange and white stripes, lighter reverse, medium, very dbl., high-centered, borne usually singly or in sprays of 3-5, no fragrance; foliage medium size, medium green, semi-glossy; bushy, spreading, low growth; [Orangeade × Pinstripe]; int. by Sequoia Nursery, 1991

Twyford HT, op, 1939, Waterer; bud long; flowers bright salmon-pink, base gold, reverse deep salmon flushed orange; foliage dark, reddish; vigorous growth

Ty Min, dy, 2005, Tucker, Robbie; flowers non-fading yellow, 2 in., dbl., high-centered, borne mostly solitary, no fragrance; recurrent; foliage medium green, matte; prickles moderate, to ¼ in., straight with point slightly downward; growth upright, medium (to 36 in.); exhibition; [Cal Poly × Soroptimist International]; int. by Nor'East Miniature Roses, 2006

Tycoon HT, mr, 1997, Bridges, Dennis A.; flowers very dbl., 41 petals, borne mostly singly; foliage medium size, dark green, semi-glossy; medium (4ft.) upright, bushy growth; [Kardinal × Thriller]; int. by Bridges Roses

Tye-Dye MinFl, rb, 2006, Sean McCann; flowers red striped with yellow, 1½-2 in., full, borne mostly solitary; foliage medium size, medium green, semi-glossy; prickles small, straight, pointed, light green, few; growth compact, bushy, medium (3 ft.); garden decorative; [seedling × seedling]

Tylea S, dp; flowers dark pink; free-flowering; low (40 cm.), groundcover growth

Tyler HT, rb, 1988, Poor, Cuyler; bud ovoid; flowers medium to dark red, reverse lighter, 4¾ in., 30-35 petals, high-centered, borne singly, slight fragrance; recurrent; foliage medium size, dark green, matte; prickles some, medium length; upright (5 ft.), vigorous growth; hips globular, medium, orange-yellow; PP8076; [(Tamango × Red Planet) × First Prize]; int. in 1988

Tynwald HT, ly, 1979, Mattock; bud ovoid; flowers cream, center yellow, 5 in., 60 petals, moderate fragrance; bushy, very upright growth; [Peer Gynt × Isis]

Typ Kassel C, mp; flowers full, globular, moderate sweet fragrance; recurrent; foliage large, bright green; growth to 5 ft.; possibly synonymous with Lippoldsburg

Typ Kasselunk – See **Typ Kassel**, C full

Typhoo Tea HT, rb, 1974, McGredy, Sam IV; bud medium, pointed; flowers medium red, silver reverse, 4-5 in., 50 petals, classic hybrid tea, borne mostly singly, moderate citrus fragrance; recurrent; foliage small, medium olive-green, glossy; prickles several, medium to long, hooked slightly downward, brown; bushy, upright (4-5 ft.) growth; hips very few ; PP3845; [Fragrant Cloud × Arthur Bell]; int. by McGredy Ltd., 1974

Typhoon HT, op, 1972, Kordes, R.; flowers salmon, shaded yellow, 4 in., 35 petals, intense fragrance; recurrent; medium growth; [Dr. A.J. Verhage × Colour Wonder]; int. by McGredy & Son

Typhoon F, yb; flowers yellow with red petal edges, cupped, borne in large clusters; recurrent; growth to 5 ft.; int. by Kordes, 2002

Tyriana HT, dp, 1965, Meilland, Alain A.; bud pointed, ovoid; flowers rose-pink, well-formed, 4½-5 in., 40 petals, moderate fragrance; foliage leathery, dark; vigorous, upright growth; [(Happiness × Independence) × Paris-Match]; int. by URS

Tyrius HT, m, 1973, Gandy, Douglas L.; flowers Tyrian purple, 5 in., 20 petals; foliage glossy, bronze; [Bettina × Prima Ballerina]; int. by Gandy's Roses, Ltd., 1972

Tzigane HT, rb, 1955, Meilland, F.; bud ovoid; flowers rose-red, reverse yellow, large, dbl., cupped to cactus-formed, moderate fragrance; foliage dark, glossy, leathery; upright, bushy, medium growth; [Peace × J.B. Meilland]; int. by URS, 1951

Tzigane, Climbing Cl HT, rb, 1958, Lagoona Nursery; [sport of Tzigane]; int. by Wheatcroft Bros., 1958

U. P. Hedrick HSpn, mp, 1932, Central Exp. Farm; flowers pink, open, large, single; profuse, non-recurrent bloom; foliage soft, dark; vigorous (6 ft.), bushy, compact growth; [*R. spinosissima altaica* × Betty Bland]
Ubekomachi LCl, mp
Uetersen S, mr, 1939, Tantau; flowers glowing red, semi-dbl.; recurrent bloom; upright, bushy growth; [Kitchener of Khartoum × Stammler]
Uetersen – See **Rosarium Uetersen**, LCl
Ufhoven HMult, op, 1964, Berger; flowers salmon pink, medium, full
Uhland HMsk, yb, 1916, Lambert, P.; flowers reddish-yellow, petals fringed, borne in clusters of 3-15; foliage pointed, like Tip-Top; [Geheimrat Dr. Mittweg × Tip-Top]
Ukigumo F, w, Keisei; int. by Keisei Rose Nurseries, 1998
Ukrainian Dawn – See **Ukrainskaia Zorka**, F
Ukrainskaia Zorka F, mr, 1955, Klimenko, V. N.; flowers bright cinnamon-red, medium; [Independence × unknown]
Ulla Land Misc OGR, mr
Ulmer Münster S, dr, 1982, Kordes, W.; flowers clear dark red, 12 cm., 35 petals, cupped, borne in clusters, slight fragrance; recurrent; foliage large, dark green, glossy; bushy, upright (5 ft.) growth; [Sympathie × seedling]
Ulrich Brunner fils HP, dp, 1882, Levet; flowers geranium-red to carmine, tinted light purple, large, 30 petals, cupped; sparse repeat; foliage leathery; few prickles; stems upright; growth vigorous; some sources say it is a sport of Paul Neyron, others say seedling of Anna de Diesbach
Ulrick's Buttercup F, ly, 1953, Ulrick, L.W.; bud ovoid; flowers medium, dbl., cupped, borne in clusters; foliage bronze; very vigorous, bushy growth; [Yvonne Rabier × Baby Alberic]
Ulrick's Gem F, pb, 1955, Ulrick, L.W.; flowers deep pink and white, very dbl., borne in clusters; foliage glossy; very vigorous, bushy growth; [Mrs Tom Henderson × Mrs Tom Henderson]
Ulrick's Red HT, mr, 1954, Ulrick, L.W.
Ulrick's Smokie F, m, 1953, Ulrick, L.W.; bud long, pointed; flowers smoky mauve, background white, large, very dbl., borne in clusters; foliage light green; bushy growth; [Mrs Tom Henderson × Tip-Top]
Ulrick's Yellow HT, my, 1953, Ulrick, L.W.; bud globular; flowers yellow, center darker, medium, dbl., cupped; foliage light green; bushy growth; [Mrs Pierre S. duPont × Lady Hillingdon]
Ulrike F, r
Ulster HP, mr, 1900, Dickson, A.; flowers salmon-red, large, dbl.
Ulster Gem HT, my, 1917, Dickson, H.; bud long, pointed; flowers canary-yellow, large, single; Gold Medal, NRS, 1916
Ulster Monarch HT, r, 1951, McGredy, Sam IV; flowers apricot shaded buff, high-pointed, medium, 50 petals; foliage glossy, bright green; upright growth; [Sam McGredy × (Mrs Sam McGredy × unknown)]
Ulster Queen F, ob, 1960, McGredy, Sam IV; flowers salmon-orange, well-formed, 3 in., 25 petals, borne in clusters; vigorous growth; [Cinnabar × Independence]; int. by McGredy & Son, 1960
Ulster Standard HT, dr, 1917, Dickson, H.; flowers deep crimson, with prominent yellow stamens, large, single
Ulster Volunteer HT, mr, 1918, Dickson, H.; flowers brilliant cherry-red, base clear white, 5-6 in., single
Ultimate Pink HT, lp, 1998, Zary, Dr. Keith W.; bud pointed, ovoid; flowers clear medium pink, 4½-5 in., 25-30 petals, high-centered, borne mostly singly, slight sweet fragrance; recurrent; foliage large, medium green, dull, leathery; prickles numerous, short, straight to hooked downward; stems long (18-22 in.), strong; tall (4½ ft.), upright, vigorous growth; PP11048; [(Honor × Silver Jubilee) × Fragrant Memory]; int. by Bear Creek Gardens, Inc., 1999; Rose of the Year, J&P, 1999
Ultimate Pleasure Min, pb, 1999, Bennett, Dee; flowers light pink, reverse medium pink, 1-1½ in., 25-35 petals, high-centered, cupped, borne mostly singly or in small clusters, moderate fragrance; recurrent; foliage medium size, medium green, semi-glossy; prickles moderate, slender, hooked slightly downward, reddish; extremely vigorous, bushy, upright, tall (24-36 in.) growth; PP12179; [Gene Boerner × Jean Kenneally]; int. by Tiny Petals, 1999
Ulysse HGal, mr, before 1838, Crammwell; flowers velvety crimson
Uma Rao HT, pb, Pal, Dr. B.P.; flowers pink with cream reverse, dbl., high-centered, moderate fragrance; int. in 1989
Umberglo Min, r, 1996, Williams, Ernest D.; flowers russet with red blush on edges, 1-1¼ in., full, borne mostly singly, moderate fragrance; foliage medium size, dark green, semi-glossy; few prickles; low (12-14 in.), compact, bushy growth; [seedling × Twilight Trail]; int. by Texas Mini Roses, 1996
Umilo – See **Marie Curie**, F
Una S, ly, 1900, Paul; bud sulphur yellow; flowers buff-yellow becoming creamy white, large, single to semi-dbl.; non-recurrent; vigorous growth; [Gloire de Dijon × *R. canina*]
Una Hawken F, ly, 1973, Murray, Nola; bud ovoid; flowers butter-yellow to cream, medium, dbl., cupped, moderate fragrance; foliage glossy, leathery; vigorous, upright, bushy growth; [Arthur Bell × Arthur Bell]; int. by Rasmussen's, 1972
Una Wallace HT, dp, 1921, McGredy; flowers soft, even-toned cherry-rose, well-formed, dbl., moderate fragrance; long, strong stems; vigorous, tall growth; Gold Medal, NRS, 1920
Uncle Bill HT, mp, Temple-Bourne, Rev. W.; flowers soft pink, moderate fragrance; free-flowering; [sport of Alec's Red]; int. in 1984
Uncle Joe HT, dr, 1973, Kern Rose Nursery; flowers very large, very dbl., high-centered, borne singly; recurrent; foliage large, dark green, leathery; very vigorous, upright, tall growth; [(Mirandy × Charles Mallerin) × seedling]; registered as Toro, by Melvin Wyant, in 1973; parentage stated as Karl Herbst × Big Red; int. by Kern Rose Nurs., 1971
Uncle John T, ly, 1904, Thorpe; flowers creamy yellow, large, full, moderate fragrance; [sport of Golden Gate]
Uncle John HT, mr, 2001, Hiltner, Martin; flowers medium red with lighter reverse, 3½-4 in., dbl., high-centered, borne mostly solitary, slight fragrance; recurrent; foliage medium size, medium green, semi-glossy; prickles moderate, ¼ in., hooked down; stems very red new growth; growth upright, medium (2½-3 ft.); garden decorative, exhibition; [Lynn Anderson × Dublin]
Uncle Lou HT, dp, 1997, Roth, Louis A.; flowers deep pink, medium sized, full, borne singly; foliage medium size, medium green, semi-glossy; upright, tall (4½-5 ft.) growth; [Queen Elizabeth × Christian Dior]
Uncle Sam HT, dp, 1965, Warriner, William A.; bud pointed, conical; flowers deep rose-pink, 5½-6 in., 30-35 petals, high-centered, moderate fragrance; recurrent; foliage dark, leathery, glossy; few prickles; vigorous, tall growth; PP2696; [Charlotte Armstrong × Heart's Desire]; int. by Howard
Uncle Steve HT, mr, 1995, Sheldon, John & Robin; flowers large, full, borne mostly singly, slight fragrance; foliage medium size, dark green, matte; upright, medium growth; [Pristine × Touch of Class]
Uncle Walter HT, mr, 1963, McGredy, Sam IV; flowers crimson-scarlet, 5 in., 30 petals, high-centered, borne often in clusters, slight fragrance; recurrent; foliage leathery, coppery; vigorous, tall growth; [Detroiter × Heidelberg]; int. by McGredy
Unconditional Love Min, dr, 2003, Barden, Paul; bud mossy, balsam/lemon scented; flowers deep red, reverse medium red, 1½ in., very full, borne in large clusters; foliage medium size, medium green, glossy; prickles moderate, ¼ in., straight, reddish; growth upright, tall (up to 24 in.); bedding, pots; [Sequoia Ruby × Scarlet Moss]
Unconditional Love F, ab; flowers amber-yellow, full, cupped, borne mostly in clusters; free-flowering; foliage medium green, glossy; compact, bushy, medium growth; int. by Love4Plants, 2004
Undine HT, ob, 1901, Jacobs; flowers dark orange, medium; upright, bushy growth; [L'Ideal × Sunset]
Unermüdliche Ch, m, 1904, Geschwind; flowers maroon with white center, medium, semi-dbl.; introduced by either Lambert or Chotek in about 1930
Unforgettable HT, mp, 1991, Warriner, William A.; bud long, pointed ovoid; flowers 30-35 petals, high-centered,

borne mostly singly, moderate fragrance; recurrent; foliage large, dark green, semi-glossy; prickles average, hooked downward; stems long, strong; tall (140 cm.), upright, spreading growth; PP6318; [Honor × American Dawn]; int. by Bear Creek Gardens, 1992

Unforgettable S, yb, 1992, Robinson, Thomas, Ltd.; flowers amber, 3-3½ in., dbl., borne in large clusters; repeat bloom; foliage small to medium size, dark green, glossy; some prickles; medium (90 cm.), bushy, spreading (hemisphere shape) growth; [Snow Carpet × Woodland Sunbeam]; int. by Thomas Robinson, Ltd., 1994

Unforgettable HT, dr, Tantau

Unguiculata – See **Œillet**, C

Unica Alba – See **White Provence**, C

Unica Spectabilis – See **Unique Admirable**, C

UNICEF F, ob, Cocker; int. by Cocker Roses, 1993

Union-Rose St Helena – See **St Helena**, F

Unique – See **White Provence**, C

Unique HSpn, w, about 1825, Cartier; flowers medium to large, full

Unique LCl, op, 1928, Evans; flowers bright fawn-orange-salmon, 4-5 cm., full, borne in small clusters; recurrent bloom; vigorous growth; [Tip-Top × Hybrid Perpetual]

Unique Ch, w, Laffay, M.; flowers white edged pink, compact

Unique Admirable C, dp, before 1820, Descemet; flowers rose pink, medium, full; foliage widely spaced, simply serrate

Unique Anglais – See **Rubra**, C

Unique Anglaise – See **Unique Rose**, C

Unique Blanche – See **White Provence**, C

Unique Blanche Panachée – See **Unique Panachée**, C

Unique Carnée C, lp, before 1811, Vilmorin; flowers blush pink, large, full, borne singly and in small clusters, moderate fragrance; foliage light green; prickles numerous, bristly

Unique de Provence – See **White Provence**, C

Unique de Provence – See **Unique Moss**, M

Unique Moss M, w, 1844, Robert; flowers pure white, occasionally tinted pink, well-mossed, large, dbl.; prickles shoots very spiny; [sport of Unique Blanche]

Unique Panachée – See **La Félicité**, D

Unique Panachée C, w, Chaussée, Mme; flowers white, faintly striped rose and lilac, large, dbl., globular; vigorous growth; [sport of Unique Rouge]; the synonym Mme d'Hébray was applied by Pradel; int. by Caron, 1821

Unique Rose – See **Rubra**, C

Unique Rose C, lp, before 1810, Cels; flowers light bright pink, medium to large, dbl., moderate fragrance; foliage edged pink; prickles small, ashen

Unique Rouge – See **Rubra**, C

Unique Rouge C, mp, before 1824; flowers bright pink, medium, dbl.

Unison HT, ob, Hiroshima; int. by Hiroshima Bara-en, 2004

United Nations F, op, 1949, Leenders, M.; flowers salmon-pink, open, medium, 26 petals, borne in clusters; foliage glossy; very vigorous, bushy growth; [Mev. Nathalie Nypels × Rosamunde]

United Nations Rose – See **Peacekeeper**, F

United States HT, op, 1918, Verschuren; flowers yellowish-salmon pink, large, semi-dbl.

Unity HT, dp, 1959, Sansam; flowers deep pink, reverse slightly darker, well-shaped, 5½ in., 45 petals, intense fragrance; foliage dark; vigorous, upright growth; [sport of Red Ensign]; int. in 1957

Universal Favorite HWich, mp, 1898, Horvath; flowers soft rose, fading to white, 2½ cm., dbl., borne in large clusters, moderate fragrance; vigorous, climbing growth; [*R. wichurana* × Pâquerette]; int. by W.A. Manda

Université d'Orléans Pol, mr, 1966, Hémeray-Aubert; bud globular; flowers semi-dbl., cupped, borne in large clusters; vigorous growth; [unknown × Ronde Endiablee]

Unn F, dp, 1972, Lundstad; bud ovoid; flowers deep pink, open, medium, semi-dbl.; foliage glossy; dwarf, moderate growth; [Rimosa × Fidélio]

Unser Stolz HT, dr, 1965, Verschuren, A.; flowers bright crimson-scarlet, large, dbl.; foliage leathery, dark, glossy; upright growth; [Ena Harkness × seedling]; int. by van Engelen, 1961

Unveiled Min, pb, 2001, Jones, Ken; flowers light pink, medium yellow reverse, 1½ in., dbl., high-centered, borne mostly solitary, slight fragrance; foliage medium size, medium green, semi-glossy; prickles small, few; growth upright (24-36 in.); garden decorative, exhibition; [sport of Incognito]

Uppingham School HT, dy, 1999, Cowlishaw, Frank; flowers golden yellow, reverse yellow, 4 in., full, borne in large clusters; foliage medium size, dark green, glossy; prickles moderate; upright, medium (to 5 ft.) growth; [Ann Harkness × (Diamond Jubilee × Picadilly)]

Upright Multiflora Sp; a clone of *R. multiflora* used for understock

Upstart Min, mr, 1982, Warriner, William A.; flowers small, semi-dbl.; foliage small, medium green, semi-glossy; upright growth; [Merci × Fire Princess]; int. by J&P, 1984

Uptown Min, m, 1991, Taylor, Pete & Kay; flowers lavender, edges darker violet, reverse lighter, yellow base, medium, full, exhibition, borne mostly singly, no fragrance; foliage medium size, medium green, semi-glossy; some prickles; medium (46 cm.), upright, bushy growth; [Azure Sea × Party Girl]; int. by Taylor's Roses, 1992

Urania HP, dr, 1906, Walsh; flowers bright crimson, dbl.; recurrent bloom; [American Beauty × Suzanne-Marie Rodocanachi]

Urara F, dp, 1999, Hirabayashi, Hiroshi; flowers pale purplish pink, 3-4 in., 25-30 petals, cupped, no fragrance; foliage dark green, leathery; growth to 2-3 ft.; [Mimi × Minuette]; int. by Keisei Rose Nurseries, 1995; Gold Medal, Japan Rose Concours, 1995

Urdh HP, mp, 1933, Tantau; bud long, pointed; flowers large, 45 petals, high-centered, intense fragrance; recurrent; vigorous growth; [Victor Verdier × Papa Lambert]; int. by C-P, 1930

Urmibala HT, ob, Ghosh, Mr. & Mrs. S.; flowers blend of orange-yellow and pink; int. in 2004

Ursel Pol, mr, 1938, Vogel, M.; flowers carmine red, medium, semi-dbl.

Ursel Tgarth HFt, yb, 1938, Ketten, Gebrüder; flowers yellow and red, medium, dbl.

Ursula HT, mr, 1970, Laperrière; bud ovoid; flowers clear red, open, medium, dbl.; foliage glossy; vigorous, upright growth; [Jeunesse × (Peace × Independence)]; int. by EFR

Uschi F, dp, 1973, Tantau, Math.; flowers medium, dbl.; foliage glossy, dark; vigorous, bushy growth; [sport of Marimba]

Usha F, dr, 1976, IARI; bud ovoid; flowers deep red, open, 1½ in., 35-40 petals; foliage soft; compact, bushy growth; [Orangeade × unknown]; int. in 1975

Usmev HT, op, Strnad

Usuzumi HT, r, Hiroshima; int. by Hiroshima Bara-en, 1995

Usvit F, op, Urban, J.; flowers salmon-pink, medium, dbl.; int. in 1978

UT Tyler Rose Gr, ob, 1984, Weeks, O.L.; flowers orange, medium, 35 petals; foliage large, medium green, matte; upright growth; [seedling × seedling]; int. by University of Texas at Tyler

Uta Maro HT, mr; flowers red with silvery reverse, large, dbl.

Utage HT, w, 1977, Ota, Kaichiro; bud pointed; flowers very large, 30-35 petals, high-centered; foliage leathery; vigorous, upright growth; [Edith Krause × Bridal Robe]

Utage HT, dr, Keisei; int. in 1979

Utano HT, w; flowers white with orange tones; int. in 1985

Utopia HT, rb, Select; flowers creamy yellow base, edged and suffused red, 4 in., 35-45 petals, high-centered, borne mostly singly; recurrent; stems long; int. by Terra Nigra BV, 2003

Utro Moskvy HT, mp, 1952, Shtanko, E.E.; flowers soft rose tinted carmine, large, 60 petals, slight fragrance; foliage leathery, grayish; spreading growth; [Frau Karl Druschki × Independence]; Gold Medal, International Exhibition, 1961

Uttam HT, lp, 1971, IARI; bud pointed; flowers pastel pink, large, dbl.; foliage glossy; vigorous, upright growth; [Elite × Open pollination]; int. in 1969

Uwe Seeler F, ob, 1973, Kordes, R.; bud ovoid; flowers salmon-orange, large, semi-dbl., high-centered, moderate fragrance; recurrent; foliage large, glossy, bronze, leathery; vigorous, upright, bushy growth; [Queen Elizabeth × Colour Wonder]; int. by Kordes, 1970

V

V for Victory HT, ly, 1941, Brownell; bud ovoid, long, pointed; flowers yellow faintly tinted orange, 45 petals, high-centered, intense fragrance; foliage glossy; vigorous, bushy, compact to open growth; [Golden Glow × Condesa de Sástago]
V G Glowing HT HT, rb
V O N Canada F, ob
V Y F Rose HT, mr
V. Viviand-Morel T, dr, 1887, Bernaix; bud long; flowers rich crimson shaded dark red and carmine, large, dbl.; foliage leathery, glossy; growth upright, robust; [Red Safrano × unknown]
V. Vivo É Hijos T, rb, 1894, Bernaix; flowers carmine pink, paler at center and base, tinted with yellow, salmon & apricot, med
Vabene HT, my, 1979, Meilland, Mrs. Marie-Louise; bud conical; flowers medium, 30 petals, high-centered; very vigorous, upright growth; [Arthur Bell × (MEIgold × Kabuki)]; int. by Meilland & Co SNC, 1977
Vagabonde F, ob, 1966, Lens; bud long, pointed; flowers salmon-orange, 25 petals, high-centered, borne in clusters of 3 or more; foliage dark, glossy; vigorous, bushy growth; [Mannequin × Fashion]; int. by Wheatcroft Bros., 1963
Vahine HT, or, 1964, Combe; flowers dark cardinal-red tinted orange; strong stems; vigorous, upright growth; int. by Vilmorin-Andrieux
Vainqueur HT, m, 1937, Heizmann, E.; bud ovoid, dark red; flowers velvety purple, reverse dark red, very large, very dbl.; foliage bright green; long, strong stems; very vigorous growth; [Sensation × unknown]; int. by A. Meilland
Vainqueur de Goliath HP, mr, 1862, Moreau, F.; flowers brilliant crimson-scarlet, very large, dbl.
Vainqueur de Solférino – See **Cardinal Patrizzi**, HP
Vaire – See **Château de Vaire**, S
Vaishnavi HT, or, K&S; flowers vibrant vermilion, broad petals, dbl., high-centered; vigorous growth; int. by KSG Son, 1992
Vajont F, Galesso, G.; int. in 1966
Val Boughey – See **Valerie Boughey**, HT
Val d'Authion HT, mp, Minier; flowers Neyron pink, undertones of bluish and silver, large, full, cupped, moderate fragrance; recurrent; foliage rich green, glossy; strong, bushy (1 m.) growth; int. in 1967
Val De Mosa HT, my, 1970, Ellick; flowers 70 petals, moderate fragrance; foliage dark, glossy; vigorous growth; [La Jolla × Cynthia Brooke]
Val Johnston S, mp, 2004, Johnston, Graeme; flowers full, cupped, opening flat, borne in large clusters, moderate fragrance; foliage medium size, semi-glossy; prickles medium, 1½-2 cm., straight; growth upright, tall (to 2 m); garden decorative; hips none; [Frau Dagmar Hastrupp × unknown]; int. by Graeme Johnston, 1992
Valdemar HMult, mp, Back
Valdemossa HT, Dot, Simon; int. in 1991
Vale of Clwyd F, pb, 1983, Bees; flowers yellow, pink petal edges, medium, dbl.; foliage large, medium green, glossy; upright growth; [Handel × Arthur Bell]
Valence Dubois HGal, mp, 1880, Fontaine; flowers medium, dbl.
Valencia HT, ab, 1967, Kordes, R.; bud large, pointed ovoid; flowers apricot-orange, 6 in., 40-45 petals, high-centered, borne singly and several together, moderate tea fragrance; recurrent; foliage large, glossy, leathery; prickles ordinary, medium, hooked downward; stems long, strong; vigorous, upright growth; hips none ; PP2651; [Golden Sun × Chantré]; int. by J&P
Valencia HT, ab, 2006; bud large, oval; flowers warm copper yellow, 12 cm., full, high-centered, borne mostly solitary, intense fragrance; recurrent; foliage fresh green, leathery; bushy, upright, medium growth; int. by W. Kordes' Söhne, 1989; Henry Edland Fragrance Medal, 1989
Valencia 89 – See **Valencia**, HT, 2006
Valencia Kordana Min, yb, Kordes; container rose; int. by W. Kordes Söhne
Valenciennes LCl, dr, 1960, Robichon; bud long, pointed; flowers crimson, fading to cherry red, 8 cm., semi-dbl., borne in clusters, slight fragrance; good repeat; foliage dark, glossy; very vigorous growth; [Paul's Scarlet Climber × seedling]
Valentin Beaulieu HWich, m, 1902, Barbier; flowers violet-pink, darker at center, aging lighter, 5-7 cm., dbl., borne in small clusters; foliage dark green; prickles fine, slightly curved, red; [*R. wichurana* × Souv de Catherine Guillot]
Valentina – See **Valentina Hit**, Min
Valentina Borgatti HT, Borgatti, G.; int. in 1969
Valentina Cortese F, Cazzaniga, F. G.; int. in 1976
Valentina Hit Min, mr, Poulsen; flowers medium red, 5-8 cm., 25-30 petals, borne mostly solitary, no fragrance; foliage dark green, glossy; growth bushy, low (40-60 cm.); PP14798; int. by Poulsen Roser, 2001
Valentine F, mr, 1951, Swim, H.C.; flowers bright red, 2½-3 in., 18 petals, borne in large clusters, slight fragrance; free-flowering; foliage dark olive-green; spreading, bushy, compact growth; [China Doll × World's Fair]; int. by Armstrong Nursery
Valentine Cupido Min, mr, Pouw; bud ovoid; flowers 4 cm., 35 petals, rosette, borne in tight sprays, slight fragrance; free-flowering; foliage dark green, glossy; prickles few, 3 mm, linear; upright (12 in), spreading growth; PP12862; [unnamed seedling × seedling]; container rose; int. by Greenheart Farms, 2003
Valentine Heart F, mp, 1990, Dickson, Patrick; flowers pale pink with hint of lilac, serrated edges, dbl., high-centered, borne in clusters, intense fragrance; recurrent; foliage large, medium green, glossy, purple when young; bushy growth; [Shona × Pot 'o Gold]; int. by Dickson Nurseries, Ltd., 1990
Valentine Surprise Mini Brite Min, rb, J&P; flowers striped; int. by Bear Creek Gardens, 2000
Valentine's Day Cl MinFl, dr, 2004, Carruth, Tom; flowers deep velvet red, 5-7 cm., 30 petals, cupped, borne in small clusters, slight fragrance; recurrent; foliage medium size, dark green, semi-glossy; prickles moderate, small, almost straight; growth spreading, climbing canes, tall, canes of 180 to 220 cm.; garden decoration; [Amalia × Raven]; int. by Weeks Roses, 2006
Valeria Sykes F, rb, 1999, Horner, Colin P.; flowers red splashed white, reverse silver, 2 in., single, borne in small clusters; foliage small, medium green, semi-glossy; few prickles; bushy, low (2 ft.) growth; [Champagne Cocktail × Robin Redbreast]; int. by Battersby Roses, 2000
Valerie F, w, 1932, Chaplin Bros.; bud pointed, yellow; flowers cream, large, borne in large clusters; foliage glossy, dark; bushy growth; Gold Medal, NRS, 1931
Valerie HT, mp, Select; florist rose; int. by Terra Nigra BV, 1994
Valerie Ann F, dy, 2005, Paul Chessum Roses; flowers dbl., borne in large clusters, moderate fragrance; foliage medium size, dark green, matte; prickles medium, flat, red, moderate; growth upright, medium (36 in.); bedding, containers; [seedling × seedling]; int. by World of Roses, 2005
Valerie Boughey HT, op, 1960; flowers coppery salmon-pink, high pointed, 6 in., 36 petals, moderate fragrance; foliage leathery, glossy; vigorous, upright growth; [sport of Tzigane]; int. by Fryers Nursery, Ltd., 1960
Valerie Howard HT, or, 2004, Bossum, Bill; flowers orange/red, reverse straw, 3 in., dbl., borne in small clusters, slight fragrance; foliage medium size, medium green, semi-glossy; prickles few, 3 mm.; growth upright, medium (3 ft.); garden; [Oreana × seedling]; int. in 2004
Valerie Jeanne Min, dp, 1981, Saville, F. Harmon; bud globular; flowers deep magenta pink, 1½-2 in., very full, high-centered, borne mostly singly, and in clusters of up to 20, slight fragrance; recurrent; foliage dark green, very glossy; prickles few, long, straight, thin; vigorous, upright growth; PP4811; [Sheri Anne × Tamango]; int. by Nor'East Min. Roses; AOE, ARS, 1983
Valerie June HT, lp, Allender, Robert William
Valerie Kathleen F, yb, 1997, Horner, Colin P.; flowers medium, dbl., borne in small clusters; foliage large, dark green, glossy; some prickles; bushy, medium (2½ ft.) growth; [(Silver Jubilee × Pink Favorite) × Amber Queen]
Valerie Purves HT, mp, 1940, Clark, A.; flowers pink, well-formed; vigorous growth
Valerie Swane – See **Crystalline**, HT
Valeta F, or, 1960, deRuiter; flowers red shaded vermilion, open, dbl., borne in clusters (up to 20); foliage dark; vigorous growth; [Signal Red × Fashion]
Valette – See **Lavalette**, D
Valfleury F, or, Croix; flowers geranium red, borne in clusters; free-flowering; vigorous, medium growth; int. by Roseraie Paul Croix, 1971; Gold Rose, Orleans, Cerf. of Merit, Monza
Valia Balkanska – See **Buffy Sainte-Marie**, HT
Valiant HT, mr, 1948, Boerner; bud long, pointed; flowers bright red, large, 30 petals, high-centered; foliage dark, leathery; vigorous, upright, branching growth; [Poinsettia × Satan]; int. by J&P
Valiant Heart F, dr, Olesen; flowers deep red, dbl., cupped, borne in large trusses, very slight fragrance; free-flowering; foliage green, glossy; bushy, upright (60-100 cm.) growth; int. by Poulsen Roser, 2000
Validé M, lp, 1857, Robert & Moreau; flowers light pink, shaded carmine, 2½-3 in., full, rosette; some repeat
Valkita – See **Mariska**, F
Valldemose F, mr, 1958, Dot, M.; flowers fiery red, large, 20 petals, globular; foliage glossy; vigorous, open growth; [Magrana × Radar]; int. in 1956
Vallée de Chamonix T, yb, 1872, Ducher; bud pink and orange-pink; flowers pinkish yellow, lightly coppery at center, medium, very dbl., flat
Valour HT, dr; flowers velvety dark red, dbl., cupped, borne mostly singly, intense fragrance; recurrent; stems long, strong; medium (4-5 ft.) growth
Valrose LCl, w, 1964, Mondial Roses; flowers white suffused pink at edges, medium, semi-dbl., borne in clusters of 3; recurrent bloom
Valse des Neiges – See **Schneewalzer 87**, LCl
Valstar HT, dp, 1962, Mondial Roses; flowers deep pink, well-formed, large, dbl.; foliage leathery; strong stems
Vamp Min, dr, 1980, Gatty, Joseph; flowers 5 petals,

cupped, borne 3 per cluster, no fragrance; foliage dark; prickles pointed; angular growth habit; [Fairy Moss × Fairy Moss]; int. in 1981

Van Artevelde HGal, dp, before 1847, Parmentier; flowers deep pink, petals imbricated in whorls, large, very dbl.

Van Bergen S, ly, 1980, James, John; bud pointed; flowers light yellow fading to white, 48 petals, borne in clusters of 3, 5 or 7, slight fruity fragrance; repeat bloom; foliage small, glossy, dark; prickles hooked, red; vigorous, compact, bushy growth; [(*R. wichurana* × Baronne Prevost) × Fun Jwan Lo]

Van Gogh S, rb, 1996, Williams, J. Benjamin; flowers red and white striped, reverse pale whitish pink with stripes, 3½-4 in., dbl., high-centered, borne in large clusters; foliage large, dark green, semi-glossy; prickles moderate; bushy, medium (3-3½ ft.) growth; [Spinning Wheel × Handel]; int. by J.B. Williams & Associates, 1997

Van Huysum – See **Celsiana**, D

Van Huysum D, dr, before 1841, Parmentier; flowers violet pink, large, dbl.; occasionally recurrent; sometimes classed as HGal or HCh

Van Nes – See **Permanent Wave**, F

Van Rossem's Jubilee HT, op, 1937, Van Rossem; flowers bright carmine or coral; foliage glossy, bronze; vigorous growth

Van Spaendonck C, dp, 1821, Cartier; flowers medium to large, full

Vanamali HT, m, 1979, Viraraghavan, M.S. Viru; bud long, pointed; flowers orchid-mauve, 6 in., 35-40 petals, high-centered, moderate fragrance; foliage dark, leathery; tall, vigorous, bushy growth; [Lady X × ((Gruss an Teplitz × unknown) × (Lake Como × Angel Face))]; int. by KSG Roses, 1978

Vancouver HT, pb, Twomey, Jerry

Vancouver Belle S, lp, 2004, Jalbert, Brad; flowers pink, reverse lighter pink, 3-4 in., dbl., borne in small clusters, slight fragrance; recurrent; foliage medium size, medium green, glossy; prickles medium, green, moderate; growth bushy, medium (2-3 ft.); hedge, container, garden decoration; [Thelma's Glory × Sexy Rexy]; int. in 1999

Vancouver Centennial – See **Jan Wellum**, Min

Vanda Beauty – See **Golden Bouquet**, HT

Vandael M, m, 1850, Laffay, M.; bud well mossed; flowers rich purple, edged lilac, large, dbl.; vigorous growth

Vanessa HT, pb, 1946, Leenders, M.; bud ovoid; flowers coral, reverse yellow, 4½ in., 25 petals; foliage bright green; vigorous growth; [Arch. Reventos × Lord Baden-Powell]; int. by Longley

Vanessa HT, mr, Taschner, Ludwig; flowers cherry red, medium, dbl., high-centered; free-flowering; stems long; vigorous, tall growth; [sport of Esther Geldenhuys]; int. by Ludwig's Roses, 1998

Vanessa HT, ob, Dräger; int. in 2000

Vanessa Belinda F, yb, 1993, Bracegirdle, A.J.; flowers yellow blend, 3-3½ in., dbl., borne in small clusters; foliage medium size, dark green, glossy; some prickles; medium (100 cm.), bushy growth; [(Champagne Cocktail × seedling) × (Glenfiddich × Priscilla Burton)]; int. by Bracegirdle, 1993

Vanessa Campello Gr, lp, Roses Noves Ferrer, S L; flowers 32 petals, high-centered, no fragrance; PP11529; [Lambada × K-881543-02]

Vanguard HRg, op, 1932, Stevens, G.A.; flowers bronze-orange-salmon, large, full, moderate fragrance; foliage light, very glossy, leathery; vigorous (to 10 ft.) growth; [(*R. wichurana* × *R. rugosa alba*) × Eldorado]; int. by J&P; Dr. W. Van Fleet Medal, ARS, 1933, David Fuerstenberg Prize, ARS, 1934

Vanhuisson – See **Van Huysum**, D

Vanilla F, w, Kordes; flowers light yellow to ivory, outer petals have green tinge, medium, dbl., high-centered, borne mostly singly; recurrent; stems medium to long; florist rose; int. by W. Kordes Söhne, 1994

Vanilla Cream F, ly, Lens; flowers light, creamy yellow, dbl., cupped, borne in clusters, slight fragrance; recurrent; foliage clear green, glossy; moderate (2 ft.) growth; int. by Louis Lens Roses, 2000

Vanilla Kordana Min, ly, Kordes; flowers light, creamy yellow, dbl.; int. by Bear Creek Gardens, 2000

Vanilla Kordana Mini Brite – See **Vanilla Kordana**, Min

Vanilla Meidiland S, w, Meilland; flowers vanilla white, dbl., cupped, borne in clusters; recurrent; low (2 ft.) growth; int. in 2005

Vanilla Perfume HT, ab, 1999, Zary, Dr. Keith W.; bud plump, ovoid; flowers light cream, blushed apricot/pink, reverse light apricot, 4-4½ in., 35 petals, high-centered, borne mostly singly and in small clusters, intense sweet, spicy vanilla fragrance; recurrent; foliage medium size, dark green, semi-glossy to glossy; prickles moderate, medium, hooked downward, brown; stems strong; upright, tall (5 ft.) growth; PP12464; [Anne Morrow Lindbergh × (Honor × Silver Jubilee)]; int. by Bear Creek Gardens, Inc., 1999

Vanilla Sky HT, w, Kordes; flowers cream, large, full, high-centered, borne mostly singly; recurrent; stems long; florist rose; int. by W. Kordes Söhne, 2005

Vanille-Groseille S, pb, Delbard; int. by Georges Delbard SA, 2001

Vanity T, my, 1911, Halstead; flowers canary yellow

Vanity HMsk, dp, 1920, Pemberton; flowers rose-pink, medium to large, single, borne in large, loose sprays, intense fragrance; recurrent bloom; foliage rich green, leathery; very vigorous (to 8 ft.), bushy growth; [Château de Clos Vougeot × seedling]

Vanity HT, mp, Select Roses BV; flowers 30-35 petals, high-centered; int. by Terra Nigra BV, 1999

Vanity Fair HT, lp, 1942, Roberts; bud long, pointed; flowers cameo-pink, large, 19 petals, high-centered; foliage soft; long stems; very vigorous, upright growth; [Better Times × Golden Rapture]; int. by Totty, 1944

Vannie F, dp, 2000, French, Bryan; flowers dark pink, reverse slightly lighter, 3 in., semi-dbl., borne singly or in clusters of 3-4, slight fragrance; recurrent; foliage medium size, dark green, semi-glossy; prickles moderate, brown-red; growth upright, medium (3-4 ft.); int. by Valley View Gardens

Van's Choice F, ob, Williams, J. Benjamin; flowers light, soft orange, dbl., cupped; free-flowering; strong growth; int. in 1998

Vanto Pol, dr, 1955, Nanto, Mikko; flowers borne in clusters; very hardy; [sport of Dick Koster]

Varenna Allen F, ab, Harkness; flowers golden apricot, semi-dbl., cupped, borne in clusters, slight fragrance; recurrent; medium, robust growth; int. by R. Harkness & Co., 2006

Variant F, op, VEG; flowers medium, dbl.

Variegata C, pb, about 1845; flowers ivory white, striped rose pink, very dbl.; foliage ovate, pointed, toothed; there is much confusion about this rose, and there may be 2 or 3 cultivars under this name; the one in commerce today is probably that found about 1845, near Angers, France

Variegata – See **Panachée**, M

Variegata HWich, w, about 1915, possibly Conard & Jones; foliage variegated green and white, occasionally tinted pink

Variegata di Bologna B, rb, 1909, Bonfiglioli; flowers white, striped purplish red, large, dbl., globular, borne in clusters of 3-5, moderate fragrance; vigorous (6-8 ft.) growth

Variegata di Bologna Rouge B, dr, Lowe

Variegated Damask – See **Panachée**, D

Varieté F, m, VEG; flowers purple/pink with lighter shading, large, dbl.; int. in 1987

Variety Club F, yb, 1965, McGredy, Sam IV; flowers yellow marked rose-red, well-formed, 48 petals, borne in clusters; foliage dark; [Columbine × Circus]; int. by McGredy

Variety Club Min, or; flowers bright orange-vermilion, dbl., cupped, rosette; recurrent; vigorous (28 in.) growth; int. by Harkness, 1999

Varin – See **Sarah**, C

Varna S, dy, GPG Bad Langensalza; flowers large, dbl.; int. in 1979

Varo Iglo HT, w, Verbeek; flowers medium, dbl.; int. in 1969

Varo Rania HT, Verbeek; int. in 1969

Varsha F, w, K&S; flowers pure white, margined rose pink; free-flowering; medium growth; [Nicole × Not stated]; int. by KSG Son, 1992

Vasant HT, yb, 1981, Division of Vegetable Crops and Floriculture; bud pointed; flowers yellow edged pink, high-centered, borne in clusters of 10, slight spicy fragrance; foliage dark; prickles straight, brown; upright, bushy growth; [Sweet Afton × Delhi Princess]; int. in 1980

Vasavi HT, dr, Kasturi; flowers deep blackish red, dbl., high-centered; int. by KSG Son, 1976

Vasco da Gama F, mr, Moreira da Silva; flowers velvety red; [Pinocchio × Alain]

Vassar Centennial HT, pb, 1961, Meilland, Mrs. Marie-Louise; flowers peach to shell-pink, 4½-5 in., 30 petals, high-centered, moderate fragrance; foliage dark, leathery; upright, branching growth; PP2031; [Helene de Roumanie × Confidence]; int. by C-P, 1961

Vater Rhein HT, dr, 1922, Kiese; flowers very dark red, dbl.; [Kynast × seedling]

Vaterland HT, dr, 1928, Berger, V.; flowers dark red with coppery reflexes, large, dbl.; foliage bronze, leathery; vigorous growth; [National Emblem × Earl Haig]; int. by Pfitzer

Vatertag Pol, ob, 1959, Tantau, Math.; flowers salmon-orange, small, globular, borne in clusters; recurrent; bushy growth; [sport of Muttertag]; int. by Rosen Tantau, 1959

Vatertag, Climbing Cl Pol, ob; [sport of Vatertag]; int. after 1959

Vatican HT, ab, 1970, Delbard-Chabert; bud ovoid; flowers apricot-yellow shaded carmine, medium, dbl., high-centered, slight fragrance; foliage glossy; moderate, bushy growth; [Grande Premiere × (Sultane × Mme Joseph Perraud)]; int. by Laxton & Bunyard, 1967

Vaucresson A, lp, before 1885; flowers flesh pink, medium, full

Vavoom F, ob, 2005, Carruth, Tom; flowers bright orange yellow, ruffled, 7-9 cm., 35 petals, high-centered, borne mostly solitary, moderate fragrance; recurrent; foliage medium size, dark green, glossy; prickles moderate, average, almost straight, brown; compact, bushy, medium growth; [Julie Newmar × Top Notch]; int. by Weeks Roses, 2007

Vedette HT, mr, 1951, Gaujard; flowers brilliant red, large, 28 petals; foliage leathery; [(Frau Karl Druschki × George Dickson) × seedling]

Vee Bryan F, w, 1998, Jones, L.J.; flowers cream, edged pink maroon, 2 in., full, borne in large clusters, moderate fragrance; [Solitaire × Solitaire]; int. by Haynes Roses, 1997

Vee Marie Min, dp, 1993, Bell, Judy G.; flowers bright deep pink, slight white on reverse, yellow stamens, medium, full, borne in small clusters, no fragrance; foliage small, dark green, glossy; few prickles; low (15 in.), bushy, spreading, compact growth; [Dale's Sunrise × Angel Face]; int. by Michigan Mini Roses, 1993

Vegesacker Charme S, pb; flowers pink with white eye, golden stamens, medium, single, shallow cup, borne in clusters, slight fragrance; foliage dark green, semi-glossy; strong, upright (4 ft.) growth; int. by Kordes, 2003

Veilchenblau HMult, m, 1909, Schmidt, J.C.; bud purplish-pink; flowers violet, petals streaked with white, center white, yellow stamens, 1¼ in., semi-dbl., cupped, moderate fragrance; non-recurrent; foliage large, pointed, glossy, light; prickles very few; stems short; vigorous, climbing (10-15 ft.) growth; [Crimson Rambler × Erinnerung an Brod]

Velay-Rose LCl, op, Croix; flowers salmon-pink; free-flowering; int. by Paul Croix, 1972; 1st Certificate, Roeulx & Saverne Intl. Show

Veldfire HT, ab, 1988, W. Kordes Söhne; flowers orange, reverse chrome-yellow, medium, 38 petals, high-centered, borne singly, slight fragrance; recurrent; foliage glossy, medium green; prickles concave, yellow-brown; upright, well-branched, free-flowering growth; [seedling × seedling]; int. by Ludwigs Roses Pty. Ltd., 1988

Velindre HT, mr, 1998, Poole, Lionel; flowers red-pink with peach reverse, high-centered, 5½ in., full, borne singly, moderate fragrance; foliage large, dark green, semi-glossy; some prickles; upright, bushy, medium growth; [Solitaire × seedling]

Velingstorprosen HGal, m

Velizy HT, ab, 1986, Delbard; flowers well-formed, large, 30 petals, slight fragrance; bushy, branching growth; [((Peace × Marcelle Gret) × (Michele Meilland × Tahiti)) × (Peace × Grand Premiere)]; int. in 1973

Velluto HMoy, dr, 1934, San Remo Exp. Sta.; bud long, pointed; flowers velvety dark crimson, stamens red, medium, semi-dbl.; intermittent bloom; foliage dark; [*R. moyesii* × J.C. Thornton]

Velour F, mr, 1967, Boerner; bud ovoid; flowers dbl., flat; foliage glossy; vigorous, upright, bushy growth; [(Garnette × unknown) × Hawaii seedling]; int. by J&P

Velours Épiscopal HCh, m, before 1908, Roseraie de l'Hay; flowers violet purple/pink, large, dbl., globular, moderate fragrance; non-remontant; some suggest it may have been introduced before 1863, but no other support found for that dating

Velours Parfumé – See **Velvet Fragrance**, HT

Velours Pourpre HGal, dr, before 1811, from Holland; flowers crimson, tending towards violet, lighter purple center, 1½-2 in., very dbl., pompon; foliage elongated; prickles numerous, small, brown

Velours Pourpre HP, m, 1866, Verdier; flowers velvety carmine with violet reflections, large, full

Velouté d'Orléans B, m, 1852, Dauvesse; flowers light purple, large, full

Velsheda HT, lp, 1936, Cant, F.; flowers softest rose-pink, well-formed, large, dbl.; foliage dark; strong, erect stems; vigorous growth

Velutina HGal, m, 1810, Van Eeden; flowers velvety purple shaded violet, golden stamens, three rows of

Veluwezoom HT, dp, 1909, Pallandt; flowers brilliant carmine passing to deep rose, large, dbl., moderate fragrance; [Mme Caroline Testout × Soleil d'Or]

Velvet Abundance – See **Red Abundance**, F

Velvet Alibi – See **Rouge Adam**, HT

Velvet Arrow HT, dr

Velvet Beauty – See **Barkhatnaia Krasavitsa**, HT

Velvet Beauty, Climbing Cl Min, dr, Bell; flowers very deep velvet red, hybrid tea; int. by Bell Roses, 2003

Velvet Beauty HT, mr, Fisher, G.; bud high pointed; flowers currant-red, 5-5½ in., 40-55 petals, high-centered, moderate clove fragrance; vigorous, upright growth; PP2100; [Happiness × New Yorker]; int. by Arnold-Fisher Co.

Velvet Cloak Min, dr, 1999, McCann, Sean; flowers burgundy red, very prominent yellow stamens, 2 in., dbl., borne mostly singly, slight fragrance; foliage medium size, medium green, semi-glossy; prickles moderate; bushy, medium (20-24 in.) growth; [Lady in Red × Ain't Misbehavin]; int. by Justice Miniature Roses, 1998

Velvet Cover – See **Burlington**, S

Velvet Dreams Min, dr, 1982, Lyon; flowers small, semi-dbl.; foliage small, medium green, semi-glossy; very miniature, upright, bushy growth; [seedling × seedling]

Velvet Flame HT, dr, 1974, Meilland; flowers 5-5½ in., 30 petals, slight fragrance; foliage dark; vigorous growth; [Tropicana × Papa Meilland]; int. by URS, 1972

Velvet Flame, Climbing Cl HT, Orard, Joseph; int. in 1981

Velvet Flower Carpet S, mr, Noack; flowers velvety red, single, shallow cup, borne in clusters, no fragrance; low (2 ft.), spreading growth; int. in 2002

Velvet Fragrance HT, dr, 1989, Fryers Nursery, Ltd.; flowers deep, velvety crimson, 4½ in., 25 petals, high-centered, intense raspberry/clove fragrance; recurrent; foliage large, dark green, semi-glossy; upright (4½ ft.) growth; [seedling × seedling]; int. in 1988; Fragrance Prize, Baden-Baden, 1990, Edland Fragrance Medal, ARS, 1987

Velvet Hour HT, dr, 1978, LeGrice; flowers oxblood-red, 3 in., 44 petals, high-centered, quilled, moderate fragrance; recurrent; foliage dark; vigorous, upright growth

Velvet Lady HT, dr, 1995, Davidson, Harvey; flowers very dark, velvet red, 5 petals, borne in small clusters; foliage medium size, dark green, very glossy; numerous prickles; spreading, medium growth; [Shining Ruby × Precious Platinum]; int. by Coiner Nursery, 1995; Silver Medal, ARCTG, 1995

Velvet Lustre – See **Happy Day**, HT

Velvet Mist HT, m, 1990, Christensen, Jack E.; flowers deep lavender, medium, 25-35 petals, high-centered, borne usually singly, moderate fruity fragrance; foliage large, medium green, matte, disease-resistant; upright, bushy, medium to tall growth; [Blue Ribbon × Shocking Blue]; int. by Jack E. christensen, 1984

Velvet Queen HT, dr, 1965, Herholdt, J.A.; flowers blood-red, pointed, 4 in.; moderate growth; [Fandango × seedling]

Velvet Robe – See **Atombombe**, HEg

Velvet Rose – See **Holoserica**, HGal

Velvet Ruby HT, mr, 1990, McGredy, Sam IV; bud small, pointed ovoid; flowers medium to dark red, reverse lighter, 11-12 cm., full, imbricated, borne singly and in small clusters, slight fragrance; recurrent; foliage large, medium green, matte; prickles ordinary, medium, slightly curved downward, brown; upright, bushy growth; PP8953; [Candella × Auckland Metro]; int. by McGredy Roses International

Velvet Ruby LCl, mr

Velvet Soft Touch HT, dr, 2001, Coiner, Jim; flowers 3½ in., semi-dbl., borne mostly solitary, no fragrance; recurrent; foliage medium size, medium green, semi-glossy; prickles numerous, small, fin-shaped; upright, vigorous, tall (5½ ft.) growth; int. by Coiner Nursery, 2001

Velvet Star LCl, mr, Barni, V.; flowers velvety red, dbl., high-centered, cupped, intense fragrance; vigorous, tall growth; int. by Rose Barni, 1998

Velvet Star HT, w, Tantau

Velvet Times HT, dr, 1960, Peters, Lincoln & Norman; bud pointed; flowers rose-red, 4½-5 in., 40-50 petals, high-centered, intense fragrance; foliage leathery; vigorous, upright growth; PP1858; [sport of Better Times]; int. by J&P, 1959

Velvet Touch Min, mr, 1993, Saville, F. Harmon; bud medium, pointed; flowers medium red, reverse darker, 1¼ in., 27-32 petals, high-centered, then flat, borne mostly singly, very slight fragrance; recurrent; foliage medium size, medium green, semi-glossy; prickles some, short, slightly curved, reddish brown; medium, bushy, compact growth; hips globular, orange; PP8919; [Rainbow's End × Acey Deucy]; int. by Nor'East Min. Roses, 1994

Velvet Treasure HT, dr; int. by J&P, 1992

Velveteen – See **Graf Lennart**, HT

Velvetier HT, dr, 1946, Brownell; bud long, pointed; flowers deep velvety red, 4-5 in., 28-35 petals, high-centered, moderate fragrance; foliage glossy; vigorous, upright growth; hardy for the class; [Pink Princess × Crimson Glory]

Velvia F, mr, 1992, Harkness, R., & Co., Ltd.; flowers 3-3½ in., full, borne in small clusters, slight fragrance; recurrent; foliage medium size, dark green, semi-glossy; some prickles; medium, bushy growth; [Dr. Darley × Trumpeter]; int. by Harkness New Roses, Ltd., 1991

Vendée Globe HT, yb, Dorieux; flowers yellow with carmine tints, large, dbl., cupped, intense fragrance; recurrent; strong, medium growth; int. by Roseraies Dorieux, 2000; Silver Medal, Rome, 2000, Gold Medal, Genoa, 2000, Gold Medal, Courtrai, 2000

Vendée Globe, Climbing Cl HT, yb, Dorieux; [sport of Vendée Globe]; int. by Roseraies Dorieux, 2005

Vendée Impériale HT, ob, Adam; flowers buff-yellow with bright orange edges, suffused down the petals when opening, large, dbl., cupped, moderate fragrance; recurrent; moderate, compact growth

Vendela HT, w, Evers, Hans J.; bud long, pointed ovoid; flowers ivory white, 4-4½ in., 30-35 petals, high-centered, borne singly, slight fragrance; recurrent; foliage large, dark green; prickles normal, medium, hooked downward; stems long, strong; vigorous, upright (6 ft.) growth; PP10999; [unnamed seedling × Tanweisa]; florist rose; int. by Tantau, 1997

Vendôme HWich, mr, 1923, Mouillère; flowers dbl., borne in clusters of 5-15; foliage dark green, glossy

Vendôme F, ob, 1958, Gaujard; bud long; flowers bright salmon, medium, dbl., moderate fragrance; foliage dark, glossy; bushy growth; [Comtesse Vandal × (Fashion × Vogue)]; int. in 1957

Vendulka F, mp, Vecera, L.; flowers large, dbl.; int. in 1974

Venere F, mp, Delbard; flowers brilliant pink, dbl., borne in clusters of 5-7; recurrent; foliage glossy, new growth red; strong (1 m.) growth; int. by Rose Barni, 1991

Venerie – See **Scouts Honor**, F

Venezuela F, op, 1959, Silva; flowers salmon, edged dull red; very vigorous growth; [Joanna Hill × Pinocchio]; int. by Booy Rose Nurs., 1957

Venice S, w, Noack; bud soft salmon-pink; flowers white, stamens golden with red base, 6 cm., single, shallow cup, borne in clusters; recurrent; foliage dark green, glossy; bushy (80-100 cm.) growth; hips decorative; int. by Noack Rosen, 2004

Venise HT, rb, 1946, Meilland, F.; flowers red with silvery white reverse flushed salmon-carmine, large, dbl.; spreading growth; [Joanna Hill × Margaret McGredy]

Venise Min, op, Adam; flowers orange-salmon, small, full, rosette, borne in clusters; recurrent; low (12-16 in.) growth; int. in 1997

Venlo F, or, 1960, Leenders, G.; bud pointed; flowers medium, semi-dbl., flat, borne in compact clusters; foliage dark; moderate, compact growth; [Cinnabar × Fashion]

Venrosa HT, mr, St Zila; flowers large, dbl.; int. in 1973

Vent des Indes F, op

Vent d'Été – See **Surrey**, S

Venture S, mp, 1984, James, John; flowers semi-dbl., borne in clusters, moderate fragrance; foliage medium size, light green, glossy; upright, slender growth; [(Charlotte Armstrong × (Cecilia × China Belle)) × Prevue]; originally registered as Pol

Venu-Vaishali HT, pb, 1970, Deshpande; bud ovoid; flowers light pink, striped white, base yellow, large, dbl.; foliage large, soft; very vigorous, upright growth; [sport of Astree]

Venus HGal, w, 1845, Vibert; flowers white with pink tints, medium to large, full

Vénus A, w, before 1846; flowers pure white, medium, full, cupped

Venus HP, dr, 1895, Kiese; flowers purple-red, large, full; [Général Jacqueminot × Princesse de Béarn]

Venus M, mr, 1904, Welter; flowers fiery red, large to very large, very full; occasional repeat; [Mme Moreau × Deuil de Paul Fontaine]; the rose in commerce today does not match older descriptions

Venus HT, dp, 1921, Bees; bud long, pointed; flowers carmine, edge flushed cream, very dbl.; [J. Barriot × Sunburst]; Gold Medal, NRS, 1922

Venus F, w, 1955, Maarse, G.; flowers pure white, well-shaped, borne in large trusses; long stems; vigorous, bushy growth; [Pinocchio × unknown]

Venus F, lp; PP10449; int. by J&P, 1997

Venus Min, yb, 2001, Ferrer, Fco.; flowers cream yellow, 2 cm., very dbl., borne mostly solitary, slight fragrance; foliage dark green; [Yellow Meillandina × seedling]; int. by Roses Noves Ferrer S.L., 2001

Venus T, m, Schmidt, J.C.; flowers carmine purple

Vénus Mère – See **Bouquet Charmant**, HGal

Venusic HT, my, 1970, Delbard-Chabert; flowers saffron-yellow, medium, dbl., cupped, moderate fragrance; foliage dark, glossy; vigorous, upright, bushy growth; [(Queen Elizabeth × Provence) × (Mme Joseph Perraud × Bayadere)]; int. in 1966

Venusta P, lp, before 1814, Descemet; flowers delicate rosy pink, very dbl.; probably extinct

Venusta A, w; flowers flesh-white, becoming yellowish-white, medium, semi-dbl.

Venusta Pendula Ayr, w; bud pink; flowers blush white, fading to creamy white, 6-8 cm., semi-dbl., borne in clusters, no fragrance; early flowering; numerous prickles; vigorous (to 15 ft.) growth; origin unknown; reintroduced by Kordes in 1928

Venustus HGal, m, about 1835, Calvert; flowers dark purple, medium, full

Vera HT, op, 1922, Paul, W.; flowers deep salmon, shaded coral-red, dbl.

Vera Allen HT, op, 1939, Dickson, A.; flowers salmon-pink, well-formed, large, dbl.; compact growth

Vera Brown F, ab, 2000, Rawlins, R.; flowers apricot, reverse pink, 5 in., full, borne in small clusters, moderate fragrance; foliage medium size, medium green, semi-glossy; prickles moderate; upright, medium (36 in.) growth; [Golden Future × Sharifa Asma]

Vera Cruz HT, pb, 1938, Moreira da Silva; bud long, pointed; flowers pink shaded mauve, flushed red and yellow, large, dbl., high-centered; foliage soft; vigorous growth; [Frank Reader × Johanniszauber]

Vera Dalton F, mp, 1961, Norman; bud pointed; flowers soft pink, 4 in., 24 petals, cupped, borne in clusters, moderate fragrance; foliage glossy, dark; vigorous, bushy growth; [(Paul's Scarlet Climber × Paul's Scarlet Climber) × (Mary × Queen Elizabeth)]; int. by Harkness

Vera Johns Gr, or, 1978, Kordes, R.; bud ovoid, pointed; flowers large, 40 petals, high-centered, slight fragrance; recurrent; foliage glossy, dark, leathery; vigorous, upright growth; [unknown × Prominent]; int. by Ludwigs Roses Pty. Ltd., 1977

Vera Johns F, ob, 1990, Kordes; buds pointed, salmon; flowers deepening to orange, dbl., high-centered, star-shaped, borne mostly singly, slight fragrance; recurrent; foliage glossy green; well-branched, medium to tall growth; int. in 1990

Vera Parker Min, mr, 2001, Parker, William David; flowers medium red, reverse lighter, 2 in., full, borne in large clusters, slight fragrance; foliage medium size, medium green, semi-glossy; prickles moderate, straight; growth bushy, medium (18-24 in.); garden decorative; [Sexy Rexy × Winsome]

Vera Roberta Carver MinFl, mp, 2005, Paul Chessum Roses; flowers dbl., borne in small clusters; foliage medium size, dark green, semi-glossy; prickles large, sharp, red, numerous; growth compact, medium (24 in.); bedding, containers; [seedling × seedling]; int. by World of Roses, 2005

Verano HT, ob; flowers orange with red petal edges and lighter reverse, high-centered; int. by Carlton Rose Nursery, 2002

Verastella HT, mp, 1958, Giacomasso; flowers rose, center deeper; strong stems; vigorous growth; int. in 1954

Verbeeka F, ob

Verbessert Mme Norbert Levavasseur – See **Verdun**, Pol

Verbesserte Tantau's Triumph – See **Cinnabar Improved**, F

Vercors HT, or, 1946, Mallerin, C.; flowers brilliant orient red, large, dbl., globular; vigorous growth; [(Mme Arthaud × Mme Henri Guillot) × (Comtesse Vandal × Brazier)]; int. by A. Meilland

Vercors – See **Savoy Hotel**, HT

Verdi HT, rb, 1960, Dorieux; bud ovoid; flowers brick-red, reverse veined darker, medium, dbl.; foliage dark, glossy; very vigorous, bushy growth; [Cafougnette × Independence]; int. by Pin, 1960

Verdi HMsk, m, 2000, Lens, Louis; flowers 2-3 cm., semi-dbl., borne in large clusters, slight fragrance; foliage medium size, dark green, glossy, disease-resistant; prickles moderate; upright, medium (100 cm.) growth; [Mr Bluebird × Violet Hood]; int. by Louis Lens N.V., 1984

Verdi HT, rb; flowers white with burgundy red edges, dbl., high-centered, borne mostly singly; recurrent; stems long; florist rose

Verdun Pol, m, 1918, Barbier; flowers vivid carmine-purple, large, dbl., globular, borne in clusters of 25-50; vigorous, dwarf growth

Verdun Superior Pol, m; flowers somewhat lighter than Verdun, and borne in larger clusters

Verena F, dr, 1975, Hetzel; bud ovoid; flowers dark velvety red, center lighter, medium, dbl., intense fragrance; foliage glossy, bluish green; upright, bushy growth; [Lucy Cramphorn × Inge Horstmann]; int. by GAWA, 1973

Vergenal HP, w

Verhaux – See **Rose Verreux**, D

Verlaine HT, w; flowers white with greenish tint

Vermilion Patio Min, or

Vermillon HT, or, 1929, Barbier; flowers scarlet tinged orange, base yellow, semi-dbl.; [Constance × Paul's Scarlet Climber]; int. by Dreer

Vermont T, mp, about 1840, Béluze; flowers carmine pink, medium, full

Vermont Vérité S, mp, 2000, Cunningham, David F.; flowers dbl., borne in large clusters, slight fragrance; foliage medium size, purplish to dark green, glossy; numerous prickles; spreading, medium growth; very hardy; [*R. macrantha* × William Baffin]; int. by White Flower Farm

Verna Mackay HT, ly, 1912, Dickson, A.; flowers buff to bright lemon-yellow, medium, dbl., borne mostly solitary

Vernon Love HP, mp, 2001, Greenwood, Chris; bud large; flowers old-fashioned, dusky pink, light pink reverse, 5-6 in., very full, borne mostly solitary, moderate fragrance; foliage large, dark green, semi-glossy; prickles few, medium, hooked downward, green; growth bushy, tall (5-6 ft.); garden decorative, exhibition; [Baronne Edmond de Rothschild × Silverado]

Verona F, lp, 1963, Swim & Weeks; bud long, pointed, conspicuous neck; flowers 2½-3 in., 32-50 petals, high-centered, borne singly and in small clusters, slight tea fragrance; abundant bloom; foliage leathery, dark green; prickles very few, medium, straight, brown; stems long for the class; vigorous, bushy growth; PP2282; [Spartan × Garnette]; greenhouse rose

Veronèse HT, mp, Richardier; flowers full, cupped; moderate (80-100 cm) growth; int. by Meilland Richardier, 2004

Veronica HT, w, 1950, Prosser; bud pale yellow; flowers snow-white, imbricated, 4½ in., 32 petals, intense fragrance; recurrent; vigorous growth

Veronica – See **Flamingo**, HT

Veronica 92 F, mp, Noack, Werner

Veronica Arnott S, my, Harkness; flowers medium yellow, outer petals fading lighter, full, cupped, moderate fragrance; medium (1 m.) growth; int. by R. Harkness & Co., 2004

Veronica Kay Min, pb, Welsh, Eric

Veronique F, mr, 1961, Delforge; flowers bright raspberry-red, 4 in., 9 petals, borne in clusters; foliage dark, glossy; vigorous, bushy growth; [Sumatra × Philippe]

Véronique B. S, op, Guillot-Masad; flowers salmon-pink in center, white outer petals, very full, cupped, intense fragrance; foliage disease-resistant; medium (80 cm.) growth; int. by Roseraie Guillot, 2002

Verrystata HT, ob, Kordes

Versailles HT, lp, 1970, Delbard-Chabert; bud ovoid; flowers soft pink, medium, dbl., cupped, slight fragrance; recurrent; foliage dark, glossy, leathery; vigorous, upright, bushy growth; [(Queen Elizabeth × Provence) × (Michele Meilland × Bayadere)]; int. in 1967; Gold Medal, Geneva, 1966, Gold Medal, Bagatelle, 1966, Gold Medal, Baden-Baden, 1965

Versailles – See **Versailles Palace**, F

Versailles S, or, Poulsen; flowers orange-red, 8-10 cm., dbl., no fragrance; growth bushy, 40-60 cm.; int. by Poulsen Roser, 2001

Versailles Blanca HT, w; int. after 1967

Versailles Palace F, or, Olesen; bud pointed ovoid; flowers more orange in greenhouse, more red outdoors, 3 in., 40-45 petals, cupped, borne in small clusters, no fragrance; recurrent; foliage large, dark green, glossy; prickles few, 5-7 mm, linear to curved; bushy (2 ft.) growth; PP11501; [(Gavno × Red Minimo) × (Red Minimo × Absolute Hit)]; int. by Poulsen, 1999

Verschuren HT, lp, Verschuren; flowers clear light pink, cupped, moderate fragrance; recurrent; foliage variegated; strong growth; int. in 1904

Verschuren's Glow Pol, mr, 1939, Verschuren; flowers medium, semi-dbl.

Verschuren's Pink HT, op, 1950, Verschuren; flowers salmon-pink with darker reflections, reflexed, 3-4 in., 42 petals, high-centered; foliage glossy, dark; very vigorous growth; [Mme Butterfly × Pink Pearl]; int. by Gregory; Gold Medal, NRS, 1949

Versigny S, ob, Guillot-Massad; flowers orange in center, orange pink outer petals, full, cupped, moderate fragrance; growth to 4 ft.; int. by Roeraie Guillot, 1998

Versilia HT, op; bud pointed, green tinted; flowers coral and apricot blend, outer petals tinted green, large, dbl., high-centered; recurrent; sturdy, medium growth; int. by NIRP, 1996

Very Busy Min, pb, 1974, Moore, Ralph S.; bud long, pointed; flowers pink and yellow, small, dbl.; foliage small, leathery; dwarf, bushy growth; [Perle d'Or × Fairy Princess]; int. by Sequoia Nursery, 1973

Very Cherry Min, mr, 1999, Walden, John K.; bud short, pointed ovoid; flowers bright red, darken with age, 2-2½ in., dbl., cupped, borne singly and in small clusters, very slight fragrance; recurrent; foliage large, medium green, glossy; prickles moderate. short, angled slightly down, brown; upright, compact, globular, medium (20-26 in.) growth; hips light green; PP12618; [seedling × New Year]; int. by Bear Creek Gardens, Inc., 1999

Vesely HT, pb

Vesenii Aromat HT, or, 1955, Klimenko, V. N.; flowers red tinted orange, base lighter, medium, 73 petals; foliage dark, glossy; very vigorous, spreading growth; [Crimson Glory × Peace]

Vesna HT, mp, Vecera, L.

Vesper F, ob, 1966, LeGrice; flowers orange, reverse burnt orange, medium, dbl., scrolled, borne in clusters, slight fragrance; recurrent; foliage small, blue-gray; moderate growth

Vesta – See **Temple d'Apollon**, HGal

Vesta – See **Feu de Vesta**, HGal

Vesta F, mr, 1946, Leenders, M.; flowers currant-red, semi-dbl.; [Irene × Donald Prior]

Vestal's Coral Gem HT, op, 1939, Vestal; flowers soft salmon-pink, reverse glowing carmine with coppery sheen, dbl.; foliage leathery, light; vigorous growth; [Betty Uprichard × unknown]

Vestal's Red HT, mr, 1937, Vestal; flowers clear red, large, dbl., cupped; foliage leathery, light; vigorous growth

Vestal's Torchlight HT, rb, 1939, Vestal; bud long, pointed; flowers red and gold, open, large, dbl.; foliage leathery, bronze; vigorous growth; [Pres. Herbert Hoover × seedling]

Vesuv F, mr, Vilmorin; flowers medium, dbl.; int. in 1963

Vésuve – See **Le Vésuve**, Ch

Vesuvia – See **Red Flower Carpet**, S

Vesuvius HT, dr, 1923, McGredy; bud long, pointed; flowers dark velvety crimson, golden stamens, large, 6 petals, cupped, moderate fragrance; recurrent; foliage light, leathery; vigorous growth

Vesuvius F, or, 1963, Vilmorin-Andrieux; flowers geranium-red, large; very vigorous growth; Gold Medal, Bagatelle, 1963

Veterans' Honor HT, dr, 1999, Zary, Dr. Keith W.; bud furled, pointed, 2 in.; flowers bright red, 5-5½ in., 25-30 petals, high-centered, borne mostly singly, slight raspberry fragrance; recurrent; foliage medium size, dark green, semi-glossy; prickles moderate; upright, spreading, tall (5 ft.) growth; [Showstopper × (seedling × Royalty)]; Rose of the Year, J&P, 2000

Véturie D, mp, 1842, Vibert; flowers rose pink, medium, full

Véturine – See **Véturie**, D

Vevey HT, my, 1953, Heizmann & Co.; flowers sun-yellow, large, dbl.

Vi Ambler HMult, m; int. in 1994

Via Mala HT, w, 1977, W. Kordes Söhne; bud long, pointed; flowers creamy white, 4 in., 33 petals, high-centered, slight fragrance; foliage glossy, dark, leathery; vigorous, upright, bushy growth; [Silver Star × Peer Gynt]

Via Romana – See **Ljuba Rizzoli**, HT

Vianden HT, pb, 1932, Ketten Bros.; flowers reddish old-rose and pink, reverse ochre-yellow and raw sienna, 90-100 petals; vigorous, bushy growth; [George C. Waud × Ruth]

Viborg F, dy, Poulsen; flowers deep yellow, 8-10 cm., full, cupped, borne in clusters, slight wild rose fragrance; recurrent; foliage dark green, glossy; bushy, medium (60-100 cm.) growth; int. by Poulsen Roser, 2000

Vice-President Curtis – See **Autumn Queen**, HT

Vice Versa MinFl, rb, 2006, Tucker, Robbie; flowers red, reverse white, 1 in., dbl., borne mostly solitary; foliage medium size, medium green, glossy; prickles ½-¾ in., curving downward, red to brown, moderate; growth compact, medium (to 30 in.); exhibition, cut flower, landscape; [seedling × Soroptimist International]; int. by Rosemania, 2007

Viceroy Gr, dp, 1997, Brown, Ted; flowers medium, dbl., borne in large clusters; foliage medium size, dark green, glossy; growth upright, medium (4½ ft.); [Esprit × Harmonie]

Vicki Buck F, yb, Hiroshima; int. by Hiroshima Bara-en, 1996

Vicki Kennedy HT, pb, 1976, Murray & Hawken; bud globular; flowers deep rose-pink, center yellow, 4 in., 53 petals; foliage large, bronze, upright, bushy growth; [Queen Elizabeth × Red Lion]; int. by Rasmussen's

Vickie Thorne HT, lp, 1972, Thorne; flowers 4-4½ in., 25 petals; foliage dark; vigorous growth; [sport of Prima Ballerina]

Vick's Caprice HP, pb, 1891, Vick; flowers lilac-rose, striped white and carmine, large, dbl., cupped, moderate fragrance; repeat bloom; upright, medium growth; [sport of Archiduchesse Elisabeth d'Autriche]

Vicky HT, or, 1978, Gaujard; bud long, pointed; flowers orange-vermilion, moderate fragrance; [Canasta × Peace]; int. in 1972

Vicky F, or, Noack, Werner; int. by Noack Rosen, 1994; ADR, 1993

Vicky Brown HT, rb; int. by Select, 1994

Vicky I S, mp, 2001, Horner, Colin P.; flowers dbl., borne in large clusters, moderate fragrance; foliage very large, dark green, very glossy, tough; prickles few, small, curved; growth upright, bushy, tall (160 cm.); garden decorative; [(Baby Love × Flower Carpet) × Liliana]; int. by Battersby Roses, 2003

Vicky Marfá HT, mp, 1959, Dot, Simon; bud ovoid; flowers begonia-pink, center yellow, large, 32 petals, high-centered, moderate fragrance; strong stems; upright, compact growth; [(Soraya × Ellinor LeGrice) × Henri Mallerin]; int. in 1958

Vicomte de Lauzières HP, m, 1889, Liabaud; flowers purplish red, very large, full, cupped; recurrent; foliage dark green; growth erect

Vicomte Fritz de Cussy B, me, 1845, Margottin; sepals narrow and long; flowers cherry red, tinged with purple, 7-8 cm., very dbl.; foliage dark green, deeply toothed; prickles large, slightly hooked, light red

Vicomte Maison HP, mr, 1868, Fontaine; flowers cherry-red, large, full

Vicomte Maurice de Mellon HT, ab, 1921, Ketten Bros.; flowers apricot and yellowish-salmon with coppery reflexes, washed pink, dbl.; [Earl of Warwick × Sunburst]

Vicomte Vigier HP, dr, 1861, Verdier, V.; flowers dark red, shaded violet, large, full

Vicomtesse d'Avesnes N, mp, 1848, Roeser; flowers light salmon-rose, 3 cm., full, borne in clusters; recurrent; growth to 3-4 ft.

Vicomtesse de Bernis T, op, 1884, Nabonnand, G.; flowers coppery rose to fawn and deep salmon, large, dbl.

Vicomtesse de Chabannes HWich, rb, 1921, Buatois; flowers purplish crimson, center white, forming a distinct eye, 5-6 cm., semi-dbl., borne in small clusters, moderate fruity fragrance; foliage dark green, glossy; vigorous, climbing growth

Vicomtesse de Grassin T, pb, 1899, Levrard; flowers carmine, striped lighter pink

Vicomtesse de Montesquieu HP, op, 1861, Quétier

Vicomtesse de Vautier – See **Vicomtesse de Wauthier**, T

Vicomtesse de Vezins HP, mp, 1867, Gautreau; flowers bright glossy pink, large, full

Vicomtesse de Wauthier T, rb, 1886, Bernaix; bud long; flowers bright carmine red, center and reverse silver rose, large, full

Vicomtesse d'Hautpoul T, w, 1881, Brassac; flowers white with salmon, large, very full

Vicomtesse Laure de Gironde HP, mp, 1852, Pradel; flowers clear delicate pink, medium, full

Vicomtesse Marie de Bourges – See **Comtesse Marie de Bourges**, HP

Vicomtesse Pierre du Fou Cl HT, op, 1923, Sauvageot, H.; flowers red aging to deep coral pink, 3-4 in., dbl., borne singly or in small clusters, intense fragrance; recurrent bloom; foliage large, glossy, bronze; vigorous, climbing growth; [L'Ideal × Joseph Hill]

Vicomtesse R. de Savigny T, pb, 1899, Guillot; flowers varying from dark China pink to deep dawn pink, base yellowish-white, large, full, moderate fragrance

Victoire Fontaine B, m, 1882, Fontaine; flowers satiny purple pink, medium to large, very full

VIctoire Modeste HBc, pb, before 1835, Guérin; flowers yellowish-pink, large, full

Victor HT, dp, 1918, E.G. Hill, Co.; bud long, pointed; flowers deep rose, often red, semi-dbl.; [(Ophelia × unknown) × Killarney Brilliant]

Victor Borge HT, ob, Olesen; bud medium, pointed ovoid; flowers orange-pink, yellow reverse, 9-11 cm., 40-50 petals, high-centered, borne singly, moderate piquant fragrance; recurrent; foliage medium size, dark green, leathery, semi-glossy; prickles some, short, wing-shaped, curved downward; upright, vigorous, medium growth; PP9357; [unnamed seedling × seedling]; int. by Poulsen Roser, 1991; Certificate of Merit, Belfast, 1992

Victor-Emmanuel B, dr, 1859, Guillot père; flowers velvety black carmine, ruffled, large, dbl., rosette to quartered, intense fragrance; recurrent; growth to 130 cm.

Victor Ferrant HT, dp, 1933, Ketten Bros.; flowers carmine changing to purplish pink, base Indian yellow, very, 60-70 petals; vigorous growth; [C.W. Cowan × Pres. Cherioux]

Victor Hugo HCh, m, about 1840; flowers lilac-pink, very large, full, globular

Victor Hugo HP, dr, 1885, Schwartz, J.; flowers carmine-red shaded purple, medium, 30 petals, globular, moderate fragrance; recurrent; vigorous growth; [Charles Lefebvre × unknown]

Victor Hugo – See **Senator Burda**, HT

Victor le Bihan HP, mp, 1868, Guillot père; flowers bright carmine pink, very large, full; recurrent; moderate growth

Victor Lemoine HP, dr, 1888, Lévêque; flowers dard red nuanced purple, brown, and violet, large, dbl.; foliage dark green

Victor Magnin Pol, mr, 1930, Van Gelderen; flowers bright red, dbl., borne in large clusters; vigorous growth

Victor Mayer HT, dr, 1921, Buatois; bud long, pointed; flowers blood-red, reflexes deeper

Victor Morlot HP, mr, 1906, Chauvry; flowers velvety scarlet, becoming poppy red, shaded darker red, very large, very full, moderate fragrance

Victor Parmentier HGal, mp, before 1847, Parmentier; flowers medium, dbl., cupped to flat, borne singly and in small clusters, moderate fragrance; non-remontant; upright (1 m.), arching growth

Victor Pulliat T, ly, 1870, Ducher; bud long; flowers pale yellow, medium, full, flat, borne in small clusters; [Mme Mélanie Willermoz × unknown]

Victor Teschendorff HT, w, 1920, Ebeling; flowers almost pure white on pale greenish yellow ground, very large, dbl., high-centered; foliage glossy, dark; long stems; vigorous growth; [Frau Karl Druschki × Mrs Aaron Ward]; int. by Teschendorff

Victor Veladin T, w; flowers lemon-white, large, with very large petals, somewhat nodding, moderate fragrance; recurrent

Victor Verdier B, mr, 1852, Dorisy

Victor Verdier HP, dp, 1859, Lacharme, F.; flowers bright rose, center carmine, reverse lighter, large, 50 petals, globular, moderate fragrance; vigorous growth; [Jules Margottin × Safrano]; arguably the first Hybrid Tea

Victor Verdier, Climbing Cl HP, mp, 1871, Paul, G.; [sport of Victor Verdier]

Victor Verne HP, mr, 1871, Damaizin; flowers currant red, large, full

Victor Waddilove HT, dp, 1923, McGredy; bud long, pointed; flowers bright carmine-pink, base yellow, large, very dbl.

Victoria – See **Antoinette**, A

Victoria HFt, yb, before 1846, Guérin; flowers salmon blush, buff center, large, semi-dbl., cupped

Victoria HT, dp, 1924, Prince; bud long, pointed; flowers deep rose-pink, center darker, dbl.; [Isobel × unknown]

Victoria F, pb, 1946, Leenders, M.; flowers carmine, center white, large, semi-dbl.; [Irene × Donald Prior]

Victoria HT, ly, 1947, Robinson, H.; flowers pale lemon-yellow, large, moderate fragrance; foliage dark green; vigorous growth; [Golden Dawn × Phyllis Gold]; int. by Baker's Nursery

Victoria – See **Victoria de los Angeles**, HT

Victoria – See **Glad Tidings**, F

Victoria HT, lp; int. by Le Jardin de Florimon, 2003

Victoria Cl F, or, Moreira da Silva; flowers clear geranium-red; [seedling × Alain]

Victoria de los Angeles HT, or, 1952, Dot, Pedro; bud ovoid; flowers velvety geranium-red, medium, 35 petals; vigorous, compact growth; [Cynthia × Manuelita]

Victoria Girls S, my, Taschner, Ludwig; flowers clear yellow, dbl., globular, to shallow cup, borne mostly singly; recurrent; foliage glossy green, disease-resistant; vigorous, neat, medium growth; int. by Poulsen, 1997

Victoria Gold F, my, Welsh; bud deep golden yellow; flowers bright yellow, petals can be edged deeper, medium, dbl., shallow cup, borne in clusters, moderate fragrance; recurrent; foliage dark green, glossy; moderate (2-3 ft.) growth; one report says Gold Bunny is one of parents; int. in 1999

Victoria Harrington HT, rb, 1931, Thomas; flowers very dark red shaded orange-brown, center lighter, large, full, intense spicy fragrance; recurrent; foliage leathery, dark; vigorous growth; [Diadem × Hadley]; int. by H&S

Victoria Harrington, Climbing Cl HT, rb, 1938, Mordigan Evergreen Nursery

Victoria Hyland HT, op, 1976, Golik; bud ovoid; flowers red-pink to coral, 4 in., 34 petals, moderate fruity fragrance; foliage glossy; moderate, compact growth; [seedling × Colour Wonder]; int. by Dynarose, 1973

Victoria Park HT, op, Pink; flowers salmon-pink, dbl., high-centered, borne singly; recurrent; int. in 1994

Victoria Regina HT, yb, 1938, Hillock; flowers golden yellow, reverse brownish yellow, sometimes blushed peach, 40 petals; vigorous, compact growth; [Nellie E. Hillock × Golden Dawn]

Victorian Charm S, lp, Clements, John; flowers 4 in., 50-60 petals, cupped to flat, borne in large clusters; recurrent; foliage glossy, oval shaped, dark green; stems long; vigorous (5 ft.) growth; PPAF; int. by Heirloom Roses, 2000

Victorian Gold HMsk, my, Clements, John; flowers double; upright, spreading growth; int. by Heirloom Roses, 2004

Victorian Lace HT, w, 1995, Marciel, Stanley G.; flowers 1½-2½ in., full, borne mostly singly, no fragrance; foliage medium size, medium green, semi-glossy; some prickles; tall (60 in.), upright growth; [unnamed seedling × seedling]; int. by Young's American Rose Nursery, 1995

Victorian Spice F, lp, 1999, Harkness, Robert & Philip; flowers soft peach pink, old-fashioned, 3½-4 in., very dbl., cupped, borne in large clusters, intense damask fragrance; recurrent; foliage medium size, dark green, glossy; prickles moderate; spreading, mounding, bushy, medium (3½ ft.) growth; Fragrance Award, Paris, 1991, Fragrance Award, Glasgow, 1998, Edlund Fragrance Award, RNRS, 1992

Victoriana F, ob, 1976, LeGrice; flowers orange, reverse silver, 5 in., 28 petals, slight anise fragrance; foliage dark green; compact, low to medium growth; int. in 1977

Victoria's Pride S, mp, Lassig, Rob; flowers medium pink, outer petals fade lighter, 4-5 cm., dbl., cupped to loose, borne in clusters of 5-15; recurrent; thornless; strong (4 ft.) growth; int. by Trewallyn Nursery, 2004

Victoria's Secret HT, w, Martin; int. by Rasmussen's Nursery, 2003

Victoria's Song HT, w, 1997, Ortega, Carlos; flowers large, dbl., borne mostly singly; foliage medium size, medium green,semi-glossy; upright, tall (6½-7ft.) growth; [Moonlight × seedling]; int. by Aebi Nursery

Victorine HT, w, 2002, McCall, Sharan; flowers cream with pink blush, white reverse, 5 in., dbl., borne mostly solitary, moderate fragrance; foliage medium size, medium green, semi-glossy; prickles moderate, ¼ in., slanting downwards; growth upright, tall (5 ft.); garden decorative, exhibition; [Thriller × Dorothy Anne]

Victorine Helfenbein HP, mp, 1850, Guillot; flowers bluish pink, medium, full

Victorine la Couronnée HGal, pb, before 1811; bud round; flowers light pink, striped red, medium, full, slight fragrance; foliage nearly round, deeply serrated; nearly thornless; Agathe group

Victory HWich, dp, 1918, Undritz; flowers deep pink, center darker, 7-8 cm., dbl., borne in small clusters, moderate fragrance; foliage glossy; numerous prickles; vigorous, climbing growth; [Dr. W. Van Fleet × Mme Jules Grolez]

Victory HT, dr, 1920, McGredy; flowers scarlet-crimson, dbl.; Gold Medal, NRS, 1919

Victory Min, mr; flowers medium red, medium, dbl., moderate fragrance; foliage dark; growth narrow, bushy, 20-40 cm.; int. by Poulsen, 1996

Victory Parade – See **Victory**, Min

Victory Red HT, dp, 1939, Elliott; flowers rose-red; [sport of Pink Delight]

Victory Rose HP, mp, 1901, Dingee-Conard

Victory Stripe HT, rb, 1942, Grillo; flowers cerise-red variegated white and light pink, 5 in., 50 petals; [sport of Jewel]

Victory Year S, mp, 1951, Wright, Percy H.; bud ovoid; flowers clear pink, open, medium, semi-dbl.; profuse, non-recurrent bloom; foliage leathery; very vigorous, upright growth; [Betty Bland × unknown]

Vida Beglan F, ly, 1993, Beglan, M.; flowers lemon yellow with very small traces of salmon, medium, full, borne in small clusters, intense fragrance; foliage medium size, medium green, matte; numerous prickles; medium (90 cm.), upright growth; [sport of Elizabeth of Glamis]; int. by Beglan, 1992

Vidal Sassoon – See **Spiced Coffee**, HT

Vidiago HT, mr, 1962, Dot, Simon; flowers currant-red, reverse geranium-red, large, 26 petals; very vigorous growth; [Baccará × (S'Agaro × Peace)]

Vidyut F, dp, 1984, Yadava, U.N.; flowers deep pink; [sport of Europeana]; int. by Tata Electric Co., 1983

Vie en Rose – See **Rosy Life**, HT

Vie en Rose F, lp, 1994, Kameyama, Yasushi; flowers bright pink, white reverse, medium, semi-dbl., borne in large clusters, moderate fragrance; foliage medium size, medium green, semi-glossy; some prickles; medium, spreading growth; [Charleston × Friesia]; int. by Kameyama, 1991

Vienna Charm HT, ob, 1963, Kordes, R.; bud large, pointed; flowers coppery, orange, 6 in., 27-35 petals, high-centered, borne singly and several together, moderate tea fragrance; recurrent; foliage dark green, leathery; prickles ordinary, short, hooked downward; stems long, strong; vigorous, tall growth; PP2550; [Chantré × Golden Sun]; int. by McGredy, 1963

Vienna Charm, Climbing Cl HT, ob, 1972, Gandy, Douglas L.; int. by Gandy Roses, Ltd.

Vienna Maid F, my, 1958, deRuiter; flowers empire-yellow, 2½ in., 30 petals, borne in large clusters; foliage dark, glossy; moderately bushy growth; int. by Blaby Rose Gardens, 1957

Vienna Woods – See **Wienerwald**, HT

Vierge – See **Alba Semi-plena**, A

Vierge – See **Rose des Peintres**, C

Vierge HSpn, w, 1820, Prévost

Vierge de Cléry – See **Vierge**, HSpn

Vierge de Cléry C, w, 1888, Baron-Veillard; sepals long; flowers pure white, medium to large, full, cupped; foliage medium green, large; prickles moderate; sometimes thought to be synonymous with White Provence, but it is not

Vierge Folle – See **My Fifi**, S single

Vierge Ivryenne HT, w, 1909, Lévêque; flowers pure white with yellow tints, large, full

Vierlanden – See **Pink Delight**, HT

Vierländerin F, mp, 1983, Kordes, W.; flowers medium salmon-pink, large, 35 petals; foliage medium size, medium green, matte; upright growth; [(Zorina × Zorina) × Rosenelfe]; int. by Kordes Roses, 1982

Vieux Chateau Certan F, ab, Dorieux; int. by Roseraies Dorieux, 1994

View Pol, dp, 1986, Lens, Louis; flowers deep pink, 2 in., 7-15 petals, borne in clusters of 3-32, no fragrance; foliage greenish-brown; prickles hooked, brown; low, bushy growth; [Britannia × *R. multiflora*]; int. in 1980; Gold Medal, The Hague, 1978

Vif Eclat HMsk, mr, 2000, Lens, Louis; flowers bright red with white eye and yellow stamens, 2 cm., single, cupped, borne in large, pyramidal clusters; recurrent; foliage medium size, medium green, semi-glossy, disease-resistant; prickles moderate; upright, medium (60-80 cm.) growth; hedge, border; [(*R. multiflora adenocheata* × Ballerina) × Ravel]; int. by Louis Lens N.V., 1992

Vigane HT, rb, 1962, Buyl Frères; flowers red and light yellow bicolor, dbl.

Vigilance Min, w, 1995, Williams, Ernest; flowers 1½-1¾ in., full, borne in small clusters, no fragrance; foliage medium size, medium green, glossy; numerous prickles; spreading (6 ft.), climbing growth; [sport of Jeanne Lajoie]; int. by Texas Mini Roses, 1995

Vigilant HT, dr, 1941, Clark, A.; flowers very dark red; [Night × unknown]

Vigo F, Moreira da Silva, A.

Vigoro HT, op, 1958, Dot, Pedro; flowers salmon-pink, large, 30 petals, high-centered, moderate fragrance; foliage clear green; very vigorous, upright, compact growth; [Ophelia × Federico Casas]; int. in 1953

Vigorosa S, pb, Wagner, S.; bud short; flowers medium sized, 12 petals, flat, moderate fragrance; foliage medium-large, dark green, semi-glossy; [(Frankfurt am Main × Maria Callas) × Dr Faust]; int. by Res. Stn. f. Horticulture, Cluj, 1994

Viking HT, dr, 1965, Moro; bud large, pointed ovoid; flowers crimson, 4½-5½ in., 45-50 petals, high-centered, becoming flat, borne singly, moderate fragrance; recurrent; foliage leathery, dark green; prickles numerous, medium, hooked downward; stems long, strong; vigorous, upright growth; hips globular, scarlet, with conspicuous neck; PP2333; [Volcano × Happiness]; int. by Ball Seed Co.

Viking – See **Rody**, S

Viking Princess – See **Countess Celeste**, S

Viking Queen LCl, mp, 1965, Phillips; flowers medium to deep pink, 3-4 in., 60 petals, globular, borne singly or in small clusters, intense fragrance; recurrent bloom; foliage dark, glossy, leathery; vigorous growth; [White Dawn × L.E. Longley]; int. by Farmer Seed and Nursery, 1963

Viktoria Adelheid HT, yb, 1932, Kordes; flowers golden yellow edged and shaded nasturtium-red, large, dbl.; foliage leathery, glossy; dwarf growth; [Charles P. Kilham × Mev. G.A. van Rossem]

Vilia F, op, 1960, Robinson, H.; flowers bright coral-pink, 2½ in., single, borne in large clusters; foliage dark, glossy; moderate growth; int. by Gregory; Gold Medal, NRS, 1958

Villa de Bilbao HT, mr, 1933, La Florida; flowers cardinal-red, large, dbl., cupped; vigorous growth; [O. Junyent × Margaret McGredy]

Villa de Madrid HT, or, 1965, Dot, Pedro; flowers vermilion-red to poppy-red, large, 60 petals, moderate musk fragrance; strong stems; upright growth; PP2462; [Baccará × Peace]; int. by C-P; Gold Medal, Madrid, 1961

Villa de Sitges HT, op, 1930, Munné, B.; flowers pink shaded salmon; very vigorous, spreading growth; [Frau Karl Druschki × Mme Edouard Herriot]

Villa des Tybilles HRg, mr, 1899, Gravereaux; flowers large, single

Villa Pia HT, dr, 1926, Leenders Bros.; bud long, pointed; flowers velvety deep red, almost black, dbl.; [Pres. Vignet × Château de Clos Vougeot]

Villa Rosa LCl, dp, 2002, Eve, André; flowers deep pink, lighter reverse, medium, dbl., borne in small clusters, slight fragrance; recurrent; foliage medium size, medium green, glossy; prickles moderate; tall (4-5 m.) growth; int. by Les Roses Anciennes de Andre Eve, 2004

Villa Rosa HT, op, Taschner, Ludwig; bud pointed, coral pink; flowers salmon-pink, large, dbl., high-centered, star-shaped, borne mostly singly; recurrent; stems strong; tall, sturdy growth; int. by Ludwig's Roses, 2005

Village Charm HMult, lp, McLeod, J.; int. in 1990

Village de Taradeau F, lp, RvS-Melle; [Kanegem × Sonja]; int. by RVS Melle, 1995

Village Festival – See **Piñata**, LCl

Village Lass Min, mr; flowers deep, rich cherry red, moderate fragrance; short growth

Village Maid – See **La Rubanée**, HGal

Villandessa HT, ob, 1978, W. Kordes Söhne; bud long, pointed; flowers orange-blend, 4½ in., 33 petals, high-centered; vigorous, upright, bushy growth; [Peer Gynt × seedling]; int. by Willemse, 1977

Villaret de Joyeuse HP, mp, 1874, Damaizin; flowers bright pink, shaded darker, very large, full, moderate fragrance

Ville d'Angers HT, mr, 1934, Delaunay; bud long, pointed; flowers pure currant-red, large, semi-dbl., cupped; foliage leathery, dark; vigorous, bushy growth; [Souv. de Georges Pernet × Souv. de Claudius Denoyel]

Ville d'Arcis sur Aube HT, op, Vially

Ville d'Asnières S, ob, Croix; flowers orange-red with silvery cast to reverse, spiral; free-flowering; foliage disease-resistant; int. by Roseraie Paul Croix, 2000; Silver Medal, Buenos Aires, 2000

Ville de Bâle – See **Rustica**, F

Ville de Bar sur Seine HT, my, Orard; int. by Ets Orard, 1996

Ville de Bordeaux HT, dr, 1955, Privat; bud long; flowers dark scarlet-red, dbl.; very vigorous growth

Ville de Brest HT, or, 1942, Gaujard; flowers fiery orange veined reddish-copper, medium, semi-dbl., globular; foliage bronze, glossy; vigorous growth

Ville de Bruxelles – See **La Ville de Bruxelles**, D

Ville de Chalons HT, or, 1938, Champion; flowers reddish-orange shaded darker, dbl.

Ville de Chine – See **Chinatown**, F

Ville de Doué F

Ville de Gand HT, op, 1951, Gaujard; flowers deep salmon, well-formed, large, 25 petals; foliage bronze; very vigorous, upright growth; [(Georges Chesnel × unknown) × ((Mme Joseph Perraud × unknown) × *R. foetida bicolor*)]; Gold Medal, Geneva, 1950

Ville de Grenoble HT, mr, 1927, Mallerin, C.; flowers clear scarlet, large, 30-40 petals, high-centered, slight spicy fragrance; foliage thick; very vigorous growth; [Capt. F. Bald × Mme Van de Voorde]; int. as Grenoble, C-P, 1931

Ville de Liffre HT, dp, Adam; flowers clear, strong pink, large, dbl., high-centered, intense fragrance; vigorous (100-150 cm.) growth

Ville de Londres HGal, dp, 1850, Vibert or Robert

Ville de Lorgues F, pb, RvS-Melle; [seedling × Pernille Poulsen]; int. in 1992; Gold Medal, Baden-Baden, 1991

Ville de Lyon HP, mp, 1866, Ducher; flowers metallic rose and wilvery-white, large, full

Ville de Malines HT, yb, 1929, Lens; bud long, pointed, yellow shaded cherry-red; flowers orange to pink shaded yellow, large, full; vigorous growth

Ville de Moulins HT, mr, Orard

Ville de Nancy HT, pb, 1940, Gillot, F.; bud long, pointed, old-rose shaded gold; flowers buff-pink, edges penciled white, reverse light pink, base yellow, 50-55 petals, cupped; foliage leathery, dark; vigorous, upright growth; [Souv. de Claudius Pernet × Federico Casas]; int. by C-P

Ville de Paris HT, my, 1925, Pernet-Ducher; flowers clear bright yellow, large, dbl., globular; foliage reddish green, glossy; vigorous, growth; [Souv. de Claudius Pernet × seedling]; Gold Medal, Bagatelle, 1925

Ville de Paris, Climbing Cl HT, my, 1935, Armstrong, J.A. (also Cognet)

Ville de Prague HT, or, 1940, Chambard, C.; bud long, bright coral-red; flowers scarlet and copper, very large; foliage bright green; bushy growth; int. by Orard

Ville de Roanne HT, Dorieux; int. in 1966

Ville de Romilly Sur Seine HT, ob, Orard; int. in 1994

Ville de Saint Denis HP, mp, 1853, Thomas; flowers rosey carmine, large, full, globular; [sport or seedling of La Reine]

Ville de St Maur Ayr, w, 1909, Denis; flowers medium, borne in corymbs; stems very flexile

Ville de Saverne HT, or, 1937, Heizmann, E.; flowers orange-scarlet, tinted brownish red, reverse tinted yellow, dbl.

Ville de Toulouse HGal, pb, 1876, Brassac; flowers carmine pink, reverse near white, medium, full, loosely quartered, slight fragrance; non-remontant

Ville de Troyes HT, dr

Ville de Valenciennes HT, or, 1954, Gaujard; flowers orange-copper, well-formed, very large, dbl.; vigorous growth; [Peace × seedling]

Ville de Villeurbanne HT, op, Guillot; flowers strong pink with lemon-cream reverse, large, dbl., turbinate, moderate fragrance; moderate (4 ft.) growth

Ville de Zurich F, or, 1970, Gaujard; flowers well-formed, 25 petals, moderate fragrance; foliage bright green; vigorous, bushy growth; [Miss France × Nouvelle Europe]; int. by Roseraies Gaujard, 1967

Ville d'Ettelbruck S, dr, 1986, Lens, Louis; flowers deep red, 2 in., 20 petals, borne in clusters of 5-18, moderate fruity fragrance; foliage dark, leathery; prickles hooked, green; upright, bushy growth; [Satchmo × Skyrocket]; int. in 1983; Bronze Medal, Baden-Baden, 1982

Ville du Havre HT, w, 1931, Cayeux, H.; flowers cream-white, washed rose-pink, base yellow, very dbl.; foliage dark; very vigorous growth; [Kitchener of Khartoum × Souv. de Claudius Pernet]; int. by Turbat

Ville du Perreux F, pb, 1989, Delbard & Chabert; flowers pink with white and cream, long, large, 28 petals; foliage bright; bushy, vigorous growth; [seedling × (Milrose × Legion d'Honneur)]; int. in 1988

Ville du Roeulx F, dp, RvS-Melle; flowers dark pink with lighter shadings, 6 cm., 19 petals, borne in clusters; strong (2.5 ft.) growth; [Melflor × Esperanza]; int. in 1990; Gold Medal, Geneve, 1989, Gold Medal, Bagatelle, 1990

Vilmorin M, lp, about 1805, Vilmorin; flowers pale blush pink, medium to large, full, cupped

Vilmorin – See **Unique Carnée**, C

Vim HT, mp, 1963, Wyant; bud pointed; flowers pink, medium, single; moderate bloom; foliage soft; moderate, bushy growth; [Charlotte Armstrong × Applause]

Vin Rosé HT, mp, 1969, Boerner; bud long, pointed; flowers light coral-pink, large, 30-35 petals, high-centered; foliage glossy; vigorous, upright growth; PP3018;

[Revelry × Hawaii]; int. by J&P

Vince Butterworth F, rb, 2006, Rawlins, Ronnie; flowers red, reverse gold, 2½ in., full, borne in small clusters; foliage medium size, dark green, glossy; prickles ½ in., triangle, moderate; growth upright, tall (48 in.); garden decoration; [Chinatown × Ingrid Bergman]; int. in 2006

Vincent Godsiff Ch, mr; flowers deep luminous rosy-red, yellow stamens, 2 in., 10 petals, cupped; foliage dark; compact, upright (to 3 ft.) growth; discovered in Bermuda.

Vincent-Hippolyte Duval HP, mp, 1879, Duval, H.; flowers bright carmine pink, large, full

Vincent van Gogh Pol, or, 1969, Buisman, G. A. H.; bud ovoid; flowers medium, dbl., cupped, borne in clusters; recurrent; foliage dark; [Allotria × Hobby]

Vincente Peluffo HP, mr, 1902, Lévêque; flowers light cerise pink nuanced darker, very large, dbl.; very remontant

Vincenz Bergers Weisse HT, w, 1943, Berger, V.; bud long, pointed, sulphur; flowers open, very large, dbl., high-centered; foliage glossy, bronze; very vigorous, upright growth; [Mrs Sam McGredy × seedling]; int. by Kordes

Vindonissa F, rb, Huber; flowers bright cerise with yellow eye and reverse, 8 cm., 21-30 petals, cupped, borne singly and in clusters; recurrent; foliage green, matte; upright (2 ft.), bushy growth; int. by Richard Huber, 1986

Vinesse F, op, Noack; flowers pink with orange and apricot tones, fading to yellow-orange, 6 cm., dbl., cupped, borne in clusters; recurrent; foliage dark green, glossy; moderate (2 ft.) growth; int. by Noack Rosen, 2002

Vineyard Song S, m, 1999, Moore, Ralph S.; flowers 1-1½ in., dbl., borne in large clusters, moderate fragrance; foliage dark green, glossy; some prickles; medium (12-16 in.) growth; [Seedling × Self]; int. by Sequoia Nursery, 1999

Vino Delicado HT, m, 1973, Raffel; bud long, pointed; flowers mauve, edged purple-red, well-formed, large, dbl., slight incense fragrance; recurrent; foliage large, leathery; upright, strong growth; [seedling × Mauve Melodee]; int. by Port Stockton Nursery, 1972

Vino Rosso HT, rb, Tantau; bud pointed ovoid; flowers bordeaux-red, reverse pink, slow opening, 4½ in., 29 petals, high-centered, globular, borne singly, slight red wine fragrance; recurrent; foliage large, dark green, leathery; prickles numerous on main canes, few on laterals, straight, brown; stems long, strong; upright (110 cm.), bushy growth; no hips; PP15628; [seedling × seedling]; int. by Rosen-Tantau, 2002

Vinoca HT, mp, 1906, Amaury-Fonseca

Vintage Visalia F, mp, 1992, Moore, Ralph S.; flowers pink, reverse of outer petals deeper pink than inside surface, large, very dbl., borne mostly singly, slight fragrance; foliage large, medium green, semi-glossy; few prickles; medium (50-60 cm.), upright, bushy growth; [Pink Petticoat × Lulu]; int. by Sequoia Nursery, 1993

Vintage Wine Cl HT, rb, 1983, Poulsen, Niels D.; flowers burgundy red, straw-yellow reverse, large, 40 petals, high-centered, slight old rose fragrance; foliage large, moss green; prickles red when new, then tan; pillar (8-10 ft.) growth; [Royal Dane × Arthur Bell]; int. by Roses by Fred Edmunds, 1983

Vinzens Berger's Weisse – See **Vincenz Bergers Weisse**, HT

Viola HT, m, 1956, Gaujard; flowers lilac-pink, very large, dbl., intense fragrance; foliage leathery; vigorous, upright growth; [Orange Triumph × (Peace × unknown)]

Viola HT, m, Ghosh, Mr. & Mrs. S.; flowers deep mauve with reddish petal edges, large, full, high-centered, borne mostly singly; recurrent; stems strong; int. in 1998

Viola Lougheed Gr, pb, 1997, Lougheed, Larry; flowers large, very dbl., borne in large clusters; foliage medium size, medium green, semi-glossy; numerous prickles; tall, spreading growth; [Pristine × Peter Frankenfeld]; int. by Lougheed Roses International

Violacea – See **La Belle Sultane**, HGal

Violacée M, m, 1876, Soupert & Notting; flowers purple, shaded violet to grayish pink, large, dbl.

Violacée – See **Purpurea**, (*R. roxburghii* hybrid)

Violaine HT, m, 1968, Gaujard; bud long, pointed; flowers large, dbl., high-centered; foliage leathery; tall, vigorous growth; [Eminence × Simone]; int. by Ilgenfritz Nursery

Violante S, Michler, K. H.; int. in 1991

Viola's Diamond Gr, w, 2004, Williams, J. Benjamin; flowers white, reverse white, 3-3½ in., dbl., borne in small clusters, moderate fragrance; foliage medium size, medium green, semi-glossy, disease-resistant; prickles few, small, curved down, light tan; growth spreading, vigorous, medium; border, hedge, garden; [Mount Shasta × Sea Foam]; int. in 2004

Violet – See **Violet Hit**, MinFl

Violet Bengal – See **Reversa**, Bslt

Violet Bengal – See **Purple Bengal**, Ch

Violet Blue – See **Veilchenblau**, HMult

Violet Brillant – See **Rouge Formidable**, HGal

Violet Carson F, op, 1964, McGredy, Sam IV; flowers peach-pink, reverse silvery, well-formed, 35 petals, borne in large clusters, moderate fragrance; foliage dark, glossy; compact, bushy growth; [Mme Léon Cuny × Spartan]; int. by McGredy

Violet Dawson HT, m, 1991, Sheldon, John & Jennifer; flowers mauve blend, medium, full, borne in small clusters, moderate fragrance; foliage medium size, dark green, disease-resistant; medium, bushy growth; winter hardy; [Paradise × seedling]

Violet Fontaine S, m, 1972, Tantau, Math.; bud ovoid; flowers violet-purple, large, dbl.; abundant, continuous bloom; foliage large, soft; vigorous, upright, bushy growth; [unknown × unknown]; int. by Ahrens & Sieberz

Violet Hit MinFl, m; flowers 5-8 cm., no fragrance; foliage dark; growth bushy, 40-60 cm.; PP10164; int. by Poulsen, 1995

Violet Hood S, m, 1979, Lens, Louis; bud ovoid; flowers dark violet, 1 in., 18 petals, pompon, intense fragrance; recurrent; foliage ribbed, brownish; very vigorous, overhanging growth; [Robin Hood × Baby Faurax]; int. in 1976

Violet Liddell HT, pb, 1904, Schwartz, A.; flowers light pink to white, center and reverse coppery salmon

Violet Messenger LCl, lp, 1973, Cadle's Roses; flowers shell-pink, base yellow, reflexed, 6 in., 30 petals, intense fragrance; foliage large, matte green; [Spek's Yellow, Climbing × Masquerade]; int. in 1974

Violet Mist MinFl, m, 1993, Bennett, Dee; flowers pale soft lavender, medium, full, borne mostly singly, slight fragrance; recurrent; foliage small, medium green, semi-glossy; some prickles; medium, bushy growth; [Lagerfeld × Ernie]; int. by Tiny Petals Nursery, 1994

Violet Paillette – See **Violet Hit**, MinFl

Violet Parncutt HT, yb, 1923, Easlea; bud small, pointed; flowers brownish gold, semi-dbl.

Violet Queen HP, m, 1892, Paul, G.; flowers marbled crimson and violet

Violet Queen HT, m, 1970, Northfield; flowers deep violet-pink, pointed, 4 in., 35-40 petals; foliage dark; upright, free growth; [seedling × Violette Dot]

Violet Ruffles HT, m, Davidson; flowers violet with ruffled edges, semi-dbl.; int. in 1997

Violet Simpson HT, op, 1930, Simpson; flowers vivid prawn-pink, base yellow, dbl.; foliage purple; int. by Laxton Bros.

Violet Wilton HT, mp, 1930, Ketten Bros.; bud very long, pointed; flowers bright rose-pink on flesh-white ground, tinted yellow, large, 35-40 petals; vigorous growth; [Gen. MacArthur × Mme Charles Lutaud]

Violetera HT, m, 1981, Dot, Simon; bud ovoid; flowers reddish-mauve, 30 petals, shallow cupped, borne singly to 3 per cluster, intense fragrance; foliage medium size, light green, matte; prickles curved, reddish-green; bushy growth; int. by Rose Barni-Pistoia, 1980

Violett Satina S, dp, Tantau; flowers medium, dbl.; int. in 1994

Violetta – See **Violette**, HMult

Violetta Pol, m, Bruant; flowers dark, smoky magenta, small, 25 petals, flat, borne in clusters; recurrent; low, bushy growth; int. in 1924

Violetta HT, m, 1957, Croix, A.; foliage glossy; vigorous growth; [Peace × Guinee]

Violetta – See **International Herald Tribune**, F

Violette HMult, m, 1921, Turbat; flowers pure deep violet, 3 cm., very dbl., slightly cupped, borne in large clusters, slight fragrance; vigorous growth

Violette Agréable HGal, m, before 1815, Descemet

Violette Bouyer HP, w, 1881, Lacharme, F.; flowers pinkish white, large, cupped; [Jules Margottin × Mlle de Sombreuil]

Violette Bronzée – See **Charles de Mills**, HGal

Violette de Crémer HGal, m, 1824, from Douai; flowers dark violet, large, very full

Violette Dot HT, m, 1960, Dot, Simon; flowers ageratum-blue, medium, 20 petals; strong stems; spreading growth; [Rosa de Friera × Prelude]

Violette et Rouge HGal, rb, before 1908; flowers violet over red

Violette Fire HMult, m; flowers violet-pink with white eye, moderate fragrance; very tall (10 m.) growth; int. in 1980

Violette Niestlé – See **Savoy Hotel**, HT

Violette Parfum – See **Blue Parfum**, HT

Violette Parfumee – See **Melody Parfumée**, Gr

Violette Parfumee, Climbing – See **Melodie Parfumée, Climbing**, Cl HT

Violina HT, pb, Tantau; bud long, pointed, dark pink; flowers shell pink, outer petals lighter with darker, thin margin, large, dbl., borne mostly singly, intense fragrance; free-flowering; foliage large, medium green, glossy; upright, strong growth; int. in 1997; Gold Medal, Monza, 1998

Violine S, m, 1986, Lens, Louis; flowers lilac, pink, white blend, 2 in., 20 petals, borne in clusters of 5-28, moderate fruity fragrance; foliage light green; prickles few, small, brown; upright, bushy growth; [(Little Angel × Picasso) × Skyrocket]; int. in 1985

Violinista Costa HT, rb, 1936, Camprubi, C.; flowers red to deep purplish red, well-formed, large, full, moderate fragrance; foliage glossy; vigorous growth; [Sensation × Shot Silk]

Violiniste Emile Lévêque HT, lp, 1897, Pernet-Ducher; bud long; flowers bright flesh pink nuanced yellow with orange reflections, large, dbl.; foliage purplish green

Violon d'Ingres HT, yb; bud large, globular; flowers clear yellow, nuanced salmon on petal edges, 5 in., very dbl., cupped, borne singly or in clusters of 3, no fragrance; recurrent; foliage dark green, matte; prickles numerous, large, curved slightly downward, tan; vigorous, bushy (70-90 cm) growth; hips round,

2 cm. ; PP12876; [Pigalle × (Paloma Blanca × Carefree Beauty)]; int. by Meilland, 2003

Violoncelliste Albert Fourès HT, ab, 1920, Croibier; flowers orange-yellow, shaded buff-yellow, dbl.; [Joseph Hill × unnamed variety]

Viorita – See **International Herald Tribune**, F

Víra HRg, mr, 1936, Böhm, J.; flowers bright red; very vigorous growth

Virago HSet, lp, 1887, Geschwind, R.; flowers deep flesh, 6 cm., semi-dbl., cupped, opening flat, borne in small clusters, no fragrance; foliage large

Virgen de Farnés HT, mp, 1960, Dot, M.; flowers bright rose, reverse lighter, well-formed, 26 petals; strong stems; vigorous growth; [Queen Elizabeth × Virgo]

Virgin F, w, 1972, E. G. Hill Co.; flowers dbl, 30-35 petals, globular, borne several together and in trusses; foliage large, leathery, dull; growth vigorous, upright; [Seventeen × Jack Frost]; int. by URS, 1971

Virgin Min, w, Lens, Louis; flowers small, dbl.

Virginal – See **White Bath**, M

Virginale – See **Beauté Virginale**, D

Virginale HP, w, 1858, Lacharme, F.; flowers pearly white, with pale flesh center, medium, dbl.

Virginale C, w; flowers pure white, often touched pink on one petal, abundant bloom, moderate fragrance; non-remontant; arching growth

Virginia T, dy, 1894, Dingee & Conard; [Safrano × Maréchal Niel]

Virginia LCl, ob, 1934, Nicolas; flowers brilliant flame, suffused gold, open, large, dbl.; non-recurrent; foliage large, dark; vigorous, climbing (9 ft.) growth; [Magnafrano × Eldorado]; int. by C-P

Virginia HT, w, Pekmez, Paul; flowers pure white, large, dbl., urn-shaped, borne usually in clusters; recurrent; foliage dark green, glossy, disease-resistant; vigorous, medium to tall growth; int. in 1994

Virginia Baker HT, mr, 2004, Baker, Larry Sr.; flowers medium red, reverse lighter, 2½-3 in., full, high-centered, borne mostly solitary, intense fragrance; good repeat bloom; foliage large, medium green, semi-glossy; growth bushy, tall (4 ft.); exhibition; [sport of Uncle Bill]

Virginia Dare HT, dp, 1934, Thompson's, J.H., Sons; bud long, pointed; flowers deep cerise-pink, large, dbl.; foliage leathery, dark; long stems; very vigorous growth; [Joanna Hill × unnamed seedling (dark red)]

Virginia Dare MinFl, w, Clements, John K.

Virginia Lass HSet, w, about 1846, Pierce; flowers blush white, medium, full

Virginia Lee Min, yb, 1989, Williams, Michael C.; bud ovoid; flowers creamy yellow with pink border, reverse creamy yellow, aging pink, medium, 30 petals, cupped, borne usually singly, no fragrance; recurrent; foliage medium size, dark green, glossy; prickles straight, green; slightly spreading, medium growth; hips globular, green to orange-yellow; [Rise 'n' Shine × Baby Katie]; int. by The Rose Garden & Mini Rose Nursery

Virginia R. Coxe – See **Gruss an Teplitz**, HCh

Virginia R. Coxe, Climbing – See **Gruss an Teplitz, Climbing**, Cl HCh

Virginia Reel S, dp, 1975, Buck, Dr. Griffith J.; bud ovoid, pointed; flowers light red, 4-4½ in., 35-45 petals, cupped, borne both singly and in clusters of 5-10, moderate sweet fragrance; recurrent; foliage large, dark green, leathery; erect, bushy growth; [Tickled Pink × Prairie Princess]; int. by Iowa State Univ.

Virginia Rose – See ***R. virginiana*** (Miller)

Virginian Rambler Ayr, lp, before 1855, from U.S.A.; flowers whitish pink, 6 cm., dbl.; nearly thornless

Virginie HGal, mp, 1825, Vibert; flowers rose pink, large, full, cupped

Virginie Ch, pb, before 1866; flowers flesh pink, centers dawn-pink, large, very full

Virginie S, lp, Schultheis; flowers mother of pearl pink, fading quickly almost to white, medium, dbl., rosette, slight fragrance; free-flowering; robust (60-100 cm.) growth; [Bonica × unknown]; int. by Rosen von Schultheis, 1999

Virginie Baltet HP, dp, 1854, Baltet

Virginie Demont-Breton N, op, 1902, Cochet; flowers coppery pink; [Isabella Gray × unknown]

Virgo HT, w, 1947, Mallerin, C.; flowers white, sometimes blush-pink, 5 in., 30 petals, high-centered; foliage dark, leathery; vigorous growth; [Blanche Mallerin × Neige Parfum]; int. by Meilland-Richardier; Gold Medal, NRS, 1949

Virgo, Climbing Cl HT, w, 1957, Mondial Roses

Virgo F, my, Burston; flowers golden yellow, lightening to medium yellow, dbl., cupped, borne in large clusters; recurrent; foliage medium green; compact (80 cm) growth; int. by Burston Nursery, 2004

Virgo Liberationem – See **Virgo**, HT

Virolay HT, ob, Camprubi, C.; flowers edges orange-red, base deep yellow, large, high-centered; vigorous growth

Vi's Violet Min, m, 1991, Moore, Ralph S.; bud lavender pink; flowers soft lavender, small, full, slight fragrance; free-flowering; foliage small, medium green, matte; upright, bushy, compact growth; [seedling × Angel Face]

Visa HT, mr, 1972, Meilland; flowers turkey-red, 5 in., 38 petals, high-centered; foliage large, leathery; vigorous, upright growth; [(Baccará × Queen Elizabeth) × Lovita]

Visalia Gold S, ly, Moore, Ralph; flowers creamy yellow; low, groundcover growth

Viscount Carlow HT, mp, 1911, Dickson; flowers carmine pink, base cream, moderate fragrance

Viscount Southwood HT, pb, 1949, Cobley; flowers China-pink shaded creamy peach to copper, 4-5 in., 35-40 petals, high-centered; vigorous growth; [Walter Bentley × Aribau]; int. by Harkness

Viscountess Charlemont HT, mp, 1937, McGredy; bud salmon-rose; flowers satiny rose-pink, base deep buttercup-yellow, large, dbl.; foliage dark cedar green; branching growth; Gold Medal, NRS, 1936

Viscountess Devonport HT, dy, 1923, Hicks; flowers rich Indian yellow, dbl.

Viscountess Enfield HT, pb, 1910, Pernet-Ducher; flowers coppery old-rose, shaded yellow; [unknown × (Soleil d'Or × unknown)]

Viscountess Falmouth HT, pb, 1879, Bennett; flowers deep pink, mottled, reverse silvery, very large, dbl., globular, moderate fragrance; numerous prickles; growth dwarf, slender; [Adam × Soupert et Notting's Perpetual Moss]

Viscountess Folkestone HT, pb, 1886, Bennett; flowers creamy silver-pink, center deep salmon-pink, dbl., moderate fragrance; recurrent

Viscountesse Folkestone, Climbing – See **Gainsborough**, Cl HT

Vision HT, pb, 1967, Dickson, A.; flowers gold and pink, 5½ in., dbl.; foliage glossy; [Kordes' Perfecta × Peace]

Vision HT, op, 1977, Poulsen, Niels D.; flowers medium salmon red, well-formed, large, 22 petals, borne 1-3 per stem; foliage dark, glossy; vigorous, spreading growth; PP6939; int. by Poulsen's Roses, 1978

Vision Blanc – See **Ice White**, F

Vision Blanc, Climbing – See **Ice White, Climbing**, Cl F

Visqueuse – See **Bourbon**, HGal

Visse Min, op, Delbard; flowers pure salmon pink, hybrid tea; free-flowering; bushy, medium growth

Vista Min, m, 1994, Saville, F. Harmon; bud short, pointed; flowers soft lavender, 1¾-2 in., 22-25 petals, high-centered, becoming flat, borne mostly singly, some small clusters, very slight fragrance; recurrent; foliage medium size, medium green, semi-glossy; prickles some, thin, straight; medium (16 in.), compact growth; hips globular, orange; PP9031; [Sachet × Copper Sunset]; int. by Nor'East Min. Roses, 1994

Vital HT, dr, Kordes; flowers clear, deep red, dbl., high-centered, borne mostly singly; recurrent; foliage dark green; few prickles; stems long, strong; [sport of Corvette]; int. in 1997

Vital Min, my, Olesen; bud long, pointed ovoid; flowers golden yellow, 4-5 cm., 25-30 petals, borne singly; recurrent; foliage dark green, glossy; prickles numerous, 3-5 mm, concave, grey-brown; upright, compact growth; PP13491; [seedling × Easter]; int. in 2000

Vital Parade – See **Vital**, Min

Vital Spark F, ab, 1982, Cocker, James; flowers gold, flushed coral, medium, 35 petals; foliage medium size, medium green, semi-glossy; bushy growth; [(Anne Cocker × (Sabine × Circus)) × Yellow Pages]; int. by Cocker & Sons

Vitality S, or, Williams, J. Benjamin; flowers bright orange-red, single to semi-dbl., shallow cup to flat, slight fragrance; recurrent; growth to 4 ft.; int. by Hortico, Inc., 2006

Vitex Spinosa – See **Rouge de Belgique**, HGal

Vittonville-Rose HT, ob, 1945, Mallerin, C.; flowers orange, base yellow, reverse lighter; vigorous growth; int. by A. Meilland

Viuda Verdaguer HT, ob, 1934, Dot, Pedro; flowers orange, open, very large, dbl.; foliage glossy, dark; very vigorous growth; [Shot Silk × Mari Dot]

Viva F, dr, 1973, Warriner, William A.; bud ovoid; flowers medium, dbl., high-centered; foliage glossy, dark; vigorous, upright growth; PP3579; [seedling × seedling]; int. by J&P, 1974; Gold Medal, Portland, 1984

Viva Min, my, Olesen; int. in 1999

Viva Romana HT, rb, Dot; flowers crimson red, slight fragrance

Vivacé F, or, 1974, Kordes; flowers large, dbl., high-centered; foliage large, leathery; very vigorous, upright growth; [Klaus Stortebeker × unknown]

Vivacious F, mp, 1971, Gregory; flowers phlox-pink, 4 in., 35 petals; very free growth; [Tropicana × unknown]

Vivacious Dianne HT, or, 1990, Christensen, Jack E.; flowers medium, 33 petals; foliage medium size, medium green, semi-glossy; upright, bushy growth; [Voodoo × Hello Dolly]; int. in 1989

Vivacity – See **Temperament**, F

Vivaldi S, mr, 1986, Lens, Louis; flowers raspberry red, 1 in., 5 petals, shallow cup, borne in clusters of 7-50; free-flowering; foliage small; prickles very hooked, greenish-brown; bushy (2 ft.), spreading growth; [(*R. multiflora* × unknown) × (seedling × Robin Hood)]; int. in 1984

Vivaldi HT, lp; bud medium, pointed, ovate; flowers creamy light pink, 14 cm., 24-28 petals, cupped, becoming flat, borne singly, very slight fragrance; recurrent; foliage dark green, weakly glossy; prickles some, straight, slanted slightly downward; upright, bushy, vigorous growth; hips large, pitcher-shaped ; PP7362; [Flamingo (Korflug) × Madelon]; greenhouse rose; int. by deRuiter, 1988

Vivarose HT, mr, Croix; flowers bright red; free-flowering; vigorous growth; int. by Roseraie Paul Croix

Vivastella HT, dp, Aicardi, D.; flowers laque de Robbie color (possibly carmine), well-shaped; [Julien Potin × Sensation]; int. by Giacomasso

Vive la France HT, rb, 1944, Mallerin, C.; bud pointed, well formed; flowers purplish red, reverse yellow, large, dbl.; foliage glossy; vigorous growth; [Shining Star × Mme Arthaud]; int. by A. Meilland; Gold Medal, Bagatelle, 1943

Vive La Suisse F, Tschanz, E.

Vivian Vivio Stolaruk HT, rb, 2004, Burks, Larry; flowers red blend, pastel at base, reverse pink blend, 5 in., full, borne mostly solitary, slight fragrance; foliage medium size, medium green, semi-glossy; prickles average, curved; upright, medium (5 ft.) growth; garden decoration; [seedling × (King of Hearts × unknown)]; int. in 2004

Viviand-Morel T, mp, 1888, Bernaix; flowers carmine pink; [Rote Safrano × unknown]

Vivid B, m, 1853, Paul, A.; flowers brilliant magenta to magenta-pink, small to medium, dbl., moderate fragrance; foliage glossy; robust, prickly growth; growth to 6 ft.

Vivid F, or, 1951, LeGrice; flowers brilliant orange-scarlet, large, 5-7 petals, borne in huge clusters; compact growth

Vivid Mason HT, dp, 1934, Mason, J.A.; flowers vivid dark pink, base yellow, large, dbl.; foliage leathery, glossy; very vigorous growth; [Premier × Mme Alexandre Dreux]; int. by McLellan Co.

Vivien HT, dp, 1922, Paul, W.; flowers deep rose-pink, dbl.

Vivien Leigh HT, mr, 1963, McGredy, Sam IV; flowers crimson, 5 in., 35 petals, high-centered; foliage dark; very free growth; [Queen Elizabeth × Detroiter]; int. by Fisons Horticulture

Vivienne Maire D, mp

Vivre HT, mp, Delbard-Chabert; int. in 1974

Vixen Min, or, 1989, Warriner, William A.; bud ovoid, pointed, green with reddish-brown; flowers red-orange with yellow base, aging red-orange to pink orange, 28 petals, cupped, no fragrance; foliage medium size, medium green, semi-glossy, small; prickles small, straight, reddish-brown; bushy, spreading, low growth; [Petticoat × Red Minimo]; int. by Bear Creek Gardens, 1990

Vlam HT, or, 1956, Leenders, M.; flowers fiery red, dbl.; vigorous growth; [Tawny Gold × Sarie Mareis]

Vlammenspel LCl, mr

Vlasta Burian Pol, m, 1937, Böhm, J.; flowers purple/pink, small, dbl.

Vlatava HMult, dr, 1936, Böhm; flowers violet red, medium, full

Vltava LCl, m, 1936, Böhm, J.; flowers violet, passing to purplish red, 4-5 cm., dbl., globular, borne in small clusters, no fragrance; foliage glossy; very vigorous, climbing growth; [Veilchenblau × unknown]

Voeux de Bonheur HT, pb, 1960, Delbard-Chabert; bud very large, long, pointed; flowers creamy white, petals edged cerise-pink, reverse white, large, 30-35 petals, high-centered, borne several together on long stem, moderate violet fragrance; foliage dark green, glossy, leathery; growth vigorous, bushy; [Michèle Meilland × Chic Parisien]; int. as Bon Voyage, Stark Bros., 1969

Voeux de Bonheur – See **Rotary Sunrise**, HT

Vogelpark Walsrode S, lp, 2006; flowers light pink, shaded peach, darker at edges, 8 cm., semi-dbl., cupped, borne in airy clusters, slight fragrance; occasional repeat; foliage tiny, medium green, glossy; wide, bushy, medium growth; int. by W. Kordes' Söhne, 1988

Vogue F, pb, 1951, Boerner; bud ovoid; flowers cherry-coral, 3½-4½ in., 25 petals, high-centered, borne in clusters, moderate fragrance; recurrent; foliage glossy; vigorous, upright, bushy, compact growth; [Pinocchio × Crimson Glory]; int. by J&P; Gold Medal, Portland, 1950, Gold Medal, Geneva, 1950

Vogue HT, pb, Pekmez, Paul; flowers light pink with darker pink edges, dbl., high-centered, borne mostly singly; recurrent; int. in 1997

Voice of Thousands F, yb, 1993, Horner, Heather M.; flowers yellow edged cherry red, medium, dbl., cupped, borne in small clusters; foliage medium size, medium green, semi-glossy; some prickles; medium (80 cm.), bushy growth; [Playgroup × Bright Smile]; int. by Horner, 1994

Voie Lactée Cl HT, w, 1949, Robichon; bud globular, creamy white; flowers pure white, 8 cm., dbl., intense fragrance; foliage glossy; very vigorous, climbing (10-14 ft.) growth; [Frau Karl Druschki × Julien Potin]

Voie Romaine HT, Dot, Simon; int. in 1977

Voila F, or, Croix; flowers borne in clusters of 6 or 7; free-flowering; foliage green, disease-resistant; int. by Paul Croix, 1969; Certificate of Merit, Madrid

Voila HT, op, Spek; florist rose; int. by Jan Spek Rozen, 2005

Vol de Nuit HT, m, 1983, Delbard, Georges; flowers deep lilac, large, 33 petals, high-centered, borne mostly singly, intense fragrance; recurrent; foliage medium size, light green, matte; prickles bronze-red; bushy growth; [(Holstein × (Bayadere × Prelude)) × Saint-Exupery]; int. in 1970; Gold Medal, Rome, 1970

Volare HT, dr, 1977, McDaniel, Earl; bud ovoid; flowers bright red, large, 38-44 petals, high-centered; foliage leathery; bushy, upright growth; PP4172; int. by Carlton Rose Nurseries, 1976

Volare F, or, 1988, McGredy, Sam IV; flowers medium, dbl.; foliage large, medium green, glossy; upright growth; [Julischka × Matangi]; int. by McGredy Roses International, 1988

Volcano HT, dp, 1950, Moro; bud long, pointed; flowers cherry-red, 6½ in., 25 petals, cupped, moderate fruity fragrance; foliage dark; vigorous, upright growth; [Charles P. Kilham × Rome Glory]; int. by J&P

Volki – See **Angelika**, F

Volumineuse HGal, mp, before 1828; flowers large, full

Volunteer F, yb, 1985, Harkness, R., & Co., Ltd.; flowers washed soft apricot yellow in center, creamy white on edges, large, 35 petals, informal, slight fragrance; recurrent; foliage medium size, light green, glossy; bushy growth; [Dame of Sark × Silver Jubilee]; int. in 1986

Volunteer Spirit S, rb, Williams, J.B.; int. by Hortico, Inc., 2005

Volupté – See **La Volupté**, HGal

Voluptuous! HT, dp, 2005, Zary, Keith W.; bud long, pointed ovoid; flowers fuchsia, reverse fuchsia, 4½-5 in., 35 petals, high-centered, borne mostly solitary, some small clusters, moderate spicy fragrance; recurrent; foliage large, dark green, glossy; prickles several, ½ in., slightly curved downward, brown; stems strong, medium; upright, medium (5 ft.) growth; PP16498; [Tournament of Roses × Trumpeter]; int. by Jackson & Perkins Wholesale, Inc., 2005

Von Hötzendorf HP, pb, 1916, Schmidt, J.C.; flowers golden rose-pink, richly tinted coppery red, dbl.; vigorous growth; [Frau Karl Druschki × Beauté de Lyon]

Von Liliencron HFt, pb, 1916, Lambert, P.; bud yellowish red; flowers yellowish light pink with white, reverse salmon-pink, dbl., high-centered, moderate fragrance; profuse bloom, sometimes recurrent; foliage glossy, dark, bronze; vigorous (6 ft.) growth; [Geheimrat Dr. Mittweg × Mrs Aaron Ward]

Von Scharnhorst S, ly, 1921, Lambert, P.; bud medium, ovoid; flowers yellow to yellowish-white, medium to large, semi-dbl., loose, open, borne in small clusters on short laterals, slight fragrance; occasional repeat; vigorous (6-8 ft.) growth; [Frau Karl Druschki × Gottfried Keller]

Vonava Elysium HT, Strnad

Voodoo HT, ob, 1984, Christensen, Jack E.; bud pointed; flowers salmon, yellow, orange and pink blend, 5-6 in., 30-35 petals, high-centered, borne mostly singly, can have 2-3 per cluster, intense rich, sweet fragrance; recurrent; foliage medium size, dark green, very glossy; prickles numerous, short, hooked slightly downward; stems long, strong; upright, bushy, tall growth; hips ovoid to globular, yellow; PP6121; [((Camelot × First Prize) × Typhoo Tea) × Lolita]; int. by Armstrong Nursery, 1986

Voorburg F, op, 1959, Buisman, G. A. H.; flowers salmon-pink, semi-dbl., borne in large clusters; foliage bronze to dark; vigorous growth; [Sangerhausen × Vogue]

Vorace B, mr, 1849, Lacharme (possibly Foulard); flowers bright crimson, medium, full

Vobergii HSpn, w, before 1902, Zabel; flowers creamy white with a faint tint of yellow, single; [*R. foetita* × *R. spinosissima*]

Vox Populi HT, dr, 1945, Mallerin, C.; flowers velvety dark red, semi-dbl.

Voyage HT, pb, Tantau; flowers medium pink, reverse lighter, medium to large, dbl., high-centered, borne mostly singly, slight fragrance; recurrent; prickles few to none; stems long; florist rose; int. by Rosen Tantau, 2003

Voyager Min, yb, 1996, Williams, Michael C.; flowers yellow blend, at times touch of pink, large, full, borne mostly singly, no fragrance; recurrent; foliage medium size, dark green, semi-glossy; medium (50 cm.), upright growth; [seedling × unknown]; int. by The Mini Rose Garden, 1997

Vrouefederasie Roos HT, pb, Taschner, Ludwig; flowers medium pink with cream reverse, full, high-centered, deep cup, moderate fragrance; recurrent; medium growth; int. by Ludwig's Roses, 2004

Vrystaat HT, ob, Tantau; flowers bright orange, dbl., high-centered; recurrent; medium growth; int. in 1992

Vulcain HP, dr, 1861, Verdier, V.; flowers rich dark crimson, well-formed, dbl.

Vulcain Pol, mr, 1921, Turbat; flowers deep cherry-red, dbl.; vigorous growth

Vulcana LCl, dr, 1964, Mondial Roses; flowers blood-red, semi-dbl., borne in clusters; vigorous growth

Vulcania HT, mr, 1948, Giacomasso; bud long; flowers purplish red, well-formed, overlarge; foliage dark; [Matador × Principe di Piemonte]

Vulcanie B, mp, 1840, Bizard; flowers medium, full

Vulgens Pol, mr, 1942, Koster; flowers medium, semi-dbl.

Vulkan HT, dr, VEG; flowers large, dbl.

Vuurbaak F, or, 1946, Leenders, M.; flowers scarlet, open, 4 in., 15 petals, borne in clusters; foliage reddish green; vigorous, upright growth; [Florentina × World's Fair]; int. by Longley

Vydehi F, ob, Datt, Braham

Vyslanek Kalina HP, mr, 1935, Böhm, J.; flowers large, dbl.

W. A. Bilney HT, ab, 1927, Easlea; flowers pale apricot suffused cerise, reverse yellow tinted pink, large; foliage dark, leathery; vigorous growth

W. A. Willet HT, pb, Kernovski, V.R.; int. in 1959

W. C. Gaunt HT, dr, 1916, Dickson, A.; bud long, pointed; flowers velvety crimson-scarlet, reflexed petals tipped scarlet, rev, dbl.

W. E. Chaplin HT, dr, 1929, Chaplin Bros.; flowers crimson, deepening to maroon, large, dbl., high-centered; vigorous growth; Gold Medal, NRS, 1930

W. E. Chaplin, Climbing Cl HT, dr, 1936, Heizmann, E.

W. E. Lippiat HT, dr, 1907, Dickson, A.; flowers deep crimson shaded maroon, large, full

W. E. Wallace HT, dy, 1922, Dickson, H.; flowers deep golden yellow, well-formed, large, dbl.; [sport of Gorgeous]; Gold Medal, NRS, 1922

W. Freedland Kendrick HT, pb, 1920, Thomas; flowers pink with peach tones, large, dbl.

W. Freeland Kendrick LCl, lp, 1920, Thomas; flowers flesh, center peach, 8-9 cm., very dbl., borne in small clusters, moderate fragrance; some repeat; foliage dark, bronze, leathery, glossy; vigorous, semi-climbing growth; [Aviateur Blériot × Mme Caroline Testout]; int. by B&A

W. G. Pountney F, or, 1964, Bennett, H.; flowers scarlet; tall growth; [Moulin Rouge × Mrs Inge Poulsen]; int. by Pedigree Nursery

W. H. Cotton HT, ab, 1946, Cobley; flowers orange shaded gold, large; foliage dark; vigorous, upright growth; [Mrs Beatty × Mrs Sam McGredy]; int. by Leicester Roses

W. H. Dunallan HT, mr, 1939, Clark, A.; flowers very rich bright red, flushed darker, semi-dbl.; vigorous growth; [Edith Clark × unknown]; int. by NRS Victoria

W. H. Troy HT, op, 1906, Dickson, A.; flowers salmon

W. J. Matthews T, mp, Matthews, W.J.

W. R. Hawkins HT, op, 1948, Toogood, F D; bud ovoid; flowers tango-pink, large, very dbl., high-centered, intense fragrance; foliage glossy; vigorous, upright growth; [(Crimson Glory × unknown) × Silver Jubilee]

Waanrode Gr, op, 2000, Lens, Louis; flowers salmon, 10 cm., full, borne in small clusters; recurrent; foliage medium size, dark green, semi-glossy, disease-resistant; numerous prickles; upright, medium (100 cm.) growth; [((*R. wichurana* × Floradora) × Coloranje) × Papillon Rose]; int. by Louis Lens N.V., 1990

Waban T, dp, 1891, Wood; flowers deep, bright pink; otherwise identical to its parent; [sport of Catherine Mermet]

Wabash Dawn S, op, 1978, Williams, J. Benjamin; bud tapered; flowers bright orange-pink, 4-4½ in., 34 petals, high-centered; repeat bloom; foliage large, glossy; vigorous, upright growth; [(Queen Elizabeth × Gladiator) × (Aztec × Little Darling)]; int. by Krider Nursery

Wachhilde Misc OGR, 1910, Geschwind; flowers large, full

Wadei HRg, mp; flowers single; foliage rich green; weak, prostrate growth; [*R. rugosa* × unknown]

Wagbi F, ob, 1981, Barrett, F.H.; bud pointed; flowers orange-pink, 20 petals, hybrid tea, opening flat, borne 3-5 per cluster, moderate fragrance; free-flowering; foliage large, dark green; prickles large, red; vigorous, upright growth; int. by John Mattock, Ltd.

Wageningen Pol, my, 1970, Buisman, G. A. H.; bud ovoid; flowers medium, dbl.; foliage dark; [Golden Giant × Peace]; int. in 1968

Wagtail – See **White Magic Carpet**, S

Wagtail Cover – See **White Magic Carpet**, S

Waiheke Gr, op, 1987, McGredy, Sam IV; bud long, pointed; flowers coral-pink with lighter reverse, fading lighter, 2 in., 30 petals, high-centered, borne in sprays of 5-9, slight spicy fragrance; recurrent; foliage medium size, dark green, glossy; prickles few, small, pointed, green; upright, bushy growth; hips ovoid, small, rare, tan-orange; PP5429; [Tony Jacklin × Young Quinn]; int. by McGredy International, 1985

Waikato – See **Velvet Ruby**, HT

Waikiki – See **Los Angeles Beautiful**, Gr

Waikiki – See **Waiheke**, Gr

Waimarie HT, m, Matthews; int. in 2001

Waipounamu HT, yb, 1983, Cattermole, R.F.; flowers creamy yellow, shaded mauve-pink on outer petals, 50 petals, high-centered, intense fragrance; foliage bronze green, glossy; upright growth; [Peace × Blue Moon]

Wait 'n' See Min, ab, Geytenbeek

Waitemata Min, rb, 1978, McGredy, Sam IV; flowers medium, 42 petals; foliage light green, glossy; bushy growth; [Wee Man × Matangi]; int. by McGredy Roses International, 1980

Waitziana S, dp, before 1849; flowers deep rose, 2½ in., single, borne mostly solitary; growth tall (8 ft.); [*R. canina* × *R. gallica*]

Walburga S, m, Scholle; flowers magenta, large, full, cupped, to almost pompon, borne usually in clusters, slight fragrance; recurrent; foliage green, glossy; strong, upright (5 ft.), broad growth

Waldfee HP, mr, 1960, Kordes, R.; flowers blood-red, 4 in., dbl., camellia-shaped, borne in small clusters, moderate fragrance; recurrent bloom; foliage glossy; vigorous, tall (10 ft.), dense growth; [Independence × Mrs John Laing]

Waldtraut Nielsen M, dp, 1932, Nielsen; flowers clear deep pink, large, full, globular, moderate fragrance; non-remontant; tall, arching growth; [Cristata × Arabella]

Walferdange HMsk, dp, 2000, Lens, Louis; flowers deep pink, reverse lighter, 4-5 cm., dbl., cupped, borne in large clusters, moderate fragrance; recurrent; foliage medium size, medium green, semi-glossy, disease-resistant; few prickles; bushy, medium (60-80 cm.) growth; [(*R. multiflora adenocheata* × Ballerina) × Felicia]; int. by Louis Lens N.V., 1990

Walko F, dr, 1957, Delbard-Chabert; flowers dark crimson, small, 23 petals, cupped to flat, borne in clusters of 6-8, moderate Damask fragrance; recurrent; [(Incendie × Holstein) × Rouge Chabert]

Walküre S, lp, 1909, Geschwind, R.; flowers whitish pink, darker at center, 6 cm., full, quartered, flat, borne in small clusters, nodding, moderate fragrance; non-remontant; tall growth; [*R. canina* × a Tea]

Walküre HT, w, 1919, Ebeling; bud long, pointed; flowers cream-white, center ochre-yellow, dbl.; [Frau Karl Druschki × Mme Jenny Gillemot]

Walkyrie HT, dr, 1959, Moro, L.; bud urn shaped or ovoid; flowers low-centered, large; bushy growth; [Happiness × Volcano]

Wall Street HT, op, Barni, V.; flowers orange pink, yellow reverse, large, dbl., classic hybrid tea, borne mostly singly, moderate fragrance; recurrent; foliage bright green; vigorous, medium growth

Wallflower – See **The Wallflower**, HMult

Walsham Gold HT, my, 1965, LeGrice; flowers yellow with burnished gold and copper overtones in cool weather; int. by Wayside Gardens Co.

Walsh's Rambler – See **America**, HMult

Walter HT, dp, 1949, Lens; bud long, pointed; flowers pink, reverse vivid rosy red, open, very large, 20 petals; foliage bronze, leathery; very vigorous, bushy growth; [Charles P. Kilham × Comtesse Vandal]

Walter Bentley HT, op, 1938, Robinson, H.; bud long, pointed; flowers coppery orange shaded pink, very large, dbl., high-centered; foliage leathery, glossy, dark, bronze; vigorous growth; [Mrs Sam McGredy × Dame Edith Helen]; int. by Wheatcroft Bros.; Gold Medal, NRS, 1937

Walter Butt S, dp, 1905, Butt; hybrid micrugosa; int. in 1905

Walter C. Clark HT, dr, 1917, Paul, W.; bud long, pointed; flowers deep maroon-crimson, shaded black, large, dbl., high-centered; foliage dark, leathery; vigorous growth

Walter Rieger S, dp, 1978, Hetzel; bud pointed; flowers pink to reddish, medium, dbl.; continuous bloom; foliage glossy; vigorous growth; [Carina × Molde]; int. in 1977

Walter Ross HT, my, 1970, Morey, Dennison; bud ovoid; flowers large, dbl., high-centered, moderate fragrance; foliage large, glossy, dark, bronze, leathery; vigorous, upright, bushy growth; [Mme Marie Curie × King's Ransom]; int. by General Bionomics

Walter Sisulu – See **Grande Amore**, HT

Walter Speed HT, dy, 1909, Dickson, A.; flowers deep lemon-yellow, passing to milk-white, dbl.

Waltham Bride HMult, w, 1905, Paul, W.; flowers snow-white, 3-4 cm., semi-dbl., borne in small to medium clusters, moderate fragrance; virtually thornless; sometimes classed as HWich or LCl

Waltham Climber No. 1 Cl HT, mr, 1885, Paul, W.; flowers rosy crimson, imbricated, large, dbl., borne singly or in small clusters, intense fragrance; recurrent bloom; nearly thornless; vigorous, climbing growth; [Gloire de Dijon × unknown]

Waltham Climber No. 2 Cl HT, or, 1885, Paul, W.; flowers flame-red, tinted crimson, large, dbl., borne singly or in small clusters; recurrent bloom; nearly thornless

Waltham Climber No. 3 Cl HT, mr, 1885, Paul, W.; flowers deep rosy crimson, imbricated, large, dbl.; recurrent bloom; vigorous, climbing growth

Waltham Crimson HT, dr, 1922, Chaplin Bros.; flowers deep crimson

Waltham Cross HT, dr, 1927, Chaplin Bros.; flowers glowing crimson-scarlet, semi-dbl.

Waltham Flame HT, 1921, Chaplin Bros.; flowers deep terra-cotta, shaded bronzy orange

Waltham Rambler HMult, dp, 1903, Paul, W.; flowers deep rosy pink, center paler, stamens bright yellow, single; early; vigorous, climbing growth

Waltham Scarlet HT, dr, 1914, Paul, W.; flowers crimson-scarlet, single

Waltham Standard HP, dr, 1897, Paul, W.; flowers Rich carmine, shaded scarlet and violet, medium

Waltraud Nielsen – See **Waldtraut Nielsen**, M

Waltz Min, ob, Benardella, Frank; flowers orange with white eye and reverse, high-centered, moderate fragrance; recurrent; int. by Treloar Roses, 1999

Waltz LCl, w, Poulsen; flowers white with yellow tones in center, 5-8 cm., full, cupped, borne in clusters, slight wild rose fragrance; recurrent; foliage dark green, glossy; bushy (150-200 cm.) growth; int. by Poulsen Roser, 2000

Waltz Time – See **Saint-Exupéry**, HT

Waltz Time Min, w, Benardella, Frank; flowers ivory

white with tonings of shrimp pink along the outer edges; free-flowering; bushy growth

Waltzing Calumet Min, yb; flowers light cream yellow, rich buttercup yellow along petal edges; bushy, medium growth

Waltzing Matilda HT, rb, 1965, Jack, J.; flowers red splashed light to dark pink, well-shaped, large, dbl.; vigorous growth; [sport of Christian Dior]; int. by Girraween Nursery

Walzertraum HT, mr, 1968, Tantau, Math.; flowers dbl.; foliage dark; int. by Buisman, 1968

Walzertraum HT, dp, Tantau; flowers strong, stable, deep pink, 4-5 in., very full, cupped, borne mostly singly, slight fragrance; recurrent; upright, strong growth; int. by Rosen Tantau, 2004

Wanaka Min, or, 1978, McGredy, Sam IV; flowers bright scarlet, small, 40 petals, borne several together, slight fragrance; free-flowering; foliage light green; low, bushy growth; [Anytime × Trumpeter]; int. by McGredy Roses International

Wanda HT, mp, 1953, Joseph H. Hill, Co.; bud short, pointed; flowers rose, 3½-4½ in., 28-30 petals, high-centered; foliage leathery; vigorous, upright growth; [Pink Bountiful × Celebrity]

Wanda HT, dr

Wanderer S, mp, 1997, Horner, Colin P.; flowers medium pink, reverse lighter, 3-4 cm., semi-dbl., globular, borne in large clusters, slight fragrance; recurrent; foliage small, dark green, semi-glossy; spreading, low (50-60cm.) growth; [Sea Foam × Eyeopener]; int. by Bill LeGrice Roses

Wanderin' Wind S, lp, 1972, Buck, Dr. Griffith J.; flowers two-toned light pink, medium, dbl., high-centered, intense fruity fragrance; free-flowering; foliage large, glossy, dark, leathery; very vigorous, upright, bushy growth; [Dornroschen × Andante]; int. by Iowa State University, 1973

Wandering Minstrel F, op, 1986, Harkness; flowers pink shaded orange, large, 28 petals, borne in clusters; foliage dark green, glossy; medium, bushy growth; [Dame of Sark × Silver Jubilee]

Wang-Jang-Ve – See **Fortune's Double Yellow**, Misc OGR

Wanguafong HT, m, Shanghai; sepals striped sport of Shi-un, pale pink with purplish pink; [sport of Shi-un]; int. in 1993

Waon F, ly, Keisei; int. by Keisei Rose Nurseries, 2005

Wapex Pol, my, 1968, Buisman, G. A. H.; bud pointed; flowers medium, semi-dbl., borne in clusters; foliage dark; [Golden Showers × Fata Morgana]

Wapiti F, rb, Meilland; flowers medium red with silver reverse, small, dbl., cupped, borne in trusses, slight fragrance; free-flowering; Gold Medal, Rome, 1987, Gold Medal, Monza, 1987, Gold Medal, Geneva, 1987

War Dance Gr, or, 1961, Swim & Weeks; bud ovoid; flowers dark orange-red, 4-4½ in., 34 petals, high-centered; foliage leathery; vigorous, bushy growth; PP2017; [Roundelay × Crimson Glory]; int. by C-P, 1962

War Dance F, mr, 1998, McGredy, Sam IV; bud small; flowers medium red, handpainted in cool weather, 2½ in., 9-10 petals, borne in small clusters, slight fruity fragrance; foliage small, medium green, semi-glossy; prickles moderate, curved downward; compact, low (30 cm.) growth; hips globose, green with orange at top; PP10699; [Howard Morrison × Sue Lawley]; int. by McGredy, 1997

War Paint LCl, mr, 1930, Clark, A.; flowers large, dbl., globular; vigorous, pillar or climbing (8 ft.) growth; [(Rhea Reid × unknown) × unknown]; int. by Hackett

Warabeuta F, op, Keisei; int. by Keisei Rose Nurseries, 1999

Warana Festival HT, mp, 1963, Jack, J.; flowers rich pink, base rich apricot, well-formed, dbl.; vigorous growth; [sport of Christian Dior]; int. by Langbecker

Warbler S, my, Olesen; flowers medium yellow, small, dbl., slight wild rose fragrance; recurrent; foliage dark green, glossy; broad, bushy (60-100 cm.) growth

Wardlip – See **Pillar Box**, F

Warley Jubilee F, mp, Warley Rose Gardens

Warleyensis S, mp; sepals persistent; flowers borne mostly solitary; numerous prickles; hips bright red, 1/2 in.; [*R. blanda* × *R. rugosa*]

Warm & Fuzzy Min, mr, 2007, Carruth, Tom; bud fragrant, mossy, well-shaped; flowers even medium red, 3-4 cm., dbl., borne in small clusters; foliage medium size, dark green, matte; prickles mixed, almost straight, tan, numerous; growth compact, short (40-50 cm.); garden decoration; [(seedling × Santa Claus) × Danny Boy]; int. by Weeks Roses, 2009

Warm Rain Min, mr, 1985, Hardgrove, Donald L.; flowers medium coral-red, medium, 70 petals, high-centered; foliage small, medium green, semi-glossy; vigorous, upright, bushy growth; [Fragrant Cloud × Orange Honey]; int. by Rose World Originals

Warm Welcome Cl Min, or, 1992, Warner, Chris; bud pointed; flowers orange vermilion, yellow base, 1½ in., 10 petals, opens quickly to flat, borne singly and in medium clusters, moderate spicy fragrance; recurrent; foliage small, dark green (red when young), semi-glossy; prickles few, pointed slightly downward, brown; tall (200+ cm.), upright growth; PP9356; [(Elizabeth of Glamis × (Galway Bay × Sutter's Gold)) × Anna Ford]; int. in 1990

Warm Wishes – See **Sunset Celebration**, HT

Warrawee HT, mp, 1935, Fitzhardinge; bud long, pointed; flowers flesh-pink shaded rose-pink, large, 30 petals, high-centered, moderate fragrance; foliage glossy; vigorous growth; [Padre × Rev. F. Page-Roberts]; int. by C-P

Warrior HT, mr, 1906, Paul, W.; flowers bright scarlet-vermilion, large, dbl., moderate fragrance

Warrior F, or, 1976, LeGrice; flowers scarlet-red, 3-4 in., 32 petals, cupped, borne in trusses, slight fragrance; recurrent; foliage light green, semi-glossy; [City of Belfast × Ronde Endiablee]; int. in 1977

Warszawa HT, ob, 1957, Grabczewski; flowers bright orange, reverse golden yellow; foliage dark, glossy; [sport of Carioca]

Wartburg HMult, mp, 1910, Kiese; flowers pink to magenta, twisted and reflexed petals, 3-4 cm., dbl., cupped, borne in large, open clusters, moderate sweet fragrance; normally non-recurrent; foliage large, light green; thornless; strong stems; very vigorous, climbing (15-20 ft.) growth; [Tausendschön × unknown]

Wartburg 77 S, my, Berger; flowers bright yellow, lightening to cream, large, dbl., borne mostly in clusters, slight fragrance; recurrent; stems long; upright, arching growth; int. in 1977

Warwhoop Min, or, 1974, Williams, Ernest D.; bud ovoid; flowers brilliant orange-red, small, very dbl.; foliage small, glossy, dark; vigorous, bushy growth; [Baccará × Little Chief]; int. by Mini-Roses, 1973

Warwick Castle S, dp, 1992, Austin, David; flowers rose pink, 3-3½ in., very full, rosette, borne in small clusters, moderate Bourbon fragrance; recurrent; foliage small, medium green, matte; some prickles; stems slender, arching; low (75 cm.), spreading growth; [The Reeve × Lilian Austin]; int. by David Austin Roses, Ltd., 1986

Warwickshire S, pb, Kordes; flowers white with rosy pink painted on the petals, single, flat, borne in clusters; recurrent; foliage dark green, glossy; short (30 in.), spreading growth; int. in 1991

Wasagaming HRg, mp, 1939, Skinner; flowers clear rose pink, dbl., moderate spicy fragrance; recurrent; vigorous growth; [(*R. rugosa* × *R. acicularis*) × Gruss an Teplitz]

Wasastiernan – See **Polstjärnan**, LCl

Waskasoo HRg, dr, 1963, Erskine; flowers dbl., high-centered, borne mostly singly, intense fragrance; recurrent; growth typical rugosa; [Little Betty × Hansa]

Watarase HT, m, 2005, Kobayashi, Moriji; flowers full, borne mostly solitary, moderate fragrance; foliage medium green, matte; prickles medium; growth upright, 160 cm.; cutting, garden; [seedling × seedling]; int. in 2005

Watchfire Min, or, 1998, Williams, Ernest D.; flowers bright coral-red with deep yellow base, 1¼-1½ in., 35 petals, high-centered, borne mostly singly; foliage medium size, medium green, semi-glossy; prickles moderate; upright, compact, bushy, medium (18 in.) growth; [Sue Jo × Twilight Trail]; int. by Texas Mini Roses, 1997

Watchung HT, yb, 1932, Didato; flowers yellow tipped pink, large, 24-26 petals; [sport of Pres. Herbert Hoover]

Water Lily MinFl, w, 2004, Jalbert, Brad; flowers cream white, 2 in., dbl., borne in very large clusters, slight fragrance; foliage medium size, medium green, semi-glossy; prickles moderate, medium, green; growth upright, tall (2 ft.); cut flower, garden rose; [Pink Petticoat × Alexander HT.]; int. in 1998

Water Music LCl, dp, 1983, Bell, Ronald J.; flowers deep pink, darker on petal edges, medium, 20 petals, slight fragrance; foliage dark, medium size, glossy; spreading, climbing growth; [Handel × unknown]; int. in 1982

Watercolor Min, mp, 1976, Moore, Ralph S.; bud long, pointed; flowers bright pink, 1½ in., 22-26 petals, high-centered, borne singly and in small clusters, slight sweet fragrance; recurrent; foliage small, glossy, leathery; prickles few, small, straight, inclined downward, brown; stems sturdy, wiry, medium; vigorous, upright, bushy growth; PP4031; [Rumba × (Little Darling × Red Germain)]; int. by Sequoia Nursery

Watercolors S, yb, 2006, Carruth, Tom; flowers yellow edged pink blushing all pink, reverse similar but with less blush color, 6-8 cm., single, shallow cup, borne in small clusters; recurrent; foliage medium size, dark green, semi-glossy; prickles average, slightly hooked, beige, moderate; growth bushy, to slightly spreading, medium (75-90 cm.); garden decoration; [(Santa Claus × Flower Carpet) × Betty Boop]; int. by Weeks Roses, 2007

Watercolour – See **Watercolor**, Min

Waterloo HMsk, w, Lens, Louis; flowers creamy white, 2-3 cm., dbl., cupped, borne in clusters; recurrent; foliage dark green; upright (4-5 ft.), arching, rounded growth; int. in 1996

Watermelon Ice S, dp, 1998, Zary, Dr. Keith W.; flowers dark lavender pink, lighter reverse, 1½ in., single, borne in large clusters, slight fragrance; repeats quickly; foliage small, dark green, semi-glossy; prickles moderate, straight; spreading, bushy, low (1½ ft.) growth; PP10229; [The Fairy × seedling]; int. by Bear Creek Gardens, Inc., 1997

Waterwise Blush S, w, Kordes; bud small, blush pink; flowers open white, yellow stamens, small, semi-dbl., cupped, borne in clusters; free-flowering; foliage hardy, disease-resistant; low, spreading growth; int. in 2002

Watsoniana – See ***R. watsoniana*** (Crépin)

Wave of Flame – See **Ho-No-o-no-nami**, LCl

Waverland HT, yb, 1986, Lens, Louis; flowers deep yellow, edged orange-red, large, 30 petals, high-centered, borne singly, intense fragrance; recurrent; foliage dark, leathery; prickles brown; upright, bushy growth; [Peer Gynt × Peace]; int. in 1982; Gold Medal, Monza, 1980

Waverley F, dr, Norman; flowers crimson-scarlet, large, 22 petals, borne in trusses; foliage glossy, dark; vigorous, bushy, compact growth

Waverley Garden Club HT, pb, Dawson; int. in about 1983

Waverley Triumph Pol, mp, 1951, Poulter; flowers bright pink, base yellow, small, semi-dbl., cupped, borne in clusters; foliage glossy, light green; vigorous, bushy growth; [sport of Orange Triumph]

Waves HT, mp, 1944, Dickson, A.; bud ovoid, pointed; flowers rose-pink, open, 4½ in., 35 petals, cupped, intense fragrance; recurrent; foliage dark, leathery, wrinkled; vigorous growth; [(seedling × (deep salmon)) × Lucie Marie]; int. by J&P

Waves of Flame – See **Ho-No-o-no-nami**, LCl

Wavria F, or, 1979, Lens, Louis; flowers orange-crimson; [sport of Europeana]; int. in 1973

Waxwing – See **Newport**, S

Wayside Garnet Min, dr, 1956, Wayside Gardens Co.; flowers garnet-red, small, dbl.; dwarf, compact growth; [sport of Oakington Ruby]

We Salute You HT, op, 2005, Carruth, Tom; buds long; flowers opening orange, aging to pink, 12-14 cm., 30-35 petals, high-centered, classic, borne mostly solitary, moderate fragrance; recurrent; foliage large, very dark green, glossy; prickles moderate, average, slightly hooked, beige; upright, medium (110 to 130 cm) growth; PPAF; [Voodoo × Sunset Celebration]; int. by Weeks Roses, 2006

We Zair C, pb; flowers two-tone pink

Wedded Bliss Min, mp, 1985, Saville, F. Harmon; flowers semi-dbl., borne in clusters, slight fragrance; foliage small, medium green, glossy; groundcover; very spreading growth; [(Yellow Jewel × Tamango) × Nozomi]; int. by Nor'East Min. Roses

Weddigen HT, lp, 1916, Lambert, P.; flowers silver-pink, large, full, moderate fragrance; [General MacArthur × Goldelse]

Wedding Bells HMult, w, 1906, Walsh; flowers white, outer half of petals soft pink, 3 cm., dbl., cupped, opening flat, borne in clusters of 10-20, no fragrance; foliage light; short stems; very vigorous, climbing (12-15 ft.)growth; [Crimson Rambler × unknown]

Wedding Cake F, w, 2007, Moore, Ralph S.; flowers pink changing to green/white, reverse pale pink to white, medium, 3 in., very full, borne in small clusters; foliage medium green, semi-glossy; prickles small, straight, brown, moderate; growth upright, 3-4 ft.; specimen, large containers; [Sheri Anne × unknown]; int. by Sequoia Nurs., 2006

Wedding Celebration – See **Isabella Rossellini**, HT

Wedding Day LCl, w, 1950, Stern, Sir Frederich; bud pale apricot; flowers yellow to white, flushed pink, 3 cm., single, borne in large clusters, intense fruity fragrance; non-remontant; foliage pewter-green; growth to 20 ft.; hips round, orange; [*R. longicuspis* × *R. moyesii*]

Wedding Garland LCl, w, Taschner, Ludwig; flowers pure white, dbl., cupped, moderate fragrance; recurrent; tall, arching growth; Iceberg is one ancestor; int. by Ludwig's Roses, 2003

Wedding Night S, Ping Lim; int. by Bailey Nurseries, 2005

Wedding Pink HT, lp, 1990, Nakashima, Tosh; bud ovoid; flowers light pink, reverse slightly paler pink, large, very dbl., high-centered, urn-shaped; foliage medium size, dark green, matte; prickles long, very narrow, reddish-brown; upright, tall growth; [sport of Bridal White]; int. by Bear Creek Gardens, 1990

Wedding Ring HT, my, 1958, Shepherd; bud long, pointed; flowers golden yellow, 4-4½ in., 25-35 petals, slight fragrance; foliage dark green, glossy, leathery; vigorous, upright, compact growth; [Ville de Paris × Mrs Sam McGredy]; int. by Bosley Nursery, 1957

Wedding Song HT, w, 1972, Whisler, D.; upright growth; [Virgo × Ivory Fashion]; int. by Gro-Plant Industries, 1971

Weddingen – See **Weddigen**, HT

Wee Ack Min, lp, 1995, Rennie, Bruce F.; flowers 1 in., dbl., borne mostly singly; foliage small, light green, semi-glossy; few prickles; medium (15-18 in.), upright growth; [seedling × Pink Sheri]; int. by Rennie Roses International, 1994

Wee Barbie Min, w, 1981, Jellyman, J.S.; bud globular; flowers cream-white, 43 petals, borne 10-20 per cluster, moderate fragrance; foliage dark; bushy growth; [seedling × seedling]; int. in 1980

Wee Benny Pol, mp, Williams, J.B.; dwarf, polyantha-like growth; int. by Hortico, Inc., 2005

Wee Beth Min, op, 1981, Cherry, R. & Welsh, E.; bud pointed, mossy; flowers salmon-pink, 11 petals, borne in clusters of 3-20, moderate sweetbriar fragrance; foliage small, dark, bristles on reverse; prickles red; bushy growth; [Orange Silk × Fairy Moss]; int. by Roy H. Rumsey, Pty. Ltd.

Wee Butterflies Pol, pb, 1990, Jerabek, Paul E.; bud pointed; flowers medium pink with white eye, small, single, borne in sprays of 3-35, slight fragrance; foliage medium size, light green, glossy; prickles straight, pink; bushy, low growth; hips round, small, red; [The Fairy × seedling]; int. in 1989

Wee Cracker F, or, 1996, Cocker, James & Sons; flowers orange vermilion, medium, dbl., borne in large clusters, slight fragrance; recurrent; foliage small, medium green, semi-glossy; some prickles; low (46-60 cm.), bushy, compact growth; [Len Turner × Jean Thomson Harris]; int. by James Cocker & Sons, 1995

Wee Jock Min, mr, 1980, Cocker, James; bud pointed; flowers small, 50 petals, borne 9-15 per cluster; recurrent; foliage small, fairly glossy, medium green; prickles red; low, compact growth; [National Trust × Wee Man]

Wee Lass Min, mr, 1975, Moore, Ralph S.; bud pointed; flowers blood-red, ½-1 in., 18 petals; foliage small, dark; upright, bushy growth; [Persian Princess × Persian Princess]; int. by Sequoia Nursery, 1974

Wee Man Min, mr, 1975, McGredy, Sam IV; flowers scarlet, 2 in., 14 petals; foliage glossy, dark; [Little Flirt × Marlena]; int. in 1974

Wee Matt – See **Waitemata**, Min

Wee One Min, mp, Tantau; int. in 1994

Wee Snowflake S, w, 2001, Weeks, Michael; flowers dbl., borne in large clusters, intense fragrance; non-remontant; foliage medium size, medium green, semi-glossy; prickles moderate, medium, hooked; growth spreading, tall (20-25 ft.); climber; fences, walls, pergolas; [Kiftsgate × unknown]; once-blooming

Wee Topper Min, mr, 1988, Anderson's Rose Nurseries; flowers small, dbl.; foliage small, light green, semi-glossy; bushy growth; [sport of Starina]

Week End HT, pb, Ghosh, Mr.&Mrs. S.; bud pointed; flowers light pink with apricot tones, reverse darker, petals prominently veined, large, dbl., high-centered, moderate sweet fragrance; recurrent; int. in 1998

Week-End S, dp

Weeping China Doll – See **China Doll, Climbing**, Cl Pol

Weepy S, pb, 2000, Lens, Louis; flowers pink, white center, reverse lighter, 2-3 cm., single, borne in large clusters, slight fragrance; recurrent; foliage small, medium green, glossy, disease-resistant; prickles moderate; growth spreading, medium (60 cm.); [*R. wichurana yakachinensis* × *R. multiflora adenocheata*]; int. by Louis Lens N.V., 1996

Weetwood HWich, lp, Bawden; flowers delicate rose pink, touched buff in heart, 4-5 cm., full, rosette, borne in hanging clusters, slight fragrance; some repeat; foliage dark green; vigorous (20-25 ft.) growth; int. in 1983

Weggis HT, pb, Huber; int. by Richard Huber AG, 2001

Wehrinsel S, dr, Berger, W.; flowers medium, semi-dbl., cupped, borne in clusters, slight fragrance; recurrent; strong, upright (2 m.) growth; int. in 1959

Weidenia S, lp, 1927, Alfons; flowers medium, single; hybrid canina

Weigand's Crimson Rambler – See **Non Plus Ultra**, HMult

Weight Watcher Success HT, yb, 1999, Zary, Dr. Keith W.; bud long, pointed ovoid; flowers light creamy yellow edged pink, 4½-5 in., 35 petals, high-centered, borne mostly singly, intense sweet and spicy fragrance; recurrent; foliage medium size, dark green, semi-glossy; prickles few, medium, hooked downward, tan; stems medium, strong; upright, spreading, tall (4-4½ ft.) growth; PP11838; [Henry Fonda × French Perfume]; int. by Bear Creek Gardens, Inc., 1999

Weihenstephan S, dp, 1964, Kordes; flowers rich pink, small, semi-dbl., borne in large clusters, slight fragrance; recurrent; vigorous (4½ ft.) growth

Weisse aus Sparrieshoop S, w, 1962, Kordes; flowers white, add pink tones in cool weather, 4 in., single, borne in large clusters, moderate fragrance; free-flowering; robust, tall growth; [sport of Sparrieshoop]

Weisse Better Times HT, w, 1940, Wirth; flowers large, dbl.

Weisse Echo Pol, w, 1925, Kiese; flowers medium, semi-dbl.

Weisse Gruss an Aachen F, w, 1944, Vogel; bud ovoid; flowers snow-white, large, very dbl., borne in clusters, moderate fragrance; recurrent; upright, bushy growth; [sport of Gruss an Aachen]

Weisse Immensee S, w, 1983, Kordes, W.; bud light pink; flowers small, 5 petals; foliage small, dark, glossy; spreading (10 ft.) growth; groundcover; [The Fairy × (*R. wichurana* × unknown)]; int. by Kordes Roses, 1982

Weisse Margo Koster Pol, w, 1939, Teschendorff; flowers small to medium, dbl.

Weisse Max Graf S, w, 1983, Kordes, W.; flowers white with yellow stamens, medium, semi-dbl., shallow cup, intense fragrance; foliage small, dark green, glossy; spreading (10 ft.) growth; groundcover; [seedling × (*R. wichurana* × unknown)]; int. by Kordes Roses

Weisse Nelkenrose HRg, w, Münster; flowers white, petals frayed, medium, dbl., cupped, borne in large clusters, slight fragrance; recurrent; strong (1 m.) growth; [sport of F.J. Grootendorst]; int. in 1966

Weisse New Dawn LCl, w, Berger; bud crimson-tipped; flowers medium, full, moderate fragrance; [sport of New Dawn]; int. in 1959

Weisse Repandia S, w, 1983, Kordes, W.; flowers small, semi-dbl.; foliage small, dark, glossy; spreading (7 ft.) growth; groundcover; [The Fairy × (*R. wichurana* × unknown)]; int. by Kordes Roses

Weisse Seerose – See **Nymphaea Alba**, HT

Weisse Tausendschön HMult, w, 1909, Kiese; bud pale yellow; flowers pure white; [sport of Tausendschön]

Weisse Woge HSpn, w, Strobel; flowers single; int. by BKN Strobel, 1999

Weisse Wolke S, w, Kordes; flowers pure white, yellow stamens, large, semi-dbl. to double, cupped, borne in clusters, moderate fragrance; recurrent; foliage dark green, glossy; bushy (3 ft.) growth; int. by W. Kordes' Söhne, 1993

Weisser Engel F, w, Verschuren; flowers clean white, dbl., cupped, borne in clusters, slight fragrance; recurrent; bushy (2 ft.), broad growth; int. in 1966

Weisser Herumstreicher HMult, w, 1899, Kiese; flowers pure white, large, dbl., borne in clusters; vigorous, climbing growth; [Daniel Lacombe × Pâquerette]

Weisser Maréchal Niel N, w, 1896, Deegan; flowers pure creamy-white, large, full, moderate tea fragrance

Weisserote Mme de Sancy de Parabère HSem, pb, Grimm, Wernt; flowers pink with a white center; int. in 1980

Weisses Meer F, w, VEG; flowers medium, semi-dbl.

Welch's Multiflora (strain of *R. multiflora*), w; thornless; growth sometimes used as understock; used for understock; int. by Mt. Arbor Nursery

Welcome HT, mp, 1948, Dickson, A.; bud ovoid; flowers glistening rose-pink, very large, 35 petals, high-centered; foliage leathery; vigorous, upright, bushy growth

Welcome Guest HT, ab, 1985, Cox, Arthur George; flowers apricot with a tinge of pink around edges of petals; [sport of Jan Guest]; int. in 1984

Welcome Home F, mr, 1984, Anderson's Rose Nurseries; flowers 20 petals; foliage medium size, light green, semi-glossy; upright growth; [Orange Sensation × Michelle]

Welcome Home LCl, pb, Kordes; int. by Mattock's Roses, 2002

Welcome Home HT, ly, 2007, Zary, Keith W.; flowers full, blooms borne mostly solitary; foliage medium size, dark green, glossy; prickles 8-10 mm., straight, greyed-orange, moderate; growth upright, tall, 5½ ft.; [Sun Goddess × O Sole Mio]; int. by Jackson & Perkins Wholesale, Inc., 2007

Welcome Stranger F, my, 1968, Fankhauser; flowers large, single; foliage extra large, glossy, leathery; very vigorous, compact growth; [Ophelia, Climbing × Allgold]; int. by A. Ross & Son

Well-Being S, yb, Harkness; flowers yellow centers blushed orange towards the rim, 4 in., 30 petals, open, cupped, borne in clusters of about five blooms, intense citrus, licorice and cloves fragrance; growth upright, tall (4-5 ft.); PPAF; int. by Harkness & Co., 2004; International Grand Prize for Perfume, Nantes, 2006

Well Done Min, my; flowers magnolia yellow, full, cupped, borne in clusters, moderate fragrance; free-flowering; robust (24 in.) growth

Wellesley HT, dp, 1905, Montgomery, A.; flowers dark rosy pink, large, dbl.; [Bridesmaid × Liberty]

Wellington C, m, 1832, Calvert; flowers crimson-rose, medium, full, cupped; growth branching; sometimes classed as HGal; int. by Int. prior to 1848

Well's Climber LCl, pb, Wells; int. in 1994

Well's Pink and White Climber – See **Well's Climber**, LCl

Wells' White Climber – See **Mme d'Arblay**, HMult

Wells's Garland – See **The Garland**, HMult

Wellworth HT, pb, 1949, LeGrice; flowers peach shaded gold, pointed, 5 in., 40 petals; foliage grayish green; vigorous growth; [Leontine Contenot × Golden Dawn]

Welsh Gold – See **Welwyn Garden Glory**, HT

Weltmeister 90 HT, dp, Dräger; int. in 1990

Welwyn Garden Glory HT, ab, Harkness; bud short; flowers amber-apricot, large, dbl., cupped, flared, moderate fragrance; recurrent; upright growth; int. in 1996

Wembley Stadium F, dp

Wenche HT, mr, 1997, Poole, Lionel; flowers large, very dbl., borne mostly singly; foliage medium size, dark green, semi-glossy; upright, medium growth; [Silver Jubilee × Loving Memory]

Wenche HT, w, 2006, Jaksland, Roger; flowers edged light red, 9 cm., full, borne mostly solitary; foliage medium size, medium green, semi-glossy; prickles 1 cm., sharp, red/brown, moderate; growth upright (80 × 80 cm.); bedding, borders, containers; [Sekel × Memoire]; int. by Roger Jaksland, 2003

Wendelien F, mr, 1946, Leenders, M.; flowers cardinal-red, 4 in., 22 petals, globular, borne in clusters; foliage bright green; vigorous, branching growth; [Donald Prior × seedling]; int. by Longley

Wendy – See **Para Ti**, Min

Wendy Pol, mp, 1949, Heers; flowers pink, open, medium, dbl., borne in clusters; foliage soft, light green; moderately vigorous, upright growth; RULED EXTINCT 11/91; [Tip-Top × Dorothy Perkins]; int. by Pacific Nursery

Wendy F, mp, 1991, Zipper, Herbert; flowers medium, dbl., exhibition, borne in small clusters, intense fragrance; foliage medium size, dark green, semi-glossy; few prickles; medium (75 cm.), upright growth; [Wendy Cussons × High Spirits]; int. by Magic Moment Miniature Roses, 1992

Wendy F, w, 1999, Schuurman, Frank B.; flowers 1½ in., full, borne in large sprays, no fragrance; foliage medium size, medium green, glossy; numerous prickles; upright, medium growth; int. by Franko Roses New Zealand, 1993

Wendy Ackerman Rose HT, ob; int. by J&P, 1998

Wendy Barrie Pol, op, 1936, Beckwith; flowers orange-salmon, well-formed, dbl.; vigorous, dwarf growth

Wendy Cussons HT, mr, 1960, Gregory; bud long, pointed; flowers rose-red, 5-6 in., 30 petals, high-centered, borne mostly singly, intense fragrance; recurrent; foliage leathery, glossy, dark; vigorous, well-branched growth; PP2104; believed to be Independence × Eden Rose; int. by Gregory & Son, 1960; Gold Medal, Portland, 1964, President's International Trophy, NRS, 1959, Golden Rose, The Hague, 1964, Gold Medal, NRS, 1959

Wendy Cussons, Climbing Cl HT, mr, 1967, Follen; int. by Gregory

Wendy Duckett F, mr, 1999, Jones, L.J.; flowers red cream, striking color, 1¼ in., full, borne in small clusters, slight fragrance; foliage small, medium green, glossy, impervious to rain; few prickles; upright, compact, medium growth; [Sheri Anne × (Whippet × Party Girl)]

Wendy Pease HT, yb, 1985, Bracegirdle, Derek T.; flowers medium, 35 petals; foliage medium size, medium green, semi-glossy; upright growth; [John Waterer × Tenerife]; int. in 1986

Wendy van Wanten F, ob, RvS-Melle; [Madelon × Patricia]; int. in 1994

Wenlock S, mr, 1985, Austin, David; flowers crimson, 5 in., very full, cupped, intense Old Rose & citrus fragrance; recurrent; foliage large, dark, semi-glossy; vigorous, bushy growth; shrub or low climber; [The Knight × Glastonbury]; int. in 1984

Wenzel Geschwind HT, m, 1902, Geschwind, R.; flowers purple/pink, medium to large, dbl., cupped, moderate fragrance; recurrent; upright (100 cm.), branching growth; [Princesse de Sagan × Comte de Bobrinsky]

Wenzel Geschwind, Climbing Cl HT, m, 1940, Vogel, M.; flowers purple/pink, medium to large, dbl.; [sport of Wenzel Geschwind]

Werner Dirks LCl, w, 1937, Kordes; bud long, pointed; flowers ivory-white, 4 in., dbl., high-centered, borne in clusters, moderate fragrance; foliage large, leathery, wrinkled; numerous prickles; long, strong stems; very vigorous, climbing growth; [Mrs Pierre S. duPont × Daisy Hill]

Werner Otto HT, my, 1995, Mungia, Larry; flowers medium yellow, 4-4½ in., 56 petals, borne mostly singly; foliage large, dark green, glossy; few prickles; medium, upright growth; [sport of Golden Fantasie]; int. by Montebello Rose Co., 1994

Werner Teschendorff F, op, 1949, Tantau; bud ovoid; flowers medium, dbl., cupped, borne in clusters; foliage glossy; vigorous, upright, bushy growth; [Swantje × Hamburg]; int. by Teschendorff

Werner von Blon S, m, Hetzel; flowers bright lilac-pink, moderate fragrance; good repeat; int. in 1993

Wesnianka HT, w, 1941, Costetske; flowers white, base carmine-yellow; [Mme Butterfly × Mrs T. Hillas]

Wessie Roos HT, mr, Kordes; bud pointed; flowers velvet red, brilliant red reverse, large, dbl., high-centered, slight fragrance; recurrent; foliage glossy; medium, rounded growth; int. by Ludwig's Roses, 1993

West Coast HT, mp, 1988, McGredy, Sam IV; flowers clear medium pink, large, dbl., urn-shaped, borne singly and in clusters, slight fragrance; recurrent; foliage large, light green, matte; medium to tall, bushy growth; [((Yellow Pages × Kabuki) × Golden Gate) × (unnamed Poulsen seedling × Picasso)]; int. by McGredy Roses International, 1986

West Country F, rb, Gandy; flowers red and gold, borne in large trusses; recurrent; foliage light green; bushy, medium growth; int. by Gandy's Roses, 2002

West Grove HT, 1914, Dingee & Conard; [Liberty × Kaiserin Auguste Viktoria]

Westbroekpark F, or, 1968, deRuiter; flowers medium, dbl., borne in clusters; foliage dark; [Orange Sensation × Kimono]

Westerland S, ab, 1976, Kordes; bud ovoid; flowers apricot-orange, 3-5 in., 20 petals, cupped, borne in clusters, intense rose, clove, spice fragrance; recurrent; foliage large, dark green, soft; vigorous, upright, climbing growth; [Friedrich Worlein × Circus]; int. in 1969; ADR, 1974

Western Gold HT, my, 1932, Western Rose Co.; flowers clear yellow; [sport of Talisman]

Western Sun HT, dy, 1965, Poulsen, Niels D.; flowers deep yellow, 5 in., 40 petals, no fragrance; free-flowering; foliage dark green; moderate growth; [(Golden Scepter × unknown) × Golden Sun]; int. by McGredy & Son

Western Sunlight HT, ab, 1990, Davidson, Harvey D.; bud pointed; flowers apricot-orange, aging to yellow, large, 31 petals, high-centered, borne usually singly, slight fruity fragrance; foliage medium size, dark green, glossy, serrated; prickles hooked downward, light brown; upright, medium growth; hips inverted, orange; does not set seed readily; PP7442; [((Honey Favorite × Irish Mist) × (San Francisco × Prima Ballerina)) × Just Joey]; int. by Hortico Roses, 1990

Western Sunset F, yb, 1958, Silva; bud pointed; flowers yellow tipped pink, becoming pink and then mahogany-red, bor, 1½-2 in., 35 petals, cupped; foliage leathery; vigorous, upright growth; PP2191; [Maxine × Masquerade]

Westfalen S, Scholle, E.; int. in 1969

Westfalengold F, Noack, Werner; int. in 1979

Westfalengruss F, mr, 1978, Hubner; bud ovoid; flowers fire-red, medium, dbl.; foliage glossy; low, bushy growth; int. by O. Baum

Westfalenpark S, ab, 1987, Kordes, W.; flowers large, full, cupped, moderate fragrance; recurrent; foliage large, dark green, glossy; bushy (5 ft.), spreading growth; [seedling × Las Vegas]

Westfield Beauty HT, ab, 1923, Morse; bud long, pointed; flowers deep coppery apricot, tinted golden and salmon-pink, dbl.; [Lady Pirrie × Mme Edouard Herriot]

Westfield Flame HT, or, 1925, Morse; bud long, pointed; flowers very deep flame, dbl.; [Mme Edouard Herriot × Diadem]

Westfield Gem HT, dr, 1925, Morse; flowers dark maroon-crimson, dbl.; [sport of Col. Oswald Fitzgerald]

Westfield Scarlet HT, mr, 1931, Morse; flowers clear scarlet, open, very large, dbl.; foliage leathery, dark; bushy growth; [sport of Lady Inchiquin]; Gold Medal, NRS, 1932

Westfield Star HT, w, 1922, Morse; bud sulphur yellow; flowers cream, fading white, flat, moderate fragrance; recurrent; strong, vigorous growth; [sport of Ophelia]

Westfriesia F, dp, 1965, deVries; bud ovoid; flowers pink-red, small, very dbl., borne in clusters

Westminster HT, rb, 1960, Robinson, H.; flowers red, gold base and reverse, large, 35 petals, loose, intense fragrance; recurrent; foliage dark; vigorous, tall growth; [Gay Crusader × Peace]; Gold Medal, NRS, 1961

Westminster 50th Anniversary HT, mr, 2007, Aguilar, Sergio; flowers medium red, reverse lighter, fading to dark pink, 5 in., dbl., borne mostly solitary; foliage medium size, dark green, semi-glossy; prickles medium, hooked, moderate; growth upright, compact, medium (4 ft.); cutting, garden decoration; [Elizabeth Taylor × New Zealand]; int. in 2007

Westminster Pink HT, mp, Fryer, Gareth; flowers pink with touch of coral, large, dbl., high-centered, borne mostly singly, moderate fragrance; recurrent; foliage dark green, glossy; medium, rounded growth; int. by Fryers, 1998

Westmont Min, mr, 1959, Moore, Ralph S.; bud pointed; flowers bright red, 1½ in., semi-dbl.; foliage leathery, semi-glossy; small vigorous (12-18 in.), bushy growth; PP1950; [(*R. wichurana* × Floradora) × (Oakington Ruby × Floradora)]; int. by Sequoia Nursery, 1958

Westward Ho! HT, rb, 1964, Allen, E.M.; flowers mahogany-red, reverse silver, 4½ in., 42 petals; foliage very dark; vigorous, upright, compact growth; [Karl Herbst × Pink Charming]; int. by Sanday

Westzeit F, ob, Noack; flowers orange with apricot and pink tones, 6 cm., dbl., cupped, borne in clusters; fast repeat; foliage dark green (new growth reddish), glossy; medium growth; int. by Noack Rosen, 2006

Wetteriana F, or

Wettra F, mr, 1985, Rijksstation Voor Sierplantenteelt; flowers large, 20 petals, cupped, borne 4-15 per cluster, no fragrance; foliage dark, matte; prickles red; upright growth; [Pink Puff × Barcarolle]; int. in 1976

Wettra, Climbing Cl F, mr

What a Peach S, ab, 2000, Warner, Chris; bud pointed, ovoid; flowers clear apricot, retaining color well, 5-6 cm., 26-32 petals, cupped, borne in small clusters, slight tea fragrance; free-flowering; foliage small, dark green, glossy; prickles numerous, 5-10 mm, straight, angled down, brown; stems new shoots dark red; growth very upright, bushy, tall (140-180 cm.); garden decoration; hips globular to urn-shaped, orange; PP15287; [Laura Ford × Sweet Magic]; int. by Weeks' Roses, 2002

What A Surprize Min, op, 2004, Graham, Susan Brandt; flowers orange pink with yellow base, 2-2½ cm., dbl., borne mostly solitary; foliage medium size, dark green, semi-glossy; prickles moderate, medium, curved; growth upright, medium (24-30 in.); containers, borders, exhibition; [sport of Hot Tamale]; int. by Susan Brandt Graham, 2005

Wheatcroft Giant HT, lp, 1962, Wheatcroft Bros.; flowers pearly pink, well-formed, large; vigorous growth

Wheatcroft's Baby Crimson – See **Perla de Alcañada**, Min

Wheatcroft's Golden Polyantha – See **Goldene Johanna Tantau**, F

Wheato F, dp, Rearsby Roses, Ltd.

Wheaton's Red LCl, dr, Williams, J.B.; flowers dark red blend; good repeater; foliage disease-resistant; nearly thornless; int. by Hortico, 2004

Wheel Horse Classic F, dr, Harkness; flowers deep, intense, crimson red, medium, hybrid tea; int. by R. Harkness & Co., 1996

Where The Heart Is HT, dp, 2002, Cocker, Anne G.; bud long; flowers cerise pink, 2½ in., full, borne mostly solitary, moderate fragrance; foliage large, medium green, glossy; prickles moderate, 9 mm., straight; growth bushy, tall (2½-3 ft.); garden decorative; [National Trust × Silver Jubilee]; int. by James Cocker & Sons, 2002

Whickham Highway F, r, 1992, Horner, Heather M.; flowers brick red, medium, 6-14 petals, borne in large clusters; foliage medium size, medium green, glossy; some prickles; tall (120 cm.), upright growth; [Mary Sumner × (KORp × Southampton)]; int. in 1993

Whimsical Min, pb, 1980, Strawn, Leslie E.; bud pointed; flowers either light pink or deeper peach-pink on same plant at same time, 48 petals, high-centered, borne singly, no fragrance; foliage medium green; upright, bushy growth; [Tiki × Baby Betsy McCall]; int. by Pixie Treasures Min. Roses

Whipped Cream Min, w, 1968, Moore, Ralph S.; bud pointed, ivory; flowers small, dbl.; foliage light green, leathery; vigorous, bushy, dwarf growth; [(*R. wichurana* × Carolyn Dean) × White King]; int. by Sequoia Nursery

Whippet HT, pb, 1973; flowers salmon-pink, reverse lighter, 5 in., 35 petals, high-centered, slight fragrance; moderate growth; int. by D. H. Scott, 1972

Whirlaway MinFl, w, 2005, Clemons, David E.; flowers pure white, 2 in., full, high-centered, borne mostly solitary, no fragrance; foliage medium size, medium green, semi-glossy; prickles few, small, straight, very thin, light green; stems long; growth upright, tall (36-48 in); exhibition, garden decoration; [Merlot × Foolish Pleasure]; int. in 2006

Whirlygig Min, pb, 1999, Justice, Jerry G.; flowers soft pink and white, reverse darker, 2 in., single, slight fragrance; foliage medium size, dark green, semi-glossy; upright, medium (20-22 in.) growth; [(seedling × Magic Carrousel) × unknown]; int. by Justice Miniature Roses, 1999

Whisky F, yb, 1964, Delforge; flowers yellow shaded orange-bronze, open, large, dbl., borne in clusters; foliage glossy, light green; very vigorous, upright growth; [Cognac × Arc-en-Ciel]

Whisky – See **Whisky Mac**, HT

Whisky, Climbing – See **Whisky Mac, Climbing**, Cl HT

Whisky Gill HT, ob, 1973, Colby; flowers burnt-orange to bright orange; [sport of Whisky Mac]; int. in 1972

Whisky Mac HT, yb, 1969, Tantau, Math.; bud ovoid; flowers bronze-yellow, well-formed, large, 30 petals, urn-shaped, borne mostly singly, intense sweet fragrance; free-flowering; foliage dark green, glossy; vigorous, upright, bushy growth; int. by Rosen Tantau, 1967

Whisky Mac, Climbing Cl HT, yb, 1984, Anderson's Rose Nurseries; [sport of Whisky Mac]; int. in 1985

Whisper Pol, Jelly, R. G.; PP3402

Whisper F, lp, 1971, Cants of Colchester, Ltd.; flowers pale pink, 3-3½ in., 10 petals; foliage light; vigorous growth; [Queen Elizabeth × Monique]

Whisper HT, w, Dickson; bud pointed, ovoid; flowers ivory, 5 in., 30-35 petals, high-centered, borne singly, slight musk fragrance; recurrent; foliage semi-glossy, dark green; prickles some, 5-8 mm, straight, brown; stems strong; vigorous (5-6 ft.) growth; PP14596; [Solitaire × Elina]; int. in 2003

Whisper Louise Pol, lp, Robinson; flowers soft clear pink, dbl., cupped, opening flat, moderate musk fragrance; recurrent; [Kathleen × Unknown]; int. in 1994

Whistle Stop Min, rb, 1989, McGredy, Sam IV; flowers red blend (striped), small, semi-dbl., slight fragrance; foliage small, medium green, semi-glossy; bushy growth; [Mighty Mouse × Hurdy Gurdy]; int. in 1989

White Aachen F, ly, 1937, Western Rose Co.; flowers buff-yellow to pure white; [sport of Gruss an Aachen]

White Alaska HT, w, 1960, Hartgerink; bud long, pointed; flowers pure white, 4½-5 in., 20 petals, high-centered; foliage leathery, dark; vigorous, upright growth; PP1862; [White Ophelia × seedling]; int. by Armacost & Royston

White America LCl, w

White American Beauty – See **Frau Karl Druschki**, HP

White American Beauty, Climbing – See **Freedom**, LCl

White Angel Min, w, 1973, Moore, Ralph S.; bud long, pointed; flowers white, yellow tints in center, 1 in., 30 petals, high-centered, borne singly and several together, slight fragrance; recurrent; foliage small, light green, semi-glossy; prickles few, medium, hooked slightly downward; stems sturdy, wiry; vigorous, dwarf, bushy growth; hips none ; PP3538; [(*R. wichurana* × Floradora) × (Little Darling × Red Miniature seedling)]; int. by Sequoia Nursery, 1971; AOE, ARS, 1975

White Arrow F, ab, Teranishi; int. by Itami Rose Garden, 2005

White Aster Min, w, Moore; bud long-pointed, small, soft pink; flowers white, small, full, borne in small clusters; foliage foliate leathery, glossy, disease-resistant; growth vigorous, bushy dwarf (10 in.); PP1767; [(*R. wichurana* × Floradora) × (Carolyn Dean × Tom Thumb)]; int. by Sequoia Nursery, 1957

White Avalanche S, w, 1988, Williams, J. Benjamin; flowers cream, opening to pure white, small, dbl., borne in clusters; foliage medium size, medium green, glossy, disease-resistant; spreading, compact, uniform., winter hardy growth; [Sea Foam × The Fairy]

White Baby Rambler – See **Katharina Zeimet**, Pol

White Baby Star Min, w, 1965, Spring Hill Nursery; [sport of Baby Gold Star]; int. by Wyant

White Banksia – See ***R. banksiae banksiae*** (Aiton)

White Baroness HP, w, Paul & Son; flowers pure white, large, full; [sport of Baroness Rothschild]

White Bath M, w, 1817, Slater; flowers pure white, occasionally striped carmine, large, full, globular; [sport of Common Moss]

White Beauty HT, w, 1965, Brooks, M.L.; bud large, pointed; flowers pure white, 4½-5½ in., 30-35 petals, high-centered, cupped, borne singly, moderate spicy fragrance; recurrent; foliage medium green, semi-glossy; prickles several, medium, straight; stems strong, medium; bushy growth; hips short, globular, green; PP1825; [sport of The Doctor]; int. by Texas Rose Research Foundation, 1964

White Beauty – See **My Fifi**, S single

White Bella Rosa – See **Bella Weiss**, F

White Belle of Portugal LCl, w

White Bells Min, w, 1984, Poulsen Roser APS; bud bright yellow; flowers pale yellow to white, 35 petals, rosette, borne in clusters, slight fragrance; scattered repeat; foliage small, medium green, semi-glossy; groundcover; spreading growth; [Mini-Poul × Temple Bells]; int. by John Mattock, Ltd, 1983

White Bianca – See **Fair Bianca**, S

White Blush A, w, Sievers, Rolf; flowers cream white, full, cupped, moderate fragrance; non-remontant; medium growth; int. in 1988

White Bon Silène – See **Bon Silène Blanc**, T

White Bonnet F, w

White Bougère T, w, 1898, Dunlop; flowers pure white

White Bouquet F, w, 1957, Boerner; bud ovoid; flowers 45 petals, gardenia-like, borne in irregular clusters, moderate spicy fragrance; foliage dark green, glossy; bushy growth; PP1415; [Glacier × (Pinocchio × unknown)]; int. by J&P, 1956

White Boursault – See **Blush Boursault**, Bslt

White Briarcliff HT, w, 1932, Lens; bud long, pointed; flowers pure white, large, dbl., high-centered; foliage leathery; vigorous growth; [(Briarcliff × Kaiserin Auguste Viktoria) × (Briarcliff × MrsHerbert Stevens)]; int. by J&P

White Butterfly HT, w, 1954, Spanbauer; bud long, pointed; flowers white, inner petals pale chartreuse, center, 3½-4½ in., 24 petals, cupped, moderate fragrance; foliage leathery; vigorous, compact growth; PP1337; [Ophelia × Curly White]; John Cook Medal, ARS, 1957

White Cap Cl HT, w, Brownell; bud medium, pointed; flowers nearly pure white, 3½-4 in., 60 petals, high-centered, then open, borne both singly and in small clusters, moderate fragrance; recurrent; prickles several; stems long, stiff; upright, tall growth; PP1273; [unnamed wichurana seedling × Break O' Day, Climbing]; int. in 1954

White Captain HRg, w, Spek/Captain

White Carpet – See **Natchez**, Min

White Cascade HT, w, 1993, Strahle, B. Glen; flowers large, white, 3-3½ in., very dbl., borne mostly singly; foliage medium size, medium green, semi-glossy; some prickles; medium, upright growth; [Coquette × Jack Frost]; int. by Carlton Rose Nurseries, 1984

White Castle – See **Ledreborg**, F

White Cécile Brünner Pol, w, 1909, Fraque; flowers white, sulfur yellow and buff; [sport of Mlle Cécile Brunner]

White Chariot Min, w, Williams, J. Benjamin; bud light apricot; flowers open to almost white, small, slight fragrance; recurrent; int. by Hortico, Inc., 2005

White Charm F, w, 1959, Swim & Weeks; bud long, pointed; flowers white, base yellow-green, 2½-3 in., 17-22 petals, high-centered, moderate fragrance; foliage leathery; bushy, upright growth; RULED EXTINCT 10/88; [Pinocchio × Virgo]; int. in 1958

White Charm Min, w, 1989, Williams, Ernest D.; bud long; flowers near white to soft yellow, sweetheart, 33 petals, high-centered, intense fragrance; foliage small, medium green, glossy; bushy, medium to tall growth; [Tom Brown × Over the Rainbow]; int. in 1988

White Chateau HT, w, 1999, Teranishi, K.; bud ivory; flowers pure white, 5 in., full, high-centered, slight fragrance; growth to 4½ ft.; [Ophelia × seedling]; int. by Itami Rose Nursery, 1996

White Chatillon Pol, w; bud pale pink, fading to white.; [probably a sport of Chatillon Rose]

White Chipper Min, w

White Chocolate Min, w, 2001, Bennett, Dee; flowers cream, dbl. to full, high-centered, borne mostly solitary, slight fragrance; recurrent; foliage medium size, medium green, semi-glossy; prickles moderate; stems long; growth upright, tall (2½-3 ft.); garden decorative, exhibition, cutting; [sport of Jean Kenneally]; int. by Tiny Petals Nursery, 2001

White Christmas HT, w, 1953, H&S; bud long, pointed; flowers pure white, medium, dbl., high-centered; foliage leathery, light green; moderate, upright growth; [Sleigh Bells × seedling]

White Christmas, Climbing Cl HT, w, Nakasuji; int. in 1968

White Clair Matin S, w; growth large shrub or low (2 m.) climber; [sport of Clair Matin]; int. by Mistydowns, 2004

White Cloud – See **Hakuun**, F

White Cloud Min, w, 1988, Saville, F. Harmon; flowers white with pale pink; PP6876; [sport of Buttons 'n' Bows]; int. by Nor'East Min. Roses

White Cloud – See **Weisse Wolke**, S

White Clouds Cl HT, w, 1953, Silva; bud long, pointed; flowers 4½ in., 50 petals; foliage leathery, dark; vigorous growth; RULED EXTINCT 8/88; [Frau Karl Druschki × Kaiserin Auguste Viktoria]

White Cochet – See **White Maman Cochet**, T

White Cockade LCl, w, 1969, Cocker; flowers 8 cm., dbl., borne in small clusters, moderate fragrance; foliage dark green, glossy; numerous prickles; vigorous, low, climbing growth; [New Dawn × Circus]

White Colorado F, w; int. by Select, 1998

White Columbia, Climbing Cl HT, w, 1934, Clark's Rose Nursery

White Comet – See **Blanche Comète**, HT dbl.

White Cover – See **Kent**, S

White Cross LCl, w, 1950, Hester; bud ovoid; flowers white, center tinted lemon, large, very dbl.; foliage leathery, glossy; very vigorous growth; [sport of Mrs Arthur Curtiss James]

White Crystal HMsk, w, 2000, Lens, Louis; flowers white, shaded pink, reverse white, 3 cm., single, borne in large clusters, moderate fragrance; foliage medium size, dark green, glossy, disease-resistant; prickles moderate; upright, tall (150-200 cm.) growth; [(*R. multiflora adenocheata* × Ballerina) × Felicia]; int. by Louis Lens N.V., 1992

White Cupido Min, w, deRuiter; int. by Greenheart Farms, 2004

White Daily Rose – See **Indica Alba**, Ch

White Dawn – See **White New Dawn**, LCl

White de Meaux – See **Rose de Meaux White**, C

White Decumba S, w; flowers pure white, yellow stamens, small, single, flat, borne in small clusters, moderate fragrance; recurrent; foliage glossy; low, spreading, groundcover growth; hips small; int. by Belle Epoque, 2003

White Delight HT, w, 1989, Warriner, William A.; bud ovoid, pointed; flowers white with pink blush, 4½ in., 35-40 petals, high-centered, borne usually singly, slight fragrance; recurrent; foliage medium size, dark green, matte; prickles moderate, hooked, medium, brown; stems long, strong; upright, medium growth; PP6664; [White Masterpiece × Futura]; int. by J&P, 1990

White Demure F, w, 1952, Boerner; bud ovoid; flowers 2-2½ in., 30-35 petals, flat; foliage leathery; vigorous, compact, bushy growth; [sport of Demure]

White Diamond S, w; flowers bright white, 2½ in., double, cupped, moderate honey/sweet fragrance; recurrent; foliage dark green, glossy; medium (4 ft.) growth; int. by Interplant, 1994

White Dian Min, w, 1965, Moore, Ralph S.; flowers white, sometimes light pink; [sport of Dian]; int. by Sequoia Nursery

White Dick Koster Pol, 1946, Grootendorst, F.J.

White Dog S, w

White Dog Rose – See ***R. arvensis*** (Hudson)

White Dorothy HWich, w, 1908, Cant, B. R.; flowers creamy white, small, 30-40 petals, pompon, borne in large clusters, no fragrance; recurrent; [sport of Dorothy Perkins]

White Dorothy Perkins – See **White Dorothy**, HWich

White Dream Min, w, 1986, Lens, Louis; flowers small, 36 petals, high-centered, borne in clusters of 3-28; prickles hooked, greenish-brown; low, bushy growth; [seedling × seedling]; int. in 1982

White Drift S, w, Meilland, Alain; bud small, ovoid; flowers bright white, 2-4.5 cm., 6 petals, flat, borne usually in clusters, moderate fragrance; free-flowering; foliage medium green, glossy; prickles several, small, hooked downward, green; low, spreading, mounded growth; PP15960; [(*R. wichurana* × The Fairy) × Iceberg]; int. in 2004

White Duchess HT, w, 1964, Herholdt, J.A.; bud spiral, pointed; flowers snow-white, medium; foliage glossy; strong stems; vigorous growth; int. by Herholdt's Nursery

White Duchesse de Brabant – See **Mme Joseph Schwartz**, T

White Eden LCl, w, 2004, Meilland International; bud medium, globular; flowers creamy white, 12-13 cm., very full, cupped, borne in small clusters, slight fragrance; recurrent; foliage large, dark green, glossy; prickles very few, short, straight, brown; growth spreading, tall (to 12 ft.); garden; hips round, yellow-green; PP16739; [sport of Pierre de Ronsard]; int. by The Conard-Pyle Company, 2004

White Edge HRg, w; int. by Roses d'Antan, 2003

White Elegance HT, w, Hiroshima; int. by Hiroshima Bara-en, 1996

White Elfe Pol, w, 1954, Holmes, V.E.; bud pointed; flowers white faintly tinted pink, 2-2½ in., 40-45 petals, high-centered, borne in clusters of 3-7; foliage dark, leathery; vigorous growth; PP1377; [sport of Rosenelfe]; int. by Avansino-Mortensen & Co., 1954

White Ensign HT, w, 1925, McGredy; flowers creamy white, large, very dbl., rosette, slight fragrance; free-flowering; foliage leathery, dark green, glossy; vigorous growth

White Ensign F, w, J&P; flowers creamy white, double, high-centered, borne in clusters; medium growth; int. by De Boer Roses, 2005

White Esteem HT, w, K&S; flowers clear white, medium, double, high-centered, borne mostly singly; recurrent; int. by KSG Son, 2001

White Euphoria S, w, Interplant; int. in 1999

White Fairy Min, w, 1952, Moore, Ralph S.; flowers small, very dbl., borne in clusters; int. by Sequoia Nursery

White Fairy Pol, w, Martin, John & Gina; flowers pure white, pompon, borne in large clusters; foliage dark green; low growth; int. by Egmont Nursery, 1998

White Feather Min, w, 1986, Moore, Ralph S.; flowers pure white, small, 15 petals, loose, borne in clusters of 3-5, slight fragrance; foliage small, light green, semi-glossy; prickles very few; medium, bushy growth; no fruit; [(*R. wichurana* × Floradora) × Peachy White]; int. by Moore Min. Roses, 1980

White Festival – See **Springwood White**, Min

White Finch Pol, w, 1937, Stielow, F.C.; flowers white, tinted pink; [sport of Mrs R.M. Finch]

White Fleurette S, w, Briant; flowers pure white, yellow stamens, medium, single, flat, borne in small clusters; recurrent; bushy growth; int. in 1989

White Flight – See **White Mrs Flight**, HMult, 1916

White Floorshow S, w; flowers pure white, 3 in., 30 petals, slight fragrance; profuse; foliage mid-green; growth spreading, mounding, 2½ × 3½ ft.; int. by Harkness, 2001

White Flower Carpet F, w, Noack, Werner; flowers clear white, yellow stamens, 6 cm., semi-double, shallow cup, borne in large clusters; recurrent; foliage medium to dark green, glossy; erect growth; int. in 1991; Golden Rose, The Hague, 1995, Gold Medal, RNRS, 1991, ADR, 1991

White Forcer Pol, w, 1926, Spek; flowers larger and

borne in larger trusses than parent; [sport of Jesse]

White Four Seasons Rose D, w, before 1785; flowers very pale blush; not dependably remontant

White Fragrant Mist HT, w, 1990, Oregon Roses, Inc.; bud pointed; flowers white with slight lavender tinge, large, dbl., cupped, borne mostly singly, heavy fruity fragrance; foliage medium size, dark green, glossy; growth upright, tall; [sport of Lavande]; int. by DeVor Nurseries, Inc.

White Garnette F, w, 1952, Boerner; flowers white tinged cream, 2 in., 30-35 petals, borne in clusters; foliage rich green; bushy growth; [(Pinocchio × unknown) × Garnette]; int. by J&P

White Gem Min, w, 1976, Meilland; bud long; flowers soft ivory, shaded pale tan, 1½ in., 90 petals, slight fragrance; foliage large, glossy, dark green; upright, bushy growth; [Darling Flame × Jack Frost]; int. by C-P

White Gene Boerner F, w, 1978, Takatori, Yoshiho; [sport of Gene Boerner]; int. by Japan Rose Nursery

White Gold LCl, w, 1943, Brownell; bud long, pointed; flowers white, center yellow, petals reflexed, dbl., high-centered; foliage dark, glossy; vigorous, climbing (20 ft.) growth; [Glenn Dale × Mrs Arthur Curtiss James]

White Gold F, w, 1998, Cocker, Ann G.; flowers white with golden yellow center, opens wide and flat, 3 in., full, borne in large clusters, moderate fragrance; foliage large, medium green, semi-glossy; prickles moderate, medium, slightly hooked; tall, bushy growth; [Morning Jewel × Myriam]; int. by James Cocker & Sons, 1998

White Gold 98 – See **White Gold**, F

White Golden Gate – See **Ivory**, T

White Grootendorst HRg, w, 1962, Eddy; flowers small, full, moderate fragrance; [sport of Pink Grootendorst]

White Gruss an Aachen – See **Weisse Gruss an Aachen**, F

White Haze S, w, Tantau; flowers shining white, guard petals may have violet-red stripe, yellow stamens, semi-double, shallow cup, borne in clusters; recurrent; foliage dark green, very glossy; compact, spreading, bushy growth; int. by Rosen Tantau, 2006

White Hedge HRg, w; flowers pure white, small yellow stamens, large, single, shallow cup, moderate fragrance; recurrent; foliage light green; upright, closely packed growth; possibly from Nyveldt, 1955

White Heritage – See **Rose-Marie**, S

White Hermosa – See **Marie Lambert**, T

White Hero S, w, Rex, Dr. Robert W.

White House HT, w, 1951, Silva; bud high-centered to ovoid; flowers satiny white; foliage thick, light green; [McGredy's Yellow × Frau Karl Druschki]

White House HT, w, 1995, Sheldon, John & Robin; flowers white with pink tinge, medium, full, borne mostly singly; foliage medium size, medium green, matte; upright, medium growth; [Pristine × (Spirit of Glasnost × Lanvin)]

White Ivory HT, w, 2003, Wells, Verlie W.; flowers ivory white, 4½ in., full, borne mostly solitary, intense fragrance; foliage medium size, dark green, semi-glossy; prickles in., straight; growth upright, tall; garden, exhibition; [seedling × seedling]; int. by Wells MidSouth Roses, 2003

White Jacques Cartier P, w; flowers clean white, very full, intense fragrance; recurrent; strong (5 ft.) growth; [sport of Jacques Cartier]

White Jewel F, w, 1960, Boerner; flowers 4 in., 33 petals, cupped, borne in clusters, moderate fragrance; vigorous, bushy growth; PP1628; [(Starlite × unknown) × Glacier seedling]; int. by J&P, 1957

White Joy HT, w, 1952, Spanbauer; bud pointed; flowers pure white, 4-5 in., 55-65 petals, flat; foliage leathery; bushy, upright growth

White Junior Miss Gr, w; flowers dainty white

White Killarney HT, w, 1909, Waban Conservatories; flowers snowy white, with enormous petals, large, semi-dbl., moderate fragrance; recurrent; [sport of Killarney]

White Killarney, Climbing Cl HT, w, 1920, Conard & Jones; [sport of Killarney]

White King Min, w, 1961, Moore, Ralph S.; bud pointed, ovoid; flowers cream-white, 1½ in., 45 petals, moderate fragrance; foliage leathery; bushy (12 in.) growth; PP2366; [Golden Glow × Zee]; int. by Sequoia Nursery

White Knight HT, w, 1957, Meilland, F.; bud long, pointed; flowers clear white, 4 in., 28-35 petals, high-centered, opens cupped, borne singly, no fragrance; recurrent; foliage leathery, light green; prickles several, medium, straight, pointed downward; vigorous, upright growth; hips none ; PP1359; [(Virgo × Peace) × Virgo]; int. by URS, 1955

White Knight, Climbing Cl HT, w, 1967, Meilland (also Komatsu, 1959); int. by Kakujitsuen

White Knights – See **White Nights**, S

White La France – See **Augustine Guinoiseau**, HT

White La Vie en Rose F, w

White Lace S, w; flowers creamy white, double, rosette, borne in clusters; recurrent; foliage glossy; compact (20 in.) growth

White Lady HT, w, 1889, Paul; [sport of Lady Mary Fitzwilliam]

White Lady – See **Dame Blanche**, HT

White Lafayette – See **Dagmar Späth**, F

White Lightnin' Gr, w, 1979, Swim, H.C. & Christensen, J.E.; bud ovoid, pointed; flowers clear white, ruffled, 3½-4 in., 30 petals, high-centered, borne in small clusters, intense citrus fragrance; recurrent; foliage glossy, medium green; prickles few, short, straight to hooked slightly downward, brown; upright, bushy growth; PP4670; [Angel Face × Misty]; int. by Armstrong Nursery, 1980

White Linen HT, w, 2005, Adlong, Paula; flowers white with pale pink edges, reverse white, 4-4½ in., full, borne mostly solitary, intense fragrance; foliage medium size, medium green, matte; prickles moderate, average, straight, green; upright, tall (4-5 ft.) growth; [Chrystalline × Louise Estes]

White Look HT, w

White Love HT, w, 1978, Buisman, G. A. H.; bud long; flowers ivory-white, large, intense fragrance; foliage dark; bushy growth; [Frau Karl Druschki × (Peace × Unknown seedling)]; int. in 1973

White Ma Perkins F, w, 1962, McDonald; bud long, pointed; flowers snow white, large, 20-40 petals, borne in clusters, intense fragrance; recurrent; foliage light green; very vigorous, upright growth; PP1965; [sport of Ma Perkins]; int. by Hennessey, 1962

White Madonna Min, w, 1975, Moore, Ralph S.; bud long, pointed; flowers white to pale pink, 1 in., 33 petals, slight fragrance; foliage glossy, leathery; upright, bushy growth; PP3844; [(*R. wichurana* × Floradora) × (Little Darling × Unnamed red Miniature)]; int. by Sequoia Nursery, 1973

White Magic – See **Class Act**, F

White Magic HMsk, w, 2000, Lens, Louis; flowers white with yellow stamens, 2-3 cm., single, flat, borne in large clusters, moderate fragrance; recurrent; foliage medium size, medium green, semi-glossy, disease-resistant; prickles moderate; bushy, medium (120 cm.), arching growth; [Ravel × *R.* × *dupontii*]; int. by Louis Lens N.V., 1989

White Magic HT, w; int. by Certified Roses, 1998

White Magic Carpet S, w; flowers white, less than 2 in., dbl., borne in clusters, slight wild rose fragrance; recurrent; foliage dark green, glossy; broad, bushy (40-60 cm.) growth; int. as Wagtail Cover, Poulsen, 1994

White Majesty HT, w, Meilland; flowers pure white, 15-20 petals, high-centered, borne mostly singly, no fragrance; recurrent; foliage dark green, glossy; stems long, strong; upright, medium growth; PPAF; [sport of Paris d'Yves St. Laurent]; int. by Meilland Richardier, 2006

White Majesty HT, w, Meilland

White Maman Cochet T, w, 1896, Cook, J.W.; flowers white, often flushed pink; [sport of Maman Cochet]

White Maman Cochet, Climbing Cl T, w, 1907, Knight, G.; flowers white streaked pink, very large, dbl.; [sport of White Maman Cochet]; int. by Leedle & Co., 1911

White Marie Curie F, w, Meilland; flowers white; free-flowering; int. by Roses du Temps Passé, 2006

White Masterpiece HT, w, 1969, Boerner; bud long, pointed; flowers satiny white, long peduncle, 5½-6 in., 50-60 petals, high-centered, borne mostly singly, slight tea fragrance; recurrent; foliage large, dark green, leathery; prickles some, angled downward; stems long, strong; upright, spreading growth; PP2998; [(Revelry × Pink Masterpiece) × seedling]; int. by J&P

White Masterpiece, Climbing Cl HT, w, Sakagami; int. in 1982

White Max Graf – See **Weisse Max Graf**, S

White Meidiland S, w, 1987, Meilland, Mrs. Marie-Louise; bud oval; flowers white with slight pink edge, slight yellow cast at times, 8 cm., 60 -70 petals, cupped, borne in clusters, no fragrance; recurrent; foliage medium size, dark green, glossy; large, spreading growth; PP6088; [Temple Bells × Coppélia 76]

White Meillandina Min, w, 1984, Meilland, Mrs. Marie-Louise; flowers medium, semi-dbl., no fragrance; foliage small, light green, semi-glossy; bushy growth; [Katharina Zeimet × White Gem]; int. by Meilland Et Cie, 1983

White Meilove F, w; int. in 2003

White Merveille – See **White Tausendschön**, HMult

White Midinette Cl Min, w, Taschner, Ludwig; flowers white with yellow stamens, small, double, pompon, borne in clusters; free-flowering; tall (10 ft.), arching growth; int. by Ludwig's Roses, 2003

White Mikado F, w, Tantau; florist rose; int. by Rosen Tantau

White Mimollet F, w, 1985, Ota, Kaichiro; [sport of Mimollet]; int. in 1984

White Mini-Wonder Min, w, 1988, Meilland, Alain A.; bud conical, small; flowers clear white, thin petals, 1½ in., 40 petals, flat cup, borne in small clusters, no fragrance; free-flowering; foliage small, medium green, matte; prickles few, very small; short (12 in.), bushy growth; PP7276; [White Gem × Cinderella]; int. by SNC Meilland & Cie

White MiniJet Min, w, Meilland; flowers double, cupped; container rose

White Minimo Min, w, Interplant; int. in 1989

White Mite Min, w, 1991, Frock, Marshall J.; flowers small (micro-mini), full, slight fragrance; foliage small, medium green, semi-glossy; upright growth; [Baby Katie × seedling]

White Moss – See **Comtesse de Murinais**, M

White Moss Rose – See **Shailer's White Moss**, M

White Mothersday – See **Morsdag Alba**, Pol

White Mountains LCl, w, 1960, Risley; bud globular; flowers white, becoming greenish, small, dbl., borne in clusters; profuse, intermittent bloom; foliage glossy; vigorous growth; quite hardy; [Skinner's Rambler × Skinner's Rambler]; int. in 1958

White Mrs Flight HMult, w, 1916, Rockford; flowers

bone white, medium, semi-dbl., cupped, open, borne in large clusters, slight fragrance; non-remontant; foliage small, medium green; tall, vigorous growth; [sport of Mrs F. W. Flight]

White Mrs Flight HMult, w, 1916, T. Rockford; flowers pure white; [sport of Mrs F.W. Flight]

White Mystery HT, w, 1984, deVor, Paul F.; [sport of Paul's Pink]; int. by DeVor Nurseries, Inc., 1982

White Neverland S, w, Hiroshima; int. by Hiroshima Bara-en, 2005

White New Dawn LCl, w, 1949, Longley, L.E.; flowers pure white, 3-3½ in., 30-35 petals, gardenia-shaped, borne in small to medium clusters, moderate sweet fragrance; recurrent; foliage glossy, dark green; numerous prickles; very vigorous, climbing growth; [New Dawn × Lily Pons]; often thought to be the same as 'Weisse New Dawn', but the flowers of 'White Dawn' are pure white whereas those of 'Wiesse New Dawn' are tinted crimson; int. as White Dawn, Univ. of Minn.

White Nights S, ly, 1985, Olesen, Pernille & Mogens N.; bud long, pointed; flowers light, creamy yellow to white, 10-15 cm., full, high-centered, urn-shaped, borne singly and in clusters of up to 5, moderate fragrance; recurrent; foliage large, leathery, dark, glossy; tall, upright, bushy growth; [seedling × Kalahari]; int. as Armorique Nirpaysage, Poulsen's Roses, 1985

White Noblesse HT, w, Tantau; florist rose; int. by Rosen Tantau, 1998

White Nun HT, w, 1970, Pal, Dr. B.P.; flowers open, medium, dbl.; foliage glossy; vigorous, upright growth; [Virgo × unknown]; int. by Indian Agric. Research Inst., 1968

White Ophelia HT, w, 1920, Cleveland Cut-Flower Co.; flowers white, center faintly tinted pink, becoming white, well-formed, semi-dbl.; [sport of Ophelia]; int. by E.G. Hill Co.

White Orléans Pol, w, 1920, Van Eyk; [sport of Orléans Rose]

White Pacific HT, w

White Pagode MinFl, w, Poulsen; flowers white, 5-8 cm., dbl., borne in clusters, no fragrance; foliage dark; cascading growth, hanging basket type; PP13453; int. by Poulsen Roser, 2000

White Patio Wonder Min, w, 2004, Jalbert, Brad; flowers white, edges turning pink in cool weather, 1½ in., very full, borne in small clusters, no fragrance; foliage medium size, dark green, glossy; prickles moderate, small, hooked, dark; spreading, wide, medium (14 in.) growth; [Thelma's Glory × Sexy Rexy]; int. in 1999

White Pavement HRg, w, Uhl, J.; bud pale pink, pointed; flowers opening soft white, large, double, cupped, moderate fragrance; recurrent; foliage dark green, disease-resistant; moderate (2½ ft.), spreading growth; hips rose-red; int. in 1989

White Peach Ovation Min, w, deRuiter

White Pearl T, w, 1889, Ritter/Nanz & Neuner; foliage large; growth upright; [sport of Perle des Jardins]

White Pearl HT, w, 1948, Totty; bud long, pointed; flowers glistening white, well-formed, large, 45-50 petals, open; foliage large, soft; very vigorous, upright growth; RULED EXTINCT 4/85

White Pearl Min, w, Totty, Charles; [sport of Minnie Pearl]; int. in 1993

White Pearl in Red Dragon's Mouth Ch, rb; flowers cerise to cherry red, white eye, semi-dbl. to double, cupped, slight spicy fragrance; recurrent; moderate (3-4 ft.) growth

White Penthouse Gr, Fineschi, G.; int. in 1995

White Perfection – See **Pristine Pavement**, HRg

White Pet Pol, w, 1879, Henderson, P.; flowers small, dbl., pompon, borne in large clusters, slight fragrance; recurrent; very dwarf, mounded growth; [sport of Félicité et Perpétue]

White Pet, Climbing Cl Pol, w, 1894, Corboeuf; flowers snowy white, borne in large clusters; [sport of White Pet]; probably synonymous with Félicité-Perpétue

White Pillar LCl, w, 1958, Hay; flowers silvery white with button eye, large, very dbl., quartered rosette, borne in clusters, moderate fragrance; recurrent; pillar (8 ft.) growth; [William F. Dreer × unknown]; int. by Marsh's Nursery

White Pinocchio F, w, 1950, Boerner; bud ovoid; flowers 2½ in., 50 petals, globular; vigorous growth; [Mrs R.M. Finch × Pinocchio]; int. by J&P

White Popcorn S, w, Williams, J. Benjamin; flowers small, double, cupped, borne in large clusters, slight fragrance; recurrent; foliage bluish-green; low (2 ft.), spreading growth; int. by Hortico, Inc., 2005

White Prince HT, w, 1961, Von Abrams; bud pointed; flowers creamy white, 5-6 in., 50-80 petals, globular, borne usually singly, slight fragrance; recurrent; foliage large, leathery, glossy; prickles numerous, medium, hooked downward, brown; stems long, strong; vigorous, upright growth; hips large, globose, variable orange; PP2246; [(Blanche Mallerin × Peace) × (Peace × Frau Karl Druschki)]; int. by Peterson & Dering, 1961

White Provence C, w, 1775, Grimwood; bud rounded, deep pink; flowers white, sometimes tinged pink, green eye, large, dbl., cupped, incurved petals, moderate fragrance; foliage doubly serrated; erect, low (3 ft.) growth; [sport of *R.* × *centifolia*]

White Queen HT, w, 1959, Boerner; bud long; flowers white, center creamy, 5 in., 30 petals, cupped, borne singly and several together, moderate tea fragrance; recurrent; foliage large, leathery; prickles numerous, medium, straight or hooked downward; stems medium, strong; vigorous, upright growth; hips none ; PP1762; [(Starlite × unknown) × Glacier seedling]; int. by J&P, 1958

White Queen Elizabeth F, w, 1965, Banner; flowers creamy white, 4 in., borne in clusters, moderate fragrance; recurrent; foliage light green, leathery; vigorous, tall growth; [sport of Queen Elizabeth]; int. by North Hill Nursery

White Quill MinFl, w, Williams, J.B.; flowers white with creamy center, double, globular to cupped; recurrent; int. by Hortico, 2003

White Radiance – See **Mary Nish**, HT

White Radox Bouquet S, w, 1989, Melville Nurseries Pty., Ltd.; bud small, rounded; flowers white with pink tinge in center, large, 50 petals, borne in sprays of 5 or more, moderate fragrance; foliage dark green, leathery; prickles hooked, small, beige; tall, shrub to semi-climber growth; [sport of Radox Bouquet]

White Rain Min, w, 1991, Moore, Ralph S.; flowers small, dbl., borne in large clusters, moderate fragrance; foliage small, light green, semi-glossy; some prickles; low (22 cm.), spreading, groundcover growth; [Papoose × Renae]; int. by Sequoia Nursery, 1992

White Rambler – See **Thalia**, HMult

White River – See **Shirakawa**, HT

White Roadrunner S, w, Uhl; flowers pure white, 5 cm., semi-double, cupped, borne in clusters, intense fragrance; recurrent; foliage dark green, leathery, very disease-resistant; bushy, compact (2 ft.) growth; int. by W. Kordes' Söhne, 2003

White Rock LCl, w, Barni, V.; flowers pure white, double, cupped, moderate fragrance; tall growth; int. by Rose Barni, 1996

White Rosamini Min, w

White Rose de Meaux – See **Rose de Meaux White**, C

White Rose of Finland – See **Polstjärnan**, LCl

White Rose of York A, w, before 1600; sepals leafy; flowers white, medium, single to dbl., borne usually several together, moderate hyacinth fragrance; summer bloom; foliage medium size, grayish, blunt, composed of 5-7 leaflets; prickles hooked, mixed with bristles, distributed irregularly; stems clear green; growth to 5 ft.; hips ovoid, large, scarlet; [*R. gallica* × *R. canina*]; probably known to the Romans (Pliny) before 77 A.D.

White Rose of York – See **Duc d'York**, A

White Russian HT, w, 2000, Giles, Diann; flowers medium, dbl., high-centered, borne mostly singly, moderate fragrance; foliage medium size, medium green, matte; prickles moderate; upright, tall (5 ft.) growth; [Sheer Bliss × unknown]; int. by Giles Rose Nursery

White Satin HT, w, 1965, Swim & Weeks; bud short pointed, conspicuous neck; flowers white, center light greenish yellow on lower half of petals, 4-4½ in., 60-80 petals, high-centered, borne singly, moderate tea fragrance; recurrent; foliage upper dark green, under light gray-green, leathery; prickles some, medium, straight, brown; stems long; vigorous, tall, bushy growth; hips long, flat at top, yellow; PP2648; [Mount Shasta × White Butterfly]; int. by Carlton Rose Nurseries

White Scotch HSpn, w, from Scotland; flowers pure white

White Seduction Pol, w; [sport of Seduction]

White Sheen F, w, 1960, Boerner; bud ovoid; flowers 2 in., 25-30 petals, borne in clusters, intense fragrance; foliage dark, glossy; upright growth; [(Ma Perkins × unknown) × Demure seedling]; int. by J&P, 1960

White Simplicity F, w, Warriner ; bud pointed ovoid; flowers clear white, 3-3½ in., 20 -25 petals, high-centered, then flattens, borne singly and several together in clusters, slight fragrance; recurrent; foliage dark green, glossy; prickles moderate, hooked downward; upright, vigorous growth; PP6666; [Sun Flare × Simplicity]; int. by J&P, 1991

White Skyliner LCl, w, Cowlishaw; flowers pure white with yellow stamens, small, semi-double, cupped, borne in clusters; recurrent; tall (6-8 ft.) growth; freestanding shrub or small climber; int. by C&K Jones, 2003

White Sparrieshoop – See **Weisse aus Sparrieshoop**, S

White Spire HT, w, Kordes; bud pointed; flowers double, high-centered, borne in small clusters, moderate fragrance; recurrent; upright, tall growth; int. by Ludwig's Roses, 1994

White Spray F, w, 1968, LeGrice; bud creamy white; flowers pure white, well-formed, small, double, borne in clusters, moderate fragrance; recurrent; stems long; vigorous, compact growth; [seedling × Iceberg]; int. by Roseland Nurs.

White Spray S, w, 2000, Lens, L.; flowers 2 cm., single, borne in large clusters, very slight fragrance; recurrent; foliage small, medium green, glossy, evergreen; prickles moderate; growth spreading, low (40-60 cm.); [*R. wichurana yakachinensis* × *R. multiflora adenocheata*]; int. by Louis Lens N.V., 1980

White Star HWich, w, 1901, Manda; flowers borne in clusters of 20-30; [Jersey Beauty × Manda's Triumph]

White Star HT, w, 1920, Morse; flowers ivory-white, base shaded lemon-yellow; [sport of Ophelia]

White Star of Finland – See **Polstjärnan**, LCl

White Stream LCl, w, Teranishi; int. by Itami Rose Garden, 2003

White Success HT, w, 1986, Jelly; bud long ovoid; flowers clear white, 5 in., 55 petals, high-centered, borne singly, no fragrance; recurrent; foliage large, dark green, semi-glossy; prickles numerous, medium, straight, brown; stems strong; upright growth; PP5632;

[Bridal Pink × seedling]; originally a greenhouse rose.; int. by E.G. Hill Co., 1985

White Sunsation S, w, Kordes; flowers white with yellow stamens, semi-double, flat; recurrent; low, spreading, groundcover growth; int. by Ludwig's Roses

White Sunshine Min, w, 1998, Jones, Steve; flowers white, like My Sunshine, single; foliage medium size, medium green, semi-glossy; compact, bushy, medium, 2 ft. growth; [Sarabande × Peggy T]

White Supreme HT, w, Williams, J.B.; flowers white, large, moderate fragrance; recurrent; growth to 5 ft.; int. by Hortico, 2004

White Surprise HBc, w, 2000, Lens, Louis; flowers white, green stamens, 10-12 cm., single, borne in small clusters, moderate fragrance; foliage large, medium green, glossy, evergreen; numerous prickles; bushy, tall (200 cm.) growth; [*R. bracteata* × *R. rugosa rubra*]; int. in 1987; Gold Medal, Le Roeulx, 1985

White Swan HT, w, 1951, Verschuren-Pechtold; bud ovoid; flowers pure white, 4½-5 in., 30 petals, high-centered, moderate fragrance; foliage glossy, dark; vigorous, upright growth; [(Kaiserin Auguste Viktoria × unknown) × White seedling]; int. by J&P

White Sweetheart F, w, 1941, J&P; flowers white flushed blush-pink when half open, small, dbl., high-centered; foliage leathery; short, strong stems; vigorous, upright, bushy growth; [sport of Rosenelfe]

White Symphonie HT, w, RvS-Melle; flowers 4 in., 59 petals; foliage matte; strong growth; int. in 1991

White Tausendschön HMult, w, 1913, Paul, W. (also Roehrs, 1918); flowers white, sometimes flaked pink; [sport of Tausendschön]

White Timeless – See **Timeless**, HT

White Timeless HT, w; flowers dbl.; [sport of Timeless]

White Treasure HT, w, 1995, Davidson, Harvey D.; flowers white, slight cast of light yellow in center, 4¾ in., full, borne mostly singly, moderate fragrance; foliage large, dark green, semi-glossy; few prickles; upright, medium (100 cm.) growth; [Smooth Sailing × Sunset Jubilee]; int. by Hortico Roses, 1995

White Valerie HT, w; int. by Select, 1998

White Wedding LCl, w, Scarman; flowers creamy white with yellow stamens, single, shallow cup, borne in large clusters; free-flowering; vigorous (8 ft.) growth; int. in 1995

White Week-end F, w

White Wine HT, w, 1995, Sheldon, John & Robin; flowers white with pink tinge, medium, full, borne mostly singly; foliage medium size, medium green, matte; upright, medium growth; [Pristine × (Spirit of Glasnost × Lanvin)]

White Wings HT, w, 1947, Krebs; bud long, pointed; flowers ivory white, wine colored stamens, anthers chocolate-colored, large, 5 petals, borne in large clusters, moderate fragrance; recurrent; foliage leathery, dark green; vigorous, upright, bushy growth; [Dainty Bess × seedling]; int. by H&S

White Wings HT, w, Poulsen; flowers pure white with crimson stamens, single; growth to 2½ ft.; int. in 1979

White Woge HSpn, w; flowers white, single; recurrent; low (50 cm.) growth; int. in 1997

Whitecap F, w, 1960, Boerner, E. S.; bud medium; flowers pure white, medium, dbl., cupped; foliage medium size, abundant; growth vigorous, upright, bushy; PP1910; int. by Stark Bros., 1959

Whiteout Min, w, 1989, McGredy, Sam IV; flowers small, 20 petals, cupped, slight fragrance; foliage small, medium green, semi-glossy; bushy, medium growth; [Sexy Rexy × Popcorn]; int. by Justice Miniature Roses, 1989

Whitfield Wonder LCl, mp, Scarman; flowers old-fashioned, borne in clusters, slight fragrance; foliage disease-resistant; tall (8 ft.) growth; int. in 2001

Whitley Bay F, w, 1989, Horner, Colin P.; bud ovoid; flowers cream with pink splashes, reverse cream, loose, medium, cupped; foliage medium size, medium green, semi-glossy; prickles medium, brown; spreading, medium growth; hips ovoid, medium, yellow; [Champagne Cocktail × (Colour Wonder × (Vera Dalton × Vera Dalton × Piccadilly))]; int. by Battersby Roses, 1990

Whitney Min, w, 1994, Bridges, Dennis A.; bud blush pink; flowers near white with a hint of pink, medium, dbl., vase-shaped, borne mostly singly or in small clusters, moderate fragrance; foliage small, medium green, semi-glossy; few prickles; medium (38 cm.), upright, spreading growth; [Jennifer × unknown]; int. by Bridges Roses, 1994

Whitsuntide Rose – See ***R. majalis*** (Herrmann) dbl.

Who Dat HT, pb, 2005, Edwards, Eddie & Phelps, Ethan; flowers striped, 4-5 in., full, high-centered, borne mostly solitary, slight fragrance; foliage dark green, glossy; prickles small, hooked; growth upright, medium (5-6 ft.); exhibition; [unknown]; int. in 2005

Whoop De Doo Min, rb, 2004, Moe, Mitchie; flowers red with yellow on lower portion of petals and somewhat on reverse, 1½-1¾ in., dbl., high-centered, borne mostly solitary, slight fragrance; recurrent; foliage medium size, medium green, semi-glossy; prickles medium, straight; growth upright, medium (18-20 in.); exhibition, garden; [Olympic Gold × Finest Hour]; int. by Mitchie's Roses and More, 2005

Whoopi Min, rb, 1991, Saville, F. Harmon; flowers white with red edges, suffused more with red as blooms age, medium, 28-32 petals, high-centered, borne mostly singly or in small clusters, slight spicy fragrance; foliage medium size, dark green, semi-glossy; bushy, medium growth; PP8176; [(Yellow Jewel × Tamango) × Party Girl]; int. by Nor'East Min. Roses, 1992

Why Not Min, rb, 1984, Moore, Ralph S.; bud long, pointed; flowers medium red, yellow eye, reverse yellow, 3 cm., 7 petals, shallow cup, borne singly and in clusters, very slight fragrance; recurrent; foliage small, medium green, matte to semi-glossy; prickles moderate, slender, curved slightly downward, brown; upright, bushy growth; hips small, globe-shaped ; PP5676; [Golden Angel × seedling]; int. by Moore Min. Roses, 1983

Why Not Cerise HT, dp, 2001, Coiner, Jim; flowers very showy, large, full, borne mostly solitary, no fragrance; foliage medium size, light green, matte; few prickles; growth compact, medium (48 in.); [seedling × seedling]; int. by Coiner Nursery, 2001

Whytewold S, w, 1961, Skinner; flowers dbl., cupped; non-recurrent; growth to 3 ft.

Wichmoss HWich, lp, 1911, Barbier; bud long, pointed, mossed; flowers pale blush-pink fading to white, 2 in., semi-dbl., borne in clusters of 6-15; foliage dark, leathery; vigorous, climbing growth; [*R. wichurana* × Salet]

Wicking HMlt, pb, 1909, Geschwind; flowers yellowish carmine-pink, center white, medium, full

Wickwar S, w, Steadman; flowers creamy white, 5 cm., single, moderate musk fragrance; foliage grayish; hips small, red; probably *R. soulieana* × *R. brunonii*; int. in 1960

Wiener Blut F, or, 1961, Horstmann; bud globular; flowers salmon-red, 30 petals, borne in clusters; vigorous, upright growth

Wiener Charme – See **Vienna Charm**, HT

Wiener Donaupark F, lp

Wiener Walzer F, mr, 1965, Tantau, Math.; bud pointed; flowers velvety bright red, large, 25-30 petals; foliage glossy; very vigorous, upright growth

Wienerwald HT, op, 1974, Kordes; bud long, pointed; flowers pink flushed with salmon, large, dbl., borne singly and several together, moderate fragrance; recurrent; foliage large, dark green, leathery; vigorous, upright, bushy growth; [Colour Wonder × seedling]

Wieteke van Dordt – See **Potifar**, HT

Wife of Bath S, pb, 1969, Austin, David; flowers deep rose-pink, reverse blush, outer petals fading blush, small to medium, very full, cupped, borne in clusters, intense myrrh fragrance; recurrent; foliage small, medium green; bushy, twiggy (3 ft.) growth; [Mme Caroline Testout × (Ma Perkins × Constance Spry)]

Wiggy F, or, 1993, Kenny, David; flowers orange-red with cerise, medium, full, borne in small clusters; foliage medium size, dark green, semi-glossy; some prickles; tall (90 cm.), upright, bushy growth; [(Prominent × Kiskadee) × (Mary Sumner × Kiskadee)]; int. by Kenny, 1993

Wijhe F, or, 1961, Buisman, G. A. H.; flowers dbl., borne in clusters; foliage dark; moderate growth; [seedling × Alpine Glow]

Wil Pink Supreme S, op

Wilberforce C, dr, about 1840; flowers dark crimson, large, dbl.; [probably *R. centifolia* × *R. gallica*]

Wild Amazone HT, dp

Wild 'n' Rare Min, m

Wild at Heart S, dp, 1993, W. Kordes Söhne; flowers deep pink, 3-3½ in., dbl., borne in large clusters; foliage large, medium green, glossy; medium (120-130 cm.), bushy, spreading (180 cm.) growth; [Bonanza × seedling]; int. by Bear Creek Gardens, 1994

Wild Banks Rose – See ***R. banksiae normalis*** (Regel)

Wild Berry Breeze HRg, m, 1999, Zary, Dr. Keith W.; flowers lavender-pink, veined petals, large, single, borne in clusters, intense spicy clove fragrance; recurrent; foliage medium size, dark green, semi-glossy, deeply rugose; numerous prickles; upright, bushy, medium (3½ ft.) growth; hips round, large, orange; PP12055; [Buffalo Gal × seedling]; int. by Bear Creek Gardens, Inc., 1999

Wild Blue Yonder Gr, m, 2004, Carruth, Tom; flowers lavender with a broad red–purple border, 9-11 cm., 25-30 petals, cupped, ruffled, borne in large clusters, intense spicy fragrance; recurrent; foliage large, dark green, semi-glossy; prickles almost straight; growth bushy, medium (100-130 cm.), upright; garden decoration; [((International Herald Tribune × *R. soulieana* derivative) × (Sweet Chariot × Blue Nile)) × (Blueberry Hill × Stephen's Big Purple)]; int. by Weeks Roses, 2006; AARS, 2006

Wild Cherry HT, mr, 1985, Bridges, Dennis A.; flowers large, dbl., moderate fragrance; foliage large, dark, glossy; bushy growth; [King of Hearts × Granada]; int. by Bridges Roses, 1985

Wild Child S, lp, 1980, Hall, William W.; bud small, pointed; flowers 5 petals, borne 3-15 per cluster, moderate tea fragrance; repeat bloom; foliage small, light green, 9 leaflet, slightly rugose; prickles curved, thin; vigorous, erect, some arching growth; [*R. rugosa rubra* × Dortmund seedling]; int. in 1982

Wild Dancer S, dp, 1998, Walden, John K.; bud short, pointed ovoid; flowers bright magenta-pink, reverse lighter, 1½ in., single, cupped, flattens, borne in large clusters, slight spicy fragrance; recurrent; foliage small, medium green, matte, leathery; prickles moderate, short, hooked downward; stems short; compact, arching, low (2½ × 2.5 ft.) growth; PP10962; [China Doll × Sweet Chariot]; int. by Bear Creek Gardens, Inc, 1998

Wild Edric S, dp, 2006; flowers deep pink with shades of purple and mauve, yellow stamens, 9½ cm., double, cupped, borne in small clusters, intense fragrance; recurrent; foliage medium size, dark green, matte; prickles numerous, medium to large, linear, light green; growth bushy, vigorous, medium (120 cm.); garden decorative, hedging; [seedling × seedling]; int. by David Austin Roses, Ltd., 2005

Wild Flame HT, or, 1974, Meyer, C.; bud ovoid; flowers medium, dbl., moderate fragrance; foliage leathery; vigorous, upright growth; [Granada × South Seas]; int. by Ball Seed Co., 1973

Wild Flower – See **Wildflower**, S

Wild Flower HT, ob; int. by Moffett Nursery, 2004

Wild Flower Min, rb; flowers white, heavily striped and splashed red, double, cupped, moderate fragrance; large growth

Wild Ginger Gr, ob, 1976, Buck, Dr. Griffith J.; bud ovoid, pointed; flowers ginger, apricot orange, 4-4½ in., 30-35 petals, cupped, borne in clusters of 4-10, moderate fruity fragrance; recurrent; foliage dark green, leathery; upright, bushy growth; winter hardy; [(Queen Elizabeth × Ruth Hewitt) × Lady Elgin]; int. by Iowa State University

Wild Honey HT, ab, 1978, Weeks; bud long, pointed; flowers coral and peach, 3-5 in., 40-50 petals, high-centered, cupped, borne singly and in small clusters, intense spicy fragrance; recurrent; foliage medium size, leathery, dark green; prickles some, short, hooked slightly downward; tall, vigorous growth; PP4357; [unknown]; int. in 1977

Wild One Min, mr, 1982, Lyon; flowers medium red, lighter center, medium, semi-dbl.; foliage medium size, dark, semi-glossy; bushy, upright growth; [Merry Christmas × seedling]

Wild Plum Min, m, 1998, Zary, Dr. Keith W.; flowers lavender blend, darker reverse, 1½-2 in., 25 petals, high-centered, borne in large clusters, slight fragrance; recurrent; foliage medium size, dark green, glossy; prickles few, straight; growth bushy, tall (3 ft.); hedging; PP9493; [Winsome × Elegance]; int. by Bear Creek Gardens, Inc., 1995

Wild Spice HRg, w, 1999, Zary, Dr. Keith W.; flowers snowy white, delicate, ruffled, large, single, borne in small clusters, intense clove fragrance; foliage dark green, semi-glossy, deeply rugose; upright, bushy, medium (3½ ft.) growth; PP11575; [Buffalo Gal × seedling]; int. by Bear Creek Gardens, Inc., 1999

Wild Spirit S, mr, 1985, James, John; flowers bright medium red, small, 5 petals; non-recurrent; foliage small, dark, matte; vigorous, upright, branched growth; [Alika × *R. moyesii*]

Wild Thing Min, ob, 1992, Bennett, Dee; flowers bright orange-yellow, large, dbl., borne mostly singly, moderate fruity fragrance; foliage small, medium green, semi-glossy, disease-resistant; some prickles; medium (60-80 cm.), bushy growth; [Gingersnap × Baby Katie]; int. by Tiny Petals Nursery, 1993

Wild Thing S, dp, 2007, Zary, Keith W.; flowers hot pink, 3 in., semi-dbl., blooms borne in large clusters; foliage medium size, dark green, glossy; prickles 4-6 mm., hooked downward, greyed-orange, moderate; growth bushy, arching, medium (3½ ft.); landscape, bedding; [seedling × Footloose]; int. by Jackson & Perkins Wholesale, Inc., 2007

Wild West F, or, 1993, Evers, Hans & Rosen Tantau; three sepals very slightly bearded; flowers orange-red, medium, very dbl., borne in large clusters; foliage large, medium green, glossy, resistant to powdery mildew; prickles small, soft, glandular on peduncles; medium (85-95 cm.), bushy growth; [Showbiz × seedling]; int. by Bear Creek Gardens, 1993

Wildenfels Gelb HFt, w, 1929, Dechant; flowers soft yellow, large, single, moderate Rosa foetida fragrance; recurrent; foliage basil-green; vigorous, strong growth

Wildenfels Rosa HFt, mp, 1928, Dechant; flowers rose pink, yellow stamens, medium, single, flat, slight fragrance; early, free flowering; upright, robust growth

Wildest Dreams Min, yb, 1992, Taylor, Franklin "Pete" & Kay; flowers yellow blending to deep pink edges, aging lighter, reverse yellow, large, dbl.; foliage small, medium green, semi-glossy; few prickles; medium (40 cm.), upright, bushy growth; [Poker Chip × unknown]; int. by Taylor's Roses, 1993

Wildeve S, pb, 2004; flowers medium pink, touched apricot, in center, outer petals and reverse lighter, 7½ cm., very full, cupped, rosette, borne in small clusters, slight fresh fragrance; foliage large, dark green, semi-glossy; prickles medium, deeply concave; bushy, medium (100 cm.), arching growth; garden decorative; seedling (medium pink English-type shrub) × Golden Celebration; int. by David Austin Roses, Ltd., 2003

Wildfang S, mp, Noack, Werner; flowers intensive, clear pink, 5 cm., double, cupped, borne in clusters; recurrent; foliage medium to dark green, glossy; mounding growth; int. by Noack Rosen, 1991

Wildfeuer S, mr, 1953, Kordes; flowers fiery red, 4½ in., semi-dbl.; non-remontant; bushy, tall growth

Wildfire F, mr, 1956, Swim, H.C.; bud ovoid; flowers bright red, 3 in., 8-10 petals, borne in clusters; foliage leathery; vigorous, bushy, compact growth; PP1381; [World's Fair × Pinocchio]; int. by Armstrong Nursery, 1955

Wildfire HT, ob, 2005, Zary, Keith W.; bud long, pointed ovoid; flowers strong orange, 9 cm., 35-40 petals, high-centered, quills, borne mostly solitary, very slight fragrance; recurrent; foliage dark green, glossy; prickles numerous, 5 mm., hooked slightly downward, brown; stems strong; upright, angular branching, vigorous (180 cm.) growth; PP16186; [seedling × Elina]; int. by Jackson & Perkins Wholesale, Inc.

Wildfire Min, ob, Fryer's; flowers flame orange, double, pointed, moderate fragrance; free-flowering; compact (2 ft.) growth; int. by Fryer's Roses, 2005

Wildfire 2000 F, yb, 2000, Thomson, George L.; flowers yellow with blazing orange overtones, reverse lighter, 2 in., dbl., borne in small clusters, moderate fragrance; foliage medium size, medium green, glossy; prickles moderate; compact, medium (3-4 ft.) growth; [Remember Me × Tequila Sunrise]; int. by Ross Roses, 1999

Wildflower S, ly, 1994, Austin, David; flowers pale yellow, 1½ in., 5 petals, shallow cup, borne mostly singly, slight fragrance; recurrent; foliage small, light green, semi-glossy; some prickles; low (2 ft.), bushy, spreading growth; [Canterbury × seedling]; int. as Wild Flower, David Austin Roses, Ltd., 1986

Wildlife S, pb, Dickson, Patrick

Wildwood HT, op, 1937, H&S; bud long, pointed; flowers gold, salmon and bronze, semi-dbl.; foliage glossy, wrinkled; vigorous growth

Wilf Taylor HT, ab, 1982, Bracegirdle, A.J.; flowers large, 35 petals, high-centered; foliage large, dark, matte; upright growth; [Gavotte × Red Lion]; int. in 1981

Wilfred Dion HT, dr; int. by J.C. Bakker and Sons, 2006

Wilfred H. Perron Min, mp, 1988, Laver, Keith G.; flowers clear shrimp-pink, aging paler, rosea, large, 70-80 petals, borne singly, no fragrance; foliage very small, medium green, matte; prickles straight out, very slender, greenish-red; bushy, low growth; hips round, very rare, green-red; [(Dwarfking '78 × Baby Katie) × Painted Doll]

Wilfred Norris HT, mp, 1973, Harkness; flowers medium salmon-pink, large, 23 petals; foliage matte; [Tropicana × Elizabeth of Glamis]; int. in 1972

Wilfred Pickles HT, op, 1939, Mee; flowers peach shaded gold, well-formed, 6 in., 26 petals; foliage glossy, dark; stems red; very vigorous growth; [Mrs Charles Lamplough × Edith Mary Mee]; int. by Fryer's Nursery, Ltd.

Wilhelm – See **Skyrocket**, HMsk

Wilhelm Breder – See **Glowing Sunset**, HT

Wilhelm Hansmann HKor, dr, 1958, Kordes; bud ovoid; flowers deep crimson, 6-7 cm., dbl., high-centered, borne in large clusters, slight fragrance; recurrent; foliage dark green, leathery; very vigorous growth; [(Baby Château × Else Poulsen) × *R.* × *kordesii*]; int. in 1955

Wilhelm Hartmann T, rb, 1902, Brauer; flowers shining red with fresh pink, base tinted yellow, full; [Marie van Houtte × Papa Gontier]

Wilhelm Kauth HT, ly, 1930, Kauth; flowers large, very dbl.

Wilhelm Kordes HT, op, 1922, Kordes, H.; bud long, pointed; flowers salmon, copper and golden blend, large, dbl., high-centered; foliage bronze, leathery, glossy; bushy growth; [Gorgeous × Adolf Koschel]

Wilhelm Kordes, Climbing Cl HT, op, 1927, Wood & Ingram; flowers salmon and copper yellow, large, full, moderate fragrance; [sport of Wilhelm Kordes]

Wilhelm Marx S, mr, 1939, Vogel, M.; flowers medium, dbl.

Wilhelm May HT, dr, Michler, K. H.; flowers velvety dark red, dbl.; int. in 1989

Wilhelm Teetzmann F, mr, 1943, Kordes; flowers intense crimson, open, large, semi-dbl., borne in clusters; very vigorous, upright, bushy growth; [Holstein × Crimson Glory]

Wilhelm Tell F, mr, Meilland

Wilhelm III – See **William III**, HSpn

Wilhire Country – See **Willhire Country**, F

Will Alderman HRg, mp, 1954, Skinner; flowers clear rose-pink, well-shaped, large, dbl.; repeat bloom; erect (4 ft.), bushy growth; [(*R. rugosa* × *R. acicularis*) × unknown HT]

Will-o'-the-Wisp MinFl, pb, Clements, John K.; flowers satiny pink yellow eye and deep amber stamens, 2-2½ in., single, flat, moderate sweet/honey fragrance; recurrent; foliage small, dark green; compact, bushy growth; int. by Heirloom Roses, 1998

Will Rogers HT, dr, 1936, Howard, F.H.; flowers velvety maroon-crimson, base almost black, burning in sun, 3 in., 65 petals, intense damask fragrance; recurrent; foliage leathery, light; vigorous, bushy, spreading growth; [seedling × (Hadley × Crimson Glory)]; int. by H&S

Will Rogers, Climbing Cl HT, dr, 1940, H&S

Will Scarlet HMsk, mr, 1948, Hilling; flowers scarlet, golden stamens, medium, semi-dbl., cupped, ruffled, slight to moderate fragrance; recurrent; [sport of Skyrocket]; int. by Wayside Gardens Co., 1956

Willhire Country F, ob, 1981, Beales, Peter; flowers flat-topped, 25 petals, borne 6-8 per cluster; foliage glossy, round, dark; prickles broad, hooked, brown; tall, upright growth; [Elizabeth of Glamis × Arthur Bell]; int. by Beales Roses, 1979

Willi Maass – See **Red Ripples**, F

William A. Bilney HT, pb, 1927, Easlea; flowers pink with light orange, large, very dbl.

William Allen Richardson N, yb, 1878, Ducher, Vve.; bud pointed; flowers orange-yellow, usually white at petal edges, medium to large, dbl., borne in small to medium clusters; early bloom, repeating; foliage dark green, glossy; very vigorous, climbing (12 ft.) growth; [Reve d'Or × unknown]

William and Mary S, rb, Beales, Peter; flowers deep silvery-pink with crimson and carmine highlights, large, double, cupped, borne singly and in clusters, slight fragrance; recurrent; foliage greyish-green, matte; bushy, upright (5-6 ft.) growth; int. by Peter Beales Roses, 1988

William Baffin HKor, dp, 1983, Svedja, Felicitas; bud ovoid; flowers deep strawberry-pink touched white near the center, 2½ in., 20 petals, flat, borne in clusters of up to 30, slight fragrance; free-flowering; foliage small, medium green, glossy; vigorous, climbing growth; [*R.* × *kordesii* × unknown]; int. by Agriculture Canada

William Booth – See **William-Booth**, HKor

William-Booth HKor, mr, 1999, Agriculture et Agroalimentaire Canada, Ogilvie; bud pointed; flowers medium red, reverse medium pink, 2 in., single, flat, borne in large clusters, slight to moderate fragrance; foliage medium size, dark green, semi-glossy; prickles moderate, long, concave, green touched red; arching, tall growth; hips round, abundant, shiny orange-red; very hardy; PP11629; [(*R.* × *kordesii* × Max Graf O.P.) × (Arthur Bell × Applejack)]

William Bowyer HT, mr, 1924, Chaplin Bros.; bud long, pointed; flowers velvety red; [Hadley × Hoosier Beauty]

William C. Egan HWich, lp, 1900, Dawson; flowers flesh-pink, 7-8 cm., very dbl., quartered, borne in large clusters, moderate fragrance; non-recurrent; foliage bright, glossy; prickles long; long stems; vigorous, semi-climbing growth; [*R. wichurana* × Général Jacqueminot]; int. by Hoopes, Bro. & Thomas

William Carroll Gr, m, 1995, Williams, J. Benjamin; flowers mauve, medium, full, borne mostly singly and in small clusters, slight fragrance; foliage large, dark green, semi-glossy; some prickles; tall (4-5 ft.), upright growth; [Queen Elizabeth × Angel Face]

William Carter HT, dp, 1957, Carter; flowers deep pink; very vigorous growth; [sport of Red Ensign]

William Christie S, mp, Guillot-Massad; flowers rose pink, very full, cupped, borne in clusters, moderate fragrance; recurrent; vigorous (4-5 ft.) growth; int. by Roseraie Guillot, 2000

William Cooper HT, dr, 1914, Dickson, H.; flowers dark laquered red, very large, full

William Corbett F, dp, 1968, Seale Rose Gardens; flowers claret-rose, semi-dbl., borne in trusses, slight fragrance; vigorous growth; [sport of Dorothy Wheatcroft]

William David – See **Goldfinger**, F

William E. Nickerson HT, or, 1928, Easlea; flowers glowing orange-cerise, large, dbl.; foliage light; vigorous growth; [Priscilla × William F. Dreer]

William F. Dreer HT, lp, 1920, H&S; flowers shell-pink, base yellow, sometimes suffusing the entire flower, dbl., high-centered; [Mme Segond Weber × Lyon Rose]

William F. Ekas HT, op, 1935, Cremer; bud cupped; flowers salmon-orange, suffused pink, 4 in., 45-50 petals; [sport of Souvenir]

William Francis Bennett HT, mr, 1886, Bennett; bud long; flowers crimson, large, dbl., moderate fragrance; foliage very dark; [Adam × Xavier Olibo]

William Godfrey S, lp, 1954, Skinner; bud white; flowers pale pink, well-shaped, large, very dbl.; intermittent bloom all season; moderately vigorous, erect growth; [Altalaris × Hybrid Perpetual]

William Grant HGal, dp

William Griffith HP, pb, 1850, Portemer; flowers glossy pink, changing to light satin-rose, medium, very full, cupped; foliage dark green, slightly rugose; prickles large, slightly hooked, reddish

William Griffith HP, m, 1850, Portemer; flowers lilac pink, tinted fawn, medium to large, full

William Grow M, dr, 1858, Laffay, M.; flowers velvety violet/red, medium, dbl., borne in clusters of 6-8; foliage dark green; numerous prickles

William Hansmann – See **Wilhelm Hansmann**, HKor

William Harvey HT, mr, 1948, Norman; flowers scarlet, 4-6 in., dbl., high-centered; vigorous, bushy growth; [Crimson Glory × Southport]; int. by Harkness

William III HSpn, m, before 1910; flowers magenta-crimson, changing to rich plum, fading to dark lilac, reverse paler, small, single to semi-dbl., cupped, borne mostly singly, moderate spicy/sweet fragrance; non-remontant; foliage tiny, dark leaden green; modest, arching growth; hips round, shiny black

William IV HSpn, w, before 1838, from England; flowers small to medium

William Jesse HCh, mr, 1838, Laffay, M.; flowers red suffused violet, large, dbl., flat; unreliable repeat; growth erect; [probably Mme Desprez × uncertain]; sometimes classed as B

William K. Harris HWich, lp, 1903, Hoopes & Thomas; flowers light flesh pink, large, dbl.; [*R. wichurana* × Bon Silène]

William Leech HT, yb, 1989, Horner, Colin P.; bud ovoid; flowers yellow edged red, reverse light yellow, large, dbl., high-centered, borne usually singly; foliage medium size, medium green, glossy; prickles medium, red; bushy, medium growth; hips ovoid, large, orange; [Royal Dane × Piccadilly]; int. by Battersby Roses, 1989

William Lobb M, m, 1855, Laffay, M.; bud heavily mossed; flowers dark crimson-purple, reverse lilac-pink, fading to grayish-lilac, large, semi-dbl., flat, moderate fragrance; non-remontant; foliage medium size, dark grey-green; extremely prickly; vigorous, tall, arching growth; sometimes attributed to Portemer

William McGown S, ob, Peden, G.H.

William Moore HT, mp, 1935, McGredy; bud long, pointed; flowers soft, even-toned pink, becoming deeper, large, dbl., cupped; foliage soft, light; bushy growth

William Morris S, ab, 1999, Austin, David; flowers apricot blend, reverse light pink, large, 120 petals, cupped, quartered, borne in small clusters, intense fragrance; recurrent; foliage medium size, dark green, glossy; prickles moderate; branching, medium (5 × 4 ft.) growth; [Abraham Darby × seedling]; int. by David Austin Roses, Ltd, 1998

William Notting HT, rb, 1904, Soupert & Notting; bud long; flowers salmon-red, center brighter, large, dbl., moderate fragrance; foliage dark green; [Mme Abel Chatenay × Antoine Rivoire]

William Orr HT, mr, 1930, McGredy; bud long, pointed; flowers crimson-scarlet, large, 45 petals, high-centered, intense fragrance; recurrent; foliage light, glossy, leathery; vigorous growth

William Paul HP, mp, 1862, Guillot; flowers carmine, medium, full

William Quarrier F, ab, 1997, Cocker, Ann G.; flowers medium, very dbl., borne in large clusters; foliage medium size, light green, dull; some prickles; compact, tall (2½-3ft.) growth; [Silver Jubilee × Geraldine]; int. by James Cocker & Sons

William R. Smith T, pb, 1908, Bagg; bud pointed; flowers center pale pink, outer petals creamy flesh, base citron-yellow, large, dbl.; foliage rich green, leathery; vigorous growth; [Maman Cochet × Mme Hoste]; int. by P. Henderson

William Rollison HP, mr, 1865, Verdier, E.; flowers bright cherry-red, aging to scarlet, large, full, globular

William Saunders HT, 1918, Byrnes

William Shakespeare S, dr, 1987, Austin, David; flowers deep crimson-purple, fading rich purple, small, dbl., rosette, borne in sprays of 3-7, intense damask fragrance; repeat bloom; foliage large, dark green, semi-glossy; prickles broad based, straight, medium, red; upright, tall growth; no fruit; [The Squire × Mary Rose]; int. by David Austin Roses, 1987

William Shakespeare 2000 S, mr, 2001, Austin, David; bud pointed ovoid; flowers velvety crimson, changing to deep purple-red, 10-11 cm., very full, cupped, borne singly and in small clusters, intense Old Rose fragrance; recurrent; foliage medium size, medium green, matte; prickles moderate, 10 mm., hooked downward, dark red-purple; stems strong; growth bushy, medium (105 cm.); garden, decorative; hips none ; PP13993; [seedling × The Dark Lady]; int. by David Austin Roses, Ltd., 2000

William Shean HT, mp, 1906, Dickson, A.; bud long, tapering; flowers clear rose-pink, veined darker, very large, dbl.; Gold Medal, NRS, 1906

William Silva HT, 1951, Silva; prickles few at base; vigorous growth; [Étoile de Hollande × Radiance]

William Stubbs S, dr, 1996, Bossom, W.E.; flowers 3¼ in., dbl., borne in small clusters; early flowering (may); foliage small, medium green, glossy; prickles moderate; spreading (10 × 12 ft.) growth; [seedling × Guinee]

William Thomson Pol, pb, 1921, Leenders, M.; flowers salmon-carmine and bright rose, small, borne in clusters; compact, bushy growth; [Maman Turbat × Ellen Poulsen]

William Tyndale LCl, m, Marshall; int. in 1990s

William Walker HT, dy, 1985, Bracegirdle, Derek T.; flowers medium, 20 petals, no fragrance; foliage medium size, medium green, semi-glossy; upright growth; [Western Sun × Circus]; int. in 1984

William Warden HP, op, 1878, Mitchell; flowers salmon-pink, very large, full, slight fragrance; recurrent; [sport of Mme Clémence Joigneaux]

William Wright Walcott HT, lp, 1921, McGorum; flowers outer petals darker, dbl.; [Richmond × Ophelia]

Williams' Double Yellow HFt, my, before 1819, Williams, John; flowers pine-yellow with green carpels in center, 2 in., semi-dbl., borne mostly singly, intense sweet fragrance; very free blooming in spring; foliage tiny, dark green; growth free but spindly; often classed as a HSpn

William's Evergreen HSem, w, 1850, William; flowers white, center rosy flesh, borne in large clusters; possibly synonymous with Flore

Williamsburg HT, lp, 1965, Howard, A.P.; bud long, pointed; flowers rose-pink, medium, dbl., cupped, moderate fragrance; foliage dark, glossy; vigorous, upright growth; PP2730; [Contrast × Queen Elizabeth]; int. by Great Western Rose Co.

Williamsburg Days S, rb, Williams, J. Benjamin; flowers red with varying number of pink stripes, yellow stamens, semi-double, flat; recurrent; int. in 1998

Williams's Sweetbriar HEg, lp, about 1800, Williams of Turnham Green; flowers dbl.

Willie Mae Min, mr, 1966, Moore, Ralph S.; flowers small, dbl.; foliage dark, glossy, leathery; vigorous, bushy, dwarf growth; PP2834; [(*R. wichurana* × Carolyn Dean) × Little Buckaroo]; int. by Mini-Roses

Willie Winkie Min, lp, 1955, deVink; flowers light rose-pink, small, dbl., globular; small, micro-mini growth; [Katharina Ziemet × Tom Thumb]; int. by T. Robinson, Ltd.

Willing Min, yb, 2006, Tucker, Robbie; flowers yellow and red, ¾ in., dbl., borne mostly solitary; foliage dark green, semi-glossy; prickles 1/4 to ? in., straight, red to brown, moderate; growth upright, tall (to 48 in.); exhibition, cut flower, garden; [Cal Poly × Dancing Flame]; int. by Rosemania, 2007

Willits Crescendo LCl, lp

Williwaw HT, m, 1978, RvS. Melle; bud pointed; flowers red-purple, yellow at base, 60 petals, cupped, moderate fragrance; foliage glossy, dark; prickles hooked; upright growth; [Silver Lining × Duke of Windsor]

Willowmere HT, op, 1913, Pernet-Ducher; bud long, pointed, coral-red; flowers rich shrimp-pink, center yellow, large, dbl., cupped; foliage light green; prickles red, numerous, strong; medium, spreading growth; [seedling × Lyon Rose]

Willowmere, Climbing Cl HT, op, 1924, Mermet; flowers shrimp-red, shaded yellow at center, large, full; [sport of Willowmere]

Willy Chapel HT, yb, 1930, Delhaye; flowers coppery yellow, shaded salmon and shrimp-pink; vigorous growth

Willy Den Ouden Pol, or, 1938, Den Ouden; flowers intense orange, small, rosette, borne on trusses; dwarf, compact growth

Wilshire HT, mp, 1991, Woodard, Joe M.; bud pointed; flowers medium, 25 petals, high-centered, moderate fragrance; foliage medium size, medium green, glossy; upright, tall growth; [sport of Don Juan]; int. by Kimbrew Walter Roses, 1991; Bronze Medal, ARC TG, 1985

Wilton S, w, Tantau ?; groundcover?; int. in 2002

Wiltshire S, mp, Kordes; flowers bright rose pink, double, cupped, borne in clusters, slight fragrance; recurrent; foliage medium green, glossy; growth low, spreading plant; int. in 1993

Wiltshire Pride HT, rb, 1988, Sanday, John; flowers scarlet with yellow at base, reverse yellow with red edging, 28 petals, high-centered; foliage large, dark green, semi-glossy; prickles slightly hooked, dark brown; upright, tall growth; [Bristol × Piccadilly]; int. by John Sanday Roses, Ltd., 1989

Wilvang S, pb, Williams, J.B.; flowers pink and white; int. by Hortico, 2004

Wim Oudshoorn F, pb; flowers soft, pastel pink, yellow stamens, semi-dbl. to double, high-centered, flattens, borne mostly in clusters; recurrent; foliage fresh green; low, broad growth

Wimi HT, pb, 1985, Tantau, Math.; flowers shiny pink, silver reverse, well-formed, large, 20 petals, intense fragrance; foliage large, dark, semi-glossy; bushy growth; int. in 1983

Win Win – See **Rosie O'Donnell**, HT

Winchester Cathedral S, w, 1995, Austin, David; flowers white, with a tendency to revert to pink, 2-2 3/4 in., very dbl., cupped, borne in small clusters, moderate sweet fragrance; recurrent; foliage medium size, medium green, semi-glossy; some prickles; medium (4 ft.), upright, bushy growth; PP8141; [sport of Mary Rose]; int. by David Austin Roses, Ltd., 1988

Wind Chimes HMsk, mp, 1946; flowers rosy pink, 1 in., single, borne in large clusters, intense fragrance; recurrent; vigorous (15-20 ft.) growth; hips flattened, orange; int. by Lester Rose Gardens, 1949

Wind Rhythm MinFl, ob, Jalbert; flowers blend of oranges and yellows, large, full, hybrid tea; low (12-14 in.) growth

Wind Song HT, ab, 1970, Morey, Dennison; flowers orange, large, dbl., moderate fragrance; foliage leathery; bushy growth; [Royal Sunset × Sierra Sunset]; int. by Country Garden Nursery, 1968

Windekind F, mr, 1976, Institute of Ornamental Plant Growing; bud pointed; flowers 3 in., 34 petals, cupped; foliage matte, dark; upright growth; [Colour Wonder × Geisha]; int. in 1974

Windermere HWich, dp, 1932, Chaplin Bros.; flowers carmine-rose, 6-7 cm., semi-dbl., borne in small clusters, slight fragrance; foliage dark green, glossy; numerous prickles; vigorous growth

Windermere S, w, 2006; flowers very full, borne in small clusters; foliage medium size, dark green, matte; prickles medium, concave, curved inward, medium red, few; growth compact, medium (100 cm.); garden decorative; [seedling × seedling]; int. by David Austin Roses, Ltd., 2006

Windflower S, lp, 1997, Austin, David; flowers soft lilac-pink, medium, double, cupped, borne in small clusters, moderate Old Rose, apple and cinnamon fragrance; recurrent; foliage medium size, medium green, semi-glossy, disease-resistant; stems wiry; bushy, medium (120 cm.) growth; very disease resistant; int. by David Austin Roses, Ltd., 1994

Winding Road Min, w, 2003, Taylor, Franklin & Kay; flowers white with red edges, 1 1/2 in., full, borne in small clusters, no fragrance; foliage medium size, dark green, semi-glossy; prickles moderate, medium, straight, brown; growth climber, tall (6 to 7 ft.); pillar; [Nicole × Chelsea Belle]; int. in 2003

Windjammer Min, dp, 1982, Saville, F. Harmon; flowers deep pink, reddened by sun, small, 35 petals; foliage medium size, medium green, semi-glossy; [Sheri Anne × Watercolor]; int. by Nor'East Min. Roses

Windlass HCh, m, Sutherland, P; [sport of Simon Robinson seedling]; int. by Golden Vale Nursery, 1995

Windmill Gr, rb, 1992, Williams, J. Benjamin; flowers burgundy with ivory white on reverse, 3-3 1/2 in., single, borne singly; foliage medium size, medium green, semi-glossy; few prickles; medium (3-5 ft.), bushy, spreading growth; [Handel × (Love × Double Feature)]; originally registered as S; int. in 1994

Windrose S, lp, Noack, Werner; flowers soft pink, yellow stamens, 4 cm., single, shallow cup, borne in clusters; recurrent; foliage dark green, glossy; upright, arching growth; int. by Noack Rosen, 1993; ADR, 1995

Windrush S, ly, 1985, Austin, David; flowers soft yellow, large, semi-dbl., shallow cup, intense spicy musk fragrance; recurrent; foliage medium size, light green, matte; vigorous, branching growth; [seedling × (Canterbury × Golden Wings)]; int. in 1984

Windsor HT, mr, 1929, Chaplin Bros.; flowers rich crimson-scarlet; vigorous growth

Windsor Castle – See **Constance Finn**

Windsor Charm HT, lp, 1978, LeMire, Walter; bud long, tulip shaped; flowers light pink to ivory, 5-5 1/2 in., 27-30 petals; foliage leathery; vigorous, bushy growth; [sport of First Prize]

Windsounds HT, lp, 1977, Scoggins; [sport of First Prize]; int. by American Rose Foundation, 1976

Windstar – See **Pink Bowie**, S

Windy City Min, dp, 1974, Moore, Ralph S.; bud long, pointed; flowers deep pink, reverse lighter, small, 3-3 1/2 cm., dbl., high-centered, borne singly and several together, slight sweet fragrance; recurrent; foliage small, bronze early, then medium green, semi-glossy; prickles few, medium, hooked downward, brown; stems strong, medium; upright, bushy growth; hips none ; PP3792; [Little Darling × (Little Darling × (*R. wichuraiana* × seedling))]; int. by Mini-Roses

Wine and Dine S, dp, 1999, Dickson, Colin; flowers rose red, ivory white eye, 2 1/4 in., single, borne in small clusters, moderate fragrance; foliage small, medium green, glossy; numerous prickles; groundcover; spreading, medium (3 ft.) growth; [seedling × seedling]; int. by Dickson Nurseries, Ltd., 1999

Wine and Roses HMsk; dr, Clements, John K.; flowers dark wine red, semi-double, borne in large trusses; foliage rich green, glossy, long, narrow; bushy (3 1/2 ft.) growth; PPAF; int. by Heirloom Roses, 1999

Wine Buff F, yb, Benny, David; flowers peach/chardonnay, dbl; foliage reddish green when young, aging to medium green, glossy; int. by Camp Hill Roses

Winefred Clarke HT, my, 1964, Robinson, H.; flowers 5 1/2 in., 34 petals, high-centered; foliage dark, glossy; [Peace × Lydia]

Wing-Ding Pol, mr, 2006, Carruth, Tom; flowers scarlet orange-red, 2-4 cm., single, shallow cup, borne in large clusters, very slight fragrance; foliage medium size, dark green, semi-glossy; prickles average, slightly hooked, brown, moderate; growth spreading, medium (45 to 60 cm.); garden decoration; [Red Fairy × Raven]; like The Fairy in habit, very large clusters, somewhat spreading, bright long lived color; int. by Weeks Roses, 2007

Winged Fellowship F, or, 1989, Horner, Heather M.; bud ovoid; flowers vermillion orange, reverse lighter, medium, 28 petals, urn-shaped; foliage medium size, medium green, matte; prickles small, brown; bushy, medium growth; hips globular, medium, red-orange; [Guitare × Prominent]; int. by Rosemary Roses, 1989

Wingthorn Rose – See ***R. sericea pteracantha*** (Franchet)

Wini Edmunds HT, rb, 1974, McGredy, Sam IV; bud ovoid; flowers red, reverse blush white, 5 1/2-6 in., 20-24 petals, high-centered, spiral, borne singly, slight sweet fragrance; recurrent; foliage large, dark green, leathery; prickles few, large, recurved; vigorous, upright (5 ft.) growth; hips round, flattened, yellow; PP3822; [Red Lion × Hanne]; int. by Edmunds Roses, 1973

Winifred HT, yb, 1930, Chaplin Bros.; flowers deep yellow, shaded peach to old-gold, large, dbl.; vigorous growth; RULED EXTINCT 4/81

Winifred Gr, mp, 1981, Jerabek, Paul E.; bud pointed; flowers bright medium pink, 23 petals, slight fragrance; foliage reddish when young; prickles slightly hooked, red; vigorous, tall growth; [Queen Elizabeth × seedling]

Winifred Coulter F, rb, 1962, Kemple; bud pointed; flowers vermilion-scarlet, reverse silvery, 2 1/2-3 1/2 in., 18-26 petals, flat, borne in clusters, intense fragrance; recurrent; foliage leathery, glossy, dark green; prickles several, hooked downward; vigorous, bushy growth; hips globular, orange-red; PP2219; [Baby Chateau × Contrast]; int. by Van Barneveld, 1962; David Fuerstenberg Prize, ARS, 1968

Winifred Coulter, Climbing Cl F, rb, Jarvis; int. in about 1968

Winkfield Crimson Emperor LCl, dr, 1960, Combe; flowers dark crimson, large, 27 petals, borne in clusters; recurrent bloom; foliage leathery; vigorous, pillar growth; [Red Empress × Surprise]; int. by Winkfield Manor Nursery, 1958

Winners All HT, dp, 1990; bud ovoid; flowers carmine pink with a touch of orange in center, loose, large, dbl., cupped, slight fruity fragrance; foliage medium size, medium green, semi-glossy; bushy, medium growth; [sport of Cherry Brandy]; int. by Rearsby Roses, Ltd., 1986

Winner's Choice HT, pb; int. by J&P, 1992

Winnie Davis T, mp, 1892, Little; bud long, pointed; flowers pink with lighter reflexes, semi-dbl., moderate fragrance; [Devoniensis × Mme de Watteville]

Winnie Renshaw Min, lp, 1991, Rennie, Bruce F.; flowers small, dbl., borne in small clusters, moderate fragrance; foliage small, medium green, semi-glossy; medium growth; [Lavonde × Party Girl]; int. by Rennie Roses International, 1991

Winning Colors Gr, ob, 1990, Twomey, Jerry; bud ovoid; flowers yellow with deep orange margins, 4 in., 60 petals, cupped, borne mostly singly, moderate musk fragrance; recurrent; foliage medium size, dark green, glossy; prickles declining, yellow-green; stems long, sturdy; upright, medium (5 ft.) growth; PP7907; [Gingersnap × Marina]; int. by DeVor Nurseries, Inc., 1990

Winnipeg Parks S, dp, 1991, Collicutt, Lynn M.; bud slender, pointed; flowers dark pink-red, 7-10 cm., 22 petals, cupped, borne singly or in sprays of 2-4, slight fragrance; repeat bloom; foliage medium size, medium green, matte; prickles some, 4-6 mm, linear, angled downward, reddish; medium (2-3 ft.), bushy growth; winter hardy ; PP9122; [(Prairie Princess × Cuthbert Grant) × (seedling × Morden Cardinette)]; int. by Agriculture Canada, 1990

Winschoten – See **Winshoten**, S

Winshoten S, dr, Meilland; flowers large, red, full, intense fragrance; int. by Meilland, 2000

Winsome HT, dp, 1924, E.G. Hill, Co.; flowers cherry-rose, dbl.; RULED EXTINCT 1/85; [Premier × Hoosier Beauty]; int. by Vestal

Winsome Cl HT, mr, 1931, Dobbie; bud long, pointed; flowers cherry-red, 3-3½ in., dbl., borne in small clusters, strong tea fragrance; foliage leathery; very vigorous growth; ruled extinct ARA 1985

Winsome Min, m, 1985, Saville, F. Harmon; flowers lilac-lavender with red tinge, 1¾-2 in., 30 -35 petals, high-centered, borne singly and in sprays, no fragrance; recurrent; foliage medium size, dark green, semi-glossy; prickles some, medium, straight, purplish; upright, bushy growth; PP5691; [Party Girl × Shocking Blue]; int. by Nor'East Min. Roses, 1985; AOE, ARS, 1985

Winsome Native S, w, 1980, Stoddard, Louis; bud ovoid, pointed; flowers 20 petals, cupped, borne singly, no fragrance; sparse, repeat bloom; foliage finely serrated, 5 leaflet; no prickles; rounded, medium growth; [Gene Boerner × *R. suffulta*]

Winspit LCl, w, Bates; int. in 2001

Winter Cheer HMsk, mr, 1914, Pemberton; flowers crimson, medium, semi-dbl.

Winter Gem T, lp, 1898, Childs; flowers creamy pink, large, dbl.

Winter Haven F, lp, 2006, Castillo, Angel; flowers dbl., borne in large clusters; foliage medium size, medium green, semi-glossy; prickles medium, straight, moderate; growth spreading, medium (34 in.); garden decorative, exhibition; [Carefree Beauty × orange-red Floribunda seedling]; int. by Angel Roses, 2007

Winter King S, dp, 1985, James, John; flowers bright deep pink, 11 petals, borne singly; repeat bloom; foliage medium size, dark, leathery, matte; compact, branching growth; hardy; [(((McGredy's Scarlet × Polly) × Frau Karl Druschki) × Northlander]

Winter Magic Min, m, 1986, Jacobs, Betty A.; flowers light lavender-gray, golden stamens, large, 30 petals, cupped, borne usually singly or in small sprays, moderate citrus tea fragrance; recurrent; foliage medium size, medium green, semi-glossy; prickles medium, slender, straight, red; medium, upright, bushy growth; hips medium, globular, orange-red; [Rise 'n' Shine × Blue Nile]; int. by Four Seasons Rose Nursery

Winter Princess Min, w, 1997, Giles, Diann; flowers medium, dbl., borne in small clusters; foliage medium size, medium green, semi-glossy; upright, medium (2½ ft.) growth; [Little Darling × select pollen]; int. by Giles Rose Nursery

Winter Sunset S, yb, 1997, Buck, Dr. Griffith J.; flowers amber-orange, 4 in., 30-40 petals, high-centered, borne in small clusters, moderate fruity fragrance; recurrent; foliage large, dark green, glossy; upright, bushy, medium growth; [Serendipity × (Country Dancer × Alexandra)]; int. by Sam Kedem Nursery, 1985

Winter Wheat Min, ly, 1995, Williams, Ernest; flowers 1¼ in., full, borne mostly singly; foliage medium size, medium green, semi-glossy; some prickles; upright (16-18 in.), bushy growth; [seedling × Twilight Trail]

Wintonbury Parish Min, w, 1988, Berg, David H.; flowers white with top third of petal light red, medium, 14 petals, high-centered, borne usually singly; foliage medium size, medium green, semi-glossy; prickles curved, large, light greenish-white; upright, medium growth; PP6843; [Poker Chip × Lady X]

Wintoniensis HMoy, mp, 1935; sepals long, leafy; flowers rosy pink, single, shallow cup, borne in large clusters; foliage with sweetbriar (apple) fragrance; vigorous (2 m.) growth; hips bristly, flagon-shaped; [*R. moyesii* × *R. setipoda*]

Wisbech Gold HT, yb, 1964, McGredy, Sam IV; flowers golden yellow edged pinkish, well-formed, 4 in., 35 petals, cupped; vigorous, compact growth; [Piccadilly × Golden Star]; int. by McGredy

Wisbech Rose Fragrant Delight – See **Fragrant Delight**, F

Wise Portia S, m, 1983, Austin, David; flowers rich magenta, large, dbl., intense fragrance; foliage medium size, dark, semi-glossy; bushy growth; [The Knight × seedling]

Wishful Thinking Min, rb, 1996, McCann, Sean; flowers medium red light yellow eye, heavy mass of yellow stamens, 1½ in., dbl., petals very reflexed, intense fragrance; foliage medium size, dark green to light orange, glossy; upright, medium (16-20 in.) growth; PPRR; [seedling × Wit's End]; int. by Justice Miniature Roses, 1997

Wishing F, op, 1984, Dickson, Patrick; flowers medium peachy pink, large, 35 petals, pointed, slight fragrance; foliage medium size, medium green, semi-glossy; bushy growth; [Silver Jubilee × Bright Smile]; int. by Dickson Nurseries, Ltd., 1984

Wishing Well HT, w, Zary, Keith; int. by Bear Creek Gardens, 1999

Wisley S, dp, 2004; flowers very full, borne in small clusters, moderate fragrance; foliage large, dark green, semi-glossy; prickles medium, hooked downward; growth bushy, vigorous, medium (125 cm.); garden decorative; [Unnamed seedling (apricot English type shrub) × Golden Celebration]; int. by David Austin Roses, Ltd., 2004

Wisteria Maiden – See **Fujimusume**, HT

Wistful Min, m, 1994, Saville, F. Harmon; bud pointed, ovate; flowers lilac lavender, 1½ in., 20-24 petals, high-centered, becoming flat, borne singly and in small clusters, slight fragrance; recurrent; foliage small, dark green, semi-glossy; prickles some, short, straight, angled slightly downward; medium (16-22 in.), upright, bushy growth; PP9562; [Sachet × Rainbow's End]; int. by Nor'East Min. Roses, 1995

Witchcraft F, yb, 1961, Verschuren; bud ovoid; flowers yellow, reverse scarlet, 2-2½ in., 45-50 petals, borne in large clusters; foliage dark, glossy; vigorous growth; [Masquerade × seedling]; int. by Blaby Rose Gardens, 1961

Witching Hour F, dr, 1967, Morey, Dennison H., Jr.; bud ovoid; flowers dark red, almost black, medium, dbl.; vigorous, bushy, compact growth; [Rapture × (F.W. Alesworth × Charles Mallerin)]; int. by General Bionomics

With All My Love HT, or, 2005, Cocker, A.G.; flowers orange/salmon/vermilion, large, very full, borne mostly solitary, slight fragrance; foliage medium size, dark green, glossy; prickles 9 mm., straight; growth upright, bushy, medium (2½-3 ft.); garden decoration; [Fragrant Cloud × Christopher]; int. in 2005

With Love HT, yb, 1983, Anderson's Rose Nurseries; flowers yellow, petal edges pink; foliage medium size, medium green, semi-glossy; upright growth; [Irish Gold × Daily Sketch]

With Thanks HT, yb, 1995, Cowlishaw, Frank; flowers deep pink, yellow eye and reverse, medium, full, high-centered, then flattens, borne in clusters, moderate fragrance; recurrent; foliage medium size, medium green, glossy; medium (2-3 ft.), upright growth; [(Southampton × Prominent) × Summer Love]; int. by Rearsby Roses, Ltd., 1996

Withersfield F, ob, 2000, Horner, Heather M.; flowers orange, reverse yellow, 8 cm., dbl., slight fragrance; foliage medium size, medium green, semi-glossy; prickles moderate; growth upright, tall (1¼ m.); [City of Portsmouth × (Prominent × Southampton)]

Wit's End Min, rb, 1989, McCann, Sean; flowers red with yellow reverse, small, 20 petals, borne in sprays of 3-5, slight fragrance; foliage small, medium green, semi-glossy; bushy growth; [Rise 'n' Shine × Siobhan]

Wizard F, or, 1998, McGredy, Sam IV; flowers orange-red with white eye, 2½ in., semi-dbl., borne in large clusters; foliage small, medium green, semi-glossy; prickles moderate; bushy, low (30 cm.) growth; [seedling × Genesis]; int. by McGredy, 1996

Wizo HT, ob, 1972, Kriloff, Michel; flowers salmon-red, reverse darker, 40 petals, high-centered; foliage reddish-green, matte; PP3139; [Tropicana × (Gamine × Romantica)]; int. by Domaine Agricole de Cronenbourg, 1968

Woburn Abbey F, ob, 1962, Sidey & Cobley; bud ovoid; flowers orange, 3½ in., 25 petals, cupped, borne singly and in irregular clusters, moderate tea fragrance; recurrent; foliage medium size, dark green, leathery; prickles average, medium, hooked downward; stems medium, strong; moderate, upright growth; hips none ; PP2319; [Masquerade × Fashion]; int. by Harkness, 1962

Woburn Abbey, Climbing Cl F, ob, Brundrett, S; int. in 1972

Woburn Gold F, dy, 1970, Robinson, H.; flowers soft golden yellow; modest growth; [sport of Woburn Abbey]

Wodan HMult, mr, 1890, Geschwind, R.; flowers carmine-red with white at petal base, lighter reverse, large, semi-dbl., cupped, borne in clusters of 5-10, slight fragrance; foliage rounded; numerous prickles; [Gloire des Rosomanes × possibly *R. multiflora*]

Wolfe's Glorie Pol, op, 1943, Wolf, Van der; flowers salmon-pink to deep orange; vigorous growth; [sport of Orléans Rose]; int. by Hage

Wolfgang von Goethe HP, pb, Weigand, L.; bud very long; flowers delicate bright yellowish-pink, very large, dbl., high-centered; vigorous growth; [Frau Karl Druschki × Souv. de Claudius Pernet]

Wolley-Dod's Rose – See **Duplex**, Misc OGR

Wollongong Gold Gr, ly, 1997, Walsh, Richard Bruce; flowers light creamy yellow, flushed pink, 1½-3 in., full, borne in small clusters, slight fragrance; foliage medium size, light green, semi glossy; low (1 m.) bushy growth; [Violet Carson × Arizona]

Woman HT, w; flowers ivory white with pink flush towards the center, full, high-centered, moderate fragrance

Woman and Home HT, ob, 1976, Gregory; flowers orange, pointed, 5 in., 33 petals; foliage glossy, dark; [Apricot Silk × (Piccadilly+I6171 × unknown)]

Woman O'th North F, lp, 1993, Kirkham, Gordon Wilson; flowers shell pink, medium, dbl., hybrid tea, borne in small clusters, moderate fragrance; foliage medium size, medium green, semi-glossy; few prickles; low (1½ × 1½ ft.), bushy growth; int. by Kirkham, 1994

Woman Pioneer – See **Pionerka**, F

Woman's Day HT, or, 1970, Armbrust; bud ovoid; flowers scarlet-orange, medium, semi-dbl., high-centered; foliage leathery; vigorous, upright growth; [Queen Elizabeth × Karl Herbst]; int. by Langbecker, 1966

Woman's Day F, pb, Welsh, Eric; flowers light pink with medium pink edges, sometimes flushed rose pink, large, full, cupped, informal, borne in clusters, slight fragrance; free-flowering; medium growth; [Avandel × WELpa]; int. in 1993

Woman's Hour F, pb, Beales, Peter; flowers satin pink, large white eye, semi-double, shallow cup, borne in clusters; recurrent; foliage light green; compact, bushy growth; int. by Peter Beales Roses, 1997

Woman's Own Min, mp, 1973, McGredy, Sam IV; flowers pink, 1½ in., 45 petals; foliage dark; [New Penny × Tip-Top]; int. by McGredy

Woman's Realm HT, mr, 1966, Gregory; flowers scarlet, 3½-4 in.; foliage glossy; upright growth; [Chrysler Imperial × unknown]

Woman's Value HT, op, 1985, Kordes, R.; bud pointed; flowers cream to soft coral, deepening to deep salmon, 42 petals, star-shaped, slight fragrance; free-flowering; foliage glossy, deep green; prickles straight, brown; medium, bushy, well-branched growth; [(Sonia × ((Dr. A.J. Verhage × Colour Wonder) × Zorina)) × Asso di Cuori]; int. by Ludwigs Roses Pty. Ltd., 1984

Women in Military S, mr, 1993, Jerabek, Paul E.; flowers bright red, large, 20-30 petals, borne in small clusters, moderate fragrance; foliage medium size, medium green, glossy; some prickles; medium (135 cm.), upright growth

Women O'th North – See **Woman O'th North**, F

Women's Institute HT, pb, Kordes; flowers cream with outer petals bordered and suffused deep pink, 4 in., double, high-centered, borne mostly singly; recurrent; medium (4-5 ft.) growth; int. as Panthea, Willhelmse, 1991

Wonder – See **Wonder Parade**, Min

Wonder of Woolies F, ab, 1978, Bees; flowers deep apricot, 4½ in., 30 petals; vigorous growth; [Arthur Bell × Elizabeth of Glamis]

Wonder Parade Min, pb, Poulsen; flowers pink blend, medium, dbl., no fragrance; foliage dark; growth bushy, 20-40 cm.; PP10934; int. by Poulsen Roser, 1996

Wonderful MinFl, pb, 2003, Wells, Verlie W.; flowers pink with yellow base, 3 in., full, borne mostly solitary, intense fragrance; foliage medium size, medium green, semi-glossy; prickles ¼ in., hooked; growth upright, tall (36 in.); garden, exhibition; [seedling × seedling]; int. by Wells MidSouth Roses, 2002

Wonderful HT, my, Poulsen; flowers yellow that lasts, 10-15 cm., full, borne one to a stem, slight fragrance; recurrent; foliage reddish green; bushy (60-100 cm.) growth; hips none; int. by Poulsen Roser, 2005

Wonderful News Min, rb, Jones, Chris; flowers cherry red with white eye and creamy white reverse, double, slight fragrance; free-flowering; foliage small, medium green, glossy; compact (12 in.), rounded growth; int. by C&K Jones, 2001

Wonderglo Min, r, 1994, Williams, Ernest D.; flowers unusual russet with red highlights, medium, very dbl., borne mostly singly, moderate fragrance; foliage small, medium green, semi-glossy; few prickles; medium (18 in.), bushy growth; [seedling × Twilight Trail]; int. by Texas Mini Roses, 1994

Wonderland S, yb, Dickson, Patrick; int. by Dickson Roses, 1994

Wonderstar F, my, 1960, Mondial Roses; flowers bright yellow, large, semi-dbl.; low, bushy growth; [Goldilocks × seedling]

Wonderstripe S, pb, Clements, John K.; flowers deep, smoky pink striped with creamy yellow and white, 4 in., very dbl., cupped, moderate fruity myrrh fragrance; recurrent bloom; foliage dark green; compact (4 ft.) growth; int. by Heirloom Roses, 1997

Wood Lawn HT, mp, 1985, Fiamingo, Joe; flowers clear medium pink; [sport of Fontainebleau]

Woodland Sunbeam Min, my, 1984, Robinson, Thomas, Ltd.; flowers patio, medium, 23 petals; foliage small, dark, glossy; few prickles; vigorous, bushy growth; [Orange Sensation × Calay]

Woodlands Lady Min, mp, 1982, Robinson, Thomas, Ltd.; flowers medium salmon-pink, small, 15 petals, borne in large clusters; foliage small, dark, glossy; compact, bushy growth; [seedling × New Penny]

Woodlands Sunrise Min, yb, 1982, Robinson, Thomas, Ltd.; flowers small, 35 petals; foliage small, dark, glossy; upright, bushy growth; [Rumba × Darling Flame]

Woodrow Sp, lp; flowers 60 petals; fall bloom; low growth; collected in Sask., Canada; a form of *R. suffulta*; int. by P.H. Wright, 1936

Wood's Garland – See **The Garland**, HMult

Woods of Windsor – See **Belami**, HT

Woods Rose – See ***R. woodsii*** (Lindley)

Woodstock Min, yb, 1999, Moore, Ralph S.; flowers bright yellow, aging red, 1-1½ in., full, borne mostly singly, slight fragrance; recurrent; foliage small, medium green, semi-glossy; few prickles; low (8-12 in.), bushy, compact growth; [seedling × Clytemnestra]; int. by Sequoia Nursery, 1999

Woody HMsk, mr, Lens

Worcestershire S, my, Kordes; flowers bright yellow, yellow stamens, semi-double, shallow cup, borne in clusters, no fragrance; recurrent; foliage glossy; low (2 ft.), spreading growth; int. in 2000

Worjackie HT, pb, 1993, Kirkham, Gordon Wilson; flowers pink blend, 2¾-3 in., full, borne mostly singly, moderate fragrance; foliage medium size, dark green, semi-glossy; numerous prickles; medium, upright growth; [Solitaire × Brandy Butter]; int. by Battersby Roses, 1994

Work of Art Cl Min, ob, 1989, Moore, Ralph S.; bud short; flowers orange blended with yellow, reverse slightly more yellow, 4-5 cm., 35 petals, high-centered, borne in loose sprays of 3-7, slight fruity fragrance; recurrent; foliage medium size, bronze aging to medium green, semi-glossy; prickles few, slender, nearly straight, average, brown; stems slender, wirey; upright, spreading, tall growth; hips globular, medium, orange; PP7617; [(Little Darling × Yellow Magic) × Gold Badge]; int. by Sequoia Nursery

World Class F, ab, Harkness; flowers golden amber, large; free-flowering; int. in 1996

World Peace HT, pb, 1987, Perry, Anthony; flowers pink blend suffused with cream, tips of petals tinged dark pink, large, 30-35 petals, high-centered, moderate fruity fragrance; foliage large, medium green, semi-glossy, disease-resistant; prickles average; upright, tall growth; hips globular, orange; [First Prize × Gold Glow]; int. by Co-Operative Rose Growers, 1991

World Peace 2000 HT, my, Pearce; int. by Pocock's Roses, 2000

World Rose – See **Die Welt**, HT

World War II Memorial Rose HT, m, 2000, Weeks, O.L.; bud large, pointed; flowers white with pinkish-lavender tones toward the petal edges, 4-5 in., 20-32 petals, high-centered, borne mostly singly; recurrent; foliage medium size, medium green, semi-glossy; prickles moderate, 5 mm., nearly straight, tan; upright (4 ft.) growth; PP14433; [Silver Spoon × Paradise]; int. by Conard-Pyle Co., 2001

World's Fair F, dr, 1939, Kordes; flowers deep crimson fading to scarlet, 4 in., 19 petals, borne in clusters, moderate spicy fragrance; foliage leathery; vigorous, bushy growth; [Dance of Joy × Crimson Glory]; int. by J&P

World's Fair, Climbing Cl F, dr, 1941, J&P

World's Fair Salute HT, mr, 1964, Morey, Dr. Dennison; bud ovoid; flowers crimson-red, 5½ in., 33 petals, high-centered, moderate fragrance; foliage leathery; vigorous, upright growth; PP2558; [Mardi Gras × New Yorker]; int. by J&P

Wörlitz S, yb, Berger, W.; flowers coral-orange with cream yellow center, large, dbl., borne singly, slight fragrance; recurrent; stems strong; int. in 1962

Worthington (natural variation of *R. setigera*), lp; flowers clear pink

Worthwhile HT, ob, 1973, LeGrice; flowers orange, reverse lighter, pointed, 5-6 in., 33 petals, pointed, slight fragrance; foliage matte, olive-green; [Gavotte × Vienna Charm]

Woschod HT, w, Bülow; flowers large, dbl.; int. in 1973

Wow! Min, ob, 1985, Strawn, Leslie E.; bud pointed; flowers bright orange, reverse more red tones, small, 25-35 petals, cupped, borne singly, slight fragrance; recurrent; foliage small, dark green, glossy; prickles few, needle, declining slightly; stems upright, slender; bushy, rounded growth; PP6469; [Ann Cocker × (Puerto Rico × Darling Flame)]; int. by Pixie Treasures Min. Roses

Wow HT, ob, deRuiter; flowers dusty orange, 11 cm., 30 petals, high-centered, borne mostly singly, no fragrance; recurrent; prickles moderate; stems long; int. by DeRuiter's Roses, 2004

Wretham Rose C, dp, Hoellering; flowers cerise pink, very full, heavy early summer bloom, moderate clove fragrance; non-remontant; numerous prickles; sturdy, tall growth; chance seedling found in Mrs. Hoellering's garden; int. in 1997

Wright's Salmon HT, op, 1960, Wright & Son; flowers salmon, 5 in., 32 petals, high-centered; [sport of Opera]

Wurzburg – See **Veldfire**, HT

Wyanda F, mp, 1968, Heidemy; bud ovoid; flowers pink, medium, dbl.; foliage dark; [United Nations × seedling]

Wyrala HT, dr, Heers, C W; [Lemania × Ami Guinard]

Wyralla HT, dr, 1949, Heers; bud ovoid; flowers large, semi-dbl., high-centered; vigorous, bushy growth; [Lemania × Ami Quinard]; int. by Pacific Nursery

X-Rated Min, pb, 1993, Bennett, Dee; flowers creamy white, edges blush a soft coral to pink, medium, 4-5 cm., 25-35 petals, cupped, borne mostly singly, moderate fragrance; recurrent; foliage small, medium green, semi-glossy; prickles some, slender, hooked slightly downward, reddish; medium, bushy growth; PP9375; [Tiki × Baby Katie]; int. by Tiny Petals Nursery, 1994

Xanadu S, op, 2003, Manners, Malcolm M.; flowers 3½ in., dbl., borne mostly solitary, slight fragrance; foliage medium size, medium green, semi-glossy; prickles moderate; bushy, medium growth; [Carefree Beauty × unknown]; plant closely resembles Carefree Beauty but flower is much more double and deeper pink; int. in 2002

Xavier Olibo HP, dr, 1865, Lacharme, F.; flowers velvety deep crimson shaded purplish; [sport of Général Jacqueminot]

Xaviere – See **Traviata**, HT, 1998

Xénia – See **Sommermärchen**, F, 2006

Xerxes S, yb, 1990, Harkness, R., & Co., Ltd.; bud pointed; flowers rich yellow with scarlet-red eye at base, reverse yellow, 5 petals, cupped; foliage small, grayish-green, matte; prickles narrow, small, reddish; upright, medium to tall growth; fruit not observed; [H. persica × Canary Bird]; int. in 1989

Xiang Fen Lian – See **Souv d'Elise Vardon**, T

Xu Gui Hua Gr, ab, 2006, Newman, Laurie; flowers dbl., borne in small clusters; foliage medium size, dark green, glossy; prickles medium, regular, maroon, moderate; growth upright, medium (1½ m.); garden decoration; [Parador × Buff Beauty]; int. by Treloar Roses, 2008

XXL – See **Parole**, HT

Y2K Min, dy, 1999, Saville, F. Harmon; flowers deep yellow with coating of coral, reverse medium yellow, 1½-2 in., dbl., borne mostly singly, slight fragrance; recurrent; foliage medium size, dark green, glossy; few prickles; bushy, low (12-15 in.) growth; [Cal Poly × New Zealand]; int. by Nor'East Miniature Roses, 2000

Ya Ya's Girl HT, pb, 2003, Sievers, Maryanne; flowers pink and cream with yellow base, 4 in., full, borne mostly solitary, slight fragrance; foliage medium size, medium green; prickles moderate, 16 mm., triangular; growth bushy, medium; garden decorative, exhibition; [sport of Mon Cheri]

Yabadabadoo HT, dy, 1982, McGredy, Sam IV; flowers large, 20 petals, high-centered, slight fragrance; foliage medium size, medium green, semi-glossy; bushy growth; [Yellow Pages × Bonfire Night]; int. by McGredy International, 1981

Yabadabadoo HT, or, Spek; flowers bright orange-red, 10-11 cm., 30-35 petals, high-centered, borne mostly singly; recurrent; few prickles; stems long; florist rose; int. by Jan Spek Rozen, 2005

Yabusame HT, mr, 1999, Ohtsuki, Hironaka; flowers crimson, 6 in., 35 petals, high-centered; growth to 6 ft.; [Big Chief × Papa Meilland]; int. in 1998

Yachiyo-Nishiki F, ob, 1987, Suzuki, Seizo; flowers orange, reverse yellow, medium, 28 petals, borne 2-5 per stem, moderate fragrance; recurrent; foliage dark green, semi-glossy; prickles curved downwards; upright, compact growth; [(Maxim × Myo-Joh) × Duftwolke]; int. by Keisei Rose Nursery, 1984

Yakachinensis – See ***R. wichurana yakachinensis***

Yakiman F, m, Adam; flowers fuchsia, full, moderate lemon fragrance; prickles very few; upright (2 ft.) growth; int. before 1997

Yakimour HT, rb, Meilland; flowers red with yellow reverse, full; int. by Sauvageot, 1986; Gold Medal, Baden-Baden, 1985

Yametsu-Hime Min, pb, 1961, Hebaru; flowers white edged pink, small, semi-dbl.; foliage glossy, light; dwarf growth; [Tom Thumb × seedling]; int. by Itami Rose Nursery

Yamini Krishnamurti HT, m, 1971, Singh; flowers lilac, medium, dbl., high-centered; foliage glossy; moderate growth; [Sterling Silver, Climbing × unknown]; int. by K. S. G. & Son, 1969

Yanina F, op, 1964, Yeoman & Sons; flowers salmon-pink, large, 16 petals; foliage glossy; vigorous growth; [Fashion × Queen Elizabeth]

Yanka S, mp, 1927, Hansen, N.E.; flowers semi-dbl., borne in clusters; non-recurrent; growth to 3-4 ft.; very hardy

Yankee Doodle HT, yb, 1975, Kordes, R.; bud pointed ovoid; flowers apricot to peachy pink, with butter-yellow reverse, 4-5 in., 65-75 petals, high-centered, cupped, borne mostly singly, slight tea fragrance; recurrent; foliage glossy, dark olive green, leathery; prickles moderate, medium, hooked slightly downward, brown; stems strong, medium; upright, bushy growth; PP3957; [Colour Wonder × King's Ransom]; int. by Armstrong Nursery, 1976

Yankee Lady – See **Pierette**, HRg semi-dbl. to dbl.

Yantai MinFl, yb, 1989, Bennett, Dee; bud ovoid; flowers pastel yellow, deeper yellow in center and pink blush on outer petals, 25-30 petals, high-centered, cupped, borne usually singly, moderate fruity fragrance; recurrent; foliage medium size, medium green, semi-glossy; prickles some, hooked downward, yellow to red; bushy, spreading, tall, vigorous growth; PP7962; [Portrait × Party Girl]; int. by Tiny Petals Nursery, 1988

Yardley Baroque HT, ly, 1999, Beales, Peter; flowers soft, primrose yellow, 4½ in., full, cupped, borne mostly singly, moderate fragrance; recurrent; foliage medium size, dark green, semi-glossy; numerous prickles; upright, medium (2-3 ft.) growth; [sport of Alpine Sunset]; int. by Peter Beales Roses, 1997

Yardley English Rose HT, mp, Kordes; flowers double, high-centered; recurrent; int. in 1990

Yaroslavna HT, mp, 1958, Sushkov & Besschetnova; flowers large, 60 petals; foliage dark; vigorous growth; [La Parisienne × Peace]

Yasaka HT, op, Keihan; int. in 1972

Yasaka, Climbing Cl HT, op, 1978; int. in 1978

Yashwant HT, rb, 1987, Patil, B.K.; flowers red, striped white and yellow, reverse yellow, striped red, 55-60 petals, high-centered; foliage glossy; prickles pale, green, curving downwards; vigorous, upright, bushy growth; [sport of Suspense]; int. by K.S.G. Sons Roses, 1985

Yasnaya Poliana HT, op, 1958, Shtanko, I.; flowers salmon-pink, well-formed, large, 45-50 petals; foliage dark; vigorous, compact growth; [Independence × Luna]

Yaswanth HT, rb; flowers red with white reverse, double

Yatkan S, mp, 1927, Hansen, N.E.; flowers 2½ in., dbl.; non-recurrent; very hardy; [probably Gruss an Teplitz × La Mélusine]

Yawa S, op, 1940, Hansen, N.E.; flowers light coral-pink, 2 in., 58 petals, borne in clusters of 4-12 on 8-12 in. stems; free, non-recurrent bloom; tall, wide spreading (pillar to 9 ft.) growth; very hardy; [Anci Bohmova × *R. blanda*]

Yayoi F, lp, Fujii

Ye Hamstead HT, dr, Drummond; int. in 1991

Ye Primrose Dame T, yb, 1886, Bennett; flowers yellow with apricot-pink center, large, full, globular

Year 2000 Min, yb, 2004, Jalbert, Brad; flowers yellow with scarlet petal edges, reverse yellow, 1¼ in., full, high-centered, borne in small clusters, no fragrance; recurrent; foliage medium size, very dark green, glossy, heavy; prickles moderate, medium, green-brown; growth bushy, medium (14-16 in.); garden and container; [Laura Ford × Kristen]; int. in 2000

Yeller Rose O'Texas HT, dy, 1987, Wambach, Alex A.; flowers medium, full, intense fragrance; foliage medium size, medium green, semi-glossy; upright growth; [sport of Arizona]

Yello Yo Yo, Climbing Cl F, dy, 1976, Weeks, O. L.; buds slender, medium, long, globular; flowers 20 petals, high-centered, borne singly and in small clusters, slight tea fragrance; foliage medium green; upright (6-8 ft.) growth; PP4048; [sport of Yello Yo Yo]

Yello Yo Yo F, dy, 1980, Weeks; bud slender, long; flowers 2½-3 in., 20-25 petals, high-centered, becoming open, borne singly and in clusters, slight tea fragrance; recurrent; foliage medium green, semi-glossy, leathery; prickles numerous, long, angled slightly downward, brown; bushy, upright growth; PP4047; [Arlene Francis × seedling]

YelloGlo – See **Jean de la Lune**, F dbl.

Yellow – See **Yellow Paillette**, MinFl

Yellow Altai HSpn, my, 1950, Wright, Percy H.; flowers bright yellow, becoming lighter, small, borne in clusters; profuse, non-recurrent bloom; foliage light green, soft; stems reddish-brown; vigorous (7 ft.), upright growth; hardy (to -60F); [*R. spinosissima altaica* × Persian Yellow]

Yellow Amer F, dy

Yellow and Fragrant HT, dy; int. by Bakker France, 2006

Yellow Angel – See **Gelber Engel**, F

Yellow Baby Rambler – See **George Elger**, Pol

Yellow Bantam Min, ly, 1960, Moore, Ralph S.; bud pointed, yellow; flowers yellow to white, very small, ½ in., 25 petals; foliage glossy; bushy (10 in.) growth; [(*R. wichurana* × Floradora) × Fairy Princess]; int. by Sequoia Nursery, 1960

Yellow Bantam, Climbing Cl Min, ly, 1965, Rumsey, R.H.

Yellow Beauty HT, my, 1945, Ruzicka's; bud longer, more pointed, clear golden yellow; more uniform growth than its parent; [sport of Golden Rapture]

Yellow Bedder HT, ly, 1923, Van Rossem; flowers clear yellow to cream, dbl.; [Mr Joh. M. Jolles × Mme Edouard Herriot]

Yellow Belinda F, dy, 1973, Tantau, Math.; bud long, pointed; flowers orange-yellow, medium, dbl.; [sport of Belinda]; int. in 1972

Yellow Belle HT, dy, Bell; flowers unfading golden yellow, small to medium, moderate fragrance; foliage disease-resistant; short growth; int. by Bell Roses

Yellow Bird HT, dy, 1974, McGredy, Sam IV; bud ovoid; flowers large, 42 petals; upright growth; [Sunlight × Arthur Bell]; int. in 1973

Yellow Bird MinFl, my, 2004, Verlie W. Wells; flowers medium yellow, reverse light yellow, 2-2½ in., full, high-centered, borne in small clusters, slight fragrance; foliage medium size, medium green, semi-glossy; prickles moderate, ¼ in., straight; bushy, medium growth; garden decoration, exhibition; [seedling × seedling]; int. by Wells Mid-South Roses, 2003

Yellow Blaze – See **Sun Flare, Climbing**, Cl F, 1987

Yellow Blush A, ly, Sievers; int. in 1988

Yellow Bouquet Min, dy, 1993, Laver, Keith G.; flowers deep yellow, medium, dbl., borne in small clusters; foliage small, medium green, matte; few prickles; low

(15-20 cm.), compact growth; [June Laver × Potluck Gold]; int. by Springwood Roses, 1994

Yellow Butterfly HT, ob, 1927, Scott, R.; flowers orange-yellow; RULED EXTINCT 1/89; [sport of Mme Butterfly]

Yellow Butterfly S, ly, 1989, Moore, Ralph S.; bud pointed; flowers light yellow, aging to near white, medium, 5 petals, informal, borne in sprays of 3-7, no fragrance; foliage medium size, light green, semi-glossy; prickles slender, inclined downward, small, brownish; bushy, spreading, medium, clean growth; hips ovoid, small, yellowish-orange; [Ellen Poulsen × Yellow Jewel]; int. by Sequoia Nursery, 1989

Yellow Button S, yb, 1981, Austin, David; bud globular; flowers medium yellow, deeper in center, rosette, 90 petals, flat, borne singly and in clusters of up to 15; repeat bloom; foliage dark; prickles straight, red; bushy growth; [Wife of Bath × Chinatown]; int. in 1975

Yellow Cécile Brünner – See **Perle d'Or**, Pol

Yellow Cécile Brünner, Climbing – See **Perle d'Or, Climbing**, Cl Pol

Yellow Charles Austin S, ly, 1981, Austin, David; flowers lemon-yellow, very full, cupped, moderate frutiy fragrance; recurrent; tall (5 ft.) growth; [sport of Charles Austin]; int. in 1979

Yellow Cluster F, my, 1949, deRuiter; flowers mimosa-yellow; spreading growth; [Golden Rapture × Polyantha seedling]; int. by Spek

Yellow Cochet – See **Alexander Hill Gray**, T

Yellow Colette – See **Yellow Romantica**, S

Yellow Condesa de Sastago – See **Jean Bostick**, HT

Yellow Condesa de Sástago – See **Yellow Sástago**, HT

Yellow Contempo F, dy, 1985, Gupta, Dr. M.N., Datta, Dr. S.K. & Banerji, Shri B; [sport of Contempo]; int. by National Botanical Research Institute, 1983

Yellow Coral F, my; florist rose; int. by Meilland Intl., 2005

Yellow Cover – See **Lexington**, S

Yellow Creeping Everbloom LCl, my, 1953, Brownell; recurrent bloom; growth very vigorous; pillar or ground-cover; [((Orange Everglow × New Dawn) × seedling) × Free Gold]

Yellow Curls HT, my, 1947, Brownell; flowers open, dbl., moderate fragrance; foliage glossy; vigorous growth; [Golden Glow × Golden Glow]

Yellow Cushion F, my, 1966, Armstrong, D.L.; bud pointed ovoid; flowers light to medium yellow, paling with age, 3-4 in., 30-40 petals, high-centered, cupped, borne in small clusters, slight to moderate fragrance; recurrent; foliage medium size, glossy, leathery; prickles several, medium, hooked slightly downward, brown; stems strong, short to medium; vigorous, bushy growth; hips globular, rough, orange to brown; PP2849; [Fandango × Pinocchio]; int. by Armstrong Nursery, 1962

Yellow Dagmar Hastrup – See **Topaz Jewel**, HRg

Yellow Dazzler – See **Yellowhammer**, F

Yellow Delight – See **Mme Chiang Kai-shek**, HT

Yellow Doll Min, ly, 1962, Moore, Ralph S.; bud pointed ovoid; flowers clear yellow to cream, 1½ in., 55-75 petals, high-centered, opening flat, borne singly and in small clusters, moderate tea rose fragrance; recurrent; foliage medium green, leathery, glossy; prickles several, medium, hooked slightly downward; vigorous, bushy (12 in.) growth; no hips; PP2450; [Golden Glow × Zee]; int. by Sequoia Nursery, 1962

Yellow Doll, Climbing Cl Min, ly, 1976, Kirk; [sport of Yellow Doll]; int. by Sequoia Nursery

Yellow Dot HT, ob, 1938, Joseph H. Hill, Co.; bud short, pointed; flowers light orange-yellow, reverse coral-red, small, dbl.; foliage soft, dark; short stems; vigorous growth; [Rapture × Betsy Ross]

Yellow Dot F, ly, Ilsink; PP10700; int. by Interplant, 1995

Yellow Dream Min, my; flowers dull medium yellow, outer petals fading lighter, double, globular, borne in clusters, slight fragrance; recurrent; foliage healthy green, glossy; low (12 in.), broad growth

Yellow Faïence HT, my, 1942, C-P; flowers lemon-yellow; [sport of Faience]

Yellow Fairy S, my, 1989, Olesen, Pernille & Mogens N.; flowers medium yellow, outer petals fading lighter, 5-8 cm., double, cupped, borne in clusters, very slight fragrance; recurrent; foliage small, light green, semi-glossy; bushy (60-100 cm.) growth; no hips; [Texas × The Fairy]; int. by Poulsen Roser ApS, 1988; Gold Medal, Madrid, 1988

Yellow Festival – See **Living Bouquet**, Min

Yellow Fleurette S, ly; flowers yellow with yellow stamens, semi-dbl., borne in sprays, no fragrance; foliage medium size, dark green, glossy; strong, bushy (2½ ft.) growth; int. by Interplant, 1992

Yellow Floorshow S, yb; flowers soft yellow with pink rim, fading to blush, semi-dbl. to double, cupped, slight to moderate fragrance; recurrent; erect, compact, wide growth; int. by Harkness, 1999

Yellow Flower Carpet – See **Celina**, S

Yellow Folies F, my, Keisei; flowers bright yellow, medium, double, cupped; recurrent; florist rose; int. by Meilland Intl., 2005

Yellow Fontaine S, my, 1972, Tantau, Math.; bud ovoid; flowers large, dbl.; free, continuous bloom; foliage large, glossy; vigorous, upright growth; [unknown × unknown]; int. by Ahrens & Sieberz

Yellow Fru Dagmar Hartopp – See **Topaz Jewel**, HRg

Yellow Gamette Pol, my

Yellow Gloria HT, my, 1936, Bertanzel; bud long, pointed; flowers golden yellow, base saffron, large, dbl., high-centered; foliage leathery; long, strong stems; vigorous growth; [sport of Talisman]

Yellow Goddess F, dy, Zary; PPAF; int. by Bear Creek Gardens

Yellow Gold HT, dy, 1957, Boerner; bud ovoid; flowers deep golden yellow, 5 in., 30-35 petals, cupped, intense fragrance; foliage leathery, glossy; strong stems; vigorous growth; PP1643; int. by J&P

Yellow Hammer – See **Yellowhammer**, F

Yellow Hammer, Climbing Cl F, my, Dorieux; int. in 1976

Yellow Herriot – See **Florence Chenoweth**, HT

Yellow Hit Min, dy, 1988, Olesen, Pernille & Mogens N.; flowers small, dbl.; foliage small, dark green, semi-glossy; bushy, compact, even growth; PP6860; [seedling × seedling]; int. by Poulsen Roser ApS; Gold Medal, International Exhibition, 1986

Yellow Holstein – See **Gelbe Holstein**, F

Yellow Hoover HT, my, 1933, Western Rose Co.; flowers pure yellow; [sport of President Herbert Hoover]

Yellow Hybrid Musk HMsk, my

Yellow Island HT, ly, Brill; flowers large, double, high-centered; stems long; florist rose; int. by Carlton Rose Nursery, 2002

Yellow Jacket S, dy, 1992, Christensen, Jack E.; flowers rich yellow, loose, 2 in., full, cupped, borne mostly singly or small clusters, slight fragrance; free-flowering; foliage medium size, dark green, glossy, very disease-resistant; some prickles; vigorous, medium (2½-3 ft.), upright, bushy growth; [seedling × seedling]; int. by Bear Creek Gardens, 1992

Yellow Jewel Min, my, 1973, Moore, Ralph S.; bud long, pointed; flowers clear yellow, red eye, 1¼ in., 10 petals, open, loose, borne singly and in small clusters, slight to moderate fragrance; recurrent; foliage small, dark green, glossy, leathery; prickles moderate, slender, hooked slightly downward, brown; compact, bushy growth; hips few, round, greenish to orange; PP3627; [Golden Glow × (Little Darling × seedling)]; int. by Sequoia Nursery

Yellow Joanna Hill HT, my, 1932, White, C.N.; bud long, pointed; flowers well-formed, 28 petals; foliage light; long stems; vigorous growth; [sport of Joanna Hill]; int. by White Bros.

Yellow Kaiserin Auguste Viktoria – See **Franz Deegen**, HT

Yellow Lady Banks' Rose – See ***R. banksiae lutea*** (Rehder)

Yellow Light HMsk, ly, 2000, Lens, Louis; flowers light yellow to white, reverse white, 1½-2 cm., single, borne in large, pyramidal-shaped clusters; recurrent; foliage small, medium green, semi-glossy; prickles moderate; spreading, medium (60 cm.) growth; [Trier × Seagull]; int. by Louis Lens N.V., 1994

Yellow Mme Albert Barbier HP, my, 1937, Lens; flowers sunflower-yellow; [sport of Mme Albert Barbier]

Yellow Magic Min, my, 1970, Moore, Ralph S.; bud long, pointed; flowers small, semi-dbl.; foliage small, glossy, dark, leathery; vigorous, dwarf, upright, bushy growth; [Golden Glow × (Little Darling × seedling)]; int. by Sequoia Nursery

Yellow Magic – See **Randilla Jaune**, Min

Yellow Maman Cochet – See **Mme Derepas-Matrat**, T

Yellow Maman Cochet – See **Alexander Hill Gray**, T

Yellow Meillandina Min, yb, 1982, Meilland, Mrs. Marie-Louise; flowers yellow, petals edged pink, 20 petals; foliage medium size, dark, semi-glossy; bushy growth; [(Poppy Flash × (Charleston × Allgold)) × Gold Coin]; int. by Meilland Et Cie, 1980

Yellow Mellow Min, my, 1985, Bridges, Dennis A.; flowers small, 35 petals; foliage large, dark, glossy; bushy growth; [Rise 'n' Shine × unknown]; int. by Bridges Roses, 1985

Yellow Mermet – See **Muriel Grahame**, T

Yellow Mikado F, my, Tantau; florist rose; int. by Rosen Tantau

Yellow Mini-Wonder – See **Potluck Yellow**, Min

Yellow Miniature Min, my, Wayside Gardens Co.; flowers bright yellow, small; [sport of Rosina seedling]; int. in 1961

Yellow Minijet – See **Potluck Yellow**, Min

Yellow Minnehaha HWich, w, before 1933, Cant, F.; flowers white with yellow centers

Yellow Moss M, dy, 1932, Walter, L.; bud ovoid, slightly mossed, deep yellow; flowers yellow, edges tinted pink, semi-dbl., cupped, moderate fragrance; intermittent bloom; foliage thick; vigorous growth; [Old Moss × Mme Edouard Herriot]; int. by J&P

Yellow Mozart S, my, Kordes; flowers darker in center with pale, creamy yellow outer petals, double; foliage medium green; vigorous (4 ft.), bushy growth

Yellow Nature S, my; recurrent; moderate (100 cm.) growth; int. by Verschuren-Pechtold, 1999

Yellow Necklace Min, ly, 1965, Moore, Ralph S.; bud pointed; flowers straw-yellow, small, dbl.; foliage leathery; vigorous, dwarf growth; [Golden Glow × Magic Wand]; int. by Sequoia Nursery

Yellow Nugget Mega Brite MinFl, dy, Walden; bud short, pointed ovoid; flowers pure deep yellow, 2½ in., 40-50 petals, quartered to cupped, borne singly and in clusters of 3-7, slight fragrance; recurrent; foliage dark green, glossy, leathery; prickles ordinary, long, straight, brown; stems short; upright (24 in.) growth; PP11143; [Sunsplash × Ferris Wheel]; int. by Bear Creek Gardens, 1998

Yellow Ocean LCl, my

Yellow Ophelia – See **Silvia**, HT

Yellow Pages HT, yb, 1973, McGredy, Sam IV; flowers dbl., 50 petals, high-centered, moderate fragrance; foliage small, glossy; [Arthur Bell × Peer Gynt]; int. by McGredy, 1972

Yellow Pagode MinFl, my, Poulsen; flowers medium

yellow, 5-8 cm., borne in clusters, no fragrance; foliage dark; cascading growth, hanging basket type; PP13471; int. by Poulsen Roser, 2000

Yellow Paillette MinFl, my, Poulsen; flowers medium yellow, 5-8 cm., slight fragrance; foliage dark; growth narrow, bushy, 40-60 cm.; int. by Poulsen Roser, 1998

Yellow Parade – See **Rainbow Yellow Parade**, Min

Yellow Pastel Min, dy, 1997, Williams, J. Benjamin; flowers bright butter yellow, reverse slightly darker, medium, dbl., borne mostly singly, slight fragrance; foliage medium size, medium green, semi-glossy; upright, compact, medium (13-18in.) growth; [Sunnydew × Rise'n'Shine]; int. by Paramount Roses

Yellow Patio Min, my; flowers golden yellow, double, cupped, very slight fragrance; vigorous (18 in.) growth

Yellow Perfection HT, ly, 1952, Joseph H. Hill, Co.; bud long, pointed, lemon-yellow; flowers canary-yellow, medium, 25-30 petals, high-centered; foliage leathery, dark; vigorous, upright growth; [Pearl Harbor × Golden Rapture]

Yellow Perle d'Or – See **Ravensworth**, Pol

Yellow Petals HT, my, 1972, Robinson, H.; flowers 5½ in., 30 petals, high-centered, moderate fragrance; foliage large, light; [King's Ransom × Dorothy Peach]; int. by Victoria Nurs., 1971

Yellow Pigmy F, my, 1964, Moore, Ralph S.; flowers small, dbl.; foliage small, glossy; dwarf, spreading growth; containers; [seedling × (Eblouissant × Goldilocks)]; int. by Sequoia Nursery

Yellow Pinocchio F, my, 1949, Boerner; bud ovoid; flowers apricot-yellow, fading to cream, 3 in., 45 petals, cupped, borne in clusters, moderate fragrance; recurrent; foliage dark green; vigorous, bushy growth; [Goldilocks × Marionette]; int. by J&P

Yellow Pinocchio, Climbing Cl F, my, 1961, Palmer; int. in 1959

Yellow Pompon – See **Pompone Jaune**, Misc OGR

Yellow Président Carnot HP, my, 1910, California Rose Co.; [sport of Président Carnot]

Yellow Provence – See ***R. hemisphaerica*** (Herrmann)

Yellow Queen Elizabeth Gr, my, 1964, Vlaeminck; flowers orange-yellow, fading to primrose yellow, outer petals lighter; [sport of Queen Elizabeth]; int. by Fryer's Nursery, Ltd.

Yellow Quill MinFl, my, Williams, J. Benjamin; int. in 1998

Yellow Rambler – See **Aglaia**, HMult

Yellow Rambler – See **Brownell Yellow Rambler**, HMult

Yellow Ribbon F, dy, 1977, Dickson, Patrick; flowers deep golden yellow, medium, 23 petals, cupped; foliage medium green, semi-glossy; vigorous, compact, bushy growth; [Illumination × Stroller]; int. by A. Dickson

Yellow Ribbons S, dy, Warner; bud pointed, ovoid; flowers light yellow to near white, 2 in., 20-25 petals, borne in clusters, slight fresh fragrance; recurrent; foliage glossy, dark green; growth speading, groundcover, 1-2 ft. tall, 2 ft. wide; PPAF; int. by Jackson & Perkins, 2005

Yellow River HT, my, 1972, Timmerman's Roses; flowers pointed, large, 30 petals; foliage glossy; vigorous growth; [sport of Bettina]

Yellow River F, my, Olij, H.W.; bud conical; flowers bright yellow, 8 cm., double, cupped, borne singly and in small clusters; recurrent; foliage dark green, glossy; prickles average, medium, light brown; erect, low (18 in.) growth; PP9512; [Frisco × Vivaldi]

Yellow Robusta HRg, ly, Maarse, J.D.; bud medium yellow; flowers light yellow, fading as they open, large, flat, moderate fragrance; non-remontant; [sport of Robusta]; int. in 1992

Yellow Romantica S, my, Meilland; flowers Naples yellow, outer petals lighter, very dbl., shallow cup, borne in clusters, moderate fragrance; recurrent; bushy (5 ft.) growth

Yellow Rose of Texas – See **Lemon Chiffon**, HT

Yellow Rose of Texas LCl, yb, Thomson; int. by Thomson for Roses

Yellow Ruffles HT, my, 1953, Brownell; flowers 4-5 in., 35-50 wavy petals, moderate fragrance; foliage dark, glossy; compact growth; PP1405; [sport of Orange Ruffels]

Yellow Sástago HT, my, 1939, Howard Rose Co.; [sport of Condesa de Sástago]

Yellow Sea LCl, my, 1978, Fong; bud long, pointed; flowers lemon-yellow, 6 in., 18-20 petals, high-centered, intense honey spice fragrance; [seedling × Ivory Fashion]; int. by United Rose Growers, 1977

Yellow Shot Silk HT, my, 1944, Beckwith; [sport of Shot Silk]

Yellow Simplicity S, dy, 1998, Zary, Dr. Keith W.; bud long, pointed ovoid; flowers deep yellow, 3 in., 15-20 petals, cupped to globular, borne in small clusters, slight fragrance; free-flowering; foliage medium size, dark green, glossy, leathery; prickles moderate, long, hooked downward; stems medium, strong; vigorous, upright (4.5 ft.) growth; hedging; PP10283; [seedling × seedling]; int. by Bear Creek Gardens, Inc., 1997

Yellow Splendor F, my; int. by Select, 1998

Yellow Springs HSpn, ly, Monteith; int. by Brentwood Bay Nurseries, 2006

Yellow Star F, my, 1965, deRuiter; flowers well-shaped, medium; foliage glossy; moderate growth

Yellow Submarine S, my, Lim, Ping; bud slender; flowers bright lemon yellow aging to pale yellow and white, 2 in., 32 petals, borne in clusters of about 5, moderate fragrance; recurrent; foliage medium green, semi-glossy; prickles several, long, triangular, slightly hooked; very upright (2-3½ ft.), bushy growth; hips ellipsoid, green with splotches of purple-brown; PP16659; [Singin' in the Rain × shrub rose]; int. by Bailey Nurseries, 2004

Yellow Sunbeam Min, my

Yellow Sunblaze – See **Yellow Meillandina**, Min

Yellow Sunblaze – See **Yellow Sunblaze 2004**, Min

Yellow Sunblaze 2004 Min, my, 2004, Meilland International; bud ovoid, medium; flowers bright lemon yellow, 4-6 cm., 44-46 petals, cupped, borne in small clusters, no fragrance; free-flowering; foliage medium size, medium to dark green, semi-glossy; prickles 5 mm, straight, yellow-green; growth compact, short (18-24 in.); garden decoration, containers; PP14274; [(Cumba Meillandina × seedling) × Good Morning America]; int. as Gold Symphonie 2002, Meilland, 2002

Yellow Sunsation S, ly, Kordes

Yellow Sunset HT, my, Dawson, George; int. in 1997

Yellow Sweet Dreams MIn, dy, Scott; flowers quite deep yellow, 1¼ in.; [sport of Sweet Dreams]; int. by Scott Nurseries, 2000

Yellow Sweet Magic Min, my, Dickson; [sport of Sweet Magic]; int. by Dickson Roses, 2004

Yellow Sweetbrier – See ***R. foetida*** (Herrmann)

Yellow Sweetheart – See **Rosina**, Min

Yellow Sweetheart F, my, 1952, Boerner; bud pointed; flowers lemon-yellow, reverse sulfur-yellow, becoming, 3½-4 in., 35 petals, globular; foliage leathery; vigorous, branching growth; [Pinocchio × seedling]; int. by J&P

Yellow Sweetheart, Climbing Cl F, ly, 1952, Moore, Ralph S.; flowers apricot-yellow to creamy -yellow, small, 26 petals, high-centered; foliage leathery, glossy; vigorous, climbing (12 ft.) growth; [(Étoile Luisante × unknown) × Goldilocks]; int. by Marsh's Nursery

Yellow Taifun – See **Yellow Typhoon**, F double

Yellow Talisman HT, ly, 1929, Amling Co.; flowers bright, clear yellow, paling with age; [sport of Talisman]

Yellow Talisman HT, ly, 1935, Eddie; flowers pale sulfur-yellow; [sport of Talisman]

Yellow Talisman, Climbing Cl HT, ly, Stocking

Yellow Tausendschön – See **Madeleine Seltzer**, HMult

Yellow Tiffany HT, yb, 1976, Floradale Nurs.; flowers yellow tinted pink; [sport of Tiffany]

Yellow Timeless HT, yb, Ammerlaan; bud ovate; flowers bright yellow with orange tint, reverse lighter, 5 in., 25 petals, high-centered, spiral, borne singly, slight fruity fragrance; recurrent; foliage dark green, glossy; prickles ordinary, concave, cinnamon; stems long; vigorous, narrow (6 ft.), bushy growth; hips pitcher-shaped ; PP10890; [sport of Timeless]; florist rose; int. by de Ruiter's New Roses, 1999

Yellow Tombola HT, dy, Spek; flowers 11 cm., 30-35 petals, high-centered, borne mostly singly; recurrent; thornless; stems long; int. by Jan Spek Rozen, 2005

Yellow Treasure HT, dy; int. by InterState Nurseries, 2001

Yellow Triumph HT, Herholdt

Yellow Typhoon F, my, Kordes; flowers double, cupped, borne in sprays of up to 20; recurrent; growth to 5 ft.; int. by Palatine Roses, 2006

Yellow Unique HT, dy, de Ruiter ; bud medium, ovate; flowers deep yellow, reverse lighter, 9 cm., 25 petals, pointed, spiral, borne singly, slight sweet, fruity fragrance; recurrent; foliage medium size, dark green, semi-glossy; prickles numerous, concave, red-brown; stems long; vigorous, narrow to bushy (6 ft.) growth; hips funnel-shaped, orange-yellow; PP10530; [seedling × seedling]; florist rose; int. in 1997

Yellow Wings S, my, 1987, James, John; flowers light-medium yellow, fading to cream, large, 16 petals, borne in clusters, moderate fragrance; foliage medium size, light green, glossy, disease-resistant; prickles straight, brown; bushy growth; [((Will Scarlet × Sutter's Gold) × Paula) × Golden Wings]; int. in 1986

Yellow Wonder – See **Young Quinn**, HT

Yellowcrest HT, ly, 1935, LeGrice; bud small, pointed; flowers clear canary-yellow, dbl.; foliage light, glossy, small; vigorous growth

Yellowhammer F, my, 1956, McGredy, Sam IV; bud medium, pointed ovoid; flowers golden yellow to light yellow, 3-3½ in., 45-50 petals, open, flat, borne in clusters, moderate fruity (apple) fragrance; free-flowering; foliage large, dark green, glossy; prickles ordinary, medium, hooked downward; stems medium; vigorous, upright, bushy growth; no hips; PP1667; [Poulsen's Yellow × seedling]; Gold Medal, NRS, 1954

Yellowhammer, Climbing Cl F, my, Dorieux; int. in 1976

Yellowstone HT, my, 1975, Weeks; bud pointed; flowers soft tawny yellow to lighter yellow, 3½-4 in., 38-44 petals, moderate tea fragrance; foliage glossy, dark, leathery; tall, upright growth; [seedling × seedling]

Yellowstone F, my, Olesen; bud short, globular; flowers medium yellow in center, lighter at outer edges, 7-10 cm., 60-75 petals, cupped, open, borne singly and in small clusters, moderate old rose fragrance; recurrent; foliage medium green, semi-glossy; prickles numerous, 8-12 mm., deeply concave, brown; vigorous, bushy (3-4 ft.) growth; PP12534; [seedling × seedling]; int. as Marselisborg, Poulsen Roser, 1996

Yesterday Pol, mp, 1974, Harkness; flowers lilac pink, golden stamens, 1½ in., 13 petals, borne in trusses, slight fragrance; foliage small, glossy; bushy growth with poly-antha characteristics; [(Phyllis Bide × Shepherd's Delight) × Ballerina]; Gold Medal, Monza, 1974, Gold Medal, Baden-Baden, 1975, ADR, 1978

Yesterday Reef HT, w, 1984, Stoddard, Louis; flowers

white, faintly tinted pink and yellow, large, 35 petals, high-centered; foliage large, medium green, matte; narrowly upright growth; [(Tiffany × Sunblest) × Irish Gold]

Yesterday's Garden S, pb, 1992, Moore, Ralph S.; flowers medium, very dbl., borne in small clusters, no fragrance; foliage medium size, medium green, semi-glossy; tall to medium (over 50 cm.), upright, bushy, spreading growth; [Shakespeare Festival × Belle Poitevine]; int. by Sequoia Nursery, 1993

Yesteryear HT, ab, Harkness; flowers soft peachy-apricot, large, full, cupped, borne singly, intense fragrance; quick repeat; foliage dark green, glossy; stems long, strong; vigorous (4 ft.) growth; [Just Joey × unknown]

Yeswant HT, rb, Patil, B.K.

Yi Bang Fĕn Ch, mp

Yi-Hong Yuan HT, rb, 1995, Hong-Quan, Li; flowers yellow, edged salmon, reverse lighter, 4½ in., very dbl., borne mostly singly; foliage medium size, dark green, semi-glossy; some prickles; upright, medium growth; [Osiria × New Bal]

YKH 501 – See **Arashiyama**, HT

Yoimatsuri F, ob, 1989, Kikuchi, Rikichi; bud ovoid; flowers orange and yellow tinged, medium, 5 petals, cupped, borne in large sprays; foliage small, light green, glossy; prickles ordinary; spreading, medium growth; [Masquerade × Subaru]; int. in 1990

Yolande d'Aragon P, m, 1843, Vibert; flowers purple-rose, tinted lilac, small eye at center, very large, very dbl., flat-cupped, quartered, borne in clusters, strong fragrance; foliage medium green, large, rounded; growth vigorous, tall (1½-2 m.), strongly branching; sometimes classed as HP; the cultivar currently in commerce under this name is probably not correct

Yolande Fontaine B, m, 1840; flowers dark violet, medium, full

Yongjoon S, lp, 2005, Ogawa, Hiroshi; flowers light pink, reverse silver pink, 7 cm., dbl., borne in small clusters, intense fragrance; foliage small, light green, matte; prickles thin; growth upright, medium (120 cm.); garden decoration, containers; [Peach Blossom × Pearl Ring]; int. in 2005

Yoriko Pol, lp, 1997, Ohmori, Yoriko; flowers light pink, reverse white, 1½ in., single, slight fragrance; foliage small, light green, semi-glossy; few prickles; spreading (45 cm.) growth; hips oval, 6-7 mm, deep orange; [seedling × seedling]

York and Lancaster D, pb, before 1867; flowers petals blush white and light pink, sometimes all one color, dbl., moderate fragrance; foliage downy light gray-green, oval with pointed ends; prickles mixed; tall growth; [sport of *R. damascena*]; first described by Monardes in 1551

York et Lancastre – See **York and Lancaster**, D

Yorkshire S, w, Kordes; flowers pure white, yellow stamens, semi-double, shallow cup, borne in small clusters, slight fragrance; recurrent; low (2 ft.), spreading growth; int. in 1998

Yorkshire – See **Innocencia**, F, 2006

Yorkshire Bank HT, w, 1981, de Ruiter, George; flowers ivory with shades of pink that fade as they open, 36 petals, borne 3-5 per cluster, moderate fragrance; recurrent; foliage bright green; prickles pointed, brown; stems long; vigorous, medium, bushy growth; [Pascali × Peer Gynt]; int. by Fryer's Nursery, Ltd., 1979; Gold Star of the South Pacific, Palmerston North, NZ, 1979, Gold Medal, Geneva, 1979

Yorkshire Lady HT, ly, 1992, Thompson, Robert; flowers soft primrose yellow to linen white, medium, full, high-centered, borne mostly singly, moderate fragrance; foliage medium size, medium green, glossy; few prickles; upright (95-100 cm.) growth; [((Red Lion × Royal Highness) × Yellow Petals) × Piccadilly]; int. by Battersby Roses, 1992

Yorkshire Provence C, mp, before 1821; flowers bright rose pink

Yorkshire Sunblaze – See **White Meillandina**, Min

Yorokobi Pol, mp, Suzuki; int. in 1955

Yosemite HT, ob, 1934, Nicolas; bud long, pointed; flowers scarlet-orange, reverse suffused carmine, dbl., cupped; foliage leathery; vigorous growth; [Charles P. Kilham × Mrs Pierre S. duPont]; int. by J&P

Yoshino HT, w, 1997, Ohtsuki, Hironaka; flowers dbl.; foliage medium size, medium green, semi-glossy; some prickles; tall (200 cm.) growth; [Confidence × Garden Party]

Yoshodama's Rose LCl, my; flowers clear pastel yellow, ruffled petals, 5-7 in., double; int. in 2007

Yosooi Min, w, Keisei; int. by Keisei Rose Nurseries, 1991

You S, pb, Takatori

You 'n' Me Min, w, 1985, McCann, Sean; flowers white, light apricot center, small, dbl., high-centered; foliage small, medium green, semi-glossy; bushy growth; [Avandel × Party Girl]

Youki San HT, w, 1965, Meilland; flowers clear white, large, 40 petals, intense sweet fragrance; foliage light green; tall growth; [Lady Sylvia × White Knight]; int. by Wheatcroft Bros.; Gold Medal, Baden-Baden, 1964

Youki San, Climbing Cl HT, w; int. in 1972

Young America HT, dr, 1902, E.G. Hill, Co.; flowers medium, dbl.; [Duke of Edinburgh × The Meteor]

Young at Heart – See **Origami**, F

Young Cale – See **Wanaka**, Min

Young France HT, lp, 1945, Meilland, F.; bud long, pointed; flowers apple-blossom-pink, base flushed orange, tipped silvery pink, high-centered; foliage soft, dark; vigorous, upright growth; [Joanna Hill × Mme Joseph Perraud]; int. by C-P

Young Hearts Min, dr

Young Love Min, ob, 1980, Lyon; bud medium-long, pointed; flowers orange, yellow-center, 18 petals, borne singly and in small clusters; foliage tiny, dark; prickles tiny, curved; compact, bushy growth; [seedling × seedling]; int. in 1979

Young Love Min, rb, Williams, J. Benjamin; flowers red and white; int. in 1994

Young Mistress – See **Regensberg**, F

Young Mistress Min, lp, Kordes; flowers bright pink, full, borne in clusters; int. in 1988

Young 'n' Innocent Min, w, 1993, Rennie, Bruce F.; flowers small, white, very dbl., borne in small clusters, moderate fragrance; foliage small, medium green, semi-glossy; some prickles; low, spreading growth; [Hap Renshaw × Tooth of Time]; int. by Rennie Roses International, 1994

Young Quinn HT, my, 1976, McGredy, Sam IV; bud small, short, pointed ovoid; flowers bright yellow, fading with age, sometimes red blush on petal edges, 8-11 cm., 20-30 petals, high-centered, to cupped, borne singly and in small clusters, slight fragrance; recurrent; foliage heavily veined, medium green, semi-glossy; prickles several, medium, almost straight, brown; stems strong, short to medium; upright, tall, bushy growth; hips globular, yellow-green; PP4063; [Peer Gynt × Kiskadee]; int. in 1975; Gold Medal, Belfast, 1978

Young Venturer F, ab, 1979, Mattock; bud ovoid; flowers rich apricot, 4½ in., 30 petals; foliage dark, glossy, leathery; vigorous, upright growth; [Arthur Bell × Cynthia Brooke]

Young Venturer, Climbing Cl F, ab, Fineschi, Gianfranco

Youpi Min, my, 1979, Lens; bud ovoid; flowers lemon-chrome, 1 in., 12-19 petals, cupped, moderate fruity fragrance; foliage light green; vigorous, compact growth; [*R. wichurana* × Pour Toi]; int. in 1966

Your Family HT, pb, Taschner, Ludwig; bud pointed, urn-shaped; flowers mother of pearl, touched with more pink when touched by the sun, large, full, classic hybrid tea form, borne singly, moderate sweet fragrance; recurrent; vigorous, tall growth; int. by Ludwig's Roses, 2004

Your Garden – See **Tino Rossi**, HT

Your Smile HT, my, 1999, Ohata, Hatsuo; flowers 6 in., 35 petals, high-centered; foliage medium green; growth to 3 ft.; [Miss Harp × Golden Sun]; int. by Komaba Rose Garden, 1997; Gold Medal, Japan Rose Concours, 1995

Yours Always HT, or, Delbard; flowers luminous orange-red, medium, full, high-centered; tall growth; int. by Bell Roses, 2003

Yours Truly HT, mp, 1945, Morris; bud long, pointed; flowers rose-pink, base golden yellow, open, 4½ in., 48 petals, intense spicy fragrance; foliage leathery; very vigorous, upright growth; [seedling × Texas Centennial]; int. by Germain's

Youth HT, w, 1935, Cook, J.W.; bud ovoid; flowers creamy, suffused pink, very large, 60 petals, high-centered; foliage dark; long stems; [Souv. de Claudius Pernet × My Maryland]

Youth – See **Molodost**, HT

Youth – See **Seishun**, HT

Youth of the World HT, mr; flowers large, dbl.

Yoyo Min, rb, 2003, Graham, Susan Brandt; flowers deep red with orange markings, each different; white eye; golden stamens, 1½-2 in., single, borne mostly solitary, no fragrance; foliage medium size, medium green, semi-glossy; prickles medium, straight, green, moderate; growth compact, medium (16-20 in.); containers, borders; [sport of Gizmo]; int. in 2003

Ypsilanté – See **Ypsilanti**, HGal

Ypsilanti HGal, m, 1821, Vibert; flowers lilac pink, fading to violet, small eye at center, very large, dbl., quartered, borne singly or in clusters of 2-3; non-remontant; foliage light green, oval; few prickles; vigorous growth

Yu-Ai HT, rb, 1973, Suzuki, Seizo; bud ovoid; flowers bright red, base yellow, large, dbl., cupped; foliage dark, leathery; very vigorous, bushy growth; [(Sarabande × unknown) × (Peace × unknown)]; int. by Keisei Rose Nursery, 1970

Yueh Yueh Hong – See **Slater's Crimson China**, Ch

Yugiri HT, pb, Suzuki, Seizo; int. in 1987

Yuhla HSet, mr, 1927, Hansen, N.E.; flowers crimson, large, semi-dbl.; non-recurrent; very hardy; [wild rose from Lake Oakwood (SD) × Général Jacqueminot]; perhaps hybrid Macounii rather than hybrid Setigera

Yuka F, lp, Keisei; int. by Keisei Rose Nurseries, 2005

Yuki Akari Cl Min, w, Komatsu; int. by Komatsu Garden, 2004

Yuki-Matsuri HT, w, 1989, Yokota, Kiyoshi; bud ovoid; flowers large, 42 petals, high-centered, urn-shaped, borne usually singly; foliage medium size, dark green, glossy; prickles sparse; medium growth; hips large, light orange; [(Dolce Vita × Royal Highness) × Nobility]

Yukihime Min, w, Kubota

Yukon – See **Sun Valley**, HT

Yuletide HT, mr, 1956, Joseph H. Hill, Co.; bud ovoid; flowers currant-red, 3½-4½ in., 43 petals, high-centered; foliage leathery, semi-glossy; vigorous, upright, bushy growth; PP1391; [Hill Crest × Silver Kenny]

Yume HT, ab, Keisei; int. by Keisei Rose Nurseries, 1994

Yumeotome Min, lp, 1989, Tokumatsu, Kazuhisa; bud ovoid; flowers pink changing to white, 38 petals, slight fragrance; foliage small, dark green; lower part of prickles hollow, about 15 on a stem; bushy growth; [sport of Miyagino]

Yusai HT, yb, 1989, Ota, Kaichiro; bud ovoid; flowers bright yellow with reddish fringe, reverse changing to red, 30 petals, high-centered; foliage medium size, dark green with bronze tinge, slightly dentate; bushy, spreading growth; [((American Heritage × unknown) × Christian Dior) × Miss Ireland]

Yuubae HT, op, Hiroshima; int. by Hiroshima Bara-en, 1996

Yuzen Gr, pb, 1986, Suzuki, Seizo; flowers pink, blending deeper at petal edges, urn-shaped, large, 50 petals, high-centered, moderate fragrance; foliage dark, glossy; prickles slanted downward; upright growth; [seedling × Confidence]; int. by Keisei Rose Nursery, 1982

Yvan Meneve HT, dp; int. by RVS, 1998

Yvan Mission Pol, mp, 1922, Soupert & Notting; flowers peach-blossom-pink, borne in large clusters; [Jeanny Soupert × Katharina Zeimet]

Yves Druhen HT, dr, 1920, Buatois; flowers dark velvety red, dbl.; [Gen. MacArthur × Château de Clos Vougeot]

Yves Latieule – See **Mme Yves Latieule**, HT

Yves Piaget HT, mp, 1985, Meilland, Mrs. Marie-Louise; bud globular, fairly large; flowers Neyron pink, 5 in., 80 petals, globular, then cupped, borne mostly singly, intense fragrance; good repeat; foliage medium size, dark green, semi-glossy; upright (3 ft.) growth; PP6895; [((Pharaoh × Peace) × (Chrysler Imperial × Charles Mallerin)) × Tamango]; int. by Meilland Et Cie, 1983; Golden Rose & Fragrance Award, Geneve, 1982, Gold Medal & Fragrance Award, LeRoeulx, 1982, Fragrance Award, Bagatelle, 1992

Yves Piaget, Climbing Cl HT, mp, Meilland; int. by Keisei Rose Nurseries, 2006

Yvette HT, op, 1921, Buatois; flowers salmon-yellow; [Mrs T. Hillas × Mme Edouard Herriot]

Yvette Pol, lp, Scarman; flowers pale pink; free-flowering; moderate (2 ft.) growth; [Yvonne Rabier × Unknown]; int. in 1996

Yvette Gayraud F, op; flowers orange salmon, small, semi-double, cupped; free-flowering; foliage medium green, glossy, disease-resistant; strong (3 ft.) growth; int. by Roses du Temps Passé, 2004

Yvette Horner HT, pb, Sauvageot; int. by Roseraies Barth, 2006

Yvon Cléroux – See **Little Deb**, MinFl

Yvonne HWich, pb, 1921, Cant, F.; flowers blush-pink, base deep pink shaded yellow, 4 cm., dbl., borne in large clusters, moderate fragrance; foliage dark olive green, glossy; very vigorous growth; Gold Medal, NRS, 1920

Yvonne Alexander F, rb, 2002, Fleming, Joyce L.; flowers medium red, reverse light red, 1¼-1½ in., single, borne in small clusters; foliage medium size, medium green, matte, disease-resistant; prickles in., triangular; growth spreading, medium (12-15 in.); bedding, hanging baskets; hardy; [Red Hot × Lavender Friendship]; int. by Hortico Nursery, Inc., 2002

Yvonne Caret HT, ob, 1965, Gaujard; flowers orange-red, reverse golden yellow, 4½ in., 25 petals; foliage bright green; int. by Gandy's Roses, 1963

Yvonne Corboeuf HP, mr, 1900, Corboeuf; flowers cherry red; [Mme Ferdinand Jamin × John Hopper]

Yvonne d'Huart HT, rb, 1932, Ketten Bros.; bud long, pointed; flowers coral-red to Lincoln red, base chrome yellow, large, dbl.; very vigorous growth

Yvonne Kenny HT, pb; flowers soft pink, palest pink at outer edges, soft yellow at base, cup and saucer, ruffled petals; medium growth; int. in 2003

Yvonne Millot HT, ab, 1936, Mallerin, C.; bud pointed; flowers apricot-yellow, large, dbl., high-centered; foliage glossy; vigorous growth; [(Pharisaer × Constance) × Feu Joseph Looymans]; int. by C-P

Yvonne Plassat HT, or, 1941, Moulin-Epinay; flowers coppery orange to glowing red, dbl.; int. by Nonin

Yvonne Printemps HT, or, 1939, Gaujard; bud long, almost red; flowers orange, veined copper, reverse bright yellow

Yvonne Rabier Pol, w, 1910, Turbat; flowers pure white, center slightly tinted sulfur, dbl., borne in clusters; recurrent; foliage rich green, glossy; vigorous growth; [*R. wichuraiana* hybrid × unknown]

Yvonne Vacherot HT, w, 1905, Soupert & Notting; bud long, pointed; flowers porcelain-white, strongly flushed rose-pink, imbricated, large, dbl., high-centered; vigorous growth; [Antoine Rivoire × Souv. d'un Ami]

Yvonne Virlet HT, my, 1936, Walter, L.; flowers golden yellow, large, dbl.

Zabeth HEg, mp, before 1813, Dupont; flowers bright pink, medium, semi-dbl.; foliage oblong ovate, very fragrant; prickles long, recurved, almost absent from blooming shoots; growth small (2-3 ft.); hips globose, bright red

Zabeth Bombifera – See **Zabeth**, HEg

Zach F, or, 2005, Rickard, Vernon; flowers orange, 3 in., dbl., borne mostly solitary, no fragrance; foliage medium size, dark green, glossy, disease-resistant; prickles moderate, ½ in., straight, brown; growth bushy, medium (48 in.); hedges, garden decoration; [Playboy × Orangeade]; int. by Almost Heaven Roses, 2005

Zacharley Rose HT, pb, 1998, Poole, Lionel; flowers pink, shaded peach at base, 4½ in., very dbl., high-centered, borne mostly singly; foliage medium size, medium green, semi-glossy; few prickles; long stems; very floriferous, upright, tall (4½ ft.) growth; [Hazel Rose × Loving Memory]; int. by David Lister, Ltd, 1998

Zagreb HT, pb, 1995, Rogin, Josip; flowers pink striped, medium, full, borne mostly singly, intense fragrance; foliage large, medium green, matte; few prickles; tall (150 cm.), upright growth; [sport of Eiffel Tower]

Zahov Hatabor F, yb, Fischel

Zaïd S, rb, 1937, Chambard, C.; bud bright yellow and copper-red; flowers coppery flame-red, semi-dbl.; non-recurrent; foliage glossy, bright green; vigorous growth; [*R. foetida bicolor* × (*R. wichurana* × unknown)]

Zaida HT, op, 1922, Lippiatt; flowers pale coral-pink, large, dbl.

Zaiga HRg, dp, Rieksta, Dr. Dz.; flowers bright pink to rose pink, fading after opening, large, semi-double to double, shallow cup to flat, slight fragrance; recurrent; foliage disease-resistant; bushy (4 ft.), arching growth; winter hardy; originated in Latvia

Zaïre M, dp, 1849, Vibert; flowers 3 in., full, shallow cup to flat; non-remontant; growth to 4 ft.

Zambra F, ob, 1961, Meilland, Mrs. Marie-Louise; bud ovoid, pointed; flowers vermilion orange, reverse yellow, 2½-3 in., 10-15 petals, high-centered early, then flat, borne in clusters, slight sweetbriar fragrance; recurrent; foliage leathery, glossy, light green; prickles several, reddish-brown; vigorous, well-branched, low to medium growth; hips globular, reddish; PP2140; [(Goldilocks × Fashion) × (Goldilocks × Fashion)]; int. by URS, 1961; Gold Medal, Rome, 1961, Gold Medal, Bagatelle, 1961

Zambra, Climbing Cl F, ob, 1969, Meilland; [sport of Zambra]; int. by URS

Zambra '80 – See **Capella**, HT

Zambra 93 F, op, Meilland, Alain A.; flowers coral pink, medium, dbl., high-centered; free-flowering; foliage dark green, semi-glossy; low (70 cm) growth; int. in 1993; Gold Medal, Bagatelle, 1992, Gold Medal, Baden-Baden, 1993

Zandrina HT, Zandri, R.; int. in 1977

Zani S, mr, 1927, Hansen, N.E.; flowers dark crimson, with a white streak through center petals, semi-dbl.; non-recurrent; growth to 6-8 ft.; very hardy; [(*R. rugosa* × Anna de Diesbach) × Tetonkaha]

Zansho HT, rb, 1978, Takahashi, Takeshi; bud ovoid; flowers scarlet and yellow, 6 in., 45 petals, high-centered; foliage dark, leathery; upright, bushy growth; [Garden Party × Christian Dior]; int. in 1975

Zanta Hofmeyer HT, pb, Laver; flowers porcelain pink, deeper pink in center, dbl., high-centered, borne mostly singly; recurrent; foliage dark green; medium growth; int. by Ludwig's Roses, 2003

Zanzibar F, mr, 1964, Leenders, J.; flowers bright red; [Paradis × Circus]

Zara Hore-Ruthven HT, mp, 1932, Clark, A.; flowers rich pink, large, dbl., cupped, slight fragrance; foliage medium green; [Mme Abel Chatenay × Scorcher]; int. by NRS South Australia

Zaria HT, w, Meilland; flowers clear white, full, cupped, borne mostly singly; recurrent; foliage medium green, matte; florist rose; int. by Meilland Intl., 2004

Zärtlichkeit S, lp, Wänninger, Franz; flowers small, single; int. in 1992

Zaryellow HT, my, Zary, Dr. Keith; PP15955

Zauberlehrling F, op, 1963, Kordes, R.; flowers light salmon, well-formed, large, dbl.; strong stems; bushy, low growth

Zborov Pol, dr, 1935, Böhm, J.; flowers blood-red, very dbl., borne in large clusters; foliage glossy, dark; vigorous growth; [sport of Corrie Koster]

Zburlici F, dp, Wagner, S.; flowers 15 petals, rosette, slight fragrance; foliage medium large, light green, glossy; [Bonica '82 × La Sevillana]; int. by Res. Stn. f. Fruit Growing, Cluj, 1995

Zebra HT, rb, Benardella, Frank A.; bud small, ovoid; flowers red with white stripes, fading to medium pink with yellowish-white, 9-11 cm., 43-46 petals, high-centered, borne singly, moderate fragrance; recurrent; foliage medium size, dark green, semi-glossy; prickles few, medium, slightly curved downward; stems long; upright, compact growth; PP10148; [Picasso × seedling]; int. in 1995

Zee Cl Min, mp, 1940, Moore, Ralph S.; flowers pink, very small; recurrent bloom; foliage very small; nearly thornless; growth to 30 in.; [Carolyn Dean × Tom Thumb]

Zeiber House Red – See **Laurent Carle**, HT

Zelda Lloyd Min, mp, 1988, Bennett, Dee; flowers medium pink, reverse deep pink, 2-3 cm., 5 petals, shallow cup to flat, borne usually singly, slight fruity fragrance; recurrent; foliage medium size, medium green, semi-glossy; prickles hooked slightly downward, reddish; bushy, medium growth; hips globular, green-yellow-brown; PP7190; [Deep Purple × Blue Mist]; int. by Tiny Petals Nursery

Zélia Pradel T, w, 1861, Pradel; flowers pure white, center yellow, large, full, moderate fragrance; sometimes classed as N

Zell Min, pb, 2000, Tucker, Robbie; flowers dbl., high-centered, borne singly and in small clusters, no fragrance; foliage small, light green, matte; some prickles; growth bushy, compact, low (12-18 in.); groundcover; [Chelsea Belle × seedling]; int. by Nor'East Min. Roses, 2001

Zen HT, w, 2004, Ohtsuki, Hironaka; flowers pure white, 15 cm., full, borne mostly solitary, intense fragrance; foliage large, dark green, semi-glossy; prickles moderate, medium, downward; growth upright, tall (120-180 cm.); cutting, exhibition; [Honor × Hoshizakuyo]; int. by Komaba Rose Garden, 2004

Zena HT, dr, 1985, Plumpton, E.; flowers dark crimson, large, 25 petals, borne singly or several together; foliage medium size, medium green, semi-glossy; upright growth; [seedling × New Style]; int. in 1986

Zena HT, lp, 2006, Poole, Lionel; flowers light pink with apricot, 5 in., full, borne in small clusters; foliage medium size, medium green, glossy; prickles large, triangular, dark brown, moderate; growth bushy, tall (3 ft.); beds, borders, exhibition; [Hazel Rose × Cardiff Bay × Solitaire × Silver Jubilee]; int. in 2007

Zénaïre HGal, m, before 1828, Dubourg; flowers purple, speckled white

Zenaitta Pol, rb, 1991, Jerabek, Paul E.; bud ovoid; flowers bright medium red with small white area at petal base, small, dbl., cupped, borne in sprays of 3-65, no fragrance; foliage small, medium green, glossy; bushy, medium growth; [seedling × seedling]

Zenith – See **Uetersen**, S

Zenith LCl, or, 1985, Delbard, Georges; flowers vermilion, semi-dbl., borne in clusters; climbing (to 8 ft.) growth; [(Spectacular × (Tenor × unknown)) × (Floradora × Incendie)]; int. by Delbard Roses, 1982

Zenobia M, mp, 1892, Paul, W.; bud well mossed; flowers satiny pink, 4 in., full, cupped, moderate Damask fragrance; non-remontant; foliage large; vigorous, tall, slender growth

Zénobie A, lp, before 1844, Vibert; flowers pale rose, medium, full

Zephelene Min, w; flowers white, petal edges turning bright coral as they open, relatively large, double, cupped; recurrent; strong, rounded, medium growth; int. by Kordes, 1994

Zéphirine Drouhin B, mp, 1868, Bizot; bud long, pointed; flowers cerise pink, base white, 3 in., 25-30 petals, borne mostly singly, moderate damask fragrance; recurrent bloom; foliage soft, light; vigorous, semi-climbing growth

Zephyr T, yb, 1895, Paul, W.; flowers sulphur yellow with white reflections, large, full, cupped

Zephyr F, yb, 1961, Verschuren; flowers yellow tipped pink, 2½-3 in., 64 petals, borne in clusters; foliage glossy, light; very vigorous growth; [Goldilocks × seedling]; int. by Blaby Rose Gardens, 1961

Zest For Life MinFl, ob, 2005, Paul Chessum Roses; flowers medium, dbl., borne in small clusters, moderate fragrance; foliage medium size, medium green, semi-glossy; prickles medium, sharp, pink, few; growth compact, medium (18 in.); bedding, containers; [seedling × seedling]; int. by World of Roses, 2005

Zesty Min, ab, Benardella, Frank; flowers deep apricot with golden yellow blendings; medium growth

Zeus HSet, my, 1959, Kern, J. J.; bud long, pointed; flowers 4-6 cm., 25 petals, loose, slight fragrance; recurrent; foliage leathery, dark; vigorous (15-20 ft.) growth; [Doubloons × unknown]

Zhang Zuo Shuang – See **China Sunrise**, HT

Zi Yan Fei Wu Ch, mp

Zig-Zag Min, rb, 1993, Chaffin, Lauren M.; flowers white with dark red picotee edge, large, very dbl., high-centered, borne mostly singly; foliage similar to Peaches 'n' Cream, medium size, medium green; some prickles; low (30 cm.), upright, bushy, compact growth; [Osiria × Pink Petticoat]; int. by Pixie Treasures Min. Roses, 1993

Zigeunerbaron F, dr, 1954, Baron, W.; flowers large, dbl.

Zigeunerblut Bslt, dr, 1889, Geschwind, R.; flowers purple-red, large, full, cupped, moderate fragrance; [*R. pendulina* × a Bourbon]

Zigeunerknabe – See **Gipsy Boy**, B

Ziggy Stardust Min, r, 1995, Rennie, Bruce F.; flowers 1¼ in., dbl., borne mostly singly; foliage medium size, medium green, semi-glossy; few prickles; medium (15 in.), upright growth; [Silver Phantom × Party Girl]; int. by Rennie Roses International

Zigri LCl, m

Zika S, lp, 1927, Hansen, N.E.; flowers shell-pink, semi-dbl.; non-recurrent bloom; very hardy; [(*R. rugosa* × Anna de Diesbach) × Tetonkaha]

Zilda Villaboin Pol, 1910, Amaury Fonseca

Zilia Pradel – See **Zélia Pradel**, T

Zingaro F, mr, 1964, Sanday, John; flowers bright crimson, 2 in., 12 petals, borne in clusters; foliage dark; compact, low growth; [Masquerade × (Independence × unknown)]

Zinger Min, mr, 1978, Schwartz, Ernest W.; bud long, pointed; flowers crimson, shaded scarlet, yellow stamens, 1½ in., 11 petals, flat, moderate fragrance; recurrent; very vigorous, spreading growth; PP4293; [Zorina × Magic Carrousel]; int. by Nor'East Min. Roses; AOE, ARS, 1979

Zita Pol, mr, 1965, Delforge; bud ovoid; flowers red shaded dark geranium, open, single; foliage dark, leathery; [Amoureuse × seedling]

Zitkala S, mr, 1942, Hansen, N.E.; flowers brilliant velvety red, 3 in., 25 petals, intense fragrance; non-recurrent; almost thornless; stems red; very hardy; [*R. blanda* × Amadis]

Zitronenfalter HSpn, ly, 1940, Berger, V.; flowers brimstone color; [(*R. spinosissima altaica* × Star of Persia) × Golden Ophelia]; int. by Teschendorff

Zitronenfalter HMsk, my, 1959, Tantau, Math.; bud ovoid; flowers golden yellow, large, 20 petals, borne in clusters, moderate fruity fragrance; recurrent; foliage dark green, leathery; prickles few, curved; upright, bushy growth; hips globular, slightly flattened on top; [Marchenland × Peace]; int. in 1956

Zitronenjette HT, my, 1987, Kordes, W.; flowers large, dbl.; foliage large, medium green, glossy; spreading growth; [Sutter's Gold × Sunblest]; int. in 1986

Zizi F, dr, 1963, Delbard-Chabert; flowers garnet-red, medium, 15 petals, borne in clusters of 3-10, moderate fragrance; vigorous, bushy growth; [Walko × Souv. de J. Chabert]

Zlata F, dy, Vecera, L.

Zlatá Praha HT, my, 1931, Böhm, J.; flowers golden yellow; [sport of Kardinal Piffl]

Zlaté Jubileum HT, dy, 1938, Böhm, J.; flowers large, dbl.

Zlaty Dech HT, dy, 1936, Böhm, J.; flowers orange-yellow, large, semi-dbl.

Zluta Zorina HT, my, Strnad

Zodiac F, mr, 1961, Verschuren; flowers dbl., 74 petals, camellia-like, borne in clusters; foliage leathery, light green; very vigorous growth; [Red Favorite × seedling]; int. by Blaby Rose Gardens, 1961

Zodiac F, pb, 1963, Kordes, R.; flowers begonia-pink, base yellow, dbl., borne in clusters of 25-30; low, bushy growth; [Masquerade × Karl Herbst]

Zoé HGal, mp, before 1826, Miellez; flowers bright pink at center, pale at edges, large, very dbl., moderate fragrance

Zoé M, lp, before 1829, Forest; sepals mossy, 3 foliaceous; flowers large, full, cupped, moderate fragrance; foliage ovoid, dentate at the tip; prickles numerous, long; all parts of plant are mossed

Zoé M, mp, 1861, Pradel; flowers large, full, moderate fragrance

Zoé F, op, Spek; int. by Jan Spek Rozen, 2005

Zoé Barbet – See **Zoé**, M

Zoë Zorab F, yb, Kordes; flowers blend of old gold and copper apricot, very full, cupped, borne in clusters, slight fragrance; recurrent; stems short; short growth; int. by Ludwig's Roses, 2001

Zola S, dy, 1979, Sanday, John; bud pointed; flowers golden yellow, 2½ in., 18 petals; foliage dark; vigorous, upright growth; [Spek's Yellow × Magenta]

Zola Budd F, rb, 1987, Kordes, R.; flowers white with ruby red painted over the petals, 5-7 petals, borne 1-3 per cluster, slight fragrance; recurrent; foliage deep green, leathery; prickles straight, light brown; vigorous, bushy, densely-branched growth; [Mabella × ((Dr. A.J. Verhage × Colour Wonder) × Zorina)]; int. by Ludwigs Roses Pty. Ltd., 1985

Zoltan Kodaly HT, Mark

Zonnekeild – See **Sonnychild**, HT

Zonnekind HT, my, 1941, Leenders, M.; flowers buttercup-yellow, large, dbl.; [Arch. Reventos × Amalia Jung]

Zonta Rose – See **Princess Alice**, F

Zora F, yb, 1985, Staikov, Prof. Dr. V.; flowers yellow, deep pink petal edges, aging deep pink, 18 petals, borne in clusters; foliage dark; vigorous growth; [Masquerade × Rumba]; int. by Kalaydjiev and Chorbadjiiski, 1974

Zorba LCl, yb, Olesen; bud broad-based, pointed-ovoid; flowers yellow with orange reverse, 3½ cm., 25-30 petals, rosette, borne in large clusters, very slight fragrance; recurrent; foliage dark green, glossy; prickles moderate, 10 mm., deeply concave, dark reddish; vigorous, upright (5-7 ft.) growth; PP15771; [seedling × Aspen]; int. by Poulsen Roser, 2003; Honorable Mention, Hradec Králové, 2006

Zorina F, or, 1965, Boerner; bud ovoid; flowers 3 in., 25 petals, cupped, moderate fragrance; foliage glossy; vigorous, upright growth; PP2321; [(Pinocchio × unknown) × Spartan]; int. by J&P, 1963; Gold Medal, Rome, 1964

Zorina, Climbing Cl F, or

Zorina HT, my, Strnad

Zorka F, rb, Vecera, L.; flowers carmine-red with white; int. in 1974

Zuccariniana – See **Kaiserin des Nordens**, HRg

Zukunft F, or, 1951, Verschuren; flowers scarlet-red; [sport of Lafayette]

Zulu Queen HT, dr, 1939, Kordes; bud long, pointed; flowers dark maroon, large, dbl., high-centered, moderate fragrance; recurrent; foliage leathery; short, bushy growth; [(Cathrine Kordes × E.G. Hill) × Fritz Hoger]; int. by J&P

Zulu Queen, Climbing Cl HT, dr, 1961, Moore

Zulu Royal – See **Melody Parfumée**, Gr

Zulu Warrior F, rb, 1980, Hawken, Una; flowers burgundy red, silver reverse, 9 petals, blooms borne 3-20 per cluster; foliage dark, tough; prickles large, reddish; medium growth; [Arthur Bell × Flaming Peace]

Zurella F, mp, Meilland

Zweibrücken HKor, dr, 1958, Kordes; bud ovoid; flowers deep crimson, large, 5-6 cm., dbl., borne in large clusters, slight fragrance; recurrent; foliage dark green, leathery; very vigorous, climbing growth; [*R. × kordesii* × Independence]; int. in 1955

Zwemania Gr, or, 1976, Zwemstra; flowers light vermilion, 25-30 petals, high-centered, moderate fruity fragrance; foliage dark; very vigorous growth; PP4049; [sport of Sweet Promise]; int. by Meilland, 1974

Zwerg – See **Rosa Zwerg**, HRg

Zwerg-Rubin Pol, mr, 1924, Schmidt, J.C.; flowers bright ruby-red, small, cupped, borne in clusters; dwarf growth; [(Rubin × unknown) × Erna Teschendorff]

Zwerg Teplitz – See **Alsterufer**, HT

Zwergeliebe Min, Delforge; int. in 1986

Zwergenfee Min, or, 1979, Kordes, W.; bud globular; flowers 2 in., 29 petals, cupped, moderate fragrance; free-flowering; foliage small, glossy; dwarf, vigorous, upright growth; [miniature seedling × Traumerei]; int. by Dehner & Co.

Zwergkönig – See **Dwarfking**, Min

Zwergkönig 78 MinFl, mr, 2006; flowers vivid deep red, 5 cm., semi-dbl., borne in small clusters; foliage dark green, dense; growth compact, medium (50 cm.); int. by W. Kordes' Söhne, 1978

Zwergkönigin – See **Queen of the Dwarfs**, Min

Zwergkönigin '82 – See **Dwarf Queen '82**, Min